Taber's 22

brings meanings to life!

Taber's *Plus*

Use your *Plus* Code to unlock the interactive world of Taber's.

- **Explore through Sight & Sound**
- **Taber's Audio**
- **Videos and Animations**
- **Brain Teaser Activities**
- **Bonus Appendices**

 The **Taber's Plus** icon throughout the book indicates a corresponding image, video, or animation online at **Taber's Plus**.

Access your Taber's *Plus* resources today!

1. Visit Davis*Plus*.FADavis.com.
2. Log in or create a new student account.
3. Enter your *Plus* Code listed below.
4. Download or view your Taber's 22 resources.

If your *Plus* Code has already been used, visit Davis*Plus*.FADavis.com.

Taber's®

CYCLOPEDIC

MEDICAL

DICTIONARY

EDITION
22

ILLUSTRATED IN FULL COLOR

Taber's®

CYCLOPEDIC
MEDICAL
DICTIONARY

F. A. DAVIS COMPANY   PHILADELPHIA

NOTE: As new scientific information becomes available through basic and clinical research, recommended treatments and drug therapies undergo changes. The author and publisher have done everything possible to make Taber's accurate, up to date, and in accord with accepted standards at the time of publication. The author, editors, and publisher are not responsible for errors or omissions or for consequences from application of the book, and make no warranty, expressed or implied, in regard to the contents of the book. Any practice described in this book should be applied by the reader in accordance with professional standards of care used in regard to the unique circumstances that may apply in each situation. The reader is advised always to check product information (package inserts) for changes and new information regarding dose and contraindications before administering any drug. Caution is especially urged when using new or infrequently ordered drugs.

Library of Congress Cataloging in Publication Data

Taber's cyclopedic medical dictionary. -- Ed. 22, illustrated in full color / editor, Donald Venes.
  p.; cm.
Cyclopedic medical dictionary
Includes bibliographical references and index.
  ISBN 978-0-8036-2977-6 (indexed : alk. paper) — ISBN 978-0-8036-2978-3 (plain : alk. paper) — ISBN 978-0-8036-2979-0 (deluxe : alk. paper)
  I. Venes, Donald, 1952- II. Taber, Clarence Wilbur, 1870- III. Title: Cyclopedic medical dictionary.
  [DNLM: 1. Medicine--Dictionary--English. W 13]
610.3--dc23
2012034064
00-064688

CONTENTS

INTRODUCTION TO EDITION 22

I grew up reading dictionaries; well, one dictionary in particular. I can't recall how or where I found it, but I do remember finding myself one day, at about age 11, stretched across my bed, reading a dictionary, and laughing.

The book that tickled me was a collection of the satirical aphorisms of Ambrose Bierce, culled from his inordinately successful newspaper columns of the late-1800s. It was known at the time as *The Cynic's Word Book,* and the columns were later collected and published as *The Devil's Dictionary.* In it, Bierce, who had fought in the Civil War and found his view of life profoundly altered by combat, decided to tell the truth about the meaning of words, and therefore, about life's combatants (us). He would define words not for what they were said conventionally to signify, but for what they really were. He would glance behind all the layers, all the petticoats, and tell you what was actually there, not what we were meant to see.

An Academy, said Bierce, was "A modern school where football is taught". English was defined as "A language so haughty and reserved that few writers succeed in getting on terms of familiarity with it"; a Noncombatant was "A dead Quaker" and a Medicine was "A stone flung down the Bowery to kill a dog on Broadway."

Somehow, years later, I found myself in an *Academy,* and a *Quaker* one at that, as a student at Swarthmore College, studying *English,* and later, in New York, near the Bowery and Broadway, studying and practicing *Medicine,* delivering stony pills into the mouths of the *Diseased.*[1] Many of them, despite my failings, recovered and lived long lives.[2]

I took (and still take) a lot of Bierce's perspective to heart, now that I am myself someone who drafts definitions for a dictionary ("A harmless drudge," according to Samuel Johnson, the noted English lexicographer). I have worked all the while to try to keep *Taber's Cyclopedic Medical Dictionary* from falling into what one might call the Dictionary[3] Trap. I have tried to capture the constant evolution of the words we use in contemporary health care. In this project I have had the friendship, support, and guidance of an absolutely perfect team of co-conspirators: notably Robert H. Craven, Jr., Brigitte Fenton, Arthur Biderman, Alison Enright, and Joseph Patwell, as well as a wonderful cadre of consultants and consulting editors, all of whom not only speak and use English better than I do, but who also know their share of computerese, technical and professional jargon, Latin, Greek, and how to get a book of this size actually published.

The revelation[4] that drives this and every edition of *Taber's* forward is that the harder our editorial team works (the more meanings, images, and tables that we put into the text), the greater is our desire and our burden to do better tomorrow. Not a day passes that we do not try to find more to share with you, and a clearer method of expressing it.

We sincerely hope, therefore, that this 22nd Edition will meet your educational[5] needs whether you are student of the health professions, a librarian, a professor, or just a professional cynic.

So far as I know, Ambrose Bierce never married. I did and am glad for it. I want to express, therefore, my unique thanks to my wife for her support of the *Taber's* project. Many were the tempestuous coastal nights when, with the rain blowing sideways, my lovely wife (herself a lifelong health care educator) would awaken, not to the ravening storm, but to the annoying *click-click-click* of my keyboard. "Don't you realize it's not even five yet?" she would mumble, diving beneath the covers. With no small measure of diplomacy[6], may I say words that Bierce never got to write or utter. "Thank you dear, for your patience, your willingness to sacrifice, and your pre-dawn understanding".

Donald Venes, MD, MSJ, FACP
Brookings, Oregon
January 2013

---

[1]*Disease*: "Nature's endowment of medical schools."

[2]*Longevity*: "Uncommon extension of the fear of death."

[2]*Dictionary*: "A malevolent literary device for cramping the growth of a language and making it hard and inelastic."

[4]*Revelation*: "Discovering late in life that you are a fool."

[5]*Education*: "That which discloses to the wise and disguises from the foolish their lack of understanding."

[6]A consul, said Bierce, of the *Diplomat*, is "a person who having failed to secure a position from the people, is given one by the administration, on the condition that he leave the country."

[All quotations are from *The Enlarged Devil's Dictionary*, by Ambrose Bierce, edited by Ernest J. Hopkins, New York: Doubleday, 1967]

CONSULTANTS AND REVIEWERS

CONSULTANTS

Richard Branson, MS, RRT
Richard R. Carlton, MS, RT(R), FAERS
Neal R. Chamberlain, PhD
Charles Christiansen, EdD, OTR, OT(C), FAOTA
Christine Chung, MD
Robert Elling, MPA, REMT-P
Jacqueline Fawcett, PhD, FAAN
Maxine Goldman, BSHC, RN
Joellen W. Hawkins, RN, WHNP-BC, PhD, FAAN
Brenda Holloway, CRNP, FNP, MSN
Olga A. C. Ibsen RDH, MS
Michael J. Katz, MD, PhD
Carol Kelly, MS, RNC, NP
Judith E. Meissner, RN, BSN, MSN
Robert F. Moran, PhD, FCCM, FAIC, FACP
Helen Rasmussen, MS, RD, FADA
Valerie C. Scanlon, PhD
Victor S. Sierpina, MD
Chad Starkey, PhD, ATC
Mary Ann Wharton, PT, MS

REVIEWERS

Naomi Adams, RN, AA, BN
Sandra Anderson, BA, NCTMB, LMT, ABT
Rick Beck, MS, NREMT-P
Jo Ann Beine, PTA, MLS
Jeannie Bower, BS
Kim O'Connell Brock, MS, ATC/L
Linda Campbell, PhD, RN, CNS, CNE
Laura Clark, MS, ATC
Lisa Conry, MA, RRT
Virginia S. Cowen, PhD, LMT
Ashlyn Cunningham, MA, OTR/L
Beth Diehl-Svrjcek / BDS Consultants, DNP, CCRN, NNP, LNCC
Rebecca Duff, PTA
Nancy Edwards, PT
Barbara Foster, MSN, RN
Geana Gaasch, MS, ATC
Heather Grable, MS, RRT
Janice Jones, PhD, RN, CNS
Joanne Carmella Klossner, PhD, LAT, ATC
Kathleen Krov, PhD, RN, CNM, CNE
Neeraj Kumar, PT, PhD
Heather MacKrell, PT, PhD
Barbara Marchelletta, BS, CMA(AAMA), RHIT, CPC, CPT
Cheryl Miller, MBA/HCM
Sandra Moaney-Wright, PhD

viii

Tamara E. Mottler, BA, CMA(AAMA)
Patrice Pierce, RN, MSN
Rosita Rodriguez, PhD, MSN, APN, ANP-BC, NP-C
Bonnie Ross, MA, RN
Marjorie Simon, RN (Canada)
Beryl Stetson, RNBC, MSN, CNE, LCCE, CLC
Elliot Stetson, RN-BC, MSN, CCRN
Brenda Windemuth, DNP, CRNP

(Material supplied by the consultants has been reviewed and edited by Donald Venes, MD, MSJ, FACP, editor, with whom final responsibility rests for the accuracy of the content.)

ix

Taber's Feature Finder

ILLUSTRATION CROSS REFERENCE

abduction (ăb-dŭk´shŭn) **1.** Lateral movement of the limbs away from the median plane of the body, or lateral bending of the head or trunk. SEE: illus. **2.** Movement of the digits away from the axial line of a limb. **3.** Outward rotation of the eyes.

— MAIN ENTRY

acanthosis Increased thickness of the prickle cell layer of the skin.

Taber's *Plus* MULTI-MEDIA CONTENT

a. nigricans A skin disorder in which dark brown or gray velvety plaques appear on the skin, typically under the arms, in the groin or upper thighs, on the neck, or near the genitalia.

— SUBENTRY

acetaminophen (ă-sĕt″ă-mĭn´ō-fĕn) A drug with antipyretic and analgesic effects similar to those of aspirin, but with limited anti-inflammatory or antirheumatic effects.

⚠ Acute overdose may cause fatal hepatic necrosis.

— CAUTION/ SAFETY

ABBREVIATION —— **ACH** *adrenocortical* **hormone**.

PRONUN-CIATION

achloropsia (ă-klō-rŏp´sē-ă) ["+ *chloros*, green, + *opsis*, vision] Color blindness in which green cannot be distinguished. SYN: *deuteranopia.*

— ETYMOLOGY
— SYNONYM

BIOGRAPHICAL INFORMATION

Addison disease [Thomas Addison, Brit. physician, 1793–1860] A rare illness marked by gradual and progressive failure of the adrenal glands and insufficient production of steroid hormones.

ENCYCLOPEDIC ENTRY

ETIOLOGY —— ETIOLOGY: Adrenal failure typically results from autoimmune destruction of the adrenal glands, chronic infections, or cancers that metastasize to the adrenal glands from other organs.

SYMPTOMS —— SYMPTOMS: The patient may be symptom-free until the majority of adrenal tissue is destroyed. Early complaints are usually nonspecific: a feeling of weakness or fatigue, lack of appetite, weight loss, nausea, vomiting, abdominal pain, and dizziness.

TREATMENT —— TREATMENT: Chronic adrenal insufficiency is managed with corticosteroids, such as prednisone, usually taken twice a day. SEE: *adrenal* **crisis**.

VOCABULARY CROSS REFERECE bolded headword for easy locating

PROGNOSIS —— PROGNOSIS: If untreated, the disease will continue a chronic course with progressive but usually relatively slow deterioration; in some patients the deterioration may be rapid. Patients treated properly have an excellent prognosis.

PATIENT CARE —— PATIENT CARE: Patients with primary adrenal insufficiency who are suffering other acute conditions are assessed frequently for hypotension, tachycardia, fluid balance, and electrolyte and glucose levels. SEE: *Nursing Diagnoses Appendix.*

NURSING DIAGNOSES CROSS REFERENCE

adenoma (ăd″ĕ-nō´mă) *pl.* **adenomata** ["+ *oma*, tumor] A benign tumor made of epithelial cells. **adenomatous** (-nō´mă-tŭs), *adj.*

— PLURAL
— ADJECTIVAL FORM

Not an actual page.

FEATURES AND THEIR USE

This section describes the major features found in *Taber's* and provides information that may help you use the dictionary more efficiently. The Feature Finder on page x is a graphic representation of many of the features described below.

1. **Taber's*Plus*:** Taber's*Plus* features a wealth of interactive, multi-media resources for nursing, allied health, and medical students and professionals. Use the promotional code on the first page of the book to access the Taber's*Plus* resources.

   Explore through Sight & Sound features over 1,200 images (465 unique to Taber's*Plus*) with short definitions and audio pronunciations that enhance the learning experience. The corresponding images, animations, or videos are indicated by the Taber's*Plus* icon. 🐦

   Taber's Audio provides pronunciations for almost 32,000 terms found in *Taber's*.

   Brain Teasers are word-building activities that increase understanding of medical terminology.

   Bonus Appendices include valuable educational and clinical healthcare resources, tools, and reference materials.

   Taber's Online, powered by Unbound Medicine offers FREE one-year access to all of the Taber's content online at www.tabers.com. Use the promotional code on the inside front cover of *Taber's* to activate your subscription.

2. **Vocabulary:** The extensive vocabulary defined in *Taber's* has been updated to meet the ongoing needs of health care students, educators, and clinicians, as well as interested consumers. The medical editor, nursing editor, and the nursing and allied health consulting editors and consultants have researched and written new entries, revised existing entries, and deleted obsolete ones, reflecting the many changes in health care technology, clinical practice, and patient care. American, rather than British, spellings are preferred.

3. **Entry Placement:** *Taber's* combines two systems for the placement and organization of entries: (a) main entries in strict alphabetical order; and (b) a main entry–subentry format. All single-word terms (e.g., **cell**) are main entries, as are some compound, or multiple word, terms, e.g., **acid-reflux disorder; nucleic acid test**. However, many compound terms, especially those in anatomy and physiology, are treated as subentries and are placed using the main entry–subentry format, e.g., arteries, veins, ligaments, and types of respiration. Entries having a considerable number of subentries are tinted in a yellow background for ease in finding them. This melding of two systems combines the best features of both: compound terms that share an important common element or classification, e.g., arteries, are subentries under the main entry (or headword). Terms that tend to be sought under the first word, e.g., diseases, disorders, tests, and

syndromes, appear as main entries under the first word. Also names of individuals and organizations are listed as main entries. All main entries are printed in **bold type**; subentries are indented under the main entry and are printed in ***bold italic type***. All entries are listed and defined in the singular whenever possible.

4. **Alphabetization:**

   Main entries are alphabetized letter by letter, regardless of spaces or hyphens that occur between the words; a comma marks the end of a main entry for alphabetical purposes, e.g., **skin, tenting of** precedes **skin cancer**.

   Subentries are listed in straight-ahead order following the same letter-by-letter alphabetization used for main entries; a comma marks the end of a subentry for alphabetical purposes. The headword is often abbreviated in subentries (such as ***preterm l.*** under **labor** or ***pulmonary i.*** under **infarction**).

5. **Eponyms:** Included as main entries are the names of individuals who were the first to discover, describe, or popularize a concept, a microorganism, a disease, a syndrome, or an anatomical structure. A brief biography appears in brackets after the pronunciation. Biographical information includes the person's professional designation, the country in which the person was born or worked, and the date of birth and death if known.

6. **Pronunciations:** Most main entries are spelled phonetically. Such spellings appear within parentheses after the boldface main entry and are given as simply as possible. The vowel *a* stands for the sounds in at, ant, or care; the vowel *e* for the sound in bed or set; *i* as in it or hid; *o* as in got, god, or lawn; *u* as in foot or put. *Taber's* also uses two *diacritics,* or marks over vowels. The macron ‾ shows the long sound of vowels, as the *a* in mate, the *e* in meet, the *i* in might, the *o* in mote, and the *u* in mute. The breve ˘ shows the short, obscure vowel, called *schwa,* which is pronounced like the *a* in sofa, the *e* in butter, the *i* in maudlin the *o* in senator, and the *u* in up. The letter combinations *oo* are pronounced as in food, *ow* as in now, *ch* as in chin, *sh* as in shin, *th* as in thin or then, and *zh* as in vision. *Accents* are marks used to indicate stress upon certain syllables. A single accent ′ marks the primary accent. A double accent ″ marks a secondary accent. Both kinds of stress can be seen in *an″ĕs-thē′zhă.* Syllables are separated by either an accent mark or a hyphen.

7. **Singular/Plural forms:** When the spelling of an entry's singular or plural form is a nonstandard formation (e.g., **villus** *pl.* **villi,** or **viscera** *sing.* **viscus**), the spelling of the singular or plural form appears in boldface after the pronunciation for the main entry. Nonstandard singular and plural forms appear as entries themselves at their normal alphabetical positions.

8. **Etymologies:** An etymology indicates the origin and historical development of a term. For most health care terms the origin is Latin or Greek. An etymology is given for most main entries and appears in brackets following the pronunciation.

9. **Abbreviations:** Standard abbreviations for entries are included with the definition, and many are also listed alphabetically as separate entries throughout the text. Additional abbreviations used for

charting and prescription writing are listed in the Appendices. A list of nonmedical abbreviations used in text appears on page xxxiv.

10. **Encyclopedic entries:** Detailed, comprehensive information is included with entries that require additional coverage because of their importance or complexity. Often this information is organized into several sections, each with its own subheading. The most frequently used subheadings are Etiology, Symptoms, Diagnosis, Treatment, and Patient Care.

11. **Patient Care:** Patient Care sections provide information for the health care worker in clinical situations. These sections have proven invaluable to health care professionals by providing patient teaching and wellness information. There are now more than 800 Patient Care sections in *Taber's*.

12. **Illustrations:** This edition of *Taber's* includes 800 illustrations in the print, 500 of which are new to this edition. In addition, there are over 400 additional, ancillary illustrations in the electronic versions of this edition. The existence of each of these ancillary illustrations in Taber's*Plus* is indicated by placement of the icon (▟▙) next to the entry with which the illustration is associated. The images were carefully chosen to complement the text of the entries with which they are associated. Each illustration is cross-referenced from its associated entry. A complete list of illustrations begins on page xv.

13. **Tables:** This edition contains 150 color-screened tables located appropriately throughout the Vocabulary section. A complete list of tables begins on page xxxi.

14. **Adjectives:** The adjectival forms of many noun main entries appear at the end of the definition of the noun form or, if the entry is long, at the end of the first paragraph. Pronunciations for most of the adjectival forms are included. Many common adjectives appear as main entries themselves.

15. ⚠ **Caution/Safety statements:** This notation is used to draw particular attention to information that may affect the health and/or safety of patients or the professionals who treat them. The information is of more than routine interest and should be considered when delivering health care. These statements are further emphasized by colored rules above and below the text.

16. **Synonyms:** Synonyms are listed at the end of the entry or, in encyclopedic entries, at the end of the first paragraph. The abbreviation SYN: precedes the synonymous term(s). Terms listed as synonyms have their own entries in the Vocabulary, which generally carry a cross-reference to the entry at which the definition appears.

17. **Cross-references:** Illustrations, tables, appendices, or other relevant vocabulary entries may be given as cross-references. These are indicated by SEE: or SEE: under followed by the name(s) of the appropriate element(s) in italics. Cross-references to the Nursing Diagnoses Appendix are highlighted in color at the end of the entry as SEE: *Nursing Diagnoses Appendix.* Entries at which an illustration appears carry the color-highlighted SEE: illus. When a SEE: refers to subentry, the main entry will appear in **boldface,** for easy reference. E.g., SEE: *temporal **line,*** where "line" is the main entry.

18. **Appendices:** The Appendices contain detailed information that can be organized or presented more easily in one section rather than interspersed throughout the Vocabulary. The entire appendix section has been reviewed and appropriately updated. Among the revised appendices are Standard Precautions, Nutrition, and Nursing Diagnoses. For a complete listing of all the Appendices, see Contents on pages v–vi. For a complete listing of all the Nursing Appendices, see page 2525.

19. **Nursing Diagnoses Appendix:** This appendix has been updated through the 2012–2014 Conference of NANDA-I (North American Nursing Diagnosis Association-International). It is divided into several sections, including two lists of NANDA-I's nursing diagnoses organized into Doenges and Moorhouse's Diagnostic Divisions and Gordon's Functional Health Patterns; an at-a-glance look at the most recent diagnoses approved by NANDA; nursing diagnoses commonly associated with almost 300 diseases/disorders (cross-referenced from the body of the dictionary); and a complete description of all NANDA-approved diagnoses through the 2012–2014 conference in alphabetical order. Included are the diagnostic division, definition, related factors, and defining characteristics for each nursing diagnosis. See the *Quick View of Contents* on page 2683 for further explanation.

LIST OF ILLUSTRATIONS

Illustrations are listed according to the main entry or subentry that they accompany. Information in parentheses indicates the source of the illustration; a list of sources appears at the end of this list. Bonus multimedia content (illustrations and videos) are listed with and can be found in Taber's*Plus*.

✈ Illustrations

Splinter hemmorrhage
Sponge
Cervical sprain
Stevens-Johnson syndrome
Reaction to a bee sting
Stomatitis
Striae
Hemorrhagic stroke
Stryker frame
Subluxation
Suicide
Sway-back
Synapse
Syphilis
Paroxysmal supraventricular tachycardia (PSVT)
Skin tags
Elaborate tattoo
Telangiectasia
Temperature regulation
Flexor tendons of the wrist
Thoracentesis
Thymus in a young child
Thyroid gland and related structures
Tinea capitis
Tinea versicolor
Bone tissue
Connective tissues
Pet scan of brain
Tonometry
Total hip replacement
Tracheostomy tube
Biliary tract

Traction
Trapezium
Foot trauma
Facial trauma
Trichinella spiralis
Trigger finger
Trypanosoma in blood
Tuberculosis
Brain tumor
Uric acid crystals
Urinary system
Urine
Urticaria
Vasculitis
Venous cutdown
Verruca vulgaris
Vitiligo
Vulva
Common warts
Genital warts on penis
Plantar wart
Common warts
Parotid gland asymmetry
Wasting interosseous tissues of hand
Components of waves
Joy stick
Splint and compression wrap
Wrapping ankle
Xerosis
Budding yeast
Yergason test
Z-plasty method of correcting a deforming scar

▆ Videos and Animations

Abduction
Adduction
Rheumatoid arthritis
Circular bandage
Figure-of-eight bandage
Spica bandage
Bandage
Bedpan
Blood group
Blood transfusion
Transfer board
Adhesive capsulitis
Tracheostomy care

Walking cast
Condom catheter
Urinary bladder catheterization
Fetal circulation
Portal circulation
Coronary artery disease
Crutch
Cardiac cycle
Denture
Descent
Sequential compression device
Venous access device
Digestion

DNA
Active drainage
Dry dressing
Hydrocolloid dressing
Nose drops
Ear
Eardrops
Elbow
Elevation
Enema
Engagement
Enteral tube feeding
Erythroblastosis fetalis
Codman exercise
Range-of-motion exercise
Expulsion rate
Extension
Eyedrops
Face mask
Fertilization
Cerebrospinal fluid
Fracture
Four-point gait
Two-point gait
Gait
Pituitary gland
Glove
Capillary blood glucose
Goniometer
Hearing
Heart
Homeostasis
Hand hygiene
Cellular immunity
Humoral immunity
Inclinometer
Metered-dose inhaler
Intradermal injection
Subcutaneous injection
Z-track injection
Active insufficiency
Passive insufficiency
Intake and output
Craniomandibular joint
Myoneural junction
Kidney
Lung
Lymphatic system
Sublingual medication
Cardinal movements of labor
Agonist muscle

Nasogastric tube
Ostomy
Ovulation
Oximeter
Pain
Personal protective equipment
Physical therapy
Presentation
Apical pulse
Brachial pulse
Carotid pulse
Dorsalis pedis pulse
Femoral pulse
Popliteal pulse
Radial pulse
Infusion pump
Sodium pump
Passive range of motion
Refraction of eye
Respiration
External respiration
Internal respiration
Thoracic respiration
Trochanter roll
External rotation
Plane of scapula
Scoliosis
Shoulder
Skin
Spermatogenesis
Sprain of ankle
Stocking
Closed suction
Nasogastric suction
Suction
Suppository
Sympathetic nervous system
Synapse
Axillary temperature
Oral temperature
Rectal temperature
Tympanic temperature
Toothbrushing
Tracheostomy care
Transdermal infusion system
Transfer board
Trochanter
Ultrasonic
Urinal
Venipuncture

ILLUSTRATION SOURCES

Barankin and Frieman: Derm Notes: Clinical Dermatology Pocket Guide. FA Davis, Philadelphia, 2006.

Centers for Disease Control and Prevention; Dr. Lucille K. Georg; Frank Collins, PhD; James Gathany (2006); Carl Washington, MD; Emory University. School of Medicine; Mona Saraiya, MD, MPH.

Chambers, K and Roche, V: Surgical Technology Review certification and professionalism. FA Davis, Philadelphia, 2010.

Chapman, L and Durham, R: Maternal-Newborn Nursing : The Critical Components of Nursing Care..FA Davis, Philadelphia, 2009.

Chung, Christine A, MD, Philadelphia, PA.

Dillon, PM: Nursing Health Assessment: A Critical Thinking, Case Studies Approach. FA Davis, Philadelphia, 2003.

Eagle, Sharon: The Professional Medical Assistant. FA Davis, Philadelphia, 2009.

Eickhoff, L, Portland, OR.

Enright, AD, Havertown, PA.

Goldsmith, LA, Lazarus, GS and Tharp, MD: Adult and Pediatric Dermatology: A Color Guide to Diagnosis and Treatment, FA Davis, Philadelphia, 1997.

Gylys, B and Masters, R: Medical Terminology Simplified: A Programmed Learning Approach by Body Systems, ed 4. FA Davis, Philadelphia, 2010.

Gylys, B and Wedding, M: Medical Terminology Systems: A Body Systems Approach, ed 6. FA Davis, Philadelphia, 2009.

Harmening, D: Clincal Hematology & Funadmentals of Hemostasis. Ed 5. FA Davis, Philadelphia, 2009.

Hatch, H, Gold Beach, OR.

Hawkins, J, Chestnut Hill, MA.

Holloway, B et al: OB/GYN & Peds Notes: Nurse's Clincial Pocket Guide, ed 2. FA Davis, Philadelphia, 2011.

Hopkins, T: Lab Notes: Guide to Lab and Diagnostic Tests, ed 2. FA Davis, Philadelphia, 2009.

Hurst, J: Anatomy & Physiology in a Flash. FA Davis, Philadelphia, 2010.

Kintz, J, Eugene, OR.

Kisner, C and Colby, L: Therapeutic Exercise, ed 5. FA Davis, Philadelphia, 2007.

Klein, A, Portland, OR.

Kloth, LC: Wound Healing: Alternatives in Management, ed 3. FA Davis, Philadelphia, 2002.

Levangie, P andNorkin, C: Joint Structure and Function: A Comprehensive Analysis, ed 5. FA Davis, Philadelphia, 2011.

Lentner, C (ed): Geigy Scientific Tables, ed 8. Ciba Geigy, Basle, Switzerland, 1981.

Leventhal, R and Cheadle, RF: Medical Parasitology: A Self-Instructional Text, ed 5. FA Davis, Philadelphia, 2002.

Lippert, L: Clinical Kinesiology and Anatomy, ed 5. FA Davis, Philadelphia, 2011.

Myers, E: EMS Notes: EMT and Paramedic Field Guide. FA Davis, Philadelphia, 2009.

Owens, April, Eugene, OR.

Prajer, R and Gross, G: DH Notes: Dental Hygienist's Chairside Pocket Guide. FA Davis, Philadelphia, 2011.

Roberts, John, MD.

Scanlon, VC and Sanders, T: Essentials of Anatomy and Physiology, ed 5& 6. FA Davis, Philadelphia, 2007 & 2010.

http://www.shapeup.org.

Speroff, L: A Clinical Guide for Contraception, ed 3. Lippincott, Williams & Wilkins.

Starkey, C: Examination of Orthopedic & Athletic Injuries, ed. 3. FA Davis, Philadelphia, 2010.

Stevens, CD: Clinical Immunology and Serology: A Laboratory Perspective. FA Davis, Philadelphia, 1996.

Strasinger, S and Di Lorenzo M: Urinalysis & Body Fluids, ed 5. FA Davis, Philadelphia, 2008.

Strauss, W. Robert, Jr. ,Cherry Hill, NJ.

Tamparo, C. and Lewis, M: Diseases of the Human Body, ed 5. FA Davis, Philadelphia, 2011.

Thompson, G: Understanding Anatomy & Physiology: A Visual, Auditory, Interactive Approach. FA Davis, Philadelphia, 2012.

Venes, D, Brookings, OR.

Ward, S and Hisley, S: Maternal-Child Nursing Care, F.A.Davis, Philadelphia, 2009.

White, G: Respiratory Notes: Respiratory Therapist's Pocket Guide, FA Davis, Philadelphia, 2008.

Wilkinson, JM and Van Leuven, K: Fundamentals of Nursing, ed 1 & 2. FA Davis, Philadelphia, 2007 & 2011.

Williams, LS and Hopper, PD (eds): Understanding Medical-Surgical Nursing, ed 4. FA Davis, Philadelphia, 2011.

World Health Organization (WHO): http://www.who.int.

LIST OF TABLES

ABBREVIATIONS USED IN TEXT*

ABBR	abbreviation	Ger.	German
Amerind	American Indian	Gr.	Greek
approx.	approximately	i.e.	id est (that is)
at. no.	atomic number	L.	Latin
at. wt.	atomic weight	pert.	pertaining
Brit.	British	pl.	plural
e.g.	exempli gratia (for example)	sing.	singular
		Sp.	Spanish
esp.	especially	SYMB	symbol
Fr.	French	SYN	synonym
fr.	from		

---

*Additional abbreviations are listed in the Units of Measurement Appendix and the Medical Abbreviations Appendix.

α Alpha, the first letter of the Greek alphabet.

Å angstrom unit.

a accommodation; ampere; anode; anterior; area; artery.

ā [L.] ante, before.

A₂ aortic second sound.

a- SEE: ¹an-.

AA Achievement *age*; Alcoholics Anonymous; amino acid; arteriae; arteries.

AAA abdominal aortic aneurysm; acne-associated arthritis; American Academy of Allergists; American Ambulance Association; American Association of Anatomists.

AAAS American Association for the Advancement of Science.

AAb Autoantibody.

AABB American Association of Blood Banks.

AACC American Association for Clinical Chemistry.

AACN American Association of Critical-Care Nurses; American Association of Colleges of Nursing.

AACVPR American Association of Cardiovascular and Pulmonary Rehabilitation.

AAFP American Academy of Family Physicians.

AAg Autoantigen.

AAHN American Association for the History of Nursing.

AAL anterior axillary line.

AAMA American Association of Medical Assistants.

AAMI Association for the Advancement of Medical Instrumentation; age-associated memory impairment.

AAMS Association of Air Medical Services.

AAMT American Association for Medical Transcription.

AAN American Academy of Nursing.

AANA American Association of Nurse Anesthetists.

AANN American Association of Neuroscience Nurses.

AANP American Academy of Nurse Practitioners.

AAOHN American Association of Occupational Health Nurses.

AAOMS American Association of Oral and Maxillofacial Surgeons.

AAOS American Academy of Orthopedic Surgeons.

AAP American Academy of Pediatrics; American Association of Pathologists.

AAPA American Academy of Physician Assistants.

AAPMR American Academy of Physical Medicine and Rehabilitation.

a/A ratio The ratio of arterial oxygen partial pressure (a) to alveolar oxygen partial pressure (A), a measure of oxygen transfer across the lung. This figure is normally greater than 0.9.

AARC American Association for Respiratory Care.

AARP American Association of Retired Persons.

AAS atomic absorption spectroscopy.

AASECT American Association of Sex Educators, Counselors, and Therapists.

AATB American Association of Tissue Banks.

Ab Antibody.

ab-, abs- [L. ab, from] Prefixes meaning *from, away from, negative, absent*. The variant abs- is used before t, e.g., *abstract*.

¹Abadie sign (ă-bad′ē) [Jean Abadie, Fr. neurologist, 1873–1946] In tabes dorsalis, insensibility to pressure over the Achilles tendon.

²Abadie sign (ă-bad′ē) [Charles A. Abadie, Fr. ophthalmologist, 1842–1932] In exophthalmic goiter, spasm of the levator palpebrae superioris.

abandonment (ă-ban′dŏn-mĕnt) [Fr. *abandoner*, to surrender] Premature termination of the professional treatment relationship by the health care provider without adequate notice or the patient's consent.

abarticulation (ab″ar-tik-yŭ-lā′shŏn) [*ab-* + *articulation*] 1. Diarthrosis. 2. An ambiguous term meaning dislocation of a joint; aparthrosis.

abasia (ă-bā′zh(ē-)ă) [¹*an-* + Gr. *basis*, step] 1. Motor incoordination in walking. 2. Inability to walk due to impairment of coordination. **abasic, abatic,** *adj.*

a.-astasia Lack of motor coordination with inability to stand or walk. SYN: astasia-abasia.

paralytic a. Abasia in which the leg muscles are paralyzed.

paroxysmal trepidant a. Abasia caused by trembling and sudden stiffening of the legs on standing, making walking impossible. It may be related to hysteria.

abate (ă-bāt′) [Fr. *abattre*, to beat down] 1. To lessen or decrease. 2. To cease or cause to cease. **abatement** (mĕnt), *n.*

abaxial, abaxile (a-bak′sē-ăl, -sĭl) [*ab-* + *axial*] 1. Not within the axis of a body or part. 2. At the opposite end of the axis of a part.

Abbe-Wharton-McIndoe operation, McIndoe operation (a′bē-whar′tŏn-mak′-in-dō) A surgical procedure performed to create a vagina in patients who do not have one. This is achieved by creating adequate space between the rectum and bladder; the inlaying of a split-thickness graft; and most importantly, continuous and prolonged dilatation during the healing stage when tissues are most likely to contract.

PATIENT CARE: The health care team supports the patient medically and psychologically by helping the patient learn about her condition and the procedure by answering questions, providing comfort, and alleviating anxiety.

Abbott method (ab'ŏts) [Edville G. Abbott, U.S. orthopedic surgeon, 1871–1938] A treatment for scoliosis that is no longer used, in which a series of plaster jackets were applied to straighten the spine.

ABC *American Botanical Council; antigen-binding capacity; airway, breathing, circulation* (the former mnemonic for assessing the status of emergency patients)

ABCD *asymmetry, border, color, diameter* (a mnemonic to aid health care providers in the recognition of malignant melanoma). Pigmented lesions on the skin with irregularities of growth and color and diameters greater than 6 mm have a considerable likelihood of being melanomas and should be professionally examined. Additional characteristics of melanomas include the sudden change of an existing mole or sudden appearance of pigmented moles. In some cases an existing mole that was flat elevates above the skin. The letter *E* is used as a mnemonic for this *expansion* or *evolution* of skin lesions (thus the mnemonic is sometimes referred to as *ABCDE*). SEE: illus.; *melanoma*.

ABCDE SEE: *ABCD*.

ABCD prediction rule ABCD score.

ABCD rule ABCD score.

ABCD score A clinical prediction value that estimates the likelihood of stroke in a patient who has had a transient ischemic attack. Its elements include: A (age greater than or less than 60); B (blood pressure above 140 mm Hg systolic or 90 diastolic); C (clinical features such as one-sided body weakness or speech disturbance); and D (duration of symptoms: 60 min, 10-60 min, or less

than 10 min). SYN: *ABCD prediction rule; ABCD rule*.

abdiction (ab-dik'shŏn) [*ab-* + *(ad)diction*] The intolerance or avoidance of drugs or chemicals.

abdomen (ab-dō'měn, ab'dŏ-měn) [L. *abdomen,* belly] The portion of the trunk lying between the thorax and the pelvis. It contains the stomach, lower part of the esophagus, small and large intestines, liver, gallbladder, and spleen. The parietal peritoneum lines the abdominal cavity. The organs within this cavity are enveloped by the visceral peritoneum. The kidneys, adrenal glands, ureters, prostate, seminal vesicles, and greater vascular structures are located behind the peritoneum (retroperitoneal or extraperitoneal). **abdominal** (ab-dom'ĭ-năl), adj. SEE: *abdominal quadrants* for illus.

INSPECTION: Visual examination of the abdomen is best done while the patient is supine with the knees slightly bent. In a healthy person the abdomen is oval-shaped, with elevations and depressions corresponding to the abdominal muscles, umbilicus, and to some degree the forms of underlying viscera. Relative to chest size, it is larger in children than in adults; it is more rotund and broader inferiorly in males than in females.

Disease can alter the shape of the abdomen. A general, symmetrical enlargement may result from ascites; a partial and irregular enlargement may result from tumors, hypertrophy of organs such as the liver or spleen, or intestinal distention caused by gas. Retraction of the abdomen may occur in extreme emaciation and in several forms of cerebral disease, esp. tubercular meningitis of children.

The respiratory movements of the abdominal walls are related to movements of the thorax and are often increased when the latter are arrested and vice versa; thus, abdominal movements are increased in pleurisy, pneumonia, and pericarditis but are decreased or wholly suspended in peritonitis and disease-caused abdominal pain.

The superficial abdominal veins are sometimes visibly enlarged, indicating an obstruction of blood flow in either the

  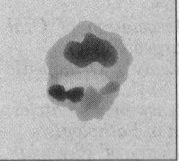 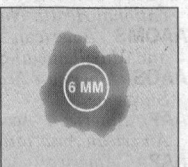

Asymmetry   Border irregularity   Color   Diameter

ABCD'S OF MELANOMA

portal system (as in cirrhosis) or the inferior vena cava.

AUSCULTATION: Listening to sounds produced in abdominal organs provides useful diagnostic information. Absent or diminished bowel sounds may indicate paralytic ileus or peritonitis. High-pitched tinkling sounds are associated with intestinal obstruction. Bruits may indicate atherosclerosis or an abdominal aortic aneurysm. During pregnancy, auscultation enables identification and evaluation of the fetal heart rate and vascular sounds from the placenta.

PERCUSSION: For the practitioner to obtain the greatest amount of information, the patient should be supine with the head slightly raised and knees slightly flexed. Percussion should be carried out systematically over the anterior surface of the abdomen. A combination of audible or tactile sensation will be perceived by the examiner according to underlying structures (e.g., gaseous distended organs versus solid organs). A large abdominal aneurysm gives dullness or flatness over it unless a distended intestine lies above it.

PALPATION: The abdomen may be palpated with fingertips, the whole hand, or both hands; pressure may be slight or forceful, continuous or intermittent. The head is supported to relax the abdominal wall. On occasion, the patient may be examined in a standing position (e.g., palpation of groin hernias that might not be palpable in the supine position).

Palpation is helpful in detecting the size, consistency, and position of viscera; the existence of tumors and swellings; and whether the tumors change position with respiration or are movable. It is necessary to ascertain whether there is tenderness in any portion of the abdominal cavity, whether pain is increased or relieved by firm pressure, and whether pain is accentuated by sudden release of firm pressure (i.e., rebound tenderness).

An arterial impulse, if one exists, is systolic and expansive. A thrill accompanying a bruit may occasionally be palpated. The surface of a tumor is usually firm and smooth but may be nodular. Inflammatory masses are typically firm and reproducibly tender. Effusion of blood into tissues (e.g., hematoma) may produce a palpable mass.

acute a. An abnormal condition of the abdomen in which there is a sudden, abrupt onset of severe pain. It requires urgent evaluation and diagnosis because it may indicate a need for immediate surgical intervention. SYN: *surgical a.*

pendulous a. An abdomen with folds of fatty tissue that drape over the pubis.

scaphoid a. An abdomen that on ex-amination appears hollowed, sunken, or emaciated.

surgical a. Acute **a.**

abdominalgia (ab″dom-ĭn-al′j(ē-)ă) [*abdomino-* + *-algia*] Pain in the abdomen.

abdominal migraine SEE: under *migraine*.

abdominal muscles SEE: under *muscle*.

abdominal quadrants Four parts or divisions of the abdomen determined by drawing imaginary vertical and horizontal lines through the umbilicus. The quadrants and their contents are:

Right upper quadrant (RUQ): right lobe of liver, gallbladder, part of transverse colon, part of pylorus, hepatic flexure, right kidney, and duodenum; *Right lower q. (RLQ):* cecum, ascending colon, small intestine, appendix, bladder if distended, right ureter, right spermatic duct in the male, right ovary and right tube, and uterus if enlarged in the female; *Left upper q. (LUQ):* left lobe of liver, stomach, small intestine, transverse colon, splenic flexure, pancreas, left kidney, and spleen; *Left lower q. (LLQ):* small intestine, left ureter, sigmoid flexure, descending colon, bladder if distended, left spermatic duct in the male; left ovary and left tube, and uterus if enlarged, in the female. SEE: illus.

abdominal reflex SEE: under *reflex*.

abdominal regions SEE: under *region*.

abdominal rescue SEE: under *rescue*.

abdominal rings The apertures in the abdominal wall. *External inguinal* or *superficial:* An interval in the aponeurosis of the external oblique muscle, just above and to the outer side of the crest of the pubic bone.

abdominal thrust maneuver Heimlich maneuver. SEE: under *Heimlich, Henry Jay*.

abdomino-, abdomin- [L. *abdomen*, stem *abdomin-,* belly] Prefixes meaning *abdomen.*

abdominocentesis (ab-dom″i-nō-sen-tē′sis) [*abdomino-* + *-centesis*] Puncture of the abdomen with an instrument for withdrawal of fluid from the abdominal cavity.

abdominocyesis (ab-dom″in-ō-sī-ēs′is) [abdomino- + Gr. *kuēsis,* pregnancy] Abdominal **pregnancy.**

abdominocystic (ab-dom″i-nō-sis′tik) [*abdomino-* + *cystic*] Pert. to the abdomen and bladder.

abdominohysterectomy (ab-dom″i-nō-his-tĕr-ek′tŏ-mē) [*abdomino-* + *hysterectomy*] Abdominal hysterectomy.

abdominohysterotomy (ab-dom″i-nō-his-tĕr-ot′ŏ-mē) [*abdomino-* + *hysterotomy*] Abdominal hysterotomy.

abdominoperineal (ab-dom″i-nō-per″ĭ-nē′ăl) [*abdomino-* + *perineal*] Pert. to the abdomen and perineal area.

abdominoplasty (ab-dom′i-nō-plas″tē)

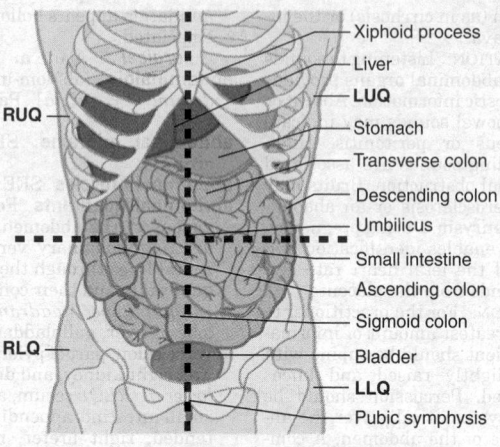

Labels: Xiphoid process, Liver, LUQ, Stomach, Transverse colon, Descending colon, Umbilicus, Small intestine, Ascending colon, Sigmoid colon, Bladder, LLQ, Pubic symphysis, RUQ, RLQ

ABDOMINAL QUADRANTS

[*abdomino-* + *-plasty*] Plastic surgery on the abdomen.

abdominoscopy (ab-dom″i-nos′kŏ-pē) [*abdomino-* + *-scopy*] An outdated term for laparoscopy.

abdominovaginal (ab-dom″i-nō-vaj′i-năl) [*abdomino-* + *vaginal*] Pert. to the abdomen and vagina.

abdominovesical (ab-dom″i-nō-ves′i-kăl) [*abdomino-* + *vesical*] Pert. to the abdomen and urinary bladder.

abducens (ab-dū′senz″) [L., *abducere*, to draw away] Pert. to drawing away from the midline of the body.

a. oculi Musculus rectus lateralis bulbi, the lateral rectus muscle, one of the extraocular muscles.

abducens nerve SEE: under *nerve*.

abducent (ab-dū′sĕnt) [L. *abducere*, to draw away] **1.** Abducting; leading away. **2.** Abducens.

abduct (ab-dŭkt′) [L. *abducere*, to lead away] To draw away from the median plane of the body or one of its parts.

abduction (ab-dŭk′shŏn) [L. *abducere*, to lead away] **1.** Lateral movement of a limb away from the median plane of the body. **2.** Lateral movement of a digit away from the median plane of the limb. **3.** Outward rotation of an eyeball.

abduction stress test SEE: under *stress test*.

abductor (ab-dŭk′tor) SEE: under *muscle*.

Abernethy fascia (ab′ĕr-nē″thēz) [John Abernethy, Brit. surgeon, 1764–1831] A layer of areolar tissue separating the external iliac artery from the iliac fascia over the psoas muscle.

aberrant (a-ber′ănt) [L. *aberrare*, to wander] Deviating from normal. SYN: *abnormal*.

aberratio (ab-ĕr-ā′sh(ē-)ō) [L.] Aberration.

aberration (ab″ĕ-rā′shŏn) [L. *aberrare*, to wander] **1.** Deviation from the nor-

mal. **2.** Imperfect refraction of light rays.

chromatic a. Unequal refraction of different wavelengths of light through a lens, producing a colored image.

chromosomal a. An abnormality in chromosomes regarding number (aneuploidy, polyploidy) or chromosomal material (translocation, deletion, duplication).

higher order a. In ophthalmology, a refractive error that cannot be corrected by bending light into the eye with eyeglasses or contact lenses.

lateral a. Deviation of a ray from the focus measured on a line perpendicular to the axis.

longitudinal a. Deviation of a ray from the direction parallel to the optic axis.

spherical a. Aberration or distortion of an image due to rays entering the peripheral portion of a spherical mirror or lens being refracted differently from those closer to the center. Thus the peripheral rays are focused on the optical axis at a different point from the central rays.

aberrometry (a″bĕr-om′ĕ-trē) [L. *aberrare*, to wander + *-metry*] The measurement of refractive errors of the eye.

Abeta Amyloid beta peptide. It is the toxic peptide that causes damage to neurons in patients having Alzheimer disease.

abetalipoproteinemia (ā″bāt″ă-lip″ŏ-prō″tēn-ē′mē-ă) [²*an-* + *beta* + *lipoprotein* + *-emia*] An inherited disorder marked by an absence of beta lipoproteins in the blood and low levels of cholesterol, fatty acids, and chylomicrons. The patient's red blood cells have a thorny or spiked appearance (acanthocytosis). The condition is most often seen in Ashkenazi Jews. Symptoms include retinal macular degeneration and chronic progressive neurological deficits, which usually begin in childhood. Affected infants develop steatorrhea and growth retardation. Later clinical manifestations include ataxia; by adolescence, many patients are unable to walk. Vitamin E may be helpful in arresting the progression of neurological aspects. SYN: *Bassen-Kornzweig syndrome.* SEE: *acanthocyte.*

abeyance (ă-bā′ăns) [Fr. *abeance,* expectation] A temporary suspension of activity, sensation, or pain.

abfraction (ab″frak′shŏn) [*ab-* + *fraction*] A wedge-shaped area in the region of the cementoenamel junction of the tooth resulting from biomechanical forces.

ABG *arterial blood gas.*

ability (ă-bi′li-tē) [Fr. *habileté,* fr L. *habilitas,* skill] The capacity to perform a task.

   cognitive a. The ability of the brain to process, retrieve, and store information. Impairment of these brain functions is common in patients with dementia, drug intoxication, or head injury.

   constructional a. The ability to copy or draw shapes, figures, or lines (e.g., with a pen and paper). This nonverbal ability depends on the integration of several higher brain functions, including perception, planning, and motor coordination. It is lost in organic brain syndromes.

   crystallized a. A learned skill, e.g., the ability to read or write or use a piece of equipment, such as a keyboard

   fluid a. The ability to reason or draw inferences, to understand new information, or to cope with new problems, environments, or experiences.

   functional a. The ability to perform activities of daily living, including bathing, dressing, and other independent living skills, such as shopping and housework. Many functional assessment tools are available to quantify functional ability. SEE: *activities of daily living.*

   impaired transfer a. Limitation of independent movement between two nearby surfaces. SEE: *Nursing Diagnoses Appendix.*

   verbal a. The ability to use words, spoken or written, to communicate.

abiogenesis (ā″bī″ō-jen′ĕ-sis) [*a-* + *biogenesis*] Spontaneous generation of life; theoretical production of living organisms from nonliving matter. **abiogenetic, abiogenous** (ā″bī″ō-jĕ-net′ik, ā″bē-oj′ĕ-nŭs), *adj.*

abiosis (ā″bī-ō′sis) [*a-* + *bio-* + *-osis*] Absence of life. **abiotic,** *adj.*

abiotrophy (ā″bī-o′trŏ-fē) [*a-* + *bio-* + *-trophy*] Premature loss of vitality or degeneration of tissues and cells with consequent loss of endurance and resistance. **abiotrophic** (ā″bī-o′trō-fik), *adj.*

ablactation (ab-lak-tā′shŏn) [*ab-* + *lactation*] **1.** The cessation of milk secretion. SEE: *wean.*

ablate (a-blāt′) [L. *ablatus,* taken away] To remove.

ablatio (a-blā′sh(ē-)ō) [L., carrying away] Ablation, removal, detachment.

   a. placentae Abruptio placentae.

   a. retinae Detachment of the retina. SEE: *retina.*

ablation (a-blā′shŏn) [L. *ablatio,* a taking away] Removal of a body part, a pathway, or a function, e.g., by chemical or physical destruction, or by surgery. Particular ablations are listed under the first word. SEE: e.g., *endometrial ablation; radiofrequency ablation; tissue ablation.*

ABLEDATA (ā′bĭl-dā′tă) A searchable Internet database of assistive technology information maintained by the National Institute on Disability and Rehabilitation Research of the U.S. Department of Education. The Web site address is www.abledata.com

ablepharia (ā″blĕ-far′ē-ă) [*a-* + Gr. *blepharon,* eyelid] Congenital absence of or reduction in the size of the eyelids. **ablepharous** (-blĕf′ă-rŭs), *adj.*

ablution (ă-bloo′shŏn) [L. *abluere,* to wash away] A cleansing or washing.

ABMS *American Board of Medical Specialties.*

abnormal (ab″nor′măl) [*ab-* + *normal*] ABBR: abnl. **1.** Diverging from a known standard or mean. SYN: *aberrant.* **2.** Exceptional. **3.** Unexpected. **abnormally** (-mă-lē), *adv.*

Abnormal Involuntary Movement Scale test ABBR: AIMS test. A system used to assess abnormal involuntary movements, such as hand tremors or rhythmic movements of the tongue and jaw, that may result from the long-term administration of psychotropic drugs. The test is often given before patients are started on antipsychotic drugs and then readministered periodically to monitor side effects.

abnormality (ab″nŏr-mal′ĭt-ē) [*ab-* + *normality*] Deviation from the normal. SYN: *aberration.*

aborad (a-bŏr′ad″) [*ab-* + *oro-* + *-ad*] Away from the mouth.

aboral (a-bŏr′ăl) [*ab-* + *oral*] Opposite to, or away from, the mouth. **aborally** (-ă-lē), *adv.*

aboriginal healing (a″bŏ-ri′jĭ-năl) [L. *ab origine,* from the beginning] SEE: under *healing.*

abort (ă-bort′) [L. *aboriri,* to miscarry] **1.** To expel an embryo or fetus prior to viability. **2.** To arrest the progress of disease. **3.** To arrest growth or development. **4.** To discontinue an effort or project before its completion.

aborted myocardial infarction   SEE: under *myocardial infarction*.

abortifacient (ă-bort-ĭ-fā'shĕnt) [*abort* + *-facient*] Anything used to cause or induce an abortion. Examples of abortifacients include prostaglandins, among other agents.

abortion (ă-bor'shŏn) [L. *abortio*] The spontaneous or induced termination of pregnancy before the fetus reaches a viable age. The legal definition of viability (usually 20 to 24 weeks) differs from state to state. Some premature neonates of less than 24 weeks or 500 g are viable. Symptoms of spontaneous abortion include abdominal cramps and vaginal bleeding, sometimes with the passage of clots or bits of tissue.

ETIOLOGY: The most common spontaneous causes are faulty development of the embryo resulting from chromosomal anomalies, abnormalities of the placenta, endocrine disturbances, acute infectious diseases, severe trauma, and shock. Other causes include problems related to the uterus, immunologic factors, and use of certain drugs.

PATIENT CARE: Assessment includes monitoring vital signs, fluid balance, and abortion status and progress. Historical data must include duration of pregnancy; Rh status; and time of onset, type, and intensity of abortion symptoms. Character and amount of vaginal bleeding are noted, and any passed tissue (embryonic or fetal) is preserved for laboratory examination. The patient is evaluated for shock, sepsis, and disseminated intravascular coagulation.

A health care professional remains with the patient as much as possible to help allay anxiety, is aware of the patient's coping mechanisms, and is alert for responses such as grief, anger, guilt, sadness, depression, relief, or happiness.

If an elective abortion or surgical completion of the abortion is needed, the procedure and expected sensations are explained, and general perioperative care is provided. If the patient is Rh negative and Coombs test negative (not isoimmune), and if the pregnancy exceeded 8 weeks' gestation, Rho(D) is administered as prescribed within 72 hr of the abortion. Prescribed fluids, oxytocics, antibiotics, and transfusions are administered as required.

After abortion, the patient is instructed to report excessive bleeding (clots greater than dime-size), pain, inflammation, or fever and to avoid intercourse, tampon use, douching, or placing anything else in the vagina until after a follow-up examination.

   complete a. An abortion in which the total products of conception have been expelled.

   elective a. Voluntary termination of a pregnancy for other than medical reasons. The procedure may be recommended when the mother's mental or physical state would be endangered by continuation of the pregnancy or when the fetus has a condition incompatible with life. It may also be performed as a result of rape, incest, or at the mother's request.

   habitual a. Three or more consecutive spontaneous abortions.

   imminent a. Impending abortion characterized by bleeding and colicky pains. The cervix is usually effaced and patulous.

   incomplete a. An abortion in which part of the products of conception has been retained in the uterus.

   induced a. The intentional termination of a pregnancy by means of dilating the cervix and evacuating the uterus. Methods used during the first trimester include cervical dilation with a laminaria tent or a cannula, vacuum aspiration, or dilation and curettage (D & C). In the second trimester, abortion may be induced with methotrexate, RU 486, prostaglandins, or the instillation of hypertonic saline into the uterus. SEE: *uterine* **curettage***; mifepristone*.

   inevitable a. An abortion that cannot be halted.

   infected a. Abortion accompanied by infection of retained fetal tissue.

   medical a. Abortion induced with a drug or drugs, e.g., the combination of mifepristone and a prostaglandin.

   missed a. Abortion in which the fetus has died before completion of the 20th week of gestation but the products of conception are retained in the uterus for 8 weeks or longer.

   partial-birth a. An abortion performed in the second or third-trimester, in which the products of conception are removed by suction curettage and forceps and the cranial contents of the fetus are evacuated before the removal of the fetus from the uterus. SYN: *dilation and evacuation*.

   septic a. Abortion in which there is an infection of the products of conception and the endometrial lining of the uterus.

   spontaneous a. Abortion occurring without apparent cause. SYN: *miscarriage*. SEE: *Nursing Diagnoses Appendix*.

   suction a. The removal of the products of conception from the uterus using a device that sucks the tissues away from the lining of the uterus.

   therapeutic a. Abortion performed when the pregnancy endangers the mother's mental or physical health or when the fetus has a known condition incompatible with life.

   threatened a. The appearance of signs and symptoms of possible loss of the fetus. Vaginal bleeding with or without intermittent pain is usually the first sign. If the fetus is still alive and attachment to the uterus has not been interrupted, the pregnancy may continue. Absolute bedrest is recommended, with avoidance of coitus, douches, stress, or cathartics.

tubal a. 1. A spontaneous abortion in which the fetus has been expelled through the distal end of the uterine tube. **2.** The escape of the products of conception into the peritoneal cavity by way of the uterine tube.

abortionist (ă-bor′shŏn-ist) One who performs an abortion.

abortive (ă-bor′tĭv) [L. *abortivus*] **1.** Preventing the completion of something. **2.** Abortifacient; that which prevents the normal continuation of pregnancy.

abortus (ă-bor′tŭs) [L. miscarriage] A fetus born before 20 weeks' gestation or weighing less than 500 g.

abrachia (ā-brā′kē-ă, -brāk′) [*a-* + *brachium*] Congenital absence of arms.

abrachiocephalia (ā-brā′kē-ō-sĕ-fāl′ē-ă) [*a-* + *brachium* + Gr. *kephalē*, head] Congenital absence of arms and head.

abradant (ă-brād′ănt) [*abrade*] An abrasive.

abrade (ă-brād′) [L. *abradere,* to scrape] **1.** To chafe. **2.** To roughen or remove by friction.

abrasion (ă-brā′zhŏn) [L. *abradere,* to scrape] **1.** Wearing away of the substance of a tooth. It usually results from mastication but may be produced by mechanical or chemical means. **2.** Scraping away of skin or mucous membrane as a result of injury or by mechanical means, as in dermabrasion for cosmetic purposes. SEE: illus.; *avulsion; bruise.*

pleural a. Mechanical **pleurodesis.**

abrasive (ă-brā′siv) [L. *abradere* , to scrape] **1.** Producing abrasion. **2.** That which abrades.

abreaction (ab″rē-ak′shŏn) [*ab-* + *reaction*] In psychoanalysis, the release of emotion by consciously recalling or acting out a painful experience that had been forgotten or repressed. The painful or consciously intolerable experience may become bearable as a result of the insight gained during this process. SEE: *catharsis* (2). **abreact** (-akt′), *v.*

abrin (ā′brin) [L. fr. Gr. *habros,* graceful, delicate + *-in*] A powerful cellular toxin derived from the seeds of the jequirty pea (*Abrus precatorius*), also called the Rosary Pea. Abrin prevents cells from making necessary proteins and may cause death or poisoning after it is inhaled, consumed, or applied to the skin.

abruptio (ă-brŭp′shē-ō) [L. *abruptio,* a breaking away] A tearing away from.

PATHOLOGY: Three types of placental abruption occur: *a. centralis:* a par-

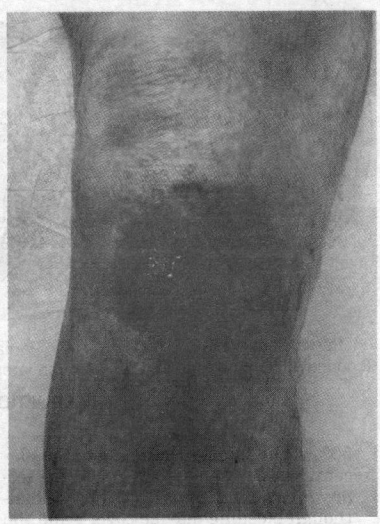

ABRASION

tial central detachment with hidden bleeding between the placenta and the uterine wall; occasionally, blood will invade the myometrium (Couvelaire uterus); *a. complete:* total placental detachment, marked by profuse vaginal bleeding, profound fetal distress, and rapid fetal demise; *a. marginalis:* partial separation of an edge of the placenta, as evidenced by vaginal bleeding. The large amount of circulating thromboplastin may cause a coagulation defect to occur, resulting in hypofibrinogenemia. SEE: *Couvelaire uterus; disseminated intravascular coagulation.*

a. placentae The sudden, premature, partial, or complete detachment of the placenta from a normal uterine site of implantation. The incidence of abruptio placentae is 1:120 births, and the risk of recurrence in later pregnancies is much higher than that for cohorts. SYN: *ablatio placentae.* SEE: illus.; *placenta.*

ETIOLOGY: The cause is unknown; however, the condition is most commonly associated with pregnancy-induced hypertension (PIH). It may occasionally be related to abdominal trauma, substance abuse (cigarette, alcohol, or cocaine), or sudden premature rupture of membranes.

SYMPTOMS: Abruptio placentae is classified according to type and severity. *Grade 1:* vaginal bleeding with possible uterine tenderness and mild tetany; neither mother nor baby is in distress; approximately 10% to 20% of placental surface is detached. *Grade 2:* uterine tenderness; tetany, with or without uterine bleeding; fetal distress; mother is not in shock. Approximately 20% to

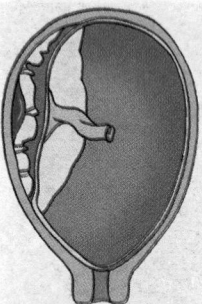 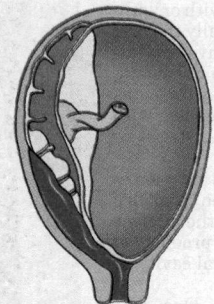 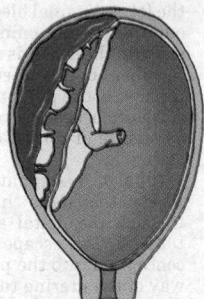

| Partial separation (concealed hemorrhage) | Partial separation (apparent hemorrhage) | Complete separation (concealed hemorrhage) |

ABRUPTIO PLACENTAE

50% of the total surface area of the placenta is detached. *Grade 3*: Uterine tetany is severe; the mother is in shock, although bleeding may be covert; and the fetus is dead. Often the patient develops coagulopathy. More than 50% of the placental surface is detached.

PATHOLOGY: Extravasation of blood occurs between the placenta and the uterine wall, occasionally between muscle fibers of the uterus. Hemorrhage can be concealed or covert, causing consumptive coagulopathy (disseminated intravascular coagulopathy).

TREATMENT: This varies with the type and extent of abruption. Women experiencing only a small marginal separation of the placenta from the uterine wall may be confined to bed and monitored closely for signs of further threat to maternal or fetal status. If prematurity also is a factor, the woman may be given betamethasone to expedite development of fetal pulmonary surfactant. If the woman is at or near term, induction of labor and vaginal delivery may be an option. SEE: *betamethasone*.

Supportive treatment and prompt surgical intervention are indicated for women who have moderate to severe abruptions. Complete detachment calls for immediate cesarean delivery, concomitant treatment of shock and, sometimes, management of a coagulation defect. The massive loss of blood jeopardizes the mother's survival; fetal mortality is 100%. If the uterus fails to contract after the surgical delivery, immediate hysterectomy may be necessary. SEE: *Couvelaire uterus*.

PROGNOSIS: Although maternal mortality is unusual, other than as noted, the perinatal mortality is between 20% and 30%.

PATIENT CARE: Early recognition and prompt management of the event and any associated complications are vital. The woman's vital signs, fundal height, uterine contractions, labor progress, and fetal status data are monitored, including heart rate and rhythm. Any changes are noted, such as prolonged decelerations in fetal heart rate or alterations in baseline variability; uterine tetany; complaints of sudden, severe abdominal pain; and the advent of or increase in vaginal bleeding. Vaginal blood loss is estimated by weighing perineal pads and subtracting the known weight of dry pads. The interval between pad changes, the character and amount of the bleeding, and the degree of pad saturation are noted. Prescribed IV fluids and medications are administered through a large-bore catheter. A central venous pressure line may be placed to provide access to the venous circulation, and an indwelling catheter is inserted to monitor urinary output and fluid balance. A calm atmosphere is maintained, and the patient's verbalization is encouraged. The patient is assisted in coping with her fears and anxiety. Questions are answered truthfully, comfort measures are implemented, and reassurance is provided as possible and consistent with the current situation and prognosis. All procedures are explained, and the woman and her family are prepared for induction of labor, vaginal delivery, or cesarean birth, as appropriate. The woman must be assured that everything is being done for the neonate's survival, which depends primarily on gestational age, blood loss, and associated hypertensive disorders. SEE: *Nursing Diagnoses Appendix.*

abs A colloquial term for the rectus abdominis muscles.

abscess (ab'ses) [L. *abscessus,* a going away] A localized collection of pus in any body part, resulting from invasion of a pyogenic bacterium or other pathogen. *Staphylococcus aureus,* e.g., methicillin-resistant *S. aureus* (MRSA), is a common cause. The abscess is surrounded by a membrane of variable strength created by macrophages, fibrin, and granulation tissue. Abscesses can disrupt function in adjacent tissues and can be life threatening in some circumstances, e.g., in the lung or within the peritoneal cavity. SEE: illus; *inflammation; pus; suppuration; Standard Precautions Appendix.*

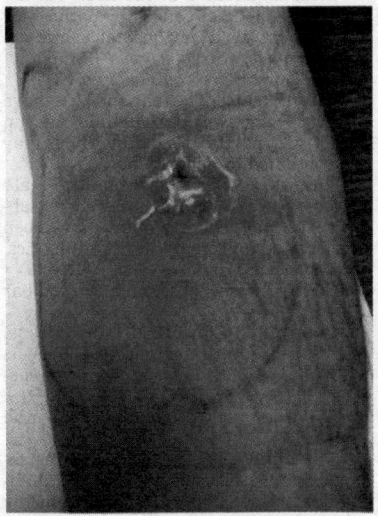

ANTECUBITAL ABSCESS

Antecubital abscess opened to allow drainage of infection

acute a. An abscess associated with significant inflammation, producing intense heat, redness, swelling, and throbbing pain. The tissue over the abscess becomes elevated, soft, and eventually unstable (fluctuant) and discolored as the abscess comes to a head (points). An abscess can rupture spontaneously or be drained via an incision. If it is left untreated, the pathogens may spread to adjacent tissues or to other parts of the body via the bloodstream. Appearance of or increase in fever may indicate sepsis.

alveolar a. An abscess around the root of a tooth in the alveolar cavity. It is usually the result of necrosis and infection of dental pulp following dental caries. SEE: *periapical a.*

amebic a. An abscess caused by *Entamoeba histolytica.* SYN: *endamebic a.*

anorectal a. An abscess in the ischiorectal fossa. It may occur in patients with Crohn disease, diabetes mellitus, or anal fissures more often than in other patients. Incision, drainage, and antibiotics usually provide effective treatment. SYN: *rectal a.*; SYN: *ischiorectal a.*

apical a. **1.** An abscess at the apex of a lung. **2.** Periapical **a.**

appendicular a. An abscess around an inflamed or ruptured vermiform appendix.

axillary a. An abscess or multiple abscesses in the axilla, e.g., in patients with hidradenitis suppurativa.

Bartholin a. SEE: under *Bartholin, Caspar (the younger).*

bicameral a. An abscess with two pockets.

bile duct a. An abscess of the bile duct. SYN: *cholangitic a.*

biliary a. An abscess of the gallbladder. It is an infrequent complication of cholangitis or obstruction of the bile duct.

bone a. **Brodie abscess.**

brain a. An intracranial abscess involving the brain or its membranes. It is seldom primary but usually occurs secondary to infections of the middle ear, nasal sinuses, face, or skull or from contamination from penetrating wounds or skull fractures. It may also have a metastatic origin arising from septic foci in the lungs (bronchiectasis, empyema, lung abscess), in bone (osteomyelitis), or in the heart (endocarditis). Infection of nerve tissue by the invading organism results in necrosis and liquefaction of the tissue, with edema of surrounding tissues. Brain abscesses may be acute, subacute, or chronic. Their clinical manifestations depend on the part of the brain involved, the size of the abscess, the virulence of the infecting organism, and other factors. SYN: *cerebral a.; intracranial a.* SEE: *Nursing Diagnoses Appendix.*

SYMPTOMS: Symptoms may include headache, fever, vomiting, malaise, irritability, seizures, or paralysis.

TREATMENT: The usual treatment is chemotherapy. Surgical drainage may be required.

breast a. Mammary **a.**

Brodie a. SEE: under *Brodie, Sir Benjamin Collins.*

bursal a. An abscess in a bursa.

canalicular a. A breast abscess that discharges into the milk ducts.

caseous a. An abscess in which the pus has a cheesy appearance.

cerebral a. Brain **a.**

cholangitic a. Biliary **a.**

chronic a. An abscess with pus but without signs of inflammation. It usually develops slowly as a result of liquefaction of tuberculous tissue. It may occur anywhere in or on the body but more frequently in the spine, hips, genitourinary tract, and lymph glands. Symptoms may be very mild. Pain, when present, is caused by pressure on surrounding parts; tenderness is often absent. Chronic septic changes accompanied by afternoon fever may occur. Amyloid disease may develop if the abscess persists for a prolonged period. SYN: *cold a.*

circumtonsillar a. Peritonsillar **a.**

cold a. Chronic **a.**

collar-button a. Two pus-containing cavities, one larger than the other, connected by a narrow channel.

dental a. An acute inflammatory infection within the maxilla or mandible. SEE: *periapical a.; periodontal a.*

dentoalveolar a. Periapical **a.**

diffuse a. An abscess not circumscribed by a well-defined capsule.

dry a. An abscess that disappears without pointing or breaking.

embolic a. Metastatic **a.**

emphysematous a. An abscess containing air or gas, produced by organisms such as *Clostridium perfringens.* SYN: *gas a.; tympanitic a.*

endamebic a. Amebic **a.**

epidural a. Extradural **a.**

extradural a. An abscess on the dura mater, an occasional cause of back pain in febrile patients, usually in those who inject drugs. SYN: *epidural a.*

fecal a. An abscess containing both pus and stool. SYN: *stercoraceous a.; stercoral a.*

filarial a. An abscess caused by parasitic infection with microfilariae.

follicular a. An abscess in a follicle.

fungal a. An abscess caused by a fungus, e.g., mycetoma. SYN: *mycotic a.*

gas a. Emphysematous **a.**

gingival a. An abscess of the gum.

helminthic a. Worm **a.**

hemorrhagic a. An abscess containing blood.

hepatic a. Liver **a.**

hot a. Acute **a.**

hypostatic a. Metastatic **a.**

idiopathic a. An abscess of unknown cause.

iliac a. An abscess in the iliac region.

iliopsoas a. An abscess in the psoas and iliacus muscles. It typically results from a local or regional spread of an intestinal or renal abscess or from a blood-borne infection, e.g., after a drug injection. SYN: *psoas a.*

intracranial a. Brain **a.**

intradural a. An abscess within the layers of the dura mater.

intraperitoneal a. Peritoneal **a.**

ischiorectal a. Anorectal **a.**

kidney a. An abscess in the kidney, typically following pyelonephritis or a blood-borne infection. The most common causative organisms are gram-negative bacteria from the lower urinary tract that spread to the kidneys and *Staphylococcus aureus* from a blood-borne infection. Immunocompromised patients may develop abscesses caused by *Nocardia, Candida,* or *Aspergillus.* Occasionally, *Mycobacterium tuberculosis* and *Echinococcus* are responsible agents. SYN: *renal a.*

TREATMENT: Antimicrobial agents are used in combination with surgical drainage. Occasionally, nephrectomy or retroperitoneal exploration is required.

lacrimal a. An abscess in a lacrimal gland or in a lacrimal duct.

lateral alveolar a. An abscess in periodontal tissue.

liver a., abscess of the liver An abscess in the liver caused by pathogenic organisms such as those of species of *Bacteroides, Streptococcus, Staphylococcus,* or *Entamoeba histolytica.*

SYMPTOMS: The patient will have high fevers; sweats and chills; and an enlarged, painful, tender liver. Pus may be obtained by aspiration.

PROGNOSIS: Embolic (multiple) abscesses are generally fatal. Liver abscesses may heal after they have been evacuated and treated with antibiotics. SEE: *hepatic a.*

lumbar a. An abscess in the lumbar region.

lung a. An abscess in lung tissue, caused by anaerobic bacteria such as *Staphylococcus aureus* or *Nocardia* species.

lymphatic a. An abscess of a lymph node.

mammary a. An abscess in the female breast, esp. one involving the glandular tissue. It usually occurs during lactation or weaning. SYN: *breast a.*

mastoid a. An abscess of the mastoid portion of the temporal bone.

metastatic a. A secondary abscess at a distance from the focus of infection. SYN: *embolic a.; hypostatic a.; wandering a.*

miliary a. Multiple small embolic abscesses.

milk a. A mammary abscess during lactation.

mycotic a. Fungal **a.**

nocardial a. An abscess caused by *Nocardia,* e.g., in the lung.

orbital a. An abscess in the orbit of the eye.

palatal a. An abscess in a maxillary tooth, erupting toward the palate.

palmar a. An abscess in the tissues of the palm of the hand.

pancreatic a. An abscess of pancreatic tissue, usually as a complication of acute pancreatitis or abdominal surgery.

parafrenal a. An abscess on the side of the frenulum of the penis.

parametric a. An abscess between the folds of the broad ligaments of the uterus.

paranephric a. An abscess in the tissues around the kidney. SYN: *perinephric a.*

parapancreatic a. An abscess in the tissues adjacent to the pancreas. SYN: *peripancreatic a.*

parietal a. A periodontal abscess

arising in the periodontal tissue other than the orifice through which the vascular supply enters the dental pulp.

parotid a. An abscess of the parotid gland.

pelvic a. An abscess of the pelvic peritoneum, esp. in the pouch of Douglas. It may arise as a complication of a sexually transmitted disease or diverticulitis.

perianal a. An abscess of the skin around the anus. It usually results from obstruction of intestinal crypts and subsequent fistula formation in the skin. SYN: *periproctic a.*

periapical a. An abscess at the apex of a tooth, usually resulting from dental caries or tooth trauma. It may be classified further as an acute periapical abscess, a chronic periapical abscess, a periapical granuloma, or a radicular cyst. SYN: *apical a.* (2); *dentoalveolar a.*

pericemental a. An alveolar abscess not involving the apex of a tooth.

pericoronal a. Pericoronitis.

peridental a. An abscess of periodontal tissue.

perinephric a. Paranephric **a.**

periodontal a. An acute or chronic abscess found in the gingiva, periodontal pockets, or periodontal ligament.

peripancreatic a. Parapancreatic **a.**

peripleuritic a. An abscess in the tissue surrounding the parietal pleura.

periproctic a. Perianal **a.**

peritoneal a. An abscess within the peritoneal cavity usually following peritonitis. It is usually caused by enteric bacteria, e.g., *Escherichia coli*, enterococci, or *Klebsiella*. SYN: *intraperitoneal a.*

peritonsillar a. An abscess of the tissue around the tonsillar capsule. Needle aspiration of the abscess, with subsequent antibiotic therapy, is an effective treatment in 90% of cases. SYN: *circumtonsillar a.*

periureteral a. An abscess in the tissue around a ureter.

periurethral a. An abscess in tissue surrounding the urethra.

perivesical a. An abscess in tissue around the urinary bladder.

pneumococcic a. An abscess due to infection with pneumococci.

premammary a. A subcutaneous or subareolar abscess of the mammary gland.

prostatic a. An abscess within the prostate gland.

protozoal a. An abscess caused by a protozoon.

psoas a. Iliopsoas **a.**

pulp a. 1. An abscess in the pulp chamber of a tooth. 2. An abscess of the tissues of the pulp of a finger.

pyemic a. A metastatic abscess, usually multiple, due to pyogenic organisms.

rectal a. Anorectal **a.**

renal a. Kidney **a.**

retrocecal a. An abscess located behind the cecum. It is an occasional, severe complication of a ruptured appendix or Crohn disease.

retromammary a. An abscess between the mammary gland and the chest wall.

retroperitoneal a. An abscess located between the peritoneum and the posterior abdominal wall. It may arise from an abscess in the kidney or from the spread of an intraperitoneal infection posteriorly.

retropharyngeal a. An abscess of the lymph nodes in the walls of the pharynx. It sometimes simulates diphtheritic pharyngitis.

ETIOLOGY: *Staphylococcus aureus* and group A hemolytic streptococcus are the most common pathogens.

SYMPTOMS: Typically, a history of pharyngitis is elicited. This is followed by high fever, dysphagia, and refusal to eat. The condition progresses to respiratory distress with hyperextension of the head ("sniffing position"), tachypnea, labored breathing, and drooling. An exquisitely tender bulge in the pharyngeal wall is usually evident.

TREATMENT: A retropharyngeal abscess, if fluctuant, should be treated with incision and drainage. If recognized before becoming fluctuant, the abscess should be treated with antibiotics, intravenously administered if the patient is unable to swallow.

retrovesical a. An abscess behind the bladder.

root a. A colloquial and veterinary term for periapical abscess.

runaround a. A colloquial term for a bacterial infection that surrounds a fingernail; a paronychia.

sacrococcygeal a. An abscess over the sacrum and coccyx.

septicemic a. An abscess resulting from septicemia.

spermatic a. An abscess of the seminiferous tubules.

spinal a. An abscess due to necrosis of a vertebra.

splenic a. An abscess of the spleen. It may arise either from the spread of infection from a neighboring organ (that is, a diverticular abscess or a ruptured gastric ulcer) or from hematogenous spread in patients with infective endocarditis.

stercoraceous a. Fecal **a.**

stercoral a. Fecal **a.**

sterile a. An abscess from which microorganisms cannot be cultivated, an occasional complication of intramuscular injection.

stitch a. An abscess formed about a stitch or suture.

streptococcal a. An abscess caused by streptococci.

subaponeurotic a. An abscess beneath an aponeurosis or fascia.

subarachnoid a. An abscess of the midlayer of the covering of the brain and spinal cord.

subareolar a. An abscess underneath the areola of the mammary gland, sometimes draining through the nipple.

subdiaphragmatic a. An abscess beneath the diaphragm, e.g., a hepatic, splenic, or interperitoneal abscess. SYN: *subphrenic a.*

subdural a. An abscess beneath the dura of the brain or spinal cord.

subfascial a. An abscess beneath the fascia.

subgaleal a. An abscess beneath the galea aponeuroticai (the epicranial aponeurosis).

subpectoral a. An abscess beneath the pectoral muscles.

subperiosteal a. A bone abscess below the periosteum.

subperitoneal a. An abscess between the parietal peritoneum and the abdominal wall.

subphrenic a. Subdiaphragmatic **a.**

subscapular a. An abscess between the serratus anterior and the posterior thoracic wall.

subungual a. An abscess beneath the fingernail. It may follow injury from a pin, needle, or splinter.

sudoriparous a. An abscess of a sweat gland.

suprahepatic a. An abscess in the suspensory ligament between the liver and the diaphragm.

syphilitic a. An abscess occurring in the tertiary stage of syphilis, esp. in bone.

thecal a. A spinal epidural abscess.

thymus a. An abscess of the thymus.

tonsillar a. Acute suppurative tonsillitis.

tooth a. Alveolar **a.**

tropical a. An amebic abscess of the liver.

tuberculous a. Chronic **a.**

tubo-ovarian a. An abscess involving both the fallopian tube and the ovary. It is typically transmitted sexually.

tympanitic a. Emphysematous **a.**

tympanocervical a. An abscess arising in the tympanum and extending to the neck.

tympanomastoid a. An abscess of both the tympanum and the mastoid.

urethral a. An abscess in the urethra.

urinary a. An abscess caused by escape of urine into the tissues.

urinous a. An abscess that contains pus and urine.

verminous a. Worm **a.**

wandering a. Metastatic **a.**

warm a. Acute **a.**

worm a. An abscess caused by or containing insect larvae, worms, or other animal parasites. SYN: *helminthic a.; verminous a.*

abscissa (ab-sis′ă) [L. *abscindere,* to cut off] The horizontal line, or x-axis, in a graph of a two-dimensional coordinate system in which perpendicular horizontal and vertical lines are used in order to provide a frame of reference. The ordinate is the vertical line, or y-axis.

abscission (ab-si′zhŏn) [L. *abscindere,* to cut off] Removal by excision.

abscopal (ab-skō′păl) Concerning the effect of radiation on tissues at some distance from the actual radiation site or target.

absence (ab′sĕns) [Fr. fr. L. *absentia*] **1.** Brief temporary loss of consciousness, as may occur in petit mal epilepsy. **2.** Lack of development of a structure.

absenteeism (ab″sĕn-tē′izm) [*absentee* + *-ism*] Prolonged or repeated absence from work, school, or assigned duties.

Absidia (ab-sid′ē-ă) A genus of pathogenic fungi of the order Phycomycetes and the family Mucoraceae.

absinthe, absinth (ab′sinth) [L. fr. Gr*apsinthion,* wormwood] A liquor containing oil of wormwood, anise, and other herbs. It is highly toxic, esp. to the nervous system.

absinthism (ab′sin-thizm) [*absinthe* + *-ism*] Deterioration of the nervous system following excessive use of absinthe.

absolute (ab′sŏ-loot′) [L. *absolvere,* to set free] **1.** Unrestricted, complete, total. **2.** Pureor highly concentrated.

absolute benefit increase ABBR: ABI. The beneficial effect of an intervention or treatment in a clinical trial. It consists of the number of events observed in the experimental cohort minus the number of events in the control group. The term is the opposite of the "absolute risk increase."

absolute refractory period SEE: under *period*.

absolute risk increase ABBR: ARI. A measure of the negative effect of an intervention or treatment in a clinical trial. It consists of the number of adverse events found in the experimental group minus the number of adverse events in the control group. It is the opposite of the "absolute benefit increase."

absorb (ăb-sorb′) [Fr. fr. L. *absorbere,* to suck in] To take in, suck up, or imbibe. SEE: *absorption; adsorb; adsorption.*

absorbance (ăb-sor′băns) **1.** In health care, the ability of a material or a tissue to absorb electromagnetic radiation, esp. ionizing radiation. **2.** In chemistry, the negative logarithm of the transmittance of radiation through a substance or solution.

absorbent (ăb-sor′bĕnt) [*absorb*] **1.** A substance that absorbs. **2.** Having the power to absorb.

absorptiometry (ăb-sorp″shē-ŏm′ĕ-trē)

[*absorptiometer*] The measurement of the dissipation of x-rays as they pass through substances (e.g., body tissues).
   dual energy x-ray a. ABBR: DEXA; DXA. A radiographic technique used to measure the average density of the mineral concentration of bone (e.g., at the femur, the heel, or the forearm). It is used primarily in the diagnosis of osteopenia and osteoporosis.
absorption (ăb-sorp′shŏn) [L. *absorptio*] **1.** The taking up of liquids by solids or of gases by solids or liquids. **2.** The taking up of light or its energy by black or colored rays. **3.** The taking up by the body of radiant energy, causing a rise in body temperature. **4.** The reduction in intensity of an x-ray photon as it passes through a substance or a beam of light as it passes through a solution (used in clinical photometry as well as nuclear methods). **5.** The passage of a substance through some surface of the body into body fluids and tissues, such as the diffusion of oxygen from the alveolar air into the blood, or the active transport of amino acids from food through the epithelium of the small intestine.
   carbohydrate a. The taking up of the monosaccharides by the brush border of the small intestine.
   colonic a. The uptake of water, electrolytes such as sodium, amino acids, and some drugs by the mucosa of the large bowel.
   cutaneous a. Absorption through the skin. SYN: *percutaneous a.*
   external a. Absorption of material by the skin and mucous membrane.
   fat a. The taking up of glycerols and fatty acids, suspended in bile salts, into the villi of the small intestine.
   gastric a. Absorption of water, alcohol, and some salts through the gastric mucosa.
   mouth a. Oral or buccal absorption of materials or medicines such as nicotine or nitroglycerin. Alkaloids are better absorbed through the oral mucosa than acidic chemicals.
   parenteral a. Absorption of fluids, electrolytes, and nutrients from a site other than the gastrointestinal tract.
   pathological a. Absorption of a substance normally excreted (e.g., urine) or of a product of disease processes (e.g., pus) into the blood or lymph.
   percutaneous a. Cutaneous **a.**
   protein a. The taking up of amino acids—singly, or linked as dipeptides or tripeptides—by the brush border of the small intestine.
   small intestinal a. The uptake of water, fatty acids, monosaccharides, amino acids, vitamins, and minerals from the lumen of the gut into the capillary networks and lacteals of the villi. The small intestine is the major site of nutrient absorption in the body.

absorption lines In spectroscopy, dark lines of the solar spectrum.
absorptive (ăb-sorp′tiv) Absorbent. **absorptively,** *adv.* **absorptiveness,** *n.*
abstinence (ăb′sti-nĕns) [Fr. fr. L. *abstinere,* to abstain] Going without something voluntarily, esp. refraining from indulgence in food, alcoholic beverages, or sexual intercourse. **abstinent,** *adj.* **abstinently,** *adv.*
abstract (ăb′străkt, ab′strakt, ab-strakt′) [L. *abstrahere,* to draw away] **1.** A summary or abridgment of an article, book, or address. **2.** Intangible.
   discharge a. Discharge summary.
abstraction (ăb-strak′shŏn) [L. *abstractio,* separation] **1.** Removal or separation of a constituent from a mixture or compound. **2.** Distraction of the mind; inattention or absent-mindedness. **3.** The process whereby thoughts and ideas are generalized and dissociated from particular concrete instances or material objects.
abulia, aboulia (ă-bū′lē-ă) [*a-* + Gr. *boulē,* will + *-ia*] **1.** Absence of or decreased ability to exercise willpower or initiative or to make decisions. **2.** A syndrome marked by slow reaction, lack of spontaneity, and brief spoken responses. It may be part of the clinical picture that accompanies injuries to or diseases of the internal capsules, basal ganglia, or frontal lobes of the brain.
abuse (ă-būs′) [L. *abusus,* wasting, misuse] **1.** Excessive or improper use, e.g., of alcohol; misuse. **2.** Injurious, pathological, or malignant treatment of another person or living thing, e.g., verbal, physical, or sexual assault.
   child a. Emotional, physical, or sexual injury to a child. It may be due either to an action or to an omission by those responsible for the child. In domestic situations in which a child is abused, it is important to examine other children and infants living in that home; about 20% will have signs of physical abuse. The examination should be done without delay. An infant or child must never be allowed to remain in an environment where abuse has occurred. SEE: *battered child syndrome; shaken baby syndrome.*
   PATIENT CARE: All health care providers, teachers, and others who work with children are responsible for identifying and reporting abusive situations as early as possible. Risks for abuse may be assessed by identifying predisposing parental, child, and environmental characteristics, but these are not by themselves predictors of actual abuse. A detailed history and thorough physical examination should be carried out. Findings should be assessed not only in comparison to known indicators of maltreatment but also in light of diseases or cultural practices that can simulate

abuse. Nurses play an important role in identifying child abuse since they often are the first health care contacts for child and family, e.g., in the emergency department, physician's office, clinic, or school.

Physical neglect may be evidenced by failure to thrive, signs of malnutrition, poor personal hygiene, dental neglect, unclean or inappropriate dress, frequent injuries from lack of supervision, enuresis, and sleep disorders.

Emotional abuse (belittling, rejection) and neglect may be suspected but are difficult to substantiate. Physical abuse is not always obvious and may be difficult to diagnose. Overt evidence of abuse includes bruises and welts, imprint burns (forming the shape of a cigarette tip or other item), immersion burns (socklike on feet and legs or donut-shaped on buttocks or genitalia), spiral fractures and dislocations of limbs, facial and rib fractures, abrasions and lacerations in various stages of healing, human bite marks (with tissue compression and contusion), and chemical poisonings. Behavioral indicators include self-stimulating behaviors; lack of social smile and stranger anxiety during infancy; withdrawal; unusual wariness; antisocial behavior (destructiveness, cruelty, stealing); being indiscriminately friendly or displaying unexpected affection; developing only superficial relationships; acting out to seek attention; being overly compliant, passive, aggressive, or demanding; delays in emotional, language, and intellectual developmental; and suicide attempts.

Symptoms in the older child include begging or stealing food, frequent school absences, vandalism, shoplifting, or substance abuse.

When sexual abuse is suspected, a thorough but gentle physical examination must be conducted. Physical indicators may include any injury to the external genitalia, anus, mouth, and throat; torn, stained, or bloody undergarments; pain on urination or recurrent urinary tract infections; pain, swelling, unusual odor, and itching of the genitalia; vaginal or penile discharge, vaginitis, venereal warts, or sexually transmitted diseases; difficulty with walking or sitting; or pregnancy in the young adolescent. In most cases, the child knows the sexual abuser; in about half the cases the abuser is a caregiver or parent.

Abuse should be suspected in the presence of physical evidence, including old injuries; conflicting stories about an accident or injury from parents or others; injury blamed on siblings or another party; injury inconsistent with the history given; a history inconsistent with the child's developmental age; a chief complaint not associated with physical evidence; inappropriate level of parental concern (absence or an exaggerated response); refusal of parents to sign for needed tests or treatments; excessive delay in seeking treatment; absence of parents for questioning; inappropriate response of the child (little or no response to pain, fear of being touched, excessive or deficient separation anxiety); previous reports of abuse in the family; and/or repeated visits to emergency facilities with injuries (this may require checking with other facilities). Suspicions may be aroused by a feeling that behaviors are "not right."

The first priority of care for the abused child is prevention of further injury. This usually involves removing the child from the abusive situation by reporting the situation to local authorities. All U.S. states and Canadian provinces have laws for mandatory reporting of such mistreatment. If evidence of abuse is supported, further action is taken. Care consistent with that for a rape victim is provided when sexual abuse is present. All needs of the abused child are considered as they would be for any other child. Caregivers act as role models for parents, helping them to relate positively to their child and fostering a therapeutic environment: there is no accusation or punishment, only concern and treatment to help parents recognize and change abusive behavior. Referral to self-help groups, resources for financial aid, improved housing, and child care are important to help families deal with overwhelming stress.

Educational programs in the prenatal period, infancy home visits, and outpatient parent groups provide opportunities for health care providers to inform families about normal growth and development and routine health care. Families can also share their concerns, gain support from others, and obtain referrals to appropriate services when needs are identified. Prevention of sexual abuse focuses on teaching children about their bodies, their right to privacy, and their right to say no. Parents and school nurses can discuss such topics with children, using "what if" questions to explore potentially dangerous situations. Everyone ought to know that "nice" people can be sexual abusers and that a change in a child's behavior toward a person requires investigation. The child must always be reassured that whatever happened was not his or her fault. Prevention of false accusations is also important. Caregivers play an important role by carefully documenting all evidence of abuse and recording exactly what they observed on examination and what behaviors occurred without interpreting their meaning.

For further information on abuse or reporting abuse, contact: U.S. Department of Health and Human Services Children's Bureau: Childhelp USA's National Child Abuse Hotline at 1-800-4 A CHILD (http:/ /www.acf.dhhs.gov/programs/cb/); Prevent Child Abuse America at 1-800-CHIL-DREN or 312-663-3520 (http://www .preventchildabuse.org); or National Clearinghouse on Child Abuse and Neglect Information at 1-800-394-3366 or 703-385-7565 (http://nccanch.acf.hhs.gov).

domestic a. Abuse of people in a domestic setting. Such abuse includes physical violence (such as striking or raping a family member), passive abuse (such as withholding access to health care), psychological or emotional abuse (such as intimidation, or threatening physical harm or abandonment), and economic abuse by imposing financial dependency. Domestic abuse is common: more than two million Americans are abused or assaulted each year.

PATIENT CARE: Domestic violence should be considered in any patient who presenting with unexplained bruises, lacerations, burns, fractures, or multiple injuries in various stages of healing, esp. in areas normally covered by clothing; delays seeking treatment for an injury; has a partner who is reluctant to leave the patient alone or is uncooperative or domineering; indicates that he or she has a psychiatric history or drug or alcohol problems; presents with injuries inconsistent with the "accident" reported; expresses fear about returning home or for the safety of children in the home; or talks about harming himself or herself. Professional health care providers should screen such patients privately to ensure confidentiality and patient safety. "Do you feel safe at home?" may elicit a history of abuse. A sympathetic and nonjudgmental manner helps victims communicate. Scrupulous documentation of evidence of abuse is critical. Reporting is mandatory in many states.

drug a. The use or overuse, usually by self-administration, of any drug in a manner that deviates from the prescribed pattern.

Health care workers, many of whom have easy access to narcotics, are at high risk of abusing analgesics. Increased awareness of this problem has led hospitals to establish special programs for identifying these individuals, esp. physicians, nurses, and pharmacists, in order to provide support and education in an attempt to control the problem and prevent loss of license.

In the U.S., the abuse or misuse of prescription drugs has been identified by the Centers for Disease Control and Prevention (CDC) as a growing problem. In 2007, for example, the CDC reported that more than 27,500 Americans died of drug overdose, an increase of more than 100% in the preceding ten years. More than five times as many people died from misuse of prescribed opioids as from heroin.

elder a. Abuse of someone over 65. It includes physical violence, financial exploitation, intimidation, humiliation, isolation, and neglect. Elders may be exploited by individuals and organizations. SYN: *elder mistreatment*.

PATIENT CARE: The assessment of older people thought to have been abused includes looking for evidence of impairment in caregiver relationships to the aged and in finding unusual patterns of injuries or illnesses unlikely to occur from disease. When abuse is suspected, questions such as "Do you feel safe and well cared for at home?" or "Has someone hurt you?" or "Did someone do this to you?" may elicit a history of abuse if the patient is mentally competent. Careful documentation of historical and physical findings (including discrepancies between patient and caregiver reports) and notification of legal authorities (such as a local adult protective services agency, long-term-care ombudsman, or the police) are mandated in most jurisdictions. Resources for health care providers include the National Center on Elder Abuse Phone (202-898-2586; www .elderabusecenter.org); Adult Protective Services (www.elderabusecenter.org/ default.cfm?p=apsstate.cfm); The National Long Term Care Ombudsman Resource Center (202-332-2275; www .ltcombudsman.org); The U.S. Administration on Aging Elder Care Locator (1-800-677-1116; www.eldercare.gov/Eldercare/Public/Home.asp).

Health care providers can also help the elderly by educating them about the potential for abuse (such as in community education and outreach programs), explaining that abuse can be physical, emotional, or financial, and that even people who appear to be kind can be abusive. Talking points include recommendations that the elderly remain active and engaged with others in the community and that they get help and representation from ombudsmen or family lawyers who can be trusted to represent their interests.

fiduciary a. Unlawful appropriation and misuse of money held in custody on behalf of a dependent.

inhalant a. The deliberate inhalation of dusts, gases, gasolines, paints, solvents or other chemicals in order to alter perception or consciousness. Many inhalants used for this purpose may damage the upper or lower respiratory tracts or cause brief or long-lasting injuries to the central nervous system.

laxative a. The ingestion of cathartic drugs to relieve perceived constipation when none is present or to prevent the absorption of nutrients, e.g., in bulimia. Patients who consume excessive quantities of laxatives may complain of chronic diarrhea or may present with illnesses caused by electrolyte deficiencies.

psychoactive substance a. Substance **a.**

sexual a. Fondling, rape, sexual assault, or sexual molestation. The abuser may be a male or female, adult or child. The victim may be of the same sex or the opposite sex as the abuser. SEE: *incest; rape.*

spouse a. Emotional, physical, or sexual mistreatment of one's spouse.

substance a. A maladaptive pattern of behavior marked by the use of chemically active agents, e.g., prescription or illicit drugs, alcohol, and tobacco. Substance abuse is pervasive and causes half of all annual deaths in the U.S. About 33% of Americans smoke cigarettes, 6% use illicit drugs regularly, and about 14% are alcoholics. The consequences of substance abuse include heart disease, cancer, stroke, chronic obstructive lung disease, cirrhosis, trauma, and familial, social, legal, and economic difficulties. SYN: *chemical dependence; psychoactive substance a.* SEE: *alcoholism; drug dependence; nicotine; tobacco; Nursing Diagnoses Appendix.*

vocal a. Any activity that traumatizes the vocal folds and alters speech quality and production, e.g., yelling, forceful coughing, or inducing vomiting.

abutment (ă-bŭt′mĕnt) [Fr. *abouter,* to place end to end] **1.** A structure that provides support for fixed restorations and prosthetic devices. Examples of dental abutments include natural teeth and implants. **2.** In dentistry, natural teeth or implants serving to support fixed restorations (bridges or prosthetic devices).

ABVD A*(driamycin),* b*(leomycin),* v*(inblastine),* and d*(acarbazine),* a combination of chemotherapeutic agents for treating Hodgkin's lymphoma.

abzyme (ab′zīm″) [*ab,* abbr. for *antibody* + *(en)zyme*] A monoclonal antibody that acts as a catalyst. SYN: *catalytic antibody; catmab.*

AC *acromioclavicular; adrenal cortex; air conduction; alternating current; anodal closure; axiocervical.*

Ac Symbol for the element actinium.

-ac [L. *-acus,* Gr. *-akos,* adj. suffix] **1.** A variant of the suffix *-ic,* used with Greek nouns whose stems end in *-i,* e.g., *cardiac,* from *cardi-* and *maniac,* from *mani-.* **2.** In pharmacology, a suffix designating an anti-inflammatory drug derived from acetic acid.

a.c. L. *ante cibum,* before meals.

acacia (ă-kā′shē-ă) [L. fr. Gr. *akakia,* Egyptian thorn] Gum arabic. A dried gummy exudation from the tree *Acacia senegal,* it is used as a suspending agent in pharmaceutical products.

academic dishonesty Intentional participation in deceptive practices in one's academic work or the work of others. Examples include cheating, fraud, plagiarism, or falsification of research results.

acalculia (ā″kal-kū′lē-ă) [*a-* + L. *calculare,* to reckon] A learning or speech disorder characterized by the inability to perform simple arithmetic operations.

acampsia (ă-kamp′sē-ă) [*a-* + Gr. *kamptein,* to bend] Inflexibility of the joints of a limb; rigidity; ankylosis.

acantha (ă-kan′thă) [Gr. *akantha,* thorn] **1.** The spine. **2.** A vertebral spinous process.

acanthamebiasis (ă-kan″thă-mē-bī′ă-sis) [*acanth-* + *amebiasis*] A rare infection of the brain and meninges caused by free-living amebae. The organisms invade the nasal mucosa of persons swimming in fresh water, the natural habitat of *Acanthamoeba* and *Naegleria fowleri.* The organisms invade the central nervous system through the olfactory foramina. The symptoms begin after an incubation period of 2 to 15 days and are those of acute meningitis. Debilitated or immunocompromised persons are esp. susceptible. Diagnosis is made by finding the amebae in the spinal fluid. Treatment is virtually ineffective and most patients die within a week of onset. Swimming pools adequately treated with chlorine are not a source of the amebae. SEE: *meningoencephalitis, primary amebic.*

acanthesthesia (ă-kan″thes-thē′zē-ă) [*acanth-* + *-esthesia*] A sensation as of a pinprick; a form of paresthesia.

acanthion (ă-kan′thē-on″, -ŏn) [Gr. *akanthion,* little thorn] The tip of the anterior nasal spine.

acantho-, acanth- [Gr. *akantha,* thorn] Combining forms meaning *thorn, spine.*

Acanthocephala (ă-kan″thŏ-sef′ă-lă) [*acantho-* + Gr. *kephalē,* head] A phylum of parasitic worms. Their usual hosts are fish and birds. SYN: *proboscis worms; spiny-headed worms; thorny-headed worms.*

acanthocyte (ă-kan′thŏ-sīt″) [*acantho-* + *-cyte*] An abnormal red blood cell with spines or thorns sticking out from its cell membrane.

acanthocytosis (ă-kan″thŏ-sī-tō′sĭs) [*acanthocyte* + *-osis*] Acanthocytes in the blood.

acanthoid (ă-kan′thoyd″) [*acanth-* + *-oid*] Thorny; spiny.

acanthokeratodermia (ă-kan″thŏ-ker″ă-tō-dĕr′mē-ă) [*acantho-* + *kerato-derma*] Hypertrophy of the horny portion of the skin of the palms of the hands and soles of the feet and thickening of the nails.

acantholysis (ak″an″thol′ĭ-sis) [*acantho-* + *-lysis*] Any disease of the skin accompanied by degeneration of the cohesive elements of the cells of the outer or horny layer of the skin.

acanthoma (ak″an″thō′mă) [*acanth-* + *-oma*] A benign tumor of the skin. It was previously used to denote skin cancer.

   a. adenoides cysticum (ad″ĕn-o′ĭ-dēz sis′tĭ-kŭm) A cystic tumor, often familial, occurring on the chest and face and in the axillary regions. The tumor contains tissues resembling sweat glands and hair follicles. SYN: *epithelioma adenoides cysticum.*

acanthopelvis (ă-kan″thŏ-pel′vis) [*acantho-* + *pelvis*] A prominent and sharp pubic spine on a rachitic pelvis. SYN: *acanthopelyx.*

acanthopelyx (ă-kan″thŏ-pel′iks) [*acantho-* + Gr. *pelyx,* wooden bowl, pelvis] Acanthopelvis.

acanthosis (ak″an″-thō′sis) [*acantho-* + *-sis*] Increased thickness of the prickle cell layer of the skin. **acanthotic** (ak″an″thot′ik), *adj.*

   a. nigricans A skin disorder in which dark brown or gray velvety plaques appear on the skin, typically under the arms, in the groin or upper thighs, on the neck, or near the genitalia. They usually appear in patients with relative insulin excess, such as adults with obesity, type 2 diabetes mellitus, or polycystic ovaries. The condition may rarely be associated with internal malignancy. SYN: *keratosis nigricans.*

   a. palmaris Tripe palm.

acarbia (ă-kar′bē-ă, ā″) [*a-* + L. *carbo,* charcoal + *-ia*] Decrease of bicarbonate in the blood.

acardia (ā″kar′dē-ă) [*a-* + Gr. *kardia,* heart] Congenital absence of the heart (e.g., in a monozygotic twin supported by the circulatory system of the other fetus). **acardiac** (ā″kar′dē-ak), *adj.*

acariasis (ak″ă-rī′ă-sis) [*acarus* + *-iasis*] Any disease caused by a mite or acarid. SYN: *acarinosis; acaridiasis.*

   demodectic a. Infection of hair follicles with *Demodex folliculorum.*

   sarcoptic a. Infestation with a burrowing mite, *Sarcoptes scabiei,* which deposits its eggs in the burrows. SEE: *scabies.*

acaricide (ă-kar′ĭ-sīd″) [*acarus* + *-cide*] **1.** An agent that destroys acarids. **2.** Destroying a member of the order Acarina. **acaricidal** (-sīd′ăl), *adj.*

acarid, acaridan (ak′ă-rĭd, ă-kar′ĭ-dăn) [*acarus*] A tick or mite of the order Acarina.

Acaridae (ă-kar′ĭ-dē) [*acarus*] A family of mites that irritate the skin. SEE: *itch, grain; itch, grocer's.*

acaridiasis (ak″ă-rĭ-dī′ă-sis) [*acarus* + *¹-id* + *-iasis*] Acariasis.

Acarina (ak″ă-rī′nă, rē′) [*acarus*] An order of arachnids that includes many ticks and mites. Most are ectoparasites whose bites or burrowing cause localized dermatitis and itching. Systemic reactions are rare. Some may be vectors of disease. SEE: *Ixodidae; Lyme disease; Sarcoptidae; scabies; tick.*

acarinosis (ă-kăr″ĭ-nō′sĭs) Acariasis.

acarodermatitis (ak″ă-rō-dĕr″mă-tī′tis) [*acarus* + *dermatitis*] Skin inflammation caused by a mite.

acaroid (ak′ă-royd″) [*acarus* + *-oid*] Resembling a mite.

acarology (ak″ă-rol′ō-jē) [*acarus* + *-ogy*] The study of mites and ticks.

acarophobia (ak″ă-rō-fō′bē-ă) [*acarus* + *-phobia*] Abnormal fear of small objects such as pins, needles, worms, mites, and small insects.

Acarus (ak′ă-rŭs) [L., mite] A genus of mites.

   A. folliculorum **Demodex** folliculorum.

   A. scabiei **Sarcoptes** scabiei. SEE: *Sarcoptes; scabies; Sarcoptidae.*

acarus Any mite or tick.

acatalasemia (ā″kat″ă-lă-sē′mē-ă) [*a-* + *catalase* + *-emia*] Acatalasia.

acatalasia (ā″kat-ă-lā′zh(ē-)ă) [*a-* + *catalase* + *-ia*] A rare inherited disease in which there is an absence of the enzyme catalase. The gingival and oral tissues are particularly susceptible to bacterial invasion with subsequent gangrenous changes and alveolar bone destruction. SYN: *acatalasemia.*

acatastasia (ā″kat-ă-stā′zh(ē-)ă) [Gr. *akatastasis,* disorder] Irregularity; deviation from the normal.

accelerated death benefit Accelerated living benefit.

accelerated drug approval The bringing of a drug to market more rapidly than most other drugs, typically because the drug serves a compelling public health interest.

accelerated living benefit Payments from a life insurance policy maker to the beneficiary before the insured person's death to help defray medical expenses that arise during a terminal illness. SYN: *accelerated death benefit; living needs benefit.*

acceleration (ak-sel″ĕ-rā′shŏn) [L. *accelerare,* to speed up] **1.** An increase in the speed of an action or function, such as pulse or respiration. **2.** The rate of change in velocity for a given unit of time.

   angular a. Rate of change in velocity per unit of time during circular movement.

   central a. Centripetal **a.**

centripetal a. Rate of change in velocity per unit of time while on a circular or curved course. SYN: *central a.*

fetal heart rate a. **1.** The increase in heart rate associated with fetal movement. **2.** A reassuring sign during labor that the fetus is not experiencing intrauterine hypoxemia.

linear a. Rate of change in velocity per unit of time while on a straight course.

negative a. Decrease in the rate of change in velocity per unit of time.

positive a. Increase in the rate of change in velocity per unit of time.

standard a. of free fall The rate of change in velocity of a freely falling body as it is acted on by gravity to travel to the earth. It is 9.81 m (or 32.17 ft)/sec^2.

acceleration fractionation SEE: under *fractionation.*

accelerator (ak-sel′ĕ-rā″tŏr) [L. *accelerare,* to speed up] **1.** Anything that increases action or function. **2.** In chemistry, a catalyst. **3.** A device that speeds up charged particles to high energy levels to produce x-radiation and neutrons.

accelerometer (ak″sel-ĕ-rom′ĕ-tĕr) [*acceler(ation)* + *-meter*] An instrument that detects a change in the velocity of the object to which it is attached. The device may be designed to record the changes and indicate the direction(s) of the acceleration.

acceptable daily intake (ak-sep′tă-bl) [L. *acceptabilis*] ABBR: ADI. That quantity of chemical residue contained in food and thought to be harmless even when consumed daily for life. The chemical residue may be a food additive, e.g., a preservative, or an antibiotic, antifungal, or a small quantity of pesticide. ADIs apply solely to residues of chemicals used intentionally by agricultural businesses in food production. ADI is expressed as mg/kg (bw)/d (milligrams of residue per kilogram body weight per day). Chemicals that enter the human food supply unintentionally are called contaminants, not residues.

acceptance (ak-sep′tăns) **1.** According to Dr. Elisabeth Kübler-Ross, the fifth and final stage of dying. Individuals who reach this stage (not all do) come to terms with impending death and await the end with quiet expectation. **2.** In organ transplantation, the harmonious integration of grafted tissue into the body of the transplant recipient. **3.** Approval or acquiescence (e.g., of a recommended treatment or a functional impairment produced by an illness).

acceptor (ak-sep′tŏr) [L. *accipere,* to accept] A compound that unites with a substance freed by another compound, called a donor.

hydrogen a. A substance that combines with hydrogen and is reduced

when a substrate is oxidized by an enzyme.

oxygen a. A substance that combines with oxygen and is oxidized when a substrate is reduced by an enzyme.

access (ak′ses) [Fr. fr. L. *accedere,* to approach] **1.** The ability or the technique of obtaining data from a specific source by a specific user. **2.** The ability of patients to see their health care providers in a timely fashion. **3.** A device, such as a catheter used in hemodialysis, that penetrates the body and is used for a therapeutic purpose.

accessible (ak-ses′ĭ-bĕl) [L. *accedere,* to approach] **1.** Able to be used or entered. In the U.S., under the requirements of the Americans with Disabilities Act (ADA), public places and places of employment must be accessible to individuals with disabilities through architectural design (such as ramps, wheelchair-wide doorways) and/or the use of assistive technologies. SEE: *barrier-free design.*

2. In surgery or clinical laboratory science, easy to obtain. It is said of blood or some body fluids (such as saliva), or tissue samples. **3.** In clinical medicine, easy to approach or to obtain an appointment with.

accessory (ak-ses′ŏ-rē) [*accessorius*] Auxiliary; assisting. This term is applied to a lesser structure that resembles in structure and function a similar organ.

accessory muscle of respiration Any of the muscles that are recruited to increase ventilation by patients with labored breathing. The sternocleidomastoids, scalenes, and pectoralis minors may be used for a more forceful inhalation; the abdominal muscles may be used for a more forceful exhalation. Their use represents an abnormal or labored breathing pattern and is a sign of respiratory distress.

accident (ak′sĭ-dĕnt) [L. *accidere,* to happen] **1.** An unforeseen, unfortunate occurrence. **2.** An unexpected complication of a disease or treatment. **accidental** (-den′tăl), *adj.*; **accidentally,** *adv.*

cerebrovascular a. ABBR: CVA. Stroke.

radiation a. Undesired excessive exposure to ionizing radiation.

accident-prone Frequently injured or at risk for traumatic injury. The validity of this concept is questionable.

acclimation (ak″lĭ-mā′shŏn) [Fr. *acclimater,* acclimate] The act of becoming adapted and adjusted to a new or unfamiliar environment. SYN: *acclimatization.* **acclimate** (ak′lĭ-māt″), *v.*

acclimatization (ă-klī″măt-ĭ-zā′shŏn) Acclimation.

a. to heat The adjustment of an organism to heat in the environment. Ex-posture to high environmental temperature requires a period of adjustment in order for the body to function efficiently. The amount of time required depends on the temperature, humidity, and duration of daily exposure. Significant physiological adjustments occur in 5 days and are completed within 2 weeks to a month. **acclimatize** (ă-klī′mă-tīz″), v.

accommodating intraocular lens SEE: under *lens*.

accommodation (ă-kom″ă-dā′shŏn) [L. *accommodare,* to suit] ABBR: a; acc. **1.** Adjustment or adaptation. **2.** In ophthalmology, a phenomenon noted in receptors in which continued stimulation fails to elicit a sensation or response. **3.** The adjustment of the eye for various distances whereby it is able to focus the image of an object on the retina by changing the curvature of the lens. In accommodation for near vision, the ciliary muscle contracts, causing increased rounding of the lens, the pupil contracts, and the optic axes converge. These three actions constitute the accommodation reflex. The ability of the eye to accommodate decreases with age. SYN: *ocular accommodation; visual accommodation.* SEE: illus. **4.** In the learning theory of Jean Piaget, the process through which a person's schema of understanding incorporates new experiences that do not fit existing ways of understanding the world. SEE: *adaptation.*

absolute a. Accommodation of one eye independently of the other.

binocular a. Coordinated accommodation of both eyes jointly.

excessive a. Greater-than-needed accommodation of the eye.

mechanism a. A method by which curvature of the eye lens is changed in order to focus close objects on the retina.

negative a. Relaxation of the ciliary muscle to adjust for distant vision.

ocular a. Accommodation (3).

positive a. Contraction of the ciliary muscle to adjust for near vision.

reasonable a. An employer's responsibility to provide necessary workplace changes in reassignment, equipment modification, devices, training materials, interpreters, and other adjustments for disabled employees.

relative a. The extent to which ac-

commodation is possible for any specific state of convergence of the eyes.

subnormal a. Insufficient accommodation.

visual a. Accommodation (3).

accommodative/convergence accommodation ratio (ă-kom′ŏ-dāt″ĭv) ABBR: A/CA. The amount of inward turning of the eyes that accompanies each diopter of accommodation. Normally the A/CA ratio is 1:4 or 1:5.

accommodative excess (ă-kom′ŏ-dāt″ĭv) Overfocusing of the eye. It causes blurry vision when one views distant objects.

accommodative fatigue (ă-kom′ŏ-dāt″ĭv) SEE: under *fatigue*.

accommodative inertia (ă-kom′ŏ-dāt″ĭv) SEE: under *inertia*.

accountability (ă-kown″tă-bil′ĭ-tē) Responsibility of health care professionals for their decisions, judgments, and acts.

ACCP *American College of Chest Physicians.*

accreditation (ă-kre″ĭ-tā′shŏn) [L. *accredere,* to give credence to] Formal recognition by an impartial body that an educational faculty or health care institution has met established quality benchmarks. In the U.S. there are two types of educational accreditation: institutional and specialized. The former recognizes the institution for having facilities, policies, and procedures that meet accepted standards. The latter recognizes specific programs of study within institutions for having met established standards.

Accredited Record Technician ABBR: A.R.T. A person who, as a result of training and experience, is competent to process, maintain in a secure place, compile, and report information in a patient's medical record. This is done according to rules set by the health care facility to comply with medical, administrative, ethical, legal, and accreditation considerations.

accretio (ă-krē′sh(ē-)ō) [L. growth] Adhesion of parts normally separate from each other.

accretion (ă-krē′shŏn) [*accretio*] **1.** An increase by external addition; accumulation. **2.** The growing together of parts naturally separate. **3.** Accumulation of foreign matter in a cavity. **accretionary** (-shŏ-ner″ē), *adj.*

acculturation (ă-kŭl″chŭ-rā′shŏn) The process by which a member of one cul-

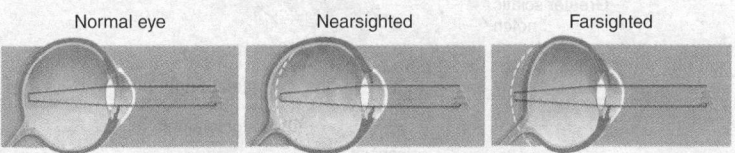

Normal eye   Nearsighted   Farsighted

VISUAL ACCOMMODATION

ture assumes the values, attitudes, and behavior of another. **acculturate** (rāt″), *v.*; **acculturational** (shŏ-năl), *adj.*; **acculturative** (ă-kul′chŭ-rā″tiv), *adj.*

accumulate (ă-kūm′yŭ-lāt″) [L. *accumulare*, to pile up] **1.** To grow in number or mass. **2.** To store or incorporate.

Accupril (ak′yŭ-pril″) Quinapril.

accuracy (a″kyŭ-ră-sē) [L. *accurare*, to take care of] **1.** The ratio of the error of measurement to the true value. **2.** The state of being free of error. **3.** The sum of the true-positive and true-negative test results, divided by the total number of tests performed.

ACD sol Citric acid, trisodium citrate, dextrose solution; an anticoagulant used in collecting blood.

ACE *Adriamycin (doxorubicin), cyclophosphamide, etoposide* (a regimen of chemotherapeutic drugs used to treat small cell lung cancer); *angiotensin-converting enzyme.*

-aceae [Feminine pl. of L. adjectival suffix-*aceus*] Suffix used in formation of names of plant families, e.g., *Solanaceae*.

acellular (ā-sel′yŭ-lăr) [¹*an-* + *cellular*] **1.** Not containing cells. **2.** Having cellular antigens, but no whole cells. The term is used to describe some vaccines.

acentric (ā″sen′trik) [²*an-* + L. fr. Gr. *kentron*, needle, pivot point, center] **1.** Not central; peripheral. **2.** In genetics, lacking a centromere.

ACEP *American College of Emergency Physicians.*

acephalia, acephalism (ā″sĕ-fāl′yă, ā″sef′ă-lizm) [*a-* + *cephalo-*, head] Congenital absence of the head.

acephalocardia (ā″sef″ă-lō-kar′dē-ă)

[*acephal(ia)* + *cardio-* + *-ia*] Congenital absence of the head and heart.

acephalochiria (ā″sef″ă-lō-kī′rē-ă) [*acephal(ia)* + *cheiro-* + *-ia*] Congenital absence of the head and hands.

acephalocyst (ā″sef″ă-lō-sist″) [*acephal(ia)* + *cyst*] A sterile hydatid cyst.

acephalopodia (ā″sef″ă-lō-pō′dē-ă) [*acephal(ia)* + *pod-* + *-ia*] Congenital absence of the head and feet.

acephalostomia (ā″sef″ă-lō-stō′mē-ă) [*acephal(ia)* + *stoma* + *-ia*] Congenital absence of the head. An opening resembling a mouth is present on the superior portion of the body.

acephalothoracia (ā″sef″ă-lō-thō-rā′sē-ă) [*acephal(ia)* + *thorac-* + *-ia*] Congenital absence of the head and chest.

acephalus (ā″sef″ă-lŭs) [*a-* + *cephalo-*] A fetus lacking a head.

acetabulectomy (as″ĕ-tab″yŭ-lek′tŏ-mē) [*acetabul(um)* + *-ectomy*] Surgical removal of the acetabulum.

acetabuloplasty (as″ĕ-tab″yŭ-lō-plas″tē) [*acetabul(um)* + *-plasty*] Surgical repair or reconstruction of the acetabulum.

acetabulum (as″ĕ-tab′ū-lŭm) [L., a little saucer for vinegar] The cavity or depression on the lateral surface of the innominate bone (hip bone). This bone is composed of the three bones ilium, ischium, and pubis, and provides the socket into which the head of the femur fits. **acetabular** (-lăr), *adj.* SEE: illus.

acetal (as′ĕ-tăl″) [L. *acetum*, vinegar + *-al*] Chemical combination of an aldehyde with alcohol.

acetaldehyde (as″ĕ-tal′dĕ-hīd″) [L. *acetum*, vinegar + *aldehyde*] CH_3CHO; an intermediate in yeast fermentation

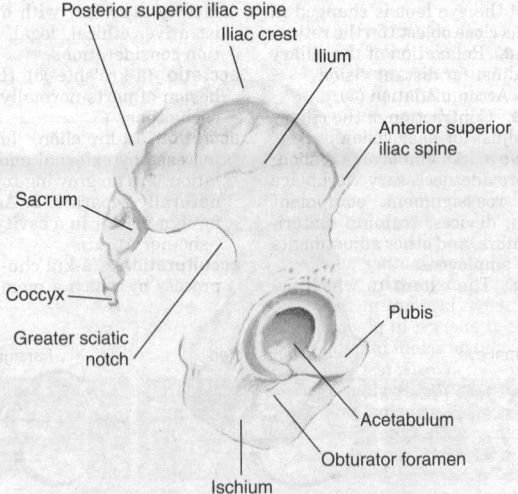

ACETABULUM OF RIGHT HIP BONE (FEMALE)

Posterior superior iliac spine

Iliac crest

Ilium

Anterior superior iliac spine

Sacrum

Coccyx

Greater sciatic notch

Pubis

Acetabulum

Ischium

Obturator foramen

and alcohol metabolism. SYN: *acetic aldehyde.*

acetamide (ă″set-ă-m′īd″, as″ĕt-am′īd″) [L. *acetum,* vinegar + *amide*] Acetic acid amide, CH_3CONH_2, used in industry for synthesis of chemicals and as a solvent.

acetaminophen (ă-sĕt″ă-min′ŏ-fĕn, as″ĕt-) [Abbr. of *N-acetyl-p-aminophenol*] ABBR: APAP. $C_8H_9NO_2$, a crystalline substance with antipyretic and analgesic effects like those of aspirin but with limited anti-inflammatory or antirheumatic effects. It is used to treat mild to moderate pain. Unlike aspirin and related drugs, it does not irritate the stomach.

⚠ Overdose may cause necrosis of the liver or fulminant hepatic failure. An acetaminophen level should routinely be checked on all patients who come to an emergency department because of medication overdose.

acetanilid, acetanilide (as″ĕ-tan′ĭl-ĭd, -īd″, as″ĕ-tan′ĭl′ĭd″) [L. *acetum,* vinegar + *anilide*] A white powder or crystalline substance obtained by interaction of glacial acetic acid and aniline.
   ACTION/USES: Acetanilid has analgesic, antipyretic, and anti-inflammatory effects. Acute or chronic poisoning may develop as a result of prolonged administration or drug idiosyncrasy. Because of its toxicity, it is rarely used.

acetate (as′ĕ-tāt′) A salt of acetic acid.

acetic (ă-sĕt′ik) [L. *acetum,* vinegar + *-ic*] Pert. to vinegar; sour.

acetic aldehyde Acetaldehyde.

aceto-, acet- [L. *acetum,* vinegar] Prefixes meaning *vinegar, acetic acid, acetyl group.*

Acetobacter (ă-sēt″ō-bak′tĕr) [L. *acetum,* vinegar, + Gr. *bakterion,* little rod] A genus of gram-negative bacilli that produce vinegar from plant matter.

acetone (as′ĕ-tōn″) [*aceto-* + *-one*] Dimethyl ketone, C_3H_6O, a colorless, volatile solvent produced by the body in excessive amounts in diabetic ketoacidosis, alcoholic ketoacidosis, and starvation. It has a sweet, fruity odor and is found in the blood and urine of diabetics, in those with other metabolic disorders, and after lengthy fasting. It is produced when fats are metabolized for their stored energy, in place of sugars, because of insufficient insulin. SEE: *ketone; ketonuria; ketosis; test, acetone.*
   a. in urine, test for A simple urine screening test, used principally in monitoring patients with type 1 diabetes mellitus, to determine the presence of ketoacidosis. To perform the test, the patient wets a specially treated paper or dipstick with urine. If ketones are present, the paper will change color within a specified time.

acetone body SEE: under *body.*

acetonemia (as″ĕ-tō-nē′mē-ă) [*acetone* + *-emia*] An excess of acetone in the blood. It causes altered mental status, abdominal pain, and anorexia.

acetone test A test for the presence of acetone in the urine; made by dribbling urine on a dipstick. The presence of acetone causes a color change on the dipstick, which can be compared to calibrated standards.

acetonitrile (as″ĕ-tō-nī′trĭl, ă-sĕt′ō) [*aceto-* + *nitrile*] Methyl cyanide, CH_3CN, an ingredient of some commercially available nail care products. When ingested, it produces a toxic reaction similar to cyanide poisoning. The onset is delayed 9 to 12 hr or more. It is also found in the urine of cigarette smokers. Treatment for poisoning is the same as for cyanide poisoning. SEE: *cotinine; cyanide poisoning.*

acetonuria (as″ĕ-tō-noor′ē-ă, -nūr′) [*acetone* + *-uria*] Ketonuria.

acetowhite test (ă-sēt′-ŏ-hwīt″) A means of examining a genital or anal lesion for the presence of human papillomavirus infection and atypical cells suggestive of cancer. The lesion (e.g., an irregularity on the surface of the uterine cervix or a wart found on the penis) is coated with 5% acetic acid. The epithelium is then examined for a change in color (e.g., from pink or red to white). This color change in the presence of acetic acid suggests a pathologically significant lesion that may require biopsy or other intervention.

acetyl (as′ĕt-ĭl, ă-sĕt′ĭl) [*aceto-* + *-yl*] CH_3CO, a univalent radical.
   a. CoA Acetylcoenzyme A.
   a.L-carnitine A dietary supplement (a form of L-carnitine) promoted for its positive effects on fat (esp. triglyceride) metabolism and Alzheimer's disease.

acetylation (ă-sĕt″ĭ-lā′shŏn) [*acetyl*] The introduction of one or more acetyl groups into an organic compound.

acetylcholine (ă-sĕt″ĭl-kō′lēn″) [*acetyl* + *choline*] ABBR: ACh. An ester of choline that is the neurotransmitter at somatic neuromuscular junctions, the entire parasympathetic nervous system, sympathetic preganglionic fibers (cholinergic fibers), and at some synapses in the central nervous system. It is inactivated by the enzyme cholinesterase. SEE: *cholinergic fiber.*
   a. chloride A salt solution of acetylcholine used in irrigation of the iris to produce contraction of the pupil after cataract surgery. The sterile solution is instilled in the anterior chamber of the eye before suturing.

acetylcholinesterase (ă-sĕt″ĭl-kō″lĭ-nes′tĕ-rās″) [*acetyl* + *cholinesterase*] ABBR: AChE. An enzyme that stops the action of acetylcholine. It is present in various body tissues, including muscles, nerve cells, and red blood cells.

acetylcoenzyme A (ă-sēt″ĭl-kō″ĕn′zīm″) [*acetyl* + *coenzyme*] A condensation product of coenzyme A and acetic acid.

acetylene (ă-set′ĭl-ēn″, ĭl-ĕn) [*acetyl* + *-ene*] C_2H_2, a colorless explosive gas, with a garlic-like odor, used as a fuel in welding. Its systematic name is ethyne. It is an asphixiant.

acetyltransferase (ă-sēt″ĭl-trans′fĕr-ās″) [*acetyl* + *transferase*] An enzyme that is effective in the transfer of an acetyl group from one compound to another.

ACGME *Accreditation Council for Graduate Medical Education.*

ACH *adrenocortical hormone; acetylcholine; achondroplasia.*

ACh *acetylcholine.*

achalasia (ā″kă-lā′zh(ē)-ă) [²*an- + chalasia*] Failure to relax; said of smooth muscles, such as those positioned between the lower esophagus and the stomach. In advanced cases, dysphagia is marked, and dilation of the esophagus may occur. SYN: *a. of the cardia; cardiospasm*. SEE: *Nursing Diagnoses Appendix.*

   a. of the cardia Achalasia.

   cricopharyngeal a. Failure of the lower pharyngeal muscles to relax during swallowing. The condition may cause dysphagia or aspiration of food or gastric contents.

   pelvirectal a. Congenital absence of ganglion cells in the distal large bowel, resulting in failure of the colon to relax.

   secondary a. Pseudoachalasia.

   sphincteral a. Failure of the intestinal sphincters to relax.

AChE *acetylcholinesterase.*

ache (āk) **1.** Pain that is persistent rather than sudden or spasmodic. It may be dull or severe. **2.** To suffer persistent pain.

acheilia (ā″kī′lē-ă) [*a-* + *chilo-* + *-ia*] Congenital absence of one or both lips.

acheiria, achiria (ā″kī′rē-ă) [*a-* + *chiro-* + *-ia*] **1.** Congenital absence of one or both hands. **2.** A loss of sensation in one or both hands. This may result from temporary or permanent injury or malfunction of the sensory mechanism, or it may occur in hysteria. **3.** Inability to determine to which side of the body a stimulus has been applied.

Achilles jerk Achilles tendon reflex.

Achilles tendon The tendon of insertion of the gastrocnemius and soleus muscles on the calcaneus; one of the strongest tendons in the body. SYN: *calcaneal tendon*. SEE: *rupture of the Achilles tendon.*

Achilles tendon reflex (ă-kil′ēz) [*Achilles*, hero of the *Iliad*, whose vulnerable spot was his heel] Plantar flexion resulting from contraction of the calf muscles after a sharp blow to the Achilles tendon, activating the S1 spinal reflex. The variations and their significance correspond closely to those of the knee jerk. It is exaggerated in upper motor neuron disease and diminished or absent in lower motor neuron disease. SYN: *Achilles jerk; ankle reflex; triceps surae jerk; triceps surae reflex.*

achillobursitis (ă-kil″ŏ-bŭr-sīt′ĭs) [*Achilles* + *bursitis*] Inflammation of the bursae lying over the Achilles tendon. SYN: *Albert's disease.*

achillodynia (ă-kil″ŏ-din′ē-ă) [*Achilles* + *-odynia*] Nondescript pain arising from the Achilles tendon.

achillorrhaphy (ă-iĭl-or′ă-fē) [*Achilles* + *-rrhaphy*] Suture of the Achilles tendon.

achillotenotomy (ă-kil″ŏ-tĕn-ot′ŏ-mē) [*Achilles* + *teno-* + *-tomy*] Achillotomy.

achillotomy (ă-kil-ot′ŏ-mē) [*Achilles* + *-tomy*] Division of the Achilles tendon, e.g., surgically or traumatically. SYN: *achillotenotomy.*

achlorhydria (ā″klor-hī′drē-ă) [*a-* + *chlor-* + *hydr-* + *-ia*] Absence of free hydrochloric acid in the stomach. It may be associated with gastric carcinoma, gastric ulcer, pernicious anemia, adrenal insufficiency, or chronic gastritis. SEE: *achylia.*

   histamine-proved a. Absence of free acid in gastric secretion even after subcutaneous injection of histamine hydrochloride.

achondrogenesis (ā″kon″drō-jen′ĕ-sis) [*a-* + *chondro-* + *-genesis*] Failure of bones and cartilage to grow, esp. the bones of the extremities.

achondroplasia (ā″kon″drō-plā′zh(ē)-ă) [*a-* + *chondro-* + *-plasia*] The most common form of short-limbed dwarfism. It is caused by a point mutation in a fibroblast growth receptor and characterized by impairment in the formation of cartilage at the epiphyses of long bones. SYN: *chondrodystrophy.*

ACHRN *Advanced Certified Hyperbaric Nurse.*

achroma (ā″krō′mă) [*a-* + *chrom-*] An absence of color or normal pigmentation as in leukoderma, albinism, and vitiligo.

achromasia (ā″krō-mā′zh(ē)-ă) [*a-* + *chrom-* + *-ia*] **1.** Absence of normal pigmentation of the skin as in albinism, vitiligo, or leukoderma. **2.** Pallor. **3.** Inability of cells or tissues to be stained.

achromate (ā″krō′māt″) [Gr. *achrōmatikos*, colorless] A person who is color-blind.

achromatic (ăk″rŏ-mat′ik) [Gr. *achrōmatikos*, colorless] **1.** Colorless. **2.** Not dispersing light into constituent components. **3.** Not containing chromatin. **4.** Difficult to stain, with reference to cells and tissues.

achromatically (-i-k(ă-)lē), *adj.*

achromatin (ā″krō′măt-ĭn) [*achromat(ic)*

+ *-in*] The weakly staining nucleoplasm of a cell nucleus.

achromatism (ā″krō′mă-tĭzm) [*achromat(ic)* + *-ism*] Colorlessness.

achromatolysis (ā″krō″mă-tol′ĭ-sĭs) [*achromat(ic)* + *-lysis*] Dissolution of cell achromatin.

achromatophil, achromophil (ā″krō-mat′ŏ-fĭl″, ā″krō′mŏ-fĭl) [*achromat(ic)* + *-phil*] A cell or tissue not stainable in the usual manner.

achromatopsia (ā″krō″mă-top′sē-ă) [*achromat(ic)* + Gr. *opsis*, vision + *-ia*] Complete color blindness.

achromatosis (ā″krō″mă-tō′sis) [*achromat(ic)* + *-osis*] The condition of being without natural pigmentation. SEE: *achroma*.

achromatous (ā″krō′mă-tŭs) [*achromat(ic)* + *-ous*] **1.** Without color. **2.** Deficient in color; lighter than normal.

achromia (ā″krō′mē-ă) [*a-* + *chrom-* + *-ia*] **1.** Absence of color; pallor. **2.** Achromatosis. **3.** Condition in which erythrocytes have large central pale areas; hypochromia. **achromic,** *adj.*

congenital a. Albinism.

Achromobacter (ā″krō″mŏ-bak′tĕr) [*¹an-* + *chromo-* + *bacter(ium)*)] A genus of gram-negative bacilli that may inhabit the lower gastrointestinal tract; may cause nosocomial infections.

A. xylosoxidans Alcaligenes xylosoxidans.

achromocyte, achromatocyte (ā″krō′mŏ-sīt″, krō-mat′ŏ-sīt″) [*¹an-* + *chromo-* + *-cyte*] Red cell ghost.

achromotrichia (ā″krō″mŏ-trik′ē-ă) [*a-* + *chromo-* + *trich-* + *-ia*] Lack of color or graying of the hair. SYN: *canities.*

nutritional a. Grayness of the hair due to dietary deficiency.

achylia, achylosis (ā″kī′lē-ă, ā″kī-lō′sis) [*¹an-* + *chyle* + *-ia*] Absence of chyle or other digestive enzymes, as in atrophic gastritis. **achylous** (ā″kī′lŭs), *adj.*

a. gastrica A dated term for the complete absence or marked decrease in the amount of gastric juice. SEE: *achlorhydria.*

a. pancreatica Absence or deficiency of pancreatic secretion; usually a sign of chronic pancreatitis.

acicular (ă-sik′yŭ-lăr) [L. *aciculus,* little needle] Needle-shaped.

acid (as′id) [L. *acidus,* sour] **1.** Any substance that liberates hydrogen ions (protons) in solution; a hydrogen ion donor. An acid reacts with a metal to form a salt, neutralizes bases, and turns litmus paper red. **2.** A substance that can accept a pair of electrons; a Lewis acid. SEE: *alkali; base; indicator;* **Lewis** *acid; pH.* **3.** A sour substance. **4.** Slang term for lysergic acid diethylamide (LSD).

acetic a. $C_2H_4O_2$, the acid that gives the sour taste to vinegar. It is also used as a reagent. Glacial (highly purified) acetic acid contains at least 99.5% acetic acid by weight.

acetoacetic a. $C_4H_6O_3$, a ketone body formed when fats are incompletely oxidized. It was formerly called acetylacetic acid. SYN: *diacetic a.; diacetic a.*

acetylsalicylic a. ABBR: ASA. Aspirin (1).

acrylic a. $C_3H_4O_2$, a colorless corrosive acid used in making acrylic polymers and resins.

adenylic a. **Adenosine** monophosphate.

alpha-hydroxy a. ABBR: AHA. Any of a class of water-soluble acids derived from fruit or milk, having a hydroxyl moiety in the first position in the molecule. AHAs are used in chemical peels and other skin care products to remove the outer layer of the epidermis. This chemical exfoliation is promoted for its cosmetic effects on wrinkled or sun-damaged skin.

alpha-linolenic a. $C_{18}H_{30}O_2$, an omega-3 fatty acid derived from plants, esp. seeds (canola oil, flaxseed, walnuts and pumpkins) and from some fish (salmon and mackerel).

alpha-lipoic a. $C_8H_{14}O_2S_2$, a natural coenzyme and antioxidant, used for short-term treatment of peripheral neuropathies.

amino a. SEE: *amino acid.*

aminoacetic a. Glycine.

aminocaproic a. $C_6H_{13}NO_2$, a hemostatic drug. It is a specific antidote for an overdose of a fibrinolytic agent.

arachidonic a. $C_{20}H_{32}O_2$, an omega-6 fatty acid formed by the action of enzymes on phospholipids in cell membranes. The acid is found in many foods. It is metabolized primarily by the cyclooxygenase or 5-lipoxygenase pathways to produce prostaglandins and leukotrienes, which are important mediators of inflammation. Corticosteroids inhibit formation of arachidonic acid from phospholipids when cell membranes are damaged. Nonsteroidal anti-inflammatory agents such as salicylates, indomethacin, and ibuprofen inhibit the synthesis of prostaglandins and leukotrienes.

argininosuccinic a. $C_{10}H_{18}N_4O_6$, a compound intermediate in the synthesis of arginine, formed from citrulline and aspartic acid.

aristolochic a. $C_{17}H_{11}NO_7$, an acid derived from *Aristolochia,* a genus of flowering plants, and used as an herbal remedy. It is promoted as an aphrodisiac, a weight loss agent, and an anticonvulsant.

⚠ The acid is a known carcinogen, and its use has been associated with and may cause end-stage renal disease and cancers of the urinary tract that may occur many years after usage has stopped.

---

ascorbic a. Vitamin C.

aspartic a. $C_4H_7NO_4$, a nonessential amino acid that is a product of pancreatic digestion.

barbituric a. $C_4H_4N_2O_3$, a crystalline acid from which phenobarbital and other barbiturates are derived.

benzoic a. $C_7H_6O_2$, a white crystalline acid having a slight odor. It is used in keratolytic ointments and in food preservation. Saccharin is a derivative of this acid.

bile a. Any of the complex acids that occur as salts in bile, e.g., cholic, glycocholic, and taurocholic acids. They give bile its foamy character, are important in the digestion of fats in the intestine, and are reabsorbed from the intestine to be used again by the liver. SEE: *enterohepatic* **circulation**.

binary a. An acid containing hydrogen and one other element.

boric a. H_3BO_3, a white crystalline acid that in water forms a very weak acid solution poisonous to plants and animals. It is soluble in water, alcohol, and glycerin. SEE: *boric acid poisoning*.

⚠️ Boric acid is toxic and should be used only rarely. It is particularly dangerous because it can be accidentally swallowed by children or used in food because of its resemblance to sugar.

---

butyric a. $C_4H_8O_2$, a viscous fatty acid with a rancid odor, derived from butter but rare in most fats. It is used in disinfectants, emulsifying agents, and pharmaceuticals.

carbolic a. Phenol (1).

carbonic a. H_2CO_3, an acid formed when carbon dioxide is dissolved in water.

carboxylic a. Any acid containing the carboxyl group –COOH. The simplest examples are formic and acetic acids.

cholic a. $C_{24}H_{40}O_5$, a bile acid formed in the liver by hydrolysis of other bile acids. It is formed from the breakdown of cholesterol and helps digest consumed fats.

cinnamic a. $C_9H_8O_2$, an insoluble white powder derived from cinnamon. It is used as a flavoring agent in cooking and in the preparation of perfumes and medicines.

citric a. $C_6H_8O_7$, an acid found naturally in citrus fruits or prepared synthetically. It acts as a sequestrant, helping to preserve food quality.

conjugated linoleic a. ABBR: CLA. Any of the isomers of linoleic acid effective against cancer, obesity, diabetes, and atheromata in laboratory rodents. CLAs have not been shown to have similar beneficial effects in humans.

cysteic a. $C_3H_7NO_5S$, an acid produced by the oxidation of cysteine. Further oxidation produces taurine.

deoxycholic a. $C_{24}H_{40}O_4$, a crystalline acid found in bile.

deoxyribonucleic a., desoxyribonucleic acid SEE: *DNA*.

diacetic a. Acetoacetic **a.**

2,4-dichlorophenoxyacetic a. 2,4-D.

docosahexaenoic a., docosahexanoic ABBR: DHA. $C_{22}H_{32}O_2$, an omega-3 fatty acid found in the oils of cold-water fish and in algae. DHA plays a role in the development of nerve cell membranes and is required for the normal growth and development of the infant brain. Lack of DHA has been linked to growing numbers of people suffering from depression.

domoic a. $C_{15}H_{20}NO_6$, a toxin that resembles glutamate, the main excitatory amino acid of the brain. When ingested, it may cause continuous seizures.

eicosapentaenoic a. ABBR: EPA. $C_{20}H_{30}O_2$, an omega-3 fatty acid found in fish oils, containing 20 carbons and five double bonds.

endogenous uric a. Uric acid derived from purines undergoing metabolism from the nucleic acid of body tissues.

essential fatty a. ABBR: EFA. A fatty acid (alpha-linoleic and linoleic) that is essential for health and must be present in the diet because it cannot be synthesized in the body. SEE: *digestion*.

ethylenediaminetetraacetic a. ABBR: EDTA. $C_{10}H_{16}N_2O_8$, a chelating agent that, in its calcium or sodium salts, is used to remove metallic ions such as lead and cadmium from the body and as a food preservative. SEE: *chelation*.

fatty a. Any of numerous monobasic acids with the general formula C_nH_{2n+1} —COOH (an alkyl radical attached to a carboxyl group).

Fatty acids are insoluble in water. This insolubility would prevent their being absorbed from the intestines, but the action of bile salts on the fatty acids enable thems to be absorbed. Fatty acids include acetic, butyric, capric, caproic, caprylic, formic, lauric, myristic, palmitic, and stearic acids. Unsaturated fatty acids have one or more double or triple bonds in the carbon chain. They include those of the oleic series (oleic, tiglic, hypogeic, and palmitoleic) and the linoleic or linolic series (linoleic, linolenic, clupanodonic, arachidonic, hydrocarpic, and chaulmoogric). SEE: *fat*.

folic a. $C_{19}H_{19}N_7O_6$, a water-soluble B complex vitamin needed for DNA synthesis and amino acid metabolism. It is present in green leafy vegetables, beans, and yeast. It is used to treat megaloblastic and macrocytic anemias and to prevent neural tube defects (NTDs) and cardiovascular disease in adults. The U.S. Public Health Service recommends that all women of childbearing age who may become or are pregnant should consume 0.8 mg of folic acid daily to reduce their risk of having a child affected with spina bifida or other NTDs. SEE: *neural tube **defect***. SYN: *folate; vitamin B₉*.

⚠️ Folic acid should not be used to treat pernicious anemia (a vitamin B_{12} deficiency) because it does not protect patients against the development of changes in the central nervous system that accompany this type of anemia.

folinic a. $C_{20}H_{23}N_7O_7$, the active form of folic acid. It is used to counteract the effects of folic acid antagonists and to treat folic acid deficiency anemia.

formic a. HCOOH, the first and strongest member of the monobasic fatty acid series. It occurs naturally in certain animal secretions, e.g., the sting of insects such as bees and ants, and in muscle, but it is also prepared synthetically.

formiminoglutamic a. $C_6N_2O_4H_{10}$, an intermediate product in the metabolism of histidine.

free fatty a. ABBR: FFA. The form in which a fatty acid leaves the cell to be transported for use in another part of the body. FFAs are not esterified and may be unbound (not bound to protein). In the plasma, the nonesterified fatty acids released immediately combine with albumin to form bound free fatty acids.

fumaric a. $C_4H_4O_4$, one of the organic acids in the Krebs cycle. It is used as a substitute for tartaric acid in beverages and baking powders.

gadolinium-diethylenetriamine pentaacetic a. ABBR: Gd-DTPA. A radiographic contrast agent, used in magnetic resonance imaging to enhance the appearance of blood vessels.

⚠️ Contrast agents containing gadolinium should not be given to patients with diminished renal function.

gallic a. $C_6H_2(OH)_3COOH$, a colorless crystalline acid. It occurs naturally as an excrescence on the twigs of trees, esp. oaks, as a reaction to the deposition of gall wasp eggs. It is used as a skin astringent and in the manufacture of writing inks and dyes.

gamma-aminobutyric a. ABBR: GABA. $C_4H_9NO_2$, the principal inhibitory neurotransmitter of the brain.

gamma-linolenic a. ABBR: GLA. $C_{18}H_{30}O_2$, an essential fatty acid promoted by alternative medicine practitioners as a treatment for skin and inflammatory disorders, cystic breast disease, and hyperlipidemia.

glucuronic a. $CHO(CHOH)_4COOH$, an oxidation product of glucose that is present in the urine. Toxic products (salicylic acid, menthol, phenol) that have entered the body through the intestinal tract are detoxified in the liver by conjugation with glucuronic acid.

glutamic a. $HOOC \cdot (CH_2)_2 \cdot CH(NH_2) \cdot COOH$, an amino acid formed in protein hydrolysis and an excitatory neurotransmitter in the central nervous system.

glyceric a. $CH_2OH \cdot CHOH \cdot COOH$, an intermediate product of the oxidation of fats.

glycocholic a. $C_{26}H_{43}NO_6$, a bile acid that hydrolyzes to glycine and cholic acid.

glycolic a. $C_2H_4O_3$, an alpha-hydroxy acid derivative used to remove the outer layer of skin to rejuvenate its appearance.

glyoxylic a. $C_2H_2O_3$, an acid produced by the action of glycine oxidase on glycine or sarcosine.

hippuric a. $C_6H_5CONHCH_2COOH$, an acid formed and excreted by the kidneys. It is formed from the combination of benzoic acid and glycine. The synthesis takes place in the liver and, to a limited extent, in the kidneys.

homogentisic a. $C_8H_8O_4$, an intermediate product of tyrosine catabolism. It is found in the urine in alkaptonuria. SYN: *alkapton*.

hyaluronic a. ABBR: HA. $(C_{14}H_{21}NO_{11})_n$, an acid mucopolysaccharide found in the extracellular matrix of connective tissue that acts as a binding and protective agent. It is found in synovial fluid and in the vitreous and aqueous humors of the eye. Patients with osteoarthritis have elevated serum levels of HA. SYN: *hyaluronan*.

hydrochloric a. HCl, an inorganic acid normally present in gastric juice. It destroys fermenting bacteria that might cause intestinal tract disturbances.

hydrocyanic a. HCN, a colorless, extremely poisonous, highly volatile acid that occurs naturally in plants but is also produced synthetically. It acts by preventing cellular respiration. Hydrocyanic acid is used in electroplating, fumigation, and in producing dyes, pigments, synthetic fibers, and plastic. Exposure of humans to 200 to 500 parts of hydrocyanic acid per 1,000,000 parts of air for 30 min is fatal. SYN: **hydrogen** *cyanide*. SEE: *Poisons and Poisoning Appendix*.

hydrofluoric a. HF, a corrosive solution of hydrogen fluoride in water. It can be used in dentistry to etch composites and porcelain surfaces and is used industrially to etch glass. SEE: *hydrogen fluoride*.

⚠️ Exposure to the skin and aerodigestive tract causes severe burns with local necrosis and systemic manifestations resulting from disordered calcium and potassium metabolism. Treatments with calcium gluconate can be beneficial.

hydroxy a. Any of the acids containing one or more hydroxyl (–OH) groups in addition to the carboxyl (–COOH) group, e.g., lactic acid, $CH_3COHCOOH$).

hydroxybutyric a. $C_4H_8O_3$, any of the acids present in the urine, esp. in diabetic ketoacidosis, when the conversion of fatty acids to ketones increases.

hydroxycitric a. $C_6H_8O_8$, an herbal extract promoted for the treatment of weight loss. Placebo-controlled studies have not found any benefit to the treatment.

hypochlorous a. HClO, an acid used as a disinfectant, deodorant, and bleaching agent. It is usually used in the form of one of its salts.

imino a. An acid formed as a result of oxidation of amino acids in the body.

inorganic a. An acid containing no carbon atoms. SYN: *mineral a.*

iopanoic a. $C_{11}H_{12}I_3NO_2$, a radiopaque contrast medium used in radiographic studies of the gallbladder.

keto a. Any organic acid containing the ketone CO (carbonyl radical).

lactic a. $C_3H_6O_3$, an organic acid formed in muscles during anaerobic cell respiration in strenuous exercise. It is also formed during anaerobic muscle activity when glucose cannot be changed to pyruvic acid in glycolysis. It contributes to muscle aches and fatigue. SYN: *lactacid*.

levulinic a. $CH_3COCH_2CH_2COOH$, an acid formed when certain simple sugars are acted on by dilute hydrochloric acid.

lignoceric a. $C_{24}H_{48}O_2$, a saturated, naturally occurring fatty acid present in certain foods, including peanuts. It is also found in wood tar, various cerebrosides, and in small amounts in most natural fats. The acid is also a by-product of lignin production.

linoleic a. $C_{18}H_{32}O_2$, an omega-6 fatty acid found in vegetables, nuts, grains, seeds, fruits and their oils. Oils rich in linoleic acid include (in descending order) safflower, sunflower, corn, soybean and cottonseed.

linolenic a. $C_{18}H_{30}O_2$, an omega-6 fatty acid, thought to be cardioprotective. It reduces the production of cytokines and down-regulates serum cell adhesion molecules thought to be intermediates in atherosclerosis.

lysergic a. $C_{16}H_{16}N_2O_2$, a crystalline acid derived from ergot. Its derivative, lysergic acid diethylamide (LSD), is a potent hallucinogen. SEE: *LSD*.

lysophosphatidic a. ABBR: LPA. $C_{21}H_{41}O_7P$, an acid purified from the ascitic fluid of patients with ovarian cancer. LPA stimulates the growth of ovarian cancer and may be a useful screening test for the disease.

malic a. $C_4H_6O_5$, an acid found in sour fruits such as apples and apricots and active in the aerobic metabolism of carbohydrates.

malonic a. $C_3H_4O_4$, a dibasic acid formed by the oxidation of malic acid and active in the Krebs cycle in carbohydrate metabolism. Malonic acid is found in beets. Its inhibition of succinic dehydrogenase is the classic example of competitive inhibition.

mandelic a. $C_8H_8O_3$, a colorless hydroxy acid. Its salt is used to treat urinary tract infections.

methacrylic a. $C_4H_6O_2$, a colorless acid used to make methyl methacrylate.

mineral a. Inorganic **a.**

monounsaturated fatty a. A fatty acid containing one double bond between carbon atoms. It is found in olive oil and is the predominant fat in the Mediterranean diet. It is thought to reduce low-density lipoprotein levels without affecting high-density lipoprotein levels. SEE: *Mediterranean diet*.

n-3 fatty a. Omega-3 fatty **a.**

n-6 fatty a. Omega-6 fatty **a.**

nicotinic a. Niacin.

nitric a. HNO_3, a colorless, poisonous, fuming corrosive acid, widely used in industry and in chemical laboratories.

nitrous a. HNO_2, a weak acid chemical reagent used in biological laboratories.

nonvolatile a. An acid, such as lactic acid or sulfuric acid, that accumulates in the body as a result of digestion, disease, or metabolism. It cannot be excreted from the body by ventilation but must be excreted by organs other than the lungs, e.g., by acidification of the urine.

nucleic a. Any of the high-molecular-weight molecules that carry the genetic information crucial to the replication of cells and the manufacturing of cellular proteins. They have a complex structure formed of sugars (pentoses), phosphoric acid, and nitrogen bases (purines and pyrimidines). Most important are ribonucleic acid (RNA) and deoxyribonucleic acid (DNA). SEE: illus.

octadecanoic a. Stearic **a.**

oleic a. $C_{18}H_{34}O_2$, a monounsaturated fatty acid found in most organic fats and oils.

omega-3 fatty a., ω-3 fatty acid Any

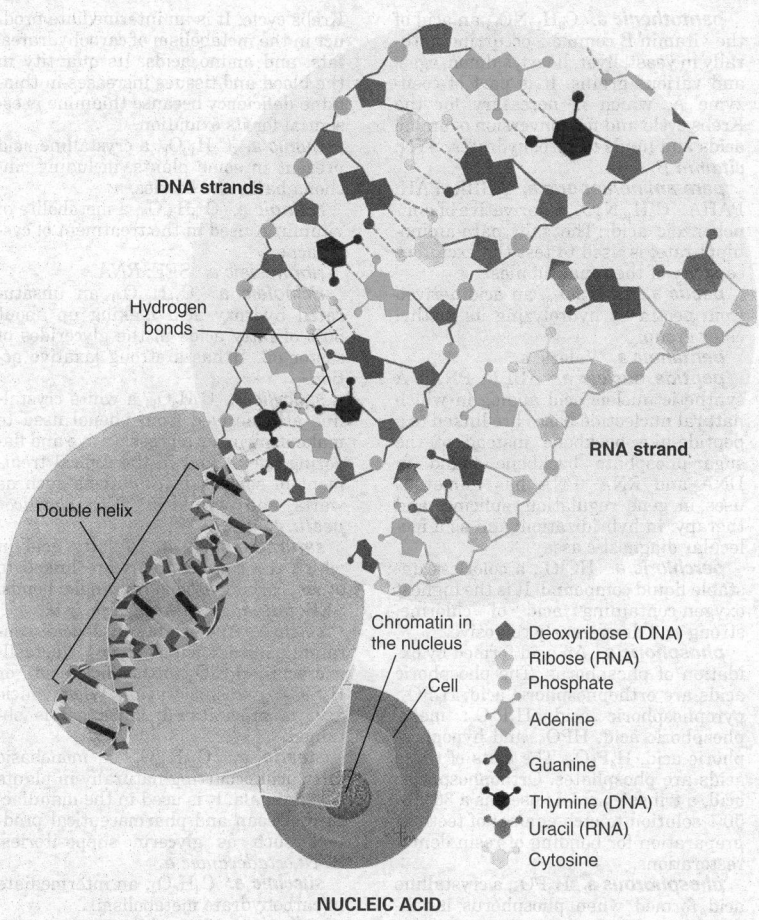

DNA strands

Hydrogen bonds

RNA strand

Double helix

Chromatin in the nucleus

Cell

◆ Deoxyribose (DNA)

Ribose (RNA)

Phosphate

Adenine

Guanine

Thymine (DNA)

Uracil (RNA)

Cytosine

NUCLEIC ACID

DNA and RNA

of the long-chain polyunsaturated fatty acids found in the oils of some saltwater fish, and in canola, flaxseed, walnuts, and some vegetables. These acids include eicosapentaenoic acid (EPA) and docosahexaenoic acid (DHA). Alpha-linolenic acid (found in flaxseed and chia) can be metabolically converted to omega-3 fatty acids in the body. People whose diets are rich in omega-3 fatty acids have a reduced incidence of cardiovascular disease. SYN: *n-3 fatty a.*

omega-6 fatty a., ω-6 fatty acid Any of the long-chain polyunsaturated fatty acids, such as linoleic acid and arachidonic acid, thought to influence cardiovascular and growth function when balanced with omega-3 fatty acids in eicosanoid production. Linoleic acids are derived from vegetable oils; arachidonic acids, from animal fats. SYN: *n-6 fatty a.*

organic a. An acid containing the carboxyl radical, –COOH. Organic acids include acetic acid, formic acid, lactic acid, and all fatty acids.

orotic a. $C_5H_4N_2O_4$, a crystalline acid occurring in milk. It is a precursor in the formation of pyrimidine nucleotides.

osmic a. Osmium tetroxide.

oxalic a. $C_2H_2O_4$, the simplest dibasic organic acid. Its potassium or calcium salts occur naturally in rhubarb, wood sorrel, and other plants. It is the strongest organic acid and is poisonous. When properly diluted, it removes ink or rust stains from cloth. It is used also as a reagent.

oxaloacetic a., oxalacetic acid $C_4H_4O_5$, a product of carbohydrate metabolism resulting from oxidation of malic acid during the Krebs cycle. It may be derived from other sources.

palmitic a. $C_{16}H_{32}O_2$, a saturated fatty acid occurring as esters in most natural fats and oils.

pantothenic a. $C_9H_{17}NO_5$, an acid of the vitamin B complex, occurring naturally in yeast, liver, heart, salmon, eggs, and various grains. It is part of coenzyme A, which is necessary for the Krebs cycle and for conversion of amino acids and lipids to carbohydrates. SYN: *vitamin B₅*.

para-aminohippuric a. ABBR: PAH, PAHA. $C_9H_{10}N_2O_3$, a derivative of aminobenzoic acid. The salt, para-aminohippurate, is used to test the excretory capacity of the renal tubules.

pectic a. $C_{17}H_{24}O_{16}$, an acid derived from pectin by hydrolyzing its methyl ester group.

pentanoic a. Valeric **a.**

peptide nucleic a. ABBR: PNA. A synthetic nucleic acid analog in which natural nucleotide bases are linked to a peptide-like backbone instead of the sugar-phosphate backbone found in DNA and RNA. PNA has numerous uses in gene regulation, splicing, and therapy; in hybridization; and as a molecular diagnostic assay.

perchloric a. $HClO_4$, a colorless unstable liquid compound. It is the highest oxygen-containing acid of chlorine, strong and dangerously corrosive.

phosphoric a. An acid formed by oxidation of phosphorus. The phosphoric acids are orthophosphoric acid, H_3PO_4; pyrophosphoric acid, $H_4P_2O_7$; metaphosphoric acid, HPO_3; and hypophosphoric acid, $H_4P_2O_6$. The salts of these acids are phosphates. Orthophosphoric acid, a tribasic acid, is used as a 30% to 50% solution to etch enamel of teeth in preparation for bonding of resin dental restorations.

phosphorous a. H_3PO_3, a crystalline acid formed when phosphorus is oxidized in moist air.

phytic a. $C_6H_{18}P_6O_{24}$, a pale, water-soluble acid that is found in cereal grains and, if ingested, may interfere with the absorption of calcium and magnesium.

picric a. $C_6H_2(NO_2)_3OH$, a yellow crystalline powder that precipitates proteins and explodes when heated or charged. It is used as a dye and a reagent. Its salts are used in the Jaffé reaction (used to measure serum creatinine). SYN: *trinitrophenol*.

polyglycolic a. $(C_2H_2O_2)_n$, a polymer of glycolic acid anhydride units. It is used to manufacture surgical sutures, clips, and mesh.

polylactic a. Polylactide.

propionic a. $C_3H_6O_2$, a carboxylic acid present in sweat.

4-pyridoxic a. $C_8H_9NO_4$, a crystalline acid that is the principal end product of pyridoxine metabolism, excreted in human urine.

pyruvic a. $C_3H_4O_3$, an organic acid that plays an important role in the Krebs cycle. It is an intermediate product in the metabolism of carbohydrates, fats, and amino acids. Its quantity in the blood and tissues increases in thiamine deficiency because thiamine is essential for its oxidation.

quinic a. $C_7H_{12}O_6$, a crystalline acid present in some plants, including cinchona bark, and berries.

retinoic a. $C_{20}H_{28}O_2$, a metabolite of vitamin A used in the treatment of cystic acne.

ribonucleic a. SEE: *RNA*.

ricinoleic a. $C_{18}H_{34}O_3$, an unsaturated hydroxy acid making up about 80% of fatty acids in the glycerides of castor oil. It has a strong laxative action.

salicylic a. $C_7H_6O_3$, a white crystalline acid derived from phenol used to make aspirin, as a preservative and flavoring agent, and in the topical treatment of some skin conditions such as warts and wrinkles. SEE: *chemical peeling*.

saturated fatty a. A fatty acid in which the carbon atoms are linked to other carbon atoms by single bonds. SEE: *fatty **a.**; unsaturated fatty **a.***

silicic a. Any of a family of acids containing silica, such as H_2SiO_3 (metasilicic acid), H_4SiO_4 (orthosilicic acid), or H_2SiO_7 (pyrosilicic acid). When silicic acid is precipitated, silica gel is obtained.

stearic a. $C_{18}H_{36}O_2$, a monobasic fatty acid occurring naturally in plants and animals. It is used in the manufacture of soap and pharmaceutical products such as glycerin suppositories. SYN: *octadecanoic **a.***

succinic a. $C_4H_6O_4$, an intermediate in carbohydrate metabolism.

sulfonic a. Any of the organic compounds having the general formula SO_2OH, derived from sulfuric acid by replacement of a hydrogen atom.

sulfosalicylic a. $C_7H_6O_6S_3$, a crystalline acid soluble in water or alcohol. It is used as a reagent for precipitating proteins, as in testing for albumin in urine.

sulfuric a. H_2SO_4, a colorless, corrosive, oily, viscous acid prepared from sulfur dioxide and used in many industrial processes and in clinical laboratories. Industrial accidents involving sulfuric acid through contact with skin or inhalation of aerosols are common.

sulfurous a. H_2SO_3, an inorganic acid and a powerful chemical reducing agent used commercially, esp. for as a bleach.

tannic a. $C_{76}H_{52}O_{46}$, a mixture of digallic acid esters of D(+) glucose prepared from oak galls and sumac. It yields gallic acid and glucose on hydrolysis.

tartaric a. $C_4H_6O_6$, an acid obtained from by-products of wine fermentation.

It is widely used in industry in the manufacture of carbonated drinks, flavored gelatins, dyes, and metals. It is also used as a reagent. It is thought to be an allergen.

taurocholic a. $C_{26}H_{45}NO_7S$, a bile acid that hydrolyzes to cholic acid and taurine.

teichoic a. Any of the polymers found in the cell walls of some gram-positive bacteria, such as the staphylococci.

trans-fatty a. The solid fat produced by heating liquid vegetable oils in the presence of hydrogen and certain metal catalysts. Partial hydrogenation changes some of the unsaturated bonds to saturated ones. The more trans-fatty acids in the diet, the higher the serum cholesterol and low-density lipoprotein cholesterol.

2,4,5-trichlorophenoxyacetic a. 2,4,5-T.

unsaturated fatty a. An organic acid in which some of the carbon atoms are linked to other carbon atoms by double bonds, thus containing less than the maximum possible number of hydrogen atoms, e.g., unsaturated oleic and linoleic acids as compared with the saturated stearic acid. Polyunsaturated fatty acids include linoleic acid and alpha-linoleic acid. SEE: *fatty a.; saturated fatty a.*

uric a. $C_5H_4N_4O_3$, a crystalline acid occurring as an end product of purine metabolism. It is formed from purine bases derived from nucleic acids (DNA and RNA). It is a common constituent of urinary stones and gouty tophi. SEE: illus.

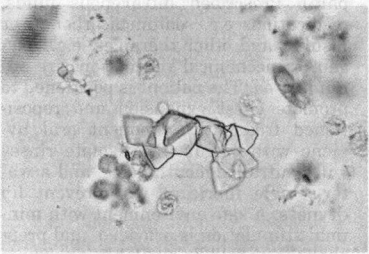

CLUMP OF URIC ACID CRYSTALS (×400)

OUTPUT: Uric acid must be excreted because it cannot be metabolized. Uric acid output should be between 0.8 and 1g/day if the patient is on an ordinary diet.

Increased elimination is observed after ingestion of proteins and nitrogenous foods, after exercise, after administration of cytotoxic agents, and in gout and leukemia. Decreased elimination is observed in kidney failure, lead poisoning, and in those who eat a protein-free diet.

valeric a. $C_5H_{10}O_2$, an oily fatty acid having a distinctly disagreeable odor, existing in four isomeric. SYN: *pentanoic a.*

valproic a. ABBR: VPA. $C_8H_{16}O_2$, an acid used to treat seizure disorders.

vanillylmandelic a., vanilmandelic acid ABBR: VMA. $C_9H_{10}O_5$, a principal metabolic product of catecholamines. VMA makes up approx. 90% of the metabolites of the catecholamines epinephrine and norepinephrine and is secreted in the urine. People with pheochromocytoma produce excess amounts of catecholamines; therefore there are increased amounts of VMA in their urine.

volatile a. An acid produced from carbon dioxide (CO_2). It can be excreted by the body by ventilation (colloquially, "blowing off CO_2").

xanthurenic a. $C_{10}H_7NO_4$, an acid excreted in the urine of pyridoxine-deficient animals after they have been fed tryptophan.

acid-citrate-dextrose ABBR: ACD sol. An anticoagulant solution used in blood collection (and in plasmaphoresis, in place of heparin). Its components are citric acid, sodium citrate, and dextrose.

acidemia (as"ĭ-dē'mē-ă) [*acid* + *-emia*] A decrease in the arterial blood pH below 7.35. The hydrogen ion concentration of the blood increases, as reflected by a lowering of serum pH values. SEE: *acid-base balance; acidity; acidosis.*

isovaleric a. A rare autosomal recessive metabolic disease affecting leucine metabolism. Isovaleric acid accumulates in the blood during periods of increased amino acid metabolism. Coma and death may occur.

lactic a. Lactacidemia.

methylmalonic a. An inherited metabolic disease caused by inability to convert methylmalonic acid to succinic acid. The clinical signs are failure to grow, mental retardation, and severe metabolic acidosis. One form of the disease will respond to vitamin B_{12} given either in utero or to the mother before delivery.

acid-fast (as'id-fast') In bacterial staining, pert. to bacteria that do not decolorize after application of acid-alcohol but keep a dark stain. Microorganisms that are acid-fast include Mycobacteria and Nocardia species.

acid hemolysin test Ham test.

acid hydrolase Any hydrolytic enzyme found in a lysosome that performs optimal catalysis at a pH of about 5.

acidify (ă-sid'ĭ-fī") [*acid* + *-ify*] 1. To make a substance acid. 2. To become acid.

acidifiable (ă-sid"ĭ-fī'ă-bl), *adj.* **acidification** (-fī-kā'shŏn), *n.* **acidifier** (-fī"ĕr), *n.*

acidity (ă-sid'ĭ-tē) [*acid*] 1. The quality of possessing hydrogen ions (protons).

SEE: *acid; hydrogen ion; pH*. **2.** Sourness.

a. of the stomach The lowered pH of the gastric contents, due to hydrogen ion release by parietal cells.

acid lipase disease Acid lipase deficiency.

acidophil, acidophile (ă-sĭd′ŏ-fĭl″, ă-sĭd′ŏ-fĭl″) **1.** Acidophilic (2). **2.** A tissue, organism, or substance that stains readily with acid stains.

acidophilic (ă-sĭd″ō-fĭl′ĭk) **1.** Having affinity for acid or pert. to certain tissues and cell granules. **2.** Pert. to a cell capable of being stained by acid dyes. SYN: *acidophil (1)*.

acidoresistant (as″ĭ-dō-rĕ-zis′tănt) Acid-resisting; said about bacteria.

acidosis (as″ĭ-dō′sis) [*acid* + *-osis*] An actual or relative increase in the acidity of blood due to an accumulation of acids (as in diabetic acidosis or renal disease) or an excessive loss of bicarbonate (as in renal disease). The hydrogen ion concentration of the fluid is increased, lowering the pH. SEE: *acid-base balance; acidemia; buffer; pH*. **acidotic** (-dot′ik), *adj*.

carbon dioxide a. Respiratory acidosis.

compensated a. Acidosis in which the pH of body fluids has returned to normal. Compensatory mechanisms maintain the normal ratio of bicarbonate to carbonic acid (approx. 20:1) in blood plasma even though the bicarbonate level is decreased or the carbon dioxide level is elevated.

diabetic a. Diabetic ketoacidosis.

dialysis a. Metabolic acidosis due to prolonged hemodialysis in which the pH of the dialysis bath has been inadvertently reduced by the action of contaminating bacteria.

hypercapnic a. Respiratory acidosis.

hyperchloremic a. Acidosis in which there is an abnormally high level of chloride in the blood.

lactic a. An accumulation of lactic acid in the blood, often due to inadequate perfusion and oxygenation of vital organs (e.g., in cardiogenic, ischemic, or septic shock), drug overdoses (commonly, salicylates or ethanol), skeletal muscle overuse (e.g., after heavy exercise or seizures), or other serious illnesses (some cancers; diabetes mellitus). Lactic acid is produced more quickly than normal when there is inadequate oxygenation of skeletal muscle and other tissues. Thus any disease that leads to tissue hypoxia, exercise, hyperventilation, or some drugs (e.g., oral hypoglycemic agents) may cause this condition. In general, when blood pH is less than 7.35 and lactate is greater than 5 to 6 mmol/L (5 to 6 mEq/L), lactic acidosis is present.

metabolic a. Any process that causes a decrease in the pH of the body as a result of the retention of acids or the loss of bicarbonate buffers. Metabolic acidosis is usually categorized by the presence or absence of an abnormal anion gap. The anion gap metabolic acidoses include diabetic, alcoholic, and lactic acidoses; the acidosis of renal failure; and acidoses that result from the consumption of excess acids e.g., salicylates, methanol, or ethanol. Non-anion gap metabolic acidoses occur in diarrhea, renal tubular acidosis, and multiple myeloma.

ETIOLOGY: Possible causes include excessive ingestion of acids, salicylates, methanol, or ethylene glycol; failure of the kidneys to excrete acids, e.g., in renal failure or renal tubular acidosis; ketoacidosis (diabetic, alcoholic, owing to starvation); severe dehydration; diarrhea; rhabdomyolysis; seizures; and shock.

PATIENT CARE: A history is obtained, focusing on the patient's urine output, fluid intake, dietary habits (including recent fasting), associated disorders (e.g., diabetes mellitus and kidney or liver dysfunction), and the use of medications (including aspirin) and alcohol. Arterial blood gas values, serum potassium level, and fluid balance are monitored. The patient is assessed for lethargy, drowsiness, and headache, diminished muscle tone, and deep tendon reflexes. The patient is also evaluated for hyperventilation, cardiac dysrhythmias, muscle weakness and flaccidity, and gastrointestinal distress (e.g., nausea, vomiting, diarrhea, and abdominal pain). Prescribed intravenous fluids, medications, e.g., sodium bicarbonate or insulin, and other therapies, e.g., oxygen or mechanical ventilation, are administered. The patient is positioned to promote chest expansion and repositioned frequently. Frequent oral hygiene with sodium bicarbonate rinses will neutralize mouth acids, and a water-soluble lubricant will prevent lip dryness. A safe environment with minimal stimulation is provided, and preparations should be available if seizures occur. Both patient and family are given oral and written information about prescribed medication and managing related diseases. SEE: *Nursing Diagnoses Appendix*.

renal a. Acidosis caused either by kidney failure, in which phosphoric and sulfuric acids and inorganic anions accumulate in the body, or by renal tubular diseases. The acidosis is induced by urinary wasting of bicarbonate and inability to excrete phosphoric and sulfuric acids.

PATIENT CARE: Renal acidosis due to one of the renal tubular acidoses responds to treatment either with sodium bicarbonate or with citrated salts (e.g., potassium citrate). The acidosis of chronic renal failure may require therapy with sodium bicarbonate or may be treated by dialysis with a bicarbonate-rich dialysate. Diets are adjusted for patients with renal failure to limit the metabolic production of acids (these usually rely on limitations of daily dietary protein). Foods rich in potassium and phosphate are restricted. Patients with renal failure should be monitored for signs and symptoms of renal acidosis, including loss of appetite, changes in levels of consciousness, or alterations in respiratory rate or effort. Laboratory monitoring may include frequent assessments of arterial blood gas values, serum electrolytes, carbon dioxide levels, and blood urea nitrogen and creatinine. Prescribed intravenous fluids are given to maintain hydration.

renal tubular a. ABBR: RTA. Any of a group of non-anion gap metabolic acidoses marked by either loss of bicarbonate or failure to excrete hydrogen ions in the urine. Type I (distal RTA) is marked by low serum potassium, elevated serum chloride, a urinary pH greater than 5.5, nephrocalcinosis, and nephrolithiasis. Alkalis such as sodium bicarbonate or Shohl's solution are effective treatments.

Type II (proximal RTA) is caused by impaired reabsorption of bicarbonate by the proximal tubules. Its hallmarks include preserved glomerular filtration, hypokalemia, excessive bicarbonate excretion in the urine during bicarbonate loading, and a urinary pH less than 5.5. Osteopenia and osteomalacia are common. Treatments include volume restriction and potassium and bicarbonate supplementation.

Type IV (hyperkalemia RTA) is usually associated with hyporeninemic hypoaldosteronism due to diabetic nephropathy, nephrosclerosis associated with hypertension, or chronic nephropathy. Patients have high serum potassium levels and low urine ammonia excretion but no renal calculi. The hyperkalemia may be managed by mineralocorticoids with furosemide. Glomerular filtration is reduced in this disorder.

respiratory a. Acidosis caused by inadequate ventilation and the subsequent retention of carbon dioxide. SYN: *carbon dioxide a.; hypercapnic a.*

PATIENT CARE: The patient suspected of developing acute respiratory acidosis is monitored using arterial blood gases, level of consciousness, and orientation to time, place, and person. The patient is also evaluated for diaphoresis, a fine or flapping tremor (asterixis), depressed reflexes, and cardiac dysrhythmias. Vital signs and ventila-

tory effort are monitored, and ventilatory difficulties such as dyspnea are documented. Prescribed intravenous fluids are given to maintain hydration. The patient is oriented as often as necessary, and information and reassurance are given to allay the patient's and family's fears and concerns. Prescribed therapies for associated hypoxemia and underlying conditions are provided, responses are evaluated, and related patient education is given.

The respiratory therapist (RT) works with the attending physician to determine when to intubate and mechanically ventilate the patient with acute respiratory acidosis. Once the patient is intubated and is receiving mechanical ventilation, the RT monitors and maintains the patient's airway and tolerance of the positive pressure ventilation. This requires the RT to perform frequent q1-2m assessments of the patient and the ventilator and report side effects to the attending physician. Some patients with advanced chronic obstructive lung disease develop chronic respiratory acidosis (as a result of CO_2 retention), usually with a compensatory metabolic (renal) alkalosis.

⚠ Acute respiratory acidosis is a medical emergency in which immediate efforts to improve ventilation are required.

acid rain Rain that, in passing through the atmosphere, is contaminated with acid substances, esp. sulfur dioxide and nitrogen oxide. These pollutants are oxidized in the atmosphere to sulfuric acid and nitric acid. Rainwater is considered abnormally acidic if the pH is below 5.6. It may damage ecosystems or individual plants and animal species.

acid reflux test Any of several methods for diagnosing gastroesophageal reflux disease, including endoscopy and direct measurement of esophageal pH.

PATIENT CARE: In esophageal pH monitoring, after mild sedation and topical pharyngeal anesthesia, an electrode is placed in the stomach and a reading taken; then the electrode is withdrawn until it is in the esophagus. Normally, the pH will become more alkaline (i.e., rise) as the electrode is moved from the stomach into the esophagus. If there is acid reflux, the pH will be acid in both the stomach and esophagus.

acidulate (ă-sij'ŭ-lāt") [L. *acidulus,* slightly acid] To make somewhat sour or acid. **acidulation** (-sij"ŭ-lā'shŏn), *n.*

acidulous (ă-sij'ŭ-lŭs) [L. *acidulus,* slightly acid] Slightly sour or acid.

aciduria (as-ĭ-door'ē-ă, -dūr') [*acid* + *-uria*] The presence of any organic or inorganic acid in the urine.

glutaric a. An inherited disorder marked by multiple neurological deficits in childhood, including motor dysfunction, developmental delay, and brain atrophy. It is caused by defective manufacture of glutaryl-coenzyme A dehydrogenase.

orotic a. A rare autosomal recessive disorder of pyrimidine metabolism in which orotic acid accumulates in the body. Clinically, children fail to grow and have megaloblastic anemia and leukopenia. The disease responds to administration of uridine or cytidine.

aciduric (as″ĭ-doo′rik, -dūr′) [*acid* + L. *durare*, to endure + *-ic*] Pert. to bacteria that are able to survive moderate acidity.

acinar (as′ĭ-nar″) [L. *acinus,* grape] Pert. to an acinus.

acinar cell carcinoma of the pancreas SEE: under *carcinoma.*

Acinetobacter (a″ĭ-nēt″ŏ-bak′tĕr) [Gr. *akinētos,* immovable, + *bacter(ium)*] A genus of gram-negative, aerobic coccobacilli that is an increasingly important cause of serious infections, esp. in hospitalized patients. It is commonly found in water, soil, and on the skin of healthy humans.

acini (as′ĭ-nī″) Pl. of acinus.

aciniform (ă-sin′ĭ-form″) [*acinus* + *-form*] **1.** Resembling a cluster of grapes. **2.** Acinous.

acinitis (as″ĭ-nīt′is) [*acinus* + *-itis*] Inflammation of glandular acini.

acinous, acinose (as′ĭ-nŭs, as′ĭ-nōs″) [*acinus*] Consisting of acini. SYN: *aciniform.*

acinus (as′ĭ-nŭs, -nī″) *pl.* **acini** [L., grape] **1.** The smallest division of a gland; a group of secretory cells surrounding a cavity. **2.** The terminal respiratory gas exchange unit of the lung, composed of airways and alveoli distal to a terminal bronchiole.

ACIP *The Advisory Committee on Immunization Practices of the U.S. Public Health Service.*

AC joint *Acromioclavicular joint.*

ACL *Anterior cruciate ligament.*

acladiosis (ă-klad″ē-ō′sis) [*Acladium* + *-osis*] An ulcerative skin disease believed to be caused by fungi of the genus *Acladium.*

aclasis, aclasia (ak′lă-sis, ă-klā′zē-ă) [*a-* + Gr. *klasis,* a breaking] Abnormal tissue arising from and continuous with a normal structure, as in achondroplasia.

diaphyseal a. Imperfect formation of cancellous bone in cartilage between diaphysis and epiphysis.

ACLS *Advanced Cardiac Life Support.*

acme (ak′mē) [Gr. *akmē,* point] **1.** The highest point; peak. **2.** Apogee. **3.** The segment of uterine labor contraction during which muscle tension is greatest.

acne (ak′nē) [Ult. fr. *acme*] An inflam-matory disease of the sebaceous follicles of the skin, marked by comedones, papules, and pustules. It is exceptionally common in puberty and adolescence. Acne usually affects the face, chest, back, and shoulders. In severe cases, cysts, nodules, and scarring occur. SYN: *common a.; a. vulgaris.*

ETIOLOGY: The cause is unknown, but predisposing factors include hereditary tendencies and disturbances in the androgen-estrogen balance. Acne begins at puberty when the increased secretion of androgen in both males and females increases the size and activity of the pilosebaceous glands. Specific inciting factors may include food allergies, endocrine disorders, therapy with adrenal corticosteroid hormones, and psychogenic factors. Vitamin deficiencies, ingestion of halogens, and contact with chemicals such as tar and chlorinated hydrocarbons may be specific causative factors. The fact that bacteria are important once the disease is present is indicated by the successful results following antibiotic therapy. The lesions may become worse in women and girls before the menstrual period.

SYMPTOMS: Acne vulgaris is marked by either papules, comedones with black centers (pustules), or hypertrophied nodules caused by overgrowth of connective tissue. In the indurative type, the lesions are deep-seated and cause scarring. The face, neck, and shoulders are common sites. Acne may be obstinate and recurrent.

TREATMENT: Treatments include skin cleansing, topical agents (e.g., azelaic acid or benzoyl peroxide or vitamin A derivatives), and oral or topical antibacterial drugs.

PATIENT CARE: The patient is instructed to wash the skin thoroughly but gently, avoiding intense scrubbing and skin abrasion; to keep hands away from the face and other sites of lesions; to limit the use of cosmetics; and to observe for, recognize, and avoid or modify predisposing factors that may cause exacerbations. The need to reduce sun exposure is explained, and the patient is advised to use a sunscreen agent when vitamin A acid or tetracycline is prescribed. Information is provided to fill knowledge gaps or correct misconceptions, and emotional support and understanding are offered, particularly if the patient is an adolescent. Patients (and others) need to be aware that extensive use of antibiotic treatment for acne increases the prevalence of antibiotic-resistant facial bacteria and can affect treatment response. Most improvement occurs during the first 6 weeks of therapy, whatever the regimen. More than half of all patients respond to therapy. Colonization with tetracycline-resistant propionibacteria diminishes response to all oral antibiotic regimens. Skin irritation as an adverse effect to treatment occurs most commonly with topical benzoyl peroxide alone, which is the most cost-effective treatment. Adding topical erythromycin may help reduce irritation and increase efficacy.

⚠️ Because of the teratogenicity of some acne medications (such as isotretinoin), pregnancy must be avoided during their use.

a. atrophica Acne with residual pitting and scarring.

bromide a. The characteristic acne caused by bromide.

a. ciliaris Acne that affects the edges of the eyelids.

common a. Acne.

a. conglobata Acne vulgaris with abscesses, cysts, and sinuses that leave scars.

cystic a. Acne with cysts containing keratin and sebum. SEE: illus.

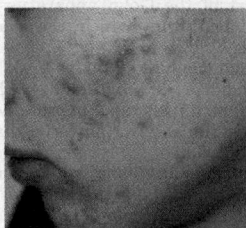

CYSTIC ACNE

TREATMENT: Isotretinoin, a vitamin A derivative, has been effective in treating this condition. For Caution concerning its use, SEE: *isotretinoin*.

a. fulminans A rare type of acne in teenage boys, marked by inflamed, tender, ulcerative, and crusting lesions of the upper trunk and face. It has a sudden onset and is accompanied by fever, leukocytosis, and an elevated sedimentation rate. About half of the cases have inflammation of several joints.

halogen a. Acne due to exposure to halogens such as bromine, chlorine, or iodine.

a. indurata Acne vulgaris with chronic, discolored, indurated surfaces.

keloid a. Acne keloidalis nuchae.

a. keloidalis nuchae Chronic follicular infection of the skin at the occiput (base of the skull) and the neck. It occurs most often in men of African heritage and causes scars and thickening of the skin. SYN: *keloid a.*

a. keratosa Acne in which suppurating nodules crust over to form horny plugs. These occur at the corners of the mouth.

a. neonatorum Acne occurring in newborns. It is common, appearing about the second to fourth week of life. Comedones, inflamed papules, and pustules may be seen (the latter yield staphylococcal species when cultured). The rash typically resolves spontaneously by the third or fourth month of life. Lesions are typically seen on the chin, cheeks, and forehead. Usually no treatment is required, but keratolytic agents may be used for severe cases.

a. papulosa Acne characterized by formation of papules with very little inflammation. SEE: illus.

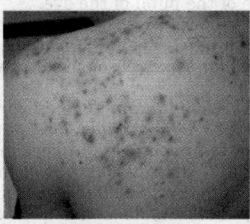

ACNE PAPULOSA

petroleum a. Acne that may occur in those who work with petroleum and oils.

a. pustulosa Acne with pustule formation and subsequent deep scars.

a. rosacea Rosacea.

steroid a. Acne caused by systemic or topical use of corticosteroid drugs.

summer a. Acne that appears only in hot, humid weather or that is much worse in such weather. Although the exact cause is unknown, the condition is not caused by increased exposure to the sun's rays.

tropical a. Severe acne caused by or aggravated by living in a hot, humid climate. The skin of the thorax, back, and legs is most commonly affected.

a. urticaria An acneiform eruption of itching wheals.

a. varioliformis Vesiculopustular folliculitis that occurs mostly on the temples and frontal margins of the scalp but may be seen on the chest, back, or nose.

a. vulgaris Acne.

acne-associated arthritis SEE: under *arthritis*.

acnegenic (ak″nē-jen′ik) [*acne* + *-genic*] Causing acne.

acneiform, acneform (ak-nē′ĭ-form″, ak-nē′form″) [*acne* + *-form*] Resembling acne.

acnemia (ăk-nē′mē-ă) [*a-* + Gr. *knēmē*, lower leg + *-ia*] Wasting of the calves of the legs.

ACNM *American College of Nurse Midwives.*

ACOG *American College of Obstetricians and Gynecologists.*

aconite (ak'ŏ-nīt") [Gr. *akoniton*, wolfsbane] The dried tuberous root of *Aconitum*, esp. *A. napellus* (monkshood) and *A. lycoctonum* (wolfsbane); a poisonous alkaloid that may cause life-threatening cardiac arrhythmias. Aconite is believed to have been used as an arrow poison early in Chinese history and perhaps also by the inhabitants of ancient Gaul. It was also used as an herbal remedy in traditional Chinese medicine.

aconitine (ă-kon'ĭ-tēn", -tĭn) [*aconite* + *-ine*] $C_{34}H_{47}NO_{11}$, a poisonous white crystalline alkaloid that is the active ingredient in aconite.

acorea (ā"kor'-ē-ă) [*a-* + Gr. *korē*, maiden, pupil of the eye + *-ia*] Absence of the pupil of the eye.

acoria (ă-kor'ē-ă) [*a-* + Gr. *koros*, satiety + *-ia*] Feeling unsatisfied after a meal for some reason other than hunger.

ACOTE *Accreditation Council for Occupational Therapy Education.*

acousmatamnesia (ă-kooz"măt-ăm-nē'zē-ă) [Gr. *akousma*, something heard + amnesia*amnesia*, forgetfulness] Inability to recall and identify sounds.

acoustic (ă-koos'tĭk) [Gr. *akoustikos*, pert. to hearing] Pert. to sound or to the sense of hearing.

acoustic apparatus Auditory apparatus; the anatomical structures essential for hearing.

acoustic area A part of the brain that lies over the vestibular and cochlear nuclei.

acousticophobia (ă-koos"tĭ-kō-fō'bē-ă) [*acoustic* + *-hobia*] Abnormal fear of loud sounds.

acoustic reflectometry Diagnostic technique for the detection of middle ear effusion. It measures the level of sound transmitted and reflected from the middle ear to a microphone located in a probe tip placed against the ear canal and directed toward the tympanic membrane.

acoustics (ă-koos'tiks) [*acoustic*] The science of sound, its production, transmission, and effects.

acousto-, acoust-, acous- [Gr. *akoustikos*, pert. to hearing, fr. *akouein*, to hear] Prefixes meaning *hearing*.

ACP *American College of Physicians; American College of Pathologists; American College of Phlebology; American College of Prosthodontists.*

acquired (ă-kwīrd') [Fr. fr. L. *acquirere*, to get] Not hereditary or innate.

acquired brain injury SEE: under *injury*.

acquired immunodeficiency syndrome SEE: *HIV/AIDS.*

acquisition (ak"wĭ-zĭsh'ŏn) [L. *acquirere*, to get] The measurement of image data during a radiological study and of its subsequent storage in memory.

acquisitus (ă-kwis'ĭ-tŭs) [L. *acquirere*, to get] Acquired.

ACR *American College of Radiology.*

acral (ak'răl) [acro- + -l] Pert. to the extremities.

acrania (ā"krā'nē-ă) [a- + crani- + -ia] Partial or complete congenital absence of the cranium.

acrid (ak'rĭd) [L. *acer*, sharp] Burning, bitter, irritating.

acridine (ak'rĭ-dēn") [acrid + -ne] A coal tar hydrocarbon from which certain dyes are prepared.

acrimony (ak'rĭ-mō"nē) [L. *acer*, sharp] Quality of being pungent, acrid, irritating, rancorous, or caustic.

acritical (ā"krit'ĭ-kăl) [a- + critical] Not marked by a crisis.

ACRM *American Congress of Rehabilitation Medicine.*

ACRN *AIDS Certified Registered Nurse.*

acro- [Gr. *akron*, extremity] Prefix meaning *extremity, top, extreme point.*

acroagnosis (ak"rō-ăg-nō'sis) [acro- + a- + Gr. *gnōsis*, knowledge] Absence of feeling of one's limb.

acroanesthesia (ăk"rō-ăn-ĕs-thē'zē-ă) [" + *an-*, not, + *aisthesis*, sensation] Lack of sensation in one or more of the extremities.

acroblast (ak'rŏ-blast") [acro- + -last] A part of the Golgi apparatus in the spermatid from which the acrosome arises.

acrobrachycephaly (ak"rō-brak"ĭ-saf'ă-lē) [acro + brachycephaly] The condition of having an abnormally short head in the anterior-posterior diameter due to fusion of the coronal suture.

acrocentric (ak"rō-sen'trik) [acro- + center + -c] Pert. to a chromosome in which the centromere is located near one end. At metaphase it has the appearance of a wishbone. **acrocentric,** *n.*

acrocephalosyndactylia, acrocephalosyndactyly (ak"rō-sef"ă-lō-sin-dak-til'ē-ă, -sin-dak'til-ē) [acro- + cephalo- + syndactyly] A congenital condition marked by a peaked head and webbed fingers and toes. SYN: *Apert syndrome.*

acrocephaly, acrocephalia (ak"rō-sef'ă-lē, ak"rō-sĕ-fāl'yă) [acro- + Gr. *kephalē*, head] The condition of having a malformed cranial vault with a high or peaked appearance and a vertical index above 77. It is caused by premature closure of the coronal, sagittal, and lambdoidal sutures. This defect may be seen in Apert syndrome. SYN: *acrocephalia*. **acrocephalic** (-sĕ-faliĭk), *adj.*

acrochordon (ak"rō-kor'don") [acro- + Gr. *chordē*, cord] A small, benign, polyp-shaped growth composed of skin and subcutaneous tissue; typically found on the neck, in the axilla, or near the eyelids. SYN: *fibroepithelial polyp; skin tag.* SEE: illus.

acrocontracture (ak"rō-kŏn-trak'chĕur) [acro- + contracture] Contracture of the hands or feet.

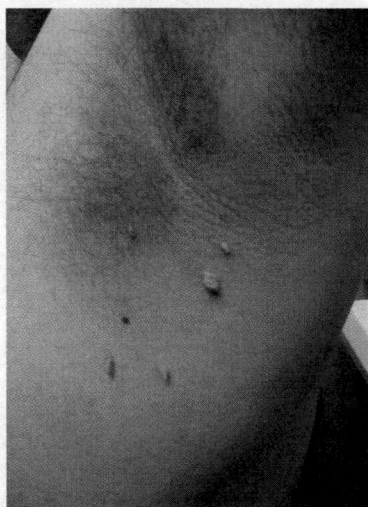

ACROCHORDON

(in the axilla)

acrocyanosis (ak″rō-sī-ă-nō′sĭs) [acro-
+ cyanosis] A blue or purple mottled
discoloration of the extremities, esp. of
the fingers, toes, and/or nose. This finding is associated with many diseases
and conditions, e.g., anorexia nervosa,
autoimmune diseases, cold agglutinins,
or Raynaud's disease or phenomenon.
Acrocyanosis is commonly observed in
newborns and in others after exposure
to cold temperatures and in patients
with reduced cardiac output. In patients
with suspected hypoxemia, it is an unreliable sign of diminished oxygenation.
(Instead of relying on this sign, pulse oximetry or arterial blood gases should be
measured.) **acrocyanotic** (-not′ik), *adj.*
acrodermatitis (ak″rō-dĕr-mă-tīt′ĭs)
[*acro-* + *dermatitis*] Dermatitis of the
extremities.
   a. chronica atrophicans Dermatitis
of the hands and feet that progresses
slowly upward on the affected limbs.
   a. continua An obstinate eczematous
eruption confined to the extremities.
   a. enteropathica A rare disease in
children aged 3 weeks to 18 months that
may be fatal if untreated. The genetically determined cause is malabsorption of zinc. Onset is insidious with failure to thrive, diarrhea, loss of hair, and
development of vesiculobullous lesions,
particularly around body orifices. SYN:
zinc deficiency syndrome.
   TREATMENT: Zinc sulfate is given
orally to the affected children.
   a. hiemalis Dermatitis that occurs in
winter and affects the extremities. It
tends to disappear spontaneously.

   a. perstans **Acrodermatitis** continua.
acrodermatosis (ak″rō-dĕr″mă-tō′sĭs)
[acro- + dermatosis] Any skin disease
that affects the hands and feet.
acrodolichomelia (ak″rō-dol″ĭ-kō-mēl′ē-
ă) [acro- + Gr. *dolichos,* long + Gr.
melos, limb] A condition in which the
hands and feet are abnormally long.
acrodynia (ak″rō-din′ē-ă) [acro- +
-ynia] A disease of infants and young
children caused by chronic mercury poisoning. It may have a prolonged clinical
course with various grades of severity.
SYN: *pink disease.*
   TREATMENT: Treatment consists of
removing the source of the mercury with
dimercaprol (BAL) antidote and supportive therapy. **acrodynic** (-din′ik),
adj.
acrodysesthesia (ak″rō-dis″es-thē′zh(ē-)ă)
[acro- + dysesthesia] Dysesthesia in
the arms and legs.
acroesthesia (ak″rō-es-thē′zh(ē-)ă)
[acro- + -sthesia] **1.** Abnormal sensitivity of the extremities. **2.** Pain in the
extremities.
acrofacial (ak″rō-fā′shăl) Pert. to the
hands, feet, and face.
acrogeria (ak″rō-jēr′ē-ă) [acro- + Gr.
gerōn, old man] A condition in which
the skin of the hands and feet shows
signs of premature aging.
acrognosis (ak″rog-nō′sis) [acro- + Gr.
gnōsis, knowledge] Sensory perception
of limbs.
acrohyperhidrosis (ak″rō-hī″pĕr-hī-drō′sis)
[acro- + hyperhydrosis] Excessive perspiration of the hands and feet.
acrohypothermy, acrohypothermia (ak″rō-
hī′pŏ-thĕr′mē, thĕr′mē-ă) [acro- +
hypothermia] Abnormal coldness of the
extremities.
acrokeratosis verruciformis (ak″rō-
ker″ă-tō′sis vĕ-roo′sĭ-for″mis) [acro- +
keratosis + L. *verruca,* wart, -form]
Hereditary disease of the skin characterized by warty growths on the extremities, principally on the backs of the
hands and on the feet.
acrokinesia (ak″rō-kĭ-nē′sē-ă) [acro- +
-inesi + -a] Excessive motion of the
extremities.
acromegaly (ak″rō-meg′ă-lē) [*acro-* +
-*megaly*] A chronic syndrome of growth
hormone excess, most often caused by a
pituitary macroadenoma. It produces a
bony enlargement, resulting in significant changes in facial and oral features.
The diagnosis is confirmed by elevated
levels of serum insulin-like growth factor 1 (IGF-1), or by a growth hormone
level that does not suppress after oral
glucose tolerance testing. SYN: *Marie's
disease.*
   ETIOLOGY: Overproduction of
growth hormone by somatotroph cells of
the anterior pituitary is responsible in
most cases.

SYMPTOMS: The onset is often so gradual that patients and their close associates may not notice a change in appearance or function. Increased sweating, decreased libido, somnolence, mood disorders, muscular pain, weakness, and loss of vision may eventually occur. Signs include a coarsening of facial features, often with frontal bossing (protuberance of the skull); enlargement of hands and feet; deepening of the voice; and increased separation of the teeth. A quarter of patients develop diabetes mellitus.

TREATMENT: Transsphenoidal resection of a growth-hormone secreting adenoma is the primary therapy.

acromelalgia (ak″rō-mĕ-lăl′j(ē-)ă) [acro- + Gr. *melos,* limb + -lgia] Erythromelalgia.

acromelic (ak″rō-mel′ik) [*acro-* + *¹melo-* + *-ic*] Pert. to the ends of the extremities.

acrometagenesis (ak″rō-met″ă-jen′ĕ-sis) [acro- + meta- + -enesis] Abnormal growth of the extremities.

acromicria (ak″rō-mik′rē-ă, -mĭk′) [acro- + micr- + -a] Congenital shortness or smallness of the extremities and face.

acromioclavicular traction test (ă-krō″mē-ō-klă-vik′yŭ-lăr) [acromion + clavicular] A maneuver used to identify acromioclavicular and costoclavicular ligament sprains. As the patient sits or stands with the affected shoulder hanging in the neutral position, the clinician pulls the humerus down. A positive test result is marked by a visible separation between the acromion and distal clavicle. SEE: illus.

acromiohumeral (ă-krō″mē-ŏ-hū′mĕr-ăl) [acromion + humeral] Pert. to the acromion and humerus.

acromion (ă-krō′mē-ŏn″) [acro- + Gr. *ōmion,* (little) shoulder] The lateral triangular projection of the spine of the scapula that forms the point of the shoulder and articulates with the clavicle. **acromial** (-ē-ăl), *adj.* SYN: *acromial process.* SEE: *acromioclavicular joint.*

acromioplasty (ă-krō′mē-ō-plas″tē) [acromion + -lasty] The surgical removal of the distal inferior acromion process of the scapula to relieve impingement of soft tissues in the subacromial space, esp. the supraspinatus tendon. This is usually performed with release of the coracoacromial ligament, arthroscopically or through open incision.

acromyotonia (ăk″rō-mī-ō-tō′nē-ă) [acro- + myotonia] Myotonia of the extremities, causing spasmodic deformity. **acromyotonus** (-ot′ŏ-nŭs), *adj.*

acroneurosis (ăk″rō-nu-rō′sis) [acro- + Gr. *neuron,* sinew, tendon + -sis] Any peripheral neuropathy affecting the extremities.

acro-osteolysis (ăk″rō-ŏos″tē-ŏl′ĭ-sis)

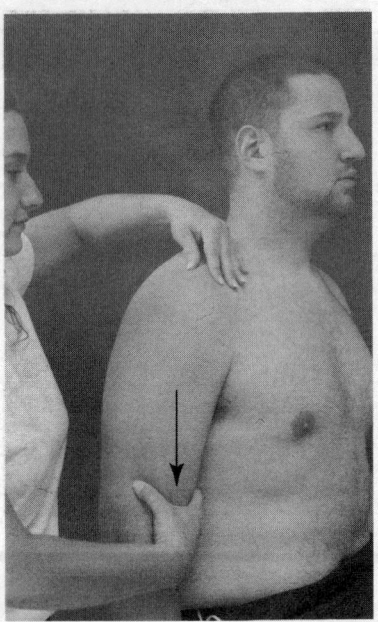

ACROMIOCLAVICULAR TRACTION TEST

[acro- + osteolysis] **1.** A familial disease causing dissolution of the tips of the bones in the extremities of young children. There is no history of trauma, and spontaneous amputation does not occur. Its cause is unknown. **2.** An occupational disease seen in workers who come in contact with vinyl chloride polymerization processes. It is marked by Raynaud's phenomenon, scleroderma-like skin changes, and radiological evidence of bone destruction of the distal phalanges of the hands. Recovery follows removal from exposure. SEE: *Raynaud's disease.*

acropachyderma (ăk″rō-pak″ē-děr′mă) [acro- + pachyderma] Clubbing of the fingers, deformation of the long bones, and thickening of the skin of the scalp, face, and extremities.

acroparalysis (ăk″rō-pă-ral′ĭ-sis) [acro- + paralysis] Paralysis of one or more extremities.

acroparesthesia (ăk″rō-par″es-thē′zh(ē-)ă) [acro- + paresthesia] A sensation of prickling, tingling, or numbness in the extremities.

acropathology (ak″rō-pă-thŏl′ŏ-jē) [acro- + pathologyn] Any disease of the extremities (e.g., the fingers or toes).

acrophobia (ăk″rō-fō′bē-ă) [acro- + -hobia] Morbid fear of high places. **acrophobe** (-fōb″), *n.*; **acrophobic** (-bik), *adj.* SYN: *hypsophobia.*

acroscleroderma (ăk″rō-skler″ŏ-děr′mă) [acro- + scleroderma] Hard, thickened skin of toes and fingers. SYN: *sclerodactylia*.

acrosclerosis (ăk″rō-skle-rō′sis) [acro- + sclerosis] A scleroderma of the upper extremities. It sometimes extends to the neck and face after Raynaud's disease.

acrosomal reaction (ak″rŏ-sō′măl) The release of enzymes from the acrosome on the head of the sperm. This process causes the sperm to penetrate the zona pellucida of the egg and begin fertilization.

acrosome (ak′rŏ-sōm″) [*acro-* + *-some*] A specialized lysosome on the head of a sperm cell that contains enzymes to digest the membrane of an egg cell. **acrosomal** (ak″rŏ-sō′măl), *adj.* SEE: *spermatozoon* for illus.

acrotrophoneurosis (ak″rō-trof″o-nu-rō′sis) [acro- + trophoneurosis] Trophoneurosis of the extremities with trophic, neuritic, and vascular changes. It is usually caused by prolonged immersion in water.

acrylamide (ak″rĭ-la′mīd″, ă-krĭl′ă-mīd) [*acrylic (acid)* + *amide*] **1.** The amide of acrylic acid, C₃H₅NO. Acrylamide is used in many types of gel electrophoresis to separate and identify proteins. **2.** A chemical by-product formed in foods cooked at high temperatures. Acrylamides cause cancer and have adverse effects on reproduction. SEE: *carcinogen*.

⚠ Acrylamide, a suspected carcinogen, found in starchy foods prepared at high temperatures, e.g., potato chips, french fries, and bread.

acrylate (ak′rĭ-lāt″) [acrylic (acid) + -te] A salt or ester of acrylic acid.

acrylonitrile (ak″rĭ-lō-nī′trĭl, trēl″) C₃H₃N; a toxic compound used in making plastics. SYN: *vinyl cyanide*.

ACS *American Cancer Society; American Chemical Society; American College of Surgeons; acute confusional state*.

ACSM *American College of Sports Medicine*.

act (akt) [L. *agere*, to drive, do] **1.** To accomplish a function. **2.** The accomplishment of a function. **3.** Legislation that has been passed and made law; a statutory law.

  compulsive a. The repetitive, ritualistic performance of an act. This may be done despite the individual's attempts to resist the act.

  impulsive a. A sudden, unexplained action, esp. one that may potentially cause danger to oneself or to others.

ACTH *adrenocorticotropic hormone; Association of Canadian Teaching Hospitals*.

ACTH stimulation test A test to determine the presence of adrenal insufficiency.

  PATIENT CARE: Synthetic adrenocorticotropic hormone (ACTH) is injected intravenously, and the serum cortisol level is measured at timed intervals (30 or 60 min after the injection). A patient with normal adrenal function will respond to the test with increased serum cortisol levels above 18 μg/dl. Serum cortisol levels <15 μg/dl are diagnostic of adrenal insufficiency. The test has been traditionally performed with an injection of 250 μg of ACTH, but studies have shown that 1 μg is an equally effective test dose. SYN: *Cortrosyn stimulation test; cosyntropin stimulation test*.

actigraphy (ak-tig′ră-fē) [acti(vity) + -raphy] The monitoring of body movements with a small device usually attached to the wrist or foot, used in sleep medicine (and sometimes in anesthesia or critical care medicine) to determine whether and how well a person is resting or sleeping. In sleep medicine, actigraphy can aid in the diagnosis of insomnia, obstructive sleep apnea, and periodic limb movements. It is used in anesthesia to determine depth of sedation (e.g., during recovery from surgery).

actin (ak′tĭn) [*act* + *-in*] One of the contractile proteins that make up the sarcomeres of muscle tissue. During contraction, the actin filaments are pulled toward the center of the sarcomere by the action of myosin filaments, and the sarcomere shortens. Actin is also found in the cytoskeleton of many kinds of cells, where it contributes to cell shape and movement.

  filamentous a. The polymerized form of actin.

  globular a. The monomeric form of actin.

acting out Expressing oneself through actions rather than speech.

  neurotic a.o. **1.** A form of transference, in which tension is relieved when one responds to a situation as if it were the same situation that originally gave rise to the tension; a displacement of behavioral response from one situation to another. **2.** In psychoanalysis, a form of displacement, in which the patient relives memories rather than expressing them verbally.

actinic (ak-tin′ik) [Gr. *aktis*, ray] **1.** Pert. to radiant energy, such as x-rays, ultraviolet light, and sunlight, esp. the photochemical effects. **2.** Pert. to the ability of radiant energy to produce chemical changes. **actinically** (-i-k(ă)lē), *adv.*

actinide (ak′tĭ-nīd″) [*actin-* + *-ide*] Any of the radioactive heavy metals designated on the periodic table of elements with atomic numbers 89–103.

The actinides include naturally occurring elements, e.g., actinium and uranium, and artificial elements, e.g., fermium.

actinism (ak′tĭ-nĭzm) [actin- + -sm] The property of radiant energy that produces chemical changes, as in photography or heliotherapy.

actinium (ak-tin′ē-ŭm) [actin- + -ium] SYMB: Ac. A radioactive element, atomic mass (weight) (most stable isotope) 227, atomic number 89.

actino-, actin- [Gr. aktis, stem aktin-, ray] **1.** Prefixes meaning ray or radiation. **2.** Prefixes meaning having a radiating structure, e.g., Actinomyces.

Actinobacillus (ak″tĭ-nō″bă-sil′ŭs) [actino- + bacillus] A genus of gram-negative coccobacilli that are parasites of hoofed mammals, and, rarely, of humans. SEE: HACEK.

A. actinomycetemcomitans A bacterium that is an important cause of periodontal infection and is sometimes implicated in endocarditis.

actinodermatitis (ak″tĭ-nō-dĕr-mă-tīt′is) [actino- + dermatitis] Dermatitis caused by exposure to radiation.

actinogenic (ak″tĭ-nō-jen′ĭk) [actino- + -enic] Radiogenic.

Actinomyces (ak″tĭ-nō-mī′sēz, ak-tin″ō) [actino- + Gr. mykēs, mushroom, fungus] A genus of bacteria of the family Actinomycetaceae that contains gram-positive staining filaments. These bacteria usually cause disease in the cervicofacial (lumpy jaw), thoracic, and abdominal areas of humans.

A. antibioticus A species from which the actinomycin antibiotics are obtained.

A. bovis A species that causes actinomycosis in cattle.

A. israelii A species that causes actinomycosis in humans. It is a normal inhabitant of the mouth, but can cause abscesses in the gingiva or the jaw, as well as in the abdominal or thoracic cavities. Viewed microscopically material from these abscesses contain purulent material within which are found yellow-colored sulfur granules.

Actinomycetales (ak″tĭ-nō-mī″sĕ-tā′lēz″) [Actinomyces] An order of bacteria that includes the families Mycobacteriaceae, Actinomycetaceae, Actinoplanaceae, Dermatophilaceae, Micromonosporaceae, Nocardiaceae, and Streptomycetaceae.

actinomycete (ak″tĭ-nō-mī′sēt″) [Actinomyces] Any bacterium of the order Actinomycetales.

actinomycetic (-mī-sĕt′ĭk), adj. **actinomycetous** (-mī-sĕt′ŭs), adj.

actinomycetoma (ak″tĭ-nō″mī-sĕ-tō′mă) [actino- + mycetoma] Mycetoma caused by an actinomycete. SEE: mycetoma.

actinomycin (ak″tĭ-nō-mīs′ĭn) [Actinomyc(es) + -in] Any of the frequently toxic drugs obtained from the species of soil bacteria Streptomyces antibioticus (Actinomyces antibioticus).

a. D Dactinomycin.

actinomycoma (ak″tĭ-nō-mī-kō′ma) [actinomycosis + -ma] A tumor produced by actinomycosis.

actinomycosis (ak″tĭ-nō-mī-kō′sĭs) [Actinomyces + -osis] An infectious bacterial disease in animals and humans. Infection may be of the cervicofacial, thoracic, or abdominal regions, or it may be generalized. Microscopic analysis of actinomycotic pus reveals characteristic sulfur granules. **actinomycotic** (ak″tĭ-nō-mī-kot′ĭk), adj.

ETIOLOGY: Causative organisms are Actinomyces bovis in cattle and Actinomyces israelii (which is normally present in the mouth) in humans. SEE: nocardiosis.

TREATMENT: Prolonged administration of high-dose penicillin is usually effective. Alternative antibiotics include erythromycins, tetracyclines, and clindamycin. Surgical incision and drainage of accessible lesions are helpful when combined with chemotherapy.

actinoneuritis (ak″tĭ-nō-nu-rīt′is) [actino- + neuritis] A rare term for nerve damage caused by radiation.

actinophytosis (ak″tĭ-nō-fi-tō′sis) [actino- + phytosis] Infection due to Actinomyces.

actinotherapy (ak″tĭ-nō-ther′ă-pē) [actino- + therapy] Treatment of disease by rays of light, esp. actinic or photochemically active rays, or by x-rays or radium.

action (ak′shŏn) [L. actio, fr. agere, to drive, do] **1.** Performance of a function or process. **2.** In pathology, a morbid process.

adipokinetic a. The action of substances to promote formation of free fatty acids from body fat stores.

antagonistic a. The ability of a drug or a muscle to oppose or resist the action or effect of another drug or muscle; opposite of synergistic action.

bacteriocidal a. Action that kills bacteria.

ball-valve a. Intermittent obstruction of a passageway or opening so that the flow of fluid or air is prevented from moving in and out in equal amounts. A common example is a mucus plug in a distal airway. During inspiration the airway widens allowing gas to flow past the plug. During expiration the airway narrows and gas is trapped. This mechanism can be responsible for a pneumothorax in ventilated patients.

calorigenic a. Heat produced by the metabolism of food.

capillary a. A surface tension effect shown by the elevation or depression of a liquid at the region of contact with a solid, as in capillary tubes. SYN: *capillarity*.

cumulative a. Sudden increased action of a drug after several doses have been given.

cumulative drug a. The action of repeated doses of drugs that are not immediately eliminated from the body. For example, preparations containing lead, silver, and mercury tend to accumulate in the body and gradually produce symptoms of poisoning.

drug a. The function of a drug in various body systems.

Local: When the drug is applied locally or directly to a tissue or organ, it may combine with the cell's membrane or penetrate the cell. Its action may be (1) astringent when the drug causes the cell or tissue to contract, (2) corrosive when the drug is strong enough to destroy cells, or (3) irritating when too much of the drug combines with cells and impairs them.

General, or systemic: This type of action occurs when the drug enters the bloodstream by absorption or direct injection, affecting tissues and organs not near the site of entry. Systemic action may be (1) specific, when it cures a certain disease; (2) substitutive or replenishing, when it supplies substances deficient in the body; (3) physical, when some cell constituents are dissolved by the action of the drug in the bloodstream; (4) chemical, when the drug or some of its principles combine with the constituents of cells or organs to form a new chemical combination; (5) active by osmosis, caused by dilution of salt (also acids, sugars, and alkalis) in the stomach or intestines by fluid withdrawn from the blood and tissues; or by diffusion, when water is absorbed by cells from the lymph; (6) selective, when action is produced by drugs that affect only certain tissues or organs; (7) synergistic, when one drug increases the action of another; (8) antagonistic, when one drug counteracts another; (9) physiological, when the drug exerts a potentially beneficial effect similar to that which the body normally produces; (10) therapeutic, when the effect is to treat or repair diseased organs or tissues; (11) side active, creating an undesired effect; (12) empirical, producing results not proved by clinical or laboratory tests to be effective; or (13) toxicological, having a toxic or undesired effect, generally the result of overdose or long-term usage.

Cumulative: Some drugs are slowly excreted or absorbed so that with repeated doses an accumulation in the body produces a toxic effect. Such drugs should not be administered continuously.

Incompatible: Undesired side effects occur when some drugs are administered together. This may be due to the antagonistic action of one drug on others or to a physical interaction of the drugs that inactivates one of them (e.g., precipitation of some drugs mixed in intravenous fluids).

reflex a. Involuntary movement produced by sensory nerve stimulation.

sparing a. The effect of a nonessential nutrient in the diet such that it decreases the requirement for an essential nutrient. For example, protein is esp. important for tissue growth and development in children. If protein intake is sufficient but caloric intake is inadequate, a protein deficiency will develop. In this situation, the addition of sufficient carbohydrates to the diet is said to spare the protein.

specific a. The particular action of a drug on another substance or on an organism or part of that organism.

specific dynamic a. Stimulation of the metabolic rate by ingestion of certain foods, esp. proteins.

synergistic a. The ability of a drug or muscle to aid or enhance the action or effect of another drug or muscle; opposite of antagonistic action.

tendon a. Passive movement of a joint when a two-joint or multijoint muscle is stretched across it.

thermogenic a. Action of a food, drug, or physical agent to cause a rise in output of body heat.

action study SEE: under *study*.

activate (ak'tĭ-vāt″) [active] To make active.

activated carrier A term sometimes used as a synonym for coenzyme.

activated partial thromboplastin time SEE: under *time*.

activated protein C ABBR: APC. An inhibitor of thrombin, and a fibrinolytic and anti-inflammatory agent produced in the bloodstream during sepsis.

activation (ak″tĭ-vā'shŏn) [activate] **1.** In immunology, the process that stimulates resting (nonfunctional) white blood cells to assume their role in the immune response. The process involves recognition of an antigen or a response to cytokines. **2.** In neuropsychology, arousal. **3.** In physiology, the triggering of a cell response, as when a neurotransmitter causes ionic channels to open in an excitable cell membrane, setting up an action potential. SEE: *antigen processing; cytokine; immune response*.

activator (ak'tĭ-vāt″ŏr) [*activate*] **1.** A substance in the body that converts an inactive molecule into an active agent, such as the conversion of pepsinogen into pepsin by hydrogen ions. **2.** Any substance that specifically induces an activity, such as an inductor or organizer in embryonic development or in a trophic hormone. **3.** A removable orthodontic appliance that transmits force passively from muscles to the teeth and alveolar process in contact with it. Also called *myofunctional appliance*.

urokinase-type plasminogen a. ABBR: uPA. A protein that degrades extracellular tissues. It has been linked to the spread of some cancers by invasion and metastasis.

tissue plasminogen a. ABBR: tPA, TPA. **1.** A natural enzyme that helps degrade blood clots by freeing plasmin from plasminogen. Plasmin in turn breaks down fibrin. **2.** A recombinant enzyme, produced in the laboratory by *Escherichia coli,* for the treatment of thrombosis, esp. in myocardial infarction and ischemic stroke. Recombinant tPA is one of several thrombolytic drugs that can be given to patients during myocardial infarction (MI) to restore the flow of blood through occluded coronary arteries. Restoring perfusion keeps heart muscle from dying, reduces the damage caused by the infarction, and reduces the subsequent risk of congestive heart failure and death. SYN: *recombinant tPA.* SEE: *thrombolysis.*

active assistive range of motion ABBR: AAROM. An exercise in which a manual or mechanical external force assists specific muscles and joints to move through their available excursion. The force is graded according to the patient's strength. AAROM exercises are used when the patient has difficulty moving or when tissue forces need to be reduced.

active compression decompression cardiopulmonary resuscitation ABBR: ACD CPR. The use of a handheld suction device applied to the chest wall during CPR to depress and then decompress the chest. The technique has not been shown to improve outcomes consistently.

active electrode In electrosurgery, the electrode used for cutting or coagulating tissue; the lead where the electrical current concentrates.

active heat and moisture exchanger An addition to a ventilator circuit that uses a passive heat and moisture exchanger and a heated component to filter, heat, and humidify the gases supplied to the ventilated patient.

active range of motion ABBR: AROM. The amount of joint motion produced by voluntary muscle contraction.

active treatment Treatment directed specifically toward cure of a disease or the resolution of injury.

activin (ak'tĭ-vin) [*active* + *-in*] Any of a family of polypeptide growth factors that help regulate various biological functions, esp. fertility. SEE: *inhibin.*

activities of daily living ABBR: ADL. Tasks performed by people in a typical day that allow independent living. Basic activities of daily living (BADL) include feeding, dressing, hygiene, and mobility. Instrumental activities of daily living (IADL) include more advanced skills such as managing personal finances, using transportation, telephoning, cooking, performing household chores, doing laundry, and shopping.

The ability to perform activities of daily living may be hampered by illness or accident resulting in physical or mental disability. Health care rehabilitation workers play a significant role in teaching people to maintain or relearn these skills so that they can achieve the highest possible degree of independence.

PATIENT CARE: The nurse and other members of the rehabilitation team, including occupational and physical therapists, assess the patient's ability to perform ADLs. The rehabilitation team instructs and trains the patient in techniques to relearn the skill, or to accommodate for inability to perform the task. Where appropriate, family members are involved in the rehabilitation program. Referrals to community agencies are arranged when specific tasks cannot be performed independently. SEE: table.

electronic aids to a.d.l. ABBR: EADLs. Computerized or electronic devices that help people with functional limitations gain entry to and exit from buildings, use telephones and other household items, and enjoy leisure activities.

extended a.d.l. Instrumental activities of daily living.

instrumental a.d.l. ABBR: IADL. Those activities and tasks beyond basic self-care that are necessary for living independently. These activities include communication, mobility, cooking, using the telephone, cleaning the house, doing laundry, shopping, going to the bank, and managing medications. SYN: *extended a.d.l.* SEE: *activities of daily living; self-care.*

Activities-Specific Balance Confidence Scale SEE: under *¹scale.*

activity (ak-tiv'ĭt-ē) [Fr. *activité,* fr L. *activitas*] **1.** The production of energy or motion; the state of being active. In the medical sciences, activity applies to various conditions: enzyme activity to the rate of influence of an enzyme on a particular system; radiation activity to the energy produced by a source of radiation. **2.** A person's use of time.

graded a. In occupational therapy, a principle of therapeutic intervention in which tasks are classified and gradually presented according to the patient's level of function and the challenge or degree of skill (physical, social, or cognitive) required by the task.

Activities of Daily Living and Factors Affecting Them

Category	Activities	Affecting Factors
Personal care	Climbing stairs, moving into and out of chair or bed, feeding oneself, opening containers, dressing, using toilet, maintaining hygiene, taking medication	Altered mobility, physical, mental, or emotional illness, elimination problems
Family responsibilities	Shopping, cooking, doing laundry, cleaning, caring for yard, caring for family and pets, managing money	Altered mobility, heavy work schedule, insomnia, physical, mental, or emotional illness
Work or school	Fulfilling work responsibilities or school assignments, getting to and from work or school	Altered mobility, stress, heavy family demands, job dissatisfaction, difficulties in school, physical, mental, or emotional illness
Recreation	Pursuing hobbies and interests, exercising, reading, watching television	Altered mobility, physical, mental, or emotional illness
Socialization	Using the telephone, traveling, visiting family and friends, joining group activities, expressing sexuality	Altered mobility, physical, mental, or emotional illness, relocation

leisure a. An activity chosen for pleasure, relaxation, or other emotional satisfaction, typically after work and other responsibilities are done.

meaning of a. The meaning, value, or representation conveyed by an act, activity, or daily occupation. In occupational health theory, activities or daily occupations are more than acts: they are personal expressions and often have symbolic significance.

optical a. In chemistry, the rotation of the plane of polarized light when the light passes through a chemical solution. Measurement of this property is useful in the determining optically active substances such as dextrose (sugars are classified by this method). Optical activity of a substance in solution can be detected by placing it between polarizing and analyzing prisms.

pulseless electrical a. ABBR: PEA. Cardiac arrest in which the continuation of organized electrical activity in the heart is not accompanied by a palpable pulse or effective circulation of blood. SEE: *cardiopulmonary **resuscitation***.

ETIOLOGY: PEA may be caused by severe acidosis, cardiac ischemia or infarction, hyperkalemia, hypothermia, hypoxia, hypovolemia (such as bleeding or dehydration), massive pulmonary embolism, cardiac tamponade, and tension pneumothorax.

SYMPTOMS: The patient is unresponsive, pulseless, and apneic.

TREATMENT: Chest compressions are started. Intravenous fluids are given, and potentially correctable conditions are addressed, e.g., when cardiac tamponade is suspected, pericardiocentesis is performed; for tension pneumothorax, needle decompression of the chest is performed. Epinephrine is the only drug proven to resuscitate patients from PEA. Nasmyth membrane.

purposeful a. The goal-directed use of time, energy, or attention that involves a person's active participation. Purposeful activity often involves a social environment (others), a physical environment (objects, tools, and materials), and a process.

activity analysis The process used by occupational therapists to determine the social, symbolic, physical, cognitive, and developmental characteristics of a task or activity. Typical characteristics of interest include safety, cost, gradability, required space, tools or supplies, complexity, and social or cultural significance or meaning.

activity intolerance Inadequate mental or physical energy to accomplish daily activities. Risk factors include debilitating physical conditions such as anemia, obesity, musculoskeletal disorders, neurological deficits (such as those following stroke), severe heart disease, chronic pulmonary disease, metabolic disorders, and prolonged sedentary lifestyle. SEE: *Nursing Diagnoses Appendix.*

activity intolerance, risk for A state in which an individual is at risk of experiencing insufficient physiological or psychological energy to endure or complete required or desired daily activities. SEE: *Nursing Diagnoses Appendix.*

activity therapist An allied health professional who assists patients or residents of care facilities with activities for leisure, recreation, habilitation, or rehabilitation purposes.

actomyosin (ak″tŏ-mī′ŏ-sĭn) [act(in)- + myosin] The combination of actin and myosin in a muscle.

Actos Pioglitazone.

actual (ak′choo-ăl) [Fr. fr. L. *actualis,* active, practical] Real, existent.

actuator (ak′choo-āt″ŏr) A component of a mechanical or electronic device that initiates a given action.

acu- [L. *acus,* needle] Prefix meaning *clarity, sharpness,* or *needle.*

acuity (ă-kū′ĭt-ē) [Fr. fr. L. *acuere,* to sharpen] **1.** Clearness, sharpness of a sensory function (e.g., visual acuity). **2.** In emergency and critical care medicine, the severity of a hospitalized patient's illness and the level of attention or service he or she will need from professional staff.

     distance a. The ability to register optical details of objects that are far from the eye, e.g., on a chart positioned 20 ft away from the viewer in a test of visual acuity.

     near a. The ability to register optical details when objects are only 12–14 in from the eye.

     visual a. A measure of the resolving power of the eye. It is usually determined by one's ability to read letters of various sizes at a standard distance from the test chart. The result is expressed as a comparison: 20/20 is normal vision, meaning the subject has the ability to see from a distance of 20 ft (6.1 m) what a person with normal vision should see at that distance. Visual acuity of 20/40 means that a person sees at 20 ft (6.1 m) what a person with normal vision sees from a distance of 40 ft (12.2 m).

     DIAGNOSIS: The Snellen chart used for most purposes ranges from 20/10 to 20/200. People who can see no better than 20/200 are said to be legally blind. People with worse vision (e.g., 20/400 or worse) are said to have "count fingers" (CF) vision: they may not be able to read any of the letters or figures on an eye chart, but they can often see (and count) how many fingers are held in front of them from a specified distance. Those who cannot identify fingers from any distance may still see "hand motion" (HM), or they may have light perception (LP). People who are completely blind are said to have "no light perception" (NLP).

     Young children or people who do not know the Roman alphabet may be able to demonstrate their visual acuity with eye charts on which symbols (e.g., of animals or other commonly recognized shapes) are drawn to similar sizes and specifications.

     PATIENT CARE: A health care professional should conduct an initial visual acuity test on all patients who come to the Emergency Department, clinic, or health care provider's office with a visual complaint or disorder. Visual acuity should be tested with an illuminated Snellen eye chart. The visual acuity of each eye is checked independently with and without the patient's distance glasses or contact lenses; then the acuity of both eyes is checked.

acuminate (ă-kū′mĭ-nit, -nāt″) [L. *acuminatus,* sharpened] Conical; pointed.

acupoint (ak′yŭ-point″) [*acu-* + *point*] A specific location on the body where an acupuncture needle is inserted or pressure is applied for therapeutic purposes, e.g., the control of postoperative nausea and vomiting.

acupressure (ak′yŭ-presh″ŭr) [*acu-* + *pressure*] Finger pressure applied therapeutically at selected points on the body. In traditional Chinese medicine, the pressure points follow lines along the body called meridians. Techniques include shiatsu, tsubo, jin shin yutsu, and jon shin do.

acupuncture (ak′yŭ-pŭngk″chŭr) [*acu-* + *puncture*] A technique for treating pain, producing regional anesthesia, treating acute or chronic illness (such as hormonal, immune, or orthopedic), or preventing disease by passing thin needles through the skin into specific points on the body. The free ends of the needles are manually twirled, heated by moxa or moxibustion, or connected to a weak electrical current. They are then typically left in place for about 20 min. Although acupuncture has a variety of uses in Asia and Europe, in the U.S. it is principally considered a treatment for local pain. It is often used in combination with other therapies, including massage, meditation, and herbal remedies. Research suggests that acupuncture relieves pain by stimulating the release of endogenous opioids, other neurotransmitters (such as serotonin), and by directly affecting afferent nerve fibers. Acupuncture has also been found to be effective in veterinary applications. In the U.S. professional proficiency in acupuncture is attained by passing an examination administered by the National Commission for the Certification of Acupuncture and Oriental Medicine of the American Academy of Medical Acupuncture. **acupuncturist** (-chŭ-rist), *n.*

⚠ It is important that the acupuncturist use sterile or disposable needles and that care be taken to prevent puncturing adjacent organs.

acute (ă-kūt′) [L. *acutus,* sharp, sharpened] **1.** Of pain, sharp, severe. **2.** Of disease, having rapid onset, severe symptoms, and a short course. SEE: *chronic* (2). **3.** Of the senses, perceiving keenly and accurately.

acute care SEE: under *care.*

acute chest syndrome A complication of sickle cell disease resulting from vascular occlusion or infection in the lungs and marked by chest pain, tachypnea, fever, rales and rhonchi, leukocytosis, and lobar consolidation.

acute confusional state SEE: *confusional state, acute.*

acute coronary syndrome ABBR: ACS. Any circumstance that suddenly impairs blood flow through the coronary arteries. Acute coronary syndrome includes all forms of acute myocardial infarction (i.e., those that cause Q waves on the electrocardiogram and those that do not, as well as those that cause S-T segment elevation and those that do not), and unstable angina pectoris.

PATIENT CARE: On admission the focus of immediate care is stabilizing the patient's condition, relieving pain caused by ischemia, and administering all medications as prescribed, including thrombolytic therapy when indicated. In the first 48 hours monitoring and treating arrhythmias, and identifying and correcting exacerbating factors such as electrolyte imbalances, hypoxemia, acidosis or drugs are priorities in care.

acute effect Any adverse effect of a transient exposure to a noxious agent, such as an infectious microorganism, ionizing radiation, or a toxin.

acute generalized exanthematous pustulosis SEE: under *pustulosis.*

acute kidney injury ABBR: AKI. Acute renal **failure**

acute panmyelosis with myelofibrosis ABBR: APMF. A form of acute leukemia in which multiple cell lines develop aberrantly, infiltrate internal organs, e.g., the spleen, and cause extensive bone marrow fibrosis.

acute phase reaction The release of physiologically active proteins by the liver into the blood in response to interleukin-6 or other cytokines that participate in the destruction of pathogens and promote healing during inflamma-

tion. This results in fever, an increase in circulating neutrophils, and activation of the hypothalamus, pituitary gland, and adrenal glands. The acute phase response involves the production of plasma proteins as well as other metabolic, hematological, and neuroendocrine events. Cytokines, produced by white blood cells, esp. macrophages, stimulate the liver's production of acute phase proteins: interleukin-6, interleukin-1β, tumor necrosis factor α, interferon-γ, and transforming growth factor β. These proteins, which increase or decrease in the blood by at least 25%, include C-reactive protein, complement, and coagulation factors; they enhance the immune response and tissue repair. Cytokines also stimulate systemic changes, producing diverse beneficial effects including fever, which enhances the immune response and stabilizes cell membranes; increased adrenal cortisol and catecholamine production, which helps maintain hemodynamic stability; thrombocytosis and leukocytosis; and increased gluconeogenesis and lipolysis, which provide nutrients for cells. There are also negative effects, however, including decreased production of erythropoietin, causing anemia; impaired growth; anorexia; lethargy; and, if prolonged, the loss of skeletal muscle and fat (cachexia). SYN: *acute phase response.* SEE: *cytokine; inflammation; interleukin-6; protein, acute phase.*

acute respiratory distress syndrome ABBR: ARDS. Respiratory insufficiency marked by progressive hypoxemia due to severe inflammatory damage causing abnormal permeability of the alveolocapillary membrane. The alveoli fill with fluid, which interferes with gas exchange. SEE: *disseminated intravascular coagulation; sepsis; systemic inflammatory response syndrome; Nursing Diagnoses Appendix.*

ETIOLOGY: ARDS may result from direct trauma to the lungs (e.g., near drowning, aspiration of gastric acids, severe lung infection) or systemic disorders (e.g., shock, septicemia, disseminated intravascular coagulation [DIC], cardiopulmonary bypass, or reaction to blood transfusions). Widespread damage to the alveolocapillary membranes is initiated through the aggregation and activity of neutrophils and macrophages and the activation of complement. Cytokines, oxygen-free radicals, and other inflammatory mediators damage the walls of capillaries and alveoli, producing diffuse inflammatory interstitial and alveolar edema, fibrin exudates, and hyaline membranes that block oxygen delivery to the blood.

DIAGNOSIS: Diagnosis is based on a history of a recent event associated with the onset of ARDS, the presence of noncardiogenic pulmonary edema on the chest radiograph, and persistent hypoxemia and a PaO_2/FIO_2 ratio of < 200.

SYMPTOMS: Dyspnea and tachypnea are followed by a progressive hypoxemia that, despite oxygen therapy, is the hallmark of ARDS. Diffuse, fluffy infiltrates can be seen on chest radiographs as inflammation increases alveolar permeability, causing visible alveolar flooding and collapse.

TREATMENT: Endotracheal intubation, mechanical ventilation with positive end-expiratory pressure (PEEP), supplemental oxygen, and tidal volumes of 4 to 8 ml/kg optimize respiratory outcomes. PEEP increases intrathoracic pressure, keeping alveoli open during exhalation. This reduces the pressure required to open alveoli during inhalation, improves gas exchange, and reduces oxygen need. The patient should be monitored and treated for acidosis, cardiac arrhythmias, DIC, oxygen toxicity, renal failure, and sepsis.

PROGNOSIS: Mortality is high, approx. 50% to 60%, depending on the amount of lung tissue affected and the ability to maintain adequate oxygen flow to vital organs. After resolution of the inflammation, the damaged lung tissue becomes fibrotic and can cause chronic restrictive lung disease. Prolonged use of more than 50% oxygen increases the risk of residual lung damage.

PATIENT CARE: To avert ARDS, respiratory status must be monitored in at-risk patients. Recognizing and treating early signs and symptoms can be crucial to a patient's survival. Ventilation rate, depth, and rhythm must be monitored and subtle changes noted. The onset of ARDS is marked by the onset of a rapid, shallow breathing pattern, and pulse oximetry must be monitored continuously for subtle changes. If shock ensues and blood is shunted away from body surfaces, resulting in cool skin, O_2 readings may become inaccurate, necessitating use of arterial blood gas monitoring for respiratory alkalosis (early) and mixed metabolic and respiratory acidosis (later). Serial chest x-rays should be obtained to assess for bilateral consolidation progressing to lung "whiteout." The patient must also be observed for chest wall retractions on inspiration, use of accessory breathing muscles, and level of dyspnea. The patient's consciousness level, cardiac rate and rhythm, blood pressure, arterial blood gas (ABG) values, serum electrolyte levels, and chest radiograph results must be monitored. Fluid balance must be closely watched by 1) measuring intravenous (IV) fluid intake, urinary output, and central venous pressure; 2) weighing the patient daily; and 3) assessing for peripheral edema. A patent airway must be maintained, and oxygen therapy with continuous positive airway pressure or mechanical ventilation with PEEP must be provided by the respiratory therapist as prescribed by the attending physician. Routine management of a mechanically ventilated patient includes 1) monitoring breath sounds, chest wall movement, vital signs and comfort, and ventilator settings and function; 2) suctioning the endotracheal tube and oropharynx; and 3) assessing changes in pulse oximetry and ABG values.

Cardiac output may be decreased because PEEP increases intrathoracic pressure and reduces venous return. For this reason, health care professionals must monitor blood pressure, urine output, mental status, peripheral pulses, and pulmonary capillary wedge pressure to determine the effects of positive-pressure ventilation on hemodynamics. Inotropic drugs must be administered as prescribed if cardiac output falls. Hemoglobin levels and oxygen saturation values must also be monitored closely because packed red blood cell transfusion may be required if hemoglobin is inadequate for oxygen delivery. The nurse and respiratory therapist (RT) must observe for signs and symptoms of barotrauma, e.g., subcutaneous emphysema, pneumothorax, and pneumomediastinum. If mechanical ventilation is used, sedation may help calm the patient and reduce the incidence of poor synchronization between the patient and the ventilator. Nutritional support should begin early to promote pulmonary cell regeneration and to provide proteins needed for successful weaning from a ventilator. Enteral nutrition is preferred over parenteral because it reduces the risk of infection. A formula that is lower in carbohydrates helps decrease CO_2 formation during metabolism in ARDS patients retaining CO_2. Fluid replacement should maintain sufficient circulating volume without causing overhydration as determined by central venous pressure readings. Nursing measures must be used to prevent problems of immobility. Prone positioning may be prescribed to improve oxygenation while lessening the risk of barotrauma, but it complicates some elements of nursing care. Prone positioning, if prescribed (usually for 4 to 6 hours daily), is often labor-intensive and requires several staff members to position the patient and therefore is best accomplished on day shift when more staff are available in an emergency. To limit the patient's fear and isolation, the procedure should be explained to the patient, assuring him or her of its safety. Sedation or analgesia are prescribed 30 to 60 minutes before turning the patient on his or her abdomen. To reduce compression of the lungs by the heart and mediastinum, a specialty bed may be used, or a pronator device (a padded metal frame that is placed against the patient's chest and abdomen, with belt buckles that secure and protect the head, chest, and abdomen during the procedure) is strapped to the patient. To use this device, the side rails on the patient's bed are lowered, and the patient is pulled close to the edge of the bed farthest from the ventilator. The patient's face is turned away from the ventilator, his or her arm tucked under the body, and the leg farthest from the ventilator crossed over the other leg at the ankle to aid in turning the patient. The patient can then be turned by one staff member on each side of the bed and one (usually an RT) at the head, who protects the endotracheal tube, IV lines, and other attachments. The prone patient's blood pressure and heart and respiratory rates must be closely monitored for evidence of position tolerance, and the RT may confirm correct endotracheal tube position by capnography. Vital signs should return to baseline within 5 min after prone positioning, repositioning the patient in the supine position if there is any drop in O_2 saturation, deterioration in ABG results, or uncontrollable patient anxiety. Once in the prone position, the patient's feet and elbows should be padded to prevent pressure injuries. The patient's head should be repositioned every hour to prevent necrosis of facial skin and to provide oral care and airway suctioning. Range of motion exercises should be performed at least every 2 hr. The patient should be repositioned to the supine position after 4 or 6 hr, as prescribed. Strict asepsis must be observed in dressing changes, suctioning, hand hygiene, and oral care. The patient must be routinely assessed for fever, changes in sputum color, and elevated white blood cell count. Response to therapy must be evaluated and adverse reactions noted. The family must be encouraged to talk to the patient even though he or she may not be able to respond verbally.

RTs play a key role in the care of patients with ARDS. They initiate mechanical ventilation as prescribed by the attending physician and monitor arterial blood gases and pulse oximetry to ensure adequate oxygenation. They adjust the tidal volume, respiratory rate, and PEEP levels to optimize tissue oxygenation. They also help determine when the patient may be ready for weaning from mechanical ventilation by periodic assessment of the patient's cardiopulmonary status.

acute respiratory failure   SEE: under *failure*.

acute retroviral syndrome   The period of initial infection with HIV when the virus first replicates, often causing a flulike or mononucleosis-like syndrome, and typically lasting for 2 to 4 weeks.

acute stress disorder   ABBR: ASD. The emotional and behavioral consequences of a sudden alteration in one's sense of safety. They include intense anxiety, fear or helplessness, or dissociative symptoms.

acute urethral syndrome   Syndrome experienced by women, marked by acute dysuria, urinary frequency, and lack of significant bacteriuria; pyuria may or may not be present. The cause is unknown, but it is important to determine whether a specific bacterial infection of the bladder or vagina is present to ensure that appropriate drugs are given as needed. The syndrome is referred to colloquially as "honeymoon cystitis" because it may occur during periods of increased sexual activity.

    PATIENT CARE: A history of the illness, including events that increase or decrease symptoms, is obtained. The degree and nature of the patient's pain, its location and possible radiation, and its frequency and duration are ascertained. The patient is instructed in the procedure for collecting a clean-catch, midstream urine specimen and is prepared for vaginal examination. If a bladder or vaginal bacterial, fungal, or protozoal infection is diagnosed, prescribed treatment measures are explained and demonstrated.

acyanoblepsia   (ā″sī″ă-nō-blep′sē-ă) [*a-* + *cyano-* + Gr. *blepsis*, sight] Inability to discern blue colors. SYN: *acyanopsia*.

acyanopsia   (ā″sī″ă-nop′sē-ă) [*a-* + *cyano-* + *-opsia*] Acyanoblepsia.

acyanotic   (ā″sī″ă-not′ik) [*a-* + *cyanotic*] Pert. to the absence of cyanosis.

acyclic   (ā″sī′klĭk, sik′lik) [*a-* + *cyclic*] **1.** Without a cycle. **2.** In chemistry, aliphatic.

acyl   (as′ĭl, ēl″, ā′sĭl) [*ac(id)* + *-yl*] General formula RC=O; in organic chemistry, the radical derived from an organic acid when the hydroxyl group (OH) is removed.

acylate   (as′ĭ-lāt″) [*acyl*] To incorporate an acyl (alkanoyl) group into a chemical compound. **acylation** (as″ĭ-lā′shŏn), *n.*

acystia   (ā″sis′tē-ă) [*a-* + *cyst-* + *-ia*] Congenital absence of the bladder.

acystinervia   (ā″sis″tĭ-něr′vē-ă) [*a-* + *cysti-* + L. *nervus*, nerve + *-ia*] Defective nerve supply to or paralysis of the bladder. SYN: *acystineuria*.

acystineuria   (ā″sis″tĭ-noor′ē-ă) Acystinervia.

AD *Alzheimer disease; anodal duration; average deviation.*

ad [L., to] In prescription writing, an indication that a substance should be added to the formulation up to a specified volume.

ad- [L. *ad*, to] Prefix indicating *adherence, increase, toward,,* e.g., adduct.

-ad [L. *ad*, to] Suffix meaning *toward* or *in the direction of*, e.g., cephalad.

a.d. [L.] *auris dextra*, right ear.

ADA *American Dental Association; American Diabetes Association; American Dietetic Association; Americans with Disabilities Act.*

ADAA *American Dental Assistants Association.*

ADAAG *Americans with Disabilities Act Accessibility Guidelines.*

Adacel (ad′ă-sel″) Tetanus toxoid, diphtheria, and acellular pertussis, adsorbed vaccine.

adactylia, adactylism, adactyly (ā″dak″ tĭl′ē-ă, ā-dak′tĭ-lĭzm, -lē) [*a-* + *dactyl-*] Congenital absence of digits of the hand or foot.

adamantine (ad″ă-man′tēn″, tī″, -mant′ĭ) [Gr. *adamantinos*, pert. to the hardest metal or to a diamond] Pert. to the enamel of teeth, very hard.

adamantinoma (ad″ă-man″tī-nō′mă) [*adamantine* + *-oma*] Ameloblastoma.

adamantoblast (ad″ă-man′tŏ-blast″) [*adamantine* + *-blast*] Ameloblast.

adamantoblastoma (ad″ă-man″tŏ-blastō′mă) [*adamantine* + *blastoma*] Overgrowth of an adamantoblast.

Adam's apple (ad′ămz) The laryngeal prominence formed by the two laminae of the thyroid cartilage at the top of the trachea along the front (ventral surface) of the neck. It is more prominent in men than in women. SYN: *pomum adami*.

Adams-Stokes syndrome (ad′ămz-stōks′) SEE: *Stokes-Adams syndrome*.

adaptation (ad″ap″tā′shŏn) [L. *adaptare*, to adjust] **1.** Adjustment of an organism to a change in internal or external conditions or circumstances. **2.** Adjustment of the eye to various intensities of light, accomplished by changing the size of the pupil and accompanied by chemical changes occurring in the rods. **3.** In psychology, a change in quality, intensity, or distinctness of a sensation that occurs after continuous stimulation of constant intensity. **4.** In dentistry, the proper fitting of dentures or bands to the teeth or closeness of a filling to the walls of a cavity. **adaptational** (-shŏ-năl), *adj.* **adaptationally** (-lē), *adv.*

chromatic a. A change in hue or saturation, or both, resulting from pre-exposure to light of other wavelengths.

color a. The fading of intensity of color perception after prolonged visual stimulation.

dark a. Adjustment of the eyes for vision in dim light. SYN: *scotopia*.

light a. Changes that occur in a dark-adapted eye in order for vision to occur in moderate or bright light. Principal changes are contraction of the pupil and breakdown of rhodopsin. Bright sunlight has 30,000 times the intensity of bright moonlight, but the eye adapts so that visual function is possible under both conditions. SEE: *night vision; vision.*

occupational a. ABBR: OA. A practice model used by the occupational therapist to provide strategies for interpreting and enhancing observed patient performance and for facilitating mastery for the patient over performance challenges. SEE: *conceptual model; occupational therapy.*

postural a. The ability to maintain balance and remain upright during changes in position and challenges to stability. SEE: *postural control.*

retinal a. Adjustment of the rods and cones of the retina to ambient light.

Adaptation Model A conceptual model of nursing developed by nursing theorist Sister Callista Roy that is based on the individual's adaptation to environmental stimuli. In this model, the goal of nursing is to promote adaptive physical, physiological, self-concept, and group identities; role function, and interdependence responses. SEE: *Nursing Theory Appendix.*

adapter, adaptor (ă-dap′tĕr) **1.** A device for joining one part of an apparatus to another. **2.** A device to facilitate connecting electrical supply cords to different receptacles. **3.** A device for adapting one type of electrical supply source to the specific requirements of an instrument.

adaptive therapy (ă-dap′tiv) Any of the services, techniques, and technologies used in occupational and physical therapy to help patients with functional disabilities overcome environmental barriers.

adaptive trial SEE: under *trial.*

adaptogen (ă-dap′tŏ-jen″) [*adapt* + *-gen*] Any agent, e.g., an herb or a nutrient, that stimulates immunity or provides resistance to disease.

adaptometer (ad″ap″tom′ĕt-ĕr) [*adapt* + *-meter*] A device to determine the time required for visual adaptation to darkness.

adaxial (ad″ak′sē-ăl) [*ad-* + *axial*] Toward the main axis.

ADCC *Antibody-dependent cellular cytoxicity.*

add (ad) A treatment for presbyopia in which a plus lens is added to the lower segment of eyeglasses to improve near vision, e.g., for reading.

addict (ad′ikt) [L. *addictus*, given over] **1.** One who cannot control the need or craving for a substance or a behavior, esp. when the craving results in adverse consequences or a decline in one's ability to function effectively. **2.** To make someone dependent or to become dependent on a substance or behavior.

addiction (ă-dik'shŏn) [*addict*] A compulsive, abnormal dependence on a substance (such as alcohol, cocaine, opiates, or tobacco) or on a behavior (such as gambling). The dependence typically has adverse psychological, physical, economic, social, or legal ramifications.

   drug a. A compulsive and maladaptive dependence on a drug that has adverse psychological, physical, economic, social, or legal ramifications. SEE: *substance abuse; substance dependence.*

   exercise a. A pattern of obsessive physical training that impairs health, produces excessive weight loss, results in injury, or has adverse economic, familial, psychological or social consequences.

addiction ministry A method of recovery from addiction managed and supervised by a religious agency.

addictionologist (ă-dik″shŏn-ol′ŏ-jĭst) [*addiction* + *-logy*] A specialist in the diagnosis, study, and treatment of psychological dependence.

Addison disease (ad'ĭ-sŏnz) [Thomas Addison, Brit. physician, 1793–1860] A rare illness marked by gradual, progressive failure of the adrenal glands and by insufficient production of steroid hormones. Patients with Addison disease are deficient in both glucocorticoids, e.g. cortisol, and mineralocorticoids, e.g. aldosterone. Cortisol is important to glucose metabolism, affects the metabolism of proteins, carbohydrates and fats, and helps maintain blood pressure and cardiovascular function. Hypovolemia and hypotension may result from aldosterone deficiency. SEE: *primary adrenal insufficiency.*

   ETIOLOGY: Primary adrenal failure typically results from autoimmune destruction of the adrenal glands (80% of cases), chronic infections; e.g., tuberculosis, cytomegalovirus, other viruses such as Lyme disease, or histoplasmosis; or cancers that metastasize to the adrenal glands from other organs, e.g., of the lungs or breast. Secondary adrenal insufficiency is related to suppression of hypothalamic-pituitary-adrenal axis function.

   SYMPTOMS: The patient may be symptom-free until the majority of adrenal tissue is destroyed. Early complaints are usually nonspecific, e.g., a feeling of weakness or fatigue. Subsequently patients may notice lack of appetite, weight loss, nausea, vomiting, abdominal pain, craving for salt, and dizziness. Physical findings may include

postural hypotension and increased skin pigmentation. Laboratory studies may reveal hyponatremia and hyperkalemia. If these findings are present, a cosyntropin stimulation test may be performed to establish the diagnosis.

   TREATMENT: Chronic adrenal insufficiency is managed with corticosteroids, e.g., hydrocortisone or prednisone, usually taken twice a day, at the lowest effective dose to replace cortisol. If the patient requires mineralocorticoid replacement, fludrocortisone is prescribed. Because of the vital role of cortisol in the body's response to stress, the maintenance dose of these medications during episodic illnesses or stresses, e.g., surgeries, is increased and then tapered over several days back to baseline levels. SEE: *adrenal crisis.*

   PROGNOSIS: Untreated patients may develop progressive problems with abdominal pain, nausea, vomiting, low blood pressure, electrolyte disturbances, or shock during major illnesses. Patients treated with corticosteroids have an excellent prognosis.

   PATIENT CARE: Patients with primary adrenal insufficiency who are suffering other acute conditions are assessed frequently for hypotension, tachycardia, fluid balance, and electrolyte and glucose levels. Prescribed adrenocortical steroids, with sodium and fluid replacement, are administered. The patient is protected from stressors, e.g., infection, noise, and light and temperature changes. Extra time for rest and relaxation is planned.

   For chronic maintenance therapy: Both patient and family are taught about the need for lifelong replacement therapy and medical supervision. Patients are taught about self-administration of steroid therapy (typically two thirds of the dose is given in the A.M. and one third in the P.M. to mimic diurnal adrenal activity). Symptoms of overdosage and underdosage and the course of action if either occurs are explained. The patient and family also are taught how to monitor blood pressure, heart rate, and blood glucose level. A medical alert tag should be worn (or a card carried) indicating that the person has Addison disease and requires a 100 mg cortisol injection if found severely injured or incapacitated. Patient and family should learn how to administer hydrocortisone by injection and should have a prepackaged syringe and needle with the drug readily available at all times. The patient also should be taught to recognize physical or mental stressors and how to adjust the usual dosage to prevent a crisis. The patient is instructed to increase fluid and salt replacement if perspiring and to follow a diet high in sodium, carbohydrates, and protein, with small, frequent meals if hypoglycemia or anorexia occurs. Measures to help prevent infection include getting adequate rest, avoiding fatigue, eating a balanced diet, and avoiding people with infections. Verbalization of feelings and concerns is encouraged. The patient is assisted in developing coping strategies and is referred for further mental health or stress management counseling if warranted. Educational materials and support are available from the National Adrenal Diseases Foundation http:// www.nadf.us/ or the National Institutes of Health at http://endo-crine.niddk.nih.gov/pubs/addison/addi-son.htm. SEE: *Nursing Diagnoses Appendix.*

Addison planes (ad′ĭ-sŏn) [Christopher Addison, Brit. anatomist, 1869–1951] Imaginary planes that divide the abdomen into nine regions to aid in the location of internal structures. SEE: *abdominal* **regions**.

addition (ă-dĭ′shŏn) [L. *addere,* to add] In chemistry, a reaction in which two substances unite without loss of atoms or valence.

addition silicone impression material An elastic final impression material used to construct cast restorations, dental prostheses, and other appliances. It is made from a vinyl polysiloxane paste mixed with a platinum salt catalyst.

⚠️ Wearing latex gloves inhibits the setting of addition silicone impression material. The contamination is so pervasive that touching the tooth with the latex will inhibit setting.

additive (ad′ĭ-tiv) [L. *additivus*] **1.** In pharmacology, the effect that one drug or substance contributes to the action of another drug or substance. **2.** Any substance that changes the composition or action of another when it is added or combined with the first; an adulterant.

color a. Any dye, pigment, or substance that can impart color when added or applied to a food, drug, or cosmetic. Use of color additives in the U.S. is regulated by the FDA. Food Drug and Cosmetic (FDC) colors certified for food use are FDC Blue No. 1, No. 2, and No. 3; Green No. 3; Red No. 3 and No. 40; and Yellow No. 5 and No. 6.

food a. A substance added to food to maintain or impart a certain consistency, to improve or maintain nutritive value, to enhance palatability or flavor, to produce a light texture, or to control pH. Food additives are used to help bread rise during baking, to keep bread mold-free, to color margarine, to prevent discoloration of some fruits, and to

prevent fats and oils from becoming rancid. The FDA regulates their use.

additive effect The therapeutic effect of a combination of two or more drugs that is equal to the sum of the individual drug effects.

add-on therapy Any treatment given to bolster or enhance the effectiveness of a previous one, esp. when the first treatment proved not to be fully effective.

adducent (ă-doo′sĕnt) [L. *adducere,* to bring toward] Causing adduction.

adduct (ă-dŭkt′) [L. *adductus,* brought toward] **1.** In physiology, to draw toward the long axis of the body or a limb. **2.** In chemistry, a compound formed by the addition of one chemical structure to another.

adduction (ă-dŭk′shŏn) [*adduct*] **1.** Lateral movement of a limb toward the median plane of the body. SEE: *abduction* for illus. **2.** Lateral movement of a digit toward the median plane of the limb. **3.** Inward rotation of an eyeball.

convergent-stimulus a. Convergence of the eyes when the gaze is fixed on an object at the near point of vision.

adenalgia (ad″ĕn-al′j(ĕ-)ă) [*aden-* + *-algia*] Adenodynia.

adenase (ad′ĕ-nās) [aden- + *-ase*] An enzyme secreted by the pancreas, spleen, and liver that converts adenine into hypoxanthine.

adendric, adendritic (ā″den′drik, ā″den-drit′ik) [*a-* + Gr. *dendritēs,* pert. to a tree] Without dendrites, as in certain cells in the spinal ganglia.

adenectomy (ad″ĕn-ek′tŏ-mē) [aden- + *-ctomy*] Excision of a gland.

adenectopia (ad″ĕ-nek-tō′pē-ă) [aden- + ectopia] Abnormal position of a gland.

adenia (ă-dē′nē-ă) [aden- + *-ia*] Chronic inflammation and enlargement of a lymph gland.

Adenia digitata (ă-dēn′ē-ă dĭj″ĭ-tā′tă) [L] A broad-leafed plant native to SE Africa. The tubers contain concentrated modeccin, a protein toxic to mammalian ribosomes.

adenine (ad′ĕ-nēn″) [aden- + *-ine*] A purine base, $C_5H_5N_5$, that is part of the genetic code of DNA and RNA. In DNA it is paired with thymine; in RNA, with uracil.

adenitis (ad″ĕ-nīt′is) [aden- + *-itis*] Inflammation of lymph nodes or a gland.

adeno-, aden- [Gr. *adēn,* gland] Prefixes meaning *gland.*

adenoacanthoma (ad″ĕ-nō-ak″an″thō′mă) [adeno- + acanthoma] Adenocarcinoma in which some cells have undergone squamous metaplasia.

adenoameloblastoma (ad″ĕ-nō-am″ĕ-lō-blas-tō′mă) [adeno- + ameloblastoma] A benign tumor of the jaw originating from ameloblasts. SYN: *adenomatoid odontogenic* **tumor**.

adenoblast (ad′ĕ-nō-blast″) [adeno- +

-blast] Any tissue that produces secretory or glandular activity.

adenocarcinoma (ad″ĕ-nō-kar″sĭn-ō′mă) [*adeno-* + *carcinoma*] A malignant tumor that originates in glandular tissues, e.g., the breast, the pancreas, or the prostate. SYN: *glandular carcinoma*. **adenocarcinomatous** (-măt-ŭs), *adj*.

　acinar a. Adenocarcinoma in which the cells are in the shape of alveoli. SYN: *alveolar a.*

　alveolar a. Acinar a.

　fetal a. A rare form of adenocarcinoma of the lung, resembling fetal lung tissue when examined microscopically. It consists of columnar cells that have a clear cytoplasm and oval nuclei.

　a. in situ ABBR: AIS. A localized cluster of malignant appearing cells found in a gland but not yet spreading outside the basement membrane of the gland.

adenocele (ad′ĕ-nō-sēl″) [*adeno-* + *-cele*] **1.** A cystic tumor arising from a gland. **2.** A tumor of glandular structure.

adenocellulitis (ad″ĕ-nō-sel″yŭ-līt′is) [*adeno-* + *cellulitis*] Inflammation of a gland and adjacent cellular tissue.

adenocyst (ad′ĕ-nō-sist″) [*adeno-* + *-cyst*] A cystic tumor arising from a gland.

adenodynia (ăd″ĕ-nō-dĭn′ē-ă) [*aden-* + *-odynia*] Pain in a gland. SYN: *adenalgia*.

adenoepithelioma (ad″ĕ-nō-ep″ĭ-thēl″ē-ō′mă) [*adeno-* + *epithelioma*] A tumor consisting of glandular and epithelial elements.

adenofibroma (ad″ĕ-nō-fĭ-brō′mă) [*adeno-* + *fibroma*] A tumor of fibrous and glandular tissue. It is frequently found in the uterus or breast.

adenofibrosis (ad″ĕ-nō-fĭ-brō′sis) [*adeno-* + *fibrosis*] The abnormal growth of fibrous or connective tissue within glandular tissue.

adenogenous (ad″ĕ-noj′ĕ-nŭs) [*adeno-* + Gr. *gennan,* to produce] Originating in glandular tissue.

adenohypophysis (ad″ĕ-nō-hī-pof′ĭ-sis) [*adeno-* + *hypophysis*] The portion of the pituitary gland containing secretory cells that release the hormones adrenocorticotropic hormone (ACTH), follicle-stimulating hormone (FSH), growth hormone (GH), luteinizing hormone (LH), prolactin, and thyroid-stimulating hormone (TSH). The adenohypophysis makes up 80% of the pituitary gland. It is an epithelial tissue that develops from the roof of the embryonic mouth. SYN: *anterior lobe; anterior lobe of pituitary gland; anterior pituitary.* **adenohypophyseal** (-hī″po″fĭ-sē′ăl), *adj*. **adenohypophysial** (-hī″pŏ-fiz′ē-ăl), *adj*.

adenoid (ad′(ĕ-)noyd″) [*aden-* + *-oid*] **1.** Having the appearance of a gland;

lymphoid. **2.** Pert. to the adenoids **3.** Pert. to or affected with enlarged adenoids.

adenoidal (ad′(ĕ-)noyd″ăl) **1.** A colloquial term for pert. to or affected with abnormally enlarged pharyngeal tonsils in children. **2.** A colloquial term for pert. to a nasal tone in the voice.

adenoidectomy (ad″ĕ-noy″dek′tŏ-mē) [*adenoid* + *-ectomy*] Excision of the adenoids. SEE: *tonsillectomy; Nursing Diagnoses Appendix.*

　PATIENT CARE: Vital signs are monitored, and the patient is observed for signs of shock. The mouth and pharynx are checked for bleeding, large clot formation, or oozing; the patient is observed for frequent swallowing, which indicates bleeding or large clot formation. Clots should be prevented from obstructing the oropharnyx. The patient is placed in either a prone position with the head turned to the side or in a lateral recumbent position to promote drainage. When the operative wound has healed sufficiently, the oral intake of cool (not hot or iced) fluids and soft foods is encouraged. The patient is also advised not to gargle until the surgical site has healed.

　Young patients: The child is reassured about routines and procedures in care. Emotional support is provided, and parental presence is encouraged. The child is evaluated for vomiting swallowed blood and is monitored for ability to swallow fluids.

adenoiditis (ad″ĕ-noyd-īt′is) [*adenoid* + *-itis*] Inflammation of adenoid tissue.

adenoids (ad′(ĕ-)noydz″) [*aden-* + *-oid*] **1.** Lymphatic tissue forming a prominence on the wall of the pharyngeal recess of the nasopharynx. **2.** A colloquial term for enlarged pharyngeal tonsils in children. SEE: *pharyngeal tonsil.*

adenolipoma (ad″ĕ-nō-li-pō′mă) [*adeno-* + *lipoma*] A benign tumor having glandular characteristics but composed of fat.

adenolymphocele (ad″ĕ-nō-lim″fō-sēl″) [*adeno-* + *lymphocele*] Cystic dilatation of a lymph node from obstruction.

adenolymphoma (ad″ĕ-nō-lim-fō′mă) [*adeno-* + *lymphoma*] A lymph gland adenoma.

adenoma (ad″ĕ-nō′mă, ′mă-tă) *pl.* **adenomas, adenomata** [*aden-* + *-oma*] A benign tumor made of epithelial cells, usually arranged like a gland. **adenomatous** (-nō′mă-tŭs), *adj*.

　PATIENT CARE: Initial care focuses on identifying the sites of tumors, performing biopsies or noninvasive studies to determine if they are benign or malignant, and discussing findings with the patient, the patient's family, and significant others. Disease-specific education is provided to explain diagnostic options and support the patient. Malignant adenomata may need surgical removal; they may be treated with a combination of therapies, including surgical removal, radiation therapy, hormone therapy or chemotherapy. Patient education, esp. with respect to the side effects of therapies and implementing strategies to ameliorate the side effects, is crucial. General emotional support of the patient eases anxiety, isolation, and suffering.

   acidophilic a. An adenoma of the pituitary gland in which cells stain with acid dyes. Such staining was formerly used to suggest the presence of growth hormones, the cause of acromegaly and gigantism. Immunocytochemistry is the modern means of classifying pituitary tumors. SYN: *eosinophil a.*

   adrenocorticotrophin-secreting a. A pituitary adenoma that secretes adrenocorticotropic hormone, the releasing hormone responsible for Cushing's syndrome.

   basophil a., basophilic a. An adenoma of the pituitary gland in which cells stain with basic dyes. The term was formerly used to suggest tumors that secreted adrenocorticotrophin (ACTH), the cause of Cushing syndrome. Those tumors are now identified more directly by the identification (by immunocytochemistry) of ACTH in tumor cells. The use of hematoxylin and eosin staining to identify pituitary tumors is obsolete.

   chromophobe a. An adenoma of the pituitary gland composed of cells that do not stain readily. The term has more historical value than descriptive value and is no longer in use.

   cystic a. Cystadenoma.

   eosinophil a., eosinophilic a. Acidophil **a.**

   fibroid a. Fibroadenoma.

   follicular a. An adenoma of the thyroid.

   gonadotroph-cell a. The most common macroadenoma of the pituitary gland. It secretes either luteinizing hormone or follicle-stimulating hormone.

   Hürthle cell a. SEE: under *Hürthle, Karl W.*

   malignant a. Adenocarcinoma.

   papillary a. An adenoma with nipple-shaped glands.

   pituitary a. An adenoma of the pituitary gland, often of one of its functional cell types. It may produce excessive amounts of hormones such as prolactin, growth hormone, or adrenocorticotrophic hormone, or it may be clinically silent.

   sebaceous a. Enlarged sebaceous glands, esp. of the face. SYN: *a. sebaceum.*

   a. sebaceum Sebaceous **a.**

   somatotroph a. A growth-hormone-secreting tumor of the anterior pituitary that causes acromegaly or giantism.

   villous a. A large polyp of the mucosal surface of the large intestine. It has the potential to develop into cancer.

adenomatome (ad″ĕ-nō′mă-tōm″) [*adenoma* + *-tome*] An instrument for removing adenoids.

adenomatosis (ad″ĕn-ō″mă-tō′sis) [*adenoma* + *-osis*] The condition of multiple glandular tissue overgrowths.

adenomectomy (ad″ĕn-ō-mek′tŏ-mē) [*adenoma* + *-ectomy*] Surgical excision of a glandular tumor.

adenomyoma (ad″ĕn-ō″mī-ō′mă) [*adeno-* + *myoma*] A benign complex tumor containing glandular and smooth muscular tissue.

adenomyometritis (ad″ĕ-nō-mī″ŏ-mĕ-trīt′is) [*adeno-* + *myometritis*] Adenomyosis.

adenomyosarcoma (ad″ĕ-nō-mī″ŏ-sar-kō′mă) [*adeno-* + *myosarcoma*] Adenosarcoma that includes muscle tissue.

adenomyosis (ad″ĕ-nō-mī-ō′sis) [*adeno-* + *myo-* + *-sis*] Benign invasive growth of the endometrium into the muscular layer of the uterus. SYN: *adenomyometritis.* SEE: *endometriosis* for illus.

adenopathy (ad-ĕ-nop′ă-thē) [*adeno-* + *-pathy*] Any abnormal enlargement of a lymph node, e.g., as a result of infection or metastasized cancer.

adenopharyngitis (ad″ĕ-nō″far″in-jīt′is) [*adeno-* + *pharyngitis*] Inflammation of the tonsils and pharyngeal mucous membrane.

adenophthalmia (ad″ĕ-nof-thal′mē-ă) [*adeno-* + *ophthalmia*] Meibomitis.

adenosarcoma (ad″ĕ-nō″sar-kō′mă) [*adeno-* + *sarcoma*] A tumor with adenomatous and sarcomatous characteristics.

adenosclerosis (ad″ĕ-nō-sklĕ-rō′sis) [*adeno-* + *sclerosis*] Glandular hardening.

adenose, adenous (ad′ĕ-nōs″, ad′ĕ-nŭs) Glandlike.

adenosine (ă-den′ŏ-sēn″) [Ger. blend of *adenine* + *ribose*] A nucleotide containing adenine and ribose.

   a. 3′,5′-cyclic monophosphate ABBR: AMP. A cyclic form of adenosine. Its synthesis from adenosine triphosphate (ATP) is stimulated by an enzyme, adenylate cyclase (also called cyclic AMP synthetase). Adenosine 3′,5′-cyclic monophosphate is important in a wide variety of metabolic responses to cell stimuli.

   a. diphosphate ABBR: ADP. A compound of adenosine containing two phosphoric acid groups. ADP is used to synthesize ATP with the energy released in cell respiration. When ATP is used for cellular functions such as protein synthesis, ADP is reformed.

a. monophosphate ABBR: AMP; 5'-AMP. A substance formed by condensation of adenosine and phosphoric acid. It is one of the hydrolytic products of nucleic acids and is present in muscle, red blood cells, yeast, and other nuclear material. SYN: *adenylic acid.*

a. triphosphatase ABBR: ATPase. An enzyme that splits adenosine triphosphate to yield phosphate and energy.

a. triphosphate ABBR: ATP. A compound of adenosine containing three phosphoric acid groups. Its chemical formula is $C_{10}H_{16}N_5O_{13}P_3$. ATP is present in all cells and is formed when energy is released from food molecules during cell respiration. Cells contain enzymes to hydrolyze ATP into ADP, phosphate, and energy, which is then available for cellular functions such as mitosis.

adenosis (ad"ĕ-nō'sis) [*aden-* + *-osis*] Any disease of a gland or of glandular tissue.

vaginal a. Disordered growth of the glandular cells of the vagina. It is a common finding in women whose mothers were exposed to diethylstilbesterol (DES) during pregnancy. Close follow-up of women with vaginal adenosis is needed because the condition is occasionally a sign of glandular cancer.

adenosquamous (ad"ĕn-ō-skwā'mŭs) [*adeno-* + *squamous*] Pert. to or containing a cellular architecture that is partly glandular and partly epithelial (squamous cell). It refers to some lung carcinomas.

adenotome (ad'ĕ-nō"tōm") [*adeno-* + *-tome*] A device for excising a gland, esp. the adenoid glands.

adenotonsillectomy (ad"ĕ-nō"ton"sĭ-lek'tŏ-mē) [*adeno-* + *tonsillectomy*] Surgical removal of the tonsils and adenoids.

adenovirus (ad'ĕ-nō-vī'rŭs) [*adeno-* + *virus*] Any of a group of double-stranded DNA viruses that can cause infections of the upper respiratory tract. A large number have been isolated. **adenoviral** (-răl), *adj.*

adenyl (ad'ĕ-nil) [*aden-* + *-yl*] The radical $C_5H_4N_5$; present in adenine.

a. cyclase An enzyme that catalyzes the production of cyclic AMP (adenosine 3',5'-cyclic monophosphate) from ATP (adenosine triphosphate). It is present on most cell surfaces.

adenylate cyclase (ă-den'ĭ-lăt sī'klăs) An enzyme important in the synthesis of cyclic AMP (adenosine 3',5'-cyclic monophosphate) from adenosine triphosphate. SYN: *cyclic AMP synthetase.*

adermia (ă-dĕr'mē-ă) [*a-* + *derm-* + *-ia*] Congenital or acquired defect in or lack of skin.

adermogenesis (ă-dĕr"mō-jen'ĕ-sis) [*a-* + *dermo-* + *-genesis*] Imperfect development of skin.

ADH *antidiuretic hormone* (vasopressin). SEE: under *hormone.*

ADHA *American Dental Hygienists' Association.*

adherence (ad'hēr-ĕns) [L. *adhaerere,* to stick] **1.** Stickiness. **2.** The extent to which a patient's behavior coincides with medical advice. Adherence may be estimated by carefully questioning the patient and family members; evaluating the degree of clinical response to therapy or the presence or absence of side effects from drugs; measuring serum drug levels or testing for excretion of the drug in the urine; and counting remaining pills. SYN: *compliance* (1). SEE: tables.

adherent (ăd-hē'rĕnt) [L. *adhaerere,* to stick] Attached to.

Factors That May Decrease Patient Adherence to Therapy in the U.S.

Communication difficulties with health care providers
Cultural barriers between patient and provider
Dementia and other forms of cognitive dysfunction
Denial of illness
Depression or anxiety
Lack of finances; excessive expense associated with obtaining care
Lack of time to arrange, wait for, and get to and from appointments
Lack of social support
Language barriers
Male gender
Marital status (unmarried)
Medical transportation difficulties
Mistrust of health care institutions or specific forms of therapy
Personality disorders
Psychoses
Religious proscriptions against particular forms of treatment
Substance abuse

Strategies that Improve Patient Adherence to Medical Regimens

Use of medications within a therapeutic class that the patient prefers
Use of medications that the patient can afford
Use of medications with the simplest dosing regimens
Use of medications with the fewest drug interactions or side effects
Patient education that is geared to the patient's level of health literacy
Follow-up by health care providers, to identify barriers to adherence and discuss patient concerns

adhesin (ăd-hēz'in) [*adhes(ion)* + *-in*] **1.** In conjugation of some bacteria, a protein on the cell surface that causes aggregation of cells. **2.** A protein found on the cell wall of bacteria such as *Escherichia coli* that enables the bacteria to bind to the host's cells.

adhesio interthalamica (ăd-hē'zē-ō in"těr-thă-lăm'ĭ-kă) [L. interthalamic adhesion] ABBR: AI. The massa intermedia that connects the two lobes of the thalamus.

adhesiolysis (ăd-hēz"ē-ol'ĭ-sĭs) [*adhesion* + *-lysis*] Surgery to cut or remove intraperitoneal adhesions.

adhesion (ad-hē'zhŏn) [L. *adhaerere*, to stick] **1.** A holding together or uniting of two surfaces or parts, as in wound healing. **2.** A fibrous band holding parts together that are normally separated. **3.** An attraction to another substance, e.g., of molecules or blood platelets to each other or to dissimilar materials.

   abdominal a. Scar tissue within the peritoneum that links hollow and/or solid organs. These strands of fibrous tissue usually form as a result of inflammation, surgery, or trauma. When they cause infertility, intestinal obstruction or pain that does not respond to medical therapies, surgery is used to cut or remove them.

   pericardial a. Sticking of the pericardium to the myocardium, e.g., after heart surgery. Extensive adhesions may lead to restriction of the normal contraction of the heart. SEE: *pericarditis*.

adhesiotomy (ad-hē"zē-ot'ŏ-mē) [*adhesi(on)* + *-otomy*] Surgical division of adhesions.

adhesive (ad-hē'siv) [L. *adhaerere*, to stick] **1.** Causing adhesion. **2.** Sticky; adhering. **3.** A substance that causes two bodies to adhere.

adiaphoresis (ā"dī"ă-fŏ-rē'sis) [*a-* + *diaphoresis*] Deficiency or absence of sweat.

Adie, William John (ā'dē) Brit. neurologist, 1886–1935.

   A. pupil A usually unilateral ocular condition in which the affected pupil is larger than the normal one, dilates slowly in accommodation-convergence reflexes, and reacts slowly and only after lengthy exposure to light or dark. It may be part of Adie syndrome if deep tendon reflexes are diminished. SYN: *tonic pupil*.

   A. syndrome An ocular syndrome marked by Adie pupil and absent or lessened Achilles tendon reflex and knee-jerk reflex. The absent or lessened deep tendon reflexes are permanent and may progress over time.

adipectomy (ad"ĭ-pek'tŏ-mē) [*adip-* + *-ectomy*] Excision of usually a large quantity of fat or adipose tissue. SEE: *liposuction*.

adipic (ă-dip'ik) Rel. to adipose tissue.

adipo-, adip- [L. *adeps*, stem *adip-*, fat] Prefixes meaning *fat*.

adipocellular (ad"ĭ-pō-sel'yŭ-lăr) [*adipo-* + *cellular*] Containing fat and cellular tissue.

adipocere (ad'ĭ-pō-sēr") [*adipo-* + L. *cera*, wax] A brown, waxlike substance composed of fatty acids and calcium soaps. It is formed in animal tissues postmortem. **adipocerous** (ad"ĭ-pos'ě-rŭs), *adj*.

adipocyte (ad'ĭ-pō-sīt") [*adipo-* + *-cyte*] Fat cell.

adipocytokine, adipokine (ad"ĭ-pō-sīt'ŏ-kīn", ad"ĭ-pŏ-kīn") [*adipo-* + *cytokine*] A molecule secreted by fat cells that affects the physiology of cells in other parts of the body. Some of these molecules influence appetite, the storage of fat in the body, and systemic inflammation.

adipofibroma (ad"ĭ-pō-fī-brō'mă) [*adipo-* + *fibroma*] A fibroma and adipoma.

adipogenous, adipogenic (ad"ĭ-poj'ěn-ŭs, ad"ĭ-pŏ-jen'ik) [*adipo-* + *-genic*] Inducing the formation of fat.

adipoid (ad'ĭ-poyd") [*adip-* + *-oid*] Fatlike; lipoid.

adipokinesis (ăd"ĭ-pō-kĭ-nē'sis, -kī-) [*adipo-* + *kinesis*] **1.** Metabolism of fat with production of free fatty acids. **2.** Mobilization and metabolism of body fat.

adiponecrosis (ad"ĭ-pō-ně-krō'sis) [*adipo-* + *necrosis*] Necrosis affecting fatty tissue.

adiponectin (ad"ĭ-pŏ-nek'tĭn) A protein derived from adipose tissue that circulates in the blood. It reduces inflammation and insulin resistance.

adipose (ad'ĭ-pōs") [L. *adiposus*, fatty] Pert. to fat; fatty.

adiposis (ad"ĭ-pō'sis) [*adipo-* + *-sis*] Obesity.

adipositis (ad"ĭ-pō-sīt'ĭs) [*adipose* + *-itis*] Inflammation in and beneath adipose tissue.

adiposity (ăd"ĭ-pŏs'ĭ-tē) Obesity.

adiposogenital syndrome (ad"ĭ-pō"sō-jen'ĭ-tăl) Fröhlich's syndrome.

adipsia, adipsy (ă-dip'sē-ă, -sē) [*¹an-* + Gr. *dipsa*, thirst + *-ia*] Absence of thirst. SYN: *aposia*.

adjudicate (ă-jood'ĭ-kāt") [L. *adjudicare*, to award a judgment, judge] To issue or make a judgment in a court of law, e.g., regarding malpractice. **adjudication** (-jood"ĭ-kā'shŏn), *n.* **adjudicator** (-jood'ĭ-kāt"ŏr), *n.*

adjunct (ad'jŭngkt") [L. *adjungere*, to join] **1.** A nonessential addition to the principal procedure or course of therapy. **2.** An assistant or associate, esp. one without full employment or professional status at a hospital, college, or university. **adjunct,** *adj.*

adjust (ă-jŭst') [Fr. *ajuster*, to gauge] **1.** To adapt to a different environment;

to cope with new conditions or stressors. **2.** To change or modify something, esp. to improve its function or condition. **3.** To manipulate a part of the body, e.g., with physical force.

adjustable gastric banding (ă-jŭs′tă-bl) A bariatric surgical treatment for obesity in which a Silastic belt encircles the proximal portion of the stomach, restricting the flow of food. The rest of the gastrointestinal tract is left unmodified. The belt initially permits the proximal stomach to hold just an ounce of food. The restriction gives patients a feeling of premature fullness after a small meal, which keeps them from overeating. It can be loosened after significant weight loss has occurred to permit slightly increased food intake. Weight loss with gastric banding, which results purely from limitations on food intake, tends to be less than what can be achieved with surgery, e.g., Roux-en-Y gastric bypass. Relatively common complications of banding include nausea and vomiting, erosion of the band into the stomach, and wound infections. Some patients learn to eat slowly but continuously and fail to lose weight.

adjuster (ă-jŭs′tĕr) A device for holding together the ends of the wire forming a suture.

adjustment (ă-jŭst′mĕnt) **1.** Adaptation to a different environment; a person's relation to the environment and the self. **2.** A change to improve function or condition. **3.** A modification made to a tooth or a dental prosthesis to enhance fit, function, or the patient's acceptance.

   occlusal a. SEE: *equilibration.*

   long-lever a. In chiropractic or osteopathy, the movement of a bone into normal position or alignment by applying a force to the most distal bone in a joint on a palpable point of resistance. SYN: *long-lever **manipulation**.*

   chiropractic a. Manipulation of a body part with applied force to bring the whole body into better or healthier alignment. Adjustments may be performed by hand or with mechanical aids.

   cost of living a. ABBR: COLA. In determining Social Security payments and other financial benefits, a change in compensation based on the rate of inflation, as demonstrated by the U.S. Consumer Price Index.

   short-lever a. In chiropractic, the movement of a single subluxed bone into normal position or alignment by changing its position relative to a neighboring bone held firmly. The adjustment is made with a forceful or explosive thrust. SYN: *short-lever **manipulation**.*

adjustment, impaired Inability to modify lifestyle/behavior in a manner consist-

ent with a change in health status. SEE: *Nursing Diagnoses Appendix.*

adjustment disorder A maladaptive reaction to an identifiable psychological or social stress that occurs within 3 months of the onset of the stressful situation. The reaction is characterized by impaired function or symptoms in excess of what would be considered normal for that stress. The symptoms are expected to remit when the stress ceases.

adjustment sleep disorder Any transient sleep disorder, e.g., insomnia, hypersomnia, that occurs during periods of psychosocial upheaval or emotional stress.

adjuvant (ad′jŭ-vănt) [L. *adjuvare,* to help] **1.** That which assists, esp. a drug added to a prescription to hasten or increase the action of a principal ingredient. **2.** In immunology, a chemical such as aluminum hydroxide or aluminum phosphate added to an antigen to increase the body's immunologic response. The adjuvants increase the size of the antigen, making it easier for B lymphocytes and phagocytes to recognize it, promote chemotaxis, and stimulate the release of cytokines. Adjuvants are not effective with all antigens and do not stimulate T-cell activity.

adjuvant therapy The use of additional therapy in addition to the primary therapy. In cancer care, for example, surgery to remove a tumor may be the primary treatment, and radiation therapy to destroy neighboring cells and tissues an adjuvant therapy.

ADL *activities of daily living.*

Adler, Alfred (ad′lĕr) Austrian psychiatrist, 1870–1937, founder of the school of individual psychology. SEE: *psychology, individual.*

ad lib (ad lib) SEE: *ad libitum.*

ad libitum (ad lib′ĭ-tŭm) [L. *ad libitum*] ABBR: ad lib. *As desired,* used as a direction in writing prescriptions.

ADMA *asymmetrical dimethylarginine.*

ADMET An acronym for *absorption, distribution, metabolism, excretion,* and *toxicity.* These are key elements that determine the safety, uptake, elimination, metabolic behavior, and effectiveness of drugs.

administration (ăd-min″ĭ-strā′shŏn) [L. *administrare,* to assist, serve] **1.** The dispensing or application of a therapeutic agent. **2.** The managers and management of a health care institution.

Administration on Aging ABBR: AOA. An agency of the U.S. Department of Health and Human Services that conducts research in the field of aging and assists federal, state, and local agencies in planning and developing programs for the aged.

administrative order (ăd-mi-nĭ-strā′tiv) A ruling by the executive or judicial branch of government compelling an action to prevent the spread of disease or to reduce an imminent public health hazard.

admission (ăd-mish′ŏn) [L. *admissio,* fr *admittere,* to send to, allow to come or go] **1.** Acceptance of a student into a program of study. **2.** Hospitalization of a patient.

admission of fact (ăd-mi′shŏn) A written request to accept or deny mutually agreed upon deeds, statements, or assertions of a lawsuit.

admix (ad-miks′) [L. *admixtus,* mixed] To blend or combine.

ad nauseam (ad no′zē-ăm) [L. to (sea)sickness] Of such degree or extent as to produce nausea.

adnexa (ad-nek′să) [L. *adnectere, annectere,* to attach] **1.** The accessory parts of a structure. **2.** The accessory structures to the uterus, namely, the ovaries and fallopian tubes. **adnexal** (ad-nek′săl), *adj.*

dental a. Tissues surrounding the tooth, i.e., periodontal ligament and alveolar bone proper.

a. oculi Lacrimal **gland**.

adnexitis (ăd″nek″sīt′is) [*adnexa* (2) + *-itis*] Inflammation of the ovaries and fallopian tubes. SYN: *annexitis.*

-adol A suffix used to designate an *opiate receptor agonist*/*antagonist.*

adolescence (ăd″ŏl-es′ĕns) [Fr. fr. L. *adolescentia*] The period from the beginning of puberty until maturity. Because the onset of puberty and maturity is a gradual process and varies among individuals, it is not practical to set exact age or chronological limits in defining the adolescent period.

prolonged a. Emerging adulthood.

adolescent (ăd″ŏl-es′ĕnt) [L. *adolescere,* to grow up] **1.** Pert. to adolescence. **2.** A young man or woman not fully grown.

adolescent turmoil In psychoanalytic theory, the belief that adolescence is invariably accompanied by behavioral or psychological upheaval. This is no longer thought to be inevitable or even the usual case.

adoption (ă-dop′shŏn) [L. *adoptare,* to choose] Assumption of responsibility for the care of a child by a person or persons who are not the biological parents.

ADP *Adenosine* diphosphate.

ADR *adverse drug reaction; alternative dispute resolution.*

adrenal (ă-drē′năl) [*ad-* + *renal*] Pert. to the adrenal gland or its secretions.

adrenalectomy (ă-drē″nă-lek′tŏ-mē) [*adrenal* + *-ectomy*] Excision of one or both adrenal glands.

PATIENT CARE: Vital signs, central venous pressure, and urine output must be monitored frequently. Signs and symptoms of hypocorticism must be assessed hourly for the first 24 hr; significant changes must be reported to the

surgeon immediately. Additional IV glucocorticoids are given as prescribed. The patient must be monitored for early indications of shock or infection and for alterations in blood glucose and electrolyte levels. To counteract shock, IV fluids and vasopressors must be administered as prescribed, and the patient's response evaluated every 3 to 5 min. Increased steroids to meet metabolic demands are needed if additional stress, e.g., infection, occurs. Other medications, including analgesics, are given as prescribed, and the patient's response is evaluated. The room must be kept cool and the patient's clothing and bedding changed often if he or she perspires profusely (a side effect of surgery on the adrenal gland). The abdomen must be assessed for distention and return of bowel sounds. Physical and psychological stresses must be kept to a minimum. Steroid medications may not be needed or may be discontinued in a few months to a year after unilateral adrenalectomy, but lifelong replacement therapy will be needed after bilateral adrenalectomy. The patient must learn to recognize the signs of adrenal insufficiency, that sudden withdrawal of steroids can precipitate adrenal crisis, and that continued medical follow-up will be needed so that steroid dosage can be adjusted during stress or illness. Patients should take steroids in a two-thirds A.M. and one-third P.M. dosing pattern to mimic diurnal adrenal activity, with meals or antacids to minimize gastric irritation. Adverse reactions to steroids, e.g., weight gain, acne, headaches, diabetes, and osteoporosis, must be explained. SEE: *Nursing Diagnoses Appendix.*

cortical-sparing a. An operation on the adrenal gland(s) in which the cortex of the gland is left in place and only the diseased portion of the gland is removed. This subtotal adrenal surgery leaves the corticosteroid-producing portion of the gland in place, increasing the probability that the patient will be able to produce his or her own steroids after the surgery.

adrenal hyperandrogenism SEE: under *hyperandrogenism.*

adrenaline (ă-drĕn′ă-lĭn) [*adrenal* + *-in*] Epinephrine. The*British Pharmaceutical Code* recognizes "adrenaline" as the preferred term in the UK for "epinephrine."

adrenalinemia (ă-dren″ă-lĭ-nē′mē-ă) [*adrenaline* + *-emia*] Epinephrine in the blood.

adrenalinuria (ă-dren″ă-lĭn-ūr′ē-ă) [*adrenalin* + *-uria*] Epinephrine in the urine.

adrenalitis, adrenitis (ă-drē″nă-līt′is, ăd″rē-nīt′is) Inflammation of the adrenal glands.

adrenalo-, adrenal-, adreno-, adren- [*ad-*

+ L. *ren,* kidney] Prefixes meaning *adrenal glands.*

adrenarche (ad″rĕ-nar′kē) [*adren-* + Gr. *archē,* beginning] Changes that occur at puberty as a result of increased secretion of adrenocortical hormones. SEE: *menarche; pubarche.*

adrenergic (ad″rĕ-nĕr′jik) [*adren-* + *ergo-* + *-ic*] Pert. to nerve fibers that release norepinephrine or epinephrine at synapses. **adrenergically** (ji-k(ă-)lē), *adv.* SEE: *sympathomimetic.*

adrenoceptive (ă-drē″nŏ-sep′tiv) [*adreno-* + L. *recipere,* to receive] Pert. to the sites in organs or tissues that are acted on by adrenergic transmitters.

adrenochrome (ă-drē′nŏ-krōm″) [*adreno-* + Gr. *chrōma,* color] $C_9H_9NO_3$; a red pigment obtained by oxidation of epinephrine.

adrenocortical (ă-drē″nō-kor′tĭ-kăl) [*adreno-* + *cortical*] Pert. to the adrenal cortex.

adrenocorticosteroid (ă-drē″nō-kor″tĭ-kō-stēr′oyd″) [*adreno-* + *corticosteroid*] A hormone produced by the adrenal cortex or a synthetic derivative of such a hormone.

adrenocorticotropic (ă-drē″nō-kor″tĭ-kō-trō′pik, -trop′ik) [*adreno-* + *corticotropic*] Having a stimulating effect on the adrenal cortex.

adrenocorticotropin (ă-drē″nō-kor″tĭ-kō-trō′pin) Adrenocorticotropic hormone.

adrenogenital (ă-drē-nō-jen′ĭ-tăl) [*adreno-* + *genital*] Pert. to the adrenal glands and the genitalia.

adrenogenital syndrome A syndrome marked by abnormally early puberty in children, overmasculinization in adults, virilism, and hirsutism, caused by the excessive production of adrenocortical hormones. SEE: *Cushing's syndrome.*

adrenogenous (ad″rĕ-noj′ĕ-nŭs) Originating in or produced by the adrenal gland.

adrenoleukodystrophy (ă-drē″nō-loo″kō-dis′trŏ-fē) [*adreno-* + *leukodystrophy*] An X-linked recessive disease in which inability to metabolize very long chain fatty acids results in Addison's disease. Treatments include replacement of adrenal hormones, administration of Lorenzo's oil, or bone marrow transplantation.

adrenolytic (ă″drēn-ŏ-lit′ik) [*adreno-* + *lytic*] Sympatholytic.

adrenomedullin (ă-drē″nō-mĕ-dŭl′ĭn) [*adreno-* + *medullin,* a renal prostaglandin] ABBR: AM. A 52–amino acid regulatory peptide that influences many body functions. These functions include blood vessel dilation (lowering blood pressure), cellular growth, circulation, electrolyte balance, kidney function, and neurotransmission. The level of adrenomedullin in the blood is elevated above normal in patients with congestive heart failure, kidney failure, and di-

abetes mellitus complicated by vascular disease.

adrenomegaly (ă-drēn″ō-meg′ă-lē) [*adreno-* + *-megaly*] Enlargement of the adrenal gland or glands.

adrenomimetic (ă-drē″nō-mĭ-met′ik) [*adreno-* + *mimetic*] Sympathomimetic.

adrenomyeloneuropathy (ă-drē″nō-mī″ĕ-lō-noo-rop′ă-thē, -nū-) [*adreno-* + *myelo-* + *neuropathy*] ABBR: AMN. A noninflammatory form of adrenoleukodystrophy in which the long tracts of the spinal cord are diseased, with limited involvement of peripheral nerves and, in most instances, no evidence of cerebral disease. It is a disease of adults, who gradually become weaker as their nerves accumulate excessive quantities of very long-chain fatty acids.

adrenosterone (ădrē-nō-stĕ-rōn′) [*adreno-* + *-sterone*] An androgenic hormone secreted by the adrenal cortex.

adrenotoxin (ă-drē″nō-tok′sin) [*adreno-* + *toxin*] A substance toxic to the adrenal glands.

adrenotropic (ă-drē″nō-trō′pik, -trop′) [*adreno-* + *-tropic*] Nourishing or stimulating the adrenal glands. The term applies esp. to hormones that stimulate adrenal gland function.

Adson, Alfred Washington (ad′sŏn) U.S. neurosurgeon, 1887–1951.

    A. maneuver A test for thoracic outlet compression syndrome. The patient's arm is moved back into extension and external rotation with the elbow extended and forearm supinated. The radial pulse is palpated while the patient is asked to tuck the chin, side-bend the head toward the opposite side, and rotate the chin toward the side of the extended arm. The patient is then asked to inhale. A positive sign of numbness or tingling in the hand or diminished pulse indicates the brachial plexus or blood vessels are compromised at the site of the scalene muscle.

    A. forceps A surgical forceps used primarily for grasping skin.

adsorb (ad-sŏrb′, zŏrb′) [*ad-* + L. *sorbere,* to suck in] In chemistry, to take up and hold by adsorption. SEE: *absorb; absorption.*

adsorbate (ad-sor′băt) [*adsorb* + *-ate*] Anything that is adsorbed.

adsorbent (ad-sor′bĕnt) [*adsorb*] 1. Pert. to adsorption. 2. A substance (e.g., activated charcoal) that readily draws other substances out of the body or out of solution.

adsorption (ad-sorp′shŏn) [*adsorb*] 1. In chemistry, adhesion by a gas or liquid to the surface of a solid. 2. Viral entry into a host cell.

ADT *admission, discharge, and transfer.*

adtorsion (ad-tor′shŏn) [*ad-* + *torsion*] Esotropia.

adult (ă-dŭlt′, ad′ŭlt″) [L. *adultus,*

grown up] The fully grown and mature organism.

adulteration (ă-dŭl″tĕ-rā′shŏn) [L. *adulterare,* to pollute] **1.** The addition or substitution of an impure, weaker, cheaper, or possibly toxic substance in a formulation or product. **2.** An impurity.

adult polyglucosan body disease (pŏl″ē-gloo′kŏ-săn) A rare neurological syndrome that results in peripheral nerve injury, upper motor neuron signs, bowel and bladder dysfunction, and sometimes, familial early-onset dementia. It is caused by the deposition of polyglucosan bodies in skin, central nervous system tissues, peripheral nerves, or sweat glands.

adult respiratory distress syndrome The former name for acute respiratory distress syndrome. SEE: *acute respiratory distress syndrome.*

advance (ăd-vans′) [Fr. *avancer,* to set forth] To carry out the surgical procedure of advancement.

advanced (ăd-vanst′) **1.** Placed or being ahead. **2.** Of a disease, in a late or critical stage of development. **3.** Far along in time or age; old or elderly.

Advanced Cardiac Life Support A training course in resuscitation techniques for health care providers offered by the American Heart Association. SEE: *life support* for illus.

advanced cardiac life support SEE: under *life support.*

advanced glycation end products ABBR: AGE. Proteins that have been nonenzymatically modified by the addition of sugar residues to lysine. These altered proteins increase with aging and in patients with hyperglycemia and diabetes mellitus.

advance directive A written document in the form of a living will or durable power of attorney prepared by a competent person and specifying what, if any, extraordinary procedures, surgeries, medications, or treatments the patient desires in the future if the patient should become incompetent to make such decisions SEE: *living will; power of attorney, durable, for health care.*

Advanced Medical Life Support ABBR: AMLS. A course offered by the National Association of Emergency Medical Technicians that teaches health care providers how to recognize and respond effectively to common medical complaints and crises.

Advanced Research Projects Agency Network ABBR: ARPANET. Designed in 1969 as a network to link certain U.S. Department of Defense computers with university computers on campuses performing defense-related research. The ARPANET network became the basis for the Internet.

advanced sleep-phase syndrome Sleep-phase syndrome.

Advanced Trauma Life Support A course offered by the American College of Surgeons to prepare physicians to manage critical trauma patients.

advancement (ăd-vans′mĕnt) Surgical detachment of a segment of tissue with reattachment to a position beyond the initial site. An example is the operation to remedy strabismus in which an extrinsic ocular muscle is severed and reattached farther from its origin.

adventitia (ad″vĕn-tĭsh′(ē-)ă) [L. *adventicius,* coming from abroad] The outermost part or layer of a structure or organ (e.g., the tunica adventitia).

adventitious (ad″ven-tĭsh′ŭs) **1.** Acquired; accidental. **2.** Arising sporadically. **3.** Pert. to adventitia.

adventitious breath sounds Abnormal lung sounds heard when listening to the chest as the person breathes. These may be wheezes, crackles (rales), or stridor. They do not include sounds produced by muscular activity in the chest wall or friction of the stethoscope on the chest.

adverse drug event Adverse drug reaction.

adverse drug reaction (ad-vĕrs′, ad′vĕrs″) ABBR: ADR. An unwanted response to a therapeutic drug. Health professionals must report all adverse events related to drugs or medical devices to the manufacturer and the FDA to aid in monitoring the safety of marketed medical products. SYN: *adverse drug event.* SEE: *drug reaction; MedWatch; post-marketing surveillance.*

ADRs are expensive and hazardous, accounting for more than 2 million injuries and 100,000 deaths related to prescription drugs annually.

PATIENT CARE: Documentation of adverse drug reactions should include: 1) patient information, including date of birth, sex, race, weight, pre-existing or coexisting medical conditions, other medications taken, tobacco or alcohol use, allergies, relevant diagnostic and laboratory study results; 2) date and time of the event; 3) specific patient outcomes attributed to the ADR, e.g., extended hospital stay; 4) history of the problem or event, including assessment findings and interventions, all persons notified and their responses, dates and times of these notifications, actions taken by those informed, and patient's response to such interventions; 5) name of the drug, its manufacturer, lot number, and expiration date on the packaging (if available), dosage, frequency, duration, route, and times of administration (any packaging or containers should be retained or returned to the pharmacy as evidence, depending on the facility's policy); 6) name, title, and credentials of person making the report; and 7) others who received the report, e.g., FDA MedWatch, pharmaceutical distributor, manufacturer. The FDA requires MedWatch reports for serious ADRs that cause death or are life-threatening or cause initial or prolonged hospitalization, disability, congenital anomaly or birth defect, or medical or surgical intervention.

adverse event Adverse reaction.

adverse reaction In pharmacology and therapeutics, an undesired side effect or toxicity caused by a treatment. Adverse reactions may be due to drug therapies, physical therapy, radiation, or surgery. The onset of the unwanted effect may be immediate or may take days or months to develop. SYN: *adverse event*. SEE: *adverse drug reaction; drug interaction; drug reaction.*

adverse selection SEE: under *selection*.

advisory (ăd-vī′zĕ-rē) A report issued by a drug manufacturer or government agency about a medical product that may cause serious injury or death to patients.

advocacy (ad′vŏ-kă-sē) [Fr. fr. L. *advocare,* to call to aid] In health care, pleading or representation for a desired goal or interest group (e.g., patients, staff, providers, or biomedical researchers).

adynamia (ā″dī-nām′ē-ă) [¹*an-* + Gr. *dynamis,* strength] Asthenia. **adynamic** (-nam′ik), *adj.*

AE *above elbow;* term refers to the site of amputation of an upper extremity proximal to the elbow.

Aeby plane (ā′bē) [Christopher T. Aeby, Swiss anatomist, 1835–1885] A plane perpendicular to the median plane of the cranium through the basion and nasion.

AED *antiepileptic drug; automated external defibrillator.*

Aedes (ā″ē′dēz″) [Gr. *aēdēs,* unpleasant] A genus of mosquitoes belonging to the family Culicidae. Many species are troublesome pests, and some transmit disease.

    A. aegypti A species that transmits yellow fever and dengue.

    A. triseriatus A species that transmits Jamestown Canyon virus, La Crosse virus, and other California encephalitis viruses.

AEL *acute erythroleukemia.*

-aemia SEE: *-emia*.

aerated (ar′āt″ĕd) [Gr. *aēr,* air] Containing air or gas.

aeration (ar″ā′shŏn) **1.** Act of airing. **2.** A process in which carbon dioxide and oxygen are exchanged between the pulmonary blood and the air in the lungs. **3.** Saturating or charging a fluid with gases.

aero-, aer- [Gr. *aēr,* air] Prefixes meaning *air* or *gas.*

aeroallergen (ar″ō-al′ĕr-jen) [*aero-* + *allergen*] A particle of dust, pollen, or powder that stimulates an immune response in a sensitive person.

aerobe (ar′ōb″) [*aero-* + Gr. *bios,* life] A microbe that is able to live and reproduce in the presence of oxygen.

    facultative a. A microorganism that prefers an environment devoid of oxygen but has adapted so that it can live and reproduce in the presence of oxygen.

    obligate a. A microorganism that can live and reproduce only in the presence of oxygen.

aerobic (ar-ō′bik) [*aerobe* + *-ic*] **1.** Taking place in the presence of oxygen. **2.** Pert. to an organism that lives and reproduces in the presence of oxygen.

aerobiosis (ar″ō-bī-ō′sĭs) [*aero-* + Gr. *biōsis,* mode of living] Life in an atmosphere containing oxygen. **aerobiotic** (-ot′ik), *adj.* **aerobiotically** (-ik(-ă)-lē), *adv.*

aerocele (ar′ō-sēl″) [*aero-* + *-cele*] Distention of a cavity with gas.

aerocoly (ar″ŏk′ŏ-lē) [*aero-* + Gr. *kōlon,* colon] Distention of the colon with gas.

aerocystoscopy (ar″ō-sis-tos′kŏ-pē) [*aero-* + *cystoscopy*] Examination with a cystoscope of the bladder distended by air.

aerodontalgia (ar″ō-don-tal′j(ē-)ă) [*aero-* + *odontalgia*] Toothache caused by a change in atmospheric pressure. **aerodontalgic** (jik), *adj.*

aerodontia (ar″ō-don′ch(ē-)ă) [*aero-* + *odont-* + *-ia*] The branch of dentistry concerned with the effect of changes in atmospheric pressure on the teeth.

aerodynamics (ar″ō-dī-nam′iks) [*aero-* + *dynamics*] The science of air or gases in motion. **aerodynamic,** *adj.* **aerodynamically** (-i-k(ă-)lē), *adv.*

aeroembolism (ar″ō-em′bŏ-lizm) [*aero-* + *embolism*] A condition in which nitrogen bubbles form in body fluids and tissues due to an excessively rapid decrease in atmospheric pressure, occurring either during ascent to high altitudes or in resurfacing from deep-sea diving or in hyperbaric oxygen therapy.

SYMPTOMS: Symptoms include a boring, gnawing pain in the joints, itching of skin and eyelids, unconsciousness, convulsions, and paralysis. Symptoms are relieved by recompression (i.e., return to lower altitudes or placement of the patient in a hyperbaric pressure chamber). Even though oxygen by masks may be available, ascents above 25,000 ft should be avoided except in aircraft with pressurized cabins. SEE: *hyperbaric chamber.*

aerogenesis (ar″ō-jen′ĕ-sis) [*aero-* + *-genesis*] Formation of gas. **aerogenic, aerogenous** (ar″ō-jen′ik, ar″oj′ĕ-nŭs), *adj.*

aerometer (ar-om′ĕ-tĕr) [*aero-* +

-meter] A device for measuring gas density.

Aeromonas (a(-ĕ)r″ō-mō′năs) A genus of gram-negative, facultatively anaerobic, non–spore-forming, motile bacilli found in water and soil. It may cause wound infections or gastroenteritis, e.g., travelers' diarrhea.

    A. hydrophilia A species that is pathogenic for humans; it is sensitive to chloramphenicol, trimethoprim-sulfamethoxazole, and some quinolones.

aeroparotitis (ar″ō-par″ŏ-tīt′ĭs) [*aero-* + *parotitis*] Swelling of one or both parotid glands due to introduction of air into the glands. This may occur in those who play wind instruments; it also occurs in nose blowing and Valsalva's maneuver if done too vigorously.

aerophagia, aerophagy (ar″ŏ-fā′j(ē-)ă, ar″of′ă-jē) [*aero-* + Gr. *phagein,* to eat] Swallowing of air.

aerophilic, aerophilous (ar″ō-fil′ik, -of′ĭ-lŭs) [*aero-* + Gr. *philein,* to love] Requiring oxygen for growth and reproduction. SYN: *aerobic.*

aerophobia (ar-ŏ-fōb′ē-ă) [*aero-* + *-phobia*] Morbid fear of a draft or of fresh air. **aerophobic** (-bik), *adj.*

aerosinusitis (ar″ō-sī″nŭ-sīt′ĭs) [*aero-* + *sinusitis* inflammation] Chronic inflammation of nasal sinuses due to changes in atmospheric pressure.

aerosol (ar′ŏ-sol″) [*aero-* + *sol*(*ution*)] **1.** A solution dispensed as a mist. **2.** Any suspension of particles in air or gas.

aerosolization (ar″ŏ-sol″ĭ-zā′shŏn) The suspension of minute solid or liquid particles in a gas.

aerosol therapy The use of medicated mists, such as bronchodilators, antivirals, corticosteroids, or mucolytic agents, to treat lung or bronchial diseases. SEE: *inhalation therapy.*

aerotitis, aero-otitis (ar-ŏ-tīt′is, ar-ō-ŏ-tīt′-is) [*aero-* + *otitis*] Inflammation of the ear, esp. the middle ear, due to failure of the eustachian tube to remain open during sudden changes in barometric pressure. It may occur during flying, diving, or working in a pressure chamber. SYN: *barotitis.*

aerotropism (ar-o′trŏ-pizm) [*aero-* + *trop-* + *-ism*] The tendency of organisms, esp. bacteria and protozoa, to move toward air (positive aerotropism) or away from it (negative aerotropism).

aerourethroscope (ar-ō-ū″rē′thrŏ-skōp″) [*aero-* + *urethroscope*] An apparatus for visual examination of the urethra after dilatation by air. **aerourethroscopy** (thros′kŏ-pē), *n.*

Aesculapius (es″kyŭ-lā′pē-ŭs) [L. *Aesculapius,* fr Gr. *Asklēpios*] The Latin form of *Asklēpios,* the Greek god of medicine, son of Apollo and the nymph Coronis.

    staff of A. A rod or crude stick with a snake wound around it, signifing the art of healing and adopted as the emblem of some medical organizations, e.g., American Medical Association. Snakes were sacred to Aesculapius because they were believed to have the power to renew their youth by shedding their old skin and growing a new one. SEE: *caduceus.*

Aesculus hippocastanum (es″kŭ-lŭs hip″ō-kas′tă-nŭm) [L. *aesculus hippocastanum,* horse-chestnut oak] SEE: *horse chestnut.*

aesthesi- SEE: *esthesi-.*

aesthetics, esthetics (es-thet′iks) [Gr. *aisthētikos,* pert. to sensation] A philosophy or theory of beauty and the fine arts. Aesthetics are important in dental restorations and in plastic and cosmetic surgery.

aetio- SEE: *etio-.*

AF *atrial flutter. atrial fibrillation.*

afebrile (ā″-feb′rīl″, -fēb′) [*a-* + *febrile*] Without fever; apyretic.

affect (af′ekt″) [L. *affectus,* acted on; mental or emotional state] In psychology, the emotional reaction associated with an experience. SEE: *mood.*

    blunted a. Greatly diminished emotional response to a situation or condition.

    flat a. Virtual absence of emotional response to a situation or condition.

    pseudobulbar a. ABBR: PBA. The labile expression of emotions (as by pathological or inappropriate laughing or crying) out of proportion to the feelings experienced by the patient. PBA is characteristic of patients with amyotrophic lateral sclerosis, multiple sclerosis, and other brain diseases.

affection (ă-fek′shŏn) [Fr. fr. L. *affectio,* disposition] **1.** A feeling of attachment; fondness. **2.** Physical or mental disease.

affective (a-fek′tiv) Pert. to an emotion or mental state. **affectively** (-lē), *adv.* **affectivity** (a″fek″ti′vĭ-tē), *n.*

affective disorder A group of disorders marked by a disturbance of mood accompanied by a full or partial manic or depressive syndrome that is not caused by any other physical or mental disorder. SEE: *Nursing Diagnoses Appendix.*

afferent (af′ĕ-rĕnt, a-fer′ĕnt) [L. *afferre,* to carry to] Transporting toward a center. It applies, for example, to a sensory nerve that carries impulses toward the central nervous system or to some blood vessels and lymphatic vessels. SEE: *efferent.*

afferent loop syndrome A group of gastrointestinal symptoms that occur in some patients who have had partial gastric resection with gastrojejunostomy. The condition is caused by partial obstruction of an incompletely draining segment of bowel. In some cases there is bacterial overgrowth in the afferent loop. Symptoms include abdominal bloating, nausea, vomiting, and pain after eating.

affidavit (af″ĭ-dā′vit) [L. *affidare,* to swear an oath] A voluntary written or printed statement submitted to an officer of the court and whose truthfulness is asserted by an oath or affirmation.

affiliated clinical site (ă-fil′ē-āt″id) SEE: under *site.*

affiliation (ă-fi-lē-ā′shŏn) [L. *affiliare,* to adopt as one's child] **1.** Membership in a larger organization. **2.** Association. In nursing or medical education, the administrative merger of two hospitals or schools of nursing. This enables students to obtain specialized training and experience that might not otherwise be available to them.

affinity (ă-fin′ĭ-tē) [L. *affinis,* neighboring, related by marriage] Attraction.
  chemical a. The force causing certain atoms to combine with others to form molecules. SEE: *chemoreceptor.*

affix (a′fiks″) [L. *affixus,* fastened to] An element attached to a word that alters its meaning, e.g., a prefix or a suffix.

A fiber SEE: under *fiber.*

afibrinogenemia (ā″fi-brin″ŏ-jĕ-nē′mē-ă) [*a-* + *fibrinogen* + *-emia*] Absence or deficiency of fibrinogen in the bloodstream.

aflatoxicosis (af″lă-tok″sĭ-kō′sis) [*A(spergillus) fla(vus)* + *toxicosis*] Poisoning caused by ingestion of aflatoxin. Farm animals and humans are susceptible to this toxicosis. SYN: *x-disease.*

aflatoxin (af″lă-tok″sin) [*A(spergillus) fla(vus)* + *toxin*] A toxin produced by some strains of *Aspergillus flavus* and *A. parasiticus* that causes cancer in laboratory animals. It may be present in peanuts and other seeds contaminated with *Aspergillus* molds.

AFO *ankle-foot orthosis.*

AFP *alpha-fetoprotein.*

African tick bite fever SEE: under *fever.*

AFRRI *Armed Forces Radiobiological Research Institute.*

afteraction (af″ tĕr-ak′shŏn) Continued reaction after the stimulus ceases, esp. in nerve centers. In the sensory centers this action gives rise to aftersensations. SEE: *aftersensation.*

afterbirth (af′tĕr-bĭrth″) The placenta and membranes expelled from the uterus after the birth of a child. SYN: *secundines.*

afterburn (af′tĕr-bŭrn″) An increase in the resting metabolic rate that occurs after exercising.

aftercare (af′tĕr-kar″) Continuing rehabilitation offered to a patient after inpatient treatment in a hospital, mental-health care institution, or other health care facility.

aftercataract (af″tĕr-kat′ă-rakt″) **1.** Secondary cataract. **2.** An opacity of the lens capsule that develops after cataract removal.

afterdamp (af′tĕr-damp″) A gaseous mixture formed by the explosion of methane and air in a mine. It contains a large percentage of carbon dioxide, nitrogen, and carbon monoxide.

afterdepolarization (af″tĕr-dē-pō″lă-rĭ-zā′shŏn) Abnormal electrical activity that occurs during repolarization of the pacemaker cells of the heart. This activity may prolong the action potential and trigger abnormal atrial or ventricular rhythms.

afterdischarge (af″tĕr-dis″charj″) The discharge of impulses from a reflex center after stimulation of the receptor has ceased. It results in prolongation of the response.

aftereffect (af′tĕr-ĕ-fekt″) A response occurring some time after the original stimulus or condition has produced its primary effect.

afterimage (af′tĕr-im′ăj) An image that persists subjectively after cessation of the stimulus. If colors are the same as those of the object, it is called positive; it is called negative if complementary colors are seen. In the former case, the image is seen in its natural bright colors without any alteration; in the latter, the bright parts become dark, while dark parts are light.
  negative a. An afterimage in which the colors and light intensity are reversed.
  positive a. An afterimage in which the colors and light intensity are unchanged.

afterload (af′tĕr-lōd″) In cardiac physiology, the force that impedes the flow of blood out of the heart. The heart contracts against a resistance primarily composed of the pressure in the peripheral vasculature, the compliance of the aorta, and the mass and viscosity of blood. SEE: *preload.*

afterloading (af′tĕr-lōd″ing) In brachytherapy, the insertion of the radioactive source after the placement of the applicator has been confirmed.

aftermovement (af′tĕr-moov″mĕnt) Persistent, spontaneous contraction of a muscle after a strong contraction against resistance has ceased. This is seen when a person forcibly pushes an arm against a wall while standing with the frontal plane perpendicular to the wall. When this is stopped and the person moves away from the wall, the arm abducts involuntarily and is elevated by the deltoid muscle.

afterpain (af′tĕr-pān″) Uterine cramping caused by contraction of the uterus and commonly seen in multiparas during the first few days after childbirth. The pains are more severe during breast-feeding but rarely last longer than 48 hr postpartum.

PATIENT CARE: Emptying the bladder can relieve pain. Nonsteroidal anti-inflammatory drugs (NSAIDs) may be useful; they should be given with food before nursing. Some women obtain relief lying on their stomachs. Aspirin should not be given if there is a tendency to bleed. The sooner an analgesic is given, the less is needed.

aftersensation (af″ tĕr-sen-sā′shŏn) A sensation that persists after the stimulus causing it has ceased. SEE: *afteraction, afterimage.*

aftertaste (af′tĕr-tāst″) **1.** Persistence of a flavor or taste after the stimulus ends. **2.** Persistence of an emotion, esp. an unfavorable one, after the event or experience.

aftertreatment (af′tĕr-trēt″mĕnt) Secondary care following the primary treatment regimen. SEE: *aftercare.*

AFUD *American Foundation for Urologic Disease.*

Ag [L. *argentum*] Symbol for the element silver.

AGA *American Gastroenterological Association; appropriate for gestational age.*

against medical advice ABBR: AMA. A patient's refusal of medically recommended treatments, esp. in the hospital. Dropping out of care or leaving a hospital AMA typically occurs when patients are dissatisfied with the pace or course of their care, carry substance abuse diagnoses, or have a history of multiple hospitalizations. The action may result in an increase in both morbidity and rehospitalization.

PATIENT CARE: The patient is asked to sign a release form indicating that the health care facility and those responsible for medical care are not liable for any adverse outcome that may result from the termination of care.

agamic (ā″gam′ĭk) [*a-* + *gam-* + *-ic*] Asexual.

agammaglobulinemia (ā″gam″ă-glob″yŭ-lĭ-nē′mē-ă) [*a-* + *gamma globulin* + *-emia*] Any of the disorders marked by an almost complete lack of immunoglobulins or antibodies. Agammaglobulinemias are caused by abnormal B lymphocyte function; they cause severe immunodeficiencies, with recurrent infections. Treatments include immunoglobulins, antibiotics, and bone marrow transplantation.

agamogenesis (ā″gam″ŏ-jen′ĕ-sĭs) [*a-* + *gamogenesis*] **1.** Asexual reproduction. **2.** Parthenogenesis. **agamogenetic** (-jĕ-net′ik), *adj.* **agamogenetically** (-ĭ-k(ă-)lē), *adv.*

agape (ă-ga′pā, a′gă-pā″) [Gr. *agapē,* love] Unselfish, unconditional love for another, without sexual or romantic feelings.

agar, agar-agar (ag′ăr, ag′ăr-ag′ăr) [Malay, gelatin] **1.** A dried mucilaginous product obtained from certain species of algae, esp. of the genus *Gelidium.* Agar is unaffected by bacterial enzymes and therefore is widely used as a solidifying agent for bacterial culture media. It is used as a laxative because of its great increase in bulk on absorption of water. It is also used by vegetarians when recipes call for gelatin. **2.** A culture medium containing agar. **3.** A constituent of dental hydrocolloid impression materials.

agaric (ag′ă-rik, ă-gar′ik) [L. fr. Gr. *agarikon,* a sort of fungus] A toxic or hallucinogenic mushroom, esp. species of the genus *Agaricus.*

agastria (ā″gas′trē-ă) [*a-* + *gastr-* + *-ia*] Absence of the stomach. **agastric** (gas′trĭk), *adj.*

Agatson score (ag′ăt-sŏn) [Arthur Agatson, U.S. cardiologist, b. 1947] A measurement of the amount of calcium in a coronary artery.

AGC *atypical glandular cells.*

AgCl Symbol for silver chloride.

AGE *advanced glycation end products.*

age (āj) [Fr. *age,* fr. L. *aetas*] **1.** The time, measured in seconds, minutes, hours, days, months, or years that an organism has lived since its birth. **2.** A particular period of life (e.g., middle age or old age). **3.** To grow old. **4.** In psychology, the degree of development of an individual as compared or contrasted with another of comparable development or accomplishment.

    achievement a. ABBR: AA. The age of a person with regard to level of acquired learning; determined by a proficiency test and expressed in terms of the chronological age of the average person showing the same level of attainment.

    advanced maternal a. ABBR: AMA. A term used to describe the age of women for whom pregnancy presents increased risks either to the fetus or to the mother. In the medical literature this age is variably stated as being over 35.

    anatomical a. An estimate of age as judged by the stage of development or deterioration of the body or tissue as compared with persons or tissues of known age.

    biological a. One's present position in regard to the probability of survival. Determination of biological age requires assessment and measurement of the functional capacities of the life-limiting organ system, e.g., the cardiovascular system.

    bone a. An estimate of biological age based on radiological studies of the developmental stage of ossification centers of the long bones of the extremities. SEE: *epiphysis.*

    chronological a. ABBR: CA. Age as determined by years since birth.

    conceptional a. The estimated gestational age as referenced from the actual time of conception. It is usually considered to be at least 14 days after the first day of the last menstrual period. SYN: *ovulation a.*

a. of consent The age at which a minor may legally engage in voluntary sexual intercourse or no longer requires parental consent for marriage. It varies among states but is usually between ages 13 and 18.

developmental a. An index of maturation expressed in months or years, which represents a value obtained by comparing performance with scaled norms for a particular age group. SEE: *achievement a.*

emotional a. Judgment of age with respect to the stage of emotional development.

functional a. Age defined in terms of physical or functional capacity; frequently applied to older adults.

gestational a. The age of an embryo or fetus as timed from the date of onset of the last menstrual period. Gestational age is specified numerically by the following convention: 360/7 indicates an age of *36 weeks, 0 days.* 295/7 indicates an age of *29 weeks, 5 days.* The first two numbers are the number of weeks of gestation. The number designated as *X/7* is the number of days since the completion of the last full week. SYN: *menstrual a.*

menarcheal a. Elapsed time expressed in years from menarche.

menstrual a. Gestational **a.**

mental a. ABBR: MA. The age of a person with regard to mental ability, determined by a series of mental tests devised by Binet and expressed in terms of the chronological age of the average person showing the same level of attainment.

middle a. An imprecise term that refers to the period of life that begins roughly at age 40 and ends at about age 64. During middle age in Western societies, many medical problems begin to increase in frequency, including degenerative arthritis, cancer, diabetes mellitus, high blood pressure, myocardial ischemia and infarction, obesity, and visual accommodative disorders.

ovulation a. Conceptional **a.**

physiological a. The relative age of a person, esp. when comparing that individual's physical status with those of other persons of the same chronological age.

aged (ājd, ā′jĕd) **1.** To have grown older or more mature. **2.** Persons who have grown old. SEE: *aging.*

Age Discrimination Act Also known as Age Discrimination in Employment Act, 29 U.S.C. subsection 621 (1967), a law that prohibits unfair and discriminatory treatment in hiring, promotion, compensation, discharge, terms, conditions, or privileges of employment by an employer against anyone 40 years old or older. In health care, this act has been used to challenge the termination of mature employees. Enforced by the Equal Employment Opportunity Commission (EEOC).

ageism (ā′jĭzm) [Coined by Robert Butler, U.S. physician, in 1968] Discrimination against older people.

Agency for Healthcare Research and Quality ABBR: AHRQ. An office of the U.S. Department of Health and Human Services dedicated to supporting, conducting, and disseminating research; promoting improvements in clinical practice; and enhancing the quality, organization, financing, and delivery of health care services.

agenesia, agenesis (ā″jĕ-nē′zh(ē-)ă, ā″jen′ĕ-sis) [*a-* + *-genesis*] **1.** Failure of an organ or part to develop or grow. **2.** Lack of potency.

agenitalism (ā″jen′ĭ-tăl-ĭzm) [*a-* + *genital* + *-ism*] Absence of genitals.

agent (ā′jĕnt) [L. *agere,* to do] Someone or something that causes an effect. For example, bacteria that cause disease are agents of the specific diseases they cause, and medicine is a therapeutic agent.

alkylating a. Any substance that introduces an alkyl radical into a compound in place of a hydrogen atom. Alkylating agents are used to treat cancer because they interfere with cell metabolism and growth. Examples include cisplatinum and cyclophosphamide.

alpha-adrenergic blocking a. A substance that interferes with the transmission of stimuli through pathways that normally allow sympathetic nervous excitatory stimuli to be effective. Agents from this class are used to treat hypertension and prostatic hyperplasia. SEE: *beta-adrenergic blocking a.*

anabolic a. Any of a class of steroid hormones resembling testosterone. These agents stimulate the growth or manufacture of body tissues. They have been used, sometimes in high doses, by male and female athletes to improve performance. This use has been judged to be illegal by a number of organizations that supervise sports, including the International Olympic Committee and the U.S. Olympic Committee. These agents are also used to treat patients with wasting illnesses. SEE: *doping; ergonomic aid.*

⚠️ Indiscriminate use of anabolic agents is inadvisable because of the undesirable side effects they may produce, e.g., in women, hirsutism, masculinization, and clitoral hypertrophy; in men, aggressiveness and testicular atrophy.

antianxiety a. Anxiolytic.

antiulcer a. A drug used to prevent or treat ulcers of the stomach or small intestine.

beta-adrenergic a. A synthetic or natural drug that stimulates beta (sympathetic) receptors, e.g., epinephrine and norepinephrine.

beta-adrenergic blocking a. Any drug that inhibits the activity of the sympathetic nervous system and of adrenergic hormones.

Members of this class of drugs are used to treat hypertension, angina pectoris, myocardial infarction, aortic dissection, arrhythmias, glaucoma, and other conditions. Commonly prescribed beta blockers include atenolol, carvedilol, metoprolol, nadolol, propranolol, and pindolol.

> ⚠ Side effects of beta blockers include worsening of asthma, blunting of the cardiovascular symptoms of hypoglycemia, bradycardia, and heart block. Rapid withdrawal from a beta-blocking drug by a patient accustomed to its use may produce tachycardia or other arrhythmias, rebound hypertension, or myocardial ischemia or infarction.

SYN: *beta blocker.*

buffering a. Buffer.

CBRNE a. Any chemical, biological, radiologic, nuclear, or explosive agent that may be used as a weapon in military or terrorist activities.

ceruminolytic a. An agent that dissolves cerumen in the external ear canal. Obstruction of the ear canal with cerumen can cause itching, pain, and temporary conductive hearing loss. The first approach to treatment should be removal of the obstruction manually with a blunt curet or loop or by irrigation. Cerumen solvents are not always recommended because they often do not eliminate the problem and frequently cause maceration of the skin of the canal and allergic reactions.

cervical-ripening a. Any drug that promotes dilation of the cervix in anticipation of childbirth.

chaotropic a. An ion that disrupts membranes, nucleic acids, and proteins.

chelating a. A drug, such as calcium disodium edetate, used to chelate substances, esp. toxic chemicals in the body.

cholinergic blocking a. Anticholinergic (2).

clearing a. **1.** A substance that increases the transparency of tissues prepared for microscopic examination. **2.** In radiographic film processing, the active agent in the fixer that clears undeveloped silver bromide crystals from

the film. The most common agent is ammonium thiosulfate. SYN: *fixing a.*

colon-cleansing a. A medication to force the bowels to evacuate, e.g., in preparation for colonoscopy.

cytotoxic a. A drug that destroys cells or prevents them from multiplying. Cytotoxic agents are used to treat cancers and severe immunological disorders, e.g., vasculitis, some forms of glomerulonephritis. An ideal agent would destroy proliferating cells without injuring the normal cells of the body.

disclosing a. A diagnostic aid used in dentistry to stain areas of the teeth that are not being cleaned adequately. A dye such as erythrosine sodium is used to color dental plaque so that inadequately brushed surfaces can be shown to patients.

Eaton a. SEE: *Eaton agent.*

erythropoiesis-stimulating a. ABBR: ESA. Any drug that binds to cellular receptors for erythropoietin and encourages red blood cell production by the bone marrow. Members of this class of drugs, which include epoietin and darbopoietin, are used to treat anemia, e.g., in patients with chronic kidney disease, cancer, or aplastic anemia. ESAs are used as an alternative to red blood cell transfusions. Potential side effects of treatment include high blood pressure and an increased risk of blood clots.

filling a. Filler.

fixing a. SEE: *clearing a.*

differentiating a. A medication such as all-trans-retinoic acid, used in differentiation therapy.

immunobiological a. Immunobiological.

immunosuppressive a. SEE: *immunosuppressant.*

luting a. Lute.

nasal drying a. Any anticholinergic, antihistaminic, or drug of a related class that decreases watery discharge from the nose, e.g., in rhinitis.

Norwalk a. SEE: under *virus.*

ocular hypotensive a. A drug that reduces intraocular pressure, e.g., in glaucoma.

oral hypoglycemic a. ABBR: OHA. Any drug taken by mouth that lowers or maintains blood glucose (as opposed to insulin, a drug taken parenterally to control blood sugar). In addition to diet and exercise regimens, OHAs are typically used to control blood glucose levels in type 2 diabetes mellitus. Commonly used oral agents for diabetes include metformin (a biguanide), sulfonylureas (such as glyburide), alpha-glucosidase inhibitors (acarbose), and thiazolidinediones (pioglitazone). Used appropriately, OHAs lower hemoglobin A1c levels by about 0.5 to 1.5%. SEE: table.

progestational a. Progestin (1).

radioprotective a. Any substance

Oral Agents That Lower Blood Glucose*

Class of Drug	Activity	Adverse Features	Approximate Cost
Alpha-glucosidase inhibitors, e.g., acarbose	Delay absorption of glucose from intestinal tract	Flatulence and other abdominal side effects	Expensive
Biguanides, e.g., metformin	Improve sensitivity to insulin; decrease glucose production by the liver	Less weight gain than with other agents; avoid in patients with renal failure	Very expensive
Sulfonylureas, 1st generation, e.g., tolazamide	Cause beta cells to release insulin	Resistance to drug may develop over time	Inexpensive
Sulfonylureas, 2nd generation, e.g., glipizide, glyburide, others	Same as 1st generation; also increase sensitivity to insulin	Same as 1st generation	Moderately expensive
Thiazolidinediones, e.g., pioglitazone	Improve sensitivity to insulin; improve lipid profile	Monthly monitoring of liver functions needed for some drugs in this class due to risk of toxicity. Heart failure and other heart diseases.	Very expensive

* Combinations of these drugs, either with each other or with insulin, may be used in patients with poorly controlled diabetes mellitus.

that shields the body from damage by radioactivity.

reducing a. A substance that loses electrons easily and therefore causes other substances to be reduced (such as hydrogen sulfide, sulfur dioxide). SYN: *reducing substance*.

sclerosing a. A substance used to cause sclerosis, esp. of the lining of a vein. SEE: *varicose **vein***.

surface-active a. Surfactant.

thermal a. Heat or cold used to promote healing. SEE: *physical agent **modality***.

thrombolytic a. Any drug that degrades blood clots. Examples include streptokinase, tenecteplase, tissue plasminogen activator, and urokinase. Such drugs are used to treat the abnormal blood clotting that occurs in heart attacks, some strokes, and pulmonary emboli. They are informally called "clot busters."

⚠ Thrombolytic drugs should not be given to patients with active bleeding, a history of surgery or major trauma within the preceding two weeks, a brain tumor, or other known risks for intracerebral hemorrhage.

topical hemostatic a. Any substance that can be applied to a wound or an incision to keep it from bleeding. Examples include adhesives derived from collagen or glutaraldehyde, cellulose-based products, fibrin sealants, hydrogels, and thrombin.

uricosuric a. A drug, e.g., probenecid or sulfinpyrazone, that increases the urinary excretion of uric acid by blocking renal tubular absorption, thereby reducing the concentration of uric acid in the blood. It is used to treat gout.

PATIENT CARE: Probenecid and sulfinpyrazones are used to treat gout. Side effects of both include headache, gastrointestinal upset, epigastric pain, kidney stone formation, and peptic ulcer. These drugs should be avoided by patients with diminished renal function. Any uricosuric agent should be taken with milk, food, or antacids to reduce gastric distress. Patients should drink large volumes of water. Sodium bicarbonate (or potassium citrate) is prescribed simultaneously with these agents to alkalinize urine and keep uric acid crystals in solution.

vascular disrupting a. Any of a class of medications used to destroy the blood supply of malignant tumors.

wetting a. 1. Any agent, such as a surfactant, that allows a fluid to spread over and coat a surface to which it is applied. **2.** In radiographic wet film processing, a solution used after washing to reduce surface tension and accelerate water flow from the film to speed drying.

Agent Orange A defoliant used extensively by U.S. military forces in the Vietnam War. It was composed of 2,4-D and 2,4,5-T. The 2,4,5-T was discovered to be contaminated with TCDD. The defoliant was stored in 55-gallon drums painted with an orange stripe. SEE: *chloracne* for illus; *TCDD*.

agent study SEE: under *study*.

agerasia (ā″jě-rā′zh(ē-)ă) [*a-* + Gr. *geras,* old age] Healthy, vigorous old age; youthful appearance of an old person.

age retardation Life extension.

age-specific (āj′spě-sif′ik) Pert. to conditions that vary with different stages of development or years of life.

ageusia, ageustia (ă-gū′zē-ă, ă-gū′stē-ă) [*a-* + Gr. *geuesthai,* to taste] Absence, partial loss, or impairment of the sense of taste. SEE: *dysgeusia; hypergeusesthesia; hypogeusia.*

ETIOLOGY: Ageusia may be caused by disease of the chorda tympani or of the gustatory fibers, excessive use of condiments, the effect of certain drugs, aging, or lesions involving sensory pathways or taste centers in the brain.

central a. Ageusia due to a cerebral lesion.

conduction a. Ageusia due to a lesion involving sensory nerves of taste.

peripheral a. Ageusia due to a disorder of taste buds of the mucous membrane of tongue.

agglomerate (ă-glom′ě-rāt″) [L. *agglomerare,* to roll into a ball] To congregate; form a mass. **agglomeratio** (-rā′shŏn), *n.*

agglutin-, agglutino- [L. *agglutinare,* to glue to] Prefixes meaning *clumping* or *gluing.*

agglutinant (ă-gloot′ĭn-ănt) [L. *agglutinare,* to glue] 1. A substance causing adhesion. 2. Causing union by adhesion, as in the healing of a wound. 3. Agglutinin.

agglutination (ă-gloot″ĭn-ā′shŏn) [L. *agglutinare,* to glue to] 1. A type of antigen-antibody reaction in which a solid cell or particle coated with antigens drops out of solution when it is exposed to a previously soluble antibody. The particles involved commonly include red blood cells, bacteria, and inert carriers such as latex. Agglutination also refers to laboratory tests used to detect specific antigens or antibodies in disease states. When agglutination involves red blood cells, it is called hemagglutination. 2. Adhesion of surfaces of a wound.

direct a. The formation of an insoluble network of antigens and their antibodies, when the antigen is mixed with specific antiserum. Direct agglutination reactions are used, for example, in typing blood or in assessing the presence of antibodies against microorganisms.

passive a. A test for the presence of a specific antibody in which inert particles or cells with no foreign antigenic markers are coated with a known soluble antigen and mixed with serum. If clumping occurs, the patient's blood contains antibodies specific to the antigen. In the past, red blood cells were used as the carriers after they were washed to remove any known antibodies; currently, latex, bentonite, and charcoal also are used.

platelet a. Clumping of platelets in response to immunological reactions.

vulvar a. Adhesion of the vaginal labia to each other, e.g., after inflammatory ulceration of the skin.

agglutination test A widely used test in which adding an antiserum containing antibodies to cells or bacteria causes them to agglutinate.

agglutinative (ă-gloot′ĭn-ā″tiv, -ă-tiv) Causing or capable of causing agglutination.

agglutinin (ă-gloot′ĭn-ĭn) [L. *agglutinare,* to glue to + *-in*] An antibody present in the blood that attaches to an antigen present on cells or solid particles. The antibody causes the cells or particles to agglutinate. Agglutinins cause transfusion reactions when blood from a different group is given. These antibodies are present at birth and require no exposure to an antigen to be created since they are genetically determined.

anti-Rh a. An antibody produced by people with Rh-negative blood who are exposed to blood containing the Rh antigen. This antibody develops in Rh-negative people who receive Rh-positive blood and in Rh-negative women carrying an Rh-positive fetus. The antibody may cause hemolytic disease of the newborn in subsequent Rh-positive pregnancies.

cold a. An antibody in the serum of patients with certain diseases that causes the agglutination of erythrocytes (usually from sheep) at low temperatures by the serum of these patients.

warm a. An agglutinin effective only at normal body temperature.

agglutinogen (ă-gloot-ĭn′ŏ-jěn) [*agglutin-* + *-gen*] An antigen that stimulates the production of an agglutinin. Agglutinogens are used primarily in laboratory testing for antibodies against specific blood types. SEE: *blood group.* **agglutinogenic, agglutogenic** (ă-gloot″ĭn-ŏ-jen′ĭk, ă-gloot″ŏ-jen′ik), *adj.*

A and B a. SEE: *blood group; ABO incompatibility.*

M and N a. Antigenic substances found on the membranes of human red blood cells. Anti-M and anti-N agglutinins are rarely found in normal serum. The red blood cells may contain M or N, or both M and N agglutinogens, resulting in blood types M, N, or MN, respectively. SEE: *blood group*.

Rh a. SEE: *Rh factor*.

agglutinophilic (ă-gloot″ĭn-ŏ-fĭl′ik) [*agglutin* + *-philic*] Readily agglutinating.

aggrecan (ag′rĕ-kan″) [*aggre(gate)* + *(proteo)glycan*] A large glycoprotein that provides stiffness and structural strength to many tissues including joint cartilage, tendons, and the aorta.

aggregate (ag′rĕ-gāt″) [L. *aggregare*, to flock together] **1.** A sum or mass of units or substances. **2.** To cluster or come together.

aggregation (ag″rĕ-gā′shŏn) A clump, cluster, collection, or group of things.

    cellular a. Clumping together of blood cells, esp. platelets or red cells.

    familial a. Multiple instances of a disease in a group of related individuals, due to shared genetic susceptibility, shared environmental exposure, or chance.

aggregometry (ag″rĕ-gom′ĕ-trē) [*aggregate* + *-metry*] The measurement of the degree to which objects, e.g., platelets, stick together.

aggression (ă-grĕsh′ŏn) [L. *aggredi*, to attack] **1.** A forceful physical or verbal act. **2.** In psychiatry, hostility, either innate or due to frustration, and directed against oneself or against another person or thing. The aggression may be appropriate and self-protective, indicating healthy self-assertiveness, or it may be inappropriate, disproportional, or illegal.

aggressive (ă-gres′iv) **1.** Pert. to or showing aggression. **2.** More intensive or concentrated than usual (e.g., chemotherapy). **3.** Rapidly developing or growing (e.g., cancer).

aging (āj′ing) **1.** Growing older. Most authorities confine the term to the maturation and physiological changes in organ systems that occur after the 30th year of life. **2.** Maturing. **3.** Any physiological, cellular, or biochemical change that occurs over time rather than from injury or disease.

    primary a. Any of the universal changes in structure and function that occur naturally during normal processes of growing older, independent of disease or excessive environmental stress.

    secondary a. Any of the changes in structure and function due to diseases prevalent in aging rather than to universal aging processes.

    successful a. **1.** Aging in which emotional, intellectual, physical, social, or spiritual interests are optimally maintained or developed. **2.** Health or well-being in aging. SYN: *life satisfaction*.

aging in place, age in place Any services provided to elderly patients that allow them to continue to live independently

rather than relocating them to care facilities.

agitation (aj″ĭ-tā′shŏn) [L. *agitare*, to drive] **1.** Excessive restlessness, increased mental, and, esp., physical activity.

    PATIENT CARE: Agitation may complicate many medical and psychiatric conditions and make patient management difficult, frustrating, and sometimes dangerous. Agitation is esp. common in the elderly, patients with dementia, and in those with organic brain syndromes. The agitated patient should always be addressed with respect; attempts should be made to calm the patient with supportive listening, a composed affect, and genuine reassurance. The presence of a calm and respected family member may be helpful. Reorientation of the patient to his or her surroundings and the reason for health care interventions or hospitalization should be provided. Medical therapies, including antipsychotic drugs, sometimes in combination with benzodiazepines or other sedatives, are variably effective.

    ⚠ Health care professionals who work with agitated patients are at a significant risk of being injured at work. Institutional programs to limit staff injury may decrease this hazard. Protocols for defusing violent situations and de-escalating interpersonal tensions may also decrease the risk.

    2. Tremor. **3.** Severe motor restlessness, usually nonpurposeful, associated with anxiety. **4.** Shaking of a container so that the contents are rapidly moved and mixed.

agitographia (aj″ĭ-tō-graf′ē-ă) [agitation + *-grapho* + *-ia*] Writing with excessive rapidity, with unconscious omission of words and syllables.

agitophasia (aj″ĭ-tō-fā′zh(ē-)ă) [*agitation* + Gr. *phasis*, speech] Excessive rapidity of speech, with slurring, omission, and distortion of sounds.

aglaucopsia, aglaukopsia (ā″glo-kop′sē-ă) [¹*an-* + Gr. *glaukos*, green, blue, gray + *-opsia*] Color blindness in which there is a defect in the perception of green. SYN: *green **blindness***. SEE: *color **blindness***.

aglossia (ā″glos′ē-ă) [*a-* + *glossa* + *-ia*] Congenital absence of the tongue.

aglossostomia (ā″glos-ŏ-stō′mē-ă) [*a-* + *glosso-* + *stoma*] Congenital absence of the tongue and mouth.

aglutition (ā″gloo-tish′ŏn) [*a-* + L. *glutire*, to swallow] Difficulty in swallowing or inability to swallow.

aglycemia (ā″glī-sē′mē-ă) [*a-* + *glycemia*] Lack of sugar in the blood.

aglycon, aglycone (a-glī′kon″, a-glī′kōn″) [¹*an-* + *glyco-* + *-one*] An isoflavone attached to the chemical structure of digitalis glycosides. It is responsible for the cardiotonic activity of those agents.

aglycosuric (ā″glī″kō-shoor′ik) [*a-* + *glycosuria* + *-ic*] Free from glycosuria.

agnathia (ag-nā′thē-ă) [*a-* + *gnath-* + *-ia*] Absence of the mandible.

agnea (ag′nē-ă) Inability to recognize objects.

AgNO₃ Formula for silver nitrate.

agnogenic (ag″nō-jen′ik) [*'an-* + Gr. *gnōsis,* knowledge + *-genic*] Idiopathic.

agnosia (ag-nō′zhă, shă) [*a-* + Gr. *gnōsis,* knowledge + *-ia*] Inability to recognize or comprehend sights, sounds, words, or other sensory information.

   auditory a. Word **deafness.**

   color a. Inability to recognize or name specific colors.

   finger a. Inability to identify the fingers of one's own hands or of others.

   optic a. Inability to interpret seen images.

   tactile a. Inability to distinguish objects by touch. SYN: *stereoagnosis.*

   time a. Unawareness of the sequence and duration of events.

   unilateral spatial a. SEE: *unilateral inattention.*

   visual object a. Loss of the ability to visually recognize presented objects even though there is some degree of ability to see.

agnostic (ag-nos′tik) [G. *agnōstos,* unknown, not capable of being known + *-ic*] Uncertain or doubtful of the ability to prove the existence of something, but esp. of God. **agnostic,** *n.* **agnosticism** (tĭ-sĭzm), *n.*

-agogue [Gr. *agōgos,* leading, inducing] Suffix meaning *producer, secretor, or promoter of the excretion of a specific substance.*

agonad, agonadal (ā″gō′nad, ā″gō-nād′ăl) [*a-* + *gonad*] Lacking gonads.

agonal (ag′ŏ-năl) [*agon(y)* + *-al*] Pert. to agony, esp to that just before death.

agonist (ăg′ŏ-nist) **1.** The muscle that directly produces a specific action. In bending the elbow, the biceps brachii is the agonist and the triceps the antagonist. SYN: *agonist muscle.* **2.** In pharmacology, a drug that binds to the receptor and stimulates the receptor's function.

   adrenergic a. Any of a group of therapeutic agents, e.g. epinephrine, that mimic or stimulate the sympathetic nervous system.

   beta a. A drug that stimulates adrenergic receptors in the lungs, heart, uterus, and other organs. Beta agonists are used to treat asthma and chronic obstructive lung diseases and to manage pregnancy.

   beta-2 a. A medication that stimulates bronchodilation. Examples include albuterol, salmeterol, terbutaline, and many others. SEE: *bronchodilator.*

   PATIENT CARE: Beta-2 agonists are used to treat patients with asthma or any pulmonary disease associated with bronchospasm. Patients given such medications need to be monitored for side effects such as tremor, tachycardia, and nausea.

   dopamine a. A drug that stimulates dopamine receptors in the brain. Some of these agents, such as ropinirole and pramipexole, are used to treat Parkinson disease.

   long-acting beta a. ABBR: LABA. A class of medications used to treat asthma. Examples include: formoterol and salmeterol.

   short-acting beta a. A group of bronchdilators used to treat acute exacerbations of asthma or chronic obstructive pulmonary disease, e.g., albuterol, metaproterenol, and pirbuterol.

agonistic antibody (ăg″ŏ-nis′tik) SEE: *antibody.*

agony (ag′ŏ-nē) [L. fr. Gr. *agōnia,* anguish, struggle] **1.** Extreme mental or physical suffering. **2.** The death struggle.

agoraphobia (ag″(ŏ)-ră-fō′bē-ă) [Gr. *agora,* marketplace + *-phobia*] A form of social phobia in which one feels overwhelming symptoms of anxiety on leaving home. The symptoms may occur in everyday situations (e.g., standing on line, eating in public) in which a person may be unable to escape or get help and may be embarrassed. Symptoms include rapid heartbeat, chest pain, difficulty in breathing, gastrointestinal distress, faintness, weakness, sweating, or fear of impending doom or of dying. People with these symptoms often avoid phobic situations by rarely or never leaving home. **agoraphobe** (ag′(ŏ)-ră-fōb″), *n.* **agoraphobic** (ag″(ŏ)-ră-fō′bik), *n.* **agoraphobic,** *adj.*;

-agra [Gr. *agra,* a seizure] Suffix meaning *sudden, severe pain.*

agrammatism (ā″gram′ă-tĭzm) [*a-* + Gr. *gramma,* stem *grammat-,* letter + *-ism*] A language disturbance marked by the misuse of grammar, esp. the inability to make subjects and verbs agree or to use conjunctions, pronouns, verb tenses, or word endings appropriately.

agranulocyte (ā″gran′yŭ-lō-sīt″) [*a-* + *granulocyte*] A nongranular, mononuclear white blood cell (a lymphocyte or a monocyte). SYN: *agranular leukocyte; lymphoid leukocyte; nongranular leukocyte.*

agranulocytosis (ā″gran″yŭ-lō-sī″tō′sis) [*agranulocyte* + *-osis*] An acute disease marked by a deficit or absence of granular leukocytes. It may occur in some leukemias or after exposure to certain drugs (e.g., clozapine) or radiation.

SYN: *agranulosis; granulocytopenia; malignant* **neutropenia**. **agranulocytic** (-sit′ik), *adj*.

agranuloplastic (ā″gran″yŭ-lō-plas′tik) [*a-* + *granulo(cyte)* + *-plastic*] Unable to form granular cells.

agranulosis (ā″gran″yŭ-lō′sis) [*agranulo(cyte)* + *-osis*] Agranulocytosis.

agraphesthesia (ā″graf″es-thē′zh(ē-)ă) [*a-* + *-graph* + *esthesi-* + *-ia*] Inability to recognize letters or numbers drawn by the examiner on skin. SEE: *graphesthesia*.

agraphia (ā″graf′ē-ă) [¹*an-* + *-graph* + *-ia*] Loss of the ability to write. SEE: *motor* **aphasia**. **agraphic** (ā″graf′ik), *adj*.

   absolute a. Complete inability to write.

   acoustic a. Inability to write words that are heard.

   amnemonic a. Inability to write sentences although letters or words can be written.

   cerebral a. Inability to express thoughts in writing.

   motor a. Inability to write due to muscular incoordination.

   optic a. Inability to copy words.

   verbal a. Inability to write words although letters can be written.

A/G ratio Albumin-globulin ratio.

Agrobacterium radiobacter (ag″rō-bak-tēr′ē-ŭm rā″dē-ō-bak′tĕr) [L. fr. Gr.] The former name of the bacterium now called *Rhizobium radiobacter*. It is a gram-negative rod-shaped bacterium. It is an opportunistic pathogen that is a rare cause of bacteremia, endocarditis, and peritonitis mostly in mostly in immunocompromised patients, and is a rare cause of urinary tract infection.

agrypnocoma (ă-grip″nŏ-kō′mă) [Gr. *agrypnos*, sleepless + *coma*] Coma in which the person is partially awake as if in an extreme lethargic state. It may be associated with delirium and lack of sleep.

agrypnotic (ā″grip-not′ik) [Gr. *agrypnos*, sleepless] **1.** Afflicted with insomnia. **2.** Causing wakefulness.

AGS *American Geriatrics Society*.

AGUS *atypical glandular cells of undetermined significance*. SEE: *atypical glandular cells*.

agyria (ā″jī′rē-ă) [*a-* + *gyro-* + *-a*] Incompletely developed convolutions of the cerebral cortex. **agyric** (-rik), *adj*.

AHA *alpha-hydroxy* **acid**; *American Heart Association; American Hospital Association*.

AHF *antihemophilic factor*, coagulation factor VIII. SEE: *coagulation* **factor**.

AHFV *Alkhurma hemorrhagic* **fever**.

AHG *antihemophilic globulin*, coagulation factor VIII. SEE: *coagulation* **factor**.

AHIMA *American Health Information Management Association*.

AHRQ *Agency for Healthcare Research and Quality*.

ah-shi point (ah-shē, -shĭr) [Chinese *ah, shì,* ah, yes! (referring to the point of pain)] SEE: under *point*.

AI *aortic* **insufficiency**; *artificial* **insemination**; *artificial* **intelligence**; *axioincisal*.

Aicardi-Goutières syndrome (e-kar-dē′-goo-tyer′) [Jean François Marie Aicardi, Fr. pediatrician, b. 1926; Françoise Goutières] A rare inherited mental retardation in which affected infants also have both encephalopathy and liver disease. It may mimic TORCH or toxoplasmosis. SYN: *pseudo-TORCH syndrome*.

Aicardi syndrome (ī-kar′dē) [Jean François Marie Aicardi, Fr. neurologist, b. 1926] A rare cause of childhood seizures, due to the congenital absence of the corpus callosum. The disease is only found in children with two X chromosomes or in those with Klinefelter's syndrome.

aichmophobia (āk″mō-fō′bē-ă) [Gr. *aichmē,* spear point + *-phobia*] Morbid fear of being touched by pointed objects or fingers.

AID *Agency for International Development; artificial insemination* **donor**.

aid (ād) **1.** Assistance provided to a person, esp. one who is sick, injured, or troubled. **2.** A resource used by a person to improve functioning; an assistive device.

   bone conduction hearing a., bone-conduction hearing aid A hearing aid that amplifies sounds and transmits them through the skull or through an implant anchored in the skull.

   button a. An assistive technology device permitting button closure by persons with the functional use of only one extremity.

   decision a. An educational tool to assist patients or health care professionals in making choices about aspects of care. SYN: *decision rule*.

   electronic travel a. ABBR: ETA. An electronic assistive technology device that makes it easier for the blind or visually impaired to move safely in busy or unfamiliar environments.

   ergogenic a. In sports medicine, the questionable and often harmful use of various substances to try to enhance performance. Some of these materials, e.g., blood transfusions, anabolic steroids, amphetamines, amino acids, and human growth hormone, are standard medicines approved for uses other than those intended by the athlete. Others are not only not indicated for any illness but may be harmful, esp. when the amount of the active ingredient in the product is unknown. Included in this latter group are cyproheptadine, taken to increase appetite, strength, and, allegedly, testosterone production; ginseng; pangamic acid; octacosanol, a 28-carbon straight-chain alcohol obtained from wheat germ oil, the biological effects of which are unknown; guarana, prepared from the seeds of the *Paullinia cupana* tree, used for its alleged ability to increase energy; gamma-oryzanol, an isomer of oryzanol extracted from rice bran oil, allegedly useful in decreasing recovery time after exercise; proteolytic enzymes, e.g., chymotrypsin, trypsin-chymotrypsin, and papain, the safety and efficacy of which have not been established, esp. when used with oral anticoagulants or by pregnant or lactating women; and bee pollen, which has shown no evidence of improving athletic performance. SEE: *anabolic agent; blood doping*.

   ergonomic a. Any engineered enhancement that makes human beings more comfortable, healthy, or productive while performing tasks in which people and technology interact.

   hearing a. An electroacoustical sound-amplifying apparatus used by those with impaired hearing. Common forms of hearing aids are those that fit within the ear ("in the ear" [ITE]), or within the auditory canal ("in the canal" [ITC]); those that are worn behind the ear (BTE), and those that are carried on the body. The modern hearing aid may simply amplify sound or may be designed to attenuate certain portions of the sound signal and amplify others. The cost may vary from several hundred dollars to more than a thousand dollars. There are a variety of hearing aids available, and therefore it is important that patients buy the type most suitable for their needs and comfort. Patients should have a trial period before making the final decision to purchase the device.

   robotic a. Any electronically controlled device that assists a person to perform tasks of living, locomotion, or to systematically guide movement of the extremities to regain movement.

   travel a. A device that makes it easier for people with sensory impairments to move freely in busy or unfamiliar environments.

aide (ād) [Fr. *aide,* helper] **1.** Assistant. **2.** A nurse's aide or nursing assistant.

   certified medication a. ABBR: CMA. An unlicensed health care worker who can administer oral and topical medications in long-term or chronic care facilities after successfully completing a state-approved medication administration course. SYN: *certified medication technician*.

   physical therapy a. A person trained by a physical therapist or physical therapist assistant to provide clinical support services in physical therapy for tasks that do not require clinical decision making or problem solving in patient care. Physical therapy aides should function with continuous on-site supervision.

AIDS (ādz) An advanced stage of infection with the human immunodeficiency virus (HIV). AIDS was unrecognized before 1981, but it is now one of the most common causes of death worldwide. Most people with AIDS are between 15 and 44 years old, poor, and heterosexual. Most have limited access to good care and live in resource-poor nations in Africa and Asia. Worldwide about 2.6 million new HIV infections occur each year. More than 33 million people live with HIV infection. Annual mortality is about 5.5 percent, and about 1.8 million people die of HIV/AIDS annually. In the U.S. more than a million people with HIV/AIDS have been identified; about 500,000 HIV-infected Americans are alive today. The primary risk groups for current HIV/AIDS are people who have unprotected sexual intercourse, injection drug users, men who have sex with men, women and men with multiple sexual partners, and children of infected mothers.

   ETIOLOGY: Two human immunodeficiency viruses, HIV-1 and HIV-2, have been identified. Both cause AIDS, but infection with HIV-2 has been primarily limited to West Africa. Infection occurs when a viral envelope glycoprotein (gp120) binds to CD4 receptors and coreceptors (called CXCR4 and CCR5) on lymphocytes, macrophages, and other immune system cells, causing viral uptake and eventual cellular destruction and immune system dysfunction. HIV is a retrovirus that uses the enzyme reverse transcriptase to convert its viral RNA to viral DNA. The viral DNA incorporates into the host cell DNA and is transcribed and translated by host cells. New viral proteins are created and assembled into virions by the viral enzyme protease. About 100 billion virions, many with minor but protective mutations, are created during each reproductive cycle of HIV. Most newly formed viruses quickly infect circulating immune cells or take up residence in body reservoirs that are relatively inaccessible to drug therapy. The ability of HIV to mutate and evade treatment has made drug management of the disease complicated and has hindered development of a vaccine. Nonetheless, treatment with combinations of drugs (see below) decreases both the severity of infection and the development of drug-resistant clones and prolongs disease-free survival. The destruction of cells needed for normal immunological function produces susceptibility to diseases that the body normally resists.

This susceptibility is the hallmark of AIDS. In the U.S., common opportunistic infections that infect AIDS patients include *Pneumocystis carinii* pneumonia (also known as *P. jiroveci*), *Mycobacterium avium intracellulare* (MAI), cytomegalovirus, *Toxoplasma gondii, Candida albicans, Cryptosporidium,* and *Histoplasma capsulatum*. AIDS patients also are subject to nonopportunistic infections (such as tuberculosis, syphilis, herpesviruses, papillomaviruses, and streptococcal pneumonia) at rates and with a virulence far exceeding those in the general population.

SYMPTOMS: Initial infection with HIV-1 may cause a mononucleosis-like syndrome, with fevers, sore throat, swollen glands, and muscle and joint aches. The opportunistic infections that accompany AIDS cause fatigue, fevers, chills, sweats, breathlessness, oral ulceration, difficulties with swallowing, pneumonia, diarrhea, skin rashes, anorexia, weight loss, confusion, dementia, and strokelike symptoms. Many people are so incapacitated by AIDS that they are unable to carry out normal activities of daily living; others have very few limitations but may periodically experience life-threatening illnesses. SEE: table.

DIAGNOSIS: The presence of antibodies to HIV indicates HIV infection. Criteria for the diagnosis of AIDS include HIV infection with 1) a CD4+ helper T-cell count of less than 200 cells/mL, in addition to 2) infection with an opportunistic pathogen, and/or 3) the presence of an AIDS-defining malignancy. Enzyme-linked immunosorbent assays (ELISA) or enzyme immunoassays (EIA) are the primary tests used to screen for HIV antibodies. These tests are sensitive but not specific for HIV infection. If antibodies are detected by enzyme immunoassays, a more specific Western blot test is required for confirmation. Point-of-care tests for HIV (in which samples of whole blood, plasma, or oral fluids are used) provide rapid HIV test results. Nucleic acid amplification testing (NAAT), polymerase chain reaction (PCR) tests, and monoclonal antibodies to viral p24 antigen can also be used to detect HIV infection. Measurement of the absolute levels of helper T cells (CD4+ T lymphocytes) and the level of HIV viremia (the viral load) are the principal tests used to monitor the course of established infection and the effectiveness of administered therapies. Many health care agencies, such as the Centers for Disease Control and Prevention and the U.S. Veterans Administration recommend routine screening for HIV/AIDS in broad segments of the population to identify and diagnose the disease in asymptomatic patients. Mass screening in the U.S. is likely to be most cost-effective in large urban areas where the vast majority of Americans infected with HIV live.

NATURAL HISTORY: Between 60% and 80% of HIV-infected patients develop AIDS within 10 years of seroconversion.

PREVENTION: HIV infection is spread by direct contact with the blood or bodily secretions of those infected, usually through a break in the skin or across mucous membranes. In most cases, it has been transmitted from person to person by one of three modes: sexually, by injection of blood products, or

Clinical Conditions and Opportunistic Infections Indicating AIDS

AIDS wasting syndrome	Kaposi sarcoma
Candida infections (candidiasis) of the trachea, bronchi, lungs, or esophagus	Leukoencephalopathy, progressive multifocal
Cervical cancer, invasive	Lymphoma: Burkitt; immunoblastic; non-Hodgkin; primary brain
Cryptococcus neoformans: Extrapulmonary infections	*Mycobacterium avium* complex or *M. kansasii:* Extrapulmonary or disseminated infections
Cryptosporidium: Chronic (lasting more than a month) infections of the gastrointestinal tract	*Mycobacterium tuberculosis*: Pulmonary or extrapulmonary infections
Cytomegalovirus: Infections other than those in liver, spleen, or lymph nodes; cytomegalovirus retinitis with loss of vision	*Mycobacterium,* other species: Extrapulmonary infections or disseminated
Encephalopathy, HIV-related	Pneumonia, *Pneumocystis carinii*
Herpes simplex: Chronic (lasting more than a month) oral ulcers, bronchitis, pneumonitis, or esophagitis	Pneumonia, recurrent
Histoplasma capsulatum: Extrapulmonary or disseminated histoplasmosis infections	*Toxoplasma gondii*: Infections (toxoplasmosis) of the brain, heart, or lung
Isosporiasis, chronic (lasting more than a month) intestinal	

Adapted from CDC:MMWR 41 (RR-17):2-3, 15, 1992.

from mother to fetus (or mother to infant). All pregnant women should be counseled about testing for the presence of HIV antibodies to prevent maternal-child disease transmission. Antiretroviral therapies during and immediately after pregnancy greatly reduce the vertical transmission of HIV. Those who engage in unsafe sex or inject drugs with contaminated needles are at the greatest risk for contracting the disease. Abstinence from risky behavior prevents the spread of the disease. Scrupulous screening of the blood supply and of organ donors has dramatically reduced iatrogenic HIV transmission.

TREATMENT: The use of highly active antiretroviral therapies (HAART), typically including two drugs that block viral nucleoside reverse transcriptases (NRTI), in addition to a non-NRTI, an integrase inhibitor, or a protease inhibitor) has revolutionized the treatment of HIV/AIDS. Expensive combination-drug "cocktails" can decrease viral loads to undetectable levels and restore a level of immunological function to AIDS patients that, although imperfect, defends against most opportunistic infections. The timing of the initiation of antiretroviral therapy depends on the public health resources available for HIV/AIDS treatment and the stage and patient-specific disease presentation. In developed nations, antiretroviral therapy should begin when CD4+ cell counts fall below 350 cells/mL of blood, when an AIDS-defining illness is experienced, when HIV-related renal disease is detected, or in patients who are coinfected with hepatitis B virus. The promise of antiretroviral therapies is realized only when patients strictly adhere to their prescription regimens and avoid behavior that may place others at risk for disease transmission. Treatments for established AIDS are also directed against the opportunistic infections of AIDS. These include drugs such as trimethoprim/sulfamethoxazole or pentamidine for *Pneumocystis carinii* (*P. jiroveci*), clarithromycin and other antimicrobial agents for *Mycobacterium avium intracellare,* valganciclovir and/or other antivirals for cytomegalovirus, and antifungal drugs (such as intraconazole and amphotericin) for histoplasmosis. Treatment for AIDS-related malignancies includes antiretroviral therapy (augmented with anthracyclines or paclitaxel) for Kaposi sarcoma, and combination chemotherapies (administered systemically or regionally) for non-Hodgkin lymphoma. About 10% of patients with HIV/AIDS die of cardiovascular disease. Cardiovascular risk factor reduction, including the use of lipid-lowering therapies, is a necessary component of therapy for those living with the disease.

OCCUPATIONAL CONCERNS: Standard infection control precautions prevent the spread of HIV/AIDS to health care providers. Occupational exposure to body fluids from AIDS patients is relatively common in health care, but transmission of the disease is rare. The risk of HIV infection after a puncture wound from a contaminated needle is estimated to be about 0.3%; the risk of seroconversion after mucous membranes are splashed with contaminated blood or body fluids is 0.09%. The virus does not proliferate or readily survive outside the body, i.e., on counters or other surfaces.

PATIENT CARE: Health care professionals should contribute actively to the education of patients about preventing the spread of HIV. Complex treatment regimens make management of the disease a burden for many patients, but these patients must be encouraged to adhere to these complicated drug regimens because failure to do so may result in the evolution of drug-resistant viruses. Health care providers should anticipate, assess, and assist patients to collaborate in helping to prevent inconsistent drug dosing or abandonment of treatment. The cost of drug therapy and other services may be a factor in adhering to medication. Health care providers should be aware of referral agencies and resources for help in obtaining social service support; information about the disease; funds for housing, food, and medication; and inpatient, outpatient, and hospice care (when it is appropriate). Health care providers should also be familiar with support groups for partners and families of people with HIV/AIDS.

immunologic A. Severe immunosuppression in HIV infection evidenced only by a very low CD4 helper cell count (less than 200 cells/mm³). Patients have not yet had an opportunistic infection but are highly likely to contract one.

perinatal A. Infection with HIV as a result of vertical transmission of the virus from an infected mother. Worldwide, in 2002, 1500 children were infected every day by maternal to child transmission of the disease; the overwhelming majority of these children live in developing nations. In the U.S. between 1992 and 1997, testing pregnant women to identify HIV infection and treating affected people with zidovudine decreased the risk of perinatal AIDS by about 70%.

TRANSMISSION: Transmission of HIV to infants occurs in utero, during labor and delivery, and through breastfeeding. Approx. 50% to 70% of infants are infected during childbirth, esp. during preterm birth with prolonged rupture of membranes; 30% to 50% are infected in utero; 20% of HIV-positive mothers can transmit the infection through breastfeeding.

DIAGNOSIS: The diagnosis is made through two positive blood test results for the presence of HIV or the growth of HIV in culture. Transmission is unlikely to occur in women whose viral load of HIV RNA has been reduced by effective antiretroviral therapy. The Centers for Disease Control and Prevention (CDC) recommends that all adults, aged 13 to 64, should be offered routine HIV testing (with the choice to opt out), rather than testing only those patients with known risk factors for the disease.

SYMPTOMS: Infants may be asymptomatic even when infected with HIV. Infection is monitored by measuring the absolute CD4+ T-cell count, measuring the amount of virus in the blood (viral load), and assessing for the presence of opportunistic infections in infancy or early childhood. Over time, the infected infant may present with *Pneumocystis carinii* (*P. jiroveci*) pneumonia, chronic diarrhea, recurrent bacterial infections, failure to thrive, developmental delays, and recurrent *Candida* and herpes simplex infections. The majority of perinatally infected children develop an AIDS-defining illness by the age of 4. Anemia and neutropenia may occur as side effects of drug therapy.

TREATMENT: Zidovudine (AZT) is given for 6 weeks to all infants born of HIV-positive mothers. Prophylaxis for *P. carinii* (*P. jiroveci*) pneumonia with trimethoprim-sulfamethoxazole begins at 6 weeks and continues for 6 months in children whose HIV test results are negative and for 1 year in infected infants. The use of highly active highly active antiretroviral therapy (HAART) is being studied. Breastfeeding is contraindicated for all HIV-infected mothers to minimize the risk of transmission of the virus.

PATIENT CARE: Women in their childbearing years who engage in high-risk behavior and women whose husbands or primary sexual partner may engage in high risk behavior should be counseled to be tested for HIV before becoming pregnant or as soon as they know they are pregnant in order to reduce the risk of infection the baby. Women who are HIV-positive should begin antiretroviral therapy immediately. Standard precautions are used with babies born of HIV-positive mothers until diagnostic tests indicate that they are not infected. Mothers and other care providers must be instructed in the use of these precautions and to watch for and quickly report respiratory infections.

AIDS-dementia complex   SEE: under *complex.*

AIDS-related complex   SEE: under *complexAIDS.*

AIDS wasting syndrome   Malnutrition in the HIV-infected patient, including both starvation (weight loss from lack of food) and cachexia (loss of lean body mass). SEE: *cachexia; cytokine; starvation.*

PATHOPHYSIOLOGY: The mechanisms by which HIV causes malnutrition include decreased nutritional intake, metabolic abnormalities, and the combination of diarrhea and malabsorption. Decreased oral intake may be related to loss of appetite, oral or esophageal ulcers (esp. from *Candida* or herpes simplex virus), difficulty chewing, fatigue, changes in mental status, or inadequate finances. Metabolic abnormalities include elevated serum cortisol, decreased anabolism, micronutrient deficiencies (vitamin B_{12}, pyridoxine, vitamin A, zinc, and selenium), and decreased antioxidants. Malabsorption and diarrhea affect 60% to 100% of patients with AIDS. Primary gastrointestinal pathogens that contribute to malnutrition include *Cryptosporidia, Microsporidia,* and *Mycobacterium avium intracellulare.* Concerns about diarrhea and fecal incontinence may underlie a patient's decreased oral intake.

PATIENT CARE: Assessment and education of patients must begin as soon as they are diagnosed as having HIV infection. Obtaining a careful history of the patient's normal nutritional intake and activity level provides the baseline for nutritional instruction. Patients are encouraged to maintain the recommended daily allowance (RDA) for all foods by following MyPyramid; protein intake of 1 to 2 g/kg of ideal body weight and vitamin and mineral intake three to four times the RDA are also encouraged. Small frequent feedings, good oral hygiene, limited fluids with meals, and the use of preferred foods are helpful strategies in countering anorexia. A written schedule may help the patient adhere to the recommended plan for intake. Any increase in exercise or activity must be accompanied by an increase in food intake.

AIH   *artificial insemination by husband* (homologous insemination).

AIHA   *American Industrial Hygiene Association; autoimmune hemolytic **anemia**.*

ailment (al'mĕnt) A complaint, disease, or physical disorder, esp. a mild or chronic one.

ailurophobia (ī-loor″ŏ-fō'bē-ă) [Gr. *ailouros,* cat + *-phobia*] Morbid fear of cats. **ailurophobe** (-fōb'), *n.*

ainhum (ān'hŭm) [East African, to saw] Spontaneous loss of fingers or toes, typically occurring in Africa, due to the formation of a fissured, constricting band forming around the digit. SYN: *spontaneous dactylolysis*.

air (ār) [Gr. *aēr*, air] The invisible, tasteless, odorless mixture of gases surrounding the earth. Air at sea level consists of approx. 78% nitrogen and 21% oxygen by volume. The remaining constituents are water vapor, carbon dioxide, and traces of ammonia, argon, helium, neon, krypton, xenon, rare gases, and some pollutants.

   alveolar a. Air in the alveoli. It is involved in the pulmonary exchange of gases between air and the blood. Its content is determined by sampling the last portion of a maximal expiration.

   liquid a. Air liquefied by great pressure and/or low temperature. It produces intense cold on evaporation.

   mechanical dead space a. Dead space air provided by artificial means. Such means include mechanical ventilation or the addition of plastic tubing to a ventilator circuit.

   minimal a. The small volume of air trapped in the alveoli when lungs collapse.

   reserve a. Expiratory reserve **volume**.

   room a. Unmodified, ambient air. The typical oxygen concentration is 21%.

air evacuation SEE: under *evacuation*.
air gap principle SEE: under *principle*.
air medical transportation The use of helicopters or fixed-wing aircraft to transport patients from the scene of an incident or local hospital to a regional trauma or specialty care center.
airsickness (ar′sik″nĕs) A form of motion sickness marked by dizziness, nausea, vomiting, headache, or drowsiness that occurs during travel in aircraft. SEE: *motion sickness; seasickness*. **airsick,** *adj.*
airway (ar′wā″) **1.** A natural passage for air to enter and exit the lungs. **2.** A device to prevent or correct an obstructed respiratory passage, esp. one inserted into the trachea and used during anesthesia or cardiopulmonary resuscitation. An open airway is essential to oxygenation and ventilation. Methods for opening the airway are described in the following entries: cardiopulmonary resuscitation; chin-lift airway technique; head tilt; jaw thrust; tracheostomy. The following subentries highlight commonly used airways in advanced cardiac life support. None of them have been proven to enhance the survival of patients who suffer sudden death in the field. SEE: *jaw **thrust***.

⚠ If a patient has a mechanism of injury involving potential trauma to the clavicles or above, the airway should

be opened only with the jaw thrust maneuver.

   Combitube a. A trademark for a dual-lumen airway consisting of a tracheal tube linked to an esophageal tube. It may be inserted blindly into the oropharynx as an airway control device when an endotracheal tube is not available or when tracheal intubation with direct visualization of the vocal cords is challenging.

   difficult a. An airway that is challenging or impossible to intubate. Intubation is increasingly difficult in: older patients, patients with head or neck trauma, obese patients, and patients with craniofacial abnormalities.

   laryngeal mask a. ABBR: LMA. An airway that can be blindly inserted into the hypopharynx to use when advanced airway control is needed during procedures that require brief anesthesia. It consists of an airway tube with a proximal cuff, which holds the middle of the tube in place at the base of the tongue, and a distal cuff to fix the end of the tube in the trachea.

⚠ It should not be used in patients at high risk of aspiration.

SYN: *laryngeal tracheal a.*
   laryngeal tracheal a. ABBR: LTA. Laryngeal mask **a.**
   nasopharyngeal a. ABBR: NPA. A soft, flexible, uncuffed tube placed through the nasal passages so that the distal tip rests in the nasopharynx. It is used to maintain the free passage of air to and from the lungs in patients with facial trauma or lockjaw or in nearly comatose patients who are breathing spontaneously. Before the tube is inserted, the proper length is determined by comparing it to the distance from the tip of the patient's nose to the earlobe. The diameter should match that of the patient's pinkie. Nasopharyngeal airways are often used by respiratory therapists to reduce the trauma from repetitive nasotracheal suctioning. SYN: *nasal trumpet*. SEE: illus.; *Standard Precautions Appendix*.

⚠ Bleeding from the nasopharynx may occur during emergency placement of this airway.

   oropharyngeal a. ABBR: OPA. A curved plastic device used to establish an airway in a patient by displacing the tongue from the posterior wall of the oropharynx. The device should be equal in length to the distance either from the corner of the mouth to the earlobe or

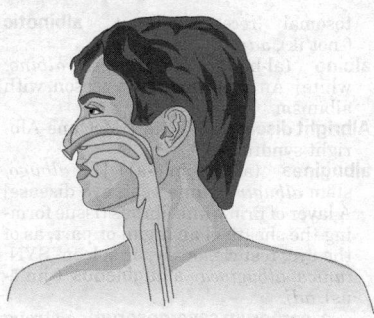

NASOPHARYNGEAL AIRWAY

A nasopharyngeal airway in proper position

from the center of the mouth to the angle of the jaw. It has a flange on the end that remains outside the mouth to keep it from being swallowed or aspirated. This device is used only in unconscious patients who do not have a gag reflex. SEE: *cardiopulmonary* **resuscitation**; illus.; *Standard Precautions Appendix*.

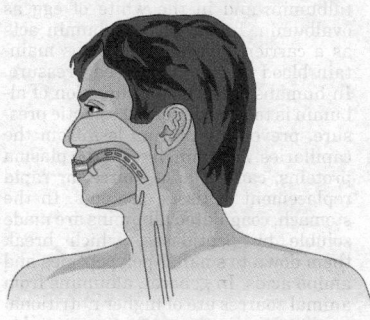

OROPHARYNGEAL AIRWAY

An oropharyngeal airway in place

⚠ The head of an unconscious patient should be stabilized before the airway is inserted to reduce the likelihood of cervical spinal cord injury and paralysis.

supraglottic a. Supralaryngeal **a.**
supralaryngeal a. A device used as an alternative to tracheal intubation in the ventilation of the critically ill. It contains both an esophageal and a tracheal lumen and may be inserted without visualization of the vocal cords. SYN: *supraglottic **a.***

airway clearance, ineffective The inability to clear secretions or obstructions from the upper respiratory tract, and thus, to maintain an open, effective airway. SEE: *Nursing Diagnoses Appendix*.

airway opening pressure SEE: under *pressure*.

AIVR *Accelerated idioventricular **rhythm**.*

Ajellomyces (a″jĕ-lō-mī′sēs″) A genus of fungi of the family Ajellomycetaceae.

A. capsulatus The sexual, perfect, form of the yeast *Histoplasma capsulatum* in its asexual form.

A. dermatiditis The sexual form of the pathogenic yeast *Blastomycosis dermatidis*.

AK *above the knee*. The term is used to refer to the site of an amputation of a lower extremity.

akathisia, acathisia (ā″ka-thi′zh(ē-)ă) [¹*an-* + Gr. *kathizein*, to sit] Intolerance of inactivity; motor restlessness. The symptom may appear as a side effect of antipsychotic drug therapy (e.g., treatment with phenothiazines).

SYMPTOMS: Affected people cannot sit still, are jumpy or fidgety, and may appear distracted.

TREATMENT: The urge to move resolves when the offending drug is withdrawn. Propranolol is also used to reduce motor restlessness.

akee, ackee (ak′ē, ă-kē′) [Liberian] The tropical tree *Blighia sapida*, of the soapberry family. Ingestion of its unripe fruit can cause severe hypoglycemia.

akinesia, akinesis (ā″kī-nē′zh(ē-)ă, kī-nē′sis) [¹*an-* + *-kinesia*] Partial or complete loss or suppression of muscle movement. **akinetic** (-net′ik), *adj.*

a. algera Akinesia with intense pain caused by voluntary movement.

Al Symbol for the element aluminum (British: aluminium).

-al [L. adj. suffix *-al-*] **1.** A suffix meaning *relating to*, as in abdominal, intestinal. **2.** In chemistry, a suffix indicating an *aldehyde*.

ala (ā′lă) *pl.* **alae** [L., wing] An expanded or winglike structure or appendage.

a. nasi Wing of the nose; broad portion forming the lateral wall of each nostril.

a. of sacrum Broad projection on each side of the base (the superior end) of the sacrum. The alae of the sacrum join the main plates (alae) of the ilium bones along the sacroiliac joints.

alacrima (ā-lak′rĭ-mă) [*a-* + *lacrima*] Dry eye.

Alagille syndrome (a-la-zhēl′) [Daniel Alagille, Fr. physician, b. 1925] A rare congenital syndrome in which arteriohepatic dysplasia is associated with developmental anomalies of the face, heart, kidneys, muscle, and nervous system.

alalia (ā″lā′lē-ă, ă-lal′) [*a-* + Gr. *lalein*, to talk] Inability to speak due to a defect in or a paralysis of the vocal organs; aphasia. An organic brain disease is usually responsible.

alanine (al′ă-nēn″) [al(dehyde) + -ne] A naturally occurring amino acid, $C_3H_7NO_2$, considered nonessential in human nutrition.

alanine aminotransferase ABBR: ALT. SEE: under *aminotransferase.*

Al-Anon (al′ă-non″) A nonprofit organization that provides group support for the family and close friends of alcoholics. SEE: *Alateen; Alcoholics Anonymous; Nar-Anon; 12-step program.*

alar (ā′lăr) [L. *ala,* wing] **1.** Pert. to or like a wing. **2.** Axillary.

ALARA *as low as reasonably achievable.*

alarmin (ă-lar′min) Any molecule released from a damaged or diseased cell that stimulates an immune response. Heat-shock proteins, interleukin-1a, and nucleosomes are examples.

alarm reaction The first stage in the general adaptation syndrome, which includes changes occurring in the body when subjected to stressful stimuli. Physiological changes that occur are direct results of damage, shock, or both, or reactions of the body to defend itself against shock.

alarm therapy A behavioral treatment for nighttime bed-wetting in which urine in the patient's bed or diaper triggers an electrical circuit that makes an irritating sound, awakening and alerting the patient to stop voiding.

ALARP *as low as reasonably practicable.*

alarplasty (ā′lăr-plas″tē) [*alar* + *-plasty*] Plastic surgery to correct defects in or reduce the width of the nostrils.

alaryngeal speech (ā″lă-rin′j(ē-)ăl) [¹*an-* + *laryngeal*] SEE: under *speech.*

alastrim (al′ă-strim″) Variola minor.

Alateen (al′ă-tēn″) A nonprofit organization that provides support for children of alcoholics. SEE: *Al-Anon; Alcoholics Anonymous; Nar-Anon; 12-step program.*

alb- [L. *albus,* white] Prefix meaning *white.*

alba (al′bă) [L. *albus,* white] The white matter of the brain.

albedo (al-bē′dō) [L. whiteness] Whiteness. Reflection of light from a surface.

    a. unguium Lunula.

Albers-Schönberg disease (al′bĕrz-shĕrn′bĕrg″) [Heinrich Ernst Albers-Schönberg, Ger. radiologist, 1865–1921] SEE: *osteopetrosis.*

Albert disease (al′bĕrt) [Eduard Albert, Austrian surgeon, 1841–1900] Achilloburistis.

albicans (al′bĭ-kanz″) [L. *albicare,* to make or become white] White; whitish.

albinism (al′bĭ-nizm) [*albino* + *-ism*] An inherited partial or total absence of pigment in skin, hair, and eyes. It is often accompanied by astigmatism, photophobia, and nystagmus because the choroid is not sufficiently protected from light. It is usually transmitted as an au-

tosomal recessive trait. **albinotic** (-not′ik), *adj.*

albino (al-bī′nō) [Portuguese *albino,* white] An organism, esp. a person, with albinism.

Albright disease (al′brīts″) McCune-Albright syndrome.

albuginea (al″byŭ-jin′ē-ă) [L. *albugo,* stem *albugin-,* white spot, eye disease] A layer of firm white fibrous tissue forming the sheath of an organ or part, as of the eye, testicle, ovary, or spleen. SYN: *tunica albuginea.* **albugineous** (-jin′ē-ŭs), *adj.*

    a. corporum cavernosorum A strong elastic white fibrous sheath of both corpora cavernosa of the penis.

    a. oculi The sclera.

    a. testis The thick, unyielding layer of white fibrous tissue lying under the tunica vaginalis.

albumen (al-bū′mĕn) [L. *albumen,* white of egg] **1.** The white of an egg. **2.** Albumin.

albumin (al-bū′mĭn) [L. *albumen,* white of egg] Any of a group of simple proteins widely distributed in plant and animal tissues. Albumin is found in the blood as serum albumin, in milk as lactalbumin, and in the white of egg as ovalbumin. In the blood, albumin acts as a carrier molecule and helps maintain blood volume and blood pressure. In humans the principal function of albumin is to provide colloid osmotic pressure, preventing plasma loss from the capillaries. Albumin, like all the plasma proteins, can act as a source for rapid replacement of tissue proteins. In the stomach, coagulated albumins are made soluble by peptidases, which break them down to smaller polypeptides and amino acids. In general, albumins from animal sources are of higher nutritional quality than those from vegetable sources because animal proteins contain greater quantities of essential amino acids. SYN: *albumen* (2). SEE: *amino acid; peptone.*

    blood a. Serum **a.**

    circulating a. Albumin present in body fluids.

    egg a. Ovalbumin.

    human a. A sterile solution of serum albumin obtained from healthy blood donors. It is administered intravenously to restore blood volume.

    ovi a. Ovalbumin.

    serum a. The main protein found in the blood. SYN: *blood **a**.* SEE: *blood; simple protein.*

    urinary a. Albumin in urine, a finding in glomerular diseases.

    vegetable a. Albumin in, or derived from, plant tissue.

albuminate (al-bū′mĭ-nāt″, năt) [*albumin* + *-ate*] A compound formed when albumin combines with an acid or alkali.

albumin-globulin ratio ABBR: A/G r. The ratio of albumin to globulin in blood plasma or serum. Normally this value is 1.3:1 to 3.0:1.

albuminocytologic dissociation (al-bū″mĭ-nō-sīt″ŏ-loj′ik) SEE: under *dissociation*.

albuminolysis (al-bū″mĭ-nol′ĭ-sis) [*albumen* + *-lysis*] An uncommon synonym for proteolysis. SEE: *proteolysis*.

albuminosis (al-bū″mĭ-nō′sis) [*albumen* + *-osis*] An abnormal increase of albumin in blood plasma.

albuminous, albuminose (al-bū′mĭ-nŭs, al-bū′mĭ-nōs″) Pert. to, resembling, or containing albumin.

albumin reaction The presence (positive reaction) or absence (negative reaction) of albumin in the sputum. A positive reaction was formerly used to indicate inflammation of the lungs.

albumin test Any chemical test for the presence of albumin, usually with electrophoresis, chromatography, spectrophotometry, spectrometry, or immunoassay, and sometimes by simple chemical reactions on dipsticks.

albuminuria (al-bū-mĭ-noo′rē-ă) [*albumen* + *-uria*] The presence of easily detectable amounts of albumin in the urine. Albuminuria is a common sign of renal impairment, e.g., nephrotic syndrome; it also occurs in fever, malignant hypertension, and in healthy people after vigorous exercise. SEE: *microalbuminuria; nephritis; nephrosis*. **albuminuretic** (noo-rĕt″ik), *adj.*, **albuminuric** (-noor′ik), *adj.*

cyclic a. Presence of small amounts of albumin in the urine at regular diurnal intervals, esp. in childhood and adolescence.

orthostatic a. Postural **a.**

postural a. Transient albuminuria in normal people who have been erect for a long time. SYN: *orthostatic* **a.**

albuterol (al-bū′tĕr-ŏl′) A beta-2 receptor agonist used to treat bronchospasm, e.g. in patients with asthma or related conditions. It is primarily administered by inhalation, but is sometimes given as a tablet.

Alcaligenes (al″kă-lij′ĕ-nēz″) [L. fr. Fr. *alcali,* alkali + *-gen*] A genus of gram-negative, aerobic bacilli normally found in the human intestinal tract, in dairy products, and in soil.

A. faecalis A species normally found in the human intestine. It has been associated with hospital-acquired septicemia and urinary tract infections.

A. xylosoxidans A species that does not ferment glucose. It has been implicated rarely in lung infections in patients with cystic fibrosis and in other health care associated infections in patients with immunosuppressing or malignant illnesses. SYN: *Achromobacter xylosoxidans*.

ALCL *Anaplastic large cell lymphoma*.

Alcock canal (al′koks″) [Benjamin Alcock, Irish anatomist, 1801– ?] Pudendal **canal**.

alcohol (al′kŏ-hol″) [L. *alcohol,* fr Arabic *al-kuh'l,* powdered antinomy, distillate] **1.** A class of organic compounds that are hydroxyl derivatives of hydrocarbons. **2.** Ethyl alcohol (C_2H_5OH), a colorless, volatile, flammable liquid. Its molecular weight is 46.07; its boiling point is 78.5°C. It is present in fermented or distilled liquors and is obtained, in its pure form, from grain by fermentation and fractionation distillation. SYN: *ethanol; grain a.*

absolute a. A solution that contains 99% ethyl alcohol and not more than 1% water.

cetyl a. A white insoluble solid substance, $C_{16}H_{34}O$, used in the manufacture of ointments.

dehydrated a. Alcohol containing not less than 99.2% by weight of ethyl alcohol. This corresponds to 99.5% by volume of ethyl alcohol.

denatured a. Alcohol rendered unfit for use as a beverage or medicine by the addition of toxic ingredients; used commercially as a solvent.

diluted a. A mixture of water and alcohol containing not less than 41% and not more than 42% by weight of ethyl alcohol. It is used as a solvent. SYN: *diluted* **ethanol**.

ethyl a. C_2H_5OH; grain alcohol. SYN: *ethanol.* SEE: *alcohol* (2); *Poisons and Poisoning Appendix*.

grain a. Ethyl **a.** SEE: *alcohol*(2).

isopropyl a. C_3H_7OH; a clear flammable liquid similar to ethyl alcohol. It is used in medical preparations for external use, antifreeze, cosmetics, and solvents. SYN: *isopropanol.* SEE: *Poisons and Poisoning Appendix*.

 Isopropyl alcohol is toxic when taken internally.

methyl a. CH_3OH; a colorless, volatile, flammable liquid obtained from distillation of wood. Even though its physical properties are similar to those of ethyl alcohol, it is not fit for human consumption. Ingestion of methyl alcohol can lead to blindness and death. It is used as a solvent, for fuel, as an additive for denaturing ethyl alcohol, as an antifreeze agent, and in the preparation of formaldehyde. SYN: *methanol; wood* **a.** SEE: *Poisons and Poisoning Appendix*.

polyvinyl a. A water-soluble synthetic resin used in preparing medicines, esp. ophthalmic solutions.

rubbing a. A preparation containing not less than 68.5% and not more than

71.5% dehydrated alcohol by volume. The remainder consists of water and denaturants and may or may not contain color additives and perfume oils. It is used as a rubefacient. Rubbing alcohol is packaged, labeled, and sold in accordance with the regulations issued by the U.S. Treasury Department, Bureau of Alcohol, Tobacco and Firearms.

⚠️ Because of the added denaturant, rubbing alcohol is poisonous if taken internally.

tertiary a. Alcohol containing the trivalent group ≡COH.

wood a. Methyl **a.**

Alcohol, Drug Abuse, and Mental Health Administration ABBR: ADAMHA. A U.S. government agency that is part of the National Institutes of Health. The agency administers grant programs supporting research, training, and service programs in alcoholism, drug abuse, and mental health.

alcohol-dependent sleep disorder Inability to sleep without consuming alcohol. The alcohol is used as a sedative/hypnotic drug.

alcoholic (al-kŏ-hol'ik) [*alcohol* + *-ic*] **1.** Pert. to alcohol. **2.** One afflicted with alcoholism.

Alcoholics Anonymous ABBR: AA. An organization consisting of alcoholics and recovering alcoholics who are trying to help themselves and others abstain from alcohol by offering encouragement and discussing experiences, problems, feelings, and techniques. The organization has groups in most U.S. cities; local chapters are listed in the telephone directory. SEE: *Al-Anon; Alateen; Nar-Anon; 12-step program.*

alcoholism (al'kŏ-hol"izm) [*alcohol* + *-ism*] A chronic, frequently progressive, and sometimes fatal disease marked by impaired control over consumption of alcohol despite its adverse effects. Dependence on alcohol, tolerance of its effects, and remissions and relapses are common. Psychological features include preoccupation with consuming alcohol and denial of addiction even against evidence to the contrary.

Alcohol abuse is one of the major threats to health in the U.S., where it is estimated to affect between 2 and 9% of the population. Each year 10% of all deaths are related to alcohol. Chronic alcoholism and alcohol-related disorders can be physically, psychologically, and economically devastating to patients and their families. SEE: *substance abuse; fetal alcohol syndrome;* table.

ETIOLOGY: Psychological, physiological, genetic, familial, and cultural factors play parts in alcoholism. Family members of alcoholics and males are most likely to be predisposed to the disease. Underage drinkers are more likely to become alcohol-dependent than are those who do not use alcohol before 21, with youths who start drinking before 15 having the highest risk of alcohol addiction.

SYMPTOMS: Pathological effects of alcoholism are found in almost any organ of the body but most commonly in the nervous system, bone marrow, liver, pancreas, stomach, and the other organs of the gastrointestinal tract. Symptoms arise both from organ-specific damage and from the psychological effects of the drug. Alcoholics are more likely than nonalcoholics to suffer falls, fractures, automotive accidents, job loss, and imprisonment. They also suffer from hypertension, gastritis, pancreatitis, hepatitis, cirrhosis, portal hypertension, memory disturbances, and oropharyngeal and pancreatic cancers at higher rates than the general population. In severe alcoholism, abstinence results in withdrawal symptoms and, occasionally, hallucinosis, delirium tremens, or withdrawal seizures. The life expectancy of alcoholics is shorter than that of nonalcoholics.

DIAGNOSIS: Alcoholism is diagnosed clinically. Although some alcoholics have many abnormal laboratory findings, none of these is definitively diagnostic. In severe hepatic disease, blood urea nitrogen is elevated, and serum glucose levels are decreased. Elevated liver function studies may indicate liver damage; and elevated serum amylase levels may indicate acute pancreatitis. Anemia, thrombocytopenia, leukopenia, increased prothrombin time, and increased partial thromboplastin time may be noted from hematologic studies.

Screening for alcoholism is best undertaken with questionnaires, like the Michigan Alcohol Screening Test (MAST) and the Alcohol Use Disorders Identification Test (AUDIT). CAGE, a widely used screening questionnaire, asks the questions: Do you feel the need to cut down on drinking? Are you *an*noyed by people who complain about your drinking? Do you feel *g*uilty about your drinking? Do you need an *eye*opener when you wake up? These tests are designed to determine when alcohol use has become physically, behaviorally, or emotionally problematic. Denial is a major concern, and patients may give false information in their health histories and deny physical problems associated with alcoholism. The usefulness of the assessment instrument depends upon the patient's honesty and trust in the clinicians. The assessor should be aware that indirect information obtained from the history and phys-

Levels of Alcohol Consumption: A Guide to Contemporary Usages

Type of drinking	Definition	Comment
Non-problematic drinking	< 1 standard drink daily (see definition of "standard drink" below)	Some evidence suggests that this level of alcohol consumption is healthful
Moderate drinking	≤ 2 drinks a day for males under age 65. ≤ 1 drink daily for women and people > 65	
At-risk drinking	Males: >4 drinks in any day or 14 drinks a week. Females: > 3 drinks in a day or 7 drinks a week	Also called "hazardous" drinking or "problematic alcohol use" by some agencies.
Binge drinking	> 5 drinks on any single occasion	Binge drinking carries an increased risk of adverse consequences, including motor vehicle accidents, assaults or aggressive behaviors, and alterations in consciousness.
Harmful drinking	*Any quantity* of drinking that produces physical or psychological injury. Any drinking during pregnancy, for example.	See "problem drinking" below.
Heavy drinking	Males: >2 drinks a day on average Females: > 1 drink a day on average	Note that "heavy drinking" begins at the upper limit of "moderate drinking" and overlaps with "at-risk drinking."
Problem drinking	Drinking that causes life problems for the drinker, e.g. health-related, legal, relationship, or occupational difficulties.	"Problem drinking" is also called "alcohol abuse," or "alcoholism" when it persists for > 12 months.
Underage drinking	Drinking before reaching age 21	Varies from one legal jurisdiction to another.
Driving while intoxicated (DWI)	A legal term, defined by the states, for the crime defined as operating a motor vehicle while influenced by alcohol (or other drugs).	Most states rely on both a standard that includes observable impairment in motor function, speech, and balance, and a blood alcohol level (adults) of 0.8. Also called "DUI" ("driving under the influence").

Standard drink: ½ oz alcohol (12 oz beer, 5 oz wine, 1.5 oz distilled spirits). Many habitual users of alcohol drink larger quantities of alcohol, e.g., 8 oz of wine, 16 oz beer, mistakenly believing these to represent a single drink.

ical examination often reveals more than does direct questioning.

TREATMENT: Abstinence from alcohol remains the cornerstone of treatment for alcoholism. Support groups for alcoholics, such as Alcoholics Anonymous (AA), have reported the highest rates of treatment success. SEE: *Alcoholics Anonymous*.

PATIENT CARE: During acute intoxication or withdrawal, the patient is carefully monitored. Assessments should include mental status, temperature, heart rate, breath sounds, and blood pressure. Medications prescribed for symptom relief are administered, and desired and undesired effects are evaluated. Evaluation for signs of inadequate nutrition and dehydration is also necessary. Patients require orientation to reality because they may have hallucinations or may try to harm themselves or others. A calm environment with minimal noise and shadows reduces the incidence of delusions and hallucinations. Seizure precautions are instituted; mechanical restraint is avoided. Health care professionals should approach patients in a nonthreatening way and explain all procedures. Even if patients are verbally abusive, apathetic, or uninterested, care providers should listen attentively and reply with empathy. Patients are also monitored for signs of depression or impending suicide.

In long-term care of alcoholism, patients are assisted to accept their drinking problem and the need for abstinence. Patients should be confronted about alcohol-related behavior and urged to examine actions. Patients taking disulfiram (or who have taken it within the last 2 weeks) must be warned of the effects of alcohol ingestion, which may last from 30 minutes to 3 hr or longer. Even a small amount of alcohol will induce adverse reactions (e.g., nausea, vomiting, facial flushing, headache). The longer the patients drink alcohol, the greater their sensitivity; therefore, they must be warned to avoid medicinal or hygienic sources of alcohol (e.g., cough syrups, cold remedies, and mouthwashes).

The entire family is assisted to develop a long-term plan for follow-up and relapse prevention, including referral to organizations such as AA, Al-Anon, and Alateen. Family involvement in rehabilitation helps reduce family stressors and tensions. If the alcoholic patient has lost contact with family and friends and has a long history of unemployment, trouble with the law, or financial difficulties, social services or other appropriate agencies may assist with rehabilitation efforts. These may involve job training, sheltered workshops, and halfway houses.

acute a. Intoxication (2).

chronic a. Alcoholism.

alcohol septal ablation A treatment for hypertrophic obstructive cardiomyopathy in which coronary artery catheterization is used to isolate the septal artery that supplies blood to the hypertrophied myocardium. Pure alcohol is injected into the artery, causing it to obstruct. The thickened heart muscle nourished by the septal artery is deprived of oxygen and dies. The procedure is a controlled and monitored myocardial infarction (heart attack), designed to eliminate the overdeveloped muscle blocking blood flow out of the heart. It is used in carefully selected patients as an alternative to surgical removal of the obstructing muscle (surgical myectomy).

alcoholuria (al″kŏ-hol-ūr′ē-ă) [*alcohol* + *-uria*] The presence of alcohol in the urine.

Alcohol Use Disorders Identification Test ABBR: AUDIT. A survey of ten questions to diagnose those people whose alcohol consumption has become harmful to their health. The AUDIT questionnaire includes three questions about a person's possible dependence on alcohol, three that determine the amount and frequency of alcohol consumption, and four that delve into any problems that may have been caused by a person's alcohol consumption in the past.

alcohol withdrawal syndrome The neurological, psychiatric, and cardiovascular signs and symptoms that result when a person accustomed to consuming large quantities of alcohol suddenly becomes abstinent. Alcohol withdrawal usually follows a predictable pattern. In the first hours of abstinence, patients are often irritable, anxious, tremulous, and easily startled. Their blood pressure and pulse rise, but they remain alert and oriented. If they do not consume alcohol (or receive drug treatment) in the first 12 to 48 hours, they may suffer an alcohol withdrawal seizure. Abstinence for 72 to 96 hours may result in severe agitation, hallucinations, and marked fluctuations in blood pressure and pulse. This stage of withdrawal is known as delirium tremens, or alcoholic delirium; it may prove fatal in as many as 15% of patients. SYN: *alcohol* **withdrawal**. SEE: *delirium tremens*.

PATIENT CARE: Benzodiazepines, e.g., chlordiazepoxide, are the preferred agents for managing alcohol withdrawal although other agents, e.g., carbamazepine, may be useful in treating mild cases. The patient should be comforted and reoriented as needed. Familiar objects and people may aid reality orientation. Every effort should be made to prevent unintentional injury; bedrails should be padded to protect against seizures and trauma, and patients should be protected from falling. Excessive stimulation of the patient should be avoided. Patients who are suffering delirium tremens are typically cared for in an Intensive Care Unit, where minute-to-minute monitoring of vitals signs and invasive management is readily available.

aldehyde (al′dĕ-hīd″) [L. *alcohol dehydrogenatum*] **1.** Oxidation product of a primary alcohol. It has the characteristic group —CHO. **2.** Acetaldehyde, CH_3CHO. It is an intermediate in yeast fermentation and alcohol metabolism.

Alder-Reilly anomaly (al′dĕr-rī′lē) [Albert von Alder, Swiss hematologist, 1888–1951; William Anthony Reilly, U.S. pediatrician, b. 1901.] Large dark leukocyte granules that stain lilac. They consist of mucopolysaccharide deposits and are indicative of mucopolysaccharidosis.

aldolase (al′dŏ-lās″) [*aldol* + *-ase*] An enzyme present in skeletal and heart muscle and the liver. It is important in converting glycogen into lactic acid. Its serum level is increased in certain muscle diseases and in hepatitis.

aldopentose (al″dŏ″pen′tōs″) A five-carbon sugar with the aldehyde group, —CHO, at the end. Arabinose is an aldopentose.

aldose (al′dōs″) [*ald(ehyde)* + *-ose*] A carbohydrate of the aldehyde group (—CHO).

aldose reductase An enzyme that makes up part of the metabolic pathway that converts glucose to fructose and sorbitol. Fructose and sorbitol may damage nerves, the retina, and the lens of the eye when they accumulate excessively, e.g., in poorly controlled diabetes mellitus.

aldosterone (al-dos′tĕ-rōn″, al″dō-stēr′ōn″) [*ald(ehyde)* + *-sterone*] The most biologically active mineralocorticoid hormone secreted by the adrenal cortex. Aldosterone increases sodium reabsorption by the kidneys, thereby indirectly regulating blood levels of potassium, chloride, and bicarbonate, as well as pH, blood volume, and blood pressure. SEE: *adrenal gland*.

aldosteronism (al″dos′tĕ-rō″nĭzm) [*aldosterone* + *-ism*] An uncommon cause of hypertension in which the blood contains abnormally high levels of aldosterone. The syndrome results from sodium retention and excretion of potassium by the kidneys. Although it is frequently asymptomatic, patients may occasionally experience frequent urination, nocturia, or headache. If potassium losses are severe, muscular weakness, cramps, tetany, or cardiac arrhythmias may occur. SYN: *hyperaldosteronism*.

    primary a. Aldosteronism due to excess secretion of mineralocorticoid by the adrenal gland. An aldosterone-secreting adenoma is frequently responsible. Removal of the adenoma will cure hypertension in some patients. SYN: *Conn's syndrome*. SEE: *Nursing Diagnoses Appendix*.

    secondary a. Aldosteronism due to extra-adrenal disorders.

aldrin (al′drĭn) [Kurt *Alder,* Ger. chemist, 1902–1958 + *-in*] A derivative of chlorinated naphthalene used as an in-

secticide. SEE: *Poisons and Poisoning Appendix*.

alemmal (ā″lem′ăl) [*a-* + *(neuri)-lemma*] Without a neurilemma, as in a nerve fiber.

alendronate (ă-len′drŏ-nāt″) A biphosphonate that stops osteoclasts from absorbing bone. It increases the density of bone and is used to treat and prevent osteoporosis and the fractures it causes.

⚠ Alendronate is administered as a pill, which should be given to patients with a large glass of water to prevent it from lodging in the upper gastrointestinal tract and causing esophagitis. Patients should also maintain an upright posture for at least 30 min after taking the medicine.

Aleppo boil (ă-lep′ō) [*Aleppo,* a city in NW Syria] Cutaneous **leishmaniasis.**

aleukemia (ā″loo-kē′mē-ă) [*a-* + *leukemia*] A deficiency of white blood cells in the circulating blood.

aleurone (al′yŭ-rōn″) [Gr. *aleuron,* flour] The protein granules present in the outer layer of the endosperm of cereal grain.

Aleve Naproxen.

Alexander disease (al″ek-san′dĕr) [W. S. Alexander, 20th-cent. New Zealand pathologist] A rare neurodegenerative disorder characterized by early-onset dementia or encephalopathy and spasticity. It usually results from a mutation in the gene that codes for glial fibrillary acidic protein (GFAP). Brain specimens from affected patients show the accumulation of abnormal inclusion bodies within astrocytes.

Alexander technique (al″ek-san′dĕr) [Frederick Matthias Alexander, Australian actor, 1869–1955] A form of bodily training that promotes postural health, esp. of the spine, head, and neck.

alexia (ă-lek′sē-ă) [¹*an-* + Gr. *lexis,* word + *-ia*] A loss of the ability to understand written or printed words. **alexic** (ă-lek′sik), *adj.* SYN: *visual aphasia; word blindness*.

    motor a. Inability to read aloud while remaining able to understand what is written or printed.

    musical a. Inability to read music. It may be sensory, optic, or visual, but not motor.

    optic a. Inability to understand what is written or printed.

alexithymia (ă-lek″sē-thī′mē-ă) [*a-* + Gr. *lexis,* word + *-thymia*] The inability to identify and articulate feelings, including those brought on by unpleasant mental or physical experiences. It is often found in patients with a history of child abuse, post-traumatic stress disorder (PTSD), drug abuse, and some somatoform disorders.

ALG *antilymphocyte globulin.*

algae (al′jē) [Pl. of L. *alga,* seaweed] Photosynthetic organisms of several phyla in the kingdom Protista. They are nonparasitic and lack roots, stems, or leaves. They contain chlorophyll and vary in size from microscopic forms to massive seaweeds. They live in fresh or salt water and in moist places. Some serve as a source of food or as nutritional supplements, e.g., kelp and Irish moss.

blue-green a. Cyanobacteria; photosynthetic organisms in the kingdom Monera. Blooms may impart a disagreeable taste to freshwater and may cause the death of fish.

algesia (al-jē′zē-ă, zhă) [Gr. *algesis,* sense of pain] A form of hyperesthesia marked by hypersensitivity to pain. **algesic, algetic** (al-jēz′ik, al-jet′ik), *adj.* SYN: *algesthesia.*

algesthesia (al″jĕs-thē′zē-ă, zhă) [Gr. *algos,* pain + *-esthesia*] **1.** Perception of pain. **2.** Algesia.

-algia, -algesia [Gr. *algos,* pain] Suffixes meaning *pain.* SEE: *-dynia.*

algicide (al′jĭ-sīd″) [*algae* + *-cide*] A substance that kills algae. **algicidal** (al″jĭ-sīd′ăl), *adj.*

algid (al′jĭd) [L. *algidus,* cold] Cold; chilly.

alginate (al′jĭ-nāt″) Any salt of alginic acid. It is derived from kelp and is used as a thickener in foods and as a pharmaceutical aid. In dentistry it is used as a material for taking impressions.

alginate slime A polysaccharide polymer that coats the surface of colonies of the bacterium, *Pseudomonas aeruginosa.* The slime forms a matrix which anchors bacteria to their environment and protects them from host defenses such as antibodies, complement, lymphocytes, phagocytes, and respiratory cilia. Strains of *P. aeruginosa* that produce alginate slime (called mucoid strains) are frequently isolated from the lungs of patients with cystic fibrosis.

algiomotor (ăl″j(ē-)ŏ-mō′tŏr) [Gr. *algos,* pain + *motor*] Causing painful contraction of muscles, particularly during peristalsis. SYN: *algiomuscular.*

algiomuscular (ăl″j(ē-)ŏ-mŭs′kyŭ-lăr) [Gr. *algos,* pain + *muscular*] Algiomotor.

algodystrophy (al″gō-dis′trŏ-fē) [Gr. *algos,* pain + *dystrophy*] Reflex sympathetic **dystrophy**.

algolagnia (al″gō-lag′nē-ă) [Gr. *algos,* pain, + *lagneia,* lust] Sexual satisfaction derived by experiencing pain or by inflicting pain on others. **algolagniac** (nē-ak″), *n.*; **algolagnist** (nist), *n.*; **algolagnic** (nik), *adj.*

active a. Sadism.

passive a. Masochism.

algometer (al″gom′ĕ-tĕr) [Gr. *algos,* pain + *-meter*] An instrument for measuring the degree of sensitivity to pain. **algometry** (ĕ-trē), *n.*

algophobia (al″gŏ-fō′bē-ă) [Gr. *algos,* pain + *-phobia*] An unusually pronounced fear of pain.

algorithm (al′gŏ-rithm) [Ult. fr. Arabic] A formula or set of instructions for solving a particular problem. In health care, a set of steps used in diagnosing and treating a disease. Appropriate use of algorithms in medicine may lead to more efficient and accurate patient care as well as reduced costs. **algorithmic** (al″gŏ-rith′mik), *adj.* **algorithmically** (mik(ă-)lē), *adv.*

algor mortis (al′gor″ mor′tis) [L. coldness of death] The lowering of body temperature after death.

aliasing (ā′lē-ăs-ing) [L. *alias,* at another time, elsewhere] A jagged distortion in a digitally generated visual image. It may be produced during image reconstruction in magnetic resonance imaging or Doppler ultrasonography, e.g., the wrap-around artifact seen on magnetic resonance images when a portion of the body extends beyond the imaged field of view.

Alice in Wonderland syndrome [Alice, from Lewis Carroll's *Alice in Wonderland*] Perceptual distortions of the size and/or shape of objects. It is often characterized by the hallucination that things are smaller than they really are and is sometimes experienced by patients suffering from migraine, infectious mononucleosis, or an overdose of hallucinogenic drugs.

alicyclic (al-ĭ-sī′klik, -sik′lik) [*ali(phatic)* + *cyclic*] Having properties of both aliphatic (open-chain) and cyclic (closed-chain) compounds.

alienate (āl′ē-ĕ-nāt″) [L. *alienus,* someone else's, alien] To isolate, estrange, or dissociate.

alienation (āl″ē-ĕ-nā′shŏn) [*alienate*] Isolation, estrangement, or dissociation, esp. from society.

occupational a. The sense of isolation or estrangement a person may experience when employed in a job that is not personally meaningful or fulfilling.

alien hand syndrome Alien limb phenomenon.

alien limb phenomenon A rare disorder of movement and sensation in which sudden unexpected movements of a hand or foot occur and are felt by the patient experiencing them to be either involuntary or initiated by others. SYN: *alien hand syndrome; Dr. Strangelove syndrome.*

aliform (al′ĭ-form″) [*ala* + *-form*] Wing-shaped.

aligner (ă-līn′ĕr) A transparent plastic mold used in orthodontics to move teeth from one position to another. SYN: *invisible* **brace**.

alignment, alinement (ă-līn'mĕnt) [Fr. *aligner*, to put in a straight line] **1.** The act of arranging in a straight line. **2.** The state of being arranged in a straight line. **3.** In orthopedics, the placing of portions of a fractured bone into correct anatomical position. **4.** The anatomical presentation of one structure to another, such as opposing joint surfaces. **5.** In dentistry, bringing teeth into correct position. **6.** In radiography, the positioning of a body part in correct relation to the radiographic source and receiver. **7.** In chiropractic, the manipulation of the spine to restore it to a healthy anatomic position.

aliment (al'ĭ-mĕnt) [L. *alimentum*, nourishment] Nutriment; food.

alimentary (al″ĭ-men'tă-rē) [*aliment*] Pert. to food, nutrition, or the digestive tract.

alimentary system Digestive system.

alimentation (al″ĭ-mĕn-tā'shŏn) [*aliment*] The process of nourishing the body, including mastication, swallowing, digestion, absorption, and assimilation. SEE: *hyperalimentation; total parenteral nutrition.*

    artificial a. Provision of nutrition, usually intravenously or by a tube passed into the gastrointestinal tract of a patient unable to take or utilize normal nourishment. SEE: *total parenteral nutrition.*

    forced a. 1. Feeding a patient unwilling to eat. **2.** Forcing a person to eat a greater quantity than desired.

    rectal a. Feeding by nutrient enemas.

alimentotherapy (al″ĭ-men″tō-ther'ă-pē) [*aliment + therapy*] Treatment of disease by dietary regulation. SYN: *dietotherapy.* SEE: *dietetics.*

aliphatic (al″ĭ-fat'ik) [Gr. *aleiphar*, stem *aleiphat-*, fat, oil] Pert. or belonging to that series of organic chemical compounds characterized by open chains of carbon atoms rather than by rings.

aliquot (al'ĭ-kwot″) [L. some, several] In pharmacy and chemistry, a known fraction, constituting a sample of a whole.

alizarin, alizarine (ă-liz'ă-rĭn, -rēn″) [Fr. *alizarine*, fr Arabic *alasāra*, extract, juice + -ine] A red dye obtained from coal tar or madder and used as a histological stain.

alkalemia (al″kă-lē'mē-ă) [*alkal(i) + -emia*] An increase in the arterial blood pH above 7.45 due to a decrease in the hydrogen ion concentration or an increase in hydroxyl ions. The blood is normally slightly alkaline (pH 7.35 to 7.45).

alkali (al'kă-lī″) *pl.* **alkalis, alkalies** [Ult. fr. Arabic *al-qalī*, ashes of salt wort] A strong base, esp. the metallic hydroxides. Alkalies combine with acids to form salts, combine with fatty acids to form soap, neutralize acids, and turn litmus paper blue. SEE: *acid; base; pH.*

    corrosive a. A strongly basic metallic hydroxide, most commonly of sodium, ammonium, and potassium, as well as carbonates. Because of their great combining power with water and their action on the fatty tissues, they cause rapid and deep tissue destruction. They have a tendency to gelatinize tissue, turning it a somewhat grayish color and forming a soapy, slippery surface, accompanied by pain and burning. SEE: *corrosion; corrosive poisoning.*

alkali denaturation test A quantitative test for hemoglobin F (fetal hemoglobin, HbF). The test uses the spectrophotometric absorbance of a mixture of saline-diluted and alkali-diluted blood.

alkalimetry (al″kă-lim'ĕ-trē) [*alkali + -metry*] Measurement of the alkalinity of a mixture.

alkaline (al'kă-lin, -līn″) [*alkali + -ine*] Pert. to or having the reactions of an alkali, esp. of having a pH greater than 7. **alkalinity** (lin'ĭ-tē), *n.*

alkaline earth Any of the oxides of the alkaline earth metals calcium, strontium, magnesium, and barium.

alkalinuria (al″kă-lĭ-noor'ē-ă) [*alkali + -uria*] Alkaline urine, i.e., urine with a pH above 7.

alkalize, alkalinize (al'kă-līz″, -lĭ-nīz″) To make alkaline. **alkalinization** (al″kă-lin″ĭ-zā'shŏn), *n.* **alkalization** (al″kă-lĭ-zā'shŏn), *n.*

alkaloid (al'kă-loyd″) [*alkali + -oid*] Any of a group of organic alkaline substances, e.g. morphine or nicotine, obtained from plants. Alkaloids react with acids to form salts that are used for medical purposes. **alkaloidal** (al″kă-loyd'ăl), *adj.*

    beta-carboline a. Any of a group of neurologically active compounds similar in structure to the amino acid L-tryptophan, the neurotransmitter serotonin, and the hallucinogen dimethyltryptamine. They increase levels of serotonin in the central and peripheral nervous system and inhibit the action of monoamine oxidase.

    vinca a. A drug made from vinca plants and used in cancer therapy.

alkalosis (al″kă-lō'sis) [*alkali + -osis*] An actual or relative increase in blood alkalinity due to an accumulation of alkalies or reduction of acids. SEE: *acid-base balance.* **alkalotic** (-lot'ik), *adj.*

    altitude a. Alkalosis due to the increased respiratory rate associated with exposure to the decreased oxygen content of air at high altitudes. This causes respiratory alkalosis. SEE: *respiratory alkalosis.*

    compensated a. Alkalosis in which the pH of body fluids has been returned to normal. Compensatory mechanisms maintain the normal ratio of bicarbonate to carbonic acid (approx. 20:1) even though the bicarbonate level is increased.

hypochloremic a. Metabolic alkalosis due to loss of chloride and produced by severe vomiting, gastric tube drainage, or massive diuresis.

hypokalemic a. Metabolic alkalosis associated with an excessive loss of potassium. It may be caused by diuretic therapy.

metabolic a. Any process in which plasma bicarbonate is increased. This is usually the result of increased loss of acid from the stomach or kidney, potassium depletion accompanying diuretic therapy, excessive alkali intake, or severe adrenal gland hyperactivity. SEE: *acid-base balance.*

SYMPTOMS: There are no specific signs or symptoms, but if the alkalosis is severe, there may be apathy, confusion, stupor, and tetany as evidenced by a positive Chvostek's sign.

TREATMENT: Therapy for the primary disorder is essential. Saline solution should be administered intravenously and, in patients with hypokalemia due to diuretic therapy, potassium is administered. Only rarely is it necessary to administer acidifying agents intravenously.

PATIENT CARE: Arterial blood gas values, serum potassium level, and fluid balance are monitored. The patient is assessed for anorexia, nausea and vomiting, tremors, muscle hypertonicity, muscle cramps, tetany, Chvostek's sign, seizures, mental confusion progressing to stupor and coma, cardiac dysrhythmias due to hypokalemia, and compensatory hypoventilation with resulting hypoxia. Prescribed oxygen, oral or IV fluids, sodium chloride or ammonium chloride, and potassium chloride if hypokalemia is a factor, along with therapy prescribed to correct the cause, are administered. Seizure precautions are observed; a safe environment and reorientation as needed are provided for the patient with altered thought processes. The patient's response to therapy is evaluated, and the patient is taught about the dangers of excess sodium bicarbonate intake if that is a factor. The ulcer patient is taught to recognize signs of metabolic alkalosis, including anorexia, weakness, lethargy, and a distaste for milk. If potassium-wasting diuretics or potassium chloride supplements are prescribed, the patient's understanding of the regimen's purpose, dosage, and possible adverse effects is ascertained.

respiratory a. Alkalosis with an acute reduction of carbon dioxide followed by a proportionate reduction in plasma bicarbonate.

ETIOLOGY: Hyperventilation (whether it is caused by hypoxia, anxiety, panic attacks, fever, salicylate intoxication, exercise, or excessive mechanical ventilation) is the primary cause of respiratory alkalosis.

SYMPTOMS: Patients may develop paresthesias; air hunger; dry oral mucosa; numbness or tingling of the nose, circumoral area, or extremities; muscle twitching; tetany and hyperreflexia; lightheadedness; inability to concentrate; mental confusion and agitation; lethargy; or coma.

TREATMENT: Therapy is given for the underlying cause. In acute hyperventilation produced by panic or anxiety, treatment includes coaching a patient to breathe in a slow, controlled, and relaxed fashion by providing reassurance and support.

PATIENT CARE: Preventive measures are taken, such as having the hyperventilating patient breathe in a slow controlled fashion, using cues provided by caregivers. The respiratory therapist prevents or corrects respiratory alkalosis in patients receiving mechanical ventilation by increasing dead space or decreasing volume. Arterial blood gas values, vital signs, and neurological status are monitored. In severe cases, serum potassium level is monitored for hypokalemia and cardiac status for dysrhythmias. Prescribed therapy is administered to treat the cause. The patient is reassured, and a calm, quiet environment is maintained during periods of extreme stress and anxiety. The patient is helped to identify stressors and to learn coping mechanisms and anxiety-reducing techniques, such as guided imagery, controlled breathing, or meditation.

alkalotherapy (al″kă-lō-ther′ă-pē) [*alkali + therapy*] Therapeutic use of alkalies.

alkapton, alcapton (al-kap′ton) [*al(kali) + Gr. kaptein, to gulp*] $C_8H_8O_4$; homogentisic acid; a yellowish-red substance sometimes occurring in urine as the result of the incomplete oxidation of tyrosine and phenylalanine.

alkaptonuria, alcaptonuria (al″kap-tŏ-noor′ē-ă) [*alkapton + -uria*] A rare inherited disorder marked by the excretion of large amounts of homogentisic acid in the urine, due to incomplete metabolism of tyrosine and phenylalanine. Presence of the acid is indicated by the darkening of standing or alkalinated urine and the dark staining of diapers or other linen. **alkaptonuric** (-noor′ik), *adj.* SEE: *ochronosis.*

alkene (al′kēn″) [*alk(yl) + -ene*] A bivalent aliphatic hydrocarbon containing one double bond.

alkyl (al′kĭl) [*al(cohol) + -yl*] Any hydrocarbon radical with the general formula C_nH_{2n+1}. The resulting substances are called alkyl groups or alkyl radicals.

alkylate (al'kĭ-lāt") **1.** To introduce one or more alkyl groups into a compound. **2.** To provide therapy with an alkylating agent.

alkylation (ăl"kĭ-lā'shŭn) A chemical process in which an alkyl radical replaces a hydrogen atom.

ALL *acute lymphocytic leukemia.*

allachesthesia (al"ă-kes-thē'zh(ē-)ă) [Gr. *allachē*, elsewhere + *-esthesia*] Perception of tactile sensation as being remote from the actual point of stimulation.

allantochorion (ă-lan"tō-kōr'ē-on") An embryonic membrane in which the allantois and chorion are fused into one structure.

allantoic (al"ăn-tō'ik) Pert. to the allantois.

allantoid (ă-lan'toyd") [Gr. *allantos*, sausage, + *-oid*] **1.** Sausage-shaped. **2.** Pert. to the allantois.

allantoin (ă-lan'tō-ĭn) [*allanto(is)* + *-in*] $C_4H_6N_4O_3$; a white crystalline substance in allantoic fluid, amniotic fluid, and fetal urine. It is the end product of purine metabolism in mammals other than primates. It is produced synthetically by the oxidation of uric acid and is used in some cosmetics, mouthwashes, and pharmaceuticals.

allantoinuria (ă-lan"tō-wĭ-noor'ē-ă) [*allantoin* + *-uria*] Allantoin in the urine.

allantois (ă-lan'tō-wĭs, al"ăn-tō'ĭ-dēz") *pl.*
allantoides [L. fr. Gr. *allantoeidēs*] A transient embryonic structure that is the tubular outpouching from the bottom of the caudal end of the 3-week-old human embryo. Later, the allantois, its adjacent connecting stalk, and the yolk stalk merge to form the umbilical cord. The walls of the allantois give rise to the umbilical vein and arteries, and part of the cavity of the allantois remains as a tube (the urachus) that connects the developing bladder with the umbilical cord.

allayed (ă-lād') Diminished in severity; mitigated, moderated.

Allegra Fexofenadine.

allele (ă-lēl', ă-lel') [Gr. *allēlōn*, of one another] Any of two or more different genes containing specific inheritable characteristics that occupy corresponding loci on paired chromosomes. A pair of alleles is usually indicated by a capital letter for the dominant and a lowercase letter for the recessive. An individual with a pair of identical alleles, either dominant or recessive, is said to be homozygous for this gene. The union of a dominant gene and its recessive allele produces a heterozygous individual for that characteristic. Some traits may have more than two alleles, but an individual has only two of them. For ex-

ample, the genes for blood type, A, B, and O, are at the same position on the chromosome pair, but an individual has only two of these genes, which may be the same or different. SYN: *allelic gene; allelomorph.* **allelic** (ă-lel'ik), *adj.*

   histocompatibility a. Any of many different forms of the histocompatibility gene. Each allele creates specific antigenic markers on the surface of cells. SEE: *histocompatibility locus antigen.*

   intermediate a. Premutation.

   prothrombin 20210A a. A guanine-to-adenine substitution at nucleotide 20210 in the prothrombin gene that increases the risk for venous clotting. The gene is usually found in people of European ancestry.

allelic gene Allele.

allelomorph (ă-lel'ŏ-morf", -lē'lŏ) [*allele* + Gr. *morphē*, form] Allele.

Allen Cognitive Level Screen A standardized method of assessing information processing based on a theory that postulates six levels of cognitive function. It is used widely by occupational therapists.

Allen test (ăl'ĕn) **1.** A bedside test used to evaluate the patency of the arteries of the hand before arterial puncture. The patient elevates the hand and repeatedly makes a fist while the examiner places digital occlusive pressure over the radial and ulnar arteries at the wrist. The hand will lose its normal pink color. Digital pressure is released from one artery (usually the ulnar), while the other (i.e., the radial) remains compressed. If there is normal blood flow through the unobstructed artery, color should return to the hand within 10 sec. The return of color indicates that the hand has a good collateral supply of blood and that arterial puncture of the compressed artery can be safely performed. **2.** A procedure to identify the presence of thoracic outlet compression syndrome caused by tightness of the pectoralis minor muscle. With the patient seated, the examiner abducts the involved shoulder to 90° and flexes the elbow to 90°. While palpating the radial pulse, the examiner externally rotates the humerus while the patient actively rotates the head to the opposite side. A diminished or absent radial pulse is indicative of the pectoralis minor muscle's compressing the neurovascular bundle. This procedure often produces false-positive results. SEE: illus.; *thoracic outlet compression syndrome.*

allergen (al'ĕr-jĕn) [*aller(gy)* + *-gen*] Any substance that causes a hypersensitivity reaction or abnormal immune response. Allergens do not stimulate an immune response in everyone, only in those sensitized to them. Common allergens include inhalants (dusts, pollen), foods (wheat, eggs), drugs (aspirin, se-

ALLEN TEST

rum), infectious agents (e.g., bacteria, viruses), contactants (chemicals, animals), and physical agents (heat, cold). SEE: *allergy; antigen; irritation; sensitization;* table.

   polymerized a. A chemically altered allergen made into a macromolecule, used in immunotherapy to stimulate a blocking antibody response stronger than the allergen's normal allergic response.

allergenic (al″ĕr-jen′ik) Producing allergy. **allergenicity** (-jĕ-nis′ĭt-ē), *n.*

allergic (ă-lĕr′jik) Pert. to, sensitive to, or caused by an allergen.

allergic reaction A reaction resulting from hypersensitivity to an antigen. SEE: *allergy* for illus.; *hypersensitivity.*

allergic salute A colloquial term for wiping the fingers or the hand upward across the nose, a sign of nasal inflammation resulting from allergies.

allergist (al′ĕr-jist) A physician who specializes in diagnosing and treating allergies.

allergoid (al′ĕr-goyd″) [*allergy* + -*oid*] A chemically altered allergen used in immunotherapy to induce tolerance to an antigen. Allergoids differ from the allergens they derive from in that they produce an IgG antibody response stronger than an IgE (hypersensitivity) response.

allergy (al′ĕr-jē) [*allo-* + Gr. *ergon,* work] An immune response to a foreign antigen that results in inflammation and organ dysfunction. Allergies range from annoying to life-threatening. They include systemic anaphylaxis, urticaria, eczematous dermatitis, hay fever, and rhinitis. They affect about 20% of Americans and can be triggered by inhalation (pollen, dust mites), direct contact (poison ivy), ingestion (drugs, foods), or injection (stinging insects, drugs). Allergic responses may be initiated and sustained by occupational exposure to allergens, and by foods, animals, fungal spores, metals, and rubber products. The most severe cases are often associated with Hymenoptera stings, penicil-

lin products, radiological contrast media, and latex. SYN: *hypersensitivity reaction.* SEE: *allergen; atopy.*

ETIOLOGY: The immune system has two main functions: first, to identify germs and parasites that may harm the body; and second, to use toxic defenses against attacks by these organisms. Allergic reactions occur when immune functions are turned on by an agent richly endowed with alien antigens. Once the immune system has been sensitized, subsequent exposure results in the binding of specific immunoglobulins (esp. IgE) or the activation of immunologically active cells (mast cells, basophils, or T cells). These can release inflammatory chemicals (histamines, kinins, interleukins) that create allergic symptoms.

SYMPTOMS: Nasal inflammation), mucus production, watery eyes, itching, rashes, tissue swelling, bronchospasm, stridor, and shock are all symptoms of allergy.

DIAGNOSIS: A history of exposure and reaction is crucial to the diagnosis of allergy. Tests for specific allergies include skin prick tests, intradermal injections, or blood tests (measurements of antigen-specific immunoglobulins).

TREATMENT: Avoiding allergens is the first step in treatment. Effective drugs for allergic symptoms include antihistamines, corticosteroids, and epinephrine. Which of these is given depends on the severity of the reaction. Antigen desensitization (immunotherapy) may be used by experienced professionals, but this technique may occasionally trigger severe systemic reactions.

PATIENT CARE: Before any drug is given, the health care provider should determine if the patient has a history of allergy. Patients receiving injected drugs or blood products are closely observed for rash, itch, wheezing, or hypotension. If an allergic reaction begins, medications prescribed for immediate management are given to the patient. Patients are taught to identify and avoid common allergens and to identify an allergic reaction. The use of drugs for the chronic management of allergies is explained, and the patient is advised about potential adverse effects. If a patient needs injectable epinephrine for emergency outpatient treatment of anaphylaxis, both the patient and family are instructed in its use.

   atopic a. Atopy.

   contact a. A type IV hypersensitivity reaction following direct contact with an allergen, usually affecting the skin. SEE: *contact dermatitis.*

   drug a. A type I, IgE-mediated hypersensitivity reaction to an administered drug, e.g., penicillin.

Common Allergies and Allergens

Common Name	Scientific Name(s)	Allergen Designation	Allergen Class	Representative Illnesses
Aspirin	Acetylsalicylic acid; other nonsteroidal anti-inflammatory drugs	Asa	Drug allergen	asthma, rhinitis, anaphylaxis
Birch	*Betula*	Bet	Aeroallergen (inhaled, or "outdoor" allergen)	hay fever
Cat	*Felis domesticus*	Fel	Pet-associated (indoor)	asthma, atopy, hives
Cockroach	*Blatella germanica*	Bla g	Pest-associated allergen (indoor)	asthma, atopy, hives
Dog	*Canis familiaris*	Can	Pet-associated (indoor)	asthma, atopy, hives
Dust mite	*Blomia tropicalis; Dermatophagoides farinae; Euroglyphus*	Blo t; Der f; Eur	Indoor	allergic rhinitis; contact dermatitis; asthma
Egg	Apovitellin; ovalbumin; ovomucoid	Gad d Gal	Food allergen	
Imported fire ant	*Solenopsis invicta*	Sol i	Insect venom	anaphylaxis
Iodine	Radiologic contrast	Io	Drug allergen	anaphylaxis
Latex (rubber)	*Hevea brasilensis*	Hev b	Occupational exposures	asthma, contact dermatitis, rhinitis
Molds	*Alternaria alternata; Aspergillus fumigatus; Cladosporium herbarum; Penicillium notatum*	Alt a; Asp f; Cla h; Pen n	Indoor and outdoor	allergic rhinitis, asthma
Mugwort	*Artemisia vulgaris*	Art v	Outdoor allergen	hay fever
Olive	*Olea europaea*	Ole e	Food allergen	anaphylaxis
Peanut	*Arachis hypogaea*	Ara h	Food allergen	anaphylaxis
Penicillin	Beta-lactam	Pcn	Drug allergen	anaphylaxis; rashes
Ragweed	*Ambrosia artemisiifolia* and others	Amb	Outdoor allergen	hay fever
Timothy grass	*Phleum pratense*	Phl p	Outdoor allergen	hay fever
Yellow jacket venom	*Vespula vulgaris* and others	Ves v	Insect venom	anaphylaxis
Wheat	*Gliadins glutens*	Tri a	Food allergy	anaphylaxis, "Baker's asthma," rhinitis

food a. An immunologic reaction to a food to which a patient has become sensitized. Sensitivity to almost any food may develop, but it develops most frequently to milk, eggs, wheat, shellfish, and chocolate. Because food allergies are type I reactions, symptoms can appear within minutes. Mild symptoms urticaria, abdominal cramps, and gastrointestinal upset) are most common, but food allergies can also cause systemic anaphylaxis and vasovagal syncope.

Food allergies are identified by eliminating any foods suspected of causing symptoms and reintroducing them one at a time. Blood tests for IgE are useful in separating food allergies from abnormal metabolic or digestive responses to food. Desensitization to food allergies is impossible, and use of antihistamines, epinephrine, and corticosteroids cannot be used for prophylaxis. Many adverse reactions to foods are not allergic in nature but may be caused by toxic, metabolic, or pharmacological reactions. SEE: *anaphylaxis; desensitization.*

glove a. A colloquial term for *latex a.*

latex a. An immune reaction resulting from contact with products derived from the rubber tree, *Hevea brasiliensis,* or the chemicals added to latex in manufacturing. Latex antigens can be inhaled or absorbed through the skin. The allergic reaction may be mild (rashes, reddened skin) or severe (bronchospasm, anaphylaxis). In health care workplaces, where wearing latex gloves is common, nonlatex products have been substituted for latex to reduce exposure. A nonallergic contact dermatitis caused by the powder used in latex gloves may be mistaken for a true latex allergy and is much more common.

peanut a. An IgE-mediated immediate hypersensitivity reaction to the consumption of peanuts (the seeds of *Arachis hypogaea*). Peanut allergens are designated *Ara* by the World Health Organization. Peanut allergy is the most important food allergy in the U.S., affecting more than a million people. Reactions range from mild (rashes) to life-threatening (closure of the airway, cardiac dysrhythmias, coma). About 50 people die of peanut allergy in the U.S. each year.

PATIENT CARE: People with known allergies to peanuts must avoid eating raw or processed peanuts and also products containing or prepared with peanut oil. Those affected by peanut allergy should learn to watch for the signs of anaphylaxis (hives, pruritus, rashes in the skin creases, shortness of breath, choking, wheezing, stridor). People with known anaphylaxis to peanuts should carry epinephrine injectors and use them at the onset of a hypersensitivity reaction. (Repeated use may be necessary in persistent reactions.) Cross-reactivity to other legumes (peas, soy products) may affect some people and pose important health risks. Affected people should wear medical alert bracelets or necklaces identifying their condition. Densensitization can be accomplished with modified peanut allergens.

penicillin a. A hypersensitivity reaction to penicillin, present in about 0.5% to 8% of the population. Although different types of hypersensitivity reactions may occur, the most common and potentially dangerous are the type I (immediate) reactions mediated by immunoglobulin E. If a patient reports a history of signs of local anaphylaxis (such as urticaria) or systemic anaphylaxis (such as bronchoconstriction, vasodilation) after taking penicillin, no penicillin or other beta-lactam antibiotics (such as cephalosporins) should be given to that patient ever again. In those very rare situations in which an infection is susceptible to no other antibiotic and the infection is serious enough to risk the danger of anaphylaxis, the patient may be desensitized with gradually increasing doses of penicillin.

allergy response, latex An allergic response to natural latex rubber products. SEE: *Nursing Diagnoses Appendix.*

allergy response, risk for latex At risk for allergic response to natural latex rubber products. SEE: *Nursing Diagnoses Appendix.*

allesthesia, alloesthesia (al″es-thē′zh(ē-)ă, al″ō-es-thē′zh(ē-)ă) [*allo-* + *-esthesia*] Perception of stimulus in the limb opposite the one stimulated. SYN: *allochesthesia; allochiria.*

alleviate (ă-lē′vē-āt″) [L. *alleviare,* to lighten] To lessen the effect of. **alleviation** (-lē″vē-ā′shŏn), *n.*

allicin (al′ĭ-sĭn) [L. *allium,* garlic + *-in*] A yellow oil released from garlic when it is bruised, crushed, or chewed. The oil is antibacterial and antifungal and used to treat hyperlipidemia.

allied health professional One who has received professional training and credentials in an allied health field, such as clinical laboratory science, radiology, emergency medical services, physical therapy, respiratory therapy, medical assisting, athletic training, dental hygiene, or occupational therapy.

alliesthesia (al″ē-es-thē′zh(ē-)ă) The perception of an external stimulus as pleasant or unpleasant, depending upon internal stimuli. A stimulus may be perceived as pleasant at one time and unpleasant at another.

Allis, Oscar (al′ĭs) Oscar Huntington Allis, U.S. surgeon, 1836–1921.

A. forceps Forceps with curved, serrated edges. They are used to grasp tissue firmly.

A. sign A clinical finding in patients with a fractured or dislocated femoral head, in which a finger can be inserted into the fascia lata femoris between the greater trochanter and the iliac crest

alliteration (ă-lit″ĕ-rā′shŏn) [L. *alliteratio*] A speech disorder in which words beginning with the same consonant sound are used to excess.

Allium sativum (al′ē-ŭm să-tē′vŭm, tī′) [L., planted garlic] The scientific name for garlic.

allo-, all- [Gr. *allos*, other, another] Prefixes meaning *divergence, difference from,* or *opposition to the normal.*

alloantigen (al″ō-an′tĭ-jĕn) [*allo-* + *antigen*] An antigen in the blood or tissue of a donor that is not present in the recipient. The alloantigen can trigger an immune response. **alloantigenic** (-an″tĭ-jĕn′ik), *adj.*

allocation (al″ŏ-kā′-shŏn) The assignment or distribution of assets or duties.

allocative efficiency (al′ŏ-kāt″ĭv) In economics and sociology, the extent to which a product or a service, e.g., hemodialysis, is provided to an entire community, rather than just to a subgroup of that community.

allochesthesia (al″ŏ-kes-thē′zh(ē-)ă) [Gr. *allachē*, elsewhere + *-esthesia*] Allesthesia.

allochiria, allocheiria (al″ŏ-kir′ē-ă) [*allo-* + *cheiro-*] Allesthesia.

allochroism (ă-lōk′rō-ĭzm, al″ŏ-krō′ĭzm) [*allo-* + Gr. *chroa*, color, + -sm] A change in color.

allochromasia (al″ŏ-krō-mā′zē-ă, -mā′zh(ē-)ă) A change in the color of hair or skin.

allodiploidy (al″ŏ-dip′loyd″ē) [*allo-* + *diploid*] Possession of two sets of chromosomes, each from a different species, like a hybrid.

allodynia (al″ŏ-din′ē-ă) [*allo-* + *-odynia*] The perception of an ordinarily painless stimulus as painful.

alloeroticism, alloerotism (al″ŏ-ĕ-rot′ĭ-sĭzm, -er′ŏ-tĭzm) [*allo-* + *eroticism*] Sexual urges stimulated by and directed toward another person. **alloerotic** (-rot′ik), *adj.*

allogeneic, allogenic (al″ŏ-jĕ-nē′ik, al″ō-jĕn′ik) Having a different genetic constitution but belonging to the same species. SEE: *isogeneic.*

allograft (al′ŏ-graft″) [*allo-* + *graft*] An organ or tissue transplanted from one member of a species to another genetically dissimilar member of the same species. Common transplanted organs include the cornea, bone, artery, cartilage, kidney, liver, lung, heart, and pancreas. Recipients of allografts take immunosuppressive drugs to prevent tissue rejection. SYN: *allogeneic graft;* *homograft.* SEE: *autograft; heterograft; transplantation.*

alloimmune (al″ō-i-mūn′) [*allo-* + *immune*] Pert. to the immune response to antigens on blood or tissue cells received from a donor of the same species.

Alloiococcus otitis, Alloiococcus otitidis (ăl-oy″ō-kŏk′ŭs) [Gr. *alloios*, another kind of + *coccus*] A species of aerobic gram-positive bacteria often found in patients with otitis media with effusion.

allokinesis (al″ō-kĭ-nē′sĭs) [*allo-* + *kinesis*] Passive or reflex movement; involuntary movement. **allokinetic** (al″ŏ-kĭ-net′ik), *adj.*

allolalia (al″ō-lā′lē-ă) [*allo-* + Gr. *lalia*, talk] A speech defect or impairment in which words are spoken unintentionally or inappropriate words are used for appropriate ones.

allomerism (ă-lom′ĕr-ĭzm) [*allo-* + *-mere* +-*ism*] A change in chemical constitution without a change in crystalline composition. SEE: *allomorphism.*

allomorphism (al″ŏ-mor′fĭzm) [*allo-* + *morph-* + *-ism*] A change in form without a change in chemical constitution. SEE: *allomerism.*

allopath (al′ŏ-path″) One who practices allopathy.

allopathy (ă″lop′ă-thē) [*allo-* + *-pathy*] **1.** A system of treating disease by inducing a pathological reaction antagonistic to the disease being treated. **2.** A term erroneously used for the regular practice of medicine to differentiate it from homeopathy. **allopathic** (al″ŏ-path′ik), *adj.* **allopathically** (al″ŏ-path′ik(ă-)lē), *adv.*

alloplasia (al″ō-plā′zh(ē-)ă) [*allo-* + *-plasia*] Heteroplasia.

alloplasty (al′ŏ-plas″tē) [*allo-* + *-plasty*] **1.** Plastic surgery using inert materials or those obtained from a tissue bank (e.g., cornea, bone). **2.** In psychiatry, adaptation by altering the external environment rather than changing oneself. SEE: *autoplasty.*

alloploidy (al″ŏ-ployd′ē) [*allo-* + *ploidy*] The state of having two or more sets of chromosomes derived from different ancestral species.

allopolyploidy (al″ŏ-pol′ē-ployd″ē) [*allo-* + *polyploidy*] The state of having more than two sets of chromosomes derived from different ancestral species.

allopsychic (al″ŏ-sī′kĭk) [*allo-* + *psychic*] Pert. to mental processes in relation to the external environment.

allopurinol (al″ō-pūr′ĭ-nol″) A drug that inhibits the enzyme xanthine oxidase. Because allopurinol causes a reduction in both serum and urine levels of uric acid, it is used in the treatment of gout and of renal calculi caused by uric acid.
A potentially fatal rash is a rare but significant side effect

alloreactive (al″ō-rē-ak′tiv) [*allo-* + *reactive*] Pert. to certain classes of T lymphocytes, immunologically reactive against a transplanted tissue or organ.

allostasis (ă-los'-tă-sĭs) Physiological adaptation to stress.

allostatic load SEE: under *load*.

allostery (al"ō-ster'ē) [*allo-* + *steric*]
1. In bacteria, alteration of a regulatory site on a protein that changes its shape and activity. This change is important in altering the way the organism responds to its molecular environment.
2. In enzymology, the ability of a factor to bind to a site on an enzyme other than its substrate-binding site and cause a change in the conformation of the enzyme and its ability to catalyze a chemical reaction. **allosteric** (-ster'ik), *adj.*

allotransplantation (al"ō-trans"plan"tā'shŏn) [*allo-* + *transplantation*] Grafting or transplantation of tissue from one individual into another of the same species. **allotransplant** (-trans'plant"), *v.*

allotriogeustia (ă-lot"rē-ō-jŭst'ē-ă, -gū'stē-ă) [Gr. *allotrios,* strange + *geusis,* taste] Perverted appetite or sense of taste.

allotriophagy (ă-lo"trē-ŏf'ă-jē) [Gr. *allotrios,* strange + *phag-*] Pica.

allotropic (al"ō-trop'ik) [*allo-* + *-tropic*]
1. Pert. to the existence of an element in two or more distinct forms with different physical properties. **2.** Altered by digestion so as to be changed in its nutritive value. **3.** Concerned with the welfare and interests of others; disinterested.

allotype (al'ŏ-tīp") [*allo-* + *type*] Any of the genetic variants of protein that occur in a single species. The serum from a person with one form of allotype could be antigenic to another person. **allotypic** (al"ŏ-tip'ik), *adj.* **allotypically** (-i-k(ă-)lē), *adv.*

allow natural death An alternative to "do not resuscitate" or "do not attempt resuscitation" in which a patient or family permits a person's vital functions to cease without medical intervention, such as the maintenance of an artificial airway or the provision of advanced cardiac life support. SEE: *do not attempt resuscitation; do not resuscitate.*

alloxan (ă-lok'săn) [*all(antoin)* + *oxa(lic)*] $C_2H_2N_2O_4$; an oxidation product of uric acid. In laboratory animals it causes diabetes by destroying the islet cells of the pancreas.

alloy (ăl'oy", ă-loy') [Fr. *aloyer,* to combine] **1.** A metal, e.g., brass, that is the fusion or mixture of two or more metals. **2.** A metal, e.g., steel, that is the fusion or mixture of a metal and a nonmetal. In dentistry, several alloys are used to restore teeth. Alloys used to construct cast restorations are often gold- and copper-based alloys. Common "silver fillings" are alloys of silver, copper, tin,

and mercury. The silver-tin-mercury alloys are called amalgams.

base metal a. An alloy that does not contain noble metals such as gold or silver. Stainless steel is the most common base metal alloy used in dentistry.

⚠ Base metal alloys should not be cleaned with sodium hypochlorite solutions.

dental casting gold a. A hard or extra-hard alloy used to manufacture crowns, inlays, and onlays.

noble-metal a. An alloy of which one metal is noble (gold, silver, platinum, or palladium). Noble-metal alloys are generally nonreactive and corrosion-resistant.

allozyme (al'ŏ-zīm") [*allo-* + *(en)zyme*] An enzyme that has small substitutions in its genetic coding and protein structure.

allyl (al'ĭl) [L. *allium,* garlic + *-yl*] C_3H_5; a univalent unsaturated radical found in garlic and mustard. **allylic** (ă-lil'ik), *adj.*

ALOC *altered level of consciousness.*

alochia (ā'lō'kē-ă) [*a-* + *lochos,* childbirth] Absence of lochia.

aloe (al'ō) [L. fr. Gr. *aloē*] The dried juice of one of several species of plants of the genus *Aloe,* used to treat skin conditions. The most common species is *Aloe vera.*

alogia (ā''lō'j(ē-)ă) [*a-* + *-logia*]
1. Complete speechlessness. **2.** Poverty of speech. It is one of the "negative symptoms" of schizophrenia.

aloin (al'ŏ-ĭn) [*aloe* + *-in*] A yellow crystalline substance obtained from aloe.

alopecia (al"ŏ-pē'sh(ē-)ă) [Gr. *alōpekia,* fox mange] Absence or loss of hair, esp. of the head.

ETIOLOGY: Alopecia may result from serious illness, drugs, endocrine disorders, dermatitis, hereditary factors, radiation, or physiological changes during aging.

TREATMENT: Treatments include drugs, such as minoxidil or finasteride; surgeries, such as hair transplantation; or prostheses (wigs).

a. areata Loss of hair in sharply defined patches usually involving the scalp or beard. SEE: illus.

a. capitis totalis Complete or near complete loss of hair on the scalp. SEE: illus.

cicatricial a. Loss of hair due to formation of scar tissue.

a. congenitalis Baldness due to absence of hair bulbs at birth.

a. follicularis Baldness due to inflammation of the hair follicles of the scalp.

a. liminaris Loss of hair along the

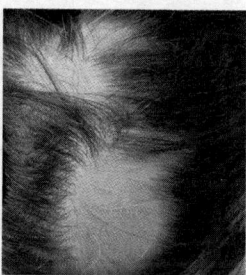

ALOPECIA AREATA OF SCALP

hairline, both front and back, of the scalp.

   male-pattern a. Male-pattern **baldness**.

   a. medicamentosa Loss of hair as a result of medical treatment, esp. treatment with drugs used in chemotherapy for cancer.

   a. pityroides Loss of both scalp and body hair accompanied by desquamation of branlike scales.

   a. prematura Premature baldness.

   a. symptomatica Loss of hair after prolonged fevers or during the course of a disease. This baldness may be due to systemic or psychogenic factors.

   a. totalis **Alopecia** capitis totalis.

   a. toxica Loss of hair thought to be due to toxins of infectious disease.

   a. universalis Loss of hair from the entire body.

alpha (al′fă) **1.** A or α, the uppercase and lowercase symbols, respectively, for the first letter of the Greek alphabet. In chemistry, the first in a series of isomeric compounds or the position adjacent to a carboxyl group. **2.** First in a series. **3.** Prototype. **4.** The dominant figure, personality, or role.

alpha-adrenergic blocking agent SEE: under *agent*.

alpha-D-galactosidase An enzyme, derived from *Aspergillus niger,* used in treating intestinal gas or bloating. SEE: *flatus*.

alpha-fetoprotein ABBR: AFP. An antigen present in the human fetus and in

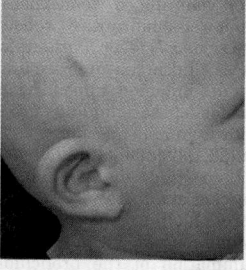

ALOPECIA CAPITIS TOTALIS

pathological conditions in the adult. The maternal serum level should be evaluated at 15 to 22 weeks' gestation. During pregnancy, elevated levels are associated with open neural tube defects, anencephaly, omphalocele, gastroschisis, and fetal death. Decreased levels may indicate an increased risk of having a baby with Down syndrome. If an abnormal level of AFP is found, further tests such as ultrasound or amniocentesis need to be done. Elevated serum levels of AFP are found in adults with hepatic carcinomas or chemical injuries. Examination results also may be abnormal in persons with diabetes, multiple pregnancies, or obesity.

alpha-fetoprotein kit ABBR: AFP test. A monoclonal antibody test for the presence of alpha-fetoprotein (AFP) in vaginal secretions, used in cases of suspected premature rupture of membranes. In healthy pregnancies AFP is detectable in the amniotic fluid but is present only in very low concentrations in vaginal secretions. If there is leakage of amniotic fluid into the vagina as a result of premature rupture of membranes, AFP levels in the vagina rise significantly.

alpha-globulin Any of the serum globulins. It is so named because of its position as it migrates in a buffered electrified solution. Alpha globulins include many clinically important proteins, e.g., alpha-1-antitrypsin, angiotensinogen, ceruloplasmin and haptoglobin. SEE: *globulin, serum*.

alpha granule deficiency syndrome A rare autosomal dominant bleeding disorder in which the alpha granules of platelets lack adenosine diphosphate, which is critical for proper platelet targeting and clumping in response to injury. The platelet count may be abnormally decreased, and the bleeding time is usually prolonged. The abnormality in platelet granulation is visible with an electron microscope. The most common clinical evidence of the disease is easy bruising in response to injury. SYN: *gray platelet syndrome*.

alpha-hydroxy acid (al′fă-hī-drok′sē) SEE: under *acid*.

alpha-linolenic acid (al′fă-lin″ŏ-lē′nik) SEE: under *acid*.

alpha-lipoic acid SEE: under *acid*.

alpha-methylacyl-CoA racemase ABBR: AMACR. An antibody that is primarily used in histopathology to stain tissues suspected of representing carcinoma of the prostate gland. Its presence substantiates the diagnosis. AMACR is also present in some colonic and some kidney cancer specimens.

alpha-methyltryptamine (al″fă-meth″ĭl-trip′tă-mēn″, mĭn) [*alpha* + *methyl* + *tryptamine*] ABBR: AMT. A hallucinogenic compound derived from tryptamine, a crystalline amine formed from tryptophan. It is known colloquially as "spirals."

alpha particles, alpha rays Radioactive, positively charged particles, equivalent to a helium nucleus (two protons and two neutrons), ejected at high speeds in certain atomic reactions.

alpha-rhythm In electroencephalography, rhythmic oscillations in electric potential occurring at an average rate of 10/sec. SYN: *alpha-wave*.

alpha-tocopherol The most active form of vitamin E found in food.

Alphavirus (al'fă-vī'rŭs) A genus of the family of Togaviridae viruses (e.g. Eastern Equine Encephalitis virus, Western Equine Encephalitis virus) transmitted to humans by mosquito bite. The bites may cause fever, rash, or central nervous system infection.

alpha-wave Alpha-rhythm.

Alport syndrome (al'port") [Arthur Cecil Alport, South African physician, 1880–1959] Congenital glomerulonephritis associated with deafness and a decrease in large thrombocytes. Occasionally there are eye abnormalities such as cataracts. Although there is no specific treatment for this condition, dialysis or kidney transplantation is used to treat affected patients with kidney failure. SYN: *hereditary* **nephritis**. SEE: *macrothrombocyte*.

alprazolam (al-prā'zŏ-lam") A benzodiazepine and antianxiety agent, administered orally to treat anxiety and panic attacks. Trade name is Xanax.

alprostadil (al-pros'tă-dĭl) A synthetic prostaglandin used to treat erectile dysfunction.

ALS *amyotrophic lateral sclerosis.*

Alstrom syndrome (ol'strom") [Carl-Henry Alström, Swedish psychiatrist, 1907–1993] A rare autosomal recessive syndrome marked by blindness resulting from retinal dystrophy, type 2 diabetes mellitus, hearing loss, heart failure, insulin resistance, obesity, and renal failure.

ALT *alanine aminotransferase.*

alternans (al-ter'nans") [L. *alternare,* to alternate] **1.** Alternation, as in contractions of the heart. **2.** Alternating, as in contractions of the heart.

Alternaria (al"tĕr-na'rē-ă) A genus of fungi of the Dematiaceae family. These fungi cause phaeohyphomycosis. They can also cause onychomycosis, sinusitis, ulcerated cutaneous infections, and keratitis, visceral infections and osteomyelitis in immunocompromised persons. In immunocompetent patients, Alternaria colonizes the paranasal sinuses, leading to chronic hypertrophic sinusitis.

alternator (al-tĕr-nā'tŏr) An electrical generator that produces alternating current.

altitude sickness SEE: under *sickness.*

altretamine (al-trĕ'tă-mĭn") A drug used for treating persistent or recurrent ovarian cancer.

altricious (al-trĭsh'ŭs) [L. *altrix,* stem *altric-,* nourisher] **1.** Slow in developing. **2.** Requiring long-term nursing care.

altruism (al'troo-ĭz-ĭm) [Fr. *altruisme*] Acting for the benefit of others regardless of the consequences for oneself.

    involuntary a. An action that is taken on behalf of others not because of one's own choosing but because of coercion, fiat, or legislation. **altruist** (al'troo-ist"), *n.* **altruistic** (al"troo-is'tik), *adj.*

alum (al'ŭm) [Fr. *alum,* fr L. *alumen,* alum] **1.** A double sulfate of aluminum and potassium or aluminum and ammonia; used as an astringent and styptic. **2.** Any of a group of double sulfates of a trivalent metal and a univalent metal.

aluminosis (ă-loo"mĭ-nō'sis) [*aluminum* + *-osis*] Chronic inflammation of the lungs in alum workers due to alum particles in inspired air.

aluminum (ă-loo'mĭ-nŭm) SYMB: Al. A silver-white metal used to filter low-energy radiation out of the x-ray beam; atomic mass (weight) 26.9815, atomic number 13.

    a. acetate A salt formed by the reaction between aluminum sulfate and lead acetate. Its aqueous solution (Burow solution) is used as a local astringent.

    a. chloride $AlCl_3$, an astringent and antiperspirant.

    a. potassium sulfate Potassium alum.

    a. sulfate $Al_2(SO_4)_3$, an antiperspirant.

aluminum poisoning SEE: under *poisoning.*

Alvarado score (al-vă-rod'ō) [A. Alvarado, U.S. physician] A diagnostic tool to estimate the likelihood that a patient with abdominal pain has appendicitis. It includes the following clinical features: 1) an elevated white blood cell count (esp. when associated with a left shift); 2) abdominal pain that migrates to the right lower quadrant of the abdomen; 3) loss of appetite; 4) nausea and/or vomiting; 5) tenderness in the right lower quadrant; 6) rebound tenderness; and 7) fever. Patients with few of these clinical features are unlikely to have an inflamed appendix; patients with most of these findings are likely to benefit from appendectomy.

alveoalgia, alveolalgia (al"vē-ŏ-ăl'j(ē-)ă, -lăl'j(ē-)ă) [*alveoli-* + *-algia*] Pain in the socket of a tooth.

alveobronchiolitis, alveobronchitis (al"vē-ō-brong"kē-ŏ-lī'tis, -brong-kī'tis) Inflammation of the bronchioles and pulmonary alveoli.

alveolar (ăl-vē′ŏ-lăr) Pert. to an alveolus.

alveolar echinococcosis SEE: under *echinococcosis*.

alveolar hydatid disease Alveolar **echinococcosis**.

alveolar pressure SEE: under *pressure*.

alveolate (al-vē′ŏ-lăt, -lāt″) Honeycombed; pitted.

alveolectomy (al″vē-ŏ-lek′tŏ-mē) [*alveoli-* + *-ectomy*] Surgical removal of all or part of the alveolar process of the mandible or maxilla. It is usually performed in treatment of neoplasms.

alveoli-, alveolo- Prefixes meaning *alveolus*.

alveolitis (al″vē-ŏ-līt′ĭs) [*alveoli-* + *-itis*] Inflammation of the alveoli.

  allergic a. Inflammation of the bronchial tree, interstitial tissue, and alveoli of the lung caused by a hypersensitivity reaction to an inhaled antigen. With repeated exposure, large numbers of macrophages form granulomas, which damage and scar lung tissue. The inhaled allergens that most often trigger allergic alveolitis are molds and other fungi, vegetables, mushrooms and mushroom compost, flour, tree bark, detergents, and contaminated humidifiers. In the acute stage, patients may present with cough, fever, chills, malaise, and shortness of breath. In the subacute and chronic forms, the onset of symptoms is gradual and prolonged. Farmer's lung and bagassosis are two common names for forms of allergic alveolitis. SYN: *hypersensitivity pneumonitis*.

alveoloclasia (al-vē″ŏ-lō-klā′zh(ē-)ă) [*alveoli-* + *-clasis* + *-ia*] Destruction of a tooth socket.

alveolodental (al-vē″ŏ-lō-den′tăl) [*alveoli-* + *dental*] Pert. to the alveoli of the tooth.

alveololingual (al-vē″ŏ-lō-ling′gwăl) [*alveoli-* + *lingual*] Pert. to the alveolar process and tongue.

alveoloplasty (al-vē″ŏ-lō-plas′tē) [*alveoli-* + *-plasty*] Surgical reconstruction of the alveolus.

alveolotomy (al″vē-ŏ-lot′ŏ-mē) [*alveolo-* + *-tomy,* incision] Surgical incision of the alveolus of a tooth.

alveolus (al-vē-ŏ-lŭs, al-vē′ŏ-lī″, -lē″) *pl.* **alveoli** [L. *alveolus,* small hollow, cavity] **1.** A small hollow. **2.** The bony socket of a tooth. **3.** An air sac of the lungs. SEE: illus. **4.** Any of the honeycombed depressions of the gastric mucous membrane. **5.** A follicle of a racemose gland.

  alveoli of the breast Glandular structures arranged in clusters throughout the breast and the site of milk synthesis.

  ⚓ **pulmonary a.** Any of the terminal epithelial sacs of an alveolar duct where gases are exchanged in respiration. It is informally called an "air sac." SYN: *alveolar sac*.

  alveoli pulmonis Pulmonary alveoli.

alveus (al′vē-ŭs) [L. hollow vessel, basket] A channel or groove.

  a. hippocampi A layer of white matter covering the ventricular surface of the hippocampus. The axons forming the alveus are from the hippocampus and subicular cortex. The axons of the alveus collect to form the fimbria (the beginning of the fornix).

alymphia (ā″lim′fē-ă) [*a-* + *lymph* + *-ia*] Complete or partial deficiency of lymph.

alymphocytosis (ā″lim″fŏ-sī′tō′sĭs) [*a-* + *lymphocytosis*] Decreased number or absence of lymphocytes in the blood.

alymphoplasia (ā″lim″fŏ-plā′zh(ē-)ă) [*′an-* + *lympho-* + *-plasia*] Failure of lymphatic tissue to develop.

  thymic a. Thymic aplasia.

Alzheimer, Alois (alts′hī″měr) Ger. neurologist, 1864–1915.

  A. disease ABBR: AD. A chronic, progressive, degenerative cognitive disorder that accounts for more than 60% of all dementias. The most common form occurs in people over 65; the rate of incidence increases with age. The illness affects more than 4 million older Americans, causes significant functional disability, and costs $80 billion to $100 billion for health care and lost wages in the U.S. annually. The number of patients is expected to more than triple in the next 30 years (14 million by 2050) as more people live into their 80s and 90s. SYN: *senile dementia of the Alzheimer type.* SEE: *positron emission tomography* for illus.; *Nursing Diagnoses Appendix.*

  ETIOLOGY: In most cases of Alzheimer disease, a number of factors seem to interact to cause the disease, and there are certain heritable risk factors. The central biochemical problem in the disease appears to be a defect in the metabolism of alpha-amyloid precursor protein.

  SYMPTOMS: The disease begins with a mild memory loss (Stage I), which then progresses to deterioration of intellectual functions, personality changes, and speech and language problems (Stage II). In the terminal stage (Stage III), patients depend on others for activities of daily living. Seizures, hallucinations, delusions, paranoia, or depression can occur in either Stage II or III. Persons with Alzheimer disease will eventually develop macular degeneration SEE: table.

  DIAGNOSIS: The diagnosis is usually made by ruling out other causes of cognitive dysfunction although a variety of laboratory tests are also employed in some settings.

  PATHOPHYSIOLOGY: Characteristic

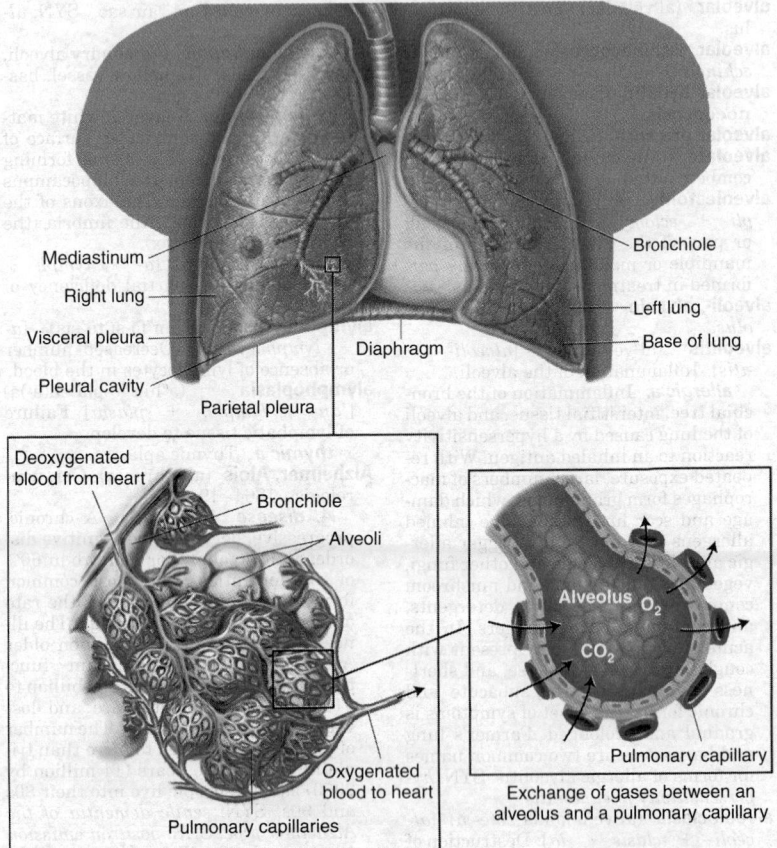

Mediastinum

Right lung

Visceral pleura

Pleural cavity

Parietal pleura

Bronchiole

Left lung

Base of lung

Diaphragm

Deoxygenated blood from heart

Bronchiole

Alveoli

Oxygenated blood to heart

Pulmonary capillaries

Alveolus O_2

CO_2

Pulmonary capillary

Exchange of gases between an alveolus and a pulmonary capillary

ALVEOLUS OF LUNGS

pathophysiological changes in the brain include neuritic plaques, neurofibrillary tangles, and marked cerebral atrophy. In addition to structural changes, abnormalities in cranial neurotransmitters may occur. Acetylcholine, for example, may be reduced by as much as 75%, contributing to cognitive impairment.

TREATMENT: The treatment of Alzheimer disease includes environmental structuring and drug therapy. Environmental structuring means provision of a safe, stimulating milieu that offers consistency and comfort for the patient. Drug therapy is to improve memory rather than cure the disease. Several cholinergic drugs, e.g., donepezil HCl (Aricept), are used to slow the decline in cognitive function. Antidepressants and psychotropic medications are used to treat patients who have secondary diagnoses such as depression and hallucinations.

PATIENT CARE: Reality orientation is helpful for patients in early stages of the disease. Validation therapy is most appropriate for patients in Stage II or III.

In collaboration with the physical and occupational therapists, the nurse assesses the patient's need for assistance with activities of daily living. Self-care, exercise, and other activities are encouraged as much as possible. If sleep disturbances occur, the patient should rest between daytime activities, but sleeping during daytime hours is to be discouraged. Neurological function, including mental and emotional states and motor capabilities, is monitored for further deterioration. Vital signs and respiratory status are assessed for pneumonia and other infections. The patient is evaluated for gastrointestinal or urinary problems (anorexia, dysphagia, and urinary or fecal incontinence); fluid and food intake is monitored to detect imbalances. The nurse or assistive nursing personnel takes the patient to

Stages of Alzheimer Disease

Stage	Common Behaviors
Stage I (early stage, mild dementia)	Loss of short-term memory
	Decreased judgment (safety concern)
	Inability to perform mathematical calculations
	Inability to comprehend abstract ideas
Stage II (middle stage, moderate dementia)	Difficulty with speech and language (aphasia, anomia)
	Labile personality changes
	Changes in usual grooming habits
	Inability to remember purpose of items (apraxia)
	Urinary incontinence
	Wandering
	Seizures
	Psychotic behaviors, such as hallucinations and paranoia
	Depression
Stage III (late stage, severe dementia)	Inability to perform activities of daily living, such as eating, dressing, and bathing; requires total care
	Inability to walk, toilet, swallow
	Minimal or no communication
	Eventually becomes bedridden and develops complications of immobility, such as pneumonia, pressure ulcers, and constipation

the bathroom or bedside commode before and after meals and every 2 hr in between. Skin is inspected for evidence of trauma. The occupational therapist, home health nurse, or case manager assesses the patient's living environment to eliminate hazards and teaches the family to monitor the patient's activity to prevent falls, burns, and other injuries. Expectations should not exceed the patient's ability to perform tasks. Because the patient may misperceive the environment, health professionals should speak softly and calmly and allow sufficient time for answers because of the patient's slowed thought processes and impaired ability to speak. The case manager or nurse evaluates the caregiver's ability to manage the patient at home and makes the appropriate referrals to available local resources such as counseling, support groups, and respite care.

Loneliness, helplessness, and boredom, all associated with institutionalization, can be reduced by incorporating into the environment plants, pets, aviaries, and children as well as opportunities to handle objects having different tactile surfaces. A decor similar to the patient's familiar surroundings may provide comfort. Music therapy may enhance emotional and physical well-being, cognitive skills, ability to communicate, and social functioning. Activity therapy should include the patient's known earlier interests and preferences. Such activities benefit the patient by encouraging interaction with others and by providing intellectual stimulation.

If mild cognitive impairment or early stage Alzheimer disease is suspected, the person should be evaluated by his physician or referred to a neurologist or gerontologist for evaluation. Early diagnosis allows family members to plan and prepare for the future. The physical and emotional health of the primary caregiver is an additional concern for the health team. Support groups can be a great help to family members by discussing care issues and exchanging information and by considering the caregivers' feelings and coping skills in an accepting atmosphere. Caregivers experience grief and loss during and after the illness and need help in expressing their grief and pain. Some male caregivers may face unique challenges in taking over many of the tasks traditionally done by an ill wife or mother. All caregivers share the struggle with the common elements of acceptance: accepting the diagnosis, the devastating changes, the limited understanding of others, the progression of the disease, and the need for placement in a nursing home if this becomes necessary. Support groups can help with this process. Respite care can give life-sustaining relief to both partners. Friends who want to help may not even know what to offer, and caregivers must learn how to ask for help with specific tasks.

The local chapter of the Alzheimer's Disease and Related Disorders Association (ADRDA), sometimes simply referred to as the Alzheimer's Association, is an excellent resource. A list of local chapters can be found through the national ADRDA at 919 N. Michigan Avenue, Suite 1000, Chicago, IL 60611-1676 or at their web site at www.alz.org.

early-onset A. disease Alzheimer disease that occurs before the age of 65.

late-onset A. disease ABBR: LOAD. Alzheimer disease occurring after the age of 65. It is the most common form of the disease

Alzheimer Disease Cooperative Study A research initiative of the National Institute on Aging and the University of California (San Diego) to assess treatments for the behavioral and cognitive symptoms of Alzheimer Disease.

Am 1. *mixed astigmatism.* 2. *ametropia.* 3. Symbol for the element americium.

AMA *against medical advice; Aerospace Medical Association; American Medical Association.*

amaas (a′mas) [Afrikaans] Variola minor.

AMACR *alpha-Methylacyl-CoA racemase.*

amacrine, amacrinal (-krīn″ăl, am′ă-krīn″) [*a- macr-* + Gr. *is,* stem *-in-,* fiber] Lacking a long process.

amadosha (a″mă-dō′shă) [Sanskrit *āma,* uncooked, undigested (food) + *dosha,* body-mind composition] In Ayurvedic medicine, undigested food waste that fills the intestinal tract.

amalgam (ă-mal′găm) [L. fr. Arabic fr. Gr. *malagma,* soft mass] An alloy used in dentistry to restore teeth. It is made predominantly of silver and mercury.

    dental a. A dental restorative material made by mixing approx. equal parts of elemental liquid mercury (43% to 54%) and an alloy powder (57% to 46%) composed of silver, tin, copper, and sometimes smaller amounts of zinc, palladium, or indium. Dental amalgam has been used for over 150 years. A fraction of the mercury in amalgam is absorbed by the body, and people with amalgam restorations in their teeth have higher concentrations of mercury in tissues (including the blood, urine, kidneys, and brain) than those without amalgam fillings. In 1993 the Public Health Service of the U.S. Department of Health and Human Services published a report acknowledging that scientific data are insufficient to conclude that amalgam fillings have compromised health. There is no evidence that removal of amalgam fillings has a beneficial effect on health. A dental amalgam is colloquially called a *silver amalgam* or a *silver filling.*

    silver a. A colloquial term for *dental amalgam.*

amalgamate (ă-mal′gă-māt″) To combine mercury with silver, tin, and copper to produce amalgam. **amalgama-**

tion (-mā′shŏn), *n.* **amalgamator** (-māt″ŏr), *n.*

amalgam condenser SEE: under *condenser.*

amalgam tattoo A benign blue, gray, or black macule on the oral mucosa resulting from the unintentional introduction of silver amalgam into a filling for a prepared cavity. It resembles a melanoma but is not cancerous.

amanita (am″ă-nīt′ă, -nēt′ă) [Gr. *amanitai,* mushrooms] Any of various mushrooms of the genus *Amanita* (e.g., *A. muscaria* and *A. phalloides*). Most are toxic to the liver. SEE: *Poisons and Poisoning Appendix.*

amastia (ā″mas′tē-ă) [*a-* + *mast-* + *-ia*] Absence of breast tissue. It may be due to a rare congenital anomaly or, more often, a bilateral mastectomy. SEE: *amazia.*

amastigote (ā″mas′tĭ-gōt″) [*a-* + *mastigote*] Leishman-Donovan bodies.

amatoxin (am″ă-tok′sin) [*ama(nita)* + *toxin*] The chemical component of poisonous mushrooms that causes early onset of gastrointestinal upset. Liver failure follows about 36 hr later

amaurosis (am″ŏ-rō′sis) [Gr. *amaurōsis,* darkening] Complete loss of vision.

amaurotic (-rot′ik), *adj.*

    albuminuric a. Amaurosis caused by kidney disease.

    congenital a. Amaurosis present at birth.

    diabetic a. Amaurosis associated with diabetes.

    epileptoid a. Sudden blindness after an epileptic seizure and lasting up to 2 weeks.

    a. fugax Transient monocular blindness.

    lead a. Amaurosis caused by lead poisoning.

    a. partialis fugax Sudden transitory blindness with symptoms like those of migraine.

    reflex a. Amaurosis due to reflex action caused by irritation of a remote part.

    saburral a. Amaurosis together with acute gastritis.

    toxic a. Amaurosis from optic neuritis caused by toxins that may be endogenous (as in diabetes) or exogenous (as in alcohol or tobacco).

    uremic a. Amaurosis due to acute renal failure.

amaxophobia (ă-mak″sŏ-fō′bē-ă) [Gr. *hamaxa* wagon + *-phobia*] Fear of being in or riding in a vehicle.

amazia (ā″mā′zē-ă) [*a-* + Gr. *mazos,* breast] Absence of all breast tissue except the nipple. SEE: *amastia.*

ambi- [L. *ambi-,* on both sides] Prefix meaning *both, both sides,* or *around.*

ambidextrous (am″bi-dek′strŭs) [*ambi-* + L. *dexter,* right, on the right] Being able to work equally well with either

hand. **ambidexterity** (-dek-ster′ĭ-tē), *n*.
ambidextrously (-dek′strŭs-lē), *adv*.
Ambien (am′bē-ĭn) SEE: *zolpidem*.
ambient (am′bē-ĕnt) [L. *ambiens,* going
around] On all sides; surrounding.
ambient temperature and pressure, saturated ABBR: ATPS. In respiratory
physiology, the physical characteristics
of a gas after its expiration from the airways, as found at the barometric pressure and temperature present in the
room in which the measurements are
made. The ATPS differs from the gas
conditions at "body temperature and
pressure, saturated" in that the temperature of the expired gas has decreased
from body temperature to ambient temperature. The expired gas remains fully
saturated with water vapor. SYN: *atmospheric temperature and pressure,
saturated*. SEE: *body temperature and
pressure, saturated*.
ambiguous (am-big′ū-ŭs) [L. *ambiguus,*
uncertain] **1.** Having more than one
meaning. **2.** Having confusing or conflicting meanings because of obscurity
or lack of clarity. **3.** In anatomy, difficult
to classify, e.g., the genitalia of a newborn whose sexual organs are difficult to
distinguish as a clitoris or a penis.
ambilevous (am-bi-lē′vŭs) [*ambi-* + L.
laevus, left, on the left] Awkward in the
use of either hand. SYN: *ambisinister*.
ambisexual (am″bi-seksh′ŭ-ăl) [*ambi-*
+ *sexual*] Sexually attracted and responsive to both sexes. **ambisexuality**
(-sek″shŭ-al′ĭ-tē), *n*. SEE: *bisexual*.
ambisinister (am″bi-sin′is-tĕr) [*ambi-*
+ L. *sinister,* left, on the left] Ambilevous.
ambitendency (am″bi-ten′dĕn-sē)
[*ambi-* + L. *tendere,* to stretch] In
psychology, a tendency due to opposing
motivations to act in contradictory
ways. SEE: *ambivalence*.
ambivalence (am-biv′ă-lĕns) [*ambi-* +
L. *valentia,* strength] In psychology, coexistence of contradictory feelings about
an object, person, or idea. **ambivalent**
(-lĕnt), *adj*.
ambivert (am′bi-vĕrt″) [*ambi-* + (*extro*)*version* or (*intro*)*version*] A person
whose personality type shows tendencies of both introversion and extroversion. **ambiversion** (am″bi-vĕr′zhŏn),
n.
amblyacousia (am″blē-ă-koo′sē-ă) [*ambly-* + *-acousia*] Dullness of hearing.
amblychromasia (am″blē-krō-
mā′zh(ē-)ă) [*ambly-* + Gr. *chroma,*
color] The state in which the cell nucleus stains faintly. **amblychromatic**
(-mat′ik), *adj*.
ambly-, ambly- [Gr. *amblys,* dull] Prefixes meaning *dull* or *dim*.
Amblyomma (am″blē-om′ă) [*ambly-* +
Gr. *omma,* eye] A genus of ticks that
includes the Lone Star tick (*A. americanum*) and the Gulf Coast tick (*A. ma-*

culatum). Some ticks from this genus
cause tick bite paralysis and are vectors
of tularemia and human ehrlichiosis.
amblyopia (am″blē-ō′pē-ă) [*ambly-* +
-opia] Unilateral or bilateral decrease
of best corrected vision in an otherwise
healthy eye, commonly due to asymmetric refractive error or strabismus. **amblyopic** (-ō′pik), *adj*.
  crossed a. Amblyopia of one eye with
hemianesthesia of the opposite side of
the face. SYN: *a. cruciata*.
  a. cruciata Crossed amblyopia.
  deprivation a. Amblyopia resulting
from nonuse of the eye. It is usually secondary to an organic problem such as
cataract or ptosis.
  a. ex anopsia Amblyopia resulting
from disuse. It usually occurs in one eye
and is associated with convergent
squint or very poor visual acuity.
  refractive a. Unequal vision resulting from large refractive errors between
the two eyes.
  strabismic a. Amblyopia secondary
to malalignment of the eyes. In this condition the brain suppresses the visual
image from the deviating eye to prevent
double vision. About 50% of childhood
amblyopia is strabismic.
  toxic a. Amblyopia due to the effects
of alcohol, tobacco, lead, drugs, or other
toxic substances.
  uremic a. Amblyopia during a uremic attack.
amblyoscope (am′blē-ŏ-skōp″) [*amblyo-* + *-scope*] An instrument for measuring binocular vision. It is used to stimulate vision in an amblyopic eye.
amboceptor unit (am′bō-sep″tŏr) [*ambi-* + (*re*)*ceptor*] The smallest quantity of
anti−red blood cell (anti-RBC) antibody
needed to hemolyze in an excess of complement.
ambos (am′bos″) [Ger. *Amboss,* anvil]
Incus or anvil bone of the middle ear.
Ambrosia (am-brō′zh(e-)ă) [Gr., food of
the gods, immortality] A genus of
weeds commonly known as ragweed.
Ambrosia species include *A. artemisiaefolia* and *A. trifida* ("giant ragweed")
and are a major source of seasonal pollen and allergies in North America. *Ambrosia* allergens are abbreviated *Amb*
by the World Health Organization.
ambulance (am′byŭ-lăns) [*ambulate*] A
vehicle for transporting the sick or injured. It is staffed with certified or licensed personnel and equipped with
such out-of-hospital emergency supplies
as are dictated by local or regional laws,
e.g. adjunctive airway devices, bandages, defibrillator, patient-carrying devices, and oxygen.
ambulant, ambulatory (am′byŭ-lănt, -lă-
tor″ē) [*ambulate*] Able to walk; not
confined to bed.
ambulate (am′byŭ-lāt″) [L. *ambulare,* to

move about] To walk or move about freely. **ambulation** (am″byŭ-lā′shŏn), *n.*

ambulatory surgery center SEE: under *center.*

Ambystoma mexicanum (am-bis′tŏ-mă mek″sĭ-ka′nŭm) SEE: *axolotl.*

ameba Variant of "amoeba." SEE: *amoeba.*

amebiasis (am″ĕ-bī′ă-sis) [*ameba* + *-iasis*] Infection or colonization with amebas, esp. *Entamoeba histolytica.* About 500 million people in tropical countries are infected. The infection typically begins in the colon but may spread to other organs, e.g., the liver or, less often, the skin or lungs. SYN: *amebic dysentery; amebic colitis.* SEE: *amoebapore; cyst; dysentery.*

ETIOLOGY: Amebiasis is acquired by ingesting contaminated food or drink that contains *E. histolytica* cysts, which gastric acid does not destroy. The cysts enter the intestines, where they release trophozoites, the feeding form of the organism, which may invade the walls of the colon or spread to the liver by the portal vein. Trophozoites divide to form new cysts, which may subsequently be excreted in stool.

DIAGNOSIS: The diagnosis of amebiasis is based on the detection of cysts or trophozoites of *E. histolytica* in stools and the presence of antibodies to the amebas in the blood. Antiamebic antibodies appear by the seventh day of infection. A colonoscopy may be performed to obtain tissue samples to differentiate amebiasis from inflammatory bowel disease. A liver abscess is diagnosed when a patient has right upper quadrant pain, jaundice, and fever; a mass in the liver (found by ultrasonography or computed tomography); and positive serological tests for *E. histolytica.*

SYMPTOMS: Most infected patients have no tissue invasion and are asymptomatic. Acute colitis, when it occurs, is marked by bloody diarrhea, abdominal pain, tenesmus, and weakness. The symptoms may be confused with those of ulcerative colitis. The dysentery lasts 3 to 4 weeks. Complications occasionally include toxic megacolon and ulcer perforation. Patients who develop liver abscesses present with severe upper right quadrant pain and fever. Massive diarrhea is not usually present.

TREATMENT: Asymptomatic patients are treated with paromomycin (500 mg orally tid for 7 days) or iodoquinol (650 mg orally tid for 20 days). Dysentery and liver abscess are treated with metronidazole (750 mg orally tid for 10 days), followed by iodoquinol (650 mg orally tid for 20 days).

PATIENT CARE: People traveling to developing countries, esp. India and Mexico, should avoid unboiled water, ice, and fresh fruits and vegetables, all of which may be infected with amebic cysts.

    hepatic a. Infection of the liver by *E. histolytica,* resulting in hepatitis and abscess formation, and usually a sequel to amebic dysentery.

amebic (ă-mē′bik) [Gr. *amoibē,* change + *-ic*] Caused by amoebas, e.g., "amebic dysentery." SYN: *amoebic* (2).

amebic carrier state A state in which a person harbors a form of pathogenic ameba but has no clinical signs of the disease.

amebicide, amebacide (ă-mē′bĭ-sīd″) [*ameba* + *-cide*] An agent that kills amebas. **amebicidal,** *adj.* **amebacidal** (-mē″bĭ-sīd′ăl), *adj.*

amebiform (ă-mē′bĭ-form″) [*ameba* + *-form*] Shaped like an ameba.

amebocyte (ă-mē′bŏ-sīt″) [*ameba* + *-cyte*] A cell showing ameboid movements.

ameboid (ă-mē′boyd″) [*ameba* + *-oid*] Resembling an ameba.

ameboidism (ă-mē′boyd″ĭzm) [*ameboid* + *-ism*] **1.** Ameba-like movements. **2.** A condition shown by certain white blood cells.

ameboma (am″ĕ-bŏ′mă) [*ameba* + *-oma*] A tumor composed of inflammatory tissue caused by amebiasis.

ameburia (am″ĕ-būr′ē-ă) [*ameba* + *-uria*] The presence of amebas in the urine.

amelanotic (ā″mel″ă-not′ik) [*a-* + *melanotic*] Lacking melanin; unpigmented.

amelia (ă-mē′lē-ă) [*a-* + *¹melo-* + *-ia*] Congenital absence of one or more limbs. SEE: *phocomelia.*

amelification (ă-mel″ĭ-fĭ-kā′shŏn) [Fr. *amel,* enamel + L. *facere,* to make] Formation of dental enamel by ameloblasts.

amelioration (ă-mēl″yŏ-rā′shŏn) [Fr. *amélioration*] Improvement of a condition. **ameliorate** (-rāt″), *v.*

ameloblast (am′ĕ-lō-blast″) [Fr. *émail,* enamel + *-blast*] A cell from which tooth enamel is formed. SYN: *adamantoblast.* **ameloblastic** (am″ĕ-lō-blas′tik), *adj.*

ameloblastic fibro-odontoma, ameloblastic fibroodontoma (fī″brō″ō-don″tō-mă) [*fibro-* + *odontoma*] A benign dental hamartoma consisting of histologically and radiographically well-differentiated tooth structures. This developmental dental lesion is most often found in the anterior maxilla. SYN: *ameloblastic odontoma; compound odontoma.*

ameloblastoma (am″ĕ-lō-blas-tō′mă) [*ameloblast* + *-oma*] A benign, slow growing, locally aggressive tumor of the jaws. It is most often found in the posterior mandible or ramus area and can be involved with a dentigerous cyst. SYN: *adamantinoma.*

amelogenesis (am″ĕ-lō-jen′ĕ-sis) [Fr. *émail,* enamel + *-genesis*] The formation of dental enamel by ameloblasts.

a. imperfecta ABBR: AI. Any of several hereditary disorders that produce inadequately mineralized enamel. There are four types of AI: hypoplastic, hypocalcified, hypomaturation, and hypoplastic-hypomaturation. The clinical appearances range from pitted enamel throughout the dentition, snow-capped incisal/occlusal thirds of the teeth (except mandibular anteriors), and a yellow to brown pitted enamel.

⚠️ Acidulated phosphate fluoride may further damage enamel in patients with amelogenesis imperfecta.

SYMPTOMS: Symptoms include enamel that may be pitted, local, smooth, rough, or lacking. Enamel may also be of normal thickness but poorly calcified or with a mottled appearance.

amelus (am′ĕ-lŭs) [*a-* + *¹mel-*] An individual with congenitally absent arms and legs.

amenity (ă-men′ĭ-tē) [L. *amoenitas,* pleasantness] In medicine, an element of health care delivery that increases patient satisfaction, whether or not it improves clinical outcomes.

amenorrhea (ā″men″ō-rē′ă) [*a-* + *meno-* + *-rrhea*] Absence of menstruation or menarche. Amenorrhea may be either primary, i.e., a failure to begin menstruating by age 16; or secondary, i.e., an absence of menstruation for more than 3 months in women who used to menstruate and who are not pregnant. Amenorrhea may be classed as physiological when it occurs during pregnancy, early lactation, after menopause, or when caused by medications, e.g., by some forms of hormonal contraception. Pathological, secondary, amenorrhea is caused by several conditions. **amenorrheic** (-rē′ĭk), *adj.*

ETIOLOGY: The primary causes of secondary amenorrhea are related either to an underlying hypothalamic-pituitary-endocrine dysfunction or to congenital or acquired abnormalities of the reproductive tract. Common abnormal diagnoses include metabolic disorders, e.g., diabetes, polycystic ovarian syndrome (PCOS), malnutrition, or obesity; emotional and stress-related disorders, e.g., anorexia nervosa; and systemic diseases, e.g., cancer, lupus, or tuberculosis.

TREATMENT: The underlying cause should be determined and corrected. If hormone deficiencies exist, substitutional therapy is recommended. Reproductive age and need for contraception must also be considered for treatment.

PATIENT CARE: The patient is assessed for other symptoms and is encouraged to seek medical attention if absence of menses is not related to pregnancy, menopause, or hormonal therapy.

dietary a. The cessation of menstrual periods in women of reproductive age due to inadequate nutrition.

emotional a. Amenorrhea resulting from shock, fright, or hysteria.

exercise a. Amenorrhea due to physical stress. It is often seen in women who participate in intensive workouts or exercise programs. SEE: *stress a.*

hyperprolactinemic a. Amenorrhea due to an excessive secretion of prolactin by the pituitary. SEE: *prolactin.*

hypothalamic a. Amenorrhea related to interference with release of gonadotropin-releasing hormone (GnRH) or with pituitary release of follicle-stimulating hormone or luteinizing hormone. Hypothalamic dysfunction may be drug-induced, e.g., related to abuse of marijuana or tranquilizers; psychogenic, e.g., related to chronic anxiety; functional, e.g., related to excessive exercise, anorexia, or obesity; or related to chronic medical illness, head injuries, or cancer.

lactational a. Suppression of normal cyclic hormonal changes resulting from breast-feeding. The advent of postpartum ovulation and menses is related to the amount of time the mother breastfeeds. Even after the resumption of menses, 50% of initial cycles are anovulatory. Women who stop nursing within 30 days usually experience the return of menstruation between 6 and 10 weeks after delivery. Among those who continue to nurse, ovulation usually occurs between postpartum weeks 17 and 28, with menstruation 30 to 36 weeks after the birth.

pathological a. Amenorrhea due to organic damage, disease, or dysfunction. Common causes include hypothalamic-pituitary dysfunction; ovarian dysfunction; alteration or obstruction of the genital outflow tract; congenital abnormalities; neoplasms; and injuries. Disease-related amenorrheas include Ascherman's syndrome, Savage's syndrome, Sheehan's syndrome, and Turner's syndrome.

physiological a. Amenorrhea due to normal body function. The amenorrhea may be due to immaturity in the prepubescent girl, aging in the postmenopausal woman, or hormonal interruptions in the gonadotropic feedback loop as occur during pregnancy and lactation; it is not related to organic disease.

postpartum a. Amenorrhea following childbirth. The amenorrhea may last for only a month or two and thus be within normal limits, or it may be permanent and therefore abnormal. *NOTE:* The onset of menstruation after childbirth may be delayed by continued breast-feeding. SEE: *Sheehan's syndrome*.

primary a. Delay of menarche until after age 16 or the absence of secondary sex characteristics after age 14. Typical causes include congenital abnormalities of reproductive structures, e.g., the müllerian ducts; absence of the uterus and/or vagina; imperforate hymen; or ovarian failure secondary to chromosomal abnormalities, as in Turner's syndrome.

secondary a. Cessation of menses in women who have menstruated previously but have not had a period in 6 months. Pregnancy is the single most common cause of secondary amenorrhea and should be excluded before other causes are sought.

stress a. Cessation of menses secondary to extreme mental or physical stress. The condition was first identified in women inmates in concentration camps and has been observed in female athletes undergoing intensive, rigorous training. It may be related to hormonal changes caused by stress or to the concomitant alteration in the ratio of muscle to fat as training intensity increases. SEE: *pseudocyesis*.

amentia (ā″men'ch(ē-)ă) [L. *amentia*, madness, insanity] **1.** Congenital mental deficiency; mental retardation. **2.** Mental disorder characterized by confusion, disorientation, and occasionally stupor. SEE: *dementia*.

nevoid a. Sturge-Weber syndrome.

phenylpyruvic a. Mental retardation due to phenylketonuria.

American Academy of Nurse Practitioners A national professional advocacy group that represents the interests of nurse practitioners in the U.S. website: www.aanp.org

American Academy of Nursing An organization formed by the American Nurses' Association. Membership in this honorary association indicates that the person selected has contributed significantly to nursing. A member is titled Fellow of the American Academy of Nursing, abbreviated FAAN.

American Association of Blood Banks ABBR: AABB. The professional organization, more commonly referred to as the AABB, whose mission is to promulgate standard practices in immunohematology.

American Association of Cardiovascular and Pulmonary Rehabilitation A professional association made up of a network of nurses, exercise physiologists, nutritionists, physical therapists, respiratory therapists, and physicians who aim to improve the health and survival of patients with cardiovascular and lung diseases.

American Association for Clinical Chemistry ABBR: AACC. A U.S.-based international association of clinical laboratory scientists including clinical chemists, microbiologists, pathologists, hematologists, and medical technologists.

American Association for Respiratory Care ABBR: AARC. The professional association for respiratory care practitioners in the U.S.

American Association of Retired Persons ABBR: AARP. The largest voluntary association of older adults (retired or not) in the U.S., with a membership of more than 30 million. The association lobbies on behalf of its members, sponsors research on aging, operates a mail-order pharmaceutical service and insurance plan, and publishes magazines and other literature for older adults.

American Board of Internal Medicine ABBR: ABIM. The professional oversight group in the U.S. that sets the standards for the training and professional certification of internists and subspecialists in internal medicine.

American Botanical Council ABBR: ABC. A nonprofit organization that disseminates information about herbal medicines to the media, the public, and the scientific and professional communities. ABC publishes HerbalGram, a quarterly journal, among other reference material.

American College of Rheumatology ABBR: ACR. An organization of health care professionals and scientists whose primary goals are to study and treat arthritis and other diseases of bones and joints. The organization also educates the public and the profession about rheumatological diseases and works as an advocate in the formulation of public policy pert. to the care of rheumatic and arthritic patients.

American College of Sports Medicine An organization that promotes and integrates scientific research, education, and practical applications of sports medicine and exercise science to maintain and enhance physical performance, fitness, health, and quality of life.

American College of Toxicology The current name of the American Board of Medical Toxicology.

American Federation for Aging Research ABBR: AFAR. An association of physicians, scientists, and other individuals involved or interested in research on biological aging and associated diseases. Its purpose is to encourage and fund research on aging.

American Geriatrics Society ABBR: AGS. An association of health care professionals interested in the problems of older adults. It encourages the study of geriatrics and stresses the importance of medical research in the field of aging.

American Holistic Medical Association A professional and advocacy group for U.S. physicians, osteopaths, and their students, who conduct research, educate others, or practice holistic medicine.

American Holistic Nursing Association A professional and advocacy group for U.S. nurses and their students who conduct research, educate others, or practice holistic nursing.

American Nurses Association ABBR: ANA. The only full-service professional organization representing the 3.1 million registered nurses in the U.S. It comprises 53 State Nurses Associations. The organization fosters high standards of nursing practice, promotes the economic and general welfare of nurses in the work environment, projects a realistic, positive view of nursing, and lobbies Congress and regulatory agencies about health care issues affecting nurses and the public. SEE: *Code for Nurses.*

American Nurses Association Network ABBR: ANA*NET. A wide-area computer network linking the 53 constituent State Nurses Associations with the national headquarters. It provides databases pert. to workplace and practice issues and various databases and services related to nursing practice. Future plans include subscriber service for all nurses, nursing organizations, and nursing schools.

American Occupational Therapy Association ABBR: AOTA. A national professional organization concerned with establishing and promoting education, research, and standards of practice for occupational therapy. The Web site is www.aota.org

American Physical Therapy Association ABBR: APTA. The national professional association that establishes and promotes standards of practice for physical therapists and physical therapist assistants.

American Psychiatric Nurses Association ABBR: APNA. An organization that provides leadership to advance psychiatric-mental health nursing practice; improve mental health care for individuals, families, groups, and communities; and shape health policy for the delivery of mental health services.

American Red Cross A branch of the international philanthropic organization Red Cross Society. It provides emergency aid during civil disasters such as floods and earthquakes, offers humanitarian services for armed forces personnel and their families, and operates centers for collecting and processing blood and blood products.

American Sign Language ABBR: ASL. A nonverbal method of communicating in which the hands and fingers are used to indicate words and concepts. SYN: *Ameslan.*

American Society for Biochemistry and Molecular Biology ABBR: ASBMB. A nonprofit organization composed of scientists and educators who seek to advance the sciences of biochemistry and molecular biology.

American Society of Clinical Oncology ABBR: ASCO. A not-for-profit professional organization of physicians who treat cancer. The group includes medical, radiological, and surgical oncologists. Website: www.asco.org

American Society for Clinical Pathology ABBR: ASCP. A professional, educational, and advocacy group for pathologists, clinical laboratory scientists, and technologists.

American Society of Hematology ABBR: ASH. An organization of professional hematologists that provides care to patients with diseases of the blood and promotes education, research, and training within the field. ASH also serves as an advocacy group for the profession.

American Standard Safety System ABBR: ASSS. Any of the specifications that govern the manufacture and use of threaded systems that link high-pressure, medical gas cylinders and the pressure-reducing valves that release the gases for clinical use to the patient. ASSS specifications differ for each type of medical gas in order to prevent medical errors, for example, to keep users from administering nitrogen or carbon dioxide to a patient for whom oxygen has been prescribed.

⚠️ Whenever gases, e.g., anesthetics, nebulized medications, oxygen are administered to patients, care should be taken to definitively identify the source gas and to monitor its concentration and flow rate.

Americans with Disabilities Act ABBR: ADA. Legislation passed by the U.S. Congress in 1990 and amended in 2008 to ensure the rights of persons with disabilities and to prohibit discrimination on the basis of disability in employment, public services, transportation, public accommodation, communications, state and local governments, and the U.S. Congress. An individual with a disability is defined by ADA as one who has a physical or mental impairment that limits one or more major activities, a person with a history or record of an impairment, or a person perceived by others to have such an impairment. Also called *Public Law 101-336.*

American Type Culture Collection ABBR: ATCC. A nonprofit scientific organization dedicated to maintainin⌐

collections of microorganisms and other biological resources for use in academic, governmental, or industrial laboratories. The ATCC also provides educational and technical support about microbiology and biological resources. Phone: 703–365–2700.

americium (a″mē-ris(h)′ē-ŭm) [*America* + *-ium*] SYMB: Am. A metallic radioactive element, atomic weight (mass) (longest-lived isotope) 243, atomic number 95.

Ameslan (a′měs-lan″) American Sign Language.

Ames test (āmz) [Bruce Nathan Ames, U.S. biochemist, b. 1928] A laboratory test of the mutagenicity of chemicals. Special strains of organisms are incubated with the test chemical, and their growth is an indicator of the mutagenicity of the substance. Most chemicals that test positive are carcinogens. Use of the test has helped reduce the use of mammals for tests of mutagenicity.

ametria (ā″mē′trē-ă) [*a-* + *metra-* + *-ia*] Congenital absence of the uterus.

ametrometer (am″ĕ-trom′ĕ-tĕr) [*ametro(pia)* + *-meter*] An instrument for measuring the degree of ametropia.

ametropia (am″ĕ-trō′pē-ă) [Gr. *ametros*, disproportionate, + *-opia*] Imperfect refractive powers of the eye in which the principal focus does not lie on the retina, as in hyperopia, myopia, or astigmatism.

ametropic, *adj.*

AMI *acute myocardial infarction.*

amicrobic (ā″mī-krō′bik) [*a-* + *microbe*] **1.** Lacking microbes. **2.** Not caused by microbes.

amidase (am′ĭ-dās″) [*amide* + *-ase*] An enzyme that catalyzes the hydrolysis of amides; a deamidizing enzyme.

amide (am′īd″) [*am(monia)* + *-ide*] Any organic substance that contains the monovalent radical —$CONH_2$. It is usually formed by replacing the hydroxyl (—OH) group of the —COOH by the —NH_2 group.

amidin (am′ĭ-din) [L. *amidum, amylum,* starch + *-in*] The soluble component of starch. SEE: *amylopectin.*

amido- Prefix indicating the presence of the radical $CONH_2$.

amidulin (ă-mid′yŭ-lin) [Fr. *amidon,* starch] Soluble starch.

Amies transport medium A phosphate-buffered, balanced salt solution used to collect and carry patient specimens for microbiological analysis to the clinical laboratory.

amikacin sulfate (am″ĭ-kā′sĭn) An aminoglycoside antibiotic.

amimia (ā″mim′ē-ă) [*a-* + *mimos,* a mime, actor + *-ia*] Loss of power to express ideas by signs or gestures.

   amnesic a. Loss of the ability to express oneself with signs or gestures or to understand them.

amine (ă-mēn′, am′ēn″) [*am(monium)* + *-ine*] Any of a group of nitrogen-containing organic compounds formed when one or more of the hydrogens of ammonia have been replaced by one or more hydrocarbon radicals.

amino- [Fr. *amine*] Prefix meaning the *presence of an amino group* (NH_2).

amino acid (ă-mē′nō) [amino-] Any of a large group of organic compounds marked by the presence of both an amino (NH_2) group and a carboxyl (COOH) group. Amino acids are the building blocks of proteins and the end products of protein digestion.

Approximately 80 amino acids are found in nature, but only 20 are necessary for human metabolism or growth. Of these, some can be produced by the liver; the rest, the "'essential' amino acids," must be supplied by food. Oral preparations of amino acids may be used as dietary supplements.

Arginine is nonessential for adults but cannot be formed quickly enough to supply the demand in infants and thus is classed as essential in early life.

Some proteins containing all the essential amino acids are called complete proteins. Examples are milk, cheese, eggs, and meat. Proteins that do not contain all the essential amino acids are called incomplete proteins. Examples are vegetables and grains. Amino acids pass unchanged through the intestinal wall into the blood, then through the portal vein to the liver and into the general circulation, from which they are absorbed by the tissues according to the specific amino acid needed by that tissue to make its own protein. Amino acids, if not otherwise metabolized, may be converted into urea. SEE: *deamination; digestion; protein.*

   branched-chain a.a. ABBR: BCAA. The essential amino acids, leucine, isoleucine, and valine. "Branched-chain" refers to their chemical structure. They are therapeutically valuable because they bypass the liver and are available for cellular uptake from the circulation. Parenteral administration, alone or mixed with other amino acids, is thought to be beneficial whenever catabolism due to physiological stress occurs. Skeletal muscles use BCAAs for their anticatabolic effects.

   conditionally dispensable a.a. An amino acid that becomes essential under specific clinical conditions, e.g., when their rate of synthesis is limited.

   essential a.a. An amino acid that is required for growth and development but that cannot be produced by the body and must be obtained from food. The essential amino acids are histidine, isoleucine, leucine, lysine, methionine, cysteine, phenylalanine, tyrosine, threonine, tryptophan, and valine. SYN: *indispensable a.a.*

    indispensable a.a. Essential amino acid.

    nonessential a.a. An amino acid that can be produced by the body and is not required in the diet. The nonessential amino acids are alanine, aspartic acid, arginine, citrulline, glutamic acid, glycine, hydroxyglutamic acid, hydroxyproline, norleucine, proline, and serine.

    semi-essential a.a. An amino acid of which an adequate amount must be consumed in the diet to prevent the use of essential amino acids to synthesize it. An example is tyrosine. Without adequate dietary intake, the essential amino acid phenylalanine is used to make tyrosine.

aminoacidemia (ă-mē″nō-as″ĭ-dē′mē-ă, ăm″ĭ-nō-) [*amino acid* + *-emia*] An excess of amino acids in the blood.

amino acid group SEE: under *group.*

aminoacidopathy (am″ĭ-nō-as″ĭ-dop′ă-thē) [*amino acid* + *-pathy*] Any of about 100 disorders of amino acid metabolism, including cystinuria, alkaptonuria, and albinism.

aminoaciduria (ă-mē″nō-, ă-mē″nō-a″sĭ-doo′rē-ă) [*amino acid* + *-uria*] An excess of amino acids in the urine.

aminobenzene (ă-mē″nō-ben′zēn, ăm″ĭ-nō-, ben-zēn′) Aniline.

aminoglutethimide (ăm″ĭ-nō-gloo-teth′ĭ-mīd″) $C_{13}H_{16}N_2O_2$, a derivative of glutethimide ($C_{13}H_{15}NO_2$) that interferes with the production of adrenocortical hormone. It has been used to decrease the hypersecretion of cortisol by adrenal tumors and to treat cancer of the adrenal gland and breast cancer that is sensitive to adrenal hormone stimulation.

aminoglycoside (ă-mē″nō-glī′kŏ-sīd″) [*amino-* + *glycoside*] Any of a class of antibiotics derived from *Streptomyces* that prevent bacterial cells from making proteins necessary for their survival. Examples include gentamicin and tobramycin.

⚠ Monitoring of drug levels is required during the use of parenteral aminoglycosides because they may cause permanent hearing loss and kidney damage.

aminolysis (am″ĭ-nol′ĭ-sis) [*amine* + *-lysis*] Metabolic transformation of amino-containing compounds by removal of the amino group. **aminolytic** (ă-mē″nŏ-lit′ik), *adj.*

aminophylline (am″ĭ-nof′ĭ-lĭn) [*amino-* + Gr. *phyllon,* plant + *-ine*] A mixture of theophylline and ethylenediamine. It is used to treat patients with reactive airway disease that does not respond to safer medications, e.g., beta-agonist drugs, other bronchodilators, or inhaled or injected corticosteroids. Besides stimulating diaphragmatic movement, it is a bronchodilator and increases heart rate. Common side effects include gastrointestinal upset and tachycardia. SYN: *theophylline ethylenediamine.*

aminopterin (am-ĭ-nop′tĕr-ĭn) A folic acid antagonist used to treat acute leukemia.

aminopurine (ă-mē″nō-pū′rĭn, ăm″ĭ-nō) [*amino-* + *purine*] An oxidation product of purine. It includes adenine and guanine. SEE: *methyl purine; oxypurine.*

aminotransferase (ă-mē″nō-trans′fĕ-rās″) [*amino* + *transferase*] An enzyme that transfers an amino group from one molecule to another. Aminotransferases, e.g., aspartate aminotransferase and alanine aminotransferase, are important, frequently measured liver enzymes. SEE: *transaminase.*

    alanine a. ABBR: ALT. An intracellular enzyme involved in amino acid and carbohydrate metabolism. It is present in high concentrations in muscle, liver, and brain. An increased level of ALT in the blood indicates necrosis or disease in these tissues. Its measurement is most commonly used as part of the differential diagnosis of liver disease and in tracking the disease. SYN: *glutamic-pyruvic transaminase; serum glutamic-pyruvic transaminase.*

    aspartate a. ABBR: AST. An intracellular enzyme involved in amino acid and carbohydrate metabolism. It is present in high concentrations in muscle, liver, and brain. An increased level of this enzyme in the blood indicates necrosis or disease in these tissues. SYN: *glutamic-oxaloacetic transaminase.*

aminuria (am-ĭ-noor′ē-ă) [*amine* + *-uria*] Presence of amines in urine.

amiodarone (ă-mē-ō′dă-rōn″) An antiarrhythmic drug with a complex pharmacology that is effective in the treatment of both atrial and ventricular rhythm disturbances. Its side effects include pulmonary fibrosis and thyroid dysfunction.

amitosis (ā″mī-tō′sis) [*a-* + *mitosis*] Simple division of the nucleus and cell without the changes in the nucleus that characterize mitosis; direct cell division. **amitotic** (-tot′ik), *adj.*

amitriptyline hydrochloride (am″ĭ-trip′tĭ-lēn″) [*am(ino)-* + *trypt(ophan)* + *(meth)yl* + *-ine*] A tricyclic antidepressant administered orally or intramuscularly. Common side effects are drowsiness, sedation, and dry mouth.

AML *acute myelocytic leukemia.*

amlodipine (am-lō′dĭ-pēn″) A calcium channel blocker and antihypertensive, administered orally to control high blood pressure, angina pectoris, and variant angina.

AMLS *Advanced medical life support.*

amma therapy (am'ă) [Chinese, push-pull] A traditional Chinese massage composed of pushing and pulling movements, percussion, and stretching applied to acupressure points on the body.

ammeter (am'mĕt-ĕr) [*am(pere)* + *-meter*] An instrument, calibrated in amperes, that measures the quantity (number of electrons) in an electric current. SEE: *milliammeter.*

Ammi visnaga (am'ē vis-nag'ă) A perennial herb with a taproot, related to Queen Anne's lace, used in traditional Egyptian medicine as a diuretic and treatment for kidney stones. It is also used as a coronary vasodilator but is poorly tolerated when given orally. Compounds developed from its furan ring include amiodarone (an antiarrhythmic drug).

ammoaciduria (am″ō-as″ĭ-door'ē-ă) [*ammo(nia)* + *aciduria*] An abnormal amount of ammonia and amino acids in the urine.

ammonia (ă-mōn'yă) [L. *sal ammoniacum,* ult. fr. *Ammon,* Egyptian deity near whose temple it was originally obtained] An alkaline gas, NH_3, formed by decomposition of nitrogen-containing substances such as proteins and amino acids. Ammonia is converted into urea in the liver. It is related to many poisonous substances but also to the proteins and many useful chemicals. Dissolved in water, it neutralizes acids and turns litmus paper blue.

 blood a. SEE: *ammoniemia.*

ammoniacal (am″ō-nī'ă-kăl) Pert. to or having the characteristics of ammonia.

ammoniated (ă-mō'nē-āt″ĕd) Containing ammonia.

ammoniemia, ammonemia (ă-mō″nē-ē'mē-ă, ă-mō-nē'mē-ă) [*ammonia* + *-emia*] Excessive ammonia in the blood. Normally, only faint traces of ammonia are found in the blood. Increased amounts are due to a pathological condition such as impaired liver function.

ammonium (ă-mō'nē-ŭm) [*ammonia* + *-ium*] NH_4^+, a radical that forms salts analogous to those of alkaline metals.

 a. alum $(NH_4)Al(SO_4)_2 \cdot {}_{12}H_2O$, an astringent and styptic. SYN: *aluminum ammonium sulfate.*

 a. carbonate $(NH_4)_2CO_3$, a compound used in preparing aromatic ammonia spirit (smelling salt).

 a. chloride NH_4Cl, a compound used as an expectorant and as an acidifier in treating acid-base balance. SYN: *sal ammoniac.*

 a. hydroxide NH_4OH, a solution of ammonia gas in water, used as a household cleaner and a refrigerant. SYN: *ammonia water.* SEE: *Poisons and Poisoning Appendix.*

 a. thiosulfate The chemical in fixing solution that removes unexposed silver bromide crystals from radiographic film during the development process.

ammoniuria (ă-mō″nē-ūr'ē-ă) [*ammonia* + *-uria*] Excessive ammonia in the urine.

amnesia (am-nē'zhă) [Gr. *amnēsia,* oblivion] Partial or total, permanent or transient loss of memory. The term is often applied to episodes during which patients forget recent events although they may conduct themselves appropriately, and after which no memory of the period persists. Such episodes are often caused by strokes, seizures, trauma, senility, alcoholism, or intoxication. The cause is often unknown.

 anterograde a. Amnesia for events that occurred after a precipitating event or medication.

> ⚠ Short-term memory loss may be induced in people who use benzodiazepine drugs (e.g., triazolam, lorazepam, or flurazepam).

 SYN: *anterograde memory.*
 auditory a. Word deafness.
 dissociative a. Inability to recall important personal information, usually of a traumatic or stressful nature, that is too extensive to be explained by ordinary forgetfulness. SYN: *psychogenic a.*
 lacunar a. Loss of memory for isolated events.
 posttraumatic a. ABBR: PTA. A state of agitation, confusion, and memory loss that the patient with traumatic brain injury (TBI) enters soon after the injury or on awakening from coma. Edema, hemorrhage, contusions, shearing of axons, and metabolic disturbances impair the ability of the brain to process information accurately, resulting in unusual behaviors that are often difficult to manage. Trauma patients with normal brain scans may have mild TBI and display some of the symptoms of PTA. Posttraumatic amnesia can last for months but usually resolves within a few weeks. During PTA, the patient moves from a cognitive level of internal confusion to a level of confusion about the environment. SEE: *Rancho Los Amigos Guide to Cognitive Levels.*
 SYMPTOMS: Symptoms include restlessness, moaning or crying out, uninhibited behavior (often sexual or angry), hallucinations (often paranoid), lack of continuous memory, confabulation, combative behavior, confused language, disorientation, perseveration, and sleep disturbances. Problem-solving ability, reasoning, and carrying out planned motor movements (as in activities of daily living) may also be impaired.
 PATIENT CARE: The patient is con-

tinually reoriented by a large calendar and clock within sight; each interaction with the patient begins with a repetition of who is in attendance, why the attendant is present, and what activity is planned; and the patient is kept safe and comfortable and is allowed as much freedom of movement as possible.

As the patient becomes confused, he may show agitation. Health care professionals can limit agitation and confusion by speaking softly in simple phrases, using gestures as necessary, and allowing time for the patient to respond. Regular visits from family are important; the family should be prepared for the patient's appearance and behavior; they should be encouraged to help the patient with activities of daily living.

Equipment for agitated patients is used; wrist restraints are avoided if possible. Urinary catheters may increase agitation due to physical discomfort (incontinence briefs can be used during the training period of a toileting program). The patient's swallowing function is evaluated as soon as possible to avoid feeding tubes, but swallowing precautions are observed. A list of stimulations that increase or decrease the patient's agitation is posted for the use of everyone in contact with the patient. Distance is maintained during aggressive outbursts. The patient's personal space should not be invaded without warning (e.g., the patient should be told in advance that his body parts are going to be touched or washed). The patient should be approached from the front, and items should be placed where the patient can best see them.

Health care professionals should watch closely for impulsive movement that can jeopardize the patient. They should warn others that the patient cannot monitor his own behavior and that words and actions may occur without awareness or forethought. Independent behavior and self-care are encouraged. The patient is engaged in short activities with a motor component. One action at a time should be monitored if the patient performs several actions that interfere with treatment. To promote abstract reasoning, humor should be used if the patient understands it. A consistent daily schedule provides structure. The patient is taught to use compensatory cues (a watch or written activity schedule) to aid memory. The patient is also assessed for posttraumatic headache, which is treated with prescribed medications.

psychogenic a. Dissociative amnesia.

retrograde a. Amnesia for events that occurred before a specific precipitant (e.g. a drug overdose, surgical op-eration, stroke, or trauma). SYN: _retrograde memory_.

selective a. Inability to remember events that occurred at the same time as other experiences that are recalled.

tactile a. Astereognosis.

transient global a. Short-term memory loss in otherwise healthy people. Remote memory is retained.

traumatic a. Amnesia caused by sudden injury to the brain.

visual a. Inability to remember the appearance of objects or to be cognizant of printed words.

amnesiac, amnesic (am-nē′z(h)ē-ak″, am-nē′zik) **1.** Pert. to, affected with, or caused by amnesia. **2.** A person who has amnesia.

amnestic (am-nes′tik) **1.** A drug that impairs memory. **2.** Pert. to, or caused by, amnesia.

amnestic disorder (am-nes′tik) Any of a group of disorders marked by memory disturbance that is due either to the direct physiological effects of a general medical condition or to the persistent effects of a drug, toxin, or similar substance. Affected patients are unable to recall previously learned information or past events. Social or occupational functioning is significantly impaired.

amniocentesis (am″nē-ō-sen-tē′sĭs) [_amnion_ + _-centesis_] Transabdominal puncture and aspiration of the amniotic sac by ultrasound to remove amniotic fluid. The sample is studied chemically and cytologically to detect genetic and biochemical disorders and maternal-fetal blood incompatibility and, later in the pregnancy, to determine fetal maturity. The procedure also allows for transfusion of the fetus with platelets or blood and instillation of drugs for treating the fetus.

This procedure is usually performed no earlier than at 14 weeks' gestation. It is important that the analysis be done by experts in chemistry, cytogenetics, and cell culture. Cell cultures may require 30 days, and, if the test has to be repeated, the time required may be insufficient to allow corrective action. SEE: illus.

⚠ The procedure can cause abortion or trauma to the fetus.

PATIENT CARE: The patient's knowledge about the procedure is evaluated, misconceptions corrected, and information provided as necessary. The patient is informed about sensations that she may experience and signs a consent form. The amniocentesis equipment is assembled; amber-colored test tubes are used (or clear test tubes covered with aluminum foil) to shield the fluid from light, which could break down bilirubin.

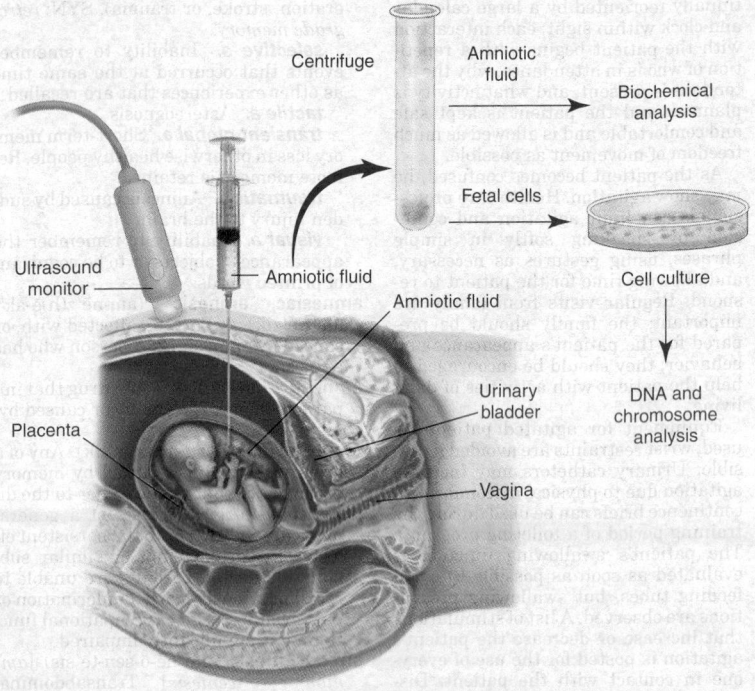

Centrifuge

Amniotic fluid

Biochemical analysis

Fetal cells

Ultrasound monitor

Amniotic fluid

Amniotic fluid

Cell culture

Placenta

Urinary bladder

DNA and chromosome analysis

Vagina

AMNIOCENTESIS

Baseline vital signs and fetal heart rate are obtained, and the fundus is palpated for fetal position and fetal and uterine activity for 30 min before, during, and 30 min after the procedure. The patient is assessed for light-headedness, nausea, and diaphoresis as well as for anxiety, pain, and labor onset. During the procedure, emotional support is provided. After the procedure, the patient is positioned on her left side and is instructed to report unusual fetal hyperactivity or hypoactivity, clear or bloody vaginal drainage, uterine contractions, abdominal pain, or fever and chills, any of which is indicative of complications. Rh-negative women with an Rh-positive fetus should be given RhoGam. SEE: *chorionic villus sampling.*

    therapeutic a. Amniodrainage.

amniochorial, amniochorionic (am″nē-ō-kō′rē-ăl, -kō-rē-on′ik) Pert. to both the amnion and chorion.

amniodrainage (am″nē-ō-drān′ăj) [*amnio-* + *drainage*] Withdrawal of amniotic fluid to treat fetal diseases and conditions such as twin-to-twin transfusion syndrome. SYN: *therapeutic **amniocentesis.***

amniogenesis (am″nē-ō-jen′ĕ-sĭs) [*amnion* + *-genesis*] Formation of the amnion.

amniography (am″nē-og′ră-fē) [*amnion*

+ *-graphy*] Radiography of the fetus for abnormalities after injection of a water-soluble contrast medium into the amniotic sac. It is an obsolete technique replaced by ultrasonography.

amnioinfusion (am″nē-ō-in-fū′zhŏn) The instillation of fluid, usually normal saline, into the amniotic sac to increase the amniotic fluid volume. This is usually done after rupture of membranes, with a catheter passed through the cervix into the uterus.

    INDICATIONS: The main indication for amnioinfusion is the treatment of repeated severe variable decelerations and fetal bradycardia unresponsive to conventional therapies. It may also be used to reduce the risk of meconium aspiration syndrome in labors where thick meconium flow is noted or to protect against cord compression due to oligohydramnios. There is controversy whether the benefits of performing this procedure outweigh the risks in the latter two cases. Several other clinical applications are being investigated.

    CONTRAINDICATIONS: Contraindications include amnionitis, known fetal or uterine anomaly, placenta previa or abruption, severe fetal distress, polyhydramnios, hypertonic uterus, and multiple gestation.

    COMPLICATIONS: Complications are

rare but include uterine overdistention and increased uterine resting tone, amniotic fluid embolus, umbilical cord prolapse, and disruption of a previous uterine scar.

PATIENT CARE: Consult local protocols for amnioinfusion because these vary from hospital to hospital.

amnion (am′nē-on″, -ŏn) [Gr. *amnion*, lamb] The innermost fetal membrane. It is a thin, transparent sac that holds the fetus suspended in amniotic fluid. The amnion grows rapidly at the expense of the extraembryonic coelom, and by the end of the third month it fuses with the chorion, forming the amniochorionic sac. SYN: *bag of waters*.

amniotic (am″nē-ot′ik), *adj.* SEE: *oligohydramnios*.

a. nodosum A mass of rounded or oval opaque elevations in the placenta, 1 to 6 mm in diameter, seen in the part of the amnion in contact with the chorionic plate and near the insertion of the cord into the placenta. They are usually associated with prolonged oligohydramnios.

amnionitis (am″nē-ō-nī′tis) Chorioamnionitis.

amniorrhea (am″nē-ŏ-rē′ă) [*amnion* + *-rrhea*] Rupture of membranes.

amniorrhexis (am″nē-ŏ-rek′sis) [*amnion* + *-rrhexis*] Rupture of the amnion.

amnioscope (am′nē-ŏ-skōp″) [*amnion* + *-scope*] An endoscope for observing the fetus and amniotic fluid through the intact amniotic membrane.

amnioscopy (am″nē-os′kŏ-pē) Direct visual examination of the fetus through an endoscope inserted into the amniotic cavity.

amniote (am′nē-ōt″) [*amnion*] Any of the vertebrate group Amniota, comprising reptiles, birds, and mammals, whose members develop an amnion.

amniotic band disruption sequence syndrome (am″nē-ot′ik) Any of several fetal malformations associated with multiple fibrous strands of amnion that appear to develop or entangle fetal parts in utero. The disrupted sequence leads to structural malformations and deformations and disruption of function. The defects include limb defects and amputations; abnormal dermal ridge patterns; simian creases; clubbed feet; craniofacial defects, including cleft lip and palate; and visceral defects such as gastroschisis and omphalocele. Failure to understand the cause of this condition can lead to misdiagnosis and inappropriate family and genetic counseling. SEE: *multiple malformation syndrome*.

amniotitis (am″nē-ŏ-tīt′ĭs) Chorioamnionitis.

amniotome (am′nē-ŏ-tōm″) [*amnion* + *-tome*] An instrument for puncturing fetal membranes.

amniotomy (am″nē-ot′ŏ-mē) [*amnion* + *-tomy*] The intentional rupture of the amniotic sac with a sterile amniohook, Allis' forceps, or amniotome to stimulate or augment labor. SYN: *artificial rupture of membranes*.

PATIENT CARE: The procedure is explained to the patient. The patient is positioned and draped correctly, and the perineum is thoroughly cleaned. Before the procedure, baseline information is obtained on fetal heart rate (FHR) and uterine contractions, which are monitored during and after the procedure. Immediately after the amniotomy, the FHR is auscultated, or the electronic recording of FHR is checked because the procedure increases the risk of cord compression or prolapse. The color, odor, consistency, and approximate amount of amniotic fluid expelled are assessed and documented. If any question exists as to its origin (amniotic fluid versus urine), the pH of the fluid is tested with nitrazine paper, which will turn blue in the presence of amniotic fluid. Bloody show or insufficient amniotic fluid can cause a false test result. The patient is evaluated for onset of labor, which should begin within 12 hr of rupture, and for fever or other signs of infection in prolonged rupture. Oxytocin induction is often used with amniotomy to limit this possibility.

amobarbital (am″ō-bar′bĭ-tol″) An odorless white crystalline powder used as a sedative; $C_{11}H_{18}N_2O_3$.

a. sodium An odorless white granular powder used as a sedative; $C_{11}H_{17}N_2NaO_3$. It is absorbed and inactivated rapidly in the liver.

A-mode (ā′mōd″) A-mode **ultrasound**.

A-mode (amplitude modulation) display A-mode **ultrasound**.

Amoeba (ă-mē′ba) [Gr. *amoibē*, change] A large genus of protozoa of the class Sarcodina, in the kingdom Protista, found in fresh and salt water and moist soil. Some species are parasitic in humans, but most parasitic species have been reclassified in the genus *Entamoeba*. SEE: *amoeba*.

amoeba, ameba (ă-mē′bă, ă-mē′bē) *pl.* **amoebae, amoebas, amebas, amebae** [Gr. *amoibē*, change] Any member of the genus *Amoeba* or of related genera, e.g., *Entamoeba*. It has pseudopodia, by which it constantly changes its shape. Oxygen and carbon dioxide are exchanged by simple diffusion through the cell membrane. Reproduction is by binary fission. Some species of *Entamoeba* are parasitic in humans. SEE: *Amoeba*.

amoebapore, amebapore (ă-mē′bă-por″) [*amoeba* + *pore*] A family of three pore-forming peptides (amoebapore A [AP-A], AP-B, and AP-C). They insert into the membranes of bacteria or eukaryotic cells and form tiny holes that result in lysis of the target cells.

amoebic (ă-mē'bĭk) [*amoeba* + *-ic*] **1.** Pert. to or resembling an amoeba. **2.** Amebic.

amok, amuck (ă-mok', ă-mŭk') [Malay, *āmok*, to engage furiously in battle] **1.** A culture-bound, one-time outburst of murderous frenzy observed chiefly in Malaysia. **2.** Pert. to or being in a murderous frenzy. **3.** Pert. to or being in an uncontrolled state.

amotivational syndrome (ā"mōt"ĭ-vă'shŏn-ăl) [¹*an-* + *motivational*] Lack of interest in activities, reduced attention and concentration, apathy, and passivity. It has been reported in association with some neuropsychiatric disorders, e.g., depression, schizophrenia, and traumatic brain injury, and with use of drugs, e.g., marijuana and selective serotonin reuptake inhibitors.

amoxicillin (ă-moks"ĭ-sĭl'ĭn) A semisynthetic penicillin used primarily to treat infections of the sinuses and the middle ear.

Amoxil (ă-mok'sĭl) SEE: *amoxicillin*.

AMP *adenosine monophosphate*

amperage (am'pě'răj, am-pēr'ăj) The rate of flow of electrons in an electrical circuit.

ampere (am'pēr") [André-Marie Ampère, Fr. physicist, 1775–1836] ABBR: amp. The basic unit of current, defined as the flow of 6.25×10^{-18} electrons per sec (1 coulomb of charge flowing per sec). SEE: *electromotive force*.

amphetamine (am-fet'ă-mēn", -mĭn) [*a(lpha)* + *m(ethyl)* + *ph(enyl)* + *th(hyl)* + *amine*] **1.** A colorless liquid that volatilizes slowly at room temperature. It is a central nervous system stimulant. The preparation most commonly used is the sulfate form, marketed as tablets or capsules. SEE: *a. sulfate*. **2.** An adrenergic administered orally to treat narcolepsy. Its therapeutic class is central nervous system stimulant.

   a. sulfate A synthetic white crystalline substance that acts as a central nervous system stimulant; $(C_9H_{13}N)_2SO_4$. It is used to treat narcolepsy and certain types of mental depression. Use of amphetamine sulfate to control appetite is contraindicated. High doses are toxic, and prolonged use may cause drug dependence.

amphi-, amph- [Gr. *amphi*, on both sides] Prefixes meaning *on both sides, on all sides, double*. In chemistry, it denotes certain positions or configurations of molecules. SEE: *ampho-*.

amphiarthrosis (am"fē-ar-thrō'sĭs) [*amphi-* + *arthrosis*] A form of articulation in which the body surfaces are connected by cartilage. Mobility is slight but may be exerted in all directions. The articulations of the bodies of the verte-

brae are examples. **amphiarthrodial** (-thrōd'ē-ăl), *adj.*

amphiaster (am"fē-as'tĕr) [*amphi-* + *aster*] Diaster.

Amphibia (am-fĭb'ē-ă) [Gr. *amphibia (zōia),* (animals) living a double life] A class of cold-blooded animals that live on land and in water; includes salamanders, frogs, and toads. They breathe through gills during their aquatic larval stage but through lungs in their adult stage.

amphibian (am-fĭb'ē-ăn) An animal of the class Amphibia. **amphibian,** *adj.*

amphibious (ăm-fĭb'ē-ŭs) Able to live or function both on land and in water.

amphiblastula (am"fĭ-blas'chŭ-lă) [*amphi-* + *blastula*] A form of blastula in which the blastomeres are of unequal size, as seen in sponges. **amphiblastic** (-blas'tĭk), *adj.*

amphibolism (am"fĭb'ŏ-lĭzm) [Gr. *amphibolos,* doubtful, ambiguous + *-ism*] The sum of the metabolic pathways that lead to both catabolic and anabolic outcomes, such as beta-oxidation of fatty acids by the liver. The resulting acetyl groups may enter the citric acid cycle for energy production or be used for the synthesis of other lipids or steroids.

amphicyte (am'fĭ-sīt") [*amphi-* + *-cyte*] SEE: *cell, satellite* (2).

amphidiarthrosis (am"fĭ-dī"ar-thrō'sĭs) [*amphi-* + *diarthrosis*] An articulation containing an amphiarthrosis and a diarthrosis, as of the lower jaw.

amphipathic (am"fĭ-path'ik) [*amphi-* + *-pathic*] In chemistry, having polar and nonpolar (water-soluble and water-insoluble) regions within a single molecule. This two-part structure allows these chemicals to link, or to segregate, oils and water. Phospholipids, bile salts, and detergents are amphipathic molecules.

amphitheater (am"fĭ-thē'ă-tĕr) [*amphi-* + *theater*] An auditorium with tiers of seats around it for students and other observers.

amphitrichate, amphitrichous (am-fĭ'trĭ-kăt", -kăt, -kŭs) [*amphi-* + *trich-*] Of microorganisms, having a flagellum or flagella at both ends.

ampho- [Gr. *amphō,* both] Prefix meaning *both, on both sides, of both kinds,* or *double.* SEE: *amphi-*.

amphocyte (am'fŏ-sīt") [*ampho-* + *-cyte*] A cell that stains with either acid or basic stains. SYN: *amphophil*.

amphodiplopia (am-fŏ-dĭ-plō'pē-ă) [*ampho-* + *diplopia*] Double vision in each eye. SYN: *amphoterodiplopia*.

ampholyte (am'fŏ-līt") [*ampho-* + *(electro)lyte*] A substance that acts as a base or an acid, depending on the pH of the solution into which it is introduced. **ampholytic** (-lit'ik,), *adj.*

amphophil (am'fŏ-fil) [*ampho-* + *-phile*] Amphocyte.

amphoric (am-for'ĭk) [Gr. *amphora* + *-ic*] Pert. to a sound like that produced by blowing across the mouth of a bottle; resonant; cavernous. Percussion of a pulmonary cavity produces such a sound. **amphoricity** (am″fŏ-ris'ĭt-ē), *n.*

amphorophony (am″fŏ-rof'ŏ-nē) [*amphor(ic)* + Gr. *phōnē*, voice] An amphoric voice sound.

amphoteric, amphoterous (am″fŏ-ter'ĭk, am-fot'ĕr-ŭs) [Gr. *amphoteros*, each or both of two] Being able to react as both an acid and a base. **amphoterism** (am″fŏ-ter'ĭzm), *n.*

amphotericin B (am″fŏ-ter'ĭ-sĭn) [*amphoteric* + *-in*] An antibiotic obtained from a strain of *Streptomyces nodosus*. The drug is usually administered intravenously to treat deep-seated fungal infections. Premedication with antipyretics, antihistamines, or corticosteroids is often necessary to decrease febrile hypersensitivity reactions. Patients must be monitored for hypokalemia or renal failure.

amphoteric reaction Reaction in which a compound reacts as both an acid and a base.

ampicillin (am″pĭ-sĭl'ĭn) A semisynthetic penicillin. Trade names include Amcill, Omnipen, Polycillin, and Principen.

amplicon (am'plĭ-kon″) An amplified segment of specific DNA or RNA sequences in which multiple copies of the nucleic acid sequences are found. Amplicons can be made during polymerase chain reactions or may occur spontaneously, e.g., in the nucleic acid content of certain organisms or tumors.

amplification (am″plĭ-fĭ-kā'shŏn) [L. *amplificatio*, making larger] Enlargement, magnification, expansion.

amplifier (am'plĭ-fi″ĕr) **1.** That which enlarges, extends, increases, or makes more powerful. **2.** In electronics, a device for increasing the electric current or signal.

amplitude (am'plĭ-tood″) [L. *amplitudo*] **1.** Amount, extent, size, abundance, or fullness. **2.** In physics, the extent of movement, as of a pendulum or sound wave. The maximum displacement of a particle, as that of a string vibrating, as measured from the mean to the extreme. **3.** Magnitude of an action potential. **4.** In radiography, the extent of tube travel during tomography.

    a. **of accommodation** The difference in the refractive power of the eye when accommodating for near and far vision. It is measured in diopters (D) and normally diminishes progressively from childhood to old age. It is approx. 16 D at age 12, 6.5 D at age 30, and 1 D at age 50.

amplitude modulation Altering the height (amplitude) of an electrical or acoustical wave. SEE: A-mode *ultrasound*.

ampule (am'pūl″) [Fr. *ampoule*] A small glass container for containing hypodermic solutions. It can be sealed and its contents sterilized.

ampulla (am-pu'lă) *pl.* **ampullae** [L. *ampulla*, little jar] Saclike dilatation of a canal or duct.

    a. **ductus deferentis** An irregular nodular dilatation of the vas deferens just before its junction with the secretory duct of the seminal vesicle. SYN: *a. of vas deferens.*

    hepatopancreatic a. SEE: *papilla of Vater.*

    a. **of lacrimal duct** The slight dilatation of the lacrimal duct medial to the punctum.

    a. **of rectum** The slight dilatation of the rectum proper just before continuing as the anal canal.

    a. **of semicircular canal** In the inner ear, any of the dilations at the ends of the three bony semicircular canals that house an ampulla of a semicircular duct. These dilations house the corresponding ampullae of the semicircular ducts inside the canals.

    a. **of semicircular ducts** The dilatation of semicircular ducts near their junction with the utricle. In the walls of the ducts are the cristae ampullares.

    a. **of uterine fallopian tube** The dilated distal end of a uterine tube terminating in a funnel-like infundibulum.

    a. **of vas deferens** Ampulla ductus deferentis.

    a. **of Vater** SEE: under *Vater, Abraham.*

ampullitis (am″pŭ-līt'ĭs) [*ampulla* + *-itis*] Inflammation of an ampulla, esp. of the ductus deferens.

amputation (am″pyŭ-tā'shŏn) [L. *amputare*, to cut around] Removal of a limb, body part, or organ, usually as a result of surgery but, occasionally, of trauma. In western countries during peacetime, the most common reason for loss of a limb is peripheral vascular disease, e.g., a blockage to blood flow to the legs caused by cigarette smoking, hypertension, high cholesterol, physical inactivity, or uncontrolled diabetes mellitus. Amputation can also result from injuries occurring accidentally, e.g., in battle or while working.

    PATIENT CARE: Immediately after amputation, vital signs are assessed; the dressing is observed for bleeding at least every 2 hr; drain patency is checked; and the amount and character of drainage are documented. Limb circulation is ascertained by checking pulses, skin color, and temperature. Postoperative pain is managed by intravenous and, later, by oral analgesics. To prevent formation of contractures, the patient is encouraged to walk, change position, rest in proper body alignment with the residual limb extended rather than bent, do range-of-motion exercises (esp. extensions), and, finally, muscle-strengthening exercises as soon as these are prescribed. Residual limb-conditioning exercises and correct residual limb bandaging (application of graded, moderate pressure to mold the residual limb into a cone shape that allows a good prosthesis fit) assist limb shrinkage. The residual limb may initially have a rigid cast. The patient is instructed in skin hygiene; to massage the limb; to examine the entire limb daily, using a mirror to see hidden areas; and to report symptoms such as swelling, redness, excessive drainage, increased pain, and residual limb skin changes (rashes, blisters, or abrasions). The patient is taught to bandage the residual limb or, when it is dry, to apply a residual limb shrinker (a custom-fitted elastic stocking that fits over the residual limb) and is advised against applying body oil or lotion because it can interfere with proper fit of a prosthesis. The need for constant bandaging until edema subsides and the prosthesis is properly fitted, the use of a residual limb sock, and proper care of the prosthesis are explained. The patient is encouraged to verbalize anger and frustration; to cope with grief, self-image, and lifestyle adjustments; and to deal with phantom limb sensation if this occurs. The patient may require referral to a local support group or for further psychological counseling. SEE: *Nursing Diagnoses Appendix.*

Chopart a. SEE: under *Chopart, François.*

congenital a. Amputation of parts of the fetus in utero. It was formerly believed to be caused by constricting bands but is now believed to be a developmental defect.

double-flap a. Amputation in which two flaps of soft tissue are formed to cover the end of the bone.

a. in contiguity Amputation at a joint.

a. in continuity Amputation at a site other than a joint.

Jaboulay a. SEE: *Jaboulay amputation.*

Pirogoff a. SEE: *Pirogoff amputation.*

primary a. Amputation performed before inflammation or infection sets in.

pulp a. The technique of removing the coronal portion of an exposed or involved vital pulp in an effort to retain the radicular pulp in a healthy, vital condition. SYN: *pulpotomy.*

secondary a. Amputation performed after onset of infection.

spontaneous a. Nonsurgical separation of an extremity or digit. SEE: *ainhum.*

traumatic a. The sudden amputation

of some part of the body due to an accidental injury.

Tripier a. SEE: *Tripier amputation.*

amputee (am″pyŭ-tē′) A person who has lost all or part of one or more limbs as a result of amputation. The amputation may be congenital or acquired through trauma or surgery.

AMS *Anticoagulation management service; anticoagulation monitoring service.*

Amsler grid (omz′lĕr) [Marc Amsler, Swiss ophthalmologist, 1891–1968] A grid of lines with a center black dot used by patients with macular degeneration to detect early worsening of their disease. Loss of vision in part of the grid or distortion of the lines (metamorphopsia) requires emergent evaluation for possible fluid or blood in the macula.

Amsterdam criteria (am′stĕr-dam″) A means of screening family members for evidence of a hereditary predisposition to colorectal cancer. People in families with nonpolyposis colorectal cancer are screened for evidence of other malignancies of the skin, endometrium, and stomach. Those who meet the Amsterdam criteria should be closely followed, e.g., with regular colonoscopies.

AMT *American Medical Technologists.*

amusia (ă-mū′zē-ă, zhă) [Gr. *amousia,* lack of refinement] Inability to produce or appreciate musical sounds.

motor a. Inability to produce musical sounds.

sensory a. Inability to appreciate musical sounds.

vocal a. Inability to sing.

amychophobia (ă-mī″kŏ-fō′bē-ă) [Gr. *amychē,* scratch + *-phobia*] Morbid fear of being scratched; fear of the claws of any animal.

amyelencephaly (ā″mī″ĕl-ĕn-sef′ā′lē) [*a-* + *myel-* + *encephalon,* brain] Congenital absence of the brain and spinal cord.

amyelia (ā″mī″ē′lē-ă) [*a-* + *myelo-* + *-ia*] Congenital absence of the spinal cord.

amyelinic (ā″mī″ē-lĭn′ik) [*a-* + *myelin* + *-ic*] Not possessing a myelin sheath; unmyelinated.

amyelus (ā″mī′ĕ-lŭs) An individual with congenital absence of the spinal cord.

amygdala (ă-mig′dă-lă) *pl.* **amygdalae** [L. fr. Gr. *amygdalē,* almond] A spherical collection of nuclei lying inside the front tip of the temporal lobe of each cerebral hemisphere. The amygdala is a central part of the limbic system. It receives inputs from the primary olfactory cortex, the inferior temporal cortex, the hypothalamus, and the lower brainstem; it innervates the inferior temporal cortex, the orbital surface of the frontal cortex, the striatum, the mediodorsal nucleus of the thalamus, the hypothalamus, and the lower brainstem. In humans, stimulation of the amygdala produces fear or anger, accompanied by a "stomach churning" sensation; sometimes, there is also urination. SYN: *amygdaloid* **complex**; *amygdaloid* **nucleus**. SEE: *limbic system* for illus.

amygdalin (ă-mĭg'dă-lĭn) [*amygdala* + *-in*] A bitter glycoside derived from the pit or other seed parts of several plants, including almonds and apricots. Amygdalin, from which the poisonous hydrocyanic acid can be produced by enzymatic action, is known in the U.S. as Laetrile. SEE: *Laetrile*.

amygdaline (ă-mĭg'dă-lĭn, -lĭn″) [*amygdala* + *-ine*] **1.** Pert. to a tonsil. **2.** Pert. to or shaped like an almond.

amygdaloid (ă-mĭg'dă-loyd″) [*amygdala* + *-oid*] **1.** Resembling an almond. **2.** Pert. to or affecting an amygdala.

amygdalolith (ă-mĭg'dă-lō-lĭth″) [*amygdala* + *lith-*] A stone in a distended crypt of a tonsil.

amygdalopathy (ă-mĭg″dă-lop'ă-thē) [*amygdala* + *-pathy*] Any disease of a tonsil.

amygdalotome (ă-mĭg'dă-lŏ-tōm″) [*amygdala* + *-tome*] An instrument for excision of a tonsil.

amyl (am'ĭl) [Gr. *amylon*, starch] A hypothetical univalent radical, C_5H_{11}, nonexistent in a free state.

   a. nitrite $C_5H_{11}NO_2$; a volatile and highly flammable clear liquid used as a vasodilator, esp. in the past for anginal pain.

amylaceous (am″ĭ-lā'shŭs) An outdated term formerly used to mean "pert. to starch; starchy."

amylase (am'ĭ-lās″) [*amyl* + *-ase*] Any of a class of enzymes that split or hydrolyze starch. Those found in animals are called alpha-amylases; those in plants, beta-amylases. Serum levels of amylase become elevated in mumps, pancreatitis, and intraperitoneal organ rupture, among other diseases and conditions. SEE: *macroamylase*.

   pancreatic a. Amylopsin.
   salivary a. Ptyalin.
   vegetable a. Diastase.

amylasuria (am″ĭ-lās-ū'rē-ă) [*amylase* + *-uria*] An increased amount of amylase in the urine. It occurs in pancreatitis

amylin (am'ĭ-lĭn) [*amyl* + *-in*] A peptide made of 37 amino acids that is secreted at the same time as insulin by the beta cells of the pancreas. It is secreted in response to a meal. Amylin has been shown to 1. inhibit appetite; 2. slow gastric emptying; 3. decrease the secretion of glucagons; and 4. inhibit the activity of osteoclasts. SYN: *islet amyloid polypeptide*.

amylo-, amyl- [Gr. *amylon*, starch] Prefixes meaning *starch* or *polysaccharide*.

amylodextrin (am″ĭ-lō-deks'trĭn) [*amylo-* + *dextrin*] A soluble substance produced during the hydrolysis of starch into sugar.

amylogenesis (am″ĭ-lō-jen'ĕ-sĭs) [*amylo-* + *-genesis*] The production of starch.

amylogenic (-jen'ĭk), *adj.*

amyloid (am'ĭ-loyd″) [*amyl-* + *-oid*] **1.** Resembling starch; starchlike. **2.** A protein-polysaccharide complex produced and deposited in tissues during some chronic infections, malignancies, and rheumatological disorders. It is a homogeneous substance staining readily with Congo red. It is associated with a variety of chronic diseases, particularly tuberculosis, osteomyelitis, leprosy, Hodgkin's disease, and carcinoma. SEE: *amyloidosis; amyloid degeneration*.

amyloid disease Amyloidosis.

amyloidosis (am″ĭ-loy″dō'sĭs) [*amyloid* + *-osis*] Any of a group of imperfectly understood metabolic disorders resulting from the insidious deposition of amyloidin tissues. Amyloidosis may cause localized or widespread organ failure. Amyloid may infiltrate many organs, including the heart and blood vessels, brain and peripheral nerves, kidneys, liver, spleen, skin, endocrine glands, or intestines. As a result, the clinical manifestations of amyloidosis are varied, and the disease may mimic other conditions ranging from nephrotic syndrome to dementias or congestive heart failure. Amyloidosis of the tongue may cause it to become markedly enlarged, interfering with speech or swallowing. Amyloid infiltration of endocrine organs can cause pituitary, thyroid, or pancreatic dysfunction.

Primary amyloidosis is present when amyloid proteins are deposited throughout the body because of their overproduction by malignant clones of immune cells. Multiple myeloma and B-cell lymphoma are the two hematological malignancies associated with primary amyloidosis.

Secondary amyloidosis is the production and deposition of amyloid in patients with chronic inflammatory conditions, e.g., rheumatoid arthritis. This is also known as *reactive, systemic amyloidosis*.

Localized amyloidosis is present when amyloid infiltrates an isolated organ (e.g., the pancreas).

DIAGNOSIS: Amyloid in tissues can be demonstrated by its characteristically green appearance when stained with Congo red stain and viewed under a polarizing microscope.

TREATMENT: Corticosteroids and melphalan or veryhigh-dose chemotherapy followed by stem-cell transplantation has been used to treat primary amyloidosis. In secondary amyloidosis, controlling the primary inflammatory illness may arrest the progress of the disease.

AA a. Amyloidosis in which amyloid A protein, a protein manufactured by the liver in chronic inflammatory diseases, deposits in tissues and causes organ dysfunction.

AL a. Amyloidosis in which immunoglobulin light chains (or parts of light chains) circulate in serum and deposit in tissues such as the kidneys. They may cause significant organ dysfunction; e.g., in the kidneys they can cause nephrotic-range proteinuria and end-stage disease.

dialysis-related a. ABBR: DRA. The accumulation of beta-2-microalbumin, a type of albumin, in the blood of patients undergoing hemodialysis. The molecule is not readily removed from the blood by some dialysis membranes, and, when the protein builds up in joints and bones, it can cause pain and loss of function, esp. at the wrist, where it produces carpal tunnel syndrome.

familial a. The only inherited form of amyloidosis. In this variant of the disease, transthyretin is manufactured by the liver and deposits in a wide variety of tissues, causing them to malfunction.

lichen a. Amyloidosis limited to the skin.

localized a. Amyloidosis in which isolated amyloid tumors are formed.

primary a. Amyloidosis not associated with a chronic disease.

secondary a. Amyloidosis associated with a chronic disease, e.g., tuberculosis, syphilis, or Hodgkin disease, and with extensive tissue destruction. The spleen, liver, kidneys, and adrenal cortex are most frequently involved.

amylolysis (am″ĭ-lol′ĭ-sĭs) [*amylo-* + *-lysis*] Hydrolysis of starch into sugar in the process of digestion. **amylolytic** (-ō-lit′ik), *adj.*

amylopectin (am″ĭ-lō-pek′tĭn) [*amylo-* + *pectin*] The insoluble component of starch. SEE: *amidin.*

amylophagia (am″ĭ-lō-fā′jă) [*amylo-* + *phag-* + *-ia*] An abnormal craving for starch.

amylopsin (am″ĭ-lop′sin) An enzyme in pancreatic juice that hydrolyzes starch into achroodextrin and maltose. SYN: *pancreatic amylase.* SEE: *digestion; duodenum; enzyme.*

amylose (am′ĭ-lōs″) [*amylo-* + *-ose*] Any of a group of carbohydrates that includes starch, cellulose, and dextrin.

amylosuria (am″ĭ-lō-sūr′ē-ă) [*amylose* + *-uria*] Amylose in the urine.

amyluria (am″ĭl-ūr′ē-ă) [*amyl-* + *-uria*] Starch in the urine.

amyoplasia (ā″mī″ō-plā′zhă) [*¹an-* + *myo-* + *-plasia*] The most common form of arthrogryposis multiplex congenita. SEE: *arthrogryposis multiplex congenita.*

amyosthenia (ā″mī″os-thē′nē-ă) [*a-* + *myo-* + *sthenia*] Muscular weakness. SEE: *myasthenia.* **amyosthenic**, *adj.*

amyotonia (ā″mī″ŏ-tō′nē-ă) [*a-* + *myotonia*] Deficiency or lack of muscular tone.

a. congenita Myotonia congenita.

amyotrophy, amyotrophia (ā″mī″o′trŏ-fē, ā″mī″ŏ′trō′fē-ă) [*¹an-* + *myotrophy*] Muscular atrophy. **amyotrophic** (-trof′ik, -trō′fik), *adj.*

monomelic a. ABBR: MMA. A pure movement disorder characterized by degeneration and death of motor neurons, resulting in atrophy of a limb, typically one arm. SYN: *Hirayama syndrome.*

neuralgic a. Idiopathic brachial **plexopathy**.

progressive spinal a. Progressive muscular **atrophy**.

amyxia (ā″miks′ē-ă) [*a-* + *myx-* + *-ia*] Absence or deficiency of mucus.

amyxorrhea (ā″miks-ŏ-rē′ă) [*a-* + *myxo-* + *-rrhea*] Lack of normal secretion of mucus.

An 1. Symbol for actinon. **2.** *anisometropia.* **3.** *anode.* **4.** *antigen.*

¹an-, a- [Gr. *a-, an-,* not, rel. to L. *in-,* Eng. *un-*] Prefixes meaning *without, away from, not* The variant *an-* is usually used before a vowel or h, e.g. *anesthesia, anhydrous;* the variant*a-* is usually used before a consonant, e.g., *acardia.*

²an- SEE: *ana-.*

ANA *American Nurses Association; antinuclear antibody.*

ana-, an- [Gr. *ana,* up, back, again] Prefixes used in words derived from Greek meaning*up, back, again, against, back* or *"re-".* The variant *an-* is used before vowels and h, e.g., *anion.*

anabiosis (an″ă-bī-ō′sĭs) [*ana-* + Gr. *biōsis,* mode of life] Resuscitation.

anabolic agent SEE: under *agent.*

anabolism (ă-na′bŏ-lĭzm) [Gr. *anabolē,* a building up + *-ism*] The building up of body tissues. It is the constructive phase of metabolism by which cells take from the blood nutrients required for repair or growth and convert these inorganic chemicals into cell products or parts of living cells. SYN: *constructive metabolism.* SEE: *catabolism; metabolism.* **anabolic** (a″nă-bo′lik), *adj.*

anabolite, anabolin (ă-nab′ŏ-līt″, -lĭn) [*anabol(ism)* + *-ite*] Any product of anabolism.

anacamptometer (an″ă-kamp-tom′ĕ-tĕr) [*ana-* + Gr. *kamptos,* bent, + *-meter*] A device for measuring the intensity of deep reflexes.

anacatesthesia (an″ă-kat″es-thē′zē-ă) [*ana-* + *cata-* + *-esthesia*] A sensation of hovering.

anacidity (an″ă-sid′ĭt-ē) [*¹AN-* + *acidity*] Abnormal deficiency of acidity, esp. of hydrochloric acid in the gastric juice.

anaclasis (ă-nāk′lă-sĭs) [*ana-* + *-clasis*] **1.** Refraction or reflection of light. **2.** Refraction of light in the interior of the eye. **3.** Reflex action. **4.** Refraction for therapeutic reasons. **5.** Forcible movement of a joint in order to treat fibrous ankylosis. **anaclastic** (an″ă-klas′tik), *adj.*

anaclitic (an″ă-klit′ik) [Gr. *anaklitikos,* pert. to reclining] In psychoanalysis, pert. to the dependence of an infant on the mother figure for care. **anaclisis** (-klī′sis), *n.*

anacrotic (an″ă-krot′ĭk) [*ana-* + Gr. *krotos,* stroke] **1.** Pert. to the ascending or vertical upstroke of a sphygmogram. **2.** Pert. to a pulse wave tracing with a notched appearance near its summit. **3.** Pert. to two heartbeats traced on the ascending line of a sphygmogram. SEE: *pulse.*

anacusia, anacusis, anakusis (an″ă-kū′sē-ă, -sis) [¹*an-* + *-acousia*] Total deafness.

anadidymus (an″ă-did′ĭ-mŭs) [*ana-* + *didymos*] A developmental abnormality in which the upper parts of the bodies of twins are fused, but the buttocks and legs are free.

anadipsia (an″ă-dip′sē-ă) [*ana-* + Gr. *dipsa,* thirst] Intense thirst.

anadrenalism (an″ă-drēn′ă-lĭzm) [¹*an-* + *adrenal* + *-ism*] Failure of the adrenal gland to function.

anadromous (ă-na′drŏ-mŭs) [Gr. *anadromos,* running upward] Pert. to the migration of fish from seawater to freshwater.

anaerobe (an′ĕ-rōb″) [¹*an-* + *aerobe*] A microorganism that can live and reproduce in the absence of oxygen.

   facultative a. An organism that can live and reproduce with or without oxygen.

   obligate anaerobe An organism that can live and reproduce only in the absence of oxygen.

anaerobic (an″ĕ-rō′bik) [*anaerobe* + *-ic*] **1.** Taking place in the absence of oxygen. **2.** Pert. to an organism that lives and reproduces in the absence of oxygen.

anaerobiosis (an″ĕ-rō-bī-ō′sĭs) [¹*an-* + *aero-* + Gr. *biōsis,* life, way of life] **1.** Life in an oxygen-free atmosphere. **2.** Functioning of an organ or tissue in the absence of free oxygen.

Anaerococcus (an″ĕ-rō-kok′ŭs) [¹*an-* + *aero-* + *coccus*] A genus of anaerobic gram-positive cocci, formerly classified as members of the genus *Peptostreptococcus.* They are butyrate-producing saccharolytic bacteria, sometimes pathogenic to humans.

anagen (an′ă-jen″) [*ana-* + *gen(esis),* generation, birth] The growth stage of hair development. SEE: *catagen; telogen.*

anakatadidymus (an″ă-kat″ă-did′ĭ-mŭs) [*ana-* + *cata-* + *didymus*] A congenital anomaly in which twins are separated above and below but joined at the trunk.

anal (ān′ăl) [L. *analis*] Rel. to the anus or outer rectal opening.

anal dynamic graciloplasty The construction of a "new" anal sphincter to treat severe intractable fecal incontinence. The gracilis muscle tendon is detached at its insertion, mobilized, and reattached by wrapping it around the sphincter. Some patients can be trained to make the sphincter functional. If necessary a sustained contraction can be stimulated by implanted electrodes, closing the anus. Additional procedures have been employed as gluteal muscle mobilization. An implantable artificial sphincter has been employed. The functional result of all of these procedures is variable.

analeptic (an″ă-lep′tik) [Gr. *analeptikos,* restorative] **1.** A drug that stimulates the central nervous system. **2.** A restorative agent.

anal erotism Anal eroticism.

analgesia (an″ăl-jē′zh(ē-)ă) [Gr. *analgēsia,* painlessness] **1.** Absence of a normal sense of pain. **2.** The relief of pain, e.g. with medications such as anesthetic drugs. **3.** The administration of a pain reliever.

   audio a. SEE: *audioanalgesia.*

   a. algera Spontaneous pain with loss of sensibility in a part.

   continuous caudal a. Analgesia to reduce the pain of childbirth. The anesthetic is injected continuously into the epidural space at the sacral hiatus.

   electrical dental a. ABBR: EDA. The treatment of oral pain or the administration of oral anesthesia with electrode pads applied to the cheeks or the oral mucosa. SEE: *audioanalgesia.*

   epidural a. A technique of managing pain in which narcotics are infused into the peridural space through an indwelling catheter. Administration may be at a continuous basal infusion rate or self-administered within programmed limits.

   USES: Epidurally administered medications diffuse across the dura mater, through the arachnoid and pia mater to provide pain relief, and are indicated to treat pain in the thoracic, lumbar, or sacral areas, e.g., in patients in labor or those undergoing thoracic surgeries, and the acute and chronic pain of chronic lumbosacral radiculopathy, cancer pain, phantom limb pain, pancreatic pain, and incisional pain. Epidural anesthesia can be used for surgeries such as cholecystectomy, coronary artery bypass grafting, hysterectomy, arthroplasty, or even abdominal aortic aneurysm repair. Epidural needles and catheters can be inserted at spinal levels C7 to T1 to treat patients with chronic pain symptoms or for surgeries of the arms and shoulders; from T4 to T5 for thoracic surgery; from T8 to T10 for upper abdominal surgery; and at L2 to L3 for lower abdominal surgery and labor and delivery. Drugs for epidural anesthesia include anesthetics such as lidocaine, analgesics such as morphine, or steroids such as methylprednisolone acetate. Epidural anesthesia is contraindicated in patients receiving systemic anticoagulation and antiplatelet therapy, e.g., aspirin products or NSAIDs, patients with abnormal or reduced concentrations of clotting factors, patients in hypovolemic shock, with abruptio placentae, and whenever there is evidence of active infection near the site of the insertion of the epidural catheter. Relative contraindications include history of headaches or backaches, chronic neurological disorders, and allergy to drugs being used.

PATIENT CARE: The anesthesia provider discusses the procedure, benefits, and risks with the patient and answers any questions. An informed consent form must be signed by the patient. The nurse may reinforce or clarify information as necessary and witness the patient's signature on the consent form. Before the procedure the patient should have an IV line infusing lactated Ringer's solution or 0.9% sodium chloride solution and should have supplemental oxygen via a nasal cannula or simple face mask. Blood pressure and oxygen saturation should be monitored throughout the procedure. The health care professional helps position the patient in the preferred sitting position with head down, shoulders slumped, and arms out in front to bend the back forward and open the vertebral spaces. Legs may be extended forward or hang over the side of the bed or table. If this position cannot be tolerated, the patient is positioned laterally with chin tucked against chest and knees in a fetal position. The patient is assisted to remain still and kept as comfortable as possible; reassurance and emotional support are provided. Once inserted, the epidural catheter is labeled according to the facility's policy, and properly and prominently identified so that only epidural drugs are administered through it (these are pure, preservative-free medications, not the same formulation as for usual intravenous preparations of the same drug). The patient should then be assisted to a comfortable position or positioned for surgery. Administration of epidural medication and the removal of the catheter are determined by state nursing laws, which nurses must know. Epidural medications are usually administered by a certified registered nurse anesthetist or by an anesthesiologist and are managed by a staff nurse.

Drugs given epidurally must be administered with a sterile technique. The dose is determined by the patient's response as the desired level of anesthesia is reached.

The patient should be assessed periodically according to the facility's policy. His blood pressure, heart rate, respiratory rate, and oxygen saturation should be documented. The insertion site and dressing are examined periodically for bleeding or medication leakage. The patient is assessed for pain from the catheter or from the infusion and for breakthrough pain related to the surgery or for the painful condition being managed. Continuous infusion via a pump or patient-controlled analgesia pump also must be checked for correct functioning. Muscle weakness and sensory loss may be indicators of epidural bleeding and nerve impingement, which requires emergency surgery to prevent permanent tissue and nerve damage. Any problems encountered should be called to the attention of the anesthesia provider. Hypotension is commonly experienced. The patient's IV fluid infusion rate may need to be increased dramatically to manage hypotension, or a vasoactive agent may be administered as prescribed. Respiratory distress will occur if the needle or catheter enters the subarachnoid space, causing high spinal anesthesia with increased loss of respiratory muscle function. The anesthesia provider and rapid response team should be notified immediately, and basic life support guidelines followed to maintain airway, breathing, and cardiovascular status.

The catheter may migrate into an epidural vein as a result of the patient's movement, causing epidural medication to enter the bloodstream and produce an overdose. Prevention of this complication involves slow, careful movement and repositioning by a caregiver team, with the patient providing minimal aid. If the dura mater is torn by the large needle or catheter during epidural insertion, a cerebrospinal fluid leak into the epidural space can occur. This complication should be suspected if the patient experiences severe and sudden headache when upright. The patient should be kept supine, the anesthesia provider notified, and the patient treated, which may involve administration of additional IV fluid, caffeine, analgesics, or an epidural blood patch. Infection is a rare complication: it is prevented by maintaining sterile technique throughout the insertion, management, and removal of the epidural device.

⚠ Excessive sedation, hypotension, respiratory depression, and coma may occur if patients receiving epidural analgesia are also given other central nervous system depressant drugs.

---

hypnotic a. The use of hypnotic suggestion to alter a patient's perception of noxious sensations, e.g., the pain of childbirth or coronary artery disease.

infiltration a. Anesthesia produced in a local area by injecting an anesthetic agent into operative sites or wounds.

interpleural a. The introduction of pain-relieving drugs into the space between the visceral and parietal pleura, e.g., to relieve the pain of thoracotomy. It is also known, incorrectly, as intrapleural anesthesia. SYN: *interpleural* **block***; interpleural* **blockade***.

intrathecal a. The injection of pain-relieving medications into the subarachnoid space. It is used to control severe pain, e.g., the pain of vertebral compression fracture or metastatic bone disease. SYN: *intrathecal* **anesthesia***.

paretic a. Complete analgesia of an upper limb in conjunction with partial paralysis.

patient-controlled a. ABBR: PCA. A drug administration method that permits the patient to control the rate of drug delivery for the control of pain. It is usually accomplished by the use of an infusion pump.

PATIENT CARE: An adult or child who is cognitively and physically able to use the equipment and who understands that pressing a button can result in pain relief is an appropriate candidate to administer his own pain medications when they are needed. Safety is secured because opioid and opiate drugs, the analgesics most often administered by PCA, cause sedation before respiratory depression. A sedated patient will drop rather than push the PCA button, preventing delivery of more drug and respiratory concerns. This safeguard can be circumvented when some unauthorized person, well-meaning though that person may be, presses the PCA button for the patient. Health care professionals should advise patients, family members, and other visitors that the PCA should be used only by the patient. When patients are unable to use PCA appropriately, a family member or nurse may be authorized to manage the system. This primary pain manager must be taught how to assess for pain and its relief, using an appropriate method for the specific patient, and how to recognize and manage the adverse effects of opioids and opiates (nausea, vomiting, constipation, sedation, and respiratory depression). The manager also needs to know how to assess the patient's sedation level using a sedation scale, such as the following: S = sleep, easy to arouse (awaken patient to determine arousability before administering a bolus); 1 = awake and alert (acceptable, may administer bolus); 2 = slightly drowsy, easily aroused (acceptable, may administer bolus); 3 = frequently drowsy, arousable, drifts off during conversation (unacceptable, notify primary nurse or health care provider); 4 = somnolent, minimal, or no response to physical stimulation (unacceptable, notify primary care provider immediately). In some cases, a secondary or even tertiary pain manager should be appointed for those times when the primary manager needs a respite. Nurse-activated dosing is appropriate for patients who have no family members who can manage pain and is useful in the intensive care unit, where the patient is usually critically ill. Health care agencies should develop criteria for selecting appropriate patients for PCA, family-controlled analgesia, and nurse-activated dosing. Patients, family members, and visitors should be taught about proper PCA use. If the patient's pain appears to be unrelieved, the patient or concerned visitor should notify the patient's primary nurse. Patients receiving PCA should be monitored at least every 2 hr for the first 24 hr, assessing vital signs, pain level, and sedation level. If sedation is at a level of 3, the opioid or opiate dose should be decreased and the basal infusion (if in use) stopped; monitoring should be increased until the sedation level is 2 or lower; and the patient's or pain manager's ability to manage the pain safely should be evaluated. If high sedation levels are found to be related to the inability to safely manage the pain using PCA, an alternative approach to pain management should be used.

perineural a. The injection of a pain-relieving drug, such as bupivacaine or lidocaine, around or near a nerve, to induce regional anesthesia. SYN: *perineural anesthesia; perineural block; perineural blockade*.

preemptive a. The administration of anesthetic before surgery in an attempt to abort postoperative pain and disability.

analgesic (an″ăl-jē′zik) [¹an-+ -algia] **1.** Relieving pain. **2.** A drug that relieves pain. Analgesic drugs include nonprescription drugs, such as aspirin and other nonsteroidal anti-inflammatory agents, and those drugs classified as controlled substances and available only by prescription. SYN: *analgetic*.

analgesic ladder, World Health Organization analgesic ladder A framework for the treatment of pain in patients with cancer and other disorders, in which the patient is treated first with anti-inflammatory analgesics such as ibuprofen or mild, non-narcotic pain relievers such as acetaminophen but subsequently may be treated with narcotic analgesics of increasing strengths if anti-inflammatory drugs or adjunctive therapies do not alleviate pain.

analgetic (an″ăl-jet′ik) Analgesic.

anal intraepithelial neoplasia SEE: under *neoplasia*.

analogous (ă-nal′ŏ-gŭs) [Gr. *analogos*, analogy, proportion] In biology, similar in function but different in origin or structure, such as the wings of a bee and the wings of an owl. SEE: *homologous*.

analogue, analog (an′ă-log″) [Gr. *analogos*, analogy, proportion] 1. In biology, an organ in different species similar in function but different in structure, such as the wings of a fly and the wings of a bird. 2. In chemistry, a compound structurally similar to another but slightly different in composition. 3. Capable of representing an infinite number of values; the opposite of digital.

   estrogen a. A compound that mimics the effects of estrogens.

   gonadotropin-releasing hormone a. A medication that mimics the action of gonadotropins and inhibits the ovaries or the testicles so that they cannot produce female or male hormones.

   insulin a. A synthetic insulin in which small changes in the amino acid structure of the polypeptide result in changes in the onset, peak effect, or duration of the molecule's physiological effects. Insulin aspart, glargine, and lispro are all insulin analogues.

analogy (ă-nal′ŏ-jē) [Gr. *analogos*, analogy, proportion] 1. Likeness between similar features of two things, allowing a comparison. 2. In biology, similarity in function but difference in structure or origin. SEE: *homology*.

anal personality SEE: under *personality*.

anal stage SEE: under *stage*.

anal wink Contraction of the anal sphincter in response to pinprick stimulus of the perineum. This reflex is evidence of normal motor function at S4–S5. It is also known as the anal or anocutaneous reflex.

analysand (ă-nal′ĭ-sand″) [L. *analysandus*, to be analyzed] A patient undergoing psychoanalysis.

analysis (ă-nal′ĭ-sĭs) *pl.* **analyses** [*ana-* + Gr. -*lysis*] 1. Separation of anything into its constituent parts. 2. Psychoanalysis. Particular analyses are listed under the first word. SEE: e.g., *blood gas analysis; continuous-flow analysis; hair specimen analysis*. **analytic** (an″ăl-it′ik), *adj.* **analytically** (i-k(ă-)lē), *adv.*

analysis of occupational performance That part of the occupational therapy evaluation that determines a person's ability to carry out activities of daily living.

   It identifies performance skills and patterns, activity demands, barriers, and contextual factors as a precursor to the selection of more specific performance assessment tools.

analysis of variance ABBR: ANOVA. A statistical technique for defining and segregating the causes of variability affecting a set of observations. Use of this technique provides a basis for analyzing effects of various treatments or variables on subjects or patients being investigated. In an experimental design in which several samples or groups are drawn from the same population, estimates of population variance between samples should differ from each other only by chance. ANOVA provides a method for testing the hypothesis that several random and independent samples are from a common, normal population.

analyst (an′ăl-ĭst) [*analysis* + -*ist* an agent suffix] 1. One who analyzes. 2. Psychoanalyst.

analyte (an′ă-līt″) [*anal(yze)* + -*ite*] A substance being analyzed, esp. a chemical. SEE: *measurand*.

analytical reading Thinking carefully, critically, and deeply while reading. One attempts to understand an author's writing by comparing and contrasting it with one's own experiences, feelings, thoughts, and knowledge.

analyze (an′ăl-īz″) [Ult. fr. Gr. *analyein*, to loose, loosen, analyze] To separate into parts; to examine methodically.

analyzer (an′ăl-īz″ĕr) Any device that determines some characteristic of an object or process, e.g., its chemical composition, cellularity, mass, oxygen content, or particle content.

   automated a. A chemical instrument to perform assays with a minimum of human intervention.

   batch a. An automated chemical analyzer in which the instrument system sequentially performs a single test or multiple tests on each of a group of samples.

   continuous flow a. An automated chemical analyzer in which the samples and reagents are pumped continuously through a system of modules interconnected by tubing.

   discrete a. An automated chemical analyzer in which the instrument performs tests on samples that are kept in discrete containers.

   field a. In visual field perimetry, a device used to assess central and peripheral visual acuity.

   pulse height a. ABBR: PHA. A circuit that differentiates between pulses of varying sizes. It is used in scintillation, blood cell, and particle counters.

anamnesis (an″am″nē′sĭs) [Gr. *anamnēsis*, recalling] 1. The faculty of remembering; recollection. 2. That which is remembered. 3. A medical history, as recalled by the patient. SEE: *catamnesis.*

anamnestic (an"am"nes'tik) [Gr. *anamnēstikos,* easily recalled] **1.** Pert. to anamnesis. **2.** Pert. to the medical history of a patient. **3.** Assisting the memory.

anamnestic reaction The rapid reappearance in the blood of antibodies to an antigen after re-exposure to the antigen. Anamnesia is a cell-mediated phenomenon caused by the presence of antigen-specific memory B lymphocytes.

anamniotic (an"am"nē-ot'ik, -ōt'ik) [¹*an-* + *amnion*] Lacking an amnion. SEE: *amniote.*

anamorph (an'a-morf") [*ana-* + *morphē,* form] The asexual state of fungi, in which they reproduce by mitosis rather than by the union of two cell nuclei and meiosis. Fungi that reproduce anamorphically are said to be "imperfect" fungi. Fungi that reproduce sexually are said to be "perfect." **anamorphic** (an"ä-mor'fik), *adj.* SEE: *teleomorph.*

anandamide (ă-nan'dă-mīd") [Sanskrit *ananda,* endlessness, eternal bliss + *amide*] A neurotransmitter that binds to and activates cannabinoid receptors on brain cells.

ANA*NET *American Nurses Association Network.*

anangioplasia (ăn-an"jē-ŏ-plā'zh(ē-)ă) [¹*an-* + *angi-* + *-plasia*] Imperfect vascularization of a part. **anangioplastic** (-plas'tik), *adj.*

anankastic, anancastic (an"ăn-kas'tik) [Gr. *anankastikos,* compulsory] Pert. to compulsion, esp. to obsessive-compulsive disorder.

anaphase (an'ă-fāz") [*ana-* + *phase*] The third stage in meiosis and mitosis,, in which there is longitudinal bisection of chromatids, which separate and move toward their respective poles.

anaphoresis (an"ă-fŏ-rē'sis) [*ana-* + *-phoresis*] The flow of electrically positive particles toward the anode (positive pole) in electrophoresis.

anaphoria (an"ă-for'ē-ă) [*ana-* + *-phoria*] The tendency of the eyeballs to turn upward. SYN: *anatropia.*

anaphrodisia (an"af"rŏ-dē'zh(ē-)ă) [¹*an-* + Gr. *aphrodisia,* sexual desire] Diminished or absent desire for sex. SEE: *aphrodisiac.* **anaphrodisiac,** *adj.* **anaphrodisiac** (-dē'zē-ak"), *n.*

anaphrodite (an"af'rŏ-dīt") [¹*an-* + *Aphrodite,* Gr. goddess of love] A person with impaired or absent sexual desire.

anaphylactic (an"ă-fĭ-lak'tik) Pert. to anaphylaxis. **anaphylactically** (-ti-k(ă-)lē), *adv.*

anaphylactic reaction Anaphylaxis.

anaphylactogenic (an"ă-fĭ-lak"tŏ-jen'ik) [*anaphylactic* + *-genic*] Producing anaphylaxis. **anaphylactogenic,** *n.*

anaphylactoid reaction (an"ă-fĭ-lak"toyd") [*anaphylact(ic)* + *-oid*] A reaction that resembles anaphylaxis, e.g., by hives, laryngeal edema, or shock, but does not involve IgE antibodies or allergens and therefore is has no allergic basis.

ETIOLOGY: This relatively uncommon type of reaction can be caused by exercise; as the result of the release of histamine when body temperature rises; by elevated endorphin levels; by ionic compounds such as contrast media that contain radiographic iodine or polymyxin B antibiotic; by solutions containing polysaccharides such as dextran; by morphine, codeine, or meperidine; and by NSAIDs. The term should not be used as a synonym for mild anaphylaxis produced by IgE-allergen reactions.

SYMPTOMS: Anaphylactoid reactions produce hives and itching identical to those of anaphylaxis. Very rarely, severe anaphylaxis or anaphylactic shock occurs. Anaphylactoid reactions are treated with the same drugs used to treat anaphylaxis.

anaphylatoxin (an"ă-fil-ă-tok'sĭn) [*anaphyla(xis)* + *toxin*] Complement components C3a, C4a, and C5a, which cause degranulation of mast cells and release of chemical mediators that promote the smooth muscle spasm, increased vascular permeability, increased mucus secretion, and attraction of neutrophils and eosinophils associated with systemic anaphylaxis.

anaphylaxis (an"ă-fĭ-lak'sĭs) [*ana-* + *(pro)phylaxis*] A sudden, severe allergic reaction between an allergenic antigen and immunoglobulin E (IgE) bound to mast cells, which stimulates the sudden release of immunological mediators locally or throughout the body. The first symptoms occur within minutes, and a recurrence may follow hours later (late-stage response). Anaphylaxis can only occur in someone previously sensitized to an allergen because the initial exposure causes immunoglobulin E (IgE) to bind to mast cells. Anaphylaxis may be local or systemic. Local anaphylactic reactions include hay fever, hives, and allergic gastroenteritis. Systemic anaphylaxis produces peripheral vasodilation, bronchospasm, and laryngeal edema and can be life-threatening. **anaphylactic** (-lak'tik), *adj.*

ETIOLOGY: IgE antibodies react when the allergen is introduced a second time. The mast cells release packets containing chemical mediators (degranulators) that attract neutrophils and eosinophils and stimulate urticaria, vasodilation, increased vascular permeability, and smooth muscle spasm, esp. in the bronchi and gastrointestinal tract. Chemical anaphylactic mediators include histamine, proteases, chemotactic factors, leukotrienes, prostaglandin

D, and cytokines, e.g., TNF-α and interleukins 1, 3, 4, 5, and 6. The most common agents triggering anaphylaxis are food, drugs, and insect stings. Local anaphylactic reactions are also commonly triggered by pollens, e.g., hay fever, allergic rhinitis, allergic asthma. SEE: *anaphylactic shock.*

SYMPTOMS: Local anaphylaxis causes such signs as urticaria (hives), edema, warmth, and erythema to appear at the site of allergen-antibody interaction. In systemic anaphylaxis the respiratory tract, cardiovascular system, skin, and gastrointestinal system are involved. The primary signs are urticaria, angioedema, flushing, wheezing, dyspnea, increased mucus production, nausea and vomiting, and feelings of generalized anxiety. Systemic anaphylaxis may be mild or severe enough to cause shock when massive vasodilation is present.

TREATMENT: Local anaphylaxis is treated with antihistamines or, occasionally, epinephrine if the reaction is severe. Treatment for systemic anaphylaxis includes protection of the airway and administration of oxygen; antihistamines, e.g., diphenhydramine or cimetidine to block histamine H_1 and H_2 receptors; IV fluids to support blood pressure; and vasopressors, e.g., epinephrine or dopamine, to prevent or treat shock. Epinephrine is also used to treat bronchospasm. Generally, drugs are given intravenously; drugs may also be given intramuscularly, e.g., diphenhydramine, or endotracheally, e.g., epinephrine. In mild cases they may be given subcutaneously. Corticosteroids may be used to prevent recurrence of bronchospasm and increased vascular permeability.

PATIENT CARE: *Prevention:* A history of allergic reactions, particularly to drugs, blood, or contrast media, is obtained. The susceptible patient is observed for reaction during and immediately after administration of any of these agents. The patient is taught to identify and avoid common allergens and to recognize an allergic reaction.

Patients also should be taught to always wear tags identifying allergies to medications in order to prevent inappropriate treatment during an emergency. Those who have had an anaphylactic reaction and are unable to avoid future exposure to allergens should carry a kit containing a syringe of epinephrine and be taught how to administer it. Patients allergic to the venom of Hymenoptera (bees, wasps, hornets) can receive desensitization.

active a. Anaphylaxis resulting from injection of an antigen.

aggregate a. Anaphylaxis stimulated by antigen-antibody complexes in the blood, which in turn cleave complement and degranulate mast cells and basophils.

biphasic a. Protracted anaphylaxis.

exercise-induced a. Anaphylactoid reaction.

idiopathic a. Anaphylaxis of uncertain cause. Some evidence suggests it may occasionally result from exposure to food allergens.

local a. Arthus reaction.

passive a. Anaphylaxis induced by injection of serum from a sensitized animal into a normal one. After a few hours the latter becomes sensitized.

passive cutaneous a. ABBR: PCA. A laboratory test of antibody levels in which serum from a sensitized person is injected into the skin. Intravenous injection of an antigen accompanied by Evan's blue dye at a later time reacts with the antibodies produced in response to the antigen, creating a wheal and blue spot at the site, indicating local anaphylaxis.

protracted a. A recurrence of anaphylactic symptoms (bronchospasm, hypotension) several hours after successful treatment for anaphylaxis, in the absence of a new exposure to a triggering antigen. SYN: *biphasic a.*

systemic a. A reaction between IgE antibodies bound to mast cells and an allergen that causes the sudden release of immunological mediators in the skin, respiratory, cardiovascular, and gastrointestinal systems. The consequences may range from mild, e.g., itching, hives, to life-threatening (airway obstruction and shock).

anaplasia (an"ă-plā'zh(ē-)ă) [*ana-* + *-plasia*] Loss of cellular differentiation and function characteristic of most malignancies. **anaplastic** (-plas'tik), *adj.*

Anaplasma phagocytophilum (an"ă-plaz'mă fag"ō-sī-tof'ĭ-lŭm) A small gram-negative coccus that is an obligate intracellular parasite. It can be transmitted to humans by tick bite and is the cause of the disease formerly known as human granulocytic ehrlichiosis (now known as anaplasmosis). It was formerly called *Ehrlichia phagocytophila.*

anaplasmosis (an"ă-plaz-mō'sĭs) [*Anaplasma* + *-osis*] Infection with species of *Anaplasma.* Although the disease is usually found in cattle, humans may sometimes contract it after a tick bite. Anaplasmosis is characterized by fevers, chills, muscle aches, headache, and interstitial pneumonia.

anapnea (an"ap-nē'ă) [*ana-* + *-pnea*] 1. Respiration. 2. Restoration of breath.

anapneic (ăn"ăp-nē'ĭk) Pert. to anapnea or relieving dyspnea.

anapophysis (an"ă-pof'ĭ-sis) [*ana-* + *apophysis*] An accessory spinal process of a vertebra, esp. a thoracic or lumbar vertebra.

Anaprox, Anaprox DS Naproxen.

anapyrexia (an"ă-pī-rek'sē-ă) [*ana-* + *pyrexia*] A decrease in body temperature below normal. SEE: *hypothermia*.

anarthria (an-ar'thrē-ă) [¹*an-* + *arthro-* + *-IA*] Loss of motor power to speak distinctly. It may result from a neural lesion or a muscular defect. SYN: *aphemia*.

anasarca (an"ă-sar'kă) [*ana-* + *sarco-*] Generalized accumulation of serous fluid; generalized edema. **anasarcous** (-sar'kŭs), *adj.*

anaspadias (an"ă-spā'dē-ăs) [*ana-* + Gr. *spadōn*, a eunuch] Epispadias.

anastole (ă-nas'tŏ-lē) [Gr. *anastolē*, a pushing back] Shrinking away or retraction of the edges of a wound.

anastomose (ă-nas'tŏ-mōz" -mōs") [Gr. *anastomōsis*, an opening] **1.** To communicate directly or by means of connecting two parts together, esp. nerves or blood vessels. **2.** To connect parts, esp. tubular parts, surgically.

anastomosis (ă-nas"tŏ-mō'sĭs, -mō'sēz") *pl.* **anastomoses** [Gr., *anastomōsis*, opening] **1.** A natural communication between two vessels. The communication may be direct or through connecting channels. **2.** The surgical or pathological connection of two tubular structures. **anastomotic** (-mot'ĭk), *adj.*

antiperistaltic a. Anastomosis between two parts of the intestine so that the peristaltic flow in one part is the opposite of that in the other.

arteriovenous a. Anastomosis between an artery and a vein by which the capillary bed is bypassed.

crucial a. An arterial anastomosis on the back of the thigh, formed by the medial femoral circumflex, inferior gluteal, lateral femoral circumflex, and first perforating arteries.

end-to-end a. Anastomosis in which the ends of two structures are joined.

Galen a. SEE: under *Galen, Claudius*.

heterocladic a. Anastomosis between branches of different arteries.

homocladic a. Anastomosis between branches of the same artery.

Hyrtl a. SEE: *Hyrtl anastomosis*.

ileal pouch anal a. A reservoir constructed in the terminal ileum of patients who have undergone colectomy, designed to create fecal continence. The pouch is anastomosed to the anus. A concurrent temporary proximal ileostomy is most often performed. The pouch may be sewn or stapled together in a J-, W-, or S-shape. The procedure is complicated by inflammation ("pouchitis") in about 50% of patients or by stricture formation in about 10% of patients.

intestinal a. Surgical connection of two portions of the intestines. SYN: *enteroenterostomy*.

isoperistaltic a. Anastomosis between two parts of the intestine such that the peristaltic flow in both parts is in the same direction.

magnetic ring a. A surgical instrument that holds two segments of resected bowel together with progressively increasing magnetic force. It is used to help restore bowel continuity in patients who have had colonic resection. It consists of two cobalt magnetic circles embedded in polyester and applied to the bowel so that the submucosal layers of the resected bowel segments are brought into tight apposition. After 7 to 12 days of intestinal healing, the submucosal and intermediate layers of bowel necrose, and the intestines expel the magnets by peristalsis.

PATIENT CARE: The patient is observed for evidence of dehiscence. Stools are examined for unusual amounts of bleeding and for the passage of the magnetic ring.

portal-systemic a. Any of the venous connections between the portal circulation and the main systemic circulation. These veins provide alternative routes by which venous blood normally shunted through the liver can reach the inferior vena cave and then the heart. Veins in the portal circulation have no valves; thus blood can travel backwards in the portal system if the pressure becomes greater than in the systemic system.

precapillary a. Anastomosis between small arteries just before they become capillaries.

side-to-side a. Anastomosis between two structures lying or positioned beside each other.

terminoterminal a. Anastomosis between the peripheral end of an artery and the central end of the corresponding vein and between the distal end of the artery and the terminal end of the vein.

ureteroureteral a. Anastomosis between two parts of the same ureter.

uterotubal a. Anastomosis between the uterus and fallopian tube.

anatomic, anatomical (ăn"ă-tom'ik, i-kăl) [Gr. *anatomikos*, pert. to dissection] Pert. to the anatomy of an organism. **anatomically** (-i-k(ă-)lē), *adv.*

anatomic snuffbox, anatomical snuffbox A depression in the skin formed at the posterior base of the thumb when the thumb is extended from the hand. The lateral (outer) wall of the snuff box is formed from the tensed tendons of the abductor pollicis longus and extensor pollicis brevis; the medial wall is formed by the tensed tendon of the extensor pollicis longus; the proximal wall is formed by the styloid process of the radius, and the distal wall is formed by the base of the first metacarpal. Under the floor of the snuff box, the scaphoid and trapezium wrist bones can sometimes be felt, and the radial artery runs under the snuff box as it loops laterally around the thumb. SEE: illus.

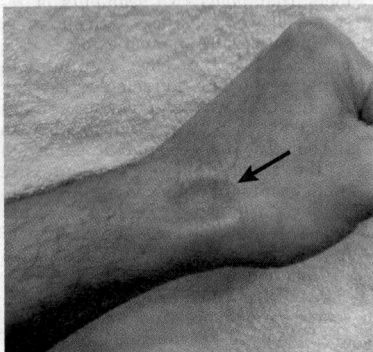

ANATOMIC SNUFFBOX

anatomist (ă-nat′ŏ-mĭst) A student of or specialist in anatomy.

anatomy (ă-nat′ŏ-mē) [Gr. *anatomē*, cutting up, dissection] **1.** The structure of an organism. **2.** The branch of science dealing with the structure of organisms.

applied a. **1.** The study of body structures to determine how they influence the body's performance and its susceptibility to disease. **2.** The study of the body's construction for guiding endoscopy, surgery, or other forms of invasive therapy.

comparative a. The comparison of similar body structures as they are found both in embryos and in the adult forms of different animals. Comparative anatomy is used to explore the hypothesis that through natural selection organisms evolved from one another.

descriptive a. Description of individual parts of the body. SYN: *systematic a.*

developmental a. The study of the development of an organism's body structures from the moment of fertilization of the egg, through the embryonic period, the fetal period, birth, childhood, adolescence, and adulthood.

gross a. The study of body structures that are visible with the naked eye, including muscles, tendons, bones, nerves, blood vessels, and viscera. SYN: *macroscopic a.*

macroscopic a. Gross a.

microscopic a. Study of structure by use of a microscope. SYN: *histology.*

morbid a. Pathological a.

pathological a. The anatomy of abnormal, diseased, or injured tissue. SYN: *morbid a.*

radiological a. Anatomy based on the radiological appearance of tissues and organs.

sectional a. Study of anatomy from

transverse, sagittal, coronal, or oblique sections.

surface a. The study of the form and markings of the surface of the body, esp. as they relate to underlying structures.

systematic a. Descriptive anatomy.

topographic a., topographical anatomy The anatomy of a portion of the body and of the relationships of the parts to each other.

anatoxin (an″ă-tok′sĭn) [*ana- + toxin*] **1.** Toxoid. **2.** A powerful nerve toxin produced by certain blue-green algae. **anatoxic** (-toks′ĭk), *adj.*

anatropia (an″ă-trō′pē-ă) [*ana- + -tropia*] Anaphoria.

anaxon, anaxone (ă-nak′son″, sōn″) [*¹an- + axon*] A nerve cell, as of the retina, having no axon.

ANC *absolute neutrophil count; Army Nurse Corps.*

anchor (ang′kŏr) [L. *ancora, anchora,* fr Gr. *ankyra,* anchor] **1.** Any structure that provides stability for a prosthetic dental appliance, e.g., a crown, bridge, or denture. The anchor may be a metal implant, a natural tooth, or part of a fixed bridge. **2.** In emergency medicine, to tie or attach a rope or sling so it will not move and can support the weight of the rescuers, basket, and patient. **3.** A tree, rock, door casing, or other strong stable device that will not move when a rescuer and patient's weight are attached to it. **4.** In cell biology, a scaffold within the cell or its membranes, on which enzymes or other important molecules are suspended.

anchorage (ang′kŏ-răj) **1.** Surgical fixation, as of prolapsed abdominal organs. **2.** The fixation of a prosthesis to a fixed support structure or anchor.

anchoring error SEE: under *error.*

ancillary (an′sĭ-ler″ē) [L. *ancillaris,* pert. to a handmaid] **1.** Subordinate, secondary. **2.** Auxiliary, supplementary.

anconal, anconeal (ang′kŏn-ăl, kŏ′nē-ăl) [Gr. *ankōn,* elbow + *-al*] Pert. to the elbow.

anconeus (ang-kō′nē-ŭs) [L. fr. Gr. *ankōn,* elbow] The short extensor muscle of the forearm, located on the back of the elbow. It arises from the back portion of the lateral epicondyle of the humerus, and its fibers insert on the side of the olecranon and upper fourth of the shaft of the ulna. It extends the forearm and stabilizes the ulna in pronation of the wrist.

ancrod (an′krod″) An enzyme purified from the venom of a Malayan pit viper and used as an anticoagulant.

Ancylostoma (ang″kĭ-los′tŏ-mă, an″sĭ-) [Gr. *ankylos,* crooked + *stoma,* mouth] A genus of nematodes of the family Ancylostomatidae whose members are intestinal parasites and include the hookworms. SYN: *Ankylostoma.*

A. braziliense A species of hookworm

that infests dogs and cats and may cause cutaneous larva migrans in humans. SEE: *larva migrans, cutaneous*.

A. caninum A species of hookworm that infests dogs and cats and may cause cutaneous larva migrans in humans. SEE: *larva migrans, cutaneous*.

A. duodenale A species of hookworm widely found in the Caribbean, South America, Africa, and Asia that causes ancylostomiasis in humans. SEE: *Necator americanus*.

Ancylostomatidae (ang″kĭ-lō″stō″mat′ĭ-dē, an″sĭ-) [*Ancyclostoma* + *-idae*] A family of nematodes belonging to the suborder Strongylata. It includes the genera *Ancylostoma* and *Necator*.

ancylostomiasis, ankylostomiasis (ang″kĭ-lō-stŏ-mī′ă-sĭs, an″sĭ-) [*Ancylostoma* + *-iasis*] Hookworm disease or infestation. It often produces iron-deficiency anemia because of the blood lost to the parasite from the gastrointestinal tract. SEE: *hookworm*.

ancyroid, ankyroid (ansī′royd″, ang-kĭ′royd″) [Gr. *ankyra*, anchor + *-oid*] Shaped like the fluke of an anchor.

Andersen disease (an″dĕr-sĕn) [Dorothy H. Andersen, U.S. pediatrician, 1901–1963] Glycogen storage disease, type IV. SEE: *glycogen storage disease*.

Andersen syndrome, Andersen-Tawil syndrome (an′dĕr-sĕn) An autosomal dominant channelopathy in which abnormal potassium release by cardiac or somatic cells results in a triad of symptoms, including life-threatening ventricular irritability. Affected patients are prone to periodic paralysis, prolonged QT syndrome with cardiac dysrhythmias, and subtle facial findings, e.g., broad forehead with narrow maxilla or chin.

andragogy (an′dră-gō-jē, goj-) [*andro-* + *(ped)agogy*] The study of adult education and how it differs from the education of children.

andro (ăn′drō) The colloquial term for *androstenedione*.

andro-, andr- [Gr. *anēr*, stem *andr-*, man (as opposed to a woman)] Prefixes meaning *man, male,* or *masculine*.

androgalactozemia (an″drō-gă-lak″tō-zē′mē-ă) [*andro-* + *galacto-* + Gr. *zēmia*, loss] Oozing of milk from a man's breast.

androgen (an′drŏ-jĕn) [*andro-* + *-gen*] A substance that produces or stimulates the development of male characteristics. Androgens include testosterone, androsterone, and dehydroandrosterone and are secreted by the interstitial tissue of the testis and by the adrenal cortex of both sexes. **androgenic** (-jen′ik), *adj.* SYN: *androgenic hormone*.

adrenal a. Any of the male sex hormones produced and released by the adrenal glands instead of by the testes. In

women, they may cause subfertility, infertility, or other conditions.

androgenetic (an″drō-jĕ-net′ik) [*andro-* + *genetic*] Pert. to or caused by male hormones.

androgen excess Hyperandrogenism.

androgen insensitivity syndrome ABBR: AIS. A relatively rare X-linked intersex condition occurring in about 1 in 20,000 births, in which individuals who have both an X and a Y chromosome and are therefore genotypically male are resistant to the effects of male hormones and appear phenotypically female. AIS can be complete or partial. In those affected with AIS, variations in the structure of the androgen receptor, which binds circulating testosterone and other androgens, block the uptake of these hormones and the transcription of genes that promote a masculine body type. SYN: *testicular feminization*.

androgenism (an″drŏj′ĕ-nizm) [*androgen* + *-ism*] Hyperandrogenism.

androgen receptor antagonist SEE: under *antagonist*.

androgen suppression therapy Treatment of prostate cancer by reducing the circulating levels of testosterone. It may be accomplished by continuously or intermittently blocking male hormone production.

androgyne (ăn′dră-jĭn″) [″ + *gyne,* woman] A female pseudohermaphrodite.

androgynoid (ăn-drŏj′ĭ-noyd) [″ + ″ + *eidos,* form, shape] A person possessing female gonads (ovaries) but secondary sex characteristics of a male (a female pseudohermaphrodite). Term is less commonly used for a person possessing male gonads (testes) but secondary sex characteristics of a female (a male pseudohermaphrodite).

androgynous (an-drŏj′ĭ-nŭs) [*andro-* + Gr. *gynē,* woman + *-ous*] **1.** Resembling or pert. to an androgynoid. **2.** Having both male and female sexual characteristics.

androgynus (ăn-drŏj′ĭ-nŭs) A female pseudohermaphrodite. SYN: *androgyne*.

android (ăn′droyd) [″ + *eidos,* form, shape] Resembling a male; manlike.

andrology (an-drol′ŏ-jē) [*andro-* + *-logy*] The scientific study of men's health. It examines the effects of male hormones on men's aging, body structure, psychology, reproductive capacity, and sexual performance.

andromimetic (an″drō-mĭ-met′ik) [*andro-* + *mimetic*] Imitating an androgen or the effect of one.

andromorphous (an″drŏ-mor′fŭs) [*andro-* + *morph-*] Resembling a male in physical structure and appearance.

andropause (an′drŏ-powz″) [*andro-* + *pause*] Any of the psychological and physiological changes caused in aging men by the gradual decrease in male hormones. Andropause is thought by some researchers to be a male equivalent of menopause. Its signs and symptoms include bone loss, loss of lean body mass, depression, fatigue, and diminished sexual interest and decreased sexual potency. It is treated with testosterone.

androphobia (an″drŏ-fō′bē-ă) [*andro-* + *-phobia*] Morbid fear of men.

androstane (an′drō-stān″) A steroid hydrocarbon, $C_{19}H_{32}$, that is the precursor of androgenic hormones.

androstenedione (an-drŏ-stēn″dī′ōn″, -stēn′dē-ōn″) A precursor of testosterone used orally by some athletes to enhance performance or increase body bulk. Androstenedione is banned by most sporting organizations.

androsterone (an-dros′tĕ-rōn″) [*andro-* + *-sterone*] $C_{19}H_{30}O_2$; an androgenic steroid found in the urine. It is a metabolite of testosterone and androstenedione and has been synthesized. As one of the androgens, androsterone contributes to the characteristic changes of growth and development of the genitals and axillary and pubic hair, deepening of the voice, and development of the sweat glands in the male.

-ane [L. *-anus*, adj. suffix] Suffix in chemistry used in naming *saturated hydrocarbons*, e.g., *butane*.

anecdote (a′nek-dōt″) [L. *anecdota*, unpublished items fr Gr. *anekdoton*, unpublished] A brief report of an isolated or unique observation. **anecdotal** (a″nek-dō′tălt), *adj.*

anechoic (a″nĕ-kō′ik) Sonolucent.

anejaculation (an″ĕ-jak″yŭ-lā′shŏn) [*ʹan-* + *ejaculation*] The inability to release semen. Spinal cord injury is a frequent cause.

anemia (ă-nē′mē-ă) [*ʹan-* + *-emia*] A reduction in the mass of circulating red blood cells. People are considered anemic when their hemoglobin levels are more than two standard deviations below the mean level in their hospital's laboratory. The diagnosis of anemia is influenced by variables such as the patient's age (neonates are anemic at levels of hemoglobin that would be considered polycythemic in some adults), gender (men have higher hemoglobin levels than women), pregnancy status (hemodilution in pregnancy lowers measured hemoglobin), residential altitude, and ethnic or racial background. **anemic** (-nē′mik), *adj.* **anemically** (mik(ă-)lē), *adv.*

Symptomatic anemia exists when hemoglobin content is less than that required to meet the oxygen-carrying demands of the body. If anemia develops slowly, however, there may be no functional impairment even though the hemoglobin is less than 7 g/100/dL of blood.

Anemia is not a disease but rather a symptom of other illnesses. It is classified on the basis of mean corpuscular volume as microcytic (80), normocytic (80–94), and macrocytic (>94); on the basis of mean corpuscular hemoglobin as hypochromic (27), normochromic (27–32), and hyperchromic (>32); and on the basis of etiological factors.

ETIOLOGY: Anemia may be caused by bleeding, e.g., from the gastrointestinal tract or the uterus; vitamin or mineral deficiencies, esp. vitamin B_{12}, folate, or iron; decreases in red blood cell production, e.g., bone marrow suppression in kidney failure or bone marrow failure in myelodysplastic syndromes; increases in red blood cell destruction as in hemolysis due to sickle cell anemia; or increases in red blood cell sequestration by the spleen (as in portal hypertension), or administration of toxic drugs (as in cancer chemotherapy).

SYMPTOMS: Anemic patients may experience weakness, fatigue, lightheadedness, breathlessness, palpitations, angina pectoris, and headache. Signs of anemia may include a rapid pulse or rapid breathing if blood loss occurs rapidly. The chronically anemic may have pale skin, mucous membranes, or nail beds and fissures at the corners of the mouth.

TREATMENT: Treatment of anemia must be specific for the cause. The prognosis for recovery from anemia is excellent if the underlying cause is treatable.

Anemia due to excessive blood loss: For acute blood loss, immediate measures should be taken to stop the bleeding, to restore blood volume by transfusion, and to combat shock. Chronic blood loss usually produces iron-deficiency anemia.

Anemia due to excessive blood cell destruction: The specific hemolytic disorder should be treated.

Anemia due to decreased blood cell formation: For deficiency states, replacement therapy is used to combat the specific deficiency, e.g., iron, vitamin B_{12}, folic acid, ascorbic acid. For bone marrow disorders, if anemia is due to a toxic state, removal of the toxic agent may result in spontaneous recovery.

Anemia due to renal failure, cancer chemotherapy, HIV, and other chronic diseases: Erythropoietin injections are helpful.

PATIENT CARE: The patient is evaluated for signs and symptoms, and the results of laboratory studies are reviewed for evidence of inadequate erythropoiesis or premature erythrocyte destruction. Prescribed diagnostic studies are scheduled and carried out. *Rest*: The patient is evaluated for fatigue; care and activities are planned and regular rest periods are scheduled. *Mouth care*: The patient's mouth is inspected daily for glossitis, mouth lesions, or ulcers. A sponge stick is recommended for oral care, and alkaline mouthwashes are suggested if mouth ulcers are present. A dental consultation may be required. *Diet*: The patient is encouraged to eat small portions at frequent intervals. Mouth care is provided before meals. The nurse or a nutritionist provides counseling based on type of anemia. *Medications*: Health care professionals teach the patient about medication actions, desired effects, adverse reactions, and correct dosing and administration. *Patient education*: The cause of the anemia and the rationale for prescribed treatment are explained to the patient and family. Teaching should cover the prescribed rest and activity regimen, diet, prevention of infection, including the need for frequent temperature checks, and the continuing need for periodic blood testing and medical evaluation. SEE: *Nursing Diagnoses Appendix*.

achlorhydric a. A hypochromic, microcytic anemia associated with a lack of free hydrochloric acid in gastric juice.

aplastic a. Anemia caused by a severe decrease in the number of stem cells and/or white blood cell ancestors. SEE: illus.

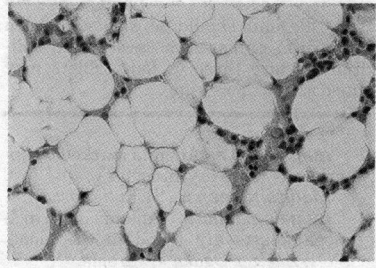

APLASTIC ANEMIA

(×200)

TREATMENT: Many patients can be treated effectively with bone marrow transplantation or immunosuppressive drugs.

PATIENT CARE: The patient and family are educated about the cause and treatment of the illness. Measures to prevent infection are explained, and the importance of adequate rest is emphasized. In the acute phase, prescribed treatment is carried out; side effects of drugs and transfusions are explained, and a restful environment for the patient is ensured. If the patient's platelet count is low (less than 20,000/cu mm), the following steps are taken to prevent hemorrhage: avoiding parenteral injec-

tions, suggesting the use of an electric razor, use of humidifying oxygen to prevent dry mucous membranes, and promoting regular bowel movements with stool softeners and dietary measures. Pressure is applied to all venipuncture sites until bleeding has stopped, and bleeding is detected early by checking for occult blood in urine and stools and by assessing the skin for petechiae and ecchymoses. Standard precautions and careful handwashing (and protective isolation if necessary) are used; a diet high in vitamins and protein is provided, and meticulous oral and perianal care are provided. The patient is assessed for life-threatening hemorrhage, infection, adverse effects of drug therapy, or blood transfusion reactions. Throat, urine, and blood cultures are performed when indicated to identify infection. SEE: *protective **isolation***.

autoimmune hemolytic a. ABBR: AIHA. Anemia caused by antibodies produced by the patient's own immune system that destroy red blood cells. They are classified by the thermal properties of the antibody involved; the *warm* form is most common and may be associated with viral infections. Drug-induced hemolytic anemias are clinically indistinguishable from AIHA and are therefore classified with this disorder.

a. of chronic inflammation Inflammatory **a.**

congenital hemolytic a. Any of a group of inherited chronic diseases marked by disintegration of red blood cells, jaundice, splenomegaly, and gallstones. Hereditary spherocytosis is the most common of these hemolytic diseases. Other such anemias include congenital elliptocytosis, hereditary stomatocytosis, and hemolytic anemias caused by enzymatic defects of the red cell, of which glucose-6-phosphate dehydrogenase and pyruvate kinase deficiency are the most important. SYN: *hemolytic **icterus**; hemolytic **jaundice***. SEE: *glucose-6-phosphate dehydrogenase*.

congenital hypoplastic a. Diamond-Blackfan anemia.

Cooley a. SEE: *Cooley anemia*.

deficiency a. Anemia due to lack of an essential ingredient such as iron or vitamins in the diet or the inability of the intestine to absorb them. SYN: *nutritional **a***.

Diamond-Blackfan a. SEE: *Diamond-Blackfan anemia*.

erythroblastic a. Anemia resulting from inheritance of a recessive trait responsible for interference with hemoglobin synthesis. SYN: ***thalassemia*** major.

folic acid deficiency a. Anemia resulting from a deficiency of folic acid. It is a cause of megaloblastic anemia and is common in patients with nutritional deficiencies, e.g., alcoholics, patients with malabsorption, and during hemolysis or pregnancy. Folate deficiency during pregnancy increases the risk of thrombocytopenia, hemorrhage, infection, and fetal neural tube defects.

PATIENT CARE: Fluid and electrolyte balance is monitored, particularly in the patient with severe diarrhea. The patient can obtain daily folic acid requirements by including an item from each food group in every meal; a list of foods rich in folic acid (green leafy vegetables, asparagus, broccoli, liver and other organ meats, milk, eggs, yeast, wheat germ, kidney beans, beef, potatoes, dried peas and beans, whole-grain cereals, nuts, bananas, cantaloupe, lemons, and strawberries) is provided. The rationale for replacement therapy is explained, and the patient is advised not to stop treatment until test results return to normal. Periods of rest and correct oral hygiene are encouraged.

hemolytic a. Anemia resulting from the destruction of erythrocytes by drugs, artificial heart valves, toxins, snake venom, infections, and antibodies. Drugs may either destroy the erythrocyte membrane directly or stimulate production of autoantibodies that lyse the erythrocytes. Children may develop hemolytic anemia in response to destruction of erythrocytes by viral and bacterial organisms. Artificial valves cause physical damage to the erythrocyte membrane during the circulation of blood through the heart. SEE: *hemolytic uremic syndrome.*

hyperchromic a. Anemia in which mean corpuscular hemoglobin concentration is higher than normal. The red blood cells are darker staining than normal.

hypochromic a. Anemia in which hemoglobin is deficient and mean corpuscular hemoglobin concentration is lower than normal.

hypoplastic a. A term for aplastic anemia. If anemia caused by failure of formation of red blood cells is meant, pure red blood cell aplasia is the proper term.

inflammatory a. Anemia due to chronic disease. SYN: *a. of chronic inflammation.*

iron-deficiency a. ABBR: IDA. Anemia resulting from a greater demand on stored iron supplies than can be provided. The erythrocyte count may sometimes be normal, but there is insufficient hemoglobin. Erythrocytes are hypochromic and show poikilocytosis. IDA is present in about 8% of men and 14% of women ages 3 to 74 years in the U.S.

ETIOLOGY: IDA is caused by inadequate iron intake, malabsorption of iron, blood loss, pregnancy and lactation, intravascular hemolysis, or a combination of these factors.

SYMPTOMS: Chronically anemic patients often complain of fatigue and dyspnea on exertion. Iron deficiency resulting from rapid bleeding may produce palpitations, orthostatic dizziness, or syncope.

DIAGNOSIS: Laboratory studies reveal decreased iron levels in the blood, with elevated iron-binding capacity and a diminished transferrin saturation. Ferritin levels are low. The bone marrow does not show stainable iron.

ADDITIONAL DIAGNOSTIC STUDIES: Adult nonmenstruating patients with IDA should be evaluated to rule out a source of bleeding in the gastrointestinal tract.

TREATMENT: Dietary iron intake is supplemented with oral ferrous sulfate or ferrous gluconate (with vitamin C to increase iron absorption). Oral liquid iron supplements should be given through a straw to prevent staining of the teeth. Iron preparations cause constipation; laxatives or stool softeners should be considered as concomitant treatment. When underlying lesions are found in the gastrointestinal tract, e.g., ulcers, esophagitis, cancer of the colon, they are treated with medications, endoscopy, or surgery.

⚠️ Parents should be warned to keep iron preparations away from children because three or four tablets may cause serious poisoning.

macrocytic a. Anemia marked by abnormally large erythrocytes.

Mediterranean a. SEE: *thalassemia.*

megaloblastic a. Anemia in which megaloblasts are found in the blood. SYN: *Zuelzer-Ogden syndrome.*

microcytic a. Anemia marked by abnormally small red blood cells. SEE: *iron-deficiency a.; thalassemia.*

milk a. In a young child, iron-deficiency anemia caused by consistent consumption of milk in amounts greater than 1 qt daily. This excessive milk intake displaces iron-rich foods in the diet.

a. of the newborn Hemoglobin levels less than 14 g/dL in term newborns. Common causes include peripartum bleeding, hemolytic disease of the newborn, twin-to-twin transfusion (15% to 30% of all monochorionic twins with abnormalities of placental blood vessels), and impaired red cell manufacture caused by glucose-6-phosphate dehydrogenase deficiency.

normochromic a. Anemia in which

the red blood cells contain the normal amount of hemoglobin.

normocytic a. Anemia in which the size and hemoglobin content of red blood cells remain normal (the mean corpuscular volume is 80–100 fL).

nutritional a. Deficiency **a.**

pernicious a. A chronic, macrocytic anemia marked by achlorhydria. It occurs most often in 40- to 80-year-old northern Europeans with fair skin but has been reported in other races and ethnic groups. It is rare in Africans and Asians.

ETIOLOGY: Pernicious anemia is an autoimmune disease. The parietal cells of the stomach lining fail to secrete enough intrinsic factor to ensure intestinal absorption of vitamin B_{12}, the extrinsic factor. This is the result of atrophy of the glandular mucosa of the fundus of the stomach and is associated with absence of hydrochloric acid.

SYMPTOMS: Symptoms include weakness, sore tongue, paresthesias (tingling and numbness) of the extremities, and gastrointestinal symptoms such as diarrhea, nausea, vomiting, and pain; in severe anemia, there may be signs of cardiac failure.

TREATMENT: Vitamin B_{12} is given parenterally or, in patients who respond, intranasally or orally.

physiological a. of pregnancy Pseudoanemia of pregnancy due to an increase of plasma that exceeds the production of red blood cells. SEE: **pseudoanemia** of pregnancy.

a. of prematurity Anemia that gradually develops in the first months of life in an infant born before the 37th week of gestation. It is caused by insufficient production of erythropoietin. Treatment may include red blood cell transfusions to increase iron stores and/or recombinant human erythropoietin.

runner's a. Mild hemolysis with hematuria, hemoglobinemia, and hemoglobinuria produced by strenuous exercise, including running. The anemia may be caused by the destruction of red blood cells during repeated striking of the ground by the runner's feet, by plasma volume expansion, and by intestinal blood loss. Blood may be lost in the feces, presumably due to transient ischemia of the gut during vigorous exercise.

septic a. Anemia due to severe infection.

sickle cell a. An autosomal recessive disorder that causes an abnormality of the globin genes in hemoglobin. The frequency of the genetic defect responsible for this chronic anemia disorder is highest among African American, native African, and Mediterranean populations. The disease also affects people from the Caribbean and Central and South America. Approximately 75,000 people in the U.S. have sickle cell anemia. The illness affects 1 of every 500 African American babies. Roughly 8% of the African American population carry the sickle cell trait. Sickle cell anemia during pregnancy increases the risk of crisis, preeclampsia, urinary tract infection, congestive heart failure, and pulmonary infarction. Use of supplemental oxygen during labor is recommended. SEE: *hemoglobin S disease; Nursing Diagnoses Appendix.*

ETIOLOGY: When both parental genes carry the same defect, the person is homozygous for hemoglobin S, i.e., HbSS, and manifests the disorder. When exposed to a decrease in oxygen, hemoglobin S becomes viscous. This causes the red cells to become crescent-shaped (*sickled*), rigid, sticky, and fragile, increasing red-cell destruction (hemolysis). When sickled red blood cells clump together, circulation through the capillaries is impeded, causing obstruction, tissue hypoxia, and further sickling. In infants younger than 5 months old, high levels of fetal hemoglobin inhibit the reaction of the hemoglobin S molecule to decreased oxygen.

SYMPTOMS: The shortened life span of the abnormal red cells (10 to 20 days) results in a chronic anemia; pallor, weakness, and fatigue are common. Jaundice may result from hemolysis of red cells. Crisis may occur as a result of sickling, thrombi formation, vascular occlusion, tissue hypoxia, and infarction. People with sickle cell anemia are at increased risk of bacterial infections relative to the general population. Specific risks include osteomyelitis, meningitis, pneumonia, and sepsis from agents such as *Streptococcus pneumoniae, Mycoplasma,* and *Chlamydia.* Sickle cell patients with fever, cough, and/or regional pain should begin antibiotic therapy immediately after cultures for blood and urine and diagnostic x-rays are obtained. Sickle cell anemia also increases the risk for ischemic organ and tissue damage. Intensely painful episodes (crises) affecting the extremities, back, chest, and abdomen can last from hours to weeks and are the most frequent cause of hospitalization. Crises can be triggered by hypoxemia, infection, dehydration, and worsening anemia. Sickle cell crisis should be suspected in the sickle cell patient with pale lips, tongue, palms, or nail beds; lethargy; listlessness; difficulty awakening; irritability; severe pain; or temperature over 104°F (37.8°C) lasting at least 2 days. Life-threatening complications may arise from damage to specific internal organs, including splenic infarcts, myocardial infarction, acute chest syndrome, liver injury, aplastic anemia, and multiorgan dysfunction syndrome. SEE: *sickle cell crisis.*

TREATMENT: Supportive therapy includes supplemental iron and blood transfusion. Administration of hydroxyurea stimulates the production of hemoglobin F and decreases the need for blood transfusions and painful crises. Prophylactic daily doses of penicillin have demonstrated effectiveness in reducing the incidence of acute bacterial infections in children. Life-threatening complications require aggressive transfusion therapy or exchange transfusion, hydration, oxygen therapy, and the administration of high doses of pain relievers. Bone marrow transplantation, when a matched donor is available, can cure sickle cell anemia.

PATIENT CARE: During a crisis, patients are often admitted to the hospital to treat pain and stop the sickling process. Adequate pain control is vital. Morphine is the opioid of choice to manage pain because it has flexible dosing forms, proven effectiveness, and predictable side effects. It should be administered using patient-controlled analgesia, continuous low-dose intravenous infusions, or sustained-release pain relievers to maintain consistent blood levels. Supplemental short-acting analgesics may be needed for breakthrough pain. Side effects of narcotic pain relievers should be treated with concurrent administration of antihistamines, antiemetics, stool softeners, or laxatives. When administering pain relievers, care providers should assess pain using a visual analog scale to evaluate the effectiveness of the treatment. Other standard pain-reduction techniques, such as keeping patients warm, applying warm compresses to painful areas, and keeping patients properly positioned, relaxed, or distracted may be helpful. Patients and families are to be advised never to use cold applications for pain relief because this treatment aggravates sickling. If transfusions are required, packed red blood cells (leukocyte-depleted and matched for minor antigens) are administered, and the patient is monitored for transfusion reactions. Scheduled deep breathing exercises or incentive spirometry helps to prevent atelectasis, pneumonia, and acute chest syndrome. During remission, the patient can prevent some exacerbations with regular medical checkups; the use of medications such as hydroxyurea; consideration of bone marrow transplantation; avoiding hypoxia (as in aircraft or at high altitudes); excessive exercise; dehydration; vasoconstricting drugs; and exposure to severe cold. The child must avoid restrictive clothing, strenuous exercise and body-contact sports but can still enjoy most activities. Additional fluid should be consumed in hot weather to help prevent dehydration. Patients and families should be advised to seek care at the onset of fevers or symptoms suggestive of infectious diseases. Annual influenza vaccination and periodic pneumococcal vaccination may prevent these common infectious diseases. Affected families should be referred for genetic counseling regarding risks to future children and for psychological counseling related to feelings of guilt. Screening of asymptomatic family members may determine whether some are heterozygous carriers of the sickling gene. Families affected by sickle cell anemia may gain considerable support in their communities or from national associations such as the American Sickle Cell Anemia Association, www.ascaa.org.

splenic a. Enlargement of the spleen due to portal or splenic hypertension with accompanying anemia, leukopenia, thrombocytopenia, and gastric hemorrhage. SEE: *Banti syndrome; congestive* **splenomegaly.**

transfusion-dependent a. Anemia for which the only effective therapy is repeated blood transfusions.

⚠ Iron overload may be a complication of therapy, esp. after the transfusion of over 10 units of blood.

anemometer (a″nĕ-mom′ĕ-tĕr) [Gr. *anemos,* wind + *-meter*] In pulmonary function studies, a device for measuring the rate of air flow through a tube. The rate at which air flows into or out of the lung may be measured by using a calibrated anemometer.

anemophobia (a″nĕ-mō-fō′bē-ă) [Gr. *anemos,* wind, + *-phobia*] Morbid fear of drafts or of the wind.

anencephaly (an″en-sef′ă-lē) [Gr. *an-,* not, + *enkephalos,* the brain] Congenital absence of the brain and cranial vault, with the cerebral hemispheres missing or reduced to small masses. This condition is incompatible with life. In the U.S., it is present in about 11 of 100,000 births. This defect results from the lack of closure of the anterior neural tube. Like other neural tube defects, the risk for anencephaly can be reduced with folic acid supplementation (800 mg daily) taken by women before and during pregnancy. SEE: *neural tube defect.* **anencephalic, anencephalus** (an″en-sĕ′făl-ik, an″en-sef′ă-lŭs), *adj.*

anephric (ă-nef′rik, ā″) [¹*an-* + *nephric*] Without kidneys.

anephrogenesis (ā″nef″rō-jen′ĕ-sĭs) [¹*an-* + *nephro-* + *genesis*] Congenital absence of the kidneys.

anergasia (an″ĕr-gā′zh(ē-)ă) [¹*an-* +

Gr. *ergasia,* work] Functional inactivity, or an organic psychosis resulting from a structural lesion of the central nervous system.

anergia (ă-nĕr'jē-ă) [¹*an-* + Gr. *ergon,* work + *-ia*] Inactivity; lack of energy.

anergy (an'ĕr-jē) Impairment in cell-mediated immune responsiveness to stimulation by an antigen. **anergic** (ă-nĕr'jik, an'ĕr), *adj.*

aneroid (an'ĕ-royd″) [¹*an-* + Gr. *nēros,* wet, fluid + *-oid*] Operating without fluid, such as an aneroid barometer that uses atmospheric pressure instead of a liquid such as mercury.

anerythroplasia (an″ĕ-rith″rō-plā′zh(ē-)ă) [¹*an-* + *erythroplasia*] Absence of red blood cell formation in the bone marrow. **anerythroplastic** (-plas′tik), *adj.*

anerythropsia (an″er-ĭ-throp′sē-ă) [¹*an-* + *erythropsia*] Inability to distinguish clearly the color red.

anesthecinesia, anesthekinesia (ă-nes″thĭ″sĭ-nē′zh(ē-)ă, -kĭ-nē′zh(ē-)ă) [¹*an-* + *esthesi-* + *-kinesia*] Sensory and motor paralysis.

anesthesia (an″ĕs-thē′zhă) [¹*an-* + *esthesi-* + *-ia*] **1.** Partial or complete loss of sensation, with or without loss of consciousness, as a result of disease, injury, or administration of an anesthetic agent, usually by injection or inhalation.

PATIENT CARE: *Preoperative:* Before induction of anesthesia, contact lenses, hearing aids, dentures (partial plates as well as full sets), wristwatches, and jewelry are removed. The anesthesiologist or nurse-anesthetist interviews and examines the patient briefly, assessing general respiratory and cardiovascular health. The patient is questioned regarding compliance with prescribed preoperative fasting. The American Society of Anesthesiologists Guidelines recommend minimum fasting as follows: 2 hours for clear liquids, 4 hours for breast milk, 6 hours for formula, nonhuman milk, or a light meal (tea and toast), and 8 hours for a regular meal (easily remembered as "2-4-6-8"). These guidelines may be modified by individual surgeons for particular patients and their conditions. Baseline vital signs are assessed and recorded. An ECG, CBC, serum chemistries, and urinalysis are ordered for many general surgeries unless results of recent tests are available. Allergies, previous surgeries, and any untoward responses to anesthetic agents are reviewed, along with any special patient restrictions. If a menstruating female is using a tampon, it is removed and replaced with a perineal pad. Depending on the patient's health status and the planned procedure, nasal oxygen, monitoring electrodes, and graduated compression stockings are applied. An intravenous route is established, and, after determining that the proper informed consent form has been signed, induction relaxation medication is administered.

Postoperative: During emergence from general anesthesia, the patient's airway is protected and vital signs monitored. Level of consciousness, status of protective reflexes, motor activity, and emotional state are evaluated. The patient is reoriented to person, place, and time; this information is repeated as often as necessary. For patients who have received ketamine, a quiet area with minimal stimulation is provided. Children may be disoriented, hallucinatory, or physically agitated as they emerge from general anesthesia. A security toy and the presence of parents may help them maintain orientation and composure. The temperatures of elderly patients should be monitored, heat loss prevented, and, as necessary, active rewarming provided. The mental status and level of consciousness of each patient should be carefully observed for changes. Patients' eyeglasses and hearing aids are returned to them as soon as possible. Before nerve block anesthesia, an intravenous infusion is established to ensure hydration. The patient is protected with side rails and other safety measures, and the anesthetized body part is protected from prolonged pressure. For regional anesthesia, sympathetic blockade is assessed by monitoring sensory levels along with vital signs (the block will wear off from head to toe, except for the sacrum and perineum, which wear off last). In obstetrics, maternal hypotension results in diminished placental perfusion and potential fetal compromise; therefore, hydration and vital signs must be closely monitored. Outcomes indicating returned sympathetic innervation include stable vital signs and temperature, ability to vasoconstrict, perianal pinprick sensations ("anal wink"), plantar flexion of the foot against resistance, and ability to sense whether the great toe is flexed or extended. The patient must tolerate oral fluids (unless restricted) and urinate before discharge. If the patient is at risk for postanesthesia headache, oral or intravenous hydration is administered, and the patient is encouraged to remain flat in bed. Prescribed analgesics are administered, and comfort measures, breathing exercises, abdominal support, and position changes are provided.

2. The science and practice of anesthesiology.

basal a. A level of unconsciousness just above the level of complete surgical anesthesia. The patient does not respond to verbal stimuli but does react to noxious stimuli (e.g., a pinprick). Basal anesthesia may be combined with local or regional anesthesia in some forms of surgery.

block a. A regional anesthetic injected into a nerve (intraneurally) or immediately around it (paraneurally). SYN: *conduction a.; neural a.*

bulbar a. Anesthesia produced by a lesion of the pons.

caudal a. Anesthesia produced by insertion of a needle into the sacrococcygeal notch and injection of a local anesthetic into the epidural space. SYN: *caudal catheter.*

central a. Pathological anesthesia due to a lesion of the central nervous system.

closed a. A method of inhalation anesthesia in which exhaled gases are rebreathed. This requires appropriate treatment of the exhaled gas to absorb the expired carbon dioxide and to replenish the oxygen and the anesthetic.

conduction a. Block **a.**

crossed a. Anesthesia of the side opposite to the site of a central nervous system lesion.

dissociative a. A type of anesthesia marked by catalepsy, amnesia, and marked analgesia. The patient experiences a strong feeling of dissociation from the environment.

a. dolorosa 1. Pain or reduced sensation limited to either the occipital nerve or a branch of the trigeminal nerve. **2.** Pain in an anesthetized zone, as in thalamic lesions.

electric a. Anesthesia induced with electric current.

electronic dental a. ABBR: EDA. In dentistry, the use of low levels of electric current to block pain signals en route to the brain. The patient controls the current through a handheld control. The current creates no discomfort and, unlike local anesthesia, leaves no numbness to wear off once the dental work is completed. SEE: *audioanalgesia; patient-controlled analgesia.*

endotracheal a. Anesthesia in which gases are administered via a tube inserted into the trachea.

epidural a. Anesthesia produced by injection of a local anesthetic into the peridural space of the spinal cord. SYN: *peridural a.* SEE: illus.

ethylene a. Ethylene given as a combination of oxygen 20%, cyclopropane 10%, and ethylene 70%. Because it is a rather weak anesthetic, volatile and inflammable, it is rarely, if ever, used.

general a. Anesthesia that produces complete loss of consciousness. General anesthesia is a medically controlled coma. Patients under general anesthesia do not respond to words or touch and cannot breathe spontaneously or protect their airway.

hypotensive a. Anesthesia during which the blood pressure is lowered.

hypothermic a. General anesthesia during which the body temperature is lowered.

hysterical a. Bodily anesthesia occurring in conversion disorders.

inadequate a. Anesthesia in which the patient is not comfortably sedated or relieved of pain. Common findings are spontaneous eye opening, grimacing, swallowing, or sweating. Vital signs may reveal unexpected hypertension or tachycardia.

infiltration a., infiltrative a. Local anesthesia produced by an injection of an anesthetic directly into the tissues.

inhalation a. General anesthesia produced by the inhalation of vapor or gaseous anesthetics, e.g., ether, nitrous oxide, and methoxyflurane.

insufflation a. Instillation of gaseous anesthetics into the inhaled air.

intrapleural a. SEE: *interpleural analgesia.*

intrathecal a. Intrathecal **analgesia.**

intratracheal a. Anesthesia administered through a catheter advanced

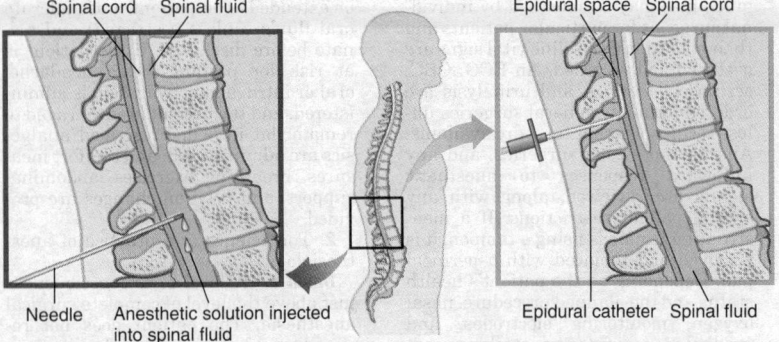

Spinal cord   Spinal fluid

Epidural space   Spinal cord

Needle   Anesthetic solution injected into spinal fluid

Epidural catheter   Spinal fluid

EPIDURAL ANESTHESIA

through the upper airway and vocal cords into the trachea.

local a. The pharmacological inhibition of nerve impulses in a body part. It is typically used to facilitate treatment of a small lesion or laceration or to perform minor surgery. Commonly used agents include lidocaine, bupivacaine, or novocaine. All local anesthetic agents work by decreasing the flow of sodium ions into nerve cells, blocking the action potential of the cells. SEE: *block a.; infiltration a.*

mixed a. General anesthesia produced by more than one drug, such as propofol for induction, followed by an inhaled drug for maintenance of anesthesia.

neural a. Block **a.**

neuraxial a. Caudal, epidural, or spinal anesthesia.

open a. Application, usually by dropping, of a volatile anesthetic agent onto gauze held over the nose and mouth.

paravertebral a. Injection of a local anesthetic at the roots of spinal nerves.

peridural a. Epidural **a.**

peripheral a. Local anesthesia produced when a nerve is blocked with an appropriate agent.

primary a. The first stage of general anesthesia, before unconsciousness.

pudendal a. Local anesthesia used primarily in obstetrics (e.g., to facilitate pelvic surgery or childbirth). The pudendal nerve on each side, near the spinous process of the ischium, is blocked.

rectal a. General anesthesia produced by introduction of an anesthetic agent into the rectum, used esp. in managing pediatric patients.

regional a. Nerve or field blocking, causing loss of sensation in a dermatome innervated by a specific nerve. SEE: *block a.; infiltration a.*

saddle block a. Anesthesia produced by introducing the anesthetic agent into the fourth lumbar interspace to anesthetize the perineum and the buttocks.

segmental a. Anesthesia due to a pathological or surgically induced lesion of a nerve root.

sexual a. Loss of genital sensation, with accompanying secondary sexual dysfunction.

spinal a. **1.** Anesthesia resulting from disease or injury to conduction pathways of the spinal cord. **2.** Anesthesia produced by injection of anesthetic into the subarachnoid space of the spinal cord.

SIDE EFFECTS: Common adverse reactions to spinal anesthesia include backache, bradycardia, headache, lowered blood pressure, and urinary retention. SYN: *subarachnoid block*. SEE: illus.

splanchnic a. Anesthesia produced

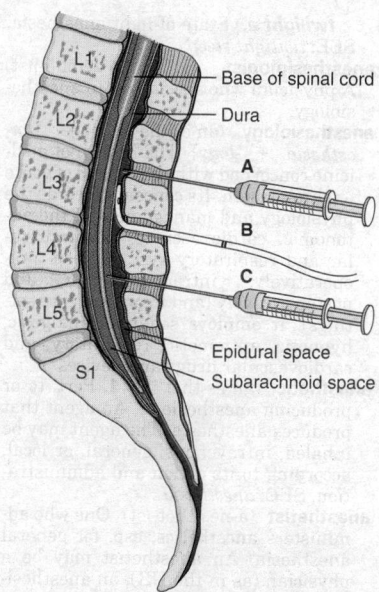

INJECTION OF SPINAL ANESTHESIA

(A) Epidural anesthesia, (B) epidural catheter, (C) spinal anesthesia

by injection of an anesthetic into the splanchnic ganglion.

stages of a. The distinct series of steps through which anesthesia progresses. The first stage of pharmacologically induced general anesthesia includes preliminary excitement until voluntary control is lost. Because hearing is the last sense to be lost, the conversation of operating room staff should be guarded during this stage. The second stage consists of loss of voluntary control. In the third stage there is entire relaxation, no muscular rigidity, and deep regular breathing.

surgical a. Depth of anesthesia at which relaxation of muscles and loss of sensation and consciousness are adequate for the performance of surgery.

tactile a. Loss of sense of touch.

topical a. Local anesthesia induced by application of an anesthetic directly onto the surface of the area to be anesthetized.

total intravenous a. ABBR: TIVA. The sole use of intravenous drugs without any inhalational agents for operative or procedural anesthesia.

traumatic a. Loss of sensation resulting from nerve injury.

tumescent a. The injection of large volumes of diluted lidocaine, bicarbonate, and epinephrine subcutaneously for use in local anesthesia. This procedure is most often used before liposuction to limit blood loss and pain.

twilight a. State of light anesthesia. SEE: *twilight sleep.*

anesthesiologist (an″ĕs-thē″zē-ol′ŏ-jĭst) A physician who specializes in anesthesiology.

anesthesiology (an″ĕs-thē″zē-ol′ŏ-jē) [*anesthesia* + *-logy*] The branch of medicine concerned with the control of acute or chronic pain. Its concerns include the physiology and management of the autonomic, cardiovascular, neuromuscular and respiratory systems, esp. preoperatively, intraoperatively, and postoperatively (and in critical care settings). It employs sedative, analgesic, hypnotic, antiemetic, respiratory, and cardiovascular drugs and devices.

anesthetic (an″ĕs-thet′ik) **1.** Pert. to or producing anesthesia. **2.** An agent that produces anesthesia. The agent may be inhaled, intravenous, general, or local, according to its action and administration. SEE: *anesthesia.*

anesthetist (ă-nes′thĕt-ĭst) One who administers anesthetics, esp. for general anesthesia. An anesthetist may be a physician (as in the UK), an anesthesiologist, or a specially trained nurse.

anesthetize (ă-nes′thĕ-tīz″) To give anesthetic drugs in order to block or relieve pain. **anesthetization** (-tĭ-zā′shŏn), *n.*

anetoderma (ă″nĕ-tō-dĕr′mă) [Gr. *anetos,* relaxed, + *derma,* skin] Localized laxity of the skin with protruding, saclike areas. These lesions are due to loss of normal skin elasticity and can be excised. SYN: *macular atrophy.*

aneuploidy (an′ū-ployd″ē) [¹*an-* + *eu-* + Gr. *-ploos, -fold* + *-oid*] Condition of having an abnormal number of chromosomes for the species indicated. **aneuploid** (an′ū-ployd″), *adj.*

aneuploidy screening The testing of embryos for evidence of sex-linked diseases and structural chromosomal defects before their implantation in the uterus during assisted reproduction. Aneuploidy screening is one means of decreasing the risk of genetic diseases in implanted embryos.

aneurysm, aneurism (an′yŭ-rizm) [Gr. *aneurysma,* a widening] Localized abnormal dilatation of a blood vessel, usually an artery, due to a congenital defect or weakness in the wall of the vessel. As aneurysms dilate, they become more and more vulnerable to rupture. **aneurysmal** (an″yŭ-riz′măl), *adj.*

ETIOLOGY: As people age, the combined effects of high blood pressure and atherosclerotic weakening of arteries produce most aneurysms in the aorta. Congenital malformations of arteries in the circle of Willis are relatively common causes of aneurysms in the brain. Aneurysms in the chest or peripheral arteries are sometimes caused by blunt trauma or by bacterial or mycotic infection.

abdominal aortic a. ABBR: AAA. A localized dilatation (saccular, fusiform, or dissecting) of the wall of the abdominal aorta. It is generally found to involve the renal arteries and frequently the iliac arteries. Occasionally the dilatation can extend upward through the diaphragm.

The patient is usually asymptomatic, and diagnosis is made accidentally during a routine physical examination or abdominal x-ray or during screening of the elderly hypertensive male. Serial ultrasounds confirm the diagnosis and determine the size, shape, and location of the aneurysm. Small, asymptomatic aneurysms may be followed over time, rather than repaired (see below). Computed tomography, magnetic resonance imaging, or aortography may assist in confirming the diagnosis and the condition of proximal and distal vessels.

SYMPTOMS: Symptoms include generalized abdominal pain, low back pain unaffected by movement, and sensations of gastric or abdominal fullness. Sudden severe lumbar or abdominal pain radiating to the flank and groin, esp. if associated with tachycardia and hypotension, may indicate enlargement or imminent rupture. Signs can include a pulsating mass in the periumbilical area and a systolic bruit over the aorta.

TREATMENT: Untreated abdominal aortic aneurysms gradually enlarge and in some instances rupture. The likelihood of rupture increases for aneurysms that are larger than 5.5 cm. Surgical repair is recommended for all aneurysms larger than 6 cm. If an aneurysm is tender and known to be enlarging rapidly (no matter what its size), surgery is strongly recommended. Surgical therapy consists of replacing the aneurysmal segment with a synthetic fabric (Dacron) graft. Immediate surgery is indicated for a ruptured aortic abdominal aneurysm. An alternative treatment to traditional laparotomy is to insert a bypass graft percutaneously into the aorta.

PATIENT CARE: In acute dissection of an abdominal aortic aneurysm, oxygenation, blood pressure, and cardiac rhythm are closely monitored, and a pulmonary artery line may be inserted to monitor hemodynamics. The patient is observed for signs of rupture, which may be fatal. He or she will require an intravenous line via a large-bore catheter, a urinary catheter, and an arterial line and pulmonary artery catheter to monitor fluid and hemodynamic balance. Additionally, cardiac monitor electrodes will be placed, and a nasogastric tube inserted.

Prescribed medications are administered to manage contributory factors such as hypertension and hypercholesterolemia; a beta-adrenergic blocking agent may be prescribed to reduce the risk of expansion and rupture. The patient is instructed in their use and taught about adverse effects that should be reported. In acute aortic rupture, admission to the intensive care unit is arranged, a blood sample is obtained for typing and cross-matching, and a large-bore (14G) venous catheter is inserted to facilitate blood replacement. The patient is prepared for and informed about elective surgery if indicated or emergency surgery if rupture occurs. The patient will require an intravenous line via a large-bore catheter, a urinary catheter, and an arterial line and pulmonary artery catheter to monitor fluid and hemodynamic balance. Additionally, cardiac monitor electrodes will be placed, and a nasogastric tube inserted. During surgery the patient will be intubated and mechanically ventilated, and such therapies will most likely still be in place postoperatively in the ICU.

Desired outcomes include the patient's ability to express anxiety, use support systems, and perform stress-reduction techniques that assist with coping; to demonstrate abatement of physical signs of anxiety; to avoid activities that increase the risk of rupture; to understand and cooperate with the prescribed treatment regimen; to identify indications of rupture and to institute emergency measures; to maintain normal fluid and blood volume in acute situations; and to recover from elective or emergency surgery with no complications. Generally post-operative patients are assisted to ambulate by the second day after surgery. Pain management and psychological support are extremely important during the acute postoperative period.

PREVENTION: Because of the relatively high incidence of AAA in men over age 60 (esp. smokers or men with intermittent claudication) and patients with myesthenia gravis, screening for AAA is recommended for these people.

aortic a. An aneurysm affecting any part of the aorta from the aortic valve to the iliac arteries. The dilated artery is usually asymptomatic, detected as an incidental finding during imaging. SEE: illus.

arteriovenous a. An aneurysm of congenital or traumatic origin in which an artery and vein become connected. Symptoms may include pain, expansive pulsation, and bruits or, occasionally, high-output heart failure.

atherosclerotic a. Aneurysm due to degeneration or weakening of the arterial wall caused by atherosclerosis.

Bérard a. SEE: *Bérard aneurysm.*

berry a. A small saccular congenital aneurysm of a cerebral vessel. It communicates with the vessel by a small opening. Rupture of this type of aneurysm may cause subarachnoid hemorrhage, a devastating form of stroke.

cerebral a. Aneurysm of a blood vessel in the brain.

Charcot-Bouchard a. SEE: *Charcot-Bouchard aneurysm.*

cirsoid a. A dilatation of a network of vessels commonly occurring on the scalp. The mass may form a pulsating subcutaneous tumor. SYN: *racemose a.*

compound a. Aneurysm in which some of the layers of the vessel are ruptured and others dilated.

dissecting a. Aneurysm in which the blood makes its way between the layers of a blood vessel wall, separating them; a result of necrosis of the medial portion of the arterial wall. SEE: *aortic aneurysm* for illus.

fusiform a. Aneurysm in which all the walls of a blood vessel dilate more or less equally, creating a tubular swelling. SEE: *aortic a.* for illus.

mycotic a. Aneurysm due to bacterial infection.

racemose a. Cirsoid **a.**

sacculated a. Aneurysm in which there is weakness on one side of the vessel; usually due to trauma. It is attached to the artery by a narrow neck. SEE: *aortic a.* for illus.

varicose a. Aneurysm forming a blood-filled sac between an artery and a vein.

venous a. Localized expansion and weakening of the wall of a vein.

aneurysmectomy (an″yŭ-riz-mek′tŏ-mē) [*aneurysm* + *-ectomy*] Surgical removal of the sac of an aneurysm.

aneurysmoplasty (an″yŭ-riz′mŏ-plas″tē) [*aneurysm* + *-plasty*] Surgical repair of an aneurysm.

aneurysmorrhaphy (an″yŭ-rĭz-mor′ă-fē) [*aneurysm* + *-rrhaphy*] Surgical closure of the sac of an aneurysm in con-

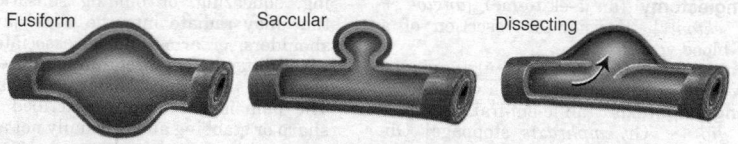

Fusiform   Saccular   Dissecting

AORTIC ANEURYSMS

junction with additional maneuvers such as bypass grafting.

aneurysmotomy (an″yū-rĭz-mot′ŏ-mē) [*aneurysm* + *-tomy*] Incision of the sac of an aneurysm.

ANF *American Nurses Foundation.*

angel dust SEE: *phencyclidine hydrochloride.*

Angelica sinensis (an-jel′ĭ-kă sĭ-nen′sĭs) [L., Chinese angelic (plant)] The scientific name for dong quai.

Angelman syndrome (ān′jĕl-măn, ăn′) [Harry Angelman, Brit. pediatrician, 1915–1996] A rare genetic condition marked by severe mental retardation, microcephaly, and paroxysms of laughter. It is due to an abnormal chromosome 15 of maternal origin. SEE: *Prader-Willi syndrome.*

angel's trumpet *Datura ruaveolens,* a flowering shrub native to the southeastern U.S. Portions of the plant are used for hallucinogenic effects. The flowers are made into a stew or tea, and the leaves are eaten. The flowers contain large quantities of the alkaloids atropine, hyoscyamine, and hyoscine. Ingestion of the plant produces intense thirst, visual disturbances, flushing, central nervous system hyperexcitability, sensory flooding, delirium, and paranoia. This is followed by hyperthermia, tachycardia, hypertension, visual hallucinations, disturbed consciousness, clonus, and subsequent convulsions. If the condition is untreated, death may occur.

TREATMENT: Treatment consists of gastric lavage, followed by 1 to 4 mg of intravenous physostigmine sulfate. This dosage should reverse the acute delirious state in 1 to 2 hr, but it may need to be repeated several times.

Angelucci syndrome (an″jĕ-loo′chē) [Arnaldo Angelucci, Italian ophthalmologist, 1854–1934] Psychological excitement, palpitations, and vasomotor disturbances associated with vernal conjunctivitis.

angel's wing Winged scapula.

anger (ang′gĕr) Extreme displeasure or exasperation in reaction to a person, a situation, or an object. Anger is instrumental in mobilizing and enhancing the ability to respond to adverse situations; for that reason, it may be essential to survival in some situations. Occasionally, anger may be a reaction to disease or dying and may be directed toward friends or family and those responsible for a patient's medical care.

angiectomy (an″jē-ek′tŏ-mē) [*angio-* + *-ektomy*] Excision or resection of a blood vessel.

angiectopia (ăn″jē-ek′tō′pē-ă) [*angio-* + *ectopia*] Displacement of a vessel.

angiemphraxis (an″jē-em-frak′sĭs) [*angio-* + Gr. *emphraxis,* stoppage] Obstruction of a vessel.

angiitis (an″jē-īt′ĭs) [*angio-* + *-itis*] In-

flammation of blood vessels. SYN: *vasculitis.*

angina (an-jī′nă, an′jĭ-) [L. *angina,* quinsy, fr. *angere,* to choke] **1.** Angina pectoris. **2.** Acute sore throat. **anginal** (an-jī′năl, an′jĭ-năl), *adj.*

abdominal a. Abdominal pain that occurs after meals, caused by insufficient blood flow to the mesenteric arteries. This symptom typically occurs in patients with extensive atherosclerotic vascular disease and is often associated with significant weight loss. SYN: *intestinal **a.**; bowel **ischemia.***

PATIENT CARE: Medical intervention for abdominal angina can include supportive care including anticoagulant therapy. Surgical intervention includes angioplasty and partial colectomy (removing the ischemic section of the bowel and reconnecting the remaining ends). It may be necessary to create a colostomy or ileostomy and to correct blockages in the mesenteric arteries. The patient must be monitored for signs and symptoms of peritonitis and/or sepsis. As the patient recovers, patient education focuses on prevention of further episodes, recognition of signs and symptoms including cramping abdominal pain after eating, blood in the stool, red or black stools, diarrhea and/or constipation. It also includes instructions and support for living with permanent or temporary colostomy or ileostomy.

a. decubitus Attacks of angina pectoris occurring while a person is in a recumbent position.

a. of effort Angina pectoris with onset during exercise. SYN: *exertional **a.***

exertional a. **A.** of effort.

intestinal a. Abdominal **a.**

Ludwig a. SEE: *Ludwig angina.*

a. pectoris An oppressive pain or pressure in the chest caused by inadequate blood flow and oxygenation to heart muscle. It is usually due to atherosclerosis of the coronary arteries and, in Western cultures, is one of the most common emergent complaints bringing adult patients to medical attention. It typically occurs after (or during) events that increase the heart's need for oxygen, e.g., increased physical activity, a large meal, exposure to cold weather, or increased psychological stress. SEE: illus.; table.

SYMPTOMS: Patients typically describe a pain or pressure located behind the sternum and having a tight, burning, squeezing, or binding sensation that may radiate into the neck, jaw, shoulders, or arms and be associated with difficulty in breathing, nausea, vomiting, sweating, anxiety, or fear. The pain is not usually described as sharp or stabbing and is usually not aggravated by deep breathing, coughing, swallowing, or twisting or turning the

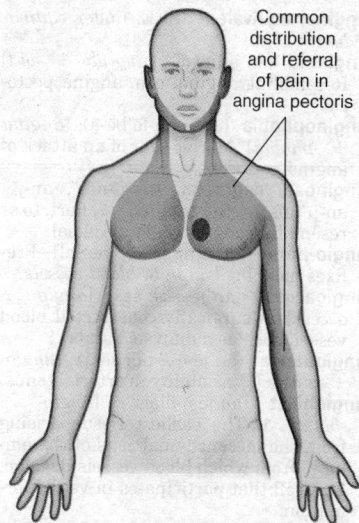

Common distribution and referral of pain in angina pectoris

ANGINA PECTORIS

muscles of the trunk, shoulders, or arms. Women, diabetics, and the elderly may present with atypical symptoms, such as shortness of breath without pain.

TREATMENT: In health care settings, oxygen, nitroglycerin, and aspirin are provided, and the patient is placed at rest. Morphine sulfate is given for pain that does not resolve after about 15 min of treatment with that regimen. Beta-blocking drugs (such as propranolol or metoprolol) are used to slow the heart rate and decrease blood pressure. They are the mainstay for chronic treatment of coronary insufficiency and are indispensable for treating unstable angina or acute myocardial infarction. At home, patients should rest and use short-act-

ing nitroglycerin. Patients with chronic or recurring angina pectoris may get symptomatic relief from long-acting nitrates or calcium channel blockers. Patients with refractory angina may be treated with combinations of all of these drugs in addition to ranolazine, a sodium channel blocker.

PATIENT CARE: The pattern of pain, including OPQRST (onset, provocation, quality, region, radiation, referral, severity, and time), is monitored and documented. Cardiopulmonary status is evaluated for evidence of tachypnea, dyspnea, diaphoresis, pulmonary crackles, bradycardia or tachycardia, altered pulse strength, the appearance of a third or fourth heart sound or mid- to late-systolic murmurs over the apex on auscultation, pallor, hypotension or hypertension, gastrointestinal distress, or nausea and vomiting. The 12-lead electrocardiogram is monitored for ST-segment elevation or depression, T-wave inversion, and cardiac arrhythmias. A health care provider should remain with the patient and provide emotional support throughout the episode. Desired treatment results include reducing myocardial oxygen demand and increasing myocardial oxygen supply. The patient is taught the use of the prescribed form of nitroglycerin for anginal attacks and the importance of seeking medical attention if prescribed dosing does not provide relief. Based on his needs, the patient should be encouraged and assisted to stop smoking, maintain ideal body weight, lower cholesterol by eating a low-fat diet, keep blood glucose under control (if the patient is diabetic), limit salt intake, and exercise (walking, gardening, or swimming regularly for 45 min to an hour every day). The patient is also taught about prescribed beta-adrenergic or calcium channel

Stages of Angina Pectoris

Class	Description
I	Ordinary physical activity, such as walking or climbing stairs, does not cause angina. Angina occurs with strenuous, rapid, or prolonged exertion at work or recreation.
II	Slight limitation of ordinary activity. Angina occurs on walking or climbing stairs rapidly, walking uphill, walking or stair climbing after meals, in cold, or in wind, under emotional stress, only during the few hours after awakening, or walking more than two level blocks and climbing more than one flight of stairs at a normal pace and in normal conditions.
III	Marked limitation of ordinary physical activity. Angina occurs on walking one to two level blocks and climbing one flight of stairs in normal conditions at a normal pace.
IV	Inability to carry on any physical activity without discomfort—angina symptoms may be present at rest.

SOURCE: Campeau, L: Grading of Angina Pectoris [letter]. Circulation 54(3), 522. Copyright 1976, American Heart Association.

blockers and any other needed interventions should they become necessary.

Four major forms of angina are identified: 1. *stable*: predictable frequency and duration of pain that is relieved by nitrates and rest; 2. *unstable*: pain that is more easily induced and increases in frequency and duration; 3. *variant*: pain that occurs from unpredictable coronary artery spasm; and 4. *microvascular*: impairment of vasodilator reserve that causes angina-like chest pain even though the patient's coronary arteries are normal. Severe and prolonged anginal pain is suggestive of a myocardial infarction. SEE: *Nursing Diagnoses Appendix.*

   preinfarction a. Angina pectoris occurring in the days or weeks before a myocardial infarction. The symptoms may be unrecognized by patients without a history of coronary artery disease.

   silent a. Unrecognized angina pectoris that presents with symptoms other than chest pain or pressure. The patient may experience dyspnea on exertion, heartburn, nausea, pain in the arm, jaw pain, tenderness in back or arms (in women), or other atypical symptoms. Silent angina pectoris occurs most often in older adults, in women, in postoperative patients who are heavily medicated, or in patients with diabetic neuropathy.

   stable a. Angina that occurs with exercise and is predictable. It is usually promptly relieved by rest or nitroglycerin.

   unstable a. ABBR: UA. Angina that has changed to a more frequent and more severe form. Its symptoms include chest pain that occurs with minimal exertion (or that progresses from pain with exertion to pain occurring with minimal exertion or at rest) and may be an indication of a severe obstruction in a coronary artery and impending myocardial infarction. It is a medical emergency, and should be aggressively managed.

   variant a. Angina due to spasm of the coronary arteries rather than from exertion or other increased demands on the heart. The pain typically occurs at rest. During coronary catheterization the spasm is usually found near an atherosclerotic plaque, often in the right coronary artery. Infusions of ergonovine may provoke it. On the electrocardiogram, the diagnostic hallmark is elevation of the ST segments during episodes of resting pain. Treatments include nitrates and calcium channel blocking drugs. Beta-blocking drugs, frequently used as first-line therapy in typical angina pectoris, are often ineffective with this angina. SYN: *Prinzmetal angina.*

   Vincent a. Necrotizing ulcerative **gingivitis**.

anginal equivalent SEE: under *equivalent.*

anginoid (an'jĭ-noyd") [*angina* + *-oid*] Resembling angina, esp. angina pectoris.

anginophobia (an"jĭ-nō-fō'bē-ă) [*angina* + *-phobia*] Morbid fear of an attack of angina pectoris.

anginose, anginous (an'jĭ-nōs", an-jī', an-jī'nŭs, an'jĭ-) [*angina*] **1.** Pert. to or resembling angina. **2.** Pharyngeal.

angio-, angi- [Gr. *angeion,* vessel] Prefixes meaning *lymph* or *blood vessels.*

angioaccess (an"jē-ō-ak'ses) [*angio-* + *access*] A surgically constructed blood vessel, such as a dialysis fistula.

angioataxia (an"jē-ō-ă-tak'sē-ă) [*angio-* + *ataxia*] Variability in arterial tonus.

angioblast (an'jē-ō-blast") [*angio-* + *-blast*] **1.** The earliest tissue arising from the mesenchymal cells of the embryo, from which blood vessels develop. **2.** A cell that participates in vessel formation.

angioblastoma (an"jē-ō-blas-tō'mă) [*angio-* + *blastoma*] Hemangioblastoma.

angiocardiogram (an"jē-ō-kar'dē-ō-gram") [*angio-* + *cardiogram*] The image of the heart and great blood vessels obtained by angiocardiography.

angiocardiography (an"jē-ō-kard"ē-og'ră-fē) [*angio-* + *cardiography*] Serial imaging, usually cineradiography, of the heart and great blood vessels after intravascular or intracardiac injection of a water-soluble contrast medium. **angiocardiographic** (ē-ō-graf'ik), *adj.*

angiocardiopathy (an"jē-ō-kar"dē-op'ă-thē) [*angio-* + *cardiopathy*] Disease of the blood vessels of the heart.

angiocarditis (an"jē-ō-kard-īt'ĭs) [*angio-* + *carditis*] Inflammation of the heart and large blood vessels.

angiocavernous (an"jē-ō-kav'ĕr-nŭs) [*angio-* + *cavernous*] Pert. to angioma cavernosum.

angiocholecystitis (an"jē-ō-kō"lĕ-sis-tīt'ĭs) [*angio-* + *cholecystitis*] Inflammation of the gallbladder and bile vessels.

angiocholitis (an"jē-ō-kō-līt'ĭs) [*angio-* + *cholitis*] Inflammation of the biliary vessels. SYN: *cholangitis.*

angiodysplasia (an"jē-ō-dis-plā'zh(ē-)ă) [*angio-* + *dysplasia*] Vascular ectasis in the mucosa of the intestine, usually the cecum, an occasional cause of lower gastrointestinal bleeding. Lesions increase with advancing age and can cause occult or obvious blood loss. SYN: *angioectasia; arteriovenous malformation.*

angioectasia (an"jē-ō-ek-tā'zh(ē-)ă) [*angio-* + *ectasia*] Angiodysplasia.

angioedema (an"jē-ō-ĕ-dē'mă) [*angio-* + *edema*] A condition marked by the development of edematous areas of skin, mucous membranes, or internal organs. It is frequently associated with urticaria. It is benign when limited to the skin but can cause respiratory distress when present in the mouth, pharynx, or larynx. It is usually the result of a type I hypersensitivity reaction. Histamine released during an immunoglobin E antibody reaction to ingested allergens such as food or drugs causes vasodilation and increased vascular permeability, producing the characteristic nonpitting, nondependent swelling that distinguishes it from regular edema. The nonallergic forms of angioedema are hereditary angioedema, which is caused by a complement deficiency, and anaphylactoid reactions. SYN: *angioneurotic edema; Quincke's disease.* SEE: *urticaria.*

TREATMENT: Antihistamines are used first for immediate relief. Epinephrine is used if swelling of the upper airways compromises breathing.

hereditary a. ABBR: HAE. A rare autosomal dominant disease marked by episodic bouts of subcutaneous and submucosal edema, esp. of the gastrointestinal tract or the upper airways. It is caused by the hereditary lack of a protein (C1 INH) that inactivates complement or by the malfunction of this protein. Physical trauma or psychological stress may precipitate attacks. The symptoms usually worsen after puberty. Anabolic steroids are typically used to treat HAE.

angioendothelioma (an″jē-ō-en″dō-thē″lē-ō′mă) *pl.* **angioendotheliomas, -mata** [*angio-* + *endothelioma*] A tumor consisting of endothelial cells, commonly occurring as single or multiple tumors of bone.

angiofibroma (an″jē-ō-fī-brō′mă) [*angio-* + *fibroma*] A tumor consisting of vascular and fibrous tissue.

angiogenesis (an″jē-ō-jen′ĕ-sĭs) [*angio-* + *-genesis*] Development of blood vessels. **angiogenic** (-jen′ik), *adj.*

angiogenic growth factor SEE: under *growth factor.*

angioglioma (an″jē-ō-glī-ō′mă, -glē′) [*angio-* + *glioma*] A tumor consisting of vascular and glial cells.

angiogram (an′jē-ŏ-gram″) [*angio-* + *-gram*] Radiographic imaging of the size, shape, and luminal structure of blood vessels after introduction of a radiopaque contrast medium. A catheter is usually inserted into a peripheral vessel and guided to the affected area by use of the Seldinger technique.

aortic a. An angiogram of the aorta; used in diagnosing aneurysms or tumors that contact and deform the aorta.

cardiac a. An angiogram of the coronary arteries, as well as the cardiac ventricles and valves.

cerebral a. An angiogram of blood vessels of the brain.

angiograph (an′jē-ŏ-graf″) [*angio-* + *-graph*] A kind of sphygmograph.

angiography (an″jē-og′ră-fē) [*angio-* + *-graphy*] **1.** A description of blood vessels and lymphatics. **2.** Diagnostic or therapeutic radiography of the heart and blood vessels with a radiopaque contrast medium. Types include magnetic resonance angiography, interventional radiology, and computed tomography.

PATIENT CARE: **Before the procedure:** health care professionals explain to the patient how a needle or catheter will be used to penetrate a blood vessel, and that a contrast agent will be injected into it to highlight the course of the vessel (map the vessel) and any abnormalities in it or associated with it. These abnormalities may include widenings and weaknesses in the blood vessels (aneurysms); narrowings of the vessel (stenoses or obstructions); abnormal connections between arteries and veins (fistulae); or unusual networks of vessels (arteriovenous malformations or in some cases, the complex blood supply of malignant tumors). Complications of angiography include damage to the blood vessel or neighboring tissues, bleeding or bruising, cardiac arrhythmias, syncope, infection, or, in very rare instances, death. These potential complications should be fully reviewed with the patient during the informed consent that precedes the procedure.

During the procedure: the patient's heart rate and rhythm are closely monitored, along with his or her blood pressure, oxygenation, mental status, and, in critically ill patients, urinary output. The patient may experience a hot flush during the injection of contrast, palpitations, or other unusual sensations. These sensations should be explained to the patient before they occur to minimize anxiety. Anxiolytics or sedatives may sometimes be administered to patients as needed.

After the procedure: the puncture site is tamponaded and bandaged and then monitored for signs of bleeding or bruising. The part of the body distal to the puncture site is periodically assessed for pulse, color, warmth, sensation, and movement. The patient is permitted to mobilize only after the puncture site is stabilized and institutional protocols are completed.

3. Recording of arterial pulse movements with a sphygmograph. **angiographic** (-ŏ-graf′ik), *adj.* **angiographically,** *adv.*

aortic a. Angiography of the aorta and its branches.

cardiac a. Angiography of the heart and coronary arteries.

catheter a. Angiography performed after a small tube is placed in a blood vessel and a contrast medium is injected to outline the internal structure of the blood vessel.

cerebral a. Angiography of the vascular system of the brain.

coronary a. Angiography of the coronary arteries to determine any pathological obstructions to blood flow to the heart muscle. It is used to provide definitive images of the coronary arteries that reveal atherosclerotic blockage to blood flow so that those blockages can be surgically bypassed, opened (with angioplasty or stenting, for example), or treated with medications. SEE: illus.

⚠️ Potential hazards of the procedure include coronary artery dissection, kidney failure resulting from exposure to angiographic contrast, and radiation exposure.

CT pulmonary a. The best contemporary test to assess a patient suspected of having a pulmonary embolism The test uses computed tomographic imaging of the pulmonary arteries to identify blood clots in the right ventricular outflow tracts or the pulmonary arteries. The presence of a clot indicates the need for treatment with anticoagulant drugs. It is used as the preferred alternative to invasive pulmonary angiography (which is accurate but requires right ventricular catheterization), or to ventilation/perfusion scanning of the lungs (which often yields indeterminate results).

⚠️ Potential hazards of the test include its radiation exposure, its risk for renal failure (esp. in patients with predisposing conditions for kidney injury), and the risk of allergy to the radiological contrast agent used in the test.

digital subtraction a. Use of a computer to investigate arterial blood circulation. A reference image is obtained by fluoroscopy. Then a contrast medium is injected intravenously. Another image is produced from the fluoroscopic image, after which the computer technique subtracts the image produced by surrounding tissues. The third image is an enhanced view of the arteries.

intravenous fluorescein a. ABBR: IVFA. The optimal diagnostic test to evaluate the vascular status of the retina and choroid. Fluorescein dye is injected into an arm vein and sequential photographs are taken of the fundus as the dye circulates at different time intervals. SEE: illus.

magnetic resonance a. ABBR: MRA. Noninvasive imaging of blood vessels by magnetic resonance imaging. The tech-

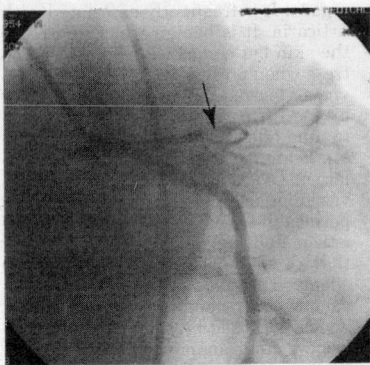

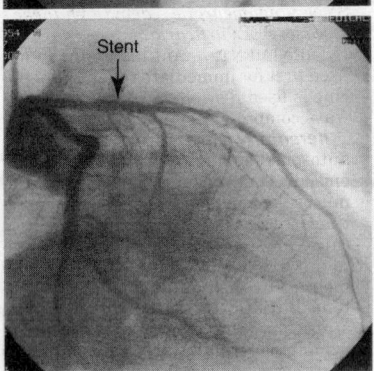

CORONARY ANGIOGRAPHY

A. tight stenosis; B. artery reopened with a stent

nique does not expose patients to ionizing radiation and avoids catheterization of the vessels. It has been used to study aneurysms, blockages, and other diseases of the carotid, coronary, femoral, iliac, and renal arteries. Studies may be done with or without contrast agents.

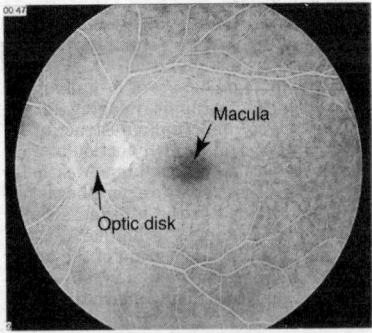

INTRAVENOUS FLUORESCEIN ANGIOGRAM

(Courtesy of Christine Chung, M.D.)

PHI-motion a. A laser imaging test to identify abnormal blood vessels in the choroidal layer beneath the retina. These abnormal vessels may leak, causing central visual field loss in age-related macular degeneration.

pulmonary a. Angiography of the pulmonary vessels (e.g., in the diagnosis of pulmonary embolism).

selective a. Angiography in which a catheter is introduced directly into the vessel to be visualized.

angiohyalinosis (an″jē-ō-hī″ă-lĭ-nō′sĭs) [*angio-* + *hyalinosis*] Hyaline degeneration of blood vessel walls.

angiohypotonia (an″jē-ō-hī″pō-tō′nē-ă) [*angio-* + *hypotonia*] Angioparalysis; angioparesis; vascular dilatation.

angioid (an′jē-oyd″) [*angio-* + *-oid*] Resembling a blood vessel.

angioid streak SEE: under *streak*.

angiokeratoma (an″jē-ō-ker″ă-tō′mă) [*angio-* + *keratoma*] A skin disorder occurring chiefly on the feet and legs, marked by formation of telangiectases or warty growths accompanied by thickening of the epidermis along the course of dilated capillaries.

angiokinetic (an″jē-ō-kĭ-net′ĭk) [*angio-* + *kinetic*] Pert. to constriction and dilation of blood vessels. SEE: *vasomotor*.

angioleukitis (an″jē-ō-loo-kīt′ĭs) [*angio-* + *leuko-* + *-itis*] Inflammation of lymphatics.

angiolipoma (an″jē-ō-lĭ-pō′mă) [*angio-* + *lipoma*] A tumor consisting of vascular and fatty cells.

angiolith (an′jē-ō-lith″) [*angio-* + Gr. *lithos,* stone] A calcified deposit in the wall of a blood vessel.

angiology (an″jē-ol′ŏ-jē) [*angio-* + *-logy*] The study of blood vessels and lymphatics.

angiolymphitis (an″jē-ō-lim-fīt′ĭs) [*angio-* + *lymph-* + *-itis*] Lymphangitis.

angiolysis (an″jē-ol′ĭ-sĭs) [*angio-* + *-lysis*] Obliteration of blood vessels, as in the umbilical cord when it is tied just after birth.

angioma (an″jē-ō′mă, ′mă-tă) *pl.* **-mas, -mata** [*angio-* + *-oma*] A usually benign tumor consisting principally of blood vessels (hemangioma) or lymph vessels (lymphangioma). It is considered to represent remnants of fetal tissue misplaced or undergoing disordered development. SEE: *epithelioma; hamartoma; nevus.* **angiomatous** (-ō′măt-ŭs), *adj.*

capillary a. A congenital, superficial hemangioma appearing as an irregularly shaped, red discoloration of otherwise normal skin, and caused by overgrowth of capillaries. SYN: **a.** *simplex.*

a. cavernosum Cavernous **a.**

cavernous a. A congenital hemangioma appearing as an elevated dark red benign tumor, ranging in size from a few millimeters to several centimeters. It may pulsate. It commonly involves the subcutaneous or submucous tissue and consists of blood-filled vascular spaces. Small cavernous angiomas may disappear without therapy. SYN: *a. cavernosum.*

cherry a. A benign, dome-shaped cherry-red papule on the trunk, consisting of a compressible mass of blood vessels measuring about 0.5 mm to 6.0 mm, and occurring esp. in people over 30. SYN: *Campbell de Morgan spot; ruby spot; senile* **a.**

senile a. Cherry **a.**

serpiginous a. An angioma marked by small red vascular dots arranged in rings, caused by proliferation of capillaries.

a. simplex Capillary **a.**

spider a. A branched growth of dilated capillaries on the skin, resembling a spider. This abnormality may be associated with cirrhosis of the liver. SYN: *nevus araneus; spider nevus.*

stellate a. A skin lesion in which numerous telangiectatic vessels radiate from a central point; commonly associated with liver disease, hypertension, or pregnancy. SYN: *spider nevus.*

telangiectatic a. An angioma composed of abnormally dilated blood vessels.

a. venosum racemosum Swelling associated with severe varicosities of superficial veins.

angiomalacia (an″jē-ō-mă-lā′sh(ē-)ă) [*angio-* + *malacia*] Softening of blood vessel walls.

angiomatosis (an″jē-ō″mă-tō′sĭs) [*angioma* + *-osis*] Condition of having multiple angiomas.

bacillary a. An acute infectious disease caused by *Bartonella quintana* or *B. henselae.* It is characterized by skin lesions that may vary from small papules to pyogenic granulomas or pedunculated masses. These occur anywhere on the skin and may involve mucous membranes. If the lesions ulcerate, they may extend to and destroy underlying bone. In addition, the organisms are disseminated to the liver, spleen, bone marrow, and lymph nodes. In the liver there may be painful, multiple, cystic, blood-filled spaces (peliosis hepatitis). Most patients with this disease are immunocompromised or infected with HIV. In the untreated immunocompetent patient, recovery may be prolonged but is usually complete. In the untreated immunocompromised patient, death is likely. When the organisms are disseminated, treatment for several months with oral doxycycline or oral erythromycin will help alter the course of the disease. Culture of the organism provides diagnosis. SEE: *cat scratch disease; trench fever.*

angiomegaly (an″jē-ō-meg′ă-lē) [*angio-* + *-megaly*] Enlargement of blood vessels, esp. in the eyelid.

angiomyocardiac (an″jē-ō-mī″ō-kard′ē-ak″) [*angio-* + *myocardiac*] Pert. to blood vessels and cardiac muscle.

angiomyolipoma (an″jē-ō-mī″ō-lĭ-pō′mă) [*angio-* + *myo-* + *lipoma*] A benign tumor containing vascular, fatty, and muscular tissues.

angiomyoma (an″jē-ō-mī-ō′mă) [*angio-* + *myoma*] A tumor composed of blood vessels and muscle tissue. SYN: *myoma telangiectodes.*

angiomyoneuroma (an″jē-ō-mī″ō-noo-rō′mă) [*angio-* + *myoneuroma*] Glomangioma.

angiomyosarcoma (an″jē-ō-mī″ō-sar-kō′mă) [*angio-* + *myosarcoma*] A malignant tumor composed of blood vessels, muscle tissue, and connective tissue.

angioneurectomy (an″jē-ō-noo-rek′tŏ-mē) [*angio-* + *neurectomy*] Excision of vessels and nerves.

angioneuromyoma (an″jē-ō-noo″rō′mī-ō′mă) [*angio-* + *neuro-* + *myoma*] Glomangioma.

angioneurotomy (an″jē-ō-noo-rot′ŏ-mē) [*angio-* + *neutotomy*] Cutting of vessels and nerves.

angionoma (an″jē-ŏ-nō′mă) [*angio-* + Gr. *nomē,* ulcer] Ulceration of a vessel.

angioparalysis (an″jē-ō-pă-ral′ĭ-sĭs) [*angio-* + *paralysis*] Vasomotor relaxation of blood vessel tone.

angiopathology (an″jē-ō-pă-thol′ŏ-jē) [*angio-* + *pathology*] Morbid changes in diseases of the blood vessels.

angiopathy (an″jē-op′ă-thē) [*angio-* + *-pathy*] Any disease of blood or lymph vessels. SYN: *angiosis.*

    amyloid a. An abnormality of cerebral blood vessels in which amyloid is

deposited in the walls of small arteries and arterioles. It may occur in those with chronic infectious and inflammatory disorders or B-cell lymphoma and is a common contributor to intracerebral hemorrhage or Alzheimer's disease in the elderly.

    cerebral proliferative angiopathy ABBR: CPA. A type of cerebral arteriovenous malformation in which normal brain tissue spaces are found within a network of abnormal capillaries. Cerebral proliferative angiopathies shunt blood away from parts of the brain and may cause headaches and /or seizures.

angiophacomatosis, angiophakomatosis (an″jē-ō-fak″ō-mă-tō′sĭs) [*angio-* + *phacomatosis*] Hippel's disease.

angioplasty (an′jē-ō-plas″tē) [*angio-* + *-plasty*] Any endovascular procedure that reopens narrowed blood vessels and restores forward blood flow. Most often angioplasties are performed on coronary, carotid, or peripheral arteries occluded by atherosclerosis. Some common angioplasty techniques include the following: *atherectomy,* which opens occluded, scarred, or calcified vessels by removing atherosclerotic plaques with rapidly rotating drills; *balloon angioplasty,* which uses the inflation of high-pressure balloons within blocked arteries to force them open; *laser and radiofrequency angioplasties,* which vaporize or ablate atherosclerotic plaques; *endovascular stents,* which hold vessels open with expandable lattices inserted across the narrowed section of the artery SEE: illus.; *percutaneous transluminal coronary a.*

    facilitated a. The treatment of acute

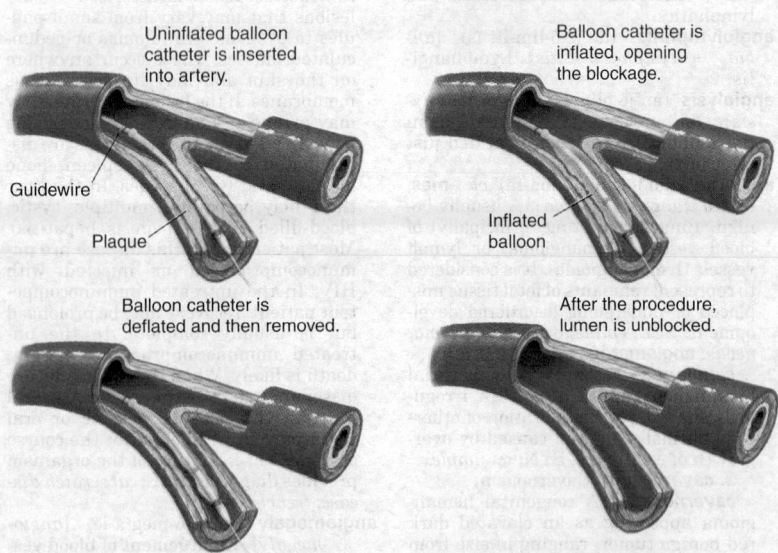

Uninflated balloon catheter is inserted into artery.

Balloon catheter is inflated, opening the blockage.

Guidewire

Plaque

Inflated balloon

Balloon catheter is deflated and then removed.

After the procedure, lumen is unblocked.

ARTERIAL BALLOON ANGIOPLASTY

myocardial infarction with small doses of clot-busting and antiplatelet drugs, followed immediately (within 1 hr) by balloon angioplasty.

laser-assisted a. The use of laser energy to vaporize an atherosclerotic plaque in a diseased coronary or peripheral blood vessel. SEE: *percutaneous transluminal coronary a.*

percutaneous transluminal coronary a. ABBR: PTCA. A percutaneous method of treating localized coronary artery narrowing without sternotomy. A special double-lumen catheter, designed so that a cylindrical balloon surrounds a portion of the vessel, is inserted through the skin into the right femoral artery. Repeated inflation and deflation of the balloon with pressure between 9 and 15 atmospheres (approximately 135 to 225 psi) dilates the narrowed vessel.

In the U.S. alone, hundreds of thousands of coronary angioplasties are performed each year. Modifications in this technique may be used to open blocked arteries in many regions of the circulation, e.g., renal, iliac, or femoral arteries.

PATIENT CARE: *Preoperative*: Angiography is used to confirm the presence and location of arterial occlusions. The cardiologist's explanation of the procedure is reinforced. The patient is encouraged to state feelings and concerns, and misconceptions are clarified. The patient is prepared physically for the procedure according to the surgeon's orders. Baseline data needed for comparison with postoperative assessment data are gathered.

Postoperative: Vital signs, cardiac rate and rhythm, and neurovascular status distal to the catheter insertion site are monitored. A Doppler stethoscope should be used if peripheral pulses are difficult to palpate. The catheter site is inspected periodically for hematoma formation, ecchymosis, or hemorrhage. The dressing is marked, and the health care provider is notified of any rapid progression. If bleeding occurs, direct pressure is applied to the catheter site. The patient should keep the punctured leg straight and limit head elevation to no more than 15° to prevent hip flexion and potential catheter migration. The patient is assessed for chest pain, which may indicate vasospasm or reocclusion of the ballooned vessel. Intravenous fluids are administered as prescribed to promote excretion of contrast medium. The patient is assessed for signs and symptoms of fluid overload, i.e., dyspnea, pulmonary crackles, distended neck veins, tachycardia, bounding pulse, hypertension, gallop rhythms. Pharmacological therapy is continued as prescribed (IV nitroglycerin, heparin). Catheter removal is explained to the patient, and direct pressure is applied to the insertion site for 30 min, followed by a pressure dressing. Vital signs continue to be monitored until it is certain that no occult hemorrhage is occurring. Discharge instructions are provided to the patient and family regarding the scheduled return visit with the cardiologist, follow-up exercise, stress testing or angiography, and any exercise prescriptions or activity restrictions (usually patients can walk 24 hr after the procedure and return to work in 2 weeks). The importance of drug regimens, including desired effects and potential adverse reactions, is reinforced.

rescue a. The use of angioplasty to open coronary arteries that remain occluded after intravenous thrombolytic therapy for acute myocardial infarction.

angiopoiesis (an″jē-ō-poy-ē′sĭs) [*angio-* + *-poiesis*] The formation of blood vessels. **angiopoietic** (-poy-et′ik), *adj.*

angiopoietin (an″jē-ō-poy-ē′tĭn; -poy′ĕ-tĭn) [*angio-* + *-poiet(ic)* + *-in*] Any of several genes (or the proteins they encode) that stimulate new blood vessel formation. The proteins encoded by angiopoietin are found in healthy cardiac endothelium and in diseased tissues such as arthritic joints and malignant tumors.

angiopressure (an′jē-ŏ-prĕsh″ŭr) [*angio-* + *pressure*] Pressure applied to a blood vessel to arrest hemorrhage.

angiorrhaphy (an″jē-or′ă-fē) [*angio-* + *-rrhaphy*] Suture of a vessel, esp. a blood vessel.

angiorrhexis (an″jē-ŏ-rek′sĭs) [*angio-* + *-rrhexis*] Rupture of a vessel, esp. a blood vessel.

angiosarcoma (an″jē-ō-sar-kō′mă) [*angio-* + *sarcoma*] A malignant neoplasm originating from blood vessels. SYN: *hemangiosarcoma*.

angiosclerosis (an″jē-ō-sklĕ-rō′sĭs) [*angio-* + *sclerosis*] Hardening of the walls of the vascular system.

angioscope (an′jē-ŏ-skōp″) [*angio-* + *-scope*] A slender fiber-optic catheter inserted directly into a blood vessel, e.g., a coronary artery, to visualize its interior.

angioscopy (an″jē-os′kŏ-pē) [*angio-* + *-scopy*] Visual examination of the inside of a blood vessel with a fiber-optic catheter. It is used primarily in the coronary arteries.

angioscotoma (an″jē-ō-skŏ-tō′mă) [*angio-* + *scotoma*] A defect in the visual field produced by the shadows of the retinal blood vessels.

angiosis (an″jē-ō′sĭs) [*angio-sn* + *-osis*] Angiopathy.

angiospasm (an′jē-ō-spazm) [*angio-* + *spasm*] Spasmodic contraction of blood vessels; may cause cramping of muscles or intermittent claudication. **angiospastic** (ăn″jē-ō-spas′tik), *adj.*

angiostatin (an″jē-ō-stat′ĭn) [*angio-* + *statin*] A protein fragment of plasminogen that inhibits the growth of blood vessels, possibly by blocking the enzyme adenosine triphosphate synthase on the endothelium. It may shrink malignant tumors by decreasing their blood supply.

angiostenosis (an″jē-ō-stě-nō′sĭs) [*angio-* + *stenosis*] Narrowing of a vessel, esp. a blood vessel.

angiosteosis (an″jē-os″tē-ō′sĭs) [*angio-* + *osteosis*] Calcification of a vessel.

angiostomy (an″jē-os′tŏ-mē) [*angio-* + *-stomy*] An operation for forming an artificial fistulous opening into a blood vessel.

angiostrongyliasis (an″jē-ō-stron″jĭ-lī′ă-sĭs) [*Angiostrongylus* + *-iasis*] Infection with *Angiostrongylus* species, a parasite commonly known as the rat lungworm.

Angiostrongylus (ăn″jē-ō-stron′jĭ-lŭs) [*angio-* + Gr. *strongylos,* round] A genus of roundworms that can cause eosinophilic meningitis in humans. This roundworm is sometimes called *rat lungworm.* Species include *A. cantonensis* and *A. costaricensis.*

angiotelectasis (an″jē-ō-tĕ-lek′tă-sĭs) [*angio-* + *tel-* + *ectasis*] Dilatation of terminal arterioles.

angiotensin (an″jē-ō-ten′sĭn) A vasopressor formed when renin is released from the kidney. It promotes the release of aldosterone.

    a. I The physiologically inactive form of angiotensin. It is converted to angiotensin II in the lungs.

    a. II ABBR: ATII. The physiologically active form of angiotensin. It raises blood pressure and stimulates production and secretion of aldosterone.

    a. amide A vasoconstricting compound of angiotensin.

angiotensin-converting enzyme inhibitor SEE: under *inhibitor.*

angiotensinogen (an″jē-ō-ten″sin″ŏ-jen″) [*angiotensin* + *-gen*] A serum globulin fraction formed in the liver; converted to angiotensin as a result of hydrolysis by renin.

angiotherapy (an″jē-ō-ther′ă-pē) [*angio-* + *therapy*] Treatment applied directly into a catheterized blood vessel. Angiotherapy is used to dissolve thrombi within arteries or veins or to infuse drugs directly into the blood supply of a tumor.

angle (ang′gĕl) [L. *angulus,* corner, angle] **1.** The figure or space outlined by the diverging of two lines from a common point or by the meeting of two planes. **2.** A projecting or sharp corner.

    A a. The orientation of the patella relative to the tibial tubercle. The angle is formed by the intersection of a line

bisecting the long axis of the patella and a passed through the tibial tubercle to the apex of the inferior pole of the patella. SEE: illus.

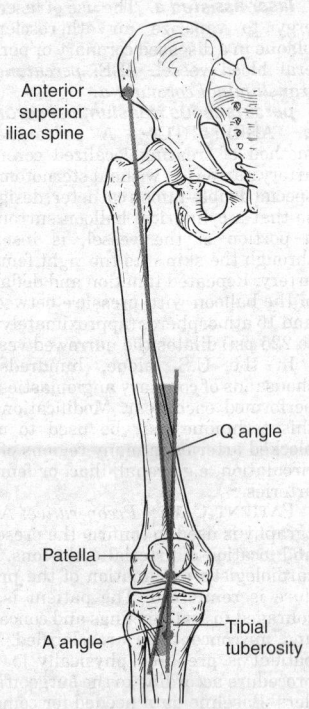

A ANGLE

The A angle is the relationship between the long axis of the patella and the tibial tuberosity; the Q angle describes the relationship between the long axis of the femur, measured from the anterior superior iliac spine.

    acromial a. The angle formed by the junction of the lateral and posterior borders of the acromion.

    acute a. An angle less than 90°.

    alpha a. The angle formed by intersection of the visual line with the optic axis.

    alveolar a. The angle between the horizontal plane and a line drawn through the base of the nasal spine and the middle point of the alveolus of the upper jaw.

    anterior chamber a. The angle between the cornea and iris at the periphery of the anterior chamber of the eye.

    biorbital a. The angle formed by the meeting of the axes of the orbits.

    cardiophrenic a. The medial inferior corner of the pulmonary cavity bordered by the heart and diaphragm.

    carrying a. The angle in the sagittal plane made at the elbow by extending the long axis of the forearm and the upper arm. This obtuse angle is more pronounced in women than in men.

caudal a. In radiology, angulation of the central ray toward the patient's feet.

cavity a. The angle formed by two or more walls of a cavity preparation in restorative dentistry.

cephalic a. In radiology, angulation of the central ray toward the patient's head.

cephalometric a. The angle formed by intersecting anthropometric lines. It is used in studies of the skull and for the diagnosis of malocclusions of dental, skeletal, and dentoskeletal origin.

cerebellopontine a. The angle formed by the junction of the cerebellum and the pons. SYN: *pontine a.*

cervicofemoral a. SEE: *a. of inclination.*

Cobb a. SEE: *Cobb angle.*

a. of convergence The angle between the visual axis and the median line when an object is looked at.

costal a. The meeting point of the lower border of the false ribs with the axis of the sternum.

costophrenic a. The lateral inferior corner of the pulmonary cavity bordered by the ribs and diaphragm.

costovertebral a. The angle formed on each side of the trunk by the junction of the last rib with the lumbar vertebrae.

craniofacial a. The angle formed by the basifacial and basicranial axes at the midpoint of the sphenoethmoidal suture.

facial a. The angle made by lines from the nasal spine and external auditory meatus meeting between the upper middle incisor teeth.

flat a. The angle between two lines that join at an angle of almost 180°.

gamma a. The angle between the line of vision and the optic axis.

gonial a. **A.** of jaw.

Hilgenreiner epiphyseal a. SEE: *Hilgenreiner epiphyseal angle.*

a. of incidence The angle between a ray striking a surface and a line drawn perpendicular to the surface at the point of incidence.

a. of inclinication (of the hip) The angle between the femoral neck and the shaft of the femur. This angle is normally 35° in infancy; with maturation of the skeleton it increases to 45°.

a. of jaw The angle formed where the vertical back edge of the ramus of the mandible meets the horizontal edge along the bottom. SYN: *gonial a.; a. of mandible.*

a. of mandible **A.** of jaw.

metafacial a. The angle between the base of the skull and the pterygoid process.

obtuse a. An angle greater than 90°.

occipital a. The angle formed at the

opisthion by the intersection of lines from the basion and from the lower border of the orbit.

ophryospinal a. The angle formed at the anterior nasal spine by the intersection of lines drawn from the auricular point and the glabella.

parietal a. The angle formed by the meeting of a line drawn tangent to the maximum curve of the zygomatic arch and a line drawn tangent to the end of the maximum frontal diameter of the skull. If these lines are parallel, the angle is zero; if they diverge, a negative angle is formed.

pontine a. Cerebellopontine **a.**

prophy a. In dentistry, a wheel containing pieces of wire. It is used for cleaning metal surfaces.

pubic a. The angle formed by the junction of the rami of the pubic bones.

Q a. The acute angle formed by a line from the anterior superior iliac spine of the pelvis through the center of the patella and a line from the tibial tubercle through the patella. The angle describes the tracking of the patella in the trochlear groove of the femur. In women, the Q angle should be less than 22° with the knee in extension and less than 9° with the knee in 90° of flexion. In men, the Q angle should be less than 18° with the knee in extension and less than 8° with the knee in 90° of flexion. SEE: *A a.* for illus.

a. of refraction The angle formed by a refracted ray of light with a line perpendicular to the surface at the refraction point.

right a. An angle of 90°.

sacrolumbar a. The angle formed by articulation of the last lumbar vertebra and the sacrum.

sacrovertebral a. The angle formed by the base of the sacrum and the fifth lumbar vertebra.

sphenoid a. The angle formed at the top of the sella turcica by the intersection of lines drawn from the nasal point and the tip of the rostrum of the sphenoid.

sternal a. The angle formed by the junction of the manubrium and the body of the sternum.

a. of Treitz The sharp curve at the duodenojejunal junction.

venous a. The angle formed by the junction of the internal jugular and subclavian veins.

visual a. The angle between the line of sight and the extremities of the object seen.

Angle classification (ang′gĕl) [Edward Hartley Angle, U.S. dentist, 1855–1930] **Classification** of malocclusion.

angor (ang′gŏr) [L. *angor,* strangling] Violent distress, as in angina pectoris.

angor animi (ang′gŏr an′ĭ-mē) [*angor* + L. *animus,* rational soul] The feeling that one is dying, as may occur in connection with angina pectoris.

angstrom unit (ang′ström) [Anders J. Ångström, Swedish physicist, 1814–1874] ABBR: A. SYMB: Å. U. An internationally adopted unit of length equal to 10^{-10} m, or 0.1 nm; used esp. to measure radiation wavelengths, including light energy.

anguidine (ang′gwĭ-dēn″) Diacetoxyscirpenol.

angular (ang′gyŭ-lăr) [L. *angularis,* having corners or angles] Having corners or angles.

angular cheilosis A disorder marked by fissures and epithelial desquamation at the corners of the mouth, esp. seen in children. The condition may be due to oral candidiasis or may be a symptom of dietary deficiency, esp. riboflavin deficiency. SYN: *perleche.*

angulation (ang″gyŭ-lā′shŏn) **1.** Abnormal formation of angles by tubular structures such as the intestines, blood vessels, or ureter. **2.** In radiology, the direction of the primary beam in relation to the film and the object being imaged. **3.** The angular relationship formed at a joint between two long bones.

    horizontal a. The position of the dental x-ray tube head in the horizontal plane. To avoid errors in x-ray interpretation, the central ray is directed perpendicular to the curve of the dental arch and film. Correct horizontal angulation produces a radiograph with "open" contacts. Incorrect horizontal angulation produces a radiograph with "overlapped" contacts.

    vertical a. The position of the dental x-ray tube head in the vertical plane, measured in degrees. The central ray is directed perpendicular to the film and the tooth when using the paralleling imaging technique. When using the bisecting angle technique, the central ray is directed perpendicular to the bisector. Errors in calculating the vertical angulation produce elongated or foreshortened images.

anhedonia (an″hē-dō′nē-ă) [¹*an-* + Gr. *hēdonē,* pleasure + -IA] Lack of pleasure in acts that are normally pleasurable. SEE: *hedonism.* **anhedonic** (-don′ik), *adj.*

anhidrosis, anidrosis (an″hi-drō′sĭs, hī-) [¹*an-* + *hidrosis*] Diminished or complete absence of secretion of sweat. It may be generalized or localized, temporary or permanent, disease related or congenital.

    TREATMENT: Treatment consists of therapy for the cause or accompanying conditions. The patient should wear soft, nonirritating clothing and use bland, soothing skin ointments and lubricants. Air conditioning provides comfort in most instances.

anhidrotic, anidrotic (an″(h)i-drot′ik,

(h)ī-) [¹*an-* + *hidrotic*] Antiperspirant.

anhydrase (an-hī′drās″) [¹*an-* + *hydaser*] An enzyme that promotes the removal of water from a chemical compound.

anhydride (an″hī′drīd″) [¹*an-* + *hydride*] A compound formed by removal of water from a substance, esp. from an acid.

anhydrous (ăn-hī′drŭs) [¹*an-* + *hydrous,* water] Lacking water. It is usually used with reference to water that could be present as an absorbed species rather than the water of crystallization.

anianthinopsy (ăn-ē-ăn′thĭn-ŏp″sē) [″ + *ianthinos,* violet, + *opsis,* vision] Inability to recognize violet or purple.

anicteric (ăn″ĭk-tĕr′ĭk) [″ + *ikteros,* jaundice] Without jaundice.

aniline (an′ĭ-lĭn) [Ult. fr. Sanskrit *nīlī,* indigo plant] The simplest aromatic amine, C_6H_7N; an oily, toxic liquid derived from benzene. It is a precursor of acetaminophen and is used to manufacture several other drugs. SYN: *aminobenzene; phenylamine.*

anilingus (ā″ni-ling′gŭs) [L. *anus* + *lingere,* to lick] Oral stimulation of the anus with the tongue or lips. SEE: *cunnilingus.*

anilinism, anilism (an′ĭl-ĭ-nizm, an′ĭl-ĭzm) [*aniline,* the indigo plant, + -*ism*] Chronic aniline poisoning. Findings include intermittent heart block, muscular weakness, cyanosis, and dizziness or vertigo.

anima (an′ĭ-mă) [L. *anima,* breath, soul] **1.** Soul. **2.** According to Carl Jung, an individual's inner self as distinguished from the external personality (persona). **3.** Jung's term for the feminine inner personality present in men. SEE: *animus.*

animal (an′ĭ-măl) [L. *animalis,* living] **1.** A living organism that requires oxygen and organic foods, is incapable of photosynthesis, has limited growth, and is capable of voluntary movement and sensation. **3. 2.** Any animal other than humans. **3.** Pert. to or from an animal.

    assistance a. Service **a.**

    cold-blooded a. An animal whose body temperature varies according to the temperature of the environment. SYN: *ectotherm; poikilotherm.*

    control a. In medical research involving the use of animals, an animal that is not treated, but is housed and cared for under the same conditions as the treated animal(s). SEE: *control* (2).

    service a. Any animal (often a dog) specially trained to assist a person who is blind, deaf, or disabled in some way. SYN: *assistance a.*

    warm-blooded a. An animal whose body temperature remains constant regardless of the temperature of the environment. SYN: *endotherm.*

animation (an″ĭ-mā′shŏn) [L. *animatio,* bestowal of life, quickening] State of being alive or active.

    suspended a. Temporary cessation of vital functions with loss of consciousness; state of apparent death.

animatism (ăn′ĭ-mă-tĭzm) [*animate* + *-ism*] Attribution of, an impersonal consciousness to everything in nature, animate and inanimate.

animism (an′ĭ-mizm) [*anima* + *-ism*] Attribution of spiritual qualities and mental capabilities to nonhuman living creatures, e.g., animals or trees, or to inanimate objects, e.g., mountains.

animus (an′ĭ-mŭs) [L. *animus,* breath, mind, soul] **1.** An animating or energizing motive or intention. **2.** A feeling of bitter hostility; a grudge. **3.** According to Carl Jung, the masculine inner personality present in women. SEE: *anima.*

anion (an′ī′ŏn) [*ana-* + Gr. *iōn,* going] An ion carrying a negative charge. It is attracted by and travels to the anode. Examples are acid radicals and corresponding radicals of their salts. SEE: *cation; electrolyte; ion.*

anionic (an″ī′ŏn′ik), *adj.*

aniridia (an″ĭ-rid′ē-ă) [¹*an-* + *irid-* + *-ia*] Congenital absence of all or part of the iris.

anisakiasis (an″ĭ-să-kī′ă-sis) [*Anisak(is)* + *-iasis*] A disease of the gastrointestinal tract accompanied by intestinal colic, fever, and abscesses. It is caused by eating the flesh of crustaceans, fish, or sea mammals infested with larval nematodes of the family Anisakidae without adequate cooking or freezing or used in raw dishes such as sashimi or sushi.

Anisakis simplex (an″ĭ-să′kis sim′pleks) A species of the genus *Anisakis,* a nematode that is an intestinal parasite typically infesting crustaceans, fish, or sea mammals. It causes anisakiasis in humans. SYN: *herring worm.*

anise (an′ĭs) [L. fr. Gr. *anison*] An annual herb, *Pimpinella anisum,* cultivated for its licorice-flavored seeds. It is used as a culinary herb, an aromatic, and a digestive aid.

aniseikonia, anisoiconia (an″ī′sī″kō′nē-ă, an″ī′sō-ī″) [*aniso-* + Gr. *eikōon,* image + *-ia*] A condition in which the size and shape of the image seen by one eye differ from the image seen by the other.

aniseikonic (kon′ik), *adj.*

anismus (ă-nĭz′mŭs) Excessive contraction of external sphincter of rectum.

aniso- [Gr. *anisos,* unequal] Prefix meaning *unequal, asymmetrical,* or *dissimilar.*

anisoaccommodation (an″ĭ′sō-ă-kom″ŏ-dā′shŏn) [*aniso-* + *accommodation*] Difference in the ability of the eyes to accommodate. SEE: *accommodation.*

anisochromatic (an″ī′sō-krō-mat′ik) [*aniso-* + *chromatic*] Not of uniform color.

anisocoria (an″ī′sō-kōr′ē-ă) [*aniso-* + Gr. *korē,* young girl, pupil (of the eye) + *-ia*] Inequality of the size of the pupils. It may be congenital or associated with aneurysms, head trauma, diseases of the nervous system, brain lesion, paresis, or locomotor ataxia. In physiologic (or benign) anisocoria the unequal size of the pupils is seen at all times, whether they are examined in well-lit or in a dark environment.

anisocytosis (an″ī′sō-sī-tō′sĭs) [*aniso-* + *cyto-* + *-sis*] A condition of excessive inequality in the size of cells, esp. erythrocytes.

anisophoria (an″ī′sō-fōr′ē-ă) [*aniso-* + *-phoria*] An eye muscle imbalance in which the horizontal visual plane of one eye is different from that of the other.

ankle (ang′kĕl) **1.** The joint between the leg and foot; the articulation of the tibia, fibula, and talus. The ankle is a hinge synovial joint. **2.** In popular usage, the region of this joint, including the tarsus and lower end of the leg. SEE: *foot* for illus. SYN: *talocrural joint.*

ankle clonus SEE: under *clonus.*

ankylo-, ankyl- [Gr. *ankylos,* crooked] Prefixes meaning *crooked, bent,* or *a fusion or growing together of parts.*

ankyloblepharon (ang″kĭ-lō-blef′ă-ron″) [*ankylo-* + *blepharo-*] Blepharosynechia.

ankylochilia (ang″kĭ-lō-kī′lē-a) [*ankylo-* + *chilo-* + *-ia*] Adhesion of the upper and lower lips.

ankylodactylia (ang-kĭ-lō-dak-til′ē-a) [*ankylo-* + *dactylo-* + *-ia*] Fusion of two or more fingers or toes.

ankyloglossia (ang″kĭ-lō-glos′ē-ă) [*ankylo-* + *glosso-* + *-ia*] Abnormal shortness of the frenulum of the tongue. SEE: *tongue-tie.*

ankylopoietic (ang″kĭ-lō-poy-et′ik) [*ankylo-* + Gr. *poiein,* to make] **1.** Indicating the presence of ankylosis. **2.** Causing ankylosis.

ankylosed (ang′kĭ-lōzd″) [*ankylo-*] **1.** Fixed; stiffened; held by adhesions. **2.** Affected with ankylosis.

ankylosis (ang″kĭ-lō′sĭs) [*ankylo-* + *-sis*] Immobility of a joint. The condition may be congenital (sometimes hereditary), or it may be the result of disease, trauma, surgery, or contractures resulting from immobility.

    PATIENT CARE: Immobility-induced contractures that can result in ankylosis can be prevented by putting joints through their normal range of motion passively whenever they cannot be exercised actively. If a nonsurgical ankylosis is present, the joint is maintained in a functional position, splints are used for patients with spastic muscles, passive range-of-motion exercises to affected joints are initiated, and appropriate physical therapy is prescribed. Orthopedic intervention may be required. If an ankylosis is surgically created, the joint is immobilized until the bone has healed (usually in 6 to 12 weeks), and correct body alignment is maintained. SEE: *ankylosing spondylitis*.

   artificial a. The surgical fixation of a joint.

   bony a. The abnormal union of the bones of a joint. SYN: *true a.*

   dental a. A condition in which dental ligaments that bind teeth to bone are lost, and the root cementum fuses directly with the adjacent alveolar bone. It is usually found in primary mandibular molars.

   extracapsular a. Ankylosis caused by rigidity of parts outside a joint.

   false a. Fibrous **a.**

   fibrous a. Ankylosis due to the formation of fibrous bands within a joint. SYN: *false a.; ligamentous a.*

   intracapsular a. Ankylosis due to undue rigidity of structures within a joint.

   ligamentous a. Fibrous **a.**

   true a. Bony **a.**

Ankylostoma (ăng″kĭ-lŏs′tō-mă) Ancylostoma.

ankylotia (ang″kĭ-lō′shē-ă) [*ankylo-* + *oto-* + *-ia*] Stricture or imperforation of the external auditory meatus of the ear.

ankylotome (ang′ki-lō-tōm″) [*ankylo-* + *-tome*] An instrument for cutting the frenulum of the tongue in tongue-tie.

ankylurethria (ang″ki-loo-rē′thrē-ă) [*ankylo-* + *urethra* + *-ia*] Stricture, imperforation, or adhesions of the urethra.

ankyrin (ang′kĭ-rin) A structural protein in red blood cells that binds cell membrane transport molecules to spectrin.

anlage (on′lŏg″ĕ) [Ger. *Anlage*, a laying on] In an embryo, an accumulation of cells destined to form a specific part of the organism; the beginning of an organized tissue, organ, or part. SYN: *primordium.*

ANNA *American Nephrology Nurses' Association.*

anneal (ă-nēl′) [Old English *anaelan*, to burn] **1.** To soften a material, e.g., glass, metal, or wax, by heating and cooling to remove internal stresses and to make it more easily adapted or swaged, as in preparation of materials for restorative dentistry. **2.** To allow a strand of nucleic acid to bond to a complementary strand, e.g., during the amplification of a desired gene in the polymerase chain reaction.

annectant, annectent (ă-nek′tănt) [L. *annectens*, tying or binding to] Linking; connecting.

Annelida (ă-nel′ĭ-dă) [L. *anellus*, little ring] The phylum that includes earthworms, leeches, and other segmented worms. Some annelids are intermediate hosts for parasitic worms. Leeches are ectoparasites. The medicinal leech, *Hirudo medicinalis*, is the source of an anticoagulant that is used to treat myocardial infarction and other conditions caused by blood clots.

annexitis (ă-neks-īt′ĭs) Adnexitis.

annular (an′yŭ-lăr) [L. *a(n)nularis,* pert. to a ring] Circular; ring-shaped.

annuloplasty (an′yŭ-lō-plas′tē) [*annulus* + *-plasty*] **1.** Surgical repair of a ring-shaped structure (e.g., a heart valve, an intervertebral disk). **2.** A device used to repair a ring-shaped structure. **annuloplastic** (an″′yŭ-lō-plas′tik), *adj.*

annulorrhaphy (an″yŭ-lor′ă-fē) [*annulus* + *-rrhaphy*] Closure of a hernial ring by suture.

annulus, anulus (an′yŭ-lŭs, -lī″) *pl.* **annuli, anuli** [L. *annulus, anulus,* a ring] A ring-shaped structure; a ring.

anococcygeal (ā″nō-kok-sij′ē-al) [*anus* + *coccygeal*] Pert. to both the anus and coccyx.

anococcygeal body SEE: under *body.*

anodal opening contraction SEE: under *contraction.*

anode (ān′ōd″) [*ana-,* + Gr. *hodos,* way] **1.** The positive pole of an electrical source. **2.** In radiography, the target of the x-ray tube. SEE: *cathode.* **anodal** (a-nōd′ăl), *adj.*

anoderm (ā′nŏ-dĕrm″) [*anus* + *derm-*] The thin, pale, shiny squamous epithelium covering the lower half (below the pectinate line) of the anal canal. This epithelium is hairless and has no glands. SEE: *anal canal.*

anodmia (a-nod′mē-ă) [*¹an-* + Gr. *odmē,* stench] Anosmia.

anodontia (an″ō-don′sh(ē-)ă) [*¹an-* + *odont-* + *-ia*] Congenital absence of the teeth.

anodyne (an′ŏ-dīn″) [*¹an-* + Gr. *odynē,* pain] **1.** Relieving pain. **2.** A drug that relieves pain.

anogenital (ā″nō-jen′ĭ-tăl) [*anus* + *genital*] Pert. to the anal and genital areas.

anoikis (ă-ny′-kis) [*¹an-* + Gr. *oikia,* house + *-(s)is*] Programmed cell death occurring in epithelial cells. It is associated with loss of the normal ability to establish contacts between the cell and the extracellular matrix. SEE: *apoptosis.*

anomalad (ă-nom′ă-lad″) [*anomaly* + Gr. *-ad,* a suffix denoting a group or unit of a number] A closely related group of developmental disorders or congenital findings, specifically ones that have a common or unifying cause.

anomaloscope (ă-nom′ă-lŏ-skōp″) [*anomaly* + *-scope*] A device used to assess color perception (color blindness). The patient is asked to adjust red and green lights to match another color, e.g., a yellow light.

anomalous (ă-nom′ă-lŭs) [Gr. *anomalos*, uneven] Deviating from or contrary to normal; irregular.

anomalous perception SEE: under *perception*.

anomaly (ă-nom′ă-lē) [Gr. *anomalia*, irregularity] A deviation from an established norm.

   Alder-Reilly a. SEE: *Alder-Reilly anomaly*.

   congenital a. Intrauterine development of an organ or structure that is abnormal in form, structure, or position. SEE: *birth* **defect**.

   Ebstein a. SEE: *Ebstein anomaly*.

   May-Hegglin a. SEE: *May-Hegglin anomaly*.

   Pelger-Huët a. SEE: *Pelger-Huët anomaly*.

anomia (ă-nom′ē-ă, -nō-mē-) [¹*an-* + L. *nom(en)*, name + *-ia*] Inability to remember names of objects.

anomie, anomy (an′ō-mē) [Fr. from Gr. *anomia*, lawlessness] A term coined by the French sociologist Emile Durkheim (1858–1917) to indicate a condition similar to alienation. The individual feels there has been a disintegration of his or her norms and values. Durkheim felt such individuals were prone to take their lives because of the anxiety, isolation, and alienation that they experience. **anomic** (ă-nom′ik, ă-nō′mik), *adj*.

anonychia (an″ō-nik′ē-ă) [¹*an-* + Gr. *onyx*, nail + *-ia*] Absence of the nails.

anonymous (ă-non′ĭ-mŭs) [Gr. *anōnymos*, nameless] **1.** Unidentified or unnamed. **2.** Shielded from the view of others; private.

anonymous testing Confidential testing for the presence of a disease or condition, e.g., for hepatitis or pregnancy.

anoperineal (ā″nō-per-ĭ-nē′ăl) [*anus* + *perineal*] Pert. to both the anus and perineum.

Anopheles (ă-nof′ĕ-lēz″) [Gr. *anophelēs*, harmful, useless] A genus of mosquitoes belonging to the family Culicidae, order Diptera. It is a vector of many infectious diseases, including malaria, dengue, and filariasis.

   A. stephensi A species found primarily on the Indian subcontinent and a vector for falciparum malaria.

anophthalmia (an″ŏf-thal′mē-ă) [¹*an-* + *ophthalmo-* + *-ia*] Congenital absence of one or both eyes. SYN: *anopia*(1).

anopia (ă-nō′pē-ă) [¹*an-* + *-opia*] **1.** Anophthalmia. **2.** Hyperphoria.

anoplasty (ā′nŏ-plas″tē) [*anus* + *-plasty*] Reconstructive surgery of the anus.

Anoplura (an″ŏ-ploor′ă) [Gr. *anoplos*, unarmed + Gr. *oura*, tail] Blood-feeding ectoparasites of mammals. They can cause localised skin irritations and are vectors of several blood-borne diseases, e.g., trench fever, epidemic typhus, epidemic relapsing fever. SEE: *louse; pediculosis*.

anopsia (ă-nop′sē-ă) [¹*an-* + *-opsia*] **1.** Hyperphoria. **2.** Inability to use the vision, as occurs in strabismus, cataract, or refractive errors or in those confined in the dark.

anorchidism, anorchia, anorchism (ă-nor′kĭ-dizm, -nor′kē-ă, -nor′kizm) [¹*an-* + *-orchid* + *-ism*] Congenital absence of one or both testes.

anorectal (ā″nō-rek′tăl) [*anus* + *rectal*] Pert. to both the anus and rectum.

anorectic, anoretic (an″ŏ-rek′tik, -ret′ik) [Gr. *anorektos*, having no appetite] **1.** Having no appetite. SYN: *anorexic*. **2.** Anorexic. (2) **3.** Causing a lack of appetite, e.g., by a drug. SYN: *anorexiant; anorexic; anorexigenic*. **4.** Something, e.g., a drug, that suppresses appetite; an anorexiant. Such drugs include amphetamines, fenfluramine, and phentermine. **5.** Anorexic. (3)

anorexia (an″ŏ-rek′sē-ă) [¹*an-* + Gr. *orexis*, appetite + *-ia*] Loss of appetite. Anorexia is seen in depression, malaise, the onset of fevers and illnesses, disorders of the alimentary tract, esp. of the stomach, and alcoholism and drug addiction, esp. cocaine addiction. Many medicines and medical procedures have the undesired side effect of causing the suppression of appetite.

   PATIENT CARE: Oral hygiene is provided before and after eating. The patient's food preferences are determined, and only preferred foods are offered. Small, frequent meals or smaller meals with between-meal and bedtime nutritional snacks are provided. The patient area is kept free of odors, and a quiet atmosphere is provided for meals. Family and friends are encouraged to bring favorite home-cooked meals and to join the patient for meals. Mealtime conversation should focus on pleasant topics and should not involve the patient's food intake. Actual intake is documented, indicating food types, amounts ingested, and approximate caloric and nutrient intake.

   a. athletica, athletic a. A compulsion to exercise, often coupled with reduced caloric intake, and, ultimately, failing health, recurrent injuries, and other impairments. The condition is more common in women than in men but not exclusively found in women. SEE: *a. nervosa; female athlete* **triad**.

   holy a. A. mirabilis.

   a. mirabilis A culture-bound illness found principally among devout women who forgo food to achieve purification of the soul. In Western nations this kind of anorexia is considered an eating disorder. SYN: *holy a.*

   a. nervosa An eating disorder marked by weight loss, emaciation, a disturbance in body image, and a fear of weight gain that results in self-imposed starvation. Patients with the disorder lose weight either by excessive dieting, compulsive exercising, self-induced vomiting, or abuse of laxatives or diuretics to purge themselves. The illness is typically found in industrialized nations and usually begins in the teenage years. Young women are 10 to 20 times more likely than boys or men to suffer from the disorder. Weight loss of greater than 15% of body weight is typical, often with significant metabolic consequences. These may include severe electrolyte disturbances, hypoproteinemia with associated edema, and endocrine dysfunction. Immune disturbances, anemia, and secondary cardiac arrhythmias may occur. In women, amenorrhea is also characteristically accompanied by infertility and loss of libido. Repeated vomiting can cause esophageal erosion, ulceration, tears, and bleeding as well as dental caries and tooth and gum erosion. The disease often resists therapy.

Diagnosis is made by the following criteria: by the patient's intense fear of becoming obese (this fear does not diminish as weight loss continues); by the patient's claims of feeling fat even when emaciated, even though a loss of 25% of original weight may occur; by there being no known physical illness accounting for the weight loss; and by the patient's refusal to maintain body weight over a minimal normal weight for age and height.

Psychiatric therapy in a hospital is usually required if the patient refuses to eat. The patient may need to be fed parenterally. SEE: *bulimia; Nursing Diagnoses Appendix.*

PATIENT CARE: The nurse, nutritionist, and physician monitor the patient's vital signs and electrolyte balance; daily fluid intake and output; food types, amounts, and approximate nutrient intake; and laboratory values. The patient is weighed daily or weekly as prescribed. If necessary, the patient's body orifices, underarm area, and hair are checked for hidden weights before being weighed. Small, frequent meals and nutritionally complete fluids are provided; the patient may accept the latter more readily. If tube feeding or parenteral nutrition is required, the procedure is explained to the patient and family. Edema or bloating, if present, is also explained, and the patient is reassured of its temporary nature. The patient's activities are strictly monitored as a precaution against vomiting, catharsis, or excessive exercise. The patient is taught that improved nutrition can correct abnormal laboratory findings. Arguments about food or related subjects are avoided. The patient

is encouraged to recognize and express feelings; assertive behavior is supported. Assistance is offered to the family and close friends in dealing with their feelings about the patient and the patient's behavior, and they are instructed not to discuss food or weight with the patient. Individual, group, and family psychotherapy or behavior modification therapy are employed. The patient and family are encouraged to continue professional counseling on an outpatient basis and are referred to local and national support and information organizations such as the Anorexia Nervosa and Related Eating Disorders Organization. Stable weight and eating patterns, the ability to express feelings, and the establishment of healthier patient-family relationships are indicators of successful intervention.

reverse a. Muscle dysmorphia.

anorexiant (an″ŏ-rek′sē-ănt) An appetite suppressant; an anorectic.

anorexic (an″ŏ-rek′sik) [*anorex(ia)* + *-ic*] **1.** Anorectic. 1, 3) **2.** Pert. to or affected by anorexia nervosa. SYN: *anorectic.* **3.** Someone affected with anorexia, esp. anorexia nervosa. SYN: *anorectic.*

anorexigenic (an″ŏ-rek″sĭ-jen′ik) [*anorexia* + *-genic*] Anorectic. (3)

anorgasmia (a″nor-gaz′-mē-ă) Inability to experience orgasm. **anorgasmic** (mik), *adj.*

anorgasmy (an′or-gaz″mē) [*¹an-* + *orgasm*] Failure to reach orgasm during sexual intercourse or masturbation.

anorthopia (an″or-thō′pē-ă) [*¹an-* + *ortho-* + *-opia*] **1.** An infrequently used term for vision in which straight lines do not appear straight and symmetry and parallelism are not properly perceived. An infrequently used term for strabismus.

anoscope (ā′nŏ-skōp″) [*anus* + *-scope*] A speculum for examining the anus and lower rectum. **anoscopic** (ā″nŏ-skop′ik), *adj.* **anoscopy** (ā-nos′kŏ-pē), *n.*

anosigmoidoscopy (ā″nŏ-sig″moy″dos′kŏ-pē) [*anus* + *sigmoidoscopy*] Proctosigmoidoscopy.

anosmatic (an″oz-mat′ik) [*¹an-* + *osmatic*] Lacking the sense of smell.

anosmia (a-noz′mē-ă) [*¹an-* + Gr. *osmē*, stench] Absence or loss of the sense of smell. **anosmic** (mik), *adj.*, **anosmous** (mŭs), *adj.* SYN: *anodmia; anosphrasia.*

anosognosia (ă-nō″sog-nō′zē-ă, zhă) [*¹an-* + *noso-* + Gr. *gnōsis,* knowledge + *-ia*] The apparent denial or unawareness of one's own neurological defect. **anosognosic** (-nō′zik), *adj.*

visual a. A neurological syndrome in which patients who cannot see deny that they are blind. An excuse such as "I lost my glasses" may be offered. The lesion is in the visual association areas of the cortex of the brain. SYN: *Anton's syndrome.*

anospinal (ā″nō-spīn′ăl) [*anus* + *spinal*] Pert. to the anus and spinal cord or to the center in the spinal cord that controls the contraction of the anal sphincter.

anostosis (an″os-tō′sis) [*¹an-* + *osteo-* + *-sis*] A defective formation or development of bone; failure to ossify.

anotia (an-ō′shē-)ă) [*¹an-* + *oto-* + *-ia*] Congenital malformation with absence of the ears.

anotropia (an″ō-trō′pē-ă) [Gr. *anō*, upwards + *-tropia*] Tendency of the eyes to turn upward and away from the visual axis.

ANOVA *analysis of variance.*

anovaginal (ā″nō-vaj′ĭn-ăl) [*anus* + *vaginal*] Pert. to the anus and vagina.

anovarism (a-nō′vă-rizm) [*¹an-* + *ovario* + *-ism*] Absence of ovaries.

anovesical (ā″nō-ves′ĭ-kăl) [*anus* + *vesical*] Pert. to both the anus and urinary bladder.

anovular, anovulatory (a-nov′yŭ-lăr, -lă-tor″ē) [*¹an-* + *ovular*] Without ovulation.

anovulation (an″ov″yŭ-lā′shŏn) [*¹an-* + *ovulation*] Failure to ovulate. This commonly occurs during the reproductive cycle, beginning in puberty when ovulation is irregular, and recurring after pregnancy and during menopause. Diseases causing anovulation include polycystic ovary syndrome. SEE: *ovulation.*

   hyperandrogenic a. Failure to ovulate as a result of excessive levels of male hormones. Polycystic ovary syndrome is the most common form of hyperandrogenic anovulation.

anoxia (ă-nok′sē-ă) [*¹an-* + *²oxy-* + *-ia*] Absence of oxygen; complete oxygen deprivation. This term is often used incorrectly to indicate hypoxia. **anoxic** (sik), *adj.*

anoxygenic (ă-nok″si-jen′ik) [*¹an-* + *oxygenic*] **1.** Not reliant on oxygen for the electrons used in photosynthesis. **2.** Not productive of oxygen during photosynthesis.

ANP *advanced nurse practitioner; atrial natriuretic peptide.*

ANS *autonomic nervous system.*

ansa (an′să, an′sē″) *pl.* **ansae** [L. *ansa*, a handle] In anatomy, a structure in the form of a loop or arc. SEE: *nerve.*

   a. cervicalis A loop of interconnected nerves in the neck that descends along and outside of the carotid sheath. It is composed of nerve branches from cervical spinal nerves C1-C3 and the hypoglossal nerve (CN XII); its branches innervate infrahyoid muscles (the sternohyoid, sternothyroid, and omohyoid muscles).

   a. lenticularis An output tract from the internal segment of the globus pallidus in the basal ganglia; it curves

around the posterior limb of the internal capsule and synapses in the ventral anterior and ventral lateral nuclei of the thalamus.

   a. peduncularis An output tract from the amygdala to the dorsomedial nucleus of the thalamus.

   a. subclavia A loop of interconnected autonomic nerves from the cervicothoracic sympathetic trunk that encircles the subclavian artery deep in the root of the neck.

ANSER system A group of questionnaires for evaluating developmental dysfunction in children.

ANSI *American National Standards Institute.*

ansiform (an′sī-form″) [*ansa* + *-form*] Shaped like a loop or an arc.

ant (ant) A small social insect of the order Hymenoptera and family Formicidae, distributed worldwide. Ants live in highly organized colonies whose members specialize in performing specific tasks. Because some ants secrete formic acid, their sting can be hazardous.

   fire a. An aggressive, stinging species that often forms large colonies. Its sting may cause itchy, painful rashes, and, in some cases, anaphylactic shock.

ant- SEE: *anti-.*

ant. *anterior* (in anatomy).

Antabuse (ant′ă-būs″) Proprietary name for disulfiram; administered orally in treatment of alcoholism. Drinking alcohol after taking this drug causes severe reactions, including nausea and vomiting, and may endanger the life of the patient. SEE: *Poisons and Poisoning Appendix.*

antacid (ant″as′ĭd) [*anti-* + *acid*] An agent that neutralizes acidity, esp. in the stomach and duodenum. Examples are calcium carbonate and magnesium oxide.

antagonism (an-tag′ŏ-nizm) [Gr. *antagōnisma*, a struggle against] **1.** Neutralization or suppression of an action by an opposing force or chemical effect. **2.** In psychology, hostility or dislike for, or resistance to another person.

   microbial a. The inhibition of one bacterial organism by another. Through microbial antagonism, the normal bacterial flora of the body provides some defense against disease-causing organisms. SEE: *opportunistic infection.*

antagonist (an-tag′ŏ-nĭst) [Gr. *antagōnistēs*, struggler] Something that blocks, undoes, or produces the opposite effect of an action, e.g., in a cellular receptor for a drug.

   adenosine diphosphate a. Thienopyridine.

   adenosine diphosphate receptor a. Thienopyridine.

   aldosterone a. Any of a class of drugs (such as spironolactone or eplerenone) that blocks mineralocorticoid receptors. These drugs are used as diuretics, e.g., in treating heart failure.

androgen-receptor a. Any drug that blocks cellular receptors for male hormones. Spironolactone is a drug in this class.

dental a. The tooth in the opposite arch against which a tooth occludes.

dihydropyridine calcium a. A calcium channel blocking drug that resembles or is based on pyridine. It is a potent relaxer of smooth muscle cells and is used to treat hypertension, angina pectoris, and other conditions. Examples of dihydropyridines include amlodipine, felodipine, and nifedipine.

drug a. A drug that prevents receptor stimulation. An antagonist drug has an affinity for a cell receptor and, by binding to it, prevents the cell from responding to an agonist.

endothelin-receptor a. A medicine that lowers blood pressure by opposing the vasoconstricting effects of endothelins.

growth hormone receptor a. Any agent that blocks the effects of growth hormone on its cellular receptors, e.g., in treating diseases such as acromegaly or diabetes mellitus.

H_2-receptor a. Any of the drugs that inhibit gastric acid secretion by blocking the effects of histamine or acetylcholine on receptors found on parietal cells. Such drugs are used to treat peptic ulcers and gastroesophageal reflux disease. SYN: *H_2 blocker*.

H_3-receptor antagonist Any of the drugs that block H_3 receptors in the central nervous system. Such drugs may be used to treat disorders of sleep and arousal, wakefulness, and attention.

leukotriene-receptor a. Any of several medications (such as zafirlukast and montelukast) that block the inflammatory effects of leukotrienes and are used to treat patients with asthma. These medications help to reduce the dependence of asthmatic patients on corticosteroids and beta-agonist inhalers.

muscular a. A muscle that opposes the action of the prime mover and produces a smooth movement by balancing the opposite forces.

narcotic a. A drug that prevents or reverses the action of a narcotic. SEE: *nalorphine hydrochloride*.

neurokinin-receptor a. Any of a group of drugs, e.g., aprepitant and fosaprepitant, that block nausea and vomiting caused by chemotherapy. They are often used in conjunction with other antiemetic drugs.

nondihydropyridine calcium a. Any calcium channel blocker that is not based on a pyridine molecule, e.g., verapamil and diltiazem. Compared to di-

hydropyridines, these agents are more negatively inotropic and are more likely to slow the conduction of the electrical activity of the heart, e.g., by prolonging the P−R interval.

platelet-activating factor a. Any drug that blocks the effects of platelet-activating factor on inflammatory or allergic diseases and conditions.

serotonin a. Any of a class of medications used to treat or prevent nausea and vomiting. Examples are ondansetron (Zofran) and granisetron (Kytril).

vasopressin-receptor a. Any of the drugs (such as conivaptan and tolvaptan) that block cellular receptors to antidiuretic hormone and increase the excretion of water by the kidneys. These agents are used to treat hyponatremia in patients with syndrome of inappropriate antidiuretic hormone.

ante- [L. *ante,* before] Prefix meaning *before.*

antebrachium, antibrachium (ant″tē-brā′kē-ŭm) [*ante-* + *brachium*] The forearm. **antebrachial, antibrachial** (-ăl), *adj.*

antecedent (ant″ē-sēd′ĕnt) [L. *antecedere,* to precede] Something that comes before something else; a precursor.

plasma thromboplastin a. ABBR: PTA. Blood coagulation factor XI, a coagulation factor active only in the intrinsic pathway of coagulation, circulating in the blood as a dimer linked by a disulfide bond with high molecular weight kininogen (HMWK), and activating blood coagulation factor IX. SYN: *Christmas factor*. SEE: *blood coagulation*; *coagulation factor*.

ante cibum (an′tē sē′bŭm) [L. before food] ABBR: a.c. Used in prescription writing to indicate *before meals.*

antecubital (ant″ē-kū′bĭt-ăl) [*ante-* + *cubital*] In front of the elbow; at the bend of the elbow.

antecurvature (ant″ē-kŭr′vă-chŭr) [*ante-* + *curvature*] An abnormal bending forward. SEE: *anteflexion*.

anteflect (ăn″tē-flĕkt) [″ + *flectere,* to bend] To bend or cause to bend anteriorly (forward).

anteflexion (ăn″tē-flĕk′shŭn) The abnormal bending forward of part of an organ, esp. of the uterus at its body and neck. SEE: *anteversion*.

antegrade (ăn′tē-grād) Moving forward or in the same direction as the flow.

antemortem (ăn′tē-mor′tĕm) [L.] Before death.

antenatal (ant″ē-nāt′ăl) [*ante-* + *¹natal*] Prenatal.

antepartal, antepartum (ăn″tē-păr′tăl, -tŭm) [L.] Period of pregnancy between conception and onset of labor; used with reference to the mother.

anterior (an-tēr′ē-ŏr) [L. *anterior,* former, previous] Before; in front of. In anatomical nomenclature, it refers to the ventral or abdominal side of the body

anterior drawer test 1. *Knee:* A test for anterior cruciate ligament rupture. It is positive if anterior glide of the tibia is increased. **2.** *Ankle:* A test for stability of the anterior talofibular ligament of the ankle. It is positive if movement is increased as the examiner grasps the heel with one hand and the distal tibia with the other and draws the heel forward. SYN: *anterior drawer sign.*

anterior horn cell SEE: under *cell.*

antero- [L. *anter(ior),* before] Prefix meaning *anterior, front, before.*

anterograde (ant″ĕ-rō-grād″) [*antero-* + L. *gradi,* to step, go] Moving to the front; in a forward direction.

anteroinferior (ant″ĕ-rō-in-fēr′ē-ŏr) [*antero-* + *inferior*] In anatomy, located in front and below. **anteroinferiorly,** *adv.*

anterolateral (ant″ĕ-rō-lat′ĕ-răl) [*antero-* + *lateral*] In anatomy, located in front and to one side. **anterolaterally,** *adv.*

anteromedial (ant″ĕ-rō-mēd′ē-ăl) [*antero-* + *medial*] In anatomy, located in front and toward the center.

anteroposterior (ant″ĕ-rō-pos-tēr′ē-ŏr, -pō′stir-) [*antero-* + *posterior*] ABBR: AP. Extending from front to rear. **anteroposteriorly,** *adv.*

anterosuperior (ant″ĕ-rō-soo-pēr′ē-ŏr) [*antero* + *superior*] In anatomy, located in front and above. **anterosuperiorly,** *adv.*

anteversion (ant″ē-vĕr′zhŏn) [*ante-* + *version*] A tipping forward of an organ as a whole, without bending. SEE: *anteflexion.*

   femoral a. Excessive anterior angulation of the neck of the femur, leading to excessive internal rotation of the femur. The normal value for femoral neck anteversion is approx. 15°.

anteverted (ant″ĭ-vĕrt′ĕd) Tipped forward, esp. of a position of the uterus. **antevert** (ant′ĭ-vĕrt″), *v.*

anthelmintic, anthelminthic, antihelmintic (ant″hel-min′tik, -thik, ant″ĭ-) [*anti-* + *helminthic*] **1.** Purging or destroying parasitic worms. **2.** An agent that purges or destroys parasitic worms. SYN: *vermicide.*

Anthemis (an′thĕ-mĭs) [L. *anthemis* fr Gr. *anthemis,* chamomile] A genus of approx. 100 species of aromatic flowering plants. The entire genus is commonly called chamomile. SEE: *chamomile.*

   A. nobilis SEE: *chamomile.*

anthocyanin (an″thŏ-sī′ă-nĭn) [Gr. *anthos,* flower + *cyano-* + *-in*] Any of several water-soluble pigments found in berries, grapes, and other fruits and vegetables as they ripen. All of them are antioxidants and belong to a class of compounds called flavonoids.

anthophobia (an″thŏ-fō′bē-ă) [Gr. *an-*

thos, flower + *-phobia*] Morbid dislike or fear of flowers.

anthrac-, anthraco- [Gr. *anthrax,* stem *anthrac-,* coal, carbuncle] Prefixes meaning *coal, carbon,* or *carbuncle.*

anthracene (an′thră-sēn″) [*anthrac-* + *-ene*] $C_{14}H_{10}$; an aromatic hydrocarbon obtained from distilling coal tar. It is used to manufacture the dye alizarin and insecticides.

anthracoid (an′thră-koyd″) [*anthrac-* + *-oid*] Pert. to or resembling anthrax.

anthracosilicosis (an″thră-kō″sil″ĭ-kō′sĭs) [*anthrac-* + *silicosis*] Black **lung**.

anthracosis (an″thră-kō′sĭs) [*anthrac-* + *-osis*] A benign accumulation of carbon deposits in the lungs due to inhalation of smoke or coal dust. **anthracotic** (-kot′ik), *adj.* SEE: *black* **lung**.

anthracycline (an″thră-sī′klēn″) [*anthrac-* + *-cycline*] Any of several antibiotic-based drugs that block DNA synthesis in tumors. They are used to treat solid organ cancers, e.g., breast cancer, and leukemias. Examples include daunorubicin, doxorubicin, and mitoxantrone.

anthrax (an′thraks″) [Gr. *anthrax,* coal, carbuncle] An acute infectious disease caused by contact with, ingestion of, or inhalation of the spores of *Bacillus anthracis.* People who work with contaminated textiles or animal products usually contract it from skin contact with animal hair, hides, or waste (the most common form of the disease, accounting for 95% of cases), but the bacilli may cause a fatal pneumonia if they are inhaled. SEE: illus.

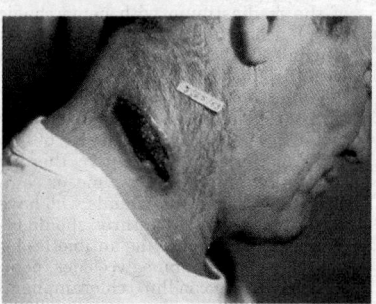

ANTHRAX

Cutaneous anthrax lesion on the neck
(SOURCE: Centers for Disease Control and Prevention)

   IMMUNIZATION: The anthrax bacillus has been prepared in aerosol form for use in biological warfare. As a result, some American troops have been vaccinated against the disease during their military training with one of several evolving vaccines. The effectiveness of the vaccine in disease prevention remains uncertain. Vaccination is also given to patients affected by active anthrax to prevent relapses. SEE: *biological warfare; Standard Precautions Appendix*.

DIAGNOSIS: Diagnosis is made by isolating *B. anthracis* from blood, sputum, or skin lesion cultures.

SYMPTOMS: Signs and symptoms usually occur within 1 to 7 days after exposure, but can take up to 60 days. Early treatment helps to reduce fatalities. Cutaneous anthrax presents with small, pruritic lesions similar to insect bites that progress to malignant pustules (large, painless boils), vesicles, or skin ulcers with necrotic centers and surrounding brawny edema, usually on an exposed body surface, such as the skin of the hand. Mortality is about 20% from untreated cutaneous anthrax and is less than 1% when treated with an antibiotic (penicillin, doxycycline, ciprofloxacin). GI anthrax involves acute inflammation of the intestinal tract from ingestion of anthrax spores. Symptoms include nausea and vomiting, decreased appetite and fever, progressing to abdominal pain, vomiting blood, and severe to bloody diarrhea. Antibiotic therapy limits mortality to from 25% to 60%. Inhalation anthrax (also called pulmonary anthrax or Woolsorter's disease) is marked by flulike symptoms progressing to fevers, sweats, cough, weakness, and rapidly developing respiratory failure, septic shock, and/or meningitis. Infection of the lungs may be suggested by the rapid onset of respiratory symptoms and chest x-ray or CT findings that may include widening of the mediastinum with hemorrhagic lymph nodes, hilar fullness, and pleural effusion. The disease is often fatal even with the appropriate antibiotic therapy.

TREATMENT: Persons exposed to anthrax (e.g., after its dissemination by bioterrorists) should receive a 60- to 100-day course of preventive therapy with ciprofloxacin, doxycycline, or penicillin G procaine. Individuals who have active infection with anthrax should receive two of the following antibiotics for a 60-day period: aminoglycosides, penicillin G (or amoxicillin), chloramphenicol, ciprofloxacin, doxycycline, imipenem or meropenem, rifampin, tetracycline, or vancomycin. Patients with pleural effusion benefit from drainage of the effusion with a chest tube.

PATIENT CARE: Health supervision is provided to at-risk employees, along with prompt medical care of all lesions. Terminal disinfection of textile mills contaminated with *B. anthracis* is supervised, using vaporized formaldehyde or other recommended treatment. All cases of anthrax (in livestock or people) are reported to local health authorities. Isolation procedures (mask, gown, gloves, hand hygiene, and incineration of contaminated materials) are maintained to protect against drainage secretions for the duration of illness in inhalation, GI, and cutaneous anthrax. For patients with inhalation anthrax, vital signs are monitored and respiratory support is provided. For patients with cutaneous anthrax, lesions are kept clean and covered with sterile dressings. Prescribed antibiotics are administered and the patient is assessed for desired and adverse effects. Frequent oral hygiene and skin care are provided. Oral fluid intake and frequent small, nutritious meals are encouraged.

anthropo- [Gr. *anthrōpos,* human being] Prefix meaning *human being* or *human life.*

anthropobiology (an″thrŏ-pō″bī-ol′ŏ-jē) [*anthropo- + biology*] Study of the biology of human beings and the great apes.

anthropogenic (an″thrŏ-pŏ-jen′ik) [*anthropo- + -genic*] Caused or produced by human beings or by human economic and social activities. The term is often used to describe human activities that have a detrimental effect on the environment or on health.

anthropoid (an′thrŏ-poyd″) [*anthropo- + -oid*] **1.** Resembling humans. **2.** Pert. to the higher primates, e.g., apes and Old World and New World monkeys. **3.** An ape. **4.** Pert. to an anomaly in the female pelvis. SEE: *anthropoid pelvis.*

anthropological baseline (an″thrŏ-pŏ-loj′ĭ-kăl) An imaginary line that passes from the lower border of the orbit to the superior margin of the external auditory meatus.

anthropology (an″thrŏ-pol′ŏ-jē) [*anthropo- + -logy*] The scientific study of human origins, including the development of physical, human cultural, religious, and social attributes. **anthropologist** (ŏ-jist), *adj.*

   medical a. The study of the impact of biology, culture, ecology, economics, environment, language, politics, and society on healing, health, health care, illness, and treatment.

   physical a. The branch of anthropology concerned with physical measurement of human beings (as living subjects or skeletal remains).

anthropometer (an″thrŏ-pom′ĕt-ĕr) [*anthropo- + -meter*] A device for measuring the human body and its parts.

anthropometry (an″thrŏ-pom′ĕ-trē) [*anthropo- + -metry*] The science of measuring the human body, including craniometry, osteometry, skin fold evaluation for subcutaneous fat estimation, and height and weight measurements; usually performed by an anthropologist. **anthropometric** (-pŏ-me′trik), *adj.*

anthropomorphism (an″thrŏ-pŏ-mor′

fizm) [*anthropo-* + *morph-* + *-ism*] Attributing human qualities to nonhuman organisms or objects. **anthropomorphic** (mor′fik), *adj.* **anthropomorphically** (mor′fi-k(ă-)lē), *adv.*

anthropophilic,   **anthropophilous** (an″thrŏ-pŏ-fĭl′ik, -pof′ĭ-lŭs) [*anthropo-* + *-phile*] Preferring humans. It is used of parasites that prefer a human host to another animal.

anthropozoonosis (an″thrŏ-pō″zō″ŏ-nō′sĭs) [*anthropo-* + *zoonosis*] An infectious disease acquired by humans from vertebrate hosts of the causative agents. Examples are rabies and trichinosis.

anti-, ant- [Gr. *anti*, opposite, in place of] Prefixes meaning *against, opposing, counteracting.*

antiadrenergic (ant″ē-ad″rĕ-nĕr′jik) [*anti-* + *adrenergic*] **1.** Preventing or counteracting adrenergic action. **2.** An agent, e.g., a beta blocker, that counteracts adrenergic effects.

antiagglutinin (ănt″ē-ă-gloot′ĭn-ĭn) [*anti-* + *agglutinin*] A specific antibody opposing the action of an agglutinin.

antiamebic (ant″ē-ă-mē′bik) [*anti-* + *amebic*] A medicine used to prevent or treat amebiasis.

antianaphylaxis (ant″ē-an″ă-fĭ-laks′ĭs) [*anti-* + *anaphylaxis, protection*] Desensitization.

antiandrogen (ant″ē-an′drŏ-jĕn) [*anti-* + *androgen*] A substance that inhibits the production of, or blocks cellular receptors for, male hormones. **antiandrogenic** (-an″drŏ-jen′ik), *adj.*

antianemic (ant″ē-ă-nē′mik) [*anti-* + *anemic*] Preventing or curing anemia.

antianginal (ant″ē-an-jīn′ăl, -an′jĭn-ăl) [*anti-* + *anginal*] **1.** Preventing or relieving angina pectoris. **2.** Any agent used to relieve angina pectoris. Drugs in this class include long-and short-acting nitrates (e.g. nitroglycerin), beta-adrenergic blocking agents, aspirin, and supplemental oxygen.

antiangiogenesis (ant″ē-an″jē-ō-jen′ĕ-sĭs) [*anti-* + *angiogenesis*] Prevention of the formation of new blood vessels, esp. the blood vessels that grow under the influence of malignant tumors. Agents causing antiangiogenesis include angiostatin, endostatin, tetracyclines, and paclitaxel. They are useful in the treatment of cancer. SEE: *angiogenesis.*

antiantibody (ant″ē-ant′i-bod-ē) [*anti-* + *antibody*] An antibody that blocks the binding site of another antibody. Blocking the site inhibits antibody-antigen binding because the antigen must compete with the antiantibody for the receptor site.

antiantitoxin (ant″ē-ant″i-tok′sin) [*anti-* + *antitoxin*] An antibody that acts against an antitoxin. SEE: *antibody; antitoxin.*

antiarrhythmic (ant″ē-ă-rith′mik) [*anti-* + *arrhythmic*] **1.** Controlling or preventing cardiac arrhythmias. **2.** An agent that controls or prevents cardiac arrhythmias.

antiarthritic (ant″ē-ar-thrit′ik) [*anti-* + *arthritic*] **1.** Relieving arthritis. **2.** An agent that relieves arthritis.

antiasthmatic (ant″ē-az-mat′ik) [*anti-* + *asthmatic*] **1.** Preventing or relieving asthma. **2.** An agent that prevents or relieves an asthma attack.

antibacterial (ant″i-bak-tēr′ē-ăl) [*anti-* + *bacterial*] **1.** Destroying or stopping the growth of bacteria. **2.** An agent that destroys or stops the growth of bacteria.

antibiogram (ant″i-bī′ō-gram″) [*anti-* + *bio-* + *-gram*] A record of the susceptibility of specific pathogenic bacteria to antibiotics. Such susceptibility varies from hospital to hospital, state to state, and country to country. Antibiograms are constructed from cultural and other data accumulated in clinical laboratories. They help clinicians decide which antibiotics to use when treating suspected infections and help public health agencies track the antibiotic resistance of microorganisms over time.

antibiosis (ant″i-bī-ō′sĭs) [*anti-* + *bio-* + *-sis*] An association or relationship between two organisms in which one is harmful to the other.

antibiotic (ant″i-bī-ot′ik) [*anti-* + *biotic*] **1.** Destructive to life. **2.** Pert. to antibiosis. **3.** A natural or synthetic substance that destroys microorganisms or inhibits their growth. Antibiotics are used extensively to treat infectious diseases in plants, animals, and humans. SEE: *antimicrobial* **drug***; bacterium.*

    bactericidal a. An antibiotic that kills microorganisms.

    bacteriostatic a. An antibiotic that inhibits the growth of microorganisms.

    beta-lactam a. Any of the antimicrobial drugs, such as penicillins or cephalosporins, that kill germs by interfering with the synthesis of bacterial cell walls. SYN: *beta-lactam.*

    beta-lactamase-resistant a. Any of the antibiotics resistant to the action of beta-lactamase. This property makes these antibiotics effective against microbial organisms that produce beta-lactamase. SEE: *beta-lactamase-resistant penicillin.*

    broad-spectrum a. An antibiotic that is effective against a wide variety of microorganisms.

    glycopeptide a. Any antibiotic composed of a short amino acid chain linked to a carbohydrate. Vancomycin and teicoplanin are glycopeptide antibiotics.

    narrow-spectrum a. An antibiotic that is specifically effective against a limited group of microorganisms.

oxyimino beta lactam a. A third-generation cephalosporin.

antibiotic-impregnated polymethacrylate beads Vehicles for delivering high-concentration antibiotic therapy to a specific area. The antibiotic-impregnated beads are implanted in open wounds with loss of tissue substance, such as open fractures.

antibiotic resistance SEE: under *resistance.*

antibiotic stewardship Antimicrobial stewardship.

antibody (ant′i-bod″ē) [*anti-* + *body*] ABBR: Ab. A substance produced by B lymphocytes in response to a unique antigen. Each Ab molecule combines with a specific antigen to destroy or control it. All antibodies, except natural antibodies (antibodies to different blood types), are made by B cells stimulated by a foreign antigen, typically a foreign protein, polysaccharide, or nucleic acid. SYN: *immunoglobulin.* SEE: illus.; *antigen; autoantibody; cytokine; isoantibody.*

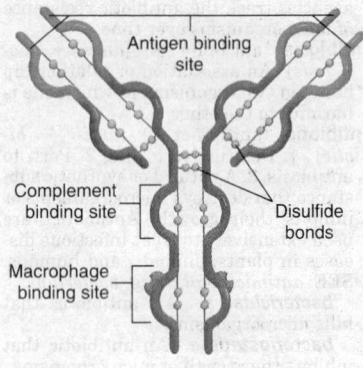

ANTIBODY

Structure of one igG molecule

Antibodies neutralize or destroy antigens in several ways. They can initiate lysis of the antigen by activating the complement system; neutralize toxins released by bacteria, coating (opsonizing) the antigen or forming a complex to stimulate phagocytosis; promote antigen clumping (agglutination); or prevent the antigen from adhering to host cells.

An antibody molecule consists of four polypeptide chains (two light and two heavy), which are joined by disulfide bonds. The heavy chains form the complement-binding site, and the light and heavy chains form the site that binds the antigen.

acetylcholine-receptor binding a. ABBR: AChR-Ab. An autoantibody against acetylcholine receptors in the neuromuscular junction. Binding, blocking, or modulating antibodies against this receptor are found in the blood of most patients with generalized myasthenia gravis and in about half of all patients with ocular forms of the disease.

agonistic a. An antibody that stimulates or activates an organ. For example, agonistic antibodies against the thyrotropin receptor in Graves disease stimulate the thyroid gland to release thyroid hormones that produce hyperthyroidism.

anticardiolipin a. ABBR: aCLa. An autoantibody against the cell membrane lipid, diphosphatidyl glycerol. It produces abnormal and sometimes life-threatening blood clotting. The antibody is found in a variety of autoimmune and infectious diseases, including in patients with the antiphospholipid antibody syndrome and syphilis.

anticyclic citrullinated peptide a. ABBR: anti-CCP. An antibody found in the serum of patients with rheumatoid arthritis but not in those with other joint or soft tissue diseases.

anti–DNase B a. An antibody formed during infection with group A beta-hemolytic streptococci. It is used, retrospectively, to help diagnose recent streptococcal infections.

antiendomysial a. An antibody that cross-reacts with smooth muscle collagen and the gluten in wheat, found in the serum of people with celiac sprue and some related autoimmune diseases.

antiendothelial cell a. An autoantibody present in the serum of patients with a variety of autoimmune diseases, including scleroderma (systemic sclerosis), systemic lupus erythematosus, interstitial lung diseases, and sarcoidosis. These cells attach to antigens on the cells that line blood vessels and injure those cells, producing blood vessel injury and inflammation (vasculitis).

antifibrillarin a. An autoantibody to the nucleolar protein fibrillarin, found in patients with diffuse systemic sclerosis (scleroderma), esp. those with relatively severe disease. It is identified more often in men than in women with the disease and in people of African descent as opposed to Europeans or Asians.

antiganglioside a. An antibody formed against the chemical components of nerves, found in the serum of those with Guillain-Barré syndrome.

antigliadin a. An antibody formed against the gluten in wheat, found in the serum of people with celiac sprue.

antileukocyte a. Any antibody found in plasma that, when donated and infused into a recipient, damages the recipient's white blood cells. Leukocyte injury after plasma exchange or infusion is the event that triggers transfusion-related acute lung injury.

anti-Hu a. An autoantibody associated with paraneoplastic encephalomyelitis. It is also known as ANNA-1 (antineuronal nuclear antibody-1).

antimicrosomal a. An autoantibody found in the plasma of patients with thyroid injury, e.g., in several forms of thyroiditis and other rheumatologic or autoimmune diseases.

antimyeloperoxidase a. An antibody found in patients with several autoimmune vasculitides, such as microscopic polyangitis. SYN: *perinuclear antineutrophil cytoplasmic a.*

antineuronal nuclear a. ABBR: ANNA. Any of several antibodies that bind to neuronal targets in the cerebrum and cerebellum, producing paraneoplastic neurological dysfunction. The antibodies are typically released by cancers such as small-cell carcinoma of the lung (also known as ANNA-1 and ANNA-2), testicular cancer (anti-Ta antibody), or breast cancer (ANNA-2).

antineutrophil cytoplasmic a. ABBR: ANCA. An autoantibody found in the blood of patients with certain forms of vasculitis (such as Churg-Strauss syndrome, microscopic polyangiitis, Wegener granulomatosis) esp. when it affects small blood vessels.

antinuclear a. ABBR: ANA. Any of a group of autoantibodies that react against normal components of the cell nucleus. These antibodies are present in a variety of immunologic diseases, including systemic lupus erythematosus, progressive systemic sclerosis, Sjögren syndrome, scleroderma, polymyositis, and dermatomyositis, and in some patients taking hydralazine, procainamide, or isoniazid. In addition, ANA is present in some normal people. Tests for ANAs are used in the diagnosis and management of autoimmune diseases.

antiphospholipid a. ABBR: aPLa. Any of a group of immunoglobulin autoantibodies that react with phospholipids, which are one of the primary components of the cell membrane (the other components are glycolipids and steroids). These antibodies are found in patients with a variety of connective tissue and infectious disorders, including systemic lupus erythematosus, the antiphospholipid antibody syndrome, syphilis, and malaria. They cause abnormal blood clotting, thrombocytopenia; and in women of childbearing age, repeated miscarriages. The anticardiolipin antibodies are one type of antiphospholipid antibody.

antiproliferating cell nuclear antigen (PCNA) a. ABBR: anti-PCNA. An antibody found in the blood of patients with diseases in which cells replicate

rapidly. Such conditions include autoimmune and inflammatory diseases and malignancies.

antiproteinase-3 a. An autoantibody found in patients with small blood vessel vasculitides, such as Wegener granulomatosis. SYN: *diffusely cytoplasmic antineutrophil a.*

antireceptor a. An antibody that reacts with the antigen receptor on a cell rather than with an antigen itself.

antiribosomal P a. An autoantibody found in patients with systemic lupus erythematosus, esp. those with neurological or psychiatric manifestations of the disorder.

anti–scl-70 a. Antitopoisomerase I a.

antithyroperoxidase a. ABBR: TPOAb. A serum marker of autoimmune thyroid destruction, i.e., of Graves disease or Hashimo tothyroiditis.

antititin a. An antibody that reacts with striated muscle cells. It is found principally in people with myasthenia gravis who also have thymoma.

antitopoisomerase I a. An autoantibody found in the serum of patients with progressive systemic sclerosis, silicosis, and systemic lupus erythematosus. Higher levels of the antibody correlate with worsening kidney, lung, and skin disease. SYN: *anti-scl-70 a.*

blocking a. An antibody that prevents an antigen from binding with a cellular receptor.

catalytic a. Abzyme.

cross-reacting a. An antibody that reacts with antigens other than its specific antigen because they contain binding sites that are structurally similar to its specific antigen. SEE: *antigenic determinant.*

cytotoxic a. An antibody that lyses cells by binding to a cellular antigen and activating complement or killer cells.

diffusely cytoplasmic antineutrophil cytoplasmic a. ABBR: C-ANCA. Antiproteinase-3 a.

direct fluorescein-conjugated a. ABBR: DFA. Direct fluorescent a.

direct fluorescent a. ABBR: DFA. A fluorescent antibody test performed on sputum to detect microorganisms that invade the respiratory tract, e.g., *Legionella, Mycoplasma,* or *Bacillus anthracis.* SYN: *direct fluorescein-conjugated a.; direct immunofluorescence test.*

Donath-Landsteiner a. SEE: *Donath-Landsteiner antibody.*

fluorescent a. ABBR: FA. An antibody that has been stained or marked by a fluorescent material. The fluorescent antibody technique permits rapid diagnosis of various infections.

glutamic acid decarboxylase a. ABBR: GADA. An antibody to glutamic acid decarboxylase. It is a serum marker of type 1 diabetes mellitus and is found in the blood of patients with stiff-person syndrome.

immune a. An antibody produced by immunization or as a result of transfusion of incompatible blood.

maternal a. An antibody produced by the mother and transferred to the fetus in utero or during breastfeeding.

monoclonal a. ABBR: MoAB. A type of antibody, specific to a certain antigen, created in the laboratory from hybridoma cells. Because monoclonal antibodies are derived from a single cell line and raised against a single antigen, they are highly specific. Diagnostically, they are used to identify microorganisms, white blood cells, hormones, and tumor antigens. In patient care, they are used to treat transplant rejection, certain cancers, and autoimmune diseases.

Hybridoma cells, used to produce monoclonal antibodies, are formed by the fusion of a spleen cell from a mouse immunized with an antigen and a multiple myeloma cell (a cancerous plasma B cell). The fused cells are screened to identify those that secrete antibodies against a specific antigen. A continuous supply of these antigen-specific monoclonal antibody secreting cells can then be grown in cultures. SEE: *antibody; B cell; hybridoma.*

natural a. An antibody present in a person without known exposure to the specific antigen, such as an anti-A antibody in a person with B blood type.

panel reactive a. ABBR: PRA. A measure of an organ transplant recipient's level of sensitization to antigens on donated organs. It is the percentage of cells taken from a broad selection of blood donors against whose antigens the organ recipient's serum reacts. The higher the panel reactive antibody, the more challenging it is to match a donor organ to the recipient.

perinuclear antineutrophil cytoplasmic a. Antimyeloperoxidase **a.**

p504s a. Alpha-methylacyl-CoA racemase.

polyclonal a. An antibody that reacts with many different antigens.

protective a. An antibody produced in response to an infectious disease. SEE: *immunity.*

radionuclide-linked monoclonal a. A monoclonal antibody to which a radioisotope has been attached. The antibody attaches to receptors on the surface of undesired cells (e.g., cancer cells) and delivers a dose of radiation directly to those cells, leaving healthy cells and tissues relatively unaffected.

sensitizing a. Reagin.

toxin-linked monoclonal a. A monoclonal antibody to which a cell-killing drug has been attached. The antibody combines preferentially with receptors on undesired cells (such as cancer cells)

and delivers its lethal drug to those cells but not to healthy cells and tissues. To increase their effectiveness and decrease immune responses to these cells, genes for antigen binding sites from human antibodies are added, creating humanized monoclonal antibodies.

warm a. Warm autoagglutinin.

antibody combining site SEE: under *site.*

antibody-dependent cellular cytotoxicity ABBR: ADCC. The process by which phagocytes and natural killer cells bind with receptors on antibodies to destroy the antigens to which the antibodies are bound. SEE: *natural killer cell.*

antibody-mediated rejection SEE: under *rejection.*

antibody therapy The creation of antibodies that target specific antigens; used to treat immunological deficiencies, some cancers, and organ transplant rejection. The antibodies are given by injection. SEE: *monoclonal* **antibody.**

anticancer (ant″i-kan′sĕr) [*anti-* + *cancer*] Pert. to any treatment to combat, prevent, or treat cancer, e.g., an anticancer protein or an anticancer drug.

anticarcinogenic (ant″i-kars″ĭn-ō-jen′ik) [*anti-* + *carcinogenic*] **1.** Tending to delay or prevent tumor formation. **2.** A substance or action that prevents or delays tumor formation.

anticariogenic (ant″i-kar″ē-ō-jen′ik) [*anti-* + *cariogenic*] A substance or action that interferes with the development of dental caries.

anticarious (ant″i-kar′ē-ŭs) [*anti-* + *carious*] Preventing tooth decay.

anticholinergic (ant″i-kō″lĭ-nĕr′jik) [*anti-* + *cholinergic*] **1.** Impeding the impulses of cholinergic, esp. parasympathetic, nerve fibers. **2.** An agent that blocks parasympathetic nerve impulses. The side effects, which include dry mouth and blurred vision, are seen in phenothiazine and tricyclic antidepressant drug therapy. SYN: *parasympatholytic.*

anticholinesterase (ant″i-kō-lĭ-nes′tĕ-rās″, rāz″) [*anti-* + *cholinesterase*] A chemical, e.g., an enzyme or drug, that opposes the action of cholinesterase.

anticipate (an-tis′ĭ-pāt″) [L. *anticapare* , to take before] **1.** To occur before the usual time of onset (of a particular illness or disease). **2.** In nursing and medicine, to expect, predict, or prepare for something outside the routine.

anticipation (an-tis″ĭ-pā′shŏn) **1.** Appearance of a symptom or disease before the usual time. **2.** In inherited illnesses, the expression of a trait at earlier and earlier ages as the trait passes from one generation to the next. Some studies suggest this effect results from enhanced surveillance of offspring as opposed to earlier onset of the disease.

anticipatory grief SEE: under *grief.*

anticipatory guidance SEE: under *guidance*.

anticipatory vomiting SEE: under *vomiting*.

anticlinal (ant″i-klī′năl) [*anti-* + Gr. *klinein*, to lean] Inclined in opposite directions, as the facing sides of a valley.

anticoagulant (ant″i-kō-ag′yŭ-lănt) [*anti-* + *coagulant*] **1.** Delaying or preventing blood coagulation. **2.** An agent that prevents or delays blood coagulation. Common anticoagulants include heparin, sodium citrate, and warfarin sodium. SEE: illus.

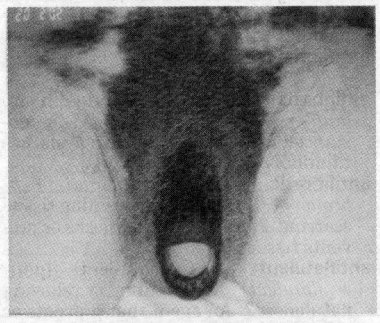

ANTICOAGULATION

Bruising and bleeding, common side effects of anticoagulation.

   coumarin a. Any of a group of natural and synthetic compounds that inhibit blood clotting by antagonizing the biosynthesis of vitamin K–dependent coagulation factors in the liver. SEE: *dicumarol; warfarin sodium*.

   warfarin sodium a. SEE: *warfarin sodium*.

anticoagulant therapy The use of drugs (e.g., heparin, low-molecular-weight heparin, or warfarin) that inhibit or interrupt coagulation, inhibit or deactivate thrombin, prevent conversion of fibrinogen to fibrin, and inhibit blood clot formation. It is used to prevent or treat disorders, such as pulmonary embolism, that result from vascular thrombosis. SEE: *heparin; thrombosis; warfarin sodium*.

⚠ Anticoagulant therapy increases the risk of bleeding.

   PATIENT CARE: The patient is observed closely for desired and adverse effects of anticoagulation therapy. This includes assessing the results of laboratory tests (protime, international ratio [INR], activated partial thromboplastin time [aPTT]) specific to the anticoagulant drug being used to regulate dosing and assessing the patient for signs or symptoms of bleeding. Patients requiring long-term use of anticoagulant therapy (usually warfarin) should wear a medic-alert device or carry a card to identify increased bleeding risk. The patient and family are taught the importance of correct dosing and follow-up testing. Patients should inspect themselves regularly for bleeding gums, bruising, petechiae, nosebleed, tarry stools, and blood in urine or vomitus and report such bleeding to the prescribing physician. Patients should avoid OTC products containing aspirin or other salicylates and should discuss other prescribed drugs (or herbal remedies, such as ginkgo biloba) with the prescriber or pharmacist to be sure these will not interfere with their anticoagulant therapy. Patients should use a soft toothbrush and shave with an electric razor. They need to read labels of food and nutritional products and learn about foods and drinks containing vitamin K in order to maintain consistent intake levels and thus avoid altering the desired anticoagulant effect.

anticoagulation (ant″i-kō-ag″yŭ-lā′shŏn) [*anti-* + *coagulation*] The prevention or hindering of the coagulation of blood, esp. by an anticoagulant drug. **anticoagulate** (-kō-ag′yŭ-lāt″), *v.*

   prophylactic a. The administration of anticoagulant drugs to patients who have a high risk for venous thromboembolism, e.g., patients admitted to medical wards of hospitals or undergoing certain forms of surgery, esp. on the hips or knees.

⚠ The practice reduces the likelihood of the formation of blood clots but increases the risk of bleeding.

anticoagulation management service (ant″ē-kō-ag″yŭ-lā′shŏn) [*anti-* + *coagulation*] ABBR: AMS. A team of specialized personnel who dedicate themselves to tracking and adjusting patient anticoagulation parameters, esp. for patients who need to take drugs like warfarin or heparins chronically. An AMS often includes pharmacists, nurses, and/or physicians, and other health care professionals. SYN: *anticoagulation monitoring service*.

anticoagulation monitoring service ABBR: AMS. Anticoagulation management service.

anticodon (ant″i-kō′do″n) [*anti-* +*codon*] A triplet of nucleotide bases on transfer RNA that complements the corresponding codon on messenger RNA.

anticonvulsant (ant″i-kŏn-vŭl′sănt) [*anti-* + *convulsant*] **1.** Preventing or relieving convulsions. **2.** An agent that prevents or relieves convulsions.

anticyclic citrullinated peptide antibodies SEE: under *antibody*.

anticytotoxin (ant″i-sīt″ŏ-tok′sĭn) [*anti-*

+ *cytotoxin*] An agent that opposes the action of a cytotoxin.

antidepressant (ant″i-dē-pressănt) [*anti-* + *depressant*] **1.** Preventing, curing, or alleviating mental depression. **2.** An agent or therapy that acts to prevent, cure, or alleviate mental depression.

    tetracyclic a. Any of a class of antidepressant agents whose chemical structure has four fused rings. These drugs block the reuptake of norepinephrine and serotonin at nerve endings.

    tricyclic a. Any of two classes of antidepressant agents whose chemical structure has three fused rings. These drugs block the reuptake of norepinephrine and serotonin at nerve endings.

antidiabetic (ant″i-dī″ă-bet′ik) [*anti-* + *diabetic*] **1.** Preventing or treating diabetes. **2.** An agent that prevents or treats diabetes. SEE: *oral hypoglycemic agent.*

antidiarrheal (ant″i-dī″ă-rē′ăl) [*anti-* + *diarrheal*] An agent for preventing or treating diarrhea.

antidiuretic (ant″i-dī″yŭ-ret′ik) [*anti-* + *diuretic*] **1.** Lessening formation of urine. **2.** An agent that decreases formation of urine.

antidote (ant′i-dōt″) [Gr. *antidoton,* given against] A substance that neutralizes poisons or their effects. **antidotal** (ant″i-dōt′ăl), *adj.*

    chemical a. An antidote that reacts with the poison to produce a harmless chemical compound. Table salt precipitates silver nitrate and forms the much less toxic silver chloride. Chemical antidotes should be used sparingly and, after their use, should be removed from the stomach by gastric lavage because they may produce serious results if allowed to remain there.

    mechanical a. An antidote such as activated charcoal that prevents gastrointestinal absorption of a poison.

    physiological a. An antidote that produces physiological effects opposite to the effects of the poison, e.g., sedatives for convulsants and stimulants for hypnotics. These should not be given without a physician's instructions.

    universal a. An antidote once used in poisoning where the specific antidote was unknown or not available, consisting of two parts activated charcoal, one part tannic acid, and one part magnesium oxide.

⚠️ The idea that there is a "universal antidote" for poisonings is flawed.

antidromic (ant″i-drom′ik, -drōm′) [*anti-* + Gr. *dromos,* running + *-ic*] Pert. to nerve impulses that travel in the opposite direction from normal. **antidromically** (-i-k(ă-)lē), *adv.*

antiembolism (ant″i-em′bŏ-lizm) [*anti-* + *embolism*] Preventing or inhibiting thrombus. The correct term is "antithrombotic." SEE: *antithrombotic.*

antiemetic (ant″ē-ĕ-met′ik) [*anti-* + *emetic*] **1.** Preventing or relieving nausea and vomiting. **2.** An agent that prevents or relieves nausea and vomiting.

antienzyme (ant″i-en′zīm″) [*anti-* + *enzyme*] An agent that opposes the action of an enzyme.

antiepileptic (ant″ē-ep″ĭ-lep′tik) [*anti-* + *epileptic*] **1.** Opposing epilepsy. **2.** A procedure or therapy that treats epilepsy.

antiestrogen (ant″ē-es′trŏ-jĕn) [*anti-* + *estrogen*] A substance that blocks or modifies the action of estrogen.

antifebrile (ant″i-fe′brĭl″, -fē′brīl″) [*anti-* + *febrile*] Antipyretic.

antifibrinolysin (ant″i-fī″brĭn-ŏ′lī′sĭn) [*anti-* + *fibrinolysi(s)* + *-in*] A substance that counteracts fibrinolysis. **antifibrinolytic** (-lit′ik), *adj.*

antifibrotic (ant″i-fi-brot′ik) [*anti-* + *fibrotic*] **1.** Blocking or preventing tissue scarring. **2.** An agent that blocks or prevents tissue scarring.

antiflatulent (ant″i-flach′ŭ-lĕnt) [*anti-* + *flatulent*] **1.** Preventing or relieving flatulence. **2.** An agent that prevents or relieves flatulence.

antifungal (ant″i-fŭng′găl) [*anti-* + *fungal*] **1.** Destroying or inhibiting the growth of fungi. **2.** An agent that destroys or inhibits the growth of fungi. SYN: *antimycotic.*

antigalactic (ant″i-gă-lak′tik) [*anti-* + *galactic*] **1.** Preventing or diminishing the secretion of milk. **2.** An agent that prevents or diminishes the secretion of milk.

antigen (ant′i-jĕn) [*anti-* + *-gen*] Any substance capable of eliciting an immune response or of binding with an antibody. Cellular antigens are proteins or oligosaccharides that mark and identify the cell surface as *self* or *nonself.* Cell surface antigens can stimulate the production of antibodies by B lymphocytes and cytotoxic responses by white blood cells, e.g., granulocytes, monocytes, and lymphocytes.

    Antigens on the body's own cells are called autoantigens. Antigens on all other cells are called foreign antigens. Matching certain types of tissue antigens is important for the success of an organ transplant. Inflammation occurs when neutrophils, monocytes, and macrophages encounter an antigen from any source during bodily injury. The antigen may be foreign or an autoantigen that has been damaged and therefore appears to be foreign. Reactions to antigens by T and B cells are part of the specific immune response. SEE: *autoantigen; cytokine; histocompatibility locus a.*

allogeneic a. An antigen that occurs in some individuals of the same species. Examples are the human blood group antigens.

alpha-fetoprotein a. SEE: *alpha-fetoprotein*.

bladder tumor a. ABBR: BTA. A protein released into the urine by malignant cells in the bladder, studied as a possible marker of cancer of the urinary bladder. Because of the low prevalence of bladder cancer in the population at large, and the low positive predictive value of the test, the U.S. Preventive Services Task Force (2006) discouraged health care professionals and patients from using this screening test.

cancer antigen ABBR: CA. A protein or carbohydrate that is either expressed by cancerous cells but not by healthy cells or is expressed by cancerous cells in much greater concentrations than by healthy cells. Cancer antigens are used in clinical medicine to screen body fluids for tumors or to follow the response of tumors to treatment. Since they stimulate the immune response, they are also used in the manufacture of antitumor vaccines. SEE: table.

carcinoembryonic a. ABBR: CEA. A molecular marker found on normal fetal cells and in the bloodstream of patients with cancers of the colon, breast, lung, and other organs. Assays for CEA are used both to monitor the effectiveness of treatments for cancer and to provide prognostic information to patients.

CD a. SEE: *cluster of differentiation*.

class I a. Any of the major histocompatibility molecules present on almost all cells except human red blood cells. These antigens are important in the re-

jection of grafts and transplanted organs.

class II a. Any of the major histocompatibility molecules present on immunocompetent cells.

cross-reacting a. An antigen having the ability to react with more than one specific antibody.

D a. The protein marker in the Rh group of antigens that stimulates the greatest immune response. SEE: *Rh blood group*.

H a. A flagellar protein present on the surface of some enteric bacilli such as *Escherichia coli*. The antigen is important in classifying these bacilli.

hepatitis a. The original term for the Australian antigen, now called hepatitis B surface antigen (HBsAg). Its discovery made possible the differentiation of hepatitis B from other forms of viral hepatitis.

hepatitis B core a. ABBR: HBcAg. A protein marker found on the core of the hepatitis B virus (HBV). HBV antigen does not circulate in the blood but is found only in liver cells infected by HBV. HBcAg stimulates the production of a protective antibody, immunoglobulin M (IgM-anti-HBc), which appears in the blood shortly before the onset of symptoms. Tests for this antibody are used with other blood tests in the diagnosis of acute and chronic hepatitis B infection. During the convalescent stage of hepatitis B infection, IgM anti-HBc is replaced by another antibody, IgG anti-HBc, which remains in the blood for years. SEE: *hepatitis B e a.; hepatitis B surface a.*

hepatitis B e a. ABBR: HBeAg. A polypeptide from the hepatitis B viral core that circulates in the blood of in-

Cancer Antigens Used as Tumor Markers

Antigen name or designation	Abbreviation	The tumor it detects
Alpha-fetoprotein	AFP	Nonseminomatous germ cell tumor
CA 15–3		Breast cancer
CA 19–9		Pancreatic cancer
CA 50		Gastrointestinal tract tumors
CA 125		Ovarian/peritoneal cancer
Carcinoembryonic antigen	CEA	Gastrointestinal tract tumors and tumors of solid internal organs
Human chorionic gonadotropin	HCG	Nonseminomatous germ cell tumors; choriocarcinoma
Microglobulin-beta 2 subunit	b2–M	Multiple myeloma
Neuron-specific enolase	NSE	Broad variety of cancers, including small-cell carcinoma of lung
NY-BR-40 and others		Breast cancer
Prostate specific antigen	PSA	Prostate cancer
Urinary tumor associated antigen	UTAA	Melanoma

Note: several antigens on this list also detect benign diseases and conditions.

fected people and indicates that the patient is highly infectious. It is released when viral DNA is actively replicating.

hepatitis B surface a. ABBR: HBsAg. The glycoprotein found on the surface of the hepatitis B viral envelope. It is the first marker of infection with the hepatitis B virus. If HBsAg is still found in blood samples 6 months after infection with the virus, chronic and potentially contagious infection with hepatitis B is present. SEE: *hepatitis B core a.; hepatitis B e a.*

hepatitis C core a. A protein released by the hepatitis C virus (HCV) into the bloodstream of infected patients. Because hepatitis C core antigen is detectable in the blood before HCV antibodies are produced, it can be used as a marker of early infection, e.g., in donated blood or plasma. It can also measure the response of HCV infection to treatment protocols; antigen levels drop with effective treatment.

histocompatibility locus a. ABBR: HLA. Any of the multiple antigens present on all nucleated cells in the body that identify the cells as self. Immune cells compare these antigens to foreign antigens, which do not match the self and therefore trigger an immune response. These markers determine the compatibility of tissue for transplantation.

They are derived from genes at seven sites (loci) on chromosome 6, in an area called the major histocompatibility complex (MHC); each histocompatibility antigen is divided into one of two MHC classes.

In humans, the proteins created in the MHC are called human leukocyte antigens (HLA) because these markers were originally found on lymphocytes. Each gene in the MHC has several forms or alleles. Therefore, the number of different histocompatibility antigens is very large, necessitating the identification and matching of HLAs in donors and recipients involved in tissue and organ transplantation. (The identification of HLAs is called tissue typing.)

The identification of HLA sites on chromosome 6 has enabled researchers to correlate the presence of specific histocompatibility and certain autoimmune diseases (e.g., insulin-dependent diabetes mellitus, multiple sclerosis, some forms of myasthenia gravis, rheumatoid arthritis, and ankylosing spondylitis). SYN: *human leukocyte a.* SEE: *major histocompatibility complex.*

human leukocyte a. Histocompatibility locus **a.**

H-Y a. A histocompatibility antigen located on the cell membrane. It has a primary role in determining the sexual differentiation of the male embryo.

K a. A capsular antigen present on the surface of some enteric bacilli. The antigen is important in classifying these bacilli.

lymphogranuloma venereum a. An antigen used in a skin test for lymphogranuloma venereum.

mumps skin test a. A standardized suspension of sterile formaldehyde-inactivated mumps virus. It is used in diagnosing mumps.

nuclear a. An antigen present in the cells of patients with certain types of connective tissue disorders. Corticosteroids can be very helpful in treating patients with high concentrations of nuclear antigen.

O a. A surface antigen of some enteric bacilli. The antigen is important in classifying these bacilli.

oncofetal a. An antigen that is normally expressed in the fetus and may reappear in the adult in association with certain tumors. Examples include alpha-fetoprotein and carcinoembryonic antigens. SYN: *oncofetal protein.*

onconeural a. An antigen found on the surface of cancer cells that closely resembles antigens found on nerve cells. Antibodies formed by immune cells against onconeural antigens cause paraneoplastic syndromes.

p24 a. The core protein of HIV. The presence of p24 antigen in the blood is a marker of uncontrolled HIV replication. p24 antigenemia is encountered in the acute retroviral syndrome before host immune response and in advanced AIDS when the immune system has been destroyed. When p24 antigen is detected in the blood, the HIV viral load is high and the person is highly infectious.

proliferating cell nuclear a. ABBR: PCNA. A protein complex released by cells actively synthesizing DNA. In the blood, PCNAs can be used as markers of disease activity in autoimmune and inflammatory illnesses, malignancies, and other conditions marked by rapid cell replication.

prostate-specific a. ABBR: PSA. A nonspecific marker of abnormalities in the prostate gland, including prostatic infection, inflammation, and prostate cancer. PSA circulates in the blood and can be detected by blood tests. PSA levels have been used to screen for prostate cancer, but are neither sensitive nor specific for detecting the disease.

⚠️ Elevations in PSA levels may prompt invasive testing (such as with biopsies) that may detect indolent cancers as well as aggressive ones. Side effects of prostate biopsy include urinary incontinence and erectile dysfunction.

SEE: *prostate cancer.*
protective a. The protein made by

Bacillus anthracis, which binds to cell membranes and allows the lethal components of anthrax toxin to enter and kill cells.

soluble a. An antigen dissolved in a liquid. A soluble antigen is recognized by B lymphocytes but cannot be detected by T lymphocytes until it has been processed by an antigen-presenting cell. SEE: *T cell*.

T-dependent a. An antigen that can stimulate an antibody response only in the presence of helper T cells.

thymus-dependent a. Any of the foreign antigens that require B lymphocyte stimulation by T cells before production of antibodies and memory cells can occur.

thymus-independent a. Any of the foreign antigens capable of stimulating B cell activation and the production of antibodies without T cell interaction. Most of these antibodies fall into the IgM class. A few memory cells are created.

T-independent a. ABBR: TI. Either of two types of antigens that stimulate B-cell production of antibodies without the presence of T cells. TI-1 antigens (e.g., lipopolysaccharides from gram-negative organisms) stimulate production of both specific (monoclonal) and nonspecific (polyclonal) antibodies and promote the release of cytokines from macrophages that enhance the immune response. TI-2 antigens, which result in monoclonal antibody production, may require the presence of cytokines. SEE: *B cell; T cell*.

transplantation a. The commonly used term for any of the histocompatibility antigens that cause the immune system of one individual to reject transplanted tissue.

tumor-specific a. An antigen produced by certain tumors. It appears on the tumor cells but not on normal cells derived from the same tissue. **antigenic** (-jen′ik), *adj.* **antigenically** (-i-k(ă-)lē), *adv.* **antigenicity** (-jĕ-nis′ĭ-tē), *n.*

antigen-antibody reaction The combination of an antigen with its specific antibody. It may result in agglutination, precipitation, neutralization, complement fixation, or increased susceptibility to phagocytosis. The antigen-antibody reaction forms the basis for B-cell—mediated immunity.

antigen binding site Antigenic determinant.

antigenemia (ăn″tĭ-jĕ-nē′mē-ă) The presence of an antigen in the bloodstream.

antigenic determinant The specific area of an antigen that binds with an antibody combining site and determines the specificity of the antigen-antibody reaction. SEE: *antigen*.

epitope a.d. The simplest form of an antigenic determinant within a complex antigenic marker. The epitope links with a paratope, one area of an antibody combining site.

antigen processing SEE: under *processing*.

antigen unit The smallest quantity of antigen required to fix one unit of complement.

antiglobulin (ant″ĭ-glob′yŭ-lĭn) [*anti-* + *globulin*] An antibody that binds with globulin and makes it precipitate out of solution. Antiglobulins are used in Coombs test to detect the presence of a particular antibody or to type blood groups.

antiglobulin test A test for the presence in human blood of antibodies. The antibodies present in the blood do not, themselves, cause agglutination. It is the addition of an antibody made in animals (antiglobulin) that stimulates red blood cell clumping. The direct antiglobulin test (DAT) is used to diagnose autoimmune hemolytic anemia and hemolytic disease of the newborn. The indirect antiglobulin test (IAT), or Coombs test, is used to identify blood types. SEE: *Coombs test*.

direct a. t. ABBR: DAT. A laboratory test for the presence of complement or an antibody that is bound to a patient's red blood cells (RBCs). The test is used in patients with autoimmune hemolytic anemia, hemolytic disease of the newborn, and transfusion reactions. After the patient's RBCs are washed to remove unbound antibodies, they are mixed with antihuman globulin serum containing polyvalent antibodies that bind with the antibody or complement on the RBCs and cause them to agglutinate (clump). Monoclonal antibodies can be used to identify the specific class of antibody or complement component causing RBC destruction. SEE: *Coombs′ test*.

antigoitrogenic (ant″ĭ-goy″trŏ-jen′ik) [*anti-* + *goitrogen* + *-ic*] Preventing the formation of a goiter.

anti-HAV Serum antibody to hepatitis A virus. The presence of anti-HAV in the blood is an indicator either of a successful immune response to vaccination or a current or previous hepatitis A infection.

anti-HBc Antibody to hepatitis B core antigen. The presence of anti-HBc in a sample of serum is an indication of infection (past or present) with hepatitis B virus.

anti-HCV Antibody to hepatitis C virus. The presence of anti-HCV in a blood sample indicates past or present infection with the virus.

anti-HDV *Antibody to hepatitis delta virus.*

antihelix, anthelix (ant″ĭ-hē′liks, anth-ē′liks, -hel′ĭ-sēz″, -hē-lĭ-) *pl.* **antiheli-**

ces, antihelixes [*anti-* + *helix*] The inner curved ridge of the external ear parallel to the helix.

antihemolysin (ant″i-hē″mŏ-lis′ĭn, mol′ĭ-sĭn) [*anti-* + *hemolysin*] An agent that opposes the action of hemolysin.

antihemophilic factor SEE: under *factor*.

antihemorrhagic, **anthemorrhagic** (ant″i-hem″ŏ-raj′ik, ant″hem-ŏ-raj′ik) [*anti-* + *hemorrhagic*] **1.** Preventing or arresting hemorrhage. **2.** An agent that prevents or arrests hemorrhage.

antihidrotic (ant″i-hi-drot′ik, hī-) [*anti-* + *hidrotic*] Antiperspirant.

antihistamine (ant″i-his′tă-mēn″, -mĭn) **1.** Opposing the action of histamine. **2.** An agent that opposes the action of histamine. Although there are two classes of histamine-blocking drugs, the term *antihistamine* is typically used to describe agents that block the action of histamines on H_1 receptors. These agents are used to treat allergies, hives, and other local and allergic reactions. Side effects of first-generation antihistamines, e.g, chlorpheniramine, include sedation, drying of mucous membranes, and urinary retention. Some first-generation antihistamines can also be used to treat insomnia, motion sickness, or vertigo. Second-generation agents (e.g., loratadine) tend to be less sedating but have beneficial effects in the treatment of allergies. **antihistaminic** (-his″tă-min′ik), *adj.* SYN: *histamine blocking agent.* SEE: *Poisons and Poisoning Appendix; histamine.*

antihormone (ant″i-hor′mōn″) [*anti-* + *hormone*] An agent that interferes with the action of a hormone.

antihypercholesterolemic (ant″i-hī″pĕr-kŏ-les″tĕ-rŏ-lē′mik) [*anti-* + *hyper-cholesterolem(ia)* + *-ic*] **1.** Preventing or controlling elevation of the serum cholesterol level. **2.** An agent that prevents or controls elevation of the serum cholesterol level.

antihyperglycemic (ant″i-hī″pĕr-glī-sē′mik) [*anti-* + *hyperglycemic*] **1.** Tending to lower elevated blood glucose levels. **2.** An agent that lowers elevated blood glucose levels.

antihyperprolactinemic (ant″i-hī″pĕr-prō-lak″tĭ-nē′mik) [*anti-* + *hyperpro-lactinem(ia)* + *-ic*] **1.** Preventing or controlling the effects of high blood levels of prolactin. **2.** An agent that lowers high blood levels of prolactin.

antihypertensive (ant″i-hī″pĕr-ten′siv) [*anti-* + *hypertensive*] **1.** Preventing or controlling high blood pressure. **2.** An agent that prevents or controls high blood pressure.

antihypnotic (ant″i-hip-not′ik) [*anti-* + *hypnotic*] **1.** Preventing or inhibiting sleep. **2.** An agent that prevents or inhibits sleep.

anti-infective (ant″ē-in-fek′tiv) [*anti-* + L. *inficere,* to corrupt, to infect] **1.** Tend-

ing to combat infection. **2.** An agent, such as an antibiotic, antifungal, or antiviral drug, that combats infection.

anti-inflammatory (ant″ē-in-flam′ă-tor-ē) [*anti-* + *inflammatory*] **1.** Counter-acting inflammation. **2.** An agent that suppresses or treats inflammation.

anti-inhibitor coagulant complex SEE: under *complex*.

antiketogenesis (ant″i-kēt″ō-jen′ĕ-sĭs) [*anti-* + *ketogenesis*] The prevention or inhibition of formation of ketone bodies. In starvation, diabetes, and other conditions, production of ketones is increased, but they accumulate in the blood because cells do not use them as rapidly as they would use carbohydrates. Carbohydrates are antiketogenic, and increased carbohydrate intake will help prevent or treat antiketogenesis. In ketonemia due to diabetes, both insulin and carbohydrates are needed to allow carbohydrate metabolism to proceed at a rate that would control ketone formation. **antiketogenetic, antiketogenic** (ant″i-kēt″ō-jĕ-net′ik, ant″i-kēt″ō-jen′ik), *adj.*

anti-kickback statute (ant″i-kik′bak″) ABBR: AKBS. A U.S. law that prohibits health care providers from receiving bribes, payments, or rebates in exchange for the referral of patients to a health care facility or for the purchase of health-related products or services.

antilactase (ant″i-lak′tās″) [*anti-* + *lactase*] An agent that opposes the action of lactase.

antileukocyte antibody (ant″i-loo′kŏ-sīt) SEE: under *antibody*.

antilipemic (ant″i-li-pē′mik) [*anti-* + *lipemic*] **1.** Preventing or counteracting the accumulation of fatty substances in the blood. **2.** An agent that prevents or counteracts the accumulation of fatty substances in the blood.

antilithic (ant″i-lith′ik) [*anti-* + Gr. *lithos,* stone + *-ic*] **1.** Preventing or relieving calculi. **2.** An agent that prevents or relieves calculi.

anti-LKM An antibody against liver and kidney cells, sometimes found circulating in the blood of people with autoimmune hepatitis.

antilysin (ant″i-līs′ĭn) [*anti-* + *lysin*] An antibody that opposes the action of lysin.

antilysis (ant″i-lī′sĭs) [*anti-* + *lysis*] Prevention of cell death (lysis). **antilytic** (-lit′ik), *adj.*

antimalarial (ant″i-mă-ler′ē-ăl) [*anti-* + *malarial*] **1.** Preventing or relieving malaria. **2.** An agent that prevents or relieves malaria.

antimanic (ant″i-man′ik) [*anti-* + *manic*] **1.** Preventing or relieving bipolar disorder. **2.** An agent that prevents or treats bipolar disorder.

antimere (ant′i-mēr″) [*anti-* + *-mere*] One of the symmetrical, corresponding parts of the body on the opposite side of its long axis.

antimetabolite (ant″i-mĕ-tab′ŏ-līt″) [*anti-* + *metabolite*] **1.** A substance that opposes the action of or replaces a metabolite and is structurally similar to it. Certain antibiotics are effective because they act as antimetabolites. **2.** Any of a class of antineoplastic drugs to treat cancer. Antimetabolites are structurally similar to vitamins, coenzymes, or other substances essential for growth and division of normal and neoplastic cells. These drugs are most effective against rapidly growing tumors. A drug-induced block of DNA synthesis occurs when the cells take in the antimetabolite rather than the necessary nutrient or enzyme.

antimicrobial, antimicrobic (ant″i-mī-krō′bē-ăl, ant″i-mī-krō′bik) [*anti-* + *microbe*] **1.** Destructive to or preventing the development of microorganisms. **2.** An agent that destroys or prevents the development of microorganisms.

antimicrobial prophylaxis in surgery The use of antibiotics before and sometimes during procedures that are prolonged or involve potential risk of infection. This practice has been shown to prevent infectious complications in colorectal surgery, gynecological and obstetric surgeries, and some cardiac, cancer, and orthopedic procedures. The type of antibiotic administered depends on the surgical procedure. This practice is best suited to procedures involving contaminated areas or implantation of prosthetic material. SEE: *antibiotic resistance*.

antimicrobial sensitivity test A laboratory method of determining the susceptibility of bacteria to antibiotics. The specimen obtained is cultured in various liquid dilutions or on solid media containing various concentrations of antimicrobial drugs in disks placed on the surface of the media. The disk-type test is not completely reliable. SYN: *culture and sensitivity test*.

antimicrobial stewardship Any of the practices and protocols that ensure that antibiotics are used prudently and appropriately. Such practices are designed to reduce unnecessary use of antibiotics and to limit the spread of antibiotic resistance in bacteria. SYN: *antibiotic stewardship*.

antimitotic (ant″i-mī-tot′ik) [*anti-* + *mitotic*] **1.** Interfering with or preventing cell division by mitosis. **2.** An agent that interferes with or prevents cell division by mitosis.

antimonial (ant″ĭ-mō′nē-ăl) [*antimony* + *-al*] **1.** Pert. to or containing antimony. **2.** A substance containing antimony

antimony (ant′ĭ-mō″nē) [L. *antimonium*] SYMB: Sb. A crystalline metalloid element, atomic weight (mass) 121.75, atomic number 51. Its compounds are used in alloys and medicines and may form poisons. SYN: *stibium*. SEE: *Poisons and Poisoning Appendix*.

antimuscarinic (ant″i-mŭs″kă-rin′ik) [*anti-* + *muscarinic*] **1.** Opposing the action of muscarine. **2.** An agent that opposes the action of muscarine. Atropine and scopolamine are antimuscarinic drugs.

antimutagenic (ant″i-mūt″ă-jen′ik) [*anti-* + *mutagenic*] Having the ability to block or prevent mutations.

antimyasthenic (ant″i-mī″ăs-then′ik) [*anti-* + *myasthenic*] **1.** Preventing or relieving muscle weakness. **2.** An agent that prevents or relieves muscle weakness, e.g., in treating myasthenia gravis.

antimycotic (ant″i-mī-kot′ik) [*anti-* + *mycotic*] Antifungal.

antinarcotic (ant″i-nar-kot′ik) [*anti-* + *narcotic*] **1.** Opposing the action of a narcotic. **2.** An agent, such as naloxone, that opposes the action of a narcotic.

antinatriuresis (ant″i-nā″trē-yŭ-rē′sĭs) [*anti-* + *natriuresis*] A decrease in the excretion of sodium in the urine.

antinauseant (ant″i-no′zē-ănt) [*anti-* + *nauseant*] **1.** Preventing or relieving nausea. **2.** An agent that prevents or relieves nausea.

antineoplastic (ant″i-nē″ŏ-plas′tik) [*anti-* + *neoplastic*] **1.** Preventing the development, growth, or proliferation of malignant cells. **2.** An agent that prevents the development, growth, or proliferation of malignant cells.

antinephritic (ant″i-nĕ-frit′ik) [*anti-* + *nephritic*] **1.** Preventing or relieving inflammation of the kidneys. **2.** An agent that prevents or relieves inflammation of the kidneys.

antineuralgic (ant″i-noor-al′jik) [*anti-* + *neuralgic*] **1.** Relieving neuralgia. **2.** An agent that relieves neuralgia.

antineuritic (ant″i-noor-it′ik) [*anti-* + *neurit(is)* + *-ic*] **1.** Preventing or relieving inflammation of a nerve. **2.** An agent that prevents or relieves inflammation of a nerve.

antineuronal nuclear antibody SEE: *antibody*.

antinuclear (ant″i-noo′klē-ăr) [*anti-* + *nuclear*] Reacting with or destroying the nucleus of a cell.

antinutrient (ant″ē-noo′trē-ĕnt) [*anti-* + *nutrient*] A food or chemical that either interferes with the absorption and metabolism of other food sources or prevents the normal growth and development of an organism.

antiobsessive (ant″i-ob-ses′iv) [*anti-* + *obsessive*] **1.** Preventing or treating obsession or obsessive-compulsive disorder. **2.** An agent for treating obsession or obsessive-compulsive disorder.

antiodontalgic (ant″i-ō″don″tal′jik)

[*anti-* + *odontalgic*] **1.** Relieving toothache. **2.** An agent that relieves toothache.

antioncogene (ant″i-ong″kō-jēn″) [*anti-* + *oncogene*] A gene that inhibits or prevents the growth of tumor cells.

antiovulatory (ant″i-ov′yŭ-lă-tŏr″ē) [*anti-* + *ovulatory*] Inhibiting or preventing ovulation.

antioxidant (ant″ē-ok′sĭ-dănt) [*anti-* + *oxidant*] **1.** Preventing or inhibiting oxidation. **2.** An agent that prevents or inhibits oxidation. Antioxidants may protect cells from the damaging effects of oxygen radicals, some forms of cancer, and reperfusion injuries.

antiparallel (ant″i-par′ă-lel″) [*anti-* + *parallel*] Parallel but pointing in opposite directions, as in the characteristic sequencing of the deoxyribonucleotides on one strand of the DNA helix, matched by the opposite sequencing on the other strand.

antiparalytic (ant″i-par″ă-lit′ik) [*anti-* + *paralytic*] **1.** Relieving paralysis. **2.** An agent that relieves paralysis.

antiparasitic (ant″i-par″ă-sit′ik) [*anti-* + *parasitic*] **1.** Destructive to parasites. **2.** An agent that destroys parasites.

antiparkinsonian (ant″i-par″kĭn-sō′nē-ăn) [*anti-* + *parkinsonian*] **1.** Effective against parkinsonism. **2.** An agent effective against parkinsonism.

antipathy (an-tip′ă-thē) [*anti-* + *-pathy*] **1.** A feeling of strong aversion. **2.** An object of strong aversion. **antipathic** (ant″i-path′ik), *adj.*

antipedicular (ant″i-pĕ-dik′yŭ-lăr) [*anti-* + *pedicular*] Effective against pediculosis.

antiperistalsis (ant″i-per″ĭ-stal′sĭs) [*anti-* + *peristalsis*] A wave of contraction in the gastrointestinal tract moving toward the oral end; reversed peristalsis. In the duodenum, it is associated with vomiting; in the ascending colon it occurs normally. **antiperistaltic** (-stal′tik), *adj.*

antiperspirant (ant″i-pĕr′spī-rănt) [*anti-* + *perspire*] **1.** Inhibiting perspiration. **2.** A substance that inhibits perspiration. SYN: *anhidrotic; antihidrotic.*

antiphagocytic (ant″i-fag″ŏ-sit′ik) [*anti-* + *phagocytic*] Preventing or inhibiting phagocytosis.

antiphospholipid antibody syndrome (ant″i-fos″fō-lip′ĭd) [*anti- phospholipid*] ABBR: APAS. A condition characterized by hypercoagulability associated with high blood levels of IgG antibodies against phospholipids. Many affected patients have a systemic autoimmune disease, e.g., systemic lupus erythematosus, but others present only with a history of frequent arterial and venous thrombi or pregnancy loss. Recent evidence suggests that antiphospholipid antibodies play a role in approx. 20% of strokes, esp. in patients who do not have common risk factors for stroke. Antiphospholipid antibodies include lupus anticoagulant and anticardiolipins; the presence of the latter causes these patients to test positive for syphilis.

Thromboses caused by the syndrome are treated and prevented with heparin, warfarin, corticosteroids, or, in some instances, immunosuppressant drugs such as cyclophosphamide.

⚠ Warfarin should not be used during pregnancy because of the risk of fetal malformations.

antiplastic (ant″i-plas′tik) [*anti-* + *plastic* (2)] **1.** Preventing or inhibiting wound healing. **2.** An agent that prevents or inhibits wound healing by preventing formation of granulation tissue.

antiplatelet (ant″i-plāt′lĕt) [*anti-* + *platelet*] **1.** Destructive to platelets. **2.** An agent that destroys or inactivates platelets, preventing them from forming blood clots.

antipodal (an-tip′ŏ-dăl) [Gr. *antipous,* with feet opposite] Located at opposite positions, e.g., at the north and south poles.

antiporter (ant′i-port″ĕr) A cell membrane protein that moves two substances in opposite directions through the membrane. SEE: *symporter.*

antiprostaglandin (ant″i-pros″tă-glan′dĭn) [*anti-* + *prostaglandin*] Any agent that blocks the release or action of prostaglandins. Antagonists of prostaglandins are primarily used to relieve pain and inflammation. SEE: *nonsteroidal anti-inflammatory drug.*

antiprostatitis (ant″i-pros″tă-tīt′ĭs) [*anti-* + *prostatitis*] Inflammation of Cowper gland.

antiprotease (ant″i-prōt′ē-ās″) [*anti-* + *protease*] A chemical that interferes with the hydrolysis of proteins by a protease enzyme.

antiprotozoal (ant″i-prōt″ŏ-zō′ăl) [*anti-* + *protozoal*] **1.** Destructive to protozoa. **2.** An agent that destroys protozoa.

antipruritic (ant″i-proo-rit′ik) [*anti-* + *pruritic*] **1.** Preventing or relieving itching. **2.** An agent that prevents or relieves itching.

antipsoriatic (ant″i-sŏr″-at′ik) [*anti-* + *psoriatic*] **1.** Preventing or relieving psoriasis. **2.** An agent that prevents or relieves psoriasis.

antipsychotic (ant″i-sī″kot′ik) [*anti-* + *psychotic*] **1.** Preventing or treating psychosis, e.g., schizophrenia. **2.** A medication to treat psychosis.

   atypical a. Second-generation **a.**

   first-generation a. A neuroleptic drug. They treat psychotic disorders and other psychiatric diseases. Side effects include extrapyramidal (Parkinsonian) reactions. SYN: *conventional a.* SEE: *neuroleptic* (1).

conventional a. First-generation **a.**

second-generation a. An antipsychotic drug that causes increased appetite, weight gain, and adverse effects on lipids. They differ from first-generation antipsychotics in that they are less likely to cause extrapyramidal side effects or tardive dyskinesia. SYN: *atypical a.*

antipyresis (ant″i-pī″rē′sĭs) [*anti-* + *pyre(tic)* + *-sis*] Use of drugs to prevent or treat fever.

antipyretic (ant″i-pī-ret′ik) [*anti-* + *pyretic*] **1.** Reducing fever. **2.** An agent that reduces fever. SYN: *antifebrile.*

antipyrotic (ant″i-pī″rot′ik) [*anti-* + *pyrotic*] **1.** Promoting the healing of burns. **2.** An agent that promotes the healing of burns.

antirachitic (ant″i-ră-kit′ik) [*anti-* + *rachitic*] **1.** Helping to cure rickets. **2.** An agent for treating rickets.

antirejection therapy (ant″i-rĕ-jek′shŏn) [*anti-* + *rejection*] Any of the drugs that suppress the immune system in patients who have undergone organ transplantation.

⚠ These agents decrease the likelihood that the transplant recipient will react against the transplanted organ but increase the likelihood of some infectious diseases and cancers.

antiresorptive (ant″i-rē-sorp′tiv, -zorp′) [*anti-* + L. *resorbere,* to suck in] **1.** Blocking or opposing the destruction of bone by osteoclasts. **2.** An agent that prevents or slows the progress of osteoporosis. SEE: *osteoporosis.*

antiretroviral (ant″i-re″trō-vī′răl) [*anti-* + *retroviral*] An agent that acts against retroviruses such as HIV.

antiretroviral treatment-related lipodystrophy syndrome HIV-related fat redistribution syndrome.

antirheumatic (ant″i-roo-mat′ik) [*anti-rheumatic*] **1.** Preventing or relieving rheumatism. **2.** An agent that prevents or relieves rheumatism.

antiscabietic (ant″i-skā″bē-et′ik) [*anti-* + *scabietic*] **1.** Preventing or relieving scabies. **2.** An agent that prevents or relieves scabies.

antiscorbutic (ant″i-skor-būt′ik) [*anti-* + *scorbutic*] **1.** Preventing or relieving scurvy. **2.** An agent that prevents or relieves scurvy.

antiseborrheic (ant″i-seb″ŏ-rē′ik) [*anti-* + *seborrheic*] **1.** Counteracting or treating seborrhea. **2.** An agent that counteracts or relieves seborrhea.

antisecretory (ant″i-sē′krĕ′tor″ē) [*anti-* + *secretory*] **1.** Inhibiting secretion of a gland or organ. **2.** An agent that inhibits secretion of a gland or organ.

antiself (ant″i-self′) [*anti-* + *self* (2)] The abnormal reaction of antibodies or lymphocytes with antigens present in the host. SEE: *autoantibody; autoimmune disease.*

antisense (an″tĭ″-sens′) [*anti-* + *sense* (6)] Pert. to strands of genetic material having a matching but reversed order of nucleic acids. In a typical double-stranded molecule of DNA, one strand, called the "sense" strand, codes for the messenger RNA; the matching strand of DNA is the antisense strand.

antisepsis (ant″i-sep′sĭs) [*anti-* + *sepsis*] Prevention of infection by preventing or inhibiting the growth of causative microorganisms.

antiseptic (ant″i-sep′tik) [*anti-* + *septic*] **1.** Pert. to antisepsis. **2.** Preventing or inhibiting growth of microorganisms. **3.** Protecting or acting like a germicide. **4.** Cleansed or free of microorganisms. **5.** An agent producing antisepsis. Alcohols, chlorhexidine, iodine, and triclosan are some commonly used antiseptics.

antiserum (ant″i-sēr′ŭm) [*anti-* + *serum*] A serum that contains antibodies for a specific antigen. It may be of human or animal origin. SYN: *immune serum.*

monovalent a. Antiserum containing antibodies specific for one antigen.

polyvalent a. Antiserum containing antibodies specific for more than one antigen.

antishock garment (ant″i-shok′) A three-compartment garment that can be placed quickly on a patient with severe hypovolemia or a suspected pelvic fracture. When the compartments are inflated, they compress the abdomen and legs, limiting the blood flow into these areas and preventing pooling of blood and fluid in the underlying tissues. The value of the device in improving long-term survival has been questioned; therefore, these garments are no longer used as frequently as they were in the past. Also known as MAST (*military antishock trousers*). SYN: *pneumatic antishock garment.*

⚠ The garment is contraindicated in cardiogenic shock, penetrating abdominal or chest trauma with hemorrhage, or congestive heart failure. In patients who are bleeding as a result of penetrating trauma, the pressure in the garment may raise systemic vascular resistance (SVR) and increase the rate and volume of blood loss.

PATIENT CARE: Inflatable compartments are filled to appropriate pressure (approx. 104 mm Hg or until the pop-off valves begin to leak), from the bottom up, and inflation is maintained until venous access and fluid resuscitation are initiated. Compartments are then deflated from top to bottom; the patient's blood pressure and pulse are monitored frequently for evidence of hypotension. SEE: *anti-G suit*.

antisialagogue (ant″i-sī″ăl′ă-gog″) [*anti-* + *sialagogue*] An agent, such as atropine, that lessens or prevents production of saliva. **antisialagogic** (ăl″ă-goj′ik), *adj.*

antisialic (ăn″tī-sī-ăl′ĭk) **1.** Inhibiting the secretion of saliva. **2.** An agent that inhibits the secretion of saliva.

antisocial (an″tī-sō′shăl) [*anti-* + *social*] Pert. to a person whose outlook and actions are socially negative and whose behavior is repeatedly in conflict with what society perceives as the norm. SEE: *asocial*.

antispasmodic (an″tī-spaz-mod′ik) [*anti-* + Gr. *spasmōdēs,* spastic] **1.** Preventing or relieving spasm. **2.** An agent that prevents or relieves spasm.

antistreptococcic, antistreptococcal (an″tī-strep″tŏ-kok′sik, -kok′săl) [*anti-* + *streptococcic*] Destructive to streptococci.

antistreptolysin (an″tī-strep-tŏ-lī′sĭn) [*anti-* + *streptolysin*] An antibody that opposes the action of streptolysin.

   a. O ABBR: ASLO. An antibody against streptolysin O that is used retrospectively to diagnose infections with group A beta-hemolytic streptococci.

antisynthetase syndrome (ant″sin′thĕ-tās″) A syndrome identified in a subset of patients with inflammatory myopathies (dermatomyositis or polymyositis). It includes the scaling and cracking of the radial and palmar surfaces of the fingers, Raynaud phenomenon, joint inflammation, interstitial lung disease, fever, and generalized weakness.

antisyphilitic (an″tī-sif″ĭ-lit′ik) [*anti-* + *syphilitic*] **1.** Curing or relieving syphilis. **2.** An agent that cures or relieves syphilis.

antithenar (ant″i-thē′năr) [*anti-* + *thenar*] The eminence on the ulnar side of the palm, formed by the muscles of the little finger. SYN: *hypothenar eminence*.

antithrombin (ant″i-throm′bĭn) [*anti-* + *thrombin*] An agent that prevents the action of thrombin.

   a. III A plasma protein that inactivates thrombin and inhibits coagulation factors IX, X, XI, and XII, preventing abnormal clotting.

antithrombotic (ant″i-throm-bot′ik) [*anti-* + *thrombotic*] Interfering with or preventing thrombosis.

antithyroid, antithyroidal (ant″i-thī′royd″, -thī′royd′ăl) [*anti-* + *thyroid*] **1.** Preventing or inhibiting the functioning of the thyroid gland. **2.** An agent (e.g., methimazole) that prevents or inhibits the functioning of the thyroid gland.

antitoxigen (ant″i-tok′sĭ-gĕn) [*antitoxi(n)* + *-gen*] Antitoxinogen.

antitoxin (ant″i-tok′sĭn) [*anti-* + *toxin*] An antibody that is produced in response to a specific biologic toxin, e.g., *Corynebacterium diphtheriae,* which causes diphtheria, and is capable of neutralizing it. Antitoxins are used for prophylactic and therapeutic purposes. SEE: *antivenin.* **antitoxic** (-tok′sik), *adj.*

antitoxinogen (ant″i-tok-sin′ŏ-jĕn) [*antitoxin* + *-gen*] An antigen that stimulates production of antitoxin. SYN: *antitoxigen.*

antitoxin unit A unit for expressing the strength of an antitoxin. Originally, the various units were defined biologically, but now they are compared with a weighed standard specified by the US Public Health Service and the World Health Organization.

antitragicus (ant″i-traj′ĭ-kŭs) [*anti-* + *tragicus*] A small muscle in the pinna of the ear.

antitragus (ant″i-trā′gŭs) [*anti-* + *tragus*] A projection on the ear of the cartilage of the auricle in front of the tail of the helix, posterior to the tragus.

antitrichomonal (ant″i-trik′ŏ-mō′-năl) [*anti-* + *trichomonal*] **1.** Resistant to or lethal to trichomonads. **2.** A medicine effective in treating trichomonal infections.

antitrismus (ant″i-triz′mŭs) [*anti-* + *trismus*] A condition in which the mouth cannot close because of tonic spasm (trismus).

antitrypsin (ant″i-trip′sĭn) [*anti-* + *trypsin*] A substance that inhibits the action of trypsin. **antitryptic** (-trip′tik), *adj.*

anti-tTG The serum antitissue transglutaminase antibody. Patients with celiac disease have elevated levels of anti-tTG.

antitubercular, antituberculous (ant″i-too-bĕr′kyŭ-lăr, kyŭ-lŭs) [*anti-* + L. *tubercle*] **1.** Preventing or treating tuberculosis. **2.** An agent used to prevent or treat tuberculosis.

antitumor (ant″ē-too″mŏr) [*anti-* + *tumor*] Inhibiting the growth or development of cancer.

antitussive (ant″i-tŭs′iv) [*anti-* + *tussive*] **1.** Preventing or relieving coughing. **2.** An agent that prevents or relieves coughing.

   centrally acting a. An agent that depresses medullary centers, suppressing the cough reflex.

antivenereal, anti-venereal (ant″i-vĕ-nĕr′ē-ăl) [*anti-* + *venereal*] Preventing or curing sexually transmitted diseases.

antivenin, antivenene, antivenom (ant″i-ven′ĭn, ant″ve″nēn′, ant″ven′ŏm) [*anti-* + *venin, venom*] A serum that contains antitoxin specific for an animal or insect venom. Antivenin is prepared from the sera of immunized animals.

PATIENT CARE: Antivenins are foreign proteins that often induce allergic reactions in patients who receive them. The likelihood of allergic reactions is reduced by prior administration of epinephrine.

black widow spider a. Antitoxic serum obtained from horses immunized against the venom of the black widow spider (*Latrodectus mactans*) and used specifically to treat bites of the black widow spider.

antivenomous (ant″ĭ-ven′ŏ-mŭs) [*anti- + venomous*] Opposing the action of venom.

antiviral (ant″ĭ-vi′răl) [*anti- + viral*] **1.** Opposing the action of a virus. **2.** A drug used to treat viral infections. Examples of antiviral drugs include: acyclovir or famciclovir (for herpes simplex virus infections); oseltamivir (for influenza virus infection); pegylated interferon and ribavirin (for hepatitis C viral infection); and ritonavir or tenofovir (for HIV infection).

antivitamin (ant″ĭ-vīt′ă-mĭn) [*anti- + vitamin*] A substance that makes a vitamin ineffective; a vitamin antagonist.

antivivisection (ant″ĭ-viv′ĭ-sek″shŏn) [*anti- + vivisection*] Opposition to vivisection or the use of live animals in experimentation. **antivivisectionist** (-viv″ĭ-sek′shŏn-ist), *n.*

antixerotic (ant″ĭ-zĕ-rot′ĭk) [*anti- + xerotic*] Preventing dryness of the skin.

antizymotic (ant″ĭ-zī-mot′ĭk) [*anti- + zymotic*] An agent that prevents or arrests fermentation (e.g., of alcohol or salicylic acid).

Antley-Bixler syndrome (ant′lē-biks′lĕr) [Ray M. Antley, contemporary U.S. physician; David Bixler, U.S. dentist and geneticist, b. 1929] A rare autosomal recessive disorder of bone and connective tissue in which malformations of both the long and the cranial bones are present.

Anton syndrome (an′ton″) [Gabriel Anton, Ger. psychiatrist, 1858–1933] Visual **anosognosia**.

antra (an′tră) Pl. of antrum.

antrectomy (an-trek′tŏ-mē) [*antro- + -ectomy*] Excision of the walls of an antrum.

antritis (an″trīt′ĭs) [*antro- + -itis*] Inflammation of an antrum, esp. the maxillary sinus.

antro-, antr- [L. *antrum*, fr. Gr. *antron*, cave, cavity] Prefixes meaning *antrum*.

antroatticotomy (an″trŏ-at″ĭ-kot′ŏ-mē) [*antro- + atticotomy*] An operation to open the maxillary sinus and the attic of the tympanum.

antrobuccal (an″trŏ-bŭk′ăl) [*antro- + buccal*] Pert. to the maxillary sinus and the cheek.

antrocele (an′trŏ-sēl″) [*antro- + -cele*] Fluid accumulation in a cyst in the maxillary sinus.

antrochoanal (an″trŏ-kō′ă-năl) [*antro- + choanal*] Pert. to both the maxillary antrum and the cavity that connects the nasopharynx and nasal cavity.

antroduodenal (an″trŏ-dū-ō-dē′năl) [*antro- + duodenal*] Pert. to the gastric antrum and the proximal region of the small bowel.

antroduodenectomy (an″trŏ-doo-ō-od″ĕn-ek′tŏ-mē) [*antro-, + duodenectomy*] Surgical removal of the pyloric antrum and the upper portion of the duodenum.

antronasal (an″trŏ-nā′zăl) [*antro + nasal*] Pert. to the maxillary sinus and nasal fossa.

antroscope (an′trŏ-skōp″) [*antro- + -scope*] An instrument for visual examination of a cavity, esp. the maxillary sinus.

antrostomy (an-tros′tŏ-mē) [*antro- + -stomy*] **1.** An operation to form an opening in an antrum. **2.** Surgical incision into an antrum.

antrotomy (an″trot′ŏ-mē) [*antro- + -otomy*] Surgical incision through an antral wall.

antrotympanic (an″trŏ-tim-pan′ik) [*antro- + tympanic* (1)] Pert. to the mastoid antrum and the tympanic cavity.

antrotympanitis (an″trŏ-tim″pă-nīt′ĭs) [*antro- + tympanitis*] Chronic inflammation of the tympanic cavity and mastoid antrum.

antrum (an′trŭm, ′tră) *pl.* **antra** [L. *antrum* fr. Gr. *antron*, cave] Any nearly closed cavity or chamber, esp. in a bone. **antral** (-trăl), *adj.*

duodenal a. The duodenal cap; a dilatation of the duodenum near the pylorus. It is seen during digestion.

gastric a. Distal non–acid-secreting segment of the stomach or pyloric gland region that produces the hormone gastrin.

maxillary a. The maxillary sinus; a cavity in the maxillary bone communicating with the middle meatus of the nasal cavity.

pyloric a. A bulge in the pyloric portion of the stomach along the greater curvature on distention.

ANTU *Alpha-naphthylthiourea,* a powerful rat poison.

anuclear (ā″-nū′klē-ăr) [¹*an- + nuclear*] Of erythrocytes, lacking a nucleus.

ANUG *acute necrotizing ulcerative gingivitis.*

anulus, annulus (an′yŭ-lŭs) *pl.* **anuli** [L. *anulus,* finger ring] A ring-shaped structure; a ring.

a. conjunctivae Conjunctival **ring**.

a. fibrosus The outer portion of the intervertebral disk, consisting of concentric rings of collagen fibers (lamellae) oriented in varying directions and designed to withstand tensile and compressive loads on the spine as it transmits weight.

anuria (ă-noor'ē-ă) [¹*an-* + *-uria*] Absence of urine formation. **anuric** (-noor'ik), *adj.*

anus (ā'nŭs) [L. *anus*, ring, anus] The outlet of the rectum lying in the fold between the buttocks.

    artificial a. An opening into the bowel formed by colostomy.

    imperforate a. A condition in which the anus is closed. SYN: *anal atresia*.

    vulvovaginal a. A congenital anomaly in a female in which the anus is imperforate, but there is an opening from the rectum to the vagina.

anvil (an'vĭl) Incus.

anxiety (ang-zī'ĕt-ē) [L. *anxietas*, distress] An uneasy feeling of discomfort or dread accompanied by an autonomic response; a feeling of apprehension caused by anticipation of danger. The source of the anxiety is often nonspecific or unknown to the individual. It is a potential signal that warns of impending danger and enables the individual to take measures to deal with threat. Recurrence of such reactions that disrupt the ability to function when immediate danger is not perceptible to others is characteristic of anxiety disorders. These include generalized anxiety disorder, panic disorder, social anxiety disorder or phobia, posttraumatic stress disorder, obsessive-compulsive disorder and procedural anxiety. SEE: *anxiety disorder; Nursing Diagnoses Appendix.*

PATIENT CARE: Health care providers evaluate the patient's level of anxiety and document related behavior and physical characteristics, e.g., sympathetic nervous system arousal, effects on the patient's perceptual field, and ability to learn and solve problems. Coping and defense mechanisms, a family history of similar problems, avoidance behavior, sleep history, depression, the use of alcohol, caffeine, tobacco, herbal supplements, prescription and over-the-counter drugs are reviewed. A calm, caring, quiet, and controlled atmosphere can prevent progression of the patient's anxiety and even reduce it by lessening feelings of isolation and instability. Patients with mild anxiety are helped to identify and eliminate stressors, if possible. Appropriate outlets are provided for excess energy. Health care providers establish a trusting relationship with the patient and encourage the patient to express feelings and concerns. False reassurance is never offered. Care for patients with severe anxiety focuses on reducing environmental stimuli. Clear, simple validating statements are used to communicate with the patient and

are repeated as often as necessary, and reality is reinforced if distortion is evident. The patient's physical needs are addressed, and activity is encouraged to help the patient discharge excess energy and relieve stress.

If the anxiety is ongoing, the patient should be referred to a care provider who specializes in treatment of anxiety disorders. Relaxation therapy, counseling, psychotherapy, and/or pharmacologic therapies may be required. Drug types used include benzodiazepines, selective serotonin reuptake inhibitors, serotonin and norepinephrine reuptake inhibitors, and tricyclic antidepressants. Desired effects of the specific prescribed drug are explained and when the patient may expect to see these results; adverse effects to watch for and report are described. The patient is advised that, in general, antianxiety drugs should not be stopped abruptly or without the prescriber's agreement. The patient also may benefit from referral to a support group such as the Anxiety Disorders Association of America.

    castration a. Anxiety about the possibility of injury to or loss of the testicles or ovaries.

    death a. The apprehension, worry, or fear related to death or dying. SEE: *Nursing Diagnoses Appendix.*

    free-floating a. Anxiety unrelated to an identifiable condition, situation, or cause.

    separation a. Distress, agitation, or apprehension expressed by toddlers or others when they are removed from mother, family, home, or other familiar surroundings.

anxiety attack SEE: under *attack*.

anxiety disorder Any of a group of mental conditions that include panic disorder with or without agoraphobia, agoraphobia without panic disorder, simple (specific) phobia, social phobia, obsessive-compulsive disorder, posttraumatic stress disorder, acute stress disorder, generalized anxiety disorder, anxiety caused by a general medical condition, and substance-induced anxiety disorder. The symptoms vary widely but interfere significantly with normal functioning. SYN: *anxiety neurosis; expectation neurosis*. SEE: *Nursing Diagnoses Appendix.*

    generalized a.d. Excessive anxiety and worry predominating for at least 6 months. Restlessness, easy fatigability, difficulty in concentrating, irritability, muscle tension, and disturbed sleep may be present. Adults with this disorder often worry about everyday, routine circumstances such as job responsibilities, finances, the health of family members, misfortune to their children, or minor matters such as being late or completing household chores. The intensity, duration, or frequency of the anxiety and worry is far out of proportion to the actual likelihood or impact of the feared event.

anxiety reaction Anxiety disorder.

anxiety state A condition marked by more or less continuous anxiety and apprehension. SEE: *anxiety disorder*.

anxiolytic (ang″zē-ō-lit′ik, angk″sē-) [*anxi(ety)*, + *-lytic*] **1.** Counteracting or relieving anxiety. **2.** A drug that counteracts or relieves anxiety. SYN: *antianxiety agent*.

any willing doctor Any provider of health care services (not just a physician) who agrees to the terms of the Medicare program.

AOA *Alpha Omega Alpha* (an honorary medical fraternity in the U.S.); *American Optometric Association; American Osteopathic Association.*

AoA *Administration on Aging.*

A.O.C. *anodal opening* **contraction**.

AOCN *Advanced Oncology Certified Nurse.*

AODA *alcohol and other drug abuse.*

AORN *Association of periOperative Registered Nurses.*

aort-, aorto- [L. fr. Gr. *aortē*, the large artery] Prefixes meaning *aorta*.

aorta (ā-ort′ă, ā-ort′ē) *pl.* **aortaeaortas** [L. *aorta* fr Gr. *aortē*, the large artery] The main trunk of the arterial system of the body. **aortic** (ā-or′tĭk), *adj.*

The aorta is about 3 cm in diameter at its origin in the upper surface of the left ventricle. It passes upward as the ascending aorta, turns backward and to the left (arch of the aorta) at about the level of the fourth thoracic vertebra, and then passes downward as the thoracic aorta to the diaphragm, and below the diaphragm as the abdominal aorta. The latter terminates at its division into the two common iliac arteries. At the junction of the aorta and the left ventricle is the aortic semilunar valve, which contains three cusps. This valve opens when the ventricle contracts and is closed by the backup of blood when the ventricle relaxes. SEE: illus.

The divisions of the aorta are as follows:

Ascending aorta (two branches): Two coronary arteries (right and left) provide blood supply to the myocardium.

Aortic arch (three branches): The brachiocephalic artery divides into the right subclavian artery, which provides blood to the right arm and other areas, and right common carotid artery, which supplies the right side of the head and neck. The left common carotid artery supplies the left side of the head and neck. The left subclavian artery provides blood for the left arm and portion of the thoracic area.

Thoracic aorta: Two or more bronchial arteries provide blood for bronchi.

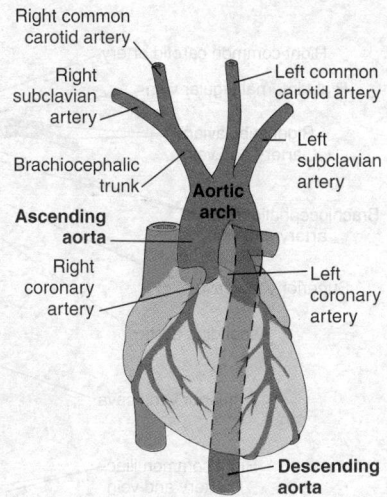

MAIN PARTS OF AORTA

Esophageal arteries provide blood to the esophagus. Pericardial arteries supply the pericardium. Nine pairs of intercostal arteries supply blood for intercostal areas. Mediastinal branches supply lymph glands and the posterior mediastinum. Superior phrenic arteries supply the diaphragm.

Abdominal aorta: The celiac artery supplies the stomach, liver, and spleen. The superior mesenteric artery supplies all of the small intestine except the superior portion of the duodenum. The inferior mesenteric artery supplies all of the colon and rectum except the right half of the transverse colon. The middle suprarenal branches supply the adrenal (suprarenal) glands. The renal arteries supply the kidneys, ureters, and adrenals. The testicular arteries supply the testicles and ureter. The ovarian arteries (which correspond to internal spermatic arteries of the male) supply the ovaries, part of the ureters, and the uterine tubes. The inferior phrenic arteries supply the diaphragm and esophagus. The lumbar arteries supply the lumbar and psoas muscles and part of the abdominal wall musculature. The middle sacral artery supplies the sacrum and coccyx. The right and left common iliac arteries supply the lower pelvic and abdominal areas and the lower extremities.

aortalgia (ā″or-tal′j(ē-)ă) [*aort-*, + *-algia*] Pain in the aortic area.

aortarctia (ā″or-tark′sh(ē-)ă) [*aort-* + L. *arctare*, to narrow] Aortic narrowing. SEE: *coarctation*.

aortectasia (ā″ort-ek-tā′zh(ē-)ă) [*aort-* + *ectasia*] Dilatation of the aorta.

aortectomy (ā″or″tek′tŏ-mē) [*aort-* + *-ectomy*] Excision of part of the aorta.

aortic arch syndrome Partial or complete

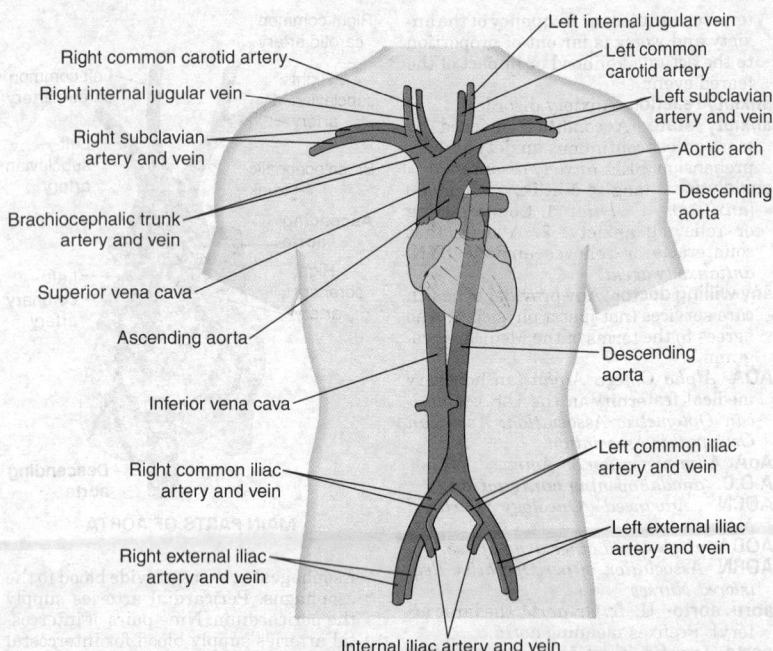

Right common carotid artery

Right internal jugular vein

Right subclavian artery and vein

Brachiocephalic trunk artery and vein

Superior vena cava

Ascending aorta

Inferior vena cava

Right common iliac artery and vein

Right external iliac artery and vein

Left internal jugular vein

Left common carotid artery

Left subclavian artery and vein

Aortic arch

Descending aorta

Descending aorta

Left common iliac artery and vein

Left external iliac artery and vein

Internal iliac artery and vein

MAJOR BRANCHES OF AORTA AND VENA CAVAE

blockage of the main arteries that arise from the aortic arch. Diminished blood flow to the parts of the body supplied by those arteries may lead to stroke, retinal infarct, or arm pain and weakness. One cause of this rare syndrome is Takayasu's arteritis.

aortic body A chemoreceptor in the wall of the aortic arch that detects changes in blood gases, esp. oxygen, and pH. It is innervated by the vagus nerve and stimulates reflex changes in heart rate, respiration, and blood pressure that restore normal blood oxygen levels.

aortic branch disease Takayasu's arteritis.

aortic dissection SEE: under *dissection*.

aortitis (ā″or″tīt′ĭs) [*aort-* + *-itis*] Inflammation of the aorta, It occurs in patients with syphilis, autoimmune vasculitis, giant cell arteritis, Takayasu's arteritis, or rheumatoid arthritis. Symptoms (fever, chills, myalgias, and malaise) are usually nonspecific.

aortoclasia (ā″or″tŏ-klā′zh(ē-)ă) [*aort-* + *-clas(is)* + *-ia*] Aortic rupture.

aortocoronary (ā″or″tŏ-kor′ŏ-ner-ē) [*aort-* + *coronary*] Pert. to both the aorta and the coronary arteries.

aortogram (ā-or′tŏ-grăm″) [*aort-* + *-gram*] An image of the aorta obtained through radiography, computed tomography, or magnetic resonance imaging, usually after the injection of a contrast agent.

aortography (ā″or″tog′ră-fē) [*aort-* + *-graphy*] Radiography of the aorta after injection of a contrast medium. **aortographic** (-grsf′ik), *adj.*

 retrograde a. Aortography by injection of a contrast medium into the aorta via one of its branches, and thus against the direction of the blood flow.

 translumbar a. Aortography by injection of a contrast medium into the abdominal aorta through a needle inserted into the lumbar area near the level of the 12th rib.

aortoiliac (ā″or″tŏ-ĭl′ē-ak) [*aort-* + *iliac*] Pert. to both the aorta and the iliac arteries.

aortolith (ā″or″tŏ-lith″) [*aort-* + *lith-*] Calcified deposit in the aortic wall.

aortomalacia (ā″or″tŏ-mă-lā′sh(ē-)ă) [*aort-* + *-malacia*] Softening of the walls of the aorta.

aortoplasty (ā″or″tŏ-plas″tē) [*aort-* + *-plasty*] Surgical repair of the aorta, frequently requiring a graft.

aortorrhaphy (ā″or″tor′ă-fē) [*aort-* + *-rrhaphy*] Suture of the aorta.

aortosclerosis (ā″or″tŏ-sklĕ-rō′sĭs) [*aort-* + *sclerosis*] Arteriosclerosis in the aorta.

aortostenosis (ā″or″tŏ-stĕ-nō′sĭs) [*aort-* + *stenosis*] Aortic stenosis.

aortotomy (ā″or″tot′ŏ-mē) [*aort-* + *-tomy*] Incision of the aorta.

AOTA *American Occupational Therapy Association.*

AP, A-P *anteroposterior.*

A.P. *anteroposterior.*

APA *American Pharmaceutical Association; American Podiatry Association; American Psychiatric Association; American Psychological Association.*

APACHE II *Acute Physiology and Chronic Health Evaluation,* a classification system for severity of disease.

apallesthesia (ă-pal″es-thē′zh(ē-)ă) [*¹an- + pallesthesia*] Inability to sense vibrations.

apallic syndrome (ā″pal′ĭk) [*¹an- + pall(ium) + -ic*] Persistent vegetative state.

apancreatic (ā″pang″krē-at′ĭk, pan-) [*¹an- + pancreatic*] **1.** Caused by absence of the pancreas. **2.** Pert. to noninvolvement of the pancreas.

APAP acetominophen SEE: *N-acetyl-p-aminophenol.*

APAP with codeine SEE: *acetaminophen.*

aparalytic (ā″par″ă-lit′ĭk) [*¹an- + paralytic*] Marked by lack of paralysis.

aparathyrosis (ā″par″ă-thī-rō′sĭs) [*¹an-+ parathyr(oid) + -osis*] Parathyroid deficiency.

apareunia (ā″pă-roo′nē-ă) [*¹an- + pareunos,* lying beside + *-ia*] Inability to accomplish sexual intercourse. SEE: *dyspareunia.*

aparthrosis (ap″ar-thrō′sĭs) [*apo- + arthrosis*] **1.** Diarthrosis. **2.** An ambiguous term meaning dislocation of a joint; abarticulation.

apathetic (ap″ă-thet′ĭk) [*apath(y) + (path)etic*] Indifferent; without interest. SYN: *apathic.* **apathetically** (i-k(ă-)lē), *adv.*

apathic (ā″path′ĭk) [*¹an- + patho- + -ic*] Apathetic.

apathism (ap′ă-thizm) [*¹an- + patho- + -ism*] Slowness to react to stimuli. SEE: *erethism.*

apathy (ap′ă-thē) [Gr. *apatheia,* insensibility] Indifference; insensibility; lack of emotion.

apatite (ap′ă-tīt″) [Ger. *Apatit,* "the deceptive stone," fr. Gr. *apatē,* deception + *-ite*] A mineral containing calcium and phosphate ions and a univalent anion in a specific ratio. It is the major constituent of teeth and bones.

APC **1.** *absolute phagocyte count.* **2.** *activated protein C.* **3.** *antigen-presenting cell.*

APE *anterior pituitary extract.*

apellous (ă-pel′ŭs) [*¹an- + L. pellis,* skin] **1.** Lacking skin. **2.** Lacking a foreskin; circumcised.

apepsia (ā″pep′sē-ă) [*¹an- + Gr.pepsis,* digestion *+-ia*] Cessation of digestion.

apepsinia (ā″pep″sin′ē-ă) [*¹an- + pepsin + -ia*] Absence of pepsin in the gastric juice.

aperient (ă-pēr′ē-ĕnt) [L. *aperire,* to open] **1.** Having a mild laxative effect. **2.** A mild laxative. SYN: *aperitive* (2).

aperiodic (ā″pēr″ē-od′ĭk) [*¹an- + periodic*] Occurring other than periodically.

aperistalsis (ā″per-ĭ-stal′sĭs) [*¹an- + peristalsis*] Absence of peristalsis.

apéritif (ă-pĕr′ĭ-tēf′) [L. *aperire,* to open] An alcoholic beverage, such as wine, taken before a meal to stimulate the appetite.

aperitive (ă-per′ĭt-ĭv) [L. *aper(i)tivus,* fr. *aperire,* to open] **1.** Stimulating the appetite. **2.** Aperient.

Apert syndrome (ă-pār′) [Eugene Apert, Fr. pediatrician, 1868–1940] A congenital condition marked by premature closure of the sutures of the skull causing malformations of the head. Other manifestations include webbed fingers and toes, cleft palate or uvula, prognathic mandible, and maxillary hypoplasia, resulting in extreme malocclusion. It is sometimes mistakenly called *Alpert syndrome.*

apertura (ap″ĕr-choor′ă) *pl.* **aperturae** [L. *apertura,* an opening] An opening.

aperture (ap′ĕr-choor″) [L. *apertura,* an opening] An orifice or opening, esp. to anatomical or bony spaces or canals.

apex (ā′peks″, ā′pĭ-sēz″) *pl.* **apexes,** **apices** [L. *apex,* tip] The pointed extremity of a conical structure.

  a. of the heart The tip of the left ventricle, opposite the base of the heart. The apex of the heart moves considerably with each heartbeat, and the point of maximal impulse (PMI) can be felt on the chest wall above the apex.

  a. of the lung The superior, subclavicular portion of the lung.

  root a. The end of the root of a tooth. The anatomical landmark in the apical region is the apical foramen.

apexcardiogram (ā″peks″kar′dē-ŏ-gram″) [*apex + cardiogram*] A graphic record of chest wall movements produced by the apex beat.

apexigraph, apexograph (ā″peks′ĭ-graf″) [*apex + -graph*] An instrument used to determine the position of the apex of the root of a tooth.

Apgar score (ap′gar″) [Virginia Apgar, U.S. anesthesiologist, 1909–1974] A system for evaluating an infant's physical condition at birth. The infant's heart rate, respiration, muscle tone, response to stimuli, and color are rated at 1 min, and again at 5 min after birth. Each factor is scored 0, 1, or 2; the maximum total score is 10. *Interpretation of scores:* 7 to 10, good to excellent; 4 to 6, fair; less than 4, poor condition. A low score at 1 min is a sign of perinatal asphyxia and the need for immediate assisted ventilation. Infants with scores below 7 at 5 min should be assessed again 5 more min; scores less than 6 at any time may indicate need for resuscitation. In depressed infants, a more accurate determination of the de-

Apgar Score

Sign	Score		
	0	1	2
Heart rate	Absent	Slow (less than 100)	Greater than 100
Respiratory effort	Absent	Slow, irregular	Good; crying
Muscle tone	Limp	Some flexion of extremities	Active motion
Reflex irritability	No response	Grimace	Cry
Color*	Blue, pale	Body pink; extremities blue	Completely pink

* Skin color or its absence may not be a reliable guide in infants with dark complexions although melanin is less apparent at birth than later.

gree of fetal hypoxia may be obtained by direct measures of umbilical cord blood oxygen, carbon dioxide partial pressure, and pH. Although the Apgar score is eponymous, some practitioners recall its elements with the mnemonic *Appearance, Pulse, Grimace, Activity, Respiration*. SEE: table.

APHA *American Public Health Association.*

aphagia (ă-fā′j(ē-)ă) [¹*an-* + *phago-* + *-ia*] Inability to swallow.

aphakia, aphacia (ă-fā′kē-ă, ă-fā′sē-ă) [¹*an-* + *phaco-*l] Absence of the crystalline lens of the eye. **aphakic, aphacic** (ă-fā′kik, ă-fā′sik), *adj.*

aphalangia (ā″fă-lan′j(ē-)ă) [¹*an-* + *phalango-* + *-ia*] Absence of fingers or toes.

aphanisis (ā″fan′ĭ-sĭs) [Gr. *aphanisis,* disappearance] Fear or apprehension that sexual potency will be lost.

aphasia (ă-fā′zh(ē-)ă) [Gr. *aphasia,* speechlessness] Absence or impairment of the ability to communicate by speech, writing, or signs because of brain dysfunction. It is considered complete or total when both sensory and motor areas are involved. SEE: *alalia.*

   acquired epileptiform a. Landau-Kleffner syndrome.

   amnesic a. Anomic **a.**

   anomic a. Inability to name objects; loss of memory for words.

   auditory a. Word **deafness.**

   Broca a. Motor **a.**

   conduction a. Aphasia marked by an inability to repeat what one has heard and by impaired writing and word finding.

   crossed a. Aphasia that develops paradoxically in a right-handed person after a stroke or lesion affecting the right hemisphere.

   executive a. Motor **a.**

   fluent a. Aphasia in which words are easily spoken but are incorrect and may be unrelated to the content of the other words spoken.

   gibberish a. Utterance of meaningless phrases.

   global a. Total aphasia involving failure of all forms of communication.

   infantile acquired a. Landau-Kleffner syndrome.

   jargon a. Communication that results in the use of jargon or disconnected words.

   mixed a. Combined receptive and expressive aphasia.

   motor a. Aphasia in which patients know what they want to say but cannot say it because of their inability to coordinate the muscles controlling speech. It may be complete or partial. Broca area is disordered or diseased. SYN: *aphemia; Broca a.; executive a.*

   nominal a. Inability to name objects.

   optic a. A form of agnosia marked by inability to name an object recognized by sight without the aid of sound, taste, or touch.

   primary progressive a. ABBR: PPA. A form of dementia marked by the inability to recall the names of things, to read, or to express oneself with speech The disorder gradually worsens and may ultimately produce other cognitive deficits. Early in the course of the disease, other brain functions of daily living are preserved, e.g., understanding speech, behaving properly, and practicing hobbies. PPA is associated with nonspecific degeneration of neurons in the left hemisphere of the brain. SYN: *progressive nonfluent a.*

   progressive nonfluent a. Primary progressive **a.**

   semantic a. Inability to understand the meanings of words.

   sensory a. Inability to understand spoken words if the auditory word center is involved (auditory aphasia) or written words if the visual word center is affected (word blindness). If both centers are involved, the patient will understand neither spoken nor written words.

   syntactic a. Inability to use proper grammatical constructions.

   transcortical a. Aphasia in which the ability to repeat words is preserved, but other language functions are impaired.

   traumatic a. Aphasia caused by head injury.

   visual a. Alexia.

Wernicke a. SEE: under *Wernicke, Carl.*

aphasiac (ă-fā′z(h)ē-ak″) Someonel affected with aphasia.

aphasic (ă-fā″zik) **1.** Pert. to aphasia. **2.** Someone affected with aphasia.

aphemia (ă-fē′mē-ă) [¹*an-* + Gr. *phēmē,* speech + -IA] **1.** Motor aphasia. **2.** Anarthria.

aphephobia (af″ě-fō′bē-ă) [Gr. *(h)aphē,* touch, + -*phobia*] Morbid fear of being touched.

apheresis (a″fē-rē′sĭs, ′sēz″) *pl.* **aphereses** [Gr. *aphairesis,* separation] Removal of unwanted or pathological components from a donor's or patient's blood by a continuous-flow separator. Apheresis is similar to hemodialysis because the treated blood is returned to the donor or patient. It has been used to treat blood hyperviscosity, cold agglutinin hemolytic anemia, posttransfusion purpura, thrombotic thrombocytopenic purpura, myasthenia gravis, sickle cell anemia, Guillain-Barré syndrome, familial hypercholesterolemia, and certain drug overdoses. SYN: *pheresis.* SEE: *cytapheresis; leukapheresis; plateletpheresis; plasmapheresis.*

aphonia (ā-fō′nē-ă) [¹*an-* + *phon-*+ -*ia*] Loss of speech sounds from the larynx, as may occur in chronic laryngitis. It may be caused by diseases of the vocal cords, paralysis of the laryngeal nerves, or pressure on the recurrent laryngeal nerve, or it may be functional (due to psychiatric causes). **aphonic** (-fon′ik), *adj.*

hysterical a. Aphonia due to somatoform disorders. There is no organic defect.

a. paranoica Obstinate silence in the mentally ill.

postoperative a. Loss of speech after a laryngectomy. Restoration of speech is accomplished with speech synthesizers and speech therapy.

spastic a. Aphonia due to spasm of the vocal muscles, esp. that initiated by efforts to speak.

aphonogelia (ā-fō″nō-jēl′ē-ă) [¹*an-* + *phono-* + Gr. *gelōs,* laughter] Inability to laugh out loud.

aphose (ăf′ōz) [¹*an-* + Gr. *phōs,* light] A subjective visual perception of darkness or of a shadow.

aphrodisiac (af″rŏ-dē′zē-ak″, -diz′ē-) [Gr. *aphrodisiakos,* pert. to sexual love or desire, fr. *Aphrodite,* goddess of love] **1.** Stimulating sexual desire. **2.** A drug, food, environment, or other agent that arouses sexual desire.

aphtha (af′thă, af′thē) *pl.* **aphthae** [Gr. *aphtha,* small ulcer] A small ulcer on a mucous membrane of the mouth, as in thrush. **aphthic** (-thik), *adj.*

Bednar a. SEE: *Bednar aphthae.*

cachectic a. A lesion formed beneath the tongue and accompanied by severe constitutional symptoms.

aphthoid (af′thoyd″) [*aphtha* + -*oid*] Resembling aphthae.

aphthong (af′thong″) [¹*an-* + Gr. *phthongos,* sound, voice] A silent letter or combination of letters in a written word.

aphthosis (af-thō′sĭs) [*aphtha* + -*osis*] Any condition characterized by aphthae.

aphthous (af′thŭs) [*aphtha*+ -*ous*] Pert. to or characterized by aphthae.

Apiaceae (ā″pē-ās′ē-ē″) [L. *Apium,* parsley (the name of the type genus) + -*aceae*] The family of spices and vegetables that includes anise, carrots, celery, and parsley. They are an occasional source of food allergy when consumed.

apical (ap′ĭ-kăl, ā′pĭ-kăl) [L. *apex,* stem *apic-,* tip] Pert. to the apex of a structure.

apical ballooning syndrome Takotsubo **cardiomyopathy.**

apical heave Visible heaving of the chest over the apex of the heart. This usually indicates left ventricular hypertrophy. SEE: *substernal* **thrust.**

apicectomy (ā″pĭ-sek′tŏ-mē) [*apex* + -*ectomy*] Excision of the apex of the petrous portion of the temporal bone.

apices (ā′pĭ-sēz) [L.] Pl. of apex.

apicitis (ā-pĭ-sīt′ĭs) [*apex* + -*itis*] Inflammation of the apex of a structure, as of the apex of a tooth root, or the petrous portion of the temporal bone, or the patella.

apicoectomy (ā-pĭ-kō-ek′tŏ-mē) [*apex* + -*ektomy*] Excision of the apex of the root of a tooth.

apicolocator (ā″pĭ-kō-lō′kā-tŏr) [*apex* + *locator*] An instrument for locating the apex of the root of a tooth.

apicolysis (ap″ĭ-kol′ĭ-sĭs) [*apex* + -*lysis*] **1.** Destruction of a dental root apex. **2.** Surgical excision or collapse of the pulmonary apex.

PATIENT CARE: During and after pulmonary surgery, the patient is assessed for symptoms of tension pneumothorax (increased pulse and respirations, cyanosis, and marked dyspnea, along with severe sharp pain, tympanic resonance to percussion, and absent breath sounds on auscultation of the affected side) and for symptoms of a mediastinal shift (cyanosis, severe dyspnea, distended neck veins, increased pulse and respiratory rate, and excessive, uncontrollable coughing). After the procedure, the patient is positioned as prescribed, usually on the affected side.

Apicomplexa (ap″ĭ-kŏm-plek′să) A phylum of the kingdom Protista (formerly a division of protozoa called *Sporozoa*); named for a complex of cell organelles (apical microtubule complex) at the apex of the sporozoite form that can penetrate host cells. It includes the medically important genera *Plasmodium, Toxoplasma, Cryptosporidium,* and *Isospora.*

apicostomy (āp″ĭ-kos′tŏ-mē) [*apex* + *-stomy*] Surgical removal of the mucoperiosteum and bone to expose the apex of the root of a tooth.

apicotomy (ap″ĭ-kot′ŏ-mē) [*apex* + *-tomy*] Incision into an apical structure.

apinealism (ā-pin′ē-ă-lĭzm) [*¹an-* + L. *pinea,* pine cone + *-ism*] Absence of the pineal gland.

apiphobia (ā″pĭ-fō′bē-ă) [L. *apis,* bee + *-phobia*] Unrealistic fear of bees.

apitherapy (āp″ĭ-ther′-ă-pē) [L. *apis,* bee + *therapy*] In alternative medicine, the application of bee stings or their chemical constituents for their putative anti-inflammatory effects. Apitherapy has been used by some health care practitioners to treat arthritis and multiple sclerosis.

aplanatic (ap″lă-nat′ik, ā″plă-) [*¹an-* + Gr. *planētos,* wandering] Free from or correcting spherical aberration.

aplasia (ă-plā′zh(ē-)ă) [*¹an-* + *-plasia*] Failure of an organ or tissue to develop normally. **aplastic** (ă-plas′tĭk), *adj.*

   a. axialis extracorticalis congenita Congenital defect of the axon formation on the surface of the cerebral cortex.

   a. cutis congenita Defective development of a localized area of the skin, usually on the scalp. The area is usually covered by a thin, translucent membrane.

   germ cell a. A cause of male infertility in which Sertoli cells are present in the seminiferous tubules, but no other reproductive cells capable of producing spermatozoa are found.

   pure red cell a. Anemia due to an isolated defect in the production of red blood cells. One common cause is parvovirus B19 infection.

   thymic a. A sometimes fatal disorder in which the thymus fails to develop, causing a deficiency of gamma globulin. There is a deficiency of lymph tissue throughout the body. SYN: *thymic alymphoplasia.*

Apley, Alan Graham (ap′lē) Brit. orthopedic surgeon, 1914–1996.

   A. compression/distraction test A test of shoulder function (with several variations) designed to detect asymmetries in range of motion observed during adduction, abduction, flexion, extension, internal rotation, and external rotation. The patient performs instructed movements involving positioning the hand to touch the opposite shoulder in front, behind the head, and behind the back onto or toward the opposite scapula.

   A. scratch test A test of shoulder function with several variations designed to detect asymmetries in range of motion observed during adduction,

flexion, extension, internal rotation, and external rotation. The patient performs instructed movements involving positioning the hand to touch the opposite shoulder in the scapular region from behind the back and over the shoulder.

APMA *American Podiatric Medical Association,* (formerly called the *American Podiatry Association*).

APMPPE *Acute posterior multifocal placoid pigment epitheliopathy.*

APN *advanced practice nurse.*

APNA *American Psychiatric Nurses Association.*

APN-CS *advanced practice nurse–clinical specialist.*

apnea (ap-nē′ă, ap′nē-) [*¹an-* + *-pnea*] Temporary cessation of breathing and, therefore, of the body's intake of oxygen and release of carbon dioxide. It is a serious symptom, esp. in patients with other potentially life-threatening conditions. SEE: *apnea monitoring; Cheyne-Stokes respiration; sleep a.; sudden infant death syndrome.*

   central a. Apnea during sleep that occurs when the respiratory center of the brainstem does not send normal periodic signals to the muscles of respiration. Observation of the patient reveals no respiratory effort (no movement of the chest, and no breath sounds).

   deglutition a. Apnea while swallowing.

   mixed a. Dysfunctional breathing during sleep that combines elements of obstructive and central sleep apneas.

   obstructive a. Absent or dysfunctional breathing that occurs when the upper airway is intermittently blocked during sleep. Observation of the patient reveals vigorous but ineffective respiratory efforts, often with loud snoring or snorting.

   obstructive sleep a. ABBR: OSA. Sleep a.

   a. of prematurity ABBR: AOP. A condition of the premature newborn, marked by repeated episodes of apnea lasting longer than 20 sec. The diagnosis of AOP is one of exclusion, made when no treatable cause can be found. Increased frequency of apneic episodes directly relates to the degree of prematurity. AOP is not an independent risk factor for sudden infant death syndrome. Apneic episodes may result in bradycardia, hypoxia, and respiratory acidosis.

   TREATMENT: There is no specific treatment. Initial efforts should begin with the least-invasive method. Tactile stimulation is often successful with early recognition. When gentle stimulation does not produce a response, bag and mask ventilation is initiated. Methylxanthines such as caffeine, theophylline, and aminophylline are helpful.

PATIENT CARE: Care includes maintenance of a neutral thermal environment, avoidance of prolonged oral feedings, use of tactile stimulation early in the apneic episode, and ventilatory support as needed. The infant who has experienced and survived an episode of apnea is maintained on cardiac and respiratory monitoring devices. Before discharge, parents are taught cardiopulmonary resuscitation, use of monitoring equipment, and how to recognize signs of medication toxicity if medications are used.

sleep a. The temporary absence of breathing during sleep. This common disorder affects about 10% of all middle-aged men and about 5% of middle-aged women in the U.S. and is classified according to the mechanism involved and by whether or not it is associated with daytime sleepiness. SYN: *obstructive sleep a.*

In obstructive sleep apnea, vigorous respiratory efforts are present during sleep but the flow of air in and out of the airways is blocked by upper airway obstruction. Patients with obstructive apnea are usually middle-aged, obese men who make loud snorting, snoring, and gasping sounds during sleep. By contrast, central sleep apnea is marked by absence of respiratory muscle activity. Patients with central apnea may exhibit excessive daytime sleepiness, but snorting and gasping during sleep are absent. Occasionally life-threatening central apneas occur as a result of strokes.

Mixed apnea begins with absence of respiratory effort, followed by upper airway obstruction. Whenever apneas are prolonged, oxygenation drops and carbon dioxide blood levels rise. Patients often awaken many times during the night or have fragmented sleep architecture. In the morning, many patients complain of headache, fatigue, drowsiness, or an unsatisfying night's rest. In addition, these individuals often have hypertension, arrhythmias, type 2 diabetes mellitus, or signs and symptoms of right-sided heart failure. Although these findings may suggest the diagnosis, formal sleep studies in a laboratory are needed to document the disorder and to measure the effects of apneas on oxygenation and other physical parameters.

SYMPTOMS: Partners of patients with sleep apnea are often the first to notice the patient's disordered breathing during sleep. Occasionally patients see their health care providers because of hypersomnolence: they may report falling asleep during the daytime in unusual circumstances, e.g., at traffic lights or whenever seated in a quiet room.

TREATMENT: Optimal therapy of obstructive sleep apnea is to assist breathing with continuous positive airway pressure (CPAP) if the patient cannot correct the condition by losing weight. CPAP provides a pneumatic splint that maintains airway patency during sleep. Palatal obstruction, a finding in a small number of patients, can be surgically corrected. Medroxyprogesterone may be of some benefit but is clearly less effective than CPAP.

apnea monitoring Monitoring the respiratory movements, esp. of infants. This may be done by use of an apnea alarm mattress, or devices to measure the infant's thoracic and abdominal movements and heart rate.

PATIENT CARE: Apnea is usually detected by placing electrodes (linked to a cardiorespiratory monitor) on the skin overlying the abdomen and thorax of the patient. SEE: *sudden infant death syndrome.*

apnea test A test used to determine whether a comatose person receiving life support has suffered brain death.

PATIENT CARE: The patient's ventilator is set to deliver no breaths per minute, and the carbon dioxide level of the blood is allowed to rise 20 mmg Hg to a level that is at least above 60 mm Hg. If apnea (no spontaneous breathing) occurs, brain death is confirmed. The test should not be performed if the person has recently received sedative, narcotic, or paralytic drugs; those drugs may suppress spontaneous breathing, falsely suggesting brain death.

apneumatosis (ap″noo-mă-tō′sĭs) [¹*an-* + *pneumatosis*] Noninflation of air cells of the lung; congenital atelectasis.

apneumia (ap-noo′mē-ă) [¹*an-* + Gr. *pneumōn,* lung] Congenital absence of the lungs.

apneusis (ap-noo′sĭs) [¹*an-* + Gr. *pneusis,* breathing] Abnormal respiration marked by sustained inspiratory effort. It is caused by surgical removal of the upper portion of the pons.

¹**apo** In Ayurvedic medicine, water, one of the five essential elements. It stimulates the tongue. Its special sense is that of taste.

²**apo** *apolipoprotein.*

apo-, ap- [Gr. *apo,* from] Prefixes meaning *separated from* or *derived from.*

apocamnosis (ăp″ŏ-kam-nō′sĭs) [Gr. *apokamnein,* to grow weary] Weariness; easily induced fatigue.

apochromatic (ap″ŏ-krō-mat′ik) [*apo-* + *chromatic*] Free from spherical and chromatic aberrations.

apocrine (ap′ŏ-krĕn, -krīn″, -krēn″) [*apo-* + *krinein,* to separate] Pert. to secretory cells that contribute part of their protoplasm to the material secreted. SEE: *eccrine; holocrine; merocrine.*

apodal, apodous (ap′ŏd-ăl, ap′ŏd-ŭs) [¹*an-* + *pod-*] Lacking feet.

apodia (ă″pō′dē-ă) [^1an- + pod- + -ia] Congenital absence of one or both feet.

apodization (ap″ŏ-dĭ-zā′shŏn) **1.** Alteration of a surface by removal of its irregularities. **2.** Introduction of a gradual change into a mathematical function that would otherwise be discontinuous. It is used in radiology to smooth out choppy signals, and in optics, to blend diffractive steps.

apoenzyme (ap″ō-en′zīm″) [apo- + enzyme] The protein portion of an enzyme. SEE: holoenzyme; prosthetic group.

apoferritin (ap″ŏ-fer′ĭt-ĭn) [apo- + ferritin] A protein that combines with iron to form ferritin. In the body, it is always bound to iron.

apogee (ap′ŏ-jēé) [apo- + Gr. gaia, gē, earth] The climax or period of greatest severity of a disease. SYN: acme (2).

apolar (ā″pō′lăr) [^1an- + polar] Without poles or processes. Some nerve cells are apolar.

apolipoprotein (ap″ŏ-lī″pō-prō′tē(-ĭ)n) [apo- + lipoprotein] ABBR: apo. Any of the proteins imbedded in the outer shell of lipoproteins. The apolipoproteins are designated apo A-I, apo A-II, apo A-IV; apo B-48 and apo B-100; apo C-I, apo C-II, apo C-III; and apo E. Except for apo A-II and apo A-IV, they metabolize and transport lipoproteins. The functions of apo A-II and apo A-IV are not fully understood. All are synthesized in the liver.

a. E ABBR: apo E. A protein that regulates lipid concentrations in plasma and may repair neuronal damage in the central nervous system. The apo E-4 allele is associated with familial late-onset Alzheimer disease, possibly because it protects neurons less effectively than other apo E alleles.

a. J Clusterin. SEE: lipoprotein.

apolipoprotein B—apolipoprotein A-I ratio ABBR: apo B—apo A-I ratio. The ratio between the primary structural components of unhealthy lipoproteins (apo A-I) and high-density lipoproteins (apo B). It is a known risk factor for coronary artery disease.

apology law (ă-pol′ŏ-jē) [Gr. apologia, (verbal) self-defense] SEE: under law.

aponeurosis (ap″ŏ-noo-rō′sĭs) pl. **aponeuroses** [apo- + neurosis] A flat, fibrous sheet of connective tissue that attaches muscle to bone or other tissues; may sometimes serve as a fascia. **aponeurotic** (-rot′ĭk), adj.

epicranial a. The fibrous membrane connecting the occipital and frontal muscles over the top of the skull. SYN: galea aponeurotica.

lingual a. Connective tissue sheet of the tongue to which lingual muscles attach.

palatine a. Connective tissue sheet of the soft palate to which palatal muscles attach.

pharyngeal a. The sheet of connective tissue lying between the mucosal and muscular layers of the pharyngeal wall. SYN: pharyngobasilar fascia.

plantar a. The sheet of connective tissue investing the muscles of the sole of the foot. SYN: plantar fascia.

aponeurositis (ap″ŏ-noo-rō-sīt′ĭs) [aponeurosis + -itis] Inflammation of an aponeurosis.

aponeurotomy (ap″ŏ-noo-rot′ŏ-mē) [apo- + neurotomy] Incision of an aponeurosis.

apophysis (ă-pof′ĭ-sĭs, ă-pof′ĭ-sēz″) pl. **apophyses** [Gr. apophysis, offshoot] A projection, esp. from a bone; an outgrowth without an independent center of ossification. **apophyseal, apophysial** (ă-pof″ĭ-sē′ăl), adj.

basilar a. The basilar process of the occipital bone.

lenticular a. The lenticular process of the incus, which articulates with the stapes.

a. raviana The anterior process of the malleus.

temporal a. The mastoid process of the temporal bone.

apophysitis (ă-pof″ĭ-sīt′ĭs) [apophysis + -itis] Inflammation of an apophysis.

apoplectic (ap″ŏ-plek′tik) [Gr. apoplēktikos, crippled by stroke] Pert. to apoplexy.

apoplectiform (ap″ŏ-plek′tĭ-form″) [apoplecti(c) + -form] Resembling apoplexy. SYN: apoplectoid.

apoplectoid (ap″ŏ-plek′toyd″) [apoplect(ic) + -oid] Apoplectiform.

apoplexia (ap″ŏ-plek′sē-ă) [Gr. apoplēktikos, crippled by a stroke + -ia] Apoplexy.

apoplexy (ap′ŏ-plek″sē) [Gr. apoplēktikos, crippled by a stroke] **1.** Copious effusion of blood into an organ, as in abdominal apoplexy or pulmonary apoplexy. **2.** An obsolete term for stroke, esp. of a rupture of a blood vessel in the brain.

esophageal a. An intramural hematoma of the esophagus.

pituitary a. Hemorrhage into or necrosis of the pituitary gland. Symptoms may include sudden headache, oculomotor palsy, peripheral visual deficits, and altered mental status. Treatment usually includes prompt administration of adrenal steroids.

uteroplacental a. Couvelaire uterus.

apoptosis (ap″ŏp-tō′sĭs) [apo- + ptōsis, a dropping] Programmed cell death; genetic limitation of the lifespan of cells. The process may be important in limiting growth of tumors.

aporepressor (ap″ŏ-rē-pres′ŏr) [apo- + repressor] A protein whose synthesis is directed by a regulator gene and that functions only when bound with core-pressors.

aposia (ă-pōz'ē-ă) [¹*an-* + Gr. *posis,* drink] Adipsia.

apotemnophilia (ap″ŏ-tem″nō-fil′ē-ă) [Gr. *apotemnein,* , to cut off, sever + *-philia*] A form of paraphilia character-ized by the individual requesting amputation of an extremity for erotic reasons.

apothecaries' weights and measures (ă-pŏth′ĕ-kăr″ēz) An outdated and obsolete system of weights and measures formerly used by physicians and pharmacists; based on 480 grains to 1 oz and 12 oz to 1 lb. It has been replaced by the metric system. SEE: *Weights and Measures Appendix.*

apothecary (ă-pŏth′ĕ-ker-ē) [L. *apothecarius,* shopkeeper fr. Gr. *apothēkē,* storehouse] **1.** A druggist or pharmacist. In England and Ireland, one licensed by the Society of Apothecaries of London or the Apothecaries' Hall of Ireland as an authorized dispenser of drugs. **2.** A pharmacy or drugstore.

apotripsis (ap″ŏ-trip′sĭs) [Gr. *apotribein,* to abrade] Removal of a corneal scar or opacity.

apovitellin (ap″ŏ-vī-tel′ĭn) [*apo-* + *vitellin*] One of several components of the lipoprotein in egg yolks. It is a source of food allergies in susceptible people.

apparatus (ap″ă-rāt′ŭs, -răt′ŭs) [L. *apparare,* to prepare] **1.** A number of parts that act together to perform a special function. **2.** A group of structures or organs that work together to perform a common function. **3.** A mechanical device or appliance used in operations and experiments.

Particular apparatuses are listed under the first word. SEE: e.g., *dental apparatus; Golgi apparatus; vocal apparatus.*

apparent (ă-par′ĕnt) [L. *apparens,* appearing] **1.** Obvious and easily seen; not disguised or hidden. **2.** Appearing at first to be true but, with greater knowledge or closer examination, may not be valid.

appearance (ă-pēr′ăns) [L. *apparere,* to appear] The visible presentation of an object.

appendage (ă-pen′dij) Anything attached to a larger or major body part, such as a tail or a limb. SEE: *appendix.*

   atrial a. A small muscular pouch attached to each atrium of the heart. SYN: *auricular a.* (1).

   auricular a. 1. Atrial **a. 2.** Additional tissue attached to the ear.

   a. of the eye The eyelid, eyelashes, eyebrow, lacrimal apparatus, and conjunctiva.

   a. of the fetus The amnion, chorion, and umbilical cord.

   a. of the skin The nails, hair, and the sebaceous and sweat glands.

   uterine a. The ovaries, fallopian tubes, and uterine ligaments.

appendectomy (ap″ĕn-dek′tŏ-mē) [*appendix* + *-ectomy*] Surgical removal of the vermiform appendix.

   incidental a. Removal of the appendix during another surgical procedure within the abdomen or pelvis.

appendiceal, appendical (ă-pen″dĭ-sē′ăl, ă-pen′dĭ-kăl) [*appendix* + *-al*] Pert. to a vermiform appendix. SYN: *appendicular* (1).

appendicectasis (ă-pen″dĭ-sek′tă-sĭs) [*appendix* + *-ectasis*] Dilatation of the vermiform appendix.

appendicitis (ă-pen″dĭ-sīt′ĭs) [*appendix* + *-itis*] Inflammation of the vermiform appendix, caused by blockage of the lumen of the appendix followed by infection. It may be acute, subacute, or chronic and occasionally is difficult to diagnose because many other illnesses may cause acute abdominal pain.

TREATMENT: Surgery is typically required. Preoperative intravenous hydration and antibiotics are given in most instances.

   acute a. A common presentation of appendiceal inflammation. Inflammation can result in infection, thrombosis, necrosis, and perforation or rupture of the intestine. Peritonitis may follow as the contents of the lower gastrointestinal tract enter the abdominal cavity. Classic presentations, which occur about 60% of the time, include abdominal pain (initially diffuse, gradually localizing to the right lower quadrant), loss of appetite, nausea, fever, and an elevated white blood cell count. The disease is more common in males and generally occurs in the young, usually between the ages of 10 and 20, but rarely before age 2 and less often after age 50. It is nevertheless important in the differential diagnosis of abdominal pain in older adults.

DIAGNOSIS: Diagnosis is simple when pain eventually localizes to the right lower quadrant, with rebound tenderness and rigidity over the right rectus muscle or McBurney's point. Walking bent over or lying with the right knee flexed are maneuvers the patient may use instinctively to reduce discomfort. If the abdominal pain suddenly stops, perforation or infarction may have occurred. Diagnostic difficulties may arise because the anatomical location of the appendix can vary; as a result, pain may be present in the pelvis, in the right upper quadrant, or in other locations. Tachycardia and moderate to severe discomfort are common. The differential diagnosis of acute appendicitis includes flares of inflammatory bowel disease, mesenteric adenitis, and pelvic inflammation. When this diagnosis is considered in a woman, it must be differentiated from pain associated with ovulation (mittelschmerz), ruptured ectopic pregnancy, torsion of the ovary, and pelvic inflammatory disease. To aid preoperative diagnosis, imaging studies, such as ultrasound or computed tomography, are often performed. SEE: table.

The greater the delay in diagnosis, the higher the incidence of complications, such as abscess formation, appendiceal rupture, sepsis, and death.

PATIENT CARE: *Preoperative:* The patient is assessed for signs and symptoms of appendicitis, e.g., elevated temperature; nausea or vomiting; onset, location, quality, and intensity of pain; rebound tenderness; constipation or diarrhea; and a moderately elevated white blood cell count (12,000 to 15,000/μl) with an increase in immature white blood cells. Abdominal ultrasound or CT scan may be used to confirm the diagnosis. The patient is positioned for comfort and kept nihil per os; intravenous fluids are started for hydration, and he or she is prepared physically and emotionally for surgery.

⚠️ To prevent possible rupture of an inflamed appendix, cathartics or enemas should not be used.

Postoperative: Vital signs, the status of bowel sounds, abdominal flatus, lung sounds, and intake and output, including prescribed intravenous fluids, are monitored and documented. The patient is positioned comfortably (Fowler's position in the case of a ruptured appendix or peritonitis). Prescribed analgesics and noninvasive comfort measures are provided. Position changes, incentive spirometry for deep breathing and coughing, and early ambulation are encouraged. The patient's ability to urinate is ascertained and documented. If required, antibiotics are administered. The dressing is inspected for any bleeding or drainage and the findings documented. Possible surgical complications include abscess formation (evidenced by continued pain and fever postoperatively) and wound dehiscence (reopening of the surgical incision after it has been closed). Nasogastric drainage may be required for decompression of the gastrointestinal tract and for prevention of nausea and vomiting if peritonitis occurs as a complication. The patient is prepared for return to home, work, and other activities.

chronic a. Appendicitis that may follow an acute but untreated attack, leaving fibrosis and narrowing of the lumen of the appendix. Some authorities question the existence of this entity, as those pathological changes can result from other inflammatory conditions or simply from a gradual narrowing of the lumen.

gangrenous a. Appendicitis in which inflammation is extreme, blood vessels are blocked in the mesentery, circulation to the appendix is cut off, and diffuse peritonitis ensues.

stump a. Inflammation occurring in the surgical remnant (the proximal portion of the appendix) after appendectomy.

tip a. Inflammation that involves

Some Severe Illnesses That May Mimic Appendicitis

Disease	Clinical Findings That May Suggest the Diagnosis
Abdominal aortic aneurysm, rupture	Pulsatile abdominal mass; abdominal bruits; mature patient; imaging studies
Colic caused by kidney stone	Blood present in the urine; visualization of stone by pyelography or computed tomography
Crohn's disease, flare	History of inflammatory bowel disease; pus or blood in stools
Diverticulitis, right-sided	May be difficult to distinguish without imaging studies, laparotomy, or laparoscopy
Ectopic pregnancy	Positive pregnancy test; abdominal ultrasound
Gastroenteritis	Others at home also ill; recent travel abroad; vomiting and diarrhea present
Ischemia of the GI tract	Pain more notable than physical findings; metabolic acidosis; blood in stools; mature patient; smoker
Perforation of an internal organ	Abdominal rigidity; free air under the diaphragm on abdominal x-ray studies
Pyelonephritis	Leukocytes and bacteria in catheterized urine specimen
Salpingitis	Sexually active woman; cervical purulence; tenderness of pelvic organs on examination
Typhlitis	History of leukemia

NOTE: Surgical consultation and abdominal imaging (e.g., with computerized tomography) will lower the likelihood of missed diagnoses or inappropriate surgery.

only the most distal portion of the appendix. It may be difficult to visualize radiographically; e.g., during CT scanning.

appendicoenterostomy (ă-pen″dĭ-kō-etn″ĕ-ros′tŏ-mē) [*appendix* + *enterostomy*] The establishment of an anastomosis between the appendix and intestine.

appendicolysis (ă-pen″dĭ-kol′ĭ-sĭs) [*appendix* + *-lysis*] Surgery to free the appendix from adhesions.

appendicopathy (ă-pen″dĭ-kop′ă-thē) [*appendix* + *-pathy*] Any disease of the vermiform appendix.

   a. **oxyurica** A lesion of the appendical mucosa supposedly due to oxyurids (intestinal parasitic worms).

appendicostomy (ă-pen″dĭ-kos′tŏ-mē) [*appendix* + *-stomy*] Surgical opening and fixation of the appendix onto the skin. The opening is employed as a vent to an obstructed colon though it is less efficient than a colostomy or cecostomy. A tube can be passed through the appendiceal lumen to instill medication (as in cases of colitis) or fluids, e.g., to relieve fecal impaction in infants with Hirschsprung's disease or in the infirm or elderly patient. The opening can also be used to remove foreign bodies from the intestinal lumen.

appendicular (ap″ĕn-dik′yŭ-lăr) [*appendix*] **1.** Appendical. **2.** Pert. to an appendage. **3.** Pert. to a limb or limbs.

appendix (ă-pen′diks, ′dĭ-sēz) *pl.* **appendixes, appendices** [L. *appendix,* appendage, addition] An appendage, esp. the appendix vermiformis. SYN: *appendage*. SEE: *digestive system* and *omentum* for illus.

   a. **epididymidis** A cystic structure attached to the epididymis, It is a vestigial remnant of the mesonephric duct.

   a. **epiploica** Any of numerous pouches of the peritoneum, filled with fat and attached to the colon.

   a. **testis** A small bladder-like structure at the upper end of the testis. It ia a vestigial remnant of the cephalic portion of the müllerian duct

   vermiform *a.* A long, narrow, worm-shaped tube connected to the back of the cecum. It varies in length from less than 1 in to more than 8 in (2.5 to 20.3 cm) with an average of about 3 in (7.6 cm). Its distal end is closed. It is lined with mucosa similar to that of the large intestine. The appendix contains many lymph nodules. It is commonly referred to simply as *the appendix*. SYN: *vermiform process*.

   a. **vermiformis** SEE: *vermiform a.*

apperception (ap″ĕr-sep′shŏn) [Fr. L. *apperceptio*] The perception and interpretation of sensory stimuli; awareness of the meaning and significance of a particular sensory stimulus as modified by one's own experiences, knowledge, thoughts, and emotions.

apperceptive (a″pĕr-sep′tiv), *adj.* **apperceptively** (a″pĕr-sep′tiv-lē), *adv.*

apperceptive personality test (a″pĕr-sep′tiv) ABBR: APT. A test used to assess attitudes, moods, and perceptions. The person tested examines a series of images and is asked to construct a story about each of them.

appestat (ap′ĕ-stat″) [*appe(tite)* + *-stat*] The area of the brain that is thought to control appetite and food intake.

appetite (ap′ĕ-tīt″) [L. *appetitus,* longing for] A strong desire, esp. for food. Appetite differs from hunger in that the latter is an uncomfortable sensation caused by lack of food, whereas appetite is a pleasant sensation based on previous experience that causes one to seek food for the purpose of tasting and enjoying. **appetitive** (-tīt″iv), *adj.*

   perverted *a.* Pica.

appetizer (ap′ĕ-tī″zĕr) A small portion of something, esp. food or drink, that stimulates desire for more. In Western societies, it is an item that usually precedes the main food offering.

applanation (ap″lă-nā′shŏn) [L. *applanare,* to flatten] Flattening, esp. of the corneal surface. **applanate** (ap′lă-nāt″, a-plā′nāt″), *v.*

applanometer (ap″lă-nom′ĕt-ĕr) [*applan(ation)* + *-meter*] Applanation tonometer.

apple packer's epistaxis SEE: under *epistaxis*.

apple picker's disease Bronchitis resulting from a fungicide used on apples.

apple sorter's disease Contact dermatitis caused by chemicals used in washing apples.

appliance (ă-plī′ăns) **1.** In dentistry, a device to provide or facilitate a particular function. The functions include dentures (to replace one or more teeth), a mandibular advancement splint (to open the airway in patients with obstructive sleep apnea), a mouth guard (to protect the teeth during sports), or a night guard (to protect teeth from clenching and grinding during sleep). SEE: *dental prosthesis*. **2.** A device for influencing a specific function, e.g., a cane, crutch, or walker to assist walking, or an appliance to discourage thumb sucking. SEE: *prosthesis*.

   colostomy *a.* Colostomy **bag**

   urinary director *a.* A hollow hand-held plastic device that fits over the vulva, enabling a woman to urinate while standing. The device collects urine and allows it to be directed away from the user through an outlet spout. Its intended use is for women who are active outdoors and need to urinate without partially disrobing. Medically, the appliance has been found to be useful in patients who have had a radical vulvectomy.

Other devices for use by women in collecting urine are available. Some of these have the capacity to contain the specimen for disposal rather than merely redirecting the flow.

application (ap″lĭ-kā′shŏn) [L. *applicare,* to apply] A program designed to perform a specific function directly for the user or, in some cases, for another program.

application of heat Placing an object, warmed above body temperature, on a body part to increase blood flow or provide relief of pain.

⚠️ Do not apply heat to extremities with reduced blood supply, which is often the case in most forms of arteriosclerosis or advanced diabetes. Do not use electric heating devices next to moist dressings.

Dry or moist heat sources may be used. Dry applications include hot water bottles, radiant heat, electric pads, and microwavable fabric heat pads filled with uncooked rice, wheat, feed corn, buckwheat hulls, barley, beans, flax seed, or other similar dry materials. Moist heat is considered more penetrating than dry heat, but this is because water-soaked materials lose heat slower than dry ones. The application should be at approx. 120°F (48.9°C). Compresses may be kept warm by keeping hot water bottles at the proper temperature next to them. Devices that force hot water at a selected temperature through soft flexible tubing surrounding a part are available. These may be used to heat wet or dry compresses.

application service provider SEE: under *provider.*

applicator (ap′lĭ-kāt″ŏr) [L. *applicare,* to apply] A device, usually a slender rod with a pledget of cotton on the end, for making local applications.

applied ethics SEE: under *ethics.*

applied kinesiology SEE: under *kinesiology.*

appointment (ă-poynt′mĕnt) **1.** A scheduled meeting between a patient and a health care professional. **2.** Assignment to the teaching staff of an academic institution.

apposition (ap″ŏ-zĭsh′ŏn) [L. *apponere,* to place alongside] **1.** The condition of being positioned side by side or fitted together. SYN: *contiguity.* **2.** Addition of one substance to another, as one layer of tissue upon another. **3.** Development by means of accretion, as in the formation of bone or dental cementum.

apprehension test (ap″rē-hen′shŏn) [L. *apprehendere,* to grasp] A test of joint instability. If instability is present, the patient displays concern or discomfort when a joint is put in a position of risk for dislocation. The patient will attempt to resist the maneuver by muscle contraction.

Patella: The patient lies supine with a relaxed quadriceps, and the examiner places digital pressure on the patella, attempting to locate it laterally.

Shoulder: The arm is abducted to 90° and rotated externally. With continued external rotation, the patient with an unstable shoulder expresses fear of dislocation.

approach (ă-prōch′) [Fr *aprocher* fr. L. *appropiare,* to draw near to] The surgical procedure for exposing an organ or tissue.

appropriate (ă-prō′prē-ăt) [L. *appropriatus,* made one's own] **1.** In psychiatry, pert. to behavior that is suitable and congruent. **2.** In medical practice, pert. to care that is expected to yield health benefits that considerably exceed risk.

appropriate for gestational age ABBR: AGA. Born with a normal height, weight, head circumference, and body mass index; being neither abnormally large nor abnormally small at birth. Because pregnancies sometimes end before 38 or after 42 weeks, the judgment of what is the appropriate size for a newborn infant is adjusted to reflect the number of weeks that the mother was pregnant and the sex of the child. Babies born after a pregnancy of 38 to 42 weeks' duration are AGA if they weigh between 2.5 and 4 kg.

approximal (ă-prok′sĭ-măl) [*ad-* + *proximal*] Contiguous; next to.

approximate (ă-prok′sĭ-māt″) [L. *approximare,* to come near to] To place or bring objects close together.

apractagnosia (ā″prak″tag-nō′zh(ē-)ă) [Gr. *apraktos,* ineffectual, unsuccessful + *agnosia*] Agnosia marked by the inability to use common instruments or tools whether they are being used on the individual's body or in the environment. This is usually due to a lesion in the parietal area of the brain.

apraxia (ā-prak′sē-ă) [*′an-* + *-praxis* + *-ia*] **1.** Inability to perform purposive movements although there is no sensory or motor impairment. **2.** Inability to use objects properly. **apractic** (-prak′tik), *adj.,* **apraxic** (-prak′sik), *adj.*

akinetic a. Inability to carry out spontaneous movements.

amnesic a. Inability to produce a movement on command because the command is forgotten, although the ability to perform the movement is present.

buccofacial a. Inability to use the muscles of the face or mouth (e.g., to whistle a tune or suck liquids through a straw).

constructional a. Inability to draw or construct two- or three-dimensional forms or figures and impairment in the ability to integrate perception into kinesthetic images.

developmental a. A disorder of motor planning and execution occurring in developing children; thought to be due to central nervous system immaturity.

dressing a. Inability to dress due to patient's deficient knowledge of the spatial relations of his or her body.

ideational a. Misuse of objects due to inability to perceive their correct use. SYN: *sensory a.*

limb a. Inability to use the arms or legs to perform previously learned movements, such as combing one's hair or kicking a ball, despite having normal muscle strength in those body parts.

motor a. Inability to perform movements necessary to use objects properly, although the names and purposes of the objects are known and understood.

sensory a. Ideational apraxia.

verbal a. The inability to form words or speak, despite the ability to use oral and facial muscles to make sounds.

visual-constructional a. The inability to assemble or draw an object after seeing its image or a model of it. This form of apraxia is commonly seen in patients with brain injuries or dementias with parietal lobe lesions.

aproctia (ā″prŏk′sh(ē-)ă) [¹*an-* + *procto-* + *-ia*] Absence or imperforation of anus. **aproctous** (prok′tŭs), *adj.*

apron (ā′prŏn) [Fr. *naperon,* cloth] **1.** An outer garment covering the front of the body for protection of clothing during surgery or certain nursing procedures. **2.** Part of the body resembling an apron, e.g., redundant skin and underlying adipose tissue of the lower abdomen.

lead a. An apron that contains lead or equivalent material and is sufficiently pliable to wear as protection from ionizing radiation. It is used to shield patients and personnel during radiological procedures.

aprosody (ā″pros′ŏ-dē) [¹*an-* + *prosody*] Absence of normal variations of pitch, rhythm, and stress in the speech.

aprosopia (ā″pros-ō′pē-ă) [¹*an-* + Gr. *prosopon,* face + *-ia*] A congenital defect in which part or all of the face is absent.

aprotes Chemical substances that are either cations such as sodium, calcium, potassium, and magnesium that carry a positive charge, or anions such as chloride and sulfate that carry a negative charge. These chemicals are unable to donate or accept protons; thus they are not acids, bases, or buffers.

aprotinin (ā″prŏt′ĭ-nin) [¹*an-* +

prot(e)in(ase) + *-in*] A serine protease inhibitor obtained from bovine pancreas. Its action is believed to be inhibition of plasmin and kallikrein. It is used to decrease blood loss and thus transfusion requirements during surgery.

APRV *airway pressure release ventilation.*

APTA *American Physical Therapy Association.*

APTA Code of Ethics A code of ethics that sets forth ethical principles for the physical therapy profession. According to its preamble, all physical therapists are responsible for maintaining and promoting ethical and competent practice and establishing a standard of conduct. This code of ethics, adopted by the American Physical Therapy Association (APTA), sets forth principles that define the roles of physical therapists as clinicians, educators, researchers, consultants, and health care administrators.

aptamer (ap′tă-měr) [L. *aptus,* fitted, appropriate + *-mere*] A chemical, usually a protein or a nucleic acid, that can fashion itself into numerous shapes, e.g., the configuration of a cell surface receptor.

aptitude (ap′tĭ-tood) [L. *aptitudo,* fitness] Inherent ability or skill in learning or performing physical or mental endeavors.

aptitude test A mental and/or physical test to evaluate skill or ability to perform certain tasks or assignments.

APTT *Activated partial thromboplastin time.*

Apt test [Leonard Apt, U.S. pediatric ophthalmologist] A test used originally to identify the source of black (bloody) stools in newborn infants; it is now used in modified form to distinguish fetal from maternal hemoglobin in blood samples from any source, e.g., the umbilical cord or the gastrointestinal tract. SEE: *swallowed blood syndrome.*

aptyalia, aptyalism (ā″tī-āl′yă, -āl′ē-ă, -tī′ă-lĭzm) [¹*an-* + Gr. *ptyalon,* saliva] Asialia.

APUD cells *amine precursor uptake and decarboxylation* cells. A class of cells, derived from the neural crest of the embryo, that produce hormones (such as insulin, ACTH, glucagon, and thyroxine) and amines (such as dopamine, serotonin, and histamine). These cells are involved in multiple endocrine neoplasia, types I and II.

apudoma (ap″oo-dō′mă) [*APUD (cells)* + *-oma*] A tumor of APUD cells.

apulmonism (ā″-pool′mŏ-nĭzm) [¹*an-* + *pulmo-* + *-ism*] Congenital absence of part or all of a lung.

apus (ā′pŭs) [¹*an-* + Gr. *pous,* foot] A person who has apodia.

apyknomorphous (ā″pik″nō-mor′fŭs) [¹*an-* + *pyknomorphous*] Pert. to a cell that does not stain deeply because its stainable material is not compact.

apyogenous (ā-pī-oj'ĕ-nŭs) [*¹an-* + *pyogen(ic)* *+-ous*] Not producing pus.

apyretic (ā-pī-ret'ĭk) [*¹an-* + *pyretic*] Without fever; afebrile.

apyrexia, apyrexy (ā″pī″rek'sē-ă, ā″pī′rek″sē) [*¹an-* + *pyrexis,* fever] Absence of fever. **apyrexial** (rek'sē-ăl), *adj.*

apyrogenetic, apyrogenic (ā″pī″rō-jĕ-net′ĭk, -jen′ĭk) [*¹an-* + *pyrogenic*] Not causing fever.

AQ *achievement quotient.*

aq [L *aqua,* water] A chemical symbol used as a term in a chemical equation, usually as a subscript or in parenthesis and adjacent to the symbol for a material dissolved in water.

aqua (ak'wă) *pl.* **aquae** [L. *aqua,* water] ABBR: aq. Water.

   medicated a. An aqueous solution of a volatile substance. It usually contains only a comparatively small percentage of the active drug. Some of these solutions are merely water saturated with a volatile oil and are used mostly as vehicles to give odor and taste to solutions.

aquagenic (ak″wă-jen'ĭk) [*aqua* + *-genic*] Caused by water.

aquaphobia (ak″wă-fō'bē-ă) [*aqua* + *-phobia*] A morbid fear of water. SYN: *hydrophobia* (2).

aquaporin (ak″wă-por'ĭn) [*aqua* + *porin*] A cell membrane protein that lets water flow into and out of cells.

aquapuncture (ak″wă-pŭngk'chŭr) [*aqua* + *puncture*] Subcutaneous injection of water to produce counterirritation.

aqua running A form of low-impact aerobic exercise for conditioning or recovery from weight-bearing injuries to the limbs. It is typically done in a pool, involves repetitive movements of both the legs and the arms that are similar to running motions on land, and may be done in a supervised class or physical therapy session.

aquatic (ă-kwot'ĭk) [L. *aquaticus,* pert. to water] **1.** Pert. to water. **2.** Inhabiting water.

aquatic therapy Exercises performed in or under water for conditioning or rehabilitation (e.g., in injured athletes or patients with joint diseases).

aque-, aqueo- [L. *aqua,* water] Prefixes meaning *water.*

aqueduct (ak'wĕ-dŭkt″) [*aque-* + *duct*] A canal or channel.

   cerebral a. A narrow tube in the roof of the midbrain that carries cerebrospinal fluid between the third and fourth ventricles.aqueduct of Sylvius, Sylvian aqueduct.

   a. of Sylvius cerebral aqueduct

   vestibular a. A small passage reaching from the vestibule to the posterior

surface of the petrous section of the temporal bone. SYN: *aqueductus vestibuli.*

aqueductus (ak″wĕ-dŭk'tŭs) A canal or channel; an aqueduct.

aqueous (ā'kwē-ŭs) [*aque-* + *-ous*] **1.** Of the nature of water; watery. **2.** The aqueous humor.

aqueous chamber SEE: under *chamber.*

aqueous flare During slit lamp examination of the eye, an abnormal appearance of the beam of light as it travels through the anterior chamber. The flare is caused by light reflecting off proteins in the aqueous humor. It is found in patients with inflammation in the anterior chamber.

aquiparous (ă-kwip'ă-rŭs) [*aque-* + *-par(a)* + *-ous*] Producing water.

AR *achievement ratio; alarm reaction.*

Ar Symbol for the element argon.

ara-A Vidarabine.

arabinose (ă-rab'ĭ-nōs″) [*(gum) arab(ic)* + *-in* + *²-ose*] Gum sugar, a pentose obtained from plants; sometimes found in urine.

arabinosuria (ă-rab″ĭ-nōs-ū'rē-ă) [*arabinose* + *-uria*] Arabinose in the urine.

Ara-C Cytarabine, an antineoplastic drug of the antimetabolite class.

arachnid (ă-rak'nĭd) [*Arachnida*] A member of the class Arachnida. **arachnidan** ('nĭ-dăn), *adj.*

Arachnida (ă-răk'nĭ-dă) [Gr. *arachnē,* spider, spider web + *-ida*] A class of the Arthropoda, including the spiders, Opiliones (harvestmen or daddy longlegs), scorpions, ticks, and mites.

arachnidism (ă-rak'nĭ-dizm) [*arachnid* + *-ism*] Systemic poisoning from a spider bite. SYN: *arachnoidism.* SEE: *spider bite.*

arachnitis (ar″rk-nīt'ĭs) [Gr. *arachnē,* spider, spider web + *-itis*] Arachnoiditis.

arachnodactyly (ă-rak″nō-dak'tĭ-lē) [Gr. *arachnē,* spider, spider web + *-dactyly*] Spider fingers; a state in which fingers and sometimes toes are abnormally long and slender. SEE: *Marfan syndrome.*

arachnoid (ă-rak'noyd″) [Gr. *arachnē,* spider, spider web + *-oid*] **1.** Resembling a web. **2.** Arachnoid **membrane**.

   cranial a. Arachnoidea encephali.

   spinal a. Arachnoidea spinalis.

arachnoidea (ă-rak″noyd'ē-ă) [L. fr. Gr. *arachnoeidēs*] Arachnoid **membrane**.

   a. encephali The part of the arachnoidea enclosing the brain. SYN: *cranial arachnoid.*

   a. spinalis The part of the arachnoidea enclosing the spinal cord. SYN: *spinal arachnoid.*

arachnoidism (ă-rak'noyd″izm) [*arachnoid* + *-ism*] Arachnidism.

arachnoiditis (ă-rak″noyd-īt'ĭs) [*arachnoid* + *-itis*] Inflammation of the arachnoid membrane. SYN: *arachnitis.*

arachnolysin (ă-rak″nō-lī'sĭn) [Gr. *ar-*

achnē, spider, spider web + *lysin*] The hemolysin present in spider venom.

arachnophobia (ă-rak″nō-fō′bē-ă) [Gr. *arachnē,* spider, spider web + *-phobia*] Morbid fear of spiders.

Ara h2 A protein in peanuts that triggers allergic responses, including life-threatening immunoglobulin E–mediated anaphylaxis.

Aran-Duchenne disease (ă-ran′dŭ-shĕn′) [F. A. Aran, Fr. physician, 1817–1861; G. B. A Duchenne, Fr. neurologist, 1807–1875] Spinal muscular **atrophy**.

Arantius, Julius Caesar (ă-ran′shē-ŭs, ′tē-ŭs) Italian anatomist and physician, 1530–1589

   A. body A small nodule at the center of each of the aortic valve cusps. SYN: *A. nodule.*

   A. nodule **A.** body.

   ventricle of A. The terminal depression of the median sulcus of the fourth ventricle of the brain.

ARB *angiotensin II receptor blocker.*

arbitration (ar-bi-trā′shŏn) [L. *arbitratio,* decision] **1.** A legal procedure for settling a dispute outside the courts, in which the parties select and agree to abide by the decision of a neutral third party (the arbiter or arbitrator). **2.** In radiology, the interpretation of images by two or more readers, who determine and report their findings after conferring together.

arbor (ar′bŏr) A structure resembling a tree with branches.

arborescent (ar″bŏ-res′ĕnt) [L. *arborescere,* to grow into a tree] Branching; treelike.

arborization (ar″bŏ-rĭ-zā′shŏn) [*arbor*] Ramification; branching, esp. terminal branching of nerve fibers and capillaries. SEE: *ferning; nerve.*

arbor vitae (ar′bŏr vī′tē) [L. tree of life] **1.** A treelike structure; a treelike outline seen in a section of the cerebellum. **2.** A tree or shrub of the genus *Thuja* or *Thujopsis.* **3.** A series of branching ridges within the cervix of the uterus.

arbovirus (ar″bŏ-vī′rŭs) [*ar(thropod-)-bo(rne) virus*] Any of a large group of viruses that multiply in both vertebrates and arthropods such as mosquitoes and ticks. Arboviruses cause diseases such as yellow fever and viral encephalitis. SEE: *arenaviruses; Togaviridae.*

ARC *AIDS-related complex.* SEE: under *AIDS.*

arc (ark) [L. *arcus,* bow] **1.** A curved line; a portion of a circle. **2.** An electric spark, esp. in defibrillation or cardioversion, that follows an unwanted or potentially hazardous pathway.

   nuclear a. Spiral patterns on the surface of the lens due to a concentric pattern of fiber growth.

   painful a. A portion of the range of motion in which pain is perceived during active movement of an extremity. Pain is usually due to pinching of soft tissues at only a specific portion of the range of motion and may be caused by tendonitis or bursitis.

   reflex a. The path followed by a nerve impulse to produce a reflex action. The impulse originates in a receptor at the point of stimulation, passes through an afferent neuron or neurons to a reflex center in the brain or spinal cord, and from the center out through efferent neurons to the effector organ, where the response occurs. SEE: illus.

arcade (ar-kād′) [Fr. *arcade,* fr. Italian *arcata,* arch] Any anatomic structure composed of a series of arches.

   Flint a. The arteriovenous anastomoses at the bases of the pyramids of the kidney.

Arcanobacterium haemolyticum (ar-kă″nō-bak-tēr′ē-ŭm hē″mŏ-lit′ĭ-kŭm) A species of gram-positive, facultatively anaerobic bacteria that grow well in carbon dioxide–enriched environments. They may cause several infectious diseases, including exudative pharyngitis/ tonsillitis, osteomyelitis, and sepsis.

arcate (ar′kāt″) [L. *arcuatus,* bow-shaped] Bow-shaped; arched; arcuate.

ARCF *American Respiratory Care Foundation.*

arch (arch) [L. *arcus,* a bow] An anatomical structure having a curved or bowlike outline. SEE: *arcus.*

   abdominothoracic a. The anterior and lateral boundary between the line dividing the thorax and the abdomen. SYN: *costal a.*

   alveolar a. The arch of the alveolar process of either jaw (maxillary and mandibular arch).

   aortic a. Any of a series of six pairs of vessels that develop in the embryo and connect the aortic sac with the dorsal aorta. During the fifth to seventh weeks of gestation, the arches undergo transformation, some persisting as functional vessels, others persisting as rudimentary structures, and some disappearing entirely.

   branchial a. Any of five pairs of arched structures that form the lateral and ventral walls of the pharynx of the embryo. The first is the mandibular arch; the second is the hyoid arch; the third, fourth, and fifth arches are transitory. They are partially separated from each other externally by the branchial clefts and internally by the pharyngeal pouches. They are important in the formation of structures of the face and neck. SYN: *pharyngeal a.*

   costal a. Abdominothoracic **a.**

   crural a. The inguinal ligament, which extends from the anterior superior iliac spine to the pubic tubercle. SYN: *Poupart's ligament.*

   deep crural a. A band of fibers arch-

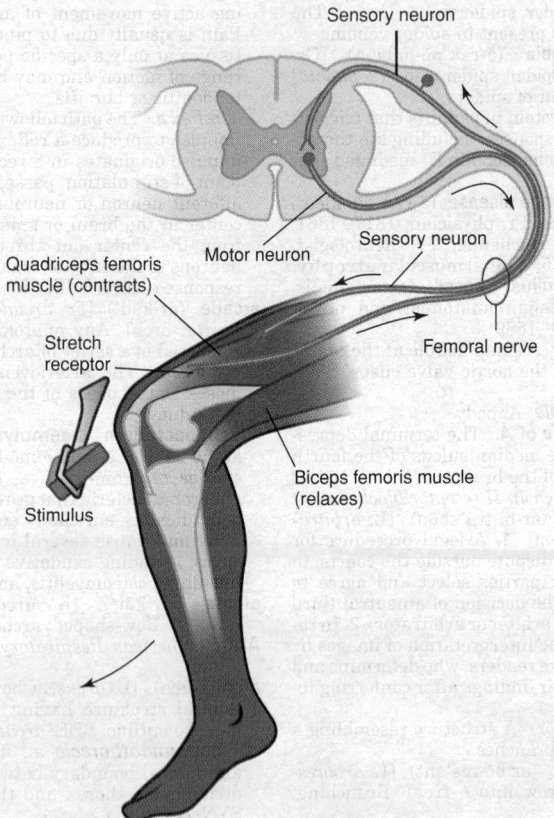

Sensory neuron

Motor neuron

Sensory neuron

Quadriceps femoris
muscle (contracts)

Femoral nerve

Stretch
receptor

Biceps femoris muscle
(relaxes)

Stimulus

REFLEX ARC FOR PATELLAR TENDON REFLEX

ing in front of the sheath of femoral vessels; the downward extension of the transversalis fascia.

deep palmar a. An arch formed in the palm by the communicating branch of the ulnar and the radial artery.

dental a. The arch formed by the alveolar process and teeth in each jaw (maxillary and mandibular arch). SYN: *arcus dentalis*.

a. of foot Any of the four vaulted structures in the foot: the internal (medial) longitudinal, the outer (lateral) longitudinal, and two transverse.

glossopalatine a. The anterior pillar of the fauces; one of two folds of mucous membrane extending from the soft palate to the sides of the tongue.

hemal a. 1. In lower vertebrates, extensions from the lateral areas of the caudal vertebrae that fuse to enclose the caudal artery and vein. In humans these are represented by the costal processes of the vertebrae. 2. An arch formed by the body and dorsal processes of a vertebra.

hyoid a. The second branchial arch,

which gives rise to the styloid process, the stylohyoid ligament, and the lesser cornu of the hyoid bone.

longitudinal a. The anteroposterior arch of the foot; the medial portion is formed by the calcaneus, talus, navicular, the three cuneiform bones, and the first three metatarsals; the lateral portion is formed by the calcaneus, cuboid, and the fourth and fifth metatarsals.

mandibular a. 1. The curved composite structure of natural dentition and supporting tissues of the mandible. 2. The residual bony ridge after teeth have been lost from the mandible.

maxillary a. The curved composite structure of the natural dentition and supporting tissues of the upper jaw (maxillary and mandibular arch); the residual bony ridge after teeth have been lost from the upper jaw.

nasal a. An arch formed by the nasal bones and by the nasal processes of the maxilla.

neural a. Vertebral **a.**

palatopharyngeal a. Pharyngopalatine **a.**

palmar a. SEE: *deep palmar a.; superficial palmar a.*

pharyngeal a. Branchial **a.**

pharyngopalatine a. The posterior pillar of the fauces; one of two folds of mucous membrane extending from the soft palate to the sides of the pharynx. The palatine tonsil lies in the front of the pharyngopalatine and behind the palatoglossal arch. SYN: *palatopharyngeal a.*

plantar a. The arch formed by the external plantar artery and the deep branch of the dorsalis pedis artery.

pubic a. The arch formed by the rami of the ischia and pubic bones. It forms the anterior portion of the pelvic outlet.

pulmonary a. The fifth aortic arch on the left side. It becomes the pulmonary artery.

superciliary a. A curved process of the frontal bone lying just above the orbit, subjacent to the eyebrow, and directly above the supraorbital notch. SYN: *superciliary ridge.*

superficial palmar a. An arch in the palm forming the termination of the ulnar artery.

superior tarsal a. The arch of the median palpebral artery that supplies the upper eyelid.

supraorbital a. A bony arch formed by the upper margin of the orbit.

transverse a. The transverse arch of the foot formed by the navicular, cuboid, cuneiform, and metatarsal bones.

vertebral a. The arch formed by the posterior projection of a vertebra that, with the body, encloses the vertebral foramen. SYN: *neural a.*

zygomatic a. The formation, on each side of the cheeks, of the zygomatic process of each malar bone articulating with the zygomatic process of the temporal bone.

Archaebacteria, Archaeobacteria (ar″kē-bak-tēr′ē-ă, ar″kē-ō-) [Gr. *archaios,* ancient + *bacteria*] A group of single-celled organisms, classified by some microbiologists as a type of bacteria and by others as a separate kingdom or domain of life. Unlike Eubacteria, they lack peptidoglycans in their cell walls. Their ribosomal RNA base sequences also differ from those found in Eubacteria. There are three divisions of archaebacteria: methanogens (organisms that produce methane); thermophiles (organisms that can live in extremely hot, acidic environments, e.g., sulfur springs); and halophiles (organisms that can only live in bodies of concentrated salt water, e.g., Dead Sea).

archetype (ar′kĕ-tīp″) [*archi-* + *type*] **1.** The original type, from which other forms have developed by differentiation. **2.** An ideal or perfect anatomical type; used as a theoretical standard in judging other individuals. **archetypal** (ar″kĕ-tīp′ăl), *adj.*

archi-, arche-, arch- [Gr. *archē,* beginning] Prefixes meaning *first, principal, beginning,* or *original.*

archiblastoma (ar″kĭ-blas-tō′mă) [*archi-* + *blastoma*] A tumor of archiblastic tissue.

archicerebellum (ar″kĭ-ser″ĕ-bel′ŭm) [*archi- cerebellum*] The flocculonodular lobe of the cerebellum. It is tied into the vestibular system and is the phylogenetically oldest segment of the cerebellum.

archipallium (ar″kĭ-pal′ē-ŭm) [*archi-* + *pallium*] The area of the brain comprising the hippocampus, the dentate gyrus, the fasciolar gyrus, and the indusium griseum. SEE: *rhinencephalon.*

architis (ar-kīt′ĭs) [Gr. *archos,* anus + *-itis*] Proctitis.

archive (ar′kīv″) [Fr. fr. L. fr. Gr. *archeia,* public offices] **1.** A database; a bank of stored information. **2.** A location in which documents, images, or records are preserved. **archival** (ar-kī′văl), *adj.* **archivist** (ar′kĭ-vist), *n.*

arch width The measured distance between the canines, bicuspids, and the first molars. These distances establish the shape and size of the dental arch.

arciform (ar′sĭ-form″) [*arcus* + *-form*] Arcuate.

arctation (ărk-tā′shŭn) [L. *arctatus,* pressing together] Stricture of any canal opening.

Arctium lappa (ark′shē-ŭm lap′ă) SEE: *greater burdock.*

arcuate (ar′kū-ăt, -āt″) [L. *arcuatus,* bowed] Shaped like an arc; bowed. SYN: *arciform.* **arcuation** (ar″kū-ā′shŏn), *n.*

arcus (ar′kŭs) *pl.* **arcus** [L. *arcus,* a bow] In anatomy, an arch. SEE: *arch.*

a. alveolaris mandibulae The arch formed by the alveolar process of the body of the mandible.

a. dentalis Dental **arch.**

a. juvenilis An opaque ring about the periphery of the cornea similar to arcus senilis but occurring in the young. It may be due to hypercholesterolemia, corneal irritation or inflammation, or a congenital anomaly.

a. senilis An opaque white ring about the periphery of the cornea, seen in the aged. It is caused by the deposit of fat granules in the cornea or by hyaline degeneration. SEE: illus.

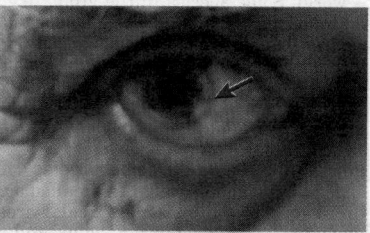

ARCUS SENILIS

ardor (ar'dŏr) [L. *ardor,* heat] Burning; great heat.

ARDS *acute respiratory distress syndrome; adult respiratory distress syndrome.*

area (ar'ē-ă) [L. *area,* an open space, threshing floor] **1.** A space having definite boundaries. **2.** A part of an organ that performs a specialized function. Particular areas are listed under the first word. SEE: e.g., *body surface area; effective radiating area; performance area.*

Area Agency on Aging ABBR: AAA. An agency that develops, coordinates, and in some cases provides a wide range of community-based services for persons aged 60 or older.

areal bone mineral density (ar'ē-ăl) SEE: under *density.*

area of rescue assistance ABBR: ARA. A safe haven near or linked to a building's evacuation route where people escaping an emergency can rest fully protected from hazards such as fire, smoke, or heat.

areata, areatus (ar"ē-āt'ă, ar"ē-āt'ŭs) [*area*] Occurring in circumscribed areas or patches.

area under the curve ABBR: AUC. The integrated quantity of drug (the serum drug concentration with respect to time after taking a single dose).

areca nut (ă-rē'kă) [L. fr. Malayalam *ataykka*] Betel nut.

arecoline (ă-rek'ŏ-lēn") [*areca* + *-ol* + *-ine*] An alkaloid found in the betel nut that causes cholinergic toxicity when the nut is chewed. Arecoline also causes periodontal disease and cancer of the upper gastrointestinal tract.

areflexia (ā"rĕ-flek'sē-ă) [*¹an-* + *reflex* + *-ia*] Absence of reflexes. **areflexic** (-flek'sik), *adj.*

arenaceous (ar"ĕ-nā'shŭs) [L. *arenaceus,* sandy] Resembling sand or gravel. SYN: *arenoid.*

Arenaviridae (ar"ĕ-nă-vēr'-ĭ-dē) [*arenavirus* + *-idae*] A family of single-stranded RNA viruses comprising the arenaviruses.

arenavirus (ar"ĕ-nă-vī'rŭs) *pl.* **arenaviruses** [*arena* + *virus*] Any of the single genus of viruses of the family Arenaviridae. These viruses are a source of zoonotic infections throughout the world. Some species in the group (e.g., Guanarito, Junin, Machupo, and Sabia virus) cause hemorrhagic fevers. Others (e.g., lymphocytic choriomeningitis virus) cause aseptic meningitis. SEE: *Lassa fever.*

arenoid (ar'ē-noyd") [*arena* + *-oid*] Arenaceous.

areola (ă-rē'ŏ-lă) *pl.* **areolae, areolas** [L. *areola,* a small space] **1.** A small space or cavity in a tissue. **2.** A circular area of different pigmentation, as around a wheal, around the nipple of the breast, or the part of the iris around the pupil. **areolar** (-lăr), *adj.*

Chaussier a. SEE: *Chaussier areola.*

a. mammae The pigmented area surrounding the nipple. SYN: **a. papillaris.**

a. papillaris A. mammae.

second a. A pigmented area surrounding the areola mammae during pregnancy.

a. umbilicalis A pigmented area surrounding the umbilicus.

areolitis (ar"ē-ŏ-līt'ĭs) [*areola* + *-itis*] Inflammation of a mammary areola.

arevareva (ă-rē"vă-rē'vă) [Tahitian, skin rash] A severe skin disease marked by scales and general debility. Arevareva is thought to be caused by excess use of kava, an intoxicating beverage whose use should be discontinued. SEE: *kava.*

ARF *acute respiratory failure; acute renal failure.*

Argasidae (ar-gas'ĭ-dē) [*Argas,* a genus name + *-idae*] A family of soft ticks that usually infest birds but may attach to humans, and occasionally infect them with relapsing fever.

argentaffin, argentaffine (ar-jent'ă-fĭn, -fĭn, -fēn") [*argentum* + L. *affinis,* associated with] Pert. to cells that react with silver salts, thus taking a brown or black stain.

argentaffinoma (ar"jent-ă"fĭ-nō'mă) [*argentaffin* + *-oma*] Carcinoid.

argentum (ar-jent'ŭm) [L. *argentum,* silver] SYMB: Ag. Silver.

arginase (ar'jĭ-nās") [*argin(in)* + *-ase*] A liver enzyme that converts arginine into urea and ornithine.

arginine (ar'jĭ-nēn") [*argen(tum)* + *-ine*] A crystalline basic amino acid, $C_6H_{14}N_4O_2$, obtained from the decomposition of vegetable tissues, protamines, and proteins. It is a guanidine derivative, yielding urea and ornithine on hydrolysis. It may also be produced synthetically. Dietary supplementation with arginine is used to treat urea cycle disorders. SEE: *amino acid.*

a. glutamate The L(+)—arginine salt of L(+)—glutamic acid.

a. hydrochloride The L(+)—arginine salt of hydrochloric acid.

suberyl a. A combination of suberic acid and arginine. It forms a portion of the molecule of various bufotoxins (toad poisons).

argininosuccinicaciduria (ar"jĭn-ĭ-nō"sŭk"sĭ"nĭk-as"ĭ-dūr'ē-ă) [*argininosuccin(ase)* + *aciduria*] A hereditary metabolic disease caused by excessive excretion, and thus deficiency, of argininosuccinase, an enzyme required to metabolize argininosuccinic acid. Findings include mental retardation, friable tufted hair, convulsions, ataxia, liver disease, and epilepsy.

argon (ar'gon") [Gr. *argos,* inactive]

SYMB: Ar. A chemical element, one of the noble gases, atomic weight (mass) 39.948, atomic number 18. It makes up approx. 1% of the atmosphere. SEE: *noble gas*.

argon plasma coagulation SEE: under *coagulation*.

Argyll Robertson pupil (ar-gīl′ rob′ĕrt-sŏn) [Douglas Argyll Robertson, Scottish ophthalmologist, 1837–1909] A symptom often present in paralysis and locomotor ataxia (due to syphilis), in which the light reflex is absent but there is no change in the power of contraction during accommodation. SYN: *luetic pupil; Robertson pupil; stiff pupil*.

argyria (ar-jir′ē-ă) [Gr. *argyros,* silver + *-ia*] Bluish discoloration of the skin and mucous membranes due to of prolonged administration of silver. SYN: *argyrosis*.

argyric (ar-jir′ik) [Gr. *argyros,* silver + *-ic*] Pert. to silver.

argyrophil, argyrophilic, argyrophile (ar′jĭ′rō″fil″, fil′ik, fĭl″) [Gr. *argyros,* silver + *-phile*] Pert. to cells that bind with silver salts, which can then be reduced to produce a brown or black stain. **argyrophilia** (fil′ē-ă), *n*.

argyrosis (ar″jĭ-rō′sĭs) [Gr. *argyros,* silver + *-osis*] Argyria.

arhinencephaly (ā″rĭn-ĕn-sef′ă-lē) [¹*an-* + *rhinencephalon*] Incomplete formation of the anterior cerebral hemispheres of the brain and related or neighboring structures.

Arias-Stella reaction (ar″yas-ste′yă) [Javier Arias-Stella, Peruvian pathologist, b. 1924] A reaction marked by decidual changes in the endometrial epithelium. These changes consist of hyperchromatic cells with large nuclei; they may be associated with ectopic pregnancy.

ariboflavinosis (ā″rī″bŏ-flā″vĭ-nō′sĭs) [¹*an-* + *riboflavin* + *-osis*] Vitamin B₂ (riboflavin) deficiency. Symptoms include lesions on the lips, stomatitis, and later, fissures in the angles of the mouth, seborrhea around the nose, and vascularization of the cornea.

arise time SEE: under *time*.

Aristolochia (a-ris″tŏ-lō′kē-ă) [L. *aristolochia* fr Gr. *aristolocheia,* birthwort] A large genus of over 500 plants, from several of which derivatives are promoted as dietary supplements, e.g., *A. serpentaria,* Virginia snakeroot, and *A. serpentaria,* Texas snakeroot.

aristolochic acid (a-ris″tŏ-lok′ik) [*Aristolochia* + *-ic*] SEE: under *acid*.

arm (arm) **1.** In anatomy, the upper extremity from shoulder to elbow. **2.** In clinical experimentation or research science, a treatment protocol in which subjects are enrolled. **3.** In popular usage, the entire upper extremity, from shoulder to hand. SEE: illus. **3.** In research on a therapeutic agent, one of several possible interventions. Most clinical trials include an active treatment arm, in which participants are exposed to the agent that is under study, and a placebo arm, a sham therapy used for the purpose of contrast or comparison.

    articulated a. A jointed instrument used in imaging and in therapeutic procedures (e.g., to permit stereotactic localization of deep anatomical structures; to guide the collection of ultrasonic images; or to focus or direct laser energy).

    Boston a. SEE: *Boston arm*.

    brawny a. Hard, swollen arm caused by lymphedema after mastectomy.

    carrying angle of a. Carrying **angle**.

    Saturday-night a. A colloquial term for musculospiral paralysis.

armamentarium (ar″mă-měn-tar′ē-ŭm) [L. *armamentarium,* armory] The total equipment of a physician or institution, such as instruments, drugs, books, and supplies.

armature (ar′mă-chŭr) [L. *armatura,* armor] **1.** In biology, a structure that serves to protect or is used to attack a predator (e.g., a stinger). **2.** A part of an electrical generator, consisting of a coil of insulated wire mounted around a soft iron core.

arm board SEE: under *board*.

Armed Forces Health Longitudinal Technology Application ABBR: AHLTA. The electronic health record used by the U.S. Department of Defense.

Armed Forces Radiobiological Research Institute ABBR: AFRRI. A branch of the American government that focuses on providing national defense against a military or terrorist attack that may employ ionizing radiation or an accidental release of radioactive material. Research investigations at the Institute concentrate on efforts to detect, block, and treat injuries and illnesses caused by the adverse effects of radioactive material on living organisms.

Armillifer (ar″mil′ĭ-fĕr) [L. *armillifer,* bracelet-wearing] A genus of blood-sucking, endoparasitic arthropods. The natural hosts are reptiles; humans are accidental hosts.

    A. moniliformis A species whose larvae are parasitic in human beings in the Philippines and China.

arm lift A colloquial term for brachioplasty.

armpit (arm′pit″) The hollow under the arm. SYN: *axilla*.

arm ratio In chromosomes, the relation of the length of the long arm of the mitotic chromosome to that of the short arm.

Arndt-Schultz principle (arnt′shoolts′) [Rudolf Arndt, Ger. psychiatrist, 1835–1900; Hugo Paul Friedrich Schultz, Ger. pharmacologist, 1853–1932] The rule that therapeutically applied energy (e.g., thermal agents, ultrasonic energy)

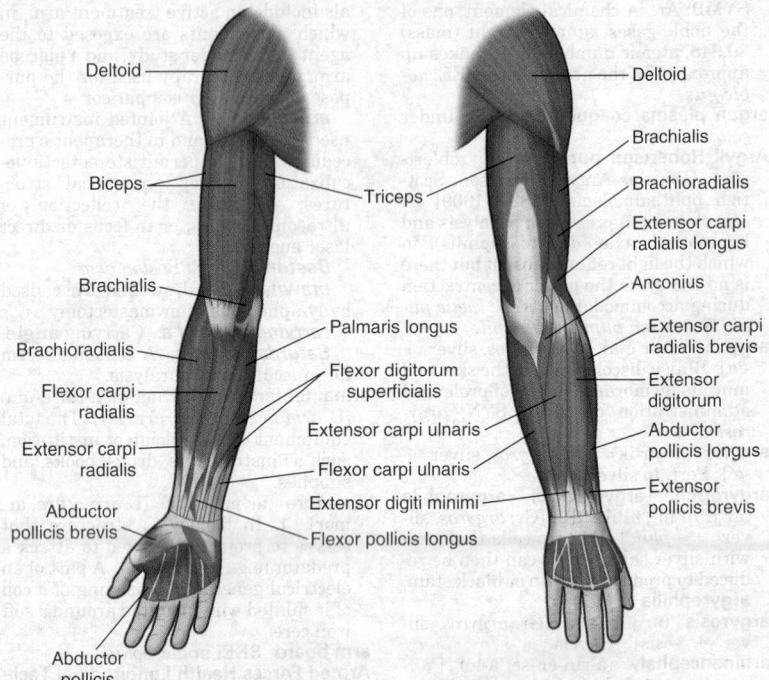

Deltoid

Biceps

Triceps

Brachialis

Brachioradialis

Flexor carpi radialis

Extensor carpi radialis

Abductor pollicis brevis

Palmaris longus

Flexor digitorum superficialis

Extensor carpi ulnaris

Flexor carpi ulnaris

Extensor digiti minimi

Flexor pollicis longus

Abductor pollicis

Deltoid

Brachialis

Brachioradialis

Extensor carpi radialis longus

Anconius

Extensor carpi radialis brevis

Extensor digitorum

Abductor pollicis longus

Extensor pollicis brevis

MUSCLES OF THE ARM

Anterior and posterior views.

must be of the proper intensity per unit of time to stimulate the desired physiological response.

Arneth, Joseph (ar′net″) German physician, 1873–1955.

A. classification of neutrophils A classification of polymorphonuclear neutrophils based on the number of lobes (one to five) in the nucleus, termed stages one to five, respectively.

arnica (ar′ni-kǎ) A perennial herb, *Arnica montana,* used in ointments and as a homeopathic remedy to promote healing, for pain, inflammation, and bacterial infection.

⚠ Oral ingestion at pharmacological (not homeopathic) dosages can be toxic.

Arnold-Chiari deformity (ar′nŏld-kē-ar′ē) [Julius Arnold, Ger. pathologist, 1835–1915; Hans Chiari, Austrian pathologist, 1851–1916] A condition in which the inferior poles of the cerebellar hemispheres and the medulla protrude through the foramen magnum into the spinal canal. It is one of the causes of hydrocephalus and is usually accompanied by spina bifida cystica and meningomyelocele.

AROM *active range of motion; artificial rupture of membranes.*

aroma (ă-rō′mă) [Gr. *arōma,* spice] An agreeable odor.

aromatherapy (ă-rō′mă-ther′ă-pē) [*aroma* + *therapy*] The therapeutic use of essential oils distilled from plants in baths, as inhalants, or during massage to treat skin conditions, anxiety and stress, headaches, and depression.

aromatic (ar″ō-mat′ik) [*aroma* + *-ic*] **1.** Having an agreeable odor. **2.** Pert. to an organic chemical compound in which the carbon atoms form closed rings (as in benzene). **3.** A plant, drug, or organic compound with a pleasant odor.

arousal (ă-row′zăl) **1.** The state of being prepared to act; alertness. **2.** Erotic excitement. **3.** Awakening from sleep.

arousal level An individual's degree of alertness or responsiveness to stimuli. The level of arousal is important in testing a newborn's behavior. These levels are deep sleep; sleep with rapid eye movements; drowsy state; a quiet, alert state; an awake and active state; and a state of active, intense crying. The infant is capable of the most responsive and complex interactions with the environment in the quiet and alert states. SEE: *psychomotor and physical development of infant.*

arraignment (ă-rān′mĕnt) A procedure in which an accused person is brought before the court to plead to a criminal charge. A person may plead guilty, not guilty, or nolo contendere ("no contest"). The judge then sets bail.

arrector pili (ă-rek′tŏr pī′lī″, pil′ē, ar″ek′tŏr′ēz pī″lōr′ŭm, pil-ōr′) *pl.* **arrectores pilorum** [L. *arrector,* raiser + *pilus*] One of the involuntary muscle fibers arising in the skin and extending down to connect with the hair follicles on the side toward which the hair slopes. After certain stimuli, including cold or fright, the muscle fibers contract, straighten the follicles, and raise the hairs, resulting in piloerection.

arrest (ă-rest′) [Fr. *arester* fr L. *arrestare,* to stop] **1.** The state of being stopped. **2.** To bring to a stop.

   bradyasystolic a. Cardiac arrest marked by an extremely slow pulse, usually less than 30 beats/min. This can be due to increased vagal stimulation, progressive heart block, hypoxemia, drugs such as beta blockers, or other causes.

   cardiac a. Sudden cessation of functional circulation. In the U.S., about 1000 people die daily as a result of cardiac arrest. SYN: *cardiopulmonary **a.**; sudden cardiac **a.** SEE: arrhythmia; myocardial infarction.*

   ETIOLOGY: Coronary artery disease is present in most victims. Cardiac arrest is usually caused by myocardial infarction or ventricular arrhythmias. Contributing causes include cardiomyopathies, valvular heart disease, diseases of the electrical conducting system of the heart (such as the long QT syndrome or the Wolff-Parkinson-White syndrome), myocarditis, chest trauma, severe electrolyte disturbances, and intoxications with drugs of abuse or prescribed agents, e.g., digitalis. Physical exertion or extreme emotional stress sometimes precipitates cardiac arrest.

   SYMPTOMS: Abrupt loss of consciousness, followed by death within an hour of onset, is the typical presentation of cardiac arrest.

   TREATMENT: Opening the airway, establishing effective respiration, and restoring circulation (with chest compression and defibrillation) are the keys to treating cardiac arrest. The effectiveness of treatment depends upon the speed with which resuscitation begins and upon the patient's underlying condition. Because most episodes of sudden cardiac arrest are unwitnessed, most patients die without treatment (spontaneous recovery from cardiac arrest in the absence of advanced cardiac life support is very rare). For resuscitated patients, therapies include implantable defibrillators, beta blockers, antiarrhythmic drugs, and, in patients with coronary artery disease, modification of risk factors, i.e., treatment of hypertension, smoking cessation, and lipid-lowering diets and drugs. SEE: table, *advanced cardiac **life support**.*

   cardiopulmonary a. Cardiac **a.**

   cleavage a. In embryology, an obstruction to or a halt in cell division.

   deep hypothermic circulatory a. ABBR: DHCA. The induction of profoundly low body temperatures, e.g. 20°C (68°F), during surgery to reduce the impact of low organ perfusion and ischemic damage.

   epiphyseal a. Cessation of the growth of long bones.

   pelvic a. A condition in which the presenting part of the fetus becomes fixed in the maternal pelvis.

   respiratory a. Cessation of spontaneous respiration.

   sinus a. A condition in which the sinus node of the heart does not initiate impulses for heartbeat. If this condition persists, it usually requires implantation of a permanent cardiac pacemaker. SEE: *artificial cardiac **pacemaker**.*

   sudden cardiac a. Cardiac **a.**

Arrhenius equation (ă-rā′nē-us) [Svante Arrhenius, Swedish chemist and Nobel laureate, 1859–1927] A mathematical formula that specifies the influence of temperature on the rate of a chemical reaction. In general, a higher temperature produces a faster reaction. The equation is used in industry and pharmacy to predict shelf life of reagents and pharmaceuticals.

arrhenoblastoma (ar″ĕ-nō″blas-tō′mă) [Gr. *arr(h)ēn,* male + *blastoma*] An ovarian tumor that secretes male sex hormone, causing virilization in the female.

arrhinia, arhinia (ă-rin′ē-ă, -rī′nē-) [*¹an-* + *rhino-* + *-ia*] Congenital absence of the nose.

arrhythmia (ā″rith′mē-ă) [*¹an-* + *rhythm* + *-ia*] Irregularity or loss of rhythm, esp. of the heart. SEE: *dysrhythmia.* **arrhythmic** (-mik), *adj.*

   atrial a. A disturbance in cardiac rhythm, including atrial fibrillation, atrial flutter, multifocal atrial tachycardia, paroxysmal supraventricular tachycardia, and premature atrial contractions.

   cardiac a. An abnormal rhythm of the heart caused by physiological or pathological disturbances in the discharge of cardiac impulses from the sinoatrial node or their transmission through conductive tissue of the heart. SEE: *bradycardia; cardioversion; artificial cardiac **pacemaker**; sick sinus syndrome; tachycardia; Nursing Diagnoses Appendix.*

   reperfusion a. Cardiac arrhythmia that occurs as the infarcted heart is re-

Routes of Drug Administration During Cardiac Arrest

Route	Pros	Cons
Peripheral IV	Easiest to insert during chest compressions; least traumatic to the patient.	Drugs infused into a peripheral vein take several minutes to reach the heart.
Central IV	Drugs and fluids infused into central veins reach the heart in seconds.	Insertion may be difficult during chest compressions, intubation, and defibrillation. Arterial injury, pneumothorax, hemothorax, and other complications are common in emergency insertions.
Intraosseous	Drugs and fluids infused into marrow reach the central circulation rapidly.	Clinical experience with IO* insertion is limited relative to IV† insertion.
Endotracheal	May be used for drug administration when an airway is present, but other forms of access have not been established.	Double or triple the IV† dose is needed to achieve similar drug effect. Drugs given ET‡ should be diluted in 5–10 ml of sterile water. Correct placement of the ET tube must be confirmed before use. Unlike the other modes of access, this route cannot be used to infuse high volumes of fluids.

* IO=intraosseous
† IV=intravenous cannula
‡ ET=endotracheal

supplied with blood after angioplasty or thrombolysis.

sinus a. Cardiac irregularity marked by variation in the interval between sinus beats and evident on the electrocardiogram as alternately long and short intervals between P waves. Sinus arrhythmia may occur with respiration (evidenced as an increased heart rate during inspiration and a decreased heart rate on expiration) or may result from the use of digitalis glycosides. In older patients, presence of sinus arrhythmia is common and is statistically linked with an increased risk of sudden death.

ventricular a. A disturbance of the (cardiac) ventricular rhythms, including torsades de pointes, ventricular fibrillation, ventricular flutter, ventricular tachycardia, or frequent premature ventricular contractions. SYN: *ventricular dysrhythmia.*

arrhythmogenic (ā-rith″mŏ-jen′ik) [*arrhythmia* + *-genic*] Tending to produce or promote cardiac arrhythmias.

arrhythmogenic right ventricular dysplasia/cardiomyopathy (ā-rith″mŏ-jen′ik) ABBR: ARVD/C. Arrhythmogenic right ventricular **dysplasia**.

ARRT *American Registry of Radiologic Technologists.*

arseniasis (ar″sĕ-nī′ă-sĭs) [*arsen(ium)* + *-iasis*] Chronic arsenic poisoning. SYN: *arsenicalism.*

arsenic (ar′sĕ-nik, ars′nik) [L. *arseni-*

cum, fr Gr. *arsenikon,* yellow orpiment] SYMB: As. A poisonous, grayish-white metallic element, atomic weight (mass) 74.922, atomic number 33, specific gravity 5.73. It is used in the manufacture of dyes and medicines.

Arsenic may be present in soil, water, and air as a common environmental toxicant. Minute traces of arsenic are found in vegetable and animal life (and in eggs). Many household and garden pesticides contain various forms of arsenic. All of these are toxic if ingested or inhaled in sufficient quantity. An accumulation of arsenic in the body will cause alimentary tract disorders, nausea, vomiting, diarrhea, dehydration, neuritis, and paralysis of the wrist and ankle muscles. SYN: *arsenium.*; SEE: *arsenic poisoning; Poisons and Poisoning Appendix.*

a. trioxide As_2O_3, a white powder, toxic in dosages greater than 0.20 mg per kilogram, but useful in lower doses to treat acute promyelocytic leukemia and other cancers.

arsenical (ar-sen′ĭ-kăl) [*arsenic* + *-al*] **1.** Pert. to or containing arsenic. **2.** A drug containing arsenic.

arsenicalism (ar-sen′ĭ-kă-lĭzm) [*arsenical* + *-ism*] Arseniasis.

arsenicophagy (ar″sen-ĭ-kof′ă-jē) [*arsenic* + *-phagia*] Habitual eating of arsenic.

arsenic poisoning SEE: under *poisoning.*

arsenium (ar-sē′nē-ŭm) Arsenic.

arsine (ar-sēn′) [*ars(enic)* + *-ine*] A poisonous gas formed from the interaction of arsenic and acid. It may be used as an agent of chemical warfare.

ART *Accredited Record Technician; antiretroviral therapy; assisted reproduction* **technology**.

artefact British spelling of *artifact*. SEE: *artifact*.

Artemisia (art″ĕ-mēzh′(ē-)ă) [L. *artemisia* fr. Gr *Artemis*, Artemis (the goddess) + *-ia*] A large genus of plants belonging to the daisy family.

    A. annua A Chinese herb used as a source of artesunate (an antimalarial drug).

    A. vulgaris SEE: *mugwort*.

arterectomy, arteriectomy (art″ĕ-rek′tŏ-mē, ar-tēr″ē-ek′tŏ-mē) [*arter(io)-* + *-ectomy*] Excision of an artery or arteries.

arteria (ăr″tē′rē-ă) *pl.* **arteriae** The Latin word for artery.

arterial (ăr-tē′rē-ăl) Pert. to one or more arteries.

arterial blood gas SEE: under *gas*.

arteriectasis, arteriectasia (ăr″tĕ-rē-ĕk′tă-sĭs, -ĕk-tā′zē-ă) [″ + *ektasis*, a stretching out] Arterial dilatation.

arterio-, arteri- [L. fr. Gr. *artēria*, windpipe, artery] Prefixes meaning *relationship to an artery*.

arteriocapillary (ar-tēr″ē-ō-kap′ĭ-ler″ē) [*arterio-* + *capillary*] Pert. to both arteries and capillaries.

arteriofibrosis (ar-tēr″ē-ō-fī-brō′sĭs) [*arterio-* + *fibrosis*] Arteriocapillary **fibrosis**.

arteriogram (ar-tēr′ē-ŏ-gram″) [*arterio-* + *-gram*] A radiograph of an artery after injection of a radiopaque contrast medium, usually directly into the artery or near its origin. SEE: *angiogram*.

arteriography (ar″tēr-ē-og′ră-fē) [*arterio-* + *-graphy*] **1.** A radiographic procedure for obtaining an arteriogram. SEE: *angiography*. **2.** A description of arteries. **arteriographic** (-ē-ŏ-graf′ik), *adj.* **arteriographically** (i-k(ă-)lē), *adv.*

arteriol-, arteriolo- [L. f. Gr. *artēria*, windpipe, artery + diminutive suffix *-ole*] Prefixes meaning *arteriole*.

arteriola (ar-tēr″ē-ō′lă) *pl.* **arteriolae** [L. *arteriola*, small artery] A small artery; an arteriole.

    a. recta One of the small arteries of the kidney that supply the renal pyramids.

arteriole (ar-tēr′ē-ōl″) [*arteriola*] A minute artery, esp. one that, at its distal end, leads into a capillary. SEE: *arteriola*. **arteriolar** (-tēr″ē-ō′lar), *adj.*

arteriolith (ar-tēr′rē-ŏ-lith″) [*arterio-* + *litho-*] An arterial calculus.

arteriolitis (ar-tēr″ē-ŏ-līt′ĭs) [*arteriole* + *-itis*] Inflammation of the arteriolar wall.

arteriolonecrosis (ar-tēr″ē-ō″lō-nĕ-krō′sĭs) [*arteriole* + *necrosis*] Destruction of an arteriole.

arteriolopathy (ar-tēr″ē-ō-lop′ă-thē) [*arteriole* + *-pathy*] Any disease of the arterioles, esp. a disease that affects arterioles throughout the body.

    calcific uremic a. Calciphylaxis.

arteriolosclerosis (ar-tēr″ē-ō″lō-sklĕ-rō′sĭs) [*arteriole* + *sclerosis*] Thickening of the walls of the arterioles, with loss of elasticity and contractility. **arteriolosclerotic** (ar-tēr″ē-ō″lō-sklĕ-rot′ĭk), *adj.*

arteriomotor (ar-tēr″ē-ŏ-mōt′ŏr) [*arterio-* + *motor*] Causing changes in the interior diameter of arteries by dilatation and constriction.

arteriomyomatosis (ar-tēr″ē-ō-mī″ō-mă-tō′sĭs) [*arterio-* + *myomatosis*] Thickening of arterial walls due to overgrowth of muscle fibers.

arterionecrosis (ar-tēr″ē-ō-nĕ-krō′sĭs) [*arterio-* + *necrosis*] Necrosis of an artery or of arteries.

arteriopathy (ar″tēr-ē-op′ă-thē) [*arterio-* + *-pathy*] A disease of the arteries.

    obliterative a. In organ transplantation, diffuse concentric stenosis of the arteries of the graft due to immunologic rejection. It is characterized pathologically by hyperplastic scarring of the intima of affected arteries and infiltration by foam cells.

arterioplasty (ar-tēr″ē-ō-plas′tē) [*arterio-* + *-plasty*] Repair or reconstruction of an artery.

arteriopressor (ar-tēr″ē-ō-pres′or″, ŏr) [*arterio-* + *pressor*] Causing increased arterial blood pressure.

arteriorrhaphy (ar-tēr″ē-or′ă-fē) [*arterio-* + *-rrhaphy*] Suturing of an artery.

arteriorrhexis (ar-tēr″ē-ō-rek′sĭs) [*arterio-* + *-rrhexis*] Rupture of an artery.

arteriosclerosis (ar-tēr″ē-ō-sklĕ-rō′sĭs) [*arterio-* + *sclerosis*] A disease of the arterial vessels marked by thickening, hardening, and loss of elasticity in the arterial walls. Three forms of arteriosclerosis are generally recognized: atherosclerosis, arteriolosclerosis, and Mönckeberg's calcification. Atherosclerosis is the single most important cause of disease and death in Western societies. **arteriosclerotic** (-rot′ik), *adj.* SEE: *atherosclerosis*.

    a. obliterans Arteriosclerosis in which the lumen of the artery is completely occluded.

arteriospasm (ar-tēr′ē-ō-spazm″) [*arterio-* + *spasm*] Spasm of an artery. **arteriospastic** (-tēr″ē-ō-spas′tik), *adj.*

arteriostenosis (ar-tēr″ē-ō-stĕ-nō′sĭs) [*arterio-* + *stenosis*] Narrowing of the lumen of an artery. The stenosis may be temporary or permanent.

arteriostosis (ar-tēr″ē-os-tō′sĭs) [*arterio-* + *osteo-* + *-sis*] Calcification of an artery.

arteriosympathectomy (ar-tēr″ē-ō-sim″pă-thek′tŏ-mē) [*arterio-* + *sympathectomy*] Removal of the arterial sheath containing sympathetic nerve fibers.

arteriotomy (ar″tēr-ē-ot′ŏ-mē) [*arterio-* + *-tomy*] Surgical division or opening of an artery.

arteriovenous (ar-tēr″ē-ō-vē′nŭs) [*arterio-* + *venous*] ABBR: A-V, AV. Pert. to both arteries and veins.

arteriovenous access Use of a shunt to connect an artery to a vein. This may be used in renal dialysis.

arteriovenous oxygen difference ABBR: C (a-v) O_2. The difference between the oxygen content of arterial and venous blood.

arteritis (art″ĕ-rīt′ĭs) [*arter(io)-* + *-itis*] Inflammation of an artery. **arteritic** (-rit′ik), *adj.* SEE: *endarteritis.*

    giant cell a. Temporal **a.**

    a. nodosa Widespread inflammation of adventitia of small and medium-sized arteries with impaired function of the involved organs. SYN: *periarteritis nodosa; polyarteritis nodosa.*

    a. obliterans Endarteritis obliterans.

    rheumatic a. An obsolete term for inflammation of small arteries as a result of rheumatic fever.

    Takayasu a. SEE: *Takayasu arteritis.*

    temporal a. A chronic inflammation of large arteries, usually the temporal, occipital, or ophthalmic arteries, identified on pathological specimens by the presence of giant cells. It causes thickening of the intima, with narrowing and eventual occlusion of the lumen. It typically occurs after age 50. Symptoms include headache, tenderness over the affected artery, loss of vision, and facial pain. The cause is unknown, but there may be a genetic predisposition in some families. Corticosteroids are usually administered. SYN: *giant cell a.*

artery (art′ĕ-rē) *pl.* **arteries** [Gr. *artēria,* windpipe, artery] A vessel carrying blood from the heart to the tissues.. Pulmonary arteries carry deoxygenated blood from the right ventricle to the lungs to pick up oxygen and to release carbon dioxide; in contrast, systemic arteries carry oxygenated blood from the left ventricle to the rest of the body. SEE: illus. (Systemic Arteries).

    ANATOMY: Structurally, a typical artery has three tissue layers: the inner layer (tunica intima) has endothelial tissue; the middle layer (tunica media) has smooth muscle and elastic connective tissue; and the outer layer (tunica externa) has connective tissue. SEE: illus. (Structure of an Artery).

    accessory meningeal a. The fourth branch of the first segment of the maxillary artery. It enters the cranial cavity through the foramen ovale.

    adrenal a. The superior, the middle, or the inferior adrenal artery, all of which supply blood to the adrenal glands. The superior adrenal artery is a branch of the inferior phrenic artery, the middle adrenal artery is a branch of the aorta, and the inferior adrenal artery is a branch of the renal artery. SYN: *suprarenal a.*

    alveolar a. The superior or the inferior alveolar artery (branches of the maxillary artery), which supply blood to the bones, gingivae, and teeth of the upper and lower jaws.

    anterior cerebral a. An artery that supplies blood to the medial side of the cerebral hemisphere and the corpus callosum; it is part of the circle of Willis, and it branches from the internal carotid artery at the base of the brain. The anterior cerebral artery anastomoses with the contralateral anterior cerebral artery via the anterior communicating artery. SEE: *brain* (Major arteries of the brain) and *circle of Willis* for illus.

    anterior communicating a. The front-most link in the arterial loop called the circle of Willis; it interconnects the right and left anterior cerebral arteries. SEE: *brain* (Major arteries of the brain) and *circle of Willis* for illus.

    anterior inferior cerebellar a. A branch of the basilar artery; it runs dorsally along the posterior edge of the pons and supplies blood to the hindbrain, the superior and middle cerebellar peduncles, and portions of the ventral cerebellum. SEE: *brain* (Major arteries of the brain) for illus.

    anterior interosseous a. A branch of the common interosseous artery; it runs through the forearm on the anterior interosseous membrane.

    anterior interventricular a. Left anterior descending coronary **a.**

    anterior spinal a. The left and right anterior spinal arteries are initially branches from the vertebral arteries, but as they descend to the hindbrain-spinal cord junction, they merge into a single midline artery that runs along the ventral surface of the spinal cord (in the anterior median sulcus). At each intervertebral foramen, radicular arteries join the anterior spinal artery, which supplies blood to the ventral half of the spinal cord.

    anterior tibial a. The terminal branch of the popliteal artery or the initial branch of the posterior tibial artery; it runs along the front of the leg alongside the peroneal (fibular) nerve. Its branches include the anterior and posterior tibial recurrent arteries and anterior medial and anterior lateral malleolar arteries; in the foot, it continues as the dorsalis pedis artery. SEE: *aorta* for illus.

    appendicular a. A branch of the il-

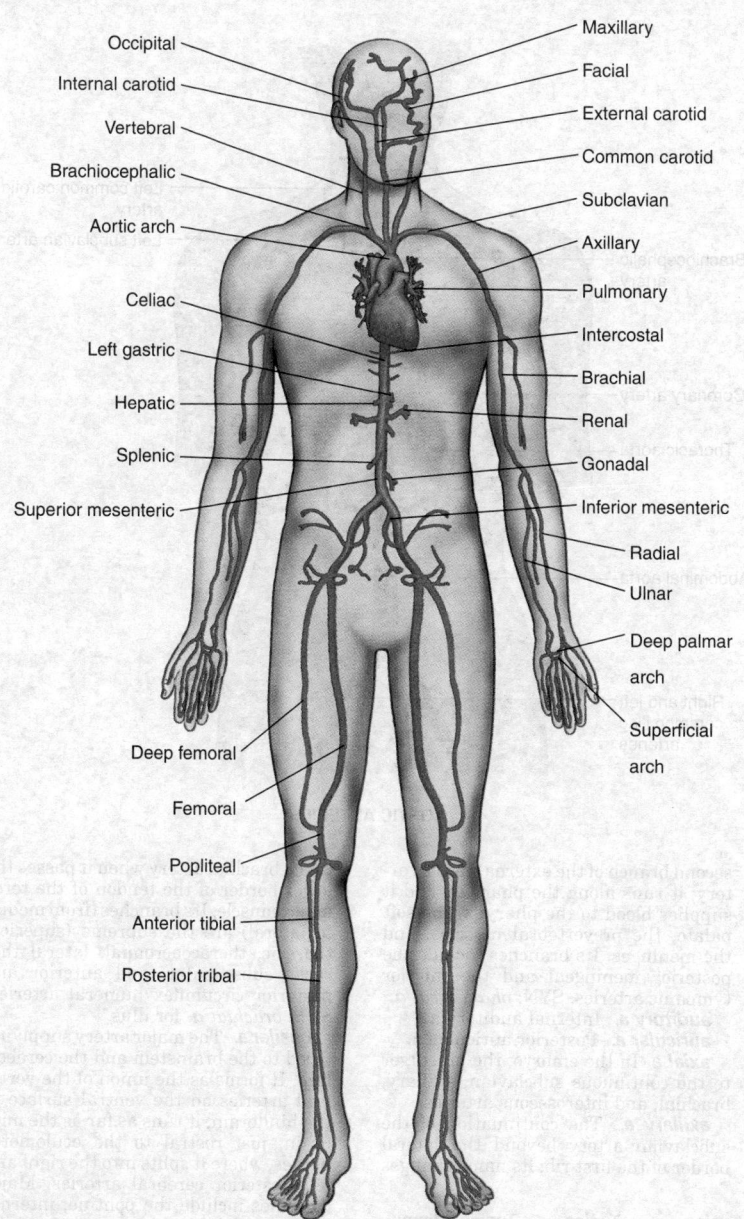

Occipital
Internal carotid
Vertebral
Brachiocephalic
Aortic arch
Celiac
Left gastric
Hepatic
Splenic
Superior mesenteric

Maxillary
Facial
External carotid
Common carotid
Subclavian
Axillary
Pulmonary
Intercostal
Brachial
Renal
Gonadal
Inferior mesenteric
Radial
Ulnar
Deep palmar arch
Superficial arch

Deep femoral
Femoral
Popliteal
Anterior tibial
Posterior tribal

SYSTEMIC ARTERIES

eocolic artery; it supplies blood to the terminal ileum and appendix.

arcuate a. In the kidneys, a branch of the interlobar arteries that runs along the base of the pyramids. Branches of the arcuate arteries are called the interlobular arteries, and these give rise to the afferent glomerular arteries.

ascending cervical a. A small branch of the inferior thyroid artery; it runs up along the cervical vertebrae and provides blood to adjacent neck muscles.

ascending pharyngeal a. The first or

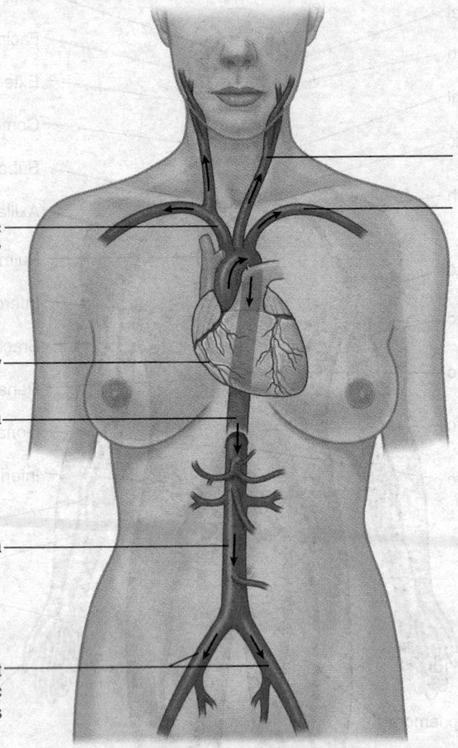

Left common carotid artery

Left subclavian artery

Brachiocephalic artery

Coronary artery

Thoracic aorta

Abdominal aorta

Right and left common iliac arteries

AORTIC ARTERIES

second branch of the external carotid artery; it runs along the pharynx, and it supplies blood to the pharynx, the soft palate, the prevertebral muscles, and the meninges. Its branches include the posterior meningeal and the inferior tympanic arteries. SYN: *pharyngeal a.*

auditory a. Internal auditory **a.**

auricular a. Posterior auricular **a.**

axial a In the embryo, the precursor to the continuous subclavian, axillary, brachial, and interosseous arteries.

axillary a. The continuation of the subclavian artery beyond the lateral border of the first rib; its name changes

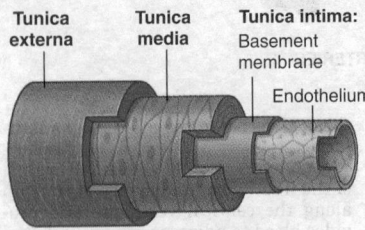

Tunica externa

Tunica media

Tunica intima:
Basement membrane

Endothelium

STRUCTURE OF AN ARTERY

to the brachial artery when it passes the lower border of the tendon of the teres major muscle. Its branches (from medial to lateral) are the supreme (superior) thoracic, thoracoacromial, lateral thoracic, subscapular, and anterior and posterior circumflex humeral arteries. SEE: *brachial a.* for illus.

basilar a. The major artery supplying blood to the brainstem and the cerebellum. It forms as the union of the vertebral arteries on the ventral surface of the hindbrain; it runs as far as the midbrain, just rostral to the oculomotor nerves, where it splits into the right and left posterior cerebral arteries. Major branches include the pontine, internal auditory (labyrinthine), anterior inferior cerebellar, and superior cerebellar arteries. Strokes involving the basilar artery can produce damage to the cerebellum and to regions of the hindbrain regulating essential vegetative functions, such as consciousness and respiration. SEE: *brain (Major arteries of the brain); circle of **Willis**;* and *head (Arteries and veins of the head)* for illus.

brachial a. The main artery of the arm. The brachial artery is a continuation of the axillary artery and it runs on the inside (medial side) of the arm; it terminates by splitting into the radial and ulnar arteries. Its main branches include the deep brachial (profunda brachii) artery and the superior and inferior ulnar collateral arteries. SEE: illus.

brachiocephalic a. Innominate **a.**

bronchial a. A branch of the thoracic aorta or the upper intercostal arteries; usually there are two left bronchial arteries and one right bronchial artery. The bronchial arteries follow the arborization of the bronchial tree and supply oxygenated blood to the walls of the bronchi and bronchioles and to the connective tissue of the lungs. The first branches of the bronchial arteries include small arteries to the esophagus, pericardium, and mediastinum. SEE: *aorta* for illus.

carotid a. The common, the internal, or the external carotid artery.

celiac a. The first unpaired midline artery branching from the abdominal aorta. It supplies blood to the foregut, i.e., the stomach, liver, spleen, pancreas, and proximal half of the duodenum. The celiac artery is short and wide; its branches include the left gastric, the splenic, and the common hepatic arteries. SYN: *celiac* **trunk**. SEE: *aorta* for illus.

central retinal a. A branch of the ophthalmic artery that enters the optic nerve in the rear of the orbit. The central retinal artery then emerges (usually as four branches, the superior and inferior temporal, and the superior and inferior nasal arteries) into the retina through the optic disc amidst the optic axons.

cerebellar a. The anterior inferior, the posterior inferior, or the superior cerebellar artery.

cerebral a. The anterior, the middle, or the posterior cerebral artery.

cervical a. The ascending cervical, the deep cervical, the superficial cervical, or the transverse cervical artery.

choroidal a. The anterior choroidal artery or one of the posterior choroidal arteries. The anterior choroidal artery it is a branch of the internal carotid artery; it supplies blood to the choroid plexus of the lateral ventricle, the optic tract, the lateral geniculate body, the posterior limb of the internal capsule, the globus pallidus, and parts of the thalamus. The posterior choroidal arteries are branches of the posterior cerebral artery; they supply blood to the choroid plexus of the third ventricle.

ciliary a. The anterior ciliary, the short posterior ciliary, or the long posterior ciliary arteries, which supply blood to the walls, intraocular structures, and choroid layer of the eye.

circumflex coronary a. Left circumflex **a.**

circumflex femoral a. The lateral or the medial circumflex femoral artery, both of which are branches of the deep femoral artery and innervate thigh muscles.

circumflex humeral a. The anterior or the posterior circumflex humeral artery, both of which are branches of the axillary artery. The anterior and posterior circumflex humeral arteries anastomose and supply blood to the surgical neck of the humerus and the deltoid, the coracobrachialis, and the heads of the biceps muscles. SYN: *humeral circumflex* **a.** SEE: *brachial* **a.** for illus.

circumflex iliac a. The deep circumflex iliac artery. It is a branch of the external iliac artery and it innervates the transversus abdominis and internal oblique muscles.

circumflex scapular a. A branch of the subscapular artery. It supplies blood to the infraspinatus and subscapularis muscles and it anastomoses with the transverse cervical and suprascapular arteries.

coccygeal a. Any of the branches of the internal iliac artery that supply blood to the coccyx and its surrounding tissues.

colic a The right, the middle, or the left colic artery.

collateral a. The radial collateral, the median collateral, or the ulnar collateral artery, all of which are branches of the brachial artery and supply blood to the arm.

common carotid a. A major artery to the head. The left common carotid usually arises from the aortic arch proximal to the left subclavian; the right common carotid is a branch of the brachiocephalic artery. Each common carotid artery runs rostrally in the carotid sheath and enters the neck (behind the sternocleidomastoid muscle) without branching; in the neck, between the level of the top of the trachea and the floor of the mouth, each common carotid artery divides into an internal and an external carotid artery. SEE: *head (Arteries and veins of the head); aorta (Branches of aorta); heart (The heart)* for illus.

common hepatic a. A branch of the celiac artery. It runs forward and to the right. After giving off the gastroduodenal artery, the common hepatic artery continues toward the liver as the hepatic artery.

common iliac a. Either of the pair of terminal branches of the abdominal aorta, each supplying blood to one side of the pelvis, abdominal wall, and lower limbs. Its two branches are the external and the internal iliac arteries. SEE: *aorta (Branches of aorta)* for illus.

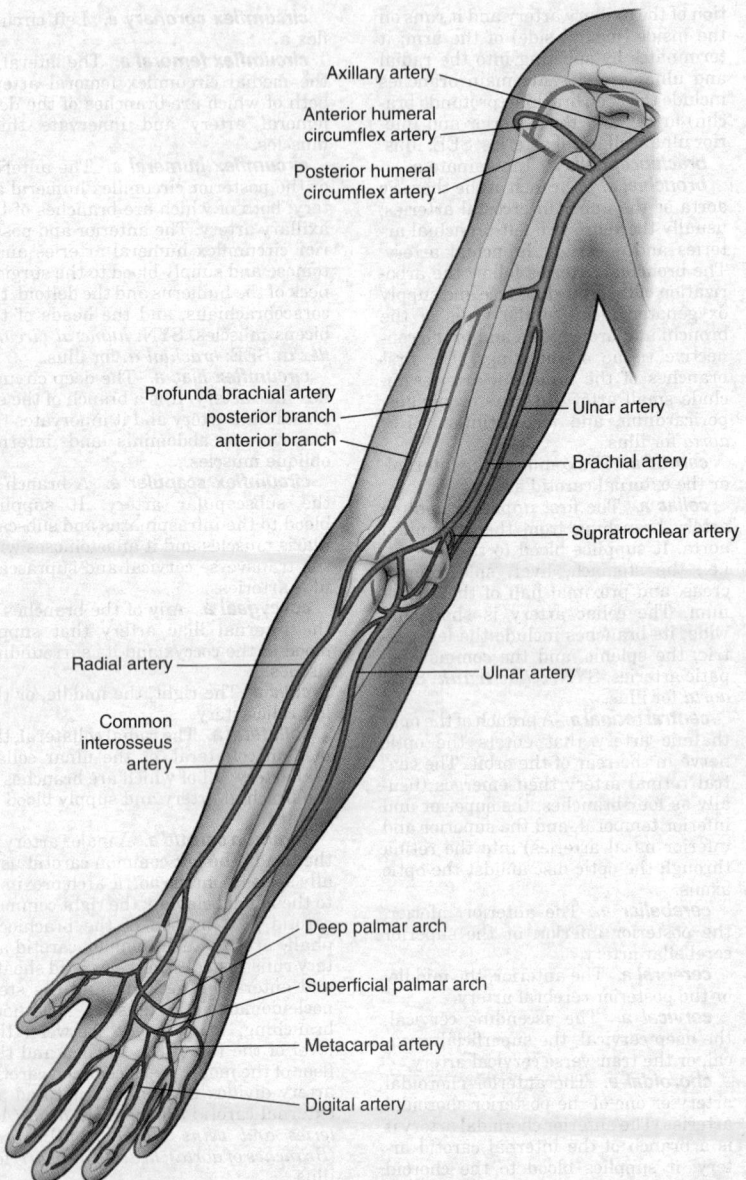

Axillary artery

Anterior humeral circumflex artery

Posterior humeral circumflex artery

Profunda brachial artery
posterior branch
anterior branch

Ulnar artery

Brachial artery

Supratrochlear artery

Radial artery

Ulnar artery

Common interosseus artery

Deep palmar arch

Superficial palmar arch

Metacarpal artery

Digital artery

BRACHIAL ARTERY

common interosseous a. A branch of the ulnar artery; the branches of the common interosseous artery include the posterior and the anterior interosseous arteries. SEE: *brachial a.* for illus.

communicating a. The anterior or the posterior communicating artery in the circle of Willis at the base of the brain.

coronary a. The right coronary ar-

tery, the left coronary artery, or their main branches. SEE: illus.

cremasteric a. A branch of the inferior epigastric artery. In the male, it runs with and supplies blood to the spermatic cord; in the female, it runs with the round ligament.

cystic a. A branch of either the hepatic or the right hepatic artery. It follows the cystic duct to the gallbladder.

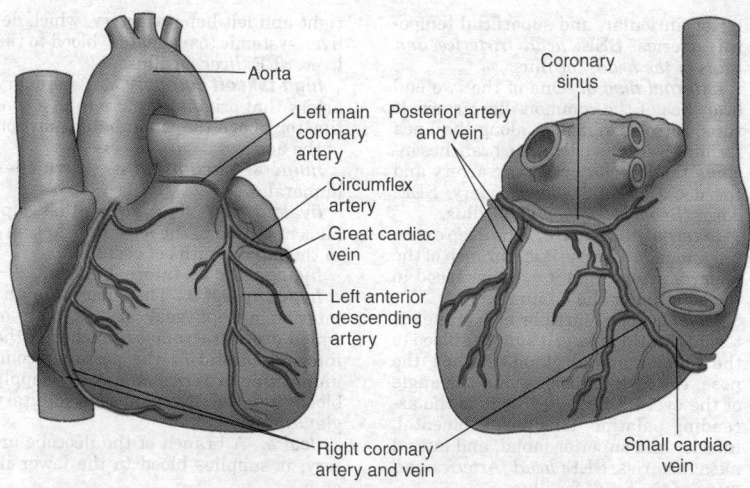

CORONARY ARTERIES

deep brachial a. Profunda brachii **a.**

deep cervical a. A branch of the costocervical trunk (from the subclavian artery). It runs to the cervical vertebrae, it supplies blood to the semispinalis cervicis muscles, and it anastomoses with the descending branch of the occipital artery.

deep femoral a. A branch of the femoral artery; it originates from the posterior side of the femoral artery and it runs in the posterior thigh. Its branches include the medial circumflex femoral and the lateral circumflex femoral arteries. SYN: *profunda femoris a.* SEE: *aorta (Branches of aorta)* for illus.

deep temporal a. The posterior or the anterior deep temporal artery, which are the second and fifth branches of the second segment of the maxillary artery. These arteries supply blood to the temporalis muscle.

descending palatine a. A branch of the maxillary artery; it runs downward in the greater palatine canal. Its branches include the lesser and the greater palatine arteries.

digital a. The digital arteries run with the digital nerves along the medial and lateral sides of each finger. SEE: *brachial a.* for illus.

dominant a. In cardiology, the coronary artery that supplies the posterior descending artery (PDA) of the heart. The coronary circulation is said to be "right dominant" when the PDA receives its blood flow from the right coronary artery, and "left dominant" when its flow comes from the left coronary artery, via the left circumflex artery.

dorsalis pedis a. The continuation of the anterior tibial artery beyond the ankle; it supplies blood to the foot.

dorsal a. of the penis A branch of the internal pudendal artery; the dorsal arteries run inside the Buck fascia along the dorsal surface of the penis, on either side of the deep dorsal vein.

dorsal scapular a. A branch of the subclavian artery; it runs with the dorsal scapular nerve and supplies blood to the rhomboid, latissimus dorsi, and trapezus muscles.

elastic a. A large artery in which elastic connective tissue is predominant in the middle layer (tunica media). Elastic arteries include the aorta and its larger branches (brachiocephalic, common carotid, subclavian, and common iliac), which conduct blood to the muscular arteries.

end a. An artery whose branches do not anastomose with those of other arteries, e.g., arteries to the brain and spinal cord. SYN: *terminal a.*

epigastric a. The superior or the inferior epigastric artery.

esophageal a. The superior or the inferior epigastric artery. Both types of esophageal arteries anastomose with each other.

ethmoidal a. The anterior or the posterior ethmoidal artery, both of which are branches of the ophthalmic artery and supply blood to the paranasal sinuses and the walls of the nasal cavity.

external carotid a. One of the two terminal divisions of the common carotid artery; it supplies blood to the extracranial parts of the head. The external carotid arises from the common carotid artery at about the level of the top of the trachea; it then runs behind the neck of the mandible toward the rear of the parotid gland. Its major branches are (from bottom to top): the ascending pharyngeal, superior thyroid, lingual, facial, maxillary, occipital, posterior auricular, and superficial temporal arteries. SEE: *head (Arteries and veins of the head)* for illus.

external iliac a. One of the two end branches of the common iliac artery; it runs, retroperitoneally, along the linea terminalis of the pelvis. Its branches include the inferior epigastric artery and the deep circumflex iliac artery. SEE: *aorta (Branches of aorta)* for illus.

external pudendal a. The deep external pudendal artery; it is a branch of the femoral artery, and it supplies blood to the scrotum or the labium majus.

facial a. The fourth branch of the external carotid artery; it supplies blood to the submandibular gland, the lips, the nose, the facial muscles, and the angle of the eye. Its branches include the ascending palatine, tonsillar, submental, inferior and superior labial, and lateral nasal arteries. SEE: *head (Arteries and veins of the head)* for illus.

femoral a. The continuation of the external iliac artery beyond the inguinal ligament; it runs in the femoral sheath between the femoral nerve (laterally) and the femoral vein (medially). Branches of the femoral artery include the superficial epigastric, the superficial circumflex iliac, the external pudendal, the deep femoral, and the descending genicular arteries. Behind the knee, the femoral artery continues as the popliteal artery. SEE: *aorta (Branches of aorta)* for illus.

fibular a. Peroneal **a.**

gastric a. The left or the right gastric artery,, or a short gastric artery.

gastroduodenal a. A branch of the common hepatic artery; it runs behind the duodenum and branches into the right gastroepiploic artery and the superior pancreaticoduodenal artery.

gastroepiploic a. The right or the left gastroepiploic artery.

genicular a. The descending genicular artery, which is a branch of the femoral artery; or the lateral superior, medial superior, lateral inferior, medial inferior, or middle genicular arteries, which are branches of the popliteal artery.

gluteal a. The inferior or the superior gluteal artery.

greater palatine a. A branch of the maxillary artery; it runs in the roof of the mouth and supplies blood to the palate, the incisive canal, and the nasal septum.

hemorrhoidal a. Rectal **a.**

hepatic a. The continuation of the common hepatic artery past the point from which the gastroduodenal artery branches off. The single (unpaired) hepatic artery gives off a branch to the gallbladder, i.e., the cystic artery and a branch to the stomach, i.e., the right gastric artery, before it divides into a right and left hepatic artery, which deliver systemic (oxygenated) blood to the liver. SEE: *liver* for illus.

high-takeoff coronary a. A coronary artery that originates more than a centimeter above the sinotubular junction of the aorta.

humeral circumflex a. Circumflex humeral **a.**

hyaloid a. A fetal artery that supplies nutrition to the lens. It disappears in the later months of gestation.

hypogastric a. Internal iliac **a.**

hypophyseal a. The superior or the interior hypophyseal artery, both of which are intracranial branches of the internal carotid or the posterior communicating arteries and both supply blood to the hypophysis (pituitary gland).

ileal a. A branch of the ileocolic artery; it supplies blood to the lower ileum.

ileocolic a. A lower branch of the superior mesenteric artery; it runs down and to the right to supply blood to the lower portion of the ascending colon and the ileocolic junction. Its inferior branch gives rise to the ascending colic, cecal, appendicular, and ileal arteries.

iliac a The common, the external, or the internal iliac artery.

iliolumbar a. A branch of the internal iliac artery; it supplies blood to the iliacus, psoas major, and quadratus lumborum muscles.

infarct-related a. An artery whose obstruction has resulted in the death of tissue, typically, in the heart or brain.

inferior alveolar a. The fifth branch of the first segment of the maxillary artery. With the inferior alveolar nerve, the inferior alveolar artery enters the mandibular canal through the mandibular foramen. Before entering the foramen, the inferior alveolar artery gives off the mylohyoid artery; the terminal branch of the inferior alveolar artery is the mental artery.

inferior epigastric a. A branch of the external iliac artery, just above the inguinal ligament; it runs upward and medially along the anterior abdominal wall medial to the internal inguinal ring. It then continues upward in the rectus sheath and eventually anastomoses with the superior epigastric artery, which is running downward in the sheath.

inferior gluteal a. A branch of the internal iliac artery; it leaves the pelvic cavity through the greater sciatic foramen, below the piriformis muscle, and it supplies blood to the gluteus maximus muscle. Its branches include the sciatic and coccygeal arteries, and it anastomoses with the lateral and medial circumflex femoral arteries.

inferior labial a. A branch of the facial artery; it runs beneath the muscles of the lower lip and anastomoses with the mental artery and the contralateral inferior labial artery.

inferior mesenteric a. The third unpaired midline artery that branches from the abdominal aorta; it originates 3 to 4 cm proximal to the aortic bifurcation. It supplies blood to the hindgut, i.e., the distal half of the transverse colon, the descending colon, the sigmoid colon, and the rectum. Its branches include the left colic, sigmoid, and superior rectal arteries. SEE: *aorta (Branches of aorta), circulation (Circulation of blood through heart and major vessels)* for illus.

inferior pancreatic a. A branch of the superior mesenteric artery; it supplies blood to the proximal duodenum and the head of the pancreas, and it anastomoses with the superior pancreaticoduodenal artery.

inferior phrenic a. A branch of the abdominal aorta just below the diaphragm; it supplies blood to the diaphragm. Its branches include the superior adrenal arteries. SYN: *phrenic a.* SEE: *aorta (Branches of aorta)* for illus.

inferior rectal a. A branch of the pudendal artery; its two or three branches supply blood to the anus.

inferior thyroid a. A branch of the thyrocervical trunk (from the subclavian artery); it winds upward behind the carotid sheath and then runs medially toward the thyroid gland. Its branches include the ascending cervical, pharyngeal, inferior laryngeal, and superior and inferior thyroid arteries.

infraorbital a. A branch of the maxillary artery; it enters the rear of the orbit through the inferior orbital fissure, it runs in the infraorbital groove, and it emerges on the face through the infraorbital foramen. It supplies blood to the canine and incisor teeth, the lower eyelid, upper lip, and cheek.

innominate a. The large artery arising from the arch of the aorta, deep to the manubrium of the sternum, and running to the right. It ends by dividing into the right subclavian and the right common carotid arteries. SYN: *brachiocephalic a.; brachiocephalic trunk.* SEE: *aorta (Branches of aorta); circulation (Circulation of blood through heart and major vessels); head (Arteries and veins of the head)* for illus.

intercostal a. Any of the nine pairs of arteries that originate from the dorsal side of the thoracic aorta and run horizontally between the ribs to supply blood to the skin, muscles, and bones of the chest wall. These aortic intercostal arteries run in interspaces 3 to 11. The intercostal arteries of the first two interspaces are branches of the superior intercostal artery (a branch of the cos-

tocervical trunk of the subclavian artery). The anterior (sternal) segments of the upper nine intercostal spaces receive their blood supplies from the anterior intercostal arteries, which are branches of the internal mammary artery. SYN: *posterior intercostal a.* SEE: *aorta (Branches of aorta)* for illus.

interlobar a. A branch of the lobar artery of the kidney; it runs between the kidney pyramids and toward the cortex of the kidney. The interlobar arteries give rise to the arcuate arteries, which run along the bases of the pyramids.

interlobular a. A branch of the arcuate artery in the kidney. The interlobular arteries run in the cortex of the kidney and give rise to the afferent glomerular arteries.

internal auditory a. A branch of the basilar artery; it enters the internal auditory meatus, with the facial (CN VII) and vestibuloacoustic (CN VIII) nerves, and supplies blood to the cochlea, the labyrinth, and the facial nerve.

internal carotid a. One of the two divisions of the common carotid artery. After branching from the common carotid, the internal carotid continues in the carotid sheath to the carotid foramen in the base of the skull just anterior to the jugular foramen. The internal carotid then turns forward and runs in the carotid canal inside the petrous part of the temporal bone. Passing over the foramen lacerum, the internal carotid emerges from its canal and follows the carotid groove upward along the medial wall of the middle cranial fossa, passing through the cavernous sinus. Just below the optic nerve, the internal carotid loops back and turns upward to become the middle cerebral artery of the circle of Willis. As it passes the optic nerve, the internal carotid puts out its first major branch, the ophthalmic artery.

Each internal carotid artery supplies blood to the ipsilateral eye and about 80% of the ipsilateral brain, including most of the frontal, parietal, and temporal lobes and the basal ganglia. These regions include the primary motor and sensory cortices; therefore, a blockage of the internal carotid artery circulation, e.g., a unilateral ischemic stroke, often produces unilateral motor weakness or sensory loss on the opposite side of the body.

In the neck, the internal carotid artery contains two receptor sites, the carotid body, a chemoreceptor for the oxygen concentration of the blood, and baroreceptors that detect and respond to arterial pressure. SEE: *head (Arteries and veins of the head); brain (Major arteries of the brain);* and *circle of Willis* for illus.

internal iliac a. One of the two branches of the common iliac artery; it arises at the level of the lumbosacral disc.hypogastric artery. SEE: *aorta (Branches of aorta)* for illus.

internal mammary a. ABBR: IMA. A branch of the subclavian artery that runs down the anterior wall of the thorax lateral to the sternum. Its branches include the anterior intercostal arteries, which supply blood to the anterior (sternal) segments of the upper nine intercostal spaces, and the musculophrenic arteries, which supply blood to the anterior (sternal) segments of intercostal spaces 7 to 11. The internal mammary artery continues in the abdominal wall as the superior epigastric artery. The left internal mammary artery is the artery most commonly used in coronary artery bypass graft surgery. SYN: *internal thoracic a.*

internal pudendal a. A branch of the internal iliac artery. The internal pudendal artery leaves the pelvic cavity through the greater sciatic foramen alongside the inferior gluteal artery, below the piriformis muscle; the artery then reenters the pelvis, running into the ischiorectal fossa via the lesser sciatic foramen. Its branches include the posterior scrotal, posterior labial, perineal, and inferior rectal arteries and the deep artery of the penis or clitoris, the dorsal artery of the penis or clitoris, and the artery of the bulb of the penis.

internal spermatic a. Testicular **a.**

internal thoracic a. ABBR: ITA. Internal mammary **a.**

interosseous a. The anterior, the common, or the posterior interosseous artery.

intersegmental a. In the embryo, any one of the ladders of arteries branching from the dorsal aorta and running with the spinal nerves.

interventricular a. The left anterior descending coronary artery or the posterior descending coronary artery.

jejunal a. Any of the branches of the superior mesenteric artery that supply blood to the jejunum.

labial a. The superior or the inferior labial artery.

labyrinthine a. A branch of the basilar or the anterior inferior cerebellar artery; it enters the internal acoustic meatus and supplies blood to the inner ear.

lateral plantar a. One of the two terminal branches of the posterior tibial artery; it runs in an arc on the plantar side of the foot, first coursing laterally from the medial side of the calcaneus bone and then curving medially to form the plantar arterial arch.

lateral thoracic a. A branch of the axillary artery; it supplies blood to the pectoralis minor muscle and to the mammary gland.

laryngeal a. The superior laryngeal artery (a branch of the superior thyroid artery) or the inferior laryngeal artery (a branch of the inferior thyroid artery), which supply blood to the larynx.

left anterior descending a. ABBR: LAD. Left anterior descending coronary **a.**

left anterior descending coronary a. ABBR: LAD coronary artery. One of two major branches of the left coronary artery. It runs down the anterior interventricular groove, and it supplies blood to the anterior walls of the right and left ventricles and to the interventricular septum. SYN: *anterior interventricular a.; left anterior descending a.; left descending a.; left descending coronary a.* SEE: *heart* for illus.

left circumflex a. ABBR: LCx. An artery that branches from the left main coronary artery and runs to the left, in the atrioventricular groove, i.e., the coronary sulcus, around the lateral and posterior sides of the heart. It supplies blood to portions of the left ventricle and left atrium. SYN: *circumflex coronary a.; left circumflex coronary a.* SEE: *heart (The heart)* for illus.

left circumflex coronary a. Left circumflex **a.**

left colic a. An upper branch of the inferior mesenteric artery; it runs to the left, it supplies blood to the descending colon, and it anastomoses with the middle colic artery and the upper sigmoid artery.

left common carotid a. The second branch of the aortic arch; it supplies blood to the left side of the neck and head.

left coronary a. ABBR: LCA. One of the two main epicardial arteries that feed the heart muscle. It originates from the left aortic sinus, a dilation in the aorta just behind one of the leaflets of the aortic valve. At the level of the junction between the atria and the ventricles, the left coronary splits into the circumflex artery, which runs to the left along the outside of the heart in the atrioventricular groove, and the left anterior descending artery, which continues down the interventricular groove. Among the heart regions it supplies are most of left atrium, the left ventricle, and the interventricular septum. SYN: *left main coronary a.* SEE: *aorta (Branches of aorta)* for illus.; *heart (The heart)* for illus.

left descending a. Left anterior descending coronary **a.**

left descending coronary a. Left anterior descending coronary **a.**

left gastric a. A branch of the celiac artery that runs along the lesser curvature of the stomach, to which it supplies blood; its esophageal branches supply blood to the esophagus below the diaphragm. SEE: *circulation (Circula-*

tion of blood through heart and major vessels) for illus.

left gastroepiploic a. A branch of the splenic artery; it runs down along the greater curvature of the stomach, to which it supplies blood.

left main coronary a. Left coronary a.

lenticulostriate a. A branch of the middle or the anterior cerebral artery that supplies blood to the basal ganglia and much of the internal capsule.

lingual a. The third branch of the external carotid artery; it supplies blood to the tongue, the suprahyoid region of the neck, the sublingual gland, and the palatine tonsils. Its branches include the suprahyoid, dorsal tongue, and sublingual arteries.

lobar a In the kidney, a branch of the segmental artery (which is a branch of the renal artery). Each pyramid of the kidney has one lobar artery; lobar arteries branch into two or three interlobar arteries.

lumbar a. One of several branches of the abdominal aorta that run toward the lumbar spine; they supply blood to the vertebral bodies, the muscles of the lower back and the posterior wall of the abdomen. The lumbar arteries anastomose with each other and with the lower intercostal, the subcostal, and the superior and the inferior epigastric arteries.

mammary a. The internal mammary artery, which is a branch of the subclavian artery, or the lateral mammary artery, which is a branch of the lateral thoracic artery. SEE: *aorta (Branches of aorta)* for illus.

marginal a. An arching feeder artery for the colon; it is composed of anastomoses of branches of the superior and inferior mesenteric arteries, and it runs in the mesentery parallel to the colon.

maxillary a. A major end branch of the external carotid artery; it arises behind the neck of the mandible and it passes behind the facial bones. Its branches include the deep auricular, anterior tympanic, middle meningeal, petrosal, superior tympanic, frontal, parietal, accessory meningeal, inferior alveolar, mylohyoid, mental, masseteric, pterygoid, buccal, posterior superior alveolar, infraorbital, descending palatine, pterygoid, and sphenopalatine arteries. SEE: *head (Arteries and veins of the head)* for illus.

medial plantar a. One of the two terminal branches of the posterior tibial artery; it runs along the medial side of the foot.

median sacral a. The final unpaired midline artery branching from the aorta; it originates 1 cm proximal to the aortic bifurcation, and it ends in the coccyx. Its branches include a pair of lumbar arteries and a number of small arteries to the rectum. SYN: *middle sacral a.*

meningeal a. The accessory, the anterior, the middle, or the posterior meningeal artery.

mental a. The terminal branch of the inferior alveolar artery; it exits the mandible through the mental foramen to supply blood to the chin.

mesenteric a. The superior or the inferior mesenteric artery.

middle cerebral a. ABBR: MCA. The continuation of the internal carotid artery beyond the circle of Willis. It runs along the lateral (Sylvian) fissure between the frontal and temporal lobes. Branches of the middle cerebral artery supply blood to the frontal, orbital, parietal, and temporal lobes of the brain. Strokes involving the middle cerebral artery often result in sensory deficits and muscle weakness on the contralateral side of the body; when a middle cerebral artery stroke is in the dominant side of the brain, the patient can also have aphasia. SEE: *brain (Major arteries of the brain)* and *circle of Willis* for illus.

middle colic a. An upper branch of the superior mesenteric artery; it runs to the right, it supplies blood to the transverse colon, and it anastomoses with the right colic artery and with branches of the left colic artery.

middle meningeal a. The third branch of the first segment of the maxillary artery. It enters the cranial cavity through the foramen ovale and runs dorsally in the dura, branching widely along the side of the skull. It divides into a frontal and a parietal branch.

middle rectal a. A branch of the internal iliac artery or the inferior vesical artery; it supplies blood to the lower rectum and upper anal canal.

middle sacral a. Median sacral **a.**

muscular a. A medium-sized artery with more smooth muscle than elastic tissue in the tunica media. Most named arteries are muscular arteries.

nasal a The dorsal, the lateral, the posterior, or the septal nasal artery, which are branches of either the ophthalmic artery or the maxillary artery.

nodal a The branch of the right coronary artery that supplies blood to the sinoatrial node.

nutrient a. An artery providing the blood supply to a bone.

obturator a. A branch of the internal iliac artery; it runs along the inner wall of the pelvis and then leaves the pelvic cavity through the obturator canal. Its branches include the pubic artery.

occipital a. An end branch of the external carotid artery; it runs up the back of the scalp and supplies blood to the sternocleidomastoid muscle, the meninges, and the scalp. Its branches include the sternocleidomastoid, meningeal, auricular, and mastoid arteries.

omental a. Any of the branches of the gastroepiploic arteries that supply blood to the omentum.

ophthalmic a. A branch of the internal carotid artery; it leaves of the cranial cavity through the optic foramen with the optic nerve. In the orbit, it branches to form the lacrimal, supraorbital, anterior and posterior ethmoidal, medial palpebral, supratrochlear, dorsal nasal, meningeal, muscular, and ciliary arteries. In addition, it gives rise to the central retinal artery.

orbital a. Any of the branches of the infraorbital artery that supply the extraocular muscles.

ovarian a. In females, a branch of the abdominal aorta; it arises below the renal artery and it runs in the suspensory ligament of the ovary, supplying blood to the ovaries, their ligaments, the fallopian tubes, and the distal ureters. The ovarian artery anastomoses with the uterine artery.

palatine a. The descending palatine artery or one of its branches, the lesser or the greater palatine arteries.

pancreatic a. Any of the many small branches of the splenic or the superior mesenteric artery that supplies blood to the pancreas.

pancreaticoduodenal a. The superior or the inferior pancreaticoduodenal artery.

perineal a. A branch of the internal pudendal artery; it supplies blood to the urogenital diaphragm, the perineal muscles, and the skin of the scrotum or labium majus.

peroneal a. A branch of the posterior tibial artery; it runs in the back of the lateral side of the leg, between the tibialis posterior and flexor hallucis longus muscles. Its branches include the lateral calcaneal artery. SYN: *fibular a.*

pharyngeal a. Ascending pharyngeal a.

phrenic a. Inferior phrenic a.

plantar a. The medial or the lateral plantar artery.

popliteal a. The continuation of the femoral artery after it leaves the adductor canal. Its branches include the medial and lateral superior genicular, middle genicular, and medial and lateral inferior genicular arteries.

posterior auricular a. An end branch of the external carotid artery; it supplies blood to the external ear, the tympanic membrane, and the posterior temporal scalp. Its branches include the stylomastoid, mastoid, and posterior tympanic arteries. SYN: *auricular a.*

posterior cerebral a. The end branch of the basilar artery; it runs around the sides of the midbrain, through the tentorium cerebelli, and along the temporal and occipital lobes to end in the calcarine fissure (the primary visual cortex). Its branches supply blood to the posterior hypothalamus, subthalamus, the choroid plexus of the third ventricle, the internal capsule, the ventral (inferior) surfaces of the temporal and occipital lobes, and parts of the thalamus and the midbrain. The posterior cerebral artery anastomoses with the circle of Willis via the posterior communicating artery. SEE: *brain (Major arteries of the brain)* and *circle of Willis* for illus.

posterior communicating a. An artery interconnecting the posterior cerebral and middle cerebral arteries at the base of the brain. SEE: *brain (Major arteries of the brain)* and *circle of Willis* for illus.

posterior descending a. ABBR: PDA. Usually (in 85% of people), a branch of the right coronary artery. It runs in the posterior interventricular groove and supplies the right ventricle and the apex of the heart. SYN: *posterior descending coronary a.; posterior interventricular a.*

posterior descending coronary a. Posterior descending a.

posterior inferior cerebellar a. A branch of the vertebral arteries; it runs dorsally along the edge of the hindbrain and supplies the choroid plexus of the fourth ventricle, the lateral hindbrain, the inferior cerebellar peduncle, and posterior regions of the cerebellum. SEE: *brain (Major arteries of the brain)* for illus.

posterior interosseous a. A branch of the common interosseous artery; it descends through the forearm between the superficial and deep layers of muscle.

posterior intercostal a. Intercostal a.

posterior interventricular a. Posterior descending a.

posterior meningeal a. The terminal branch of the ascending pharyngeal artery; it enters the skull through the jugular foramen to supply the meninges of the cerebellar fossa.

posterior spinal a. The left and right posterior spinal arteries run separately along the dorsal surface of the spinal cord and supply blood to the dorsal half of the spinal cord. At the top of the spinal cord, the posterior spinal arteries are branches of the vertebral arteries; at each intervertebral foramen, radicular arteries anastomose with the posterior spinal arteries.

posterior tibial a. The continuation of the popliteal artery below the popliteus muscle. Its branches include the peroneal (fibular), the posterior medial malleolar, and the medial calcaneal arteries. The posterior tibial artery continues into the foot behind the medial malleolus; beside the calcaneus bone, it branches into the medial and lateral plantar arteries, which run in the plantar side of the foot.

profunda brachii a. A branch of the brachial artery that dives to the back of the arm and runs beside the radial nerve. Its branches include the radial collateral and medial collateral arteries. SYN: *deep brachial a.* SEE: *brachial a.* for illus.

profunda femoris a. Deep femoral **a.**

pudendal a. The external or the internal pudendal artery.

pulmonary a. The right and left pulmonary arteries branch from the pulmonary trunk. They carry deoxygenated blood (from the right ventricle) into the lungs to exchange respiratory gases at the capillaries that surround the alveoli. SEE: *circulation (Circulation of blood through heart and major vessels)* and *heart (The heart)* for illus.

radial a. A branch of the brachial artery that begins at the level of the cubital fossa and ends in the deep palmar arterial arch of the hand. It supplies blood to the forearm, the lateral side of the wrist, and the palm, and its branches include the radial recurrent, superficial palmar, palmar carpal, dorsal carpal, dorsal metacarpal, and dorsal digital arteries. SEE: *brachial a.* for illus.

radicular a. Any of the arteries that are branches of the vertebral, deep cervical, ascending cervical, inferior thyroid, posterior intercostal, lumbar, or lateral sacral arteries and that enter the vertebral canal through the intervertebral foramina to divide and then to join the posterior and anterior spinal arteries.

rectal a. The superior, the middle, or the inferior rectal artery. SYN: *hemorrhoidal a.*

renal a. A branch of the abdominal aorta; it supplies blood to the kidneys, the adrenal gland, and the superior portion of the ureter. The right renal artery is longer than the left and passes behind the inferior vena cava and the right renal vein. Branches of the renal artery include segmental arteries of the kidney, ureteric arteries, and inferior adrenal arteries. SEE: *aorta (Branches of aorta)* for illus.

right colic a. A branch of the superior mesenteric artery; it runs to the right, it supplies blood to the ascending colon, and it anastomoses with the middle colic artery and branches of the ileocolic artery.

right common carotid a. A branch of the brachiocephalic artery supplying blood to the right side of the neck and the head.

right coronary a. ABBR: RCA. One of the two main epicardial arteries that feed the heart muscle. It originates from the right aortic sinus, a dilation in the aorta just behind one of the leaflets of the aortic valve. It runs to the right along the outside of the heart in the atrioventricular groove, i.e., the coronary sulcus, between the atria and the ventricles. Usually, its two main branches are the right marginal artery and the posterior descending artery. Among the heart regions it supplies are the sinoatrial and atrioventricular nodes, the right ventricle, the right atrium, and often, the inferior or posterior wall of the left ventricle. SYN: *right main coronary a.* SEE: *aorta (Branches of aorta)* and *heart (The heart)* for illus.

right gastric a. A branch of the common hepatic artery that runs along the lesser curvature of the stomach, beginning in the pyloric region, and that meets and anastomoses with the left gastric artery.

right gastroepiploic a. A terminal branch of the gastroduodenal artery; it runs up along the greater curvature of the stomach from the pyloric region.

right main coronary a. Right coronary **a.**

sacral a. The median sacral artery, which is the last unpaired branch of the aorta, or the lateral sacral artery, which is a branch of the internal iliac artery.

scapular a. The circumflex scapular or the dorsal scapular artery.

sciatic a. A branch of the inferior gluteal artery that runs alongside the sciatic nerve.

short gastric a One of the five to seven small branches of the splenic artery that innervate the fundus and the upper region of the greater curvature of the stomach.

sigmoid a. Any of three branches of the inferior mesenteric artery; they run to the left, they supply blood to the sigmoid colon, and they anastomose with the left colic and superior rectal arteries.

spermatic a. Testicular **a.**

sphenopalatine a. An end branch of the maxillary artery; it runs into the posterior nasal cavity and it also supplies blood to the frontal, maxillary, ethmoidal, and sphenoidal sinuses. Its branches include the posterior lateral nasal and posterior septal arteries, and it anastomoses with the ethmoidal, greater palatine, and superior labial arteries.

spinal a. The anterior or the posterior spinal artery.

spiral a. The coiled terminal branch of a uterine artery. It supplies the superficial two thirds of the endometrium, and, in a pregnant uterus, it empties into intervillous spaces, supplying blood that bathes the chorionic villi at the placental site. SYN: *coiled a.*

splenic a. A branch of the celiac artery; it runs to the left, under the stomach and along the pancreas to the hilum of the spleen where it divides into six or more branches. It supplies blood to the spleen, stomach, omentum, and pancreas. SEE: *circulation (Circulation of blood through heart and major vessels)* for illus.

striate a. A lenticulostriate or a thalamostriate artery (a branch of the posterior cerebral artery) that supplies blood to the striate nucleus of the brain.

subclavian a. The large horizontal artery at the base of the neck that supplies blood to the neck, shoulder, upper chest, and arm. The right subclavian artery originates from the brachiocephalic artery; the left subclavian artery originates from the aortic arch. The branches of the subclavian (beginning at its origin) are the vertebral artery (on the right side only), the thyrocervical trunk, the internal mammary artery, the costocervical trunk, and the transverse (descending) scapular artery. SEE: *head (Arteries and veins of the head); aorta (Branches of aorta);* and *heart (The heart)* for illus.

sublingual a. A branch of the lingual artery that supplies blood to the sublingual gland.

submental a. A branch of the facial artery; it supplies blood to the submandibular gland and the chin.

subscapular a. A large branch of the axillary artery; it supplies blood to the back wall of the thorax and the latissimus dorsi and subscapularis muscles. Its branches include the thoracodorsal and circumflex scapular arteries.

superficial epigastric a. A branch of the femoral artery; it supplies blood to the superficial fascia of the lower abdomen and the inguinal lymph nodes, and it anastomoses with the inferior epigastric artery.

superficial temporal a. An end branch of the external carotid artery; it supplies blood to the scalp in front of the ear and to the parotid glands. Its branches include the transverse facial, middle temporal, anterior auricular, zygomaticoorbital, frontal, and parietal arteries.

superior cerebellar a. A branch of the basilar artery; it sends branches to the midbrain, pons, medial cerebellum, and deep cerebellar nuclei. SEE: *brain (Major arteries of the brain)* for illus.

superior epigastric a. The terminal branch of the internal thoracic artery. The superior epigastric artery runs downward through the anterior diaphragm and enters the rectus sheath; it anastomoses with the upward traveling inferior epigastric artery.

superior gluteal a. A large branch of the internal iliac artery; it leaves the pelvic cavity through the greater sciatic foramen, above the piriformis muscle. Its branches include a superficial branch, which supplies blood to the gluteus maximus muscle, and a deep branch, which supplies blood to the other gluteus muscles and to the greater trochanter of the femur. The superior gluteal artery anastomoses with the inferior gluteal, the deep circumflex iliac, and the lateral femoral circumflex arteries.

superior intercostal a. A branch of the costocervical trunk (from the subclavian artery) that divides to form the intercostal arteries that run in the first two intercostal spaces.

superior laryngeal a. A branch of the superior thyroid artery; it follows the internal laryngeal branch of the superior laryngeal nerve, it supplies blood to the larynx, and it anastomoses with the inferior laryngeal artery.

superior labial a. A branch of the facial artery; it supplies blood to the upper lip and the rostral nasal cavity and nasal septum.

superior mesenteric a. ABBR: SMA. The second unpaired midline artery branching from the abdominal aorta; it originates 1 to 2 cm distal to the celiac artery. It supplies blood to the midgut, i.e., the distal half of the duodenum, the jejunum, the ileum, the ascending colon, and the proximal half of the transverse colon. Its branches include the inferior pancreaticoduodenal, jejunal, ileal, ileocolic, marginal, and right and middle colic arteries. SEE: *aorta (Branches of aorta)* and *circulation (Circulation of blood through heart and major vessels)* for illus.

superior pancreaticoduodenal a. A branch of the gastroduodenal artery; it supplies blood to the proximal duodenum and the head of the pancreas, and it anastomoses with the inferior pancreaticoduodenal artery.

superior rectal a. The terminal branch of the inferior mesenteric artery; it supplies blood to the upper rectum.

superior thyroid a. The first branch of the external carotid artery; it supplies blood to the surrounding muscles, the infrahyoid region of the neck, the larynx, and the thyroid gland, where it anastomoses with the inferior thyroid artery. Its branches include the infrahyoid, superior laryngeal, sternocleidomastoid, and cricothyroid arteries.

supraorbital a. A branch of the ophthalmic artery; it supplies blood to the forehead, frontal sinus, and frontal scalp.

suprarenal a. Adrenal **a.**

suprascapular a. A branch of the thyrocervical trunk (from the subclavian artery); it runs over the superior transverse scapular ligament in the scapular notch and supplies blood to the supraspinous and infraspinous fossae. Its branches include the acromial arteries and it anastomoses with the subscapular and transverse cervical arteries.

supratrochlear a. A branch of the ophthalmic artery; it supplies blood to the frontal and medial scalp.

sural a A large branch of the popliteal artery that supplies blood to the gastrocnemius, soleus, and plantaris muscles.

temporal a. The deep, the middle, or the superficial temporal artery.

terminal a. End **a.**

testicular a. In males, a long slender branch of the abdominal aorta arising below the renal artery; it supplies blood to the testes, epididymis, cremasteric muscles, and lower ureters. SYN: *spermatic a.; internal spermatic a.* SEE: *aorta (Branches of aorta)* for illus.

thoracic a. The internal or the lateral thoracic artery.

thoracoacromial a. A branch of the axillary artery; its branches run to the acromion, the clavicle, and the deltoid and pectoral muscles.

thoracodorsal a. A branch of the subscapular artery; it supplies blood to the back wall of the thorax and the latissimus dorsi muscle.

thyroid a. The inferior or the superior thyroid artery.

tibial a. The anterior or the posterior tibial artery.

transverse cervical a. A branch of the thyrocervical trunk (from the subclavian artery); it runs posteriorly through the lower neck. Its branches supply blood to the trapezius muscle and to the medial scapula.

transverse facial a. A branch of the superficial temporal artery; it supplies blood to the parotid gland, parotid duct, masseter muscle, and overlying skin, and it anastomoses with the facial, masseteric, buccal, lacrimal, and infraorbital arteries.

tympanic a. The anterior, the inferior, or the superficial tympanic artery, which are branches of the maxillary or the ascending pharyngeal arteries and which supply blood to the tympanic cavity.

ulnar a. A branch of the brachial artery originating in the cubital fossa and ending in the deep palmar and superficial palmar arterial arches of the hand. It supplies blood to the forearm, the medial side of the wrist, the palm, and the hand, and its branches include the common interosseous, the anterior and posterior ulnar recurrent, the palmar carpal, and the dorsal carpal arteries. SEE: *brachial a.* for illus.

umbilical a. In the embryo, either of a pair of arteries that originate in the embryonic aortas (the dorsal aortas) and that carry blood from the embryo to the yolk sac and the chorion. In the adult, the lumen of the umbilical arteries disappears and the arteries become fibrous cords, called the medial umbilical ligaments, along the inner surface of the abdominal wall.

uterine a. A branch of the anterior division of the internal iliac artery; it supplies blood to the upper vagina, cervix, uterus, and fallopian tubes.

vaginal a. A branch of the internal iliac; it supplies blood to the uterus and, with the uterine artery, forms the azygos artery of the vagina. The vaginal artery in females is a homologue of the inferior vesical artery in males.

vertebral a. ABBR: VA. The first branch of the subclavian artery; it runs up the back of the neck via foramina in the transverse processes of the cervical vertebrae and enters the cranial cavity through the foramen magnum. The right and left vertebral arteries merge along the ventral surface of the hindbrain to become the basilar artery. Branches of the vertebral artery include the anterior and posterior spinal arteries and the posterior inferior cerebellar artery.

The vertebral arteries carry about 20% of the brain's blood supply, feeding the brainstem, cerebellum, and most of the posterior cerebral hemispheres. Blockages of the vertebral circulation, e.g., an ischemic stroke, can produce problems in vegetative functions, such as consciousness and respiration, and problems of balance, hearing, motor coordination, and visual perception. SEE: *head (Arteries and veins of the head)* and *brain (Major arteries of the brain)* for illus.; *circle of Willis* for illus.

vesical a. The superior or the inferior vesical artery, which is a branch of the internal iliac artery and which supplies blood to the urinary bladder, the lower ureter, and in males, the ductus deferens.

arthralgia (ar-thral′j(ē-)ă) [*arthro-* + *-algia*] Pain in a joint. **arthralgic** (-jik), *adj.*

    a. saturnina Joint pain resulting from lead poisoning.

arthrectomy (ar-threk′tŏ-mē) [*arthro-* + *-ectomy*] Surgical excision of a joint.

arthresthesia (ar″thres-thē′zh(ē-)ă) [*arthr-* + *esthesia*] The perception of articular motions; joint sensibility.

arthritic (ar-thrit′ik) [*arthro-*) + *-itic*] **1.** Pert. to arthritis. **2.** A person afflicted with arthritis. **arthritically** (i-k(ă-)lē), *adv.*

arthritis (ăr-thrī′tĭs) *pl.* **arthritides** [*arthro-* + *-itis*] Joint inflammation, often accompanied by pain, swelling, stiffness, and deformity. Arthritis is very common, affecting millions. The most prevalent type, osteoarthritis or degenerative arthritis, increases in incidence with age but is not considered a part of normal aging. Other forms of arthritis include rheumatoid arthritis, ankylosing spondylitis, and psoriatic arthritis. *Arthritis* differs from *rheumatic disease* in that arthritis is a disease of joints whereas rheumatic disease may also affect other tissues and organs. **arthritic** (-thrit'ik), *adj.*

ETIOLOGY: Arthritis may result from infections (e.g., rheumatic fever, staphylococcal infections, gonorrhea, tuberculosis), metabolic disturbances (e.g., gout, calcium pyrophosphate crystal disease), multisystem autoimmune diseases (e.g., psoriasis, rheumatoid arthritis, systemic lupus erythematosus), neuropathies (e.g., Charcot's joint), joint trauma, or endocrine diseases (e.g., acromegaly). SEE: *bursitis; monoarthritis; osteoarthritis; polyarthritis; rheumatism.*

TREATMENT: Anti-inflammatory drugs, corticosteroids, monoclonal antibodies, antibiotics, joint aspiration, surgery, and occupational or physical therapies may play a role in treating arthritis, depending on the cause and severity of the illness.

acne-associated a. ABBR: AAA. Joint inflammation accompanying acne fulminans, typically in adolescent boys. It is a rare type of spondyloarthropathy. The joint disease in AAA commonly involves the acromioclavicular and sacroiliac joints. Painful hyperostosis of the sternum and clavicles are typical findings. The syndrome is also known as SAPHO syndrome (synovitis, acne, pustulosis, hyperostosis, and osteomyelitis). Affected boys are HLA-B27 negative. SYN: *synovitis acne pustulosis hyperostosis and osteomyelitis syndrome.*

acute suppurative a. Septic arthritis.

adjuvant a. ABBR: AA. An experimental model of arthritis in rodents induced by injection of foreign substance, such as Freund's adjuvant, into the tail vein or paw. This model can be used to study new agents for human arthritis treatment. SEE: *Rheumatoid a.*

allergic a. Arthritis occurring in serum sickness or, occasionally, as a result of food allergies. SEE: *serum sickness.*

bacterial a. Infection of joints associated with fever and other systemic symptoms. Joint destruction occurs if the infection is not treated expeditiously. Removal of pus from the joint is necessary. In older or immunosuppressed patients, the most common causative organism is *Staphylococcus aureus.* Staphylococci, anaerobes, or gram-negative bacteria are found in prosthetic joint infections. Gonococci and *Borrelia burgdorferi,* the spirochete that causes Lyme disease, differ from other forms of bacteria that cause joint infection in that they tend to affect younger and more active people. SYN: *acute suppurative a.; septic a.*

cricoarytenoid a. One of the causes of dysphonia and vocal fold immobility that does not involve laryngeal nerve damage. It is caused by degenerative changes of the cricoarytenoid joints.

degenerative a. Osteoarthritis.

enteropathic a. Joint disease associated with inflammatory bowel disease.

epidemic a. Infectious arthritis, often accompanied by a rash, caused by the Ross River virus.

experimental a. Any form of arthritis induced in laboratory animals, used to study pathophysiology, or to foster improvements in diagnosis or treatment of the disease.

gonococcal a. Arthritis, often with tenosynovitis and/or rash, caused by gonococcal infection. The joints of the knees, wrists, and hands are most commonly affected. The disease may affect any sexually active person and may follow infection of a mucous membrane by gonorrhea. This presentation of gonorrhea is usually called "disseminated gonococcal infection" (DGI).

TREATMENT: It is treated with intravenous ceftriaxone. A tetracycline antibiotic is usually given at the same time to treat possible co-infection with *Chlamydia* species.

gouty a. Arthritis caused by gout.

hypertrophic a. Osteoarthritis.

juvenile idiopathic a. ABBR: JIA. The preferred name for juvenile rheumatoid arthritis.

juvenile rheumatoid a. ABBR: JRA. Any of a group of chronic, inflammatory diseases involving the joints and other organs in children under 16. The age of onset is variable, as are the extra-articular manifestations. JRA affects about 1 in 1000 children (150,000 to 250,000 in the US alone) with overall incidence twice as high in females and is the most common form of arthritis in childhood. At least five subgroups are recognized. SYN: *Still's disease; juvenile idiopathic a.* SEE: *Nursing Diagnoses Appendix.*

SYMPTOMS: Signs and symptoms depend on the type of JRA that is present.

TREATMENT: Anti-inflammatory agents are the mainstay of palliation but have little effect on the outcome of the disease. Corticosteroids may have adverse effects on bone growth; therefore most rheumatologists try to minimize their use. Disease-modifying drugs, such as methotrexate or leflunomide are current mainstays of treatment. Hematopoietic stem cell transplantation may be used in specialized treatment centers. Surgery is used to release ankylosed joints once the child reaches physical maturity and is able to carry out vigorous rehabilitation. Physical and occupational therapy are needed to maintain muscle strength and joint range of motion to prevent contractures, deformities, and disability. Gait training and joint protection also are helpful. Splinting joints in correct alignment reduces pain and prevents contractures. Regularly scheduled slit-lamp examinations help in the early diagnosis of iridocyclitis, which should be managed by an ophthalmologist, usually with corticosteroids and mydriatics. Other extra-articular manifestations should be referred to medical and surgical specialists.

PATIENT CARE: The child and family are instructed about the disease, treatment, and coping strategies, and are encouraged to express concerns. A well-balanced diet, regular exercise and rest periods, and avoidance of overexertion are encouraged. The child should be encouraged to be independent and involved in education and have an active social life. Moist heat helps relieve pain and stiffness. Placing the child in a warm bath, immersing painful hands and feet in pans of warm water for 10 min two to three times daily, or using daily whirlpool baths, a paraffin bath, or hot packs provide temporary relief of acute swelling and pain. Swimming and aerobic exercise in warm water are recommended to strengthen muscles and maintain mobility. Good posture and body mechanics are important; sleeping on a firm mattress without a pillow or with only a thin pillow is recommended to maintain proper body alignment. The patient should lie prone to straighten the hips and knees when resting or watching television. When braces or splints are required, their use is explained and demonstrated. Activities of daily living and playing provide opportunities to maintain mobility and incorporate therapeutic exercises using assistive and safety devices. The child with photophobia due to iridocyclitis should wear sunglasses. The child and family are referred to local and national support and information groups like the Arthritis Foundation (404-872-7100) (www.arthritis.org). Desired outcomes include the child's ability to achieve and maintain optimal health with joints that are movable, flexible, and free of deformity; to move with minimal or no discomfort; to engage in activities suitable to his or her interests, capabilities, and developmental level; and to perform self-care activities to maximum capabilities.

Lyme a. The large-joint arthritis that develops in approx. 35% to 80% of patients with Lyme disease, caused by the spirochete *Borrelia burgdorferi*. It appears 2 weeks to 2 years after infection and is marked by periodic episodes of pain that move among different joints; the shoulders, knees, elbows, and ankles are involved most commonly. Approx. 10% of patients develop permanent deformities. The likelihood of chronic arthritic complaints is markedly diminished if patients are treated with amoxicillin or other appropriate antibiotics. SEE: *Lyme disease.*

a. mutilans Severe joint destruction, a characteristic of several inflammatory joint diseases, including some instances of psoriatic arthritis.

neuropathic a. Arthritis associated with diseases of the nervous system. It occurs most commonly as a result of diabetes but can occur in tabes dorsalis, syphilis, and syringomyelia.

oligoarticular type I juvenile idiopathic a. A form of JIA that accounts for about 33% of all cases; 80% of cases occur in girls, usually presenting in early childhood. Only a few joints are involved, typically the large joints of the knee, ankle, or elbow. One third of cases develop chronic iridocyclitis. Results of rheumatoid factor evaluation are usually negative. Ultimately, 10% of these children develop ocular damage, and 20% go on to develop polyarthritis.

oligoarticular type II juvenile idiopathic a. A form of JIA that 90% of the time occurs in boys. As with type I, few joints are involved in this form of JIA; the hip girdle is usually involved. Sacroiliitis and acute iridocyclitis are the important extra-articular manifestations; an unknown percentage of children develop chronic spondyloarthropathy.

palindromic a. Transient recurrent arthritis, of unknown cause, usually affecting large joints, such as the knees and elbows.

polyarticular juvenile idiopathic a., rheumatoid factor−negative A form of JIA that accounts for about 25% of all cases; 90% of cases occur in girls. It may involve multiple joints. Iridocyclitis, its most severe extra-articular manifestation, is rare. Severe arthritis develops in 10% to 15% of these children.

polyarticular juvenile idiopathic a., rheumatoid factor−positive A form of JIA that accounts for 5% to 10% of all cases; 80% of cases occur in girls. Typically presenting later in childhood, this arthritis may affect multiple joints. There are few extra-articular manifestations but 50% or more of these children develop severe arthritis.

psoriatic a. Arthritis associated with psoriasis. The exacerbations and remissions of arthritic symptoms do not always parallel those of psoriasis. "Sausage-shaped" deformities of the fingers and toes are often present.

reactive a. Arthritis that occurs shortly after an infection of the urinary or gastrointestinal tract. It often affects large joints in the lower extremities, usually in people under 50. Reiter's syndrome may be a form of reactive arthritis.

rheumatoid a. A chronic systemic disease marked by inflammation of multiple synovial joints. The disease usually affects similar groups of joints on both sides of the body and can create bony erosions that can be seen radiographically. Subcutaneous nodule formation and elevated serum rheumatoid factor levels are common. Patients typically complain of joint stiffness in the morning rather than after activities. Women are affected three times more often than men. Members of some ethnic groups, such as certain Native Americans, have higher rates of this disease than the general population. The illness usually begins in mid-life, but any age group can be affected. SEE: illus.

ETIOLOGY: Factors implicated in the development and the severity of this disease include genetics (e.g., HLA haplotypes), autoimmune phenomena, and environmental influences.

SYMPTOMS: Joint pains, morning stiffness, gelling, malaise, and fatigue are often present. Systemic disease marked by pleural effusions, pericarditis, pulmonary fibrosis, neuropathies, and ocular disorders may occur. Symptoms usually develop gradually over the course of several months but may begin abruptly in some patients.

TREATMENT: Most rheumatologists recommend aggressive therapy with disease-modifying antirheumatic drugs (DMARDs) early in the course of the illness to prevent bony erosions and loss of joint function. Drugs in this class include agents like methotrexate. Nonsteroidal anti-inflammatory drugs, e.g., ibuprofen or corticosteroids are often prescribed for palliation. Many patients may continue to take low-dose corticosteroids for years, but the benefits of long-term steroid use must be weighed against the risks, such as diabetes, osteoporosis, and adrenal suppression. Gold compounds can be used, but they are weaker than DMARDs and newer agents. Newer agents include antibodies to tumor necrosis factor and other immunomodulatory drugs. Powerful immunosuppressive agents like cyclosporine, azathioprine, and mycophenolate may also be used. Combination therapies involving several agents from different classes can be used. Joint replacement surgery can be helpful for some patients. Homeopathic substances such as black currant (gamma linolenic acid) and fish oil have demonstrated efficacy in rheumatoid arthritis

PATIENT CARE: All joints are assessed for inflammation, deformities, and contractures. The patient's ability to perform activities of daily living (ADLs) is evaluated. The patient is assessed for fatigue. Vital signs are monitored, and weight changes, pain (location, quality, severity, inciting and relieving factors), and morning stiffness (esp. duration) are documented. Use of moist heat is encouraged to relieve stiffness and pain. Prescribed anti-inflammatory and analgesic drugs are admin-

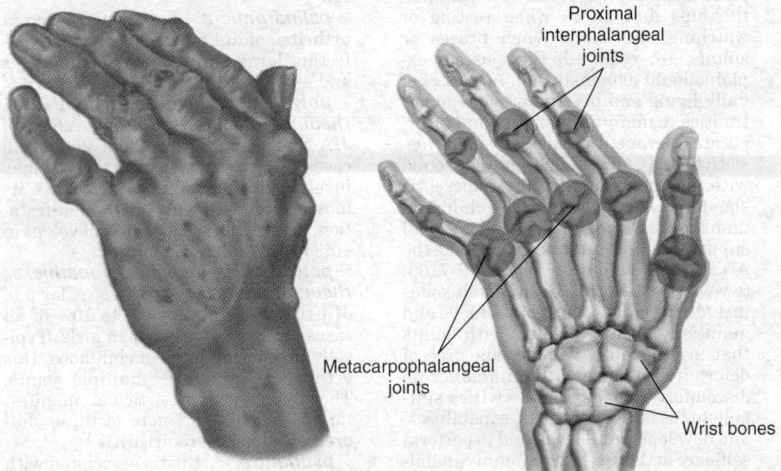

Proximal interphalangeal joints

Metacarpophalangeal joints

Wrist bones

RHEUMATOID ARTHRITIS

istered and evaluated; the patient is taught about the use of these medications. Patient response to all medications is evaluated, esp. after a change in drug regimen, and the patient and family are taught to recognize the purpose, schedule, and side effects of each. Over-the-counter drugs and herbal remedies may interact with prescribed drugs and should not be taken unless approved by physicians or pharmacists. Inflamed joints are occasionally splinted in extension to prevent contractures. Pressure areas are noted, and range of motion is maintained with gentle, passive exercise if the patient cannot comfortably perform active movement. Once inflammation has subsided, the patient is instructed in active range-of-motion exercise for specific joints. Warm baths or soaks are encouraged before or during exercise. Cleansing lotions or oils should be used for dry skin. The patient is encouraged to perform ADLs, if possible, allowing extra time as needed. Assistive and safety devices may be recommended for some patients. The patient should pace activities, alternate sitting and standing, and take short rest periods. Referral to an occupational or physical therapist helps keep joints in optimal condition as well as teaching the patient methods for simplifying activities and protecting joints. The importance of keeping PT/OT appointments and following home-care instructions should be stressed to both the patient and the family. A well-balanced diet that controls weight is recommended (obesity further stresses joints). Both patient and family should be referred to local and national support and information groups. Desired outcomes include cooperation with prescribed medication and exercise regimens, ability to perform ADLs, slowed progression of debilitating effects, pain control, and proper use of assistive devices. For more information and support, patient and family should contact the Arthritis Foundation (404-872-7100) (www.arthritis.org). SEE: *Nursing Diagnoses Appendix.*

septic a. Inflammation of the synovial tissues in a joint as the result of a pyogenic bacterial infection. Once infection occurs, cartilage is destroyed and the joint space narrows. Patients at greatest risk are those with pre-existing arthritis, joint trauma, or immune deficiencies and those who use intravenous drugs. SYN: *bacterial a.; acute suppurative a.*

ETIOLOGY: The primary site of infection is usually elsewhere, with joint infection occurring as the result of bacteremia or spread from osteomyelitis in an adjacent bone. The most common pathogen for those 16 to 40 years old is *Neisseria gonorrhoeae;* other common bacteria include *Staphylococcus aureus,* group B streptococci, and gram-negative bacilli such as *Escherichia coli* and *Salmonella* spp.

SYMPTOMS: Suppurative arthritis is marked by an acutely painful, warm, swollen joint with limited range of motion and fever; the white blood cell count and erythrocyte sedimentation rates are increased. Except in gonococcal arthritis, only one joint is affected, most commonly the knee, hip, or shoulder.

TREATMENT: Prompt treatment is necessary, including drainage of the joint and antimicrobial drug therapy (intravenous penicillinase-resistant penicillins and third-generation cephalosporins). The affected joint is supported with a sling or pillows, and the patient's pain is treated with mild opioids and nonsteroidal anti-inflammatory agents. Without vigorous treatment, significant joint destruction can occur.

syphilitic a. Arthritis occurring in the secondary and tertiary stages of syphilis and marked by tenderness, swelling, and limitation of motion.

systemic juvenile idiopathic a. A form of JIA that accounts for 20% of all cases; boys are affected 60% of the time. Fever and rash may be the presenting symptoms, either with or without joint involvement. Ultimately, 25% of these children develop severe arthritis.

tuberculous a. Chronic, slowly progressive arthritis of hips, knees, ankles, or intervertebral disks caused by *Mycobacterium tuberculosis.* The organism usually spreads via the blood or from osteomyelitis in an adjacent bone. The macrophage and lymphocyte response to the mycobacterium destroys the bone along the joint margins, resulting in progressive pain, fibrosis, and restricted movement. SEE: *granuloma.*

arthritis mutilans SEE: under *arthritis.*

arthritogenic (ar-thrit″ŏ-jen″ik) [*arthrit(is)* + *-genic*] Capable of causing or accelerating joint disease. **arthritogenicity** (-jĕ-nis′it-ē), *n.*

arthro-, arthr- [Gr. *arthron,* joint] Prefixes meaning *joint.*

arthrocentesis (ar″thrŏ-sen-tē′sĭs) [*arthro-* + *centesis*] Entry into a joint space with a needle to remove fluid. SEE: illus.

arthrochalasia (ar″thrŏ-kă-lā′zhă) [*arthro-* + *chalasia*] Pathological loosening of the joints. Arthrochalasia causes dislocations. SEE: *hypermobility.*

arthrochondritis (ar″thrŏ-kon-drīt′ĭs) [*arthro-* + *chondritis*] Inflammation of an articular cartilage.

arthroclasia (ar″thrŏ-klā′zh(ē-)ă) [*arthro-* + *-clasis* + *-ia*] The inten-

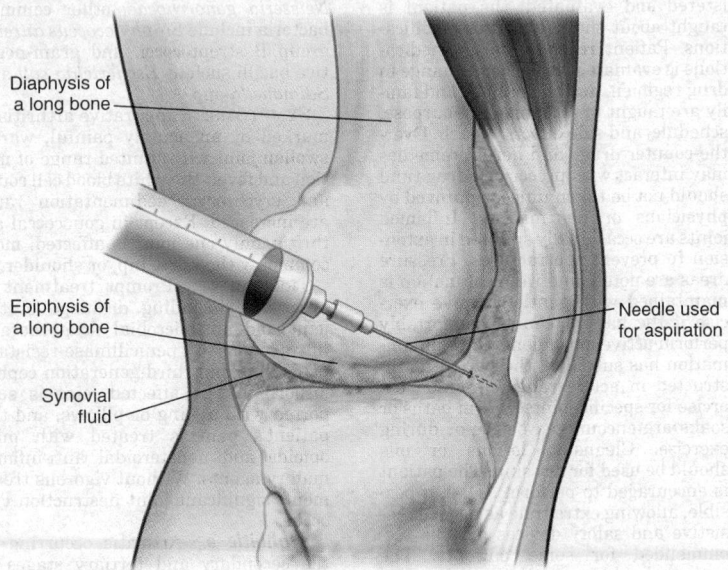

ARTHROCENTESIS

(Labels in figure: Diaphysis of a long bone; Epiphysis of a long bone; Synovial fluid; Needle used for aspiration)

tional breaking of adhesions of an ankylosed joint to provide movement.

arthrodesis (ar-throd′ĕ-sĭs) [*arthro-* + *-desis*] The fusion of two bones.

arthrodia (ar-thrōd′ē-ă) [Gr. *arthrōdēs*, well jointed, well knit + *-ia*] A type of synovial joint that permits only simple gliding movement within narrow limits imposed by ligaments.

arthrodynia (ar″thrō-din′ē-ă) [*arthro-* + *-dynia*] Pain in a joint.

arthrodysplasia (ar″thrō-dis-plā′zh(ē-)ă) [*arthro-* + *dysplasia*] A hereditary condition marked by deformity of various joints.

arthroendoscopy (ar″thrō-en-dos′kŏ-pē) [*arthro-* + *endoscopy*] An obsolete term for arthroscopy.

arthrogenic muscle inhibition SEE: under *inhibition*.

arthrogram (ar′thrŏ-gram″) [*arthro-* + *-gram*] Visualization of a joint by radiographic study after injection of a contrast medium into the joint space.

arthrography (ar-throg′ră-fē) [*arthro-* + *-graphy*] **1.** Radiography of a joint. **2.** Radiography of a synovial joint after injection of a contrast medium. The medium may be radiolucent (air), radiopaque, or both. **arthrographic** (ar″thrŏ-graf′ik), *adj*.

    magnetic resonance a. Imaging of joint diseases with magnetic resonance technologies, typically after the injection of a contrast agent into the affected joint.

arthrogryposis (ar″thrō″grĭ-pō′sĭs) [arthro- + gryposis] Fixation of a joint in a flexed or contracted position. The

gryposis may be due to adhesions in or around the joint.

    a. multiplex congenita A congenital generalized fixation or ankylosis of joints. The condition may be due to a variety of changes in the spinal cord, muscles, or connective tissue.

arthrokinematics (ar″thrō-kin″ĕ-mat′iks) [*arthro-* + *kinematics*] Description of the movement of the joint surfaces when a bone moves through a range of motion. Arthrokinematic movements include rolling and gliding of a joint **arthrokinematic,** *adj.*

arthrology (ar-throl′ŏ-jē) [*arthro-* + *-logy*] The scientific study of joints.

arthrolysis (ar-throl′ĭ-sĭs) [*arthro-* + *-lysis*] An operation to restore mobility to an ankylosed joint.

arthrometer (ar-throm′ĕt-ĕr) [*arthro-* + *-meter*] Goniometer.

arthroneuralgia (ar″thrō-nū-ral′j(ē-)ă) [*arthro-* + *neuralgia*] Pain in or around a joint.

arthropathology (ar″thrŏ-pă-thol′ŏ-jē) [*arthro-* + *pathology*] The pathology of joint disease.

arthropathy (ar-throp′ă-thē) [*arthro-* + *-pathy*] Any joint disease.

    Charcot a. SEE: under *Charcot, Jean M.*

    inflammatory a. An inflammatory joint disease, such as rheumatoid arthritis.

    neuropathic a. Bone, cartilage, and joint disruption or destruction that occurs because of diminished sensation in a limb (e.g., Charcot's joint).

arthroplasty (ar'thrŏ-plas″tē) [*arthro-* + *-plasty*] Surgery to reshape, reconstruct, or replace a diseased or damaged joint. This may be done to alleviate pain, to permit normal function, or to correct a developmental, accidental, or hereditary joint defect.

PATIENT CARE: *Preoperative*: The patient is prepared physically and emotionally for the procedure. Baseline data are gathered (usually including CBC, serum chemistry screen, urinalysis, prothrombin time and partial thromboplastin time, and chest x-ray and ECG for those over 40). Anesthesia is usually general, epidural, or a combination of the two. The patient is taught about postoperative care, patient-controlled analgesia, and any orthopedic equipment that may be prescribed.

Postoperative: The surgeon may prescribe traction or other immobilization devices, such as splints, pillows, or casts, or a continuous passive motion device. Bedrest is maintained for the prescribed period, with assisted ambulation usually beginning by the evening of surgery or the following day. The patient is positioned as prescribed. The affected joint is maintained in proper alignment; immobilization devices are inspected for pressure, and frequent neurovascular and motor checks are made on the involved limb distal to the operative site. Prescribed analgesics are administered, often with a patient-controlled device, and the patient is taught about self-administration. When oral analgesics become appropriate (usually 24 to 48 hr after surgery), care is taken to ensure that dosing provides equal analgesic effects. Noninvasive measures are used to reduce pain and anxiety. Vital signs are monitored for hypovolemic shock due to blood loss, and the patient is assessed for other complications such as thromboembolism, fat embolism, and infection. Incentive spirometry helps the patient's deep breathing and coughing, mobilizing secretions. Frequent changes in position and adequate fluid intake are encouraged. Rehabilitation therapists help the patient with exercise and activity, with appropriate measures taken to prevent dislocation of the prosthesis and to reinforce prescribed activity restrictions. The patient is taught to report symptoms such as fever, pain, and increased joint stiffness, and is referred for home care and outpatient rehabilitation. Acute care and rehabilitation may require about 10 days for standard procedures. Patients with minimally invasive procedures may be discharged to home care within 24 to 48 hr. General patient care concerns apply throughout. SEE: *Nursing Diagnoses Appendix*.

   cup a. of hip Surgical technique for remodeling the femoral head and acetabulum and then covering the head with a metal cup. It is rarely used in treating arthritis of the hip. Total hip replacement is usually the procedure of choice in the elderly as well as in young adults on a selective basis.

   minimally invasive total knee a. Total replacement of the knee joint without severing the quadriceps tendon, everting the kneecap, or dislocating the tibiofemoral joint. The surgery is better tolerated in the short run than traditional total knee replacement. Convalescence is shorter, and the need for narcotic analgesics is lessened. Long-term evaluations comparing traditional and minimally invasive arthroplasty are needed.

arthropneumoradiography (ar″thrō-nū″mō-rā-dē-og′rǎ-fē) [*arthro-* + *pneum-* + *radiography*] Radiography of a synovial joint after injection of a radiolucent contrast medium such as air or helium. SEE: *arthrogram*.

arthropod (ar'thrŏ-pod″) [*arthro-* + *podo-*] A member of the phylum Arthropoda.

Arthropoda (ar-throp′ŏd-ǎ) [*arthro-* + *podo-*] A phylum of invertebrate animals marked by bilateral symmetry, a hard exoskeleton, segmented bodies, and jointed paired appendages. It includes the crustaceans, insects, myriapods, arachnids, and similar forms. It is the largest animal phylum, containing over 900,000 species. Many are of medical importance because of their bites or stings, as parasites, and as vectors of microbial diseases.

arthroscope (ar'thrŏ-skōp″) [*arthro-* + *-scope*] An endoscope for examining the interior of a joint.

arthroscopic wand An electrosurgical device consisting of a radiofrequency (RF) generator linked to a bipolar electrode. The electrode is inserted into a body part, such as a joint, and then bathed in an electrically conductive fluid. When RF energy stimulates the active electrode, it generates voltage gradients between it and the return electrode that are able to cut away or disintegrate tissue. Arthroscopic wands are used in joint surgery to shave damaged menisci or cartilage, for example.

arthroscopy (ar-thros′kŏ-pē) [*arthro-* + *-scopy*] Direct joint visualization by an arthroscope, usually to remove, repair, or replace tissue, such as cartilage fragments or torn ligaments, or to anneal injured tissues. **arthroscopic** (ar″thrŏ-skop′ik), *adj.* illus.

PATIENT CARE: *Preoperative*: The patient is prepared physically and emotionally for the procedure. Baseline data (e.g., range of motion, girth measurements) are gathered. The operative site

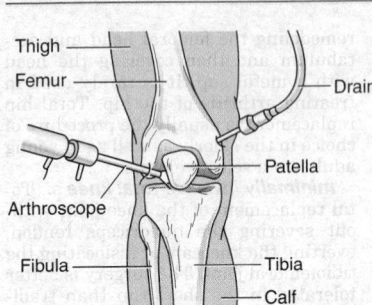

Thigh
Femur
Drain
Patella
Arthroscope
Fibula
Tibia
Calf

ARTHROSCOPY OF KNEE

is prepared according to protocol and type of anesthesia.

Postoperative: Vital signs are monitored until stable, and intravenous or oral fluids are provided, depending on the type of anesthesia used. Neurovascular status is assessed. The surgical dressing is inspected for drainage, and the presence of any drainage devices and their contents are documented. Postoperative teaching stresses expected sensations, such as joint soreness and grinding; the application of ice to relieve pain and swelling; use of analgesics; restrictions on activity or walking; weight-bearing exercises; and use of crutches or other such devices. The patient is instructed to report any unusual drainage, redness, joint swelling, unusual softness in the joint, severe or persistent pain, or fever, because these may indicate infection, effusion, hemarthrosis, or a synovial cyst. The patient is referred for outpatient follow-up care as necessary. SEE: *Nursing Diagnoses Appendix*.

arthrosis (ar-thrō'sĭs) [*arthro-* + *-sis*] **1.** Joint. **2.** A joint disorder caused by trophic degeneration.

arthrospore (ar'thrŏ-spor″) [*arthro-* + *spore*] A fungal spore formed by segmentation. *Coccidiodes immitis* is a fungus that produces a highly infectious arthrospore when grown at room temperature.

arthrostomy (ar-thros'tŏ-mē) [*arthro-* + *-stomy*] A surgical opening into a diseased joint.

arthrotome (ar'thrŏ-tōm″) [*arthro-* + *-tome*] A knife used for joint surgery.

arthrotomy (ar-throt'ŏ-mē) [*arthro-* + *-tomy*] Cutting into a joint.

arthrotropic (ar″thrŏ-trō'pĭk) [*arthro-* + *-tropic*] Attracted to joints; tending to grow in or to invade joints.

arthroxesis (ar-throk'sĕ-sĭs) [*arthro-* + Gr. *xesis*, scraping] Scraping of diseased tissue from a joint.

Arthus phenomenon Arthus reaction.

Arthus reaction (ar-toos') [Nicholas Maurice Arthus, Fr. bacteriologist, 1862–1945] A severe local inflammatory reaction that occurs at the injection site of an antigen in someone previously sensitized. Arthus reactions are a form of type III allergy reactions producing an antigen-antibody immune complex. SYN: *Arthus phenomenon; local ana-phylaxis*.

artichoke (art'ĭ-chōk″) [Italian *articiocco*] The edible head of a thistle-like vegetable (*Cynara scolymus*), which is rich in dietary fiber, vitamins A and K, and trace minerals.

articulate (ar-tik'yŭ-lāt″) [L. *articulatus*, jointed] **1.** To join (two bones) together in a joint. **2.** In dentistry, to arrange teeth on a denture. **3.** To speak clearly.

articulation (ar″tik″yŭ-lā'shŏn) [*articulatio*] **1.** A joint; the site of close approximation of two or more bones. It may be immovable (as in synarthrosis), slightly movable (amphiarthrosis), or freely movable (diarthrosis). Cartilage or fibrous connective tissue lines the opposing surfaces of all joints. **2.** The relative position of the tongue and palate necessary to produce a given sound. **3.** Enunciation of words and sentences. **4.** The movement of articulating surfaces through their available joint play or range of motion, used to determine joint mobility or to treat joint pain. **articular** (ar-tik'yŭ-lăr), *adj.*

   confluent a. Speech in which syllables are run together.

   dental a. The contact relationship between upper and lower teeth when moving against each other or into or out of centric position.

   talocrural a. The ankle joint; a ginglymoid or hinge joint.

   working a. The occlusion of teeth on the side toward which the mandible is moved. SYN: *working bite*.

articulation disorder Inability to produce speech sounds (phonemes) correctly because of imprecise placement, timing, pressure, speed, or flow of movement of the lips, tongue, or throat.

articulator (ar-tik'yŭ-lāt″ŏr) In dentistry, a device for maintaining casts of the teeth in a precise and natural relationship.

articulo mortis (ar-tik'yŭ-lō mort'ĭs) SEE: *in articulo mortis*.

artifact (art'ĭ-fakt) [L. *ars*, art + *facere*, to make] **1.** Anything artificially produced. **2.** In histology and radiography, a structure or feature produced by the technique used and not occurring naturally. **3.** In electronics, the appearance of a spurious signal inconsistent with results expected from the signal being studied. For example, an electrocardiogram may contain artifacts produced by a defective machine, electrical interference, patient movement, or loose electrodes.

artificial life The scientific study of the

means of simulating living systems, e.g., *in silica, in vitro,* or *in vivo.*

artificial rupture of membranes ABBR: AROM. Amniotomy.

artificial urinary sphincter SEE: under *sphincter.*

art therapy The use of creative arts such as drawing or painting to express oneself, and the exploration of one's attempts at self-expression as means of holistic healing.

arum family poisoning SEE: under *poisoning.*

ARVD/C *Arrhythmogenic right ventricular dysplasia/cardiomyopathy.* SEE: *arrhythmogenic right ventricular dysplasia.*

aryepiglottic (ar″ĕ-ep″ĭ-glot′ik) [*ary(tenoid)* + *epiglott(is)* + *-ic*] Pert. to the arytenoid cartilage and epiglottis.

aryl- [*ar(omatic)* + *-yl*] Prefix denoting a radical derived from an aromatic hydrocarbon as a result of the removal of a hydrogen ion.

arytenoid (ar″ĭ-tē′noyd″) [Gr. *arytaina,* ladle + *-oid*] **1.** Resembling a ladle or pitcher mouth. **2.** Pert. to the arytenoid cartilages or muscles of the larynx. SEE: *larynx* for illus.

arytenoidectomy (ar″ĭ-tē″noy″dek′tŏ-mē) [*arytenoid* + *-ectomy*] Surgical excision of arytenoid cartilage.

arytenoiditis (ar″ĭ-tē′noy″dīt′ĭs) [*arytenoid* + *-itis*] Inflammation of arytenoid cartilage or muscles.

arytenoidopexy (ar″ĭt-ĕ-noyd′ŏ-pek″sē) [*arytenoid* + *-pexy*] Surgical fixation of the arytenoid muscle or cartilage.

AS *ankylosing spondylitis; aortic stenosis;* L., *auris sinistra,* left ear.

As **1.** *astigmatic; astigmatism.* **2.** Symbol for the element arsenic.

ASA *acetylsalicylic acid; American Society of Anesthesiologists.*

asafetida, asafoetida (as-ă-fet′ĭd-ă) [L. *asafoetida* fr. Persian *āzā,* gum, mastic + L. *f(o)etida,* fetid, smelly] A gum resin, obtained from the roots of *Ferula asafoetida,* with a characteristic strong odor and garlic taste. Although this substance is no longer used in medicine, it has historical interest. Until the early 20th century, it was used as a carminative and as an amulet to ward off disease. It is used in Asia as a condiment and food flavoring and as an animal repellent in veterinary medicine.

ASAHP *Association of Schools of Allied Health Professions.*

asana (os′ă-nă) [Sanskrit *āsana,* sitting down] Any yoga posture employed in traditional Indian healing for flexibility, strength, relaxation, and mental discipline.

ASAP *as soon as possible.* SEE: *stat.*

asbestos (az-bes′tŏs) [Gr. *asbestos,* unquenchable] A fibrous, incombustible form of magnesium and calcium silicate used in insulating materials. Although asbestos fibers are commercially useful, they have been implicated in several diseases, including fibrosis of the lung and cancers of the respiratory and gastrointestinal systems. Because of these health hazards, they are no longer sold or manufactured in the U.S.

asbestos body A beaded, dumbbell-shaped body formed when a macrophage engulfs asbestos fibers.

asbestosis (az″bes″tŏ′sĭs) [*asbestos* + *-osis*] A pneumoconiosis due to protracted inhalation of asbestos particles, which penetrate bronchioles and alveolar walls causing diffuse interstitial fibrosis.

SYMPTOMS: Symptoms include exertional dyspnea or, with extensive fibrosis, dyspnea at rest. In advanced disease, the patient may complain of a dry cough (productive in smokers), chest pain (often pleuritic), and recurrent respiratory tract infections.

PATIENT CARE: A history of occupational, family, or neighborhood exposure to asbestos fibers is obtained. The chest is auscultated for tachypnea and fine crackles in the lung bases, and the fingers are inspected for clubbing. Changes in quality and quantity of sputum, restlessness, increased tachypnea, and changes in breath sounds are monitored and documented. Complications such as cor pulmonale or pulmonary hypertension are noted. Diagnosis includes characteristic changes on chest x-rays, lung CT scans, pulmonary function testing, and arterial blood gas analysis.

Oxygen is administered when arterial blood gas levels or pulse oximetry indicates hypoxemia in ordinary air. Administering aerosolized therapies and increasing fluid intake may improve the respiratory function of some patients. . Chest physiotherapy (controlled coughing, percussion and vibration) helps relieve respiratory symptoms. Antibiotics are usually not needed unless the patient develops a secondary lung infection with excessive secretions.

The patient is advised to avoid crowds and those with known respiratory infections and to obtain influenza and pneumococcal immunizations. Instruction by the respiratory therapist is given in the use and care of oxygen and aerosol equipment, inhalers, or transtracheal catheters. Patients who smoke tobacco are encouraged to join smoking cessation programs because cigarettes and asbestos damage the lungs and the damage from the exposure to these agents is more than additive. Exposure to asbestos has been linked with lung cancer, including bronchogenic carcinoma and esp. mesothelioma. The latency period may be 20 years or more.

ascariasis (as″kă-rī′ă-sĭs) [*ascaris* + *-asis*] Infestation by *Ascaris lumbricoides*.

ascarid (as′kă-rĭd) [*ascar(is)* + *-id(ae)*] A nematode worm of the family Ascaridae. **ascarid,** *adj.*

Ascaris (as′kă-rĭs) [Gr. *askaris,* pinworm] A genus of worms belonging to the family Ascaridae. They inhabit the intestines of vertebrates.

    A. lumbricoides A species of *Ascaris* that lives in the human intestine; adults may grow to 12 in long. Eggs are passed with the feces and require at least 2 weeks' incubation in the soil before they become infective. After being swallowed, the eggs hatch in the intestinal tract, and the larvae enter the venous circulation and pass to the lungs. From there they migrate up the respiratory passages, are swallowed, and reach their site of continued residence, the jejunum. In a 1- to 2-year life span, the female is capable of producing 200,000 eggs a day. The eggs are passed with the feces, and a new cycle is started. Children up to the ages of 12 to 14 are likely to be infected. Intestinal obstruction may be a complication in children under 6 years of age.

    TREATMENT: Albendazole and mebendazole are the drugs most commonly used to treat infection with Ascaris.

ascaris (ă-skar′ĭ-dēz″) *pl.* **ascarides** A worm of the genus *Ascaris.*

    raccoon a. Baylisascaris procyonis.

ascend (ă-send′) [L. *ascendere,* to climb up] To move from the lower part of the body toward the head. Guillain-Barré syndrome is an example of an ascending paralysis, which begins in the feet and progresses upward to the muscles of the legs, abdomen, and chest.

ASC-H An abbreviation for *atypical squamous cells.* The finding cannot exclude a high-grade squamous intraepithelial lesion, an abnormal finding on a Papanicolaou smear in which a high-grade (precancerous or cancerous) lesion is suspected but not definitively identified cytologically. Patients with ASC-H cell findings are referred for colposcopy.

Aschner phenomenon (ash′nĕr) [Bernhard Aschner, Austrian gynecologist, 1883–1960] Slowing of the heart rate after pressure is applied to the eye or the carotid sinus. It was formerly used to slow the heart in patients with supraventricular tachycardia or angina pectoris. Also called Aschner's reflex and sign. SYN: *oculocardiac reflex.*

Aschoff, Ludwig (ash′of″) German pathologist, 1866–1942.

    A. body One of microscopic foci of fibrinoid degeneration and granulomatous inflammation found in the interstitial tissues of the heart in rheumatic fever.

    A.'s cell A large cell with basophilic

cytoplasm and a large vesicular nucleus, often multinucleated.

asci (as′(k)ī″, (k)ē″) Pl. of ascus.

ascia (as′(k)ē-ă) [L. *ascia,* ax] A form of spiral bandage with each turn overlapping the previous one for a third of its width.

ascites (ă-sīt′ēz) [Gr. *askitēs* from *askos,* a leather bag] Edema marked by excess serous fluid in the peritoneal cavity. SYN: *hydroperitoneum;* **hydrops** *abdominis;.* SEE: *edema; peritonitis;* illus. **ascitic** (-sit′ik), *adj.*

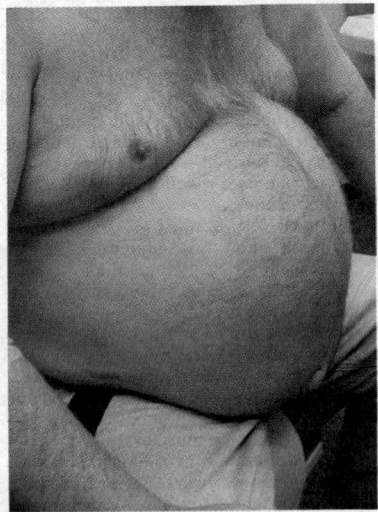

ABDOMINAL GIRTH CAUSED BY MASSIVE ASCITES

    ETIOLOGY: Ascites may be caused by interference in venous return of the heart (as in congestive heart failure), obstruction of flow in the vena cava or portal vein, obstruction in lymphatic drainage, disturbances in electrolyte balance (as in sodium retention), depletion of plasma proteins, cirrhosis, malignancies (such as ovarian cancer), or infections within the peritoneum.

    PATIENT CARE: Ventilatory effort, appetite and food intake, fluid intake and output, and weight are assessed. The patient should be advised to limit fluid intake to about 1.5L daily and be educated about a low-sodium diet. Both of these interventions may limit or slow the reaccumulation of fluid in the peritoneum. Abdominal girth is measured at the largest point, and the site marked for future measurements. Paracentesis, if necessary, is explained to the patient. Emotional and physical support are provided to the patient throughout the procedure. Desired outcomes include eased ventilatory effort, improved appetite, improved general comfort, and identification of the cause of the accumulated fluid.

a. chylosus Chyle in the ascitic fluid, usually due to rupture of the thoracic duct.

diuretic-resistant a. Ascites in the peritoneal cavity that cannot be eliminated with diuretic medications such as furosemide and spironolactone. It must be managed with high-volume paracentesis or a transjugular intrahepatic portosystemic shunt.

hemorrhagic a. Bloody ascites, usually due to malignancy or, occasionally, by tuberculosis.

ASCLS _American Society for Clinical Laboratory Science,_ formerly American Society for Medical Technology.

ASCO _American Society of Clinical Oncology._

Ascoli, Alberto (as-kō'lē) Alberto Ascoli, Italian serologist, 1877–1957

A.'s reaction A thermoprecipitation test for anthrax; used for detection of anthrax bacilli. SYN: _Ascoli test._

A.'s test Ascoli reaction.

Ascomycetes (as″kō-mī″sēt′ēz″) [Gr. _askos,_ leather bag + _mycetes_] In one system of taxonomy, a class of the true fungi that includes the genera _Histoplasma, Micosporum, Penicillium,_ and the yeast _Saccharomyces._ This class is equivalent to the phylum Ascomycotina in another system of taxonomy.

Ascomycotina (as″kō-mī″kō-tī′nă) In one system of taxonomy, a phylum of the true fungi. It is synonymous with the class Ascomycetes in another system of taxonomy.

ascospore (as′kō-spor″) [_ascus_ + _spore_] A spore produced within an ascus. **ascosporic** (as″kŏ-spor′ik), _adj._

ASCOT _A severity characterization of trauma._

ascus (as′kŭs, as′(k)ī″, (k)ē″) _pl._ **asci** [Gr. _askos,_ leather bag] A saclike spore case in which ascospores, typically eight, are formed; characteristic of the Ascomycetes.

ASC-US, ASCUS _atypical squamous cells of uncertain significance_ It is a finding on some abnormal PAP smears in which frankly dysplastic lesions are not found, but cell nuclei demonstrate minor histopathological abnormalities.

ASD _Adapted seating **device.**_

-ase [Fr. fr. (_diast_)ase] A suffix used in chemistry for naming _enzymes._ It is added to the name of the substance upon which it acts (e.g., _lipase_).

asemia (ā″sē′mē-ă) Asymbolia.

asepsis (ā″sep′sĭs) [¹_an-_′ + _sēpsis,_ decay] A condition free of viable microorganisms. SEE: _antisepsis; sterilization._ **aseptic** (-tik), _adj._

aseptic-antiseptic (ā″sep′tik-ant″ĭ-sep′tik) Both aseptic and antiseptic.

aseptic technique SEE: under _technique._

a severity characterization of trauma

ABBR: ASCOT. An assessment tool for predicting the likelihood that an injured patient will survive after serious trauma. It includes the patient's age, whether the trauma was blunt or penetrating, the Glasgow Coma Scale, and the initial blood pressure and respiratory rate.

asexual (ā″sek′shŭ-ăl) [¹_an-_ + _sexual_] **1.** Lacking sex organs or functional sex organs. **2.** Produced or reproduced without sex. SYN: _agamic._ **asexuality** (shŭ-al′ĭt-ē), _n._ **asexually,** _adj._

asexualization (ā″sek″shŭ-ăl-ĭ-zā′shŏn) Sterilization, esp. by ablation of the ovaries or testes.

ash (ash) Incombustible powdery residue of a substance or body that has been incinerated or cremated.

soda a. **Sodium** carbonate.

ASHD _atherosclerotic heart disease._

Asherman syndrome (ash′ĕr-măn) [Joseph G. Asherman, Czech physician, b. 1889] Presence of adhesions in the endometrial lining of the uterus, often causing secondary amenorrhea, infertility, or repeated spontaneous abortion. Its causes include endometritis, aggressive curettage used for the treatment of menorrhagia, removal of retained placental fragments, or termination of pregnancy.

ashwagandha, ashvagandha (ăsh-wă-găn′dă, -vă-) [Sanskrit _aśvagandha,_ horse smell] An herbal extract of _Withania somnifera,_ employed in ayurvedic medicine as an adaptogen, an aphrodisiac, an immune stimulant, and a tonic.

ASIA _American Spinal Injury Association._

asialia (ā″sī-āl′ē-ă) [¹_an-_ + _sialo-_ + _-ia_] Absence or deficiency of saliva. The condition may be caused by disease (mumps, typhoid fever), dehydration, drugs, radiation therapy to the salivary glands, old age, obstruction of salivary ducts, or Sjögren's syndrome, in which there is deficient function of lacrimal, salivary, and other glands. SYN: _ptyalia._

Asian lady beetle Harmonia axyridis.

asiderosis (ā″sid″ĕ-rō′sĭs) [¹_an-_ + _sidero-_ + _-sis_] Deficiency of iron reserve in the body.

ASIL _Anal intraepithelial **neoplasia;** anal squamous intraepithelial **lesion.**_

ASIS _anterior superior iliac spine._ Radiographic palpation point on the skin on each side of the front of the pelvis.

-asis Suffix meaning _condition, state._

ASLO _antistreptolysin-O._

as low as reasonably achievable, as low as reasonably practicable ABBR: ALARA; ALARP. In radiology and toxicology, the term is used to express the desire to reduce to a minimum the exposure of living organisms to hazards and toxins.

asocial (ā-sō′shăl) [¹_an-_ + _social_]

1. Withdrawn from society. **2.** Inconsiderate of the needs of others.

asoma (ā″sō′mă) [¹an- + soma] A deformed fetus with an imperfectly formed trunk and head.

asparaginase (as″pă-raj′ĭ-nās″, -nāz″) [asparagine + -ase] An antineoplastic agent derived from the bacterium Escherichia coli.

asparagine (ă-spar′ă-jēn″) [asparagus + -ine] Aminosuccinic acid, a nonessential amino acid.

Asparagus (ă-spar′ă-gŭs) [L. fr. Gr. asparagos] A genus of liliaceous herbs. A. officianalis is cultivated as a vegetable for its edible shoots, which are a source of fiber, carotenoids, and vitamins C and K.

aspartame (as″păr-tām″, ă-spar′tām″) [aspart(yl) + (phenyl)a(linine) + m(ethyl) + e(ster)] A low-calorie artificial sweetener made of aspartic acid and phenylalanine. It should not be consumed by those with phenylketonuria. It is unsuitable for cooking because its flavor is changed when heated. Trade names are Equal and NutraSweet.

aspartate aminotransferase (ă-spar′tāt″) [aspart(ic acid) + -ate] ABBR: AST. SEE: under aminotransferase.

aspastic (ā″spas′tik) [¹an- + spastic] Not subject to convulsions.

aspecific (ā″spĕ-sif′ik) [¹an- + specific] Not specific.

aspect (as′pekt″) [L. aspectus, appearance] **1.** The part of a surface facing in any designated direction. **2.** Appearance, looks.

ASPEN American Society for Parenteral and Enteral Nutrition.

Asperger disorder (as′pĕr″gĕr) [Hans Asperger, Austrian psychiatrist, 1844–1954] A severe, sustained impairment of social interaction and functioning. In contrast to autism, there are no clinically significant delays in language, cognitive, or developmental age-appropriate skills.

aspergillin (as″pĕr-jil′ĭn) [Aspergillus + -in] A pigment produced by Aspergillus niger.

aspergillosis (as″pĕr-jil-ō′sĭs) [Aspergillus + -osis] Infection caused by the Aspergillus fungus or one of its mold species, of which A. fumigatus is the most common. Colonizing aspergillosis involves growth of the fungus within the body, without tissue invasion. Invasive aspergillosis is an opportunistic infection that affects people with immunodeficiencies; the primary infection is usually pneumonia, but the brain, kidney, and heart valves may also be affected. It is treated with voriconazole, amphotericin B or caspofungin.

allergic bronchopulmonary a. A disease in which a patient with asthmatic bronchitis develops a hypersensitivity to Aspergillus colonizing (not invading) the airways.

SYMPTOMS: Worsening of asthma, fleeting infiltrates, eosinophilia, and positive aspergillus precipitants are clues to diagnosis.

TREATMENT: The mainstay of therapy is the use of steroids to suppress the hypersensitivity.

aural a. Otomycosis caused by Aspergillus.

pulmonary a. Lung disease caused by Aspergillus.

Aspergillus (as″pĕr-jil′ŭs) [L. aspergere, to sprinkle] A genus of fungi comprising more than 600 species of molds, some of which cause human disease. The principal human pathogens are Aspergillus fumigatus and, less often, A. flavus, A. nidulans, and A. niger. SEE: aspergillosis.

A. clavatus A species found in soil and manure. It can cause an occupational hypersensitivity pneumonitis known as malt worker's lung.

A. concentricus A species once thought to be the cause of tinea imbricata ringworm.

A. flavus A species found on corn, peanuts, and grain. It is a plant, animal and human pathogen. After A. fumigatus, A. flavus is the second most common cause of aspergillosis of the lung. Other common clinical syndromes associated with A. flavus include chronic granulomatous sinusitis, keratitis, cutaneous aspergillosis, wound infections and osteomyelitis following trauma and inoculation. This species of Aspergillus can produce significant quantities of aflatoxin, a carcinogenic and acutely toxic compound.

A. fumigatus The species that is the most common cause of aspergillosis in humans and birds. It is found in soil and manure.

A. glaucus A species with blue pigment found on dried fruit.

A. nidulans A species common in soil, causing one form of white mycetoma.

A. niger A pathogenic species with black spores, frequently present in the external auditory meatus. It may cause pneumonia in immunocompromised patients, and otomycosis. The presence of localized oxalate crystals within necrotic tissue from the external auditory canal suggests the diagnosis.

A. ochraceus A species that produces the characteristic odor of brewing coffee.

A. versicolor A species that produces a mycotoxin called sterigmatocystin. A. versicolor has been reported as an agent of cutaneous disease, onychomycosis, otomycosis, osteomyelitis, and pulmonary disease.

aspermatogenesis (ā″spĕr″mat″ō-jen′ĕsĭs) [¹an- + spermatogenesis] Absence of spermatogenesis.

aspermia (ā″spĕr′mē-ă) [¹*an-* + *sperm* + *-ia*] Failure to form semen or to ejaculate. **aspermic** (-mik), *adj.*

asphalgesia (as″fal-jē′z(ē-)ă) A burning sensation sometimes felt on touching certain articles during hypnosis.

asphyxia (ăs-fik′sē-ă) [¹*an-* + Gr. *sphyxis,* pulse] An insufficient intake of oxygen. **asphyxial** (-sē-ăl), *adj.*

ETIOLOGY: Extrinsic causes include choking, toxic gases, exhaust gas (principally carbon monoxide), electric shock, drugs, anesthesia, trauma, crushing injuries of the chest, compression of the chest, injury of the respiratory nerves or centers, diminished environmental oxygenation, and drowning.

Intrinsic causes include hemorrhage into the lungs or pleural cavity, foreign bodies in the throat, swelling of the airways, diseases of the airways, ruptured aneurysm or abscess, edema of the lung, cardiac deficiency, tumors such as goiter, and pharyngeal and retropharyngeal abscesses. Other causes include paralysis of the respiratory center or of respiratory muscles, anesthesia, pneumothorax, narcotic drugs, electrocution, and child abuse.

SYMPTOMS: In general, symptoms range in severity from dyspnea, palpitations, and impairment of consciousness, to coma, seizures, permanent brain injury, and death.

autoerotic a. Autoerotic hypoxia.

fetal a. Asphyxia occurring in a fetus. It results from interference in placental circulation, umbilical cord compression, or premature separation of the placenta, as in abruptio placentae.

local a. Asphyxia affecting a limited portion of the body (e.g., fingers, hands, toes, or feet) due to insufficient blood supply. It is a symptom usually associated with Raynaud's disease.

sexual a. Autoerotic hypoxia.

asphyxiant (ăs-fik′sē-ănt) An agent, esp. a gas, that produces asphyxia.

chemical a. An agent that prevents the delivery of oxygen from the bloodstream to cells, or that disables the biochemistry of cellular respiration even in the presence of adequate oxygen levels in the blood. Chemical asphyxiants include agents such as carbon monoxide and cyanide. Initial treatment consists of the administration of 100% inspired oxygen, usually by nonrebreather mask.

simple a. A gas that displaces oxygen from the atmosphere, thereby reducing the amount of oxygen available during inhalation.

asphyxiate (ăs-fik′sē-āt″) To cause asphyxiation or asphyxia. **asphyxiation** (-fik″sē-ā′shŏn), *n.* **asphyxiator** (-fik′sē-āt″ŏr), *n.*

aspirate (as′pĭ-rāt″) [L. *aspirare,* to breathe upon] **1.** To draw in or out by suction. **2.** To make a sound like that of the letter *h.*

aspiration (as″pĭ-rā′shŏn) [*aspirate*] **1.** Drawing in or out by suction. Foreign bodies may be aspirated into the nose, throat, or lungs on inspiration. **2.** Withdrawal of fluid from a cavity by suctioning with an aspirator. The purpose of aspiration is to remove fluid or air from an affected area (as in pleural effusion, pneumothorax, ascites, or an abscess) or to obtain specimens (such as blood from a vein or serum from the spinal canal).

EQUIPMENT: Aspiration equipment includes disinfecting solution for the skin; local anesthetic; two aspirating needles; a vacuum bottle or other closed system for receiving the fluid; a sterile receptacle for the specimen; sterile sponges, towels, and basins; sterile gloves, face masks, and gowns; and surgical dressings as the case may require.

PATIENT CARE: The nurse assists with the aspiration procedures by assembling necessary equipment, by explaining the procedure and expected sensations to the patient, and by ascertaining that a consent form has been signed. The patient is draped to ensure privacy and warmth as well as emotional comfort. Emotional support is provided throughout the procedure. The operator is assisted in obtaining and processing specimens. The type and amount of any drainage or aspirated material is observed and documented. The operative site is dressed, and patient outcomes and any complications are monitored.

The respiratory therapist is primarily responsible for aspirating excessive airway secretions. This procedure may be done as a therapeutic maneuver to ease breathing or as a diagnostic procedure to collect a sputum sample for analysis of the microbes associated with the infection.

fetal meconium a. Meconium aspiration syndrome.

microsurgical epididymal sperm a., micro-epididymal sperm aspiration ABBR: MESA. SEE: *testicular sperm a.*

percutaneous epididymal sperm a. ABBR: PESA. SEE: *testicular sperm a.*

suction a. Vacuum **a.**

suprapubic a. of urine A procedure for draining the bladder when it is not possible to use a urethral catheter. The skin over the lower abdominal area is cleansed. An incision in the abdominal wall is made with a needle or trocar to gain access to the bladder. To prevent complications during the procedure, it is important to observe the following guidelines: The patient should be positioned in the marked Trendelenburg position. The bladder should be distended with 400 ml of fluid. Any previous abdominal wall incisions that may have left the bladder or bowel adherent to the scar tissue should be noted. The incision should be no more than 3 cm above the pubic symphysis. The trocar should be inserted 30° toward the bladder, i.e., away from the pubic symphysis (if in doubt, a small-gauge needle should be inserted for orientation); the trocar should not be placed in a vertical direction. The depth of trocar insertion should be monitored, using gentle pressure on the trocar to prevent damage to the bladder base.

⚠️ The needle may pierce a loop of bowel that is lying over the anterior surface of the bladder.

testicular sperm a. ABBR: TESA. The procurement of sperm directly from the testes, e.g., by surgery or needle aspiration. Similar techniques include microsurgical aspiration of sperm by micro-epididymal sperm aspiration (MESA) or percutaneous epididymal sperm aspiration (PESA).

transbronchial needle a. ABBR: TBNA. A method of sampling abnormal tissue masses found in the mediastinum. A needle is guided into the mass during bronchoscopy, and cells are dislodged with a sawing motion. Suction is applied to gather specimens. TBNA is typically used to determine whether the mass represents a malignancy, such as a bronchogenic carcinoma or lymphoma.

vacuum a. Evacuation of the contents of the uterus by a curet or catheter attached to a suction apparatus. The procedure is performed before the 12th week of gestation. It is the most common form of surgical abortion. SYN: *suction a.*

aspiration, risk for The state in which an individual is at risk for entry of gastric secretions, oropharyngeal secretions, or exogenous food or fluids into tracheobronchial passages due to dysfunction or absence of normal protective mechanisms. Pathological respiratory aspiration is prevented by placing the unconscious patient (or any other patient without a gag reflex) on his or her left side with the head turned laterally. A head-low position protects the airway, prevents silent regurgitation, and promotes evacuation of mucus or vomitus, e.g., by suctioning the nasopharynx as necessary. SEE: *Nursing Diagnoses Appendix.*

aspirator (as′pĭ-rāt″ŏr) [*aspirate*] An apparatus for evacuating the fluid contents of a cavity. Varieties are piston pump, compressible rubber tube, rubber bulb, and siphon, a trocar and cannula, and hypodermic needle and syringe.

dental a. An aspirator that suctions water, saliva, blood, or tissue debris from the oral cavity.

aspirin (as′p(ĕ-)rĭn) [Ger. *Aspirin,* originally a trademark] **1.** $C_9H_8O_4$, a nonsteroidal anti-inflammatory drug that is a derivative of salicylic acid. It occurs as white crystals or powder. It is one of the most widely used and prescribed analgesic-antipyretic and anti-inflammatory agents. Because of its ability to bind irreversibly to platelets and inhibit platelet aggregation, aspirin in a dose of 75 to 325 mg/day is used as prophylactic to prevent coronary artery disease, transient ischemic attacks, and thromboembolic disease of the cerebral vessels. Aspirin causes prolongation of the bleeding time. A single dose of 65 mg approx. doubles the bleeding time of normal people for a period of 4 to 7 days. This same antiplatelet effect can cause the undesired effects of intestinal bleeding and peptic ulceration. SYN: *acetylsalicylic acid.*

⚠️ Children with viral infections such as varicella or influenza should not be given aspirin because of the possibility of increasing their risk of developing Reye's syndrome.

2. An aspirin tablet.

aspirin poisoning SEE: under *poisoning.*

asplenia (ă-splē′nē-ă) [¹*an-* + L. *splen,* spleen + *-ia*] Absence of the spleen.

asplenic (-splē′nik, -splen′ik), *adj.*

asplenia syndrome A rare disorder of fetal development that occurs before the fifth gestational week and results in congenital anomalies of the left hemibody, including absence of the spleen.

asporin A protein found in the extracellular matrix that decreases cartilage production and the accumulation of proteoglycans.

asporogenic, asporogenous (ā″spōr-ŏjen′ik, ā″spŏ-roj′ĕ-nŭs) [¹*an-* + *sporogen-*] Not reproducing by spores.

asporous (ā″spōr′ŭs) [¹*an-* + *spore*] Having no spores.

ASRT *American Society of Radiologic Technologists.*

assailant (ă-sāl′ănt) One who violently attacks and injures another person.

assault (ă-solt′) [L. *assaltus, assultus,* jumped on] **1.** A sudden, vehement attack, whether physical or verbal. A military assault is an attack against enemy forces, with the expectation of close, hand-to-hand combat. **2.** In law, the unlawful threat or attempt to touch or harm another. SEE: *battery.* **3.** Sexual assault.

sexual a. Actual or attempted oral, anal, or vaginal penetration against the victim's will. It includes sexual intercourse, forced penetration of another person's body, and grasping of the victim's breasts, buttocks, or genitals. SEE: *rape*.

assay (as'ā″, a-sā′) [Fr. *assai*, trial] The analysis of a substance or mixture to determine its constituents and the relative amount of each.

anti-Xa a. A test that monitors blood clotting in patients taking anticoagulant drugs, such as low molecular weight heparin or unfractionated heparin. Heparins bind to antithrombin, which inhibits clotting factor Xa. The degree to which factor Xa is inhibited is measured by this assay.

biological a. Bioassay.

enzyme-linked immunosorbent a. ABBR: ELISA. The former name for "enzyme immunoassay." SEE: *enzyme immunoassay*.

fetal fibronectin a. ABBR: fFN. A screening test that identifies the probability of preterm labor. Fibronectin, a cold insoluble globulin, is usually found in cervicovaginal fluid during the first 20 weeks of pregnancy. It is then undetectable until about gestational week 34. A positive fFN test result in women with symptoms of threatened preterm labor indicates the probability of delivery within 1 week. Aggressive treatment of threatened preterm labor with tocolytics and corticosteroids increases potential for fetal survival.

gel mobility shift a. Electrophoretic study in a gel that permits the identification of interactions between DNA and other molecules, such as receptor proteins, based on their differential movement.

hormone a. A blood test to assess endocrine system status.

immunodot a. An antigen detection tool in which droplets containing antibodies to a specific antigen are dried on strips of nitrocellulose. Samples of body fluids from patients are exposed to these antibodies. A chemical or fluorescent reaction from binding of the antigen is used to suggest its presence in the tested sample. Immunodot assays are used, e.g., in rapid tests for the presence of influenza, pneumococcal pneumonia, malaria, and strep throat.

immunoradiometric a. ABBR: IRMA. Radioassay in which an antibody is labeled with a radioactive tracer. Antigens are detected when they bind, reversibly, to the antibody.

intracellular killing a. A laboratory test of bacterial ingestion by phagocytes. Neutrophils or macrophages are placed in a culture with bacteria. After 30 min, the remaining bacteria are killed with an antibiotic, and the phagocytes are stained and examined for the number of bacteria they have ingested. This assay is only accurate if the phagocytes have been tested previously for the ability to ingest bacteria. SYN: *neutrophil microbicidal a.*

neutrophil microbicidal a. Intracellular killing **a.**

plasma very long-chain fatty acid a. ABBR: VLCFA assay. A blood test to detect adrenoleukodystrophy in infants or adrenomyeloneuropathy in adults with progressive paraparesis.

serotonin release a. A laboratory test for diagnosing heparin-induced thrombocytopenia. Platelets from a patient suspected of having the disease are mixed with healthy platelets labeled with radioactive serotonin. The release of radiolabeled serotonin after exposure to therapeutic doses of heparin constitutes a positive test.

sperm penetration a. A test to evaluate male fertility in which a sample of sperm is added to hamster eggs whose zona pellucida has been removed. The number of sperm that penetrate each egg is measured and compared to a normal value. SYN: *hamster zona-free ovum test*.

tandem mass a. Tandem mass **spectrometry.**

telomeric repeat amplification protocol a. ABBR: TRAP. A means of detecting telomerase activity in laboratory specimens. Telomerase can be used as a biomarker for the presence of malignant cells. TRAP has been used to detect abnormal telomerase activity in urine (a marker of bladder cancer) and in tissue and cell extracts, e.g., in lymphomas or renal tumors.

assertive community treatment (ă-sĕr′tiv) A community-based multidisciplinary treatment approach in mental health that includes case management, team-based group decision-making, and client/family involvement.

assessment (ă-ses′mĕnt) [L. *assessare*, to assess a tax] **1.** An appraisal or evaluation of a patient's condition by a physician, nurse, or other health care provider, based on clinical and laboratory data, medical history, and the patient's account of symptoms. **2.** The process by which a patient's condition is appraised or evaluated.

comprehensive a. A detailed, systematic physical examination of a patient.

comprehensive geriatric a. ABBR: CGA. A multidisciplinary process to evaluate the medical, functional, psychiatric, and social strengths and limitations in older patients. CGA provides a focus on the interrelated factors that contribute to illness. By addressing the complexity of needs, in some studies CGA improves survival and decreases the frequency of acute care hospitalization.

external quality a. ABBR: EQA. Proficiency testing.

fetal a. Estimating the health status of a fetus by a variety of techniques in order to prevent developmental injuries or death. SEE: *amniocentesis; chorionic villus sampling; deceleration; Doppler echocardiography; fetal heart rate monitoring; fetal (vibratory) acoustic stimulation;* table.

Techniques for Assessing Fetal Health

amniocentesis
amniotic fluid volume measurement
biophysical profile
chorionic villus sampling
contraction stress testing
Doppler velocimetry
fetal movement counting (with ultrasound correlation)
monitoring of fetal heart rate
nonstress test

functional a. In rehabilitation, the determination of a person's ability to perform everyday tasks and requirements of living. Functional assessment scales vary greatly with respect to the number, type, and scoring of the tasks used to determine performance levels, their degree of standardization, and their predictive validity. SEE: *activities of daily living.*

functional gait a. Functional ambulation **profile**.

gait a. An analysis of a person's ability to walk, esp. to identify those deficits that limit safe walking. It involves evaluations of the patient's muscular strength, joint movement, balance, posture, sensory perception, and spatial orientation.

⚠️ During gait assessments, care should be taken to anticipate and prevent injuries that may occur if the patient falls.

SYN: *gait analysis.*

gestational age a. **1.** Estimation of the prenatal age of the fetus, typically by reviewing the pregnant woman's menstrual history, making measurements of fundal height, or by making ultrasonic measurements of fetal parts. This information is essential so that appropriately timed obstetrical care can be provided and the pregnancy's progress can be compared with normal standards. SEE: *amniocentesis; fundal height.* **2.** Estimation of newborn maturity; comparison of newborn assessment findings against the expected physical and neuromuscular characteristics consistent with a given point in gestation. SEE: *Dubowitz tool; large for gestational age; small for gestational age.*

Kitchen Task A. ABBR: KTA. A performance-based measure of cognitive function in which a subject is asked to follow a pudding recipe, and the amount of support needed to complete the task is measured. The test has been used to assess the ability of demented patients to make their own meals and to demonstrate to caregivers the amount of support that cognitively impaired individuals may need when performing simple household tasks.

needs a. An analysis of what is necessary to solve an administrative or clinical problem, and what resources must be used to accomplish the task.

nursing a. SEE: *nursing assessment.*

pain a. A determination of the character, duration, intensity, and location of a patient's pain, including its effects on his or her ability to function.

primary a. The first evaluation of the patient in the field, conducted after it is clear that the scene is safe. This preliminary evaluation is designed to locate and manage life-threatening injuries or illness and to determine the patient's triage priority. The initial assessment follows the sequence of mental status, airway, breathing, and circulation.

rapid trauma a. ABBR: RTA. The evaluation of a trauma patient's head, neck, chest, abdomen, pelvis, extremities, and posterior, conducted after the initial assessment in patients with a forceful mechanism of injury, such as a car crash. SYN: *rapid trauma exam.*

risk a. An estimate of the hazards people face, made by compiling data about disease and death rates during specified periods of time.

secondary a. The more thorough evaluation of a patient after the initial examination of his ABCs (airway, breathing, and circulation).

Assessment of Motor and Process Skills ABBR: AMPS. A performance test of complex tasks required for activities of daily living, used in rehabilitation. It is one of the first of a generation of functional performance assessments designed to accommodate differences in settings and raters through statistical mechanisms. SEE: *functional assessment.*

Assessment of Occupational Functioning ABBR: AOF. A standardized test of functional capacity for persons ages 13 and older who reside in long-term care settings. The test measures instrumental activities of daily living and other activity-related characteristics.

assignment (ă-sīn'mĕnt) [L. *assignamentum,* marking out, designation] The amount of money Medicare approves for specific health care services. Health care providers who "accept assignment" from Medicare agree to provide medical services in exchange for

Medicare's monetary reimbursement and do not seek additional payments from patients.

assimilable (ă-sim′ĭ-lă-bl) [L. *assimilabilis*] Capable of assimilation. **assimilability** (-sim″ĭ-lă-bil′it-ē), *n.*

assimilate (ă-sim′ĭ-lāt″) [L. *assimilare,* to make like, liken] **1.** To absorb digested food. **2.** In psychology, to absorb newly perceived information into the existing subjective conscious structure.

assimilation (ă-sim″ĭ-lā′shŏn) [L. *assimilatio,* likeness, similarity] **1.** The transformation of food into living tissue; anabolism. **2.** In psychology, the absorption of newly perceived information into the existing subjective conscious structure.

assistant (ă-sis′tănt) [L. *assistere,* to stand by, help] One that aids or supports. SYN: *aide.* Particular assistants are listed under the first word. SEE: e.g., *nursing assistant; personal digital assistant; physical therapist assistant.*

assisted birth SEE: under *birth.*

assisted death SEE: under *death.*

assisted hatching In assisted reproduction, the separation of the blastocyst from the zona pellucida in the laboratory using artificial means (e.g., lasers or chemicals).

assisted living A group residence for adults, in which tenants live in individual apartments but receive some personal-care services, including shared meals, day and night supervision, assistance with medications, and other benefits, which vary according to state regulations.

assisted reproduction technology SEE: under *technology.*

assisted suicide SEE: under *suicide.*

assistive listening system (ă-sis′tiv) Any technology that enhances the understanding of speech by people with hearing impairments in acoustic environments in which speech is distorted, muffled, or obscured by background noise.

assistive technology SEE: under *technology.*

assistive technology model Any of several conceptual models that describe the interface between individuals with disabilities and assistive technology devices that guide therapeutic application or intervention. Examples include the HAAT (Human, Activity, Assistive Technology) Model, the HETI (Human Environment/Technology Interface) Model, and the HIA (Human Interface Assessment) Model.

associated reaction Involuntary and nonfunctional spontaneous movements associated with the performance of difficult or stressful intentional motion. SEE: *associated **movement**.*

association (ă-sō″s(h)ē-ā′shŏn) [L. *associare,* to ally with] **1.** The act of joining or uniting; coordination with another idea or structure; a relationship. In psychiatry, association refers in particular to the relationship of conscious and unconscious ideas or feelings. **2.** In genetics, the occurrence of two characteristics at a frequency greater than would be predicted by chance. **3.** In clinical epidemiology, the relationship of the occurrence of two events, without evidence that the event being investigated actually causes the second condition. For instance, malaria may possibly occur in warm climates with proper breeding conditions for certain types of tropical plants, but the actual *cause* is *Plasmodium,* the malaria parasite.

clang a. A speech disorder marked by the use of words grouped by their sound or rhyme rather than by their meaning.

controlled a. Induced **a.**

controlled word a. Verbal fluency task.

free a. **1.** The trend of thoughts when one is not under mental restraint or direction. **2.** In psychoanalysis, the procedure that requires the patient to speak his or her thought flow aloud, word for word, without censorship.

genetic a. Evidence that a particular gene is responsible, or partly responsible, for a disease.

a. of ideas The linking in memory of two or more ideas because of their similarity, relationship, or timing.

induced a. The idea suggested when the examiner gives a stimulus word. SYN: *controlled **a.*** SEE: *association test.*

association area Area of the cerebral cortex connected to motor and sensory areas of the same side, to similar areas on the other side, and to other regions of the brain (e.g., the thalamus). It integrates motor and sensory functions.

Association for Gerontology in Higher Education ABBR: AGHE. An agency that promotes the education and training of persons preparing for research or careers in gerontology and geriatrics. It is committed to the development of education, research, and public service and works to increase public awareness of the needs of gerontological education.

association of ideas SEE: under *association.*

association test A test used to determine an individual's response to verbal stimuli. The nature of the response and time required may provide insight into the subject's personality and previous experiences.

assonance (as′ŏ-năns) [L. *assonare,* to sound to, answer to] **1.** Similarity of sounds in words or syllables. **2.** Abnormal tendency to use alliteration. **assonant** (-nănt), *adj.*

assumption (ă-sŭmp′shŏn) [L. *assumere,* to take up] An idea that is not subjected to logical or empirical study; a supposition.

assumption of risk A doctrine of law whereby the plaintiff assumes the risk of medical treatment or procedures and may not recover damages for injuries sustained as a result of the known and described dangers and risks.

AST *aspartate aminotransferase.*

astasia (ă-stā′zh(ē-)ă) [Gr. *astasia*, instability] Inability to stand or sit erect due to motor incoordination.

astasia-abasia An isolated inability to stand or walk although all leg movements can be performed while sitting or lying down. It is often described as a conversion or somatoform disorder.

astatine (as′tă-tēn″) [Gr. *astatos*, unstable + -*ine*] SYMB: At. A radioactive chemical element, a member of the halogen family, atomic number 85, atomic weight (mass) 210.

asteatosis (ās″tē-ă-tō′sĭs, ă-stē″ă-) [¹*an-* + *steatosis*] Drying, cracking, and scaling of the skin.

    a. cutis Winter **itch**.

aster (as′tĕr) [Gr. *astēr*, star] An intracellular brace or support composed of microtubules that extend from the centrioles to the cell membrane during mitosis.

astereognosis (ă″ster″ē-og-nō′sĭs) [¹*an-* + *stereognosis*] Inability to distinguish objects by sense of touch. SYN: *tactile amnesia.*

asterion (as-tēr′ē-on″) *pl.* **asteria** [Gr. *asterios*, starry] A craniometric point at the junction of the lambdoid, occipitomastoid, and parietomastoid sutures.

asterixis (as″tĕ-rik′sĭs) [¹*an-* + Gr. *sterixis*, fixed position] Abnormal muscle tremor consisting of involuntary jerking movements, esp. in the hands, but also seen in the tongue and feet. It may be due to various diseases, but is usually found in patients with diseases of the liver. SYN: *flapping tremor; liver flap.* SEE: *alcoholism; hepatic encephalopathy.*

asternia (ā″stĕrn′ē-ă) [¹*an-* + *sterno-* + -*ia*] Congenital absence of the sternum.

asteroid (as′tĕ-royd″) [*aster* + -*oid*] Star-shaped.

asthenia (as-thē′nē-ă) [Gr. *astheneia*, weakness] Lack or loss of strength; debility; any weakness, but esp. one originating in muscular or cerebellar disease. SYN: *adynamia.*

    neurocirculatory a. A somatoform disorder marked by mental and physical fatigue, dyspnea, giddiness, precordial pain, and palpitation, esp. on exertion. The cause is unknown but the condition occurs in those under stress. It is common among soldiers in combat. Psychotherapy and removal of the stress situation are needed. SYN: *cardiac*

neurosis. SEE: *chronic fatigue syndrome; posttraumatic stress disorder.*

-asthenia [Gr. *astheneia*, weakness, sickliness] Suffix meaning *weakness* or *debility.*

asthenic (as-then′ik) [Gr. *asthenikos*, wek] **1.** Pert. to asthenia; weak. **2.** Pert. to a body build marked by a narrow, shallow thorax, a long thoracic cavity, and a short abdominal cavity; ectomorphic.

asthenobiosis (as″thĕ-nō-bī-ō′sĭs) [Gr. *asthenēs*, weak + *bio-* + -*sis*] A condition of reduced biological activity of an animal, resembling hibernation but not related to temperature or humidity.

asthenocoria (as″thĕ-nō-kōr′ē-ă) [Gr. *asthenēs*, weak + Gr. *korē*, pupil (of the eye) + -*ia*] A sluggish pupillary light reflex.

asthenope (as′thĕ-nōp″) [Gr. *asthenēs*, weak + ²*opo-*] One affected by asthenopia.

asthenopia (as″thĕ-nō′pē-ă) [Gr. *asthenēs*, *weak* + -*opia*] Weakness or tiring of the eyes accompanied by pain, headache, and dim vision. Symptoms include pain in or around the eyes; headache, usually aggravated by using the eyes for close work; fatigue; vertigo; and reflex symptoms such as nausea, twitching of facial muscles, or migraine. **asthenopic** (-nop′ik), *adj.* SYN: *eyestrain.*

    accommodative a. Asthenopia due to strain of the ciliary muscles.

    muscular a. Asthenopia due to weakness of the extrinsic ocular muscles.

asthenospermia (as″thĕ-nō-spĕr′mē-ă) [Gr. *asthenēs*, weak + *sperm* + -*ia*] Loss or reduction of motility of spermatozoa in semen. It is associated with infertility.

asthma (az′mă) [Gr. *asthma*, panting, shortness of breath] An inflammatory disorder of the airways that causes periodic and reversible obstruction to airflow, usually in response to an allergen, a chemical irritant, an infection, or physical stimuli such as cold air or exercise. **asthmatic** (az-mat′ik), *adj.*

Clinically, most patients present with episodic wheezing, shortness of breath, and/or cough. Between attacks the patient may or may not have normal respiratory function. Although most asthmatics have mild disease, in some cases the attacks become continuous. This condition, called *status asthmaticus,* may be fatal.

ETIOLOGY: The recurrence and severity of attacks are influenced by several triggers, of which exposure to tobacco smoke and viral illnesses are the most frequently identified factors. Other respiratory exposures (e.g., to air pollution, allergens, dust, cold air, exercise, fumes, or medicines) may contribute to asthma attacks. Autonomic and inflammatory mediators (esp. arachidonic acid derivatives such as leukotrienes) play important roles.

TREATMENT: Mild episodic asthma is well managed with intermittent use of short-acting inhaled beta-2 agonists, such as albuterol. Patients with more severe disease or frequent exacerbations rely on medications to control the disease, such as inhaled corticosteroids, mast cell stabilizing drugs (e.g., cromolyn), long-acting beta-2 agonists (e.g., salmeterol), inhibitors of leukotrienes (e.g., montelukast), and short-acting beta-2 agonists. IgE blockade with omalizumab, a monoclonal antibody, may be used for severe allergic asthma; its routine use is limited by its cost. Salmeterol and formoterol, both long-acting beta-2 agonists, have been linked to an increased risk of death and carry a black box warning.

Acute asthmatic attacks may require high doses or frequent dosing of beta agonists and steroids. Supplemental oxygen is provided. Increased fluid intake is encouraged to help thin secretions and ease removal. Antibiotics are used only for bacterial infection. The patient is observed closely to see how well he or she adapts to the demands imposed by airway obstruction. Key elements of the patient's response are subjective sense of breathlessness, fatigue during breathing, and whether the attack is worsening or improving with treatment. Monitoring of the acute asthmatic includes regular assessments of peak air flow, oxygen saturation, blood gases, and cardiac rhythms. Exhaustion or altered mental status may be signs of impending respiratory failure, which may warrant close noninvasive ventilatory support or endotracheal intubation.

PATIENT CARE: When the acute attack subsides, the nurse or respiratory therapist instructs the patient in the proper use of inhaled medications, paying special attention to how well the patient uses metered dose inhalers. A spacer device is often used to improve the inhalation of medications into the lower airways.

Patients whose breathing is labored are seated in an upright (high-Fowler's) position to ease ventilatory effort and are given low-flow oxygen and other prescribed medications. Purulent sputum should be sent to the laboratory for culture and sensitivity, gram stain, or other ordered studies. The health care provider educates the patient about eliminating exposure to allergens or irritants (e.g., secondhand smoke, cold air) and teaches home measures to prevent or decrease the severity of future attacks. Caregivers ascertain that patient and family understand the prescribed maintenance regimen, including the reasons for the order in which inhalers are to be used and any adverse effects to be reported, as well as the use of emergency treatment if an attack threatens.

In the U.S. at least 5% of the population has asthma. Asthma is normally evident during spirometry as a decrease in the amount of air a person can exhale in one second during a maximal exhalation (the FEV_1 and as a decrease in the total forced expiratory volume divided by the forced vital capacity (the FEV_1/FVC ratio). These deficits reverse by at least 12% after the administration of beta-agonist drugs like albuterol. When the diagnosis is uncertain, it can be determined with the use of a methacoline challenge, a test in which a provocative concentration of this muscarinic agonist is given to the patient to inhale and airway responsiveness is measured.

Further information on asthma and this and other tests can be obtained from the National Heart, Lung, and Blood Institute (www.nhlbi.nih.gov); National Asthma Education and Prevention Program (http://www.nhlbi.nih.gov/guidelines/asthma/asthupdt.htm; and the American Lung Association (http://www.lungusa.org). SEE: *Nursing Diagnoses Appendix.*

allergic a. Bronchial asthma.

bakers' a. A colloquial term for reactive airway disease caused by inhalation of airborne wheat proteins in occupational settings.

bronchial a. A common form of asthma due to hypersensitivity to an allergen. SYN: *allergic a.*

cardiac a. Wheezing that results from heart disease, esp. acute or chronic heart failure.

exercise-induced a. Asthmatic attacks that occur during physical exertion.

extrinsic a. Reactive airway disease triggered by an allergic (hypersensitivity) response to an antigen.

intrinsic a. Asthma assumed to be due to some endogenous cause because no external cause can be found.

nocturnal a. An increase in asthmatic symptoms during sleep. Nocturnal asthma may be caused by a variety of conditions, including gastroesophageal reflux, allergens in the bedroom, circadian variations in circulating hormone levels, or inadequate doses of antiasthmatic medications at night. Treatment is tailored to the underlying cause.

occupational a. Airway narrowing resulting from exposures in the workplace to environmental dusts, fibers, gases, smoke, sprays, or vapors.

stable a. Asthma in which there has been no increase in symptoms or need for additional medication for at least the past 4 weeks.

unstable a. An increase in asthmatic symptoms during the past 4 weeks.

TREATMENT: Usually the dosage of the patient's bronchodilator or other medications needs to be increased.

PATIENT CARE: The patient must be monitored closely for signs of respiratory failure such as abnormal sensorium and severe tachypnea and tachycardia.

asthmagenic, asthmogenic (az″mă-jen′ĭk) [*asthma* + *-genic*] Producing asthma.

astigmatism (ă-stig′mă-tizm) [¹*an-* + Gr. *stigma*, point, + *-ism*] ABBR: As. A form of ametropia in which the refraction of a ray of light is spread over a diffuse area rather than sharply focused on the retina. It is due to differences in the curvature in various meridians of the cornea and lens of the eye. The exact cause is unknown. Some types show a familial pattern. **astigmatic** (as″tig-mat′ik), *adj.* SYN: *astigmia*.

against-the-rule a. Astigmatism in which the eye has greater refractive power in the horizontal than in the vertical meridian.

compound a. Astigmatism in which both horizontal and vertical curvatures are involved.

index a. Astigmatism resulting from inequalities in the refractive indices of different parts of the lens.

mixed a. Astigmatism in which one meridian is myopic and the other hyperopic.

simple a. Astigmatism along one meridian only.

with-the-rule a. Astigmatism in which the eye has more refractive power in the vertical meridian than in the horizontal meridian.

astigmatometer, astigmometer (as″tig-mă-tom′ĕt-ĕr, -mom′ĕt-ĕr) [*astigmatism* + *-meter*] An instrument for measuring astigmatism.

astigmia (ă-stig′mē-ă) Astigmatism.

-astine A suffix used in pharmacology for an antihistamine that blocks H₁ histamine receptors.

astomatous, astomous (ā″tŏm′ă-tŭs, ă-stō′mŭs) [¹*an-* + *stoma*] In certain protozoa, without a mouth or oral aperture.

astomia (ă-stōm′ē-ă) [¹*an-* + *stoma* + *-ia*] Congenital absence of the mouth.

astragalectomy (ă-strag-ă-lek′tŏ-mē) [*astragalus* + *-ectomy*] Surgical removal of the ankle bone.

astragalus (ă-strag′ă-lŭs) [Gr. *astragalos,* ball of the ankle joint] An obsolete term for the talus of the ankle. SEE: *talus.*

Astragalus membranaceus (mem″bră-nā′s(h)ē-ŭs) A flowering perennial plant of the legume family, from whose roots a brew is concocted that is used in traditional Chinese medicine as an herbal remedy as immune stimulant and as a treatment for colds and flu.

astraphobia (as″tră-fō′bē-ă) [Gr. *astrapē,* flash of lightning + *-phobia*] Fear of thunder and lightning.

astriction (ă-strik′shŏn) [L. *astrictio,* tightening] Action of an astringent.

astringent (ă-strin′jĕnt) [L. *astringere,* to bind fast] **1.** Drawing together, constricting, binding. **2.** An agent that has a constricting or binding effect (i.e., one that checks bleeding or secretion of body fluids by coagulation of proteins on a cell surface). The principal astringents are salts of metals such as lead, iron, zinc (ferric chloride, zinc oxide), permanganates, and tannic acid. SEE: *styptic.*

astro- [Gr. *astron,* star] Prefix meaning *star,* or *star-shaped.*

astrobiology (as″trō-bī-ol′ŏ-jē) [*astro-* + *biology*] Study of extraterrestrial life. **astrobiologic** (-bī-ŏ-loj′ik), *adj.* **astrobiologist** (-bī-ol′ŏ-jist), *n.*

astroblast (as′trō-blast″) [*astro-* + *-blast*] A cell that develops from a primitive radial glial cell and gives rise to an astrocyte. **astroblastic** (as″trō-blas′tik), *adj.*

astroblastoma (as″trō-blas-tō′mă) [*astro-* + *blastoma*] A grade II astrocytoma, composed of cells with abundant cytoplasm and two or three nuclei.

astrocyte (as′trō-sīt″) [*astro-* + *-cyte,* cell] A common, asterisk-shaped glial cell with many radiating cell processes. Astrocytes are neuroectodermal cells that begin as radial glia that later mature into multipolar cells. Astrocytes are spread homogeneously throughout the central nervous system and each astocyte occupies its own compartment of neuropil. The cell processes of an astrocyte are covered with "leaflets" of cytoplasm that contact axons, synaptic structures, blood vessels, and neighboring glia. Touching astrocytes are electrically coupled and can propagate calcium potentials and within its microdomain of neuropil, each astrocyte regulates the extracellular concentration of certain molecules, including neurotransmitters. In areas of injury, astrocytes can proliferate. SYN: *astroglial cell.* SEE: illus. **astrocytic** (as″trō-sit′ik), *adj.*

astrocytoma (as″trō-sī-tō′mă) [*astro-* + *cyt-* + *-ma*] Tumor of the brain or spinal cord composed of astrocytes. Tumors are graded according to how many mitoses are found in a biopsy specimen, how necrotic they are, and how aggressively they invade surrounding tissues, esp. blood vessels. The least invasive of these tumors are known, according to the World Health Organization (WHO) grading system as (grade I) pilocytic astrocytomas, pleomorphic xanthoastrocytomas, and subependymal giant cell astrocytomas. The average survival for

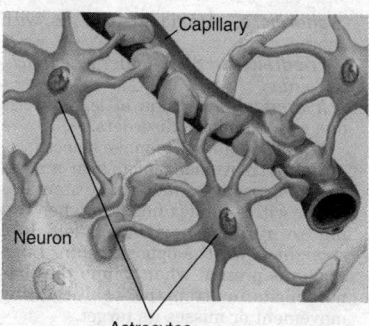

ASTROCYTES

patients with grade 1 astrocytoma is about a decade. The most aggressive (grade IV) astrocytomas are called glioblastoma multiforme. These tumors have a poor prognosis, typically less than a year.

anaplastic a. A relatively aggressive and invasive brain tumor derived from supporting cells in the brain. It typically is diagnosed in people aged 30-50, in whom it often causes symptoms such as headache and seizures. Anaplastic astrocytomas are known as grade III astrocytomas under the WHO grading system.

fibrillary a. A relatively slow growing astrocytoma histologically composed of cells with many fibrils. It usually is found in adolescents and young adults. Although its cells are moderately well differentiated, they tend to invade neighboring tissues.

intraventricular a. Subependymal giant cell astrocytoma.

low-grade a. A relatively slow-growing brain cancer made up of glial cells that have an atypical cellular appearance when viewed microscopically. They are known under the WHO grading system as grade II astrocytomas. The median survival after diagnosis is 7 to 8 years.

pilocytic a. A low-grade (relatively slow growing) tumor made of supporting cells of the brain. It usually found in the cerebellum of children, in whom it causes symptoms of headache, nausea, vomiting, and difficulty with balance.

subependymal giant cell a. An astrocytoma that arises from the cells that line the ventricles of the brain. It is the typical tumor affecting children with tuberous sclerosis. SYN: *intraventricular astrocytoma*.

astroglia (as-trog'lē-ă, as"trŏ-glī'ă) [*astro- + glia*] Astrocytes. **astroglial** (-ăl), *adj.*

astrokinetic motion (as"trŏ-kĭ-net'ĭk) [*astro- + kinetic*] SEE: under *motion*.

astrophobia (as"trŏ-fō'bē-ă) [*astro- + -phobia*] Morbid fear of stars and celestial space.

Astroviridae (as"trŏ-vēr'ĭ'dē) [*astrovir(us) + -idea*] A family of spherical or star-shaped, single-stranded RNA viruses distributed worldwide. The virus causes epidemic viral gastroenteritis in adults and children. The incubation period has been estimated to be 3 to 4 days. The outbreaks are self-limiting and in the absence of coexisting pathogens, the intestinal signs and symptoms last 5 days or less. Treatment, if required, is supportive and directed to maintaining hydration and electrolyte balance.

astrovirus (as'trŏ-vī"rŭs) [*astro- + virus*] A member of the single genus of the virus family Astroviridae. They are an important cause of gastrointestinal illnesses and diarrhea, esp. in children. Clinical symptoms include anorexia, headache, fever, diarrhea, and vomiting. SYN: *human astrovirus*.

asyllabia (ā"sĭ-lā'bē-ă) [*¹an- + Gr. syllabē*, syllable + *-ia*] A form of alexia in which the patient recognizes letters but cannot form syllables or words.

asymbolia (ā"sim-bō'lē-ă) [*¹an- + symbolon*, a token, sign + *-ia*] Inability to comprehend words, gestures, or any type of symbol. SYN: *asemia*. SEE: *aphasia*.

asymmetrical dimethylarginine (dī"meth"ĭl-ar'jĭ-nēn") An endogenous inhibitor of nitric acid synthase, an enzyme found in endothelial cells. Its concentration is elevated in patients with chronic kidney disease. It has been proposed as a biomarker of and risk factor for cardiovascular disease.

asymmetric cell division Cell division in which the daughter cells have differing quantities of cytoplasm.

asymmetry (ā"-sim'ĕ-trē) [*¹an- + symmetry*] Lack of symmetry. **asymmetric, asymmetrical** (ā"sĭ-me'trik, ā"sĭ-me'trĭkăl), *adj.* **asymmetrically** (ā"sĭ-me'trĭk(ă-)lē), *adv.*

asymptomatic (ā"simp-tŏ-mat'ĭk) [*¹an- + symptomatic*] ABBR: asx. Without symptoms. **asymptomatically** (-k(ă-)lē), *adv.*

asynchronism (ā"sing'krŏ-nizm) [*¹an- + synchronism*] **1.** The failure of events to occur in time with each other as they usually do. **2.** Incoordination. **asynchronous** (-nŭs), *adj.*

asynchronous communication SEE: under *communication*.

asynclitism (ā"sin'klĭ-tizm, sing') [*¹an- + synclitism*] An oblique presentation of the fetal head in labor. SEE: *presentation* for illus.

anterior a. Anterior parietal presentation. SYN: *Naegele's obliquity*.

posterior a. Posterior parietal presentation. SYN: *Litzmann's obliquity*.

asyndesis (ā″sin′dĕ-sĭs) [¹*an-* + *syn-desis*] A cognitive defect in which related thoughts cannot be assembled to form a comprehensive concept.

asynechia (ā″sĭ-nek′ē-ă, -nēk′) [¹*an-* + *synechia*] Lack of continuity of structure in an organ or tissue.

asynergia, asynergy (ā″sĭ-nĕr′j(ē-)ă, ā″sin′ĕr-jē) [¹*an-*+ *synergy*] Lack of coordination among parts or organs normally acting together. In neurology, it is lack of coordination between muscle groups. **asynergic** (ā″sĭ-nĕr′jik), *adj.*

asyntaxia (ā″sin-tak′sē-ă) [¹*an-* + Gr. *syntaxis*, arrangement + -*ia*] Failure of the embryo to develop properly.

asystematic (ā″sis″tĕ-mat′ik) [¹*an-* + *systematic*] Not systematic; not limited to one system or set of organs.

asystole, asystolia (ā″sis′tŏ-lē, ā″sis-tō′lē-ă) [¹*an-* + *systole*] Cardiac standstill; absence of electrical activity and contractions of the heart evidenced on the surface electrocardiogram as a flat (isoelectric) line during cardiac arrest. In most instances, asystole is an electrocardiographic confirmation that a patient has died. **asystolic** (ā″sis-tol′ik), *adj.*

At Symbol for the element astatine.

ATA **1.** One atmosphere absolute, i.e., the air pressure found at sea level on earth. **2.** *American Telemedicine Association.* **3.** *American Tinnitus Association.* **4.** *Alliance for Technology Access.*

atactiform (ā″tak′tĭ-form″) [*ataxia* + -*form*] Resembling ataxia.

ataractic, ataraxic (at″ă-rak′tik, -rak′sik) [*ataraxia* + -*ic*] **1.** Pert. to ataraxia. **2.** Pert. to tranquilizers. **3.** A tranquilizer.

ataraxia, ataraxy (at″ă-rak′sē-ă, at′ă-rak″sē) [Gr. *ataraxia*, calmness, quiet] A state of complete mental calm and tranquility, esp. without depression of mental faculties or clouding of consciousness.

atavism (at′ă-vizm) [L. *atavus*, ancestor + -*ism*] The appearance of a characteristic presumed to have been present in some remote ancestor, due to chance recombination of genes or environmental conditions favorable to their expression in the embryo. **atavistic** (at″ă-vis′tik), *adj.* **atavistically** (ti-k(ă-)lē), *adv.*

ataxia (ă-tak′sē-ă, ā″) [Gr. *ataxia*, lack of order] Defective muscular coordination, esp. that manifested when voluntary muscular movements are attempted. **atactic, ataxic** (ă-tak′tik, ā″, ă-tak′sik, ā″), *adj.*

   alcoholic a. In chronic alcoholism, ataxia due to a loss of proprioception.

   bulbar a. Ataxia due to a lesion in the medulla oblongata or pons.

   cerebellar a. Ataxia due to cerebellar disease.

   choreic a. Ataxia in patients with chorea.

   Friedreich a. SEE: under *Friedreich, Nikolaus.*

   hysterical a. Ataxia of leg muscles due to somatoform disorders.

   limb a. Inability to make smooth, coordinated movements of an arm or a leg, as when trying to touch an examiner's finger with an index finger or when trying to run one's right or left heel straight down the opposite shin. Limb ataxia is present when a limb that has no deficits in strength wobbles during movement or misses its target.

   locomotor a. **Tabes** dorsalis.

   Marie a. SEE: under *Marie, Pierre Marie.*

   motor a. Inability to perform coordinated muscle movements.

   optic a. Loss of hand-eye coordination in reaching for an object one has seen, due to damage to visually dedicated regions of the cerebral cortex.

   sensory a. Ataxia due to interference in conduction of sensory responses, esp. proprioceptive impulses from muscles. The condition becomes aggravated when the eyes are closed. SEE: *Romberg sign; spinal a.*

   spinal a. Ataxia due to spinal cord disease.

   static a. Loss of deep sensibility, causing inability to preserve equilibrium in standing.

ataxiagram (ă-tak′sē-ă-gram″) [*ataxia* + -*gram*] A record or tracing produced by an ataxiagraph.

ataxiagraph (ă-tak′sē-ă-graf″) [*ataxia* + -*graph*] Ataxiameter.

ataxiameter (ă-tak″sē-am′ĕt-ĕr) [*ataxia* + -*meter*] An instrument for measuring the degree and direction of swaying in ataxia. SYN: *ataxiagraph.*

ataxiamnesia (ă-tak″sē-ăm-nē′zh(ē-)ă) [*ataxia* + *amnesia*] A condition marked by ataxia and amnesia.

ataxiaphasia, ataxaphasia (ă-tak″sē-ă-fā′zh(ē-)ă, tak″să-) [*ataxia* + *aphasia*] Inability to arrange words into sentences.

ataxia-telangiectasia A degenerative brain disease of children, marked by cellular and humoral immunodeficiency, progressive cerebellar degeneration, telangiectasis of the bulbar conjunctiva, and increased risk of malignancy. It is transmitted as an autosomal recessive trait. Death usually occurs in adolescence or early adulthood. Parents should be informed that subsequent children have a 25% risk of having this condition. SYN: *Louis-Bar syndrome.*

ataxophobia (ă-tak″sŏ-fō′bē-ă) [Gr. *ataxia*, lack of order + -*phobia*] Fear of disorder or untidiness.

ATBCB *Architectural and Transportation Barriers Compliance Board,* a federal agency charged with enforcing legislation requiring that federal buildings and transportation facilities be accessible to the disabled.

ATC *Athletic Trainer, Certified.*

ATCC *American Type Culture Collection.*

-ate [L. *-atum,* adj. suffix] Suffix in chemistry used in naming a *salt or an ester of an acid* ending in *-ic,* e.g., **nitrate.**

atelectasis (at″ĕl-ek′tă-sĭs) [*atelo-* + *-ectasis*] **1.** A collapsed or airless condition of the lung. **2.** A condition in which the lungs of a fetus remain partially or totally unexpanded at birth (hyaline membrane disease/respiratory distress syndrome).

ETIOLOGY: It also may be caused by obstruction of one or more airways with mucus plugs; by hypoventilation secondary to pain (e.g., from fractured ribs or related to surgery) or to ventilation with inadequate tidal volumes; by inadequate surfactant production; or by compression of the lung externally or the lung or bronchi by tumors, aneurysms, or enlarged lymph nodes. It is sometimes a complication following abdominal or thoracic surgery, caused by splinting. Thoracic and high abdominal surgery poses extra risks because of the location of the incision. It occurs in patients with chronic obstructive pulmonary disease, bronchiectasis, or cystic fibrosis, and also in those who smoke tobacco heavily. Chronic atelectasis, called *middle lobe syndrome,* results from compression of the middle lobe bronchus by surrounding lymph nodes.

SYMPTOMS: Symptoms may not be present if the atelectasis is minor and the patient has previously healthy lungs. Dyspnea is common when the atelectasis is severe.

TREATMENT: Treatment varies with the cause. The patient with atelectasis due to persistent ventilation with small tidal volumes is given lung expansion therapy such as incentive spirometry. During mechanical ventilation, the patient should receive appropriate tidal volume, and positive end-expiratory pressure (PEEP) to increase FRC. Oxygen should be administered at the lowest setting that will prevent hypoxemia. The patient should be weaned from the ventilator and extubated as soon as possible. The patient with atelectasis due to mucus plugging needs bronchial hygiene therapy to assist with mucus removal. Artificial surfactant may be useful for the infant with premature lungs and atelectasis.

PATIENT CARE: Patients at risk (esp. those who have had chest or high abdominal surgeries or those with underlying chronic problems with ventilation) are evaluated for dyspnea, decreased chest wall movement, inspiratory substernal or intercostal retractions, dia-

phoresis, tachypnea, tachycardia, and pleuritic chest pain. Lung fields are percussed for decreased resonance, and the chest is auscultated for abnormal breath sounds (diminished breath sounds, bronchial breath sounds in areas of consolidation, and fine, late-inspiratory crackles). Pulse oximetry and arterial blood gas values are monitored for evidence of hypoxemia. Bronchial hygiene therapies are useful for the patient with atelectasis due to retained pulmonary secretions. Positioning the patient in semi-Fowler's and occasionally high-Fowler's position (unless specifically contraindicated) helps increase lung capacity and encourage deeper breathing. The patient should also be encouraged and helped to sit in a chair and walk as soon as possible. The nurse or respiratory therapist instructs and monitors the patient on the use of incentive spirometry to prevent or correct existing atelectasis. Using this calibrated device, the patient takes slow, sustained maximal inspirations to total lung capacity, holds the breath for 5 seconds, and exhales passively to help keep the alveoli open. This should be done about 10 times an hour while the patient is awake. Adequate pain control, frequent coaching, reinforcement, and praise are essential to be sure that the appropriate technique is employed. Patients anticipating surgery should be taught correct use of incentive spirometry preoperatively to allow time for practice. SEE: *incentive spirometry.*

Adequate fluid intake is encouraged, inspired air is humidified as necessary, and the patient is assisted to mobilize and clear secretions. Intubated or obtunded patients are suctioned as necessary.

absorption a. Alveolar collapse secondary to the washout of nitrogen, an inert gas that normally helps maintain alveolar volume.

passive a. Collapse of a portion of the distal lung units due to persistent breathing with small tidal volumes.

TREATMENT: The patient must be stimulated to breathe deeply and ambulate when possible.

resorption a. Collapse of distal lung units due to plugging of the airway with mucus.

TREATMENT: Airway suctioning or chest physiotherapy.

atelectotrauma, atelectrauma (at″ĕl-ek″tŏ-tro′mă, -ek″tro′mă) [*atelectasis* + *trauma*] Injury to the lung caused by shearing forces as alveoli that are next to each other collapse and re-expand during mechanical ventilation. The condition may be prevented by applying enough positive end-expiratory pressure to limit alveolar collapse at end expiration.

atelencephalia, ateloencephalia (ă-tel″en-sĕ-fāl′ē-ă, -tel″ō-en-) [*atelo-* + *encephalon* + *-ia*] A congenital anomaly with imperfect development of the brain.

atelia (ă-tēl′ē-ă) [Gr. *ateleia,* incompleteness] Imperfect or incomplete development.

ateliosis (ă-tel″ē-ō′sĭs, tēl′ē) [*atelia* + *-osis*] A form of infantilism due to pituitary insufficiency, in which there is arrested growth but no deformity. The voice and face may resemble those of a child. **ateliotic** (-ot′ik), *adj.*

atelo- [Gr. *atelēs,* imperfect] Prefix meaning *imperfect* or *incomplete.*

atelocardia (at″ĕl-ō-kar′dē-ă) [*atelo-* + Gr. *kardia,* heart] Congenital incomplete development of the heart.

atelocephaly (at″ĕl-ō-sef′ă-lē) [*atelo-* + *cephalo-* + *-ia*] Incomplete development of the head.

atenolol (ă-ten′ŏ-lol″, -lōl″) A beta-blocking agent.

athelia (ă-thē′lē-ă) [*¹an-* + *thel-* + *-ia*] Congenital absence of the nipples.

atherectomy (ath″ĕr-ek′tŏ-mē) [*athero-* + *-ectomy*] The removal of atherosclerotic plaque from arteries with rotating drills or lasers.

athermic (ā″thĕr′mĭk) [*¹an-* + *thermic*] Lacking heat.

athero-, ather- [Gr. *athērē,* gruel, porridge] Prefixes meaning *fatty plaque.*

atherogenesis (ath″ĕ-rō-jen′ĕ-sĭs) [″ + *genesis,* generation, birth] Formation of atheromata in the walls of arteries. **atherogenic** (-jen′ik), *adj.* **atherogenicity** (-jĕ-nis′ĭt-ē), *n.*

atheroma (ath″ĕ-rō′mă) *pl.* **atheromata** [*athero-* + *-oma*] Fatty degeneration or thickening of the walls of the larger arteries occurring in atherosclerosis. SEE: *arteriosclerosis.* **atheromatous** (-ō′măt-ŭs), *adj.*

atheromatosis (ath″ĕ-rō″mă-tō′sĭs) [*atheroma* + *-osis*] Generalized atheromatous disease of the arteries.

atheronecrosis (ath″ĕ-rō″nĕ-krō′sĭs) [*athero-* + *necrosis*] Necrosis or degeneration accompanying arteriosclerosis.

atherosclerosis (ath″ĕ-rō″sklĕ-rō′sĭs) [*athero-* + *sclerosis*] The most common form of arteriosclerosis, marked by cholesterol-lipid-calcium deposits in the walls of arteries that may restrict blood flow. **atherosclerotic** (sklĕ-rot′ik), *adj.* SEE: *coronary artery disease* for illus.

PATHOLOGY: The initial pathological changes, called fatty streaks, are visible on the endothelial surfaces of major blood vessels by the age of 10. These lesions may progress to thickening of the lining of arteries (a process called intimal thickening) if risk factors for atherosclerosis are not addressed. Whether these lesions in turn progress to advanced lesions, called fibrous plaques, depends on hemodynamic forces (e.g., hypertension) and abnormal plasma levels of lipoproteins (e.g., high levels of total and LDL cholesterol; low levels of HDL cholesterol). Ultimately, arteries affected by the disease may become nearly completely blocked, a condition that causes ischemia. If a plaque within a blood vessel suddenly ruptures, the blood vessel may close and organs or tissues may infarct. SEE: *myocardial infarction; peripheral vascular disease; stroke.*

ETIOLOGY: Risk factors for atherosclerosis include use of tobacco, diabetes mellitus, elevated blood lipid concentrations, hypertension, family history, male gender, menopause, microalbuminuria, chronic kidney disease, age, sedentary lifestyle, and obesity. The role of vascular inflammation due to chronic infections or elevated homocysteine levels are topics of active research.

SYMPTOMS: Symptoms may develop in any organ system with a blood supply diminished by atherosclerosis. These symptoms commonly include angina pectoris, intermittent claudication, strokes, transient ischemic attacks, and renal insufficiency.

TREATMENT: Treatment includes regular exercise, stopping smoking, and a dietary regimen of low-cholesterol and low-fat foods. Medical treatment of hypertension, lipid disorders, and diabetes mellitus is also helpful. Angioplasty, atherectomy, or arterial bypass graft operations are beneficial for some patients.

PATIENT CARE: The patient and family are taught about risk factors associated with atherosclerosis, and the health care professionals help the patient modify these factors. Patients who smoke cigarettes are encouraged to enroll in smoking cessation programs. Community-based plans and programs to change sedentary activity patterns, reduce stress, control obesity, and decrease saturated fat intake to control triglyceride and cholesterol levels are explored with the patient. The nurse or other health care professional refers the patient for medical treatment to control hypertension and diabetes mellitus and supports the patient's efforts to cooperate with lifestyle and health care changes. Regular exercise of a type and extent appropriate for the patient's health and adequate rest are prescribed. The patient is informed of the need for long-term follow-up care to prevent a variety of body system complications.

athetoid (ath′ĕ-toyd″) [Gr. *athetos* unfixed, changeable + *-oid*] **1.** Resembling or affected with athetosis. **2.** A person affected with athetosis.

athetosis (ath-ĕ-tō′sĭs) [Gr. *athetos* + *-osis*] A condition in which slow, irregular, twisting, snakelike movements occur in the upper extremities, esp. in the hands and fingers. These involuntary movements prevent sustaining the body, esp. the extremities, in one position. All four limbs may be affected, or the involvement may be unilateral. The symptoms may be due to encephalitis, cerebral palsy, hepatic encephalopathy, drug toxicity, or Huntington's chorea or may be an undesired side effect of prolonged treatment of parkinsonism with levodopa.

There are several types of athetosis. In *athetosis with spasticity,* muscle tone fluctuates between normal and hypertonic; often there is moderate spasticity in the proximal parts and athetosis more distally. Modified primitive spinal reflex patterns are often present. In *athetosis with tonic spasms,* muscle tone fluctuates between hypotonic and hypertonic. Excessive extension or flexion is evident. There are strong postural asymmetry and frequent spinal or hip abnormalities or deformities.

In *choreoathetosis,* muscle tone fluctuates from hypotonic to normal or hypertonic. There are extreme ranges of motion. Deformities are rare, but subluxation of the shoulder and finger joints often occurs. *Pure athetosis* is much rarer than the others. Muscle tone fluctuates between hypotonic and normal. Deformities are rare. Twitches and jerks of muscles or individual muscle fibers are seen, along with slow, writhing, involuntary movements that are more proximal than distal.

PATIENT CARE: Muscle tone and joint range of motion are assessed; joints are inspected for involuntary movements, spasticity, and joint deformities and subluxations. Degree of interference with activities of daily living and self-image is evaluated. Prescribed therapies are administered and evaluated for desired effects and adverse reactions. Emotional support and acceptance are provided, and the patient is informed about local and national groups and services offering support and information. **athetotic** (-tot′ik), *adj.*

athletic trainer (ath-let′ik) A person who has completed educational and clinical experiences and is capable of working with athletes and others involved in strenuous physical activity and their environment to help prevent injuries, advise them concerning appropriate equipment, clinically diagnose injuries, administer emergency treatment, determine if specialized medical care is required, and rehabilitate those with injuries. Athletic trainers work under the direction of licensed physicians. In most states, athletic trainers must be licensed to practice.

athletic training SEE: under *training.*

athrepsia, athrepsy (ă-threp′sē-ă, -sē) [¹*an-* + Gr. *threpsis,* nourishment] Marasmus. **athreptic** (-threp′tik), *adj.*

athyroidemia (ā″thī″roy″dē′mē-ă, ă-thī″roy-) [¹*an-* + *thyroid* + *-emia*] Absence of thyroid hormone in the blood.

athyroidism (ā″thī′roy-dizm, ă-thī′) [¹*an-* + *thyroid* + *-ism*] Suppression of thyroid secretions, or absence of the thyroid gland. SEE: *hypothyroidism.*

ATII *Angiotensin II.*

Ativan (at′ĭ-van″) SEE: *lorazepam.*

Atlanta Classification of Acute Pancreatitis A clinical risk stratification tool to gauge the severity of disease in patients with acute pancreatitis. It consists of measurements of the patient's blood pressure, serum creatinine level, and oxygenation. These are combined with evidence of hemorrhage, abscess formation, pseudocyst formation, or necrosis along with Ranson criteria, C-reactive protein levels, and APACHE-III scores.

atlantal (ăt-lant′ăl, at-) [*atlanto-* + *-al*] Pert. to the atlas.

atlanto- [Gr. *atlas,* stem *atlant-,* Atlas] A prefix meaning the *atlas.*

atlantoaxial (ăt-lant″ō-ak′sē-ăl) [*atlanto-* + *axial*] Pert. to the atlas and the axis.

atlanto-occipital, atlantooccipital (ăt-lan″tō-ok-sip′tĭ-ăl) [*atlanto-* + *occipital*] Pert. to the atlas and the occipital bones.

atlas (at′lăs) [In Gr. mythology a Titan condemned to support the heavens on his shoulders] **1.** The first cervical vertebra by which the spine articulates with the occipital bone of the head. **2.** A comprehensive map, e.g., of an anatomical structure, an organ, or a tissue.

ATLS *advanced trauma life support.*

atm *atmosphere; atmosphere, standard.*

atmosphere (at′mŏs-fēr″) [Gr. *atmos,* vapor + *sphere*] **1.** The gases surrounding the earth. **2.** Climatic condition of a locality. **3.** In physics, the pressure of the air on the earth at mean sea level, approx. 14.7 lb/sq in (101,325 pascals or 760 torr). **4.** In chemistry, any gaseous medium around a body. **atmospheric** (at″mŏs-fēr′ik), *adj.*

standard a. The pressure of air at sea level when the temperature is 0°C (32°F). This is equal to 14.7 lb/sq in., or 760 torr, or 101,325 pascals.

atmospheric temperature and pressure, saturated ABBR: ATPS. Ambient temperature and pressure, saturated.

ATN *acute tubular necrosis.*

ATNR *asymmetrical tonic neck reflex.*

atom (at′ŏm) [Gr. *atomos,* indivisible] The smallest part of an element. An atom consists of a nucleus and surrounding electrons. The nucleus is positively charged, and this determines the atomic number of an element. A large number of entities in the atomic nucleus have been identified, and the search for others continues. Dimensions of atoms are of the order of 10^{-8} cm. SEE: *atomic theory; electron.* **atomic** (ă-tom′ik), *adj.*

tagged a. Tracer.

atomic mass number SEE: under *number.*

atomic mass unit ABBR: AMU. Dalton.

atomic theory SEE: under *theory.*

atomize (at′ŏm-īz″) To convert a liquid to a spray or vapor. **atomization** (at″ŏ-mī-zā′shŏn), *n.*

atomizer (at′ŏ-mī″zĕr) An apparatus for atomizing.

atonicity (ā″tō-nis′ĭt-ē) [¹*an-* + *tonicity*] The state of being atonic or without tone, esp. muscle tone; atony.

atony, atonia (at′ŏn-ē, ā″tō′nē-ă) [Gr. *atonos*, toneless, languid + *-ia*] Lack of normal tone or strength; debility. **atonic** (ā″ton′ik, ă-), *adj.*

a. of bladder Inability to urinate due to lack of muscle tone. It is frequently seen after traumatic deliveries or after the use of epidural anesthesia.

gastric a. Atony in the stomach and failure to contract normally, causing a delay in movement of food out of the stomach.

atopen (at′ŏ-pĕn, -pen″) An infrequently used synonym for allergen.

atopic (ā″top′ik, tŏ′pik) **1.** Pert. to atopy. **2.** Displaced; malpositioned.

atopognosis (ā″top″og-nō′sĭs, tōp″) [¹*an-* + *topognosis*] Inability to locate a sensation of touch or feeling.

atopy (at′ŏ-pē) [Gr. *atopia*, strangeness] A type I hypersensitivity or allergic reaction for which there is a genetic predisposition. Normal allergic reactions are not genetically determined. The basis for atopy lies in the histocompatibility genes. The child of two parents with atopic allergy has a 75% chance of developing similar symptoms; if one parent is affected, the child has a 50% chance of developing atopy. Hay fever and asthma are two of the most commonly inherited allergies; contact dermatitis and gastrointestinal reactions also may be inherited. As with all type I hypersensitivity reactions, IgE is the primary antibody involved. Atopy is often associated with asthma. SYN: *atopic allergy.* SEE: *allergy; immunity; reagin.*

atorvastatin (ă-tor″vă-stăt′ĭn) A lipid-lowering drug of the statin class, used to treat elevated total serum cholesterol and LDL cholesterol levels.

atoxic (ā″toks′ik) [¹*an-* + *toxic*] Nonpoisonous.

ATP *adenosine triphosphate.*

ATPase *adenosine triphosphatase.*

ATPS *Ambient temperature and pressure, saturated; atmospheric temperature and pressure, saturated.*

atraumatic (ā″tro-mat′ik) [¹*an-* + *trau-*

matic] **1.** Not causing trauma. **2.** Not caused by trauma.

atresia (ă-trē′zhă) [¹*an-* + Gr. *trēsis,* a perforation] Congenital absence or closure of a normal body opening or tubular structure. **atresic, atretic** (ă-trē′zik, ′sik, ă-tret′ik), *adj.*

anal a. Imperforate anus.

aortic a. Congenital closure of the aortic valvular opening into the aorta.

biliary a. Closure or absence of some or all of the major bile ducts.

choanal a. A congenital occlusion of the passage between the nose and pharynx by a bony or membranous structure.

congenital aural a. Failure of the external ear canal to develop in utero. When this condition affects both ears, the child may suffer permanent hearing loss and have difficulty speaking and acquiring language skills. Unilateral cases require no specific therapy.

duodenal a. Congenital closure of a portion of the duodenum.

esophageal a. Congenital failure of the esophagus to develop.

follicular a. Normal death of the ovarian follicle following failure of the ovum to be fertilized.

intestinal a. Congenital closure of any part of the intestine.

mitral a. Congenital closure of the mitral valve opening between the left atrium and ventricle.

prepyloric a. Congenital closure of the pyloric end of the stomach.

pulmonary a. Congenital closure of the pulmonary valve between the right ventricle and the pulmonary artery.

urethral a. Absence or closure of the urethral orifice or canal.

vaginal a. Congenital closure or absence of the vagina.

atria (ā′trē-ă) Pl. of atrium.

atrial (ā′trē-ăl) Pert. to the atrium.

atrial natriuretic factor SEE: under *factor.*

atrichia (ā″trik′ē-ă) [¹*an-* + *tricho-* + *-ia*] **1.** Absence of hair. **2.** Lack of cilia or flagella.

atrichosis (ā″tri-kō′sĭs) [*atrich(ia)* + *-osis*] Congenital absence of hair.

atrichous (a′trĭ-kŭs, ā″trik′ŭs) **1.** Without flagella. **2.** Without hair.

atriopeptin (ā″trē-ō-pep′tin) Atrial natriuretic factor.

atrioseptopexy (ā″trē-ō-sep′tŏ-pek″sē) [*atrium* + *septum* + *-pexy*] Surgical repair of an interatrial septal defect.

atrioventricular (ā″trē-ō-ven″trik′yŭ-lăr) [*atrium* + *ventricular*] ABBR: A-V, AV. Pert. to both the atrium and the ventricle.

atrioventricularis communis (ā″trē-ō-ven-trik″yŭ-lar′ĭs kŏ-mū′nĭs) Persistence of the common atrioventricular canal. In this congenital anomaly of the heart, the division of the common atrioventricular canal in the embryo fails to occur. This causes atrial septal defect and atrioventricular valve incompetence.

atriplicism (ă-trĭp′lĭ-sĭzm) [*Atriplex* + *-ism*] Poisoning due to eating a kind of spinach, *Atriplex littoralis*.

at-risk drinking (ăt′rĭsk″) The consumption of a potentially unhealthy amount of alcohol. Men are said to participate in at-risk drinking when they consume more than four alcoholic drinks a day (or 14 or more drinks a week). At-risk drinking for women consists of the consumption of more than three drinks a day, or seven or more drinks a week.

atrium (ā′trē-ŭm) *pl.* **atria** [L. *atrium,*corridor] A chamber or cavity communicating with another chamber or passageway.

  a. **of the ear** The portion of the tympanic cavity lying below the malleus; the tympanic cavity proper.

  a. **of the heart** The upper chamber of each half of the heart. The right atrium receives deoxygenated blood from the entire body (except lungs) through the superior and inferior venae cavae and coronary sinus; the left atrium receives oxygenated blood from the lungs through the pulmonary veins. Blood passes from the atria to the ventricles through the atrioventricular valves. In the embryo, the atrium is a single chamber that lies between the sinus venosus and the ventricle.

atrophoderma (ă″trŏ-fō-dĕr′mă) [*atroph(y)* + *derma*] Atrophy of the skin.

atrophy (a′trŏ-fē) [*ʲan-* + *-trophy*] **1.** A decrease in size of an organ or tissue; wasting. Atrophy may result from death and resorption of cells, diminished cellular proliferation, pressure, ischemia, malnutrition, decreased activity, or hormonal changes. **2.** To degenerate; lose size, strength, or vitality. **atrophic** (ā″trŏ′fĭk, trŏf′ĭk), *adj.*

  brown *a.* Atrophic tissue that is yellowish-brown rather than its normal color. It is seen principally in the heart and liver of the aged. The pigmentation is due to the presence of lipofuscin, the "wear and tear" pigment that may be associated with aging. Its presence in tissue is a sign of injury from free radicals. SEE: *lipofuscin; free* **radical**.

  compression *a.* Decrease in size, function, or physiologic activity of a body part due to constant pressure.

  correlated *a.* Atrophy of a part following destruction of a correlated part, e.g., of a nerve that supplies a muscle.

  Cruveilhier *a.* Spinal muscular **a.**

  denervation *a.* Atrophy caused by inhibition of a motor nerve.

  disuse *a.* Partial or complete atrophy of a body part or tissue from immobilization or failure to move a body part.

  group *a.* A change in the appearance

of muscle fibers that have lost their nerve supply. It is marked by an increase in the size of the motor unit and a decrease in the fibers within to a uniformly small size.

  macular *a.* Anetoderma.

  microvillous *a.* Microvillus inclusion disease.

  multiple systems *a.* A neurological syndrome marked by Parkinson disease, autonomic failure (loss of sweating, urinary incontinence, dizziness or syncope on arising, miosis), and ataxia.

  muscular *a.* Atrophy of muscle tissue, esp. due to lack of use or denervation.

  myelopathic *a.* Muscular atrophy resulting from a lesion of the spinal cord.

  myotonic *a.* **Myotonia** congenita.

  olivopontocerebellar *a.* A disease characterized by degeneration of neurons in the cerebellum, pons, and inferior olives of the brain, typically resulting in ataxia.

  optic *a.* Atrophy of the optic disk as a result of degeneration of the optic nerve.

  pathological *a.* Atrophy that results from the effects of disease processes.

  peroneal muscular *a.* Charcot-Marie-Tooth disease.

  physiological *a.* Atrophy caused by the normal aging processes in the body. Examples are atrophy of embryonic structures; atrophy of childhood structures on reaching maturity, as the thymus; atrophy of structures in cyclic phases of activity, as the corpus luteum; atrophy of structures following cessation of functional activity, as the ovary and mammary glands; and atrophy of structures with aging.

  postmenopausal vaginal *a.* Drying and shrinking of the vaginal tissues, related to the hormonal changes associated with menopause. Menopausal women who continue to engage in sexual intercourse during and following menopause have less vaginal atrophy than do those women who become sexually inactive. SEE: *hormone replacement therapy.*

  postpoliomyelitis muscular *a.* ABBR: PPMA. Postpolio syndrome.

  progressive hemifacial *a.* A rare disorder usually affecting females, in which cheek tissues on one side of the face gradually waste or deteriorate. There is no treatment. The disease is often associated with local hair loss and may be accompanied by seizures or trigeminal neuralgia. The progression usually lasts between 2 and 10 years but then enters a stable phase, at which time cosmetic surgery may be possible. SYN: *Parry-Romberg syndrome.*

  progressive muscular *a.* Spinal muscular **a.**

  spinal muscular *a.* An autosomal recessive disorder in which motor neurons in the spinal cord die, leading to muscle paralysis. There are three types. Type 1 usually is fatal by age 4; the cause of death is respiratory paralysis. Types 2 and 3 are slower to progress. Treatments aim to prevent nutritional deficiencies, orthopedic deformities, and respiratory infections. SYN: *Aran-Duchenne disease;* **Hoffmann** *atrophy; progressive muscular **a.**; Werdnig-Hoffmann disease; wasting **palsy**; wasting **paralysis**.*

trophoneurotic a. Atrophy due to disease of the nerves or nerve centers supplying the affected muscles.

unilateral facial a. Progressive atrophy of one side of the facial tissues.

urogenital a. Atrophic **vaginitis**.

atropine sulfate (a′trŏ-pēn″) [*Atrop(a belladonna),* a species name + *-ine*] A salt of an alkaloid obtained from belladonna. A parasympatholytic agent, it counteracts the effects of parasympathetic stimulation. It is used primarily to treat potentially life-threatening bradycardias and heart blocks. SEE: *atropine sulfate poisoning.*

atropinism, atropism (a″trŏ-pē-nizm, a′trŏ-pizm) [*atropine* + *-ism*] Atropine sulfate poisoning.

atropinization (a″trŏ-pē-nĭ-zā′shŏn) Administration of atropine until the desired pharmacologic effect is achieved.

atropinize (a′trŏ-pĭ-nīz″), *v.*

ATS *American Thoracic Society.*

attachment (ă-tach′mĕnt) [Fr. *atachier,* to fasten] **1.** A device or anatomical structure linked to another. **2.** In dentistry, a plastic or metal device used for retention or stabilization of a dental prosthesis, such as a partial denture. **3.** An enduring psychological bond of affection.

epithelial a. The link between the reflection of the junctional (gingival) epithelium and the enamel, cementum, or dentin of the tooth.

parent-newborn a. The unconscious incorporation of the infant into the family unit. Characteristic parental behavior includes making eye contact with the infant, touching the infant with their fingertips, calling the infant by name, and recognizing of physical and behavioral similarities with other family members. Attachment is enhanced or impeded by the infant's responses. SEE: *bonding, mother-infant; engrossment; position, en face.*

attachment, risk for impaired parent/infant/child Disruption of the interactive process between parent or significant other and infant that fosters the development of a protective and nurturing reciprocal relationship. SEE: *Nursing Diagnoses Appendix.*

attachment apparatus The cementum, periodontal ligament, and alveolar bone

that serve to attach the tooth to the bone.

attack (ă-tak′) [Italian *attacare,* to attach, attack] **1.** The onset of an illness or symptom, usually dramatic (e.g., a heart attack or an attack of gout). **2.** An assault.

anxiety a. An imprecise term for sudden onset of anxiety, sometimes accompanied by a sense of imminent danger or impending doom and an urge to escape.

brain a. A term proposed by the National Stroke Association for the sudden loss of neurological function that constitutes a stroke. The term is meant to be similar to "heart attack" in order to convey the emergent nature of strokes and the need for affected patients to seek care immediately when treatment may do the most good.

drop a. A sudden fall with loss of muscular tone and loss of consciousness. Drop attacks may occur in patients with arrhythmias, autonomic failure, epilepsy, narcolepsy, and strokes. Treatment depends on the underlying cause.

heart a. Myocardial infarction.

panic a. A discrete period of intense fear or discomfort accompanied by at least four of the following symptoms: palpitations, sweating, trembling or shaking, sensations of shortness of breath or smothering, feeling of choking, chest pain or discomfort, nausea or abdominal distress, dizziness or lightheadedness, feeling of unreality or being detached from oneself, feeling of losing control, fear of dying, paresthesias, and chills or hot flushes. The onset is sudden and builds to a peak usually in 10 min or less. It may include a sense of imminent danger or impending doom and an urge to escape.

PATIENT CARE: Precautions are taken to ensure the patient's safety. A calm, quiet, and reassuring environment helps the patient overcome anxious feelings. Speaking slowly in short, simple sentences, giving one direction at a time, and avoiding giving explanations for using these to relieve stress help the patient feel less overwhelmed. If the patient is hyperventilating, the caregiver demonstrates slow, deep breathing. Touch may not be reassuring to the patient and should be avoided until trust is established. Once the attack has subsided, the patient is encouraged to discuss fears and helped to identify situations or events that act as triggers for an attack. Relaxation techniques may be taught, with explanations given regarding using them to relieve stress or avoid an attack. The patient may be referred for behavioral therapy, supportive psychotherapy, or pharmacologic therapy (antianxiety agents, antidepressants, beta-blockers), separately or in combination.

transient ischemic a. ABBR: TIA. A neurologic deficit, having a reversible vascular cause, that produces stroke symptoms that resolve within 24 hr. Most TIAs resolve within an hour of onset. Patients who have suffered a TIA have an increased risk of peripheral and coronary artery atherosclerosis and an increased risk of subsequent heart attack and stroke. SEE: *stroke*.

SYMPTOMS: TIAs and strokes have similar symptoms. These vary depending on the blood vessel affected but may include weakness of one half of the face or half of the body, confusion, dizziness, aphasia, monocular visual loss, hemibody sensory loss, sudden trouble walking, loss of balance, or severe headache with no known cause. A person who develops any of these symptoms should seek emergency medical assistance immediately. He should not attempt to drive or be driven to the emergency center but should call or have a family member call 911 for help.

ETIOLOGY: TIAs usually occur in patients with underlying atherosclerosis, esp. of the carotid arteries, intracranial arteries, or the aorta. Emboli to the brain caused by atrial fibrillation, cerebrovascular vasospasm, transient episodes of hypotension, cerebral vasculitis, polycythemia vera, and other illnesses may occasionally produce TIAs.

TREATMENT: Studies involving large numbers of patients have shown that the risk of subsequent stroke in those who have suffered TIAs can be substantially reduced with antiplatelet or anticoagulant drugs (e.g., aspirin, clopidogrel, or warfarin) and with drugs that control blood pressure and lipids. Carotid endarterectomy or balloon angioplasty and stenting are better options than medical therapy for stroke prevention in TIA patients with extensive carotid artery blockages, provided their surgeons have an operative mortality rate of less than 5%.

PATIENT CARE: Because symptoms of TIA may resolve by the time the patient reaches the emergency care center, an accurate history of the event should be obtained, questioning not only the patient but also family, first-responders, and any other witnesses. Carotid arteries are assessed for bruits, the heart for evidence of atrial fibrillation, and the cranial nerves, speech and motor strength for signs of functional loss. The patient may have brain imaging studies (e.g., CT or MRI) to exclude other intracerebral disorders. Baseline laboratory studies including serum chemistries, glucose level and coagulation factors are obtained. The health care professional supports the patient and family during diagnostic procedures by explaining the procedures and expected sensations and by encouraging verbalization of feelings and concerns. Therapeutic interventions are provided, and the patient is instructed about desired effects and adverse reactions of prescribed drugs.

The patient also is encouraged to follow preventive measures: stopping smoking and avoiding second-hand smoke, exercising regularly (walking at a moderate pace for 30 min daily), losing weight if obesity is a concern, eating a heart-healthy diet, drinking no more than one (women) or two (men) alcoholic drinks daily, seeking medical management for elevated cholesterol or blood pressure, and more tightly controlling glucose levels if diabetes mellitus is present.

vagal a. Vasodepressor syncope.

attendant (ă-ten'dănt) A paramedical hospital employee who assists in the care and personal support of patients.

attending (ă-tend'ing) Pert. to or being the physician or surgeon having primary responsibility for a patient.

attention (ă-ten'shŏn) Direction of the consciousness to a person, thing, perception, or thought.

attentional bias (ă-ten'shŏn-ăl) An error in diagnosis or other form of analysis in which a person is unable to see the truth because he or she does not perceive a critical piece of data.

attention-deficit hyperactivity disorder ABBR: ADHD. A persistent pattern of inattention, hyperactivity and impulsivity, or both, occurring more frequently and severely than is typical in those at a comparable level of development. ADHD is the most commonly reported neurobehavioral disorder of childhood. The illness may begin in early childhood but may not be diagnosed until after the symptoms have been present for many years. The prevalence is estimated to be 3% to 5% in children; 4% in adults.

SYMPTOMS: Signs may be minimal or absent when the person is under strict control or is engaged in esp. interesting or challenging situations. They are more likely to occur in group situations. Although behaviors vary widely, affected people typically exhibit motor restlessness, impulsivity, and difficulty concentrating on a single task or chore. They tend to do more poorly in school than one might predict based on assessments of their intelligence alone. While characteristics of ADHD are found in many people at one time or another, a key feature of ADHD is the excessive or unusual pattern of behavior outside normal bounds of exuberance or excitement. The findings must be severe enough to be maladaptive and inconsistent with specified levels of development, and last at least six months.

> ⚠ ADHD may sometimes be confused with other disorders.

DIAGNOSIS: The disorder is difficult to diagnose in children under age 5. It is important to distinguish ADHD from age-appropriate behavior in active children and from disorders such as mental retardation, primary learning disabilities, alteration of mood, anxiety, petit mal seizures, or personality changes caused by illness, family stress, or drugs. The criteria determined by the American Psychiatric Association include specific limits concerning the duration and severity of symptoms of inattention and hyperactivity-impulsivity. The findings must be severe enough to be maladaptive and inconsistent with specified levels of development.

TREATMENT: In both children and adults, the domestic, school, social, and occupational environments are evaluated to determine contributing factors and their relative importance. Standard treatment includes behavioral and psychological therapy, environmental changes, and medication. Medications commonly used to treat ADHD include methylphenidate, dextroamphetamine, atomoxetine, and pemoline. These agents, with the exception of atomoxetine, are central nervous system (CNS) stimulants. Adverse reactions to CNS stimulants include decreased appetite, difficulty sleeping, anxiety, stomach ache, headache, jitteriness, and social withdrawal (the latter in children).

Behavior therapy for patients with ADHD includes positive reinforcement, time-out, response cost (loss of rewards or privileges for problem behaviors) and token economy (a combination of positive reinforcement and response cost). Combinations of drug therapy and behavioral therapies, or drug therapies alone, appear to have a more beneficial effect than behavioral therapy, psychotherapy, or parent skills training alone.

attenuation (ă-ten″ū-ā′shŏn) [L. *attenuare,* to thin, reduce] **1.** Dilution. **2.** The lessening of virulence. Bacteria and viruses are made less virulent by being heated, dried, treated with chemicals, passed through another organism, or cultured under unfavorable conditions. **3.** A weakening or reduction in the strength of a previously observed measurement or trend. **4.** In technology, engineering, and physics, acoustics, radiology, and optics, the reduction in amplitude, magnitude, strength, or intensity of matter, radiation, energy, a

beam, or a signal In electronics, it is the opposite of amplification. **attenuate** (ă-ten′ū-āt″), *v.* **attenuated** (ă-ten′ū-āt″ĕd), *adj.*

attic (at′ik) [L. *atticus*] Epitympanic recess.

attic disease Chronic inflammation of the attic of the ear.

atticitis (at″ĭ-sīt′is) [*attic* + *-itis*] Inflammation of the attic of the ear.

atticoantrotomy (at″ĭ-kō-an-trot′ŏ-mē) [*attic* + *antrotomy*] Surgical opening of the attic and mastoid antrum of the ear.

atticotomy (at″ĭ-kot′ŏ-mē) [*attic* + *-tomy*] Surgical opening of the tympanic attic of the ear.

attitude (at′ĭ-tood″, -tūd″) [L. *aptitudo,* fitness] **1.** Bodily posture or position, esp. of the limbs. A particular attitude may be a symptom of disease (e.g., the stereotyped posturing assumed by catatonics). **2.** A long-standing point of view that guides or influences one's behaviors; a predisposition to think about things and respond to them in internally consistent or patterned ways.

crucifixion a. A position in which the body is rigid with the arms at right angles to the long axis of the body; seen in catatonia.

defense a. A position automatically assumed to avert pain.

fetal a. The relationship of the fetal parts to one another (e.g., the head and extremities flexed against the body).

forced a. An abnormal position due to disease or contractures.

frozen a. Stiffness of gait, seen in amyotrophic lateral sclerosis.

stereotyped a. A position taken and held for a long period, seen frequently in mental diseases.

atto- [Danish, *atten,* eighteen] Symbol: a. In the International System of Units (SI), a prefix meaning 10^{-18}.

attraction (ă-trak′shŏn) [L. *attrahere,* to draw toward] A force that causes particles of matter to be drawn to each other.

chemical a. The tendency of atoms of one element to unite with those of another to form compounds.

molecular a. The tendency of molecules with unlike electrical charges to attract each other. SEE: *adhesion; cohesion.*

attribute (ă-tri′būt″) [L., *attribuere,* to assign, ascribe] **1.** To assign a cause. **2.** To explain, e.g., a phenomenon or an event. **3.** To predicate, e.g., a theory on a piece of evidence.

attrition (ă-trish′ŏn) [L. *attritio,* a rubbing against] **1.** The act of wearing away by friction or rubbing. **2.** Any friction that breaks the skin. **3.** The process of wearing away, as of teeth, in the course of normal use. **4.** In research, the progressive loss of study subjects with each passing year because of, e.g., relocation, lack of interest, failure of outreach, or death. **attritional** (ŏn-ăl), *adj*.

at. wt. *Atomic weight*.

atypia (ā-tip′ē-ă) [¹*an-* + Gr. *typos,* type + *-ia*] **1.** Deviation from a standard or regular type. **2.** In a histological or pathological specimen, a suggestion of aberrant cellular behavior; e.g., a precancerous or cancerous appearance.

atypical (ā-tip′ĭ-kăl) [¹*an-* + *typical*] Deviating from the normal; not conforming to type. **atypically** (tip′ĭ-k(ă-)lē), *adv*.

atypical ductal hyperplasia SEE: under *hyperplasia*.

atypical glandular cells ABBR: AGC. SEE: under *cell*.

atypical squamous cells of uncertain significance ABBR: ASC-US. An abnormal finding on a Papanicolaou test in which squamous cells from the endocervix have enlarged nuclei with irregular nuclear membranes and hyperchromasia. These pathological changes are more prominent than those typically seen with inflammation alone. ASC-US is often associated with infection of the cervix with human papillomavirus. In some cases the abnormality resolves on its own; in others, it is associated with higher-grade lesions of the uterine cervix.

ATZ *Anal transition zone*.

AU *angstrom unit; aures unitas,* both ears; *auris uterque,* each ear.

Au [L. *aurum*] Symbol for the element gold.

AUC *area under the curve*.

Au.D. *Doctor of Audiology*.

audi-, audio- [L. *audire,* to hear] Prefixes meaning *hearing*.

audible (od′ĭ-bl) Capable of being heard. **audibility** (od″ĭ-bil′ĭt-ē), *n*. **audibly** (od′ĭ-blē), *adv*.

audible sound SEE: under ¹*sound*.

audile (o′dī″l) [*aud(itory)*] **1.** Pert. to hearing; auditory. **2.** A person who retains more auditory information than information received through other senses. **3.** In psychoanalysis, one whose mental perceptions are auditory. SEE: *motile; visile*.

audioanalgesia, audio-analgesia, audio analgesia (od″ē-ō-an″ăl-jē′zhă, -z(h)ē-ă) [*audio-* + *analgesia*] The use of music or electronic masking noise to reduce anxiety, disruptive behavior, or pain during unpleasant procedures, e.g., during dentistry. SYN: *music distraction*. SEE: *electronic dental anesthesia*.

audioanesthesia (od″ē-ō-an″ĕs-thē′zh(ē-)ă) [*audi-* + *anesthesia*] Anesthesia or analgesia produced by sound. It is used by dentists to help prevent perception of pain.

audio clip A brief recorded file, linked to a website or to an electronic message, used to relay audible information from one user to another.

audiogenic (od″ē-ō-jen′ik) [*audi-* + *-genic*] Originating in sound.

audiogram (od′ē-ō-gram″) [*audi-* + *-gram*] A graphic record produced by an audiometer.

audiology (od″ē-ol′ō-jē) [*audi-* + *-logy*] The study of hearing disorders through identification and evaluation of hearing loss, and the rehabilitation of those with hearing loss, esp. that which cannot be improved by medical or surgical means. **audiologist** (od″ē-ol′ŏ-jĭst), *n*.

audiometer (od″ē-om′ĕt-ĕr) [*audi-* + *-meter*] An instrument for testing hearing.

audiometry (od″ē-om′ĕ-trē) [*audi-* + *-metry*] A test that measures the ability to detect sounds of varying frequencies and varying levels of loudness. **audiometric** (-ē-ō-me′trik), *adj.*; **audiometrist** (-om′ĕ-trist), *n*. SEE: *spondee threshold*.

> ***averaged electroencephalic a.*** A method of testing the hearing of children who cannot be adequately tested by conventional means. The test is based on the electroencephalogram's being altered by perceived sound without the need for a behavioral response; therefore, the test may be done on an autistic, severely retarded, or hyperkinetic child who is asleep or sedated. SEE: *auditory evoked response*.

> ***behavioral observational a.*** ABBR: BOA. A hearing test for individuals (such as children aged 6–8 months) who may not be able to signal their responses to sounds with speech or gestures, but who may reorient their eyes or bodies in response to sounds. Interpretation of BOA results is subjective and may not be reproducible.

> ***brainstem evoked response a.*** Evoked response **a.**

> ***evoked response a.*** A computer-aided technique to average the brain's response to latency of auditory stimuli. Auditory brainstem evoked response (ABER), one kind of this type of audiometry, is used to test the hearing of those, esp. children, who cannot be tested in the usual manner. SYN: *brainstem evoked response a.*

> ***immittance a.*** Audiometry that combines acoustic reflex testing, a reflex decay test, and tympanometry. Formerly called impedance or tympanometry testing, it is a test that measures the structural integrity and normal functioning of the tympanic membrane and the middle ear.

> ***play a.*** A hearing test of preschool children (ages 3 and up) in which the child is asked to drop a toy into a pail whenever he or she hears a tone.

> ***pure tone a.*** A test to determine hearing sensitivity and hearing loss in

response to different sound frequencies. The test subject is exposed to sounds of specific frequencies within the normal range of human speech (about 250–8000 Hz). Each tonal frequency is presented to the subject at different increasing intensities or decibels of sound until he or she identifies the frequency. A chart is constructed representing the range of detectable frequencies and the sound intensity (loudness) required to elicit a response from the subject.

speech a. A test of the ability to hear and understand speech. The threshold of detection is measured in decibels.

visual reinforcement a. A method of testing the hearing of children under 3 in which the child is rewarded when he or she looks toward a sound source.

audioscope (od′ē-ō-skōp″) [*audi-* + *-scope*] A device to test hearing, esp. in the 500 to 4000 Hz range (the range of human speech). It combines an otoscope (for identifying cerumen impaction or abnormalities that may cause conductive hearing loss) with an audiometer (set at 40 dB) to assess the ability to hear particular tones.

PATIENT CARE: Hearing loss occurs in about 25% to 40% of all people older than 65. The Canadian Task Force on Preventive Health Care recommends audioscopic screening of all older adults for hearing loss. Patients whose hearing loss is demonstrated by screening should be referred for formal audiological testing.

audit (od′it) [L. *auditus*, hearing] In medical care facilities, an official examination of the record of some or all aspects of patient care. This is done by trained staff who are not usually affiliated with the institution. The purpose of an audit is to compare and evaluate the quality of care provided with accepted standards.

audit-, audito- [L. *auditus*, past participle of *audire*, to hear] Prefixes meaning *hearing*.

audition (o-dish′ŏn) [L. *auditio*, hearing] Hearing.

chromatic a. A condition in which certain color sensations are aroused by sound stimuli. SYN: *colored a.*

colored a. Chromatic audition.

gustatory a. A condition in which certain taste sensations are aroused by sound stimuli.

mental a. Recollection of a sound based on previous auditory impressions.

auditory (od′ĭ-tōr″ē) [L. *auditorius*, pert. to hearing] Pert. to the sense of hearing.

auditory area The hearing center of the cerebral cortex; located in the floor of the lateral fissure and surfacing on the dorsal surface of the superior temporal gyrus. It receives auditory fibers from the medial geniculate body.

auditory defensiveness Excessive attention to sounds that do not disturb others.

auditory dyssynchrony SEE: under *dyssynchrony*.

auditory evoked response SEE: under *response*.

auditory tube Eustachian tube.

audit trail A software tracking notation system used for data security. An audit trail is attached to a computer file each time it is opened so that an operator can determine when a file has been accessed and by whom.

Auenbrugger sign (ow-ĕn-broog′ĕr) [Leopold Joseph Auenbrugger, Austrian physician, 1722–1809] Epigastric prominence due to marked pericardial effusion.

Auerbach plexus (ow′ĕr-boks″) [Leopold Auerbach, Ger. anatomist, 1828–1897] Myenteric **plexus**.

Auer bodies (ow′ĕr) [John Auer, U.S. physician, 1875–1948] Rod-shaped structures, present in the cytoplasm of myeloblasts, myelocytes, and monoblasts, found in leukemia. Also called *Auer rods*.

Aufrecht sign (owf′rekt″) [Emanuel Aufrecht, Ger. physician, 1844–1933] Diminished breathing sound that is heard above the jugular fossa, indicative of tracheal stenosis.

augmentation (og″mĕn-tā′shŏn) [L. *augmentare,* to increase, grow] **1.** The act of adding to or increasing the shape, size, function, or strength of something. **2.** In obstetrics, the use of pharmacological or surgical interventions to help the progression of a previously dysfunctional labor. SYN: *a. of labor.*

breast a. Augmentation **mammaplasty**.

a. of labor Augmentation (2).

localized alveolar ridge a. Dental surgery to repair defects in the jaw due to the extraction or loss of a tooth. A bone graft is placed into the socket formed at the base of the extracted tooth. Alternatives to a bone graft include a soft-tissue graft or bone substitutes. The surrounding gum is sutured in place to cover the graft. The grafted bone can repair aesthetic defects or be used as a foundation for dental implants. Results generally include an increase in the width and/or height of the alveolar ridge. SYN: *ridge a.*

percutaneous vertebral a. ABBR: PVA. Any surgical treatment for spinal fractures that corrects the defect produced by the fracture, e.g., kyphoplasty or vertebroplasty.

ridge a. Localized alveolar ridge a.

augmentative (og-men′tă-tiv) [L. *augmentare,* to increase, grow] Able to enlarge or increase.

Augmentin (og-ment′ĭn) SEE: *amoxicillin*.

augnathus (og-nā'thŭs) [Gr. *au*, again + Gr. *gnathos*, jaw] A fetus with a double lower jaw.

aur-, auro- [L. *auris*, ear] Prefixes meaning *ear*.

aura (or'ă) [L. fr. Gr. *aura*, breeze] **1.** A subjective but recognizable sensation that precedes and signals the onset of a convulsion or migraine headache. In epilepsy the aura may precede the attack by several hours or only a few seconds. An epileptic aura may be psychic, or it may be sensory with olfactory, visual, auditory, or taste hallucinations. In migraine the aura immediately precedes the attack and often consists of ocular sensory phenomena. **2.** An electromagnetic field that psychics and some alternative medical providers assert they can sense around living beings.

aural (or'ăl) [L. *auris*, the ear] **1.** Pert. to the ear. **2.** Pert. to an aura. **aurally** (ă-lē), *adv.*

aural acoustic admittance ABBR: Y$_a$. The relative ease of passage of a sound wave through the ear and its components.

aural acoustic immittance ABBR: AAI. The electrical impedance plus the admittance of the ear to sound.

aural rehabilitation SEE: under *rehabilitation*.

aurantiasis cutis (or"ăn-tī'ă-sĭs kū'tĭs) [L. *aurantium*, orange + *-iasis*] Yellow pigmentation of skin due to ingestion of excessive amounts of food that contain carotene, such as carrots, oranges, and squash. SEE: *carotenemia*.

aureola (or-ē'ō-lă) [Latin *aureola* (*corona*), golden (crown)] The ring of pigmented tissue that surrounds the nipple of the breast. It has a greater diameter in women than in men.

auriasis (or-ī'ă-sĭs) [*aur-* + *-iasis*] Chrysiasis.

auric (or'ik) [L. *aurum*, gold + *-ic*] Pert. to gold, esp. in its trivalent state.

auricle (or'ĭ-kl) [*auricula*] **1.** Pinna (2). **2.** A small conical pouch forming a portion of the right and left atria of the heart. Each projects from the upper anterior portion of each atrium. **3.** An obsolete term for the atrium of the heart.

auricul-, auriculo- [L. *auricula*, the external ear, earlobe, diminutive of *auris*, ear] Prefixes meaning *ear*.

auricula (or-ik'yŭ-lă) *pl.* **auriculae** [L. *auricula*, little ear] Auricle, esp. the auricular (atrial) appendage.

auricular (or-ik'yŭ-lăr) [L. *auricularis*, pert. to the ear] Pert. to an auricle, e.g., of the ear or of the cardiac atria.

auriculare (or-ik"yŭ-lār'ē) *pl.* **auricularia** [L. *auricularis*, pert. to the ear] A craniometric point at the center of the opening of the external auditory canal.

auricular therapy Acupuncture in which needles are inserted into specific points on the ear said to map or connect to other parts of the body. It is used in traditional Chinese medicine and alternative and complementary medicine to treat a variety of conditions, including sciatica and tobacco addiction. SYN: *auriculotherapy*.

auriculotemporal (or-ik"yŭ-lō-tem'pŏ-răl) [*auricul-* + *temporal*] Pert. to the ear and the area around the temple.

auriculotemporal syndrome Frey syndrome.

auriculotherapy (or-ik"yŭ-lō-ther'ă-pē) [*auricul-* + *therapy*] Auricular therapy.

auris (ow'ris, or'is, ow'rēz, or'ēz) *pl.* **aures** [L. *auris*, ear] Ear.
  a. dextra Right ear.
  a. sinistra Left ear.

aurotherapy (or"ō-thĕr'ă-pē) [*aur-* + *therapy*] Chrysotherapy.

aurum (or'ŭm, aur') [L. *aurum*, gold] SYMB: Au. Gold.

auscultate (os'kŭl-tāt") [L. *auscultare*, to listen to] To examine by listening. **auscultatory** (os-kŭl'tă-tōr"ē), *adj.*

auscultation (os"kŭl-tā'shŏn) [*auscultate*] Listening for sounds within the body, esp. from the chest, neck, or abdomen.

PATIENT CARE: A stethoscope is typically used. It is applied to the patient's skin surface gently but firmly to eliminate any environmental noises that may be present. Auscultation is used to detect heart rate and rhythm and any cardiac murmurs, rubs, or gallops; crackles or wheezes in the lungs; pleural rubs; movement of gas or food through the intestines; vascular or thyroid bruits; fetal heart tones; and other physiological phenomena.

five-point a. Auscultaton of breath sounds over the stomach, lung apices, and axillae. It is used as one of several relatively effective methods of confirming that an endotracheal tube is properly placed in the trachea and not in the esophagus. Capnography is a more precise form of confirmation of appropriate tube placement.

immediate a. Auscultation in which the ear is applied directly to the skin.

mediate a. Auscultation in which sounds are conducted from the surface to the ear through an instrument such as a stethoscope.

Austin Flint murmur (os'tĭn-flint') [Austin Flint, U.S. physician, 1812–1886] A presystolic or late diastolic heart murmur best heard at the apex of the heart. It is present in some cases of aortic insufficiency. It is thought to be due to the vibration of the mitral valve caused by the backward-flowing blood from the aorta meeting the blood flowing in from the left atrium.

Australian X disease Former name of Murray Valley encephalitis.

Austrian triad (os'trē-ăn) [First described by Richard Ladislas Heschl, Austrian pathologist, 1824–1881] Systemic infection with *Streptococcus pneumoniae*, producing endocarditis, meningitis, and pneumonia at the same time.

autacoid (ot'ă-koyd″) [*auto-* + Gr. *akos*, remedy + *-oid*] **1.** A term originally used by the British physiologist Edward Sharpey-Shafer as a substitute for the word *hormone*. **2.** A prostaglandin or a related compound that forms rapidly, acts, and then decays or is destroyed enzymatically.

authority gradient SEE: under *gradient*.

authorization (o″thŏr-ĭ-zā'shŏn) [L. *auctorizare*, to give surety for] **1.** Permission, esp. official permission. **2.** Legal empowerment.

authorization to request or release information A document approved and signed by a patient or legal representative on behalf of the patient that legally permits a health care facility to send specified confidential elements of the patient's medical records to another facility.

autism (o'tizm) [*auto-* + *-ism*] **1.** In classic psychiatry, mental introversion in which the attention or interest is thought to be focused on the ego. Objective validation of this concept is lacking. **2.** Withdrawal from communication with others, often accompanied by repetitive or primitive behaviors. **autistic** (o-tis'tik), *n.* **autistic,** *adj.* SEE: *Nursing Diagnoses Appendix*.

    infantile a. A syndrome appearing in childhood with symptoms of self-absorption, inaccessibility, aloneness, avoidance of eye contact, inability to relate, highly repetitive play, rage reactions if interrupted, rhythmical body movements, and many language disturbances. The cause is unknown, but some research suggests that anomalies in serotonin transport increase the likelihood of the disease.

    regressive a. Autism that develops in a child after normal development during the first 24–30 months of life. SYN: *Heller dementia*. SEE: *childhood disintegrative disorder*.

    spectrum disorder a. A synonym for pervasive developmental disorder, i.e., any of the group of illnesses known as classical autism, Asperger disorder, childhood disintegrative disorder (regressive autism), and Rett syndrome.

auto- [Gr. *autos*, self] Prefix meaning *self*, *same (one)*

autoactivation (ot″ō-ak″tĭ-vā'shŏn) [*auto-* + *activation*] Autocatalysis.

autoagglutination (aw″tō-ă-gloo″tĭ-nā'shŭn) [*auto-* + L. *agglutinare*, adhere to] Agglutination, or clumping of red blood cells, in response to an autotransfusion (e.g., the transfusion of a person's

own blood that has been removed by phlebotomy or during surgery).

autoagglutinin (aw″tō-ă-glū'tĭ-nĭn) A substance present in an individual's blood that agglutinates that person's red blood cells.

    cold a. An IgM class autoantibody that is activated only when the temperature falls below 100°C. These antibodies may destroy the patient's red blood cells and are one cause of autoimmune hemolytic anemia. They are found in the serum of patients (esp. those older than 50 years) with atypical (e.g., mycoplasma) pneumonia, infectious mononucleosis, cytomegalovirus infections, mumps, and certain blood diseases. The complement-mediated, autoimmune hemolysis that results is an example of a type II hypersensitivity reaction. SYN: *cold agglutinin*. SEE: *autoantibody; hemolytic anemia*.

    warm a. An IgG class autoantibody that is activated at a temperature of 37°C. These antibodies damage the membranes on the patient's own red blood cells, which results in their destruction by the spleen, producing an autoimmune hemolytic anemia. The source of the autoantibodies is unclear in 50% of the cases. In the other 50% of patients, they are related to a drug reaction; autoimmune diseases, esp. systemic lupus erythematosus; or malignancies. SYN: *warm antibody*. SEE: *autoantibody; hemolytic anemia*.

autoamputation (aw″tō-ăm″pū-tā'shŭn) Spontaneous amputation of a part or limb. SEE: *ainhum*.

autoanalysis (aw″tō-ă-năl'ĭ-sĭs) [″ + *analyein*, break down] A patient's own insights into the elements underlying his or her mental disorder.

autoantibody (ot″ō-ant'ĭ-bod″ē) ABBR: AAb. An antibody, produced by B cells in response to an altered autoantigen on one type of the body's own cells, that attacks and destroys these cells. Autoantibodies are the basis for autoimmune diseases such as rheumatoid arthritis and diabetes mellitus. Several theories exist about why autoantibodies are formed. The most common theory proposes that AAbs develop as the result of a combination of hereditary and environmental risk factors that cause an autoantigen to be seen as foreign by B cells; as a result, antibodies are produced for its destruction. SEE: *antibody; antigen; autoimmune disease; autoimmunity; immunoglobulin*.

autoantigen (ot″ō-ant'ĭ-jen″) [*auto-* + *antigen*] ABBR: AAg. An antigen on the body's own cells. AAgs on the cell surface of body tissues are part of the process in which an immune response by B lymphocytes or self-reacting T lymphocytes damages the tissues with the autoantigen. SYN: *self-antigen*.

autoantitoxin (aw″tō-ăn″tĭ-tŏk′sĭn) [″ + ″ + *toxikon,* poison] Antitoxin produced by the body itself.

autocatalysis (ot″ō-kă-tal′ĭ-sĭs) [*auto-* + *aatalysis*] Increase in the rate of a chemical reaction resulting from products that are produced in the reaction acting as catalysts. SYN: *autoactivation.* SEE: *catalyst.* **autocatalytic** (-kat-ă-lit′ik), *adj.*

autocatharsis (ot″ō-kă-thar′sĭs) [*auto-* + *catharsis*] A form of psychotherapy in which patients discuss their issues in order to unburden themselves.

autocatheterization (ot″ō-kath″ĕt-ĕr-ĭ-zā′shŏn) [*auto-* + *catheterization*] Catheterization of oneself, esp. urinary catheterization.

autochthonous (o-tok′thŏ-nŭs) [Gr. *autochthōn,* from the very earth] **1.** Found where developed, as in the case of a blood clot or a calculus. **2.** Pert. to a tissue graft to a new site on the same individual. **autochthonously** (-lē), *adv.*

autocinesia, autocinesis (ot″ō-sĭ-nē′zh(ē-)ă, -nē′sĭs) Autokinesia.

autoclasis (o″tok′lă-sĭs) [*auto-* + *-clasis*] Destruction of a part from internal causes.

autoclave (ot′ō-klāv″) [*auto-* + L. *clavis,* a key] A device that sterilizes by steam pressure, usually at 250°F (121°C) and 15 lbs per square inch for a specified length of time. SEE: *sterilization.* **autoclave,** *v.*

autocrine (ot′ō-krin″, -krīn″, -krēn″) [*auto-* + *-crine*] Secreting macromolecules that influence the secreting cell from the outside. One of three general mechanisms (the others being endocrine and paracrine) by which ductless glands regulate or control the activities of cells.
     a. regulation The secretion of self-regulatory macromolecules, such as certain growth factors.
     a. signaling Autocrine regulation.

autocystoplasty (ot″ō-sis′tŏ-plas″tē) [*auto-* + *cystoplasty*] Plastic repair of the bladder with grafts from one's own body.

autocytolysis (ot″ō-sī-tol′ĭ-sĭs) [*auto-* + *cytolysis*] Self-digestion or self-destruction of cells.

autodermic (ot″ō-dĕr′mik) [*auto-* + *dermic*] Pert. to one's own skin, esp. to dermatoplasty with a patient's own skin.

autodigestion (ot″ō-dī-jes′chŏn, -dĭ-) [*auto-* + *digestion*] Digestion of tissues by their own secretions, e.g., the digestion of the pancreas during severe pancreatitis.

autodiploid (ot″ō-dip′loyd″) [*auto-* + *diploid*] Having two sets of chromosomes; caused by redoubling the chromosomes of the haploid cell.

autodrainage (ot″ō-drā′nij) [*auto-* + *drainage*] Drainage of a cavity by the fluid passing through a channel in one's own tissues or to the outside of the body.

autoecholalia (ot″ō-ek-ō-lā′lē-ă) [*auto-* + *echolalia*] Repetition of the last portion of one's own statements.

autoeczematization (ot″ō-eg-zē-măt-ĭ-zā′shŏn, -zem″ăt-) [*auto-* + *eczema*] The dissemination to broad areas of skin of a previously localized dermatitis. It is an autoimmune reaction, apparently triggered by T lymphocytes sensitized to keratinocyte antigens.

autoerotism, autoeroticism (ot″ō-er′ŏ-tizm, ot″ō-ĕ-rot′ĭ-sizm) [*auto-* + *erot(ic)ism*] **1.** Self-gratification of the sexual instinct, usually by manual stimulation of erogenous areas, esp. the penis or clitoris. SEE: *masturbation; autoerotic hypoxia.* **2.** Self-admiration combined with sexual emotion, such as that obtained from viewing one's naked body or one's genitals. **autoerotic** (ot″ō-ĕ-rot′ik), *adj.* **autoerotically** (ot″ō-ĕ-rot′i-k(ă-)lē), *adv.*

autofluorescence endoscopy (ot″ō-floo″(ŏ-)res′ĕns) SEE: under *endoscopy.*

autogenesis (ot-ō-jen′ĕ-sĭs) [*auto-* + *genesis*] Self-generation. SYN: *abiogenesis.* **autogenetic** (-jĕ-net′ik), *adj.*

autogenous (o-toj′ĕ-nŭs) **1.** Originating within the body; self-producing. **2.** Pert. to a vaccine from a culture of the patient's own bacteria. **autogenously,** *adv.*

autograft (ot′ō-graft″) [*auto-* + *graft*] A graft transferred from one part of a patient's body to another. **autograft,** *v.*
     limbal cell a. Limbal stem cell autograft.
     limbal stem cell a. The transfer of healthy limbal tissue from a patient's donor eye to repair damaged ocular epithelium in the other eye, esp. after that caused by a chemical burn or congenital defect. SYN: *limbal cell a.; stem cell a.*
     pulmonary a. Ross procedure.
     stem cell a. Limbal stem cell autograft.

autohemagglutination (ot″ō-hē″mă-gloot″ĭ-nā′shŏn) [*auto-* + *hemagglutination*] Agglutination of one's own red cells.

autohemic (ot″ō-hē′mĭk) [*auto-* + *hemic*] Performed with one's own blood.

autohemolysin (ot″ō-hē-molīs′ĭn) [*auto-* + *hemolysin*] An antibody that acts on the blood cells of the individual in whose blood it is formed.

autohemolysis (ot″ō-hē-mol′ĭ-sĭs) [*auto-* + *hemolysis*] Hemolysis of one's blood cells by one's own serum.

autohemolysis test A test of the rate of hemolysis of sterile defibrinated whole blood incubated at 37°C. Normal cells hemolyze at a certain rate, but red blood cells from persons with certain types of disease (such as hereditary spherocytosis) hemolyze at a faster rate.

autohemotherapy (ot″ō-hē″mō-ther′ă-pē)

[*auto-* + *hemo-* + *therapy*] Treatment by withdrawal and intramuscular injection of one's own blood.

autohypnosis (ot″ō-hip-nō′sĭs, -nō′sēz) *pl.* **autohypnoses** [*auto-* + *hypnosis*] Self-induced **hypnotism. autohypnotic** (-not′ik), *adj.*

autoimmune adrenalitis (ot″ō-im-ūn″) [*auto-* + *immune*] ABBR: AA. Destruction of the adrenal cortex by circulating autoantibodies. The disease is more common in women than in men; its cause is unknown. In industrialized countries it is the most common cause of Addison's disease. The adrenal medulla is spared. Patients with autoimmune adrenalitis often have other autoimmune conditions, esp. thyroiditis, vitiligo, and pernicious anemia.

autoimmune disease A disease produced when the body's normal tolerance of the antigens on its own cells (autoantigens [AAg] or self-antigens) is disrupted. Current theories are that the loss of self-tolerance is the result of damage to AAgs by microorganisms, a strong similarity in appearance between the AAg and a foreign antigen, or a foreign antigen linking with an AAg. Autoantibodies (AAbs) produced either by B lymphocytes or self-reacting T lymphocytes attack normal cells whose surface contains an autoantigen destroying the tissue. Both inherited risk factors and environmental factors are considered significant in the development of autoimmune disease. Researchers have found links between AAb production and the inheritance of certain histocompatibility antigens, indicating that genetic susceptibility is probably a component in autoimmune diseases. Other unknown factors within the immune system may prevent it from stopping the abnormal inflammatory process once it has begun.

Many diseases are based on AAb-AAg reactions. Systemic lupus erythematosus and rheumatoid arthritis are autoimmune diseases in which multiple tissues are affected. Some autoimmune disorders manifest themselves primarily in only one or two tissues even though they, too, are systemic. The damage to cardiac valves in rheumatic fever occurs because AAgs on the valves are similar in structure to antigens on Group A beta-hemolytic streptococci. Insulin-dependent diabetes mellitus is caused by AAb destruction of the islets of Langerhans, and multiple sclerosis is caused by AAb destruction of the myelin sheath covering nerves. Hemolytic anemia, some forms of glomerulonephritis, myasthenia gravis, chronic thyroiditis, Reiter syndrome, and Graves disease are also autoimmune diseases. SEE: *antigen; autoantibody; autoantigen; autoimmunity; histocompatability locus antigen; inflammation; molecular mimicry.*

autoimmune polyglandular syndrome Polyglandular autoimmune syndrome.

autoimmune theory of aging SEE: under *theory.*

autoimmunity (ot″ō-im-ū′nĭt-ē) [*auto-* + *immunity*] The body's tolerance of the antigens present on its own cells, i.e., autoantigens or self-antigens. It is theorized that autoreactive T lymphocytes are destroyed in the thymus by negative selection or in peripheral blood. Autoreactive T cells that escape destruction in the thymus may become tolerant because they are exposed to thousands of autoantigens as they circulate in the blood.

The loss of self-tolerance is believed to be due to many hereditary and environmental factors and occurs when autoantigens are damaged, when they link with a foreign antigen, when the structure of a autoantigen is very similar to that of a foreign antigen (molecular mimicry), or when autoreactive T cells are not adequately controlled or are activated by nonspecific antigens. The changes in the appearance of the autoantigen or activation of autoreactive T-cells result in autoantigens being perceived as foreign. Inflammation and destruction of the tissues bearing the antigen occur because of the production of autoantibodies by B cells or the cytotoxicity of autoreactive T cells, which attack the autoantigens. SYN: *autoreactivity.* SEE: *antigen; autoantibody.*

autoinduction (ot″ō-in-dŭk′shŏn) [*auto-* + *induction*] Self-regulation of a biochemical, enzymatic, genetic, metabolic, or pharmacological process.

autoinfusion (ot″ō-in-fū′zhŏn) [*auto-* + *infusion*] Returning blood or body fluids from blood vessels, cavities, or surgical fields to the patient.

autoinjector (ot″ō-in-jek′tŏr) [*auto-* + *injector*] A syringe that contains a spring-loaded needle with a preloaded dose of medication. When forced against the body with a stabbing motion, the device activates and administers a calculated dose of medication. Autoinjectors are commonly used for self-administration of epinephrine (to mitigate anaphylaxis); by migraine sufferers (to achieve prompt relief of headache); or by military and emergency services workers to combat the effects of nerve agents.

autoinoculation (ot″ō-in-ok″yŭ-lā′shŏn) [*auto-* + *inoculation*] Inoculation with organisms obtained from one's own body.

autointoxication (ot″ō-in-tok″sĭ-kā′shŏn) [*auto-* + *intoxication*] Endogenous toxicosis.

autoisolysin (ot″ō-ī-sol′ĭ-sĭn, -ī″sō-lī′) [*auto-* + *iso-* + *lysin*] An antibody that causes dissolution of cells of the individual from which it was obtained and of other individuals of the same species.

autokeratoplasty (ot″tō-ker′ă-tō-plas″tē) [*auto-* + *keratoplasty*] Grafting of corneal tissue taken from the patient's other eye.

autokinesis (ot″ō-kĭ-nē′sĭs) [*auto-* + *kinesis*] Voluntary movement. SYN: *autocinesia*. **autokinetic** (-net′ik), *adj*.

visual a. The illusion that an object in space, esp. at night, moves as one continues to look at it. Thus, an aviator looking at a distant light may perceive that the light has moved even though it is stationary.

autolesion (ot″ō-lē′zhŏn) [*auto-* + *lesion*] A self-inflicted injury.

autologous (o-tol′ŏ-gŭs) [*auto-* + *(homo)logous*] Originating within an individual, esp. a factor present in tissues or fluids.

autologous chondrocyte implantation SEE: under *implantation*.

autologous chondrocyte transplantation Autologous chondrocyte implantation.

autologous endometrial coculture (kō′kŭl″chŭr) An assisted reproduction technique in which a zygote created by in vitro fertilization is incubated in endometrial tissue harvested from an infertile woman's uterus through the pre-embryonic period before transfer.

autolysate (o-tol′ĭ-sāt″, ot″ŏ-lī′sāt″) [*auto-″* + *lysate*] A specific product of autolysis.

autolysis (o-tol′ĭ-sĭs) [*auto-* + *lysis*] **1.** The self-dissolution or self-digestion that occurs in tissues or cells by enzymes in the cells themselves, as occurs after death and in some pathological conditions. **2.** Hemolysis. **autolytic** (ot″ŏ-lit′ik), *adj*.

autolysosome (ot″ŏ-lī′sŏ-sōm″) [*auto-* + *lysosome*] Any of the lysosomes that enable digestion of injured portions of the cell in which they are located.

automated decision support system 1. Software used in clinical medicine to suggest diagnoses and treatments based on the clinical data and algorithms for their interpretation. **2.** Any computer system that supports human decision-making.

automated dispensing cabinet ABBR: ADC. A cabinet or drug storage device or that electronically dispenses medications in a controlled fashion and tracks their use, replacing or supporting the traditional unit-dose drug delivery system.

automatic (ot″ŏ-mat′ik) [Gr. *automatos,* self-acting] Spontaneous; involuntary. **automatically** (-mat′i-k(ă-)lē), *adv*.

automatic drug dispenser A computer-driven medication cabinet that monitors orders for prescription drugs and releases the drugs one at a time. It is used to prevent medication errors such

as double dosing. SYN: *automatic medication dispensing system*.

automatic exposure control ABBR: AEC. In radiology, an ionization chamber or solid-state device that terminates the radiation exposure at a preset level. It is used to optimize radiographic technique and maximize patient safety. SYN: *phototimer*.

automaticity (ot″tŏ-mă-tis′it-ē) **1.** The unique property of cardiac muscle tissue to contract without nervous stimulation. **2.** The ability to perform a task without conscious attention. **3.** The habitual response or behavior associated with a given stimulus. SEE: *habit*.

automatic medication dispensing system Automatic drug dispenser.

automatic movement reaction Automatic reaction.

automatic obedience In catatonia, an exaggerated attempt to cooperate with a request or a command made by another person.

automatic reaction A category of reflexes that includes righting and equilibrium reactions. SYN: *automatic movement reaction*.

automatic tube compensation SEE: under *compensation*.

automation (ot″ŏ-mā′shŏn) An automatically controlled operation of an apparatus or system by mechanical or electronic devices that take the place of human elements of observation, effort, and decision making.

laboratory a. The use of clinical laboratory instruments that assay large numbers of samples with minimal human intervention.

automatism (o-tom′ă-tizm) [Gr. *automatismos,* a happening by itself] **1.** An automatic action or behavior without conscious volition or knowledge. **2.** A tic (stereotyped movement disorder) such as lip smacking, chewing, or gesturing that is not controlled consciously.

automotive restraint SEE: under *restraint*.

autonomic (ot″ŏ-nom′ik) [*autonom(y)* + *-ic*] **1.** Self-controlling; functioning independently. **2.** Pert. to the autonomic nervous system. **autonomically** (-nom′i-k(ă-)lē), *adv*.

autonomic dysreflexia (aw″tō-nŏm′ĭk dĭs-rē-flēk′sē-ă) The state in which a person with a spinal cord injury at T7 or above experiences a life-threatening uninhibited sympathetic response of the nervous system to a noxious stimulus. SEE: *Nursing Diagnoses Appendix*.

autonomic dysreflexia, risk for A lifelong threatening uninhibited response of the sympathetic nervous system for an individual with a spinal cord injury or lesion at T8 or above who has recovered from spinal shock. SEE: *Nursing Diagnoses Appendix*.

autonomic hyperreflexia SEE: under *hyperreflexia.*

autonomic nervous system ABBR: ANS. The parts of the nervous system that control unconscious, involuntary, and visceral body functions. The autonomic nervous system reflexively balances the body's smooth muscle tone, blood pressure, temperature, fluid composition, state of digestion, metabolic activity, and sexual activation. In the central nervous system (CNS), the activities of the autonomic nervous system (ANS) are coordinated in the brainstem (especially in the nucleus of the tractus solitarius) and in the hypothalamus. In the peripheral nervous system (PNS), the ANS comprises the visceral motor axons, the visceral sensory axons, and the enteric nervous system (a neural net within the walls of the gastrointestinal tract). Compared to peripheral somatic axons, the peripheral autonomic axons tend to be small (less than 3 μm in diameter), slowly conducting, and sparsely myelinated. The autonomic motor circuits also differ from somatic motor pathways. Peripheral somatic motor pathways, i.e., the circuitry sending signals to skeletal muscles, are only one axon long; axons of somatic motor neurons in the spinal cord and brainstem synapse directly on the effector cell, a muscle cell. In contrast, peripheral autonomic motor pathways are two axons long. First, an axon (a preganglionic axon) of a visceral motor neuron in the spinal cord or brainstem synapses on a neuron in a peripheral ganglion. Second, the axon (a postganglionic axon) of the ganglion neuron synapses on the effector cell, a smooth muscle cell, a cardiac muscle cell, or a secretory cell.

This autonomic motor circuitry is further subdivided into two parallel subsystems; the sympathetic and the parasympathetic. The subsystems differ in two major ways:

1. In the sympathetic system, the central (preganglionic) neurons are located only in the thoracic and lumbar segments of the spinal cord; in the parasympathetic system, the central neurons are located only in the brainstem and in a short segment of the caudal end of the spinal cord.

2. In the sympathetic system, norepinephrine is the characteristic neurotransmitter of the postganglionic axons; in the parasympathetic system, acetylcholine is the characteristic neurotransmitter of the postganglionic axons.

In both the sympathetic and parasympathetic systems, the characteristic neurotransmitter of the preganglionic axons is acetylcholine. Besides their characteristic neurotransmitters, autonomic nerves influence surrounding tissues through the release of other active chemicals including ATP, nitric oxide, and a range of peptides, e.g., substance P and vasoactive intestinal peptide. As a result of their different final transmitters, the effects of the two subsystems differ. Sympathetic stimulation readies an animal for interaction with the outside world and prepares the animal for "fight or flight"; e.g., activation of sympathetic axons increases heart rate and decreases gastrointestinal peristalsis. On the other hand, parasympathetic stimulation relaxes and quiets an animal; e.g., activation of parasympathetic axons decreases heart rate and increases gastrointestinal peristalsis. The accompanying table compares the effects of sympathetic and parasympathetic stimulation on specific tissues. SEE: *parasympathetic nervous system; sympathetic nervous system;* illus.; table.

PATHOLOGY: The ANS is distributed throughout the body, and autonomic dysfunction can produce a wide range of symptoms, such as bladder malfunction, blood pressure abnormalities, breathing difficulty, gastrointestinal motility problems, heart arrhythmias, impotence, nasal congestion, sweating disorders, syncope, and visual symptoms. Drugs that act on or mimic autonomic neurotransmitters are commonly used to alleviate these symptoms as well as other conditions, such as glaucoma, heart failure, shock, and thyroid storm. To assess the overall functioning of the ANS, physicians often begin with simple measurements of the reflexive responses of the cardiovascular system; specifically, they measure the changes of blood pressure and heart rate as a person stands from sitting and exercises.

autonomous (o-ton'ŏ-mŭs) Independent of external influences. **autonomously** (-lē), *adv.*

autonomy (o-ton'ŏ-mē) [*autonomia,* independence] Independent functioning.

AutoPap A computerized method of screening and analyzing Pap smears for abnormal cells.

auto-PEEP The inadvertent application of positive end-expiratory pressure (PEEP) to the lungs of a patient receiving mechanical ventilation. It occurs most often in patients with obstructive lung disease whose mechanical ventilator is set at an insufficient expiratory time.

ETIOLOGY: Auto-PEEP is caused by air trapping during mechanical ventilation.

PATIENT CARE: It may cause the patient to "fight" the ventilator, breathing at the wrong time in the respiratory cycle. It is treated by reducing tidal volume and increasing the expiratory time during ventilation.

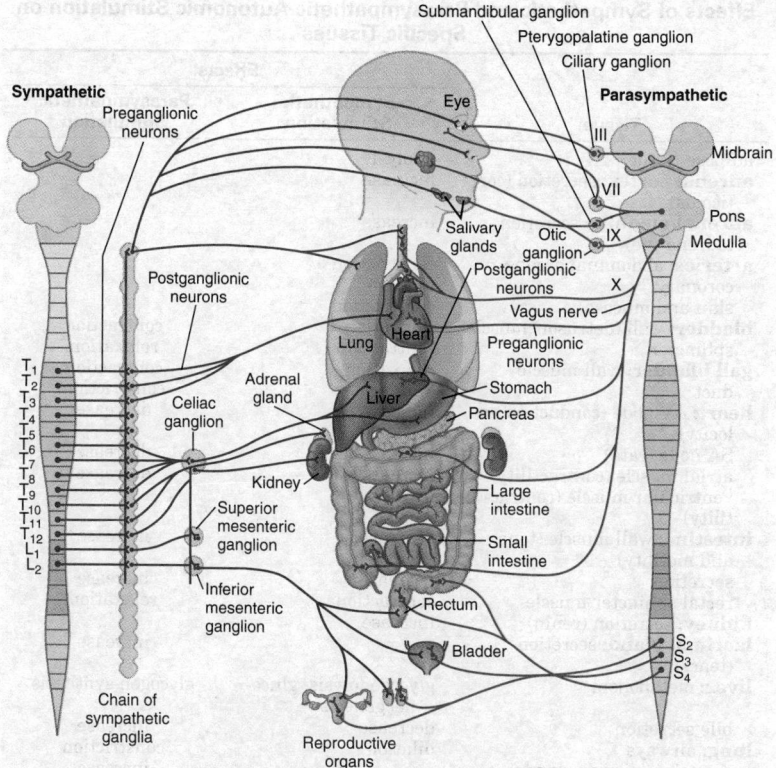

AUTONOMIC NERVOUS SYSTEM

autophagia, autophagy (ot″ŏ-fā′j(ē-)ă, o-tof′ă-jē) [*auto-* + *-phagy*] **1.** Biting oneself. **2.** Self-consumption by a cell. **autophagic** (ot″ŏ-fā′jik), *adj.*

autophagocytosis (ot″ŏ-fag″ŏ-sĭ-tō′sĭs, -sī-) [*auto-* + *phagocytosis*] In a cell, the digestion of portions of cell organelles or mitochondria injured or atrophied. This digestive process is essential to the survival of the cell. SEE: *endocytosis; phagocytosis; pinocytosis.*

autophil (ot′ŏ-fil″) [*auto-* + *-phil*] A person who has a sensitive autonomic nervous system.

autophilia (ot″ŏ-fil′ē-ă) [*auto-* + *-philia*] Narcissism; self-love.

autophobia (ot″ŏ-fō′bē-ă) [*auto-* + *-phobia*] **1.** A neurotic fear of being alone. **2.** Abnormal fear of being egotistical.

autophony (o-tof′ŏ-nē) [*auto-* + Gr. *phōnē*, sound, voice] The vibration and echolike reproduction of one's own voice, breath sounds, and murmurs; usually due to diseases of the middle ear and auditory tube.

autoplasty (ot′ŏ-plas″tē) [*auto-* + *-plasty*] Plastic surgery using grafts from the patient's body. **autoplastic** (-plas′tik), *adj.*

autopolyploidy (ot″ŏ-pol′ē-ployd″ē) [*auto-* + *polyploidy*] The condition of having more than two complete sets of chromosomes. **autopolyploid**, *adj.*

autoprecipitin (ot″ŏ-pri-sip′ĭt-ĭn) [*auto-* + *precipitin*] Precipitin active against the serum of the animal in which it was formed.

autopsy (o′top-sē) [Gr. *autopsia*, seeing with one's own eyes] Postmortem examination of the organs and tissues of a body to determine the cause of death or pathological conditions. SYN: *necropsy; necroscopy.*

psychological a. An attempt to determine what, if any, emotional or psychological factors caused or contributed to an individual's suicide.

virtual a. A determination of the factors that contributed to or caused the death of a person, employing imaging devices, e.g., CT scans, MRI, or ultrasonography instead of surgical dissection of the corpse.

autopsychic (ot″ŏ-sī′kik) [*auto-* + *psychic*] Aware of one's own personality.

Effects of Sympathetic and Parasympathetic Autonomic Stimulation on Specific Tissues

Tissue:	Sympathetic Stimulation	Parasympathetic Stimulation
adipose tissue	lipolysis	
adrenal cortex: secretion (corticoids)	increase	
adrenal medulla: secretion (adrenaline)	increase	
arteries: abdominal organs	constriction	
coronary	dilation	
skin and mucosa	constriction	
bladder: wall (detrusor) muscle	relaxation	contraction
sphincter	contraction	relaxation
gall bladder: wall muscle	relaxation	contraction
duct	dilation	constriction
heart: AV node (conduction velocity)	increase	decrease
SA node (rate)	increase	decrease
atrial muscle (contractility)	increase	decrease
ventricular muscle (contractility)	increase	
intestine: wall muscle (tone and motility)	decrease	increase
secretion	decrease	increase
rectal sphincter muscle	contraction	relaxation
kidney: secretion (renin)	increase	
lacrimal gland: secretion (tears)		increase
liver: metabolism	glycogenolysis, gluconeogenesis	glycogen synthesis
bile secretion	decrease	increase
lung: airways	dilation	constriction
secretion (airway glands)		increase
nasopharynx: secretion (mucosal glands)		increase
pancreas: secretion (enzymes and insulin)	decrease	increase
secretion (glucagon)	increase	
pineal gland: melatonin synthesis	stimulation	
pupil	dilation	constriction
reproductive tract: muscles	contractions	
blood vessels	constriction	dilation, erection
salivary gland: secretion	decrease	increase
skeletal muscle	increase contractility, glycogenolysis	
skin: pilomotor muscle	contraction	
secretion (sweat)	increase	
spleen: capsule	contraction	
stomach: wall muscle (tone and motility)	decrease	increase
secretion	decrease	increase
uterus: pregnant	contraction	
nonpregnant	relaxation	

autopsychosis (ot″ō-sī-kō′sĭs) [*auto-* + *psychosis*] A mental illness in which patients have disordered ideas about themselves.

autoradiogram (ot″ō-rād′ē-ŏ-gram″) Autoradiograph.

autoradiograph (ot″ō-rād′ē-ŏ-graf″) A radiograph formed by radioactive materials present in a tissue or an individual. An image is made by injecting radiochemicals into the target of interest and then exposing x-ray film or an image receptor to that target. SYN: *autoradiogram; radioautograph.*

autoradiography (ot″ō-rād″ē-og′ră-fē) [*auto-* + *radiography*] The use of autoradiographs in investigating disease. **autoradiographic** (ē-ŏ-graf'ĭk), *adj.*

autoreactive (ot″ō-rē-ak'tĭv) [*auto- reactive*] Exhibiting an immune response against the body's own antigens.

autoreactivity (ot″ō-rē″ak-tĭv'ĭt-ē) [*auto- + reactivity*] Autoimmunity.

autoreceptor (ot″ō-ri-sep'tŏr) [*auto- + receptor*] A cellular receptor that influences how the cell manufactures and releases the same neurotransmitter that stimulated the receptor.

autoregulation (ot″ō-reg″yŭ-lā'shŏn) [*auto- regulation*] Control of an event such as blood flow through a tissue (e.g., muscle) by alteration of the tissue. If blood flow is insufficient, precapillary sphincters dilate; when blood flow increases, precapillary sphincters constrict. **autoregulate** (-reg″yŭ-lāte″), *v.*

autoreinfusion (ot″ō-rē″in-fū'zhŏn) [*auto- + reinfusion*] Intravenous injection of a patient's blood that has been collected from a site in which bleeding had occurred, such as the abdominal or pleural cavity. SEE: *autologous blood transfusion.*

autosensitization (ot″ō-sen″sĭt-ĭ-zā'shŏn) [*auto- + sensitization*] Sensitivity to one's own cells, fluids, or tissues. SEE: *autoimmune disease.*

autosepticemia (ot″ō-sep″tĭ-sē'mē-ă) [*auto- + septicemia*] Septicemia from resident bacterial flora or their toxins.

autoserodiagnosis (ot″ō-sir″ō-dī″ăg-nō'sĭs) [*auto- + serodiagnosis*] Diagnosis through serum from the patient's blood.

autosite (ot'ŏ-sīt″) [*auto- + Gr. sitos,* food] The relatively normal member of asymmetrically conjoined twins, the other twin being dependent on the autosite for its nutrition.

autosmia (o-toz'mē-ă) [*auto-+ osmia*] Awareness of the odor of one's own body.

autosomal dominant Pert. to or characteristic of an autosomal dominant gene. SEE: *autosomal dominant* **gene**.

autosomal recessive Pert. to or characteristic of an autosomal recessive gene. SEE: *autosomal recessive* **gene**.

autosomatognosis (ot″ō-sō″mă-tog-nō'sĭs) [*auto- + somato- + Gr. gnōsis,* knowledge] The feeling that a part of the body that has been removed is still present. SEE: *phantom limb.*

autosome (ot'ŏ-sōm″) [*auto- + soma*] Any chromosome other than the sex (X and Y) chromosomes. SEE: *chromosome.* **autosomal** (-sō'măl), *adj.*

autosplenectomy (ot″ō-spli-nek'tŏ-mē) [*auto- + splenectomy*] Multiple infarcts of the spleen that cause it to become fibrotic and nonfunctioning; seen in sickle cell anemia.

autostimulation (ot″ō-stim″yŭ-lā'shŏn) [*auto- + stimulation*] **1.** In immunology, stimulation by antigens present in the organism. **2.** Stimulation or motivation of oneself.

autosuggestibility (ot″ō-sŭg-jes″tĭ-bil'ĭt-ē) [*auto- + suggestible*] Peculiar lack of resistance to any suggestion originating in one's own mind. **autosuggestible** (-sŭg-jes'tĭ-bl), *adj.*

autosuggestion (ot″ō-sŭg-jes'chŏn) [*auto- + suggestion*] The acceptance of an idea or thought arising from within one's own mind, bringing about some physical or mental action or change. **autosuggest** (-sŭg-jest'), *v.*

autotomography (aw″tō-tō-mŏg'ră-fē) [″ + Gr. *tome,* incision, + *graphein,* to write] Radiographic tomography in which the patient rather than the x-ray tube is moved.

autotopagnosia (aw″tō-tŏp-ăg-nō'zē-ă) [″ + *topos,* place, + *a-,* not, + *gnosis,* knowledge] Inability to orient various parts of the body correctly; occurs in lesions of the thalamoparietal pathways of the cortex.

autotoxemia (aw″tō-tŏk-sē'mē-ă) Endogenous toxicosis.

autotoxin (aw″tō-tŏk'sĭn) Poison generated within the body on which it acts.

autotransfusion (aw″tō-trăns-fū'zhŭn) [″ + L. *trans,* across, + *fundere,* pour] A method of returning the patient's own extravasated blood to the circulation. Blood shed during surgery, e.g., during the repair of a ruptured spleen, is collected during the operation and returned intravenously into the circulation of the patient.

autotransplantation (aw″tō-trăns″plăn-tā'shŭn) [″ + ″ + *plantare,* to plant] Surgical transfer of tissue from one part of the body to another part.

autotrophic (aw″tō-trō'fĭk) [″ + *trophe,* nourishment] Self-nourishing; capable of growing in the absence of organic compounds; pert. to green plants and bacteria, which form protein and carbohydrate from inorganic salts and carbon dioxide.

autovaccination (aw″tō-văk″sĭ-nā'shŭn) [″ + *vacca,* cow] **1.** Vaccination with autogenous vaccine or autovaccine. **2.** A vaccination resulting from virus or bacteria from a sore of a previous vaccination, as may occur when a smallpox vaccination sore is scratched and the virus is subsequently transferred to a break in the skin elsewhere.

autovaccine (aw″tō-văk'sēn) Vaccine prepared from a virus in the patient's own body.

autumn crocus (o'tŭm) [L. *autumnus,* season of abundance, autumn] A perennial lily (*Colchicum autumnale*), that produces colchicine.

auxiliary (ăwg-zĭl'ē-ār-ē) [L. *auxiliarius,* help] **1.** Providing additional aid. **2.** A person who aids.

dental a. A person who assists in the care and treatment of dental patients.

Responsibilities vary according to the needs of the dentist, training and capabilities of the individual, and state regulations. Common dental auxiliaries include receptionist, dental assistant, dental hygienist, and dental lab technician.

auxin (awk′sĭn) [Gr. *auxe*, increase] A substance that promotes growth in plant cells and tissues.

auxology (og″zol′ŏ-jē, ok″sol′) [Gr. *auxanein, auxein*, to grow + *-logy*] The study of growth (the increase in height, weight, and head circumference, in childhood and adolescence).

auxotroph (awk′sō-trōf) [″ + *trophe*, nutrition] An auxotrophic organism.

auxotrophic (awk-sō-trō′fĭk) Requiring a growth factor that is different from that required by the parent organism.

A-V, AV *arteriovenous; atrioventricular.*

A-V access *Arteriovenous access.*

availability (ă-vāl″ă-bĭl′ĭ-tē) In nutrition, the extent to which a nutrient is present in a form that can be absorbed and used by the body.

availability heuristic A nonsystematic form of reasoning based on how easily a solution to a problem is encountered in thought rather than in logic or careful analysis.

avalvular (ă-văl′vū-lăr) Without valves.

avascular (ă-văs′kū-lăr) [Gr. *a-*, not, + L. *vasculum*, little vessel] Lacking in blood vessels or having a poor blood supply, said of tissues such as cartilage.

avascularization (ă-văs″kū-lăr-ĭ-zā′shŭn) **1.** Deprivation of blood to tissues by interference with its arterial supply. **2.** Expulsion of blood from tissues, esp. the extremities, as in the use of Esmarch's bandage.

A-V block *Atrioventricular block.*

Avellis paralysis syndrome (ă-věl′ēz) [Georg Avellis, Ger. laryngologist, 1864–1916] Paralysis of half of the soft palate, pharynx, and larynx and loss of pain, heat, and cold sensations on the opposite side.

average Arithmetic mean.

aversion (ă-věr′zhŏn, shŏn) [L. *aversio*, a turning away from] A strong feeling of dislike or repugnance.

aversion therapy A form of behavior therapy designed to reduce or extinguish unwanted or hazardous behaviors. The goal of aversion therapy is to have the patient associate the undesirable behavior with something noxious, such as a foul taste, a headache, a hot flash, nausea or vomiting, or profuse sweating. In chemical aversion therapy, for example, a patient may be treated with a drug that makes the consumption of another substance, such as alcohol, extremely unpleasant. The use of chemical aversion therapy is controversial because in some cases it produces side effects that may themselves be in-

jurious or life-threatening. Aversion therapy also has been used to treat other forms of drug dependence, eating disorders, paraphilias, self-mutilation, and tobacco abuse. SEE: *disulfiram.*

avian (ā′vē-ăn) Concerning birds.

aviation physiology SEE: under *physiology.*

avidin (ăv′ĭ-dĭn) [L. *avidus*, greedy] A protein in egg whites that binds biotin and inhibits its absorption. Avidin is destroyed by cooking. SEE: *biotin.*

avidity (ăv-ĭd′ĭ-tē) **1.** Eagerness; a strong attraction for something. **2.** The net or relative affinity of antibodies to bind with their receptors, antigens, or ligands.

avirulent (ă-vĭr′ū-lĕnt) [Gr. *a-* not, + L. *virus*, poison] Without virulence.

avitaminosis (ā-vī″tă-mĭ-nō′sĭs) [″ + *vitamin* + *osis*, condition] Disease caused by vitamin deficiency. SEE: *vitamin.* **avitaminotic** (-mĭ-nŏt′ĭk), *adj.*

avivement (ă-vēv-mŏn′) [Fr.] Surgical trimming of wound edges before suturing them.

Avogadro, Amedeo (ov″ŏ-god′rō) Italian physicist and chemist, 1776–1856.

A. law Equal volumes of gases at the same pressure and temperature contain equal numbers of molecules.

A. number The number of molecules, 6.0221367×10^{23}, in one gram molecular weight of a compound.

avoidable (ă-voyd′ă-bĕl) Preventable.

avoidable decline A preventable decrease in the functional abilities of a person, e.g., a resident of a care facility.

avoidance (ă-voyd′ăns) The conscious or unconscious effort to escape from situations or events perceived by the individual to be threatening to personal comfort, safety, or well-being.

avoirdupois measure (av″ĕr-dĕ-poyz′, -pwa′) [Fr. *avoir du pois*, to have (some) weight] A system of weighing or measuring articles in which 7000 grains equal 1 lb. SEE: *Weights and Measures Appendix.*

AVPU An acronym used by health care providers to standardize the way of describing a patient's mental status. It stands for **a**lert (oriented to person, place and day); responds to **v**erbal stimuli (appropriate or inappropriate); responds to **p**ainful stimuli (localizes, withdraws or demonstrates decorticate or decerebrate neurological posturing); or totally **u**nresponsive.

avulse (ă-vŭls′) [L. *avulsus*, torn away] Of a muscle or tendon, to tear away or separate, usually by accident.

avulsion (ă-vŭl′shŭn) [Gr. *a-*, not, + L. *vellere*, to pull] **1.** A tearing away forcibly of a part or structure. If surgical repair is necessary, a sterile dressing may be applied while surgery is awaited. Avulsed fingers, toes, limbs or other separated tissue should be recovered if possible. **2.** The complete separation of a tooth from its alveolus, which under appropriate conditions may be reimplanted. The term usually refers to dental injuries resulting from acute trauma. SYN: *evulsion*. SEE: illus.

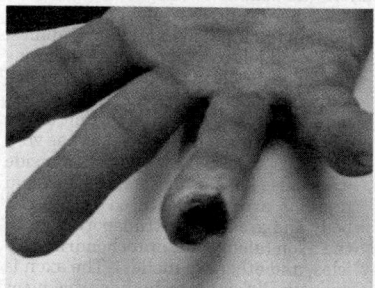

AVULSED FINGERTIP

award (ă-ward′) **1.** An amount of money paid to the party prevailing in a lawsuit. **2.** A formal public recognition of excellence.

awareness (ă-war′nĕs) In psychology or neurology, the conscious perception of one's environment or of oneself.

   cost a. In the economics of medical care, knowledge and consideration of the comparative costs of preventive actions versus the treatment of avoidable illness and disability.

   fertility a. The identification of the days in a woman's menstrual cycle during ovulation when her potential for conception is highest. SYN: *natural family planning*. SEE: *basal temperature chart; cervical mucus; mittelschmerz*.

   intraoperative a. A complication of anesthesia in which insufficient anesthetic is administered and the patient feels pain or has other unpleasant perceptions of events that occur in the operating room. SYN: *a. with recall*.

AWHONN *Association of Women's Health, Obstetric, and Neonatal Nurses.* Formerly Nurses' Association of the American College of Obstetrics and Gynecology (NAACOG).

axanthopsia (ăk″săn-thŏp′sē-ă) [″ + *xanthos,* yellow, + *opsis,* vision] Yellow blindness.

Axenfeld-Rieger syndrome (ăk′sĕn-fĕld-rē′gĕr) [Karl Theodor Paul Polykarpus Axenfeld, German ophthalmologist, 1867–1930; Herwigh Rieger, Austrian ophthalmologist, 1898–1986] ABBR: A-R syndrome. A congenital disorder of the anterior chamber of the eye with anomalous development of the iris. The ocular manifestations are always present in both eyes. Glaucoma develops in nearly half of all patients. Patients with A-R syndrome may also have developmental anomalies in other or-

gans, including the skin, heart, facial bones, teeth, and pituitary gland.

axenic (ă-zĕn′ĭk) [″ + *xenos,* stranger] Germ free, as pert. to animals, or pure, as pert. to cultures or microorganisms; sterile.

axial (ăk′sē-ăl) [L. *axis,* axle] Situated in or pert. to an axis.

axilemma (ăk″sĭ-lĕm′ă) [″ + Gr. *lemma,* husk] Axolemma.

axilla (ak-sil′ă) *pl.* **axillae** [L. *axilla,* armpit] Armpit.

axilla conformer A splint designed to prevent adduction contractures after severe burns to the axillary region.

axillary (ăk′sĭ-lār-ē) Pert. to the axilla.

axillary node dissection The surgical removal of lymph nodes that drain a breast affected by breast cancer to debulk the tumor or to evaluate the nodes for evidence that the tumor has spread.

axio- (ăk′sē-ō) [L. *axis,* axle] Combining form meaning *relating to an axis;* in dentistry, the long axis of the tooth.

axiobuccal (ăk″sē-ō-bŭk′kăl) [L. *axis,* axle, + *bucca,* cheek] Concerning the angle formed by the long axis of the tooth and the buccal walls of a cavity of the tooth.

axioincisal (ăk″sē-ō-ĭn-sī′zăl) [″ + *incisor,* a cutter] Concerning the angle formed by the long axis of the tooth and the incisal walls of a cavity in the tooth.

axiolabial (ăk″sē-ō-lā′bē-ăl) [″ + *labialis,* pert. to the lips] Concerning the angle formed by the long axis of the tooth with the labial walls of a cavity in the tooth.

axiolingual (ăk″sē-ō-lĭng′gwăl) [″ + *lingua,* tongue] Concerning the angle formed by the long axis of the tooth and the lingual walls of a cavity in the tooth.

axiomesial (ăk″sē-ō-mē′zē-ăl) [″ + Gr. *mesos,* middle] Concerning the angle formed by the long axis of a tooth and the mesial walls of a cavity in the tooth.

axio-occlusal, axioocclusal (ăk″sē-ō-ŏk-klū′zăl) [″ + *occlusio,* closure] Concerning the angle formed by the long axis of the tooth and the occlusal walls of a cavity in the tooth.

axioplasm (ăk′sē-ō-plăzm) [″ + LL. *plasma,* form, mold] The cytoplasm of an axon.

axiopulpal (ăk″sē-ō-pŭl′păl) [″ + *pulpa,* pulp] Concerning the angle formed by the long axis of a tooth and the pulpal walls of a cavity in the tooth.

axis (ak′sĭs) [L. *axis,* axle, axis] **1.** A real or imaginary line that runs through the center of a body or about which a part revolves. **2.** The second cervical vertebra (epistropheus). It bears the odontoid process (dens), about which the atlas rotates. SYN: *odontoid vertebra*.

   basicranial a. The axis connecting the basion and gonion.

   basifacial a. The axis from the subnasal point to the gonion.

cardiac a. A graphic representation of the main conduction vector of the heart, determined through measurements of direction and amplitude of the complexes in several leads on a 12-lead electrocardiogram. Normal axis is zero to +90°.

cerebrospinal a. The central nervous system.

condylar a. A projected line connecting the condyles of the mandible. Movement of the mandible is rotation around this imaginary line. SYN: *hinge a.; mandibular a.; transverse mandibular a.*

coronal a. Frontal **a.**

enteroinsular a. The hormones and neurotransmitters from the gastrointestinal tract that regulate the secretion of hormones by the pancreas (esp. insulin).

hinge a. Condylar **a.**

mandibular a. Condylar **a.**

neural a. Central nervous system.

optic a. A line that connects the anterior and posterior poles of the eye.

phlebostatic a. An anatomic reference point on the surface of the body, used to approximate the position of the right atrium and pulmonary artery in critical care.

PATIENT CARE: The line is identified by drawing two lines on the supine body: one, in the right mid-axillary position, descending from head to foot; and the other, from the anterior to the posterior of the chest, at the level of the fourth intercostal space. The intersection of the these two lines constitutes the axis. It is used in critical care to provide a reproducible location for the zeroing and leveling of hemodynamic monitoring systems such as pulmonary artery catheters.

principal a. In optics, a line that passes through the optical center or nodal point of a lens perpendicular to the surface of the lens.

sagittal a. Imaginary line running anterior-posterior, about which frontal plane motion occurs.

transverse mandibular a. Condylar **a.**

visual a. The line of vision from the object seen through the pupil's center to the macula lutea.

axis cylinder Axon (2).

axo-, ax-, axi- [Gr. *axōn*, L. *axis* axle, axis] Prefixes meaning *axis* or *axon.*

axoid (ak'soyd") [*axis* (2) + *-oid*] Pert. to the axis (2).

axolemma (ăk"sō-lĕm'ă) [" + *lemma*, husk] The cell membrane of an axon. SYN: *axilemma.*

axolotl (ak'sŏ-lot"ĕl) [Nahuatl *āxōlōtl*] A Mexican salamander, *Ambystoma mexicanum,* studied in experimental medicine because of its ability to regenerate severed nerves.

axolysis (ăk-sŏl'ĭ-sĭs) [" + *lysis*, disso-

lution] Destruction of the axis cylinder of a nerve.

axometer (ăk-sŏm'ĕ-tĕr) [" + *metron,* measure] Measuring device for adjusting eyeglasses so that the lenses are suitable for the optic axes of the eyes.

axon (ăk'sŏn, -sōn) [Gr. *axon,* axis] The nontapering process of a neuron that contains neurofilaments, microtubules, and organelles.. Axons make neurons the longest cells in the body; in humans, a microscopically thin axon can be >2 ft long. Axons arise from a portion of the cell body, the axon hillock, that has very few ribosomes, and the cytoplasm inside axons also has no ribosomes. All axonal proteins are manufactured in the cell body and are actively transported down the axon (along with mitochondria, vesicles, and other organelles). The axon is structurally similar whether growing or stationary; however, when an axon is elongating, its end becomes a specialized motile organelle, the growth cone. When the axon stops at a target cell, its end turns into a secretory organelle, the presynaptic terminal.

Axons carry electrochemical impulses and are the "wires" of the nervous system. Inside the central nervous system, axons follow stereotypically-located paths called tracts; in the peripheral nervous system, axons run inside stereotypically-located nerves. Most axons conduct impulses anterogradely, i.e., away from their neuronal cell body. The notable exception is the dorsal root ganglion cell. This neuron has an axon that branches, and, while one branch carries impulses anterogradely, the other branch carries impulses toward the cell body and acts like a dendrite. SYN: *nerve fiber.* SEE: *nerve.* **axonal** (ăk'sŏn-ăl), *adj.*

axonal transport SEE: under *transport.*

axoneme (ăk'sōn-nēm) [" + *nema,* a thread] The core filament of a cilium or a flagellum.

axonometer (ăk-sō-nŏm'ĕ-tĕr) [" + *metron,* measure] Device for determining the axis of astigmatism.

axonotmesis (ăk"sŏn-ŏt-mē'sĭs) [" + *tmesis,* incision] Nerve injury that damages the nerve tissue without actually severing the nerve.

axoplasm (ak'sŏ-plazm) [*axo-* + *plasm*] The cytoplasm (neuroplasm) of an axon that encloses the neurofibrils. **axoplasmic** (ak"sŏ-plaz'mik), *adj.*

ayahuasca (a"yä-wos'kă) [Sp. *ayahuasca* fr Quechua *aya,* spirit + *huasca, waska,* vine] Any of several psychotropic brews consumed by indigenous peoples of South America in shamanistic ceremonies. The drinks are teas made from a variety of plants rich in harmaline alkaloids and other hallucinogens.

Ayurveda (ī"yŭr-vād'ă, -ved') [Sanskrit

ayus, life, lifespan + *veda,* knowledge, science] An ancient Indian medical system, promoted as a means of restoring balance and health by harmonizing mind and body. Ayurveda uses herbal remedies, massage therapy, yoga, and pulse diagnosis. It bases its beliefs on five elements (fire, air, earth, water, and sky), which combine to influence a classification of body types that must be harmonized with nature to maintain well-being. SYN: *Ayurvedic medicine; vedic medicine.* **Ayurvedic** (-văd', -ved'), *adj.*

azalide A derivative of the macrolide antibiotics, modified by the addition of nitrogen to the macrolide ("large ring") structure. An example is azithromycin.

azithromycin (ā-zīth'rō-mī-sīn) A macrolide antibiotic related to erythromycin. It is used primarily to treat infections caused by respiratory pathogens, such as *Haemophilus influenzae, Moraxella catarrhalis, Streptococcus pneumoniae,* and *Legionella pneumophila,* and urethritis caused by gonococci and chlamydia.

azo-, az- [Gr. *azōtos,* lifeless] Prefix indicating the presence of —N:N— group in a chemical structure. This group is usually connected at both ends to carbon atoms. SEE: *azo compounds.*

azo compounds (a'zō") SEE: under *compound.*

azoospermia (ă-zō-ō-spĕr'mē-ă) [" + *zoon,* animal, + *sperma,* seed] Absence of spermatozoa in the semen.

Azorean disease (ā-zor'ē-ăn) A form of hereditary ataxia present in Portuguese families whose ancestors lived in the Azores. It is a degenerative disease of the nervous system. Symptoms vary but may include gait ataxia, limitation of eye movements, widespread muscle fasciculations, mild cerebellar tremor, loss of reflexes in lower limbs, and extensor plantar reflex response.

azotemia (ăz"ō-tē'mē-ă) [" + " + *haima,* blood] Presence of increased amounts of nitrogenous waste products, esp. urea, in the blood. SEE: *uremia.*

Azotobacter (ă-zō"tō-băk'tĕr) A genus of gram-negative, aerobic bacilli that fixes atmospheric nitrogen in soil and water.

azoturia (ăz"ō-tū'rē-ă) [" + " + *ouron,* urine] An increase in nitrogenous compounds, esp. urea, in urine.

AZT *Azidothymidine,* the former name for zidovudine.

azure lunulae (ăz'ŭr loo'nū-lē) [O.Fr. *azur,* blue, + L. *lunula,* little moon] Blue discoloration of the base, or lunulae, of the fingernails. It may be seen in patients with hepatolenticular degeneration (Wilson's disease). Blue discoloration of the entire nail may be present in argyria and following therapy with quinacrine hydrochloride.

azurophil(e) (ăz-ū'rō-fĭl) [" + Gr. *philein,* to love] Staining readily with azure dye. **azurophilic** (ăz-ū'rō-fĭl'ĭk), *adj.*

azurophilia (ăz"ū-rō-fĭl'ē-ă) Condition in which some blood cells have azurophil granules.

azygography (ăz"ĭ-gŏg'ră-fē) [Gr. *a-,* not, + *zygon,* yoke, + *graphein,* to write] Radiography of the azygos veins by the use of an intravenous contrast medium.

azygos (ā-zī'gŏs) [" + *zygon,* yoke] **1.** Occurring singly, not in pairs. **2.** An unpaired anatomical part. **azygos, azygous** (ā-zī'gŏs), *adj.*

azygos vein SEE: under *vein.*

azymia (ă-zī'mē-ă) [" + *zyme,* ferment] Condition of absence of an enzyme.

β (bā′tă) Beta, second letter of the Greek alphabet. SEE: *beta*.

B **1.** Symbol for the element boron. **2.** *Bacillus; Balantidium; barometric; base; bath; behavior; buccal.*

BA *basophil,* (clinical laboratory).

Ba Symbol for the element barium.

BAAM *Beck airway airflow monitor.*

babble (bab′ĕl) **1.** The meaningless sounds made by an infant before he or she is able to generate mature speech. **2.** Any incomprehensible vocalization.

   multitalker b. Background noise made by several speakers talking at the same time. It competes with and may mask or disguise sounds or voices that a person, esp. one with hearing loss, wishes to hear.

Babesia (bă-bē′zē-ă) [Victor Babès] Genus of protozoa of the family Babesiidae that causes babesiosis, a febrile illness that causes symptoms similar to those found in influenza, accompanied by hemolytic anemia. *Babesia microti* is the principal human pathogen, transmitted to humans by tick bite. Other hosts include cattle, sheep, horses, and dogs.

   B. bigemina The causative organism of Texas fever in cattle.

   B. bovis The causative organism of hemoglobinuria and jaundice (red-water fever) in cattle. It is a tick-borne protozoan parasite that infects cattle in tropical and sub tropical regions of the world and can cause huge losses of livestock.

babesiosis (bab″ĕ-sī′ŏ-sĭs, bă-bē″zē-ō′sĭs) [Victor *Babes,* Romanian bacteriologist, 1854–1926 + *-osis*] A rare, usually self-limited disease caused by an intraerythrocytic protozoan, *Babesia microti,* and perhaps other Babesia species. The disease is transmitted by deer ticks, and occurs most often in New England in the U.S. It has also been reported elsewhere. Severe forms are most likely to occur in elderly people and in people without functioning spleens. Rarely, the infection is transmitted by blood transfusion from an asymptomatic carrier. The incubation period may last from weeks to months.

   SYMPTOMS: Symptoms include fever, chills, headache, sweats, myalgia, arthralgia, and nausea and vomiting.

   DIAGNOSIS: The diagnosis is suggested when a patient with an appropriate outdoor exposure presents with typical symptoms, plus hemolytic anemia. Thick and thin blood smears and other laboratory techniques (e.g., the polymerase chain reaction) may be used for definitive confirmation.

   PREVENTION: The skin should be protected from tick exposure. Asplenic persons should avoid endemic areas. After possible exposure, removal of ticks or their nymphs may prevent infection.

   TREATMENT: Drugs used include atovaquone and quinine plus clindamycin or azithromycin, both given orally. Asplenic patients may require exchange transfusion.

Babinski, Joseph-François-Felix (bă-bin′skē) Fr. neurologist, 1857–1932.

   B. reflex Dorsiflexion of the great toe when the sole of the foot is stimulated. Normally, when the lateral aspect of the sole of the relaxed foot is stroked, the great toe flexes. If the toe extends instead of flexes and the outer toes spread out, Babinski reflex is present. It is a normal reflex in infants under the age of 6 months but indicates a lesion of the pyramidal (corticospinal) tract in older people. Care must be taken to avoid interpreting voluntary extension of the toe as Babinski reflex. SYN: *Babinski sign.*

   B. sign Babinski reflex.

baby (bā′bē) Infant.

   battered b. A baby or child whose body provides evidence of physical abuse such as bruises, cuts, scars, fractures, or abdominal visceral injuries that have occurred at various times in the past. SEE: *battered child syndrome.*

   blue b. An infant born with cyanosis, which may be caused by anything that prevents proper oxygenation of the blood, esp. a congenital anomaly that permits blood to go directly from the right to the left side of the heart without going through the lungs. The most common cyanotic congenital heart defects are tetralogy of Fallot, transposition of the great vessels, and hypoplastic left heart syndrome.

   boarder b. An infant kept in a hospital nursery until status permits discharge to family care or transfer to another agency for maintenance or adoption.

   cocaine b. An infant exposed to cocaine in utero through maternal use of the drug. Cocaine crosses the placenta by simple diffusion and enters the fetal circulation. This occurs because of its high lipid solubility, low molecular weight, and low ionization at physiological pH.

   CONSEQUENCES: Cocaine is vasoconstrictive and decreases blood flow to the placenta and fetus. Cocaine abuse during pregnancy has been correlated with birth defects, intrauterine growth retardation, and perinatal death related to premature separation of the placenta (abruptio placentae), preterm labor and delivery, low birth weight, and sudden infant death syndrome.

Cocaine use by the father at the time of conception may have a negative effect on sperm quality.

PATIENT CARE: Cocaine-dependent newborns often experience a significant, agonizing withdrawal syndrome that can last 2 to 3 weeks and require continual assessment and evaluation. During the withdrawal period, patient care measures are instituted to effect the following outcomes: that the infant maintain an open airway and breathe easily, with adequate oxygen intake, independent respiratory effort, and adequate tissue perfusion; that the infant relax and sleep; that crying diminish; that the infant be able to remain asleep for 3- to 4-hr periods; that the infant recover from seizures with minimal or no sequelae; that the infant ingest and retain sufficient fluids for hydration and nutrients for growth; and that the infant's skin remain intact and free from infection.

The parents and significant others are an important part of the care plan. The mother requires considerable support because her need for and abuse of drugs result in decreased coping abilities. The newborn's withdrawal symptoms, decreased consolability, and poor interactive behavior put even more stress on the mother's ability to cope. Home health care, treatment for addiction, and education are important considerations. Health care providers explore, with the mother, options for care of herself and her infant and for future fertility management, employing a sensitive approach that communicates respect for the patient and her ability to make responsible decisions. Depending on the scope of the patient's drug abuse problem, total prevention may be unrealistic; however, the parent is referred for education and social supports to provide opportunities for detoxification and abstinence. If the infant is in the mother's care, inclusion in the support program has been shown to be beneficial to both. Because the newborn's dependence is physiological, not psychological, no predisposition to later dependence is thought to be present. The psychosocial environment in which the infant is raised, however, may predispose the baby to addiction. The infant must be referred for child welfare follow-up assessment, evaluation, and action, which may include removing the infant from the birth mother's care temporarily or permanently. SEE: *infant of substance-abusing mother.*

   collodion b. A newborn covered with a collodion-like layer of desquamated skin; may be due to ichthyosis vulgaris.

   crack b. An infant exposed to crack cocaine in utero owing to the mother's use of the drug during pregnancy. SEE: *cocaine b.*

   test-tube b. A colloquial term for a baby born to a mother whose ovum was removed, fertilized outside her body, and then implanted in her uterus. SEE: *gamete intrafallopian transfer; in vitro fertilization.*

baby boomer Any person born in the years immediately following the end of World War II (usually defined as the years 1946–1964) when birth rates in the U.S. were unusually high.

baby bottle syndrome Decay of primary teeth in older infants and toddlers due to taking a feeding bottle to bed and retaining liquid in the mouth. This creates massive caries. SYN: *bottle mouth caries; nursing-bottle syndrome.*

Baby Doe regulations Federal, state, and hospital policies insuring that handicapped infants will receive nourishment, warmth, and life-saving treatment without regard to the quality of life.

babygram A colloquial term for an entire radiologic skeletal survey of an infant, including the long bones and the bones of the cranium, face, pelvis, and thorax.

baby lung hypothesis In neonatal critical care medicine, the loss of functioning alveoli in acute lung injury or the acute respiratory distress syndrome. In both of these diseases large sections of the lungs lose their compliance, collapse, or fill with fluids, leaving only a remnant of the lung available for ventilation. Ventilatory strategies designed for fully operational, adult-sized lungs may provide too much air at too high a volume and pressure to the limited lung tissue that can be potentially recruited. This hypothesis suggests that overtaxing an infant-sized lung with adult ventilation can result in further injury to an already damaged lung.

BAC *blood alcohol concentration.*

bacciform (băk′sĭ-form) [″ + *forma,* form] Berry-shaped; coccal.

Bach flower therapy [Edward Bach, British physician, 1886–1936] A form of aromatherapy in which the essences of wildflowers are used to promote wellness.

Bacillaceae (băs-ĭ-lā′sē-ē) A family of rod-shaped, usually gram-positive bacteria of the order Eubacteriales that produce endospores and are commonly found in soil. Genera of this family include *Bacillus* and *Clostridium.*

bacillar, bacillary (băs′ĭl-ăr, băs′ĭl-ăr-ē)

1. Pert. to or caused by bacilli. **2.** Rod-like.

bacille Calmette-Guérin (bă-sēl′) An organism of the strain *Mycobacterium bovis*, weakened (attenuated) by long-term cultivation on bile-glycerol-potato medium. SEE: *BCG vaccine*.

bacillemia (băs-ĭ-lē′mē-ă) [L. *bacillus*, rod, + Gr. *haima*, blood] The presence of rod-shaped bacteria in the blood.

bacilliform (bă-sĭl′ĭ-form) [″ + *forma*, form] Resembling a bacillus in shape.

bacillosis (băs″ĭ-lō′sĭs) [″ + Gr. *osis*, infection] Infection by rod-shaped bacteria.

Bacillus (bă-sil′ŭs) [L. *bacillus*, diminutive of *baculum*, a staff, walking stick] A genus of gram-positive, spore-forming, often aerobic, rod-shaped bacteria in the family Bacillaceae; they grow singly or in chains. Most inhabit soil and water. Some, such as *Bacillus anthracis* and *Bacillus cereus*, cause serious human diseases. SEE: *bacterium*.

   B. anthracis A large, spore-forming bacterial rod that is the causative agent of anthrax. It is one of two bacteria that produces a protein capsule and the only pathogenic bacterium to have the edema factor. The other bacterium that produces a protein capsule is *Yersinia pestis*. SEE: *edema factor*.

   B. cereus A gram-positive spore-forming food pathogen that causes two types of food poisoning syndromes: emesis and diarrhea. Type 1, the emetic syndrome, is caused by the production of a heat-stable cereulide (a small, heat-stable dodecadepsipeptide), which can damage the host cell mitochondria and in rare cases cause liver damage. Foods containing large amounts of rice are more likely to cause the type 1 syndrome. The emetic toxin may not be destroyed by brief cooking. Type 2, the diarrheal syndrome, is caused by production of the heat-labile enterotoxins hemolysin BL and nonhemolytic enterotoxin. These enterotoxins stimulate the adenylate cyclase-cyclic adenosine monophosphate system in intestinal epithelial cells, leading to profuse watery diarrhea. Foods commonly associated with type 2 syndrome are meat and vegetables.

   B. stearothermophilus A spore-forming bacillus that may survive disinfection or sterilization. Its presence on a clinical instrument or surface is used as an indicator of inadequate sterility.

bacillus (bă-sil′ŭs, bă-sil′ī″, ē″) *pl.* **bacilli** [L. *bacillus*, diminutive of *baculum*, a staff, walking stick] **1.** A rod-shaped microorganism. **2.** A rod-shaped microorganism belonging to the class Schizomycetes. SEE: *Bacillus; bacterium*.

   acid-fast b. ABBR: AFB. A bacillus not readily decolorized by acids or other means when stained. *Mycobacterium tuberculosis* is an acid-fast bacillus.

   Hansen b. SEE: *Hansen bacillus*.

   Koch b. SEE: under *Koch, Heinrich Herman Robert*.

   Pfeiffer b. SEE: under *Pfeiffer, Richard F*.

   Shiga bacillus SEE: under *Shiga, Kiyoshi*.

   Welch b. SEE: under *Welch bacillus*.

Bacillus species ABBR: *Bacillus* spp. All of the species of *Bacillus*.

bacitracin (băs-ĭ-trā′sĭn) An antibiotic obtained from a strain of *Bacillus subtilis*. Its antibacterial actions are similar to those of penicillin. It treats gram-positive cocci and bacilli and some gram-negative organisms. Because bacitracin is toxic when used parenterally, it is usually applied topically in ointment form.

back 1. The dorsum. **2.** The posterior region of the trunk from neck to pelvis.

   Health care workers often strain their backs; therefore, it is important to learn basic concepts in back care.

backache (băk′āk″) [″ + ″] Back pain.

back board SEE: under *board*.

backbone (băk′bōn″) The vertebral column; spinal column. SEE: *vertebra*.

backcross (băk′krŏs″) In genetics the pairing of a first filial generation hybrid with an organism whose genotype is identical to the parental strain.

backflow Abnormal backward flow of fluids.

background level The concentration of a substance in the air, soil, or water; independent of or prior to any artificial contamination of the environment.

back pain SEE: under *pain*.

backrest An adjustable device that supports the back in bed.

backscatter (băk″skăt′ĕr) In radiation physics, the deflection of ionizing radiation back more than 90° from interactions with intervening matter.

back school A term for educational programs, often sponsored by industry, that emphasize body mechanics and ergonomic principles with the goal of preventing initial or recurring injuries to the spine.

backup Anything that serves to replace a function or system that fails.

backwash A reverse flow; reflux.

-bactam [From *b(eta)* + *(l)actam(ase)*] A suffix used to designate an antibiotic that inhibits bacterial beta-lactamase.

bacteremia (băk-tĕr-ē′mē-ă) [Gr. *bakterion*, rod, + *haima*, blood] Bacteria in the blood. SEE: *sepsis*.

¹bacteria (bak-tēr′ē-ă) Pl. of bacterium.

²bacteria In popular and nontechnical usage, a singular noun commonly misused for *bacterium*. The plural *bacterias* is also common.

bacterial interference The limitation of the growth of one bacterium by another, e.g., in a culture or in a susceptible organism.

bacterial plasmid SEE: *plasmid.*

bacterial synergism The interaction of indigenous flora to allow a strain of bacteria to become pathogenic when it would normally be harmless.

bacterial vaginosis SEE: under *vaginosis.*

bactericidal (băk″tĕr-ĭ-sī′dăl) Capable of killing bacteria.

bactericide (băk-tĕr′ĭ-sīd) [Gr. *bakterion*, rod, + L. *caedere*, to kill] An agent that destroys bacteria, but not necessarily their spores.

bactericidin, bacteriocidin (băk-tĕr′ĭ-sīd′ĭn) Anything lethal to bacteria. One example of a bactericidin is an antibody lethal to bacteria in the presence of complement.

bacteriemia (băk-tĕr-ē-ē′mē-ă) Bacteremia.

bacterio-, bacteri- [Gr. *baktērion*, little staff] Prefixes meaning *bacteria.*

bacterioagglutinin (băk-tē″rē-ō-ă-gloo′tĭ-nĭn) [″ + L. *agglutinans*, gluing] An antibody in serum that causes agglutination, or clumping, of bacteria in vitro.

bacteriocidal (băk″tĕr-ē-ō-sī′dăl) Bactericidal.

bacteriocin (băk-tē′rē-ō-sĭn) Protein produced by certain bacteria that exerts a lethal effect on closely related bacteria. In general, bacteriocins are more potent but have a narrower range of activity than antibiotics.

bacteriogenic (băk-tē″rē-ō-jĕn′ĭk) [″ + *gennan*, to produce] **1.** Caused by bacteria. **2.** Producing bacteria.

bacteriohemagglutinin (băk-tē″rē-ō-hĕm″ă-gloo′tĭ-nĭn) [″ + *haima*, blood, + L. *agglutinans*, gluing] A bacterial toxin that clumps (agglutinates) red blood cells.

bacteriohemolysin (băk-tē″rē-ō-hē-mŏl′ĭ-sĭn) [″ + ″ + *lysis*, dissolution] A bacterial toxin that destroys (lyses) red blood cells.

bacteriologic, bacteriological (băk-tē″rē-ō-lŏj′ĭk, -ăl) [″ + *logos*, word, reason] Pert. to bacteriology.

bacteriologist (băk-tēr″ē-ŏl′ō-jĭst) An individual trained in the field of bacteriology.

bacteriology (băk-tēr″ē-ŏl′ō-jē) Scientific study of bacteria.

bacteriolysin (băk-tē″rē-ŏl′ĭ-sĭn) [″ + *lysis*, dissolution] A substance, esp. an antibody produced within the body of an animal, that is capable of bringing about the lysis of bacteria.

bacteriolysis (băk-tē″rē-ŏl′ĭ-sĭs) The destruction or dissolution of bacteria. **bacteriolytic** (-ō-lĭt′ĭk), *adj.*

bacteriophage (băk-tē′rē-ō-fāj″) [Gr. *bakterion*, rod, + *phagein*, to eat] A virus that infects and lyses bacteria. It consists of a head that contains either DNA or RNA and a tail by which it at-

taches to the host cell. SYN: *bacterial virus; phage.* SEE: *virus* for illus.

bacteriophytoma (băk-tē″rē-ō-fī-tō′mă) [″ + *phyton*, plant, + *oma*, tumor] A tumor-like growth caused by bacteria.

bacterioprecipitin (băk-tē″rē-ō-prē-sĭp′ĭ-tĭn) Antibodies that bring about precipitation of bacterial antigens.

bacterioprotein (băk-tē″rē-ō-prō′tē-ĭn) Any of the proteins within the cells of bacteria.

bacteriopsonin (băk-tē″rē-ŏp′sō-nĭn) An opsonin, acting on bacteria.

bacteriosis (băk-tē″rē-ō′sĭs) [″ + *osis*, condition] Any disease caused by bacteria.

bacteriostasis (bak-tēr″ē-ō-stā′sĭs) [*bacterio-* + *stasis*] Inhibition or retardation of the growth of bacteria without their destruction.

bacteriostatic (bak-tēr-ē-ō-stat′ik) [*bacterio-* + *static*] Pert. to bacteriostasis. SYN: *microbiostatic.*

bacteriotherapy (bak-tēr″ē-ō-ther′ă-pē) [*bacterio-* + *therapy*] Administration of live bacteria, e.g., the probiotic *Lactobacillus acidophilus*, to someone in order to restore health or cure disease. **bacteriotherapeutic** (-ther″ă-pūt′ik), *adj.*

bacteriotoxic (bak-tēr″ē-ō-tŏk′sĭk) **1.** Toxic to bacteria. **2.** Due to bacterial toxins.

bacteriotoxin (băk-tē″rē-ō-tŏk′sĭn) [″ + *toxikon*, poison] Toxin specifically produced by or destructive to bacteria.

bacteriotropin (băk-tē″rē-ŏt′rō-pĭn) [″ + *tropos*, a turn] An opsonin or a substance that enhances the ability of phagocytes to engulf bacteria.

bacteristatic (bak-tēr″ē-stăt′ĭk) Inhibiting the growth of bacteria. SEE: *bactericidal.*

bacterium (bak-tēr′ē-ŭm, -tēr′ē-ă) *pl.* **bacteria** [L. *bacterium*, fr Gr. *baktērion*, a small staff] A one-celled organism without a true nucleus or cell organelles, belonging to the kingdom Procaryotae (Monera). The cytoplasm is surrounded by a rigid cell wall composed of carbohydrates and other chemicals that provide the basis for the Gram stain. Some bacteria produce a polysaccharide or polypeptide capsule, which inhibits phagocytosis by white blood cells. Bacteria synthesize DNA, RNA, and proteins, and they can reproduce independently but may need a host to provide food and a favorable environment. Millions of nonpathogenic bacteria live on human skin and mucous membranes; these are called *normal flora.* Bacteria that cause disease are called *pathogens.* **bacterial** (-ăl), *adj.* SEE: table.

    CHARACTERISTICS: *Shape:* There are three principal forms of bacteria. *Spherical* or *ovoid* bacteria occur as single cells (micrococci) or in pairs (diplococci), clusters (staphylococci), chains (strep-

Common Bacterial Infections

Organism	Type and/or Site of Infection
Gram-Positive Bacteria	
Clostridium difficile	Pseudomembranous colitis
Staphylococcus aureus	Pneumonia, cellulitis, boils, impetigo, toxic shock, postoperative bone/joints, eyes, peritonitis
Staphylococcus epidermidis	Postoperative bone/joints, IV line–related phlebitis
Streptococcus pneumoniae (pneumococcus)	Pneumonia, meningitis, otitis media, sinusitis, septicemia
Streptococcus pyogenes	Scarlet fever, pharyngitis, impetigo, rheumatic fever, erysipelas
viridans group streptococci	Endocarditis
Gram-Negative Bacteria	
Campylobacter jejuni	Diarrhea (most common worldwide cause)
Escherichia coli	Urinary tract, pyelonephritis, septicemia, gastroenteritis, peritonitis
Haemophilus influenzae	Pneumonia, meningitis, otitis media, epiglottitis
Klebsiella pneumoniae	Pneumonia, wounds
Legionella pneumophilia	Pneumonia
Neisseria gonorrhoeae	Gonorrhea
Neisseria meningitidis (meningococcus)	Meningitis
Pseudomonas aeruginosa	Wounds, urinary tract, pneumonia, IV lines
Salmonella enteritidis	Gastroenteritis, food poisoning
Salmonella typhi	Typhoid fever
Shigella dysenteriae	Dysentery
Vibrio cholerae	Cholera

tococci), or cubical groups (sarcinae). *Rod-shaped* bacteria are called bacilli, more oval ones are called coccobacilli, and those forming a chain are called streptobacilli. *Spiral* bacteria are rigid (spirilla), flexible (spirochetes), or curved (vibrios). SEE: illus.

Size: On average, bacilli measure about 1 μm in diameter by 4 μm in length. They range in size from less than 0.5 to 1.0 μm in diameter to 10 to 20 μm in length for some of the spirilla.

Reproduction: Binary fission is the usual method of reproduction, but some bacteria exchange genetic material with members of the same species or different species. Reproductive rate is affected by changes in temperature, nutrition, and pH. If the environment becomes unfavorable, some bacilli form spores, in which their genetic material is condensed and surrounded by a thick wall. Spores are highly resistant to heat, drying, and disinfectants. When the environment again becomes favorable, the spores germinate.

Mutation: Bacteria, like all living things, undergo mutations, and the environment determines which mutations are beneficial and have survival value. Certainly beneficial to bacteria, though not at all to humans, are the mutations that provide resistance to the potentially lethal effects of antibiotics.

Motility: None of the cocci are capable of moving, but most bacilli and spiral forms can move independently. Locomotion depends on the possession of one or more flagella, slender whiplike appendages that work like propellers.

Food and oxygen requirements: Most bacteria are heterotrophic (require organic material as food). If they feed on living organisms, they are called *parasites;* if they feed on nonliving organic material, they are called *saprophytes.* Bacteria that obtain their energy from inorganic substances, including many of the soil bacteria, are called *autotrophic* (self-nourishing). Bacteria that require oxygen are called aerobes; those that grow only in the absence of oxygen are called anaerobes. Bacteria that grow both with and without oxygen are facultative anaerobes. Most bacteria in the human intestines are anaerobic. SEE: *infection, opportunistic.*

Temperature requirements: Although some bacteria live at very low or very high temperatures, the optimum temperature for most human pathogens is 97° to 99°F (36° to 38°C).

ACTIVITIES: *Enzyme production:* Bacteria produce enzymes that act on

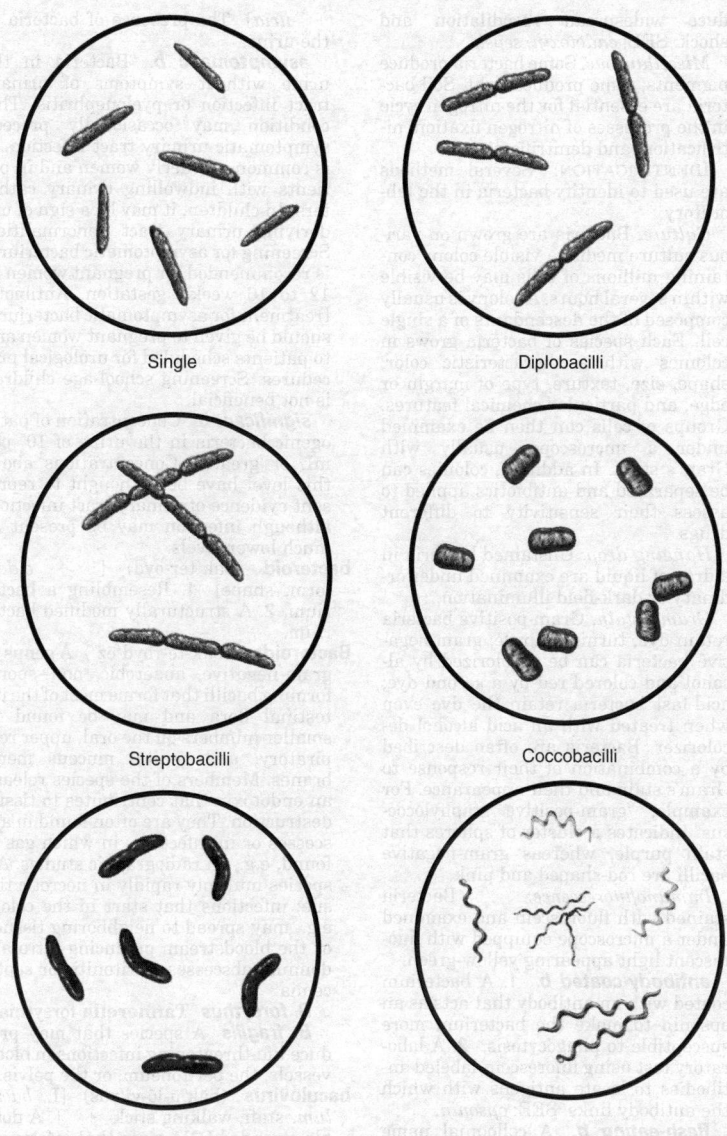

Single

Diplobacilli

Streptobacilli

Coccobacilli

Vibrio

Spirochetes

BACTERIA SHAPES AND STRUCTURES

complex food molecules, breaking them down into simpler materials; they are the principal agents of decay and putrefaction. Putrefaction, the decomposition of nitrogenous and other organic materials in the absence of air, produces foul odors. Decay is the gradual decomposition of organic matter exposed to air by bacteria and fungi.

Toxin production: Cell wall molecules called *adhesins* bind bacteria to the host cells. Once attached, the bacteria may produce poisonous substances called toxins. There are two types: exotoxins, enzymes that are released by bacteria into their host, and endotoxins, which are parts of the cell walls of gram-negative bacteria and are toxic even after the death of the cell. Exotoxins include hemolysins, leukocidins, coagulases, and fibrinolysins. Endotoxins stimulate production of cytokines that can produce widespread vasodilation and shock. SEE: *endotoxin; sepsis.*

Miscellaneous: Some bacteria produce pigments; some produce light. Soil bacteria are essential for the nitrogen cycle in the processes of nitrogen fixation, nitrification, and denitrification.

IDENTIFICATION: Several methods are used to identify bacteria in the laboratory:

Culture: Bacteria are grown on various culture media; a visible colony containing millions of cells may be visible within several hours. A colony is usually composed of the descendants of a single cell. Each species of bacteria grows in colonies with a characteristic color, shape, size, texture, type of margin or edge, and particular chemical features. Groups of cells can then be examined under a microscope, usually with Gram's stain. In addition, colonies can be separated and antibiotics applied to assess their sensitivity to different drugs.

Hanging drop: Unstained bacteria in a drop of liquid are examined under ordinary or dark-field illumination.

Gram's stain: Gram-positive bacteria retain dye, turning purple; gram-negative bacteria can be decolorized by alcohol and colored red by a second dye; acid-fast bacteria retain the dye even when treated with an acid alcohol decolorizer. Bacteria are often described by a combination of their response to Gram's stain and their appearance. For example, "gram-positive staphylococcus" indicates a cluster of spheres that stain purple, whereas gram-negative bacilli are rod-shaped and pink.

Immunofluorescence: Bacteria stained with fluorescein and examined under a microscope equipped with fluorescent light appearing yellow-green.

antibody-coated b. 1. A bacterium coated with an antibody that acts as an opsonin to make the bacterium more susceptible to phagocytosis. 2. A laboratory test using fluorescein-labeled antibodies to locate antigens with which the antibody links. SEE: *opsonin.*

flesh-eating b. A colloquial name given in the popular media to a rare invasive infection of the skin and underlying soft tissue by group A streptococcus. The infection is difficult to treat with antibiotics alone because it progresses rapidly through tissue planes. Emergency surgical debridement is required. SEE: *necrotizing fasciitis.*

heterotrophic b. Any of the bacteria that rely on organic compounds to grow and reproduce.

probiotic b. A bacterium that prevents illness, e.g., the *Lactobacillus.* species found in yogurt.

bacteriuria (bak-tēr″ē-ū′rē-ă) [*bacterio-* + *-uria*] The presence of bacteria in the urine.

asymptomatic b. Bacteria in the urine without symptoms of urinary tract infection or pyelonephritis. This condition may occasionally precede symptomatic urinary tract infection. It is common in elderly women and in patients with indwelling urinary catheters. In children, it may be a sign of underlying urinary tract abnormalities. Screening for asymptomatic bacteriuria is recommended for pregnant women at 12 to 16 weeks' gestation. Antibiotic treatment for asymptomatic bacteriuria should be given to pregnant women and to patients scheduled for urological procedures. Screening school-age children is not beneficial.

significant b. Concentration of pathogenic bacteria in the urine of 10^5 per mL or greater. Concentrations above this level have been thought to represent evidence of urinary tract infection, although infection may be present at much lower levels.

bacteroid (băk′tĕr-oyd) [″ + *eidos,* form, shape] 1. Resembling a bacterium. 2. A structurally modified bacterium.

Bacteroides (bak-tĕ-royd′ēz″) A genus of gram-negative, anaerobic, non–spore-forming bacilli that forms most of the intestinal flora and may be found in smaller numbers on the oral, upper respiratory, and genital mucous membranes. Members of the species release an endotoxin that contributes to tissue destruction. They are often found in abscesses or in infections in which gas is found, e.g., on radiographic studies. All species multiply rapidly in necrotic tissue; infections that start in the colon, e.g., may spread to neighboring tissues or the bloodstream producing intra-abdominal abscesses, peritonitis or septicemia.

B. forsythus **Tannerella** forsythia.

B. fragilis A species that may produce life-threatening infections in blood vessels, the peritoneum, or the pelvis.

baculovirus (băk″ū-lō-vī′rŭs) [L. *baculum,* staff, walking stick + ″] A double-stranded DNA virus that infects insects. It has been used experimentally in recombinant DNA technology, e.g., in manufacturing vaccines.

bad breath SEE: under *breath.*

bad debt SEE: under *debt.*

Baer plane [Karl Ernst von Baer, Prussian-Estonian anatomist, 1792–1876] A plane through the upper border of the zygomatic arches.

baffle (băf′ĭl) In respiratory care, a component of a nebulizer designed to remove large aerosol particles.

bag (bag) 1. A sack or pouch. 2. A colloquial term meaning to support a patient's respirations with a face mask and a manually compressible source of air or oxygen. **3.** To place a specimen or a used or potentially infectious item in a flexible plastic container, either for delivery to the lab or for disposal.

    colostomy b. A watertight receptacle that holds the discharge from a colostomy site. SYN: *colostomy **appliance**; colostomy **pouch***.

     Douglas b. SEE: *Douglas bag*.

     hot water b. Hot water bottle

     🔊 **ice b.** A flexible, watertight bag with a sealable opening large enough to permit ice cubes or chipped ice to be added. It is used in any condition requiring local application of cold. In an emergency any sturdy, flexible plastic bag can be used, with the open end sealed by a knot. A simple ice pack can be made at home by mixing 3 cups of water and 1 cup of rubbing alcohol in a resealable plastic bag and placing the sealed mixture in the freezer for 8 to 12 hours. The solution will not freeze but will attain a gel-like consistency that molds to the body part on which it is used. Alternatively, a bag of frozen peas may be used as a conforming ice bag. The usual application time for an ice bag is alternating 10 min on, 20 min off.

⚠️ Dry ice should not be placed in an ice bag.

---

    b. of waters Amnion.

    Politzer b. SEE: *Politzer bag*.

    Voorhees b. SEE: *Voorhees bag*.

bagassosis (băg-ă-sō′sĭs) [Sp. *bagazo*, husks, + Gr. *osis*, condition] A form of hypersensitivity pneumonitis, due to inhalation of bagasse dust, the moldy, dusty fibrous waste of sugar cane after removal of the sugar-containing sap. The dust contains antigens from thermophilic actinomycetes.

Baghdad boil (bag′dad) [Baghdad, the capital of Iraq] Cutaneous leishmaniasis.

bag mask device SEE: under *device*.

Bailey, Harriet (bā′lē) [U.S. nurse educator, 1875–1953] The first nurse educator to write a textbook on psychiatric nursing. *Nursing Mental Diseases* was published by Macmillan in 1920 and was the standard text for psychiatric nursing for two decades.

Bainbridge, Francis Arthur (bān′brij″) Brit. physician, 1839–1896.

    B. effect Bainbridge reflex.

    B. reflex An increase in heart rate caused by an increase in blood pressure or distention of the heart. SYN: ***Bainbridge** effect*.

baker [AS. *bacan*, cook by dry heat] Two or more electric lamps mounted in semicircular containers used for applying heat to various parts of the body. They are also called *electric light bakers*.

Baker cyst [William M. Baker, Brit. surgeon, 1839–1896] A synovial cyst arising from the synovial lining of the knee. It occurs in the popliteal fossa.

BAL *British antilewisite; bronchoalveolar lavage.*

Balamuthia mandrillaris (băl″ă-mooth′ē-ă măn″drĭl-ār′ĭs) [NL.] An opportunistic amoeba that lives in soil and water. It can cause a potentially fatal infection of the brain and meninges, esp. in those with immunosuppressive illnesses.

balance (bal′ăns) [Fr. *balance* fr. L. *bilanx, bilancia,* double scale] **1.** A device for measuring weight; a scale. **2.** A condition in which the intake and output of substances such as water and nutrients are approx. equal; a state of equilibrium. SEE: *homeostasis*. **3.** Coordination and stability of the body in space. Normal balance depends on information from the vestibular system in the inner ear, from other senses such as sight and touch, from proprioception and muscle movement, and from the integration of these sensory data by the cerebellum.

    acid-base b. The chemical equilibrium that maintains the body's pH at about 7.40; i.e., at the concentration of hydrogen ions that is most favorable to routine cellular metabolic processes. The equilibrium is maintained by the action of buffer systems of the blood and the regulatory (homeostatic) functions of the respiratory and urinary systems. Disturbances in acid-base balance result in acidosis or alkalosis. SEE: *pH*.

    analytical b. A very sensitive scale used in chemical analysis.

    energy b. The number of calories consumed as food, minus the calories expended, e.g., during exercise.

    PATIENT CARE: When consumption exceeds expenditure, a positive energy balance is present, and weight is gained. When consumption is less than energy expenditure, a negative energy balance is present, weight is lost, and risk factors for cardiovascular disease diminish.

    fluid b. Regulation of the amount of liquid in the body. A negative fluid balance (fluid deficit) may occur when fluids are lost by vomiting, diarrhea, bleeding, or diaphoresis. Fluid overload may result from the excessive administration of intravenous fluids, or in diseases marked by impaired fluid excretion, such as congestive heart failure, cirrhosis, or renal failure. SEE: *dehydration; diuresis; fluid replacement;* and entries beginning with the words *fluid volume*.

    Treatment of fluid imbalances depends on the cause; the patient's cardiac, renal, and hepatic function; measured serum electrolytes; and acid-base balance.

    Useful means of gauging changes in fluid balance are 1) to measure fluid inputs and outputs; or 2) to measure day-to-day variations in body weight.

life b. A harmonious blend of occupational, familial, social, and leisure pursuits. SYN: *role b.; work-family b.; work-life b.*

metabolic b. Comparison of the intake and excretion of a specific nutrient. The balance may be negative when an excess of the nutrient is excreted or positive when more is taken in than excreted.

nitrogen b. The difference between the amount of nitrogen ingested and that excreted each day. If protein intake is greater than the nitrogen excreted, a positive balance exists; if protein intake is less, there is a negative balance. SYN: *nitrogen equilibrium; nitrogenous equilibrium.*

protein b. Equilibrium between protein intake and anabolism, and protein catabolism and elimination of nitrogenous products. SEE: *nitrogen equilibrium.*

role b. Life **b.**

static b. Static **equilibrium**.

work-family b. Life **b.**

work-life b. Life **b.**

balance beam SEE: under *beam.*

balance disorder Any condition that affects a person's ability to feel steady while walking, sitting, standing, resting, working, or turning. Some common examples include disease of the labyrinth of the ear, cerebellar strokes, and seasickness.

Balance Error Scoring System ABBR: BESS. A modification of the Romberg test that assesses a patient's ability to maintain postural stability following traumatic brain injury. The test is performed in two stages. The first is performed on a solid surface; the second is performed on a soft surface such as thick foam. Points are deducted for "errors" (loss of balance or sway) during testing. Pre-injury test results are compared to post-injury test results to determine the magnitude of impairment following injury.

balance training SEE: under *training.*

balanic (bă-lăn′ĭk) [Gr. *balanos,* glans] Pert. to the glans clitoridis or glans penis.

balanitis (bal″ă-nīt′ĭs) [*balano-* + *-itis*] Inflammation of the skin covering the glans penis.

b. circinata A clearly defined, painless red lesion on the skin of the glans penis. It often accompanies polyarthritis and conjunctivitis as part of a triad sometimes seen in Reiter syndrome. SEE: *Reiter syndrome.*

b. circumscripta plasmacellularis **Zoon** balanitis.

plasma cell b. **Zoon** balanitis.

b. xerotica obliterans ABBR: BXO. Sclerotic and atrophic patches on the skin of the penis that can cause narrowing of the urinary meatus and phimosis. The cause is chronic balanoposthitis, and the condition is associated with penile lichen sclerosis, e.g., circumcision for phimosis.

TREATMENT: High-dose topical steroids or long courses of antibiotics are given.

balano-, balan- [Gr. *balanos,* acorn, glans (penis)] Prefixes meaning *glans penis* or *glans clitoridis.*

balanocele (băl′ă-nō-sēl″) [″ + *kele,* tumor, swelling] Protrusion of the glans penis through a rupture of the prepuce.

balanoplasty (băl′ă-nō-plăs″tē) [″ + *plassein,* to form] Plastic surgery of the glans penis.

balanoposthitis (bal″ă-nō-pos-thīt′ĭs) [*balano-* + *posthitis*] Inflammation of the glans and the foreskin of the penis.

balanopreputial (băl″ă-nō-prē-pū′shē-ăl) Pert. to the glans penis and prepuce.

balanorrhagia (băl″ă-nō-rā′jē-ă) [″ + *rhegnynai,* burst forth] Balanitis with pus formation.

Balans chair SEE: *kneeling chair.*

balantidial (băl-ăn-tĭd′ē-ăl) Pert. to *Balantidium,* a genus of protozoa.

balantidiasis (băl″ăn-tĭ-dī′ă-sĭs) Infection of the large intestine by *Balantidium coli.*

SYMPTOMS: Symptoms include abdominal pain, diarrhea, vomiting, weakness, and weight loss.

TREATMENT: Treatment consists of tetracyclines, metronidazole, or paromomycin.

Balantidium (băl-ăn-tĭd′ē-ŭm) [Gr. *balantidion,* a bag] A genus of ciliated protozoa. A number of species are found in the intestines of both vertebrates and invertebrates.

B. coli A normal parasite of swine and the largest protozoan parasite of humans. It causes balantidiasis. SEE: illus.

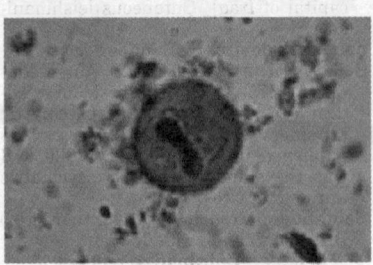

├───────────┤ 50μm

BALANTIDIUM COLI CYST

(×400)

balanus (băl′ă-nŭs) [Gr. *balanos,* glans] The glans penis or glans clitoridis.

baldness (bald′nĕs) Lack of or partial loss of hair on the head. SEE: *alopecia.*

male-pattern b. The typical pattern of baldness in males in which the baldness begins in the frontal area and proceeds until only a horseshoe area of hair remains in the back and at the temples. It is due to testosterone, but genetic predisposition is also a factor. Baldness does not usually occur in males having no familial tendency to become bald. Minoxidil or finasteride has helped stimulate growth of hair in some individuals. SYN: *male-pattern alopecia*. SEE: illus.

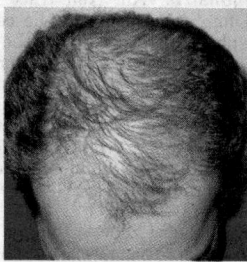

MALE PATTERN BALDNESS

Balint syndrome (bal'int) [Rudolph Balint, Hungarian physician, 1874–1929] Inability to scan the peripheral visual field and to grasp an object under visual guidance, and visual inattention; usually due to bilateral occipitoparietal lesions of the brain.

Balke test (bălk) [Bruno Balke, contemporary Ger.-born U.S. physician] A test to determine maximum oxygen utilization. The subject walks on a flat (0% grade) treadmill at a constant rate of 3.5 miles/hr for 2 min. The treadmill is inclined 1% each successive minute until the subject is exhausted and unable to continue. Oxygen utilization is measured throughout the test.

⚠️ The test is not suitable for those with impaired musculoskeletal, cardiovascular, or respiratory systems.

ball (bal) A spherical object.
   balance b. Swiss **b.**
   fitness b. Swiss **b.**
   food b. Phytobezoar.
   freeze b. Ice **b.**
   fungus b. The growth of a mold, often *Aspergillus,* in a body cavity without the invasion of tissue. Most common sites are the nasal cavities, paranasal sinuses, kidneys, and lungs.
   ice b. Tissue that has been frozen during cryoablation or cryosurgery. SYN: *freeze* **b.**
   b. of the foot The padded portion of the anterior extremity of the sole of the foot.
   b. of the thumb The thenar eminence of the thumb.

   stability b. Swiss **b.**
   Swiss b. An inflatable vinyl or rubber ball, used in exercise training, rehabilitation, and sports to treat low back pain or to strengthen the muscles of the abdomen and chest. SYN: *balance* **b.**; *fitness* **b.**; *stability* **b.**

Ballard tool, Ballard score (bal'ărd) [Jeanne Ballard, U.S. neonatologist] A system for estimating newborn gestational age by rating physical and neuromuscular characteristics of maturity. For infants born between 20 and 28 weeks' gestation, Ballard tools are more accurate than other systems of estimating gestational age. Six neuromuscular markers are assessed: posture, square window (degree of wrist flexion), arm recoil, popliteal angle (degree of knee flexion); scarf sign (ability to extend infant's arm across the chest past the midline); and heel-to-ear extension. Seven physical characteristics are also evaluated: skin; lanugo; plantar creases; breast; eye and ear; and genitals. Each factor is scored independently, and then an overall sum is used to determine the gestational age. The tool is most accurate if performed within the first 12 to 20 hr of life or as soon as the baby's condition stabilizes.

ballistics (bă-lĭs'tĭks) [Gr. *ballein,* to throw] The science of the motion and trajectory of projectiles, including bullets, bombs, rockets, and guided missiles.

ballistocardiograph (bă-lĭs″tō-kăr'dē-ō-grăf) [″ + *kardia,* heart, + *graphein,* to write] A mechanism for measuring and recording the impact caused by the discharge of blood from the heart at each beat and the resulting recoil. The minute movements of the body with each heartbeat are recorded as they are transmitted to the special platform that supports the subject.

balloon (bă-loon') [Fr. *ballon,* big ball] **1.** To expand, dilate, or distend, as to expand a cavity by filling it with air or water in a bag. **2.** A flexible, expandable object that can be placed inside a vessel or cavity to expand it or at the end of a catheter to prevent its removal. SEE: *catheter; percutaneous transluminal coronary angioplasty.*
   intragastric b. An inflatable device in inserted into the stomach to induce satiety, used to treat morbid obesity.

ballottable (bă-lŏt'ă-bl) Capable of identification by ballottement.

ballottement (băl-ŏt-mŏn') [Fr. *balloter,* to toss about] **1.** A palpatory technique used to detect or examine a floating object in the body, such as an organ. It is used in examining the abdomen esp. when ascites is present, and joint effusions. **2.** A diagnostic maneuver in pregnancy. The fetus or a fetal part rebounds when displaced by a light tap of the examining finger through the vagina.

balm (bom) [Ult. fr the same source as *balsam*] **1.** A soothing or healing ointment, esp. one from the resins of plants of the genus *Commiphora*. SEE: *Commiphora*. **2.** Any soothing, restorative ointment or preparation. SYN: *balsam* (2).

   b. of Gilead 1. The balm or balsam carried from Gilead by the caravan of merchants to whom Joseph was sold by his brothers, probably balsam from *Commiphora opobalsamum* (*C. gileadensis*), and probably the biblical myrrh. SYN: *balsam of Gilead; Mecca* **balsam**. **2.** The balsam fir, *Populus candicans,* or its resin, used as an expectorant and an ointment.

balneology (băl-nē-ŏl′ō-jē) [L. *balneum,* bath, + Gr. *logos,*word, reason] The science of baths and bathing.

balneotherapy,   **balneotherapeutics** (băl″nē-ō-thĕr′ă-pē, -thĕr″ă-pū′tĭks) [″ + Gr. *therapeia,* treatment] The use of baths in treatment of disease.

Balo disease A rare, rapidly progressing form of multiple sclerosis. It differs from other multiple sclerosis variants, in that it is not characterized by relapses and remissions.

balsam (bol′săm) [L. *balsamum,* fr Gr. *balsamon,* balsam, fr Semitic] **1.** A fragrant, resinous, oily exudate from various trees and plants. It is used in topical preparations to treat irritated skin or mucous membrane. **2.** Balm (2).

   Mecca b. Balm of Gilead

   b. of Gilead Balm of Gilead

   b. of Peru A balsam obtained from the bark of the tree *Myroxylon perierae* or *M. balsamum,* used as a topical ointment.

BALT *bronchus-associated lymphoid tissue.*

banana sign An anterior curvature of the cerebellar hemispheres in a developing fetus, with obliteration of the cisterna magna. It is an ultrasonic sign found in the second trimester of pregnancy and is a marker of a neural tube defect, e.g., spina bifida.

Bancroft filariasis (ban′kroft″, bang′) [Joseph Bancroft, Brit. physician, 1836–1894] A filarial infection caused by *Wuchereria bancrofti.* SEE: *elephantiasis.*

band (band) **1.** A cord or tapelike tissue that connects or holds structures together. SEE: *bundle; ligament; tract.* **2.** Any appliance that encircles and applies pressure around a body part or structure. **3.** A segment of a myofibril. **4.** A metal strip or seamless band for attaching orthodontic appliances to teeth. **5.** An immature, unsegmented neutrophil seen in some illnesses on a peripheral blood smear. An increase in bands indicates that all mature neutrophils have been released from the bone marrow, usually during severe inflammation or infection, and that the marrow is releasing immature cells.

   A b. The darker of the two alternating stripes seen along muscle fibers (myofibrils) when viewed with a polarization microscope. The A bands are regions in which the thin (actin) filaments overlap the thick (myosin) filaments. The alternating regions, lighter in color, are the I bands and contain only actin fibrils. SYN: *anisotropic b.; anisotropic disk*.

   anisotropic b. A **b.**

   diagonal b. An axon tract in the basal forebrain region of the cerebral hemisphere. It interconnects the septal area and the substantia inominata. SYN: *diagonal band of Broca; tractus diagonalis.*

   H b. A narrow band in the center of the A band of a sarcomere; it contains only thick (myosin) filaments and is bisected by the M line. SYN: *Engelmann disk; H zone.*

   I b. In muscle fibers, the light band segment of a sarcomere, containing lateral ends of thin (actin) filaments. There is one to either side of the medial A band. SYN: *isotropic b.*

   iliotibial b. A thick, wide fascial layer from the iliac crest along the lateral thigh to the fascia around the lateral aspect of the knee joint. Fibers from the tensor fascia lata and gluteus maximus muscles insert into the proximal band.

   isotropic b. I **b.**

   M b. M **line**.

   oligoclonal b.s Immunoglobulins found in the cerebrospinal fluid of patients with multiple sclerosis (MS) and, occasionally, in other neurological conditions. They are used as a marker of MS when magnetic resonance imaging studies of the brain are not diagnostic.

   Z b. Z **line**.

bandage (ban′dăj) **1.** A piece of soft, usually absorbent gauze or other material applied to a limb or other part of the body as a dressing. **2.** To cover by wrapping with a piece of gauze or other material.

   Bandages are used to hold dressings in place, apply pressure to a part, immobilize a part, obliterate cavities, support an injured area, and check hemorrhages. Types of bandages include roller, triangular, four-tailed, many-tailed (Scultetus), quadrangular, elastic (elastic knit, rubber, synthetic, or combinations of these), adhesive, elastic adhesive, newer cohesive bandages under various proprietary names, impregnated bandages (plaster of Paris, water-glass [silica], starch), and stockinet. Use of a self-adhering, form-fitting roller bandage facilitates bandaging by eliminating the special techniques needed when ordinary gauze roller bandages are used. SEE: illus.; *sling.*

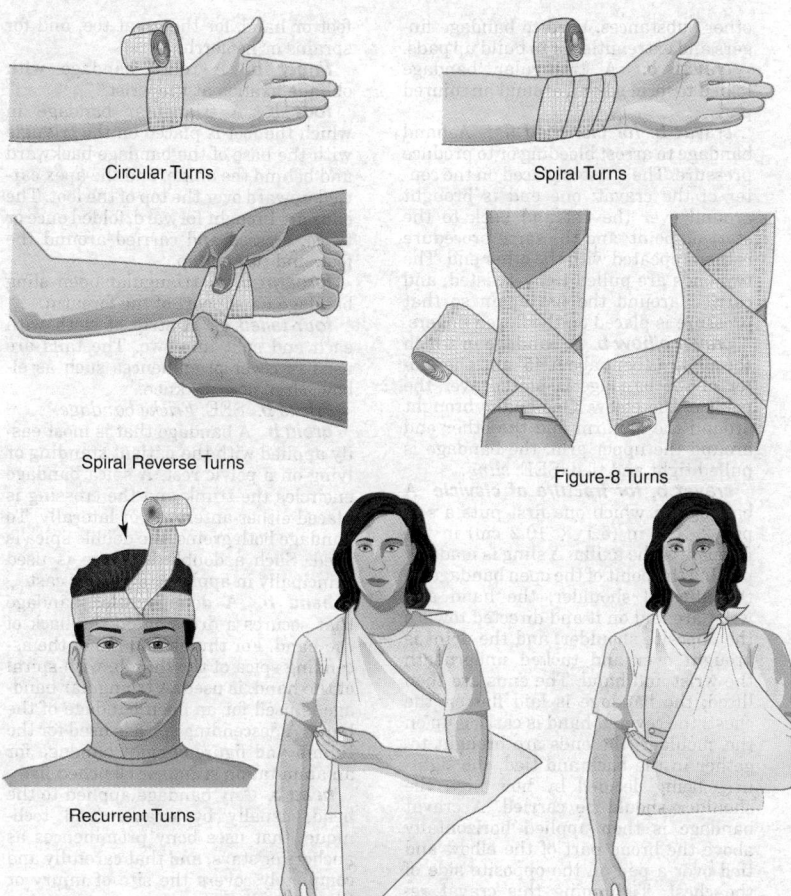

Circular Turns

Spiral Turns

Spiral Reverse Turns

Figure-8 Turns

Recurrent Turns

APPLYING BANDAGES

⚠ Skin-to-skin contact will, if continuous, cause ulceration or infection.

abdominal b. A single wide cravat or several narrow ones used to hold a dressing in place or to exert moderate pressure.

adhesive b. A bandage made of adhesive tape.

amputation-stump b. An elastic bandage applied to an amputation stump to control postoperative edema and to shape the stump. The elastic bandage is applied in a recurrent or figure-of-eight fashion with more pressure applied to the distal, rather than the proximal, portion of the limb.

ankle b. A bandage in which one loop is brought around the sole of foot and the other around the ankle and is secured in front or on the side.

axilla b. A bandage with a spica-type turn starting under the affected axilla, crossing over the shoulder of the affected side, and making the long loop under the opposite armpit.

back b. An open bandage to the back, applied like a chest bandage, the point placed above the scapula of the injured side.

Barton b. SEE: *Barton bandage*.

breast b. A suspensory bandage and compress for the breasts.

butterfly b. An adhesive bandage used in place of sutures to hold wound edges together. Filmy sterile adhesive strips have replaced the butterfly bandage.

buttocks b. T b.

circular b. A bandage applied in circular turns about a part.

cohesive b. A bandage made of material that sticks to itself but not to other substances, used to bandage fingers and extremities or to build up pads.

cravat b. A triangular bandage folded to form a band around an injured part.

cravat b. for clenched fist A hand bandage to arrest bleeding or to produce pressure. The wrist is placed on the center of the cravat; one end is brought around over the fist and back to the starting point, and the same procedure is then repeated with the other end. The two ends are pulled tight, twisted, and carried around the fist again so that pressure is placed on the flexed fingers.

cravat elbow b. A bandage in which the elbow is bent about 45° and the center of the bandage is placed over the point of the elbow. One end is brought around the forearm and the other end around the upper arm; the bandage is pulled tight and tied. SEE: *sling*.

cravat b. for fracture of clavicle A bandage in which one first puts a soft pad 2 × 4 in (5.1 × 10.2 cm) in the forepart of the axilla. A sling is made by placing the point of the open bandage on the affected shoulder; the hand and wrist are laid on it and directed toward the opposite shoulder, and the point is brought over and tucked underneath the wrist and hand. The ends are then lifted; the bandage is laid flat on the chest; the covered hand is carried up on the shoulder; the ends are brought together in the back and tied, the tightness being decided by how high the shoulder should be carried. A cravat bandage is then applied horizontally above the broad part of the elbow and tied over a pad on the opposite side of the chest. Tightening this cravat retracts the shoulders and scapulae.

crucial b. SEE: *T b.*

demigauntlet b. A bandage that covers the hand but leaves the fingers uncovered.

ear b. A T bandage for the ear. A piece is sewn across the right angle of the T bandage.

elastic b. A bandage that can be stretched to exert continuous pressure. It usually is made of special weaves or of material containing rubber and is used on swollen extremities or joints, on the chest in empyema, on fractured ribs, or on the legs to support varicose veins.

Esmarch b. SEE: *Esmarch bandage.*

eye b. A bandage for retaining dressings. The simple roller bandage for one eye or the monocle or crossed bandage. The binocular or crossed bandage for both eyes is 2 in × 6 yd (5.1 cm × 5.49 m).

figure-of-eight b. A bandage in which the turns cross each other like the figure eight, used to retain dressings, to exert pressure for joints (or to leave the joint uncovered), to fix splints for the

foot or hand, for the great toe, and for sprains or hemorrhage.

finger b. A roller bandage with oblique fixation at the wrist.

foot b. A triangular bandage in which the foot is placed on the triangle with the base of the bandage backward and behind the ankle, and the apex carried upward over the top of the foot. The ends are brought forward, folded once or twice, crossed and carried around the foot, and tied on top.

forearm b. A triangular open sling bandage for support of the forearm.

four-tailed b. A strip of cloth with each end split into two. The tails are used to cover prominences such as elbow, chin, nose, or knee.

Fricke b. SEE: *Fricke bandage.*

groin b. A bandage that is most easily applied with the patient standing or lying on a pelvic rest. A spica bandage encircles the trunk and the crossing is placed either anteriorly or laterally. To bandage both groins, the double spica is used. Such a double bandage is used principally in applying a plaster cast.

hand b. A demigauntlet bandage that secures a dressing on the back of the hand. For thumb and hand, the ascending spica of the thumb, with spiral of the hand, is used. A triangular bandage is used for an open bandage of the hand. A descending spica is used for the thumb and figure-of-eight bandage for an amputation stump or clenched fist.

head b. Any bandage applied to the head, usually by wrap-around technique, that uses bony prominences as anchors or stays, and that carefully and completely covers the site of injury or the suture line.

heel b. A triangular bandage used for the heel.

hip b. A triangular open bandage of the hip. A cravat bandage or other band is tied around the waist; the point of another bandage is slipped under and rolled or pinned directly above the position of the wound. The base is rolled up and the ends are carried around the thigh, crossed, and tied.

impregnated b. A wide-meshed bandage used to make molds or immobilize parts of the body. The material is impregnated with a substance such as plaster of Paris, which is applied wet and hardens after drying.

knee b. A knee cravat in which triangular and the figure-of-eight bandages are used.

leg b. A bandage applied by fixing the initial end by a circular or oblique fixation at the ankle or with a figure-of-eight of the foot and ankle.

many-tailed b. A bandage with split ends used for the trunk and limbs; a piece of roller to which slips are stitched in an imbricated fashion. SEE: *four-tailed b.; Scultetus, Johannes*.

Martin b. SEE: *Martin bandage*.

neck b. *Neck spica*: Bandage 2½ in × 8 yd (6.4 cm × 7.3 m). *Bandage following thyroid gland surgery*: Roller bandage 2½ in × 9 yd (6.4 cm × 8.2 m). *Adhesive plaster bandage for thyroidectomy*: Used to hold dressing on wound in place. A small dressing is applied to center of strip and then applied to back of neck. *Special bandage*: A double-loop bandage of the head and neck made by using a figure-of-eight turn.

oblique b. A bandage applied obliquely to a limb, without reverses.

plaster b. A bandage stiffened with a paste of plaster of Paris, which sets and becomes very hard. SEE: *cast* (4).

pressure b. A bandage for applying pressure, usually used to stop hemorrhage or prevent edema.

protective b. A bandage that covers a part or keeps dressings in place.

quadrangular b. A towel or large handkerchief, folded variously and applied as a bandage of head, chest, breast, or abdomen.

recurrent b. A bandage over the end of a stump.

reversed b. A bandage applied to a limb in such a way that the roller is inverted or half twisted at each turn so as to make it fit smoothly and resist slipping off the limb. SEE: *spiral reverse b.*

roller b. A long strip of soft material, usually from ½ to 6 in (1.3 to 15.2 cm) wide and 2 to 5 yd (1.83 to 4.57 m) long, rolled on its short axis. When rolled from both ends to meet at the center, it is called a double-headed roller.

rubber b. A rubber roller bandage used to apply pressure to prevent swelling or hemorrhage of a limb. SEE: *Esmarch b.*

Scultetus b. SEE: under *Scultetus, Johannes*.

shoulder b. An open bandage of the shoulder (spica bandage); a shawl bandage of both shoulders and neck.

spica b. A bandage in which a number of figure-of-eight turns are applied, each a little higher or lower, overlapping a portion of each preceding turn so as to give an imbricated appearance. This type of bandage is used to support, to exert pressure, or to retain dressings on the breast, shoulder, limbs, thumb, great toe, and hernia at the groin.

spiral b. A roller bandage to be applied spirally.

spiral reverse b. A technique of twisting, in its long axis, a roller bandage on itself at intervals during application to make it fit more uniformly. These reverse folds may be necessary every turn or less often, depending on the contour of the part being bandaged.

stellate b. A bandage that is wrapped crosswise on the back.

suspensory b. A bandage for supporting any part but esp. the breast or scrotum.

T b. A bandage shaped like the letter T and used for the female perineum and, in certain cases, the head. SYN: *buttocks b.; T binder*.

tailed b. A bandage split at the end.

triangular b. A square bandage folded diagonally. When folded, the several thicknesses can be applied to afford support.

Velpeau b. SEE: under *Velpeau, Alfred*.

bandemia (băn-dē′mē-ă) [Band shape of cell nucleus + Gr. *haima*, blood] The presence of more than 6% of immature neutrophils (band cells) in the blood. This finding indicates infection, inflammation, or some other significant physical stress.

banding 1. The use of chemicals to stain chromosomes so that the characteristic bands may be visualized. **2.** The use of an appliance to encircle and apply pressure around a body part or structure.

bandster (ban(d)′stĕr) An informal term for a person who has had gastric banding for weight loss.

bandwagon effect (band′wag″ŏn) A method of making decisions based on people's perceptions of what others have decided whether or not they have made a thoughtful choice. It is decision making based on peer pressure.

bandwidth 1. In electronics the range of frequencies within which performance with respect to some characteristic falls within specified limits. **2.** A measurement describing how much information can be transmitted at once through a communications medium.

Banisteriopsis caapi A tropical vine indigenous to South America whose bark is boiled with other plants to make hallucinogenic drinks, such as ayahuasca, or yage.

bank (bangk) [Italian *banca*, counter, (moneychanger's) table] In medicine and biology, a stored supply of body fluids or tissues for use in another individual (e.g., blood bank, eye bank, kidney bank, tissue bank).

blood b. A place in which whole blood and certain derived components are processed, typed, and stored until needed for transfusion. Blood is mixed with adenine-supplemented citrate phosphate dextrose and is stored at 4°C (39°F). Heparin may be used as a preservative. Banked blood should be used as soon as possible because the longer it is stored, the fewer red blood cells survive in usable form. Ninety percent of the red cells survive up to 14 days of storage, but only 70% remain after 24 days.

⚠ It is mandatory that appropriate quality assurance measures be undertaken to ensure that patients are properly identified at the bedside and at the blood bank in order to prevent the transfusion of mismatched blood. Blood banking measures are designed to minimize the risk of communicable illnesses, including hepatitis viruses and HIV.

---

cell b. A facility for keeping cells frozen at extremely low temperatures. These cells are used for investigating hereditary diseases, human aging, and cancer. Collections of banked cells are kept by the National Institutes of Health (the Human Genetic Mutant Cell Repository and the Aging Cell Repository) and at the Cornell Institute for Medical Research.

eye b. An organization that collects and stores corneas for transplantation.

serum b. A laboratory or storage facility where samples of serum are kept, typically at subfreezing temperatures, for their future value in the retrospective study of important or emerging diseases. The JANUS serum bank, in Norway, has one of the largest and best organized national collections of stored serum; its specimens have been used primarily in studies of tumor markers.

sperm b. A repository for the storage of semen used for artificial insemination. In some banks the specimen is frozen. SEE: *Standard Precautions Appendix.*

tissue b. A facility for collecting, processing, and storing tissue for later transplantation. Tissue stored includes bone, skin, nerve, fascia, tendon, heart valve, dura mater, cornea, and bone marrow. These are tested for microbial pathogens and stored either in a freeze-dried or frozen state.

Bankart lesion (bang′kärt) [Arthur Sidney Blundell Bankart, Brit. orthopedic surgeon, 1879–1951] An avulsion injury of the anterior capsule and labrum of the glenoid rim of the glenohumeral joint. This lesion is a common cause of recurrent anterior glenohumeral dislocations or anterior glenohumeral instability.

Banna virus (ban′na″, ban′ä) [Xishuang *Banna,* Yunnan province, China] SEE: under *virus.*

Banting, Sir Frederick Grant (bant′ing) Canadian scientist, 1891–1941; co-discoverer of insulin, with Charles Herbert Best and John J. R. Macleod in 1922; Nobel laureate 1923.

Banti syndrome (ban′tē) [Guido Banti, It. physician, 1852–1925] A syndrome combining anemia, splenic enlargement, hemorrhage, and, ultimately, cirrhosis; secondary to portal hypertension.

bar (bar) [Fr. fr. L. *barra,* rod] **1.** A metal piece attaching two or more units of a removable dental prosthesis. **2.** A rigid component of a splint or brace. **3.** A section of tissue that connects two similar structures.

C b. The curved part of a hand splint that maintains the thumb web space.

grab b. A bar attached to the wall to assist in basic activities of daily living.

lumbrical b. A component of a hand splint that rests on the dorsal surface of the proximal phalanges to prevent hyperextension of the metacarpophalangeal joints.

median b. Contracture or constriction of the vesical neck of the bladder caused by benign hypertrophy or fibrosis of the prostate. It may obstruct the flow of urine from the bladder.

Mercier b. SEE: *Mercier bar.*

swivel trapeze b. Trapeze b.

T-b. T-piece.

trapeze b. A triangular device suspended above a bed to facilitate transferring and positioning the patient. SYN: *swivel trapeze b.*

Bárány caloric test [Robert Bárány, Austrian physician and physiologist, 1876–1936. Awarded Nobel Prize in medicine in 1914] Evaluation of vestibular function by irrigation of the ear canal with either warm or cold water. Normally when warm water is used, rotatory nystagmus toward the irrigated ear is observed; with cold water, the normal response is rotatory nystagmus away from the irrigated ear. If vestibular function is impaired, the response may be absent or diminished. If one ear is normal and the other is not, a comparison between the two may be made.

-barb [Fm. *barb(iturate)*] Suffix used in pharmacology to name a *barbiturate.*

barbiturate poisoning SEE: under *poisoning.*

barbiturates (băr-bĭt′ū-rāts, băr-bĭ-tū′rāts) A group of organic compounds derived from barbituric acid (e.g., amobarbital, phenobarbital, secobarbital) that are used to treat and prevent convulsions, relieve anxiety, or aid sleep. Side effects include drowsiness, depressed respirations, decreased blood pressure, and decreased body temperature. These drugs can also cause tolerance and dependence. SEE: *Poisons and Poisoning Appendix.*

barbotage (băr-bō-tŏzh′) [Fr. *barboter,* to dabble] Repeated injection and withdrawal of fluid, as in gastric lavage, or the administration of an anesthetic into the subarachnoid space by alternate injection of anesthetic and withdrawal of cerebrospinal fluid into the syringe.

barbula hirci (băr′bū-lă hĭr′sī) [L. *barbula,* little beard, + *hircus,* goat] **1.** Hairs present on the ears. **2.** Axillary hair.

bar code SEE: under *code*.

bar code-enabled point of care technology ABBR: BPOC. A form of keyless data entry that facilitates automatic identification and collection of data and allows real-time confirmation of patient identity, medication taken, and dosage, time, and route of administration of the medication.

baresthesia (băr-ĕs-thē′zē-ă) [Gr. *baros*, weight, + *aisthesis*, sensation] Sense of weight or pressure; pressure sense.

bariatrics (băr″ē-ă′trĭks) [″ + *iatrike*, medical treatment] The branch of medicine that deals with prevention, control, and treatment of obesity.

baricity (bă-rĭs′ĭ-tĭ) The relative pressure, density, or concentration of a gas or a solution. *Hyperbaric* solutions have an increased density relative to a reference substance (e.g., hyperbaric oxygen has a greater oxygen concentration than the air we normally breathe). *Hypobaric* solutions are less concentrated than a reference solution (e.g., an injected drug can be made hypobaric relative to serum or plasma by diluting it with sterile water).

baritosis (băr″ĭ-tō′sĭs) A relatively benign form of pneumoconiosis caused by inhalation of barium dust.

barium (bar′ē-ŭm) SYMB: Ba. A soft metallic element of the alkaline earth group, atomic weight (mass) 137.373, atomic number 56. Barium is used as an intraluminal contrast agent in gastrointestinal radiography.

    b. sulfate BaSO₄, a radiopaque contrast medium used in radiographic studies of the gastrointestinal tract. SYN: *barite*.

barium compounds SEE: under *compound*.

barium meal The ingestion of barium sulfate to outline the esophagus, stomach, and small intestines during x-ray or fluoroscopic examination. The exam may be used as an alternative to endoscopy to diagnose reflux, dysphagia, peptic disease, or other upper gastrointestinal conditions. Also called *upper G.I. series*.

    PATIENT CARE: If the exam or procedure does not follow a barium enema, the patient should receive nothing by mouth after midnight on the night before the examination. No food or liquids should be taken by mouth until the last image is produced. If the exam is done within a few days after a barium enema examination, it is important to be sure the colon is free of barium, which could interfere with visualization of the stomach and intestines. A cleansing enema the evening before the exam may remove residual barium from the colon.

barium swallow Radiographic examination of the esophagus during and after introduction of a contrast medium consisting of barium sulfate. Structural ab-

normalities of the esophagus (such as strictures or tumors) and vessels (such as esophageal varices) may be demonstrated. SEE: *esophagram*.

Barlow disease (bahr′lō) [Sir Thomas Barlow, Brit. physician, 1845–1945] A deficiency disease due to lack of vitamin C (ascorbic acid). It occurs in both breast-fed and bottle-fed babies (usually between 6 and 12 months of age) who fail to receive adequate supplements of vitamin C. SEE: *scurvy, infantile*.

    TREATMENT: Therapy includes vitamin C and adequate daily intake of fruit juices (orange, grapefruit, tomato).

Barlow test A maneuver designed to detect subluxation or dislocation of the hip. The examiner adducts and then extends the legs while keeping a hand over the head of the femur. A dysplastic joint will be felt to dislocate as the femur leaves the acetabulum.

Barmah Forest virus (bar′mă) [*Barmah* Forest, southeastern Australia] SEE: under *virus*.

barn (bărn) [Special use of *barn*] ABBR: bn. A unit of area, employed chiefly in chemistry and physics, approximating the size of the nucleus of a uranium atom. One barn = 10^{-24} sq cm.

baro-, bar- [Gr. *baros*, weight] Prefixes meaning *weight* or *pressure*.

barognosis (băr-ŏg-nō′sĭs) [″ + *gnosis*, knowledge] The ability to estimate weights; the opposite of baragnosis.

barograph (băr′ō-grăf″) A device used to measure and record changes in atmospheric pressure.

baroreceptor (băr″ō-rē-sĕp′tor) A sensory nerve ending stimulated by changes in pressure. Baroreceptors are found in the walls of the cardiac atria, the vena cava, aortic arch. The baroreceptors of the lung are stretch receptors that are stimulated by inflation. SYN: *barostat; pressoreceptor*. SEE: illus.

baroreflex (băr″ō-rē′flĕks) [″ + L. *reflexus*, bent back] Any of the reflexes mediated or activated through a group of nerves located in various blood vessels in the intrathoracic and cervical areas and in the heart and its great vessels.

baroscope (băr′ō-skōp) [″ + *skopein*, to examine] An instrument that registers changes in the density of air.

barostat (băr′ō-stăt″) Baroreceptor.

barotitis (bar″ō-tīt′is) [bar- + otitis] Aerotitis.

barotrauma (băr″ō-traw′mă) [″ + *trauma*, wound] Any injury caused by a change in atmospheric pressure between a potentially closed space and the surrounding area. SEE: *aerotitis; barotitis; bends*.

barratry (băr′ă-trē) The practice of encouraging or sponsoring legal actions, esp. frivolous or unnecessary lawsuits.

Barr body (băr) [Murray L. Barr, Cana-

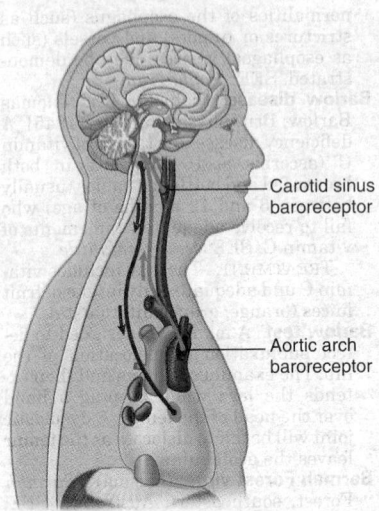

Carotid sinus baroreceptor

Aortic arch baroreceptor

BARORECEPTOR

dian anatomist, 1908–1995] Sex chromatin mass seen within the nuclei of normal female somatic cells. According to the Lyon hypothesis, one of the two X chromosomes in each somatic cell of the female is genetically inactivated. The Barr body represents the inactivated X chromosome.

barrel chest SEE: under *chest*.

barren [O. Fr. *barhaine*, unproductive] Sterile; incapable of producing offspring.

Barrett esophagus (bar'ĕt) [Norman R. Barrett, Brit. surgeon, 1903–1979] Replacement of the squamous epithelium of the distal esophagus with metaplastic columnar epithelium as a result of chronic exposure of the esophagus to stomach acid. It is diagnosed via endoscopy. The pathological changes usually occur after many years of gastroesophageal reflux disease and are occasionally followed by adenocarcinoma of the distal esophagus. SEE: *gastroesophageal reflux disease*.

barrier (bar'ē-ĕr) [Fr. *barriere*, a bar] **1.** An obstacle, impediment, obstruction, boundary, or separation. **2.** A device, e.g., a glove, mask, or drape, used to limit potentially infectious contact between health care providers and patients.

    architectural b. Any limitation in the design of facilities that restricts their access and use by persons with disabilities.

    blood-brain b. ABBR: BBB. Any of the special characteristics of the capillary walls of the brain that prevent potentially harmful substances (including many medications) from moving out of the bloodstream into the brain or cerebrospinal fluid. It consists of either the perivascular glial membrane or the vascular endothelium or both.

    blood-nerve b. A physiological barrier between nerves and capillaries that partially blocks the flow of ions from the blood across the perineurium.

    chemical b. **1.** The chemical characteristics of certain areas of the body that oppose colonization by microorganisms. The acidity of gastric juice, for example, prevents colonization by most disease-causing germs. **2.** A contraceptive cream, foam, jelly, or suppository that contains chemical spermicides.

    glomerular filtration b. The structure of the renal glomerulus that prevents the loss of proteins in the urine, thereby preserving albumin and globulins in the plasma instead of letting them leach into the urine.

    language b. Any of the difficulties in communication that arise when patients and their health care providers do not share fluency in a common language.

    PATIENT CARE: Professionally trained health care interpreters should be employed to bridge communication gaps. The interpreters are known to have better communication with the patient than do family members, concerned lay people, or incompletely trained staff members.

    mucus b. A thick, slippery coating of glycoproteins and other secreted organic chemicals that line and protect the intestinal epithelium. SYN: *mucus layer*.

    placental b. The selective ability of the placental membranes to limit the exchange of substances between the maternal and fetal circulations. Although water, oxygen and other gases, drugs, necessary nutrients, e.g., glucose and amino acids, maternal antibodies, and viruses cross the barrier unimpaired, large molecules, red blood cells, bacteria, and protozoa cross it only through breaks in placental integrity.

    primary radiation b. A wall or partition that shields the radiographer and others from direct exposure to x-rays. It must be capable of adequate lead equivalency to reduce the maximum possible x-ray beam strength to the level of background exposure.

    secondary radiation b. A wall or partition that shields against scattering or leakage of x-rays.

barrier cream A topical compound for limiting or preventing contact with irritants such as allergens, parasites, or toxins.

barrier-free design An approach to planning and designing living environments that emphasizes accessibility and use by persons with functional limitations. SEE: *universal design*.

Barthel index (bar'thĕl) [D.W. Barthel, 20th-cent. U.S. psychiatrist] A widely used functional assessment of activities of daily living. It assesses a person's ability to perform feeding, transfers, personal grooming and hygiene, toileting, walking, negotiating stairs, and controlling bowel and bladder functions.

Bartholin, Caspar (the younger) (bar-tul'in, bart'ŏ-lĭn, bar'thŏ-) Danish anatomist, 1655–1738.

   B. abscess An infection that develops when the Bartholin glands become occluded in an acute inflammation.

   B. cyst A cyst commonly formed in chronic inflammation of the Bartholin glands.

   B. ducts Large ducts of the sublingual salivary gland, parallel to the Wharton duct.

   B. gland Either of two small compound mucous glands located one in each lateral wall of the vestibule of the vagina, near the vaginal opening at the base of the labia majora. SYN: *vulvovaginal gland*.

bartholinitis (băr″tō-lĭn-ī′tĭs) [*Bartholin* + Gr. *itis,* inflammation] Inflammation of Bartholin's gland.

Barth syndrome (bărth) [P.G. Barth, b. 1944] A rare X-linked disorder in which affected boys have reduced muscle tone, cardiomyopathy, learning disabilities, a low white blood cell count, and a diminished ability to fight infections.

Bartlett-Biedel syndrome (bărt'lĕt-bēd'ĭl) An inherited cause of obesity that usually manifests itself in childhood. It is caused by a mutation in a single gene.

Barton, Clara (băr'tŏn) U.S. nurse, 1821–1912. Founder of the American National Red Cross. She aided the wounded in the Civil War and was a contemporary of Florence Nightingale.

Barton bandage (bart'ŏn) [John Rhea Barton, U.S. surgeon, 1794–1871] A double figure-of-eight bandage for the lower jaw.

Bartonella (bart″ŏn-el'ă) [Alberto L. Barton, Peruvian physician, 1871–1950] A genus of gram-negative bacteria of the family Bartonellaceae, that cause infections transmitted to humans from animal hosts.

   B. bacilliformis A species that causes bartonellosis. SEE: *bartonellosis*.

   B. elizabethae The organism previously known as *Rochalimaea elizabethae,* which causes an infection most often identified in immunocompromised patients with HIV infection. It has been implicated as a cause of bacteremia and endocarditis.

   B. henselae A species that, together with *B. quintana,* causes acute and persistent bacteremia and localized tissue infection, which may lead to bacillary angiomatosis, bacillary peliosis, and other inflammatory responses. This infection can occur in the immunocompromised and immunocompetent but is seen most frequently in patients with HIV infection. *B. henselae,* previously named *Rochalimaea henselae,* is the causative agent of cat scratch disease. Therapy for bacillary angiomatosis is oral antibiotics. SEE: *bacillary angiomatosis; disease, cat scratch; peliosis, bacillary*.

   B. quintana The species previously known as *Rochalimaea quintana,* spread by the body louse. During World War I, it caused epidemics of trench fever in battlefield troops. Together with *B. henselae,* it may cause bacillary angiomatosis, bacillary peliosis, and other inflammatory diseases. Treatment includes oral antibiotics. SEE: *trench fever*.

bartonellosis (bart″ŏn-el″ō′sĭs) [*Bartonella* + *-osis*] Any disease caused by *Bartonella* species. *B. bacilliformis* causes Oroya fever, *B. henselae* cat scratch fever, and *B. quintana* trench fever.

Barts hemoglobin (bart) [*Barts,* nickname of St. Bartholomew's Hospital (London)] Abnormal hemoglobin occurring in a form of thalassemia in which the affected person carries two copies of the alpha thalassemic globin gene from each parent. This condition causes erythroblastosis fetalis.

Bartter syndrome (bart'ĕr) [Frederic Crosby Bartter, U.S. physician, 1914–1983] Hyperplasia of the juxtaglomerular cells of the kidney, hypokalemic alkalosis, and hyperaldosteronism without a rise in blood pressure. It usually occurs in children and may be accompanied by growth retardation. Etiology is unknown. Affected patients are treated with potassium supplements and angiotensin-converting enzyme inhibitors or potassium-sparing diuretics.

bary- [Gr. *barys,* heavy] Prefix meaning *heavy, dull, hard*.

baryglossia (băr-ĭ-glŏs′ē-ă) [Gr. *barys,* heavy, + *glossa,* tongue] Slow, thick utterance of speech.

barylalia (bar-ĭ-lā′lē-ă) [*bary-* + *-lalia*] Indistinct, husky speech due to imperfect articulation.

baryophobia (băr″ĭ-ō-fō′bē-ă) The unreasonable fear that one's child will become obese. The allowed diet may be insufficient to support the child's growth and development needs.

basal (bā′săl) [*base* + *-al*] **1.** Pert. to the base. **2.** Of primary importance. **3.** Continuously active or present (e.g., basal insulin secretion). **4.** Located at the origin or underpinning of a structure.

basal body SEE: under *body*.

basal-bolus insulin therapy An insulin

regimen for diabetic patients in which patients use short- or rapid-acting insulins before each meal (bolus doses) and a long-acting insulin once a day (basal dose).

PATIENT CARE: A typical regimen uses approximately equal doses of long-acting insulin (such as glargine) and short- or rapid-acting insulins. The total dose of premeal insulin is either divided into thirds (if a patient consumes roughly equal amounts of carbohydrates at each meal) or is adjusted so that the meal with the greatest carbohydrate load is covered by a proportionately larger dose of rapid-acting insulin

basal cell nevus syndrome A rare autosomal dominant disorder which causes basal cell carcinomas to develop at an early age, a propensity for medulloblastomas, skeletal anomalies, and other findings.

basal ganglia Four masses of gray matter located deep in the cerebral hemispheres: caudate, lentiform, and the claustrum. Parkinsonism and Huntington's chorea are diseases of the basal ganglia, which are key components in the formation of habits and unconscious motor programs. The caudate and lentiform nuclei and the fibers of the internal capsule that separate them constitute the corpus striatum. The function of the basal ganglia is complex. They contribute to some of the subconscious aspects of voluntary movement such as accessory movements and inhibiting tremor. They do not initiate movement but rather provide coordination of complex motor circuits. Neurotransmitters that affect the basal ganglia are acetyl-

choline, dopamine, gamma-aminobutyric acid (GABA), and serotonin.

basal metabolic rate SEE: under *rate*.

basal rate In patient-controlled analgesia (PCA), the amount of pain reliever that is infused independent of any demands made by the patient.

PATIENT CARE: The basal rate of drug infusion in PCA is often set at zero to ensure that all doses of pain medication are dictated by the patient's individual needs for pain control. High basal rates may occasionally result in narcotic overdose. Basal rates above zero are used under carefully controlled circumstances to facilitate rest or sleep.

basal ridge An eminence on the lingual surface of the incisor teeth, esp. the upper ones. It is situated near the gum. SYN: *cingulum* (2).

basal temperature chart A daily chart of temperature obtained upon awakening. Some women are able to predict the time of ovulation by carefully analyzing the character and rhythm of the temperature chart. This information and other data can be used to establish that the woman is ovulating. Use of this method to control conception by predicting time of ovulation is unreliable in most cases. SEE: illus.; *conception; luteal phase **defect***.

base (bās) [Fr. *base*, L. *basis*, fr Gr. *basis*, step, pedestal] **1.** The lower part of anything; the supporting part. **2.** The principal substance in a mixture. **3.** Any substance that combines with hydrogen ions (protons); a hydrogen ion acceptor (Bronsted base). Strong bases, e.g., sodium hydroxide or lye, are corrosive to human tissues. Whether an unknown

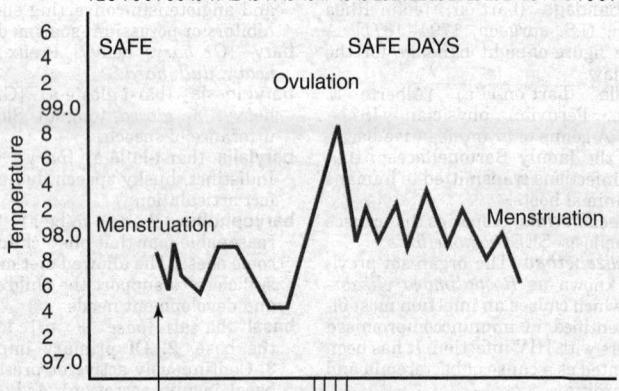

Days of Menstrual Cycle

1 2 3 4 5 6 7 8 9 10 11 12 13 14 15 16 17 18 19 20 21 22 23 24 25 26 27 28 1 2 3 4 5 6 7

SAFE   SAFE DAYS

Ovulation

Temperature

99.0   98.0   97.0

Menstruation   Menstruation

Example line only   1234 (Not safe)

BASAL TEMPERATURE CHART

chemical compound is a base or an acid may be determined by the color produced when it is added to a solution containing an indicator or by measurement of pH by an electrometer and suitable pH electrode. SYN: *alkali.* SEE: *acid; pH.* **4.** A substance that can donate a pair of electrons; a Lewis base. SEE: *Lewis base.*

   cavity b. In dentistry, the lining material placed in a cavity preparation, such as zinc phosphate cement, zinc oxide-eugenol cement, glass ionomer cement, or calcium hydroxide along with small amounts of other medicinal or adhesive materials.

   denture b. That part of the denture made of metal or resin, or both, that supports the artificial teeth and rests on abutment teeth or the residual alveolar ridge.

   nucleic b. In molecular biology, a ring-shaped chemical (either a purine or a pyrimidine) that specifies the coded genetic structure of DNA and RNA. DNA is made up of the bases adenosine, cytosine, thymine, and guanine; RNA contains uracil, in place of thymine.

Basedow disease (boz′ĕ-dō″) [Karl A. von Basedow, Ger. physician, 1799–1854] Graves disease.

base excess The difference between the normal and the actual buffer base concentration in a blood sample when titrated by strong acid at pH = 7.40 and PCO_2 = 40 mm Hg. The base excess is usually determined indirectly using measured values for pH and PCO_2 and then calculated using known relationships.

   b. e. of blood The substance concentration of base in whole blood determined at a pH of 7.40 and PCO_2 of 40 mm Hg. This measurement helps one assess the relative contribution of respiratory versus metabolic components in acid-base imbalances in the blood.

   b. e. of extracellular fluid ABBR: BE (ecf). The substance concentration of base in extracellular fluid determined at a pH of 7.40 and PCO_2 of 40 mm Hg. Because this quantity cannot be determined directly, a model of extracellular fluid is used as a basis. The model consists of one volume of blood plus two volumes of plasma. As with the base excess of blood, this quantity helps one assess the respiratory versus metabolic components in acid-base balance. In contrast to the base excess of blood, the base excess of extracellular fluid is said to be more representative of the acid-base status of the accessible fluid compartment and thus more appropriate for deciding on and evaluating therapy.

baseline (bās′līn″) A known or initial measurement used as a starting point against which future measurements can

be contrasted (e.g., temperature or blood pressure).

baseplate (bās′plāt) A temporary, preformed shape made of wax, metal, or acrylic resin that represents the base of a denture; used in assessing the relations of maxillary-mandibular teeth or for placement of artificial teeth in denture preparation.

basiarachnoiditis (bā″sē-ă-răk″noy-dī′tĭs) [Gr. *basis,* base, + *arachne,* spider, + *eidos,* form, shape, + *itis,* inflammation] Inflammation of the arachnoid membrane at the base of the brain.

basic **1.** In chemistry, possessing the properties of a base. **2.** Fundamental.

Basidiobolus (băs″ĭd-ē-ŏb′ŏ-lŭs) [NL] A genus of filamentous fungi (of the class Zygomycetes) found in soil, decaying vegetation, and the spore of amphibians, bats, and reptiles. It can cause cutaneous, subcutaneous, gastrointestinal, and blood vessel infections in humans. Human infections are reported mostly from Africa, South America, and tropical Asia.

Basidiomycetes (bă-sĭd″ē-ō-mī-sē′tēz) In one system of taxonomy, a class of the true fungi that contains mushrooms, bracket fungi, the plant parasites rusts and smuts, and the human parasite *Cryptococcus.* This class is equivalent to the phylum Basidiomycotina in another system of taxonomy. Mushroom toxins may be lethal to humans if ingested, and spores of these fungi may cause allergic asthma.

Basidiomycotina (băs″ĭd-ē-ō-mī″kō-tēn′ă) [NL.] In one system of taxonomy, a phylum of the true fungi. It is equivalent to the class Basidiomycetes in another system of taxonomy.

basilar (băs′ĭ-lăr) [L. *basilaris*] Basal (1).

basilateral (bā″sē-lăt′ĕr-ăl) [″ + L. *lateralis,* pert. to the side] Both lateral and basilar.

basilic (bă-sil′ik) [L. *basilicus* fr Gr. *basilikos,* royal] Prominent, important.

basin (bās′ĭn) An open, bowl-like container for holding liquids. It may be shaped to fit around a structure.

   emesis b. A kidney-shaped basin that can fit close to the neck so vomitus may be collected.

   lymph node b. The lymph nodes, considered collectively, into which lymph channels drain from a particular region of the body. Lesions on an arm, for example, drain into the axillary basin; those on a leg drain into the groin. Similarly, prostate cancers drain into pelvic and periaortic basins.

basio-, basi- [Gr. *basis,* base] Prefixes meaning *base* or *foundation.*

basion (bā′sē-ŏn) The midpoint of the anterior border of the foramen magnum.

basiphobia (bā″sē-fō′bē-ă) [Gr. *basis,* a

stepping, + *phobos,* fear] Fear of walking.

basis (bā′sĭs) *pl.* **bases** [L., Gr.] The base of a structure or organ.

basket [ME.] A netlike terminal arborization of an axon (or its collateral) of a basket cell that forms a network about the cell body of a Purkinje cell.

basophil, basophile (bā′sō-fĭl, -fīl″) [*basic (dye)* + *-phile*] ABBR: BA. **1.** A cell or part of a cell that stains readily with basic dyes such as methylene blue. **2.** A type of cell found in the anterior lobe of the pituitary gland. It usually produces corticotropin (ACTH), the hormone that stimulates the adrenal cortex to secrete cortisol. **3.** One type of granulocytic white blood cell. Basophils make up less than 1% of all leukocytes but are essential to the innate immune response of inflammation because they release histamine and other chemicals that dilate blood vessels and make capillaries more permeable. SYN: *basophilic **leukocyte**.* SEE: *blood* for illus.

basophilia (bā-sō-fĭl′ē-ă) **1.** A pathological condition in which basophilic erythrocytes are found in the blood. **2.** A condition marked by a high number of basophilic leukocytes in the blood.

basophilic (bā-sō-fĭl′ĭk) Pert. to basophils or to the propensity to stain with basic dyes.

basophilism (bā-sŏf′ĭ-lĭzm) A condition marked by an excessive number of basophils in the blood.

   pituitary b. Cushing's syndrome.

Bassen-Kornzweig syndrome (băs′ĕn-kŏrn′zvīg) [Frank A. Bassen, U.S. physician, 1903–2003; Abraham L. Kornzweig, U.S. physician, 1900–1982] Abetalipoproteinemia.

Bassini operation (bă-sē′nē) [Edoardo Bassini, It. surgeon, 1844–1924] A specific surgical procedure for inguinal hernia.

BAT *brown adipose tissue; blunt abdominal trauma.*

batch analysis An analysis in which all of the samples collected for a specific, nonemergent assay undergo the same testing process at the same time or sequentially. By contrast, samples collected for stat analyses are not saved in batches. These analyses are performed instead whenever individual specimens are received.

Bates method, Bates exercise (bāts) [W.H. Bates, U.S. physician, 1860-1931] An alternative medical practice for disorders of visual accommodation that includes blinking, covering the eyes with the palms of the hands, moving the eyes rapidly from side to side, exposing them to sunlight, and discarding eyeglasses.

bath (bath) The medium and method of cleansing the body or any part of it, or treating it therapeutically as with air, light, vapor, or water. The temperature

of the cleansing bath for a bed patient should be about 95°F (35°C) with a room temperature of 75° to 80°F (23.9° to 26.7°C).

THERAPEUTIC EFFECT: Warm and hot baths and applications soothe both the mind and the body. Gradually elevated hot tub and vapor baths relax all the muscles of the body. Hot baths promote vasodilation in the skin, drawing blood from the deeper tissues, and also help to relieve pain and stimulate nerves. Cold baths and applications abstract heat and stimulate reaction, esp. if followed by brisk rubbing of the skin. Cold constricts small blood vessels when applied locally. SEE: *hydrotherapy.*

   alcohol b. Application of a diluted alcohol solution to the skin as a stimulant and defervescent.

   alkaline b. A bath in which 8 oz (227 g) of sodium bicarbonate or washing soda is added to 30 gal (114 L) of water.

   alum b. A bath using alum in washing solution as an astringent.

   aromatic b. A bath to which some volatile oil, perfume, or herb is added.

   astringent b. Bathing in liquid containing an astringent, such as alum or tannic acid.

   bed b. A bath for a patient confined to bed.

PATIENT CARE: All necessary equipment is assembled, the room temperature is adjusted to a comfortable level, and the room is checked for drafts. While shielding the patient, the health care provider removes the top covers and replaces them with a bath blanket for the patient's physical warmth. The patient's ability to bathe independently is assessed, and the patient is encouraged to do so to the extent possible and permitted. Bathing may be accomplished using prepackaged disposable cloths impregnated with a no-rinse cleansing agent (heated in the microwave), various sized towels wet in warm water and wrung well prior to application or a basin of water which should be comfortably warm, 110° to 120°F (43.3° to 48.1°C), and changed as often as necessary to maintain the desired temperature and to permit thorough rinsing. The entire body, including the perineal area and genitalia, is washed, rinsed (if soap used), and dried thoroughly, one area at a time. Although traditional bathing has been done from the head downward toward the toes, with genitalia bathed last, use of prepared disposable cloths or towels for separate areas allows the care provider to bathe the patient in any order desired: for instance, demented patients may become upset by having their faces washed but accept bathing that begins with upper or lower extremities. Whatever method is employed, the patient should remain covered except for the area being bathed. After the bath, lotion may be applied to the skin (if not contraindicated), a clean gown is applied, and the patient's hair is combed or brushed. Oral hygiene is performed in conjunction with bathing. The bed is usually remade with clean linens at this time or following removal of the patient from bed to chair. The health care provider assists as needed with any part of this care. When bathing obese patients, drying of skin folds may be facilitated by using a handheld hair dryer on warm, taking care not to injure the skin in any way. Researchers have shown that bathing patients in ICU settings with disposable clothes saturated with 2% chlorhexidine gluconate reduces contamination rates from vancomycin-resistant enterococci (VRE), a common nosocomial infection, for both patients' skin and the ICU environment (object surfaces, health care providers' hands, et al), leading to less frequent infection. Additional hair care (shampoo, wet and dry shampoo products, styling) is provided as necessary, following protocols.

bland b. Bath containing substances such as starch, bran, or oatmeal for the relief of skin irritation; an emollient bath.

brine b. Saline **b.**

bubble b. A bath in which the water contains many small bubbles produced mechanically as by an air pump or chemically by bubble bath preparations.

⚠ Perfumes used in bubble baths may cause cystitis, skin irritation, and vaginitis, esp. in children.

carbon dioxide b. An effervescent saline bath consisting of water, salts, and carbon dioxide (CO_2). The natural CO_2 baths are known as Nauheim baths.

cold b. A bath in water at a temperature below 65°F (18.3°C).

colloid b. Emollient bath.

complete bed b. A bath in which the entire patient is bathed. SYN: *full b.*

continuous b. A bath administered for an extended period but seldom for longer than several hours. It is used in treating hypothermia or hyperthermia and certain skin diseases.

contrast b. Alternate immersion of hands or feet in hot water (1 min) then cold water (30 sec) for a prescribed length of time to promote circulation. The initial water temperature should be maintained throughout the bath, and the bath should end with immersion in cold water.

emollient b. A bath used for irritation and inflammation of skin and after

erysipelas. SYN: *colloid b.* SEE: *glycerin b.; oatmeal b.; powdered borax b.; starch b.*

foam b. A tub bath to which an extract of a saponin-containing vegetable fiber has been added. Oxygen or carbon dioxide is driven through this mixture to create foam.

foot b. Immersion of the feet and legs to a depth of 4 in (10 cm) above the ankles in water at 98°F (36.7°C).

full b. Complete bed bath.

glycerin b. A bath consisting of 10 oz (300 mL) of glycerin added to 30 gal (114 L) water.

herb b. A full bath to which is added a mixture of 1 to 2 lb (454 to 907 g) of herbs such as chamomile, wild thyme, or spearmint tied in a bag and boiled with 1 gal (3.8 L) of water.

hip b. Sitz bath.

hot b. A tub bath with the water covering the body to slightly above the nipple level. The temperature is gradually raised from 98°F (36.7°C) to the desired degree, usually to 108°F (42.2°C).

hot air b. Exposure of the entire body except the head to hot air in a bath cabinet.

hyperthermal b. A bath in which the whole body except the head is immersed in water from 105° to 120°F (40.6° to 48.9°C) for 1 to 2 min.

lukewarm b. A bath in which the patient's body except the head is immersed in water from 94° to 96°F (34.4° to 35.6°C) for 15 to 60 min.

medicated b. A bath to which substances such as bran, oatmeal, starch, sodium bicarbonate, Epsom salts, pine products, tar, sulfur, potassium permanganate, and salt are added.

milk b. A bath taken in milk for emollient purposes.

mud b. The use of mud in order to apply moist heat.

mustard b. A stimulative hot foot bath consisting of a mixture of 1 tablespoon (15 mL) of dry mustard in a quart (946 mL) of hot water added to a pail or large basin filled with water of 100° to 104°F (37.8° to 40°C).

Nauheim b. A bath in which the body is immersed in warm water through which carbon dioxide is bubbled.

needle b. Whirlpool bath.

neutral b. A bath in which no circulatory or thermic reaction occurs, temperature 92° to 97°F (33.3° to 36.1°C).

neutral sitz b. Same as sitz bath, except temperature is 92° to 97°F (33.3° to 36.1°C) or for hot bath 104° to 110°F (37.8° to 40°C), duration 15 to 60 min.

oatmeal b. A bath consisting of 2 to 3 lb (907 g to 1.4 kg) oatmeal added to 30 gal (114 L) water.

oxygen b. A bath given by introducing oxygen into the water through a special device that is connected to an oxygen tank.

paraffin b. A bath used to apply topical heat to traumatized or inflamed limbs. The limb is repeatedly immersed in warm paraffin, 118° to 126°F (47.8° to 52.2°C), and quickly withdrawn until it is encased in layers of the material. Paraffin may be applied with a paintbrush for larger joints.

powdered borax b. Bath consisting of ½ lb (227 g) added to 30 gal (114 L) water; 5 oz (150 mL) glycerin may be added.

saline b. Bath given in artificial seawater made by dissolving 8 lb (3.6 kg) of sea salt or a mixture of 7 lb (3.2 kg) of sodium chloride and ½ lb (227 g) of magnesium sulfate in 30 gal (114 L) of water. SYN: *brine b.; salt b.; seawater b.*

salt b. Saline bath.

sauna b. A hot, humid atmosphere created in a small enclosed area (often paneled in cedar) by pouring water on rocks heated, e.g., by an electric heater.

seawater b. Saline b.

sedative b. A prolonged warm bath. A continuous flow of water as well as an air cushion or back rest may be used.

sheet b. A bath given by wrapping the patient in a sheet previously dipped in water 80° to 90°F (26.7° to 32.2°C), and by rubbing the whole body with vigorous strokes on the sheet.

sitz b. The immersion of thighs, buttocks, and abdomen below the umbilicus in water. In a hot sitz bath the water is first 92°F (33.3°C) and then elevated to 106°F (41.1°C). SYN: *hip b.*

sponge b. A bath in which the patient is not immersed in a tub but washed with a washcloth, sponge, or antibacterial wipes.

starch b. A bath consisting of 1 lb (454 g) of starch mixed into cold water, with boiling water added to make a solution of gluelike consistency, then added to 30 gal (114 L) of water.

stimulating b. A bath that increases cutaneous blood flow. SEE: *cold b.; mustard b.; saline b.*

sun b. Exposure of all or part of the nude body to sunlight.

⚠️ Direct exposure of the skin to sunlight or other sources of ultraviolet energy increases the risk of skin cancer.

sweat b. A bath given to induce perspiration.

towel b. A bath given by applying towels dipped in water 60° to 70°F (15.6° to 21.1°C) to the arms, legs, and anterior and posterior surfaces of trunk, and then removing the towels and drying the parts.

whirlpool b. A therapeutic stainless steel, fiberglass, or plastic tank that uses turbines to agitate and aerate water into which the body, or part of it, is immersed. Tanks come in various sizes to accommodate treatment of different body parts (Hubbard and "low boy" tanks for full-body treatments or extremity tanks for arm or leg treatments). Water temperature selection varies depending on the condition of the patient and the desired therapeutic outcome. Cold whirlpools (ranging from 50°–79°F) are useful in treating acute inflammation. Tepid whirlpools (79°–92°F) are used to facilitate early therapeutic exercise. Neutral temperatures (92°–96°F) are generally indicated for treatment of wounds or for patients who have circulatory, cardiac, or sensory disorders or neurological changes in muscle tone. Hot whirlpools (99°–110°F) are beneficial in relieving pain, increasing soft tissue extensibility, and treating chronic conditions such as arthritis. In general, whirlpool temperatures should not exceed 110° to 115°F because of risk of burns. SYN: *needle b.*

bath bench Bathtub seat (1).

bathmotropic (bath″mŏ-trop′ik) [Gr. *bathmos,* a step +*-tropic*] Pert. to the excitability of nerves or muscles, esp. to the ability of heart muscles to be stimulated by the nerves that innervate them.

bathophobia (băth″ō-fō′bē-ă) [Gr. *bathos,* deep, + *phobos,* fear] Abnormal fear of depths; commonly refers to fear of height or of looking down from a high place.

bathyanesthesia (băth-ē-ăn″ĕs-thē′zē-ă) [″ + *an-,* not, + *aisthesis,* sensation] Loss of deep sensibility.

bathyesthesia (băth″ē-ĕs-thē′zē-ă) [″ + *aisthesis,* sensation] A consciousness or sensibility of parts of the body beneath the skin.

bathyhyperesthesia (băth-ē-hī″pĕr-ĕs-thē′zē-ă) [″ + *hyper,* above, + *aisthesis,* sensation] Excessive sensitivity of muscles and other deep body structures.

bathyhypesthesia (băth″ē-hīp″ĕs-thē′zē-ă) [″ + *hypo,* under, + *aisthesis,* sensation] Impairment of sensitivity in muscles and other deep body structures.

bat lyssavirus (bat) A single-stranded RNA virus that causes encephalitis. It can be transmitted to humans by an animal bite. SEE: *Lyssavirus.*

Batten disease (Băt′ĕn) [Frederick E. Batten, English ophthalmologist, 1865–1918] The most common of the neuronal ceroid lipofuscinoses (NCLs). This eponym is sometimes used as a synonym for the entire class of NCLs. The disease is an autosomal recessive, neurodegenerative disorder that results from the excessive accumulation of lipid-protein complexes in the brain and eye. Early symptoms include the sudden onset of visual impairment and seizures in childhood. Regression of developmental milestones and dementia precede premature death.

battered child syndrome Physical abuse of a child by an adult, family member, or friend. The abuse may be frequent and recurring. SEE: *child* **abuse***; shaken baby syndrome; Nursing Diagnoses Appendix.*

battered woman A woman who has been physically or sexually assaulted by her husband, partner, or former partner. Typically verbal abuse precedes physical violence. An escalating pattern of intimidation and injury often results, sometimes ending in death. Frequently women are reluctant to report this type of abuse because they feel trapped or isolated. Women from any socioeconomic level may be affected. Shelters and support for battered women are available in many locations.

battery [Fr. *baterie*, a beating] **1.** A device for generating electric current by chemical action. **2.** A series of tests, procedures, or diagnostic examinations given to or done on a patient. **3.** In law, the unlawful touching, beating, striking, or wounding of another person without consent, justification, or excuse. In legal medicine, battery occurs if a medical or surgical procedure is performed without proper consent. SEE: *assault* (2); *sexual harassment.*

Battle sign (bat′ĕl) [William Henry Battle, Brit. surgeon, 1855–1936] Ecchymosis behind the ear; a physical finding in patients with basilar skull fracture.

bay (bā) An anatomical recess or depression filled with liquid.

Bayes theorem (bāz) [Thomas Bayes, Brit. mathematician, 1702–1761] A statistical theorem concerned with analyzing the probability that a patient may have a specific condition after diagnostic testing. The theorem states that if a disease is very rare (the pretest probability is low), the patient is unlikely to have that condition even with a positive diagnostic test. Conversely, when the pretest probability of a specific condition is very high, a negative test result does not rule out the condition.

Bayley Scales of Infant Development (Bā′lē) A standardized battery of tests used to provide information about the developmental status of children aged 2 to 42 months. The battery is designed to indicate motor, mental, and behavioral levels based on performance and parental reports.

Baylisascaris procyonis (bāl″ĭ-sas′kă-rĭs prō″sē-ōn′ĭs, sē′ŏn-ĭs) [L. *procyon*, raccoon fr. Gr.] The raccoon roundworm. Accidental consumption of roundworm eggs (such as by children who put contaminated soil in their mouths) can re-

sult in encephalitis. SYN: *raccoon* **ascaris***.*

Bazin disease (bă-zin′) [Antoine P. E. Bazin, Fr. dermatologist, 1807–1878] A chronic skin disease occurring in young adult females; characterized by hard cutaneous nodules that break down to form necrotic ulcers that leave atrophic scars. The disease is almost invariably preceded by tuberculosis, but the etiological relationship to that disease is debated. SYN: *erythema induratum.*

BBT *baby's blood type; basal body temperature.*

BCAA *branched-chain amino acids.*

BCG *bacille Calmette-Guérin.*

bcl-2 Member of a family of oncogenes that is involved in tumor suppression. *Bcl-2* is an oncogene that is responsible for some of the ability of certain tumors to elude the host organism's defenses. *Bcl-2* suppresses apoptosis, permitting the metastasis of tumors. When referring to the protein product of the gene, the term "Bcl-2" is used. SEE: *apoptosis; oncogene.*

b.d. L. *bis die,* twice a day.

Bdellovibrio (dĕl″ō-vĭb′-rē-ō″) [Gr. *bdello*, leech, + *vibrio*] A genus of gram-negative bacteria that parasitize other bacteria by living and reproducing inside them.

Be Symbol for the element beryllium.

B.E. *below elbow,* referring to the site of amputation of an arm; *barium enema.*

BEACOPP *Bleomycin, etoposide, Adriamycin (doxorubicin), cyclophosphamide. Oncovin (vincristine), procarbazine, prednisone* (chemotherapeutic agents to treat Hodgkin disease).

bead (bēd) [ME. *bede,* prayer, prayer bead (on a rosary), bead] A small spherical object, typically made of glass, plastic, or metal. Beads have numerous uses in health care. They are employed in sterilization equipment and in some diagnostic and therapeutic injections.

beaded (bēd′ĕd) Referring to disjointed colonies along the inoculation line in a streak or stab culture.

beading (bēd′ĭng) Alternating stretches of dilation and stenosis within an artery, usually only seen during angiography.

beads, rachitic (bēdz) Visible swelling where the ribs join the costal cartilages, seen in rickets. SYN: *rachitic rosary.*

beaker (bē′kĕr) A widemouthed glass vessel with vertical sides, a closed circular base and circular opening for mixing or holding liquids.

beam (bēm) **1.** Photons, atomic particles, or sound waves aligned in parallel rays. In radiology and nuclear medicine, these rays may originate from a point-source and be directed toward an object in order to image or treat the object. **2.** The part of an analytical balance to

which the weighing pans are attached.
3. A long, slender piece of wood, metal, or plastic resin that acts as a support, e.g. in a dental appliance or other applications.

    balance b. In occupational and physical therapy, a plank 4 inches or more wide used to assess and improve balance and motor coordination, usually elevated several inches from the floor.

beam nonuniformity ratio ABBR: BNR. A measure of the homogeneity of a therapeutic ultrasound wave, expressed as a ratio between the ultrasound unit's average intensity (the metered output) and the peak intensity within the output wave. A completely homogeneous wave is represented by a 1:1 BNR.

⚠ FDA regulations require that the BNR be clearly labeled on therapeutic ultrasound units. A BNR of greater than 8:1 is considered to be potentially harmful.

beard The hair on a man's face and throat.
bearing down The expulsive effort of a parturient woman in the second stage of labor. Valsalva's maneuver is used, causing increased pressure against the uterus by increasing intra-abdominal pressure.
beat (bēt) A pulsation or throb (e.g., as in contraction of the heart).

    apex b. The impulse of the heart felt by the hand when held over the fifth or sixth intercostal space in the left midclavicular line.

    artificially paced b. A heartbeat stimulated by an artificial pacemaker.

    captured b. A ventricular contraction directly stimulated by an electrical impulse either from the sinus node or from the pulse generator of a pacemaker.

    complex ectopic b. Any electrical activation of the heart that originates outside the sinoatrial node.

    dropped b. A single interruption in the regular pacing of the electrical and mechanical activity of the heart.

    ectopic b. An electrical impulse that begins at any place in the heart other than the sinoatrial node.

    escape b. A depolarization of the heart that occurs after a prolonged pause or after failure of the sinus node to generate an electric impulse. Most escape beats are generated in the ventricles.

    extra b. Extrasystole.

    forced b. Extrasystole brought on by artificial heart stimulation.

    premature b. An electrical impulse that arises from a site other than the sinus node in the heart, occurring before the expected sinus beat.

Bechterew, Vladimir Mikhailovich, Bekhterev, Bechterev (bek'tĕ-ref″) Russian neuropathologist, 1857–1927

    B.-Mendel reflex SEE: *Mendel-Bechterew reflex.*

    B. reflex **1.** Contraction of the facial muscles due to irritation of the nasal mucosa. **2.** Dilatation of the pupil on exposure to light. **3.** Contraction of the lower abdominal muscles when the skin on the inner thigh is stroked.

Beck airway airflow monitor (bĕk) ABBR: BAAM. A device that is attached to the nasotracheal tube to help the intubator locate the sound of the air movement through the vocal cords.

Becker muscular dystrophy (bek'ĕr) [Peter E. Becker, Ger. geneticist, 1908–2000] ABBR: BMD. An X-linked recessive form of muscular dystrophy, typically first becoming evident in adolescence as difficulty with gait or with pelvic girdle muscle strength. It is characterized pathologically by inadequate production of dystrophin and thus is similar to, but usually milder than, Duchenne muscular dystrophy.

Beck triad (bek) [Claude S. Beck, U.S. surgeon, 1894–1971] Hypotension, distended neck veins, and muffling of heart sounds, the physical findings in cardiac tamponade.

Beckwith-Wiedeman syndrome (bĕk' wĭth-vēd'ĕ-măn) An autosomal dominant syndrome whose hallmarks are enlargement of the tongue and visceral organs, gigantism, and umbilical hernia, often with neonatal hypoglycemia.

becquerel (bĕk'rĕl) [Antoine Henri Becquerel, Fr. physicist, 1852–1908] SYMB: Bq. An SI-derived unit of activity of a radionuclide equal to the quantity of the material having one spontaneous nuclear transition, i.e., disintegrations, per second. One curie has 3.7×10^{10} transitions per second. Thus, one curie is equivalent to 3.7×10^{10} becquerels. SEE: *curie;* SI Units Appendix.

bed (bed) **1.** A supporting structure or tissue. **2.** A couch or support for the body during sleep.

    air b. **1.** A large inflated cushion used as a mattress. **2.** An air-fluidized bed.

    air-fluidized b. A bed consisting of a mattress filled with tiny glass or ceramic spheres that are suspended by a continuous flow of warm air. The patient "floats" on the mattress with only minimal penetration. Because of the even distribution of weight, the bed is particularly useful in treating or preventing pressure sores.

    capillary b. A network of capillaries.

    circular b. A bed that allows a patient to be turned end-over-end while held between two frames. This permits turning the patients without disturbing them by turning the two frames inside a circular apparatus that holds the ends of the frames. It is useful in treating paralyzed or immobilized patients.

Gatch b. SEE: *Gatch bed.*

hydrostatic b. Water **b.**

kinetic b. A bed that constantly turns patients side to side through 270°. It is used to prevent the hazards of immobility in patients requiring prolonged bedrest, as in multiple trauma and some neuromuscular diseases.

low air-loss b. A mattress composed of inflatable air cushions that is used to relieve pressure on body parts, esp. in patients who are being hospitalized for a long time or who have skin breakdown or to prevent skin breakdown.

metabolic b. A bed arranged to facilitate collection of feces and urine of a patient so that metabolic studies can be done.

nail b. The skin that lies beneath a nail at the tip of a digit.

open b. A bed available for assignment to a patient.

rocking b. An obsolete form of body ventilation that shifts the patient's position to move the diaphragm and facilitate gas exchange.

surgical b. A bed equipped with mechanisms that can elevate or lower the entire bed platform, flex or extend individual components of the platform, or raise or lower the head or the feet of the patient independently.

tonsillar bed The mucosal layer between the palatoglossal and palatopharyngeal arches that is filled with the palatine tonsil.

tumor b. The vascular and stromal tissue that surrounds a cancerous tumor and provides it with oxygen, growth factors, and nutrients.

water b. A rubber mattress partially filled with warm water (100°F or 37.8°C). It is used to prevent and treat pressure sores. SYN: *hydrostatic b.*

wound b. The base or floor or a burn, laceration, or chronic ulcer. To heal properly, it should have a rich supply of capillary blood, be free of necrotic debris, and be uninfected.

bed-bound, bedbound (bed'bownd") Bedridden.

bedbug A flat, reddish-brown insect, *Cimex lectularius* of the family *Cimicidae.* Its bite causes an itchy, red, hive-like rash and, occasionally, other allergic reactions. The adult bugs are about 5 to 7 mm long and survive for up to a year without feeding. Bedbugs may transmit bloodborne infections (such as hepatitis B or Chaga's disease) to humans. Treatment for bites consists of application of antipruritic lotions. In heavy infestations, an appropriate insecticide should be used to spray furniture, mattresses, floors, baseboards, and walls.

bed entrapment Hospital bed entrapment.

bedewing Clouding of vision resulting from edema of the cornea.

bedfast (bed'fast") Bedridden.

bed hold A reservation that allows one to stay in, or return to, a care facility. The reservation is usually made just before relocation to the facility or during furloughs away from it (e.g., in hospital or on family visits).

bedlam [From Hospital of St. Mary of Bethlehem, pronounced "bedlem" in Middle English.] **1.** An asylum for the insane. **2.** Any place or situation characterized by a noisy uproar.

bed management Daily hospital utilization review, esp. as it affects the length of a patient's stay and the planning of his or her discharge.

bed mobility, impaired Limitation of independent movement from one bed position to another. SEE: *Nursing Diagnoses Appendix.*

Bednar aphthae (bed'nar") [Alois Bednar, physician in Vienna, 1816–1888] Infected, traumatic ulcers appearing on the hard palate of infants; usually caused by sucking contaminated objects.

bedpan (bed'pan") A pan placed under a bedridden patient for collecting feces and urine.

PATIENT CARE: Using a bedpan is uncomfortable and awkward and requires more exertion from the patient than using a bedside toilet. Patients, esp. those recovering from myocardial infarction, should not be forced to use a bedpan if it is possible for them to use a bedside toilet.

bed rail Side rail.

bedrest **1.** A device for propping up patients in bed. **2.** The confining of a patient to bed for rest.

bedridden Unable or unwilling to leave the bed. SYN: *bed-bound; bedfast.*

bed rope ladder Rope ladder.

Bedsonia (bed-sō'nē-ă) [Sir Samuel Phillips Bedson, Brit. bacteriologist, 1886-1969] A term formerly used for the genus *Chlamydia.*

bedsore [AS. *bedd,* bed, + *sare,* open wound] Pressure sore.

bedtime fading A behavioral treatment for childhood insomnia, in which the sleep-resistant child is allowed to go to sleep late for a few nights and then gradually guided to sleep at earlier and earlier hours until the desired time of sleep is reached. The treatment limits conflicts with the child over bedtime and creates a more rapid onset of sleep because the late hour at which the child is initially put to rest means he or she will go to bed tired.

bedtime resistance SEE: under *resistance.*

bed-wetting (bed'wet"ing) Enuresis,

esp. nocturnal enuresis. SEE: *enuresis*.
bed-wetter ("ĕr), *n.*
BEE *basal energy expenditure.*
bee An insect of the order Hymenoptera and superfamily Apoidea. Included is the common honeybee, *Apis mellifera,* which produces honey and beeswax. SEE: *bee sting*.
bee bread Bee **pollen**.
Beer law (bēr) [August Beer, Ger. physicist, 1825–1863] The basic law that is the foundation for all absorption photometry. It predicts the linear relationship between the monochromatic light absorbance (A) of a solution and its concentration (c). The law is given as $A = \varepsilon lc$, where A = absorbance, ε = molar absorptivity, l = path distance, and c = concentration. It is also known as the Beer-Lamber or Bougher-Beer law.
Beer operation [Georg Joseph Beer, Ger. ophthalmologist, 1763–1821] A flap operation for cataract or artificial pupil.
Beers, Clifford Whittingham (bērz) U.S. mental health advocate and writer 1876–1943. Beers helped to found the American mental hygiene movement with the publication of his book "A Mind that Found Itself" (1908), a personal account of his treatment for mental illness, which brought attention to the inadequacies of institutionalized psychiatric care in the early 20th century.
Beers, Mark Howard (bērz) U.S. geriatrician, 1954–2009.
  B. criteria A list of medications that frequently cause side effects when administered to elderly patients. Among the medications on the list are those that cause prominent neuropsychiatric, renal, and anticholinergic side effects. SYN: *Beers list*.
  B. list Beers criteria.
bee sting therapy Apitherapy.
beeswax (bēz'wăks) Yellow wax obtained from the honeycomb of bees. A purified form is used in ointments.
beeturia (bēt-ū'rē-ă) Deep red or pink coloration of urine caused by betanin, the pigment in beets. This condition is common in iron-deficient adults and children and can occur after ingestion of even one beet.
Beevor sign (bē'vŏr) [C. E. Beevor, Brit. neurologist, 1854–1908] Upward (cephalad) movement of the umbilicus when the neck of a patient with paralysis of the lower rectus abdominis muscles is flexed. It is one marker of fascioscapular muscular dystrophy and is found in other conditions (e.g., in some patients who have suffered trauma to the trunk, abdomen, or spinal cord).
behavior (bi-hā'vyĕr) **1.** The manner in which one acts; the actions or reactions of individuals under specific circumstances. **2.** Any response elicited from an organism.

  caring b. The actions or responses of providing patient services.
  PATIENT CARE: The following are the 10 highest-ranked caring behaviors, derived from nursing literature, then selected by nurses as evident in caring situations with patients: attentive listening, comforting, honesty, patience, responsibility, providing information so the patient can make an informed decision, touch, sensitivity, respect, addressing the patient by name.
  illness b. Any of the ways in which an individual acts or reacts to his or her own illness or the illness of a family member. Common reactions include frustration, anxiety, denial, anger, and withdrawal.
  self-consoling b. Any of the self-quieting actions of infants, such as sucking on their fists and watching mobiles and other moving objects.
  self-injurious b. ABBR: SIB. Maladaptive behavior of various types, including self-scratching, illicit drug use, head banging, and tobacco use. The cause is unknown, but one theory is that the behavior is self-stimulatory.
  type A b. A behavior pattern marked by the characteristics of competitiveness, aggressiveness, easily aroused hostility, and an overdeveloped sense of urgency. Although some studies have suggested that this behavior pattern is important in coronary artery disease and hypertension, the evidence supporting this claim is controversial. The risk of accidents, suicide, and murder is higher in type A individuals.
  type B b. A behavior pattern marked by the lack of competitiveness, hostility, and time pressure.
behavior, risk-prone health Inability to modify lifestyle/behaviors in a manner consistent with a change in health status. SEE: *Nursing Diagnoses Appendix.*
behavioral genetics SEE: under *genetics*.
behavioral science SEE: under *science*.
behavioral system model A conceptual model of nursing developed by Dorothy Johnson. The person is regarded as a behavioral system with seven subsystems—attachment, dependency, ingestion, elimination, sexuality, aggression, achievement. The goal of nursing is to restore, maintain, or attain behavioral system balance and stability. SEE: *Nursing Theory Appendix.*
behaviorism (bē-hāv'yŏr-ĭzm) A theory of conduct that regards normal and abnormal behavior as the result of conditioning rather than choice or will.
behavior therapy Techniques used to change maladaptive behaviors, based on principles of learning theory. Cigarette smoking, eating disorders, and alcohol abuse are commonly treated through behavior therapy, which may

include the use of positive reinforcement, aversive conditioning, discrimination, and modeling.

Behçet disease Behçet syndrome.

Behçet syndrome (bā'sĕt, be-chet') [Hulusi Behçet, Turkish dermatologist, 1889–1948] A rare, multisystem, chronic, recurrent disease of unknown cause, marked by ulceration of the mouth and genitalia and by uveitis. The central nervous system, blood vessels, joints, and intestinal tract may be involved. It is genetically associated with HLA-B51. The disease occurs worldwide but is most common in the eastern Mediterranean and eastern Asia, where it occurs mostly in young men and is a leading cause of blindness. In the western world, where the disease is less severe, it affects men twice as frequently as it does women but is not a leading cause of blindness. The period between attacks is irregular but may be as short as days or as long as years. SYN: *Behçet disease; cutaneomucouveal syndrome.*

TREATMENT: Therapy depends on the severity of the clinical findings. Mild disease of skin and joints may be treated with topical steroids or nonsteroidal anti-inflammatory drugs. Involvement of the central nervous system or gastrointestinal tract may require high dose steroids or cytotoxic drugs, such as chlorambucil, cyclophosphamide, or methotrexate.

bejel (bĕj'ĕl) A nonvenereal form of syphilis endemic in Central and Western Africa and Eastern Mediterranean countries; children are especially susceptible.

bel (bĕl) SYMB: B. A unit of measurement of the intensity of sound. It is expressed as a logarithm of the ratio of two sounds of acoustic intensity, one of which is fixed or standard; the ratio is expressed in decibels.

belay (bĕ-lāy') To protect with a rope. A rescuer can belay a stokes basket as it is being lowered to a safe position.

belch (belch) **1.** To expel gas from the stomach through the mouth; to eructate. **2.** An act of belching; eructation.

belching (belch'ing) Raising of gas from the stomach and expelling it through the mouth and nose. For belching to occur, there is first an increase in gastric pressure; then the lower esophagus sphincter relaxes to allow equalization of pressure in the stomach and esophagus. Relaxation of the upper esophagus sphincter allows the gas to escape through the pharynx and mouth. SEE: *water brash.*

ETIOLOGY: Belching may be caused by gastric fermentation, air swallowing, or ingestion of carbonated drinks or gas-producing foods.

Bell, Sir Charles (bĕl) Scottish physiologist and surgeon, 1774–1842.

B. palsy Paralysis of the facial nerve. Bell palsy is usually caused by a reactivation of herpes simplex virus although other infections (such as syphilis or Lyme disease) are sometimes implicated. Complications may include corneal drying and ulceration and mild dysarthria. Either side of the face may be affected. Attacks recur in about 10% of cases. SYN: *Bell paralysis; facial palsy; facial nerve palsy; facial nerve paralysis; facial paralysis.*

SYMPTOMS: Paralysis of the facial nerve typically results in an asymmetrical facial appearance. The affected patient is unable to raise one side of the mouth to smile or to wrinkle or raise the eyebrow on the same side. This peripheral nerve dysfunction is distinguished from strokes that alter facial movement by the involvement of both the forehead and the mouth. Paralysis of the face caused by strokes usually only limits movement of the oral muscles. SEE: illus.

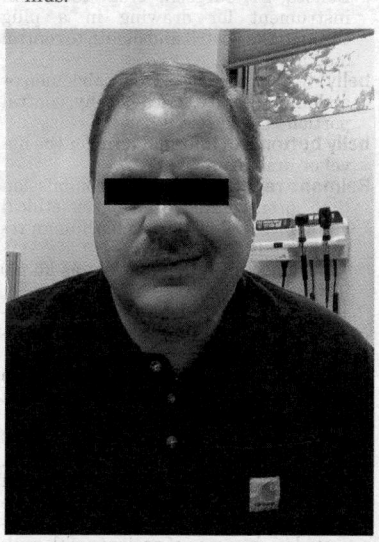

BELL PALSY
Asymmetrical smile in patient with Bell Palsy

TREATMENT: Tapering doses of prednisone without antiviral drugs provide the most effective results. In addition, the affected eye should be protected from drying with artificial tears or unmedicated ointments. Some practitioners advise wearing sunglasses during the palsy or patching the eye to protect it from foreign bodies or drying.

PROGNOSIS: Partial facial paralysis is usually resolved within several months. The likelihood of complete recovery after total paralysis varies from 20% to 90%.

B. paralysis Bell palsy.

Bell phenomenon Rolling of the eyeball upward and outward when an attempt is made to close the eye on the side of the face affected in peripheral facial paralysis.

belladonna (bĕl″ă-dŏn′ă) [It., beautiful lady] An anticholinergic derived from *Atropa belladonna,* a poisonous plant with reddish flowers and shiny black berries. Belladonna is the source of various alkaloids (stramonium, hyoscyamus, scopolamine, and atropine) and is used mainly for its sedative and spasmolytic effects on the gastrointestinal tract. All alkaloids derived from belladonna are toxic. SEE: *atropine in Poisons and Poisoning Appendix.*

Bellini, Lorenzo (bĕ-lē′nē) Italian physician and anatomist, 1643–1704.

B. tubule A papillary duct of the kidney; the union of several collecting tubules.

Bellocq cannula (bel-ok′) [Jean Jacques Bellocq, Fr. surgeon, 1732–1807] An instrument for drawing in a plug through the nostril and mouth to control epistaxis.

belly [AS. *baelg,* bag] **1.** The abdomen or abdominal cavity. **2.** The fleshy, central portion of a muscle.

belly button An informal term for the navel or umbilicus.

Belmont report A national commission that promulgated the basic ethical guidelines and principles for human research in the U.S.

belonoskiascopy (bĕl″ō-nō-skī-ăs′kō-pē) [Gr. *belone,* needle, + *skia,* shadow, + *skopein,* to examine] Subjective retinoscopy by means of shadows and movements to determine refraction.

benazepril An ACE inhibitor used to treat hypertension and congestive heart failure.

Bence Jones protein (Bĕns Jōnz) [Henry Bence Jones, Brit. physician, 1814–1873] The light chain portion of immunoglobulin molecules that may be deposited in the renal tubules and excreted in the urine of patients with multiple myeloma. The protein is involved in renal amyloidosis and renal failure.

benchmark (bench′mark″) **1.** A criterion of quality or service in health care, usually expressed as a measurable standard. **2.** A reference standard or basis for comparison that serves as a definition of a norm.

Bender Visual Motor Gestalt test (ben′dĕr) [Lauretta Bender, U.S. psychiatrist, 1897–1987] A test in which the subject copies a series of patterns. The results vary with the type of psychiatric disorder present.

bends, the (bĕndz) A lay term for decompression illness. SEE: *decompression illness; hyperbaric chamber.*

Benedict solution (ben′ĕ-dikt″) [Stanley R. Benedict, U.S. chemist, 1844–1936] A solution formerly used to test for the presence of sugar. To 173 g sodium or potassium citrate and 100 g anhydrous sodium carbonate (dissolved in 700 mL water) is added 17.3 g crystalline copper sulfate that has been dissolved in 100 mL of water. Sufficient water is added to the mixture to make 1000 mL. SEE: *Benedict's test.*

Benedikt syndrome (ben′ĕ-dikt) [Moritz Benedikt, Austrian physician, 1835–1920] Hemiplegia with oculomotor paralysis and clonic spasm or tremor on the opposite side. Benedikt's syndrome is caused by lesions that damage the third nerve and involve the red nucleus and corticospinal tract.

beneficence (bĕn-ĕf′ă-sĕns) **1.** An ethical principle that emphasizes doing what is best for the patient. **2.** Choosing to do good; acting kindly or charitably.

beneficiary (ben″ĕ-fish′ē-er″ē, -fish′ĕ-rē) [L. *beneficiarius,* pert. to a favor] One who receives or is entitled to receive a benefit, e.g., from a contract, a health insurance policy, or an estate.

benefit **1.** Something that promotes health. **2.** A term for service stipulations of an insurance policy, esp. a medical policy.

benefit trigger, trigger A set of conditions or self-care deficits used by a health insurer as criteria for the initiation of insurance payouts. In the care of elderly patients, benefits for certain residential services may be linked to the documentation of new deficits in self-care, e.g., the inability to perform two or more activities of daily living.

benevolence (bĕ-nĕv′ŏ-lĕns) [L. *benevolentia,* good will] The desire to act in a good, kindly manner toward others.

benign (bē-nīn′) [L. *benignus,* mild] Not recurrent or progressive; nonmalignant.

benign forgetfulness A memory defect marked by the inability to immediately recall a name or date. The item, whether recent or remote, is eventually recalled. SYN: *benign senescent forgetfulness.*

benign senescent forgetfulness Benign forgetfulness.

Bennett, Edward Hallaran (ben′ĕt) Irish surgeon, 1837–1907.

B. double-ring splint A metal splint that slips on the finger and limits hyperextension of the proximal interphalangeal joint.

B. fracture An intra-articular fracture at the base of the first metacarpal with dislocation of the carpometacarpal joint due to traction of the abductor pollicis longus muscle on the first metacarpal. This fracture usually requires percutaneous pinning to maintain reduction.

Bentall procedure (ben′tal″) [Hugh Bentall, Brit. cardiac surgeon] The replacement of the aortic valve, root of the aorta, and the ascending aorta in patients with diseases of both the valve and the proximal aorta. The procedure involves the use of a graft to replace the diseased vessel, and reimplantation of the coronary arteries arising from the proximal aorta into the graft.

bentonite (bĕn′tŏn-īt) [Fort Benton, U.S.] A hydrated aluminosilicate that forms a thick, slippery substance when water is added. It is used as a suspending and clarifying agent. It may be heat-sterilized.

benzaldehyde (bĕn-zăl′dĕ-hīd) A pharmaceutical flavoring agent derived from oil of bitter almond.

benzamide (ben-zam′īd) [*benzoin* + *amide*] Any of a class of drugs, including domperidone, metoclopramide, and trimethobenzamide, that block dopamine and serotonin receptors and stimulate acetylcholine receptors in smooth muscle. They are principally used to treat nausea and vomiting.

benzene, benzin, benzine (ben′zēn″, ben-zēn′) [*benz(oin)* + *-ene*] C_6H_6, a highly flammable volatile organic compound that is the simplest member of the aromatic series of hydrocarbons. It is composed of six carbon atoms in a ring and has one hydrogen atom attached to each carbon atom. It is immiscible with water, dissolves fats, and is used as a solvent and in the synthesis of dyes and drugs. SYN: *benzol*. SEE: *Poisons and Poisoning Appendix*.

 It is a carcinogen.

   ethenyl b. SEE: *ethenylbenzene*.

benzoate (bĕn′zō-āt) A salt of benzoic acid.

benzocaine (bĕn′zō-kān) Ethyl aminobenzoate, a local anesthetic used topically.

benzodiazepine (bĕn″zō-dī-ăz′ĕ-pēn) Any of a group of chemically similar psychotropic drugs with potent hypnotic and sedative action; used predominantly as antianxiety and sleep-inducing drugs. Side effects of these drugs may include impairment of psychomotor performance; amnesia; euphoria; dependence; and rebound (i.e., the return of symptoms) transiently worse than before treatment, upon discontinuation of the drug.

benzoic acid (ben-zō′ik) SEE: under *acid*.

benzoin (bĕn′zoyn, -zō-ĭn) [Fr. *benjoin*] A balsamic resin. It is used as a solution applied to the skin to prepare it for application of adhesives, esp. adhesive tapes.

benzol (bĕn′zŏl″) Benzene.

benzonatate (bĕn-zō′nă-tāt) A sub-

stance chemically related to procaine and used to suppress cough.

benzoylecgonine (bĕn-zoyl-ĕk′gō-nīn) The principal metabolite of cocaine. Screening tests for cocaine determine its presence or absence.

benzoyl peroxide (bĕn′zŏwl″) A topical agent used for the treatment of acne vulgaris. It is usually considered as a first-line treatment for mild to moderate acne. Common side effects include drying of the skin and skin discomfort.

benztropine mesylate (bĕnz′trō-pēn) An antiparasympathomimetic agent usually used with other drugs in treating parkinsonism.

benzyl (bĕn′zēl″) $C_6H_5COOCH_2C_6H_5$; the hydrocarbon radical of benzyl alcohol and various other compounds.

   b. benzoate An aromatic, clear, colorless oily liquid with a sharp, burning taste. It is used as a topical scabicide.

benzylpenicillin procaine (bĕn″zĭl-pĕn-ĭ-sĭl′ĭn) Penicillin G procaine.

benzylpenicilloyl polylysine, benzylpenicilloyl poly-L-lysine (ben′zēl″pen″ĭ-sĭl′ō-il″pol″i-lī′sēn, ′zĕl-) [*benzyl* + *penicilloyl-polylysine*] ABBR: PPL. Penicilloyl-polylysine.

BEP *bleomycin, etoposide, cisplatin.* (chemotherapeutic agents to treat cancers of the testes and ovaries).

Bérard aneurysm (bā-rar′) [Auguste Bérard, Fr. surgeon, 1802–1846] An arteriovenous aneurysm in the tissues surrounding an injured vein.

bereavement (bē-rēv′mĕnt) The expected reactions of grief and sadness upon learning of the loss of a loved one. The period of bereavement is associated with increased mortality. It is useful for those who care for the bereaved to emphasize human resilience and the power of life rather than the stress that accompanies bereavement.

bergamot phototoxicity (bĕr′gă-mot″) Berlock **dermatitis**.

Berg balance test (bĕrg) A 14–item evaluation of physical activities, including; sit-to-stand, reaching, turning, and single leg stance. The activities are assessed on a 5–point scale (0 to 4). This test has been shown to be highly predictive of patient falls.

Berger disease (bĕr′jĕr, ber-zhā′) [Jean Berger, contemporary Fr. nephrologist] Immunoglobulin A **nephropathy**.

Bergeron chorea (ber′jĕ-ron″) Electric chorea.

Bergman triad (berg′măn, ′man″) Dyspnea, axillary or thoracic petechiae, and diminished mental status, the classic findings in patients with fat embolism.

Bergmeister papilla (bĕrg′mīst′-ĕr) A veil in front of the retina of the eye. It is made of a conical mass of glial remnants that are the developmental tissue of the eye that has not been reabsorbed.

beriberi (bĕr′ē-bĕr′ē) [Singhalese, reduplication of *beri*, weakness] A disease marked by peripheral neurologic, cerebral, and cardiovascular abnormalities and caused by a lack of thiamine. Early deficiency produces fatigue, irritability, poor memory, sleep disturbances, chest pain, anorexia, abdominal discomfort, and constipation. Beriberi is endemic in Asia, the Philippines, and other islands of the Pacific.

ETIOLOGY: Deficiency is caused by subsistence on highly polished rice, which has lost all thiamine content through the milling process. Secondary deficiency can arise from decreased absorption, impaired absorption, or impaired utilization of thiamine.

TREATMENT: Treatment consists of oral or parenteral administration of thiamine and eating a balanced diet.

shoshin b. Shoshin syndrome.

berkelium (bĕrk′lē-ŭm) [University of California at *Berkeley*, where first produced + *-ium* (1)] SYMB: Bk. A transuranic element; atomic weight (mass) 247, atomic number 97.

Berlin edema (bĕr′lĭn) [Rudolf Berlin, Ger. ophthalmologist, 1833–1897] Commotio retinae.

berloque dermatitis SEE: under *dermatitis*.

Bernard glandular layer (ber-nar′, -nard′) The layer of cells lining the acini of the pancreas.

Bernard puncture (ber-nar′) [Claude Bernard, Fr. physiologist, 1813–1878] Puncture in the floor of the fourth ventricle of the brain an experimental animal in order to induce glycosuria.

Bernard-Soulier syndrome (bĕr-när′sool-yā′) [Jean A. Bernard, Fr. hematologist, 1907–2006; Jean-Pierre Soulier, Fr. hematologist, 1915–2003] An autosomal recessive bleeding disorder marked by an inherited deficiency of a platelet glycoprotein. The platelets are large. Bleeding results from defective adhesion of platelets to subendothelial collagen and is disproportionate to the reduction in platelets.

Bernhardt-Roth syndrome Meralgia paresthetica.

Bernheim effect (bern′hīm″, ber-nem′) [P. Bernheim, 20th-cent. Fr. physician] The effect of elevated pressures in the left ventricle of the heart on right ventricular performance, or of elevated pressures in the right ventricle on left ventricular contraction (the *reverse Bernheim effect*).

Bernstein test (bĕrn′stīn) [Lionel Bernstein, U.S. physician, b. 1923] Test to reproduce the pain of heartburn. This is done by swallowing a dilute solution (0.1 N) hydrochloric acid. This is compared with a placebo infusion of normal saline into the esophagus. The latter does not cause heartburn.

berylliosis (bĕr″ĭl-lē-ō′sĭs) [*beryllium* +

Gr. *osis*, condition] Beryllium poisoning, usually of the lungs. The beryllium particles cause fibrosis and granulomata at any site, whether inhaled or accidentally introduced into or under the skin.

beryllium (bĕ-ril′ē-ŭm) [Gr. *bēryllos*, beryl (a mineral) + *-ium* (1)] SYMB: Be. A metallic element, atomic weight (mass) 9.0122, atomic number 4, specific gravity 1.848. It is used as a window in some x-ray tubes to produce a soft (low kilovoltage) beam appropriate for imaging soft tissue (mammography or specimen radiography) or for forensic and industrial radiography of extremely thin objects, e.g., a postage stamp or fingerprint.

Best disease (best) [Franz Best, Ger. pathologist, 1878–1902] Vitelliform macular dystrophy that begins in childhood or adolescence, worsens in adulthood, and is characterized by degeneration of the pigment epithelium of the macula. SEE: *macular* **dystrophy**; *vitelliform macular* **dystrophy**.

bestiality (bĕs-tē-ăl′ĭ-tē) [L. *bestia*, beast] The use of animals (e.g., snakes, poultry, and nonhuman mammals) for sexual enjoyment.

best interest standard The ethical requirement that people who care for others will do so in good faith, placing their assessment of that person's best interests above their own. The standard particularly applies to the care of incompetent or dependent people, e.g., infants or patients who are so ill that they cannot make decisions on their own.

best supportive care SEE: under *care*.

beta (bāt′ă) **1.** B or β, the uppercase and lowercase symbols, respectively, for the second letter of the Greek alphabet. **2.** In chemistry, a prefix to denote isomeric variety or position in compounds of substituted groups.

beta blocker SEE: under *blocker*.

beta-carboline alkaloid (bāt″ă-kar′bō-lēn″) SEE: under *alkaloid*.

beta carotene A yellow-orange pigment found in fruits and vegetables; it is the most common precursor of vitamin A. The daily human requirement for vitamin A can be met by dietary intake of beta carotene.

TOXICITY: Ingestion of large doses of vitamin A either acutely or chronically causes skin and liver damage, among other injuries. Beta carotene supplements increase the risk of death among smokers and have no known beneficial effects on nonsmokers. Beta carotene occurring naturally in foods has no known toxicity.

BENEFITS: A diet rich in beta carotene has been associated with a decreased risk of certain cancers.

DOSING: Vitamin A activity in foods is expressed as retinol equivalents (RE).

Six mg of beta carotene equals 1 μg of retinol or 1 RE. SEE: *vitamin A; retinol.*

beta cell SEE: under *cell.*

betacism (bā'tă-sĭzm) [Gr. *beta,* the letter b, + *-ismos,* condition] Speech in which other letters of the alphabet are inappropriately pronounced like the letter *b.*

beta cryptoxanthin Cryptoxanthin.

beta-glucan, β-glucan (bāt'ă-gloo'kăn) Any of a class of complex carbohydrate nutrients, derived from yeast, with immune-stimulating and antimicrobial activity in laboratory experiments. They are promoted as dietary supplements.

beta-glucuronidase, β**-glucuronidase** (bāt'ă-gloo"kū-ron'ĭ-dās") An enzyme found in lysosomes. It is involved in the breakdown of glycosaminoglycan.

beta-lactam (bā'tă lăk'tăm) Beta-lactam antibiotic.

beta-lactamase, β**-lactamase** (bāt"ă lak'tă-mās", -māz") An enzyme that destroys the beta-lactam ring of penicillin-like antibiotics and makes them ineffective.

> ***extended-spectrum b. l.*** ABBR: ESBL. Any enzyme that makes bacteria (esp. gram-negative bacteria such as the Enterobacteriaceae) resistant to the effects of broad-spectrum beta-lactam antibiotics.

beta-lactamase resistance (bāt"ă lak'tă-mās", -māz") SEE: under *resistance.*

beta-lactamase-resistant antibiotic, β**-lactamase-resistant antibiotic** (bāt"ă lak'tă-mās", -māz") SEE: under *antibiotic.*

betamethasone (bā"tă-mĕth'ă-sōn) A powerful, synthetic glucocorticoid used to treat many conditions including dermatitis, arthritis, inflammatory bowel disease, reactive airways disease, and respiratory distress syndrome in preterm infants, among others.

beta$_2$ microglobulin (mī"krō-glŏb'ū-lĭn) ABBR: β_2-m. A polypeptide that is one of the class I major histocompatibility markers on cell surfaces; it is grouped into chains of low molecular weight called light chains. The β_2-m chain may be affected by the *nef* gene in HIV, preventing CD8+ T lymphocytes from recognizing the virus. SEE: *acquired immunodeficiency syndrome; major histocompatibility complex.*

beta subunit Glycoprotein hormones containing two different polypeptide subunits designated α and β chains. Analysis of the units of these hormones (e.g., follicle-stimulating, luteinizing, chorionic gonadotropin, and thyrotropin) enables early diagnosis of such conditions as pregnancy and ectopic pregnancy.

betatron (bā'tă-trŏn) A circular electron accelerator that produces either high-energy electrons or x-ray photons.

betel nut (bēt'ĭl) [Portuguese *betele*] The nut of the tropical Asian palm *Areca catechu,* chewed for its stimulant and euphoric effects. SYN: *areca nut.*

⚠️ Chewing betel nut causes cholinergic effects, which some people may not tolerate well. Chewing betel nut has also been associated with oral and esophageal cancers, esp. in those who also smoke cigarettes or drink alcohol.

Bethesda System, The (bĕ-thez'dă) ABBR: TBS. A system for reporting cervical or vaginal cytologic diagnoses. Use of TBS replaces the numerical designations (Class 1 through 5) of the Papanicolaou smear with descriptive diagnoses of cellular changes. Cellular changes are identified as benign; reactive, such as those due to inflammation, atrophy, radiation, or use of an intrauterine device; or malignant. Hormonal evaluation of vaginal smears is provided. Low-grade squamous intraepithelial lesions include what was previously called grade 1 cervical intraepithelial neoplasia (CIN 1) and cellular changes due to human papilloma virus, that is, koilocytosis. High-grade squamous intraepithelial neoplasia includes what was once identified as CIN 2 and CIN 3. SEE: *cervical **cancer***; *cervical intraepithelial **neoplasia**.*

Bethlem myopathy A rare, autosomal dominant form of limb-girdle muscular dystrophy that becomes clinically obvious in early childhood. It is usually slowly progressive, gradually resulting in weakness that may limit the ability to walk independently. Muscle contractures, e.g., of the hands, ankles, and elbows, are characteristic.

Betulaceae (bech"ŭ-lās'ē-ē") [*Betula* + *-aceae*] The family of flowering trees that include birches and beeches. Tree pollen from members of this family produces allergic reactions in many people in the early spring.

Betula verrucosa (bĕch'oo-lă, bĕ'tū-lă vĕ-roo-kō'să) [L. "rough birch"] The scientific name for the European white birch tree. European white birch pollen, abbreviated *Bet* by the World Health Organization, contains allergens that cause allergies in the spring in the northern hemisphere.

Betz cells (Bĕts) [Vladimir A. Betz, Russ. anatomist, 1834–1894] A type of giant pyramidal cell in the cortical motor area of the brain. The axons of these cells are included in the pyramidal tract.

bevel (bĕv'ĕl) **1.** A surface slanting from the horizontal or vertical. **2.** In dentistry, to produce a slanting surface in the enamel margins of a cavity preparation, named according to the surface resulting.

bezoar (bē'zor) [Arabic *bazahr*, protecting against poison] A hard mass of entangled material sometimes found in the stomachs and intestines of animals and humans, such as a hairball (trichobezoar), a hair and vegetable fiberball (trichophytobezoar), or a vegetable foodball (phytobezoar).

Bezold, Friedrich (bē'zold″, bāt'solt″) Ger. otologist, 1842–1908.

   B. mastoiditis Abscess underneath insertion of the sternocleidomastoid muscle due to pus breaking through the mastoid tip.

   B. perforation A perforation on the inner surface of the mastoid bone.

BFP *biologically false positive.*

BFU *burst-forming-unit.*

Bi Symbol for the element bismuth.

bi- [L. *bis,* twice] Prefix meaning *two, double, twice.*

biarticular (bī″ăr-tĭk'ū-lăr) [″ + *articulus,* joint] Pert. to two joints; diarthric (e.g., temporomandibular joints).

bias (bī'ăs) [Fr. *biais,* oblique] In experimental medicine, statistics, and epidemiology, any effect or interference tending to produce results that depart systematically from the true value. Particular biases are listed under the first word. SEE: e.g. *citation bias; geographical bias; spectrum bias.*

bibasilar (bī-băs'ĭ-lăr) Pertaining to both lung bases.

bibliographic manager (bĭb″lē-ō-grăf'ĭk măn'ă-jĕr) Software products to manage textbook and journal references, create databases, and format information for search and retrieval.

bibulous (bĭb'ū-lŭs) [L. *bibulus,* from *bibere,* to drink] Absorbent. SYN: *hydrophilous; hygroscopic.*

bicameral (bī-kăm'ĕr-ăl) [L. *bis,* twice, + *camera,* a chamber] Having two cavities or chambers.

bicarbonate (bī-kăr'bō-nāt) Any salt containing the HCO₃⁻ (bicarbonate) anion. SEE: *carbonic acid.*

   blood b. Measured HCO_3^- in the blood. The amount present is an indicator of the alkali reserve and is best understood when comparison is made of the blood bicarbonate, pH, PCO_2, and base excess, using the Henderson-Hasselbalch equation.

   b. of soda Sodium bicarbonate.

bicellular (bī-sĕl'ū-lăr) [″ + *cellularis,* little cell] **1.** Composed of two cells. **2.** Having two chambers or compartments.

biceps (bī'sĕps) [″ + *caput,* head] A muscle with two heads.

   b. brachii The muscle of the upper arm that flexes the elbow and supinates the forearm. SEE: illus.

   b. femoris One of the hamstring muscles lying on the posterior lateral side of the thigh. It flexes the leg, ro-

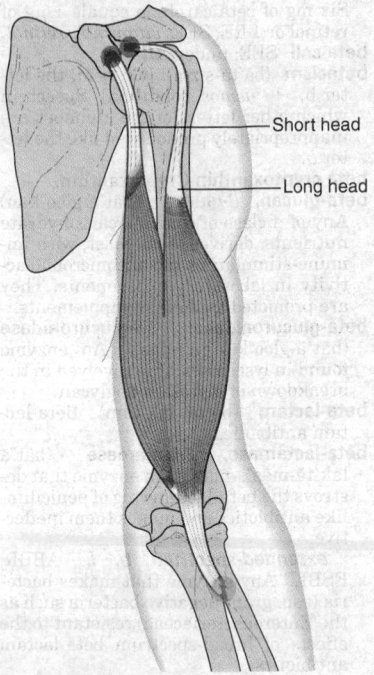

Short head
Long head

BICEPS BRACHII

tates it outward, and also extends the thigh.

bicipital (bī-sĭp'ĭ-tăl) [L. *biceps,* two heads] **1.** Pert. to a biceps muscle. **2.** Having two heads.

bicistronic (bī″sĭs-trŏn'ĭk) [″ + *cistron*] Capable of making two proteins from a single messenger RNA molecule.

biconcave (bī-kŏn'kāv) [L. *bis,* twice, + *concavus,* concave] Concave on each side, esp. as a type of lens.

biconvex (bī-kŏn'vĕks) [″ + *convexus,* rounded raised surface] Convex on two sides, esp. as a type of lens. SEE: *biconcave* for illus.

bicornate, bicornis (bī-kor'nāt, -nĭs) [″ + *cornutus,* horned] Having two processes or hornlike projections.

bicoronal (bī″kŏr'ă-năl) [″ + L. *corona,* garland, crown fr. Gr. *korone,* curved object, crown] **1.** Pert. to both areas of the corona radiata. **2.** Pert. to the articulations on either side of the skull that join to form a crown-shaped structure during normal fetal development.

bicorporate (bī-kor'pō-rāt) [″ + *corpus,* body] Having two bodies.

bicuspid (bī-kŭs'pĭd) [*bi-* + *cuspid*] Having two cusps or projections or having two cusps or leaflets.

b.i.d. L. *bis in die,* twice daily.

bidet (bē-dā') [Fr., a small horse] A basin used for cleaning the perineum.

bidi (bē'dē) [Hindi *bīdī,* a compound in

betel leaf] A hand-rolled, often flavored cigarette imported from India or Southeast Asia. It is popular with young smokers but has a higher nicotine and tar content than most commercially available cigarettes in the U.S. Like other brands of tobacco in the U.S., it causes cancers, an increased risk of fetal death during pregnancy, heart disease, peripheral vascular disease, chronic obstructive lung disease, and genetic mutations.

Bier, August Karl Gustav (bēr) Ger. surgeon, 1861–1949.

   B. block Regional anesthesia induced by the injection of a local anesthetic into a vein. It is typically used for surgeries on a limb (such as to repair a distal fracture) after placement of a tourniquet on the limb to hold the anesthetic in place.

   PATIENT CARE: The limb is exsanguinated before the injection of the anesthetic either by milking blood from its distal end to the tourniquet and placing an Esmarch bandage to keep the blood from flowing back into it or by elevating it above the heart. The tourniquet (such as a blood pressure cuff) is then inflated, and the anesthetic is injected distally.

Bietti crystalline dystrophy (bē-et′ē) [G. B. Bietti, 20th-cent. Italian ophthalmologist] A rare, autosomal-recessive eye disease that causes gradually worsening night blindness and peripheral vision loss. It results from the deposition of crystals in the cornea and retina, with gradual atrophy of the choroid and retina. This condition is more common in Asians than in other ethnic groups.

bifacial (bī-fā′shăl) [″ + *facies,* face] Having similar opposite surfaces.

bifid (bī′fĭd) [″ + *findere,* to cleave] Cleft or split into two parts.

Bifidobacteria (bī″fĭd-ō-băk-tēr′ē-ă) [″ + ″] Pl. of Bifidobacterium.

Bifidobacterium (bī″fĭd-ō″bak-tēr′ē-ŭm, -tēr′ē-ă) *pl.* **bifidobacteria** [*bifid* + *bacterium*] A genus of gram-positive, nonmotile anaerobic bacteria that live in the intestines and vagina. Two species are used clinically as probiotics. *Bifidobacterium* and *Lactobacillus* species (such as *B. longum, B. infantis,* and *L. acidophilus*) are used clinically as probiotic bacteria, i.e., they contribute to human health. They have been used to treat antibiotic-associated diarrhea, irritable bowel syndrome, and inflammatory bowel diseases and are also used in dairies to produce fermented milks and yogurt. The use of antibiotics to treat infectious diseases may decrease the concentration of *Bifidobacterium* in the gastrointestinal tract, allowing disease-causing bacteria to multiply.

bifocal (bī-fō′kăl) [″ + *focus,* hearth] Having two foci, as in bifocal eyeglasses.

bifocal eyeglasses A corrective lens containing upper and lower segments, each with a different power. The main lens is for distant vision; the secondary lens is for near vision.

bifurcate, bifurcated (bī′fŭr-kāt, bī-fŭr′kāt′d) [″ + *furca,* fork] Having two branches or divisions; forked.

bifurcation (bī-fŭr-kā′shŭn) **1.** A separation into two branches; the point of forking. **2.** Furcation.

bigemina (bī-jĕm′ĭ-nă) [L.] Pl. of bigeminum.

bigeminal (bī-jĕm′ĭ-năl) [L. *bigeminum,* twin] Double; paired.

bigeminum (bī-jĕm′ĭ-nŭm) *pl.* **bigemina** [L.] A bigeminal body.

bigeminy (bī-jĕm′ĭ-nē) Occurring in pairs or couplets. **bigeminal,** *adj.*

   junctional b. Cardiac arrhythmia in which every other beat is a junctional ectopic or premature junctional contraction. SYN: *nodal b.*

   nodal b. Junctional **b.**

   ventricular b. Cardiac arrhythmia in which every other beat is a ventricular ectopic or premature ventricular contraction.

bigorexia (big″ō-rek′sē-ă) [*big* + *(an)orexia*] SEE: *muscle dysmorphia.*

biguanide (bī-gwŏn′īd″) A member of the class of oral antihyperglycemic agents that works by limiting glucose production and glucose absorption, and by increasing the body's sensitivity to insulin. Glucophage is one member of this drug class.

bi-ischial (bī-ĭs′kē-ăl) Concerning both ischial tuberosities of the pelvis.

bilabe (bī′lāb″) [*bi-* + *labium*] A long, thin surgical instrument with a hinged lower jaw. It is inserted into the bladder via the urethra to remove small calculi from the bladder.

bilateral (bī-lat′ē-răl) [*bi-* + *lateral*] Pert. to or affecting two sides. **bilaterally** (răl-ē), *adv.*

bilateralism (bī-lăt′ĕr-ăl-ĭzm) [″ + ″ + Gr. *-ismos,* condition] Bilateral symmetry.

bilayer (bī″lā′ĕr) [*bi-* + *layer*] A two-component layer.

   lipid b. The two layers of phospholipid molecules included within the outer membrane of most cells. These layers are arranged so their two hydrophilic (water-soluble) sides face the interior and the exterior of the cell, and their hydrophobic (nonpolar) core is in between. The membrane is relatively impermeable to molecules such as glucose and amino acids but very permeable to lipid-soluble molecules such as oxygen, carbon dioxide, and alcohol. SEE: *cell* for illus.

bilberry (bĭl′bĕr″ē) The European huckleberry (*Vaccinium myrtillus*). It is promoted as a treatment for ocular and circulatory disorders and as a treatment for diarrhea. Its mechanisms of action are: antioxidant, astringent, collagen stablizer, and vasoprotector.

bile (bīl) [L. *bilis,* bile] A thick, viscid, bitter-tasting fluid secreted by the liver. It passes from the hepatic duct of the liver either to the cystic duct of the gallbladder or to the common bile duct to the duodenum. The bile from the liver is straw-colored; that from the gallbladder varies from yellow to brown to green.

Bile is stored in the gallbladder, where it is concentrated, and discharged into the duodenum when fatty chyme enters from the stomach. Contraction of the gallbladder is brought about by cholecystokinin-pancreozymin (a hormone produced by the duodenum); its secretion is stimulated by the entrance of fatty foods into the duodenum. Added to water, bile decreases surface tension, providing a foamy solution favoring the emulsification of fats and oils. This action is due to the bile salts, mainly sodium glycocholate and taurocholate.

COMPOSITION: Bile pigments (principally bilirubin and biliverdin) are responsible for the variety of colors observed. In addition, bile contains cholesterol, lecithin, mucin, and other organic and inorganic substances.

FUNCTION: The function of bile in digestion is to emulsify fats, facilitating their digestion in the small intestine by pancreatic lipase. Bile also stimulates peristalsis. Normally the ejection of bile occurs only during duodenal digestion. About 800 to 1000 ml/24 hr are secreted in the normal adult. SEE: *gallbladder.*

PATHOLOGY: Interference with the flow of bile causes jaundice and the presence of unabsorbed fats in the feces. SEE: *jaundice.*

cystic b. Bile stored in the gallbladder. It is concentrated, as opposed to hepatic bile.

hepatic b. Bile secreted by the liver cells. It is relatively dilute, is collected in the bile ducts, and flows to the gallbladder.

lithogenic b. Bile that favors gallstone production. This may be associated with several conditions: the most important is increased secretion of cholesterol in the bile (e.g., in obesity, high-caloric diets, or drugs such as clofibrate).

bile acid sequestrant SEE: under *sequestrant.*

Bilharzia (bil-har′zē-ă) [Theodor Maximilian Bilharz, Ger. helminthologist, 1825–1862] Former name for *Schistosoma,* the human blood fluke. SEE: *Schistosoma.*

bilharzial, bilharzic (bil-har′zē-ăl, bil-har′zĭk) Pert. to *Bilharzia* (*Schistosoma*).

bilharziasis (bĭl″hăr-zī′ă-sĭs) Schistosomiasis. SEE: *Bilharzia.*

bili- [L. *bilis,* bile] Prefix meaning *bile.*

biliary (bĭl′ē-ār-ē) Pert. to bile.

biliary apparatus Structures concerned with secretion and excretion of bile; includes liver, gallbladder, and hepatic, cystic, and common bile ducts.

bilicyanin (bĭl″ĭ-sī′ă-nĭn) [L. *bilis,* bile, + *cyaneus,* blue] A blue or purple pigment, an oxidation product of biliverdin.

biliflavin (bĭl″ĭ-flā′vĭn) [″ + *flavus,* yellow] A yellow pigment derived from biliverdin.

bilifuscin (bĭl″ĭ-fŭs′ĭn) [″ + *fuscus,* brown] A dark brown pigment from bile and gallstones.

biligenesis (bĭl″ĭ-jĕn′ĕ-sĭs) [″ + Gr. *genesis,* generation, birth] The formation of bile.

bilingual (bī′lĭng′gwĭl) Being able to speak and write in a semantically correct and fluent style in two languages.

biliopancreatic diversion (bĭl″ē-ō-păn″krē-ăt′ĭk) [″ + ″] ABBR: BPD. A bariatric surgical treatment for obesity in which most of the stomach is removed. The remaining proximal pouch is anastomosed to the distal ileum bypassing the duodenum and proximal small intestine. The proximal small intestinal segment is anastomosed to the ileum distal to the gastroileal anastomosis. The procedure restricts the intake of nutrients and causes malabsorption, both of which lead to weight loss. Successful procedures result in sustained weight loss of about 25% of body weight, a result as good as any other surgical treatment for overweight. Common complications of the procedure include iron-deficiency anemia, deficiencies in the absorption of vitamins A, D, E, and K and the minerals calcium and magnesium, gradual bone loss, foul-smelling stools, and failure of surgical anastomoses. The operation takes more time to perform than other bariatric surgeries and tends to have more immediate postoperative complications. The procedure is infrequently performed because of its many complications.

bilious (bĭl′yŭs) [L. *bilosus*] **1.** Pert. to bile. **2.** Afflicted with biliousness.

biliousness (bĭl′yŭs-nĕs) **1.** An obsolete term for symptoms ascribed to liver disorders. **2.** An excess of bile.

bilirubin (bĭl-ĭ-roo′bĭn) [″ + *ruber,* red] $C_{33}H_{36}O_6N_4$; the orange-colored or yellowish pigment in bile. It is derived from hemoglobin of red blood cells that have completed their life span and are destroyed and ingested by the macrophage system of the liver, spleen, and red bone marrow. When produced elsewhere, it is carried to the liver by the blood. It is changed chemically in the liver and excreted in the bile via the duodenum. As it passes through the intestines, it is converted into urobilinogen by bacterial enzymes, most of it being excreted through the feces. If urobilinogen passes into the circulation, it is excreted through the urine or re-excreted in the bile. The pathological accumulation of bilirubin leads to jaundice in many cases, such as physiological jaundice of the newborn.

   direct b. Bilirubin conjugated by the liver cells to form bilirubin diglucuronide, which is water-soluble and excreted in urine.

   indirect b. Unconjugated bilirubin that is present in the blood. It is fat-soluble.

bilirubinate (bĭl-ĭ-roo'bĭn-āt) A salt of bilirubin.

bilirubinemia (bĭl″ĭ-roo-bĭn-ē′mē-ă) [″ + *ruber*, red, + Gr. *haima*, blood] Bilirubin in the blood, usually in excessive amounts. Bilirubin normally is present in the blood in small amounts. It increases, however, in diseases in which there is excessive destruction of red blood cells or interference with bile excretion; the amount is also increased when the liver is diseased or damaged. Also called *hyperbilirubinemia*. SEE: *jaundice*.

bilirubinometry (bĭl″ĭ-roo-bĭn-ŏm′ĭ-trē) The laboratory technique of measuring bilirubin levels in blood, skin, cerebrospinal fluid, or urine. These measurements are used esp. in the treatment of hyperbilirubinemia in neonates. SEE: *hyperbilirubinemia; kernicterus.*

bilirubinuria (bĭl″ĭ-roo-bĭn-ū′rē-ă) [″ + ″ + Gr. *ouron,* urine] Presence of bilirubin in urine. SYN: *biliuria.*

biliuria (bĭl-ĭ-ū′rē-ă) Bilirubinuria.

biliverdin (bĭl-ĭ-vĕr′dĭn) [″ + *viridis,* green] $C_{33}H_{34}O_6N_4$; a greenish pigment in bile formed by the oxidation of bilirubin.

bill of health (bil) [L. *billa,* variant of *bulla*] A public health certificate stating that passengers on a public conveyance or ship are free of infectious disease.

Billings method (bil′ingz) [John Billings, Australian neurologist, 1918–2007] A method of family planning in which observations about the thickness and slipperiness of cervicovaginal mucus are used to determine when a woman is more (or less) likely to conceive a child.

billion [Fr. *bi,* two, + *million,* million] **1.** In the U.S., billion is a number equal to 1 followed by 9 zeros (1,000,000,000) or (10^9). **2.** In Europe, billion is a number equal to 1 followed by 12 zeros (10^{12}), that is, bi-million, or twice the number of zeros in a million (10^6).

Billroth, Christian A.T. (bil′rōt″, roth″) Prussian-born Austrian surgeon, 1829–1894.

   B. I operation Partial gastrectomy with gastroduodenostomy.

   B. II operation Partial gastrectomy with gastrojejunostomy.

bilobate (bī-lō′bāt) [L. *bis,* twice, + *lobus,* lobe] Having two lobes.

bilocular (bī-lŏk′ū-lăr) [″ + *loculus,* cell] **1.** Having two cells. **2.** Divided into compartments.

biloma An abnormal collection of bile outside the gallbladder, usually resulting from injury to the right upper quadrant during trauma or surgery.

bimanual (bī-măn′ū-ăl) [″ + *manus,* hand] With both hands, as in bimanual palpation.

bimaxillary (bī-măk′sĭ-lĕr″ē) [″ + *maxilla,* jawbone] Pert. to or afflicting both jaws.

bimodal (bī″mō′dăl) [*bi-* + *modal*] **1.** Pert. to a graphic presentation that contains two peaks. **2.** Pert. to a set of data that has two distinct maximum values.

binary (bī′nă-rē) [L. *binarius,* of two] **1.** Composed of two elements. **2.** Separating into two branches.

binary system A numbering system well suited to use by computers. All of the information placed into a computer is in binary form, i.e., numbers made up of zeros and ones (0s and 1s). In this system each place in a binary number represents a power of 2 (i.e., the number of times 2 is to be multiplied by itself). SYN: *binary code.*

binaural (bī′nawr′ăl) [L. *bis,* twice, + *auris,* ear] Pert. to both ears.

binauricular (bĭn″aw-rĭk′ū-lăr) [″ + *auricula,* little ear] Binaural; pert. to both auricles of the ear.

bind 1. To fasten, wrap, or encircle with a bandage. **2.** In chemistry and immunology, the uniting or adherence (i.e., bonding) of one molecule or chemical entity to another (e.g., the joining of a toxin to an antitoxin or of a hormone to its receptor on a cell surface).

binder (bĭn′dĕr) **1.** A broad bandage most commonly used as an encircling support of the abdomen or chest. SEE: *bandage.* **2.** In dentistry, a substance that holds a mixture of solid particles together.

   abdominal b. A wide band fastened snugly about the abdomen for support. SEE: *Scultetus binder* under Scultetus, Johannes.

   chest b. A broad band that encircles the chest and is used for applying heat, dressings, or pressure and for supporting the breasts. Shoulder straps may be used to keep the binder from slipping.

   double-T b. A horizontal band about the waist to which two vertical bands are attached in back, brought around the leg, and again fastened to the horizontal band.

   obstetrical b. A binder that extends

from the ribs to the pelvis, providing support for a markedly pendulous abdomen. Such support may be rarely required for severe diastasis recti or for marked separation and mobility of the pubic symphysis during pregnancy.

   phosphate b. Any of various medications used to prevent hyperphosphatemia in patients with end-stage renal disease. Calcium carbonate taken with meals is the most commonly employed agent. In the past aluminum-containing antacids were used for this purpose, but this practice is now avoided because of the toxic accumulation of aluminum in patients with renal failure.

   Scultetus b. SEE: under *Scultetus, Johannes.*

   T b. T bandage.

   towel b. A towel that encircles the abdomen or chest and whose ends are pinned together.

Binder syndrome A syndrome related to facial growth, with hypoplasia of the maxillae and nasal bones resulting in a flattened face, elongated nose, and smaller maxillary arch with crowding of the teeth and malocclusions.

binge drinking (binj) The consumption of more than four or five alcoholic drinks in a row (the lower number applies to women; the higher number applies to men). The behavioral consequences of this practice frequently include impaired driving impaired driving, sexual assaults, and other forms of violence. SEE: *alcoholism.*

binge eating An eating disorder marked by rapid consumption of large amounts of food in a short period of time. SEE: *bulimia.*

bingo card A method of packaging medications in which a blister pack is enclosed in a folded-over card, usually printed with proprietary advertising for the medication inside.

binocular (bĭn-ŏk′ū-lăr) [L. *bis,* twice, + *oculus,* eye] Pert. to both eyes.

binocularity (bĭn-ŏk-ū-lăr′ĭ-tē) [″] The coordinated use of both eyes. It is also known as eye teaming.

binomial (bī-nō′mē-ăl) [″ + *nomen,* name] In mathematics and statistics, an equation containing two variables.

binotic (bĭn-ŏt′ĭk) [″ + Gr. *ous,* ear] Pert. to or having two ears.

binovular (bĭn-ŏv′ū-lăr) Biovular.

Binswanger, Otto (bĭn′svang″ĕr) Swiss psychiatrist and neurologist, 1852–1929.

   B. dementia Binswanger disease.

   B. disease A form of vascular dementia in which insufficient blood flow to focal areas of the white matter of the brain just beneath the cerebral cortex produces slow thinking, memory loss, unsteady gait and clumsiness, personality changes, altered behavior, and sometimes, urinary incontinence. SYN:

*Binswanger dementia; subcortical arteriosclerotic **encephalopathy;** subcortical vascular **dementia**.*

binuclear, binucleate (bī-nū′klē-ăr, -āt) [″ + *nucleus,* kernel] Having two nuclei.

bio- [Gr. *bios,* life] Prefix meaning *life.*

bioabsorbable (bī″ō-ăb-sor′bă-bĕl) Capable of being assimilated into the body. SYN: *bioresorbable.*

bioaccumulation (bī″ō-ă-kū″mū-lā′shŭn) The gradual incorporation of chemicals, drugs, pollutants, or other agents into living cells.

bioactive (bī″ō-ăk′tĭv) Affecting living tissues.

bioactive food component SEE: under *component.*

bioactive glass A biologically compatible synthetic material used surgically in bone grafting and periodontal applications. It consists of varying amounts of silicates, sodium and calcium oxides, and phosphates.

bioartificial (bī″ō-ăr″tĭ-fĭsh′ăl) [″ + ″] Composed of both living and manufactured components, typically a collection of cells held within a scaffolding or membrane. Bioartificial organs can be used to assist patients with organ failure (e.g., end-stage heart, kidney, liver, or pancreatic disease).

bioassay (bī″ō-ăs′ā) [″ + O. Fr. *asaier,* to try] In pharmacology, the determination of the strength of a drug or substance by comparing its effect on a live animal or an isolated organ preparation with that of a standard preparation.

bioastronautics (bī″ō-ăs″trō-naw′tĭks) The study of the effects of space travel on living plants and animals.

bioavailability (bī″ō-ă-vāl″ă-bĭl′ĭt-ē) [*bio-* + *availability*] The rate and extent to which an active drug or metabolite enters the body, permitting access to the site of action. Bioavailability is determined either by measurement of the concentration of the drug in body fluids or by the magnitude of the pharmacologic response. **bioavailable** (-ă-vāl′ă-bĭl), *adj.*

biobank (bī′ō-băngk″) [″ + ″] An institution that stores human tissues, e.g., autopsy specimens, blood, or organ biopsies, for research.

bioburden (bī′ō-bŭr′dĕn) The number of contaminating microorganisms present on an object (e.g., on the surface of a surgical glove, endoscope, or body part). Reduction of the bioburden is the goal of infection control programs and protocols.

biocatalyst (bī-ō-kăt′ă-lĭst) [″ + *katalyein,* to dissolve] An enzyme; a biochemical catalyzer.

biochemical (bī″ō-kem′ĭ-kăl) Pert. to biochemistry.

biochemical pregnancy SEE: under *pregnancy.*

biochemistry [" + *chemeia*, chemistry] The chemistry of living things; the science of the chemical changes accompanying the vital functions of plants and animals.

biochemorphology (bī″ō-kĕ-mor-fŏl′ō-jē) [" + " + *morphe*, shape, + *logos*, word, reason] The science of the relationship between chemical structure and biological action. SEE: *stereochemistry*.

biocide (bī′ō-sīd) [" + L. *caedere*, to kill] A substance, esp. a pesticide or an antibiotic, that destroys living organisms.

bioclimatology (bī″ō-klī-mă-tŏl′ō-jē) [" + *klima*, climate, + *logos*, word, reason] Study of the relationship of climate to life.

biocolloid (bī″ō-kŏl′oyd) [" + *kollodes*, glutinous] A colloid from animal, vegetable, or microbial tissue.

biocompatibility (bī″ō-kŏm-păt″ă-bĭl′ĭ-tē) The condition of being harmonious with living systems.

biocontainment (bī″ō-kŏn-tān′-mĕnt) In infectious disease laboratories, the process and procedures used to confine harmful microorganisms to the areas in which they are being investigated. The precise regulations vary with the pathogenicity of the organisms. SEE: *biosafety level*.

biodefense (bī″ō-dĕ-fĕns′) [" + "] National or international efforts to prevent the spread of biologically destructive agents, esp. when they are used in terrorism or warfare.

biodegradable (bī″ō-dē-grād′-ă-bĕl) Susceptible to degradation by biological processes, such as bacterial or enzymatic action.

biodegradation (bī″ō-dĕg″rĕ-dā′shŭn) The breakdown of organic materials into simple chemicals by biochemical processes. SYN: *biological degradation*.

biodynamics (bī″ō-dī-năm′ĭks) [Gr. *bios*, life, + *dynamis*, force] Pertaining to the kinetics of chemical or mechanical processes in biological systems.

bioelectrical (bī″ō-ĕ-lĕk′trĭ-kĭl) Pert. to the electrical activities of living organisms.

bioelectrical impedance analysis (bī″ō-ĭ-lĕk′trĭ-kĭl) ABBR: BIA. A method of body composition analysis useful in measuring the total body water and other components. BIA relies on the changes in electrical current as it travels through body fluids and tissues. The results obtained may vary with ambient temperature and humidity, the subject's hydration, and other variables.

bioelectronics (bī″ō-ē″lĕk-trŏn′ĭks) The study of the transfer of electrons between molecules in biological systems.

bioenergetics (bī″ō-ĕn″ĕr-jĕt′ĭks) The study of energy transfer and relationships among living systems.

bioengineering (bī″ō-ĕn″jĭ-nēr′ĭng) The application of engineering concepts, equipment, skills, and techniques to solving medical problems. SEE: *biomedical engineering*.

bioequivalent (bī″ō-ē-kwĭv′ă-lĕnt) **1.** Biologically equivalent to another agent, esp.*another drug or therapeutic agent.* **2.** A drug whose effects on the body are indistinguishable from the effects of another.

bioethics (bī″ō-eth′iks) [*bio-* + *ethics*] Moral inquiry into issues raised by advances in medicine and the life sciences, e.g., genetics or biomedical engineering.

bioethics committee Any local, regional, national, or international group that reviews the moral implications of biomedical research, e.g., research into cloning, human enhancement, biotechnology, or life extension.

biofeedback (bī″ō-fēd′bak″) [*bio-* + *feedback*] A training program to develop one's ability to control the autonomic (involuntary) nervous system. After learning the technique, the patient may be able to control heart rate, blood pressure, and skin temperature or to relax certain muscles. The patient learns by using monitoring devices that sound a tone when changes in pulse, blood pressure, brain waves, and muscle contractions occur. Then the patient attempts to reproduce the conditions that caused the desired changes.

 thermal b. A form of biofeedback in which a person applies a temperature sensor to his skin (usually on a peripheral body part) and then tries to improve blood flow to that part, thereby raising the temperature detected. It is used to treat psychological stress, headaches, and other somatic symptoms exacerbated by anxiety.

biofilm (bī′ō-film″) A thin coating of bacteria embedded in a moist, adhesive matrix that may cover mucous membranes and devices placed inside the body, including catheters and stents. Bacteria thriving in a biofilm are resistant both to phagocytosis by white blood cells and to destruction by antibiotics. SYN: *microbial mat*.

bioflavonoid (bī″ō-flā′vŏ-noyd″) [*bio-* + *flavonoid*] Flavonoid.

biogenesis (bī″ō-jĕn′ĕ-sĭs) [" + *genesis*, generation, birth] The theory that life can originate only from pre-existing life and never from nonliving material. **biogenetic** (-jĕ-nĕt′ĭk), *adj.*

biogenic (bī-ō-jĕn′ĭk) Produced by living organisms.

 b. amines A group of chemical compounds, most of which are important in neurotransmission. Included are norepinephrine, histamine, serotonin, and dopamine.

biogerontology (bī″ō-jĕ-rŏn-tŏl′ō-jē) [″ + ″] The study of the fundamental biological processes that result from aging.

biohazard (bī″ō-haz″ĕrd) Anything that is harmful or potentially harmful to humans, other species, or the environment. SEE: *biosafety level.*

bioidentical (bī′ō-ī-dĕn′tĭ-kĭl) [″ + ″] Having the same chemical structure and function as a molecule found in nature.

bioinequivalent (bī″ō-ĭn-ē-kwĭv′ă-lĕnt) Differing in physiological or pharmacological action from another agent.

bioinstrument (bī″ō-ĭn′stroo-mĕnt) A device placed in the body to record or transmit data.

biokinetics (bī″ō-kĭ-nĕt′ĭks) [″ + *kinetikos,* moving] The study of growth changes and movements in developing organisms.

biologic, biological (bī″ŏ-loj′ĭk, -loj′ĭ-kăl) **1.** Pert. to biology. **2.** An agent derived from or made of living tissues or cells and used in health care.
   follow-on b. Biosimilar.

biological intelligence Those components of intelligence that can be directly attributed to the anatomy and physiology of the central nervous system. Biological intelligence is sometimes distinguished from artificial intelligence, i.e., intelligence demonstrated by computer behavior, and from psychometric intelligence or intelligence as documented by the performance of subjects on IQ tests.

biological therapy Therapy with immunologically active agents.

biological value (of protein) A measure of the efficiency of a consumed protein, esp. its nitrogen or amino acid content.

biological warfare ABBR: BW. Warfare in which disease-producing microorganisms, toxins, or organic biocides, e.g., *Bacillus anththracis* or *Yersinia pestis* are deliberately used to destroy, injure, or immobilize livestock, vegetation, or human life, as by causing diseases, e.g., anthrax or plague. SYN: *biowar.* SEE: *chemical warfare.*

biologist (bī-ŏl′ō-jĭst) A specialist in biology.

biology (bī-ol′ō-jē) [*bio-* + *-logy*] The science of life and living organisms and their structures and processes.
   molecular b. The study of DNA, proteins, and other molecular constituents of cells.
   radiation b. The study of the effects of radiation on living organisms.

bioluminescence (bī″ō-loo″mĭ-nĕs′ĕns) [″ + L. *lumen,* light] Emission of visible light from living organisms, (e.g., cold light produced by fireflies).

biolysis (bī-ŏl′ĭ-sĭs) [″ + *lysis,* dissolution] The chemical decomposition of living tissue by the action of living organisms. **biolytic** (bī-ō-lĭt′ĭk), *adj.*

biomarker (bī′ō-mahrk′ĕr) **1.** A signal that serves as an indicator of the state of a living organism. **2.** A biochemical, genetic, or molecular indicator that can be used to screen diseases, such as cancer.

biomarker of susceptibility A biomarker used to indicate that a cell, organism, or tissue can be influenced by a specific agent or toxin.

biomass (bī′ō-măs) [″ + L. *massa,* mass] All of the living organisms in a specified area.

biomaterial (bī″ō-mă-tēr′ē-ĭl) [″ + ″] An inert substance used to replace a body part or to be made compatible with living tissue.

biome (bī′ōm) [″ + *oma,* mass] A major type of environment, such as tundra, forest, or swamp, marked by its climate, flora, fauna, and pathogens.

biomechanics (bī″ō-mĕ-kăn′ĭks) The application of engineering and physical science to the movement of living organisms. SEE: *kinesiology.*

biomedical (bī′ō-mĕd′ī-kĭl) Biological and medical; pert. to application of natural sciences to the study of medicine.
   b. engineer A certified design engineer, usually with a Bachelor of Science degree, who designs and/or maintains medical equipment. Also referred to as a *clinical engineer.*
   b. engineering Application of the principles and practices of engineering to biomedical research and health care, as seen in the development of devices such as cardiac pacemakers, hearing aids, and artificial limbs and joints.
   b. engineering technologist A certified technical specialist who repairs and maintains medical equipment.

biometeorology (bī″ō-mē″tē-or-ŏl′ō-jē) [″ + *meteoros,* raised from off the ground, + *logos,* word, reason] The study of the effects of weather on living organisms.

biometric identifier (bī″ō-mĕ′trĭk ī-dĕn′tĭ-fī″ĕr) Biologically unique data (e.g., fingerprint data, genetic data, and voiceprints) that identify a person. Under provisions of the Health Insurance Portability and Accountability Act, biometric identifiers are protected health information that must be held in strict confidence by health care agencies and professionals.

biometrics (bī″ō-mĕt′rĭks) Biometry (1).

biometry (bī-ŏm′ĕ-trē) [″ + *metron,* measure] **1.** The application of statistics to biological science. SYN: *biometrics; biostatistics.* **2.** The computation of life expectancy. **3.** Identification of living things by precise anatomical or physiological measurements.
   ophthalmic b. Measurement of any part of the eye, from the cornea to the retina, with an ophthalmic ultrasound.

biomicroscope (bī″ō-mī′krŏ-skōp) A microscope used with a slit lamp for viewing segments of the eye.

biomicroscopy (bī″ō-mī-krŏs′kŏ-pē) [″ + ″] The examination of tissues with an illuminated low-powered microscope, e.g., in slit lamp examinations of the eyes or in cervical colposcopy.

biomolecule (bī″ō-mol′ĕ-kūl″) [bio- + molecule] An organic chemical produced by a living organism, e.g., a carbohydrate or polysaccharide, a nucleic acid sequence, or a polypeptide or protein. **biomolecular** (-mŏ-lek′yŭ-lăr), adj.

bion (bī′ŏn) [Gr. bios, life] Any living organism.

bionics (bī-ŏn′ĭks) The study of biological functions and mechanisms and the application of these findings to the design of machines, esp. computers.

biopharming (bī′ō-fărm″ĭng) [″ + Gk. pharmakon, poison + pun on farming] The genetic alteration of a plant or animal so that its cells can be used to manufacture medications.

biophysics (bī″ō-fīz′ĭks) [″ + physikos, natural] Application of physical laws to biological processes and functions. **biophysical** (-ĭ-kăl), adj.

biopolymer (bī″ō-pol′ĭ-mĭr) [bio- + polymer] **1.** A polymer made of biologically compatible or biodegradable components. **2.** A naturally occurring polymer produced by living organisms, e.g., a starch, or polypeptide.

bioprosthesis (bī″ō-pros-thē′sĭs) [bio- + prosthesis] A replacement body part made with living tissues, such as tissues derived from cows or pigs.

biopsy (bī′op″sē) [bio- + -opsy] ABBR: bx. A tissue sample removed from the body for microscopic examination, usually to establish a diagnosis. The tissue can be obtained surgically or by aspiration. The procedure can be guided by computed tomography, ultrasonography, magnetic resonance imaging, or radiography, or it can be performed without imaging, i.e., "blindly".

    aspiration b. Needle **b.**

    blind b. A biopsy taken without radiographic guidance or strong evidence of localized disease.

    brush b. The removal of cells from an organ by rubbing them loose.

    cone b. Removal of a cone shaped piece of tissue from the uterine cervix to diagnose or treat cervical diseases. The procedure may be performed with a scalpel, carbon dioxide (CO_2) laser, or Loop Electrosurgical Excision Procedure (LEEP).

    endometrial b. The removal of a sample of uterine endometrium for microscopic study. The procedure is commonly used in fertility assessment to confirm ovulation and to determine the cause of dysfunctional or postmenopausal bleeding.

    fine needle aspiration b. ABBR: FNA biopsy. The removal of cells or tissue through a long, narrow-gauge nee-

dle with or without radiological guidance. SEE: illus.

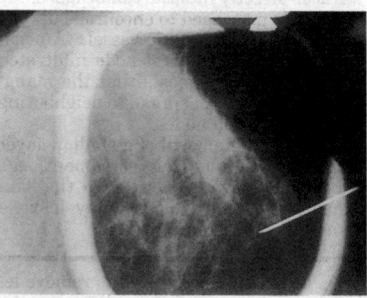

FINE NEEDLE BREAST BIOPSY

    fine-needle nonaspiration b. Fine-needle capillary **sampling**.

    liver b. 1. The percutaneous removal of tissue from the liver with a large-bore needle that captures a core of tissue. **2.** A wedge of the liver obtained during laparotomy or laparoscopy.

    muscle b. The removal of muscle tissue for microscopic examination and chemical analysis.

    needle b. The withdrawal of fluid or tissue by means of negative pressure applied with needle and syringe. SYN: aspiration biopsy.

    percutaneous breast b. Use of a directional, high-speed, rotating cutter attached to a vacuum source to gather multiple contiguous core samples of breast tissue through a single point of insertion. This minimally invasive procedure is usually performed under local anesthesia, using stereotactic imaging or real-time ultrasonography.

    percutaneous renal b. Obtaining renal tissue for analysis with a needle inserted through the skin, usually done after the kidney has been localized by ultrasound, computed tomography, or angiography. This technique is used to establish a diagnosis of renal dysfunction, determine prognosis in patients with renal disease, evaluate the extent of renal injury, and determine appropriate therapy. The most common complication is urinary bleeding, which tends to clear gradually over several days.

    percutaneous transthoracic needle aspiration b. Use of a radiographically guided aspiration needle to obtain a sample of tissue in cases of suspected pulmonary malignancies or other unknown lesions. Because of the risk of pneumothorax, the procedure is usually contraindicated in patients receiving mechanical ventilation.

    punch b. The removal of a small piece of tissue (usually of the skin) with a hollow, round cutting tool.

    sentinel node b. A technique for

identifying the initial site of cancer metastasis. After injection of a radioactive tracer directly into the tumor mass, the tissue is massaged to encourage uptake of tracer by lymphatic vessels. A negative biopsy of the first node infiltrated by the tracer suggests that the malignancy has not yet spread to neighboring regional lymph nodes.

shave b. Removal of a shallow layer of skin with a cutting instrument, e.g., a scalpel, sawing parallel to the skin surface. A shave biopsy may leave a small depression in the skin.

⚠ It should not be used to remove lesions suspected for melanoma or lesions that seem to have significant depth.

suction b. A technique for obtaining tissue by aspiration, e.g., to obtain tissue from the mucosa of the stomach and intestines.

vacuum-assisted biopsy A biopsy technique in which a hypodermic probe is placed through the skin into an organ of the body (such as the breast), and negative pressure is used to draw one or more samples into a chamber, where they are captured and removed for analysis under a microscope.

biopsychosocial (bī″ō-sī″kō-sō′shăl) Biological, psychological, and social; pert. to the application of knowledge from the biological and behavioral sciences to study or solve human problems.

biopterin (bī-ŏp′tĕr-ĭn) 2-amino-4-hydroxy-6-(1,2-hydroxypropyl) pteridine, important in metabolizing phenylalanine. A deficiency of biopterin is a rare cause of phenylketonuria.

bioptome (bī-ŏp′tōm) A tool used to obtain biopsies of the endomyocardium. It consists of a forceps (with small tissue-cutting jaws) that is advanced into the ventricle along a catheter or guidewire.

bioremediation (bī″ō-rĕ-mē″dē-ā′shŭn) The conversion of hazardous wastes and pollutants into harmless materials by microorganisms.

bioresorbable (bī″ō-rē-sor′bă-bĕl) Bioabsorbable.

biorhythm (bī′ō-rĭth″ŭm) [″ + *rhythmos,* rhythm] A cyclic phenomenon (e.g., circadian rhythm, sleep cycle, and menstrual cycle) that occurs with established regularity in living organisms. SEE: *clock, biological.*

bios (bī′ŏs) [Gr., life] **1.** Organic life. **2.** A group of substances (including inositol, biotin, and thiamine) necessary for the most favorable growth of some yeasts.

biosafety level (bī″ō-sāf′tē) ABBR: BSL. A classification system to indicate the safety precautions required when investigating microorganisms, esp. viruses known to be dangerous or lethal to those exposed to them. There are four BSLs, with BSL-4 requiring the highest level of security.

bioscience (bī″ō-sī′ĕns) [Gr. *bios,* life, + L. *scientia,* knowledge] Life science.

biosensor (bī′ō-sen″sor″) [*bio-* + *sensor*] **1.** A device that senses and analyzes biological information, including temperature, heart rate, blood pressure, or the chemical composition of body fluids. **2.** A device that incorporates some biologic agent (e.g. an enzyme) as a part of its sensing capability.

biosignature (bī″ō-sig′nă-chŭr) [*bio-* + *signature*] A particular group of proteins found in body fluid or tissue that identifies the tissue type or a molecular disease.

biosimilar (bī″ō-sim′ĭ-lăr) [*bio-* + *similar*] **1.** A generic version of a biologically active pharmaceutical agent, e.g., of a manufactured antibody or hormone. **2.** Pert. to such a generic version. SYN: *follow-on biologic.* **biosimilarity,** *n.*

biospectrometry (bī″ō-spĕk-trŏm′ĕ-trē) [″ + L. *spectrum,* image, + Gr. *metron,* measure] Use of a spectroscope to determine the amounts and kinds of substances in tissues.

biospectroscopy (bī″ō-spĕk-trŏs′kō-pē) [″ + ″ + Gr. *skopein,* to examine] Examination of tissue by use of a spectroscope.

biosphere (bī′ō-sfēr″) [″ + *sphaira,* ball] The parts of earth's land, water, and atmosphere in which living organisms can exist.

biostatistics (bī″ō-stă-tĭs′tĭks) Biometry (1).

biosynthesis (bī″ō-sĭn′thĕ-sĭs) [″ + *synthesis,* a putting together] The formation of chemical compounds by a living organism.

biota (bī-ō′tă) [Gr. *bios,* life] The combined animal and plant life in an area.

biotaxis (bī″ō-tăk′sĭs) [″ + *taxis,* arrangement] Movement of an organism in response to an external stimulus.

Biot breathing (bē-ō′) [Camille Biot, Fr. physician, b. 1878] Breathing marked by several short breaths followed by long, irregular periods of apnea. It is seen in patients with increased intracranial pressure. SEE: *Cheyne-Stokes respiration.*

biotechnology (bī″ō-tĕk-nŏl′ō-jē) The use of living organisms or biological processes in technical industrial applications.

biotelemetry (bī″ō-tĕl-ĕm′ĕ-trē) [Gr. *bios,* life, + *tele,* distant, + *metron,* measure] Recording physiological parameters such as temperature, heart rate, ECG, and EEG in subjects remote from the investigator. This is done by transmitting and receiving by telephone or other electronic methods.

bioterrorism (bī″ō-ter′ŏr-ĭ″zĭm) [*bio-* + *terrorism*] The use of biological warfare agents (such as anthrax or smallpox) against civilian rather than military targets.

biotherapy (bī′ō-thĕr′ă-pē) In complementary medicine and in oncology, the use of biological response modifiers (e.g., interleukins, phytochemicals, or phytonutrients) to enhance the immune response, alter hormone levels, or assist in the treatment of cancer.

biothesiometer (bī″ō-thēz″ē-ŏm′ĕt-ĕr) An instrument used to measure vibration perception.

biotic (bī-ot′ik) [Gr. *biōtikos,* pert. to life]
1. Pert. to life or living organisms.
2. Produced or caused by living organisms. **3.** Pert. to the biota.

biotics (bī-ŏt′ĭks) [Gr. *biotikos,* living] The science that deals with the functions of life.

biotin (bī′ō-tĭn) A vitamin that is a co-enzyme involved in gluconeogenesis and fat synthesis. It is commonly found in egg yolks, peanut butter, liver, kidney, cauliflower, and yeast. Deficiencies occur when people consume large amounts of raw egg white, which contains avidin. Deficiency is also common among alcoholics. Children with biotin deficiency have delayed mental and physical development, alopecia, impaired immunity, and anemia. SYN: *vitamin H.*

biotoxin (bī-ō-tŏk′sĭn) [Gr. *bios,* life, + *toxikon,* poison] A toxin produced by or found in a living organism.

biotransformation (bī″ō-trăns″fŏr-mā′shŭn) The chemical alteration that a substance undergoes in the body.

biotrauma (bī″ō-traw′mă) [″ + ″] Injury to the lungs during mechanical ventilation resulting from excessive inflammation (i.e., from the systemic release of damaging cytokines). Biotrauma is one type of ventilatory-induced lung injury. SEE: *inflammation* for illus.

biotype (bī′ō-tīp) [″ + *typos,* mark]
1. Individuals possessing the same genotype. **2.** In microbiology, the former name for biovar. SEE: *biovar.*

biovar (bī′ō-văr) [*biol*ogical *var*iation] In microbiology, a term for variants within a species. These are usually distinguished by certain biochemical and physiological characteristics.

biovular (bī-ŏv′ū-lăr) [L. *bis,* twice, + *ovum,* egg] Derived from or pert. to two ova. SYN: *binovular.*

biowar (bī-ō-wăr′) Biological warfare.

BiPAP A trade name for a device that provides pressure support during non-invasive ventilation.

biparental (bī″pă-rĕn′tăl) [″ + *parere,* to bring forth, to bear] Derived from two parents, male and female.

biparietal (bī″pă-rī′ĕ-tăl) Concerning the parietal bones or their eminences.

biparous (bĭp′ă-rŭs) Producing two ova or offspring at one time.

biped (bī′pĕd) [″ + *pes,* foot] An animal with two feet.

bipenniform (bī-pĕn′ĭ-form) [″ + *penna,* feather, + *forma,* shape] Muscle fibers that come from each side of a tendon in the manner in which barbs come from the central shaft of a feather.

biphasic (bī-fāz′ĭk) Consisting of two phases. SYN: *diphasic.*

bipolar (bī-pōl′ăr) [″ + *polus,* a pole]
1. Having two poles or processes.
2. Pert. to the use of two poles in electrotherapeutic treatments. The term *bi-terminal* should be used when referring to an alternating current. **3.** A two-poled nerve cell. **4.** A term used as a synonym for the more formal psychiatric term, mood disorder, bipolar.

bipolar disorder A psychological disorder marked by manic and depressive episodes. Bipolar disorders are divided into four main categories: bipolar I, bipolar II, cyclothymia, and nonspecified disorders. Mania is the essential feature of bipolar I, whereas recurrent moods of both mania and depression mark bipolar II. SEE: *mood disorder; Nursing Diagnoses Appendix.*

TREATMENT: Often the first-line choice of medication is lithium carbonate. If there are concerns about the side effects of lithium or it is found to be ineffective, valproate, carbamazepine, or other anticonvulsant agents may be tried.

⚠ Bipolar disorder should not be managed with agents that solely treat unipolar depression. Such treatment may trigger manic or hypomanic episodes.

Bipolaris (bī″pō-lār′ĭs [″ + L. *polaris,* polar]) A genus of filamentous pigment-producing fungi that can cause disease in immunosuppressed and immunocompetent patients. Bipolaris species are found in soils and vegetation, and have been identified in brain, lung, and sinus infections.

BIRADS (bī″rădz″) [Acronym fm. *Breast Imaging Reporting and Data System*] A classification system developed by the American College of Radiology to characterize findings obtained during breast imaging. Breast imaging may be done by mammography, magnetic resonance imaging, and/or ultrasonography. Category 1 findings are considered normal. Categories 2 and 3 are considered to have minor abnormalities, and those in category 3 require follow-up testing within a half year. Categories 4 and 5 are "suspicious" and "worrisome" for cancer, respectively.

biramous (bī-rā′mŭs) [″ + *ramus,* a branch] Possessing two branches.

birefractive (bī″rē-frăk′tĭv) [″ + *refrangere*, to break up] Pert. to or having birefringence.

birefringence (bī″rē-frĭn′jĕns) The splitting of a ray of light in two. **birefringent** (-jĕnt), *adj.*

birth (bĭrth) The act of being born; passage of a child from the uterus.

   assisted b. Any birth in which delivery of the neonate is accomplished with instruments, e.g., forceps of vacuum extraction, or by operation, e.g. cesarean section. SYN: *assisted **delivery***.

   cesarean b. Cesarean section.

   complete b. The instant of complete separation of the body of the infant from that of the mother, regardless of whether the cord or placenta is detached.

   cross b. Crossbirth.

   dry b. A colloquial and imprecise term for a birth that follows premature rupture of membranes.

   live b. An infant of any gestational age showing one of the three evidences of life (breathing, heart action, movements of a voluntary muscle) after complete birth. In some countries a live birth is considered not to have occurred if the infant dies during the 24 hr following delivery. Which of these two definitions is used has considerable effect on various vital statistics concerned with the viability of the fetus at time of delivery.

   multiple b. The birth of two or more offspring produced in the same gestation period.

   out-of-hospital b. A birth that takes place in a setting where is no access to anesthesia or surgery, e.g. in the home, at a birthing center, or in a hospital without operating capabilities. Many out-of-hospital births are managed by midwives.

   premature b. Preterm **b.**

   preterm b. Delivery occurring between 20 and 38 weeks' gestation. Neonatal morbidity and mortality are high because of physiological immaturity. Preterm neonates are at high risk for developing respiratory distress syndrome; intraventricular hemorrhage; sepsis; patent ductus arteriosus; retinopathy of prematurity; and necrotizing enterocolitis. SYN: *premature **b.*** SEE: *prematurity; preterm **labor***.

   TREATMENT: When there is a risk of birth occurring between 24 and 34 weeks' gestation, corticosteroid therapy to stimulate fetal lung maturation and production of pulmonary surfactant should be considered; however, birth must occur in no less than 24 hr after administration. Therapy should be repeated weekly until 34 weeks' gestation. There is no evidence that this treatment is harmful to fetuses of either gender.

   CONTRAINDICATIONS: Corticosteroid therapy should not be administered if the mother has chorioamnionitis or if there is evidence that the drug will have an adverse effect on the mother. Caution is recommended in women who have diabetes mellitus and/or hypertension.

birth canal SEE: under *canal*.

birth center SEE: under *center*.

birth certificate A legal written record of the birth of a child, as required by U.S. law.

birth control Prevention of conception or implantation of the fertilized ovum, or termination of pregnancy. Methods of birth control may be temporary and reversible or permanent. Temporary methods to avoid conception include physical barriers (e.g., male and female condoms, diaphragms, cervical caps, and vaginal sponges) that are most effective when used in conjunction with chemical barriers (such as spermicidal vaginal suppositories, creams, jellies, or foams). Hormonal methods include oral contraceptive pills and progestin implants to suppress ovulation. Fertility awareness methods, such as rhythm, involve identification of and abstinence during ovulation, graphing basal body temperature and changes in cervical mucus consistency and estimation of the day of ovulation. Intrauterine devices (IUD) prevent zygote implantation. Sterilization techniques include male vasectomy and female tubal ligation. Sterilization usually is permanent but may be reversible.

birth control pill SEE: under *pill*.

birth defect SEE: under *defect*.

birthing chair (bĭrth′ĭng) A chair designed for use during childbirth. The mother is in a sitting or semireclining position, which facilitates the labor process and is more comfortable than the supine position.

birth labor support Continuous support in labor.

birthmark (bĭrth′mark″) Nevus (1).

birth mother SEE: under *mother*.

birth parent(s) SEE: under *parent*.

birth spacing Birth **interval**.

birth weight SEE: under *weight*.

bisacodyl (bĭs-ăk′ō-dĭl; bĭs″ă-kō′dĭl) A cathartic drug that acts by its direct effect on the colon. It may be administered orally or by rectal suppository. Trade names are Dulcolax and Theralax.

bisection (bī-sĕk′shŭn) [″ + *sectio*, a cutting] Division into two parts by cutting.

bisexual (bī″seksh′ŭ-ăl) [bi- + sexual] 1. Pert. to both sexes. 2. Having imperfect genitalia of both sexes in one individual; hermaphroditic. 3. An animal or plant having genitalia of both sexes; a hermaphrodite. 4. An individual sexually active with others of either sex. SEE: *heterosexual; homosexual; lesbian.*

bisferious (bĭs-fĕr'ē-ŭs) [" + *ferire,* to beat] Having two beats; dicrotic.

Bishop score (bĭsh'ŏp) A system for evaluating the potential for successful elective induction of labor. Factors assessed include fetal station, cervical position, effacement, dilation, and consistency. Each factor receives a score of 0, 1, 2, or 3, for the maximum predictive total score of 15. The lower the score, the greater the possibility that labor induction will fail.

bishop's weed Ammi visnaga.

bisiliac (bĭs-ĭl'ē-ăk) [" + *ilium,* ilium] Pert. to the two iliac crests or any corresponding iliac structures.

bis in die (bĭs ĭn dī'ē, dē'ā) [L.] ABBR: b.d.; b.i.d. Twice in a day.

bismuth (biz'mŭth) [Ger. *Wismuth, Bismut,* white mass] SYMB: Bi. A silvery metallic element, atomic weight (mass) 208.980, atomic number 83. Its compounds are used as a protective for inflamed surfaces. Its salts are used as an astringent and as a treatment for diarrhea.

bisphenol A (bĭs-fēn'ŏl) [L. *bis,* twice + "] ABBR: BPA. A chemical used in many consumer products to increase their durability and toughness. Its chemical formula is 2,2–bis (4,4'-hydroxyphenyl) propane. It is used principally in manufacturing polycarbonates and epoxy resins. It has estrogen-like effects in animal tissue. Some studies have suggested that BPA has negative hormonal effects on adults and the developing fetus.

bisphosphonate (bĭs-fos'fŏ-nāt") Any of a class of medications that inhibit the resorption of bones by osteoclasts. Medications in this class are used to treat osteoporosis, hypercalcemia, and metastatic bone cancers. Examples include pamidronate, etidronate, clodronate, and alendronate.

⚠️ Drugs from this class occasionally cause osteonecrosis of the jaw, esp. in cancer patients. Drugs from this class may increase the risk of fractures in patients with osteopenia and should not be used.

bit depth The number of shades of gray in a digital image. Bit depth is defined as 2^n, where the multiplier 2 indicates that the image is in black and white and n represents the power to which the computer can multiply this function. Therefore a bit depth of 2^1 would produce 2 shades of gray; a bit depth of 2^{12} would produce 4096 shades of gray. Digital radiography, CT, and MR images are produced with bit depths of 10 or 12.

bite (bīt) **1.** To cut with the teeth. **2.** An injury in which the body surface is torn by an insect or animal, resulting in abrasions, punctures, or lacerated wounds. There may be evidence of a wound, usually surrounded by a zone of redness and swelling, often accompanied by pain, itching, or throbbing. This type of wound often becomes infected and may contain specific noxious materials such as bacteria, toxins, viruses, or venom. SEE: *sting.* **3.** In dentistry, the angle and manner in which the maxillary and mandibular teeth occlude. SEE: *occlusion.*

cat b. A wound inflicted by the teeth of a cat, typically a puncture wound on the hand or the arm. A cat bite is usually infected with several aerobic and anaerobic organisms, including *Pasteurella multocida.* Broad-spectrum antibiotics are required. About 20% of the time, the wound does not respond to antibiotic therapy and needs incision and drainage or débridement.

check b. A sheet of hard wax used to make an impression of teeth to check articulation.

closed b. Overbite.

cross b. A form of dental malocclusion in which the cusps of one tooth, e.g., arising from the maxilla, close within the cusps of the tooth arising in the mandible (or vice versa).

deep b. In orthodontics, a colloquial term for a pathological overbite.

dog b. A laceration or puncture wound made by the teeth of a dog. The dog should be observed for 10 days to determine the presence of rabies. SEE: *Capnocytophaga canimorsus; rabies.*

TREATMENT: The wound must be cleansed thoroughly. It should be washed vigorously with soap and water for at least 10 min to remove saliva. Flushing with a viricidal agent should be followed with a clear rinse. Bleeding, unless it is massive, should not be stopped because blood flow helps to cleanse the wound. Routine tetanus prophylaxis should be provided and information obtained about the animal, its location, and its owner. These data should be included in a report to public health authorities. Appropriate antirabies therapy must be initiated if the animal is known to have rabies.

end-to-end b. A bite in which the incisors of both jaws meet along the cutting edge when the jaw is closed.

fire ant b. Injury caused by he venom of the fire ant, resulting in local redness and tenderness, and occasional episodes of life-threatening anaphylaxis.

TREATMENT: The area, which may contain multiple bites, should be washed with soap and water. Epinephrine, 0.3 to 0.5 ml of a 1:1000 aqueous solution, should be given subcutaneously every 20 to 30 min in cases complicated by anaphylaxis. Use of a tourniquet slows absorption of the venom. Application of ice packs to the area relieves pain. Oxygen, endotracheal intubation, and vasopressors, as well as corticosteroids and antibiotics, may be required.

flea b. A hemorrhagic punctum surrounded by erythematous and urticarial patches and caused by the injection of flea saliva.

TREATMENT: Ice applied to the site decreases the pain. Application of a corticosteroid cream may decrease the inflammatory response.

PREVENTION: Flea bites serve as vectors for *Yersinia pestis,* the bacterium that causes plague. The skin should be treated with an insect repellent available as a powder, spray, or oil for topical use.

human b. A laceration or puncture wound caused by the teeth of a human. The aerobic and anaerobic organisms transmitted from the mouth may cause cellulitis, and, occasionally, infections of other soft tissues and bones.

TREATMENT: The wound should be irrigated thoroughly and may require surgical débridement. A moist dressing should be applied and tetanus prophylaxis administered. A penicillin with a beta-lactamase inhibitor usually provides adequate antibiotic coverage.

insect b. An injury in which the body surface is torn by an insect, resulting in abrasions, punctures, or lacerated wounds. Insect bites cause more deaths than do snake bites. For more information, see entries for individual insects.

SYMPTOMS: The reaction of a previously sensitized person is a potentially life-threatening medical emergency that requires prompt, effective therapy. Symptoms may include hives, itching and swelling in areas other than the site of the bite, tightness in the chest and difficulty in breathing, hoarse voice, swelling of the tongue, dizziness or hypotension, unconsciousness, and cardiac arrest.

FIRST AID: If the wound is suspected of containing venom, a bandage sufficiently tight to prevent venous return is applied if the bite is on an extremity. The wound is washed with saline solution thoroughly and a dry sterile dressing is applied. Appropriate antitetanus therapy is applied. Treatment for shock may be needed.

Some insect bites contain an acid substance resembling formic acid and consequently are relieved by topically applied alkalies, such as ammonia water or baking soda paste. For intense local pain, injection of local anesthetic may be required. Systemic medication may be needed for generalized pain.

Individuals who have had an allergic reaction to an insect bite may benefit from venom immunotherapy. This treatment involves administration of very small amounts of the insect venom over several weeks until immunity develops. Immunity is then maintained by periodic venom boosters.

Persons who have a history of an anaphylactic reaction to insect bites should avoid exposure to insects by wearing protective clothing, gloves, and shoes. Cosmetics, perfumes, and hair sprays should be avoided because they attract some insects, as do brightly colored and white clothing. Because foods and odor attract insects, care should be taken when cooking and eating outdoors.

open b. A bite in which a space exists between the upper and lower incisors when the mouth is closed.

snake b. A puncture wound made by the fangs of a snake. All snakes should be considered poisonous, although only a few secrete enough venom to inoculate poison deeply into the tissues.

PATIENT CARE: When snake bite, esp. from a venomous snake, is confirmed or strongly suggested, the patient's airway, breathing, and circulation should be assessed, and he should be transported immediately to a medical facility equipped and staffed to handle snake bites. In the hospital, the patient is attached to a cardiac monitor, an automatic noninvasive blood pressure monitoring machine, and a pulse oximeter. If necessary, oxygen administered at 4 L/min via nasal cannula, and an intravenous infusion of Ringer's lactate or normal saline should be started. Pulses below the wound and capillary refill time in the wounded limb are assessed and compared to the unaffected limb. The circumference of the affected limb should be measured at the bite and at equal distances above and below it, to monitor the spread of edema and inflammation. Lung sounds are auscultated for clarity, and the patient is asked about medical history, allergies, and history of previous snakebite. Snakebite symptoms can range from mild swelling, pain, and erythema to hypotension, shock, and a disseminated intravascular coagulation-like syndrome. In all cases the affected limb should be placed in a neutral, resting position.

If the patient has actually received venom from the snake bite (only about 50% of patients have), the appropriate antivenin should be administered intravenously, appropriately diluted. If the required antivenin is prepared from horse serum, the patient should be tested for sensitivity before administering the antivenin. The antivenin should be infused slowly, over about an hour in most cases, and the patient monitored for adverse reactions for at least another hour. Resuscitation equipment for treating anaphylaxis should be readily available throughout the infusion. Children require a higher dosage of antivenin than do adults. A blood sample should be drawn from the patient for complete blood count, coagulation profile, BUN, creatinine, creatine kinase, and blood type and cross-match. A urine specimen should be obtained to test for myoglobinuria.

The wound should be cleaned with cool soap and water. Analgesics and other prescribed treatments (antibiotics, methylprednisolone, antihistamines) should be administered, as well as tetanus prophylaxis if indicated.

Snake antivenin information is available from the nearest Poison Control Center. The patient should be observed for potential complications such as compartment syndrome, coagulopathy, rhabdomyolysis, renal failure, and wound infection. Prior to discharge, the signs and symptoms of delayed adverse reactions to antivenin should be explained to the patient, and he or she should be advised to immediately report fever, malaise, joint pain, rash, or unusual body bruising.

FIRST AID: The patient should be transported immediately to a medical facility equipped and staffed to handle snake bites. In the hospital, an intravenous infusion of Ringer's lactate or normal saline should be started.

A polyvalent antivenin serum for bites by pit vipers is prepared by Wyeth Lab. Inc. Antivenin for coral snake bite is also available from Wyeth. The use of antibodies to treat pit viper bites is being used experimentally.

⚠ Alcoholic stimulants must not be taken, and nothing should be done to increase circulation. One should not cauterize with strong acids or depend on home remedies. Tetanus prophylaxis is essential.

spider b. Punctures of the skin and/or envenomation by the fangs of a spider. SEE: *black widow spider; brown recluse spider.*

stork b. Colloquial term for telangiectasia.

tick b. A wound produced by a bloodsucking tick. Adult ticks (and immature nymphs) may be vectors for infectious diseases, including Rocky Mountain spotted fever, Q fever, tularemia, borreliosis, babesiosis, ehrlichiosis, anaplasmosis, and Lyme disease. They can also produce tick paralysis, a disease that may mimic Guillain-Barré syndrome.

The bite itself may produce a localized reddened area of skin, which is typically of little importance. This area may be raised or slightly itchy.

PATIENT CARE: People who are exposed to environments where ticks proliferate (hikers, hunters, surveyors, or children and adults with more casual environmental exposures) should be educated about the importance of wearing clothing that leaves little skin exposed. The clothing should be pretreated with insect repellents or insecticides like permethrin. Adults and children over two should also apply repellent products like DEET, lemon eucalyptus oil, or picaridin directly to exposed skin. These products will prevent not only tick attachment but also other insect bites, e.g., by disease-causing mosquitoes. Attached ticks should be removed from the skin by taking a pair of small tweezers or forceps, grasping the tick firmly by the mouth parts, and pulling the insect directly out of the skin, leaving no body parts embedded.

⚠ Ticks should not be removed by burning them with matches, by soaking them in petroleum jelly, or by injecting the subcutaneous tissue beneath their mouth parts with lidocaine. None of these methods is effective, and some may be hazardous.

working b. Working **articulation**.
bitelock (bīt′lŏk) A device used in dentistry for retaining bite rims outside the mouth in the same position as they were inside the mouth.
bitemporal (bī-tĕm′pō-răl) [L. *bis,* twice, + *temporalis,* pert. to a temple] Pert. to both temples or temporal bones.
biteplate (bīt′plāt) A dental device used to correct or diagnose malocclusion. It is worn in the palate, usually on a temporary basis.
Bitot spots (bē′tō) [Pierre A. Bitot, Fr. physician, 1822–1888] Triangular shiny gray spots on the conjunctiva seen in vitamin A deficiency.
bitrochanteric (bī″trō-kăn-tĕr′ĭk) Pert. to both greater trochanters of the two femurs.
bitter (bĭt′ĕr) [AS. *biter,* strong] Having a caustic, sharp, or disagreeable taste. It is one of the five taste senses (bitter, salty, savory, sour, and sweet).
bitter melon A bitter-tasting tropical vegetable (*Momordica charantia*) popular in Asian countries, also known as balsam apple, balsam pear, bitter gourd, cerasee, karela, ku gua, and squirting cucumber. It is promoted in complementary and alternative medicine for its effects on diabetes mellitus, HIV infection, and obesity. SYN: *karela.*
bitter orange A citrus tree, *Citrus auran-*

tium, whose oils are used in some cultures as an oral remedy for gastrointestinal conditions such as constipation or nausea. Bitter orange is commonly used in dietary supplements as an aid to fat loss and as an appetite suppressant.

⚠ Bitter orange can worsen cardiovascular disease and glaucoma.

biuret (bī″yŭ-ret′, bī′yŭ-ret″) [*bi-* + *urea*] NH₂CONHCONH₂, a crystalline decomposition derivative of urea.

biuret reaction (bī″yŭ-ret′, bī′yŭ-ret″) A method for detecting or measuring protein in body fluids, e.g., serum or saliva. The presence of biuret can be detected by the addition of sodium hydroxide and copper sulfate solutions to the sample. A rose to violet color indicates the presence of protein, and a pink and finally blue color indicates the presence of urea. SYN: *biuret test.*

biuret test (bī″yŭ-ret′, bī′yŭ-ret″) Biuret reaction.

BiVAD *Biventricular assist* **device**.

bivalent (bī-vā′lĕnt) [″ + *valens,* powerful] **1.** In chemistry, having a valence of two. **2.** In cytology, a structure consisting of two paired homologous chromosomes, each split into two sister chromatids during meiosis.

bivariate (bī-văr′ē-ĭt, āt″) [″ + ″] Pertaining to two variables.

bixel (bĭks′ĕl) [Fr. *b(eam)* + *(pi)xel*] A beam element or ray in radiation oncology.

bizygomatic (bī″zī-gō-măt′ĭk) Pert. to the most prominent point on each of the two zygomatic arches.

Bjerrum, Jannik Petersen (byer′um) Danish ophthalmologist, 1851–1920.

   B. screen Tangent **screen**.

   B. scotoma A sickle- or comet-shaped blind spot usually found in the central zone of the visual field; seen in glaucoma.

BK *below knee,* a term used to refer to the site of amputation of a lower extremity.

Bk Symbol for the element berkelium.

black (blăk) [AS. *blaec*] **1.** Devoid of color or reflecting no light. **2.** Marked by dark pigmentation.

black blood magnetic resonance imaging SEE: under *imaging.*

black box warning A written advisory supplied by a pharmaceutical company to health care professionals whenever a medication causes any serious side effect(s). Under U.S. federal regulations, this advisory is mandatory and must be highlighted by "a prominently displayed box."

black cohosh (kō′hosh″) A perennial herb, *Cimicifuga racemosa* (also *Actaea racemosa*), of eastern North America whose rootstock preparations are promoted as a treatment for menstrual and menopausal discomfort. SYN: *black* **snakeroot**; *bugbane.* SEE: *blue cohosh.*

blackhead An open comedo. SEE: *comedo.*

black heel Subcutaneous bleeding into the skin behind the calcaneus typically caused by repetitive trauma, for example, in runners or other athletes.

black membrane SEE: under *membrane.*

blackout (blăk′owt″) Sudden loss of consciousness. SYN: *syncope.* SEE: *red-out.*

   alcoholic b. An episode of forgetting all or part of what occurred during or following a period of alcohol intake.

blackwater fever SEE: under *fever.*

bladder (blad′ĕr) A membranous sac or receptacle for a secretion, as the gallbladder; commonly used to designate the urinary bladder. SEE: *urinary b.; genitourinary system.*

   autonomous b. A bladder in which there is interruption in both the afferent and efferent limbs of the reflex arcs. Bladder sensation is absent; dribbling is constant; residual urine amount is large.

   cord b. Distention of the bladder without discomfort. Symptoms include a tendency to void frequently and dribbling after urination. The condition is caused by a lesion affecting the posterior roots of the spinal column at the level of bladder innervation above the sacrum.

   fallen b. A colloquial term for a cystocele.

   hypertonic b. **1.** A bladder with excessive muscle tone. **2.** Increased muscular activity of the bladder.

   irritable b. Bladder condition marked by increased frequency of contraction with an associated desire to urinate.

   motor paralytic b. A neurogenic bladder caused by defective nerve supply to the bladder. In the acute form urination is not possible. In the chronic form there is difficulty in urinating, which may lead to recurrent urinary tract infections.

   nervous b. A condition marked by the repeated desire to urinate, but doing so fails to empty the bladder.

   neurogenic b. Any dysfunction of the urinary bladder caused by lesions of the central nervous system or nerves supplying the bladder.

   nonneurogenic neurogenic b. SEE: *Hinman syndrome.*

   overactive b. A sudden, intense urge to urinate that may or may not lead to loss of urine (urinary incontinence).

   spastic b. Neurogenic bladder due to complete transection of the spinal cord above the sacral segments.

   urinary b. A muscular, membranous, distensible reservoir that holds urine situated in the pelvic cavity. It receives urine from the kidneys through the ureters and discharges it from the body through the urethra. SEE: *urinary system.*

ANATOMY: The bladder is situated in the anterior inferior portion of the pelvic cavity. In the female it lies in front of the anterior wall of the vagina and the uterus; in the male it lies in front of the rectum. The lower portion of the bladder, continuous with the urethra, is called the neck; its upper tip, connected with the umbilicus by the median umbilical ligament, is called the apex. The region between the openings of the two ureters and the urethra is the trigone. The wall of the bladder has three major layers. The mucous membrane lining is transitional epithelium. The middle layer is three sheets (longitudinal, circular, longitudinal) of smooth muscle, called the detrusor muscle. The outer layer on the superior surface is the visceral peritoneum; on the lateral and inferior surfaces it is areolar connective tissue. The bladder is supported by numerous ligaments; it is supplied with blood by the superior, middle, and inferior vesical arteries, and drained by numerous veins and lymphatics; and it is innervated by branches of the third and fourth sacral nerves by way of the hypogastric plexus.

The bladder has a normal storage capacity of 500 ml (about 16 oz) or more. In disease states it may be greatly distended. A frequent cause of distention of the bladder in older men is interference with urination due to hypertrophy of the prostate gland, which surrounds the urethra and neck of the bladder.

PHYSIOLOGY: An average of 40 to 50 oz (about 1.2 to 1.5 L) of urine is excreted in a 24-hr period, but this varies with the amount of fluid ingested and the amount lost through exhalation, sweat, and the bowels. Inability to empty the bladder is known as retention and may require catheterization. Sphincter muscles are part of the mechanism that controls retention within the bladder.

For patients who need help in managing bladder elimination problems there are a variety of options: indwelling urethral catheters, Kegel exercises, intermittent catheterization, suprapubic indwelling catheters, external collecting devices (urinals and specially designed bedpans), medications for promoting bladder emptying (such as bethanechol, phenoxybenzamine, diazepam, dantrolene, or baclofen), and medicines to promote bladder storage (such as imipramine, oxybutynin, propanthelene, pseudoephedrine, or phenylpropanolamine). For men, a condom designed to collect and contain urine is available. SEE: *bladder training.*

The force of urination is much greater in a child than in an adult because in the child the bladder is more an abdominal organ than a pelvic one. The child's abdominal muscles help to expel the urine.

EXAMINATION: *Palpation:* The bladder cannot be palpated when empty. When full it appears as a tumor in the suprapubic region that is smooth and oval on palpation.

Percussion: When it is distended with urine, the rounded superior margin is easily made out by observing the tympanic sound of the intestines on one hand and dull sound of the bladder on the other.

bladder augmentation Surgical enlargement of the urinary bladder with a segment of bowel. The technique enlarges the reservoir of the bladder and enhances the compliance of the detrusor muscles. It is used esp. in patients with neurogenic bladder problems refractory to medical therapy. When a major portion of the bladder is resected (due to a malignancy), an isolated intestinal pouch is used as a substitute for the bladder (neoenterocystoplasty). SYN: *enterocystoplasty.*

bladder drill Bladder **training**.

bladder infection SEE: under *infection.*

bladder training SEE: under *training.*

bladder tumor antigen SEE: under *antigen.*

bladderwrack, bladder wrack (blăd′ĕr-răk″) A yellow-brown seaweed, *Fucus vesiculosus,* which contains significant quantities of iodine. It is used as an alternative medicine for a variety of proposed cures, e.g., of hypothyroidism, but its effectiveness has not been documented in controlled trials. SYN: *Fucus vesiculosus.*

Blalock-Hanlon procedure (blā′lŏk″-hăn′lŏn) [Alfred Blalock, U.S. surgeon, 1899–1965; C. Rollins Hanlon, U.S. surgeon, b. 1915] The surgical creation of an atrial septal defect or enlargement of the foramen ovale in an infant with transposition of the great arteries. This procedure helps to improve oxygenation until total repair is undertaken.

Blalock-Taussig shunt (blā′lŏk″-tăw′sig″) [Alfred Blalock, U.S. surgeon; 1899–1965; Helen B. Taussig, U.S. pediatrician; 1898–1986] ABBR: B-T shunt. An anastomosis of a subclavian artery to the pulmonary artery on the same side. This procedure increases blood flow to the lungs in children with cardiac defects. The modified Blalock-Taussig shunt involves the use of synthetic graft material to create the anastomosis.

blanch (blănch) **1.** To lose color, esp. of the face, usually suddenly and in the context of being frightened or saddened. **2.** To briefly scald a vegetable or nut-fruit in order to facilitate removal of the skin, peel, or covering. **3.** To bleach.

blanch test, blanching test A test of the integrity of the circulation performed by applying and then quickly releasing pressure to a fingernail or toenail. After losing color, the blanched nail normally regains a pink appearance within 2 seconds or less. Failure to do so suggests impaired blood flow to the extremity. SYN: *capillary nail refill test.* SEE: illus.

blank (blănk) A surrogate analytical sample that either has no analyte present or is subject to only part of the analytical process. The purpose of the blank is to assess the contribution of nonspecific effects on the final reaction, and thus be able to eliminate those effects from the final analytical results. The term "blank" may be modified by a word indicating the type of effect being evaluated, with the resultant complete term being, for example, "reagent blank," a blank containing only reagents.

¹blast (blast) [Gr. *blastos,* sprout, shoot] A cell that produces something (e.g., osteoblast, fibroblast).

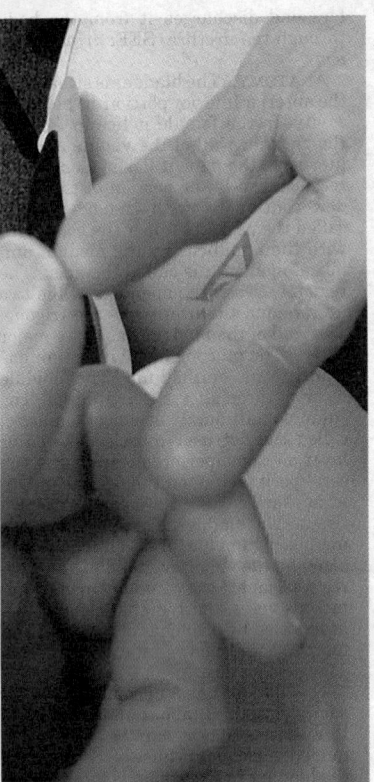

Color returns to the digit; the normal delay in color return is 2 seconds or less

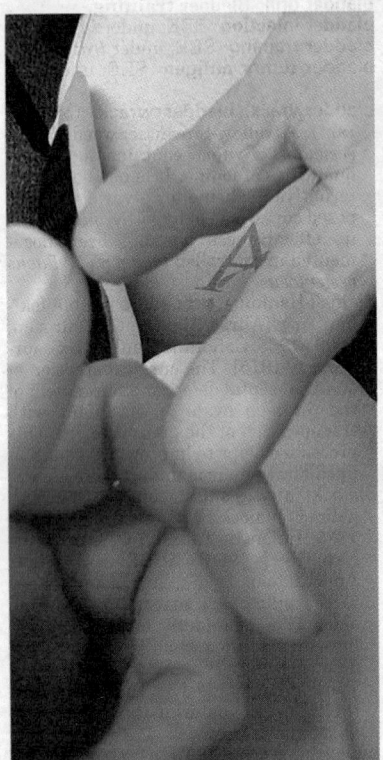

BLANCH TEST

Blanching of the finger after compression

²blast (blast) [Old English *blæst,* puff of wind] A sudden, violent movement of air such as accompanies the explosion of a shell or bomb; or a violent sound, as the blast of a horn. It often causes damage to blast-sensitive organs such as the tympanic membrane, lung, or colon. It may also forcibly move people and objects, resulting in unpredictable injuries to unprotected body parts. SYN: *blast wind.*

blast- [Gr. *blastos,* sprout, shoot] Prefix meaning *an embryonic state of development.*

-blast [Gr. *blastos,* sprout, shoot] Suffix meaning *an embryonic state of development* or *the creator of a type of cell,* e.g., an osteoblast or a lymphoblast.

blastema (blăs-tē′mă) [Gr. *blastema,* sprout] The undifferentiated cells from which the specialized tissues of organs are formed.

blastid (blăs′tĭd) [Gr. *blastos,* germ] The site of the nucleus of a fertilized ovum.

blast lung SEE: under *lung*.

blastochyle (blăs′tō-kīl) [″ + *chylos*, juice] Fluid contained in the blastocele.

blastocoel, blastocoele, blastocele (blas′tŏ-sēl″) [*blast-* + *-coele*] The fluid-filled cavity within the blastula of the developing embryo.

blastocyst (blăs′tō-sĭst) [″ + *kystis*, bag] In mammalian embryo development, the stage that follows the morula. It consists of an outer layer, or trophoblast, and an inner cell mass, from which the embryo will develop. The enclosed cavity is the blastocele. At this stage, implantation in the endometrium (lining of the uterus) occurs. SEE: *fertilization* for illus.

Blastocystis hominis (blăs′tō-sĭs″tĭs hŏm′ĭn-ĭs) A protozoan once thought to be a harmless commensal in the human gastrointestinal tract but now believed to be an intestinal parasite that produces diarrhea, abdominal pain, bloating, and weight loss in some people.

blastocystosis (blăs″tō-sĭs-tō′sĭs) Intestinal infection with *Blastocystis hominis*.

blastocyte (blăs′tō-sīt) [″ + *kytos*, cell] An undifferentiated embryonic cell.

blastocytoma (blăs-tō-sī-tō′mă) [″ + ″ + *oma*, tumor] Blastoma.

blastoderm (blăs′tō-dĕrm) [″ + *derma*, skin] A disk of cells (germinal disk or blastodisk) that develops on the surface of the yolk in an avian or reptilian egg from which the embryo develops; also, in mammalian embryos a disk of cells lying between the yolk sac and the amniotic cavity from which the embryo develops. From the blastoderm, the three germ layers (ectoderm, mesoderm, and endoderm) arise.

blastokinin (blăs″tō-kī′nĭn) A globulin found in the uterine lumen of some mammals near the time of blastocyst implantation.

blastolysis (blăs-tŏl′ĭ-sĭs) [″ + *lysis*, dissolution] Lysis or destruction of a germ cell or a blastoderm.

blastoma (blăs-tō′mă) *pl.* **blastomata** [″ + *oma*, tumor] A neoplasm composed of immature, undifferentiated cells derived from the blastema of an organ or tissue. SYN: *blastocytoma*. SEE: *blastema*.

blastomere (blas′tŏ-mēr″) [*blast-* + *-mere*] Any of the cells resulting from the cleavage of a fertilized ovum. SYN: *cleavage cell*.

blastomerotomy (blăs″tō-mēr-ŏt′ō-mē) [″ + ″ + *tome*, incision] Destruction of blastomeres.

Blastomyces (blast-ŏ-mī′sēz″) [*blasto-* + Gr. *mykēs*, fungus] A genus of yeast-like budding fungi pathogenic to humans. At room temperature these fungi grow in a moldlike mycelial form, and at body temperature in a yeastlike form.

    B. dermatitidis The species that causes North American blastomycosis, a rare fungal infection in humans.

blastomycete (blăs″tō-mī′sēt) Any organism of the genus *Blastomyces*.

blastomycosis (blas″tō-mī-kō′sĭs) [*blasto-* + *mycosis*] A rare fungal infection caused by inhalation of the conidia of *Blastomyces dermatitidis*. This infection may produce inflammatory lesions of the skin (cutaneous form) or lungs or a generalized invasion of the skin, lungs, bones, central nervous system, kidneys, liver, and spleen. SYN: *North American b.*

    TREATMENT: Treatment consists of amphotericin B or the less toxic itraconazole.

    keloidal b. Lobomycosis.

    North American b. Blastomycosis.

    South American b. Paracoccidioidomycosis.

blastopore (blăs′tō-por) [″ + *poros*, passageway] In the embryo of mammals, the small opening into the archenteron made by invagination of the blastula.

blastospore (blăs′tō-spor) [″ + *sporos*, seed] A spore formed by budding from a hypha, as in yeast.

blastula (blăs′tū-lä) *pl.* **blastulae** [L.] An early stage in the development of a zygote into an embryo; it consists of a hollow sphere of cells enclosing a cavity, the blastocele. In large-yolked eggs, the blastocele is reduced to a narrow slit. In mammalian development, the blastocyst corresponds to the blastula of lower forms.

blast wind ²Blast

Blatella (blă-tel′ă) [L. diminutive of *blatta*] A genus of cockroaches (family Blattidae). SEE: *cockroach*.

    B. germanica SEE: *German cockroach*.

Blatta (blat′ă) [L. *blatta*, cockroach] A genus of cockroaches (family Blattidae). SEE: *cockroach*.

    B. orientalis SEE: *oriental cockroach*.

Blau syndrome (blow) A rare autosomal dominant disease characterized by camptodactyly and granulomatous involvement of joints, skin, and uvea.

bleb (blĕb) An irregularly shaped elevation of the epidermis; a blister or a bulla. Blebs may vary in size from less than 1 cm to as much as 5 to 10 cm; they may contain serous, seropurulent, or bloody fluid. Blebs are a primary skin lesion that may occur in many disorders, including dermatitis herpetiformis, pemphigus, and syphilis. SEE: *bulla*.

bleeder (blēd′ĕr) [AS. *bledan*, to bleed] **1.** A colloquial term for one whose ability to coagulate blood is either deficient or absent, so that small cuts and injuries lead to prolonged bleeding. SEE: *he-*

mophilia. **2.** A colloquial term for a small artery that has been cut or torn.

bleeding (blēd′ing) **1.** The emission of blood, as from an injured vessel. **2.** The process of emitting blood, as a hemorrhage or the operation of letting blood.

Normally, when blood is exposed to air, it changes to allow fibrin to form. This entangles the cells and forms a blood clot. SEE: *coagulation, blood; coagulation factor; hemorrhage.*

arterial b. Bleeding in spurts of bright red blood from an artery.

EMERGENCY CARE: Arterial bleeding may be controlled by applying pressure with the fingers at the nearest pressure point between it and the heart. The artery is located and digital pressure is applied above it until bleeding stops or until the artery is ligated or repaired. When a pressure point is ineffective in controlling arterial bleeding on an extremity, a tourniquet may be needed. SEE: table.

breakthrough b. Intermenstrual spotting or bleeding experienced by some women who are taking oral contraceptives.

clinically significant b. Bleeding that causes hemodynamic instability (blood pressure less than 100 mm Hg or pulse more than 100 beats per min) or requires a transfusion of more than 2 units of blood in 24 hours.

dysfunctional uterine b. ABBR: DUB. A diagnosis of exclusion in which there is abnormal bleeding from the uterus not caused by tumor, inflammation, or pregnancy. These causes of bleeding must be ruled out before DUB may be diagnosed. The condition may occur with ovulatory cycles, but most often occurs with anovulation. It is common in women with polycystic ovary syndrome. Endometrial hyperplasia followed by sloughing of the endometrium may occur in women with repeated anovulatory cycles.

ETIOLOGY: The absence of the luteal progesterone phase interferes with normal endometrial preparation for implantation or menstruation. Prolonged constant levels of estrogen stimulate uneven endometrial hypertrophy so that some areas slough and bleed before others, causing intermittent bleeding.

functional b. **1.** Loss of blood from the uterus caused by an organic lesion, such as a cyst, fibroid, or malignant tumor. **2.** Metrorrhea.

gastrointestinal b. Bleeding from anywhere in the gastrointestinal tract. SYN: *gastrointestinal hemorrhage.* SEE: Medical Emergencies.

herald b. Spontaneous hemorrhage from the gastrointestinal tract in a patient with an aortic bypass graft. The hemorrhage typically stops suddenly,

Control of Arterial Bleeding

Artery	Course	Bone Involved	Spot to Apply Pressure
For Wounds of the Face			
Temporal	Upward ½ in (13 mm) in front of ear	Temporal bone	Against bony prominence immediately in front of ear or on temple
Facial	Upward across jaw diagonally	Lower part of lower maxilla	1 in (2.5 cm) in front of angle of lower jaw
For Wounds of the Upper Extremity			
Axillary	Downward across outer side of armpit to inside of humerus	Head of humerus	High up in armpit against upper part of humerus
Brachial	Along inner side of humerus under edge of biceps muscle	Shaft of humerus	Against shaft of humerus by pulling aside and gripping biceps, pressing tips of fingers deep down against bone
For Wounds of the Lower Extremity			
Femoral	Down thigh from pelvis to knee from a point midway between iliac spine and symphysis pubis to inner side of end of femur at knee joint	Brim of pelvis	Against brim of pelvis, midway between iliac spine and symphysis pubis
Posterior tibial	Downward to foot in hollow just behind prominence of inner ankle	Inner side of tibia, low down above ankle	For wounds in sole of foot, against tibia in center of hollow behind inner ankle

only to recur massively days or weeks later. It is sometimes a clinical hallmark of bleeding from an aortoenteric fistula.

internal b. Hemorrhage from an internal organ or site, esp. the gastrointestinal tract.

menstrual b. SEE: *menstruation.*

nasal b. Epistaxis.

nuisance b. Loss of a few drops of blood from minor cuts and scratches; or bruising of the skin after minor trauma. It is a potential complication of treatment with anticoagulant or antiplatelet drugs, and an occasional cause of drug discontinuation by treated patients.

occult b. Inapparent bleeding, esp. that which occurs into the intestines and can be detected only by chemical tests of the feces. SYN: *Internal hemorrhage.*

uterine b. Bleeding from the uterus. Physiological bleeding via the vagina occurs in normal menstruation. Abnormal forms include excessive menstrual flow (hypermenorrhea, menorrhagia) or too frequent menstruation (polymenorrhea). Nonmenstrual bleeding is called metrorrhagia. Pseudomenstrual or withdrawal bleeding may occur following estrogen therapy. Breakthrough bleeding is the term used for intermenstrual bleeding that sometimes occurs in women who take progestational agents such as birth control pills or receive estrogen-progesterone replacement therapy. SEE: *amenorrhea; dysfunctional uterine **b.**; menstruation; Nursing Diagnoses Appendix.*

variceal b. SEE: *esophageal **varix**.*

venous b. A continuous flow of dark red blood.

FIRST AID: Venous bleeding may be controlled by firm, continuous pressure applied directly to the bleeding site. If bleeding is from an area over soft tissues, a large, compress bandage should be held firmly against the site.

⚠ A tourniquet should not be used. If the bleeding is over a bony area, as in the case of a ruptured varicose vein of the leg, pressure held firmly against the vein will provide immediate control of the blood loss. The patient should be taken to a health care provider as soon as possible if bleeding does not stop.

---

withdrawal b. Uterine bleeding following discontinuation of treatment with cyclic hormone replacement therapy. It is caused by sloughing of the endometrium but is not technically considered menstruation because it is not associated with an ovulatory cycle.

blennadenitis (blĕn"ăd-ĕ-nī'tĭs) [" + *aden,* gland, + *itis,* inflammation] Inflammation of the mucous glands.

blenno-, blenn- [Gr. *blennos,* slime, mucus] Prefixes meaning *mucus.*

blennoid (blĕn'oyd) [" + *eidos,* form, shape] Mucoid (2).

blennorrhagia (blĕn"ō-rā'jē-ă) [" + *rhegnynai,* to break forth] Any excessive discharge from mucous membranes.

blennorrhea (blĕn"ō-rē'ă) [Gr. *blennos,* mucus, + *rhoia,* flow] Any discharge from mucous membranes. SYN: *blennorrhagia.*

inclusion b. Chlamydial conjunctivitis.

blepharadenitis (blĕf"ăr-ăd-ĕ-nī'tĭs) [Gr. *blepharon,* eyelid, + *aden,* gland, + *itis,* inflammation] Inflammation of the meibomian glands.

blepharal (blĕf'ăr-ăl) Pert. to an eyelid.

blepharectomy (blĕf"ăr-rĕk'tō-mē) [" + *ektome,* excision] Surgical excision of all or part of an eyelid.

blepharedema (blĕf"ăr-ĕ-dē'mă) [" + *oidema,* swelling] Edema of the eyelids, causing swelling and a baggy appearance.

blepharism (blĕf'ăr-ĭ-zĭm) [" + *-ismos,* condition] Twitching or blinking of the eyelids. SEE: *blepharospasm.*

blepharitis (blĕf"ăr-ī'tĭs) [" + *itis,* inflammation] Ulcerative or nonulcerative inflammation of the hair follicles and glands along the edges of the eyelids.

SYMPTOMS: The eyelids become red, tender, and sore with sticky exudate and dry or waxy scales on the edges; there may be itching or burning, watering of the eyes and loss of eyelashes. Styes and meibomian cysts are associated with the condition.

ETIOLOGY: The ulcerative type is usually caused by infection with staphylococci. The cause of the nonulcerative type is often unknown; it may be due to allergy or exposure to dust, smoke, or irritating chemicals, or in association with seborrhea of the scalp, eyebrows and ears.

PATIENT CARE: Patients are taught how to keep their scalp, eyebrows, and eyelids clean and to avoid rubbing their eyes with their hands. Warm compresses four times a day, lid hygiene, and antibiotic ointment at bedtime will improve symptoms with two weeks. In severe cases, systemic antibiotics are indicated, with culture of the lid margin and antibiotic sensitivity studies are used to determine the appropriate regimen.

angular b. An infection often involving the lateral canthus of the eyelid. Often caused by the bacterium Moraxella

b. ciliaris Inflammation affecting the ciliary margins of the eyelids. SYN: **b.** *marginalis.*

b. marginalis **Blepharitis** ciliaris.

b. parasitica Blepharitis caused by parasites such as mites or lice.

seborrheic b. A nonulcerative form of blepharitis in which waxy scales form on the eyelids. It is usually associated with seborrheic dermatitis of the surrounding skin.

b. squamosa Chronic blepharitis with scaling.

b. ulcerosa Blepharitis with ulceration.

blepharo-, blephar- [Gr. *blepharon*, eyelid] Prefixes meaning *eyelid*.

blepharoadenoma (blĕf″ăr-ō-ăd-ĕ-nō′mă) [″ + ″ + *oma*, tumor] A glandular tumor of the eyelid.

blepharoatheroma (blĕf″ăr-ō-ăth″ĕ-rō′mă) [″ + *athere*, thick fluid, + *oma*, tumor] A sebaceous cyst of the eyelid.

blepharochalasis (blĕf″ăr-ō-kăl′ă-sĭs) [″ + *chalasis*, relaxation] Hypertrophy of the skin of the upper eyelid due to loss of elasticity following edematous swellings as in recurrent angioneurotic edema of the lids. The skin may droop over the edge of the eyelid when the eyes are open.

blepharoclonus (blĕf″ă-rŏk′lō-nŭs) [″ + *klonos*, tumult] Clonic spasm of the muscles that close the eyelids (orbicularis oculi).

blepharoconjunctivitis (blĕf″ă-rō-kŏn-jŭnk″tĭ-vī′tĭs) [″ + L. *conjungere*, to join together, + Gr. *itis*, inflammation] Inflammation of the eyelids and conjunctiva.

blepharodiastasis (blĕf-ă-rō-dī-ăs′tă-sĭs) [″ + *diastasis*, separation] Excessive separation of the eyelids, causing the eyes to open wide.

blepharoncus (blĕf″ă-rŏn′kŭs) [″ + *onkos*, tumor] A tumor of the eyelid.

blepharopachynsis (blĕf″ă-rō-pă-kĭn′sĭs) [″ + *pachynsis*, thickening] Abnormal thickening of the eyelid.

blepharoplast (blĕf′ă-rō-plăst) Basal body.

blepharoplasty (blĕf′ă-rō-plăs″tē) Plastic surgery upon the eyelid.

blepharoplegia (blĕf″ă-rō-plē′jē-ă) [Gr. *blepharon*, eyelid, + *plege*, a stroke] Paralysis of an eyelid.

blepharoptosis (blĕf″ă-rō-tō′sĭs) [″ + *ptosis*, a dropping] Drooping of the upper eyelid; may be congenital or acquired.

blepharopyorrhea (blĕf″ă-rō-pī-ō-rē′ă) [″ + *pyon*, pus, + *rhoia*, flow] Purulent discharge from the eyelid.

blepharorrhaphy (blĕf″ă-ror′ă-fē) [″ + *rhaphe*, seam, ridge] Tarsorrhaphy.

blepharorrhea (blĕf″ă-rō-rē′ă) [″ + *rhoia*, flow] Discharge from the eyelid.

blepharospasm (blĕf′ă-rō-spăsm) [″ + *spasmos*, a convulsion] A twitching or spasmodic contraction of the orbicularis oculi muscle due to tics, eyestrain, or nervous irritability.

essential b. Blepharospasm of unknown cause. It may be so severe as to be debilitating. Surgery has helped some patients. Botulinum toxin A injected into the muscles that control the spasm has been of benefit. This treatment will need to be repeated after 2 to 3 months.

blepharosphincterectomy (blĕf″ă-rō-sfĭnk″tĕr-ĕk′tō-mē) [″ + *sphinkter*, a constrictor, + *ektome*, excision] Excision of part of the orbicularis palpebrarum to relieve pressure of the eyelid on the cornea.

blepharostat (blĕf′ă-rō-stăt) [″ + *histanai*, cause to stand] A device for separating the eyelids during an operation.

blepharosynechia (blef″ă-rō″sĭ-nē′kē-ă) [*blepharo-* + *synecheia*] Adhesion of the edges of the upper eyelid to the lower one. SYN: *ankyloblepharon*.

blepharotomy (blĕf-ă-rŏt′ō-mē) [″ + *tome*, incision] Surgical incision of the eyelid.

Bleuler, Eugen (bloy′lĕr, oy′gĕn) [1857–1939] Swiss psychiatrist known for studies on schizophrenia.

blind (blīnd) **1.** Having no sight or defective sight; visually impaired. **2.** Pert. to a method, study, or clinical trial in which neither the subject nor the investigator knows the hypothesis, problem, or condition being tested. Blinding reduces the potential for bias. SYN: *blinded; masked* (2). SEE: *double-blind; single-blind.*

blind bronchoalveolar lavage The use of a catheter inserted without bronchoscopic visualization into the tracheobronchial tree to obtain lower respiratory specimens of fluid for culture. A relatively low-cost alternative to bronchoscopically obtained cultures or brushings in patients suspected of having ventilator-associated pneumonia.

blinded (blīnd′ĕd) Blind (2).

blind loop syndrome A condition caused by intraluminal growth of bacteria in the upper portion of the small intestine. Conditions associated with this syndrome are anatomical lesions that lead to stasis such as diverticula or surgically created blind loops; diseases associated with motor function of the small intestine; and any condition that decreases gastric acid secretion. The syndrome is diagnosed by the clinical signs and symptoms of malabsorption and the use of breath tests for detecting overgrowth of bacteria in the intestine.

TREATMENT: Antimicrobial therapy and nutritional support are needed. Surgery may be indicated to correct certain anatomical presentations.

blindness (blīnd′nĕs) Inability to see. The leading causes of blindness in the U.S. are age-related macular degeneration, diabetic retinopathy, and glaucoma.

Blindness may be caused by diseases of the lens, retina, or other eye structures; diseases of the optic nerve; or lesions of the visual cortex or pathways of the brain. A small number of infants are born blind, but far more people become blind during life. In the U.S., blindness due to infection is rare, but worldwide diseases like trachoma and onchocerciasis are relatively common causes of severe visual impairment. In malnourished people, vitamin A deficiency is an important cause of blindness.

A variety of free services are available for the blind and physically handicapped. Talking Books Topics, published bimonthly in large-print, cassette, and disc formats, is distributed free to the blind and physically handicapped who participate in the Library of Congress free reading program. It lists recorded books and magazines available through a national network of cooperating libraries and provides news of developments and activities in library services. Subscription requests may be sent to Talking Books Topics, CMLS, P.O. Box 9150, Melbourne, FL 32902-9150.

amnesic color b. Inability to remember the names of colors.

color b. A genetic or acquired abnormality of color perception. Complete color blindness, a rare disease, is called achromatopsia. Red-green color blindness, which affects about 8% of the male population, is an X-linked trait. Although *color blindness* is the term most commonly used, it is inaccurate: *color deficiency* and *color vision deficiency* are preferred. SEE: illus.

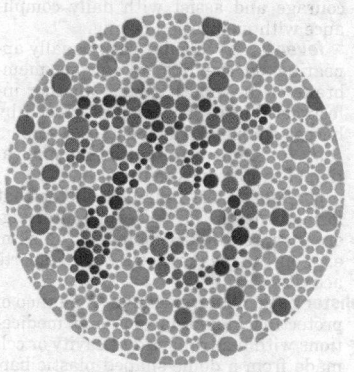

TEST FOR COLOR BLINDNESS

cortical b. Blindness due to lesions in the left and right occipital lobes of the brain. The eyes are still able to move, and the pupillary light reflexes remain, but the blindness is as if the optic nerves had been severed. The usual cause is oc-clusion of the posterior cerebral arteries. Transitory cortical blindness may follow head injury. SYN: *cerebral visual impairment*.

day b. Hemeralopia.

eclipse b. Blindness due to burning the macula while viewing an eclipse without using protective lenses. Looking directly at the sun at any time can damage the eyes. SYN: *solar b.; solar maculopathy*.

green b. Aglaucopsia.

hysterical b. An inaccurate term for functional blindness, i.e., blindness caused by psychological disorders rather than by demonstrable organic pathology.

legal b. A degree of loss of visual acuity that prevents a person from performing work requiring eyesight. In the U.S. this is defined as corrected visual acuity of 20/200 or less, or a visual field of 20° or less in the better eye. In the U.S. there are about three quarters of a million blind people, and about 8 or 9 million people with significant visual impairment.

letter b. A form of aphasia marked by an inability to understand the meaning of letters.

night b. Nyctalopia (1).

note b. The inability to recognize musical notes. It is due to a lesion of the central nervous system.

object b. A disorder in which the brain fails to recognize things even though the eyes function normally. SEE: *apraxia*.

psychic b. Sight without recognition due to a brain lesion.

red-green b. Red-green color **b.**

red-green color b. Inability to see red hues. It is the most common kind of color blindness. SYN: *red-green b.*

river b. SEE: *onchocerciasis*.

snow b. Blindness, usually temporary, due to the glare of sunlight on snow. It may result in photophobia and conjunctivitis, the latter resulting from effects of ultraviolet radiation.

solar b. Eclipse **b.**

taste b. An inability to taste certain substances such as phenylthiocarbamide. This inability is due to an autosomal recessive trait.

transient monocular b. A temporary loss of vision affecting one eye. In older adults it is usually a form of transient ischemic attack, caused by carotid atherosclerosis, and is therefore a harbinger of stroke. In young adults it may be caused by migraine. SYN: *amaurosis fugax*.

ETIOLOGY: In older adults, causes of carotid atherosclerosis include smoking, diabetes mellitus, hypertension, obesity, and hypercholesterolemia. When atherosclerotic plaques form within the carotid artery, they may ulcerate. The exposed endothelium within the artery becomes a focus of inflammation and blood clotting. Blindness occurs when tiny clots from the carotid arteries embolize to the ophthalmic arteries.

SYMPTOMS: Patients often describe a dark shade descending into the field of vision. At the same time they may have other stroke symptoms, e.g., difficulty with speech or weakness of the hand on the side opposite the affected eye.

TREATMENT: A patient who may have carotid atherosclerosis should begin taking aspirin or other antiplatelet drugs if these are tolerated. Blood pressure and lipid levels should be controlled. The patient should be referred for noninvasive evaluation of blood flow through the carotid arteries, e.g., ultrasonography. If the carotid arteries are significantly blocked, the patient and physician should consider the risks and benefits of carotid endarterectomy.

violet b. Inability to see violet tints.

word b. Alexia.

blink To open and close the eyes involuntarily; to wink rapidly. Blinking, which normally occurs about 12 to 20 times a minute, helps protect the cornea against microscopic injury. It occurs less often in neurodegenerative diseases, such as Parkinson's disease, and more often in meningitis and corneal irritation. SEE: *reflex, blink.*

blip (blip) A temporary deviation in a measurement from its baseline or its expected range.

blister (blis'tĕr) **1.** A collection of fluid below or within the epidermis. **2.** To form a blister.

TREATMENT: The area should be cleansed with mild soap and a protective dressing applied. Unless a blister is painful or interferes with function because of its size, it should not be punctured. If puncturing is required, it should be done aseptically, with the skin left in place. A sterile pressure bandage should then be applied. SEE: *Standard Precautions Appendix.*

⚠ If infection develops, treatment is the same as for any other wound, including tetanus prophylaxis or booster as required.

blood b. A small subcutaneous or intracutaneous extravasation of blood resulting from the rupture of blood vessels. SEE: illus.

TREATMENT: A firm dressing should be applied with moderate pressure to prevent extravasation and hasten absorption of blood. In some cases it is desirable to puncture the wound aseptically and aspirate the contents.

calendar b. A blister pack in which each dose of a medication is labeled with

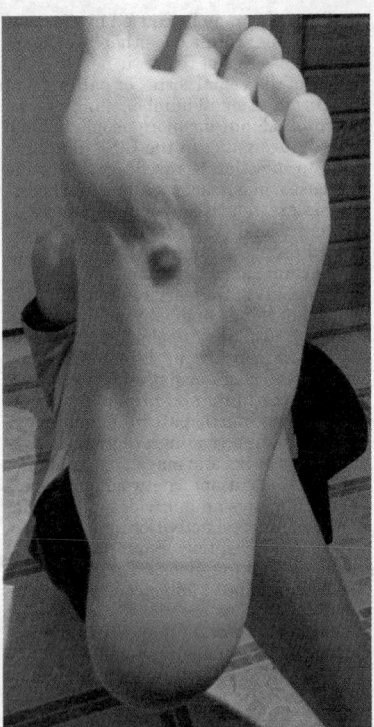

BLOOD BLISTER
On the sole of the foot after cryotherapy for a plantar wart

a specific day of the week (e.g., M, T, W) or of the month (1st, 2nd, 3rd) to encourage and assist with daily compliance with medication dosing.

fever b. A vesicular rash usually appearing on the lips or mucous membrane of the mouth during another infectious illness. The rash is caused by herpes simplex virus. SEE: *cold sore.*

fly b. A blister produced by application of cantharides to the skin.

friction b. An inflamed blister that forms beneath the epidermis after vigorous or repeated rubbing of the skin, e.g., on the toes or heels during sports activities.

blister pack, blister package A method of protecting individual doses of medications within a transparent cavity or cell made from a dome-shaped plastic barrier. The barrier separates one dose from another, protects the medication from moisture, and keeps it from being crushed or damaged during transportation or storage. Each dose of the medication can be individually released or unwrapped without affecting the integrity of the neighboring doses.

bloated (blōt'ĕd) [AS. *blout*] Swollen or

distended beyond normal size as by serum, water, or gas.

bloating (blōt) Abdominal discomfort related to disorders of intestinal motility and intestinal sensitivity to distention. This symptom is often presumed to be related to the retention of fluid or gas in the bowel, but it also may be produced by disorders of the ovaries or other genitourinary organs.

block (blok) **1.** Obstruction or stoppage of a passage or an opening. **2.** A method of regional anesthesia to stop the passage of sensory impulses in a nerve, a nerve trunk, the dorsal root of a spinal nerve, or the spinal cord, depriving a patient of sensation in the area involved SEE: *anesthesia.* **3.** To obstruct a passage or opening. **4.** Hardened, preserved tissue, prepared for thin slicing and mounting on a slide to make it suitable for microscopic viewing.

air b. Leakage of air from the respiratory passageways and its accumulation in connective tissues of the lungs, forming an obstruction to the normal flow of air.

atrioventricular b. ABBR: A-V block. A condition in which the depolarization impulse is delayed or blocked at the atrioventricular (A-V) node or a more distal site, as in the A-V bundle or bundle branches. A-V block can be partial or complete. There are several degrees: *First-degree* block is due to prolonged A-V conduction; electrocardiograms show a characteristic prolonged P-R interval. *Second-degree* blocks are intermittent, i.e., some, but not all A-V impulses are transmitted to the ventricles. *Third-degree* block, also known as complete A-V block, is present when no atrial impulses are conducted to the ventricles.

A-V block may be caused by age-related degenerative changes; drugs such as digoxin, beta blockers, and calcium channel blockers; hyperkalemia; hypokalemia; increased vagus nerve activity; local hypoxia; and scarring from myocardial infarction.

bed b. A block made of sturdy material, such as wood, to elevate one end of a bed relative to the other. Bed blocks may be used in the home, e.g., to treat people with gastroesophageal reflux disease. Most beds in health care institutions are built with devices that separately raise or lower the feet, legs, trunk, or head.

bite b. **1.** A wedge of sturdy material used to maintain space between the two jaws. **2.** A film holder held between the teeth for stable retention of the film packet during dental radiology.

bundle branch b. SEE: *bundle branch block.*

Bunnell b. SEE: *Bunnell block.*

complete atrioventricular b. Third-degree atrioventricular block. SEE: *atrioventricular b.*

digital b. Injection of a regional anesthetic into the proximal portion of a finger or toe.

ear b. Blockage of the auditory tube to the middle ear. It may result from trauma, infection, or an accumulation of cerumen. SEE: *aerotitis; otitis media.*

epidural b. SEE: *epidural anesthesia.*

field b. Regional anesthesia in which a limited operative area is walled off by an anesthetic.

first-degree atrioventricular b. Delayed conduction through or from the atrioventricular node, marked on the electrocardiogram by a prolonged P-R interval. Usually no treatment is necessary. SYN: *first-degree heart block.*

heart b. SEE: *bundle branch block; heart block.*

infranodal block The Mobitz II variety of second-degree heart block. SEE: *second-degree heart block.*

mandibular b. Regional anesthesia of the lower face and mandibular tissues by infiltration of the mandibular division of the trigeminal nerve.

interpleural b. Interpleural **analgesia.**

maxillary b. Second division **b.**

nerve b. The induction of regional anesthesia by preventing sensory nerve impulses from reaching the central nervous system. This is usually done by injecting an anesthetic solution (such as lidocaine) into a peripheral nerve or by electrically stimulating the nerve.

neuromuscular b. A disturbance in the transmission of impulses from a motor endplate to a muscle. It may be caused by an excess or deficiency of acetylcholine or by drugs that inhibit or destroy acetylcholine. SYN: *neural blockade.*

paravertebral b. Infiltration of the stellate ganglion with a local anesthetic.

patchy anesthetic b. Partial numbness after administration of a spinal anesthetic that was incomplete or inadequate to perform an operation painlessly.

saddle b. SEE: *saddle block anesthesia.*

second division b. Regional anesthesia of the upper face and maxillary tissues by infiltration of the maxillary division of the trigeminal nerve. SYN: *maxillary b.*

sinoatrial b. **1.** Sinoatrial **heart block.** **2.** Heart block in which there is interference in the passage of impulses between the sinus node and the atria.

spinal b. Blockage in the flow of cerebrospinal fluid within the spinal canal.

subarachnoid b. Spinal **anesthesia.**

ventricular b. Interference in the flow of cerebrospinal fluid between the ventricles or from the ventricles through the foramina to the subarachnoid space.

blockade (blo-kād′) Prevention of the action of something, such as a drug or a body function.

    adrenergic b. Inhibition of responses to adrenergic sympathetic nerve impulses and to agents such as epinephrine.

    cholinergic b. Inhibition of cholinergic nerve stimuli or cholinergic agents.

    ganglionic b. Blocking of the transmission of stimuli in autonomic ganglia. Pharmacologically, this is done by using drugs that occupy receptor sites for acetylcholine and by stabilizing the postsynaptic membranes against the actions of acetylcholine liberated from presynaptic nerve endings. The usual effects of drugs that cause ganglionic blockade are vasodilatation of arterioles with increased peripheral blood flow; hypotension; dilation of veins with pooling of blood in tissues, decreased venous return, and decreased cardiac output; tachycardia; mydriasis; cycloplegia; reduced tone and motility of the gastrointestinal tract with consequent constipation; urinary retention; dry mouth; and decreased sweating. Ganglionic blocking drugs are not often used to treat hypertension but are used to treat autonomic hyperreflexia and to produce controlled hypotension during certain types of surgery. Several drugs are available for ganglionic blocking.

    interpleural b. Interpleural **analgesia**.

    lymphatic b. A local defense mechanism in which minute bits of material, such as fibrinous exudate from injured tissue, enter local lymphatic vessels, obstructing them and preventing foreign substances, esp. bacteria, from passing through them.

    neural b. Neuromuscular **block**.

    neuraxial b. Spinal or epidural anesthesia.

blockbuster drug A drug that generates more than a billion dollars in sales.

block design A neuropsychological test involving the placement of wooden blocks according to three-dimensional drawings. The test assesses the presence of constructional apraxia, often exhibited in patients with brain lesions.

blocker (blok′ĕr) A drug that prevents the normal action of a system or cell receptor. SEE: *antagonist; blockade; inhibitor*.

    beta b. Beta-adrenergic blocking agent.

    bronchial b. ABBR: BB. A device for facilitating single-lung ventilation during thoracic surgery or thoracoscopy. The bronchial blocker is placed into the mainstem bronchus on the side of the chest where the operation is being per-

formed, and its balloon is inflated within the airway. Potential complications of the device include dislodgement, misplacement, or accumulation of fluid behind the blockade.

    calcium channel b. ABBR: CCB. Any of a group of drugs that slow the influx of calcium ions into smooth muscle cells, resulting in decreased arterial resistance and oxygen demand. These drugs are used to treat angina, hypertension, vascular spasm, intracranial bleeding, congestive heart failure, and supraventricular tachycardia. Because hypotension occurs as both an intended and, occasionally, an unwelcome effect, blood pressure must be monitored especially closely during the initial treatment period.

    H_2 b. SEE: H_2-*receptor* **antagonist**.

blocking (blŏk′ĭng) **1.** Obstructing. **2.** In psychoanalysis, a sudden break in free association as a defense against unpleasant ideas.

Blomia tropicalis (blō′mē-ă trŏp-ĭ-kăl′ĭs) The scientific name for a common house mite found in South and Central America. Allergens derived from this mite cause allergic reactions, including asthma and atopy. It is abbreviated Blot by the World Health Organization.

blood (blŭd) The cell-containing fluid that circulates through the heart, arteries, veins, and capillaries, carrying nourishment, electrolytes, hormones, vitamins, antibodies, heat, and oxygen to the tissues and taking away waste matter and carbon dioxide. SEE: *erythropoietin*.

    CHARACTERISTICS: Blood has a distinctive, somewhat metallic, odor. Arterial blood is bright red or scarlet and usually pulsates if the artery has been cut. Venous blood is dark red or crimson and flows steadily from a cut vein.

    COMPOSITION: Human blood is about 52% to 62% plasma and 38% to 48% cells. The plasma is mostly water, ions, proteins, hormones, and lipids. The cellular components are the erythrocytes (red blood cells [RBCs]), leukocytes (white blood cells [WBCs]), and thrombocytes (platelets). The leukocytes comprise neutrophils, eosinophils, basophils, lymphocytes, and monocytes. SEE: illus. (Blood Composition) and (Types of Blood Cells); *buffy coat; plasma; serum*.

    An adult weighing 70 kg has a blood volume of about 5 L or 70 ml/kg of body weight. Blood constitutes about 7% to 8% of the body weight. The pH of the blood is from 7.35 to 7.45. The specific gravity of blood varies from 1.048 to 1.066, the cells being heavier and plasma lighter than this. Blood is of slightly higher specific gravity in men than in women. Specific gravity is higher after exercise and at night. SEE:

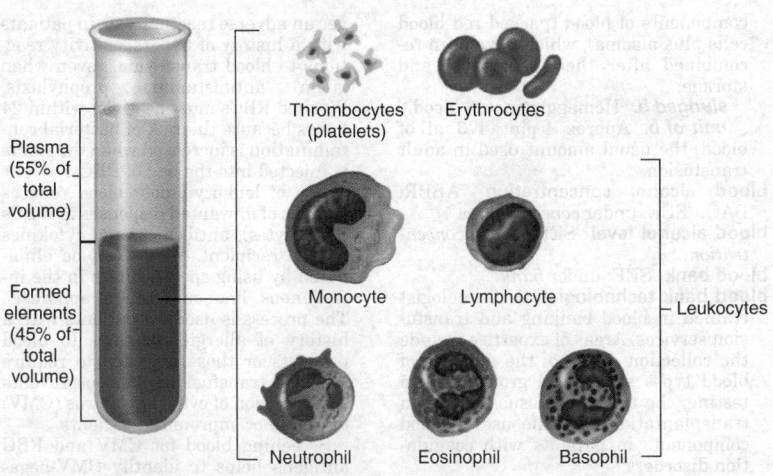

BLOOD COMPOSITION

Components of blood and relationship to other body tissues

blood count; cell; erythrocyte; leukocyte; plasma; platelet.

FUNCTION: In passing through the lungs, the blood gives up carbon dioxide and absorbs oxygen; after leaving the heart, it is carried to the tissues as arterial blood and then returned to the heart in the venous system. It moves in the aorta at an average speed of 30 cm/sec, and it makes the circuit of the vascular system in about 60 seconds. RBCs carry oxygen; WBCs participate in the immune response to infection; platelets are important in blood clotting. The plasma transports nutrients, waste products, hormones, carbon dioxide, and other substances, and contributes to fluid-electrolyte balance and thermal regulation.

FORMATION: RBCs are produced in the red bone marrow at the rate of about 2,400,000/sec, and each RBC lives for about 120 days. In healthy individuals, the concentration of RBCs in the blood remains stable over time. Platelets and WBCs are also produced in the red bone marrow, and agranular WBCs are produced in lymphatic tissue.

clotting of b. SEE: *coagulation, blood.*

cord b. The blood present in the umbilical vessels connecting the placenta to the fetus. Because cord blood is immunologically immature, it is esp. useful in transfusion therapy and hematological transplantation.

defibrinated b. Whole blood from which fibrin has been removed. It does not clot.

formed elements of b. Blood cells, as opposed to blood proteins or other chemical constituents of blood.

fresh b. Blood that has been collected less than 48 hours prior to its use in a transfusion.

occult b. SEE: under *occult.*

oxygenated b. Blood that has been exposed to oxygen in the lung; sometimes referred to as arteriolized blood.

predonation of b. autologous blood transfusion.

reconstituted blood A blood product used in transfusion therapy composed of

TYPES OF BLOOD CELLS

Cell types found in smears of peripheral blood from normal individuals.

components of blood (packed red blood cells plus plasma), which have been recombined after their separation and storage.

sludged b. Hemagglutinated blood.

unit of b. Approx. 1 pint (473 ml) of blood, the usual amount used in adult transfusion.

blood alcohol concentration ABBR: BAC. SEE: under *concentration.*

blood alcohol level SEE: under *concentration.*

blood bank SEE: under *bank.*

blood bank technologist A technologist trained in blood banking and transfusion services. Areas of expertise include the collection of blood; the analysis of blood types with blood group antigen testing; the typing of tissues for organ transplantation; and the use of blood components in patients with coagulation disorders.

blood cell casts SEE: under *cast.*

blood component therapy Transfusion of one or more of the components of whole blood. The blood components may have been taken from the patient previously (autologous transfusion) or donated by someone else (homologous transfusion). Except in the case of acute hemorrhage, the transfusion of whole blood is rarely needed. Use of a component rather than whole blood permits several patients to benefit from a single blood donation. Blood components used in clinical medicine include packed red blood cells (RBCs); leukocyte-poor RBCs; frozen glycerolized RBCs; thawed deglycerolized RBCs; washed RBCs; whole blood; heparinized whole blood; granulocytes; platelets; and plasma and plasma fractions. The latter include antihemophilic factor (Factor VIII), prothrombin complex (Factors VII, IX, and X), gamma globulin, and albumin.

PATIENT CARE: Irradiation of blood by gamma rays (gamma irradiation) incapacitates donor lymphocytes in whole blood, RBCs, platelets, or granulocytes. These lymphocytes are blocked from proliferating in response to foreign antigens, esp. those in the bone marrow, of immunocompromised recipients, causing transfusion-associated graft-versus-host disease. In patients who are not immunocompromised, the donor white blood cells (WBCs) are destroyed. Irradiated blood is given to patients who are donating or receiving bone marrow transplants or who have hematological or lymphatic cancers. In addition, blood used for intrauterine or neonatal exchange transfusions and blood donated by a biological relative also is irradiated.

Washing blood (RBCs, platelets) in 0.9% sodium chloride removes most, but not all, of the antibodies that could trigger an adverse reaction, esp. in patients with a history of hypersensitivity reactions to blood transfusions, even when given antihistamine prophylaxis. Washed RBCs must be given within 24 hours because the risk of bacterial contamination is increased when the saline is injected into the bag of RBCs.

Use of leukocyte-poor blood reduces the risk of unwanted responses to WBCs (leukocytes), antibodies, and cytokines by the recipient. WBCs can be eliminated by using special filters in the intravenous line or through aphoresis. The process is used for patients with a history of allergic reactions to blood products or those expected to require multiple transfusions. It also prevents transmission of cytomegalovirus (CMV) to immunocompromised patients.

Screening blood for CMV and RBC antigens helps to identify CMV-negative blood, which is needed for high-risk patients. More than half of persons over 35 years of age have been infected with CMV. However, this screened blood is beneficial for premature infants; infants under age 4 weeks; recipients of intrauterine transfusion regardless of the mother's CMV status; any patient who requires a bone marrow or organ donor transplant if the marrow or organ donor also is CMV-negative; and CMV-negative patients who are potential transplant candidates, pregnant, about to undergo splenectomy, or have AIDS/HIV or congenital immune deficiency. SEE: table; *blood transfusion; Standard Precautions Appendix.*

blood corpuscle SEE: under *corpuscle.*

blood count SEE: under *count.*

blood crossmatching Crossmatching.

blood donor deferral (dĭ-fŭr′ăl) [L. *deferre,* to carry down, report, accuse] The postponement or permanent exclusion of blood donation by a person suspected of having an infectious or hematological disease.

blood draw Phlebotomy.

blood gas analysis Chemical analysis of the pH, carbon dioxide and oxygen concentrations, and oxygen saturation of the blood. This analysis is used to diagnose serious metabolic and respiratory disorders. It may be performed using arterial or venous blood, although only arterial blood gas analysis evaluates lung function; the specimen may be obtained from numerous sites. Mixed venous samples may be obtained from the right atrium of the heart. The blood sample is usually collected in a heparinized syringe, with care being taken to ensure that the specimen is immediately placed on ice (to avoid misinterpretations caused by metabolism) and not exposed to air (to prevent oxygenation of the sample). SEE: *Allen test; blood gas.*

Blood Components Used in Transfusion Therapy

Component	When it is used	Approximate volume (in mL) infused or typical preparation	Storage/ viability	Expected outcome
Packed red blood cells	When needed to restore the oxygen-carrying capacity of the blood of the patient	470	Refrigerated or frozen; may last as long as 42 days	An increase in hemoglobin of 1 g/dL
Platelets	In severely thrombocytopenic patients, e.g., < 40,000/dL in hemorrhaging patients, or < 10,000, in patients who are not yet bleeding	"Five-pack" (i.e., a pooled concentrate from five donors); single-donor apheresis pack	Stored at room temperature (72° F); needs constant agitation; may last 5 days	An increase in platelet counts of > 20,000/dL
Fresh-frozen plasma (FFP)	To replace missing coagulation factors	225	Must be frozen within 6 hours of donation; useful for up to a year	Improvement in prothrombin time/INR
Cryoprecipitate	To supply blood components; esp., fibrinogen, Factors VIII and XIII, fibronectin, and von Willebrand Factor	Prepared from the insoluble proteins that remain when FFP is thawed for use. Ten-donor pack usually used	Can be refrozen and stored after use of FFP; usually useful for 28 days	Increase in fibrinogen level by 2-5 mg

Abbreviations: dL=deciliter; INR=international normalized ratio; mL=milliliter

⚠️ Rarely, arterial punctures taken from the wrist may damage the radial artery or compromise the blood supply of the hand.

blood gases SEE: under *gas*.

blood glucose, unstable, risk for Risk for variation of blood glucose/sugar levels from the normal range. SEE: *Nursing Diagnoses Appendix*.

blood group A genetically determined system of antigens located on the surface of the erythrocyte. There are a number of human blood group systems; each system is determined by a series of two or more genes that are allelic or closely linked on a single autosomal chromosome. The ABO system is of prime importance in blood transfusions. The Rhesus (Rh) system is esp. important in obstetrics. There are about 30 Rh antigens. SEE: illus.; *Rh factor*.

The population can be phenotypically divided into four ABO blood groups: A, B, AB, and O. Individuals in the A group have the A antigen on the surface of their red cells; B group has the B antigen on red cells; AB group has A and B antigens on red cells; and O group has neither A nor B antigens on red cells. The individuals in each group have in their sera the corresponding antibody to the red cell antigens that they lack. Thus, a group A person has the anti-B antibody; group B has anti-A antibodies; group AB has no antibodies for A and B; and group O individuals have anti-A and anti-B antibodies in their sera.

Blood group factors are important in blood banking. Analysis of blood groups

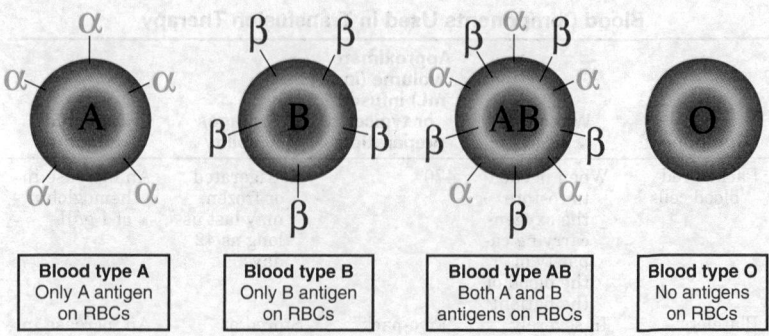

Blood type A Only A antigen on RBCs	**Blood type B** Only B antigen on RBCs	**Blood type AB** Both A and B antigens on RBCs	**Blood type O** No antigens on RBCs

ABO BLOOD TYPES

is important in identification of bloodstains for medicolegal purposes, in genetic and anthropological studies, and, formerly, in determination of the probability of fatherhood in paternity suits.

   Kell b.g. SEE: *Kell blood group.*

   Rh b.g. A group of antigens on the surface of red blood cells present to a variable degree in human populations. When the Rh factor (an antigen often called D) is present, an individual's blood type is designated Rh⁺ (Rh positive); when the Rh antigen is absent, the blood type is Rh⁻ (Rh negative). If an individual with Rh⁻ blood receives a transfusion of Rh⁺ blood, anti-Rh antibodies form. Subsequent transfusions of Rh⁺ blood may result in serious transfusion reactions (agglutination and hemolysis of red blood cells). A pregnant woman who is Rh⁻ may become sensitized by entry of red blood cells from an Rh⁺ fetus into the maternal circulation after abortion, ectopic pregnancy, or delivery. In subsequent pregnancies, if the fetus is Rh⁺, Rh antibodies produced in maternal blood may cross the placenta and destroy fetal cells, causing erythroblastosis fetalis. SEE: *Rh immune globulin.*

blood in stool The presence of visible or clinically detectable hemoglobin in feces. Bright red blood in stool is known as hematochezia. It may be produced by anorectal disorders, such as hemorrhoids, or by bleeding from diverticuli, cancers, some forms of dysentery, or angiodysplasia of the bowel (among other causes). It sometimes results from massive bleeding from the upper gastrointestinal tract. SEE: *hematochezia; hematemesis; melena;* Emergency Situations.

bloodless (blŏd′lĕs) **1.** Without blood. **2.** Without the loss of blood, e.g., bloodless surgery.

bloodletting (blŏd′lĕt″ĭng) Removal of blood from the body as a therapeutic measure, usually by venipuncture. It is used to treat hemochromatosis, polycy-

themia vera, and infants born with excessively high hemoglobin levels.

blood level The concentration of anything, esp. a drug, in the plasma, serum, or blood.

blood-nerve barrier SEE: under *barrier.*

blood patch SEE: under *patch.*

blood pressure ABBR: BP. The tension exerted on the walls of arteries by: the strength of the contraction of the heart; the resistance of arterioles and capillaries; the elasticity of blood vessels; the blood volume; and blood viscosity.

   Normal blood pressure is defined as a systolic BP between 100 and 120 mm Hg and a diastolic BP below 80 mm Hg (in adults over age 18). Prehypertension is present when measured blood pressures are between 120 and 140 mm Hg systolic or between 80 and 90 mm Hg diastolic. When either the systolic pressure exceeds 140 mm Hg or the diastolic exceeds 90 mm Hg, and these values are confirmed on two additional visits, stage I hypertension (high blood pressure) is present. SEE: illus.

   Low blood pressure is sometimes present in healthy individuals, but it indicates shock in patients with fever, active bleeding, allergic reactions, active heart disease, spinal cord injuries, or trauma. Blood pressure should be checked routinely whenever a patient sees a health care provider because controlling abnormally high blood pressure effectively prevents damage to the heart and circulatory system as well as the kidneys, retina, brain, and other organs.

   PATIENT CARE: Elevated blood pressures should first be addressed by giving advice to patients about lifestyle modifications, such as limiting the intake of alcohol, following a diet approved by the American Heart Association, and increasing the level of physical exercise. Weight loss in obese patients is also advisable. Medications are added to lifestyle instructions most of the time. Antihypertensive medications are used according to evidence-based guidelines

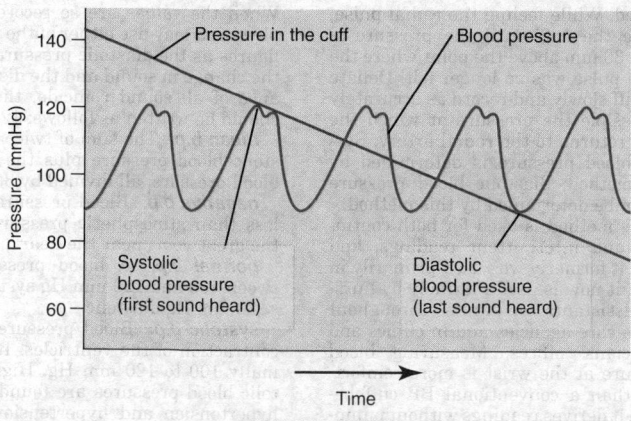

BLOOD PRESSURE

Relationship of blood pressure to changes in cuff pressure and the first and fifth Korotkoff sounds (BP 120/80)

and the side effects these drugs may cause in particular patients. Diuretics, for example, are esp. helpful in blacks and elderly patients (but may be inadvisable in patients with gout); beta blockers are the drugs of choice in patients with a history of myocardial infarction (but would be contraindicated in patients with advanced heart block); alpha blockers are well suited for men with prostatic hypertrophy; and angiotensin-converting enzyme inhibitors prevent kidney disease in patients with diabetes mellitus. Other antihypertensive drug classes include the angiotensin II receptor antagonists, centrally active alpha antagonists, and calcium channel blockers. Low blood pressure is not treated in healthy patients; in patients with acute illnesses, it is often corrected with hydration or pressor agents.

augmented diastolic b.p. An increase in diastolic pressure, usually by an artificial device, such as an intra-aortic balloon pump. SEE: *intra-aortic balloon counterpulsation.*

central b.p. Blood pressure in the heart chambers, in a great vein, or close to the heart. If determined in a vein, it is termed central venous pressure; if in the aorta or a similar large artery close to the heart, it is designated central arterial pressure.

chronic low b.p. A condition in which the systolic blood pressure is consistently less than 100 mm Hg. In the absence of associated disease, low blood pressure is often a predictor of longevity and continued health. SEE: *hypotension; orthostatic hypotension.*

diastolic b.p. The blood pressure when the ventricles of the heart are filling with blood. In health this equals about 60 to 80 mm Hg.

direct measurement of b.p. Determination of the blood pressure within the lumen of an artery or within a chamber of the heart with a catheter introduced into the organ and attached to a pressure-monitoring transducer. It is done by placing a sterile needle or small catheter inside an artery and having the blood pressure transmitted through that system to a suitable recorder. As the blood pressure fluctuates, the changes are recorded graphically.

high b.p. Hypertension.

indirect measurement of b.p. A simple external method for measuring blood pressure.

Palpation method: The same arm, usually the right, should be used each time the pressure is measured. The arm should be raised to heart level if the patient is sitting, or kept parallel to the body if the patient is recumbent. The patient's arm should be relaxed and supported in a resting position. Exertion during the examination could result in a higher blood pressure reading. Either a mercury-gravity or aneroid-manometer type of blood pressure apparatus may be used. The blood compression cuff should be the width and length appropriate for the size of the subject's arm: narrow (2.5 to 6 cm) for infants and children and wide (13 cm) for adults. The inflatable bag encased in the cuff should be 20% wider than one third the circumference of the limb used. The deflated cuff is placed evenly and snugly around the upper arm so that its lower edge is about 1 in above the point of the brachial artery where the bell of the electronic sensor will be applied. While feeling the radial pulse, inflate the cuff until the pressure is about 30 mm above the point where the radial pulse was no longer felt. Deflate the cuff slowly and record as accurately as possible the pressure at which the pulse returns to the radial artery. Systolic blood pressure is determined by this method; diastolic blood pressure cannot be determined by this method.

This method is used for both continuous and intermittent readings, and while it formerly was used primarily in ICUs, it now is used routinely by nursing assistants on units throughout health care agencies and in clinics and physicians' offices. Measuring blood pressure at the wrist is more comfortable than a conventional BP cuff because it derives readings without pumping a bladder full of air, and with accuracy rivaling direct measurement from an arterial catheter. The sensor is placed directly over the radial artery and connected to an electronic monitor. Pressure is monitored every 15 heartbeats and systolic, diastolic, mean arterial pressure, waveforms, and pulse rate are displayed. The first reading appears in 15 seconds, and the sensor measures pressures from 40 to 240 mm Hg, with preset alarms to alert the nurse to extreme highs and lows. Results are not affected by low cardiac output, arrhythmias, hypothermia, or obesity, and this method is being used increasingly on adults in hospital special care units where frequent serial readings are required.

Auscultatory method: Begin as above. After inflating the cuff until the pressure is about 30 mm above the point where the radial pulse disappears, place the bell of the stethoscope over the brachial artery just below the blood pressure cuff. Then deflate the cuff slowly, about 2 to 3 mm Hg per heartbeat. The first sound heard from the artery is recorded as the systolic pressure. The point at which sounds are no longer heard is recorded as the diastolic pressure. For convenience the blood pressure is recorded as figures separated by a slash. The systolic value is recorded first.

Sounds heard over the brachial artery change in quality at some point prior to the point the sounds disappear. Some physicians consider this the diastolic pressure. This value should be noted when recording the blood pressure by placing it between the systolic pressure and the pressure noted when the sound disappears. Thus, 120/90/80 indicates a systolic pressure of 120 with a first diastolic sound change at a pressure of 90 and a final diastolic pressure of 80. The latter pressure is the point of disappearance of all sounds from the artery.

When the values are so recorded, the physician may use either of the last two figures as the diastolic pressure. When the change in sound and the disappearance of all sound coincide, the result should be written as follows: 120/80/80.

   mean b.p. The sum of twice the diastolic blood pressure plus the systolic blood pressure, all divided by 3.

   negative b.p. Blood pressure that is less than atmospheric pressure, as in the great veins near the heart.

   normal b.p. A blood pressure between 100 and 120 mm Hg systolic and < 80 mm Hg diastolic.

   systolic b.p. Blood pressure during contraction of the ventricles. It is normally 100 to 120 mm Hg. Higher systolic blood pressures are found in prehypertension and hypertension. SYN: *systolic pressure.*

blood pressure load During ambulatory (outpatient) blood pressure monitoring, the amount of time that a patient's systolic or diastolic blood pressure exceeds normal values.

blood pressure monitoring, ambulatory The measurement with a portable blood pressure monitor of blood pressure of outpatients. It is used to record the patient's diastolic and systolic pressures during activity and rest throughout the day.

blood product Blood **component**.

blood salvage A collection of the siphoned blood that has escaped from the operative site of non-contaminated surgeries so that after appropriate filtration it may be returned to the patient. SEE: *autologous blood transfusion; cell saver.*

bloodshot (blŭd′shot″) Local congestion of the smaller blood vessels of a part, as when the vessels of the conjunctiva are dilated and visible.

blood shunting Shunting.

bloodstream (blŏd′strēm″) The blood that flows through the circulatory system of an organism.

blood test A test to determine the chemical, physical, or serological characteristics of the blood or some portion of it.

blood thinner A popular but erroneous name for an anticoagulant.

blood transfusion SEE: under *transfusion.*

blood typing The classification of red blood cells by the proteins and carbohydrates (antigens) found on the surface of the erythrocyte membrane.

blood urea nitrogen ABBR: BUN. Nitrogen in the blood in the form of urea, the metabolic product of the breakdown of amino acids used for energy production. The normal concentration is about 8 to 18 mg/dL. The level of urea in the blood provides a rough estimate of kidney function. Blood urea nitrogen levels may be increased in the presence of dehydration, decreased renal function, upper gastrointestinal bleeding, or treatment with drugs such as steroids or tetracyclines. SEE: *creatinine*.

blood vessels The veins, arteries, and capillaries.

blood warmer A device that raises refrigerated blood or intravenous fluids to a desired temperature, usually 98.6°F (37.0°C), or a little above.

⚠ Testing the device for temperature control on a regular basis is important to avoid transfusion errors.

Bloom syndrome (bloom) [David Bloom, U.S. dermatologist, b. 1892] An autosomal recessive disease, found predominantly but not exclusively in persons of Jewish ancestry, marked by chromosomal abnormalities, facial rashes, dwarfism, and a propensity to develop leukemia.

blotch (blŏtch) A blemish, spot, or area of discoloration on the skin.

blotting method SEE: under *method*.

Blount disease [Walter Putman Blount, U.S. surgeon, 1900–1992] **Tibia** vara.

blow-by (blō′bī″) An imprecise method of oxygen delivery in which an oxygen source (such as a tube connected to a pressurized gas canister) discharges oxygen in front of the nostrils or mouth of the patient.

PATIENT CARE: It is used primarily to supply supplemental oxygen to infants, neonates, and toddlers, who may not tolerate wearing other oxygen delivery systems (such as a nasal cannula or face mask).

blowfly (blō′flī″) Any of the flies belonging to the family Calliphoridae. Most blowflies are scavengers. Their maggots (larvae) live in decaying flesh or meat, but occasionally they may live in decaying or suppurating tissue. One species, the screw-worm fly, *Callitroga hominivorax*, attacks living tissue, laying its eggs in the nostrils or open wounds of its domestic animal or human host, giving rise to myiasis.

sheep b. A common blowfly found worldwide, and a cause of myiasis in humans. The maggots (larvae) of the fly feed esp. on sheep. Sterile maggots of this species are necrophagous and have been used to debride wound infections. SYN: *green bottlefly*. SEE: *Calliphora vomitoria; myiasis*.

blowpipe (blō′pīp″) A tube through which a gas or current of air is passed under pressure and directed upon a flame to concentrate and intensify the heat.

BLS *basic life support.*

blue (bloo) [O. Fr. *bleu*] **1.** A primary color of the spectrum; sky color; azure. **2.** Cyanotic.

blue bloater A person with chronic bronchitis who demonstrates evidence of cyanosis and pedal edema. SEE: *chronic bronchitis*.

ETIOLOGY: It is most often the result of long-term cigarette smoking.

TREATMENT: The patient often benefits from oxygen therapy, bronchial hygiene (e.g., clearing of the lungs), and smoking cessation.

bluebottle fly SEE: under *fly*.

blue cohosh (kō′hosh″) A North American herb, *Caulophyllum thalictroides*, that produces blue berries. It is sometimes used by Native American women to induce labor.

⚠ Maternal use of the herb in late pregnancy has been associated with stroke, heart attack, and congestive heart failure in newborns.

SYN: *squaw root*. SEE: *black cohosh*.

Blue Cross A nonprofit medical care insurer in the U.S. The insurance is mostly for hospital services. SEE: *Blue Shield*.

blue diaper syndrome A rare autosomal recessive syndrome in which the amino acid tryptophan is not absorbed from the gastrointestinal tract.

blues (blooz) A colloquial term for depression or a depressed mood.

postpartum b. A period of heightened maternal emotions that follow the birth of a baby, typically beginning in the first three to five days after childbirth. Common symptoms are irritability, emotional lability, and tearfulness although exaggerated happiness may also be reported. Unlike postpartum depression, postpartum blues typically resolves in a week to ten days.

Blue Shield A nonprofit medical care insurer in the U.S. The insurance is for that part of medical care provided by health care professionals. SEE: *Blue Cross*.

Blumberg sign (bloom′bĕrg″) [Jacob Moritz Blumberg, Ger. surgeon and gynecologist, 1873–1955] Rebound **tenderness**.

blunt (blŭnt) **1.** Of surgical instruments, having a smooth or rounded end. **2.** Having no sharp angles, edges, or points.

blunt end In a health care institution, the administrative or bureaucratic apparatus that supports and often directs patient care. Individuals actually providing the care (aides, midlevel pesonnel, nurses, and physicians) are said to work at the "sharp end" of health care.

blush (blŭsh) [AS. *blyscan*, to be red] Redness of the face and neck due to vasodilation caused by emotion or heat. Blushing may also be associated with certain diseases, including carcinoid syndrome, pheochromocytoma, and Zollinger-Ellison syndrome.

BMA *British Medical Association.*

BMD *bone mineral **density**.*

BME *Biomedical Engineer.*

BMET *Biomedical Engineering Technologist.*

BMI *body mass index.*

B-mode (brightness mode) display B-mode **ultrasound**.

BMR *basal metabolic **rate**.*

BMT *bone marrow transplant.*

BNA *Basle Nomina Anatomica.*

board (bōrd) [Old English *bord,* board, table] **1.** A long, flat piece of a substance such as wood or firm plastic. **2.** A governing or oversight committee, such as one that directs the affairs of a hospital, clinic, company, or other organization.

American B. of Internal Medicine SEE: *American Board of Internal Medicine.*

arm b. **1.** A board placed under and attached to the arm for stabilization during intravenous administration. **2.** A device attached to the sides of a wheelchair to permit support or positioning of the arm, esp. for persons with upper-extremity paralysis.

back b. A stiff board on which an individual with a known or suspected spinal or pelvic injury is secured so that the patient's neuraxis is splinted in-line during transport. The device should be used with a head immobilization device and a cervical collar.

balance b. Rocker **b.**

bed b. A firm board placed beneath a mattress to keep it from sagging. It is used to treat some persons with back difficulties. It is also used in cardiopulmonary resuscitation to improve the effectiveness of chest compressions.

communication b. Any device with letters, pictures, or words that lets patients with impaired physical and verbal ability express themselves.

foot b. A flat piece of material placed at the foot end of a patient's bed. It is angled slightly away from the patient and extends up above the mattress. When used properly it helps to prevent footdrop. The patient should be positioned in bed so that when the legs are fully extended the soles of the feet just touch the padded board.

b. of health A public body, appointed or elected, concerned with administering the laws pert. to the health of the public.

institutional review b. ABBR: IRB. A medical oversight committee that governs or regulates medical investigations involving human subjects. The purpose of the board is to protect the rights and health of participants in clinical trials. SEE: *informed consent.*

lap b. A tray or platform that is placed over the lap. When such a device is designed to be attached to a wheelchair in order to support the hands and arms or to permit manual activities, it is known as a wheelchair lap board.

long back b. A flat or slightly concave board approx. 6 ft long and 2 ft wide, often made of laminated wood or plastic, that is used to immobilize a patient with a mechanism for a potential neck or back injury. This device is used together with a cervical/head immobilization device or blanket roll and a rigid extrication collar.

message b. An Internet-based forum for posts and discussions about, e.g., a specific disease or condition.

National Athletic Trainers' Association B. of Certification, Inc. SEE: *National Athletic Trainers' Association Board of Certification, Inc.*

National B. for Certification in Occupational Therapy SEE: *National Board for Certification in Occupational Therapy.*

National B. for Respiratory Care SEE: *National Board for Respiratory Care.*

rocker b. A board with rockers or a partial sphere on the undersurface so that a rocking motion occurs when a person stands on it. It is commonly used in therapy with children having central nervous system deficits to facilitate the development of appropriate equilibrium-related postural reflexes. It is also used in patients/clients of all ages to stimulate lower extremity and trunk proprioception and kinesthetic sense. SYN: *balance **b.**; *wobble **b.***

short back b. A flat board, approx. 3 ft long and 2 ft wide, often made of laminated wood or plastic that is used to immobilize a seated patient with a mechanism for a potential neck or back injury. This device is used together with a cervical/head immobilization device or blanket roll and a rigid extrication collar. The short backboard is used to remove a stable injured patient from a vehicle onto a long backboard. Most ambulance services have moved to a more modern vest-style device such as a Kendrich extrication device (KED).

sliding b. Transfer board.

spine b., spineboard Back board.

transfer b. A device used to bridge the space between a wheelchair and a bed, toilet, or car seat; used to facilitate independent or assisted transfer of the patient from one of these sites to another. SYN: *sliding **b**.* SEE: illus.

wobble b. Rocker board.

board-certified (bord'sĕrt'ĭ-fīd") SEE: *board **certification**.*

board eligible A designation that signifies that a professional has completed all the requirements for admission to a special board certification examination

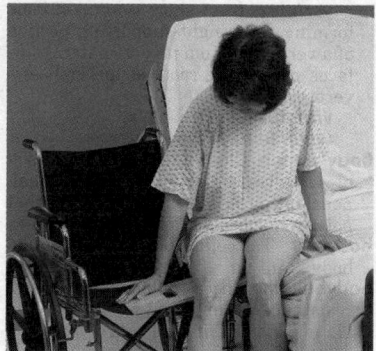

TRANSFER BOARD

Use of a transfer board to move from bed to chair.

but has not yet taken and passed the examination. SEE: *certification, board*.

boarder A patient no longer requiring hospitalization who is provided with meals and lodging in a hospital, usually until other living arrangements can be made.

Bochdalek, Vincent (bok'da-lek) Vicent Alexander Bochdalek, Bohemian anatomist 1810–1883.

foramen of B. A fetal diaphragmatic opening that may not close completely; a site for a congenital diaphragmatic hernia.

B. ganglion A ganglion of the plexus of the dental nerve in the maxilla above the canine tooth.

Bodo (bō'dō) A genus of nonpathogenic, flagellate protozoa of the family Bodonidae often found in stale feces or urine and sometimes in the urinary bladder.

body (bod'ē) **1.** A complete organism, living or dead; the sum of its physical components. SYN: *soma* (1). **2.** Trunk (1). **3.** The principal mass of any structure. **4.** A distinct mass. **5.** The largest or most important part of any organ. SEE: *limbic system* for illus.

acetone b. Ketone body.

anococcygeal b. The muscle and fibrous tissue lying between the coccyx and the anus.

aortic b. A chemoreceptor in the wall of the aortic arch that detects changes in blood gases, esp. oxygen, and pH. It is innervated by the vagus nerve and stimulates reflex changes in heart rate, respiration, and blood pressure that restore normal blood oxygen levels.

asbestos b. A beaded, dumbbell-shaped body formed when a macrophage engulfs asbestos fibers.

Barr b. SEE: *Barr body*.

basal b. A small granule usually present at the base of a flagellum or cilium in protozoa. SYN: *basal granule; blepharoplast*.

chromaffin b. One of a number of bodies composed principally of chromaffin cells, arranged serially along both sides of the dorsal aorta and in the kidney, liver, and gonads. They are ectodermal in origin, having the same origin as cells of the sympathetic ganglia. SYN: *paraganglion*.

ciliary b. A structure directly behind the iris of the eye. It secretes the aqueous humor and contains the ciliary muscle that changes the shape, and thus the refractive power, of the lens by tightening and relaxing the tension on the lens zonule. SYN: *ciliary apparatus*. SEE: *eye* for illus.

coccygeal b. An arteriovenous anastomosis at the tip of the coccyx formed by the middle sacral artery. SYN: *glomus coccygeum*.

Donovan b. SEE: *Donovan body*.

foreign b. Anything present at a site where it would not normally be found. Slivers, cinders, dirt, or small objects may lodge in the skin, ears, eyes, or nose or may be taken internally. If not removed, they may cause unsightly marks or tattooing of the skin and inflammation and infection of the tissue involved. SEE: *foreign bodies in ear; foreign bodies in the esophagus; foreign body in nose; foreign bodies in the skin; foreign bodies in vagina*.

carotid b. The chemoreceptors at the bifurcation of each common carotid artery, which detect changes in blood gases (esp. oxygen) and pH. They stimulate reflex changes in heart rate, respiration, and blood pressure that restore normal blood oxygen levels. They are innervated by the glossopharyngeal nerves.

hyaline b. A homogeneous substance resulting from colloid degeneration; found in degenerated cells. SEE: *degeneration, hyaline*.

ketone b. One of a number of substances that increase in the blood as a result of faulty carbohydrate metabolism. Among them are β-hydroxybutyric acid, acetoacetic acid, and acetone. They increase in persons with untreated or inadequately controlled diabetes mellitus and are the primary cause of acidosis. They may also occur in other metabolic disturbances. SYN: *acetone b.*

lateral geniculate b. One of two bodies forming elevations on the lateral portion of the posterior part of the thalamus. Each is the termination of afferent fibers from the retina, which it receives through the optic nerves and tracts.

Lewy b. Lewy body.

loose b. A fragment of bone or cartilage within the joint of a patient with severe degenerative or neuropathic arthritis.

Luys b. SEE: *Luys body*.

Mallory b. SEE: *Mallory body.*

mammillary b. A spherical complex of hypothalamic nuclei that bulges out of the base of the brain behind the pituitary gland on either side of the midline. The mammillary body is an integral component of the limbic circuitry, receiving signals from the hippocampus via the fornix and sending signals to the anterior thalamus via the mammillothalamic tract. SEE: *medial mammillary **nucleus**; limbic system* for illus.

medial geniculate b. One of two bodies lying in the posterior part of the dorsal thalamus. Each receives fibers from the acoustic tract of the pons and the inferior colliculus through the brachium.

Nissl b. SEE: under *Nissl, Franz.*

perineal b. A mass of tissue that separates the anus from the vestibule and the lower part of the vagina.

pineal b. SEE: *pineal gland.*

pituitary b. Obsolete term for the pituitary gland.

polar b. A small nonfunctional cell produced in oogenesis resulting from the divisions of the primary and secondary oocytes.

psammoma b. A laminated calcified body seen in certain types of tumors and sometimes associated with chronic inflammation.

restiform b. One of the inferior cerebellar peduncles of the brain, found along the lateral border of the fourth ventricle. These two bands of fibers, principally ascending, connect the medulla oblongata with the cerebellum.

Russell body SEE: *Russell body.*

striate b. The corpus striatum, composed of the cordate and lenticular nuclei of the brain.

trachoma b. A mass of cells present as an inclusion body in the conjunctival epithelial cells of individuals with trachoma.

trapezoid b. A transverse sheet of secondary sensory axons that originate in the cochlear nuclei and that cross the midline just dorsal to the pons in the rostral hindbrain. About half of the cochlear axons remain ipsilateral and ascend toward the inferior colliculus via the lateral lemniscus. Those cochlear axons that cross the cross the midline in the trapezoid body also join the (contralateral) lateral lemniscus and run toward the inferior colliculus.

ultimobranchial b. One of two embryonic pharyngeal pouches usually considered as rudimentary fifth pouches. They become separated from the pharynx and incorporated into the thyroid gland, where they give rise to parafollicular cells that secrete calcitonin, a hormone that lowers the blood calcium level.

vertebral b. A short column of bone forming the weight-supporting portion of a vertebra. From its dorsolateral surfaces project the roots of the arch of a vertebra.

vitreous b. Vitreous (2).

wolffian b. Mesonephros.

body armor Clothing designed to resist blast waves, blunt force trauma, heat, penetrating objects, shrapnel, and other potential sources of physical injury.

body art Tattooing, body piercing, and body painting.

bodybuilding (bod´ē-bild″ing) The use of resistance training and weight training along with nutritional and/or pharmacological methods to increase muscle size in an effort to alter physical appearance.

body burden The amount of a substance present in an organism. The term is usually reserved for descriptions of infectious or toxic substances. It may be represented arithmetically as the concentration of the substance multiplied by the mass of the tissues that store it.

body composition The relative percentages of bony minerals, cell mass, lean body mass, body fat, and body water in an organism, and their distribution through the body. Determination of the specific gravity of the body is done to estimate the percentage of fat. This may be calculated by various methods, including underwater weighing, which determines the density of the individual; use of radioactive potassium, ^{40}K; measuring the total body water by dilution of tritium; and use of various anthropometric measurements such as height, weight, and skin fold thickness at various sites. None of these methods is free of the potential for error. Underwater weighing is useful but may provide misleading information when used in analyzing body composition of highly trained athletes. The obese person has a lower body density than does the lean person, because the specific gravity of fat tissue is less than that of muscle tissue. The fat content for young men will vary from about 5% to 27% and for women from about 18% to 35%.

body contouring Any form of cosmetic surgery used to shape, sculpt, or reshape body lines. It includes "lifts," e.g., face-lift, and abdominoplasty.

body dysmorphic disorder ABBR: BDD. A preoccupation with one or more imagined defects in appearance. The disorder is also known colloquially as *athletica nervosa.* SEE: *muscle dysmorphia.*

body image, disturbed Disruption in the way one perceives one's body image (e.g., after an injury or illness) or an incongruity between one's actual appearance and the way one perceives it (e.g., in anorexia nervosa). SEE: *body dys-*

morphic disorder; *Nursing Diagnoses Appendix.*

body jewelry Any adornment placed through and attached to a body part, e.g., belly or nipple rings, nose studs, or tongue bars.

⚠️ Foreign objects placed in body parts may interfere with radiological imaging or invasive procedures or may conduct electricity during surgery. The body jewelry, as well as rings, necklaces, eyeglasses or lenses, and dentures, may have to be removed before surgery for the patient's safety.

body language The revelation of attitude or mood through physical gestures, posture, or proximity; nonverbal communication. A grimace, shrug, silence, smile, wink, raised eyebrows, avoidance, turning away, or even fighting are examples of nonverbal communication. SYN: *gestural communication; nonverbal communication.* SEE: *kinesics.*

body map SEE: under *map.*

body packer syndrome Drug overdose as a result of the ingestion of multiple small packages, usually containing drugs of abuse (esp. cocaine), to transport them illegally. Inadvertent overdose may occur if the packages rupture.

body packing The ingestion of a container, e.g., a plastic bag, filled with an illegal drug. This technique is used by drug smugglers to evade detection while carrying small amounts of cocaine, methamphetamines, or narcotics through security points. The container passes through the gastrointestinal tract and is recovered after defecation. If it ruptures, dissolves, or is punctured, it may release dangerous quantities of drug into the carrier. SYN: *body stuffing.*

body piercing Placing an object, usually a metal or plastic ornament, into a body part such as the ears, navel, nose, lips, tongue, nipple, or genitalia. Piercing may be associated with problems such as local skin infections, the transmission of blood-borne infections, and allergic reactions to the object.

body rocking SEE: under *rocking.*

body scheme Knowledge of one's body parts and their relative positions. SEE: *proprioception.*

body snatching Robbing a grave of its body, which was done in the past to obtain bodies for anatomical study in medical schools.

body stuffing Body packing.

body surface area The surface area of the body expressed in square meters. Body surface area is an important measure in calculating pediatric dosages and drug dosages in chemotherapy, managing burn patients, and determining radiation doses. Nomograms for accurately determining body surface area are available for both pediatric and adult patients. SEE: *burn; rule of nines.*

body temperature, risk for imbalanced At risk for failure to maintain body temperature within normal range. SEE: *Nursing Diagnoses Appendix.*

body temperature and pressure, saturated ABBR: BTPS. In respiratory physiology, the volume of gas in the lung and the flow of gas from the airways, adjusted for the body temperature of the patient, the barometric pressure at sea level, and the saturation of the gas with water vapor (respiratory gases, unlike gases circulating in the environment, are fully humidified). SEE: *ambient temperature and pressure, saturated.*

body type SEE: under *type.*

body weight ratio Body weight in grams divided by body height in centimeters.

bodywork (bod′ē-wŏrk) Any musculoskeletal manipulation such as massage, stretching, postural alignment, and breathing exercises that are used to relieve stress, treat pain, and promote a sense of wellness.

Boeck sarcoid (bek) [Caesar P. M. Boeck, Norwegian dermatologist, 1845–1917] Former name for sarcoidosis.

Boerhaave syndrome (boor′hav″ĕ) [Hermann Boerhaave, Dutch physician, 1668–1738] Spontaneous rupture of the esophagus usually associated with violent retching or vomiting. SEE: *Mallory-Weiss syndrome;* .

Bohr effect (bōr) [Christian Bohr, Danish physiologist, 1855–1911] The effect of an acid environment on hemoglobin; hydrogen ions alter the structure of hemoglobin and increase the release of oxygen. It is esp. important in active tissues producing carbon dioxide and lactic acid.

boil (boyl) [AS. *byl,* a swelling] A tender, dome-shaped skin lesion, typically caused by infection around a hair follicle with *Staphylococcus aureus.* Boils usually arise on the face, neck, axilla, or buttocks (i.e., on body surfaces that frequently perspire and chafe). When they first appear they are often superficial, but as they mature they form localized abscesses with pus and necrotic debris at their core. On rare occasions they spread to deeper tissues, sometimes with tragic consequences (e.g., a boil on the neck or face may spread to the brain or meninges). SYN: *furuncle.* SEE: illus.; *carbuncle.*

TREATMENT: Warm moist compresses relieve pain and encourage drainage of the infected nodule to the skin surface. Oral antistaphylococcal antibiotics, such as trimethoprim/sulfamethoxazole or clindamycin, are given when the lesion is surrounded by

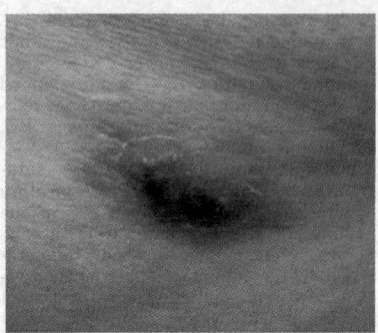

BOIL

local cellulitis. Incision and drainage is sometimes needed.

boiled rice water SEE: under *water.*

boiling (boyl'ĭng) Process of vaporizing a liquid. Boiling water destroys most microorganisms (but may not destroy spores or viruses), solidifies (denatures) albumin, weakens fibrin and muscle proteins in meat, bursts starch granules, and softens cellulose in cereals and vegetables.

-bol [Fm. *(ana)bol(ic)*] A suffix used in pharmacology to designate an *anabolic steroid.*

bolus (bō'lŭs) [L. *bolus* fr Gr. *bolos,* a lump] **1.** A mass of masticated food ready to be swallowed. **2.** A rounded preparation of medicine for oral ingestion. **3.** A concentrated mass of a diagnostic substance given rapidly intravenously, such as an opaque contrast medium or an intravenous medication. **4.** In radiology, a tissue-equivalent material placed on the surface of the body to minimize the effects of an irregularly shaped body surface. The dose at the skin surface tends to increase, minimizing the skin-sparing effect of megavoltage radiation.

   alimentary b. A mass of masticated food in the esophagus that is ready to be passed into the stomach.

   correction bolus An injection of a short-acting insulin, used to bring an unexpectedly high blood sugar back to normal. Correction boluses are often given based on a prescribed sliding scale.

bombesin (bom'bĕ-sĭn) ABBR: BBS. A neuropeptide present in the gut and brain tissue of humans. It has antiulcer, anti-inflammatory, appetite-suppressing, and trophic effects. It has been identified in a number of malignancies and has been used in oncology as an biological marker of disease progression.

Bombus (bom'bŭs) [L. *bombus,* humming] The genus of stinging insects (family Apidae) that includes the bumblebees.

bona fide (bō'nă, bŏ'nă, fīd, fĭd'ē, fē'dā)

[L.] Carried out in good faith; honest, without fraud or deception.

bond (bond) **1.** A force that binds ions or atoms together. It is represented by a line drawn from one molecule or atom to another as in H—O—H, in which the lines represent a pair of electrons. **2.** An interpersonal connection or tie.

   covalent b. Chemical bond formed when atoms share one, two, or three pairs of electrons. This is the type of bond found in organic molecules. SEE: *ionic b.; polar covalent b.*

   disulfide b. A covalent bond between two sulfur-containing amino acids, which helps maintain the shape of proteins such as insulin, keratin, and antibodies. SYN: *disulfide bridge.*

   hydrogen b. The weak attraction of a covalently bonded hydrogen to nearby oxygen or nitrogen atoms in the same or a different molecule. Hydrogen bonds give water its cohesiveness and its surface tension. These bonds also help maintain the three-dimensional shape of proteins and nucleic acids; such shape is essential to their functioning.

   ionic b. A chemical bond formed by the loss and gain of electrons between atoms. This type of bond is found in inorganic acids, bases, and salts.

   nonpolar covalent b. A covalent bond in which the pair of electrons is shared equally between two atoms.

   polar covalent b. A covalent bond in which one atom attracts the shared pair of electrons more strongly than does the other atom, and thus has a slightly negative charge. The atom with the weaker attraction has a slightly positive charge.

bonding (bond'ĭng) **1.** In dentistry, the use of a low-viscosity polymerizable adhesive to provide mechanical retention of cast restorations, autopolymerizing restorations, and orthodontic appliances. **2.** Development of a strong emotional attachment between individuals (e.g., a mother and child) after frequent or prolonged close contact.

   mother-infant b. The emotional and physical attachment between infant and mother that is initiated in the first hour or two after normal delivery of a baby who has not been dulled by anesthetic agents or drugs. It is believed that the stronger this bond, the greater the chances of a mentally healthy infant-mother relationship in both the short- and long-term periods after childbirth. For that reason, the initial contact between mother and infant should be in the delivery room and the contact should continue for as long as possible in the first hours after birth. It is also called mother-infant attachment.

bone (bōn) **1.** Osseous tissue, a specialized form of dense connective tissue consisting of bone cells (osteocytes) embedded in a nonliving matrix. Bone matrix is made of calcium carbonate, calcium phosphate, and collagen fibers. SYN: *os*. **2.** A unit of the skeleton; the human skeleton has 206 bones. Bones surround and protect some vital organs, and give points of attachment for the muscles, serving as levers and making movement possible. In the embryo, the bones of the skull are first made of fibrous connective tissue, which is gradually replaced by bone matrix. The remainder of the skeleton is first made of hyaline cartilage, which is also replaced by bone matrix, beginning during the third month of gestation. The outer surface of a bone is compact bone, and the inner more porous portion is cancellous (spongy) bone. The shafts of long bones are made of compact bone that surrounds a marrow canal. Compact bone is made of haversian systems, which are precise arrangements of osteocytes, blood vessels, and lymphatics within the bony matrix. All of these contribute to the maintenance and repair of bone. The periosteum is the fibrous connective tissue membrane that covers a bone. It has blood vessels that enter the bone, and it provides a site of attachment for tendons and ligaments. Bones are classified according to shape as long, short, flat, or irregular. In the elderly, esp. women, osteoporosis may develop, a condition in which bones become brittle and break easily. SEE: illus.; *skeleton* for names of principal bones.

Femur

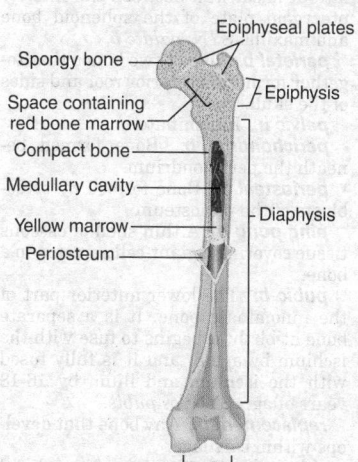

Epiphyseal plates

Spongy bone —

Epiphysis

Space containing
red bone marrow—

Compact bone—

Medullary cavity—

Yellow marrow—

Periosteum —

Diaphysis

Epiphysis

PARTS OF A LONG BONE

alveolar b. The bony tissue or process of the maxilla or mandible that supports the teeth. SYN: *alveolar process*.
breast b. Sternum.

brittle b. Bone that is abnormally fragile, as in osteogenesis imperfecta.
cancellous b. A spongy bone in which the matrix forms connecting bars and plates, partially enclosing many intercommunicating spaces filled with bone marrow. SYN: *spongy b.*
carpal bone One of the eight wrist bones, which are aligned in two rows. The proximal row contains (from the thumb to the little finger) the scaphoid, lunate, triquetral, and pisiform bones. The distal row contains (from thumb to little finger) the trapezium, trapezoid, capitate, and hamate bones.
cartilage b. A bone formed by endochondral ossification developing from the primary centers of bone formation. SYN: *endochondral b.*
cavalry b. Rider **b.**
collar b. Clavicle.
compact b. The hard, dense bone made of haversian systems that forms the surface layer of all bones and the shafts of long bones, in contrast to spongy bone that forms the bulk of the short, flat, and irregular bones and the ends of long bones.
cotyloid b. A bone that forms a part of the medial portion of the acetabulum during fetal development. It subsequently fuses with the pubis.
cranial b. A bone of the skull or brain case.
cuboid b. The outer bone of the instep bones of the foot that articulates posteriorly with the calcaneus and anteriorly with the fourth and fifth metatarsals.
cuneiform b. One of the bones of the internal, middle, and external tarsus.
dermal b. Membrane **b.**
ear b. One of the ossicles of the tympanic cavity: the malleus, incus, and stapes. SEE: *ear* for illus.
endochondral b. Cartilage **b.**
ethmoid b. A complex thin-walled bone, roughly cuboidal in shape, located in the middle of the skull above the nasal cavities and below the anterior fossa of the cranial cavity. Its flat upper surface is the cribriform plate, which forms much of the roof of the nasal cavities; its upper surface has a midline bony keel that projects up into the cranial cavity and on both sides of which are perforated valleys through which the olfactory nerves project up from the olfactory epithelium. In the midline under the cribriform plate is a mirror-image (to the crista galli) keel, the perpendicular plate, which projects down between the nasal cavities as part of the bony nasal septum. The right and left sides of the ethmoid bone are the ethmoidal labyrinths, composed of ethmoidal air cells; the inner surfaces of the labyrinths form the middle nasal conchae, while the lateral surfaces form the orbital plates,

which are part of the mosaic of bones that form the inner walls of the orbits.

frontal b. The forehead bone.

funny b. A colloquial term for the groove along the inner back side of the elbow (behind and underneath the medial epicondyle of the humerus) in which the ulnar nerve runs. Pressure on the groove compresses the ulnar nerve, producing a tingling discomfort on the inside of the forearm as well as the 4th and 5th fingers.

hamate b. The most medial wrist (carpal) bone in the distal row. It has a hooked process on its palmar side. The hamate articulates with the 4th and 5th metacarpals. SYN: *hamatum; os hamatum; unciform bone.*

heel b. Calcaneus.

hip b. Innominate **b.**

hyoid b. The horseshoe-shaped bone at the base of the tongue. It is mobile and its ends hang by the stylohyoid ligaments from the styloid process on each side of the base of the skull. The hyoid bone is suspended by many muscles (the hyoid muscles): the suprahyoid muscles (geniohyoid, mylohyoid, digastric, and hyoglossus) attach the hyoid bone to the mandible and the floor of the mouth; the infrahyoid muscles (omohyoid, sternohyoid, and thyrohyoid) attach it to the larynx and the thoracic cage. The hyoid bone anchors and moves with the jaw, tongue, pharynx, and larynx. SEE: illus.

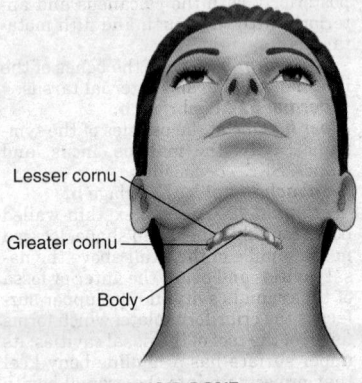

Lesser cornu

Greater cornu

Body

HYOID BONE

innominate b. The hip bone or os coxae, composed of the ilium, ischium, and pubis. It is united with the sacrum and coccyx by ligaments to form the pelvis. SYN: *pelvic b.; os coxae.*

interradicular b. The alveolar bone between the roots of multirooted teeth.

intramembraneous b. Membrane bone.

ivory b. Marble **b.**

lacrimal b. A thin, irregularly shaped bone on the medial side of the orbit.

lesser multangular b. The second in

distal row of carpal bones. SYN: *trapezoid b.*

lunate b. Semilunar **b.**

malar b. A four-pointed bone on each side of the face, uniting the frontal and superior maxillary bones with the zygomatic process of the temporal bone. SYN: *cheekbone; zygoma; zygomatic b.*

marble b. An abnormally calcified bone with a spotted appearance on a radiograph. SYN: *ivory b.* SEE: *osteopetrosis.*

membrane b. Bone formed within embryonic fibrous connective tissue, in which fibroblasts differentiate into osteoblasts. Such bone is formed without a cartilage model and includes the bones of the face and cranium. SYN: *dermal b.; intramembraneous b.*

metatarsal b. Any of the bones of the metatarsus. SEE: *foot* for illus.

mosaic b. Bone appearing as small pieces fitted together, characteristic of Paget's disease.

nasal b. Either of the two small bones forming the bridge of the nose.

occipital b. The bone that forms the lower, posterior skull; it articulates with the parietal and temporal bones anteriorly, and the atlas inferiorly.

orbicular b. The rounded end of the long process of the incus, a middle ear ossicle. It probably represents a secondary ossification center in the long or lenticular process.

palate b. Palatine **b.**

palatine b. One of the bones forming the posterior part of the hard palate and lateral nasal wall between the interior pterygoid plate of the sphenoid bone and maxilla. SYN: *palate b.*

parietal b. One of two bones that together form the posterior roof and sides of the skull.

pelvic b. Innominate **b.**

perichondrial b. Bone formed beneath the perichondrium.

periosteal b. Bone formed by osteoblasts of the periosteum.

ping pong b. A thin shell of osseous tissue covering a giant-cell sarcoma in a bone.

pubic b. The lower anterior part of the innominate bone. It is a separate bone at birth; it begins to fuse with the ischium by age 8, and it is fully fused with the ischium and ilium by 16-18 years of age. SYN: *os pubis.*

replacement b. Any bone that develops within cartilage.

rider's b. Ossification of the distal end of the adductor muscles of the thigh, as may be seen in horseback riders. SYN: *cavalry b.*

sacral b. Sacrum.

scaphoid b. The largest carpal bone in the first row of wristbones. It is on the thumb side of the hand and articulates directly with the radius. SYN: *os sca-phoideum*.

semilunar b. Crescent-shaped bone of the carpus. SYN: *lunate b.*

sesamoid b. A type of short bone occurring in the hands and feet and embedded in tendons or joint capsules.

Soemmering b. SEE: *Soemmering bone.*

sphenoid b. The large bone at the base of the skull that has the ethmoid bone in front of it, the occipital bone behind it, and the parietal and temporal bones at the sides. It is shaped like a large moth. Its two broad, curved wings form the front walls of the middle cranial fossae, and its two "tails," the pterygoid processes, which hang in front of the neurocranium in the pterygoid fossa behind the facial skeleton. Between the wings, in the center of the body of the sphenoid bone, there is a deep, concave pocket (the sella turcica), in which the pituitary gland lies.

spongy b. Cancellous **b.**

squamous b. The upper anterior portion of temporal bone.

stirrup b. Stapes.

sutural b. Wormian **b.**

tabular b. A flat bone, or one with two compact bone portions enclosing a center of spongy bone.

tarsal b. One of the seven bones of the ankle, hind-foot, and midfoot, consisting of the talus, calcaneus, navicular, cuboid, and three cuneiform bones.

temporal b. A bone on both sides of the skull at its base. It is composed of squamous, mastoid, and petrous portions, the latter enclosing the receptors for hearing and equilibrium. SYN: *os temporale.* SEE: *Arnold's canal; mastoid; petrosa; styloid process.*

thigh b. Femur.

trapezoid b. The second bone in the distal row of carpal bones. It lies between the trapezium and capitate bones.

triquetral b. The third carpal bone in the proximal row, enumerated from the radial side. SYN: *triquetrum.*

wormian b. One of the small, irregular bones found along the cranial sutures. SYN: *sutural b.*

woven b. Embryonic or rapidly growing bone characterized microscopically by a prominent fibrous matrix.

zygomatic b. The cheekbone; the bone on either side of the face below the eye. SYN: *malar b.*

bone densitometry A method of determining the density of bone by use of radiographic techniques. The use of dual photon absorptiometry provides density data of the axial skeleton with a precision of 97% to 98%. It is used in testing for degree of osteoporosis. SEE: *osteoporosis; dual energy x-ray absorptiometry.*

bone fracture, nonunion, electrical stimulation for A method of stimulating a nonunion bone fracture to heal through an invasive or noninvasive electromagnetic field. Invasive electrical stimulation involves the implantation of electrodes into the bone proximal and distal to the fracture site. Surface electrodes are placed on the skin over the area of fracture for the noninvasive technique. SEE: *nonunion.*

bonelet (bōn'lĕt) Ossicle.

bone marrow SEE: under *marrow.*

bone marrow aspiration and biopsy The removal of a small amount of tissue (bone marrow biopsy) and fluid filled with blood cells (bone marrow aspiration) from the central core of a bone. The aspiration and biopsy are used to diagnose blood disorders such as anemias and cancers, infectious diseases that affect the marrow, or to gather cells for later infusion into a patient (e.g., in bone marrow transplantation).

PATIENT CARE: The purpose of the test is explained to the patient (and family as necessary). The patient is advised that some discomfort or pressure may be felt, e.g., a crunching or popping sound may be heard as the needle penetrates the bone. A signed, informed consent must be obtained before the procedure. The patient's history is reviewed, including risk for bleeding, coagulation studies, platelet count, anticoagulant therapy, and use of drugs or supplements that interfere with clotting. The patient is also assessed for allergies to antiseptic or anesthetic solutions. The patient is advised that he or she must remain still throughout the procedure, and the ability to do so is assessed. Baseline signs are recorded, and a sedative is administered as prescribed. The patient is assisted to the appropriate position for the insertion site: the lateral decubitus position for the posterior iliac crest and the supine position for the sternum or anterior iliac crest. The health care provider helps the patient maintain the desired position. The patient is encouraged to take deep breaths and use relaxation techniques during the procedure.

A sterile prepackaged set is used for the aspiration, and the practitioner is assisted as necessary. The patient is assessed throughout the procedure for pallor, diaphoresis, or other changes. After the aspiration, direct pressure is applied to the puncture site for 5 to 10 minutes or according to agency policy until bleeding is controlled; the wound is then covered with a sterile dressing. The patient is helped into a comfortable position, and vital signs are checked. The puncture site is reassessed as necessary for bleeding. All specimens are labeled and transported to the laboratory. Postprocedure pain intensity is evaluated, and analgesia is provided as prescribed. The patient is advised to watch for and report any signs of infection and is warned to avoid any drugs containing acetylsalicylic acid (aspirin), which may cause bleeding.

Specimens of marrow and aspirate are sent to the cytology or pathology laboratory for microscopic analysis, to the microbiology laboratory if cultures are needed, and/or to the clinical laboratory for chromosomal analysis or staining. A biopsy or aspirate that does not yield adequate material for analysis is known colloquially as a "dry tap."

bone mineral density SEE: under *density*.

bone morphogenetic protein (mor″fō-jĕ-net′ĭk) SEE: under *protein*.

bone paste One of several composite materials that can be used to repair defects in bones during orthopedic surgery.

bone–patellar tendon–bone ABBR: B-PT-B. An autologous graft used to repair a ruptured anterior cruciate ligament. It consists of the central portion of the patellar tendon linked to a segment of bone taken from the patella (colloquially the kneecap) and a segment extracted from the tibia (the shin).

bony (bō′nē) Resembling or of the nature of bone. SYN: *osseous*.

bony prominence A part of the body with limited subcutaneous tissue over a bone. Examples include the heels, the iliac crests, and the sacrum. The skin that overlies a bony prominence is more prone to pressure ulceration than more padded body parts.

bonzo (bŏn′zō) A receptor found on the surface of cellular membranes that facilitates the entry of the human immunodeficiency virus.

Boophilus (bō-ŏ′fil-ŭs) [L. *bos,* ox, cow, Gr. *philein,* to love] A genus of ticks that parasitizes humans and cattle and other animals. SEE: *Ixodes*.

boost (boost) In radiation oncology the delivery of a large dose of radiation to a tumor in addition to the radiation supplied by an external beam.

booster (boo′stĕr) An additional dose of an immunizing agent to increase the protection afforded by the original series of injections. The booster is given some months or years after the initial immunization.

booster effect **1.** A strong immune response generated by a second exposure to an antigen. **2.** An increase in the size of the reaction to intradermally injected tuberculin when a second injection is given 7 to 21 days after the first.

BOOSTRIX (boos′trĭks) Tetanus toxoid, reduced diphtheria toxoid, and acellular pertussis vaccine, adsorbed.

boot A special shoe, brace, or bandage for covering, protecting, and/or immobilizing the foot, ankle, and lower leg.

   walking b., walker boot Walking cast.

borate (bō′rāt) Any basic salt of boric acid. SEE: *Poisons and Poisoning Appendix.* **borated,** *adj.*

borax (bor′ăks) [L., from Arabic, from Persian *burah*] Sodium borate, used as a detergent, a water softener, and a weak antiseptic.

borborygmus (bor″bō-rĭg′mŭs) *pl.* **borborygmi** [Gr. *borborygmos,* rumbling in the bowels] A gurgling, splashing sound normally heard over the large intestine; it is caused by passage of gas through the liquid contents of the intestine. Its absence may indicate paralytic ileus or obstruction of the bowels due to torsion, volvulus, or strangulated hernia.

border (bawr′dĕr) The outer part or edge; boundary.

   brush b. The microvilli on the free surface of the cells lining the small intestine and the proximal convoluted portion of the renal tubules. Microvilli are folds of the cell membrane and greatly increase the surface area for absorption.

   ruffled b. A series of wavy or finger-like folds of the plasma membrane of osteoclasts.

   vermilion b. The red boundary of the lips that represents the highly vascular, hyalinized, keratinized epithelial covering between the outer skin and the moist oral mucosa of the mouth.

borderline (bor′dĕr-līn″) An incomplete state, as in a borderline diagnosis, in a patient who has some of the requirements for a definite diagnosis but not enough for certainty; a condition judged numerically (e.g., high blood pressure in which the value is close to a hypertensive level but not at a diagnostic level).

Bordetella (bord″ĕ-tel′ă) [Named after Jules *Bordet*] A genus of hemolytic gram-negative coccobacilli of the family Alcaligenaceae. Some species are parasitic and pathogenic in warm-blooded animals, including humans.

   B. pertussis The causative agent of whooping cough. SEE: *pertussis*.

Bordet-Gengou medium (bor-dā′zhon-goo′) [Jules Jean Baptiste Vincent Bordet, Belgian immunologist, 1870–1961; Octave Gengou, Fr. bacteriologist, 1875–1957] ABBR: BG medium. A culture medium used to isolate *Bordetella pertussis* from clinical specimens.

bore **1.** The internal diameter of a tube. **2.** To drill, e.g. into the surface of a bone or tooth.

boredom (bor′dŏm″) A feeling of fatigue, depression, or disinterest caused by a lack of challenging or meaningful work or stimulation. SEE: *apathy*.

borescope, bore scope (bor′skōp″) Any

device used to look inside small spaces or internal organs. It has three basic parts: an eyepiece on one end, a lens on the other, and a medium (such as a fiberoptic cable) that transmits light from the lens to the eyepiece.

Borg dyspnea scale (borg) A system used to document the severity of the patient's shortness of breath using numbers anchored with verbal descriptions (e.g., 10 = completely out of breath; 5 = somewhat breathless; 1 = breathing easily). The patient or athlete chooses the number that best corresponds to his or her current perceived respiratory effort.

boric acid poisoning SEE: under *poisoning*.

borism (bawr′ĭ-zĭm) The symptoms caused by the internal use of borax or boron compounds. These include dry skin, eruptions, and gastric disturbances.

Bornholm disease (born′hōm) [named for the Danish island Bornholm] An epidemic disease marked by sudden intense pleuritic or abdominal pain and fever. It is caused by various coxsackie viruses. SYN: *epidemic pleurodynia*.

TREATMENT: Nonsteroidal anti-inflammatory agents and local application of heat may control symptoms.

boron (bōr′on″) [*bor(ax)* + *(carb)on*] SYMB: B. A metalloid element, atomic weight (mass) 10.81, atomic number 5. It is found only in compounds, e.g., boric acid or borax.

Borrelia (bor-rē′lē-ă) A genus of spirochetes, some of which cause disease in humans.

  B. burgdorferi The causative agent of Lyme disease.

  B. duttonii The causative agent for East African tick-borne relapsing fever. Other causes of endemic relapsing fever include *Borrelia hermii*.

  B. lonestari The causative agent of Southern tick-associated rash illness.

  B. recurrentis The causative agent of louse-borne relapsing fever.

borreliosis (bo-rel″ē-ō′sĭs) Any of several arthropod-borne diseases caused by spirochetes of the genus *Borrelia*.

boss (bŏs) [O. Fr. *boce*, a swelling] A round circumscribed swelling or growth (e.g., a tumor) that becomes large enough to produce swelling.

bosselated (bŏs′ĕ-lāt-ĕd) Marked by numerous bosses.

bossing (bŏs′ĭng) Protuberance of the frontal areas of the skull.

Boston brace SEE: under *brace*.

Boston Naming Test ABBR: BNT. A neuropsychiatric test to measure aphasia and naming ability. In the test the subject must name 60 line drawings of common and rarely seen objects. It is frequently used to assess patients with autism, brain injuries, or strokes.

Boswellia (boz-wel′ē-ă) A genus of trees found in the Middle East and India. The trees produce an oleoresin used in ayurvedic medicine as anti-inflammatory treatment for arthritis and asthma.

Botallo duct (bō-tal′ō) [Leonardo Botallo, Italian anatomist, 1530–1600] Ductus arteriosus.

botanical (bō-tă′nĭ-kl) 1. Relating to botany or plants. 2. A plant extract used to maintain health, treat, or prevent illness.

botany (bot′ăn-ē, bot′nē) [From L. *botanicus*, fr Gr. *botanikos*, pert. to plants, fr *botanē*, plants, fodder] The division of biology that studies plants.

botfly (bot′flī″) Any of several flies of the family Oestridae and other families whose maggots (larvae) are parasitic on the skin of mammals. SEE: *Dermatobia; myiasis*.

Bothrops (bō′throps″) [Gr. *bothros*, pit, hole + Gr. *ōps*, face, eye] A genus of venomous pit vipers found mostly in the Central and South American tropics. It includes the fer-de-lance, one of the deadliest snakes known.

botryoid (bŏt′rē-oyd) [Gr. *botrys*, bunch of grapes, + *eidos*, form, shape] Resembling a bunch of grapes.

botryomycosis (bŏt″trē-ō-mī-kō′sĭs) [Gr. *botrys*, bunch of grapes + ″] A boil or furuncle, resembling an actinomycotic mass, but composed instead of bacteria, specifically *Staphylococcus aureus*.

bottle propping Feeding an infant milk or formula by supporting the fluid container with an inanimate object rather than the parent's hand.

⚠ Unsupervised feeding of infants decreases their bonding with parents and increases the risk of both aspiration and ear infections.

botuliform (bŏ-chū′lĭ-form″) [L. *botulus*, sausage, + ″] Shaped like a sausage.

botulin (bŏch-ă-lĭn) The protein neurotoxin that causes the clinical disease botulism. It may be used to efface skin wrinkles, and to treat neurological conditions such as torticollis.

botulism (bŏt′ū-lĭzm) [″ + Gr. *-ismos*, condition] A paralytic and occasionally fatal illness caused by exposure to toxins released from *Clostridium botulinum*, an anaerobic, gram-positive bacillus. In adults, the disease usually occurs after food contaminated by the toxin is eaten, after gastrointestinal surgery, or after the toxin is released into an infected wound. In infants (usually between 3 and 20 weeks of age), the illness results from intestinal colonization by clostridial spores (perhaps related to honey or corn syrup ingestion), then production of the exotoxin within the intestine. Because the toxin is extraordinarily lethal and easy to manufacture and distribute, concern has been raised regarding its use as an agent of biological warfare.

Foodborne botulism may result from consumption of improperly cooked and canned meals, in which the spores of the bacillus survive and reproduce. Wound botulism may begin in abscesses, where an anaerobic environment promotes the proliferation of the bacterium and absorption of its poison. In either case cranial nerve paralysis and failure of the autonomic and respiratory systems may occur; however, gastrointestinal symptoms are likely only in foodborne outbreaks.

The poison responsible for botulism damages the nervous system by blocking the release of acetylcholine at the neuromuscular junction. This is the cause of the paralysis associated with the illness.

SYMPTOMS: Nausea, diarrhea, vomiting, ptosis, double vision, slurred speech, and swallowing difficulties are all common in adults. Constipation, poor feeding, and flaccidity (floppy baby syndrome) may occur in children. The spectrum of illness is broad; some patients suffer other complications, including generalized paralysis and respiratory failure, the usual cause of death (25% mortality).

DIAGNOSIS: Positive serum, gastric contents, stool, or suspected food cultures for botulinum toxin, or a positive mouse inoculation test (using samples from suspected food sources), will make the diagnosis in patients in whom other neurological evaluations are negative. Because the clinical presentation is similar to stroke and Guillain-Barré and Eaton-Lambert syndromes, neural imaging and spinal fluid analysis are generally performed; results are negative in botulism.

TREATMENT: Trivalent antitoxin (ABE), an antitoxin made from horses, should be administered IV or IM early in patients suspected of having botulism. Early usage decreases mortality and morbidity associated with the illness. Botulinum antitoxin is available from the Centers for Disease Control and Prevention by calling (404) 639-2206 (daytime) or (404) 639-2888 (evening). SEE: *Poisons and Poisoning Appendix.*

PATIENT CARE: Patients who have ingested tainted foods may benefit from gastrointestinal decontamination (lavage and enema to remove unabsorbed toxin). IV fluids provide hydration. Very close monitoring of affected patients, preferably in intensive care units, is indicated so that prompt intubation and mechanical ventilation can begin if respiratory failure develops. Vital signs,

respiratory effort, and respiratory distress are documented and reported. Arterial blood gases are monitored. Neuromotor function is carefully and repeatedly assessed. Before botulinum antitoxin is administered, a history of the patient's allergies, esp. to horse serum, is obtained and a skin sensitivity test performed. After antitoxin administration, the patient must be closely watched for anaphylaxis. Epinephrine 1:1,000 (SC) and airway equipment should be readily available for such an emergency. Other hypersensitivity reactions and serum sickness can also occur.

If relatives or other close contacts of the patient have eaten similar foods or shown similar symptoms, they should be carefully assessed and treated. Botulism is a reportable illness in every state in the U.S. Health care professionals can help to prevent botulism by explaining proper food processing and preserving techniques. Food obtained from a bulging container or food with a peculiar odor should always be avoided.

infant b. A form of botulism that affects infants less than 1 year old who ingest soil or food (esp. honey) containing *Clostridium botulinum* spores. The infant's protective intestinal flora is not yet established, and the spores germinate into active bacteria that produce the neurotoxin. It is treated with oral amoxicillin.

SYMPTOMS: The symptoms include constipation, lethargy, listlessness, poor feeding, ptosis, loss of head control, difficulty in swallowing, hypotonia, generalized weakness, and respiratory insufficiency. The disease may be mild or severe.

intestinal b. Botulism caused by production of botulinum toxin in the colon following ingestion of spores of *Clostridium botulinum.* Most cases occur in infants. SEE: *infant b.*

wound b. Botulism acquired when spores of the bacteria contaminate an anaerobic wound, germinate, and produce the neurotoxin.

bouba Yaws.

Bouchard nodes (boo-shar′, -shard) Bony enlargements or nodules, located at the proximal interphalangeal joints, that result from osteoarthritis or degenerative joint disease.

bougie (boo′zhē) [Fr. *bougie,* candle] A slender, flexible, tapered instrument used to explore and dilate tube-shaped organs, such as the male urethra or the esophagus.

PATIENT CARE: Typically, a narrow diameter bougie is inserted into a stricture in the organ first, followed by instruments of larger and larger diameter until the organ's internal lumen expands.

gum elastic b. A small, flexible instrument used to locate the trachea. It is used as an intubation aid, esp. when intubation with standard techniques is difficult.

bouillon (boo-, bool-yŏn′) [Fr.] A clear broth made from meat or vegetables. It may be used as a culture medium for bacteria.

Bouin fluid (boo-an′, bwon) [Paul Bouin, Fr. anatomist, 1870–1962] A fixative for embryological and histological tissue. It consists of formaldehyde, glacial acetic acid, picric acid, and water.

bound (bownd) **1.** In chemistry, the holding in combination of one molecule by another. SEE: *bind* (2). **2.** Contained, not free.

bouquet (boo-kā′) [Fr., nosegay] A cluster or bunch of structures, esp. blood vessels.

Bourdon gauge A low-pressure flow metering device.

Bourneville disease Tuberous sclerosis.

boutonnière (boo-tŏn-yār′) [Fr., buttonhole] A surgically produced or spontaneously occurring buttonhole-like opening in a structure, such as a membrane or tendon.

boutonnière deformity SEE: under *deformity.*

boutons terminaux (boo-tŏn′ tĕr-mĭ-nō′) [Fr., terminal buttons] The bulblike expansions at the tips of axons that come into synaptic contact with the cell bodies of other neurons.

Bouveret syndrome (boo-vrā′) [Leon Bouveret, French internist, 1850-1929] Gastric outlet obstruction resulting from impaction of a gallstone in the duodenum.

bovine (bō′vīn) [L. *bovinus*] Pert. to cattle; derived from cattle.

bovine somatotropin A ABBR: BST A. A growth hormone used to increase milk production in cows.

bowel (bow′ĕl) [O. Fr. *boel*, intestine] Intestine.

bowel bypass syndrome A febrile illness occurring after intestinal bypass surgery for morbidly obese patients. Affected patients typically report aching joints and muscles, and have pustules and papules on the arms, legs, and or chest.

bowel incontinence Change in normal bowel habits characterized by involuntary passage of stool. SEE: *Nursing Diagnoses Appendix.*

bowel rest The intentional restriction of oral nutrition, typically used with other therapies for patients with gastrointestinal diseases such as bowel obstruction, ileus, pancreatitis, or acute abdomen.

bowel sounds SEE: under *sound.*

bowel training SEE: under *training.*

bowel transit time SEE: under *time.*

Bowie-Dick test (bō′ē-dik′) A technique in the flash sterilization of surgical instruments to ensure that residual air in the sterilizer has been removed before use of the equipment.

bowleg (bō′leg″) Valgus knee.

Bowman, Sir William (bō′măn) Brit. anatomist, physiologist, and ophthalmologist, 1816–1892.

   B. capsule Part of the renal corpuscle. It consists of a visceral layer of podocytes closely applied to the glomerulus and an outer parietal layer. SYN: *glomerular capsule*. SEE: *kidney* for illus.

   B. lamina **B.** membrane.

   B. membrane The thin homogeneous membrane separating the corneal epithelium from the corneal substance. SYN: *anterior elastic **lamina**; **Bowman** lamina.*

box and block test A standardized, timed test of manual dexterity and endurance, used in rehabilitation, in which the subject transfers small blocks from one side of a box to another.

box-and-whiskers plot A graph representing data in quartiles, in which the data points above the 25th percentage and below the 75th are included in a box, the data points below the 25th percentage and above the 75th are represented by lines ("whiskers") below and above the box, and the median is shown by a line within the box. The median is the value that has an equal number of data points above it and below it.

boxing (bŏks′ĭng) In dentistry, the building up of vertical walls, usually in wax, around an impression to produce the desired size and form of the base of the cast and to preserve certain landmarks of the impression.

box jellyfish Any of several species of jellyfish of the class Cubozoa, known for their extremely lethal venom. SEE: *Cubozoa; sea wasp.*

box-note In emphysema, a hollow sound heard on percussion.

Boyden chamber (boyd′ĕn) A chamber used to measure chemotaxis. Cells are placed on one side of a membrane and chemotactic material on the other. The number of cells migrating to the filter quantitates the chemotactic effect.

Boyer bursa (bwa-yā′) [Baron Alexis de Boyer, Fr. surgeon, 1757–1833] A bursa anterior to the thyrohyoid membrane.

Boyer cyst A painless and gradual enlargement of the subhyoid bursa.

Boyle's law (boylz) [Robert Boyle, Brit. physicist, 1627–1691] A law stating that, at a constant temperature, the volume of a gas varies inversely with the pressure.

BP *blood pressure; British Pharmacopoeia.*

b.p. *boiling point.*

BPD *biparietal diameter; bronchopulmonary dysplasia.*

BPH *benign prostatic hypertrophy.*

BPP *Biophysical profile.*

Bq *becquerel.*

Br **1.** Symbol for the element bromine. **2.** *Brucella.*

brace (brās) **1.** Any of a variety of devices used in orthopedics for holding joints or limbs in place. **2.** In the plural, a colloquial term for temporary dental prostheses used to align or reposition teeth.

    back b. A common term for *spinal orthosis.*

    Boston b. A low-profile plastic thoracolumbosacral orthosis (spinal jacket) with no metal suprastructure, used to treat mild to moderate lower thoracic and lumbar scoliosis.

    invisible b. Aligner.

    Milwaukee b. A brace made of strong, lightweight materials. It extends from a chin cup with neck pad to the pelvis, and is used to correct minimal-curve scoliosis.

    Taylor b. SEE: *Taylor brace.*

    unloader knee b. A brace that produces a valgus force on the knee to reduce compressive forces on the medial articular surfaces. It is used to treat patients with deformity and pain caused by osteoarthritis of the knee.

brachial (brā′kē-ăl) [L. *brachialis*] Pert. to the arm.

brachialgia (brā″kē-ăl′jē-ă) [L. *brachialis*, brachial, + Gr. *algos*, pain] Intense pain in the arm.

brachialis (brā″kē-ăl′ĭs) [L. *brachialis*, brachial] A muscle of the arm lying immediately under the biceps brachii. It flexes the forearm. SEE: illus.

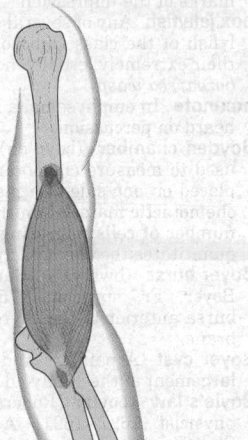

BRACHIALIS

brachio-, brachi- [L. *bracchium*, arm] Prefixes meaning *arm.*

brachiocephalic (brā″kē-ō-sĕ-făl′ĭk) [L. *brachium*, arm, + Gr. *kephale*, head] Pert. to the arm and head.

brachiocrural (brā″kē-ō-kroo′răl) [″ + *cruralis*, pert. to the leg] Pert. to the arm and thigh.

brachiocubital (brā″kē-ō-kū′bĭ-tăl) [″ + *cubitus*, forearm] Pert. to the arm and forearm.

brachioplasty (brăk″ē-ō-plăs′tē) [″ + ″] Cosmetic surgery to remove unwanted skin and fat from the upper arm. SEE: *arm lift.*

brachioradialis (brā″kē-ō-rā″dē-ā′lĭs) [″ + *radialis*, radius] A muscle lying on the lateral side of the forearm. It flexes the forearm.

brachium (brā′kē-ŭm) *pl.* **brachia** [L., arm, from Gr. *brakhion*, shorter, hence "upper arm" as opposed to longer forearm] **1.** The upper arm from shoulder to elbow. **2.** Anatomical structure resembling an arm.

    b. conjunctivum Superior cerebellar peduncle.

    b. pontis Middle cerebellar peduncle.

brachy- [Gr. *brachys*, short] Suffix meaning *short.*

brachybasia (brăk-ē-bā′sē-ă) [″ + *basis*, walking] A slow, shuffling gait.

brachycephalic,   **brachycephalous** (brak″i-sĕ-fal′ĭk, -sef′ă-lŭs) [*brachy-* + Gr. *kephalē*, head] Having a short, broad head with a cephalic index > 80. This is considered a short head but not abnormal, because this index falls within the standard range of variation among humans. **brachycephaly** (-sef′ă-lē), *n.*

brachycheilia (brăk″ē-kī′lē-ă) [″ + *cheilos*, lip] Abnormal shortness of the lips.

brachydactylia (brăk″ē-dăk-tĭl′ē-ă) [″ + *daktylos*, finger] Abnormal shortness of the fingers or toes.

brachygnathia (brăk-ĭg-nā′thē-ă) [″ + *gnathos*, jaw] Abnormal shortness of the lower jaw.

brachymorphic (brăk″ē-mor′fĭk) [″ + *morphe*, form] Shorter and broader than usual, with reference to body type.

brachyphalangia (brăk″ē-fă-lăn′jē-ă) [″ + *phalanx*, closely knit row] Shortness of a bone or bones of a finger or toe.

Brachyspira (brā″kē-spī′ră) [″ + *spir(ochete)*] A genus of spirochete that occasionally colonizes the lower gastrointestinal tract. It causes dysentery in animals such as dogs or pigs and has been identified as a cause of human disease, e.g., abdominal cramping, diarrhea, and rectal bleeding.

brachytherapy (brăk″ē-ther′ă-pē) [*brachy-* + *therapy*] In radiation therapy, the use of implants of radioactive materials such as radium, cesium, iridium, or gold at the treatment site, e.g., an internal organ with a malignant lesion. It is classified by dose (low, medium, high, or pulsed); by duration (temporary or permanent); and by placement (contact or interstitial). SYN: *endocurietherapy;*

implant radiation therapy; internal radiation therapy.

⚠️ The treated patient can emit radiation and can endanger others. If the radiation source is dislodged, it is removed by a radiation safety officer using special long-handled tongs and is placed in a lead container. All linens and dressings are considered contaminated. Pregnant women and children younger than 16 should not visit the patient.

PATIENT CARE: Before treatment, patient care focuses on explanation of the therapy, including a discussion of its planned duration, potential side effects, expected limitations on the patient's lifestyle, and typical efficacy. After implantation, patient care includes comfort care, radiation protection for staff and visitors, monitoring the patient for any untoward effects, and concluding the therapy, with an explanation of any expected sequella or activity restrictions.

vascular b. Temporary implantation of radioactive material within the lumen of a blood vessel. It is used to prevent blood vessels opened by stents or other invasive cardiovascular procedures from closing again after invasive cardiovascular procedures, e.g., stent placements.

bracket (brǎ′kĕt) A support of wood, metal, or some durable material. In orthodontics, brackets may be bonded to teeth or attached to them indirectly. Orthodontic brackets are used to attach arch wires, which apply pressure to the teeth to realign them.

Braden scale (brād′ĕn) [Barbara Braden, contemporary U.S. nurse] A validated assessment tool commonly used to quantify a patient's degree of risk for developing a pressure ulcer. Each assessment parameter is measured on a scale from high risk of 1 to low risk of 3 or 4. The parameters include sensory perception, moisture, activity, mobility, nutrition, and friction and shear, with a possible total score range of 4 to 23. The lower the total score, the higher the risk for pressure ulcer development. Patients are at risk for developing pressure ulcers if the total score is less than 17. Patients need to be assessed on a regular basis.
PATIENT CARE: For optimal risk assessment the scale should be used repeatedly.

Bradford frame (brǎd′fĕrd) [Edward H. Bradford, U.S. orthopedic surgeon, 1848–1926] An oblong frame, about 7 × 3 ft (2.13 × 0.91 m), that allows patients with fractures or disease of the hip or spine to urinate and defecate without moving the spine or changing position.

brady- [Gr. *bradys,* slow] Prefix meaning *slow.*

bradyacusia (brǎd″ē-ă-koo′sē-ă) [″ + *akouein,* to hear] An abnormally diminished hearing acuity.

bradyarrhythmia (brǎd″ē-ă-rǐth′mē-ă) [″ + *a-,* not, + *rhythmos,* rhythm] A heart rate of less than 60 beats per minute found in an adult. SYN: *bradydysrhythmia.*

bradycardia (brǎd″i-kard′ē-ă, brad″) [*brady-* + *-cardia*] A slow heartbeat marked by a pulse rate below 60 beats per minute in an adult.
athletic b. Athlete's heart.
fetal b. Persistent fetal heart rate slower than 110 beats per minute.
relative b. A heart rate that is too slow for a person's immediate physiological needs, although it may be more than 60 beats per minute. Heart rates are said to be relatively slow when they do not allow adequate circulation of blood to the brain, coronary arteries, or other vital organs.
sinus b. A slow sinus rhythm with an atrial rate below 60 beats per minute in an adult or 70 beats per minute in a child.

bradycrotic (brǎd″ē-krŏt′ĭk) [″ + *krotos,* pulsation] Pert. to slowness of pulse.

bradydiastole (brǎd″ē-dī-ăs′tō-lē) [″ + *diastole,* dilatation] Prolongation of the diastolic pause.

bradydysrhythmia (brǎd″ē-dĭs-rǐth′mē-ă) Bradyarrhythmia.

bradyecoia (brǎd″ē-ē-koy′ă) [Gr. *bradyekoos,* slow to hear] Partial deafness.

bradyesthesia (brǎd″ē-ĕs-thē′zē-ă) [″ + *aisthesis,* sensation] Slowness of perception.

bradykinesia (brǎd″ē-kĭ-nē′sē-ă) [″ + *kinesis,* movement] Extreme slowness of movement.

bradykinin (brǎd″ē-kī′nĭn) A plasma kinin. SEE: *kinin.*

bradylexia (brǎd″ē-lĕks′ē-ă) [Gr. *bradys,* slow, + *lexis,* word] Abnormal slowness of reading that cannot be attributed to lack of intelligence. SEE: *dyslexia.*

bradylogia (brǎd″ē-lō′jē-ă) [″ + *logos,* word, reason] Slow speech due to mental impairment.

bradyphagia (brǎd″ē-fā′jē-ă) [″ + *phagein,* to eat] Abnormal slowness in eating or swallowing.

bradyphrenia (brǎd″ē-frēn′ē-ă) [″ + Gr. *phren,* mind] Slowness of thought and information processing, seen in some forms of dementia.

bradypnea (brǎd″ĭp-nē′ă, brǎd″ĭ-nē′ă) [″ + *pnoe,* breathing] Abnormally slow breathing.

bradyrhythmia (brǎd″ē-rǐth′mē-ă) [″ + *rhythmos,* rhythm] **1.** Slowness of heart or pulse rate. **2.** In electroencephalography, slowness of brain waves (1 to 6 per sec).

bradytachycardia (brăd″ē-tăk″ē-kăr′dē-ă) [″ + *tachys*, swift, + *kardia*, heart] Increased heart rate alternating with slow rate. SEE: *sick sinus syndrome*.

Bragard test [K. Bragard, 20th-cent. Ger. orthopedic surgeon] Lasègue sign.

braille (brāl) [Louis Braille, blind Fr. educator, 1809–1852] A system of reading and printing that enables the blind to read by using the sense of touch. Raised dots arranged in patterns represent numerals and letters of the alphabet and can be identified by the fingers.

   contracted b. A version of braille in which abbreviations, contractions and other short forms of words are used in addition to the use of the standard alphabet and standard punctuation marks.

   noncontracted b. A type of braille in which only the regular alphabet and punctuation marks are used. SEE: *contracted b.*

brain (brān) A large highly-organized complex of neuron cell bodies, axons, dendrites, and glia filling the cavity inside the skull; the brain is enwrapped by fluid-filled protective membranes called meninges.

ANATOMY: The brain is a soft, compact organ responsible for consciousness, planned neural programs, and cognition. The brain is continually active, and, although it is only 2% of the body's mass, it receives 17% of the heart's output and consumes 20% of the body's oxygen supply. The brain receives its blood through four arteries: two large arteries, the right and left internal carotid arteries, run up from the chest in the front (anterior half) of the neck; and two smaller arteries, the right and left vertebral arteries, run in the back (posterior half) of the neck. The carotid arteries supply blood to about 80% of the brain, including most of the frontal, parietal, and temporal lobes of the cerebral hemispheres and the basal ganglia. The vertebral arteries supply blood to the remaining 20% of the brain, including the brainstem, cerebellum, and most of the posterior lobes of the cerebral hemispheres. SEE: illus. (Major arteries of the brain).

The most basic divisions of the brain are (from rostral to caudal) the forebrain (prosenchephalon), midbrain

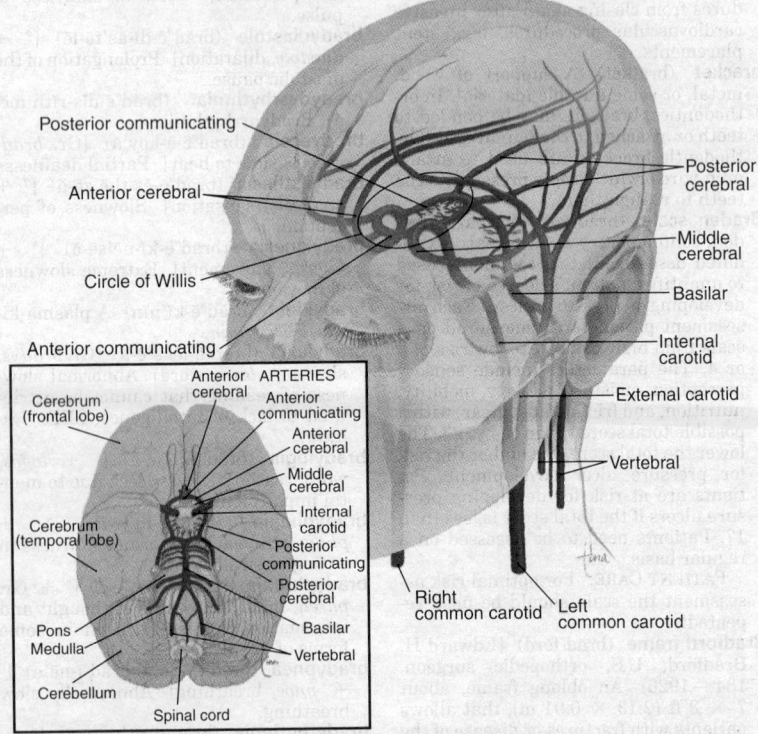

Posterior communicating
Anterior cerebral
Circle of Willis
Anterior communicating
Posterior cerebral
Middle cerebral
Basilar
Internal carotid
External carotid
Vertebral
Right common carotid
Left common carotid

ARTERIES
Cerebrum (frontal lobe)
Anterior cerebral
Anterior communicating
Anterior cerebral
Middle cerebral
Internal carotid
Posterior communicating
Posterior cerebral
Cerebrum (temporal lobe)
Pons
Medulla
Basilar
Vertebral
Cerebellum
Spinal cord

MAJOR ARTERIES OF THE BRAIN

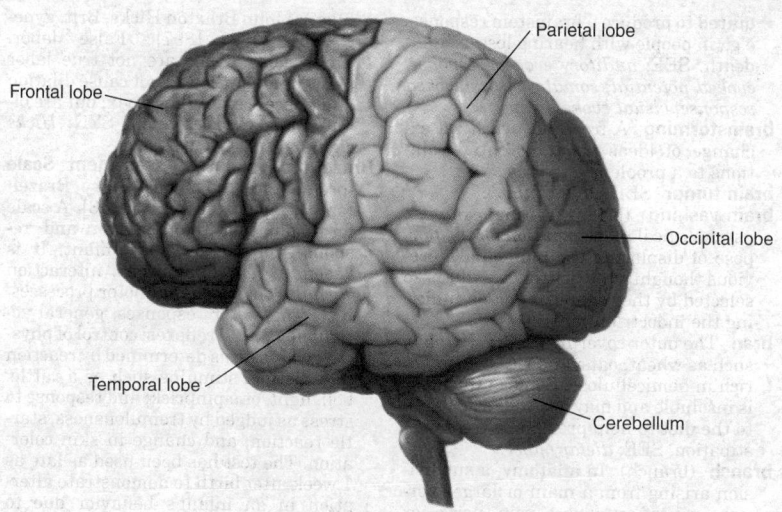

BRAIN STRUCTURES

(mesencephalon), and hindbrain (rhombencephalon). Physically, the forebrain dominates: the rostral end of the forebrain comprises the two cerebral hemispheres, which grow over much of the remaining brain (the brainstem) and fill the skull with their wavy infolded cortices. Between the cerebral hemispheres lies the caudal portion of the forebrain, the diencephalon, which contains the thalami, collections of nuclei that are way-stations and gatekeepers for signals to and from the cerebral cortices, and the hypothalamus, a center of visceral signals and the site of the pituitary gland. Caudal to the diencephalon is the midbrain, marked by two pairs of bulges (the tectum or colliculi) on its dorsal surface. The final segment of the brainstem, the hindbrain, has a rostral division, the pontine region (metencephalon), from the dorsal side of which bulges the cerebellum. The most caudal portion of the hindbrain is the medulla oblongata (myelencephalon or, in older literature, the bulb), which smoothly grades into the spinal cord. SEE: *fasciculus; tract* illus. (Brain Structures).

brain attack SEE: under *attack*.

brain mapping Cortical mapping.

Brain reflex (brān) [Walter Russell Brain, Brit. physician, 1895–1966] Extension of the flexed arm when the quadrupedal posture is assumed. SYN: *quadrupedal extensor **reflex***.

brainstem (brān'stĕm″) The stemlike part of the brain that connects the cerebral hemispheres with the spinal cord. It includes the diencephalin, midbrain, and hindbrain. Some anatomists

do not include the diencephalon in the brainstem. SEE: illus.

brainstem auditory evoked potential ABBR: BAEP. Brainwaves that are produced in response to sounds, i.e., stimulation of the cochlear nerve. Tests of auditory evoked potential are used to determine the threshold of sound re-

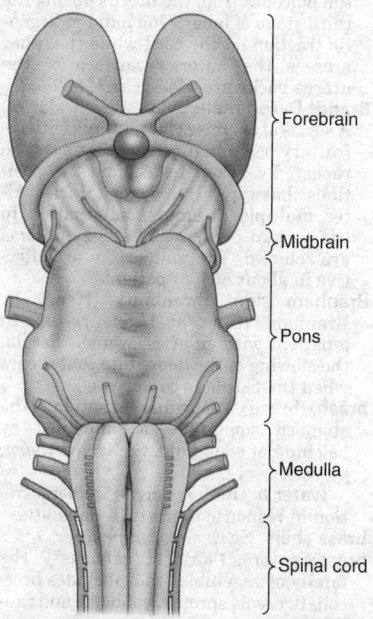

BRAINSTEM

quired to produce a brainstem response, e.g., in people with hearing loss or brain death. SEE: *auditory evoked response; evoked potential; somatosensory evoked response; visual evoked response.*

brainstorming A free and uncritical exchange of ideas about potential solutions to a problem.

brain tumor SEE: under *tumor.*

brainwashing (brān'wăsh-ĭng) Intense psychological indoctrination for the purpose of displacing the individual's previous thoughts and attitudes with those selected by the regime or person inflicting the indoctrination.

bran The outer covering of cereal grains, such as wheat, oats, and rice, which are rich in hemicellulose. Some of this fiber is insoluble and may be used to add bulk to the diet to help prevent or treat constipation. SEE: *dietary fiber.*

branch (brănch) In anatomy, a subdivision arising from a main or larger portion, esp. of an artery, vein, nerve, or lymphatic vessel.

branchial (brăng'kē-ăl) [L. *branchia,* gills] Pert. to or resembling gills of a fish or a homologous structure in higher animals.

branchioma (brăng″kē-ō′mă) [″ + Gr. *oma,* tumor] A tumor derived from the branchial epithelium.

branchiomeric (brăng″kē-ō-mĕr′ĭk) [″ + Gr. *meros,* part] Pert. to the branchial arches.

Brandt-Andrews maneuver (brăndt-ăn′drĕwz) A technique for expressing the placenta from the uterus during the third stage of labor. One hand puts gentle traction on the cord while the other presses the anterior surface of the uterus backward. SEE: *Credé method.*

Brandt-Daroff maneuvers (brănt′ dăr′ŏf) A series of exercises for patients with refractory positional vertigo. Patients are repeatedly asked to assume the positions that typically trigger attacks. After multiple attempts, habituation to the vertigo occurs, and the symptoms are relieved. The maneuvers are effective in about 80% of patients.

Branham sign (bran′ăm) [Henry H. Branham, 19th-cent. U.S. surgeon] In a patient with an arteriovenous fistula, the slowing of the heart rate that occurs when the fistula is compressed.

brash (brăsh) A burning sensation in the stomach sometimes accompanied by belching of sour fluid. SYN: *heartburn; pyrosis.*

> **water b.** Reflex salivary hypersecretion in response to peptic esophagitis.

brass chills SEE: *metal fume fever.*

brassica (brăs′ĭ-kă) [L. "cabbage"] The family of vegetables that includes broccoli, Brussels sprouts, cabbage, and cauliflower.

Braxton Hicks contractions (brăk′stŏn-hĭks″) [John Braxton Hicks, Brit. gynecologist, 1823–1897] False labor. These contractions are not true labor pains because they do not cause dilation and effacement of the cervix, but are often interpreted as such. SYN: *Hicks sign.*

Brazelton Neonatal Assessment Scale (brā′zĕl-tŏn″) [Thomas Berry Brazelton, U.S. pediatrician, b. 1918] A scale for evaluating the behavior and responses of the newborn infant. It is based on four dimensions: interaction with the environment; motor processes, including motor responses, general activity level, and reflexes; control of physiological state as determined by reaction to a distinct stimulus such as a rattle, bell, light, or a pinprick; and response to stress as judged by tremulousness, startle reaction, and change in skin coloration. The test has been used as late as 1 week after birth to demonstrate alteration in an infant's behavior due to drugs administered to the mother while the infant was in utero.

BRBPR *bright red blood per rectum.* SEE: *hematochezia.*

BRCA1 gene SEE: under *gene.*

BRCA2 gene SEE: under *gene.*

break (brāk) **1.** In orthopedics, a fracture. **2.** To interrupt the continuity in a tissue or electric circuit or the channel of flow or communication.

breakaway (brāk′ă-wā″) In orthodontics, a device to apply tension or force to a facebow.

breakpoint (brāk′poynt″) Cutoff level.

breakthrough disease (brāk′throo″) Any disease that occurs in spite of adequate vaccination to prevent it, (e.g., "breakthrough varicella" or "breakthrough influenza").

breakthrough pain SEE: under *pain.*

breast (brest) **1.** The upper anterior aspect of the chest. **2.** The mammary gland, a compound alveolar gland consisting of 15 to 20 lobes of glandular tissue separated from each other by interlobular septa. Each lobe is drained by a lactiferous duct that opens onto the tip of the nipple. The mammary gland secretes milk used for nourishment of the infant. For purposes of description, the female breast is divided into four quadrants: upper inner (the top medial quarter), lower inner (the bottom medial quarter), upper outer (the top lateral quarter), and the lower outer (the bottom lateral quarter). The tail of the breast extends up and away from the upper outer quadrant. SEE: illus.; *mammary gland; milk.*

DEVELOPMENT: During puberty, estrogens from the ovary stimulate growth and development of the duct system. During pregnancy, progesterone secreted by the corpus luteum and placenta acts synergistically with estro-

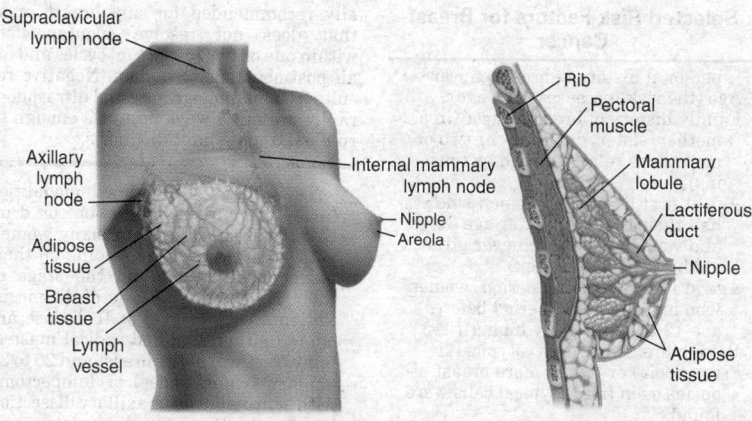

BREAST

Structure of mammary glands

gens to bring the alveoli to complete development. After parturition, prolactin in conjunction with adrenal steroids initiates lactation, and oxytocin from the posterior pituitary induces ejection of milk. Sucking or milking reflexly stimulates both milk secretion and discharge of milk.

CHANGES IN PREGNANCY: During the first 6 to 12 weeks, there is fullness and tenderness, erectile tissue develops in the nipples, nodules are felt, pigment is deposited around the nipple (primary areola) (in blondes the areolae and nipples become darker pink; in brunettes they become dark brown and sometimes even black), and a few drops of fluid may be squeezed out. During the next 16 to 20 weeks, the secondary areola shows small whitish spots in pigmentation due to hypertrophy of the sebaceous glands (glands of Montgomery).

caked b. An accumulation of milk in the secretory ducts of the breast after delivery, causing a large area to become inflamed, hard, and tender.

chicken b. A deformity in which the sternum projects anteriorly; caused by rickets or obstructed respiration in childhood. SYN: *pigeon b.*

pigeon b. Chicken breast.

breast cancer A malignant neoplasm (usually an adenocarcinoma) of the breast; the most common malignancy of American women and the leading cause of death in American women aged 40 to 55. In 2011 the American Cancer Society estimated that 230,000 women would be newly diagnosed with invasive breast cancer and that more than 39,000 women would die of the disease. Breast cancer usually presents as a dominant mass in one breast, although the malignancy may first become evident when nipple discharge, nipple retraction, skin dimpling, or asymmetrical swelling of the breast occurs. In most cases breast cancers are first identified by women performing breast self-examination. A smaller but considerable number are detected by professional examination or mammography. About 1000 men are diagnosed with breast cancer annually. Breast cancer has several pathological variants. Carcinoma in situ, the most localized form of the disease, represents a preinvasive stage confined to a duct or lobule. Other presentations include lobular carcinoma, infiltrating ductal carcinoma, inflammatory carcinoma, and Paget disease of the nipple.

ETIOLOGY: There are several known risk factors for breast cancer. SEE: table.

SYMPTOMS: A dominant breast mass; bloody, brown, or serous discharge from a nipple; and/or breast nodularity or lumpiness are the most common symptoms of breast cancer.

DIAGNOSIS: Regular breast self-examination, professional breast examination, and mammography are the keys to screening for breast cancer. All these screenings identify many more benign lesions than malignant ones, esp. in younger patients, and none of these techniques can definitively exclude breast cancer. Many mammographically detected lesions are benign, and about 15% of the time mammography will fail to detect lesions that are truly malignant. Digital mammography provides significantly better detection in women with dense breasts, those under age 50, and those who are premenopausal or perimenopausal. If a suspicious mass is identified, fine needle aspiration, core biopsy, or excisional biopsy must be used to ob-

Selected Risk Factors for Breast Cancer

A personal history of breast cancer

Age (the risk increases with age)

Family history of breast cancer (in a mother, sister, daughter, or two or more close relatives such as cousins)

Age at first live birth (women who had their first child after age 30 and women who have never given birth are at higher risk)

Age at first menstrual period (women who had their first period before age 12 are at slightly higher risk)

Benign breast changes (atypical hyperplasia) or two or more breast biopsies even if no atypical cells were found

Race (white women are more likely to develop breast cancer than black women, but blacks are more likely than whites to die of it; Hispanic and Asian women have a lower risk of developing the disease)

Genetics: Several genes (including BRCA1 and BRCA2, among others) increase a woman's chance of developing breast cancer

Oral contraceptive pills and hormone replacement therapy may both slightly increase the risk of a woman's developing breast cancer

Obesity increases the risk of a woman's developing breast cancer

Alcohol use: The greater the alcohol intake of a woman, the greater the risk of breast cancer

SOURCE: Adapted from the National Cancer Institute and other sources.

tain tissue for analysis. Ultrasonography can be used before biopsy to identify solid masses and cysts. Solid breast masses have a much greater chance of being malignant than cysts. Other imaging techniques used to help identify breast cancers include magnetic resonance imaging, positron emission tomography, and ductal imaging. SEE: table. SEE: *breast self-examination; double reading; mammography.*

STAGING: The size of tumors and their possible metastasis to the chest wall, skin, axillae, or distant sites all determine the stage of breast cancer. Lymphatic mapping during cancer surgery can be used to find metastases to sentinel lymph nodes and guide therapies. Staging provides important information about the need for particular forms of therapy and the prognosis. SEE: illus.

⚠️ A biopsy (obtained by fine needle aspiration, with a stereotactic core needle, or by surgical lumpectomy) is usu-

ally recommended for any breast mass that does not resolve spontaneously within one or two menstrual cycles and for all postmenopausal women. Negative results from mammography and ultrasonography are not always accurate enough to rule out a malignant diagnosis.

TREATMENT: Combined modalities (including surgery, radiation, or drug therapies) are offered to many women with breast cancer, depending on their menopausal status and the stage of their disease at the time of diagnosis. Patients with stage I or II disease are offered either modified radical mastectomy (removal of the breast and 20 to 30 axillary lymph nodes) or lumpectomy with sentinal node or axillary dissection (as required) and radiotherapy, provided they have no contraindications to either of these choices. A variety of radiotherapy options are available, depending upon the individual patient's cancer. In premenopausal women with tumors larger than a centimeter, adjuvant chemotherapy prolongs survival, probably by eliminating microscopic metastases. Chemotherapeutic regimens commonly used include CMF (cyclophosphamide, methotrexate, and fluorouracil), CAF (cyclophosphamide, doxorubicin [Adriamycin], and fluorouracil), AC (doxorubicin [Adriamycin] and cyclophosphamide), doxorubicin (Adriamycin) followed by CMF, or FEC (fluorouracil, epirubicin, and cyclophosphamide). All of these agents are given several times in cycles of treatment. These same regimens are offered to vigorous postmenopausal women whose cancer has spread to axillary lymph nodes. Hormonal therapies like tamoxifen or raloxifene (two estrogen-receptor blockers) are also beneficial in patients with estrogen-receptor–positive tu-

Common and Experimental Techniques used in Breast Imaging

Mammography: Computed tomographic laser mammography; digital mammography

Ductography

Elastography

Electrical impedance imaging (T-scan)

Magnetic resonance imaging (MRI)

Microwave imaging

Nuclear scanning

Optoacoustic tomography

Scintimammography (molecular breast imaging)

Thermography

Tomosynthesis

Ultrasonography

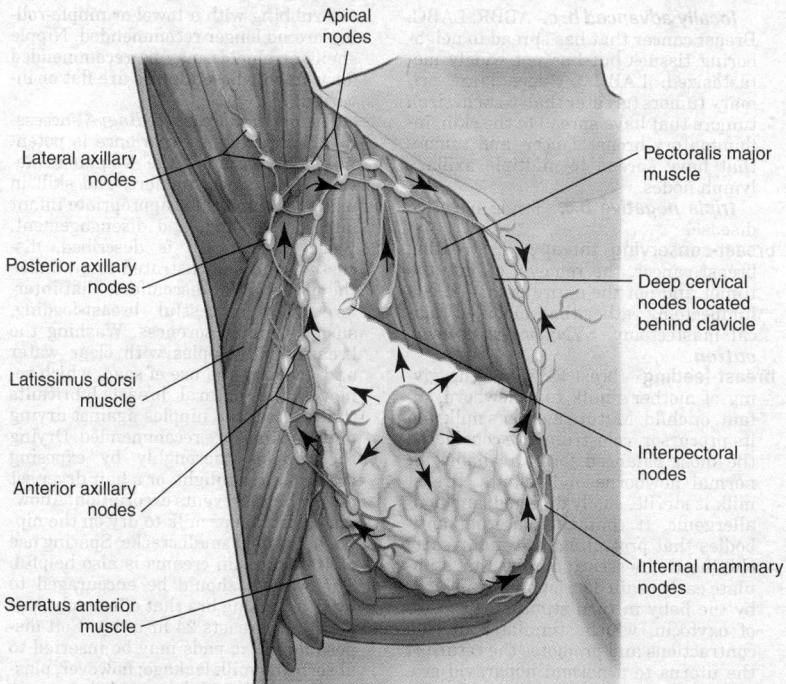

Apical
nodes

Lateral axillary
nodes

Posterior axillary
nodes

Latissimus dorsi
muscle

Anterior axillary
nodes

Serratus anterior
muscle

Pectoralis major
muscle

Deep cervical
nodes located
behind clavicle

Interpectoral
nodes

Internal mammary
nodes

BREAST CANCER

Possible paths of lymphatic spread

mors. Aromatase inhibitors (such as letrozole), and monoclonal antibodies (such as trastuzumab) may be prescribed to selected patients. After breast surgery, some women choose to have cosmetic restoration of the breast, either with saline- or silicone-filled implants or with tissue reconstructions made from the abdominal muscles. If breast cancer recurs after treatment, very high-dose chemotherapies are prescribed and peripheral stem cell transplantation is occasionally considered, but only in research settings. Bone metastases may be treated with monthly dosing of intravenous zoledronic acid (Zometa). SEE: *ductal carcinoma in situ of breast*.

PATIENT CARE: The patient's feelings and level of knowledge about her disease are determined. She is encouraged to express fears and concerns, and her family, supporters, or health care professionals stay with her during periods of anxiety or anguish. If surgery is planned, the procedure, postoperative care, and expected outcomes are explained.

While undergoing chemotherapy, the patient is monitored for adverse reactions (such as nausea, vomiting, ano-

rexia, stomatitis, gastrointestinal ulceration, anemia, leukopenia, thrombocytopenia, and bleeding), so that they can be managed early. Weight and nutrition status are evaluated. Skin is inspected for redness, irritation, or breakdown if radiation therapy is prescribed, and aloe or a prescribed cream is applied. Bisphosphate drugs (such as alendronate or zolendronic acid) are administered to prevent or treat bone metastases or hypercalcemia, but their use may be associated with osteonecrosis of the jaw.

Comfort measures are used to promote relaxation and rest and to relieve anxiety. If immobility develops late in the disease, careful repositioning, excellent skin care, respiratory toilet, and low-pressure mattresses are used to prevent complications, e.g., skin breakdown, respiratory problems, pathological fractures. The patient's and family's coping abilities are evaluated, and referral for counseling and support services may be necessary. End-stage disease patients benefit from hospice care. Women judged to be at highrisk for breast cancer may have tamoxifen or ralozifene prescribed as preventative therapy.

locally advanced b. c. ABBR: LABC. Breast cancer that has spread to neighboring tissues but has not widely metastasized. LABC includes large primary tumors (greater than 5 cm in size), tumors that have spread to the skin, inflammatory breast cancer, and tumors that have spread to multiple axillary lymph nodes.

triple negative b.c. Triple negative disease.

breast-conserving therapy In treating breast cancer, the removal of only the tumor and not the entire breast. It is a lumpectomy rather than modified radical mastectomy. SYN: *breast conservation*.

breast-feeding (brest′fēd″ing) The giving of mother's milk to a newborn, infant, or child. Mature mother's milk and its precursor, colostrum, are considered the most balanced foods available for normal newborns and infants. Breast milk is sterile, easily digested, and non-allergenic. It contains maternal antibodies that protect against many early childhood illnesses and lipids that stimulate early brain development. Suckling by the baby in turn stimulates release of oxytocin, which stimulates uterine contractions and promotes the return of the uterus to a normal nongravid size and state. Breast-feeding may engender or strengthen early bonding. The World Health Organization and the American Academy of Pediatrics (AAP) encourage health care professionals to promote, protect, and support breast-feeding as the exclusive nourishment for the first 6 months of life, followed by gradual supplementation with iron-rich foods for the next 6 months, with continuation of breast-feeding for as long as the mother and child desire. When breast-feeding must be interrupted for even a short time, the breasts should be pumped every 3 hr for 10 to 15 min to preserve lactation, and the colostrum or milk fed to the infant unless contraindicated. Exclusive breast-feeding for 6 months helps prevent infant ear infections, diarrhea, and other GI problems, and respiratory illness such as asthma and pneumonia. It also may reduce excessive childhood weight gain and obesity and reduce the mother's risk for breast and ovarian cancer.

PATIENT CARE: *Prenatal preparations*: During the last trimester of pregnancy, techniques that increase the potential for successful breast-feeding are discussed with women who have selected that infant-feeding option. Very little preparation is required for the breast and nipples. During pregnancy, the nipple and aerola thicken, and glands on the aerola, which contain a lubricant to keep the nipple from drying, enlarge. Toughening nipples by vigorous rubbing with a towel or nipple-rolling are no longer recommended. Nipple shells or shields may be recommended for women whose nipples are flat or inverted.

Postpartum breast-feeding: A successful breast-feeding experience is potentiated by assisting the woman to develop confidence, comfort, and skill in using techniques for appropriate infant latch-on, feeding, and disengagement. Basic breast care is described, discussed, and demonstrated to minimize the potential for discomforts that interfere with successful breast-feeding, such as nipple soreness. Washing the breasts and nipples with clear water and avoiding the use of soap, which removes the natural breast lubricants that protect the nipples against drying and cracking, are recommended. Drying the nipples thoroughly by exposing them to air, sunlight, or a hair dryer set on low heat prevents excoriation. Allowing colostrum or milk to dry on the nipple helps heal small cracks. Sparing use of 100% lanolin creams is also helpful. The woman should be encouraged to wear a nursing bra that effectively supports her breasts 24 hr a day. Soft disposable fabric pads may be inserted to absorb any milk leakage; however, plastic liners should be avoided because they retain moisture and body heat, which softens and macerates the nipple. Skin-to-skin contact is encouraged and is associated with longer periods of breast-feeding, better temperature regulation, less crying, enhanced maternal responsiveness, and skill competence.

Positioning: Positioning is a fundamental component of successful breast-feeding and the greatest deterrent to sore nipples. Both mother and infant should be positioned for comfort and convenience of nursing. Mother and infant should face each other in the chest-to-chest position, and the mother's nipple should be at the level of the infant's nose. Positions include cross cradle, football hold, and side-lying.

Latching-on: To elicit nipple erection and to facilitate latch-on, the mother cups her hand under her breast and either places her thumb (C-hold) or her index finger (scissors-hold) above the areola with the other three fingers below the areola, supporting the weight of the breast. The infant should grasp the whole nipple with its gums on the areola. Suckling then compresses the milk ducts and effectively ejects milk. Preventing the infant from suckling only on the end of the nipple reduces potential for nipple soreness, erosion, and cracking.

Feeding: Infants should be allowed to feed until they exhibit signs of satisfaction. Feeding from a single breast is allowable as long as the infant nurses approximately every 2 hr and feeds until satisfied; this encourages the intake of the higher-calorie, high-fat hind milk.

Disengaging: The mother should gently insert her fingers between the infant's gums to break the suction and withdraw the breast from the baby's mouth.

Engorgement: Feeding the newborn on demand usually prevents the development of engorgement. Should it occur, the mother either may apply warm wet compresses or stand beneath a shower of warm water to stimulate the let-down reflex and initiate milk flow. The mother also should be taught how to manually express enough milk to relieve the pressure and soften the areola to encourage latch-on when feeding.

Nipple soreness: Some discomfort is common during the first few breastfeeding days. The mother's first actions should be to check the infant's feeding position and grasp of the nipple. Altering her position for feeding also alters the stress points on the nipple as the infant suckles and enhances breast emptying. If soreness is related to the newborn's vigorous sucking because of hunger, the mother may elect to nurse more frequently. The mother is encouraged to continue with breast-feeding; however, if the suggested measures prove ineffective and discomfort persists throughout the feeding interval or does not subside by the end of the first postpartum week, the mother should be assisted to seek consultation with a lactation specialist.

Breast reduction: Successful breastfeeding after breast reduction is decreased due to a greater risk of insufficient milk supply, esp. if the nerves to the nipple have been compromised. Some milk ducts are lost, which decreases the potential to produce milk. It is important to support a woman's decision to breast-feed and assist her with supplemental systems if needed.

Breast augmentation: There is increased success with breast-feeding with augmentation as long as the nipple has not been surgically altered. Compression of glandular tissue can increase the risk of decreased milk supply. Support and use of supplemental systems, if needed, are helpful.

⚠️ Women who are infected with the human immunodeficiency virus (HIV) may transmit it to their children by breast-feeding.

In most instances, however, maternal illness does not contraindicate breastfeeding, or does so only for a short time until treatment is initiated. If maternal surgery is anticipated, the mother can be encouraged to pump and store milk in advance, then assisted to pump or breast-feed directly as soon as possible after surgery. Many medications required by mothers are safe for their infants either because drug concentration in breast milk will be insignificant or because the infant's gut will absorb only a minimal amount of the drug. Resources containing information on breast-feeding and breast-feeding/medications include: the AAP's "Transfer of Drugs & Other Chemicals into Human Milk" (170 usually compatible drugs, effects on milk production, minor adverse effects on mother or infant, drugs requiring temporary cessation of breast-feeding, "caution" drugs) (http://aappolicy .aappublications.org/cgi/content/full/ pesiatrics:108/3/776); International Lactation Consultant Association (www .ilca.org); National Center for Chronic Disease Prevention and Health Promotion: Breastfeeding (www.cdc.gov/breast-feeding); La Leche League International (www.llli.org).

Health care professionals should carefully examine and question policies that limit women's rights, abilities, or opportunities to breast-feed.

breastfeeding, effective The state in which the mother-infant exhibit appropriate proficiency and satisfaction with breastfeeding. In addition to maternal satisfaction and infant contentment, expected outcomes include successful latch-on and appropriate weight gain. Infant weight gain proceeds within expected parameters. SEE: *Nursing Diagnoses Appendix.*

breastfeeding, ineffective The state in which a mother, infant, or child experiences dissatisfaction or difficulty with breastfeeding process. SEE: *Nursing Diagnoses Appendix.*

breastfeeding, interrupted A break in the continuity of the breastfeeding process as a result of inability or inadvisability to put a baby to breast for feeding. SEE: *Nursing Diagnoses Appendix.*

breast implant SEE: under *implant.*

breast self-examination ABBR: BSE. A technique that enables a woman to detect changes in her breasts. The accompanying illustration explains the specific steps to be followed. The examination should be done each month soon after the menstrual period ends because normal physiological changes that may confuse results occur in the premenstrual period. SEE: illus.; *mammography.*

breath (breth) [Old English*brǣth,* odor, exhalation] The air inhaled and exhaled in respiration.

   bad b. Halitosis.

   liver b. The mousy odor of the breath characteristic of those with severe liver disease. SEE: *hepatic coma.*

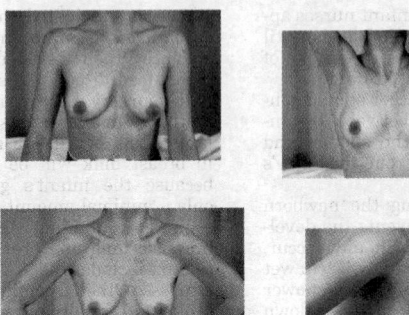

Inspection

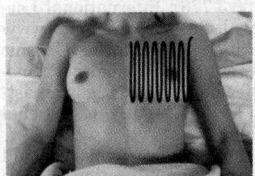 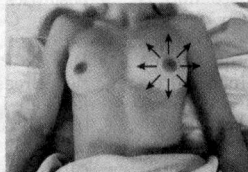 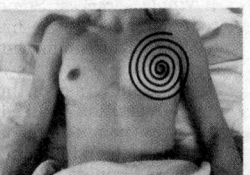

BREAST SELF-EXAMINATION

Palpation

uremic b. The fishy, ammoniacal breath odor characteristic of those with uremia.

breathability (brĕth″ă-bil′ĭt-ē) The ability of a fabric or woven coating to allow moisture and gases to travel through its pores. It is an important feature in the design of clothing liners, transdermal medication patches, and wound coverings.

breath actuation (ăk″chŭ-ā′shŭn) The release by inspiration of a substance to a patient. Breath-actuated inhalers are used in respiratory medicine to increase the probability that a patient will deliver a dose of inhaled medication to the lungs when the airway is open.

breath-holding (brĕth-hōl′dĭng) The voluntary or involuntary stopping of breathing may be seen in children who use this to attempt to control the behavior of their parents.

breathing (brĕth′ing) The act of inhaling and exhaling air. SEE: *chest; respiration.*

    apneustic b. An abnormal breathing pattern marked by prolonged inspiration followed by an inspiratory pause. This is usually associated with brainstem injuries.

    assisted b. Any technique that improves respiration. Such breathing includes the provision of supplemental oxygen, bag-valve-mask ventilation, noninvasive ventilation, mechanical ventilation, and mouth-to-mouth ventilation.

    asthmatic b. Harsh breathing with prolonged wheezing heard throughout expiration.

    ataxic b. An irregular, uncoordinated breathing pattern common in infants.

    belly b. Abdominal **respiration**.

    Biot b. SEE: *Biot breathing.*

    bronchial b. Bronchial sounds.

    Cheyne-Stokes b. SEE: *Cheyne-Stokes respiration.*

    continuous positive-pressure b. A method of mechanically assisted pulmonary inflation. A device administers air or oxygen to the lungs under a continuous pressure that is always greater than zero. SYN: *continuous positive-pressure ventilation.*

    diaphragmatic b. Abdominodiaphragmatic **b.**

    frog b. A respiratory pattern in which the air in the mouth and pharynx is forced into the lungs by gulping and swallowing it. This may be observed in patients whose respiratory muscles are weak or paralyzed.

    glossopharyngeal b. A technique of breathing in which the patient with inspiratory muscle weakness increases the volume of air breathed in by taking several gulps of air, closing the mouth, and forcing air into the lungs.

inspiratory resistive b. Inspiration with an added workload to increase the strength and endurance of the inspiratory muscles.

intermittent positive-pressure b. ABBR: IPPB. A mechanical method for assisting pulmonary ventilation with a device that administers air or oxygen for the inflation of the lungs under positive pressure. Exhalation is usually passive. SYN: *intermittent positive-pressure ventilation.*

Kussmaul b. SEE: under *Kussmaul, Adolph.*

mouth b. Inhaling and exhaling through the oral cavity instead of the nose. It occurs in people who have abnormal facial bone structure, as well as in individuals with nasal or sinus congestion. It has been associated with and may cause developmental abnormalities of the facial structure, esp. elongation of the facial bones.

periodic b. An irregular respiratory pattern marked by alternating periods of rapid and slow respirations and by apneic periods lasting 15 sec or less. It is a commonly observed breathing pattern in neonates and infants and in some individuals having sleep apnea.

pursed-lip b. An expiratory maneuver in which the patient exhales through puckered lips to slow expiratory flow and to create slight back pressure. This action may prevent premature closure of intrapulmonary airways, esp. in the patient with chronic obstructive lung disease.

shallow b. Breathing in which the volume of inspired and expired air is diminished (e.g., 200 ml per breath in adults). It is common in elderly patients, patients with rib or pleural pain, or restrictive lung diseases.

yogic b. Pranayama.

breathing pattern, ineffective Inspiration and/or expiration that does not provide adequate ventilation. SEE: *Nursing Diagnoses Appendix.*

breathlessness (brĕth'lĕs-nĕs") Dyspnea.

breath test A test that to detect a specific substance in the breath to help explain metabolic changes. Breath tests are used to detect evidence of bacterial overgrowth in the intestines, to investigate the causes of malabsorption, to detect *Helicobacter pylori* in the stomach, and to estimate alcohol in the tissues, due to micro-organisms in the patient. SYN: *sniff test* (2).

carbon-urea b.t. A diagnostic test in which the patient ingests 13C-labeled or 14C-labeled urea, which binds to and can be measured in exhaled carbon dioxide. It is used to diagnose infection with *Helicobacter pylori*, a common cause of peptic ulcer. SEE: *Helicobacter pylori; peptic ulcer.*

breath test for lactase deficiency The measurement of hydrogen in the breath after ingestion of a standard amount (50 g) of lactase. SEE: *lactase deficiency syndrome.*

breath work, breathwork The conscious control of the rate, rhythm, and depth of breathing, a technique used in relaxation and meditative practices in order to reduce psychological stress, control anxiety and emotion, and focus thoughts.

breech (brēch) [AS. *brec,* buttocks] The nates, or buttocks.

bregma (brĕg'mă) *pl.* **bregmata** [Gr., front of head] The point on the skull where the coronal and sagittal sutures join. The anterior fontanel in the fetus and young infant. **bregmatic** (-măt'ĭk), *adj.*

Brenner tumor (bren'ĕr) [Fritz Brenner, Ger. pathologist, 1877–1969] A rare, usually benign tumor of the ovary composed of fibrous and epithelial elements.

Breuer-Hering reflex Hering-Breuer reflex.

brevetoxin (brev'ĕ-tok"sin) [(*Karenia*) *brevis* + *toxin*] A potent, lipid-soluble, neurotoxic compound produced by marine dinoflagellates, such as *Karenia brevis,* an organism initially identified in "red tides" in coastal Florida.

brevicollis (brĕv'ĭ-kŏl'ĭs) [L. *brevis,* short, + *collum,* neck] Shortness of the neck.

bridge (brij) **1.** The upper part of the external nose formed by the junction of the nasal bones. **2.** The curved part of a pair of eyeglasses that rests on the bridge of the nose. **3.** A narrow band of tissue. **4.** A cast dental restoration that replaces missing teeth. The restoration is usually made of gold alloy, with or without a porcelain exterior, and is attached to adjacent or abutment teeth for support. **4.** The use of a short-acting drug when treatment with a longer-acting drug must be temporarily interrupted or during the initiation of the long-acting drug before it reaches full therapeutic effectiveness.

PATIENT CARE: Bridging is commonly used for perioperative anticoagulation. In patients who have atrial fibrillation or a history of blood clotting, warfarin, which has a relatively long half-life, is withheld several days before surgery. The bridge consists of the administration of low-molecular-weight heparins (LMWHs), which have a shorter half-life, until about 12 hr before the procedure in order to prevent clotting. At a safe time after the operation, LMWHs are reinstituted until warfarin reaches therapeutic levels, e.g., an international normalized ratio of 2 or more. The duration of bridging therapy varies but is typically between 2 days and 1 week.

5. An exercise for activating the abdominal and hip extensor muscles. The patient lies on his back with knees flexed and feet flat against a horizontal surface, such as a floor, bed, or plinth (treatment table). The patient then lifts his hips while his feet, shoulders, and head maintain contact with the surface. Bridging is often recommended as part of preprosthetic training for patients with transtibial or transfemoral lower extremity amputations. SEE: illus.

BRIDGING

⚠ Bridging should always be performed while the prosthesis is removed.

> ***disulfide b.*** Disulfide **bond**.
bridgework (brĭj'wŏrk) A partial denture held in place by attachments other than clasps.
> ***fixed b.*** A cast restoration or bridge cemented to natural teeth.
> ***removable b.*** Partial denture.
bridle (brī'dl) In anatomy, a frenum.
brief (brēf) [Fr. *bref* fr L. *brevis,* short, brief, a catalogue] **1.** A condensed legal argument in legal format and style. **2.** A written or spoken summary of an important or complex topic; an abstract. **3.** To make a written or spoken summary of. **4.** To conduct a short session of instruction or preparation for a person, crew, or staff on how to accomplish an upcoming operation. SEE: *debrief.*
briefing (brēf'ing) A short session of instruction or preparation for a person, crew, or staff on how to accomplish an upcoming operation.
Bright disease (brīts) [Richard Bright, Brit. physician, 1789–1858] A vague and obsolete term for kidney disease. It usually refers to nonsuppurative inflammatory or degenerative kidney disease marked by proteinuria and hematuria and sometimes by edema, hypertension, and nitrogen retention. SEE: *nephritis.*
Bright Futures A set of health supervision guidelines and recommendations for the promotion of health and the prevention of disease in infants, toddlers, children, and adolescents.
bright light therapy Treatment of sleep and/or mood disorders by exposure to bright fluorescent lights (typically

10,000 lux) for at least 2 hours a day. Bright light therapy has been used as an alternative to drug therapy for seasonal affective disorder and insomnia (e.g., in shift workers).
brightness (brīt'nĕs) **1.** The perceived brilliance of an image, e.g., its clarity, how light it is (rather than how dark it looks), and the intensity of the light that it emits. **2.** In imaging technology, e.g., radiology, the luminous intensity, measured in candelas, of a display monitor's visible emissions. Such brightness is solely a function of the monitor and is not related to the magnitude of exposure of the image receptor.
brightness gain SEE: under *gain.*
brim 1. The upper edge of a bowl-shaped object or region. **2.** An edge or margin.
> ***pelvic b.*** The bony upper edge of the true (lesser) pelvis, which is the rim of the pelvic inlet (superior pelvic aperture). The pelvic brim comprises the pubic crest and pectineal line of each pubis, the arcuate line of each ilium, the inner edge of the alae of the sacrum, and the sacral promontory. The pelvic brim is oval shaped in females and heart shaped in males. SYN: ***linea*** *terminalis* *(1); pelvic* ***opening.***
Briquet syndrome (brĭ-kā') [Paul Briquet, Fr. physician, 1796–1881] **1.** A personality disorder in which alcoholism and somatization disorder occur. **2.** Somatization disorder. **3.** An old term for hysterical personality disorder.
Brissaud, Édouard (brē-sō') Fr. physician and pathologist, 1852–1909.
> ***B. reflex*** Contraction of the tensor fasciae latae muscle when the sole of the foot is stroked or tickled. It is a component of the extensor plantar response.
British antilewisite ABBR: BAL. Trade name for dimercaprol, a compound used as an antidote in poisoning due to heavy metals such as arsenic, gold, and mercury.
British Pharmacopoeia ABBR: B.P. The standard reference on drugs and their preparations used in Great Britain.
British thermal unit ABBR: BTU. The amount of heat necessary to raise the temperature of 1 lb of water from 39°F to 40°F.
brittle diabetes SEE: under *diabetes.*
broach (brōch) [ME. *broche,* pointed rod] **1.** A dental device used to remove the arteries, veins, lymph vessels, and nerves in the pulp of a tooth. **2.** A technique used for preparing the intramedullary canal of a bone by using a cutting device. This is done in preparation for a prosthetic replacement.
Broadbent sign (brod'bent″) [Sir William Henry Broadbent, Brit. physician, 1835–1907] A visible retraction of the left side and back in the region of the 11th and 12th ribs synchronous with

the cardiac systole in adhesive pericarditis.

Broca, Pierre-Paul (brō-ka′, brō′kǎ) Fr. surgeon and anthropologist, 1824–1880.

   B. aphasia Motor **aphasia**.

   B. area The area of the left hemisphere of the brain at the posterior end of the inferior frontal gyrus. It contains the motor speech area and controls movements of tongue, lips, and vocal cords. Loss of speech may follow any stroke affecting this area. SYN: *Broca center; Broca convolution; motor speech area; speech center*. SEE: *motor aphasia*.

   B. center Broca area.

   diagonal band of B. Diagonal **band**.

Brodie, Sir Benjamin Collins (brō′dē) Brit. surgeon, 1783–1862.

   B. abscess A localized infection of bone, esp. of one of the long bones of the lower extremities. SYN: *bone abscess*.

   B. knee Osteomyelitis of the knee.

brodifacoum A long-acting warfarin-like anticoagulant used to kill mice and other rodents.

Brodmann areas (brōd′man″) [Korbinian Brodmann, Ger. neurologist, 1868–1918] The division of the cerebral cortex into 47 areas. This was originally done on the basis of cytoarchitectural characteristics, but the areas are now classified according to their functions.

broken-heart syndrome SEE: *takotsubo cardiomyopathy*.

brom-, bromo- [Gr. *brōmos,* stench] Prefixes indicating the *presence of bromine*.

bromelain (brō′mĕ-lān) A group of protein-digesting enzymes derived from pineapples. Its applications include tenderizing meat.

bromide (brō′mīd) [Gr. *bromos,* stench] A binary compound of bromine combined with an element or a radical. It is a central nervous system depressant, and overdosage can cause serious mental disturbance.

bromide poisoning SEE: under *poisoning*.

bromidrosiphobia (brō″mĭ-drō-sĭ-fō′bē-ǎ) [″ + *hidros,* sweat, + *phobos,* fear] An abnormal fear of personal odors, accompanied by hallucinations.

bromidrosis, bromhidrosis (brō″mĭ-drō′sĭs) Sweat that is fetid or offensive due to bacterial decomposition. It occurs mostly on the feet, in the groin, and under the arms.

   PATIENT CARE: The axillae, groin, and feet should be cleansed daily with soap and water, rinsing well and drying thoroughly. Deodorant preparations should be used; and clothing and shoes changed, aired, and cleaned frequently. SYN: *kakidrosis*.

bromine (brō′mēn) [*brom-* + *-ine*] SYMB: Br. A gaseous chemical element, a halogen, in group 17 of the periodic table, atomic weight (mass) 79.904, atomic number 35. It is obtained from natural brines from wells and sea water; its compounds are used in medicine and photography. SEE: *bromide*.

bromism (brō′mĭzm) [″ + *-ismos,* condition] Poisoning that results from prolonged use of bromides. SEE: *Poisons and Poisoning Appendix*.

bromobenzylcyanide A toxic gas used as a riot control agent.

bromocresol green (brō″mō-krē′sŏl) [″ + ″] A stain used in histologic and pathologic studies to stain cellular components with a pH of 3.8 to 5.4, and in microbiology as a culture medium for yeasts.

bromoderma (brō″mō-dĕr′mǎ) [″ + *derma,* skin] An acne-like eruption due to allergic sensitivity to bromides.

bromoiodism (brō″mō-ī′ō-dĭzm) [″ + *ioeides,* violet colored, + *-ismos,* condition] Poisoning from bromine and iodine or their compounds.

bromomenorrhea (brō″mō-mĕn-ō-rē′ǎ) [″ + *men,* month, + *rhoia,* flow] Menstrual discharge marked by an offensive odor.

bronchi (brong′kī″, brong′kē″) Plural of bronchus.

   foreign bodies in b. Any materials that are aspirated into the lower airways, such as beans, nuts, seeds, or coins. These items, which usually lodge in the right bronchus because of its anatomical relation to the trachea, may cause pneumonia, airway inflammation, abscess formation, or atelectasis.

   TREATMENT: They are typically removed with bronchoscopy.

bronchial (brŏng′kē-ǎl) Pert. to the bronchi or bronchioles.

bronchial blocker SEE: under *blocker*.

bronchial breath sounds SEE: *sound, bronchial*.

bronchial thermoplasty The reduction in the amount of smooth muscle mass in the airways when heat energy is applied to the airways bronchoscopically. The procedure uses heat energy generated with radiofrequency technology to ablate smooth muscle. It has been used as an experimental treatment for asthma.

bronchial tube One of the smaller divisions of the bronchi.

bronchial washing Irrigation of one or both bronchi to collect cells for cytologic study or to help cleanse the bronchi.

bronchiectasis (brong″kē-ek′tǎ-sĭs) [*broncho-* + *ectasis,*] Chronic dilation of a bronchus or bronchi, usually in the lower portions of the lung, caused by the damaging effects of a long-standing infection.

   SYMPTOMS: Chronic cough, foul-smelling, mucopurulent sputum production, dyspnea, and wheezing are common.

ETIOLOGY: The condition may be acquired or congenital and may occur in one or both lungs. Bronchiectasis has three forms (cylindrical, varicose, and saccular), which may occur individually or together. Acquired bronchiectasis usually occurs secondary to an obstruction or an infection such as bronchopneumonia, chronic bronchitis, tuberculosis, cystic fibrosis, or whooping cough. The incidence has decreased with antibiotic treatment of acute infections.

DIAGNOSIS: Radiography is used to assist in the diagnosis, either with chest x-rays, or computed tomography of the lung; the disease may be visualized and cultures taken during bronchoscopy.

TREATMENT: Therapy consists of oral or IV antibiotics for 7 to 10 days, pulmonary hygiene, and postural drainage. Resection of affected areas may be done in selected patients. Aerosols may be useful for bronchodilation if bronchospasm is present. SEE: *postural drainage.*

PATIENT CARE: The patient is assessed for the presence or increased severity of respiratory distress. Ventilatory rate, pattern, and effort are observed, breath sounds are auscultated, and sputum is inspected for changes in quantity, color, or viscosity. The respiratory therapist evaluates gas exchange by monitoring arterial blood gas values and administers oxygen according to protocol or as prescribed. The patient is observed for complications such as cor pulmonale. The patient should increase oral fluid intake and be shown how to use a humidifier or nebulizer to help thin inspissated secretions. The patient is also taught to breathe deeply and cough effectively. Chest physiotherapy is most effective and least disruptive if carried out in the morning, 1 or 2 hr before meals, and at bedtime. The patient is taught to remain in each prescribed position for at least 10 min; then percussion is performed, followed by two-stage coughing to remove secretions. The nurse or respiratory therapist suctions the oropharynx if the patient is unable to clear the airway and teaches the patient and family how to do this. The need for frequent oral hygiene to remove foul-smelling secretions and help prevent anorexia is explained. The patient is taught to dispose of secretions, to cleanse items contaminated by secretions, and to wash hands thoroughly to avoid spreading infection. Air pollutants and people with upper respiratory infections should be avoided. If the patient smokes, he may need referral to a smoking cessation program or nicotine patches . Pre-

scribed medications (antibiotics, bronchodilators, and expectorants) are given, and both patient and family are instructed in their use, action, and side effects. The patient is advised not to take over-the-counter drugs without the health care provider's approval and to have respiratory infections treated promptly. Supportive care is provided to help the patient adjust to the lifestyle changes that irreversible lung damage requires. Balanced, high-protein meals (in frequent, small amounts if necessary) aid tissue healing. If surgery is scheduled, the patient is prepared physically and emotionally. Preoperative and postoperative teaching and care are conducted, and the patient's status is monitored to prevent complications.

    capillary b. Bronchiolectasis.

    saccular b. Dilated bronchi of saccular or irregular shape. The proximal third to fourth branches of the bronchi are severely dilated and end blindly with extensive collapse.

    varicose b. Dilated bronchi that resemble varicose veins; irregular dilatation and constriction as seen in cystic fibrosis.

bronchiloquy (brŏng-kĭl′ō-kwē) [″ + L. *loqui,* to speak] Unusual vocal resonance over a bronchus surrounded by consolidated lung tissue.

bronchiocele (brŏng′kē-ō-sēl) [″ + *kele,* tumor, swelling] Circumscribed dilatation of a bronchus.

bronchiogenic (brŏng″kē-ō-jĕn′ĭk) [″ + *gennan,* to produce] Having origin in the bronchi.

bronchiole (brŏng′kē-ōl) *pl.* **bronchioles** [L. *bronchiolus,* air passage] One of the smaller subdivisions of the bronchial tubes. Bronchioles have no cartilage in their walls; they also have few glands in their mucosa.

    respiratory b. The last division of the bronchial tree. Respiratory bronchioles are branches of terminal bronchioles and continue to the alveolar ducts, which lead to the alveoli.

    terminal b. The next-to-last subdivision of a bronchiole, leading to the respiratory bronchioles.

bronchiolectasis (brong″kē-ō-lek′tă-sĭs) [*bronchiolo-* + *ectasis*] Dilatation of the bronchioles. SYN: *capillary bronchiectasis.*

bronchiolitis (brong″kē-ō-līt′ĭs) [*bronchiole* + *-itis*] Inflammation of the bronchioles, particularly as an acute process in children during the first 2 years of life, with peak incidence around 6 months of age. Most cases occur during the winter and early spring months.

ETIOLOGY: The respiratory syncytial virus (RSV) accounts for 50% of cases. Other viruses (parainfluenza, adenoviruses) and mycoplasma species make up the remaining cases. There is no evidence that bacteria cause the illness, or that antibiotics cure it.

SYMPTOMS: URI symptoms (runny nose, sneezing) appear first, quickly replaced by the hallmarks of the disease, respiratory distress, nasal flaring, retractions, tachypnea, cyanosis, and wheezing. The wheezing is what gives the disease its commonly used name, "baby asthma." Some infants, especially those a few months old, develop severe respiratory distress with hypoxia and gasping respirations, requiring hospitalization, oxygen, and assisted ventilation. Chest x-ray films show hyperinflation of the lungs with scattered areas of pneumonia and/or atelectasis.

TREATMENT: Infants with moderate or worse respiratory distress should be admitted to the hospital for observation, respiratory therapy, and oxygen. Whether bronchodilators such as nebulized albuterol have any value in the treatment is still debated, but they are often used. Ribavirin, a nebulized antiviral agent, is used in severe cases of bronchiolitis due to proven RSV infection in children under age 2.

PROGNOSIS: The case fatality rate is less than 1%, but a significant proportion of affected infants develop reactive airway disease (i.e., asthma) in later childhood.

PREVENTION: Preventive drugs have been developed for infants with bronchopulmonary dysplasia and other congenital cardiac or pulmonary diseases. These include palivizumab, a monoclonal antibody, and an RSV immune globulin.

PATIENT CARE: The infant requires close observation regarding the demands imposed by airway obstruction at the bronchiolar level. The infant is observed for gradually increasing respiratory distress, paroxysmal cough, dypsnea and irritability, as well as for tachypnea with flaring nostrils and intercostal and subcostal retractions, and shallow respiratory excursion.

The infant should be percussed for hyperresonance and scattered consolidation and auscultated for fine crackles, prolonged expiratory phase, and diminished breath sounds by the nurse, respiratory therapist, and physician. Audible or auscultatory wheezing may be present, as well as hyperinflation leading to increased A-P diameter and depressed diaphragm.

The parents are educated regarding the need for hospitalization, and treatments that will be employed are explained. The use of a mist tent and oxygen are discussed as well as assisted ventilation if this becomes necessary, and the parents are taught how to maintain contact with their infant. The parents also need to understand that tachypnea, weakness, and fatigue limit the infant's ability to obtain fluids in sufficient amounts to provide adequate hydration, thus intravenous fluids will be used until symptoms abate. Since parents expect medications to be prescribed for their infant, the nurse explains why various drugs (antibiotics, bronchodilators, corticosteroids, cough suppressants, and expectorants) are not employed and helps them to understand why sedatives are contraindicated although rest is an important part of therapy. Hospitalization of an infant is traumatic to parents and to the child depending on his or her age and severity of illness, so emotional support is provided to all throughout this crisis. The parents are helped to provide love, touch, and care for their infant, are instructed on how they can contact the nurse if they must be absent from the crib-side, and are assisted to understand and deal with behavioral regression that may occur.

b. **exudativa** Bronchiolitis with fibrinous exudation and grayish sputum; often associated with asthma.

b. **obliterans** Bronchiolitis in which the bronchioles and, occasionally, some of the smaller bronchi are partly or completely obliterated by nodular masses that contain granulation and fibrotic tissue.

bronchiolo-, bronchiol- [L. *bronchiolus,* fr. *bronchus,* air passage] Prefixes meaning *bronchiole.*

bronchiolus (brŏng-kē'ō-lŭs) *pl.* **bronchioli** [L.] Bronchiole.

bronchiospasm (brŏng'kē-ō-spăzm) [Gr. *bronchos,* windpipe, + *spasmos,* a convulsion] Bronchospasm.

bronchiostenosis (brŏng"kē-ō-stĕn-ō'sĭs) [" + *stenosis,* act of narrowing] Narrowing of the bronchial tubes.

bronchitis (brong-kīt'ĭs) [*broncho-* + *-it is*] Inflammation of the mucous membranes of the bronchial airways, caused by irritation or infection, or both, by pathogen. Bronchitis can be acute or chronic. SEE: *Nursing Diagnoses Appendix.*

ETIOLOGY: Bronchitis is caused by infectious agents such as viruses (particularly rhinoviruses, influenza A and B, parainfluenza, adenoviruses, and respiratory syncytial virus) or, less often, mycoplasma, Chlamydia, streptococcus, haemophilus, bramhamella, or staphylococcus. Infection is often indistinguishable from the common cold and is usually treated as such unless pneumonia is also present. Acute bronchial irritation (noninfectious bronchitis) may also be caused by exposure to various physical and chemical agents such as dust, fumes, or pollens. Allergies and pre-existing conditions such as asthma or chronic obstructive lung disease may be important cofactors.

PATIENT CARE: A history is obtained documenting tobacco use, including type, duration, and frequency. Calculation of pack-year history gives useful information. The health care provider assesses for other known respiratory irritants and allergens, exertional or worsening dyspnea, and productive cough. The patient is evaluated for changes in baseline respiratory function such as the use of accessory muscles in breathing, cyanosis, neck vein distention, pedal edema, prolonged expiratory time, tachypnea, and wheezes or crackles. The color (gray, white, or yellow) and characteristics of sputum are often documented (but may have little diagnostic significance). Tests such as arterial blood gas analysis, chest x-rays, oximetry, peak flow measurements, pulmonary function testing, and sputum Gram stain are occasionally employed. They are explained to the patient if they have been ordered. Prescribed antihistamines, bronchodilators, corticosteroids, decongestants, expectorants, and other medications are administered and the response is documented. Antibiotics are rarely indicated. Daily activities are interspersed with rest periods to conserve energy and to prevent fatigue. Patients with comorbid conditions should be hospitalized, in which case all general patient care concerns apply. Patients needing help to quit smoking are given counseling and support and referred to smoking cessation programs and for adjunctive drug therapy when prescribed.

acute b. **1.** An infection of the bronchi that may be indistinguishable from the common cold, often associated with repetitive coughing or sputum production. It is usually caused by viruses (particularly rhinoviruses, influenza A or B, parainfluenza, adenoviruses, or respiratory syncytial virus) or less often by *Mycoplasma pneumoniae,* Chlamydia, streptococci, *Haemophilus spp, Moraxella lacunata, Bordetella pertussis,* or staphylococci. **2.** Noninfectious inflammation of the bronchi caused by exposure to such irritants as dusts, fumes, or pollens.

PATIENT CARE: Patients are treated with bedrest, increased fluid intake, and antipyretics and analgesics for comfort. Antibiotics are rarely indicated (even if purulent sputum is present), unless bacterial infection is determined by culture or the symptoms continue for more than 10 days or there is an underlying disease such as congestive heart failure, chronic obstructive lung disease, or an immunodeficiency. Some prolonged cases of acute bronchitis will eventually prove to be caused by pertus-

sis, which will respond to erythromycin-based drugs. A chest x-ray examination to check for pneumonia is indicated when clinically suspected (the presence of severe respiratory symptoms, fever, tachycardia, hypoxia, or abnormal lung sounds).

asthmatic b. Bronchitis compounded by wheezing, caused by spasm of hyperreactive airways.

chronic b. Bronchitis marked by increased mucus secretion by the tracheobronchial tree. A productive cough must be present for at least 3 months in two consecutive years for the clinical diagnosis of chronic bronchitis to be made; also, other bronchopulmonary diseases (such as bronchiectasis, tuberculosis, tumor) must be excluded. SEE: *chronic obstructive pulmonary disease.*

ETIOLOGY: Chronic irritation by inhaled irritants (esp. cigarette smoking) and repeated infections are the primary risk factors. Chronic bronchitis is 4 to 10 times more common in heavy smokers; cigarette smoke interferes with the movement of cilia and inhibits the activity of white blood cells in the bronchi and alveoli. The predominant pathological changes are hypertrophy and hyperplasia of the mucus-secreting glands of the large and small airways. Some patients also have hyperreactive airways with widespread inflammation, narrowing and distortion. The changes in the respiratory epithelium may increase the risk of lung cancer.

DIAGNOSIS: Diagnostic studies may include chest x-ray, pulmonary function or peak flow testing, arterial blood gas studies, and ECG.

SYMPTOMS: Although the disease begins earlier, signs and symptoms may not appear until patients are 40 to 50 years old. A chronic cough producing copious amounts of sputum occurs early, and patients have frequent respiratory problems, often as a result of acute bronchopulmonary infections. Dyspnea is generally moderate and occurs relatively late in the disease process. Over time, right-sided heart failure (cor pulmonale) develops, marked by dependent edema, distended neck veins, pulmonary hypertension, and an enlarged right ventricle.

TREATMENT: Bronchodilators, inhaled steroids, and other drugs are used to prevent bronchospasm, improve airflow, and aid in the removal of secretions. Increased fluid intake (about 3 L/day), ultrasonic or mechanical nebulizer treatments, and chest physiotherapy may be needed to help thin, loosen and remove secretions. Acute respiratory infections are treated with empirical antibiotics such as azithromycin or trimethoprim/sulfamethoxazole, among others. Patients with underlying chronic bronchitis should receive pneumococcal and influenza vaccines. Other treatments are symptom based. Cessation of smoking is an important part of the overall treatment. Oxygen therapy is frequently needed.

PATIENT CARE: The initial history and assessment covers tobacco use, presence of other known respiratory irritants and allergens, degree of dyspnea, use of accessory muscles for breathing, presence of wheezes or rhonchi, color, sputum characteristics, nutritional status, and the effect of the disease on desired activity. Patients who smoke are referred to a smoking cessation program. The patient's lungs are auscultated before and after aerosol therapy to assess the effectiveness of bronchodilators.

The patient/family need extensive education and ongoing psychosocial support to cope with this chronic disease. Simple pathophysiology of the disease process is taught and used as a basis for explanations about diagnostic tests (such as pulmonary function tests) and all interventions to increase patient cooperation in the complex care regimen. Written materials usually augment verbal instruction. Patients and families are taught how to ensure and document adequate fluid intake (about 3 L/day unless otherwise restricted) to loosen secretions; to schedule small, frequent, high-protein meals to combat anorexia and weight loss; to use pursed-lip breathing and controlled cough to increase airflow and prevent fatigue from coughing spasms; to provide oral care frequently to minimize anorexia and the risk of infection; and to maintain muscle strength by continuing to exercise, but with a plan to pace activities to avoid fatigue. They also are taught to watch for and report signs of possible heart failure (such as dependent edema, or weight gain of more than 1 kg/day) or acute respiratory infection, e.g., increased dyspnea and changes in sputum characteristics such as color or amount. As the disease progresses, the family is assisted to make decisions about how routines may be modified to best meet individual needs.

The respiratory therapist delivers bronchodilators and other inhaled medications, e.g., steroids, as indicated by the presence of wheezing or evidence of retained airway secretions. Chest physical therapy may prove useful when the patient cannot easily cough the secretions out. Oxygen therapy is administered based on evidence of hypoxemia, inadequate perfusion of vital organs, or cor pulmonale.

chronic desquamating eosinophilic b. Asthma.

eosinophilic b. Bronchitis marked by chronic cough, eosinophils in sputum, and improvement in symptoms after the administration of corticosteroids. It is similar to asthma, but there is no wheezing or airway reactivity, and the airways are not infiltrated by mast cells.

plastic b. Bronchitis marked by violent cough and paroxysms of dyspnea in which casts of the bronchial tubes are expectorated.

putrid b. Chronic bronchitis with foul-smelling sputum.

vegetal b. Bronchitis resulting from lodging of foods of vegetable origin in the bronchus.

wheezy b. Bronchiolitis.

broncho-, bronch-, bronchi- [L. fr. Gr. *bronchos,* windpipe] Prefixes meaning *airway.*

bronchoblennorrhea (brŏng″kō-blĕn″ō-rē′ă) [″ + *blennos,* mucus, + *rhoia,* flow] Chronic bronchitis in which sputum is copious and thin.

bronchocele (brŏng′kō-sēl) [″ + *kele,* tumor, swelling] A localized dilatation of a bronchus.

bronchoconstriction (brŏng″kō-kŏn-strĭk′shŭn) [″ + L. *constringere,* to draw together] Constriction of the bronchial tubes.

bronchodilatation (brŏng″kō-dĭl-ă-tā′shŭn) [″ + L. *dilatare,* to open] Expansion or relaxation of the large airways.

bronchodilator (brŏng′kō-dī-lā′tor) A drug that expands the bronchi by relaxing bronchial muscle. There are three classes of bronchodilators: beta$_2$ adrenergic-receptor agonists, methylxanthines, and anticholinergic agents. The beta$_2$ adrenergic-receptor agonists produce the greatest bronchodilation in patients with bronchial asthma. The beta$_2$ adrenergic-receptor agonists are the best drugs for patients with mild, intermittent asthma and for acute attacks of reactive airway disease. SEE: table.

bronchoedema (brŏng″kō-ĕ-dē′mă) [″ + *oidema,* swelling] Edematous swelling of the mucosa of the bronchial tubes, reducing the size of air passageways and inducing dyspnea.

bronchogenic (brŏng-kō-jĕn′ĭk) [″ + *gennan,* to produce] Having origin in a bronchus.

broncholith (brŏng′kō-lĭth) [″ + *lithos,* stone] A calculus in a bronchus.

broncholithiasis (brŏng″kō-lĭth-ī′ă-sĭs) [″ + *lithos,* stone, + *-iasis,* state] Bronchial inflammation or obstruction caused by calculi in the bronchi.

bronchomotor (brŏng″kō-mō′tor) [″ + L. *motus,* moving] Causing dilation or constriction of the bronchi.

bronchomycosis (brŏng″kō-mī-kō′sĭs) [″ + *mykes,* fungus, + *osis,* condition] Any fungal infection of the bronchi or bronchial tubes, usually caused by fungi of the genus *Candida.*

Features of Bronchodilator Drugs

Drug Class	Route	Uses	Common Side Effects
Beta$_2$ agonists (e.g., albuterol, salmeterol)	Orally or by inhalation	Intermittent attacks of wheezing; exercise-induced asthma; prevention of asthma	Palpitations, tachycardia, nervousness
Methylxanthines (e.g., theophylline)	Orally, intravenously	Asthma; COPD	Palpitations, tachycardias, nausea, vomiting, seizures
Anticholinergics (e.g., ipratropium)	By inhalation	COPD; acute asthma (when combined with beta-agonist drug)	Dry mouth, cough, nausea

bronchophony (brŏng-kŏf′ō-nē) [″ + *phone,* voice] An abnormal increase in tone or clarity in vocal resonance.

bronchoplasty (brŏng′kō-plăs″tē) [″ + *plassein,* to form] Surgical repair of a bronchial defect.

bronchopleural (brŏng″kō-ploor′ăl) [″ + *pleura,* side, rib] Pert. to the bronchi and the pleural cavity.

bronchopneumonia (brŏng″kō-noo-mō′nē-ă) [broncho- + pneumonia] A type of pneumonia marked by scattered consolidation (areas filled with inflammatory exudate) in one or more lobes of the lung. It occurs primarily in infants and in the elderly, both of whom have decreased resistance to bacterial and viral infections. It is often a complication of bronchitis.

bronchopulmonary lavage SEE: under *lavage.*

bronchoreactivity (brŏng″kō-rē″ak-tiv′it-ē) [*broncho-* + *reactivity*] The responsiveness of the airways to allergens, provocative chemicals, or inflammation.

bronchorrhagia (brŏng″kor-ā′jē-ă) [″ + *rhegnynai,* to break forth] A bronchial hemorrhage.

bronchorrhaphy (brŏng″kor′ă-fē) [*broncho-* + *-rrhaphy*] The suturing of a bronchus.

bronchorrhea (brŏng-kō-rē′ă) [″ + *rhoia,* flow] An abnormal secretion from the bronchial mucous membranes.

bronchorrhoncus (brŏng″kor-ŏn′kŭs) [″ + *rhonchos,* snore] A bronchial crackle.

bronchoscope (brŏng′kō-skōp) [″ + *skopein,* to examine] An endoscope designed to pass through the trachea for visual inspection of the tracheobronchial tree. The device can be used for lavage, or to remove tissue for biopsy or foreign bodies from the tracheobronchial tree.

bronchoscopy (bron-kos′kŏ-pē, brong-) [*broncho-* + *-scopy*] Examination of the bronchi through a bronchoscope.

    autofluorescence b. Bronchoscopy in which tissues are illuminated with pure blue laser light. The wavelength of blue light enhances the difference in appearance between normal and malignant tissues, since malignant and premalignant surfaces glow (fluoresce) when compared with healthy tissues.

    standard b. White light bronchoscopy.

    white light b., white-light bronchoscopy ABBR: WLB. Bronchoscopy in which tissues are illuminated with only the normal light spectrum available for use in fiber-optic evaluation of tissues. SYN: *standard b.*

bronchosinusitis (brŏng″kō-sī″nŭs-ī′tĭs) [″ + L. *sinus,* a hollow, + Gr. *itis,* inflammation] Infection of a bronchus and a sinus at the same time.

bronchospasm (brŏng′kō-spăzm) [″ + *spasmos,* a convulsion] An abnormal narrowing with partial obstruction of the lumen of the bronchi due to spasm of the peribronchial smooth muscle. Clinically this is accompanied by coughing and wheezing. Bronchospasm occurs in reactive airway diseases such as asthma and bronchitis. Treatment may include bronchodilators and corticosteroids. SYN: *bronchiospasm.* SEE: *asthma.*

bronchospirometer (brŏng″kō-spī-rŏm′ĕ-tĕr) [″ + L. *spirare,* to breathe, + Gr. *metron,* measure] An instrument for determining the volume of air inspired from one lung and for collecting air for analysis.

bronchostaxis (brŏng″kō-stăk′sĭs) [″ + *staxis,* dripping] Hemorrhage from the walls of a bronchus.

bronchostenosis (brŏng″kō-stĕn-ō′sĭs) [″ + *stenosis,* act of narrowing] Stenosis of a bronchus.

bronchostomy (brŏng-kŏs′tō-mē) [″ + *stoma,* mouth] The surgical formation of an opening into a bronchus.

bronchotomy (brŏng-kŏt′ō-mē) [″ + *tome,* incision] Surgical incision of a bronchus, the larynx, or the trachea.

bronchovesicular (brŏng″kō-vĕ-sĭk′ū-lăr)

[" + L. *vesicula,* a tiny bladder] Pert. to bronchial tubes and alveoli with special reference to sounds intermediate between bronchial or tracheal sounds and vescicular sounds.

b. breath sounds SEE: *sound, bronchovesicular.*

bronchus (brong′kŭs, brong′kī″, brong′kē″) *pl.* **bronchi** [Gr. *bronchos,* windpipe] One of the two large branches of the trachea. The trachea divides opposite the third thoracic vertebra into the right and left main bronchi. The point of division, called the carina trachea, is the site where foreign bodies too large to enter either bronchus would rest after passing through the trachea. The right bronchus is shorter and more vertical than the left one. After entering the lung each bronchus divides further and terminates in bronchioles.

tracheal b. An accessory bronchus that branches off directly from the trachea, the carina, or another bronchus. It is an ectopic malformation of the respiratory tract that usually runs to the right upper lobe of the lung. SYN: **b. suis.** SEE: illus.; *bronchi.*

Broselow pediatric emergency tape (brōz′lō″, bros′) [James Broselow, contemporary U.S. emergency physician] ABBR: BT. A color-coded strip of paper, 58.6 in (146.5 cm) in length, inscribed at length-based intervals with information on the use of fluids, pressors, anticonvulsants, and resuscitation equipment. It is used to provide a quick estimate of the weight of pediatric patients, (because the lean body mass of children is roughly proportional to their height). It provides a rapid means of determining the dosages of medications and the size of the equipment that should be used in pediatric resuscitations, up to children who weigh 36 kg.

⚠ The correlations between the length of a child and his or her mass were derived from American data and may not apply to children of other nationalities.

broth (brawth) [ME.] **1.** A liquid nutrient made from simmering any food (cereals, meats, vegetables) in liquid. **2.** A

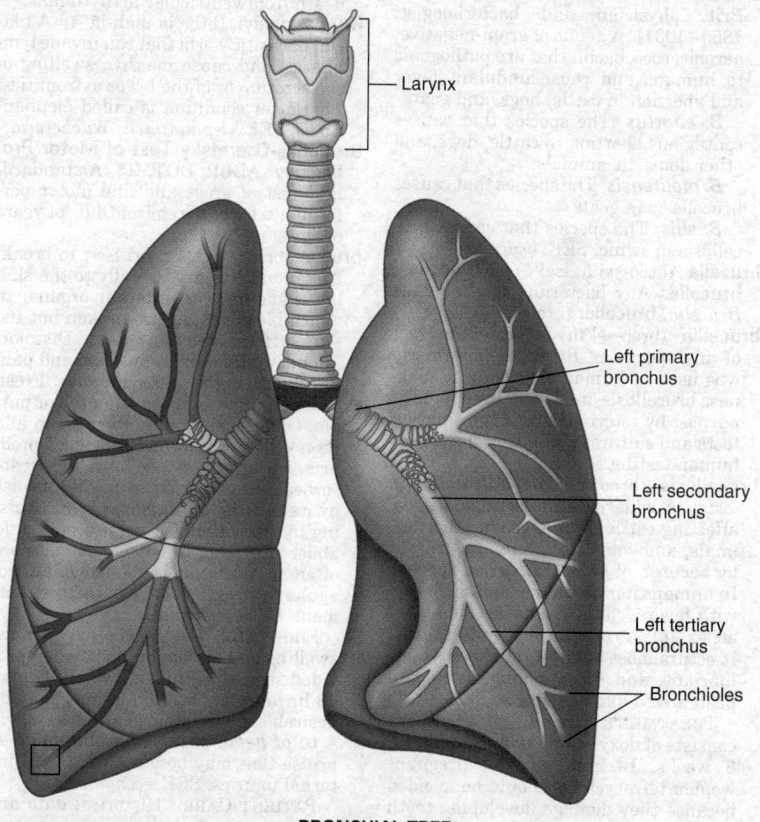

Larynx

Left primary bronchus

Left secondary bronchus

Left tertiary bronchus

Bronchioles

BRONCHIAL TREE

liquid nutrient medium used to facilitate the growth of microorganisms.

Broviac catheter (brō'vē-ak″) A tunneled central venous catheter that is similar to a Hickman catheter but with a smaller tube diameter that allows it to be used for pediatric patients.

brow The forehead.

browlift (brow'lift″) [″ + ″] A colloquial term for ophryplasty.

brown baby syndrome The dark grayish brown skin color seen in infants undergoing extensive phototherapy for hyperbilirubinemia. The condition may last for months but is not known to produce permanent harm.

brownian movement (brown'ē-ăn) [Robert Brown, Brit. botanist, 1773–1858] SEE: under *movement*.

Brown-Séquard syndrome (brown'sā-kar') [Charles E. Brown-Séquard, Fr. physician, 1817–1894] Hemisection of the spinal cord with: paralysis, loss of position and vibratory sense, and ataxia on the same side of the body as the lesion; and loss of pain and temperature sensitivity on the side opposite the lesion.

Brucella (broo-sel'ă) [Sir David Bruce, Brit. physician and bacteriologist, 1855–1931] A genus of gram-negative, aerobic, coccobacilli that are pathogenic to humans and cause undulant fever and abortion in cattle, hogs, and goats.

   B. abortus The species that causes contagious abortion in cattle, dogs, and other domestic animals.

   B. melitensis The species that causes brucellosis in goats.

   B. suis The species that causes brucellosis in swine. SEE: *brucellosis*.

brucella (broo-sel'ă, -sel'ē) *pl.* **brucellae, brucellas** Any bacterium of the genus *Brucella*. **brucellar** (broo-sel'ăr), *adj.*

brucellin (broo-sĕl'ĭn) A protein extract of any species of *Brucella*. It formerly was used in human skin tests to diagnose brucellosis and is still used for that purpose by veterinarians. Agglutination tests and cultures are now preferred for human testing.

brucellosis (broo″sĕ-lō'sĭs) [*Brucella* + *-osis*] A widespread infectious disease affecting cattle, swine, goats, other animals, and sometimes humans, caused by bacteria of several *Brucella* species. In humans it is an influenza-like illness, with fevers, chills, headache, and body aches. It is a rare cause of endocarditis. It occurs most often in ranchers, veterinarians, and those who consume unpasteurized dairy products.

   TREATMENT: In adults, treatment consists of doxycycline and rifampin for 6 weeks. In children and pregnant women tetracyclines should be avoided because they damage developing teeth and bones. SYN: *Malta fever; Mediter-*

ranean fever; undulant fever. SEE: *Brucella.*

Bruch, Karl (brook, brookh) Karl Wilhelm Ludwig Bruch, Ger. anatomist, 1819–1884.

   Bruch g. Any of the conjunctival lymph nodes in the lower lids.

   B. membrane A glassy membrane of the uvea of the eye, lying between the choroid membrane and the pigmented epithelium of the retina. SYN: *lamina basalis choroideae; lamina vitrea; vitreous lamella.*

Bruck disease (brook) [Alfred Bruck, Ger. physician, b. 1865] Osteogenesis imperfecta.

Brudzinski sign (broo-jin'skē, -zin') [Józef Brudzinski, Polish physician, 1874–1917] Flexion of the hips when the neck is flexed from a supine position. It occurs in patients with meningeal inflammation. SEE: *Kernig's sign; meningitis.*

Brugada syndrome (broo-gŏd'ă) A rare hereditary syndrome, occasionally autosomal dominant, marked by right bundle branch block, S-T segment elevation in the right precordial leads of the ECG, and a high risk of sudden death from ventricular arrhythmias.

Brugia malayi (broo'jă mah-lā'-ī) A filarial parasitic worm that can invade lymphatics and cause massive swelling of the scrotum or of the lower extremities. The latter condition is called elephantiasis. SEE: *elephantiasis; Wuchereria.*

Bruininks-Oseretsky Test of Motor Proficiency ABBR: BOTMP. A standardized test of gross and fine motor performance for children from 4 to 14 years of age.

bruise (brooz) [O. Fr. *bruiser,* to break] A traumatic injury (usually to the skin but sometimes to internal organs) in which blood vessels are broken but tissue surfaces remain intact. Discoloration, swelling, inflammation, and pain are typical signs and symptoms. Fresh bruises on the skin are often red or purple. Older bruises may turn green and then yellow or brown, as the blood products within them age and are reabsorbed, but gauging the age of a bruise by its color is imprecise, at best. Bruising in infants may suggest occult child abuse. Bruising in the elderly is more often an indication of the use of anticoagulant drugs than of physical mistreatment. SYN: *ecchymosis.*

   FIRST AID: Cold packs may reduce swelling and discomfort, esp. when provided soon after injury. Twenty-four to 48 hr later, application of heat may be desirable, followed by gentle massage.

   b. of head, chest, and abdomen A bruise that may be associated with internal injuries. SEE: *ecchymosis.*

   PATIENT CARE: Historical data are collected regarding the exact cause and location of the injury. The possibility of an abusive injury is investigated if the history given does not seem consistent with the injury, or if the related details change. The bruised area is inspected, and the location, color, size, discomfort, and other pertinent characteristics are documented. The patient is assessed for other injuries dependent on the specific location and severity of the original injury. Related skin abrasions are cleansed thoroughly. Neurological status (AVPU) is monitored hourly or as needed for any patient with a suspected head injury.

stone b. A pain perceived of the bottom of the foot, often the result of metatarsalgia or plantar fasciitis.

bruit (brwē, broot) [Fr., noise] An adventitious sound of venous or arterial origin heard on auscultation.

placental b. Placental souffle.

Brunner glands (brun'ĕr) [Johann C. Brunner, Swiss anatomist, 1653–1727] Compound glands of the duodenum and upper jejunum that are similar to the pyloric glands of the stomach. They are embedded in the submucosa and lined with columnar epithelium. They secrete alkaline mucus which neutralizes the hydrochloric acid entering the duodenum from the stomach. SYN: *duodenal glands.*

Brunner's syndrome (brŭn'ĕr) [H.G. Brunner, D. geneticist] A rare X-linked deficiency of monoamine oxidase A. Mild mental retardation and impulsive or aggressive behaviors are characteristically found in affected children.

brush A tool with bristles on its end designed to remove debris or damaged cells from a body part.

Brushfield spot (brŭsh'fēld") [Thomas Brushfield, Brit. physician, 1858–1937] Any of the gray or pale yellow spots sometimes present at the periphery of the iris. They may be an isolated finding but are sometimes found in Down syndrome.

brushing (brŭsh'ĭng) **1.** A technique of tactile stimulation using small brushes over selected dermatomes to elicit muscular responses in the rehabilitation of persons with central nervous system damage. **2.** Cleaning with a brush, as in toothbrushing. **3.** A clinical specimen obtained by rubbing a body part with a brush. The tissue or cells obtained are examined microscopically for evidence of disease. **4.** In massage therapy, superficial stroking performed with the fingertips.

bruxism (brŭk'sĭzm) [Gr. *brychein,* to grind the teeth, + *-ismos,* condition] The grinding of the teeth, esp. in children, during sleep.

ETIOLOGY: Psychological stress or abnormalities of tooth occlusion are the principal causes.

TREATMENT: If the condition is due to psychological causes, tension, anxiety, and stress should be reduced. The teeth should be treated for caries, malocclusion, or periodontal disease. Occlusal guards for the teeth may be of benefit. SYN: *oromandibular sleep movement disorder.*

Bryant traction (brī'ănt) [Sir Thomas Bryant, Brit. surgeon, 1828–1914] Traction applied to the lower legs with the force pulling vertically. It is used esp. in treating fractures of the femur in children.

B.S. *Bowel sounds.*

B-scan B-mode **ultrasound**.

BSE 1. *breast self-examination.* **2.** *bovine spongiform encephalopathy.*

BT *Broselow pediatric emergency tape.*

BTPS *Body temperature and pressure, saturated.*

BTU *British thermal unit.*

bubo (boo'bō) *pl.* **buboes** [Gr. *boubon,* groin, swollen gland] An inflamed, swollen, or enlarged lymph node often exhibiting suppuration, occurring commonly after infective disease due to absorption of infective material. The nodes most commonly affected are those of the groin and axilla.

axillary b. A bubo in the armpit.

indolent b. A bubo in which suppuration does not occur.

inguinal b. A bubo in the region of the groin. SYN: *buboadenitis.*

venereal b. A bubo resulting from a venereal disease. SEE: *lymphogranuloma venereum.*

bubonadenitis (boo-bŏn-ăd-ĕ-nī'tĭs) [" + *aden,* gland, + *itis,* inflammation] Inguinal bubo.

bucca (bŭk'ă) *pl.* **buccae** [L., cheek] The cheek.

buccal (bŭk'ăl) Pert. to the cheek or mouth.

bucco-, bucc- [L. *bucca,* cheek] Prefixes meaning *cheek.*

buccocervical (bŭk"kō-sĕr'vĭ-kăl) Concerning the buccal surface and cervical margin of a tooth.

Buck extension (bŭk) [Gurdon Buck, U.S. surgeon, 1807–1877] A method of producing traction by applying regular or flannel-backed adhesive tape to the skin and keeping it in smooth close contact by circular bandaging of the part to which it is applied. The adhesive strips are aligned with the long axis of the arm or leg, the superior ends being about 1 in. (2.5 cm) from the fracture site. Weights sufficient to produce the required extension are fastened to the inferior end of the adhesive strips by a rope that is run over a pulley to permit free motion. SYN: *Buck's traction.*

Bucky, Gustav P. (bŭk'ē) German-born U.S. radiologist, 1880–1963.

B. diaphragm A specialized film holder with a moving grid located immediately beneath the radiographic table or upright apparatus. It decreases the effects of scatter and secondary radiation during a radiographic exposure. SYN: *Potter-Bucky diaphragm.*

B. factor A measure of the amount of radiation absorbed by the Bucky diaphragm. This indicates the amount by which to increase the technical factors when a grid is being used.

Bucky factor SEE: *Bucky, Gustav P.*

bud [ME. *budde,* to swell] **1.** In anatomy, a small structure resembling a bud of a plant. **2.** In embryology, a small protuberance or outgrowth that is the anlage or primordium of an organ or structure.

    limb b. In the embryo, a clump of cells that is the precursor of one of the four limbs.

    lung b. In the embryo, a pouch that grows out of each side of the developing foregut tube beginning at stage 12 (26 days). It pushes into the primitive pleural coeloms and continues to elongate and branch to become the embryonic lung.

    taste b. Any of the primary sensory cells that are found mainly on the margins and the back of the tongue and respond to a range of chemicals introduced into the mouth. Sensory cells of the taste buds live for approx. 10 days and are then replaced from basal stem cells. SEE: *taste.*

    tooth b. The earliest evidence of tooth development. The tooth buds form in the dental lamina. Tooth buds for the deciduous teeth develop first (6 weeks of gestation) and more superficially; tooth buds for the permanent teeth develop later (10 weeks of gestation) and deeper in the dental lamina. SEE: *enamel organ.*

Budd-Chiari syndrome (bŭd′kē-ār′ē) SEE: *thrombosis, hepatic vein.*

budding (bŭd′ing) **1.** A method of asexual reproduction in which a small offshoot or sprout grows from the side or end of the parent and develops into a new organism, which in some cases remains attached and in others separates and lives an independent existence. Budding is common in sponges and coelenterates. The budding of yeasts is mitosis with unequal division of cytoplasm. **2.** The release of human immunodeficiency virions from an infected cell.

buddy taping Securing a digit to the one next to it. It is a form of splinting used to treat toe and finger injuries.

Buerger, Leo (bŭr′ĕr) Austrian-born U.S. surgeon, pathologist, and urologist, 1879–1943.

    B.-Allen exercise Buerger postural exercise.

    B. disease ABBR: BD. A chronic, recurring, inflammatory, but nonatheromatous vascular occlusive disease, chiefly of the peripheral small and medium-sized arteries (and sometimes veins) of the extremities causing decreased blood flow to the feet and legs. Occasionally the hands are also affected, causing painful ulceration of the fingertips. The disease is seen most commonly in males 20 to 40 years of age who smoke cigarettes or chew tobacco. SYN: *thromboangiitis obliterans.*

SYMPTOMS: Symptoms include paresthesias of the foot, easy fatigability, and foot and leg cramps. In patients with severely limited blood flow to the legs, skin ulceration or moist gangrene of the extremities may develop. Amputation is sometimes needed to remove dead tissue.

TREATMENT: Absolute, permanent abstinence from tobacco in all forms is crucial. The patient should avoid excessive use of the affected limb, exposure to temperature extremes, use of drugs that diminish the blood supply to extremities, trauma, and fungus infections. Aspirin and vasodilators may be prescribed. If gangrene, pain, or ulceration is present, complete bedrest is advised with a padded foot-board or bed cradle to prevent pressure on the extremities; if these are absent, the patient should walk at a comfortable pace for 30 min twice daily. For arterial spasm, blocking of the sympathetic nervous system by injection of various drugs or by sympathectomy may be done.

PATIENT CARE: The history should document occurrences of painful, intermittent claudication of the instep, calf, or thigh, which exercise aggravates and rest relieves; the patient's walking ability (distance, time, and rest required); the patient's foot response to exposure to cold temperatures (initially cold, numb, and cyanotic; later reddened, hot, and tingling); and any involvement of the hands, such as digital ischemia, trophic nail changes, painful fingertip ulcerations, or gangrene. Peripheral pulses are palpated, and absent or diminished radial, ulnar, or tibial pulses documented. Feet and legs are inspected for superficial vein thrombophlebitis, muscle atrophy, peripheral ulcerations, and gangrene, which occur late in the disease. Soft padding is used to protect the feet, which are washed gently with a mild soap and tepid water, rinsed thoroughly, and patted dry with a soft towel. The patient is instructed in this daily care routine and advised to inspect tissues for injury such as cuts, abrasions, and signs of skin breakdown (redness or soreness) and to report all injuries to the health care provider for treatment. The patient is advised to avoid wearing tight or restrictive clothing, sitting or standing in one position for long periods, and walking barefoot;

also, shoes and cotton or woolen stockings should be carefully fitted, but stockings should not be tight enough to hinder venous return from the legs. He should obtain medical care following any local trauma. Extremities must be protected from temperature extremes, esp. cold. The patient is taught the Buerger postural exercises if prescribed and is cautioned to avoid use of over-the-counter drugs without the attending health care provider's approval. The patient who smokes is referred to a smoking cessation program, but nicotine patch therapy should not be prescribed given the patient's associated hypersensitivity to nicotine. For the patient with ulcers and gangrene, bedrest is prescribed; a padded footboard or cradle is used to prevent pressure from bed linens. If hospitalization is required for treatment of ulcers or gangrene, or if amputation is required, rehabilitative needs are considered, esp. regarding changes in body image, and the patient is referred for physical and occupational therapy and for social services as appropriate.

    B. postural exercise An exercise used for circulatory disturbances of the extremities. SYN: *Buerger-Allen exercise*.

    B. test A noninvasive bedside test used to assess the adequacy of arterial blood flow into the legs. While the patient is lying flat on his back, both legs are elevated to an angle of 45°. Loss of the normal perfused color of either leg suggests that its arterial blood flow is compromised since a normal artery can pump blood against gravity without difficulty.

buffalo hump (bŭf′ă-lō hŭmp) A deposit of fat in the lower midcervical and upper thoracic area of the back. It is usually caused by excessive adrenocortical hormone production or therapy. SYN: *dorsocervical fat pad*.

buffer (bŭf′ĕr) **1.** Any of several molecules that react with strong acids or bases to prevent large changes in the pH of, for example, body fluids. **2.** A substance tending to offset reaction of an agent administered in conjunction with it.

    blood b. A chemical present in the blood that prevents rapid changes in pH. The principal buffers are carbonic acid, carbonates and bicarbonates, monobasic and dibasic phosphates, and proteins such as hemoglobin.

buffer stock An inventory of stored vaccine that allows a nation or an institution to respond quickly to emergent needs. The buffer stock usually consists of a three-month supply of a vaccine. SYN: *vaccine buffer stock*.

buffy coat A light stratum of blood seen when the blood is centrifuged or allowed

to stand in a test tube. The red blood cells settle to the bottom and, between the plasma and the red blood cells, a light-colored layer contains mostly white blood cells. Platelets are at the top of this coat; the next layers, in order, are lymphocytes and monocytes; granulocytes; and reticulocytes. In normal blood, the buffy coat is barely visible; in leukemia and leukemoid reactions, it is much larger. SEE: illus.

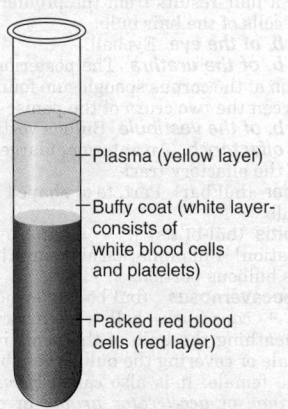

Plasma (yellow layer)

Buffy coat (white layer consists of white blood cells and platelets)

Packed red blood cells (red layer)

BUFFY COAT

bufotoxin (bū″fō-tŏks′ĭn) [L. *bufo,* toad, + Gr. *toxikon,* poison] A general term for any toxin present in the skin of a toad.

bug (bŭg) **1.** A colloquial term for any small insect or arthropod, esp. of the order Hemiptera, that has sucking mouth parts, incomplete metamorphosis, and two pairs of wings, the fore pair being half membranous. SEE: *bedbug; chigger.* **2.** A colloquial term for a disease-causing germ or microorganism.

    assassin b. Any member of the family Reduviidae. Many are predaceous; others are bloodsucking. *Panstrongylus, Triatoma,* and *Rhodnius* are vectors of Chagas disease. SEE: *conenose; trypanosomiasis.*

    cone-nose b., cone-nosed bug Conenose.

    kissing b. Conenose.

    red b. Chigger.

bugbane (bŭg′bān″) Black cohosh.

bugleweed (bū′g′l-wēd″) A perennial herb of the genus *Lycopus,* principally found in moist habitats in Europe and North America. It is used mainly in homeopathic remedies for cardiac and thyroid disorders. It contains cardiac glycosides and iodine.

built environment SEE: under *environment.*

built-up handle The portion of an implement that has been increased in diameter to accommodate its use by people with limited or weak grasp.

bulb (bŭlb) [L. *bulbus,* bulbous root; Gr. *bolbos*] **1.** Any rounded or globular structure. Medulla (3).

aortic b. The dilated portion of the truncus arteriosus in the embryo that gives rise to the roots of the aorta and pulmonary arteries.

duodenal b. The upper duodenal area just beyond the pylorus.

hair b. The expanded portion at the lower end of the hair root. The growth of a hair results from the proliferation of cells of the hair bulb.

b. of the eye Eyeball.

b. of the urethra The posterior portion of the corpus spongiosum found between the two crura of the penis.

b. of the vestibule Bulbus vestibuli.

olfactory b. An anterior enlargement of the olfactory tract.

bulbar (bŭl′bar) Pert. to or shaped like a bulb.

bulbitis (bŭl-bī′tĭs) [″ + Gr. *itis,* inflammation] Inflammation of the urethra in its bulbous portion.

bulbocavernosus (bŭl″bō-kăv″ĕr-nō′sŭs) [″ + *cavernosus,* hollow] A muscle ensheathing the bulb of the penis in the male or covering the bulbus vestibuli in the female. It is also called *ejaculator urinae* or *accelerator urinae* in males and *sphincter vaginae* in females.

bulboid (bŭl′boyd) [″ + Gr. *eidos,* form, shape] Shaped like a bulb.

bulbonuclear (bŭl″bō-nū′klē-ăr) [″ + *nucleus,* kernel] Pert. to the nuclei in the medulla oblongata.

bulbospongiosus (bŭl″bō-spŏn″jē-ō′sŭs) One of the three voluntary muscles of the penis. It acts to empty the canal of the urethra after urination and to assist in erection of the corpus cavernosum urethrae. The anterior fibers contribute to penile erection by contracting to compress the deep dorsal vein of the penis.

bulbous (bŭl′bŭs) [L. *bulbus*] Bulb-shaped; swollen; terminating in an enlargement.

bulbus [L.; Gr. *bolbos*] Bulb.

b. cordis In the embryo, the segment of the heart tube destined to be partitioned and to form the two ventricular outflow segments, to the aorta on the left and to the pulmonary trunk on the right.

bulge sign An assessment maneuver used to identify a joint effusion, esp. at the knee. The examiner tugs or "milks" the soft tissues medial to the joint laterally and superiorly and then presses on the lateral surface of the joint in the opposite direction. If a fluid collection bulges on the medial surface, joint fluid is present.

bulgur, bulghur (bŭl′gŭr, bul′) [Turkish, *bulğur* fr Persian] Wheat kernels that have been boiled and then allowed to dry. It is a cereal grain with a lowglycemic index.

bulimia, boulimia (bū-lim′ē-ă, boo-, -lē′mē) [Gr. *boulimia,* ravenous hunger, fm. *bous,* ox + *limos,* hunger] Excessive and insatiable appetite. **bulimic** (bū-lim′ik, boo-, -lē′mik), *adj.*

b. nervosa A disorder marked by recurrent episodes of binge eating followed by feelings of humiliation, guilt, shame, and self-deprecation, and resulting in self-induced vomiting and diarrhea, excessive exercise, strict dieting or fasting to reverse the effects of binging, and an exaggerated concern about body shape and weight. These behaviors must be present at least twice a week for 3 months to establish this diagnosis. SEE: *anorexia nervosa.*

PATIENT CARE: Early recognition and intervention may sometimes prevent this disorder from increasing in severity and duration or producing harm.

Health history includes a weight history (frequency of weighing, premorbid weight, menstrual threshold, history of weight fluctuations). Changes are graphed to help identify stress-related patterns. The patient should be questioned about perceptions of ideal weight and total body appearance, as well as specific areas (e.g., hips, thighs, abdomen). Having the patient draw self-portraits may help to communicate this information. Any dieting behaviors are determined, including cause, onset, type, frequency, duration, and the presence of external influences (e.g., peer pressure). Characteristically, patients with bulimia demonstrate difficulty with controlling impulses, chronic depression, poor self esteem, low tolerance of frustration , recurrent anxiety, alienation , self-consciousness, difficulty in expressing feelings of anger, and impaired social or occupational adjustment.

Laboratory testing includes serum electrolyte studies and complete blood count to detect hypochlorhidria, hypokalemia, metabolic acidosis, or dehydration.

Assessments for psychologic, sexual, and physiologic manifestations of bulimia, including depression, suicidal ideation, and substance abuse, are important. Family history should include information concerning psychiatric problems, existence of physical or sexual abuse, communication patterns, and quality of relationships.

The patient with bulimia nervosa should be referred for cognitive behavioral therapy, and/or treatment with antidepressant drugs, such as selective serotinin reuptake inhibitors. Bupropion should be avoided.

bulk 1. In nutrition, a substance that absorbs water in the intestinal tract. The increased mass helps to stimulate peristalsis. Bulk materials include bran cereals, cellulose, lignins, and psyllium. They are used therapeutically to treat constipation and other bowel disorders. **2.** A mass; a large volume of cells, such as might be found in a tumor.

bulla (bŭl′ă) *pl.* **bullae** [L. *bulla,* bubble, knob] **1.** A large blister or skin vesicle filled with fluid SEE: illus.; *pompholyx.* **2.** A bleb.

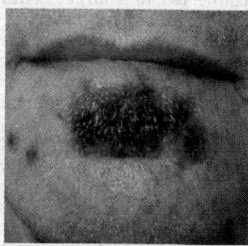

BULLAE OF IMPETIGO

  b. ethmoidalis A rounded, thin-walled, bony projection into the middle meatus of the nose underneath the middle turbinate bone, formed by an anterior ethmoid sinus.

bullectomy (bul-ek′tŏ-mē) [*bulla* + *-ectomy*] Surgical removal of a giant bulla from an emphysematous lung to allow the remaining normal lung tissue to expand and contract more effectively during respiration. It is used in selected circumstances as a treatment for severe chronic obstructive lung disease.

bullous (bŭl′ŭs) [L. *bulla,* bubble] Like a blister or vesicle.

bully A person who uses physical or psychological means or force to get his or her way, esp. by intimidating or hurting others who may be smaller or weaker.

BUN *Blood urea nitrogen.*

bundle (bŭn′dĕl) A group of fibers. SYN: *fasciculus.*

  Arnold b. SEE: under *Arnold, Friedrich.*

  atrioventricular b. A bundle of fibers of the impulse-conducting system of the heart. From its origin in the atrioventricular node, it enters the interventricular septum, where it divides into two branches whose fibers pass to the right and left ventricles respectively, the fibers of each trunk becoming continuous with the Purkinje fibers of the ventricles. SYN: *A-V bundle.* SEE: *heart block.*

  A-V b. Atrioventricular **b.**

  cingulate b. Cingulum.

  cingulum b. Cingulum.

  efferent cochlear b. Olivocochlear **b.**

  b. of His SEE: under *His, Wilhelm Jr.*

  b. of Kent Kent bundles.

  medial forebrain b. A diffuse limbic tract of lightly myelinated and unmyelinated axons interconnecting the forebrain, hypothalamus, and brainstem. Along with the dorsal longitudinal fasciculus, the medial forebrain bundle is the main pathway by which monoaminergic axons from cells in the hindbrain and midbrain reach the striatum, the limbic system, and the cerebral cortices of the forebrain.

  medial longitudinal b. Medial longitudinal **fasciculus.**

  nigrostriate b. A dopaminergic axon tract from the substantia nigra to the striatum in the basal ganglia. Activation of the nigrostriate bundle inhibits the striatum, which normally lowers the activity of motor programs. In Parkinson's disease, neurons in the substantia nigra are damaged, and their effect on the striatum is reduced; the result is unchecked activity of the striatum and an excessive damping of motor programs, i.e., hypokinetic behavior. SYN: *nigrostriatal fibers.*

  olivocochlear b. An axon tract that originates in the superior olivary nuclei of the hindbrain. The tract exits the brainstem and runs in the vestibulocochlear nerve (CN VIII), eventually synapsing on hair cells in the cochlea in the inner ear. The olivocochlear bundle is one pathway by which the auditory system can modify its perception of sound. SYN: *efferent cochlear b.*

  ventilator b. A cluster of four evidenced-based safety measures that decrease the risk to patients of mechanical ventilation while in the intensive care unit. The elements of the bundle may include elevating the head of the patient's bed, administering medications to prevent deep venous thrombosis, administering medications to reduce the incidence of GI bleeding, and giving the ventilated patient periodic intermissions from sedation.

bundle branch block ABBR: BBB. A defect in the electrical conduction system of the heart in which there is failure of conduction down one of the main branches of the bundle of His. On the surface electrocardiogram, the QRS complex is >0.12 sec. and its shape is altered. SYN: *bundle branch heart block; interventricular heart block.*

  left b.b.b. ABBR: LBBB. A defect in the conduction system of the heart in which electrical conduction down the left bundle branch is delayed. On the 12-lead EKG, it gives the QRS complex a widened QS complex in lead V_1 (0.12 sec.).

  right b.b.b. ABBR: RBBB. A defect in the conductive system of the heart in which electrical conduction down the right bundle branch is delayed. On the 12-lead EKG, it gives the widened QRS complex an RSR appearance in leads V_1 and V_2.

bundling (bŭn′dlĭng) A mandatory system of drug distribution involving monitoring and reporting side effects to the U.S. Food and Drug Administration.

bung (bŭng) [ME. *bunge,* stopper] A stopper or diaphragm that covers a vial and prevents fluids from escaping.

bunion (bŭn′yŭn) Inflammation and thickening of the first metatarsal joint of the great toe, usually associated with marked enlargement of the joint and lateral displacement of the toe.
   ETIOLOGY: Bunions may be caused by heredity, degenerative bone or joint diseases such as arthritis, but most often are produced by tight-fitting shoes and high heels that force toes together and displace weight onto the forefoot.

Bunnell block (bŭn′nĕl) An orthotic device used after surgical repair of flexor tendon hand injuries. It prevents flexion at joints proximal to the one being exercised during the rehabilitation regimen.

Bunsen burner (bŭn′sĕn) [Robert W. E. von Bunsen, Ger. chemist, 1811–1899] A gas burner used primarily in laboratories, in which gas and air are mixed in variable concentrations to facilitate combustion. The burner consists of a port that allows main gas flow to enter, a controlling gas valve (needle valve), and a vertical barrel or tube with vents that allow the air flow to be controlled.

Bunyaviridae (bŭn″yă-vĭr′ĭ-dē) A family of RNA viruses that are transmitted to people by insect bite and may cause fevers, rashes, central nervous system infections, and widespread bleeding.

buphthalmos (bŭf-thal′mos) [Gr. *bous,* ox + Gr. *ophthalmos,* eye] Enlargement of the eyeball due to elevated intraocular pressure, seen in congenital glaucoma.

bupropion (bū-prŏp′ē-ŏn) An antidepressant medication that is also moderately effective in aiding smoking cessation, esp. when used along with cognitive and behavioral therapies.

bur, burr (bŭr) A rotating tool to cut tissue, e.g, to shave fatty deposits from arteries or to cut or abrade tooth structure, bone, and other dental materials.

Burch procedure (bŭrch) Surgery in which a sling is sutured around the urethra and neck of the bladder to the iliopectineal ligament. It is used to alleviate stress urinary incontinence in women.
   PATIENT CARE: Vital signs, suprapubic catheter, and wound drainage are checked. The patient is helped to void as needed. Fluid intake and output is measured and recorded.

burdock (bŭr′dok″) Any of several biennial thistles of the genus *Arctium,* of the daisy family, esp. *A. lappa.*
   greater b. A biennial thistle, *Arctium lappa,* cultivated for its edible root, and promoted as a treatment for arthritis, constipation, diabetes, fluid retention, and hair loss. The plant has shown no effectiveness as an herbal remedy.

buret, burette (bū-rĕt′) [Fr.] **1.** A special hollow glass tube usually with a stopcock at the lower end. It is used in chemical analysis to measure the amount of liquid reagent used. **2.** A calibrated chamber used to ensure accurate measurement of small amounts of intravenous fluid and to prevent fluid infusion overload. The chamber is usually connected to a larger container of fluid. SYN: *volume controller.*

buried bumper syndrome Erosion of the internal flange of a percutaneously placed feeding tube into the organ in which it resides, e.g., the stomach or jejunum.

Burkholderia (bĕrk″hōl-dār′ē-ă) [NL.] A genus of aerobic gram-negative rod-shaped bacteria (family Burkholderiaceae) that includes some species that are significant animal and plant pathogens and many other species that are environmentally active in biodegradation.
   B. cepacia A species that causes nosocomial infections, esp. in intensive care units. Most susceptible are patients on mechanical ventilation and those with cystic fibrosis or chronic granulomatous disease. It is resistant to aminoglycosides and many cephalosporin antibiotics.
   B. gladioli A species of multiply drug-resistant bacteria that may cause ocular infections, pneumonia (esp. in patients with cystic fibrosis), skin abscesses, and other infections.
   B. mallei A species that causes glanders and farcy. It has been used as a biological weapon. It was formerly called *Pseudomonas mallei.*
   B. pseudomallei A species that causes meliodosis.

Burkitt lymphoma (bŭrk′kĭt) [Denis P. Burkitt, Ugandan physician, 1911–1993] A rapidly growing, B-cell, non-Hodgkin's lymphoma. It is rare in the U.S. but common in equatorial Africa, where it often afflicts children aged 5 to 10 years. There is a strong association of this malignancy with Epstein-Barr virus.

burn (bŭrn) Tissue injury resulting from excessive exposure to thermal, chemical, electrical, or radioactive agents. The effects may be local, resulting in cell injury or death, or both local and systemic, involving primary shock (which occurs immediately after the injury and is rarely fatal) or secondary shock (which develops insidiously following severe burns and is often fatal). In the U.S. about 1.25 million people receive medical care for burns annually. More than 50,000 of these burn victims are hospitalized as a result of severe burn injury. Burns are usually classified as:
   First degree: a superficial burn in which damage is limited to the outer

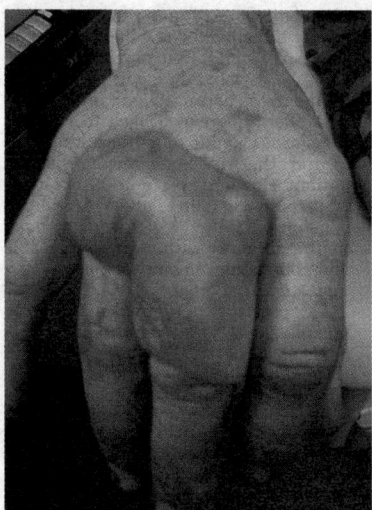

SECOND DEGREE BURN

layer of the epidermis and is marked by redness, tenderness, and mild pain. Blisters do not form, and the burn heals without scar formation. A common example is sunburn.

Second degree: a burn that damages partial thickness of the epidermal and some dermal tissues but does not damage the lower-lying hair follicles, sweat, or sebaceous glands. The burn is painful and red; blisters form, and wounds may heal with a scar. SEE: illus. (Second Degree Burn).

Third degree: a burn that extends through the full thickness of the skin and subcutaneous tissues beneath the dermis. The burn leaves skin with a pale, brown, gray, or blackened appearance. The burn is painless because it destroys nerves in the skin. Scar formation and contractures are likely complications.

Fourth degree: a burn that extends through the full thickness of the skin and into underlying bone, fat, muscles, and tendons. Third- and fourth-degree burns are best managed at specialized burn centers. SEE: illus. (Burns).

COMPLICATIONS: Sloughing of skin, gangrene, scarring, erysipelas, nephritis, pneumonia, immune system impairment, or intestinal disturbances are possible complications. Shock and infection must always be anticipated with higher-degree or larger burns. The risk of complication is greatest when more than 25% of the body surface is burned.

ETIOLOGY: Burns may result from ultraviolet radiation, bursts of steam, heated liquids and metals, chemical fires, electrocution, or direct contact with flame or flammable clothing.

PRECAUTIONS: A person in burning clothing should never be allowed to run. The individual should lie down and roll. A rug, blanket, or anything within reach can be used to smother the flames. Care must be taken so that the individual does not inhale the smoke. The clothing should be cut off carefully so that the skin is not pulled away. Synthetic fabrics that have melted into the burn wound are best removed later in the emergency department or burn center. Jewelry should be removed even if not near the burn wounds due to concerns for fluid shifts and swelling. Blisters should not be opened, as this increases the chance for infection. Patients with large burn areas or third- and fourth-degree burns must receive appropriate tetanus prophylaxis.

NOTE: In severe, widespread burns, the patient must be transferred to a burn center as soon as is practical.

TREATMENT: The first responsibility in the care of the burn patient is to assess the patency of the airway and to ensure that breathing is unimpaired. If smoke inhalation or airway injury is suspected, intubation should be performed before edema makes this impossible. Airway injury is most likely to occur after facial burns or smoke inhalation in closed spaces. A cough productive of soot or charred material in-

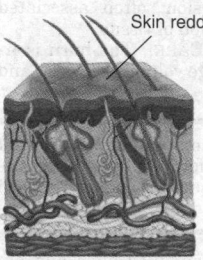

Skin reddened

First degree
Superficial

Blisters

Second degree
Partial thickness

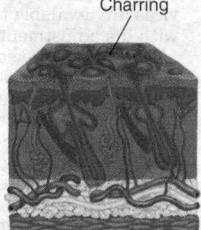

Charring

Third degree
Full thickness

BURNS

creases the likelihood of inhalational injury.

The second task in burn care is to ensure cardiac output and tissue perfusion. Volume resuscitation with crystalloid is given per standard protocols; at the same time, urinary output, blood pressure and pulse, body weights, and renal function are closely monitored to ensure adequate hydration.

The immediate care of the burn itself involves the removal of any overlying clothing and jewelry and the irrigation of the affected tissues with cool water, taking care to avoid excessively cooling the body. To help prevent hypothermia and infection, cover the burn wounds with sterile dressings if available, or a clean sheet, separating burn wound surfaces. Gentle tissue débridement should be followed by application of nonadherent dressings, skin substitutes, topical antiseptics, or autografts, as dictated by circumstances. Tetanus prophylaxis is routinely given, usually with both tetanus toxoid and tetanus immune globulin.

In specific circumstances, additional interventions such as hyperbaric oxygen therapy for carbon monoxide intoxication, escharotomy for circumferential burns, antibiotic therapy for infections, pressor support for hypotension, or nutritional support may be needed.

Patients with large or complex burn injuries should be transferred to regional burn centers or to the care of surgeons with special interest in burn management.

PATIENT CARE: During rehabilitation, individually fitted elastic garments are applied to prevent hypertrophic scar formation, and joints are exercised to promote a full range of motion. The patient is encouraged to increase activity tolerance, obtain adequate rest, strive for physical and emotional independence, and resume vocational and social functioning. Referrals for occupational therapy, psychological counseling, support groups, or social services are often necessary. Reconstructive and cosmetic surgery may be required. Support groups and services are available to assist the patient with life adjustments.

Patients' previous psychological states may predispose them to injury and may have an adverse effect on recovery. Patients with burn injuries demonstrate a wide range of emotional responses including anger, frustration, irritability, and psychological states (delirium, anxiety, depression, and grief). Posttraumatic stress disorder (PTSD) may occur after a burn injury. Often, the PTSD patient will need help from primary or specialized care providers to recover psychologically. Explain patient needs and care concerns to family to help alleviate their cares and concerns (and varied psychological responses). Involve them with you in patient care as permissible. Family members should be encouraged to sit with the patient, and to touch, speak to, read to, and otherwise communicate with the patient. Providing patients with a sense of purpose will help to alleviate feelings of helplessness and will provide both patient and family with more comfortable and comforting memories. SEE: *Nursing Diagnoses Appendix.*

The provision of optimal nutrition to burn patients is an important component of recovery. Because of protein losses, the total protein consumed by a burn patient should be at least 2.5 g/kg of body weight daily. Total caloric needs may exceed 30 kcal/kd/daily. The risk of infections may be reduced by the provision of dietary supplements, esp. arginine and glutamine.

acid b. A burn caused by exposure to corrosive acids such as sulfuric, hydrochloric, and nitric.

PATIENT CARE: The burn area should be flushed with large volumes of water. For further details of definitive treatment, see under *sulfuric acid poisoning.*

actinic b. Burns caused by ultraviolet or sun rays. Treatment is the same as for dry heat burns.

b. of aerodigestive tract Necrosis of the oral mucosa, trachea, or esophagus due to the ingestion of caustic substances. After an assessment of the patient's airway, breathing, and circulation, the medical team determines the severity of the exposure by physical examination or laryngoscopy. Some patients may require hospitalization for local care and the administration of intravenous steroids, histamine antagonists, and antibiotics. Late complications may include strictures of the affected internal organs.

alkali b. A burn caused by caustic alkalies such as lye, caustic potash (potassium hydroxide), and caustic soda (sodium hydroxide), and marked by a painful skin lesion, often associated with gelatinization of tissue.

EMERGENCY CARE: The burn is irrigated with large volumes of water and dressed.

⚠️ Be careful to brush dry powder off the skin before applying water, as some chemicals, such as lye, react with water.

brush b. A combined burn and abrasion resulting from friction.

TREATMENT: Loose dirt is carefully brushed away and the area is cleansed with soap and water. An antiseptic solution or ointment is applied and covered with a dressing. Tetanus toxoid or antitoxin is given if required. A brush burn is also informally called a "road rash" as in the case of a motorcyclist who slid across the pavement.

chemical b. Tissue destruction caused by corrosive or irritating chemicals such as strong acids or bases, phenols, pesticides, disinfectants, fertilizers, or chemical warfare agents.

TREATMENT: Irrigate with large quantities of water.

electric b. Tissue destruction caused by the passage of electrical current through the body, usually as a result of industrial accidents or lightning exposures. Entry and exit wounds are usually present; significant internal organ damage may be found along the path of the current through the body.

b. of eye A burn of the eyeball due to contact with chemical, thermal, electrical, or radioactive agents.

EMERGENCY CARE: The eye should be washed immediately with the nearest available supply of water, even if it is not sterile. Irrigation may need to be continued for hours if burn is due to lye. Care must be taken to prevent runoff from draining into the uninjured eye.

fireworks b. Injury from explosives; usually a burn, often with embedded foreign bodies and a high incidence of infection and tetanus, which should be prevented by meticulous care of injury and use of antitetanus toxoid and immune globulin.

flash b. A burn resulting from an explosive blast such as occurs from ignition of highly inflammable fluids, or in war from a high-explosive shell or a nuclear blast.

gunpowder b. A burn resulting from exploding gunpowder, usually at very close range. It is often followed by tetanus, which should be prevented by administration of antitetanus toxoid and immune globulin and meticulous care of the injury area.

inhalation b. Inhalation injury.

radiation b. A burn resulting from overexposure to radiant energy as from x-rays, radium or other radioactive elements, sunlight, or nuclear blast.

respiratory b. A burn to the components of the respiratory system usually caused by inhaling superheated gases. SEE: *inhalation injury.*

thermal b. A burn resulting from contact with fire, hot objects, or fluids. SEE: illus.

x-ray b. SEE: *radiation burn.*

burn center A hospital-based health care facility staffed with specialists essential to the comprehensive care of burn patients.

burner (bŭrn'ēr) A lay term for trauma

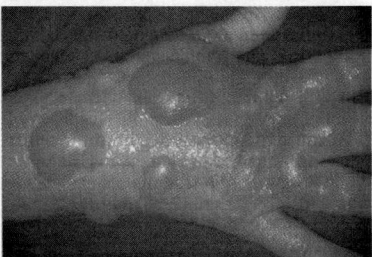

BLISTERED PARTIAL THICKNESS THERMAL BURN

to the brachial plexus, marked by a fiery sensation in the neck that radiates down the arm, esp. when the neck is deviated from the involved side and the contralateral shoulder is depressed. This condition, which is esp. prevalent in contact sports, causes the cervical nerve root to become compressed between two vertebrae. Weakness and numbness follow the burning sensation but are usually transient. Repeated brachial plexus trauma can result in permanent neuropathy. SYN: *stinger.*

⚠ The presence of a vertebral fracture should be ruled out (as with x-rays) before testing for brachial plexus trauma.

Burnett syndrome [Charles Hoyt Burnett, U.S. physician, 1913–1967] Milk-alkali syndrome.

burning mouth syndrome A burning sensation in one or several parts of the mouth. It occurs in older adults and is generally related to menopausal or psychological factors. Identified causes are denture irritation, yeast infection, decreased salivary production, systemic factors such as nutritional and estrogen deficiencies, and sensory neuropathies. It is also called *oral dysesthesia.* Treatment consists of therapy for the causative condition. SYN: *burning tongue.*

burnish (bĕr'nĭsh) To condense or polish a metal surface with a smooth metal instrument.

burnisher (bĕr'nĭsh-ĕr) An instrument with a blade or nib for smoothing the margins of a dental restoration.

burnout (bŭrn'owt) **1.** Rendering unserviceable by excessive heat. **2.** Exhaustion due to chronic job stress. It is characterized by physical and emotional fatigue and sometimes physical illness. Frustration from a perceived inability to end the stresses and problems associated with powerlessness in one's job contribute to loss of concern for patients or good job performance. Health care professionals are esp. prone to burnout, particularly those working in highly stressful conditions.

wax b. Removal of an invested wax pattern from a mold by heating, thereby creating the mold space for casting metal.

Burow's solution (boo'rōz) [Karl August von Burow, Ger. surgeon, 1809–1874] A dilute solution of aluminum acetate; used in dermatology as a drying agent for weeping skin lesions.

burp **1.** To belch. **2.** To hold a baby against the chest and pat it on the back to induce belching.

BURP maneuver The application of *b*ackward, *u*pward, and *r*ightward *p*ressure to the larynx as part of an effort to facilitate endotracheal intubation, e.g., during advanced cardiac life support.

burr SEE: *bur.*

burrow (bŭr'rō) A tunnel made in or under the skin (e.g., by an insect or a parasite). SEE: *cutaneous larva migrans; scabies.*

burrowing (bŭr'ō-ĭng) The formation of a subcutaneous tunnel made by a parasite or of a fistula or sinus containing pus.

bursa (bŭr'să) *pl.* **bursae** [Gr., a leather sack] **1.** A padlike sac or cavity found in connective tissue usually in the vicinity of joints. It is lined with synovial membrane and contains a fluid (synovia) that reduces friction between tendon and bone, tendon and ligament, or between other structures where friction is likely to occur. **2.** A blind sac or cavity.

Achilles b. A bursa located between the Achilles tendon and the calcaneus.

adventitious b. A bursa not usually present but developing in response to friction or pressure.

calcaneal b. The bursa between the Achilles tendon and the heel bone.

Calori's b. SEE: *Calori's bursa.*

olecranon b. A bursa at the elbow joint lying between the olecranon process and the skin.

omental b. The lesser peritoneal cavity; the cavity of the great omentum. It communicates with the greater or true peritoneal cavity via the vestibule and epiploic foramen.

patellar b. Formed by several bursae located in the region of the patella; includes the suprapatellar, infrapatellar, and prepatellar bursae. Some communicate with the cavity of the knee joint.

pharyngeal b. A small, median, blind sac found in the lower portion of the pharyngeal tonsil.

subacromial b. The large bursa lying between the acromion and the coracoacromial ligament above and the insertion of the supraspinatus muscle below. It is also known as the subdeltoid bursa.

bursal (bŭr'săl) Pert. to a bursa.

bursectomy (bŭr-sĕk'tō-mē) [Gr. *bursa,* a leather sack, + *ektome,* excision] Excision of a bursa.

bursitis (bŭr-sīt'ĭs) [*bursa* + *-itis*] Inflammation of a bursa, esp. between bony prominences and muscle or tendon, as in the shoulder and knee. It is typically caused by repeated stresses placed on a joint during work or play, but sometimes results from sudden trauma, from inflammatory joint disease, or bacteria. Common forms include rotator cuff, miner's or tennis elbow, and prepatellar bursitis. Fluid accumulation in the bursa results in irritation, inflammation, sudden or gradual pain, and symptoms such as impaired joint movement. SEE: *Nursing Diagnoses Appendix.*

TREATMENT: Therapy includes rest and immobilization of the affected part during the acute stage. Active mobilization as soon as acute symptoms subside will help to reduce the likelihood of adhesions. Nonsteroidal anti-inflammatory drugs, analgesics, local application of cold then heat, and diathermy are helpful. Fluid removal (aspiration of the bursa) and injection of local anesthetics and cortisone into bursae may be required to reduce inflammation and relieve pain. In chronic bursitis, surgery may be necessary.

PATIENT CARE: Rest is prescribed, and movement of the affected part is restricted during the acute phase if pain and limited range of joint motion are present. If pain and loss of function are severe and do not improve with rest, the patient is referred for medical evaluation; physical therapy may also be needed to maintain joint mobility and prevent neighboring muscle atrophy.

anserine b. Inflammation of the sartorius bursa located over the medial side of the tibia just below the knee.

prepatellar b. An inflammation of the bursa anterior to the patella, with accumulation of fluid. It may be seen in those who have to kneel frequently or continually while working. SYN: *carpetlayer's* ***knee;*** *housemaid's* ***knee;*** *roofer's knee.* SEE: illus.

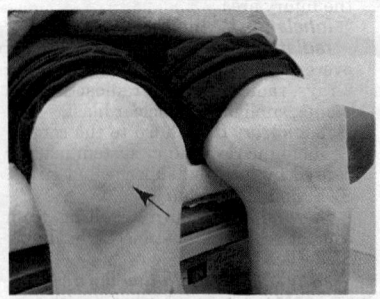

PREPATELLAR BURSITIS

septic b. Bursitis caused by bacterial invasion of the joint.

bursolith (bŭr′sō-lĭth) [″ + *lithos,* stone] A calculus formed in a bursa.

bursopathy (bŭr-sŏp′ă-thē) [″ + *pathos,* disease, suffering] Any pathological condition of a bursa.

bursotomy (bŭr-sŏt′ō-mē) [″ + *tome,* incision] Incision of a bursa.

burst (bŭrst) To undergo mitosis and proliferate rapidly, e.g., in response to a cytokine or hormone.

burst-forming-unit, burst-forming unit ABBR: BFU. A stem cell that produces red blood cell progeny and not blood cells of other lineages.

Buruli ulcer (bŭ-rool′ē) [Fm. the Buruli (now Nakasongola) District in Uganda] SEE: under *ulcer.*

Buschke scleredema (boosh′kĕ, kē) [Abraham Buschke, Ger. dermatologist, 1868–1943] Generalized nonpitting edema that begins on the head or neck and spreads to the body. This lasts a year or less and leaves no sequelae. The cause is unknown. SYN: *scleredema adultorum.*

bushmaster (bush′mas″tĕr) A long and powerful poisonous snake *Lachesis muta,* a member of the pit viper family, that lives in Central America and in northernmost South America. SYN: *Lachesis muta.*

butane (bū′tān) C_4H_{10}; a gaseous, inflammable hydrocarbon derived from petroleum.

Buthidae (bū′thĭ-dē) [*Buthus,* the type genus + *-idae*] The family of the class Arachnida that comprises most of the venomous scorpions.

butt [ME. *butte,* end] To join the ends of two objects together.

butterbur (bŭt′ĕr-bŭr″) An herb from which an herbal remedy is made for treatment of migraine headache and allergic rhinitis. SYN: *Petasites hybridus.*

butterfly (bŭt′ĕr-flī″) An adhesive bandage used in place of sutures to hold wound edges together.

buttermilk (bŭt′ĕr-mĭlk″) The liquid left after the separation of butter from milk or cream. It contains 2% fat. Cultured buttermilk is made by adding streptococci to milk to give it a sour flavor.

buttocks (bŭt′ŭks) [AS. *buttuc,* end] The external prominences posterior to the hips; formed by the gluteal muscles and underlying structures. SYN: *nates.*

button (bŭt′n) An anatomical or pathological structure that resembles a button.

buttonhole (bŭt′ŏn-hōl″) An incision (sometimes inadvertent) into the wall of a cavity or membrane. This term may be applied to surgical procedures on hollow organ systems such as the gastrointestinal, urinary tract, and cardiovascular systems and to some of myocutaneous grafts.

butyl-2-cyanoacrylate (būt′ĭl-too″sī″ă-nō-ak′rī-lāt″, sī-an″ō-) A tissue adhesive used for wound closure. SEE: *cyanoacrylate adhesive.*

butylene (bū′tĭ-lēn) A hydrocarbon gas, C_4H_8.

butyraceous (bū″tĭ-rā′shŭs) [L. *butyrum,* butter] Containing or resembling butter.

butyrate (būt′ĭ-rāt″) A salt of butyric acid. Butyrates form a class of short chain fatty acids and are the primary nutritional source for colonocytes.

butyrin (bū′tĭr-ĭn) A soft, yellow semiliquid fat that is present in butter.

butyroid (bū′tĭ-royd) [″ + Gr. *eidos,* form, shape] Having the appearance or consistency of butter.

butyrometer (bū″tĭ-rŏm′ĕ-tĕr) [″ + Gr. *metron,* measure] A device for estimating the amount of butterfat in milk.

butyrophenone (bū″tĭ-rō-fē′nōn) A class of drugs, some of which are used to treat psychoses, acute agitation, Tourette's syndrome, and other disorders. Tardive dyskinesia may be a side effect of prolonged use.

BV *Bacterial vaginosis.*

BW *Biological warfare; body weight.*

bx *Biopsy.*

BXO *Balanitis xerotica obliterans.*

Byler disease (bī′lĕr) An inherited disorder with a defect on chromosome 18 in which infants develop cholestatic jaundice and eventually cirrhosis. A high incidence of retinitis pigmentosa is associated with this disease, and mental retardation is frequently seen in affected children. Death from liver disease occurs by adolescence. SYN: *progressive familial intrahepatic cholestasis.*

bypass (bī″păs′) A means of circumvention; a shunt. It is used surgically to install an alternative route for the blood to flow past an obstruction if a main or vital artery, e.g., the abdominal aorta or a coronary artery, becomes obstructed. The various procedures are named according to the arteries involved, e.g., coronary artery, aortoiliac, or femoropopliteal bypasses. The circulation of the heart may be bypassed by providing an extracorporeal device to pump blood while a surgical procedure is being done on the coronary arteries or cardiac valves.

aortocoronary b. Coronary artery bypass.

coronary artery b. Surgical establishment of a shunt that permits blood to travel from the aorta or internal mammary artery to a branch of the coronary artery at a point past an obstruction. It is used to treat coronary artery disease.

Traditional surgery requires opening the chest and sternum, spreading the ribs, and use of external heart/lung oxygenation. Less invasive techniques use several small incisions (keyhole surgery), smaller surgical instruments, and fiber-optic cameras. Recovery time is reduced and there are fewer postoperative complications. SEE: illus.

PATIENT CARE: *Preoperative:* The surgical procedure and the equipment and procedures used in the postanesthesia and intensive care units are explained. If possible, a tour of the facilities is arranged for the patient. The nurse assists with insertion of arterial and central lines and initiates cardiac monitoring when the patient enters the operating room.

Postoperative: Initially the postoperative patient will be intubated, mechanically ventilated, and will undergo cardiac monitoring. He will also have a nasogastric tube, a chest tube and drainage system, an indwelling urinary catheter, arterial and venous lines, epicardial pacing wires, and, often, a pulmonary artery catheter.

Signs of hemodynamic compromise, e.g., severe hypotension, decreased cardiac output, and shock, are monitored; vital signs are obtained and documented according to protocol until the patient's condition stabilizes. Disturbances in heart rate or rhythm are monitored; any abnormalities are documented and reported. Preparations are made to initiate or assist with epicardial pacing, cardioversion, or defibrillation as necessary. Pulmonary artery, central venous, and left atrial pressures are monitored, and arterial pressure is maintained within prescribed guidelines (usually between 110 and 70 mm Hg). Peripheral pulses, capillary refill time, and skin temperature and color

are assessed frequently; the chest is auscultated for changes in heart sounds or pulmonary congestion. Any abnormalities are documented and reported to the surgeon. Tissue oxygenation is monitored by assessing breath sounds, chest excursion, symmetry of chest expansion, pulse oximeter, and arterial blood gas (ABG) values. Ventilator settings are adjusted as needed. Fluid intake and output and electrolyte levels are assessed for imbalances. Chest tube drainage is maintained at the prescribed negative pressure (usually −10 to −40 cm H_2O); chest tubes are inspected for patency. The patient is assessed for hemorrhage, excessive drainage (>200 ml/hr), and sudden decrease or cessation of drainage. Prescribed analgesics and other medications are administered.

Throughout recovery the patient is evaluated for changes in oxygenation, ventilation, neurological status, and urinary output. After the patient is weaned from the ventilator and extubated, chest physiotherapy and incentive spirometry are used, and the patient is encouraged to breathe deeply and to cough to prevent atelectasis of the lung and to clear mucus from the airway. The patient is helped to change position frequently. Help is also given with range-of-motion exercises and with active leg movement and gluteal and quadriceps setting exercises.

Before discharge the patient is instructed to report any signs of infection (fever, sore throat, redness, swelling, or drainage from the leg or chest incisions) or cardiac complications (angina, dizzi-

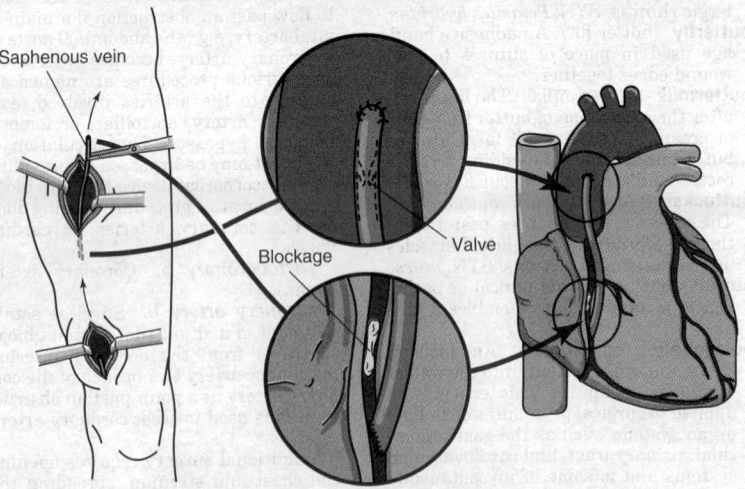

Saphenous vein

Blockage

Valve

CORONARY ARTERY BYPASS
Myocardial reperfusion by coronary artery bypass graft surgery

ness, rapid or irregular pulse, or increasing fatigue or prolonged recovery time after activity or exercise). Postpericardiotomy syndrome often develops after open heart surgery. Postoperative depression may also develop weeks after discharge; both patient and family are reassured that this is normal and usually passes quickly. The patient is advised to observe any tobacco, sodium, cholesterol, fat, and calorie restrictions, which may help reduce the risk of recurrent arterial occlusion. The patient needs to maintain a balance between activity and rest and should schedule a short afternoon rest period and plan to get 8 hr of sleep nightly. Frequent rest should also follow any tiring activity. Participation in the prescribed cardiac rehabilitative exercise program is recommended, and any activity restrictions (avoiding lifting heavy objects, driving a car, or doing strenuous work until specific permission is granted) are reinforced. Appropriate reassurance is offered that the patient can climb stairs, engage in sexual activity, take baths or showers, and do light chores. The patient is referred to local information and support groups or organizations, such as the American Heart Association. SYN: *aortocoronary b.*

extra-anatomic vascular b. Surgical revascularization for peripheral vascular disease of the limbs, using a prosthetic graft (e.g., axillofemorally or femorofemorally) to divert blood to a site distal to an arterial obstruction.

PATIENT CARE: Postoperatively, it is important to monitor the patient's vital signs for changes, esp. of pulse and rhythm, and to assess the patient for symptoms of angina pectoris or arrhythmias. Cardiac monitoring and frequent ECGs are routine aspects of care. The surgical wound is checked for bleeding or hematoma formation, or signs of infection or dehiscence. Peripheral pulses are palpated using a doppler, if necessary, to determine peripheral perfusion.

gastric b. Any surgical procedure in which the stomach, or most of the stomach, is isolated and disconnected from the rest of the upper gastrointestinal tract. SEE: *Roux-en-y gastric b.*

jejunoileal b. A surgical procedure for decreasing absorption of nutrients from the small intestine by anastomosing the proximal jejunum to the distal ileum. Although it can be used to treat obesity, jejunoileal bypass has been replaced by gastric bypass procedures because of the significant complications of jejunoileal bypass surgery.

minimally invasive direct coronary artery b. ABBR: MIDCAB. The placement of a coronary artery graft without stopping the heart or using a cardiopulmonary bypass (heart-lung machine). A thoracotomy rather than a medial sternotomy is used to access the heart, which is then stabilized by use of a compression or suction device to decrease movement. The procedure is used primarily for grafting a single vessel, usually the left or right internal mammary artery. Although MIDCAB has the advantages of lower surgical costs and possibly a decreased risk of complications, it has the disadvantages of limited surgical visibility and more difficult suturing. SYN: *off-pump coronary artery b.*

off-pump coronary artery b. Minimally invasive direct coronary artery bypass

Roux-en-y gastric b. A bariatric surgical procedure in which the superior portion of the stomach is isolated from the rest of the stomach and the jejunum is connected to it. As a result, food passes directly from the proximal stomach into the middle of the small intestine. It bypasses the majority of the stomach, which is isolated from the working portion of the stomach and from the duodenum. An opening is made in the duodenum and the jejunum, and the two organs are connected via a surgical stoma. This permits drainage into the jejunum of gastric secretions from the isolated greater curvature of the stomach. This form of gastric bypass is the most common bariatric surgical procedure and among the most successful. Since the duodenum absorbs many important vitamins and nutrients, including iron, vitamin B_{12}, and calcium, nutritional deficiencies and iron-deficiency anemia are common complications. Others include nausea, vomiting, ulcers, and anastomotic leaks. SEE: *Nursing Diagnoses Appendix.*

byssinosis (bĭs″ĭ-nō′sĭs) [Gr. *byssos,* cotton, + *osis,* condition] Reactive airways disease of cotton, flax, and hemp workers. Byssinosis is caused by the inhalation of dust and foreign materials, including bacteria, mold, and fungi. The disease does not occur in textile workers who work with cotton after it is bleached. It is marked by symptomatic wheezing and tightness in the chest. Symptoms are usually more pronounced at the beginning of each work week than later on. SEE: *pneumonoconiosis.*

bystander CPR Cardiopulmonary resuscitation (CPR) that is performed by a layperson who is not part of the organized emergency-response system in a community.

C **1.** Symbol for the element carbon. **2.** *Celsius; centigrade; cervical vertebra* (C1 to C7); *kilocalorie* (large calorie).

c *calorie; centum* (a hundred); *circa* (about); *clonus; closure; compound; congius* (gallon).

c̄ [L.] *cum,* with.

¹⁴C Carbon-14.

CA *cancer-associated antigen.*

Ca Symbol for the element calcium.

CA 125 An antigen produced by tissues derived from coelomic epithelium. It is associated with various epithelial cancers, including ovarian cancer. It may be used to assess response to treatment in women with known ovarian cancer.

CA19-9 Cancer antigen 19-9; a carbohydrate (oligosaccharide) antigen found in patients with cancers of several internal organs, including adenocarcinomas of the pancreas, gallbladder, stomach, colon, and ovaries.

CA 72-4 An immunoassay that detects tumor-associated glycoprotein 72, an antigen found on many mucin-secreting gastrointestinal cancers.

CAAHEP *Commission on Accreditation for Allied Health Educational Programs.*

C-A-B *compressions—airway—breathing* (a mnemonic for the preferred order of interventions in the basic life support of the unresponsive patient, according to the American Heart Association's 2010 guidelines for emergency cardiac care).

CABG *coronary artery bypass graft.*

Cabot rings (kab'ŏt) [Richard C. Cabot, U.S. physician, 1868–1939] Blue-staining threadlike inclusions of unknown origin, found in the red blood cells in severe anemia. They may appear as rings, figures-of-eight, or twists. They seem to be parts of the nucleus, with histones and iron but no DNA.

Cabrera sign (kă-brā'ră) Electrocardiographic evidence of myocardial infarction in patients with left bundle branch block or ventricular pacing, in which there is a 0.04 second notch in the ascending limb of the S wave of leads V3, V4, or V5.

CAC *Coronary artery calcification.*

cacao (kă-kā'ō, kă-kaw'ō) [Mex.-Sp. from Nahuatl *cacahuatl,* cacao beans] **1.** The seed of *Theobroma cacao* used to prepare cacao butter (theobroma oil), chocolate, and cocoa. **2.** A reddish to brown powder prepared from the roasted ripe seeds of *Theobroma cacao* (family Sterculiaceae), having a chocolate odor and taste. It is used as a syrup

base, as a flavoring for certain medications, and in beverages and confections.

Cacchi-Ricci syndrome (kŏk'kē rĭ'chē, rē') [Roberto Cacchi, Vincenzo Ricci, 20th-cent. Ital. radiologists] Sponge kidney.

cachectin (kă-kĕk'tĭn) Tumor necrosis factor alpha.

cachexia (kă-kek'sē-ă) [*caco-* + Gr. *hexis,* condition] A state of ill health, malnutrition, and wasting. It may occur in many chronic diseases, malignancies, and infections. **cachectic** (-kek'tik), *adj.*

PATIENT CARE: Activities should be interspersed with frequent rest periods and the patient's response to activity monitored to prevent fatigue. Oral hygiene is provided before and after eating. Small, frequent meals of high-calorie, high-nutrient, concentrated soft foods are offered along with fluids to reduce the effort required in eating. The patient is repositioned frequently to prevent skin breakdown. The skin is inspected for breakdown, and tissues are protected from pressure with flotation pads or mattresses and other assistive devices. When moved, the patient is handled gently, and the joints are supported to prevent pain and pathological fractures. Assisted passive or active range-of-motion exercises are provided to maintain joint mobility. Elimination is monitored to prevent retention of urine or stools, and the patient is assisted with toileting. If incontinence occurs, steps are taken to protect skin integrity and to preserve the patient's self-esteem.

   cancerous c. Wasting caused by cancer.

   cardiac c. Muscle wasting and weight loss occurring in persons with congestive heart failure, and linked with excess circulating levels of tumor necrosis factor and other inflammatory cytokines. It has a poor prognosis.

   malarial c. Wasting due to chronic malaria.

cachinnation (kak-ĭ-nā'shŏn) [L. *cachinnare,* to laugh aloud] Excessive, inappropriate, loud laughter. It may be associated with schizophrenia.

CaCl₂ Calcium chloride.

CaCO₃ Calcium carbonate.

caco-, cac- [Gr. *kakos,* bad] Prefixes meaning *bad* or *ill.*

CaC₂O₄ Calcium oxalate.

cacodylate (kak″ŏ-dil'āt) [Gr. *kakōdēs,* foul-smelling] A salt of cacodylic acid.

cacosmia, kakosmia (kă-kŏz'mē-ă) [" + *osme,* smell] **1.** An unpleasant odor.

2. Subjective perception of a disagreeable odor. SEE: *parosmia*.

CAD *computer-aided dispatch; computer-assisted design; computer-aided detection; coronary artery disease.*

cadaver (kă-dav′ĕr) *pl.* **cadavera** [L. *cadaver,* dead body] A dead body; a corpse.

cadaveric, cadaverous (kă-dav′ĕ-rĭk, kă-dav′ĕ-rŭs), *adj.*

cadence (kād′ĕns) [Fr. fr Italian *cadenza,* a falling] The number of movements of a body part, e.g., the number of revolutions made by a foot pushing the crank of a bicycle, or the number of steps taken per unit of time.

cadherin (kad-hēr′in, -her′) Any of several cellular adhesion molecules (molecules that hold cells together). In cancer cells, mutations in cadherins keep cells from sticking together normally. As a result, malignant cells grow irregularly, invade other tissues, and metastasize to distant locations.

cadmium (kad′mē-ŭm) [L. *cadmia,* calamine, fr Gr. *kadmeia* (gē), Cadman [Theban] earth + *-ium* (1)] SYMB: Cd. A soft bluish-white metal present in zinc ores, atomic number 48, atomic weight (mass) 112.40, specific gravity 8.65. It is used industrially in electroplating and in atomic reactors. Its salts are poisonous. SEE: *Poisons and Poisoning Appendix.*

caduceus (kă-dū′sē-ŭs) [L., a herald's wand] In mythology, the wand or staff that belonged to Apollo and was given to Hermes, or Mercury. It consists of two serpents entwined around a staff, surmounted by two wings, and is used as the medical insignia of certain groups such as the U.S. Army Medical Corps. Although the caduceus is sometimes used to symbolize the medical profession, the staff of Aesculapius is considered the more appropriate symbol.

caecum (sē′kŭm) Cecum.

caelotherapy (sē″lō-ther′ă-pē) [L. *caelum,* heaven, + therapy] Therapy using religion or religious symbols.

Caenorhabditis elegans (sē″nō-răb-dīt′ĭs ĕl′ă-gănz, -găns) A roundworm, about 1 mm long. It is the first multicellular organism for which the full genome was sequenced. Its cells are used in studies of the molecular basis of development, aging, and fat metabolism.

café au lait macules (ka-fā′ ō lā′) SEE: under *macule.*

cafestol (kaf′ĕ-stol″) The oily, aromatic hydrocarbon in coffee that raises serum cholesterol levels. It is largely removed when coffee is filtered.

caffeine (kăf′ēn, kă-fēn′) $C_8H_{10}N_4O_2$; an alkaloid present in coffee, chocolate, tea, many cola drinks, cocoa, and some over-the-counter medicines. The amount of caffeine in beverages varies from 40 to 180 mg in 6 oz (180 mL) of coffee, from 2 to 5 mg in decaffeinated coffee, and from 20 to 110 mg in 5 oz (150 mL) of tea. The caffeine in cola drinks ranges from 30 to 90 mg in a 360-mL (12-oz) serving. The pharmacological action of caffeine includes stimulation of the central nervous system and of gastric acid and pepsin secretion, elevation of free fatty acids in plasma, diuresis, basal metabolic rate increase, total sleep time decrease, and possible blood glucose level increase. Caffeine is considered an ergogenic aid in athletics because it tends to enhance endurance and improves reaction time. Adverse effects include drug dependence and withdrawal in some habitual users. SEE: *caffeine intoxication; caffeine withdrawal.*

caffeine intoxication SEE: under *intoxication.*

caffeinism (kăf′ēn-ĭzm) Caffeine intoxication.

Caffey, John (kaf′ē) U.S. pediatric radiologist, 1895–1966. He was a pioneer in pediatric radiology.

　　C.'s disease Infantile cortical hyperostosis.

CAGE-AID The CAGE screening technique *adapted to include drugs.* The patient is asked if he or she has ever had to cut down his or her use of alcohol or drugs or been annoyed by criticism of alcohol or drug use.

caged molecule A molecule that can become activated by particular wavelengths of light.

CAG repeat disease A group of neurodegenerative diseases characterized by the repetition of the nucleotides cytosine-adenine-guanine in specific genes. Diseases in this group include Huntington's chorea.

CAH *congenital adrenal hyperplasia.*

CAI *computer-assisted instruction.*

caida mollera, caida de la mollera (kă-ē′thă, -dă mō-yā′ră, -lyă′) [Sp., fallen fontanel] Severe dehydration in infancy. In some Hispanic cultures *caida mollera* applies to any severe illness in infancy attributed to incorrect care or handling. Causes include diarrhea, decreased appetite, and an inability to nurse (similar to those found in acute gastroenteritis with dehydration). Findings include fever, irritability, restlessness, and sunken fontanels. Folk remedies for this illness include inserting a finger into the child's mouth and pushing up on the palate or applying substances to or sucking on the fontanel.

-caine [Fr. *(co)caine*] A suffix used in pharmacology to name *local anesthetics.*

caisson disease (kā′sŏn″) Decompression illness.

CAKUT *congenital anomalies of the kidneys and urinary tract.*

Cal Large *calorie.*

cal Small *calorie.*

calamine (kăl′ă-mīn) A pink powder,

containing zinc oxide with a small amount of ferric oxide. It is used externally in various skin conditions as a protective and astringent, an ointment, or a lotion.

calamus scriptorius (kal'ă-mŭs) [L.] The inferior portion of the floor of the fourth ventricle of the brain. It is shaped like a pen and lies between the restiform bodies.

Calan, Calan SR SEE: *verapamil.*

calcaneoapophysitis (kăl-kā″nē-ō-ă-pŏf″ē-zī′tĭs) [L. *calcaneus,* heel, + Gr. *apophysis,* offshoot, + *itis,* inflammation] Pain and inflammation of the posterior portion of the calcaneus at the place of insertion of the Achilles tendon.

calcaneodynia (kăl-kā″nē-ō-dĭn′ē-ă) [″ + Gr. *odyne,* pain] Pain in the heel.

calcaneofibular (kăl-kā″nē-ō-fĭb′ū-lăr) [″ + *fibula,* pin] Pert. to the calcaneus and fibula.

calcaneonavicular (kăl-kā″nē-ō-nă-vĭk′ū-lăr) [″ + *navicula,* boat] Pert. to the calcaneus and navicular bone.

calcaneoscaphoid (kăl-kā″nē-ō-skă′foyd) [″ + Gr. *skaphe,* skiff, + *eidos,* form, shape] Pert. to the calcaneus and scaphoid bone.

calcaneotibial (kăl-kā″nē-ō-tĭb′ē-ăl) [″ + *tibia,* shinbone] Pert. to the calcaneus and tibia.

calcaneum (kăl-kā′nē-ŭm) *pl.* **calcanea** [L. *calcaneus,* heel] Calcaneus.

calcaneus (kăl-kā′nē-ŭs) *pl.* **calcanei** [L. *calcaneus,* heel] The heel bone. It articulates with the cuboid bone and with the talus. SYN: *os calcis.* SEE: *leg* for illus.

calcaneal, calcanean (kăl-kā′nē-ăl, kăl-kā′nē-ăn), *adj.*

calcar (kal′kar) [L., a spur] A spurlike process. **calcarine,** *adj.*

   c. femorale A bony spur that strengthens the femoral neck.

calcareous (kăl-kā′rē-ŭs) [L. *calcarius,* of lime] Having the nature of lime; chalky.

calcemia (kăl-sē′mē-ă) [L. *calx,* lime, + Gr. *haima,* blood] Hypercalcemia.

calci-, calc-, calco- [L. *calx,* stem *calc-,* lime, limestone, quicklime] Prefixes meaning *calcium, calcite* or *calcium salt.*

calcic (kăl′sĭk) [L. *calcarius*] Pert. to calcium or lime.

calcicosis (kăl″sĭ-kō′sĭs) [L. *calx,* lime, + Gr. *osis,* infection] Pneumoconiosis caused by inhaling dust from limestone (marble).

calcidiol (kăl-sĭ-dī′ŏl) 25-hydroxyvitamin D. It is the stored form of vitamin D that circulates in the body.

calciferol (kăl-sĭf′ĕr-ŏl) Vitamin D₂. A synthetic vitamin D. It has the most vitamin D activity of those substances derived from ergosterol. It is used for prophylaxis and treatment of vitamin D deficiency, rickets, and hypocalcemic tetany. SYN: *ergocalciferol.*

calciferous (kăl-sĭf′ĕr-ŭs) [″ + *ferre,* to carry] Containing calcium, chalk, or lime.

calcific (kăl-sĭf′ĭk) [″ + *facere,* to make] Forming or composed of lime.

calcification (kăl″sĭ-fĭ-kā′shŏn) [*calcific*] The process in which organic tissue becomes hardened by the deposition of calcium salts in the tissues.

   arterial c. Calcium deposition in the arterial walls.

   coronary artery c. ABBR: CAC. Calcium phosphate (hydroxyapatite) in coronary arteries, an indicator of coronary artery atherosclerosis. CAC is found in diseased but not healthy coronary arteries. During ultrafast CT scanning of the heart, tissue densities that exceed 130 Hounsfield units typically contain significant amounts of deposited calcium. The total amount of calcium present in a person's coronary arteries can be measured by assessing the length of calcified artery and the density of the calcium identified. These factors together are used to generate a "calcium score." A calcium score > 100 is often cited as a measurement indicative of a moderately high risk of future myocardial infarction or ischemia. People with scores > 100 should begin taking daily aspirin and should actively modify atherosclerotic risk factors such as smoking, high blood pressure, hyperlipidemia, and diabetes mellitus. A score greater than 400 is often cited as indicating an urgent need for stress testing with radionuclide imaging, e.g., thallium or sestamibi.

> ⚠ Caution is needed to interpret raw calcium scores. The test is not perfectly sensitive: a small number of people without coronary artery calcium deposits still may have plaque rupture and myocardial infarction. Also, the score is just one of several markers of atherosclerosis, all of which should be factored into a risk assessment for coronary artery disease.

   dystrophic c. The deposition of calcium salts in dead, dying, or necrotic tissues.

   eggshell c. The presence of a thin ring of calcium surrounding a soft tissue mass. It is seen, e.g., in lymph nodes affected by silicosis, and in some cases of sarcoidosis, fungal sinusitis, or follicular thyroid carcinoma.

   familial idiopathic basal ganglia c. Fahr syndrome. SEE: under *Fahr, Karl Theodor.*

   metastatic c. Calcification of soft tissue with transference of calcium from bone, as in osteomalacia and disease of the parathyroid glands.

Mönckeberg c. SEE: *Mönckeberg calcification.*

pathological c. Calcinosis.

placental c. The deposition of calcium in the placenta as a result of placental abruption, infarction, or aging. This form of placental degeneration may contribute to preterm labor and fetal distress. SEE: *abruptio placentae; infarction.*

popcorn c. In radiologic imaging, the appearance of calcium deposits in lesions in irregularly lobulated or scalloped clusters rather than in concentric circles, straight lines, or dense masses. The lesions may appear in pulmonary hamatomas and in the growth plates and metaphyses of bones in some benign diseases, e.g., osteogenesis imperfecta.

calcific tendinitis SEE: under *tendinitis.*

calcigerous (kal-sij′ĕ-rŭs) [calc- + L. *gerere,* to bear] Containing calcium or lime salts.

calcimimetic Any drug that acts like calcium, for example, that lowers serum parathyroid hormone levels.

calcination (kăl″sĭ-nā′shŭn) [L. *calcinare,* to char] Drying by roasting to produce a powder.

calcine (kăl′sĭn) **1.** To expel water and volatile materials by heating to a high temperature. **2.** A powder produced by roasting.

calcinosis (kăl″sĭ-nō′sĭs) [L. *calx,* lime, + Gr. *osis,* condition] A condition marked by abnormal deposition of calcium salts in tissues. SYN: *pathological **calcification.***

c. circumscripta Subcutaneous calcification.

calcipexis, calcipexy (kăl″sĭ-pĕk′sĭs, -pĕk′sē) [″ + Gr. *pexis,* fixation] Fixation of calcium in body tissues. **calcipectic** (-pĕk′tĭk), *adj.*

calciphylaxis (kal″sĭ-fĭ-lak′sĭs) [*calci- + phylaxis*] A disease of small blood vessels in which calcium is deposited within the medial layer of the vessel wall. Gangrenous changes occur in organs that rely on blood flow through the affected vessels, esp. in the skin and in internal organs. The disease is usually found in patients with end-stage renal disease on hemodialysis but may occasionally occur in other patients. SYN: *calcific uremic **arteriolopathy.***

calciprivia (kăl″sĭ-prĭv′ē-ă) [″ + *privus,* without] Deficiency or absence of calcium.

calcitonin (kăl″sĭ-tō′nĭn) A hormone produced by the human thyroid gland that is important for maintaining a dense, strong bone matrix and regulating the blood calcium level. In patients with medullary carcinoma of the thyroid, calcitonin levels are markedly increased and serve as a tumor marker. Given na-sally, salmon calcitonin can be used to treat osteoporosis.

calcitriol (kăl-sĭ′trē-ŏl″) The active hormone form of vitamin D that promotes the absorption of calcium and phosphate in the intestines, decreases calcium excretion by the kidneys, and acts along with parathyroid hormone to maintain bone homeostasis. It is also known as 1,25-dihydroxycholecalciferol or 1,25-dihydroxyvitamin D3.

calcium (kal′sē-ŭm) [*calci- + -ium*] SYMB: Ca. A silver-white metallic chemical element, atomic number 20, atomic weight (mass) 40.08. Lime (calcium oxide), CaO, is its oxide. Calcium is a major component of limestone. Hydroxylapatite, a calcium phosphate, makes up about 75% of body ash and about 85% of mineral matter in bones.

FUNCTION: Calcium is important for blood clotting, enzyme activation, and acid-base balance. It gives firmness and rigidity to bones and teeth. It is essential for lactation, the function of nerves and muscles (including heart muscle), and maintenance of membrane permeability. Most absorption of calcium occurs in the duodenum and is dependent on the presence of calcitriol. Dietary factors affecting calcium absorption include phytic acid, consumption of too much phosphorus, and polyphenols found in tea. Approximately 40% of the calcium consumed is absorbed. Blood levels of calcium are regulated by parathyroid hormone; deficiency of this hormone produces hypocalcemia. The serum level of calcium is normally about 8.5 to 10.5 mg/dL. Low blood calcium causes tetany. Blood deprived of its calcium will not clot. Calcium is deposited in the bones but can be mobilized from them to keep the blood level constant when dietary intake is inadequate. At any given time, the body of an adult contains about 700 g of calcium phosphate; of this, 120 g is the element calcium. Adults should consume at least 1 g of calcium daily. Pregnant, lactating, and postmenopausal women should consume 1.2–1.5 g of calcium per day.

SOURCES: Excellent sources of calcium include milk and milk products (but not cottage cheese), and calcium-fortified orange juice. Good sources include canned salmon and sardines, broccoli, tofu, rhubarb, almonds, figs, and turnip greens.

SEE: *Recommended Daily Dietary Allowances Appendix.*

⚠ 1. Laboratory error and variation may sometimes cause inaccurate or inconsistent values in evaluating calcium levels.

⚠️ 2. Excessive calcium supplementation has been associated with a small increased risk of vascular calcification and heart attack.

SEE: *hypercalcemia; hypocalcemia; osteoporosis.*

c.-45 SYMB: ^{45}Ca. A radioactive isotope of calcium, half-life 164 days.

c. chloride $CaCl_2 \cdot 2H_2O$, a salt used to raise the calcium content of the blood in disorders such as hypocalcemic tetany or overdose of calcium channel blocker or beta blocker. It is used in solution and administered intravenously. It is incompatible with epinephrine.

c. cyclamate $C_6H_{12}NNaO_3S$, an artificial sweetening agent. SEE: *cyclamate.*

c. disodium edetate A substance used to bind metallic ions, such as lead or zinc. It is used to treat poisoning caused by those metals.

c. gluconate $C_{12}H_{22}CaO_{14}$, a granular, white, odorless, and flavorless powder used to treat hypocalcemia, or overdose by calcium channel blocker or by beta blocker.

c. glycerophosphate $C_3H_7CaO_6P$, the calcium salt of glycerophosphoric acid. It is used as a dietary supplement, in drug formulation, and to prevent dental caries.

c. hydroxide $Ca(OH)_2$, a white powder used as an astringent applied to the skin and mucous membranes and in dentistry as cavity liner or a pulp-capping material under a layer of zinc phosphate. It induces tertiary dentin formation for bridging or root closure, but it may be related to a chronic pulpitis and pulp necrosis after pulp capping.

c. oxalate CaC_2O_4, a compound containing calcium, present in urine in crystalline form. It is a constituent of some kidney stones. SEE: illus.

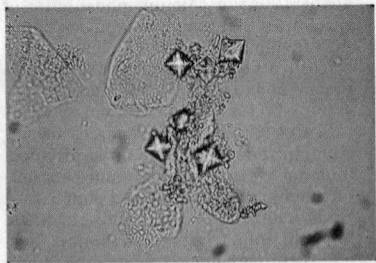

**CLASSIC DIHYDRATE CALCIUM OXALATE
CRYSTALS**

(Orig. mag. ×400)

c. pantothenate A salt of pantothenic acid, commonly used in vitamin supplements. Biochemically, it transfers acetyl groups from one compound to another. Egg yolks, liver, and yeasts are nutritional sources.

c. saccharin An artificial sweetening agent. SEE: *saccharin.*

total serum c. The sum of the soluble and protein-bound calcium in the blood.

calcium pyrophosphate dihydrate crystal deposition disease Pseudogout.

calciuria (kăl″sē-ū′rē-ă) [″ + Gr. *ouron,* urine] Calcium in the urine.

calcofluor white stain (kal″kō-floo′ŏr) SEE: under *stain.*

calcospherite (kăl″kō-sfē′rīt) [″ + Gr. *sphaira,* sphere] A small, calcified body found in specimens of the prostate, the thyroid, and some tumors.

calculogenesis (kăl″kū-lō-jěn′ě-sĭs) [″ + Gr. *genesis,* generation, birth] The formation of stones.

calculus (kal′kyŭ-lŭs, -lī″, -lē″) *pl.* **calculi** [L. *calculus,* pebble] A stone. It is usually composed of mineral salts. Stones can occur in the gallbladder, kidneys, ureters, bladder, or urethra. SEE: *gallstone; kidney stone.*

biliary c. Gallstone.

dendritic c. A renal stone molded in the form of the pelvis and calyces.

dental c. Mineralized dental plaque, located above or below the gums.

hemic c. A calculus formed from coagulated blood.

pancreatic c. A calculus in the pancreas, made of calcium carbonate with other salts and inorganic materials.

prostatic c. A stone in the prostate.

renal c. A calculus in the kidney that may block urine flow. If the ureter is blocked by the stone, there is sudden, severe, and paroxysmal renal colic often with chills, fever, hematuria, and frequency of urination. If stones do not pass spontaneously, they should be removed.

TREATMENT: Pain relief should be a priority, as should forcing fluids unless passage is completely blocked by the calculus. Smooth muscle relaxants help in passing the stone and relieving pain. If the stone is preventing urine flow or continues to grow and cause infection, surgery must be performed. Alternatively, the stone may be disintegrated ultrasonically. SYN: *kidney stone; urolith.* SEE: *extracorporeal shock-wave lithotriptor; laser treatment for kidney stone removal.*

salivary c. Salivary stone.

urinary c. A stone formed in the urinary tract, but usually found in the renal pelvis and/or kidney calyces. These vary in composition but may contain urates, calcium, oxalate, calcium carbonate, phosphates, and cystine. SEE: *lithotriptor.*

SYMPTOMS: Predisposing factors include dehydration, infection, obstruction, and metabolic factors. In the U.S., urinary stones develop in 2% to 10% of people, more often in southeastern states than in other parts of the country. Males have a 3 times higher rate than females, esp. between ages 30 and 40. Struvite calculi, which account for about 15% of all stones, are found primarily in females, usually related to urinary tract infections. Pain related to obstruction is the primary symptom. Classic renal colic travels from the costovertebral angle to the suprapubic region and external genitalia. Its intensity fluctuates, but is excruciating at its peak. Nausea and vomiting usually accompany the most severe pain. Diagnosis is based on the clinical picture plus CT scan or MRI, excretory urography, KUB x-rays, and stone analysis.

PATIENT CARE: The patient is encouraged to verbalize anxieties and concerns about the severe pain. Pain relief measures are instituted as prescribed: they include analgesics, antispasmodics, and warm, moist heat. All urine is strained for stones, and any calculus is sent for laboratory analysis. Vigorous hydration with oral or intravenous fluids helps in passage of small stones (90% are smaller than 5 mm in diameter). If a lithotriptor is to be used to shatter the calculus for removal by suction or natural passage, the duration of the procedure and follow-up care are explained. Procedures for surgical removal depend on the location of the calculus; they include cystoscopy with ureteral manipulation, or a flank or lower abdominal laparoscopic or open approach. All diagnostic studies are explained, and the patient is encouraged to verbalize fears and concerns. Urine is observed for hematuria, and specimens are tested for specific gravity and pH. Vital signs are monitored. If temperature is elevated, antipyretic measures are instituted as ordered, and antibiotics specific to cultured organisms are prescribed. Fluids are forced (PO/IV) to enhance dilution of urine, and intake and output are monitored. Fruit juices, specifically cranberry juice or cranberry tablets, help to acidify urine. The health care professional stays alert for complications such as infection, stasis, and retention. A catheter is inserted as ordered. Dietary management is based on the composition of the stone. If phosphate stones are present, patients should increase their intake of acid-ash foods such as cereals, eggs, meat, and cranberry and grape juices. Those prone to uric acid stones should consume an alkaline-ash diet of green vegetables and fruits and avoid foods high in purine. To minimize urinary tract infections, esp. for females, the patient is taught proper perineal hygiene, and the need for increased fluid intake is emphasized.

After surgery, the patient usually has an indwelling catheter or a nephrostomy tube in place. Bloody drainage is expected, and this tube should never be irrigated without a physician's order. If the kidney was removed, the patient should be reassured that the body can adapt well to one kidney. Pulmonary hygiene with an inspirometer is stressed in the presence of flank or abdominal incisions. Dressings are assessed for drainage and are changed per protocol, and signs of hemorrhage or infection are reported promptly. SEE: *Nursing Diagnoses Appendix.*

vesical c. A kidney stone that has lodged or formed in the urinary bladder.

calefacient (kăl″ĕ-fā′shĕnt) [L. *calere,* to be warm, + *facere,* to make] Conveying a sense of warmth when applied to a part of the body; something that conveys such a sense.

calendar blister SEE: under *blister.*

Calendula officinalis (kă-len′jŭ-lă) The pot marigold, a flowering plant of the marigold family from whose flowers extracts are made for a topical anti-inflammatory, bactericide, and antiseptic.

calf (kăf) [AS. *cealf*] The thick muscular back part of the leg below the knee, formed by the gastrocnemius and soleus muscles.

caliber (kăl′ĭ-bĕr) [Fr. *calibre,* diameter of bore of gun] The diameter of any orifice, canal, or tube.

calibration (kăl-ĭ-brā′shŭn) **1.** Determination of the accuracy of an instrument by comparing its output with that of a known standard or an instrument known to be accurate. **2.** Measuring of size, esp. the diameter of vessels or the caliber of an orifice.

    c. of instruments A procedure in which the mechanical functioning or electrical circuitry of a device is brought into alignment with a known standard. SEE: *calibration; calibrator.*

calibrator (kăl′ĭ-brā-tor) **1.** An instrument for measuring the inside diameter of tubes or orifices. **2.** Any material or tool used to ensure that a laboratory device, test specimen, or sample matches known standards and performs accurately.

caliceal (kăl″ĭ-sē′ăl) [Gr. *kalyx,* cup of a flower] Pert. to a calix.

calicectasis (kăl″ĭ-sĕk′tă-sĭs) [″ + *ektasis,* dilatation] Dilatation of the renal calyx. SYN: *caliectasis.*

calices (kā′lĭ-sēz″) Pl. of calix.

Caliciviridae (kăl-ĭ-sĕ-vī′rĭ-dā) [L. *chalice, calyx,* "cuplike" appearance of viral particles under electron microscopy] A family of positive-stranded RNA viruses that includes the Noroviruses (a member of which is Norwalk virus, a common cause of diarrhea in humans). SEE: *Astroviridae; Calicivirus.*

Calicivirus (kăl-ĭs′ĭ-vī″rŭs) A genus of

the family Caliciviridae that causes epidemic viral gastroenteritis in adults and children. Genera are classed in accordance with the geographic areas in which they have been identified. SEE: *Norwalk agent.*

caliculus (kă-lik′yŭ-lŭs) *pl.* **caliculi** [L., small cup] A cup-shaped structure.

   c. ophthalmicus Optic cup.

caliectasis (kăl″ē-ĕk′tă-sĭs) [Gr. *kalyx,* cup of a flower, + *ektasis,* dilatation] Dilatation of the renal calyx. SYN: *caliectasis.*

California Verbal Learning Test ABBR: CVLT. A neuropsychiatric test to measure the ability to remember heard words and the categories in which they belong. The subject listens to 16 items (four items in each of four categories) and then repeats as many of those items as he or she can recall. The subject is assessed on the number of terms retained and on the ability to recall that a particular item that he or she failed to recall may be from a particular category, e.g., a fruit or a color. A second set of 16 items is then presented. Finally, after performing a series of tasks lasting 20 minutes, the subject is asked to recall the first 16 items again.

californium (kal″ĭ-for′nē-ŭm) [University of *California* (Berkeley) + *-ium*] SYMB: Cf. A synthetic radioactive element prepared by bombardment of curium with alpha particles, atomic weight (mass) 251, atomic number 98. It has properties similar to dysprosium.

caligo (kă-lī′gō) [L., darkness] Dimness of vision.

caliper(s) (kăl′ĭ-pĕr) [Fr. *calibre,* diameter of bore of gun] A hinged instrument for measuring thickness or diameter.

calisthenics (kăl″ĭs-thĕn′ĭks) [Gr. *kalos,* beautiful, + *sthenos,* strength] An exercise program that emphasizes development of gracefulness, suppleness, and range of motion and the strength required for such movement.

call center SEE: under *center.*

Call-Exner bodies (kall′eks′nĕr) [Emma Louise Call, U.S. physician, 1847–1937; Siegmund. Exner, Austrian physiologist, 1846–1926] Eosinophilic follicles present inside tumors of the ovary, e.g., granulosa cell tumors.

Calliphora vomitoria (kă-lif′ŏ-ră vom″ĭ-tōr′ē-ă) One of the species of common blowfly, whose maggots (larvae) sometimes infest human wounds, causing myiasis. SEE: *blowfly; myiasis.*

call light SEE: under *light.*

callosal (kă-lō′săl) [L. *callus,* hardened skin] Pert. to the corpus callosum.

callosity, callositas (kă-lŏs′ĭ-tē, -ĭ-tăs) [L. *callosus,* hard] Callus.

callosomarginal (kă-lō″sō-măr′jĭ-năl) [L. *callus,* hardened skin, + *margo,* margin] Pert. to the corpus callosum and marginal gyrus; marking the sulcus between them.

callosotomy (ka-los′tŏ-mē) [*(corpus) callosum* + *-tomy*] The surgical separation of the cerebral hemispheres by cutting the corpus callosum. It is used to treat refractory seizures and usually decreases their severity by preventing the spread of seizure activity from one side of the brain to the other.

callosum (kă-lō′sŭm) [L. *callosus,* hard] Corpus callosum.

callous (kăl′ŭs) Hard; like a callus.

callous-unemotional personality SEE: under *personality.*

call system Communications technology that allows patients to signal caregivers when they are urgently needed and allows caregivers to communicate with each other at a distance.

call to stool A feeling that one will soon need to defecate.

callus (kal′ŭs) [L., hardened skin] **1.** A circumscribed thickening and hypertrophy of the horny layer of the skin. It may be oval or elongated, gray or brown, slightly elevated, with a smooth burnished surface. It appears on the flexor surfaces of hands and feet and is caused by friction, pressure, or other irritation. SEE: illus. SYN: *callosity.*

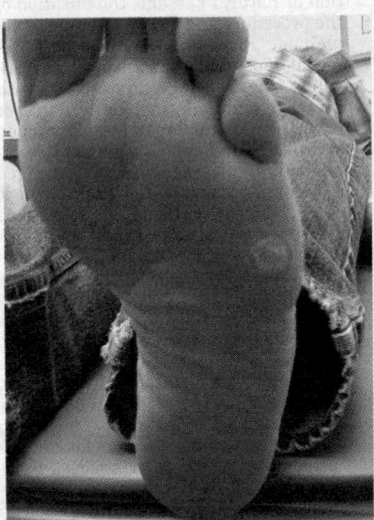

CALLUS

(on the weight-bearing portion of the foot)

   TREATMENT: Salicylic acid or careful shaving will remove the callosity temporarily. Removal is made permanent only by elimination of the cause.

   2. The osseous material woven between the ends of a fractured bone that is ultimately replaced by true bone during healing. SEE: *porosis.*

   definitive c. The exudate found between two ends of a fractured bone that develops into true bone.

provisional c. A temporary deposit between the ends of a fractured bone that is reabsorbed when true bone develops.

calmative (kă′mă-tĭv) **1.** Sedative; soothing. **2.** An agent that acts as a sedative.

calmodulins (kal″mŏdj′i-lĭnz) Intracellular proteins that combine with calcium ions to activate the contraction of smooth muscle and other processes.

calor (kā′lor) [L., heat] **1.** Heat. **2.** The heat of fever. It is one of the five classic signs of inflammation, the others being redness (rubor), swelling (tumor), pain (dolor), and loss of function (functio laesa).

Calori bursa (kă-lō′rē) [Luigi Calori, It. anatomist, 1807–1896] The bursa found between the arch of the aorta and the trachea.

caloric (kă-lor′ĭk) [L. *calor,* heat] Relating to heat or to a calorie.

caloric cost The net energy consumed by an activity, esp. an athletic activity in which muscles contract repeatedly.

caloric expenditure, calorie expenditure The number of kilocalories used during an activity or during a specific length of time. It increases with the difficulty of the activity (how many muscles are used and how hard they work) and with the duration of the activity.

caloric method SEE: under *method.*

caloric source A colloquial term for any artificial or natural food, e.g., amino acids, carbohydrates, fats, or proteins.

caloric test A procedure used to assess vestibular function in patients who complain of dizziness or exhibit standing balance disturbances or unexplained sensorineural hearing loss. With the patient supine, each ear canal is irrigated with warm (44°C) water for 30 sec, followed by irrigation with cold (30°C) water. Warm water elicits rotatory nystagmus to the side being irrigated; cold water produces the opposite reaction (i.e., nystagmus to the opposite side). SYN: *oculovestibular test; Bárány's caloric test.*

calorie (kăl′ŏ-rē) [L. *calor,* heat] A unit of heat. A calorie may be equated to work or to other units of heat measurement. Small calories are converted to joules by multiplying by 4.1855.

gram c. Small **c.**

kilogram c. Large calorie; one thousand calories.

large c. ABBR: C, Cal, or kcal. The amount of heat needed to change the temperature of 1 kg of water from 14.5°C to 15.5°C. It is commonly used in metabolic studies and in reference to human nutrition. It is always capitalized to distinguish it from a small calorie. SYN: *kilogram c.; kilocalorie.*

small c. ABBR: c, cal. The amount

of heat needed to change the temperature of 1 g of water 1°C. SYN: *gram c.*

calorie restriction, caloric restriction Limiting the consumption of food to less than what an organism would eat if given free access to nutrients. In laboratory animals, esp. mice and rodents, limiting the quantity of food ingested, while maintaining adequate levels of essential nutrients, prolongs life. Calorie restriction in humans decreases body mass index, improves serum lipid levels, and lowers blood pressure (with other potentially beneficial effects), but its effect on longevity is speculative. SEE: *calorie; Food Guide Pyramid; food requirements.*

calorifacient (kă-lor″ĭ-fā′shĕnt) [L. *calor,* heat, + *faciens,* making] **1.** Producing heat. **2.** A food that is calorically rich.

calorific (kăl″ō-rĭf′ĭk) Producing heat.

calorigenic (kă-lor″ĭ-jĕn′ĭk) [″ + Gr. *gennan,* to produce] Pert. to the production of heat or energy.

calorimeter (kăl″ō-rĭm′ĕ-tĕr) [″ + Gr. *metron,* measure] An instrument for determining the amount of heat exchanged in a chemical reaction or by the animal body under specific conditions.

bomb c. An apparatus for determining potential food energy. Heat produced in combustion is measured by the amount of heat absorbed by a known quantity of water in which the calorimeter is immersed.

respiration c. An apparatus for measuring heat produced from exchange of respiratory gases.

calorimetry (kăl″ō-rĭm′ĕ-trē) Measurement of quantities of heat.

calponin (kal-pō′nĭn) A smooth-muscle binding protein. It is used in immunohistochemistry to identify tumors that contain myoepithelial cells, and it regulates the contraction of smooth muscle.

calprotectin (kăl′prō-tĕk′tĭn) A water-soluble, 36.5 kD protein found in the cytosol of neutrophils. Laboratory assays that detect fecal calprotectin (FC) are used as screening tests for colorectal cancer, diverticulitis, dysentery, and inflammatory bowel diseases. FC levels are not elevated in patients with functional or noninflammatory bowel disorders.

calretinin (kal-ret′ĭn-ĭn) A calcium-binding protein used in immunohistochemical studies to identify the presence of neuronal cells or several specific tumors, e.g., malignant mesotheliomas.

calsequestrin (kăl-sĕ-kwĕs′trĭn) A protein in the sarcoplasmic reticulum of muscle cells that regulates the concentration of calcium ions.

calvaria (kăl-vā′rē-ă) [L., skull] The domelike superior portion of the cranium, composed of the superior portions of the frontal, parietal, and occipital bones. SYN: *skullcap.*

calx (kălks) [L.] **1.** Lime. **2.** Heel.

calyces (kā'lĭ-sēz″) Pl. of calyx.

calyciform (kă-lĭs'ĭ-form) [Gr. *kalyx,* cup of a flower, + L. *forma,* shape] Cup-shaped.

Calymmatobacterium granulomatis (kă-lĭm″mă-tō-băk-tē'rē-ŭm) SEE: under *Klebsiella.*

calyx (kā'lĭx) *pl.* **calyces** [Gr. *kalyx,* cup of a flower] **1.** Any cuplike organ or cavity. **2.** A cuplike extension of the renal pelvis that encloses the papilla of a renal pyramid; urine from the papillary duct is emptied into it.

CAM *Cell adhesion molecule; complementary and alternative medicine.*

camera (kăm'ĕr-ă) [Gr. *kamara,* vault] In anatomy, a chamber or cavity.

Cameron ulcer (kam'ĕr-ŏn, -rŏn) An ulcer or a linear erosion found in a hiatal hernia. It is found in about 5% of patients with hiatal hernia, and sometimes causes acute or chronic upper gastrointestinal bleeding.

camomile (kam'ō-mīl″) Chamomile.

cAMP *cyclic adenosine monophosphate.*

Campbell de Morgan spot, Campbell de Morgan lesion (kam'bĕl dĕ mor'găn) [Campbell Greig De Morgan, Brit. surgeon, 1811–1876] Cherry **angioma**.

Camper's fascia The upper layer of the superficial fascia of the abdomen that overlies Scarpa's fascia and consists of a layer of fatty tissue.

camphor (kăm'for) [Malay, *kapur,* chalk] A gum obtained from an evergreen tree native to China and Japan.

camphorated (kăm'fō-rāt″ĕd) Combined with or containing camphor.

campimeter (kămp-ĭm'ĕ-tĕr) [L. *campus,* field, + Gr. *metron,* measure] A device for measuring the field of vision.

campimetry (kămp-ĭm'ĕ-trē) Perimetry (2).

campospasm (kăm'pō-spăzm″) Camptocormia.

camptocormia (kămp″tō-kor'mē-ă) [Gr. *kamptos,* bent, + *kormos,* trunk] A deformity marked by habitual forward flexion of the trunk when the individual is standing. SYN: *camptospasm.*

camptodactylia (kămp″tō-dăk-tĭl'ē-ă) [″ + *dactylos,* finger] Permanent flexion of the fingers or toes.

camptomelic dwarfism A form of dwarfism characterized by bowing of the bones of the lower extremities.

camptospasm (kămp'tō-spăzm) [″ + *spasmos,* spasm] Camptocormia.

camptothecin (kămp'tō-thē'sĭn) ABBR: CPT. An inhibitor of the enzyme topoisomerase I. Medications derived from this agent (including irinotecan and topotecan) are used to treat a variety of cancers.

Campylobacter (kăm'pĭ-lō-băk'tĕr) [Gr. *kampylos,* curved, + *bakterion,* little rod] A genus of gram-negative, spirally curved, rod-shaped bacteria of the fam-

ily Spirillaceae that are motile and non–spore-forming. One or both ends of the cell have a single polar flagellum.

   C. coli A species of *Campylobacter* that normally infects dogs but can cause intestinal infection and diarrhea in immunocompromised humans.

   C. fetus A species with several subspecies that can cause disease in both humans and animals. It is a food borne bacterial infection which may vary in severity from mild to severe. This organism is less likely to cause gastrointestinal symptoms such as diarrhea when compared with the other Campylobacter species, but is prone to cause infection in other parts of the body such as the appendix, abdominal cavity, central nervous system (meningitis), gallbladder, urinary tract, and bloodstream.

   C. jejuni A subspecies of *C. fetus* formerly called *Vibrio fetus.* It is the most frequent bacterial cause of gastroenteritis in the U.S. The disease is usually self-limiting. Treatment consists of fluid and electrolyte replacement and administration of the antibiotic to which the organism is sensitive. Infection with *Campylobacter jejuni* is strongly associated with Guillain-Barré syndrome.

   C. pylori The former name of the bacterium now called *Helicobacter pylori.*

campylobacteriosis (kăm″pĭ-lō-băk-tēr″ē-ō'sĭs) [″ + ″] Any infection caused by *Campylobacter* species, esp. one that causes gastrointestinal disease.

CAMRSA An abbreviation for community-acquired methicillin-resistant *Staphylococcus aureus.*

Canadian C-spine rule A prediction rule consisting of a cluster of signs and symptoms that help to rule out the need for a radiograph to diagnose a spinal fracture in a patient who comes to the emergency department after receiving an injury to the head or neck.

Canadian Institutes of Health Research ABBR: CIHR, CIHR-IRSC. The Canadian government's federal agency that funds and oversees scientific research into diseases, health outcomes, and health technologies. The French Canadian version is *Instituts de recherche en Santé du Canada,* abbreviated IRSC. Its website is http://www.cihr-irsc.gc.ca.

Canadian Nurses Association ABBR: CNA. The official national organization for professional nurses from the 10 provinces of Canada and the Northwest Territories. All services provided by the organization are offered in English and French.

Canadian Nurses Association Testing Service ABBR: CNATS. An organization affiliated with the Canadian Nurses Association that is responsible for administering the nursing licensure examination to graduates of approved nursing schools. Successful completion of the examination qualifies the candidate as a registered nurse. The examination is analogous to the National Council Licensure Examination (NCLEX) in the U.S.

Canadian Occupational Performance Measure ABBR: COPM. An individualized and standardized outcome measure designed for use by occupational therapists to assess clients' perceptions of change in their ability to perform the activities and tasks of daily living. The client identifies problems in daily function that are then measured on the basis of performance and client satisfaction.

Canadian Transport Emergency Centre ABBR: CANUTEC. A Canadian telephone hotline, similar to CHEMTREC in the U.S., that provides information to teams handling hazardous materials at the site of toxic spills or mass casualties.

canal (kă-nal′) [L. *canalis,* channel] A narrow tube, channel, tunnel, or passageway. SEE: *duct; foramen; groove; space.*

   adductor c. A connective tissue channel, through which the femoral artery, femoral vein, and saphenous nerve pass inside the lower half of the inner thigh between the femoral triangle and the popliteal fossa. The channel is surrounded by the vastus medialis, adductor longus, and adductor magnus muscles, and it is covered by the sartorius

muscle. SYN: *Hunter canal; subsartorial c.*

   Alcock c. Pudendal **c.** SEE: *Alcock canal.*

   alimentary c. The digestive tract from the mouth through the anus.

   alveolar c. In the skull, any of the two or three channels leading from small holes along the middle of the infratemporal surface of the maxilla. These channels transmit the posterior superior alveolar blood vessels and nerves, which supply the upper molars and their surrounding gums. SYN: *superior alveolar **canal**; maxillary c.*

   anal c. The 4 cm long terminal section of the large intestine, beginning where the rectum passes downward and forward through the pelvic diaphragm and ending in the anus. The entire length of the anal canal is surrounded by sphincter muscles, and the canal remains closed except during defecation and passage of flatus. SEE: illus.

   Arnold c. SEE: under *Arnold, Friedrich.*

   auditory c. Either the external auditory canal or the internal auditory canal. SEE: *external auditory **c.**; internal auditory **c.***

   birth c. The passageway comprising the cervix, vagina, and vulva, through which the products of conception, including the fetus, pass during labor and birth.

   carotid c. The channel followed by

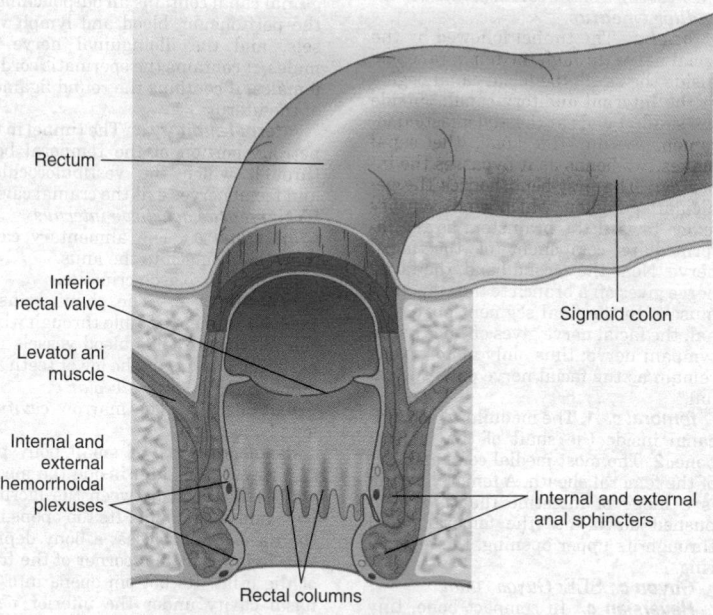

Rectum

Inferior rectal valve

Levator ani muscle

Internal and external hemorrhoidal plexuses

Sigmoid colon

Internal and external anal sphincters

Rectal columns

ANAL CANAL

the internal carotid artery (and its accompanying sympathetic nerves) as it passes through the bone of the skull. The oval external opening is in the petrous portion of the temporal bone just in front of the opening to the jugular canal. The carotid canal runs forward until, passing over the foramen lacerum, it turns up and opens into the middle cranial fossa along a groove at the base of the sella turcica.

central c. of spinal cord The remnant of the lumen of the neural tube. Largely obliterated in the adult spinal cord.

cervical c. The passageway through the center of the cervix.

condylar c. A hole in the occipital bone of the skull for passage of the emissary vein from the transverse sinus. It opens anterior to the occipital condyle.

c. of Corti SEE: under *Corti*.

craniopharyngeal c. In the embryo, a temporary tubular space in the cartilage of the base of the sphenoid bone, enclosing the developing pituitary gland.

Dorello c. SEE: *Dorello canal*.

external auditory c. The open, tubular passageway from the pinna (auricle) of the ear to the tympanic membrane (ear drum). It is lined by thin, sensitive skin, which continues as the outer covering of the tympanic membrane. Its outer edge is a channel in the temporal bone of the skull. The cartilage inside the pinna extends as a middle layer between the skin and the bone in the first third of the canal. SEE: *external auditory* **meatus**.

facial c. The tunnel followed by the facial nerve through the temporal bone. Inside the skull, the facial canal begins in the internal auditory canal; outside the skull, it ends at the stylomastoid foramen. Within the bone, the canal makes two bends as it bypasses the inner ear. The first bend houses the geniculate ganglion, which sends sensory axons toward the brainstem as the intermediate component of the facial nerve. Near the second bend, the facial nerve gives off a branch to the stapedius muscle. In the final segment of the canal, the facial nerve gives off the chorda tympani nerve; thus, only motor axons remain as the facial nerve exits the canal.

femoral c. 1. The medullary (central) canal inside the shaft of the femoral bone. **2.** The most medial compartment of the femoral sheath. A femoral hernia is a bulge of intestine that has been pushed down into the femoral canal through its upper opening, the femoral ring.

Guyon c. SEE: *Guyon canal*.

Haversian c. In compact bone, tiny channels in the center of concentric cylinders of mineralized tissue. Nerves and blood vessels run through these channels, all of which interconnect. Each Haversian canal is the center of an osteon. SEE: *bone; Havers, Clopton*.

Huguier c. SEE: *Huguier canal*.

Hunter c. Adductor **c.** SEE: *Hunter canal*.

Huschke c. SEE: under *Huschke, Emil*.

hypoglossal c. A hole in the skull, just above the foramen magnum in the occipital bone, through which the hypoglossal nerve and a branch of the ascending pharyngeal artery pass. SYN: *anterior condyloid* **foramen**.

inferior alveolar c. Mandibular **c.**

infraorbital c. An anterior-posterior bony canal or groove in the floor of the orbit. The infraorbital artery and nerve run in this canal, which opens anteriorly as the infraorbital foramen.

inguinal c. A tube made of the transversalis fascia and the aponeuroses of the abdominal wall muscles just above the inguinal ligament. The inguinal canal is a cylindrical passageway 4 cm long from the retroperitoneal space to the subcutaneous fascia. It begins at the deep (internal) inguinal ring inside the abdominal wall, approx. halfway between the anterior superior spine of the iliac bone and the pubic symphysis, 0.50 in (1.25 cm) above the inguinal ligament. It continues downward and toward the midline, and it ends at the superficial (external) inguinal ring under the skin at the pubic crest. The inguinal canal contains an outpouching of the peritoneum, blood and lymph vessels, and the ilioinguinal nerve. In males, it contains the spermatic cord; in females, it contains the round ligament of the uterus.

internal auditory c. The tunnel in the petrous portion of the temporal bone through which the vestibulocochlear and facial nerves exit the cranial cavity. SYN: **meatus** *acusticus internus*.

intestinal c. The alimentary canal from the stomach to the anus.

lacrimal c. Nasolacrimal **c.**

mandibular c. The channel inside the body of the mandible through which the inferior alveolar blood vessels and nerve pass to supply the lower teeth and gums. SYN: *inferior alveolar* **c.**

medullary c. The marrow cavity of long bones.

nasolacrimal c. A small bony passageway in the skull inside the medial wall of the orbit between the lacrimal bone and the maxilla. Its top opens into the nasolacrimal fossa, a bony depression in lower medial corner of the front of the orbit. Its bottom opens into the nasal cavity under the inferior nasal concha. It contains the membranous nasolacrimal duct, which drains tears from the eye. SYN: *lacrimal* **c.**

neurenteric c. A temporary canal in the vertebrate embryo between the neural and intestinal tubes. It is the temporary communication between cavities of the yolk sac and the amnion.

Nuck c. SEE: *Nuck canal.*

nutrient c. In bone, a tiny tubular space filled by vessels and nerves running to and from the osteons and the other basic metabolic and growth units. SEE: *bone.*

obturator c. An opening in the obturator membrane of the hip bone that transmits the obturator vessels and nerve.

optic c. In the skull, a roughly spherical opening through the lesser wing of the sphenoid bone connecting the middle cranial fossa and the superior-medial edge of the back of the orbit. The optic nerve and the ophthalmic artery pass through the optic canal. SYN: *optic foramen.*

pericardioperitoneal c. Pleuroperitoneal **c.**

pterygoid c. In the skull, a small horizontal channel beginning inside the canal of the foramen lacerum (in the middle cranial fossa), passing through the root of the pterygoid process of the sphenoid bone, and opening into the pterygopalatine fossa behind and below the medial wall of the orbit. It transmits the pterygoid nerve and vessels to the pterygopalatine ganglion. SYN: *vidian* **c.**

pudendal c. A tunnel inside the obturator fascia along the lower pelvic surface of the internal obturator muscle and running along the inner lower edge of the ramus of the ischium. It contains the pudendal nerve and vessels. SYN: *Alcock canal.*

pulp c. Root **c.** (1).

Rivinus c. SEE: *Rivinus, August Quirinus.*

root c. **1.** The channel inside the tooth that extends from the pulp chamber to the apical foramen. It contains arteries, veins, lymphatic vessels, and sensory nerve endings. SYN: *pulp* **c.** **2.** Colloquially, the procedure for preserving a tooth by removing its diseased pulp cavity.

sacral c. The continuation of the vertebral canal into the sacrum.

semicircular c. One of the three perpendicular tubular hollows, each forming two-thirds of a circle, that extend from the vestibule of the labyrinth in the inner ear. The semicircular canals are the bony shells that contain the similarly shaped semicircular ducts, membranous sensory organs that detect the angular acceleration and the orientation of the head.

spinal c. Vertebral **c.**

subsartorial c. Adductor **c.**

uterine c. The cavity of the uterus.

vaginal c. The cavity of the vagina. The vaginal walls can expand but are normally in contact with each other; thus, this cavity is a potential space.

vertebral c. The continuous channel through the central foramina in the vertebrae, which contains the spinal cord and the spinal nerve roots in their meningeal coverings. SYN: *spinal* **c.**

vidian c. Pterygoid **c.**

canaliculitis (kăn″ă-lĭk″ū-lī′tĭs) A relatively rare infection of the tear duct of the eye. It is usually found in one eye rather than both, and in people over age 50. It may be caused by chronic infection with *Actinomyces, Aspergillus, Candida,* or *Nocardia* species.

canaliculus (kăn″ă-lĭk′ū-lŭs) *pl.* **canaliculi** [L. *canalicularis*] A small channel or canal. In bone or cementum, such channels radiate out from lacunae and anastomose with canaliculi of neighboring lacunae.

lacrimal canaliculus In the eye, one of two short curved ducts, inferior and superior, beginning at the lacrimal punctum along the edge of each eyelid and carrying tears from the lacrimal lake into the lacrimal sac.

canalicular (-lĭk′ū-lăr), *adj.*

canalis (kă-nā′lĭs) *pl.* **canales** [L., channel] Canal.

canalithiasis Benign paroxysmal positional vertigo.

canalith repositioning maneuver Use of the Hallpike maneuver to reposition a canalith in the semicircular canal(s) to relieve benign positional vertigo. SYN: *Epley maneuver.* SEE: *Hallpike maneuver.*

canalization (kăn″ăl-ī-zā′shŭn) Formation of channels in tissue.

canaloplasty (kă-nal′ŏ-plas″tē) [*canal* + *-plasty*] **1.** Surgery for glaucoma in which the drainage through the canal of Schlemm is improved by opening the ostia and stretching the trabecular meshwork. **2.** Spinal surgery to alleviate lumbar spinal stenosis. **3.** Canalplasty.

canalplasty (kan′ăl-plas″tē) [*canal* + *-plasty*] Surgery to reopen a narrow, closed, or clogged external auditory canal. It is used, for example, in patients with external otitis that has not responded to medical therapy. SYN: *canaloplasty* (3).

Canavan disease (kăn′ă-van″) [Myrtle May Moore Canavan, U.S. pathologist, 1879–1953] An autosomal recessive disorder of infants, marked by spongy white matter with Alzheimer type II cells. SYN: *Canavan–van Bogaert–Bertrand disease.*

canavanine (kă-năv′ă-nĭn) An amino acid produced by some leguminous plants, such as the jack bean. It is used primarily for feeding stock. It is structurally related to L-arginine. It prevents the growth of some bacteria.

Canavan-van Bogaert-Bertrand disease (kan'ă-van"van-bō'gĕrt) Canavan disease.

cancellated (kăn'sĕ-lāt"ĕd) [L. *cancellus,* lattice] Reticulated; said of a lattice-like structure.

cancelled cycle In assisted reproduction technology, a month during which the ovary is stimulated but no follicles are aspirated.

Cancell/Entelev Distilled water containing chemicals such as catechol, inositol, nitric acid, potassium hydroxide, sodium sulfite, and sulfuric acid. It has been promoted as an alternative treatment for cancer and HIV/AIDS. The mixture has not been proven to work, and is not approved for use in the U.S. by the Food and Drug Administration.

cancellous (kăn'sĕl-ŭs) Having a reticular or latticework structure, as the spongy tissue of bone.

cancellus (kan-sel'ŭs, kan-sel'ī", 'ē") *pl.* **cancelli** [L.] An osseous plate composing cancellous bone; any structure arranged as a lattice.

cancer (kan'sĕr) [L. *cancer,* crab, suppurating ulcer] Malignant neoplasia marked by the uncontrolled growth of cells, often with invasion of healthy tissues locally or throughout the body. Cancer is the second leading cause of death in the U.S. after cardiovascular disease. In 2006 the American Cancer Society (ACS) reported that 564,830 Americans died of cancer and that twice that number were newly diagnosed with one form or another of the disease. The most common cancers in the U.S. are lung, breast, colon, prostate, and skin. Because most cancers occur in patients who are 65 or older, the incidence of cancer is expected to increase as the population ages. More than 200 kinds of cancer have been identified. Cancers that arise from epithelial tissues are called *carcinomas;* from mesenchymal tissues, *sarcomas;* from glial cells, *gliomas;* from lymphatic cells, *lymphomas;* from blood-forming cells, *leukemias;* from pigmented skin cells, *melanomas;* from plasma cells, *myelomas.* SYN: *malignancy* (2). SEE: *carcinoma; leukemia; lymphoma; oncogene; sarcoma.*

Cancer cells have several reproductive advantages over normal cells. They can make proteins that stimulate their own growth or new blood vessels to bring them nourishment. They can produce enzymes that prevent their chromosomes from aging. They can invade the lymphatic system and bloodstream and find places to grow in new tissues (metastasis).

Usually, as cancer cells proliferate, they become increasingly abnormal and require more of the body's metabolic output for their growth and development. Damage caused by their invasion of healthy tissues results in organ malfunction, pain, and, often, death. SEE: table (Estimated New Cancer Cases and Deaths by Sex, U.S. 2008).

ETIOLOGY: Ionizing radiation, ultraviolet light, some viruses, and drugs that damage nucleic acids may initiate the genetic lesions that result in cancers. The best-known and most widespread type of carcinogen exposure, however, is consumption of tobacco. The ACS estimates that one third of the cancer deaths that occur annually in the U.S. are related to nutrition and other lifestyle factors. Some cancers are familial, i.e., genetic; others result from occupational exposures to carcinogens. Ironically, chemotherapeutic drugs used to treat some cancers may damage chromosomes and occasionally cause secondary malignancies.

SYMPTOMS: Symptoms of widespread cancer include pain, malnutrition, weakness, fatigue, bone fractures, and strokelike syndromes. Early warning signs of cancer may be remembered by the mnemonic CAUTION: *C*hange in bowel or bladder habit; *A* sore that does not heal; *U*nusual bleeding or discharge; *T*hickening or mass in the breast or other body parts; *I*ndigestion or difficulty in swallowing; *O*bvious change in a wart or a mole; *N*agging cough or hoarseness. People should seek prompt medical attention if they observe any of these signs.

DIAGNOSIS: The location of a suspected lesion often dictates the means to diagnose cancer: men with urinary symptoms may be screened for prostate cancer with a prostate specific antigen (PSA) test; an alpha-fetoprotein (AFP) test may be used to screen for liver cancer. Several other tumor markers (such as the CA 125 test for ovarian cancer) are used only after a diagnosis has already been made by other means. Endoscopy and radiography are typically used to locate and assess the extent of the disease, but definitive diagnosis still rests on the examination of cytological specimens (such as the Papanicolaou [Pap] test) or the pathological review of biopsy specimens. SEE: illus. (Cancer); table (Controversies in Cancer Screening in the General Population).

Screening for cancers can identify some malignancies before they have invaded neighboring tissues or become widespread. The most widely used screening tests include the Pap test for cervical cancer, mammography for breast cancer, prostate specific antigen tests for prostate carcinoma, and occult blood tests and colonoscopy for intestinal cancers.

TREATMENT: Surgery, chemother-

Estimated New Cancer Cases and Deaths by Sex, U.S., 2008*

	Estimated New Cases		Estimated Deaths	
	Male	Female	Male	Female
All sites	745,180	692,000	294,120	271,530
Oral cavity & pharynx	25,310	10,000	5,210	2,380
Esophagus	12,970	3,500	11,250	3,030
Stomach	13,190	8,310	6,450	4,430
Colon & rectum	77,250	71,560	24,260	25,700
Liver & intrahepatic bile duct	15,190	6,180	12,570	5,840
Pancreas	18,770	18,910	17,500	16,790
Lung & bronchus	114,690	100,330	90,810	71,030
Melanoma-skin	34,950	27,530	5,400	3,020
Breast	1,990	182,460	450	40,480
Uterine corpus		40,100		7,470
Ovary		21,650		15,520
Prostate	186,320		28,660	
Urinary bladder	21,230	17,580	9,950	4,150
Kidney & renal pelvis	33,130	21,260	8,100	4,910
Brain & other nervous system	11,780	10,030	7,420	5,650
Thyroid	8,930	28,410	680	910
Non-Hodgkin lymphoma	35,450	30,670	9,790	9,370
Leukemia	25,180	19,090	12,460	9,250

*Excludes basal and squamous cell skin cancers and in situ carcinomas except urinary bladder.
Carcinoma in situ of the breast accounts for about 67,770 new cases annually, and melanoma
in situ accounts for about 54,020 new cases annually. Estimates of new cases are based on
incidence rates from the NCI SEER program, 1995 to 2004.
SOURCE: ©2008, American Cancer Society, Inc., Surveillance Research

apy, immunotherapy, hormone therapy, radiation therapy, and combined-modality therapies often are effective methods for treating patients with cancer. The specific treatment used depends on the type, stage, and location of the cancer and the patient's general health.

The pain associated with cancer is often severe. Cancer patients may suffer depression and anxiety and have nutritional deficits. Guidelines addressing these issues are readily available, e.g., from the U.S. Department of Health and Human Services' Agency for Health Care Policy and Research. Publications may be obtained by calling 1-800-4-CANCER or from websites such as from the ACS (www.cancer.org). SEE: *chemotherapy.*

PATIENT CARE: There must be close collaboration among the entire health care team and the patient and family must be encouraged to participate in care . The patient's knowledge of the disease is determined, misinformation corrected, and information supplied about the disease, its progression, its treatment, and expected outcome. Such information should be updated regularly. The patient's and family's coping mechanisms are supported, and verbalization of feelings and fears, esp. with changes in body image, pain and suffering, and dying and death, is encouraged. Participation in local support groups is

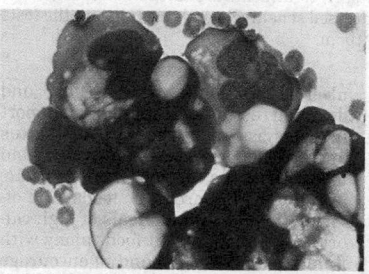 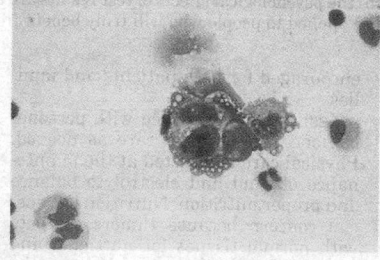

CANCER

(A) Ovarian carcinoma cells and (B) adenocarcinoma of the prostate (orig. mag. ×500)

Controversies in Cancer Screening in the General Population[*]

Test	To Detect	Discussion
Breast self-examination	Breast cancer	Monthly self-examination by women is a noninvasive way to screen for changes in the breast. This method detects many benign and cancerous lumps, but its ability to prolong life is still debated.
Mammography	Breast cancer	Mammography is clearly effective screening in women over 50. Most mammograms are obtained by women in their 40s. The incidence of cancer is higher in later life, when mammography use tends to decline.
Digital rectal examination (DRE)	Colorectal cancer, prostate cancer	DRE is easy to perform and inexpensive but its cancer screening value is unproven; and, when it detects cancers, there is no proof that the test results in better patient outcomes. In addition, DRE detects a very small number of cancers, only those within the reach of the examiner.
Fecal occult blood test	Colorectal cancer	In people over 50, testing stool specimens for hidden bleeding detects many cancers; this detection results in earlier treatment and prolongation of life. The accuracy and value of the test relative to sigmoidoscopy and colonoscopy are uncertain.
Chest x-ray, sputum cytology, CT of the chest	Lung cancer	Prospective studies have yielded conflicting results for any method of screening for lung cancer in smokers, and the costs of screening, e.g., with computed tomography of the chest, may be prohibitive. The tests are of no value to nonsmokers.
Prostate specific antigen (PSA)	Prostate cancer	PSA testing detects many previously undetected prostate cancers but may result in increased death and disease due to complications from subsequent surgery. Refinements in its application may improve its usefulness as a screening tool.
Genetic testing	For predisposition to a variety of cancers	The predictive value of genetic testing for cancer is very small. Experts are debating the emotional and ethical consequences of genetic cancer screening tests.

[*]Note: Cancer screening tests are most likely to be useful when: (1) the cancer is common and deadly; (2) the test reliably distinguishes between healthy and diseased people; (3) early detection of the disease leads to improved treatments; (4) treatments are safe and well-tolerated; (5) the psychological effects of test results are addressed sensitively and carefully; (6) the tests are applied to people who will truly benefit from them.

encouraged for both patients and families.

Assistance is provided with personal hygiene and physical care as needed. Physical care is directed at the maintenance of fluid and electrolyte balance and proper nutrition. Nutrition is a special concern because tumors compete with normal tissues for nutrients and grow at their expense and because the disease or treatments can cause anorexia, altered taste sensations, mouth ulcerations, vomiting, diarrhea, and draining fistulas. Nutritional support includes assessing the patient's status and problems, experimenting to find foods that the patient can tolerate, avoiding highly aromatic foods, and offering frequent small meals of high-calorie, high-nutrient soft foods along with fluids to limit fatigue and to encourage overall intake. Intake of noncaffeinated liquids should be encouraged: 2 quarts per day of juices or other caloric beverages in frequent, small amounts rather than water alone. Elimination is maintained by administering stool softeners as necessary if analgesic drugs result in constipation.

Using careful and gentle handling, the health care professional assists with range-of-motion exercises, encourages ambulation and mobility, and turns and repositions the immobile patient frequently to decrease the deleterious multisystemic effects of immobilization. The patient is made comfortable by correct body alignment, noninvasive measures (such as guided imagery and cutaneous stimulation), and medication (preferably administered on a regular schedule to prevent pain, with additional dosing to relieve breakthrough pain). Emotional assistance includes allaying the patient's fears of helplessness and loss of control; providing hope for remission or long-term survival but avoiding giving false hope; and providing the patient with realistic reassurance about pain control, comfort, and rest. Psychological counseling and antidepressant therapies may be helpful.

Hospice care (at home or in a dedicated center), if needed, is discussed with the patient and family. The goal is to provide good quality of life with minimal discomfort, pain, and restrictions rather than to continue specific therapy. Family members are encouraged to assume an active role in caring for the patient. Communication is fostered between patient and family and other health care providers, and the patient is helped to maintain control and to carry out realistic decisions about issues of life and death.

To provide effective emotional support to the patient and family, health care professionals must understand and cope with their own feelings about terminal illness and death and seek assistance with grieving and in developing a personal philosophy about dying and death. They will then be better able to listen sensitively to patients' concerns, to offer genuine understanding and comfort, and to help patients and family work through their grief. SEE: *Nursing Diagnoses Appendix.*

bladder c. A malignancy that arises in the cells of the urinary bladder. In Western nations, most of the cases are transitional cell carcinomas. Common causes include cigarette smoking, occupational exposure to carcinogens, or chronic bladder infection. Symptoms of bladder cancer may include painful urination, bloody urination, or frequent or urgent urination. Depending on the extent of invasion or spread of the tumor, it may be treated with endoscopy, surgery, chemotherapy, or immunotherapy.

bone c. Any malignancy of bone tissue. Primary bone tumors (such as osteosarcomas) are rare in adults; they are seen more often in children and adolescents. Secondary or metastatic bone tumors are far more common. Tumors arising in other areas of the body that metastasize to the bones most often spread from organs such as prostate or breast.

breast c. SEE: *breast cancer.*

cervical c. A malignant neoplasm of the cervix of the uterus. With an incidence of 15:100,000, it is the third most common cancer of the female reproductive tract and causes 5% of all cancer deaths among women. Although it may occur in younger women, the average age at diagnosis is 54. The disease is insidious, asymptomatic in the early stages, and best treated when recognized at an early stage.

ETIOLOGY: Some strains of the human papillomavirus (HPV) are carcinogenic to cervical epithelium. While there are other risk factors (such as tobacco smoking, early age at first intercourse, and having multiple sex partners), HPV is the major factor responsible for the development of this cancer.

DIAGNOSIS: Periodic Pap tests are recommended for all sexually active women. The tests identify cellular changes with 95% accuracy. Dilatation and curettage, punch biopsy, and colposcopy may be done if Pap test findings raise the suspicion of cancer. If abnormal cells are detected, HPV testing is often performed to screen for presence of one of the high risk types of the virus. SEE: *Bethesda System, The; cervical intraepithelial neoplasia; colposcopy; cryosurgery; loop electrode excision procedure; Papanicolaou test.*

TREATMENT: Management varies from cryotherapy or laser therapy for low-grade squamous intraepithelial lesions, conization for carcinoma in situ, to hysterectomy for preinvasive cervical cancer in women who are not planning to have children. Stage-related management of invasive cervical carcinoma includes radiation and/or hysterectomy.

PREVENTION: Vaccination against human papillomavirus virus (HPV). SEE: *HPV vaccine.*

chimney sweeps' c. Cancer of the skin of the scrotum due to chronic irritation by coal soot.

colorectal c. ABBR: CRC. A malignancy of the colon or rectum. It is the second leading cause of cancer deaths in the U.S. At some time during their lives 6% of Americans will be diagnosed with the disease. In 2008 the ACS estimated that 154,000 Americans would be newly diagnosed with colorectal cancer and that it would cause 50,500 deaths.

ETIOLOGY: The cancer occurs more often in people with a family history of the disease, those with familial adenomatous polyposis, and in those with inflammatory bowel diseases such as ulcerative colitis. It also occurs more often in people who are obese than in those who are not and in those who consume a high fat, low-fiber diet.

SYMPTOMS: Symptoms may be absent or may include change in the usual pattern of bowel habits, esp. in those over 40; recent onset of constipation, diarrhea, or tenesmus in an older patient; bright red or dark blood in the stool. Laboratory findings may include iron-deficiency anemia or positive fecal occult blood tests.

DIAGNOSIS: Diagnosis may be suggested by findings on digital rectal examination, anoscopy, flexible or rigid sigmoidoscopy, colonoscopy, virtual colonoscopy, or barium enema examination. It is confirmed by biopsy of suspicious lesions. Prevention includes screening of asymptomatic men and women of average risk starting at age 50, annual home fecal occult blood testing (over a three-day period), and colonoscopy every 10 years. During colonoscopy, removal of benign polyps prevents progression to malignant tumors. If polyps are found, colonoscopy should be repeated in 3 to 5 years (depending on the presence of other risk factors). Detection of colorectal cancer at an early stage via colonoscopy offers patients a very high likelihood of cure rate at 5 years. Neither digital rectal examination nor testing of a single stool specimen from the digital exam provides adequate screening. Patients at increased risk for colorectal cancer (those who have had previous colorectal adenomas or resected cancers or a history of ulcerative colitis or of colon cancer in a first-degree relative younger than 60) should undergo screening more frequently and at an earlier age. When colorectal carcinoma is diagnosed, additional tests are conducted to determine the stage of the disease (chest radiographs, CT, MRI, and blood studies, including carcinoembryonic antigen levels, and liver function studies).

TREATMENT: Surgical resection performed by laparotomy, minimally invasive surgery, microsurgery, or laparoscopy can cure localized colorectal cancer. Whatever procedure is used, the type of surgery depends on the location of the tumor, and the goal of the surgery is removal of the malignant tumor and adjacent tissue and any lymph nodes that may contain cancer cells. Adjuvant therapies may include chemoembolization of blood vessels that feed the primary tumor or metastases; radiation therapy; brachytherapy; chemotherapy; or monoclonal antibody therapy. Carcinoembryonic antigen is helpful in monitoring patients during and following treatment to determine effectiveness and detect recurrence or metasasis.

PATIENT CARE: Health care providers should teach patients the importance of colorectal screening and indicate applicable lifestyle modifications (a low-fat diet, maintenance of a normal body mass index). Patients with familial colon cancer syndromes, such as familial adenomatous polyposis, should be counseled about the need for close surveillance by professional gastroenterologists.

Aspirin and other nonsteroidal antiinflammatory drugs appear to reduce the number of colon polyps, thus decreasing the risk of developing colorectal cancer. Patients interested in such therapy should discuss its potential risks and benefits with their health care providers.

Patients diagnosed with colorectal cancer who undergo surgery need counseling about the operation, the duration of recovery, and, in many cases, the use of a postoperative colostomy. Before surgery, a stomal therapist consults with the surgeon regarding appropriate stoma location, and the abdomen is marked. The therapist answers questions from the patient and family and begins to develop a relationship that will support the patient through postoperative care and teaching. Patient and family are encouraged to access the ACS (800-ACS-2345 or www.cancer.org) for additional information. SYN: *carcinoma of the colon; colorectal carcinoma*.

   epithelial c. Basal cell **carcinoma**.
   epithelial c. of the ovary SEE: *ovarian c.*
   esophageal c. SEE: *esophageal cancer.*
   fallopian tube c. A malignancy that begins to grow in the cells that form the inner surfaces of the fallopian tubes, usually an adenocarcinoma. It is the least common form of gynecological cancer.
   familial medullary thyroid c. ABBR: FMTC. A rare, autosomal, dominantly inherited predisposition to medullary carcinoma of the thyroid. The disease is genetically related to the multiple endocrine neoplasia (MEN) syndromes. However, families affected by FMTC rarely develop hyperparathyroid tumors or pheochromocytoma.
   gastric c. Adenocarcinoma of the stomach. About 50% to 60% of all carcinomas of the stomach occur in the pyloric region. About 20% occur along the lesser curvature; the rest are located in the fundus, particularly along the greater curvature. Although this form of

cancer is common throughout the world in people of all races, the incidence of gastric cancer exhibits unexplained geographic, cultural, and gender differences, with the highest incidence in men over 40 and higher mortality in China, Korea, Japan, Taiwan, Iceland, Chile, and Austria.

From 1930 to the 1990s, the incidence of gastric cancer declined from about 38 cases per 100,000 to about 6 cases per 100,000. In 2010, the ACS estimated there would be 21,000 new cases of gastric cancer in the U.S. and 10,570 deaths from this disease. The prognosis for a particular patient depends on the stage of the disease at the time of diagnosis, but overall the 5-year survival rate is about 19%.

PREDISPOSING CAUSES: Although the cause of gastric cancer is unknown, predisposing factors include a diet rich in pickled or smoked foods, a history of gastric surgery, and a history of infection by *Helicobacter pylori*. The disease runs in some families; therefore, there may also be a genetic component.

COMPLICATIONS: Malnutrition occurs as a result of impaired eating, the metabolic demands of the growing tumor, or obstruction of the GI tract. Iron deficiency anemia results as the tumor causes ulceration and bleeding. The tumor can interfere with the production of the intrinsic factor needed for vitamin B_{12} absorption, resulting in pernicious anemia. As the cancer spreads to regional lymph nodes and nearby structures and metastasizes to other structures, related complications occur.

SIGNS AND SYMPTOMS: In the early stages, the patient may occasionally experience pain in the back or in the epigastric or retrosternal areas that is relieved with nonprescription analgesics. As the tumor grows, the patient may notice a vague feeling of fullness, heaviness, and abdominal distention after meals. Depending on the progression of the cancer, the patient may report weight loss due to disturbance of the appetite; nausea; and vomiting. There may be dysphagia and coffee-ground vomitus if the tumor is located in the cardia and slowly bleeds. Weakness and fatigue are common. Because early symptoms include chronic dyspepsia and epigastric discomfort, patients may self-treat with OTC antacids or histamine blockers, delaying prescribed therapies and allowing the cancer to progress.

Palpation of the abdomen may disclose a mass. A skilled examiner may be able to palpate enlarged lymph nodes, esp. in the supraclavicular and axillary regions.

DIAGNOSTIC STUDIES: Gastric cancer is diagnosed by fiber-optic endoscopy with biopsy. Studies to rule out specific organ metastases include endoscopic ultrasonography, computed tomography scans, chest radiographs, liver and bone scans, and liver biopsy.

TREATMENT: Radical surgery to remove the tumor is possible in more than one third of patients. Even in the patient whose disease is not considered surgically curable, resection may temporarily ease symptoms and improve the patient's response to chemotherapy and radiation therapy. The nature and extent of the lesion determine the type of surgery. Surgical procedures include gastroduodenostomy, gastrojejunostomy, partial gastric resection, and total gastrectomy. If metastasis has occurred, the omentum and spleen may have to be removed.

Chemotherapy for GI tumors may help control signs and symptoms and prolong survival. Gastric adenocarcinomas respond to several agents, including fluorouracil, carmustine, doxorubicin, and mitomycin. Tumors that express HER2 antigens respond to treatment with trastuzumab (a monoclonal antibody that targets the human epidermal growth factor). Antispasmodics, antacids, and proton pump inhibitors may help relieve GI acidity and reflux symptoms. Antiemetics can control nausea, which intensifies as the tumor grows. Analgesics, sedatives, and tranquilizers are used to control pain and anxiety.

PATIENT CARE: Nutritional intake is monitored, and the patient is weighed periodically. The health care provider initiates comprehensive clinical and laboratory investigations, including serial studies as indicated, if these have not already been done. The patient is prepared physically and emotionally for surgery, chemotherapy, or radiotherapy. During hospitalization, all general patient care concerns apply.

Throughout the course of the illness, a high-protein, high-calorie diet with vitamin supplementation helps the patient avoid or recover from weight loss, malnutrition, and anemia, and promote wound healing. Frequent small meals are offered.

To stimulate a poor appetite, antidepressant or steroid drugs may be administered. The patient is instructed in use of all drugs and the expected adverse effects of treatment, as well as in management strategies for these effects.

Radiation therapy may cause nausea, vomiting, local skin damage, malaise, diarrhea, and fatigue. Chemotherapy may cause bone marrow suppression, infection, nausea, vomiting, mouth ulcers, and hair loss. During radiation or chemotherapy, oral intake is encouraged to remove toxic metabolites. Bland fruit juices, ginger ale, or other fluids, and prescribed antiemetics are provided to minimize nausea and vomiting; comfort and reassurance are offered as needed. The patient is advised to report persistent adverse reactions.

The patient is encouraged to follow a normal routine as much as possible after recovery from surgery and during radiation therapy and chemotherapy. He should stop activities that cause excessive fatigue (at least temporarily) and incorporate rest periods. The patient should avoid crowds and people with known infections. Home-health care is provided as necessary. If curative treatment fails, palliative care and psychological support continues, with questions answered honestly but tactfully. Home or in-patient hospice care referrals are suggested as available.

SYN: *stomach c.*

hard c. A cylindrical cancer composed of fibrous tissue. SYN: *scirrhous c.; scirrhous* **carcinoma**.

head and neck c. Squamous cell carcinoma usually arising in the pharynx, oral cavity, or larynx. Research has shown links between human papillomavirus infection, tobacco smoking, and excessive alcohol use and head and neck cancers.

interval c. A cancer whose presence is diagnosed in the time between scheduled screening tests, e.g., a breast cancer that is not detected by regular periodic mammography, professional examination, and self-breast exams.

kidney c. Renal cell **carcinoma**.

latent c. A cancer that grows slowly and has no important health effect on the patient.

lip c. A squamous cell carcinoma of the lower lip usually seen in men or smokers.

liver c. Malignancy of the liver that results either from spread from a primary source or from primary tumor of the liver itself. The former is the more frequent cause. Male sex, hepatitis B or C, cirrhosis, and other liver diseases are predisposing factors. The liver is the most common site of metastatic spread of tumors that disseminate through the bloodstream. The prognosis for survival is from a few months to 1 yr.

SYMPTOMS: The disease may cause severe pain and tenderness; cachexia (loss of weight); and encephalopathy. Jaundice is common. The liver is enlarged, its surface is nodular, and a central depression or umbilications can often be detected.

lung c. The deadliest form of cancer in the U.S., responsible for about 159,000 deaths a year, according to statistics published by the ACS in 2011. The term includes four cell types: squamous cell (epidermoid) carcinoma, ade-nocarcinoma, large cell (anaplastic) cancer, and small cell (oat cell) cancer. The vast majority are caused by carcinogens in tobacco smoke, including second-hand smoke. Other risks include exposure to carcinogenic industrial and air pollutants (asbestos, uranium, arsenic, nickel, chromium, iron oxides, coal dust and radioactive dusts), radon gas concentrations, and familial susceptibility. Survival after diagnosis is poor: only one of seven patients lives for 5 years. However, if detected early (before spreading from the lungs), survival rates rise for most people. Radiofrequency ablation (RFA) is a promising therapy for patients with small lung tumors. SYN: *bronchogenic carcinoma*. SEE: illus.

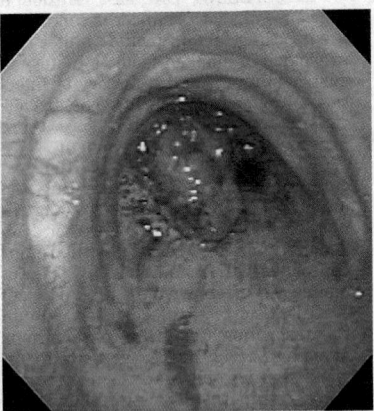

LUNG CANCER

Lung cancer seen endoscopically. The tumor is bleeding after being biopsied.

TREATMENT: Treatment includes lung surgery, radiation therapy, and chemotherapy usually in combination.

PATIENT CARE: Staging determines the extent of the disease and aids in planning treatment and predicting the prognosis. Lung cancer is relatively difficult to cure but much easier to prevent. Children and adolescents should be discouraged from smoking tobacco products, and current smokers should be assisted in their efforts to quit, e.g., through referrals to local branches of the ACS, smoking-cessation programs, individual counseling, or group therapy.

SCREENING AND PUBLIC HEALTH: Chest x-rays do not show small, early cancers, but CT scanning can be used to screen people who have a long history of smoking and who are 50 to 60 years old. In this high-risk group, screening detects the disease in its early stages when it is most likely to be curable. However, since screening is very expensive, and since there are millions of smokers, the public health costs of mass screening are high compared with the cost of encouraging smokers to quit or of teaching teenagers not to start smoking.

oral cavity c. Squamous cell carcinoma of the mouth or tongue. Oral cavity cancers are only rarely caused by salivary gland tumors or sarcomas.

ovarian c. Any malignant growth in an ovary. About 85% to 90% of ovarian cancers arise from the surface epithelium of the ovary. In the U.S. in 2008, the ACS estimated there would be about 21,600 new patients diagnosed with ovarian cancer and about 15,200 deaths from the disease. Most cases (70%) are diagnosed when the disease is already at an advanced stage because early detection methods are still unsatisfactory. The early symptoms of the disease are often nonspecific and often mimic irritable bowel (constipation, vague abdominal pain, bloating). Initial laboratory studies (routine blood tests and x-rays) are often unremarkable.

Currently, more women die of epithelial ovarian cancer than of all other gynecological cancers combined. A small percentage of patients with ovarian cancer may have a hereditary predisposition, e.g., they have BRCA-1 or BRCA-2 genes. High-risk women include those with multiple first-degree relatives (mother, sister, daughter) or second-degree relatives (aunt, grandmother, cousin) with histories of breast or ovarian cancer. Preventive surgery to remove the ovaries and fallopian tubes is the only way such women can significantly reduce their risk.

PATIENT CARE: Ovarian cancer patients may feel threatened or vulnerable. They benefit from pretreatment support and education. Health care professionals address the patient's psychosocial needs while preparing her for treatment and manage the potential adverse reactions and the treatment and changes related to advancing disease.

The first step in care is typically surgical debulking of the tumor. In this phase of care, the surgical oncologist attempts to remove not only the primary tumor, but also as many small tumorlets found within the peritoneum. The patient and family should be taught about the extensive surgical procedure and what to expect after surgery. After surgery, the patient is monitored for infection, circulatory complications, fluid and electrolyte imbalances, and pain. The patient who is to receive chemotherapy should be taught about major adverse reactions to the usual medications employed, taxanes and platinum-based drugs, such as fatigue, nausea and vomiting, hair loss, diarrhea, constipation, mucositis, neuropathy, arthralgia and myalgia, difficulty concentrating (*chemobrain*), and myelosuppression, as well as about measures to be taken to prevent and manage these problems. Chemotherapy may be given directly into the peritoneum or intravenously. Depression, anger, frustration, and anxiety are common.

After the acute phase of treatment, the patient may undergo premature menopause; loss of fertility; alterations in body image, sexual function, and family relationships; impaired functional capacity; financial difficulties; and loss of spiritual well-being. The patient should be assessed for mood changes, inability to concentrate, fatigue, insomnia, and other symptoms of depression. Her medical history, current medications and treatments, nutritional status, pain rating, elimination pattern, and sexual history should be reviewed for factors that contribute to depression. Participating in a support group, meeting with mental health professionals, and taking an antidepressant or anti-anxiety medication can help alleviate depression and anxiety.

Advancing or relapsing ovarian cancer may cause complications. These may include development of ascites, intestinal obstruction, deep vein thrombosis, malnutrition and cachexia, lymphedema, and pleural effusion. Current five-year survival rates for ovarian cancer are about 30% to 40%. If ovarian cancer recurs after treatment or fails to regress with treatment, palliative and end-of-life care may aid both patients and their families.

c. of the pancreas Pancreatic **c.**

pancreatic c. Carcinoma of the pancreas. The American Cancer Society estimated there would be 37,700 new cases of the disease in the U.S. in 2008, with 34,300 deaths caused by the illness that year. Although the causes of pancreatic cancer are unknown, it has been found in more men than women, more blacks than whites, more smokers than nonsmokers, and more patients with a history of chronic pancreatitis and diabetes mellitus than without. When cancer occurs in the head of the pancreas, where it may obstruct the bile ducts and cause jaundice, the disease is most likely to be diagnosed at an early stage, when it may be most responsive to therapy. Surgical excision of the tumor and treatment with chemotherapy or radiotherapy may prolong survival in some patients. Only 4% of victims of pancreatic cancer survive 5 years. SYN: *carcinoma of the pancreas; c. of the pancreas; pancreatic carcinoma.*

primary c. The original cell or tissue type from which a metastatic cancer arises.

prostate c. SEE: *prostate cancer.*

scirrhous c. Hard c.

skin c. A broad term that includes basal cell carcinomas, squamous cell carcinomas, and melanomas. Together, these skin cancers are the most common cancers in the U.S. They are all associated with excessive exposure to ultraviolet light, e.g., sun exposure. SEE: *basal cell carcinoma; squamous cell carcinoma; melanoma.*

PATIENT CARE: According to the U.S. Preventative Services Task Force (USPSTF), benefits from routine screening for skin cancers with a total body skin examination are unproven, even in high-risk patients.

stomach c. Gastric c.

terminal c. Widespread or advanced cancer, from which recovery is not expected.

testicular c., germ-cell Any of a group of testicular cancers that include choriocarcinomas, embryonal carcinomas, seminomas, spermatocytic seminomas, sex cord tumors, teratomas, and tumors with mixtures of several different malignant cell types.

c. of unknown primary site Disseminated cancer in which the original tissue type is uncertain. Such cancers generally have poor prognoses.

ETIOLOGY: Patients with such cancers are usually evaluated for tumors that might respond well to therapy, such as a lymphoma, a thyroid cancer, a germ cell tumor, or neoplasms of the breast or prostate.

c. of uterus A malignant neoplasm of the uterus, usually of the endometrium, found most often in women over 50. Other uterine cancers include those that arise in the muscular wall of the uterus (sarcomas), cervical cancers, and trophoblastic cancers. Symptoms may include post menopausal bleeding, bleeding between periods, and irregular, long, heavy periods. Pain during urination and during intercourse may be reported. Diagnosis of endometrial cancer is made by endometrial biopsy. The most common treatment is hysterectomy, although radiation and hormone therapy may be used. SEE: *Bethesda System, The; cervical cancer; cervical intraepithelial* **neoplasia.**

vulvar c. Any malignant neoplasm of the vulva. Of these, 90% are squamous cell carcinomas; the rest are caused by adenocarcinomas, sarcomas, or Paget's disease.

Vulvar cancer accounts for 4% of all gynecological malignancies. More than 50% of cases occur in postmenopausal women between 65 and 70. Generally, vulvar cancers are localized, slow-growing, and marked by late metastasis to the regional lymph nodes. Treatment may include surgery and/or radiation therapy. SEE: *vulvectomy.*

cancer antigen SEE: under *antigen.*

cancer cell SEE: under *cell.*

cancer cluster SEE: under *cluster.*

cancer grading and staging The standardized procedure for expressing cancer cell differentiation, called grading, and the extent of dissemination of the cancer, called staging. This procedure is very helpful in comparing the results of various forms of therapy. Cancer is graded on the differentiation of the tumor cells and the number of mitoses present. These are thought to be correlated with the ability of the tumor to grow and spread. Some cancers are graded I to IV, the latter being the most anaplastic and having the least resemblance to normal tissue.

Cancers are staged according to size, amount of local spread (metastases), and whether blood-borne metastasis has occurred. There are two major staging systems. The TNM judges the size of primary tumor (T), evidence of regional extension or nodes (N), and evidence of metastases (M). Another system classifies cancers as Stage 0 to IV according to the size of the tumor and its spread.

It is not possible to determine the site of the primary malignancy for some metastatic cancers. The most frequent cell types are adenocarcinoma, melanoma, lymphoma, sarcoma, and squamous cell carcinoma. Even though the prognosis is poor for affected patients, their response may be improved if the cell type is specifically identified.

cancericidal (kăn″sĕr-ĭ-sī′dăl) [L. *cancer,* crab, + *cidus,* killing] Lethal to malignant cells.

cancerigenic (kăn″sĕr-ĭ-jĕn′ĭk) [″ + Gr. *gennan,* to produce] Carcinogenic.

Cancer Information Service A program sponsored by the National Cancer Institute that provides cancer information to patients and their families, health professionals, and the general public. Information may be obtained by calling the toll-free number 1-800-4-CANCER.

CANCERLIT (kan′sĕr-lit″) [*cancer* + *lit(erature)*] A database of published information about cancer, including its causes, pathophysiology, diagnosis, and treatment.

cancerogenic (kăn″sĕr-ō-jĕn′ĭk) [″ + Gr. *gennan,* to produce] Carcinogenic.

cancerophobia (kăn″sĕr-ō-fō′bē-ă) [″ + Gr. *phobos,* fear] Unreasonable fear of cancer.

cancerous (kăn′sĕr-ŭs) Pert. to malignant growth.

cancer screening SEE: under *screening.*

cancer worry A person's psychological perception of the risk of succumbing to cancer. It is considered a means of motivating health-protective behavior in some people in that it may drive them to undergo appropriate screening tests and to follow health promotional guidelines. But it may also reflect a form of unwarranted anxiety in others, esp. when it does not motivate actions that promote better health, or when it results in unwarranted fear or pessimism.

cancra (kăng′kră) Pl. of cancrum.

cancroid (kăng′kroyd) [″ + Gr. *eidos,* form, shape] **1.** Like a cancer. **2.** A type of keloid. **3.** Epithelioma.

cancrum (kăng′krŭm)*pl.* **cancra** [L. *cancer,* crab, creeping ulcer] A rapidly spreading ulcer.

   c. nasi A gangrenous inflammation of the nasal membranes.

   c. oris Gangrenous destruction of oral and facial tissues occurring as a consequence of an infection of the gums (necrotizing ulcerative gingivitis), usually with anaerobic bacteria or herpesviruses. The disease is most commonly found in children who live in extremely impoverished circumstances, are severely malnourished, have poor oral hygiene, or a recent measles infection. It is usually found in children from underdeveloped nations. SYN: *noma.*

   c. pudendi Ulceration of the vulva.

candela (kăn-dĕl′ă) [L. *candela,* candle] SYMB: cd. The SI base unit of the intensity of light.

Candida (kan′dĭd-ă) [L. *candidus,* bright white] A genus of yeasts of the family Cryptococcaceae that develop a pseudomycelium and reproduce by budding. *Candida* (formerly *Monilia*) species are part of the normal flora of the mouth, skin, intestinal tract, and vagina.

   C. albicans A *Candida* species that is the principal cause of candidiasis (moniliasis).

   C. dubliniensis A *Candida* species that resembles *Candida albicans* and is capable of causing thrush. It differs from *C. albicans* in its inability to grow in the laboratory at temperatures exceeding 94° F (42° C).

   C. glabrata A *Candida* species that is usually nonpathogenic in humans but may cause serious illness in immunocompromised patients. It was formerly called *Torulopsis glabrata.*

   C. krusei A *Candida* species responsible for bloodborne, cardiac, and ocular infections, esp. in immunocompromised patients. It is resistant to fluconazole.

   C. lusitaniae A *Candida* species that causes serious infections in immunocompromised (e.g., neutropenic) patients. It is often resistant to treatment with amphotericin B.

   C. parapsilosis A *Candida* species that causes serious infections, most often identified in surgical or traumatic wound patients, critically ill newborns, and patients with indwelling devices.

   C. rugosa A *Candida* species that causes azole-resistant infections, esp. in patients in medical or surgical ICUs. It

is more commonly isolated in Latin American hospitals than in other locations around the world.

   C. tropicalis A *Candida* species that, unlike *C. albicans,* does not produce germ tubes and does not hydrolyze urea. It is responsible for bloodborne infections in patients with diabetes mellitus, leukemias and lymphomas.

candidate gene (kăn′dĭ-dāt″) A gene that is suspected of being responsible for a particular trait or illness.

candidemia (kăn″dĭ-dē′mē-ă) The presence of yeast from the genus *Candida* in the blood.

candidiasis (kan″dĭ-dī′ă-sĭs) [*Candida* + *-iasis*] Fungal infection of the skin or mucous membrane with any species of *Candida,* but chiefly *Candida albicans. Candida* species are part of the body's normal flora. *Candida* grows in warm, moist areas, causing superficial infections of the mouth, vagina, nails, and skinfolds in healthy people. In patients with immunodeficiencies, central venous lines, and burns, or those receiving peritoneal dialysis, it can invade the bloodstream, causing disseminated infections. SEE: illus.; *normal flora; thrush.*

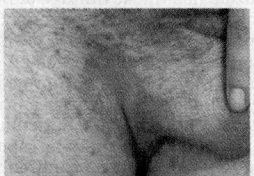

CANDIDIASIS

ETIOLOGY: *Candida* infections are due to a disruption in the composition of normal flora or a change in host defenses. Antibiotic therapy, which destroys the bacteria in normal flora, and inhaled or systemic corticosteroid therapy, which decreases white blood cell activity, are common treatments that may cause candidiasis. Vulvovaginal candidiasis is common during pregnancy, possibly as the result of increased estrogen levels. Infections of the nail beds (paronychia) can occur in those whose hands are frequently in water or who wear occlusive gloves or who are receiving chemotherapy. Elevated glucose levels can be the predisposing factor in patients with diabetes mellitus. Chronic mucocutaneous candidiasis is common in patients with AIDS or other immunosuppressant illnesses. Systemic fungal infections may be present in any organ, including the brain, heart, kidneys, and eyes.

SYMPTOMS: Oral lesions (thrush) are raised, white patches on the mucosa and tongue that can be easily scraped off, revealing an underlying red, irritated surface. Skin lesions are red and macerated, and are usually located in skinfolds of the groin or abdomen and under pendulous breasts. Vaginal infections are characterized by itching and a thick, cheesy discharge. Blurred vision is the first symptom noticed in ocular candidiasis. The symptoms produced in systemic infections depend on the extent of the infection and the organs affected, i.e., whether *Candida* invades the heart, esophagus, meninges, kidneys, or lungs. *Candida* septicemia can cause chills, fever, and shock with oliguria leading to renal failure.

TREATMENT: Oral candidiasis is treated with a single dose of fluconazole or with clotrimazole lozenges or nystatin oral solution (which must be held in the mouth for several minutes before swallowing) for 14 days. Topical forms of amphotericin B, clotrimazole, econazole, nystatin, or miconazole are effective for skin infections. Fluconazole is used for oral or vaginal infections in patients with AIDS. Amphotericin B, fluconazole, flucytosine, ketaconazole, and newer antifungal agents are used to treat patients with systemic infections. For patients with kidney disease, ketaconazole has the advantage of liver metabolism and fecal excretion. Some strains of *C. albicans* are resistant to fluconazole. Pregnant women should consult their health care providers before taking or applying these drugs.

PATIENT CARE: Patients with thrush need explanations about the need to swish nystatin solution in their mouths for several minutes before swallowing to obtain maximum benefit. A nonirritating mouthwash and a soft toothbrush are provided to loosen tenacious secretions without causing irritation. A topical anesthetic helps relieve mouth discomfort, and a soft diet may be helpful. The patient's intake is monitored: mouth pain may interfere with nutritional intake, esp. in those recovering from surgery, trauma, or severe infection. The patient is weighed twice a week to assess nutritional status.

Patients who are obese or incontinent of urine are at special risk for *Candida* infection, esp. if they are receiving antibiotics. Skin folds should be carefully washed and dried, and antifungal cream or powder applied, usually 3 to 4 times a day. When possible, the affected area should be exposed to the air.

Patients with vulvovaginal candidiasis should be reminded not to wear constricting clothing such as panty hose and to wear cotton underwear. If there is pain after intercourse (dyspareunia), the patient is counseled that sexual impairment should resolve as the infection subsides, and to complete the full course of medication as prescribed. Although the sexual partners of infected patients usually will not need treatment, partners of patients with recurrent vaginal infections should be examined and treated if indicated to prevent ongoing reinfections.

Patients with systemic candidiasis require inpatient care for intravenous or intrathecal drug administration, monitoring of laboratory findings, and assessment to identify and manage adverse drug effects and to treat infection extension to other sites and complications. Vital signs are monitored because of the risk of septic shock. Supportive care includes premedication with antipyretics, antihistamines, or corticosteroids to minimize hypersensitivity reactions if the patient is receiving intravenous amphotericin B. Multiple factors affect whether or not immunocompromised patients will develop or die from candidiasis. These include the severity of their underlying illness, nutritional status, history of alcohol abuse, diabetes mellitus, renal or liver failure, illicit drug use, or other comorbid conditions. Immunosuppressed individuals should be encouraged to or reduce risk factors for infection. The patient should be encouraged to eat a nutritious diet, balance activity with rest, reduce stressors, and manage time realistically. All high-risk hospitalized patients, esp. those receiving antibiotic therapies, should be assessed for indications of candidiasis superinfection.

oropharyngeal c. Thrush.

pseudomembranous c. Thrush.

candiru (kăn-dēr-oo′, -dēr′oo) *Vandellia cirrhosa.*

cane (kān) An assistive device prescribed to provide support during ambulation and transfers for individuals with weakness, instability, pain, or balance loss. It also may be used to unload a lower extremity joint or to partially eliminate weight-bearing. Standard (conventional) canes are made from wood or aluminum and have a variety of hand grip styles. Other styles include tripod canes, quadruped (quad) canes, and walk ("hemi") canes. Canes should be used on the unaffected (stronger) side of the body.

canine (kā′nīn‴) [L. *caninus,* pert. to a dog, dog's] **1.** Pert. to a dog. **2.** Any of four teeth, two in the maxilla and two in the mandible, located between the lateral incisor and the first premolar in permanent dentition. SYN: *cuspid; eyetooth.* SEE: *dentition* for illus.

Canis familiaris (kā′nĭs fă-mĭl″ē-âr′ĭs) [L., family dog] The scientific name for the domestic dog. Dogs are often used as guides for people with sensory impairments and as companions for older or institutionalized people. Dog allergens, abbreviated *Can* by the World Health

Organization, are a common source of indoor allergies.

canities (kăn-ĭsh′ē-ēz) [L., gray hair] Congenital (rare) or acquired whiteness of the hair. The acquired form may develop rapidly or slowly and be partial or complete.

   c. unguium Gray or white streaks in the nails. SYN: *leukonychia.*

cannabinoid (kan′ă-bĭ-noyd″, kă-nab′ĭ-noyd″) [*cannabis* + *-oid*] A compound that is either extracted from or synthesized to resemble *Cannabis sativa* (marijuana).

   synthetic c. K2.

Cannabis sativa (kan′ă-bĭs) [L. *cannabis,* fr Gr. *kannabis,* hemp] A species of annual herb native to Central and South Asia, whose tough fiber (hemp) is used for making rope and its oils, resins, and seeds used medicinally and as a psychoactive, recreational drug. SEE: *hashish; marijuana; tetrahydrocannabinol.*

cannibalism (kăn′ĭ-băl-ĭzm″) The human consumption of human flesh. SEE: *kuru.*

Cannon, Walter B. (kan′ŏn) U.S. physiologist, 1871–1954.

   C. ring A contracted band of muscles in the transverse colon near the hepatic flexure.

   fight-or-flight reaction of C. The generalized response to an emergency situation. This includes intense stimulation of the sympathetic nervous system and the adrenal gland. The heart and respiratory rates, blood pressure, and blood flow to muscles are increased. This response prepares the body either to flee or to fight.

cannula (kăn′ū-lă) [L., a small reed] A tube or sheath that encloses a trocar. After the device is inserted into a blood vessel, body cavity, duct, or hollow organ, withdrawal of the trocar lets fluid drain (so that it can be collected or sampled) or escape. SEE: illus.

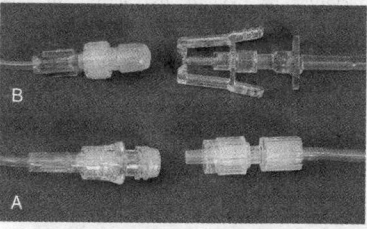

NEEDLELESS CANNULAE USED TO CONNECT AN ADDITIVE TO PRIMARY INTRAVENOUS INFUSIONS

(A) Threaded-lock cannula; (B) Lever-lock cannula

   Bellocq's c. SEE: *Bellocq's cannula.*

   nasal c. Tubing used to deliver oxygen at levels from 1 to 6 L/min. The na-

sal prongs of the cannula extend approx. 1 cm into each naris and are connected to a common tube, which is then connected to the oxygen source. It is used to treat conditions in which a slightly enriched oxygen content is needed, such as emphysema. The exact percentage of oxygen delivered to the patient varies with respiratory rate and other factors.

cannulate (kăn′ū-lāt) To introduce a cannula.

cannulation of large veins, venous cannulation (kăn″ū-lā′shŭn) Gaining access to venous circulation by placing a flexible catheter into one of the large veins, usually the femoral, subclavian, or jugular vein. The cannula may be used to provide hyperalimentation; to administer drugs; or to replace fluids, among other uses.

> ⚠ Potential complications of venous cannulation include bleeding, infection, pneumothorax, arterial puncture, and injury to internal organs, among others.

canonical Standard; generally accepted.

cantharides (kăn-thăr′ĭ-dēz) *sing.,* **cantharis** [Gr. *kantharis,* beetle, + *eidos,* form, shape] Dried insects of the species *Cantharis vesicatoria;* poisonous if taken internally in large doses. It was formerly used externally as a counterirritant and vesicant, and internally for its supposed aphrodisiac effect. It is no longer used. SYN: *Spanish fly.* **cantharidal** (-thăr′ĭ-dăl), *adj.*

Cantharis (kăn′thă-rĭs) A genus of beetles, *C. vesicatoria,* known as Spanish fly. SEE: *cantharides.*

canthectomy (kăn-thĕk′tō-mē) [Gr. *kanthos,* angle, + *ektome,* excision] Excision of a canthus.

canthi (kăn′thī) Pl. of canthus.

canthitis (kăn-thī′tĭs) [″ + *itis,* inflammation] Inflammation of a canthus.

cantholysis (kăn-thŏl′ĭ-sĭs) [″ + *lysis,* dissolution] Incision of an optic canthus of an eye to widen the palpebral slit.

canthoplasty (kăn′thō-plăs″tē) [″ + *plassein,* to form] **1.** Plastic surgery of an optic canthus. **2.** Enlargement of the palpebral fissure by division of the external canthus.

canthorrhaphy (kăn-thor′ă-fē) [″ + *rhaphe,* seam, ridge] Suturing of a canthus.

canthotomy (kăn-thŏt′ō-mē) [″ + *tome,* incision] Surgical division of a canthus.

canthus (kăn′thŭs) *pl.* **canthi** [Gr. *kanthos,* angle] The angle at either end of the slit between the eyelids; the lateral canthus (commissura palpebrarum lateralis) and the medial canthus (commissura palpebrarum medialis). **canthal** (-thăl), *adj.*

Cantor tube (kăn'tĕr toob, tūb) Intestinal tube.

Cantrell pentalogy (kan'trĕl) A rare congenital condition developing during embryogeny in which defects occur in the formation of the upper abdomen and lower chest, resulting in omphalocele, ectopic location of the heart, sternal malformation, and other anomalies. The defects are sometimes amenable to surgical repair.

CANUTEC *Canadian Transport Emergency Centre.*

CaO Calcium oxide.

CaO₂ The content of oxygen in arterial blood.

cao gio (kow' jē'ō) [Vietnamese] Coining.

Ca(OH)₂ Calcium hydroxide.

CAOT *Canadian Association of Occupational Therapists* (a professional society for promoting occupational therapy through education, research, certification programs, and standards of practice).

CAP *College of American Pathologists.*

¹cap [L. *capere,* to take] *capiat,* let (the patient) take, used as a direction in writing prescriptions.

²cap (kap) [L. *cappa,* hood] **1.** A covering. SYN: *tegmentum.* **2.** The first part of the duodenum. **3.** The protective covering of a developing tooth. **4.** The artificial covering of a tooth, used for cosmetic reasons. SEE: *enamel organ.*

> **cervical c.** A contraceptive barrier that is inserted into the vagina and placed over the uterine cervix prior to intercourse. It prevents conception by keeping sperm from entering the womb.

> **cradle c.** Seborrheic dermatitis of the newborn, usually appearing on the scalp, face, and head. Thick, yellowish, crusted lesions develop on the scalp, and scaling, papules, or fissuring appears behind the ears and on the face. SEE: *seborrhea.*
>
> TREATMENT: The head is cleansed with a mild shampoo daily. Corticosteroid cream is applied to the affected area twice daily.

> **fibrous c.** A layer of connective tissue, including smooth muscle cells and macrophages, that forms on an atherosclerotic plaque. Rupturing of the cap into the underlying plaque is the cause of acute arterial obstruction during myocardial infarction.

> **knee c.** Patella.

capacitance (kă-păs'ĭ-tăns) [L. *capacitas,* holding] **1.** The ability to store an electrical charge. **2.** The ratio of the charge transferred between a pair of conductors to the potential difference between the conductors.

capacitation (kă-păs"ĭ-tā'shŭn) A natural process that helps sperm cells to fertilize ova. As they travel through the female reproductive tract, the plasma membranes of sperm cells break down, exposing the acrosomes to the acidic environment surrounding the corona radiata of the ovum. This attracts the sperm to the ovum and releases spermatic enzymes responsible for penetration. The process requires about 7 hr.

capacitor (kă-pas'ĭt-ŏr) [*capacit(y)*] An electronic device for storing electric charges by using two conducting surfaces and a nonconductor. SYN: *condenser (3); electrical **condenser**.*

capacity (kă-pas'ĭ-tē) [Fr. fr L. *capacitas,* capacity] **1.** The potential ability to contain; the potential power to do something. **2.** Cubic content. **3.** The ability to perform mentally. **4.** The measure of the electrical output of a generator.

> **forced vital c.** ABBR: FVC. The volume of gas exhaled from the completely inflated lungs during a maximal expiratory effort.
>
> PATIENT CARE: Patients with a significantly reduced vital capacity are prone to respiratory failure, esp. during the immediate postoperative period.

> **functional bladder c.** SEE: *functional c. (2).*

> **functional c.** **1.** In cardiovascular medicine, the ability of a person to perform aerobic work during maximum oxygen intake. **2.** The largest amount of urine a patient can comfortably hold before feeling the urge to urinate. It may be estimated by recording how much urine a patient voids on each occasion during a two- or three-day period. The largest volume is called the *functional bladder capacity.*

> **maximum aerobic c.** ABBR: $VO_{2\,max}$ BP. The maximum amount of physiological work that an individual can do, as measured by oxygen consumption. $VO_{2\,max}$ is determined by the combination of aging and cardiovascular conditioning and is associated with the efficiency of oxygen extraction in the tissues. SYN: *maximal oxygen uptake.*

> **mental c.** The ability of a person to make legally valid decisions.
>
> PATIENT CARE: This ability can be tested with assessment tools such as the Aid to Capacity Evaluation (ACE) test, available on the Internet at www.jointcentreforbioethics.ca/tools/documents/ace.pdf

> **testamentary c.** The ability of a person to make a will or living will.

> **timed vital c.** A test of vital capacity of the lungs expressed with respect to the volume of air that can be quickly and forcibly breathed out in a certain amount of time. SEE: FEV_1.

> **total lung c.** ABBR: TLC. The volume of air in the lungs after a maximal inspiration. This amount is important in evaluating the ability of the lung to

exchange oxygen and carbon dioxide. SEE: *pulmonary function test; vital c.; volume, residual.*

vital c. The volume of air that can be exhaled from the lungs after a maximal inspiration. This amount is important in evaluating the ability of the lung to exchange oxygen and carbon dioxide. SEE: *pulmonary function test; total lung c.; volume, residual.*

CAPD *continuous ambulatory peritoneal dialysis.*

Capgras syndrome [Jean Marie Joseph Capgras, Fr. psychiatrist, 1873–1950] The patient's delusion that a close relative or friend has been replaced by an impostor. SEE: *delusion of substitution.*

capillarectasia (kăp″ĭ-lăr″ĕk-tā′sē-ă) [L. *capillaris,* hairlike, + Gr. *ektasis,* dilatation] Distention of capillary vessels.

Capillaria (kăp″ĭ-lăr′ē-ă) A genus of parasitic nematodes.

C. philippinensis A species of roundworm discovered in the Philippines. It causes severe diarrhea, malabsorption, and enteric protein loss in humans; mortality is high.

capillariasis (kă-pĭl″ă-rī′ă-sĭs) [*Capillaria* + *-iasis*] Infestation of the large intestine with the roundworm *Capillaria.* Treatment is with mebendazole or albendazole.

capillaritis (kap″ĭ-lăr-ī′tĭs) [″ + Gr. *itis,* inflammation] An inflammation of the capillaries.

capillarity (kăp″ĭ-lăr′ĭ-tē) Capillary action.

capillaropathy (kăp″ĭ-lăr-ŏp′ă-thē) [″ + Gr. *pathos,* disease] A capillary disorder or disease.

capillaroscopy (kăp″ĭ-lăr-ŏs′kō-pē) [″ + Gr. *skopein,* to examine] Examination of capillaries for diagnostic purposes.

capillary (kap′ĭ-ler″ē) *pl.* **capillaries** [L. *capillaris,* hairlike] **1.** Any of the minute blood vessels, averaging 0.008 mm in diameter, that connect the ends of the smallest arteries (arterioles) with the beginnings of the smallest veins (venules). **2.** Pert. to a hair; hairlike.

arterial c. One of the very small vessels that are the terminal branches of the arterioles or metarterioles.

blood c. One of the minute blood vessels that convey blood from the arterioles to the venules and form an anastomosing network that brings the blood into intimate relationship with the tissue cells. Its wall consists of a single layer of squamous cells (endothelium) through which oxygen diffuses to the tissue and products of metabolic activity enter the bloodstream. Blood capillaries average about 8 μm in diameter.

lymphatic c. A thin-walled lymphatic vessel at the beginning of a branch of the lymphatic system. Lymphatic capillaries have closed ends, but have no basement membranes and are more permeable than blood capillaries. Fluids, salts, proteins, large molecules, particles, debris, microorganisms, and migrating cells can pass from the interstitial spaces into lymphatic capillaries. Lymphatic capillaries lead to larger lymphatics that transport the lymph to lymph nodes. SEE: illus.

secretory c. Any of the very small canaliculi that are part of the secretory

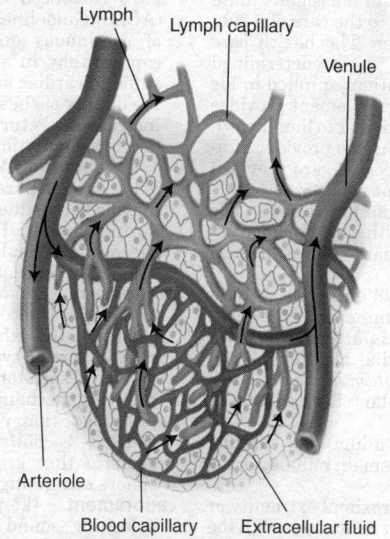

Lymph

Lymph capillary

Venule

Arteriole

Blood capillary

Extracellular fluid

LYMPHATIC CAPILLARY

Located in extracellular matrix

outflow path receiving secretion discharged from gland cells.

venous c. One of the minute vessels that convey blood from a capillary network into the small veins (venules).

capillary attraction Capillary action.

capillary nail refill test Blanch test.

capillus (kă-pĭl′ŭs) *pl.* **capilli** [L., a hair]
1. A hair, esp. of the head. 2. A filament.
3. A hair's breadth.

capita (kop′ĭ-ta″, kap′ĭt-a) [L.] Plural of caput.

capital (căp′ĭ-tăl) [L. *capitalis*] Pert. to the head.

capital punishment Sentencing a criminal to death and carrying out the sentence via a legal method such as hanging, electrocution, or lethal injection.

PATIENT CARE: Whether or not to participate in capital punishment raises challenging ethical concerns for health care professionals. The decision may need to be individually considered in the context of personal, religious, or institutional philosophies. Guidance can be gained by consulting professional position statements on roles and responsibilities, such as those promulgated by the American Nurses Association and the International Council of Nurses; various Church organizations; and State Boards that govern health care; among others.

capitate (kăp′ĭ-tāt) [L. *caput,* head]
1. Head-shaped; having a rounded extremity. 2. The central and largest of the eight carpal (wrist) bones. It articulates with the third metacarpal.

capitation (kăp″ĭ-tā′shŭn) A form of reimbursement for health care services in which the health insurer assigns a finite number of patients to the care of a subcontracting provider. The health care provider is paid a predetermined amount for each patient enrolled in his or her care. This arrangement provides incentives to the provider to limit health care costs, by placing the provider at financial risk if the cost of care provided exceeds the payment received.

capitation fee (kăp″ĭ-tā′shŭn) The amount paid a health care provider annually from each patient in a medical group plan.

capitellum (kăp″ĭ-těl′ŭm) [L., small head] The round eminence at the lower end of the humerus articulating with the radius; the radial head of the humerus. SYN: *capitulum humeri.*

capitular (kă-pĭch′ă-lăr) Pert. to a capitulum.

capitulum (kă-pĭch′ă-lŭm) *pl.* **capitula** [L., small head] A small, rounded articular end of a bone.

c. fibulae The proximal extremity or head of the fibula. It articulates with the tibia.

c. humeri Capitellum.

c. of the malleus In the middle ear, the head (the large rounded extremity) of the malleus. It carries the facet for the incus.

Caplan syndrome (kap′lăn) [Anthony Caplan, Brit. physician, 1907–1976] Rheumatoid arthritis and pneumoconiosis with progressive massive fibrosis of the lung in coal workers. SYN: *pneumoconiosis.*

Capnocytophaga (kăp″nō-sī-tŏf′ă-gă) [NL] A genus of gram-negative, facultatively anaerobic bacilli that may be isolated from the oral cavity of humans and canines and are associated with serious systemic infections, esp. in asplenic patients.

C. canimorsus The main pathogen for humans from dog bites. This organism causes septicemia, meningitis, endocarditis, and rare ocular infections. Those at increased risk of developing *C. canimorsus* infections include patients who have undergone a splenectomy and those who abuse alcohol.

TREATMENT: Treatments may include penicillins, or in penicillin-allergic patients, doxycycline and metronidazole.

capnography (kap″nog′ră-fē) [Gr. *kapnos,* smoke + *-graphy*] Continuous recording of the concentration of carbon dioxide (CO_2) in inhaled and exhaled air. Measurements of the level of (CO_2) are used to ensure that airway adjuncts (such as endotracheal tubes) are correctly placed in the trachea (and not in the esophagus) of a mechanically ventilated patient.

The American Heart Association 2010 Advanced Cardiac Life Support (ACLS) Guidelines recommend the use of continuous quantitative waveform capnography in all patients who have suffered cardiac arrest to evaluate both the quality of chest compressions and to indicate the return of a patient's spontaneous circulation.

volumetric c. ABBR: VCap. The plot of the expired partial pressure of carbon dioxide versus the expired tidal volume during a breath. It may help determine the optimal tidal volume for the mechanically ventilated patient.

capnometry (kăp-nŏm′ĕ-trē) The measurement of the concentration of carbon dioxide in the exhaled breath of a critically ill person, typically a victim of cardiac or respiratory arrest or a patient receiving mechanical ventilation.

capnophilic (kăp-nō-fĭl′ĭk) [Gr. *kapnos,* smoke, + *philein,* to love] Pert. to bacteria that grow best in an atmosphere containing carbon dioxide.

capotement (kă-pōt-mŏn′) [Fr.] A splashing sound that may be heard when the dilated stomach contains air and fluid.

capping (kap′ing) 1. **Pulp** capping.

2. Placing an artificial crown on a tooth for cosmetic purposes. **3.** In immunology, the aggregation of living B lymphocytes that have reacted with fluorescein-labeled anti-immune globulin cells to form a polar cap.

pulp c. The technique and material for covering and protecting from external conditions a vital, exposed pulp while the pulp heals and secondary or tertiary dentin forms to cover it. SYN: *capping* (1).

capsaicin (kăp-sā′ĭ-sĭn) [Fr. caps(icum)] The chemical ingredient in chili peppers that provides their pungency, also used as a topical analgesic.

capsicum (kăp′sĭ-kŭm) The genus of pepper plants, of which there are more than 200 varieties, including jalapeño and tabasco.

capsid (kap′sĭd) [L. *capsa,* box + ²-*id*] The protein covering around the central core of a virus. The capsid develops from protomers (protein units), protects the nucleic acid in the core of the virus from the destructive enzymes in biological fluids, and promotes attachment of the virus to susceptible cells. SYN: *coat protein.*

capsomer, capsomere (kăp′să-mēr, kăp′să-mēr″) [″ + Gr. *meros,* part] Short ribbons of protein that make up a portion of the capsid of a virus.

capsula (kăp′sŭ-lă) *pl.* **capsulae** [L., little box] A sheath or continuous enclosure around an organ or structure.

capsular (kăp′sŭ-lar) Pert. to a capsule.

capsular pattern In a joint, the proportional loss or limitation of passive range of motion that suggests inflammation in that joint (e.g., the capsular pattern of the glenohumeral joint, in order of most restriction, is lateral rotation, abduction, and medial rotation).

capsular switching A change in the polysaccharide capsule that encloses a bacterium, typically as a result of gene transfer between related organisms. It alters the susceptibility of encapsulated bacteria (such as meningococci and pneumococci) to antibiotic therapy.

capsulation (kăp″sŭ-lā′shŭn) Enclosure in a capsule.

capsule (kap′sŭl, sool″) [L. *capsula,* little box] **1.** A sheath or continuous enclosure around an organ or structure; a capsula. **2.** A special container made of gelatin, sized for a single dose of a drug. The enclosure prevents the patient from tasting the drug.

articular c. Joint capsule.

auditory c. The embryonic cartilaginous capsule that encloses the developing ear.

bacterial c. The polysaccharide or polypeptide layer that surrounds the cell wall of some bacteria; it provides resistance to phagocytosis. Capsules are antigenic. Their antigens are used to manufacture several common vaccines.

Bowman c. SEE: under *Bowman, Sir William.*

brood c. A cystlike body that develops within a hydatid cyst of *Echinococcus granulosus.*

cartilage c. The layer of matrix that forms the innermost portion of the wall of a lacuna enclosing a single cell or a group of cartilage cells. It is basophilic.

Crosby c. SEE: *Crosby capsule.*

Glisson's c. SEE: under *Glisson, Francis.*

glomerular c. SEE: *Bowman, Sir William.*

internal c. A large bidirectional fiber tract connecting the cerebral cortex with the ipsilateral thalamus and sending axons from the cerebral cortex to the brainstem and spinal cord.

joint c. The sleevelike membrane that encloses the ends of bones in a diarthrodial joint. It consists of an outer fibrous layer and an inner synovial layer and contains synovial fluid. SYN: *articular c.*

c. of the kidney Renal capsule.

lens c. A transparent, elastic, connective tissue membrane that surrounds and encloses the lens of the eye.

M2A c. A plastic container, measuring about 1 x ½ in, that holds a video camera, batteries, antennas, and flash. It is swallowed and allowed to pass through the intestinal tract, where it is used to obtain images of the small intestine.

PATIENT CARE: The device is typically used to find the cause of gastrointestinal blood loss in patients who have no evidence of bleeding in the esophagus, stomach, duodenum, and colon.

nasal c. The cartilaginous capsule that develops in the embryonic skull to enclose the nasal cavity.

optic c. The cartilaginous capsule that develops in the embryonic skull to enclose the eye.

otic c. The cartilaginous capsule that develops in the embryonic skull to enclose the ear.

renal c. The fibrous membrane on the outer surface of a kidney, which is in turn enclosed by adipose tissue that cushions the kidney. SYN: *c. of the kidney.*

suprarenal c. A tough connective tissue capsule that encloses the adrenal gland.

temporomandibular joint c. The fibrous covering of the synovial joint between the skull and mandible on each side of the head.

Tenon c. SEE: under *Tenon, Jacques R.*

capsulectomy (kăp″sū-lĕk′tō-mē) [L. *capsula,* little box, + Gr. *ektome,* excision] Surgical removal of a capsule.

capsule endoscopy SEE: under *endoscopy*.

capsulitis (kap″syŭ-līt′ĭs) [*capsule* + *-itis*] Inflammation of a capsule.

   adhesive c. Fibrosis surrounding a joint that severely limits movement. It can result from arthritis, inflammation, or trauma. Adhesive Capsulitis.

   adhesive c. of shoulder A condition that causes shoulder pain, with restricted movement even though there is no obvious intrinsic shoulder disease. This may follow bursitis or tendinitis of the shoulder or may be associated with systemic conditions such as chronic pulmonary disease, myocardial infarction, or diabetes mellitus. Prolonged immobility of the arm favors development of adhesive capsulitis. The condition is more common in women after age 50. It may resolve spontaneously 12 to 18 months after onset or may result in permanent restriction of movement. Treatment includes injection of glucocorticoids; use of nonsteroidal anti-inflammatory agents and physical therapy may provide symptomatic relief; early range-of-motion exercises following an injury may prevent development of the disease; and manipulation of the shoulder while the patient is anesthetized may be of benefit. SYN: *frozen shoulder; pericapsulitis*.

capsulolenticular (kăp″sū-lō-lĕn-tĭk′ū-lăr) [″ + *lenticularis*, pert. to a lens] Pert. to the capsule of the eye and the lens.

capsuloplasty (kăp′sū-lō-plăs″tē) [″ + Gr. *plassein*, to mold] Plastic surgery of a capsule, esp. a joint capsule.

capsulorhexis (kăp″sū-lor-ĕk′sĭs) A common method of cataract extraction in which a circular incision is made in the anterior capsule to permit lens extraction.

capsulorrhaphy (kăp″sū-lor′ă-fē) [″ + Gr. *rhaphe*, seam, ridge] Suture of a joint capsule or of a tear in a capsule.

capsulotome (kăp′sū-lō-tōm″) [″ + Gr. *tome*, incision] An instrument for incising the capsule of the crystalline lens.

capsulotomy (kăp″sū-lŏt′ō-mē) Cutting of a capsule of the lens or a joint.

   laser c. The use of a laser to make a hole in the capsule surrounding the lens of the eye to let light pass. Extracapsular removal of a cataract allows the capsule surrounding the lens to remain in the eye; however, if the capsule becomes cloudy, laser capsulotomy is used to restore vision.

Captain of the Ship Doctrine SEE: under *doctrine*.

captation Capture or uptake by cells or tissues; said especially of chemicals or radioactive isotopes.

captioning The display of spoken words as text on a television or a movie screen, to improve the comprehension of dialogue by hearing-impaired individuals.

captopril (kăp′tŏ-prĭl) A drug that blocks the conversion of angiotensin I to angiotensin II. It is used primarily to treat high blood pressure and congestive heart failure. It also can be used in the diagnosis of renovascular hypertension and in the management of the renal crises that occur in systemic sclerosis (scleroderma). Important side effects of the medication are cough, angioedema, and hypotension.

capture 1. In atomic physics, the joining of an elementary particle such as an electron or neutron with the atomic nucleus. 2. In electrophysiology, the mechanical beating of the heart in response to an electrical stimulus.

   ventricular c. The normal contraction of the myocardium after electrical depolarization.

caput (kop′ut″, ′ŭt, kap′ŭt, kop′ĭ-ta″, kap′ĭt-a) *pl.* **capita** [L. *caput*, the head] 1. The head. 2. The chief extremity of an organ.

   c. medusae A plexus of dilated veins around the umbilicus, seen in patients with portal hypertension (usually as a result of cirrhosis of the liver). It may be seen in newborns. SEE: illus.

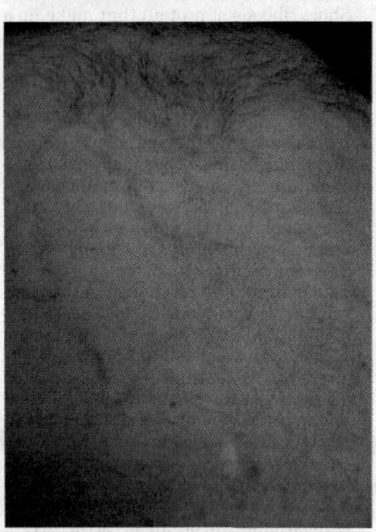

CAPUT MEDUSAE

Prominent superficial abdominal veins seen on a patient with cirrhosis and portal hypertension.

   c. succedaneum Diffuse edema of the fetal scalp that crosses the suture lines. Head compression against the cervix impedes venous return, forcing serum into the interstitial tissues. The swelling reabsorbs within 1 to 3 days.

Carabelli cusp (kar-ă-bel′ē) [Georg Carabelli, Hungarian-born Austrian dentist and professor of dental surgery, 1787–1842] An accessory cusp found on the lingual aspect of the mesiolingual cusp of the maxillary first upper molar that may be unilateral or bilateral.

carbacephem (kăr-bă-sĕph'ĕm) A class of broad-spectrum antibiotic drugs, derived from cephalosporins, that resist degradation by bacterial beta-lactamases. One drug in this class is loracarbef.

carbamazepine (kăr-bă-măz'ĕ-pēn) A drug used to treat trigeminal neuralgia, temporal lobe epilepsy, bipolar disorder, and chronic pain.

carbamide (kar'bă-mīd″, kar-bam'ĭd) [*carbo-* + *amide*] $CO(NH)_2$; urea in an anhydrous powder.

carbaminohemoglobin (kăr-băm″ĭ-nō-hē″mō-glō'bĭn) A chemical combination of carbon dioxide and hemoglobin.

carbanion (kăr-băn'ī-ŏn) A carbon ion with a negative electrical charge.

carbapenem A class of antibiotics with a broad spectrum of action against grampositive, gram-negative, and anaerobic germs. The carbapenems include imipenem and meropenem.

carbidopa (kăr″bĭ-dō'pă) A drug used with levodopa to treat parkinsonism.

carbinolamine dehydratase (kăr″bĭn-ōl'ă-mĭn dē-hī'drĭ-tās″) An enzyme that hydroxylates phenylalanine. Deficient concentrations of the enzyme are a potential cause of phenylketonuria.

carbo-, carb- [L. *carbo*, stem *carbon-*, coal (dead or burning), charcoal] Prefixes meaning *carbon*.

carbohydrase (kăr″bō-hī'drās) One of a group of enzymes (such as amylase and lactase) that hydrolyze carbohydrates.

carbohydrate (kăr″bō-hī'drāt) [L. *carbo*, carbon, + Gr. *hydor*, water] One of a group of organic chemicals, including sugars, glycogen, starches, dextrins, and celluloses, that contain only carbon, oxygen, and hydrogen. Usually the ratio of hydrogen to oxygen is 2 to 1. Glucose and its polymers (including starch and cellulose) are estimated to be the most abundant organic chemical compounds on earth, surpassing in quantity even the great stores of fuel hydrocarbons beneath the earth's crust. Carbohydrates are one of the six classes of nutrients needed by the body (the others are proteins, fats, minerals, vitamins, and water).

Green plants use the sun's energy to combine carbon dioxide and water to form carbohydrates. Most plant carbohydrates (celluloses) are unavailable for direct metabolism by vertebrates. However, the bacteria present in the intestinal tracts of some vertebrates break down cellulose to molecules that can be absorbed. The human intestinal tract lacks the enzyme that splits cellulose into sugar molecules, but humans do split starch into maltose by means of their salivary and pancreatic amylases.

CLASSIFICATION: Carbohydrates are grouped according to the number of carbon atoms they contain and how many of the basic types are combined into larger molecules. The most common simple sugars, monosaccharides, contain five or six carbon atoms and are called pentoses and hexoses, respectively. Two monosaccharides linked together are called a disaccharide. A series (chain) of monosaccharides or disaccharides is called a polysaccharide. Ribose and deoxyribose are the most important pentoses; glucose, fructose, and galactose are the most important hexoses in human metabolism. The disaccharide sugars in the diet are maltose (2 D-glucose molecules), sucrose or cane sugar (glucose and fructose), and lactose or milk sugar (D-glucose and D-galactose). These sugars are split and eventually converted to glucose by enzyme action. The two important polysaccharides are starch and glycogen; the latter is called animal starch. The basic monosaccharide building block for both of these large polymers is glucose. Dietary starch and glycogen are metabolized first to glucose and then to carbon dioxide and water in humans. SEE: table (Classification of Important Carbohydrates).

FUNCTION: Carbohydrates are a basic source of energy. They are stored in the body as glycogen in virtually all tissues, but principally in the liver and muscles. Glucose, an important source of reserve energy, can be mobilized from these sites.

DIGESTION AND ABSORPTION: Cooked but not raw starch is broken down to disaccharide by salivary amylase. Both cooked and raw starches are split in the small intestine by pancreatic amylase. Disaccharides cannot be absorbed until they have been split into monosaccharides by the enzymes present in the brush border of cells lining the intestinal tract. Glucose and galactose are the actively absorbed sugars. Fructose is absorbed by diffusion. SEE: table (Digestion of Carbohydrates).

METABOLISM: Although very complex at the molecular level, carbohydrate metabolism can be explained as follows. Carbohydrates are absorbed as glucose, galactose, or fructose. Fructose and galactose are converted to glucose by the liver and are then available for energy production, or they may be stored after conversion to glycogen. The glycogen is available for metabolism to glucose whenever reserve energy is needed. SEE: *muscle metabolism*.

SOURCES: Carbohydrates are present in food in digestible and indi-

Classification of Important Carbohydrates

Classification	Formula	Examples	Some Properties
Monosaccharides	$C_6H_{12}O_6$	Glucose	Crystalline, sweet, very soluble, readily absorbed
Pentoses	$C_5H_{10}O_5$ or $C_5H_{10}O_4$	Ribose	Part of nucleic acid, RNA
		Deoxyribose	Part of nucleic acid, DNA
Disaccharides	$(C_6H_{10}O_5)_2 \cdot H_2O$ or $C_{12}H_{22}O_{11}$ hydrolyzed to simple sugars	Sucrose	Crystalline, sweet, soluble, digestible
		Lactose	
		Maltose	Present in milk
Polysaccharides	$(C_6H_{10}O_5)_n$ composed of many molecules of simple sugars. (Since polysaccharides can be composed of various numbers of monosaccharides and disaccharides, n refers to an unknown number of these groups.)	Starch	Amorphous, little or no flavor, less soluble. Vary in solubility and digestibility.
		Dextrin	
		Cellulose	
		Glycogen	

gestible forms. The digestible type are an important source of energy. Those that cannot be used, usually some form of cellulose, are beneficial in adding bulk to the diet. Whole grains, vegetables, legumes (peas and beans), tubers (potatoes), fruits, honey, and refined sugar are excellent sources of carbohydrate. Calories derived from sugar and candy have been termed "empty" calories because these foods lack essential amino acids, vitamins, and minerals. SEE: *fiber, dietary*.

NUTRITION: Carbohydrates contain 4.1 kcal/g and are esp. useful as a quick source of energy as they are readily digested.

complex c. 1. A starch. 2. A molecule made of several linked saccharides; a polysaccharide.

carbohydrate-deficient **transferrin** ABBR: CDT. A serum protein used as a clinical marker of occult alcohol abuse. Frequent heavy use of alcohol depletes transferrin of carbohydrate moieties that are normally attached to it.

carbohydrate loading SEE: under *loading*.

carbolfuchsin A solution composed of basic fuchsin and phenol that is used in microscopy primarily as a stain for bacteria and mycobacteria.

carbon (kar′bŏn) [L. *carbo*, coal (dead or burning), charcoal] SYMB: C. The nonmetallic element that is the characteristic constituent of organic compounds, average atomic weight (mass) 12.0111, atomic number 6.

The isotope containing six protons and six neutrons (Carbon-12) is used as the basic for all atomic masses of all elements and by international agreement has a mass of 12.0000 amu (12.0000 g/mol). Carbon occurs in two pure forms, diamond and graphite, and in impure forms in charcoal, coke, and soot. Its compounds are constituents of all living tissue. Carbon combines with hydrogen,

Digestion of Carbohydrates

Enzyme	Produced in	Carbohydrates Digested	End Product
Sucrase (invertase)	Small intestine	Sucrose	Glucose and fructose
Maltases	Small intestine and mucosal cells of small intestine	Maltose	Two D-glucose
Lactase	Small intestine	Lactose	D-glucose and D-galactose
Salivary amylase	Saliva (mouth)	Cooked starch, glycogen, and dextrins	Maltose
Pancreatic amylase	Pancreas	Raw and cooked starch and glycogen	Maltose

nitrogen, and oxygen to form the basis of all organic matter. Organic carbon compounds provide energy in foods.

impregnated c. An electrode having a carbon shell with a core of various metals or salts of metals for use in a carbon arc lamp.

carbon-14 SYMB: ^{14}C. A radioactive isotope of carbon with a half-life of 5600 years; mass number 14; atomic mass (weight) 14. It is used as a tracer in metabolic studies and in archaeology to date materials containing carbon.

carbonate (kar'bŏ-nāt″) [L. *carbo,* carbon] Any salt of carbonic acid.

c. of soda Sodium carbonate used commercially in crude form, such as washing soda. The free alkali present is irritating and in strong concentrations has the effect of sodium hydroxide.

carbonated drink A fluid infused with carbon dioxide and consumed for hydration or refreshment, such as a cola or other soft drink.

carbon dioxide SYMB: CO_2. A colorless gas heavier than air and produced in the combustion or decomposition of carbon or its compounds. It is the final metabolic product of carbon compounds in food. The body eliminates CO_2 through the lungs. If CO_2 accumulates in body fluids, the pH will decrease. It is also given off by decomposition of vegetable and animal matter and is formed by alcoholic fermentation as in rising bread. Green plants absorb it directly from the air and use it in photosynthesis. Approx. 1 sq m of leaf surface can absorb the CO_2 from 2500 L of air in 1 hr. An acre of trees uses an estimated 4½ tons (4082 kg) of CO_2 a year. Commercially, CO_2 gas is used in carbonated drinks, and the solid form is used to make dry ice.

carbon dioxide combining power The amount of carbon dioxide (CO_2) that the blood can hold in chemical combination. CO_2 in aqueous solution forms carbonic acid. The amount of carbonic acid that the serum can take up is a measure of its reserve power to prevent acidosis. The normal amount is 50 to 70 mL/dL of blood (usually expressed as 50 to 70 vol%). Values below 50 indicate acidosis; above 70, alkalosis.

carbon dioxide inhalation Providing the patient with a mixture of oxygen and carbon dioxide. It can be used as an accessory to artificial respiration when resuscitation equipment is not available. In the past, it also was used to stimulate breathing and to treat persistent hiccups.

carbon dioxide solid therapy Solid carbon dioxide (CO_2 snow) used for therapeutic refrigeration. Solid CO_2 has a temperature of −112°F (−80°C). Its application to the skin for 1 to 2 sec causes superficial frostbite; 4 to 5 sec, a blister;

10 to 15 sec, superficial necrosis; and 15 to 45 sec, ulceration. It is used mostly for removal of certain nevi and warts, occasionally for telangiectasia.

carbon disulfide (dī-sŭl'fĭd) A colorless liquid, CS_2, that is toxic when it touches the skin or is inhaled or consumed. It may cause an alcohol-like intoxication, burns, stupor, coma, or death. It is used principally in the manufacture of products such as cellophane or rayon and sometimes causes occupational health-related illnesses in workers who produce these substances.

carbonemia (kăr″bŏ-nē'mē-ă) [L. *carbo,* carbon, + Gr. *haima,* blood] An excess accumulation of carbonic acid in the blood.

carbonic (kăr-bŏn'ĭk) Pert. to carbon.

c. anhydrase An enzyme that catalyzes union of water and carbon dioxide to form carbonic acid, or performs the reverse action. It is present in red blood cells.

carbonize (kăr'bŏn-īz) To char or convert into charcoal.

carbon monoxide SYMB: CO. A poisonous gas resulting from the inefficient and incomplete combustion of organic fuels. CO is colorless, tasteless, and odorless and cannot be detected by the senses. Carbon monoxide is distributed widely; it is found in the exhaust gas from the internal combustion engines in most motor-powered vehicles, and in sewers, cellars, and mines.

carbon tetrachloride (tĕt″ră-klō'rīd) SYMB: CCl_4. A clear, colorless liquid, not flammable, with an odor like that of chloroform. Although having narcotic and anesthetic properties resembling chloroform, it is too toxic to be suitable as an anesthetic or for any medical use. Inhalation of a small quantity can produce death due to the toxic damage to the liver and kidney.

c.t. poisoning SEE: under *poisoning.*

carbonyl (kăr'bŏn-ĭl) [″ + Gr. *hyle,* matter] The divalent radical carbon monoxide, characteristic of aldehydes and ketones.

carboxyhemoglobin (kăr-bŏk″sē-hē″mō-glō'bĭn) [″ + Gr. *oxys,* acid, + *haima,* blood, + L. *globus,* sphere] A compound formed by carbon monoxide and hemoglobin in carbon monoxide poisoning. SEE: table.

carboxyhemoglobinemia (kăr-bŏk″sē-hē″mō-glō-bĭn-ē'mē-ă) The presence of carboxyhemoglobin in the blood. SEE: *carbon monoxide poisoning.*

carboxyhemoglobin fraction SEE: under *fraction.*

carboxyl (kăr-bŏk'sĭl) The characteristic group (—COOH) of organic carboxylic acids such as acetic acid (CH_3COOH) and all of the amino acids.

carboxylase (kăr-bŏk'sĭ-lās) An enzyme that catalyzes the addition of a carboxyl

Effects of Carboxyhemoglobin

Carboxyhemoglobin levels*	Comments (Symptoms/Signs)
<1%	Healthy nonsmokers (None)
2%	Level found in urban exercisers
2–4%	May cause subtle effects in some persons with coronary disease
3–15%	Typical levels found in light to heavy smokers
5%	Typical levels found in people who smoke one pack of cigarettes a day

*Carboxyhemoglobin levels above 10–25% are typically considered potentially significant, that is, capable of causing long-lasting neurological consequences. However, brain injury may occur at higher or lower levels. The significance of carboxyhemoglobin levels in the blood can only be determined by the clinical setting/exposure and physical examination.

group to a molecule. Found in brewer's yeast, it catalyzes the decarboxylation of pyruvic acid by producing acetaldehyde and carbon dioxide. In the body, this process requires the presence of vitamin B_1 (thiamine), which acts as a coenzyme.

carboxylation (kăr-bŏk″sē-lā′shŭn) In chemistry, the replacement of hydrogen by a carboxyl (—COOH) group.

carboxymethylcellulose (kar-bok″sē-meth″ĭl-sel′yŭ-lōs″) SEE: *carboxymethylcellulose sodium.*

carboxypeptidase E (kar″bok″sē-pep′tĭ-dās″, -dāz″) [*carbo-* + *²oxy-* + *peptidase*] An enzyme that helps synthesize peptide hormones and neuropeptides. An N-terminal truncated protein variant of carboxypeptidase E (CPE-ΔN) influences the growth and metastasis of cancer cells.

carbuncle, carbunculus (kăr′bŭng″k′l, kăr-bŭng′kū-lŭs) [L. *carbunculus,* small glowing ember] A painful, deep abscess of the skin involving multiple hair follicles, formed by the merger of two or more boils (furuncles) and draining through multiple follicular openings. **carbuncular** (-bŭng′kū-lăr), *adj.* SEE: *boil.*

ETIOLOGY: Staphylococci, including methicillin–resistant staph, are the usual cause. They may be introduced into the skin by chafing, pressure, shaving, or by pits or cracks that result from dermatitis and commonly occur on the neck, face, axillae or buttocks.

SYMPTOMS: The lesions are often tender, red, warm, and swollen, enlarge over a period of days, then may rupture, exuding pus and necrotic material.

TREATMENT: Warm compresses, incision and drainage, and topical, and/or systemic antibiotics (sulfa drugs, cephalosporins, or clindamycin are usually effective). Recurrence is an indication that the patient should be assessed for some underlying disease or immunodeficiency.

PATIENT CARE: Patients and caregivers are taught proper hand and skin hygiene and to change the dressings at least twice a day to remove infected material, and to prevent the spread of infection in the home by avoiding contact with wound drainage, disposing of dressings in sealed bags, and washing contaminated linens separately in very hot water. SEE: *Standard Precautions Appendix.*

carbunculosis (kăr-bŭng″kū-lō′sĭs) [″ + Gr. *osis,* condition] The appearance of several carbuncles in succession or simultaneously.

carcass (kăr′kăs) A dead body; the term is usually used to describe nonhuman bodies such as the remains of a steer or a sheep.

carcino-, carcin- [Gr. *karkinos,* crab, ulcerating sore] Prefixes meaning *cancer.*

carcinogen (kăr′sĭn-, kăr-sĭn′ō-jĕn) Any substance or agent that produces cancer or increases the risk of developing cancer in humans or animals. SEE: table.

chemical c. Any chemical substance capable of causing cancer.

carcinogenesis (kar″sĭ-nō-jen′ĕ-sĭs) [*carcino-* + *genesis*] The transformation of normal cells into cancer cells, often as a result of chemical, viral, or radioactive damage to genes.

field c. The transformation of healthy cells into cancer cells within an entire region of the body rather than just within a single locale or tissue. Tobacco smoke, which diffusely pervades the oral and respiratory tract, may cause cancer not just in the mouth, but also in the entire field into which smoke is inhaled, e.g., the nose, throat, larynx, trachea, bronchi, lungs, and esophagus. SYN: *field effect.*

carcinogenic (kăr″sĭ-nō-jĕn′ĭk) Producing cancer.

carcinoid (kar′sĭn-oyd″) [*carcino-* + *-oid*] A tumor derived from the neuroendocrine cells in the intestinal tract, bile ducts, pancreas, bronchus, or ovary. It secretes serotonin and other vasoactive substances. SYN: *argentaffinoma.*

carcinoid syndrome A group of symptoms produced by carcinoid tumors that

Carcinogens

Carcinogen	Type of Agent	Organs or Tissues Commonly Damaged	Comments
Alcohol consumption	Consumer toxin	Upper aerodigestive tracts, esp. mouth and pharynx and larynx	Effect is most pronounced in people who smoke
Arsenic	Chemical	Blood, bone marrow, digestive tract, skin, urinary bladder, other organ systems	May contaminate water supply
Asbestos	Mineral	Respiratory tract, pleura and peritoneum	Associated with lung cancers and mesotheliomas. Effect is most pronounced in people who have smoked
Cigarette smoke	Consumer toxin	Aerodigestive tracts, other organs	Also a major cause of cardiovascular disease
Formaldehyde	Chemical	Nasopharynx, blood and bone marrow	Used as an embalming agent
Hepatitis B	Virus	Liver	Exposure to blood or body fluids
Hepatitis C	Virus	Liver	Exposure to blood or body fluids
Human Papillomavirus	Virus	Epithelial cells of the oropharynx and genitalia	Interpersonal contact, e.g., sexually transmitted
Mustard Gas	Chemical	Blistering agent	First used in WWI
Smokeless tobacco	Consumer toxin	Oropharynx, gastrointestinal tract	Retained in the buccal mucosa. Also known as "spit tobacco"
Sunshine (solar radiation/ ultraviolet radiation)	Physical	Skin, mucous membranes	Cause of basal cell, squamous cell carcinomas, melanoma. Outdoor exposures or indoor (tanning booths)
Vinyl chloride	Chemical	Liver, possibly brain	Used in the chemical industry to make plastic/polymers
X-rays and other forms of ionizing radiation	Physical	Many organs, depending on those that are penetrated	Used in diagnostic applications in health care; exposure to radioactive elements

secrete excessive amounts of serotonin, bradykinin, and other powerful vasoactive chemicals.

SYMPTOMS: One or more of the following may occur: brief episodes of flushing, esp. of the face and neck, tachycardia, facial and periorbital edema, hypotension, intermittent abdominal pain with diarrhea, valvular heart lesions, weight loss, hypoproteinemia, and ascites. When carcinoid tumors are found in the bronchi, intermittent bronchospasm may be the presenting symptom. Endocardial fibrosis and symptoms of pellagra may occasionally occur.

DIAGNOSIS: The diagnosis is based on clinical presentation, greatly increased excretion of 5-HIAA in urine, and uptake by tumors of specific radioisotopes, such as MIBG or pentreotide.

TREATMENT: Isolated tumors can be surgically removed. Multiple metastatic tumors can be treated with arterial embolization and with variable success with chemotherapy.

carcinolysis (kăr″sĭ-nŏl′ĭ-sĭs) [Gr. *karkinos,* crab, + *lysis,* dissolution] Destruction of carcinoma cells. **carcinolytic** (-nō-lĭt′ĭk), *adj.*

carcinoma (kar″sĭn-ō′mă) [*carcin-* + *-oma*] A malignant tumor that occurs in epithelial tissue and may infiltrate local tissues or produce metastases. It may affect almost any organ or part of the body and spread by direct extension, through lymphatics, or through the bloodstream. The causes vary with tumor type.

PATIENT CARE: Optimal patient care includes: identifying and explaining to patient and family the type of cancer and its typical natural history; options for treatment, side effects of treatments, expected response of the cancer to the treatment, best predictions for recovery and life expectancy, availability of clinical trials, alternative and complementary therapies, and the potential benefit of referral to specialty cancer centers.

acinar cell c. of the pancreas A rare carcinoma that arises from pancreatic cells that manufacture digestive proteins, such as lipase, chymotrypsin, or alpha-1-antitrypsin.

alveolar cell c. A type of lung carcinoma.

basal cell c. ABBR: BCC. The most common human cancer, typically found on skin exposed to sun or other forms of ultraviolet light. Although it is sometimes locally invasive, it rarely metastasizes to other organs. Typically it begins as a small, shiny papule. The lesion enlarges to form a whitish border around a central depression or ulcer that may bleed. When the lesion reaches this stage, it is often called a rodent ulcer. After biopsy, the removal method used is determined by the size, location, and appearance of the lesion. SYN: *basal cell epithelioma; epithelial cancer.* SEE: illus.

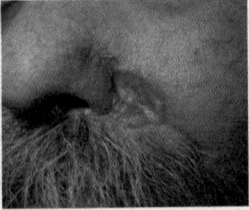

BASAL CELL CARCINOMA

bronchioloalveolar c. A relatively rare form of non-small cell lung cancer consisting of columnar cells, and in which the tumor arises in the periphery of the lung within the septal borders of the alveoli, which the tumor tends to preserve. The tumor cells frequently produce mucin.

bronchogenic c. Lung **cancer**.

chorionic c. Choriocarcinoma.

choroid plexus c. A cancer that arises from the cells that line the fluid-filled cavities (ventricles) of the brain.

c. of the colon SEE: *colorectal cancer.*

colorectal c. Colorectal **cancer**.

c. cuniculatum Any slowly growing squamous cell carcinoma of the skin, typically presenting as a gradually enlarging warty tumor.

ductal c. in situ of breast SEE: *ductal carcinoma in situ of breast.*

embryonal c. An aggressive germ cell tumor that may metastasize widely. It can occur in young adults of either sex.

epidermoid c. Squamous cell carcinoma.

c. erysipelatoides Metastatic spreading of cancer, usually from an internal organ to the skin, to which the spreading tumor gives a red, inflammatory appearance.

giant cell c. Carcinoma marked by the presence of unusually large cells.

glandular c. Adenocarcinoma.

keratinocyte c. A cancer arising from cells in the epidermis. It includes basal cell carcinomas, keratoacanthomas, and squamous cell carcinomas of the skin. Most keratinocyte carcinomas arise in sun-exposed areas of the body, such as the ears, the temples, the forehead or the nose.

c. in situ ABBR: CIS. Malignant cell changes in the epithelial tissue that do not extend beyond the basement membrane.

medullary c. Carcinoma in which there is a predominance of cells and little fibrous tissue.

melanotic c. Carcinoma containing melanin.

mucinous c. Carcinoma in which the glandular tissue secretes mucin.

neuroendocrine c. Any of a diverse group of malignancies, such as carcinoid, islet cell tumors, neuroblastoma, and small-cell carcinomas of the lung. All have dense core granules and produce polypeptides that can be identified by immunochemical methods.

oat cell c. A poorly differentiated carcinoma of the bronchus that contains small oat-shaped cells. SYN: *small cell c.*

c. of pancreas Pancreatic **cancer**.

pancreatic c. Pancreatic **cancer**.

papillary c. of the thyroid SEE: *papillary carcinoma of the thyroid.*

renal cell c. A carcinoma that arises from the proximal tubular cells of the kidney. In 2008 the American Cancer Society estimated there would be about 56,700 new patients diagnosed with renal cell carcinoma and about 13,700 deaths from it. SYN: *hypernephroma; kidney* **cancer**.

SYMPTOMS: Because of its location in the retroperitoneum, renal cell carcinoma may grow to a relatively large size before it manifests obvious symptoms. The most common findings are blood in the urine (hematuria), flank pain, or a flank mass. Some patients develop fevers, weight loss, or symptoms caused by hormones excreted by the tumor. These hormones (parathyroid-like hormone or erythropoietin) occasionally cause hypercalcemia or abnormal increases in the red blood cell count (erythrocytosis).

TREATMENT: Surgical removal of the affected kidney may be curative for those patients whose tumor has not spread outside the perirenal fascia. Treatment options are less successful for patients with metastatic disease because renal cell carcinomas are relatively resistant to chemotherapy.

sarcomatoid c. A carcinoma that contains both epithelial and mesenchymal components. This cancer may arise from cells in the kidney, urinary bladder, or lung.

scirrhous c. Hard **cancer**.

small cell c. Oat cell **c.**

squamous cell c. Carcinoma that develops primarily from squamous cells, e.g., of the skin or in the mouth, lungs, bronchi, esophagus, or cervix. SYN: *epidermoid c.* SEE: illus.

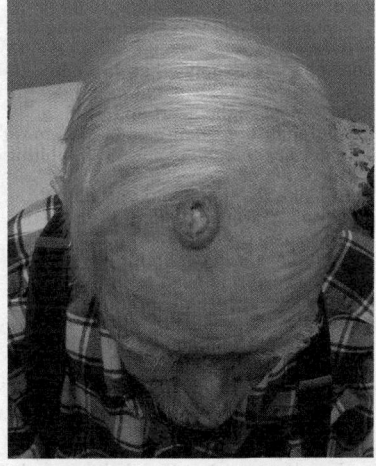

SQUAMOUS CELL CARCINOMA

thymic c. A carcinoma found in the anterior mediastinum, usually a squamous cell carcinoma, spindle cell carcinoma, or lymphoepithelioma. Many of these tumors release chemically active substances that cause paraneoplastic syndromes.

transitional cell c. A carcinoma that originates in cells that line the urinary tract, e.g., in cells that line the inner kidney, the ureters, or the urinary bladder. SYN: *urothelial c.*

urothelial c. Transitional cell **c.**

carcinomatosis (kar″sĭn-ō″mă-tō′sĭs, ′sēz) *pl.* **carcinomatoses** [*carcinoma* + *-osis*] Widespread dissemination of carcinoma in the body. SYN: *carcinosis.*

carcinosarcoma (kăr″sĭ-nō-săr-kō′mă) [″ + *sarx,* flesh, + *oma,* tumor] A malignant tumor containing the elements of both carcinoma and sarcoma.

embryonal c. A malignant germ-cell tumor derived from embryonic cells.

carcinosis (kăr″sĭ-nō′sĭs) [″ + *osis,* condition] Carcinomatosis.

cardamom, cardamon (kăr′dă-mŭm) [Gr. *kardamomon*] The dried ripe fruit of an herb, *Elettaria repens* or *E. cardamomum.* It is used as an aromatic and carminative.

Cardarelli sign (kar″dă-rel′ē) [Antonio Cardarelli, Italian physician, 1831–1926] Pulsating movement of the trachea to one side. It may be present with thoracic aortic aneurysm.

cardia (kăr′dē-ă) [Gr. *kardia,* heart] The upper orifice of the stomach connecting with the esophagus. **cardial,** *adj.*

-cardia [Gr. *kardia,* heart] Suffix meaning *location or action of the heart,* esp. when it is anomalous or undesirable.

cardiac (kăr′dē-ăk) [L. *cardiacus*] **1.** Pert. to the heart. **2.** Pert. to the cardia.

cardiac arrest SEE: under *compensation*arrest.

cardiac calcium score A measurement of the amount of calcium present on CT scanning of the coronary arteries. It is a radiological marker of coronary artery atherosclerosis. A high score (>400) predicts a high coronary artery atherosclerotic burden. Patients with scores in this range should promptly undergo some form of stress testing. A score between 100 and 399 predicts moderately high risk of coronary events. People with scores in this range should actively modify cardiac risk factors. Scores between 11 and 99 indicate some atherosclerosis; patients in this range should have regular follow up and management of cardiac risk factors. Scores between 1 and 10 suggest less than 10% probability of coronary artery disease. A score of 0 implies that there is no calcified plaque within the coronary arteries.

cardiac compensation SEE: under *compensation.*

cardiac failure SEE: under *failure.*

cardiac output SEE: under *output.*

cardiac reflex SEE: under *reflex.*

cardiac resynchronization therapy Resynchronization therapy.

cardiac silhouette The shadow on the

chest radiograph created by the heart. A large cardiac silhouette is consistent with cardiac hypertrophy. A narrow silhouette is often seen in patients with emphysema.

cardiac surgery SEE: under *surgery*.

cardiac syndrome X Ischemic chest pain in patients with normal coronary angiography results but abnormal findings on stress testing or myocardial imaging.

cardialgia (kăr″dē-ăl′jē-ă) [Gr. *kardia*, heart, + *algos*, pain] Pain at the pit of the stomach or region of the heart, usually occurring in paroxysms.

cardiectasia, cardiectasis (kăr″dē-ĕk-tā′sē-ă, -ĕk′tă-sĭs) [″ + *ektasis*, dilatation] Dilatation of the heart.

cardiectomy (kăr″dē-ĕk′tō-mē) [″ + *ektome*, excision] **1.** Excision of the gastric cardia. **2.** Harvesting of the heart and adjacent great vessels for transplantation.

Cardiff Count-to-Ten chart (kăr′dif) A way to assess intrauterine well-being in which the expectant woman records fetal movement during her usual activities. There should be at least 10 movements within a 12-hour period; if fewer than 10 movements are perceived, further medical evaluation is needed.

cardinal (kăr′dĭ-năl) [LL. *cardinalis*, important] Of primary importance, as in the cardinal signs: temperature, pulse, respiration, and blood pressure.

cardio-, cardi- [Gr. *kardia*, heart] Prefixes meaning *heart*.

cardioaccelerator (kăr″dē-ō-ăk-sĕl′ĕr-ā-tor) [″ + L. *accelerare*, to hasten] Something that increases the rate of the heartbeat.

cardioactive (kăr″dē-ō-ăk′tĭv) [″ + L. *activus*, acting] Acting on the heart.

cardioangiography (kăr″dē-ō-ăn″jē-ŏg′ră-fē) [″ + *angeion*, vessel, + *graphein*, to write] Angiocardiography.

cardioangiology (kăr″dē-ō-ăn″jē-ŏl′ō-jē) [″ + ″ + *logos*, word, reason] The science of the heart and blood vessels.

cardioaortic (kăr″dē-ō-ā-or′tĭk) [″ + *aorte*, aorta] Pert. to the heart and the aorta.

Cardiobacterium hominis (kăr″dē-ō-băk-tēr′ĭ-ŭm hŏm′ĭ-nĭs) [NL] A gram-negative, rod-shaped bacterium. It is a member of the HACEK group of bacteria and is part of the normal flora of the oral cavity and upper airway. It is an occasional cause of culture-negative endocarditis.

cardiocele (kăr′dē-ō-sēl) [″ + *kele*, tumor, swelling] A herniation or protrusion of the heart through an opening in the diaphragm or through a wound.

cardiocentesis (kăr″dē-ō-sĕn-tē′sĭs) Cardiopuncture.

cardiochalasia (kăr″dē-ō-kă-lā′zē-ă) [″ + *chalasis*, relaxation] Relaxation of the muscles of the cardiac sphincter of the stomach.

cardiodiaphragmatic (kăr″dē-ō-dī″ă-frăg-măt′ĭk) Concerning the heart and the diaphragm.

cardiodilator (kăr″dē-ō-dī′lā-tor) [″ + L. *dilatare*, to enlarge] A device for dilating the cardia of the gastroesophageal junction.

cardiodynamics (kăr″dē-ō-dī-năm′ĭks) The science of the forces involved in propulsion of blood from the heart to the tissues and back to the heart.

cardiodynia (kăr″dē-ō-dĭn′ē-ă) [Gr. *kardia*, heart, + *odyne*, pain] Pain in the region of the heart.

cardioesophageal (kăr″dē-ō-ĕ-sŏf″ă-jē′ăl) Pert. to the junction of the esophagus and the stomach.

cardiogenesis (kăr″dē-ō-jĕn′ĕ-sĭs) [″ + *genesis*, generation, birth] Formation and growth of the embryonic heart.

cardiogenic (kăr″dē-ō-jĕn′ĭk) [″ + *gennan*, to produce] Originating in the heart.

cardiograph (kăr″dē-ō-grăf″) [″ + *graphein*, to write] A device for registering the electrical activity of the heart muscle. **cardiographic** (-ō-grăf′ĭk), *adj*.

cardiography (kard″ē-og′ră-fē) [*cardio-* + *-graphy*] The recording and study of the electrical activity of the heart.

   impedance c. ABBR: ICG. A noninvasive means of determining cardiac output in which the stroke volume of each cardiac contraction is determined by measuring beat-to-beat changes in the electrical impedance of the chest and neck. SYN: *electrical impedance plethysmography*.

cardiohepatic (kăr″dē-ō-hĕ-păt′ĭk) [″ + *hepatos*, liver] Pert. to the heart and liver.

cardiohepatomegaly (kăr″dē-ō-hĕp″ă-tō-mĕg′ă-lē) [″ + ″ + *megas*, large] Enlargement of the heart and liver.

cardioinhibitory (kăr″dē-ō-ĭn-hĭb′ĭ-tō-rē) [″ + L. *inhibere*, to check] Inhibiting the action of the heart.

cardiokinetic (kăr″dē-ō-kĭ-nĕt′ĭk) [″ + *kinesis*, movement] Pert. to the action of the heart.

cardiolipin (kăr″dē-ō-lĭp′ĭn) [″ + *lipos*, fat] Previously used term for diphosphatidylglycerol.

cardiolith (kăr′dē-ō-lĭth″) [″ + *lithos*, stone] A concretion or calculus in the heart.

cardiologist (kăr-dē-ŏl′ō-jĭst) [″ + *logos*, word, reason] A physician specializing in treatment of heart disease.

cardiology (kăr-dē-ŏl′ō-jē) The study of the physiology and pathology of the heart.

   nuclear c. A noninvasive method for studying cardiovascular disease by use of nuclear imaging techniques. These examinations are usually done while the individual is exercising. Coronary artery disease can be investigated as can damage to the myocardium following coronary infarction. The size and function of the ventricles can be evaluated using these techniques.

cardiolysin (kăr″dē-ŏl′ĭ-sĭn) [″ + *lysis*, dissolution] An antibody acting destructively on the heart muscle.

cardiolysis (kăr-dē-ŏl′ĭ-sĭs) An operation that separates adhesions constricting the heart in adhesive mediastinopericarditis.

cardiomalacia (kăr″dē-ō-mă-lā′shē-ă) [Gr. *kardia*, heart, + *malakia*, softening] Softening of the heart muscle.

cardiomegaly (kăr″dē-ō-měg′ă-lē) [″ + *megas*, large] Enlargement of the heart.

cardiomotility (kăr″dē-ō-mō-tĭl′ĭ-tē) [″ + L. *motilis*, moving] The ability of the heart to move.

cardiomyocyte (kar″dē-ō-mī′ŏ-sīt″) [*cardio-* + *myocyte*] A cardiac muscle cell. The cell is striated, containing thick and thin proteins arranged linearly. These filaments are composed, like other striated muscle cells, largely of actin and myosin. The cell has an abundant supply of mitochondria that supply the energy needed by the cell for regular muscular contraction.

cardiomyoliposis (kăr″dē-ō-mī″ō-lĭp-ō′sĭs) [″ + *mys*, muscle, + *lipos*, fat, + *osis*, condition] Fatty degeneration of the heart.

cardiomyopathy (kard″ē-ō-mī-op′ă-thē) [*cardio-* + *myopathy*] ABBR: CMP. Any disease that affects the heart muscle, diminishing cardiac performance.

   alcoholic c. Cardiomyopathy caused by years of heavy alcohol abuse. Affected patients have enlarged hearts and left ventricular failure. Abstinence from alcohol may halt or reverse the course of the illness in some people.

   arrhythmogenic right ventricular c. ABBR: ARVC. Arrhythmogenic right ventricular **dysplasia**.

   congestive c. Cardiomyopathy associated with enlargement of the left ventricle of the heart and congestive heart failure.

   constrictive c. Restrictive **c.**

   eosinophilic c. Löffler endocarditis.

   hypertrophic c. ABBR: HCM. An autosomal dominant cardiomyopathy marked by excessive and disorganized growth of myofibrils, impaired filling of the heart (diastolic dysfunction), a reduction in the size of ventricular cavities, and, often, ventricular arrhythmias and sudden death. Examination of the heart by echocardiography or other modalities may show the enlargement of the heart to be most pronounced in the interventricular septum. Hypertrophy in that location may limit the flow of blood (and increase pressure gradients) from the left ventricle to the aorta. Abnormal anterior motion of the mitral valve during systole also may be found.

These two findings are often designated on echocardiographic reports of patients with HCM by the abbreviation ASH-SAM (*asymmetric septal hypertrophy–systolic anterior motion* [of the mitral valve]). Other forms of HCM may affect only the cardiac apex or cause diffuse enlargement of the heart muscle. The mass of the left ventricle in HCM is > 500 g. SEE: illus.

Normal

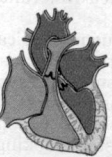

Comparison to normal
Note normal size of chambers and thickness of ventricle walls for comparison with cardiomyopic heart changes

Dilated (or congestive)

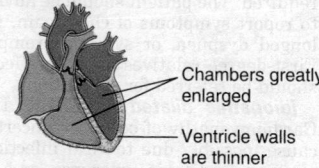

Chambers greatly enlarged

Ventricle walls are thinner

Hypertrophic

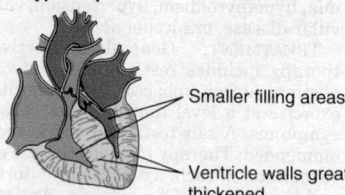

Smaller filling areas

Ventricle walls greatly thickened

Restrictive

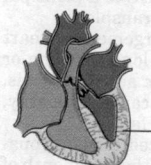

Muscle layers are stiff and resist stretching for filling

CARDIOMYOPATHIES

SYMPTOMS AND SIGNS: Although patients may be asymptomatic for many years, they commonly report shortness of breath (particularly on exertion), fatigue, atypical chest pain (at rest and after meals), orthopnea, dizziness, and other symptoms of congestive heart failure after the heart muscle markedly enlarges. An S4 and a harsh crescendo-decrescendo systolic murmur, best heard at the left lower sternal border, may be present. Ventricular arrhythmias are common and may result in palpitations, syncope, or sudden death.

TREATMENT: Drug therapies include

beta blocking and calcium channel blocking drugs (such as verapamil) to slow heart rate, control arrhythmias, and reduce myocardial oxygen demand. Anticoagulants and antiarrhythmic agents are also occasionally used. For patients with marked enlargement of the ventricular septum and high outflow tract pressure gradients (>50 mm Hg), surgical removal of the enlarged muscle or ablation often produces favorable improvements in exercise tolerance and breathing.

PATIENT CARE: Strenuous physical exercise should be discouraged because it may produce breathlessness, presyncope, or frank loss of consciousness. If applicable, the patient should be encouraged to lose weight, stop smoking, and limit alcohol intake. An implanted cardioverter/defibrillator (ICD) may be required. The patient should be advised to report symptoms of chest pain, prolonged dyspnea, or syncope promptly. First-degree relatives of those affected should be referred for evaluation.

idiopathic dilated c. ABBR: IDC. Cardiomyopathy of occult or uncertain cause, possibly due to viral infections, unrecognized toxic exposures, or a genetic predisposition, but not to ischemia, hypothyroidism, hypertension, valvular disease, or alcohol abuse.

TREATMENT: General supportive therapy includes rest, weight control, abstinence from tobacco, and moderate exercise at a level that does not cause symptoms. A salt-restricted diet is recommended. Therapy includes the use of vasodilators, such as ACE inhibitors, and diuretics like furosemide. Anticoagulants are important to prevent thrombus formation. IDC is a principal indication for cardiac transplant.

c. of overload Enlargement of heart muscle resulting from long-standing or severe hypertension or aortic stenosis. Like all other forms of cardiomyopathy, the end result is heart failure.

peripartum c. Dilated cardiomyopathy occurring either in the last month of pregnancy or in the six months after delivery. Its cause is unknown, but it occurs more often in older and multiparous women.

primary c. Cardiomyopathy of unknown cause.

restrictive c. Cardiomyopathy associated with lack of flexibility of the ventricular walls. Common causes include amyloidosis, hemochromatosis, sarcoidosis, and other diseases in which the heart is infiltrated by foreign material or scarred. SYN: *constrictive c.*

secondary c. Any cardiomyopathy in which the cause is either known or associated with a well-defined systemic disease. Included are cardiomyopathies associated with inflammation, toxic chemicals, metabolic abnormalities, and inherited muscle disorders.

stress-induced c. Takotsubo c.

tachycardia-induced c. Cardiac remodeling and dysfunction that results from a chronically increased heart rate, usually a supraventricular arrhythmia. It is treated with medications such as beta blockers that slow the heart rate.

takotsubo c. Reversible dysfunction of the left ventricle. It may be the cause of transient heart failure that occurs after exceptionally stressful events. The heart in such instances takes on a rounded shape with a narrow neck, resembling a traditional Japanese lobster trap (*takotsubo*). It is informally called *broken-heart syndrome.* SYN: *apical ballooning syndrome; stress-induced c.; transient left ventricular apical ballooning.*

cardiomyopexy (kăr′dē-ō-mī′ō-pĕk″sē) [″ + ″ + *pexis,* fixation] Surgical fixation of a vascular tissue such as pectoral muscle to the cardiac muscle and pericardium to improve blood supply to the myocardium.

cardiomyoplasty (kăr″ dē-ō-mī′ō-plăs″tē) Surgical implantation of skeletal muscle to either supplement or replace myocardial muscle.

cardiomyotomy (kăr″dē-ō-mī-ŏt′ō-mē) Surgical therapy for achalasia. The muscles surrounding the cardioesophageal junction are cut, while the underlying mucous membrane is left intact.

cardionecrosis (kăr″dē-ō-ně-krō′sĭs) [″ + *nekros,* dead, + *osis,* condition] Death of heart tissue.

cardionephric (kăr″dē-ō-nĕf′rĭk) [″ + *nephros,* kidney] Pert. to the heart and kidney.

cardioneural (kăr″dē-ō-nū′răl) [″ + *neuron,* nerve] Pert. to nervous control of the heart.

cardioneurosis (kăr″dē-ō-nū-rō′sĭs) [″ + ″ + *osis,* condition] Functional neurosis with cardiac symptoms.

cardiopathy (kăr″dē-ŏp′ă-thē) [″ + *pathos,* disease, suffering] Any disease of the heart.

cardiopericarditis (kăr″dē-ō-pĕr″ĭ-kăr-dī′tĭs) [″ + *peri,* around, + *kardia,* heart, + *itis,* inflammation] Inflammation of the myocardium and pericardium.

cardiophobia (kăr″dē-ō-fō′bē-ă) [″ + *phobos,* fear] An abnormal preoccupation with or fear of heart disease.

cardioplasty (kăr″dē-ō-plăs′tē) [″ + *plassein,* to form] An operation on the cardiac sphincter of the stomach to relieve cardiospasm.

cardioplegia (kăr″dē-ō-plē′jē-ă) [″ + *plege,* stroke] Intentional, temporary arrest of cardiac function by means of hypothermia, medication, or electrical stimuli to reduce the need of the myocardium for oxygen, or to facilitate surgery on the heart by making it move less.

cardiopneumograph (kăr″dē-ō-nū′mō-grăf) [″ + ″ + *graphein,* to write] A device for recording the motion of the heart and lungs.

cardioprotective (kăr″dē-ō-prō-těk′tĭv) [Gr. kardia, heart, + L. *protectus,* shielding] Capable of shielding the heart from damage caused by, e.g., electrolyte disturbances, infections, ischemia, or toxins.

cardioptosis (kăr″dē-ŏp-tō′sĭs) [″ + *ptosis,* a dropping] Prolapse of the heart.

cardiopulmonary (kăr″dē-ō-pŭl′mō-něr-ē) [″ + L. *pulmo,* lung] Pert. to the heart and lungs.

cardiopulmonary arrest SEE: under *arrest.*

cardiopuncture (kăr″dē-ō-pŭnk′chŭr) [″ + L. *punctura,* piercing] Surgical incision or puncture of the heart. SYN: *cardiocentesis.*

cardiopyloric (kăr″dē-ō-pī-lor′ĭk) [″ + *pyloros,* gatekeeper] Pert. to the cardiac and pyloric ends of the stomach.

cardiorenal (kăr″dē-ō-rē′năl) [Gr. *kardia,* heart, + L. *renalis,* pert. to kidney] Pert. to both the heart and the kidneys.

cardiorenal syndrome Injury to the kidneys resulting from insufficient blood flow to the kidneys in patients with heart failure.

cardiorrhaphy (kăr″dē-or′ă-fē) [″ + *rhaphe,* seam, ridge] Suturing of the heart muscle.

cardiorrhexis (kăr″dē-ō-rĕk′sĭs) [″ + *rhexis,* rupture] Rupture of the heart.

cardiosclerosis (kăr″dē-ō-sklē-rō′sĭs) [″ + *sklerosis,* hardening] Hardening of the cardiac tissues and arteries.

cardioselectivity (kard″ē-ō-sě″lek″tiv′ĭt-ē) [*cardio-* + L. *seligere,* to separate, select] A stronger action on receptors in the heart than on those in the lungs. It is said of beta-adrenergic blocking agents that selectively block beta-1 receptors and thus do not cause bronchospasm.

PATIENT CARE: Patients with asthma or chronic obstructive pulmonary disease should avoid high doses of nonselective beta-adrenergic drugs because they can cause wheezing and shortness of breath. Patients with mild or moderate obstructive lung disease can safely use cardioselective beta blockers. SEE: *beta-adrenergic blocking agent.* **cardioselective** (kard″ē-ō-sě″lěk′tiv), *adj.*

cardiospasm (kard′ē-ō-spazm) [*cardio-* + *spasm*] Achalasia.

cardiotachometer (kăr″dē-ō-tăk-ŏm′ĕ-těr) [Gr. *kardia,* heart, + *tachos,* speed, + *metron,* measure] An instrument for measuring the heart rate over a long period.

cardiotherapy (kăr″dē-ō-thěr′ă-pē) [″ + *therapeia,* treatment] The treatment of cardiac diseases.

cardiothoracic ratio (kăr″dē-ō-thō-răs′ĭk) [″ + ″] The relation of the overall diameter of the heart to the widest part of the inside of the thoracic cavity. Usually the heart's diameter is half or less than half that of the thoracic cavity.

cardiothyrotoxicosis (kăr″dē-ō-thī″rō-tŏk″sĭ-kō′sĭs) [″ + *thyreos,* shield, + *toxikon,* poison, + *osis,* condition] Heart disease due to hyperthyroidism.

cardiotocography (kar″dē-ō-tō-kog′ră-fē) [*cardio-* + *tocography*] The monitoring of intrauterine fetal heart rate and uterine contraction.

PATIENT CARE: Two transducers are used, one to measure fetal heart rate and the other to measure uterine contractions. The transducers are most often strapped to the maternal abdomen. When transducers are used internally, a scalp electrode is applied to the fetus, and a pressure catheter is inserted into the uterine cavity to measure contractions. The internal method is believed to provide a more accurate reading in complicated deliveries.

cardiotomy (kăr″dē-ŏt′ō-mē) [″ + *tome,* incision] Incision of the heart.

cardiotonic (kăr″dē-ō-tŏn′ĭk) [″ + *tonos,* tone] Increasing the tonicity of the heart. Various drugs, including digitalis, are cardiotonic. SEE: *inotropic.*

cardiotoxic (kăr″dē-ō-tŏk′sĭk) [″ + *toxikon,* poisoning] Poisonous to the heart.

cardiovalvulitis (kăr″dē-ō-văl″vū-lī′tĭs) [″ + L. *valvula,* valve, + Gr. *itis,* inflammation] Inflammation of the heart valves.

cardiovalvulotome (kăr″dē-ō-văl′vū-lō-tōm″) [″ + ″ + Gr. *tome,* incision] An instrument for excising part of a valve, esp. the mitral valve.

cardiovascular (kăr″dē-ō-văs′kū-lăr) [″ + L. *vasculum,* small vessel] Pert. to the heart and blood vessels.

cardiovascular collapse Sudden loss of blood flow to the brain and other organs, causing altered mental status and hypotension. This may be caused by conditions such as anaphylaxis, cardiogenic shock, vasovagal syncope, or postural hypotension.

cardiovascular disease ABBR: CVD. Any disease of the heart or blood vessels, including atherosclerosis, cardiomyopathy, coronary artery disease, peripheral vascular disease, and others.

cardiovascular reflex SEE: under *reflex.*

cardiovascular system The heart and blood vessels (aorta, arteries, arterioles, capillaries, venules, veins, venae cavae).

cardiovascular technologist A technologist with specialized training in both invasive and noninvasive cardiac techniques. These include physical examination of the patient with heart disease, history taking, drug therapy, and some or all of the following tests or procedures (under professional supervision): blood gas analysis, Doppler ultrasonography, electrocardiography, exercise stress testing, echocardiography, and cardiac catheterization.

cardioversion (kăr′dē-ō-vĕr″zhŭn) [″ + L. *versio*, a turning] The restoration of normal sinus rhythm by chemical or electrical means. When performed medicinally, the procedure relies on the oral or intravenous administration of antiarrhythmic drugs. Electrical cardioversion relies instead on the delivery of synchronized shock of direct electrical current across the chest wall. It is used to terminate arrhythmias such as atrial fibrillation, atrial flutter, supraventricular tachycardia, and well-tolerated ventricular tachycardia. Unlike defibrillation, which is an unsynchronized shock applied during dire emergencies, electrical cardioversion is timed to avoid the T wave of cardiac repolarization to avoid triggering malignant arrhythmias. A patient will almost always require sedation and analgesia before the procedure. SEE: illus.

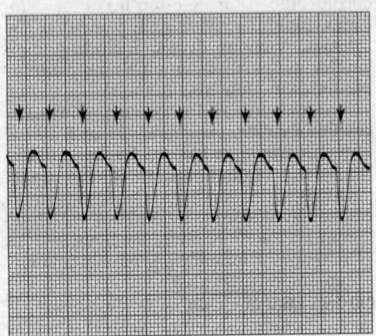

CARDIOVERSION

Synchronization during cardioversion of ventricular tachycardia; an arrow above each QRS complex denotes the period in cardiac depolarization when a shock will be delivered to terminate the rhythm

⚠ Electrical cardioversion should not be used in patients who have recently eaten (because of the risk of regurgitation of stomach contents), in patients with severe electrolyte abnormalities, in patients with some drug overdoses, or in patients unable or unwilling to give informed consent. Patients need to be advised of the risks of cardioversion, including the rare precipitation of ventricular fibrillation and ventricular tachycardia, the development of bradyarrhythmias or heart blocks, and the possibility of embolic stroke.

PATIENT CARE: The procedure, expected sensations, complications, and risks are explained to and clarified for the patient. Emotional support is provided throughout the procedure and at its conclusion. The patient's medication history is reviewed, and cardiac glycoside use is reported to the health care provider, along with the patient's electrolyte levels. Emergency equipment (including ACLS drugs, a bag mask device, supplemental oxygen, suction, laryngoscope and appropriate size ET tube, defibrillator, and supplies for intravenous injection) are assembled at the bedside. In the hospital setting, emergency personnel (respiratory technicians, anesthesiologists, nurses, and paramedics) may assist the attending physician. The patient's vital signs are checked, an intravenous infusion is started, and the patient is connected to a continuous ECG monitor. Dentures are removed from the mouth, and necklaces or pendants, as well as nitroglycerin patches, are removed from the chest and neck. Chest electrodes are placed to facilitate recording of tall R waves without interfering with paddle placement. A 12-lead ECG is obtained and the patient is given enriched oxygen to breathe. The patient is placed in a supine position, and adequate ventilation and oxygenation are ensured by observation and oximetry. A sedative, such as diazepam, is provided as prescribed unless the patient is profoundly hypotensive. The defibrillator leads are attached to the patient. The cardioverter/defibrillator is set to synchronize with the patient's QRS complex, and the recording is checked to ensure that each R wave is marked. The control is set to the energy level prescribed by the health care provider or by protocol. The defibrillation pads for hands-free operation (or manual paddles) are placed in prescribed positions on the chest wall. All personnel in attendance are cleared from direct contact with the patient or his or her bed. After this is carefully verified, the electrical current is discharged. The monitor is immediately analyzed to ensure that the dysrhythmia has resolved. If it has not, the procedure is repeated, usually with a higher energy setting. After successful cardioversion, health care personnel monitor the posttreatment rhythm and vital signs until the patient's stability is assured. The patient's skin is inspected for burns. SEE: *defibrillation.*

cardioverter (kăr′dē-ō-vĕr″tĕr) A device used to administer electrical shocks to the heart through electrodes placed on the chest wall or on the surface of the heart itself. It is used in the emergency management of cardiac dysrhythmias such as ventricular or supraventricular tachycardias. Changing the dysrhythmia to normal sinus rhythm is called cardioversion. SEE: *defibrillator*.

automatic implantable c. An implantable device for detecting and terminating ventricular tachycardia or fibrillation.

carditis (kăr-dī'tĭs) [" + *itis*, inflammation] Inflammation of the layers of the heart. It usually involves two of the following: pericardium, myocardium, or endocardium.

Coxsackie c. Carditis or pericarditis that may occur in infections with enteroviruses of the Coxsackie groups, and also with echovirus groups.

Lyme c. The acute onset of atrioventricular conduction block, often in association with myocarditis, in a patient with Lyme disease. It is treated with antibiotics. Temporary cardiac pacing is infrequently required.

rheumatic c. Inflammation of cardiac tissue as a result of acute rheumatic fever. Mitral insufficiency is a prominent feature, and aortic insufficiency is sometimes present as well.

Cardizem SEE: *diltiazem*.

Cardura (kahr-door'ă) Doxazosin.

care (kar) In health care, the application of professional skill, often including love, support, and concern, to provide health benefits to a person or a community.

acute c. Health care delivered to patients who have experienced sudden illness or injury, or who are recovering from a procedure or operation. Acute care generally occurs in the prehospital or hospital setting or in the emergency department and is usually focused on the immediate, critical problems of the patient.

adult day c. ABBR: ADC. A licensed agency where the chronically ill, disabled, or cognitively impaired can stay during the day under health care supervision. Most people attending adult day care are older and need some assistance. They are able to participate in structured activities and to walk with or without an assistive device. Most day care centers operate 5 days a week for 8 to 12 hr a day.

adult foster c. Long-term care for adults who are unable to live alone due to physical, emotional, or developmental impairments. This care is offered in a variety of settings, including a facility that resembles a family residence. Such a facility may have fewer regulations than a nursing home.

best supportive c. Ideal patient care, e.g., health care that meets the patient's nutritional, philosophical, psychologi-cal, physical, medical, surgical, and social needs.

charity c. Care provided to patients who are not expected to be able to pay for the services they receive. SEE: *bad debt*.

cluster c. A system of home care for older adults that allows the needs of many clients who live in proximity to be met by a team of workers.

culturally competent c. The provision of health care with tolerance and respect for people of all ages, nationalities, races, beliefs, and customs.

day c. The supervision of dependents during working hours. The goals of day care are to provide adequate, affordable care for young children or dependent adults, esp. while the primary caregivers are at work.

developmentally appropriate c. Care that suits the patient's stage of life by meeting his or her cognitive, emotional, and social needs.

due c. **1.** The kind of care that a competent, responsible, and interested provider will give to an individual in need. **2.** Care that meets generally accepted community standards.

emergency cardiac c. ABBR: ECC. The basic and advanced life support assessment and treatment necessary to manage sudden and often life-threatening events affecting cardiovascular and pulmonary systems. ECC includes identifying the nature of the problem, monitoring the patient closely, providing basic and advanced life support as quickly as possible, preventing complications, reassuring the patient, and transporting the patient to the most appropriate facility for definitive cardiac care. SEE: *advanced cardiac life support*; *basic life support*; *cardiopulmonary resuscitation*.

end-of-life c. Supportive care for the dying. Such care includes invasive interventions such as advanced cardiac life support, or supportive interventions, such as educational, emotional, physical, or social assistance to the terminally ill and their families and significant others.

evidence-based health c. The concept that the practice of medicine should be based on firm data rather than anecdote, tradition, intuition, or belief. SYN: *evidence-based medicine; evidence-based practice*.

family-centered c. The integration and collaboration of family members in the patient care team, esp. in the care of dependent infants, children, or adults with complex or continuing health care needs.

PATIENT CARE: Family and friends are increasingly needed to provide patient care. Although researchers have identified the "typical caregiver" as a

46-year-old female with some college education, in actuality anyone in the infirm individual's circle may be called upon to provide care. The care provided may vary from simply helping with driving or shopping, to managing treatment and medications, to providing assistance with activities of daily living, such as bathing, feeding, toileting, and transferring the patient, or helping the patient make health care decisions and choices. The health care professional should identify the primary caregiver(s), recognize the level of strain occurring, and develop a partnership to reduce the burden of care and prevent caregiver exhaustion and burnout. In addition to psychosocial support, the family caregiver may benefit from practical instruction about how to perform caregiving activities, never assuming that the caregiver knows what to do or how to do it. Health care professionals should be available to step in when situational demands exceed the family caregiver's capabilities, and to step back when the family's support is what is needed most. Caregivers need to seek their own support from family, friends, community agencies, support groups, or/or their faith community.

foster c. The care of individuals who cannot live independently (such as children, homeless families, or frail elderly people) in a group or private home.

futile c. In clinical practice, esp. in the care of patients at the end of life, any intervention that will not improve a patient's health, well-being, comfort, or prognosis. SEE: *advance directive; hospice.*

health c. All of the services made available by medical professionals to promote, maintain, or preserve life and well-being. Its major objectives are to relieve pain; treat injury, illness, and disability; and provide comfort and hope.

home health c. The provision of equipment and services to patients in their homes to restore and maintain the patients' maximal levels of comfort, function, and health.

hospital-at-home c. A form of community-based treatment in which acute medical problems are actively addressed in the patient's home by trained health care specialists in place of similar care provided in-hospital. It has been used to treat both medical issues (such as congestive heart failure, COPD, or end-of-life) and also postoperative recuperation. Although hospital-at-home care has been proposed as a low-cost alternative to inpatient care, its cost structure is not clearly more favorable than inpatient treatment.

informal c. Care that is provided to the very young, the very old, the weak, the poor, and the sick by family, friends, neighbors, and concerned citizens, rather than by trained, licensed, or certified health care professionals.

intensive c. **1.** Care of critically ill patients by continuous monitoring of various body functions. **2.** An intensive care unit.

kangaroo c. The placing of a newborn directly onto the mother's skin to enhance bonding, regulate body temperature, improve the infant's oxygenation, or increase the mother's production of milk.

long-term c. ABBR: LTC. A range of continuous health care or social services for those with chronic physical or mental impairments, or both. LTC provides for basic needs and promotes optimal functioning. It includes care in assisted living facilities, the home, hospice, and nursing homes. SEE: *Nursing Diagnoses Appendix.* SEE: *nursing home.*

managed c. Any of the methods of financing and organizing the delivery of health care in which costs are contained by controlling the provision of benefits and services. Physicians, hospitals, and other health care agencies contract with the system to accept a predetermined monthly payment for providing services to patients who are enrolled in a managed care plan. Enrollee access to care may be limited to the physicians and other health care providers who are affiliated with the plan. In general, managed care attempts to control costs by overseeing and altering the behavior of their providers. Clinical decision making is influenced by a variety of administrative incentives and constraints. Incentives affect the health care provider's financial return for professional services. Constraints include specific rules, regulations, practice guidelines, diagnostic and treatment protocols, or algorithms. Care is overseen by quality assurance procedures and utilization reviews. SEE: *cost awareness; cost-effectiveness; gatekeeper; Health Maintenance Organization; managed competition; resource-based relative value scale.*

medical c. The use of medical skills to benefit a patient.

monitored anesthesia c. ABBR: MAC. Repeated careful evaluation of a patient's airway, breathing, blood pressure, and organ perfusion during deep sedation or general anesthesia.

mouth c. Personal and bedside care of the oral cavity including the gingivae, teeth, lips, epithelial covering of the mucosa, pharynx, and tongue. People who are normally able to provide their own oral hygiene may require help in maintaining a healthy oral environment when they are ill. The intensity and frequency of care is dictated by the patient's comfort; the severity of the ill-

Common Tests Performed Prenatally*

Name of test	Type of test	What it reveals
Alpha fetoprotein	Blood	Increased risk for fetus of Down syndrome or neural tube defects, such as meningomyelocoele
Amniocentesis	Invasive	Genetic diseases such as Down syndrome
Beta strep culture	Vaginal swab	Colonization of the vagina with group B beta streptococcus, a source of neonatal sepsis
Blood type	Blood	ABO blood type; Rh antigen
Chlamydia	Cervical swab	Infection with *Chlamydia trachomatis*
Glucose tolerance testing	Blood	Gestational diabetes mellitus
GC/Gonorrhea	Cervical swab	Infection with *Neisseria gonorrheae*
Hemoglobin	Blood	Anemia (maternal)
Hepatitis B antigen and/or antibody	Blood	Presence of chronic or active hepatitis
Human immuno-deficiency virus antibody test	Blood	HIV/AIDS infection
Pap test	Cervical sample	Cancer of the uterine cervix
Rubella antigen	Blood	Immunity to German measles
Triple or quad marker screen	Blood	Birth defects such as Down syndrome or spina bifida
Ultrasonography	Radiologic, non-invasive	Age of the fetus; multiple pregnancies; developmental abnormalities; quantity of amniotic fluid
Urinalysis	Urine	Urinary tract infection; chronic kidney disease; proteinuria, e.g. in preeclampsia
Varicella-Zoster antibody	Blood	Immunity to chickenpox
VDRL, RPR, FTA-ABS, others	Blood	Infection with syphilis

*Not all these tests are performed on all expectant mothers.

ness; potential or existing irritation or inflammation secondary to trauma or therapy; and the patient's state of consciousness, level of cooperation, and ability to care for himself or herself. SEE: *stomatitis.*

nurse-led c. Health care managed by and provided primarily by advanced practitioner nurses. Many community health centers are led by advanced practitioner nurses.

personal c. Self-care (2).

prehospital c. The care a patient receives from an emergency medical service before arriving at the hospital. This is usually done by emergency medical technicians and paramedics. SEE: *out-of-hospital.*

prenatal c. The regular monitoring and management of the health status of the pregnant woman and her fetus during gestation. Comprehensive care is based on a thorough review of the woman's medical, surgical, obstetrical and gynecological, nutritional, and social history, and that of the family for indications of genetic or other risk factors. Laboratory analyses provide important data describing the woman's current health status and indications for treatment and anticipatory guidance. Periodic visits are scheduled to evaluate changes in blood pressure, weight, fundal height, fetal heart rate, and fetal activity, and to assess for any signs of emerging health problems. To enable the patient's active participation in care and to facilitate early diagnosis and prompt treatment of emerging problems, emphasis is placed on anticipatory guidance and patient teaching. The health care professional describes and discusses nutrition and diet (including the importance of folate supplementation), self-management of common minor complaints, and signs to report promptly to the primary caregiver; helps patients gain access to resources available for preparation for childbirth, breastfeeding, newborn care, and parenting; and provides support and counseling. SEE: *pregnancy; prenatal diagnosis;* table.

prepaid c. Managed care in which a patient or group contracts for all its health care services in advance, instead of paying for each service when it is delivered.

primary c. Integrated, accessible, basic health care provided where the patient first seeks medical assistance by clinicians responsible for most of the patient's personal health care, including health maintenance, therapy during illnesses, and consultation with specialists.

relationship-centered c. Health care that explicitly recognizes the importance of patients, their supporters, their community, their providers, and their health care administrators as they jointly affect the experience of health, disease prevention, and treatment.

residential c. Care provided in a live-in facility other than the patient's home. The very young, the very old, and those with physical infirmities, or behavioral or substance abuse problems are often treated in residential care centers.

respiratory c. The evaluation, treatment, and rehabilitation of patients with cardiopulmonary disease by respiratory therapy professionals working under a physician's supervision.

respite c. Provision of short-term care to the elderly, disabled, or chronically ill of a community to allow caregivers a temporary relief from their responsibilities. The care may be provided either in the patient's home, church, community center, nursing home, or caregiver's home.

restorative c. Rehabilitation (1).

secondary medical c. Medical care of a patient by a physician acting as a consultant. The provider of primary medical care usually refers the patient for expert or specialty consultation or for a second opinion.

secondary nursing c. Nursing care aimed at early recognition and treatment of disease. It includes general nursing intervention and teaching of early signs of disease so that prompt medical care by a physician, nurse practitioner, speech therapist, or other appropriate provider can be obtained. SEE: *preventive nursing*.

simultaneous c. In patients with potentially terminal illnesses, the combined or alternating use of palliative and curative therapies.

skilled c. Medical care provided by licensed professionals working under the direction of a physician.

stepped c. Treatment that follows a predetermined or algorithmic sequence. The simplest, most affordable, or most broadly effective treatment regimen is used first. If that fails or causes side effects, other options are employed one after another until an endpoint is reached.

survivorship c. A plan for patient follow-up that links the treatments a patient has received from an oncologist and the needs of the patient after intensive cancer treatments have been completed. With about 10 million cancer survivors in the U.S., and that number rising, survivors are living longer and receiving more fragmented care. A follow-up care plan helps communicate to the patient and his or her future health care providers details of cancer staging, treatment, and disease surveillance that may otherwise be misunderstood or neglected. According to the Institute of Medicine, such a plan should include the following elements: 1. a clear, concisely written statement of the patient's diagnosis, the methods used in treatment (such as what specific chemotherapeutic drugs and what doses of radiation), and the expected or potential effects of that treatment; 2. detailed information about the need for specific follow-up services and a timetable specifying when such services should be delivered; 3. information about secondary disease prevention (including the detection of cancer recurrence and the need for monitoring for secondary cancers); 4. information about the availability of support services and agencies in the patient's community; 5. information for the patient about legal protections after diagnosis, including employment and insurance.

Survivor care plans are often drawn up and given to patients by oncologists or advanced practice nurses. They should address concerns about nutrition, physical activity, exercise, and mobility; elimination; cognition and perception; pain and discomfort; sleep, and rest; self-perception; relationships with spouse, parents, children, other family members, and friends; and sexuality and reproductive issues.

tactical combat casualty c. ABBR: TCCC. Treatment provided to military personnel while engaged in battle.

tertiary medical c. A level of medical care in a facility staffed and equipped to administer comprehensive care. This level of care is usually provided in a large hospital to which the patient has been referred or transferred. It includes techniques and methods of therapy and diagnosis involving equipment and personnel not economically feasible in a smaller institution because of underutilization.

tracheostomy c. Management of the tracheostomy wound and the airway device. The patient should be suctioned as often as necessary to remove secretions. Sterile technique is maintained throughout the procedure. Before suctioning, the patient should be aerated well, which can be accomplished by using an Ambu bag attached to a source of oxygen. The patency of the suction catheter is tested by aspirating sterile normal saline through it. The catheter is inserted without applying suction, until the patient coughs. Suction is then applied intermittently and the catheter withdrawn in a rotating motion. The lungs are auscultated by assessing the airway, and the suctioning procedure is repeated until the airway is clear. Each suctioning episode should take no longer than 15 sec, and the patient should be allowed to rest and breathe between suctioning episodes. The suction catheter is cleansed with sterile normal saline solution, as is the oral cavity if necessary. The inner cannula should be cleansed or replaced after each aspiration. Metal cannulas should be cleansed with sterile water.

An emergency tracheotomy kit is kept at the bedside at all times. A Kelly clamp is also kept at the bedside to hold open the tracheostomy site in an emergency. Unless ordered otherwise, cuffed tracheostomy tubes must be inflated if the patient is receiving positive-pressure ventilation. In other cases, the cuff is kept deflated if the patient has problems with aspiration. The dressing and tape are changed every 8 hr, using aseptic technique. Skin breakdown is prevented by covering tracheostomies with an oval dressing between the airway device and the skin. To apply neck tapes, two lengths of twill tape approx. 10 in (25 cm) long are obtained; the end of each is folded and a slit is made 0.5 in (1.3 cm) long about 1 in (2.5 cm) from the fold. The slit end is slipped under the neck plate and the other end of the tape pulled through the slit. This is repeated for the other side. The tape is wrapped around the neck and secured with a square knot on the side. Neck tapes should be left in place until new tapes are attached. Tracheal secretions are cultured as ordered; their color, viscosity, amount, and abnormal odor, if any, are observed. The site is inspected daily for bleeding, hematoma formation, subcutaneous emphysema, and signs of infection. Appropriate skin care is provided. The medical care team should help alleviate the patient's anxiety and apprehension and communicate openly with the patient. The patient's response is documented.

transitional c. Health care services provided to patients after hospitalization in an acute care facility before they are ready to return to their homes. Transitional care shortens acute hospital stays, decreases health care costs, and provides a period for recuperation for patients still unable to thrive independently. Facilities used in transitional care include rehabilitation units, long-term care hospitals, subacute care facilities, hospice services, and some home care services.

uncompensated c. Health care provided to those who are uninsured and unable to pay for the services they receive. In the U.S. most uncompensated care is provided for in a relatively small number of urban hospitals.

wound c. Any technique that enhances the healing of skin abrasions, blisters, cracks, craters, infections, lacerations, necrosis, and/or ulcers. Wound care involves 1. local care to the skin, with débridement and dressings; 2. careful positioning of the affected body part to avoid excessive pressure on the wound; 3. application of compression or medicated bandages; 4. treatment of edema or lymphedema; 5. treatment of infection; 6. optimization of nutrition and of blood glucose levels; 7. the use of supports and cushions; and 8. maximization of blood flow and oxygen. Website: Association for the Advancement of Wound Care: www.aawcone.org/patientresources.shtml

caregiver One who provides care to a dependent or partially dependent patient. In an acute care setting, the caregiver is most often a professional; however, in the home care situation, this person is often a family member. Care of caregivers is a focus of nurses, social workers, and other health care providers who manage chronically ill patients. Generally, caregivers need emotional support and comfort owing to the extreme stress of their lives. SEE: *caregiver burden*.

caregiver burden The perception of stress and fatigue caused by the sustained effort required in caring for persons with chronic illness or other conditions with special needs for care.

caregiver role strain A caregiver's felt or exhibited difficulty in performing the family caregiver role. SEE: *Nursing Diagnoses Appendix*.

caregiver role strain, risk for The vulnerability of the caregiver for difficulties felt in performing the role of family caregiver. SEE: *Nursing Diagnoses Appendix*.

Caregiver Stress Inventory ABBR: CSI. A 50-item scale specific to professionals caring for dependent patients. It is divided into three subscales measuring stress related to the patient's verbal and physical behavior, the patient's mental, emotional, and social behavior, and the resources, knowledge, and abilities of the staff.

care transition Transition (2).

CARF *Commission on Accreditation of Rehabilitation Facilities.*

caries (kar′ēz, ker′) [L. *caries,* rottenness] Gradual decay and disintegration of soft or bony tissue or of a tooth. If the decay progresses, the surrounding tissue becomes inflamed and an abscess forms, e.g., chronic abscess, tuberculosis, and bacterial invasion of teeth. In caries, the bone disintegrates by pieces, whereas in necrosis, large masses of bone are involved. SYN: *dental cavity*. **carious** (-rē-ŭs), *adj.*

arrested c. Apparent lack of progress in a carious lesion as a result of remineralization.

bottle mouth c. Baby bottle syndrome.

cervical c. Caries involving the neck of the tooth, slightly above or below the junction between the root cementum and the enamel crown.

dental c. Progressive decalcification of the enamel and dentin of a tooth; tooth decay. The condition is caused by dental infection, and the erosion of teeth by the acid by-products of bacterial metabolism on their surfaces.

PREVENTION: Minimizing the dietary intake of refined sugars and careful toothbrushing twice a day with a fluoride-containing toothpaste reduces the incidence of dental caries. Use of dental floss or tape removes plaque from between adjacent tooth surfaces; deep pits and fissures may be sealed by the application of resins. The sealant may need to be replaced periodically. Early detection and dental restorations offer the best form of control once caries has formed. Topical application of fluoride promotes resistance to dental caries. Dental caries is less likely to develop if appropriate amounts of fluoride are ingested while the teeth are developing. It is important that excess fluoride not be ingested because greater amounts than required (about 1 mg/day) cause mottling of the teeth. Fluoride in the diet does not obviate the need for topical application of fluoride to the teeth. SYN: *dental cavity*. SEE: *dental plaque*.

incipient c. One of the two distinct stages in the development of a carious dental lesion. The first stage is the incipient lesion, marked by the appearance of a white spot. Microscopic pores course through the enamel to the subsurface demineralization, where the main body of the lesion is located.

pit and fissure c. Caries in the pits and fissures of tooth enamel.

radiation c. Dental caries that develops as a side effect of treatment of malignancies of the oral cavity with ionizing radiation. The etiology is, in part, due to the dysfunction of the salivary glands.

rampant c. A sudden onset of widespread caries that affects most of the teeth and penetrates quickly to the dental pulp.

recurrent c. Dental caries that develops at the small imperfections between the tooth surface and a restoration, caused by plaque at the imperfections. SYN: *secondary c.*

root c. Caries on the root of a tooth. The root is more susceptible to decay than the rest of the tooth due to the lack of an enamel covering, difficulty in maintaining a clean root surface, and the lack of effective preventive therapies.

secondary c. Recurrent **c.**

c. sicca Bony destruction such as that caused by infection with syphilis.

spinal c. Pott's disease. SEE: under *Pott, John Percivall*.

caries activity test Any laboratory test that measures the degree of caries activity in a dental patient. The tests may identify the number of cariogenic bacteria or the acid production from saliva samples.

caries-detecting dyes Any stain or fluorescent solution used to reveal demineralized dentin. When applied to teeth, they highlight areas that may need excavation. A clinical examination of the tooth for hardness may be needed to confirm suspicious regions illuminated by dyes. Some studies suggest they are overly sensitive but not specific.

carina (kă-rī′nă) *pl.* **carinae** [L., keel of a boat] A structure with a projecting central ridge.

nasal c. Olfactory nasal sulcus.

carina of the trachea The ridge at the lower end of the trachea separating the openings of the two primary bronchi. SEE: illus.

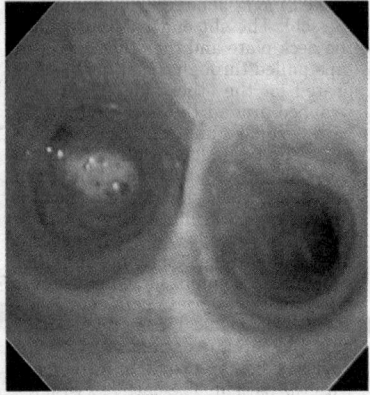

CARINA OF THE TRACHEA

seen bronchoscopically

c. of the urethra The ridge extending posteriorly from the urethral orifice and continuous with the anterior column of the vagina.

caring behaviors SEE: under *behavior*.

carioca test A side-shuffling, sport-specific functional test of agility and kinesthetic awareness that is used toward the end of a rehabilitation program to reintegrate athletes back into competition following lower extremity injuries. Derived from a Latin dance step, the carioca test involves the alternate stepping of one foot in front and then behind the other.

cariogenesis (kăr″ē-ō-jĕn′ĕ-sĭs) [L. *caries,* rottenness, + Gr. *genesis,* generation, birth] The formation of caries. SEE: *dental caries.*

cariogenic (kă″rē-ō-jĕn′ĭk) [″+Gr. *gennan,* to produce] Conducive to caries formation.

cariostatic (kā″rē-ō-stăt′ĭk) Able to prevent the formation of dental caries. Common cariostatic agents include fluoride and chlorhexidine.

carious (kar′ē-ŭs) [L. *cariosus,* decayed] **1.** Affected with or pert. to dental caries or decay. **2.** Having pits or perforations.

carminative (kăr-mĭn′ă-tĭv) [L. *carminativus,* cleanse] An agent that helps to prevent gas formation in the gastrointestinal tract.

carnal (kăr′năl) [L. *carnalis,* flesh] Pert. to the desires and appetites of the flesh; sensual.

carneous (kăr′nē-ŭs) [L. *carneus,* fleshy] Fleshy.

Carnett sign (kar″net′) [John Berton Carnett, 20th-cent. U.S. surgeon] In evaluating a surgical abdomen, decreased abdominal tenderness to palpation after the supine patient elevates his or her head from the bed. The sign indicates that acute abdominal pain originates in the rectus muscle sheath rather than the peritoneum.

Carney triad (kar′nē) [J. Aidan Carney, contemporary U.S. pathologist] The combined presence of gastric stromal tumors, paragangliomas, and pulmonary chondromas in a patient.

carnitine (kăr′nĭ-tĭn) A chemical, γ-trimethylamine-β-hydroxybutyrate, important in metabolizing palmitic and stearic acids. It has been used therapeutically in treating myopathy due to carnitine deficiency.

carnivore (kăr′nĭ-vor) An animal that eats primarily meat, particularly an animal of the order Carnivora, which includes cats, dogs, and bears.

carnivorous (kăr-nĭv′ō-rŭs) [L. *carnivorus*] Flesh-eating.

carnophobia (kăr″nō-fō′bē-ă) [″ + Gr. *phobos,* fear] An abnormal aversion to meat.

carnose (kăr′nōs) Having the consistency of or resembling flesh.

carnosine (kăr′nō-sĭn) $C_9H_{14}N_4O_3$; a chemical, β-alanylhistidine, present in brain and muscle. It has been promoted as an "anti-aging" agent.

carnosity (kăr-nŏs′ĭ-tē) [L. *carnositas,* fleshiness] An excrescence resembling flesh; a fleshy growth.

carotenase (kăr-ŏt′ĕ-nās) [Gr. *karoton,* carrot] An enzyme that catalyzes the conversion of beta-carotene to retinaldehyde.

carotene (kăr′ă-tēn) [Gr. *karoton*] One of several yellow, red, orange, or green antioxidant compounds that are biochemical precursors of Vitamin A. Many fresh fruits and vegetables (including apricots, carrots, corn, kale, oranges, spinach, squash, sweet potatoes, and tomatoes) are rich in these chemicals. They may play a part in preventing atherosclerosis, neurodegenerative diseases, cancers, and retinal degeneration.

Retinol is the form of vitamin A found in mammals. One retinol equivalent is equal to 6 μg of beta-carotene. Beta-carotene is a safer food supplement than vitamin A because the latter has much greater toxic potential in large doses.

⚠ Smokers who supplement their diet with beta carotene increase their risk of lung cancer.

carotenemia, carotinemia (kar″ŏt-ĕ-nē′mē-ă) [*carotene* + *-emia*] Carotene in the blood, marked by pseudojaundice (yellowing of the skin). It can be distinguished from true jaundice by the lack of yellow discoloration of the conjunctivae in carotenemia.

carotenoid (kă-rŏt′ĕ-noyd) [″ + *eidos,* form, shape] **1.** One of a group of more than 500 yellow, orange, green, or red fat-soluble pigments found naturally in fruits and vegetables and acting as antioxidants in the body. About 50 carotenoids are precursors of vitamin A. Carotenoids that have health benefits are alpha carotene, lycopene, cryptoxanthan, zeaxanthan, and lutein. **2.** Resembling carotene.

carotic (kă-rŏt′ĭk) [Gr. *karos,* deep sleep] **1.** Carotid. **2.** Resembling stupor; stupefying.

carotid (kă-rŏt′ĭd) [Gr. *karos,* deep sleep] **1.** Pert. to the right and left common carotid arteries, which form the principal blood supply to the head and neck. The left arises directly from the aortic arch and the right from the brachiocephalic artery. Each of these two arteries divides to form external and internal carotid arteries. **2.** Pert. to any carotid part, such as the carotid sinus.

carotid body SEE: under *body.*

carotidynia, carotodynia (kăr-ŏt″ĭ-dĭn′ē-ă) [″ + *odyne,* pain] Pain in the face, neck, or jaw. It may be produced in persons with atypical facial neuralgia by pressure on the common carotid artery. The pain is dull and referred to the same side to which pressure was applied. Treatment is with analgesics.

carpal (kăr′păl, kar′păl) [Gr. *karpalis*] Pert. to the carpus or wrist.

carpal tunnel syndrome Pain or numbness and tingling that affect some part of the median nerve distribution of the hand (the palmar side of the thumb, the index finger, the radial half of the ring finger, and the radial half of the palm) and may radiate into the arm. Patients may have a history of cumulative trauma to the wrist, e.g., as a result of overuse in carpentry, rowing, typing, computing, or the operation of vibrating tools or machinery. In addition, the condition may occur after wrist fracture, in pregnancy, or as a consequence of systemic or metabolic disorders such as diabetes mellitus, hypothyroidism, acromegaly, and amyloidosis. SEE: *repetitive motion injury*.

TREATMENT: The patient should rest the extremity, avoiding anything that aggravates the symptoms. This may require splinting of the wrist for several weeks to relieve tension on the median nerve. The patient's job requirements should be analyzed and recommendations provided for modified tools or a change in job assignment. The patient is taught how to avoid tension on the median nerve. Other treatments may include yoga, corticosteroid injections, or surgery.

PATIENT CARE: The patient is evaluated for loss of sensation on the palmar surface of the fingertips and for atrophy of the thenar muscles—both of which indicate advanced median nerve injury. If they are present, a referral to a specialist is indicated. Physical assessments of the carpal tunnel (Phalen's and Tinel's signs) have poor accuracy but are generally performed.

Most patients with pain that is thought to come from the carpal tunnel are treated with modification of work, a wrist splint to hold the affected hand(s) in a neutral position, and an anti-inflammatory drug, such as ibuprofen. Occupational counseling is suggested if the syndrome necessitates a temporary or permanent job change.

The need for diagnostic studies, such as nerve conduction tests or electromyography, and expected sensations, are explained. If surgery (carpal tunnel release) is required, the patient is prepared by explaining the procedure and expected sensations. Postoperatively, neurovascular status in the affected extremity is carefully assessed (patient and significant others should be taught this assessment), and the patient is encouraged to keep the hand elevated to reduce swelling and discomfort. The patient should perform prescribed wrist and finger exercises daily to improve circulation and to enhance muscle tone; he or she can perform these exercises in warm water if they are painful (wearing a surgical glove if dressings are still in place). He or she should avoid lifting

anything weighing more than a few ounces. The patient should report severe, persistent pain or tenderness, which may point to tenosynovitis or hematoma formation. The incision should be kept clean and dry, and dressings changed daily until the incision has healed completely. Dressings should also be checked for bleeding; any unusual bleeding or drainage should be reported. The patient is encouraged to express any concerns, and support is offered. SEE: *Nursing Diagnoses Appendix*.

carpectomy (kăr-pĕk'tō-mē) [" + *ektome*, excision] Excision of the carpus or a portion of it.

Carpentier-Edwards valve (kar-pon-tyā'ed'wärds) [Alain Carpentier, Fr. heart surgeon, b. 1933; M.L. Edwards, U.S. physician, b. 1906] An artificial heart valve made from pig (porcine) pericardium attached to an engineered ring. The ring is surgically attached to the endocardium.

carpetlayer's knee SEE: under *knee*.

carphologia, carphology (kăr-fō-lō'jē-ă, -fŏl'ō-jē) [Gr. *karphos*, dry twig, + *legein*, to pluck] Involuntary picking at bedclothes, seen esp. in febrile delirium. SYN: *floccillation*.

carpo- [Gr. *karpos*] Prefix meaning *carpus*.

carpometacarpal (kăr"pō-mĕt"ă-kăr'păl) [" + *meta*, beyond, + *karpos*, wrist] Pert. to both the carpus and the metacarpus.

carpopedal (kăr"pō-pĕd'ăl) [" + L. *ped*, foot] Pert. to both the wrist and the foot.

carpoptosis (kăr"pŏp-tō'sĭs) [" + *ptosis*, a falling] Wrist drop.

carpus (kăr'pŭs) [L.] The eight bones of the wrist joint. SEE: *skeleton*; *wrist drop*.

carrageen, carragheen (kar'ă-gēn") [*Carrageen*, a village in southeast Ireland] Dried red alga, *Chondrus crispus*, from which carrageenan is obtained. SYN: *Irish moss*. SEE: *carrageenan*; *Chondrus*.

carrageenan, carrageenin (kar'ă-gēn'ăn) [*carrageen*] The colloid extract from carrageen, used as a demulcent and thickening agent in medicines and foods. SYN: *Irish moss*. SEE: *carrageen*; *Chondrus*.

carriage (kăr'ĭj) [Old North Fr. *carier*, to transport by vehicle] The harboring, holding, or transporting of a chemical, gene, infection, or other material.

carrier (kar'ē-ĕr) [Fr. *carier*, to bear] **1.** A person who harbors a specific pathogenic organism, has no discernible symptoms or signs of the disease, and is potentially capable of spreading the organism to others. **2.** An animal, insect, or substance, e.g., food, water, feces that can transmit infectious organisms.

SYN: *vector*. SEE: *fomes; isolation; microorganism; Standard Precautions Appendix; communicable disease* for table. **3.** A molecule that when combined with another substance can pass through a cell membrane, as occurs in facilitated diffusion or some active transport mechanisms. **4.** One who carries a recessive gene together with its normal allele; a heterozygote. **5.** An instrument or apparatus for transporting something, e.g., in dentistry, an amalgam carrier.

active c. One who harbors a pathogenic organism for a clinically significant time and is able to pass the infection to others.

convalescent c. One who harbors an infective organism during recovery from the disease caused by the organism.

genetic c. One whose chromosomes contain a pathological gene that may be transmitted to offspring. In some cases, e.g., Tay-Sachs disease, this condition can be detected prenatally by a laboratory test done on amniotic fluid.

gestational c. A woman who accepts a fertilized egg from a man and woman who provide the sperm and egg. The carrier is not usually genetically related to the intended parents.

incubatory c. One who harbors and spreads an infectious organism during the incubation period of a disease before it becomes clinically evident.

infant c. Any device used to carry a newborn or young child on the chest or the back of an adult. Poor design or misuse of such devices may pose a risk of suffocation to the child.

intermittent c. One who harbors an infectious organism, e.g., methicillin-resistant *Staphylococcus aureus* in the nasal passages, from time to time but not continuously.

carrier-free (kăr′ē-ĕr-frē) Not attached to a carrier; said of radioactive isotopes.

carrier prodrug, carrier-linked prodrug A prodrug that is transiently attached to another chemical used to ferry it to its target or in other ways improve its bioavailability and kinetics.

carrier screening, carrier identification Performing genetic tests on a person to see if he or she may carry a recessive trait that might be expressed after mating with another carrier of the trait. It is used in high-risk families or populations to screen for illnesses such as cystic fibrosis, Gaucher's disease, and Tay-Sachs disease.

Carrion disease (kar-ē-ōn′) [Daniel A. Carrion, 1850–1885, a Peruvian student who died after voluntarily injecting himself with a disease] Bartonellosis.

carry-over The portion of analyte brought from one reaction segment to the next. The accuracy of laboratory test results may be altered by contaminants that are transferred from one reaction to the following one.

car surfing Crouching, kneeling, standing on, or clinging to the outside of a moving automobile or truck. It has been associated with serious and sometimes fatal trauma.

cART *Combination antiretroviral therapy.*

Cartia XT SEE: *diltiazem.*

cartilage (kart′ĭ-lăj) [L. *cartilago*, gristle] A specialized type of dense connective tissue consisting of cells embedded in a ground substance or matrix. The matrix is firm and compact and can withstand considerable pressure or tension. Cartilage is bluish-white or gray and is semiopaque; it has no nerve or blood supply of its own. The cells lie in cavities called lacunae. They may be single or in groups of two, three, or four.

Cartilage forms parts of joints in the adult skeleton, such as between vertebral bodies and on the articular surfaces of bones. It also occurs in the costal cartilages of the ribs, in the nasal septum, in the external ear and lining of the eustachian tube, in the wall of the larynx, and in the trachea and bronchi. It forms the major portion of the embryonic skeleton, providing a model in which most bones develop.

alar c. Cartilage forming the broad lateral wall of each nostril.

articular c. The thin layer of smooth, hyaline cartilage located on the joint surfaces of a bone, as in a synovial joint.

costal c. A cartilage that connects the end of a true rib with the sternum or the end of a false rib with the costal cartilage above.

cricoid c. The lowermost cartilage of the larynx; shaped like a signet ring, the broad portion or lamina being posterior, the anterior portion forming the arch. SEE: *larynx* for illus.

cuneiform c. One of two small pieces of elastic cartilage that lie in the aryepiglottic fold of the larynx immediately anterior to the arytenoid cartilage.

elastic c. Cartilage that contains elastin fibers in the matrix. Found in the epiglottis, external ear, and auditory tube, it strengthens these and maintains their shape.

fibrous c. Fibrocartilage.

hyaline c. A bluish-white, glassy, translucent cartilage. The matrix appears homogeneous although it contains collagenous fibers forming a fine network. The walls of the lacunae stain intensely with basic dyes. Hyaline cartilage is flexible and slightly elastic. Its surface is covered by the perichondrium except on articular surfaces. It is found in articular cartilage, costal cartilages, the nasal septum, the larynx, and the trachea.

Meckel c. SEE: under *Meckel, Johann Friedrich (the younger).*

nasal c. Any of the cartilages forming the principal portion of the subcutaneous framework of the nose.

palpebral c. One of the thin plates of connective tissue resembling cartilage that form the framework of the eyelid.

parachordal c. One of a pair of cartilages in the cephalic portion of the notochord of the embryo that unites in humans to form a single basal plate that is the forerunner of the occipital bone.

Reichert c. SEE: *Reichert cartilage.*

semilunar c. One of two crescentic cartilages (medial and lateral) of the knee joint between the femur and tibia.

sesamoid c. One or more small cartilage plates present in fibrous tissue between the lateral nasal and greater alar cartilages of the nose.

shark c. An alternative remedy promoted for the treatment of arthritis and cancer.

thyroid c. The largest and most anterior cartilage of the larynx, consisting of two broad laminae united anteriorly to form a V-shaped structure. It forms a subcutaneous projection called the laryngeal prominence or Adam's apple. SEE: *thyroid gland* for illus.

vomeronasal c. One of two narrow strips of cartilage lying along the anterior portion of the inferior border of the septal cartilage of the nose.

Y c. The cartilage that connects the pubis, ilium, and ischium and extends into the acetabulum.

cartilaginification   (kăr″tĭ-lă-jĭn″ĭ-fĭ-kā′shŭn) [″ + *facere,* to make] Cartilage formation or chondrification; the development of cartilage from undifferentiated tissue.

cartilaginoid (kăr″tĭ-lăj′ĭ-noyd) [″ + Gr. *eidos,* form, shape] Resembling cartilage.

cartilaginous (kăr″tĭ-lăj′ĭ-nŭs) Pert. to or consisting of cartilage.

caruncle (kăr′ŭng-kl) [L. *caruncula,* small flesh] A small fleshy growth.

lacrimal c. A small reddish elevation found on the conjunctiva near the inner canthus, at the medial angle of the eye.

sublingual c. A protuberance on each side of the frenulum of the tongue, containing the openings of the ducts from the submandibular and sublingual salivary glands.

urethral c. A small, red, papillary growth that is highly vascular and is sometimes found in the urinary meatus in females. It is characterized by pain on urination and is very sensitive to friction.

caruncula (kăr-ŭng′kū-lă) *pl.* **carunculae** [L.] Caruncle.

c. hymenales Small irregular nodules representing remains of the hymen.

Carvallo sign (kar-val′yō, -va′yō) [J. M. Rivero-Carvallo, contemporary Mexican physician] An increase in intensity of the presystolic murmur heard in patients with tricuspid stenosis during inspiration, and its decrease during expiration. This is best demonstrated with the patient in an erect position.

carvedilol (kăr-vē′dĭ-lōl) A beta- and alpha-blocking drug that can be used to treat high blood pressure and congestive heart failure.

carve-out In managed care, a service or benefit for a specific disease, condition, or population that is contracted for separately from the rest of a health insurance plan. Carve-outs typically are used in managed care contracts to identify the costs associated with esp. expensive forms of care, such as mental health or substance abuse services.

carver (karv′ĕr) **1.** A knife or other instrument used to fashion or shape an object. **2.** In dentistry, an instrument to shape dental restorations in the mouth or to fabricate teeth in a laboratory.

amalgam c. Any of several small sharp instrument of varying shapes used to carve or contour amalgam restorations to obtain optimal occlusion.

wax c. A blunt instrument of varying shape to heat and carve or shape wax patterns.

cary-, caryo- SEE: *karyo-.*

CAS *Coronary artery scan; Chemical Abstract Service.*

Casal necklace [Gaspar Casal, Sp. physician, 1691–1759] Bilaterally symmetrical lesions of the neck that represent a portion of the skin's involvement in pellagra. The lesions begin as erythemas and progress to vesiculation and crusting.

cascade (kas″kād′) [Fr. fr Italian *cascare,* to fall] The continuation of a process through a series of steps, each one initiating the next, until the final step is reached. The action may or may not become amplified as each step progresses.

prescribing c. The administration of a new drug to a patient because of side effects produced by another prescription. Later prescriptions increase the risk of further side effects, drug interactions, and patient harm. A prescribing cascade usually results from the failure of the health care prescriber to recognize a patient's presenting illness as evidence of an adverse drug reaction. In many patients, but esp. in those with diminished kidney or liver function, side effects of drugs are a common cause of drug toxicity and hospitalization.

cascara sagrada (kăs-kăr′ă să-grä′dă) The dried bark of *Rhamnus purshiana,* a small tree grown on the western U.S. coast and in parts of South America. It is the main ingredient in aromatic cascara sagrada fluid extract, a cathartic.

case [L. *casus*, happening] **1.** An occurrence of disease; incorrectly used to refer to a patient. **2.** An enclosing structure.

caseate (kā′sē-āt) [L. *caseus*, cheese] To undergo cheesy degeneration, as in certain necroses.

caseation (kā″sē-ā′shŭn) **1.** The process in which necrotic tissue is converted into a granular amorphous mass resembling cheese. **2.** The precipitation of casein during coagulation of milk.

case control A form of research in which patients with a disease are compared with closely matched individuals who do not have the disease. It is used to uncover risk factors or exposures that may produce illness.

casefinding (kās″fīnd′ĭng) An active attempt to identify persons who have a certain disease.

case history SEE: under *history*.

casein (kā′sē-ĭn) [L. *caseus*, cheese] The principal protein in milk, which forms curds at acid pH. When coagulated by rennin or acid, it becomes one of the principal ingredients of cheese.

case law SEE: under *law*.

caseload The total number of patients managed by a particular health care professional or agency.

case management An individualized approach to coordinating patient care services, esp. when clients with complex needs or chronic medical problems require multifaceted or interdisciplinary care. Case management is a particularly valuable approach to meeting the service needs of impaired older persons and others with chronic medical disabilities.

    hospital c.m. A system of patient care delivery in which a case manager, typically a registered nurse, coordinates interdisciplinary care for a group of patients. The advantages of hospital case management are improved quality, continuity of care, and decreased hospital costs.

case mix The unique characteristics of any patient population, e.g., its history of behavioral or medical illnesses, or its socioeconomic status. The unique characteristics of different groups of patients alter many variables relating to the care they receive. A group of healthy twenty-year-old men serving in the military overseas has different needs than a rural community primarily composed of retired people. Differences in case mix affect health care costs, the need for specialist care, nursing home care, hospice care, prenatal care, and specific medications.

case-mix bias (kās′mĭks″) [″ + ″] Spectrum bias.

caseous (kā′sē-ŭs) **1.** Resembling

cheese. **2.** Pert. to transformation of tissues into a cheesy mass.

case report A formal summary of a unique patient and his or her illness, including the presenting signs and symptoms, diagnostic studies, treatment course, and outcome. SYN: *case study*.

case study Case report.

caspase A protein that regulates programmed cellular death (apoptosis).

CASS *Continuous aspiration of subglottic secretions.*

cassava (kă-sah′vă) [Sp. *cazabe*] A group of perennial herbs of the genus *Manihot*. The plant is one of the most efficient converters of solar energy to carbohydrate. The root of *M. esculenta* provides an excellent source of starch and can thrive in poor, dry, acid soils. To be suitable for eating, the root is processed by one of several methods to remove or control the amount of cyanide present. Tapioca is made from cassava.

cassette (kă-set′) [Fr., *cassette*, a little box] **1.** A flat, lightproof box with an intensifying screen, for holding x-ray film. Digital radiography photostimulable phosphor (PSP) systems use cassettes to provide lightproof holders for the PSP screens while they are exposed and carried to a processing unit. **2.** A case used for film or magnetic tape.

    screen-type c. A light-tight film holder.

cast (kăst) [ME. *casten*, to carry] **1.** In dentistry, a positive copy of jaw tissues over which denture bases may be made. **2.** To make an accurate metallic reproduction of a wax pattern of a dental appliance, tooth crown, or inlay cavity preparation. **3.** Pliable or fibrous material shed in various pathological conditions; the product of effusion. It is molded to the shape of the part in which it has been accumulated. Casts are classified as bronchial, intestinal, nasal, esophageal, renal, tracheal, urethral, and vaginal; constituents are classified as bloody, fatty, fibrinous, granular, hyaline, mucous, and waxy. **4.** A solid mold of a part, usually applied in situ for immobilization of fractures, dislocations, and other severe injuries. It is carefully applied to the immobilized part and allowed to dry and harden (over 24 to 48 hr). Care is taken not to apply any pressure to the cast until after the cast is dried and hardened. Synthetic materials, such as fiberglass, are also used, esp. for non–weight-bearing parts of the body. SEE: illus.

    PATIENT CARE: Neurovascular status distal to the cast is monitored; and any deterioration in circulation and in sensory or motor abilities, such as paresthesias, paralysis, diminished pulses, pallor, coldness, or pain, is documented and reported. Pain or burning under the cast other than a transient

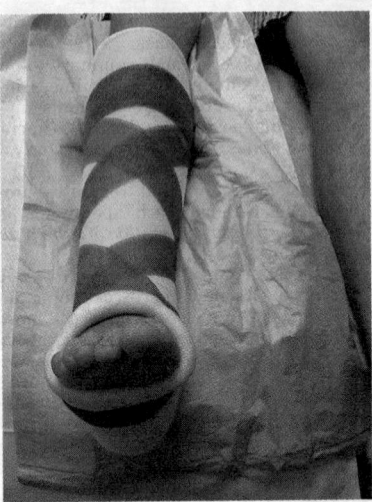

DECORATED CAST

sense of warmth (which is expected), is also documented and reported. The cast may be bivalved or removed to relieve pressure on the swollen tissues beneath it. To limit swelling the casted extremity should be supported above heart level for the first 24 hours. All casts must be kept dry to avoid maceration of the skin. Objects should not be placed inside a cast to relieve itching, but relief often can be obtained by applying cold (a well-sealed ice bag) to the cast over the area that itches, or by scratching the opposite extremity in the same area. Joints above and below the cast should be exercised to prevent stiffness and contractures. The patient is instructed in symptoms to be reported, cast care and ways to protect the cast from damage; prescribed exercises or activity limitations; and use of any assistive devices such as slings, crutches, or walker. SEE: *Nursing Diagnoses Appendix*.

blood cell c. Red blood cell cast.

body c. A cast used to immobilize the spine. It may extend from the thorax to the pelvis.

bronchial c. Mucus formed into the shape of the bronchi in which it was previously lodged.

broomstick c. A type of cast used following skin traction for (Legg-Calvé-Perthes disease. A bar is used between upper femoral casts to maintain abduction. SEE: *Legg-Calvé-Perthes disease*.

epithelial c. Tubular epithelial cells in the urine, a finding in some cases of glomerulonephritis.

fatty c. A urinary cast, consisting of a mass of fatty globules, seen in the examination of patients with nephrosis.

fibrinous c. A yellow-brown cast sometimes seen in glomerulonephritis.

granular c. A coarse or fine granule, short and plump, sometimes yellowish, similar to a hyaline cast, and soluble in acetic acid. It is seen in inflammatory and degenerative nephropathies. SEE: *cast*.

hyaline c. The most common form of cast found in the urine, transparent, pale, and having homogeneous rounded ends. It may be a benign finding, or may be present in fevers, stress, kidney disease, or unchecked hypertension.

light c. A cast used in orthopedics, made of a lightweight material that is usually applied and then hardened by treating with the heat from a light.

Minerva c. A body cast that extends from the top of the head to the iliac crests, leaving the facial features exposed, but supporting the chin and neck. It is used to treat odontoid fractures in children.

plaster c. Rigid dressing made of gauze impregnated with plaster of Paris, used to immobilize an injured part, esp. in bone fractures.

red blood cell c. A urinary cast composed principally of red blood cells strongly suggestive of glomerulonephritis. SYN: *blood cell c.*

spica hip c. A cast containing the lower torso and extending to one or both lower extremities. If only one lower extremity is included, it is called a single hip spica; if two are included, it is called a double hip spica. These are used for treating pelvic and femoral fractures.

urinary c. A cylindrical clump of cells and proteins found in the urine in a wide variety of diseases and conditions.

uterine c. Tissue or mucus from the endometrium passed in exfoliative endometritis or membranous dysmenorrhea.

walking c. A cast or boot that allows the patient to be ambulatory. SYN: *walking boot*.

waxy c. A light yellowish, well-defined urinary cast probably made up of disintegrating kidney cells, found in some chronic kidney diseases, glomerulonephritis, and uncontrolled hypertension.

white blood cell c. A leukocyte cast found in urine in acute pyelonephritis, interstitial nephritis, and at times, glomerulonephritis.

cast-brace A lower extremity cast that is open and hinged at the knee joint. It can be used to treat femoral fractures.

Castellani paint (kăs-tĕl-ăn′ē) [Aldo Castellani, It. physician, 1878–1971] Paint used to disinfect skin and to treat fungus infections of the skin. Its components are phenol, resorcinol, basic fuchsin, boric acid, and acetone.

casting (kăst′ĭng) The forming of an object in a mold.

serial c. Replacing casts on injured

extremities at specified intervals to permit progressively greater ranges of joint motion so that the maximum range needed for function may be restored.

Castle intrinsic factor (kas'ĕl) [William Bosworth Castle, U.S. physician and physiologist, 1897–1990] Intrinsic **factor**.

Castleman disease (kas'l-măn) [Benjamin Castleman, U.S. pathologist, 1906–1982] An occasionally aggressive illness marked by excessive growth of lymphoid tissue either localized in a single lymph node group or in multiple regions of the body. Although the cause is not precisely known, its associations with acquired immunodeficiency syndrome, Kaposi's sarcoma, and human herpes virus 8 infection have led some experts to propose that it has an infectious basis. Localized disease responds well to surgical resection. Widespread disease can sometimes be treated effectively with chemotherapy.

castor oil (kăs'tĕr oyl) SEE: under *oil*.

castrate (kăs'trāt) [L. *castrare*, to prune] **1.** To remove the testicles or ovaries. SEE: *spay*. **2.** To render an individual incapable of reproduction. **3.** To spay or neuter. **4.** To deprive an individual of sex hormones by medical means, esp. in the treatment of hormone-sensitive illnesses. **5.** One who has been rendered incapable of reproduction.

castrated (kăs'trāt-ĕd) Rendered incapable of reproduction by removal of the testicles or ovaries.

castration (kăs-trā'shŭn) **1.** Excision of the testicles or ovaries. **2.** Destruction or inactivation of the gonads.

   chemical c. The use of gonadotropin-releasing hormone agonists to inhibit the production of male hormones, e.g., in patients with prostate cancer.

   female c. Removal of the ovaries. SYN: *oophorectomy; spaying*.

   male c. Removal of the testes. SYN: *orchiectomy*.

   parasitic c. Destruction of the gonads by parasitic organisms early in life. It may result from direct infestation of the gonad or indirectly from effects of infestation in other parts of the body.

casualty (ka'zhĕl-tē) [L. *casualis*, accidental] **1.** An accident causing injury or death. **2.** A person injured or killed in an accident or preventable traumatic event. **3.** A military person captured, missing, injured, or killed.

casuistics (kăz-ū-ĭs'tĭks) [L. *casus*, chance] **1.** Analysis of clinical case records to establish the general characteristics of a disease. **2.** In moral questions, the determination of right and wrong by application of ethical principles to a particular case.

CAT SEE: *CT*.

cata-, cat-, cath-, kata-, kat- [Gr. *kata*, down, against, according to] Prefix meaning *down, downward, destructive,* or *against*.

catabolin (kă-tăb'ō-lĭn) Interleukin-1–beta.

catabolism (kă-tab'ŏ-lĭzm) [Gr. *katabolē*, a casting down + *-ism*] The destructive phase of metabolism. It includes all the processes in which complex substances are converted into simpler ones, often with the release of energy, and cell respiration for the formation of adenosine triphosphate (ATP) SYN: *destructive **metabolism***. SEE: *anabolism; metabolism*. **catabolic** (kat'ă-bol'ĭk), *adj*.

catabolite (kă-tăb'ō-līt) Any product of catabolism.

catacrotic (kăt''ă-krŏt'ĭk) [" + *krotos*, beat] Indicating the downstroke of pulse tracing interrupted by an upstroke.

catacrotism (kă-tăk'rō-tĭzm) [" + " + *-ismos*, condition] A pulse with one or more secondary expansions of the artery following the main beat.

catadicrotic (kăt''ă-dī-krŏt'ĭk) [" + *dis*, twice, + *krotos*, beat] Manifesting one or more secondary expansions of a pulse on the descending limb of the tracing.

catadicrotism (kăt''ă-dī-krō-tĭzm) [" + " + " + *-ismos*, condition] Two minor expansions following the main beat of an artery.

catagen (kăt'ă-jĕn) [" + *gennan*, to produce] The intermediate phase of the hair-growth cycle, between the growth or anagen stage and the resting or telogen phase.

catagenesis (kăt''ă-jĕn'ĕ-sĭs) [" + *genesis*, generation, birth] Retrogression or involution.

catalase (kăt'ă-lās) An enzyme present in almost all cells that catalyzes the decomposition of hydrogen peroxide to water and oxygen.

catalepsy (kăt'ă-lĕp''sē) [Gr. *kata*, down, + *lepsis*, seizure] A condition seen in some patients after parietal lobe strokes and some psychotic patients in which patients may appear to be in a trance or may assume rigidly held body postures. **cataleptic** (kăt''ă-lĕp'tĭk), *adj*.

cataleptoid (kăt''ă-lĕp'toyd) [" + " + *eidos*, form, shape] Resembling or simulating catalepsy.

catalysis (kă-tăl'ĭ-sĭs) [Gr. *katalysis*, dissolution] The speeding of a chemical reaction by a catalyst. **catalytic** (kăt-ă-lĭt'ĭk), *adj*.

catalyst (kăt'ă-lĭst) A substance that speeds the rate of a chemical reaction without being permanently altered in the reaction. Catalysts are effective in small quantities and are not used up in the reaction (i.e., they can be recovered unchanged). All enzymes are catalysts; the human body has thousands of enzymes, each specific for a particular reaction. For example, pepsin catalyzes the hydrolysis of protein; amylase catalyzes the hydrolysis of starch; transaminases catalyze the transfer of an amino group from one molecule to another. SYN: *catalyzer*.

homogeneous c. A catalyst that exists in the same phase as the chemicals it influences and the reactions it produces. SEE: *phase*.

catalytic RNA Ribozyme.

catalytic triad SEE: under *triad*.

catalyze (kăt′ă-līz) [Gr. *katalysis,* dissolution] To cause catalysis.

catalyzer (kăt′ă-lī-zĕr) A catalyst.

catamenia (kăt-ă-mē′nē-ă) [Gr. *kata,* according to, + *men,* month] Menstruation.

catamenial (-ăl), *adj.*

catamnesis (kăt-ăm-nē′sĭs) [Gr. *kata,* down, + *mneme,* memory] A patient's medical history after treatment; the follow-up history. SEE: *anamnesis.*

cataphasia (kăt-ă-fā′zē-ă) [″ + *phasis,* speech] A speech disorder in which a single word is uttered repeatedly.

cataphoresis (kăt″ă-fō-rē′sĭs) [Gr. *kata,* down, + *phoresis,* being carried] Transmission of electronegative ions or drugs into the body tissues or through a membrane by use of an electric current.

cataphoria (kăt″ă-fō′rē-ă) [″ + *pherein,* to bear] The tendency of visual axes to incline below the horizontal plane.

cataphoric (kăt″ă-for′ĭk) Pert. to cataphora or cataphoresis.

cataplectic (kăt-ă-plĕk′tĭk) [″ + *plexis,* stroke] Pert. to cataplexy.

cataplexy, cataplexia (kăt′ă-plĕks-ē, kăt-ă-plĕk′sē-ă) A sudden, brief loss of muscle control brought on by strong emotion or emotional response, such as a hearty laugh, excitement, surprise, or anger. Although this may cause collapse, the patient remains fully conscious. The episode lasts from a few seconds to as long as several minutes. The condition may be less severe with age. About 70% of patients with narcolepsy also have cataplexy.

cataract (kat′ă-rakt″) [L. *catar(r)acta,* fr Gr. *katarraktēs,* waterfall] An opacity of the lens of the eye, usually occurring as a result of aging, trauma, endocrine or metabolic disease, intraocular disease, or as a side effect of the use of tobacco or certain medications, e.g., steroids. Cataracts are the most common cause of blindness in adults. SEE: illus.; *visual field* for illus.

SYMPTOMS: At first, vision is distorted, particularly during night driving or in very bright light, causing light sensitivity (photophobia). As the cataract progresses, severe visual impairment develops.

PREVALENCE: Ninety percent of adults over 65 have cataracts.

TREATMENT: Removal of the lens is

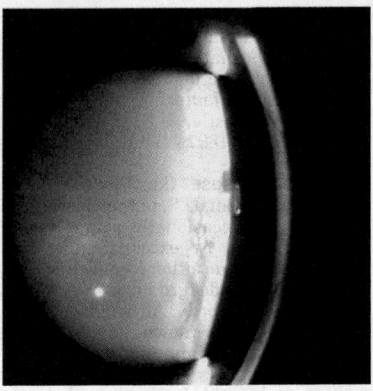

CATARACT
(Courtesy of Christine Chung, MD)

the only effective treatment. In the U.S. about a million cataract surgeries are performed annually, usually as an outpatient, same-day procedure. Typically, the lens and its anterior capsule are removed by extracapsular extraction or by phacoemulsification, leaving the posterior capsule of the lens in place, and a posterior chamber intraocular lens is inserted where the patient's own lens used to be. SEE: *extracapsular extraction; intraocular lens; phacoemulsification.*

PATIENT CARE: *Preoperative:* The procedure is explained to the patient. An antiseptic facial scrub is performed. Mydriatic and cycloplegic eye drops are instilled to dilate the pupil, followed by lidocaine jelly and betadine drops prior to surgery; osmotic diuretics may be given to reduce intraocular pressure. An intravenous access is initiated, and antibiotics, a sedative, short-acting general anesthetic, and a local anesthetic are provided.

Postoperative: The patient is instructed to wear a clear eyeshield if prescribed, and to call if experiencing pain, or loss of vision. Blurred vision the day of surgery is to be expected. Eye drops are to be placed as directed and the patient should not swim or strain himself. A postoperative checkup visit is scheduled for the day following surgery. Both patient and family are taught how to inspect the eye for redness or watering and to report these conditions as well as any photophobia or sudden visual changes; wash hands well and then to instill eye drops (antibiotic to prevent inflammation and steroids to reduce infection) as prescribed; and to maintain the eye patch and shield as prescribed by the surgeon. The patient should be taught to protect the eye from bright sunlight or glare by wearing dark glasses. The patient should not swim or strain himself or herself. SEE: *Nursing Diagnoses Appendix.*

cortical c. A cataract that develops in the cortex of the lens. It has a spiky or spoked appearance on physical examination of the eye.

hypermature c. A cataract in which the lens solidifies and shrinks. This stage follows the mature stage.

immature c. An early cataract, too poorly developed to require therapy.

lenticular c. A cataract occurring in the lens.

mature c. Sufficiently dense changes in the anterior cortex of the lens to prevent the examiner from viewing the posterior portion of the lens and the posterior portion of the eye; that is, the entire lens is opaque and ophthalmoscopic examination of the eye past the lens is not possible.

morgagnian c. SEE: *Morgagni cataract.*

nuclear c., nuclear sclerotic c. A cataract in which the central portion of the lens is opacified.

posterior cortical c. Posterior subcapsular **c.**

posterior subcortical c. Posterior subcapsular **c.**

posterior subcapsular c. ABBR: PSC. A cataract between the posterior capsule and cortex. It is more common in younger patients, diabetics, and patients who use steroids. It tends to diminish near vision before it affects distance vision. SYN: *posterior subcortical c.; posterior cortical c.*

radiation c. A cataract caused by exposure to radiation, esp. from sunlight.

senile c. A cataract occurring in an older person.

cataractogenic (kăt″ă-răk″tō-jĕn′ĭk) [L. *cataracta,* waterfall, + Gr. *gennan,* to produce] Causing or forming cataracts.

catarrh (kă-tăr′) [Gr. *katarrhein,* to flow down] Term formerly applied to inflammation of mucous membranes, esp. of the head and throat. **catarrhal** (-ăl), *adj.*

dry c. An obsolete term for a nonproductive cough.

vernal c. Allergic conjunctivitis.

catastrophizing (kă-tăs′trō-fī-zĭng) Exaggerated focus on perceived failures in one's past, present, or future; associated with mood disorders, especially depression, and chronic pain.

catatonia (kăt-ă-tō′nē-ă) [″ + *tonos,* tension] **1.** A phase of schizophrenia in which the patient is unresponsive, marked by the tendency to assume and remain in a fixed posture and the inability to move or talk. **2.** Stupor. **catatonic** (-tŏn′ĭk), *adj.*

catatricrotic (kăt″ă-trī-krŏt′ĭk) [″ + *treis,* three, + *krotos,* beat] Manifesting a third impulse in the descending stroke of the sphygmogram of the pulse.

catatricrotism (kăt″ă-trī′krō-tĭzm) A condition in which the pulse shows a third impulse in the descending stroke of a pulse tracing.

catatropia (kăt″ă-trō′pē-ă) [″ + *tropos,* turning] A condition in which both eyes are turned downward.

catcher's mask cranioplasty (kach′ĕrz mask) A surgical technique for reconstructing a traumatically injured skull in which ribs are used as autografts to provide a scaffolding over the injury and parts of the calvarium are mobilized to smooth out the intercostal spaces. The structure provided by the ribs resembles the mask worn by catchers behind home plate.

catchment area A geographical area defining the portion of a population served by a designated medical facility.

catchweed (kach′wēd″) Galium aparine.

cat's claw [Translation of Sp. *uña de gato* or Portuguese *unha de gato*] **Uncaria** tomentosa.

cat-cry syndrome SEE: *syndrome, cri du chat.*

catecholamine (kăt″ĕ-kōl′ă-mēn) One of many biologically active amines, including metanephrine, dopamine, epinephrine, and norepinephrine, derived from the amino acid tyrosine. They have a marked effect on the nervous and cardiovascular systems, metabolic rate, temperature, and smooth muscle.

Category A Agents (of bioterrorism) Those infectious agents that would produce the worst casualties if they were to be released in a biological attack on a population. The Category A agents include: anthrax, botulism, Ebola virus, Lassa virus, plague, smallpox, and tularemia.

category test One of the neuropsychological tests of abstract thinking; it assesses a patient's ability to learn strategies for sorting objects into related groups.

catelectrotonus (kăt″ē-lĕk-trŏt′ō-nŭs) [″ + *elektron,* amber, + *tonos,* tension] The increased excitability produced in a nerve or muscle in the region near the cathode during the passage of an electric current.

catenating (kăt′ĕn-āt″ĭng) [L. *catena,* chain] **1.** Pert. to a disease that is linked with another. **2.** Forming a series of symptoms.

catenation (kăt″ĕn-ā′shŭn″) Concatenation.

catenoid (kăt′ĕ-noyd) [″ + Gr. *eidos,* form, shape] Chainlike; pert. to protozoan colonies whose individuals are joined end to end.

catgut (kăt′gŭt″) Sheep intestine (primarily the submucosal layer) processed for use as an absorbable ligature.

chromic c. Catgut treated with chromium trioxide. This enhances the strength of the suture material and delays its absorption.

catharsis (kă-thar′sĭs) [Gr. *katharsis*, a purifying, cleansing] **1.** Purgative action upon the bowels. **2.** The Freudian method of freeing the mind by recalling from the patient's memory the events or experiences that were the original causes of a psychoneurosis. SEE: *abreaction*.

cathartic (kă-thart′ik) [Gr. *kathartikos*, pert. to catharsis, purifying, cleansing] **1.** Pert. to or causing evacuation of the bowel. **2.** An agent that causes evacuation of the bowel, e.g., cascara sagrada, castor oil.

   saline c. A salt, such as epsom salt, used to produce evacuation of the bowel. SEE: *purgative*.

cathepsins (kă-thĕp′sĭns) A group of protein-destroying, lysosomal enzymes found in nearly every cell in the body. Many of these enzymes are released by cancer cells in excessive amounts, a factor that contributes to the invasiveness of tumors into neighboring tissues. The detection of cathepsins in tumors is strongly correlated with metastasis.

catheter (kath′ĕt-ĕr) [Gr. *kathetēr*, a tube for insertion] A tube passed into the body for evacuating or injecting fluids. It may be made of elastic, elastic web, rubber, glass, metal, or plastic. SEE: illus.

   antimicrobial-impregnated central c. An intravenous catheter saturated with antibiotics, designed to decrease the likelihood of colonization or infection of indwelling infusion lines.

   arterial c. A catheter inserted into an artery to measure pressure, remove blood, inject medication or radiographic contrast media, or perform an interventional radiological procedure.

   balloon c. A multi-lumened catheter surrounded by a balloon. The balloon may be expanded by injecting air, saline, or contrast medium.

   Bozeman-Fritsch c. SEE: *Bozeman-Fritsch catheter*.

   Broviac catheter Broviac catheter.

   cardiac c. A long, fine catheter specially designed for passage through the lumen of a blood vessel into the arteries or chambers of the heart. SEE: *cardiac catheterization*.

   central c. A catheter inserted into a central vein or artery for diagnostic or therapeutic purposes.

   central venous c. A catheter inserted into the superior vena cava to permit intermittent or continuous monitoring of central venous pressure, to administer fluids, medications or nutrition, or to facilitate obtaining blood samples for chemical analysis. SEE: illus.

   PATIENT CARE: Health care professionals must use caution to prevent life-threatening complications when inserting and maintaining a central line. The subclavian approach to the placement of a central line is preferred, because femoral placements may be complicated by deep venous thrombosis, and internal jugular sites carry an increased risk of infection. Sterile technique is a requirement during insertion. The skin should be prepared with chlorhexidine-gluconate (2%) or povidone-iodine. Ultrasound guidance improves the likelihood

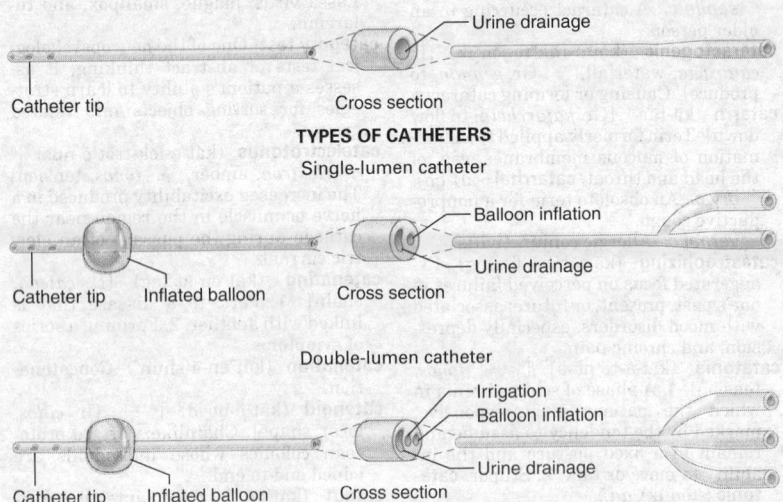

Urine drainage

Catheter tip   Cross section

TYPES OF CATHETERS

Single-lumen catheter

Balloon inflation

Urine drainage

Catheter tip   Inflated balloon   Cross section

Double-lumen catheter

Irrigation
Balloon inflation
Urine drainage

Catheter tip   Inflated balloon   Cross section

Triple-lumen catheter

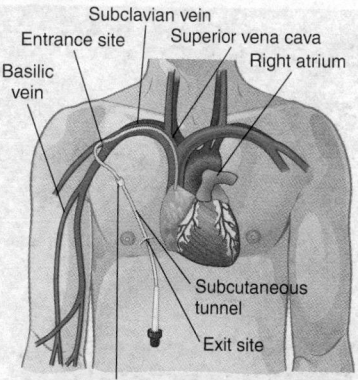

Subclavian vein
Entrance site — Superior vena cava
Basilic vein — Right atrium
Subcutaneous tunnel
Exit site
Dacron cuff

CENTRAL VENOUS CATHETER

A tunneled central venous catheter is inserted through subcutaneous tissue in the chest wall into the jugular or subclavian vein

of entering the desired vein without injury to neighboring structures. With or without radiological guidance, the best results are obtained by practitioners who perform the procedure frequently. After the catheter is inserted, it should be firmly sewn to the skin to keep it from migrating in and out of the insertion site. An antibiotic impregnated patch covered by a sterile dressing should be placed at the insertion site. The catheter should be manipulated as infrequently as possible during its use. Dressing changes are carried out using sterile technique. IV tubing and solutions and injection caps also should be changed as required by the agency's protocol. Health care professionals are responsible for preventing, assessing for, and managing central venous therapy complications (e.g., air embolism; cardiac tamponade; chylothorax, hemothorax, hydrothorax, or pneumothorax; local and systemic infections; and thrombosis). Documentation should include preprocedure and postprocedure physical assessment of the patient, catheter type and size, insertion site location, x-ray confirmation of the placement, catheter insertion distance (in centimeters), and the patient's tolerance of the procedure. Maintenance care procedures also should be fully documented. The site should be carefully inspected for inflammation, and any drainage should be cultured. When catheter-related infections are suspected, the catheter tip provides valuable information about infection sources in cases of sepsis. The tip should be cut off with sterile scissors and dropped directly into a sterile specimen container.

condom c. A specially designed condom that includes a collection tube attached to the distal end. The tubing carries urine to a collecting bag. Its use prevents men with urinary incontinence from soiling clothes or bed linens.

⚠ Continual use of this device may excoriate the skin of the penis.

double-channel c. A catheter providing for inflow and outflow.

elbowed c. Prostatic **c.**

eustachian c. A catheter passed into the eustachian tube through the nasal passages to ventilate the middle ear.

female c. A catheter about 5 in (12.7 cm) long, used to pass into a woman's bladder.

Foley c. SEE: *Foley catheter.*

glide c. A catheter inserted into the ureter to remove impacted kidney stones. A lubricated wire is advanced past the obstructing stone. The glide catheter is mounted on the wire, moved toward the kidney beyond the stone, and used to snare and retrieve the stone.

guide c. A catheter that makes it easier to enter that vessel with other devices or instruments. Guide catheters are used to facilitate the placement of lasers, stents, and balloons for angioplasty.

heparin-bonded c. A pulmonary artery catheter with a heparin coating to reduce the risk of thrombus formation.

Hickman c. SEE: *Hickman catheter.*

impregnated c. A catheter coated with a medication to prevent complications of prolonged insertion in the body. Commonly used coatings include antibiotics and antiseptics.

indwelling c. Any catheter that is allowed to remain in place in a vein, artery, or body cavity.

indwelling pleural c. Pleural **c.**

intra-aortic c. SEE: *intra-aortic balloon counterpulsation.*

intrauterine pressure c. ABBR: IUPC. A catheter inserted into the uterus of a woman during labor, when labor is protracted, arrested, or when the force of uterine contractions are difficult to monitor indirectly.

intravenous c. A catheter inserted into a vein to administer fluids or medications or to measure pressure.

Karman c. SEE: *Karman catheter.*

male c. A catheter 12 to 13 in (30.5 to 33 cm) long, used to pass into a man's bladder.

pacing c. A catheter inserted most commonly into the right side of the heart via the brachial, femoral, internal jugular, or subclavian vein for temporary pacing of the heart. The pacing wires or leads provide the electrical stimulus from an external source (a pulse generator).

peripherally inserted central venous c. ABBR: PICC, PICC line. A soft, flexible central venous catheter, inserted in a vein in the arm and advanced until the tip is positioned in the axillary, subclavian, or brachiocephalic vein. It may also be advanced into the superior vena cava. A PICC is commonly used for prolonged antibiotic therapy, total parenteral nutrition, continuous opioid infusion, or intermittent chemotherapy.

pharyngeal suction c. A rigid catheter used to suction the pharynx during direct visualization. SYN: *Yankauer suction c.*

pleural c. A small chest catheter inserted between the parietal and visceral pleura and used to drain recurrent pleural effusions, e.g., in patients with cancer. SYN: *indwelling pleural c.*

presternal c. A catheter used for peritoneal dialysis that exits the chest instead of the lower abdomen. It is made of two silicone rubber tubes joined at the implantation site by a titanium connector that links its abdominal and presternal parts.

prostatic c. A catheter, 15 to 16 in (38 to 40.6 cm) long, with a short elbowed tip designed to pass prostatic obstruction. SYN: *elbowed c.*

pulmonary artery c. A catheter inserted into the pulmonary artery to measure pulmonary artery pressures, pulmonary capillary wedge pressure, and, indirectly, left atrial pressure and cardiac output.

self-retaining c. A bladder catheter designed to remain in place (e.g., a Foley catheter).

suprapubic c. A catheter that is used to drain urine percutaneously from the urinary bladder. It permits direct drainage through the lower abdominal wall. Suprapubic urinary diversion is typically used to temporarily decompress the bladder but not exclusively used as a temporary means of decompressing the bladder when the urethra is obstructed, e.g., in children with congenital deformities of the penis or urethra, or in adults with bladder outlet obstruction. When it is used for this purpose, it is considered a bridge before definitive surgery. SEE: *suprapubic aspiration of urine;* illus.

PATIENT CARE: The nurse observes for hemorrhage or prolonged hematuria and signs of local or systemic infection. Aseptic technique is used during dressing or equipment changes. Bladder irrigation is performed as prescribed. Medications, e.g., analgesics, antispasmodics, and bowel stimulants, are administered as prescribed. The patient's ability to micturate is evaluated. Intake and output are monitored and recorded.

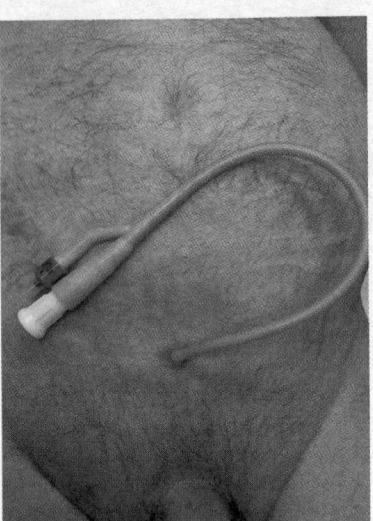

SUPRAPUBIC CATHETER

used to drain urine

Fluids are forced unless otherwise restricted to ensure passage of dilute urine.

Swan-Ganz c. SEE: *Swan-Ganz catheter.*

Tenckhoff peritoneal c. SEE: *Tenckhoff peritoneal catheter.*

triple-lumen c. ABBR: TLC. A central catheter containing three separate channels or passageways.

tunneled central venous c. An intravenous catheter inserted into the subclavian or internal jugular vein and then advanced into the right atrium or superior vena cava. The proximal end is tunneled subcutaneously from the insertion site and brought out through the skin at an exit site below the nipple line. Commonly used tunneled catheters include the Hickman and Broviac catheters.

umbilical vein c. A catheter placed in the umbilical vein of an infant to facilitate administration of medicines parenterally or to do an exchange transfusion.

vertebrated c. A catheter in sections to be fitted together so that it is flexible.

winged c. A catheter with little flaps at each side of the beak to help retain it in the bladder.

Word c. A rubber catheter with an inflatable balloon at its end, used to treat cysts or abscesses, e.g., Bartholin gland cysts in the vulva.

Yankauer suction c. SEE: *Yankauer suction catheter.*

catheter angiography SEE: under *angiography.*

catheterization   (kăth″ĕ-tĕr-ĭ-zā′shŭn)

[Gr. *katheterismos*] Use or passage of a catheter.

cardiac c. Percutaneous intravascular insertion of a catheter into the cardiac ventricles, coronary arteries, or great vessels for diagnosis, assessment of abnormalities, interventional treatment, and evaluation of the effects of pathology on the heart and great vessels. Diagnostic tests that can be performed with cardiac catheterization include:

1. Assessments of coronary artery anatomy and patency;
2. Estimates of cardiac ejection fraction and wall motion;
3. Measurements of intracardiac pressures;
4. Evaluations of the cardiac valves;
5. Biopsies of the endomyocardium.

PATIENT CARE: *Precatheterization:* The nurse prepares the patient physically and emotionally by explaining the procedure and expected sensations. The patient's vital signs, including the presence and intensity of peripheral pulses, are assessed to establish a baseline measure. Cardiac monitoring leads are applied and an intravenous infusion initiated. Anxiety and activity levels are documented, as well as the presence and pattern of any chest pain. Any known allergies, particularly to shellfish or iodine (suggestive of sensitivity to radiopaque dye), are also documented, and the cardiologist is alerted to these allergies or any changes in the patient's condition. The groin is cleansed and hair is removed locally, and the patient is informed that an oral or intravenous mild sedative (rather than general anesthesia) will probably be given before or during the procedure, so that he or she is able to cough and breathe deeply as instructed during testing. A radiopaque contrast medium is injected into the arteries and nitroglycerin may be administered to aid visualization. After the injection, the patient may feel light-headed, warm, or nauseated for a few moments. The patient will have to lie on the back for several hours after the procedure and should report chest pain immediately both during and after the procedure.

During catheterization: Support personnel assist with the procedure according to protocol by monitoring cardiac pressures and rhythm and the results of hemodynamic studies. Patient comfort and safety are assured; and changes in emotional status, level of consciousness, and verbal and nonverbal responses are assessed to determine the patient's response to the procedure and need for reassurance or medication to prevent vasovagal reactions or coronary artery spasm. Any complications, such as cardiac arrhythmias or allergic reaction to the contrast medium, are also evaluated and reported.

Postcatheterization: The nurse provides emotional support to the patient and answers questions. Cardiac rhythm and vital signs (including apical pulse and temperature) are monitored until stable according to protocol (usually every 15 min for the first 1 to 2 hr) or more frequently as the patient's condition requires. The blood pressure should not be checked in any limb used for catheter insertion. The dressing is inspected frequently for signs of bleeding, and the patient is instructed to report any increase in dressing tightness (which may indicate hematoma formation). Pressure is applied over the entry site and the extremity is maintained in extension according to protocol. The patient is cautioned to avoid flexion or hyperextension of the affected limb for 12 to 24 hr depending on protocol.

Neurovascular status of the involved extremity distal to the insertion site is monitored for changes, which may indicate arterial thrombosis (the most frequent complication), embolus, or another complication requiring immediate attention. The head of the bed is elevated no more than 30 degrees, and the patient is confined to bedrest. The patient may complain of urinary urgency immediately after the procedure. Fluids are given to flush out the dense radiopaque contrast medium, and urine output is monitored, esp. in patients with impaired renal function. The patient is assessed for complications such as pericardial tamponade, myocardial infarction, pulmonary embolism, stroke, congestive heart failure, cardiac dysrhythmia, infection, and thrombophlebitis. The patient's preoperative medication regimen is resumed as prescribed (or revised).

The patient will need to be driven home, and a responsible adult should be in attendance until the next morning. Both patient and family are provided with written discharge instructions explaining the need to report any of the following symptoms to the physician: bleeding or swelling at the entry site; increased tenderness; redness; drainage or pain at the entry site; fever; and any changes in color, temperature, or sensation in the involved extremity. The patient may take acetaminophen or other nonaspirin analgesic every 3 to 4 hr as needed for pain. The entry site should be covered with an adhesive bandage for 24 hr or until sutures, if present, are removed (usually within 6 days). The patient usually is permitted to shower the day after the procedure and to take a tub bath 48 hr after the procedure (if no sutures are present).

Strenuous activity should be avoided for 24 hr after the procedure.

urinary bladder c. Introduction of a drainage tube through the urethra into the bladder to withdraw urine. Catheterization of the bladder may be performed when sterile urinary specimens are needed for laboratory analysis, when precise monitoring of urinary output is required (e.g., in the critical care unit), or when patients have chronic voiding difficulties.

Patients with chronic difficulty urinating sometimes are given indwelling urinary catheters; as an alternative, they may be given bladder training instruction, or assistance with toileting. When this is ineffective they may be instructed in the technique of clean, intermittent self-catheterization. To do this, they need to learn about their urethral anatomy and about methods they can use to avoid introducing microorganisms into the urinary bladder (handwashing, periurethral and catheter cleansing, and catheter storage). Most patients need to catheterize themselves four or five times daily. Carefully performed intermittent catheterization is less likely to cause urinary tract infection than is chronic indwelling urinary catheterization. Individuals who have difficulty retaining urine (urinary incontinence) should receive bladder training and assistance in toileting at specific intervals rather than having an indwelling urinary catheter. SEE: illus.

PATIENT CARE: After the procedure and expected sensations are explained to the patient, the proper equipment is assembled, sterile gloves are donned, a sterile field created, and the indwelling catheter is connected to a closed drainage bag, if not preconnected. The balloon at the tip of this catheter is inflated (and deflated) before its insertion to make sure that it will stay in place after

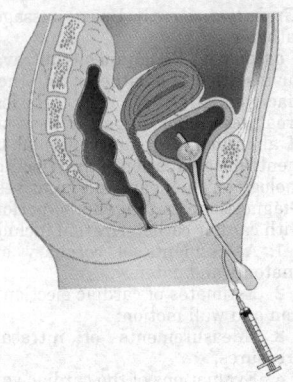

Female

entering the bladder. The patient is properly positioned and draped (see instructions for female and male patients); the urethral orifice is prepared with antiseptic solution and the catheter is gently inserted. Sterile technique is maintained throughout these procedures. The indwelling catheter is advanced beyond the point where urinary flow begins, and the balloon inflated with the specified amount of sterile water, then the catheter is permitted to slip back slightly. The drainage tube is secured to the patient's leg, then looped on the bed, and the tubing leading to the collection bag is straightened to facilitate gravity drainage. The collection bag is suspended above the floor. The drainage tube is prevented from touching a surface when the collection bag is emptied; the spout is wiped with an alcohol swab before being refastened to the bag. The meatal area should be cleansed daily and inspected for inflammation. The patient's ability to void and remain continent is periodically evaluated and catheterization is discontinued when possible. Results of the procedure, including the character and volume of urine drained and the patient's response, are observed and documented. The patient should be draped to limit embarrassment and provided warmth and privacy, exposing only the genitalia area.

Female: The patient should be in the dorsal recumbent position on a firm mattress or examining table to enhance visualization of the urinary meatus. Alternately, the lithotomy position, with buttocks at the edge of the examining table and feet in stirrups, may be used. For female patients with difficulties involving hip and knee movements, the Sims' or left lateral position may be more comfortable and allow for better visualization. Pillows may be placed un-

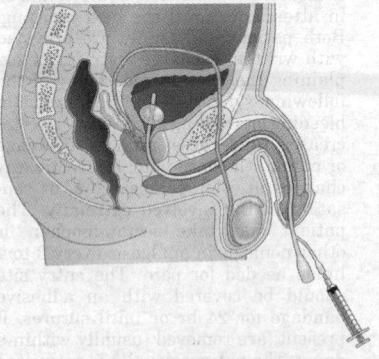

**CATHETERIZATION OF URINARY
BLADDER**

Male

der the head and shoulders to relax the abdominal muscles.

Male: The patient should be in a supine position with legs extended. Lubricant is applied to the catheter or may be instilled directly into the urethra with a prefilled syringe to facilitate passage of the tube. After the procedure, care should be taken to return the male patient's prepuce to its normal position to prevent any subsequent swelling.

Unless otherwise restricted, oral intake should be encouraged to maintain adequate urine output, and urine inspected for cloudiness and changes in color or odor, any of which indicate the need for urine culture to test for infection. When removing the indwelling catheter, the patient should be draped, the genitalia cleansed, and the balloon fully deflated using a syringe. The catheter is then gently rotated to ensure that it is not adhering to urogenital tissue, and should easily slip out into the gloved hand. Pulling the glove off over the catheter tip, then wrapping glove and catheter in a waterproof wrapper or bag, provides "double bagging" for disposal.

A high rate of morbidity and mortality is associated with long-term use of indwelling urinary catheters (7 days or longer). Indwelling urinary catheters should be used only for very brief periods or specific concerns, such as urinary retention that cannot be managed with other methods, or palliative care. Most indwelling catheters are made of latex. Silicone catheters should be used in patients with latex allergies. Silver-coated urinary catheters may result in fewer infections than silicone, silicone-coated, or the common hydrogel-coated latex catheters. Experts advocate using the smallest size catheter effective for the patient, usually 14 or 16 French, with a 5-mL balloon. Catheters 18 French or larger create discomfort, increase the risk of blocking the periurethral glands, and can lead to urinary tract infection and urethral irritation and erosion. For long-term use, inflate a 5-mL balloon with 10 mL of water, as underinflation can lead to balloon distortion and catheter deflection. The 30-mL balloon is useful for a short time following genitourinary surgery to decrease bleeding and prevent dislodgement. Urethral catheter tubing should be secured to prevent tension on the bladder neck and accidental dislodgement. For males, securing the tubing restraint on the abdomen works best; for females, the anterior medial thigh. The common practice of changing catheters monthly is based on Medicare and Medicaid reimbursement structures; however, data on the frequency for change are lacking. Thus change is probably best individualized

to the patients or carried out following manufacturer's recommendations for the various types of catheters. Drainage bags should be emptied every 4 to 6 hr (minimum) to avoid migration of bacteria to the catheter lumen. If a patient develops symptoms of a urinary tract infection (fever, chills, malodorous or cloudy urine, hematuria, and/or suprapubic pain), antibiotic therapy should be instituted and a sample of urine sent for culture. Prophylactic antibiotics are not recommended with indwelling urinary catheterization, as they lead to drug-resistant infectious agents.

catheterize (kăth'ĕ-tĕr-īz) To pass or introduce a catheter into a part of the body, e.g., the urinary bladder.

catheter-related bloodstream infection An infection caused by a bacterium or fungus that enters the blood via a device inserted into it. *Staphylococcus aureus, Candida species, Enterococci,* and *Pseudomonas* species are common causes of bacteremia and sepsis in patients with invasive catheters.

cathexis (kă-thĕk'sĭs) [Gr. *kathexis,* retention] The emotional or mental energy used in concentrating on an object or idea.

cathode (kăth'ōd) [Gr. *kathodos,* a way down] ABBR: ca. **1.** The negative electrode from which electrons are emitted; the opposite of the anode or positive pole. **2.** In a vacuum tube, the electrode that serves as the source of the electron stream.

cathode ray tube A vacuum tube with a thin window at the end opposite the cathode to allow the cathode rays (electron beams) to pass outside. More generally, any discharge tube in which the vacuum is fairly high. Cathode ray tubes were commonly used in the past to display radiologic images but have been replaced with flat screen monitors for this and other applications.

cathodic (kă-thŏd'ĭk) **1.** Pert. to a cathode. **2.** Proceeding outwardly or efferently as applied to a nerve impulse.

cation (kat'ī"ŏn) [*cata-* + Gr. *iōn,* going] An ion with a positive electric charge. It is attracted by and travels to the cathode. SEE: *anion; electrolyte; ion.* **cationic** (kat"ī"on'ik), *adj.*

catmab (kat'mab") [Abbr. for *cat(alytic) m(onoclonal) a(nti)b(ody)*] Abzyme.

catoptrophobia (kă-tŏp"tră-fō'bē-ă) [Gr. *katoptron,* mirror + "] A morbid fear of mirrors or of breaking them.

CAT scan SEE: under *scan.*

cat scratch disease A febrile disease characterized by lymphadenitis and, in some cases, conjunctivitis, uveitis, endocarditis, osteomyelitis, or central nervous system infections, transmitted to people by cats, esp. kittens. Fever, malaise, headache, and anorexia accompany the lymphadenopathy. The causative organism is *Bartonella henselae* (formerly *Rochalimaea*), which in cats usually produces asymptomatic infection. Diagnosis is based on clinical findings, a history of contact with cats, and positive results from a cat scratch antigen skin test. Antibiotics are not recommended in mild disease, but aminoglycosides, quinolones, or macrolides may be indicated for severe, disseminated disease. SEE: *bacillary angiomatosis; Bartonella; Nursing Diagnoses Appendix.*

PATIENT CARE: The patient is assessed for related symptoms and a history of cat contact. Prescribed cat scratch antigen skin testing is explained and administered. The patient is taught how to use hot compresses and handle and dispose of contaminated dressings. He is also advised to report headache, sore throat, stiff neck, and continuing fever (esp. if accompanied by chills or night sweats) because these may be indicators of rare complications. The patient is referred for further immune system evaluation if immunodeficiency is suspected because immunocompromise puts the patient at high risk for a disseminated form of this disease.

cat unit The amount of drug per kilogram of body weight just sufficient to kill a cat when injected intravenously slowly and continuously.

Caucasian (kaw'kā'zhĕn) Pert. unscientifically to individuals of European or Northern African descent. **caucasoid,** *adj.*

caud-, caudo- [L. *cauda,* tail] Prefixes meaning *tail.*

cauda (kowd'ă, kod', kow'dī", ko'dē") pl. **caudae** [L. *cauda,* tail] A tail or tail-like structure.

    c. epididymidis The inferior portion of the epididymis that is continuous with the ductus deferens.

    c. equina The terminal portion of the spinal cord and the spinal nerves below the first lumbar nerve.

    c. striati A tail-like posterior extremity of the corpus striatum.

caudad (kaw'dăd) [L. *cauda,* tail, + *ad,* toward] Toward the tail; in a posterior direction.

cauda equina syndrome (ek-wē'nă, ē-kwī'nă) Injury to or compression of the nerve roots of the spinal cord below the level of the conus medullaris (the first lumbar nerve). Hallmarks of the syndrome are loss of control of bowel or bladder function, sexual dysfunction, and paraplegia. Causes of the syndrome include compression on the spinal cord by tumors, infections, and herniated disks, or stenosis of the spinal canal.

caudal (kod'ăl) [L. *caudalis* fr. L. *cauda,* tail] **1.** Pert. to a cauda (tail) or tail-like

structure. **2.** Toward the tail end of the organism.

caudate (kaw'dāt) [L. *caudatus*] Possessing a tail.

caul (kawl) [O.Fr. *cale,* a small cap] Membranes or portions of the amnion covering the head of the fetus at birth.

Caulobacter crescentus (kawl-ŏ-băk'tĕr krĕ-sĕn'tŭs) A single-celled slightly curved bacterium that thrives in watery environments. It exists in two forms: a flagellated swarmer cell, and a stalked cell.

Caulophyllum thalictroides (kol"ŏ-fil'ŭm) SEE: *blue cohosh.*

causalgia (kaw-săl'jē-ă) [" + *algos,* pain] Intense burning pain accompanied by trophic skin changes, due to injury of nerve fibers. SYN: *complex regional pain syndrome, type 2.*

causal treatment Treatment directed toward removal of the cause of the disease.

cause (kawz) [L. *causa*] Something that brings about a particular condition, result, or effect.

    antecedent c. An event or condition that predisposes to a disease or condition.

    determining c. The final event or condition that brings about a disease or condition.

    necessary and sufficient c. In logic, an antecedent condition that is wholly and solely capable of producing an effect.

    predisposing c. Something that favors the development of a disease or condition.

    proximate c. An event that immediately precedes another and is felt to be responsible for its occurrence.

    remote c. An event or condition that is not immediate in its effect but predisposes to the development of a disease or condition.

    ultimate c. The remote event or condition that initiated a train of events resulting in the development of a disease or condition.

caustic (kaw'stĭk) [Gr. *kaustikos,* capable of burning] **1.** Corrosive and burning; destructive to living tissue. **2.** An agent, particularly an alkali, that destroys living tissue (e.g., silver nitrate, potassium hydroxide, nitric acid). SEE: *poisoning; Poisons and Poisoning Appendix.*

cauter-, cautero- [L. fr. Gr. *kautēr,* branding iron] Prefixes meaning *heat or burn.*

cauterant (kaw'tĕr-ănt) [Gr. *kauter,* a burner] **1.** Cauterizing. **2.** A cauterizing agent.

cauterization (kaw"tĕr-ī-zā'shŭn) [Gr. *kauteriazein,* to burn] Destruction of tissue with, e.g., a caustic chemical electric current, a frozen probe, a hot iron, a laser, or ultrasound.

chemical c. Cauterization by the use of chemical agents, esp. caustic substances.

electrical c. Electrocautery.

cauterize (kaw′tĕr-īz) To burn with a cautery, or a cauterizing agent, device, or technique.

cautery (kot′ĕ-rē) [L. *cauterium*, fr Gr. *kautērion*, branding iron] **1.** A device used to destroy tissue by electricity, freezing, heat, laser, ultrasound energy, or corrosive chemicals. It is used in potentially infected wounds and to destroy excess granulation tissue. Thermocautery consists of a red-hot or white-hot object, usually a piece of wire or pointed metallic instrument, heated in a flame or with electricity (electrocautery, galvanocautery). **2.** The act or effect of cauterizing.

actual c. Cauterization caused by heat or chemical reaction.

CAUTI *catheter-associated urinary tract infection.*

cava (kā′vă) The vena cava.

caval (kā′văl) Pert. to the vena cava.

caveola (kăv-ē-ō′lă) *pl.* **caveolae** A small pit or depression formed on the cell surface during pinocytosis.

cavernitis (kăv″ĕr-nī′tĭs) [L. *caverna*, hollow, + Gr. *itis*, inflammation] Inflammation of the corpus cavernosum of the penis.

cavernoma (kăv″ĕr-nō′mă) [″ + Gr. *oma*, tumor] A cavernous angioma. SEE: *angioma; hemangioma.*

cavernositis (kăv″ĕr-nō-sī′tĭs) [″ + Gr. *itis*, inflammation] Inflammation of the corpus cavernosum.

cavernosography (kă″vĕr-nō-sŏg′ră-fē) [Fr. *(corpus) cavernosum* + Gr. *graphos*, drawn, written] Radiological imaging of the corpus cavernosum.

cavernostomy (kav-ĕr-nos′tŏ-mē) [L. *caverna*, a hollow, cavern + *-stomy*]] The surgical opening of a hollow body part or cavity.

cavernous (kăv′ĕr-nŭs) [L. *caverna*, a hollow] Containing hollow spaces.

cavernous sinus syndrome The clinical consequences of a blood clot in the sinus cavernosus. Symptoms commonly include headache, unilateral or bilateral facial pain, ocular paralysis, facial edema, and retinal edema. SEE: *sinus cavernosus.*

cavitary (kăv′ĭ-tā″rē) Pert. to a cavity.

cavitation (kăv″ĭ-tā′shŭn″) [L. *cavitas*, hollow] **1.** Normal formation of a cavity, as in the formation of the amnion in human development. **2.** Pathological formation of a cavity, as in the development of cavities in lung tissue in pulmonary tuberculosis or a hole in the essential part of an organ (the parenchyma) caused by cancer or infection. **3.** The formation of gaseous bubbles in body fluids during exposure to ultra-sonic energy; known as acoustic cavitation.

cavitis (kā-vī′tĭs) [″ + Gr. *itis*, inflammation] Inflammation of a vena cava.

cavity (kăv′ĭt-ē) [L. *cavitas*, hollow] A hollow space, such as a body organ or the hole in a tooth produced by caries.

abdominal c. The ventral cavity between the diaphragm and pelvis, containing the abdominal organs. It is lined with a serous membrane, the peritoneum, and contains the following organs: stomach with the lower portion of the esophagus, small and large intestines (except sigmoid colon and rectum), liver, gallbladder, spleen, pancreas, adrenal glands, kidneys, and ureters. It is continuous with the pelvic cavity; the two constitute the abdominopelvic cavity. SEE: *abdomen; abdominal quadrants* for illus.

alveolar c. A tooth socket.

articular c. The synovial cavity of a joint.

body c. **1.** Any hollow space within the body. SEE: illus. **2.** A hidden body space that is accessible from the outside, e.g., rectum or vagina. Referred to in "body cavity search for contraband". **3.** Derivatives of the coelom, i.e., the pericardial, peritoneal, and plural sacs. SEE: *coelom.*

buccal c. Oral cavity.

cotyloid c. Acetabulum.

cranial c. The cavity of the skull, which contains the brain.

dental c. Caries.

dorsal c. The body cavity composed of the cranial and spinal cavities. SEE: *body c.* for illus.

glenoid c. Glenoid fossa (2).

joint c. The articular cavity or space enclosed by the synovial membrane and articular cartilages. It contains synovial fluid. SYN: *joint space.*

laryngeal c. The hollow inside the larynx from its inlet at the laryngopharynx to the beginning of the trachea. It has three segments (from top to bottom): vestibule of the larynx, ventricle of the larynx, infraglottic cavity.

lesser peritoneal c. Omental bursa.

medullary c. The marrow-filled space in a bone.

nasal c. One of two cavities between the floor of the cranium and the roof of the mouth, opening to the nose anteriorly and the nasopharynx posteriorly. Its lining of ciliated epithelium warms and moistens inhaled air, and traps dust and pathogens on mucus that are then swept toward the pharynx. The nasal septum (ethmoid and vomer) separates the nasal cavities, and the olfactory receptors are in the upper part of each cavity. The paranasal sinuses (frontal, maxillary, sphenoidal, and ethmoidal) open into the meatus below the conchae. The orifices of the frontal, an-

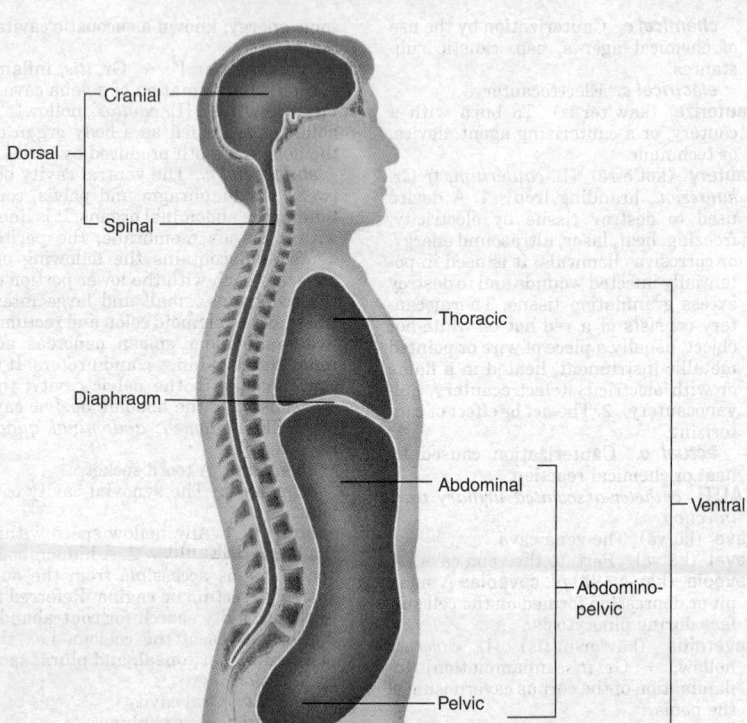

CAVITIES OF THE BODY

terior ethmoidal, and maxillary sinuses are in the middle meatus. The orifices of the posterior ethmoidal and sphenoidal sinuses are in the superior meatus. The nasal mucosa is highly vascular; blood is supplied by the maxillary arteries from the external carotid arteries and by the ethmoidal arteries from the internal carotid arteries. SEE: illus.

oral c. The space inside the teeth and gums that is filled by the tongue when the mouth is closed and relaxed. SYN: *buccal c.*

pelvic c. The bony hollow formed by the innominate bones, the sacrum, and the coccyx. The major pelvic cavity lies between the iliac fossae and above the iliopectineal lines. The minor pelvic cavity lies below the iliopectineal lines. SEE: *pelvis.*

pericardial c. The potential space between the epicardium (visceral pericardium) and the parietal pericardium. SEE: *pericardia friction rub; pericarditis.*

peritoneal c. The potential space between the parietal peritoneum, which lines the abdominal wall, and the visceral peritoneum, which forms the sur-

face layer of the visceral organs. It contains serous fluid.

pleural c. The potential space between the parietal pleura that lines the thoracic cavity and the visceral pleura that covers the lungs. It contains serous fluid that prevents friction.

pleuroperitoneal c. The ventral body cavity. SEE: *body cavity* for illus.; *coelom.*

pulp c. The cavity in a tooth containing blood vessels and nerve endings.

resonating c. The anatomic intensifiers of the human voice, including the upper portion of the larynx, pharynx, nasal cavity, paranasal sinuses, and oral cavity.

Rosenmüller c. SEE: under *Rosenmüller, Johann Christian.*

serous c. The space between two layers of serous membrane (e.g., the pleural, pericardial, and peritoneal cavities).

spinal c. The cavity that contains the spinal cord. SEE: *body c.* for illus.

thoracic c. The part of the ventral cavity above the diaphragm, the domed muscle that separates it from the abdominal cavity; it is enclosed by the chest wall. The thoracic viscera include

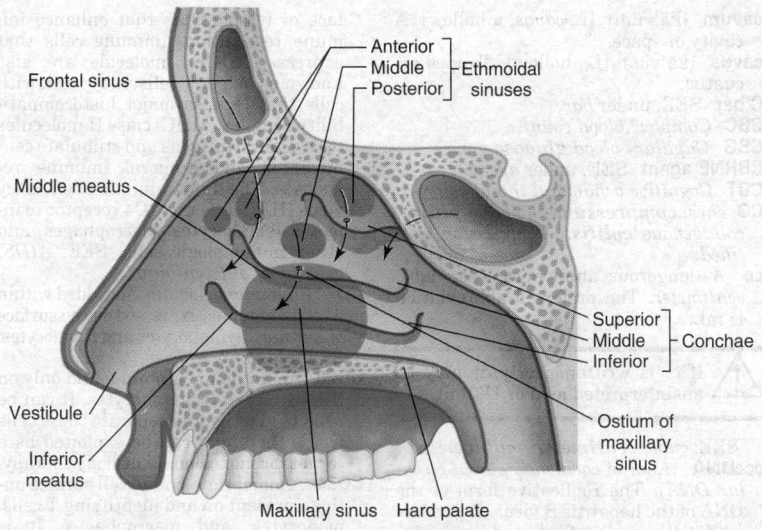

NASAL CAVITY

the pleural membranes that surround the lungs, the mediastinum between the lungs, which contains the heart and pericardial membranes, the thoracic aorta, pulmonary artery and veins, vena cavae, thymus gland, lymph nodes, trachea, bronchi, esophagus, and thoracic duct. SEE: illus.

tympanic c. Middle ear.

uterine c. The hollow space inside the body of the uterus.

visceral c. The body cavity containing the viscera (i.e., the thorax, abdomen, and pelvis).

cavity classification SEE: under *classification*.

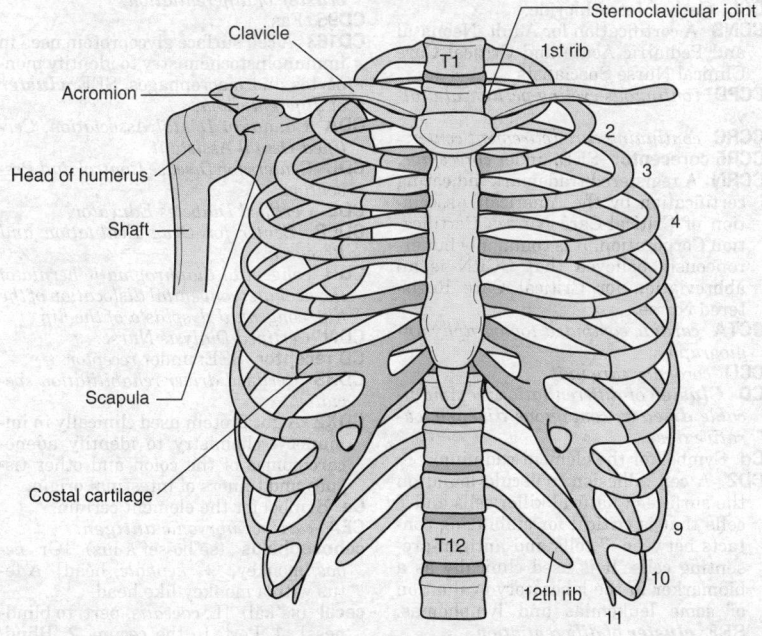

THORACIC CAVITY

cavum (kā′vŭm) [L. *cavus,* a hollow] A cavity or space.

cavus (kā′vŭs) [L., hollow] Talipes arcuatus.

C bar SEE: under *bar.*

CBC *Complete blood count.*

CBG *Capillary blood glucose*

CBRNE agent SEE: under *agent.*

CBT *Cognitive behavioral therapy.*

CC *chest compression; chief complaint; collagenous colitis; Commission Certified.*

cc A dangerous abbreviation for *cubic centimeter.* The preferred abbreviation is mL.

⚠ If cc is written poorly, it may be misinterpreted as u or U (unit).

SEE: *cubic centimeter; milliliter; mL.*

cccDNA [Abbr.of *covalently closed circular DNA*] The replicative form of the DNA of the hepatitis B virus. It persists within the nuclei of infected liver cells, produces viral RNA transcripts, and is difficult to eradicate. cccDNA is thought to be the form of the virus responsible for both chronic hepatitis B infection and persistent viral infection after antiviral treatment.

CC-CPR [*c(hest) c(ompressions)* + *c(ardio)p(ulmonary) r(esuscitation)*] CPR performed with only chest compressions but no rescue breathing. SYN: *hands-only CPR.*

CCD *Charge-coupled device.*

CCl₄ Carbon tetrachloride.

CCNS A certification for Adult, Neonatal and Pediatric Acute and Critical Care Clinical Nurse Specialists.

CCPD *continuous cycling peritoneal dialysis.*

CCRC *continuing care retirement center.*

CCR5 coreceptor SEE: under *coreceptor.*

CCRN A registered trademark indicating certification by the American Association of Critical-Care Nurses Certification Corporation. It is commonly but erroneously believed that CCRN is an abbreviation for Critical Care Registered Nurse.

CCTA *cardiac computed tomography angiography.*

CCU *coronary care unit.*

CD *Cluster of differentiation; communicable disease; contagious disease; curative dose.*

Cd Symbol for the element cadmium.

CD2 A cell adhesion molecule found on the surface of natural killer cells and T cells that is critical for stabilizing contacts between T cells and antigen-presenting cells. It is used clinically as a biomarker in the laboratory evaluation of some leukemias and lymphomas. SEE: *cluster of differentiation.*

CD4 One of a group of proteins on the surface of lymphocytes that enhance immune recognition. Immune cells that express the CD4 molecule are also known as helper T cells; they work with cells that express major histocompatibility complex (MHC) class II molecules to recognize antigens and stimulate cell-mediated and humoral immune responses. The human immunodeficiency virus (HIV) uses the CD4 receptor to infect T lymphocytes, macrophages, and other immunologic cells. SEE: *AIDS; cluster of differentiation.*

CD7 An immunoglobulin embedded within a cell membrane, expressed on the surface of mature T lymphocytes and thymocytes. SEE: *cluster of differentiation.*

CD20 An antigenic protein found only on the surface of B lymphocytes. It can be used to identify and separate those cells from others and can be exploited as a target for monoclonal antibody therapy.

CD34 A membrane-bound cell surface antigen present on and identifying T cells, monocytes, and macrophages. It is found principally on endothelial cells and blood-forming stem cells, and regulates cell-to-cell adhesion.

CD56 A cell surface glycoprotein heavily expressed by several blood and lymphatic cancers. SEE: *cluster of differentiation.*

CD57 A cell surface antigen expressed on many natural killer cells. SEE: *cluster of differentiation.*

CD68 A glycoprotein expressed on monocytes and tissue macrophages. SEE: *cluster of differentiation.*

CD95 Fas.

CD163 A cell surface glycoprotein used in immunohistochemistry to identify monocytes and macrophages. SEE: *cluster of differentiation.*

CDA *Canadian Dental Association; Certified Dental Assistant.*

CDC *Centers for Disease Control and Prevention.*

CDE *Certified Diabetes Educator.*

CDER *Center for Drug Evaluation and Research.*

CDH *congenital diaphragmatic hernia of the neonate; congenital dislocation of the hip; congenital dysplasia of the hip.*

CDN *Certified Dialysis Nurse.*

CD receptor SEE: under *receptor.*

CDRS *Certified driver rehabilitation specialist..*

CDX2 A gut protein used clinically in immunocytochemistry to identify adenocarcinomas of the colon and other tissues and tumors of intestinal origin.

Ce Symbol for the element cerium.

CEA *carcinoembryonic antigen.*

cebocephalus (sē″bō-sĕf′ă-lŭs) [Gr. *kebos,* monkey, + *kephale,* head] A fetus with a monkey-like head.

cecal (sē′kăl) [L. *caecalis,* pert. to blindness] **1.** Pert. to the cecum. **2.** Blind, terminating in a closed extremity.

cecectomy (sē-sĕk'tō-mē) [L. *caecum*, blindness, + Gr. *ektome*, excision] Surgical removal of the cecum.

cecitis (sē-sī'tĭs) [" + Gr. *itis*, inflammation] Inflammation of the cecum. It is often encountered during profound chemotherapy-induced neutropenia. SYN: *typhlitis; typhloenteritis*.

cecocolopexy (sē"kō-kō'lō-pĕk"sē) [" + Gr. *kolon*, colon, + *pexis*, fixation] Surgical fixation of the colon and the cecum.

cecocolostomy (sē"kō-kō-lŏs'tō-mē) [" + " + *stoma*, mouth] An anastomosis of the cecum to a portion of the colon.

cecoileostomy (sē"kō-ĭl"ē-ŏs'tō-mē) [" + *ileum*, ileum, + Gr. *stoma*, mouth] Surgical formation of an anastomosis between the cecum and the ileum.

cecopexy (sē'kō-pĕk"sē) [" + Gr. *pexis*, fixation] Surgical fixation of the cecum to the abdominal wall.

cecoplication (sē"kō-plĭ-kā'shŭn) [" + *plica*, fold] Suturing the cecum to the abdominal wall to prevent torsion or correct ptosis.

cecoptosis (sē"kŏp-tō'sĭs) [" + Gr. *ptosis*, a dropping] Falling displacement of the cecum.

cecosigmoidostomy (sē"kō-sĭg"moy-dŏs'tō-mē) [" + Gr. *sigmoeides*, shaped like Gr. letter Σ (sigma), + *stoma*, mouth] A surgical connection between the cecum and the sigmoid.

cecostomy (sē-kŏs'tō-mē) [" + Gr. *stoma*, mouth] Surgical formation of an artificial opening into the cecum.

cecotomy (sē-kŏt'ō-mē) [" + Gr. *tome*, incision] An incision into the cecum.

cecum, caecum (sē'kŭm) [L. *caecum*, blindness] A blind pouch or cul-de-sac that forms the first portion of the large intestine, located below the entrance of the ileum at the ileocecal valve. It averages about 6 cm in length and 7.5 cm in width. At its lower end is the vermiform appendix. SEE: *colon*.

cef- [Fr. *ceph(alosporin)*] A prefix used in pharmacology to name a *cephalosporin*.

ceftriaxone (sĕf-trī'ăks-ōn) An injectable, third-generation cephalosporin with a long half-life that can be given once daily. It is used to treat a wide spectrum of respiratory, gastrointestinal, and urinary infections.

ceiling effect The optimal potential effect of a medication. Once a therapeutic limit is reached, increases in dose may produce side effects but no further beneficial effects.

-cele [Gr. *kēlē*, tumor, swelling] Suffix meaning *swelling, hernia,* or *tumor*. SEE: *-coele*.

Celebrex (sĕl'ĕ-brĕks") SEE: *celecoxib*.

celecoxib (sel-ĕ-kok'sib) A nonsteroidal anti-inflammatory drug approved for the treatment of osteoarthritis and rheumatoid arthritis.

Celexa SEE: *citalopram*.

celiac (sē'lē-ăk) [Gr. *koilia*, belly] Pert. to the abdominal cavity.

celiac disease Malabsorption, weight loss, and diarrhea, resulting from immunological intolerance to dietary wheat products, esp. gluten and gliaden. Patients may suffer bloating, flatulence, steatorrhea, anemia, weakness, malnutrition, vitamin and mineral deficiencies, rashes, bone loss, attenuated growth, delayed puberty, or failure to thrive. The disease is common, occurring in about 1 in 110 Americans. SYN: *celiac **sprue**.* SYN: *nontropical **sprue***.

celiectomy (sē"lē-ĕk'tō-mē) [" + *ektome*, excision] **1.** Surgical removal of an abdominal organ. **2.** Excision of the celiac branches of the vagus nerve.

celiocentesis (sē"lē-ō-sĕn-tē'sĭs) [" + *kentesis*, puncture] Puncture of the abdomen.

celiocolpotomy (sē"lē-ō-kŏl-pŏt'ō-mē) [" + *kolpos*, vagina, + *tome*, incision] An incision into the abdomen through the vaginal wall.

celioenterotomy (sē"lē-ō-ĕn"tĕr-ŏt'ō-mē) [" + *enteron*, intestine, + *tome*, incision] An incision through the abdominal wall and into the intestine.

celiogastrostomy (sē"lē-ō-găs-trŏs'tō-mē) [" + *gaster*, stomach, + *stoma*, mouth] Laparogastrostomy.

celiogastrotomy (sē"lē-ō-găs-trŏt'ō-mē) [Gr. *koilia*, belly, + *gaster*, stomach, + *tome*, incision] Laparogastrotomy.

celiohysterectomy (sē"lē-ō-hĭs-tĕr-ĕk'tō-mē) [" + *hystera*, uterus, + *ektome*, excision] Removal of the uterus through an abdominal incision.

celiohysterotomy (sē"lē-ō-hĭs"tĕr-ŏt'ō-mē) [" + " + *tome*, incision] A transabdominal incision into the uterus.

celiomyomectomy (sē"lē-ō-mī"ō-mĕk'tō-mē) [" + " + *oma*, tumor, + *ektome*, excision] Excision of uterine myoma via an abdominal incision.

celiomyomotomy (sē"lē-ō-mī"ō-mŏt'ō-mē) [" + " + " + *tome*, incision] An abdominal incision into a uterine myoma.

celiomyositis (sē"lē-ō-mī"ō-sī'tĭs) [" + " + *itis*, inflammation] Inflammation of the abdominal muscles.

celiopathy (sē"lē-ŏp'ă-thē) [" + *pathos*, disease, suffering] Any disease of the abdomen.

celiorrhaphy (sē"lē-or'ă-fē) [" + *rhaphe*, seam, ridge] Laparorrhaphy.

celiosalpingectomy (sē"lē-ō-săl"pĭn-jĕk'tō-mē) [" + *salpinx*, tube, + *ektome*, excision] Removal of the fallopian tubes through an abdominal incision.

celioscope, celoscope (sē'lē-ō-skōp", sē'lō-skōp") [²*celo-* + *-scope*] An endoscope for visual examination of a body cavity.

celioscopy (sē"lē-ŏs'kō-pē) Examination of a body cavity through a celioscope.

celiotomy (sē″lē-ŏt′ō-mē) [″ + *tome,* incision] Surgical incision into the abdominal cavity.

   vaginal c. Incision into the abdomen through the vagina.

celite (sē′līt″) A chalklike powder that is a contact activator of the intrinsic system of coagulation.

cell (sel) [L. *cella,* a chamber] The basic unit of life. A cell is a group of self-sustaining biochemical reactions that are isolated from the environment by a selectively permeable lipid membrane. Among the key reactions are those that maintain a stable intracellular concentration of ions; for mammalian cells, typical internal concentrations include 140 mM K+, 5-15 mM Na+, 5-15 mM Cl-, and a pH of 7.2, which can be significantly different from their concentrations outside the cell. Other key reactions move molecules and molecular complexes within the cell, sometimes changing the cell's shape. These reactions, along with many others, require energy, and the generation of energy by breaking apart preexisting hydrocarbon molecules ("food") is the job of glycolysis and other characteristic intracellular metabolic reactions. SEE: *glycolysis; metabolism; mitochondrion.*

   STRUCTURE: Intracellular chemical reactions are controlled by enzymes that are organized in stable molecular complexes called organelles. The polymer-based organelles include centrioles and the cytoskeleton; nucleic acid-based organelles include ribosomes; and membrane-enclosed organelles include the nucleus, endoplasmic reticula, Golgi complexes, lysosomes, peroxisomes, mitochondria, and storage and transport vesicles. SEE: illus. Individual mammalian cells are usually microscopic, typically ranging from 5 μm to 50 μm in diameter. In humans, lymphocytes are small cells (6 μm in diameter), columnar epithelial cells (10 μm x 20 μm) are medium-size cells, and mature ova (120-150 μm) are some of the largest cells.

   CELL DIVISION: In mammals, all new cells arise from existing cells through cell division, and an animal's growth results largely from increases in the number of its cells, most of which differentiate into specialized cell types to form the body's various tissues. Cell division involves two major processes: karyokinesis, the division of the nucleus, and cytokinesis, the division of the remainder of the cell. When generating somatic daughter cells, karyokinesis uses a process called mitosis, which produces daughter cells with a full complement of chromosomes. When generating germ cells, karyokinesis includes a process called meiosis, which produces daughter cells with half the normal number of chromosomes. SEE: *meiosis* and *mitosis* for illus.

   A c. Alpha cell of the pancreas.

   accessory c. A monocyte or macrophage that participates in the immune response. SEE: *antigen-presenting c.; macrophage.*

   acidophilic c. Acidophil.

   acinar c. A cell present in the acinus

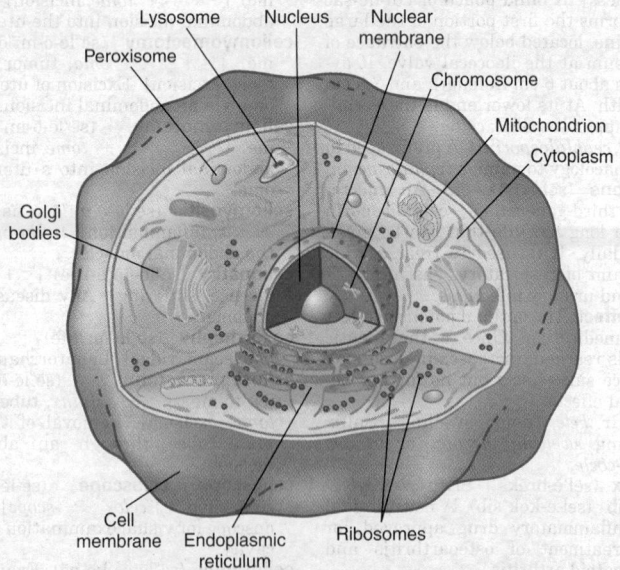

Lysosome   Nucleus   Nuclear membrane

Peroxisome

Chromosome

Mitochondrion

Cytoplasm

Golgi bodies

Cell membrane   Endoplasmic reticulum   Ribosomes

COMMON COMPONENTS AND ORGANELLES OF HUMAN CELLS

of an acinous gland, e.g., of the pancreas.

adipose c. Adipocyte..

adult stem c. A precursor cell that can also give rise to identical precursor cells: daughters of a stem cell can develop into a terminally differentiated cell type or they can remain a stem cell. Adult stem cells are found in many tissues, such as bone marrow, brain, retina, skin, intestines, liver, testis, and pancreas.somatic stem cell.embryonic stem cell.

adventitial c. A macrophage along a blood vessel, together with perivascular undifferentiated cells associated with it.

air c. An air-filled sinus cavity in a bone.

alpha c. **1.** An enteroendocrine cell that produces glucagon and is found in the pancreatic islets. A cell. **2.** An acidophil of the adenohypophysis (anterior pituitary gland).

alveolar c. **1.** In the lung, either of two types of epithelial cells lining the alveoli. Type I cells are simple thin squamous epithelial cells. Type II cells secrete pulmonary surfactant. Type II cells are smaller and more numerous than Type I cells. **2.** In the mammary glands, the milk-secreting epithelial cells, which are activated during lactation.

amacrine c. A modified nerve cell in the retina that has dendrites but no axon. SEE: *neuron*.

ameloblast c. Ameloblast.

anterior horn c. A somatic motor neuron that has its cell body in the ventral (anterior) horn of the gray matter of the spinal cord; its axon passes out through a ventral root and innervates skeletal muscle.

antigen-presenting c. ABBR: APC. A cell that breaks down antigens and displays their fragments on surface receptors next to major histocompatibility complex molecules. This presentation is necessary for some T lymphocytes that are unable to recognize soluble antigens. Macrophages are the primary antigen-presenting cells, but B cells and dendritic cells also can act as APCs. SEE: *T c.; macrophage processing cell*.

APUD c. The abbreviated name for an 'amine precursor uptake and decarboxylation cell'. These cells are the constituents of a diffuse neuroendocrine system and all have metabolic pathways that make and utilize serotonin (5-HT). APUD cells include chromaffin cells, enterochromaffin cells, and SIF cells as well as certain cells found in the parathyroid gland, thyroid gland, pituitary gland, hypothalamus, and placenta.

argentaffin c. A cell in the epithelium of the stomach, intestines, and appendix that secretes serotonin.

astroglial c. Astrocyte.

atypical glandular c. ABBR: AGC. An abnormal finding on a Pap test. This classification is divided into "favor neoplasia" or "not otherwise specified (NOS)." NOS is subdivided into endocervical or endometrial origin. Atypical endocervical cells are important because of their risk for significant disease. SYN: *atypical glandular cells of undetermined significance*.

atypical glandular c. of undetermined significance ABBR: AGUS. Atypical glandular cells.

B c. **1.** A lymphocyte that synthesizes and secretes antibodies. B lymphocytes originate and differentiate in the bone marrow and then populate the spleen, lymph nodes, and other lymphoid tissues. When exposed to an antigen, a B cell divides to form (a) plasma cells, which produce antigen-specific antibodies, and (b) a lesser number of memory B cells, which can quickly differentiate into plasma cells upon a second exposure to the original antigen. Antibody production is a key part of the humoral immune response of adaptive immunity. The humoral immune response is effective against bacteria, viruses, and other pathogens, and provides the rationale for vaccination. SYN: *B lymphocyte*. SEE: *T c.* **2.** Pancreatic beta cell.

band c. The developing leukocyte at a stage at which the nucleus is not segmented.

basal c. **1.** A rounded or cuboidal epithelial stem cell found in the bottom layer of pseudostratified epithelia, such as the epidermis and the lining of the airways of the lung. **2.** Either of two types of cell found in the bottom layer of the olfactory epithelium; one type is a flattened "basal cell proper", and the other is a rounded stem cell called a globose cell. **3.** A rounded stem cell found in the taste buds and a progenitor of the specialized taste receptor cells.

basket c. **1.** Myoepithelial cell. **2.** One of the nonspiny granule cells found in the cerebral cortex. **3.** One of the small interneurons found in the outermost layer of the cerebellar cortex along with stellate cells.

basophilic c. Basophil.

beta c. **1.** Any of the insulin-secreting cells of the pancreas that constitute the bulk of the islets of Langerhans. B cell. **2.** A basophil cell of the adenohypophysis (anterior pituitary gland).

Betz c. SEE: *Betz cells*.

bipolar c. Bipolar neuron.

blast c. **1.** A precursor cell for a specific cell type. **2.** An immature cell of a specific type.

blood c. Any cell normally found circulating in the blood stream. Blood cells include red cells and white cells; red cells generally remain inside blood vessels, while white cells can also more into the tissues outside the blood vessel walls. SEE: *blood* for illus.

bone c. An osteoblast, osteoclast, or osteocyte.

bone marrow c. Marrow cell.

brush c. An epithelial cell found sparsely in the lining of the bronchial tree. The cell's surface has long stiff microvilli, and the cell has the appearance of an absorptive cell.

cancer c. A cell present in a neoplasm and differentiated from normal tissue cells because of its degree of anaplasia, irregularity of shape, nuclear size, changes in the structure of the nucleus and cytoplasm, increased number of mitoses, and ability to metastasize.

capsule c. Satellite cell.

cartilage c. Chondrocyte.

castration c. An enlarged and vacuolated basophil cell seen in the pituitary in gonadal insufficiency or following castration.

CD3 c. T cell.

CD4 c. Helper T cell.

CD8 c. A suppressor T cell, e.g., a cytotoxic T cell.

CD 34+ c. A cell with the CD34 protein on its surface membrane. Some CD34 cells that are hemopoietic stem cells can be separated out from peripheral blood.

chemoreceptor c. Chemoreceptor.

chief c. 1. Any of the cells of the parathyroid gland that secretes the parathyroid hormone. 2. Any of the cells of the gastric glands that secretes pepsinogen.

chromaffin c. A cell that produces, stores, and secretes catecholamines (dopamine and norepinephrine). Chromaffin cells are found in the medulla of the adrenal glands and in small clusters in the sympathetic ganglia.

chromophobe c. Chromophobe.

Clara c. A cuboidal epithelial cell found in the lining of the terminal and the respiratory bronchioles of the lungs. Clara cells are nonciliated, and they secrete surfactant, like the type II alveolar epithelial cells found deeper in the bronchial tree.

cleavage c. Blastomere.

clue c. A vaginal epithelial cell, thickly coated with coccobacillary organisms. Clue cells are a hallmark of bacterial vaginosis.

columnar c. An epithelial cell with height greater than its width.

columnar epithelial c. Columnar cell.

cone c. A cell in the retina whose scleral end forms a cone that serves as a light receptor. Vision in bright light, color vision, and acute vision depend on the function of the cones. SEE: *rod c.*

cortical c. A cell in the cortex of an organ, e.g., a neuron in the cerebral cortex.

corticotroph c. Corticotroph.

cuboid c. A cell – usually epithelial – with a height about equal to its width and depth.

cytotoxic c. Cytotoxic T cell.

cytotoxic T c. A CD8+ T lymphocyte that can destroy microorganisms directly through the release of perforin and proteolytic enzymes. These cells are particularly important in the defense against viruses, rejection of allografts, and, possibly, new malignant cells. SYN: CD8 cell; cytotoxic cel; *killer T c.*

D c. An enteroendocrine cell that produces somatostatin and is found in the pancreatic islets, stomach, and small intestine. delta cell; somatostatin cell.

daughter c. A cell formed by cell division.

decoy c. A cell found in the urine with inclusion bodies in its nucleus. It indicates infection with BK virus in renal transplant recipients.

delta c. Pancreatic D cell.

dendritic c. One type of antigen-presenting cell that helps T cells respond to foreign antigens. Dendritic cells are found in epithelial tissues and include the Langerhans' cells of the skin and the interdigitating cells in lymph nodes; they also circulate in the blood.

dust c. A macrophage that migrates into the lumen of lung aveoli and ingests debris, particles of air pollution, and pathogens to keep the airspaces clear.

EC c. 1. An embryonal carcinoma cell, which is a cultured cell line. 2. An enterochromaffin cell that secretes substance P and is found in the stomach and small intestine.

effector c. A cell that carries out the final response or function of a particular process. The main effector cells of the immune system, for example, are activated lymphocytes and phagocytes— the cells involved in destroying pathogens and removing them from the body. SEE: *leukocyte.*

embryonic stem c. ABBR: ES cell. A cell from the inner cell mass of the blastocyst (the 3-5 day old mammalian embryo) that can give rise to all the somatic cells of the body. Embryonic stem cells can be maintained as pure stem cell cultures.adult stem cell.

endothelial c. The type of epithelial cell that lines blood vessels and lymph vessels; these cells are usually squamous (flattened) and form sheets one layer thick. Endothelial cells are derived from mesenchyme cells of the embryo. A sheet of endothelial cells is called an endothelium.

enterochromaffin c. ABBR: EC cell. An enteroendocrine cell that produces serotonin and is found in the small intestine. Enterochromaffin cells are very similar to the cells, found throughout the peripheral sympathetic nervous system, that are called simply 'chromaffin cells'.

enteroendocrine c. One of the scattered hormone-producing cells found in the pancreatic islets and throughout the gastrointestinal (mainly, small intestinal) mucosa.

ependymal c. Any of the epithelial cells that form a one-cell-thick layer lining the ventricles and the central canal of the central nervous system. The ventricular (apical) surfaces of many ependymal cells are covered with cilia or microvilli. In most places, the ependymal layer does not have a basal lamina. Specialized regions of ependymal cells include the covering of the blood vessels and loose connective tissue of the choroid plexuses; here, the ependyma is specialized to secrete cerebrospinal fluid.

epithelial c. Any of the cells forming the cellular sheets that cover surfaces, both inside and outside the body. Epithelial cells are closely packed and take on polyhedral shapes, from tall (columnar) through squat (cuboidal) to flat (squamous). Epithelial cells adhere strongly to one another, and one of their surfaces -- the basal surface -- sticks firmly to a thin extracellular film of fibrils called a basal lamina. A sheet of epithelial cells derived from embryonic epithelia (the ectoderm or the endoderm) is called an epithelium. SEE: *epithelium.*

ethmoid air c. Ethmoid sinus.

eukaryotic c. The type of cell composing multicellular, as well as a number of unicellular, organisms. Unlike prokaryotic cells, eukaryotic cells have many of their intracellular functions organized within structures called organelles. Some organelles -- notably, the nucleus, which contains the DNA -- are enclosed by intracellular membranes.

F c. An enteroendocrine cell that produces pancreatic polypeptide and is found in the pancreatic islets.

fat c. Adipocyte.

flame c. A bone marrow cell with a bright red cytoplasm, occasionally found in the marrow of patients with multiple myeloma.

flow c. An optical cell used in photometers and cell counters, through which the sample and any standards are passed for detection and measured or counted by optical or electrometric means. SEE: *cytometry.*

foam c. A cell that contains vacuoles; a lipid-filled macrophage.

follicle c. Follicular cell.

follicular c. 1. The secretory cell of the thyroid gland; it produces the thyroid hormones, T3 (triiodothyronine) and T4 (tetraiodothyronine or thyroxine). 2. Any of the flattened somatic cells that form a monolayer around each primary oocyte in the ovary. After puberty, when an oocyte matures, during a monthly cycle, its follicular cells divide, become cuboidal, and form a multilayered coating for the oocyte; at this stage, the follicular cells are called granulosa cells.

folliculostellate c. A supporting cell in the adenohypophysis (anterior pituitary gland); it produces bioactive peptides, including growth factors and cytokines.

foreign body giant c. Giant cell.

G c. An enteroendocrine cell found in the stomach that produces the hormone gastrin.

ganglion c. 1. Any neuron whose cell body is located within a ganglion. 2. A neuron of the retina of the eye whose cell body lies in the ganglion cell layer. The axons of ganglion cells form the optic nerve.

germ c. A cell whose function is to reproduce the organism. Early in development, primordial germ cells are found in the genital ridges of the embryo. Later, in the testis, the primordial germ cells are called spermatogonia, and in the ovary, they are called oogonia. When they mature, the germ cells (i.e., spermatogonia and oogonia) differentiate into haploid gametes (i.e., spermatozoa and ova). primordial germ cell.

giant c. 1. A multinucleated phagocyte created by several individual macrophages that have merged around a large pathogen or a substance resistant to destruction, such as a splinter or a surgical suture. SEE: *granuloma; tuberculosis.* 2. A large multinucleated (40-60 nuclei) tumor cell characteristic of certain bone and tendon tumors. 3. A large multinucleated cell that invades the walls of the aorta and its major branches in giant cell arteritis.

glial c. One of three types of nonneuronal cell in the central nervous system: astrocytes, oligodendrocytes, and microglial cells. SYN neuroglial cellneuroglial cell.

gitter c. A macrophage present at sites of brain injury. The cells are packed with lipoid granules from phagocytosis of damaged brain cells. SEE: *microglia.*

globus c. One of the two varieties of basal cell found in the olfactory epithelium. It is a rounded neuroblast or neural stem cell for the olfactory receptor cells.

goblet c. A mucous cell sitting between nonsecretory cells, such as is found in the intestinal epithelium.

Golgi c. SEE: under *Golgi, Camillo.*

gonadotroph c. Gonadotroph.

granule c. 1. Any of the small neurons that pack the granular cell layer of the cerebellar cortex, immediately below the Purkinje cell layer. Granule cells receive inputs (mossy fibers) from the spinal cord and brainstem (except the inferior olive). Axons of granule cells run perpendicular to the Purkinje cell dendrites, on which they synapse. **2.** Any of the neurons of the cerebral cortex that are not pyramidal cells. Cortical granule cells are categorized as spiny or nonspiny. stellate cell. **3.** A small axon-less neuron found in the olfactory bulb.

granulosa c. One of the many cuboidal cells that surround and nurture the maturing oocyte.follicular cell (2).

gustatory c. Taste cell.

hair c. An epithelial cell possessing stereocilia in the maculae, cristae ampullaris, and the organ of Corti. These cells are receptors for the senses of position and hearing.

heart failure c. A red-colored (from ingested red cells) lung macrophage often found in the sputum of patients with congestive heart failure.

HeLa c. A line of human epithelial cells that grows well in culture. It is an immortal cancer cell that has been maintained in continuous tissue cultures for decades from a patient with carcinoma of the cervix. It is named for the first two letters of the patient's first and last names, Henrietta Lacks. HeLa cells have been used in thousands of experiments on cell growth, differentiation, and cancer, and in virology, pharmacology, and other fields.

helmet c. A schistocyte or fragmented blood cell, seen in hemolytic anemias. SEE: illus.

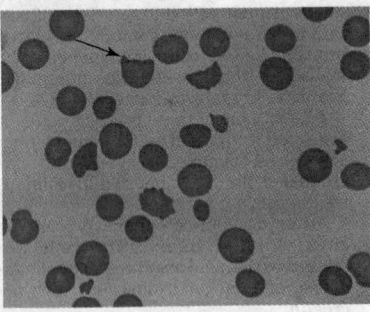

HELMET CELLS

(Orig. mag. ×640)

helper c. A type of T lymphocyte whose surface is marked by CD4 receptors; it is involved in both cell-mediated and antibody-mediated immune responses. It secretes cytokines that stimulate the activity of B cells and other T cells and binds with class II histocompatibility antigens, which are processed by macrophages and other antigen-presenting cells.helper T cell. SEE: *antigen processing; T c.; cell-mediated immunity.*

helper T c. Helper cell.

hematopoietic stem c. A progenitor cell in the bone marrow that can replicate itself as well as produce precursor cells of the various blood cell lineages.

hilus c. An androgen-producing cell found in the ovarian hilum. It is analogous to the male Leydig cell.

horizontal c. A neuron of the inner nuclear layer of the retina. The axons of these cells run horizontally and connect various parts of the retina.

Hürthle c. SEE: *Hürthle cell.*

hybridoma c. SEE: *hybridoma.*

hyperchromatic c. A cell that contains more than the normal number of chromosomes and hence stains more densely.

I c. An enteroendocrine cell that produces the enzyme cholecystokinin-pancreozymin (pancreaticozymin) and is found in the small intestine.

interdigitating c. A type of antigen-presenting cell found in lymph nodes and lymphoid tissue.

interstitial c. Any of the many cells found in connective tissue of the ovary, in the seminiferous tubules of the testes, and in the medulla and cortex of the kidney. The cells in the testes and ovaries produce hormones such as testosterone and estrogen.

intestinal absorptive c. In the small intestine, any of the tall columnar cells topped with a brush border made of thousands of microvilli.

islet c. A cell of the islets of Langerhans of the pancreas.

juxtaglomerular c. A modified smooth muscle cell in the wall of the afferent arteriole leading to a glomerulus of the kidney. This type of cell secretes renin when blood pressure decreases to activate the renin-angiotensin mechanism, which increases sodium retention, thus elevating the blood pressure.

K c. An enteroendocrine cell that produces gastric inhibitory peptide (glucose-dependent insulinotropic peptide) and is found in the small intestine. This peptide stimulates the beta cells of the pancreas to secrete insulin.

killer c. Natural killer cell.

killer T c. Cytotoxic T cell.

Kulchitsky c. An APUD cell found in the lung.

Kupffer c. SEE: *Kupffer cell.*

L c. An enteroendocrine cell that produces glucagon-like peptide-1 and is found in the small intestine. This peptide signals the pancreas to secrete insulin after a meal.

labile c. A cell that is always mitotically active, such as the epithelial cells lining the stomach and the stem cells in the red bone marrow.

lactotroph c. Lactotroph.

LAK c. Abbreviation for lymphokine-activated killer cell. These natural killer cells, obtained from the patient's blood, have been activated in culture with interleukin-2.LAK cells; the cells can then be used to treat patients with solid malignant tumors.

Langerhans c. A type of dendritic antigen-presenting cell that typically resides in the skin.

L.E. c. Historically, an abbreviation for *lupus erythematosus* cell, a polymorphonuclear leukocyte that contains the phagocytized nucleus of another cell. It is characteristic but not diagnostic of lupus erythematosus.

This distinctive cell may form when the blood of patients with systemic lupus erythematosus is incubated and further processed according to a specified protocol. The plasma of some patients contains an antibody to the nucleoprotein of leukocytes. These altered nuclei, which are swollen, pink, and homogeneous, are ingested by phagocytes. These are the L.E. cells. The ingested material, when stained properly, is lavender and displaces the nucleus of the phagocyte to the inner surface of the cell membrane. The L.E. cell phenomenon can be demonstrated in most patients with systemic lupus erythematosus but is not essential for diagnosis.

Leydig c. SEE: *Leydig's cell.*

littoral c. A macrophage found in the sinuses of lymphatic tissue.

liver c. Hepatocyte.

lutein c. A cell of the corpus luteum of the ovary that contains fatty yellowish granules. Granulose lutein cells are hypertrophied follicle cells; these lutein (paralutein) cells develop from the theca interna.

lymphoid c. An obsolete term for lymphocyte.

lymphokine-activated killer c. LAK cell.

M c. **1.** A microfold cell, which is a cell in the gastrointestinal epithelium covering patches of lymphoid tissue. M cells transport antigens from the intestinal lumen to the underlying lymphoid tissues for recognition and processing. **2.** An APUD cell that produces melanotropin and is found in the pituitary gland.

macroglial c. An astrocyte or an oligodendrocyte.

marrow c. Bone marrow cell.

mast c. A large tissue cell resembling a basophil, which is essential for inflammatory reactions mediated by immunoglobulin E (IgE) but does not circulate in the blood. Mast cells are present throughout the body in connective tissue, but are concentrated beneath the skin and the mucous membranes of the respiratory and digestive

tracts. Mast cells are covered with IgE molecules, which bind with foreign antigens and stimulate degranulation, releasing such mediators as histamine, prostaglandins, leukotrienes, and proteinases from densely packed granules within the cytoplasm. These mediators produce type I (immediate) hypersensitivity reactions (e.g., urticaria, allergic rhinitis, asthma, angioedema, and systemic anaphylaxis). SEE: illus.

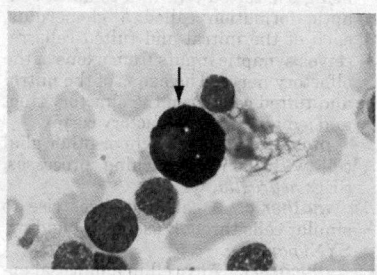

MAST CELL

mastoid c. Mastoid air cell.

mastoid air c. Any of the variable-sized, air-filled sinuses inside the mastoid antrum. About 20% of adult skulls have no mastoid air cells.

memory c. A cell derived from B or T lymphocytes that can quickly recognize a foreign antigen to which the body has been previously exposed. Memory T cells stimulate T helper lymphocytes and cytotoxic T cells; memory B cells stimulate the production of antigen-specific antibodies by B plasma cells. Both types of memory cells survive for years, providing a durable adaptive immune response against foreign antigens.

mesenchyme c. One of the two basic somatic cell lineages -- the other being epithelial cells. In contrast to epithelial cells, mesenchyme cells are not polarized and are frequently motile. In the early embryo, mesenchyme cells fill many of the spaces enclosed by epithelia. Later, mesenchyme cells will secrete the space-filling extracellular matrix molecules, such as collagen and glycoproteins, that characterize connective tissue.

mesenchymal stem c. A stem cell found in connective tissue and capable of producing cells of the connective tissue lineages, such as cartilage, bone, muscle, and fat cells.

mesothelial c. The type of epithelial cell that lines serous (pleural, peritoneal, and pericardial) cavities, blood vessels, and lymph vessels; these cells are usually squamous (flattened) and form sheets one layer thick. Mesothelial cells are derived from mesenchyme cells of the embryo. A sheet of mesothelial cells is called a mesothelium.

microglial c. A small glial cell of the central nervous system and retina. Microglia have spiky branched processes and are arranged homogeneously throughout the brain and spinal cord. They are activated by disease and injury, after which they become phagocytic and sometimes resume their embryonic motility like a macrophage.

mitral c. One of the two principal neurons of the olfactory bulb -- the other being the tufted cell. In a complex synaptic formation called a glomerulus, each of the mitral and tufted cells receives synaptic inputs from axons of the olfactory nerve. The axons of the mitral and tufted cells form the olfactory tract and synapse in the olfactory cortex.

mossy c. An astrocyte or other glial cell with many branching processes. SEE: *neuroglia.*

mother c. A cell that gives rise to similar cells through fission or budding. SYN: *parent c.*

mucosal c. Any cell in a mucosal epithelium.

mucous c. An epithelial cell that secretes mucus and IgA antibodies. Mucous cells and serous cells are the two varieties of secretory cells found in exocrine glands.mucus cell.

mucus c. Mucous cell.

multinucleated giant c. Giant cell.

multipolar c. Multipolar neuron.

muscle c. muscle.

myeloid c. Any white blood cell other than lymphocytes.

myeloma c. A cell present in the bone marrow of patients with multiple myeloma.

myoepithelial c. A smooth muscle cell found in some epithelia; it lies between glandular cells and the basal lamina of sweat, mammary, lacrimal, and salivary glands. basket cell.

natural killer c. ABBR: NK cell. A large granular lymphocyte – a defensive cell of innate immunity – that bonds to cells and lyses them by releasing cytotoxins. Natural killer cells are null cells, lymphocytes that do not have B cell or T cell surface markers, and they can be activated without previous antigen exposure. NK cells destroy cells infected with viruses and some types of tumor cells in cultures. They also secrete gamma interferon (INFγ), tumor necrosis factor alpha (TNFα), and granulocyte-macrophage colony-stimulating factor (GMCSF), enhancing the effect of T lymphocytes. SYN: *killer c.*

nerve c. Neuron.

neural crest c. Embryonic cells of the neuron-glia lineage that form along the ridges (neural folds) of the neural plate and that migrate into the developing organism to produce a variety of tissues. The migratory ability of these embryonic epithelial cells is similar to the motility of mesenchyme cells; this has led neural crest cells to be called mesectodermal cells. In the neural lineage, neural crest cells give rise to the dorsal root ganglia, the placodes that will develop into the olfactory and auditory sensory organs, the pituitary gland, the peripheral autonomic nervous system, and the neurenteric and APUD cells. In the glial lineage, neural crest cells give rise to Schwann cells and other peripheral satellite cells. In addition, neural crest cells of the cranial region give rise to certain facial connective tissue, including the bones of the nasal cavities, the roof of the mouth, and the sella turcica.

neuroglial c. Glial cell.

NK c. Natural killer cell.

null c. A large lymphocyte without the cell markers of either a T cell or a B cell. Natural killer cells are examples of null cells.

odontoblast c. Odontoblast.

oligodendroglial c. Oligodendrocyte.

olfactory c. Olfactory receptor cell.

olfactory receptor c. A cell of the olfactory mucosa that has receptors for the sense of smell. Olfactory cells are continuously replaced from stem cells throughout adult life. olfactory cell.

osteoprogenitor c. Any of the mesenchyme precursor cells committed to the bone lineage and capable of producing osteoblasts and osteocytes. Osteoprogenitor cells are found in bone, bone marrow, and other connective tissue.

oxyntic c. A parietal cell of the gastric glands; it produces hydrochloric acid and the intrinsic factor.

parent c. Mother cell.

pigment c. Any cell that normally contains pigment granules.

plasma c. A cell derived from a B lymphocyte that has been sensitized to a specific foreign antigen and produces antibodies to that particular antigen. It may be found in the blood or in tissue fluid. SYN: *plasmacyte.*

postganglionic c. Postganglionic neuron.

PP c. An enteroendocrine endocrine cell found in the pancreatic islets that produces pancreatic polypeptide.

pre-B c. The immediate precursor of a lymphocytic B cell.

preganglionic c. Preganglionic neuron.

prickle c. A cell with spiny processes that connect with similar processes of adjoining cells. These are found in the stratum spinosum of the keratinized epithelium of the epidermis.

primordial c. Primordial germ cell.

primordial germ c. A germ cell before it begins its maturation into a haploid gamete.primordial cell.

progenitor c. A cell (sometimes a stem cell) that produces cells of a particular lineage, e.g., a neuroblast.

prokaryotic c. The form of cell composing many primitive unicellular organisms, such as bacteria. Prokaryotic cells do not have nuclei, which are partitioned by an intracellular membrane; instead the DNA forms one main coil in the cell cytoplasm.

Purkinje c. SEE: under *Purkinje, Johannes E. von.*

pus c. A leukocyte present in pus. Pus cells are often degenerated or necrotic.

pyramidal c. A large, common neuron found in the cerebral cortex. Pyramidal cells are flask-shaped or triangular, and, in the parts of the cortex with six layers, they occupy the fifth layer. Pyramidal cell dendrites project up into the most superficial layer of the cortex, while pyramidal cell axons run in the opposite direction, i.e., downward and out of the cortex.

radial glial c. A structural macroglial cell that is a key component of the developing nervous system. Radial glial cells first appear in the neural tube, where their cell bodies are suspended between two thin cell processes; the apical process attaches to the inner (ventricular) surface of the neural tube, and the basal process attaches to the outer (pial) surface. Early in development, neuroblasts migrate radially along the scaffolding formed by the radial glial cell processes, and growing axons may follow the scaffolding longitudinally. Later, many radial glial cells retract their processes and differentiate into astrocytes.

red c. A small cell that is filled with hemoglobin, has no nucleus, and is shaped like a biconcave disc. Red cells transport oxygen to tissues and carbon dioxide to the lungs. Individual red cells have a life span of 3-4 months, and new red cells are continually being produced in the bone marrow. In a healthy person, 99% of the cells circulating in the blood are red cells. SYN: *erythrocyte; red blood cell; red blood corpuscle.*

red blood c. ABBR: RBC. Red cell.

Renshaw c. SEE: *Renshaw cell.*

resting c. 1. A cell that is not dividing. SEE: *interphase.* **2.** A cell not performing its normal function (i.e., a nerve cell that is not conducting an impulse or a muscle cell that is not contracting).

reticular c. 1. An undifferentiated cell of the spleen, bone marrow, or lymphatic tissue that can develop into one of several types of connective tissue cells or into a macrophage. **2.** A cell of reticular connective tissue. SEE: *reticular tissue.*

reticuloendothelial c. An out-of-date term for a cell of the mononuclear phagocytic system.

rod c. A cell in the retina of the eye whose scleral end is long and narrow,

forming a rod-shaped sensory receptor. Rods are stimulated by light and are essential for vision in dim light. SEE: *cone c.*

rosette c. A rose-shaped cluster of phagocytes surrounding lysed nuclear material or red blood cells. Rosette cells occur frequently in blood in which L.E. cells are present. Rosette cells are not diagnostic of lupus erythematosus. SEE: *L.E. c.*

S c. An enteroendocrine cell that produces secretin and is found in the small intestine.

satellite c. 1. A stem cell associated with skeletal muscle that may form a limited number of new muscle cells after injury. **2.** One of the neuroglia cells enclosing the cell bodies of sensory neurons in spinal ganglia. SYN: *capsule c.*

scavenger c. A phagocyte that cleans up disintegrating tissues or cells.

Schwann c. SEE: under *Schwann, Theodore.*

segmented c. A segmented neutrophil (i.e., one with a nucleus of two or more lobes connected by slender filaments).

sensory c. A cell that when stimulated gives rise to nerve impulses that are conveyed to the central nervous system.

septal c. A type II alveolar cell that secretes pulmonary surfactant; it is adjacent to a septum of the alveoli.

serous c. An epithelial cell that secretes a watery fluid containing proteins, glycoproteins, and often antibodies (IgA, IgG, and IgM). Serous cells and mucous cells are the two varieties of secretory cells found in exocrine glands.

Sertoli c. SEE: *Sertoli cell.*

sex c. Gamete.

sickle c. An abnormal erythrocyte shaped like a sickle. SYN: *drepanocyte.* SEE: *anemia, sickle cell.*

signet-ring c. A vacuolated cell with the nucleus off center. Mucus-secreting adenocarcinomas usually contain these cells.

skeletal muscle c. SEE: *muscle.*

smooth muscle c. SEE: *muscle.*

somatic c. Any cell that is not a germ cell.

somatic stem c. Adult stem cell.

somatostatin c. D cell.

squamous c. A flat epithelial cell.squamous epithelial cell.

squamous epithelial c. Squamous cell.

stellate c. 1. Granule cell of the cerebral cortex. **2.** One of the small interneurons found in the outer layer of the cerebellar cortex along with basket cells.

stem c. An embryonic stem cell or an adult stem cell.

Sternberg-Reed c. SEE: *Reed-Sternberg cell.*

striated muscle SEE: *muscle*.

suppressor T c. A subpopulation of regulatory T lymphocytes that develop in the thymus gland, that slows or stops a specific immune response.

sustentacular c. A supporting cell, as in the acoustic macula, organ of Corti, olfactory epithelium, taste buds, or testes.

syncytial giant c. Giant cell.

T c. A lymphocyte that responds to specific antigens, with the assistance of antigen-presenting cells (APCs). T cells arise in the bone marrow and migrate to the thymus gland, where they mature; then they circulate between blood and lymph, serving as one of the primary cells of the adaptive immune response. Immature T cells are called thymocytes. Mature T cells are antigen specific. Their surface receptors (T cell receptors, abbrev. TCRs) respond only to a single antigen. T cells are further categorized using another family of surface protein markers called clusters of differentiation (CDs). All T cells have a CD3 marker. Additional markers differentiate the subclasses of T cells. CD4 T helper cells serve primarily as regulators, secreting cytokines that stimulate the activities of other white blood cells. CD8 T cells (cytotoxic T cells) directly lyse (kill) organisms, an important defense against viruses; most CD8 T cells also produce gamma interferon (INFγ), one of the strongest stimulators of macrophage activity. SYN: *T lymphocyte*. SEE: *immune response; lymphocyte; immunological surveillance; T-cell receptor*.

A T cell can only recognize the "foreignness" of antigens after they have been modified by macrophages and other antigen-presenting cells (APCs). After this, T cells dominate the adaptive immune response by mobilizing B cells and other T cells of the cell-mediated immune pathways. T cells are responsible for type IV hypersensitivity reactions, such as graft rejection, and for tumor cell recognition and destruction. SEE: *cytokine; cell-mediated immunity*.

target c. 1. An erythrocyte with a dark rounded central area surrounded by a lightly stained clear ring, which in turn is surrounded by a dense ring of peripheral cytoplasm. It is present in certain blood disorders, such as thalassemia, and in patients who have no spleen. SEE: *hemoglobin C disease* for illus. SYN: *codocyte; leptocyte*. 2. The cell at which a signal (e.g., hormone or nerve impulse) is aimed.

tart c. A phagocyte that has ingested the unaltered nuclei of cells. These nuclei can be observed unchanged within the phagocytes.

taste c. Any of the neuroepithelial cells within a taste bud that are receptors for the sense of taste. Each possesses on the free surface a short gustatory hair that projects through the inner taste pore. SYN: *taste receptor cell*.

taste receptor cell taste cell.

tendon c. Any of the fibroblasts of white fibrous connective tissue of tendons arranged in parallel rows.

terminally differentiated c. A cell sufficiently committed to a particular function that it can no longer divide, e.g. a red cell.

thymic epithelial c. The epithelial cells that form the internal scaffolding of the thymus. These cells vary in shape and size but generally align in sheets and cords, partitioning the thymus into islands of close-packed lymphocytes in the organ's cortex. Thymic epithelial cells are not simply structural and they interact actively with adjacent lymphocytes.

thymus c. Any cell characteristic of the thymus, including thymic epithelial cells and thymocytes (thymic lymphocytes).

thyroid c. Any cell characteristic of the thyroid gland, but usually referring to a thyroid follicular cell.

totipotent c. An undifferentiated embryonic cell that has the potential to develop into any type of cell.

transitional c. The stretchable epithelial cells that compose the transitional epithelium (uroepithelium), which lines most of the urinary tract. Transitional cells are strongly interconnected. They are cuboidal when not under pressure, and they become flattened and squamous when stretched. Transitional epithelia are 4-6 cells thick, and the top transitional cells -- those on the lumenal surface -- fuse to become larger and polyploid.

trophoblast c. One of the epithelial cells forming the surface of the spherical blastocyst stage embryo. Trophoblast cells are destined to give rise to many of the extraembryonic tissues.

tufted c. SEE: *mitral cell*.

undifferentiated c. A cell resembling an embryonic cell in that it does not have the specific morphologic or functional characteristics of any particular adult cell type.

unipolar c. A cell with a single cell process.

Vero c. A lineage of cells used in cell cultures and isolated from kidney epithelial cells of the African green monkey (*Cercopithecus aethiops*).

visual c. A rod cell or cone cell of the retina.

wandering c. A rarely used term for a cell (such as a macrophage) that moves like an ameba.

white c. Leukocyte.

white blood c. ABBR: WBC. Leukocyte.

cell adhesion molecule ABBR: CAM. Any molecule that traverses the cell membrane and contains a chemical domain that binds it to other cells or to the extracellular matrix.

cell bank SEE: under *bank*.

cell-based therapy The use of living cells as therapeutic agents. Possible examples include dendritic cells, to initiate immune responses to particular cancers; stem cells, as a source for tissue replacement, repair, or gene delivery; and tumor cells, to create antigen targets for the immune system.

cell coat A colloquial term for glycocalyx.

cell counter, electronic An electronic instrument used to count blood cells, employing either an electrical resistance or an optical gating technique. SEE: *flow cytometry*.

cell division The fission of a cell. SEE: *meiosis* and *mitosis* for illus.

cell-free Pertaining to fluids or tissues that contain no cells or in which all the cells have been disintegrated by laboratory treatment.

cell growth cycle SEE: under *cycle*.

cell kill In antineoplastic therapy, the number of malignant tumor cells destroyed by a treatment.

cell line A group of identical cells that can be maintained in the laboratory indefinitely because they are able to thrive and reproduce themselves in vitro.

cell mass SEE: under *mass*.

cellobiose (sĕl′ō-bī′ōs) A disaccharide resulting from the hydrolysis of cellulose.

cellophane (sĕl′ō-fān) A thin, transparent, waterproof sheet of cellulose acetate. It is used as a dialysis membrane.

cell-penetrating peptide SEE: under *peptide*.

cell saver An apparatus that aspirates extravasated blood in an operative field; after appropriate filtration the blood may be returned to the patient. SEE: *blood salvage*.

⚠ This device cannot be used when the blood returned to the patient may be infected, e.g., in perforated diverticulitis, contaminated with certain medications, or when malignancy is present in the operative field.

cell sorting The separation of cells from one another, based on physical or chemical properties. Cell-separation techniques are used to collect uniform populations of cells from tissues or fluids in which many different cell types are present. The collected cells can then be used for transplantation or scientific study. Common methods of separating cells include cloning, centrifugation, electrophoresis, magnetism, and antibody- or fluorescent-binding. SEE: *flow cytometry*.

fluorescence-activated c. s. ABBR: FACS. A method of separating cells by selectively tagging them with colored fluorescent dyes bound to specific cellular structures or molecules.

cellula (sĕl′ū-lă) *pl.* **cellulae** [L., little cell] **1.** A minute cell. **2.** A small compartment.

cellular (sĕl′ū-lăr) Pertaining to, composed of, or derived from cells.

cellularity (sel″yŭ-lar′ĭt-ē) The number of cells in a volume of tissue or in a cytologic or histologic specimen. SEE: *hypercellularity; hypocellularity*.

cellular reprogramming The use of transcription factors to induce a differentiated somatic cell to become pluripotent.

cellulase (sĕl′ū-lās) An enzyme that converts cellulose to cellobiose. It is present in some microorganisms and marine life.

cellulifugal (sĕl″ū-lĭf′ū-găl) [″ + *fugere*, to flee] Extending or moving away from a cell.

cellulipetal (sĕl″ū-lĭp′ĭ-tăl) [″ + *petere*, to seek] Extending or moving toward a cell.

cellulite (sĕl′ū-līt″) A colloquial term for subcutaneous deposits of fat with dimpling of the skin, esp. in the buttocks and thighs.

cellulitis (sel″yŭ-līt′ĭs) [*cellula* + *-itis,*] A spreading bacterial infection of the skin and subcutaneous tissues, usually caused by streptococcal or staphylococcal infections in adults (and occasionally by *Haemophilus* species in children). It may occur following damage to skin from an insect bite, an excoriation, or other wound. The extremities, esp. the lower legs, are the most common sites. Adjacent soft tissue may be involved. Affected skin becomes inflamed: red, swollen, warm to the touch, and tender. Spread of infection up lymphatic channels may occur. Cellulitis involving the face is called erysipelas. When it affects the lower extremities, cellulitis must be differentiated from stasis dermatitis, which is associated most commonly with bilateral, chronic dependent edema and, occasionally, with deep venous thrombosis. Risk factors for cellulitis include diabetes mellitus, lymphedema, venous stasis or insufficiency, immune suppression, injection drug use, malnutrition, peripheral vascular disease, and previous skin diseases. SEE: illus.; *necrotizing fasciitis*.

ETIOLOGY: Bacteria gain access through breaks in the skin and spread rapidly, overwhelming normal body defenses; lesions between the toes from athlete's foot are common entry sites.

TREATMENT: For mild cases of cellulitis, oral antibiotics may be effective

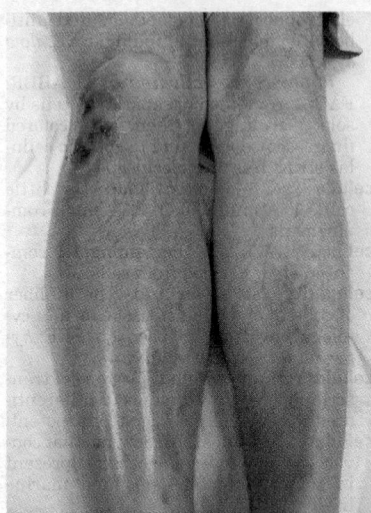

CELLULITIS

depending on the causative organism. For severe cases, intravenous penicillinase-resistant penicillins are used; surgical débridement to obtain cultures and to rule out fasciitis is recommended for patients with diabetes.

> ⚠ Rarely, group A streptococcal cellulitis may be complicated by exfoliative dermatitis or infection of the subcutaneous fat and fascia, causing necrosis (necrotizing fasciitis), a condition popularly ascribed to the action of "flesh-eating bacteria."

PATIENT CARE: Blood cultures should be obtained from patients with cellulitis to assess for sepsis before beginning therapy with antibiotics. The affected body part should be elevated above the level of the heart. Outlining the affected area with a skin marker allows the caregiver to readily determine if inflamed tissues are responding to therapy. Size, shape, color, and temperature of the affected area and surrounding tissues should be documented and any drainage described. Applying warm soaks to the area increases vasodilation, thus decreasing edema and relieving pain. Pain should be treated with prescribed oral analgesics and anti-inflammatory drugs. Blood sugars, if elevated, should be lowered to normal levels (preferably about 126 mg/dL or less). Patients on prolonged bedrest should be given heparin to prevent deep venous thrombosis as well as stool softeners to prevent constipation. Patients who develop cellulitis are often at risk for recurrence; they should learn general skin hygiene, how to clean cuts, scratches, cracked skin, and abrasions, and the importance of prompt treatment for infections.

    dissecting c. of the scalp An inflammatory pustular disease of the scalp, similar to acne conglobata or hidradenitis suppurativa. It can be treated surgically, with isotretinoin, or with laser therapy. SYN: *perifolliculitis capitis abscedens*.

    eosinophilic c. A rash marked by firm, swollen, itchy patches that appear suddenly. The patches may be oval or circular, violet or red, and are associated with abnormally high blood eosinophil levels. The cause is unknown. SYN: *Wells syndrome*.

    orbital c. Postseptal **c.**

    pelvic c. Parametritis.

    periorbital c. Preseptal **c.**

    postseptal c. Facial infection invading the orbit. SYN: *orbital* **c.**

    preseptal c. Soft tissue infection limited to the tissues anterior to the orbital septum. SYN: *periorbital* **c.**

cellulofibrous (sĕl″ū-lō-fī′brŭs) [″ + *fibra*, fiber] Both cellular and fibrous.

cellulose (sel′yŭ-lōs″) [*cellula* + *¹-ose*] A polysaccharide that forms plant fiber; a fibrous form of carbohydrate, $(C_6H_{10}O_5)_n$, constituting the supporting framework of most plants. It is composed of many glucose units. When ingested, it stimulates peristalsis and promotes intestinal elimination. When ingested by humans, cellulose provides no nutrient value because it is not chemically changed or absorbed in digestion; it remains a polysaccharide.

    Some foods that contain cellulose are apples, apricots, asparagus, beans, beets, bran flakes, broccoli, cabbage, celery, mushrooms, oatmeal, onions, oranges, parsnips, prunes, spinach, turnips, wheat flakes, whole grains, and whole wheat bread. SEE: *dietary fiber*.

    c. acetate 1. A support medium commonly used in electrophoresis. 2. A semisynthetic dialysis membrane.

    carboxymethyl sodium c. ABBR: CMC. SEE: *carboxymethylcellulose sodium*.

    oxidized c. Cellulose that has been oxidized and is made to resemble cotton or gauze. It is used to arrest bleeding by direct application to the site of hemorrhage.

    c. triacetate ABBR: TAC. A semisynthetic dialysis membrane with excellent biocompatibility that can be used in high-flux dialyzers.

cellulotoxic (sĕl″ū-lō-tŏk′sĭk) [″ + Gr. *toxikon*, poison] 1. Poisonous to cells. 2. Caused by cell toxins.

cell wall SEE: under *wall*.

¹celo-, cel- [Gr. *kēlē*, tumor, swelling] Prefixes meaning *tumor* or *hernia*.

²celo-, cel- [Gr. *koilia,* cavity] Prefixes meaning *cavity.*

celom, celoma (sē'lŏm, sē-lō'mă) [Gr. *koiloma,* a hollow] The coelom.

celosomia (sē-lō-sō'mē-ă) [" + *soma,* body] A congenital fissure of the sternum with herniation of the fetal viscera.

Celsius, Anders (sel'sē-ŭs) Swedish astronomer, 1701–1744.

   C scale A temperature scale on which the boiling point of water is 100° and the freezing point is 0°. This is the official scientific name of this temperature scale. SYN: *centigrade ¹scale.* SEE: *Fahrenheit ¹scale* for table; *thermometer* for table; Conversion Rules and Factors.

   C. thermometer A thermometer generally used in scientific notation. Temperature of boiling water at sea level is 100°C and the freezing point is 0°C. SYN: *centigrade thermometer.*

cement (sē-mĕnt') **1.** Any material that hardens into a firm mass when prepared appropriately. **2.** To cause two objects to stick together, as in using an adhesive to join a gold inlay to the cavity of a tooth and to insulate the pulp from metallic fillings. **3.** The material used to make one substance adhere to another.

   glass ionomer c. A dental adhesive made from powdered aluminosilicate glass and liquid polyacrylic acid, used as a lining for dental cavities; as a permanent dental restorative material; and, as a result of leakage, as a source of fluoride. The cement is not recommended for Class II or IV restorations.

   silicate c. A hard, translucent, tooth-colored restorative material. Silicate cement is produced by mixing aluminosilicate (an acid-based powdered glass) with liquid phosphoric acid. Because the cement is damaging to pulp of the tooth, pulp protection is required. Leakage often occurs at the margins of a silicate cement, but the fluoride released prevents caries.

⚠ Pulp protection is required.

   zinc-eugenol c. A cement and protectant used in dentistry. SEE: *zinc oxide and eugenol.*

   zinc phosphate c. The oldest of the dental cements, composed of a powder (zinc oxide and magnesium oxide) and a liquid (phosphoric acid and water). An acid-base reaction occurs when the powder and liquid are mixed. The set cement is unreacted zinc oxide particles suspended within a matrix of zinc aluminophosphate. The cement is used for inlays, crowns, bridges, and orthodontic appliances.

   zinc polycarboxylate c. Dental cement that can be used to attach cast restorations and orthodontic appliances

and as a thermal insulating base. It forms an adhesive bond with enamel. It is produced by mixing a powder containing zinc oxide and magnesium oxide with a liquid solution of polyacrylic acid.

cementation (sē"mĕn-tā'shŭn, sĕm"ĭn) The use of a plastic or moldable substance to seal joints and cement or join substances together. SYN: *luting.*

cementicle (sē-mĕn'tĭ-kl) The small calcified area in the periodontal membrane of the root of a tooth.

cementitis (sē"mĕn-tī'tĭs) [L. *cementum,* cement, + Gr. *itis,* inflammation] Inflammation of the dental cementum.

cementoblast (sē-mĕn'tō-blăst) [" + Gr. *blastos,* germ] A cell of the inner layer of the dental sac of a developing tooth. It deposits cementum on the dentin of the root.

cementoclasia (sē-mĕn"tō-klā'sē-ă) [" + Gr. *klasis,* breaking] Decay of the cementum of a tooth root.

cementoclast (sē-mĕn'tō-klăst) A very large multinucleated cell associated with the removal of cementum during root resorption, more correctly called an odontoclast.

cementogenesis (sē-mĕn"tō-jĕn'ĕ-sĭs) [" + Gr. *genesis,* generation] The development of cementum on the root dentin of a tooth.

cementoid (sē"mĕn'toyd) [" + Gr. *eidos,* form, shape] The noncalcified matrix of cementum.

cementum (si-ment'ŭm) [L. *caementum,* rubble, unhewn stone] The thin layer of calcified tissue formed by cementoblasts which covers the outer portion of the tooth root. In it are embedded the collagenous fibers of the periodontal ligament, which are also attached to the surrounding alveolar bone proper, thereby supporting the tooth. Also called *substantia ossea dentis.*

CEN *certified emergency nurse.*

censor (sĕn'sĕr) [L. *censor,* judge] In psychoanalysis, a psychic inhibition that prevents abhorrent unconscious thoughts or impulses from being expressed objectively in any form recognized at the conscious level.

census (sen'sŭs) [L. *census,* assessment] In hospital management, the number of patients currently cared for by the hospital.

Centella asiatica (sen-tel'ă ā"s(h)ē-at'ĭ-kă, "z(h)ē-) A low-lying herb native to India and East Asia. It is used for a wide variety of medicinal purposes in Ayurvedic and traditional Chinese medicine as a sedative, an antiasthmatic, a treatment for liver and skin diseases, and a promoter of longevity. SYN: *gotu kola.*

centenarian (sĕn"tĕ-nă'rē-ăn) A person over the age of 100.

center (sent'ĕr) [L. *centrum,* center fr Gr. *kentron,* point, needle, pivot] **1.** The middle point of a body. **2.** A group of nerve cells within the central nervous system that controls a specific activity or function.

acoustic c. The hearing center in the brain, located in the temporal lobe of the cerebrum.

adult day care c. A center for daytime supervision of adults. These centers provide supervised social, recreational, and health-related activities, usually in a group setting. The centers permit caregivers a respite and free them for other activities (work, play, appointments, socialization) during the day.

ambulatory surgery c. An outpatient surgical center for cardioversions, endoscopies, and other relatively minor operations that do not require prolonged confinement in a hospital.

association c. The center controlling associated movements.

auditory c. The center for hearing in the anterior gyri of the transverse temporal gyri. SEE: *auditory area*.

autonomic c. The center in the brain or spinal cord that regulates any of the activities under the control of the autonomic nervous system. Most centers are located in the hypothalamus, medulla oblongata, and spinal cord.

birth c. An alternative nonhospital facility that provides family-oriented maternity care for women judged to be at low risk of experiencing obstetrical complications.

Broca c. SEE: under *Broca, Pierre-Paul*.

call c. A communications center that manages incoming and outgoing telephone calls with customers and clients. In health care, the center may help to manage appointments and messages or may provide patients with information about illnesses, health care resources, services provided, or self-management of disease.

chondrification c. The center of cartilage formation.

ciliospinal c. The center in the spinal cord that transmits sympathetic impulses that dilate the pupils of the eyes.

day care c. A place for the care of preschool children when their parents are for any reason unable to care for them. Initially, such facilities were open during normal working hours, but many now offer early drop-off and late pickup.

defecation c. Either of two centers, a medullary center located in the medulla oblongata and a spinal center located in the second to fourth sacral segments of the spinal cord. The anospinal center controls the reflex aspects of defecation.

deglutition c. A group of structures in the brain that controls swallowing. These structures are located in the medulla oblongata and in the inferior pons.

diabetic c. 1. An area in the floor of the fourth ventricle of the brain. 2. A health care facility that provides specialized care to patients with diabetes mellitus.

epiotic c. The ossification center of the temporal bone, forming the upper and posterior part of the auditory capsule.

expiratory c. The part of the respiratory center, located dorsal to the inspiratory center, that promotes a forced exhalation.

feeding c. An area in the ventrolateral nucleus of the hypothalamus that originates signals to the cerebral cortex that stimulate eating. SEE: *satiety c.; set point weight*.

germinal c. A collection of B cells undergoing proliferation within the follicle of a lymph node or other lymphoid tissue after antigen stimulation.

gustatory c. The center, primarily in the parietal lobes, that feels and interprets taste. SYN: *taste c.; taste area*.

heat-regulating c. Either of two centers, a heat loss and a heat production center, located in the hypothalamus. They regulate body temperature.

higher c. A center in any portion of the brain, in contrast to one in the spinal cord.

independent living c. A community facility that coordinates services for the disabled, including counseling, training, rehabilitation, assistance with devices, and respite care.

inspiratory c. The respiratory center, located in the rostral half of the reticular formation overlying the olivary nuclei, that generates impulses that cause contraction of the diaphragm and external intercostal muscles.

lower c. A center in the brainstem or spinal cord.

micturition c. A center that controls the reflexes of the urinary bladder. These are located in the second to fourth and fourth to sixth sacral segments of the cord. Higher centers are present in the medulla oblongata, hypothalamus, and cerebrum. SEE: illus.

motor cortical c. An area in the frontal lobe in which impulses for voluntary movements originate.

nerve c. An area in the central nervous system or in a ganglion that is responsible for certain functions; examples include the motor areas in the frontal lobes of the cerebrum.

organization c. 1. An embryonic group of cells that induces the development of another structure. 2. A region in an ovum that is responsible for the mode of development of the fertilized ovum.

ossification c. The site or sites in bones where calcification begins and bone replaces fibrous connective tissue or cartilage. The region of bone forma-

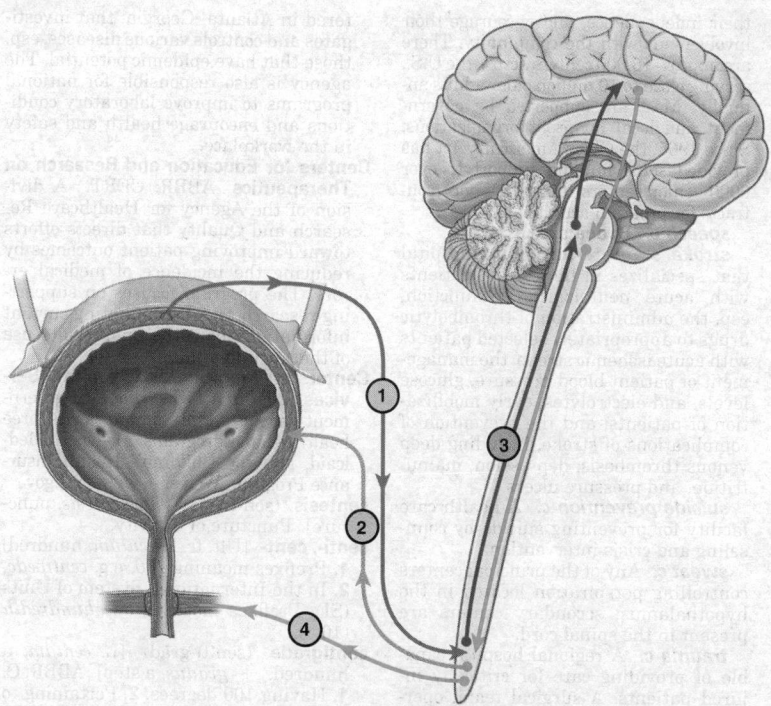

MICTURITION CENTER

(1) Afferent nerve. (2) Efferent nerve controlling bladder muscles. (3) Spinal cord and medulla oblongata. (4) Efferent nerve controlling bladder outlet.

tion at the center of the body of a long bone is called the primary (diaphyseal) ossification center. Most secondary ossification centers are found in the epiphyses.

panoramic rotational c. The axis on which the tube head and cassette of a panoramic x-ray machine rotate.

pneumotaxic c. The center in the pons that rhythmically inhibits inspiration.

poison control c., poison c. A facility meeting the staffing and equipment standards of the American Association of Poison Control Centers and recognized to be able to give information about poisoning or treatment to patients suffering from poisoning. A poison information center consists of specially trained staff and a reference library but does not have treatment facilities. More than 400 poison centers are scattered throughout the U.S., offering 24-hr service. They are commonly associated with or are part of large hospitals or medical schools. A government agency (the Bureau of Drugs Division of the Poison Control Branch of the Food and Drug Administration, U.S. Department of Health and Human Services) is also active in poison control programs

and in coordinating the efforts of individual centers. In the U.S., all poison control centers can be reached by calling 1-800-222-1222. SEE: Health Care Resources Appendix.

psychocortical c. Any of the centers of the cerebral cortex concerned with voluntary muscular contractions.

reflex c. A region within the brain or spinal cord where connections (synapses) are made between afferent and efferent neurons of a reflex arc.

respiratory c. A region in the medulla oblongata of the brainstem that regulates movements of respiration. This area consists of an inspiratory center and an expiratory center. The pons contains the apneustic center and the pneumotaxic center.

satiety c. An area in the ventromedial hypothalamus that modulates the stimulus to eat by sending inhibitory impulses, following a meal, to the feeding center. Blood levels of nutrients and gastrointestinal hormones influence its activity.

senior c. A community building or meeting room where older adults gather for education, recreation, and services and activities that reflect their interests, enhance their dignity, support their independence, and encourage their involvement with the community. There are approx. 15,000 centers across the U.S., serving close to 10 million older adults annually. Most are supported by government and local nonprofit organizations. Since 1965, the Older Americans Act has provided some funding support to over 6000 senior centers through service contracts for program activities.

speech c. Broca area.

stroke s. A tertiary care hospital that specializes in the care of patients with acute neurological dysfunction, esp. the administration of thrombolytic drugs to appropriately selected patients with acute ischemic stroke; the management of patient blood pressure, glucose levels, and electrolytes; early mobilization of patients; and the prevention of complications of stroke, including deep venous thrombosis, depression, malnutrition, and pressure ulcers.

suicide prevention c. A health care facility for preventing suicide by counseling and crisis intervention.

sweat c. Any of the principal centers controlling perspiration located in the hypothalamus; secondary centers are present in the spinal cord.

trauma c. A regional hospital capable of providing care for critically injured patients. A surgical team, operating suite, surgical subspecialties, intensive care unit, and specialized nursing team are always available.

vasoconstrictor c. The center in the medulla oblongata that brings about the constriction of blood vessels.

vasomotor c. The center that controls the diameter of blood vessels; the vasoconstrictor and vasodilator centers.

visual c. A center in the occipital lobes of the cerebrum that receives visual information transmitted from the retina.

vital c. Any of the centers in the medulla concerned with respiration, heart rate, or blood pressure.

center of excellence An educational or health care institution recognized for its superiority in education, patient care, and/or research.

Center for Drug Evaluation and Research ABBR: CDER. A division of the U.S. Food and Drug Administration that reviews and oversees the manufacture of pharmaceuticals distributed to U.S. citizens and provides clinical information about the uses and hazards of drugs. Website: www.fda.gov/cder/

centering 1. As part of meditative practice, an attempt to attain a state of self-awareness, relaxation, and psychological balance. **2.** In bodywork, focusing of the mind of the practitioner before beginning a therapeutic session with a patient.

Centers for Disease Control and Prevention ABBR: CDC. A division of the U.S. Public Health Service headquar-

tered in Atlanta, Georgia, that investigates and controls various diseases, esp. those that have epidemic potential. The agency is also responsible for national programs to improve laboratory conditions and encourage health and safety in the workplace.

Centers for Education and Research on Therapeutics ABBR: CERT. A division of the Agency for Healthcare Research and Quality that directs efforts toward improving patient outcomes by reducing the incidence of medical errors. The program focuses on supporting research and disseminating current information about the appropriate use of therapeutic agents.

Centers for Medicare and Medicaid Services ABBR: CMS. The U.S. government agency that administers three health-related programs: Medicare, Medicaid, and the Children's Health Insurance Program. Web site: www.cms.gov

centesis (sen-tē'sĭs) [Gr. *kentēsis,* puncture] Puncture of a cavity.

centi-, cent- [Ult. fr. L. *centum,* hundred] **1.** Prefixes meaning *100,* e.g. *centipede.* **2.** In the International System of Units (SI), Prefixes meaning *one hundredth* (10^{-2}).

centigrade (sĕn'tĭ-grād) [L. *centum,* a hundred, + *gradus,* a step] ABBR: C. **1.** Having 100 degrees. **2.** Pertaining to a thermometer divided into 100°. The boiling point of water is 100° and the freezing point is 0°.

centigram (sĕn'tĭ-grăm) [″ + Gr. *gramma,* a small weight] One hundredth of a gram.

centile (sen'tīl″, 'tĭl) Percentile.

centiliter (sĕn'tĭ-lē-tĕr) [″ + Gr. *litra,* measure of wt.] One hundredth of a liter. SEE: *metric system.*

centimeter (sent'ĭ-mēt″ĕr) [*centi-* + *-meter*] ABBR: cm. One hundredth of a meter.

cubic c. ABBR: cc, cm³. In the metric system, a unit of volume equal to that of a cube 1 cm on a side. It is functionally equivalent to a milliliter.

⚠ The common abbreviation cc is considered a dangerous abbreviation. The preferred abbreviation is mL.

SEE: *milliliter; mL.*

square c. ABBR: cm². In the metric system, a unit of area equal to that of a square 1 cm on a side. SEE: *metric system.*

centimeter-gram-second system ABBR: CGS. An early version of the SI units system, no longer in use.

centimorgan (sĕn'tĭ-mor″găn) ABBR: cM. One hundredth of a morgan; a measure of genetic distance that indicates the likelihood of crossover of two loci on a gene.

centipede (sĕn'tĭ-pēd″) [" + *pes,* foot] An arthropod of the subclass Chilopoda distinguished by an elongated flattened body of many segments, each with a pair of jointed legs. The first pair of appendages are hooklike claws bearing openings of ducts from poison glands. The bites of large tropical centipedes may cause severe local and sometimes general symptoms, but they are rarely fatal.

centipoise (sent'ĭ-poyz″) [*centi-* + *poise*] A unit of viscosity in SI units for one hundredth of a poise. SEE: *poise.*

Centor criteria (sent'ŏr) [R.M. Centor, contemporary U.S. physician] A clinical prediction rule used in the diagnosis of streptococcal pharyngitis (strep throat). It includes four elements: fever above 100.5°F (41°C); no cough; exudates on the tonsils; and tenderness in the anterior cervical lymph nodes. The likelihood of strep throat is greater than 40% when all four elements are present. It is less than 3% in patients with just one element. Patients with two or three of the criteria should be evaluated further with rapid antigen tests or throat culture before antibiotics are prescribed.

centrad (sĕn'trăd) [Gr. *kentron,* center, + L. *ad,* toward] Toward the center.

central (sĕn'trăl) **1.** Situated at or pertaining to a center. **2.** Principal or controlling.

central auditory processing disorder A condition, sometimes confused with attention deficit disorder or hearing disorders, in which a child has normal hearing and intelligence, but cannot interpret sounds and their correct contexts or meanings.

central cord syndrome, central cervical cord syndrome Paralysis of the hands and arms (and often of the lower limbs but to a less severe degree) resulting from an injury to the cervical spinal cord. Bladder dysfunction and sensory losses below the level of the injury often occur. The condition is typically produced by a hyperextension injury of the neck.

central core disease A rare, congenital muscle disease characterized by muscular weakness or hypotonia in infancy due to impaired release of calcium by skeletal muscle. Calcium is a crucial cofactor in muscle contraction.

central dogma of molecular biology The outdated principle which states that proteins are made from RNA, which in turn is made from DNA. Other permutations are found in nature; e.g., RNA viruses use a reverse transcriptase to make complementary DNA.

central excitatory state ABBR: CES. A condition of increased excitability in the central nervous system, esp. in the spinal cord, following an excitatory stimulus.

central inhibitory state ABBR: CIS. A condition of decreased excitability in the central nervous system, esp. in the spinal cord, resulting from an inhibitory stimulus.

central island An abnormally raised ridge of corneal tissue that may be left behind after failed photorefractive eye surgery. The lump or ridge of thick cornea may cause distorted or double vision.

central nervous system ABBR: CNS. The brain and spinal cord, as opposed to the peripheral nervous system. The central nervous system is entirely enclosed by a delicate membrane called the pia.

central serous retinopathy SEE: under *retinopathy.*

central venous oxygen saturation ABBR: ScvO$_2$. The oxygen saturation of venous blood sampled from the superior vena cava. It is slightly less than the oxygen saturation from the lower body (as measured in the inferior vena cava) because of the increased oxygen saturation that occurs in the brain and upper body.

central vision loss SEE: under *loss.*

centration (sĕn″trā'shŭn) The ability of the preschool child to focus or center attention on only one aspect or characteristic of a situation at a time.

centrifugal (sĕn-trĭf'ū-găl) [" + L. *fugere,* to flee] Receding from the center.

centrifuge (sen'trĭ-fūj″) A device that spins test tubes at high speeds. The heavy, more dense, particles in the liquid settle to the bottom of the tube, and the lighter liquid goes to the top. When unclotted blood is centrifuged, the plasma goes to the top and the heavy red cells go to the bottom of the tube. The white blood cells are heavier than the plasma but lighter than the red blood cells, so they form a thin layer between the red blood cells and the plasma. SEE: *buffy coat.*

   human c. A device that accommodates a human subject being rotated while suspended from a long arm. It is used to investigate the ability of subjects to withstand positive gravitational forces.

centriole (sĕn'trē-ōl) A minute organelle consisting of a hollow cylinder closed at one end and open at the other, found in the cell center or attraction sphere of a cell. Before mitosis it divides, forming two daughter centrioles (diplosomes). During mitosis the centrioles migrate to opposite poles of the cell, and each forms the center of the aster to which the spindle fibers are attached. SEE: *mitosis.*

centripetal (sĕn-trĭp'ĕ-tăl) [" + L. *petere,* to seek] Directed toward the axis.

centroblast (sen'trŏ-blast″) [*center* + *-blast*] A B lymphocyte that reproduces within the germinal center of a lymph node. It has a noncleaved nucleus. Unlike the centrocyte, into which it develops, it does not express immunoglobulins on its cell surface.

centrocyte (sĕn'trō-sīt) [″ + *kytos,* cell] Any of the stages of B lymphocytes found in the center of lymphatic follicles.

centrodesmus (sĕn-trō-dĕz'mŭs) [Gr. *kentron,* center, + *desmos,* a band] The matter connecting the two centrosomes in a nucleus during mitosis.

centrolecithal (sĕn″trō-lĕs'ĭ-thăl) [″ + *lekithos,* yoke] Pert. to an egg cell with the yolk centrally located.

centromere (sĕn'trō-mēr) [″ + *meros,* part] A constricted region of a chromosome, a specific sequence of about 200 nucleotides that connects the chromatids during cell division. Attached to this DNA is a protein disk called a kinetochore, which attaches the pair of chromatids to a spindle fiber.

centrosclerosis (sĕn″trō-sklĕ-rō'sĭs) [″ + *sklerosis,* a hardening] Filling of the bone marrow space with bone tissue.

centrosome (sĕn'trō-sōm) [″ + *soma,* body] A region of the cytoplasm of a cell usually lying near the nucleus, containing in its center one or two centrioles, the diplosomes. SEE: *mitosis.*

centrosphere (sĕn'trō-sfēr) [″ + *sphaira,* sphere] The cytoplasm of the centrosome.

centrostaltic (sĕn″trō-stăl'tĭk) [″ + *stellein,* send forth] Pert. to a center of motion.

centrum (sĕn'trŭm) *pl.* **centra** [L.] 1. Any center, esp. an anatomical one. 2. The body of a vertebra.

cepacia SEE: *Burkholderia cepacia.*

cephalad (sĕf'ă-lăd) [Gr. *kephale,* head, + L. *ad,* toward] Toward the head.

cephalalgia (sĕf-ă-lăl'jē-ă) [″ + *algos,* pain] Headache. SYN: *cephalodynia.* **cephalalgic** (-jĭk), *adj.*

cephalea (sĕf-ă-lē'ă) [Gr. *kephale,* head] Cephalalgia.

cephaledema (sĕf″ăl-ĕ-dē'mă) [″ + *oidema,* swelling] Edema of the head, esp. of the brain.

cephalexin (sĕf″ă-lĕk'sĭn) A first-generation cephalosporin antibiotic. It is effective against gram-positive and some gram-negative bacteria.

cephalhematocele (sĕf″ăl-hē-măt'ō-sēl) [″ + *haima,* blood, + *kele,* tumor] A bloody tumor communicating with the dural sinuses.

cephalic (sĕ-făl'ĭk) [L. *cephalicus*] 1. Pert. to the head. 2. Superior in position.

cephalic suspension The supported suspension of a patient by the head to extend the vertebral column.

cephalo-, cephal- [Gr. *kephalē,* head] Prefixes meaning *head.*

cephalocaudal pattern of development

(sĕf″ă-lō-kawd'ăl) [″ + ″] The principle of maturation that states motor development, control, and coordination progress from the head to the feet.

cephalocele (sĕf'ă-lō-sēl) [″ + *kele,* hernia] Protrusion of the brain from the cranial cavity.

cephalocentesis (sĕf″ă-lō-sĕn-tē'sĭs) [″ + *kentesis,* puncture] Surgical puncture of the cranium.

cephalodynia (sĕf″ă-lō-dĭn'ē-ă) [″ + *odyne,* pain] Headache.

cephalohematoma (sĕf″ă-lō-hē″mă-tō'mă) [″ + ″ + *oma,* tumor] A mass composed of clotted blood, located between the periosteum and the skull of a newborn. It is confined between suture lines and usually is unilateral. The cause is rupture of periosteal bridging veins due to pressure and friction during labor and delivery. The blood reabsorbs gradually within a few weeks of birth. Incidence is 1.5–2.5% of all deliveries. The overlying scalp is not discolored. If the lesion is extensive, hyperbilirubinemia may develop.

cephalohemometer (sĕf″ă-lō-hē-mŏm'ĕ-tĕr) [″ + *haima,* blood, + *metron,* measure] An instrument for determining changes in intracranial blood pressure.

cephalometer (sĕf-ă-lŏm'ĕ-tĕr) [″ + *metron,* measure] 1. A device for measuring the head. 2. In radiology, a device that maintains the head in a certain position for radiographic examination and measurement.

cephalometry (sĕf″ă-lŏm'ĕ-trē) Measurement of the head by using certain bony points directly, or by tracing radiographs made using well-established planes for linear and angular measurements. Cephalometry is used in oral, orthodontic, and plastic surgery, e.g., in the repair of cleft palate or facial asymmetries. It is also employed in dentistry to assess growth and to determine orthodontic or prosthetic treatment plans.

cephalomotor (sĕf″ă-lō-mō'tor) [Gr. *kephale,* head, + L. *motus,* motion] Pert. to movements of the head.

cephalopathy (sĕf″ă-lŏp'ă-thē) [″ + *pathos,* disease, suffering] Any disease of the head or brain.

cephalopelvic (sĕf″ă-lō-pĕl'vĭk) Pert. to the relationship between the measurements of the fetal head and the diameters of the maternal pelvis, esp. to the size of the pelvic outlet through which the fetal head will pass during delivery.

cephaloplegia (sĕf″ă-lō-plē'jē-ă) [″ + *plege,* stroke] Paralysis of head or neck muscles or both.

cephalorhachidian (sĕf″ă-lō-ră-kĭd'ē-ăn) [″ + *rhachis,* spine] Pert. to the head and spine.

cephalosporin (sef″ă-lō-spōr'ĭn) [*Cephalospor(ium)* + *-in*] Any of a group of antibiotic derivatives of cephalosporin C, obtained from the fungus *Cephalosporium.*

fifth-generation c. A broad-spectrum cephalosporin capable of treating infections with methicillin-resistant *Staphylococcus aureus* (MRSA), and many gram-negative, antibiotic-resistant enteric bacteria.

first-generation c. Any of a group of cephalosporin antibiotics capable of killing gram-positive cocci such as *Staphylococcus aureus,* streptococci, and some aerobic gram-negative rods. These agents are used to treat skin and soft tissue infections, uncomplicated respiratory tract infections, and urinary tract infections. Examples of first-generation cephalosporins are cephalothin, cephaloridine, cephapirin, cefazolin, cephradine, cephalexin, and cefadroxil.

fourth-generation c. Any of a group of cephalosporin antibiotics possessing broad-spectrum activity They are zwitterions that can penetrate the outer membranes of gram-negative bacteria. Many can cross the blood-brain barrier and are used to treat meningitis.

second-generation c. Any of a group of cephalosporin antibiotics possessing some ability to kill gram-positive cocci such as staphylococci and streptococci, as well as aerobic gram-negative rods. Some agents, i.e., cefotetan, cefoxitin, and cefmetazole, can be used to treat anaerobic infections. Examples of second-generation cephalosporins are cefamandole, cefuroxime, cefonicid, cefor-anide, cefixime, cefaclor, cefoxitin, cefotetan, and cefmetazole.

third-generation c. Any of a group of cephalosporin antibiotics capable of killing aerobic gram-negative rods. They are used to treat pneumonia and meningitis. Some agents, i.e., ceftazidime and cefoperazone, are very effective against against *Pseudomonas aeruginosa* Examples of third-generation cephalosporins are cefsulodin, cefotaxime, ceftizoxime, ceftriaxone, cefoperazone, moxalactam, and ceftazidime.

Cephalosporium (sĕf″ă-lŏ-spor′ē-ŭm) [*cephalo-* + *spore* + *-ium*] SEE: *Acremonium.*

cephalostat (sĕf′ă-lō-stăt″) A device that holds a patient's head in a fixed position. It may be used, e.g., in anesthesiology, to facilitate tracheal intubation; in dental radiography, to improve the quality of radiographs; and in ear, nose, and throat surgery to limit head movement. SYN: *craniostat.*

cephalothoracic (sĕf″ă-lō-thō-răs′ĭk) [″ + *thorakos,* chest] Pert. to the head and thorax.

cephalothoracopagus (sĕf″ă-lō-thō″ră-kŏp′ă-gŭs) [″ + ″ + *pagos,* thing fixed] A double fetus joined at the head and thorax.

-cephalus [Gr. *-kephalos,* "-headed"]

1. Suffix indicating a cephalic abnormality, e.g., *hydrocephalus.* 2. Suffix indicating an organism having a particular kind of head, e.g., *Rhipicephalus* (fan-shaped head).

cephamycin (sĕf-ă-mī′sĭn) [From *cepha(losporin)* + ″] A group of antibiotics related to the second-generation cephalosporins, having increased bacterial activity against Enterobacteriaceae but diminished effectiveness against gram-positive bacteria. Members of this class of drugs, e.g., cefoxitin, cefotetan, are often used to treat mixed aerobic/anaerobic infections.

-cept A combining form for a drug formed when a receptor is fused to the Fc portion of an immunoglobulin G molecule.

ceptor (sĕp′tor) [L. *receptor,* receiver] Receptor (2).

chemical c. A ceptor that detects chemical changes in the body.

contact c. A ceptor that receives stimuli contributed by direct physical contact.

distance c. A ceptor that perceives stimuli remote from the immediate environment.

cera (sē′ră) [L.] Wax (1).

c. alba White wax.

c. flava Yellow wax.

ceramics, dental [Gr. *keramos,* potter's clay] The use of porcelain or porcelain-like materials to manufacture esthetic dental restorations. Crowns, veneers, and inlays are some dental restorations that use porcelain.

ceramidase (sĕ-răm′ĭ-dās″, -dāz″) [*ceramide* + *-ase*] A lysosomal enzyme that partcipates in the metabolism of fatty components of cell membranes. SEE: *sphingolipid.*

ceramide (sĕr′ă-mīd) A class of lipids that do not contain glycerol. They are derived from a sphingosine. Glycosphingolipids and sphingomyelins are derived from ceramides.

c. oligosaccharides A class of glycosphingolipids.

Cerastes (sĕ-ras′tēz) [Gr. *kerastēs,* horned serpent] A genus of venomous snakes popularly known as horned vipers.

cerato-, cerat- SEE: *kerato-.*

cercaria (sĕr-kā′rē-ă) *pl.* **cercariae** [Gr. *kerkos,* tail] A free-swimming stage in the development of a fluke or trematode. Cercariae develop within sporocysts or rediae that parasitize snails or bivalve mollusks. They emerge from the mollusk and either enter their final host directly or encyst in an intermediate host that is ingested by the final host. In the latter case, the encysted tailless form is known as a metacercaria. SEE: *fluke; trematode.*

cercaricide (sĕr-kă′rĭ-sīd″) An agent that is lethal to cercaria.

cerclage (ser-klazh′) [Fr., *cerclage,* hooping] Encircling tissues with a ligature, wire, or loop.

cervical c. The use of ligatures around the cervix uteri to treat cervical incompetence during pregnancy. It is usually performed between 12–14 weeks before the cervix has begun to thin or dilate and is removed towards the end of pregnancy. SEE: *Shirodkar operation*.

Cercomonas (sĕr-kŏm′ō-năs) [Gr. *kerkos*, tail, + *monas*, unit] A genus of free-living flagellate protozoa.

cercomoniasis (sĕr″kō-mō-nī′ă-sĭs) Infestation with *Cercomonas intestinalis*.

cercus (sĕr′kŭs) *pl.* **cerci** [L., tail] A hairlike structure.

cerea flexibilitas (sē′rē-ă flĕk″sĭ-bĭl′ĭ-tăs) [L. *cera*, wax, + *flexibilitas*, flexibility] Flexibility, waxy. SEE: *catalepsy*.

cereal (sēr′ē-ăl) [L. *cerealis*, of grain] An edible seed or grain, containing approximately 70% to 80% carbohydrate by weight and 8% to 15% protein. Many cereals also provide significant dietary fiber. Common cereals include barley, oats, rice, and wheat.

cerebell-, cerebelli-, cerebello- [L. *cerebellum*, little brain, a diminutive of *cerebrum*, brain] Prefixes meaning *cerebellum* or *cerebellar*.

cerebellifugal (sĕr″ĕ-bĕl-ĭ-fū′găl) [L. *cerebellum*, little brain, + *fugere*, to flee] Extending or proceeding from the cerebellum.

cerebellipetal (sĕr″ĕ-bĕl-lĭp′ĭ-tăl) [″ + *petere*, to seek] Extending toward the cerebellum.

cerebellitis (sĕr″ĕ-bĕl-ī′tĭs) [″ + Gr. *itis*, inflammation] Inflammation of the cerebellum.

cerebellum (sĕr-ĕ-bĕl′ŭm) [L., little brain] The portion of the brain forming the largest segment of the rhombencephalon. It lies dorsal to the pons and medulla oblongata, overhanging the latter. It consists of two lateral cerebellar hemispheres and a narrow medial portion, the vermis. It is connected to the brainstem by three pairs of fiber bundles, the inferior, middle, and superior peduncles. The cerebellum is responsible for coordination of voluntary movements, the speed, trajectory, and stopping of movements, and for maintaining posture and balance. Sensory information to the cerebellum comes from the skeletal muscles and from inner ear receptors.

Although the cerebellum does not initiate movements, it interrelates with many brainstem structures in executing various movements, including maintaining proper posture and balance; walking and running; fine voluntary movements as required in writing, dressing, eating, and playing musical instruments; and smooth tracking movements of the eyes. The cerebellum controls the property of movements, such as speed, acceleration, and trajectory. **cerebellar** (-ăr), *adj*.

cerebr-, cerebri-, cerebro- [L. *cerebrum*, brain] Prefixes meaning *brain, cerebral*, or *cerebrum*.

cerebral (sĕr′ă-brĭl, să-rē′) **1.** Pert. to the intellect. **2.** Of, pertaining to, or located within the cerebrum, as cerebral palsy, cerebral aneurysm, and cerebral cortex.

cerebral dominance SEE: under *dominance*.

cerebral palsy ABBR: CP. An umbrella term for a group of nonprogressive but frequently changing motor impairment syndromes secondary to lesions or anomalies of the brain arising in the early stages of its development. CP is a symptom complex rather than a specific disease. For the vast majority of children born at term in whom CP later develops, the disorder cannot reasonably be ascribed to birth injury or hypoxic-ischemic insults during delivery. CP rarely occurs without associated defects such as mental retardation (60% of cases) or epilepsy (50% of cases).

Risk factors have been divided into three groups: those factors occurring before pregnancy, such as an unusually short interval (less than 3 months) or an unusually long interval since the previous pregnancy; those factors occurring during pregnancy, including physical malformations, twin gestation, abnormal fetal presentation, fetal growth retardation, or maternal hypothyroidism; and perinatal factors such as prematurity, premature separation of the placenta, or newborn encephalopathy. Nonetheless among infants with one or more of these risk factors, 95% do not have CP.

CP is classified by the extremities involved and the type of neurological dysfunction present, such as spastic (50%), hypotonic, dystonic, athetotic (20%), ataxic (10%), or a combination of these. It is not possible to diagnose CP in the neonatal period, and early clinical diagnosis is complicated by the changing pattern of the disease in the first year of life. Many patients have impaired swallowing and/or drooling. Impaired speech is present in about 80% of these children, and many also have dental abnormalities, deficits in vision and/or hearing, and reading disabilities.

All infants and children, esp. those at risk for CP (low birth weight, low Apgar scores at 5 min, seizures, metabolic disturbances), are assessed for delays in attaining developmental milestones. This type of assessment can provide valuable clues to recognizing CP. CP should also be suspected in infants who have difficulty sucking or keeping a nipple or food in their mouths; who seldom move voluntarily or have arm or leg tremors with voluntary movement; who cross their legs when lifted from behind rather than bicycling or pulling them up; or who have legs that are difficult to separate (making diapering problematic). Early recognition and promotion of optimal development assist the child to realize his or her potential.

INCIDENCE: In the U.S., about 10,000 children are born each year with CP.

TREATMENT: Therapy is directed to maximizing function and preventing secondary handicaps. Essential to the outcome of patients with CP is establishing good hand function, which helps compensate for other motor deficits. Broad therapeutic goals include establishing locomotion, communication, self-help and gaining optimum appearance and integration of motor functions; correcting associated deficits as effectively as possible; and providing educational opportunities adapted to the individual child's needs and capabilities. Antianxiety agents may be employed to relieve excessive motion and tension. Botulinum toxin helps to reduce contractures. Skeletal muscle relaxants may be given to decrease spasticity. Anticonvulsants are used for children experiencing seizure activity, and dextroamphetamine may improve performance in hyperactive, dyskinetic children. SEE: *Nursing Diagnoses Appendix.*

PATIENT CARE: The individualized therapeutic plan usually involves a variety of settings, facilities, and specially trained personnel, including the parents, who are taught to handle their child's condition properly. A specially trained physical therapist designs an individualized program of exercises and other treatment modalities to meet the child's specific problems and needs and to stimulate the child to achieve functional goals. A speech therapist is an important team member and initiates speech training early before the child develops poor communication habits. Eye and ear specialists deal with visual and auditory deficits. Dental care is esp. important and should start as soon as teeth erupt. Braces and other mobilizing devices help prevent or reduce deformities, control alignment, and permit self-propulsion. An orthopedic surgeon intervenes when spasticity causes progressive deformities. Nurses in pediatric facilities and community settings are involved in all aspects of therapeutic management and provide support and encouragement. They teach the child (as appropriate) and the parents about the desired and adverse effects of any medications used in the therapeutic regimen.

A wide variety of technical aids are available to help improve the child's function. They include electromechanical toys, microcomputers, voice synthesizers, and other devices the child can control. Passive range of motion, stretching, and elongation exercises are valuable at any age. Training in activities of daily living and manual skills is based on the child's developmental level and functional abilities. Manual activities are started early to improve the child's motor function and to provide sensory experiences and environmental information. The child is encouraged to feed himself or herself, using specially designed utensils and placing food well back in the mouth to aid swallowing. A high-calorie diet should be provided to meet the child's high-energy status. Thoroughly chewing food, drinking through a straw, and sucking on lollipops all help in developing muscle control, minimizing drooling. Washing and dressing independently are also encouraged, with clothing modified to aid this independence rather than carrying out these tasks for the child. Parents are taught to assist only when necessary and then in an unhurried manner because hurried movements tend to increase muscle spasticity. Play is incorporated into the therapeutic program.

The child's needs and potential determine his or her educational requirements, which range from attendance at regular school to special classes or facilities designed to meet his or her needs. The teaching team develops an individual educational prescription (IEP), which they communicate to parents and others involved in the child's learning. Special Olympics and other community programs can enable the child to participate in competitive sports, adding an extra dimension to physical activities. The child should also be encouraged to participate in artistic programs, games, and other activities. Parents should be advised against overprotection and helped to recognize the child's need to establish relationships with other children. A valuable intervention on the part of health care professionals is providing the family with emotional support, helping them to cope with the disorder and to connect with other families. Parent groups share concerns and problems and provide practical information as well as comfort. United Cerebral Palsy Association Inc. (800-872-5827; www.ucpa.org) provides a variety of services for children with CP and their families. Local chapters can be accessed through a local telephone directory or health department.

Throughout treatment, health care providers and the child's family continually reassess and evaluate the child's status by observing movements and speech, self-care and other activities, school attendance and performance, interactions with others and choice of activities, and behaviors and responses to challenges. The child and family are interviewed regularly about their feelings and concerns and are supported to cope with the condition.

cerebral salt wasting syndrome ABBR: CSW. Hyponatremia that develops in a critically ill patient who has suffered brain injury or infarction. The condition typically occurs in patients who are volume-depleted. High concentrations of sodium are found in the urine. Infusions of saline are therapeutic.

cerebration (sĕr″ĕ-brā′shŭn) [L. *cerebratio,* brain activity] Mental activity; thinking.

cerebromeningitis (sĕr″ĕ-brō-mĕn″ĭn-jī′tĭs) [″ + Gr. *meninx,* membrane, + *itis,* inflammation] Inflammation of the cerebrum and its membranes.

cerebropathy (sĕr″ĕ-brŏp′ă-thē) [″ + *pathos,* disease, suffering] Any disease of the brain, esp. the cerebrum.

cerebrophysiology (sĕr″ĕ-brō-fĭz-ē-ŏl′ō-jē) [″ + Gr. *physis,* nature, + *logos,* word, reason] The physiology of the brain.

cerebrosclerosis (sĕr″ĕ-brō″sklĕ-rō′sĭs) [″ + Gr. *sklerosis,* hardening] Hardening of the brain, esp. of the cerebrum.

cerebroside (sĕr′ĕ-brō-sīd″) A lipid or fatty substance present in nerve and other tissues.

cerebrosidosis (sĕr″ĕ-brō″sī-dō′sĭs) A form of lipoidosis with kerasin in the fatty cells. SEE: *Gaucher's disease.*

cerebrospinal (sĕr″ĕ-brō-spī′năl) [″ + *spina,* thorn] Pert. to the brain and spinal cord, as the cerebrospinal axis.

cerebrospinal axis SEE: under *axis.*

cerebrospinal fluid-to-blood glucose ratio Glucose ratio.

cerebrospinal puncture SEE: under *puncture.*

cerebrosterol A brain-derived sterol (technically: 24S-hydroxycholesterol) that is found in excessive concentrations in the bloodstream of persons with Alzheimer's disease.

cerebrotomy (sĕr″ĕ-brŏt′ō-mē) [L. *cerebrum,* brain, + Gr. *tome,* incision] **1.** Incision of the brain to evacuate an abscess. **2.** Dissection of the brain.

cerebrovascular (sĕr″ĕ-brō-văs′kū-lăr) [″ + *vasculum,* vessel] Pert. to the blood vessels of the brain, esp. to pathological changes.

cerebrovascular accident ABBR: CVA. Stroke.

cerebrum (sĕr′ĕ-brŭm, sĕr-ē′brŭm) [L.] The largest part of the brain, consisting of two hemispheres separated by a deep longitudinal fissure. The hemispheres are united by three commissures—the corpus callosum and the anterior and posterior hippocampal commissures.

The surface of each hemisphere is thrown into numerous folds or convolutions called gyri, which are separated by furrows called fissures or sulci.

EMBRYOLOGY: The cerebrum develops from the telencephalon, the most anterior portion of the prosencephalon or forebrain.

ANATOMY: Each cerebral hemisphere consists of three primary portions—the rhinencephalon or olfactory lobe, the corpus striatum, and the pallium or cerebral cortex. The cortex is a layer of gray matter that forms the surface of each hemisphere. The part in the rhinencephalon (phylogenetically the oldest) is called the archipallium; the larger nonolfactory cortex is called the neopallium. The cerebrum contains two cavities, the lateral ventricles (right and left) and the rostral portion of the third ventricle. The white matter of each hemisphere consists of three kinds of myelinated fibers: commissural fibers, which pass from one hemisphere to the other; projection fibers, which convey impulses to and from the cortex; and association fibers, which connect various parts of the cortex within one hemisphere.

Lobes: The principal lobes are the frontal, parietal, occipital, and temporal lobes and the central (the insula or island of Reil). *Basal ganglia:* Masses of gray matter are deeply embedded within each hemisphere. They are the caudate, lentiform, and amygdaloid nuclei and the claustrum. *Fissures and sulci:* These include the lateral cerebral fissure (of Sylvius), the central sulcus (of Rolando), the parieto-occipital fissure, the calcarine fissure, the cingulate sulcus, the collateral fissure, the sulcus circularis, and the longitudinal cerebral fissure. *Gyri:* These include the superior, middle, and inferior frontal gyri, the anterior and posterior central gyri, the superior, middle, and inferior temporal gyri, and the cingulate, lingual, fusiform, and hippocampal gyri.

PHYSIOLOGY: The cerebrum is concerned with sensations (the interpretation of sensory impulses) and all voluntary muscular activities. It is the seat of consciousness and the center of the higher mental faculties such as memory, learning, reasoning, judgment, intelligence, and the emotions. SEE: illus.

On the basis of function, several areas have been identified and located. Motor areas in the frontal lobes initiate all voluntary movement of skeletal muscles. Sensory areas in the parietal lobes are for taste and cutaneous senses, those in the temporal lobes are for hearing and smell, and those in the occipital lobes are for vision. Association areas are concerned with integration, analysis, learning, and memory.

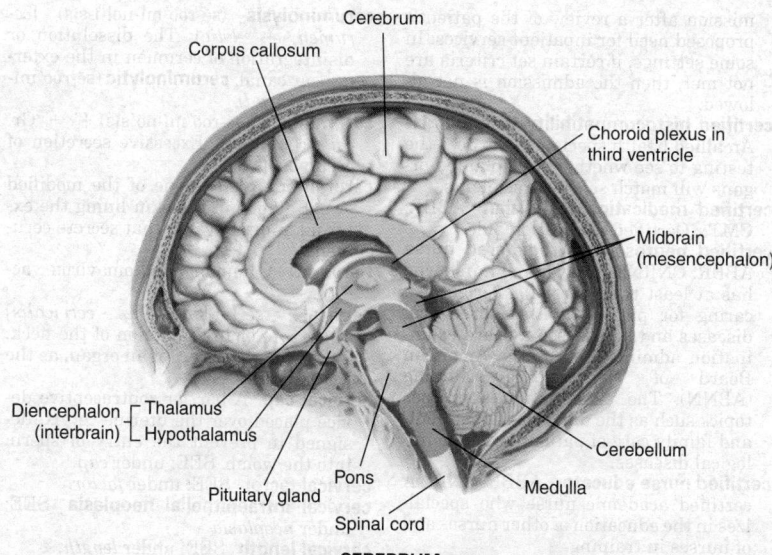

Cerebrum

Corpus callosum

Choroid plexus in third ventricle

Midbrain (mesencephalon)

Diencephalon (interbrain) ⌐ Thalamus └ Hypothalamus

Cerebellum

Pons

Medulla

Pituitary gland

Spinal cord

CEREBRUM

cereulide (sĕr′oo-līd″) The heat-stable toxin produced by *Bacillus cereus* that causes nausea and vomiting.

cerium (sir′ē-ŭm) [L. *Ceres,* a Roman goddess + *-ium*] SYMB: Ce. A metallic chemical element obtained from the rare earths, atomic mass (weight) 140.12, atomic number 58. ^{142}Ce is the most stable isotope, having a half life of 5×10^{16} years.

ceroid (sē′royd) A fatty pigment present in various tissues.

CERT *Centers for Education and Research on Therapeutics.*

certifiable (sĕr″tĭ-fī′ă-bl) **1.** Pert. to infectious diseases that must be reported or registered with health authorities. **2.** In forensic medicine, pert. to a mentally incompetent person who requires the care of a guardian or institution.

certificate of need ABBR: CON. A declaration from a government planning agency indicating that the construction or alteration of an existing health facility is justified. Designed initially in the 1970s to prevent the construction of duplicate health care facilities in local or regional markets, some analysts have suggested that CONs have instead defended existing hospitals from unwanted competition.

certification (sĕrt″ĭ-fĭ-kā′shŏn) **1.** A legal document prepared by an official body that indicates a person or institution has met certain standards, or that a person has completed a prescribed course of instruction or training. **2.** The completion of a form indicating the cause of death. **3.** The legal process of declaring a person insane or mentally incompetent on the basis of medical evidence.

board c. In health care, a process that ensures that a person has met standards beyond those of admission to licensure and has passed specialty examinations in a field, such as medical pathology or women's health care. The various medical professional organizations establish their own standards and administer their own board certification examinations. Those who successfully complete all requirements may either be called fellows (such as Fellow of the American College of Surgeons [FACS] or Fellow of the American College of Physicians [FACP]) or be called diplomates or some other title (such as registered nurse [RN] or (registered nurse, women's health nurse practitioner, board certified [WHNP-BC]). Board certification may be required by a hospital for admission to the medical staff or for determination of a staff member's rank, e.g., general staff, associate staff, or full attending status.

categorical c. A professional qualification to practice in one limited field within health care, rather than broad or unlimited certification.

medical-surgical nursing c. The validation of knowledge in medical-surgical nursing via an examination offered by one of two organizations: 1. The Medical-Surgical Nursing Certification Board (MSNCB), a partner of the Academy of Medical-Surgical Nurses (AMSN), or 2. The American Nurses Credentialing Center (ANCC), a subsidiary of the American Nurses Association.

preadmission c. Authorization granted to the patient for hospital admission after a review of the patient's proposed need for inpatient services. In some settings, if certain set criteria are not met, then the admission is not allowed.

certified histocompatibility technologist An allied health specialist who does the testing to see whether transplanted organs will match selected recipients.

certified medication technician ABBR: CMT. Certified medication aide.

certified neuroscience registered nurse ABBR: CNRN. A registered nurse who has at least two years of experience in caring for patients with neurological diseases and has passed a board examination administered by the American Board of Neuroscience Nursing (ABNN). The examination addresses topics such as the diagnosis, treatment, and family care of patients with neurological diseases.

certified nurse educator ABBR: CNE. A certified academic nurse who specializes in the education of other nurses and of nurses in training.

certified occupational therapy assistant ABBR: COTA. An occupational therapy assistant who has passed the national certification examination. SEE: *occupational therapy assistant.*

certified organic Accredited as meeting specified legal standards for food production and record keeping, i.e., grown, processed, accounted for, and transported to guarantee organic purity.

certified pulmonary function technician An individual trained to evaluate respiratory function who has passed the examination offered by the National Board for Respiratory Care.

certified respiratory therapist ABBR: CRT. An entry-level respiratory care practitioner who has passed the examination offered by the National Board for Respiratory Care.

certify (sĕrt'ĭ-fī") [L. *certus,* certain, + *facio,* to make] **1.** To confirm or verify. **2.** To make a declaration concerning the sanity of an individual. **3.** To report certain specified diseases to public health authorities.

ceruloplasmin (sĕ-roo"lō-plăz'mĭn) A blue glycoprotein to which most of the copper in the blood is attached. It is decreased in Wilson's disease.

cerumen (sĕ-roo'mĕn) [L. *cera,* wax] A substance secreted by glands at the outer third of the ear canal. Usually cerumen does not accumulate in the ear canal, but it may clog the channel in some persons; the cerumen may become impacted and must be physically removed, not by irrigation of the canal but by use of a curette. Soft cerumen is easily removed by gentle syringe instillation of water in the canal.

ceruminal, ceruminous (sĕ-roo'mĭ-năl, sĕ-roo'mĭ-nŭs), *adj.*

ceruminolysis (sĕ-roo"mĭ-nol'ĭ-sĭs) [*cerumen* + *-lytic*] The dissolution or disintegration of cerumen in the external ear canal. **ceruminolytic** (sĕ-roo"mĭ-nō-lit'ik), *adj.*

ceruminosis (sĕ-roo"mĭ-nō'sĭs) [" + Gr. *osis,* condition] Excessive secretion of cerumen.

ceruminous gland One of the modified sweat glands in the skin lining the external auditory canal that secrete cerumen.

Cervarix A human papillomavirus vaccine.

cervical (sĕr'vĭ-kăl) [L. *cervicalis*] **1.** Pert. to or in the region of the neck. **2.** Pert. to the cervix of an organ, as the cervix uteri.

cervical cap A barrier contraceptive device placed over the uterine cervix, designed to prevent the entry of sperm into the womb. SEE: under *cap.*

cervical factor SEE: under *factor.*

cervical intraepithelial neoplasia SEE: under *neoplasia.*

cervical length SEE: under *length.*

cervical motion tenderness ABBR: CMT. Pain elicited when the uterine cervix is manipulated during pelvic examination. CMT is often found in patients with pelvic inflammatory disease.

cervical rib syndrome Pain and paresthesias in the hand, neck, shoulder, or arms, usually due to compression of the brachial plexus of nerves by an accessory cervical rib.

cervical ripening The biochemical changes in the cervix that take place gradually over the last few weeks of gestation in preparation for childbirth. The cervix softens, and its potential for stretching increases. Normally this occurs naturally, but in postterm pregnancies it may be necessary to use mechanical dilators or drugs. Placement of *Laminaria digitata* or prostaglandin E analogs (e.g., misoprostol) in the vagina or cervical canal promotes cervical ripening and onset of labor but does not reduce the rate of cesarean deliveries.

PATIENT CARE: Fetal status is assessed by monitoring the heart rate for 30 min before gel insertion and for approx. 1 hr after the procedure. The woman is assessed for uterine contractions and signs of hyperstimulation, nausea, or vomiting. If hyperstimulation occurs, the gel is removed, and the primary health care provider is notified.

cervicectomy (sĕr"vĭ-sĕk'tō-mē) [L. *cervix,* neck, + Gr. *ektome,* excision] Surgical removal of the cervix uteri.

cervices (sĕr'vĭ-sēz") Pl. of cervix.

cervicitis (sĕr-vĭ-sī'tĭs) [" + Gr. *itis,* inflammation] Inflammation of the cervix uteri.

cervico-, cervic- [L. *cervix,* stem *cervic-,* neck, nape, cervix (of the uterus)] Prefixes meaning the *neck* or to the *neck of an organ.*

cervicocolpitis (sĕr″vĭ-kō-kŏl-pī′tĭs) [″ + Gr. *kolpos,* vagina, + *itis,* inflammation] Inflammation of the cervix uteri and vagina.

cervicodynia (sĕr″vĭ-kō-dĭn′ē-ă) [″ + Gr. *odyne,* pain] A pain or cramp of the neck; cervical neuralgia.

cervicofacial (sĕr″vĭ-kō-fā″shē-ăl) [″ + *facies,* face] Pert. to the neck and face.

cervicogenic (sĕr″vĭ-kō-jĕn′ĭk) Relating to, or beginning in, the upper segments of the cervical spine or neighboring soft tissues.

cervicography (sĕr″vĭ-kŏg′ră-fē) Photographic study of the uterine cervix.

cervicomedullary junction (sĕr″vĭ-kō-med′ŭ-ler″ē, -mej′, -mă-dŭl′ă-rē) [*cervico-* + *medullary*] SEE: under *junction.*

cervicovaginitis (sĕr″vĭ-kō-văj″ĭ-nī′tĭs) [″ + *vagina,* sheath, + Gr. *itis,* inflammation] Inflammation of the cervix uteri and the vagina.

cervix (sĕr′vĭks, ′vĭ-sēz″, sĕr″vĭ′sēz″) *pl.* **cervices, cervixes** [L. *cervix,* nape, neck] The neck or a part of an organ resembling a neck.

unfavorable c. A cervix that is not adequately prepared for a vaginal delivery of a newborn child (one with a Bishop's score of less than or 6). A favorable cervix is one with a Bishop's score more than 6.

c. uteri The the lower part of the uterus from the internal os outward to the external os. It is rounded and conical, and a portion protrudes into the vagina. It is about 1 in (2.5 cm) long and is penetrated by the cervical canal, through which the fetus and menstrual flow escape. It may be torn in childbirth, esp. in a primigravida.

Deeper tears may occur in manual dilatation and use of forceps; breech presentation also may be a cause. Laceration may be single, bilateral, stellate, or incomplete. Tears are repaired by suturing to prevent hemorrhage and later complications. SYN: *cervical canal; neck of the uterus.*

CES *central excitatory state.*

cesarean, Cesarean, caesarean, Caesarean, caesarian, Caesarian, cesarian, Cesarian (si-zar′ē-ăn, -zer′) [Fr the legend that such an operation was performed for the birth of Julius*Caesar*] **1.** Pert. to a cesarean section. **2.** A cesarean section. *Cesarean* is the most common spelling variant in the U.S. Both the capitalized and uncapitalized forms are acceptable. Writers should be consistent with whatever form they prefer.

cesarean birth Cesarean section.

cesarean section ABBR: CS. Delivery of the fetus by means of an incision through the abdominal wall and into the uterus. Operative approaches and techniques vary. A horizontal incision through the lower uterine segment is most common; the classic vertical midline incision may be used in times of profound fetal distress. Elective cesarean section is indicated for known cephalopelvic disproportion, malpresentations, some patients with toxemia, and active genital herpes infection. The most common reason for emergency cesarean delivery is fetal distress.

COMPLICATIONS: Potential adverse effects on the mother following cesarean delivery include bleeding, fever, abdominal pain, hospital-acquired infection (wound, respiratory, genitourinary), thromboembolic phenomena, paralytic ileus, and wound dehiscence.

PATIENT CARE: *Preoperative:* The procedure is explained to the patient (and/or her partner) and psychological support is provided. Baseline measures of maternal vital signs and fetal heart rate are obtained; maternal and fetal status are monitored until delivery according to protocol. Laboratory data, ultrasound results, or the results of other studies are available to the obstetrical team. The operative area is prepared according to the surgeon's preference, and an indwelling urinary catheter is inserted as prescribed. An intravenous infusion with a large-bore catheter is started, and oral food and fluid are restricted as time permits. Blood replacement is prepared only as the surgeon requests. The patient is premedicated to reduce anxiety and discomfort. She should be placed in a slightly lateral (15°) position to reduce vena caval compression, supine hypotension, and resultant fetal hypoxia. General or regional anesthesia is initiated depending on the extent of fetal or maternal distress.

Postoperative: As soon as possible after the delivery of the baby, the mother is allowed to see and touch her newborn. Once recovery is sufficient, the patient should have the opportunity to hold and or breast-feed the newborn. The pediatrician or nurse midwife or anesthetist assesses the newborn's status. The neonate is observed for signs of respiratory distress and resuscitative equipment kept readily available until physiologically stable. Vital signs are monitored for mother and baby. The dressing and perineal pad are assessed for bleeding. The fundus is gently palpated for firmness (avoiding the incision), and intravenous oxytocin is administered as prescribed. If general anesthesia is used, routine postoperative care and positioning are provided; if regional anesthesia is used, the anesthesia level is assessed until sensation has completely returned. Intake and output are monitored, and any evidence of blood-tinged urine is documented and reported. (The indwelling urinary catheter usually is removed within 48 hr.) For some mothers, applying a coldpack to the incision controls pain and swelling; if prescribed, analgesics are administered, and noninvasive pain-relief measures are instituted. Lochia and breasts are assessed. The mother is assisted to turn from side to side and is encouraged to breathe deeply, cough, and use incentive spirometry to improve ventilation and to mobilize secretions. When bowel sounds have returned, oral fluids and food are encouraged and bowel and bladder activity are monitored.

The patient is assisted with early ambulation to prevent pulmonary, vascular, and GI complications, and urged to visit her newborn in the nursery if the neonate is not healthy enough to be brought to her bedside. Usual postpartal instruction is provided regarding fundus, lochia, and perineal care; breast and nipple care; and infant care. Instruction is also given on incision care and the need to report any hemorrhage, chest or leg pain (possible thrombosis), dyspnea, separation of the wound's edges, or signs of infection, such as fever, difficult urination, or flank pain. Any activity restrictions after discharge are discussed with both the woman and her partner. Encourage the patient to share feelings about the experience, suggest participation in a cesarian birth sharing group if available and appropriate, and arrange for further psychological support as deemed necessary. SYN: *cesarean birth;* C-section. SEE: *Nursing Diagnoses Appendix.*

cervical c.s. Surgical removal of the fetus, placenta, and membranes through an incision in the portion of the uterus just above the cervix.

classic c.s. Surgical removal of the fetus, placenta, and membranes through an incision in the abdominal and uterine walls.

extraperitoneal c.s. Surgical removal of the fetus, placenta, and membranes through an incision into the lowest portion of the anterior aspect of the uterus. This approach does not entail entering the peritoneal cavity.

low transverse c.s. Surgical removal of the fetus, placenta, and membranes through a transverse incision into the lower uterine segment. Use of this incision is associated with a decreased incidence of maternal and fetal mortality and morbidity in future pregnancies.

postmortem c.s. Surgical removal of the fetus from the uterus immediately after maternal death.

CESD *Cholesterol ester storage disease.* SEE: *acid lipase disease.*

cesium (sē'zē-ŭm) [L. *caesius,* sky blue + *-ium* (1)] SYMB: Cs. A chemical element, atomic weight (mass) 132.905, atomic number 55. It has several isotopes. The radioactive isotope ¹³⁷Cs, which has a half-life of 30 years, is used therapeutically for irradiation of cancerous tissue.

cesspool Colloquial term for *septic tank.*

Cestan-Chenais syndrome (sĕs-tăn'shĕn-ā') [Raymond Cestan, Fr. neurologist, 1872–1934; Louis J. Chenais, Fr. physician, 1872–1950] A neurological disorder with complex hemibody deficits and cranial nerve findings produced by a lesion of the brainstem.

Cestoda (sĕs-tōd'ă) [Gr. *kestos,* girdle] A subclass of the class Cestoidea, phylum Platyhelminthes, which includes the tapeworms, having a scolex and a chain of segments (proglottids) (e.g., *Taenia,* intestinal parasites of humans and other vertebrates).

cestode (sĕs'tōd) [" + *eidos,* form, shape] A tapeworm; a member of the Cestoda family.
cestoid (-toyd), *adj.*

cestodiasis (sĕs"tō-dī'ă-sĭs) [" + " + *-iasis,* condition] Infestation with tapeworms. SEE: *Cestoda.*

Cestoidea (sĕs-toy'dē-ă) A class of flatworms of the phylum Platyhelminthes; it includes the tapeworms.

cetirizine (sĕ-tīr'ĭ-zēn) A piperazine, administered orally to relieve allergic symptoms caused by histamine release, including seasonal and perennial allergic rhinitis and chronic urticaria. Its therapeutic classes are allergy, cold, and cough remedies, and antihistamines.

CETP *Cholesteryl ester transfer protein.*

CF *characteristic frequency; Christmas factor; cystic fibrosis.*

Cf Symbol for the element californium.

CFR *Code of federal regulations.*

CFRN *Certified Emergency Flight Nurse.*

CFT *complement fixation test.*

CFU-E *Colony-forming unit committed to erythropoiesis.*

CGD *Chronic granulomatous disease.*

cGMP *Current good manufacturing practices; cyclic guanosine monophosphate.*

C.G.S. *centimeter-gram-second,* a name given to a system of units for length, weight, and time.

CH₄ Methane.

C₂H₂ Acetylene.

C₂H₄ Ethylene.

CH₅₀ A laboratory test that assesses the integrity of the entire complement system. It measures the ability of a patient's serum complement, when activated, to destroy sheep red blood cells. Diminished activity may prompt further testing, e.g., for levels of terminal complement components, for levels of C3 and C4, or for diseases in which antigen-antibody complexes circulate in the blood.

C$_6$H$_6$ Benzene.

Chaddock reflex (chad'ŏk) [Charles G. Chaddock, U.S. neurologist, 1861–1936] **1.** Extension of the great toe when the outer edge of the dorsum of the foot is stroked. It is present in disease of the corticospinal tract. **2.** Flexion of the wrist and fanning of the fingers when the tendon of the palmaris longus muscle is pressed.

CHADS score A means of predicting the likelihood that a patient in atrial fibrillation will have a stroke. CHADS is a mnemonic for *c(ongestive)* heart failure; *h(ypertension), a(ge)* over 75 years, *d(iabetes)* mellitus, and a previous history of *s(troke)* (or transient ischemic attack [TIA]).

    PATIENT CARE: A previous history of stroke or TIA is worth two points. The other variables are each worth one point. Patients with a CHADS score of 0 can be safely treated with aspirin because they have the lowest probability of stroke; Patients with one point can be treated either with aspirin or warfarin. Patients who score two or more points should be treated with warfarin as the preferred stroke prevention unless there are contraindications to the drug.

Chadwick sign (chad'wik) [James R. Chadwick, US gynecologist, 1844–1905] A deep blue-violet color of the cervix and vagina caused by increased vascularity. It is a probable sign of pregnancy that becomes evident around the fourth week of gestation.

Chaetomium (kē"tōm'ē-ŭm) [Gr. *chaitē,* hair] A genus of filamentous, pigmented fungi that decompose plants and plant materials. They are an occasional cause of nail and skin infections in normal hosts and of serious systemic infections in immunocompromised patients.

chafe (chāf) [O.Fr. *chaufer,* to warm] To injure by rubbing or friction.

chafing (chāf'ĭng) A superficial inflammation that develops when skin is subjected to friction from clothing or adjacent skin. This may occur at the axilla, groin, or anal region, between digits of hands and feet, or at the neck or wrists. Erythema, maceration, and sometimes fissuring occur. Bacterial or fungal infection may result secondarily.

Chagas disease (shag'äs) [Carlos Ribeiro Justiniano Chagas, Brazilian physician, 1879–1934] A bloodborne disease caused by *Trypanosoma cruzi* and transmitted by the biting of a reduviid bug. It is characterized by fever, lymphadenopathy, hepatosplenomegaly, and facial edema. Chronic cases may be mild or asymptomatic, or may be accompanied by myocarditis, cardiomyopathy, megaesophagus, megacolon, or death.

    ETIOLOGY: Chagas disease may be transmitted from person-to-person by needlestick injury, transfusion, organ donation, or during childbirth. SYN: *American* **trypanosomiasis;** *South American* **trypanosomiasis.** SEE: ***Trypanosoma** cruzi*.

chagoma (shă-gō'mă) A painful, red swollen lesion found at the site of inoculation of the parasite *Trypanosoma* into the skin. SEE: *trypanosomiasis, South American*.

chain (chān) [Fr. *chaine,* fr L. *catena, chain*] **1.** A related series of events or things. **2.** In bacteriology, bacterial organisms strung together. **3.** In chemistry, the linkage of atoms in a straight line or in a circle or a ring. The ring or straight-line structures may have side chains that branch off from the main compound.

    cold c. The maintenance of refrigerated temperatures for vaccines from the time they are manufactured through their shipment and delivery to health care facilities until their administration to patients.

    c. of custody A verifiable procedure that tracks the movement and location of physical evidence (e.g., medical samples taken during a rape examination) through its shipping, handling, and processing at a clinical laboratory until it is presented in court.. SEE: *rape*.

    electron transport c. The stage of cellular respiration in which the most adenosine triphosphate is generated. In this biochemical reaction, electrons are passed along the cytochromes of a cell or mitochondrial membrane and are ultimately accepted by oxygen, producing water. Hydrogen ions (protons) are transported across the membrane. The source of the protons and electrons is primarily nicotinamide adenine dinucleotide, which is recycled during the reaction. SYN: *cytochrome transport **system***.

    food c. The transfer of food energy from producers (green plants) to primary consumers (herbivores) to secondary consumers (carnivores). Dead organisms of all kinds are reduced to simpler chemicals by decomposers (bacteria and fungi), which make minerals available again for green plants.

    heavy c. The large polypeptide chains of antibodies. SEE: *heavy chain disease*.

    J c. The joining portion of a polymeric immunoglobulin, found in dimeric and polymeric IgA and pentameric IgM.

    kinematic c., kinetic c. A series of bones connected by joints. Movement of one segment influences other parts of the chain.

    light c. The small polypeptide chains of antibodies.

    c. of survival In emergency cardiac care, the notion that the survival of patients in cardiac arrest depends on the linkage of the following: 1. immediate recognition and activation, 2. early CPR, 3. rapid defibrillation, 4. effective advanced life support, and 5. integrated post-cardiac arrest care. If for any reason any one of these links is missing or delayed, the chance of survival decreases considerably. SEE: *cardiopulmonary* **resuscitation**.

chaining (chān′ĭng) A behavioral therapy in which reinforcement is given for behaviors related to established behavior. Also called *chained reinforcement*.

chain reaction A self-renewing reaction in which the initial stage triggers a subsequent reaction, which in turn causes the next, and so on.

chair, birthing SEE: *birthing chair*.

chair stand, chair-stand test (chăr) [O.Fr.] The time it takes to rise from a seated position in a straight-backed chair to a standing position unsupported. The test may be performed in several ways. In one assessment the subject gets up from a chair five times, and the time it takes to complete these maneuvers is measured. In another assessment the number of times the patient can get up and down in 30 sec is counted. The test is one of several used in physical therapy and gerontology to assess balance, endurance, mobility, and strength.

chakra, cakra (chăk′rä) [Sanskrit, *cakra*, wheel, turning] In Ayurveda, Kundalinī yoga and Tantric yoga, any of the seven energy centers running parallel to the spine that influence the conscious state of the body and therefore its health and well-being. Chakras are believed to interact directly with the endocrine and nervous systems to influence physical and emotional states.

chalasia (kă-lā′zē-ă) [Gr. *chalasis*, relaxation] Relaxation of sphincters.

chalazion (kă-lā′zē-ŏn) *pl.* **chalazia, chalazions** [Gr. *khalaza*, hailstone] A benign, granulomatous lesion analogous to a sebaceous cyst developing on the eyelids, formed by distention of a meibomian gland with secretion. SYN: *meibomian cyst*. SEE: *steatoma*.

chalicosis (kăl-ĭ-kō′sĭs) [Gr. *chalix*, limestone, + *osis*, condition] Pneumonoconiosis associated with the inhalation of dust produced by stone cutting.

challenge (chal′ĕnj) In immunology, administration of a specific antigen to an individual known to be sensitive to that antigen in order to produce an immune response.

   c. for cause A request that a prospective juror not be allowed to serve for specific reasons or causes, e.g., concerns about potential bias or prejudice.

   fluid c. The rapid infusion of fluids (crystalloids such as normal saline, or colloids, such as albumin) to resuscitate

blood pressure in a patient thought to be hypovolemic.

   PATIENT CARE: In a typical child 20 mL/kg of normal saline is given intravenously (or intraosseously) over 30 min. The volume infused into an adult is usually 250–1000 mL. The lower volume is used if there are concerns that the patient may develop pulmonary edema. The patient's blood pressure, heart rate and rhythm, oxygenation, and respirations are closely monitored during and after the infusion for evidence of a positive response, e.g., a mean arterial pressure that rises above 70 mm Hg, or deterioration, e.g., increasing dyspnea, ventricular ectopy, or hypoxia. Patients who respond favorably to a fluid challenge are typically placed on a maintenance infusion of fluids to sustain them hemodynamically.

   food c. Exposing a patient to a substance to which the patient is thought to react adversely. Ethically, the test cannot be performed without the patient's permission, but for accuracy the test foods should be disguised during the test. Typically, food challenges are performed after the patient has eliminated the suspected food from his or her diet for 1 or 2 weeks. To eliminate bias, the patient should agree to ingest several disguised foods that he or she is known to tolerate, in addition to the suspected food. SEE: *elimination* **diet**.

   nasal c. Nasal allergen challenge.

   nasal allergen c. A test to determine if a person is allergic to a particular allergen. A sample of the allergen is placed in the nose, and symptoms are evaluated. Nasal allergen tests are considered to be the best tests to use to determine whether a particular substance is a cause of a patient's allergic rhinitis. SYN: *nasal c.*

   peremptory c. A challenge to remove a juror from a prospective jury without cause.

challenge test Administering a substance in order to determine its ability to cause a response, esp. the giving of an antigen and observing or testing for the antibody response.

chalone (kăl′ōn) [Gr. *chalan*, to relax] A protein that inhibits mitosis in the tissue in which it is produced.

chamber (chām′bĕr) [Fr. *chambre*, ult. fr. Gr. *kamara*, vault] A compartment or closed space.

   altitude c. Low-pressure **c.**

   anterior c. The space between the cornea and the iris of the eye. SEE: *posterior c.*

   Boyden c. SEE: *Boyden chamber*.

   drip c. A hollow device where intravenous fluids are collected before infusion into a patient.

   hyperbaric c. An airtight enclosure strong enough to withstand high internal pressure. It is used to expose animals, humans, or an entire surgical team to increased air pressure. SYN: *pressure c.* SEE: *hyperbaric* **oxygenation**.

ionization c. A device used to measure radiation by equating ion production in a gas chamber with the intensity of an electrical charge.

low-pressure c. An enclosure designed to simulate high altitudes by exposing humans or animals to low atmospheric pressure. Such studies are essential for simulated flights into the atmosphere and space. SYN: *altitude c.*

monoplace c. A hyperbaric chamber that supplies an enriched oxygen environment to a single person (or to a small child with a family member or nurse in attendance). It may be used to treat those suspected of severe carbon monoxide exposure.

multiplace c. A hyberbaric chamber that supplies an enriched oxygen environment to several patients who have suffered severe carbon monoxide exposure. All the patients wear their own masks and have their own oxygen supply within the chamber.

posterior c. In the eye, the space behind the iris and in front of the vitreous body. It is occupied by the lens, its zonules, and the aqueous humor. SEE: *anterior c.; eye* for illus.

pressure c. Hyperbaric **c.**

pulp c. The central cavity of a tooth. The pulp canal contains arteries, veins, lymphatic vessels, and sensory nerve endings. Anatomically, the pulp chamber can be divided into the body and the pulp horns. Pulp horns correspond to the cusps of the teeth. SEE: *root canal; pulp cavity.*

suction control c. The part of a chest tube drainage system that sets the negative pressure applied to the pleural space, facilitating the drainage of gas and fluid.

valved holding c. SEE: under *metered-dose* **inhaler**.

vitreous c. The cavity behind the lens in the eye that contains the vitreous humor.

water seal c. The component of a chest tube drainage system that permits the drainage of gas from the patient's pleural space but does not permit that gas to return. It typically holds about 2 cm of sterile water.

Chamberlain procedure (chăm′bĕr-lĭn) [J. Maxwell Chamberlain, U.S. thoracic surgeon, 1908–1968] Incision into the mediastinum through an incision made next to the sternum. The procedure is used to obtain specimens for biopsy or laboratory analysis as an alternative to mediastinoscopy.

Chamberlen forceps (chăm′bĕr-lĕn) [Peter Chamberlen (senior), 1560–1631, or Peter Chamberlen (junior) 1601–1683, Fr.-born Brit. surgeons] The original obstetrical forceps.

chamomile, camomile (kam′ŏ-mīl″, -mēl″) [L. *chamaemelon,* fr Gr. *chamaimēlon,* earth apple] The dried flowering heads (blossoms) of *Anthemis nobilis* (Roman chamomile) or *Matricaria recutita* (German chamomile).

German c. An annually flowering member of the aster family (*Matricaria recutita*). Teas made from the flower are used as a mild sedative, an astringent, a cosmetic hair rinse, an analgesic, and an antispasmodic in the treatment of colic, indigestion, and irritable bowel syndrome. Oils extracted from the plant are used in alternative and complementary medicine to relieve itch. Some people are sensitive to the plant's oils and may develop contact dermatitis after exposure. SYN: *wild c.*

wild c. German **c.**

champissage (shăm-pĭ-săzh′) [Fr. fr Hindi *champo,* knead, press] An ancient Hindu technique of scalp massage. It is promoted as a means of combating hair loss. The shoulders and neck are sometimes included in the treatment.

CHAMPUS (cham′pŭs) *Civilian Health and Medical Program of the Uniformed Services.*

chance **1.** That which occurs randomly. **2.** An accident.

chancre (shang′kĕr) [Fr. *chancre,* ulcer fr. L. *cancer*] A hard, syphilitic primary ulcer, the first sign of syphilis, appearing approx. 2 to 3 weeks after infection. SEE: illus.; *syphilis.* **chancrous** (shang′krŭs), *adj.*

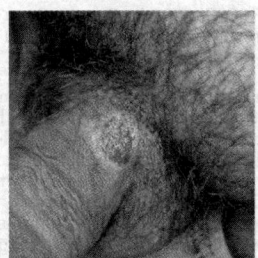

TYPICAL CHANCRE OF PRIMARY SYPHILIS

SYMPTOMS: The ulcer begins as a painless erosion or papule that ulcerates superficially. It generally occurs alone. It has a scooped-out appearance due to level or sloping edges that are adherent, and a shining red or raw floor. The ulcer heals without leaving a scar. It may appear at almost any site including the mouth, penis, urethra, hand, toe, eyelid, conjunctiva, vagina, or cervix. SYN: *hard c.; hunterian c.; true c.*

⚠️ During the chancre stage, syphilis is highly contagious. The chancre contains many spirochetes.

hard c. Chancre.
hunterian c. Chancre.
simple c. Chancroid.
soft c. Chancroid.
true c. Chancre.

chancroid (shăng′kroyd) [″ + Gr. *eidos*, form, shape] A sexually transmitted infection, caused by the *Haemophilus ducreyi* (a gram-negative bacillus). Its hallmark is the appearance on the genitals of one or more painful ulcers. The incubation period is typically 2 to 5 days, although longer incubations have been reported. The genital chancre of syphilis is clinically distinguished from that of chancroid in that the syphilitic ulcer is painless. Cultures on chocolate agar are used to confirm the diagnosis. Ceftriaxone, azithromycin, or ciprofloxacin are used to treat the infection. SEE: illus.

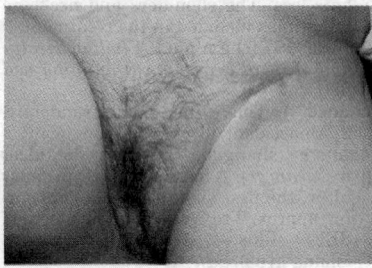

CHANCROID

(SOURCE: Centers for Disease Control and Prevention: Dr. Greg Hammond and Susan Lindsley)

SYMPTOMS: A chancroid begins with multiple pustules or ulcers having abrupt edges, a rough floor, yellow exudate, and purulent secretion. It is sensitive and inflamed. It heals rapidly, leaving a scar. Chancroids may affect the penis, urethra, vulva, or anus. Multiple lesions may develop by autoinoculation. Types include transient, phagedenic, giant, and serpiginous.

change of life Menopause.

change-of-shift That time during the working day when one group of health care professionals arrives for work and another group prepares to leave. At this juncture reports about patients are relayed from one group to another and tasks that need to be accomplished are assigned.

channel (chăn′ĕl) [Fr. fr. L. *canalis*, a waterpipe] **1.** A conduit, groove, or passageway through which various materials may flow. **2.** In cell biology, a passageway in the cell membrane through which materials may pass.

anion c. Any of the channels in red blood cells that cross the cell membrane. Chloride ions (Cl⁻) and bicarbonate ions (HCO₃⁻) are exchanged via these channels.

gated c. An ion channel in a cell membrane that opens or closes in response to a stimulus such as a neurotransmitter or to a change in pressure, voltage, or light.

ion c. A protein that spans the lipid bilayer of the cell membrane and regulates the movement of charged particles (e.g., electrolytes) into and out of cells.

leakage c. An ion channel in a cell membrane that is always open, making the membrane permeable to ions. SYN: *nongated c.*

lymph c. Lymph sinus.

nongated c. Leakage channel.

receptor-operated c. A conduit in a cell membrane through which ions pass when a neurotransmitter binds to its receptor site.

voltage c. A glycosylated protein in a cell membrane through which ions pass when the electrical potential of the membrane shifts.

voltage-gated c. Any of the gated ion channels that open in response to a change in the membrane potential of a cell membrane. These channels give muscle fibers and neurons their ability to generate and propagate impulses. SYN: *voltage-regulated c.*

voltage-regulated c. Voltage-gated channel.

channelopathy A disease that results from a mutation in an ion channel in a cell membrane (e.g., from a mutation that alters the uptake of an electrolyte such as sodium, potassium, or calcium by a cell).

chaotropic agent (kā″ŏ-trŏp′ik, -trŏp′) [Gr. *chaos* + *-tropic*] SEE: under *agent.*

chaperone (shap′ĕ-rōn″) **1.** One who accompanies a health care provider during the examination of a potentially vulnerable patient to ensure the patient's safety and comfort. **2.** Molecular chaperone.

molecular c. A protein that shapes other protein molecules so they can work optimally as receptors or can be secreted or cleared from cells.

Chapman sign (chap′măn) Electrocardiographic evidence of myocardial infarction in patients with left bundle branch block or ventricular pacing, in which the upward stroke of the R wave in leads 1, aVL, or V6 is notched. The sign has good sensitivity but only fair specificity.

chapped (chăpt) [ME. *chappen*] Inflamed, roughened, fissured, as from exposure to cold.

character (kăr'ăk-tĕr) **1.** A person's pattern of thought and action, esp. regarding moral choices. Character differs from personality, although in psychiatry the terms are often used interchangeably. **2.** The feature of an organism or individual that results from the expression of genetic information inherited from the parents.

character disorder A personality disorder manifested by a chronic, habitual, maladaptive pattern of reaction that is relatively inflexible, limits the optimal use of potentialities, and often provokes the responses from the environment that the individual wants to avoid.

characteristic (kar"ăk-tĕ-ris'tik) [Gr. *charaktēristikos*, pert. to a stamp] **1.** A trait or character typical of an organism or of an individual. **2.** In logarithmic expressions, the number to the left of the decimal point, as distinguished from the mantissa, the number to the right of the decimal point.

   acquired c. A trait or quality that was not inherited but is the result of environmental influence.

   anal c. Anal **personality**.

   dominant c. SEE: *dominant*.

   primary sex c. An inherited trait that influences the development of the reproductive organs.

   receiver operating c. Receiver operating **curve**.

   recessive c. Recessive **gene**.

   secondary sex c. A gender-related physical attribute that normally develops under the influence of sex hormones at puberty. Voice quality, facial hair, and body fat distribution are examples.

   sex-conditioned c. A genetic trait carried by both sexes but expressed or inhibited by the sex of the individual.

   sex-limited c. A trait present in only one sex even though the gene responsible is present in both sexes.

   sex-linked c. A trait controlled by genes on the sex chromosomes. The X and Y chromosomes determine sex but also carry genes unrelated to sex. SYN: *sex-linked gene*.

characterize (kăr'ăk-tĕr-īz") To mark, identify, or describe the attributes of something. This helps to distinguish an individual or material from other examples of similar individuals or materials.

charcoal (chăr'kōl) [ME. *charcole*] A black granular mass or fine powder prepared from soft charred wood.

   ACTION/USES: In treating people who have ingested organic poisons, activated charcoal is given orally as a suspension in water, using 8 mL of diluent per gram of charcoal. This may be given to infants by using a nippled bottle. The dose is 1 to 2 g/kg of body weight. Superactivated charcoal is two to three times more effective than activated charcoal. Charcoal should be administered as soon as possible after intake of the toxin. It is contraindicated in patients who have ingested corrosive chemicals. Ionized chemicals (e.g., acids, alkalis, and salts of cyanide, iron, and lithium) are not well absorbed by charcoal.

   superactivated c. A type of charcoal used in treating poisoning. It is several more times as effective as activated charcoal.

Charcot, Jean M. (shar-kō') Fr. neurologist, 1825–1893.

   C. arthropathy C. joint.

   C. foot Destruction of the joints of the feet and/or ankles in patients with diabetic neuropathy. Although the bony destruction limits the ability of the patient to walk, it is often painless. SYN: *diabetic neuroarthropathy; diabetic osteoarthropathy; diabetic osteopathy*.

   C. joint A type of diseased joint marked by hypermobility associated with tabes dorsalis, syringomyelia, or other conditions involving spinal cord disease or injury. Bone decalcification occurs on the joint surfaces, accompanied by bony overgrowth about the margins. Pain is usually absent although there are exceptions. Deformity and instability of the joint are characteristic. SYN: *C. arthropathy*.

   C. triad **1.** The combination of nystagmus, intention tremor, and scanning speech. It is frequently associated with multiple sclerosis. **2.** The combination of right upper quadrant abdominal pain, fever, and jaundice, a marker of cholangitis.

Charcot-Bouchard aneurysm (shăr-kō') [Charcot; Charles Jacques Bouchard, Fr. physician, 1837–1886] A microaneurysm in a small artery of the brain thought, in the past, to be a cause of intracranial hemorrhage.

Charcot-Leyden crystal (shăr-kō'lī'dĕn) [Charcot; Ernest V. von Leyden, Ger. physician, 1832–1910] A type of colorless, hexagonal, double-pointed, often needle-like crystal found in the sputum in asthma and bronchial bronchitis or in the feces in ulceration of the intestine, esp. amebiasis.

Charcot-Marie-Tooth disease (shar-kō"mă-rē"tooth') [Charcot; Pierre Marie, Fr. neurologist, 1853–1940; Howard Henry Tooth, Brit. physician, 1856–1925] A form of progressive neural atrophy of muscles supplied by the peroneal nerves. There are numerous variants of the disease: some are transmitted on the X chromosome; some are autosomal recessive. In all versions there is a defect in the myelination of peripheral nerves, causing motor deficits (such as footdrop) and loss of sensation. SYN: *peroneal muscular atrophy*.

charge (charj) **1.** In electricity, the amount of electrical force present. **2.** To add electrical energy to a battery. **3.** The cost to the patient and/or the third-party payer for a medical service or hospitalization.

covered c. A medical service reimbursable by a third-party payer.

customary and reasonable c. The usual cost of a service to a patient. The term is used in the medical insurance industry to determine the amount the provider will be reimbursed for the service or procedure. Under Medicare, this is the lowest customary fee charged by a physician for a service or the prevailing fee of other area physicians for the same service.

maximum allowable c. ABBR: MAC. In medical care financial management, the maximum reimbursement rate a health plan will allow for the cost of services such as prescribed medicines or professional fees.

prevailing c. The typical fee that a health care provider bills for a service, e.g., an office visit or a surgical procedure.

charity care SEE: under *care.*

charlatan (shăr′lă-tăn) [It. *ciarlatano*] A pretender to special knowledge or ability, as in medicine. SYN: *quack.*

Charles Bonnet syndrome (sharl bo-nā′) [Charles Bonnet, Swiss scientist, 1720–1793] Complex visual hallucinations typically experienced by elderly people with profound visual impairment, such as the loss of central visual acuity in macular degeneration.

charleyhorse (chăr′lē-hors″) A colloquial term for pain and tenderness in the fibromuscular tissue of the thighs, usually caused by muscle strain or tear. The condition is marked by sudden onset and aggravation on movement. Relief can be obtained from rest, local applications of cold, gentle massage, and nonsteroidal anti-inflammatory drugs.

chart (chart) [L. *charta*, paper] **1.** A form or sheet of paper used to record the course of a patient's illness. It includes records of temperature, pulse, respiratory rate, blood pressure, urinary and fecal output, and doctors' and nurses' notes. **2.** To record on a graph the sequence of events such as vital signs. SEE: *charting.* **3.** The complete clinical record of a patient, including physical and psychosocial state of health as well as results of diagnostic tests. Plans for meeting the needs of the patient are also included. SEE: *problem-oriented medical record.* **4.** To record the clinical, radiographic, and forensic findings of the teeth and surrounding tissues.

Particular charts are listed under the first word. SEE: e.g., *basal temperature chart; Cardiff Count-to-Ten chart; dental chart.*

charta (kăr′tă) [L.] A preparation intended principally for external application, made either by saturating paper with medicinal substances or by applying the latter to the surface of the paper by adding adhesive liquid.

charting (chart′ĭng) Recording a patient's progress and treatment during an illness, outpatient procedure, office visit, or hospitalization. The physician and other health care providers need detailed information about the patient that the nurse or other members of the health care team may contribute through observation and contact. These notes and flow sheet entries contain details used in planning, implementing, and evaluating patient care. SEE: *nursing process; problem-oriented medical record.*

⚠ Verbal reports are not sufficient; they may be misunderstood or forgotten.

Written documentation is considered legal evidence. It must be recorded promptly and be dated and timed, and be clear, concise, and legible. Mistakes should be corrected by noting the mistaken entry and correction, or by placing a single line through the mistaken entry and writing the correction immediately after. If an entry is made late, it should follow the most recent entry in the chart and include the date and time when it was made. Slang should not be used. Since charting procedures may differ among health care institutions, it is crucial to learn to use the system specified in one's own facility.

Mental state: The record should document the patient's alertness and awareness, cooperativeness, delirium or delusion, depression, hallucinosis, psychotic symptoms, and teaching and learning ability. Reactions to visitors and mood change after visitors depart should be reported. This is esp. important in psychiatric patients. *Miscellaneous:* Any sudden or marked change in the patient's condition is charted, as well as any subsequent notification of the patient's relatives, physician, or clergy. *Nausea:* The chart should record whether nausea was accompanied by vomiting, and whether it followed certain foods, drugs, interventions, or treatments. *Nerves:* All symptoms of nervousness or excitability should be noted. *Nursing care:* The nurse should chart and date all activities, ambulation, assessments, independent interventions, medications given, and special treatments. *Pain:* The record should include the character (e.g., sharp, dull, burning, grinding, throbbing), onset, location, duration, and any factors that exacerbate the pain or facilitate its remission. *Personal care*: Baths, personal hygiene, and the patient's reactions to these should be recorded. For women, this includes menstruation and the type of menstrual protection used. *Physician*: The physician's visit is recorded as are any verbal or telephone orders and the time they are expressed or written, and carried out. *Physical therapy*: The hour of going for treatment, the hour of return, and the condition of the patient should be charted. *Sleep*: Hours of sleep during both day and night are charted. If an accurate estimate is impossible, an approximation is made and noted as such. Abnormalities of sleep, such as apneic periods, bruxism, nightmares, and sleepwalking are recorded. *Surgery*: Documentation includes the procedure, preparation (including medications), the time, the admission and discharge from the postanesthesia care unit (PACU) or critical care unit; the transfer to the patient's room, the condition, lines, monitors, tubes, and assessment on return to the room; and the results of assessments during the first few hours after surgery. PACU and critical care nurses record treatment and condition while the patient is under their care. *Symptoms*: An accurate description of all symptoms should be given. The remarks should include both subjective and objective findings. *Time*: Everything relating to the patient's progress should be charted as it occurs. *Treatments*: The hour of treatment, the nature of the treatment, the provider of the treatment, and the patient's reaction are recorded. *Radiographic studies*: The type of study, its hour of initiation, the location of the study, the transportation involved, the practitioners, and the patient's subsequent condition are all recorded. *Visits of family or clergy*: The hour, the name of the visitor, and the rite performed are charted, as well as the patient's response.

PATIENT CARE: The following subheadings exemplify those aspects of patient care found in complete nursing records: *Vital signs*: including blood pressure, pulse, respiration, and temperature. They are recorded on admission and before the patient goes for procedures, to the operating room, or with any significant change in patient status. Recording of the blood pressure should include any differences noted between arms, and any postural changes (when bleeding, dizziness, fluid loss, or syncope are present). The pulse record should include its rate in beats per minute and any unusual characteristics such as irregularities of rhythm. Respiratory records include the rate per minute and the character (e.g. Cheyne-Stokes, deep, difficult, easy, gasping,

labored, quiet, shallow, or stertorous). The record of temperature should include the method of measurement (axillary, auditory, central, oral, rectal) and whether the temperature is accompanied by chills, diaphoresis, rigors, or localizing symptoms. Any treatment for fevers of hypothermia should be recorded. *Alterations in consciousness*: Coma, drowsiness, and obtundation as well as convulsions should be precisely described. It is important to make note of the appearance of the patient during these events, including any localizing movements, any precipitating events, and ocular and pupillary findings if abnormal. Incontinence of bowel or bladder, and unintentional injury to self during changes in consciousness should be noted, as well as any delay in recovery to normal awareness. *Diet*: The percentage of intake for each meal and type of meals consumed are recorded. If a calorie count is needed, the type and amount of each food and liquid taken are recorded. If the patient is being monitored for intake and output, the amount of each liquid consumed is documented. The following should be included in dietary records: amount of liquids taken; hours of giving; type of diet (full, light, soft, liquid, special); and appetite. The description of appetite may include remarks about special likes or dislikes, difficulties with ingestion, or alterations in digestion. *Discharge or death*: The date and hour of discharge or death and the name of the person who ordered the discharge or pronounced the death should be given. *Dressings*: This chart should include the changes of dressings on wounds and the amount and character of drainage (including the phrase "Specimen Saved," if this was done). In addition, the hour, the person who changed the dressing, the removal of stitches or drains, and the patient's reaction to the dressing change should be recorded. *Drugs*: The name of each medicine, the dosage, the route of administration, the time of administration, and the frequency should be confined to the prescribed column of the medical record. When preparations are dispensed in liquid form, the actual dose given should be recorded rather than the amount of solution. Any unfavorable, unusual, or idiosyncratic reaction from drugs or treatments should be recorded. All medicines, treatments, preparations, and the like should be charted by the nurse who administers them whether or not the nurse is in charge of the patient. *Excretions*: Time, character, and other facts are included. The chart should include a description of the stool, including whether produced spontaneously or by enema, the amount, consistency, color, presence or absence of blood, pus or mucus, the odor, and any abnormal constituents present. The chart should have a similar description of the urine, and include records of its amount, its color and general appearance, and whether the urine was obtained through a catheter. The nurse should record any urination accompanied by pain or burning, and the time any specimen of urine was sent to the laboratory. The timing of a 24-hour collection should be noted, and the amount obtained should be recorded in the chart and on the laboratory record. *General appearance*: The patient's color, mental state (see below), and mood should be documented. *Hemorrhages and discharges*: These should be described, and any unusual specimens saved for examination. *Infant feeding*: Breast versus bottle feeding are noted, and any maternal education is given. Any formula given should be recorded the first time; afterward, the amount given suffices. If infants regurgitate, the approximate amount is recorded. *Laboratory*: The date and time, type of specimen, ordering physician, method of transport, and courier are all noted. SEE: *chain of custody*.

charting and numbering of teeth Any of the various systems developed for designating teeth in a chart system including numbers, letters, or symbols. They are not uniformly accepted. Widely used are the two-digit system of Federation Dentaire Internationale (FDI system) and the American system, which numbers the permanent teeth consecutively from the upper right third molar as #1 through the maxillary teeth to #16, and then to the left mandibular third molar as #17 and through the mandibular teeth to the right third molar as #32.

chartula (kăr'tū-lă) [L., small piece of paper] A paper folded to form a receptacle containing a dose of medicine.

chasma (kăz'mă) [Gr., a cleft] An opening, gap, or wide cleft.

chaste tree berry [partial translation of L. *Vitex agnus-castus,* chaste-lamb chaste tree] An herbal remedy from the chemically active fruit of the chaste tree or hemp tree (*Vitex agnus-castus*), promoted for its relief of premenstrual symptoms (particularly swelling of the breasts) and discomfort associated with menopause and as an aid for breast enlargement.

Chaussier areola (shō-sē-ā') [François Chaussier, Fr. physician, 1746–1828] Indurated tissue that surrounds a pustule caused by anthrax.

CHB *complete heart block.*

Ch.B. *Bachelor of Surgery;* used mostly in the United Kingdom.

CHD *congenital hip dislocation; congenital heart disease; coronary heart disease.*

check [O.Fr. *eschec*] **1.** To slow down

or arrest the course of a condition. **2.** To verify.

check bite SEE: under *bite.*

checkpoint In molecular and cell biology, a process or chemical that temporarily blocks or slows a biochemical event. Checkpoint mutations are associated with the unregulated growth of some cancers.

check-up General term for a visit to a health care provider for a history and physical examination.

check valve SEE: under *valve.*

Chédiak-Higashi syndrome (shē'dē-ăk-hē-gă'shē) [M. Chédiak and O. Higashi, contemporary French and Japanese physicians, respectively] A lethal metabolic disorder, inherited as an autosomal recessive trait, in which neutrophils contain peroxidase-positive inclusion bodies. Partial albinism, photophobia, and pale optic fundi are clinical features. Children usually die by 5 to 10 years of age of a lymphoma-like disease.

cheek [AS. *ceace*] **1.** The side of the face forming the lateral wall of the mouth below the eye. SYN: *bucca.* **2.** The buttock.

cheekbone (chēk'bōn) The malar bone. SEE: *zygomatic bone.*

cheeking (chēk'ing) A colloquial term for concealing a medication in the mouth, i.e., between the teeth and the cheek, in order to avoid swallowing it.

cheek retractor SEE: under *retractor.*

cheilectomy (kī-lĕk'tō-mē) [Gr. *cheilos,* lip, + *ektome,* excision] **1.** Surgical removal of abnormal bone around a joint to facilitate joint mobility. **2.** Surgical removal of a lip.

cheilectropion (kī''lĕk-trō'pē-ŏn) [" + *ektrope,* a turning aside] Eversion of the lip.

cheilitis, chelitis, chilitis (kī-līt'ĭs) [*chilo-* + *-itis*] Inflammation or chapping of the lips, esp. at their corners. This condition may be caused by exposure to sun, wind, or other elements or it may result from habitual lip licking. SYN: *angular c.*

　actinic c. Solar **c.**

　angular c. cheilitis

　solar c. Precancerous damage to the lips (primarily the lower lip) due to excessive exposure to the sun. SYN: *actinic c.*

　c. venenata Dermatitis of the lips resulting from chemical irritants in lipsticks, lip cream, and various other materials.

cheilo-, cheil- SEE: *chilo-.*

cheilognathopalatoschisis (kī''lō-nā''thō-păl-ă-tŏs'kĭ-sĭs) [" + *gnathos,* jaw, + L. *palatum,* palate, + Gr. *schisis,* a splitting] A developmental anomaly in which there is a cleft in the hard and soft palates, upper jaw, and lip.

cheilophagia (kī''lō-fā'jē-ă) [" + *phag-*

ein, to eat] The habit of biting one's own lip.

cheiloplasty (kī'lō-plas″tē) [*cheilo-* + *-plasty*] Plastic surgery on the lips. SYN: *labioplasty (1).*

cheilorrhaphy (kī-lor'ă-fē) [″ + *rhaphe,* seam, ridge] Surgical repair of a cleft lip.

cheiloschisis (kī-lŏs'kĭ-sĭs) [″ + *schisis,* a splitting] Cleft lip.

cheilosis, chelosis (kī-lō'sĭs) [*cheilo-* + *-osis*] angular cheilosis.

cheilostomatoplasty (kī″lō-stō-mǎt'ō-plăs″tē) [″ + *stoma,* mouth, + *plassein,* to form] Plastic surgery and restoration of the mouth.

cheilotomy, chilotomy (kī-lŏt'ō-mē) [″ + *tome,* incision] Excision of part of the lip.

cheiralgia (kī-răl'jē-ă) [″ + *algos,* pain] Nontraumatic or neuralgic pain in the hand.

    c. paresthetica Numbness and pain in the hand, esp. in the region supplied by the radial nerve.

cheiro-, cheir- SEE: *chiro-.*

cheirognostic, chirognostic (kī″rŏg-nŏs'tĭk) [Gr. *cheir,* hand, + *gnostikos,* knowing] Able to distinguish the left from the right side of the body; able to perceive which side of the body is being stimulated.

cheirospasm (kī'rō-spăsm) [″ + Gr. *spasmos,* a convulsion] Chirospasm.

chelate (kē'lāt) [Gr. *chele,* claw] **1.** In chemistry, to grasp a metallic ion in a ring-shaped molecule. **2.** In toxicology, to use a compound to enclose or sequester a toxic substance, rendering it inactive or less injurious. SEE: *poisoning; Poisons and Poisoning Appendix.*

chelation (kē-lā'shŭn) [Gr. *chele,* claw] **1.** The combining of metallic ions with certain heterocyclic ring structures so that the ion is held by chemical bonds from each participating ring. **2.** An alternative or complementary medical practice that uses infusions of ethylenediaminetetra-acetic acid to remove toxic substances from the body. Its effectiveness in the treatment of human disease is unproven.

cheloid (kē'loyd) [Gr. *kele,* tumor, swelling, + *eidos,* form, shape] Keloid.

chemabrasion (kēm-ă-brā'shŭn) The use of a chemical to destroy superficial layers of skin. This technique is used to treat scars, tattoos, or abnormal pigmentation. SYN: *chemexfoliation.*

chemexfoliation (kēm'ĕks-fō'lē-ā″shŭn) Chemabrasion.

CHEMFET *chemically sensitive field effect transistor.*

chemical, biological, radiological, nuclear, and explosive agents ABBR: CBRNE. Technologically sophisticated weapons that may be used in military or terrorist activities.

Chemical Abstract Service ABBR: CAS.

A branch of the American Chemical Society that maintains a registry of chemicals, active ingredients used in drugs, and food additives. Each chemical is assigned a permanent CAS number through which current data can be traced.

chemical change A process in which molecular bonds break or form to create substances with new properties or characteristics. For example, oxygen and hydrogen combine to form water. Sodium (a metal) and chlorine (a gas) combine to form sodium chloride, or common salt. Glucose ($C_6H_{10}O_5$) is metabolized to carbon dioxide (CO_2) and water (H_2O). Oxygen combines with hemoglobin to form oxyhemoglobin when the hemoglobin in the blood comes into contact with the oxygen in the air contained in the alveoli of the lungs. A chemical change is also known as a chemical reaction.

chemical compound SEE: under *compound.*

chemical dependence Substance **abuse**.

chemical dependency counselor A health care professional who provides guidance and assistance to people addicted to drugs or alcohol and to their families and significant others. Counselors also educate the public about substance abuse and participate in addiction prevention programs.

chemical disaster SEE: under *disaster.*

chemical emergency A sudden release or spill of a potentially hazardous chemical into the environment.

chemically sensitive field effect transistor ABBR: CHEMFET. A specialized chemical sensor found in some clinical laboratory instruments.

chemical restraint SEE: under *restraint.*

chemical warfare Waging war with toxic chemical agents. Agents include nerve gases; agents that cause temporary blindness, paralysis, hallucinations, or deafness; irritants to the eyes and lungs; blistering agents, e.g., mustard gas; defoliants; and herbicides.

    PATIENT CARE: Victims of a chemical exposure or attack require decontamination, ideally on site as rapidly as possible by specially equipped and trained Emergency Medical Services (EMS)/fire personnel or hospital-based health care professionals. Decontamination includes isolation of the victim, preferably outdoors or in a sealed, specially ventilated room; removal of all of the victim's clothing and jewelry; protection of any part of the victim's body that has not been exposed to toxins; repeated irrigation and flushing of exposed skin with water (a dilute woundcleansing solution, such as Dakin's solution, may be used on skin but not on the eyes or within penetrating wounds); additional irrigation of wounded skin with sterile solution (typically for about

10 min longer than the irrigation of intact skin); irrigation of the eyes with saline solution (about 15 min); cleansing beneath the surface of exposed fingernails or toenails; and collection and disposal of effluent and contaminated clothing. To avoid secondary injuries and exposures, trained personnel who carry out decontamination must wear chemical masks with a filtered respirator, self-contained underwater breathing apparatus (SCUBA), and splash-resistant protective clothing that covers all skin and body surfaces and is impervious to all chemicals. Following decontamination, victims require triage and treatment.

Treatments for chemical exposures include both supportive care (such as the administration of oxygen, intravenous fluids, analgesics, topical remedies, and psychosocial support) and the administration of antidotes or chemical antagonists such as physostigmine. Details of the treatment for most specific exposures may be found in references such as the National Library of Medicine's website: www.sis.nlm.nih.gov/Tox/ChemWar.html. SEE: *biological warfare.*

chemiluminescence, chemoluminescence (kĕm″ĭ-loo″mĭ-nĕs′ĕns, kĕm″ō-loo″mĭ-nĕs′ĕns) Cold light or light resulting from a chemical reaction and without heat production. Certain bacteria, fungi, and fireflies produce this type of light. SEE: *luciferase.*

chemist (kĕm′ĭst) Someone who is trained in chemistry.

chemistry (kem′ĭ-strē) [Ult. fr Gr. *chēmeia,* alchemy] The science dealing with the molecular and atomic structure of matter and the composition of substances (their formation, decomposition, and transformations). **chemical** (kem′ĭ-kăl), *adj.*

   analytical c. Chemistry concerned with the detection of chemical substances (qualitative analysis) or the determination of the amounts of substances (quantitative analysis) in a compound.

   biological c. Biochemistry.

   colloid c. The chemistry of emulsions, mists, foams, and suspensions.

   combinatorial c. The manufacturing of molecules having specific sizes, shapes, or functional characteristics using computer-aided algorithms or design rules.

   computational c. The use of mathematical formulas to simulate or study a variety of chemical characteristics, including a compound's electronic structure, geometry, potential energy, and kinetic rate constants.

   general c. The study of the entire field of chemistry with emphasis on fundamental concepts or laws.

   inorganic c. The chemistry of compounds not containing carbon.

   nuclear c. Radiochemistry; the study of changes that take place within the nucleus of an atom, esp. when the nucleus is bombarded by electrons, neutrons, or other subatomic particles.

   organic c. The branch of chemistry dealing with substances that contain carbon compounds.

   pathological c. The study of chemical changes induced by disease processes (e.g., changes in the chemistry of organs and tissues, blood, secretions, or excretions).

   pharmaceutical c. The chemistry of medicines, their composition, synthesis, analysis, storage, and actions.

   physical c. Theoretical chemistry; the chemistry concerned with fundamental laws underlying chemical changes and the mathematical expression of these laws.

   physiological c. The subdivision of biochemistry concerned with chemical processes in living organisms.

chemistry panel A group of routinely performed laboratory tests that assess commonly measured electrolytes, e.g., the concentrations of sodium or potassium in the blood; kidney function, e.g., BUN or creatinine; glucose; or liver function. The term is sometimes abbreviated as CHEM7, CHEM8, or CHEM15, depending on the number of tests included in the panel. SYN: *chemistry **profile**.*

chemo A colloquial term for cancer chemotherapy.

chemo-, chemi-, chem- [Gr. *chēmia,* alchemy] Prefixes meaning *chemical, chemistry.*

chemoautotrophic (kĕm″ō-aw″tō-trŏf′ĭk, kĕm″) [″ + ″] Capable of oxidizing a reduced molecule in the presence of other inorganic materials in order to synthesize carbohydrates. Chemoautotrophy is a characteristic nutritional strategy of the Proteobacteria.

chemo brain A colloquial term for difficulties with concentration and memory that may follow the administration of some forms of cancer chemotherapy.

chemocautery (kĕm″ō-kaw′tĕr-ē) [Gr. *chemeia,* chemistry, + *kauterion,* branding iron] Cauterization by chemical agents.

chemoceptor (kĕm′ō-sĕp-tĕr) Chemoreceptor.

chemocoagulation (kē″mō-kō-ăg″ū-lā′shŭn) [″ + L. *coaglutio,* coagulation] Coagulation caused by chemical agents.

chemodectoma (kē″mō-dĕk-tō′mă) [″ + *dektikos,* receptive, + *oma,* tumor] A tumor of the chemoreceptor system. SEE: *paraganglioma.*

chemoembolization (kē″mō-em″bŏ-lĭ-zā′shŏn′) [*chemo-* + *embolization*] A treatment for a solid tumor, e.g., a malignant mass in the liver, in which a catheter is advanced through the major artery that supplies blood to the tumor, thereby administering anticancer drugs directly into the tumor. The procedure delivers chemotherapy directly into the target tissue.

chemokine (kēm″ō-kīn′) Any polypeptide cytokine that causes chemotaxis, attracting neutrophils, monocytes, and T lymphocytes; e.g., to assist in destroying an invading microorganism. SEE: *cytokine; inflammation.*

chemokinesis (kēm″ō-kĭn-ē′sĭs) The accelerated random locomotion of cells, usually in response to chemical stimuli.

chemoluminescence (kēm″ō-loo″mĭ-nĕs′ĕns) Chemiluminescence.

chemolysis (kē-mŏl′ĭ-sĭs) [″ + *lysis,* dissolution] Destruction by chemical action.

chemomechanical caries removal (kē″mō-mĕ-kăn′ĭ-kĭl) ABBR: CCR. The removal of demineralized dentin from a tooth by applying a chemical gel or solution to soften it and then scraping away the diseased tissue manually. This technique may be used as an alternative to dental drilling. It is typically used in pediatric dentistry, in phobic patients, and in patients with anesthetic allergies or contraindications to drilling.

chemoneurolysis (kē″mō-noo-rol′ĭ-sĭs) [*chemo- + neurolysis*] The destruction of a diseased peripheral nerve, usually one that causes intense pain, by injecting chemicals (such as certain alcohols) into it.

chemonucleolysis (kēm″ō-nū-klē-ŏl′ĭ-sĭs) A method of dissolving a herniated nucleus pulposus, by injecting the enzyme chymopapain into it. This procedure is controversial and is contraindicated for patients with a herniated lumbar disk in which the nucleus pulposus protrudes through the annulus.

chemopallidectomy (kē″mō-păl″ĭ-dĕk′tō-mē) [″ + L. *pallidum,* globus pallidus, + Gr. *ektome,* excision] Destruction of a portion of the globus pallidus of the brain with drugs or chemicals.

chemoprevention (kē″mō-prē-vĕn′shŭn) [Gr. chemeia, chemistry, + ME preventen, to anticipate] Chemoprophylaxis.

chemoprophylaxis (kē″mō-prō″fĭ-lak′sĭs) [*chemo- + prophylaxis*] The use of a drug or chemical to prevent a disease, e.g., the taking of a medicine by a traveler to prevent malaria. SYN: *chemoprevention.*

chemoreceptor (kē″mō-rē-sep′tŏr) [*chemo- + receptor*] A sense organ or sensory nerve ending (as in a taste bud) that is stimulated by and reacts to certain chemical stimuli and that is located outside the central nervous system. Chemoreceptors are found in the large arteries of the thorax and neck (carotid and aortic bodies), the taste buds, and the olfactory cells of the nose. SYN: *chemoceptor; chemosensor.* SEE: *carotid body; taste bud.*

chemoreflex (kē″mō-rē′flĕks) [″ + L. *reflectere,* to bend back] Any involuntary response initiated by a chemical stimulus. SYN: *chemical reflex.*

chemoresistance (kē″mō-ri-zĭs′tăns, kem″ō-) [*chemo- + resistance*] **1.** The resistance of a cell or microorganism to the expected actions of drugs or chemicals. **2.** Lack of responsiveness to chemotherapy. **chemoresistant** (′tănt), *adj.*

chemosense (kē′mō-sens″) [*chemo- + sense*] Either of the two chemical, chemosensory, senses of smell and taste.

chemosensitive (kē″mō-sĕn′sĭ-tĭv) Reacting to the action of a chemical or a change in chemical composition.

chemosensor (kē′mō-sen″sŏr) [*chemo- + sensor*] Chemoreceptor.

chemosensory (kē″mō-sen′sŏ-rē) [*chemo- + sensory*] Pert. to the sensory detection of a chemical, esp. by odor.

chemosensory disorder Any disorder of smell or taste, e.g., anosmia or ageusia.

chemosis (kē-mō′sĭs) [Gr. *cheme,* cockleshell, + *osis,* condition] Edema of the conjunctiva around the cornea. **chemotic** (-mŏt′ĭk), *adj.*

chemosterilant (kē″mō-stĕr′ĭ-lănt) **1.** A chemical that kills microorganisms. **2.** A chemical that causes sterility, usually of the male, in organisms such as insects.

chemosurgery (kēm″ō-sŭr′jĕr-ē) Destruction of tissue by the use of chemical compounds.

chemosynthesis (kē″mō-sĭn′thĕ-sĭs) The formation of a chemical compound from other chemicals or agents. In biological systems, this involves metabolism.

chemotactic (kē″mō-tăk′tĭk) Pert. to chemotaxis.

chemotaxin (kēm″ō-tăk′sĭn) A substance released by bacteria, injured tissue, and white blood cells that stimulates the movement of neutrophils and other white blood cells to the injured area. Complement factors 3a (C3a) and 5a (C5a), cytokines, leukotrienes, prostaglandins, and fragments of fibrin and collagen are common chemotaxins. SEE: *inflammation.*

chemotaxis (kē″mō-tăk′sĭs) [Gr. *chemeia,* chemistry, + *taxis,* arrangement] The movement of additional white blood cells to an area of inflammation in response to the release of chemical mediators by neutrophils, monocytes, and injured tissue. SEE: *chemotropism.*

chemothalamectomy (kē″mō-thăl-ă-mĕk′tō-mē) Chemical destruction of a part of the thalamus.

chemotherapy (kē″mō-ther′ă-pē)
[*chemo-* + *therapy*] Drug therapy used to treat infections, cancers, and other diseases and conditions. SEE: *Nursing Diagnoses Appendix*.

⚠ Chemotherapeutic agents to treat cancer are poisons and pose risks to those who handle them, primarily pharmacists and nurses. Usually, only oncology practitioners specifically trained in chemotherapy administration should perform this task. The most important factor in reducing exposure is proper protection in preparation and administration of these agents. After washing hands, the health care provider dons appropriate apparel. Protective clothing may be used if drugs are prepared under a hood, but generally only surgical powder-free or hypoallergenic latex-free chemotherapy gloves are used for most administration. He or she then gathers equipment to administer the drugs, including normal saline or 5% dextrose in water (D5W) solution as prescribed (the same solution should be used for both priming and mixing), IV tubing, the drugs, alcohol swabs, sterile gauze, required to start an IV line or enter a port, and plastic-backed absorbent pads. Hydration is provided before administration of the chemotherapy drugs, along with an antiemetic, antihistamine, or other agents. Patients may often eat or drink during the administration of chemotherapy. The drugs should be administered in a calm environment, and all chemotherapy waste and equipment must be discarded in designated waste containers. Health care providers must follow OSHA guidelines when cleaning up drug spills. Spill kits should be available and used, and spill areas cleaned three times using soap and water (for the skin) or detergent followed by clean water (for other surfaces). Gloves should also be worn when handling the patient's excreta. Exposure poses additional risks to female reproductive health, including ectopic pregnancies, spontaneous abortions, and fetal abnormalities.

PATIENT CARE: Cancer chemotherapeutic agents include alkylating agents and nitrosureas, antimetabolites, antitumor antibiotics, plant alkaloids, and steroid hormones. Antineoplastic agents kill cancer cells but also kill or injure normal cells, esp. those that normally divide rapidly and may therefore compromise the patient's comfort and safety. Bone marrow suppression is a common and potentially serious adverse reaction. Chemotherapy can decrease the numbers of leukocytes, erythrocytes, and platelets. Leukopenia increases the patient's risk for infection, esp. if the granulocyte count falls below $1000/mm^3$. The patient is given information about personal hygiene and potential sites for infection and is taught to recognize signs and symptoms, e.g., fever, cough, sore throat, or a burning sensation when urinating. The patient is cautioned to avoid crowds and people with colds or flu. Filgrastim (Neupogen) or pegfilgrastim (Neulasta) is administered as prescribed to stimulate proliferation and differentiation of neutrophils. Thrombocytopenia increases a patient's risk for bleeding when the platelet count falls below $50,000/mm^3$; the risk is highest when the platelet count falls below $20,000/mm^3$. Oprelvekin (Neumega) may be used to treat this complication. The patient is assessed and taught to observe for bleeding gums, increased bruising or petechiae, hypermenorrhea, tarry stools, hematuria, and coffee-ground emesis. He or she is advised to avoid cuts and bruises and to use a soft toothbrush and an electric razor. The patient must report sudden headaches, which could indicate intracranial bleeding. He or she should use a stool softener, as prescribed, to avoid colonic irritation and bleeding. Intramuscular injections are avoided to prevent bleeding. Anemia develops slowly over the course of treatment; therefore the patient's hemoglobin, hematocrit, and red blood cell counts are monitored. Dehydration can lead to a false-normal hematocrit, which decreases when the patient is rehydrated. The patient is assessed for and taught to report any dizziness, fatigue, pallor, or shortness of breath on minimal exertion. He or she must rest more frequently, increase dietary intake of iron-rich foods, and take a multivitamin with iron, as prescribed. Growth factors or colony-stimulating factors are administered as prescribed, e.g., epoetin alfa (Procrit) enhances erythrocyte production to increase hemoglobin levels; whole blood or packed cells are transfused as prescribed for a symptomatic patient.

Antineoplastics attack cancer cells because they divide rapidly. For the same reason, they also destroy rapidly dividing normal cells. While epithelial damage can affect any mucous membrane, the oral mucosa is the most common site of destruction. Stomatitis is a temporary but disabling phenomenon that may interfere with eating and drinking. It can range from mild and barely noticeable to severe and debilitating malnutrition. Preventive mouth care is initiated and taught to the patient to provide comfort and decrease the severity of mouth pain. Therapeutic mouth care is also provided, including topical antibiotics, if prescribed. The patient may experience nausea and vomiting from gastric mucosal irritation (from oral or parenteral chemotherapy), chemical irritation of the central nervous system (from parenteral chemotherapy), or psychogenic factors activated by sensations, suggestions, or anxiety. Chemotherapy-induced nausea and vomiting is troublesome because it can cause fluid and electrolyte imbalance, noncompliance with the treatment regimen, tears at the esophageal-gastric junction that lead to massive bleeding (Mallory-Weiss syndrome), wound dehiscence, and pathological fractures. It also reduces quality of life by interfering with the patient's ability and motivation to take an active role in his or her self-care. Such complications are assessed for and prevented as much as possible. Chemical irritation is controlled by administering prescribed combinations of antiemetics that act by different mechanisms, e.g., serotonin antagonists, prochlorperazine, diphenhydramine, droperidol, and dronabinol. Signs and symptoms of aspiration are monitored because most antiemetics are sedating. Psychogenic factors can be relieved by relaxation techniques to minimize feelings of isolation and anxiety before and during each treatment. The patient is encouraged to express feelings of anxiety, listen to music, engage in relaxation techniques, meditation, or self-hypnosis to help promote feelings of well-being and a sense of control.

Hair loss is distressing for the patient, esp. when the patient's body image or self-esteem is closely linked to his or her appearance. The patient is informed that hair loss usually is gradual, affects both men and women, and may be partial or complete, depending on the drug or drug combination employed. He or she is reassured that alopecia is reversible after treatment ends. A wig can be prescribed as a cranial prosthesis (for insurance coverage of the expense). The patient is encouraged to purchase it before hair loss begins and is informed where to acquire it and other head coverings. Although some patients prefer to expose their baldness, the scalp should be protected from exposure to the sun. Some chemotherapeutic agents have irreversible effects such as peripheral neuropathy although treatment is available to reduce these.

Chemotherapy extravasation may lead to tissue necrosis if the drug is a vesicant, and the patient is taught to immediately report any pain, stinging, burning, swelling, or redness at the injection site. Extravasation must be distinguished from vessel irritation or flare reaction. Vein irritation is felt as aching or tightness along the blood vessel, and the length of the vein may become reddened or darkened, accompanied by swelling. In flare reaction, itching is the major complaint; redness occurs in blotches along the vessel, may look like hives, and subsides within 30 min. Blood return from the IV can usually be obtained with both irritation and flare reaction. To help prevent extravasation, most known vesicant drugs are administered through a central venous catheter. If extravasation is suspected, the infusion is stopped, and any drug is aspirated. The extremity is elevated, and cold compresses are applied, except for *Vinca* alkaloids, for which heat is recommended. Depending on agency protocol, the oncologist is notified; and, if a specific antidote for the drug exists, it is administered as prescribed. The main line IV provides direct access to the patient if an undesired reaction occurs; other drugs can be administered quickly to counteract the adverse reaction. SEE: table.

Complementary and alternative therapies are often used to help patients undergoing chemotherapy to feel better and more in control of their illness and its treatment.

Important Considerations in the Administration of Chemotherapy

- Has the patient had allergic reactions to this medication in the past?
- What fluids are compatible, or incompatible, with the agent to be administered?
- What is the exact dosage for this patient's body size and weight?
- How is the drug mixed or prepared?
- What is the proper route of administration?
- How stable is the drug once prepared?
- How should it be stored?
- What other drugs is the patient taking? Are any likely to cause drug interactions?
- Can the drug cause skin or vein irritation during administration? How will these complications be managed?
- What is the anticipated schedule of administration?
- What are the specific side effects of the agent? How should the patient and health care team prepare for early or delayed effects?
- How are effects of the drug to be monitored?
- How often should the patient have physical examinations, imaging studies, or blood tests?
- What findings suggest further drug administration should be delayed or cancelled?
- Who should the patient contact with concerns?

adjuvant c. Administration of cytotoxic drugs to eradicate cancerous cells remaining in the body after surgery or radiation therapy.

combination c. The use of two or more complementary drugs to treat a disease.

consolidation c. A cycle of therapy with cytotoxic drugs after the initial treatment for a cancer. The object is to sustain a remission achieved during induction.

hyperthermic intraperitoneal c. ABBR: HIPEC. Chemotherapy for cancer that has spread to and diffusely covers the internal organs within the peritoneum. The drugs are heated before they are infused.

induction c. The initial treatment of advanced cancers or leukemias with high doses of cytotoxic drugs to produce a remission.

peritoneal c. Intraperitoneal injection of antineoplastic drugs.

topical c A cancer-fighting medication, e.g., 5-fluorouracil, applied to the skin as a cream, ointment, or paste.

chemotherapy-induced nausea and vomiting Vomiting that occurs after the administration of drugs used to treat cancer. Although its causes are complex, it appears to result from both direct irritation of the gastrointestinal tract by cytotoxic drugs, and the release of chemical mediators, such as 5-hydroxytryptamine (5-HT), from the gastrointestinal tract. 5-HT antagonists are among the most effective treatments. Dopaminergic effects in the central nervous system are also involved in chemotherapy-induced nausea and vomiting, and drugs that antagonize these effects, such as phenothiazines and other neuroleptics, can be used to treat the syndrome. Endocannabinoid drugs, corticosteroids (such as dexamethasone), antianxiety drugs (such as lorazepam) also have selected uses. Drugs that block receptors for neurokinins (such as aprepitant) are esp. effective in treating emesis that occurs more than 24 hours after chemotherapy.

chemotropism (kē-mŏt′rō-pĭzm) [″ + *tropos,* a turning] The growth or movement of an organism in response to a chemical stimulus, such as the movement of bacteria toward nutrients.

chemotx *treatment with chemotherapeutic drugs.*

CHEMTREC The Chemical Transportation Emergency Center, which provides a 24-hr hotline with product information and emergency advice to rescue personnel at the scene of a hazardous materials incident.

cherubism (chĕr′ū-bĭzm) A swollen appearance of the face of a child due to infiltration of the jaw, esp. the mandible, with masses of vascular fibrous tissue containing giant cells.

CHESS *Comprehensive Health Enhancement Support System.*

chest (chĕst) [AS. *cest,* a box] The thorax, including all the organs (e.g., heart, great vessels, esophagus, trachea, lungs) and tissues (bone, muscle, fat) that lie between the base of the neck and the diaphragm.

PHYSICAL EXAMINATION: *Inspection*: The practitioner inspects the chest to determine the respiratory rate and whether the right and left sides of the chest move symmetrically during breathing. In pneumonia, pleurisy, or rib fracture, for example, the affected side of the chest may have reduced movement as a result of lung consolidation or pain ("splinting" of the chest). Increased movements may be seen in extensive trauma ("flail" chest). The patient in respiratory distress uses accessory muscles of the chest to breathe; retractions of the spaces between the ribs are also seen when patients labor to breathe.

Percussion: The chest wall is tapped with the fingers (sometimes with a reflex hammer) to determine whether it has a normally hollow, or resonant, sound and feel. Dullness perceived during percussion may indicate a pleural effusion or underlying pneumonia. Abnormal tympany may be present in conditions such as emphysema, cavitary lung diseases, or pneumothorax.

Palpation: By pressing or squeezing the soft tissues of the chest, bony instability (fractures), abnormal masses (lipomas or other tumors), edema, or subcutaneous air may be detected.

Auscultation: Chest sounds are assessed using the stethoscope. Abnormal friction sounds may indicate pleurisy, pericarditis, or pulmonary embolism; crackles may be detected in pulmonary edema, pneumonia, or interstitial fibrosis; and wheezes may be heard in reactive airway disease. Intestinal sounds heard in the chest may point to diaphragmatic hernias. Heart sounds are diminished in obesity and pericardial effusion; they are best heard near the xiphoid process in emphysema. Lung sounds may be decreased in patients with chronic obstructive lung diseases, pleural effusion, and other conditions.

barrel c. An increased anteroposterior chest diameter caused by increased functional residual capacity, which in turn results from airway narrowing and a loss of lung elasticity. It is most often seen in patients with chronic obstructive pulmonary disease (i.e., chronic bronchitis and emphysema).

emphysematous c. A misnomer for the barrel-shaped appearance of the chest in emphysema. The thorax is short and round, the anteroposterior diameter is often as long as the transverse diameter, the ribs are horizontal, and the angle formed by divergence of the costal margin from the sternum is obtuse or obliterated.

flail c. A condition of the chest wall due to two or more fractures on each affected rib resulting in a segment of rib not attached on either end; the flail segment moves paradoxically in with inspiration and out during expiration.

flat c. A deformity of the chest in which the anteroposterior diameter is short, the thorax long and flat, and the ribs oblique. The scapula is prominent; the spaces above and below the clavicles are depressed. The angle formed by divergence of the costal margins from the sternum is very acute.

funnel c. Pectus excavatum.

pigeon c. A condition in which the sides of the chest are considerably flattened and the sternum is prominent. The sternal ends of the ribs are enlarged or beaded. Often there is a circular construction of the thorax at the level of the xiphoid cartilage. The condition is often congenital and present in mucopolysaccharidoses. SYN: **pectus** *carinatum.*

chest compression SEE: under *compression.*

chest pain observation unit ABBR: CPOU. A hospital ward equipped with continuous cardiac monitoring in which patients thought to have a relatively low or an intermediate risk of acute coronary syndromes are evaluated for myocardial ischemia or infarction before their return home or their admission, if necessary, to a coronary care unit.

chest physical therapy, chest physiotherapy ABBR: CPT, Chest PT. A type of respiratory care usually incorporating postural drainage, cough facilitation, and breathing exercises used for loosening and removing lung secretions. It may include percussion (clapping) and vibration over the affected areas of the lungs, simultaneous with postural drainage to remove secretions. Auscultation of breath sounds is done before and after the procedure.

chest PT *chest physical therapy.*

chest region SEE: under *region.*

chest tube Thoracostomy tube.

chest wiggle In high-frequency oscillatory ventilation (HFOV), the rapid movements of the chest wall of the patient in response to the delivery of small volumes of gas into the airways several times a second.

Cheyne nystagmus (chān(-ē)) [John Cheyne, Scottish physician, 1777–1836] Nystagmus whose rhythm resembles that of Cheyne-Stokes respiration. SEE: *Cheyne-Stokes respiration.*

Cheyne-Stokes respiration (chān'stōks') [John Cheyne; William Stokes] A breathing pattern marked by a period of apnea lasting 10 to 60 sec, followed by gradually increasing depth and frequency of respirations (hyperventilation). It occurs in dysfunction or depression of the cerebral hemispheres, (as in coma), in basal ganglia disease, and occasionally in congestive heart failure. It often indicates a grave prognosis in adults but may be a normal finding in children.

CHF *congestive heart failure.*

chi In biochemistry, a regulatory sequence of base pairs that participate in the repair or recombination of nucleic acid strands.

ch'i (chē) [Chinese *qì, ch'ï,* breath] SEE: *qi.*

chia (chē'ă) [Sp. *chía,* fr Nahuatl (Aztec) *chian,* oily] A member of the sage family of grains, *Salvia hispanica.* It is a rich nutritional source of amino acids and alpha-linoleic acid and has been proposed as an appetite suppressant. SYN: *salba.*

Chiari deformity (kē-ar'ē) Arnold-Chiari deformity.

Chiari-Frommel syndrome (kē-ar'ē-from'ĕl) [Hans Chiari, Austrian pathologist, 1851–1916; Richard Julius Ernst Frommel, Ger. gynecologist, 1854–1912] A rare hormonal disorder following childbirth and lasting for more than six months, when weaning does not end lactation and amenorrhea persists. A pituitary adenoma may be present.

chiasm, chiasma (kī'ăzm, kī-ăz'mă) [Gr. *khiasma,* cross] A crossing or decussation.

optic c. An X-shaped crossing of the optic nerve fibers in the brain. Past this point, the fibers travel in optic tracts. Fibers that originate in the outer half of the retina end on the same side of the brain; those from the inner half cross over to the opposite, or *contralateral,* side.

chickenpox (chĭk'ĕn-pŏks'') Varicella.

chigger, jigger (chig'ĕr, jig') [Variant of *chigoe*] A six-legged mite of the genus *Trombicula,* common in the southern U.S. During summer months, hikers, outdoor enthusiasts, and field hands may become infested with these nonscabietic mites, which tend to attach to the skin, causing an intensely itchy rash. The skin irritation results from an allergic reaction to the injected saliva of the insect; unlike some other insects, the mites do not feed on human blood. Occasionally chiggers act as vectors for rickettsial diseases, such as scrub typhus. Infestation can be prevented by applying insect repellents to outdoor clothing. SYN: *chigoe* (2); *harvest* **mite**; *red* **bug**; *red* **mite**. SEE: *Tunga.*

TREATMENT: Proprietary preparations are available to kill chiggers. They are applied topically to affected skin. One of these, Kwell, contains hexachlorohexane. Benzyl benzoate ointment and gamma benzene hexachloride are also effective.

chigoe (chig'ō, chē'gō) [Of uncertain origin] **1. Tunga** penetrans. **2.** Chigger.

chigoe infestation Infestation by the flea *Tunga penetrans*.. In humans the usual sites of invasion are the spaces between the toes, where the burrowing female swells and causes a painful open sore.

TREATMENT: The gravid flea is removed with a sterile needle. The site is treated with tincture of iodine, which is toxic to the remaining fleas and eggs. SEE: *Tunga penetrans*.

chi kung (chē goong) [Chinese *qì, ch'i*, breath, air, spirit + *gōng. kūng*, work, practice] SEE: *qi gong*.

chikungunya virus An alphavirus, typically found in Africa or Southeast Asia, that can be transmitted to humans by the bite of *Aedes* mosquitoes. After an incubation period of about a week, the virus produces high fevers, headache, nausea, vomiting, and severe joint pain, usually in the wrists or ankles.

chilblain (chĭl'blān) [AS. *cele*, cold, + *blegen*, to puff] A mild form of cold injury marked by localized redness, burning, and swelling on exposed body parts, esp. in cool, damp climates. The affected skin sometimes blisters or ulcerates. Insufficient blood flow into small blood vessels in the skin may contribute to the formation of chilblains. SYN: *pernio*.

PREVENTION: Patients with a history of chilblains should wear warm, loose-fitting clothing when outdoors in the cold.

child (chīld) [AS. *cild,* child] Any human between infancy and puberty. SEE: *pediatrics*.

child abuse SEE: under *abuse*.

childbearing (chīld'bar"ĭng) The act of carrying and being delivered of a child.

   delayed c. SEE: *elderly primigravida*.

childbearing period SEE: under *period*.

childbed Historically, the period of parturition during which women remained in bed for labor, delivery, and the traditional 6 weeks' recovery time after childbirth. SYN: *puerperium*. SEE: *childbed fever*.

childbirth (chīld'bĭrth") The act of giving birth to a child. SYN: *parturition*. SEE: *delivery; labor*.

   natural c. The delivery of a fetus without the use of analgesics, sedatives, or anesthesia and less reliance on technology (and more reliance on emotional support during labor and delivery) than may be practical during standard obstetrical care. The woman, and often her partner, go through a training period beginning months before the actual delivery. This training is called psychopro-

phylactic preparation for childbirth. SEE: *Lamaze method; psychoprophylactic preparation for childbirth*.

   prepared c. Childbirth in which the mother, and often also the father, of the baby has been educated about childbirth, anesthesia, and analgesia during labor. The mother may choose to have natural childbirth or to receive medications or regional anesthesia. SEE: *natural c.; Lamaze method; psychoprophylactic preparation for childbirth*.

childhood (chīld'hood) [AS] **1.** That stage of life that begins after infancy and ends at adolescence; physiologically, from age 1 until the onset of puberty. **2.** The stage of life that begins with the end of infancy and ends with the onset of independent living; psychologically and socially, from age 1 until a person leaves the parental home to make his or her own way in life.

childhood disintegrative disorder Disintegrative disorder.

child life specialist A health care specialist who helps children and their families cope with illnesses and injuries. Disease or injury poses unique stresses for children, their siblings, and their parents. Child life specialists help reduce these stresses and promote healthy coping skills and development through interventions that include therapeutic play, support and counseling, and patient orientation and education. In a hospital setting, child life specialists are often part of a multidisciplinary team.

child neglect Failure by those responsible for caring for a child to provide for the child's nutritional, emotional, or physical needs.

childproof Designed to prevent injury to children; used esp. of medicine containers that children cannot open.

Children's Health Insurance Program ABBR: CHIP. A state-based program providing health insurance for children whose parents have no private insurance and have incomes that exceed eligibility limits for Medicaid. Website: www.cms.gov/home/chip.asp

chilectropion (kī-"lĕk-trō'pē-ŏn) Cheilectropion.

Chiliaditi anomaly (kēl"yă-dēt'ē) [Demetrios Chilaiditi, Viennese-born Gr. radiologist, b. 1883] The abnormal positioning of the large bowel between the liver and the diaphragm.

chill (chĭl) [AS. *cele*, cold] Involuntary, rapid contraction of muscle groups (shivering) accompanied by the sensation of cold, or the sensation of being cold without shivering. It may be caused by a rising fever associated with an infection, a hypersensitivity reaction to drugs or blood transfusions, exposure to cold temperatures, or a neuroendocrine disturbance in the temperature-regulating centers of the hypothalamus. Severe chills accompanied by violent shaking of the body are called rigors.

chill therapy An informal term for *induced hypothermia*. SEE: under *hypothermia*.

chilo-, chil-, cheil-, cheilo- [Gr. *cheilos*, lip] Prefixes meaning *lip*.

Chilomastix mesnili (kī″lō-măs′tĭks měs-nĭl′ē) A species of Mastigophora that is usually nonpathogenic but can cause diarrhea in humans.

chimera (kī-mē′rǎ) **1.** A tissue in which two distinct forms of DNA are present. **2.** The conjugation of two different drugs, cells, proteins, or organisms. **3.** A double-egg twin whose blood and blast cells have been mixed in embryo with those of the other twin. Therefore, although each twin originally had a different blood group, each now has a mixed group.

chimpanzee (chĭm-păn′zē) An intelligent ape (*Pan troglodytes*) native to parts of Africa. The DNA of humans and chimps is closely matched.

chin (chin) The point of the lower jaw below the lower lip.

Chinese red rice Red yeast rice extract. SEE: under *extract*.

chin jerk Chin reflex.

CHIP *Children's Health Insurance Program.*

CHIP rule [computed tomography in head injury patients] A diagnostic prediction rule used to determine if a patient with a minor head injury would benefit from emergent CT imaging of the brain. Low-risk patients are those who have a Glascow Coma Scale (GCS) of 15 and no history of loss of consciousness, amnesia, vomiting, or generalized headache. These patients do not need neuroimaging in the Emergency Department and can be discharged home with follow-up. Patients who are over 60 or who have a history of alcohol or drug use, epilepsy, or coagulopathy are considered high risk regardless of their GCS. Those with intermediate GCS values are considered to have medium-risk mild head injuries.

chiragra (kī-răg′rǎ) [Gr. *cheir*, hand, + *agra*, seizure] Pain in the hand.

chirality (kī-răl′ĭ-tē) [Gr. *cheir*, hand] The geometric distinctness of an object from its mirror image. Examples include chemicals with "left-" and "right-handed" structures.

chiro-, chir-, cheiro-, cheir- [Gr. *cheir*, hand] Prefixes meaning *hand*.

chirokinesthesia (kī″rō-kĭn″ĕs-thē′zē-ă) [″ + *kinesis*, movement, + *aisthesis*, sensation] A subjective sensation of hand motions.

chiromegaly (kī″rō-měg′ă-lē) [″ + *megas*, large] Enlargement of the hands, wrists, or ankles.

chiroplasty (kī′rō-plăs″tē) [″ + *plas-*

sein, to form] Plastic surgery on the hand.

chiropodist (kĭ-rŏp′ō-dĭst, kĭ-) [″ + *pous*, foot] An obsolete term for podiatrist. SEE: *podiatrist*.

chiropody (kĭ-rŏp′ō-dē) Obsolete term for treatment of foot disorders. SEE: *podiatry*.

chiropractic (kī″rō-prăk′tĭk) [Gr. *cheir*, hand, + *prattein*, to do] A system of health care in which diseases are treated predominantly with manipulation or massage of spinal and musculoskeletal structures, nutritional therapies, and emotional support. Treatment is based on the premise that some illnesses are caused by misalignments of the vertebrae and that correcting vertebral subluxations helps to maintain healthy nervous and musculoskeletal systems. Prescription drugs and surgeries are not used. Chiropractic was founded in the U.S. in 1895 by Daniel D. Palmer.

⚠ Although chiropractic manipulation is usually safe, it may occasionally pose a risk of fracture or paralysis to patients with some bone or joint diseases (e.g., osteoporosis or inflammatory arthritis), metastatic cancer, or spinal infections. Manipulation of the neck has also resulted in rare instances of carotid and vertebral artery dissection, stroke, or nerve injury.

Chiropractors are the fourth largest group of health practitioners in the U.S. (at 50,000), after physicians, dentists, and nurses. Chiropractic is 1 of the 10 most commonly used complementary or alternative medicine (CAM) therapies. PATIENT CARE: Common problems treated with chiropractic are neck and shoulder pain, headaches, sports injuries, and work-related injuries such as carpal tunnel syndrome. Spinal manipulation is either performed manually, or with mechanical devices to control the force and direction of adjustments. Adjunctive therapies include massage, hot or cold applications, ultrasound, and nutrition. When manipulation is considered appropriate, a specific type of adjustment is done, depending on the patient's condition. The most common technique is the high-velocity, low-amplitude thrust (osseous adjustment), performed by moving a joint to the end point of its current normal range of motion and then imparting a swift, low-amplitude, specifically directed thrust.

chiropractor (kī″rō-prăk′tŏr) A person certified and licensed to provide chiropractic care.

chirospasm (kī′rō-spăzm) [″ + *spasmos*, spasm] A spasm of the hand muscles; writer's cramp. SYN: *cheirospasm*.

Chirurgiae Magister ABBR: ChM. Master of Surgery. A degree offered to a student who makes a significant contribution to the theory or practice of surgery.

chisel (chĭs'l) A beveled-edge steel cutting instrument used in dentistry and orthopedics.

chi-square (kī-skwār) SYMB: χ^2. A statistical test to determine the correlation between the number of actual occurrences and the expected occurrences.

chitin (kī'tĭn) [Gr. *chiton*, tunic] A polysaccharide that forms the hard exoskeleton of arthropods such as insects and crustaceans. It is also present in the cell walls of some fungi. **chitinous** (-nŭs), *adj.*

chitosan (kī'tō-săn) A polysaccharide made of glucosamine, naturally present in the exoskeleton of crustaceans. It resists digestion in the stomach but degrades in the colon. It is used to protect drugs and oral vaccines for controlled release into the gastrointestinal tract.

Chlamydia (klă-mĭd'ē-ă) [Gr. *chlamys*, cloak] A bacterial genus of intracellular parasites of the family Chlamydiaceae with several recognized species, of which only *C. trachomatis* infects humans. The organisms are characterized as bacteria because of the composition of their cell walls and their reproduction by binary fission, but they reproduce only within cells. These species cause a variety of diseases. SEE: *Chlamydophila.*

   C. trachomatis A species that causes a great variety of diseases, including genital infections in men and women. The diseases caused by *C. trachomatis* include conjunctivitis, epididymitis, lymphogranuloma venereum, pelvic inflammatory disease, pneumonia, trachoma, tubal scarring, and infertility.

   C. trachomatis is a common sexually transmitted pathogen (causing more than a million chlamydial infections in the U.S. each year). Men with chlamydial infection experience penile discharge and discomfort while urinating. Women may be asymptomatic or may experience urethral or vaginal discharge, painful or frequent urination, lower abdominal pain, or acute pelvic inflammatory disease, which may result in infertility.

   Transmission of the disease can be prevented by avoiding contact with infected people and by using condoms during intimate sex. A pregnant woman with a chlamydial infection can transmit the disease to her newborn during birth. In newborns, ophthalmic antibiotic solution should be instilled in the conjunctival sac of each eye to prevent neonatal conjunctivitis and blindness caused by *Chlamydia.*

   DIAGNOSIS: Several tests are available, including cultures, antigen detection assays, ligase chain reactions, polymerase chain reactions, and enzyme-linked immunoassays.

   TREATMENT: Erythromycin, azithromycin, or tetracycline is effective.

⚠️ Tetracyclines are generally not recommended for pregnant women or children under 8 years old.

Chlamydophila (klă-mĭ-dŏf'ĭ-lă) [Gr. *chlamys*, cloak + "] A bacterial genus of intracellular parasites of the family Chlamydiaceae, comprising six species, of which *C. pneumoniae* and *C. psittaci* infect humans. The organisms are characterized as bacteria because of the composition of their cell walls and their reproduction by binary fission, but they reproduce only within cells. These species cause a variety of diseases. SEE: *Chlamydia.*

   C. pneumoniae A species of *Chlamydophila* that is an important cause of pneumonia, bronchitis, and sinusitis. It is believed to be transmitted from person to person by respiratory tract secretions (e.g., by airborne droplets). Most cases are mild and rarely require hospitalization. It is possible that this organism is a factor in the development of coronary artery disease.

   TREATMENT: Treatment consists of daily tetracycline, macrolide, or fluoroquinolone for 14 to 21 days.

   C. psittaci A species of *Chlamydophila* common in birds and animals. Pet owners, pet shop employees, poultry workers, and workers in meat-processing plants are frequently exposed to *C. psittaci.*

   SYMPTOMS: After an incubation period of 5 to 15 days, nonspecific symptoms (e.g., malaise, headache, fever) develop; progression to pneumonia is serious and may be fatal. Alternatively, the disease may resemble infectious mononucleosis with fever, pharyngitis, hepatosplenomegaly, and adenopathy. Severity may vary from inapparent to mild to fatal systemic disease.

   PROGNOSIS: The fatality rate is approx. 20% in untreated patients.

   TREATMENT: Treatment consists of tetracycline or doxycycline for 10 to 21 days.

chloasma (klō-ăz'mă) [Gr. *chloazein*, to be green] Tan to brown, sharply defined patches of skin pigment, usually found symmetrically on the forehead, temples, cheeks, or upper lip. The excess pigmentation often occurs in pregnant women, in women using oral contraceptives, or in patients with underlying liver disease. Women are affected more often than men. Sun exposure tends to worsen the condition. SYN: *melasma.*

c. gravidarum Brownish pigmentation of the face, often occurring in pregnancy. It usually disappears after delivery. It is also seen in some women who take progestational oral contraceptives. SYN: *mask of pregnancy*. SEE: illus.

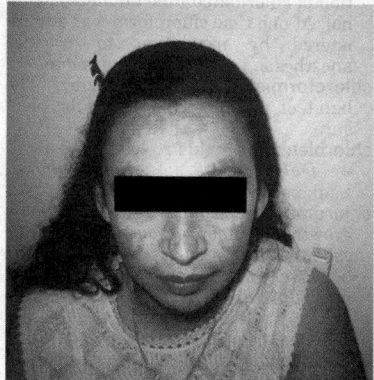

CHLOASMA GRAVIDARUM

c. hepaticum Liver spot.
idiopathic c. Chloasma caused by external agents such as sun, heat, mechanical means, and x-rays.
c. traumaticum Skin discoloration following trauma.
chloracne (klor-ăk′nē) Generalized acne that usually occurs after industrial exposure to chemicals such as polychlorinated biphenyls (PCBs) or dioxin. SEE: illus.

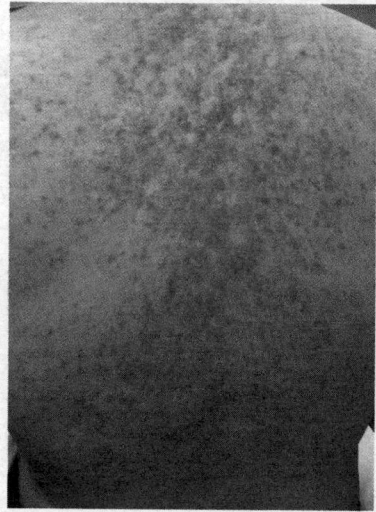

CHLORACNE
In a Vietnam veteran who was exposed to Agent Orange

chloral (klōr′ăl) [*chloro-* + *-al*] **1.** An oily liquid having a bitter taste. **2.** Chloral hydrate.
chloral hydrate A drug occasionally used as a sedative and hypnotic. Benzodiazepines (such as temazepam) have largely replaced chloral hydrate. SYN: *chloral (2)*.
chlorate (klō′rāt) A salt of chloric acid. SEE: *Poisons and Poisoning Appendix*.
chlordane (klor′dān) A organochlorine used as an insecticide. In humans it causes neurological toxicities (such as alterations in memory and motor function) among other problems. SEE: *Poisons and Poisoning Appendix*.
chlordiazepoxide hydrochloride (klor″dī-ăz″ĕ-pŏk′sīd) A benzodiazepine derivative used to treat anxiety, alcohol withdrawal syndrome, and insomnia, and occasionally as a premedication in anesthesia.
chloremia (klō-rē′mē-ă) [Gr. *chloros*, green, + *haima*, blood] Increased chloride in the blood.
chlorhexidine (klor-hek′sĭ-dīn″, -dēn″) A bisbiguanide used as a topical disinfectant and as an oral treatment for plaque and gingivitis.

⚠️ Rarely, systemic anaphylaxis can occur after exposure of the skin to this agent.

PATIENT CARE: In dentistry chlorhexidine oral rinses (0.12% solution) are used an antimicrobial before dental procedures or as a rinse used by patients twice a day to treat gingivitis. The chlorhexidine rinse should be performed after meals to minimize its impact on taste. Patients should not rinse with water after a chlorhexidine rinse. Side effects include staining of the teeth, of tooth-colored restorations, and of the tongue; bitter taste, transient loss of taste, and soft tissue ulceration. Other forms of chlorhexidine are used in topical (skin) disinfectants, e.g., in Intensive Care Units. Cleansing patients' skin in the ICU with chlorhexidine gluconate (2%) lowers the rate of vancomycin-resistant enterococci (VRE) colonization and reduces VRE environmental contamination, leading to less frequent acquisition of infection with this nosocomial pathogen.
chlorhexidine gluconate (gloo′kă-nāt″) A topical disinfectant.
chlorhydria (klor-hī′drē-ă) [″ + *hydor*, water] An excess of hydrochloric acid in the stomach.
chloride (klō′rīd) [Gr. *chloros*, green] A binary compound of chlorine; a salt of hydrochloric acid. In health, blood serum contains 100 to 110 mmol/L of chloride ions.
FUNCTION: Chloride is the major ex-

tracellular anion and contributes to many body functions including the maintenance of osmotic pressure, acid-base balance, muscular activity, and the movement of water between fluid compartments. It is associated with sodium in the blood and was the first electrolyte to be routinely measured in the blood. Chloride ion is secreted in the gastric juice as hydrochloric acid.

chloridemia (klō″rĭ-dē′mē-ă) [″ + *haima*, blood] Chlorides in the blood.

chloride-responsive (klōr′īd″ri-spon′siv) Treatable with normal saline (a 0.9% solution of sodium chloride).

chloridometer, chloridimeter (klor-ĭ-dom′ĕt-ĕr, -dim′) [*chloride* + *-meter*] An instrument for determining the amount of chloride in a body fluid.

chloriduria (klō″rĭ-dū′rē-ă) [″ + *ouron*, urine] Excess of chlorides in the urine.

chlorinated (klō′rĭn-ā-tĕd) Impregnated or treated with chlorine.

chlorination (klōr″ĭ-nā′shŏn) The addition of chlorine or one of its derivatives to water to kill microorganisms. For effective disinfection, a concentration of 0.5 to 1 part chlorine per million parts water is necessary. Some studies have suggested an association (but not a causal link) between the chlorination of drinking water and the incidence of cancers and birth defects.

chlorine (klōr′ēn) [*chloro-* + *-ine*] SYMB: Cl. A highly irritating, very poisonous gaseous chemical element, a member of the halogen family, atomic weight (mass) 35.453, atomic number 17. It is destructive to the mucous membranes of the respiratory passages, and excessive inhalation may cause death. Because of its oxidizing powers, chlorine is used as an active bleaching agent, a germicide, and a disinfectant of water supplies and sewage.

chlorite (klō′rīt) A salt of chlorous acid; used as a disinfectant and bleaching agent.

chloro-, chlor- [Gr. *chlōros*, green, greenish yellow, yellow] Prefixes meaning *green, chlorine,* or *containing chlorine.*

chloroacetophenone, w-chloroacetophenone (klō″rō-ăs′ĭ-tō-fĕ-nōn″) A toxic chemical compound, C_8H_7ClO, released as an aerosol or mist in riot control. It irritates the eyes, lungs, nose, and skin, and is a form of tear gas.

chlorobenzylidene malononitrile, o-chlorobenzylidenemalononitrile (klō″rō-bĕn-zĭl′ĭ-dēn măl-ō-nī′trĭl) A toxic white powder, $C_{10}H_5ClN_2$,/Cl-$C_6H_4CH=C(CN)_2$, released as an aerosol or mist in riot control. It irritates the eyes, lungs, nose, and skin, and is a form of tear gas.

chlorofluorocarbon (klōr″ō-floor″ō-kar′bŏn) [*chloro-* + *fluorocarbon*] ABBR: CFC. A fluorinated hydrocarbon, formerly used in metered dose inhalers as a propellant gas. CFCs accumulate in and damage the ozone layer of the stratosphere.

chloroform (klō′rō-form) [Gr. *chloros*, green, + L. *forma*, form] $CHCl_3$; a heavy, clear, colorless liquid with a strong ether-like odor, formed by the action of chlorinated lime on methyl alcohol. At one time chloroform was administered by inhalation to produce anesthesia, but this use is obsolete.

chloroformism (klō′rō-form″ĭzm) The habit of inhaling chloroform for pleasure.

chloroleukemia (klō″rō-loo-kē′mē-ă) [″ + *leukos*, white, + *haima*, blood] Leukemia with chlorosis.

chloroma (klō-rō′mă) [″ + *oma*, growth] A tumor composed of leukemic cells that may metastasize to the brain, bones, skin, or other locations. Chloromas often have a green appearance due to an abundance of the fluorescent chemical myeloperoxidase.

chloronychia (klō″rō-nĭk-ē-ă) Green nail syndrome.

chloropenia (klō″rō-pē′nē-ă) Hypochloremia.

chloropenic (-nĭk), *adj.*

chlorophane (klō′rō-fān) [″ + *phainein*, to show] A green-yellow pigment in the retina.

chlorophenothane (klō″rō-fĕn′ō-thān) An insecticide, better known as DDT, not used in the U.S. since the 1970s because of its toxic effects on animals and the environment.

chlorophyll, chlorophyl (klō′rō-fĭl) [″ + *phyllon*, leaf] The green pigment in plants that accomplishes photosynthesis. In this process, carbon dioxide and water are combined to form glucose and oxygen according to the following equation: $6\ CO_2 + 6\ H_2O + \text{light} \rightarrow C_6H_{12}O_6 + 6\ O_2$. The primary energy source for our planet is the sunlight absorbed by chlorophyll. Four forms of chlorophyll (a, b, c, and d) occur in nature.

chloropia, chloropsia (klō-rō′pē-ă, klō-rŏp′sē-ă) [″ + *opsis*, vision] A sign of digitalis toxicity in which viewed objects appear green.

chloroplast, chloroplastid (klō′rō-plăst, klō″rō-plăs′tĭd) [″ + *plastos*, formed] A small green cell organelle found in the leaves and some stems of plants. Chloroplasts are the sites of photosynthesis. They possess a stroma and contain four pigments: chlorophyll a, chlorophyll b, carotene, and xanthophyll.

chloroquine hydrochloride (klō′rō-kwĭn) A white crystalline powder used to treat both malaria and amebic dysentery. SEE: *malaria.*

chlorosis (klŏ-rō′sĭs) [*chloro-* + *-sis*] An old term for iron-deficiency anemia. SYN: *green sickness.* **chlorotic** (-rot′ik), *adj.*

chlorpheniramine maleate (klor″fĕn-ĭr′ă-mēn) An antihistamine that may be used orally or by injection. It is available under several trade names, including Chlor-Trimeton and Teldrin.

chlorpromazine (klawr-prō′mă-zēn) A tranquilizing agent used primarily in its hydrochloride form to treat schizophrenia. Its side effects may include sedation, slurred speech, and tardive dyskinesia.

ChM *chirurgiae magister,* Master of Surgery.

choana (kō′ă-nă) *pl.* **choanae** [Gr. *choanē,* funnel] A funnel-shaped opening, esp. of the posterior nares (either of the two communicating passageways between the nasal fossae and the pharynx). **choanal** (-năl), *adj.*

choke (chōk) [ME. *choken*] To prevent respiration by compressing or obstructing the larynx or trachea.

choked disk Papilledema.

chokes (chōkz) Respiratory symptoms such as substernal distress, paroxysmal cough, tachypnea, or asphyxia. These may occur in decompression illness, esp. in cases of aeroembolism resulting from exposure to pressure lower than atmospheric.

choking (chōk′ĭng) [ME. *choken,* to suffocate] Upper airway obstruction caused, for example, by a foreign body in the trachea or oropharynx, laryngeal edema or spasm, or external compression of the neck. The choking patient may have gasping or stridorous respirations, repetitive ineffective coughing, an inability to speak, or hypersalivation. Intense agitation may be present. If the airway is not rapidly cleared, asphyxia and hypoxia may produce loss of consciousness or death. SEE: *Heimlich maneuver.*

cholagogue (kō′lă-gŏg) [Gr. *chole,* bile, + *agein,* to lead forth] An agent that increases the flow of bile into the intestine (i.e., a choleretic or cholecystagogue).

cholangiectasis (kō-lăn″jē-ĕk′tă-sĭs) [″ + *angeion,* vessel, + *ektasis,* dilatation] Dilation of the bile ducts.

cholangio-, cholangi- [Gr. *cholē,* bile + Gr. *angeion,* vessel] Prefixes meaning *bile vessel.*

cholangiocarcinoma (kō-lăn″jē-ō-kăr″sĭ-nō′mă) [″ + ″ + *karkinos,* crab, + *oma,* tumor] Carcinoma of the bile ducts.

cholangioenterostomy (kō-lăn″jē-ō-ĕn″tĕr-ŏs′tō-mē) [″ + ″ + *enteron,* intestine, + *stoma,* mouth] Surgical formation of a passage between a bile duct and the intestine.

cholangiogastrostomy (kō-lăn″jē-ō-găs-trŏs′tō-mē) [″ + ″ + *gaster,* stomach, + *stoma,* mouth] Surgical formation of a passage between a bile duct and the stomach.

cholangiography (kŏ-lan″jē-og′ră-fē, kō″) [*cholangio-* + *-graphy*] Radiography of the bile ducts, now replaced by ultrasonography.

percutaneous transhepatic c. ABBR: PTC. A radiologic examination involving direct percutaneous puncture of an intrahepatic duct by a needle inserted through the eighth or ninth intercostal space into the center of the liver. Radiopaque material is injected into the dilated intrahepatic biliary tree. The procedure is useful in determining the cause of obstructive jaundice. SEE: *endoscopic retrograde cholangiopancreatography; jaundice.*

cholangiole (kō-lăn′jē-ōl) [″ + ″ + *ole,* dim. suffix] The small terminal portion of the bile duct.

cholangiolitis (kō-lăn″jē-ō-lī′tĭs) [″ + ″ + Gr. *itis,* inflammation] Inflammation of the bile ducts, occurring in various forms of hepatitis.

cholangioma (kō-lăn-jē-ō′mă) [″ + *angeion,* vessel, + *oma,* tumor] A tumor of the bile ducts.

cholangiopancreatography (kŏ-lan″jē-ŏ-pang″krē-ă-tog′ră-fē, -pan″) [*cholangio-* + *pancreat-* + *-graphy*] Radiographic visualization and examination of the bile ducts and pancreas.

endoscopic retrograde c. ABBR: ERCP. Cholangiopancreatography following injection of a radiopaque material into the papilla of Vater. This is done through a fiberoptic endoscope guided by use of fluoroscopy. The procedure is helpful in determining the cause of obstructive jaundice. SEE: *jaundice; percutaneous transhepatic cholangiography.*

magnetic resonance c. ABBR: MRCP. Cholangiopancreatography by magnetic resonance imaging, a noninvasive alternative to endoscopic retrograde cholangiopancreatography. It is used if biopsies are not needed and direct visualization of the ampulla of Vater is not required.

cholangioscopy (kŏ-lan″jē-os′kŏ-pē, kō″) [*cholangio-* + *-scopy*] Endoscopic evaluation of the lumen (the inside) of the bile ducts.

cholangiostomy (kō″lăn-jē-ŏs′tō-mē) [″ + ″ + *stoma,* mouth] Surgical formation of a fistula into the bile duct.

cholangiotomy (kō″lăn-jē-ŏt′ō-mē) [″ + ″ + *tome,* incision] Incision of an intrahepatic or extrahepatic bile duct, e.g., to remove gallstones.

cholangitis (kō″lan″jīt′ĭs) [*cholangio-* + *-itis*] Inflammation of the bile ducts.

primary sclerosing c. A chronic liver disease of unknown origin marked by inflammation and obliteration of the intrahepatic and extrahepatic bile ducts. The disease progresses silently and steadily and in most patients leads to cirrhosis, portal hypertension, and liver failure. Seventy percent of patients are men and the mean age at diagnosis is 39. Liver transplantation can be used to treat patients who develop cirrhosis from this disease.

 Ursodeoxycholic acid should not be used to treat the disease.

cholanopoiesis (kō″lă-nō-poy-ē′sĭs) [Gr. *chole*, bile, + *ano*, upward, + *poiesis*, making] Synthesis of cholic acid in the liver.

cholate (kō′lāt) Any salt or ester of cholic acid.

chole-, chol- [Gr. *cholē*, bile] Prefixes meaning *bile* or *gall*.

cholecalciferol (ko″lē-kăl-sĭf′ĕr-ŏl) Vitamin D₃; an antirachitic, oil-soluble vitamin occurring as white, odorless crystals.

cholecystagogue (kō″lē-sĭs′tă-gŏg) [″ + ″ + *agogos*, leader] A drug or action that empties the gallbladder.

cholecystangiography (kō″lē-sĭs″tăn-jē-ŏg′ră-fē) [″ + ″ + *angeion*, vessel, + *graphein*, to write] Radiographic examination of the gallbladder and bile ducts after injection of a contrast medium, a procedure replaced by ultrasonography.

cholecystectasia (kō″lē-sĭs-tĕk-tā′zē-ă) [″ + ″ + *ektasis*, dilatation] Dilatation of the gallbladder.

cholecystectomy (kō″lē-sĭs″tek′tŏ-mē) [*cholecyst-* + *-ectomy*] Removal of the gallbladder by laparoscopic or abdominal surgery. The procedure is performed for symptomatic gallbladder and bile duct disease. In the U.S. alone, more than half a million operations are performed annually, but some hospitals have reported a 20% increase in this number since the introduction of laparoscopic surgery. Surgical complications, including wound infections, adverse reactions to anesthetics, and injury to the liver, gallbladder, bile ducts, or neighboring organs, occur about 5% of the time. SEE: illus.

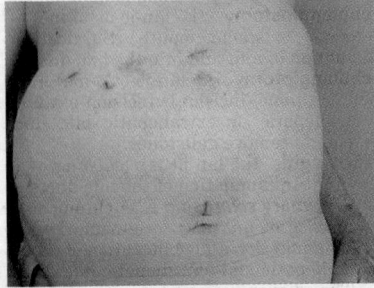

LAPAROSCOPIC CHOLECYSTECTOMY SCARS

Acute, chronic, or acalculous cholecystitis (biliary inflammation that is not caused by gallstones), repeated episodes of biliary colic, biliary dyskinesia, gallstone pancreatitis, and occasionally cholangitis are indications for the procedure. The gallbladder does not usually need to be removed for asymptomatic gallstone disease.

PATIENT CARE: *Preoperative:* The patient is informed about the procedure, including the need for drains, catheter, nasogastric tubes, etc., and taught about incentive spirometry, leg exercises, incision splinting, analgesia use, and other postoperative concerns.

Postoperative: General patient care concerns apply. Vital signs are monitored and dressings are inspected. The patient is assessed for pain and for gastrointestinal and urinary function; analgesics and antiemetics are provided as needed. Fluid and electrolyte balance is monitored, and prescribed fluid replacement therapy is administered until the patient is permitted oral intake. The patient is encouraged to breathe deeply and to perform incentive spirometry to prevent atelectasis and impaired gas exchange. The patient is assisted with early ambulation and with splinting the abdomen when moving about or coughing. Peripheral circulation is evaluated, and venous return is promoted with leg exercises and elastic stockings or pneumatic hose as prescribed.

If a laparoscopic approach is used, the patient will typically be discharged the day of or the day after surgery. Clear liquids are offered after recovery from general anesthesia, and the patient resumes a normal diet within a few days. If an open incision is used, the patient is placed in a position of comfort; a nasogastric (NG) tube is frequently required to prevent abdominal distention and ileus, and is attached to low intermittent suction; and the volume and characteristics of drainage from the NG tube and any abdominal drains or T-tube are documented. Skin care and appropriate dressings are provided around any drain site.

When peristalsis returns, the NG tube is removed as directed. Oral intake, beginning with clear liquids, is initiated. The T-tube may be clamped before and after each meal to allow additional bile to enter the intestine. Signs and symptoms of postcholecystectomy syndrome (fever, abdominal pain, and jaundice) and other complications involving obstructed bile drainage are reported; urine and stool samples are collected for analysis of bile content should any such complications occur.

Discharge teaching for the patient and family includes wound care and T-tube care if appropriate (the T-tube may remain in place up to 2 weeks); the need to report any signs of biliary obstruction (fever, jaundice, pruritus, pain, dark urine, and clay-colored stools); the importance of daily exercise such as walking; avoidance of heavy lifting or straining for the prescribed period; and any restrictions on motor vehicle operation. Although diet is not restricted, the patient may be more comfortable avoiding excessive intake of fats and gas-forming foods for 4 to 6 weeks. Arrangements for home health follow-up or care may be necessary. The patient should return to the surgeon for a post-operative evaluation visit as scheduled. If gallstones were present, the patient is taught to reduce the risk of recurrence by maintaining normal body weight, exercising regularly, and eating three well-balanced meals daily, including fiber and calcium and avoiding alcohol and foods high in saturated fat. Weight loss, if needed, should be carried out gradually, and crash dieting discouraged. SEE: *Nursing Diagnoses Appendix.*

extended c. Surgery for gallbladder cancer in which the organ and surrounding tissues (the neighboring liver and regional lymph nodes) are removed.

laparoscopic laser c. Removal of the gallbladder using a laser as a cutting tool, applied laparoscopically. This procedure may be inappropriate for patients with severe acute cholecystitis, a palpable gallbladder, or evidence of a stone in the common bile duct. The use of a laser as opposed to endoscopic electrosurgical instrument is according to the preference of the surgeon.

PATIENT CARE: The nurse or surgeon explains to the patient that this type of surgery will not be used if the patient is pregnant or has had extensive abdominal surgery (because of concern for adhesions), severe acute cholecystitis, a palpable gallbladder, evidence of a stone in the common bile duct, or a bleeding problem. The patient is also told that the surgeon, using the endoscopic technique, will be able to remove the gallbladder without unsightly scarring, leaving only four (or less) small punctures, which reduces the risk for wound complications (infection, hematoma, separation). Risks for other complications (pneumonia, thrombophlebitis, urinary retention, and paralytic ileus) are also decreased because the procedure enables early mobility and may avoid use of parenteral analgesia. Patients will experience less pain and immobility, require less narcotic analgesia, be discharged on the same or on the next day, and be able to return to their usual activities (including work) within 7 days. Preoperative preparation, which usually is similar to

that for any other abdominal surgery, is explained.

Postoperatively, the patient is stabilized during a brief stay in postanesthesia and then is transported to a surgical observation unit. The patient is offered clear liquids (carbonated beverages are avoided because they may cause distension and abdominal pressure). If the patient tolerates liquids, the IV is removed, and the patient is offered a regular diet. Analgesics are administered orally as prescribed as soon as the patient can take liquids. A parenteral narcotic (which may cause drowsiness, reduced intestinal motility, and/or vomiting) is given only if the patient continues to feel pain after taking an analgesic. Once the patient is comfortable, he is helped to walk because early ambulation speeds recovery. The patient is usually fully awake and walking within 3 or 4 hr of arrival on the unit. If he experiences shoulder pain, a heating pad may be applied. The surgeon, however, usually removes the carbon dioxide at the end of the procedure to prevent this problem. The nurse evaluates the patient's readiness for discharge, which usually can occur if the patient is afebrile, walking, eating, and voiding, and has stable vital signs with no evidence of bleeding or bile leakage. To assess for the latter risks, the patient is observed for severe pain and tenderness in the right upper quadrant, an increase in abdominal girth, leakage of bile-colored drainage from the puncture site, a fall in blood pressure, and increased heart rate

The patient is instructed to keep the adhesive bandages covering the puncture site clean and dry. He may remove them the next day and bathe or shower as usual. The patient most likely will require little analgesia, but a prescription is given for use as needed. He is reminded to pace activity according to energy level. While no special diet is required, the patient may wish to avoid excessive fat intake and gas-forming foods for 4 to 6 weeks. He should return to the surgeon for follow-up evaluation as directed and report any vomiting, abdominal distention, signs of infection, and new or worsening pain.

cholecystenterorrhaphy (kō″lē-sĭs-těn″těr-or′ă-fē) [″ + ″ + *enteron,* intestine, + *rhaphe,* seam, ridge] Suture of the gallbladder to the intestinal wall.

cholecystenterostomy (kō″lē-sĭs-těn″těr-ŏs′tō-mē) [″ + ″ + *enteron,* intestine, + *stoma,* mouth] Surgical formation of a passage between the gallbladder and the small intestine.

cholecystic (kō″lē-sĭs′tĭk) Pert. to the gallbladder.

cholecystitis (kō″lĕ-sis-tīt′ĭs) [*chole-*

cysto- + *-itis*] Inflammation of the gallbladder, usually caused by obstruction of the bile ducts by gallstones. Cholecystitis caused by gallstones occurs commonly, esp. in women, the obese, and those who have been dieting, and can occur following pregnancy. Its acute form is more common during middle age, the chronic form occurring more frequently in the elderly. The disease is marked by colicky pain developing shortly after a meal in the right upper quadrant of the abdomen.

Acalculous cholecystitis (biliary inflammation not caused by gallstones) is a disease of the critically ill. It is associated with a high likelihood of abscess formation, gallbladder perforation, gangrene, and death.

ETIOLOGY: Acute cholecystitis is usually caused by obstruction of the bile ducts, with chemical irritation and often infection of the gallbladder.

SYMPTOMS: Cholecystitis due to gallstones causes right upper quadrant pain that occurs after a fatty meal, as well as fever, chills, nausea, and vomiting. The pain of cholecystitis often radiates into the right shoulder or right side of the back. Jaundice is present in about 20% of patients, usually related to obstruction of the common bile duct by a gallstone. In patients in intensive care units, acalculous cholecystitis may present with fever and few other easily identified symptoms.

DIAGNOSIS: Ultrasonography of the right upper quadrant, the diagnostic procedure of choice, reveals cholecystitis in about 90% of patients. Oral cholecystograms, computed tomography of the abdomen, and other diagnostic tests are sometimes used when the disease is suspected clinically but ultrasonography is not diagnostic.

TREATMENT: Cholecystectomy is the usual treatment. Gallbladder drainage (cholecystostomy) is sometimes used as a temporizing procedure in unstable patients. Gallstones lodged in the ampulla of Vater can sometimes be removed with endoscopic retrograde cholangiopancreatography.

PATIENT CARE: During an acute attack, the patient's vital signs and fluid balance are monitored, oral intake is withheld, prescribed antiemetics are administered as necessary, and intravenous fluid and electrolyte therapy is maintained as prescribed. A nasogastric tube may be employed. The patient's comfort is ensured, and prescribed narcotic analgesics and anticholinergics are administered to relieve pain.

Diagnostic tests explain pretest instructions and aftercare are explained; the surgeon's explanation of any prescribed surgical interventions, including possible complications, is reinforced; and the patient is prepared physically and emotionally for such procedures.

emphysematous c. Inflammation of the gallbladder due to infection with a gas-producing microorganism, such as *Clostridium perfringens.*

cholecysto-, cholecyst- [Gr. *cholé,* bile + Gr. *kystis,* bladder] Prefixes meaning *gallbladder.*

cholecystoduodenostomy (kō″lē-sĭs″tō-dū″ō-dē-nŏs′tō-mē) [″ + ″ + L. *duodeni,* twelve, + Gr. *stoma,* mouth] Surgical formation of a passage between the gallbladder and the duodenum.

cholecystogastrostomy (kō″lē-sĭs″tō-găs-trŏs′tō-mē) [″ + ″ + *gaster,* belly, + *stoma,* mouth] Surgical formation of a passage between the gallbladder and the stomach.

cholecystogram (kō″lē-sĭs′tō-grăm) [″ + ″ + *gramma,* something written] A radiograph of the gallbladder. This procedure is being replaced by ultrasonography.

cholecystography (kō″lē-sĭs-tŏg′ră-fē) [″ + ″ + *graphein,* to write] Radiography of the gallbladder, a procedure replaced by ultrasonography.

cholecystojejunostomy (kō″lē-sĭs″tō-jĕ-jū-nŏs′tō-mē) [″ + ″ + L. *jejunum,* empty, + Gr. *stoma,* mouth] Surgical formation of a passage between the gallbladder and the jejunum.

cholecystokinin (kō″lē-sĭs″tō-kīn′ĭn) ABBR: CCK. A hormone secreted into the blood by the mucosa of the upper small intestine. It stimulates contraction of the gallbladder and pancreatic secretion.

cholecystokinin-secretin test A direct test of pancreatic function that assesses both the endocrine and exocrine functions of the pancreas. A double-lumen tube is inserted into the patient's gastrointestinal tract. One lumen samples the duodenal juices, the other removes gastric secretions. First secretin and then cholecystokinin are given to the patient intravenously; then the duodenal juices are analyzed to determine whether adequate levels of bicarbonate and trypsin are secreted. SYN: *secretin injection **test**.*

cholecystolithiasis (kō″lē-sĭs″tō-lĭ-thī′ă-sĭs) [″ + ″ + *lithos,* stone, + *-iasis,* condition] Gallstones in the gallbladder.

cholecystolithotripsy (kō″lē-sĭs″tō-lĭth′ō-trĭp″sē) [″ + ″ + ″ + *tripsis,* a rubbing] Crushing of a gallstone in the unopened gallbladder with an extracorporeal shock-wave lithotriptor; its use is primarily investigational.

cholecystomy (kō″lē-sĭs′tō-mē) [Gr. *chole,* bile, + *kystis,* bladder, + *tome,* incision] Cholecystotomy.

cholecystopathy (kō″lē-sĭs-tŏp′ă-thē) [″ + ″ + *pathos,* disease, suffering] Any gallbladder disorder.

cholecystopexy (kō″lē-sĭs′tō-pĕk″sē) [″ + ″ + *pexis*, fixation] Suturing of the gallbladder to the abdominal wall, in conjunction with cholecystostomy.

cholecystoptosis (kō″lē-sĭs-tŏp-tō′sĭs) [″ + ″ + *ptosis*, a dropping] Downward displacement of the gallbladder.

cholecystorrhaphy (kō″lē-sĭs-tor′ă-fē) [″ + *kystis*, bladder, + *rhaphe*, seam, ridge] Suturing of the gallbladder.

cholecystostomy (kō″lē-sĭs-tŏs′tō-mē) [″ + ″ + *stoma*, mouth] Surgical formation of an opening into the gallbladder through the abdominal wall.

cholecystotomy (kō″lē-sĭs″tŏt′ō-mē) [*cholecysto-* + *-tomy*] Incision of the gallbladder. It may be done for drainage or removal of gallstones.

choledochal (kō-lē-dŏk′ăl) [″ + *dochos*, receptacle] Pert. to the common bile duct.

choledochectasia (kō-lĕd″ō-kĕk-tā′zē-ă) [″ + ″ + *ektasis*, distention] Distention of the common bile duct.

choledochectomy (kō-lĕd″ō-kĕk′tō-mē) [″ + ″ + *ektome*, excision] Excision of a portion of the common bile duct.

choledochitis (kō″lē-dō-kī′tĭs) [″ + ″ + *itis*, inflammation] Inflammation of the common bile duct.

choledocho-, choledoch- [Gr. *cholēdochos*, containing bile fr. *cholē*, bile + *dechesthai*, to receive] Prefixes meaning *bile duct*.

choledochoduodenostomy (kō-lĕd″ō-kō-dū-ō-dē-nŏs′tō-mē) [″ + ″ + L. *duodeni*, twelve, + Gr. *stoma*, mouth] Surgical formation of a passage between the common bile duct and the duodenum.

choledochoenterostomy (kō-lĕd″ō-kō-ĕn-tĕr-ŏs′tō-mē) [″ + ″ + *enteron*, intestine, + *stoma*, mouth] Surgical formation of a passage between the common bile duct and the intestine.

choledochography (kō-lĕd″ō-kŏg′ră-fē) [″ + *dochos*, receptacle, + *graphein*, to write] Radiography of the bile duct following administration of a radiopaque contrast medium, a procedure replaced by ultrasonography.

choledochojejunostomy (kō-led″ō-kō″je-joo-nos′tō-mē) [*choledochojejunostomy* + *choledochojejunostomy*] Surgical joining of the common bile duct to the jejunum.

choledocholith (kō-lĕd′ō-kō-lĭth″) [″ + ″ + *lithos*, stone] A calculus, or stone, in the common bile duct.

choledocholithiasis (kō-lĕd″ō-kō-lĭ-thī′ă-sĭs) [″ + ″ + *lithos*, stone, + *-iasis*, condition] Calculi in the common bile duct.

choledocholithotomy (kō-lĕd″ō-kō-lĭth-ŏt′ō-mē) [″ + ″ + ″ + *tome*, incision] Removal of a gallstone through an incision of the bile duct.

choledocholithotripsy (kō-lĕd′ō-kō-lĭth″ō-trĭp-sē) [″ + ″ + ″ + *tripsis*, a crushing] Crushing of a gallstone in the common bile duct.

choledochoplasty (kō-lĕd′ō-kō-plăs″tē) [Gr. *chole*, bile, + *dochos*, receptacle, + *plassein*, to form] Surgical repair of the common bile duct.

choledochorrhaphy (kō-lĕd″ō-kor′ă-fē) [″ + ″ + *rhaphe*, seam, ridge] Suture repair of the common bile duct.

choledochoscope (kŏ-led′ō-kŏ-skōp″) [*choledocho-* + *-scope*] A fiber-optic endoscope for examining the interior of the common bile duct.

choledochoscopy (kŏ-led″ō-kos′kŏ-pē) [*choledocho-* + *-scopy*] Visual examination of the interior of the common bile duct.

choledochostomy (kō-lĕd″ō-kŏs′tō-mē) [″ + ″ + *stoma*, mouth] Surgical drainage of the common bile duct by T-tube or catheter exiting the abdominal wall.

choledochotomy (kō″lĕd-ō-kŏt′ō-mē) [″ + ″ + *tome*, incision] Surgical incision of the common bile duct.

cholelith (kŏl′ĭ-lĭth″) Gallstone.

cholelithiasis (kō″lē-lĭ-thī′ă-sĭs) [″ + ″ + *-iasis*, condition] The presence or formation of gallstones. SEE: *cholecystectomy; cholecystitis; colic (1); gallstone; lithotripsy.*

cholelithic (kō″lē-lĭth′ĭk) Pert. to or caused by biliary calculus.

cholelitholytic (kō″lē-lĭth″ō-lĭt′ĭk) [″ + ″] Able to dissolve or destroy gallstones.

cholelithotomy (kō″lē-lĭ-thŏt′ō-mē) [″ + *lithos*, stone, + *tome*, incision] Removal of gallstones through a surgical incision.

cholelithotripsy, cholelithotrity (kŏl″ă-lĭth′ă-trĭp″sē, kō″lē-lĭ-thŏt′rĭ-tē) [″ + ″ + *tripsis*, a crushing] Crushing of a gallstone.

cholemesis (kō-lĕm′ĕ-sĭs) [″ + *emein*, to vomit] Bile in the vomitus.

choleperitoneum (kō″lē-pĕr″ĭ-tō-nē′ŭm) [″ + *peri*, around, + *teinein*, to stretch] Bile in the peritoneum.

cholera (kol′ĕ-ră) [L. *cholera*, fr Gr. *cholera*, intestinal disease, fr. *cholē*, bile, gall] An acute infection involving the entire small intestine, marked by profuse, watery, secretory diarrhea. Without treatment the severe loss of fluids and electrolytes can cause dehydration and vascular collapse. The incubation period is from a few hours to 4 or 5 days. Cholera is endemic in India, other parts of Asia, and sub-Saharan Africa where it is a major cause of loss of life, esp. after natural disasters. **choleraic** (kol″ĕ-rā′ik), *adj.* SYN: *Asiatic c.*

ETIOLOGY: The causative organism, *Vibrio cholerae*, is a short, curved, motile gram-negative rod. Two serotypes have been identified, 01 and 0139 (Bengal). The bacteria do not invade the bowel wall but produce a potent enterotoxin that causes increased secretion of chloride, bicarbonate, and water into the small intestine, which overwhelms the large intestine's ability to reabsorb. Transmission is through water and food contaminated with excreta of infected persons.

SYMPTOMS: Approximately 80% of patients have mild disease marked by diarrhea and malaise. Severe attacks are characterized by periodic voluminous rice water stool, vomiting, and muscle cramps. Without treatment, severe dehydration develops, characterized by loss of skin turgor, dizziness, increased heart rate and respirations, decreased urinary output, and, ultimately, circulatory collapse, and hypovolemic shock. Hypoglycemia may be a problem in very young children.

TREATMENT: The use of oral solutions to replace the lost water, sodium, chloride, and bicarbonate has decreased the death rate from cholera by preventing death due to dehydration. A commercial or over-the-counter oral rehydration solution can be used or a solution made by adding 1 level tsp of salt and 1 heaping tsp of sugar to 1 L of water; patients should replace 5% to 7% of body weight, e.g., a 20-kg child would receive 1 to 1.4 L of fluid per day. Hospitalization and intravenous fluid replacement are required if the patient is already dehydrated. Quinolone antibiotics decrease the duration and severity of the disease.

PREVENTION: Several cholera vaccines are available, including oral vaccines made with recombinant DNA technology. To avoid infection with cholera, travelers to developing countries should not drink unboiled water, add ice to beverages, or eat raw or partially cooked shellfish, uncooked vegetables or salads, or fruits they have not peeled themselves. They should not assume that bottled water is safe, and they should swim only in chlorinated swimming pools.

Asiatic c. Cholera.

pancreatic c. Watery diarrhea, hypokalemia, hypochlorhydria syndrome.

choleresis (kŏl-ĕr-ē′sĭs, kō-lĕr′ĕ-sĭs) [Gr. *chole*, bile, + *hairesis*, removal] The secretion of bile by the liver.

choleretic (kŏl-ĕr-ĕt′ĭk) **1.** Stimulating excretion of bile by the liver. **2.** Any agent that increases excretion of bile by the liver.

choleric (kŏl′ĕr-ĭk) Irritable; quick-tempered without apparent cause.

choleriform (kŏl-ĕr′ĭ-form) [L. *cholera*, + *forma*, shape] Resembling cholera.

choleroid (kŏl′ĕr-oyd) [″ + Gr. *eidos*, form, shape] Resembling cholera.

cholescintigraphy (kŏl″ĭ-sĭn-tĭg′ră-fē) Imaging of the biliary tree by means of a nuclear medicine scanning examination, a HIDA scan. SEE: *HIDA scan*.

cholestasis, cholestasia (kō″lĕ-stā′sĭs, kō″lĕ-stā′zh(ē-)ă) [*chole-* + *stasis*] Arrest of the flow of bile. This may be due to intrahepatic causes, obstruction of the bile duct by gallstones, or any process that blocks the bile duct (e.g., cancer). **cholestatic** (kō″lĕ-stat′ik), *adj.*

   intrahepatic c. of pregnancy ABBR: ICP. A complication of approx. 1% of pregnancies in which elevated levels of pregnancy hormones cause obstruction to bile flow within the liver. Levels of bilirubin rise in the maternal circulation during the second and third trimesters of pregnancy, causing itching, bile staining of urine, and a lighter stool color than normal. ICP increases the risk of preterm delivery of the fetus and of bleeding disorders and loss of life of the fetus. SYN: *obstetric c.*

   obstetric c. Intrahepatic c. of pregnancy.

   progressive familial intrahepatic c. Byler disease.

cholesteatoma (kō″lē-stē″ă-tō′mă) [″ + *steatos*, fat, + *oma*, tumor] An epithelial pocket or cystlike sac filled with keratin debris. It can occur in the meninges, central nervous system, and skull, but is most common in the middle ear and mastoid area. The cyst, which is filled with a combination of epithelial cells and cholesterol, most commonly enlarges to occlude the middle ear. Enzymes formed within the sac cause erosion of adjacent bones, including the ossicles, and destroy them. Cholesteatomas are classified as congenital, primary acquired, and secondary acquired. They are common causes of conductive hearing loss and can be treated surgically.

cholesteremia, cholesterolemia (kō-lĕs″tĕ-rē′mē-ă, kō-lĕs″tĕr-ŏl-ē′mē-ă) [″ + *stereos*, solid, + *haima*, blood] Hypercholesterolemia.

cholesterol (kŏ-les′tĕ-rōl″) [*chole-* + *sterol*] $C_{27}H_{45}OH$, a monohydric alcohol; a sterol widely distributed in animal tissues and occurring in egg yolks, various oils, fats, myelin in brain, spinal cord and axons, liver, kidneys, and adrenal glands. It is synthesized in the liver and is a normal constituent of bile. It is the principal constituent of most gallstones and of atherosclerotic plaques found in arteries. It is important in metabolism, serving as a precursor to various steroid hormones (e.g., sex hormones, adrenal corticoids).

   An elevated blood level of cholesterol increases a person's risks of developing coronary heart disease (CHD). Lowering elevated total blood cholesterol levels and the levels of low-density lipoprotein cholesterol reduces the risk of heart attacks both in persons with a prior history of coronary disease and in asymptomatic individuals. Risk categories and recommended actions are included in the accompanying table. SEE: table.

Cholesterol levels may be decreased by eating a diet that is low in cholesterol and fat and high in fiber; exercising regularly; and taking medications. Drugs used to control cholesterol levels include lovastatin (and other statins); niacin; and bile-acid resins, e.g., cholestyramine.

high-density lipoprotein c. SEE: *high-density lipoprotein* under lipoprotein.

low-density lipoprotein c. SEE: *low-density lipoprotein* under lipoprotein.

non-HDL c. The total cholesterol minus the HDL cholesterol. It is a risk factor, independent of other cholesterol measurements, for atherosclerotic vascular disease, esp. in patients with diabetes mellitus, triglyceride levels > 200 mg/dL, or people with the metabolic syndrome.

total c. The sum of low- and high-density lipoproteins.

cholesterol embolization syndrome The systemic consequences that result from the splintering of cholesterol-containing plaques from the aorta; when this occurs fragments of cholesterol crystals may travel to and obstruct blood vessels throughout the body. The renal, mesenteric, and femoral arteries are most often affected; involvement of the cerebral vessels is unusual. This condition may arise after trauma to the aorta (e.g., during catheterization or cardiac surgery). It may produce renal failure, and ischemia or infarction of the bowel, toes, or skin. It may ultimately result in death in about half of all affected patients. There is no effective treatment.

cholesterol ester storage disease ABBR: CESD. SEE: *Acid lipase deficiency*.

cholesterolosis (kō-lĕs"tĕr-ō-lō'sĭs) The abnormal accumulation of cholesterol in tissues.

choleverdin (kō"lē-vĕr'dĭn) SEE: *biliverdin*.

choline (kō'lĭn, -lēn) [Gr. *chole*, bile] An amine, $C_5H_{15}NO_2$, widely distributed in plant and animal tissues. It is a constituent of lecithin and other phospholipids. It is essential in normal fat and carbohydrate metabolism. A deficiency leads to fatty liver. Choline is also involved in protein metabolism, serving as a methylating agent, and is a precursor of acetylcholine. SYN: *vitamin B_{11}*.

Choline contains six metabolites: betaine; glycerophosphocholine; phosphocholine; phosphatidylcholine; sphingomyelin; and total choline. It can be found in wheat germ, egg yolks, soy, and liver.

cholinergic (kō"lĭn-ĕr'jĭk) [" + *ergon*, work] **1.** Liberating acetylcholine; used of nerve endings. **2.** An agent that produces the effect of acetylcholine.

cholinergic blocking agent SEE: under *agent*.

cholinesterase (kō"lĭn-ĕs'tĕr-ās) Any enzyme that catalyzes the hydrolysis of choline esters, such as acetylcholinesterase, which catalyzes the breakdown of acetylcholine to acetic acid and choline. Cholinesterases are inhibited by physostigmine (eserine).

cholinoceptive (kō"lĭn-ō-sĕp'tĭv) [" + L. *receptor*, receiver] Pert. to sites on cells that are acted on by cholinergic transmitters.

cholinolytic (kō"lĭn-ō-lĭt'ĭk) [" + *lysis*, dissolution] Anticholinergic (2)..

cholinomimetic (kō"lĭ-nō-mī-mĕt'ĭk) [" + *mimetikos*, imitating] Acting in the same way as acetylcholine.

chologenic (kō"lō-jĕn'ĭk) [" + *gennan*, to produce] Promoting or stimulating bile production.

chololith (kŏl'ō-lĭth) [" + "] Obsolete term for gallstone. SEE: *cholelith*.

chololithiasis (kŏl"ō-lĭth-ī'ăs-ĭs) [" + " + *-iasis*, state] Cholelithiasis.

cholorrhea (kŏl"ō-rē'ă) [" + *rhoia*, flow] Excessive secretion of bile.

chondral (kŏn'drăl) [Gr. *chondros*, cartilage] Pert. to cartilage.

chondralgia (kŏn-drăl'jē-ă) [" + *algos*, pain] Pain in or around a cartilage.

chondralloplasia (kŏn"drăl-ō-plā'zē-ă) [" + *allos*, other, + *plassein*, to form] Cartilage in abnormal places.

chondrectomy (kŏn-drĕk'tō-mē) [" + *ektome*, excision] Surgical excision of a cartilage.

chondric (kŏn'drĭk) [Gr. *chondros*, cartilage] Pert. to cartilage.

chondrification (kŏn-drĭ-fĭ-kā'shŭn) [" + L. *facere*, to make] Conversion of other tissues into cartilage.

chondritis (kŏn-drī'tĭs) [" + *itis*, inflammation] Inflammation of cartilage.

chondro-, chondr- [Gr. *chondros*, cartilage] Prefixes meaning *cartilage*.

chondroadenoma (kŏn"drō-ăd-ē-nō'mă) [" + *aden*, gland, + *oma*, tumor] An adenoma comprised of cartilaginous tissue.

chondroangioma (kŏn"drō-ăn-jē-ō'ma) [" + *angeion*, vessel, + *oma*, tumor] An angioma containing cartilaginous elements.

chondroblast (kŏn'drō-blăst) [" + *blastos*, germ] A cell that forms cartilage. SYN: *chondroplast*.

chondroblastoma (kŏn"drō-blăs-tō'mă) [" + " + *oma*, tumor] A benign neoplasm in which the cells resemble cartilage cells and the tumor appears to be cartilaginous.

chondrocalcinosis (kŏn"drō-kăl'sĭn-ō'sĭs) [" + L. *calx*, lime, + Gr. *osis*, condition] Pseudogout; chronic, recurrent arthritis with some features that suggest gout. The crystals found in the synovial fluid are calcium pyrophosphate dihydrate and not urate crystals. The

Lipid Level Management for Cholesterol Level Reduction

Suggested Management of Patients with Raised Lipid Levels

- LDL cholesterol is the primary key to treatment. Diet is first-line therapy and drug intervention is reserved for patients considered to be at a higher risk. Continue diet for at least 6 months before initiating drug therapy; use drug therapy in conjunction with diet, not in place of diet. The greater the risk the more aggressive the intervention.
- If there is evidence of coronary heart disease (CHD), do lipoprotein analysis.
- Initially measure total cholesterol and HDL cholesterol levels; based on these results and the presence or absence of other risk factors, determine course of action or proceed to lipoprotein analysis.
- See American Heart Association (AHA) diet, Step I, and AHA diet, Step II.
- Risk factors for atherosclerosis: advanced age, diabetes mellitus, family history, hypertension, male gender, obesity, sedentary lifestyle, tobacco use.

TOTAL AND HDL CHOLESTEROL

Status and Total Cholesterol	HDL Cholesterol	≥2 Positive Risk Factors	Recommendations
Desirable (200 mg/dL)	≥35 mg/dL	N/A*	• Reassess total and HDL levels in 5 yr. • Provide information on diet, physical activity, and risk factor reduction.
	≤35 mg/dL	N/A	• Do lipoprotein analysis (see below).
Borderline high (200–239 mg/dL)	≥35 mg/dL	No	• Reassess total and HDL levels in 1–2 yr. • Reinforce diet, physical activity, and other risk factor reduction activities.
	≤35 mg/dL	Yes	• Do lipoprotein analysis (see below).
High (≥240 mg/dL)			• Do lipoprotein analysis (see below).

LIPOPROTEIN ANALYSIS
LDL cholesterol = (total cholesterol − HDL) − (triglycerides ÷ 5)

Status and LDL Cholesterol	≥2 Positive Risk Factors	Recommendations
Desirable (130 mg/dL)	N/A	• Reassess total and HDL in 5 yr. • Provide information on diet, physical activity, and risk factor reduction.
Borderline high-risk (130–159 mg/dL)	No	• Reassess total, HDL, and LDL annually. • Provide information on Step I diet and physical activity.
High-risk (≥160 mg/dL)	Yes	• Clinical workup (history, physical exam, and lab tests) to check for secondary causes or familial disorders. • Consider risk factors that can be changed. • Initiate Step I diet; if diet fails, proceed to Step II diet. • Consider drug therapy if diet fails to obtain desired levels. • **Goal** for borderline high-risk patients with ≥2 negative risk factors is LDL 130 mg/dL. • **Goal** for high-risk patients with no other risk factors is LDL 160 mg/dL.

Table continued on following page

Lipid Level Management for Cholesterol Level Reduction (Continued)

- When there is **evidence of CHD**, the **goal** of therapy is to reduce LDL to ≤100 mg/dL.
  - LDL >100—Do clinical workup and initiate diet or drug therapy.
  - LDL ≤100—Individualize instruction on diet and physical activity and repeat lipoprotein analysis annually.

---

*N/A = not applicable.

SOURCE: http://www.nhlbi.nih.gov/guidelines/cholesterol/atp3full.pdf, from the Third Report of the Expert Panel on Detection, Evaluation and Treatment of High Blood Cholesterol in Adults (Adult Treatment Panel III); National Cholesterol Education Program; National Heart, Lung, and Blood Institute; National Institutes of Health, NIH Pub. No. 02-5215, September 2002.

most commonly involved joint is the knee.

chondroclast (kŏn′drō-klăst) [″ + *klastos,* broken into bits] A giant cell involved in the absorption of cartilage.

chondrocostal (kŏn″drō-kŏs′tăl) [″ + L. *costa,* rib] Pert. to the ribs and costal cartilages.

chondrocranium (kŏn-drō-krā′nē-ŭm) [″ + *kranion,* head] The cartilaginous embryonic cranium before ossification.

chondrocyte (kon′drō-sīt) [*chondro-* + *-cyte*] A cell that creates and sustains the cartilage that cushions joints. SYN: *cartilage cell; cartilage corpuscle.*

chondrodermatitis nodularis chronica helicis (kŏn″drō-der″mă-tī′tĭs) Growth of nodules on the helix of the ear.

chondrodynia (kŏn″drō-dĭn′ē-ă) [″ + *odyne,* pain] Pain in or about a cartilage.

chondrodysplasia (kŏn″drō-dĭs-plā′zē-ă) [″ + Gr. *dys,* bad, + *plasis,* a molding] A disease, usually hereditary, resulting in disordered growth. It is marked by multiple exostoses of the epiphyses, esp. of the long bones, metacarpals, and phalanges. SYN: *dyschondroplasia.*

chondrodystrophy (kon″drō-dĭs′trŏ-fē) [*chondro-* + *dystrophy*] Achondroplasia.

chondroendothelioma (kŏn″drō-ĕn″dō-thē″lē-ō′mă) [″ + *endon,* within, + *thele,* nipple, + *oma,* tumor] An endothelioma that contains cartilage.

chondroepiphysitis (kŏn″drō-ĕp″ĭ-fĭz-ī′tĭs) [″ + *epiphysis,* a growing on, + *itis,* inflammation] Inflammation of the epiphyseal portion of the bone and the attached cartilage.

chondrofibroma (kŏn″drō-fī-brō′mă) [″ + L. *fibra,* fiber, + Gr. *oma,* tumor] A mixed tumor with elements of chondroma and fibroma.

chondrogenesis (kŏn″drō-jĕn′ĕ-sĭs) [″ + *genesis,* generation, birth] Formation of cartilage. **chondrogenic** (-jĕn′ĭk), *adj.*

chondroid (kŏn′droyd) [″ + *eidos,* form, shape] Resembling cartilage; cartilaginous.

chondroitin (kon-droyt′ĭn, -drō′ĭ-tĭn) A glycosaminoglycan (complex polysaccharide) present in connective tissue, including the cornea and cartilage. It is promoted as a dietary supplement for use in the treatment of joint pain, usually with glucosamine.

c. sulfate A glycosaminoglycan present in connective tissue, including the cornea and cartilage. It is used as a dietary supplement to treat joint pain, esp. in people and animals with degenerative joint disease, usually combined with the dietary supplement glucosamine.

chondrolipoma (kŏn-drō-lĭp-ō′mă) [″ + *lipos,* fat, + *oma,* tumor] A tumor made of cartilaginous and fatty tissue.

chondrolysis (kŏn-drŏl′ĭ-sĭs) [″ + *lysis,* dissolution] The breaking down and absorption of cartilage.

chondroma (kon-drō′mă, ′măz, ′mă-tă) *pl.* **chondromas, chondromata** [*chondro-* + *-oma*] A slow-growing, painless cartilaginous tumor. It may occur wherever there is cartilage. **chondromatous** (-ă-tŭs), *adj.*

chondromalacia (kon″drō-mă-lā′sh(ē-)ă) [*chondro-* + *malacia*] Softening of the articular cartilage, esp. of the patella.

c. patellae Chondromalacia at the front of the knee, accompanied by pain and crepitus, and often affecting younger athletes

chondromatosis (kŏn″drō-mă-tō′sĭs) [″ + *oma,* tumor, + *osis,* condition] Formation of multiple chondromas of the hands and feet; often occurs in joint spaces.

chondromucoprotein (kŏn″drō-mū″kō-prō′tē-ĭn) [″ + ″ + *protos,* first] The ground substance (the fluid or solid material) that occupies the space between the cells and fibers of cartilage.

chondromyoma (kŏn″drō-mī-ō′mă) [″ + *mys,* muscle, + *oma,* tumor] A combined myoma and cartilaginous neoplasm.

chondromyxoma (kŏn″drō-mĭks-ō′mă) [″ + *myxa,* mucus, + *oma,* tumor] A chondroma with myxomatous elements.

chondromyxosarcoma (kŏn-drō-mĭk″sō-săr-kō′mă) [″ + ″ + *sarx,* flesh, + *oma,* tumor] A cartilaginous and sarcomatous tumor.

chondro-osseus (kŏn″drō-ŏs′ē-ŭs) [″ + L. *osseus,* bony] Composed of cartilage and bone.

chondropathology (kŏn″drō-pă-thŏl′ō-jē) [Gr. *chondros,* cartilage, + *pathos,* disease, + *logos,* word, reason] The pathology of cartilage disease.

chondropathy (kŏn-drŏp′ă-thē) Any disease of cartilage.

chondroplasia (kŏn″drō-plā′zē-ă) [″ + *plassein,* to mold] The formation of cartilage.

chondroplast (kŏn′drō-plăst) Chondroblast.

chondroplasty (kŏn′drō-plăs″tē) [″ + *plassein,* to mold] Plastic or reparative surgery on cartilage.

chondroporosis (kŏn″drō-pō-rō′sĭs) [″ + *poros,* passage] The porous condition of pathological or normal cartilage during ossification.

chondroprotection (kŏn-drō-prō-tĕk′shŭn) **1.** Cartilage preservation. **2.** The potential of some drugs or nutrients to prevent the degradation of cartilage that occurs with various forms of arthritis.

chondrosarcoma (kŏn-drō-săr-kō′mă) [″ + *sarx,* flesh, + *oma,* tumor] A cartilaginous sarcoma.

chondrosis (kŏn-drō′sĭs) [″ + *osis,* condition] The development of cartilage.

chondrosternal (kŏn″drō-stĕr′năl) [″ + *sternon,* chest] **1.** Pert. to sternal cartilage. **2.** Pert. to both costal cartilage and the sternum.

chondrosternoplasty (kŏn″drō-stĕr′nō-plăs″tē) [″ + ″ + *plassein,* to mold] Surgical correction of a deformed sternum.

chondrotome (kŏn′drō-tōm) [″ + *tome,* incision] A device for cutting cartilage.

chondrotomy (kŏn-drŏt′ō-mē) Dissection or surgical division of cartilage.

Chondrus (kon′drŭs) [L. *chondrus,* fr Gr. *chondros,* grain, ganule, cartilage] A genus of red algae that includes *Chondrus crispus,* the source of carrageenan. SEE: *carrageen; carrageenan.*

choosing death Deciding to die. In particular, an individual may choose to withdraw from chronic kidney dialysis with no medical reason for withdrawing. In one study, stopping dialysis in this situation was three times more common in patients treated at home than in those treated at dialysis centers. SEE: *death; death with dignity; do not attempt resuscitation; suicide.*

CHOP *cyclophosphamide, doxorubicin (hydroxorubicin), Oncovin (vincristine), prednisone* (chemotherapeutic agents to treat non-Hodgkin lymphoma.)

Chopart, François (shō-par′) Fr. surgeon, 1743–1795.

C. amputation Disarticulation at the midtarsal joint.

C. joint The union of the remainder of the tarsal bones with the calcaneus and talus.

chorda (kor′dă) *pl.* **chordae** [L. *chorda,* intestine, rope fr Gr. *chordē,* string, gut] A cord or tendon.

c. dorsalis Notochord.

c. gubernaculum An embryonic structure forming a part of the gubernaculum testis in males and the round ligament in females.

c. tendinea One of several small tendinous cords that connect the free edges of the atrioventricular valves to the papillary muscles and prevent inversion of these valves during ventricular systole.

c. tympani A sensory branch of the facial nerve (CN VII) that carries taste information from the anterior two-thirds of the tongue. The cell bodies of its neurons lie in the geniculate ganglion inside the facial canal; the axons of these neurons synapse in the nucleus of the tractus solitarius in the brainstem. Preganglionic parasympathetic axons, en route to the submandibular ganglion, run with the chorda tympani.

c. vocalis The vocal folds of the larynx.

chordal (kor′dăl) Pert. to chorda, esp. the notochord.

Chordata (kor-dā′tă) [LL., notochord] A phylum of the animal kingdom including all animals that have a notochord during their development (i.e., all vertebrates).

chordee (kor-dē′) [Fr., corded] Painful downward curvature of the penis during erection. It occurs in congenital anomaly (hypospadia) or in urethral infection such as gonorrhea. SEE: *Peyronie's disease.*

chorditis (kor-dī′tĭs) [Gr. *chorde,* cord, + *itis,* inflammation] Inflammation of the spermatic or vocal cord.

c. nodosa Singer's node.

chordoma (kor-dō′mă) [″ + *oma,* tumor] A rare type of tumor that occurs at any place along the vertebral column. It is composed of embryonic nerve tissue and vacuolated physaliform cells. The neoplasm may cause death because of its surgical inaccessibility and the damage caused by the expanding tissue.

chordotomy (kor-dŏt′ō-mē) Cordotomy.

chorea (kō-rē′ă) [Gr. *choreia,* dance] Involuntary dancing or writhing of the limbs or facial muscles. **choreal** (kō-rē′al, kō′rē-ăl), *adj.*

acute c. Sydenham chorea.

Bergeron c. Electric **c.**

chronic c. Huntington **c.**

electric c. Sudden, rhythmic, involuntary contractions, in rapid succession, of a group or groups of muscles, starting at an extremity or half of the face, and covering a large part or all of the body. This causes violent movements as if the patient had been stimulated by an electric current. It is usually fatal. SYN: *Bergeron c.; Dubini disease;* **spasmus** *Dubini.*

epidemic c. Dancing mania; uncontrolled dancing. It was manifested in the 14th century in Europe. SYN: *dancing mania.*

c. gravidarum A form of Sydenham's chorea seen in some pregnant women, usually in those who have had chorea before, esp. in their first pregnancy. SEE: *Sydenham's chorea.*

Henoch c. SEE: *Henoch chorea.*

hereditary c. Huntington chorea.

Huntington c. SEE: *Huntington chorea.*

hyoscine c. Movements simulating chorea and sometimes accompanied by delirium, seen in acute scopolamine intoxication.

hysteric c. A form of hysteria with choreiform movements.

mimetic c. Chorea caused by imitative movements.

c. minor Sydenham's chorea.

posthemiplegic c. Chorea affecting partially paralyzed muscles subsequent to a hemiplegic attack.

sporadic c. of the elderly A mild, usually benign disorder of adults marked by chorea-like movements and mild cognitive deficits. It may be related to Huntington's chorea. SEE: *Huntington's chorea.*

Sydenham c. SEE: *Sydenham chorea.*

choreatic disorder (kō″rē-ăt′ĭk) [″] Any disease whose symptoms include rapid, involuntary body movements.

choreiform (kō-rē′ĭ-form) [Gr. *choreia,* dance, + L. *forma,* form] Of the nature of chorea.

choreoathetoid (kō″rē-ō-ăth′ĕ-toyd) [″ + *athetos,* not fixed, + *eidos,* form, shape] Pert. to choreoathetosis.

choreoathetosis (kō″rē-ō-ăth″ĕ-tō′sĭs) [″ + ″ + *osis,* condition] A type of athetosis frequently seen in cerebral palsy, marked by extreme range of motion, jerky involuntary movements that are more proximal than distal, and muscle tone fluctuating from hypotonia to hypertonia.

chori-, chorio- [Gr. *chorion,* the membrane that encloses a fetus, afterbirth] Prefixes meaning *chorion, chorionic,* or *choroid.*

chorioadenoma (kō″rē-ō-ăd″ĕn-ō′mă) [Gr. *chorion,* outer membrane enclosing an embryo, + *aden,* gland, + *oma,* tumor] A rare glandular tumor of the outermost embryonic membrane.

c. destruens A type of hydatidiform mole in which the chorionic villi penetrate the myometrium.

chorioallantois (kō″rē-ō-ă-lăn′tō-ĭs) In embryology, the membrane formed by the union of the chorion and allantois. In the human embryo, this develops into the placenta.

chorioamnionitis (kōr″ē-ō-am″nē-ō-nīt′ĭs) [*chorion* + *amnion* + *-itis*] Inflammation of the amnion, usually secondary to bacterial infection, and often associated with premature rupture of membranes. This condition is an obstetric emergency that may cause pneumonia, meningitis, or sepsis in the neonate, and bacteremia or sepsis in the mother. Symptoms include fever, rapid heart rate in both the mother and the fetus, and a tender uterus.

ETIOLOGY: The most common agents are *Bacteroides* species, *Escherichia coli,* streptococci, and *Prevotella* species.

TREATMENT: Intravenous antibiotics are given. These include ampicillin and gentamicin, vancomycin, clindamycin, or metronidazole. SYN: *amnionitis; amniotitis.*

chorioangioma (kō″rē-ō-ăn-jē-ō′mă) [″ + *angeion,* vessel, + *oma,* tumor] A vascular tumor of the chorion.

choriocapillaris (kōr″ē-ō″kap″ĭ-lar′ĭs) [*chorio-* + L. *capillaris,* hairlike] The capillary layer of choroid. It is the source of blood to cones, rods, and the pigment epithelium of the eye.

choriocarcinoma (kōr″ē-ō-kar″sĭn-ō′mă) [*chorion* + *carcinoma*] An extremely rare, very malignant neoplasm, usually of the uterus but sometimes at the site of an ectopic pregnancy. Although the actual cause is unknown, it may occur following a hydatid mole, a normal pregnancy, or an abortion. This cancer may respond dramatically to combined modality therapy using surgery and chemotherapy. SYN: *chorionepithelioma; chorionic carcinoma.* SEE: *gestational trophoblastic disease.*

choriocele (kō′rē-ō-sēl) [Gr. *choroeides,* resembling a membrane, + *kele,* tumor, swelling] A protrusion of the choroid coat of the eye through a defective sclera.

choriogenesis (kō″rē-ō-jĕn′ĕ-sĭs) [Gr. *chorion,* chorion, + *genesis,* generation, birth] Formation of the chorion.

chorioid (kō′rē-oyd) Choroid.

choriomeningitis (kō″rē-ō-mĕn″ĭn-jī′tĭs) [″ + *meninx,* membrane, + *itis,* inflammation] Inflammation of the brain, meninges, and often the choroid plexuses.

lymphocytic c. An acute viral infection of the central nervous system marked by flulike symptoms (fever, malaise, headache). The disease is transmitted to humans from house mice.

chorion (kōr′ē-on) [Gr. *chorion,* membrane (surrounding the fetus)] An extraembryonic membrane that, in early development, forms the outer wall of the blastocyst. It is the thicker, outer layer of the two fetal membranes and is formed from the trophoblast and its lining of mesoderm. From it develop the chorionic villi, which grow into the endometrium and will become the fetal portion of the placenta. SEE: *embryo*, *placenta*, and *umbilical cord* for illus.; *trophoblast*. **chorionic** (kōr″ē-on′ik), *adj*.

  c. frondosum The outer surface of the chorion. Its villi contact the decidua basalis. This is the placental portion of the chorion.

  c. laeve The smooth, nonvillous portion of the chorion.

chorionepithelioma, chorioepithelioma (kōr″ē-on″ep″ĭ-thē″lē-ō′mă, kōr″ē-ō-ep″ĭ-thē″lē-ō′mă) [*chorion* + *epithelioma*] Choriocarcinoma.

chorionicity (kōr″ē-o-nis′it-ē) In a twin or multifetal pregnancy, the number of chorions in the placenta that supply blood and nourishment to the developing fetuses. Twins sharing a common placenta may experience twin-twin transfusion syndrome; those with separate blood supplies have, on average, fewer perinatal health problems.

chorionic plate SEE: under *plate*.

chorionic villi The vascular projections from the chorion, which will form the fetal portion of the placenta. SEE: *embryo* for illus.

chorionic villus sampling SEE: under *sampling*.

chorionitis (kōr″ē-ō-nīt′ĭs) [*chorion* + *-itis*] Inflammation of the fetal chorion, often due to infection.

chorioretinal (kō″rē-ō-rĕt′ĭ-năl) Pert. to the choroid and retina. SYN: *retinochoroid*.

chorioretinitis (kō″rē-ō-rĕt″ĭn-ī′tĭs) [Gr. *chorioeides*, skinlike, + L. *rete*, network, + Gr. *itis*, inflammation] Inflammation of the choroid and retina, often caused by infections (such as toxoplasmosis, cytomegalovirus, or tuberculosis) or by multisystem diseases (such as sarcidosis).

choroid (kō′royd) [Gr. *chorioeides*, skinlike] The dark blue vascular layer of the eye between the sclera and retina, extending from the ora serrata to the optic nerve. It consists of blood vessels united by connective tissue containing pigmented cells and contains five layers: the suprachoroid, the layer of large vessels, the layer of medium-sized vessels, the layer of capillaries, and the lamina vitrea (a homogeneous membrane next to the pigmentary layer of the retina). It is a part of the uvea or vascular tunic of the eye. SYN: *chorioid*.

choroideremia (kō-roy-dĕr-ē′mē-ă) [″ + *eremia*, destitution] A hereditary primary choroidal degeneration transmitted as an X-linked trait. In males, the earliest symptom is night blindness followed by constricted visual field and eventual blindness. In females, the condition is nonprogressive and vision is usually normal.

choroiditis (kōr″oy″dīt′ĭs) [*choroid* + *-itis*] Inflammation of the choroid.

  areolar c. Choroiditis in which inflammation spreads from around the macula lutea.

  central c. Choroiditis in which exudation is limited to the macula.

  diffuse c. Choroiditis in which the fundus is covered with spots.

  exudative c. Choroiditis in which the choroid is covered with patches of inflammation.

  metastatic c. Choroiditis due to embolism.

  Tay c. SEE: under *Tay, Warren*.

choroidocyclitis (kō-roy″dō-sĭk-lī′tĭs) [Gr. *chorioeides*, skinlike, + *kyklos*, a circle, + *itis*, inflammation] Inflammation of the choroid coat and ciliary processes.

choroidoiritis (kō-royd″ō-ī-rī′tĭs) [″ + *iris*, iris, + *itis*, inflammation] Inflammation of the choroid coat and iris.

choroidopathy (kō″roy-dŏp′ă-thē) [″ + *pathos*, disease, suffering] Any disease of the choroid.

CHPN *Certified Hospice and Palliative Nurse.*

Christian Science A system of religious teaching based on Christian Scientists' interpretation of Scripture, founded in 1866 by Mary Baker Eddy. The system emphasizes healing of disease by mental and spiritual means.

Christian-Weber disease SEE: *Weber-Christian disease*.

Christmas, Stephen (kris′măs) [British-born Canadian, 1947–1993] He was the first person identified as having Christmas disease (hemophilia A).

  C. disease SEE: *hemophilia B*.

  C. factor ABBR: CF. An obsolete term for plasma thromboplastin component.

Christmas disease (krĭs′mĭs) [*Christmas*, family name of the first patient with the disease who was studied] Hemophilia B.

Christmas factor SEE: under *Christmas, Stephen*.

Christmas tree adapter A connector that links a patient to a device that collects or administers gases or liquids. It consists of a wide base onto which is mounted a cylinder with progressively smaller external threading (and looks a little like the tapering trunk of an evergreen tree). Christmas tree adapters are used to drain body fluids (for example by serving as connectors from indwelling urinary catheters to collection systems) or to administer medications (such as radiological contrast) or medical gases (such as oxygen).

⚠ When administering oxygen to a patient, all connectors used are green. Health care providers should confirm this color on the source of the gas and on all patient connections to avoid giving the wrong gas to the patient.

Christ-Siemens-Touraine syndrome (krĭst'sē'mĭns-too-rĕn') A rare congenital disease characterized by hairlessness, inability to sweat, and abnormal tooth formation.

chrom-, chromato-, chromo- [Gr. *chrōma,* stem *chrōmat-,* color] Prefixes meaning *color, pigment.*

chromaffin (krō-măf'ĭn) [Gr. *chroma,* color, + L. *affinis,* having affinity for] **1.** Staining readily with chromium salts. **2.** Denoting the pigmented cells forming the medulla of the adrenal glands and the paraganglia. SYN: *chromaphil.*

chromaffin body SEE: under *body.*

chromaffinoma (krō"mă-fĭ-nō'mă, krō-maf-ĭ-) [*chromaffi* + *-oma*] Paraganglioma.

chromaffinopathy (krō"măf-ĭn-ŏp'ă-thē) [" + " + Gr. *pathos,* disease] Any disease of chromaffin tissue.

chromaffin reaction Histological demonstration of cytoplasmic granules containing epinephrine when subjected to stains containing chromium salts. Such granules stain green with ferric chloride, yellow with iodine, and brown with osmic acid.

chromaffin system The mass of tissue forming paraganglia and medulla of suprarenal glands, which secretes epinephrine and stains readily with chromium salts. Similar tissue is found in the organs of Zuckerkandl and in the liver, testes, ovary, and heart. SYN: *chromaffin tissue.*

chromaphil (krō'mă-fĭl) [" + *philein,* to love] Chromaffin.

chromate (krō'māt) [Gr. *chromatos,* color] A salt of chromic acid. SEE: *potassium chromate.*

chromatic (krō-măt'ĭk) Pert. to color.

chromatid (krō'mă-tĭd) One of the two potential chromosomes formed by DNA replication of each chromosome before mitosis and meiosis. They are joined together at the centromere and separate at the end of metaphase; then the new chromosomes migrate to opposite poles of the cell at anaphase.

chromatin (krō'mă-tĭn) [Gr. *chroma,* color] The deeply staining genetic material present in the nucleus of a cell that is not dividing. It is the largely uncoiled chromosomes, made of DNA and protein.

sex c. Barr body.

chromatin-negative Lacking visible chromatin. It is characteristic of cell nuclei of normal human males. SEE: *Barr body.*

chromatinolysis (krō"mă-tĭn-ŏl'ĭ-sĭs) [" + *lysis,* dissolution] **1.** Destruction of chromatin. **2.** The emptying of a cell, bacterial or other, by lysis.

chromatinorrhexis (krō"mă-tĭn-or-

rĕk'sĭs) [" + *rhexis,* rupture] Splitting of chromatin.

chromatin-positive Having the sex chromatin (the Barr body); characteristic of nuclei in cells of normal females.

chromatin test A test for genetic sex in which blood or tissue cells are examined for the presence or absence of Barr bodies.

chromatism (krō'mă-tĭzm) [" + *-ismos,* condition] **1.** Unnatural pigmentation. **2.** A chromatic aberration.

chromatogram (krō-măt'ō-grăm) [" + *gramma,* something written] A record produced by chromatography.

chromatographic analysis (krō-măt'ă-grăf'ĭk ă-năl'ĭ-sĭs) Analysis of substances on the basis of the reaction of the constituents as they are differentially absorbed on one of a variety of materials such as filter paper.

chromatography (krō"mă-tŏg'ră-fē) [*chrom-* + *-graphy*] The separation of two or more chemical compounds in a liquid or gaseous mixture by their removal at different rates based on differential solubility and adsorption. This separation is often accomplished by letting the chemicals percolate through a column of a powdered adsorbent or by passing them across the surface of an adsorbent paper, among other techniques. **chromatographic** (-mat"ō-graf'ik), *adj.*

adsorption c. Chromatography accomplished by applying the test material to one end of a sheet or column containing a solid. As the material moves, the various constituents adhere to the surface of the particles of the solid at different distances from the starting point according to their chemical characteristics.

column c. A form of adsorption chromatography in which the adsorptive material is packed into a column.

gas c. An analytical technique in which a sample is separated into its component parts between a gaseous mobile phase and a chemically active stationary phase.

gas-liquid c. ABBR: GLC. Chromatography in which a gas moves over a liquid, and chemical substances are separated on the liquid by their different adsorption rates.

gel filtration c. A type of column chromatography in which chemicals are separated via pores according to their molecular size.

high-performance liquid c. ABBR: HPLC. Application of high pressure to liquid chromatography technique to increase separation speed and enhance resolution. SYN: *high pressure liquid c.*

high pressure liquid c. High-performance liquid chromatography.

paper c. Chromatography in which

paper strips are used as the porous solid medium.

partition c. Chromatography in which substances in solution are separated by being exposed to two immiscible solvents. The immobile solvent is located between the spaces of an inert material such as starch, cellulose, or silica. The substances move with the mobile solvent as it passes down the column at a rate governed by their partition coefficient.

thin-layer c. ABBR: TLC. Chromatography involving the differential adsorption of substances as they pass through a thin layer or sheet of cellulose or some other inert compound.

chromatoid (krō'mă-toyd) [Gr. *chroma*, color, + *eidos*, form, shape] Staining in the same manner as chromatin.

chromatokinesis (krō"mă-tō-kī-nē'sĭs) [" + *kinesis*, movement] The movement of chromatin during the division of a cell.

chromatolysis (krō"mă-tŏl'ĭ-sĭs) [" + *lysis*, dissolution] The dissolution of chromophil substance (Nissl bodies) in neurons in certain pathological conditions, or following injury to the cell body or axon. SYN: *chromolysis; karyolysis*.

chromatometer (krō-mă-tŏm'ĕt-ĕr) [" + *metron*, measure] A scale of colors for testing color perception.

chromatophil, chromatophilic (krō'mă-tō-fĭl", krō"mă-tō-fĭl'ĭk) [" + *philein*, to love] Staining easily.

chromatophore (krō-măt'ō-for) [" + *phoros*, bearing] A pigment-bearing cell.

chromatopsia (krō"mă-tŏp'sē-ă) [" + *opsis*, vision] Abnormally colored vision.

chromatoptometry (krō"măt-ŏp-tŏm'ĕ-trē) [" + *optos*, visible, + *metron*, measure] Measurement of color perception.

chromatosis (krō"mă-tō'sĭs) [" + *osis*, condition] 1. Pigmentation. 2. The pathological deposition of pigment in any part of the body where it is not normally present, or excessive deposition where it is normally present.

chromaturia (krō-mă-tū'rē-ă) [" + *ouron*, urine] Abnormal color of the urine.

chromesthesia (krō"mĕs-thē'zē-ă) [" + *aisthesis*, sensation] The association of color sensations with words, taste, smell, or sounds.

chromidrosis, chromhidrosis (krō"mĭd-rō'sĭs) [" + *hidros*, sweat] Excretion of colored sweat. Red sweat may be caused by an exudation of blood into the sweat glands or by color-producing microorganisms in those glands. This disorder is treated by relief of the underlying condition.

ETIOLOGY: Colored sweat may be due to ingestion or absorption of certain substances, such as pigment-producing bacteria. It may also be caused by certain metabolic disorders.

SYMPTOMS: Colored sweat may be localized in the eyelids, breasts, axillae, and genitocrural regions, and occasionally on the hands and limbs. It may be grayish, bluish, violaceous, brownish, or reddish; it collects on skin, giving a greasy, powdery appearance to parts.

chromium (krō'mē-ŭm) [Fr. *chrome*, fr. Gr. *chrōma*, color, + *-ium* (1)] SYMB: Cr. A very hard metallic element, atomic weight (mass) 51.996, atomic number 24. It is an essential trace element required for normal uptake. Chromium works with insulin to regulate the release of energy from glucose.

c. picolinate $Cr(C_6H_4NO_2)_3$, an essential nutrient involved in the metabolism of carbohydrates and lipids. It has been popularly promoted as a diet aid and to enhance lean body strength and mass.

chromium-51 A radioactive isotope of chromium. The half-life is 27.7 days. Red blood cells are labeled with this isotope in order to study their length of life in the body.

chromium poisoning SEE: under *poisoning*.

chromoblast (krō'mō-blăst) [Gr. *chroma*, color, + *blastos*, germ] An embryonic cell that becomes a pigment cell.

chromoblastomycosis (krō"mō-blăs"tō-mī-kō'sĭs) [" + "] Chromomycosis.

chromocenter (krō'mō-sĕn"tĕr) [" + *kentros*, middle] Karyosome.

chromodacryorrhea (krō"mō-dăk"rē-ō-rē'ă) [" + *dacryon*, tear, + *rhoia*, flow] A flow of blood-stained tears.

chromoendoscopy (krō"mō-en-dos'kō-pē) [*chromo- + endoscopy*] The use of tissue-staining dyes, such as methylene blue, to aid in the identification of abnormal or precancerous lesions seen inside the body during endoscopy. SYN: *chromoscopy*.

chromogen (krō'mŏ-jĕn) [*chrom- + -gen*] A chemical that changes color if it is activated, e.g., by an antibody or enzyme.

chromogenic (krō"mŏ-jen'ĭk), *adj.*

chromogenesis (krō"mō-jĕn'ĕ-sĭs) [" + *genesis*, generation, birth] Production of pigment.

chromolipoid (krō"mō-lĭp'oyd) [" + *lipos*, fat, + *eidos*, form, shape] Lipochrome.

chromolysis (krō-mŏl'ĭ-sĭs) Chromatolysis.

chromomere (krō'mō-mēr) [Gr. *chroma*, color, + *meros*, part] One of a series of chromatin granules found in a chromosome.

chromomycosis (krō"mō-mī-kō'sĭs) [" + *myxa*, mucus, + *osis*, condition] A chronic fungal skin infection marked by itching and warty plaques on the skin and subcutaneous swellings of the feet, legs, and other exposed areas. Various fungi have been implicated, including *Phialophora verrucosa, P. pedrosoi, P. compacta,* and *Cladosporium carrionii.* Some of these are also called *Fonsecaea pedrosoi* and *F. compacta.* SYN: *chromoblastomycosis.*

chromopexic, chromopectic (krō″mō-pĕk′sĭk, -pĕk′tĭk) [″ + *pexis,* fixation] Pert. to fixation of coloring matter, as the liver function in forming bilirubin.

chromophane (krō′mō-fān) [″ + *phainein,* to show] Retinal pigment of some animal species.

chromophil(e) (krō′mō-fĭl, -fīl) [″ + *philein,* to love] **1.** Any structure that stains easily. **2.** One of two types of cells present in the pars distalis of the pituitary gland. It is considered a secretory cell.

chromophilic, chromophilous (krō-mō-fĭl′ĭk, krō-mŏf′ĭl-ŭs) Staining readily.

chromophobe (krō′mō-fōb) [″ + *phobos,* fear] Any cell or tissue that stains either poorly or not at all; a type of cell found in the pars distalis of the pituitary gland.

chromophobia (krō″mō-fō′bē-ă) The condition of staining poorly. **chromophobic** (-bĭk), *adj.*

chromophore (krō′mō-for) [″ + *pherein,* to bear] Any chemical that displays color when present in a cell that has been prepared properly. **chromophoric** (-for′ĭk), *adj.*

chromophose (krō′mō-fōz) [″ + *phos,* light] A subjective sensation of a spot of color in the eye.

chromoprotein (krō″mō-prō′tē-ĭn) [″ + *protos,* first] One of a group of conjugated proteins consisting of a protein combined with hematin or another colored, metal-containing, prosthetic group (e.g., hemoglobin, hemocyanin, chlorophyll, flavoproteins, cytochromes).

chromoscopy (krō-mos′kŏ-pē) [*chromo-* + *-scopy*] Chromoendoscopy.

chromosomal breakage The disruption of a chromosome, as by radiation or toxic chemicals. When this occurs, the two fragments may rejoin, or a fragment may rejoin another broken chromosome. Unrepaired chromosome breaks are associated with many malignant and premalignant conditions.

chromosomal inversion SEE: under *inversion.*

chromosome (krō′mŏ-sōm″) [*chrom-* + *-some*] A linear strand made of DNA (and associated proteins in eukaryotic cells) that carries genetic information. Chromosomes stain deeply with basic dyes and are esp. conspicuous during mitosis. The normal diploid number of chromosomes is constant for each species. For humans, the diploid number is 46 (23 pairs in all somatic cells). In the formation of gametes (ovum and spermatozoon), the number is reduced to one half (haploid number); i.e., the ovum and sperm each contain 23 chromosomes. Of these, 22 are autosomes and one is the sex chromosome (X or Y). At fertilization, the chromosomes from the sperm unite with the chromosomes from the ovum. The sex of the embryo is determined by the sperm. The ovum always contributes an X chromosome. The sperm may contribute an X or a Y chromosome. An embryo with XX chromosomes will be female; an embryo with XY chromosomes will be male. SEE: *Barr body; centromere; chromatid; cytogenetics; dominant; gene; heredity; karyotype; mutation; recessive; telomere.*

accessory c. An unpaired sex chromosome. SEE: *sex chromosome.*

banded c. A chromosome specially stained to delineate bands of various widths on its regions or loci. This facilitates analysis and investigation of genes and gene-related illnesses.

bivalent c. A double chromosome resulting from the conjugation of two homologous chromosomes in synapsis, which occurs during the first meiotic division.

homologous c. One of a pair of chromosomes that contain genes for the same traits; one is maternal in origin, the other paternal.

Philadelphia c. An abnormal chromosome 22 in which there is translocation of the distal portion of its long arm to chromosome 9. It is found in leukocyte cultures of many patients with chronic myelocytic leukemia. The Philadelphia chromosome was the first chromosomal change found to be characteristic of a human disease.

sex c. One of two chromosomes, the X and Y chromosomes, that determine sex in humans and that carry the genes for sex-linked characteristics.

somatic c. Autosome.

X c. One of the sex chromosomes; women have two (XX) present in all somatic cells, and men have one (XY). Characteristics transmitted on the X chromosome are said to be X-linked or sex-linked. The human X chromosome, sequenced in 2005, has approximately 1100 genes.

Y c. The male-determining member of a pair of human chromosomes (XY) present in the somatic cells of all male humans.

chromotherapy (krō″mō-thĕr′ă-pē) [Gr. *chroma,* color, + *therapeia,* treatment] The use of colored light to treat disease.

chromotrichia (krō″mō-trĭk′ē-ă) [″ + *thrix,* hair] Coloration of the hair.

chromotropic (krō″mō-trŏp′ĭk) [″ + *tropikos,* turning] **1.** Being attracted to color. **2.** Attracting color.

chronaxie (krŏ′năk-sē) [Gr. *chronos,* time, + *axia,* value] A number expressing the sensitivity of a nerve to electrical stimulation. It is the minimum duration, in milliseconds, during which a current of prescribed strength must pass through a motor nerve to cause contraction in the associated muscle. The strength of direct current (rheobasic voltage) that will just suffice if given an indefinite time is first determined, and exactly double this strength is used for the final determinations.

chronic (kron′ĭk) [Gr. *chronikos,* pert. to time] **1.** Of long duration; long-lasting. **2.** Habitual; persistent. **3.** A colloquial term for *Cannabis sativa* (marijuana").

chronically neurologically impaired ABBR: CNI. Having a general level of intellectual function that is significantly below average and that exists concurrently with deficits in adaptive behavior. These behavioral changes may first appear in childhood or may develop after head trauma or stroke. This condition is sometimes called "organic brain syndrome" in adults or "mental retardation" in children. Chronically neurologically impaired children are often grouped epidemiologically with persons who have other developmental disabilities including chronic epilepsy, autism, and cerebral palsy.

chronic bullous disease of childhood A rare, self-limiting bullous disease that causes lesions beneath the epidermis, in the oral cavity, and sometimes on the conjunctiva, where scars may form. The disease is characterized by the presence of immunoglobulin A deposits lined up along the basement membrane of the epithelium.

chronic effect A consequence (of a toxic agent or of radiation) that develops slowly and/or has a long lasting course.

chronic exposure SEE: under *exposure.*

chronic fatigue syndrome ABBR: CFS. A syndrome marked by incapacitating fatigue that rest does not relieve, and decreased physical, cognitive, and social function. It affects men and women of all ages and races. It is frequently associated with decreased concentration, irritability, sleep disturbances, recurrent sore throats, low-grade temperatures, swollen glands, and bone or muscle aches. In the past, this condition has been called (without justification) chronic Epstein-Barr virus infection, myalgic encephalomyelitis, "yuppie flu," and chronic fatigue immunodeficiency syndrome (CFIDS).

ETIOLOGY: The cause of CFS is unknown. According to the Centers for Disease Control and Prevention (CDC), CFS may have many precipitating causes, all of which produce a common endpoint. These causes may include viral infection or disruptions in neurological, endocrine, or immune system function.

SYMPTOMS: The CDC has established criteria for diagnosis: the patient must have 2 major criteria and either 8 of 11 symptom criteria or 6 symptom criteria and 2 of 3 physical criteria. No definitive test exists for this disorder. Diagnostic studies should include tests to rule out other similar clinical illnesses. Data from studies suggest that approximately 50% of patients recover, although not all symptoms disappear. SEE: table.

TREATMENT: Because there is no known cause, treatment focuses on supportive care. Nonsteroidal anti-inflammatory drugs (NSAIDs) may be useful for myalgia or arthralgias; low doses of tricyclic and some other antidepressants sometimes enhance pain control and also may be useful for patients having trouble sleeping. Complex immunological or metabolic therapies have not proved effective on a consistent basis. Cognitive behavioral therapies have been helpful in some patients.

PATIENT CARE: Activity level and degree of fatigue during activities of daily living are assessed. The patient's emotional response to the illness and coping abilities are evaluated. Emotional support is provided through the long period of diagnostic testing and the protracted, sometimes discouraging course of the illness. Patients are referred for mental health or career counseling as needed and to the CFS Association and/or or a local support group if available, to help them lead as normal a life as possible. Activities should be reduced when fatigue is greatest, but bedrest other than that required for sleep should be avoided because it does not relieve disability. The patient should participate in a graded exercise program, which may be difficult to initiate and maintain but may help him or her feel better. Exercise should be carried out for short periods and slowly increased, to avoid increasing fatigue.

chronic granulomatous disease ABBR: CGD. A rare congenital, often fatal immunodeficiency marked by recurrent infections caused by a defect in white blood cells. The polymorphonuclear leukocytes of affected children are able to ingest but not kill certain bacteria. CGD occurs mostly in boys as an X-linked inheritance although an autosomal recessive variant of the disease is also known. Twenty percent of reported cases occur in girls. Manifestations of this disease include widespread granulomatous lesions of the skin, lungs, and lymph nodes. Hypergammaglobulinemia, anemia, and leukocytosis are also present.

SCREENING: The nitroblue tetrazo-

Criteria for Diagnosing CFS

Major Criteria	• New onset of persistent or relapsing debilitating fatigue in a person without a history of similar symptoms • Fatigue doesn't resolve with bed rest and is severe enough to reduce or impair average daily activity by 50% for 6 months. • Exclusion of other disorders after evaluation through history, physical examination, laboratory findings
Symptom Criteria	• The initial development of the main symptom complex over a few hours or days • Profound or prolonged fatigue, especially after exercise levels that would have been easily tolerated before • Low-grade fever • Painful lymph nodes • Muscle weakness • Muscle discomfort or myalgia • Sleep disturbances (insomnia or hypersomnia) • Headaches of a new type, severity or pattern • Migratory arthralgia without joint swelling or redness • Photophobia, forgetfulness, irritability, confusion, depression, transient visual scomata, difficulty thinking, and inability to concentrate
Physical Criteria	These criteria must be recorded on at least two occasions, at least 1 month apart: • Low-grade fever • Nonexudative pharyngitis, palpable or tender nodes

lium test is used for screening high-risk persons, e.g., family members.

SYMPTOMS: Symptoms include chronic acute infections of the skin, liver, lymph nodes, intestinal tract, and bone, often involving bacteria or other microorganisms that usually do not cause infections in patients with normal immune function.

TREATMENT: CGD may be treated with antibiotic or antifungal therapy, interferon, or definitively with bone marrow transplantation.

chronicity (krŏn-ĭs'ĭt-ē) The condition of being long lasting or of showing little or slow progress.

chronic kidney disease ABBR: CKD. Any illness in which kidney function remains diminished for a long period of time. CKD is defined as >30 mg of urinary albumin excretion per gram of urinary creatinine, or a glomerular filtration rate of <60 mL/min/1.73m^2 and includes both end-stage renal disease and improper functioning of kidney transplants. "Renal insufficiency" is a less-preferred term.

chronic lung disease ABBR: CLD. **1.** Bronchopulmonary **dysplasia**. **2.** An erroneous term for chronic obstructive lung disease.

chronic lung disease of the newborn Bronchopulmonary **dysplasia**.

chronic obstructive lung disease ABBR: COLD. Chronic obstructive pulmonary disease.

chronic obstructive pulmonary disease ABBR: COPD. Any of a group of debilitating, progressive, and potentially fa-

tal lung diseases that have in common increased resistance to air movement, prolongation of the expiratory phase of respiration, and loss of the normal elasticity of the lung. The chronic obstructive lung diseases include emphysema, chronic obstructive bronchitis, chronic bronchitis, and asthmatic bronchitis. Taken together, they make up the fourth most common cause of death in the U.S. The incidence of death from COPD is rising whereas the death rate from heart disease, cancer, and stroke (the three illnesses that currently cause more death in the U.S. than COPD) is falling. SYN: *chronic airflow obstruction.* SYN: *chronic obstructive lung disease.*

ETIOLOGY: Most patients with chronic airflow limitations are or were smokers, and their lung disease is a direct consequence of the toxic effects of tobacco smoke on the lung. A smaller number have been exposed to environmental tobacco smoke (second-hand smoke) or to dusts, chemicals, or smoke at work, or to environmental pollution. People who genetically lack the enzyme α-1 antitrypsin also develop COPD, typically at an earlier age than smokers (in their 40s instead of their 50s or 60s).

In the U.S. millions of people have COPD. About a half million Americans are admitted to hospitals each year with exacerbations of the disease.

SYMPTOMS: Diseases in this group are typically marked by difficulty breathing during exertion, as well as chronic cough and sputum.

TREATMENT: Acute exacerbations of COPD should be managed with inhaled bronchodilators, e.g., albuterol and ipratroprium, low flow oxygen (to raise the oxygen saturation to about 90%), antibiotics (if patients have more productive mucus than normal), and corticosteroids. For most patients who smoke, exacerbations occur several times a year. Patients with frequent exacerbations improve when treated with prophylactics such as azithromycin. Between exacerbations, disease management relies on smoking cessation and regular exercise (pulmonary rehabilitation), as well as supplemental oxygen, when it is needed. Additional preventive therapies include annual influenza vaccinations, and pneumococcal vaccination. Chronic management of COPD includes the use of anticholinergic agents, such as tiotropium, with long-acting beta agonists, like formoterol, and short-acting drugs, like albuterol. Corticosteroids have less benefit in chronic management (than in asthma) and can occasionally cause significant side effects. Aminophylline, a drug used extensively in the past for COPD, is now rarely used because of its interaction with other drugs and potential toxicity.

PATIENT CARE: The respiratory therapist teaches breathing and coughing exercises and postural drainage to strengthen respiratory muscles and to mobilize secretions. Breathing retraining (e.g. pursed lip breathing) slows the respiratory rate, decreases airway resistance, and decreases dyspnea. Prolonging expiration to 2 or 3 times the length of inspiration reduces air-trapping and improves ventilation. The patient is encouraged to participate in a pulmonary rehabilitation program, as well as to stop smoking and avoid other respiratory irritants. Patients are instructed to avoid contact with other people with respiratory infections and taught the use of prescribed prophylactic antibiotics and bronchodilator therapy. Good oral and hand hygiene helps prevent infections. Frequent small meals of easily digested foods and adequate fluid intake are encouraged and are taken with oxygen by nasal cannula because eating may tire the patient. The patient's schedule alternates periods of activity with rest. The patient and family are assisted with disease-related lifestyle changes and are encouraged to express their feelings and concerns about the illness and its treatment.

The respiratory therapist monitors arterial blood gases and pulmonary function studies to determine the extent of the disease and proper treatment in consultation with the attending physician. Acute exacerbation occurs when the patient acquires a respiratory infection or other complication that must be recognized and treated promptly. Aerosol and humidity therapy is useful to thin and mobilize thick sputum and promote bronchial hygiene. Low-concentration oxygen therapy (usually no more than 2 to 3L/m) is applied as needed to keep the PAO_2 between 60 and 80 mm Hg. Because COPD patients gradually develop high $PaCO_2$ levels, the chemoreceptors in their brains become less sensitive to carbon dioxide as a trigger for ventilation and more dependent on hypoxemia as their ventilatory driver. Excessive oxygen may eliminate that hypoxic drive, resulting in decreased ventilatory rate and effort, confusion, drowsiness, and other signs of carbon dioxide narcosis, leading to death. Aerosolized bronchodilators are used to reduce dyspnea and promote improved cough. Mechanical ventilation is reserved for the patient in acute respiratory failure due to a superimposed condition that is reversible and not responding to initial therapy.

⚠ 1. In hypoxic patients, oxygen therapy must be adjusted carefully to optimize arterial oxygen saturation.
2. Before traveling on airplanes, patients with COPD should consult their health care providers about special oxygen needs.

Some COPD patients (mainly emphysema patients) benefit from lung volume reduction surgery. Removal of diseased tissue, which provides little ventilation, allows the more functional tissue to expand and become useful in gas exchange. Lung transplantation is an option for selected patients with severe disease.

chronic pelvic pain syndrome Chronic abacterial prostatitis.

chronic respiratory failure SEE: under *failure*.

chronic sorrow A cyclical, recurring, and potentially progressive pattern of pervasive sadness that is experienced by a parent or caregiver, or individual with chronic illness or disability in response to continual loss, throughout the trajectory of an illness or disability. SEE: *Nursing Diagnoses Appendix*.

chronic thromboembolic pulmonary hypertension SEE: under *hypertension*.

chronic wasting disease A prion disease of deer and elk that resembles mad cow disease (bovine spongiform encephalitis). SEE: *prion disease*.

chrono-, chron- [Gr. *chronos*, time] Prefixes meaning *time* or *timing*.

chronobiology (krŏn″ō-bī-ŏl′ō-jē) [Gr. *chronos*, time, + *bios*, life, + *logos*, word, reason] The study of the effects of time on biochemistry, the release of hormones, sleeping and waking cycles, and related aspects of plant and animal life. SEE: *circadian; clock, biological.*

chronognosis (krŏn″ŏg-nō′sĭs) [″ + *gnosis,* knowledge] The subjective realization of the passage of time.

chronograph (krŏn′ō-grăf) [″ + *graphein,* to write] A device for recording intervals of time.

chronological (krŏn″ō-lŏj′ĭ-kăl) [″ + *logos,* word, reason] Occurring in natural sequence according to time.

chronopharmacology (krŏn″ō-făr″mă-kŏl′ō-jē) A method used in pharmacokinetics to describe the diurnal changes in plasma drug concentrations.

chronophobia (krŏn″ă-fō′bē-ă, krŏn″) [Gr. *chronos,* time + ″] Fear of time or its perceived duration, esp. in prisoners.

chronotaraxis (krō-nō-tăr-ăk′sĭs) [″ + *taraxis,* without order] Being unable to orient oneself with respect to time.

chronotherapy (krŏn″ō-thĕr′ă-pē) [″ + ″] **1.** The timing of treatments for specific disorders (e.g., cancer, hypertension) with drugs given to coincide with circadian body rhythms. **2.** A treatment for sleep disorders in which a person goes to bed later and later until the desired bedtime hour is reached.

chronotropic (krŏn″ō-trŏp′ĭk) [″ + *tropikos,* turning] Influencing the rate of occurrence of an event, such as the heartbeat. SEE: *inotropic.*

chronotropism (krŏn″ō-trō′pĭzm) [″ + ″ + *-ismos,* condition] Interference with periodic events such as the heartbeat.

   negative c. Deceleration of the rate of an event such as the heartbeat.

   positive c. Acceleration of the rate of an event such as the heartbeat.

CHRPE *Congenital hypertrophy of the retinal pigment epithelium.*

chrysarobin (krĭs″ă-rō′bĭn) [Gr. *chrysos,* gold, + Brazilian *araraba,* bark] A mixture of neutral principles obtained from goa powder, which is deposited in the wood of Araroba, a leguminous tree of South America. It is used topically as an ointment for treatment of certain skin disorders. It promotes the growth of skin tumors in laboratory animals.

Chryseobacterium (krĭs″ē-ō-bak-tēr′ē-ŭm) [Gr. *chryseos, chryous,* golden + *bacterium*] A genus of nonfermentative, glucose-oxidizing, yellow gram-negative rod-shaped bacteria. Some species cause opportunistic infections in severely immunosuppressed people.

chrysiasis (krĭ-sī′ă-sĭs) [Gr. *chrysos,* gold + *-iasis*] **1.** Gray patches of skin discoloration after therapeutic administration of gold. **2.** Deposition of gold in tissues. SYN: *auriasis.*

chrysoderma (krĭs″ō-dĕr′mă) [″ + *derma,* skin] Discoloration of the skin due to deposition of gold.

chrysotherapy (krĭs″ō-thĕr′ă-pē) [Gr. *chrysos,* gold + *therapy*] Treatment of disease by administration of gold salts. It used in the treatment of rheumatoid arthritis and autoimmune bullous disease, esp. pemphigus vulgaris. The advisability of using gold in treating rheumatoid arthritis is controversial.

  ⚠ Side effects, including toxicity to the kidneys and bone marrow, are significant. The patient will need frequent monitoring of blood and urine.

  SYN: *aurotherapy.*

chunk (chŭnk) In neurology, informatics, and psychology, a single unit of memory. A chunk is typically a number, name, fact, or other discrete informational element.

chunking (chŭngk′ĭng) A strategy for improving memory and learning, in which information is arranged into manageable clusters ("chunks") of data.

Churg-Strauss syndrome (chŭrg-strŏws) [Jacob Churg, U.S. pathologist, 1910–2005; Lotte Strauss, U.S. pathologist, 1913–1985] A rare systemic vasculitis affecting the respiratory, musculoskeletal, cardiac, and peripheral nervous systems. It typically develops in patients with a history of asthma or allergy and is marked by hypereosinophilia.

Chvostek sign (vos′tek, kvos′) [Franz Chvostek, Austrian surgeon, 1835–1884] A spasm of the facial muscles following a tap on the facial nerve; seen in hypocalcemic tetany.

chylangioma (kī″lăn-jē-ō′mă) [Gr. *chylos,* juice, + *angeion,* vessel, + *oma,* tumor] A tumor of the intestinal lymph vessels containing chyle.

chyle (kīl) [Gr. *chylos,* juice] A fluid absorbed by the lacteals, i.e., the lymphatic capillaries in the small intestines.. Chyle contains interstitial fluid from local arterial capillaries, chylomicrons formed of triglycerides from recent meals, lymphocytes, immunoglobulins, and fat soluble vitamins from the intestines. After a fatty meal, the high concentration of chylomicrons makes chyle thick and milky. Chyle is bacteriostatic.

chylemia (kī-lē′mē-ă) [″ + *haima,* blood] Chyle in the peripheral circulation.

chyliferous (kī-lĭf′ĕr-ŭs) [″ + L. *ferre,* to carry] Carrying chyle.

chyliform (kī′lĭ-form) [″ + L. *forma,* shape] Resembling chyle.

chyloderma (kī″lō-dĕr′mă) [″ + *derma,* skin] Lymph accumulated in the enlarged lymphatic vessels and thickened skin of the scrotum. SYN: *elephantiasis, scrotal.*

chylomediastinum (kī″lō-mē″dē-ăs-tī′nŭm) [″ + L. *mediastinum,* median] Chyle in the mediastinum.

chylomicron (kī″lō-mī′krŏn) [″ + *mikros*, small] A lipoprotein molecule formed in the small intestine from digested fats for transport of fats to other tissues.

chylomicronemia syndrome (kīl″ō-mī″krō-nēm′ē-ă) [″ + ″ + ″] A disorder of lipid metabolism in which massively elevated levels of triglycerides are accompanied by the presence of chylomicrons in the blood, even after a fast. It results in abdominal pain, eruptive xanthomas, hepatosplenomegaly, memory loss, and occasionally, life-threatening pancreatitis. The syndrome may result from congenital deficiencies or inhibition of lipoprotein lipase; from apolipoprotein deficiency; or from diseases or conditions that elevate plasma triglyceride levels (poorly controlled diabetes mellitus; excessive ingestion of alcohol; the use of some drugs).

chylopericardium (kī″lō-pĕr″ĭ-kăr′dē-ŭm) [″ + L. *peri*, around, + Gr. *kardia*, heart] Chyle in the pericardium.

chyloperitoneum (kī″lō-pĕr″ĭ-tō-nē′ŭm) [″ + *peritonaion*, peritoneum] Chyle in the peritoneal cavity.

chylopneumothorax (kī″lō-nū″mō-thō′răks) [″ + *pneumon*, air, + *thorax*, chest] Chyle and air in the pleural space.

chylorrhea (kī″lō-rē′ă) [Gr. *chylos*, juice, + *rhoia*, flow] Escape of chyle resulting from rupture of the thoracic duct.

chylothorax (kī″lō-thō′răks) [″ + *thorax*, chest] Chyle in the pleural cavities.

chylous (kī′lŭs) Pert. to or of the nature of chyle.

chyluria (kī-lū′rē-ă) [″ + *ouron*, urine] The presence of chyle in the urine, giving it a milky appearance.

chymase (kī′mās) An enzyme in gastric juice that accelerates the action of the pancreatic enzymes.

chyme (kīm) [Gr. *chymos*, juice] The mixture of partly digested food and digestive secretions found in the stomach and small intestine during digestion of a meal. It is a varicolored, thick, nearly liquid mass.

chymopapain (kī-mō-pă′pā-ĭn) An enzyme related to papain.

chymosin (kī′mō-sĭn) [Gr. *chymos*, juice] An enzyme that curdles milk; present in the gastric juice of young ruminants. It is the preferred term for rennin because of possible confusion with the term renin.

chymotrypsin (kī″mō-trĭp′sĭn) [″ + *tryein*, to rub, + *pepsis*, digestion] A digestive enzyme produced by the pancreas and functioning in the small intestine that, with trypsin, hydrolyzes proteins to peptones or amino acids. It can be synthesized and given orally to patients with pancreatic insufficiency.

CI *chemotherapeutic index* (parasitology); *color index.*

Ci *curie.*

CIAI *Complicated intraabdominal infections.*

cib Abbreviation for L. *cibus,* food.

cibophobia (sī″bō-fō′bē-ă) [L. *cibus,* food, + Gr. *phobos*, fear] A morbid aversion to or fear of food.

cicatricial pemphigoid SEE: under *pemphigoid.*

cicatricotomy (sĭk″ă-trĭk-ŏt′ō-mē) [″ + Gr. *tome*, incision] Incision of a cicatrix or scar.

cicatrix (sĭk′ă-triks″, sĭ-kā′triks, sik-ă-trī′sēz″, sĕ-kā″trĭ-sēz″) [L. *cicatrix,* scar] A scar left by a healed wound. Lack of color is due to an absence of pigmentation. Cicatricial tissue is less elastic than normal tissue and therefore usually appears contracted. SEE: *keloid.*
cicatricial (sĭk″ă-trish′ăl), *adj.*

cicatrizant (sĭk-ăt′rĭ-zănt) [L. *cicatrix,* scar] Favoring or causing cicatrization; an agent that aids in scar formation.

cicatrization (sĭk″ă-trĭ-zā′shŭn) Healing by scar formation.

cicatrize (sĭk′ă-trīz) To heal by scar tissue.

cicutism (sĭk′ū-tĭzm) Poisoning resulting from ingestion of *Cicuta maculata* or *C. virosa,* water hemlock.

-cide [L. *-cidere,* to kill] Suffix meaning *killing* or *destroying.*

ciguatoxin (sē″gwă-tŏk′sĭn) The toxic substance (acyclic polyether) that causes ciguatera poisoning. The toxin interferes with nerve impulse transmission by altering cell membrane sodium channel polarization.

cilia (sil′ē-ă, sil′ē-ŭm) *sing.,* **cilium** [L. *cilium,* eyelid] 1. Eyelashes. 2. Threadlike projections from the free surface of certain epithelial cells such as those lining the trachea, bronchi, and some reproductive ducts, e.g., the fallopian tubes. They propel or sweep materials, such as mucus or dust, across a surface, such as the respiratory tract.

ciliarotomy (sĭl″ē-ă-rŏt′ō-mē) [″ + Gr. *tome*, incision] Surgical section of the ciliary zone in glaucoma.

ciliary (sil′ē-er″ē) [L. *ciliaris,* pert. to an eyelid] 1. Pert. to a cilium or to cilia. 2. Pert. to certain anatomical structures of the eye, e.g., the ciliary muscle.

ciliary apparatus Ciliary **body.**

ciliary body SEE: under *body.*

ciliary nerve, long One of the two or three branches of the nasal nerves supplying the ciliary muscle, iris, and cornea.

ciliary nerve, short One of the several branches of the ciliary ganglion supplying the ciliary muscle, iris, and tunics of the eyeball.

Ciliata (sĭl″ē-ă′tă) Formerly a class of protozoa characterized by locomotion by cilia. Now called Ciliophora, a phylum of the kingdom Protista.

ciliate (sĭl′ē-āt) [L. *cilia,* eyelids] Ciliated.

ciliated (sĭl′ē-ā-tĕd) Possessing cilia.

ciliectomy (sĭl″ē-ĕk′tō-mē) [″ + Gr. *ektome,* excision] Excision of a portion of the ciliary body or ciliary border of the eyelid.

ciliogenesis (sĭl″ē-ō-jĕn′ĕ-sĭs) Formation of cilia.

ciliopathy (sil″ē-op′ă-thē) [*cilia* (threadlike projections) + *-pathy*] Any inherited disease, such as the polycystic kidney diseases, caused by mutations in genes that impair ciliary function or ciliary links to centrosomes within cells.

Ciliophora (sĭl″ē-ō-fōr′ă) A phylum of the kingdom Protista that includes unicellular and colonial forms possessing cilia for locomotion. Some are free living and others are parasitic species such as *Balantidium coli.*

ciliospinal (sĭl″ē-ō-spī′năl) [″ + *spinalis,* pert. to a spine] Pert. to the ciliary body and spinal cord.

ciliostatic (sĭl″ē-ō-stăt′ĭk) [″ + Gr. *statos,* placed] Interfering with or preventing movement of the cilia.

ciliotomy (sĭl″ē-ŏt′ō-mē) [″ + Gr. *tome,* incision] Surgical cutting of the ciliary nerve.

ciliotoxicity (sĭl″ē-ō-tŏks-ĭs′ĭ-tē) The action of anything that interferes with ciliary motion.

cilium (sĭl′ē-ŭm) [L. *cilium,* eyelid] Sing. of cilia.

-cillin [Fr. (*peni*)*cillin*] A suffix used in pharmacology to name an *antibiotic related to penicillin.*

cillosis (sĭl-ō′sĭs) [L.] Spasmodic twitching of the eyelid.

cimetidine (sī-mĕt′ĭ-dēn″) An H₂-receptor antagonist that inhibits the secretion of stomach acid. It is primarily used to treat peptic ulcers and gastroesophageal reflux disease. SEE: *peptic ulcer.*

Cimex lectularius (sī′mĕks lĕk-tū-lā′rē-ŭs) The bedbug; an insect belonging to the order Hemiptera. SYN: *Acanthia lectularia.* SEE: *bedbug.*

Cimicifuga racemosa (sī-mĭ-sĭf′ū-gă ră-sē-mō-să) [NL., clustering bug-repellent] The scientific name for black cohosh.

cimicosis (sĭm″ĭ-kō′sĭs) Itching due to the bite of a bedbug.

CIN *cervical intraepithelial neoplasia.*

CINAHL *Cumulative Index to Nursing and Allied Health Literature*

cinchona (sĭn-kō′nă, -chō′nă) [Sp. *cinchon,* Countess of Cinchon] The dried bark of the tree from which the antimalarial quinine is derived.

cinchonism (sĭn′kŏn-ĭzm) [″ + Gr. *-ismos,* condition] Poisoning from cinchona or its alkaloids. SYN: *quininism.*

cinclisis (sĭn′klĭ-sĭs) [Gr. *kinklisis,* a wagging] Swift spasmodic movement of any part of the body.

cineangiocardiography (sĭn″ē-ăn″jē-ō-kăr″dē-ŏg′ră-fē) [Gr. *kinesis,* movement, + *angeion,* vessel, + *kardia,* heart, + *graphein,* to write] Cinefluorographic imaging of the heart chambers or coronary vessels after injection of a radiopaque contrast medium. SEE: *cardiac catheterization.*

   radionuclide c. The use of a scintillation camera to record and project the image of a radioisotope as it travels through the heart and great vessels.

cinematics (sĭn″ē-măt′ĭks) [Gr. *kinema,* motion] The science of motion; kinematics.

cinematoradiography (sĭn″ē-măt-ō-ră″dē-ŏg′ră-fē) [″ + L. *radius,* ray, + Gr. *graphein,* to write] Radiography of an organ in motion.

cinemicrography (sĭn″ē-mī-krŏg′ră-fē) [Gr. *kinesis,* movement, + *mikros,* small, + *graphein,* to write] A motion picture record of an object seen through a microscope.

cineplastics (sĭn″ē-plăs′tĭks) [″ + *plassein,* to form] The arrangement of muscles and tendons in a stump after amputation so that it is possible to impart motion and direction to an artificial limb.

cingulotomy (sing′gyŭ-lot′ŏ-mē) [*cingulum* + *-tomy*] Surgical excision of the anterior half of the cingulate gyrus of the brain. It may be done to alleviate intractable pain or obsessive compulsive disorder.

cingulum (sing′gyŭ-lŭm, sing′gyŭ-lă) *pl.* **cingula** [L., *cingulum,* belt, girdle] **1.** A myelinated axon tract underlying the cingulate gyrus on the medial side of the cerebral hemisphere. It is the major long association tract of the medial hemisphere and interconnects the frontal and parietal lobes with the parahippocampal and adjacent gyri of the ipsilateral temporal lobe. The cingulum is a segment of the loop of neural circuits called the limbic system. SYN: *cingulate bundle; cingulate fasciculus; cingulum bundle.* **2.** A convexity on the cervical third of the lingual aspect of incisors and canines. SYN: *basal ridge.*

cinnamic acid (sī-nam′ik) SEE: under *acid.*

cinnamon (sĭn′nă-mŏn) A volatile oil derived from the bark of *Cinnamomum zeylanicum.* It is used as a flavoring agent in cooking and in preparing pharmaceutical products.

cino-, cin- SEE: *kino-.*

CIP *Congenital insensitivity to pain.*

Cipro SEE: *ciprofloxacin.*

ciprofloxacin (sip″rō-flok′să-sĭn, ″rō-) A fluoroquinolone and anti-infective, administered orally or intravenously to treat urinary tract and gynecological infections; gonorrhea; prostatitis; infectious diarrhea; and infections of the respiratory tract, abdomen, skin, bones, and joints.

> ⚠ Ciprofloxacin should never be used by pregnant or lactating women.

circa (sĭr′kă) [L.] ABBR: c. About; used before dates or figures that are approximate.

circadian (sĭr″kă-dē′ăn, sĭr-kā′dē-ăn) [L. *circa*, about, + *dies*, day] Pert. to events that occur at approx. 24-hr intervals, such as certain physiological phenomena. SEE: *biological clock*. SEE: *night work, maladaption to*.

circinate (sĕr′sĭ-nāt) [L. *circinatus*, made round] Circular.

circle (sĭr′kĕl) [L. *circulus*, a little ring] Any ring-shaped structure.

    c. of diffusion One or more circles on the projection plane of an image not in focus of the lens of the eye.

    c. of Willis SEE: under *Willis, Thomas*.

circuit (sĕr′kĭt) [L. *circuire*, to go around] **1.** The course or path of an electric current. **2.** The path followed by a fluid circulating in a system of tubes or cavities. **3.** The path followed by nerve impulses in a reflex arc from sensory receptor to effector organ.

    ventilator c. The external or internal pneumatic delivery component of a mechanical ventilator.

circuit party A large, often elaborately produced social gathering for gay and bisexual men.

circular (sĭr′kū-lar) [L. *circularis*] **1.** Shaped like a circle. **2.** Recurrent.

circulation (sĭr″kyŭ-lá′shŏn) [L. *circulatio*, encirclement] Movement in a regular or circular course.

    arterial c. Movement of blood through the arteries. It is maintained by the pumping of the heart and influenced by the elasticity and extensibility of arterial walls, peripheral resistance in the areas of small arteries, and the quantity of blood in the body.

    assisted c. Use of a mechanical device to augment or replace the action of the heart in pumping blood.

    bile salt c. Secretion and reuptake of the sodium glycocholate and taurocholate found in hepatic bile. Bile salts enter the duodenum and emulsify fats in the small intestine. They are resorbed in the terminal ileum and returned to the liver in portal blood.

    blood c. The movement of blood through the left atrium and ventricle of the heart, aorta, arteries, arterioles, capillaries, venules, veins, vena cava, and back to the right side of the heart, into the pulmonary artery, lungs, and left side of the heart again. SEE: *artery; heart; circulatory system; vein*.

    collateral c. Circulation established through an anastomosis between two vessels supplying or draining two adjacent vascular areas. This enables blood to bypass an obstruction in the larger vessel that supplies or drains both areas or enables blood to flow to or from a tissue when the principal vessel involved is obstructed.

    coronary c. Movement of blood through the vessels of the heart, specifically from the ascending aorta to the epicardial coronary arteries to the penetrating arteries of the myocardium, the coronary arterioles, capillaries, veins, coronary sinus, and into the right atrium. A few of the small veins open directly into the atria and ventricles. SEE: illus.

    enterohepatic c. Circulation in which substances secreted by the liver pass into the intestines where some are absorbed into the bloodstream and returned to the liver and re-secreted. Bile and bile salts follow this pathway.

    extracorporeal c. Circulation of blood outside the body. This may be through an artificial kidney or a heart-lung device.

    fetal c. The course of the flow of blood in a fetus. Oxygenated in the placenta, blood passes through the umbilical vein and ductus venosus to the inferior vena cava and thence to the right atrium. It then follows one of two courses: through the foramen ovale to the left atrium and thence through the aorta to the tissues, or through the right ventricle, pulmonary artery, and ductus arteriosus to the aorta and thence to the tissues. In either case the blood bypasses the lungs, which do not function before birth. Blood returns to the placenta through the umbilical arteries, which are continuations of the hypogastric arteries. At birth or shortly after, the ductus arteriosus and the foramen ovale close, establishing the postpartum circulation. If either fails to close, the baby may be hypoxemic. SEE: illus.; *patent ductus arteriosus*.

    hypophyseal c. Superior and inferior hypophyseal arteries (slender branches from arteries of the circle of Willis) that provide blood to the pituitary gland and adjacent regions of the hypothalamus. Venous blood from the pituitary gland drains into the cavernous sinuses and, from there, into the internal jugular veins. Some of the superior hypophyseal arteries form primary capillary beds in the hypothalamus and the veins draining those beds ramify again to form secondary capillary beds in the adenohypophysis (anterior lobe of the pituitary), thus forming a portal circulation (the hypothalamic-pituitary portal circulation). Releasing factors secreted from the hypothalamus into the primary capillary beds reach the adenohypophysis via the secondary capillary beds.

    lymph c. The flow of lymph from the tissues into the lymphatic collecting system. Lymph is formed from the tis-

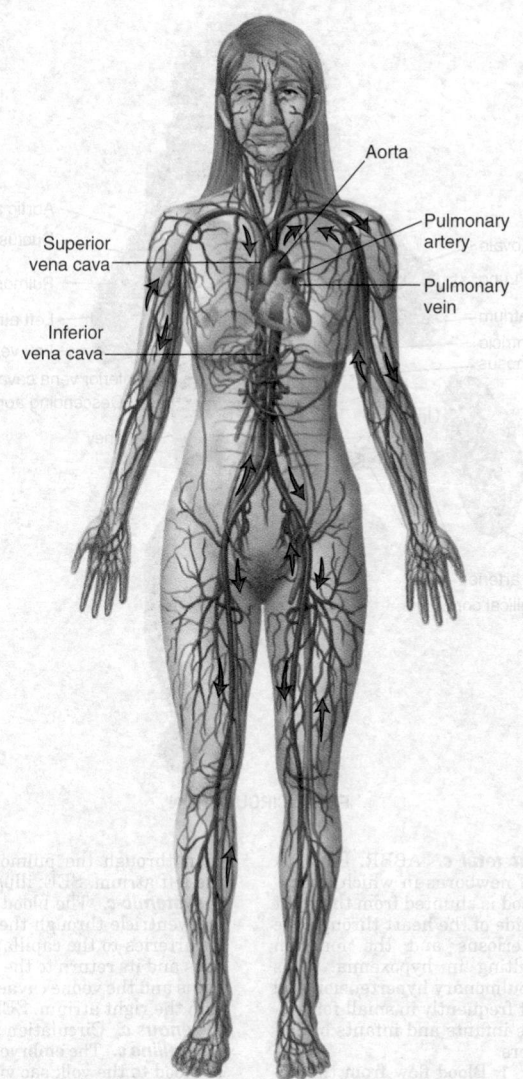

Aorta

Pulmonary artery

Superior vena cava

Pulmonary vein

Inferior vena cava

CIRCULATION OF BLOOD THROUGH HEART AND MAJOR VESSELS

sue fluid that fills the interstitial spaces of the body. It is collected into lymph capillaries, which carry the lymph to the larger lymph vessels. These converge to form one of two main trunks, the right lymphatic duct and the thoracic duct. The right lymphatic duct drains the right side of the head, neck, and trunk and the right upper extremity; the thoracic duct drains the rest of the body. The thoracic duct originates at the cisterna chyli, which receives the lymphatics from the abdominal organs and legs. It courses upward through the dia-phragm and thorax and empties into the left subclavian vein near its junction with the left interior jugular vein. The right lymphatic duct empties into the right subclavian vein. Along the course of lymph vessels are lymph nodes, which remove bacteria and other foreign materials, thus preventing their entrance into the bloodstream. Lymph flow is maintained by a difference in pressure at the two ends of the system. Important accessory factors aiding lymph flow are breathing movements and muscular activity.

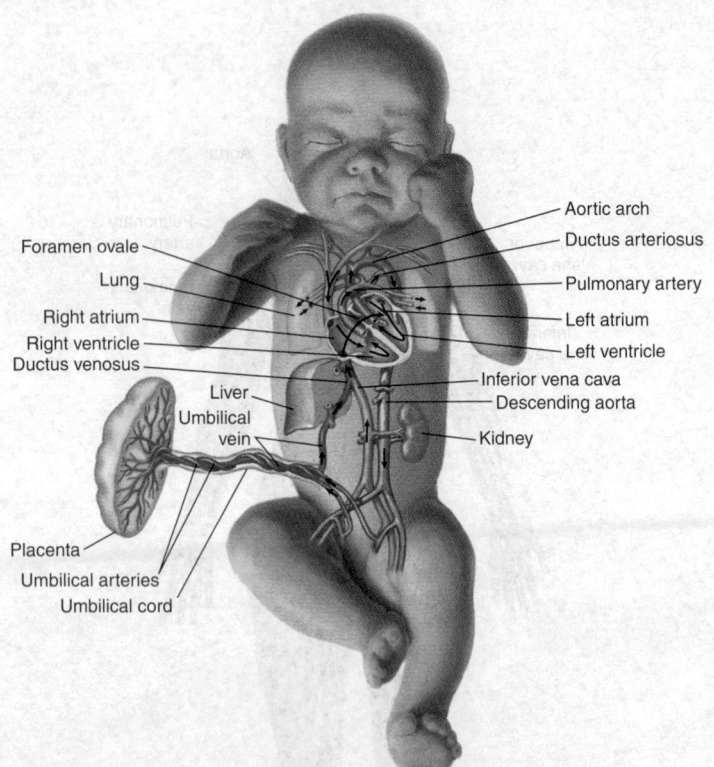

FETAL CIRCULATION

persistent fetal c. ABBR: PFC. A condition of newborns in which unoxygenated blood is shunted from the right to the left side of the heart through the ductus arteriosus and the foramen ovale, resulting in hypoxemia. It is caused by pulmonary hypertension and occurs most frequently in small-for-gestational-age infants and infants of diabetic mothers.

portal c. **1.** Blood flow from the abdominal organs that passes through the portal vein, the sinusoids of the liver, and into the hepatic vein before returning to the heart from the inferior vena cava. This pathway permits the liver to process and to detoxify substances entering the body from the gastrointestinal tract. **2.** A portal system between the hypothalamus and the anterior pituitary gland. The hypothalamus secretes releasing or inhibiting hormones into the blood; they are carried directly to the anterior pituitary and stimulate or inhibit secretion of specific hormones.

pulmonary c. The flow of blood from the right ventricle of the heart to the lungs for exchange of oxygen and carbon dioxide in the pulmonary capillaries, then through the pulmonary veins to the left atrium. SEE: illus.

systemic c. The blood flow from the left ventricle through the aorta and all its arteries to the capillaries of the tissues and its return to the heart through veins and the venae cavae, which empty into the right atrium. SEE: illus.

venous c. Circulation via the veins.

vitelline c. The embryonic circulation of blood to the yolk sac via the vitelline arteries and its return to general circulation through the vitelline veins.

circulation, motion, sensation ABBR: CMS. An assessment of the neurological and vascular health of a body part; specifically, of its capillary refill, pulses, motor function, and sense of touch. Serial assessments of CMS are particularly important to perform in certain clinical settings, such as in patients with progressive or rapidly changing neurological diseases, or in patients who have had vascular or endovascular surgery. Patients with compromised arterial blood flow to a limb, for example, may have pale or dusky extremities with delayed return of color after pressure is applied to the skin. Another ex-

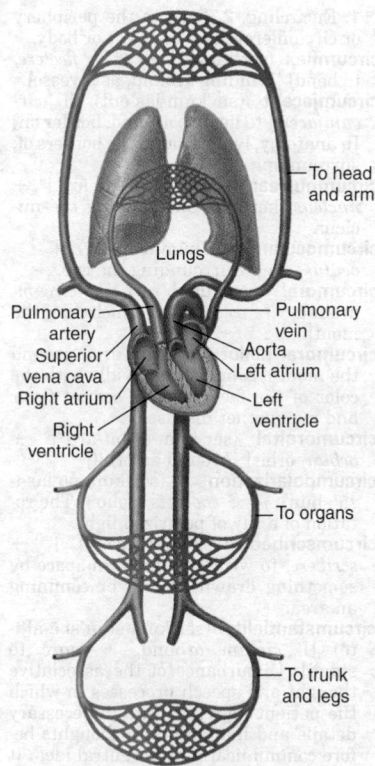

PULMONARY CIRCULATION

ample: patients with diabetic neuropathy may have diminished proprioception, or decreased awareness of vibration and light touch in their feet and sometimes their hands.

circulation path Access standards for de-signing the way of passage, whether exterior or interior, for pedestrians regardless of their ability.

circulation rate The minute volume or output of the heart per minute. In an average-sized adult with a pulse rate of 70, the amount is about 3 L/sq m of body surface each minute.

circulation time SEE: under *time*.

circulatory (sĭr″kū-lă-tōr′ē) Pert. to circulation.

circulatory failure SEE: under *failure*.

circulatory system A system concerned with circulation of body fluids. It includes the cardiovascular and lymphatic systems.

circum- [L.] Prefix meaning *around*.

circumanal (sĭr″kŭm-ā′năl) Around the anus.

circumcision (sĭr″kŭm-sizh′ŏn) [L. *circumcisio,* a cutting around] Surgical removal of genital foreskin.

   female c. Female genital cutting.

   male c. Surgical removal of the end of the foreskin of the penis. Circumcision usually is performed at the request of the parents, in some cases for religious reasons. Considerable controversy exists whether the procedure has medical benefits: some authorities suggest that circumcision is associated with a reduced risk of HIV infection, urinary tract infections, sexually transmitted diseases, and penile carcinoma. Other authorities dispute these findings, suggesting that the procedure may have adverse effects on sexual, emotional, or psychological health. If the procedure is performed, anesthesia should always be used.

   PATIENT CARE: *Preoperative:* The procedure and expected sensations are explained to the patient or his parents. Adult patients should be reassured that the procedure will not interfere with urinary, sexual, or reproductive func-

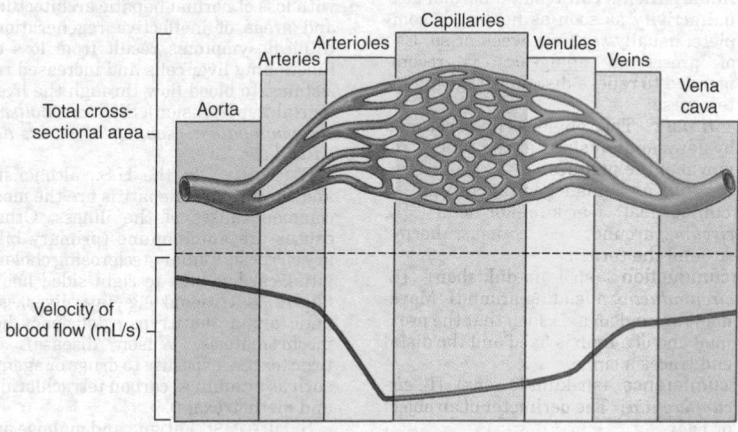

SYSTEMIC CIRCULATION

tion. Necessary equipment, including a restraining board for the newborn, and appropriate anesthetics are assembled. The newborn should not receive food within 1 hr before the procedure.

Postoperative: Vital signs are monitored, and the incision is inspected for bleeding every 15 min for the first hour, then hourly for 12 to 24 hr, as protocol directs. Bleeding is controlled by applying gentle pressure with sterile gauze sponges; any heavy or persistent bleeding should be reported, and preparations made for blood vessel ligation. A sterile petroleum gauze dressing is applied after circumcision, remains in place for 24 hr, and is replaced if it becomes dislodged during that time. The penis is gently washed at diaper change, and fresh sterile petroleum gauze is reapplied. The dressing, glans penis, and sutures, if present, are periodically examined for swelling, redness, or purulent exudate; any signs of infection are reported, and a specimen of the exudate is obtained. A plastic bell instead of petroleum gauze may be used to cover the glans and to prevent hemorrhage and contamination. The newborn is diapered loosely to avoid irritation and should not be positioned on the abdomen for the first few hours after the procedure.

For the adult patient, analgesics are provided, and a topical anesthetic ointment or spray is applied as needed. If prescribed, a sedative is given to help prevent nocturnal penile tumescence and resulting pressure on the suture line. The patient is encouraged to void within 6 hr after the procedure. Either the patient or his family is instructed how to keep the area clean and how to change and apply dressings. They are also instructed to watch for and report renewed bleeding or signs of infection. Adult patients can resume normal sexual activity as soon as healing is complete, usually within a week or so. Use of prescribed analgesics is recommended to relieve discomfort during intercourse.

ritual c. The religious rite performed by Jews and Muslims at the time of removal of the prepuce.

sunna c. Female genital cutting.

circumcorneal (sĕr″kŭm-kor′nē-ăl) [L. *circum*, around, + *corneus*, horny] Around the cornea.

circumduction (sĭr″kŭm-dŭk′shŏn) [L. *circumductio*, a leading around] Movement around an axis such that the proximal end of a limb is fixed and the distal end traces a circle.

circumference (sĭr-kŭm′fĕ-rĕns) [L. *circumferentia*] The perimeter of an object or body.

circumferential (sĕr″kŭm-fĕr-ĕn′shăl)

1. Encircling. 2. Pert. to the periphery or circumference of an object or body.

circumflex (sĕr′kŭm-flĕks) [″ + *flectere*, to bend] Winding around, as a vessel.

circumjacent (sĭr″kŭm-jās′ĕnt) [L. *circumjacere*, to lie (all) around, border on] In anatomy, lying around the borders of; surrounding.

circumnuclear (sĕr″kŭm-nū′klē-ăr) [″ + *nucleus*, kernel] Surrounding the nucleus.

circumocular (sĕr″kŭm-ŏk′ū-lăr) [″ + *oculus*, eye] Surrounding the eye.

circumoral (sĕr″kŭm-ō′răl) [L. *circum*, around, + *os*, mouth] Encircling the mouth.

circumoral pallor A white area around the mouth, contrasting vividly with the color of the face, seen in scarlet fever and many other diseases.

circumorbital (sĕr″kŭm-or′bĭt-ăl) [″ + *orbita*, orbit] Around an orbit.

circumpolarization (sĕr″kŭm-pō″lăr-ĭ-zā′shŭn) [″ + *polaris*, polar] The rotation of a ray of polarized light.

circumscribed (sĕr′kŭm-skrībd) [″ + *scribere*, to write] Limited in space by something drawn around or confining an area.

circumstantiality (sĕr″kŭm-stăn″shē-ăl′ĭ-tē) [L. *circum*, around, + *stare*, to stand] Disturbance of the associative thought and speech processes in which the patient digresses into unnecessary details and inappropriate thoughts before communicating the central idea. It is observed in schizophrenia, obsessional disturbances, and certain cases of dementia.

circumvallate (sĕr″kŭm-văl′āt) [″ + *vallare*, to wall] Surrounded by a wall or raised structure.

CIREN *Crash injury research and engineering network*.

cirrhosis (sĭ-rō′sĭs) [Gr. *kirrhos*, tawny + *-osis*] A chronic disease of the liver characterized by scarring of the liver with loss of normal hepatic architecture and areas of ineffective regeneration. Clinical symptoms result from loss of functioning liver cells and increased resistance to blood flow through the liver (portal hypertension). SEE: *alcoholism; encephalopathy; esophageal varix; hepatic; liver*.

ETIOLOGY: In the U.S., alcoholism and chronic viral hepatitis are the most common causes of the illness. Other causes are autoimmune (primary biliary cirrhosis), biliary (sclerosing cholangitis), cardiac (due to right-sided heart failure), nutritional (e.g., fatty liver), genetic (alpha-$_1$-antitrypsin deficiency, hemochromatosis, Wilson disease), or toxic (excess exposure to drugs or agents such as vitamin A, carbon tetrachloride, and methotrexate).

SYMPTOMS: Fatigue and malaise are common but nonspecific symptoms of the illness. Anorexia, early satiety, dyspepsia, altered bowel habits, and easy bruising and bleeding also are reported often. Alterations in mental status, personality, or behavior ("hepatic encephalopathy") are common but vary in severity and may not be noticed initially. Pruritus is reported when significant jaundice is present. Signs of the illness may include ascites; asterixis; bleeding from gums, nose, or gastroesophageal varices; "mousy" breath odor; edema; jaundice; and an irregular liver edge with hepatic enlargement (the liver may shrink when complete loss of function is present). Multiple skin findings may include abnormal pigmentation, palmar erythema, spider angiomas, ecchymoses, and dilated abdominal veins. Limited thoracic expansion caused by hepatomegaly or ascites and endocrine changes such as menstrual irregularities, testicular atrophy, gynecomastia, and loss of chest and axillary hair may also be present. SEE: illus.

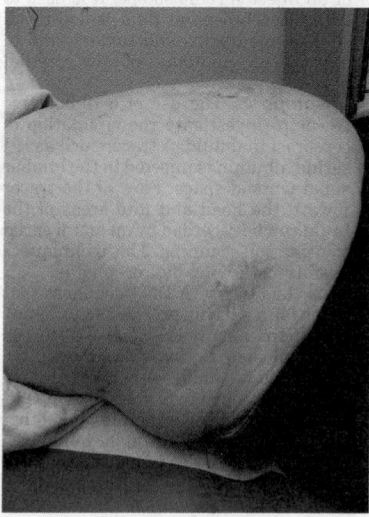

ASCITES CAUSED BY CIRRHOSIS

TREATMENT: Liver transplantation may be curative, but its use is limited by the number of donor organs available. Shunting procedures to divert blood flow from the hepatic to the systemic circulation may improve portal hypertension and its consequences.

PATIENT CARE: Daily weights are obtained, fluid and electrolyte balance is monitored, and abdominal girth is measured. The ankles, sacrum, and scrotum are also assessed for dependent edema. The stools are inspected for color, amount, and consistency. Stools and vomitus are tested for occult blood. Surface bleeding sites are monitored frequently, and direct pressure is applied

to the site if bleeding occurs. The patient is observed for indications of internal bleeding, such as anxiety, epigastric fullness, weakness, and restlessness; and vital signs are monitored as appropriate. Dependent areas are exercised and elevated, and skin breakdown is prevented by eliminating soaps and by using lubricating oils and lotions for bathing. The patient is frequently repositioned. The patient should avoid straining at stool and should use stool softeners as necessary and prescribed. Violent sneezing and nose blowing should also be avoided. A soft toothbrush or sponge stick and an electric razor are used. Aspirin, acetaminophen, or other over-the-counter medications should not be taken without the physician's knowledge. Alcohol or products containing alcohol are prohibited.

Both patient and family may require referral to alcohol cessation and related support groups. Prescribed therapies, including sodium and fluid restriction, dietary modifications, supplemental vitamin therapy, antiemetics, and diuretics, are administered. The patient's response to prescribed therapies is assessed, and he or she is instructed in their use and any adverse reactions. Care is taken to avoid drugs metabolized by the liver, as the cirrhotic liver is increasingly unable to detoxify such substances. A regimen of moderate exercise alternating with periods of rest is prescribed; energy conservation measures are explained; small, frequent, nutritious meals are recommended; and exposure to infections should be avoided. Appropriate safety measures are instituted, esp. if the patient demonstrates hepatic encephalopathy, and the patient is frequently reoriented to time and place. Salt-poor albumin is administered and paracentesis performed, if prescribed, to control ascites. The patient is physically and psychologically prepared for required medical and surgical procedures. SEE: *Nursing Diagnoses Appendix.*

alcoholic c. Cirrhosis resulting from chronic liver damage by alcoholism. Approx. 20% of chronic alcoholics develop cirrhosis.

biliary c. Cirrhosis marked by prolonged jaundice due to chronic retention of bile and inflammation of bile ducts. SEE: *obstructive biliary c.; primary biliary c.*

cardiac c. Passive congestion of the liver caused by right-sided heart failure, ultimately resulting in hepatic scarring and failure. SYN: *congestive hepatopathy.*

glissonian c. An inflammation of the peritoneal coat of the liver. SYN: *perihepatitis.*

hypertrophic c. Cirrhosis in which

connective tissue hyperplasia causes the liver to be greatly enlarged.

inactive c. End-stage scarring of the liver without ongoing inflammation. It is one of the patterns of cirrhosis of the liver that may be seen on liver biopsy.

infantile c. Cirrhosis occurring in childhood as a result of protein malnutrition. SEE: *kwashiorkor.*

Laënnec c. SEE: under *Laënnec, René.*

metabolic c. Cirrhosis resulting from metabolic disease such as hemochromatosis, glycogen storage disease, or Wilson disease.

obstructive biliary c. Cirrhosis resulting from obstruction of the common duct by a stone or tumor.

primary biliary c. A rare, progressive form of cirrhosis usually occurring in middle-aged women, marked by jaundice, pruritus, fatigue, and autoimmune destruction of the small bile ducts.

syphilitic c. Cirrhosis occurring in tertiary syphilis, in which gummas form in the liver and cause coarse lobulation on healing.

zooparasitic c. Cirrhosis resulting from infestation with hepatobiliary parasites, esp. blood flukes of the genus *Schistosoma* or liver flukes, e.g., *Clonorchis sinensis.*

cirrhotic (sĭ-rŏt'ĭk) Pert. to or affected with cirrhosis.

cirsectomy (sĕr-sĕk'tō-mē) [Gr. *kirsos,* varix, + *ektome,* excision] Excision (of a portion) of a varicose vein.

cirsoid (sĕr'soyd) Varicose.

cirsotomy (sĕr-sŏt'ō-mē) Incision of a varicose vein.

CIS *central inhibitory state.*

cis (sĭs) [L., on the same side] In organic chemistry, a form of isomerism in which similar atoms or radicals are on the same side. In genetics, a prefix meaning the location of two or more genes on the same chromosome of a homologous pair.

CISD *Critical incident stress debriefing; critical incident stress defusing.*

cisplatin, cis-platinum (sĭs'plă-tĭn) A drug used to treat cancers, esp. solid tumors such as testicular and ovarian carcinoma. Common side effects of this drug include severe nausea and vomiting and renal failure.

cis-retinal (sĭs'rĕt'ĭ-năl, rĕt″năl) [L. prefix *cis-,* this side of + ″] The form of retinal combined with a glycoprotein opsin (rhodopsin in rods) during darkness. Light striking the retina changes it to *trans*-retinal and begins the generation of a nerve impulse.

cistern (sĭs'tĕrn) A reservoir for storing fluid.

lumbar c. In the subarachnoid space of the vertebral column, the fluid-filled space between the end of the spinal cord (vertebral level L1-L2 in adults) and the end of the arachnoid-dural membrane (vertebral level S2).

subarachnoid c. Any of the spaces at the base of the brain where the arachnoid becomes widely separated from the pia, giving rise to large cavities.

cisterna (sĭs-tĕr'nă) [L.] A reservoir or cavity.

c. chyli A saclike lymphatic vessel that is anterior to the second lumbar vertebra and is the origin of the thoracic duct. Into it empty the intestinal and right and left lumbar lymphatic trunks.

c. magna The cranial subarachnoid space between the medulla and the cerebellum; the foramina of the fourth ventricle open into it. Cerebrospinal fluid flows from it into the spinal subarachnoid space.

cisternal (sĭs-tĕr'năl), *adj.*

cisternography (sĭs″tĕr-nog'ră-fē) [*cistern* + *-graphy*] Radiographic evaluation of the basal cisterns of the brain and of the flow of cerebrospinal fluid, e.g., with magnetic resonance imaging or an injected radioisotope. It is used to detect cerebrospinal fluid leaks, to visualize aneurysms and tumors, and to assess the anatomy of the cranial nerves.

isotope c. The use of a radioactive tracer to investigate the circulation of cerebrospinal fluid. A tracer such as ^{131}I serum albumin is injected in the lumbar subarachnoid space. Flow of the tracer toward the head and into areas of the brain can be recorded by means of serial scintillation scanning. This technique is useful in studying hydrocephalus.

cistron (sĭs'trŏn″) A DNA sequence that codes for a specific protein (i.e., a gene).

cisvestitism (sĭs-vĕs'tĭ-tĭzm) [L. *cis,* on the same side, + *vestitus,* dressed, + Gr. *-ismos,* condition] Wearing of clothes appropriate to one's sex but suitable for a calling or profession other than one's own. An example would be a civilian who dresses in a uniform of the armed services.

CIT *Center for Information Technology* (of the National Institutes of Health)

citalopram (sī-tăl'ō-prăm) A selective serotonin reuptake inhibitor and antidepressant. It is administered orally and may be used as an adjunct to psychotherapy.

citation bias (sī-tā'shŭn bī'ĭs) 1. The tendency for research investigations that show benefit to be quoted more often than those that are neutral or negative. 2. The tendency for a scientist to cite research articles more frequently that are published in her or his preferred journals (i.e., in those journals that are familiar because they are published in the same country or the same language as that spoken by the scientist).

Citelli syndrome (chē-tel'ē) [Salvatore

Citelli, Italian laryngologist, 1875–1947] Insomnia or drowsiness and lack of concentration associated with intelligence disorders, seen in children with infected adenoids or sphenoid sinusitis.

citrate (sĭt′rāt, sī′trāt) A compound of citric acid and a base.

   sildenafil c. SEE: *sildenafil.*

citrated (sĭt′rāt-ĕd) Combined or mixed with citric acid or a citrate.

citric acid cycle SEE: under *cycle.*

citronella (sĭt″rŏn-ĕl′ă) A volatile oil obtained from *Cymbopogon citratus,* or lemongrass, that contains geraniol and citronellal. It is used in perfumes and as an insect repellent.

citrovorum factor Leucovorin.

citrulline (sĭt-rŭl′lĭn) An amino acid, $C_6H_{13}N_3O_3$, formed from ornithine. It is sometimes used to treat patients with urea cycle defects because citrulline is not taken up by the liver but is converted to arginine in the kidney.

citrullinemia (sĭt-rŭl″lĭ-nē′mē-ă) A type of aminoaciduria accompanied by increased amounts of citrulline in the blood, urine, and spinal fluid. Clinical findings include ammonia intoxication, liver disease, vomiting, mental retardation, convulsions, and failure to thrive.

Civilian Health and Medical Program of the Uniformed Services ABBR: CHAMPUS. The former name of the health care insurer for active members of the military, their dependents, and for military retirees now known as TRICARE. SEE: *TRICARE.*

CK *Creatine kinase; cytokeratin.*

CKD *Chronic kidney disease.*

CKD-EPI creatinine equation A tool developed by the Chronic Kidney Disease Epidemiology in collaboration with the National Institutes of Diabetes, Digestive, and Kidney Diseases to estimate the glomerular filtration rate of patients with differing serum creatinine levels. The equation takes into account the patient's gender, race, age, body weight, and history of organ transplantation or of diabetes mellitus.

Cl 1. Symbol for the element chlorine. 2. *chloride; clavicle; Clostridium.*

clade (klād) [G. *klados,* branch] 1. A group of related living organisms that share specific genetic material. 2. A genetically distinct strain of a microorganism.

Cladophialophora (klăd″ō-fī″ă-lŏf′ĕ-ră) [NL.] A genus of pigmented soil fungi that sometimes cause cutaneous, subcutaneous, or intracerebral infections in humans, often in those with immunosuppressive diseases and conditions. Species within the genus include *C. bantiana, C. boppii,* and *C carrionii.*

cladosporiosis (klăd″ō-spō-rē-ō′sĭs) [Gr. *klados,* branch, + *sporos,* seed, + *osis,* condition] An infection, usually of the central nervous system, caused by the fungus *Cladosporium.*

Cladosporium (klăd″ă-spōr′ē-ŭm) A genus of fungi that infect the skin. SEE: illus.

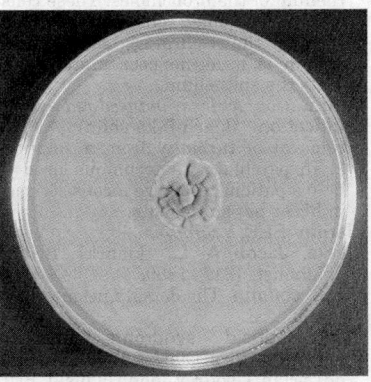

CLADOSPORIUM

(SOURCE: Centers for Disease Control and Prevention: Dr. Lucille K. Georg)

   C. herbarum A mold that is a common cause of indoor and outdoor allergies. Its allergen designation is Cla.

claim (klām) 1. An assertion of fact. 2. A request or demand for reimbursement of medical care costs.

clairvoyance (klār-voy′ăns) [Fr.] The alleged ability to be aware of events that occur at a distance without receiving any sensory information concerning those events.

clamp (klamp) A device used in surgery to grasp, join, compress, or support an organ, tissue, or vessel. SEE: *forceps.*

   rubber dam c. An attachment that fits on the cervical part of the tooth for retention of a rubber dam.

   towel c. An instrument used to hold towels or drapes in place on the surgical field.

CLAMS *Clinical Linguistic and Auditory Milestone Scale.*

clang (klăng) [L. *clangere,* to peal] A loud, metallic sound.

clang association SEE: under *association.*

clap (klăp) A colloquial term for gonorrhea.

clapotage, clapotement (kla-po-tazh′, kla-pot-mon′) [Fr.] Any splashing sound in succession of a dilated stomach.

clapping (klap′ing) 1. A technique for clearing the airway in which the therapist rhythmically strikes with his or her cupped hands the chest wall to help loosen thick secretions in the lungs. SYN: *cupping* (1). 2. A similar, rhythmic striking of any body part, used in massage therapy.

Clapton lines (klap'tŏn) Green lines on the dental margin of the gums in copper poisoning.

Clara cell (klăr'ă, klah'ră) [Max Clara, Austrian anatomist, 1899–1937] One of the secreting cells in the surface epithelium of the bronchioles. These cells, along with goblet cells, provide secretions for the respiratory tract. The secretion is a mucus-poor protein that coats the epithelium.

CLARE *Contact lens–induced red eye.*

clarification (klăr"ĭ-fĭ-kā'shŭn) **1.** The removal of turbidity from a solution. **2.** In psychiatry, a technique used to help a patient recognize inconsistencies in his or her statements.

Claritin SEE: *loratadine.*

Clarke, Jacob A. L. (klahrk) British anatomist, 1817–1880.

   C. **column** The dorsal nucleus of the spinal cord.

Clarke-Hadfield syndrome (klahrk' hăd'fēld) [Cecil Clarke, 20th-cent. Brit. physician; Geoffrey John Hadfield, Brit. pathologist, 1899–1968] An infrequently used eponym for cystic fibrosis. SEE: *cystic fibrosis.*

Clark electrode (klahrk) Oxygen electrode.

Clark rule (klark) A method of calculating pediatric drug dosages. The weight of the child in pounds is multiplied by the adult dose and the result is divided by 150. SEE: *dosage.*

-clasis, -clast [Gr. *klan,* to break] Suffixes meaning *break, breaking, breaker.*

clasmatodendrosis (klăz-măt"ō-děn-drō'sĭs) [Gr. *klasma,* fragment, + *dendron,* tree, + *osis,* condition] Breaking up of astrocytic protoplasmic expansions.

clasp (klăsp) A device for holding objects or tissues together. In dentistry, a type of wire or metal retainer or attachment used to stabilize dentures or prosthetic devices in the mouth.

clasp-knife phenomenon Increased muscle resistance to passive movement of a joint followed by a sudden release of the muscle; commonly seen in patients with spasticity.

class (klăs) [L. *classis,* division] **1.** In biology, a taxonomic group of clearly defined organisms classified below a phylum and above an order. **2.** In statistics, a group of variables that fall within certain value limits.

class effect A drug effect produced by all members of a chemically related group of medications and not only by a single drug from that class.

classification (klăs"ĭ-fĭ-kā'shŏn) The orderly grouping of similar organisms, animals, individuals, diseases, or pathological findings according to traits or characteristics common to each group.

   Angle c. **Classification** of malocclusion.

   Arneth c. of neutrophils SEE: under *Arneth, Joseph.*

   c. of caries Any of five classifications of dental caries according to the part of the tooth involved. Class I is occlusal; class II, interproximal, commonly at the dentinoenamel junction of bicuspids and molars; class III, interproximal surfaces not involving incisal surfaces; class IV, interproximal but involving an incisal surface; and class V, the faciocervical area. SYN: *cavity c.*

   cavity c. **Classification** of caries.

   Denver c. A system for classifying chromosomes based on the size and position of the centromere. SEE: *chromosome.*

   Dukes c. SEE: under *Dukes classification.*

   International C. of Diseases SEE: *International Classification of Diseases.*

   International C. of Functioning, Disability, and Health SEE: *International Classification of Functioning, Disability, and Health.*

   International C. of Nursing Practice SEE: *International Classification of Nursing.*

   Keith-Wagener-Barker c. SEE: *Keith-Wagener-Barker classification.*

   Kraepelin c. SEE: under *Kraepelin classification.*

   Lancefield c. SEE: *Lancefield classification.*

   Landsteiner c. SEE: *Landsteiner classification.*

   c. of living organisms A systematic method of assigning organisms to various groups. Living organisms are classified into five kingdoms: Monera (Prokaryota), Protista, Fungi, Plantae, and Animalia. Within a kingdom, the subdivisions usually are phylum, class, order, family, genus, and species. The genus and species names are referred to as binomial nomenclature, with the larger (genus) category first and the precise species name second. SEE: *taxonomy.*

   Mallampati c. SEE: *Mallampati classification.*

   c. of malocclusion A system for classifying the three different types of malocclusion and their subdivisions as applicable Class I shows normal anteroposterior relationship but with crowding and rotated teeth; Class II, the lower arch is distal to the upper arch on one or both sides, and the lower first molar is distal to the upper first molar; Class III, the lower arch is anterior to the upper arch on one or both sides; the lower first molar is anterior to the upper first molar. SYN: *Angle classification.*

   Schilling c. SEE: *Schilling classification.*

   TNM c. A method of classifying malignant tumors with respect to primary tumor, involvement of regional lymph *n*odes, and presence or absence of *me*-tastases.

classification of living organisms SEE: under *classification*.

class restriction The requirement of certain T lymphocytes for the presence of either class I or class II major histocompatibility complex markers on antigen-presenting cells. These markers enable the T cells to recognize and respond to foreign antigens. CD4+ T cells require class II antigens and CD8+ T cells require class I antigens. Class restriction is a type of clonal restriction. SEE: *antigen-presenting cell; clonal restriction*.

clastic (klăs′tĭk) [Gr. *klastos,* broken] Causing division into parts.

clastogen (klăs′tă-jĕn″) [Gr. *klastos,* broken + *gennan,* to produce] Any agent that can damage a chromosome. Examples of clastogens include chemotherapeutic agents (e.g., cyclophosphamide or nitrogen mustard), and many forms of electromagnetic radiation (e.g., ultraviolet light or x-rays).

clastogenic (klăs′tō-jĕn″ĭc) [″ + *gennan,* to produce] Capable of breaking chromosomes (e.g., able to cause chromosomal abnormalities).

Claude syndrome (klod) [Henri Claude, Fr. psychiatrist, 1869–1945] Paralysis of the third cranial nerve, contralateral ataxia, and tremor; caused by a lesion in the red nucleus of the brain.

claudication (klod″ĭ-kā′shŏn) [L. *claudicatio,* a limp] Cramping pain that limits movement of the legs or arms, occurring during exercise.

   intermittent c. Cramping or pain in leg muscles brought on by a predictable amount of walking (or other form of exercise) and relieved by rest. This symptom is a marker of peripheral vascular disease of the aortoiliac, femoral, or popliteal arteries. It may be present in patients with diffuse atherosclerosis, for example, with arterial insufficiency in the coronary or carotid circulations as well as the limbs. SEE: *peripheral vascular disease*.

   PHYSICAL EXAMINATION: The patient often has thin or shiny skin over the parts of the limb with decreased blood flow. Diminished pulses and bruits (audible blood flow through partially blocked arteries) may also be present.

   DIAGNOSIS: In patients with a suggestive history, the blood pressure (BP) is measured in the affected limb and divided by the BP in the arm on the same side of the body. This ratio is called the ankle-brachial index (ABI); patients with significant peripheral vascular disease have an ABI of less than 85%. If surgery is contemplated for the patient, angiography may be used to define anatomical obstructions more precisely.

   TREATMENT: Affected patients are

encouraged to begin a program of regular exercise, to try to maximize collateral blood flow to the legs. Oral pentoxifylline improves the distance patients can walk without pain. For severely limiting claudication, patients may require angioplasty or arterial bypass surgery to respectively open or bypass obstructed arteries.

   jaw c. Fatigue or cramping pain felt in the jaw, esp. while eating meats or other tough foods. About half of all patients with giant cell arteritis report this symptom.

   neurogenic c. Leg pain or numbness that occurs with standing or walking and is relieved by sitting or resting with the spine flexed. It is typically caused by lumbar disk disease.

   venous c. Claudication resulting from inadequate venous drainage.

claustrophilia (klaws-trō-fĭl′ē-ă) [L. *claustrum,* a barrier, + Gr. *philein,* to love] Dread of being in an open space; a morbid desire to be shut in with doors and windows closed.

claustrophobia (klaws-trō-fō′bē-ă) [″ + Gr. *phobos,* fear] Fear of being confined in small, closed spaces (e.g., a locked room or an enclosed MRI device).

claustrum (klŏs′trŭm) [L.] **1.** Barrier. **2.** The thin layer of gray matter separating the external capsule of the brain from the island of Reil.

clavate (klā′vāt) Club-shaped.

clavicle (klav′ĭ-kl) [L. *clavicula,* little key] A bone curved like the letter *f* that articulates with the sternum and the scapula. SYN: *collar bone*.

clavicotomy (klăv″ĭ-kŏt′ō-mē) [″ + Gr. *tome,* incision] Surgical division of the clavicle.

clavicular (klă-vĭk′ū-lăr) Pert. to the clavicle.

clavus (klā′vŭs) [L. *clavus,* a nail, spike] A corn, or callosity.

   c. hystericus A sharp pain usually localized to the vertex of the skull; said to be of psychosomatic origin.

clawfoot (klaw′ foot) A deformity of the foot marked by an excessively high longitudinal arch, usually accompanied by dorsal contracture of the toes.

clawhand, claw hand (klo′hand″) A hand marked by hyperextension of the proximal phalanges of the digits and extreme flexion of the middle and distal phalanges. Usually it is caused by injury to the ulnar and median nerves. SYN: *main en griffe*.

Clean Air Act A federal law, enacted in 1956 and amended many times since then, that empowers the administration to protect the public health and welfare by defining and attempting to control atmospheric pollutants, including automotive and factory exhausts such as sulfur dioxide, nitrogen dioxide, carbon monoxide, particulates, and lead.

clean-catch method SEE: under *method*.

cleaning, ultrasonic (klēn'ĭng) The use of high-frequency vibrations to clean instruments.

Clean Water Act An act originally passed by the federal government in 1972, and since amended several times, that gives the Environmental Protection Agency (EPA) responsibility for developing criteria for water-quality standards and controlling and regulating pollutants discharged into water sources.

clear (klēr) **1.** A colloquial term used in cardiopulmonary resuscitation to warn nearby staff that a patient is about to receive an electrical shock (during cardioversion or defibrillation) and should not be in contact with another person, so that no one involved in the resuscitation will inadvertently be injured by the shock.

    PATIENT CARE: The protection of rescuers in a resuscitation is usually ensured by the person in charge of the code. He or she should methodically examine the safe position of all participants in the event and chant (while verifying that no one is in contact with the patient): "I'm clear. You're clear. We are all clear." Only after this should a shock be administered.

    2. To remove (something) from the body or from a body compartment or body fluid. **clearing,** *n.*

clearance (klēr'ăns) In medicine, the rate of removal of a substance from the body, e.g. in feces, the urine, sweat, or exhaled gases. SEE: *renal clearance test*.

    estimated creatinine c. ABBR: CrCl. The rate of the removal of creatinine from the serum by the kidney. SEE: *creatinine clearance test*.

    lactate c. The removal of accumulated lactic acid from the blood in patients with severe sepsis or shock. Rapid lactate clearance is associated with an increased likelihood of survival in critically ill patients.

    total c. **1.** The sum of the clearances from each organ or tissue participating in the elimination of a substance from the body. **2.** The volume or mass of tissue cleared of a substance divided by the time it takes to eliminate the substance from the body.

cleavage (klē'vĕj) [AS. *cleofian*, to cleave] **1.** Splitting a complex molecule into two or more simpler ones. **2.** The series of divisions of a fertilized egg into many smaller cells or blastomeres. SYN: *segmentation*. SEE: *blastomere; embryo*.

cleavage arrest SEE: under *arrest*.

cleavers (klē'vĕrz) One of several common names for the weed having the scientific name *Galium aparine*. SEE: *Galium aparine*.

cleft (kleft) **1.** A fissure or elongated opening. **2.** Divided or split.

    alveolar c. An anomaly resulting from lack of fusion between the medial nasal process and the maxillary process. A cleft maxillary alveolar process is usually associated with a cleft lip or palate or both.

    branchial c. An opening between the branchial arches of an embryo. In lower vertebrates it becomes a gill cleft. SYN: *branchial fissure*.

    facial c. An anomaly resulting from failure of the facial processes of the embryo to fuse. Common types are oblique facial cleft, an open nasolacrimal furrow extending from the eye to the lower portion of the nose that is sometimes continuous with a cleft in the upper lip, and transverse facial cleft, which extends laterally from the angle of the mouth.

    intratonsillar c. Supratonsillar fossa.

    pudendal c. In females, the slit between the labia majora.

    synaptic c. The synapse of a neuromuscular junction (between the axon terminal of a motor neuron and the sarcolemma of a muscle fiber). Impulse transmission is accomplished by a neurotransmitter.

cleft cheek Transverse facial cleft.

cleido-, cleid- [Gr. *kleis*, stem *kleid-*, key] Prefixes meaning *clavicle, clavicular*.

cleidotomy (klī-dŏt'ō-mē) [" + Gr. *tome*, incision] Division of a fetal clavicle to facilitate delivery.

clenbuterol (klĕn-bū'tĕr-ŏl) A beta-2 agonist drug formerly used by veterinarians to promote animal growth. It has been used by athletes as a doping agent to increase muscle mass. It is also occasionally used to dilute illicit drugs such as heroin. Its toxicities include tachycardia, palpitations, hyperglycemia, hypokalemia, and chest pain.

clenching (klĕnch'ĭng) **1.** Forcible, repeated contraction of the jaw muscles with the teeth in contact. This causes pulsating, bilateral contractions of the temporalis and pterygomasseteric muscles. It may be done consciously, subconsciously while awake, or during sleep. SEE: *bruxism*. **2.** Tightly closing the fist.

clerkship (klĕrk'shĭp") A clinical experience in the education of a student of the health professions in which he or she is introduced to the practical care of patients with particular illnesses or characteristics.

CLIA (klē'ä) *Clinical Laboratory Improvement Amendments* (the U.S. legal amendments regulating and overseeing privately run medical laboratories).

click (klĭk) **1.** An abrupt, brief sound heard in listening to the heart sounds. **2.** Any brief sound but esp. one heard during a joint movement. **3.** In dentistry, a noise associated with temporomandibular joint movement, sometimes accompanied by pain or joint dysfunction.

client (klī′ĕnt) The patient of a health care professional.

client-centered approach Emphasis on a patient's or client's autonomy and right to choose goals and/or interventions based on his or her identified needs for services. SYN: *client-centered therapy.* SEE: *Patient's Bill of Rights.*

client-centered therapy Client-centered approach.

client server Network architecture that places commonly used resources on centrally accessible computers for retrieval by any individual with access to the network.

climacteric (klī-măk′tĕr-ĭk, klī-mak′tĕ-rik, klī″mak″ter′ik) [L. *climactericus,* fr Gr. *klimaktērikos,* pert. to a rung of a ladder, pert. to a critical point or turning point] In females, menopause; in males, the corresponding period of diminished sexual arousal and activity. SEE: *menopause.*

climatology, medical (klī″mă-tŏl′ō-jē) [Gr. *klima,* sloping surface of the earth, + *logos,* word, reason] The branch of meteorology that includes the study of climate and its relationship to disease. SEE: *bioclimatology.*

climatotherapy (klī″măt-ō-thĕr′ăp-ē) [″ + *therapeia,* treatment] Treatment of disease by having the patient move to a specialized climate; historically used in the treatment of diseases like tuberculosis (cold, wintry air was thought to contribute to cure).

climax (klī′măks) [Gr. *klimax,* ladder] **1.** The period of greatest intensity. **2.** The sexual orgasm.

clinic (klin′ik) [Gr. *klinikos,* pert. to a bed] **1.** A center for physical examination and treatment of ambulatory patients. **2.** Medical and dental instruction in which patients are observed directly, symptoms noted, and treatments discussed. **3.** A center where preliminary diagnosis is made and treatment given, e.g., an x-ray clinic, dental clinic, or child-guidance clinic.

    free medical c. A clinic that provides medical care without expecting payment for services. A free clinic typically combines medical services with patient education, patient empowerment, and social work.

    group medical c. Shared medical appointment.

    sex c. A clinic for the diagnosis and treatment of sexual dysfunction.

    walk-in c. A general medical care clinic open to those who do not have an appointment.

clinical (klĭn′ ĭ-kăl) **1.** Founded on actual observation and treatment of patients as distinguished from data or facts ob-

tained from other sources. **2.** Pert. to a clinic.

clinical cooperative group SEE: under *group.*

clinical data repository A computer platform that stores and consolidates data for real-time access to information about patients and patient care from a variety of internal systems.

clinical decision support system ABBR: CDSS. Interactive computer programs directly assisting physicians and other health professionals with decision-making tasks. CDSS is either a rule-based or a normative automated system consisting of a variety of elements, ranging from simple alert systems to sophisticated longitudinal administrative and clinical reporting applications. It employs evidence-based or statistically significant best-practice guidelines and alerts to promote better clinical choices and outcomes.

clinical ecology A form of medical practice based on two concepts: that a broad range of environmental chemicals and foods can cause symptoms of illness (such as malaise, fatigue, dizziness, joint discomfort) and that the immune system is functionally depressed by exposure to many synthetic chemicals in the workplace, the home, or contemporary agricultural products. The premise of clinical ecology is that these exposures are toxic or that they trigger hypersensitivity reactions, or environmental illness.

clinical education SEE: under *education.*

clinical incidence rate The number of instances of a disease divided by the number of people at risk.

clinical information system ABBR: CIS. Hospital information system.

clinical judgment The exercise of clinical knowledge and experience in the diagnosis and treatment of patients. SEE: *decision analysis.*

Clinical Linguistic and Auditory Milestone Scale SEE: under [1] *scale.*

clinically isolated syndrome A single episode of inflammation or demyelination of nerves within the central nervous system that suggests multiple sclerosis. Additional events confirm multiple sclerosis.

clinical messaging The sharing of patient information (such as laboratory or radiology reports) among health care personnel who use linked electronic medical record systems.

clinical nurse leader ABBR: CNL. A nurse who supervises and coordinates care for patients, using evidence-based methodologies to manage care plans. According to the American Association of Colleges of Nursing (AACN), the CNL requires educational preparation equal to or greater than a master's degree in nursing. Use of "CNL" also requires passing the associated certification examination. The CNL is a 2004 initiative of AACN and the Department of Veterans Affairs–Office of Nursing Services to improve the quality of patient care and prepare nurses to thrive in the health care system.

clinical pregnancy SEE: under *pregnancy*.

clinical reasoning The use of a patient's history, physical signs, symptoms, laboratory data, and radiological images to arrive at a diagnosis and formulate a plan of treatment.

clinical risk index for babies SEE: under *index*.

clinical simulation An educational model of a phenomenon or activity that allows students to rehearse behaviors without placing clients or institutional resources at risk.

PATIENT CARE: Simulation replaces or amplifies real patient experiences with guided experiences that mimic experiences that professionals may encounter during their daily work or during extraordinary circumstances. Simulations may be conducted using interactive audio or video, specially designed simulators, or live volunteer faculty members acting out predetermined scenarios. Simulated experiences may be followed by group discussions, debriefings, or more traditional forms of pedagogy.

clinical target volume SEE: under *volume*.

clinical trial SEE: under *trial*.

clinician (klĭn-ĭsh'ăn) [Gr. *klinikos*, pert. to a bed] A health professional with expertise in patient care rather than research or administration.

nonphysician c. Nonphysician **provider**.

clinicopathological (klĭn"ĭ-kō-pǎ"thō-lŏj'ĭk-ăl) Concerning clinical and pathological disease manifestations.

clinicopathological conference ABBR: CPC. A teaching conference in which clinical findings are presented to a physician previously unfamiliar with a case, who then attempts to diagnose the disease that would explain the clinical findings. The exact diagnosis is then presented by the pathologist, who has either examined the tissue removed at surgery or has performed the autopsy.

clinocephaly (klī"nō-sěf'ă-lē) [Gr. *klinein*, to bend, + *kephale*, head] Congenital flatness or saddle shape of the top of the head, caused by bilateral premature closure of the sphenoparietal sutures.

clinodactyly (klī"nō-dăk'tĭ-lē) [" + *daktylos*, finger] Hypoplasia of the middle phalanx of one or more of the fingers resulting in inward curving of these fingers.

clinoid (klī'noyd) [Gr. *kline*, bed, + *eidos*, form, shape] Shaped like a bed.

clinometer (klī-nŏm'ĕ-tĕr) [Gr. *klinein*, to slope, + *metron*, measure] An instrument formerly used for estimating torsional deviation of the eyes; used to measure ocular muscle paralysis.

clinoscope (klī'nō-skōp) Clinometer.

clip (klip) A device for holding or compressing tissues or other material together, e.g., after surgery; available in a variety of metals and slowly absorbed materials (e.g., polyglycolic acid).

clithrophobia (klĭth"rō-fō'bē-ă) [Gr. *kleithria*, keyhole, + *phobos*, fear] A morbid fear of being locked in.

clitoridectomy (klī"tō-rĭd-ĕk'tō-mē) [Gr. *kleitoris*, clitoris, + *ektome*, excision] Excision of the clitoris.

clitoriditis (klī"tō-rĭd-ī'tĭs) Clitoritis.

clitoridotomy (klī"tō-rĭd-ŏt'ō-mē) [" + *tome*, incision] Incision of the clitoris; female circumcision.

clitoris (klĭt'ă-rĭs, klĭ-tōr'ĭs) [Gr. *kleitoris*] One of the structures of the female genitalia; a small erectile body located beneath the anterior labial commissure and partially hidden by the anterior portion of the labia minora.

STRUCTURE: It consists of three parts: a body, two crura, and a glans. The body, about 1 in (2.5 cm) long, consists of two fused corpora cavernosa. It extends from the pubic arch above to the glans below. The two crura are continuations of the corpora cavernosa and attach them to the inferior rami of the pubic bones. They are covered by the ischiocavernosus muscles. The glans, which forms the free distal end, is a small rounded tubercle composed of erectile tissue. It is highly sensitive. The glans is usually covered by a hoodlike prepuce, and its ventral surface is attached to the frenulum of the labia.

clitorism (klī'tō-rĭzm) **1.** The counterpart of priapism; a long-continued, painful condition with recurring erection of the clitoris. **2.** Clitoral enlargement.

clitoritis (klī"tō-rī'tĭs) Inflammation of the clitoris. SYN: *clitoriditis*.

clitoromegaly (klī"tō-rō-měg'ă-lē) [" + *megas*, large] Clitoral enlargement. This may be caused by an endocrine disease or by use of anabolic steroids.

clivus (klī'vŭs) [L., a slope] A surface that slopes, as the sphenoid bone.

clo (klō) A unit for thermal insulation of clothing. It is the amount of insulation necessary to maintain comfort in a sitting-resting subject in a normally ventilated room (air movement at the rate of 10 cm/sec) at a temperature of 70°F (21°C) with relative humidity of less than 50%.

cloaca (klō-ā'kă) [L. *cloaca*, a sewer] **1.** A cavity lined with endoderm at the posterior end of the body that serves as a common passageway for urinary, digestive, and reproductive ducts. It exists in adult birds, reptiles, and amphibia, and in the embryos of all vertebrates. **2.** An opening in the sheath covering necrosed bone.

clock (klok) A device for measuring time.

    biological c. **1.** An internal system in organisms that influences behavior in a rhythmic manner. Functions such as growth, feeding, secretion of hormones, the rate of drug action, the wake-sleep cycle, the menstrual cycle, and reproduction coincide with certain external events such as day and night, the tides, and the seasons. Biological clocks appear to be set by environmental conditions in some animals, but if these animals are isolated from their environment they continue to function according to the usual rhythm. A gradual change in environment does produce a gradual change in the timing of the biological clock. SEE: *circadian; maladaptation to night work; zeitgeber.* **2.** A colloquial term for the decrease in fertility that accompanies aging, particularly as women approach the age of 35.

clock drawing test One of the mental status tests that assesses a person's ability to draw a complex, but frequently used, object. Persons with normal cognitive function and a normal sense of time can draw a clock face, place the hours 1 through 12 in appropriate positions, and insert the hands of the clock to demonstrate a particular time of day (e.g., "10:25"). Demented patients make several characteristic errors: the clock face may be poorly drawn; the hours may be spaced unevenly; and the hour and minute hands misplaced or left off the clock face entirely.

clonal restriction The occurrence of the same characteristics as the parent cell in all clones (offspring) of one B or T lymphocyte. For example, surface receptors are identical, so clones react to the same group of specific antigens as the parent cell does.

clonazepam (klō-năz′ĕ-păm) A benzodiazepine used to treat anxiety, panic, and seizure disorders.

clone (klōn) [Gr. *klōn*, a cutting used for propagation, twig] **1.** In microbiology, the asexual progeny of a single cell. **2.** A group of plants propagated from one seedling or stock. Members of the group are identical but do not reproduce from seed. **3.** In tissue culture or in the body, a group of cells descended from a single cell. The term often refers to the descendants of lymphocytes and to those of malignant cells. **4.** In immunology, a group of lymphocytes descended from a single sensitized T or B lymphocyte; they all respond to the same foreign antigen. **5.** In biology, the creation of an embryo from an unfertilized egg and the diploid nucleus of a somatic cell. With the full diploid number of chromosomes, the egg cell begins dividing as if fertilization had taken place. Clones of sheep, cows, cats, and many other animals have been produced. **clonal** (′ăl), *adj.*

clonicotonic (klŏn″ĭ-kō-tŏn′ĭk) [Gr. *klonos*, turmoil, + *tonikos*, tonic] Both clonic and tonic, as some forms of muscular spasm.

clonidine hydrochloride (klō′nĭ-dēn) A centrally acting alpha-agonist drug used to treat hypertension and opiate withdrawal.

clonorchiasis (klō″nor-kī′ă-sĭs) A disease caused by the Chinese liver fluke, *Clonorchis sinensis,* which infects the bile ducts of humans. Infection is caused by eating uncooked freshwater fish containing encysted larvae. Early symptoms are loss of appetite and diarrhea; later there may be signs of cirrhosis. The disease may be prevented by cooking fish thoroughly or by freezing it at −10°C (14°F) for a minimum of 5 days. The disease rarely causes death.

Clonorchis sinensis (klō-nor′kĭs sī-nĕn′sĭs) The Chinese liver fluke, an important cause of biliary disease, esp. in Asia.

clonospasm (klŏn′ō-spăzm) [″ + *spasmos*, spasm] Clonic spasm.

clonus (klō′nŭs) [L. *clonus,* fr Gr. *klonos,* turmoil, confusion] Spasmodic alternation of muscular contractions between antagonistic muscle groups caused by a hyperactive stretch reflex from an upper motor neuron lesion. Sustained pressure or stretch of one of the muscles usually inhibits the reflex.

    ankle c. Repetitive extension-flexion movement of the ankle muscles, associated with increased muscle tonus. It is a common symptom of corticospinal disease. **clonic** (klon′ik), *adj.* **clonicity** (klō-nis′ĭt-ē, klon-), *n.*

clopidogrel (clō-pĭd′ō-grĕl) A platelet aggregation inhibitor, administered orally to reduce the risk for atherosclerotic events (e.g., myocardial infarction, stroke, vascular death). Its therapeutic class is antiplatelet agent.

Cloquet, Jules G. (klō-kā′) Fr. anatomist, 1790–1883.

    C. fascia Fascia surrounding the femoral ring.

    C. hernia A type of crural hernia. SEE: *crural* **hernia***.*

closed record The completed medical chart of a patient, either after discharge from care or after the patient's death.

Clostridium (klos-trid′ē-ŭm) [Gr. *kloster,* spindle] A genus of gram-positive, anaerobic, spore-forming bacilli in the family Bacillaceae. The genus comprises more than 250 species that are inhabitants of soil, water, and the intestinal tracts of humans and animals. Many species are pathogenic in humans, including those that colonize dead tissue, secrete numerous proteolytic enzymes, and cause gas gangrene.

C. baratii A species in which some strains produce a neurotoxin that causes botulism.

C. botulinum The species that causes most cases of botulism. Under anaerobic conditions, the bacteria produce a neurotoxin that causes paralysis by blocking the release of acetylcholine at neuromuscular junctions. SEE: *botulism*.

C. butyricum A species in which some strains produce a neurotoxin that causes botulism.

C. chauvoei The organism causing blackleg or symptomatic anthrax in cattle.

C. difficile ABBR: C. diff. A species that causes watery diarrhea, fever, anorexia, and abdominal pain, sometimes accompanied by pseudomembranous colitis, esp. in patients previously treated with antibiotics or confined in health care settings. Most antibiotics (except aminoglycosides) have been associated with the development of C. diff.-associated disease, which varies in clinical significance from a relatively mild diarrheal illness, to one complicated by dehydration, electrolyte disturbances, toxic megacolon, and death.

PATIENT CARE: Outbreaks of C. diff. are found in many health care institutions, including nursing homes and hospitals. To prevent the spread of the disease in these facilities, staff should practice scrupulous hand hygiene, and patients affected by diarrheal illnesses should be isolated. Gowns and gloves should be worn by personnel attending infected patients. Linens should be disinfected, and other infection control practices followed. Surfaces potentially contaminated by clostridial spores should be treated with hypochlorite bleaches as a disinfectant. Personal patient care items should not be shared or re-used. Mild to moderately infected patients typically improve with the oral administration of metronidazole or vancomycin, although more severely ill patients may need infusions of vancomycin directly into the gastrointestinal tract. Patients with toxic megacolon may need surgery to remove damaged bowel. Fluid support intravenously, and other elements of general supportive care also apply. SEE: *pseudomembranous colitis*.

C. histolyticum A species found in cases of gas gangrene.

C. novyi A species found in many cases of gas gangrene.

C. perfringens The most common causative agent of gas gangrene. SYN: *C. welchii; gas bacillus*.

C. septicum A species found in cases of gangrene in humans, as well as in cattle, hogs, and other domestic animals.

C. sordellii A species that may cause anaerobic infections in bones, joints, soft tissues, the uterus, and elsewhere.

C. sporogenes A species frequently associated with other organisms in mixed gangrenous infections.

C. tetani The species that causes tetanus. SEE: *tetanus*.

C. welchii C. *C. perfringens*.

Clostridium botulinum C2 (boch″ĭ-lī′nŭm) A two-component protein toxin released by *C. botulinum*. One part of this binary toxin binds to receptors on the surface of cells, which permits the second component of the toxin to catalyze the destruction of the cytoskeleton.

closure (klō′shŭr) **1.** Shutting or bringing together as in suturing together the edges of a laceration wound. **2.** In psychotherapy, the resolution of an issue that was a topic in therapy and a cause of distress for the patient.

clot (klot) [Old English *clott*, lump] **1.** A mass with a jelly-like or semi-solid consistency. **2.** To coagulate.

agonal c. A clot formed in the heart after death.

antemortem c. A clot formed in the heart or its cavities before death.

blood c. A mass formed when blood solidifies into a gel. SEE: *blood coagulation*.

chicken fat c. A yellow blood clot appearing to contain no erythrocytes.

currant jelly c. A soft red postmortem blood clot found in the heart and vessels.

distal c. A clot formed in a vessel on the distal side of a ligature.

external c. A clot formed outside a blood vessel.

internal c. A clot formed by coagulation of blood within a vessel.

laminated c. A clot formed in a succession of layers filling an aneurysm.

muscle c. A clot formed in muscle tissue.

passive c. A clot formed in the sac of an aneurysm.

postmortem c. A clot formed in the heart or in a blood vessel after death.

proximal c. A clot formed on the proximal side of a ligature.

stratified c. A clot consisting of layers of different colors. SEE: *coagulation, blood; factor, coagulation; thrombosis*.

CLO test *Campylobacter*-like organism test; an assay to determine the presence of urea-splitting organisms in the upper gastrointestinal tract. The test is one of several used to diagnose whether or not ulcers or gastritis are caused by *Helicobacter pylori*.

clothing [AS. *clath*, cloth] Wearing apparel; used both functionally and decoratively. From the medical standpoint, clothes conserve heat or protect the body (e.g., gloves, sunhelmets, and shoes). Air spaces in a fabric and its texture, rather than the material alone, conserve heat. In matted woolen fabrics, the air spaces are destroyed and insulation is lost. Wool and silk absorb more moisture than other fabrics, but silk loses it more readily. Cotton and linen come next, but linen loses moisture more quickly than cotton. Knitted fabrics absorb and dry more readily than woven fabrics of the same material. The temperature inside an individual's hat may vary from 13° to 20°F (7° to 11°C) warmer than the outside temperature.

    adapted c. Garments designed with special features, such as Velcro closures, to enable persons with disabilities to dress themselves without assistance. SEE: *clo; hypothermia*.

clotrimazole (klō-trĭm′ă-zōl) An over-the-counter antifungal drug used to treat athlete's foot and other fungal skin infections, including vulvovaginal candidiasis. Intravaginal use occasionally causes burning, redness, and itching in the patient, her sex partner, or both.

clotting (klŏt′ĭng) The formation of a jelly-like plug made of platelets and plasma proteins. The plug usually stops the flow of blood. SEE: *coagulation, blood*.

clouding (klowd′ĭng) **1.** Making, becoming, or being unclear or incoherent. **2.** Making obscure or indistinct.

cloven spine Congenital defect of spinal canal walls caused by lack of union between laminae of the vertebrae. SYN: *spina bifida cystica*.

clove oil [L. *clavus,* a nail or spike] A volatile oil distilled from the dried flower buds of the clove tree, *Eugenia caryophyllus*. It is used as an antiseptic and an aromatic and is applied directly to relieve pain in teeth.

clozapine (klō′ză-pēn″) A dopamine receptor–blocking drug used to treat psychosis.

cloze (klōz) [Abbrev. of *closure*] A sentence completion test used in speech and language pathology in which a word is deleted from a sentence and the person being tested is asked to fill in the blank with an appropriate term.

CLRT *Continuous lateral rotation therapy.*

CLU *Clusterin.*

clubbing (klŭb′ĭng) An enlarged terminal phalanx of the finger. Excessive growth of the soft tissues of the ends of the fingers gives the fingers a sausage or drumstick appearance when viewed from above, and a beaked appearance when viewed from the side. Increased soft tissue is deposited beneath the cuticle, resulting in a fingertip that is thinner at the distal interphalangeal joint than at the base of the nail. Clubbing may be present in chronic obstructive pulmonary disease, interstitial fibrosis of the lungs, cyanotic congenital heart disease, carcinoma of the lung, bacterial endocarditis, and many other illnesses. SYN: *clubbed finger; hippocratic finger*. SEE: illus.

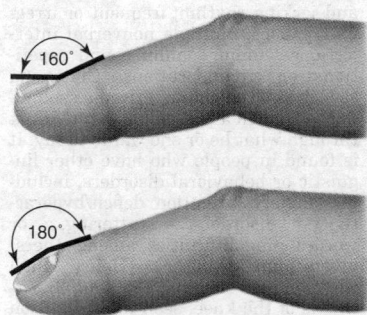

FINGERNAIL CLUBBING

club drug SEE: under *drug*.

clubfoot Talipes equinovarus.

clubhand A deformity of the hand in which it is twisted out of position.

clump (klŭmp) [AS. *clympre,* a lump] **1.** A mass of bacteria in solution; may be caused by an agglutination reaction. **2.** To gather together.

clumping (klŭmp′ĭng) Agglutination.

cluster (klŭs′tĕr) A closely grouped series of events, e.g., cases of a disease, with well-defined distribution patterns in relation to time, place, or risk factor exposure.

    cancer c. The occurrence of many cancers in a small geographical area or a defined population in much greater numbers than would be expected through chance alone.

    c. of differentiation ABBR: CD. Any of a group of cell surface protein markers on the white blood cells. These markers are used to classify immune cell types and establish international nomenclature standards. The markers are found on many blood cells and some nonblood cells but are used most often to refer to lymphocytes. The markers may be identified by specific monoclonal antibodies and are used to designate cell populations, e.g., CD4 lymphocytes as T helper cells, and CD8 lymphocytes as suppressor T cells. Each marker has a specific function in the cell, such as passing a signal from the T-cell receptor to the cytoplasm. Particular CDs are followed by numbers (CD2, CD3, etc.) and are so listed. SEE: e.g., *CD2; CD7; CD68*. SEE: *T cell*.

    suicide c. An epidemic of suicides, within a defined location or a short time.

clusterin (klŭs'tĕ-rĭn) [*cluster* + *-in*] ABBR: CLU. A multifunctional cell-protective glycoprotein (molecular weight 75-80 kDa) found in many tissues. High levels of CLU are found in cells undergoing apoptosis. SYN: *apolipoprotein J*.

cluttering (klŭt'ĕr-ĭng) A disorder of speech fluency, characterized by speech that has an abnormal, often rapid pace and jerking rhythm; frequent or irregular pauses; multiple nonverbal interjections ("umm," "ahhh"); and repetitions or circumlocutions. Cluttering speech is often characterized as sounding as though a person has not thought through what he or she wants to say. It is found in people who have other linguistic or behavioral disorders, including anxiety, attention deficit/hyperactivity disorders, stuttering, or word-finding difficulties, among others.

Clutton joint (klŭt'ŏn) [Henry Hugh Clutton, Brit. surgeon, 1850–1909] Arthritis of the knee, seen in conjunction with keratitis in congenital syphilis.

clysis (klī'sĭs) *pl.* **clyses** [Gr. *klyzein*, to cleanse] Injection of fluid into the body other than orally. Fluid may be injected into tissue spaces, the rectum, or the abdominal cavity. This technique is used to inject fluids parenterally when venipuncture is not possible. SEE: *enteroclysis; venoclysis*.

-clysis [Gr. *klysis*, washing, flushing] Suffix meaning *washing*.

CM *Certified Midwife*.

c/m *counts per minute*.

cm *Centimeter*.

Cm Symbol for the element curium.

cm² *Square **centimeter***.

cm³ *Cubic **centimeter***.

CMA *Canadian Medical Association; Certified Medication Aide; Certified Medical Assistant*.

C_max Maximum concentration of a drug achieved after dosing.

CMI *cell-mediated immunity*.

c/min *counts per minute*.

c.mm. *cubic millimeter*. This symbol (also, mm³) is no longer accepted usage in health care.

CMMS *Columbia Mental Maturity Scale*.

CMN *Curcumin*.

CMRR *common mode rejection ratio*.

CMS *Circulation, motion, sensation*.

CMS 1500 The billing form used by the Center for Medicare Services (CMS) for all claims made by physicians and other providers of health care services.

CMT *certified medical transcriptionist; certified medication technician*.

CMV *continuous mandatory ventilation; cytomegalovirus*.

CN *cyanogen*.

CNA *Canadian Nurses' Association; Certified Nursing Assistant*.

Cnidaria (nī-dar'ē-ă) [L. *cnide* fr Gr. *knidē*, nettle] The phylum of aquatic species that contain stinging cells to defend themselves or injure prey. The phylum includes the box jellyfish and Portuguese man-of-war species and thousands of others.

CNM *Certified Nurse Midwife*.

CNRN *Certified Neuroscience Registered Nurse*.

CNS *central nervous system; clinical nurse specialist; coagulase-negative staphylococci; Congress of Neurological Surgeons*.

CO Formula for carbon monoxide; *cardiac output*.

Co Symbol for the element cobalt.

CO₂ Formula for carbon dioxide.

Co1 *coccygeal spinal nerve*.

CoA *coenzyme A*.

coach (kōch) To provide suggestions, feedback, direction, training, and redirection to another person or to a group or team to improve the ability to perform a task well. **2.** One who provides such suggestions, feedback, direction, or training.

    health c. One who educates, encourages, and motivates another to achieve improved fitness or wellness.

coach's finger SEE: under *finger*.

coadaptation (kō"ăd-ăp-tā'shŭn) Mutual adaptation of two independent organisms, organs, or persons.

coadministration (cō"ăd-mĭn-ĭstrā'shŭn) The giving of two or more therapeutic agents at the same time.

coagglutination (kō"ă-gloo"tĭn-ā'shŭn) [L. *coagulare*, to curdle] Use of latex or other inert particles to which an antibody will bind in laboratory tests of agglutination.

coagula (kō-ăg'ū-lă) [L.] Pl. of coagulum.

coagulability (kō-ăg"ū-lă-bĭl'ĭ-tē) The capacity to form clots, esp. blood clots.

coagulable (kō-ăg'ū-lă-b'l) Capable of clotting; likely to clot.

coagulant (kō-ăg'ū-lănt) [L. *coagulans,* congealing] **1.** Something that causes a fluid to coagulate. **2.** Causing coagulation.

coagulase (kō-ăg'ū-lāz) [L. *coagulum,* blood clot] Any enzyme, such as thrombin, that causes coagulation.

coagulate (kō-ăg'ū-lāt) [L. *coagulare,* to congeal] To solidify; to change from a fluid state to a semisolid mass. **coagulated** (kō-ăg'ū-lāt-ĕd), *adj*.

coagulation (kō-ag"yŭ-lā'shŏn) [L. *coagulatio,* clotting] The thickening of a liquid into a gel or solid.

    argon plasma c. ABBR: APC. The destruction of tissues with heat generated by applying an electrical current to an argon plasma. The plasma distributes heat to a minimal depth so that only superficial structures are coagulated while deeper ones remain undisturbed. APC is used in several applications, e.g., in the destruction of some superficial cancers and in the treatment of some stenoses that have formed within normally hollow organs, such as the trachea.

blood c. The clumping together of blood cells to form a clot. This may occur in vitro, intravascularly, or when a laceration of the skin allows the escape of blood from an artery, vein, or capillary. Coagulation of blood may occur in two pathways, depending on the beginning of the process.

Extrinsic: The extrinsic pathway (in an abbreviated outline form) requires the blood to be exposed to a subendothelial tissue factor originating outside the blood. This factor begins a complex series of chemical reactions involving thromboplastin, factor VII, and calcium; binding to factor X, causing its conversion to factor Xa; and the resulting conversion of prothrombin to thrombin to fibrinogen and eventually fibrin.

Intrinsic: The intrinsic pathway (in abbreviated outline form) occurs when blood is drawn without contamination by tissue factor. This clotting pathway does not require an additive. It is triggered when the blood is exposed to a foreign surface and factor XII is activated. Factor XII may also be activated through limited cleavage by kallikrein. This process is accelerated by high-molecular-weight kininogen (HMWK). This leads to formation of factor XII, a process that produces more HMWK to accelerate kallikrein production. The process continues and factors XI and IX, and HMWK, in concert with calcium, generate factor Xa. The clotting cascade then continues as in the extrinsic pathway, and prothrombin is converted to thrombin, which acts on fibrinogen to produce fibrin. SEE: *coagulation factor*.

☞ **disseminated   intravascular   c.** ABBR: DIC. A life-threatening disease occurring as a complication of other conditions in which the coagulation pathways are hyperstimulated, resulting in diffuse rather than localized activation of coagulation factors. The accelerated clotting occludes small blood vessels (usually in the kidneys and extremities, but sometimes in the brain, lungs, pituitary and adrenal glands, and GI mucosa), resulting in organ necrosis. Clotting factors are consumed to such an extent that generalized bleeding may occur. SEE: *acute respiratory distress syndrome; hypofibrinogenemia; sepsis; serine protease inhibitor; systemic inflammatory response syndrome; Nursing Diagnoses Appendix.*

ETIOLOGY: DIC usually occurs acutely but may be a chronic condition in cancer patients. Various conditions have been associated with DIC, including sepsis; extensive burns or other trauma; pancreatitis; acute intravascular hemolysis; gram-negative or gram-positive septicemia; acute viral, rickettsial, or protozoal infection; abruptio placentae, septic abortion, and other obstetric complications; surgical procedures; heatstroke; certain poisonous snake bites; severe head injury; malignancy; retained dead fetus; liver disease; incompatible blood transfusion; and systemic lupus erythematosus.

SYMPTOMS: Symptoms of DIC include bleeding from surgical or invasive procedure sites and from the GI tract, oral cavity, nose, or urinary tract. The patient may also experience nausea and vomiting; dyspnea; severe muscle, back, and abdominal pain; chest pain; hemoptysis; epistaxis; seizures; and oliguria. Peripheral pulses and blood pressure may be decreased, and the patient may demonstrate confusion or other changes in mental status.

TREATMENT: The underlying illness must be recognized and treated promptly. In some cases, depending on the cause, heparins or antithrombin III may be administered; patients may receive transfusional support (blood, cryoprecipitate, fresh frozen plasma, packed RBCs, or platelets).

PATIENT CARE: In acute DIC, intake and output are monitored hourly, esp. when blood products are given, and the patient is observed for transfusion reactions and fluid overload. The blood pressure cuff is used infrequently to avoid triggering subcutaneous bleeding. Any emesis, drainage, urine, or stool should undergo a test for occult blood, and dressings and linens should be weighed to measure the amount of blood lost. Daily weights are obtained, particularly in cases of renal involvement. The patient is observed closely for signs of shock, and the abdominal girth measured every 2 to 4 hr if intra-abdominal bleeding is suspected.

The results of serial blood studies (e.g., hemoglobin, hematocrit, and coagulation studies) are monitored. All venipuncture sites are checked frequently for bleeding. Analgesics are given as prescribed, as well as heparin therapy, if prescribed (the latter is controversial). The patient is repositioned every 2 hr, and meticulous skin care is provided. Prescribed oxygen therapy is administered. Areas at risk can be washed gently with hydrogen peroxide and water to remove crusted blood. Pressure, cold compresses, and topical hemostatic agents are applied to control bleeding. Parenteral injections are avoided and venipunctures limited whenever possible; pressure should be applied to an injection site for at least 20 min after removal of a needle or intravenous catheter. The patient is protected from injury by enforcement of complete bedrest during bleeding episodes and by padding the bed rails if the patient is at risk for agitation. Frequent rest periods are provided.

The disorder, the patient's progress, and treatment options and posttreatment appearance are explained, and the patient and family are encouraged to express their feelings and concerns and are referred for further counseling or support as needed.

coagulator (kō-ăg'ū-lāt"ŏr) **1.** A surgical device that utilizes electrical current, light energy, ultrasound, etc., to stop bleeding. **2.** A pharmacological substance used to induce hemostasis or solidification of proteinaceous fluids.

argon beam c., argon plasma coagulator A surgical instrument that uses radiofrequency current in an adjustable jet of argon gas to distribute heat that cuts or coagulates tissue. The jet disperses blood and debris from the targeted tissue. It is often employed during endoscopic procedures.

⚠ The patient must be grounded when using this electrosurgical device.

infrared c. A surgical instrument that focuses infrared light energy to cut or damage tissues or to stop bleeding. The device has been used in skin surgery, hair transplantation, ablation of abnormal cardiac conduction pathways, and treatment of internal hemorrhoids, among other applications.

microwave c. A surgical instrument that focuses microwave energy through an antenna to cut or cauterize tissue. The device can be used in open or laparoscopic surgeries.

coagulometer (kō-ag"yŭ-lom"ĕt-ĕr) [*coagul(ate)* + *-meter*] A device that measures the time it takes for a sample of blood to clot. It is often used in point-of-care testing, esp. in monitoring and adjusting warfarin dosages for anticoagulated patients.

coagulopathy (kō-ag"yŭ-lop'ă-thē) [*coagul(ation)* + *-pathy*] A defect in blood-clotting mechanisms. SEE: *coagulation, blood.*

consumption c. Disseminated intravascular coagulation.

dilutional c. Depletion of clotting factors that results from major hemorrhage followed by massive transfusion with red blood cells.

coagulum (kō-ăg'ū-lŭm) *pl.* **coagula** [L. *coagulatio,* clotting] A coagulated mass, clot, or precipitate.

coalesce (kō-ăl-ĕs') [L. *coalescere*] To fuse; to run or grow together.

coalescence (kō-ă-lĕs'ĕns) **1.** The fusion or growing together of two or more body parts. **2.** The mixture or combination of fluids or particles. **3.** In speech, the blurring of two verbal sounds together, sometimes in a way that makes them unintelligible.

coal worker's pneumoconiosis ABBR: CWP. Black lung.

coapt (kō'ăpt) [L. *coaptare,* to fit together] To bring together, as in suturing a laceration.

coaptation (kō"ăp-tā'shŭn) [L. *coaptare,* to fit together] The adjustment of separate parts to each other, as the edges of fractures.

CoARC (kō'ărk") *Committee on Accreditation for Respiratory Care.*

coarctate (kō-ărk'tāt) [L. *coarctare,* to tighten] To press together; pressed together.

coarctation (kō"ark-tā'shŏn) [L. *coar(c)tatio,* a crowding together] **1.** Compression of the walls of a vessel. **2.** Shriveling. **3.** A stricture.

c. of the aorta A localized congenital malformation resulting in narrowing of the aorta, often resulting in hypertension in adolescents and young adults. On physical assessment, it produces a delayed pulse in the femoral arteries relative to the pulse perceived at the radial arteries. Chest x-rays may show rib notching. Surgical correction of the obstruction may cure high blood pressure.

coarctotomy (kō"ărk-tŏt'ō-mē) [" + Gr. *tome,* incision] Cutting or dividing of a stricture.

COart (kō'ărt") Cardiac output, measured by thermodilution methods in the aorta.

coat [L. *cotta,* a tunic] A covering or a layer in the wall of a tubular structure, as the inner coat (tunica intima), middle coat (tunica media), or outer coat (tunica adventitia) of an artery.

coating (kōt'ĭng) **1.** A layer applied to or covering a surface. **2.** A film.

Coats disease (kōts) [George Coats, Brit. ophthalmologist, 1876–1915] A congenital, unilateral nonhereditary disorder of the retina characterized by aneurysmal dilation of blood vessels with prominent subretinal exudate. This term is used to describe at least six separate retinal disorders.

cobalamin (kō-băl'ă-mĭn) Another name for vitamin B_{12}, a complex molecule containing one atom of cobalt. SEE: *cyanocobalamin.*

cobalt (kō'balt") [Ger. *Kobalt*] SYMB: Co. A hard, gray, ductile, metallic element, atomic mass (weight) 59.933, atomic number 27, specific gravity 8.9. Cobalt deficiency causes anemia in ruminants, but this has not been demonstrated in humans. Cobalt is an essential element in vitamin B_{12}. Cobalt stimulates production of red blood cells, but its use as a therapeutic agent is not advised. In children, cobalt overdose may cause death. In adults, it may cause anorexia, nausea, vomiting, deafness, and thyroid hyperplasia with resultant compression of the trachea.

cobalt-57 A radioactive isotope of cobalt with a half-life of 272 days.

cobalt-60 A radioactive isotope of cobalt, having a half-life of 5.27 years. It formerly served as a source of beta and gamma rays in radiation units used to treat malignancies. Modern radiation units have replaced cobalt-60 by higher-energy sources, e.g., linear accelerators.

cobalt machine A radiation therapy unit that uses the gamma rays emitted by radioactive cobalt-60 isotopes to treat the relatively shallow cancers of the head and neck (and other regions of the body).

Coban Trade name for a self-adherent compression bandage used for protection and edema control. Also called *Coban wrap.*

Cobb angle (kob) [J.R. Cobb, 20th-cent. U.S. orthopedic surgeon] The angle formed by the intersection of two lines drawn on a spinal radiograph of a person (usually a child or adolescent) suspected of having scoliosis. One line is drawn parallel to the lower surface of the lowest affected vertebral body, and the other is drawn parallel to the upper surface of the highest affected body. Angles of greater than 10% are diagnostic of scoliosis.

COBRA (kō'brǎ) *Consolidated Omnibus Reconciliation Act.*

cobra (kō'brǎ) [Fr Portuguese *cobra (de capello),* (hooded) snake] Any of a group of poisonous snakes of the genera *Naja, Ophiophagus* and other genera, native to parts of Africa, Asia, and Australia. SEE: *Naja; Ophiophagus.*

COCA *color, odor, consistency, amount* (for assessing drainage from the body).

coca (kō'kǎ) Dried leaves of the shrub *Erythroxylum coca,* from which several alkaloids including cocaine are obtained.

cocaine (kō-kān') Cocaine hydrochloride.

cocaine baby SEE: under *baby.*

cocaine hydrochloride (kō-kān', kō'kān) The hydrochloride of an alkaloid obtained from the shrub *Erythroxylum coca,* native to Bolivia and Peru and cultivated extensively in South America. Cocaine is classed as a drug of abuse when used for nonmedical purposes. Street names for cocaine include snow, coke, crack, lady, flake, gold dust, green gold, blow, and toot. Medically it is used as a topical anesthetic applied to mucous membranes. SYN: *cocaine.* SEE: *crack; free base; freebasing.*

cocaine hydrochloride poisoning, acute SEE: under *poisoning.*

cocainism (kō'kān-ĭzm) The habitual use of cocaine. SEE: *cocaine hydrochloride poisoning, acute.*

cocainization (kō-kān″ĭ-zā'shŏn) The use of cocaine to induce analgesia.

cocarboxylase (kō″kăr-bŏk'sĭ-lās) Thiamine pyrophosphate.

cocarcinogen (kō-kăr'sĭ-nō-jěn″) A chemical or environmental factor that enhances the action of a carcinogen, the end result being the development of a malignancy.

cocci (kŏk'sī) Pl. of coccus.

Coccidia (kŏk-sĭd'ē-ă) [Gr. *kokkos,* berry] A subclass of the phylum Apicomplexa (apical microtubule complex) of the kingdom Protista. All are intracellular parasites usually infecting epithelial cells of the intestine and associated glands.

coccidian (kŏk-sĭd'ē-ăn) **1.** Pert. to Coccidia. **2.** Any member of the order Coccidia.

Coccidioides (kok″sid″ē-oyd'ēz) A genus of pathogenic fungi with two species, *Coddidiodes immitis* and *C. posadasii. Coddidiodes immitis* and *C. posadasii* are thermally dimorphic fungi found in soil particularly in warm and dry areas with low rain fall, high summer temperatures, and low altitude. The two species are morphologically identical but genetically and epidemiologically distinct. *C. immitis* is geographically limited to California's San Joaquin valley region, whereas *C. posadasii* is found in the desert southwest of the U.S., Mexico, and South America. The two species appear to co-exist in the desert southwest and Mexico. Both cause coccidioidomycosis.

coccidioidin (kŏk″sĭd-ē-oy'dĭn) An antigenic substance prepared from *Coccidioides immitis.* It is used as a skin test in diagnosing coccidioidomycosis.

coccidioidomycosis (kok″sid″ē-oyd″ō-mī-kō'sĭs) [*Coccidioid(es)* + *mycosis*] Infection with any species of the genus *Coccidioides.* Arthroconidia (spores from the fungus) circulate in the air when the soil is disturbed, e.g., during construction, dust storms, or earthquakes. Those who inhale the spores may develop active or subclinical infection. SYN: *San Joaquin valley* **fever;** *valley* **fever.** SEE: *Nursing Diagnoses Appendix.*

Approx. 80% of people in the southwestern and western U.S. have positive skin test reactions, which identify those infected. The infection is common among migrant farm workers, construction workers, and others who disturb soil. Usually infection is asymptomatic and requires no treatment. In approx. 10% of patients, fever, cough, pleurisy, or rashes such as erythema multiforme occur. Granulomas may be seen on the chest x-ray of patients with fungal pneumonia. Systemic infection involving the skin and meninges of the brain with abscesses forming throughout the body occurs in less than 1% of patients but is often fatal. This disseminated form is more common in pregnant women and the immunosuppressed. Affected patients are treated with long-term fluconazole, itraconazole, ketoconazole, or with amphotericin B; these drugs have a 50% to 70% success rate.

DIAGNOSIS: Diagnostic testing for the disease includes collecting blood, sputum, pus from lesions, and tissue for biopsy, using strict secretion precautions. An initial skin test also is administered, as both the primary and disseminated forms produce a positive coccidioidin skin test. A rising serum or body fluid antibody titer indicates dissemination. Additional testing may involve pleural, spinal, and joint fluid for the presence of antibodies. After diagnosis, serial skin testing, blood cultures, and serological testing are performed to help document the effectiveness of therapy. The patient is cautioned not to wash off the circle marked on the skin for serial testing, as it aids in reading test results.

TREATMENT: Most patients with primary infection recover without therapy. Patients with disseminated disease may be treated with intravenous amphotericin, or with a variety of azole antifungals, such as fluconazole or voriconazole.

PROGNOSIS: For primary infection, the prognosis is favorable. Disseminated disease is often fatal.

PATIENT CARE: In mild primary disease, bedrest and adequate fluid intake are encouraged. The patient is monitored for shortness of breath. If arthralgia is present, prescribed analgesics are administered. Standard precautions are observed by health care professionals. If the patient has draining lesions, the patient and family are taught about strict secretion precautions, including the "no touch" dressing technique and careful hand hygiene. In central nervous system (CNS) dissemination, the patient is monitored closely for decreased level of consciousness or change in mood or affect.

Before intrathecal administration of amphotericin B, the procedure is explained to the patient, who is reassured that he or she will receive a local anesthetic before lumbar puncture. If the patient is prescribed amphotericin B intravenously, a test dose is administered as prescribed; if tolerated, the treatment dose is infused slowly (rapid infusion may result in circulatory collapse). The dosage (but not the rate) is increased gradually as prescribed. During the infusion, the patient's vital signs are monitored. Temperature may rise

and the patient may experience shaking chills and hypotension 1 to 2 hr after the infusion is initiated, but these should subside within 4 hr after the infusion is completed. Fluid intake and output are assessed, with any oliguria or anuria noted. Laboratory results are evaluated for elevated blood urea nitrogen and creatinine levels and hypokalemia. To ease adverse reactions to amphotericin B, antiemetics, antihistamines, and antipyretics or small doses of corticosteroids are administered as prescribed. The patient is warned to report immediately any hearing loss, tinnitus, dizziness, headache, blurred vision, diplopia, and breathing difficulty. Laboratory findings are also monitored for blood dyscrasias and liver failure. The patient is monitored for any seizures, cardiac arrhythmias, respiratory distress, hemorrhagic gastroenteritis, drug extravasation, and anaphylactoid reactions. The patient is informed that therapy may take several months, and the importance of cooperating with the treatment regimen and recommended follow-up studies is emphasized.

coccidiosis (kŏk-sĭd-ē-ō′sĭs) [″ + *osis,* condition] Any disease resulting from infestation with Coccidia. SEE: *Coccidia.*

Coccinia indica (kŏk-sĭn′ē-ă ĭn-dĭ′kă) The climbing ivy gourd, used in ayruvedic medicine to treat diabetes mellitus. Ingestion of an extract made from its dried leaves, often mixed with the dried roots of *Abroma augusta,* lowers blood sugars.

coccobacilli (kŏk″ō-bă-sĭl′ī) Bacilli that are short, thick, and somewhat ovoid. SEE: *bacterium* for illus.

coccobacteria (kŏk″ō-băk-tē′rē-ă) **1.** Spherical-shaped bacteria. **2.** Any kind of cocci.

coccogenous (kŏk-ŏj′ĕn-ŭs) [Gr. *kokkos,* berry, + *gennan,* to produce] Produced by cocci.

coccoid (kŏk′oyd) [″ + *eidos,* form, shape] Resembling a micrococcus.

coccus (kok′ŭs) *pl.* **cocci** [L. *coccus,* fr Gr. *kokkos,* berry] A bacterial type that is spherical or ovoid. When cocci appear singly, they are designated *micrococci;* in pairs, *diplococci;* in clusters like bunches of grapes, *staphylococci;* in chains, *streptococci;* in cubical packets of eight, *sarcinae.* Many are pathogenic, causing such diseases as strep throat, erysipelas, scarlet fever, rheumatic fever, pneumonia, gonorrhea, meningitis, and puerperal fever. **coccal** (′ăl), *adj.* SEE: *bacterium.*

coccyalgia, coccydynia (kŏk″sē-ăl′jē-ă, kŏk″sē-dĭn′ē-ă) [Gr. *kokkyx,* coccyx, + *algos,* pain, + *odyne,* pain] Pain in the coccyx. SYN: *coccygodynia.*

coccygeal (kŏk-sĭj′ē-ăl) Pert. to or in the region of the coccyx.

coccygeal body SEE: under *body*.

coccygeal nerve The lowest of the spinal nerves; one of the pair of nerves arising from the coccygeal section of the spinal cord and entering the pudendal plexus.

coccygectomy (kŏk″sĭ-jĕk′tō-mē) [″ + *ektome,* excision] Surgical excision of the coccyx.

coccygeus (kŏk-sĭj′ē-ŭs) Pert. to the coccyx.

coccygodynia (kŏk-sĭ-gō-dĭn′ē-ă) [″ + *odyne,* pain] Coccyalgia.

coccyx (kŏk′sĭks) [Gr. *kokkyx,* coccyx] A small bone at the base of the spinal column in humans, formed by four fused rudimentary vertebrae. It is usually ankylosed and articulated with the sacrum above.

cochineal (kŏch′ĭn-ēl) [L. *coccinus,* scarlet] A dried female insect, *Coccus cacti,* previously used as a dye.

cochlea (kŏk′lē-ă) [Gr. *kokhlos,* land snail] A winding cone-shaped tube forming a portion of the bony labyrinth of the inner ear. It contains the organ of Corti, the receptor for hearing.

The cochlea is coiled, resembling a snail shell, winding two and three quarters turns about a central bony axis, the modiolus. Projecting outward from the modiolus, a thin bony plate, the spiral lamina, partially divides the cochlear canal into an upper passageway, the scala vestibuli, and a lower one, the scala tympani. Between the two scalae is the cochlear duct, the auditory portion of the membranous labyrinth. The spiral organ (of Corti) lies on its floor. The base of the cochlea adjoins the vestibule. At the cupola or tip, the two scalae are joined at the helicotrema. SEE: illus. **cochlear** (-ăr), *adj.*

cochlear implant SEE: under *implant*.

cochlear nerve The division of the vestibulocochlear nerve (eighth cranial nerve) that supplies the cochlea. SEE: *vestibulocochlear nerve*.

cochleitis (kŏk″lē-ī′tĭs) [Gr. *kokhlos,* land snail, + *itis,* inflammation] Inflammation of the cochlea.

cochleopalpebral reflex (kō″klē-ō″pal-pē′brăl, kok″lē-) SEE: under *reflex*.

cochleovestibular (kŏk″lē-ō-vĕs-tĭb′ū-lăr) [″ + L. *vestibulum,* vestibule] Pert. to the cochlea and vestibule of the ear.

Cochrane Review (kŏk′rĭn) An evidence-based, systematic review of published health care research performed by an international group of academics who study the effectiveness of medical treatments (The Cochrane Collaboration, headquartered in Canada). Used to identify the efficacy of procedures, techniques, and devices. Website: www.cochrane.org.

Cockayne syndrome (kŏ-kān′) [Edward A. Cockayne, Brit. physician, 1880–1956] A congenital syndrome characterized by dwarfism, gait disturbance, microcephaly, ocular atrophy, photosensitivity, and premature aging.

Cockcroft-Gault formula A calculation used to estimate creatinine clearance based on age, weight, serum creatinine, and gender. Estimated creatinine clearance may be used to adjust dosages of renally excreted drugs. This formula is commonly used to adjust dosages for adult patients because their serum creatinine level may be a poor indicator of renal function. Because of decreased muscle mass in elderly patients, the serum creatinine level is a poor indicator of renal function; therefore this formula is used to adjust dosages. For men the formula is (140 − age)(weight in kg)/72 × serum creatinine. For women, this result is multiplied by the factor 0.85.

cockroach (kok′rōch″) [Sp. *cucaracha*] Any of the very common insect pests of the family Blattidae that infest homes and facilities that handle and store food. There are approx. 4500 species of cockroach, of which approx. 30 are associated with humans. The most common species in the U.S. are *Blatta, Blatella,*

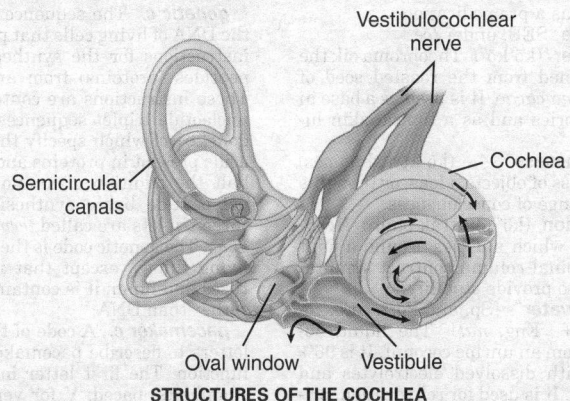

STRUCTURES OF THE COCHLEA

Eurycotis, and *Periplaneta.* Cockroaches defecate on human food, thereby transmitting to it bacteria, protozoan cysts, and helminth ova. Cockroaches are also a common cause of allergies and asthma.

American c. The largest of the common cockroaches (*Periplaneta americana*), capable of flight, native to Africa but carried worldwide on ships, and found in tropical and subtropical climates. Allergens derived from *P. americana* are abbreviated *Per a* by the World Health Organization. SYN: *waterbug.*

Australian c. A small cockroach (*Periplaneta australasiae*), similar to but smaller than the American cockroach, native to Asia but carried worldwide on ships, and found in tropical and subtropical climates.

German c. A small, flightless cockroach (*Blattella germanica*) that is a common pest in urban areas. SYN: *croton **bug**.*

oriental c. A large cockroach (*Blatta orientalis*) that prefers dark, moist places and is often be found around decaying organic matter, and in sewers, drains, and damp basements SYN: *waterbug.*

cocktail (kok′tāl″) A beverage containing several ingredients, or a combination of drugs used to treat a disease that would not respond adequately to any of them given alone.

GI c. A mixture of a topical anesthetic and antacid sometimes given to patients suspected of having noncardiac chest pain. Its use is controversial.

⚠️ Patients suffering from acute coronary ischemia may sometimes respond to the administration of a GI cocktail, confusing the diagnosis and delaying appropriate therapy.

lytic c. A mixture of analgesic and phenothiazine derivatives used in anesthesia as a premedication.

cock-up toe SEE: under *toe.*

cocoa butter (kō′kō″) Theobroma oil; the fat obtained from the roasted seed of *Theobroma cacao.* It is used as a base in suppositories and as a topical skin lubricant.

coconsciousness (kō-kŏn′shŭs-nĕs) Awareness of objects, ideas, or thoughts at the fringe of consciousness.

cocontraction (kō″kŏn-trăk′shŭn) A condition in which muscles around a joint or the spinal column contract simultaneously to provide stability.

coconut "water" [Sp. and Port. *coco,* coconut, + Eng. *nut*] The liquid obtained from an unripe coconut. It is 96% water with dissolved electrolytes and minerals. It is used for rehydration, primarily in countries where the water supply is suspect.

cocoon strategy Cocoon immunity.

code (kōd) [Fr. *code,* fr L. *codex,* book] **1.** A collection of rules and regulations or specifications. **2.** A set of symbols that communicate information or conceal it from people not familiar with the true meaning of the symbols. **3.** A form of message used in transmitting information in a hospital, esp. when the information is broadcast over a public address system (e.g., "code blue" or "code 9" could indicate a particular type of emergency to an emergency care team). SEE: table; *code cart; code drug.* **4.** A system of symbols that represents information contained in a computer data bank.

bar c. A parallel array of alternately spaced black bars and white spaces representing a coded number, numbers, or letters, depending on the format employed. It is used clinically for patient sample identification as well as analyzer and operator ID.

binary c. SEE: *Binary system.*

civil c. Comprehensive written organization of general rules and regulations authorized by the legislature, based on Roman, Spanish, and French civil law. In the U.S., the judicial system that presides over health care issues and lawsuits is governed by the civil code in Louisiana only and by common law in other states.

c. of ethics A summary (sometimes in written form) of a profession's values and standards of conduct.

c. of federal regulations ABBR: CFR. The list of U.S. government regulations that specify the way certain activities or practices must be carried out and will be enforced. For example, CFR Title 21 recount the rules and regulations that govern the manufacture, handling, and storage of food and drugs; CFR Title 49, Section 105, the general procedures for the transportation of hazardous materials.

genetic c. The sequence of bases in the DNA of living cells that provides the instructions for the synthesis of polypeptides (proteins) from amino acids. These instructions are contained in 64 nucleotide triplet sequences, called codons, 61 of which specify the 20 amino acids present in proteins and 3 of which halt the addition of amino acids to a polypeptide being synthesized. These three triplets are called *termination codons.* The genetic code is the same in all living things, except that in some viruses and fungi, it is contained in RNA rather than DNA.

pacemaker c. A code of three to five letters to describe pacemaker type and function. The first letter indicates the chamber(s) paced: V for ventricle pac-

Hospital Emergency Codes

Type of Emergency	Commonly Used Hospital Paging Terminologies	Services Needed
Adult needing life support	Code Blue; Code 99	Advanced cardiac life support
Bioterrorism alert	Code Zebra	Treat as Mass Casualty Incident; notify Department of Homeland Security and State Health Department
Bomb threat	Code Black; Code Yellow; Code 10	Evacuation of building; security staff; local police and fire departments
Doctor needed urgently	Code Green	Presence of available medical staff — often, Emergency Department or Intensive Care Unit physicians
Fire in the facility	Code Red	Available maintenance and security staff; fire extinguishers
Infant abduction	Code Stork (Sometimes called Code Pink, but see below)	Blockade of all entries to and exits from the hospital
Infant requiring life support	Code Pink	Practitioners trained in neonatal or pediatric life support
Multiple Casualty Incident	Code Triage; Code Amber	All available personnel to assist in triaging and treating the sick and wounded; hospital-wide emergency strategies implemented.
Potentially violent person on premises	Code Strong; Doctor Strong; Code Grey; Code Silver; Code North	Show of force by security personnel and others; hospital supervisor

ing, A for atrial pacing, and D for dual chamber (i.e., both atrial and ventricular) pacing. The second letter indicates the chamber from which electrical activity is sensed (i.e., A for atrium, V for ventricle, or D for dual sensing). Other notations indicate the response to a sensed electrical signal: none, inhibition, triggering of pacing, and dual response that may inhibit or trigger pacing in the atrium, ventricle, or both.

pacing c. A code of three to five letters used for describing pacemaker type and function. The first letter indicates the chamber or chambers paced: V for ventricle, A for atrium, or D for dual, i.e., for pacing of both chambers. The second letter, which may also be V, A, or D, indicates the chamber from which electrical activity is sensed. The third letter indicates the response to the sensed electrical activity: O indicates no response to the electrical activity sensed; I, inhibition of the pacing action; T, triggering of the pacemaker function; and D, that a dual response of spontaneous atrial and ventricular activity will inhibit atrial and ventricular pacing. The fourth letter, previously used to

describe programmable functions, is now used to designate variability of the pace rate with metabolic need. A fifth letter may indicate antitachycardia-pacing capability, but this is more usually incorporated into automatic implantable defibrillators. SEE: *pacemaker; artificial cardiac pacemaker.*

slow c. A colloquial term for the use of advanced cardiac life support with little if any intent to restore cardiopulmonary or neurological function. In some instances, slow resuscitative efforts are made when professional staff and moribund patients differ with respect to their interpretation of the appropriateness of end of life care. The practice, at best, rests on dubious moral and legal grounds. An alternate term, the "Hollywood Code," implies that the rescue attempt is made as a pretense.

triplet c. In DNA or mRNA, the sequence of three nucleotides that is the code for a particular amino acid. The triplet sequence controls the amino acid sequence during protein synthesis.

code cart A container or cart that can easily and quickly be moved to a patient who has suddenly developed a life-threatening emergency. Supplies should always be replenished and arranged so that the most frequently used first-line drugs and equipment are readily available. Powered equipment, such as a defibrillator, is tested regularly to be certain it is functioning properly. SEE: *basic life support; code* (3).

code of federal regulations SEE: under *code*.

Code for Nurses A statement by the American Nurses Association to guide nurses in their legal and ethical practice.

The nurse, in all professional relationships, practices with compassion and respect for the inherent dignity, worth, and uniqueness of every individual, unrestricted by considerations of social or economic status, personal attributes, or the nature of health problems.

The nurse's primary commitment is to the patient, whether an individual, family, group, or community.

The nurse promotes, advocates for, and strives to protect the health, safety, and rights of the patient.

The nurse is responsible and accountable for individual nursing practice and determines the appropriate delegation of tasks consistent with the nurse's obligation to provide optimum patient care.

The nurse owes the same duties to self as to others, including the responsibility to preserve integrity and safety, to maintain competence, and to continue personal and professional growth.

The nurse participates in establishing, maintaining, and improving health care environments and conditions of employment conducive to the provision of quality health care and consistent with the values of the profession through individual and collective action.

The nurse participates in the advancement of the profession through contributions to practice, education, administration, and knowledge development.

The nurse collaborates with other health professionals and the public in promoting community, national, and international efforts to meet health needs.

The profession of nursing, as represented by associations and their members, is responsible for articulating nursing values, for maintaining the integrity of the profession and its practice, and for shaping social policy.

[Reprinted with permission from American Nurses Association, Code of Ethics for Nurses with Interpretive Statements, ©2001 American Nurses Publishing, American Nurses Foundation/American Nurses Association, Washington, DC.]

codeine (kō′dēn″) [Gr. *kōdeia,* head, head of the poppy + *-ine*] An alkaloid obtained from opium or synthetically from morphine as methylmorphine. It is used as an analgesic, a cough suppressant, or a sedative/hypnotic drug. Common side effects include nausea, constipation, itching, or confusion. Tolerance of or dependence on codeine may develop with regular use.

codependency (kō″dē-pĕn′dĕn-sē) **1.** In psychology, unintentional or conscious reinforcement of another person's addictive or self-destructive behaviors. **2.** In biology, symbiosis.

coding (kōd′ing) **1.** In billing for medical services, the grouping of medical diagnoses within an established category, usually with standard symbols such as those in the International Classification of Diseases (ICD). **2.** The writing of computer program instructions to process data or produce a specified output. **3.** In educational research, the grouping of data into related categories or concepts.

CODIS *Combined DNA Index System.*

cod liver oil SEE: under *oil.*

Codman exercise (kod′măn) [Ernest Amory Codman, U.S. surgeon, 1869–1940] A gentle, circular exercise of the upper extremity following immobilization to reestablish glenohumeral joint range of motion and function following injury. SYN: *pendulum exercise.*

codocyte (kō′dō-sīt″) Target cell.

codon (kō′don″) A sequence of three bases in a strand of DNA or mRNA that is the genetic code for a specific amino acid.

   amber c. The nucleic acid sequence of uracil, adenine, guanine. Its abbreviation is UAG. It is one of the three codons that signals the end of transcription of an mRNA molecule.

coefficient (kō″ĕ-fish′ĕnt) **1.** In chemistry, a numeral put before a chemical formula or compound to indicate the number of molecules of that substance taking part in the chemical reaction. **2.** An expression of the ratio between two different quantities, or the effect produced by varying certain factors.

   activity c. **1.** A factor used in potentiometry to describe the activity of free ions in solution. **2.** A vitamin deficiency factor that describes the enhancement of enzyme activity after saturation with a vitamin.

   attenuation c. The calculated remainder of the x-ray beam that is received by the detectors in a computed tomography (CT) unit. This value is used to determine the CT (Hounsfield) number.

   diffusion c. The number of milliliters of gas at 1 atmosphere of pressure that will diffuse a distance of 1 μm over 1 sq cm/min.

   c. of absorption The volume of gas absorbed by a unit volume of a liquid at 0°C and a pressure of 760 mm Hg.

   c. of elastic expansion The volumetric expression in cubic centimeters of a compressed gas cylinder under hydrostatic test conditions.

   c. of refraction The quotient of the sine of the angle of incidence divided by the sine of the angle of refraction.

   c. of thermal expansion The change in the dimensions of a material when its temperature is raised 1°C. In dentistry, if the relative expansion and contraction of restorative materials, casts, or appliances are not accounted for, the patient may have problems with improper fitting, microleakage, or adhesive debonding.

   c. of variation Analytical variability expressed as the standard deviation's percentage of the mean. This mode of expressing the analytical variability enables one to determine if the variability proportion changes with the actual value. It is typically a useful tool when there is a relatively large dynamic range for the quantity being measured. It is subject to misinterpretation if applied to numbers that have already been mathematically manipulated, such as logarithms.

   ventilation c. The amount of air that must be respired for each liter of oxygen to be absorbed.

-coele, -coel, -cele [Ult. fr. Gr. *koilos,* hollow] Suffixes meaning *cavity, chamber.* SEE: *-cele.*

Coelenterata (sē-lěn″tĕr-ā′tă) A phylum of invertebrates that includes corals, hydras, jellyfish, and sea anemones. Contact with some species can result in sting injuries. SEE: *bite; sting.*

coelom (sē′lŏm) [Gr. *koiloma,* a cavity] The fluid-filled cavity in an embryo that forms in the mesoderm as a coalescence of outpouchings of the endoderm. In humans, the coelom develops into the pleural, peritoneal, and pericardial cavities. These fluid-filled cavities are enclosed sacs lined by mesodermal cells that are specialized to transport fluid into and out of the cavity. Organs, e.g., heart, lungs, digestive tract, and liver, protrude into the coelomic cavity, where the surrounding fluid partially isolates them from outside forces. SYN: *body cavity.*

   extraembryonic c. In humans, the cavity in the developing blastocyst that lies between the mesoderm of the chorion and the mesoderm covering the amniotic cavity and yolk sac.

coenocyte (sē′nŏ-sīt″) [Gr. *koinos,* common + *-cyte*] A primitive cellular structure found in some fungi, algae, and slime molds. Coenocytes are multinucleated cells that can have processes many centimeters long.

coenzyme (kō-en′zīm″) [*co-* + *enzyme*] An enzyme activator; a diffusible, heat-stable substance of low molecular weight that, when combined with an inactive protein called apoenzyme, forms an active compound or a complete enzyme called a holoenzyme (e.g., adenylic acid, riboflavin, and coenzymes I and II).

   c. A A derivative of pantothenic acid, important as a carrier molecule for acetyl groups in many reactions including the Krebs cycle (tricarboxylic acid cycle) and the oxidation of fatty acids.

   c. Q A dietary supplement promoted by alternative medicine practitioners as an antioxidant and as a treatment for gingivitis and heart diseases.

   c. Q10 Ubiquinone.

coexcitation (kō-ĕk-sī-tā′shŭn) [″ + *excitare,* to arouse] Simultaneous excitation of two parts or bodies.

cofactor (kō′făk-tor) **1.** A biochemical or physiological agent that produces an effect in conjunction with other agents. **2.** One of several agents in the development of an illness or epidemic.

coffee (kŏ′ fē) The beverage made from the seed of trees of the genus *Coffea,* called coffee beans. Coffee has a 2500-year history of consumption. It contains numerous volatile and nonvolatile compounds, including caffeine and cafestol. Moderate consumption of caffeine is not a risk factor for cardiovascular disease, birth defects, breast disease, or cancer.

coffee bean sign A radiologic sign consisting of a greatly distended, air-filled loop of sigmoid colon extending from the pelvis on abdominal radiography. The apposed medial walls of the dilated bowel form a distinct oblique line that resembles the cleft of a coffee bean. The coffee bean arises from the pelvis and may be very large, with its apex often extending above the level of T10 to the left or right of the midline. This sign is characteristic of sigmoid volvulus.

Coffin-Lowry syndrome (kŏf′ĭn low′rē) A rare, X-linked genetic syndrome characterized by abnormalities of the head, face, and axial skeleton; mental retardation; short stature; and weak muscle tone.

-cog A suffix used in pharmacology to designate a *marketed blood-clotting factor.*

Cogan syndrome (kō′găn) [David G. Cogan, U.S. ophthalmologist, 1908–1993] Interstitial keratitis associated with tinnitus, vertigo, and usually deafness.

cognition (kŏg-nĭsh′ŭn) [L. *cognoscere,* to know] Thinking skills, including language use, calculation, perception, memory, awareness, reasoning, judgment, learning, intellect, social skills, and imagination. **cognitive** (kŏg'nĭ-tĭv), *adj.*

cognitive behavioral therapy ABBR: CBT. A form of psychotherapy that challenges patients to identify and learn from their ineffective patterns of behavior by consciously choosing to make healthy changes in them.

cognitively impaired, no dementia, cognitive impairment, not dementia ABBR: CIND. Mild cognitive impairment.

cognitive processing therapy ABBR: CPT. A treatment for victims of sexual assault who have post-traumatic stress disorder. The victim is taught to identify how his or her attitudes and beliefs before the sexual assault (e.g., of safety or invulnerability) have changed because of the assault, and how the dissonance between the victim's former world and the present one creates fear, anxiety, depression, and avoidance. The victim next writes a detailed account of the sexual assault and, through repeated rereading of the event aloud to others and while alone, learns to desensitize herself or himself to the psychological impact of the assault.

cognitive psychology SEE: under *psychology*.

cognitive restructuring Any psychological method used to remove negative thoughts or irrational roadblocks that harm a person's emotional health.

cognitive retraining Restoring analytical skills, decision making, memory, and reasoning through stimulation and practice. SYN: *rehabilitation, cognitive*.

cognitive science SEE: under *science*.

Cohen syndrome A rare autosomal recessive disease characterized by small head size, mental retardation, poor muscle tone, visual disturbances, joint laxity, and low white blood cell counts.

coherent (kō-hēr'ĕnt) [L. *cohaerere*, to stick together] **1.** Sticking together, as parts of bodies or fluids. **2.** Consistent; making a logical whole.

cohesin (kō-hē'sĭn) A protein complex that binds sister chromatids to each other. It releases them during mitosis and contributes to gene expression and the repair of DNA.

cohesion (kō-hē'zhŭn) The property of adhering.

cohesive (kō-hē'sĭv) Adhesive; sticky.

Cohnheim, Julius Friedrich (kōn'hīm') Ger. pathologist, 1839–1884.

    C. areas The irregular groups of fibrils seen in a cross section of a striated muscle fiber.

cohort (kō'hort') [L. *cohors*, armed force, retinue] A selected group of people born during a particular period and traced through life during successive time and age periods.

    patient c. **1.** Any group of individuals affected by common diseases, environ-

mental or temporal influences, treatments, or other traits whose progress is assessed in a research study. **2.** Any research subjects who are linked because they have something in common and who are then studied over time.

cohort analysis Cohort **study**.

coil (koyl) **1.** A continuous material such as tubing, rope, or a spring arranged in a spiral, loop, or circle. **2.** An antenna used to generate a magnetic field (e.g., in magnetic resonance imaging devices).

coin counting A sliding movement of the tips of the thumb and index finger over each other. This may occur in Parkinson's disease. Also called *pill rolling*.

coinfection (kō'ĭn-fĕk'shĭn) [" + "] Simultaneous infection with two or more microorganisms, e.g., with the human immunodeficiency virus (HIV) and mycobacterium tuberculosis (TB). The prevalence of coinfection among humans is unknown but probably common.

coining (koy'nĭng) **1.** A traditional health practice in which a heated coin is placed or rubbed on the skin (to treat conditions such as asthma). A health care provider who is unaware of this practice could erroneously attribute the lesions caused by coining to physical abuse. SYN: *cao gio*. **2.** In biomedical engineering, a cold-working process used to improve the strength of metals used for biological purposes (e.g., nails used in orthopedic surgeries).

coinsurance (kō'ĭn-shoor'ăns) The percentage of the price of an office visit, procedure, laboratory study, pharmaceutical prescription, or hospitalization that a patient is obligated to pay under his or her health insurance plan. It differs from co-payment in that it is not a fixed cost but one that varies with the cost of the service provided. SEE: *co-payment*.

coin test A test for pneumothorax. A metal coin is placed flat on the chest and struck with another coin. The chest is auscultated at the same time. If a pneumothorax is present, a sharp, metallic ringing sound is heard.

coitarche (kō'ĭt-ăr'kē) Age at first sexual intercourse.

coition (kō-ĭsh'ŭn) [L. *coire*, to come together] Coitus.

coitophobia (kō'ĭ-tō-fō'bē-ă) [" + Gr. *phobos*, fear] Morbid fear of sexual intercourse.

coitus (kō'ĭ-tŭs) Sexual intercourse between a man and a woman by insertion of the penis into the vagina. SYN: *coition; copulation; sexual intercourse*. **coital** (-tăl), *adj.*

    c. interruptus Coitus with withdrawal of the penis from the vagina before seminal emission occurs. This is not an effective method of contraception.

c. reservatus Coitus with intentional suppression of ejaculation.

c. Saxonius Coitus with manual pressure placed either on the urethra at the underside of the penis or in the perineum to block the emission of semen at ejaculation; also called the squeeze technique. It is used to prevent premature ejaculation.

col (kŏl) The nonkeratinized, depressed gingival tissue that lies between adjacent teeth; it extends labiolingually between the interdental papillae below the interproximal contact of the teeth.

col-, coli-, colo- [Gr. *kolon*, large intestine] Prefixes meaning *colon*.

Cola, kola (kō'lă) [W. African *kola*] A genus of tropical trees that produce the kola nut. A kola nut extract is used in pharmaceutical preparations and as a main ingredient in some carbonated beverages.

colation (kō-lā'shŭn) [L. *colare*, to strain] Straining, filtering.

colchicine (kŏl'chĭ-sĭn) A medicine used principally to treat and prevent gout. One common side effect of the drug is diarrhea.

Colchicum autumnale (kol'kē-ŭm o''tŭm-nol'ē, ow'', -nol'ā) SEE: *autumn crocus.*

COLD *chronic obstructive lung disease.* SEE: *chronic obstructive pulmonary disease.*

cold (kōld) **1.** Common cold. **2.** Absence of heat or warmth; the quality or state of being at a low temperature; the opposite of heat.

chest c. Acute bronchitis.

common c. An acute infection of any or all parts of the respiratory tract from the nasal mucosa to the nasal sinuses, throat, larynx, trachea, and bronchi. Common colds occur in most people, usually at least once a year. They are more common in smokers and in children than in healthy adults. The common cold causes more loss of work and school time than any other ailment.

The contagious period begins before the onset of symptoms. Causative viruses are distributed to others by sneezing (aerosolization) and by direct contact with nasal secretions. The incubation period is typically from 12 to 72 hr.

ETIOLOGY: Most colds are caused by rhinoviruses, adenoviruses, coronaviruses, coxsackieviruses, influenza viruses, parainfluenza viruses, or respiratory syncytial viruses.

SYMPTOMS: The common cold is marked by swelling of the nasal mucosa with increased mucus production that may occlude the nasal passages. Sneezing, lacrimation, a sore or scratchy throat, hoarseness, cough, colorful sputum, headache, chills, and malaise are also common. Symptoms usually resolve within 2 days to 2 weeks. If a cold lasts longer than 10 days, or is accompanied by fever or systemic symptoms, it is advisable to consult a health care provider. Persons with chronic diseases, such as diabetes or heart or lung disease, should consult a health care provider if a cold is severe, is accompanied by fever, or lasts more than 10 days.

CONTAGIOUSNESS: The virus may be present in the nasal secretions for a week or longer after the onset of symptoms. SYN: *cold* (1).

cold agglutinin disease Any of a group of disorders marked by hemolytic anemia, obstruction of the microcirculation, or both. It is caused by agglutination of red blood cells by immunoglobulins that precipitate at cool or cold temperatures. The most common symptom is Raynaud's phenomenon. Cold agglutinin disease often occurs transiently after infection with *Mycoplasma pneumoniae* or Epstein-Barr virus. Often the cause is idiopathic.

cold chain The maintenance of refrigeration of items (esp. vaccines) from the point of their origin at the manufacturer, through their transportation, unloading, distribution, and cold storage at the site where they will be used.

cold compression therapy unit ABBR: CCT unit. A cooling jacket that simultaneously delivers cold therapy and static compression to an extremity, joint, or other body part. Water is chilled in an external container to a temperature of 45° to 55°F (7.2° to 12°C) and is then circulated through a circumferentially applied compression device. CCT units are used immediately after surgery or joint injury to control swelling and reduce pain. SYN: *controlled cold therapy unit.*

⚠ This device should not be used with patients who have known contraindications to cold application or external compression (e.g., peripheral vascular disease, Raynaud's phenomenon, advanced diabetes, or neurological insufficiency).

cold cream A water-in-oil emulsion ointment base used on the skin.

cold-damp Foggy vapor in a mine charged with carbon dioxide.

cold ischemia time SEE: under *time.*

cold knife surgery SEE: under *surgery.*

cold laser therapy Low level laser therapy.

cold pressor test A test that measures blood pressure and heart rate response to the immersion of one hand in ice water.

cold spot In radiation oncology, a tissue region that is exposed to much less radiation than neighboring tissues.

coldspray, cold spray (kōld-sprā) **1.** An aerosol used to lower the temperature and thus harden thermoplastic splinting material during fitting or molding. **2.** A vaporized chemical such as ethyl chloride or fluoromethane used to produce rapid cooling and numbness of the skin.

cold steel A colloquial term for surgery performed with a scalpel rather than with electrocautery, lasers, or radiofrequency ablation.

cold storage In organ transplantation, the refrigeration of donated organs before they are transplanted into recipients.

cold stress SEE: *hypothermia.*

colectomy (kō-lĕk′tō-mē) [Gr. *kolon,* colon, + *ektome,* excision] Excision of part or all of the colon.

Coleus forskohlii (kō′lē-ŭs for″skō′lē-ī′, ′lē-ē) A member of the mint family that is used in Ayurvedic medicine as an extract to treat diverse conditions, including weight loss and asthma.

colibacillemia (kō″lĭ-băs-ĭl-lē′mē-ă) [Gr. *kolon,* colon, + L. *bacillus,* little rod, + Gr. *haima,* blood] *Escherichia coli* in the blood.

colibacillosis (kō″lĭ-băs-ĭ-lō′sĭs) [″ + ″ + Gr. *osis,* condition] Infection with *Escherichia coli.*

colibacilluria (kō-lĭ-băs-ĭl-ū′rē-ă) [″ + ″ + Gr. *ouron,* urine] Presence of *Escherichia coli* in the urine.

colibacillus (kō″lĭ-bă-sĭl′ŭs) [″ + L. *bacillus,* little rod] The colon bacillus, *Escherichia coli.*

colic (kolik) [Gr. *kolikos,* pert. to the colon] **1.** Spasm in any hollow or tubular soft organ accompanied by pain. **2.** Pert. to the colon. SEE: *biliary colic; tormina.*

   biliary c. Right upper quadrant pain due to obstruction of a bile duct by a gallstone.

   infantile c. Colic occurring in infants, principally during the first few months of life. It may respond to substitution of a hypoallergenic formula for cow's milk or to decreased stimulation of the infant.

   intestinal c. Colic typically associated with intestinal obstruction or ileus.

   lead c. Severe abdominal colic associated with lead poisoning.

   menstrual c. Dysmenorrhea.

   renal c. Pain in the region of one of the flanks that radiates inferiorly, toward the lower abdomen, groin, scrotum, labia, or thigh. It may be associated with the passage of kidney stones.

   uterine c. Severe abdominal pain arising in the uterus, usually during the menstrual period. SEE: *dysmenorrhea.*

colica (kŏl′ĭ-kă) [L.] Colic.

colicky (kŏl′ĭk-ē) Concerning colic or affected by it.

colicoplegia (kō″lĭ-kō-plē′jē-ă) [″ + *plege,* stroke] Colic and paralysis due to lead poisoning.

colicystitis (kō″lĭ-sĭs-tī′tĭs) [″ + *kystis,* bladder, + *itis,* inflammation] Inflammation of the bladder resulting from *Escherichia coli* infection.

colicystopyelitis (kō-lĭ-sĭs″tō-pī″ĕ-lī′tĭs) [″ + ″ + *pyelos,* pelvis, + *itis,* inflammation] *Escherichia coli* inflammation of the bladder and renal pelvis.

coliform (kō′lĭ-form″, kol′ĭ-) [*coli-+-form*] **1.** Shaped like a sieve; cribriform. **2.** A general term applied to some species of the family Enterobacteriaceae, including *Escherichia coli, Enterobacter,* and *Klebsiella* species. Their presence in water, esp. that of *E. coli,* is presumptive evidence of fecal contamination.

colinephritis (kō″lĭ-nē-frī′tĭs) [″ + *nephros,* kidney, + *itis,* inflammation] Pyelonephritis caused by *Escherichia coli.*

colisepsis (kŏl″ĭ-sĕp′sĭs, kŏl″) [″ + ″] Infection caused by *Escherichia coli.*

colitis (kō-līt′ĭs) [*col-* + *-itis*] Inflammation of the colon. SEE: *dysentery; gay bowel syndrome; Crohn disease.*

   amebic c. Amebiasis.

   antibiotic-associated c. Antibiotic-induced diarrhea. SEE: *pseudomembranous c.*

   collagenous c. ABBR: CC. Chronic watery diarrhea of unknown cause, in which the appearance of the bowel during endoscopy is normal. Biopsies of the bowel wall reveal thickening of the collagen layer beneath the colonic epithelium. CC is ten times more common in women than in men and is usually diagnosed in people aged 40 to 60.

   E. coli 0157:H7 c. An infectious, bloody diarrhea caused by *Escherichia coli* 0157:H7. SEE: *E. coli 0157:H7.*

   infectious c. Colitis caused by pathogens such as amebas, bacteria, and protozoa. It may be caused by *Campylobacter, Cryptosporidium, Escherichia coli, Entamoeba histolytica, Giardia, Salmonella,,* and *Shigella.*

   lymphocytic c. ABBR: LC. Chronic watery diarrhea of unknown cause, in which the endoscopic and radiological appearance of the bowel wall is normal. Biopsies of the bowel wall reveal excessive numbers of lymphocytes within the intestinal epithelium. LC is equally common in men and women and is usually diagnosed in people aged 40 to 60.

   microscopic c. ABBR: MC. Either of two forms of colitis (collagenous and lymphocytic), in which people have chronic, watery diarrhea despite having normal-appearing bowels during endoscopy or radiologic study.

   pseudomembranous c. Colitis associated with antibiotic therapy and, sometimes, with chronic debilitating illnesses in adult patients in the community. It is caused by one of two exotoxins produced by *Clostridium difficile,* which is part of the normal intestinal flora.

Broad-spectrum antibiotics disrupt the normal balance of the intestinal flora and allow an overgrowth of strains that produce toxins. The exotoxins damage the mucosa of the colon and produce a pseudomembrane composed of inflammatory exudate. The symptoms (foul-smelling diarrhea with gross blood and mucus, abdominal cramps, fever, and leukocytosis) usually begin 4 to 10 days after the start of antibiotic therapy. The disease is treated by discontinuing previously prescribed antibiotics and beginning therapy with oral metronidazole; use of vancomycin should be limited to patients who do not respond to metronidazole. Diarrhea may reappear in approx. 20% of patients after treatment, necessitating a second course of therapy.

radiation c. Colitis due to damage of the bowel by radiation therapy. The symptoms are those of an inflamed bowel (pain, cramps, diarrhea, and rectal bleeding). Malabsorption may develop as a result of permanent injury to the mucosa.

ulcerative c. Colitis marked pathologically by continuous inflammation of the intestinal mucosa, which typically involves the anus, rectum, and distal colon, and sometimes affects the entire large intestine. It occurs most often in patients during the second or third decade of life, although a second cluster of cases occurs in patients in their sixties. The disease is associated with an increased incidence of cancer of the colon. SEE: *Crohn disease; inflammatory bowel disease; Nursing Diagnoses Appendix.*

SYMPTOMS: Bloody diarrhea and pain with the passage of stools are characteristic. In severe cases, patients may have more than 6 bloody bowel movements in a day. Iron deficiency anemia often develops as a result.

TREATMENT: Aminosalicylate drugs and corticosteroids decrease symptoms and improve inflammation. Patients with refractory disease may require colectomy.

PATIENT CARE: The patient is prepared for diagnostic studies (sigmoidoscopy, colonoscopy, barium enema, CT scan) and is told that the procedure can be uncomfortable and fatiguing. He is taught to understand and participate in treatment goals: controlling inflammation, maintaining or restoring fluid and electrolyte balance, receiving adequate nutrition and replacing nutritional losses, and preventing complications. The nurse or dietitian teaches the patient about dietary intake, which should be high-caloric, nonspicy, caffeine-free, and low in high residue foods and milk products. Actual dietary and caloric intake must be documented. If the patient is unable to take fluids by mouth, intravenous (IV) fluid and electrolyte replacement or parenteral nutrition are instituted as prescribed. Fluid intake and output are monitored, particularly for frequency, volume, and characteristics of diarrhea. The patient is monitored for dehydration and electrolyte imbalances, particularly hypokalemia, hypernatremia, and anemia.

Prescribed drug therapy is administered; the patient is evaluated for desired and adverse effects and is taught about the particulars of his regimen, which usually includes sulfasalazine (5-ASA), prescribed for its antibiotic and anti-inflammatory effects. Studies have shown that, in high-risk patients, 5-ASA given both orally and by enema appears to sustain remission better than oral therapy alone. Since 5-ASA interferes with folate metabolism, use of a folate supplement is encouraged. Corticosteroids such as prednisone often are prescribed to reduce inflammation. The patient is taught that once clinical remission is achieved, steroid therapy can be tapered gradually and discontinued, but should never be summarily stopped. If the patient requires prolonged steroid therapy, he must report gastric irritation, edema, personality changes, moon face, and hirsutism. Corticosteroids given chronically may produce many serious side effects, including bone loss, diabetes mellitus, and cataracts. Antispasmodic and antidiarrheal agents (tincture of belladonna, diphenoxylate, loperamide) are used rarely and with great caution because they can precipitate colonic dilation (toxic megacolon). Measures to prevent perianal skin breakdown are reviewed, e.g., cleaning the rectal area thoroughly but gently following each bowel movement, applying a moisture barrier such as petroleum jelly, and changing position frequently.

While surgery is considered only for patients who do not respond to pharmacological therapies, several surgical procedures are available to attempt to preserve rectal evacuation. Bowel surgeries require a special antibiotic preparation, and postoperative care includes all general patient care concerns. In addition, a temporary nasogastric tube is usually inserted, and a diet is gradually advanced after removal of the tube. The patient may have a permanent or temporary stoma or a pouch ileostomy and requires ongoing teaching and support from a stomal therapist and support groups for help and management.

colla (kŏl′lă) Pl. of collum.

collagen (kol′ă-jĕn) [Gr. *kolla*, glue, + ″] A strong, fibrous insoluble protein found in connective tissue, including the dermis, tendons, ligaments, deep fascia, bone, and cartilage. Collagen is the protein typical of dental tissues (except enamel), forming the matrix of dentin, cementum, and alveolar bone proper. Collagen fibers also form the periodontal ligament, which attaches the teeth to their bony sockets. **collagenic** (kŏl″ă-jen′ĭk), *adj.* **collagenous** (kŏ-loj′ĕ-nŭs), *adj.*

collagenase (kŏl-lăj′ĕ-nās) [″ + ″ + *-ase*, enzyme] A member of the metalloproteinase family of enzymes that degrades collagen.

collagenic (kŏl″ă-jĕn′ĭk) Producing or containing collagen.

collagenoblast (kŏl-lăj′ĕ-nō-blăst) [″ + ″ + *blastos*, germ] A fibroblast-derived cell that produces collagen when mature.

collagenolysis (kŏl″ă-jĕn-ŏl′ĭ-sĭs) [″ + ″ + *lysis*, dissolution] The degradation or destruction of collagen.

collagenosis (kŏl-lăj″ĕ-nō′sĭs) [″ + ″ + *osis*, condition] A connective tissue disease.

collagenous colitis (kŏ-loj′ĕ-nŭs) SEE: under *colitis.*

collapse (kŏ-laps′) [L. *collapsus,* fallen into ruin] **1.** A sudden exhaustion, prostration, or weakness due to decreased circulation of the blood.

SYMPTOMS: Common symptoms include alterations in mental status, an inability to stand without dizziness, and/or severe generalized weakness. Physical findings include pallor, cold clammy skin, gooseflesh, a thin or thready pulse, an increased respiratory rate, tachycardia, and hypotension.

PATIENT CARE: A patent airway is maintained, the patient's head is lowered, and the lower extremities are elevated slightly in the Trendelenburg position to enhance venous return to the heart. Vital signs and level of consciousness are assessed for signs of shock or aspiration of vomitus. High concentration oxygen by a nonrebreather mask should be administered and oxygen saturation and ventilation evaluated. The patient should be kept warm but not hot. The patient's ECG should be monitored for arrhythmias, and an intravenous (IV) line should be established. If the patient is hypotensive, IV fluids should be given. The health care provider remains with the patient, briefly and calmly orienting him or her to surroundings and explaining procedures to provide reassurance of appropriate care.

2. An abnormal retraction of the walls of an organ.

cardiovascular c. SEE: *cardiovascular collapse.*

circulatory c. 1. Shock (1). **2.** Hypoperfusion.

lung c. 1. Atelectasis. **2.** Compression of lung caused by pneumothorax, hydrothorax, or hemothorax.

TREATMENT: Bronchial hygiene, postural drainage, and percussion are used to assist in mucus removal for those patients with atelectasis due to mucus plugging. Bronchoscopy may also be useful in these patients. Chest tubes are inserted to drain air or fluid from the pleural cavity when present.

collapse therapy The production of a pneumothorax on one side to treat pulmonary tuberculosis. It allows the lung on that side to be at rest. This form of treatment was popular in the preantibiotic era, but has been superseded by newer pharmaceutical practices.

collapsing (kō-lăps′ĭng) **1.** Falling into extreme and sudden prostration resembling shock. **2.** Shrinking; disintegrating. **3.** Condensing.

collapsotherapy (kŏ-lăp″sō-thĕr′ă-pē) [L. *collapsus,* fallen to pieces, + Gr. *therapeia,* treatment] Treatment of pulmonary disorders by unilateral pneumothorax and immobilization of the affected lung.

collar (kŏl′ăr) [L. *collare,* neckband] **1.** A band worn around the neck. **2.** A structure or marking formed like a neckband. **3.** A device designed to limit movement of the neck.

cervical c. A soft or rigid band of plastic or padded foam that is designed to limit extension, flexion, and lateral movement of the neck. Soft collars usually are reserved for confirmed strains of the neck. SEE: *rigid cervical c.; cervical immobilization device; orthosis; Philadelphia collar* for illus.

extrication c. Rigid cervical collar.

Philadelphia c. A firmly constructed, lightweight collar used to restrict cervical spine movement, e.g. during extrication of injured patients from motor vehicles. SEE: illus.

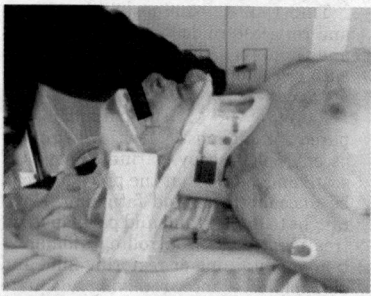

PHILADELPHIA COLLAR

rigid cervical c. A firm plastic collar applied to the neck of a patient whose mechanism of injury may lead to a neck injury. It is designed to limit flexion, extension, and lateral movement of the neck. Because no collar eliminates all movement, patients who have not yet had a fracture ruled out by x-ray examination should remain immobilized to a backboard. SYN: *extrication c.* SEE: *cervical immobilization device.*

collarette (kol″ă-ret′) The wavy boundary visible on the anterior surface of the iris between its two annular sectors, the outer, ciliary zone and the inner, pupillary zone.

collateral (kŏ-lăt′ĕr-ăl) [L. *con,* together, + *lateralis,* pert. to a side] **1.** Accompanying, side by side, as in a small side branch of a blood vessel or nerve. **2.** Subordinate or accessory.

collateral trigone SEE: under *trigone.*

collectin (kŏl-lĕk′tĭn) A plasma protein that binds carbohydrate molecules in the cell walls of microorganisms and facilitates phagocytosis. SEE: *phagocytosis.*

collectins (kō-lĕk′tĭnz) Soluble, collagen-like proteins secreted into the blood of animals. They bind carbohydrate and fatty molecules on the surface of disease-causing microorganisms and help the body agglutinate, neutralize, or opsonize them so that they may be consumed and destroyed by white blood cells. Collectins are one component of the innate immune system.

collection, spot urine The sampling of a single, untimed urine specimen, voided spontaneously by the patient. The sample is analyzed to determine its protein, creatinine, or electrolyte content. This type of specimen differs from a timed urinary specimen, which represents all the urine a patient produces over a 12- or 24-hr period. Both types of specimen are used in the diagnosis and treatment of renal disease.

collective bargaining A negotiation between an employer and employee representatives, e.g., between a health care facility and one of its employee unions.

Colles, Abraham Irish surgeon, 1773–1843.

   C. fascia The inner layer of the superficial fascia of the perineum.

   C. fracture A transverse fracture of the distal radial metaphysis with displacement of the hand posteriorly and outward, causing the characteristic "dinner fork" deformity during radiographical evaluation. Contaminant trauma to the ulnar styloid process and the triangular fibrocartilage complex may also occur.

   PATIENT CARE: A history of the injury is obtained, and the patient is assessed for pain, swelling, mobility, and any deformity of the distal forearm. The areas above and below the fracture site are inspected for color changes and palpated for pulses, temperature, and the presence of sensation. The extremity is temporarily immobilized with a splint, and cold is applied according to protocol to reduce pain and limit swelling. The patient is scheduled for radiography, all procedures are explained, and noninvasive pain relief measures are instituted to reduce discomfort. The nurse or orthopedic technician assists with closed reduction and casting if carried out in the emergency department or refers the patient to an orthopedic surgeon for treatment and follow-up care.

colliculectomy (kŏl-lĭk″ŭ-lĕk′tō-mē) [L. *colliculus,* mound, + Gr. *ektome,* excision] Removal of the colliculus seminalis.

colliculitis (kŏl-lĭk″ū-lī′tĭs) [″ + Gr. *itis,* inflammation] Inflammation of the colliculus seminalis.

colliculus (kŏl-lĭk′ū-lŭs) *pl.* **colliculi** [L.] A little eminence.

   c. seminalis An oval enlargement on the crista urethralis, an elevation in the floor of the prostatic portion of the urethra. On its sides are the openings of the ejaculatory ducts and numerous ducts of the prostate gland. SYN: *c. urethralis.*

   c. urethralis Colliculus seminalis.

collimation (kŏl″ĭ-mā′shŭn) [L. *collineare,* to align] **1.** The process of making parallel. **2.** In radiography, the process of limiting the scatter and extent of the x-ray beam to the part being radiographed.

collimator (kol′ĭ-māt″ŏr) [L. variant of *collineare,* to align, direct, aim] A radiographic device used to limit the scatter and extent of the x-ray beam.

   automatic collimator Positive beam limiting **device.**

colliquation (kŏl″ĭ-kwā′shŭn) [L. *con,* together, + *liquare,* to melt] **1.** Abnormal discharge of a body fluid. **2.** Softening of tissues to liquefaction. **3.** Wasting.

colliquative (kŏ-lĭk′wă-tĭv) Pert. to a liquid and excessive discharge, as a colliquative diarrhea.

collodion (kō-lō′dē-ŏn) [Gr. *kollodes,* resembling glue] A thick fluid coating, made of dissolved pyroxylin, that is used to dress wounds or to supply medications to the skin. When applied, it dries to form a transparent film.

   flexible c. A collodion preparation containing camphor and castor oil. It is more elastic than collodion.

   salicylic acid c. A flexible film used to remove accumulated layers of dead skin and scale (e.g., to treat psoriasis, warts, corns, or calluses).

colloid (kol′oyd″) [Gr. *kollodes,* glutinous] **1.** A gluelike substance, such as a protein or starch, whose particles (molecules or aggregates of molecules) when dispersed as much as possible in a solvent, remain uniformly distributed and do not form a true solution. **2.** The size of a microscopic colloid; particles ranging from 10^{-9} to 10^{-11} meters (1 to

100 nm). **3.** A semi-fluid gel found within the follicles of the thyroid gland and containing the thyroid hormones. **4.** A substance used as a plasma expander in place of blood. **colloidal** (kŏ-loyd′ăl), *adj.*

colloidal silver (kŏ-loyd′ăl) SEE: under *silver.*

colloid suspension A colloidal solution in which particles of the dispersed phase are relatively large. SYN: *suspensoid.*

collum (kŏl′lŭm) *pl.* **colla** [L.] **1.** The necklike part of an organ. **2.** The neck.

collyrium (kō-lĭr′ē-ŭm) [Gr. *kollyrion,* eye salve] An eyewash or lotion for the eye.

coloboma (kŏl″ō-bō′mă) *pl.* **colobomata** [Gr. *koloboma,* a mutilation] A lesion or defect of the eye, usually a fissure or cleft of the iris, ciliary body, or choroid. Sometimes the eyelid is involved. Colobomata may be congenital, pathological, or surgical.

colocalization (kō″lō″kăl-ĭ-zā′shŭn) [″ + ″] The consistent presence of two molecules at a single cellular site, as evidenced by digital or fluorescent imaging techniques.

colocecostomy (kō″lō-sē-kos′tō-mē) [*col-* + *cecostomy*] Surgical joining of the more distal colon to the cecum.

colocolostomy (kō″lō-kō-lŏs′tō-mē) [″ + *kolon,* colon, + *stoma,* mouth] The surgical formation of a passage between two portions of the colon.

colocutaneous (kō″lō-kū-tā′nē-ŭs) [″ + L. *cutis,* skin] **1.** Pert. to the colon and the skin. **2.** Pert. to a pathological or surgical connection between the colon and the skin. SEE: *colostomy.*

coloenteritis (kō″lō-ĕn″tĕr-ī′tĭs) [Gr. *kolon,* colon, + *enteron,* intestine, + *itis,* inflammation] Inflammation of the mucous membrane of the small and large intestines.

colofixation (kō″lō-fĭk-sā′shŭn) Suspension of the colon.

colography (kŏ-log′ră-fē) [*colon* + *-graphy*] Radiographic imaging of the large intestine. SYN: *virtual colonoscopy.*

colon (kō′lŏn) [L. *colon,* fr Gr. *kolon,* large intestine] The large intestine from the end of the ileum to the anal canal that surrounds the anus, about 59 in (1.5 m) long; divided into the ascending, the transverse, the descending, and the sigmoid or pelvic colon. Beginning at the cecum, the first part of the large intestine (ascending colon) passes upward to the right colic or hepatic flexure, where it turns as the transverse colon passing ventral to the liver and stomach. On reaching the spleen, it turns downward (left colic or splenic flexure) and continues as the descending colon to the brim of the pelvis, where it is continuous with the sigmoid colon and extends to the rectum. SEE: illus.

FUNCTION: *Mechanical:* The colon mixes the intestinal contents. *Chemical:* The colon does not secrete digestive enzymes. The products of bacterial action that are absorbed into the bloodstream are carried by the portal circulation to the liver before they enter the general circulation. More water is absorbed in the colon than in the small intestine. In this way, body fluids are conserved, and despite the large volumes of secretions added to the food during its progress through the alimentary canal, the contents of the colon are gradually dehydrated until they assume the consistency of normal feces or even become quite hard. SEE: *absorption, colon; defecation.*

BACTERIA OF THE COLON: The normal microbial flora in the colon, some of which may produce vitamins, esp. vitamin K; metabolize proteins and sugars; produce organic acids and ammonia; and deconjugate bile acids. Several conditions, such as use of antibiotics, corticosteroids, or dieting, may alter the normal flora. Although *Escherichia coli* is the most widely known bacterium that inhabits the colon, it is not the most common, being outnumbered by anaerobic *Bacteroides* species by a very wide margin.

   irritable c. Irritable bowel syndrome.

   sigmoid c. The part of the colon that turns medially at the left iliac crest, between the descending colon and the rectum; shaped like the letter S.

   spastic c. Irritable bowel syndrome.

colon cutoff sign The finding of colonic gas in the proximal colon but not in the part distal to the splenic flexure. It may be identified on plain radiography or computer tomographic scanning of the abdomen and is indicative of acute pancreatitis.

colonic (kō-lon′ik, kŏ-) [*colon* + *-ic*] **1.** Pert. to the colon. **2.** A common colloquial term for *colonic irrigation* or *enema.*

colonic inertia SEE: *inertia.*

colonization (kŏl″ō-nī-zā′shŭn) The growth of microorganisms, esp. bacteria, in a particular body site.

colono-, colon- [L. fr. Gr. *kolon,* large intestine] Prefixes meaning *colon.*

colonocyte (kŏ-lŏn′ō-sīt) [″ + ″] An endothelial cell of the large intestine.

colonopathy (kō″lō-nŏp′ă-thē) [Gr. *kolon,* colon, + *pathos,* disease] Any disease of the colon.

colonoscope (kō-lŏn′ō-skōp) [″ + *skopein,* to examine] An endoscope used to examine the colon. SEE: *sigmoidoscope.*

colonoscopy (kō″lŏ-nos′kō-pē) [*colon* + *-scopy*] Visualization of the lower gastrointestinal tract. The procedure usually consists of the insertion of a flexible endoscope through the anus to inspect the entire colon and terminal ileum. The

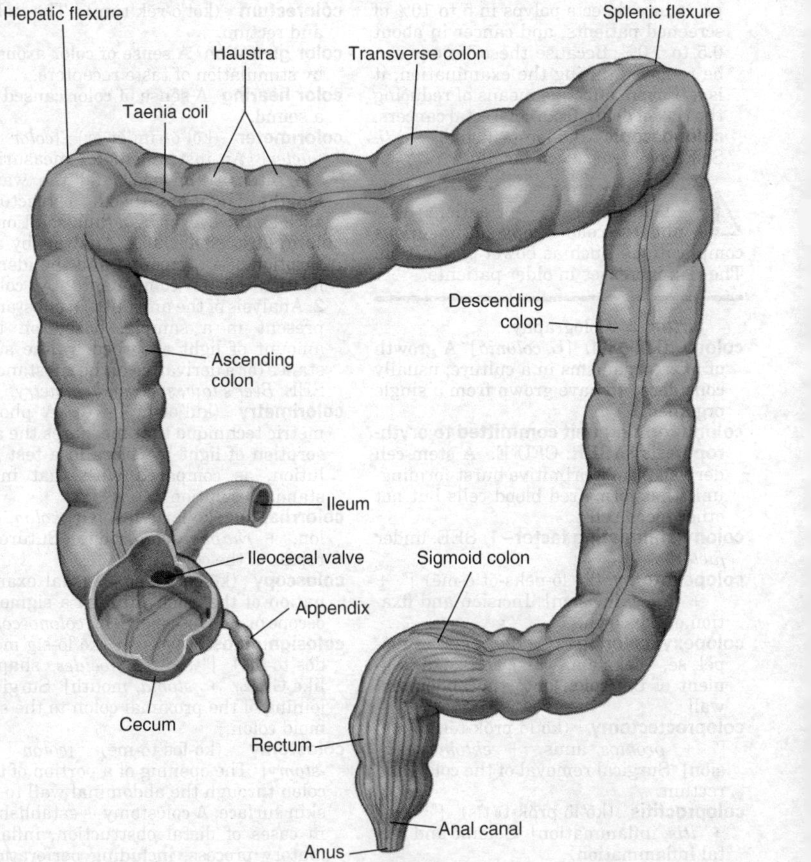

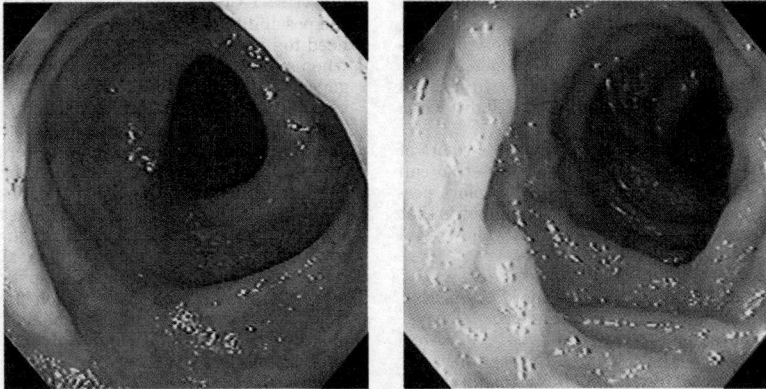

Hepatic flexure

Haustra

Taenia coil

Transverse colon

Splenic flexure

Ascending colon

Descending colon

Ileum

Ileocecal valve

Sigmoid colon

Appendix

Cecum

Rectum

Anal canal

Anus

COLON AND RECTUM

COLON
Normal colon, seen endoscopically

procedure detects polyps in 5 to 10% of screened patients, and cancer in about 0.5 to 1.0%. Because these lesions can be removed during the examination, it is a proven, effective means of reducing the risk of death from colorectal cancers.
colonoscopic (kō-lon″ŏ-skop′ik), *adj.* SEE: *coloscopy; colon* for illus.

⚠️ About 0.3 to 0.5% of patients who undergo colonoscopy suffer serious complications, such as bowel perforation. The risk increases in older patients.

    virtual c. Colography.
colony (kŏl′ō-nē) [L. *colonia*] A growth of microorganisms in a culture; usually considered to have grown from a single organism.
colony-forming unit committed to erythropoiesis ABBR: CFU-E. A stem cell derived from a primitive burst-forming-unit that forms red blood cells but not other blood cells.
colony-stimulating factor–1 SEE: under *factor.*
colopexotomy (kō″lō-pĕks-ŏt′ō-mē) [″ + ″ + *tome,* incision] Incision and fixation of the colon.
colopexy, colonopexy, colopexia (kō′lō-pĕk″sē, -pĕks′ē-ă) Fixation of a segment of the colon onto the abdominal wall.
coloproctectomy (kō″lō-prŏk-tĕk′tō-mē) [″ + *proktos,* anus, + *ektome,* excision] Surgical removal of the colon and rectum.
coloproctitis (kō″lō-prŏk-tī′tĭs) [″ + ″ + *itis,* inflammation] Colonic and rectal inflammation.
coloproctostomy (kō″lō-prŏk-tŏs′tō-mē) [″ + ″ + *stoma,* mouth] Surgical creation of a passage between a segment of the colon and the rectum.
coloptosis (kō-lŏp-tō′sĭs) A downward displacement of the colon.
color [L.] A visible quality, distinct from form, light, texture, size, brightness, and shade, that distinguishes some objects from others.
    complemental c. One of two spectral colors that produce white light when blended.
    primary c. Any of the three colors of light—red, green, and violet—that can be mixed to produce all the colors perceived by the human eye. Pigments that can be so mixed are red, yellow, and blue.
color additive SEE: under *additive.*
color blindness SEE: under *blindness.*
color deficiency SEE: under *deficiency.*
colorectal (kō″lō-rek′tăl) [*col-* + *rectal*] Pert. to the colon and the rectum.
colorectostomy (kō″lō-rĕk-tŏs′tă-mē) [″ + ″ + Gr. *stoma,* mouth] Surgical formation of a passage between the colon and rectum.

colorectum (kōl″ō-rĕk′tŭm) The colon and rectum.
color gustation A sense of color aroused by stimulation of taste receptors.
color hearing A sense of color caused by a sound.
colorimeter (kŏl″ō-rim′ĕt-ĕr) [*color* + *-meter*] An instrument for measuring the intensity of color and the wavelengths of light absorbed by a structure, such as the eye, or by a fluid solution.
colorimetric analysis 1. Analysis by adsorption of a compound and the identification of its components by color. **2.** Analysis of the amount of a substance present in a sample, based on the amount of light absorbed by the substance (or a derivative of the substance). SEE: *Beer's law; spectrophotometry.*
colorimetry (kŭl″ŏr-ĭm′ĕ-trē) A photometric technique that measures the absorption of light by colors in a test solution, as compared with that in a standard solution.
colorrhaphy (kō-lor′ă-fē) [Gr. *kolon,* colon, + *rhaphe,* seam, ridge] Suture or repair of the colon.
coloscopy (kō-lŏs′kō-pē) Visual examination of the colon through a sigmoidoscope or colonoscope. SEE: *colonoscope.*
colosigmoidostomy (kō″lō-sĭg″moy-dŏs′tō-mē) [″ + *sigmoeides,* shaped like Gr. Σ, + *stoma,* mouth] Surgical joining of the proximal colon to the sigmoid colon.
colostomy (kŏ-los′tŏ-mē) [*colon* + *-stomy*] The opening of a portion of the colon through the abdominal wall to its skin surface. A colostomy is established in cases of distal obstruction, inflammatory process, including perforation, and when the distal colon or rectum is surgically resected. A temporary colostomy is performed to divert the fecal stream from an inflamed or operative site. SEE: illus.; *ostomy* for colostomy care.
    PATIENT CARE: *Preoperative:* When the possibility exists that a patient will need to have a colostomy created (even when surgery is performed in an emergency), the patient and family are advised about the nature of the colostomy, including temporary versus permanent stoma and general principles of aftercare. The patient is assured that he or she will be able to resume a normal lifestyle with a stoma. A stomal therapist works with patient and family throughout this experience. Except in an extreme emergency (e.g., perforation, penetrating trauma, etc.), preparation for colon surgery with laxatives, enemas, and antibacterial agents is coordinated with the surgery's starting time. Intravenous hydration is instituted.
    Postoperative: Routine care, including the use of various monitors, pneumatic hose, incentive spirometry, and pulmo-

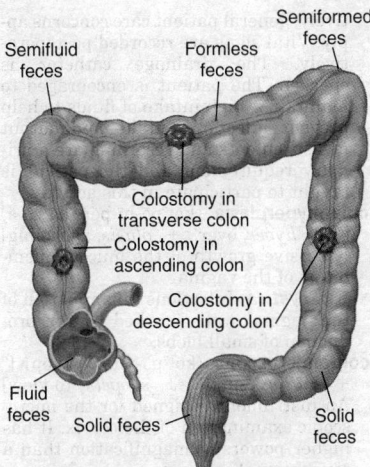

Semifluid feces   Formless feces   Semiformed feces

Colostomy in transverse colon

Colostomy in ascending colon

Colostomy in descending colon

Fluid feces   Solid feces   Solid feces

COLOSTOMY SITES

nary toilet measures, along with special attention given to inspecting the stoma for viability and the surrounding skin for irritation and excoriation. The stoma should be smooth and cherry red, and may be slightly edematous. Any discoloration or excessive swelling is documented and reported. The stoma and surrounding skin are gently cleansed and dried thoroughly. A drainage bag is applied by fitting a karaya adhesive ring (or other appliance) before the patient leaves the operating room to ensure a firm seal and to prevent leakage without constricting the stoma. Nonirritating skin barriers are used as appropriate.

Avoidance of dehydration and maintenance of electrolyte balance are emphasized until the patient is able to eat a normal diet. Stool consistency is observed. If colostomy irrigations are prescribed, the patient is advised that the procedure is similar to an enema. The patient is advised to return to a normal diet judiciously, adding new foods gradually while observing their effect. He or she should avoid gas-forming, odoriferous, spicy, and irritating foods. Colostomy requires a difficult adjustment by both patient and family; they are encouraged to verbalize their fears and concerns, and support is offered. The patient is reassured of the ability to regain continence with dietary control and bowel retraining. Usual physical activities should be gradually resumed, avoiding heavy lifting and activities that could cause injury to the stoma and surrounding tissues. Abdominal muscle strengthening should be part of a supervised exercise program. Both patient and partner are encouraged to discuss their feelings and concerns about body

image changes and about resumption of sexual relations, and they should be assured that the appliance will not dislodge if empty. The patient should avoid food and fluids a few hours before sexual activity. Participation in a local "ostomates" support group help the patient and significant others to manage the stoma and associated concerns. Depression is not uncommon after ostomy surgery, and psychological counseling is recommended if depression persists. SEE: *Nursing Diagnoses Appendix.*

   ascending c. A colostomy typically connected to the right side of the abdomen, in which the proximal large intestine (rather than the descending bowel or sigmoid) empties through a stoma fashioned in the right lower quadrant of the abdomen.

   decompressive c., decompressing colostomy A colostomy between the proximal colon and the abdominal wall. It is used to drain intestinal contents when an obstruction in the distal colon might otherwise cause the organ to perforate or rupture.

   descending c. A colostomy in which part of the descending colon or the sigmoid colon is brought to the abdominal wall to empty its contents into a collection device. It is the most common colostomy. SYN: *sigmoid c.*

   double-barrel c. Most often a temporary colostomy with two openings into the colon: one distal and one proximal. Elimination occurs through the proximal stoma, allowing the distal length of the colon to rest and heal. When healing is complete, the two ends are rejoined and returned to the peritoneal cavity, and normal bowel function resumes. In colitis, resection rather than reanastomosis is performed.

   sigmoid c. Descending **c.**

   temporary c. A colostomy between the colon and the exterior abdominal wall, used for a few months until the proximal colon and a more distal part of the large bowel can be joined safely. It is created typically when inflammation in the distal colon needs time to resolve.

   terminal c. A colostomy in which the proximal cut end of the colon is formed into a stoma and the distal colon is either resected or closed.

   wet c. **1.** A colostomy in the right side of the colon. The drainage from this type of colostomy is liquid. **2.** A colostomy in the left side of the colon distal to the point where the ureters have been anastomosed to it. Thus the urine and fecal material are excreted through the same stoma. Ureterocolostomy has been abandoned in favor of other extra-intestinal urinary diversion procedures.

colostrorrhea (kŏ-los″trŏ-rē′ă) [*colostrum* + *-rrhea*] Excessive secretion of colostrum.

colostrum (kŏ-los'trŭm) [L. *colostrum*, beestings] Breast fluid that may be secreted from the second trimester of pregnancy onward but is most evident in the first 2 to 3 days after birth and before the onset of true lactation. This yellowish fluid, which is the first milk produced by the breast after childbirth, contains abundant carbohydrates, proteins (including antibodies), and minimal fat.

colotomy (kō-lŏt'ō-mē) [Gr. *kolon*, colon, + *tome*, incision] Incision of the colon.

colpectomy (kŏl-pĕk'tō-mē) [" + *ektome*, excision] Surgical removal of the vagina.

colpitis (kŏl-pī'tĭs, kŏl-pīt'ĭs) Vaginitis (2).

   c. macularis Small red spots on the epithelium of the upper vagina and cervix. The spots are seen best with a colposcope and are called, colloquially, "strawberry spots." They are often seen in women who are infected with trichomonas. SEE: *Trichomonas vaginalis.*

colpo-, colp- [Gr. *kolpos*, fold, womb, vagina] Prefixes meaning *vagina*.

colpocele (kŏl'pō-sēl) [" + *kele*, tumor, swelling] A hernia into the vagina.

colpoceliotomy (kŏl"pō-sē"lē-ŏt'ō-mē) [" + *koilia*, belly, + *tome*, incision] An incision into the abdomen through the vagina. SEE: *culdoscopy.*

colpocleisis (kŏl"pō-klī'sĭs) [*colpo-* + Gr. *kleisis*, a closure] Surgical occlusion of the vagina. It is performed for elderly, medically fragile women with uterine or vaginal vault prolapse, who are not and do not wish to be sexually active. A total colpocleisis is performed if the woman has had a total hysterectomy; and a partial colpocleisis is done if the uterus and cervix are present, so that any abnormal bleeding from the uterus or cervix can be detected.

colpocystitis (kŏl"pō-sĭs-tī'tĭs) [" + *kystis*, bladder, + *itis*, inflammation] Inflammation of the vagina and bladder.

colpocystocele (kŏl"pō-sĭs'tō-sēl) [" + *kystis*, bladder, + *kele*, tumor, swelling] Prolapse of the bladder into the vagina.

colpocystotomy (kŏl"pō-sĭs-tŏt'ō-mē) [" + " + *tome*, incision] An incision into the bladder through the vagina. This procedure is no longer used, as better surgical approaches to the bladder are available.

colpocystourethropexy (kŏl"pō-sĭs-tō-ū-rē'thrō-pĕks-ē) The transvaginal surgical suspension of the urethra and bladder—used to treat urinary incontinence in women. The surgery restores the proper cystourethral angle for normal urinary continence.

   PATIENT CARE: The procedure and associated sensations are explained preoperatively, along with postoperative regimens and expectations. Postoperatively, general patient care concerns apply. Vital signs are recorded postoperatively. The drainage catheter is checked. The patient is encouraged to maintain a high intake of fluids to help prevent infection. Intake and output measurements and recording are a primary requirement and the patient is taught to participate in this activity.

colpohyperplasia (kŏl"pō-hī-pĕr-plā'zē-ă) [" + *hyper*, over, + *plasis*, a forming] Excessive growth of the mucous membrane of the vagina.

   c. cystica Infectious inflammation of the vaginal walls marked by the production of small blebs.

colpomicroscope (kŏl"pō-mī'krō-skōp) [" + *mikros*, small, + *skopein*, to view] An instrument designed for the microscopic examination of the cervix. It has higher powers of magnification than a conventional colposcope.

colpomyomectomy (kŏl"pō-mī"ō-mĕk'tō-mē) [" + *mys*, muscle, + *oma*, tumor, + *ektome*, excision] Removal of a fibroid tumor of the uterus through the vagina.

colpoperineoplasty (kŏl"pō-pĕr"ă-nē'ō-plăs"tē) [" + *perinaion*, perineum, + *plassein*, to form] Surgical repair of the perineum and the vagina.

colpoperineorrhaphy (kŏl"pō-pĕr"ĭn-ē-or'ră-fē) [" + " + *rhaphe*, seam, ridge] Surgical repair of tears in the vagina and perineum.

colpopexy (kŏl'pō-pĕk"sē) [" + *pexis*, fixation] Suture of a relaxed and prolapsed vagina to the pelvic wall.

colpoplasty (kŏl'pō-plăs"tē) [" + *plassein*, to form] Plastic surgery of the vagina.

colpoptosis (kŏl'pŏp-tō'sĭs) [" + *ptosis*, a dropping] Prolapse of the vagina.

colporrhaphy (kol-por'ă-fē) [*colpo-* + *-rrhaphy*] Surgical repair to the vaginal wall to treat cystocele or rectocele.

colporrhexis (kŏl"pō-rĕk'sĭs) [" + *rhexis*, rupture] Laceration or rupture of the vaginal walls.

colposcope (kŏl'pō-skōp) [" + *skopein*, to examine] An instrument used to examine the tissues of the vagina and cervix through a magnifying lens.

colposcopy (kŏl-pŏs'kō-pē) The examination of vaginal and cervical tissues by means of a colposcope. Colposcopy is used to select sites of abnormal epithelium for biopsy in patients with abnormal Pap smears. It is helpful in defining tumor extension, for evaluating benign lesions, and in postpubertal vaginal examination of diethylstilbestrol-exposed daughters.

colpostat (kŏl'pō-stăt) [" + *statikos*, standing] A device for holding an instrument, such as a radioactive implant, in place in the vagina.

colpostenosis (kŏl"pō-stĕn-ō'sĭs) [" +

stenosis, narrowing] Stenosis or narrowing of the vagina.

colposuspension (kŏl″pō-sŭs-pĕn′shŭn) Colpocystourethropexy.

colpotomy (kŏl-pŏt′ō-mē) [″ + *tome,* incision] An incision into the wall of the vagina. SYN: *coleotomy.*

coltivirus (kŏl′tĕ-vī″rŭs) A genus of viruses (family Reoviridae) that causes Colorado tick fever in the U.S., Eyach virus infection in Europe, and Banna virus infection in Asia.

coltsfoot (kŏlts′foot″) [So called from the shape of its leaves] A perennial, yellow-flowered herb *Tussilago farfara,* used traditionally to treat asthma, cough, and other respiratory ailments. Some research suggests it is carcinogenic.

Columbia mental maturity scale ABBR: CMMS. A psychometric test used to assess the ability of young children to reason, or think logically.

columella (kŏl″ū-mĕl′lă) [L., small column] **1.** A little column. **2.** In microbiology or mycology, the portion of the sporangiophore on which the spores are borne.

column (kol′ŭm) [L. *columna,* pillar] A cylindrical supporting structure.

anal c. Vertical folds of the mucous membrane in the anal canal. SYN: *rectal c.*

anterior c. Ventral column.

Clarke c. SEE: under *Clarke, Jacob A.L.*

dorsal c. The triangular (in cross-section) sector of white matter demarcated by the dorsal midline (the dorsal median sulcus) and the dorsal horn on each side of the spinal cord. The dorsal column is a large bundle of ipsilateral primary sensory axons. SYN: *dorsal funiculus; posterior c.* 2.

c. of fornix Either of two arched bands of fibers that form the anterior body of the fornix. The fibers lead to the mammillary body.

c. of Goll SEE: under *Goll, Friedrich.*

gray c. Gray matter in the anterior and posterior horns of the spinal cord.

intermediolateral cell c. Lateral horn.

lateral c. **1.** A column in the lateral portion of the gray matter of the spinal cord. It contains cell bodies of preganglionic neurons of the sympathetic nervous system. **2.** The triangular (in cross-section) sector of white matter demarcated by the dorsal and ventral horns on each side of the spinal cord. The lateral column contains axons of neurons with cell bodies inside the brain or spinal cord, not axons from the dorsal root ganglia. SYN: *lateral funiculus.* **3.** The articulation in the midfoot between the fourth and fifth metatarsal bones and the cuboid.

motor c. In the brainstem and spinal cord, a group of functionally analogous motor nuclei that are aligned longitudinally and that occupy a stereotyped position in cross-sections. The three motor columns, which run in the medial and ventral quadrants of the brainstem and spinal cord, comprise the branchial motor column (the nucleus ambiguus, the facial motor nucleus, and the trigeminal motor nucleus), the somatic motor column (the ventral horns of the spinal cord and the hypoglossal, abducens, trochlear, and oculomotor nuclei), and the visceral motor column (the lateral horns of the spinal cord and the dorsal motor nucleus of the vagus, the salivatory nucleus, and the Edinger-Westphal nucleus).

posterior c. **1.** The posterior horn of the gray matter of the spinal cord. It consists of an expanded portion or caput connected by a narrower cervix to the main portion of the gray matter. **2.** Dorsal column.

rectal c. Anal column.

renal c. Cortical material of the kidney that extends centrally, separating the pyramids.

sensory c. In the brainstem and spinal cord, a group of functionally analogous secondary sensory nuclei that are aligned longitudinally and that occupy a stereotyped position in cross-sections. The three sensory columns, which run in the lateral and dorsal quadrants of the brainstem and spinal cord, comprise the general somatic sensory column (the dorsal horns of the spinal cord and the mesencephalic, principal sensory, and spinal trigeminal nuclei), the special somatic sensory column (the cochlear and vestibular nuclei), and the visceral sensory column (the nucleus of the solitary tract).

spinal c. Vertebral column.

ventral c. The triangular (in cross-section) sector of white matter demarcated by the ventral horn and the ventral midline (the ventral median fissure) on each side of the spinal cord. The ventral column contains axons of neurons with cell bodies inside the brain or spinal cord, not axons from the dorsal root ganglia. SYN: *anterior c.; ventral funiculus.*

vertebral c. The portion of the axial skeleton consisting of vertebrae (7 cervical, 12 thoracic, 5 lumbar, the sacrum, and the coccyx) joined together by intervertebral disks and fibrous tissue. It forms the main supporting axis of the body, encloses and protects the spinal cord, and attaches the appendicular skeleton and muscles for moving the various body parts. SYN: *spinal c.* SEE: illus.

columna (kō-lŭm′nă) *pl.* **columnae** [L.] A column or pillar.

columnar (kō-lŭm′năr) **1.** In anatomy, shaped like a column or pillar. **2.** In his-

Lateral (side) spinal column

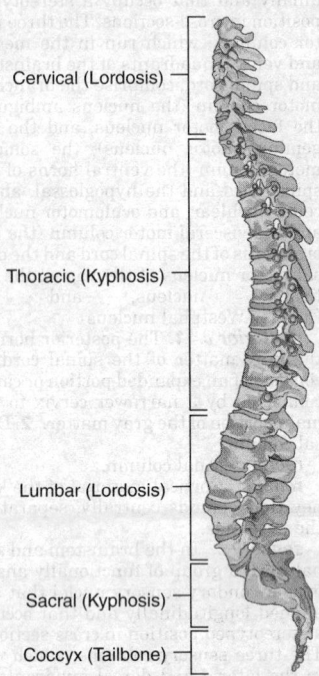

Cervical (Lordosis)

Thoracic (Kyphosis)

Lumbar (Lordosis)

Sacral (Kyphosis)

Coccyx (Tailbone)

VERTEBRAL COLUMN

View from left is anterior view

tology, composed of long, narrow, cylindrical epithelial cells.

com-, col-, con-, cor- [L. *cum,* with] Prefix meaning *together* or *with.* Com- remains com- before vowels and b, m, and p; it becomes col- before l; cor- before r; and con- before all other sounds. SEE: *syn-.*

coma (kō′mă) [Gr. *kōma,* a deep sleep] A state of unconsciousness from which one cannot be aroused. Coma is the most severe of the alterations of consciousness. It differs from sleep in that comatose patients will not awaken with stimulation. It differs from lethargy, drowsiness, or stupor (states in which patients are slow to respond) in that comatose patients are completely unresponsive. Finally, it differs from delirium, confusion, or hallucinosis (states in which patients' sense of reality is distorted and expressions are bizarre) in that comatose patients cannot express themselves at all. SEE: *Glasgow Coma Scale.*

ETIOLOGY: Two thirds of the time, coma results from diffuse brain injury or intoxication, such as may be caused by drug overdose, poisoning, hypoglycemia, uremia, liver failure, infection, or closed-head trauma. In about one third of cases, coma results from intracranial lesions, such as massive strokes, brain tumors, or abscesses. For these focal injuries to depress consciousness, the lesion must result in compression or injury to the brain's reticular activating system (the network of cells responsible for arousal). Rarely, coma is feigned by patients with psychiatric illnesses.

TREATMENT: The airway, breathing, and circulation are supported. The cervical spine is protected if there is any question of traumatic injury to the head and neck. A rapid physical examination is performed to determine whether the patient has focal neurological deficits. Simultaneously, intravenous dextrose, naloxone, and thiamine are given (to try to reverse narcotic overdose or diabetic coma). If the examination reveals focal findings, an intracranial lesion may be present and should be quickly diagnosed (with brain scans) and treated (e.g., with neurosurgery if appropriate). If the patient is neurologically nonfocal, treatment focuses on metabolic support, the administration of antidotes for any proven intoxications, and treatment for infections. Seizures, if present, should be promptly controlled with anticonvulsants. Blood-sugar levels should be tightly controlled (between 80 and 110 mg/dL). Fevers should be suppressed with antipyretics. Acid-base disturbances should be corrected.

⚠ If there is a question whether the coma is due to an overdose of insulin or to hypoglycemia, it is crucial to give glucose intravenously. Administration of naloxone is also standard care.

PATIENT CARE: A patent airway is maintained. If neck trauma is suspected (e.g., if the patient was found on the floor), the patient should not be moved, except after protecting the cervical spine. Neurological status is monitored with the Glasgow Coma Scale. Frequency of assessment depends on protocol and the patient's stability. Findings are documented, and evidence of clinical deterioration is reported.

Fluid and electrolyte balance is monitored and maintained; gastrointestinal and urinary functions are assessed; care for the indwelling urinary catheter, intravenous line, and nasogastric or PEG feeding tube is provided, as well as adequate enteral or parenteral nutrition; and bowel elimination is maintained with stool softeners, suppositories, or enemas. Ventilatory status is assessed by auscultating for abnormal lung sounds, and adequate ventilation and oxygenation are determined by arterial blood gases or oxygen saturation values. The nurse or respiratory therapist assists with intubation and provides mechanical ventilation as required. The patient is repositioned to improve aeration of lung bases, and drainage of secretions is encouraged. The oropharynx (and endotracheal tube) is suctioned gently but briefly as necessary, considering concerns for increased intracranial pressure. The corneas are protected from ulceration by applying artificial tears to moisturize the eyes and by patching the eyes closed if the patient is unable to close them. Skin status is assessed and a plan instituted to prevent or manage pressure areas; passive range-of-motion exercises are provided; the patient is repositioned frequently; distal extremities are supported and elevated to prevent dependent edema; and appropriate supportive devices are used to prevent external hip rotation, flexion and extension contractures, and footdrop. Therapy to prevent deep venous thrombosis should be given (for example, heparin, warfarin, or compression stockings). Early enteral feeding of the patient prevents malnutrition.

Verbal and tactile stimulation are provided; the patient is assessed per orders (or hospital protocol) to person, time, place, and activities; nothing is said in the patient's presence that the patient should not hear, because the unresponsive patient may occasionally be somewhat aware of his or her surroundings. Emotional and educational support is offered to family members. SEE: *shock*.

alcoholic c. A coma due to ingestion of alcohol.

apoplectic c. A coma produced by intracranial hemorrhage and its associated increase in intracranial pressure. One side of the body and one or more extremities may be paralyzed, usually on the opposite side of the injury in the brain. One pupil may be larger than the other, usually on the same side as the brain injury. SEE: *cerebral hemorrhage; diabetic c.; hypoglycemic c.*

barbiturate c. A coma caused by ingestion or injection of barbiturates. It is used clinically in the treatment of elevated intracranial pressure.

PATIENT CARE: The patient usually requires intubation and mechanical ventilation. Ventilatory status and oxygenation are monitored, adequate ventilation is maintained, and pulmonary toilet is provided. Aseptic technique is used for all procedures to prevent nosocomial infections.

diabetic c. Coma resulting from extremely low or extremely high blood sugar levels. Although both hyperglycemia and hypoglycemia can cause coma in diabetic patients, hypoglycemia is much more common. As a result, emergency treatment of hypoglycemia (with an ampule of intravenous dextrose) is always given first to comatose patients before initiating blood sugar testing. If high blood sugar levels are the cause of altered consciousness, insulin and massive hydration are usually needed.

PATIENT CARE: The primary treatment measures for diabetic ketoacidosis are replacing fluids and electrolytes and then administering insulin, which usually will resolve metabolic acidosis. The nurse or laboratory technician draws blood for glucose, acetone, complete blood count, electrolytes, and arterial blood gases and obtains urine for urinalysis. The patient is assessed for neurological signs and symptoms; aspiration precautions are instituted as warranted. Intravenous (IV) access is initiated, and 1 L or 15 mL/kg of normal saline solution (NS) is administered over the first hour. Some physicians prescribe an IV bolus of 0.1 to 0.15 units/kg of regular insulin once fluid resuscitation begins, but usually insulin is held until 1 to 2 L of fluid have been administered. The first liter of fluid is followed by NS (or 0.45% saline solution [SS] if the patient's sodium level is elevated) at 7.5 mL/kg/hr for 2 to 4 hr, then at 3.75 mL/kg/hr for 24 to 36 hr until fluid losses are corrected. The patient's lungs are auscultated every hour, then every 2 to 4 hr for crackles related to fluid overload. Regular insulin is added to all fluids after the first or second liter (depending on protocol), to infuse at a rate of 0.1 units/kg/hr, with the intent of reducing glucose levels by 75 to 100 mg/dL/hr. The patient's blood glucose is monitored hourly, and electrolyte and serum acetone studies are repeated in 4 hr. The patient's heart rhythm also is monitored for potassium-related arrhythmias, such as ventricular ectopy. Once the patient's blood glucose is below 300 mg/dL, the prescribed IV fluid is changed to D5/0.45% NS to prevent hypoglycemia. Throughout initial resuscitation and ongoing fluid and insulin therapy, health care providers search for and treat the underlying cause (infection being the most common). The patient is monitored closely until ketones are no longer present in the blood and the bicarbonate level in the serum is > 21.

When the patient is considered stable, has bowel sounds, is awake, and is able to tolerate food, insulin is administered subcutaneously as prescribed. The patient is then allowed to eat a diabetic meal. Another 2 hr pass before the patient's insulin infusion is discontinued, until the subcutaneous regular insulin is absorbed. IV insulin has a 5- to 7-min half-life, so premature discontinuance could lead to a return of ketoacidosis. Blood glucose levels are assessed every 2 to 4 hr as warranted. The dietitian assesses and evaluates the patient's nutritional needs, and helps him or her to understand the importance of meal planning for optimal glucose control. The patient is ready for discharge when normal hydration and functional digestion are present and acidosis is absent. He or she is taught how to manage blood sugars and to continue to take prescribed insulin or hypoglycemic agents even when food cannot be consumed, because illness makes blood sugars vary. The signs of hyperglycemia, how to perform glucose monitoring, and when and how to test for urine ketones are reviewed. The patient learns how to substitute liquids for solid foods during illness in order to maintain adequate carbohydrate and fluid intake, the need for more frequent glucose monitoring when ill, and when to contact the primary care provider (blood glucose above 300 mg/dL, inability to eat, or vomiting). The patient also is referred to a home care nurse for further monitoring as necessary, and to a community-based diabetic education course for enhanced understanding and control of diabetes.

hepatic c. Coma resulting from portal-systemic encephalopathy.

hyperosmolar nonketotic c. ABBR: HNC. A coma in which the patient has a relative insulin deficiency and resulting hyperglycemia, but enough insulin to prevent fatty acid breakdown. The condition occurs in individuals with type 2 diabetes and is caused by hyperosmolarity of extracellular fluids and subsequent intracellular dehydration. It often is precipitated by severe physical stress or by extreme or prolonged dehydration.

hypoglycemic c. Unconsciousness caused by very low blood sugars, usually less than 40 mg/dL. The most common cause is a reaction to insulin or an oral hypoglycemic agent. The patient typically will recognize, after reviving, that coma was preceded by heavy exercise, limited caloric intake, or a recent increase in the dose of diabetic medications. Occasionally alcoholic patients, patients with salicylate overdoses, or severely malnourished patients will present with coma and low blood sugar. Very rarely, the hypoglycemic patient will be found to have an insulin-secreting tumor of the pancreas.

irreversible c. A coma from which the patient cannot recover.

Kussmaul c. SEE: under *Kussmaul, Adolph.*

myxedema c. Unresponsiveness or lethargy that results from severe or neglected hypothyroidism. It is marked by neurological dysfunction, by respiratory depression, and by lowered body temperature, blood pressure, blood sugar, and serum sodium. The condition is an endocrinological crisis that requires treatment with thyroid and adrenocortical hormones, fluids, and glucose; gradual rewarming; ventilatory support; and intensive monitoring.

uremic c. Loss of consciousness caused by the toxic effects of the nitrogen-containing wastes and inorganic acids that accumulate in the bloodstream of patients in renal failure. Coma in renal failure usually occurs after other uremic symptoms, such as loss of appetite, confusion, lethargy, or seizures.

vigil c. Akinetic mutism.

comatose (kō′mă-tōs) In a coma.

combatant (kăm-bat′ănt, kom′bă-tănt) [Fr. *combattant*] A member of the armed forces, e.g., a soldier, sailor, marine, or airman, engaged in or prepared to be engaged in battle. **combatant,** *adj.*

combat disorder (kŏm′băt) [LL *combattere*] Any disease or condition that affects military personnel, their families, and/or victims of war.

combat support hospital SEE: under *hospital.*

combination antiretroviral therapy ABBR: cART. Highly active antiretroviral therapy.

Combined DNA Index System ABBR: CODIS. A database maintained by the FBI of DNA samples obtained from crime scenes and directly from convicted criminals. The system is used to generate investigative leads in the evaluation of criminal behavior such as sexual assaults and murders.

combined oral contraceptive (kŏm-bīnd′) ABBR: COC. A birth control pill that contains both an estrogen and a progestin.

combustion (kŏm-bŭs′chŏn) [L. *comburere,* to burn up] **1.** Any reaction in which a food or fuel source is oxidized and releases heat. **2.** In metabolism, the oxidation of food with production of heat, carbon dioxide, and water.

comedo (kŏm′ă-dō) *pl.* **comedones, comedos** [L. *comedere,* to eat up] The typical small skin lesion of acne vulgaris and seborrheic dermatitis. The closed form is called a whitehead. It consists of a papule from which the contents are not easily expressed. When inflamed these lesions form pustules and nodules. The open form of comedo, called a blackhead, is rarely inflamed. It has a dilated opening from which the oily debris is easily expressed. Both forms are usually located on the face, but the chest and back may be involved. SEE: illus.

comedocarcinoma (kŏm″ă-dō-kăr-să-nō′mă) Ductal carcinoma in situ of breast.

comet tail artifact In ultrasound imaging, an anomalous finding in which the reverberation of the ultrasound signal

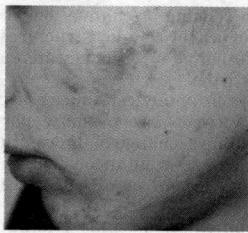

COMEDONES

within a cyst or gas bubble produces the appearance of a dense trail of echoes behind the structure.

comfort, readiness for enhanced A pattern of ease, relief, and transcendence in physical, pyschospiritual, environmental, and/or social dimensions that can be strengthened. SEE: *Nursing Diagnoses Appendix.*

comfrey (cŭm′frē) A hardy perennial, *Symphytum officinale,* whose leaves and roots and oil can be obtained. The oil is used in ointment form to promote wound healing. Because it contains known liver toxins, comfrey is not recommended for use in tea and should not be taken internally.

comity (kŏ′mĭ-tē) In interpersonal relations or social interactions, the condition of politeness, courtesy, and respect.

commando procedure SEE: under *procedure.*

commensal (kŏ-mĕn′săl) [L. *com-,* together, + *mensa,* table] Either of the two organisms of different species that live in a close but nonparasitic relationship. SEE: *commensalism; symbiosis.*

commensalism (kŏ-mĕn′săl-ĭzm″) The symbiotic relationship of two organisms of different species in which neither is harmful to the other and one gains some benefit such as protection or nourishment (e.g., nonpathogenic bacteria in the human intestine).

comment period SEE: under *period.*

comminute (kŏm′ĭ-nūt) [L. *com-,* together, + *minuere,* to crumble] To break into pieces.

comminution (kŏm″ĭ-nū′shŭn) [L. *comminutio,* crumbling] The reduction of a solid body to varying sizes by crushing, grating, hammering, pulverizing, slicing, granulating, and other processes.

Commiphora (kŏ-mif′ō-ră) [L. *Commiphora,* fr Gr. *kommiphora,* gum-bearing] A genus of nearly 200 flowering plants, shrubs, and tress, native to Africa, Arabia, and India. Several species produce fragrant resins used for incense, perfume, and medication.

C. gileadensis SEE: *balm of Gilead* (1).

C. mukul SEE: *guggul.*

C. opobalsamum SEE: *balm of Gilead* (1).

C. wightii SEE: *guggul.*

Commission on Accreditation of Allied Health Education Programs ABBR: CAAHEP. The U.S. agency that reviews the credentials and educational quality of numerous allied health professional academic programs, including those in athletic training, blood bank technology, cytotechnology, exercise physiology, medical illustration, polysomnography. Address: 1361 Park Street, Clearwater, FL 33756; Website: www.caahep.org

commissura (kŏm″mĭ-sū′ră) *pl.* **commissurae** [L.] Commissure.

commissure (kom′ĭ-shur″) [*commissura*] 1. In the central nervous system, an axon tract that crosses the midline (sagittal) plane between two homologous and symmetric structures, e.g., the corpus callosum, which interconnects the right and left cerebral cortices. 2. The meeting of two structures, as the lips, eyelids, or labia, across the midline (sagittal) plane. **commissural** (kom″ĭ-shur′ăl), *adj.*

anterior c. A symmetric axon tract running transversely through the lamina terminalis and connecting the right and left temporal cortices.

c. of the fornix Hippocampal commissure.

habenular c. A group of decussating axons of the stria medullaris. The stria medullaris contains axons projecting to the habenula from the septal nuclei, the preoptic hypothalamus, and the anterior thalamic nuclei; those stria medullaris axons that project to the contralateral habenula cross the midline plane via the habenular commissure.

hippocampal c. A thin sheet of axons from the fornix that cross the midline plane under the posterior sector of the corpus callosum and interconnect homologous fields of the right and left hippocampi. SYN: *c. of fornix.*

posterior c. An axon tract running transversely through the gray matter that forms the roof of the cerebral aqueduct in the midbrain. This tract contains commissural axons interconnecting the right and left pretectal areas; it also contains decussating axons from each pretectal area to the contralateral Edinger-Westphal nucleus.

tectal c. A symmetric axon tract running transversely through the ventral tectum of the midbrain and interconnecting the right and left superior colliculi.

commissurorrhaphy (kŏm″ĭ-shūr-or′ă-fē) [″ + Gr. *rhaphe,* seam, ridge] The surgical joining of the parts of a commissure to decrease the size of the opening.

commissurotomy (kŏm″ĭ-shūr-ŏt′ō-mē) [″ + Gr. *tome,* incision] Surgical incision of any commissure; used, for example, to treat mitral stenosis to increase the size of the mitral orifice. This is done by incising the adhesions that cause the leaves of the valve to stick together. Commissurotomy may also be used to treat certain psychiatric conditions by incising the anterior commissure of the brain.

commitment (kŏ-mĭt′mĕnt) The legal procedure for hospitalization of a patient who may not be competent to choose to be hospitalized. Confining a patient without his or her consent may be necessary, for example, to care for suicidal patients, patients with altered mental status, or persons with certain contagious diseases.

Committee on Accreditation for Respiratory Care ABBR: CoARC. An accreditation agency that works with the Commission on Accreditation of Allied Health Programs to ensure the educational quality of programs that provide professional education in respiratory care. Its website is www.coarc.com.

commode (kŏ-mōd′) [Fr. *commode*, fr L. *commodus*, convenient] A receptacle suitable for use as a toilet.
   bedside c. A portable toilet that enables a patient to sit comfortably while defecating or urinating. For many patients using a bedside commode is less stressful than using a bedpan. Using a bedside commode also reduces the risk of the Valsalva maneuver, which is more likely to occur when using a bedpan.

common law SEE: under *law*.

common mode rejection ratio ABBR: CMRR. The ability of an amplifier to amplify a signal in the presence of electrical noise. The higher the number, the better the amplification.

Common Rule SEE: under *rule*.

commotio cordis (kŏ-mō′shē-ō kŏr′dĭs) Sudden death following blunt chest trauma. At autopsy, no pathological findings are demonstrated. The syndrome is believed to be caused by ventricular fibrillation.

commotio retinae (kŏ-mō′shē-ō rĕt′ĭ-nē, kŏm-mō′tē-ō rĕ′tĭ-nī) [L. "disturbance of the retina"] Retinal edema and bleeding occurring after blunt ocular trauma.

communicable (kŏ-mūn′kă-bl) [L. *communicabilis*] Capable of being transmitted from one individual to another (human to human, animal to animal, animal to human, human to animal).

communicable period SEE: under *period*.

communicans (kŏ-mū′nĕ-kănz) [L. *communicare*, to connect with] One of several communicating nerves or arteries.

communication (kŏ-mū″nĭ-kā′shŏn) [L. *communicatio*, making common, imparting, communication] **1.** The sending of data, messages, or other forms of information from one entity to another.

2. An opening or channel between two anatomical or cellular structures.
   alternative c. Augmentative and alternative c.
   asynchronous c. A mode of interaction between two or more parties in which the exchange of information does not require simultaneous active participation. E-mail is such a communication.
   augmentative and alternative c. Any method or device that improves a person's ability to give information to or receive information from others. The term is used esp. for techniques that promote the exchange of language and symbols with the speech- and hearing-impaired. Technologies that assist communication include hearing aids, communication boards, and portable electronic (digital) devices that display, print out, or synthesize speech. SYN: *alternative c.* SEE: *communication board*.
   EMS c. A communication system that coordinates emergency medical care among ambulances, 911 (telephone) dispatch centers, and hospital emergency departments. Contact includes citizen to EMS, dispatcher to EMS crew, paramedic to doctor, and EMS crew to emergency department, as well as EMS to other public safety organizations (i.e., police, fire, and rescue). SEE: *disaster planning; EMS medical control*.
   gestural c. Body language.
   nonverbal c. Body language.
   paraverbal c. The inflection, pacing, pitch, and tone of speech; the emphasis one places on particular words, phrases, or pauses while speaking.
   privileged c. Confidential information furnished (to facilitate diagnosis and treatment) by the patient to a professional authorized by law to provide care and treatment. In some states, the person who has received this communication cannot be made to divulge it. When this is the case, communication between the patient and the recipient is classed as privileged.
      Information given by the patient with the family present may not be considered privileged.
   synchronous c. A mode of communication between parties in which messages and responses are exchanged immediately. An example of synchronous communication is talking by telephone.
   therapeutic c. An interaction between a health care professional and a patient that aims to enhance the patient's comfort, safety, trust, or health and well-being.

communication, impaired verbal The state in which a person experiences a decreased, delayed, or absent ability to receive, process, transmit, and use a system of symbols or anything that conveys meaning. SEE: *Nursing Diagnoses Appendix.*

communication, readiness for enhanced A pattern of exchanging information and ideas with others that is sufficient for meeting one's needs and life's goals and can be strengthened. SEE: *Nursing Diagnoses Appendix.*

communication board SEE: under *board.*

communication disorder Any speech or language impairment that interferes with human communication.

communicator (kŏ-mū′nĭ-kā-tor) An electronic device that permits persons with impaired verbal and physical ability to communicate through graphic or symbolic light-emitting diode (LED) displays, printed messages, or synthetic speech.

community (kŏ-mūn′ĭt-ē) [L. *communitas*, society, community] 1. A group of individuals or organisms that live together. 2. A group of human beings sharing beliefs, goals, interests, or perspectives. 3. A defined ecological niche or geographic space; a locality.

Community Integration Questionnaire ABBR: CIQ. A 15-item questionnaire that assesses how well a person who has experienced traumatic brain injury copes with home and social skills and the demands of daily living. The CIQ was developed by Barry Willer, Ph.D. and is a copyrighted assessment.

community-living Pert. to life in a community, esp. in one more strictly defined than the general population, for example, by age or disability.

community supervision Parole (2).

comorbid (kō″mor′bĭd) [*com-* + *morbid*] Pert. to a disease that exists simultaneously with and worsens or affects a primary disease. For example, the primary disease could be cancer and the comorbid disease emphysema **comorbidity** (-mor-bid′ĭt-ē), *n.*

compact (kŏm′păkt) Closely and tightly packed together; solid.

compaction (kŏm-păk′shŭn) 1. Simultaneous engagement of the presenting parts of twins in the pelvis so that labor cannot progress. 2. In dentistry, the act or process of joining or packing together powdered gold, mat gold, or gold foil in a prepared cavity in a tooth.

companion diagnostics SEE: under *diagnostics.*

companionship service (kŭm-păn′yĭn-shĭp) The provision of personal home-based protection, assistance, and company for those who cannot or do not frequently leave their residences. Companionship services include conversation, reading aloud, or running light errands and are most often provided to the aged or infirm.

comparative effectiveness research SEE: under *research.*

comparative fault Comparative negligence.

comparative negligence In forensic medicine, negligence of the plaintiff and defendant measured in terms of percentages. Damages awarded are decreased in proportion to the plaintiff's amount of negligence provided it is less than that of the defendant. SYN: *comparative fault.*

comparator (kŏm-par′ăt-ŏr) [L. *comparator*, a comparer] Something, e.g., an old drug from an established class, with which another item is compared.

comparison value A term sometimes used in public health or toxicology as a synonym for *baseline.*

compartment 1. A part of the body composed of several elements linked in a common structure, e.g. the abdominal compartment, or the muscular compartments of a limb. 2. A conceptual body part considered as an independent system when modeling the distribution or clearance of substances.

compartmentalization (kŏm-part″ment″ăl-ĭ-zā′shŏn) 1. In psychology, the division or splitting of emotions from thought; of work from leisure; or of action from logic or morality; dissociation. 2. The division of the cell or of other biological structures into distinct regions with separate functions. 3. In health care management, the splitting of a large task into smaller parts. **compartmentalize** (ment′ăl-īz″), *v.*

compartment syndrome (kŏm-part′mĕnt) Elevation of tissue pressure within a closed fascial compartment, causing a decreased arteriovenous pressure and decreased muscular perfusion. Acutely, compartment syndromes are caused by hemorrhage and/or edema within a closed space, or external compression or arterial occlusion that induces postischemic reperfusion. Health care professionals should be watchful for compartment syndrome in crushing injuries, burns, casted fractures, and wounds requiring heavy circumferential dressings. Chronic compartment syndromes (also known as exertional or recurrent compartment syndromes) may result from muscular expansion during exercise or decreased size of the anatomical compartment.

SYMPTOMS: Both types of compartment syndrome occur most frequently in the lower arm, hand, lower leg, or foot and are marked by limb pallor, swelling, and pain. The overlying skin may feel hard. As intracompartmental pressure increases, distal neurovascular function may become compromised. Chronic compartment syndrome is definitively diagnosed by measuring the intramuscular pressure while the patient is at rest and during exertion.

TREATMENT: Acute compartment

syndromes should be managed with topically applied ice and elevation of the limb. External compression should be avoided because of the risk of increasing intracompartmental pressure. Absent or diminished distal pulses require prompt surgical consultation.

PATIENT CARE: The patient with acute compartment syndrome may need a fasciotomy if symptoms are not resolved in 30 min. Fasciotomy may also be required to relieve the symptoms of chronic compartment syndrome.

abdominal c. s. ABBR: ACS. An extreme increase in pressure within the abdominal cavity that disrupts the blood flow to vital organs. It can result from any condition that causes an accumulation of blood or fluid within the abdominal space or a decrease in size of the abdominal cavity, including abdominal or pelvic trauma, intra-abdominal hemorrhage, peritonitis, extensive abdominal packing, and postoperative edema of the gastrointestinal tract.

SYMPTOMS: Clinical manifestations of ACS include hypoxemia, widened pulse pressure, and a decrease in cardiac output, urinary output, level of consciousness, and gastric pH. Intra-abdominal pressure is normally less than 5 mm Hg. Signs of organ dysfunction occur when the pressure reaches 15 to 20 mm Hg, as measured indirectly by measuring bladder pressure.

TREATMENT: ACS is treated surgically. Patients require meticulous supportive care, e.g., of blood volume status, hemodynamics, oxygenation, and ventilation.

chronic c. s. An increase in intracompartmental pressure that may occur during exercise or other forms of exertional activity. The increased intracompartmental pressure decreases blood flow to the distal extremity and impairs nerve function.

ETIOLOGY: Individuals who have herniated muscles that occlude the neurovascular network, unyielding fascia in a closed compartment, or excessive hypertrophy of muscles during exercise are predisposed to chronic compartment syndrome.

SYMPTOMS: The patient will complain of pain, numbness, and weakness in the involved extremity during exercise. Inspection may also reveal cyanosis and swelling in the distal portion of the involved limb. Symptoms may subside following activity or may lead to muscle necrosis, requiring fasciotomy.

exertional c. s. Chronic **c. s.**

recurrent anterior c. s. Chronic **c. s.**

recurrent c. s. Chronic **c. s.**

compassion (kŏm-pash′ŏn) [*comp-* + *passion*] Awareness of and feeling for the pain and suffering of others; sympathy.

compassionate use (kŏm″pash′ŏn-ăt) The administration of investigational (i.e., as yet unapproved) drugs to a patient in a special circumstance in which it is felt that the drug may be lifesaving or effective when no other therapy would be. The procedure requires the treating physician to contact either the Food and Drug Administration or the drug manufacturer to obtain permission.

compassion fatigue SEE: under *fatigue*.

compatibility (kŭm-păt-ĭ-bĭl′ĭ-tē) **1.** The ability of two or more drugs to be mixed or taken together without unfavorable or unwanted results. **2.** The ability of two individuals or groups to interact harmoniously, without undue strife or tension.

compatible (kŏm-pat′ĭ-bĕl) [L. *compatibilis,* sympathetic] **1.** In transfusions and grafting, capable of being used without immunological reaction. **2.** In pharmacology, pert. to the ability to combine two medicines without interfering with the action of either. **compatibility** (-pat″ĭ-bil′ĭt-ē), *n.*

compensable (kŏm-pĕn′sŭ-b′l) [L. *compensare,* to counterbalance] Reimbursable; entitled to or warranting compensation. Payable under the protections granted by worker's compensation or by other legal entities that give monetary awards to injured parties.

compensating (kŏm″pĕn-sāt′ĭng) Making up for a deficiency.

compensation (kom″pĕn-sā′shŏn) [L. *compensatio,* a counterbalance] **1.** The restoration of a normal physiological state by one organ when another is malfunctioning. For example, in metabolic acidosis, hyperventilation reduces the partial pressure of carbon dioxide in the body to elevate the pH back toward a normal level. **2.** In psychoanalysis, a psychic mechanism in which a person who feels himself to be inadequate (e.g., because of neuroses, character defects, or a physical disability) makes up for this perception by stressing or using other personal strengths and assets. Sublimation is often similar but differs by substituting a higher social goal to gratify the infrasocial drive by replacement rather than by only camouflaging. **3.** Restitution by payment to a person injured (e.g., in the workplace). **4.** Wages, fee, or salary for work done or services rendered.

automatic tube c. A method of overcoming the airway resistance that is required to move gas through the resistance of an endotracheal tube.

cardiac c. The ability of the heart to make up for impairments in functioning through muscular hypertrophy or other means.

workers′ c. A payment or payments made to an employee injured or disabled on the job. In most states, after a qualifying medical examination, an employee is certified as having specific functional impairments as the result of a documented injury. A predetermined amount of money, based on the severity of the injury and its consequences, is paid to the employee until the impairments improve or resolve.

competence (kom′pĕt-ĕns) [L. *competere*, to meet, agree] **1.** In psychiatry and in law, ability to manage one's affairs, and by inference, being sane; usually stated as mental competence. **2.** Performance in a manner that satisfies the demands of a situation; effective interaction with the environment.

   professional c. Proficiency in the application of the arts and sciences of healing. Such competence requires communication skills, dedication to serving others, empathy, good judgment, and technical knowledge.

competency validation program Core competency.

competition (kŏm″pĕ-tĭsh′ŭn) The simultaneous attempt of similar substances to attach to a receptor site of a cell membrane.

complaint (kŏm-plānt′) **1.** The principal reason for seeking medical assistance. **2.** The initial pleading or document that commences a legal action, states grounds for such an action, names the parties to the lawsuit, and demands for relief. SYN: *petition*.

   chief c. ABBR: CC. The symptom or group of symptoms that represents the primary reason for seeking health care.

   subjective memory c. Subjective memory **impairment**.

complement (kŏm′plĕ-mĕnt) [L. *complere*, to complete] A group of proteins in the blood that play a vital role in the body's immune defenses through a cascade of interactions. Components of complement are labeled C1 through C9. Complement acts by directly lysing (killing) organisms; by opsonizing an antigen, thus stimulating phagocytosis; and by stimulating inflammation and the B-cell–mediated immune response. All complement proteins lie inactive in the blood until activated by either the classic or the alternative pathways.

   The lack of C3 increases susceptibility to common bacterial infections, whereas deficits in C5 through C9 are usually associated with increased incidence of autoimmune diseases, particularly systemic lupus erythematosus and glomerulonephritis. Lack of C1 causes hereditary angioedema of the extremities and gastrointestinal tract. The lack of any of the more than 25 proteins involved in the complement system may affect the body's defenses adversely.

complemental (kŏm-plĕ-mĕnt′ăl) Complementary.

complementarity (kŏm″plĕ-mĕn-tăr′ĭ-tē) In individual and group interactions, the extent to which emotional requirements are met.

complementary (kom″plĭ-ment′ă-rē, -men′trē) **1.** Supplying something that is lacking in another system or entity. **2.** Having an inverse relationship with another molecule so that the two molecules attract or bind to each other perfectly. **3.** Being a reversed copy of another molecule (e.g., complementary DNA). **4.** In mathematics, any two angles that sum to 90°. SYN: *complemental*.

complement-fixation reaction A reaction seen when complement enters into combinations formed between soluble or particulate antigens and antibody. It is used to diagnose many infectious illnesses, including chlamydia, syphilis, and mycoplasma, among others. SEE: *complement; complement fixation*.

complement unit The smallest quantity of complement required for hemolysis of a given amount of red blood cells with one amboceptor (hemolysin) unit present.

complete metabolic panel ABBR: CMP. Comprehensive metabolic panel.

complex (kom′pleks″) [L. *complexus*, woven together] **1.** Intricate. **2.** Of a complicated nature. **3.** A group of interrelated biological entities. **4.** An atrial or ventricular systole as it appears on an electrocardiographic tracing. **5.** All the ideas, feelings, and sensations connected with a subject. **6.** A subconscious idea (or group of ideas) that has become associated with a repressed wish or emotional experience and that may influence behavior, although the person may not realize the connection with the repressed thoughts or actions. **7.** In Freudian theory, a grouping of ideas with an emotional background. These may be harmless, and the individual may be fully aware of them, e.g., an artist sees every object with a view to a possible picture and is said to have established a complex for art. Often, however, the complex is aroused by some painful emotional reaction such as fright or excessive grief that, instead of being allowed a natural outlet, becomes unconsciously repressed and later manifests itself in some abnormality of mind or behavior. According to Freud, the best method of determining the complex is through psychoanalysis. SEE: *Electra complex; Jocasta complex; Oedipus complex*. **8.** An anatomical or intracellular structure.

   AIDS-dementia c. ABBR: ADC. Encephalopathy caused by direct infection of brain tissue by HIV. This condition affects patients with severe immunosuppression more often than those whose immune function is stronger.

Central nervous system HIV infection affects as many as 15% of AIDS patients, but in 1997 its incidence decreased to approx. 30% of its previous occurrence because of the effectiveness of highly active antiretroviral therapy (HAART). Central nervous system HIV infections in children tend to be more pronounced than those in adults.

ETIOLOGY: The exact cause of AIDS dementia is unknown, but current theories suggest that it results from HIV infection of macrophages in the brain (microglia) and the destructive release of cytokines that disrupt neurotransmitter function.

SYMPTOMS: AIDS dementia is characterized by slow, progressive memory loss, decreased ability to concentrate, a general slowing of cognitive processes, and mood disorders. Motor dysfunction may also be present, including ataxia, bowel and bladder incontinence, and seizures. Higher levels of HIV RNA in the cerebrospinal fluid (CSF viral load) are correlated with increased problems.

TREATMENT: Treatment options may include highly active antiretroviral therapies. Since their introduction the incidence of AIDS-dementia complex has decreased.

PATIENT CARE: The patient's mental status and level of consciousness must be assessed and documented. Clear documentation is essential to track a patient's changes over time. Orientation to person, place, and time; thought processes (cognition); verbal communication skills; and memory losses can be determined through simple conversations that reveal the patient's ability to recall normal details of the day and previous teaching. Particular attention is paid to patients' abilities to comply with their complex medication regimen; inability to do so requires another person to assume responsibility for this task. The patient's affect and mood; the presence of agitated, restless, or lethargic behavior; and the extent to which clothing is clean and appropriate for the weather may reveal progressing dementia when compared with previously documented mental status assessments.

Interventions are based on clear communication. As patients develop dementia, they may become frightened, and a consistently gentle approach with positive feedback is essential. Clocks, calendars, and memory aids help the patient become reoriented. Step-by-step written instructions should be given to augment verbal instructions. Caregivers need to learn how to reorient the patient, how to recognize and treat hallucinations, how to create a safe environment, how to ensure that basic hygiene needs are met, and how to document medication schedules and intake because patients may forget to eat or drink adequately. SYN: *HIV-associated dementia*. SEE: *AIDS*.

AIDS-related c. ABBR: ARC. The symptomatic stage of infection with human immunodeficiency virus (HIV) before the onset of AIDS. Its clinical signs include fatigue, intermittent fevers, weight loss greater than 10%, chronic or persistent intermittent diarrhea, night sweats, diminished delayed hypersensitivity (skin test) response to common allergens, presence of HIV antibodies in blood, and decreased CD4+ T-lymphocyte count. SEE: *AIDS*.

amygdaloid c. Amygdala.

anti-inhibitor coagulant c. A blood product derived from human plasma, used to augment the effects of clotting factors given to patients with hemophilia. Hemophiliacs who have received repeated injections of clotting factors may develop antibodies to those factors, which decreases the effectiveness of hemophilia treatments. Anti-inhibitors are used to counteract the effect of the unwanted antibodies

castration c. A morbid fear of being castrated.

Eisenmenger c. SEE: *Eisenmenger syndrome*.

Ghon c. SEE: *Ghon complex*.

HLA c. Major histocompatibility **c.**

immune c. A substance formed when antibodies attach to antigens to destroy them. These complexes circulate in the blood and may eventually attach to the walls of blood vessels, producing a local inflammatory response. Immune complexes form in type III hypersensitivity reactions and are involved in the development of glomerulonephritis, serum sickness, arthritis, and vasculitis.

inferiority c. The condition of having low self-esteem. It is a 20th-century term stemming from Adlerian therapy.

inferior olivary c. Inferior **olive**.

major histocompatibility c. ABBR: MHC. A group of genes on chromosome 6 that code for the antigens that determine tissue and blood compatibility. In humans, histocompatibility antigens are called human leukocyte antigens (HLA) because they were originally discovered in large numbers on lymphocytes. There are thousands of combinations of HLA antigens. Class I MHC antigens (HLA-A, HLA-B, and HLA-C) are found on all nucleated cells and platelets. Class II antigens (HLA-DR, HLA-DQ, and HLA-DP) are found on lymphocytes and antigen processing cells and are important in the specific immune response. In tissue and organ transplantation, the extent to which the HLA or "tissue type" of the donor and recipient match is a major determinant of the success of the transplant. SYN:

HLA c. SEE: *histocompatibility locus antigen.*

membrane attack c. The combination of complement factors C5 through C9 that directly attack and kill the cell membranes of microorganisms during the terminal attack phase of the complement cascade. SEE: *complement; inflammation.*

Mycobacterium avium c. ABBR: MAC, MAI. An atypical mycobacterium that causes systemic bacterial infection in patients with advanced immunosuppression, esp. those with AIDS. It occasionally causes lung infections in patients with chronic obstructive lung disease. SYN: *Mycobacterium avium-intracellulare c.*

SYMPTOMS: MAC infection in AIDS patients can cause fatigue, fever, weight loss, cachexia, pancytopenia, and death.

TREATMENT: Multiple antimicrobial agents, given at the same time and for long courses, are required to treat MAC. Combination therapy may include a macrolide with drugs such as rifabutin, ethambutol, ciprofloxacin, amikacin, and/or clofazimine.

Mycobacterium avium-intracellulare c. Mycobacterium avium **c.**

nodal premature c. ABBR: NPC. Ectopic cardiac beat originating in the atrioventricular node.

nuclear pore c. A collection of membrane-associated proteins that regulate the passage of large molecules between the cytoplasm and the cell nucleus.

oculomotor c. A group of interrelated nuclei found near the midline in the rostral midbrain. They include the oculomotor nucleus and the Edinger-Westphal nucleus, and they innervate somatic muscles, e.g., inferior rectus and levator palpebrae muscles, and visceral muscles (preganglionic parasympathetic axons to the ciliary ganglia) via the oculomotor nerve (CN III).

olivary c. Olive (2).

osteomeatal c. The middle turbinate and the middle meatus of the nose.

QRS complex The pattern traced on the surface electrocardiogram by depolarization of the ventricles. In the anterior chest leads, e.g., V_1 to V_3, the complex normally consists of a small initial downward deflection (Q wave), a large upward deflection (R wave), and a second downward deflection (S wave). The normal duration of the complex is 0.06 to 0.11 sec. Longer QRS complexes are seen in premature ventricular beats and ventricular arrhythmias.

QRST c. Q-T interval.

superiority c. Exaggerated conviction that one is better than others, a pretense used to compensate for a real or imagined inferiority.

superior olivary c. Superior **olive.**

symptom c. Syndrome.

tuberous sclerosis c. Tuberous sclerosis.

complex ectopic beat SEE: under *beat.*

complexed prostate-specific antigen (kŏm-plekst′, kom′plekst″) ABBR: cPSA. A laboratory test that assays levels of prostate-specific antigen bound to alpha-1-chymotrypsin. The cPSA test is slightly more useful in the detection of prostate cancer than the simple PSA test but may not be as accurate as assessments of serum unbound or free PSA.

complexion (kŏm-plĕk′shŭn) The color and appearance of the facial skin.

complex regional pain syndrome, type 1 Reflex sympathetic dystrophy.

complex regional pain syndrome, type 2 Causalgia.

compliance (kŏm-plī′ăns) **1.** Adherence (2). **2.** Alteration of size and shape in response to application of force, weight, or release from force. The lung and thoracic cage of a child may have a high degree of compliance as compared with that of an elderly person.

dynamic c. A measure of the ease of lung inflation with positive pressure.

effective c. Patient compliance during positive-pressure breathing using a tidal volume corrected for compressed volume divided by static pressure.

frequency-dependent c. A condition in which pulmonary compliance decreases with rapid breathing; used to identify small airway disease.

myocardial c. The ease with which the heart muscle relaxes as it fills with blood.

pulmonary c. A measure of the force required to distend the lungs.

static c. A volume-to-pressure measurement of lung distensibility with exhalation against a closed system, taken under conditions of no airflow. It can be represented mathematically as: Tidal volume/Pplat-total PEEP (positive end-expiratory pressure).

tubing c. The ability of ventilator tubing to expand when pressurized. It is calculated by closing the ventilator circuit and measuring the volume under pressurization.

ventricular c. Distensibility or stiffness of the relaxed ventricle of the heart.

compliance program A corporate or institutional program that provides guidelines for the ethical and legal behavior of employees. It is used to disseminate knowledge about, supervise, and enforce the conduct of health care employees, specifically their adherence to federally mandated rules that regulate health care fraud, waste, and abuse.

complicating disease A disease that occurs during the course of another disease.

complication (kŏm″plĭ-kā′shŭn) [L. *cum*, with, + *plicare*, to fold] An added difficulty; a complex state; a disease or accident superimposed on another without being specifically related, yet affecting or modifying the prognosis of the original disease (e.g., pneumonia is a complication of measles and is the cause of many deaths from that disease).

component (kŏm-pō′nĕnt) [L. *componere*, to put together] A constituent part.

bioactive food c. A compound occurring in food that brings about a physiological effect.

blood c. Any transfusible product derived from whole blood, e.g., red blood cells, platelets, plasma, coagulation factors, immunoglobulins. SYN: *blood product*.

plasma thromboplastin c. ABBR: PTC. Blood coagulation factor IX, an enzyme precursor activated by vitamin K, binding with calcium, phospholipids, and blood coagulation factor VIII to further activate blood coagulation factor X. It was formerly called "Christmas factor." SEE: *blood **coagulation**; coagulation **factor***.

component blood therapy SEE: *blood component therapy*.

composite (kŏm-pŏz′ĭt) [L. *compositus*, put together] A material made of two (or more) parts that when linked exhibit different biological, chemical, or physical properties than either part alone.

compos mentis (kŏm″pŭs mĕn′tĭs) [L.] Of sound mind; sane. SEE: *non compos mentis*.

compound (kom′pownd″) [L. *componere*, to place together] **1.** In chemistry, a substance composed of two or more units or parts combined in definite proportions by weight and having specific properties of its own. Compounds are formed by all living organisms and are of two types, organic and inorganic. **2.** Made up of more than one part. **3.** In pharmacy, to prepare a prescription.

amphoteric c. A compound that reacts as both an acid and a base.

antisense c. Any of the manufactured compounds that may alter disease processes by blocking the production of harmful proteins by diseased cells. These molecules seek out and impede the functioning of a diseased cell's messenger RNA (a "sense" strand). Without this intervention, the RNA would carry basic directions for the production of disease-causing proteins. SYN: *antisense drug*.

aromatic c. Any of the ring or cyclic compounds related to benzene, many having a fragrant odor.

azo c. Any of the organic substances that contain the azo group. An example is azobenzene, $C_6H_5N : NC_6H_5$. They are related to aniline and include important dyes and indicators. SEE: *indicator* for table.

barium c. Any of the compounds containing barium and suitable diluents or additives. They are used in the form of insoluble barium sulfate to visualize, that is, to outline, the hollow viscera in roentgenography. Poisoning occasionally occurs when the soluble barium salts are used accidentally in place of the insoluble sulfate. SEE: *Poisons and Poisoning Appendix*.

chemical c. 1. A substance consisting of two or more chemical elements, in specific proportions and in chemical combination, for which a chemical formula can be written. Examples include water (H_2O) and salt (NaCl). **2.** A substance that can be separated chemically into simpler substances.

impression c. A nonelastic molding used in dentistry to make imprints of teeth and other oral tissues. Impression compound is a thermoplastic material, i.e., it softens when heated and solidifies without chemical change when cooled.

inorganic c. Any of numerous compounds that, in general, contain no carbon.

optimal cutting temperature c. An embedding medium for preparing tissues for sectioning and microscopic analysis.

organic c. A compound containing carbon. Such compounds include carbohydrates, proteins, and fats.

polar c. A molecule with distinct electrical charges in different regions, i.e., a positive charge in one region and a negative charge in another.

quarternary ammonium c. A salt of ammonia (NH_4^+) in which the loci held by the hydrogen ions in ammonia are held instead by alkyl groups.

saturated c. An organic compound with all carbon bonds filled. It does not contain double or triple bonds.

unsaturated c. An organic compound having double or triple bonds between the carbon atoms.

compounding (kom′pownd″ing) Combining pharmacologically active agents at a pharmacy; mixing or preparing a single active agent at a pharmacy for use by an individual patient.

> ⚠ Pharmacies that compound drugs are regulated by state and local boards of pharmacy, not by the FDA.

compounding aseptic isolator Any modular device or enclosed microenvironment used in a pharmacy to prepare sterile items for administration to patients. It may be used, e.g., to prepare antibiotics, biologic agents, or total parenteral nutrition. SYN: *compounding isolator*.

compounding isolator Compounding aseptic isolator.

comprehend (kŏm-prē-hĕnd′) To understand.

Comprehensive Health Enhancement Support System ABBR: CHESS. A computer-based system of integrated services designed to help individuals cope with a health crisis or medical concern. It was developed by a team of decision, information, education, and communication scientists at the University of Wisconsin-Madison's Center for Health Systems Research and Analysis (CHSRA). CHESS is currently being used by several major health organizations in the U.S. and Canada. Website: http://chsra.wisc.edu

comprehensive metabolic panel ABBR: CMP. A frequently ordered cluster of lab tests, comprising measurements of serum electrolytes (sodium, potassium, chloride, and calcium), renal function (blood urea nitrogen [BUN] and creatinine), acid-base balance (bicarbonate), liver functions, and glucose. The test is obtained by drawing a blood sample from a peripheral vein or, in critical care, from a central vein. SYN: *complete metabolic panel*.

¹compress (kom′pres″) [Fr. fr. L. *compressare*, to squeeze together] A cloth, wet or dry, folded and applied firmly to a body part.

   cold c. A soft, absorbent cloth, several layers thick, dipped in cold water, slightly wrung out, and applied to the part being treated. The duration of the application is usually 10 to 20 min.

   hot c. A soft, absorbent cloth folded into several layers, dipped in hot water 107° to 115°F (41.7° to 46.1°C), barely wrung out, and placed on the part to be treated. It is covered with a piece of cloth.

   wet c. Two or more folds of soft cloth wrung out of water at prescribed temperatures and covered with fabric.

²compress (kŏm-pres′) **1.** To press together into a smaller space. **2.** To close or occlude by applying pressure or squeezing together, as the edges of a wound or a vein.

compressible (kŭm-prĕs′ĭ-bĭl) Able to be pressed into a smaller space or squeezed together.

compression (kŏm-presh′ŏn) [L. *compressio*, a pressing together] The action of pressing together, or the state of being pressed together.

   breast c. Squeezing the breast between movable grids prior to mammographic or magnetic resonance imaging. Its purpose is to limit movement of the breast and optimize image detail, minimize the dose of radiation received, maximize the quantity of breast tissue in the field of view, and stabilize the breast during biopsy.

   cerebral c. Potentially life-threatening pressure on the brain produced by increased intracranial fluid, embolism, thrombosis, tumors, skull fractures, or aneurysms.

   SYMPTOMS: The condition is marked by alterations of consciousness, nausea and vomiting, limb paralysis, and cranial nerve deficits. It may present as, or progress to, brain death. SEE: *Glasgow Coma Scale*.

   PATIENT CARE: The patient is closely assessed for signs and symptoms of increased intracranial pressure, respiratory distress, convulsions, bleeding from the ears or nose, or drainage of cerebrospinal fluid from the ears or nose (which most probably indicates a fracture). Neurological status is monitored for any alterations in level of consciousness, pupillary signs, ocular movements, verbal response, sensory and motor function (including voluntary and involuntary movements), or behavioral and mental capabilities; and vital signs are assessed, esp. respiratory patterns. Any signs of deterioration are documented and reported. Seizure precautions are maintained.

   Insertion of an intracranial pressure (ICP) monitoring device permits monitoring of cerebral perfusion and draining of cerebrospinal fluid to decrease ICP and reduce intracranial volume. A brain scan may help to determine the cause. Hyperventilation reduces $PaCO_2$, causing cerebral blood vessels to constrict, thus lessening blood volume within the cranium and lowering ICP. Osmotic diuretics and hypertonic saline solutions also help to move fluid out of the brain and into the intravascular space. If these therapies fail, decompressive craniectomy, high-dose barbiturate therapy, and aggressive therapeutic hyperventilation may be instituted. All general patient care concerns apply. In addition, the patient requires aggressive pulmonary care to prevent respiratory complications; enteral or parenteral nutrition to maintain a normoglycemic state, meet hypermetabolic energy requirements, and prevent protein calorie malnutrition; and careful assessment for coagulopathies and gastrointestinal bleeding and prophylaxis for deep vein thrombosis. Physical and occupational therapists help to prevent musculoskeletal complications. Special mattresses, careful repositioning, and regular skin care help prevent skin breakdown.

   chest c. ABBR: CC. Forcible depression of the thorax during cardiopulmonary resuscitation. This technique is used to circulate the blood of a patient whose heart is no longer beating effectively enough to sustain life.

PATIENT CARE: Effective chest compressions in an adult should depress the sternum by 1.5–2 in (4–5 cm). In a child or infant, the sternum should be depressed by the rescuer to a depth of about 1/2 to 1/3 the depth of the chest.

digital c. Compression of blood vessels with the fingers to stop hemorrhage.

intermittent c. A technique for reducing edema in an extremity by pumping air (intermittent pneumatic compression) or, less commonly, chilled water through a sleeve that surrounds an extremity. Circumferential pressure applied to the arm or leg is gradually increased to enhance venous and lymphatic flow, and then the sleeve is deflated. The process is then repeated. SEE: *sequential compression device*.

c. of morbidity Shortening of the period or proportion of long-term disability by elimination of a chronic disease.

myelitis c. Compression due to pressure on the spinal cord, often caused by a tumor.

spot c. The application of local pressure to a region of the breast in which an anomaly was found during routine mammography. The locally imaged portion of breast tissue is magnified by compression and is therefore easier to view than the surrounding breast tissue because the volume of tissue in the image is minimized.

compression glove A glove made of material that stretches; used to maintain pressure on and decrease the swelling in an arm or hand. Gloves may be measured for a custom fit or ordered from a sizing chart. In the early stages, a patient will need a new garment every few months as the edema decreases and the garment loses elasticity.

compression paddle In mammography, a thin plastic device that squeezes breast tissue against the support table, in order to achieve either uniform pressure on all breast tissue or a uniform thickness.

compression-ventilation ratio In emergency cardiac care, the number of times a rescuer forcibly depresses the chest of a victim of cardiac arrest for each administered breath.

PATIENT CARE: The American Heart Association (2010) suggests a ratio of 30 chest compressions followed by 2 ventilations for an adult for each cycle of cardiopulmonary resuscitation. The same ratio is used for infants and children when a single rescuer is working alone. Two rescuers working together with an infant or child should use a ratio of 15:2. The breaths and compressions do not need to be synchronized. The breaths and compressions do not need to be synchronized.

compressor (kŏm-prĕs'ŏr) **1.** An instrument or device that applies a compressive force, as in compaction of gold. **2.** A muscle that compresses a part, as the compressor hemispherium bulbi, which compresses the bulb of the urethra.

air c. A machine that compresses air into storage tanks for use in air syringes, air turbine handpieces, and other air-driven tools.

compromised host (kom'prŏ-mīzd″) SEE: under *host*.

Compton scattering (komp'tŏn) [Arthur H. Compton, U.S. physicist and Nobel laureate, 1892–1962] An interaction between x-rays and matter in which the incoming photon ejects a loosely bound outer-shell electron. The resulting change in the direction of the x-ray photon causes scatter, increasing the dose and degrading the radiographic image. Most interactions between x-rays and matter are of this type, esp. at high energies. SEE: *scatter*.

compulsion (kŏm-pŭl'shŭn) [L. *compulsio*, compulsion] A repetitive stereotyped act performed to relieve fear connected with obsession. If denied, it causes uneasiness. SYN: *compulsion neurosis*. **compulsive** (-sĭv), *adj*.

compulsory (kŏm-pŭl'sor-ē) **1.** Compelling action against one's will. **2.** Required.

computational knowledge The use of a computer to interpret data, used as a basis for forming hypotheses, establishing trends, testing relationships, and making decisions.

computer-aided detection ABBR: CAD. Software that alerts a radiologist to abnormal or suspicious elements of a radiological image.

computer-assisted instruction SEE: under *instruction*.

computer-assisted interviewing, computer-assisted self-interviewing ABBR: CAI. The gathering of data from patients about such matters as allergies, behaviors, medical conditions and medications via direct input into an electronic health record by the patient.

computerized physician or provider order entry ABBR: CPOE. Any system that allows registered health care providers to request drugs, laboratory studies, or radiological tests by entering those requests in an electronic health care record.

computer literacy 1. The ability to acquire and apply a basic understanding of computer hardware and software to solve problems or access information. **2.** Educational programs designed to help students gain mastery in computer applications.

computer science SEE: under *science*.

computer vision syndrome ABBR: CVS.

Eye symptoms that result from excessive computer use. Commonly reported findings include blurry distance vision, visual fatigue, a sense of eye dryness, headaches, or neck or shoulder pain. CVS may be improved with special eyewear designed for computer users.

COMT Catechol-*O*-methyltransferase, an enzyme that breaks down dopamine and L-dopa in the brain and thus reduces the effectiveness of some treatments for Parkinson's disease. Drugs that inhibit COMT improve patient responsiveness to treatment with levodopa, one of the mainstays of treatment for Parkinson's disease.

CON *certificate of need.*

con-A *concanavalin-A.*

conarium (kō-nā′rē-ŭm) [L.] The pineal body of the brain.

conation (kō-nā′shŭn) [L. *conatio,* an attempt] The initiative, impulse, and drive to act. All of these may be diminished in cerebral diseases, esp. those involving the medial orbital parts of the frontal lobes. SEE: *abulia.*

concanavalin-A (kŏn″kă-năv′ĭ-lĭn) ABBR: con-A. A protein derived from the jack bean used to stimulate proliferation of T lymphocytes. SEE: *mitogen.*

concatenation (kŏn-kăt″ĭ-nā′shŭn) [L. *con,* together, + *catena,* chain] A group of events or effects acting in concert or occurring at the same time. SYN: *catenation.*

Concato disease (kon-kot′ō) [Luigi M. Concato, It. physician, 1825–1882] Polyserositis.

concave (kŏn′kāv, kŏn-kāv′) [″ + *cavus,* hollow] Having a spherically depressed or hollow surface.

concavity (kŏn-kăv′ĭ-tē) A surface with curved, bowl-like sides; a rounded depression.

concavoconcave (kŏn-kā″vō-kŏn′kāv) [″ + *cavus,* hollow, + *con,* with, + *cavus,* hollow] Concave on opposing sides.

concavoconvex (kŏn-kā″vō-kŏn′věks) [″ + ″ + *convexus,* vaulted] Concave on one side and convex on the opposite surface. SEE: *convex.*

concealment (kŏn-sēl′měnt) **1.** In medicolegal affairs, failure to provide information or evidence. **2.** In research, a technique to guarantee blinding of subjects and investigators. **3.** In patient care, shielding a patient from his diagnosis. **4.** In plastic surgery, the hiding of a structure with an undesirable appearance. **5.** In electrocardiography, the invisibility of a rhythm or conduction disturbance. **6.** In emergency or military medicine, hiding behind a curtain or bush to make it difficult for an assailant to see or direct gunfire toward one.

conceive (kŏn-sēv′) [L. *concipere,* to take to oneself] **1.** To become pregnant. **2.** To form a mental image or to bring into mind; to form an idea.

concentration (kon″sĕn-trā′shŏn) **1.** Fixation of the mind on one subject to the exclusion of all other thoughts. **2.** An increase in the strength of a fluid by evaporation. **3.** The amount of a substance in a mixture or solution expressed as weight or mass per unit volume.

   airborne c. The mass of particulate substances or fibers, or the vapor percentage of dissolved pollutants in a specific volume of air. As the concentration increases, the risk of inhalational exposure rises.

   blood alcohol c. ABBR: BAC. The weight of ethanol in a fixed volume of blood, usually expressed in the U.S. in mg/dL. Concentration depends on quantity, the rate of alcohol ingestion, metabolism, and alcohol absorption rates. BAC is used to measure the degree of a person's intoxication. The alcohol level at which a person is considered legally impaired varies by country and state. SYN: *blood alcohol level.*

   hydrogen ion c. [H^+], the molar concentration of hydrogen ions in a solution. It is the factor responsible for the acidic properties of a solution. SEE: *pH.*

   inhibitory c. ABBR: IC. The concentration of a medication in the blood that will inhibit the replication of a specified percentage of microorganisms. The abbreviation IC is often followed by a number, e.g., 50 or 90. The IC50 of a drug to treat acquired immunodeficiency syndrome is the drug concentration that will inhibit replication of 50% of all HIV virions, and IC90 is the concentration that will inhibit 90% of the virions.

   low-density lipoprotein particle c. ABBR: LDL particle concentration. The number of low-density lipoprotein particles in a specified volume of plasma. The higher the concentration, the greater the risk of atherosclerotic vascular disease. SYN: *low-density lipoprotein particle number.*

   mass c. SYMB: ρ. The amount of matter of any material divided by its volume. In the metric system, ρ is defined in kilograms per liter (kg/L). SEE: *substance c.; molar c.*

   maximum allowable c. ABBR: MAC. The upper limit of concentration of certain atmospheric contaminants allowed in the workplace.

   mean cell hemoglobin c. The average concentration of hemoglobin in a given volume (usually 100 ml) of packed red blood cells, obtained by multiplying the number of grams of hemoglobin in the unit volume by 100 and dividing by the hematocrit. SYN: *mean corpuscular hemoglobin c.*

   mean corpuscular hemoglobin c. ABBR: MCHC. Mean cell hemoglobin concentration.

   minimum alveolar c. ABBR: MAC.

A measure of the relative potency of an anesthetic agent, specifically, the concentration of the agent in exhaled air that will prevent 50% of people from moving when they are exposed to a painful or noxious stimulus, such as one they might experience during surgery.

minimum bactericidal c. The lowest concentration of an antimicrobial that kills a defined fraction of bacteria or fungi. SYN: *minimum lethal c.*

minimum inhibitory c. ABBR: MIC. The lowest concentration of an antimicrobial drug that prevents visible bacterial growth in a defined growth medium.

minimum lethal c. ABBR: MLC. Minimum bactericidal **c.**

molar c. SYMB: *c.* The number of moles of a substance in a specified volume of solution. SEE: *mass c.*

osmotic c. Osmolality.

substance c. SYMB: *c.* The amount of a specified material or the amount of substance (measured in moles) in the total volume of a system. SEE: *mass c.*

concentration test A kidney function test based on the ability of the person to produce concentrated urine under conditions that would normally cause such production, as in intentional dehydration.

concentric (kŏn-sĕn'trĭk) [" + *centrum,* center] Having a common center.

concept (kon'sept") [L. *conceptum,* something understood] A notion formed in the mind; an idea. **conceptual** (kŏn-sep'choo-ăl), *adj.*

conception (kŏn-sep'shŏn) [L. *conceptio,* comprehending, conception] **1.** The mental process of forming an idea. **2.** The onset of pregnancy marked by implantation of a fertilized ovum in the uterine endometrium. SEE: *contraception; fertilization; implantation.*

conception vessel SEE: under *vessel.*

conceptual framework Conceptual **model**.

Conceptual Level Analogies Test ABBR: CLAT. A neuropsychiatric test designed to gauge abstract verbal reasoning.

conceptual models of nursing (kŏn-sĕp'chū-ăl) Sets of abstract and general concepts and propositions that each provide a distinctive frame of reference for viewing human beings, the environment, health, and nursing goals and actions; used to guide nursing practice, research, education, and administration. SEE: *Nursing Theory Appendix.*

conceptual system Conceptual **model**.

conceptus (kŏn-sep'tŭs) [L. *conceptus,* gathering, conception, something conceived] The products of conception. They include the embryo/fetus, placenta, and membranes.

concha (kŏng'kă) *pl.* **conchae** [Gr. *konche,* shell] **1.** The outer ear or the pinna.

2. One of the three nasal conchae. SEE: *nasal concha.*

c. auriculae A concavity on the median surface of the auricle of the ear, divided by a ridge into the upper cymba conchae and a lower cavum conchae. The latter leads to the external auditory meatus.

c. bullosa A distention of the turbinate bone due to cyst formation.

nasal c. One of the three scroll-like bones that project medially from the lateral wall of the nasal cavity; a turbinate bone. The superior and middle conchae are processes of the lateral mass of the ethmoid bone; the inferior concha is a facial bone. Each overlies a meatus.

c. sphenoidalis In a fetal skull, one of the two curved plates located on the anterior portion of the body of the sphenoid bone and forming part of the roof of the nasal cavity.

conchotome (kŏng'kō-tōm) [" + *tome,* incision] A device for excising the middle turbinate bone.

concoction (kŏn-kŏk'shŭn) [L. *con,* with, + *coquere,* to cook] A mixture of two medicinal substances, usually done with the aid of heat.

concomitant (kŏn-kŏm'ĭ-tănt) [" + *comes,* companion] Accessory; taking place at the same time.

concordance (kŏn-kor'dăns) **1.** In twins, the equal representation of a genetic trait in each. **2.** In statistics, the degree to which separate observations align with, are congruent with, each other.

concrement (kŏn'krē-mĕnt) [L. *concrementum*] A concretion as of protein and other substances. If infiltrated with calcium salts, it is termed a calculus.

concrescence (kŏn-kres'ĕns) [L. *concrescere,* to grow together] **1.** The union of separate parts; coalescence. **2.** In dentistry, the attachment of a tooth to an adjacent tooth by deposition of cementum of the roots only.

concrete (kŏn'krēt, kŏn-krēt') [L. *concretus,* solid] Condensed, hardened, or solidified.

concretio cordis (kŏn-krē'shē-ō kor'dĭs) Obliteration of the pericardial space in chronic, constrictive pericarditis.

concretion (kŏn-krē'shŭn) [" + *crescere,* to grow] Calculus.

concussion (kŏn-kŭsh'ŏn) [L. *concussio,* a shaking] **1.** An injury resulting from impact with an object. **2.** Partial or complete loss of function, as that resulting from a blow or fall.

c. of brain An imprecise term for a traumatic brain injury.

cerebral c. Traumatic brain **injury**.

c. of labyrinth Deafness resulting from a blow to the head or ear.

spinal c. Loss of function in the spinal cord resulting from a blow or severe jarring.

condensation (kŏn"dĕn-sā'shŭn) [L, *con,*

with, + *densare,* to make thick]
1. Making more dense or compact.
2. Changing of a liquid to a solid or a gas to a liquid. **3.** In psychoanalysis, the union of ideas to form a new mental pattern. **4.** In chemistry, a type of reaction in which two or more molecules of the same substance react with each other and form a new and heavier substance with different chemical properties. **5.** A mechanical process used in dentistry to pack amalgam into a cavity preparation. The goal of condensation is to produce a homogeneous restorative material with an absence of voids. Condensation is also a method of placing a direct gold restoration, improving the physical properties of the gold foil used and forcing the foil to adapt to the cavity preparation.

condensation silicone impression material An elastic final impression material for constructing dental cast restorations, prostheses, and appliances. It is made of two pastes containing siloxane and stannous octoate and has a limited shelf life.

condenser (kŏn-den'sĕr) **1.** A device used to liquefy gases or vapors, or rarely to convert gases directly into solids. **2.** An instrument or tool used to compact and condense restorative materials in dental cavity preparations. SEE: *plugger.* **3.** Capacitor.

    amalgam c. In dentistry, a tool to compress amalgam into a cavity preparation.

    electrical c. Capacitor.

    substage c. In a microscope, that part of the lens system that supplies the illumination critical to the resolving power of the instrument. SYN: *Abbe condenser.*

condensin (kŏn-dĕn'sĭn) [L. *con,* with, + *densare,* to make thick, + in, into] A protein complex that compacts and organizes dividing chromosomes during mitosis.

condiment (kŏn'dĭ-mĕnt) [L. *condire,* to pickle] An appetizing ingredient added to food.

    CLASSIFICATION: *Aromatic:* vanilla, cinnamon, cloves, chervil, parsley, bay leaf. *Acrid or peppery:* pepper, ginger, tabasco, all-spice. *Alliaceous or allylic:* onion, mustard, horseradish. *Acid:* vinegar, capers, gherkins, citron. *Animal origin:* caviar, anchovies. *Miscellaneous:* salt, sugar, truffles.

    In general, with the exception of sugar, condiments have little nutritional value. They are appetizers, stimulating the secretion of saliva and intestinal juices.

condition 1. A state of health; physical, esp. athletic, fitness. **2.** To train a person or animal to respond in a predictable way to a stimulus.

conditioning (kŏn-dish'ŏn-ing) **1.** Im-

proving the physical capability of a person by an exercise program. **2.** In psychology, the use of a special and different stimulus in conjunction with a familiar one. After a sufficient period in which the two stimuli have been presented simultaneously, the special stimulus alone will cause the response that could originally be produced only by the familiar stimulus. Ivan Pavlov used dogs to demonstrate that the strange stimulus, ringing of a bell, could cause the animal to salivate if the test was done after a period of *conditioning* during which the bell and the familiar stimulus, food, were presented simultaneously. Also called *classical conditioning.* **3.** The administration of chemotherapy in preparation for bone marrow transplantation. The purpose is to eliminate cancer cells from the marrow before donor cells are infused. **4.** The treatment with heat and moisture of gases supplied to a patient through an endotracheal tube so that the gases more closely approximate those that might pass through the upper airways into the trachea and bronchi during spontaneous breathing.

    aversive c. SEE: *aversion therapy.*

    operant c. The learning of a particular action or type of behavior followed by a reward. This technique was publicized by the Harvard psychologist B. F. Skinner, who trained animals to activate (by pecking, in the case of a pigeon, or pressing a bar, in the case of a rat) an apparatus that released a pellet of food.

    work c. Work **hardening**.

condom (kon'dŏm) [origin uncertain] A thin, flexible penile sheath made of synthetic or natural materials. *Condom* typically refers to a *male condom.* Condoms are used commonly during sexual intercourse to prevent conception by capturing ejaculated semen. Latex condoms also shield against sexually transmitted diseases (STDs). Their effectiveness is affected by careful handling (to avoid punctures, tears, or slippage), usage before sexual contact (to prevent inadvertent transmission of sperm or germs), and allowing sufficient space for ejaculation (to prevent condom rupture). To avoid damage to condoms, only water-soluble lubricants should be used to facilitate vaginal entry. Condoms should not be reused. SEE: *contraception; female c.; sexually transmitted disease;* illus.

⚠ Only a water-based lubricant such as K-Y Jelly® should be used with a condom. Oil-based products begin to deteriorate latex in less than 1 min.

    female c. An intravaginal device, similar to the male condom, designed to

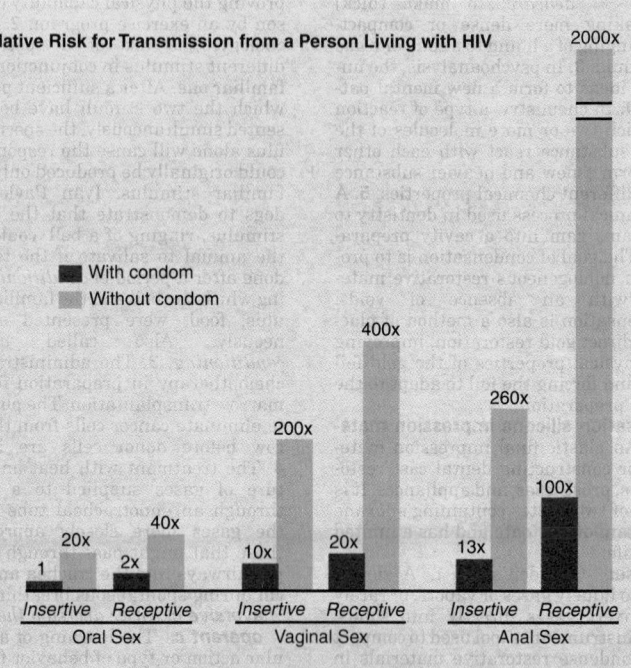

Relative Risk for Transmission from a Person Living with HIV

Legend:
■ With condom
□ Without condom

Oral Sex — Insertive: 1 / 20x; Receptive: 2x / 40x
Vaginal Sex — Insertive: 10x / 200x; Receptive: 20x / 400x
Anal Sex — Insertive: 13x / 260x; Receptive: 100x / 2000x

Types of Sexual Activity

CONDOM USE AND HIV RISK

prevent unwanted pregnancy and STDs. It consists of a soft loose-fitting polyurethane sheath closed at one end. A flexible polyurethane ring is inside the closed end, and another sheath is at the open end. The inner ring is used for insertion, covering the cervix as a contraceptive diaphragm does and also for anchoring and positioning the condom well inside the vagina. During use the external ring remains outside the vagina and covers the area around the vaginal opening. This prevents contact between the labia and the base of the penis. The female condom is prelubricated; additional lubrication is provided in the package. It is designed for one-time use. As a contraceptive, it is as effective as other barrier methods. SEE: illus.

   lambskin c. Natural membrane **c.**
   membrane c. Natural membrane **c.**
   natural membrane c. A penile condom made from lamb cecum.

⚠ Unlike condoms made from latex or polyurethane, natural membrane condoms may be porous to HIV and hepatitis B virus (HBV).

SYN: *lambskin **c.**; membrane **c.***

conductance (kŏn-dŭk′tăns) [L. *conducere,* to lead] The conducting ability of a body or a circuit for electricity. The best conductor is one that offers the least resistance such as gold, silver, or copper. When expressed as a numerical

FEMALE CONDOM

value, conductance is the reciprocal of resistance. The unit is the ohm.

airway c. ABBR: G$_{AW}$. The amount of airflow divided by the amount of pressure that produces it; a measure of the ability of the respiratory airways to maintain airflow.

conduction (kŏn-dŭk'shŭn) **1.** The process whereby a state of excitation affects adjacent portions of a tissue or cell, so that the disturbance is transmitted to remote points. Conduction occurs not only in the fibers of the nervous system but also in muscle fibers. **2.** The transfer of electrons, ions, heat, or sound waves through a conductor or conducting medium.

aberrant c. The movement of electrical impulses through the heart along diseased or accessory pathways.

air c. The conduction of sound to the inner ear via the pathway provided by the air in the ear canal.

bone c. Sound conduction through the cranial bones.

conduction system of the heart Specialized myocytes in the heart that conduct the electrical impulses throughout the heart. In order of normal conduction, the system consists of the sinoatrial node, the intra-atrial tracts, the atrioventricular node, the bundle of His, the right and left bundle branches, and the Purkinje fibers. SEE: illus.

conductivity (kŏn″dŭk-tĭv'ĭ-tē) The specific electric conducting ability of a substance. Conductivity is the reciprocal of unit resistance or resistivity. The unit is the ohm/cm. Specific conductivity is sometimes expressed as a percentage. In such cases, it is given as a percentage of the conductivity of pure copper under certain standard conditions.

conductor (kŏn-dŭk'tŏr) **1.** A medium that transmits electricity, a force, heat, or a signal. **2.** A guide directing a surgical knife or probe.

conduit (kŏn'doo-ĭt, 'dit) [Fr. *conduit,* fr L. *conductus,* pipe, channel] A channel, esp. one constructed surgically.

ileal c. A method of diverting the urinary flow by transplanting the ureters into a prepared and isolated segment of the ileum, which is sutured closed on one end. The other end is connected to an opening in the abdominal wall. Urine is collected there in a special receptacle. When feasible, the ileal conduit may be anastomosed to the urethra, reestablishing continuity of urinary flow.

condylar (kŏn'dĭ-lăr) [Gr. *kondylos,* knuckle] Pert. to a condyle.

condyle (kŏn'dīl) *pl.* **condyles** [Gr. *kondylos,* knuckle] A rounded protuberance at the end of a bone forming an articulation.

condylectomy (kŏn″dĭ-lĕk'tō-mē) [″ + *ektome,* excision] Surgical excision of a condyle.

condyloid (kŏn'dĭ-loyd) [Gr. *kondylos,* knuckle, + *eidos,* form, shape] Pert. to or resembling a condyle.

condyloma (kŏn″dĭ-lō'mă, 'mă-tă) *pl.* **condylomas, condylomata** [Gr. *kondylōma,* wart] A wart, found on the genitals or near the anus, with a textured surface that may resemble coral, cauliflower, or cobblestone. **condylomatous** ('mă-tŭs), *adj.*

c. acuminatum A wart, typically found on the genitals, the perineum, the anus, or the mucosal surfaces of the vagina or mouth, usually spread by sexual contact. It is caused by various types of human papilloma virus and may be spread by physical contact with an area containing a wart. The spread of a wart from one labium to the other by autoinoculation is possible. The virus that causes the wart is usually transmitted sexually. SYN: *genital wart.*

TREATMENT: Topically applied liquid nitrogen, imiquimod cream, fluorouracil, or podophyllin may prove effective; multiple treatments are usually needed, including occasionally surgery, electrosurgery, or laser ablation. Extremely large lesions (Buschke-Lowenstein tumor) may need radical excision.

c. latum A mucous patch, characteristic of syphilis, most often on the vulva or anus. It is flat, coated with gray exudate and has a delimited area. SYN: *moist papule.*

condylotomy (kŏn″dĭ-lŏt'ō-mē) [Gr. *kondylos,* knuckle, + *tome,* incision] Division of a condyle without its removal.

cone (kōn) [Gr. *kōnos,* pine cone] **1.** A solid or hollow three-dimensional figure with a circular base and sides sloping up to a point. **2.** In the outer layer of the retina, any of the flask-shaped cells that are stimulated by the wavelengths of light of different colors. The cones are essential for color discrimination. SYN: *retinal c.; cone cell.* SEE: *retina* for illus.; *rod; rod cell.* **3.** A hollow, tapered, cylindrical device used in upper-extremity exercise to improve grasp, coordination, and range of motion. **4.** A device on a dental radiography machine that indicates the direction of the central beam and helps to establish the desired source-to-film distance.

c. of light One of the triangular areas of reflected light on the tympanic membrane extending downward from the umbo. SEE: *umbo.*

ocular c. A cone of light in the eye with the point on the retina.

retinal c. Cone (2).

visual c. The cone whose vertex is at the eye and whose generating lines touch the boundary of a visible object.

cone cut An area of a dental radiograph that was not exposed to radiation during imaging as a result of improper aiming of the primary beam. To avoid this

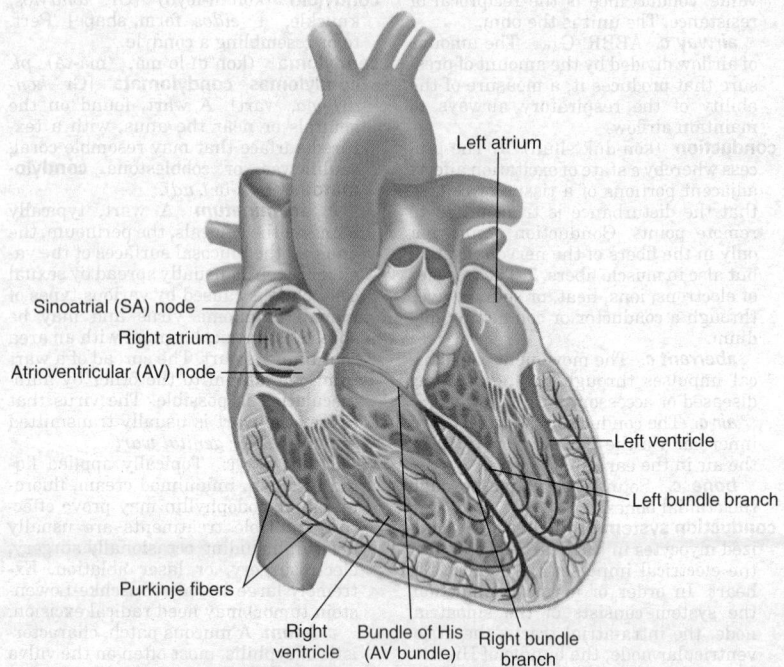

Left atrium

Sinoatrial (SA) node

Right atrium

Atrioventricular (AV) node

Left ventricle

Left bundle branch

Purkinje fibers

Right ventricle

Bundle of His (AV bundle)

Right bundle branch

CONDUCTION SYSTEM OF THE HEART

problem, the proper point of entry must be carefully calculated.

cone cutting Failure to cover or expose the whole area of a radiograph with the useful beam. The film is only partially exposed.

conenose (kōn′nōz″) Any member of the genus *Triatoma* and other genera of the family Reduviidae. Some conenoses are vectors of Chagas disease. SYN: *conenose **bug**; kissing **bug**. SEE: assassin **bug***.

conexus (kŏ-nĕk′sŭs) [L.] A connecting structure.

confabulation (kŏn-fab″yŭ-lā′shŏn) [L. *confabulari,* to talk together] A behavioral reaction to memory loss in which the patient unconsciously fills in memory gaps with inappropriate words or fabricated ideas, often in great detail. Confabulation differs from fabrication in that the patient has no desire to lie and believes he is telling the truth. It is a common finding in patients with Korsakoff's syndrome. SYN: *fabrication* (2).

confectio, confection (kŏn-fĕk′shē-ō, -shŭn) [L. *conficere,* to prepare] A sugar-like soft solid in which one or more medicinal substances are incorporated so that they can be administered agreeably and preserved conveniently. The use of confections is rare in contemporary medicine.

confidence level The probability associ-

ated with a confidence interval, and stated as a part of that interval.

confidentiality (kon″fĭ-den″shē-al′ĭt-ē) The maintenance of privacy by not sharing or divulging to a third party privileged or entrusted information.

PATIENT CARE: Patients' knowledge that they may safely discuss sensitive matters with their health care providers is necessary for successful, caring, and effective diagnosis and treatment. Matters discussed in confidence are held in secret except in the rare instances when the information presents a clear threat to the health and well-being of another person, or in cases in which public health may be compromised if the information is not revealed. In these instances it is unethical and illegal not to disclose the information. SEE: *forensic medicine; privileged communication*.

configuration (kŏn-fĭg″ū-rā′shŭn) **1.** The shape and appearance of something. **2.** In chemistry, the position of atoms in a molecule.

    activity c. An assessment approach used by occupational therapists to determine an individual's usual use of time during a typical week. The technique is designed to elicit the person's perceptions of the nature of daily activities and satisfaction with them. SEE: *time diary*.

confinement (kŏn-fīn′mĕnt) [O.Fr. *con-*

finer, to restrain in a place] **1.** Historically, the 6-week period between the day of parturition and the end of the puerperium when women were expected to absent themselves from society, remain at home to recover, and be cared for by their family members. **2.** Hospitalization, esp. for labor and delivery. **3.** The experience of being restrained to a physical space in order to limit activity.

confirm (kŏn-fĭrm′) [L. *confirmare,* to strengthen] To show by repetition of a test (or with a complementary test) that a result initially obtained is accurate.

confirmation bias (kon″fĭr-mā′shŏn) An error in diagnostic thinking in which one sees only those patterns in the data that support one's preconceptions.

confirmatory test (kŏn-fĭr′mă-tor″ē) A examination used to validate the results obtained by another. The confirmatory examination may be more sensitive or specific but must be based on different examining principles.

conflict (kŏn′flĭkt) [L. *confligere,* to contend] **1.** The opposing action of incompatible substances. **2.** In psychiatry, the conscious or unconscious struggle between two opposing desires or courses of action; applied to a state in which social goals dictate behavior contrary to more primitive desires.

conflict, decisional The state of uncertainty about the course of action to be taken when choice among competing actions involves risk, loss, or challenge to personal life values. SEE: *Nursing Diagnoses Appendix.*

conflict, parental role Parent experience of role confusion and conflict in response to crisis. SEE: *Nursing Diagnoses Appendix.*

conflict of interest Prejudice or bias that may occur when one's impartiality is compromised by opportunities for personal gain or occupational advancement, or by the chance that one's work may support a favored point of view or social agenda.

conflict resolution SEE: under *resolution.*

confluence of sinuses (kŏn′floo-ĕns) The union of the superior sagittal and transverse venous sinuses.

confluent (kŏn′floo-ĕnt) [L. *confluere,* to run together] Running together, or joined, as when adjacent rashes merge.

conformation (kŏn″for-mā′shŭn) The form or shape of a part, body, material, or molecule.

confound (kŏn-fownd′) [L. *confundere,* to confuse, to pour together] **1.** To introduce bias into a research study. **2.** To confuse, bewilder, or mystify. **confounding,** *n.*

confounding by indication **1.** The bias introduced into a study when a variable is a risk factor for a disease among nonexposed persons, even though the risk fac-

tor is not an intermediate step in the causal pathway between the exposure and the disease. **2.** The decision of researchers to make treatment assignments based on a patient's pretreatment prognosis.

confrontation (kŏn″frŭn-tā′shŭn) [L. *con,* together with, + *frons,* face] **1.** The examination of two patients together, one with a disease and the other from whom the disease was supposedly contracted. **2.** A method of determining the extent of visual fields in which that of the patient is compared with that of the examiner. **3.** In psychiatry, a feedback procedure in which a patient's behavior and apparent feelings are presented to facilitate better understanding of his or her actions.

confusion (kŏn-fū′zhŭn) [L. *confusio,* a mingling] The state or condition of not being aware of or oriented to time, place, or self.

   acute c. The abrupt onset of reversible disturbances of consciousness, attention, cognition, and perception that develop over a short period of time. SYN: *acute confusional state.* SEE: *delirium; Nursing Diagnoses Appendix.*

   chronic c. An irreversible, longstanding, and/or progressive deterioration of intellect and personality characterized by decreased ability to interpret environmental stimuli, decreased capacity for intellectual thought processes, and disturbances of memory, orientation, and behavior. SEE: *dementia; Nursing Diagnoses Appendix.*

   postictal c. Confusion that follows a seizure. It usually resolves in an hour unless complicated by head injury, hypoxia, or status epilepticus. SEE: *epilepsy.*

confusion, acute, risk for At risk for reversible disturbances of consciousness, attention, cognition, and perception that develop over a short period of time. SEE: *Nursing Diagnoses Appendix.*

confusional state, acute SEE: *acute confusion.*

congener (kŏn′jĕn-ĕr) [L. *con,* together, + *genus,* race] **1.** Two or more muscles with the same function. **2.** Something that resembles something else in structure, function, or origin. In the production of alcoholic beverages by fermentation, chemical substances termed congeners are also produced. These chemicals, more than 100 of which are known, impart aroma and flavor to the alcoholic compound. The precise role of these congeners in producing toxic effects is unknown.

congenital (kŏn-jĕn′ĭ-tăl) [L. *congenitus,* born together] Present at birth.

congenital disease A disease that is present at birth. It may be due to hereditary factors, prenatal infection, injury, or the effect of a drug the mother took during pregnancy.

congenital hypertrophy of the retinal pigment epithelium ABBR: CHRPE. A thickening of the retinal pigment epithelium present at birth. The thickening appears on funduscopic examination as an oval, black, clearly demarcated lesion within which there are atrophic areas surrounded by a halo that has no pigment. It has been associated with and has been considered to be an ocular marker of familial adenomatous polyposis.

congenital insensitivity to pain ABBR: CIP. A rare defect in perception of pain in which children are born with an inherited sensory and autonomic neuropathy and a markedly reduced ability to perceive painful experiences, e.g., bone and joint injuries, lacerations, and abrasions.

congenital rubella syndrome ABBR: CRS. Infection of the fetus early in a pregnancy, caused by transplacental transmission of the rubella virus and leading to a wide range of problems including spontaneous abortion, stillbirth, or major birth defects of the heart, eyes, or central nervous system, including deafness. Women who become pregnant and have not received rubella immunization should be advised of the risk of fetal development of CRS. For unimmunized women who develop rubella in the first trimester of pregnancy, the risk of CRS may be as high as 85%. The risk decreases sharply after the eighth week of pregnancy and is absent after the 20th week of gestation. Fetal infection can be determined by serial studies of the immunoglobulin gamma M and immunoglobulin gamma G rubella antibodies. Prevention of CRS consists of active immunization of all children and of women of childbearing age.

⚠️ Immunization with live rubella virus is contraindicated during pregnancy. It is recommended that women avoid pregnancy during the 3-month period after immunization. Infants with CRS are considered to be contagious. Only health care workers known to be immune to rubella (seropositive) should be permitted to care for infants with CRS.

congested (kŏn-jĕs'tĕd) [L. *congerere,* to heap together] Containing an abnormal amount of blood or tissue fluid.

congestion (kŏn-jes(h)'chŏn) [L. *congestio,* a gathering together] An excessive amount of blood or tissue fluid in an organ or in tissue. **congestive** (-tĭv), *adj.*

passive c. Hyperemia of an organ resulting from interference with blood flow from capillaries into venules, e.g., in congestive heart failure.

pulmonary c. The accumulation of an abnormal amount of blood in the vascular bed of the lungs. It usually occurs in association with heart failure.

conglobate (kŏn'glŏ-bāt) [L. *con,* together, + *globare,* to make round] In one mass, as lymph glands.

conglobation (kŏn"glŏ-bā'shŭn) An aggregation of particles in a rounded mass.

conglomerate (kŏn-glŏm'ĕr-āt) [" + *glomerare,* to heap] **1.** An aggregation in one mass. **2.** Clustered; heaped together.

conglutinant (kŏn-gloo'tĭ-nănt) Promoting adhesion, as of the edges of a wound.

Congo-Crimean viral hemorrhagic fever (kong'gŏ-krī-mē'ăn) SEE: under *fever.*

congregate housing (kŏng'gră-gĭt, -gāt") A group residence, usually for older persons, which encourages independence and community living. The tenants may need some medical or social assistance, but not enough to require hospitalization or nursing home care. Congregate housing can also be used by head-injured patients, spinal cord-injured patients, recovering alcoholics, and others. SEE: *assisted living.*

coniasis (kō-nī'ă-sĭs) [Gr. *konis,* dust, + -*iasis,* condition] Dustlike calculi in gallbladder and bile ducts.

conidia (kō-nĭd'ē-ă) *sing.,* **conidium-** Asexual spores of fungi.

conidiophore (kŏn-ĭd'ē-ō-for) [" + *phoros,* bearing] The stalk supporting conidia.

coning (kō'nĭng) [Gr. *konos,* cone] Herniation of the brain through the foramen magnum. This is a neurological catastrophe that almost always results in death.

coniofibrosis (kō"nē-ō-fī-brō'sĭs) [Gr. *konis,* dust, + L. *fibra,* fiber, + Gr. *osis,* condition] Pneumoconiosis produced by dust such as that from asbestos or silica. This causes fibrosis to develop in the lung.

coniology (kō-nē-ŏl'ŏ-jē) [" + *logos,* study of] The study of dust and its effects.

coniosis (kō"nē-ō'sĭs) [" + *osis,* condition] Any condition caused by inhalation of dust.

coniosporosis (kō"nē-ō-spō-rō'sĭs) [" + *sporos,* seed, + *osis,* condition] A hypersensitivity reaction consisting of asthma and pneumonitis caused by breathing the spores of *Cryptostroma corticale* or *Coniosporium corticale.* These fungi grow under the bark of some types of trees. Workers who strip the bark from these trees may develop this condition.

coniotomy (kō"nē-ŏt'ō-mē) [L. *conus,* fr Gr. *kōnos,* pine cone + -*tomy*] Cricothyrotomy.

conization (kŏn"ĭ-zā'shŭn) [Gr. *konos,* cone] SYN: *cone biopsy.*

conjecture A conclusion that is not proved but rather is assumed from incomplete evidence; a guess or speculation.

conjugata (kŏn″jū-gā′tă) Conjugate (2).

    c. diagonalis Diagonal conjugate.

    c. vera True conjugate.

conjugate (kŏn′jū-gāt) **1.** Paired or joined. **2.** An important diameter of the pelvis, measured from the center of the promontory of the sacrum to the back of the symphysis pubis. In obstetrics, the diagonal conjugate is measured and the true conjugate is estimated. SYN: *conjugata*. SEE: *diagonal c.*

    diagonal c. The distance between the sacral promontory and the lower inner surface of the symphysis pubis, usually more than 4.52 in (11.5 cm). SYN: *conjugata diagonalis*.

    external c. The diameter measured (with calipers) from the spine of the last lumbar vertebra to the front of the pubes; it is normally about 8 in (20.3 cm).

    obstetrical c. The distance between the sacral promontory and a point slightly below the upper inner margin of the symphysis pubis; the shortest diameter to which the fetal head must accommodate to descend successfully through the pelvic inlet.

    true c. In obstetrics, the distance between the midline superior point of the sacrum and the upper margin of the symphysis pubis. It is the anteroposterior diameter of the pelvic inlet, estimated by subtracting 1.5 to 2 cm from the measurement of the diagonal conjugate. SYN: *conjugata vera*.

conjugated linoleic acid SEE: under *acid*.

conjugation (kŏn″jū-gā′shŭn) **1.** A coupling. **2.** In biology, the union of two unicellular organisms accompanied by an interchange of nuclear material as in *Paramecium*.

conjunctiva (kon″jŭngk-tī′vă, -tī′vē″) *pl.* **-vae-vas** [L. *(membrana) conjunctiva*, conjunctive (membrane)] The mucous membrane that lines the eyelids and is reflected onto the eyeball.

    DIVISIONS: The palpebral conjunctiva covers the undersurface of the eyelids. The bulbar conjunctiva coats the anterior portion of the eyeball. The fornix conjunctiva is the transition portion forming a fold between the lid and the globe.

    INSPECTION: The palpebral and ocular portions should be examined. Color, degree of moisture, presence of foreign bodies or petechial hemorrhages, and inflammation should be observed.

    PATHOLOGY: Conjunctival pathology includes trachoma, pannus, and discoloration. Yellowish discoloration is seen in jaundice and pale conjunctivae are seen in anemias. Note: The skin of a person with hypercarotinemia is yellow, but the conjunctivae are not.

conjunctival test (kŏn-jŭngk-tī′văl) An outdated allergy test in which the suspected antigen is placed in the conjunctival sac; if it is allergenic for that patient, the conjunctiva becomes red and itchy and tears are produced.

conjunctivitis (kŏn-jŭnk″tĭ-vīt′ĭs) [*conjunctiva* + *-itis*] Inflammation of the conjunctiva. Treatment is directed against the specific cause.

    PATIENT CARE: Viral, gonococcal, and chlamydial conjunctivitis are highly contagious diseases spread by person-to-person contact. When an infection is present, the patient experiences itching, tearing, burning, pain and a mucopurulent discharge, along with the feeling of a foreign body in the eye. The conjunctiva becomes hyperemic, thus the common name of "pinkeye." To limit spread of the disease, patients with infectious conjunctivitis should avoid touching their eyes and should wash their hands thoroughly before and after any eye contact or treatment. If eye drops are prescribed, the patient is taught how to avoid contaminating the medication dispenser. To do this, without having the dropper tip touch the patient's eye, the patient's head should be placed backward with the eyes looking upward, and the drop or drops as prescribed placed into a pouch created by pulling downward on the lashes and tissues of the bottom eyelid. If an ophthalmic ointment is prescribed, the patient is taught to apply it to the inner aspect of the bottom eyelid in a thin ribbon, from the inner to the outer canthus. If the eye is difficult to open because of sticky discharge, the patient should rinse it with sterile saline or other ophthalmic solution or apply a moist compress to the eyelids. Hand hygiene helps prevent spread of infection from one eye to the other and transfer of the infection from the affected patient to others in the household.

⚠️ Gonococcal and chlamydial conjunctivitis are sexually transmitted diseases. All sexual partners of affected patients should be identified and treated.

    acute contagious c. Epidemic **keratoconjunctivitis**.

    acute hemorrhagic c. A contagious viral eye infection marked by rapid onset of pain. It causes swollen eyelids, hyperemia of the conjunctiva, and later subconjunctival hemorrhage. The disease, which is self-limited and for which there is no specific therapy, usually affects both eyes. Several viral agents can cause this disease, including enterovirus 70, echovirus 7, and a variant of coxsackievirus A24.

angular c. of Morax-Axenfeld An infection of the lateral canthus of the eyelid. The infection is often caused by the Moraxella species.

catarrhal c. Conjunctivitis due to causes such as foreign bodies, bacteria, or irritation from heat, cold, or chemicals.

chlamydial c. Conjunctivitis caused by *Chlamydia trachomatis*. In newborns this type of conjunctivitis is encountered more frequently than ophthalmia neonatorum caused by gonococci. Prophylaxis for chlamydial conjunctivitis is 1% topical silver nitrate. If the disease develops, drugs such as azithromycin, quinolones, or sulfa-based antibiotics are used. SYN: inclusion **c.**; inclusion **blennorrhea**.

follicular c. A type of conjunctivitis characterized by pinkish round bodies in the retrotarsal fold; can be chronic or acute.

giant papillary c. ABBR: GPC. An immune/foreign body response of the conjunctiva to contact lenses, esp. if left in place for 4 or more weeks, to nylon, or to prosthetic materials. It causes itching of the eye, redness, photophobia, swelling, and blurry vision. Examination reveals giant papillae on the superior tarsus.

PATIENT CARE: Changing or removing disposable contact lenses frequently decreases the likelihood of contracting GPC. All contact lens wearers should be advised to use good hand hygiene esp. before handling lenses, and to replace lenses according to prescribed schedule, using prescribed cleaning and storage guidelines, and a "rub and rinse" cleaning method rather than no rub. If such symptoms occur, the individual should remove the contact lens immediately and seek evaluation and treatment from the primary care provider or ophthalmologist.

gonococcal c. A severe, acute form of purulent conjunctivitis caused by *Neisseria gonorrhoeae*. SEE: *ophthalmia neonatorum*.

gonorrheal c. SEE: gonococcal **c.**

granular c. Acute contagious inflammatory conjunctivitis with granular elevations on the lids that ulcerate and scar.

inclusion c. Chlamydial **c.**

ligneous c. A rare eye disease in which fibrin deposits create woody plaques on the conjunctiva. Similar plaques may develop in the airways and genitalia. The disease often is found in patients with a deficiency in plasminogen levels.

membranous c. Acute conjunctivitis marked by a false membrane with or without infiltration.

c. of newborn Ophthalmia neonatorum.

phlyctenular c. An allergenic form of conjunctivitis common in children and marked by small white nodules on the bulbar conjunctiva often near the limbus. Can be seen in tuberculosis and staphylococcal infections.

purulent c. A form of conjunctivitis caused by organisms producing pus, esp. gonococci.

seasonal c. Allergic inflammation of the conjunctiva that occurs because of exposure to pollens, grasses, and other antigens.

vernal c. Allergic conjunctivitis associated with a papillary response, itching, thick, ropy discharge; common in young patients, esp. males.

conjunctivoma (kŏn-jŭnk″tĭ-vō′mă) [L. conjungere, to join together, + Gr. oma, tumor] A tumor of the conjunctiva.

conjunctivoplasty (kŏn″jŭnk-tĭ′vō-plăs″tē) [″ + Gr. plassein, to form] Removal of part of the cornea and replacement with flaps from the conjunctiva.

connective (kŏ-nĕk′tĭv) [L. connectere, to bind together] Connecting or binding together, as connective tissue.

connective tissue SEE: under *tissue*.

connective tissue disease ABBR: CTD. A group of diseases that affect connective tissue, including muscle, cartilage, tendons, vessels, skin, and ligaments. CTDs may be acute but are usually chronic. They may be localized or systemic and are marked by inflammatory or autoimmune injury. Examples of such diseases include systemic lupus erythematosus, rheumatoid arthritis, systemic sclerosis, and the vasculitides.

connexon (kŏn-ĕks′ŭn) A protein that forms tunnels across gap junctions, enabling ions or small molecules, such as glucose, to pass from one cell to another.

Conn syndrome (kon) [J. W. Conn, U.S. physician, 1907–1981] Primary hyperaldosteronism. Clinical findings include muscle weakness, polyuria, hypertension, hypokalemia, and alkalosis associated with an abnormally high rate of aldosterone secretion by the adrenal cortex. SEE: *Nursing Diagnoses Appendix.*

conotoxins (kō″nō-tŏks′ĭn) [Gr. konos, cone + ″] Any of a group of poisonous peptides made by mollusks known as cone snails. Conotoxins are potent nerve toxins and are considered to be potential biological or chemical warfare agents. Some conotoxins may also be used to treat neuropathic pain.

CONS, CoNS *coagulase-negative staphylococci.*

consanguinity (kŏn″săn-gwĭn′ĭ-tē) [L. consanguinitas, kinship] Relationship by blood (i.e., descent from a common ancestor).

conscience (kon'shŭntz) One's inner sense of what is right, wrong, or fair, esp. regarding relations with people or society. This sense can inhibit or reinforce the individual's actions and thoughts. SEE: *superego.*

conscious (kŏn'shŭs) [L. *conscius,* aware] Being aware and having perception; awake. SEE: *coma.*

consciousness (kon'chŭs-nĕs) Arousal accompanied by awareness of one's environment. In practice, consciousness is said to be present when a person is awake, alert, and oriented to his or her surroundings, i.e., where one is, who one is, what the date is.

Alterations of consciousness are common. Sleep is an altered state of consciousness from which one can be easily aroused. Stupor and lethargy are conditions in which one's level of arousal is diminished. In coma, one cannot be aroused. Other alterations in consciousness occur in delirium, dementia, hallucinosis, or intoxication, when persons may be fully aroused but have impaired perceptions of themselves and their environment.

altered level of c. ABBR: ALOC. A circumlocution for impaired consciousness (confusion, drowsiness, lethargy, stupor, or coma).

clouding of c. In delirium, a state in which awareness of the environment is impaired.

cost c. Awareness of economic limits in the practice of medicine.

disintegration of c. In classic psychoanalysis, disorganization of the personality. It is produced by the contents of the unconscious gradually disrupting the conscious.

levels of c. States of arousal and awareness, ranging from fully awake and oriented to one's environment to comatose. It is important to use a standardized system of description rather than vague terms such as semiconscious, semicomatose, or semistuporous.

Alert wakefulness: The patient perceives the environment clearly and responds quickly and appropriately to visual, auditory, and other sensory stimuli.

Drowsiness: The patient does not perceive the environment fully and responds to stimuli appropriately but slowly or with delay. He or she may be roused by verbal stimuli but may ignore some of them. The patient is capable of verbal response unless aphasia, aphonia, or anarthria is present. Lethargy and obtundation also describe the drowsy state.

Stupor: The patient is aroused by intense stimuli only. Loud noise may elicit a nonspecific reaction. Motor response and reflex reactions are usually preserved unless the patient is paralyzed.

Coma: The patient does not perceive the environment and intense stimuli produce a rudimentary response if any. The presence of reflex reactions depends on the location of the lesion(s) in the nervous system.

consensual (kŏn-sĕn'shū-ăl) [L. *consensus,* agreement] **1.** Pert. to reflex stimulation of one part or side produced by excitation of another part or the opposite side. **2.** Mutually agreeable. **3.** Consenting.

consensual light reflex SEE: under *reflex.*

consensual reaction 1. An involuntary action. **2.** A crossed reflex.

consensus (kŏn-sĕn'sĭs) [L. "agreement"] Agreement, esp. universal agreement.

consensus statement (stāt'mĕnt) A comprehensive summary of the opinions of a panel of experts about a particular scientific, medical, nursing, or administrative issue. Its purpose is to provide guidance to health care professionals, esp. on controversial or poorly understood aspects of care. SEE: *position statement.*

consent (kŏn-sent') [L. *consentire,* to agree] The granting of permission by the patient for another person to perform an act (e.g., permission for a surgical or therapeutic procedure or experiment to be performed by a physician, nurse, dentist, or other health care professional).

implied c. Nonverbal consent suggested by the actions by the patient, as when he or she enters the dental office and sits in a dental chair. This suggests that the patient seeks examination, diagnosis, and consultation.

informed c. A voluntary agreement made by a well-advised, mentally competent patient to be treated by a health care provider or institution, or randomized into a research study.

PATIENT CARE: The health care provider should provide full disclosure of information regarding the material risks, benefits of the proposed treatment, alternatives, and consequences of no treatment, so that the patient can make an intelligent, or informed, choice.

⚠ The information should be provided by the practitioner who will be performing the procedure. A nurse or any other health care provider who obtains informed consent for the practitioner performing the procedure exceeds his or her scope of practice and may face legal consequences.

parental c. Permission granted to a health care provider by a child's mother or father for health care services.

consent form SEE: under *form.*

consenting adult A mature individual

who agrees to participate in social or sexual activity by virtue of his or her own desire or free will.

consequence (kŏn'sē-kwĕns) **1.** Any result, conclusion, or effect. **2.** In psychology, the end result of a behavior, which may be positive, negative, or neutral.

conservation (kŏn″sĕr-vā'shŏn) [L. *conservatio,* keeping, preserving] A cognitive principle, first described by Piaget, indicating that a certain quantity remains constant despite the transformation of shape. Children develop conservation ability for number, length, liquid amount, solid amount, space, weight, and volume.

   breast c. Breast-conserving therapy.

conservation model A conceptual model of nursing developed by Myra Levine. The person is viewed as a holistic being who adapts to environmental challenges. In this model the goal of nursing is to promote wholeness through conservation of energy, structural integrity, personal integrity, and social integrity. SEE: *Nursing Theory Appendix.*

conservative (kŏn-sĕr'vă-tĭv) [L. *conservare,* to preserve] Pert. to the use of a simple rather than a radical method of medical or surgical therapy. SEE: *radical (2).*

conservative treatment 1. The withholding of treatments and management of disease by observation, or conversely, the use of surgery when observation only would depart from the usual care. **2.** In surgical cases, the preservation of the organ or part if at all possible with the least possible alteration.

conservator (kŏn-sĕr'vă-tŏr) A person appointed by the courts to manage the affairs of another person (called the conservatee), esp. if there is strong evidence that the conservatee is incapable of managing his or her own affairs. SEE: *guardianship.*

conservatorship (kŏn-sĕr'vă-tor-shĭp″) The preservation and protection of a dependent person's self and property by another individual. The term does not refer to imprisonment or confinement in a psychiatric facility. This is called *guardianship* in some states.

Consolidated Omnibus Reconciliation Act ABBR: COBRA. Federal legislation that requires employers with 20 or more employees to offer health insurance coverage to their employees for as long as 18 months after employment ends.

consolidation (kŏn-sŏl-ĭ-dā'shŭn) [L. *consolidare,* to make firm] The process of becoming solid. The term is used esp. for description of diseases of the lungs (e.g., acute pneumonia).

consort diagram (kon'sort″ dī'gram″) A graphical depiction of the enrollment, randomization, treatment, and follow-up of patients participating in a clinical trial.

conspicuity In radiology, the relative visibility of a lesion — how well it stands out against the images received from neighboring tissues.

constant (kon'stănt) [L. *constans,* standing firm] **1.** Unchanging. **2.** A condition, fact, or situation that does not change.

   rate c. The speed of a chemical reaction. It varies with absolute (Kelvin) temperature.

constellation (kŏn″stĕl-lā'shŭn) [L. *con,* together, + *stella,* star] A group, set, or configuration of objects, individuals, or conditions.

constipation (kŏn″stĭ-pā'shŭn) [L. *constipare,* to press together] A decrease in a person's normal frequency of defecation accompanied by difficult or incomplete passage of stool and/or passage of excessively hard, dry stool. SEE: *Nursing Diagnoses Appendix.*

ETIOLOGY: Predisposing factors in healthy people include a diet that lacks fiber, inadequate consumption of fluids, a sedentary lifestyle, and advancing age. Many drugs, including opiates, antidepressants, calcium channel blockers, antiemetics, and anticholinergics also cause constipation. Among metabolic illnesses, hypothyroidism and disorders of calcium metabolism occasionally contribute to difficulty with the passage of stools. Pathological lesions of the bowel (e.g., diverticular disease, anorectal gonorrhea, hemorrhoids, or obstructions due to tumors, adhesions, or incarcerated hernias) may also be responsible.

NOTE: Normal bowel frequency varies from person to person. Some people normally have three bowel movements daily, while others have a normal pattern of one or two bowel movements a week.

⚠️ A change in frequency of bowel movements may be a sign of serious intestinal or colonic disease (e.g., a malignancy). A change in bowel habits should be discussed with a physician.

TREATMENT: Consumption of fresh vegetables, fruits, and whole grains helps prevent constipation. Medications to alleviate constipation include docusate, bulk-forming laxatives (such as psyllium), magnesium-containing compounds, lactulose, and a variety of enemas.

   atonic c. Constipation due to weakness or paralysis of the muscles of the colon and rectum.

   colonic c. The state in which an individual's pattern of elimination is characterized by hard, dry stools, which results from a delay in passage of food residue.

obstructive c. Constipation due to a mechanical obstruction of the intestines, e.g., by hernias, adhesions, or tumors.

perceived c. The state in which a person makes a self-diagnosis of constipation and ensures a daily bowel movement through use of laxatives, enemas, and suppositories. SEE: *Nursing Diagnoses Appendix.*

spastic c. Constipation due to excessive tonicity of the intestinal wall, esp. the colon.

constipation, risk for Having the potential for a decrease in a person's normal frequency of defecation accompanied by difficult or incomplete passage of stool and/or passage of excessively hard, dry stool. SEE: *Nursing Diagnoses Appendix.*

constitution (kŏn-stĭ-tū'shŭn) [L. *constituere,* to establish] The physical makeup and functional habits of the body. **constitutional** (-ăl), *adj.*

constitutive (kŏn'stĭ-too"tĭv, tū") [L. *constituere,* to put together] In genetics, always expressed.

constraint-induced movement therapy ABBR: CIMT. A method of rehabilitation in which a patient is encouraged to use an injured body part by limiting the use of uninjured body parts. The technique is used, e.g., in rehabilitation from stroke and can help to overcome the nonproductive behavior of learned nonuse. SEE: *stroke.*

constriction (kŏn-strĭk'shŭn) [L. *con,* together, + *stringere,* to draw] **1.** The binding or squeezing of a part. **2.** The narrowing of a vessel or opening (e.g., blood vessels or the pupil of the eye).

constrictor (kŏn-strĭk'tor) **1.** Something that binds or restricts a part. **2.** A muscle that constricts a vessel, opening, or passageway, as the constrictors of the faucial isthmus and pharynx and the circular fibers of the iris, intestine, and blood vessels.

construct validity In a research study, the fitness of a particular research method for the use to which the study is put or its suitability for the conceptual or theoretical use for which it is employed.

consult (kŏn-sŭlt' (sense 1), kon'sŭlt" (sense 2)) [L. *consultare,* to consult] **1.** To provide professional guidance to another health care professional in the care of a patient. **2.** An informal term for consultation.

consultand (kŏn-sŭl'tănd) [L. *consultandus,* (one) to be consulted] A person who requests genetic counseling.

consultant (kŏn-sŭlt'ănt) [L. *consultare,* to counsel] In the health care professions, a health care worker, such as a nurse, physician, dentist, pharmacist,

or psychologist, who acts in an advisory capacity, often providing expert knowledge in a given specialty.

legal nurse c. A registered nurse who provides expert information to lawyers or others involved in health care legal issues. These consultants must have either an advanced degree or certification through special programs. SEE: *forensic nursing.*

consultation (kon"sŭl-tā'shŏn) Diagnosis and proposed treatment by two or more health care workers at one time, one of whom usually is specially trained in the problem confronting the patient.

Consumer Assessment of Health Plans Survey ABBR: CAHPS. A questionnaire used by American health care quality assurance agencies to evaluate customer satisfaction with health care. The survey monitors satisfaction with the accessibility, clarity, and timeliness of provided care.

Consumer Product Safety Commission A U.S. government agency charged with overseeing the safety of a wide variety of products, tools, and toys used in the home, in communities, and in the workplace.

consummation (kŏn"sŭ-mā'shŭn) The first act of sexual intercourse after marriage.

consumption (kŏn-sŭmp'shŭn) [L. *consumere,* to waste away] **1.** Tuberculosis. **2.** Wasting. **3.** The using up of anything.

consumptive (kŏn-sŭmp'tiv) [L. *consumptivus,* wasteful, destructive] **1.** Pert. to or afflicted with tuberculosis. **2.** Pert. to a decrease in a required resource resulting from disease or use. For example, a consumptive coagulopathy is a tendency to bleed resulting from use of clotting factors.

contact (kon'takt) [L. *contingere,* to touch] **1.** Mutual touching or apposition of two bodies. **2.** One who has been recently exposed to a contagious disease.

casual c. Relations between people without the sharing of blood or body fluids, such as playing games together, using the same shower, sharing meals, or living in close proximity.

complete c. The contact that occurs when the entire proximal surface of a tooth touches the entire surface of an adjoining tooth, proximally.

close c. In public health and infectious diseases, anyone who repeatedly and regularly shares the living space of someone with a contagious disease.

PATIENT CARE: The sharing of body fluids and blood with another person constitutes close contact, as does the bathing, clothing, and toileting of the sick person. Close contacts with contagious people may need prophylactic treatment, quarantine, or observation to ensure their health and the health of others. Those who have *casual* contact with a sick person typically do not require these measures.

direct c. Transmission of a communicable disease from the host to a healthy person by way of body fluids (e.g., respiratory droplets, blood, or semen), cutaneous contact, or placental transmission.

eye c. A direct look into the eyes of another.

indirect c. Transmission of a communicable disease by any medium between the host and the susceptible person. The medium may be contaminated food or water; medical supplies; the hands of a health care worker; clothing; or an arthropod vector. SEE: *fomes*.

intercuspal c. Contact between the cusps of opening teeth.

occlusal c. The normal contact between teeth when the maxilla and mandible are brought together in habitual or centric occlusion.

proximal c. Touching of teeth on their adjacent surfaces.

contactant (kŏn-tăk′tănt) A substance that produces an allergic or sensitivity response when it contacts the skin directly.

contact lens associated solution toxicity SEE: under *toxicity*.

contact surface SEE: under *surface*.

contact tracing The identification of those known to have had prolonged or close interactions with a disease vector, typically through patient interviews and analysis of laboratory specimens.

contagious (kŏn-tā′jŭs) Capable of being transmitted from one individual to another. SEE: *infectious*.

contagious disease SEE: under *disease*.

contagium (kŏn-tā′jē-ŭm) [L.] The agent causing infection.

container (kŏn-tā′něr) A receptacle for storing a medical specimen or supplies. Use of sterile disposable containers for collecting specimens is recommended, since contamination of the container may alter the results of the specimen analysis and therefore interfere with the diagnosis. SEE: *Standard Precautions Appendix*.

containment (kŏn-tān′měnt) **1.** In public health, the control or eradication of infectious diseases. **2.** In environmental health, the prevention of spread of toxic substances into the environment. **3.** In health care delivery, the management, control, and restriction of excessive spending. SYN: *cost c.*

cost c. Containment (3).

contaminant (kŏn-tăm′ĭ-nănt) A substance or organism that soils, stains, pollutes, or renders something unfit for use.

contaminate (kŏn-tăm′ĭ-nāt) [L. *contaminare*, to render impure] **1.** To soil, stain, or pollute. **2.** To render unfit for

use through introduction of a harmful or injurious substance. **3.** To make impure or unclean. **4.** To deposit a radioactive substance in any place where it is not supposed to be.

contamination (kŏn-tăm″ĭ-nā′shŭn) **1.** The act of contaminating, esp. the introduction of pathogens or infectious material into or on normally clean or sterile objects, spaces, or surfaces. **2.** In psychiatry, the fusion and condensation of words so that they run together when spoken.

radiation c. Radiation in or on a place where it is not wanted.

contamination Exposure to environmental contaminants in doses sufficient to cause adverse health effects. SEE: *Nursing Diagnoses Appendix*.

contamination, risk for Accentuated risk of exposure to environmental contaminants in doses sufficient to cause adverse health effects. SEE: *Nursing Diagnoses Appendix*.

content-specific delusion Monothematic delusion.

context of care Those elements of an individual's life or living situation that have psychological, social, and/or economic relevance to his or her use of professional health services. The context of a person's care may include such elements as that person's attitudes toward illness; belief systems (e.g., ethnic, racial, or religious); cognitive abilities; emotional states; family life; finances; and previous experiences with health care agencies, among others.

contig A continuous segment of genetic material on a chromosome.

contiguity (kŏn-tĭ-gū′ĭ-tē) [L. *contiguus*, touching] Contact or close association.

solution of c. The dislocation or displacement of two normally contiguous parts.

continence (kŏn′tĭ-něns) [L. *continere*, to hold together] Self-restraint, used esp. in reference to refraining from sexual intercourse, and to the ability to control urination and defecation. SEE: *incontinence*.

continent (kŏn′tĭ-něnt) **1.** Able to control urination and defecation. **2.** Not engaging in sexual intercourse. SEE: *continence*.

contingency fee A wage charged by a legal professional for services rendered, payable only if the injured party wins damages as a result of the successful resolution of a suit. Contingency fees usually consist of a percentage of the damages recovered by the injured party.

contingent valuation (kŏn-tin′jĕnt val″yū-ā′shŏn) A method of assigning a monetary value to a nonexchangeable condition, product, or service, e.g., health care or environmental quality. It is based on surveys of the stated preferences of people for specified conditions, asking them how much they might be willing to pay for those services.

continuing care community A type of managed care that combines health insurance, housing, and social care, usually for the elderly. The participant enters a contractual arrangement, in which he or she receives a residence and long-term care on an as-needed basis in exchange for an agreed-upon fee.

continuing education SEE: under *education*.

continuity (kŏn″tĭ-nū′ĭ-tē) [L. *continuus*, continued] The condition of being unbroken, uninterrupted, or intimately united.

continuous aspiration of subglottic secretions ABBR: CASS. Suctioning pooled oropharyngeal fluids from the subglottic region just above the cuff of an endotracheal tube. It is a technique used in mechanically ventilated patients to prevent ventilator-associated pneumonias.

continuous-flow analysis An examination with a laboratory instrument that separates samples and appropriate reagents before specimens are analyzed by placing air bubbles between individual specimens and the reagents as they are injected into a tube. Specimens are then analyzed as they flow along the tube by various analytical principles (colorimetry, electrochemistry).

continuous glucose monitoring ABBR: CGM. Moment-to-moment measurement of body glucose concentrations, e.g., with sensors placed in subcutaneous tissue.

continuous lateral rotation therapy ABBR: CLRT. The use of a moving bed that shifts patients from one side to the other; used in critical care to prevent nosocomial pneumonia in immobile patients.

continuous renal replacement therapy ABBR: CRRT. Use of a filtration or dialysate bath device to remove fluid and small waste product molecules from the blood of patients with acute renal failure who are unable to tolerate hemodialysis.

Removal of water occurs as the result of diffusion, convection, and ultrafiltration. There are four types of CRRT. In all types, blood is removed continuously for 24 hr and passed through a chamber containing a semipermeable filter. Excess fluid is removed slowly and, as a result, there is decreased risk of hemodynamic instability when compared to hemodialysis. In arteriovenous systems, blood pressure provides the force by which blood moves through the filtration system. In venovenous systems, pumps propel the blood. Anticoagulants are added to reduce clotting stimulated by blood coming in contact with a foreign surface.

In *continuous arteriovenous hemofiltration* (CAVH) and *continuous venovenous hemofiltration* (CVVH), a catheter placed in a peripheral artery carries blood at a rate of 300 to 800 ml/hr through a chamber containing a semipermeable membrane. Excess water and solutes move across the membrane and out of the blood, which is then returned to the venous system.

In *continuous arteriovenous hemodiafiltration* (CAVHDF) and *continuous venovenous hemodiafiltration* (CVVHDF), the chamber through which blood passes contains a dialysate solution in addition to a filtration membrane. Changing the concentration of the solution increases the amount of waste products and water that can be removed from the blood as it passes through the device.

continuous spectrum 1. An unbroken series of wavelengths, either visible or invisible. 2. An unbroken range of radiations of different wavelengths in any portion of the invisible spectrum.

continuous support in labor The presence of a trained professional (such as a doula), or a lay person, and/or family members at the bedside of a parturient woman, to coach, empathize with, give practical aid to, and/or inform the expectant mother about birthing. It helps alleviate anxiety, feelings of isolation, and pain. SYN: *birth labor support*.

continuum of care The range of services required by chronically ill, impaired, or elderly people. Services include, among others, preventive measures, acute medical treatments, rehabilitative and supportive care, and social services.

contortrostatin (kŏn-tŏr″trō′stă′tĭn) [NL. *contortrix* (Southern) copperhead +statin] A protein derived from snake venom that inhibits the migration of cells (e.g., of metastasizing cancer cells).

contour (kŏn′toor) [It. *contornare*, to go around] 1. The outline or surface configuration of a part. 2. To shape or form a surface, as in carving dental restorations to approximate the conditions of the original tooth surface.

    gingival c. The normal arching appearance of the gingiva along the cervical part of the teeth and rounding off toward the attached gingiva.

    gingival denture c. The form of the denture base or other materials around the cervical parts of artificial teeth.

contoured (kŏn′toord) Having an irregular, undulating surface resembling a relief map; said, e.g., of bacterial colonies.

contra- [L. *contra*, against] Prefix meaning *opposite* or *against*.

contra-aperture (kŏn″trä-ăp′ĕr-chūr″) [L. *contra*, against, + *apertura*, opening] A second opening made in an abscess.

contraception (kŏn″tră-sep′shŏn) [*contra-* + *(con)ception*] The prevention of conception.

   emergency c. Postcoital **c.**

   extended cycle c. A form of oral contraception that reduces the number of menstrual cycles in which contraceptive hormones are taken for more than 28 consecutive days (e.g., 84 days) and a placebo is taken for seven days. During the seven days of placebo, menstrual bleeding occurs.

   postcoital c. ABBR: PCC. The prevention of pregnancy in the first hours or days that follow sexual intercourse. Methods commonly used include the administration of hormones chemically related to estrogen or progesterone, or the insertion of an intrauterine device in the first five days of unprotected coitus or after known or suspected contraception failure (such as condom rupture). Levonorgestrel (Plan B) is the most commonly used progestin used in postcoital contraception and is available without prescription for patients over 17 years of age. A prescription is required for patients under age 17. Low-dose mifepristone (RU 486) is an alternative. SEE: *morning-after pill*. SEE: *emergency c.*

⚠️ Postcoital contraception will not work if the woman is already pregnant as a result of previous unprotected intercourse.

PATIENT CARE: Oral agents used for emergency contraception prevent implantation of the blastocyst into the uterine endometrium. The most common physical side effects of treatment are nausea and vomiting, menstrual changes (esp. during the cycle after the treatment), breast tenderness, dizziness, and malaise. Some of these, e.g., nausea and vomiting, are manageable with medications. Postcoital contraception is available by prescription in the U.S. and over the counter in several other countries. It neither increases the likelihood of future infertility nor future ectopic pregnancies. It also does not provide protection against sexually transmitted illnesses, such as Chlamydia, gonorrhea, or HIV. Nurses and nurse practitioners may be consulted by patients about the use of emergency contraceptives, esp. by adolescents. It is important for health care professionals to be able to provide age- and patient-specific education about pregnancy and sexuality and to be aware of the individual, familial, ethical, religious, and social aspects of treatment.

   postpartum c. The use of hormone therapies or mechanical means of contraception after delivery.

   PATIENT CARE: Women who have no risk factors for blood clotting may safely begin or resume hormonal contraception 21 days after delivery. Women who have risk factors for venous thromboembolism (such as a prior blood clot in the legs, pelvis or lungs, age over 35 years, cardiomyopathy, a history of smoking, postpartum hemorrhage, or cesarean delivery should delay hormonal contraception for at least 42 days.

   transvaginal c. Any form of contraception placed within the reproductive tract of a woman, including intrauterine devices (IUDs) and vaginal rings.

contraceptive (kŏn″tră-sep′tiv) Any process, device, or method that prevents conception. Categories of contraceptives include steroids; chemical; physical or barrier; combinations of physical or barrier and chemical; "natural"; abstinence; and permanent surgical procedures. SEE: table; *abortion*.

   STEROIDS: Oral contraceptives ("the pill)" consist of chemicals similar to the natural hormones estrogen or progesterone and act by preventing ovulation. When taken according to instructions, the pills are almost 100% effective. Other means of administering steroid compounds are by implantation of these agents under the skin, in contraceptive vaginal rings, in patches, in intrauterine devices, or by injection. Long-acting contraceptives, including the implanted Levonorgestrel, are available.

⚠️ The antibiotic rifampin decreases estrogen concentrations in women taking oral contraceptive pills. This lowers the effectiveness of the pill in preventing pregnancy. Women using oral contraceptives and rifampin at the same time should either abstain from sexual intercourse or use additional barrier methods of contraception to avoid unwanted pregnancies.

   CHEMICAL: Spermicides in the form of foam, cream, jelly, spermicide-impregnated sponge, or suppositories are placed in the vagina before intercourse. They may be used alone or in combination with a barrier contraceptive. They act by killing the sperm. Douching after intercourse is not effective.

   PHYSICAL OR BARRIER: Intrauterine contraceptive devices (IUDs) are plastic or metal objects placed inside the uterus. They are thought to prevent the fertilized egg from attaching itself to the lining of the uterus. Their effectiveness is only slightly lower than that of oral contraceptives. Diaphragms are made of a dome-shaped piece of rubber with a flexible spring circling the edge. They are available in various sizes and are inserted into the vagina so as to cover the cervix. A diaphragm must be used in conjunction with a chemical spermicide, which is applied before positioning the diaphragm. A specially fitted cervical cap is also available as a barrier-type contraceptive. A sponge impregnated with a contraceptive cream or jelly is available. It is placed in the vagina up to several hours before intercourse. The male partner can use a condom, a flexible tube-shaped barrier placed over the erect penis so that the ejaculate is contained in the tube and is not deposited in the vagina. Made of rubber or animal membranes, condoms are available in both dry and wet-lubricated forms and in various colors.Used properly, the condom is a reliable means of contraception. It is more effective if combined with a chemical spermicide. Condoms also help prevent transmission of diseases by sexual intercourse by providing a physical barrier. SEE: *condom*.

NATURAL FAMILY PLANNING: This method involves abstaining from intercourse for a specified number of days before, during, and after ovulation. The rhythm method is based on calculating the fertile period by the use of a calendar, on which the supposed infertile days are marked. In practice, this method has a high rate of failure. Other methods include determining ovulation by keeping a basal temperature chart and judging the time of ovulation by observing cyclical changes in the cervical mucus. SEE: *chart, basal temperature.*

Sophisticated home-diagnostic tests for the hormonal changes present at ovulation are available. Withdrawal, the removal of the penis from the vagina just before ejaculation, is subject to a high failure rate because sperm may be contained in the pre-ejaculatory fluid from the penis.

PERMANENT: *For women:* Tubal ligation involves surgical division of the fallopian tubes and ligation of the cut ends. This procedure does not interfere with the subsequent enjoyment of sexual intercourse. This form of sterilization is effective but virtually irreversible. *For men:* Vasectomy consists of cutting the vas deferens and ligating each end so that the sperm can no longer travel from the testicle to the urethra. The procedure must be done bilaterally and the ejaculate tested for several months postoperatively to make certain sperm are not present. Until two successive tests reveal absence of sperm, the method should not be regarded as having succeeded. Attempts to reverse this surgical procedure have succeeded in only a small percentage of cases. Vasectomy does not interfere

with the normal enjoyment of sexual intercourse.

contraceptive cream A water-soluble cream introduced into the vagina before intercourse to decrease the likelihood of conception. It is impregnated with spermicide. Like contraceptive foams, films, and gels, spermicide-laden contraceptive creams may cause transient vaginal ulceration or epithelial damage.

contract (kŏn-trăkt') [L. *contrahere*, to draw together] **1.** To draw together, reduce in size, or shorten. **2.** To acquire through infection, as to contract a disease. **3.** In psychology or psychiatry, the patient's commitment to attempt to alter behavior or to take a specific course of action. **4.** An agreement consisting of one or more legally enforceable promises among two or more parties such as people, corporations, and partnerships. Four elements are in a contractual relationship: offer, acceptance, consideration, and breach. In health care, contracts are used to govern relationships, for example, between employees and employers, insurers and the insured, or health care providers and patients.

contractile (kŏn-trăk'tĭl) Able to contract or shorten.

contractility (kŏn-trăk-tĭl'ĭ-tē) **1.** Having the ability to contract or shorten. **2.** In cardiac physiology, the force with which left ventricular ejection occurs. It is independent of the effects of preload or afterload.

contraction (kŏn-trak'shŏn) [L. *contractio*, a drawing together] A shortening or tightening, as of a muscle; a shrinking or a reduction in size.

  anodal opening c. ABBR: AOC. Contraction of the muscles at the anode when the electrical circuit is open.

  Braxton Hicks c. SEE: *Braxton Hicks contractions.*

  carpopedal c. A contraction of the flexor muscles of the hands and feet due to tetany, hypocalcemia, or hyperventilation.

  concentric muscle c. Contraction of a muscle in which the extended muscle is shortened. Pulling the body up by grasping a bar over the head is such a contraction.

  eccentric muscle c. Lengthening of the muscle as it contracts against resistance. Lowering the body from a position in which the body was supported by the flexed arms, i.e., holding onto a bar above the head, is such a contraction.

  graduated muscular c.s 1. The mechanism by which all smooth, coordinated muscle activity occurs. Normally controlled involuntarily by the central nervous system, motor units are recruited and stimulated at an intensity needed to accomplish a desired activity. **2.** Contractions accomplished by use of electric current of varying strength and

Current Contraceptive Use by Women, 15 to 44 Years of Age: 2002

Contraceptive Status and Method	All Women, 1995	All Women[12]	Age						Race/ethnicity		
			15–19 Years	20–24 Years	25–29 Years	30–34 Years	35–39 Years	40–44 Years	White only, Non-Hispanic	Black only, Non-Hispanic	Hispanic[3]
All women (1,000)	60,201	61,561	9,834	9,840	9,249	10,272	10,853	11,512	39,498	8,250	9,107
					Percent Distribution						
Using contraception (contraceptors)	64.2	61.9	31.5	60.7	68.0	69.2	70.8	69.1	64.6	57.6	59.0
Female sterilization	17.8	16.7	(—)	2.2	10.3	19.0	29.2	34.7	15.4	22.6	19.9
Male sterilization	7.0	5.7	(—)	0.5	2.8	6.4	10.0	12.7	7.6	1.3	2.6
Pill	17.3	18.9	16.7	31.9	25.6	21.8	13.2	7.6	22.2	13.1	13.0
Implant, Lunelle (T\MV)	0.9	0.8	0.4	0.9	1.7	0.5	0.5	0.2	0.5	0.6	1.8
3–month injectable (Depo-Provera) (T\MV)	1.9	3.3	4.4	6.1	4.4	2.9	1.5	1.1	2.7	5.4	4.3
Intrauterine device (IUD)	0.5	1.3	0.1	1.1	2.5	2.2	1.0	0.8	1.0	0.8	3.2
Diaphragm	1.2	0.2	(—)	0.1	0.3	0.1	(—)	0.4	0.2	0.1	(—)
Condom	13.1	11.1	8.5	14.0	14.0	11.8	11.1	8.0	10.7	11.4	10.9
Periodic abstinence– calendar rhythm	1.3	0.7	(—)	0.8	0.3	0.9	1.1	1.2	0.8	0.3	0.6
Periodic abstinence– natural family planning	0.2	0.2	(—)	(—)	0.4	0.2	0.3	0.4	0.3	0.1	0.3
Withdrawal	2.0	2.5	0.8	3.1	5.3	2.6	2.4	1.0	2.6	1.5	2.2
Other methods	1.1	0.6	0.6	0.2	0.4	0.4	0.5	1.1	0.7	0.5	0.3
Not using contraception	35.8	38.1	68.5	39.3	32.0	30.8	29.2	30.9	35.4	42.4	41.0
Surgically sterile–female (noncontraceptive)	3.0	1.5	(—)	(—)	0.4	0.9	2.1	4.9	1.6	1.6	0.9
Nonsurgically sterile–female or male	1.7	1.6	0.7	0.7	0.9	1.4	1.2	4.4	1.7	1.4	1.7
Pregnant or postpartum	4.6	5.3	3.5	9.5	8.4	6.9	3.8	0.8	4.7	5.7	6.9
Seeking pregnancy	4.0	4.2	1.2	2.8	5.5	7.0	5.1	3.3	4.0	4.3	5.2
Other nonuse	22.5	25.5	63.1	26.3	16.9	14.6	16.9	17.6	23.6	29.5	26.4

Never had intercourse or no intercourse in 3 months before interview	17.1	18.1	56.2	17.9	8.9	7.6	9.1	10.8	17.0	19.0	18.7
Had intercourse in 3 months before interview	5.2	7.4	6.9	8.4	8.0	7.0	7.7	6.7	6.5	10.4	7.7
All other nonusers	0.2	(–)	(–)	(–)	(–)	(–)	0.1	0.1	0.1	0.1	(–)

SOURCE: Adapted from U.S. National Center for Health Statistics. *Advance Data from Vital and Health Statistics*. www.census.gov/compendia/statab/cats/births-deaths marriages divorces.html

—Represents or rounds to zero.
[1] Includes other races, not shown separately.
[2] Persons who had sterilizing operation and who gave as one reason that they had medical problems with their reproductive organs.
[3] Includes all other sterilization operations and sterilization of the husband or current partner.
[4] Persons sterile from illness, accident, or congenital conditions.
[5] Douches, suppositories, and less frequently used methods.

duration. This method is used in muscles with an intact nerve supply when muscles are atonic, wasted away, or when voluntary exercise is not feasible, and in denervated muscles, as in cases following nerve injury or poliomyelitis.

hourglass c. An excessive, irregular contraction of an organ at its center. SEE: *ectasia*.

idiomuscular c. Motion produced by degenerated muscles without nerve stimulus.

incoordinate uterine c. An abnormality of the first stage of labor in which uterine contractions are too weak or too ineffective to dilate the cervix.

isoinertial muscle c. Shortening and increased tension in a muscle against a constant load or resistance.

isometric c. A muscular contraction in which the muscle increases tension but does not change its length. SYN: *static muscle c.*

isotonic c. A muscular contraction in which the muscle maintains constant tension by changing its length during the action.

lead pipe c. A cataleptic condition during which limbs remain in any position in which they have been placed.

premature ventricular c. ABBR: PVC. Contraction of the cardiac ventricle before the normal time, caused by an electrical impulse to the ventricle arising from a site other than the sinoatrial node. The PVC may be a single event or may occur several times a minute or in pairs or strings. Three or more PVCs in a row constitute ventricular tachycardia.

static muscle c. Isometric contraction.

tetanic c. 1. Continuous muscular contraction. 2. A sudden, strong, sustained uterine contraction that jeopardizes maternal and fetal status. It may occur during oxytocin induction or stimulation of labor and can cause profound fetal distress, premature placental separation, or uterine rupture.

tonic c. Spasmodic contraction of a muscle for an extended period.

contraction stress test ABBR: CST. A procedure used after 34 weeks' gestation to evaluate placental sufficiency by assessing fetal response to the physiological stress of artificially induced uterine contractions. Contractions may be generated by breast stimulation or by the oxytocin challenge test. SEE: *oxytocin challenge test*.

contract research organization ABBR: CRO. Any privately financed, for-profit entity that performs industry-sponsored biomedical research. Health research is conducted in government-sponsored laboratories, e.g., the National Institutes of Health or the Centers for Disease Control and Pre-

vention; academic medical centers (such as those affiliated with a major university hospitals); and CROs.

contracture (kŏn-trak'chŭr) [L. *contractura*, a drawing together] Fibrosis of connective tissue in skin, fascia, muscle, or a joint capsule that prevents normal mobility of the related tissue or joint. SEE: illus.

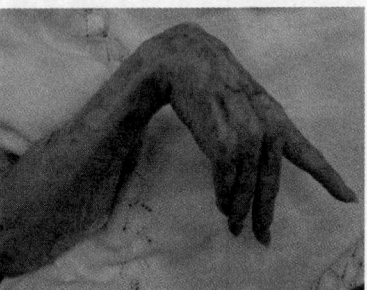

CONTRACTURE OF THE RIGHT HAND

Dupuytren c. SEE: *Dupuytren contracture*.

fibrotic c. Contraction of a muscle in which the muscle tissue has been replaced by fibrous tissue because of injury.

functional c. Contraction of a muscle that decreases during anesthesia or sleep.

myostatic c. Adaptive shortening of muscle, usually caused by immobilization and without tissue pathology.

physiological c. A temporary condition in which tension and shortening of a muscle are maintained for a considerable time although there is no tetanus. It may be induced by injury, disease, heat, drug action, or acids.

pseudomyostatic c. An apparent permanent contraction of a muscle due to a central nervous system lesion, resulting in loss of range of motion and resistance of the muscle to stretch.

Volkmann c. SEE: *Volkmann, Richard von*.

contrafissura (kŏn"tră-fĭ-shū'ră) [L. *contra*, against, + *fissura*, fissure] A skull fracture at a point opposite where the blow was received. SEE: *contrecoup*.

contraindication (kon"tră-in-dĭ-kā'shŏn) [*contra-* + *indication*] A symptom or circumstance that makes treatment with a drug or device unsafe or inappropriate.

absolute c. A contraindication for which a proposed treatment or intervention is impossible; an unqualified contraindication.

relative c. A contraindication that applies in all but a few unusual or extreme mitigating circumstances.

contralateral (kŏn"tră-lăt'ĕr-ăl) [" +

latus, side] Originating in or affecting the opposite side of the body, as opposed to homolateral and ipsilateral.

contralateral reflex SEE: under *reflex.*

contrasexual (kon"tră-sek'shoo-ăl) [*contra-* + *sexual*] Characteristic of the gender that differs from one's genotype. For example, a woman with polycystic ovaries may develop secondary sexual characteristics, e.g., facial hair, that are contrasexual.

contrast (kon'trast") In radiology, the difference between adjacent densities in an image. This is controlled by the energy of the beam and influenced by the characteristics of the part radiographed, production of scatter radiation, type of image receptor (direct or photostimulable plate, or combination of film and screen), and processing.

   image receptor c. The characteristics of an imaging medium that influence the ability of the radiologist to see differences in density between adjacent objects in the image.

   long-scale c. A radiograph that demonstrates small differences in density between adjacent areas. Long-scale contrast is a result of high kilovoltage peak (kVp). In dental radiography, for example, 80 to 90 kVp or higher is necessary to produce a radiograph with long-scale contrast.

   short-scale c. A radiograph that demonstrates large differences in density between adjacent areas. Short-scale contrast is a result of low kilovoltage peak (kVp). In dental radiography, for example, a kVp less than about 60 must be used to produce a radiograph with short-scale contrast.

   subject c. The physical characteristics of an object or imaging technique that influence how the object's image will appear on a radiographical film. The subject contrast of a radiograph can be increased or decreased by increasing or decreasing the kilovoltage peak (kVp). It may also be affected by the thickness, density, and composition of the subject.

contrast medium SEE: under *medium.*

contrast resolution SEE: under *resolution.*

contrast sensitivity The ability to distinguish objects from the background in which they are located. It is a critical component of functionally adequate vision.

contrasuppressor cell SEE: under *cell.*

contravolitional (kŏn"tră-vō-lĭ'shŭn-ăl) [L. *contra,* against, + *velle,* to wish] In opposition to or without the will; involuntary.

contrecoup (kŏn'tră-koo") An injury to parts of the brain located on the side opposite that of the primary injury, as when a blow to the back of the head forces the frontal and temporal lobes against the irregular bones of the anterior portion of the cranial vault.

control (kŏn-trōl') [Fr. *contreroller,* to keep a duplicate roll or account] **1.** To regulate or maintain. **2.** The regulation of objects or events by another agent. **3.** A standard against which observations or conclusions may be checked to establish their validity, as a control animal (e.g., one that has not been exposed to the treatment or condition being studied in the other animals). **4.** In clinical investigations, a research subject whose age, sex, race, behavior, weight, or health matches as many features of the population being studied as is possible or appropriate. When cases and controls are closely matched, the validity of results increases. SYN: *control group; reference group.* **5.** To dominate, coerce, or forcibly manage the behavior of another person.

controlled (kŏn-trōld') **1.** Supervised, overseen, or closely monitored. **2.** Effectively treated.

controlled area An area in which a protection officer oversees the occupational exposure of personnel to ionizing radiation. Controlled access, occupancy, and working conditions are necessary for radiation protection.

controlled cold therapy unit ABBR: CCT. Cold compression therapy unit.

Controlled Substance Act The Comprehensive Drug Abuse Prevention and Control Act; a law enacted in 1970 to control the distribution and use of all depressant and stimulant drugs and other drugs of abuse or potential abuse as may be designated by the Drug Enforcement Administration (DEA) of the Department of Justice.

   The act specifies record keeping by the pharmacist, the format for prescription writing, and the limit on the amount of a drug that can be legally dispensed. This limit and whether refills are allowed vary with the nature of the drug. Centrally acting drugs (such as narcotics, stimulants, and certain sedatives) are divided into five classes called schedules I through V. Schedule I drugs are experimental. Prescriptions for schedule II drugs may not be refilled. Prescriptions for schedule III and IV drugs may be refilled up to five times within 6 months of the time the initial prescription was written. Schedule V drugs are restricted only to the extent that all nonscheduled prescription drugs are regulated.

   Controlled substances are labeled with a large C followed by the Roman numeral designation. Alternatively, the Roman numeral is within the large C.

controlled word association Verbal fluency task.

contuse (kŏn-tooz') [L. *contundere,* to bruise] To bruise.

contusion (kŏn-too′zhŭn) Bruise.

myocardial c. Cardiac injury from blunt or penetrating trauma to the chest. It is an occasional cause of cardiac arrhythmia and a rare cause of rupture of the heart.

conus (kō′nŭs) [Gr. *konos*] **1.** A cone. **2.** A posterior staphyloma of a myopic eye.

c. arteriosus The smooth-walled outflow tract of the right cardiac ventricle leading to the pulmonary valve.

c. medullaris The most caudal segment of the spinal cord, found at the L1-L2 vertebral level and ending in the filum terminalis. Beyond its lumbar expansion, the spinal cord tapers and is called the conus medullaris. Injury to or lesions at the L2 vertebral level of the spine often cause conus medullaris damage, leading to loss of voluntary control of pelvic sphincters, sexual dysfunction, and loss of lower sacral sensation ("saddle anesthesia").

convalescence (kŏn″văl-ĕs′ĕns) [L. *convalescere*, to become strong] The period of recovery after a disease or an operation.

convalescent (kŏn″vă-lĕs′ĕnt) **1.** Getting well. **2.** One who is recovering from a disease or operation.

convection (kŏn-vĕk′shŭn) [L. *convehere*, to convey] **1.** The movement of solutes that occurs during ultrafiltration of a fluid. **2.** Loss of body heat by means of transfer to the surrounding cooler air.

convenience sample SEE: under *sample*.

convergence (kŏn-vĕr′jĕns) [L. *con*, with, + *vergere*, to incline] **1.** The moving of two or more objects toward the same point. **2.** In reflex activity, the coming together of several axons or afferent fibers on one or a few motor neurons; the condition in which impulses from several sensory receptors converge on the same motor center, resulting in a limited and specific response. **3.** The directing of visual lines to a nearby point.

convergent (kŏn-vĕr′jĕnt) Tending toward a common point.

conversion (kŏn-vĕr′zhŭn) [L. *convertere*, to turn round] **1.** The change from one condition to another. For example, a patient with an arrhythmia may convert from atrial fibrillation to sinus rhythm, or a patient with no evidence of tuberculosis may convert to a positive purified protein derivative status. **2.** In obstetrics, a change in position of a fetus in the uterus by the physician to facilitate delivery. SEE: *version*.

conversion disorder Somatoform disorder.

conversion reaction A type of neurosis in which loss or alteration of physical functioning suggests a physical disorder but instead expresses a psychological conflict or need. The disturbance is not under voluntary control and cannot be explained by a disease process; it is not limited to pain or sexual dysfunction. SYN: *conversion symptom*. SEE: *somatoform disorder*.

conversion study SEE: under *study*.

convert (kŏn-vĕrt′) [L. *convertere*, to turn around] In cardiology, to change an arrhythmia to a normal heart rhythm, either spontaneously or with drugs or electricity.

convex (kŏn′vĕks, kŏn-vĕks′) [L. *convexus*, vaulted, arched] Curved evenly; resembling the segment of a sphere.

convexoconcave (kŏn-vĕk″sō-kŏn′kāv, -kŏn-kāv′) Concavoconvex.

convexoconvex (kŏn-vĕk″sō-kŏn′vĕks) [″ + *convexus*, arched] Convex on two opposite faces.

convolute, convoluted (kŏn′vō-loot; -loot′ĕd) [L. *convolvere*, to roll together] Rolled, as a scroll.

convolution (kŏn″vŏ-loo′shŏn) [L. *convolvere*, to roll together] A turn, fold, or coil of something.

convulsant (kŏn-vŭl′sănt) [L. *convellere*, to pull together] **1.** An agent that produces a convulsion. **2.** Causing the onset of a convulsion.

convulsion (kŏn-vŭl′shŏn) [L. *convellere*, to tear loose] An occurrence or series of occurrences of involuntary muscular contractions and relaxations.

NOTE: It is important for the person who observes the convulsion to record on the chart the following: time of onset, duration, whether the convulsion started in a certain area of the body or became generalized from the start, type of contractions, whether the patient became incontinent, and whether the convulsion caused the patient to be injured or strike the head. This information, in addition to its medicolegal importance, is valuable in diagnosis and in caring for the patient.

ETIOLOGY: Common causes are epilepsy, eclampsia, meningitis, heat cramps, brain lesions, tetanus, uremia, hypoxemia, hypotension, and many poisonings. In children, the cause is often fever.

TREATMENT: Febrile convulsions in children are usually controlled by suppressing fever with acetaminophen. In adults a specific diagnosis should be made. Diagnostic testing may include assessments of serum chemistries, oxygenation, alcohol levels, brain scanning, or lumbar puncture. The patient should be prevented from self-injury and from the aspiration of oral or gastrointestinal contents. If fever is present, antipyretic drugs may be helpful. Sedatives or anesthesia may be ordered by the physician. Aftercare includes rest in bed. SEE: *febrile convulsion*.

clonic c. A convulsion with intermittent contractions, the muscles being alternately contracted and relaxed.

febrile c. A tonic-clonic seizure occurring in children between ages 6 months and 5 years who have no other signs of CNS infection or CNS abnormalities. About 3% to 5% of children will have this type of seizure, thought to be caused by a rapid rise in body temperature to 102.5°F (89°C) or higher. Boys are more susceptible than girls. The seizure rarely lasts more than 10 min, and repeat seizures during the same febrile episode are uncommon. The risk for a seizure during the next febrile illness is 30%, and for the episode after that 17%. A complete history and physical examination should include neurological appraisal to rule out other causes, such as epilepsy; acute lead encephalopathy; cerebral concussion, hemorrhage, or tumor; hypoglycemia; or poisoning with a convulsant drug. SEE: *epilepsy.*

TREATMENT: Appropriate therapy, such as acetaminophen or ibuprofen, should be instituted to reduce the fever. Oral diazepam (Valium) may be administered while fever is present to prevent seizure recurrence, though in many children the seizure is the first indication of fever. The measures to reduce the temperature must not be so vigorous as to cause hypothermia. Ice water baths and vigorous fanning with application of alcohol should not be used. The application of cool compresses with a gentle flow of air over the body is sufficient. A hypothermia blanket is also suitable. The efficacy and advisability of daily anticonvulsant drug therapy for children with recurrent febrile seizures have not been proven.

⚠️ 1. If the fever is due to influenza or varicella, salicylates should not be administered; their use could increase the risk for developing Reye's syndrome. 2. Prolonged treatment with phenobarbital depresses cognitive function in children and produces marked personality changes in about 15% of them.

hysterical c. An obsolete term for a pseudoseizure.

mimetic c. A facial muscle spasm.

puerperal c. Spontaneous convulsuion in the postpartum woman.

salaam c. Nodding spasm.

tetanic c. A tonic convulsion with constant muscular contraction.

tonic c. Convulsion in which the contractions are maintained for a time, as in tetany.

toxic c. Convulsion due to a toxin on the nervous system.

uremic c. Convulsion caused by the toxic effects of accumulated waste products and inorganic acids in renal failure.

convulsive (kŏn-vŭl′sĭv) Pert. to convulsions.

cooking [L. *coquere,* to cook] The process of heating foods to prepare them for eating. Cooking makes most foods more palatable and easier to chew, improves their digestibility (and sometimes their nutrient bioavailability), and destroys or inactivates harmful organisms, or toxins that may be present. Cooking releases the aromatic substances and extractives that contribute odors and taste to foods. These odors help to stimulate the appetite.

⚠️ Not all toxic substances are inactivated by heat. Most microorganisms and parasites are destroyed in the ordinary process of cooking when the food is heated to internal temperatures of 160°F to 175°F. Pork must be cooked completely throughout to kill the encysted larvae of *Trichinella.*

ACTION: *Protein:* Soluble proteins become coagulated. *Soluble substances:* These, including heat-labile vitamins, are often inactivated by boiling, and even mineral substances and starches, although insoluble to a certain extent, may be altered in this process. *Starch:* The starch granules swell and are changed from insoluble (raw) starch to soluble starch capable of being converted into sugar during digestion and of being assimilated in the system.

cooldown (kool′down″) Any low-impact, low intensity movement, such as walking, stretching, or casually performed calisthenics, performed after vigorous exercise. It allows body temperature to fall gradually, returns blood from skeletal muscles to the central circulation, and decreases muscle lactate concentrations. **cool-down,** *adj.*

Cooley anemia (kool′ē) [Thomas Benton Cooley, U.S. pediatrician, 1871–1945] Beta-thalassemia major.

Coolidge tube (koo′lĭj) [William D. Coolidge, U.S. physicist and chemist, 1873–1975] A kind of hot-cathode tube that is so highly exhausted that the residual gas plays no part in the production of the cathode stream, and that is regulated by variable heating of the cathode filament.

cooling (koo′ling) A reduction in temperature, e.g. of a patient, a laboratory sample, or a chemical reagent.

cooling blanket (koo′ling) Hypothermia blanket.

Coomassie blue (kū′mă-sē) [Kumasi, Ghana (proprietary name)] Anazolene sodium, a stain used to demonstrate proteins, e.g., in protein electrophoretic gels.

Coombs test (Koomz) [R. R. A. Coombs, Brit. immunologist, 1921–2006] A laboratory test for the presence of antibodies, usually blood type antibodies, in serum. The patient's serum is incubated with red blood cells (RBCs) with known antigenic markers; if antibodies to the antigen are present in the serum, they bind with the RBCs. When antihuman globulin is added, RBC clumping (agglutination) occurs. The test is used for crossmatching blood before transfusions to ensure that no antigen-antibody reactions will occur and to test for the presence of specific antibodies to RBCs.

cooperative learning An educational strategy in which learners join in small, structured groups to complete educational tasks, solve problems together, and further each other's understanding of material.

Cooper ligaments (Koop-ĕr) [Sir Astley Paston Cooper, Brit. surgeon, 1768–1841] Supportive fibrous structures throughout the breast that partially sheathe the lobes shaping the breast. These ligaments affect the image of the glandular tissue on a mammogram.

Coopernail sign (koop'ĕr-nāl″) [George L. Coopernail, U.S. surgeon, 1876–1962] Bruising of the skin of the perineum, scrotum, or labia. It is considered indicative of a pelvic fracture.

coordination (kō-or″dĭn-ā′shŭn) [L. co-, same, + ordinare, to arrange] **1.** The working together of various muscles to produce certain movements. The ability to produce coordinated movement is necessary to execute fine motor skills, manipulate objects, and perform gross motor tasks. Coordinated movement requires sequencing of muscle activity and stability of proximal musculature. **2.** The working together of different body systems in a given process, as the conjoint action of glandular secretion and involuntary muscles in digestion.

coordination of benefits Insurance policy provisions that govern how benefits for multiply insured parties are to be paid. The total benefits paid from different payers are linked so that the amount paid on behalf of the insured does not exceed the fee for the service provided.

COpa (kō′pă″) Cardiac output, measured by thermodilution methods in the pulmonary artery.

co-payment, co-pay (kō″pā′mĕnt, kō′pā′) The fee insured persons must pay, in addition to their health insurance premiums and deductibles, for specific medical services such as emergency department visits, appointments with primary care providers, laboratory studies, prescriptions, or x-ray examinations. SEE: *coinsurance.*

COPD *chronic obstructive pulmonary disease.*

cope (kōp) [ME. *caupen,* to contend with] **1.** To deal effectively with and handle stresses. **2.** The upper half of a flask used in casting. **3.** In dentistry, the cavity side of a denture flask.

coping (kōp′ĭng) Adapting to and managing change, stress, or opportunity (e.g., acute or chronic illness, disability, pain, death, relocation, work, changes in family structure, new relationships, or new ideas).
    c. mechanism Coping skill.
    c. skill Any characteristic or behavioral pattern that enhances a person's adaptation. Coping skills include a stable value or religious belief system, problem solving, social skills, health-energy, and commitment to a social network. SYN: *c. mechanism.*

coping, compromised family A state in which a usually supportive primary person (family member or close friend [significant other]) provides insufficient, ineffective, or compromised support, comfort, assistance, or encouragement that may be needed by the patient to manage or master adaptive tasks related to the his or her health challenge. SEE: *Nursing Diagnoses Appendix.*

coping, defensive The state in which an individual repeatedly projects a falsely positive self-evaluation based on a self-protective pattern that defends against underlying perceived threats to positive self-regard. SEE: *Nursing Diagnoses Appendix.*

coping, disabled family A state in which the behavior of a significant person (family member or other primary person) disables his or her own capacities and the patient's capacities to effectively address tasks essential to either person's adaptation to the health challenge. SEE: *Nursing Diagnoses Appendix.*

coping, ineffective Inadequate adaptive behavior and inability of a person in meeting life's demands and roles. SEE: *Nursing Diagnoses Appendix.*

coping, ineffective community A pattern of community activities for adaptation and problem solving that is unsatisfactory for meeting the demands or needs of the community. SEE: *Nursing Diagnoses Appendix.*

coping, readiness for enhanced A pattern of cognitive and behavioral efforts to manage demands that is sufficient for well-being and can be strengthened. SEE: *Nursing Diagnoses Appendix.*

coping, readiness for enhanced community A pattern of community activities for adaptation and problem solving that is satisfactory for meeting the demands or needs of the community but can be improved for management of current and future problems/stressors. SEE: *Nursing Diagnoses Appendix.*

coping, readiness for enhanced family A

state in which the family member has effectively managed adaptive tasks involved with the patient's health challenge and is exhibiting desire and readiness for enhanced health and growth in regard to self and in relation to the patient. SEE: *Nursing Diagnoses Appendix.*

copolymer (kō-pol′ĭ-mĕr) [*com-* + *polymer*] A polymer composed of two or more kinds of monomers.

copper (kop′ĕr) [L. *cuprum* fr. *cyprum,* fr *(aes) cyprium,* Cyprian (metal)] SYMB: Cu. A metallic chemical element, atomic mass (weight) 63.54, atomic number 29, specific gravity 8.96. Its salts are irritant poisons. Small quantities of copper are used by the body. Symptoms of deficiency include anemia, weakness, impaired respiration and growth, and poor use of iron. SEE: *Wilson disease; Poisons and Poisoning Appendix.*

FUNCTION: The total body content of copper is 100 to 150 mg; the amount normally ingested each day is less than 2 mg. It is found in many vegetable and animal tissues. Copper is an essential component of several enzymes, including those for hemoglobin synthesis and cell respiration. It is stored in the liver, and excess is excreted in bile or by the kidneys.

copperhead (kop′ĕr-hed″) A poisonous snake, *Agkistrodon contortrix,* common in the southern, eastern, and central U.S. SEE: *snake* **bite.**

copr-, copro- [Gr. *kopros,* dung, manure] Prefixes meaning *feces,* e.g., *coprolith* or *obscenity,* e.g., *coprolalia.*

copremesis (kŏp-rĕm′ĕ-sĭs) [Gr. *kopros,* dung, + *emesis,* vomiting] The vomiting of fecal material.

coproantibody (kŏp″rō-ăn′tĭ-bŏd″ē) Any one of a group of antibodies to various bacteria in the feces. They are of the IgA type. Their ability to protect the host has not been shown.

coprolagnia (kŏp″rō-lăg′nē-ă) [″ + *lagneia,* lust] An erotic satisfaction at the sight or odor of excreta.

coprolalia (kop″rō-lā′lē-ă) [*copro-* + *-lalia*] The use of vulgar, obscene, or sacrilegious language, seen in schizophrenia and Tourette syndrome. SYN: *eschrolalia.*

coprolith (kŏp′rō-lĭth) [″ + *lithos,* stone] Hard, inspissated feces.

coprology (kŏp-rŏl′ō-jē) [″ + *logos,* word, reason] Scientific study of the feces. SYN: *scatology* (1).

coprophagy (kŏp-rŏf′ă-jē) [″ + *phagein,* to eat] The eating of excrement.

coprophilia (kŏp″rŏ-fĭl′ē-ă) [″ + *philein,* to love] Abnormal interest in feces.

coprophilic (kŏp″rŏ-fĭl′ĭk) A term applied to organisms that normally live in fecal material.

coprophobia (kŏp″rŏ-fō′bē-ă) [″ + *pho-*

bos, fear] Abnormal fear of defecation and feces.

coproporphyria, hereditary coproporphyria (kŏp″rō-por-fĭr′ē-ă) [″ + *porphyra,* purple] An autosomal dominant error in the synthesis of heme in which an excess amount of coproporphyrin is excreted in the feces.

coproporphyrin (kŏp″rō-por′fĭr-ĭn) A porphyrin present in urine and feces. Coproporphyrins I and II are normally present in minute and equal amounts, but quantities are altered in certain diseases such as poliomyelitis and in infectious hepatitis and lead poisoning.

coproporphyrinuria (kŏp″rō-por″fĭr-ĭn-ū′rē-ă) Excess coproporphyrin in the urine.

coproscopy (kŏ-pros′kŏ-pē) [Gr. *kopros,* dung + *-scopy*] The microscopic analysis of stool specimens, usually to detect parasites, sometimes aided by molecular biological technology.

coprozoa (kŏp″rō-zō′ă) [″ + *zoon,* animal] Protozoa living in or identified within fecal matter.

copulation (kŏp″ū-lā′shŭn) [L. *copulatio*] The act of uniting in sexual intercourse. SYN: *coition; coitus.*

copy number variant A long stretch of DNA base pairs that is repeated several times in the chromosomes of some people, usually those of similar ethnic, geographic, or racial origins.

cor (kor) [L.] Heart.

coracoacromial (kor″ă-kō-ă-krō′mē-ăl) [Gr. *korax,* raven, + *akron,* point, + *omos,* shoulder] Pert. to the acromial and coracoid processes of the scapula.

coracoid (kor′ă-koyd) [″ + *eidos,* form, shape] Shaped like a crow's beak.

CO(RB) [Abbr. of *c(ardiac) o(utput),* as measured by the *r(e)b(reathing)* of an inert gas] A noninvasive method of measuring cardiac output.

cord (kord) [Gr. *khorde*] **1.** A stringlike structure. **2.** The umbilical cord. **3.** A firm, elongated structure consistent with a thrombosed vein, esp. in the extremities, where it may be felt on palpation.

nuchal c. The condition in which the umbilical cord is found wrapped around the neck of the fetus during delivery. If the cord cannot be unwrapped easily, or if there is more than one loop, the cord should be clamped and cut before delivery continues.

spermatic c. The cord by which the testis is connected to the abdominal inguinal ring. It surrounds the ductus deferens, blood vessels, lymphatics, and nerves supplying the testis and epididymis. These are enclosed in the cremasteric fascia, which forms an investing sheath.

umbilical c. The attachment connecting the fetus with the placenta. It contains two arteries and one vein surrounded by a gelatinous substance (Wharton's jelly). The umbilical arteries carry blood from the fetus to the placenta, where nutrients are obtained and carbon dioxide and oxygen are exchanged; this oxygenated blood returns to the fetus through the umbilical vein. SEE: illus.

The umbilical cord is surgically severed after the birth of the child. To give the infant a better blood supply, the cord should not be cut or tied until the umbilical vessels have ceased pulsating. However, in preterm infants, the cord should be clamped and cut before pulsation ceases to avoid maternal-newborn transfusion and reduce the risk of hypovolemia, polycythemia, and hyperbilirubinemia.

The stump of the severed cord atrophies and leaves a depression on the abdomen of the child (the navel, umbilicus, or belly button).

Willis C. SEE: under *Willis, Thomas*.
cordal (kor'dăl) Pert. to a cord (e.g., a spinal or vocal cord).
cordate (kor'dāt) [L. *cor*, heart] Shaped like a heart.
cordectomy (kor-děk'tō-mē) [Gr. *khorde*, cord, + *ektome*, excision] Surgical removal of a cord.
corditis (kor-dī'tĭs) Funiculitis.
cordocentesis (kor″dō-sen″tē'sĭs) [*cord* (2) + *centesis*] Withdrawal of a sample of fetal blood from the umbilical cord with a needle inserted through the abdominal and uterine walls into the am-

niotic sac. It is done under ultrasonic guidance after 17 weeks of pregnancy to diagnose fetal abnormalities or infections when amniocentesis, chorionic villus sampling, or fetal ultrasound have proven inconclusive.

⚠ Risks of the procedure include pain, bleeding, infection, premature rupture of membranes, and miscarriage.

SYN: *percutaneous cord blood sampling*.
cordopexy (kor'dō-pěk″sē) [″ + *pexis*, fixation] Surgical fixation of anatomical cords, esp. the vocal cords.
cordotomy (kor-dŏt'ō-mē) [″ + *tome*, incision] Spinal cord section of lateral pathways to relieve intractable pain.
core (kor) **1.** The center of a structure. **2.** A cylindrical tissue specimen.
coreceptor (kō″rē-sep'tŏr) [*com-* + *receptor*] A structure on a cell membrane that enhances the action of the cell receptor.
CCR5 c. A cell surface receptor found on macrophages that facilitates entry of HIV-1 into these cells. Chemokines released by T cells attempt to compete with HIV by blocking the receptor to prevent infection.
CXCR4 c. A cell surface receptor found on T cells that facilitates entry of HIV-1into these cells. SYN: *fusin*.
coreclisis (kor″ē-klī'sĭs) [Gr. *kore*, pupil

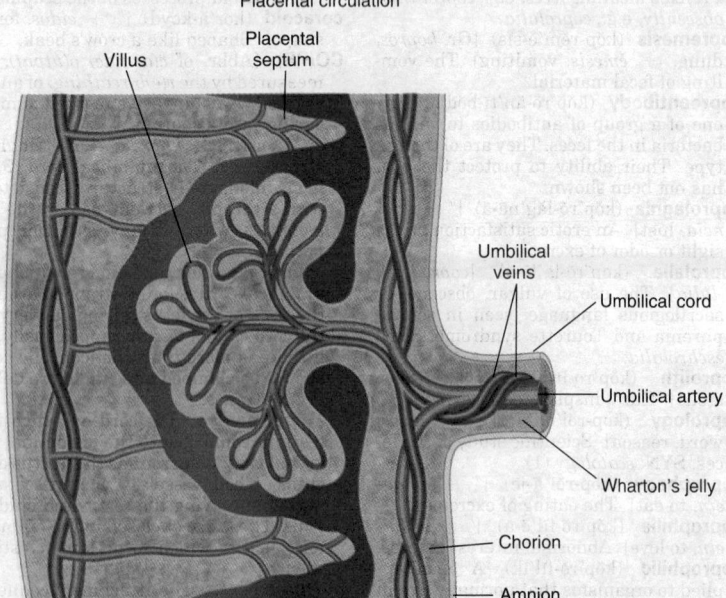

Placental circulation
Placental septum
Villus
Umbilical veins
Umbilical cord
Umbilical artery
Wharton's jelly
Chorion
Amnion

UMBILICAL CORD

of the eye, + *kleisis,* closure] Occlusion of the pupil.

core competency The basic knowledge and the fundamental set of attitudes and skills that are needed to perform in one's role as a health care professional. SYN: *competency validation program.*

corectasia, corectasis (kor-ĕk-tā′zē-ă, -ĕk′tă-sĭs) [″ + *ektasis,* dilatation] Dilatation of the pupil of the eye resulting from disease.

corectome (kō-rĕk′tōm) Iridectome.

corectopia (kor-ĕk-tō′pē-ă) [″ + *ek,* out of, + *topos,* place] A condition in which the pupil is to one side of the center of the iris.

coredialysis (kō″rē-dī-ăl′ĭ-sĭs) [″ + *dia,* through, + *lysis,* dissolution] Separation of the outer border of the iris from its ciliary attachment. SEE: *iridodialysis.*

coregistration (kō-rĕj″ĭ-strā′shŭn) The correlation of anatomical and metabolic data from different imaging techniques (e.g., from a CT scan and a PET scan of the same organ) in order to obtain enhanced images of diseased tissues.

core link In osteopathic medicine the hypothesis that manipulation of the cranial sutures results in subtle movements of the sacrum.

corelysis (kor-ĕl′ĭ-sĭs) [″ + *lysis,* dissolution] Obliteration of the pupil caused by adhesions of the iris to the cornea.

coremorphosis (kor″ē-mor-fō′sĭs) [″ + *morphe,* form, + *osis,* condition] Establishment of an artificial pupil.

coreoplasty (kō′rē-ō-plăs″tē) [″ + *plassein,* to form] Any operation for forming an artificial pupil.

corepressor (kō″rē-prĕs′sor) The substance capable of activating the repressor produced by a regulator gene.

corestenoma (kor″ē-stĕn-ō′mă) [″ + *stenoma,* contraction] Narrowing of the pupil.

    c. congenitum Partial congenital obliteration of the pupil by outgrowths from the iris that form a partial gridlike covering over the pupil.

core value A fundamental idea that unites individuals and defines the efforts and goals of the institution for which they work. In health care, core values include devotion and service to others, lifelong learning, and a dedication to ongoing quality improvement.

CORF Comprehensive outpatient rehabilitation facility.

Cori cycle (kō′rē) [Carl Ferdinand Cori, Czech-born U.S. physician and biochemist, 1896–1984; Gerty T. Cori, Czech-born U.S. biochemist, 1896–1957] The cycle in carbohydrate metabolism in which muscle glycogen breaks down, forms lactic acid, which enters the bloodstream and is converted to liver glycogen. Liver glycogen then breaks down into glucose, which is carried to muscles, where it is reconverted to muscle glycogen.

coring (kăwr′ĭng) [ME.] The operative removal of a plug or wedge of tissue (e.g., with a hollow surgical instrument).

corium (kō′rē-ŭm) *pl.* **coria** [L., skin] Dermis. SEE: *skin* for illus.

corm (korm) [Gr. *kormos,* a trimmed tree trunk] A short, bulb-shaped underground stem of a plant such as the autumn crocus, a source of colchicine.

corn [L. *cornu,* horn] A horny induration and thickening of the skin that may be hard or soft according to location. It is usually caused by the pressure or friction from poorly fitting shoes. SEE: *clavus.*

    SYMPTOMS: Hard corns on exposed surfaces have a horny, conical core extending into the dermis, causing pain and irritation. Soft corns occur between the toes and are kept soft by moisture and maceration. They may occasionally become infected.

    TREATMENT: Properly fitting shoes should be worn to reduce friction on the foot. Spongy materials or pads that limit friction prevent the foot from abrasion. Keratolytic agents are used to remove corns. A podiatrist may remove corns with a scalpel. Patients with diabetes or peripheral vascular disease who have corns need special care to prevent foot infections.

cornea (kor′nē-ă) [L. *(tela) cornea,* horny (web)] The transparent anterior portion of the sclera, about one sixth of its surface. It is anterior to the aqueous humor, the iris, pupil and lens of the eye. The cornea is the first part of the eye that refracts light. It is composed of five layers: an epithelial layer, Bowman's membrane (anterior limiting membrane), the substantia propria corneae, vitreous membrane, and a layer of endothelium. Beyond the edge of the cornea is the sclera (the white of the eye). **corneal** (kor′nē-ăl), *adj.*

    flat c. A cornea that is minimally rounded anteriorly. It focuses light behind the retina, producing hyperopia (farsightedness).

    steep c. A cornea that bulges anteriorly focusing light in front of the retina, producing myopia (nearsightedness).

corneal impression test (kor′nē-ăl) In diagnosing rabies, the immunofluorescent staining of material obtained from the corneas of patients suspected of having the disease. The rabies virus may be seen in the stained material.

corneal transplant (kor′nē-ăl) SEE: under *transplant.*

Cornelia de Lange syndrome (dĕ lăng, lahng′ă) [Cornelia de Lange, Dutch pediatrician] ABBR: CdLS. An autosomal dominant disorder marked by mental retardation, facial and limb anomalies, deafness, short stature, failure to thrive, and hirsutism. Affected children may have behavioral problems, including difficulty sleeping, hyperactivity, and a tendency to mutilate themselves.

corneoblepharon (kor″nē-ō-blĕf′ă-rŏn) [″ + Gr. *blepharon,* eyelid] Adhesion of the eyelid to the cornea.

corneomandibular reflex (kor″nē-ō-mandib′yŭ-lăr) SEE: under *reflex.*

corneosclera (kŏr″nē-ō-sklĕ′ră) [L. *corneus,* horny, + *skleros,* hard] The cornea and sclera, constituting the tunica fibrosa or fibrous coat of the eye.

corneous (kor′nē-ŭs) [L. *corneus*] Horny; hornlike.

corneum (kor′nē-ŭm) [L., horny] Stratum corneum.

corniculate (kor-nĭk′ū-lāt) Containing small horn-shaped projections.

corniculum (kor-nĭk′ū-lŭm) [L., little horn] A small hornlike process.

cornification (kor″nĭ-fĭ-kā′shŭn) Keratinization.

cornified (kor′nĭ-fīd) Changed into horny tissue.

cornu (kor′nū) *pl.* **cornua** [L., horn] Any projection like a horn. **cornual** (-ăl), *adj.*

   c. coccygeum One of the two upward-projecting processes that articulate with the sacrum.

   c. cutaneum A hornlike excrescence on the skin.

   c. of the hyoid The greater or the lesser horn of the hyoid bone.

   c. of the sacrum The two small processes projecting inferiorly on either side of the sacral hiatus leading into the sacral canal.

   c. of the uterus The entry point of the fallopian tube into the uterine cavity.

corona (kŏ-rō′nă) [Gr. *korone,* crown] Any structure resembling a crown. **coronal** (-năl), *adj.*

   c. ciliaris The circular figure on the inner surface of the ciliary body.

   c. dentis The crown of a tooth.

   c. glandis The posterior border of the glans penis.

   c. radiata 1. The ascending and descending fibers of the internal capsule of the brain that extend in all directions to the cerebral cortex above the corpus callosum. Many of the fibers arise in the thalamus. 2. A thin mass of follicle cells that adhere firmly to the zona pellucida of the human ovum after ovulation.

   c. veneris Syphilitic blotches on the forehead that parallel the hairline.

coronary (kor′ō-nă-rē) [L. *coronarius,* pert. to a crown or circle] Encircling, as the blood vessels that supply blood directly to the heart muscle; loosely used to refer to the heart and to coronary artery disease. *Coronary pain* is usually dull and heavy and may radiate to the arm, jaw, shoulders, or back. Typically, the patient describes the pain as being viselike or producing a feeling of compression or squeezing of the chest.

   café c. Chest pain, cyanosis, and collapse (or sudden death) during a meal, caused by aspiration of a bolus of food into the trachea. The Heimlich maneuver may be used to clear the obstructed airway of an adult or child who is still choking and conscious with severe obstruction.

coronary artery bypass SEE: under *bypass.*

coronary artery calcification SEE: under *calcification.*

coronary artery disease ABBR: CAD. Narrowing of the coronary arteries, usually as a result of atherosclerosis. It is the single most common cause of death in industrialized nations. In the U.S. in 2001, 460,000 people died of coronary artery disease. SEE: illus.; *angina pectoris; ischemic heart disease; myocardial infarction.*

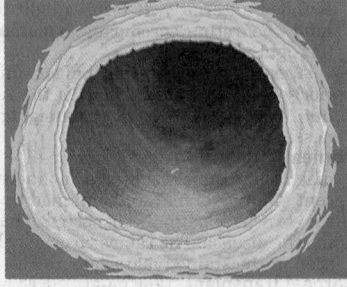

A   **B**

NORMAL AND DISEASED CORONARY ARTERIES

(A) Cross-section of normal coronary artery. (B) Cross-section of atherosclerotic coronary artery showing atherosclerosis narrowing the lumen.

Stenoses within the coronary circulation most commonly occur in people who smoke or who have diabetes mellitus, hypertension, adverse lipid profiles, or a familial predisposition to coronary heart disease. CAD tends to worsen as people age and is more common in men than in women. A person's risk for coronary artery disease can be estimated, e.g with on-line tools such as the following from the National Cholesterol Education Program Website: (http://hp2010.nhlbihin .net/atpiii/calculator.asp?usertype+prof). If blockages within the coronary arteries limit the flow of oxygenated blood to the myocardium, ischemia or infarction of the heart muscle may occur.

SYMPTOMS: Typically, patients who experience symptoms due to CAD report pain, burning, or pressure in the chest (angina pectoris) that begins or worsens with exertion, emotion, exposure to cold air, or the eating of a large meal. The pain may be described as a suffocating feeling or may be experienced as shortness of breath. It is often located beneath the sternum and can radiate to the upper chest, neck, jaw, shoulders, back, or arms. It may cause bloating, nausea, vomiting, or perspiration. However, many patients may not recognize the symptoms of coronary artery disease, a condition called "silent ischemia," or they may attribute their symptoms to another cause (e.g., indigestion).

TREATMENT: A low-fat, low-cholesterol diet, a regular program of sustained exercise, and smoking cessation all help patients to limit CAD. Medications to control hypertension, lipids, and ischemia (such as beta blockers, statins, and nitrates) also alleviate symptoms. Invasive approaches to reopen narrowed arteries are helpful in some patients. These include coronary angioplasty, stent placement, atherectomy, and coronary artery bypass surgery.

coronary artery scan SEE: under *scan*.

coronary artery spasm SEE: under *spasm*.

coronary atherectomy A technique of removing obstructions from the coronary artery with a cutting instrument inserted through a cardiac catheter.

coronary blood flow The amount of blood perfusing the heart muscle through the coronary arteries. This may be measured by one of several techniques including indicator dilution or use of radioisotopes.

coronary care unit A specially equipped area of a hospital providing intensive nursing and medical care for patients who have acute coronary thrombosis.

coronary flow reserve SEE: under *reserve*.

coronary microvascular disease ABBR: CMD. Abnormally reduced blood flow to the myocardium, resulting in ischemic chest pain in patients who have no evidence of obstruction to blood flow through the epicardial coronary arteries. It can be identified with coronary reactivity testing. CMD is more common in women than in men. Despite the normal appearance of the coronary arteries on angiography, CMD increases the risk for heart attack, heart failure, and sudden death. It can be treated with antiplatelet drugs like aspirin, beta blockers or other antianginal drugs, and statins. SYN: *coronary microvascular* **dysfunction**.

coronary microvascular syndrome Coronary microvascular disease.

coronary perfusion pressure SEE: under *pressure*.

coronary reactivity testing The measurement of blood flow inside a coronary artery after the use of IV drugs such as nitroglycerin, adenosine, or acetylcholine. The size of the arteries after the administration of these drugs and the changes in blood flow through them signal the presence of abnormal coronary artery reactivity to pharmacological stress. These findings can be used to confirm the diagnosis of microvascular coronary disease.

coronary sinus The vessel or passage that receives the cardiac veins from the heart. It opens into the right atrium. SEE: *coronary artery* for illus.

coronavirus (kor″ō-nă-vī′rŭs-ĕs) [L. *corona*, crown, + *virus*, poison] One of a group of viruses, morphologically similar, ether-sensitive, and containing RNA that are responsible for some common colds and severe adult respiratory syndrome (SARS). They are so named because their microscopic appearance is that of a virus particle surrounded by a crown.

coroner (kor′ŏ-nĕr) [L. *corona*, crown] An official (originally, English crown officer) who investigates and holds inquests concerning death from unknown or violent causes. The coroner may or may not be a physician, depending on the law in each state.

coronoid (kor′ō-noyd) [Gr. *korone*, something curved, kind of crown, + *eidos*, form, shape] Shaped like a crown.

coronoidectomy (kor″ō-noy-dĕk′tō-mē) [″ + ″ + *ektome*, excision] Excision of the coronoid process of the mandible.

coroscopy (kō-rŏs′kō-pē) [″ + *skopein*, to examine] Shadow test to determine refractive error of an eye. SYN: *retinoscopy; skiascopy*.

corpora (kor′pŏ-ră) [L. *corpora*, bodies, pl. of *corpus*] Pl. of corpus.

    c. arenacea Psammoma bodies found in the pineal body. SYN: *brain sand*.

    c. quadrigemina Lamina quadrigemina.

corporeal (kor-pō'rē-ăl) Having a physical body.

corpse (korps) [L. *corpus,* body] The dead human body.

corpsman (kor'măn) An enlisted person in the US Armed Forces who works as a member of the medical team. During duty in the armed forces he or she receives training and experience in one or more health-related fields. In wartime, a corpsman may be assigned as the only medically trained person to a field unit or a small ship. SYN: *medic; medical corpsman.*

corpulence (kor'pyŭ-lĕns) [L. *corpulentus,* fr. *corpus,* body] Obesity. **corpulent** (-lĕnt), *adj.*

cor pulmonale (pŭl-mă-nāl'ē, pool-mō-nah'lē) Hypertrophy or failure of the right ventricle resulting from disorders of the lungs, pulmonary vessels, chest wall, or respiratory control center. Living for an extended period at a high altitude may occasionally cause this condition.

SYMPTOMS: Symptoms include chronic productive cough, exertional dyspnea, wheezing, fatigue, weakness, drowsiness, and alterations in level of consciousness. On physical examination, dependent edema is present, and the neck veins are distended. The pulse is weak, and hypotension may occur due to reduced cardiac output. Tachycardia, a gallop rhythm, tricuspid insufficiency, or a right ventricular heave may be present. Sometimes an early right ventricular murmur or a systolic pulmonary ejection sound may be heard. The liver is enlarged and tender, and hepatojugular reflux is present. Pulmonary artery pressure measurements (if assessed in the cardiac catheterization lab or the intensive care unit) show increased right ventricular and pulmonary artery pressures related to increased pulmonary vascular resistance. Angiography or echocardiography documents right ventricular enlargement.

PATIENT CARE: Fluid retention is prevented by limiting the patient's intake as prescribed (usually 1 to 2 L daily) and by providing a low-sodium diet. The rationale for fluid restriction is explained, because those patients with chronic obstructive pulmonary disease would previously have been encouraged to increase fluid intake to help loosen and thin secretions. Frequent position changes are encouraged, and meticulous respiratory care is provided, including prescribed oxygen therapy and breathing exercises or chest physiotherapy. Assistance is provided to help the patient rinse the mouth after respiratory therapy.

Serum potassium levels are monitored closely if diuretics are prescribed, signs of digitalis toxicity (anorexia, nausea, vomiting) are noted, and cardiac arrhythmias are monitored. Periodically, arterial blood gas levels are measured, and signs of respiratory failure are noted. Prescribed medications are administered and evaluated for desired effects (e.g., improvements in oxygenation, ventilation, or edema), as are any adverse reactions (e.g., cardiac decompensation). A nutritious diet (limiting carbohydrates if the patient is a carbon dioxide retainer and low-sodium salt) is provided in frequent small meals to limit fatigue.

Care activities are paced and rest periods provided. The patient is encouraged to verbalize fears and concerns about the illness, and members of the health care team remain with the patient during times of stress or anxiety. The patient is encouraged to identify actions and care measures that promote comfort and relaxation and to participate in care decisions. The importance of avoiding respiratory infections and of reporting signs of infection immediately (increased sputum production, changes in sputum color, increased coughing or wheezing, fever, chest pain, and tightness in the chest) is stressed. Immunizations against influenza and pneumococcal pneumonia are recommended. Use of over-the-counter medications should be avoided unless the health care provider is consulted first. If the patient needs supplemental oxygen or suctioning at home, referral is made to a social service agency for assistance in obtaining the necessary equipment, and correct procedures are taught for equipment use. As appropriate, the patient is referred to smoking cessation programs, nicotine patch therapy, and local support groups.

corpus (kor'pŭs) *pl.* **corpora** [L., body] The principal part of any organ; any mass or body.

c. albicans A mass of fibrous tissue that replaces the regressing corpus luteum following rupture of the graafian follicle. It forms a white scar that gradually decreases and eventually disappears.

c. amylaceum A mass having an irregular laminated structure like a starch grain; found in the prostate, meninges, lungs, and other organs in various diseases. SYN: *colloid corpuscle.*

c. callosum The large commissure that interconnects the right and left cerebral hemispheres in the brain. SYN: *callosum.*

c. cavernosum Any erectile tissue, esp. the erectile bodies of the penis, clitoris, male or female urethra, bulb of the vestibule, or nasal conchae.

c. cavernosum penis One of the two columns of erectile tissue on the dorsum of the penis.

c. ciliare Ciliary body.

c. dentatum The gray layer in the white matter of the cerebellum. SYN: ***c. rhomboidale.***

c. hemorrhagicum A blood clot formed in the cavity left by rupture of the graafian follicle.

c. interpedunculare The gray matter between the peduncles in front of the pons varolii.

c. luteum The small yellow endocrine structure that develops within a ruptured ovarian follicle and secretes progesterone and estrogen. SEE: *fertilization* for illus.

c. mammillare Mammillary body.

c. spongiosum Erectile tissue surrounding the male urethra inside the shaft of the penis. SEE: *penis* for illus.

c. striatum Striatum

c. uteri The main body of the uterus, located above the cervix.

c. vitreum The vitreous part of the eye.

corpuscle (kor'pŭs-ĕl) [L. *corpusculum,* little body] **1.** Any small rounded body. **2.** An encapsulated sensory nerve ending. **3.** A blood cell. **corpuscular** (kor-pŭs'kyŭ-lăr), *adj.*

axis c. The center of a tactile corpuscle.

blood c. An erythrocyte or leukocyte.

bone c. Bone **cell.**

cancroid c. The characteristic nodule in cutaneous epithelioma.

cartilage c. Chondrocyte.

chromophil c. Nissl body.

chyle c. A corpuscle seen in chyle.

colloid c. Corpus amylaceum.

colostrum c. A cell containing phagocytosed fat globules, present in milk secreted the first few days after parturition.

corneal c. A type of connective tissue cell found in the fibrous tissue of the cornea.

genital c. An encapsulated sensory nerve ending resembling a pacinian corpuscle that is found in the skin of the external genitalia and nipples.

Gierke c. Hassall corpuscle.

Golgi-Mazzoni c. SEE: *Golgi-Mazzoni corpuscle.*

Hassall c. SEE: *Hassall corpuscle.*

Krause c. SEE: *Krause corpuscle.*

lymph c. Lymphocyte.

malpighian c. **1.** Renal corpuscle. **2.** A malpighian body of the spleen.

Mazzoni c. SEE: *Krause corpuscle.*

Meissner c. SEE: *Meissner corpuscle.*

milk c. A fat-filled globule present in milk. It represents the distal end of a mammary gland cell broken off in apocrine secretion.

pacinian c. An encapsulated nerve ending found in the dermis, subcutaneous tissue, and other connective tissue membranes; it is a sensory receptor for pressure.

Purkinje c. SEE: *Purkinje cell.*

red c. Erythrocyte.

red blood c. Erythrocyte.

renal c. A glomerulus and Bowman's capsule of the nephron of a kidney, the site of glomerular filtration. SYN: *malpighian c.* (1). SEE: illus.

reticulated c. An obsolete term for *reticulocyte.* SEE: *reticulocyte.*

Ruffini c. SEE: under *Ruffini, Angelo.*

splenic c. A nodule of lymphatic tissue in the spleen.

tactile c. A sensory receptor that responds to touch (e.g., Meissner's corpuscle). Tactile corpuscles are located in the dermal papillae just beneath the epidermis and are most numerous on the fingertips, toes, soles, palms, lips, nipples, and tip of the tongue.

terminal c. A nerve ending.

white c. Leukocyte.

white blood c. Leukocyte.

corpuscular (kor-pŭs'kū-lăr) Pert. to corpuscles.

correctable visual impairment SEE: under *impairment.*

correction The altering of a condition that is abnormal or malfunctioning.

correction bolus SEE: under *bolus.*

correction factor SEE: under *factor.*

corrective (kŏ-rĕk'tĭv) [L. *corrigere,* to correct] **1.** A drug that modifies the action of another. **2.** Pert. to such a drug.

correlation (kor″ĕ-lā'shŏn) [L. *correlatio,* report, relation] **1.** In statistics, the degree to which one variable increases or decreases with respect to another variable. A variable can have a positive or negative correlation with another variable. A positive correlation exists when the coefficient of correlation is +1 or

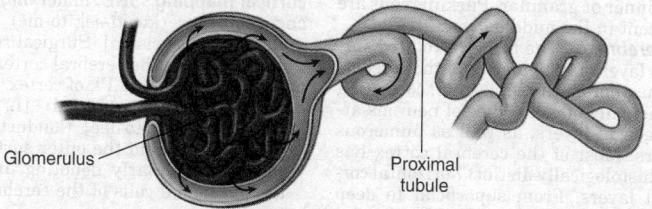

Glomerulus   Proximal tubule

RENAL CORPUSCLE

greater; a negative correlation exists when the coefficient is −1 or less; a correlation is considered to be nonexistent when the value is zero. **2.** The processes by which the various activities of the body, esp. nervous impulses, occur in relation to each other.

correspondence The act or condition of corresponding (i.e., occurring in proper relationship to other phenomena).

corresponding Agreeing with, matching, or fitting.

Corrigan pulse (kor'ĭ-găn) [Sir Dominic J. Corrigan, Ir. physician, 1802–1880] Waterhammer pulse.

corroborating (kŏr-ŏb'ō-rā-tĭng) Confirming or supporting with evidence.

corrosion (kŏ-rō'zhŭn) [L corrodere, to corrode] The slow disintegration or wearing away of something by a destructive agent.

corrosive (kŏ-rō'sĭv) Producing corrosion.

corrosive poisoning SEE: under *poisoning.*

corrugator (kŏr'ă-gāt″ĕr) [L. con, together, + rugare, to wrinkle] A muscle that lies above the orbit, arises medially from the frontal bone, and has its insertion on the skin of the medial half of the eyebrows. It draws the brow medially and inferiorly.

corrugator supercilii Corrugator **muscle**.

cortex (kor'teks″, kort'ĭ-sēz″) *pl.* **cortices** [L. *cortex,* rind] **1.** The outer layer of an organ as distinguished from the inner medulla, as in the adrenal gland, kidney, ovary, lymph node, and thymus **2.** The outer layer of a structure, as a hair or the lens of the eye. **3.** In the brain, a surface sheet of layered or laminated gray matter, as in the outermost sector of the cerebral and cerebellar hemispheres. **4.** The outer superficial portion of the stem or root of a plant.

   adrenal c. The outer layer of the adrenal gland. It has three concentric layers: the zona glomerulosa, which secretes mineralocorticoids (mainly aldosterone); and the zona fasciculata and the zona reticularis, which both secrete glucocorticoids (cortisol), androgens, and estrogens.

   cerebellar c. The surface layer of the cerebellum consisting of three layers: the outer or molecular, the middle, and the inner or granular. Purkinje cells are present in the middle layer.

   cerebral c. The thin, convoluted surface layer of gray matter of the cerebral hemispheres (the cerebrum), consisting principally of cell bodies of neurons arranged in layers, as well as numerous fibers. Most of the cerebral cortex has six histologically distinct horizontal cortical layers. From superficial to deep they are: 1. molecular layer (horizontal axons, Golgi type II cells, dendrites of

underlying pyramidal cells); 2. external granular layer (closely packed small granule cells); 3. external pyramidal layer (pyramidal neurons, granule cells, Martinotti cells); 4. internal granular layer (closely packed stellate cells); 5. internal pyramidal layer (pyramidal neurons, granule cells, Martinotti cells); and 6. multiform (fusiform) layer (spindle-shaped cells).

   entorhinal cortex The inner gyrus of the temporal lobe of the brain. It comprises the parahippocampal gyrus and the subicular cortex. In the entorhinal cortex, the five-layer structure of the ventral temporal cortex gradually merges into the single layer that is found in the dentate gyrus, the innermost edge of the temporal lobe. The entorhinal cortex receives signals from and projects back to the frontal cortex, the insula, and the cingulate cortex, and it is the key brain region funneling input to the hippocampus.

   functional c. Any of the regions of the brain that control speech, language, and other cognitive activities.

   olfactory c. The portion of the cerebral cortex concerned with the sense of smell. It includes the piriform lobe and the hippocampal formation.

   renal c. SEE: *kidney.*

   visual c. The primary visual areas of the cerebral cortex, contained in the gyri on either side of the calcarine sulcus on the medial surface of the occipital lobe. The visual cortex of one side of the brain receives input representing the opposite half of the visual fields of both eyes.

Corti, Alfonso Giacomo Gaspare (kor'tē) Italian anatomist, 1822–1876.

   canal of C. A triangular canal extending the entire length of the organ of Corti. Its walls are formed by the external and internal pillar cells.

   C. ganglion A ganglion on the cochlear nerve.

   organ of C. An elongated spiral structure running the entire length of the cochlea in the floor of the cochlear duct and resting on the basilar membrane. It contains the receptors for hearing, hair cells that are stimulated by sound waves. SYN: *organum spirale; spiral organ.* SEE: illus.; *Claudius' cell.*

cortical (kor'tĭ-kăl) Pert. to a cortex.

cortical mapping SEE: under *mapping.*

corticectomy (kor″tĭ-sĕk'tō-mē) [″ + Gr. *ektome,* excision] Surgical removal of a portion of the cerebral cortex.

cortices (kor'tĭ-sēz) Pl. of cortex.

corticifugal (kor″tĭ-sĭf'ū-găl) [L. *cortex,* rind, + *fugere,* to flee] Conducting impulses away from the outer surface, or cortex; particularly denoting axons of the pyramidal cells of the cerebral cortex.

corticipetal (kor″tĭ-sĭp'ĕ-tăl) [″ + *pe-*

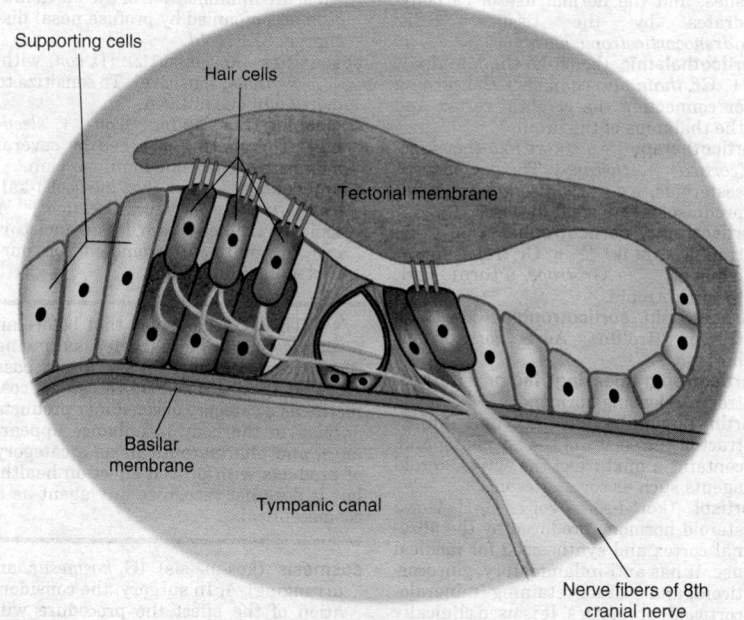

Supporting cells

Hair cells

Tectorial membrane

Basilar membrane

Tympanic canal

Nerve fibers of 8th cranial nerve

ORGAN OF CORTI

tere, to seek] Conducting impulses toward the outer surface, or cortex; particularly denoting thalamic radiation fibers conveying impulses to sensory areas of the cerebral cortex.

cortico-, cortic- [L. *cortex,* stem *cortic-,* bark, rind] Prefixes meaning *cortex.*

corticoadrenal (kor″tĭ-kō-ăd-rē′năl) [″ + *ad,* toward, + *ren,* kidney] Pert. to the cortex of the adrenal gland.

corticobasal (kŏr″tĭ-kō-bāz′ăl) Concerning the cerebral cortex and the basal ganglia.

corticobasal degeneration SEE: under *degeneration.*

corticobulbar (kor″tĭ-kō-bŭl′băr) [″ + *bulbus,* bulb] Pert. to the cerebral cortex and upper portion of the brainstem, as the corticobulbar tract.

corticoid (kor′tĭ-koyd) [″ + Gr. *eidos,* form, shape] Corticosteroid.

corticopleuritis (kor″tĭ-kō-ploo-rī′tĭs) [″ + Gr. *pleura,* rib, + *itis,* inflammation] Inflammation of the outer parts of the pleura.

corticopontine (kor″tĭ-kō-pŏn′tīn) [″ + *pons,* bridge] Pert. to or connecting the cerebral cortex and the pons.

corticostatin (kor″tĭ-kō-stă′tĭn) [L. *cortex,* bark, + *status,* stance] A peptide that inhibits adrenocorticotropic hormone–stimulated secretion of corticosteroids by the adrenal glands. Rich in arginine and cystine, it is secreted by cells in the lungs, spleen, pituitary, and other organs. It competes with cortico-

tropin for binding sites and appears to mediate the physiological response of the body to sepsis.

corticosteroid (kort″ĭ-kō-stēr′oyd″) [*cortico-* + *steroid*] Any of several steroid hormones secreted by the cortex of the adrenal gland or manufactured synthetically for use as a drug. They are classified according to their biological activity as glucocorticoids, mineralocorticoids, and androgens. Adrenal corticosteroids do not initiate cellular and enzymatic activity but permit many biochemical reactions to proceed at optimal rates. SYN: *corticoid.*

Drugs from this class are widely used to treat inflammatory illnesses, including arthritis, asthma, and dermatitis. They are also used as replacement hormones in patients with adrenal insufficiency.

⚠ Common side effects of long-term use of these agents include thinning of the skin, easy bruising, cataract formation, glucose intolerance, alterations in sleep cycles, osteoporosis, and immune suppression.

corticosterone (kor″tĭ-kŏs′tĕ-rōn) A hormone of the adrenal cortex that influences carbohydrate, potassium, and sodium metabolism. It is essential for normal absorption of glucose, the formation of glycogen in the liver and tissues, and the normal use of carbohydrates by the tissues. SEE: *adrenocorticotropic hormone.*

corticothalamic (kor″tĭ-kō-thă-lăm′ĭk) [″ + Gr. *thalamos,* chamber] Concerning or connecting the cerebral cortex and the thalamus of the brain.

corticotherapy (kort′ĭ-kō-ther′ă-pē) [*cortico-* + *therapy*] The use of corticosteroids, e.g., prednisone or methylprednisolone, to treat disease.

corticotropic, corticotrophic (kŏr″tĭ-kō-trōp′ĭk, -trōf′ĭk) [″ + Gr. *trophe,* nourishment; ″ + Gr. *trope,* a turn] Pert. to corticotropin.

corticotropin, corticotrophin (kor″tĭ-kō-trō′pĭn, -trō′fĭn) Adrenocorticotropic hormone.

corticotropin-releasing factor Corticotropin-releasing hormone.

cortin (kor′tĭn) [L. *cortex,* rind] An extract of the cortex of the adrenal gland; contains a mixture of the active steroid agents such as corticosterone.

cortisol (kort′ĭ-sōl″, -zol″) $C_{21}H_{30}O_5$, a steroid hormone produced by the adrenal cortex and synthesized for medical use. It has anti-inflammatory, glucocorticoid, and sodium-retaining (mineralocorticoid) properties. It is used clinically to reduce the pain and inflammation of various conditions, including rashes, hemorrhoids, arthritis, and inflammatory bowel disease. It also is used as steroid replacement therapy in patients with adrenal insufficiency. SYN: *17-hydroxycorticosterone;.* SYN: *hydrocortisone.*

cortisone (kor′tĭ-sōn) A hormone isolated from the cortex of the adrenal gland and also prepared synthetically. It regulates the metabolism of fats, carbohydrates, sodium, potassium, and proteins, and is also used as an anti-inflammatory agent.

Cortrosyn (kor′trŏ-sin) SEE: *Cosyntropin.*

Cortrosyn stimulation test ACTH stimulation test.

Corynebacterium (kor″ĭ-nē-bak-tir′ē-ŭm) [L. *corynebacterium* fr Gr. *korynē,* a club, + *bacterium*] A genus of gram-positive, aerobic, nonmotile bacilli of the family Corynebacteriaceae. Some are part of normal skin flora; others are pathogens for domestic animals, birds, and reptiles.

   C. diphtheriae The causative agent of diphtheria in humans. SEE: *diphtheria.*

   C. minutissimum The causative species of erythrasma.

   C. parvum An organism used as part of a nonspecific immunotherapy regimen (investigational) in the treatment of lung cancer.

   C. vaginale A former name for Gardnerella vaginalis.

coryza (kŏ-rī′ză) [Gr. *koryza,* catarrh]

An acute inflammation of the nasal mucosa accompanied by profuse nasal discharge. SEE: *cold.*

cosensitize (kō-sĕn′sĭ-tīz) [L. *con,* with, + *sensitivus,* sensitive] To sensitize to more than one antigen.

cosleeping (kō″slēp′ĭng) [*con-* + *sleeping*] The sharing of a bed by several members of the same family or clan.

cosmeceutical (koz″mĕ-soot′ĭ-kăl) [*cosme(tic)* + *(pharma)ceutical*] A topically applied cream, lotion, moisturizer, or ointment promoted for purported health benefits.

⚠ The FDA has ruled that before an agent can be marketed as having pharmaceutical properties, it must pass stringent testing. The FDA recognizes cosmetics as a category of consumer products applied to the body to enhance appearance, and pharmaceuticals as a category of products with proven effect on health, but it does not recognize any agent as a cosmeceutical.

cosmesis (kŏs-mē′sĭs) [G. *kosmesus,* an arranging] **1.** In surgery, the consideration of the effect the procedure will have on the appearance of the patient. **2.** In rehabilitation, the characteristic of orthotic and prosthetic devices that determines their acceptability (and thus their successful use) in relation to a person's body image. For example, persons with hand amputations may sometimes prefer a more cosmetically acceptable but functionally useless glove over a less appealing but highly functional artificial limb with a stainless steel terminal device.

cosmetic (kŏz-mĕt′ĭk) **1.** A preparation such as powder or cream for improving appearance. **2.** Serving to preserve or promote appearance.

cost-, costo- [L. *costa,* side, rib] Prefixes meaning *rib.*

costa (kŏs′tă) *pl.* **costae** [L.] Rib.

costal (kŏs′tăl) Pert. to a rib.

costalgia (kŏs-tăl′jē-ă) [L. *costa,* rib, + Gr. *algos,* pain] Pain in a rib or the intercostal spaces (e.g., intercostal neuralgia).

cost awareness SEE: under *awareness.*

costectomy (kŏs-tĕk′tō-mē) [″ + Gr. *ektome,* excision] Surgical excision or resection of a rib.

cost-effectiveness An assessment or determination of the most efficient and least expensive approaches to providing health care and preventive medicine services. One component, health education, focuses on helping people to assume some responsibility for their own health maintenance and avoid preventable illness and disability. Accident prevention programs, immunization drives, and safe-sex campaigns are designed to reduce the number of patients who will suffer preventable illnesses. To control costs, health care providers and health care customers must also understand the comparative value of procedures and medicines. SEE: *preventive medicine; preventive nursing.* **cost-effective,** *adj.*

Costen syndrome [James B. Costen, U.S. otolaryngologist, 1895–1961] Temporomandibular joint syndrome.

cost minimization The selection or employment of the least expensive of several health care options.

costocervical (kŏs″tō-sĕr′vĭ-kăl) Concerning the ribs and neck.

costochondral (kŏs″tō-kŏn′drăl) [L. *costa,* rib, + Gr. *chondros,* cartilage] Pert. to a rib and its cartilage.

costochondritis (kos″tŏ-kon-drīt′ĭs) [*cost-* + *chondritis*] Inflammation of the costochondral joints of the chest, which can cause chest pain. The pain of costochondritis can sometimes be distinguished from other, more serious forms of chest pain by its reproducibility on palpation of the involved joints and the absence of abnormalities on chest x-ray examinations, electrocardiograms, and blood tests. SYN: *Tietze's syndrome.* SEE: *arthritis; costochondral.*

SYMPTOMS: Symptoms include pain and tenderness over the joints lateral to the sternum.

TREATMENT: Use of a nonsteroidal anti-inflammatory agent often helps reduce the discomfort, which normally resolves spontaneously over time.

costoclavicular (kŏs″tō-klă-vĭk′ū-lăr) [″ + *clavicula,* a little key] Pert. to the ribs and clavicle.

costopneumopexy (kŏs″tō-nū′mō-pĕk″sē) [″ + Gr. *pneumon,* lung, + *pexis,* fixation] Anchoring a lung to a rib.

costosternal (kŏs″tō-stĕr′năl) [″ + Gr. *sternon,* chest] Pert. to a rib and the sternum.

costotome (kŏs′tō-tōm) [″ + Gr. *tome,* incision] Knife or shears for cutting through a rib or cartilage.

costotomy (kŏs-tŏt′ō-mē) **1.** Incision or division of a rib or part of one.

costovertebral (kŏs″tō-vĕr′tĕ-brăl) [″ + *vertebra,* joint] Pert. to a rib and a vertebra.

cost recovery A payment demanded by a professional licensing board from a practitioner found to have violated standards of practice. The fee is a reimbursement to the board for the expenses it incurs during the investigation and prosecution of its case against the practitioner.

cost sharing An approach to health insurance in which the insured party pays for some of the services received, and the insurance sponsor, usually an employer, pays the rest. Methods of sharing costs between the insured and the sponsor include copayments, deductibles, and annual out-of-pocket expenses.

cosyntropin (kō″sĭn-trō′pĭn) Synthetic adrenocorticotropic hormone (ACTH). It is used to test for adrenal insufficiency by giving the medication parenterally and checking plasma cortisol levels at timed intervals. If the levels fail to rise appropriately, adrenal insufficiency is present. Trade name is Cortrosyn.

cosyntropin stimulation test ACTH stimulation test.

Cotard delusion [J. Cotard, Fr. neurologist, b. 1840 d. 1889] Delirium of negation.

CO(TD) [Abbr. of c*(ardiac)* o*(utput),* as measured by the *t(hermo)d(ilution)* of blood] An invasive method of measuring cardiac output that relies on the advancement of a catheter through central veins into the right ventricle.

PATIENT CARE: A cool or room temperature tracer is injected, and the thermal decay (or heating of the blood followed by thermal decay) is used to determine the cardiac output.

cot death SEE: under *death.*

CO₂ therapy **1.** Therapeutic application of low temperatures with solid carbon dioxide. SEE: *cryotherapy; hypothermia* (2). **2.** Inhalation of carbon dioxide to stimulate breathing.

cotinine (kōt′ĭn-ēn″) The principal metabolite of nicotine; excreted in the urine. Its detection indicates that the individual has recently smoked cigarettes or inhaled secondhand smoke. SEE: *tobacco.*

cotransport (kō″trănz′pōrt) The transfer of two substances in the same direction across a cell membrane.

cotton [ME. *cotoun,* from Arabic *qutn,* cotton] A soft, white, fibrous material obtained from the fibers enclosing the seeds of various plants of the Malvaceae, esp. those of the genus *Gossypium.*

purified c. Cotton fibers from which the oil has been completely removed. This enhances the ability to absorb liquids.

styptic c. Cotton impregnated with an astringent.

cottonmouth (kot′ŏn-mowth″) A venomous snake, *Agkistrodon piscivorus,* common in the southern and eastern U.S. SYN: *water moccasin.* SEE: *snake bite; venomous snake.*

Cotton test (kŏt′n) A manual stress test used to identify the amount of lateral translation of the talus within the ankle mortise. The examiner stabilizes the proximal ankle while shifting the talus laterally. A positive test is marked by increased motion relative to the uninvolved side and is indicative of a sprain of the distal tibiofibular syndesmosis or the subtalar joint. SEE: illus.

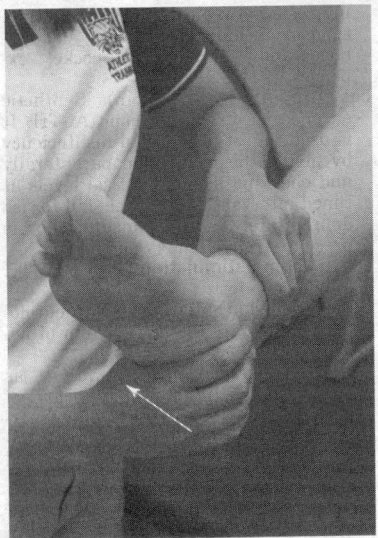

COTTON TEST

cotton-wool spot SEE: under *spot*.

co-twin (kō-twĭn) Either one of twins.

cotyledon (kŏt″ĭ-lē′dŏn) [Gr. *kotyledon*, hollow of a cup] **1.** A mass of villi on the chorionic surface of the placenta. **2.** Any of the rounded portions into which the placenta's uterine surface is divided. **3.** The seed leaf of a plant embryo.

cotyloid (kŏt′ĭ-loyd) [Gr. *kotyloeides*, cup-shaped] Shaped like a cup.

cough (kof) A forceful, sometimes violent expiratory effort preceded by a preliminary inspiration. The glottis is partially closed, the accessory muscles of expiration are brought into action, and the air is noisily expelled.

There is no one course of therapy for a cough because it may be due to a variety of conditions. Each disease is evaluated and treated accordingly. It is usually inadvisable to suppress completely coughs due to inflammation of the respiratory tract. This is particularly true if sputum is produced as a result of coughing. SEE: *expectoration*.

brassy c. A dry cough heard in patients who have pressure on the left recurrent laryngeal nerve, as in aortic aneurysm or in those with laryngeal inflammation.

bronchial c. A cough heard in patients with bronchiectasis or bronchitis. It may be provoked by a change of posture, as when getting up in the morning, and produces frothy mucus that is copious, dirty gray, and has a fetid odor. The cough is hacking and irritating in the earlier stages; in later stages it is looser and easier. Cold air can exacerbate this cough.

chronic c. A cough that occurs daily for at least three weeks.

diphtherial c. A cough heard in laryngeal diphtheria. It is noisy and brassy, and breathing is stridulous.

dry c. A cough unaccompanied by sputum production.

ear c. A reflex cough induced by irritation in the ear that stimulates Arnold's nerve.

hacking c. A series of repeated efforts, as in many respiratory infections.

harsh c. A metallic cough occurring in laryngitis.

moist c. A loose cough accompanied by production of mucus or exudate.

paroxysmal c. A persistent cough occurring with a sudden onset.

productive c. A cough in which mucus or an exudate is expectorated.

pulmonary c. A cough that is deep, seen in pneumonia. It may be hacking and irritating in the early stages of lung infection; in later stages, it is frequent and productive. SEE: *sputum*.

reflex c. A cough due to irritation from the middle ear, pharynx, stomach, or intestine. It may occur singly or coupled, or may be hacking. Stimulation of Arnold's nerve of the ear can cause it.

trigeminal c. A reflex cough from irritation of the trigeminal terminations in respiratory upper passages.

whooping c. **1.** Pertussis. **2.** The paroxysmal cough ending in a whooping inspiration that occurs in pertussis.

coulomb (koo′lŏm, -lōm) [Charles A. de Coulomb, Fr. physicist, 1736–1806] ABBR: C. A unit of electrical quantity; the quantity of electricity that flows across a surface when a steady current of 1 amp flows for 1 sec.

Coumadin (koo′mă-dĭn) A trade name for SEE: *warfarin sodium*.

coumarin anticoagulant (koo′mă-rĭn) SEE: under *anticoagulant*.

Council of Teaching Hospitals and Health Systems ABBR: COTH. A division of the American Association of Medical Colleges, consisting of 400 hospitals where clinical education is provided to health professions students.

counsel (kown′sĕl) [Fr. *conseil* fr L. *consilium*, deliberation, conclusion, resolution, plan] **1.** To advise, esp. officially or professionally. **2.** Advice, esp. official or professional. **3.** A lawyer acting as the legal representative of one of the parties in a trial.

counseling (kown′sĕl-ĭng) The providing of advice and guidance to a patient by a health professional.

count (kownt) **1.** The number of units in a sample or object. **2.** To enumerate.

absolute granulocyte c. ABBR: AGC. The total number of neutrophils, basophils, and eosinophils in a specimen of blood.

absolute neutrophil c. ABBR: ANC. The actual number of neutrophils in a cubic millimeter of blood. The approximate normal range is 3000 to 6000 cells/mm³. This figure is measured before and after drugs are given that may lower neutrophil counts, such as those used in cancer chemotherapy. Generally, chemotherapy is not given unless the patient's ANC is greater than 1000. Patients with an ANC of less than 500 cells/mm³ are at high risk for infection. SEE: *neutrophil*.

⚠️ The development of fever in a patient with neutropenia secondary to chemotherapy is an indication for urgent medical evaluation and prompt institution of broad-spectrum antibiotics.

---

absolute phagocyte c. ABBR: APC. The number of phagocytes (neutrophils and monocytes-macrophages) in a cubic millimeter of blood. The APC is the sum of the neutrophils (*segs* and *bands*), monocytes, and macrophages times one hundredth (1/100) of the white blood cell count. SEE: *absolute neutrophil c.; blood c.*

blood c. The number of red cells and leukocytes per microliter (μl) of whole blood. Normally, the number of erythrocytes in men averages 5 million/μl; in women, 4.5 million/μl. Prolonged exposure to high altitude increases the number. Leukocytes average 5000 to 10,000/μl. Platelets range from 140,000 to 400,000/μl. Hemoglobin (12 to 18 g/100 ml) and hematocrit (38% to 48%) are determined from samples of whole blood.

complete blood c. ABBR: CBC. A laboratory evaluation of all the cells that circulate in the blood, including the number and the hemoglobin content of red blood cells, the white blood cells (and their subtypes), and platelets. The typical CBC provides assessments of size and shape of red blood cells and platelets as well.

PATIENT CARE: The CBC is among the most common blood tests performed in the clinical laboratory and aids in the diagnosis of anemia and erythrocytosis, bleeding and the repletion of blood cells by transfusion, thrombocytopenia and thrombocytosis, and infections and leukemias. Blood is obtained for the test from venipuncture or aspiration from an indwelling vascular access or port. It is taken to the laboratory in a tube that contains the anticoagulant ethylenediaminetetraacetic acid (EDTA).

differential blood c. The number and type of white blood cells as determined by microscopic examination of a thin layer of blood on a glass slide stained to show the shape of the various cells. The number and variety of white cells in a sample of a given size are obtained. Even though the red cells are not counted by this method, their shape, size, and color can be evaluated. Some blood diseases and inflammatory conditions may be recognized in this way. In a differential count, the varieties of the leukocytes and their percentages normally should be: neutrophils (segmented), 40% to 60%; eosinophils, 1% to 3%; basophils, 0.5% to 1%; lymphocytes, 20% to 40%; monocytes, 4% to 8%.

pollen c. The concentration of grains of pollen found in the atmosphere on a given day in a specific location. The measurement is used by allergy sufferers to forecast the likelihood they will have allergic symptoms, e.g., sneezing, sniffling, or wheezing.

surgical c. Counting the exact number of sponges, instruments, and other materials before, during, and after an operation in order to reduce the likelihood of leaving an object inside a body cavity.

total lymphocyte c. ABBR: TLC. The number of lymphocytes in a specimen of blood. The count may be increased in clonal diseases such as chronic lymphocytic leukemia or decreased in diseases such as AIDS. In AIDS, decreases in the total lymphocyte count usually reflect a marked decline in the number of helper T4 cells.

counter (kown'tĕr) A device for counting anything.

colony c. An apparatus for counting bacterial colonies in a culture plate.

impedance c. A blood cell counter that uses cell membrane electrical impedance to determine the volume of cells in a solution.

particle c. An electronic device for counting and differentiating cells, platelets, and small particles according to their volume.

scintillation c. A device for detecting and counting radiation. Flashes of light are produced when radiation is detected.

counter- [Fr. *countre, contre,* fr. L. *contra,* against] Prefix meaning *against, in opposition to, opposite.*

counteract (kown"tĕr-ăkt') To act against or in opposition to.

countercurrent exchanger (kown"tĕr-kŭr'ĕnt) The exchange of chemicals between two streams of fluid flowing in opposite directions on either side of a permeable membrane. This permits the fluid leaving one side of the membrane to be similar to the composition of the fluid entering the other end of the other stream.

counterextension (kown"tĕr-ĕks-tĕn'shŭn) [L. *contra,* against, + *extendere,* to extend] Back pull or resistance to extension on a limb.

counterimmunoelectrophoresis (kown"tĕr-ĭm"ū-nō-ē-lĕk"trō-fō-rē'sĭs) [" + *immunis,* safe, + Gr. *elektron,* amber, + *phoresis,* bearing] The process in which antigens and antibodies are placed in separate wells and an electric current is passed through the diffusion medium. Antigens migrate to the anode and antibodies to the cathode. If the antigen and antibody correspond to each other, they will precipitate and form a precipitin band or line upon meeting in the diffusion medium.

counterincision (kown″tĕr-in-sizh′ŏn) [*counter-* + *incision*] Relaxing **incision**.

counterirritant (kown″tĕr-ĭr′ĭ-tănt) [″ + *irritare,* to excite] An agent such as mustard plaster that is applied locally to produce an inflammatory reaction for the purpose of affecting some other part, usually adjacent to or underlying the surface irritated. Three degrees of irritation are produced by the following classes of agents: 1. rubefacients, which redden the skin; 2. vesicants, which produce a blister or vesicle; and 3. escharotics, which form an eschar or slough or cause death of tissue. SEE: *acupuncture; escharotic; moxibustion; plaster, mustard.*

counterirritation (kown″tĕr-ĭr″ĭ-tā′shŭn) Superficial irritation that relieves some other irritation of deeper structures.

counteropening (kown″tĕr-ō′pĕn-ĭng) [L. *contra,* against, + AS *open,* open] Relaxing **incision.**

counterpressure instrument (kown′tĕr-presh″ŭr) SEE: under *instrument.*

counterpulsation (kown″tĕr-pŭl-sā′shŏn) [*counter-* + *pulsation*] Any of several techniques used to decrease the workload of a failing heart and increase blood flow to the coronary arteries.

   enhanced external c. ABBR: EECP. A noninvasive treatment for angina pectoris and congestive heart failure involving the use of inflatable cuffs on the patient's legs to improve myocardial perfusion and increase cardiac output. Cuffs placed on the calves, lower thighs, and upper thighs are inflated sequentially during diastole when coronary artery filling occurs. The inflated cuffs increase diastolic central aortic pressure, increase blood flow to the coronary arteries, and may enhance collateral blood flow. EECP is used to treat angina pectoris that does not respond to maximal medical therapy.

   intra-aortic balloon c. ABBR: IABC. The use of a balloon attached to a catheter inserted through the femoral artery into the proximal descending thoracic aorta to produce alternating inflation and deflation during diastole and systole, respectively. The balloon is inflated with helium. IABC lowers resistance to aortic blood flow during systole and increases resistance during diastole. It is used to treat patients with cardiogenic shock and those awaiting cardiac transplant, recovering from myocardial in-

farction, being weaned from cardiopulmonary bypass, and, rarely, those with unstable angina or intractable ventricular arrhythmias. It is contradicted in aortic valve insufficiency and dissecting aortic aneurysms. SYN: *intra-aortic balloon pump.*

   PATIENT CARE: *Patient preparation:* If time permits, the health care provider explains to the patient that the cardiologist will place a special catheter into the aorta, usually via a femoral artery to help the heart pump more easily and to provide specific procedural and sensation information. The nurse explains that the catheter will be connected to a large console beside the bed that has an alarm system and that he or she will promptly answer any alarms. The nurse further explains that the console normally makes a pumping sound and assures the patient that this does not mean that the heart is not beating. The nurse also makes clear that because of the catheter, the patient will not be able to sit up, bend the knee, or flex the hip more than 30°. The patient will remain on the cardiac monitor and have a central line (pulmonary artery catheter), arterial line, and peripheral intravenous (IV) line in place. A thorough assessment of circulation of lower extremity pulses is conducted. Most insertions are performed under fluoroscopy. If the procedure is to be performed at the bedside, the nurse gathers the appropriate equipment, including a surgical tray for percutaneous catheter insertion, heparin solution, normal saline solution, the IABP catheter, and the pump console. The nurse prepares the femoral insertion site according to protocol, ascertains that a signed informed consent for the procedure has been obtained, and provides the patient with emotional support throughout the procedure. Sedation and analgesia are administered as prescribed.

   Monitoring and aftercare: Following institutional protocol or physician orders, the nurse sets the console to regulate the rate of inflation and deflation of the balloon according to the electrocardiogram or the arterial waveform. The balloon rapidly inflates during the onset of diastole (the isometric or isovolumetric relaxation phase), as indicated by the dicrotic notch on the arterial waveform. Inflation forces blood into the coronary arteries and increases perfusion and blood flow to the kidneys, brain, and other organs and tissues. During the onset of ventricular systole, the balloon is rapidly deflated, causing a fall in aortic pressure that reduces myocardial oxygen consumption, decreases afterload, and increases stroke volume and cardiac output. (If the patient has no intrinsic heart rate, the pump may be set to its own intrinsic rate.) The nurse uses strict aseptic technique in caring for the catheter insertion site and connections and frequently inspects the site for bleeding or inflammation. If bleeding occurs at the insertion site, the nurse applies direct pressure over it and notifies the cardiologist. The nurse maintains the catheterized leg in correct body alignment and prevents hip flexion. The nurse maintains elevation of the head at no more than 30° to prevent upward migration of the catheter and occlusion of the left subclavian artery. If the balloon occludes the artery, the nurse can expect to note a diminished left radial pulse and the patient's report of dizziness. (Incorrect balloon placement may also occlude the renal artery, causing flank pain or a sudden drop in urine output.) Hemodynamic parameters are monitored according to agency protocols; urine output is monitored hourly. The nurse also periodically assesses distal pulses and documents the color, temperature, and capillary refill of the patient's extremities. The nurse also evaluates the warmth of the affected leg, color, pulses, and the patient's ability to move the toes at 30-min intervals for the first 4 hr after balloon insertion, then hourly for the duration of IABP. (Often, arterial flow to the involved extremity diminishes during insertion, but the pulse should strengthen once pumping begins.)

Even if the patient is receiving anticoagulants to inhibit thrombosis, the nurse keeps in mind that the patient may still be at risk for formation of thrombi and observes for such indications such as a sudden weakening of pedal pulses, pain in the limb, and motor or sensory loss. The nurse applies antithrombotic stockings (or pneumatic pulsatile stockings) as prescribed and encourages active range-of-motion exercises every 2 hr for the arms, the unaffected leg, and the affected ankle. The patient is also assisted with pulmonary hygiene. Meticulous skin care is provided.

An alarm on the console may detect gas leaks from a damaged or ruptured balloon. If the alarm sounds, or if the nurse observes blood in the catheter, he or she should shut down the pump console and immediately place the patient in the Trendelenburg position to prevent an air (gas) embolus from reaching the brain and then notify the cardiologist.

Once the signs and symptoms of left ventricular failure have diminished and the patient requires only minimal pharmacological support, the patient will be gradually weaned from IABP by decreasing the balloon volume, the frequency of balloon inflation and deflation, or both over a period of hours or days. To discontinue IABP, the cardiologist or a designate will deflate the balloon, clip the sutures, and remove the catheter, allowing the site to bleed for 5 seconds to expel clots. Because of the potential for blood splattering, involved personnel should wear protective coverings and eye-shields. The nurse then applies direct pressure to the site for at least 15 min (longer if anticoagulant therapy has been administered), followed by a pressure dressing with a sandbag on top. The nurse evaluates the site for bleeding and hematoma formation hourly for the next 4 hr and reports frank bleeding, local swelling, and increased patient pain. Usually the patient will be transferred to a telemetry unit for follow-up care until ready for discharge.

counterresistance (kown″tĕr-rĭ-zĭs′tăns) A term rooted in Freudian psychoanalysis that refers to resistance by a psychotherapist that corresponds to the patient's resistance to closeness and change of life patterns. Examples include coming late to sessions, avoiding certain subjects, and fascination with the patient. Three types are countertransferance, characterological resistance, and cultural resistance.

countershock (kown′tĕr-shŏk″) The application of electric current to the heart by internal paddles, external paddles, or electrodes. SEE: *cardioversion; defibrillation.*

counterstain, counter stain (kown′tĕr-stān″) A pigment used to highlight or add contrast to parts of a tissue specimen that have already been colored with a primary stain.

counterstrain (kownt′ĕr-strān″) SEE: *strain and counterstrain.*

countertraction (kown″tĕr-trăk′shŭn) The application of traction so the force opposes the traction already established; used in reducing fractures and assisting with surgical dissection.

countertransference (kown″tĕr-trăns-fĕr′ĕns) In psychoanalytic theory, the development by the analyst of an emotional (i.e., transference) relationship with the patient. In this situation, the therapist may lose objectivity.

coup (kū) SEE: *contrecoup.*

couplant (kŭp′lănt) A medium, typically a viscous, nontoxic liquid or gel, that transmits ultrasonic energy from its source to the object to be stimulated. In respiratory care, a couplant in a nebulizer transmits the ultrasonic vibrations into a chamber in which a medication is held. The ultrasonic energy aerosolizes the medication for inhalation by the patient.

couple (kŭp′ĕl) **1.** To join. **2.** To have sexual intercourse. **3.** Dyad, senses (1) and (4).

coupler Any device that joins two objects, e.g., a video endoscope to its light source.

couple-year of protection ABBR: CYP. In family planning, the number of days per year that any method of birth control will prevent conception. Abstinence from sexual intercourse, or sterilization of both members of a couple, provides absolute (365 days/year) protection. Other methods of family planning or fertility inhibition are relatively less effective. Couples that attempt penile withdrawal before male climax (coitus interruptus) have the lowest levels of CYP of any method. Condoms provide a moderate increase in contraceptive effectiveness but are less effective than intrauterine devices, contraceptive pills, or contraceptive implants.

coupling (kŭp'lĭng) **1.** In cardiology, the regular occurrence of a premature beat just after a normal heart beat. **2.** A device that holds two instruments together. **3.** A surgically constructed link between two organs or blood vessels

Courvoisier, Ludwig Georg (koor-vwa'zyā') Swiss surgeon, 1843–1918.

    C. law Disease processes associated with prior inflammation of the gallbladder (e.g., gallstones) produce scarring, which prevents enlargement of the gland. When the common bile duct is obstructed by cancer, the gallbladder becomes palpably dilated.

    C. sign Painless enlargement of the gallbladder in a jaundiced patient. The sign suggests a cancer obstructing the biliary tree.

couvade (koo-vad') [Fr. *couvade,* hatching, incubation] The custom in some cultures of the father remaining in bed as if ill during the time the mother is confined for childbirth. In other cultures, expectant fathers may experience psychosomatic pregnancy-simulating symptoms of nausea, fatigue, and backache.

Couvelaire uterus (koo-vlār') [Alexandre Couvelaire, Fr. obstetrician, 1873–1948] A potential complication of placental abruption in which blood flows into the myometrium. Such a uterus is enlarged and tense; it contracts poorly and may occasionally rupture. SYN: *uteroplacental apoplexy.*

covalence (kō-vāl'ĕns) The sharing of electrons between two atoms, which bonds the atoms. **covalent** (-ĕnt), *adj.*

covariance (kō-vā'rē-ăns) In statistics, the expected value of the product of the deviations of corresponding values of two variables from their respective means.

covariant (kō-vā'rē-ănt) In mathematics, pert. to variation of one variable

with another so that a specified relationship is unchanged.

cover (kŏ'vĕr) **1.** To provide protection from potential illnesses with drugs, e.g., to cover a patient with a fever with antibiotics pending results of cultures. **2.** A blanket or other garment to warm or reassure a patient. **3.** To provide insurance for a particular disease or its treatment.

Covera-HS SEE: *verapamil.*

covered lives The number of people (and their dependents) enrolled in a particular health insurance program.

coverslip, cover slip (kŏv'ĕr-slip") Cover glass used in microscopic examination.

COVTT *Certified Optometic Vision Therapy Technician.*

Cowden disease, Cowden syndrome (kowd'ĕn) [*Cowden,* family name of first patient described] Multiple hamartoma.

co-witness (kō'wit'nĕs) One who corroborates, amplifies, or sometimes confuses the history provided by the patient.

Cowling rule (kowl'ĭng) A method for calculation of pediatric drug dosages in which the age of the child at the next birthday is divided by 24. However, the most safe and accurate methods of pediatric dosage calculation include the weight and body surface area or both of the patient. SEE: *Clark rule.*

cowpea mosaic virus SEE: under *virus.*

Cowper gland (kow'pĕr, koo') [William Cowper, Brit. anatomist, 1666–1709] Either of two small, round, yellow glands, one on each side of the prostate gland, each with a duct about 1 in (2.5 cm) long, terminating in the wall of the urethra. They secrete a viscid fluid forming part of the seminal fluid and correspond to the Bartholin glands in the female. SYN: *bulbourethral **gland**.* SEE: *prostate; urethra.*

cowperitis (kow"pĕr-ī'tĭs) [*Cowper* + Gr. *itis,* inflammation] Inflammation of Cowper glands.

cowpox (kow'poks) Vaccinia.

COX *Cyclooxygenase.*

coxa (kok'sǎ, kok'sē", kok'sī") *pl.* **coxae** [L. *coxa,* hip, hip bone] **1.** Hip. **2.** Hip joint.

    c. plana Legg-Calvé-Perthes disease.

    c. saltans Snapping hip.

    c. valga A deformity produced when the angle of the head of the femur with the shaft is greater than 120°. SEE: *valgus.*

    c. vara A deformity produced when the angle made by the head of the femur with the shaft is less than 120°. In coxa vara the angle may be 80° to 90°. Coxa vara may occur in rickets, bone injury, or congenitally. SEE: *varus.*

coxalgia (kŏk-săl'jē-ă) [L. *coxa,* hip, + Gr. *algos,* pain] Pain in the hip.

coxarthrosis (kŏks"ărth-rō'sĭs) [" + Gr.

arthron, joint, + *osis*, condition] Arthrosis of the hip joint.

coxib (kŏk'sĭb) Any nonsteroidal anti-inflammatory drug (NSAID) used to treat pain and inflammation by inhibiting cyclooxygenase-2 (COX-2) but not cyclooxygenase-1 (COX-1). Most NSAIDs (e.g., celecoxib) inhibit both COX-2 and COX-1. Selective inhibition prevents the coxibs from forming prostaglandins, which irritate the upper gastrointestinal tract.

Coxiella (kŏk"sē-ĕl'lă) [Herold Rae Cox, U.S. bacteriologist, 1907 – 1986] A genus of bacteria of the order Legionellales.

    C. burnetii Causative organism of Q fever.

coxiellosis Infection with *Coxiella burnetti*, a disease more commonly known as Q fever.

coxitis (kŏk-sī'tĭs) [L. *coxa*, hip, + Gr. *itis*, inflammation] Inflammation of the hip joint.

coxodynia (kŏk"sō-dĭn'ē-ă) [" + Gr. *odyne*, pain] Pain in the hip joint.

coxotuberculosis (kŏk"sō-tū-bĕr"kū-lō'sĭs) [" + *tuberculum*, a little swelling, + *osis*, diseased condition] Tuberculosis of the hip joint.

coxsackievirus, coxsackie virus (kok-sak'ē-vī"rŭs) [*Coxsackie*, a town in NY state] Any of a group of viruses that are causative agents of human disease. There are 23 group A and 6 group B coxsackieviruses. Most coxsackievirus infections are mild, but the viruses produce a variety of important illnesses, including aseptic meningitis, herpangina, epidemic pleurodynia, epidemic hemorrhagic conjunctivitis, acute upper respiratory infection, and myocarditis. SEE: *picornavirus*.

Cozaar SEE: *losartan*.

cozymase (kō-zī'mās) ABBR: NAD. Nicotinamide-adenine dinucleotide.

CP *candle power; cerebral palsy; chemically pure.*

Cp50 A symbol for the measure of intravenous anesthetic potency, specifically the concentration of the agent in the blood that will prevent movement after a skin incision in half the patients to whom the agent is given.

CPA *Canadian Physiotherapy Association.*

CPAN *certified post-anesthesia nurse.*

CPAP *continuous positive air* **pressure**.

C. Ped. *Certified Pedorthist.*

CPFT *Certified Pulmonary Function Technician.*

CPK *creatine phosphokinase.*

c.p.m. *counts per minute.*

CPOE *computerized physician order entry; computerized provider order entry.*

CPOU *Chest pain observation unit.*

CPPD *calcium pyrophosphate dihydrate.*

CPPV *continuous positive pressure ventilation.*

CPR *Cardiopulmonary* **resuscitation**; *customary, prevailing, and reasonable.*

C.P.S. *cycles per second.*

CPT *chest physical therapy.*

Campylobacter pylori The former name of the bacterium now called *Helicobacter pylori*.

CR *central ray; chloroquine-resistance; chloroquine-resistant; computed radiography; crown-rump.*

Cr Symbol for the element chromium.

crabs A slang term for *pediculosis pubis*.

crack Street name for a form of cocaine prepared from an aqueous solution of cocaine hydrochloride to which ammonia (with or without baking soda) has been added. This causes the alkaloidal form of cocaine to be precipitated. Because crack is not destroyed by heating, it may be smoked. The neuropsychiatric effects of crack are very brief compared with those of ingested or injected cocaine, but more intense. Adverse physiological effects of the drug include changes in behavior, compulsive use (addiction), cardiac dysrhythmias, coronary ischemia, stroke, and damage to the fetus during pregnancy, among others. SEE: *cocaine hydrochloride poisoning, acute.*

crack baby SEE: under *baby*.

crackle An adventitious lung sound heard on auscultation of the chest, produced by air passing over retained airway secretions or the sudden opening of collapsed airways. It may be heard on inspiration or expiration. A crackle is a discontinuous adventitious lung sound as opposed to a wheeze, which is continuous. Crackles are described as fine or coarse. SYN: *rale*. SEE: *sounds, adventitious lung.*

    coarse c. Louder, rather long, low-pitched lung sounds. Coarse inspiratory and expiratory crackles indicate excessive airway secretion.

    fine c. Soft, very short, high-pitched lung sounds. Fine, late-inspiratory crackles are often heard in pulmonary fibrosis and acute pulmonary edema.

    late-inspiratory c. A discontinuous adventitious lung sound that is present in the latter half of inhalation.

    PATIENT CARE: The presence of late-inspiratory crackles is indicative of restrictive lung disorders such as atelectasis or pulmonary fibrosis.

cradle [AS. *cradel*] A lightweight frame placed over part of the bed and patient to provide protection of and prevent pressure on an injured or burned part or to contain either heat or cold.

cramp (kramp) **1.** A pain, usually sudden and intermittent, of almost any area of the body, esp. abdominal and pelvic viscera. SEE: *dysmenorrhea.* **2.** A painful, involuntary skeletal muscle contraction. SEE: *systremma.*

    TREATMENT: Therapy depends on the cause and location of the cramp. In muscular cramps, the muscle is extended and compressed, and heat and massage are applied.

artisan's c. A cramp of one of the intrinsic muscles of the hand, esp. after overuse. SEE: *focal dystonia*.

heat c. Skeletal muscle spasm caused by the excess fluid and/or electrolyte loss that occurs with profuse sweating. The usual muscles affected are those used during work, i.e., the hand, arm, or leg muscles. The cramps may come on during work or up to 18 hr after completing a work shift.

TREATMENT: The patient should be rehydrated by drinking cool water or an electrolyte-containing drink, such as diluted juice or a commercially marketed sports drink. The severity of the cramp can be decreased through passive stretching and/or massage of the muscle. Severe heat cramps may require the use of an intravenous electrolyte solution, such as normal saline or Ringer's solution.

PREVENTION: Heat cramps may be prevented by maintaining proper hydration by drinking water or commercial electrolyte drinks before and during exposure to hot, humid environments. Normal dietary amounts of electrolytes and salt should be encouraged during meals.

menstrual c. An abdominal cramp associated with menstruation. SEE: *dysmenorrhea*.

muscle c. A painful, involuntary muscle contraction. It may be due to ischemia of the muscle(s), dehydration, or electrolyte imbalance.

Cramps associated with exercise may be alleviated, if not abolished, by flexing (stretching) the involved muscle group. At the same time, gentle massage to the area will help. Quinine, methocarbamol, chloroquine, and other drugs may help to relieve recurring or unrelenting muscle cramps.

Active muscle cramps, an unwanted tonic contraction that accompanies a voluntary muscle contraction, occur when the muscle is already in its most shortened position.

occupational c. A form of focal dystonia in which agonist and antagonist muscles contract at the same time. This can occur in writers, pianists, typists, and almost any occupation; they are not considered to have an emotional basis.

TREATMENT: Rest from the specific task and administration of anticholinergics and benzodiazepine may provide temporary relief. SEE: *focal dystonia*.

pianist's c. Spasm, or occupational neurosis, of muscles of fingers and forearms from piano playing. SEE: *focal dystonia*.

shoemaker's cramp A spasm of the

muscles of the hand and arm, esp. after repetitive use.

writer's c. A cramp after prolonged writing affecting muscles of the thumb and two adjacent fingers. SEE: *focal dystonia*.

cranberry (krăn′bĕr-ē) A tart red fruit, *Vaccinium macrocarpon*, commonly used in the treatment and prevention of urinary tract infections (UTIs). Evidence supporting cranberry as treatment of UTIs is limited. Whether drinking cranberry juice is as effective in preventing UTIs as chronic antibiotic use is unknown. Its mechanism of action is to decrease adherence of some bacteria to the urothelium.

cranial (krā′nē-ăl) [L. *cranialis*] Pert. to the cranium.

cranial vault Neurocranium

craniectomy (krā-nē-ĕk′tŏ-mē) [Gr. *kranion*, skull, + *ektome*, excision] Opening of the skull and removal of a portion of it.

cranio-, crani- [L. fr. Gr. *kranion*, skull] Prefixes meaning *skull*.

craniocaudal (krā″nē-ō-kawd′ăl) [″ + L. *cauda*, tail] Direction from head to foot.

craniocele (krā′nē-ō-sēl) [″ + *kele*, tumor, swelling] Protrusion of the brain from the skull. SEE: *encephalocele*.

craniocerebral (krā″nē-ō-sĕr-ē′brăl) [″ + L. *cerebrum*, brain] Relating to the skull and brain.

craniocleidodysostosis (krā″nē-ō-klī″dō-dĭs-ŏs-tō′sĭs) [″ + *kleis*, clavicle, + *dys*, bad, + *osteon*, bone, + *osis*, condition] A congenital condition that involves defective ossification of the bones of the head and face and of the clavicles.

craniodidymus (krā″nē-ō-dĭd′ĭ-mŭs) [″ + *didymos*, twin] A congenitally deformed fetus with two heads.

craniofacial (krā″nē-ō-fā′shăl) Concerning the head and face.

craniofrontonasal syndrome (krā″nē-ō-frŭn″tō-nā′zĭl) [″ + ″ + ″] An X-linked disorder characterized by malformation of the cranial suture of the skull. Girls born with this disorder are more severely affected than boys, i.e., they are more likely to have dysmorphic facial and cranial features.

craniology (krā″nē-ŏl′ō-jē) [″ + *logos*, word, reason] The study of the skull.

craniomalacia (krā-nē-ō-mă-lā′shē-ă) [″ + *malakia*, softening] Softening of the skull bones.

craniometer (krā-nē-ŏm′ĕ-tĕr) [″ + *metron*, measure] Instrument for making cranial measurements.

craniometry (krā-nē-ŏm′ĕ-trē) [″ + *metron*, measure] Study of the skull and measurement of its bones. SEE: illus.

craniopagus (krā-nē-ō-ŏp′ă-gŭs) [″ + *pagos*, a fixed or solid thing] Twins joined at the skulls.

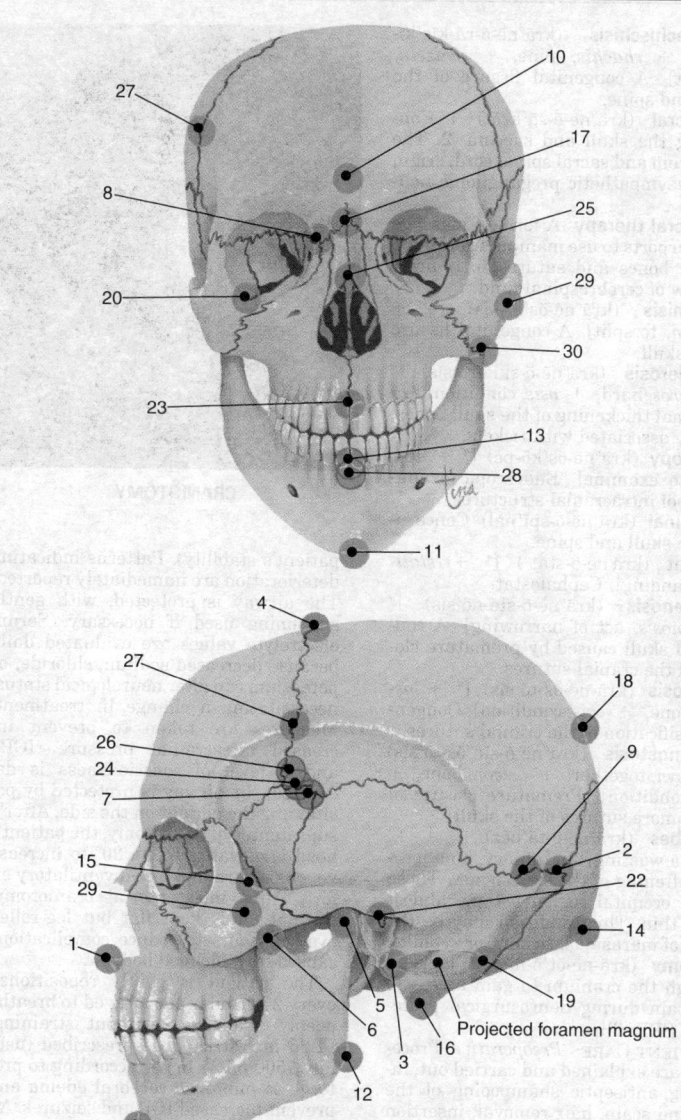

CRANIOMETRIC POINTS

These are the fixed points of the skull used in craniometry: 1) acanthion; 2) asterion; 3) basion; 4) bregma; 5) condylion; 6) coronion or koronion; 7) crotaphion; 8) dacryon; 9) entomion; 10) glabella or metopion; 11) gnathion; 12) gonion; 13) infradentale; 14) inion; 15) jugale; 6) koronion; 16) mastoidale; 10) metopion; 17) nasion; 18) obelion; 19) opisthion; 20) orbitale; 21) pogonion; 22) porion; 23) prosthion; 24) pterion; 25) rhinion; 26) sphenion; 27) stephanion; 28) symphysion; 29) zygion; 30) zygomaxillary point.

craniopharyngioma (krā″nē-ō-făr-ĭn-jē-ō′mă) [″ + ″ + *oma*, tumor] A tumor of a portion of the pituitary gland that often causes hormone deficiencies.
cranioplasty (krā′nē-ō-plăs-tē) [″ +

plassein, to form] Surgical correction of defects of the skull.
craniopuncture (krā′nē-ō-pŭnk″chūr) [″ + L. *punctura*, puncture] Puncture of the skull.

craniorhachischisis (krā″nē-ō-ră-kĭs′kĭ-sĭs) [″ + *rhachis,* spine, + *schizein,* to split] A congenital fissure of the skull and spine.

craniosacral (krā″nē-ō-sā′krăl) **1.** Concerning the skull and sacrum. **2.** The brainstem and sacral spinal cord, origin of parasympathetic preganglionic neurons.

craniosacral therapy A form of massage that purports to use manipulation of the cranial bones and sutures to redirect the flow of cerebrospinal fluid.

cranioschisis (krā″nē-ŏs′kĭ-sĭs) [″ + *schizein,* to split] A congenital fissure of the skull.

craniosclerosis (krā″nē-ō-sklē-rō′sĭs) [″ + *skleros,* hard, + *osis,* condition] An abnormal thickening of the skull bones; usually associated with rickets.

cranioscopy (krā″nē-ŏs′kō-pē) [″ + *skopein,* to examine] Endoscopic examination of intracranial structures.

craniospinal (krā′nē-ō-spī′năl) Concerning the skull and spine.

craniostat (krā′nē-ō-stăt″) [″ + *statikos,* standing] Cephalostat.

craniostenosis (krā″nē-ō-stē-nō′sĭs) [″ + *stenosis,* act of narrowing] A contracted skull caused by premature closure of the cranial sutures.

craniostosis (krā-nē-ŏs-tō′sĭs) [″ + *osteon,* bone, + *osis,* condition] Congenital ossification of the cranial sutures.

craniosynostosis (krā″nē-ō-sĭn″ŏs-tō′sĭs) [″ + *syn,* together, + *osteon,* bone, + *osis,* condition] Premature closure of one or more sutures of the skull.

craniotabes (krā″nē-ō-tā′bēz) [″ + L. *tabes,* a wasting] In infancy, an abnormal softening of the skull bones. Those in the occipital region become almost paper thin. This condition may be the result of marasmus, rickets, or syphilis.

craniotomy (krā-nē-ŏt′ō-mē) **1.** Incision through the cranium to gain access to the brain during neurosurgical procedures. SEE: illus.

PATIENT CARE: *Preoperative:* Procedures are explained and carried out, including antiseptic shampooing of the hair and scalp, hair removal, insertion of peripheral arterial and venous lines and indwelling urinary catheter, and application of pneumatic compression dressings. The patient is prepared for postoperative recovery in the neurological intensive care unit: the presence of a large bulky head dressing, possibly with drains; use of corticosteroids, antibiotics, and analgesics; use of monitoring equipment; postoperative positioning and exercise regimens; and other specific care measures.

Postoperative: Neurological status is assessed according to protocol (every 15 to 30 min for the first 12 hr, then every hour for the next 12 hr, then every 4 hr or more frequently, depending on the

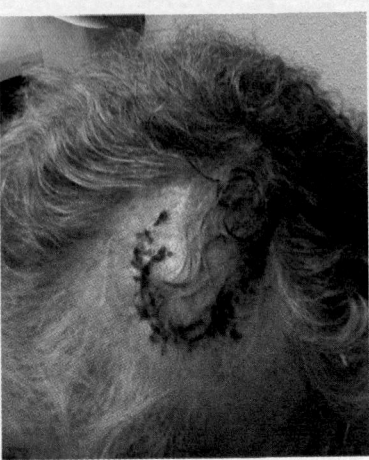

CRANIOTOMY

patient's stability). Patterns indicating deterioration are immediately reported. The airway is protected, with gentle suctioning used if necessary. Serum electrolyte values are evaluated daily because decreased sodium, chloride, or potassium can alter neurological status, necessitating a change in treatment. Measures are taken to prevent increased intracranial pressure (ICP), and if level of consciousness is decreased, the airway is protected by positioning the patient on the side. After a supratentorial craniotomy, the patient's head is elevated 15° to 30° to increase venous return and to aid ventilatory effort. After infratentorial craniotomy, the patient is kept flat but log-rolled every 2 hours to reduce complications caused by prolonged bedrest.

The patient is gently repositioned every 2 hr and is encouraged to breathe deeply and cough without straining. Fluid is restricted as prescribed (usually 1500 ml/24 hr) or according to protocol, to minimize cerebral edema and prevent increased ICP and seizures. An NPO ("nothing by mouth") protocol is maintained for 24 to 48 hr to prevent aspiration and vomiting, which can increase ICP. Wound care is provided as appropriate; dressings are assessed for increased tightness (indicative of swelling); and closed drainage systems are checked for patency and for volume and characteristics of any drainage. Excessive bloody drainage, possibly indicating cerebral hemorrhage, and any clear or yellow drainage, indicating a cerebrospinal fluid leak, is reported to the surgeon. Patients who have had a transsphenoidal procedure are restricted from nose-blowing and nasal drainage is checked for the presence of cerebrospinal fluid. The patient is observed for signs of wound infection.

Prescribed stool softeners are also administered to prevent increased ICP from straining during defecation. Before discharge, the patient and family are taught to perform wound care; to assess the incision regularly for redness, warmth, or tenderness; and to report such findings to the neurosurgeon. If self-conscious about appearance, the patient can wear a wig, hat, or scarf until the hair grows back and can apply a lanolin-based lotion to the scalp (but not to the incision line) to keep it supple and to decrease itching as the hair grows. Prescribed medications, such as anticonvulsants, may be continued after discharge.

2. After the death of a fetus, the breaking up of the fetal skull to facilitate delivery in difficult parturition.

craniotonoscopy (krā″nē-ō-tō-nŏs′kō-pē) [″ + *tonos,* tone, + *skopein,* to examine] Auscultatory percussion of the cranium.

craniotrypesis (krā″nē-ō-trĭ-pē′sis) [″ + Gr. *trypesis,* a boring] The introduction of trephine or burr holes into the cranial bones.

cranium (krā′nē-ŭm) *pl.* **crania** [L.] The portion of the skull that encloses the brain, consisting of single frontal, occipital, sphenoid, and ethmoid bones and the paired temporal and parietal bones. SEE: *skeleton.*

crank (krănk) A slang term for methamphetamine hydrochloride.

crapulous (krăp′ū-lŭs) [L. *crapulosus,* hungover] Relating to the effects of excessive drinking and eating; relating to intoxication.

crash cart (krash) A mobile medicine chest for storing and transporting the equipment, medications, and supplies needed to manage life-threatening emergencies (e.g., anaphylaxis, cardiac arrest or dysrhythmias, pulmonary edema, shock, or major trauma).

crash injury research and engineering network ABBR: CIREN. A multidisciplinary group composed of clinicians, educators, engineers, and public health officials that works to understand and prevent traumatic injuries caused by automotive collisions.

Crataegus laevigata (kră-tē′gŭs lē″vĭ-gā′tă) [L. (partly fr. Gk.), smooth thorn] Hawthorn.

crater (krā′tĕr) A circular depression with an elevated area at the periphery.

crateriform (krā-tĕr′ĭ-form) [Gr. *krater,* bowl, + L. *forma,* shape] In bacteriology, relating to colonies that are saucer-shaped, crater-like, or goblet-shaped.

craving (krāv) [AS *crafian*] An uncontrollable desire to be exposed to something, especially to an addictive agent.

Crawford Small Parts Dexterity Test A performance test that uses the manipulation of small tools under standardized conditions to measure fine motor skills and eye-hand coordination.

crawling A slow and inefficient mode of movement, such as is seen in early childhood, in which the hands and knees are on the floor, and much of the effort of forward movement is generated by the flexion and extension of the shoulders and hips.

crazing (krāz′ĭng) Minute fissures on the surface of natural or artificial teeth.

CRC *colorectal* **cancer**.

C-reactive protein SEE: under *protein.*

cream The fat portion of milk. When untreated milk is allowed to stand undisturbed, the cream rises to the top of the container. Approx. 90% of the calories in cream come from fat.

crease (krēs) A line produced by a fold.

    gluteofemoral c. The crease that bounds the inferior border of the buttocks.

    inframammary c. The attachment of the inferior edge of the breast to the chest wall; the location of the film during craniocaudal filming of the breast.

    simian c. A crease on the palm of the hand, so called because of its similarity to the transverse flexion crease found in some monkeys. Normally the palm of the hand at birth contains several flexion creases, two of which are separate and approx. transverse. When these two appear to fuse and form a single transverse crease, a simian crease is present. The crease may be present in a variety of developmental abnormalities, including Down syndrome, rubella syndrome, Turner syndrome, Klinefelter syndrome, pseudohypoparathyroidism, and gonadal dysgenesis. SEE: illus.

creatinase (krē′ă-tĭn-ās) [Gr. *kreas,* flesh, + *-ase,* enzyme] An enzyme that decomposes creatinine.

creatine (krē′ă-tĭn) [Gr. *kreas,* flesh] $C_4H_9O_2N_3$; a colorless, crystalline substance that can be isolated from various animal organs and body fluids. It combines readily with phosphate to form phosphocreatine (creatine phosphate), which serves as a source of high-energy phosphate released in the anaerobic phase of muscle contraction. Creatine may be present in a greater quantity in the urine of women than in that of men. Creatine excretion is increased in pregnancy and decreased in hypothyroidism.

creatine kinase ABBR: CK. An enzyme that catalyzes the reversible transfer of high-energy phosphate between creatine and phosphocreatine and between adenosine diphosphate (ADP) and adenosine triphosphate (ATP). Different isoforms predominate in different tissues (skeletal muscle [CK-MM], cardiac mus-

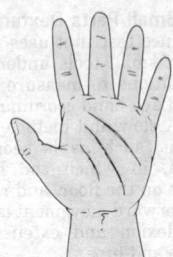

SIMIAN CREASE
Normal palmar crease

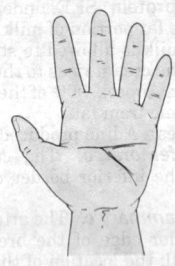

Simian crease

cle [CK-MB], and the brain [CK-BB]), aiding in differential diagnosis of conditions in which this enzyme is present in the bloodstream.

The serum level of CK-MB may be increased 10 to 25 times the normal level in the first 10 to 14 hr after myocardial infarction and return to normal within 2 to 4 days, provided that no further heart muscle necrosis occurs. Serum levels of CK-MB are also increased in progressive muscular dystrophy, in myocarditis, and following trauma to skeletal muscle. Serum CK-MB levels are not elevated in liver disease or pulmonary infarction.

creatinemia (krē″ă-tĭn-ē′mē-ă) [″ + *haima*, blood] An excess of creatine in circulating blood.

creatinine (krē-ăt′ĭn-ĭn) [*creatine* + *-ine*] $C_4H_7ON_3$; the decomposition product of the metabolism of phosphocreatine. It is a normal, alkaline constituent of urine and blood and is a source of energy for muscle contraction. Increased quantities of creatinine are found in advanced stages of renal disease. The average normal serum creatinine value is less than 1.2 mg/dL. In general, serum creatinine levels rise as kidney function worsens. SEE: *blood urea nitrogen*.

creatinine clearance test ABBR: CrCl test. A laboratory test for estimating glomerular filtration rate of the kidney. Creatinine clearance can be estimated by use of the following formula for

males: (140 − age)(body weight in kg)/72 × serum creatinine (mg/dL) For females, the formula is multiplied by 0.85. The normal creatinine clearance is about 125 ml/min. Lower levels reflect renal insufficiency and may influence the excretion of many drugs and toxins from the body.

creatinuria (krē-ă″tĭn-ū′rē-ă) [″ + *ouron,* urine] Excess concentration of creatinine in urine.

creatorrhea (krē″ă-tō-rē′ă) [″ + *rhoia,* flow] The presence of undigested muscle fibers in the feces, seen in some cases of pancreatic disease.

Credé, Carl (krē-dā′) Carl Siegmund Franz Credé, Ger. gynecologist and obstetrician, 1819–1892.
    C. maneuver SEE: *Credé method* (3).
    C. method 1. Expulsion of the placenta by downward pressure on the uterus through the abdominal wall with the thumb on the posterior surface of the fundus uteri and the flat of the hand on the anterior surface, with the pressure being applied in the direction of the birth canal. This may cause inversion of the uterus if done improperly. **2.** For treatment of the eyes of the newborn, the use of 1% silver nitrate solution instilled into the eyes immediately after birth for the prevention of ophthalmia neonatorum (gonorrheal ophthalmia). **3.** For emptying a flaccid bladder, application of pressure over the symphysis pubis for periodic expulsion of urine. This technique is sometimes used therapeutically to initiate voiding in bladder retention in those with paralysis following spinal cord injury (neurogenic bladder). SYN: *Credé maneuver.*

credential (kri-den′shăl) [L. *credentia,* trust, credit + *-al-*] **1.** Recognition by licensure, certification, or award of a degree in a field in which a person has met certain educational, professional, or occupational requirements. **2.** Evidence or testimonial, usually written, of such licensure, certification, or award of a degree. **3.** To issue or grant such licensure, certification, or award of a degree. **credentialed,** *adj.* **credentialing,** *n.*

creep (krēp) [AS.] The time-dependent plastic deformation of a material under a static load or constant stress. In dentistry, creep may be destructive to dental amalgam restoration. In osteopathic medicine, creep is used to alter the responsiveness of tissues to the application of repetitively applied tissue loads or tension.

creeping Moving slowly, and close to the surface. In pediatrics, dragging oneself along the floor, a form of locomotion that precedes crawling.

cremains (krī-mānz′) [contraction of *cremated remains*] That which remains after the body has been prepared for burial by cremation.

cremaster (krē-măs′tĕr) [L., to suspend] One of the fascia-like muscles inside the middle layer of the spermatic cord. **cremasteric** (-ĭk), *adj.*

cremate (krē′māt″, kri-māt′) [L. *cremare,* to burn to ashes] To reduce a dead body to ash by burning. **cremation** (kri-mā′shŏn), *n.*

crematorium (krē″mă-tō′rē-ŭm) [L.] A place for the burning of corpses.

crenate (krē′nāt) [L. *crenatus*] Notched or scalloped, as a crenated condition of blood corpuscles.

crenation (krē-nā′shŭn) The conversion of normally round red corpuscles into shrunken, knobbed, starry forms, as when blood is mixed with salt solution of 5% strength. SEE: *plasmolysis.*

crenocyte (krē′nō-sīt) Crenated red blood cell.

creosote (krē′ō-sōt) [Gr. *kreas,* flesh, + *sozein,* to preserve] A mixture of phenols obtained from the destructive distillation of coal or wood. This toxic substance has been used as a disinfectant and as a preserver of wood. Because creosote is a potent carcinogen, contact with it should be avoided by wearing protective garments, gloves, and masks.

crepitant (krĕp′ĭ-tănt) [L. *crepitare*] Crackling; having or making a crackling sound.

crepitation (krĕp-ĭ-tā′shŭn) **1.** A crackling sound heard in certain diseases, e.g., the crackle heard in pneumonia. **2.** A grating sound heard on movement of ends of a broken bone. **3.** A clicking or crackling sound often heard in movements of joints, such as the temporomandibular, elbow, or patellofemoral joints, due to roughness and irregularities in the articulating surfaces. SEE: *temporomandibular joint syndrome.*

crepitus (krep′ĭt-ŭs) [L. *crepitus,* creaking] A crackling or rattling sound made by a part of the body, either spontaneously or during physical examination.

    scapulothoracic c. Snapping scapula syndrome.

crepuscular (krē-pŭs′kū-lăr) [L. *crepusculum,* twilight] Pert. to twilight; used to describe a twilight mental state.

crescent (kres′ĕnt) [L. *crescere,* to grow] Shaped like a sickle or a waxing or waning moon. **crescentic** (krē-sen′tĭk), *adj.*

    c. body

    myopic c. A grayish patch around the optic disk in the fundus of the eye caused by atrophy of the choroid.

    c. of Giannuzzi SEE: under *Giannuzzi, Giuseppe.*

cresol (krē′sŏl) Yellow-brown liquid obtained from coal tar and containing not more than 5% of phenol, used as a disinfectant in a 1% to 5% solution for articles or areas that do not come in direct contact with food.

crest [L. *crista,* crest] A ridge or an elongated prominence, esp. one on a bone.

    alveolar c. The most coronal portion of the bone surrounding the tooth; the continuous upper ridge of bone of the alveolar process, which is usually the first bone lost as a result of periodontal disease.

    iliac c. The anatomical landmark for the superior margin of the pelvis, located between the anterosuperior and posterosuperior iliac spines.

    intertrochanteric c. On the posterior femoral shaft, the ridge of bone extending from the greater to the lesser trochanter. SYN: *intertrochanteric line.*

CREST syndrome The presence of calcinosis, *R*aynaud's phenomenon, *e*sophageal dysfunction, *s*clerodactyly, and *t*elangiectasia, a variant of progressive systemic sclerosis.

cretin (krē′tĭn) [Fr.] A person afflicted with congenital hypothyroidism. SEE: *cretinism.* **cretinous** (-ŭs), *adj.*

cretinism (krēt′ĭn-izm) [*cretin* + *-ism*] A congenital condition caused by a lack of thyroid hormones, characterized by arrested physical and mental development, myxedema, dystrophy of the bones and soft tissues, and lowered basal metabolism. The treatment consists of administration of synthetic thyroid hormones. SEE: *hypothyroidism; myxedema.*

cretinoid (krē′tĭ-noyd) [″ + Gr. *eidos,* form, shape] Having the symptoms of cretinism, or resembling a cretin, owing to a congenital condition.

Creutzfeldt-Jakob disease (kroyts′fĕlt-yah″kōp) [Hans Gerhard Creutzfeldt, 1885–1964; Alfons Maria Jakob, 1884–1931, Ger. psychiatrists] ABBR: CJD. A central nervous system disease that causes rapidly progressive dementia usually accompanied by muscle jerking, difficulty walking, and aphasia. The causative agent is thought to be a prion, related to the causative agent of bovine spongiform encephalopathy. It can be transmitted from person-to-person by organ transplantation, transfusion, or the donation of other products. It is uniformly fatal in less than a year.

⚠ The causative agent of CJD is extremely resistant to most sterilization procedures. SEE: *Standard Precautions Appendix.*

crevice (krĕv′ĭs) [Fr. *crever,* to break] A small fissure or crack.

    gingival c. The fissure produced by the marginal gingiva with the tooth surface. SYN: *gingival pocket; periodontal pocket; sulcus.*

crevicular (krĕv-ĭk′ū-lăr) Pert. to the gingival crevice or sulcus. SYN: *sulcus; gingival pocket; periodontal pocket.*

CRF *corticotropin-releasing factor.*

CRH *corticotropin-releasing hormone.*

CRIB *Clinical risk index for babies.*

crib (krĭb) [AS. *cribbe,* manger] **1.** A framework around a denture or a natural tooth to serve as a brace or supporting structure. **2.** A small bed with long legs and high sides for an infant or young child.

cribrate (krib'rāt', 'răt) [L. *cribratus,* passed through a sieve, sifted] Cribriform.

cribriform, cribiform (krib'rĭ-form″) [L. *cribrum,* a sieve + *-forma*] Perforated with small holes like a sieve. SYN: *cribrate.*

crick (krĭk) A muscle spasm or cramp, esp. in the neck.

cricoarytenoid (krī″kō-ă-rĭt'ĕn-oyd) [Gr. *krikos,* ring, + *arytaina,* pitcher, + *eidos,* form, shape] Extending between the cricoid and arytenoid cartilages.

cricoid (krī'koyd″) [Gr. *krikos,* a ring + *-oid*] **1.** Shaped like a signet ring. **2.** The cricoid cartilage.

cricoidectomy (krī″koyd-ĕk'tō-mē) [″ + ″ + *ektome,* excision] Excision of the cricoid cartilage.

cricoidynia (krī-koy-dĭn'ē-ă) [″ + ″ + *odyne,* pain] Pain in the cricoid cartilage.

cricopharyngeal (krī″kō-făr-ĭn'jē-ăl) [″ + *pharynx,* throat] Pert. to the cricoid cartilage and pharynx.

cricothyroid (krī-kō-thī'royd) [″ + *thyreos,* shield, + *eidos,* form, shape] Pert. to the thyroid and cricoid cartilages.

cricothyroidotomy (krī″kō″thī″royd″ot'ŏ-mē) [*cricoid* (2) + *thyroidotomy*] Cricothyrotomy.

cricothyrotomy (krī″kō″thī″rot'ŏ-mē) [*cricoid* (2) + *thyrotomy*] An emergency surgical airway procedure involving an incision between the cricoid and thyroid cartilages in the midline of the anterior neck. SYN: *coniotomy; cricothyroidotomy.*

cricotomy (krī-kŏt'ō-mē) [″ + *tome,* incision] Division of the cricoid cartilage.

cricotracheotomy (krī″kō-trā″kē-ŏt'ŏ-mē) [″ + *tracheia,* windpipe, + *tome,* incision] Division of the cricoid cartilage and upper trachea in closure of the glottis.

cri du chat syndrome (krī dĕ shah) A sporadically inherited congenital anomaly in which affected infants have mental retardation, microcephaly, dwarfism, and a laryngeal defect that results in unusual vocalizations.. An affected infant is said to cry like a cat (*cri du chat* in French). It results from a deletion of the short arm of chromosome 5.

Crigler-Najjar syndrome (krĭg'lĕr-nah'jahr) [John Fielding Crigler, U.S. physician, b. 1919; Victor A. Najjar, U.S. physician, b. 1914] One of two familial forms of congenital hyperbilirubinemia associated with brain damage as a result of bilirubin deposition in the brain (kernicterus). The syndrome is caused by an enzyme deficiency in the liver that causes faulty bilirubin conjugation. It is transmitted as an autosomal recessive trait; death may occur within 15 months after birth in the more severe form.

crimp (krĭmp) [AS. *gecrympan, to curl*] To bind or mold with applied pressure; to crease.

-crine, -crin [Gr. *krinein,* to separate] Suffixes meaning *secrete.*

crisis (krī'sis) *pl.* **crises** [Gr. *krisis,* turning point] **1.** The turning point of a disease. **2.** The sudden descent of a high temperature to normal or below. **3.** A sudden painful experience. **4.** An unstable period in a person's life characterized by the inability to adapt. SEE: *crisis intervention.*

   abdominal c. Severe pain in the abdomen caused by biliary or renal colic, testicular or ovarian torsion, ruptured ectopic pregnancy, sickle cell anemia, bowel obstruction and/or perforation, aortic dissection, hemorrhage, and trauma, among other illnesses.

   addisonian c. Acute adrenocortical insufficiency.

   adrenal c. Acute adrenocortical **insufficiency.**

   blast c. In chronic myelogenous leukemia, a rapid expansion in the clone of leukemic cells, which overrun the blood or bone marrow.

   celiac c. The rapid onset of dehydration and metabolic disarray in fulminant celiac disease. Patients are treated with intravenous hydration, electrolytes, and parenteral nutrition.

   Dietl c. SEE: *Dietl crisis.*

   hypertensive c. Any severe elevation in blood pressure (usually a diastolic pressure greater than 130 mm Hg) with or without damage to internal organs or other structures, e.g., brain, heart, aorta, kidneys. In hypertensive *emergencies,* end organs are damaged, and antihypertensive drugs usually are given intravenously to try to lower the blood pressure within an hour. Agents used in hypertensive emergencies include sodium nitroprusside, nitroglycerin, labetalol, and enalaprilat.

   In hypertensive *urgencies,* the blood pressure is extremely elevated, but there is no sign or immediate threat of organ damage. Typically, oral beta blockers, ACE inhibitors, or clonidine, alone or in combination, are given to lower pressures over 1 or 2 days.

   oculogyric c. A spasm of involuntary deviation and fixation of the eyeballs, usually upward, often occurring as an adverse reaction to the use of phenothiazine medications. It may last for only several minutes or for hours. This condition is a dystonic reaction. SEE: *dystonia*.

   rectal c. Tenesmus and rectal pain in locomotor ataxia.

   salt-losing c. Acute vomiting, dehydration, hypotension, and sudden death as a result of acute loss of sodium; may be caused by adrenal hyperplasia, salt-losing nephritis, or gastrointestinal disease.

   scleroderma renal c. The abrupt onset of kidney failure and severe hypertension in patients with progressive systemic sclerosis. It is treated by controlling blood pressure with angiotensin converting enzyme inhibitors, sometimes in association with other agents.

   sickle cell c. Vaso-occlusive c. (in sickle cell disease).

   tabetic c. Abdominal pain due to tabes dorsalis in patients with syphilis.

   thyroid c. Thyroid **storm**.

   thyrotoxic c. Thyroid **storm**.

   transient aplastic c. ABBR: TAC. A serious complication of infection with human parvovirus B-19 infection in patients with chronic hemolytic anemia such as sickle cell disease. This virus causes erythema infectiosum. SEE: *erythema infectiosum*.

   true c. Temperature drop accompanied by a fall in the pulse rate.

   vaso-occlusive c. (in sickle cell disease) Painful occlusions of blood vessels in bones, the chest, the lungs, or the abdomen in patients with sickle cell anemia. The syndrome is caused by sickling of blood cells in small blood vessels, with resulting infarction and tissue death. SYN: *sickle cell c.*

crisis intervention A problem-solving activity for correcting or preventing the continuation of an emergency, esp. one caused by psychological distress or drug overdose.

crista (krĭs'tă) *pl.* cristae [L.] **1.** A crest or ridge. **2.** A fold of the inner membrane of a mitochondrion into its fluid-filled cavity.

   c. ampullaris A localized thickening of the membrane lining the ampullae of the semicircular canals; it is covered with neuroepithelium containing hair cells that are stimulated by movement of the head.

   c. galli A ridge on the ethmoid bone to which the falx cerebri is attached.

-crit [Gr. *kritos*, fr. *krinein*, to separate] Suffix meaning *separate*.

criterion (krī-tēr'ē-ŏn, 'ē-ă) *pl.* **criteria** [L. *criterium* fr Gr. *kritērion*, a means for judging] A standard or attribute for judging a condition or establishing a diagnosis.

   eligibility c. Entry c.

   entry c. Any of a patient's characteristics that make him or her a candidate for enrollment in a clinical trial of a new treatment or therapeutic device. SYN: *eligibility c.; inclusion c.*

   inclusion c. Entry c.

critical (krĭt'ĭ-kăl) [Gr. *kritikos*, critical] **1.** Pert. to a crisis in which a dramatic change for the better or worse is probable. **2.** Pert. to a potentially fatal disease. **3.** Sufficient in quantity or quality to initiate or maintain a reaction, esp. a nuclear reaction. **4.** Pert. to the phase of the life cycle during which cells are responsive to certain regulators. **5.** Pert. to the first trimester of pregnancy when organ systems are being formed and the fetus is most vulnerable to environmental factors that may cause deformities.

critical care unit SEE: *intensive care unit*.

critical incident stress debriefing, critical incident stress defusing ABBR: CISD. A group session conducted by mental health professionals and emergency medical service peers for rescuers after a tragic incident, such as the death of a partner, serious injuries to children, a mass casualty incident, or other disaster. A CISD is not a critique but rather an open discussion about rescuers' thoughts about an incident, combined with some teaching about the effects of stress that can be expected over the next few days to weeks.

critical laboratory value, critical value A test result obtained from a clinical specimen that is so far outside the normal range that it is likely to indicate an acute risk to the health of the patient. SYN: *critical result*.

critical thinking SEE: under *thinking*.

CRKP *carapenem-resistant Klebsiella pneumoniae*.

CRM *Certified Reference Material*.

CRNA *certified registered nurse anesthetist*.

Crohn disease (krōn) [Burrill B. Crohn, U.S. gastroenterologist, 1884–1983] An inflammatory bowel disease marked by patchy areas of full-thickness inflammation anywhere in the gastrointestinal tract, from the mouth to the anus. It frequently involves the terminal ileum of the small intestine or the proximal large intestine and may be responsible for abdominal pain, diarrhea, malabsorption, formation of fistulas between the intestines and other organs, and bloody stools. Like ulcerative colitis, it is most common in the second and third decades of life. SEE: *regional enteritis; regional ileitis*. SEE: *inflammatory bowel disease; Nursing Diagnoses Appendix*.

   TREATMENT: Medical therapies include anti-inflammatory drugs (such as corticosteroids, aminosalicylates (such as mesalamine), and antibodies to tumor necrosis factor. Nutritional support of the patient may be needed during flares of the disease. Surgical removal of diseased bowel segments is often followed by relapse and may result in malnutrition.

Crosby capsule (krŏz′bē) [William Holmes Crosby, Jr., U.S. physician, 1914–2005] A device attached to a flexible tube that is introduced into the gastrointestinal tract per os. It is designed so that a sample of tissue may be obtained from the mucosal surface with which it is in contact. The capsule is then removed and the tissue examined for evidence of pathological changes.

cross [L. *crux*] **1.** Any structure or figure in the shape of a cross. **2.** In genetics, the mating or the offspring of the mating of two individuals of different strains, varieties, or species.

crossbirth Presentation of the fetus in which the long axis of the fetus is at right angles to that of the mother and requires version or cesarean delivery. Also called *transverse lie*.

crossbreeding Mating of individuals of different breeds or strains.

cross-bridge In the sarcomere of a muscle cell, the portion of the myosin filaments that pulls the actin filaments toward the center of a sarcomere during contraction.

cross-cultural Concerning the physiological and social differences and similarities of two or more cultures.

cross-dress To dress in clothing worn by members of the opposite sex.

crossed Passing from one side to the other, as the crossed corticospinal tract, in which nerve fibers cross from one side of the medulla to the other.

crossed finger technique SEE: under *technique*.

cross education SEE: under *education*.

cross-examination (kros′ĕg-zam″ĭ-nā′shŏn) The interrogation of a witness by the opposing party in a legal dispute. **cross-examine** (-zam′ĭn), *v.*

cross-eye Manifest inward deviation of the visual axis of one eye toward that of the other eye when looking at an object. SYN: *adtorsion; esotropia*. SEE: *squint; strabismus*. **cross-eyed,** *adj.*

cross-fertilization Fusion of male and female gametes from different individuals.

crosshatching (kros′hach″ing) In the surgical repair of lacerations, a cosmetic defect in which lines across the wound ("train tracks") are left on the skin after sutures are removed.

crossing over In genetics, the mutual interchange of blocks of genes between two homologous chromosomes. It occurs during synapsis in meiosis. In this process, there is no gain or loss of genetic material, but a recombination does occur.

crossmatching **1.** The process of mixing a sample of the donor's red blood cells with the recipient's serum (major crossmatching) and mixing a sample of the recipient's blood with the donor's serum (minor crossmatching). It is done before transfusion to determine compatibility of blood. **2.** The determination of the compatibility of a donated organ's human leukocyte antigens with the recipient's antigens.

crossover (kros′ō″vĕr) **1.** In genetics, pert. to an instance or a result of crossing over. **2.** Such an instance or a result. **3.** Crossover **trial**.

crossover trial SEE: under *trial*.

cross reaction A reaction between an antibody and an antigen that is similar to the specific antigen for which the antibody was created. It enables immunoglobulins to cross-link and activate B cells.

cross-sex (kros′seks″) Pert. to or involving a member of the opposite sex.

cross-tolerance The development of tolerance to all the medications within a particular class of agents rather than simply to one agent.

cross-training **1.** A cost-containment measure whereby instruction and experience are provided to enable health care workers to perform procedures and provide services previously limited to other members of the health team. **2.** In physical fitness training, the use of one or more sports to train for another. For example, training in both cycling and running strengthens all of the leg muscle groups and makes them less vulnerable to injury.

crotaline (krŏt′ăl-īn″, ′ăl-ĭn) [*Crotalus*] Pert. to poisonous snakes of the genus *Crotalus*. SEE: *pit* **viper**.

Crotalus (krŏt′ăl-ŭs) [L. *crotalum*, fr Gr. *krotalon*, rattle, castanet] A genus of venomous snakes of the family Crotalidae that includes most rattlesnakes.

crotonism (krō′tŏn-ĭzm) Poisoning from croton oil.

croton oil (krōt′ŏn) [Gr. *kroton*, a tick, castor oil plant seed (which is tickshaped)] SEE: under *oil*.

crouch (krowch) [ME. *crouchen*] To bend the knees and bring the upper body down and forward.

croup (kroop) An acute viral disease of early childhood, usually occurring from age 6 months to 5 years (and more in males than in females), marked by a resonant barking cough (described as sounding "seal-like"), stridor, and varying degrees of respiratory distress. Inflammation and spasm of the larynx, trachea, and bronchi account for most of the symptoms; thus croup is also known as *laryngotracheobronchitis*.

ETIOLOGY: Although bacterial infections of the larynx can result in "false croup," the condition is caused almost exclusively by viruses, esp. parainfluenza, respiratory syncytial, and influenza viruses.

DIAGNOSIS: Diagnosis is based on

characteristic clinical findings and x-ray examination of the neck, which may show subglottic narrowing of air within the trachea.

TREATMENT: Supportive measures include rest and supervised hydration. Positioning in an infant seat or in Fowler's position is helpful. Although cool mist is often provided via inhalation, its effectiveness is unproven. Oral corticosteroids are routinely prescribed and have proved beneficial in mild as well as moderate to severe cases (less sleep loss, better clinical outcomes in early days). Hospitalization may be necessary for more severe cases; nebulized racemic epinephrine and oxygen therapy may be needed. Intubation is rarely required unless the patient shows evidence of respiratory fatigue or hypoxia. Antibiotics are seldom needed because the viruses involved do not predispose to secondary bacterial infections. The vast majority of children, even those hospitalized, recover without complications.

PATIENT CARE: A quiet, calm environment is maintained; all procedures are explained to the family, and support and reassurance are provided to the child and family to reduce fear and anxiety. Ventilation and heart rate are monitored, as are cough, hoarseness, breath sounds, and ventilatory rate and character. The affected child is observed carefully for retractions, inspiratory stridor, cyanosis, labored breathing, and restlessness. Antipyretics and sponge baths are provided for fever; infants and young children with temperatures above 102°F (38.9°C) are observed for seizures. If the child becomes dehydrated, oral or intravenous rehydration is administered. Sore throat is relieved with water-based ices such as fruit sherbets, and thicker fluids are avoided if the child is producing thick mucus or has difficulty swallowing. Hand hygiene is scrupulously practiced when caring for the child to avoid transmitting respiratory syncytial virus (RSV) or parainfluenza infections to other children. Parents must also wash hands frequently and thoroughly. SEE: *Nursing Diagnoses Appendix.*

diphtheritic c. Laryngeal diphtheria.

membranous c. Inflammation of the larynx with exudation forming a false membrane. SYN: *croupous laryngitis.* SEE: *Nursing Diagnoses Appendix.*

SYMPTOMS: Symptoms include those of laryngitis: loss of voice; noisy, difficult, and stridulous breathing; weak, rapid pulse; livid skin; and moderate fever.

ETIOLOGY: Several viruses may cause this disease. These include parainfluenza, respiratory syncytial virus, and various influenza viruses.

TREATMENT: Antibiotics are indicated only if there is secondary bacterial infection; corticosteroids are of no benefit. If hypoxia is present, inhalation of a 40% concentration of well-humidified oxygen is indicated. This is best accomplished by a face mask.

spasmodic c. A form of croup that typically occurs in the middle of the night. The characteristic barky cough is present, but there are no other signs of viral illness. The child is perfectly fine the next morning, only to have a repeat of symptoms the next 2 or 3 nights. Hospitalization is rarely required. An allergic etiology is suspected. Antihistamines are sometimes helpful.

croupous (kroo'pŭs) Pert. to croup or having a fibrinous exudation.

Crouzon disease (kroo-zon') [Octave Crouzon, Fr. neurologist, 1874–1938] An autosomal dominantly inherited congenital disease characterized by hypertelorism (widely spaced eyes), craniofacial dysostosis, exophthalmos, optic atrophy, and divergent squint. The disease is one of the craniosynostoses.

crowd out (krowd owt) To displace or replace one population or community with elements from a competing one.

Crow-Fukase syndrome (krō″fū-kă′sē) POEMS syndrome.

crowing (krō′ĭng) A noisy, harsh sound on inspiration.

crown (krown) [L. *corona,* wreath] The top or highest part of an organ, tooth, or other structure, as the top of the head; the corona.

anatomical c. The part of the tooth covered with enamel.

clinical c. The portion of the natural tooth that is exposed in the mouth, from the gingiva to the occlusal plane or the incisal edge.

dental c. Dental restoration made of porcelain, porcelain fused to metal, stainless steel, gold alloy, and other base metal alloys. The crown usually covers the tooth from the occlusal surface to the gingival margin.

crowning (krown′ĭng) Visible presentation of the widest aspect of the fetal head at the vaginal introitus.

crown lengthening A dental procedure, often performed by a periodontist, in which the gingiva and/or bone surrounding a tooth are removed to expose enough of the base of the tooth to support a filling or a crown.

crown-rump (krown′rŭmp′) ABBR: CR. The axis for measurement of a fetus, from the tip of the head to the tip of the sacrum. SEE: illus.

crown work SEE: under *work.*

CRP *C-reactive protein.*

CRT *cathode ray tube.*

CRTT *certified respiratory therapy technician.*

crucial (kroo′shăl) [L. *crucialis*]

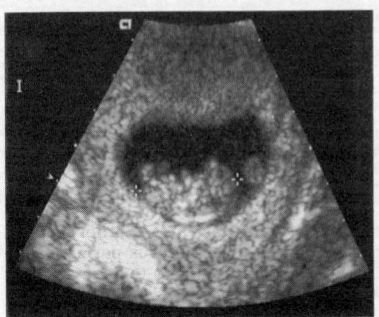

CROWN-RUMP

Ultrasonographic image of a fetus aged 9 weeks and 3 days. The crown-rump length is highlighted.

1. Cross-shaped. **2.** Decisive; of supreme importance; critical.

cruciate (kroo′shē-āt) Cross-shaped, as in the cruciate ligaments of the knee.

crucible (kroo′sĭ-b'l) [L. *crucibulum*] A dish or container for substances that are being melted, burned, or dehydrated while exposed to high temperatures.

cruciform (kroo′sĭ-form) [L. *crux*, cross, + *forma*, shape] Shaped like a cross.

crude (krood) [L. *crudus*, raw] Raw, unrefined, or in a natural state.

cruise (krooz) **1.** To walk sideways or diagonally while holding onto people or objects. It is a form of locomotion used by infants and toddlers as they begin to assume an upright posture while exploring their environment. **2.** A colloquial term for surfing the Internet. **3.** To travel for pleasure aboard a ship. Health problems associated with cruising include athletic injuries, excessive use of alcohol, failure to take prescribed medications, and epidemic diarrhea.

crura (kroo′rä) *sing.*, **crus** [L., legs] A pair of elongated masses or diverging bands resembling legs.

   c. cerebri A pair of bands joining the cerebrum to the medulla and pons.

   c. of diaphragm Two pillars connecting the spinal column and diaphragm.

crural (kroo′răl) [L. *cruralis*] Pert. to the leg or thigh; femoral.

   c. palsy Paralysis of the nerves of the legs (e.g., 12th thoracic, first to fifth lumbar, and first to third sacral spinal nerves).

crus (krŭs) *pl.* **crura** [L.] **1.** Leg. **2.** Any structure resembling the leg.

   c. cerebri Either of the two peduncles connecting the cerebrum with the pons.

crusher A surgical instrument used to flatten tissues.

crush syndrome (krŭsh) The tissue damage and systemic effects of prolonged traumatic muscle compression. Crushing injuries may cause compartment syndromes, muscle necrosis, and

leakage of muscle cell contents into the systemic circulation, especially after blood flow is restored to damaged tissues. Kidney failure may occur when myoglobin released from injured muscles blocks renal tubules. Electrolyte and acid base disturbances are common. Treatment may include local surgical care, metabolic support, hydration, and alkalinization of the urine. SEE: *renal failure, acute; reperfusion; rhabdomyolysis.*

crust, crusta (krŭst) [L. *crusta*] **1.** Dried serum, pus, or blood on the skin surface. Crusts are seen in diseases in which the skin weeps, such as eczema, impetigo, and seborrhea. They are often yellow-brown, dirty cream- or honey-colored. **2.** An outer covering or coat.

crusted scabies Widespread scabies involving large areas of the skin, usually found in people with immune-suppressing illnesses, malnutrition, or unhygienic living situations. Crusted scabies is very contagious. Scaling skin from affected persons readily distributes mites to individuals in contact with the patient.

crutch (krŭtch) [AS. *crycc*] **1.** An assistive device prescribed to provide support during ambulation and transfers for individuals with paralysis, weakness, or injury. It also may be used to provide support for balance loss or to minimize or eliminate weight bearing on lower extremities. A variety of crutches are available. The most common is the axillary crutch, which generally is constructed of wood or aluminum. This type of crutch consists of a curved surface that fits directly under the axilla, and double uprights connected by a hand grip that converge into a single contact point at the distal end. A rubber suction tip generally is fitted to this distal end for safety. The axillary crutch should be adjusted to suit the user's height. Other variations include the forearm crutch or Lofstrand crutch. This aluminum crutch consists of a single metal tube, a hand grip, and a metal cuff that surrounds the proximal forearm. Platform adaptations for forearm crutches, which allow individuals to bear weight through the forearm, are available.

   PATIENT CARE: Depending on activity restrictions, the patient is taught an appropriate gait pattern for crutch walking, including negotiating stairs and moving safely through doorways. The patient should "walk on his or her hands," not lean on the crutches during ambulation or when transferring from a standing to sitting position. Prolonged or excessive pressure in the axilla can lead to axillary nerve damage. The patient's safety and dexterity while on crutches are evaluated, and use of a walker may be recommended if safety is a concern.

2. In psychology, any mechanism used by a person to maintain balance or avoid stress.

Crutchfield tongs (krŭtch″fēld′) [William Gayle Crutchfield, U.S. surgeon, 1900–1972] A traction device whose pins are inserted into the skull to distract and/or immobilize the neck. Crutchfield tongs are used to stabilize fractures of the cervical spine.

Cruveilhier-Baumgarten murmur A murmur heard on the abdominal wall over the collateral veins connecting the caval and portal veins.

Cruveilhier-Baumgarten syndrome (kroo-vāl-yā′bŏm′găr-tĕn) [Jean Cruveilhier, Fr. pathologist, 1791–1874; Paul Clemens von Baumgarten, Ger. pathologist, 1848–1928] Cirrhosis of the liver caused by patency of the umbilical or paraumbilical veins and the resultant collateral circulation. It is associated with prominent periumbilical veins, portal hypertension, liver atrophy, and splenomegaly.

cry (krī) The production of inarticulate sounds, with or without weeping, which may be sudden, loud, or quiet, as in a sob.

cryanesthesia (krī-ăn-ĕs-thē′zē-ă) [″ + an-, not, + aisthesis, sensation] Loss of sense of cold.

cryesthesia (krī-ĕs-thē′zē-ă) [″ + aisthesis, sensation] Sensitivity to the cold.

cry for help Any attempt to reach out to others in times of distress.

cryo (krī′ō″) In informal clinical speech, a short form for cryoprecipitate.

cryo-, cry- [Gr. kryos, cold] Prefixes meaning cold. SEE: psychro-.

cryoablation (krī″ō-a-blā′shŏn) [cryo- + ablation] Destruction of tissue, e.g., of a small cancer or an abnormal electrical pathway, by freezing it to very cold temperatures.

cryoanalgesia (krī″ō-an″ăl-jē′zhă, z(h)ē-ă) [cryo- + analgesia] The relief of pain by applying a cold object to a painful part of the body or by destroying painful nerves with very cold probes.

cryoanesthesia (krī′ō-an″ĕs-thē′zē-ă, zhă) [cryo- + anesthesia] The topical cooling of body parts (e.g., with ice or liquid nitrogen) to reduce pain or permit surgery.

cryobank (krī′ō-bănk) A facility that stores and preserves refrigerated or frozen biological specimens.

cryobiology (krī″ō-bī-ŏl′ō-jē) [″ + bios, life, + logos, word, reason] The study of the effect of cold on biological systems.

cryocautery (krī″ō-kot′ĕ-rē) [cryo- + cautery] A device for application of cold sufficient to kill tissue or stop bleeding.

cryocompression (krī″ō-kŏm-prĕsh′ŭn) The squeezing of a body part in a cold device, wrap, or sleeve to prevent or reduce swelling of an extremity.

cryocrit (krī′ō-krĭt) [″ + krinein, to separate] The proportion of cold-precipitable protein in a serum sample, usually represented as a percentage. The cryocrit is used as a measure of immune complex formed in response to various agents, such as viruses.

cryoextraction (krī″ō-ĕks-trăk′shŭn) The use of a cooling probe introduced into the lens of the eye to produce an ice ball limited to the lens. The ice ball, which includes the lens, is then removed. This can be used to treat ophthalmic conditions, such as hemangiomas or cataracts.

cryofibrinogen (krī″ō-fī-brĭn′ō-jĕn) An abnormal fibrinogen that precipitates when cooled and dissolves when reheated to body temperature.

cryofibrinogenemia (krī″ō-fī-brĭn″ō-gĕnē′mē-ă) [Gr. kryos, cold, + L. fibra, fiber, + Gr. gennan, to produce, + Gr. haima, blood] The coagulation of blood in small vessels, caused by cryofibrinogens in the plasma. This rare symptomatic illness can cause ulceration, gangrene, necrosis, or purpura, esp. when the skin is exposed to cold. Cryofibrinogenemia usually develops secondarily, e.g., in patients with metastatic cancer, lymphoma, or collagen-vascular disease.

cryogen (krī′ō-jĕn) [″ + gennan, to produce] A substance that produces low temperatures.

cryogenic (krī″ō-jĕn′ĭk) Producing or pert. to low temperatures. SEE: illus.

cryoglobulin (krī″ō-glŏb′ū-lĭn) [″ + L. globulus, globule] An abnormal globulin that precipitates when cooled and dissolves when reheated to body temperature. Cryoglobulins are usually composed of IgM, or less commonly IgE or IgA molecules. They may form in response to some viral infections, esp. to chronic infection by hepatitis C virus.

cryoglobulinemia (krī″ō-glŏb″ū-lĭn-ē′mē-ă) [″ + ″ + Gr. haima, blood] The presence in the blood of an abnormal protein that forms gels at low temperatures. It is found in association with pathological conditions such as hepatitis C viral infection, multiple myeloma, leukemia, and certain forms of pneumonia.

cryohypophysectomy (krī″ō-hī″pō-fĭz-ĕk′tō-mē) [Gr. kryos, cold, + hypo, under, + physis, growth, + ektome, excision] Destruction of the hypophysis by the use of cold.

cryokinetics (krī″ō-kĭ-nĕt′ĭks) [″ + kinesis, motion] The therapeutic use of cold (such as ice packs or ice immersion) before active exercise. The application of cold increases the amount of motion that is available to a joint by decreasing

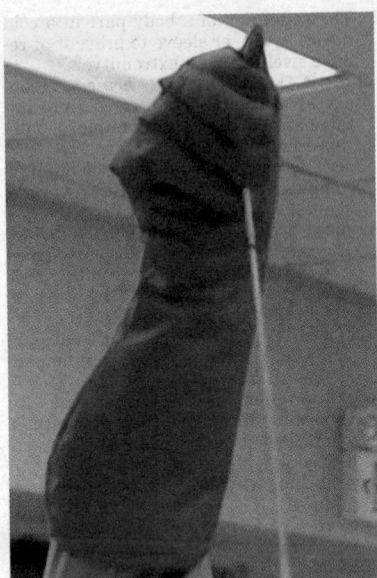

CRYOGENIC APPLICATIONS EQUIPMENT

Insulated glove for use while handling very cold materials used in cryogenic applications

pain. Active exercise increases range of motion, improves tissue tensile strength, and enhances healing. SEE: *cryotherapy*.

TREATMENT: Cold therapy is administered to the patient until skin numbness is reported. Non–weight-bearing or weight-bearing exercises are then implemented without causing pain.

⚠ This technique should not be used in patients for whom cold application cryotherapy or active exercise is contraindicated.

---

cryolesion (krī'ō-lē"zhŭn) **1.** The cooling of an area in order to injure or destroy it. SYN: *cryotherapy*. **2.** A lesion produced by exposure to cold (e.g., frostbite).

cryoneurolysis (krī"ō-noo-rol'ĭ-sĭs) [*cryo- + neurolysis*] The destruction of a nerve by applying a very cold probe to it, e.g., one whose temperature is −321°F (the temperature of liquid nitrogen). It is one of the methods of neurolysis to treat intolerable nerve pain.

cryophilic (krī"ō-fĭl'ĭk) [" + *philein*, to love] Showing preference for cold, as in psychrophilic bacteria. SYN: *psychrophilic*.

cryo-poor plasma Cryosupernatant.

cryoprecipitate (krī"ō-prē-sĭp'ĭ-tāt) **1.** The precipitate formed when serum

from patients with rheumatoid arthritis, glomerulonephritis, systemic lupus erythematosus, hepatitis C infection, and other chronic diseases in which immune complexes are found. It is stored at 4°C. **2.** A derivative of plasma that contains fibrinogen, clotting factor VIII, and fibronectin. It is used for bleeding disorders.

cryopreservation (krī'ō-prĕ"sĕr-vā'shŭn) The preservation at very low temperatures of biological materials such as blood or plasma, embryos or sperm, or other tissues. After thawing, the preserved material can be used for its original biological purpose.

cryoprobe (krī'ō-prōb) A device for applying cold to a tissue. Liquid nitrogen is the coolant frequently used. SEE: *cryoextraction*.

cryoprotectant (krī'ō-prō-tĕk"tănt) A drug that permits cells to survive freezing and thawing. **cryoprotective** (-tĕk'tĭv), *adj*.

cryoprotein (krī'ō-prō'tē-ĭn) Any protein that precipitates when cooled below body temperature. SEE: *cryofibrinogen; cryoglobulin*.

cryostat (krī'ō-stăt) A device for maintaining very low temperatures.

cryostretch (krī'ō-strĕch) [" + AS. *streccan*, extend] A technique used to reduce muscle spasm by combining cold applications to produce numbness with proprioceptive neuromuscular facilitation. The body part is numbed using an ice pack or vapocoolant spray and then muscle elongated using proprioceptive neuromuscular facilitation techniques. The ice application and exercise are repeated, to stretch and fatigue the involved muscle group.

cryosupernatant (krī"ō-soop"ĕr-nāt'ănt) The portion of fresh frozen plasma that remains after the removal of cryoprecipitate. It contains very low levels of factor VIII, fibrinogen, and von Willebrand's factor. SYN: *cryo-poor plasma*.

cryosurgery (krī"ō-sĕr'jĕ-rē) [*cryo- + surgery*] The use of extremely cold probes to destroy lesions, including cancerous or infected tissues. Cryosurgery is a minimally invasive procedure that has been used to treat metastatic liver cancer, prostate cancer, sun-induced skin cancers, warts, cutaneous leishmaniasis, and even abnormal conduction pathways in the heart or nervous system. Liquid nitrogen is often the agent used.

cryothalamotomy (krī"ō-thăl"ă-mŏt'ō-mē) [" + L. *thalamus*, inner chamber, + Gr. *tome*, incision] The destruction of a portion of the brain with a hypothermic probe. This procedure is used, rarely, to treat parkinsonism and other movement disorders.

cryotherapy (krī"ō-ther'ă-pē) [*cryo- + therapy*] **1.** The application of cold to a

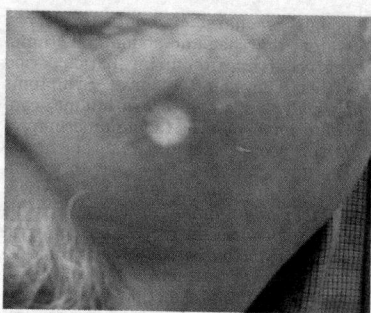

CRYOTHERAPY

Frosting of the skin at the site of actinic keratosis after treatment with liquid nitrogen

body part to decrease tissue temperature, and thereby to decrease cellular metabolism, improve cellular survival, decrease inflammation, decrease pain and muscle spasm, and promote vasoconstriction. SEE: illus.; table. **2.** Cryosurgery.

cryotolerant (krī″ō-tŏl′ĕr-ănt) [″ + L. *tolerare,* to bear] Able to tolerate very low temperatures.

cryotome (krī′ŏ-tōm″) [*cryo-* + *-tome*] A cold cutting tool for making very thin sections of tissues after they have been removed from the body and frozen for rapid microscopic analysis.

crypt (kript) [Gr. *kryptē,* hidden place] **1.** A small sac or cavity extending into an epithelial surface. **2.** A tubular gland, esp. one of the intestine.

   dental c. A space in the bony jaw occupied by a developing tooth.

   c. of iris An irregular excavation on the anterior surface of the iris near the pupillary and ciliary margins.

   synovial c. Diverticulum of a synovial membrane of a joint.

   tonsillar c. A deep indentation, lined with stratified squamous epithelium, into the lymphatic tissue of a lingual or palatine tonsil.

crypt- [Gr., *kryptos,* hidden] Prefix meaning *hidden.*

cryptdin (krĭp′dĭn) A cation released from intestinal crypts, as a defense against infection with enteric bacteria. It is part of the innate immune response. Cryptdins destroy bacteria by punching holes in their cell membranes.

cryptectomy (krĭp-tĕk′tō-mē) [″ + *ektome,* excision] Excision of a crypt.

cryptesthesia (krĭp-tĕs-thē′zē-ă) [″ + *aisthesis,* sensation] Subconscious awareness of facts or occurrences other than through the senses or rational thinking, such as through intuition or alleged clairvoyance.

cryptic (krĭp′tĭk) [Gr. *kryptikos,* hidden] **1.** Having a hidden meaning; occult. **2.** Tending to hide or disguise.

cryptitis (krip-tīt′ĭs) [*crypt* + *-itis*] Inflammation of a crypt.

cryptococcoma (krĭp″tō-kŏ-kō′mă) [*crypto-* + *cocc(us)* + *-oma*] A mass, typically in the brain, consisting of cryptococcal fungi.

cryptococcosis (krĭp″tō-kŏk-ō′sĭs) [″ + *kokkos,* berry, + *osis,* condition] Infection with the opportunistic fungus *Cryptococcus neoformans,* a spore-forming yeast present worldwide in the soil and in bird droppings. Humans contract the disease by inhalation. It may occur in healthy persons but is most common in immunosuppressed patients such as those with AIDS, leukemia, or organ transplants. Infection typically involves the brain and meninges but may affect the lungs, skin, liver, or bone. Immunecompetent persons respond to short-term treatment with amphotericin B and fluconazole, but many months of suppressive therapy with these drugs are needed in patients with AIDS. SYN: *torulosis.* SEE: *AIDS; amphotericin B.*

Cryptococcus (krĭp″tō-kok′ŭs) [*crypto-* + *coccus*] A genus of pathogenic yeast-like fungi.

Contraindications to the Topical Application of Cold to Musculoskeletal Injuries

Indications	Contraindications
Acute injury or inflammation	Anesthetic skin
Acute or chronic pain	Cold allergy/cold-induced urticaria
Acute or chronic muscle spasm	Cold-induced myocardial ischemia (or other unstable heart or lung disease)
Neuralgia	Diabetes mellitus (when complicated by vascular disease or sensory loss)
Postsurgical pain and edema	Peripheral vascular disease
Use prior to rehabilitation exercises	Raynaud's phenomenon
Small, superficial, first-degree burns	Systemic lupus erythematosus
Spasticity accompanying central nervous system disorders	Uncovered open wounds

SOURCE: Adapted from Starkey, C: Therapeutic Modalities, ed 3., F. A. Davis Co., Philadelphia, 2004.

C. gattii An encapsulated yeast, similar in structure to *C. neoformans*. It can cause meningoencephalitis and pneumonia in immunocompetent individuals who live in temperate or subtropical climates.

C. neoformans A species that is the causative agent of cryptococcosis. It is the only encapsulated yeast that causes human infection.

cryptococcus (krĭp″tŏ-kok′ŭs, -kok′sī″, -kok′sē″, -kok′ī″, -kok′ē″) *pl.* **cryptococci** [*crypto-* + *coccus*] Any fungus of the genus *Cryptococcus*. **cryptococcal** (-kok′ăl), *adj.*

cryptodidymus (krĭp-tō-dĭd′ĭ-mŭs) [″ + *didymos*, twin] A congenital anomaly in which one fetus is concealed within another.

cryptogenic (krĭp″tō-jĕn′ĭk) [″ + *gennan*, to produce] Of unknown or indeterminate origin.

cryptography (krĭp-tog′ră-fē) [*crypt-* + *-graphy*] The science and techniques of concealing or disguising information through encoding and decoding. In the health professions cryptography is used to ensure the confidentiality of medical records.

cryptolith (krĭp′tō-lĭth) [″ + *lithos*, stone] A stone within a crypt.

cryptomenorrhea (krĭp″tō-mĕn″ō-rē′ă) [″ + *men*, month, + *rhoia*, flow] Monthly subjective symptoms of menses without flow of blood; may be caused by an imperforate hymen.

cryptomerorachischisis (krĭp″tō-mē″rō-ră-kĭs′kĭ-sĭs) [″ + *meros*, part, + *rhachis*, spine, + *schisis*, a splitting] Spina bifida occulta without a tumor but with bony deficiency.

cryptophthalmus (krĭp″tŏf-thăl′mŭs) [″ + *ophthalmos*, eye] Complete congenital adhesion of the eyelid to the globe of the eye.

cryptorchid, cryptorchis (krĭpt-or′kĭd, -or′kĭs) [″ + *orchis*, testis] An individual in whom either or both testicles have not descended into the scrotum. SEE: *monorchid.*

cryptorchidectomy (krĭpt″or-kĭ-dĕk′tō-mē) [″ + ″ + *ektome*, excision] Operation for correction of an undescended testicle.

cryptorchidism, cryptorchism (krĭpt-or′kĭd-ĭzm, -kĭzm) [″ + *orchis*, testis, + *-ismos*, condition] Positioning of one or more testes outside the scrotum, e.g., a failure of the testes to descend into the scrotum.

cryptosporidiosis (krĭp″tō-spŏr-ĭd″ē-ō′sĭs) A diarrheal disease caused by protozoa of the genus *Cryptosporidium* and often transmitted to humans after exposure to water or food that has been contaminated with cysts found in animal waste. *C. parvum* is the most common species that infects humans. The typical infection in immunocompetent

people is characterized by explosive, watery diarrhea and abdominal cramping, occurring after an incubation period of between 4 and 14 days. Symptoms typically last a week or two but may continue for a month. In immunocompromised people, including cancer chemotherapy patients, those with organ transplants, and people with AIDS, chronic or fulminant infection may be found. Profuse diarrhea and dehydration or infection of the biliary tract occurs often. Treatment for people with normal immune function includes hydration and antidiarrheal drugs. Immunocompromised patients improve most when their immune status is restored. In a small percentage of people, asymptomatic carriage of the organism results in long-term shedding of the parasite in stool.

When the organism contaminates public water supplies, hundreds of thousands of those drinking that water may develop diarrhea. A water-borne infection with *Cryptosporidium* caused an estimated 400,000 cases of diarrhea in Milwaukee in the 1990s. This outbreak was attributed to contamination of the municipal water supply by grazing livestock. Resistant to chlorine, cryptosporidial cysts are incompletely removed by standard water-filtration systems. The least expensive method of killing the organism in water is to boil the water. Some types of bottled water that come from above-ground sources may contain cryptosporidia. Water filters effective against the organism are labeled "absolute 1 micron" or "National Sanitation Foundation (NSF) certified for Standard 53 cyst removal."

⚠ Stools from affected patients are highly infectious. Standard techniques must be used in handling and disposing of them. SEE: *Standard Precautions Appendix.*

Cryptosporidium (krĭp′tō-spor-ĭd″ē-ŭm) A genus of protozoa in the kingdom Protista classed as a coccidian parasite. It is an important cause of diarrhea, esp. in immunocompromised patients, but may cause large outbreaks in the general population when it contaminates supplies of drinking water. SEE: *cryptosporidiosis.*

cryptoxanthin (krĭp″tō-zăn′thĭn) A natural carotenoid pigment found in foods, such as orange and orange rind, papaya, egg yolk, butter, and apples. It can be converted to Vitamin A in the body. SYN: *beta cryptoxanthin.*

cry reflex SEE: under *reflex.*

crystal (krĭs′tăl) [Gr. *krystallos,* ice] A solid in which atoms are arranged in a specific symmetrical pattern, forming distinct lattices, with definable fixed angles, faces, walls, and interatomic relationships. Examples include ice and many salts.

apatite c. In dentistry, the hydroxyapatite crystal typical of calcified tissues; a complex of calcium phosphate and other elements, present in bone and in the cementum, dentin, and enamel layers of teeth. The most dense crystalline pattern is found in enamel, the hardest tissue of the body.

Charcot-Leyden c. SEE: *Charcot-Leyden crystal.*

Charcot-Neumann c. A spermine crystal found in semen and some animal tissues.

Charcot-Robin c. A type of crystal formed in the blood in leukemia.

c. of hemin Hemin.

liquid c. A substance that alters its color or changes from opaque to transparent when subjected to changes in temperature, electric current, pressure, or electromagnetic waves, or when impurities are present. Liquid crystals have been used to detect temperature fluctuation in infants and may be divided into two general classes: cholestric, which change color; and nematic, which can change back and forth from transparent to opaque.

crystallin (krĭs′tăl-ĭn) Globulin of the crystalline lens.

crystalline (krĭs′tă-lĭn) Resembling crystal.

c. deposits An acid group including the urates, oxalates, carbonates, and sulfates. The alkaline group includes the phosphates and cholesterin ammonium urate.

crystalline maculopathy SEE: under *maculopathy.*

crystallization (krĭs″tă-lĭ-zā′shŭn) [Gr. *krystallos,* ice] The formation of crystals.

crystallized ability (krĭs′tă-lĭzd″) SEE: under *ability.*

crystallography (krĭs″tă-log′ră-fē) [*crystal* + *-graphy*] The study of crystals. It is useful, for example, in examining complex molecules (e.g., DNA) or the components of kidney stones.

crystalloid (krĭ′stăl-oyd″) [″ + *eidos,* form, shape] **1.** Like a crystal. **2.** A substance capable of crystallization, which in solution can be diffused through animal membranes; the opposite of colloid.

crystalloiditis (krĭs″tăl-oyd-ī′tĭs) [″ + ″ + *itis,* inflammation] Inflammation of the crystalline lens.

crystalluria (krĭs-tă-lū′rē-ă) [″ + *ouron,* urine] The appearance of crystals in the urine. It may occur following the administration of many drugs, including sulfonamides. It can be prevented by adequate hydration.

C&S *Culture and sensitivity.*

CS *Cesarean section.*

Cs Symbol for the element cesium.

C-section Cesarean section.

CSF *cerebrospinal fluid.*

CSII *continuous subcutaneous insulin infusion*

CSM *circulation, sensation, and motor function* (a mnemonic for guiding the assessment of an injured limb, e.g., before and after it is splinted or casted).

CSPOMM Certification of Special Proficiency in Osteopathic Manipulative Medicine

CSR Center for Scientific Review (of the National Institutes of Health)

CST *Certified Surgical Technologist.*

C substance A complex carbohydrate present in the cell wall of pneumococcal bacteria (Streptococcus pneumoniae). SEE: *C-reactive protein.*

C-suite (sē′swēt″) [*c(hief)* + *suite*] The chief executives or officers of a health care institution or other corporation, e.g., the Chief Executive Officer or Chief Financial Officer.

CT *computed tomography.* Also abbreviated as *CAT,* for the former term *computerized axial tomography.*

CTD *connective tissue disease.*

Ctenocephalides (ten″ō-sĕ-fal′ĭ-dēz″) [Gr. *kteis,* stem *kteno-,* comb + *cephalo-*+ *-ides*] A genus of fleas of the order Siphonaptera. Common species are *C. canis* and *C. felis,* the dog flea and cat flea, respectively. The adults feed on their hosts; the larvae live on dried blood and feces of adult fleas. Adults may attack humans and other animals. They are intermediate hosts of *Dipylidium caninum,,* one of the species of dog tapeworm, and may transmit other helminth and protozoan infections. SEE: **Dipylidium** *caninum.*

CTEPH *Chronic thromboembolic pulmonary* **hypertension**.

C-terminal In chemical nomenclature, the alpha-carboxyl group of the last amino acid of a molecule.

CTICU *cardiothoracic intensive care unit.*

CTZ *chemoreceptor trigger zone.*

Cu [L. *cuprum*] Symbol for the element copper.

cubic measure A unit or a system of units used to measure volume or capacity as distinguished from liquid measure. SEE: *Weights and Measures Appendix.*

cubital (kū′bĭ-tăl) [L. *cubitum,* elbow] Pert. to the ulna or to the elbow.

cubital tunnel syndrome Medial elbow pain, hand fatigue, and sensations in the fourth and fifth fingers resulting from ulnar nerve damage in the cubital tunnel. This condition is frequently seen in throwing athletes.

cubitus (kū′bĭ-tŭs) [L] Elbow; forearm; ulna.

c. valgus A posture of the arm in which the forearm deviates laterally. It may be congenital or caused by injury or disease. In women, slight cubitus valgus is normal and is one of the secondary sex characteristics. SEE: *valgus*.

c. varus A posture of the arm in which the forearm deviates medially. SEE: *varus*.

cuboid (kū'boyd) [Gr. *kubos*, cube, + *eidos*, form, shape] Like a cube.

Cubozoa (kū″bŏ-zō'ă) [Gr. *kybos*, a die, cube + *-zoa*] A class of venomous marine invertebrates that includes the box jellyfish and sea wasp. SEE: *box jellyfish; sea wasp*.

cue (kū) In psychology, a symbol, prompt, hint, or stimulus to remind an organism to respond in a certain way or to initiate a particular set of behaviors.

cue acquisition The initial information-gathering stage during the process of clinical reasoning. The practitioner must pay attention to both objective (physical) signs and subjective (reported) symptoms as well as contextual information gathered from observation and interviews.

cued speech SEE: under *speech*.

cuff (kŭf) [ME. *cuffe*, glove] **1.** An anatomical structure encircling a part. **2.** A belt or rim positioned at the end of a structure, designed to help fasten it in place.

   attached gingival c. Attachment or junctional epithelium attached to the calcified root of the tooth apical to the gingival sulcus.

   gingival c. The most coronal portion of the gingiva around the tooth.

   rotator c. A musculotendinous structure consisting of supraspinatus, infraspinatus, teres minor, and subscapularis tendons blending with the shoulder joint capsule. The muscles, which surround the glenohumeral joint below the superficial musculature, stabilize and control the head of the humerus in all arm motions, function with the deltoid to abduct the arm, and rotate the humerus. Weakness in the cuff muscles may lead to impingement syndromes and tendinitis; tears in the cuff may lead to subluxations; and calcification may lead to immobilization of the shoulder.

cuffed endotracheal tube An airway catheter used to provide an airway through the trachea and at the same time to prevent aspiration of foreign material into the bronchus. This is accomplished by an inflatable cuff that surrounds the tube. The cuff is inflated after the tube is placed in the trachea. SEE: *endotracheal tube* for illus.

cuffing (kŭf'ĭng) A collection of inflammatory cells in the shape of a ring around small blood vessels.

cuff pressure SEE: under *pressure*.

cuirass (kwē-răs') [Fr. *cuirasse*, breastplate] A firm bandage around the chest.

cul-de-sac (kŭl″dĕ-sak') [Fr., bottom of

the sack] **1.** A blind pouch or cavity. **2.** Douglas cul-de-sac.

culdocentesis (kŭl″dō-sen″tē'sĭs) [Douglas' *cul*-de-sac + *centesis*] A procedure for obtaining specimens from the posterior cul-de-sac by aspiration or surgical incision through the vaginal wal. The procedure, performed for therapeutic or diagnostic reasons, has been replaced by ultrasound.

culdoscope (kŭl'dō-skōp) An endoscope used in performing a culdoscopic examination.

culdoscopy (kŭl-dŏs'kō-pē) Examination of the viscera of the female pelvic cavity after introduction of an endoscope through the wall of the posterior fornix of the vagina.

-cule, -cle [Fr. *-cle*, fr. L. *-culus*, adj. suffix] Suffixes meaning *little*, as *molecule* and *corpuscle*.

Culex (kū'lĕks) [L., gnat] A genus of small to medium-sized mosquitoes of cosmopolitan distribution. Some species are vectors of disease organisms.

   C. pipiens The common house mosquito; it serves as a vector of several illnesses, including *Wuchereria bancrofti* and West Nile virus.

   C. quinquefasciatus Mosquito common in the tropics and subtropics; the most important intermediate host of *Wuchereria bancrofti*.

Culicidae (kū-lĭs'ĭ-dē) A family of insects belonging to the order Diptera; includes the mosquitoes.

Cullen sign (kŭl'ĕn) [Thomas Stephen Cullen, U.S. gynecologist, 1868–1953] Bluish discoloration of the periumbilical skin caused by intraperitoneal hemorrhage. This rare finding is sometimes found in patients with acute pancreatitis, blunt trauma to the abdomen, or ruptured ectopic pregnancy.

culling (kŭl'ĭng) **1.** The process of removal of abnormal or damaged blood cells from the circulation by the spleen. **2.** In public health, slaughtering herds of potentially infected animals, to prevent the spread of diseases like avian influenza or mad cow disease to humans. SEE: *pitting; spleen*.

cult (kŭlt) [L. *cultus*, care] A group of people with an obsessive commitment to an ideal or principle or to an individual personifying that ideal.

cultivation (kŭl″tĭ-vā'shŭn) [L. *cultivare*, to cultivate] The propagation of living organisms, esp. growing microorganisms in an artificial medium.

cultural awareness Cultural competence.

cultural competence Sensitivity to the cultural, philosophical, religious, and social preferences of people of varying ethnicities or nationalities. Professional skill in the use of such sensitivities facilitates the giving of optimal patient care.

PATIENT CARE: The population of most Western nations is diverse. It includes people from every continent, many different walks of life, and many different linguistic and ethnic origins. Caregivers whose education is based solely in Western medicine may need on a daily basis to challenge their own ethical beliefs and constructs, examining their appropriateness for the people for whom they provide care. Health care providers should be aware of and trained in the National Standards on Culturally and Linguistically Appropriate Services propagated through the Office of Minority Health of the US Department of Health & Human Services, or from those nongovernmental organizations or health care providers with whom they work, to enhance their ability to communicate appropriately with young and old, rich and poor, educated and illiterate, as well as European, Asian, African, and Latin American patients. SYN: *cultural awareness; cultural sensitivity.*

cultural formulation A systematic review of a person's cultural background and the role of culture in the manifestation of symptoms and dysfunction. It includes the cultural identity of the individual, cultural explanations of the illness, cultural factors related to the environment and individual functioning, cultural elements of the clinician-patient relationship, and a general discussion of how cultural considerations may influence the diagnosis and treatment of a psychiatric illness.

cultural sensitivity Cultural competence.

culture (kŭl′chŭr) [L. *cultura,* cultivation, care] **1.** In the biological sciences, the propagation of microorganisms or of living tissue cells in special media that are conducive to their growth. **2.** Shared human artifacts, attitudes, beliefs, customs, entertainment, ideas, language, laws, learning, and moral conduct. **cultural** (′chŭ-răl), *adj.* **culturally** (-ră-lē), *adv.*

   active surveillance c. Surveillance c.

   biphasic c. A culture in which solid and liquid growth media are combined in a single container, or in which different growth media are layered.

   blood c. A culture used to identify bacteria, fungi, or viruses in the blood. This test consists of withdrawing blood from a vein under sterile precautions, placing it in or on suitable culture media, and determining whether or not microbes grow in the media. If organisms grow, they are identified by bacteriological methods. Multiple blood cultures may be needed to isolate an organism.

   cell c. The growth of cells in vitro for experimental purposes. The cells proliferate but do not organize into tissue.

   contaminated c. A culture in which

bacteria from a foreign source have infiltrated the growth medium.

   continuous flow c. A bacterial culture in which a fresh flow of culture medium is maintained. This allows the bacteria to maintain their growth rate.

   corporate c. The institutional values of a corporation, hospital, professional association, or other entity.

   gelatin c. A culture of bacteria on a gelatin medium.

   hanging block c. A thin slice of agar seeded on its surface with bacteria and then inverted on a coverslip and sealed in the concavity of a hollow glass slide.

   hanging drop c. A culture accomplished by inoculating the bacterium into a drop of culture medium on a cover glass and mounting it upside down over the depression on a concave slide.

   negative c. A culture made from suspected matter that fails to reveal the suspected organism.

   nonradiometric c. A culture medium in which the growth of microorganisms is detected without the use of radioactive isotopes.

   positive c. A culture that reveals the suspected organism.

   pure c. A culture of a single form of microorganism uncontaminated by other organisms.

   radiometric c. A method for detecting the presence of microorganisms in a sample body fluid or tissue in which the metabolism of infecting organisms is demonstrated by their incorporation or release of specifically radiolabeled chemicals in the culture medium, e.g., carbon dioxide labeled with ^{14}C. Radiometric culture media have been used to detect bacteria, fungi, mycobacteria, and viruses in clinical specimens.

   slant c. A culture in which the medium is placed in a slanted tube to allow greater surface for growth of the inoculum of bacteria.

   slice c. A means of studying living tissues by obtaining specimens from approx.100 to 400 μm in thickness and maintaining them in vitro in a nutrient bath. The technique is used in investigations of brain or liver diseases.

   stab c. A bacterial culture made by thrusting into the culture medium an inoculating needle with the bacterial specimen.

   stock c. A permanent culture from which transfers may be made.

   streak c. The spreading of the bacteria inoculum by drawing a wire containing the inoculum across the surface of the medium.

   surveillance c. The sampling of patients on admission into a hospital or an intensive care unit for the presence of particular microorganisms (such as methicillin-resistant *Staphylococcus* *aureus.* or vancomycin-resistant enterococci). SYN: *active surveillance c.*

tissue c. A culture in which tissue cells are grown in artificial nutrient media.

type c. A culture of standard strains of bacteria that are maintained in a suitable storage area. These permit bacteriologists to compare known strains with unknown or partially identified strains.

culture and sensitivity ABBR: C&S. Identification of microorganisms in a clinical specimen (as in a sample of blood, cerebrospinal fluid, sputum, or urine) and a determination of the antibiotic, antifungal, or antiviral drugs that effectively kill them.

culture and sensitivity test Antimicrobial sensitivity test.

culture-bound syndrome A recurrent, locality-specific pattern of behavior or disease; a folk illness; an illness that affects a specific ethnic group, tribe, or society.

cumulative (kū'mū-lă-tĭv) [L. *cumulus,* a heap] Increasing in effect by successive additions.

cumulative drug action SEE: under *action.*

cumulative effect A drug effect that is apparent only after several doses have been given. It is caused by excretion or metabolic degradation of only a fraction of each dose given.

Cumulative Index to Nursing and Allied Health Literature ABBR: CINAHL. A specialized literature database covering nursing, allied health, alternative health, consumer health, and selected biomedical information resources. Print volumes date back to 1956, and an electronic database dates back to 1982. The electronic database indexes almost 3000 nursing and allied health journals.

cumulative trauma disorder Overuse syndrome.

cumulative trauma syndrome Overuse syndrome.

cumulus (kū'myŭ-lŭs) [L. *cumulus,* a little mound] A small elevation; a heap of cells.

c. oophorus A solid mass of follicular cells that surrounds the developing ovarian follicle. It projects into the antrum of the graafian follicle. After ovulation this layer of cells must be penetrated by a sperm for fertilization to occur. SYN: *discus proligerus.*

cuneate (kū'nē-āt) [L. *cuneus,* wedge] Wedge-shaped; cuneiform.

cuneiform (kū-nē'ĭ-form) [" + *forma,* shape] Wedge-shaped.

cuneo- [L. *cuneus,* wedge] Prefix meaning *wedge.*

cuneus (kū'nē-ŭs) *pl.* **cunei** [L., wedge] A wedge-shaped lobule of the brain on the mesial surface of the occipital lobe.

cuniculus (kū-nĭk'ū-lŭs) *pl.* **cuniculi** [L.,

an underground passage] A burrow in the epidermis made by scabies.

cunnilinguist (kŭn-ĭ-lĭn'gwĭst) [L. *cunnus,* pudenda, + *lingua,* tongue] One who practices cunnilingus.

cunnilingus (kŭn-ĭ-lĭn'gŭs) Sexual activity in which the mouth and tongue are used to stimulate the female genitalia. SEE: *fellatio; oral sex.*

cunnus (kŭn'ŭs) [L.] The vulva; pudenda.

CUP *cancer, unknown primary* (a metastatic malignancy whose primary source is not known). Most malignant tumors having unidentified primary sources are adenocarcinomas.

cup (kŭp) [L. *cuppa,* drinking vessel] **1.** Small drinking vessel. **2.** A cupping glass. SEE: *cupping.* **3.** An athletic supporter (jock strap) reinforced with a piece of firm material to cover the male genitalia; worn to protect the penis and testicles during vigorous and contact sports. **4.** Either of the two cup-shaped halves of a brassiere that fit over a breast. **5.** A method of producing counterirritation. SEE: *cupping.*

favus c. A cup-shaped crust that develops in certain fungal infections. SEE: *favus.*

glaucomatous c. An enlargement of the normal physiological cup due to glaucomatous nerve damage.

optic c. In the embryo, a double-layered cuplike structure connected to the diencephalon by a tubular optic stalk. It gives rise to the sensory and pigmented layers of the retina.

physiological c. A depression in the center of the optic nerve through which the blood vessels pass; normal cup to disc ratios range from 0.3 to 0.5 of the disk diameter.

wet c. In traditional medicine, a cupping glass that is placed on the skin after the skin injured. It is purported to draw toxins from the body.

cup arthroplasty of hip SEE: under *arthroplasty.*

cup feeding SEE: under *feeding.*

cupola, cupula (kū'pō-lă, -pū-lă) [L. *cupula,* little tub] **1.** The little dome at the apex of the cochlea and spiral canal of the ear. **2.** The portion of costal pleura that extends superiorly into the root of the neck. It is dome-shaped and accommodates the apex of the lung.

cupping (kŭp-ing) **1.** Application to the skin of a glass or bamboo vessel from which air has been withdrawn by heat or of a special suction apparatus in order to draw blood to the surface. Cupping purportedly disperses blocked or congested energy. **2.** Clapping (1).

cupric (kū'prik, koo') [L. *cuprum,* copper + *-ic*] Pert. to divalent copper, Cu^{++}, in solution; also referred to as Cu II or copper II.

c. sulfate The pentahydrate salt of

copper, $CuSO_4 \cdot 5H_2O$, used as an antidote in treating phosphorus poisoning.

cuprous (kū′prŭs) Concerning monovalent copper, Cu^+, in a compound; also referred to as Cu I or Cu (I).

cupruresis (kū″proo-rē′sĭs) [L. *cuprum*, copper, + Gr. *ouresis*, to void urine] Excretion of copper in the urine.

CUPS *critical, unstable, potentially unstable, and stable;* patient priority classifications used during the primary assessment of a patient.

cupulolithiasis (kū″pū-lō-lĭth-ī′ă-sis) [L. dim. of *cupa*, a tub, + Gr. *lithos*, stone, + *iasis*, state or condition of] A disease of calculi in the cupula of the posterior semicircular canal of the middle ear. The condition may be associated with positional vertigo.

curanderismo (koo-ron-dah-rēs′mō, koo-ron-dă-riz′mō) [Mexican Spanish] A traditional holistic system of healing in Mexican-American folk medicine based on a belief that magic and ritual can be used to treat a broad spectrum of illnesses. Practitioners are known as *curanderas* (females) and *curanderos* (males).

curare (kū-, koo-rär′ē) [phonetic equivalent of a South American Indian name for extracts of plants used as arrow poisons] A paralytic drug, derived from natural plant resins, that is used by indigenous South American hunters to immobilize prey. Synthetic derivatives of this agent are used medicinally to relax skeletal muscles during anesthesia and critical care.

curarization (kū″rär-ī-zā′shŭn) Paralysis induced by curare or by a drug like curare (e.g., pancuronium or vecuronium).

curative (kū′ră-tĭv) [L. *curare*, to take care of] Having the ability to heal or remedy an illness.

curative ratio Therapeutic **ratio**.

curb cut, curb ramp (kĕrb) An area in which a sidewalk has been modified or designed to eliminate the vertical curb. By providing a gradual slope to the street at this point, an environmental obstacle has been removed, thus improving access for persons with wheelchairs, those who have difficulty walking, or for persons pushing wheeled vehicles.

curbside consultation (kŭrb′sīd″) An informal discussion between two health care professionals about the likely causes of a patient's illness, the natural history of the disease, possible interventions, remedies, or treatments, etc. Unlike a formal consultation, it does not involve a detailed history, physical examination, or review of laboratory and radiographic studies.

curcumin (kŭr-kŭm′ĭn) [*Curcuma*, genus name of the ginger family + *-in*] ABBR: CMN. A yellow compound (di-feruloylmethane) found in the spice turmeric. It is an anti-inflammatory and antioxidant and has been used on the Indian subcontinent for hundreds of years to treat a variety of illnesses.

curd (kĕrd) [ME] Milk that has been curdled (usually by an acid such as vinegar or rennet). This produces a mass of casein, a dairy protein. Cottage cheese and paneer are both examples of curd.

cure [L. *cura*, care] **1.** Course of treatment to restore health. **2.** Restoration to health.

curet, curette (kū-rĕt′) [Fr. *curette*, a cleanser] **1.** A spoon-shaped scraping instrument for removing tissue matter from a cavity. **2.** In dentistry, one of a variety of sharp instruments used to remove calculus and to smooth tooth roots or to remove soft tissues from a periodontal pocket or extraction site.

    Gracey c. A curet used to remove subgingival calculus from a tooth during periodontal débridement.

curettage (kū″rĕ-tăzh′) [Fr.] **1.** Scraping of a cavity. SYN: *curettement*. **2.** The use of a curet in removal of necrotic tissue from around the tooth, dental granulomata, or cysts and tissue fragments or debris from the bony socket after tooth extraction; also called débridement.

    periapical c. Use of a curet to remove pathological tissues from around the apex of the tooth root.

    suction c. Vacuum aspiration.

    uterine c. Scraping to remove the contents of the lining of the uterus. This procedure is used to evacuate the uterus following inevitable or incomplete abortion, to produce abortion, to obtain specimens for use in diagnosis, and to remove growths, such as polyps.

    PATIENT CARE: *Preoperative:* The health care provider explains and clarifies the procedure, answers any questions, and describes expected sensations. Physical preparation of the patient is completed according to protocol, and the patient is placed in the lithotomy position. Asepsis is maintained throughout the procedure.

    Postoperative: Vital signs are monitored until they are stable, and the patient is monitored until she is able to tolerate liquids by mouth and to urinate without difficulty. A perineal pad count is performed to determine the extent of uterine bleeding, and excessive bleeding is documented and reported to the health care provider. Prescribed analgesics are administered to relieve pain and discomfort. Before discharge, the patient is instructed to report profuse bleeding immediately; to report any bleeding lasting longer than 10 days; to avoid use of tampons, diaphragms, and douches; and to report severe pain and signs of infection such as fever or foul-smelling vaginal discharge. Gradual resumption of usual activities is encouraged as long as they do not result in vaginal bleeding. The woman is counseled to avoid the use of tampons or douches and to abstain from intercourse for 2 weeks or until after the follow-up examination.

curettement (kū-rĕt'mĕnt) [Fr.] Curettage.

Curie (kūr'ē, kū-rē') **1.** Marie, the Polish-born Fr. chemist, 1867–1934, who discovered the radioactivity of thorium, discovered polonium and radium, and isolated radium from pitchblende. She was awarded the Nobel Prize in physics in 1903 with her husband, and in chemistry in 1911. **2.** Pierre, Fr. chemist, 1859–1906, who, with his wife, was awarded the Nobel Prize in 1903.

curie [Marie *Curie*] ABBR: Ci. The quantity of a radioactive substance which has 3.7×10^{10} transitions, or disintegrations, per second. One gram of radium has almost exactly 3.7×10^{10} transitions per second. Thus 1 Ci of radium has a mass of almost exactly 1 g. SEE: *becquerel*.

curium (kūr'ē-ŭm) [Pierre and Marie *Curie* + *-ium* (1)] SYMB: Cm. A synthetic chemical element of the actinide series, atomic weight (mass) of the longest-lived isotope, 247, atomic number 96. The half-life of the most stable isotope is 16 million years.

Curling ulcer (kŭr'ling) [Thomas B. Curling, Brit. physician, 1811–1888] A peptic ulcer that sometimes occurs following severe burns to the body; a form of stress ulcer.

Currarino triad (kur-ä-rē'nō) [Guido Currarino, Italian-born U.S. pediatric radiologist, b. 1920] A congenital birth defect of caudal structures, characterized by malformation of the sacrum, anus, and rectum.

current (kŭr'ĕnt) [L. *currere,* to run] A flow, as of water or the transference of electrical impulses.

   alternating c. ABBR: ac; AC. A current that periodically changes its direction. It may be either sinusoidal or nonsinusoidal in form. The alternating current wave usually used therapeutically is the sinusoidal form. Alternating current from the power grid in the U.S. operates at a frequency of 60 Hz. Most other countries use 50 Hz.

   direct c. ABBR: dc; DC. A current that flows in one direction only, used medically for cardioversion and defibrillation of dysrhythmias.

   galvanic c. Direct electric current, usually from a battery.

current density SEE: under *density*.

current good manufacturing practices ABBR: cGMP. Those specifications for the manufacture, processing, packaging, storage, and shipment of drugs as promulgated by the FDA to ensure that the therapeutic agents marketed in the U.S. are made of safe, active ingredients and are free of impurities.

curriculum (kŭ-rik'yŭ-lŭm, 'yŭ-lă) *pl.* **curriculua, curriculums** [L. *curriculum,* running, a race] **1.** A course of study. **2.** An outline or summary of available courses of study in an academic discipline, an educational institution, or a particular specialty.

Curschmann spirals (kŭrsh'măn) [Heinrich Curschmann, Ger. physician, 1846–1910] Coiled spirals of mucus occasionally seen in sputum of asthma patients. SEE: *sputum*.

curse (kĕrs) **1.** To attempt to inflict injury by appeal to a malevolent supernatural power. **2.** Injury assumed to have been inflicted by a malevolent supernatural power. **3.** To use foul, offensive language.

curvature (kĕr'vă-chŭr) [L. *curvatura,* a slope] A normal or abnormal bending or sloping away; a curve.

   angular c. A sharp bending of the vertebral column.

   cervical c. The anterior curvature of the cervical vertebrae. The cervical curvature is a secondary spinal curve that begins to develop in the fetus and continues to form throughout infancy.

   c. of spine One of four normal curves or flexures of the vertebral column as seen in profile: cervical, thoracic, lumbar, and sacral. Abnormal curvatures may occur as a result of maldevelopment or disease processes. SEE: *kyphosis; lordosis; scoliosis*.

   lumbar c. The anterior curvature of the lumbar vertebrae. The lumbar curvature is a secondary spinal curve that begins to develop in the fetus and continues to form throughout infancy.

   sacral c. The posterior curvature of the sacral vertebrae. The sacral curvature is a primary spinal curve that develops during the embryonic period.

   thoracic c. Posterior curvature of the thoracic vertebrae. The thoracic curvature is a primary spinal curve that develops during the embryonic period.

curve (kŭrv) [L. *curvus,* bent, crooked] A bend, chart, or graph.

   c. of Carus SEE: *curve of Carus*.

   characteristic c. Sensitometric **c.**

   dental c. Curve of Spee.

   D log E c. Sensitometric **c.**

   dose response c. A graph charting the effect of a specific dose of drug, chemical, or ionizing radiation.

   dye-dilution c. A graph of the disappearance rate of a known amount of injected dye from the circulation; used to measure cardiac function.

   epidemic c. A chart or graph in which the number of new cases of an illness is plotted over time.

   growth c. A graph of heights and

weights, head circumference, and body mass index of infants and children of various ages. A line connecting the data points produces the curve. Usually the changes in height and weight are shown on the same chart. Growth charts are specific for age and gender.

learning c. The effect of learning or practice on the performance of an intellectual or physical task. The term describes the acquisition of competence with experience, time, and training.

normal c. Normal **distribution**.

receiver operating c. ABBR: ROC curve. A plot of the fraction of true positives test results versus the fraction of false positive test results; the sensitivity of a test versus (1-the test specificity). SYN: *receiver operating characteristic.*

sensitometric c. In radiographic film analysis, the curve derived by graphing the exposure to the film versus the film density. Analysis yields information about the contrast, speed, latitude, and maximum and minimum densities of the film or film-screen system. Digital radiography systems exhibit linear curves. SYN: *characteristic c.; D log E c.; Hurter and Driffield curve.*

c. of Spee SEE: *curve of Spee.*

Stephan c. SEE: *Stephan curve.*

survival c. In radiobiology, a dose response curve.

time-temperature cooling c. The mathematical relation that plots the physical and chemical behaviors of dental (and other) materials as their temperature decreases over time.

curve of Carus (kar′ŭs) [Carl Gustav Carus, Ger. physiologist and painter, 1789–1869] An arc corresponding to the pelvic axis. At the end of the second stage of labor, when the fetal head reaches the curve of Carus, it is directed upward toward the vaginal introitus and forced into extension by the resistance of the pelvic floor.

curve of Spee (shpā) [Ferdinand Graf von Spee, Ger. embryologist, 1855–1937] An anatomic curvature established by viewing the occlusal alignment of teeth, beginning with the tip of the lower canine and extending back along the buccal cusps of the natural premolar and molar teeth to the ramus of the mandible. SYN: *dental curve.*

curvilinear (kĕr′vĕ-lĭn″ē-ăr) Concerning or pert. to a curved line.

Cushing, Harvey (koosh′ĭng) U.S. surgeon, 1869–1939.

C. disease Cushing syndrome caused by excessive production of adrenocorticotropic hormone.

C. response A reflex due to cerebral ischemia that causes an increase in systemic blood pressure. This maintains cerebral perfusion during increased intracranial pressure.

C. syndrome The symptoms from prolonged exposure to excessive glucocorticoid hormones. Glucocorticoids are naturally excreted by the adrenal glands; however, Cushing syndrome is a side effect of the pharmacological use of steroids in the management of inflammatory illnesses, e.g., reactive airways disease or arthritis. Glucocorticoid excess from pituitary or adrenal adenomas or from the production of excess levels of adrenocorticotropic hormone by lung cancer is exceptionally rare (and is called Cushing disease).

SYMPTOMS: The affected patient may complain of muscular weakness, thinning of the skin, easy bruising due to capillary fragility, weight gain, rounding of facial features ("moon-like" facies), cervicodorsal fat (buffalo hump) on the upper back, poor wound healing related to immunosuppression, decreased sexual drive and function, menstrual irregularities, insomnia, or psychological depression. Symptoms of diabetes mellitus, e.g., thirst, polyuria, and polyphagia, may be present because glucocorticoid hormones oppose the action of insulin. On physical examination, patients may have excessive fat in the face, upper back, and trunk, but none on the limbs. The abdominal skin may be marked by purplish lines (striae). Women may have excessive hair growth on the face and extremities due to increased androgen production. Increased catabolism leads to muscle wasting and osteopenia or osteoporosis. Hypertension is often present.

TREATMENT: Cushing's syndrome caused by the chronic use of steroid hormones may improve if steroids can be given every other day or if high doses of these medications can be gradually tapered. When Cushing's disease is present, surgery to remove the causative adenoma is usually needed, sometimes with adjunctive radiation therapy. Before surgery a medication to inhibit cortisol production, e.g., mitotane, may be prescribed along with drugs to reduce blood glucose and blood pressure.

PATIENT CARE: When prolonged administration of therapeutic, as opposed to replacement, doses of adrenocortical hormones is required, the patient is monitored for development of adverse reactions. A diet is provided that is high in protein and potassium but low in calories, carbohydrates, and sodium. The patient is assisted to adjust to changes in body image and strength. Realistic reassurance and emotional support are provided, and the patient is encouraged to verbalize feelings about losses and to develop positive coping strategies. Intermittent rest periods are recommended, and assistance is provided with mobility, esp. with movements requiring arm-shoulder strength. Safety measures are instituted to prevent falls. Instruction to the patient should include information about the risk for the development of diabetes mellitus, cataracts, easy bruising, and infections. For information and support, refer the patient to The National Adrenal Diseases Foundation. SEE: *Nursing Diagnoses Appendix.*

   C. ulcer A stress ulcer in patients with increased intracranial pressure. Cushing ulcer may be caused by increased secretion of gastric acid due to vagus nerve stimulation. SEE: *stress ulcer.*

cushingoid (koosh′ĭng-oyd) Having physical characteristics that result from excess exposure to corticosteroids, such as a rounded face, weight gain, or thin, easily bruised skin.

cushion (koosh′ĭn) In anatomy, a mass of connective tissue, usually adipose, that acts to prevent undue pressure on underlying tissues or structures.

   wheelchair c. A padded surface for wheelchair seats designed to prevent pressure sores. There are several static varieties, including air-filled, polyurethane foam, and flotation, the latter filled with water or gel. Dynamic surfaces, which require an external power source, protect pressure points by alternating high and low air pressures through a system of valves and pumps. SYN: *pressure relief device.*

cusp (kŭsp) [L. *cuspis,* point] **1.** A rounded or cone-shaped point on the crown of a tooth. **2.** One of the leaflike divisions or parts of the valves of the heart. **cuspidate** (kŭs′pĭ-dāt″), *adj.* SEE: *bicuspid valve; tricuspid **valve**.*

   Carabelli c. SEE: *Carabelli cusp.*

   plunger c. A cusp of a tooth that tends to forcibly wedge food into interproximal areas, causing an impaction. Cusp points should be rounded, shortened, or reduced with a dental drill.

cuspid (kŭs′pĭd) [L. *cuspis,* point] Canine (2).

custody (kŭs′tŏ-dē) [L. *custodia,* care, protection, watch] **1.** Direct control or care by an agent or agency in charge. **2.** Legal guardianship, as for a child. **3.** Legal detention or incarceration by the police or other law enforcement agency. **4.** Safekeeping of evidence, as of illegal drugs or weapons for presentation in a trial.

custom A generally accepted practice or behavior by a particular group of people or a social group.

cut (kŭt) **1.** Separating or dividing of tissues by use of a sharp surgical instrument such as a scalpel. **2.** To dilute a substance in order to decrease the concentration of the active ingredient.

cut- [L. *cutis,* skin, hide, leather] Prefix meaning *skin.*

cutane-, cutaneo- [L. *cutaneus,* fr. *cutis,* skin] Prefixes meaning *skin.*

cutaneomucouveal syndrome (kū-tā″nē-ō-mū″kō-ū′vē-ăl) Behçet's syndrome.

cutaneous (kū-tā′nē-ŭs) [L. *cutis,* skin] Pert. to the skin. SYN: *integumentary.*

cutaneous nerves Peripheral nerves innervating the skin.

cutaneous radiation syndrome ABBR: CRS. The damaging effects of radiation exposure on the skin. In limited exposures, CRS may be limited to mild sunburning. Blistering, hair loss, necrosis, or permanent scarring may occur with more extensive exposures.

cutdown (kŭt′down) A surgical procedure for locating a vein or artery to permit intravenous or intra-arterial administration of fluids or drugs; required in patients with vascular collapse caused by shock or other conditions.

Cuterebra (kūt″ĕ-rē′bră, kū-ter′) A genus of botflies whose maggots (larvae) may infest the skin, causing myiasis. SEE: *botfly; myiasis.*

cuticle (kū′tĭ-k′l) [L. *cuticula,* little skin] A layer of solid or semisolid tissue that covers the free surface of a layer of epithelial cells. It may be horny or chitinous and sometimes is calcified. Examples include the enamel cuticle of a tooth and the capsule of the lens of the eye.

   acquired c. A layer of salivary products, bacteria, and food debris on the surface of the teeth; not a true cuticle. SYN: *pellicle.*

   attachment c. Dental **c.**

   dental c. The glycosaminoglycans layer produced by attachment epithelium on the cementum of the tooth root. It is continuous with and identical in origin and function to enamel cuticle, which is present on the enamel crown. SYN: *attachment **c**.*

   enamel c. The thin, calcified layer that covers the enamel crown of the tooth prior to eruption. Remnants that persist after decalcification of the tooth for microscopy are called Nasmyth's membrane. SYN: *cuticula dentis.*

cuticula (kū-tik′yū-lă) [L. *cutis,* skin + -*cule*] Cuticle.

   c. dentis Nasmyth membrane.

cuticularization (kū-tĭk″ū-lăr-ĭ-zā′shŭn) Growth of skin over a sore or wound.

cutin (kū′tĭn) [L. *cutis,* skin] A wax that combines with cellulose to form the cuticle of plants.

cutireaction (kū″tĕ-rē-ăk′shŭn) An inflammatory or irritative reaction appearing on the skin; skin reaction.

   von Pirquet c. The reaction of the skin after inoculation with tuberculosis toxins.

cutis (kūt′ĭs) [L. *cutis,* skin, hide, leather] The skin, consisting of the epidermis and the corium (dermis) and resting on the subcutaneous tissue.

c. anserina Piloerection.

c. aurantiasis Yellow discoloration of the skin resulting from ingesting excessive quantities of vegetables, such as carrots, which contain carotenoid pigments. SEE: *carotenemia.*

c. hyperelastica Ehlers-Danlos syndrome.

c. laxa A rare inherited condition in which there is loss of elastic fibers of the skin. The skin becomes so loose it hangs and sags. Pulmonary emphysema, intestinal diverticula, and hernias also may be present. There are at least three inheritable patterns of this disease. There is no known treatment. SYN: *c. pendula.*

c. marmorata Transient mottling of the skin caused by exposure to decreased temperature. SYN: *mottling.*

c. pendula Cutis laxa.

c. vera Dermis.

c. verticis gyrata Convoluted scalp folds 1 to 2 cm thick. It may develop any time from birth to adolescence and is more common in males. The skin cannot be flattened by traction. SYN: *bulldog scalp.*

Cutivate SEE: *fluticasone.*

cutization (kū-tī-zā'shŭn) Skinlike changes in a mucous membrane as a result of continued inflammation.

cutoff level (kŭt'of") In laboratory testing, the threshold value that distinguishes a positive test result from a negative one. SYN: *breakpoint.*

cut point SEE: under *point.*

cut throat Laceration of the throat. The seriousness of the injury depends on the angle of thrust of the cutting object, the location of the injury, and the amount of tissue damage.

PATIENT CARE: The patient should be transported to the nearest trauma center for evaluation. If there is evidence of bleeding into the airway, the patient should be positioned so that blood is not aspirated. Suction devices should be available at the bedside. If the trachea is severed, it should be kept open and free of clots. Bleeding sites should be compressed until definitive therapy is available. Vital signs and cardiac rhythms should be continuously monitored. For patients who cannot protect their airways, intubation and mechanical ventilation are required.

cuvette (kū-vĕt') [Fr. *cuve*, a tub] A small transparent glass or plastic container, esp. one used to hold liquids to be examined photometrically.

cv *coefficient of variation.*

CVA *Cerebrovascular accident.*

CVD *cardiovascular disease.*

CVP *central venous pressure.*

CVS *Chorionic villus sampling.*

cyanhemoglobin (sī"ăn-hē"mō-glō'bĭn) Hemoglobin combined with cyanide.

cyanide (sī'ă-nīd") [*cyan-* + *-ide*] A compound containing the radical −CN, such as potassium cyanide (KCN), or sodium cyanide (NaCN). It is a potent toxin that interrupts cellular respiration.

cyanide poisoning SEE: under *poisoning.*

cyanmethemoglobin (sī"ăn-mĕt"hē-mō-glō'bĭn) Combination of cyanide and methemoglobin.

cyano-, cyan- [Gr. *kyanos,* cyanus; dark blue substance] Prefixes meaning *blue.*

cyanoacrylate adhesive (sī"ă-nō-ak'rĭ-lāt", sī-an"ō-) [*cyan(ide)* + *acrylate*] Any of the monomers of *N*-alkyl cyanoacrylate used as a tissue adhesive in the repair of simple lacerations, e.g., of the arms or legs. Commercially available versions are called *superglue.*

⚠ Superglues can cause tissues to adhere firmly to each other. They should not be used near the eyes or mouth or on the hands in order to avoid bonding these tissues together.

cyanocobalamin (sī"ăn-ō-kō-băl'ă-mĭn) The form of vitamin B_{12} available for use in the U.S. SEE: *cobalamin; vitamin B_{12}.*

cyanogen (sī-ăn'ō-jĕn) [" + *gennan,* to produce] **1.** The radical CN. **2.** A poisonous gas, CN—CN.

cyanophilous (sī-ăn-ŏf'ĭl-ŭs) Having an affinity for a blue dye or stain.

cyanopia, cyanopsia (sī-ăn-ō'pē-ă, -ŏp'sē-ă) [" + *opsis,* vision] Vision in which all objects appear to be blue.

cyanosis (sī"ă-nō'sĭs) [*cyano-* + *-sis*] A blue, gray, slate, or dark purple discoloration of the skin or mucous membranes caused by deoxygenated or reduced hemoglobin in the blood. Cyanosis is found most often in hypoxemic patients and rarely in patients with methemoglobinemias. Occasionally, a bluish skin tint that superficially resembles cyanosis results from exposure to the cold. In the very young patient, cyanosis may point to a congenital heart defect. **cyanosed** (sī'ă-nōst", sī'ă-nōzd"), *adj.*

ETIOLOGY: This condition usually is caused by inadequate oxygenation of the bloodstream.

TREATMENT: Supplemental oxygenation is supplied to cyanotic patients who are proven to be hypoxemic. SEE: *asphyxia.*

⚠ Oximetry or arterial blood gas analysis should be used to determine whether a patient is adequately oxygenated. Relying only on the appearance of the skin or mucous membranes to determine hypoxemia may result in misdiagnosis.

central c. A bluish discoloration of the mucous membranes in the mouth, indicating hypoxemia and respiratory failure.

TREATMENT: If hypoxemia is confirmed by oximetry or arterial blood gas analysis, supplemental oxygen is provided.

PATIENT CARE: The patient's vital signs, blood gases, and sensorium should be monitored closely, as this sign may indicate hypoxemia accompanying impending respiratory failure. SYN: *circumoral c.*

circumoral c. Central **c.**

congenital c. Cyanosis usually associated with a birth defect, such as stenosis of the pulmonary artery orifice, ventricular septal defect, or a patent foramen ovale or ductus arteriosus. SEE: *tetralogy of Fallot.*

delayed c. Tardive **c.**

enterogenous c. Cyanosis induced by intestinal absorption of toxins or by certain drugs. SEE: *methemoglobinemia.*

peripheral c. A bluish discoloration of the digits.

PATIENT CARE: The patient's vital signs, oxygen saturation, blood gases, and mental status should be monitored closely.

c. retinae Bluish appearance of the retina seen in congenital heart disease, polycythemia, and in certain poisonings, such as dinitrobenzol.

tardive c. Cyanosis caused by congenital heart disease and appearing only after cardiac failure. SYN: *delayed c.*

cyanotic (sī-ăn-ŏt'ĭk) Of the nature of, affected with, or pert. to cyanosis.

cyanuria (sī"ă-nū're̅-ă) The voiding of blue urine.

cyber- [*cyber(netic)*] A prefix that means pertaining to computers, computing, or the Internet.

cyberknife (sī'bĕr-nīf") [*cyber-* + *knife*] A frameless stereotactic robot-controlled system for radiosurgery.

cybernetics (sī"bĕr-nĕt'ĭks) [Gr. *kybernetes*, helmsman] The science of control and communication in biological, electronic, and mechanical systems. This includes analysis of feedback mechanisms that serve to govern or modify the actions of various systems.

cyberphilia (sī"bĕr-fĭl'ē-ă) [" + *philein*, to love] Fascination with the use of machines, esp. computers, their use, and their programming.

cyberphobia (sī"bĕr-fō'bē-ă) [" + *phobos*, fear] Tension, anxiety, and stress in persons required to work with a computer.

cyberspace (sī'bĕr-spās") [*cyber-* +

space] **1.** The Internet. **2.** An electronic representation of the world as stored in data and shared among computers; the virtual world.

cycad (sī'kad", kăd) [L. *Cycas*, a genus name] A variety of palmlike evergreen plants, including *Cycas revoluta* and *C. circinalis*, from which cycasin has been isolated.

cycasin (sī'kă-sĭn) A carcinogenic substance present in cycad plants.

cyclamate (sī'klă-māt) The calcium salt of cyclamic acid, formerly used as a nonnutritive sweetener and now banned because of possible cancer-causing effects.

cyclarthrosis (sī-klär-thrŏ'sĭs) [Gr. *kyklos*, circle, + *arthron*, joint, + *osis*, condition] A lateral ginglymus or pivot joint, which makes rotation possible.

cycle (sī'kĕl) [Gr. *kyklos*, circle] A regular, complete series of movements or events.

anovular c. Menstrual cycle in which ovulation is absent.

cardiac c. The period from the beginning of one heartbeat to the beginning of the succeeding beat, including *systole* and *diastole*. Normally, the atria contract immediately before the ventricles. The ordinary cycle lasts 0.8 sec with the heart beating approx. 60 to 85 times a minute in the adult at rest. Atrial systole lasts 0.1 sec, ventricular systole 0.3 sec, and diastole 0.4 sec. Although the heart seems to be working continuously, it actually rests for a good portion of each cardiac cycle.

cell c. The cycle of the growth and development of a cell. The cell cycle consists of mitosis, during which chromosomes actively divide to form two sister cells, and the interphase, during which the cell grows, begins to synthesize DNA, and prepares for chromosomal division. The interphase consists of several gap or G phases and the S (DNA Synthesis) phase. SEE: *interphase; meiosis* and *mitosis* for illus.

cell growth c. The order of physical and biochemical events that occur during the growth of cells. In tissue culture studies, the cyclic changes are divided into specific periods or phases: the DNA synthesis or S period, the G_2 period or gap, the M or mitotic period, and the G_1 period.

citric acid c. Krebs cycle.

Cori c. SEE: *Cori cycle.*

duty c. During chest compressions of a victim of cardiac arrest, the relative amount of time that the chest is compressed compared to the time that the chest is allowed to recoil to its fully inflated position. A cycle of 50% occurs when chest compression equals chest recoil.

estrus c. The sequence from the beginning of one estrus period to the beginning of the next. It includes proestrus, estrus, and metestrus, followed by a short period of quiescence called diestrus.

gastric c. The progression of peristalsis through the stomach.

genesial c. 1. The period from puberty to menopause. **2.** The period of sexual maturity.

glycolytic c. The cycle by which glucose is broken down in living tissue.

initiated c. In assisted reproduction, any month when a woman is treated with drugs that stimulate the ovary to produce follicles.

Krebs c. SEE: *Krebs cycle.*

life c. All of the developmental history of an organism, whether in a free-living condition or in a host (e.g., as a parasite that experiences part of its cycle inside another organism).

menstrual c. The periodically recurrent series of changes occurring in the uterus and associated sex organs (ovaries, cervix, and vagina) associated with menstruation and the intermenstrual period. The human cycle averages 28 days in length, measured from the beginning of menstruation. The menstrual cycle is, however, quite variable in length, even in the same person from month to month. Variations in the length of the cycle are due principally to variation in the length of the proliferative phase. SEE: illus.

The menstrual cycle is divided into four phases characterized by histological changes that take place in the uterine endometrium. They are:

Proliferative Phase: Following blood loss from the endometrium, the uterine epithelium is restored to normal; the endometrium becomes thicker and more vascular; the glands elongate. During this period, the ovarian follicle is maturing and secreting estrogens; with the estrogen stimulation, the endometrium hypertrophies, thickening and becoming more vascular, and the glands elongate. The phase is terminated by the rupture of the follicle and the liberation of the ovum at about 14 days before the next menstrual period begins. Fertilization of the ovum is most likely to occur in the days immediately following ovulation.

Luteal or Secretory Phase: After releasing the ovum, the corpus luteum secretes progesterone. With the progesterone stimulation, the endometrium becomes even thicker; the glands become more tortuous and produce an abundant secretion containing glycogen. The coiled arteries make their appearance; the endometrium becomes edematous; the stroma becomes compact. During this period, the corpus luteum in an ovary is developing and secreting progesterone. This phase lasts 10 to 14 days.

Premenstrual or Ischemic Phase: If pregnancy has not occurred, the coiled arteries constrict and the endometrium becomes anemic and shrinks a day or two before menstruation. The corpus luteum of the ovary begins involution. This phase lasts about 2 days and is terminated by the opening up of constricted arteries, the breaking off of

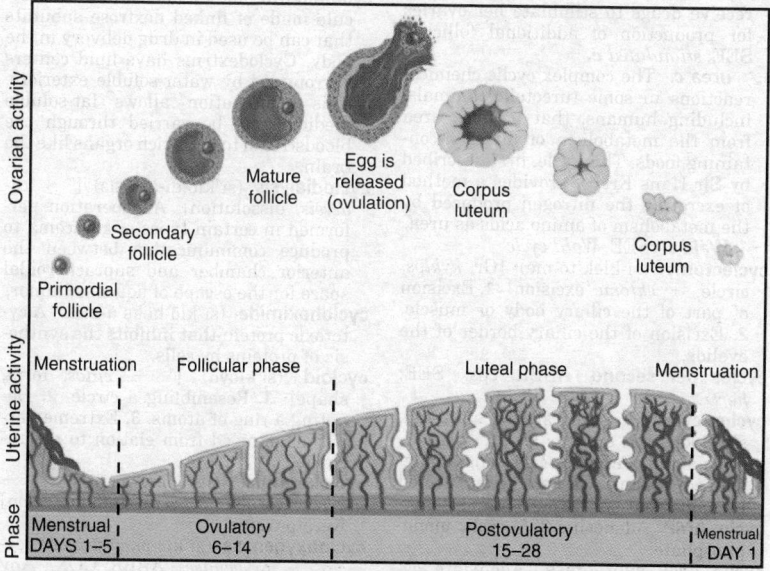

PHASES OF THE MENSTRUAL CYCLE

small patches of endometrium, and the beginning of menstruation with the flow of menstrual fluid.

Menstruation: The functional layer of the endometrium is shed.

The menstrual cycle is altered by pregnancy, the use of contraception, intercurrent illnesses, diet, and exercise.

nitrogen c. A series of natural processes in which nitrogen is discharged from animal life into the soil; the nitrogen is taken up from the soil by nitrogen-fixing bacteria and converted to nitrates usable by plants for their nourishment; and in turn nitrogen is taken up by plant-eating animals.

sleep-wake c. The amount of time spent asleep and awake and the cycle of that schedule from day to day.

stimulated c. A cycle in assisted reproduction in which a woman receives drugs to stimulate her ovaries for production of additional follicles. SEE: *unstimulated c.*

stretch-shortening c. An eccentric muscle contraction followed immediately by a concentric contraction of the same muscle group. The elastic potentiation that occurs during the eccentric phase increases the force of output of the concentric contraction. These exercises replicate functional movement patterns and are typically used in the advance phase of rehabilitation, particularly in sports rehab. Exercises incorporating this phenomenon are called plyometrics. SEE: *plyometrics.*

tricarboxylic acid c. Krebs cycle.

unstimulated c. A cycle in assisted reproduction in which a woman does not receive drugs to stimulate her ovaries for production of additional follicles. SEE: *stimulated c.*

urea c. The complex cyclic chemical reactions in some (ureotelic) animals, including humans, that produce urea from the metabolism of nitrogen-containing foods. This cycle, first described by Sir Hans Krebs, provides a method of excreting the nitrogen produced by the metabolism of amino acids as urea.

Wald c. SEE: *Wald cycle.*

cyclectomy (sī-klĕk′tō-mē) [Gr. *kyklos,* circle, + *ektome,* excision] **1.** Excision of part of the ciliary body or muscle. **2.** Excision of the ciliary border of the eyelids.

cycles per second ABBR: cps. SEE: *hertz.*

cyclic, cyclical (sī′klik, sik′lik; sī′kli-kăl, sik′li-kăl) [L. *cyclicus* fr. Gr. *kyklikos,* circular] **1.** Periodic. **2.** Having a ring-shaped structure. **3.** Pert. to or affected by menstruation.

cyclic AMP Adenosine 3′,5′-cyclic monophosphate.

cyclic AMP synthetase Adenylate cyclase.

cyclic vomiting syndrome Abdominal **migraine**.

-cycline [Fm *(tetra)cycline*] A suffix used in pharmacology to name an *antibiotic derived from tetracycline.*

cyclins (sī′klĭnz) A group of intracellular proteins that regulate the cell cycle, i.e., cell growth and division. Some cyclins, including cyclins D and E, are overexpressed in human breast cancer cells.

cyclitis (sĭk-lī′tĭs) [″ + *itis,* inflammation] An inflammation of the ciliary body of the eye.

SYMPTOMS: The patient exhibits perilimbal injection, keratic precipitates in the corneal endothelium, reduced or hazy vision, and decreased intraocular pressure. Pain in or about the eye with photophobia is present, which is worse at night and on pressure. Its course is rapid and progressively unfavorable. Complications include iritis, choroiditis, scleritis, and glaucoma.

TREATMENT: Steroid eye drops are used. Cataract surgery is helpful in some cases.

cyclo-, cycl- [Gr. *kyklos,* wheel, circle] **1.** Prefixes meaning *circular* or *cycle.* **2.** Prefixes meaning the *ciliary body of the eye.*

cyclobenzaprine (sī″klō-bĕn′ză-prēn) A tricyclic antidepressant analog and centrally acting skeletal muscle relaxant. It is administered orally to manage acute painful musculoskeletal conditions associated with muscle spasm.

cyclochoroiditis (sī″klō-kō″royd-ī′tĭs) [″ + *chorioeides,* skinlike, + *itis,* inflammation] Inflammation of the ciliary body and choroid coat of the eye.

cyclodextrin (sī-klō-dĕks′trĭn) A molecule made of linked dextrose subunits that can be used in drug delivery in the body. Cyclodextrins have lipid centers surrounded by water-soluble exteriors. This combination allows fat-soluble medicines to be carried through the bloodstream to lipid-rich organs like the brain.

cyclodialysis (sī″klō-dī-ăl′ĭ-sĭs) [″ + *dialysis,* dissolution] An operation performed in certain types of glaucoma to produce communication between the anterior chamber and suprachoroidal space for the escape of aqueous humor.

cycloheximide (sī″klō-hĕks′ă-mīd) A cytotoxic protein that inhibits the synthesis of proteins by cells.

cycloid (sī′kloyd) [″ + *eidos,* form, shape] **1.** Resembling a circle. **2.** Denoting a ring of atoms. **3.** Extreme variations of mood from elation to melancholia.

cyclokeratitis (sī″klō-kĕr-ă-tī′tĭs) [″ + *keras,* cornea, + *itis,* inflammation] Keratouveitis.

cyclooxygenase (sī″klō-ok′sĭ-jĭ-nās″) [*cyclo-* + *oxygenase*] ABBR: COX. Any of several enzymes, e.g., COX-1, COX-2, that make prostaglandins from arachidonic acids. They play a central role in inflammatory diseases, blood clotting, pain, and cellular proliferation.

cyclophoria (sī″klō-fō′rē-ă) [″ + *phoros*, bearing] Deviation of the eye around its anteroposterior axis due to weakness of the oblique muscles. SYN: *periphoria*.

cyclopia (sī-klō′pē-ă) [Gr. *kyklos*, circle, + *ops*, eye] The condition of having a single eye.

cycloplegia (sī″klō-plē′jē-ă) [″ + *plege*, a stroke] Paralysis of the ciliary muscle. This can be an anticholinergic side effect of antipsychotic or antidepressant medications.

cyclops (sī′klŏps) A fetal malformation in which there is only one eye. SYN: *monoculus* (2).

cyclosis (sī-klō′sĭs) [Gr. *kyklosis*, circulation] A streaming of cytoplasm within a cell.

cyclosporiasis (sī″klō-spŏr-ī′ă-sĭs) [Genus name + ″] Infection with any species of *Cyclospora*.

cyclotomy (sī-klŏt′ō-mē) [″ + *tome*, incision] Surgical incision of the ciliary muscle of the eye.

cyclotron (sī′klō-trŏn) A particle accelerator in which the particle is rotated between magnets, gaining speed with each rotation.

cyclotropia (sī″klō-trō′pē-ă) Manifest cyclophoria.

cyesis (sī-ē′sĭs) [Gr. *kyesis*] Pregnancy.

cylinder (sĭl′ĭn-dĕr) [Gr. *kylindros*] A hollow, tube-shaped body.

   crossed c. Two cylindrical lenses at right angles to each other; used in diagnosing astigmatism.

   extension c. A hollow tube attached to the end of the collimator apparatus of an x-ray tube. It limits the size of the beam, decreasing scatter radiation and increasing detail.

   gas c. A high-pressure, nonreactive, seamless tempered steel container for compressed gas used for medical, therapeutic, or diagnostic purposes.

   urinary c. An obsolete term for urinary casts.

cylindroadenoma (sĭ-lĭn″drō-ăd″ē-nō′mă) [Gr. *kylindros*, cylinder, + *aden*, gland, + *oma*, tumor] An adenoma containing cylindrical masses of hyaline material.

cylindroid (sĭl-ĭn′droyd) [″ + *eidos*, form, shape] 1. Cylinder-shaped. 2. A mucous, spurious cast in urine, recognized by its twists and turns, varying markedly in diameter in different places, most frequently pointed at the ends, and frequently crossing an entire field. It does not usually have cellular intrusions.

cylindroma (sĭl″ĭn-drō′mă) [″ + *oma*, tumor] A skin tumor of apocrine origin usually found on the face or forehead

containing a collection of cells forming cylinders.

cylindruria (sĭl″ĭn-drū′rē-ă) [″ + *ouron*, urine] The presence of cylindroids in the urine.

cymatic therapy (sī-măt″ĭk) [Gr. *kymatikos*, swollen, wavy] The therapeutic uses of music and sound.

cynanthropy (sĭn-ăn′thrō-pē) [Gr. *kyon*, dog, + *anthropos*, man] Insanity in which the patient behaves like a dog.

cynic spasm SEE: under *spasm*.

cynophobia (sī″nō-fō′bē-ă) [″ + *phobos*, fear] Unreasonable fear of dogs.

CYP3A4 One isoenzyme form of the cytochrome P450 system involved in the metabolism of many drugs. Drugs that alter this enzyme system can influence the metabolism of other agents taken by patients and cause unanticipated toxic effects.

cyrtosis (sĭr-tō′sĭs) [″ + *osis*, condition] Any abnormal curvature of the spine. SEE: *kyphosis; lordosis*.

cyst (sist) [Gr. *kystis*, bladder, sac] 1. A closed sac or pouch with a definite wall, containing fluid, semifluid, or solid material. It is usually an abnormal structure resulting from developmental anomalies, obstruction of ducts, or parasitic infection. 2. In biology, a structure formed by and enclosing certain organisms in which they become inactive, such as the cyst of certain protozoans or of the metacercariae of flukes.

   adventitious c. A cyst formed around a foreign body.

   alveolar c. Dilation and rupture of pulmonary alveoli to form air cysts.

   apical c. A cyst near the apex of the root of a nonvital tooth.

   arachnoid c. An abnormal collection of cerebrospinal fluid within the arachnoid membrane. The cysts may compress nearby structures within the brain. In infants, they may cause headaches, altered mental status, learning disabilities, or enlargement of the head. In adults, they are an occasional cause of epilepsy.

   Baker c. SEE: *Baker cyst*.

   Bartholin c. SEE: under *Bartholin, Caspar (the younger)*.

   blood c. Hematoma.

   blue dome c. 1. A mammary cyst containing light, straw-colored fluid, which appears blue when seen through the surrounding tissue. 2. A small dark-blue cyst in the vagina caused by retained menstrual blood seen in endometriosis.

   branchial c. Cervical **c.**

   bone c. A cystic mass in bone, usually a normal variant or a benign tumor.

   Boyer cyst SEE: *Boyer cyst*.

   cervical c. A closed epithelial sac derived from a branchial groove of its corresponding pharyngeal pouch. SYN: *branchial c.*

chocolate c. An ovarian cyst with darkly pigmented gelatinous contents.

colloid c. A cyst with gelatinous contents.

complex c. A cyst that consists of solid material and fluid-filled cavities; it may have walls of tissue inside it or internal echoes. When a complex cyst is identified on ultrasound, surgical removal is generally indicated to exclude malignancy.

congenital c. A cyst present at birth and resulting from abnormal development, such as a dermoid cyst, imperfect closure of a structure as in spina bifida cystica, or nonclosure of embryonic clefts, ducts, or tubules, such as cervical cysts.

daughter c. A cyst growing out of the walls of another cyst.

dental c. A cyst that forms from any of the odontogenic tissues.

dentigerous c. A fluid-filled, epithelial-lined cyst usually surrounding the crown of a tooth that is erupting or has not yet erupted. The tooth normally erupts through the cyst without treatment. SYN: *eruption c.; follicular c.; follicular odontoma c.*

dermoid c. **1.** An ovarian teratoma. **2.** A nonmalignant cystic tumor containing elements derived from the ectoderm, such as hair, teeth, or skin. These tumors occur frequently in the ovary but may develop in other organs such as the lungs.

distention c. A cyst formed in a natural enclosed cavity, such as a follicular cyst of the ovary.

echinococcus c. Hydatid **c.**

endometrial c. An ovarian cyst or tumor lined with endometrial tissue, usually seen in ovarian endometriosis.

epidermoid c. A cyst filled with keratin, sebum, and skin debris that may form on the scalp, the back of the neck, or the axilla. It is benign andf can be removed surgically. SYN: *sebaceous c.*

eruption c. Dentigerous **c.**

extravasation c. A cyst arising from hemorrhage or escape of other body fluids into tissues.

exudation c. A cyst caused by trapping of an exudate in a closed area.

follicular c. A cyst arising from a follicle, as a follicular cyst of the thyroid gland, the ovary, or a forming tooth. SYN: *dentigerous c.* SEE: illus.

ganglion cyst ganglion (2)

Gartner c. SEE: *Gartner cyst.*

Gorlin c. SEE: *Gorlin cyst.*

hydatid c. A cyst formed by the growth of the larval form of *Echinococcus granulosus,* usually in the liver. SYN: *echinococcus c.*

implantation c. A cyst resulting from displacement of portions of the epidermis, as may occur in injuries.

intraligamentary c. A cystic forma-

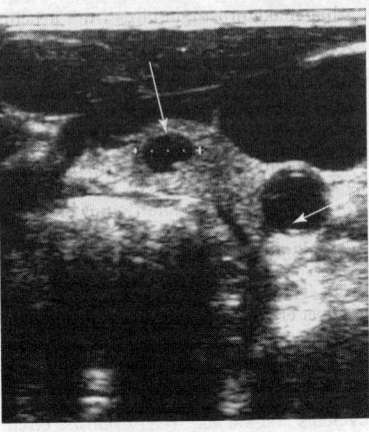

FOLLICULAR CYST

Follicular cysts seen on ultrasonography of the thyroid gland.

tion between the layers of the broad ligament.

involutional c. A cyst occurring in the normal involution of an organ or structure, as in the mammary gland.

keratin c. A cyst containing keratin.

c.s of liver Simple cysts, usually small and single; or hydatid cysts; or cysts associated with cystic disease of the liver, a rare condition usually associated with congenital cystic kidneys. SEE: *Echinococcus granulosus; hydatid.*

meibomian c. Chalazion.

meniscus c. A fluid-filled cyst often associated with a degenerative horizontal meniscal tear, more frequently seen in the lateral meniscus of the knee. This ganglion-like cyst may present with a palpable mass at the joint line of the knee and can be visualized by magnetic resonance imaging.

morgagnian c. SEE: under *Morgagni, Giovanni B.*

Morgagni c. SEE: under *Morgagni, Giovanni B.*

mother c. A hydatid cyst enveloping smaller ones.

mucous c. A retention cyst composed of mucus.

nabothian c. A cyst caused by closure of the ducts of the nabothian glands in the uterine cervix as a result of chronic cervicitis.

odontogenic c. A cyst associated with the teeth, such as a dentigerous or radicular cyst.

ovarian c. A fluid-filled cyst that develops in the ovary and consists of one or more chambers. The main types of cysts are follicular cysts, the corpus luteum, teratoma, and endometrioma. The patient's primary complaint is generally pelvic pain or pain during intercourse. The cysts may be palpated during bimanual examination but are diagnosed by ultrasound. Many cysts resolve spontaneously. Although non-malignant, the cyst may have to be removed surgically because of twisting of the pedicle, which causes gangrene, or because of pressure. SEE: *polycystic ovary syndrome*.

parasitic c. A cyst enclosing the larval form of certain parasites, such as the cysticercus or hydatid of tapeworms or the larva of certain nematodes, i.e., *Trichinella*.

parovarian c. A cyst of the parovarium.

periapical c. Radicular **c.**

pilar c. An epithelial cyst with a wall that resembles the follicular epithelium. It is filled with a homogeneous mixture of keratin and lipid. SYN: *trichilemma c.*

pilonidal c. A cyst most often in the sacrococcygeal region, usually at the upper end of the intergluteal cleft. It is due to a developmental defect that permits epithelial tissue to be trapped below the skin or may be acquired. This type of cyst may become symptomatic in early adulthood when an infected draining sinus forms. SYN: *pilonidal fistula*.

popliteal c. Baker cyst.

porencephalic c. An anomalous cavity of the brain that communicates with the ventricular system.

proliferative c. A cyst lined with epithelium that proliferates, forming projections that extend into the cavity of the cyst.

radicular c. A necrotic, inflammatory cyst that develops at the root of a non-vital tooth. The cyst is attached to the root of the tooth and may be lateral to it if the cyst is associated with a lateral pulp canal. SYN: *periapical c.; root-end c.*

retention c. A cyst retaining the secretion of a gland, as in a mucous or sebaceous cyst.

sebaceous c. Epidermoid **c.**

seminal c. A cyst of the epididymis, ductus deferens, or other sperm-carrying ducts that contain semen.

suprasellar c. A cyst of the hypophyseal stalk just above the floor of the sella turcica. Its wall is frequently calcified or ossified.

synovial c. Accumulation of synovia in a bursa, synovial crypt, or sac of a synovial hernia, causing a tumor.

theca-lutein c. Benign enlargement of the Graafian follicle, typically occurring in pregnancies (particularly in multiple pregnancies) or in other conditions that cause markedly elevated levels of serum human chorionic gonadotropin (HCG) levels, e.g., molar pregnancies or choriocarcinomas. SYN: *hyperreactio luteinalis*.

trichilemma c. Pilar **c.**

tubo-ovarian c. An ovarian cyst that ruptures into the lumen of an adherent uterine tube.

unilocular c. A cyst containing only one cavity.

vaginal c. A cyst in the vagina.

vitelline c. A congenital cyst of the gastrointestinal canal. Lined with ciliated epithelium, it is the remains of the omphalomesenteric duct.

wolffian c. A cyst lying in one of the broad ligaments of the uterus.

-cyst [Gr. *kystis*, bladder] Suffix meaning the *urinary bladder* or a *cyst*.

cystadenocarcinoma (sĭs-tăd″ē-nō-kăr″sĭ-nō′mă) [Gr. *kystis*, bladder, + *aden*, gland, + *karkinos*, crab, + *oma*, tumor] A glandular malignancy that forms cysts as it grows.

cystadenoma (sis″tăd″ĕn-ō′mă) [*cysto-* + *adenoma*] A glandular tumor that contains pockets filled with cysts. SYN: *cystic adenoma*.

papillary c. lymphomatosum Warthin's tumor.

pseudomucinous c. A cyst filled with a thick, viscid fluid and lined with tall epithelial cells.

serous c. A cyst filled with a clear serous fluid and lined with cuboidal epithelial cells.

cystalgia (sĭs-tăl′jē-ă) [″ + *algos*, pain] Pain in the bladder. SYN: *cystodynia*.

cystathionine (sĭs″tă-thī′ō-nĭn) $C_7H_{14}N_2O_4S$; an intermediate compound in the metabolism of methionine to cysteine.

cystathioninuria (sĭs″tă-thī″ō-nĭ-nū′rē-ă) A hereditary disease caused by a deficiency of the enzyme important in metabolizing cystathionine, resulting in mental retardation, thrombocytopenia, and acidosis.

cystatin C (sĭs′tăt-ĭn) A cysteine proteinase inhibitor found in the bloodstream in elevated concentrations in patients with impaired kidney function. It is a small protein composed of 120 amino acids (mass 13 kD) that is produced by nucleated cells throughout the body and easily filtered by the glomeruli of the kidneys. It is reabsorbed and catabolized by proximal tubular cells. Because levels of cystatin C do not depend on a patient's age, height, muscle mass, or weight, it is thought to be a better measure of kidney function than the creatinine clearance test, which is most often used to assess renal health.

cystectomy (sĭs-těk′tō-mē) [″ + *ektome*, excision] **1.** Removal of a cyst. **2.** Excision of the urinary bladder or a part of it.

cysteic acid (sis′tē-ĭk) SEE: under *acid*.

cysteine hydrochloride (sĭs′tĕ-ēn″) [From *cystine*] An amino acid, $C_3H_7NO_2S \cdot HCl \cdot H_2O$, containing sulfur and found in many proteins. It is valuable as a source of sulfur in metabolism.

cystic (sĭs'tĭk) [Gr. *kystis*, bladder] **1.** Of or pert. to a cyst. **2.** Pert. to the gallbladder. **3.** Pert. to the urinary bladder.

cysticercoid (sĭs"tĭ-sĕr'koyd) [" + *kerkos*, tail, + *eidos*, form, shape] The larval encysted form of a tapeworm. It differs from a cysticercus in having a much reduced bladder.

cysticercosis (sĭs"tĭ-sĕr-kō'sĭs) [" + " + *osis*, condition] Infestation with the larvae of the pork tapeworm. It occurs when ingested *Taenia solium* larvae from uncooked pork burrow through the intestinal wall and are carried to other tissues through the blood. They may encyst in the heart, eyes, muscles, or brain. In the brain, they may cause a wide variety of neurological symptoms, including seizures. A patient history of eating undercooked pork or other meats may be helpful in establishing the diagnosis, esp. in adults with new-onset seizures who are found to have multiple cystic lesions in the brain.

TREATMENT: Anticonvulsants are used to control seizures. Antiparasitic drugs such as praziquantel or albendazole are effective.

cysticercus (sĭs"tĭ-sĕr'kŭs) *pl.* **cysticerci** The encysted larval form of a tapeworm, consisting of a rounded cyst or bladder into which the scolex is invaginated. SYN: *bladder worm*.

   c. cellulosae The bladder worm that is the larva of the pork tapeworm, *Taenia solium*.

cystic fibrosis SEE: under *fibrosis*.

cysticotomy (sĭs"tĭ-kŏt'ō-mē) [" + *tome*, incision] Incision of cystic bile duct. SYN: *choledochotomy*.

cystiform (sĭs'tĭ-form) [" + L. *forma*, form] Having the form of a cyst.

cystigerous (sĭs-tĭj'ĕr-ŭs) [" + L. *gerere*, to bear] Containing cysts.

cystine (sĭs'tēn) [Gr. *kystis*, bladder] $C_6H_{12}N_2S_2O_4$; a sulfur-containing amino acid produced by the action of acids on proteins that contain this compound. It is an important source of sulfur in metabolism.

cystinemia (sĭs"tĭ-nē'mē-ă) [*cystine* + Gr. *haima*, blood] The presence of cystine in the blood.

cystine storage disease An inherited disease of cystine metabolism resulting in abnormal deposition of cystine in body tissues. The cause is disordered proximal renal tubular function. Clinically, the child fails to grow and develops rickets, corneal opacities, and acidosis.

cystinosis (sĭs"tĭ-nō'sĭs) [" + Gr. *osis*, condition] A rare, autosomal recessive disorder, one of the lysosomal storage diseases, that results in the deposition of cystine crystals in body tissues. Affected children develop growth failure, rickets, renal tubular acidosis, hypothyroidism, and kidney failure, often followed by lung disease, sexual dysfunc-

tion, and neurological disorders. SEE: *cystine storage disease*.

cystinuria (sĭs"tĭ-nū'rē-ă) [" + *ouron*, urine] **1.** The presence of cystine in the urine. **2.** A hereditary metabolic disorder characterized by excretion of large amounts of cystine, lysine, arginine, and ornithine in the urine. It results in the development of recurrent urinary calculi.

cystitis (sĭs-tī'tĭs) [Gr. *kystis*, bladder, + *itis*, inflammation] Bladder inflammation usually occurring as a result of a urinary tract infection. Associated organs (kidney, prostate, urethra) may be involved. This condition may be acute or chronic. Females are affected 10 times more than males. Adult males and children may develop lower urinary tract infections from anatomic or physiologic abnormalities such as prostatic hypertrophy (adult men) or anomalies of the ureterovesicular junction. The infection usually is ascending, caused by a gram-negative enteric bacterium (e.g., *Escherichia coli, Klebsiella, Proteus, Enterobacter, Pseudomonas,* or *Serratia*), and occasionally by gram-positives (*Staphylococcus saprophyticus* or enterococci). When an indwelling catheter is present or the patient has a neurogenic bladder, multiple pathogens may be responsible. SEE: *Nursing Diagnoses Appendix*.

SYMPTOMS: Cystitis is marked by urinary urgency, frequency, and pain. Bladder spasms and perineal aching or fullness are also reported.

TREATMENT: Antibiotics are useful in treating the infection, but more definitive therapy is required if the basic cause is a kidney stone or a structural defect in the urinary tract such as obstruction.

PATIENT CARE: The patient is assessed for pain, burning, urinary frequency, bladder spasms, chills, and fever. The urinary bladder is palpated and percussed for distention. Volume and frequency of urinary output are monitored, and urine is inspected for cloudiness and gross hematuria. A clean-catch or catheterized specimen is sent to the laboratory for urinalysis and culture and sensitivity tests. Oral fluid intake is encouraged to dilute urine and to decrease pain on voiding. Heat is applied to the lower abdomen to decrease bladder spasms. Urinary antiseptics, analgesics, and antibiotics are administered and evaluated for therapeutic effectiveness and any adverse reactions. The patient is warned that urinary antiseptics such as phenazopyridine hydrochloride (Pyridium) will color the urine reddish orange and may stain fabric. The importance of follow-up urinalysis and culture testing to ensure that the cause of cystitis has been eliminated is emphasized in cases of recurrent disease.

interstitial c. A chronically painful inflammatory bladder condition, the etiology of which is often undetermined. It sometimes occurs as a result of exposure to drugs such as cyclophosphamide or ciprofloxacin but more often is idiopathic.

Most commonly, the disease is seen in women 30 to 70 years of age. The disease is not life-threatening, but the pain it causes can make a patient's life intolerable. The most common symptoms are urinary frequency, nocturia, and suprapubic pain on bladder filling. There is no curative medical therapy, but hydraulic distention of the bladder, intravesical instillations, transcutaneous electrical nerve stimulation, and antidepressants, as well as a variety of alternative medicines, have been tried, with variable success. Some patients are treated with urinary diversion procedures or cystectomy.

cystitomy (sĭs-tĭt′ō-mē) **1.** Surgical incision of a cavity. **2.** Incision of the capsule of the crystalline lens.

cysto-, cyst- [Gr. *kystis*, bladder] Prefixes meaning the *urinary bladder* or a *cyst*.

cystoadenoma (sĭs″tō-ăd″ĕ-nō′mă) [″ + *aden*, gland, + *oma*, tumor] A tumor containing cystic and adenomatous elements.

cystocele (sis′tŏ-sēl″) [*cysto-* + *-cele*] A bladder hernia that protrudes into the vagina. It occurs when the fascia separating the two organs is weakened or damaged, e.g., as a result of obstetrical or surgical trauma. SYN: *vesicocele*.

cystodiaphanoscopy (sĭs″tō-dī″ă-făn-ŏs′kō-pē) [″ + *dia*, through, + *phanein*, to shine, + *skopein*, to examine] Transillumination of the abdomen by an electric light in the bladder.

cystodynia (sĭs″tō-dĭn′ē-ă) [″ + *odyne*, pain] Cystalgia.

cystoelytroplasty (sĭs″tō-ē-lĭt′rō-plăs-tē) [″ + *elytron*, sheath, + *plassein*, to form] Repair of a vesicovaginal fistula.

cystoepiplocele (sĭs″tō-ē-pĭp′lō-sēl) [″ + *epiploon*, omentum, + *kele*, tumor, swelling] Herniation of a portion of the bladder and the omentum.

cystoepithelioma (sĭs″tō-ĕp″ĭ-thē″lē-ō′mă) [″ + *epi*, upon, + *thele*, nipple, + *oma*, tumor] Epithelioma in the stage of cystic degeneration.

cystofibroma (sĭs″tō-fĭ-brō′mă) [″ + L. *fibra*, fiber, + Gr. *oma*, tumor] Fibrous tumor containing cysts.

cystogastrostomy (sĭs″tō-găs-trŏs′tō-mē) [″ + *gaster*, stomach, + *stoma*, mouth] Joining an adjacent cyst, usually of the pancreas, to the stomach.

cystogram (sĭs′tō-grăm) [″ + *gramma*, something written] A radiograph of the bladder.

cystography (sĭs-tŏg′ră-fē) [″ + *graphein*, to write] Radiography of any cyst into which a contrast medium has been instilled, esp. the bladder.

cystoid (sĭs′toyd) [″ + *eidos*, form, shape] Resembling a cyst.

cystojejunostomy (sĭs″tō-jē-jū-nŏs′tō-mē) [″ + L. *jejunum*, empty, + Gr. *stoma*, mouth] Joining of an adjacent cyst to the jejunum.

cystolith (sĭs′tō-lĭth) [″ + *lithos*, stone] Vesical **calculus. cystolithic** (sĭs″tō-lĭth′ĭk), *adj.*

cystolithectomy (sĭs-tō-lĭ-thĕk′tō-mē) [″ + *lithos*, stone, + *ektome*, excision] Excision of a stone from the bladder.

cystolithiasis (sĭs-tō-lĭ-thī′ă-sĭs) [Gr. *kystis*, bladder, + *lithos*, stone, + *-iasis*, condition] Formation of stones in the bladder.

cystolitholapaxy (sĭs″tō-lĭth-ŏl′ă-păk-sē) [″ + ″] The removal of a kidney stone from the bladder by crushing the particles and extracting them by irrigation.

cystolutein (sĭs″tō-loo′tē-ĭn) [″ + L. *luteus*, yellow] Yellow pigment found in some ovarian cysts.

cystoma (sĭs-tō′mă) *pl.* **cystomata, cystomas** [″ + *oma*, tumor] A cystic tumor; a growth containing cysts.

cystometer (sĭs-tŏm′ĕ-tĕr) [″ + *metron*, measure] A device for estimating the capacity of the bladder and pressure changes in it during micturition.

cystometrography (sĭs″tō-mĕ-trŏg′ră-fē) [″ + ″ + *graphein*, to write] A graphic record of the pressure in the bladder at varying stages of filling.

cystopexy (sĭs′tō-pĕk″sē) [″ + *pexis*, fixation] Surgical fixation of the bladder to the wall of the abdomen.

cystoplasty (sĭs′tō-plăs′tē) [″ + *plassein*, to form] Plastic operation on the bladder.

cystoplegia (sĭs″tō-plē′jē-ă) [″ + *plege*, stroke] Paralysis of the bladder. **cycloplegic** (sī″klō-plē′jĭk), *adj.*

cystoproctostomy (sĭs″tō-prŏk-tŏs′tō-mē) [″ + *proktos*, rectum, + *stoma*, mouth] Surgical formation of a connection between the urinary bladder and the rectum.

cystoptosia, cystoptosis (sĭs″tŏp-tō′sē-ă, -sĭs) [″ + *ptosis*, a dropping] Prolapse into the urethra of the vesical mucous membrane.

cystoradiography (sĭs″tō-rā″dē-ŏg′ră-fē) [″ + L. *radius*, ray, + Gr. *graphein*, to write] Radiography of the gallbladder or urinary bladder.

cystorrhaphy (sĭst-or′ă-fē) [″ + *rhaphe*, seam, ridge] Surgical suture of the bladder.

cystorrhea (sĭs″tō-rē′ă) [″ + *rhoia*, flow] A discharge of mucus from the urinary bladder.

cystorrhexis (sĭs″tō-rĕk′sĭs) [″ + *rhexis*, rupture] Rupture of the bladder.

cystosarcoma (sĭs″tō-săr-kō′mă) [″ + *sarx*, flesh, + *oma*, tumor] A sarcoma containing cysts or cystic formations.

cystoscope (sĭst′ō-skōp) [″ + *skopein*, to examine] An instrument for interior examination of bladder and ureter. It is introduced through the urethra into the bladder.

cystoscopy (sĭs-tos′kŏ-pē) [*cysto-* + *-scopy*] Examination of the bladder with a cystoscope, usually to evaluate the bladder for a source of bleeding or a tumor.

cystospasm (sĭs′tō-spăzm) [Gr. *kystis*, bladder, + *spasmos*, a convulsion] A spasmodic contraction of the urinary bladder.

cystostomy (sĭs-tŏs′tō-mē) [″ + *stoma*, mouth] Surgical creation of an opening into the bladder.

   suprapubic c. Surgical opening of the bladder from just above the symphysis pubis; any of several catheters are placed in the opening to facilitate drainage.

cystotome, cystitome (sĭs′tō-tōm) [″ + *tome*, incision] An instrument for incision into the sac of the crystalline lens or of the bladder.

cystotomy (sĭs-tŏt′ō-mē) [″ + *tome*, incision] Incision of the bladder.

cystotrachelotomy (sĭs″tō-trā″kē-lŏt′ō-mē) [″ + *trachelos*, neck, + *tome*, incision] Incision into the neck of the bladder.

cystoureteritis (sĭs″tō-ū-rē″tĕr-ī′tĭs) [″ + *oureter*, ureter, + *itis*, inflammation] Inflammation of the ureter and urinary bladder.

cystoureterogram (sĭs″tō-ū-rē′tĕr-ō-grăm) [″ + ″ + *gramma*, something written] A radiograph of the bladder and ureter obtained after instillation of a contrast medium.

cystourethritis (sĭs″tō-ū″rē-thrī′tĭs) [″ + *ourethra*, urethra, + *itis*, inflammation] Inflammation of the urinary bladder and urethra.

cystourethrocele (sĭs″tō-ū-rē′thrō-sēl) [″ + ″ + *kele*, tumor, swelling] Prolapse of the bladder and urethra of the female.

cystourethrography (sĭs″tō-ū″rē-throg′ră-fē) [*cysto-* + *urethrography,*] Radiography of the bladder and urethra with a radiopaque contrast medium. **cystourethrographic** (-ū-rē″thrō-graf′ik), *adj*.

   chain c. Radiography in which a sterile beaded radiopaque chain is introduced into the bladder by a special catheter so that one end of the chain is in the bladder and the other extends outside via the urethra. This examination is useful in demonstrating anatomical relationships, esp. in women with persistent urinary incontinence.

   voiding c. ABBR: VCUG. Cystourethrography done before, during, and after voiding.

PATIENT CARE: A VCUG is used to identify vesicoureteral reflux in children between the ages of 2 and 24 months if they experience two or more urinary tract infections. The test may also be used to evaluate the bladder for fistulae, foreign bodies, obstruction, trauma, or tumors. Patients, esp. children, benefit from analgesia and anxiolysis before and during the procedure. The patient, caregivers, and professional staff are shielded from radiation exposure. The patient is placed in a frog-legged, supine position. A urinary catheter is inserted into the urethra under sterile conditions. Contrast agent (warmed to body temperature) is infused into the bladder. Fluoroscopic images of the lower urinary tract are recorded during voiding, which is often accomplished with the patient standing upright after the bladder is filled.

⚠ A VCUG should not be performed during pregnancy (because of the risk of radiation exposure) or during active urinary infections. Any allergy to the contrast medium used during the procedure should be assessed before it is infused.

cystourethropexy, retropubic (sĭs″tō-ū-rē′thrō-pĕks-ē) A general term for a surgical procedure for correction of stress urinary incontinence.

cystovesiculography (sĭs″tō-vĕ-sĭk-ū-lŏg′ră-fē) Radiography of the bladder and seminal vesicles after instillation of a contrast medium.

cytapheresis (sīt″a-fĕ-rē′sĭs, ′sēz″) *pl.* **cytaphereses** [*cyto-* + *apheresis*] A kind of apheresis in which cellular material is removed from a donor's or patient's blood. SEE: *apheresis*.

-cyte (sīt) [Gr. *kytos*, cell] Suffix meaning *cell*.

cytidine (sī′tĭ-dĭn) A nucleoside that is one of the four main riboside components of ribonucleic acid. It consists of a cytosine and D-ribose.

cyto-, cyt- [Gr. *kytos*, cell] Prefixes meaning *cell*.

cytoanalyzer (sī″tō-ăn″ă-lī′zĕr) An automated device for detecting malignant cells in microscopic preparations or in fluids. It is used in conjunction with professional analysis.

cytoarchitectonic (sī″tō-ărk″ĭ-tĕk-tŏn′ĭk) [″ + *architektonike*, architecture] Pert. to structure and arrangement of cells.

cytobiology (sī″tō-bī-ŏl′ō-jē) [″ + *bios*, life, + *logos*, word, reason] Biology of cells.

cytobiotaxis (sī″tō-bī-ō-tăk′sĭs) [″ + ″ + *taxis*, arrangement] The influence of living cells on other living cells. SYN: *cytoclesis*.

cytobroom (sī′tō-broom″) [″ + *broom*] A plastic, broom-shaped device used to sample cells from the cervix and endocervix during liquid-based cytological sampling of the uterine cervix for malignant and premalignant cells.

cytobrush (sī′tō-brŭsh″) A miniature brush used to sample cells from the vagina, cervix, or endocervix for Papanicolaou testing. SEE: *Papaniculaou test* for illus.

cytocentrum (sī″tō-sĕn′trŭm) [″ + *kentron,* center] The area of cytoplasm that contains the centrioles. SYN: *centrosome.* SEE: *sphere, attraction.*

cytochalasin B (sī″tō-kăl′ă-sĭn) A chemical that destroys the contractile microfilaments in cells. This fragments cells and permits the fragments to be investigated.

cytochemistry (sī″tō-kĕm′ĭs-trē) The chemistry of the living cell.

cytochrome (sī′tō-krōm) [″ + *chroma,* color] An iron-containing protein found in the mitochondria of eukaryotic cells; each is given a letter name (a, b, c). The cytochrome transport system (electron transport chain) is the last stage in aerobic cell respiration. SEE: *c. oxidase; c. P450; cytochrome transport system.*

   c. P450 ABBR: CYP. A group of enzymes present in every type of cell in the body except red blood cells and skeletal muscle cells. They are important in metabolizing substances normally present in the body such as steroids, fat-soluble vitamins, fatty acids, prostaglandins, and alkaloids. The P450 enzymes also detoxify drugs and a great number of environmental pollutants, such as carcinogens present in tobacco smoke and charcoal-broiled meat, polychlorinated biphenyls, and dioxin. Specialized types of cytochrome P450 are involved in the synthesis of nitric oxide.

cytochrome transport system Electron transport **chain.**

cytocide (sī′tō-sīd) An agent that kills cells. **cytocidal** (sī″tō-sī′dăl), *adj.*

cytoclasis (sī″tŏk′lă-sĭs) [″ + *klasis,* destruction] Destruction of cells. **cytoclastic** (sī″tō-klăs′tĭk), *adj.*

cytoclesis (sī″tō-klē′sĭs) [″ + *klesis,* a call] Cytobiotaxis.

cytodiagnosis (sī″tō-dī″ăg-nō′sĭs) [″ + *dia,* through, + *gignoskein,* to know] Diagnosis of pathogenic conditions by the study of cells present in exudates and fluids.

cytodieresis (sī″tō-dī-ĕr′ē-sĭs) [″ + *diairesis,* division] Cytokinesis.

cytodistal (sī″tō-dĭs′tăl) [″ + *distare,* to be distant] Pert. to a neoplasm remote from the cell of origin.

cytofluorometry (sī″tō-floo″ŏr-ŏm′ĕ-trē) Flow **cytometry.**

cytogenesis (sī″tō-jĕn′ĕs-ĭs) [″ + *genesis,* generation, birth] Origin and development of the cell. **cytogenic** (sī-tō-jĕn′ĭk), *adj.*

cytogenetics (sī″tō-jĕ-nĕt′ĭks) The study of the structure and function of chromosomes. Clinically, the science of cytogenetics has been applied to the diagnosis and management of congenital disorders. The diagnosis of some fetal abnormalities can be made by chromosomal analysis of chorionic villus samples as early as 8 to 14 weeks' gestation. SEE: *amniocentesis; chorionic villus sampling.*

cytogenous (si-tŏj′ĕn-ŭs) [″ + *gennan,* to produce] Producing cells.

cytogeny (sī-tŏj′ĕ-nē) [″ + *genesis,* generation, birth] The formation and development of the cell.

cytogerontology (sī″tō-jĕ-rŏn-tŏl′ō-jē) The study of cell aging developed by Leonard Hayflick.

cytoglycopenia (sī″tō-glī-kō-pē′nē-ă) [″ + *glykys,* sweet, + *penia,* poverty] Deficient glucose of blood cells; also called cytoglucopenia.

cytohistogenesis (sī″tō-hĭs″tō-jĕn′ĕ-sĭs) [″ + *histos,* web, + *genesis,* generation, birth] The structural development of cells.

cytoid (sī′toyd) [″ + *eidos,* form, shape] Resembling a cell.

cytoinhibition (sī″tō-ĭn″hĭ-bĭsh′ŭn) [″ + L. *inhibere,* to restrain] Impairment of the growth or functioning of cells.

cytokeratin (sīt″ō-ker′ăt-ĭn) [*cyto-* + *keratin*] ABBR: CK. . Any of the intermediate-sized filament proteins found in epithelial cells. Antibodies against CKs are used to detect specific cell types. The detection of unique CKs helps in the immunohistochemical identification of the origin of specific cancers.

cytokine (sīt′ō-kīn″) Any of more than 100 proteins produced primarily by white blood cells. They provide signals to regulate immunological aspects of cell growth and function during both inflammation and specific immune response. Each cytokine is secreted by a specific cell in response to a specific stimulus. Cytokines produced by monocytes or macrophages and lymphocytes are called monokines and lymphokines, respectively. Cytokines include the interleukins, interferons, tumor necrosis factors, erythropoietin, and colony-stimulating factors. They act by changing the cells that produce them (autocrine effect) and altering other cells close to them (paracrine effect); a few affect cells systemically (endocrine effect). SEE: *granulocyte-macrophage colony-stimulating* **factor***; immune response; inflammation; interferon; interleukin; macrophage; tumor necrosis* **factor***.*

   proinflammatory c. Any of the circulating substances in the blood that deplete lean body mass in critical illness.

They include several interleukins (IL-1, IL-6, and IL-8) and tumor necrosis factor.

cytokinesis (sī″tō-kĭ-nē′sĭs) [″ + *kinesis,* movement] The separation of the cytoplasm into two parts, a process that follows the division of the cell nucleus (mitosis). SYN: *cytodieresis.*

cytokine storm (sīt′ō-kīn″) SEE: under *storm.*

cytologist (sī″tŏl′ō-jĭst) A person trained in cytology.

cytology (sī-tol′ŏ-jē) [*cyto-* + *-logy*] The science that deals with the formation, structure, and function of cells. **cytologic, cytological** (sīt″ŏ-loj′ik, ′ĭ-kăl), *adj.*

 exfoliative c. Microscopic examination of cells obtained from body excretions, e.g., from the anus or genitourinary tract.

 imprint c. The study of cellular morphology or of tissue diseases after a clinical specimen, e.g., a bone marrow biopsy, is dabbed on a microscope slide. It is used in some settings as an adjunct or alternative to fine needle aspiration biopsy, frozen sectioning, and other pathological techniques.

 liquid-based c. ABBR: LBC. A means of performing a Papanicolaou test (Pap test) in which the head of the plastic spatula used to obtain cells from the endocervix is inserted directly into a vial containing a fluid cellular preservative. The vial is spun in the laboratory, and a pellet of pure cells is obtained. This cellular layer is then deposited on a microscope slide and examined for evidence of cellular atypia or frank cancer. The liquid-based cytology differs from traditional cervical cytology in that the contents of the spatula are not smeared directly onto a microscope slide. This reduces the number of specimens received by the laboratory that are unable to be interpreted pathologically.

 sputum c. The examination of cells obtained from mucus in the upper or lower respiratory tract to see if cancer cells are present. SEE: *sputum specimen.*

cytolysin (sī-tŏl′ĭ-sĭn) [″ + *lysis,* dissolution] **1.** An antibody that causes disintegration of cells. **2.** A molecule in cytotoxic T lymphocytes that enhances their ability to kill by creating pores in the plasma membranes of microorganisms through which proteolytic enzymes pass.

cytolysis (sī-tŏl′ĭ-sĭs) Dissolution or destruction of living cells.

cytomegalovirus (sīt″ō-meg″ă-lō-vī′rŭs) [*cyto-* + *megalo-* + *virus*] A widely distributed species-specific herpesvirus; in humans, it inhabits many different tissues and causes cytomegalic inclusion disease (cytomegalovirus infec-

tion). SYN: *human herpesvirus 5.* SEE: *cytomegalovirus infection.*

cytomegalovirus infection SEE: under *infection.*

cytometaplasia (sī″tō-mĕt″ă-plā′zē-ă) [Gr. *kytos,* cell, + *metaplasis,* change] Change in form or function of cells.

cytometer (sī-tŏm′ĕ-ter) [″ + *metron,* measure] An instrument for counting and measuring cells.

 flow c. A device for measuring thousands of cells as they are forced one at a time through a focused light beam, usually a laser. Cells studied by this device need to be in an evenly dispersed suspension.

cytometry (sī-tŏm′ĕ-trē) The counting and measuring of cells.

 flow c. A technique for analyzing individual cells passing through a detector system. In one method, the cells are tagged with a monoclonal antibody carrying a fluorescent label. They pass through the detector at about 10,000 cells per second. Flow cytometry has many clinical and research applications. These include analysis of cell size, structure, and viability; examination of DNA and RNA in the cells; determination of pH in the cells; and chromosome analysis. Flow cytometry is also used to determine the percentages of cells in various stages of development in a population, making it possible to estimate the extent or controllability of a malignant tumor. Monitoring the number of populations of T cells, B cells, and T helper and suppressor cells and using that information to calculate the helper/suppressor ratio assist in determining the patient's immune status. Flow cytometry has been used in monitoring survival of transplanted organs and tissues such as bone marrow. SYN: *cytofluorometry.* SEE: *cell sorting.*

cytomitome (sī″tō-mī′tōm) [″ + *mitos,* thread] The fibrils or microtubules of the cytoplasm.

cytomix (sī′tō-mĭks) [Gr. *kytos,* cell, + L. *mistura,* mixture] A mixture of cytokines containing tumor necrosis factor, interleukin-1 beta, and gamma interferon.

cytomodulatory (sī″tō-mŏj′ŏl-ŏ-tawr″ē, -mŏ′dūl-) [″ + modulatory] Capable of altering cells, esp. their growth, immune responsiveness, or reproduction.

cytomorphology (sī″tō-mor-fŏl′ō-jē) [″ + *morphe,* form, + *logos,* word, reason] The study of the structure of cells.

cytomorphosis (sī″tō-mor-fō′sĭs) [″ + ″ + *osis,* condition] The changes in a cell during its life cycle.

cyton (sī′tŏn) [Gr. *kytos,* cell] **1.** A cell. **2.** The cell body of a neuron. SYN: *perikaryon.*

cytopathic (sī″tō-păth′ĭk) [″ + *pathos,* disease] Concerning pathological changes in cells, esp. those injured or destroyed by viruses or other microorganisms. SYN: *cytopathogenic*.

cytopathogenic (sī″tō-păth″ō-jĕn′ĭk) [″ + *pathos*, disease, + *gennan*, to produce] Cytopathic.

cytopathology (sī″tō-păth-ŏl′ō-jē) [″ + ″ + *logos*, word, reason] The study of the cellular changes in disease.

cytopenia (sī″tŏ-pē′nē-ă) [″ + *penia*, lack] Decrease in the number of the cells in blood or other tissue.

cytophagocytosis (sī″tō-făg″ō-sī-tō′sĭs) [″ + *phagein*, to eat, + *kytos*, cell, + *osis*, condition] Cytophagy.

cytophagy (sī-tŏf′ă-jē) The destruction of other cells by phagocytes. SYN: *cytophagocytosis*.

cytophotometry (sī″tŏ-fō-tŏm′ĕ-trē) SEE: *flow cytometry*.

cytophysiology (sī″tō-fĭz-ē-ŏl′ō-jē) [″ + *physis*, nature, + *logos*, word, reason] Physiology of the cell.

cytoplasm (sīt′ŏ-plazm) [*cyto-* + *-plasm*] The protoplasm of a cell outside the nucleus. SEE: *cell*. **cytoplasmic** (sīt″ŏ-plaz′mik), *adj*.

cytoplast (sī′tō-plăst) The cytoplasm of a cell as distinguished from the contents of the nucleus.

cytoprotective (sī″tō-prō-tĕk′tĭv) [Gr. *kytos*, cell, + L.L. *protegere*, to protect, to cover] Capable of shielding cells from injury, e.g., damage from electrolyte disturbance, infection, ischemia, or toxins.

cytoreduction (sīt″ō-rĕ-dŭk′shŭn) [″ + ″] Cellular killing, usually of cancerous cell clones, with chemotherapy. **cytoreductive** (-dŭk′-tĭv), *adj*.

cytoscopy (sī-tŏs′kō-pē) [″ + *skopein*, to examine] Microscopic examination of cells for diagnostic purposes.

cytosine (sī′tō-sīn) $C_4H_5N_3O$; a pyrimidine base that is part of DNA and RNA. In DNA it is paired with guanine.

cytoskeleton (sī″tō-skĕl′ĕ-tŏn) The internal structural framework of a cell consisting of three types of filaments: microfilaments, microtubules, and intermediate filaments. These form a dynamic framework for maintaining cell shape and allowing rapid changes in the three-dimensional structure of the cell.

cytosol (sī′tō-sŏl) The fluid of cytoplasm, an aqueous solution of ions and nutrients.

cytosome (sī′tō-sōm) [″ + *soma*, body] The portion of a cell exclusive of the nucleus.

cytostasis (sī-tŏs′tă-sĭs) [Gr. *kytos*, cell, + *stasis*, standing still] Stasis of white blood cells, as in the early stage of inflammation.

cytostatic (sī″tŏ-stăt′ĭk) [″ + *stasis*, standing still] Preventing the growth and proliferation of cells.

cytotactic (sī″tō-tăk′tĭk) Pert. to cytotaxia.

cytotaxia, cytotaxis (sī-tō-tăk′sē-ă, -sĭs) [″ + *taxis*, arrangement] Attraction or repulsion of cells for each other.

cytotechnologist (sī″tŏ-tĕk″nŏl′ă-jĭst) A medical laboratory technologist who works under the supervision of a pathologist to examine cells in order to diagnose cancer or other diseases.

cytotechnology (sī″tŏ-tĕk-nŏl′ō-jē) Microscopic examination of cells to identify abnormalities.

cytotherapy (sī″tŏ-thĕr′ă-pē) [″ + *therapeia*, treatment] **1.** Hormonotherapy. **2.** Use of cytotoxic or cytolytic substances or serums to treat disease.

cytotoxic agent SEE: under *agent*.

cytotoxicity, antibody-dependent cell-mediated (sī″tō-tŏk-sĭs′ĭ-tē) ABBR: ADCC. The increased ability of natural killer (NK) cells and eosinophils to bind with foreign antigens coated with IgG antibodies and destroy them. When receptors on NK cells bind to the antibody's Fc fragment, they are stimulated to produce interferon gamma and degranulate, releasing destructive enzymes that kill cells infected with a virus. The presence of antibodies differentiates ADCC from T-cell cytotoxicity, which does not require their presence.

cytotoxin (sī″tō-tŏk′sĭn) [″ + *toxikon*, poison] An antibody or toxin that attacks the cells of particular organs. SEE: *endotoxin; exotoxin; leukocidin; lysis; neurotoxin*. **cytotoxic** (sī″tō-tŏks′ĭk), *adj*.

cytotrophoblast (sīt″ŏ-trō′fŏ-blast″) [*cyto-* + *trophoblast*] The thin inner layer of the trophoblast composed of cuboidal cells and anchoring the embryonic chorion to the maternal endometrium. SYN: *Langhans layer*. SEE: *trophoblast*.

cytotropic (sī″tō-trŏp′ĭk, -trōp′ĭk) [″ + *trope*, a turn] Having an affinity for cells.

cytotropism (sī-tŏt′rō-pĭzm) [″ + *trope*, a turn, + *-ismos*, condition] The movement of cells toward or away from a stimulus such as drugs, viruses, bacteria, or physical conditions such as heat or cold.

cytozoon (sī-tō-zō′ŏn) A protozoon that lives as an intracellular parasite.

cyturia (sĭ-tū′rē-ă) [Gr. *kytos*, cell, + *ouron*, urine] The presence of any kind of cells in the urine.

Czermak spaces (cher′mak″) [Johann Czermak, Ger. physiologist, 1828–1873] The interglobular spaces in dentin caused by failure of calcification. SYN: *interglobular spaces*.

Δ, δ Uppercase and lowercase delta, respectively; the fourth letter of the Greek alphabet.

D 1. L. *da*, give; *date; daughter; deciduous;* L. *detur*, let it be given; *died; diopter; divorced; doctor; permeability.* **2.** Symbol for the element deuterium.

d *density;* L. *dexter* or *dextro*, right; L. *dies*, day; *distal; dorsal; duration.*

D1 The first diagonal artery that branches off from the left anterior descending (LAD) coronary artery. Similarly, D2 is the second diagonal branch of the LAD.

D- In biochemistry, a prefix indicating the structure of certain organic compounds with asymmetric carbon atoms. If a carbon atom is attached to four different substituent groups that can be arranged in two ways and represent nonsuperimposable mirror images, it is classed as asymmetrical. The name of such a compound is preceded by D. When there are only three dissimilar groups around the carbon atom, only one configuration in space is possible. The carbon atom is classed as symmetrical (or chiral), and the name is preceded by L.

In other chemical nomenclature, a lower-case *d-* or *l-* indicates the rotational direction of a polarized light shined through a solution of the compound. When the plane of the light is rotated to the right (i.e., is dextrorotatory), the compound's name is preceded by *d-*. When the light is rotated to the left (i.e., is levorotatory), the name is preceded by *l-*.

If a D compound that has an asymmetrical carbon can also rotate light and is dextrorotatory, its name is preceded by D(+); if levorotatory, by D(−). If the asymmetrical carbon is of the L form and is dextrorotatory, its name is prefixed by L(+); if it is levorotatory, the name is preceded by L(−).

D/A *digital to analog.*

Da *dalton.*

dacry- [Gr. *dakryon*, a tear] Prefix meaning *tears, lacrimal gland, lacrimal apparatus.*

dacryocystectomy (dăk″rē-ō-sĭs-těk′tō-mē) [″ + *kystis*, cyst, + *ektome*, excision] Excision of membranes of the lacrimal sac.

dacryocystitis (dăk″rē-ō-sĭs-tī′tĭs) [″ + ″ + *itis*, inflammation] Inflammation of a lacrimal sac, including its mucous and submucous membranes. It may occasionally extend the surrounding connective tissue and cause periorbital cel-

lulitis. It is usually secondary to prolonged obstruction of a nasolacrimal duct.

SYMPTOMS: The symptoms are profuse tearing (epiphora); redness and swelling in the lacrimal sac, which may also extend to the lids and conjunctiva; and pain, esp. on pressure over the sac.

TREATMENT: Hot compresses should be applied to the area. Appropriate topical and systemic antibiotic therapy depend on the organisms isolated from the inflamed area. The physician should incise and drain the sac if it is fluctuant; attempt to restore permeability of the duct with a probe when acute symptoms have subsided; and in chronic cases, extirpate the sac or perform an intranasal operation (dacryocystorhinostomy).

dacryocystocele (dăk″rē-ō-sĭs′tō-sēl) [Gr. *dakryon*, tear, + *kystis*, cyst, + *kele*, tumor, swelling] A herniated protrusion of a lacrimal sac.

dacryocystorhinostomy (dăk″rē-ō-sĭs″tō-rī-nŏs′tō-mē) [″ + ″ + ″ + *stoma*, mouth] Surgical connection of the lumen of a lacrimal sac with the nasal cavity.

dacryocystotomy (dăk″rē-ō-sĭs-tŏt′ō-mē) Incision of a lacrimal sac.

dacryostenosis (dăk″rē-ō-stěn-ō′sĭs) [″ + *stenosis*, act of narrowing] Obstruction or narrowing of a lacrimal or nasal duct.

dactyl (dăk′tĭl) [Gr. *daktylos*, finger] A finger or toe; a digit of the hand or foot.

-dactylia, -dactylism, -dactyly [L. *-dactylia*, fr Gr *daktylos*, finger + *-ia*] Suffix meaning *having such a kind of digit or digits or having so many digits.*

dactylitis (dăk″tĭ-lī′tĭs) [″ + *itis*, inflammation] Inflammation of the fingers or toes, resulting in a sausage-shaped appearance of the digits. Dactylitis is a common finding in reactive arthritis.

dactylo-, dactyl- [Gr. *daktylos*, finger, toe] Prefixes meaning *finger* or *toe.*

dactylus (dăk′tĭ-lŭs) [Gr. *daktylos*] Digit.

Dale reaction (dāl) [Sir Henry H. Dale, 1875–1968, Brit. scientist and Nobel Prize winner in 1936] A test formerly used to demonstrate the ability of muscle tissues from an anaphylactic organism to contract on reexposure to the antigen. SYN: *Schultz reaction.*

dalton (dolt′ŏn) [John *Dalton*] SYMB: Da. An arbitrary unit of mass equal to ¹⁄₁₂ the mass of carbon 12, or 1.657×-10^{-24} g. It is used to describe the mass of large molecules such as proteins. SYN: *atomic mass unit.*

Dalton's law [John Dalton, Brit. chemist, 1766–1844] A law that states that, in a mixture of gases, the total pressure is equal to the sum of the partial pressures of each gas.

DALY *disability-adjusted life year.*

dam **1.** A thin sheet of latex used in dentistry and oral surgery to isolate a part from the surrounding tissues and fluids. SYN: *dental d.; rubber dam.* **2.** A barrier made of flexible material, such as latex, that prevents body fluids from entering the mouth during oral sex (cunnilingus or fellatio). It is used as a shield against sexually transmitted infections.

   dental d. Dam (1).

damage-control laparotomy SEE: under *laparotomy.*

damages The compensation or payment awarded by the courts to an injured party.

   compensatory d. In a lawsuit, money awarded to an injured individual to repay that person for the actual costs that have resulted from the injury. The damages should restore the injured party to his or her preinjury status.

   punitive d. Damages awarded in an amount intended to punish the defendant for the egregious nature of the tort. The defendant's actions must be willful and wanton, and the damages are not based on the plaintiff's actual monetary loss.

damp **1.** Moist, humid. **2.** A noxious gas in a mine.

damping Steady diminution of the amplitude of successive vibrations, as of an electric wave or current.

dance therapy, dance movement therapy The use of creative dance and movement for healing.

dancing eyes–dancing feet syndrome, dancing eyes, dancing feet syndrome Opsoclonus myoclonus syndrome.

D and C *dilation and curettage.*

D and E *dilation and evacuation of the uterus.* SEE: *dilation and curettage.*

dandelion (dan′dĕl-ī″ŏn) [Fr *dent de lion,* lion's tooth] A common weed (*Taraxacum officinale*) used in folk and alternative medicine as an anti-inflammatory, a diuretic, a laxative, and as a tonic for digestive problems. It induces a contact allergy in some individuals. Dandelion water extract (DWE) made from the plant is used as an herbal antioxidant.

dander (dăn′dĕr) Small scales from the skin, hair, or feathers of animals, which may provoke allergic reactions in sensitized individuals.

dandruff Scale that exfoliates from the outer layer of the skin, esp. from the scalp.

   TREATMENT: Several over-the-counter products, including salicylic acid, pyrithione zinc, and selenium sulfide, provide effective treatment.

Dandy-Walker syndrome (dăn′dē-wawk′ĕr) [Walter E. Dandy, U.S. neurosurgeon, 1886–1946; Arthur E. Walker, U.S. surgeon, 1907–1995] A congenital brain malformation characterized by fourth ventricle (posterior fossa) cystic dilation, hydrocephalus, and improper formation of the cerebellar vermis.

   TREATMENT: Treatments sometimes include cyst drainage or ventriculoperitoneal shunting.

Dane particle (dān) [David S. Dane, contemporary Brit. virologist] The hepatitis B virus.

dangerous abbreviations, acronyms, and symbols A shortened version of a word or phrase that may be misinterpreted because of its similarity in print or cursive handwriting to another word or phrase with a different meaning. Some examples of dangerous abbreviations are cc, D/C, q.d., and U.

danshen (dahn-shĕn) [Chinese *dān shēn*] Salvia miltiorrhiza.

dardarin (dăr-dăr′ŭ) [Basque *dardara,* tremor] A protein whose presence in the body has been associated with an autosomal dominant (familial) form of Parkinson's disease. SYN: *leucine-rich repeat kinase 2.*

Darier, Ferdinand Jean (dar-yā′) French dermatologist, 1856–1938.

   D. disease A rare autosomal dominant skin disease characterized by numerous warty papules that merge into large plaques. The lesions often become infected and may have an offensive odor. SYN: *keratosis follicularis.*

   D. sign The skin change produced when the skin lesion in urticaria pigmentosa is rubbed briskly. The area usually begins to itch and becomes raised and surrounded by erythema. SEE: *mastocytosis; urticaria pigmentosa.*

dark reactions Any enzymatically mediated chemical reaction that takes place in the absence of light. One example is the series of light-independent reactions that produce glucose from carbon dioxide and cellular energy sources.

darkroom A room designed to be devoid of light. The darkroom is necessary for the development of older forms of radiographic film.

Darmstadtium (darm″stat′ē-ŭm) [*Darmstadt,* Germany + *-ium*] SYMB: Ds. A synthesized radioactive metallic element with a very short half-life; atomic mass 281; atomic number 110. The half-life of isotope ^{281}Ds is about 10 sec.

dartos (dăr′tŏs) [Gr.] The muscular, contractile tissue beneath the skin of the scrotum.

darwinism (dăr'wĭ-nĭzm) The theory of biological evolution through natural selection.

data *sing.*, **datum 1.** Individual raw facts that have not yet been interpreted, organized, or evaluated. **2.** A body of facts or information obtained by observation or research.

interim d. Scientific information that is studied part way through a medical research project to see whether there are hazards associated with the study or clear benefits from one treatment or another.

database A collection of data that is organized so that its contents can easily be accessed, managed, and updated. Databases are used to manage and archive large amounts of information.

data modeling 1. The analysis of data, e.g., to make a practical impact on health care practices or business operations. **2.** A language for describing the structure and processing of a database.

data repository 1. Computer storage. **2.** A program that optimizes storage, retrieval, and processing of very large collections of data.

data safety monitoring board, data and safety monitoring board ABBR: DSMB. An independent group of scientists and concerned community members who oversee the interim findings of a research project to determine whether the research undertaken is proceeding without evidence of harm to the subjects enrolled in the study.

data warehouse A central repository for the data collected by the various computer systems of an enterprise.

datum, data 1. A single piece or item of information, e.g., a statistic, date, or fact. **2.** Something admitted, given, or assumed, esp. as a basis for reasoning.

Datura (dă-tū'ră) A genus of plants, one member of which, *Datura stramonium*, contains constituents of hyoscyamine and scopolamine, which have anticholinergic properties.

daughter (daw'tĕr) **1.** The product of the decay of a radioactive element. **2.** A product of cell division, as a daughter cell or daughter nucleus. **3.** One's female child.

DAWN *Drug Abuse Warning Network.* The network was renamed "New DAWN" in 2003.

dawn phenomenon (don) A marked increase in insulin requirements between 6 A.M. and 9 A.M. as compared with the midnight to 6 A.M. period. It is caused by hepatic gluconeogenesis. The increased dose of insulin required during this period contrasts with the Somogyi phenomenon, which is managed by decreasing insulin during the critical period. Dawn phenomenon may occur in those with diabetes mellitus of either type and in some normal people. SEE: *diabetes mellitus.*

day care center SEE: under *center.*

daydream Mental musing or fantasy while awake.

dazzle Dimming of vision due to intense stimulus of very bright light. SEE: *glare.*

dB, db *decibel.*

DC *Dichorionic; direct* **current**; *Doctor of Chiropractic.*

dc, d/c *discontinue.*

DCIS *ductal carcinoma in situ.*

DDH *Developmental* **dislocation** *of the hip.*

D-dimer (dē'dī'mĕr) A by-product of the degradation of blood clots, specifically, of the fibrin within a clot. The presence of an elevated level of D-dimer in the setting of a suspected pulmonary embolus or deep venous thrombosis is justification for further testing. The absence of D-dimer in plasma is used to help exclude a diagnosis of deep venous thrombosis or pulmonary embolism when the test is performed with an enzyme-linked immunosorbent assay (ELISA).

DDT Dichlorodiphenyltrichloroethane, now called chlorophenothane; a powerful insecticide effective against a wide variety of insects, esp. the flea, fly, louse, mosquito, bedbug, cockroach, Japanese beetle, and European corn borer. However, many species develop resistant populations, and birds and fish that feed on affected insects suffer toxic effects. In 1972, the U.S. banned DDT except for essential public health use and a few minor uses to protect crops for which there were no effective alternatives.

When ingested orally, it may cause acute poisoning. Symptoms are vomiting, numbness and partial paralysis of limbs, anorexia, tremors, and coma, resulting in death. SEE: *Poisons and Poisoning Appendix.*

de- [L. *de,* from, down from] Prefix meaning *down* or *from.* or to signify removal (as in *decamp*) or privation (as in *delouse*).

deacidification (dē"ă-sĭd"ĭ-fĭ-kā'shŭn) [" + *acidus,* sour, + *facere,* to make] Neutralization of acidity.

deactivation (dē-ăk-tĭ-vā'shŭn) [" + *activus,* acting] The process of becoming or making inactive.

dead [AS. *dead*] Without life or life processes. SEE: *death.*

dead-end host SEE: under *host.*

dead space SEE: under *space.*

dead tooth A nonvital tooth by clinical standards, having had the pulp removed by endodontic treatment. The term is a poor choice because, if the periodontal tissues are healthy, the tooth will continue to function without symptoms.

deaf [AS. *deaf*] **1.** Partially or completely lacking the sense of hearing. **2.** Unwilling to listen; heedless.

deafferentation (dē-ăf″ĕr-ĕn-tā′shŭn) Cutting off of the afferent nerve supply. SEE: *denervation*.

deaf-mute A person who is unable to hear or speak. See http://www.nad.org/infocenter/infotogo/dcc/terms.html. According to the National Association for the Deaf, this term is offensive.

deaf-mutism The state of being both deaf and unable to speak.

deafness (def′nĕs) Complete or partial loss of the ability to hear. The deficit may be temporary or permanent. More than 20 million Americans have hearing impairment; most of them are over 65; about 5% are children. Hereditary forms of hearing impairment affect about 1 newborn in 2000. In this population hearing deficits may impair language acquisition and speech. Acquired hearing loss affects the lives of nearly half of all people over 80, in whom it may be a prominent cause of social isolation or depression. SYN: *hearing loss*.

ETIOLOGY: Hearing impairment has multiple causes. Congenital deafness occurs during pregnancy or delivery and in such syndromes as neurofibromatosis or Usher syndrome. Toxic deafness may result from exposure to such agents as salicylates, diuretics, or aminoglycoside antibiotics or be due to infections of the central nervous system (meningococcal meningitis, syphilis) or of the eighth cranial nerve. Many viruses may contribute to loss of hearing, as may prolonged or repetitive exposures to environmental noise. Otosclerosis is an example of bilateral conductive hearing loss due to progressive ossification of the annular ligaments of the ear. Presbycusis is an otologic effect of aging resulting from the loss of hair cells in the organ of Corti and leading to progressive, symmetrical, bilateral sensorineural hearing loss, esp. of high-frequency tones. Sudden hearing loss may result from ear trauma, fistulae, stroke, drug exposures, cancer, multiple sclerosis, vasculitis, or Ménière disease. Not infrequently, adult patients with unilateral conductive hearing loss have a cerumen impaction.

DIAGNOSIS: Simple bedside tests (such as assessing a patient's ability to hear a whispered phrase or the sound of rasping fingers) may suggest hearing impairment. Tuning fork tests that compare air and bone conduction of sound help clinicians identify whether hearing loss is due to conductive or sensorineural causes. Audiometry provides definitive diagnosis.

TREATMENT: The degree of hearing loss is calculated according to an American Medical Association formula: For every decibel that the pure tone average exceeds 25 dB, hearing impairment equals 1.5%. Therapy depends on the underlying condition. Cerumen impaction, for example, responds to irrigation of the external auditory canal, while otosclerosis may respond to the intraaural (surgical) placement of prostheses or laser surgery. Other forms of therapy include the use of hearing amplifiers or cochlear implants or education in lip reading or sign language.

PATIENT CARE: Patients can prevent damage to hearing from excessively loud noises by wearing sound-muffling ear plugs or muffs when exposed to loud noise from any source, esp. industrial noise, and by recognizing that loud music can be as detrimental to hearing as the noise of a jackhammer. After exposure to noise levels above 90 dB for several hours, overnight rest will usually restore normal hearing, but not in those who experience repeated exposure. Patients should avoid cleaning inside the ears or putting sharp objects in them. Many antibiotics and chemotherapeutic drugs are ototoxic and hearing should be evaluated continually when such drugs are used.

When interacting with a person with a hearing deficit, the health care professional should make his or her presence known to the patient by sight by raising or waving of the arm (as even gentle touch may startle the person) before beginning to speak. If possible, background noise should be decreased. The health care professional's face should be well lit to make the lips and facial expression easy to see. He or she should face the patient directly or direct the voice toward the side preferred by the patient. To facilitate lip reading, short words and simple sentences should be used. Clear and distinct enunciation and speaking slowly in a low tone are helpful. Exaggerated mouthing of words or loud tones and shouting should be avoided. Placing a stethoscope in the patient's ears and speaking into the bell helps to limit extraneous sounds and to direct words into the patient's ears. If the patient is literate, sign language or finger spelling may be used to communicate. Written information should be presented clearly and in large letters, esp. if the patient has poor visual acuity.

Any child in whom hearing loss is suspected or who fails a language screening examination should be referred to an audiologist or otolaryngologist for further evaluation and therapy and, as necessary, to a speech therapist for language evaluation and therapy.

Health care professionals can help

prevent hearing loss in their patients and communities by teaching about and assessing for signs of hearing impairment in anyone receiving ototoxic drugs; stressing the dangers of excessive noise exposure; explaining to pregnant women the danger to the fetus from exposure to drugs, chemicals, and infections, esp. rubella; and encouraging the use of protective devices in noisy environments and during occupational or recreational exposure to noise.

acquired d. Loss of hearing that is not present at birth but develops later in life.

central d. Deafness resulting from lesions of the auditory tracts of the brain or the auditory centers of the cerebral cortex.

conduction d. Conductive hearing loss.

cortical d. Deafness caused by a lesion of the auditory cortex of the brain rather than by a problem in the auditory nerve or the ear.

hereditary d. Hearing loss passed down through generations of a family.

high-frequency d. Inability to hear high-frequency sounds, e.g., sound frequencies just below 20 kHz.

mitochondrial d. Deafness caused by the inheritance of a mutation in mitochondrial DNA. It is transmitted from mother to child.

nerve d. Deafness due to a lesion of the auditory nerve or central neural pathways.

nonsyndromic d. Any form of hereditary hearing impairment caused by one of many genetic mutations, e.g., in somatic, mitochondrial, or X-linked genes.

occupational d. Deafness caused by working in places where noise levels are quite high. Persons working in such an environment should wear protective devices.

partial d. Deafness in which the ability to hear low-frequency sounds is preserved but high-frequencies are inaudible.

perceptive d. Deafness resulting from lesions involving sensory receptors of the cochlea or fibers of the acoustic nerve, or a combination of these.

postlingual d. Hearing impairment that develops after a patient has learned language.

prelingual d. Hearing impairment that is present in infancy and childhood, before language skills are acquired.

profound d. A level of hearing loss in which a person cannot hear a sound unless it is at least 90 decibels loud (about as loud as a lawnmower or a nearby motorcycle).

pure word d. Word **d.**

rhinogenic d. Deafness that is caused by chronic nasal or pharyngeal inflammation, with chronic otitis.

sensorineural d. Deafness due to defective function of the cochlea or acoustic nerve.

sex-linked d. A form of sensorineural deafness, found only in males, and carried as a recessive trait on the X chromosome.

sudden d. Deafness that occurs after an acute insult to the ear, e.g., after exposure to a toxin or medication (as from too high a dose of aminoglycosides), after a viral infection that damages the inner ear, or after blasts or head trauma.

tone d. The inability to detect differences in musical sounds.

tune d. The inability to detect differences in musical pitch or to appreciate differences in melodies.

word d. A form of aphasia in which sounds and words are heard but linguistic comprehension is absent. SYN: auditory **agnosia**; auditory **amnesia**; auditory **aphasia**; pure word **d.**

deamidase (dē-ăm′ĭ-dās) An enzyme that splits amides to form carboxylic acid and ammonia.

deamidation (dē″ăm-ĭ-dā′shŭn) The removal of an amide group by hydrolysis.

deaminase (dē-ăm′-ĭ-nās″) An enzyme that causes the removal of an amino group from organic compounds.

deamination, deaminization (dē-am″ĭ-nā′shŏn, dē-am″ĭ-nĭ-zā′shŏn) Loss of the NH_2 radical from amino compounds. Alanine can be deaminized to produce ammonia and pyruvic acid: $CH_3CH(NH_2)COOH + O = CH^3CO \cdot COOH + NH^3$. Deaminization may be simple, oxidative, or hydrolytic. Oxidizing enzymes are called deaminization enzymes when the oxidation is accompanied by splitting off of amino groups. Deaminization is the first step in the use of amino acids in cell respiration; the NH_2 is converted to urea.

dearterialization (dē″ăr′tēr″ē-ăl-ĭ-zā′shŭn) [L. *de*, from, + Gr. *arteria*, artery] Changing of arterial into venous blood; deoxygenation.

death (deth) Permanent cessation of all vital functions including those of the heart, lungs, and brain. SEE: table; *brain d.; euthanasia; life.*

SIGNS: The principal clinical signs of death are apnea and asystole. Other indications, including loss of cranial nerve reflexes and the cessation of the electrical activity of the brain, may be necessary for those receiving mechanical life support.

PATIENT CARE: Legal procedures and institutional protocols should be followed in the determination of death. The times of cessation of breathing and heartbeat are documented, and the physician or other legally authorized health

The Leading Causes of Death in the U.S. (2007)*

Cause of Death	Number of Deaths in 2004	Percent of Total Deaths
Heart disease	616,067	25.4
Cancer (malignant neoplasms)	562,875	23.2
Stroke (cerebrovascular diseases)	135,952	5.6
Chronic lower respiratory disease	127,924	5.3
Accidents	123,706	5.1
Alzheimer disease	74,632	3.1
Diabetes mellitus	71,382	2.9
Influenza and pneumonia	52,717	2.2
Nephritis, nephrotic syndrome, and nephrosis	46,448	1.9
Septicemia	34,828	1.4
Suicide (intentional self-harm)	34,598	1.4
Chronic liver disease and cirrhosis	29,165	1.2
Essential hypertension and hypertensive renal disease	23,965	1.0
Parkinson disease	20,058	0.8
Assault (homicide)	18,361	0.8

SOURCE: National Vital Statistics Report, Vol. 58, No. 19, May 20, 2010
*Total number of deaths: 2,423,712

care professional is notified and asked to certify death. The family is notified according to institutional policy, and emotional support is provided. Auxiliary equipment is removed, but the hospital identification bracelet is left in place. The body is cleansed, clean dressings are applied as necessary, and the rectum is packed with absorbent material to prevent drainage. The deceased is placed in a supine position with the limbs extended and the head slightly elevated. Dentures are inserted, if appropriate; the mouth and eyes are closed; and the body is covered to the chin with a sheet.

The deceased's belongings are collected and documented. Witnesses should be present, esp. if personal items have great sentimental or monetary value. The family is encouraged to visit, touch, and hold the patient's body as desired. In some situations (as in neonatal death or accidental death) and according to protocol, a photograph of the deceased is obtained to assist the family in grieving and remembering their loved one. A health care professional and a family member sign for and remove the patient's belongings.

After the family has gone, the body is prepared for the morgue. Body tags, imprinted with the patient's identification plate or card information (name, identification number, room and bed number, attending physician), along with the date and time of death, are tied to the patient's foot or wrist as well as to the outside of the shroud. The body is then transported to the morgue and placed in a refrigerated unit according to protocol.

activation-induced cell d. ABBR: AICD. Destruction of T or B lymphocytes that would otherwise be activated by contact with self-antigens. AICD maintains immunological tolerance; it is enhanced by interleukin-2 (IL-2) and inhibited by interleukin-15 (IL-15).

assisted d. Help that enables a person who wants to die to do so. The help may be counseling or providing the physical means or instruments that allow the person to commit suicide. The legal and ethical questions concerning such acts, esp. if the assisting person is a health care professional, are topics of active debate. SEE: *assisted suicide; euthanasia.*

biological d. Death due directly to natural causes.

black d. A colloquial term for bubonic plague.

brain d. The cessation of brain function. The criteria for determining brain death include lack of response to stimuli, lack of all reflexes, absent respirations, and an isoelectric electroencephalogram that for at least 30 min will not change in response to sound or pain stimuli. Other criteria sometimes used include loss of afferent cerebral evoked potentials, loss of isotope uptake during brain scans, or absence of cerebral perfusion on Doppler sonography. Before making this diagnosis, two physicians, including one experienced in caring for severely brain-damaged patients, should examine the patient. It is inadvisable for physicians associated with transplant procedures to participate in the review. The patient's body may be kept "alive" briefly by life-support devices if the patient is an organ donor.

⚠️ Some drugs (such as barbiturates, methaqualone, diazepam, meclo-qualone, meprobamate, trichloroethylene) can produce short isoelectric periods on encephalograms. Hypothermia must also be excluded as the cause of apparent brain death. Preterm infants whose gestational age is less than 37 weeks should not be diagnosed with brain death.

PATIENT CARE: The determination of brain death has both medical and legal consequences. It establishes a criterion for the withdrawal of life support from the critically ill who no longer have measurable brain function. At the same time it may initiate a discussion with family members of the deceased about organ donation. Those who have unequivocally specified that they would like to donate their organs at death currently make up a very small percentage of the population. Most of those who die have not made plans for organ donation, and some (such as those who die from trauma) may have never considered making a living will, a directive to physicians, or plans for organ donation. Discussions with family members in the immediate postmortem period may be emotionally challenging both for health care professionals and the grieving.

Brain death differs from the death of the heart, lungs, or other internal organs, and family members may often be confused about its meaning. They may wonder why they can still observe evidence of cardiac activity or effective mechanical ventilation. Family members may be unwilling to consent to withdrawal of ventilator support even when clinicians recognize that continued treatment will be of no benefit. There is a procedure to protect the rights of patients and their families in resolving disputes when family members do not agree with clinicians' decisions regarding discontinuance of life support in situations of medical futility. It is important for health care providers to explain that the brain-dead patient may still have an active heart rhythm but no longer has the ability to think, see, hear, or feel. The pulse and breath of the brain-dead patient can be artificially maintained for a short time. The central nervous system has already failed. If organ donation is being considered, an expert counselor should discuss this with the next of kin and help make the necessary arrangements. For some families, organ donation by the deceased provides some solace at a time of deep loss. If time is needed for a significant loved one to be present with the patient before he or she is removed from life-support, the involved physicians should be notified and a time arranged. It is often helpful for families to do this. If a close family member cannot be present and the family is concerned about this, it may help them to have a photograph of the patient once he or she has died that can be shared with others. After life support has been withdrawn, it is considerate to provide private time for the family to be with the deceased, supporting them as necessary. A hospital chaplain or the patient's or family's priest, rabbi, minister, or pastor will often provide spiritual comfort for survivors in addition to the support and comfort provided by professional staff. SYN: *death by brain criteria*.

cot d. The British term for sudden infant death syndrome.

crib d. Sudden infant death syndrome.

d. with dignity Death that is allowed to occur in accordance with the wishes of a patient. An individual may choose to withdraw from chronic medical therapies, as when there is little expectation of cure. Patients who choose death rather than active treatment often have advanced malignancies, poor performance status, major depression, poor social support, or a desire for a palliative approach to end-of-life care.

early neonatal d. Death of a newborn infant in the first 7 days after delivery. SEE: *intrapartum d.; stillbirth*.

fetal d. Spontaneous death of a fetus occurring after the 20th week of gestation. The cause is often unknown, but fetal death is often associated with maternal infection, diabetes mellitus, fetal and placental abnormalities, and pre-eclampsia.

functional d. Central nervous system death with vital functions being artificially supported.

good d. Death in which the rights of the person have been respected and during which the dying person was made as comfortable as possible and was in the company of persons he or she knew and loved. SEE: *living will*.

interphase cell d. The death of a cell before its next mitosis.

intrapartum d. Death of an infant occurring during its delivery.

molecular d. Death of cell life.

neocortical d. Persistent vegetative state.

pregnancy-related d. The death of a woman occurring within 6 weeks after pregnancy, conception, or termination of pregnancy.

sudden d. Death occurring unexpectedly and instantaneously or within 1 hr of the onset of symptoms in a patient with or without known preexisting heart disease. Sudden death due to cardiac conditions occurs in the U.S. at the rate of one a minute. It may be caused by cardiovascular conditions, including ventricular fibrillation or tachycardia, ischemic heart disease, aortic stenosis, coronary embolism, myocarditis, ruptured or dissecting aortic aneurysm, Stokes-Adams syndrome, stroke, pulmonary thromboembolism, and other, noncardiovascular-related, disorders, such as electrolyte imbalance and drug toxicity.

    wrongful d. Loss of life caused by negligent, illegitimate, or illegal acts.

death investigation The customary investigation of a violent, suspicious, or unexpected death or of a death unattended by a physician. The investigation is, by law, done by an officially appointed person. The investigation system includes medical examiners, coroners, or both a combined medical examiner and coroner. The system used varies from state to state. SEE: *coroner.*

debanding (dē-bănd′ĭng) [″ + ″] In orthodontics, the removal of a cemented orthodontic band from a tooth.

debarment (dē″bar′mĕnt) Disbarment

debilitate (dĭ-bĭl′ĭ-tāt″) To produce weakness or debility.

debility (dē-bil′ĭt-ē) [L. *debilitas,* weakness] Lack of strength; weakness. SEE: *asthenia.*

debonding (dē-bŏnd′ĭng) [″ + ″] In orthodontics, the removal of a bracket from a tooth.

debridement, débridement (di-brēd′mĕnt, dā-brēd-mon(t)′) [Fr. *débrider,* to remove a bridle] The removal of foreign material and dead or damaged tissue, esp. in a wound. **debride, débride** (dē-brēd′, dā-), *v.*

    autolytic d. A form of enzymatic débridement that uses the body's own enzymes to remove necrotic or nonviable tissue.

    canal d. The removal of organic and inorganic debris from a dental root canal by mechanical or chemical methods. This procedure is done in preparation for sealing the canal to prevent further decay of the tooth.

    enzymatic d. Use of proteolytic enzymes to remove dead tissue from a wound. The enzymes do not attack viable tissues.

    epithelial d. The removal of the entire epithelial lining or attachment epithelium from a periodontal pocket.

    mechanical d. The removal of necrotic or devitalized tissue from a wound using friction, hydrotherapy, scraping, or wet-to-dry dressings.

    sharp d. Removal of necrotic tissue from a wound with a scalpel or a related surgical tool.

debrief (dē″brēf′) To question carefully and thoroughly a person, crew, or staff after completion of an operation in order to find out how successful the operation was and how to improve future operations. **debriefing** (″brēf′ing), *n.* SEE: *brief.*

debris (dĕ-brē′) [Fr., remains] The remains of broken-down or damaged cells or tissue.

debt (det) [Fr. *dette,* something owed] Something owed or lacking and for which payment or performance must be made.

    bad d. Health care goods and services provided to patients who are expected to be able to pay for them, but who, for any of a variety of reasons, do not. SEE: *charity care.*

    oxygen d. After strenuous (anaerobic) physical activity, the oxygen required in the recovery period, in addition to that required while resting, to oxidize the excess lactic acid produced and to replenish the depleted stores of adenosine triphosphate and phosphocreatinase.

debulking (dē-bŭlk′ing) Surgery to remove a large portion of a tumor when complete excision is not possible. SEE: *downsizing.*

debut, début (dā′bū″, dā-bū′, deb′ū) [Fr. *débuter,* to make the first move in a game] **1.** An introductory or premiere event, e.g., the release of a new drug or device. **2.** A first experience of something, as of sexual intercourse or of a drug.

deca-, dec- [Gr. *deka,* ten] Prefixes meaning *ten.* SEE: *deka-.*

decagram (dĕk′ă″grăm) [Gr. *deka,* ten, + *gramma,* small weight] A mass equal to 10 g.

decalcification (dē″kăl-sĭ-fĭ-kā′shŭn) [L. *de,* from, + *calx,* lime, + *facere,* to make] The removal or withdrawal of calcium salts from bone or teeth.

decalcify (dē-kăl′sĭf-ī) **1.** To soften bone through removal of calcium or its salts by acids. **2.** To remove the mineral content from bones or teeth so that sections can be cut and stained for microscopic examination.

decaliter (dĕk′ă-lē″tĕr) [Gr. *deka,* ten, + Fr. *litre,* liter] A measure of 10 L, equivalent to 10,000 mL, or about 10.57 qt. SEE: *deciliter.*

decameter (dĕk′ă-mē-tĕr) [Gr. *deka,* ten, + *metron,* measure] A measure of 10 m; 393.71 in.

decannulation (dē-kăn″nū-lā′shŭn) The removal of a cannula.

decant (dē-kănt′) [L. *de,* from, + *canthus,* rim of a vessel] To pour off liquid so the sediment remains in the bottom of the container.

decantation (dē″kăn-tā′shŭn) Gentle pouring off of a liquid so the sediment remains.

decapitation (dē-kăp″ĭ-tā′shŭn) [″ + *caput,* head] **1.** Separation of the head from the body; beheading. **2.** Separation of the head from the shaft of a bone.

decapsulation (dē-kăp″sŭ-lā′shŭn) [″ + *capsula,* little box] Removal of a capsule.

decarboxylase (dē″kar-bok′sĭ-lās″) An enzyme that catalyzes the release of carbon dioxide from compounds such as amino acids.

    glutamic acid d. ABBR: GAD. An enzyme (molecular mass 65 kD) that is found in the brain and the islet cells of the pancreas and participates in the synthesis of gamma-aminobutyric acid. Antibodies to GAD are found in the blood of patients with diabetes mellitus, type 1, and stiff-person syndrome.

decarboxylation (dē″kăr-bŏks-ĭ-lā′shŭn) A chemical reaction in which the carboxyl group, —COOH, is removed from an organic compound.

decay (dē-kā′) [″ + *cadere,* to fall, die] **1.** Gradual loss of vigor with physical and mental deterioration as may occur in aging. **2.** To waste away. **3.** Decomposition of organic matter by the action of microorganisms. SEE: *caries; cementoclasia.* **4.** Disintegration of radioactive substances.

    radioactive d. The continual loss of energy by radioactive substances. Disintegration of the nucleus by the emission of alpha, beta, or gamma rays eventually results in the complete loss of radioactivity. The time required for some materials to become stable may be minutes and, for others, thousands of years. SEE: *half-life.*

    tooth d. Caries.

decay product An isotope formed during the decay of a radioactive material.

decel (dē-sel′) A colloquial term for *deceleration* of the fetal heart rate.

deceleration (dē-sĕl″ē-rā′shŭn) **1.** A rapid decrease in velocity. **2.** A fall in the baseline fetal heart rate as recorded by the fetal monitor.

    Early deceleration coincides with uterine contractions and reflects the fetal vagal response to head compression during these contractions. Normal baseline variability is evident throughout the interval between uterine contractions. *Late deceleration* occurs after contraction and reflects insufficient blood flow through the intervillous spaces of the placenta. *Variable deceleration* does not occur at any consistent point during contractions. The monitor record also exhibits different degrees and shapes. Variable deceleration indicates interference with blood flow through the umbilical vessels caused by cord compression. SEE: *fetal distress.*

deceleration injury SEE: under *injury.*

decennial (dĭ-sĕn′ē-ĭl) [L. *decennium,* period of ten years] Occurring every tenth year. Some booster vaccinations, e.g., against tetanus and diphtheria,

were traditionally administered one decade after the prior dose.

decerebrate (dē-sĕr′ē-brāt) [″ + *cerebrum,* brain] **1.** To eliminate cerebral function by decerebration. **2.** A person or animal who has been subjected to decerebration.

decerebrate posture SEE: under *posture.*

decerebration (dē-sĕr-ĕ-brā′shŭn) Removal of the brain or cutting of the spinal cord at the level of the brainstem. SEE: *pithing.*

dechlorination (dē-klōr″ĭ-nā′shŏn) [″ + Gr. *chloros,* green] Reduction in the amount of chlorides in the body by reduction of or withdrawal of salt in the diet.

deci- [L. *decimus,* tenth] In the Système International d'Unités (SI system), a prefix meaning *one tenth.*

decibel (dĕs′ĭ-bĕl) [L. *decimus,* tenth, + *bel,* unit of sound] ABBR: dB. A unit for expressing logarithmically the pressure or power (and thus degree of intensity or loudness) of sound. The dB is a tenth of a bel.

decidua (dē-sĭd′ū-ă) [L. *deciduus,* falling off] The endometrium or lining of the uterus and the tissue around the ectopically located fertilized ovum, e.g., in the fallopian tube or peritoneal cavity. The decidua has an interior compact layer and a surface spongy layer. The vasculature, glands, and interstitial cells of the endometrium undergo marked hypertrophy during pregnancy. **decidual** (-ăl), *adj.*

    d. basalis The part of the decidua that unites with the chorion to form the placenta.

    d. capsularis The part of the decidua that surrounds the chorionic sac.

    d. parietalis The endometrium during pregnancy except at the site of the implanted blastocyst.

deciduate (dē-sĭd′ū-āt″, -ĭt) [″] **1.** To shed the decidua (lining) of the uterus. **2.** A mammal that sheds the lining of the uterus during the birth of its offspring.

deciduation (dē-sĭd″ū-ā′shŭn) The loss of the decidua during menstruation.

deciduitis (dē-sĭd″ū-ī′tĭs) [″ + Gr. *itis,* inflammation] Inflammation of the decidua.

deciduoma (di-sij″oo-ō′mă) [*decidua* + *-oma*] **1.** A uterine tumor composed of chorionic membranes or decidual tissue that remain in the uterus following pregnancy. **2.** A decidual mass in the uterus caused by trauma.

deciduous (dē-sĭd′ū-ŭs) [L. *deciduus*] Falling off; subject to being shed.

decigram (dĕs′ĭ-grăm) [L. *decimus,* tenth, + Gr. *gramma,* small weight] One tenth of a gram.

deciliter (des′ĭ-lēt-ĕr) [*deci-* + *liter*] ABBR: dL. In the Système International d'Unités (SI system), a unit of volume equal to 0.1 L or 100 mL.

decimeter (dĕs′ĭ-mē″tĕr) [″ + Gr. *metron,* measure] One tenth of a meter.

decision aid SEE: under *aid.*

decision analysis A logical, consistent approach to making a medical decision when its consequences cannot be foretold with certainty. Uncertainties in medical practice are due to many factors (e.g., biological variation and limitations in the clinical data available for an individual patient). There are three steps in the analysis:

1. the consequences of each option is described schematically by the use of a decision tree;

2. probability is used to quantify the uncertainties inherent in each option; and

3. each possible outcome is designated by a number that measures the patient's preference for that outcome as compared with the others.

After the last step is completed, each outcome is assigned a "utility" value in which 1.0 indicates a perfect outcome and 0 is the worst possibility. Decision analysis may be used to help members of the health care team and the patient make logical choices concerning management of illness.

decision making The use of adequate information to come to a conclusion and make choices.

decision making, readiness for enhanced A pattern of choosing courses of action that is sufficient for meeting short- and long-term health-related goals and can be strengthened. SEE: *Nursing Diagnoses Appendix.*

decision-making capacity SEE: *capacity* (3).

decision tree SEE: under *tree.*

Declaration of Helsinki (hĕl′sĭng-kē) A guideline promulgated by the World Medical Association that governs the ethical treatment of patients enrolled in medical research.

declination (dĕk″lĭ-nā′shŭn) Cyclophoria.

decline (dē-klīn′) **1.** Progressive decrease. **2.** The declining period of a disease.

functional d. The loss of independent function that often accompanies an acute illness or the cumulative effects of a chronic illness, a restriction in activities, or a change in diet, esp. in older persons.

decoction (dē-kŏk′shŭn) [L. *de,* down, + *coquere,* to boil] A liquid medicinal preparation made by boiling vegetable substances with water. Liquid extracts obtained this way are often used in herbal medicines.

decolorize (dē-kŭl′ĕ-rīz″) [″ + colorize] To remove dye from a stained microscopic specimen, usually with an acidalcohol wash.

decompensate (dē-kom′pĕn-sāt″) [*de-* + L. *compensare,* to counterbalance] To fail or lose stability or ability to function; to suffer decompensation.

decompensation (dē-kom″pĕn-sā′shŏn) **1.** Failure of the heart to maintain adequate circulation, or failure of other organs to work properly during stress or illness. **2.** In psychology, failure of defense mechanisms such as occurs in initial and subsequent episodes of acute mental illness.

decomposer (dē″kŏm-pō′zĕr) Bacteria and fungi that degrade dead organic matter to simple organic and inorganic molecules. SEE: *biodegradation.*

decomposition (dē-kŏm-pō-zĭsh′ŭn) [″ + *componere,* to put together] **1.** The putrefactive process; decay. **2.** Reducing a compound body to its simpler constituents. SEE: *biodegradation; fermentation; resolution.*

double d. A chemical change in which the molecules of two interacting compounds exchange a portion of their constituents.

hydrolytic d. A chemical change in substances due to addition of a molecule of water.

simple d. A chemical change by which a molecule of a single compound breaks into its simpler constituents or substitutes the entire molecule of another body for one of these constituents.

decompress (dē″kŏm-prĕs′) **1.** To pass from a state of stress to tranquillity. **2.** To relieve pressure, esp. that produced by air or gas.

decompression (dē″kŏm-presh′ŏn) [*de-* + *compression*] **1.** The removal of pressure, as from gas in the intestinal tract. **2.** The slow reduction or removal of pressure on deep-sea divers and caisson workers to prevent development of nitrogen bubbles in the tissue spaces.

explosive d. In aviators or divers, decompression resulting from an extremely rapid rate of change to a much lesser pressure. This may occur if a high-altitude aircraft suddenly loses its cabin pressure or if a diver ascends rapidly. Either of these causes violent expansion of body gases. SEE: *decompression illness.*

surgical d. **1.** The freeing of a trapped body part, e.g., the operative release of a nerve from entrapment by neighboring structures. **2.** The surgical evacuation of fluids or clot from a closed space.

decompression illness SEE: under *illness.*

deconditioning (dē″kŏn-dĭsh′ŭ-nĭng) A loss of physical fitness due to failure to maintain an optimal level of physical activity or training. Inactivity for any reason may lead to deconditioning. For example, individuals placed on prolonged bedrest may experience overall deconditioning of the skeletal, muscular, circulatory, and respiratory systems.

decongestant (dē-kŭn-jĕs'tĭnt) **1.** Reducing congestion or swelling. **2.** An agent that reduces congestion, esp. nasal.

decontamination (dē-kŭn-tăm″ĭ-nā'shŭn) The use of physical, chemical, or other means to remove, inactivate, or destroy harmful microorganisms or poisonous or radioactive chemicals from persons, spaces, surfaces, or objects. Decontamination differs from sterilization. It renders a person or object mostly rather than completely free of contaminants. Decontamination of people exposed to hazardous materials should be performed in an orderly fashion. Tools and outer gloves should be removed first; surface contaminants should next be blown or washed away; any breathing apparatus, protective equipment, and clothing should then be removed, followed by careful washing and drying of the skin. Finally, the exposed person should be medically monitored until he or she is judged to be safe.

> **gastrointestinal d.** Cleansing of the gastrointestinal tract to remove toxic substances, pills taken in overdose, or microorganisms. Activated charcoal or polyethylene glycol solutions (e.g., GoLYTELY) given orally reduce the uptake of many drugs from the gastrointestinal tract. Before bowel surgery, oral antibiotics (e.g., neomycin) may be given to reduce the number of bacteria within the intestines.

> **hand d.** Hand **hygiene.**

> **selective oropharyngeal d.** ABBR: SOD. An infection-control method used in critical care units in which topical antibiotics are applied to the oral cavity (and back of the throat) as a means of reducing bacterial colonization and ventilator-associated pneumonia.

decorin A small proteoglycan that opposes the actions of transforming growth factor beta in connective tissues, esp. in the response to inflammation, injury, or scarring.

decorin-binding protein SEE: under *protein*.

decorticate posture (dē-kort″ĭ-kĭt, -kāt″) SEE: under *posture*.

decortication (dē-kort″ĭ-kā'shŏn) [*de-* + L. *cortex,* bark] The stripping away of a restrictive membrane from the surface of an entrapped organ or structure.

> **pulmonary d.** Surgical removal of restrictive tissue from the visceral pleura. It is used to treat an entrapped lung, e.g., in patients who have a malignant pleural effusion.

> **renal d.** Removal of the capsule of the kidney.

decrement (dĕk'rĕ-mĕnt) [L. *decremen-* *tum,* decrease] **1.** The period in the course of a febrile disease when the fever subsides. **2.** A reduction in the response of the nervous system to repeated stimulation. **3.** A decrease in the quantity or force of an entity. **4.** The portion of each uterine contraction between acme and baseline. The downslope is recorded by the fetal monitor.

decrepitation (dē-krĕp″ĭ-tā'shŭn) A crackling noise.

decrepitude (dē-krĕp'ĭ-tūd) A state of general feebleness and decline that sometimes accompanies old age; weakness; infirmity.

decrescendo (dā″krĕ-shen'dō, dē″) [Italian *decrescendo,* decreasing] Of heart murmurs, gradually becoming softer or quieter.

decubitus (dē-kū'bĭ-tŭs) [L., a lying down] **1.** Pressure sore. **2.** A patient's position in bed. **decubital** (-tăl), *adj.*

> **dorsal d.** Lying on the back.

> **lateral d.** Lying on the side.

> **ventral d.** Prone positioning. Also known as supine positioning.

decubitus ulcer SEE: under *ulcer.*

decussate (dē-kŭs'āt) [L. *decussare,* to make an X] **1.** To cross, as the two lines of an X. **2.** In reference to axons in the central nervous system, to cross the midplane (the sagittal plane) of the brain or spinal cord en route to a target on the contralateral side.

decussation (dē″kŭ-sā'shŭn) **1.** A crossing of structures in the form of an X. **2.** A place in which linear structures cross. SYN: *chiasm; chiasma.* **3.** In reference to axons in the central nervous system, the crossing of the midplane (the sagittal plane) of the brain or spinal cord en route to a target on the contralateral side

> **d. of the brachium conjunctivum** Decussation of the superior cerebellar peduncles.

> **dorsal tegmental d.** The crossing, in the dorsal section of the midbrain tegmentum, of descending axons from the superior colliculus to form the tectospinal tracts.

> **d. of the pyramids** Pyramidal **d.**

> **pyramidal d.** The crossing of 90% of the axons of the corticospinal tracts (the pyramidal tracts) in the ventral region of the caudal hindbrain. On the contralateral side, the crossed axons interdigitate with 10% of the corticospinal axons that have not crossed, and the full complement of axons continues into the spinal cord in the lateral funiculus. SYN: **d.** *of the pyramids.*

> **d. of the superior cerebellar peduncles** The crossing, in the rostral hindbrain, of the outflow axons from the deep cerebellar nuclei as they run towards the contralateral red nuclei.

> **supraoptic d.** Several bundles of axons crossing the midline in the hypo-

thalamus, dorsal to the optic chiasm. These crossings include the anterior hypothalamic commissure, the dorsal supraoptic decussation, and the ventral supraoptic decussation.

ventral tegmental d. The crossing, in the ventral section of the midbrain tegmentum, of descending axons from the red nucleus to form the rubrospinal tracts.

dedifferentiation (dē-dĭf″ĕr-ĕn-chē-ā′shŭn) **1.** The return of parts to a homogeneous state. **2.** The process by which mature differentiated cells or tissues become sites of origin for immature elements of the same type, as in some cancers.

deductible (dĭ-dŭk′tĭ-bĭl) An expense borne by an insured party before any obligated payments are made by the insurer.

deduction (dē-dŭk′shŭn) Reasoning from the general to the particular.

deep [AS. *deop*] Below the surface.

deepening (dēp′ĕn-ĭng) [″] In hypnotherapy, achieving a more relaxed or receptive state of mind.

deep heating, deep heat The application of radiant energy beneath the skin and beneath the subcutaneous tissue. The target of such heating is generally muscles and tendons. SEE: *diathermy; thermotherapy; ultrasound.*

deer fly SEE: under *fly.*

deer tick virus SEE: under *virus.*

de-escalate (dē-ĕs′kă-lāt″) To defuse a potentially dangerous interaction between two or more individuals.

DEET (dēt) *N,N*-diethyl-3-methylbenzamide, a potent, broad-spectrum insect repellent.

⚠ Although topically applied DEET is generally safe when applied to the skin, it should not come in contact with plastics, which it may dissolve. DEET is not recommended for use by children under the age of 2.

DEF *decayed, extracted, filled.*

defamation (dĕf″ă-mā′shŭn) In law, an act of communication that is a quasi-intentional tort (civil wrong) that occurs when one person communicates false information to another person that injures or harms a third person who, as a result, is shamed, held in contempt, ridiculed, loses status or reputation in the community, or experiences loss of employment or of earnings. Oral defamation is slander. Written defamation is libel.

defatted (dē-făt′ĕd) [L. *de,* from, + AS. *faelt,* to fatten] Freed from or deprived from fat, e.g., by trimming fat away, skimming fat from the surface of a liquid, or draining fat from a food. Defatting is a practice used by dieters to re-

duce the fat and caloric content of a meal.

defecation (dĕf-ĕ-kā′shŭn) [L. *defaecare,* to remove dregs] Evacuation of the bowels. The expulsion of a fecal mass is accompanied by coordinated action of the following: involuntary contraction of the circular muscle of the rectum behind the bowel mass, followed by contraction of the longitudinal muscle; relaxation of the internal (involuntary) and external (voluntary) sphincter ani; voluntary closure of the glottis, fixation of the chest, and contraction of the abdominal muscles, causing an increase in intra-abdominal pressure. SEE: *constipation; feces; stool.*

defecography (dĕ″fĕ-kŏg′grăfē) Radiography of the anorectal region after instillation of a barium paste into the rectum. The defecation process is imaged by direct filming or video recording.

defect (dē′fekt″, di-) [L. *defectus,* weakness, failure] A flaw or imperfection. **defective** (di-fek′tiv), *adj.*

alcohol-related birth d. A congenital abnormality that reflects the teratogenic effects of maternal alcohol use on developing fetal structures. The most common abnormalities involve the heart, eyes, kidneys, and skeleton. SEE: *fetal alcohol effects; fetal alcohol syndrome.*

aortic septal d. A congenital abnormality in which there is a communication between the ascending aorta and the pulmonary artery requiring corrective surgery.

atrial septal d. A congenital heart defect in which there is an opening between the atria, which may cause shunting of oxygenated blood from the left side of the heart to the right side.

birth d. A congenital anomaly. Birth defects are a leading cause of infant mortality in the U.S. and most developed countries. Each year in the U.S. about 150,000 babies are born with serious birth defects. About 3% of all pregnancies have some form of genotypically mild abnormality. Known causes include human teratogens, chromosomal defects, and single-gene defects. The cause is unknown in about two thirds of the cases. SEE: table.

congenital d. An anatomical or physiological abnormality that is present at birth.

congenital heart d. A structural abnormality of the heart and great blood vessels that occurs during intrauterine development. Abnormalities are commonly classified by the presence or absence of cyanosis. Acyanotic abnormalities include atrial and ventricular septal defects, coarctation of the aorta, and patent ductus arteriosus. Cyanotic defects include tetralogy of Fallot,

Common Birth Defects

Type of Defect	Examples	Approximate Prevalence per 10,000 Births	Comments
Chromosomal	Down syndrome (trisomy 21)	13	Increases with maternal age over 35 years
	Trisomy 18	2.3	
Infectious	Varicella-zoster infection (chickenpox)	7	
Metabolic	Phenylketonuria (PKU)	3.5	
Structural	Cleft lip and/or palate	10	
	Neural tube defects, including anencephaly and spina bifida	3	Folate supplementation during pregnancy prevents neural tube defects
	Transposition of the great vessels	5	
Toxic	Fetal alcohol spectrum disorders	2–15	Varies with prevalence of alcohol use in the community; preventable with abstinence
	Isotretinoin (acne medication)		Avoid all pregnancies during therapy with isotretinoin

transposition of the great vessels, and hypoplastic left-sided heart syndrome.

filling d. An interruption of the contour of a body structure revealed by radiographic contrast material. It may be due to an obstruction caused by blood clots, emboli, malignancies, or extrinsic compression.

limb reduction d. A congenital malformation in which one or more limbs develop incompletely or not at all.

luteal phase d. A deficiency in either the amount or the duration of postovulatory progesterone secretion by the corpus luteum. Insufficient hormonal stimulation results in inadequate preparation of the endometrium for successful implantation and support of the growing embryo. This condition is associated with infertility or habitual spontaneous first-trimester abortion. SEE: *menstrual cycle*.

neural tube d. ABBR: NTD. Any of a group of congenital structural disorders attributable to failure of the embryonic neural tube to close during development. Cranial fusion disorders, including anencephaly and encephalocele, or spinal fusion disorders, including spina bifida, lumbar meningomyelocele, and meningocele, may occur as a consequence of this failure. In the U.S. about 3000 children are born each year with neural tube defects. Although there may be a family history of such disorders, roughly 85% of affected infants are born to women who have not been considered at risk. Prenatal folic acid deficiency has been implicated in NTDs, but other predisposing factors may be involved. To reduce the risk of NTDs, the U.S. Public Health Service recommends a daily folic acid intake of 0.4 mg for all fertile women of childbearing age. Prior supplementation with folic acid prevents damage to the embryonic neural tube during the first 3 to 4 weeks of its development when many women are unaware that they are pregnant. The importance of an adequate intake before pregnancy is predicated on the fact that damage to the developing embryo often occurs before the woman knows she is pregnant. The neural tube develops from the neural plate at 3 weeks' gestation. At 4 weeks' gestation, closure has been achieved except at the cranial and caudal ends; cranial closure occurs at 24 days and caudal closure at 26 days' gestation. SEE: *microencephaly*; **spina** *bifida cystica*; **spina** *bifida occulta*.

Elevated levels of maternal serum alpha-fetoprotein (MSAFP) are found in NTDs such as fetal anencephaly. Screening for MSAFP is done between 15 and 19 weeks' gestation. Alpha-fetoprotein also is found in amniotic fluid. The prognosis for infants born with NTDs depends on the area and the degree of involvement. Despite supportive care, some defects (such as anencephaly) are fatal shortly after birth. Others, such as myelomeningocele, may benefit from surgery done within 24 to 48 hr after birth; in some cases, however, surgery does not improve the deformity, disability, and chronic health problems that compromise the individual's quality of life.

    prune-belly d. A colloquial, descriptive term for children with congenital absence of one or more layers of abdominal muscles. SYN: *triad syndrome*.

    retention d. The inability to recall a name, number, or fact shortly after being requested to remember it.

    septal d. A defect in one or more of the septa between the heart chambers.

    ventricular septal d. An abnormal opening in the septum between the ventricles of the heart that may produce shunting of blood from left to right or other diseases.

defendant (dĭ-fĕn'dănt) In law, the person, entity, or party charged or sued in a legal action. The defendant is the party accused of a criminal or civil wrong from whom legal relief or damages are sought. SEE: *plaintiff*.

defense [L. *defendere*, to repel] **1.** Resistance to disease. **2.** Protective action against harm or injury. SYN: *defense mechanism*.

defense reaction A mental response whose purpose (according to classical psychoanalysis) is to protect the ego.

defense reflex SEE: under *reflex*.

defensin (dē-fĕn'sĭn) [term coined by Robert I. Lehrer, U.S. physician, b. 1938] Destructive peptides (groups of amino acids) found in the granules of neutrophils and other phagocytic cells that kill bacteria and fungi by destroying their membranes. Defensins are active against bacteria, fungi, and enveloped viruses in vitro. They may contribute to host defenses against susceptible organisms.

defensive (dĕ-fen'sĭv) **1.** Defending; protecting from injury. **2.** In behavioral health, inordinately self-protective, esp. in response to criticism or inquiries by others.

¹defer (dē-fer') [Fr. *différer*, to differ, fr L. *diferre*, carry in different directions, differ] To delay or postpone a decision or action.

²defer (dē-fer') [Fr. *déférer*, fr L. *deferre*, to carry down, report, accuse] To yield respectfully to the opinions or desires of others.

deferens (dĕf'ĕr-ĕnz) [L. *deferens*, carrying away] Deferent.

deferent (dĕf'ĕr-ĕnt) Conveying something away from or downward. SEE: *afferent; efferent*.

deferential (dĕf-ĕr-ĕn'shăl) [L. *deferre*,

to bring to] Pert. to or accompanying the ductus deferens.

deferoxamine mesylate (dĕ-fĕr-ŏks'ă-mēn) A drug with a very high affinity for iron. It is used parenterally to reduce the iron overload in patients with hemochromatosis, acute iron poisoning, or multiple blood transfusions.

defervescence (dĕf'ĕr-ves'ĕns) [L. *defervescere*, to become calm] The subsidence of fever to a normal temperature.

defibrillation (dē-fĭb''rĭ-lā'shŏn) [*de-* + *fibrillation*] **1.** Termination of ventricular fibrillation (vfib) with electrical countershock(s). This is the single most important intervention a rescuer can take in patients who have suffered cardiac arrest due to vfib or pulseless ventricular tachycardia.

    PATIENT CARE: Traditional defibrillation uses a monophasic waveform: a single energy pulse. Monophasic electrical current travels in one direction from one electrode or paddle through the heart to the other electrode. In a successful attempt the energy converts the lethal rhythm to a rhythm with a pulse, and to be successful, this type of defibrillation must deliver high energy (200 or more joules).

    The biphasic defibrillator delivers current through the heart in two directions, flowing through the heart and back again to the first electrode. Biphasic defibrillation uses lower levels of electrical current than monophasic techniques. Advantages for the patient include lower risk of skin burns, less myocardial injury and dysfunction following defibrillation, and more rapid return of ejection fraction and mean arterial pressure to baseline. In addition, the lower energy levels permit the equipment to be smaller, lighter, less demanding on batteries, and easier to maintain than monophasic models. Biphasic defibrillation usually is initiated at 120 to 150 joules, with the level increased as needed. In cardioversion, only 30 joules is typically required. Health care professionals should become familiar with the type of defibrillator in their facility so that they can safely and rapidly operate defibrillators in an emergency. Staff-development sessions should be provided by the agency to ensure competency.

    2. A term formerly used to signify termination of atrial fibrillation. The contemporary terms are *conversion* or *cardioversion*.

    public access d. The use of automated external defibrillators by trained lay people who witness a sudden cardiac arrest.

defibrillator (dē-fĭb'rĭ-lāt''ŏr) [*de-* + *fibrillat(ion)*] A device that delivers an electrical shock that completely depolarizes the myocardium, producing a brief period of asystole. The goal of defibrillation is to let the sinoatrial node recover control of the heart's electrical activity and terminate potentially fatal heart rhythms, such as ventricular tachycardia and ventricular fibrillation. SEE: *cardioversion*.

A defibrillator may be used with conductive pads applied to the chest wall or may be surgically implanted in the chest, e.g., in patients who have previously been resuscitated from sudden death.

automated external d. ABBR: AED. A defibrillator that performs all functions by computer (analyzes rhythm, selects an energy level, charges the machine, and shocks the patient). The operator applies adhesive paddles and turns the machine on, then makes certain that no one is in contact with the patient. SYN: *automatic d.*

automatic d. Automated external **d.**

manual d. A defibrillator that requires the operator to assess the need for defibrillation (by reviewing monitor data and the patient's clinical condition), select an energy level, charge the machine, and deliver shock.

defibrination (dē-fib″rĭ-nā′shŏn) [L. *de*, from, + *fibra*, fiber] The process of removing fibrin, usually from blood. SEE: *blood* **coagulation**.

deficiency (di-fĭsh′ĕn-sē) [L. *deficere*, to lack] Less than the normal amount; a lack.

acid lipase d. One of two autosomal recessive illnesses in which the body lacks an enzyme for metabolizing fats, causing cholesterol, oils, or waxes to accumulate in abnormal amounts in the body. The acid lipase diseases are Wolman disease and cholesterol ester storage disease. SYN: *acid lipase disease.*

antithrombin-III d. An inherited hypercoagulable state. It is due to absent or deficient levels of antithrombin III in the blood. SYN: *hereditary thrombophilia.*

biotinidase d. An autosomal recessive disease in which affected children fail to metabolize biotin effectively. Seizures, encephalopathy, neurodevelopmental delay, spasticity or diminished muscle tone, paresis, visual disturbances, deafness, skin rash, and hair loss commonly occur. Immediate ongoing treatment with supplemental biotin can effectively suppress the symptoms of this disease.

branching enzyme d. Type IV glycogen storage disease.

ceramidase d. Farber disease.

color d. SEE: *color* **blindness**.

color vision d. SEE: *color* **blindness**.

copper d. The clinical consequences of inadequate consumption or absorption of dietary copper. Its hallmarks include an unsteady gait, neuropathy, muscle spasticity, and, occasionally, anemia. It may occur as a consequence of gastric bypass surgery or long-term parenteral nutrition.

delta storage pool d. Dense granule deficiency syndrome.

functional iron d. A deficiency of iron significant enough to affect the development of healthy red blood cells. It may precede the appearance of measurable anemia.

PATIENT CARE: Functional iron deficiency may be defined by the presence of hypochromatic red cells; by an increase in hemoglobin production after test doses of administered iron; or, most accurately, by the measurement of the mean hemoglobin content of reticulocytes. It is common in patients receiving hemodialysis and in critically ill persons.

TREATMENT: Treatments include iron and folate supplements and epoetin alpha (Procrit) to increase red blood cell production. In emergencies, infusion of fresh frozen packed cells or washed packed cells provide temporary relief.

glucose-6-phosphate dehydrogenase d. An X-linked disorder affecting the red blood cells. It is present in the U.S. in about 13% of black males and 2% of black females. The deficiency also occurs in Arab, Mediterranean, and Asian populations. The enzyme is essential to maintaining the integrity of erythrocytes; thus a deficiency of it causes nonimmune hemolytic anemia. There are many variants of the enzyme and great variation in severity of the disease. Some people do not have clinical symptoms until they are exposed to certain drugs (such as antimalarials, antipyretics, sulfonamides) or to fava beans, or when they contract an infectious disease. In others the condition is present at birth. When present at birth, anemia, hepatomegaly, hypoglycemia, and interference with growth are present. In those who have the deficiency but are not affected until exposed to certain drugs or infections, hemolytic anemia and jaundice occur.

DIAGNOSIS: Laboratory tests for evidence of the enzyme deficiency are available.

TREATMENT: The only treatment is avoidance of drugs known to cause hemolysis and avoidance of fava beans if the person is known to be sensitive to them.

immune d. Immunodeficiency.

intrinsic sphincter d. ABBR: ISD. Weakening of the urethral sphincter muscles, a frequent cause of stress urinary incontinence.

leukocyte adhesion d. ABBR: LAD. A rare autosomal recessive disorder in which white blood cells are unable to migrate out of blood vessels in response to infection. It often presents in early childhood with severe periodontal disease, premature loss of teeth, and recurrent infections.

medium-chain acyl-CoA dehydrogenase d. ABBR: MCADD. An inherited disorder of faulty nutrient oxidation in which affected infants are unable to metabolize fatty acids when their stores of blood glucose are low, e.g., between meals. The disease is common, occurring in 1 in 10,000 infants, and often fatal in infancy. Surviving infants may suffer brain damage from inadequate nutrition to the central nervous system during fasts.

muscle phosphorylase d. McArdle disease

ornithine transcarbamylase d. The most common urea cycle enzyme deficiency disorder inherited as an autosomal recessive trait, characterized by the absence of ornithine transcarbamylase (an enzyme in the urea cycle), which results in the excessive buildup of ammonia in the bloodstream. The disease is typically diagnosed in infancy and occurs in less than 1 in 8000 births.

phosphofructokinase d. ABBR: PFKM. A glycogen storage disease caused by a deficiency of muscle phosphofructokinase and characterized by muscular weakness, muscle cramps after exercise, hemolysis, hyperuricemia, and myoglobinuria. SYN: *glycogen storage disease* type VII; *Tarui disease.*

d. of sweating Anhidrosis.

ZAP70 d. *Zeta-chain associated protein kinase d.*

zeta-chain associated protein kinase 70 kDa d. ABBR: ZAP70 deficiency. A severe combined immunodeficiency disease in which CD8+ T cells are missing from the circulation and the thymus develops abnormally.

deficiency disease A condition due to lack of a substance essential in body metabolism. The deficiency may be due to inadequate intake, digestion, absorption, or use of foods, minerals, water, or vitamins. It may also be due to excess loss through excretion or to an intestinal parasite such as hookworm or tapeworm. Deficiency diseases include night blindness and keratomalacia (caused by lack of vitamin A); beriberi and polyneuritis (lack of thiamine); pellagra (lack of niacin); scurvy (lack of vitamin C); rickets and osteomalacia (lack of vitamin D); pernicious anemia (lack of gastric intrinsic factor and vitamin B_{12}).

deficit (def'ĭ-sĭt) [L. *deficit,* it lacks] A deficiency (e.g., a loss of neurological function after a stroke).

isomolar volume d. An equal proportion of loss of water and electrolytes from the body.

pulse d. A condition in which the speed of the pulse at the radial artery is less than the pulse of the heart. This is seen in atrial fibrillation.

water d. In dehydrated patients with high serum sodium levels (hypernatremia), the quantity of water that must be provided to the patient to restore normal electrolyte balance and fluid volume.

deficit syndrome of schizophrenia Negative symptoms of schizophrenia that persist or are found even during psychotic remissions. Such symptoms include social withdrawal, loss of motivation, poverty of speech, and blunting of affect.

definition [L. *definire,* to limit] **1.** The precise determination of limits, esp. of a disease process. **2.** The detail with which images are recorded on radiographic film or screens.

definitive (dĭ-fin'ĭt-iv) [L. *definitivus,* explanatory] **1.** Clear and final, as in an answer. **2.** Optimal, as in a therapy **3.** Without question; indisputable

deflection (dē-flĕk'shŭn) A turning away from a previous or usual course.

defloration (dĕf"lō-rā'shŭn) [L. *de,* from, + *flos, flor-,* flower] Rupture of the hymen during coitus, by accident, surgically, or through vaginal examination. Not many women have a hymen that is of such size or consistency as to require its surgical rupture. SEE: *hymen; virginity.*

defluvium (dē-floo'vē-ŭm) [L.] A falling or flowing out.

defocus (dē-fō'kŭs) [L. *de,* away from, + *focus,* hearth] The blurring of a visual image caused by spherical aberration, chromatic aberration, or diffraction. SYN: *optical d.*

optical d. Defocus.

defog (dē"fog') To remove moisture or mist from a surface, esp. one meant to be transparent.

deformability (dē-form"ă-bĭl'ĭ-tē) Capability of being deformed.

deformation (dē"for"mā'shŏn) **1.** The act of deforming. **2.** A disfiguration. **deformational** ('shŏ-năl), *adj.*

deformational plagiocephaly (dē"form-mā'shŏn-ăl) SEE: under *plagiocephaly.*

deformity (de-for'mĭt-ē) [L. *deformitas,* ugliness, deformity] Alteration in or distortion of the natural form of a part, organ, or the entire body. It may be acquired or congenital. If present after injury, deformity usually implies the presence of bone fracture, bone dislocation, or both. It may be due to extensive swelling, extravasation of blood, or rupture of muscles and severe contracture of scar tissue.

Arnold-Chiari d. SEE: *Arnold-Chiari deformity.*

boutonnière d. A finger position

marked by extension of the metacarpophalangeal and distal interphalangeal joints and flexion of the proximal interphalangeal joint. This condition outwardly resembles a pseudoboutonnière deformity. SEE: *pseudoboutonnière d.*

ETIOLOGY: A rupture of the central extensor tendon of the involved finger. The tendon then displaces palmarly relative to the proximal interphalangeal joint.

TREATMENT: The finger is splinted with the proximal and distal interphalangeal joints in extension. Surgery may be required for patients who do not respond to conservative treatment.

Haglund d. SEE: *Haglund deformity.*

Madelung d. SEE: *Madelung deformity.*

pencil-in-cup d. A form of osteolysis found in severe inflammatory arthritis, esp. in the finger and toe joints. The deformity is characterized by thinning of the phalangeal shaft and widening of its base proximal to the joint space.

Sprengel d. SEE: *Sprengel deformity.*

string-of-pearls d. Fusiform enlargement of the proximal and middle phalanges, seen in rickets.

swan-neck d. A finger deformity marked by flexion of the distal interphalangeal joints and hyperextension of the proximal interphalangeal joints, often seen in rheumatoid arthritis.

Volkmann d. SEE: *Volkmann, Richard von.*

defuse (dĭ-fūz′) **1.** To remove a fuse from an explosive device. **2.** To make a crisis or other situation less dangerous or inflammatory.

deg *degeneration; degree.*

degeneracy The ability of structurally differing molecules to perform overlapping, redundant, or equivalent functions. This ability is a characteristic of some nucleic acid codons (which code for the same amino acid despite having differing base pairs) and some molecules used by the immune system.

degenerate (dē-jĕn′ĕ-rāt″) [L. *degenerare,* to fall from one's ancestral quality] **1.** To deteriorate. **2.** Characterized by deterioration.

degeneration (dē-jen″ĕ-rā′shŏn) [*de-* + *generation*] Deterioration or impairment of an organ or part in the structure of cells and the substances of which they are a component. SEE: *regeneration.* **degenerative** (de-jen′ĕ-rāt″iv, -jen′ĕ-rătiv), *adj.*

age-related macular d. SEE: *macular d.*

amyloid d. Degeneration of organs or tissues from amyloid deposits. The deposits are waxy and translucent and have a hyaline appearance. The liver, spleen, and kidneys are usually involved, but any tissue may be infiltrated.

ascending d. Nerve fiber degeneration progressing to the center from the periphery.

caseous d. Cheesy alteration of tissues, as seen in tuberculosis.

colloid d. Mucoid degeneration in the protoplasm of epithelial cells.

corticobasal d. A neurological disorder in which brain cells atrophy and die in the basal ganglia and the cortex of the brain. The disease produces symptoms similar to those found in Parkinson's disease but does not respond to parkinsonian medications.

cystic d. Cyst formation accompanying degeneration.

descending d. Nerve fiber degeneration progressing toward the periphery from the original lesion.

fatty d. Deposit of abnormal amounts of fat in the cytoplasm of cells, or replacement or infiltration of tissues by fat cells.

fatty d. of the heart Fatty **infiltration** of the heart.

fibroid d. Change of membranous tissue into fibrous tissue.

frontotemporal lobar d. Pick disease.

granulovacuolar d. A pathological finding in the brain cells of some patients with Alzheimer dementia in which the neuronal cytoplasm is partly replaced by cavities that contain particles resembling grit or sand.

hepatocerebral d. Loss of nerve and supporting cells of the brain from multiple episodes of hepatic encephalopathy or coma. This condition may be caused by Wilson disease or other insults to the liver, e.g., hepatic coma produced by alcoholic, drug-induced, or viral hepatitis.

hepatolenticular d. Wilson disease.

hyaline d. A form of degeneration in which the tissues assume a homogeneous, glassy appearance. It is caused by hyaline deposits replacing musculoelastic elements of blood vessels with a firm, transparent substance that causes loss of elasticity. It is responsible for hardening of the arteries and is often followed by calcification or deposit of lime salts in dead tissue. Calcification also may result in concretions. SYN: *vitreous d.*

hydropic d. Pathological change in cells marked by the appearance of water droplets in the cytoplasm.

lattice d. Atrophy or thinning of the retina at its margins, a common condition that affects about 10% of the population. The condition is usually bilateral and is often asymptomatic although affected persons may complain of seeing sudden flashes of light.

It is an occasional cause of retinal detachment.

macular d. ABBR: MD. Loss of pigmentation in the macular region of the retina, usually affecting those over 50. MD is a common disease of unknown cause that produces central visual field loss and is the leading cause of permanent visual impairment in the U.S. By age 75, about 15% of Americans are affected. Contributing factors to MD include a family history of MD, advancing age, cataract surgery, hyperlipidemia, hypertension, obesity, smoking, and a diet low in carotenoids, vitamin C, vitamin E, and zinc. People with Alzheimer Disease will eventually develop MD, but the reverse is not true.

SYMPTOMS: There are two kinds of macular degeneration: wet and dry. In wet MD, neovascularization intrudes under the retinal pigment epithelium from the choroid, where the new blood vessels may suddenly bleed or leak fluid, distort the normal architecture of the macula, and degrade central visual acuity. The visual loss caused by wet MD is an emergency. In dry MD, the more common and more benign form, hard and soft drusen accumulate beneath the retinal pigment epithelium. They may cause slowly progressive blurring of central vision or may occasionally and gradually lead to wet MD.

The central visual loss that marks MD can make reading, working with the hands, driving, or recognizing people's faces difficult because the center of the visual field is the region of greatest loss of visual acuity (i.e., a central scotoma). Peripheral vision is preserved in this disease. SYN: *age-related macular degeneration*. SEE: *visual field* for illus.

TREATMENT: Laser photocoagulation of new blood vessel membranes can help arrest visual loss in some patients with the exudative form of age-related MD, changing the wet form to the dry form. However, this form of treatment is complicated by a high rate of recurrence and some immediate visual loss in a scotoma. Other treatments include antiangiogenic drugs, regimens with vitamins A, C, E, and zinc and copper, photodynamic therapy, radiation therapy, and retinal surgery.

PATIENT CARE: The Amsler grid, and other testing devices such as a tangent screen, can be used to test patients for visual distortions due to retinal disease, but the validity and reproducibility of Amsler grid testing is poor. Low vision optical aids improve the quality of life for patients who retain good peripheral vision. Affected patients should be referred for visual rehabilitation.

mucoid d. Mucous **d.**

mucous d. Deposition of mucus in the connective tissue of organs or in epithelial cells. SYN: *mucoid* **d.**; *myxomatous* **d.**

myxomatous d. Mucoid **d.**

pigmentary d. Degeneration in which affected cells develop an abnormal color.

polypoid d. Formation of polyp-like growths on mucous membranes.

secondary d. Wallerian **d.**

senile d. The bodily and mental changes that occur during pathological aging.

spongy d. Familial demyelination of the deep layers of the cerebral cortex. The affected area has a spongy appearance. Symptoms include mental retardation, enlarged head, muscular flaccidity, and blindness. Death usually occurs before 18 months of age.

vacuolar d. Swelling of cells with an increase in the number and size of vacuoles. SYN: *cloudy swelling*.

vitreous d. Hyaline **d.**

wallerian d. The dying back of the axons of nerves after an insult to nerve tissue, such as a toxic exposure, a metabolic change, trauma, or deprivation of blood supply. The myelin surrounding the axon deteriorates, and the ability of the axon to transmit signals diminishes. SYN: *secondary d.*

waxy d. Amyloid degeneration seen in wasting diseases.

degenerative disease (dē-jěn'ě-rǎ-tǐv) An illness resulting from aging, repetitive injury, or other pathological causes.

degenerative joint disease Osteoarthritis.

deglutition (dē"gloo-tǐsh'ŭn) The act of swallowing. **deglutitive,** *adj.*

Degos disease ABBR: DD. A rare form of vasculitis that damages small blood vessels. The disease initially results in tissue infarction within the skin, but in some instances causes widespread and occasionally fatal tissue infarction in the gastrointestinal tract and other organs. SYN: *malignant atrophic papulosis*.

degradation (deg"rǎ-dā'shŏn) [L. *degradatio,* a step down] Physical, metabolic, or chemical change from a more complex form to a less complex one. Foods are physically degraded during chewing and then are chemically degraded from complete compounds, such as proteins and starches, to amino acids and sugars, respectively. SYN: *biodegradation*.

degranulation (dē-grǎn"ū-lā'shŭn) The release of chemical mediators from preformed storage depots in cells, esp. hematological cells such as neutrophils, mast cells, basophils, macrophages, and platelets.

degree (dě-grē') [Fr. *degree* fr L. *degradus*] **1.** A unit of measurement of temperature. **2.** A unit of angular measure. **3.** A stage of severity of a disease or injury (e.g., second-degree burn). **4.** Evidence of academic attainment granted by the institution in which the individual studied.

degrees of freedom ABBR: d.f. In defining the properties of a statistical sample, the number of independent observations in a quantity. For example, if a sample contains a total of 10 children who are being classified by hair color (brown, black, or blond) and it is known that four of the children have blond hair, then there are two degrees of freedom. If, at the beginning of the investigation, the hair color of all the subjects is unknown, there are three degrees of freedom.

degustation (dē″gŭs-tā′shŭn) [L. *degustatio*] The sense of taste; the function or act of tasting.

dehiscence (dē-his′ĕns) [L. *dehiscere*, to gape] **1.** A disruption, partial or complete, particularly of a closed wound (esp. a surgical wound), or of an encapsulated anatomical entity. SYN: *wound disruption.* **2.** In dentistry, an isolated area in which the tooth root is denuded of bone from the margin nearly to the apex. It occurs more often in anterior than posterior teeth, and more on the vestibular than the oral surface.

PATIENT CARE: Dehiscence can be lessened by assessing nutritional status and risk factors such as obesity or malnourishment before surgery; by ensuring proper nutrition as time permits; and by providing support for the wound during coughing and movements that strain the incision. Surgically, stay sutures and wound bridges may minimize cases at risk. If dehiscence occurs, the surgeon is notified immediately, and the wound is covered with a sterile dressing or towel moistened with warm sterile physiological saline solution. The cov-

ering may need to be held in place by hand to keep abdominal tissues from "spilling" into the wound until a restraining bandage can be applied. The patient should flex the knees slightly to decrease tension on the abdominal muscles. The patient is kept calm and quiet, is reassured that measures are being taken to care for the wound, and is prepared physically and emotionally for surgery to close the wound. SEE: *Nursing Diagnoses Appendix.*

dehumanization (dē-hū″măn-ĭ-zā′shŭn) [L. *de,* from, + *humanus,* human] Loss of human qualities, as occurs in psychotic or in previously normal people subjected to torture or mental stress imposed by others.

dehumidifier (dē″hū-mĭd′ĭ-fī″ĕr) A device for removing moisture from the air.

dehydrate (dē-hī′drāt″) [*de-* + *hydrate*] **1.** In chemistry, to deprive of, lose, or become free of water, e.g., by removing surface or environmental water from it, or by removing bound water of crystallization. **2.** To lose or be deprived of water from the body or tissues. **3.** To become dry.

dehydration (dē″hī″drā′shŏn) [*de-* + *hydration*] **1.** The removal of water from a chemical, e.g., by surface evaporation or by heating it to release water of crystallization. **2.** The clinical consequences of negative fluid balance, i.e., of fluid intake that fail to match fluid loss. Dehydration is marked by thirst, orthostatic hypotension, tachycardia, elevated plasma sodium levels, hyperosmolality, and, in severe instances, cellular disruption, delirium, falls, hyperthermia, medication toxicity, renal failure, or death. SEE: *Nursing Diagnoses Appendix;* illus.

ETIOLOGY: Worldwide, the most common cause of dehydration is diarrhea. In industrialized nations, dehydration is also caused by vomiting, fe-

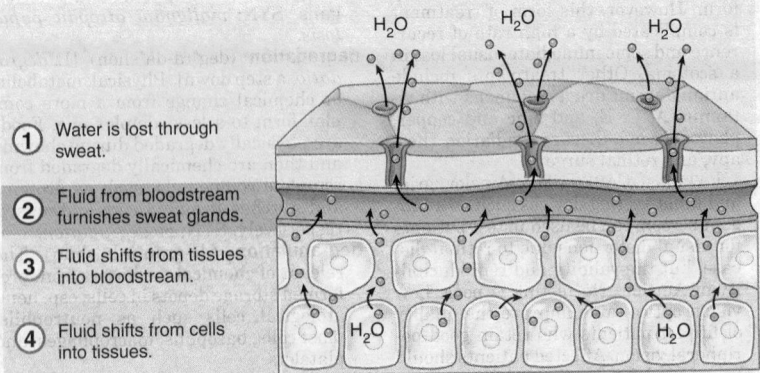

① Water is lost through sweat.

② Fluid from bloodstream furnishes sweat glands.

③ Fluid shifts from tissues into bloodstream.

④ Fluid shifts from cells into tissues.

DEHYDRATION RESULTING FROM SWEATING

vers, heat-related illnesses, diabetes mellitus, diuretic use, thyrotoxicosis, and hypercalcemia. Patients at risk for dehydration include those with an impaired level of consciousness and/or an inability to ingest oral fluids, patients receiving only high-protein enteral feedings, older adults who do not drink enough water, and patients (esp. infants and children) with watery diarrhea. The elderly (esp. those over 85) are increasingly hospitalized for dehydration. Dehydration is avoidable and preventable. Lengthy fasting before a procedure, long waits in emergency departments, or increased physical dependency (e.g., being unable to pour water from a bedside container) may place patients at risk. Nursing home residents are at higher risk for dehydration than older adults living independently, partly because of limited access to oral fluids. The elderly also are at risk because of reduced thirst-response, a decrease in total body fluids, and declining renal function. Clinical states that can produce hypertonicity and dehydration include a deficiency in synthesis or release of antidiuretic hormone (ADH) from the posterior pituitary gland (diabetes insipidus); a decrease in renal responsiveness to ADH; osmotic diuresis (hyperglycemic states, administration of osmotic diuretics); excessive pulmonary water loss from high fever (esp. in children); and excessive sweating without water replacement.

⚠️ Dehydration should not be confused with fluid volume deficit. In the latter condition, water and electrolytes are lost in the same proportion as they exist in normal body fluids; thus, the electrolyte to water ratio remains unchanged. In dehydration, water is the primary deficiency, resulting in increased levels of electrolytes or hypertonicity.

PATIENT CARE: The patient is assessed for decreased skin turgor; dry, sticky mucous membranes; rough, dry tongue; weight loss; fever; restlessness; agitation; and weakness. Cardiovascular findings include orthostatic hypotension, decreased cardiovascular pressure, and a rapid, weak pulse. Hard stools result if the patient's problem is not primarily watery diarrhea. Urinary findings include a decrease in urine volume (oliguria), specific gravity higher than 1.030, and an increase in urine osmolality. Blood serum studies reveal increased sodium, protein, hematocrit, and serum osmolality.

Continued loss of water is prevented, and water replacement is provided as prescribed, usually beginning with a 5% dextrose in water solution intra-venously if the patient cannot ingest oral fluids. Once adequate renal function is present, electrolytes can be added to the infusion based upon periodic evaluation of serum electrolyte levels. Health care professionals can prevent dehydration by quickly treating causes such as vomiting and diarrhea, measuring fluid intake (and where possible urine output) in at-risk patients, providing glasses and cups that are light and easily handled, teaching certified nursing assistants (CNAs) and family care providers to record fluid intake, observing urine concentration in incontinent patients, offering fluids in small amounts every time they interact with an at-risk patient, encouraging increased amounts of fluids (at the patient's preferred temperature) with and between meals and at bedtime (to 50 oz or 1500 mL/day unless otherwise restricted), and offering preferred fluids and a variety of fluids (including frozen juice bars, water-rich fruits and vegetables), and assessing for excessive fluid loss during hot weather and replacing it.

voluntary d. The willful refusal to eat, drink, or accept fluids from health care providers, sometimes used by the terminally ill to hasten death.

dehydroandrosterone (dē-hī″drō-ăn-drō-stĕr′ōn, -drŏs′tĕr-ōn) A previously used name for dehydroepiandrosterone.

dehydrocholesterol (dē-hī″drō-kŏ-les′tĕ-rol″) A sterol found in the skin and other tissues that forms vitamin D after activation by irradiation.

7-dehydrocholesterol reductase deficiency Smith-Lemli-Opitz syndrome.

dehydrocholic acid (dē-hī″drō-kŏl′ĭk) A bile salt that stimulates production of bile from the liver.

dehydrocorticosterone (dē-hī″drō-kor-tĭ-kōs′tĕr-ōn) A physiologically active steroid, $C_{21}H_{28}O_4$, isolated from the adrenal cortex. It is important in water and salt metabolism. Also called 11-dehydrocorticosterone.

dehydroepiandrosterone (dē-hī″drō-ĕp″ē-ăn-drŏs′tĕr-ōn) ABBR: DHEA. An androgenic substance, $C_{19}H_{28}O_2$, present in urine. It has about one fifth the potency of androsterone. The level of this hormone in plasma decreases with age. It is promoted as an antiaging, anticancer, and antiatherosclerosis agent by alternative medicine practitioners.

dehydrogenase (dē-hī-drŏj′ĕ-nās) An enzyme that catalyzes the oxidation of a specific substance, causing it to give up its hydrogen.

alcohol d. An enzyme that catabolizes ethyl alcohol (ethanol) in the liver. When ethanol is consumed in relatively large amounts, it is instead catabolized by the microsomal ethanol oxidizing system, also in the liver. SEE: *system, microsomal ethanol oxidizing.*

dehydrogenate (dē-hī″drŏj′ĕn-āt) To remove hydrogen from a chemical compound.

dehydroisoandrosterone (dĕ-hī″drō-ī″sō-ăn-drŏs′tĕr-ōn) A 17-ketosteroid excreted in normal male urine. It possesses androgenic activity.

deidentification (dē′ī-dĕn″tĭ-fĭ-kā′shŭn) The removal of personal identifying data (e.g., the patient's name, date of birth, address, phone number, social security number) from a medical record in order to ensure patient confidentiality.

deinstitutionalization (dē-ĭn″stĭ-tū″shŭn-ăl-ĭ-zā′shŭn) The placement of hospitalized psychiatric patients in the community in halfway houses, community mental health centers, residential hotels, group homes, or boarding houses.

deionization (dē-ī″ŏn-ī-zā′shŭn) Removal of ions from a substance, producing a substance free of minerals.

Deiters, Otto F.C. (dī′tĕrz) [Otto F. C. Deiters, Ger. anatomist, 1834–1863] Nineteenth century German anatomist/histologist.

    D. cell A supporting cell for the sensory-motor outer hair cells of the organ of Corti in the cochlea.

    D. nucleus Lateral vestibular **nucleus.**

déjà entendu (dā′zhà ŏn-tŏn-doo′) [Fr., already heard] **1.** Recognition of something previously understood. **2.** The illusion that what one is hearing was heard previously.

déjà vu (dā′zhà voo) [Fr., already seen] The illusion that something seen or some situation being experienced for the first time has been previously seen or experienced.

dejecta (dē-jĕk′tà) [L. *dejectio,* injection] Feces; intestinal waste.

dejection (dē-jĕk′shŭn) **1.** A cast-down feeling or mental depression. **2.** Defecation or act of defecation.

Dejerine, Joseph Jules (dĕ-zhrēn′) Swiss-born Fr. neurologist, 1849–1917.

    D. syndrome A condition in which deep sensation is depressed but tactile sense is normal, caused by a lesion of the long root fibers of the posterior spinal column.

Dejerine-Roussy syndrome (dĕ-zhrēn′roo-sē′) [Joseph Jules Dejerine; Gustave Roussy, Swiss-Fr. neuropathologist, 1874–1948] Thalamic pain syndrome.

Dejerine-Sottas disease (dā″zhĕr-ēn′ sō′tŏs) An inherited, progressive, motor, and sensory demyelinating neuropathy. Nerve roots from affected persons are hypertrophied.

deka-, dek- [Gr. *deka,* ten] In the Système International d'Unités (SI system), prefixes meaning 10¹. SEE: *deca-*.

delamination (dē-lăm″ĭ-nā′shŭn) [″ + *lamina,* plate] Division into layers, esp. that of a blastoderm into two layers—epiblast and hypoblast.

Delaney clause (dĕ-lā′nē) [After an amendment in 1958 made by James *Delaney,* Congressman from New York] A clause in the U.S. Food, Drug, and Cosmetic Act that bans any additive that causes cancer when it is consumed by animals or humans.

de Lange syndrome (dĕ lang′) [Cornelia de Lange, Dutch pediatrician, 1871–1950] SEE: *Cornelia de Lange syndrome.*

de la Tourette SEE: *de la Tourette, Georges Gilles.*

delayed hypersensitivity reaction A localized skin response mediated by T cells, which occurs 24 to 72 hr after injection of a specific antigen to which the person has been previously sensitized. It is used routinely to screen for tuberculosis infection through injection of purified protein derivative of *Mycobacterium tuberculosis.* In patients with immunodeficiency, common microbial antigens to which most people have been exposed, such as diphtheria, tetanus, measles, or *Candida,* are used to determine the presence of defects in T-cell–mediated immunity (CMI). If patients do not develop induration at the site, indicating a positive response to the antigen, a CMI defect is present. Delayed hypersensitivity is a type IV hypersensitivity reaction mediated by cytokines released by macrophages and helper T cells. SYN: *nonimmediate allergic reaction.*

delayed reaction A reaction occurring a considerable time after a stimulus, esp. a reaction such as a skin inflammation occurring hours or days after exposure to the allergen.

de-lead (dē-lĕd) To remove lead from the body or a tissue. SEE: *chelate.*

deleterious (dĕl″ē-tē′rē-ŭs) [Gr. *deleterios*] Harmful.

deletion (dē-lē′shŭn) In cytogenetics, the loss of a portion of a chromosome.

Delhi boil (del′ē) [City in N India] cutaneous leishmaniasis.

delicate Having a fine, fragile structure.

delimitation (dē-lĭm″ĭ-tā′shŭn) [L. *de,* from, + *limitare,* to limit] Determination of limits of an area or organ in diagnosis.

delinquent (dē-lĭn′kwĕnt) **1.** Someone, esp. a juvenile, whose behavior is criminal or antisocial. **2.** Of a criminal or antisocial nature. **3.** Overdue or late.

deliquescence (dĕ″lĭ-kwĕs′ĕns) The process of becoming liquefied or moist by absorbing of water from the air. Ordinary table salt has this property. **deliquescent,** *adj.*

deliriant (dē-lĭr′ē-ănt) [L. *delirare,* to leave the furrow, be frenzied] An agent that alters mental status, causing agitated confusion, e.g., atropine or other anticholinergic drugs.

delirium (di-lir'ē-ŭm) [L. *delirium,* madness, insanity] An acute, reversible state of disorientation and confusion. Delirium is marked by disorientation without drowsiness; hallucinations or delusions; difficulty in focusing attention; inability to rest or sleep; and emotional, physical, and autonomic overactivity.

ETIOLOGY: Common causes include drug and alcohol withdrawal; medication side effects; infections (esp. sepsis); pain; surgery or trauma; hypoxia; electrolyte and acid-base imbalances; sensory deprivation and sensory overload; dementia; hospitalization and/or depression, esp. but not exclusively in people 65 years or older.

TREATMENT: Treatment involves determining the cause of the delirium and removing or resolving it if possible.

PATIENT CARE: Preventive measures may sometimes reduce the risk of delirium in hospitalized patients. Such measures include providing glasses and hearing aids to patients with known sensory defects; mobilizing patients or providing range-of-motion (ROM) activities several times each day; avoiding multiple new medications; maintaining hydration by encouraging oral fluid intake; using holistic measures to promote relaxation; inducing sleep and reducing anxiety; and engaging family members or people familiar to delirious patients in their care.

The health care professional should consider delirium whenever an acute change in mental status occurs. Supportive care consists of minimizing unanticipated, frightening, or invasive procedures; integrating orienting statements into normal conversation; and providing confused patients with a calm supportive presence. When patients express deluded thoughts, it is important not to try to convince them that their perceptions are distorted. Speaking in a calm, clear voice, talking directly to the patient and using only simple statements and questions, and maintaining eye contact may be helpful. Maintaining caregiver consistency and encouraging family visiting are especially beneficial. Delirious patients should be roomed close to nursing stations so that they can be frequently observed. Physical protection from self-injury should be provided by bed alarms, wander guards, or mattresses placed on the floor to decrease the likelihood of patients' falling. Delirious patients should be permitted to sleep without interruption. Pain that they experience should be treated with analgesic drugs that do not affect mental status. Large calendars and clocks should be provided to aid orientation.

Natural light should be used to delineate day and night. Other useful preventive interventions include limiting interfacility transfers and room changes as much as possible and providing complementary therapies to decrease agitation and aggression (e.g., music therapy, massage, and shared activities). Antipsychotic drugs and benzodiazepines may be used cautiously when other nonpharmacological interventions have failed.

   acute d. Delirium that develops suddenly.

   alcoholic d. D. tremens.

   d. cordis Atrial **fibrillation**.

   emergence d. Unusually intense agitation in a patient awakening from anesthesia.

   febrile d. Delirium occurring with fever.

   toxic d. Delirium resulting from exposure to or ingestion of a psychically active agent, e.g., jimson weed, lysergic acid diethylamide (LSD), mescaline, or psilocybin.

   traumatic d. Delirium following injury or shock.

   d. tremens ABBR: DT. The most severe expression of alcohol withdrawal syndrome, marked by visual, auditory, or tactile hallucinations, extreme disorientation, restlessness, and hyperactivity of the autonomic nervous system (evidenced by such findings as pupillary dilation, fever, tachycardia, hypertension, and profuse sweating). About 15% of affected patients may die, usually as a result of comorbid illnesses. In most affected patients, recovery occurs within 3 to 5 days. SYN: *alcoholic **d.*** SEE: *alcoholism; alcohol withdrawal syndrome.*

TREATMENT: Sedation with benzodiazepines is the chief therapy. Other supportive care includes airway protection (and intubation when indicated); fluid and electrolyte resuscitation; hemodynamic support; protection of the patient from injury; and precautions against seizure. Comorbid conditions resulting from chronic alcoholism (e.g., pancreatitis, esophagitis, hepatitis, or malnutrition) may complicate therapy.

PATIENT CARE: The patient and those nearby need to be protected from harm while prescribed treatment is carried out to relieve withdrawal symptoms. The patient's mental status, cardiopulmonary and hepatic functions, and vital signs (including body temperature) are monitored in anticipation of complicating hyperthermia or circulatory collapse. Prescribed drug and fluid therapy, titrated to the patient's symptoms and blood pressure response, are administered as prescribed, or by symptom-triggered algorithms. A calm, evenly illuminated environment is provided to reduce visual hallucinations.

The patient is addressed by name; surroundings are validated frequently to orient the patient to reality, and all procedures are explained. The patient is observed closely and left alone as little as possible. Physical restraints should be reserved for patients who are combative or who have attempted to injure themselves. Patience, tact, understanding, and support are imperative throughout the acute withdrawal period. Once the acute withdrawal has subsided, the patient is advised of the need for further treatment and supportive counseling. SEE: *Nursing Diagnoses Appendix*.

⚠ It is crucial to distinguish the signs and symptoms of alcoholic delirium from those caused by intracerebral hemorrhage, meningitis, or intoxication with substances other than alcohol. Evaluation of the patient suspected of having the DTs may therefore require neuroimaging, lumbar puncture, or drug screening.

deliver (dĕ-liv′ĕr) [L. *deliberare*, to free completely] **1.** To aid in childbirth. **2.** To give birth. **3.** To remove or extract, as a tumor from a cystic enclosure or a cataract.

delivery (di-liv′ĕ-rē) [Fr. fr L. *deliberare*, to set free] **1.** Giving birth to a child, together with the placenta and membranes, by a parturient woman. SEE: *labor*. **2.** The provision and administration of a therapeutic agent to a patient.

> **abdominal d.** Delivery of a child by cesarean section.

> **assisted d.** Assisted **birth**.

> **breech d.** Delivery of the fetus that presents in the breech position, i.e., the buttocks are the first part of the body to be delivered. SYN: *breech* **extraction**. SEE: *breech* **presentation**.

> **elective d.** Aiding the birth of a newborn before the onset of uterine contractions or the spontaneous rupture of membranes.

> **forceps d.** Delivery of a child by application of forceps to the fetal head. *Outlet forceps deliveries* are performed when the scalp of the fetus is visible at the vaginal introitus and the fetal skull has descended to the pelvic floor. *Low forceps deliveries* are performed when the fetal skull is at or above station +2 cm and not on the pelvic floor. *Midforceps deliveries* are performed when the station is above +2 cm but the head is engaged. *High forceps deliveries*, performed in the past, are no longer performed.

> **operative d.** Delivery of a newborn with forceps, by surgery, e.g. cesarean section, or by vacuum extraction.

> **precipitous d.** An unexpected birth caused by swift progression through the second stage of labor with rapid fetal descent and expulsion. SEE: *precipitate* **labor**.

PATIENT CARE: Although primiparas may experience unduly rapid labor and delivery, the event is more common among multiparas. Signs to be alert for are an accelerating second stage, such as the abrupt onset of strong contractions, an intense urge to bear down, or the patient's conviction that delivery is imminent. To diminish the urge to push, the woman should be encouraged to pant.

Emergency delivery by health care professionals. If time permits, the health care provider opens the emergency delivery pack, scrubs, and gloves, and places a sterile drape under the patient's buttocks. As crowning occurs, the health care provider uses the dominant hand to gently support the oncoming fetal head and the other hand to support the woman's perineum. If the amniotic sac is intact, the membranes are to be broken. The head should be born between contractions and supported as it emerges. The health care provider immediately feels for a nuchal cord. If the cord loosely encircles the infant's neck, it should be slipped over the infant's head. If it is tightly looped, two clamps are used to occlude the cord and cut it between them; the clamp is left in place. The health care provider unwinds the cord and suctions the infant's nose and mouth. He or she places one hand on either side of the infant's head and gently exerts downward traction to deliver the anterior shoulder. Gentle upward traction assists delivery of the posterior shoulder, and the body emerges as the mother gently pushes. Standard birthing protocols are then followed, such as using a bulb syringe to suction the newborn as needed, drying the infant, and placing the newborn on the mother's abdomen (skin to skin) in a head-dependent position to facilitate drainage of mucus and fluid. The patient is assessed for signs of placental separation (small gush of blood, more cord protruding from the vagina, fundal rebound). Traction on the cord to hasten placental separation is contraindicated. The postdelivery status of the mother and newborn is assessed and recorded.

> **premature d.** Preterm **d.**

> **preterm d.** Childbirth that occurs between the date of fetal viability and the end of the 37th week of gestation. SYN: *premature d.* SEE: *preterm* **labor**.

> **site-specific d.** Any of the techniques to help a therapeutic agent concentrate in the organ where it will have the greatest effect. These include attaching a drug to a monoclonal antibody or administering prodrugs that are converted to active agents only in targeted cells.

spontaneous d. Delivery of an infant without external aid.

vaginal d. Expulsion of a child, placenta, and membranes through the birth canal.

ventouse d. Removal of the fetus from the womb with a vacuum extractor.

dellen (děl'ĕn) Thinning in the periphery of the cornea that results from locally inadequate lubrication of the corneal surface.

delouse (dē-lows') [*de-* + *louse*] To treat a person infected with ectoparasites, esp. lice or scabies.

delousing (dē-lows'ing) [L. *de,* from, + AS. *lus,* louse] Ridding the body of lice. SEE: *louse.*

Delphi method (del'fī") [After the oracle of Apollo at *Delphi*] SEE: under *method.*

delta (del'tă) **1.** Δ or δ, the uppercase and lowercase symbols, respectively, for the fourth letter of the Greek alphabet. **2.** A triangular space. **3.** In calculus, a change in value or amount of something being measured or monitored.

deltacortisone (děl"tă-kor'tĭ-sōn) Prednisone, a steroid hormone with glucocorticoid activity.

delusion (di-loo'zhŏn) [L. *deludere,* to cheat] A false belief without appropriate external stimulation and inconsistent with the individual's own knowledge and experience. It is seen most often in psychoses, in which patients may not be able to distinguish their own unverified thoughts, fears, or feelings from reality. It differs from hallucination in that the latter involves the false excitation of one or more senses. The most serious delusions are those that cause patients to harm others or themselves, e.g., fear of being poisoned may cause the patient to refuse food. Delusions may lead to suicide or self-injury. False beliefs include being persecuted or being guilty of an unpardonable sin. SEE: *hallucination; illusion.*

antichrist d. The psychotic belief that other people are devils. Patients with this delusion often react violently to those whom they suspect of being demonic.

d. of control A delusion that one's thoughts and actions are under the control of an external force.

fixed d. A delusion that remains unaltered.

d. of grandeur An unreasonable conviction of one's own power, importance, or wealth, accompanied by a feeling of well-being, seen in manic patients. SYN: *megalomania.*

d. of persecution A delusion in which patients believe people or agencies are seeking to injure or harass them.

d. of substitution Capgras syndrome.

delusional Pert. to a delusion.

demand (di-mand') [L. *demandare,* to charge, entrust] **1.** A need for something. **2.** A legal obligation asserted in courts, e.g., payment of a debt or monetary award for injuries suffered by the plaintiff and caused by the defendant. **3.** In health care delivery, the amount of care a population seeks to use. **4.** In patient-controlled analgesia, a request for a dose of a pain-relieving medication.

activity d. Any of the characteristics of tasks pertinent for analyzing how a given task must be taught and performed. These characteristics include specific actions, space requirements, objects, body functions, time requirements, and sequences.

biological oxygen d. The amount of oxygen required for a biological reaction, esp. the oxygen required to oxidize materials in natural water supplies, e.g., rivers or lakes. SEE: *eutrophication.*

metabolic d. ABBR: Q/VO₂. The cardiac output divided by the oxygen uptake.

specific adaptations to imposed d. ABBR: SAID. A principle in exercise prescription that any tissue will alter its structure to accommodate the stresses placed on it. The intensity and direction of force, type and speed of muscle contraction, frequency and duration of exercise, range of motion, and external environment influence tissue adaptation. In physical therapy, SAID is used to prescribe the best exercises to regain function in work and sports.

demand-induced ischemia SEE: under *ischemia.*

demarcation (dē"măr-kā'shŭn) [L. *demarcare,* to limit] A limit or boundary.

demasculinization (dē-măs"kū-lĭn-ĭ-zā'shŭn) Loss of male sexual characteristics. This may be caused by lack of the male hormone or by the action of certain drugs.

Dematiaceae (dē"mă-tē-ā'sē-ē) A family of fungi that contain melanin in their cell walls and have a dark color. They occasionally infect humans, esp. those who are immunocompromised. SYN: *dematiaceous fungus.*

dematiaceous (dē"mă-tē-ā'shŭs, dĕm") Pert. to fungi having a dark brown or black appearance. The dark pigment is found in the hyphae or the conidia.

demented (dē-mĕnt'ĕd) Chronically cognitively impaired. SEE: *dementia.*

dementia (di-men'chă) [L. *dementia,* madness] A progressive, irreversible decline in mental function, marked by memory impairment and, often, deficits in reasoning, judgment, abstract thought, registration, comprehension, learning, task execution, and use of language. The cognitive impairments diminish a person's social, occupational, and intellectual abilities. In the U.S., 4.5 million people are afflicted by dementia. The prevalence is esp. high in the very elderly: about 20% to 40% of those over 85 are demented. Dementia is somewhat more common in women than in men. It must be distinguished by careful clinical examination from delirium, psychosis, depression, and the effects of medications. SEE: *Alzheimer disease; Huntington chorea; Parkinson disease;* table.

SYMPTOMS: The onset of primary dementia may be slow, taking months or years. Memory deficits, impaired abstract thinking, poor judgment, and clouding of consciousness and orientation are not present until the terminal stages; depression, agitation, sleeplessness, and paranoid ideation may be present. Patients become dependent for activities of daily living and typically die from complications of immobility in the terminal stage.

ETIOLOGY: Dementia may result from many illnesses, including AIDS, chronic alcoholism, Alzheimer disease, vitamin B_{12} deficiency, carbon monoxide poisoning, cerebral anoxia, hypothyroidism, subdural hematoma, or multiple brain infarcts (vascular dementia).

TREATMENT: Some medications, e.g., donepezil, nemantidine, and tacrine, improve cognitive function in some patients.

PATIENT CARE: Demented patients deserve respectful and dignified care at all stages of their disease. Caregivers assist the demented with activities of daily living and with the cognitive and behavioral changes that accompany the disease. A variety of nursing interventions may reduce the risk of inadvertently precipitating behavioral symptoms. Health care professionals should reinforce the patient's abilities and successes rather than disabilities and failures. Caregivers can help the patient make optimal use of his or her abilities by reducing the adverse effects of other health conditions, sensory impairments, and cognitive defects while maximizing social and environmental factors that support functional capacity. Daily routines should be adjusted to focus on the person rather than the task,

e.g., the comfort of bathing rather than the perceived need to bathe in a certain way at a certain time.

Interaction and communication strategies should be adjusted to ensure that the message delivered is the one perceived (obtain attention, make eye contact, speak directly to the individual, match nonverbal communication and gestures to the message, slow the pace of speech, use declarative sentences, use nouns instead of pronouns). Commands including the word "don't" and questions beginning with "why" should be avoided. Tasks should be broken down into manageable steps. Reassurance and encouragement are provided to assist the patient to act more independently. Reality grounding is not necessary for such a patient; thus, if the patient asks to see his mother (who is dead), reminding him of her death may reinforce the pain of that loss. It may be better to redirect the conversation, asking the patient to talk about his mother, instead. Written agreements and reminders may not be as useful as they would be in the care of other patients, for a demented patient may not remember what has been negotiated and agreed upon in the past. The patient's environment should be adjusted to provide needed safety. Finding the correct balance between doing too much or too little may be difficult for the caregiver, who should recognize that the balance may shift day to day and that patience and flexibility are more helpful. Caregivers must be aware that the patient will have moments of lucidity, which should be treasured but not considered evidence that the patient is exaggerating or feigning his or her disease to obtain attention. Family members who provide care must be aware that they, too, have emotional needs and can become angry, frustrated, and impatient and that they need help to learn to forgive themselves as well as the loved one they are caring for. Finally, such caregivers must learn how to accept help and should not fear to admit that they cannot carry the burden of care by themselves.

AIDS-d. complex SEE: *AIDS-dementia complex.*

alcoholic d. A form of toxic dementia in which there is loss of memory and problem-solving ability after many years of alcohol abuse.

d. of the Alzheimer type ABBR: DAT. SEE: *Alzheimer disease.*

Binswanger d. **Binswanger** disease.

dialysis d. A neurological disturbance in patients who have been on dialysis for several years. There are speech difficulties, myoclonus, dementia, seizures, and, eventually, death.

Prevalence of Dementia, by Patient Age

Age	Prevalence
<60	0.1%
60–64	~1%
>65	3 — 11%
>85	25 — 47%

The causative agent is presumed to be aluminum in the dialysate.

epileptic d. An infrequent complication of epilepsy, presumed to result from injury to neurons during uncontrolled seizures.

frontotemporal d. A general term for any of four types of dementia: 1. frontotemporal lobar degeneration; 2. Pick's disease; 3. primary progressive aphasia; or 4. semantic dementia. Symptoms include personality changes, apathy, compulsive or repetitive behavior, lack of social inhibition, and deterioration in language use.

HIV-associated d. SEE: *AIDS-dementia* **complex**.

d. with Lewy bodies A common neurodegenerative disease characterized by gradual and progressive loss of intellectual abilities combined with a movement disorder that resembles Parkinson disease. Those affected often have marked fluctuations in their ability to stay alert and awake and also visual hallucinations. The disease is characterized pathologically by deposits of Lewy bodies. The dementia is treated symptomatically.

mixed d. Dementia in which elements of both Alzheimer disease and vascular dementia are found.

multi-infarct d. Dementia resulting from multiple small strokes. After Alzheimer disease, it is the most common form of dementia in the U.S. It has a distinctive natural history. Unlike Alzheimer disease, which develops insidiously, the cognitive deficits of multi-infarct dementia appear suddenly, in stepwise fashion. The disease is rare before middle age and is most common in patients with hypertension, diabetes mellitus, or other risk factors for generalized atherosclerosis. Brain imaging in patients with this form of dementia shows multiple lacunar infarctions. SYN: *vascular* **d.**

d. paralytica An obsolete term for tertiary syphilis.

presenile d. Dementia beginning in middle age, usually resulting from cerebral arteriosclerosis or Alzheimer disease. The symptoms are apathy, loss of memory, and disturbances of speech and gait. SEE: *Nursing Diagnoses Appendix.*

primary d. Dementia associated with Alzheimer disease.

d. pugilistica Traumatic dementia, i.e., encephalopathy or an organic brain syndrome caused by closed head injury. It is sometimes referred to colloquially as "boxer's brain."

semantic d. Any of a group of brain disorders marked by nearly complete losses in the understanding of word meanings, spelling, and the identification or recognition of facts, faces, or objects. The disease is marked pathologically by local atrophy in the neocortex of the temporal lobe of the brain.

senile d. of the Alzheimer type ABBR: SDAT. **Alzheimer** disease.

subcortical vascular d. **Binswanger** disease.

vascular d. ABBR: VaD. Multi-infarct **d.**

demi- [Fr. *demi*, fr. L. *dimidius*, half] Prefix meaning *half.*

demilune (dĕm'ĭ-loon) [L. *dimidius*, half, + *luna*, moon] A crescent-shaped group of serous cells that form a caplike structure over a mucous alveolus. They are present in mixed glands, esp. the submandibular gland.

demineralization (dē-mĭn″ĕr-ăl-ĭ-zā′shŭn) [L. *de*, from, + *minare*, to mine] Loss of mineral salts, esp. from the teeth or bones. It occurs commonly in dental caries; next to joints in people with arthritis; in bones that have been immobilized; in underutilized bones after stroke; and in osteoporosis. SEE: *decalcification.*

demise (dĕ-mīz′) [L. *dimittere*, to dismiss] Death.

demodectic (dĕm-ō-dĕk′tĭk) Concerning or caused by the mite *Demodex.*

Demodex (dem′ŏ-deks″, dĕm′) [Gr. *dēmos*, fat + *dex*, worm] A genus of mites of the class Arachnida (order Acarina).

D. folliculorum A species that infests hair follicles and sebaceous glands of various mammals, including humans. SYN: *Acarus folliculorum; follicle mite.*

demography (di-mog′ră-fē) [Gr. *dēmos*, people + *-graphy*] The study of measurable characteristics of human populations. The characteristics may include population size, growth, density, age, race, sex, or marital status. The information may be used to forecast health needs and the use of health services. **demographic** (dē″mŏ-graf′ik, dem″ŏ-), *adj.*

demoniac (dĕ-mō′nē-ak″) **1.** Concerning or resembling a demon. **2.** Frenzied, as if possessed by demons or evil spirits.

demotivate (dē-mō′tĭ-vāt) To cause loss of incentive or motivation.

demulcent (dĕ-mŭl′sĕnt) [L. *demulcens*, stroking softly] An oily or mucilaginous agent used to soothe or soften an irritated surface, esp. mucous membranes. SEE: *emollient.*

demyelinate (dē-mī′ĕ-lĭ-nāt″) [*de-* + *myelinate*] To remove the myelin sheath of nerve tissue.

demyelination Destruction or removal of the myelin sheath of nerve tissue, seen in Guillain-Barré syndrome, multiple sclerosis, and many other neurological diseases.

denature (dē-nā′chŭr) [*de-* + *nature*] **1.** In chemistry, to change the qualities of a substance, esp. to make alcohol (ethyl alcohol) unfit to drink by adding an unpleasant ingredient, e.g. methanol. **2.** In biochemistry, to make a change in conditions (temperature, addition of a substance) that causes an irreversible change in the structure of a protein, usually resulting in precipitation of the protein. **2.** In genetics, to separate double-stranded DNA into two complementary strands, usually with heat. **denatured** ('chŭrd), *adj.* **denaturation** (dē″nā″chŭ-rā′shŏn), *n.*

dendr-, dendro- [Gr. *dendron*, tree] Prefixes meaning *tree.*

dendric (dĕn′drĭk) Pert. to or possessing a dendrite.

dendriform (dĕn′drĭ-form) [″ + L. *forma*, shape] Branching or treelike.

dendrite (dĕn′drīt″) [Gr. *dendritēs*, pert. to a tree] A short spike-shaped cell process. The term usually refers to the branched, tapering cell processes of neurons. Incoming synapses form on the neuronal dendrites, which often arborize, sometimes extensively. SYN: *dendron.* SEE: illus.

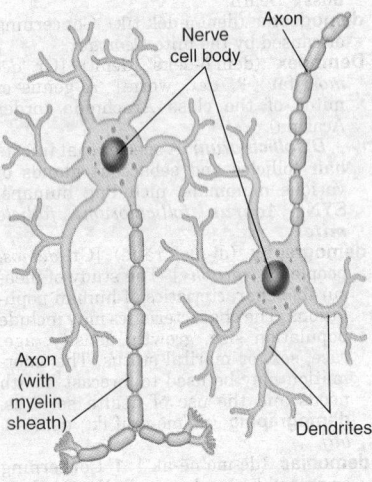

DENDRITES

dendritic (den-drit′ik), *adj.*

dendroid (dĕn′droyd) [″ + *eidos,* form, shape] **1.** Dendriform; dendritic; pert. to dendrites. **2.** Arborescent; treelike.

dendron (dĕn′drŏn) [Gr., tree] Dendrite.

denervation (dē-nĕrv-ā′shŭn) [L. *de,* from, + Gr. *neuron,* nerve] **1.** Excision, incision, or blocking of a nerve supply. **2.** A condition in which the afferent and efferent nerves are cut. SEE: *deafferentation.*

dengue (deng′gē, gā) [Sp. *dengue,* fr Swahili *dinga,* cramp] An acute febrile illness, often presenting with severe musculoskeletal pain, caused by one of four serotypes of flavivirus. The disease

is transmitted to humans by the bite of the *Aedes aegypti* mosquito. It is endemic in tropical regions of the world and a major health problem in Southeast Asia, Mexico, and Central America, where it causes periodic epidemic disease. Worldwide, tens of millions of people have been infected. Sporadic outbreaks occur in the warmer regions in the U.S., e.g., Texas and Hawaii. SYN: *dengue fever.*

SYMPTOMS: The incubation period of 5 to 7 days precedes sudden onset of fever, myalgia, arthralgias, headache, and abdominal pain; a rash may develop 3 days later. Most patients recover without a problem. About 5% of patients develop dengue hemorrhagic fever. The illness often affects children and is frequently fatal.

DIAGNOSIS: An enzyme-linked immunosorbent assay for dengue antibodies may facilitate diagnosis. SEE: *dengue hemorrhagic fever.*

dengue hemorrhagic fever SEE: under *fever.*

denial (dĕ-nī′ăl) **1.** Refusal to admit the reality of or to acknowledge the presence or existence of something; keeping of anxiety-producing realities from conscious awareness. This is a defense mechanism. **2.** In medical care reimbursement, the decision by the patient's insurer that part or all of the medical care administered was not justified. The result of the denial is that the insurer refuses to pay for all or a portion of the medical costs incurred.

denial and isolation According to Elisabeth Kübler-Ross, the initial emotional reactions to being told of impending death. Individuals refuse to accept the diagnosis and seek additional professional opinions in the hope that the predicted outcome is erroneous. When these efforts are in vain, the patient feels isolated and abandoned. SEE: *acceptance.*

denitrify (dē-nī′trĭ-fĭ) To remove nitrogen from something.

denitrogenation (dē-nī″trŏ-jĕn-ā′shŭn) In aerospace medicine, the removal of nitrogen from the body of a person preparing to fly in an environment in which the barometric pressure will be much lower than at sea level. Prior to the flight, the person breathes 100% oxygen for a variable length of time, depending on the anticipated degree of reduced barometric pressure. SYN: *preoxygenation.* SEE: *decompression illness.*

de novo (dē nō′vō, dā, nō′wō) **1.** Over again from the beginning; anew. **2.** Previously undetected. **3.** Previously untreated.

dens (denz, den′tēz″) *pl.* **dentes** [L. *dens,* tooth] **1.** A tooth. SEE: *dentition* for illus. **2.** The odontoid process of the axis, which serves as a pivot for the rotation of the atlas.

d. caninus A canine tooth.

d. incisivus An incisor tooth.

d. in dente A dental anomaly found esp. in lateral maxillary incisors, in which radiographs reveal a toothlike structure within the tooth. It may cause pulp necrosis or other periapical difficulties. Treatments include endodontics or dental extraction. SYN: **d. invaginatus; dilated compound odontoma.**

d. invaginatus Dens in dente.

densitometer (děn″sĭ-tŏm′ĕ-tĕr) **1.** An instrument that measures bacterial growth and the effect on it of antiseptics and bacteriophages. **2.** In radiology, an instrument that measures the optical density of a radiograph.

densitometry (děn″sĭ-tŏm′ĕ-trē) **1.** The determination of the density of a substance (e.g., bone). **2.** The determination of the amount of ionizing radiation to which a person has been exposed.

bone d. SEE: *bone densitometry.*

density (den′sit-ē) [L. *densitas,* thickness] **1.** The relative weight of a substance compared with a reference standard; a physical parameter of a substance that is equal to its mass per unit volume. SEE: *specific* **gravity**. **2.** The quality of being dense; a physical parameter of a substance that is equal to its mass per unit volume. **3.** The extent of exposure of image receptors; formerly known as the blackness of the metallic silver that was visible in a developed radiographic film image. **4.** In digital imaging, *density* has been replaced by *image receptor (IR) exposure.*

areal bone mineral d. ABBR: areal BMD. The bone mineral content, measured by dual-energy x-ray absorptiometry (DEXA), divided by the bone area in square centimeters.

bone mass d. ABBR: BMD. Bone mineral **d.**

bone mineral d. ABBR: BMD. The average mineral concentration of a specimen of bone; skeletal mass. BMD is reduced in osteopenia and osteoporosis. A reduction in BMD predisposes patients to fractures. SYN: *bone mass* **d.**

PATIENT CARE: BMD can be measured by techniques such as dual x-ray absorptiometry (DEXA). Postmenopausal women should be assessed for osteoporosis and receive some form of BMD measurement so that, if their bone density is inadequate, they can be given treatment to lower the risk of fractures. Postmenopausal women with risk factors for osteoporosis or who have sustained osteoporotic fractures should undergo BMD testing.

caloric d. Calories per gram of food. The number of calories in a given mass of food influences hunger and feeding behaviors in animals and humans. When a limited amount of food is available, foods of higher caloric density are more likely to satisfy hunger than equivalent amounts of food with fewer calories. Calorically dense foods that provide little in the way of micronutrients are often termed empty calories. SEE: *satiety.* SYN: *energy* **d.**

current d. The amperage divided by the surface area to which it is applied, e.g., in electrosurgery.

energy d. Caloric **d.**

mammographic breast d. A radiological appearance of the mammary glands during mammography in which the epithelial and stromal elements of the breasts are more prominent than the fatty components. Breast density increases the likelihood that a mammogram will be difficult to interpret and that a patient will subsequently develop breast cancer.

microvessel d. The concentration of small blood vessels in a malignant tumor. It reflects the amount of angiogenesis within the tumor and has been correlated with the ability of tumors to grow and metastasize.

nutrient d. The ratio of the nutrients present in a food relative to its caloric value.

optical d. The ability of a laboratory specimen to absorb or block the passage of light. The optical density of a laboratory sample can be used as an indicator of the concentration of specific components in the sample. SYN: *optical absorbance.*

population d. The number of organisms, usually people, living within a defined space, such as a city, county, or town. In the U.S., regions with greater population densities tend to have different health care problems than lightly populated ones. Conditions such as gunshot wounds, HIV/AIDS, and tuberculosis are more common in cities than in rural areas, but cities also tend to have a greater health care infrastructure and more professional resources than rural areas.

relative d. Specific **gravity**.

dental Pert. to the teeth.

dental apparatus The tooth and its supporting tissues.

dental assistant One who assists in the care and treatment of dental patients. The responsibilities vary according to the needs of the dentist, the training and capability of the individual, and the state regulations of duties.

dental chart A diagram of the teeth on which clinical and radiographic findings can be recorded. It includes existing restorations, decayed surfaces, missing teeth, periodontal pocket depth, and the conditions of all soft tissues.

dental consonant A consonant pronounced with the tongue at or near the front upper teeth.

dental emergency An acute condition affecting the teeth, such as inflammation of the soft tissues surrounding teeth or post-treatment complications of dental surgery. It is best treated by a dentist. Nevertheless, the primary care physician and other health care professionals must be familiar with these emergency conditions and their management. SEE: table.

dental engineering A field of study that includes the manufacture, testing, and use of dental materials, such as cements, metallic alloys, and dental devices.

dental geriatrics SEE: under *geriatrics*.

dental handpiece (hand'pēs") An instrument for holding dental burs to remove tooth structure or to smooth and polish restorative materials. Handpiece rotations are measured in rotations per second. Handpieces may be powered by electric motor or air turbines and are characterized as high speed or low speed depending on their rotational speed.

⚠️ Overheated dental handpieces may burn oral tissues.

contra-angle d.h. A handpiece with one or more bends so that the shaft of the rotary instrument is at an angle to the handpiece to reach less accessible areas of the mouth for dental work.

high-speed d.h. A dental handpiece that operates at speeds about 100,000 to 800,000 rpm. The high-speed or ultra-speed handpiece operates with a water spray and may have a fiber-optic light to facilitate better visibility. A water spray is necessary to reduce the temperature within the handpiece and surgical site. SYN: *turbine d.h.*

low-speed d.h. A dental handpiece that operates at speeds about 6,000 to 10,000 rpm. Low-speed handpieces are used to polish and finish dental restorations.

turbine d.h. High-speed **d.h.**

dental identification The use of the unique characteristics of a person's teeth or dental work as recorded in dental charts, radiographs, and records to establish the person's identity.

dental laboratory technician Dental technician.

dental malposition Abnormal location of the teeth with respect to each other or to the mandible or maxilla.

dental material Any of several types of colloids, plastics, resins, and metal alloys used in dentistry to take impressions, restore teeth, or duplicate dentition.

dental tape Waxed or unwaxed thin tape

used for cleaning and removing plaque from between the teeth.

dental technician A technician who constructs or manufactures fixed restorations (bridgework), crowns, and other dental restorations as authorized by dentists. SYN: *dental laboratory technician.*

dental treatment Any of a variety of treatments of the teeth and adjacent tissues to restore or maintain normal oral health and function.

dental unit **1.** A masticatory unit consisting of a single tooth and its adjacent tissues. **2.** A mobile or fixed piece of equipment, usually complete with chair, light, engine, and other accessories or utilities necessary for dental examinations or operations.

dentate (děn'tāt) [L. *dentatus,* toothed] Notched; having short triangular divisions at the margin; toothed.

dentes (děn'tēz) *sing.,* **dens** [L.] Teeth.

dentia (děn'shē-ă) [L.] Eruption of teeth.

denticle (děn'tĭ-kl) [L. *denticulus,* little tooth] **1.** A small toothlike projection. **2.** A calcified structure within the pulp of the tooth. SYN: *pulp stone.*

denticulate (děn-tĭk'ū-lăt) [L. *denticulatus,* small-toothed] Finely toothed or serrated.

dentification (děn"ĭ-fĭ-kā'shŭn) [L. *dens,* tooth, + *facere,* to make] Conversion into dental structure.

dentiform (děnt'ĭ-form) [" + *forma,* shape] Toothlike.

dentifrice (děn'tĭ-frĭs) [" + *fricare,* to rub] A paste, liquid, gel, or powder for cleaning teeth. A dentifrice may be cosmetic or therapeutic. Cosmetic dentifrices must clean and polish; therapeutic dentifrices must reduce some disease process in the oral cavity. Each dentifrice generally contains an abrasive, water, humectants, a foaming agent, a binder, a flavoring agent, a sweetener, a therapeutic agent, a coloring material, and a preservative.

dentigerous (děn-tĭj'ěr-ŭs) [" + *gerere,* to bear] Having or containing teeth.

dentin, dentine (dent'ĭn, den"tēn', dentēn') [L. *dens,* tooth] The calcified part of the tooth surrounding the pulp chamber, covered by enamel in the crown and cementum in the root area. Dentin is called primary, secondary, or reparative according to its location inside the tooth and its relative sensitivity.

interglobular d. Dentin that contains spaces or hypomineralized areas between mineralized globules or calcospheres.

dentinal (děnt'-ĭn-ăl) Pert. to dentin.

dentine hypersensitivity Tooth pain resulting from exposure to cold temperatures, osmotic agents (e.g. sugars or other sweets), or touch. It is caused by exposure of dentinal tubules when ce-

Signs and Symptoms and Recommended Emergency Management of Odontogenic (Dental) Problems

Condition	Signs and Symptoms	Management
Periodontal disease		
Periodontal abscess	Localized pain; swelling of gingivae; possible sinus tract; lack of response to percussion; periodontal pocketing	Curettage to establish drainage; antibiotics; warm saline rinses; soft diet; referral to dentist
Pericoronitis	Pain and generalized soreness; inflamed operculum over partially erupted tooth	Irrigation; warm saline rinses; gentle massage with toothbrush; antibiotics for fever and lymphadenopathy; referral to dentist for possible tissue excision or tooth removal
Necrotizing ulcerative gingivitis	Generalized pain; bleeding gums; fetid odor; generalized gingival inflammation; necrotic tissue; loss of interdental papillae; fever	General débridement; daily saline rinses; hydration; referral to dentist; antibiotics if necessary; dietary recommendations; rinse twice daily with 1.2% chlorhexidine; brushing and flossing after resolution
Primary herpetic gingivostomatitis (highly infectious)	Gingival ulceration; fever; punctate lesions of gingivae and possibly dorsum of tongue; buccal mucosa, floor of mouth, lips; malaise; headache; irritability; lymphadenopathy	Rest; diluted mouthwashes; increased fluid intake; soft diet; topical analgesics; referral to dentist
Pulpitis and periapical problems		
Reversible pulpitis	Sharp, transient pain response to cold stimuli; recent dental restoration	Analgesics; avoidance of thermal stimuli; referral to dentist
Irreversible pulpitis	Spontaneous pain; persistent or lingering pain response to thermal stimuli	Referral to dentist for removal of pulp and root canal therapy or extraction of tooth
Periapical inflammation	Acute pain on percussion	Examination for lymph node involvement, intraoral and extraoral; swelling; fever; analgesics; referral to dentist
Periapical abscess	Tooth sensitive to touch; tooth mobile; fever; swelling or sinus tract; possible fever if systemic involvement	Thorough systemic examination; incision and drainage; antibiotics; analgesics; warm water rinses; referral to dentist
Post-treatment complications		
Alveolar osteitis (dry socket)	Throbbing pain 2–4 days after extraction	Irrigation of extraction site; sedative dressing (eugenol); analgesics; gauze packs, bone wax,; referral to dentist
Tooth sensitivity	Imbalance when teeth contact; thermal sensitivity; pain on closing mouth	Referral to dentist

SOURCE: Adapted from Comer, RW, et al: Dental emergencies. Postgrad Med 85(3):63, Feb. 1989.

mentum is worn off the outer layer of a tooth, e.g. in patients who have receding gums.

dentinogenesis (děn″tĭn-ō-jěn′ĕ-sĭs) [″ + *genesis,* generation, birth] Formation of dentin in the development of a tooth.

   d. imperfecta Hereditary aplasia or hypoplasia of the enamel and dentin of a tooth, resulting in misshapen blue or brown teeth.

dentinoid (děnt′inoyd) [″ + Gr. *eidos,* form, shape] **1.** Resembling dentin. **2.** The noncalcified matrix of dentin, similar to the noncalcified matrix of bone, which is called osteoid. SYN: *predentin.*

dentinoma (děn″tǐ-nō′mǎ) [″ + Gr. *oma,* tumor] A tumor composed of tissues from which the teeth originate, consisting mainly of dentin.

dentist [L. *dens,* tooth] ABBR: DDS, DMD. One who has been professionally trained and licensed to practice dentistry.

dentistry (dent′ĭ-strē) **1.** The branch of medicine dealing with the care of the teeth and associated structures of the oral cavity. It is concerned with the prevention, diagnosis, and treatment of diseases of the teeth and gums. **2.** The art or profession of a dentist.

   esthetic d. Any of those dental treatments that improve the location, visual appearance, and function of the teeth and jaws.

   forensic d. The area of dentistry particularly related to jurisprudence; usually, the identification of unknown persons by the details of their dentition and tooth restorations.

   Whereas forensic medicine often is used to establish the time and cause of death, forensic dentistry may be used to establish identity on the basis of dental records only.

   four-handed d. Extensive use of a chairside dental assistant to facilitate and enhance the productivity of the dentist.

   geriatric d. Dental **geriatrics**.

   hospital d. The practice of dentistry in a hospital where the dentist is an integral part of the comprehensive health care team.

   operative d. The restoration of dental structure with amalgam, gold, or other suitable materials.

   preventive d. That phase of dentistry concerned with the maintenance of the normal masticatory apparatus by teaching good oral hygiene and dietary practice, and preserving dental health by early restorative procedures. SEE: table.

   public health d. The area of dentistry that seeks to improve the dental health of communities by epidemiological studies, research in preventive methods,

and better distribution, management, and use of dental skills.

dentition (děn-tǐsh′ŭn) [L. *dentitio*] The type, number, and arrangement of teeth in the dental arch. SEE: illus.; *teeth* for illus.

   heterodont d. A set of teeth of various shapes that may serve different functions (e.g., incisors, canines, and molars).

   mixed d. A set of both primary and permanent teeth, as in children between 6 and 13 years of age.

   permanent d. The 32 permanent teeth, which begin to erupt at about 6 years of age in people. These are completed by the 16th year with the exception of third molars, which appear between the 18th and 25th years. The incisors are followed by the bicuspids (premolars) and the canines; then the second molars are followed by the third molars. In some individuals the third molars, although present beneath the gingiva, do not erupt. The appearance of the first molars is highly variable, but in some instances they may be the first permanent teeth to appear. SEE: *teeth.*

   primary d. The 20 primary or deciduous teeth in children. In general, the order of eruption is two lower central incisors, 6 to 8 months; two upper central incisors, 5 to 7 months; two lower lateral incisors, 8 to 11 months; two upper lateral incisors, 7 to 10 months; four canines (cuspids), lower and upper, 16 to 20 months; four first molars, lower and upper, 10 to 16 months; four second molars, upper and lower, 20 to 30 months.

dento-, denti-, dent- [L. *dens,* stem *dent-,* tooth] Prefixes meaning *tooth* or *teeth.*

dentoalveolar (děn″tō-ăl-vē′ō-lăr) [L. *dens,* tooth, + *alveolus,* small hollow] Pert. to the alveolus of a tooth and the tooth itself.

dentofacial (děn″tō-fā′shăl) Concerning the teeth and face.

dentolabial (děn-tă-lā′bē-ăl) [″ + *labium,* lip] Pert. to both the teeth and the lips.

dentulous (děn′tū-lŭs) Having one's natural teeth. SEE: *edentulous.*

denture (děn′chūr) A partial or complete set of artificial teeth set in appropriate plastic materials to substitute for the natural dentition and related tissues. SYN: *dental prosthesis.*

   PATIENT CARE: Proper denture care involves cleansing the dentures after each meal by gently brushing them with warm water and by scrubbing them with only moderate pressure. Cleansing solutions and mixtures accepted by the American Dental Association are ammonia water 28% (2 ml in 30 ml water); trisodium phosphate (0.6 g in 30 ml water); sodium hypochlorite, or bleach (2 ml in 120 ml water). Dentures should be

Preventing Oral Diseases/Maintaining Oral Health

Disease	Prevention	Details	Special Considerations
Tooth decay	• Brush teeth regularly • Floss regularly • Avoid eating simple sugars • Use fluoride toothpastes	• Use a soft or *very* soft brush • Brush gently twice a day • Hold the brush at a 45-degree angle to the gum line • Brush for 2 min at a time • Use dentifrice with fluoride • Get annual or biannual checkups with a dental professional	• Diabetes mellitus: brush teeth after each meal and snack; maintain blood glucose levels at ≤ 125 mg/dL • Cancer patients: brush after each meal and snack; keep mouth moist with frequent fluid intake • Children: have dentist apply dental sealants regularly; begin using small amount of fluoride-containing dentifrice by 13th month
Periodontal disease	• Floss regularly • Brush teeth regularly • Avoid eating simple sugars • Consider antimicrobial rinses	• Daily or twice a day • Get annual or biannual checkups with scaling or root planing as indicated	People with established periodontitis may require: • periodontal rinses • scaling and planing • antibiotics • periodontal surgery
Oral cancer (e.g., squamous cell carcinoma)	Avoid cancer-causing agents	Get regular professional checkups	• Avoid cigarettes, pipes, and cigars • Avoid smokeless ("spit") tobacco • Limit alcohol intake

properly fitted in the patient's mouth; when stored outside the mouth, they should be placed in a well-identified, opaque, closed container. Dentures are stored wet or dry according to their particular composition and according to instructions by the dentist. Dentures are removed from comatose or moribund patients as well as from patients undergoing surgery.

fixed partial d. A dental restoration of one or more missing teeth. It may be attached to a fixed, implanted structure within the mandible or maxilla.

full d. A dental appliance that replaces all of the teeth in one arch.

immediate d. A complete set of artificial teeth inserted immediately after removal (extraction) of natural teeth. Over time this denture must be remade or relined because the soft tissues and the bone from which the extraction has been taken shrink and resorb.

partial d. A dental appliance made of an acrylic base, porcelain teeth, and a stainless steel substructure. A partial denture replaces multiple teeth within a dental arch.

denture base material The chemical resin (typically polymethylmethacrylate) from which a denture is made.

denturist (děn′chŭr-ĭst) A person licensed in some states to fabricate and fit dentures. This person is not a dentist or a dental technician.

denucleated (dē-nū′klē-āt″ĕd) [L. *de*, from, + *nucleus*, kernel] Deprived of a nucleus.

denudation (dē″nŭ-dā′shŭn) [L. *denudare*, to lay bare] Removal of a protecting layer or covering through surgery, pathological change, or trauma.

Denver classification (den′vĕr) [*Denver*, Colorado] SEE: under *classification*.

Denver Developmental Screening Test ABBR: DDST. A widely used screening test to detect the presence of any devel-

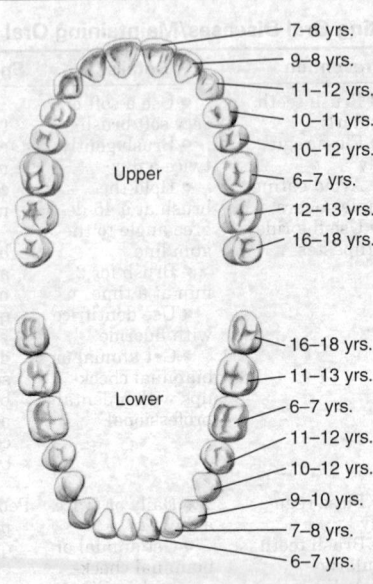

Upper

- 7–8 yrs.
- 9–8 yrs.
- 11–12 yrs.
- 10–11 yrs.
- 10–12 yrs.
- 6–7 yrs.
- 12–13 yrs.
- 16–18 yrs.

Lower

- 16–18 yrs.
- 11–13 yrs.
- 6–7 yrs.
- 11–12 yrs.
- 10–12 yrs.
- 9–10 yrs.
- 7–8 yrs.
- 6–7 yrs.

DENTITION

opmental delays of children from birth to 6 years of age.

Denver shunt 1. Pleuroperitoneal **shunt** (for relief of pleural effusion). **2.** Peritoneovenous shunt (for relief of ascites)

Denys-Drash syndrome (děn'ĭs-drăsh') A rare congenital syndrome caused by a mutation in the Wilms' tumor gene that includes male pseudohermaphroditism, progressive renal failure, and an increased risk for genitourinary tumors.

deodorant (dē-ō'dor-ănt) [" + *odorare,* to perfume] An agent that masks or absorbs foul odors.

deodorize (dē-ō'dor-īz) [" + *odor,* odor] To remove odor.

deodorizer (dē-ō'dor-īz-ĕr) Something that deodorizes.

deontology (dē"ŏn-tŏl'ō-jē) [Gr. *deonta,* needful, + *logos,* word, reason] System of ethical decision making that is based on moral rules and unchanging principles. SEE: *ethics.*

deossification (dē-ŏs"ĭ-fĭ-kā'shŭn) [L. *de,* from, + *os,* bone, + *facere,* to make] Loss or removal of mineral matter from bone or osseous tissue.

deoxy- Prefix meaning *deoxidized* or a *reduced* form of.

deoxycholic acid (dē-ok"sē-kō'lik) SEE: under *acid.*

deoxycorticosterone (dē-ok"sē-kor"tē-kŏs'tĕr-ōn) A hormone from the adrenal gland. It acts principally on salt and water metabolism.

deoxygenation (dē-ok"sĭ-jĕn-ā'shŭn) Removal of oxygen from a chemical compound or tissue.

deoxyhemoglobin (dē-ŏk"sē"hĕ'mŏ-glō"bĭn) Chemically reduced (deoxygenated) hemoglobin.

deoxypyridinoline (dē-ŏk"sē-pĭ-rĭ-dĭn'ō-lēn, -lĭn) ABBR: Dpd. A component of the structural matrix of bone, principally found in type 1 collagen as a structural cross link. It provides tensile strength to bone.

When bone resorption exceeds bone rebuilding, e.g., in osteoporosis, Dpd is released into the circulation and excreted unchanged in the urine. The detection of elevated levels of Dpd in a concentrated urine specimen is used as a marker of ongoing bone loss in osteoporosis. Reduced levels of Dpd are an indicator of the effectiveness of therapies that reduce bone resorption (e.g., bisphosphonates).

The Dpd urine test is performed by obtaining the first urine voided by a patient on awakening—this ensures that the specimen will be maximally concentrated. The level of Dpd obtained is expressed in nmol of Dpd/mmol of urinary creatinine.

deoxyribonuclease (dē-ŏk"sē-rī"bō-nū'klē-ās) ABBR: DNase. An enzyme that hydrolyzes and thus depolymerizes deoxyribonucleic acid (DNA).

deoxyribonucleoprotein (dē-ŏk"sē-rī"bō-nū"klē-ō-prō'tē-ĭn) One of a class of conjugated proteins that contain deoxyribonucleic acid.

deoxyribonucleoside (dē-ŏk"sē-rī"bō-nū'klē-ō-sīd) One of a class of nucleotides in which the pentose is 2-deoxyribose.

deoxyribose (dē-ŏk"sē-rī'bōs) A pentose sugar that is part of DNA.

deoxyribozyme (dē-ŏk″sē-rī′bō-zīm)) A DNA molecule capable of cleaving itself (i.e., of cutting itself into smaller pieces).

deoxyuridine suppression test (dē-ŏk″sē-ūr′ĭ-dēn″, -dĭn) A test primarily used in research laboratories to detect early or mild cases of vitamin B_{12} deficiency.

Department of Health and Human Services ABBR: DHHS. The U.S. agency that administers federal health programs, including the Food and Drug Administration, the Centers for Disease Control and Prevention, The National Institutes of Health, and other agencies.

dependence, dependency (dē-pen′dĕns, dē-pen′dĕn-sē) [L. *dependere*, to hang down] **1.** A form of behavior that suggests inability to make decisions. **2.** A psychic craving for a drug that may or may not be accompanied by physiological dependency. **3.** A state of reliance on another. SEE: *habituation; withdrawal*.

¹dependent (dē-pen′dĕnt) **1.** Needing or relying on something or someone else for life, support, or help. **2.** Pert. to someone with a dependency, as on drugs or alcohol. **3.** In mathematics and statistics, pert. to a variable that has values determined by one or more independent variables. **4.** In anatomy, hanging down.

²dependent, dependant (dē-pen′dĕnt) Someone or something dependent on someone else or something else.

dependent adult Any individual between the ages of 18 and 65 whose functional limitations prevent him or her from maintaining legal rights or living alone without support from others.

dependent care The support and nurturing of persons who cannot meet their own needs, such as children or functionally impaired adults.

depersonalization disorder The belief that one's own reality is temporarily lost or altered. Affected patients experience estrangement or a sense of unreality and may feel that their body parts have changed size or been otherwise altered. A feeling of being automated or as if in a dream may be present. The disorder is usually rapid in onset and usually occurs in adolescence or under extreme stress, fatigue, or anxiety.

depersonalize (dē-pĕr′sŏn-ăl-īz″) To make impersonal; to deprive of personality or individuality.

dephosphorylation (dē-fŏs″for-ĭ-lā′shŭn) [L. *de*, from, + *phosphorylation*] Removal of a phosphate group from a compound.

depigmentation (dē″pĭg-mĕn-tā′shŭn) **1.** The pathological loss of normal pigment, as in vitiligo. **2.** Removal of pigment, esp. from the skin, by chemical or physical means.

depigmented (dē″pig′mĕnt-ĕd, ″pigment′) Devoid of normal skin coloring

or lighter in color than surrounding skin, as in vitiligo. **depigmentation** (dē″pig″mĕn-tā′shŏn), *n*.

depilate (dĕp′ĭ-āt) [L. *depilare*, to deprive of hair] To remove hair.

depilation (dĕp″ĭl-ā′shŭn) Hair removal. SEE: *epilation*.

depilatory (dē-pĭl′ă-tōr″ē) An agent used to remove hair.

deplete (dē-plēt′) [L. *depletus*, emptied] To empty; to produce depletion.

depletion (dē-plē′shŭn) Removal of substances such as blood, fluids, iron, fat, or protein from the body.

deploy (di-ploy′) [Fr. *deployer*, to scatter] **1.** To prepare personnel or resources for anticipated use, e.g. in a mass casualty or a field of battle. **2.** To put into therapeutic use. **3.** To insert (e.g., prostheses, stents). **deployment** (mĕnt), *n*.

depolarization (dē-pō″lăr-ĭ-zā′shŭn) [″ + *polus*, pole] A reversal of charges at a cell membrane; an electrical change in an excitable cell in which the inside of the cell becomes positive (less negative) in relation to the outside. This is the opposite of polarization and is caused by a rapid inflow of sodium ions.

depolymerization (dē-pŏl″ĭ-mĕr-ĭ-zā′shŭn) The breakdown or splitting of polymers into their basic building blocks or monomers. The glucose monomer may be polymerized to form the large glycogen polymer and then broken down (i.e., depolymerized) to form glucose.

deponent (dē-pō′nĕnt) One who testifies under oath about the facts at issue in litigation. The testimony is transcribed by a court reporter and becomes part of the legal record.

deposit (dē-pŏz′ĭt) [L. *depositus*, having put aside] **1.** Sediment. **2.** Matter collected in any part of an organism.

 calcareous d. A deposit of calcified material, as in calculus on teeth.

deposition (dĕp″ă-zĭsh′ĭn) **1.** Pretrial discovery tool or technique in which the person being questioned (the deponent) is placed under oath and asked to testify about issues on the subject of litigation, which is then transcribed by a court reporter. **2.** The sedimentation of particles previously suspended or circulating in solution.

 diffusion d. The accumulation of aerosol particles on a surface due to their random bombardment by gas molecules.

depot (dē′pō, dĕp′ō) [Fr. *dépot*, fr L. *depositum*, put down] A place of storage, esp. in the body, such as a fat depot or a drug depot. Drugs that remain in long-term storage in the body after injection include hormonal agents (such as progesterone, testosterone, insulin, and leuprolide) and antipsychotic agents (such as haloperidol and risperidone), among others.

depravation (dĕp″ră-vā′shŭn) [L. *depravare*, completely destroyed] A pathological deterioration of function or secretion.

depressant (dē-prĕs′ănt) [L. *depressus*, pressed down] An agent that decreases the level of a body function or nerve activity (e.g., a sedative).

   cardiac d. An agent that decreases heart rate and contractility.

   cerebral d. An agent that sedates or tranquilizes.

   motor d. An agent that lessens contractions of involuntary muscles.

   respiratory d. An agent that lessens frequency and depth of breathing.

depressed (dē-prĕst′) **1.** Below the normal level, as when fragments of bone are forced below their normal level and that of surrounding portions of bone. **2.** Low in spirits; dejected. **3.** Having a decreased level of function. SEE: *depression.*

depression (dē-presh′ŏn) [L. *depressio*, a pressing down] **1.** A hollow or lowered region. **2.** The lowering of a part, such as the mandible. **3.** The decrease of a vital function such as respiration. **4.** Any of several mood disorders marked by loss of interest or pleasure in living. Disorders linked to depression include dysthymia, major depressive disorder, schizoaffective disorders, bipolar disorders, seasonal affective disorders, postpartum depressive disorders, and mood disorders caused by substance abuse or other medical conditions. Medical and psychiatric conditions that can trigger or exacerbate depression include anxiety disorders, autoimmune diseases, chronic pain, eating disorders, endocrine disorders, heart attack, infectious diseases, neurologic disorders (stroke), sleep disorders, substance abuse, and drugs (e.g., some beta blockers, calcium channel blockers, steroids, hormones, chemotherapeutic agents, appetite suppressants, and sedatives). The U.S. Preventive Services Task Force recommends screening for depression in primary care settings. Formal screening tools may be used (e.g., the Beck Depression Inventory, Hamilton Rating Scale for Depression, and Geriatric Depression Scale). A simple means of screening for depression is to ask patients: (1) Over the past 2 weeks have you felt down, depressed, or hopeless? (2) Over the past 2 weeks have you felt little interest or pleasure in doing things?

   Depressive disorders are common: about 20% of women and about 10% of men may suffer from major depression at some point during their lives. Worldwide, depression is considered to be the fourth most serious illness as far as the overall burden it imposes on people's health. Depressed patients have more medical illnesses and a higher risk of self-injury and suicide than patients without mood disorders.

SYMPTOMS: Characteristic symptoms of the depressive disorders include persistent sadness, hopelessness, or tearfulness; loss of energy or persistent fatigue; persistent feelings of guilt or self-criticism; a sense of worthlessness; irritability; inability to concentrate; decreased interest in daily activities; changes in appetite or body weight; insomnia or excessive sleep; and recurrent thoughts of death or suicide. These symptoms cause pervasive deficits in social functioning.

TREATMENT: Psychotherapies, behavioral therapies, electroconvulsive therapy (ECT, shock therapy), and psychoactive drugs are effective in the treatment of depressive disorders.

⚠ Depressed people who express suicidal thoughts should not be left alone, esp. if hospitalized.

PATIENT CARE: The patient is assessed for feelings of worthlessness or self-reproach, inappropriate guilt, concern with death, and attempts at self-injury. Level of activity and socialization are evaluated. Adequate nutrition and fluids are provided. Dietary interventions and increased physical activity are recommended to manage drug-induced constipation; assistance with grooming and other activities of daily living may be required. A structured routine, including noncompetitive activities, is provided to build the patient's self-confidence and to encourage interaction. Health care professionals should express warmth and interest in the patient and be optimistic while guarding against excessive cheerfulness. Support is gradually reduced as the patient demonstrates an increasing ability to resume self-care. Drug therapies are administered and evaluated: these may include tricyclic antidepressants (TCAs), selective serotonin reuptake inhibitors (SSRIs), selective norepinephrine and serotonin reuptake inhibitors, dopamine-norepinephrine reuptake inhibitors, and norepinephrine-serotonin modulators. Monamine oxidase (MAO) inhibitors also may be used, but these have a high risk for toxicity unless necessary dietary restrictions are strictly followed. These drugs may be used alone or in combination with specific psychotherapeutic approaches such as cognitive behavioral therapy (CBT) or brief psychosocial counseling. CBT helps patients understand how their thoughts can become distorted and contribute to depression and anxiety and helps them learn coping behaviors that reduce feelings of anxiety, distress, and helplessness caused by distorted thinking.

If ECT is required (usually for patients who have not responded well to drug therapy or for whom drugs pose a risk), the patient is informed that a series of treatments may be needed. Before each ECT session, the prescribed sedative is administered, and a nasal or oral airway inserted. Vital signs are monitored, and support is offered by talking calmly or by gentle touch. After ECT, mental status and response to therapy are evaluated. The patient may be drowsy and experience transient amnesia but should become alert and oriented within 30 min. The period of disorientation lengthens after subsequent treatments. SYN: *unipolar d.* SEE: *Nursing Diagnoses Appendix.*

agitated d. Depression accompanied by restlessness and increased psychomotor activity.

anaclitic d. Depression in infants suddenly separated from their mothers between the first months and 1 year of age. The loss of the love, affection, and nurturing usually present in the mother-child relationship may cause severe disturbances in health and in motor, language, and social development or may occasionally lead to death. Symptoms first found in affected infants include crying, panicky behavior, and increased motor activity. Later, psychologically abandoned or neglected infants manifest dejection, apathy, staring into space, and silent crying. Recovery is possible if the mother or a surrogate is available to meet the infant's needs for parental support.

atypical d. ABBR: AD. A form of depression in which overeating and oversleeping are commonly observed, often but not exclusively in association with leaden paralysis, extreme sensitivity to interpersonal rejection, and highly reactive moods. The condition typically has an earlier age of onset than typical depression, is more likely to affect women than men, and shares some features with bipolar disorder.

bipolar d. SEE: *bipolar disorder.*

double d. An episode of major depression superimposed on dysthymic disorder.

endogenous d. Depression that occurs without an apparent precipitating cause. SEE: *melancholia.*

hidden d. Masked **d.**

major d. A mood disorder characterized by a period of at least 2 weeks of depressed mood or the loss of interest or pleasure in nearly all activities.

SYMPTOMS: In children and adolescents, the mood may be irritable rather than sad. Establishing the diagnosis requires the presence of at least four of the following: (1) changes in appetite, weight, sleep, and psychomotor activity; (2) decreased energy; (3) feelings of worthlessness or guilt; (4) difficulty in thinking, concentrating, or making decisions; or (5) recurrent thoughts of death or plans for or attempts to commit suicide.The symptoms must persist for most of the day, nearly every day, for at least 2 consecutive weeks. The episode must be accompanied by clinically significant distress or impairment in social, occupational, or other important areas of functioning. Also, the disorder must not be due to bereavement, drugs, alcohol, or the direct effects of a disease such as hypothyroidism. SYN: *major depressive episode mood disorder.*

masked d. Depression in older adults that usually presents with physical symptoms or illness. SYN: *hidden d.; somatic d.*

minor d. A mood disorder lasting at least 2 weeks in which fewer symptoms of depression are present than in major depression (two to five symptoms as opposed to more than five).

postnatal d. Postpartum **d.**

postpartum d. ABBR: PPD. Depression occurring up to 6 months after childbirth and not resolving in 1 or 2 weeks. The disease occurs in about 10% to 20% of women who have recently delivered.

SYMPTOMS: Affected mothers typically report insomnia or hypersomnia, psychomotor agitation or retardation, changes in appetite, tearfulness, despondency, feelings of hopelessness, worthlessness or guilt, decreased concentration, suicidal ideation, inadequacy, inability to cope with infant care needs, mood swings, irritability, fatigue, and loss of normal interests or pleasure.

DIAGNOSIS: Two screening tools are available for PPD in English-speaking patients: the Edinburgh Postnatal Depression Scale (EPDS) and the Postpartum Depression Screening Scale (PDSS), both of which appear to be more sensitive in screening PPD than the more general Beck Depression Inventory.

TREATMENT: Drugs (e.g., tricyclic antidepressants and serotonin reuptake inhibitors), counseling, or electroconvulsive therapy are all effective therapies. PPD support groups are generally helpful to women. Online support networks include Postpartum Support International (www.postpartum.net) and Depression After Delivery (www.charityadvantage.com/depression afterdelivery/Home.asp). Carefully designed studies have shown that nursing care aids in the diagnosis, prevention, and treatment of this disorder. SYN: *postnatal d.* SEE: *postpartum blues.*

poststroke d. A dysphoric mood disorder that follows a cerebral infarction, found in about a quarter of stroke patients. Although for many years depression after strokes was thought to occur mainly in patients who had injured the nondominant hemisphere of the brain, research has shown that this phenomenon is most common in female patients and those who have had higher education.

reactive d. Depression that is usually self-limiting, following a serious event such as a death in the family, the loss of a job, or a personal financial catastrophe. The disorder is longer lasting and more marked than an expected reaction to the stress experienced.

respiratory d. a decrease in the ability to exhale and inhale. It is a common side effect of anesthetic, narcotic, and sedative drugs. SYN: *reduced ventilation.*

somatic d. Masked **d.**

unipolar d. Depression (4).

winter depression Seasonal affective disorder.

depressive disorder Depression. SEE: *Nursing Diagnoses Appendix.*

depressor (dē-prĕs′or) [L.] **1.** A variety of muscle (d. anguli oris). **2.** An agent or drug which depresses function. **3.** An instrument used to press down on tissues, e.g., on the tongue.

tongue d. A device used to draw down and displace the tongue to facilitate visual examination of the throat.

depressor reflex SEE: under *reflex.*

deprivation (dep″rĭ-vā′shŏn) [*de-* + *privare,* to remove] Loss or absence of a necessary part or function.

androgen d. 1. The chemical suppression of male sex hormones to prevent their stimulatory effects on various hormone-sensitive illnesses, including prostate cancer and predatory sexual behavior. SYN: *androgen suppression.* **2.** Orchiectomy.

emotional d. Isolation of an individual, esp. an infant, from normal emotional stimuli. In infants this impairs mental and physical development.

occupational d. Prolonged restriction from participation in necessary or meaningful activities due to circumstances outside the individual's control. Geographic isolation, incarceration, disability, or social exclusion may contribute to such circumstances.

sensory d. The absence of usual and accustomed visual, auditory, tactile, or other stimuli, e.g., in patients whose eyes are bandaged for extended periods following eye surgery, patients on respirators, astronauts, or people imprisoned in dark, soundproof cells. The long-lasting absence of normal stimuli eventually produces psychological and neurological symptoms, including auditory and visual hallucinations, anxiety, depression, and delusions.

PATIENT CARE: The patient's usual response to prolonged quiet or isolation is assessed. Patients who require more environmental stimuli (radio, TV noise, social contact) suffer more (and more quickly) than do those who prefer quiet. Stimulation is provided to replace those stimuli that the patient is deprived of. Caregivers tell those patients who cannot see or whose visual field is limited by position or equipment about weather, time of day, and surrounding colors. They also describe equipment, locations, food, and other features of the environment that the patient wants to experience but cannot see, allowing touch to help replace vision. For the patient whose hearing is reduced by location or equipment (or by effects of drug therapy), devices are used that assist the hearing-impaired to understand speech. Sensory-deprived patients are encouraged to use radio or TV as desired, and the health care professional makes frequent visits to prevent these patients from feeling abandoned. Therapies are related to time of day (such as before breakfast, after dinner, at bedtime), and a clock and calendar are provided to assist with time orientation. Reported auditory or visual hallucinations should be investigated thoroughly and a source sought that can simulate the sound or sight reported by the patient, e.g., a linen cart may sound like a passing truck; a moving curtain may look like a ghost. Caregivers validate reality for the patient by changing lighting or altering external noises to eliminate confusion.

sleep d. Prolonged periods of time without sleep (sustained natural, periodic suspension of relative consciousness). SEE: *Nursing Diagnoses Appendix.*

deprogram (dē-prō′grăm) To free an individual from some mentally harmful cult, religion, or political belief system.

depth (depth) **1.** The distance between an elevated and a depressed point; a measure of height. **2.** The quality of being deep; richness; intensity.

depth dose SEE: under *dose.*

depth psychology SEE: under *psychology.*

depuration (dĕp″ūr-ā′shŭn) The process of freeing from impurities. **depurative,** *adj.*

depurator (dĕp″ūr-ā′tor) An agent that purifies.

de Quervain disease (dĕ ker′ven) De Quervain tenosynovitis.

de Quervain tenosynovitis (dĕ ker′ven) [Fritz de Quervain, Swiss surgeon,

1868–1940] Chronic tenosynovitis of the abductor pollicis longus and extensor pollicis brevis muscles. SYN: *de Quervain disease.*

derangement (dē-rānj′mĕnt) [Fr. *deranger,* unbalance] **1.** Lack of order or organization; confusion. **2.** An injury or its structural consequences. **3.** A defect in the annulus fibrosus of the intervertebral disk allowing the nucleus pulposus to herniate.

Dercum disease (dĕrk′ŭm) [Francis X. Dercum, U.S. neurologist, 1856–1931] The appearance of multiple painful fatty nodules (lipomas) in the skin of adults, esp. overweight or postmenopausal women.

derealization (dē-rēl″ĭ-zā′shŭn) A sense that reality has changed; a sense of detachment from one's surroundings.

derivation (dĕr″ĭ-vā′shŭn) [L. *derivare,* to draw off] The source or origin of a substance or idea.

derivative (dĕ-rĭv′ă-tĭv) **1.** Something that is not original or fundamental. **2.** Something derived from another body or substance. **3.** Something that produces derivation. **4.** In embryology, anything that develops from a preceding structure, as the derivatives of the germ layers.

derma (dĕr′mă) [Gr. *derma,* skin] Dermis. **dermal** (dĕr′măl), *adj.*

dermabrasion (dĕrm′ă-brā′zhŭn) [″ + L. *abrasio,* wearing away] A surgical procedure used to resurface the skin. It may remove acne scars, nevi, tattoos, or fine wrinkles on the skin. Complications of the procedure include infection, skin pigment changes, or scarring. SYN: *planing.*

Dermacentor (dĕr″mă-sĕnt′or) A genus of ticks belonging to the order Acarina, family Ixodidae.

   D. andersoni An important North American species that is parasitic on humans or other mammals during some part of its life cycle. It may cause tick paralysis and is a vector of Rocky Mountain spotted fever, scrub typhus, tularemia, brucellosis, Q fever, and several forms of viral encephalomyelitis. SYN: *wood tick.*

   D. variabilis A species similar to *D. andersoni,* and the main vector for Rocky Mountain spotted fever in the central and eastern U.S. It is parasitic to dogs, horses, cattle, rabbits, and humans.

Dermanyssus gallinae (dĕr″mă-nĭ′sŭs găl-ī′nē) [Gr. *derma,* skin + *nyssō,* to prick + L. *gallina,* hen] A species of mite found in chickens. Its bite may cause an itchy rash, esp. prevalent in owners of infested farm animals or pets.

dermatan sulfate (dĕr′mă-tan″) A macromolecule found throughout the body that may have an important function in the formation of connective tissue by promoting cell growth. It helps fibroblasts to develop into cells, including cartilage and synovial tissue. It also promotes blood coagulation. SEE: *proteoglycans.*

dermatitis (dĕr″mă-tīt′ĭs, -tīt′ĭ-dēz″) *pl.* **dermatitides, dermatitises** [*dermato-* + *-itis*] An inflammatory rash marked by itching and redness. SEE: *eczema.*

   ETIOLOGY: Dermatitis has many causes,, including contact with skin irritants (such as the oil that causes poison ivy or oak); venous stasis, with edema and vesicle formation near the ankles; habitual scratching, as is found in neurodermatitis; dry skin, as in winter itch; and ultraviolet light, as in photosensitivity reactions.

   TREATMENT: When a source of dermatitis is identifiable (such as in contact dermatitis due to a detergent or topical cosmetic), the best treatment is to avoid the irritating substance and to cleanse the affected area immediately with mild soap and water. Once skin inflammation is established, topical corticosteroid ointments or systemic steroids (during extreme exacerbations), topical immunomodulator agents (in patients above age 2), weak tar preparations and ultraviolet B light therapy (to increase the thickness of the stratum corneum) and antihistamines may be used, with antibiotics reserved for secondary infections. Dermatologists may prescribe occlusive dressings intermittently to help clear lichenified skin.

   PATIENT CARE: The patient should avoid known skin irritants. Tepid baths, cool compresses, and astringents sometimes help relieve inflammation and itch. Moisturizing creams or lotions following bathing help to retain skin moisture, but perfumed products should be avoided. Drug therapy is administered and evaluated for desired effects and adverse reactions. The patient is taught to apply topical medications and is educated about their most common side effects. Scratching is discouraged and the fingernails kept short to limit excoriation. The patient should be made aware that drowsiness may occur with antihistamine use and that driving or operating mechanical equipment should be avoided until the extent of this effect is known. Health care professionals should be careful not to show any negative feelings when touching lesions during assessment or treatment but should follow standard precautions. Skin changes alter body image, and the patient will need assistance in accepting and coping with what he or she may view as disfigurement. Children and adolescents may require and benefit from counseling to help them deal with emotional components of their condition.

   actinic d. A chronic red or eczematous rash, usually on the face or exposed skin surfaces, that typically results from exposure and sensitization to ultraviolet rays. Adults over age 50 may be affected. SEE: illus. SYN: *photosensitivity* **d.**

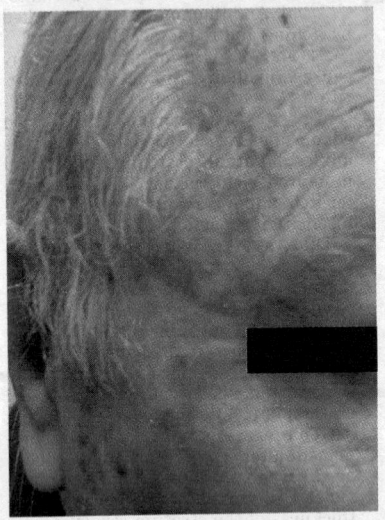

ACTINIC DERMATITIS

allergic contact d. Contact **d.**

atopic d. Chronic dermatitis of unknown cause found in patients with a history of allergy. The disease usually begins after the first 2 months of life, and those affected may experience exacerbations and remissions throughout childhood and adulthood. In many cases, there is a family history of allergy or atopy: if both parents have atopic dermatitis, the chances are nearly 80% that their children will have it, as well. Atopic dermatitis is typically found in flexural creases of the body, e.g., the antecubital and popliteal fossae. The skin lesions consist of reddened, cracked, and thickened skin that can become exudative and crusty from scratching. Scarring or secondary infection may occur. Most patients have an elevated level of immunoglobulin E in their serum. SEE: illus.

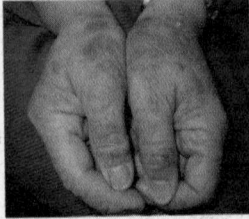

ATOPIC DERMATITIS

TREATMENT: The patient should avoid soaps and ointments. Bathing is kept to a minimum, but bath oils may help to prevent drying of the skin. Clothing should be soft textured and should not contain wool. Fingernails should be kept short to decrease damage from scratching. Antihistamines may help reduce itching at night. Heavy exercise should be avoided because it induces perspiration. A nonlipid softening lotion followed by a corticosteroid in a propylene glycol base may effectively treat acute exacerbations; when large areas of the body are involved, oral steroids may be needed. Because of the adverse effects associated with corticosteroids, topical immunosuppressants such as tacrolimus that decrease T-cell activity have been developed. Antistaphylococcal antibiotics may be needed to control secondary infection, introduced when scratching causes microfissures in the skin.

cercarial d. Swimmer's **itch**.

contact d. Dermatitis due to contact with allergens or an irritating substance. Allergic contact dermatitis is caused by a T-cell–mediated hypersensitivity reaction to natural or synthetic environmental allergens. These combine with skin proteins, altering the normal autoantigens so that new, foreign antigens are created. Nonallergic contact dermatitis, also known as irritative contact dermatitis, is usually caused by exposure to a detergent, soap, or other skin irritant. SYN: *allergic contact d.; d. venenata* (1). SEE: illus.

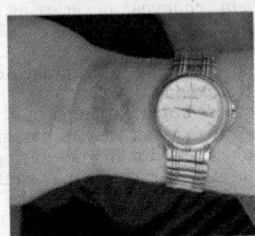

CONTACT DERMATITIS

Allergic reaction to topical anesthetic

SYMPTOMS: Skin changes, which appear 4 to 48 hr after exposure, depending on the degree of sensitivity to the allergen, consist of erythema, local edema, and blisters. The blisters may weep in severe cases. Most patients complain of intense itching. Signs and symptoms of the disease usually last 10 to 14 days. Reexposure to the cause will trigger a relapse.

TREATMENT: Tepid baths, cool compresses, topical astringents (such as solutions of aluminum acetate), antihistamines, and corticosteroids all provide some relief.

contagious pustular d. A cutaneous disease of sheep and goats transmitted to humans by direct contact. The lesion on humans is usually solitary and on the hands, arms, or face. This maculopapular area may progress to a pustule up to 3 cm in diameter and may last 3 to 6 weeks. The etiological agent is *Parapoxvirus*, a genus of poxvirus. SYN: *orf*.

diaper d. Diaper **rash**.

exfoliative d. Generalized dermatitis, often followed by scaling. It may be caused by leukemias or lymphomas that infiltrate the skin; extensive psoriasis; drug reactions (such as vancomycin); allergies, seborrhea, or atopy. The condition is often associated with systemic findings, including lymphadenopathy, hepatic and splenic enlargement, fever, anemia, eosinophilia, and decreases in serum albumin.

When the skin involvement is extensive, the patient may become depressed because of the cosmetic changes.

TREATMENT: Therapy is directed at treating the underlying cause.

factitial d. A self-inflicted irritation or injury to the skin.

d. herpetiformis A chronic dermatitis characterized by erythematous, papular, vesicular, bullous, or pustular lesions with a tendency to grouping and with intense itching and burning.

ETIOLOGY: It is associated with allergy to gluten and is often found in patients with celiac disease (gluten-sensitive enteropathy).

SYMPTOMS: The lesions develop suddenly and spread peripherally. The disease is variable and erratic, and an attack may be prolonged for weeks or months. Secondary infection may follow trauma to the inflamed areas.

TREATMENT: Oral dapsone provides substantial relief of symptoms in a few days. Sulfapyridine also may be used.

livedo-like d. Nicolau syndrome.

d. medicamentosa Drug **rash**.

photoallergic contact d. Photoallergy.

photosensitivity d. Actinic **d.**

poison ivy d. Dermatitis resulting from irritation or sensitization of the skin by urushiol, the toxic resin of plants of the genus *Toxicodendron* (*Rhus*). There is no absolute immunity; susceptibility varies greatly, even in the same individual.

Those sensitive to poison ivy may also react to contact with other plants, such as the mango rind and cashew oil. These plants contain chemicals that cross-react with the sap present in poison ivy, poison oak, and poison sumac.

SYMPTOMS: Some time elapses between skin contact with the poison and first appearance of symptoms, varying from a few hours to several days and de-

pending on the sensitivity of the patient and the condition of the skin. Moderate itching or a burning sensation is soon followed by small blisters; later manifestations vary. Blisters usually rupture and are followed by oozing of serum and subsequent crusting.

PREVENTION: Some barrier creams have been used to prevent poison ivy dermatitis. They are sprayed on the skin prior to anticipated contact with the plant.

TREATMENT: In mild dermatitis, antihistamines and a lotion to relieve itching are usually sufficient. In severe dermatitis, cool, wet dressings or compresses, potassium permanganate baths, and topical corticosteroids are often effective. In some instances, intramuscular or oral corticosteroid therapy is used. If plant leaves are burned and the smoke inhaled, or if plant leaves are ingested, the patient should be directed to an emergency care center. Demulcents, fluids, morphine, and a high-protein, low-fat diet may be prescribed.

PATIENT CARE: Prevention is important in those with known sensitivity and in those with no previous contact with or reaction to the plant. Instruction of the patient focuses on helping the patient to recognize the plant, to avoid contact with it, and to wear long-sleeved shirts and long pants in wooded areas. If contact occurs, the patient should wash with soap and water immediately to remove the toxic oil. Contaminated clothing and pets also should be promptly and thoroughly washed because contact with such items may cause poison dermatitis in other members of the household.

radiation d. Dermatitis due to radiation exposure. SYN: *radioepidermitis; radioepithelitis; radiodermatitis.*

rhus d. Contact dermatitis caused by the toxic resin in poison ivy or oak. SEE: *poison ivy d.; Toxicodendron.*

schistosome d. Swimmer's **itch**.

stasis d. Eczema of the legs with edema, pigmentation, and sometimes chronic inflammation. It is usually due to impaired return of blood from the legs. Compression stockings help the rash to resolve gradually. SEE: illus.

d. venenata **1.** Contact **d. 2.** Any inflammation caused by local action of various animal, vegetable, or mineral substances contacting the surface of the skin.

dermato-, dermat-, derm- [Gr. *derma*, stem *dermat-*, skin] Prefixes meaning *skin*.

Dermatobia (dĕr″mă-tō′bē-ă) [*dermato-* + Gr. *bios*, life] A genus of botflies belonging to the order Diptera of the family Oestridae. SEE: *botfly; myiasis.*

D. hominis A species found in parts

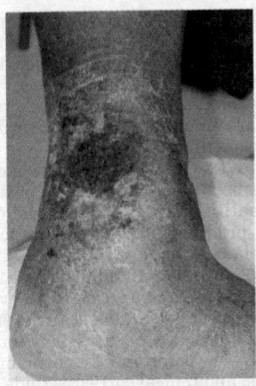

STASIS DERMATITIS

of tropical America, whose larvae infest humans and cattle.

dermatochalasis (děr″mă-tō-kă-lā′sĭs) [*dermato-* + Gr. *chalasis,* relaxation] Loose or sagging soft tissue in the eyelids, esp. the upper eyelid. It results from loss of tissue elasticity and is more prevalent in older people.

dermatofibroma (děr″mă-tō-fĭ-brō′mă) [″ + L. *fibra,* fiber, + Gr. *oma,* tumor] A firm but freely movable benign skin nodule, often found on the lower extremities. SEE: illus.; *dimple **sign***.

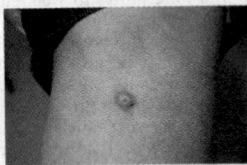

DERMATOFIBROMA

dermatofibrosarcoma (děr″mă-tō-fī″brō-sär-kō′mă) [″ + ″ + Gr. *sarx,* flesh, + *oma,* tumor] Fibrosarcoma of the skin.

dermatogen (děr-măt′ō-jěn) [″ + *gennan,* to produce] Antigen from a skin disease.

dermatoglyphics (děr″mă-tō-glĭf′ĭks) [″ + *glyphe,* a carving] Study of the surface markings of the skin, esp. those of the hands and feet, used in identification and genetic studies. SEE: *fingerprint* for illus.

dermatographism Dermographism.

dermatoheliosis (děr″mă-tō-hē″lē-ō′sĭs) Photoaging.

dermatologist (děr″mă-tŏl′ō-jĭst) [Gr. *dermatos,* skin, + *logos,* word, reason] A physician who specializes in treating diseases of the skin.

dermatology (děr″mă-tŏl′ō-jē) The science of the skin and its diseases.

dermatome (děr′mă-tōm) [Gr. *derma,* skin, + *tome,* incision] **1.** An instrument, mechanical or manual, to shave thin layers of skin for transplantation (grafting). **2.** A band or region of skin supplied by a single sensory nerve. SEE: illus. **3.** The lateral portion of the somite of an embryo, where the dermis of the skin originates; the cutis plate.

dermatomycosis (děr″mă-tō-mī-kō′sĭs) *pl.* **dermatomycoses** [″ + *mykes,* fungus, + *osis,* condition] A skin infection caused by certain fungi of the genera *Trichophyton, Epidermophyton,* and *Microsporum.* SYN: *tinea.*

C2
C3
C4
C5
T1
T2
T3
T4
T5
T6
T7
T8
T9
T10
T11
T12
L1
L2
L3
L4
L5
T1 — C6
— C5
— C6
— C7
— C8
— S2
— S3
— S1
L4   L5

☐ Cervical (C)
■ Thoracic (T)
■ Lumbar (L)
■ Sacral (S)

DERMATOME

dermatomyositis (dĕr″mă-tō-mī″ō-sī′tĭs)
[″ + ″ + *itis,* inflammation] A rare acute, subacute, or chronic disease of connective tissue, of unknown cause, marked by edema, rash, weakness, pain, and inflammation of the muscles. SEE: illus.

DERMATOMYOSITIS

SYMPTOMS: Dermatomyositis symptoms include fever, malaise, and weakness, esp. of the pelvic and shoulder girdle muscles, neck, and pharynx; skin and mucosal lesions (e.g., Gottron's papules), and joint discomfort. Performance of ordinary activities (getting up from a chair, combing one's hair, reaching above one's head, raising one's head from pillow) are affected. About one third of patients have dysphagia. Dysphonia and difficulty breathing also may be present, with death associated with respiratory disease, heart failure, associated cancers, or adverse effects of drug therapies. The disease progresses slowly, with frequent exacerbations and remissions, and occurs two times more frequently in females than in males. The prognosis worsens with aging.

TREATMENT: The treatment is symptomatic and includes bedrest, physical therapy, high-dose steroid therapy, and other anti-inflammatory agents. Cytotoxic drugs such as azathioprine, cyclophosphamide, and methotrexate are often beneficial in patients who do not respond to adrenocortical steroids. Analgesics are provided as necessary. Serum muscle enzyme levels and muscle strength usually improve after 2 to 6 weeks of vigorous therapy, allowing corticosteroid dosages to be gradually tapered down.

PATIENT CARE: The patient's level of discomfort, muscle weakness, and joint range of motion are assessed and documented daily. The patient's face, neck, upper back, chest, nail beds, eyelids, and interphalangeal joints are evaluated for rashes, and any findings are documented. Frequent assistance is provided to help the patient reposition in correct body alignment; appropriate supportive devices, frequent passive ROM exercises, and graduated exercises are used to prevent and treat muscle atrophy and joint contractures. Warm baths, moist heat, and massage are provided to relieve stiffness, and

prescribed analgesics are administered. Oral lesions are irrigated with warm saline solution, as necessary. Tepid sponge baths and compresses are used to relieve pruritus and to prevent scratching; antihistamines are also administered as prescribed. Self-care activities, with assistance if necessary, are encouraged and paced according to the patient's response. Reassuring the patient that muscle weakness during exacerbations is temporary helps to ease fears of dependence. Prescribed corticosteroid, cytotoxic, or immunosuppressant drugs are administered, and the patient's response is evaluated.

Both patient and family are educated about the disease process, treatment expectations, and possible adverse reactions to corticosteroid, cytotoxic, and immunosuppressant therapies. Good nutrition and a low-sodium diet are recommended to prevent fluid retention. The patient should be educated about the potential ongoing side effects of therapy (e.g., those associated with chronic, high-dose corticosteroids) and assisted to develop physical and emotional coping skills to deal with these. The patient is encouraged to express feelings, fears, and concerns about the illness; realistic support and encouragement are provided.

dermatopathology (dĕr″mă-tō-pă-thŏl′ō-jē) [″ + ″ + *logos,* word, reason] The study of skin diseases.

dermatopathy (dĕr″mă-tŏp′ă-thē) Any skin disease.

dermatophilosis (dĕr″mă-tō-fĭ-lō′sĭs) An actinomycotic infection that occurs in certain hooved animals and rarely in humans.

dermatophyte (dĕr′mă-tō-fīt) [″ + *phyton,* plant] A fungal parasite that grows in or on the skin. Dermatophytes rarely penetrate deeper than the epidermis or its appendages—hair and nails. They cause skin diseases such as favus, tinea, ringworm, and eczema. Important dermatophytes include the genera *Microsporum, Trichophyton,* and *Epidermophyton.*

dermatophytid (dĕr″mă-tŏf′ĭ-tĭd) A toxic rash or eruption occurring in dermatomycosis.

dermatophytosis (dĕr″mă-tō-fĭ-tō′sĭs) [″ + *phyton,* plant, + *osis,* condition] Athlete's foot.

dermatoplasty (dĕr′măt-ō-plas″tē) Transplantation of living skin to cover cutaneous defects caused by injury, operation, or disease. **dermatoplastic** (dĕr″măt-ō-plas′tĭk), *adj.*

PATIENT CARE: Techniques are employed during surgery to protect the graft from dislodgement. Postoperative measures include use of splints and dressings, which are employed to minimize trauma, prevent undue motion, prevent infection, and promote healing of both the transplant site and the donor site. Signs of infection such as fever and pain are monitored, and assistance is offered to help the patient to cope with altered mobility. Any discomfort is assessed, and pain relief is provided as indicated. Nutrition is emphasized to aid healing.

dermatosclerosis (dĕr″mă-tō-sklĕr-ō′sĭs) [″ + *sklerosis*, hardening] Infiltration of the skin with fibrous material.

dermatoscope (dĕr-mat′ŏ-skōp″) [*dermato-* + *-scope*] An instrument used to perform dermatoscopy. Older dermatoscopes consist of a low-power (10×) magnifier, a nonpolarized light source, a transparent plate, and a light layer of mineral oil between the instrument and the skin. The mineral oil allows inspection of skin lesions without reflection from the skin surface. More recent dermatoscopes use polarized light to eliminate skin surface reflections.

dermatoscopy (dĕr″mă-tos′kō-pē) [*dermato-* + *-scopy*] Inspection with a dermatoscope of a pigmented skin lesion to determine malignancy. SYN: *epiluminescence* **microscopy**.

dermatosis (dĕr″mă-tō′sĭs, -tō′sēz″) *pl.* **dermatoses** [*dermato-* + *-osis*] Any skin disease, esp. any noninflammatory skin disease. SEE: *dermatitis*.

    linear IgA bullous d. A blistering disease of the skin and mucous membranes characterized by the presence of IgA antibodies in the mucous membranes, serum, and skin. It typically arises after exposure to specific medications, such as amiodarone, captopril, phenytoin, or vancomycin.

    neutrophilic d. Any of several skin disorders characterized by abnormal collections of polymorphonuclear leukocytes (neutrophils) in the skin. Examples of such disorders are Sweet syndrome and pyoderma gangrenosum.

    d. papulosa nigra An eruption consisting of many tiny tumors, or milia, on facial skin. It is more common in blacks than in other ethnic groups.

dermatosparaxis (dĕr″mă-tō-spă-răk′sĭs) [″ + Gr. *sparassein*, to tear] Loose, sagging, fragile, and easily bruised skin. When it is caused by a deficiency of procollagen I, it is responsible for a rare variant of Ehlers-Danlos syndrome.

dermatotherapy (dĕr″mă-tō-thĕr′ă-pē) [″ + *therapeia*, treatment] Treatment of skin disease.

dermatotropic (dĕr″mă-tō-trŏp′ĭk) [″ + *trope*, a turning] Acting preferentially on the skin.

dermic (dĕr′mĭk) [Gr. *derma*, skin] Pert. to the skin.

dermis (dĕr′mĭs) [*(epi)dermis.*] The layer of the skin lying immediately under the epidermis, consisting of the papillary and reticular layers. It is composed of fibrous connective tissue made of collagen and elastin and contains numerous capillaries, lymphatics, and nerve endings. In it are hair follicles and their smooth muscle fibers, sebaceous glands and sweat glands, and their ducts. SYN: *corium; cutis vera; derma; true skin.*

dermographism (dĕr-mŏg′ră-fĭzm) A form of urticaria (hives) in which a pale raised wheal and red flare are produced on the skin when it is gently stroked or scratched. SYN: *dermatographism.* SEE: illus.

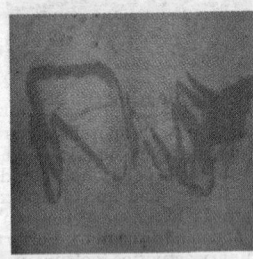

DERMOGRAPHISM

dermography, dermographia (dĕr-mŏg′ră-fē, dĕr″mō-grăf′ē-ă) A form of urticaria due to allergy.

dermoid (dĕr′moyd) [″ + *eidos*, form, shape] **1.** Resembling the skin. **2.** Dermoid **cyst**.

dermolipoma (dĕr″mō-lĭ-pō′mă) **1.** A growth of yellow fatty tissue beneath the bulbar conjunctiva. **2.** A lipoma of the skin.

dermopathy (dĕr-mŏp′pă-thē) [″ + ″] Any disease of the skin.

    diabetic d. Necrobiosis lipoidica diabeticorum.

DES *diethylstilbestrol.*

desalination (dē-săl″ĭ-nā′shŭn) Partial or complete removal of salts from a substance, as from seawater or brackish water, so that it is suitable for agricultural or household purposes but not necessarily for drinking.

desaturase (dē-sach′ŭ-rās″) [*de-* + *satur(ate)* + *-ase*] An enzyme that converts an unsaturated fatty acid chain to one that includes at least one carbon-carbon double bond.

desaturation (dē-săt″ū-rā′shŭn) [L. *de,* from, + *saturare,* to fill] **1.** A process whereby a saturated organic compound is converted into an unsaturated one, as when stearic acid, $C_{18}H_{36}O_2$, is changed into oleic acid, $C_{18}H_{34}O_2$. The product has different physical and chemical properties after this transformation. SEE: *saturated* **hydrocarbon**. **2.** The removal of a component from a chemical solution (e.g., a solute from a solvent). **3.** The dissociation of oxygen from hemoglobin.

Descemet membrane (des(-ĕ)-mā′) [Jean Descemet, Fr. anatomist, 1732–

1810] An elastic layer deep in the corneal layers formed of endothelium.

descemetocele (děs″ĕ-mět′ō-sēl) A protrusion of Descemet's membrane.

descend To move from the top of the body toward the feet; to move in a caudal direction.

descendens (dē-sĕn′děns) [L. *de*, from, + *scendere*, to climb] Descending; a descending structure.

   d. hypoglossi A branch of the hypoglossal nerve occurring at the point at which the nerve curves around the occipital artery, which passes down obliquely across (sometimes within) the sheath of the carotid vessels to form a loop just below the middle of the neck with branches of the second and third cervical nerves.

descensus (di-sen′sŭs) [L. *descensus*, descent] The process of falling; descent.

descent (di-sent′) [Fr. *descente*, a climb down] **1.** An act or instance of moving from a higher place or location to a lower one, e.g., from the testes to the scrotum. **2.** Derivation from a common ancestor; lineage; ancestry. **3.** In obstetrics, the movement of a fetus through the pelvis during labor and delivery. SEE: cardinal *movements* of labor.

desensitization (dē″sen″sĭt-ĭ-zā′shŏn) [*de-* + *sensitization*] **1.** Treatment of an allergy by repeated injections of a dilute solution containing the chemical mediators of inflammation. Gradually increasing concentrations of the antigen are used. The concentration is too weak to cause symptoms but strong enough to promote gradual immune tolerance. It increases the levels of immunoglobulin G, which blocks immunoglobulin E from binding to mast cells and initiating the release of the chemical mediators of inflammation. Although not always successful, desensitization is still commonly used, esp. for patients whose allergic response to an antigen is systemic anaphylaxis. SYN: *antianaphylaxis; hyposensitization.* SEE: *allergy; anaphylaxis; tolerance.*

⚠️ The patient must be closely monitored for signs of anaphylaxis for at least 20 min after each injection of dilute antigen. Emergency drug therapy is maintained nearby for immediate treatment of anaphylaxis. Prescribed antihistamine therapy is provided to relieve lesser allergic symptoms (e.g., urticaria, pruritus, wheezing).

   2. In psychiatry, the alleviation of an emotionally upsetting life situation.

   systematic d. A form of behavior therapy, used particularly for phobias, in which the patient is gradually exposed to anxiety-producing stimuli until they no longer produce anxiety. SEE: *implosion flooding.*

desensitize (dē-sĕn′sĭ-tīz) [L. *de*, from, + *sentire*, to perceive] **1.** To deprive of or lessen sensitivity by nerve section or blocking. **2.** To administer dilute concentrations of an allergen to block allergic responses.

desexualize (dē-sěks′ū-ăl-īz) [″ + *sexus*, sex] To castrate; to remove sexual traits.

desferrioxamine (děs-fĕr′ē-ŏks′ă-mēn) Deferoxamine mesylate.

desiccant (děs′ĭ-kănt) Causing desiccation or dryness.

desiccate (děs′ĭ-kāt) [L. *desiccare*, to dry up] To dry. To remove water from any substance, e.g., by heating or by storage with a hygroscopic materials.

desiccation (děs″ĭ-kā′shŭn) The process of drying up. SEE: *electrodesiccation.*

designated infection (and exposure) control officer ABBR: DICO. An officer working in emergency medical services charged with the responsibility of maintaining appropriate guidelines for the service with respect to exposure of clients to potentially infectious or toxic agents.

-desis [Gr. *desis*, fr. *dein*, to bind] Suffix meaning *binding, fixation.*

desmitis (děs-mī′tĭs) [″ + *itis*, inflammation] Inflammation of a ligament.

desmo- [Gr. *desmos*, fr. *dein*, to bind] Prefix meaning a *band* or *ligament.*

desmoglein (děz″mō-glē′ĭn) A cell surface molecule typically found in desmosomes that makes skin cells adhere to each other. Autoantibody disruption of cellular adhesion by desmogleins results in pemphigus. Disruption of desmogleins by staphylococcal toxins is responsible for the blistering of the skin seen in staphylococcal scalded skin syndrome.

desmoid (děs′moyd) [″ + *eidos*, form, shape] **1.** Tendon-like. SYN: *fibroid* (1). **2.** A very tough and firm fibroma.

desmoplasia (děs-mō-plā′zē-ă) [″ + Gr. *plassein*, to form] An abnormal tendency to form fibrous tissue or adhesive bands.

desmoplastic (děs″mō-plăs′tĭk) [″ + *plassein*, to form] Causing or forming adhesions.

desmopressin acetate (dez″mŏ-pres′ĭn) A synthetic antidiuretic, a vasopressin analog, with greater antidiuretic activity but less pressor activity than vasopressin. Desmopressin is used to treat central diabetes insipidus, primary nocturnal enuresis (bed-wetting), and bleeding caused by mild forms of hemophilia A or von Willebrand disease.

desmosis (děs-mō′sĭs) [″ + *osis*, condition] Any disease of the connective tissue.

desmosome (děs′mō-sōm) [″ + *soma*, body] A cellular junction made of glycoprotein that provides attachment and stability between epithelial cells and in the intercalated disks of cardiac muscle.

desmotomy (děs-mŏt′ō-mē) [″ + *tome*, incision] Dissection of a ligament.

desoxy- Older variant of "deoxy-." SEE: *deoxy-*.

desoxycorticosterone (děs-ŏk″sē-kor-tǐ-kŏs′těr-ōn) An active steroid hormone produced by the adrenal cortex. It plays an important role in the regulation of water and salt metabolism.

despair The eighth stage in Erikson's developmental theory; the opposite of ego integrity. The individual experiences sorrow over past life events and dismay over a foreshortened life.

desquamate (děs′kwă-māt) [L. *desquamare*, to remove scales] To shed or scale off the surface epithelium.

desquamation (děs″kwă-mā′shŭn) **1.** The peeling skin characteristic of postmature infants. **2.** Shedding of the epidermis. SEE: illus.

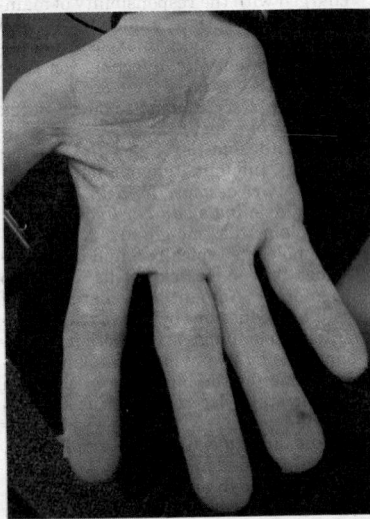

DESQUAMATION OF THE SKIN OF THE PALM

desquamative (děs-kwŏm′ă-tǐv) Of the nature of desquamation, or pert. to or causing it. SYN: *keratolytic*.

destination therapy The use of permanently implanted left ventricular assist devices to treat patients with severe end-stage heart failure. Destination therapy is typically employed for patients who either are deemed poor candidates for heart transplantation or for those who cannot obtain a heart for transplantation as a result of a shortage of organs.

destructive [L. *destructus*, destroyed] Causing ruin or destruction; the opposite of constructive.

destructive lesion SEE: under *lesion*.

desulfhydrase (dē″sŭlf-hī′drās) An enzyme that cleaves cysteine into hydrogen sulfide, ammonia, and pyruvic acid.

Desyrel SEE: *trazodone*.

DET *diethyltryptamine.*

det L. *detur*, let it be given.

detachment [O.Fr. *destachier*, to unfasten] **1.** The process of separating or the state of being separated. **2.** Avoidance of emotional or interpersonal ties. **3.** Apathy. **4.** Lack of interest.

detail **1.** The resolution of a radiologic image; the clarity or distortion of its individual elements. **2.** In pharmacology, to provide person-to-person education about the pharmacology, uses, and side effects of a drug.

detector (dě-tek′tŏr) [L. *detector*, revealer] A device for determining the presence of something, e.g., an image detector.

  flame ionization d. ABBR: FID. A device used in gas chromatography in which a sample burned in a flame changes the conductivity between two electrodes.

  image d. Any device used in radiology to receive and record energy emitted in imaging from its source. Examples of image detectors are x-ray cassettes, imaging plates, ultrasonic transducers, and flat panel detectors.

  lie d. Polygraph.

  optical d. The sensor in a typical colorimeter or photometer that senses the light transmitted by the sample.

  radiation d. An instrument used to detect the presence of radiation. SEE: *dosimeter.*

  Toftness radiation d. A device promoted as a means of detecting energy released by damaged spinal nerves. It was used in the late 20th century in chiropractic. The device has no diagnostic or therapeutic value and is illegal to use in the U.S.

detergent (dě-těr′jěnt) [L. *detergere*, to wipe off] **1.** Something that purges or cleanses; cleansing. **2.** A cleaning or wetting agent prepared synthetically from any of several chemicals. These are classed as anionic if they have a negative electric charge or cationic if they have a positive charge. SEE: *soap.*

  anionic d. A natural or synthetic chemical substance such as a soap, which does not ionize when placed in water.

deterioration [L. *deteriorare*, to deteriorate] Retrogression; said of impairment of mental or physical functions.

determinant (dē-těr′mǐ-nănt) [L. *determinare*, to limit] That which determines the character of something.

determination [L. *determinatus*, limiting] The establishing of the nature or precise identity of a substance, organism, or event.

determinism (dē-těr′mǐ-nizm) The theory that all human action is the result of predetermined and inevitable physical, psychological, or environmental conditions uninfluenced by personal choices or random events.

psychic d. The theory that mental processes are determined by conscious or unconscious motives and are never irrelevant.

deterministic effect (dē-tĕr″mĭ-nĭs′tĭk) An effect that has a threshold of chemical or radiation exposure below which are no measurable effects and above which the severity is dose-related.

deterrent (dē-tĕr′ĕnt) [L. deterrēre, to deter] **1.** An agent that inhibits the action of another agent. **2.** An agent that discourages or prevents the use of another agent.

detorsion (dē-tor′shŭn) **1.** Surgical therapy for torsion of a testicle, ureter, or volvulus of the bowel. **2.** Correction of any bodily curvature or deformity.

detox (dē′tŏks) Colloquial term for detoxification.

detoxicant (dē-tŏk′sĭ-kĭnt) [″ + ″] Any agent, e.g., activated charcoal, that removes toxins from the body.

detoxification (dē-tŏk″sĭ-fĭ-kā′shŭn) [″ + ″ + L. facere, to make] **1.** Reduction of the toxic properties of a poisonous substance. SEE: biotransformation. **2.** The process of removing the physiological effects of a drug or substance from an affected individual.

detoxify (dē-tŏk′sĭ-fī) **1.** To remove the toxic quality of a substance. **2.** To treat a toxic overdose of any medicine, but esp. of the toxic state produced by drug abuse or acute alcoholism.

detrition (dē-trĭsh′ŭn) [L. detritus, to rub away] The wearing away of a part, esp. through friction, as of the teeth. SEE: bruxism.

detritus (dĭ-trī′tŭs) [L., to rub away] Any broken-down, degenerative, or carious matter produced by disintegration.

detrusor hyperactivity with impaired contractility ABBR: DHIC. Detrusor instability.

detrusor instability SEE: under instability.

detrusor overactivity Detrusor instability.

detumescence (dē″tū-mĕs′ĕns) [L. de, down, + tumescere, to swell] **1.** Subsidence of a swelling. **2.** Subsidence of the swelling of erectile tissue of the genital organs (penis or clitoris) following erection.

deuteranopia, deuteranopsia (doo″tĕr-ă-nō′pē-ă, doo″tĕr-ă-nop′sē-ă) [″ + anopia, blindness] Green blindness; color blindness in which there is a defect in the perception of green. SEE: color blindness.

deuterate (dū′tĕr-āt) To combine with deuterium.

deuterium (doo-tēr′ē-ŭm, dū-) [deutero-

+ -ium (1)] SYMB: ²H, D. The isotope of hydrogen with an atomic weight (mass) 2. It is used in certain nuclear reactors as an absorber of neutrons. Water made from deuterium is incompatible with life if ingested exclusively because of slight differences in bond angles and distances that prevent necessary hydrogen bonding. SYN: heavy hydrogen.

d. oxide An isotope of water in which hydrogen has been displaced by its isotope deuterium. Its properties differ from ordinary water in that it has higher freezing and boiling points and is incapable of supporting life. SYN: heavy water.

deutero-, deuter- [Gr. deuteros, second] Prefixes meaning second or secondary.

deuteron (dū′tĕr-ŏn) SYMB: d. The nucleus of deuterium or heavy hydrogen.

devascularization (dē″vas″kyū-lă-rĭ-zā′shŏn) [de- + vascularization] A decrease in, or complete interruption of, the blood supply to a part of the body due to disease or surgery.

developer In radiology and photography, the solution used to make the latent image visible on the radiographic film.

development (dĕ-vel′ŏp-mĕnt) [Fr. développer, to unwrap] **1.** Growth to full size or maturity, as in the progress of an egg to the adult state. SEE: growth. **2.** Passage through a series of stages of improvement, education, or learning.

cognitive d. The sequential acquisition of the ability to learn, reason, and analyze that begins in infancy and progresses as the individual matures.

delayed d. Developmental delay.

faculty d. The use of formal programs to improve the teaching ability, scholarship, professionalism, and wellness of educators. Such programs are sometimes provided by an employer.

instructional d. Any of the programs used in health education to improve the coursework and curriculum of an educational institution.

organizational d. In academic health care, any of the initiatives used to improve the effectiveness, leadership, stability, and the structure of educational institutions.

risk for delayed d. At risk for delay of 25% or more in one or more of the areas of social or self-regulatory behavior, or cognitive, language, gross, or fine motor skills. SEE: Nursing Diagnoses Appendix.

developmental Pert. to development.

developmental coordination disorder Exceptional clumsiness, or an unusual delay in meeting motor milestones of childhood when such a delay results in functional impairment and cannot be attributed to other medical conditions.

developmental delay An impairment in

the performance of tasks or the meeting of developmental milestones that a child should achieve by a specific chronological age. The diagnosis of a developmental delay is made with testing that assesses cognitive, physical, social, and emotional development as well as communication and adaptive skills. SYN: *delayed development*.

developmental dislocation of the hip SEE: under *dislocation*.

developmental milestone An achievement or ability that has special importance in the growth, motor functioning, or social development of infants, toddlers, and older children and teens, usually associated with a particular age range, e.g., sitting, crawling, walking, language acquisition.

developmental screening SEE: under *screening*.

Developmental Test of Visual Motor Integration A test of visual perception and motor planning requiring the copying of shapes and forms.

deviance [L. *deviare*, to turn aside] A variation from the accepted norm.

deviant Something (or someone) that is variant when compared with the norm or an accepted standard.

deviant behavior Any behavior considered to be grossly abnormal.

deviate (dē′vē-āt″) [L. *deviare*, to turn aside] **1.** To move steadily away from a designated norm. **2.** An individual whose behavior, esp. sexual behavior, is so far removed from societal norms that it is classed as socially, morally, or legally unacceptable.

deviation (dē″vē-ā′shŏn) [*deviate*] **1.** A departure from the normal. **2.** Alteration of a course or direction.

   axis d. A shift of the normal electrical vectors of the heart. It is sometimes a result of conduction disease, of enlargement of the chambers of the heart, or of obstructive lung disease.

   conjugate d. Deviation of the eyes to the same side.

   eye d. In eye muscle imbalance and "crossed eyes," the abnormal visual axis of the unaligned eye.

   minimum d. The smallest deviation that a prism can produce.

   skew d. A condition in which one eyeball is directed upward and outward, the other inward and downward.

   standard d. ABBR: SD. SYMB: σ. In statistics, the commonly used measure of dispersion or variability in a distribution; the square root of the variance.

   d. of tongue Marked turning of the tongue from the midline when protruded, indicative of lesions of the hypoglossal nerve.

device (di-vīs′) [Fr. *devis*, contrivance] An apparatus, tool, or machine made for a specific function. SEE: illus.

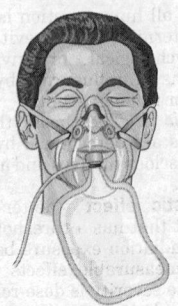

NON-REBREATHER MASK DEVICE

   abduction d. A trapezoidal pillow, wedge, or splint placed between the arm and torso to prevent adduction. It is commonly used postoperatively for patients having total joint replacement or open reduction or internal fixation of the hip or shoulder. SEE: illus.

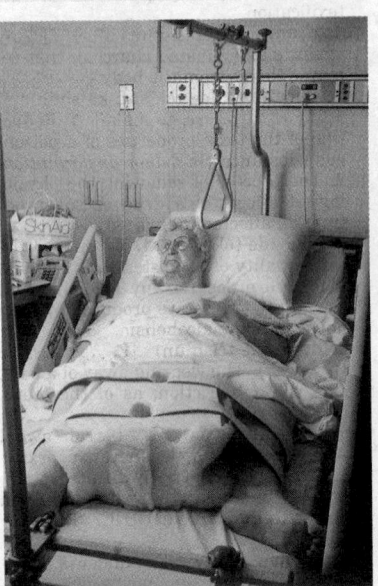

ABDUCTION DEVICE

Abductor pillow use following hip replacement surgery.

   adaptive d. Assistive **technology**.

   assistive technology d. Assistive **technology**.

   bag mask d. A manually operated resuscitator used to ventilate a nonbreathing patient or assist the ventilation of a patient who is not breathing at an effective rate or tidal volume. The device consists of a bag, an oxygen reservoir system, a one-way flow valve, and a clear face mask. It is designed to be attached to an oxygen source by tubing to deliver concentrations approaching 100%.

biventricular assist d. ABBR: BiVAD. A device that helps both ventricles of the heart contract more effectively. It is used to treat heart failure by propelling blood out of the chambers of the heart.

charge-coupled d. ABBR: CCD. A device used in video and digital imaging (such as in CT scanning) that creates electronic images from light.

femoral compression d. A device used to apply pressure to the large artery or vein in the thigh after it has been cannulated in order to reduce bleeding from the punctured vessel. Femoral compression devices are used, e.g., after angiography.

Flutter d. SEE: *Flutter device*.

head immobilization d. A device that attaches to a long back board and holds the patient's head in neutral alignment. SEE: *long back board*.

humanitarian use d. Humanitarian device exemption.

improvised explosive d. ABBR: IED. Military jargon for a homemade bomb or land mine used in unconventional warfare.

input d. In assistive technology, the device that activates an electronic device. This can be a manual switch, a remote control, or a joystick. SEE: *switch*.

inspiratory impedance threshold d. Inspiratory impedance threshold valve.

intrauterine contraceptive d. ABBR: IUCD, IUD. SEE: *intrauterine contraceptive device*.

left ventricular assist d. ABBR: LVAD. A pump surgically implanted in patients with severe heart failure to move blood from the left ventricle to the ascending aorta. The LVAD usually augments the heart's function until it heals (following a severe myocardial infarction) or until a heart transplant becomes available, e.g., for patients with heart failure with a markedly diminished ejection fraction. The LVAD also may be used permanently for a patient who does not meet criteria for transplantation.

listening d. A speech amplifier that aids the hearing-impaired in direct person-to-person communication or telephone conversation. Such devices differ from conventional hearing aids in that they reduce interference from background noises.

medical d. Any health care product that is intended for the diagnosis, prevention, or treatment of disease and does not primarily work by effecting a chemical change in the body

mobility d. Any assistive technology that aids the movement of people with physical impairments. Examples include lift chairs, scooters, or wheelchairs.

needleless d. A device that has no exposed sharp surface, used to inject drugs and fluids. It is designed to decrease the risk of needle-stick injuries by health care professionals.

oxygen-conserving d. ABBR: OCR. Any device that reduces the loss of administered oxygen into the environment, e.g., one that releases oxygen to a patient only when the patient inhales.

oxygen-powered ventilation d. A multifunction ventilation devicehat uses high-flow oxygen. This device can often be triggered by negative pressure caused by an inhaling patient; it can also be operated by a button while the operator watches the patient's chest rise.

⚠ During resuscitation, it is necessary to use the positive-pressure aspect of this device and manually trigger or compress the button because the patient cannot open the valve by inhaling. These devices should be fitted with an overinflation high-pressure alarm to avoid gastric distention and/or barotrauma.

personal flotation d. ABBR: PFD. A life vest to prevent drowning and near drowning. People engaged in water sports, such as boating or water skiing, or rescuers working on or near the water should wear PFDs at all times. The U.S. Coast Guard sets standards and establishes specifications for the manufacture and use of PFDs. PFDs may be used to provide added buoyancy for the patient during aquatic therapy.

personal assistive mobility d. Personal mobility **d.**

personal mobility d. Any assistive device that facilitates individual human transportation. Examples include powered wheelchairs, scooters, bicycles and unicycles. Although many such devices are used by people with activity or mobility restrictions, mobility aids can be employed generally, e.g., for urban transportation in place of automobiles. SYN: *personal assistive mobility* **d.**

powered mobility d. ABBR: PMD. Any assistive device (such as a powered wheelchair, a lift chair, or a scooter) that improves the movement of the functionally impaired.

pressure relief d. An appliance filled with air, water, gel, or foam, to reduce pressure points caused by the patient's body weight when seated or bedridden. Examples include wheelchair cushions and air or water flotation mattresses.

protective d. An external support applied to vulnerable joints or other body parts to guard against injury. Protective devices include helmets, braces, tape or wrapping, and padding.

sequential compression d. ABBR: SCD. A device to reduce edema or prevent the formation of blod clots in an extremity. A chambered nylon sleeve is progressively inflated from its distal segment to the proximal segment, forcing venous and lymphatic return. SCDs are inflated with air (pneumatic compression) or, less commonly, chilled water (cryocompression). SCDs are used frequently in the perioperative period. SEE: *intermittent* **compression**.

single-use d. A medical device used once for the care of a single patient and then immediately discarded.

spine arthroplasty d. A prosthesis to replace a damaged intervertebral disk.

telecommunication d. for the deaf ABBR: TDD. A device that allows the hearing-impaired to use the telephone even if they cannot comprehend speech. A keyboard and display screen are used.

venous access d. A specially designed catheter for gaining and maintaining access to the venous system. This device provides access for patients who require intravenous fluids or medications for several days or more, e.g., those having a bone marrow transplant or who are receiving long-term total parenteral nutrition. SEE: *venous port.* SEE: illus.

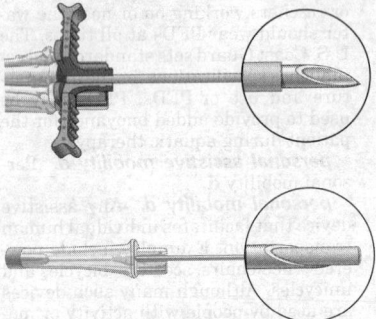

VENOUS ACCESS DEVICES

A. An over-the-needle catheter; B. An inside-the-needle catheter.

ventricular assist d. ABBR: VAD. A pump to treat heart failure. It helps the ventricles to contract and move blood to the lungs and/or the aorta. SEE: *left ventricular assist d.*

devitalize (dē-vīt′ăl-īz″) [*de-* + *vital*] **1.** To destroy or lose vitality; make or become lifeless. **2.** In biology, to deprive of a normal supply of nutrients and oxygen. **3.** In dentistry, to destroy the vitality of a tooth or the pulp of a tooth.

devitalization (-vīt″ăl-ĭ-zā′shŏn), *n.* **devitalized** (-īzd″), *adj.*

DEXA *dual energy x-ray absortiometry.*

dexamethasone (děk″să-měth′ă-sōn) A synthetic glucocorticoid drug.

dexamethasone suppression test A test performed to diagnose the cause of Cushing syndrome, in which low or high doses of dexamethasone are given to the patient, and their effect on serum cortisol levels are measured. The response to the test may indicate whether a patient has normal cortisol suppression, an adrenal adenoma, a pituitary tumor, or secretion of ACTH by a malignant tumor. SEE: *corticotropin production, Cushing syndrome; ectopic.*

dexter (děks′tĕr) [L.] On the right side. SEE: *sinister.*

dexterity Skill in using the hands, usually requiring both fine and gross motor coordination.

dextral (děks′trăl) Pert. to the right side.

dextrality (děks-trăl′ĭ-tē) Right-handedness. SEE: *sinistrality.*

dextran (děks′trăn) [L. *dexter,* right] A polysaccharide produced by the action of *Leuconostoc mesenteroides* on sucrose. It is available in various molecular weights and is used as a plasma volume expander.

dextrase (děks′trās) An enzyme that splits dextrose and converts it into lactic acid.

dextrin (děks′trĭn) [L. *dexter,* right] A carbohydrate that is an intermediate in the breakdown of starch in digestion. Further action by amylases digests dextrin to maltose. It is a carbohydrate of the formula $(C_6H_{10}O_5)^{11}$

dextro-, dextr- [L. *dexter,* stem *dextr-,* (on the) right] Prefixes meaning *right, on the right, dextrorotatory.*

dextroamphetamine sulfate (děks″trō″am-fet′ă-mēn″, -mĭn) [*dextro-* + *amphetamine*] A compound related to amphetamine sulfate (i.e., an isomer of amphetamine); sometimes written D-amphetamine sulfate or dextroamphetamine sulfate. It is used as a central nervous system stimulant in attention deficit hyperactivity disorder and occasionally as a treatment for depression in patients with terminal illnesses. Prolonged use can cause psychological dependence. Its street name is "speed."

dextrocardia (děks″trō-kăr′dē-ă) [″ + Gr. *kardia,* heart] The condition of having the heart on the right side of the body.

dextromethorphan (děk″strō-me-thor′fan″) $C_{18}H_{25}NO$, widely used as cough suppressant in over-the-counter and generic cough and cold medications. When consumed in excess, it can cause perceptual alterations and hallucinations.

dextroposition (děks″trō-pō-zĭsh′ŭn) Displacement to the right.

dextrorotatory (děks″trō-rō′tă-tor-ē) [″ + *rotare,* to turn] Causing to turn to the right, applied esp. to substances that turn polarized rays of light to the right.

dextrose (děks'trōs) Glucose.

dextroversion (děk"strō-věr'zhŭn) [" + *vertere,* to turn] Turned or located toward the right.

DFA *Direct fluorescein-conjugated **antibody;** direct fluorescent **antibody**.*

DFP *di-isopropyl fluorophosphate.* SEE: *isoflurophate.*

dg *decigram.*

DHCA *Deep hypothermic circulatory **arrest**.*

DHEA *Dehydroepiandrosterone.*

DHHS *Department of Health and Human Services.*

DHT *Dihydrotestosterone.*

di- [Gr. *dis,* twice] Prefix meaning *twice, double,* or *two.*

dia- [Gr. *dia,* through, across] Prefix meaning *(passing) through, (going) apart, completely.*

diabetes (dī"ă-bēt'ēz) [Gr. *diabētēs,* (one) passing through] A general term for diseases marked by excessive urination and elevated blood sugar, esp. diabetes mellitus (DM). SEE: *Nursing Diagnoses Appendix.*

   brittle d. DM that is exceptionally difficult to control. The disease is marked by alternating episodes of hypoglycemia and hyperglycemia. Frequent adjustments of dietary intake and insulin dosage are required.

   ETIOLOGY: Diabetes may be brittle when insulin is not well absorbed; insulin requirements vary rapidly; insulin is improperly prepared or administered; the Somogyi phenomenon is present; the patient has coexisting anorexia or bulimia; the patient's daily exercise routine, diet, or medication schedule varies; or physiological or psychological stress is persistent. SYN: *brittle **d.** mellitus.*

   brittle d. mellitus Brittle **d.**

   bronze d. Hemochromatosis.

   chemical d. 1. Asymptomatic DM, a stage in which no obvious clinical signs and symptoms of the disease are present but blood glucose measurements are abnormal. 2. Type 2 DM occurring in an obese child or adolescent. The syndrome is sometimes referred to as "mature onset diabetes of youth" (MODY).

   cystic fibrosis–related d. ABBR: CFRD. DM arising in patients with cystic fibrosis (CF). It is the most common complication of CF other than those conditions that affect the lungs. It is caused by destruction of islet cells (the cells in the pancreas that make insulin) as well as a decrease in sensitivity of the liver and muscles to the actions of insulin. The disease usually first becomes clinically obvious in young adults.

   PATIENT CARE: Although CFRD can be diagnosed with fasting glucose blood tests or hemoglobin A1c levels, many experts recommend using an oral glucose tolerance test. Fifteen to 30% of patients with CF are affected by their 20th birthday, and perhaps as many as half have the disease by age 30. CFRD is associated with more severe lung disease than is experienced by patients with CF and normal glucose tolerance. Oral hypoglycemic agents, insulin, and exercise are the primary methods of treatment. Caloric restriction, a cornerstone of treatment for other forms of diabetes, is relatively contraindicated because of the need for aggressive nutritional supplementation in CF patients.

   double d. A colloquial term for *hybrid diabetes.*

   endocrine d. DM caused by diseases of the ovaries, pituitary, thyroid, or adrenal glands.

   fibrocalculous pancreatic d. A rare form of DM caused by chronic tropical pancreatitis and destruction of insulin-producing islet cells.

   gestational d. ABBR: GDM. DM that begins during pregnancy owing to changes in glucose metabolism and insulin resistance.

   GDM affects a large percentage of pregnant American women, ranging from about 1.5% to 14%, depending on the ethnic group studied. Although gestational diabetes usually subsides after delivery, women with GDM have a 45% risk of recurrence with the next pregnancy and a significant risk of developing type 2 diabetes later in life.

   DIAGNOSIS: Although many diabetic specialists recommend universal screening for GDM, it is agreed by all diabetologists that women at risk for GDM (women over age 25 who are overweight at the start of pregnancy; have a previous history of gestational diabetes; have had a previous infant weighing 9 lb or more at birth; have a history of a poor pregnancy outcome, glycosuria, or polycystic ovary syndrome; or who are from families or ethnic groups with a high incidence of type 2 DM) should undergo oral glucose tolerance testing as soon as possible to assess blood glucose levels while fasting and after meals. Testing should be repeated at 24 to 28 weeks' gestation if the first screening is negative.

   TREATMENT: A calorically restricted diet, regular exercise, and metformin or insulin are used to treat GDM.

   PATIENT CARE: Blood glucose self-monitoring is essential to management, and patients should be taught to monitor glucose levels four times each day, obtaining a fasting level in the MORN-

ING, followed by three postprandial levels (1 hr after the start of each meal). Blood glucose levels at 1 hr after beginning a meal are considered the best predictor for subsequent fetal macrosomia. Target blood glucose levels are 90 mg/dL or less (fasting) and 120 to 140 mg/dL postprandially. The patient and her partner should be instructed that food, stress, inactivity, and hormones elevate blood glucose levels and that exercise and insulin lower them. They will need to learn about both pharmacological (measuring and injecting insulin) and nonpharmacological (menu management and physical activity) interventions to maintain a normal glycemic state (euglycemia) throughout the pregnancy, while ensuring adequate caloric intake for fetal growth and preventing maternal ketosis. Women who have no medical or obstetrical contraindicting factors should be encouraged to participate in an approved exercise program, because physical activity increases insulin receptor sensitivity. Even performing 15 to 20 min of "armchair exercises" daily (while reading or watching television) can help the pregnant woman reduce hyperglycemia without increasing the risk of inducing uterine contractions. If euglycemia is not achieved by nutrition therapy and exercise within 10 days, insulin is started. Pregnant women require three to four times the amount of insulin needed by a nonpregnant woman. Human minimally antigenic insulin should be prescribed. Often one dose of long-acting insulin at bedtime is sufficient, with rapid-acting insulins, i.e., regular insulin, insulin aspart recombinant (Novolog), or insulin lispro recombinant (Humalog) used to aid optimal glycemic control. Insulin glargine (Lantus), once used for gestational diabetes, is no longer recommended for pregnant women. Because stress can significantly raise blood glucose levels, stress management is a vital part of therapy. The woman's feelings about her pregnancy and diabetes as well as her support system should be carefully assessed. Coping strategies should be explored. The patient is taught about deep breathing and relaxation exercises and encouraged to engage in activities that she enjoys and finds relaxing. She and her partner should learn to recognize interaction tensions and ways to deal with these to limit stress in their environment.

Maternal complications associated with GDM include pregnancy-induced hypertension, eclampsia, and the need for cesarean section delivery.

hybrid d. A form of DM that has characteristics of both types 1 and 2. The patient may have episodes of diabetic ketoacidosis but marked insulin resistance and an obese body type.

iatrogenic d. DM due to administration of drugs such as corticosteroids or dextrose infusions.

idiopathic d. Type 1b **d.** mellitus.

immune-mediated d. mellitus Type 1 **d.**

d. insipidus ABBR: DI. Excessive urination caused either by inadequate amounts of circulating vasopressin (antidiuretic hormone) in the body (hypothalamic DI) or by failure of the kidney to respond to antidiuretic hormone (nephrogenic DI). Urinary output is often massive, e.g., 5 to 15 L/day, which may result in dehydration in patients who cannot drink enough liquid to replace urinary losses, e.g., those with impaired consciousness. The urine is dilute (specific gravity is often below 1.005), and typically the patient's serum sodium level and osmolality rise as free water is eliminated as urine. If water deficits are not matched or the urinary losses are not prevented, death will result from dehydration.

ETIOLOGY: DI usually results from hypothalamic injury (such as brain trauma or neurosurgery) or from the effects of certain drugs (such as lithium or demeclocycline) on the renal resorption of water. Other representative causes include sickle cell anemia (in which renal infarcts damage the kidney's ability to retain water), hypothyroidism, adrenal insufficiency, inherited disorders of antidiuretic hormone production, and sarcoidosis.

SYMPTOMS: The primary symptoms are urinary frequency, thirst, and dehydration.

TREATMENT: When DI is a side effect of drug therapy, the offending drug is withheld. DI caused by failure of the posterior pituitary gland to secrete antidiuretic hormone is treated with synthetic vasopressin.

PATIENT CARE: Fluid balance is monitored. Fluid intake and output, urine specific gravity, and weight are assessed for evidence of dehydration and hypovolemic hypotension. Serum electrolyte and blood urea nitrogen levels are monitored.

The patient is instructed in nasal insufflation of vasopressin (desmopressin acetate, effective for 8 to 20 hr, depending on dosage), the oral tablet form being more useful for bedtime or administration of subcutaneous or intramuscular vasopressin (effective for 2 to 6 hr). The length of the therapy and the importance of taking medications as prescribed and not discontinuing them without consulting the prescriber are stressed. Hydrochlorothiazide can be prescribed for nephrogenic DI not caused by drug therapy; amiloride may be used in nephrogenic DI caused by lithium administration. Meticulous skin and oral care are provided; use of a soft toothbrush is recommended; and petroleum jelly is applied to the lips and an emollient lotion to the skin to reduce dryness and prevent skin breakdown. Adequate fluid intake should be maintained.

Both the patient and family are taught to identify signs of dehydration and to report signs of severe dehydration and impending hypovolemia. The patient is taught to measure intake and output, to monitor weight daily, and to use a hydrometer to measure urine specific gravity. Weight gain should be reported because this may signify that the medication dosage is too high. Recurrence of polyuria may indicate dosing that is too low. The patient should wear or carry a medical ID tag and have prescribed medications with him or her at all times. Both patient and family need to know that chronic DI will not shorten the lifespan, but lifelong medications may be required to control the signs, symptoms, and complications of the disease. Counseling may be helpful in dealing with this chronic illness.

insulin-dependent d. mellitus ABBR: IDDM. Type 1 **d.**

juvenile-onset d. A dated term for type 1 diabetes.

latent d. DM that manifests itself during times of stress such as pregnancy, infectious disease, weight gain, or trauma. Before the stress, no clinical or laboratory findings of diabetes are present. There is a very strong chance that affected people will eventually develop overt type 2 DM.

latent autoimmune d. in adults ABBR: LADA. A form of type 1 diabetes usually diagnosed after 30 years of age, in which there are serum antibodies against insulin, pancreatic islet cells, or the protein products of those cells. Most patients affected by LADA eventually require insulin therapy, like patients with type 1 DM.

maternally inherited d. and deafness SEE: *maternally inherited diabetes and deafness.*

mature-onset d. of youth ABBR: MODY. Type 2 DM that presents during childhood or adolescence, typically as an autosomal dominant trait in which there is diminished but not absent insulin production by the pancreas. Children with this form of DM are not prone to diabetic ketoacidosis.

d. mellitus ABBR: DM. A chronic metabolic disorder marked by hyperglycemia. DM results either from failure of the pancreas to produce insulin (type 1 DM) or from insulin resistance, with inadequate insulin secretion to sustain normal metabolism (type 2 DM). Either type of DM may damage blood vessels, nerves, kidneys, the retina, and the developing fetus and the placenta during pregnancy. Type 1 or insulin-dependent DM has a prevalence of just 0.3 to 0.4%. Type 2 DM (formerly called *adult-onset* DM) has a prevalence in the general population of 6.6%. In some populations (such as older persons, Native Americans, African Americans, Pacific Islanders, Mexican Americans), it is present in nearly 20% of adults. Type 2 DM primarily affects obese middle-aged people with sedentary lifestyles, whereas type 1 DM usually occurs in children, most of whom are active and thin, although extremely obese children are now being diagnosed with type 2 diabetes as well. SEE: table; ***dawn** phenomenon; insulin; insulin pump; insulin resistance; diabetic polyneuropathy; Somogyi phenomenon.*

Type 1 DM usually presents as an acute illness with dehydration and often diabetic ketoacidosis. Type 2 DM is often asymptomatic in its early years. The American Diabetes Association (1-800-DIABETES) estimates that more than 5 million Americans have type 2 DM without knowing it.

ETIOLOGY: Type 1 DM is caused by autoimmune destruction of the insulin-secreting beta cells of the pancreas. The loss of these cells results in nearly complete insulin deficiency; without exogenous insulin, type 1 DM is rapidly fatal. Type 2 DM results partly from a decreased sensitivity of muscle cells to insulin-mediated glucose uptake and partly from a relative decrease in pancreatic insulin secretion.

SYMPTOMS: Classic symptoms of DM are polyuria, polydipsia, and weight loss. In addition, patients with hyperglycemia often have blurred vision, increased food consumption (polyphagia), and generalized weakness. When a patient with type 1 DM loses metabolic control (such as during infections or periods of noncompliance with therapy), symptoms of diabetic ketoacidosis occur. These may include nausea, vomiting, dizziness on arising, intoxication, delirium, coma, or death. Chronic complications of hyperglycemia include retinopathy and blindness, peripheral and autonomic neuropathies, glomerulosclerosis of the kidneys (with proteinuria, nephrotic syndrome, or end-stage renal failure), coronary and peripheral vascular disease, and reduced resistance to infections. Patients with DM often also sustain infected ulcerations of the feet, which may result in osteomyelitis and the need for amputation.

DIAGNOSIS: Several tests are helpful in identifying DM. These include tests of fasting plasma glucose levels, casual (randomly assessed) glucose levels, or

Comparison of Diabetic Ketoacidosis and Hypoglycemia

	Diabetic Ketoacidosis	Hypoglycemia
Onset	Gradual	Often sudden
History	Often acute infection in a diabetic or insufficient insulin intake	Recent insulin injection, inadequate meal, or excessive exercise after insulin
	Previous history of diabetes may be absent	
Musculoskeletal	Muscle wasting or weight loss	Weakness
Tremor		
Muscle twitching		
Gastrointestinal	Abdominal pains or cramps, sometimes acute	Nausea and vomiting
	Nausea and vomiting	
Central nervous system	Headache	Confusion, delirium, or seizures
Double or blurred vision		
Irritability		
Cardiovascular	Tachycardia	Variable
	Orthostatic hypotension	
Skin	Flushed, dry	Diaphoretic, pale
Respiratory	Air hunger	Variable
	Acetone odor of breath	Increased respiratory rate
	Dyspnea	
Laboratory values	Elevated blood glucose (>200 mg/dL)	Subnormal blood glucose (0–50 mg/dL)
	Glucose and ketones in blood and urine	Absence of glucose and ketones in urine unless bladder is full

glycosylated hemoglobin levels. Diabetes is currently established if patients have classic diabetic symptoms and if on two occasions fasting glucose levels exceed 126 mg/dL (>7 mmol/L), random glucose levels exceed 200 mg/dL (11.1 mmol/L), or a 2-hr oral glucose tolerance test is 200 mg/dL or more. A hemoglobin A1c test that is more than two standard deviations above normal (6.5% or greater) is also diagnostic of the disease.

TREATMENT: DM types 1 and 2 are both treated with specialized diets, regular exercise, intensive foot and eye care, and medications.

Patients with type 1 DM, unless they have had a pancreatic transplant, require insulin to live; intensive therapy with insulin to limit hyperglycemia ("tight control") is more effective than conventional therapy in preventing the progression of serious microvascular complications such as kidney and retinal diseases. Intensive therapy consists of three or more doses of insulin injected or administered by infusion pump daily, with frequent self-monitoring of blood glucose levels as well as frequent changes in therapy as a result of contacts with health care professionals. Some negative aspects of intensive therapy include a three times more frequent occurrence of severe hypoglycemia, weight gain, and an adverse effect on serum lipid levels, i.e., a rise in total cholesterol, LDL cholesterol, and triglycerides and a fall in HDL cholesterol. Participation in an intensive therapy program requires a motivated patient, but it can dramatically reduce eye, nerve, and renal complications compared to conventional therapy. SEE: *insulin pump* for illus.

Some patients with type 2 DM can control their disease with a calorically restricted diet (for instance 1600 to 1800 cal/day), regular aerobic exercise, and weight loss. Most patients, however, require the addition of some form of oral hypoglycemic drug or insulin. Oral agents to control DM include sulfonylurea drugs (such as glipizide), which increase pancreatic secretion of insulin; biguanides or thiazolidinediones (such as metformin or pioglitazone), which increase cellular sensitivity to insulin; or α-glucosidase inhibitors (such as acarbose), which decrease the absorption of

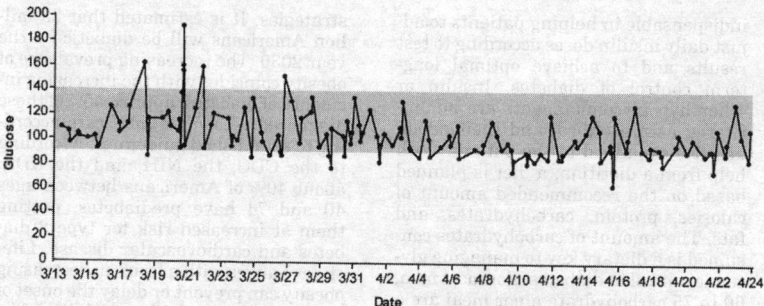

WELL-CONTROLLED DIABETES MELLITUS

Daily blood sugar abstracted from the records of a patient whose DM is well controlled (hemoglobin A1c=6.4). The average capillary blood glucose level is 104 mg/dL, and the standard deviation is 19. Sixty-five percent of the readings are between 90 and 140 mg/dL; the lowest blood sugar is 67 mg/dL (on April 15) and the highest is about 190 (on March 21).

carbohydrates from the gastrointestinal tract. Both types of diabetics also may be prescribed pramlintide (Symlin), a synthetic analog of human amylin, a hormone manufactured in the pancreatic beta cells. It enhances postprandial glucose control by slowing gastric emptying, decreasing postprandial glucagon concentrations, and regulating appetite and food intake; thus pramlintide is helpful for patients who do not achieve optimal glucose control with insulin and/or oral antidiabetic agents. When combinations of these agents fail to normalize blood glucose levels, insulin injections are added. Tight glucose control can reduce the patient's risk of many of the complications of the disease. SEE: illus.

PREVENTION OF COMPLICATIONS: Patients with DM should avoid tobacco, actively manage their serum lipid levels, and keep hypertension under optimal control. Failure to do so may result in a risk of atherosclerosis much higher than that of the general public. Other elements in care include receiving regular vaccinations, e.g., to prevent influenza and pneumococcal pneumonia.

PROGNOSIS: Diabetes is a chronic disease whose symptoms can be ameliorated and life prolonged by proper therapy. The isolation and eventual production of insulin in 1922 by Canadian physicians F. G. Banting and C. H. Best made it possible to allow people with the disease to lead normal lives.

PATIENT CARE: The diabetic patient should learn to recognize symptoms of low blood sugar (such as confusion, sweats, and palpitations) and high blood sugar (such as, polyuria and polydipsia). When either condition results in hospitalization, vital signs, weight, fluid intake, urine output, and caloric intake are accurately documented. Se-

rum glucose and urine ketone levels are evaluated. Chronic management of DM is also based on periodic measurement of glycosylated hemoglobin levels (HbA1c). Elevated levels of HbA1c suggest poor long-term glucose control. The effects of diabetes on other body systems (such as cerebrovascular, coronary artery, and peripheral vascular) should be regularly assessed. Patients should be evaluated regularly for retinal disease and visual impairment and peripheral and autonomic nervous system abnormalities, e.g., loss of sensation in the feet. The patient is observed for signs and symptoms of diabetic neuropathy, e.g., numbness or pain in the hands and feet, decreased vibratory sense, footdrop, and neurogenic bladder. The urine is checked for microalbumin or overt protein losses, an early indication of nephropathy. The combination of peripheral neuropathy and peripheral arterial disease results in changes in the skin and microvasculature that lead to ulcer formation on the feet and lower legs with poor healing. Approx. 45,000 lower-extremity diabetic amputations are performed in the U.S. each year. Many amputees have a second amputation within five years. Most of these amputations are preventable with regular foot care and examinations. Diabetic patients and their providers should look for changes in sensation to touch and vibration, the integrity of pulses, capillary refill, and the skin. All injuries, cuts, and blisters should be treated promptly. The patient should avoid constricting hose, slippers, shoes, and bed linens or walking barefoot. The patient with ulcerated or insensitive feet is referred to a podiatrist for continuing foot care and is warned that decreased sensation can mask injuries.

Home blood glucose self-monitoring is

indispensable in helping patients to adjust daily insulin doses according to test results and to achieve optimal long-term control of diabetes. Insulin or other hypoglycemic agents are administered as prescribed, and their action and use explained to the patient. With help from a dietitian, a diet is planned based on the recommended amount of calories, protein, carbohydrates, and fats. The amount of carbohydrates consumed is a dietary key to managing glycemic control in diabetes. For most men, 60 to 75 carbohydrate g per meal are a reasonable intake; for most women, 45 to 60 g are appropriate. Saturated fats should be limited to less than 7% of total caloric intake, and trans-fatty acids (unsaturated fats with hydrogen added) minimized. A steady, consistent level of daily exercise is prescribed, and participation in a supervised exercise program is recommended.

Hypoglycemic reactions are promptly treated by giving carbohydrates (orange juice, hard candy, honey, or any sugary food); if necessary, subcutaneous or intramuscular glucagon or intravenous dextrose (if the patient is not conscious) is administered. Hyperglycemic crises are treated initially with prescribed intravenous fluids and insulin and later with potassium replacement based on laboratory values.

Regular ophthalmological examinations are recommended for early detection of diabetic retinopathy. The patient is educated about diabetes, its possible complications and their management, and the importance of adherence to the prescribed therapy. The patient is taught the importance of maintaining normal blood pressure levels (120/80 mm Hg or lower). Control of even mild-to-moderate hypertension results in fewer diabetic complications, esp. nephropathy, cerebrovascular disease, and cardiovascular disease. Limiting alcohol intake to approximately one drink daily and avoiding tobacco are also important for self-management. Emotional support and a realistic assessment of the patient's condition are offered; this assessment should stress that, with proper treatment, the patient can have a near-normal lifestyle and life expectancy. Long-term goals for a patient with diabetes should include achieving and maintaining optimal metabolic outcomes to prevent complications; modifying diet and lifestyle to prevent and treat obesity, dyslipidemia, cardiovascular disease, hypertension, and nephropathy; improving physical activity; and allowing for the patient's nutritional and psychosocial needs and preferences. Assistance is offered to help the patient develop positive coping

strategies. It is estimated that 23 million Americans will be diabetic by the year 2030. The increasing prevalence of obesity coincides with the increasing incidence of diabetes; approx. 45% of those diagnosed receive optimal care according to established guidelines. According to the CDC, the NIH, and the ADA, about 40% of Americans between ages 40 and 74 have prediabetes, putting them at increased risk for type 2 diabetes and cardiovascular disease. Lifestyle changes with a focus on decreasing obesity can prevent or delay the onset of diabetes in 58% of this population. The patient and family should be referred to local and national support and information groups and may require psychological counseling. SEE: *Nursing Diagnoses Appendix.*

non–insulin-dependent d. mellitus ABBR: NIDDM. Type 2 **d.** SEE: *type 1 d.* for table.

pancreatic d. Diabetes associated with destruction of the exocrine and endocrine functions of the pancreas, such as occurs in chronic or recurrent pancreatitis.

renal d. Renal glycosuria, marked by a low renal threshold for glucose. Glucose tolerance is normal and diabetic symptoms are lacking.

secondary d. mellitus DM that results from damage to the pancreas (e.g., after frequent episodes of pancreatitis) or from drugs such as corticosteroids (which increase resistance to the effects of insulin).

steroid d. Hyperglycemia caused by the use of exogenously administered corticosteroids, e.g., prednisone, methylprednisolone, or dexamethasone.

strict control of d. Regulation of blood glucose to normal or nearly normal levels, both before and after meals. Tight control of blood sugar has been shown to improve the survival of patients in intensive-care units and to prevent long-term complications of DM, e.g., blindness, nerve damage, and kidney failure.

Patients with meticulously controlled DM typically have a hemoglobin A1c level of 6.5 to 7.0 or lower, fasting blood sugars that are less than 110 mg/dL, and after-meal blood sugar readings that are 140 mg/dL or less. SYN: *tight control of d.*

tight control of d. Strict control of **d.**

true d. **D.** mellitus.

type 1 d. DM that usually has its onset before the age of 25 years, in which the essential abnormality is related to absolute insulin deficiency. It was formerly known as *juvenile diabetes.* SEE: table.

type 1a d. mellitus The most common form of type 1 DM. It is caused by autoimmune destruction of the beta

Comparison of Type 1 (Insulin-Dependent) Diabetes Mellitus and Type 2 (Non–Insulin-Dependent) Diabetes Mellitus

	Type 1	Type 2
Age at onset	Usually under 30	Usually over 40
Symptom onset	Abrupt	Gradual
Body weight	Normal	Obese—80%
HLA association	Positive	Negative
Family history	Common	Nearly universal
Insulin in blood	Little to none	Some usually present
Islet cell antibodies	Present at onset	Absent
Prevalence	0.2–0.3%	6%
Symptoms	Polyuria, polydipsia, poly-phagia, weight loss, ketoacidosis	Polyuria, polydipsia, peripheral neuropathy
Control	Insulin, diet, and exercise	Diet, exercise, and often oral hypoglycemic drugs or insulin
Vascular and neural changes	Eventually develop	Will usually develop
Stability of condition	Fluctuates, may be difficult to control	May be difficult to control in poorly motivated patients

cells of the pancreas and inadequate insulin production. In type 1a DM, antibodies against insulin, islet cells of the pancreas, or glutamic acid decarboxylase is often present in the blood. The patient is prone to develop diabetic ketoacidosis if he or she is not treated with insulin.

type 1b d. mellitus A relatively less common form of type 1 DM (seen in only about 10% of type 1 diabetics) in which autoimmune antibodies against insulin, pancreatic beta cells, or their protein products are not found in the blood. Beta cells are nonetheless destroyed (by unknown means), and the patient develops hyperglycemia or ketoacidosis unless he or she receives insulin. SYN: *idiopathic d.*

type 2 d. A type of DM that occurs predominantly in adults. The insulin produced is sufficient to prevent ketoacidosis but insufficient to meet the total needs of the body, and resistance to the effects of insulin on peripheral tissues is often present. This type of diabetes in nonobese patients can usually be controlled by diet and oral hypoglycemic agents (e.g., sulfonylurea drugs or metformin). Eventually, insulin therapy is often required. In some patients the condition can be controlled by careful diet and regular exercise. SYN: *non–insulin-dependent d. mellitus*. SEE: *type 1 diabetes* for table.

unstable d. mellitus Brittle **d.**
diabetes educator One who is professionally certified as a diabetes educator by the National Certification Board for Diabetes Educators. The person certified is given the designation CDE.
diabetic (dī-ă-bĕt′ĭk) **1.** Pert. to or affected by diabetes. **2.** Permissible or fit

for patients with diabetes. **3.** A person with diabetes.
diabetic foot care Daily inspection, cleaning, and thorough drying of the feet of a diabetic to prevent complications.
PATIENT CARE: In-home care by the patient or a caregiver should include a daily foot inspection for cracks in the skin, calluses, abrasions, lacerations, blisters, ulcers, or ingrowing nails; changes in color or temperature; or loss of capillary refill. Any of these should be reported to a health care professional. Diabetic patients should be advised to keep their feet warm and dry, to wear clean shoes with good support, to avoid walking barefoot or without socks, and to trim nails carefully. Tobacco products, which decrease arterial blood flow, should be avoided. Professional diabetic foot care includes examination of the feet for diminished pulses (or other circulatory problems); examination of the feet for sensation (with monofilament testing); and consulting a podiatrist or diabetic care specialist at least once a year. Deficiencies in diabetic foot care can have disastrous complications, including amputations and Charcot foot.
diabetic glucose tolerance SEE: under *tolerance*.
diabetic ketoacidosis SEE: under *ketoacidosis*.
diabetogenic (dī″ă-bĕt″ō-jĕn′ĭk) [″ + *gennan*, to produce] Causing diabetes.
diabetology (dī-ă-bĕ-tol′ŏ-jē) [*diabetes* + *-logy*] The medical specialty concerned with diabetes mellitus. **diabetologist** (′ŏ-jist), *n.*
diacetate (dī-ăs′ĕ-tāt) A salt of diacetic acid.
diacetoxyscirpenol (dī″as″ĕ-toks″ĕ-

sēr'pĕ-nol") ABBR: DAS. A deadly toxin derived from *Fusarium* species. DAS may grow on and contaminate cereals and other stored crops and can be toxic to fungi, plants, and animals (including humans). It has been used in the past in chemotherapy and can be used as an agent of biological or chemical warfare. SYN: *anguidine.*

diacetylmorphine (dī"ă-sē"tĭl-mor'fēn) Heroin.

diacidic (dī-ăs'ĭd-ĭk) [Gr. *dis,* twice, + L. *acidus,* soured] Containing two acidic hydrogen ions.

diagnose (dī'ăg-nōs) [Gr. *diagignoskein,* to discern] To determine the cause and nature of a pathological condition; to recognize a disease.

diagnosis (dī"ăg-nō'sĭs, -nō'sēz") *pl.* **diagnoses** [Gr. *diagnōsis,* discernment] ABBR: dx. **1.** A disease or syndrome a person has or is believed to have. **2.** The use of scientific or clinical methods to establish the cause and nature of a person's illness or injury and the functional impairment it produces. The diagnosis forms the basis for patient care.

  antenatal d. Prenatal **d.**

  clinical d. Identification of a disease by history, physical examination, laboratory studies, and radiological studies.

  cytological d. Identification of a disease based on cells present in body tissues or exudates.

  differential d. Identification of a condition, disease, or illness by comparison with others that share some features, signs, and symptoms of the presenting disease but differ in some critical ways.

  dual d. The presence of mental illness in a patient with a history of concurrent substance abuse.

  d. by exclusion A presumptive diagnosis made by excluding diseases in the differential diagnosis, leaving one as the most likely of the alternatives even though the diagnosis is not established unequivocally.

  medical d. **1.** The identification of the cause of the patient's illness or discomfort. **2.** The process of determining the unique cause of a patient's illness.

  noninvasive prenatal d. ABBR: NIPD. Any test used to identify birth defects that relies on the analysis of blood or easily obtained body fluids.

  nursing d. SEE: *nursing diagnosis.*

  oral d. The area of dentistry devoted to the compilation and study of the patient's dental history and a detailed clinical examination of the oral tissues and radiographs to assess oral health, with the object of developing a treatment plan to restore tooth structure and proper occlusion and to promote healing and better oral health.

  pathological d. Determination of the cause or causes of an illness by examining fluids and tissues from the patient before or after death. The examination may be performed on blood, plasma, microscopic tissue samples, or gross specimens. SEE: *autopsy; pathology.*

  physical d. Identification of an illness or abnormality by looking at, listening to, percussing, or palpating the patient. In contemporary health care, amid much controversy, diagnostic imaging, e.g., ultrasound, has replaced many traditional physical diagnostic skills.

  preimplantation genetic d. In assisted reproduction, the testing of a fertilized egg for heritable illnesses before the ovum is inserted into the female.

  prenatal d. Identification of disease or congenital defects of the fetus during gestation. A growing number of pathological conditions can be diagnosed by analyses of maternal blood and such tests as chorionic villi sampling, ultrasound, embryoscopy, amniocentesis, and fetoscopy. Thus, the gender, inherited characteristics, and current status of the fetus can be identified as early as the first trimester, helping parents in their decision-making if findings indicate an incurable disorder. Mid-trimester and last trimester tests provide information regarding the physical characteristics of the fetus and placenta, and analysis of amniotic fluid allows estimation of fetal age and maturity and may improve intrauterine management of treatable disorders. SYN: *antenatal* **d.** SEE: *prenatal surgery.*

  primary d. Diagnosis of the most important disease or underlying disease afflicting a patient. SYN: *first-listed d.*

  radiographic d. Identification of an illness by the interpretation of radiographic findings.

  tongue d. In traditional Chinese medicine, the methodical evaluation of the appearance of the patient's tongue to determine the cause of a complaint or syndrome.

diagnosis-related group SEE: under *group.*

diagnostic Pert. to a diagnosis.

  in vitro d. ABBR: IVD. **1.** Any device, reagent, material, or system designed for use in the laboratory diagnosis of disease or health status. The term also refers to a general category of entities that are highly and specifically regulated by the U.S. Food and Drug Administration and other regulatory bodies. **2.** The laboratory analysis of body substances (e.g., blood, saliva, stool, or urine) for specific analytes indicative of disease.

Diagnostic and Statistical Manual of Mental Disorders (Fourth Edition) ABBR: DSM-IV. The standard nomenclature of emotional illness used by all health care practitioners. DSM-IV, published by the American Psychiatric Association, was introduced in 1994.

diagnostician (dī"ăg-nŏs-tĭsh'ŭn) [Gr. *diagignoskein*, to discern] One skilled in diagnosis.

diagnostics (dī"ăg-nos'tiks) [*diagnos(is)* + *-ics*] The science, art, or practice of diagnosis.

    companion d. Laboratory tests and test kits used to determine the suitability of patients for tailored or targeted forms of therapy, e.g., therapies that act on unique biochemical pathways or that require specific genotypes or mutations.

    molecular d. Molecular **pathology** (2).

diakinesis (dī"ă-kĭ-nē'sĭs) [Gr. *dia*, through, + *kinesis*, motion] The stage in the first prophase of meiosis, during which the homologous chromosomes shorten and thicken and the nuclear membrane disappears.

dial (dī'ăl) [L. *dialis*, daily, fr. *dies*, day] A graduated circular face, similar to a clock face, on which some measurement is indicated by a pointer that moves as the entity being measured (pressure, temperature, or heat) changes.

dialectical behavior therapy A form of psychological counseling in which patients are directed to change dysfunctional behavior patterns within a context of acceptance and compassion. It is used principally to manage personality disorders.

dialy- [Gr. *dia*, through + *lysis*, dissolution] Prefix meaning *separation.*

dialysance (dī"ă-lĭ'săns) In renal dialysis, the minute rate of net exchange of a substance between blood and dialysis fluid per unit of blood-bath concentration gradient.

dialysate (dī-ăl'ĭ-sāt) **1.** A liquid that has been dialyzed. **2.** In renal failure, the fluid used to remove or deliver compounds or electrolytes that the failing kidney cannot excrete or retain in the proper concentrations.

dialysis (dī-al'ĭ-sĭs, 'ĭ-sēz") *pl.* **dialyses** [*dia-* + *-lysis*] **1.** The passage of a solute through a membrane. **2.** The diffusion of blood across a semipermeable membrane to remove toxic materials and to maintain fluid, electrolyte, and acid-base balance in cases of impaired kidney function or absence of the kidneys. SEE: *hemodialysis; Nursing Diagnoses Appendix.*

    chronic ambulatory peritoneal d. Continuous ambulatory peritoneal **d.**

    continuous ambulatory peritoneal d. ABBR: CAPD. Dialysis in which fluid is infused into the peritoneum through an implanted catheter and then drained from the body after absorbing metabolic toxins. The peritoneal lining serves as the dialytic membrane. CAPD is an alternative to hemodialysis for patients with end-stage renal disease. It removes

fluids, electrolytes, and nitrogen-containing wastes by osmosis but is less efficient than hemodialysis. Scrupulous antiseptic technique is needed to avoid introducing infectious microorganisms into the dialysate and peritoneum. The technique has several benefits: it can be performed at home by patients (increasing their autonomy); it avoids the hypotension sometimes associated with hemodialysis; and it is better tolerated than hemodialysis because it is less likely to produce rapid shifts in the concentration of urea, electrolytes, and other solutes in the bloodstream. SYN: *chronic ambulatory peritoneal d.* SEE: *peritoneal d.*

    continuous cyclic peritoneal d. ABBR: CCPD. Dialysis performed every night with fluid remaining in the peritoneal cavity until the next night.

    intermittent peritoneal d. ABBR: IPD. Dialysis using automated equipment, often performed overnight. The fluid is drained from the peritoneal cavity at the end of the treatment.

    peritoneal d. Dialysis in which the lining of the peritoneal cavity is used as the dialyzing membrane, requiring less complex equipment and less specialized personnel than hemodialysis, little or no heparin, no blood loss, and minimal cardiovascular stress. Dialyzing fluid introduced into the peritoneal cavity is left to dwell there for a specified time and then passively drained.

    Peritoneal dialysis is used to treat renal failure and, less commonly, certain types of poisoning, hypothermia, or heatstroke. SEE: *Nursing Diagnoses Appendix.*

    ⚠ Although peritoneal dialysis may be performed anywhere by the patient, allowing him or her to be independent, regular follow-up with health care professionals is needed to optimize its safety and effectiveness.

PATIENT CARE: Strict aseptic technique is maintained throughout the procedure. The patient is observed for signs of peritonitis, pain, respiratory difficulty, and low blood pressure. Peritoneal dialysis requires a semipermanent implantation of a catheter through the abdominal wall into the peritoneum, just below the umbilicus. Patients with a history of abdominal surgeries may have scarring; they are not candidates for peritoneal dialysis and should use hemodialysis, instead. The patient's understanding of the procedure and the reason for it, care of the peritoneal catheter, and symptoms of infection are verified. Medication schedule can be changed before and after dialysis. Urea clearance is less than with hemodialysis

(60%), and excessive protein loss may necessitate a high protein diet. The patient's ability to adjust lifestyle to provide a balance of adequate rest and activity is evaluated.

renal d. Hemodialysis.

dialysis disequilibrium A disturbance in which nausea, vomiting, drowsiness, headache, and seizures occur shortly after the patient begins hemodialysis or peritoneal dialysis. The cause is related to the rapid correction of metabolic abnormalities in the uremic patient. SYN: *disequilibrium syndrome.*

dialysis-related amyloidosis (dī-al'ĭ-sĭs-rĕ-lāt'ĕd) SEE: under *amyloidosis.*

dialysis technician A technician who operates and maintains an artificial kidney machine following approved methods to provide dialysis treatment for patients with chronic kidney disease.

dialytic (dī"ă-lĭt'ĭk) Belonging to or resembling the process of dialysis.

dialyzable (dī-ă-līz'ă-b'l) Capable of receiving dialysis.

dialyze (dī'ă-līz) To perform a dialysis or to undergo one.

dialyzer (dī'ă-līz"ĕr) [*dialyze*] The apparatus used in performing dialysis. SYN: *artificial kidney; hemodialyzer.*

diameter (dī-am'ĕt-ĕr) [*dia-* + *-meter*] The distance from any point on the periphery of a surface, body, or space to the opposite point.

biparietal d. ABBR: BPD. The transverse distance between the parietal eminences on each side of the head (about 9.25 cm).

bizygomatic d. The greatest transverse distance between the most prominent points of the zygomatic arches.

buccolingual d. The measurement of a tooth from the buccal to the lingual surface.

conjugate d. Conjugate (2).

interspinous d. The distance between the two anterior superior spines of the ilia.

mesiodistal d. The measurement of a tooth from the ventral or mesial surface to the distal or dorsal surface.

occipitofrontal d. The distance from the posterior fontanel to the root of the nose.

d. of pelvis Any diameter of the pelvis found by measuring a straight line between any two points. The diameters are:*anteroposterior,* the distance between the sacrovertebral angle and the symphysis pubis; *bi-ischial,* the distance between the ischial spines; *conjugata diagonalis,* the distance between the sacrovertebral angle and the symphysis pubis; *conjugata vera,* the true conjugate between the sacrovertebral angle and the middle of the posterior aspect of the symphysis pubis (about 1.5 cm less than the diagonal conjugate); *intercristal,* the distance between the

crests of the ilia; *interspinous,* the distance between the spines of the ilium; *intertrochanteric,* the distance between the greater trochanters when the hips are extended and the legs are held together; and *obstetrical conjugate,* the distance between the promontory of the sacrum and the upper edge of the symphysis pubis. SEE: *pelvis.*

Diameter Index Safety System ABBR: DISS. A set of engineering standards preventing users of compressed gases from linking pressurized gas holding tanks to the wrong hoses or tubing. The standards designate specific-sized connectors for each different medical gas. The system is designed to prevent delivering room air or nitrogen to a patient in need of oxygen therapy.

⚠ Whenever gases, e.g., anesthetics, nebulized medications, or oxygen, are administered to patients, the identity of the source gas, and the required flow rates or concentrations should be verified and monitored.

diamid(e) (dī-ăm'ĭd, -īd) [L. *di,* two, + *amide*] A compound that contains two amine groups. The term is sometimes used incorrectly to indicate a diamine or hydrazine.

diamidine (dī-ăm'ĭ-dēn) Any chemical compound that contains two amidine, $C(NH)NH_2$, groups.

diamine (dī-ăm'ĭn, -ēn) A chemical compound with two amino, $-NH_2$, groups.

diaminobenzidine (dī"ă-mēn"ō-bĕn'zĭ-dēn") ABBR: DAB. A chromogen, $C_{12}H_{14}N_4$, used in immunocytochemistry to highlight peroxidase.

Diamond-Blackfan anemia (dī'(ă-)mŏnd-blak'fan") [Louis Klein Diamond, Ukrainian-born U.S. pediatrician, 1902–1999; Kenneth Daniel Blackfan, U.S. pediatrician, 1883–1941] A rare, severe normochromic macrocytic anemia of neonates and infants in which vitamin B_{12} and folate levels are normal or elevated and reticulocytosis is inadequately low.

TREATMENT: The anemia may respond to corticosteroid therapy or may require repeated transfusions. SYN: *congenital hypoplastic* **anemia**; *Fanconi syndrome.*

diapause (dī'ă-pawz) [Gr. *dia,* through, + *pausis,* pause] **1.** The state of metabolic inactivity that some plants, seeds, eggs, and insect forms assume to survive adverse conditions such as winter. **2.** A pause in early embryonic development. In some mammals, a fertilized egg will stop developing at the blastocyst stage until the uterine lining is receptive to implantation of the embryo. Evidence suggests that this form of delayed implantation may occur in humans.

diapedesis (dī″ă-pĕd-ē′sĭs) [″ + *pedan,* to leap] The movement of white blood cells and other cells out of small arterioles, venules, and capillaries as part of the inflammatory response. The cells move through gaps between cells in the vessel walls. SEE: illus.; *inflammation.*

diaphane (dī′ă-fān) [Gr. *dia,* through, + *phainein,* to appear] A very small electric light used in transillumination.

diaphanography (dī″ă-făn-ŏg′ră-fē) SEE: *transillumination.*

diaphanoscopy (dī″ă-făn-ŏs′kō-pē) Examination using the diaphanoscope; transillumination.

diaphorase (dī-ăf′ō-rās) Dihydrolipoamide dehydrogenase.

diaphoresis (dī″ă-fō-rē′sĭs) [″ + *pherein,* to carry] Profuse sweating.

diaphoretic (dī″ă-fō-rĕt′ĭk) [″ + *pherein,* to carry] **1.** A sudorific, or an agent that increases perspiration. **2.** Covered by sweat.

diaphragm (dī′ă-fram″) [Gr. *diaphragma,* a partition] **1.** A thin membrane as is used for dialysis. **2.** In microscopy, an apparatus located beneath the opening in the stage and permitting regulation of the amount of light passing through the object. **3.** A rubber or plastic cup that fits over the cervix uteri, used for contraceptive purposes. SEE: illus. (Contraceptive Diaphragm). **4.** The dome-shaped skeletal muscle that separates the abdomen from the thoracic cavity with its convexity upward. It contracts to promote inhalation, flattening downward and permitting the lungs to expand. It relaxes to promote exhalation, rising to its dome-shaped position and compressing the lungs.

The origin of the diaphragm is the xiphoid process, the lower six costal cartilages, and the lumbar vertebrae. The diaphragm is directly superior to the liver, the stomach, the spleen, the ad-

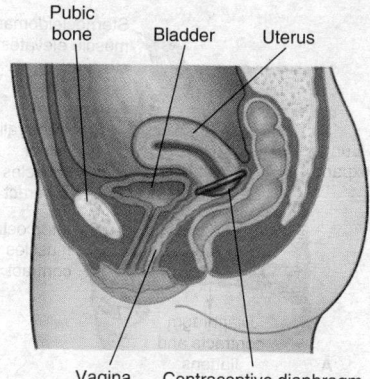

CONTRACTIVE DIAPHRAGM

Pubic bone — Bladder — Uterus

Vagina — Contraceptive diaphragm covers cervix

CONTRACEPTIVE DIAPHRAGM

renal glands, and the kidneys; the right side is slightly higher than the left. SEE: illus. (Movement of Rib Cage and Diaphragm During Respiration); *Boerhaave syndrome.*

   Bucky d. SEE: *Bucky, Gustav P.*

   pelvic d. Pelvic **floor.**

   Potter-Bucky d. Bucky diaphragm.

   slit d. A gap between the foot processes of podocytes in the renal glomerulus, composed of a filter made of proteins that holds large molecules within the plasma but allows smaller soluble chemicals to pass with water into the urine.

   urogenital d. The urogenital trigone, or triangular ligament. A musculofascial sheath that lies between the ischiopubic rami, it is superficial to the pelvic diaphragm. In males it surrounds the membranous urethra; in females, the vagina.

diaphragmatic (dī″ă-frăg-măt′ĭk) Pert. to the diaphragm.

diaphragmatic flutter Leeuwenhoek's disease.

diaphyseal (dī″ă-fĭz′ē-ăl) [Gr. *diaphysis,*

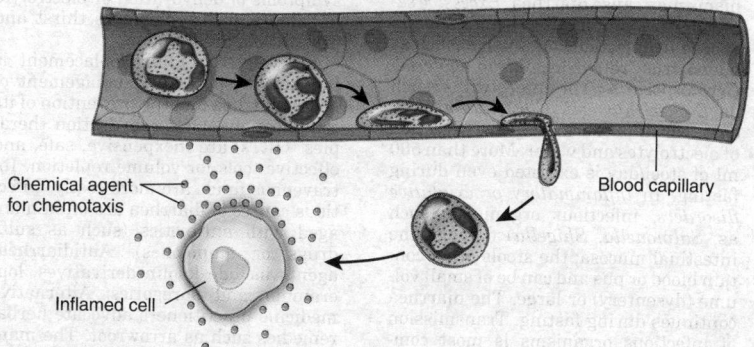

Chemical agent for chemotaxis

Blood capillary

Inflamed cell

DIAPEDESIS

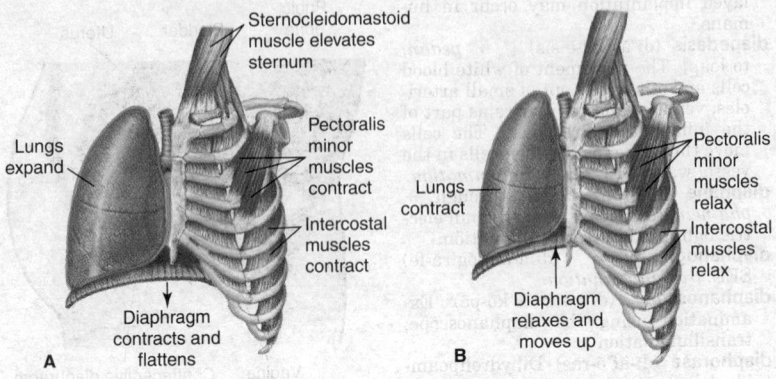

MOVEMENT OF RIB CAGE AND DIAPHRAGM DURING RESPIRATION

A. Inspiration: Air drawn into lungs; B. Expiration: Air forced out of lungs

a growing through] Part of or affecting the shaft of a long bone.

diaphysis (dī-ăf′ĭ-sĭs) The shaft or middle part of a long cylindrical bone. SEE: *apophysis; epiphysis.*

diarrhea (dī-ă-rē′ă) [*dia-* + *-rrhea*] The passage of fluid or unformed stools. In acute diarrhea, the frequency of bowel movements and the volume of fluid lost determine the severity of the illness. In tropical nations, infectious diarrheal illnesses are among the most common causes of disease and death, esp. in children, who become dehydrated easily. Diarrhea in the tropics is typically attributed to contaminated drinking water, inadequate sanitation, or poor hygiene. Worldwide, millions of children die from diarrhea each year. Diarrheal illnesses are common in Western nations as well but tend to be more benign and more effectively managed. SEE: *cholera; oral rehydration therapy; viral* **gastroenteritis**; *Nursing Diagnoses Appendix.* **diarrheal**, *adj.*

ETIOLOGY: Five general mechanisms may cause diarrhea. *Excessive secretion,* or secretory diarrhea, is usually caused by infectious organisms (such as adenovirus, rotavirus, *Vibrio cholerae, Cryptosporidium*) or enterotoxins (such as *Escherichia coli, Clostridium difficile*), which produce excessive secretion of electrolytes and water. More than 500 ml of stool/day is excreted even during fasting. In *inflammatory or exudative disorders,* infectious organisms (such as, *Salmonella, Shigella*) damage the intestinal mucosa; the stools often contain blood or pus and can be of small volume (dysentery) or large. The diarrhea continues during fasting. Transmission of infectious organisms is most commonly person-to-person or through contaminated water or food. The incubation period and duration of illness vary, depending on the organism involved. The diarrhea may be bloody.

Osmotic diarrhea occurs when highly concentrated substances that cannot be absorbed (such as antacids, lactulose, lactose) pull water from the intestinal wall into the stool. More than 500 ml of stool/day is excreted, but the diarrhea subsides during a fasting state.

Malabsorption of nutrients results in steatorrhea with high osmolarity. The diarrhea is eliminated by fasting, and both osmotic and secretory components are involved. *Abnormal intestinal motility* resulting from surgical removal of sections of the bowel, diabetic neuropathy, or irritable bowel syndrome produces alternating patterns of diarrhea and constipation.

SYMPTOMS: Frequent watery bowel movements or stools with pus, blood, oils, or mucus are characteristic of diarrhea, as are abdominal cramping, bloating, or rectal discomfort. When volume losses from diarrhea are large, symptoms of dehydration or electrolyte imbalance, such as dizziness, thirst, and prostration, are common.

TREATMENT: Fluid replacement is the key to successful management of acute diarrhea and the prevention of its complications. Oral rehydration therapies (ORTs) are inexpensive, safe, and effective tools for volume repletion. Intravenous fluids are more costly. Infectious causes of diarrhea are often managed with antibiotics (such as sulfa drugs or quinolones). Antidiarrheal agents include kaolin derivatives, loperamide, and paregorics. Alternative medicine practitioners advocate herbal remedies such as arrowroot. The management of chronic diarrhea depends on the underlying cause.

PATIENT CARE: The patient is assessed for signs and symptoms of dehydration and metabolic disarray or renal failure, such as headache, lethargy, orthostatic dizziness, decreasing level of consciousness, and compensatory hyperventilation. The frequency, consistency, color, and volume of stools are monitored, and bowel sounds auscultated for changes from normal patterns. Fluid balance, intake and output, and daily weights are also monitored. Prescribed oral or intravenous fluids and electrolyte and nutrient replacements are administered, and the patient's response is evaluated. The anal area is assessed for skin excoriation and gently but thoroughly washed and rinsed after each bowel movement, and protective ointment is applied. Standard precautions are observed for these interventions. Antidiarrheal medications are administered as prescribed. Whenever diarrhea or acute gastroenteritis of unknown cause is encountered, health professionals should consider the possibility of waterborne illness and obtain a drinking water history (such as water sources at home, school, and work, recreational water exposures, travel abroad, use of filtering system).

The spread of infectious diarrhea is prevented by practicing and teaching thorough handwashing and hygiene measures, by using standard precautions and measures of controlling infection in health care facilities, by correctly handling and refrigerating foods at risk for bacterial contamination, by appropriately filtering or treating water supplies, and by reporting diarrheal pathogens to appropriate public health authorities.

acute d. Diarrhea marked by sudden onset.

antibiotic-associated d. Mild to moderate diarrhea in individuals taking oral antibiotics. The antibiotics destroy the normal flora in the gastrointestinal tract. SEE: *pseudomembranous colitis.*

fatty d. Steatorrhea.

infantile d. Diarrhea in children under 2 years of age. Most commonly, it is caused by infectious enterocolitis due to rotavirus, Norwalk virus, or *Escherichia coli.* SEE: *enterocolitis.* SYN: *toddler's d.*

SYMPTOMS: Frequent watery stools, occasionally accompanied by evidence of dehydration, are the primary findings.

TREATMENT: Each year the deaths of thousands of children with diarrhea are prevented by the use of oral rehydration solutions consisting of clean (potable) water, salt, potassium, bicarbonate, and glucose. SEE: *oral rehydration solution.*

mucous d. Diarrhea with mucus.

osmotic d. Diarrhea caused by the retention of osmotically active solutes in the small intestine. This causes fluid to be drawn into the intestinal lumen. The retained fluid is more than the colon can resorb. The solute may be the result of maldigestion, malabsorbed nutrients, or drugs.

secretory d. Diarrhea in which there is a large volume of fecal output caused by abnormalities of the movement of fluid and electrolytes into the intestinal lumen. This can be caused by hormonal abnormalities present in disorders such as carcinoid syndrome, Zollinger-Ellison syndrome, certain types of pancreatic adenomas, and medullary carcinomas of the thyroid.

simple d. Diarrhea in which stools contain only normal excreta.

summer d. Diarrhea occurring in children during months when rotavirus is not prevalent. *Shigella, Campylobacter jejuni,* and cryptosporidia are among the most common causes.

travelers' d. ABBR: TD. Diarrhea experienced by visitors, esp. those who go to tropical countries. The most common causes are enterotoxigenic *Escherichia coli,* amebas, *Giardia, Cyclospora, Cryptosporidium, Shigella, Salmonella,* and *Campylobacter.* The disease is common, affecting as many as 40% of travelers to underdeveloped nations. There is no completely effective method of prevention, but avoidance of tap water, fresh fruits and vegetables, iced drinks, or inadequately cooked foods is helpful. Fish and shellfish may contain biotoxins even when well cooked; local residents can provide valuable advice concerning which fish to avoid. Loperamide with a quinolone antibiotic (such as ciprofloxacin) used after the passage of the first loose stool frequently aborts the illness, but children and pregnant women should not take quinolones. As with other forms of diarrhea, rehydration is crucial. Antidiarrheals are used for comfort.

weanling d. Severe gastroenteritis that sometimes occurs in infants who recently have been weaned.

diarrheagenic, diarrheogenic (dī-ă-rē'ă-jĕn'ĭk) [" + "] Producing diarrhea.

diarthrosis (dī"ar-thrō'sĭs) [*di-* + *diarthrosis*] An articulation in which opposing bones move freely (e.g., a hinge joint or a pivot joint). SYN: *abarticulation* (1); *aparthrosis* (1).

diary A personal record kept by a patient or caregiver of important outpatient observations, e.g., blood pressures; blood glucose levels; caloric intake; or the frequency of certain symptoms, such as bowel movements, crying spells, headaches, palpitations, or urination.

diaschisis (dī-ăs-kĭ'sĭs) In a person with a focal brain injury, a reduction in synaptic activity (and often, cerebral blood flow and metabolism) in a part of the brain that is remote from the injury. Brain functions that are lost as a result of diaschisis often are restored with rehabilitation or the return of blood flow.

diascope (dī′ă-skōp) [Gr. *dia*, through, + *skopein*, to examine] A glass plate held against the skin for examining superficial lesions. Erythematous lesions will show the compressed capillary bed, but a hemorrhagic area will not blanch when the glass is pressed against the skin. SEE: illus.

DIASCOPE

diascopy (dī-ă′skŏ-pē) Examination of skin lesions by means of a diascope.

diastase (dī′ă-stās″) [Gr. *diastasis*, a separation + -ase] A specific enzyme in plant cells, e.g., as in sprouting grains and malt, that converts starch into sugar. SYN: *vegetable amylase.*

diastasis (dī-as′tă-sĭs, ′tă-sēz″) *pl.* **diastases** [Gr. *diastasis*, separation] **1.** In surgery, injury to a bone involving separation of an epiphysis. **2.** In cardiac physiology, the last part of diastole. It follows the period of most rapid diastolic filling of the ventricles, consists of a period of retarded inflow of blood from atria into ventricles, lasts (in humans under average conditions) about 0.2 sec, and is immediately followed by atrial systole.

diastema (dī″ă-stē′mă) *pl.* **diastemata** [Gr. *diastema*, an interval or space] **1.** A fissure. **2.** A space between two adjacent teeth.

diastematomyelia (dī″ă-stĕm″ă-tō-mī-ē′lē-ă) [″ + *myelos*, marrow] A congenital fissure of the spinal cord, frequently associated with spina bifida cystica.

diastematopyelia (dī″ă-stĕm″ă-tō-pī-ē′lē-ă) [″ + *pyelos*, pelvis] A congenital median slit of the pelvis.

diaster (dī″as′tĕr) [*di-* + *aster*] A double star figure formed during mitosis. SYN: *amphiaster.*

diastole (dī-ăs′tō-lē) [Gr. *diastellein*, to expand] The period of cardiac muscle relaxation, alternating in the cardiac cycle with systole or contraction. During diastole, the cardiac muscle fibers lengthen and the chambers fill with blood. SEE: *blood pressure; heart; murmur; pulse; systole.*

diastolic (dī-ăs-tŏl′ĭk) Pert. to diastole.

diathermy (dī′ă-thĕr″mē) [*dia-* + *thermo-*] The therapeutic use of a high-frequency current to generate heat

within some part of the body. The frequency is greater than the maximum frequency for neuromuscular response and ranges from several hundred thousand to millions of cycles per second. It is used to increase blood flow to specific areas. It should not be used in the acute stage of recovery from trauma. **diathermal, diathermic** (dī′ă-thĕr′măl, dī′ă-thĕr′mik), *adj.* SYN: *endothermy.*

     laparoscopic ovarian d. ABBR: LOD. Laparoscopic ovarian drilling.

diathesis (dī-ăth′ĕ-sĭs) [Gr. *diatithenai*, to dispose] A constitutional predisposition to certain diseases or conditions.

diathetic (dī″ă-thĕt′ĭk) Pert. to diathesis.

diatom (dī′ă-tom″) [L. *Diatoma*, originally a genus name] Any of a group of unicellular, microscopic algae, numerous in freshwater and saltwater. The cell walls are made of silica.

diatomaceous (dī″ăt-ŏ-mā′shŭs) [L. *Diatomace(ae)*] Pert. to or consisting of diatoms or their fossilized siliceous remains.

diatomaceous earth Silica containing fossilized shells of microscopic algae with a siliceous or calcium-containing cell wall. It is used in insulating material and filters and as an absorbent. SYN: *diatomite.*

diatomic (dī″ă-tom′ik) [*di-* + *iatomic*] Containing two atoms; said of molecules.

diatomite (dī-at′ŏ-mīt″) [*diatom* + -ite] Diatomaceous earth.

diazepam (dī-ăz′ĕ-păm) An antianxiety and sedative drug used extensively in the U.S. It is used to treat status epilepticus, acute cocaine poisoning, and a variety of anxiety disorders. Prolonged use may cause dependence or tolerance.

diazo-, diaz- A prefix used in chemistry to indicate that a compound contains the —N=N— group.

diazotize (dī-ăz′ō-tīz) In chemistry, to convert NH_2 groups into diazo, —N=N—, groups.

dibasic (dī-bā′sĭk) [″ + *basis*, base] Capable of neutralizing or accepting two hydrogen ions.

DIC *disseminated intravascular coagulation.*

dicalcic, dicalcium (dī-kal′sĭk, dī-kal′sē-ŭm) [″ + L. *calx*, lime] Containing two atoms of calcium.

dicentric (dī-sĕn′trĭk) Having two centers or two centromeres.

dicephalus (dī-sĕf′ă-lŭs) [″ + *kephale*, head] A congenitally deformed fetus with two heads.

dichorionic (dī″kō-rē-ŏn′ĭk) ABBR: DC. Having two chorions. This may occur in two-egg (dizygotic) twins.

dichotomy, dichotomization (dī-kot′ŏ-mē, dī-kot″ŏ-mĭ-zā′shŏn) [Gr. *dicha*, twofold, + *tome*, incision] **1.** Bifurcation of a vein. **2.** Cutting or dividing into two parts.

dichroic (dī-krō′ĭk) Pert. to dichroism.

dichroic mirror SEE: under *mirror*.

dichroism (dī′krō-ĭzm) [Gr. *dis*, two, + *chroa*, color] The property of appearing to be one color by direct light and another by transmitted light.

dichromate (dī-krō′māt) A chemical that contains the Cr_2O_7 group.

dichromatic (dī″krō-măt′ĭk) Able to see only two colors.

dichromatism (dī-krō′mă-tĭzm) The ability to distinguish only two primary colors.

dichromic (dī-krō′mĭk) **1.** Containing two atoms of chromium. **2.** Seeing only two colors.

DICOM *Digital Imaging and Communications in Medicine.*

dicophane (dī′kō-fān) A powerful insecticide now rarely used because of its toxicity. SYN: *chlorophenothane; DDT.*

Dicrocoelium dendriticum (dī″krō-sēl′ē-ŭm den″drit′ĭ-kŭm) A species of liver flatworm that uses grazing animals (cattle, sheep) as its definitive host. Its intermediate hosts are snails and ants. It is an occasional cause of liver fluke infestation in humans. SEE: *liver* **fluke.**

dicrotic (dī-krŏt′ĭk) [Gr. *dikrotos*, beating double] Having two arterial pulsations for one heartbeat; pert. to a double pulse; bisferious.

dicrotic notch In a pulse tracing, a notch on the descending limb.

dicrotic wave SEE: under *wave*.

dicrotism (dī′krŏt-ĭzm) [″ + *-ismos*, condition] The state of being dicrotic.

dictyosome (dĭk′tē-ō-sōm) [Gr. *diktyon*, net, + *soma*, body] A cytoplasmic vesicle thought to be a secretory portion of the Golgi apparatus.

dicumarol (dī-koo′mă-rŏl) An anticoagulant drug. SEE: *warfarin sodium.*

dicyclic (dī-sī′klĭk) **1.** Having or concerning two cycles. **2.** In chemistry, containing two cyclic ring structures.

didactic (dī-dak′tik, dī-) [Gr. *didaktikos*, good at teaching] **1.** In the medical professions, pert. to classroom instruction by lectures and textbooks as opposed to clinical or bedside teaching, or laboratory sessions. **2.** In general usage, pert. to teaching or instruction.

didactylism (dī-dăk′tĭ-lĭzm) [Gr. *dis*, two, + *daktylos*, finger] The congenital condition of having only two digits on a hand or foot.

didelphic (dī-dĕl′fĭk) [″ + *delphys*, uterus] Having or pert. to a double uterus.

didymus (dĭd′ĭ-mŭs) [Gr. *didymos*, twin] **1.** Twin. **2.** A congenital abnormality involving joined twins. **3.** Testis.

die 1. To cease living. **2.** In dentistry, a positive duplicate made from an impression of a tooth.

dieldrin (dī-ĕl′drĭn) A chlorinated hydrocarbon used as an insecticide. It is toxic to humans and marine and terrestrial animals. SEE: *Poisons and Poisoning Appendix.*

dielectric (dī-ē-lĕk′trĭk) [Gr. *dia*, through, + *elektron*, amber] Insulating by offering great resistance to the passage of electricity by conduction.

diencephalon (dī″ĕn-sĕf′ă-lŏn) [Gr. *dis*, two, + *enkephalos*, brain] The second portion of the brain, lying between the telencephalon and mesencephalon. It includes the epithalamus, thalamus, metathalamus, and hypothalamus.

Dientamoeba (dī″ĕn-tă-mē′bă) A genus of parasitic protozoa marked by possession of two similar nuclei.

    D. fragilis A species of parasitic ameba inhabiting the intestine of humans. Persons infected may have diarrhea with blood or mucus, abdominal pain, and anal pruritus. This ameba has been found inside the eggs of pinworms. The eggs may act as a vector.

dieresis (dī-ĕr′ĕ-sĭs) [Gr. *diairesis*, a division] **1.** Breaking up or dispersion of things normally joined, as by an ulcer. **2.** Mechanical separation of parts by surgical means.

diet (dī′ĕt) [L. *diaeta*, fr Gr. *diaita*, way of living, diet] **1.** Liquid and solid foods regularly consumed in normal living. **2.** A prescribed allowance of food adapted for a particular state of health or disease. SYN: *eating plan*. SEE: table. **3.** To eat or drink in accordance with prescribed rules.

    acid-ash d. A diet to acidify the urine. It contains acidic foods such as meat, fish, eggs, and cereals and is lacking in fruits, vegetables, cheese, and milk.

    American Heart Association d. Any diet for optimal cardiovascular health advocated by the American Heart Association (AHA). The AHA recommends meal plans that emphasize fruits, vegetables, whole grains, and fish, but little sodium, fat, or sugar.

    American Heart Association d., Step II A diet formerly recommended by the American Heart Association to effect large changes in serum lipids and body weight. It has been replaced by the therapeutic lifestyle changes diet.

    balanced d. A diet adequate in energy-providing substances (carbohydrates and fats), tissue-building compounds (proteins), inorganic chemicals (water and mineral salts), agents that regulate or catalyze metabolic processes (vitamins), and substances for certain physiological processes, e.g., bulk for promoting peristaltic movements of the digestive tract.

    bland d. A diet to buffer gastric acidity by providing meals of palatable, non-irritating foods. The diet includes milk, cream, prepared cereals, gelatin, soup, rice, butter, crackers, eggs, lean meats,

Diseases in Which Diet Plays an Important Role

Condition	Consensus Recommendations
Celiac sprue	Avoid glutens, e.g., wheat, barley, and rye
Cholelithiasis	Avoid fatty foods
Cirrhosis	Limit sodium and protein intake; avoid alcohol and high-fat foods
Coronary artery disease	American Heart Association diets; limit saturated fats and trans fats; increase fiber
Congestive heart failure	Limit sodium
Diabetes mellitus	American Diabetic Association Diet, carbohydrate controlled, calorie restricted if overweight, limit saturated fats
Diverticulosis	Low-residue diet
Dysphagia	Special consistency diets as indicated by testing/tolerance
Esophagitis	Avoid alcohol, nonsteroidal drugs, tobacco; consume thick liquids
Gastroesophageal reflux disease (GERD)	Avoid caffeine, chocolates, mints, high-fat foods, acidic foods, alcohol, or late meals
Gout	Limit intake of alcohol, fructose, purines, and animal-based proteins
Hyperhomocysteinemia	Increase consumption of folates, vitamin B_{12}
Hyperlipidemias	National Cholesterol Education Program Diet with limited saturated fats, trans fats, and cholesterol; increase soluble fiber
Iron deficiency anemia	Iron supplements
Irritable bowel syndrome	Increase fiber content of meals, limit dairy products
Kidney stone formers	Liberal fluid intake
Nephrotic syndrome	Limit sodium intake
Obesity	Caloric restriction
Osteoporosis	Supplement calcium and vitamin D; limit alcohol and tobacco
Pernicious anemia	Supplement cyanocobalamin (vitamin B_{12})
Renal failure	Limit sodium, potassium, protein, and fluids
Consensus recommendation	After the age of eight, dietary intake of calcium should equal about 1000–1300 mg daily

fish, cottage cheese, custards, tapioca, cookies, and plain cake. Multivitamins may be a necessary adjunct. Highly seasoned foods, fried foods, foods that are gas-producing, and most raw fruits and vegetables are avoided, as are drinks containing caffeine and alcohol. A bland diet may be indicated in treatment of gastritis, peptic ulcer, and hiatal hernia.

Dietary Approaches to Stop Hypertension d. ABBR: DASH diet. A diet proven to treat stage I hypertension, consisting of generous amounts of cereals, fruits, and vegetables (for fiber, vitamins, and minerals), low-fat dairy products, nuts, and lean meats (to maximize protein intake without too much saturated fat and cholesterol). Guidelines for a diet of 2000 calories daily include seven to eight servings of grains and grain products; four to five servings of vegetables; four to five servings of fruits; two to three servings of low-fat or nonfat dairy products; two or fewer servings of lean meats, proteins, and fish. The plan also permits four to five servings of nuts, seeds, and legumes per week. It is recommended that sodium intake be less than 3000 g/day. The complete diet provides more specific recommendations for sodium. Compared with the diet recommended in the Food Guide Pyramid, this diet contains more fruits and vegetables but less fat. SEE: table.

elemental d. A diet of predigested liquid consisting of amino acids, vita-

The DASH Diet (Eating Plan)

Food Group	Daily Servings	Serving Sizes	Examples and Notes	Significance of Each Food Group to the DASH Eating Plan
Grains and grain products	7–8	1 slice bread; 1 oz dry cereal; 1/2 C cooked rice, pasta, or cereal	Whole wheat bread, English muffin, pita bread, bagel, cereals, grits, oatmeal, crackers, unsalted pretzels and popcorn	Major sources of energy and fiber
Vegetables	4–5	1 C raw leafy vegetable, 1/2 C cooked vegetable; 6 oz vegetable juice	Tomatoes, potatoes, carrots, green peas, squash, broccoli, turnip greens, collards, kale, spinach, artichokes, green beans, lima beans, sweet potatoes	Rich sources of potassium, magnesium, and fiber
Fruits	4–5	6 oz fruit juice; 1 medium fruit; 1/4 C dried fruit; 1/2 C fresh, frozen, or canned fruit	Apricots, bananas, dates, grapes, oranges, orange juice, grapefruit, grapefruit juice, mangoes, melons, peaches, pineapples, prunes, raisins, strawberries, tangerines	Important sources of potassium, magnesium, and fiber
Lowfat or fat-free dairy foods	2–3	8 oz milk, 1 C yogurt, 1.5 oz cheese	Skim (fat-free) or 1% (low fat) milk, skim or low fat buttermilk, fat-free or low fat regular or frozen yogurt, low fat and fat-free cheese	Major sources of calcium and protein
Meats, poultry, and fish	2 or less	3 oz cooked meats, poultry, or fish	Select only lean; trim away visible fats; broil, roast, or boil, instead of frying; remove skin from poultry	Rich sources of protein and magnesium
Nuts, seeds, and dry beans	4–5/week	1.5 oz or 1/3 C nuts, 1/2 oz or 2 tbsp seeds, 1/2 C dry beans	Almonds, filberts, mixed nuts, peanuts, walnuts, sunflower seeds, kidney beans, lentils	Rich sources of energy, magnesium, potassium, protein, and fiber

Table continued on following page

The DASH Diet (Eating Plan) (Continued)

Food Group	Daily Servings	Serving Sizes	Examples and Notes	Significance of Each Food Group to the DASH Eating Plan
Fats and oils	2–3	1 tsp soft margarine, 1 Tbsp low fat mayonnaise, 1 tbsp regular salad dressing, 2 tbsp light salad dressing, 1 tsp vegetable oil	Soft margarine, low fat mayonnaise, light salad dressing, vegetable oil	DASH has 27% of calories as fat, including fat in or added to foods
Sweets	5/ week	1 tbsp sugar, 1 tbsp jelly or jam, 1/2 oz jelly beans, 8 oz lemonade	Maple syrup, sugar, jelly, jam, fruit-flavored gelatin, jelly beans, hard candy, fruit punch, sorbet, ices	Sweets should be low in fat

SOURCE: National Institutes of Health. September 1998; revised May 2003. Facts about the DASH Eating Plan. http://www.nhlbi.nih.gov/health/public/heart/hbp/dash/new_dash.pdf

mins, minerals, electrolytes, and glucose.

elimination d. A method for assessing allergic responses to foods. To determine food allergies, foods suspected of causing problems are added one at a time to determine whether any of them causes an adverse reaction.

Eskimo d. A traditional diet in which marine mammals (and their blubber) are consumed. It is rich in omega-3 fatty acids and appears to be protective against atherosclerosis, immune, and inflammatory diseases. SYN: *Inuit d.*

evolution d. A diet consisting of high fiber nutrients (with little sugar) taken in small portions throughout the day. It is thought to represent the observed eating habits of primates and of humans in the past.

Feingold d. SEE: *Feingold diet.*

fluid d. Liquid **d.**

gluten-free d. A diet that excludes gluten by eliminating all products containing wheat, rye, or barley. Foods containing buckwheat, corn, oats, quinoa, and rice are generally thought to be well tolerated. Because gluten is present in many foods containing thickened sauces, the diet must be discussed with a dietitian. It is the basis of management for celiac disease. SEE: *celiac sprue; sprue.*

high-calorie d. A diet that contains more calories than normally required for a person's metabolic and energy needs and therefore places that person in positive energy balance. The diet should include three meals and between-meal snacks and exclude fermentable and bulky foods. A high-calorie diet may be used to prevent weight loss in wasting diseases, in high basal metabolism, and after a long illness; in deficiency caused by anorexia, poverty, and poor dietary habits; and during lactation (when an extra 1000 and 1200 kcal each day are indicated).

high-carbohydrate d. An imprecise term for a conventional American eating plan, e.g., one outlined on the website: www.MyPyramid.gov. SEE: *carbohydrate loading.*

high-residue d. A diet that contains considerable amounts of substances such as fiber or cellulose, which the human body is unable to metabolize and absorb. This diet is particularly useful in treating constipation and may be beneficial also in preventing certain diseases of the gastrointestinal tract. Lay people may refer to a high-residue diet as one containing a lot of roughage. SEE: *fiber.*

Inuit d. Eskimo **d.**

ketogenic d. A high-fat, high-protein, controlled-carbohydrate diet, in which the body primarily metabolizes fats instead of glucose. It has been used to treat some forms of epilepsy and has been promoted as a weight-loss diet as well.

light d. A diet consisting of all foods allowed in a soft diet, plus whole-grain cereals, easily digested raw fruits, and vegetables. Foods are not pureed or ground. This diet is used as an intermediate regimen for patients who do not require a soft diet but are not yet able to resume a full diet.

liquid d. A diet for those unable to tolerate solid food or for patients whose gastrointestinal tract must be free of solid matter. This type of diet may contain coffee with hot milk, tea, water, milk in all forms, milk and cream mixtures, cocoa, strained cream soups, fruit juices, meat juices, beef bouillon, tea, clear broths, gruels, strained meat soups, and eggnog. SYN: *fluid* **d.**

liquid protein d. A severely calorically restricted diet, lacking carbohydrates, fats, and many minerals and vitamins.

⚠️ Its use has been associated on occasion with cardiac rhythm disturbances and sudden cardiac death.

low carbohydrate, hypocaloric d. A diet that limits total calories usually to about 1200 calories per day and total carbohydrates to no more than about 25% of total calories. Although this diet does not create more weight loss than calorically restricted high-carbohydrate diets, it does reduce fasting levels of insulin and triglycerides and may be preferable for inactive or obese patients with type 2 diabetes mellitus or impaired glucose tolerance.

low-fat d. An imprecise term for a diet in which the percentage of calories derived from fatty foods is limited (usually to less than 30% of total calories).

low-protein d. A diet that contains a limited amount of protein. The principal sources of food energy are fats and carbohydrates. This diet is used to treat end-stage renal and hepatic disease.

low-salt d. Low-sodium **d.**

low-sodium d. A diet containing about 500 mg (approx. 10 mmol) of sodium daily. It is used occasionally to help manage hypertension, congestive heart failure, or renal failure. On this diet, table salt should not be added to food, and the salt content of commonly used beverages such as beer or soft drinks should be noted. To help regulate sodium consumption, sodium-containing medicines should be avoided. SYN: *low-salt* **d.**; *sodium-free diet; salt-free* **d.**

macrobiotic d. A diet consisting of vegetables and fish, advocated for the prevention and treatment of cancer. This diet is derived from the Japanese diet and features soy, rice, seaweed, pickled vegetables, and small amounts of fish. SEE: *pescovegetarian.*

Mediterranean d. A well-tolerated, palatable diet that mimics the traditional cuisine of Italy, Greece, and the islands of the Mediterranean Sea. It in-

cludes fish and other seafood, wine, and olive oil, and derives about 25% to 35% of its calories from fat, but the primary fat is olive oil, a monounsaturated fat. Additional healthy fats are supplied by grapeseed oil and fats in whole vegetables, nuts, and seeds.

Paleolithic d. A diet that mimics the food choices of modern hunter-gatherer societies or primitive human cultures. It includes nuts, fruits, vegetables, wild game, and fish and typically derives about 21% of its calories from fat. SEE: *evolution* **d.**

peptide d. A diet in which nitrogen content is provided as simple amino acids (or small strings linked by amino acids) rather than as intact proteins.

prudent d. A diet to protect against heart disease, stroke, and other common diseases. It consists of fruits, vegetables, whole grains, legumes, nuts, fish, and low-fat dairy products rather than refined or processed foods, red meats, high concentrated sweets , eggs, and butter. A multistep approach decreases fat, cholesterol, and protein.

reducing d. A diet to help people lose weight by restricting the number of calories and carefully balancing other nutrients. SYN: *calorie reduction* **d.**

salt-free d. Low-sodium **d.**

sodium-free d. Low-sodium **d.**

soft d. A diet consisting of only soft or semisolid foods or liquids, including fish, eggs, cheese, chicken, cereals, bread, toast, and butter. Excluded are red meats, vegetables, or fruits having seeds or thick skins, cellulose, raw fruits, and salads.

therapeutic lifestyle changes d. ABBR: TLC diet. A diet in which fat calories make up between 25% and 35% of total caloric intake; less than 7% of each day's total calories come from saturated fat; total cholesterol intake is less than 200 mg; and total calories are adjusted to achieve and sustain a healthy weight and serum cholesterol.

very low calorie d. A commercially available diet in which caloric intake may be from 400 to 800 kcal/day. This diet is usually in the form of a powdered supplement taken 3 to 5 times a day with large amounts of water. This diet can be effective, but the long-range efficacy in maintaining the weight loss may be discouraging. Vitamins and minerals are typically added to this diet because the small number of macronutrients consumed are inadequate for daily needs.

wellness d. Anti-inflammatory **d.**

Western d. A diet with inadequate fruits, vegetables, whole grains, legumes, fish, and low-fat dairy products and excessive amounts of refined and processed foods, alcohol, salt, red meats, sugary beverages, snacks, eggs, and butter. The Western diet, which is low in potassium, high in sodium, fats, and simple carbohydrates, has been implicated in many diseases, including atherosclerosis, type II diabetes, hypertension, and obesity.

yo-yo d. SEE: *weight cycling.*

dietary (dī′ĕ-tĕr″ē) **1.** Pert. to a diet or to the rules for a diet. **2.** A regulated food allowance for an individual or a population.

Dietary Guidelines for Americans Recommendations issued periodically and revised in 2000 from the Center for Nutrition Policy and Promotion at the U.S. Department of Agriculture for planning and eating a healthy diet. SEE: table; *Food Guide Pyramid.*

dietary portfolio A collection of foods that when taken together on a regular basis help maintain health or accomplish a nutritional goal.

Dietary Reference Intakes ABBR: DRI. In the U.S., federally recommended dietary allowances, adequate intakes, tolerable upper intake levels, and estimated average requirements for essential nutrients and other food components in the diet.

dietetic (dī″ĕ-tĕt′ĭk) **1.** Pert. to diet or its regulation. **2.** Food specially prepared for restrictive diets.

dietetics (dī″ĕ-tĕt′ĭks) [Gr. *diaitetikos*] The science of applying nutritional data to the regulation of the diet of healthy and sick individuals. Some fundamental principles and facts of this science are summarized here.

CONSERVATION OF ENERGY: To produce metabolic balance, the number of calories consumed must equal the energy required for basic metabolic needs

plus additional energy output resulting from muscular work and added heat losses. Thus a person whose basal rate is 1000 kcal per 24 hr may do work and lose heat during the day, adding about 1500 kcal to the energy output; he or she must, therefore, obtain 2500 kcal per day.

One g of fat yields approx. 9 kcal. One g of carbohydrate or protein yields about 4 kcal.

NOTE: To convert kilocalories to kilojoules, multiply them by 4.1855.

CONSERVATION OF MATTER: Everything that leaves the body, whether exhaled as carbon dioxide and water or excreted as urea and minerals, must be replaced by food. Thus, a person excreting 10 g of nitrogen daily must receive the same in his or her diet, for the element can be neither created nor destroyed. This metabolic balance may be monitored by careful chemical analysis of all that is eaten and excreted.

dietetic technician A technician who assists the food service manager and dietitian in a health care facility with planning, implementing, and evaluating food programs. The technician may train and supervise dietary aides.

dietetic treatment Treatment of disease based on regulation of diet.

di-2-ethylhexyl phthalate (dī-too-ĕth″ĭl-hĕks-ĭl fthăl′ăt) ABBR: DHEP. A plastic form of polyvinyl chloride used to manufacture intravenous (IV) tubing and containers. It may leach into IV solutions during the administration of fluids and blood products, producing toxic effects.

diethylstilbestrol (dī-ĕth″ĭl-stĭl″bĕs′trŏl) ABBR: DES. A synthetic preparation possessing estrogenic properties. It is several times more potent than natural estrogens and may be given orally. It is used therapeutically in the treatment of menopausal disturbances and other disorders due to estrogen deficiencies.

⚠ Diethylstilbestrol should not be administered during pregnancy. Such use has been found to be related to subsequent vaginal malignancies in the daughters of mothers who were given it.

This drug was once used extensively during pregnancy to treat threatened and habitual abortion. An estimated 5 million to 10 million Americans received DES during pregnancy or were exposed to the drug in utero. Those who were exposed to DES in utero were found to be at risk of developing reproductive tract abnormalities such as clear-cell cervicovaginal cancer in women and reproductive tract abnormalities in men. These findings were reported in 1970; the use of the drug dur-

---

Dietary Guidelines for Americans

AIM FOR FITNESS
Aim for a healthy weight.
Be physically active each day.
BUILD A HEALTHY BASE
Let the Food Guide Pyramid guide your food choices.
Choose a variety of grains daily, especially whole grains.
Choose a variety of fruits and vegetables daily.
Keep food safe to eat.
CHOOSE SENSIBLY
Choose a diet that is low in saturated fat and cholesterol and moderate in total fat.
Choose beverages and foods to moderate your intake of sugars.
Choose and prepare foods with less salt.
If you drink alcoholic beverages, do so in moderation.

SOURCE: U.S. Department of Agriculture, www.nal.usda.gov/fnic/dga

ing pregnancy was subsequently banned in the U.S. in 1971 and in Europe in 1978. Women who took the drug are now known as DES mothers and their daughters and sons are known as DES daughters and DES sons, respectively.

diethyltoluamide (dī-ĕth″ĭl-tŏl-ū′ă-mīd) ABBR: DEET. An effective insect repellent, esp. for repelling arthropods such as ticks and mosquitoes and flies.

diethyltryptamine (dī-ĕth″ĭl-trĭp′tă-mĭn) A hallucinogenic agent that at low doses has effects similar to those of lysergic acid diethylamide (LSD).

dietitian, dietician (dī-ĕ-tĭsh′ăn) [Gr. *diaita,* way of living] An individual whose training and experience are in the area of nutrition and who has the ability to apply that information to the dietary needs of the healthy and sick.

   registered d. ABBR: RD. A specialist in dietetics who has met the requirements for certification stipulated by the American Dietetic Association.

dietotherapy (dī″ĕ-tō-ther′ă-pē) Alimentotherapy.

diet therapy The alteration of dietary intake to treat or prevent clinical disease. SEE: *diet.*

Dieulafoy, Georges (dyu-lă-fwa′) Fr. physician, 1839–1911.

   D. lesion A vascular defect in the mucosa of the gastrointestinal tract (typically the stomach, but sometimes other organs) in which an arteriole protrudes into the lumen and bleeds briskly. Dieulafoy lesions are an uncommon cause of massive gastrointestinal blood loss. The bleeding can be controlled with cauterization, rubber banding, wedge resection, or other techniques.

differential (dĭf″ĕr-ĕn′shăl) [L. *differre,* to carry apart] Marked by or relating to differences.

differential amplifier An amplifier used to increase the difference between two signals, one of which is usually a reference.

differential lung ventilation SEE: under *ventilation.*

differentiation (dĭf″ă-rĕn″shē-ā′shŭn) **1.** In embryology, the acquiring of individual characteristics. This occurs in progressive diversification of cells of the developing pre-embryo and embryo. **2.** The distinguishing of one disease from another. **3.** In psychiatry, the integration of emotional and intellectual functions in an individual.

   lymphocyte d. The process by which immature lymphocytes are stimulated to become functional T and B cells able to recognize and respond to antigens.

differentiation therapy The use of medications to make cancer cells evolve into cells no longer capable of infinite replication.

difficult airway SEE: under *airway.*

diffraction (dif-frak′shŏn) [L. *diffractio,* a breaking up] The change occurring in light when it passes through crystals, prisms, or parallel bars in a grating, in which the rays are deflected and thus appear to be turned aside. This produces dark or colored bands or lines. The term is also applied to similar phenomena in sound. Ultrasonographic diffraction dramatically affects both lateral resolution and system sensitivity.

diffraction grating The device in a spectrophotometer that disperses white light into the colors (wavelengths) of the electromagnetic spectrum, using multiple lines precisely etched into an optically aligned material such as a specialized mirror or metal plate.

diffusate (dĭf′ū-sāt) [L. *dis,* apart, + *fundere,* to pour] In dialysis, the portion of a liquid that passes through a membrane and that contains crystalloid matter in solution. SYN: *dialysate.*

diffuse (dĭ-fūs′) Spreading, scattered, spread.

diffusible (dĭ-fūz′ĭ-bl) Capable of being diffused.

diffusion (dif-ū′zhŏn) [L. *diffusio,* pouring out, spreading out] The tendency of the molecules of a substance (gas, liquid, or solid) to move from a region of high concentration to one of lower concentration. In the body, oxygen and carbon dioxide move by diffusion. The diffusion of water to an area of greater solute concentration is called osmosis. SEE: illus.

   facilitated d. The movement of a substance (such as glucose) through a cell membrane along a concentration gradient with the help of membrane proteins acting as carrier molecules.

   water d. The movement of water into and out of cells, e.g., cells of the central nervous system after a stroke. Decreases in water diffusion are found when brain cells have been deprived of blood and oxygen.

diffusion tensor imaging ABBR: DTI. SEE: under *imaging.*

Diflucan SEE: *fluconazole.*

digastric (dī-găs′trĭk) [Gr. *dis,* twice, + *gaster,* belly] Having two bellies; said of certain muscles.

DiGeorge syndrome (dē-jŏrj′) A congenital aplasia or hypoplasia of the thymus caused by a missing gene on chromosome 22 and subsequent deficiency of competent T lymphocytes and cell-mediated immunity. Also characteristic are hypoparathyroidism and heart defects.

digest (dī-jest′, dĭ-) [L. *digerere,* to separate, force apart] **1.** To change food from its ingested form to a soft, moisturized mass broken down in the intestinal tract by chemicals, bacteria, and enzymes. SEE: *metabolism.* **2.** To make a condensation of a subject. **3.** To cleave DNA with a restriction endonuclease.

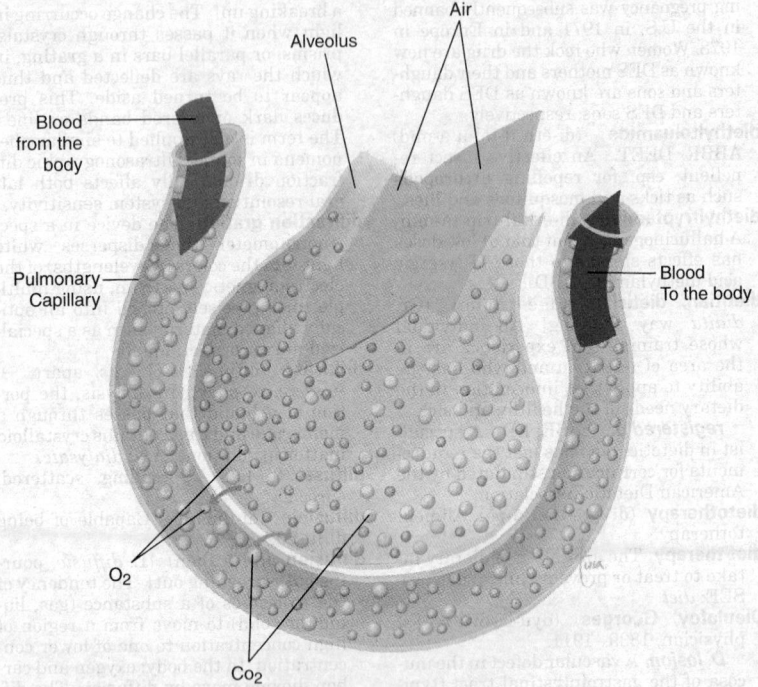

DIFFUSION OF RESPIRATORY GASES

digestant (dī-jes′tănt) **1.** An agent that digests food or aids in digestion, such as pepsin or pancreatin. **2.** A preparation made from the digestive glands or lining membrane of the stomach, classified according to the foods it digests, such as carbohydrate or protein.

digestibility (dī″jes″tĭ-bĭl′ĭt-ē, dī-) The quantity of food that the body retains after a meal. Mathematically, it is (Mass of food consumed – Mass of stool excreted)/Mass of food consumed.

digestible Capable of being digested.

digestion [L. *digestio,* a taking apart] The process by which food is broken down mechanically and chemically in the gastrointestinal tract and converted into absorbable forms. Salts (minerals), water, and monosaccharides can be absorbed unchanged, but starches, fats, and proteins must be broken down into smaller molecules. This is brought about by enzymes, each of which acts on a specific type of food and requires a specific pH to be effective. SEE: table.

Hormones released by the gastrointestinal mucosa stimulate the secretion of digestive enzymes and bile and influence the motility (peristalsis) of the stomach and intestines. Starches and disaccharides are digested to monosaccharides; fats are digested to fatty acids

and glycerol; proteins are digested to amino acids. During digestion vitamins and minerals are liberated from these large organic molecules. SEE: *intestinal hormone.*

    artificial d. Digestion occurring outside the living organism by an enzyme.

    chemical d. The conversion of complex food molecules into simpler molecules by digestive enzymes. SEE: table.

    duodenal d. That part of digestion that occurs in the duodenum where stomach contents mix with biliary and pancreatic secretions. The duodenum absorbs iron, vitamin B_{12}, and other essential nutrients. SEE: *duodenum.*

    extracellular d. Digestion outside a cell, as of tissue by bacterial enzymes (toxins).

    gastric d. That part of digestion that takes place in the stomach. SEE: *stomach.*

    intestinal d. That part of digestion that occurs in the intestine. SEE: *absorption; large intestine; small intestine.*

    intracellular d. The consumption and chemical degradation of materials ingested by cells (e.g., bacteria, viruses, or large molecules) within vacuoles in the cytoplasm.

    mechanical d. The conversion of food into small pieces by chewing, churning of the stomach, or the emulsifying ac-

Action of Digestive Enzymes on Food

Food Component	Enzyme	Secretion	Site of Action
Proteins	Pepsin	Gastric juice, acid	Stomach
	Trypsin	Pancreatic juice, alkaline	Small intestine
	Peptidases	Intestinal juice	Small intestine
Fats	Lipase	Gastric juice	Stomach
		Pancreatic juice	Small intestine
Carbohydrates	Salivary amylase	Saliva, alkaline	Mouth
	Pancreatic amylase	Pancreatic juice	Small intestine
	Sucrase, maltase, lactase	Intestinal juice	Small intestine

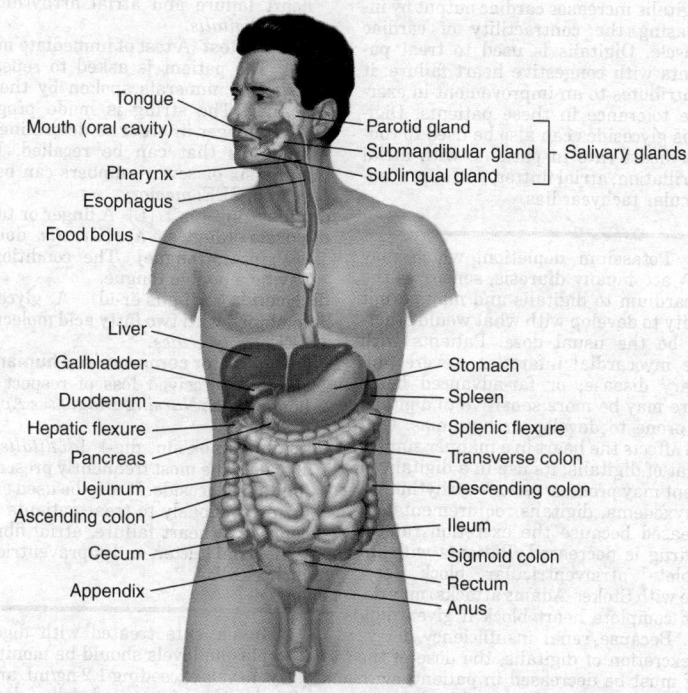

Tongue
Mouth (oral cavity)
Pharynx
Esophagus
Food bolus
Liver
Gallbladder
Duodenum
Hepatic flexure
Pancreas
Jejunum
Ascending colon
Cecum
Appendix

Parotid gland
Submandibular gland
Sublingual gland
— Salivary glands
Stomach
Spleen
Splenic flexure
Transverse colon
Descending colon
Ileum
Sigmoid colon
Rectum
Anus

THE DIGESTIVE SYSTEM

tion of bile salts, exposing more surface area to digestive enzymes.

   oral d. That part of digestion that takes place in the mouth. It includes the physical process of chewing food and the chemical process of starch splitting by the enzyme amylase, present in the saliva.

   pancreatic d. The digestion of proteins and fats by pancreatic enzymes released into the intestine.

   salivary d. Digestion of starches by salivary amylase.

   self-d. Autodigestion.

digestive (dī-jĕs′tĭv) Pert. to digestion.
digestive juice SEE: under *juice.*
digestive system The alimentary canal (oral cavity, pharynx, esophagus, stomach, small and large intestines) and the accessory organs (teeth, tongue, salivary glands, liver, and pancreas). SEE: illus.; *digestion.*
digit (dĭj′ĭt) *pl.* **digits** [L. *digitus,* finger] A finger or toe. **digital** (-ĭ-tăl), *adj.*
digital **1.** Pert. to a digit, e.g., a finger or toe. **2.** Pert. to numbers, i.e., to variables that can be assigned different numerical values.

Digital Imaging and Communications in Medicine ABBR: DICOM. The computer standard language for distributing and viewing any type of medical image.

digitalis (dĭj″ĭ-tăl′ĭs) [L. *digitus,* finger] An antiarrhythmic and cardiotonic drug, derived from the dried leaves of *Digitalis purpurea,* the common foxglove. It is also found in smaller quantities in the leaves of other plants, such as rhododendrons. SEE: *Poisons and Poisoning Appendix.*

ACTION/USES: Digitalis glycosides increase the force of myocardial contraction, increase the refractory period of the atrioventricular node, and, to a lesser degree, affect the sinoatrial node. Digitalis increases cardiac output by increasing the contractility of cardiac muscle. Digitalis is used to treat patients with congestive heart failure: it contributes to an improvement in exercise tolerance in these patients. Digitalis glycosides can also be used to control heart rate in patients with atrial fibrillation, atrial flutter, and supraventricular tachycardias.

⚠️ Potassium depletion, which may accompany diuresis, sensitizes the myocardium to digitalis and may permit toxicity to develop with what would otherwise be the usual dose. Patients with acute myocardial infarction, severe pulmonary disease, or far-advanced heart failure may be more sensitive to digitalis and prone to develop arrhythmias. Calcium affects the heart in a manner similar to that of digitalis; its use in a digitalized patient may produce serious arrhythmias. In myxedema, digitalis requirements are decreased because the excretion rate of the drug is decreased. Patients with incomplete atrioventricular block (esp. those with Stokes-Adams attacks) may develop complete heart block if given digitalis. Because renal insufficiency delays the excretion of digitalis, the dose of the drug must be decreased in patients with this problem. Digitalis glycosides interact with many other drugs used to treat patients with heart failure (e.g., warfarin and amiodarone). Patients taking agents that alter drug levels of digitalis may need frequent clinical assessment to prevent digitalis toxicity. Elderly patients, in whom the drug is most often used, are at greatest risk for digitalis toxicity.

digitalis poisoning SEE: *poisoning, digitalis.*

digitalization (dĭj″ĭ-tăl-ĭ-zā′shŭn) **1.** Subjection of an organism to the action of digitalis. **2.** Providing a loading dose of digoxin to a patient, to reach a therapeutic drug level rapidly.

digital mammography SEE: under *mammography.*

digital portfolio E-portfolio.

digital radiography ABBR: DR; DX. Radiography using computerized acquisition of data for imaging instead of conventional or analog film and intensifying screen imaging.

digitate (dĭj′ĭ-tāt″) [L. *digitus,* finger] Having finger-like impressions or processes.

digitation (dĭj-ĭ-tā′shŭn) A finger-like process.

Digitek (dĭ′jĭ-tĕk″) SEE: *digoxin.*

digiti (dĭj′ĭ-tī) Pl. of digitus.

digitoxin (dĭj-ĭ-tŏk′sĭn) A cardiotoxic glycoside obtained from various species of foxglove, used infrequently to treat heart failure and atrial arrhythmias. SEE: *digitalis.*

digit span test A test of immediate memory. The patient is asked to repeat a string of numerals spoken by the examiner. The string is made progressively longer in order to determine the numerals that can be recalled. Normally six or seven numbers can be repeated. SEE: *memory.*

digitus (dĭj′ĭ-tŭs″) [L] A finger or toe.

diglossia (dī-glŏs′ē-ă) [Gr. *dis,* double, + *glossa,* tongue] The condition of having a double tongue.

diglyceride (dī-glĭs′ĕr-īd) A glyceride combined with two fatty acid molecules. SEE: *triglycerides.*

dignity, risk for compromised human At risk for perceived loss of respect and honor. SEE: *Nursing Diagnoses Appendix.*

digoxin (dij-ok′sĭn, dig-) [*dig(italis)* + *(t)oxin*] The most frequently prescribed digitalis glycoside. It may be used orally or intravenously to treat patients with congestive heart failure, atrial fibrillation, atrial flutter, and supraventricular tachycardias.

⚠️ In patients treated with digoxin, plasma levels should be monitored closely. Levels exceeding 1.2 ng/mL are associated with an increased risk of death.

dihydrate (dī-hī′drāt″) [*di-* + *hydrate*] A compound containing two water molecules in fixed ratio to the bound molecule. SEE: *dihydric.*

dihydric (dī-hī′drik) [*di-* + *hydro-* + *-ic*] A compound containing two hydrogen atoms. SEE: *dihydrate.*

dihydrolipoamide dehydrogenase (dī″hī″drō-lĭp″ō-ăm′īd″) The flavoprotein catalyst of the reoxidation of nicotinamide-adenine dinucleotide (NAD) or nicotinamide-adenine dinucleotide phosphate (NADP) by the mitochondrial electron transport chain. SYN: *diaphorase.*

dihydropyridine calcium antagonist
SEE: under *antagonist*.

dihydrosphingosine (dī-hī″drō-sfĭng′gŏ-sēn) CH₃—[CH₂]₁₄—CHOH—CH(NH₂)—CH₂OH; a long-chain amino alcohol present in sphingolipids, also known as sphinganine. SEE: *sphingolipid; sphingosine.*

dihydrotachysterol (dī-hī″drō-tăk-ĭs′tĕr-ŏl) A hydrogenated tachysterol; a steroid obtained by irradiation of ergosterol. It aids the absorption of calcium from the digestive tract in hypoparathyroidism.

dihydrotestosterone (dī-hī″drō-tes-tos′tĕ-rōn″) [*di- + hydro- + testosterone*] ABBR: DHT. An active metabolic by-product of testosterone that contributes to hypertrophy of the prostate gland, beard growth, and male-pattern baldness. Drugs that inhibit the conversion of testosterone to DHT are used to reverse the effects of benign prostatic hyperplasia.

dihydroxycholecalciferol (dī″hī-drŏk″sē-kō″lē-kăl-sĭf′ĕ-rŏl) One of the vitamin D analogs and metabolites that influence the body's absorption and use of calcium and phosphorus. Vitamin D and its analogs prevent and are used to treat rickets, osteodystrophy, hypocalcemia, and hypophosphatemia. SEE: *Vitamins Appendix.*

3,4-dihydroxyphenylalanine (dī-hī-drŏk″sē-fĕn″ĭl-ăl′ă-nēn) 1. Dopa. 2. L-phenylalanine, the primary ingredient in the artificial sweetener, aspartame.

diisocyanate (dī-ī″sō-sī′ăn-āt″) Any of a group of low molecular weight compounds used to manufacture polyurethanes in paints, varnishes, and other industrial applications. Diisocyanates are a common cause of occupational asthma.

dilaceration (dī″lăs-ĕr-ā′shŭn) [L. *dilacerare*, to tear apart] 1. A tearing apart, as of a cataract. SEE: *discission.* 2. Bending of the root of a tooth due to injury during development.

dilatant (dī-lā′tănt) [L. *dilatare*, to enlarge] Anything that causes dilation.

dilatation (dĭl″ă-tā′shŏn) [L. *dilatatio*, a spreading out or apart] 1. Expansion of an organ or vessel beyond normal size. SYN: *dilation* (2). Dilation (1).

   balloon d. of the prostate A treatment for prostatic hyperplasia.

   cervical d. The gradual opening of the cervical os during labor to allow the fetus to leave the uterus.

   digital d. Dilatation of an opening or a cavity by use of the fingers.

   heart d. SEE: under *dilation of the heart* (under heart).

   stomach d. Distention of the stomach caused by food or gas. Acute dilatation of the stomach or acute gastromesenteric ileus may occur as a postoperative or postpartum condition and usually results from reflex spasm of the gastric outlet rather than mechanical obstruction of the organ.

   toxic d. of colon Toxic megacolon.

dilation (dī-lā′shŏn) [L. *dilatare*, to spread out] 1. Expansion of an orifice, either by normal muscular action or by a dilator. SYN: *dilatation* (2). Dilatation (1).

dilation and curettage ABBR: D and C. An outpatient surgical procedure that expands the cervical canal of the uterus (dilation) so that the surface lining of the uterine wall can be scraped or sampled (curettage). The procedure may be used to treat dysfunctional uterine bleeding or postmenopausal bleeding. It is used to evaluate endometrial tissues for evidence of cancer and to perform abortions or remove retained products of conception after incomplete miscarriages.

   PATIENT CARE: Preoperatively, the patient's understanding of the procedure is ascertained, with any misconceptions clarified. She is told what she will experience and what to expect after the procedure. The patient usually will be allowed nothing to eat or drink after midnight. Intravenous access is initiated for administration of fluids and short-acting anesthetics.

   Postoperatively, the patient's vital signs are assessed frequently until stable, and the amount and type of vaginal bleeding are monitored, with a pad count kept. Once the patient has voided and is tolerating oral intake, she is discharged to the care of her partner or other support person. She should not drive if general anesthesia or a narcotic analgesic was administered. Inpatient care is required only in the case of emergencies with severe hemorrhage or excessive blood loss.

   Postdischarge care is reviewed with the patient, including concerns to report. The patient should not need to change sanitary pads more than hourly and should keep a pad count, noticing if the pads are soaked through. She may pass a few small clots but should report any the size of a quarter or larger and bleeding that exceeds saturating one pad per hour for a total of eight over the first 8 hr. The patient then should experience only spotting, which may last a few weeks. Usually, she should not use tampons for at least 1 week after surgery. Abdominal cramping is not unusual for the first few days; it usually can be relieved by taking a mild analgesic (such as acetaminophen, aspirin) or placing a heating pad or hot water bottle on the lower abdomen. The patient should check her temperature every 4 hours for 2 days and notify her care provider of any elevation over 100°F (37.8°C). Usually, the patient is told to refrain from intercourse for 2 weeks or until her postoperative visit, scheduled according to the gynecologic surgeon's wishes. SEE: *Nursing Diagnoses Appendix.*

dilation and evacuation ABBR: D and E. Partial-birth **abortion**.

dilation of the heart Enlargement of the chambers of the heart, typically because of diseases of the heart valves or cardiomyopathy. It may result in congestive heart failure.

dilator (dī-lāt'ŏr) [L. *dilatare*, to expand] An instrument for dilating a muscular tubular structure, e.g., an esophagus, or for stretching cavities or openings.

    balloon d. A dilator that slips into a narrow structure and then inflates to widen it.

    mechanical d. A dilator that has a tapered end and a wider middle and is inserted progressively into a stricture until its widest point crosses the stricture and expands its diameter.

    vaginal d. A glass, plastic, or metal device for dilating the vagina.

dildo, dildoe (dĭl'dō) An artificial penis-shaped device to simulate sexual intercourse.

dill (dĭl) A hardy annual, *Anethum graveolens,* whose leaves and seeds are used primarily to flavor foods. It is also used as an antiflatulent and antispasmodic, but scientific evidence of its effectiveness is lacking.

diltiazem (dĭl-tī'ă-zĕm) A calcium channel blocker administered orally or intravenously to manage hypertension, angina pectoris, variant angina, supraventricular tachyarrhythmias, and rapid ventricular rates in atrial flutter or fibrillation. Its therapeutic classes are antianginal, antiarrhythmic, and antihypertensive. Trade names include Cardizem, Dilacor XR, and Diltia XT.

diluent (dĭl'ū-ĕnt) [L. *diluere*, to wash away] An agent that reduces the potency or concentration of the substance or solution to which it is added.

dilution (dī-loo'shŭn) **1.** The process of attenuating or weakening a substance. **2.** A diluted substance.

dilutional coagulopathy (dī-loo'shŏn-ăl, dī-) SEE: under *coagulopathy.*

dimension, vertical A vertical measurement of the face; used in dentistry for growth studies and for reference in denture placement.

dimer (dī'mĕr) **1.** In chemistry, esp. polymer chemistry, a combination of two identical molecules to form a single compound. **2.** In virology, a capsomer containing two subunits.

dimercaprol (dī-mĕr-kăp'rŏl) $C_3H_8OS_2$; a compound, 2,3-dimercaptopropanol, used as an antidote in poisoning from heavy metals such as arsenic, gold, and mercury. It is a colorless liquid with a disagreeable odor. Mixed with benzyl benzoate and oil, it is administered intramuscularly.

dimethylamine (dī-mĕth"ĭl-ăm'ĭn) $(CH_3)_2NH$; a malodorous product of decay of materials that contain proteins.

p-dimethylaminoazobenzene (dī-mĕth"ĭl-ăm"ĭ-nō-ăz"ō-bĕn'zēn) A carcinogenic dye, butter yellow.

4-dimethylaminopyridine (dī-mĕth"ĭl-ăm"ĭ-nō-pēr'ĭ-dēn) A catalyst used in the synthesis of organic chemicals to add acetyl groups to molecules.

dimethylmercury (dī-mĕth-ĭl-mĕr'kū-rē) An exceptionally toxic form of mercury that may cause disease and death even after minute exposures. It is readily absorbed through the skin and respiratory tract. SEE: *mercury poisoning.*

dimethyl phthalate (dī-mĕth"ĭl thăl'āt) An insect repellent.

dimethyl sulfoxide (dī-mĕth'ĭl sŭlf-ŏks'īd) ABBR: DMSO. A solvent used to treat interstitial cystitis. The drug was previously believed to improve the absorption of medications through the skin, and it was used to treat rheumatic diseases.

dimethyltryptamine (dī-mĕth"ĭl-trĭp'tă-mēn) ABBR: DMT. An agent that in low doses has hallucinogenic action like that of LSD.

dimorphous (dī-mor'fŭs) [" + *morphe,* form] Occurring in two different forms.

dimple (dimp'ĕl) A small depression in the skin, esp. of the cheek or chin.

dimple veiling Asymptomatic irregularities on the surface of the cornea due to trapping of air bubbles beneath a contact lens. The condition is visible when the cornea is stained with fluorescein sodium but is not hazardous.

dimpling The formation of slight depressions in the flesh due to retraction of the subcutaneous tissue. It occurs in certain carcinomas, such as cancer of the breast. SEE: *peau d'orange.*

dinitrogen monoxide (dī"nī'trŏ-jĕn) [*di-* + *nitrogen*] Nitrous oxide.

Dinoflagellata (dī"nō-flaj"ĕ-lā'tă) [Gr. *deinos,* fearsome, awesome + *flagellate*] A phylum of the kingdom Protista comprising photosynthetic unicellular organisms that are part of the phytoplankton in fresh and ocean water. Some marine species bloom explosively in red tides. Shellfish that feed on the dinoflagellates are toxic to humans (causing paralytic shellfish poisoning). Another species produces ciguatera toxin, which is poisonous to fish and to humans who consume such fish.

dinucleotide (dī-nū'klē-ō-tīd) The product of cleaving a polynucleotide.

Dioctophyma (dī-ŏk"tō-fī'mă) A genus of roundworms found in dogs but rarely in humans.

Diogenes syndrome (dī-oj'ĕ-nēz) [Diogenes of Sinope, Gr. philosopher, 412–323 B.C.] A lack of interest in personal cleanliness or cleanliness of the home, usually occurring in the elderly who live alone. Those affected are usually undernourished but not necessarily from poverty. This condition occurs in all socioeconomic circumstances. It may be associated with excessive saving of items, e.g., old newspapers; social retreat; and rejection of assistance.

diopter (dī-ŏp'tĕr, dī'ŏp-) [Gr. *dia*, through, + *optos*, visible] The refractive power of a lens; the reciprocal of the focal length expressed in meters. It is used as a unit of measurement in refraction. **dioptric** (-ŏp'trĭk), *adj.*

dioptrics (dī-ŏp'trĭks) The science of light refraction.

Dioscorea (dī″ŏ-skŏr'ē-ă) [NL] A genus of yams, a potato-like root vegetable used in many cultures as a source of dietary carbohydrates. There are approx. 150 species. *Dioscorea villosa*, the wild yam, is used as a source of topically applied cosmetics and plant-derived steroids.

diotic (dī-ot'ĭk) [*di-* + *otic*] Pert. to both ears; binaural.

Diovan SEE: *valsartan.*

dioxide (dī-ŏk'sīd) [Gr. *dis*, two, + *oxys*, sharp] A compound having two oxygen atoms per molecule.

dioxin (dī-ok'sĭn) Any of a family of toxic chlorinated hydrocarbons, esp. TCDD. Dioxins are unwanted pollutant by-products in the manufacture of paper and pesticides and in the incineration of waste and garbage. Dioxin-like compounds are also released by the degradation of some other organic molecules. Initial exposure to dioxins can produce chloracne, liver injury, and peripheral neuropathy. SEE: *Agent Orange; pentachlorophenol; polychlorinated biphenyls; TCDD; 2,4,5-trichlorophenoxyacetic acid.*

dioxybenzone (dī-ŏks″ĭ-bĕn'zōn) A topical sunscreen that blocks ultraviolet A and B.

DIP *distal interphalangeal.*

dipeptidase (dī-pĕp'tĭ-dās) An enzyme that catalyzes the hydrolysis of dipeptides to amino acids.

dipeptide (dī-pĕp'tĭd, -tīd) [″ + *peptein*, to digest] A derived protein obtained by hydrolysis of proteins or condensation of amino acids.

Dipetalonema perstans (dī-pĕt″ă-lō-nē'mă) The former name for the parasitic worm now called *Moasonella perstans*. SEE: *Mansonella perstans.*

diphallus (dī-făl'ŭs) [″ + *phallos*, penis] A condition in which there is either complete or incomplete doubling of the penis or clitoris.

diphasic (dī-fā'zĭk) [″ + *phasis*, a phase] Biphasic.

diphenylhydantoin sodium (dī-fĕn″ĭl-hī-dăn'tō-ĭn) Phenytoin.

diphosphatidylglycerol (dī-fŏs″fă-tĭ-dĭl-glĭs′ĕr-ŏl) An extract of beef hearts that contains phosphorylated polysaccharide esters of fatty acids. It is used in certain tests for syphilis.

2,3-diphosphoglycerate (dī″fŏs-fō-glĭs′ĕr-āt″) ABBR: 2,3-DPG. An organic phosphate in red blood cells that alters the affinity of hemoglobin for oxygen. Blood cells stored in a blood bank lose 2,3-diphosphoglycerate, but once they are infused, the substance is resynthesized or reactivated.

diphtheria (dif-thĕr'ē-ă) [Gr. *diphthera*, hide, membrane + *-ia*] A rare toxin-mediated bacterial infectious disease marked by the formation of a patchy grayish-green membrane over the tonsils, uvula, soft palate, and posterior pharynx. Occasionally the skin, conjunctiva, ears, GI and urinary tracts are involved. In cutaneous diphtheria, impetiginous lesions occur. The membrane is created by a thick, inflammatory exudate. SEE: *antitoxin; exotoxin; sepsis; diphtheria toxoid.* **diphtherial** (-thĕr'ē-ăl), *adj.*

ETIOLOGY: The causative organism is *Corynebacterium diphtheriae*. Airborne droplets transmit the organism from person to person (usually from asymptomatic carriers or convalescent patients). More people carry the disease than actually contract an active infection. An effective vaccination program has made the incidence of the disease rare in the U.S. except among groups of people who do not receive immunizations. The lack of virulent strains to reinforce immunity, however, has resulted in loss of immunity in some older adults. The incubation period is 2 to 5 days and occasionally longer.

IMMUNIZATION: Immunization is by administration of three doses at least 4 weeks apart, beginning at 2 months of age. Diphtheria toxoid (inactivated exotoxin capable of stimulating antibody production) is given in combination with pertussis vaccine (usually acellular pertussis) and tetanus toxoid; a fourth dose is given 1 year later. Booster doses are administered if a child under 6 years old or other close family member is exposed to diphtheria. Because effective immunity does not last longer than 10 years after the last vaccination, people should receive a booster of diphtheria toxoid every 10 years. Immunity to diphtheria is assessed by measuring antibody levels in the blood.

SYMPTOMS: Patients present with fever, malaise, cervical lymphadenopathy, and sore throat, raspy cough, hoarseness, and other croup-like symptoms. A tough yellow-white or gray-green pseudomembrane forms in the throat. It contains cellular debris and fibrin and, unlike the exudate caused by streptococci, is difficult to remove and can obstruct air flow, resulting in stridor, suprasternal retractions, tachypnea, cyanosis, and death by suffocation if not treated. As the bacteria multiply, they produce a potent exotoxin that prevents protein synthesis in cells. Once the exotoxin has spread to the bloodstream, signs of sepsis develop. The toxin can cause peripheral nerve paralysis, thrombocytopenia, renal and pulmonary involvement, and myocarditis, with ventricular fibrillation resulting in death.

DIFFERENTIAL DIAGNOSIS: Similar symptoms may be due to tonsillitis, scarlet fever, acute pharyngitis, streptococcal sore throat, peritonsillar abscess, infectious mononucleosis, necrotizing ulcerative gingivitis, acute moniliasis, primary HIV retroviral syndrome, and staphylococcal infections in the respiratory tract after chemotherapy. Examination of a smear from the infected area is advisable; cultures should be obtained in every instance to confirm the diagnosis. In the laryngeal type of diphtheria, edema of the glottis, foreign bodies, and retropharyngeal abscess must be considered.

TREATMENT: If an adult or unimmunized child shows signs of infection, diphtheria antitoxin, containing preformed antibodies, is administered immediately without waiting for laboratory confirmation. Because antitoxin is made from animal serum, type III hypersensitivity must first be assessed with an intradermal injection of 1:10 dilute antitoxin. If testing is positive, desensitization should be attempted even though it is time-consuming and not without risk. When antitoxin is administered, epinephrine 1:1000 and resuscitation equipment should be on standby, and the patient should be closely observed for anaphylaxis. Intravenous erythromycin administered for 7 to 14 days may decrease exotoxin production by *C. diphtheriae* and limit spread of the disease although it may sometimes cause thrombophlebitis.

PATIENT CARE: The patient is monitored for respiratory distress, sepsis, and myocardial or neural involvement. Humidified oxygen is administered to maintain saturated hemoglobin (SaO_2) above 92%, and the patient is assessed for increased ventilatory effort, use of accessory muscles, nasal flaring, stridor, cyanosis, and agitation or decreased level of consciousness. If airway obstruction occurs, intubation, tracheostomy, mechanical ventilation, or other life-support may be required. Hypotension, tachycardia, and crackles on auscultation may indicate heart failure. Sepsis may produce fever, tachycardia, and hypotension. Neuromuscular involvement is assessed through weakness, paralysis, or sensory changes. All data are clearly documented. Patients who receive antitoxin are closely observed for local or systemic anaphylaxis.

Strict isolation is maintained until two consecutive negative nasopharyngeal cultures have been obtained at least 1 week after drug therapy ceases. Unimmunized members of the patient's household are advised to receive diphtheria toxoid appropriate for age and to complete the proper series of diphtheria immunizations. Even if previously immunized, a person should receive a booster immunization if more than 10 years has passed since the last vaccination. All cases of diphtheria must be reported to local public health authorities. Families are to be prepared for a prolonged convalescence esp. if the patient has neuromuscular involvement.

    cutaneous d. A skin infection, usually at the site of a wound, caused by *C. diphtheriae*, usually occurring in humid, tropical regions with poor sanitation. It is characterized by slow healing and shallow ulcers containing a tough grayish membrane. It is treated with diphtheria antitoxin and penicillin or erythromycin.

    laryngeal d. A complication of diphtheria caused by extension of the membrane from the pharynx with gradual occlusion of the airway. The signs are restlessness, use of accessory respiration muscles, and development of cyanosis. If this condition is not remedied effectively, death results.

diphtheria antitoxin 1. The protective antibody formed after exposure to *Corynebacterium diphtheriae* or its toxoid. The object of immunization with diphtheria toxoid is to develop high enough titers of this antibody to prevent diphtheria on subsequent exposures. **2.** Solution containing preformed antibodies to *C. diphtheriae*, used to treat diphtheria. Skin tests to assess for type III hypersensitivity are necessary before administration because the solution is obtained from animal serum.

diphtheroid (dĭf′thĕ-royd) [″ + *eidos*, form, shape] **1.** Resembling diphtheria or the bacteria that cause diphtheria. **2.** A false membrane or pseudomembrane not due to *Corynebacterium diphtheriae*.

Diphyllobothrium (dī-fĭl″ō-bo′th′rē-ŭm) [L. *Diphyllobothrium,* fr *di-* + Gr. *phyllon,* leaf + Gr. *bothrion,* pit] A genus of tapeworm of the order Pseudophyllidea, marked by a scolex with two bothria (slitlike grooves). The genus was formerly called *Dibothriocephalus.*

    D. latum A species that is native to Scandinavia, the Baltics, and western Russia, and is now found in North America, esp. the Pacific Northwest, that infests fish and mammals. The adult lives in the intestine of fish-eating mammals, including humans. It is the largest tapeworm infesting humans and may reach a length of 50 to 60 ft (15.2 to 18.3 m); the average is 20 ft (6.1 m). The eggs develop into ciliated larvae that are eaten by small crustaceans called copepods. The larvae pass through several stages in the copepods and develop further after the copepods are eaten by fish, finally encysting in fish muscle. People acquire the infection by eating raw or poorly cooked fish that contains cysts. Infection can be prevented by thoroughly cooking all freshwater fish or by keeping the fish frozen at −10°C (14°F) for 48 hr before eating. SYN: *broad* **tapeworm***; fish* **tapeworm**. SEE: illus.

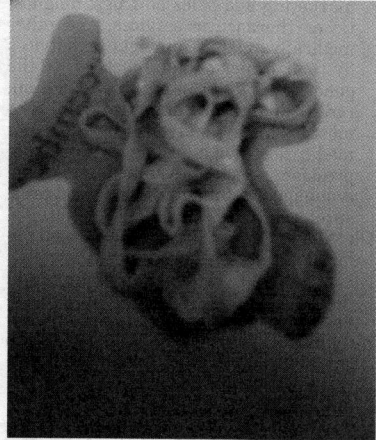

DIPHYLLOBOTHRIUM LATUM

Passed in patient's stool.

SYMPTOMS: Patients often report abdominal pain, weight loss, digestive disorders, progressive weakness, and symptoms of pernicious anemia because the worm absorbs ingested vitamin B_{12} from the gastrointestinal tract.

TREATMENT: Praziquantel is used to treat the infestation.

diphyodont (dĭf′ē-ō-dŏnt) [″ + *phyein*, to produce, + *odous*, tooth] Having two sets of teeth, a primary and a permanent set, as in humans.

diplacusis (dĭp″lă-kū′sĭs) [″ + *akousis*, hearing] A disturbed perception of pitch in which two tones are heard for every sound produced.

diplegia (dī-plē′jē-ă) [Gr. *dis*, twice, + *plege*, a stroke] **1.** Paralysis of similar parts on both sides of the body. **2.** In cerebral palsy, excessive stiffness usually occurs in all limbs but greater stiffness in the legs than in the arms. **diplegic** (-jĭk), *adj.*

spastic d. Congenital spastic stiffness of the limbs.

diplo- [Gr. *diploos*, twofold, double] Prefix meaning *double* or *twin*.

diplobacillus (dĭp″lō-bă-sĭl′ŭs) [″ + L. *bacillus*, a little stick] A pair of bacilli, linked end to end.

diplocardia (dĭp″lō-kăr′dē-ă) [″ + *kardia*, heart] A condition in which the two lateral halves of the heart are partially separated by a groove.

diplococcus (dĭp″lō-kŏk′ŭs) *pl.* **diplococci** Any of various spherical bacteria ap-

pearing in pairs. SEE: *bacterium* for illus; *Neisseria gonorrhoeae* for illus.

diploë (dĭp′lō-ē) [Gr. *diploē*, fold] Spongy bone containing red bone marrow between the two layers of compact bone of the skull bones. **diploetic** (-lō-e′tĭc), *adj.*

diploid (dĭ′ployd″) [*diplo-* + *-oid*] Of somatic cells, possessing two sets of chromosomes (46 chromosomes in humans), twice the haploid number of chromosomes in germ cells. **diploidy** (-ploy′dē), *n.* SEE: *chromosome*.

diplokaryon (dĭp″lō-kăr′ē-ŏn) [″ + *karyon*, nucleus] A diploid nucleus.

diplomyelia (dĭp″lō-mī-ē′lē-ă) [″ + *myelos*, marrow] A condition in certain types of spina bifida in which the spinal cord appears to be doubled due to a lengthwise fissure.

diplopia (dip-lō′pē-ă) [*diplo-* + *-opia*] Two images of an object seen at the same time. SYN: *ambiopia; double vision*.

binocular d. Double vision occurring when both eyes are open. It results from misalignment of the ocular muscles.

crossed d. Binocular vision in which the image is on the side opposite from the eye that sees it.

homonymous d. Uncrossed **d.**

monocular d. Double vision with one eye.

vertical d. Double vision with one of the two images higher than the other.

diplotene (dĭp′lō-tēn) The stage in the first prophase of meiosis when spindle fibers form and the homologous chromosomes begin to separate.

dipole (dī′pōl) A molecule in which each end has an equal but opposite charge. The intensity of the charge is given by its dielectric moment or constant.

dipping 1. Palpation of the liver by a quick depressive movement of the fingers while the hand is held flat on the abdomen. **2.** Immersion of an object in a solution, esp. applied to the dipping of cattle or dogs for tick control. **3.** A drop in blood pressure of 10% or more that occurs at night or during sleep. Nocturnal blood pressure dipping is a normal phenomenon. Its absence is associated with a variety of illnesses, including obstructive sleep apnea.

diprosopus (dĭp-rō-sōp′ŭs) [Gr. *dis*, twice, + *prosopon*, face] A malformed fetus with a double face.

dipstick (dip′stik″) A paper strip impregnated with chemicals, used for analysis of body fluids, esp. urine.

PATIENT CARE: Dipsticks are used in the clinical laboratory and in point-of-care testing of urinary specimens. The dipstick is not usually dipped into a urine specimen: small droplets of urine are dribbled over its colorimetric test sections. Typically these are used to provide semi-quantitative indications of the abnormal presence of albumin and other proteins, blood cells, glucose, hemoglobin, or nitrites. Dipsticks are also used to indicate pregnancy, e.g., when human chorionic gonadotropin is found in high concentration in urine. SYN: *test strip*.

Diptera (dĭp´tĕr-ă) [Gr. *dipteros,* having two wings] An order of insects characterized by sucking or piercing mouth parts, one pair of wings, and complete metamorphosis. It includes the flies, gnats, midges, and mosquitoes. It contains many species involved in the transmission of pathogenic organisms, such as malaria.

dipterous (dĭp´tĕr-ŭs) Having two wings; characteristic of the order Diptera.

Dipylidium (dī˝pī˝lid´ē-ŭm, ˝pĭ-) A genus of tapeworms (family Dipylidiae) that infests dogs and cats.

    D. caninum A species that is a common parasite of dogs and cats. Infestation in humans may occasionally occur through the accidental ingestion of lice or fleas, the intermediate hosts. SYN: *dog tapeworm*. SEE: *Ctenocephalides*.

diquat (dī´kwăt) A herbicide, chemically related to paraquat, that releases hydrogen peroxide and oxygen radicals when consumed. It can cause nausea, vomiting, renal failure, altered mental status, and cardiac arrhythmias.

directed differentiation The use of growth factors to stimulate stem cells to specialize into specific adult cells.

directed verdict (dĭ-rek´tĕd vĕr´dĭkt) A determination of the outcome of a trial solely by a judge without input from a jury.

direct immunofluorescence test Direct fluorescent antibody.

directionality The ability to perceive one's position in relation to the environment; the sense of direction. Problems with directionality are frequently found in children with learning disabilities or suspected minimal brain dysfunction.

direct light reflex SEE: under *reflex*.

directly observed therapy ABBR: DOT. Oral administration of a drug or of drugs to a patient under supervision to ensure the drug is swallowed. DOT is esp. important in treating patients with infectious diseases (e.g., HIV/AIDS or tuberculosis) in which development of drug-resistant microorganisms is likely to threaten public health if the drug is not taken exactly as prescribed.

director (dĭ-rek´tŏr) A grooved surgical instrument with an open channel into which another instrument, e.g., a knife, is placed and advanced safely into the operative field.

director of nursing ABBR: DON, DN. The nursing manager or chief executive officer.

    PROFESSIONAL ORGANIZATION: The National Association of Directors of Nursing–Long-term Care (NADONA-LTC) addresses the needs of directors and assistant directors of nursing and provides educational conferences.

direct reflex SEE: under *reflex*.

direct-to-consumer advertising (dĭ-rĕkt´ too kŏn-soo´mĕr ăd´vĕr-tī˝zĭng) The marketing and sales of drugs, diagnostic or therapeutic services, and other medically related products or services by their owner or manufacturer to the general public by means of television, radio, the Internet, and direct mail. The most commonly advertised drugs are medications for allergies, arthritis, depression, erectile dysfunction, gastroesophageal reflux, and high blood pressure.

Dirofilaria (dī˝rō-fĭ-lā´rē-ă) A genus of filarial worms.

    D. immitis Heartworm, a species of filariae that occurs in dogs but may infest humans.

dirty bomb A weapon that disperses into the environment low-level radioactive material bonded to a conventional explosive.

¹ **dis-** [L. *dis-,* apart, asunder] Prefix meaning *opposite of, reverse of, deprived of, excluded from, not*. "Dis-" must not be confused with "dys-."

² **dis-** [Gr. *dis,* twice] Prefix meaning *double* or *twice*.

disability (dis˝ă-bil´ĭt-ē) [¹*dis-* + *ability*] Any physical, mental, or functional impairment that limits a major activity. It may be partial or complete. The definition of disability is controversial. To some experts it refers to any restriction or inability to perform socially defined roles or tasks that are expected of an individual in specific social contexts. Another concept of disability is that it is any restriction or lack of ability to perform tasks or roles in the manner previously considered normal for an individual. Contemporary beliefs of disability recognize that characteristics of the environment interact with an individual's abilities to determine functional performance. In this view, the presence of disability is not entirely determined by bodily function or impairment. SYN: *activity limitation; functional limitation*. SEE: *death* for table; *handicap*.

    developmental d. A disability due to congenital abnormality, trauma, deprivation, or disease that interrupts or delays the sequence and rate of normal growth, development, and maturation.

    excess d. The discrepancy that exists when a person's functional limitations are greater than those warranted by the objective degree of impairment. Often excess disability is created by attitudes and policies that create barriers to a disabled person's full participation.

learning d. Any of several disorders characterized by difficulty in reading, writing, or mathematics that is two standard deviations below the norm for a person of otherwise normal intelligence. The condition may become apparent at an early age but usually is not recognized until the child begins formal education in school. The frequency of this condition in boys is five times that in girls. About 5% of children in school use special educational services because of learning disorders. SYN: *academic skills disorder; learning disorder.*

nonverbal learning d. Any cognitive or mood disorder that is first noticed in school-aged children in which language use is preserved, but other abilities (e.g., in affect, computation, or drawing) are adversely affected.

reading d. Dyslexia.

disability-adjusted life year ABBR: DALY. An estimate of how much a burden a disease poses to public health. The estimate includes the number of early deaths caused by the disease relative to the average life expectancy of a population and the severity and duration of the functional losses the disease causes in those who survive with it.

disability analysis The attempt to determine the relative importance of life events that contribute to functional impairments. Determining the relationship between occupational or other exposures and the development of chronic illness is often a complex task. For example, chronic obstructive lung diseases may result from nonoccupational factors such as tobacco abuse, or from genetic illnesses such as alpha$_1$-antitrypsin disease or from job-related exposures to chemicals, dusts, or asbestos. Similarly, hearing loss may occur as a natural consequence of aging or as a result of exposures to high levels of noise at work (e.g., with heavy machinery) or during recreation (motorcycle riding or snowmobiling).

Disability Rating Scale SEE: under [1] *scale.*

disaccharidase (dī-săk'ă-rĭ-dās) A group of enzymes that split disaccharides into monosaccharides.

disaccharide (dī-săk'ĭ-rĭd) [Gr. *dis,* twice, + *sakkharon,* sugar] A carbohydrate composed of two monosaccharides. SEE: *carbohydrate.*

disarticulation (dĭs″ăr-tĭk″ū-lā'shŭn) [L. *dis,* apart, + *articulus,* joint] Amputation through a joint.

disassimilation (dĭs″ă-sĭm″ĭ-lā'shŭn) [″ + *ad,* to, + *similare,* to make like] The conversion of assimilated material into less complex compounds for energy production.

disaster [″ + L. *astrum,* star, illstarred] A natural or man-made occurrence such as a flood, tornado, earthquake, forest fire, bridge or building collapse, nuclear reactor accident, war, explosion, terrorist attack or bombing, or train wreck. The need for emergency evacuation and medical services is increased during and following a disaster. It is essential that hospitals and community services have a plan for the expeditious mobilization and use of their services at such times.

chemical d. The accidental release of large amounts of toxins into the environment. The effects suffered by people in the area are determined by the toxicity of the chemical, its speed in spreading, its composition (liquid, solid, or gaseous), and the spill site, esp. its proximity to a water supply or buildings. The major effect may be due to the chemical itself or to a resulting fire or explosion. The catastrophic release of chemicals may overwhelm, at least temporarily, local or regional health care resources. SEE: *chemical warfare.*

disaster medical assistance team ABBR: DMAT. A group of specially trained and readily mobilized medical and rescue workers available to respond to a mass casualty incident on short notice. Team members include physicians, nurses, paramedics, firefighters, and other support personnel.

Disaster Mortuary Operational Response Team ABBR: DMORT. A specially trained group of citizens trained to evaluate deceased victims of natural and man-made disasters and to provide them with mortuary services. DMORT members participate in the evaluation of the cause of mass deaths, in the identification of the dead, and in the processing and disposition of remains.

disaster planning A procedure for coping with mass casualties or massive disruptions of normal health care services as a result of human or natural catastrophes. In the U.S., the Joint Commission on the Accreditation of Health Organizations (JCAHO) requires that all hospitals have a written plan in place and that drills be performed twice a year to assess the plan's usefulness. The plan should address major problems such as airplane crashes, contamination of the water supply, earthquakes, electrical power failures, explosions, famine, fire, flood, or terrorist attacks. The plan may be for a local community, region, or state and should link health care resources with other public services and the media. The Federal Aviation Administration (FAA) also requires disaster planning and drills at airports on a regular basis.

disaster recovery plan SEE: under *plan.*

disbarment (dis-bar'mĕnt) Loss of professional rights or privileges. SYN: *debarment.*

disc SEE: *disk.*

discharge (dis-charj', dis'char"j) **1.** In the medical professions, to officially release from care. The release is authorized by a physician, other medical care worker, or a medical care facility. **2.** To release pent-up energy or emotion. **3.** Release from care, confinement, or custody. **4.** Release of pent-up energy or emotion. **5.** The emission of a secretion or excretion of pus, feces, urine, and so forth. **6.** The material thus emitted.

   disruptive d. The passage of current through an insulating medium due to the breakdown of the medium under electrostatic stress.

   early supported d. Any of the methods to facilitate the return of hospitalized patients to lower levels of care, including nursing care facilities, foster care, or home. Early supported discharge optimizes the management of patient length-of-stay, relieves caregiver stress, and empowers patients to return to higher levels of functioning.

   lochial d. Uterine excretion following childbirth. SEE: *lochia.*

discharge planning Any strategy used to facilitate outpatient care for someone currently receiving inpatient health services. It may include the identification of the proposed date of hospital discharge, a program for the use of professional, institutional, or familial home health services, a review of the appropriate use of prescriptions and their side effects, instructions for the use of durable medical equipment, and a list of appointments for follow-up care.

discharge summary A document that outlines the details of the hospitalization of a patient.

   PATIENT CARE: It is prepared when the patient is released from a health care facility and incorporated in her permanent medical records. It should ideally include the explanation for the patient's admission; a record of her complaints, physical findings, laboratory results and radiographic studies while hospitalized; a list of changes in her medications at discharge; and recommendations for follow up care. For optimal patient care it should be transmitted to or reviewed with her outpatient primary care provider. SYN: *discharge abstract.*

discharging (dis'chärg"ing) The emission of or the flowing out of material, as the discharge of pus from a lesion; excretion.

discipline A branch or domain of knowledge, instruction, or learning. Nursing, medicine, physical therapy, and social work are examples of health-related or professional disciplines. History, sociology, psychology, chemistry, and physics are examples of academic disciplines.

discission (dis-sizh'ŭn) [L. *dis,* apart, + *scindere,* to cut] Rupture of the capsule of the crystalline lens in cataract surgery.

discitis, diskitis (dis(k)-īt'ĭs, disk-īt'ĭs) [*disk* + *-itis*] Inflammation of a disk, esp. an interarticular cartilage.

disclosing agent SEE: under *agent.*

discocyte (dis'kō-sīt") [" + "] A normally shaped red blood cell.

discogenic (dis"kō-jĕn'ĭk) [" + *gennan,* to produce] Caused by an intervertebral disk.

discoid (dis'koyd) Like a disk.

disconnection syndrome Disturbance of the visual and language functions of the central nervous system due to interruption of the connections between two cerebral hemispheres in the corpus callosum, occlusion of the anterior cerebral artery, or interruption of the connections between different parts of one hemisphere. These disorders also may be produced by tumors or hypoxia. They can manifest in several ways including the inability, when blindfolded, to match an object held in one hand with that in the other; the inability to execute a command with the right hand but not the left; when blindfolded, the ability to correctly name objects held in the right hand but not those in the left; and the inability to understand spoken language while being able to speak normally. SEE: *inattention, unilateral.*

discoplacenta (dis"kō-plă-sĕn'tă) [Gr. *diskos,* quoit, + *plakous,* a flat cake] A disklike placenta.

discordance (dis-kor'dăns) In genetics, the expression of a trait in only one of a twin pair. SEE: *concordance.*

discordant (dis-kord'ănt) [L. *discordare,* to be at variance, quarrel] **1.** Pert. to or showing dissimilarity; disagreeing. **2.** In genetics, pert. to or showing discordance. **3.** In twins, differing in one or more characteristics, e.g., growth. **4.** In psychology, Resulting from or producing conflict with one's self image.

discordant couple A couple in a sexual relationship, only one of whom is infected with a sexually transmitted pathogen, e.g., herpesvirus or HIV/AIDS.

discovery Pretrial device used to obtain or discover all information, facts, and circumstances surrounding the allegations at issue in the lawsuit. Techniques include interrogatories, requests for production of documents and things, admissions of facts, physical and mental examinations, and depositions.

discrete (dis-krēt') [L. *discretus,* separated] Separate; said of certain eruptions on the skin. SEE: *confluent.*

discrete analysis An automated methodology in which samples are held in separate containers to be assayed. In a continuous flow system, all samples flow through the same tubing.

discriminant function (dis-krim'ĭ-nănt) SEE: under *function.*

discrimination (dĭs-krĭm″ĭ-nā′shŏn) [L. *discriminatio,* a contrast] **1.** The process of distinguishing or differentiating. **2.** Unequal and unfair treatment or denial of rights or privileges without reasonable cause. Federal statutes prohibit discrimination based on age, sex, sexual preference, religion, race, national origin, and disability. **3.** The accuracy with which risk factors separate a population into the healthy and the sick.

   figure-ground d. The ability to see the outline of an object as distinct from visually competing background stimuli. This ability is often impaired following central nervous system damage.

   genetic d. Unequal treatment of persons with either known genetic abnormalities or the inherited propensity for disease. Genetic discrimination may have a negative effect on employability, insurability, and other socioeconomic variables.

   spatial d. The ability to perceive as separate points of contact the two blunt points of a compass when applied to the skin.

   speech d. The ability to recognize a spoken word if it is uttered loudly enough for the hearer to detect it as a sound.

   tactile d. Two-point discrimination.

   tonal d. The ability to distinguish one tone from another. This is dependent on the integrity of the transverse fibers of the basilar membrane of the organ of Corti.

   two-point d. The ability to localize two points of pressure on the surface of the skin and to identify them as discrete sensations. SYN: *tactile d.* SEE: *two-point discrimination test.*

discus (dĭs′kŭs) [Gr. *diskos,* quoit] Disk.

   d. proligerus Cumulus oophorus.

disease (dĭz-ēz′) [Fr. *desaise,* fr. *des,* from + *aise,* ease] A condition marked by subjective complaints, a specific history, clinical signs and symptoms, and laboratory or radiographic findings. Disease and illness differ in that disease is usually objective and tangible or measurable, whereas illness (and associated pain, suffering, or distress) is subjective and personal. Thus, a person may have a serious but symptom-free disease (such as hypertension) without illness. Conversely, a person may be extremely ill (such as with post-traumatic stress disorder) but have no obvious evidence of disease.

   Particular diseases are listed under the first word. SEE: e.g., *chronic obstructive pulmonary disease; foot and mouth disease; inflammatory bowel disease;* table.

   communicable d. ABBR: CD. A disease that may be transmitted directly or indirectly from one person to another.

SEE: table; *Standard Precautions Appendix.*

   complex d. A disease that appears to run in families but whose expression also appears to be influenced by environmental factors.

   contagious d. ABBR: CD. Any disease, usually an infectious disease, readily transmitted from one person to another.

   hereditary d. A disease caused by genetic factors transmitted from parent to offspring. Also known as an inherited disease. SEE: table.

   hypokinetic d. Any illness produced by lack of physical exercise.

   monogenic d. A disease that is inherited from one generation to the next in classic mendelian fashion.

   neglected d. Any disease affecting a large number of people, esp. in developing nations, who receive little attention from governments, medical researchers, and pharmaceutical companies. The term is used to raise social awareness of the illness among public health practitioners and citizens of Western nations. Examples of neglected diseases include Chagas disease, leishmaniasis, malaria, malnutrition, sleeping sickness, and tuberculosis.

   orphan d. A illness that is so rare that it receives little attention from medical researchers or the pharmaceutical industry. In the U.S., it is an illness that affects less than 200,000 people. SEE: *National Organization for Rare Disorders.*

   secondary d. A disease caused by another disease, e.g., diseases of the joints and muscles of the lower limbs caused by obesity because of the increased trauma of transporting and supporting the added weight.

   stable d. In oncology, cancer that neither responds to treatment nor worsens significantly during treatment.

   subacute d. A disease in which symptoms are less pronounced but more prolonged than in an acute disease, intermediate between acute and chronic disease.

   systemic d. A generalized disease rather than a localized or focal one.

disease burden The total effect of a disease on an individual or on a society.

disease progression A change in the way an illness affects a patient as it moves from its earliest stages to its peak and then to its resolution. SEE: *natural history (of disease).*

diseasome (dĭz-ēz′sōm″) [*disease* + *-some*] The entire complement of inheritable diseases, including their underlying genes and the ways those genes are expressed.

disenfranchisement (dĭs″en-fran″chĭz′mĕnt) [¹*dis-* + *enfranchisement*] Deprivation of a person's legal rights

Fungal Diseases

Disease Name	Fungus	Presentation	Susceptibility
Aspergillosis	*Aspergillus fumigatus* (and other aspergillus species)	Allergic bronchopulmonary aspergillosis (ABPA); aspergilloma; invasive or disseminated (bloodstream) infection	Persons with asthma, other allergic diseases, cystic fibrosis. Aspergilloma/invasive disease: most affected persons are immunosuppressed
Blastomycosis	*Blastomyces dermatitidis*	Pneumonia; skin infections; disseminated infections	Endemic in the Central U.S. Infection most common after camping, fishing, hunting
Candidiasis	*Candida albicans, C. glabrata* (and other *Candida* species)	Diaper rash; oral thrush; vaginitis; esophagitis; sepsis with dissemination to multiple organs	People with burns; recent antibiotic therapy; diabetes mellitus; indwelling catheters; immunosuppressant diseases, therapies, or conditions
Coccidioidomycosis	*Coccidioides immitis*	Pneumonia; bone infection; skin abscesses; meningitis	Endemic in the Southwestern U.S. and parts of Central America. Infection common near construction projects; after earthquakes or other soil disturbances
Cryptococcosis	*Cryptococcus neoformans*	Meningitis; pneumonia; skin infections	Found in soil and pigeon droppings. Most affected persons are immunosuppressed
Dermatophytosis	*Tinea* species	Athlete's foot *(Tinea pedis)*; beard *(Tinea barbae)*; chest and back *(Tinea corporis)*; groin *(Tinea cruris)*; scalp *(Tinea capitis)*; others	Infection often develops on warm, moist skin
Histoplasmosis	*Histoplasma capsulatum*	Pneumonia	Endemic in the Mississippi and Ohio River Valleys and parts of Central America; near caves; poultry farms

Table continued on following page

Fungal Diseases (Continued)

Disease Name	Fungus	Presentation	Susceptibility
Phaeohyphomycosis	Various dematiaceous fungi, e.g., *Cladophialophora, Bipolaris, Exophiala, Wangiella* species	Skin infections; brain infections	Endemic in tropical countries; local skin disease may result from cuts or scratches; disseminated disease occurs in the immunosuppressed
Pneumocystosis	*Pneumocystis carinii*	Pneumonia; disseminated infections	Most affected persons are immunosuppressed
Sporotrichosis	*Sporothrix schenckii*	Skin infections; lung, bone, joint, and disseminated infections	Outdoor skin exposures, e.g., gardening, landscaping Lung and disseminated infections most common in alcoholics, persons with COPD, diabetes mellitus, or immunosuppression
Mucormycosis; Zygomycosis	*Absidia, Mucor, Rhizopus* and other species	Skin infections; pneumonia; invasive sinus and brain infections	Persons with poorly controlled diabetes mellitus or immune suppressing diseases, therapies, or conditions

or privileges, such as the right to citizenship, the right to vote, and the right to participate in activities or options available to others. SEE: *enfranchisement*.

disengagement (dĭs″ĕn-gāj′mĕnt) [Fr. *desengager*] **1.** The emergence or release of the fetal head from within the maternal pelvis. **2.** Any withdrawal from participation in customary social activity. **3.** In psychiatry, autonomous functioning with little or no emotional attachment and a distorted sense of independence.

disentanglement (dĭs″ĕn-tăn′gl-mĕnt) A rescue technique used to free a trapped victim that involves removing the wreckage from around the patient (rather than removing the patient from the wreckage). For example, freeing a person trapped in a crushed car often requires the car to be pried apart with heavy rescue tools capable of cutting through metal.

disequilibrium (dĭs-ē″kwĭ-lĭb′rē-ŭm) [L. *dis*, apart, + *aequus*, equal, + *libra*, balance] An unequal and unstable equilibrium.

disequilibrium syndrome Dialysis disequilibrium.

disharmony (dĭs″hăr′mō-nē) Lack of harmony; discord.

disinfect (dĭs-ĭn-fĕkt′) [″ + *inficere*, to corrupt] To free from infection by physical or chemical means.

disinfectant A substance that prevents infection by killing bacteria. Most disinfectants are used on equipment or surfaces rather than in or on the body. Common disinfectants are halogens; salts of heavy metals; organic compounds such as formaldehyde, or alcohol 70%, iodoform, hydrogen peroxide, or ethylene oxide. The term is usually applied to a chemical or physical agent that kills vegetative forms of microorganisms.

disinfection (dĭs″ĭn-fĕk′shŭn) The application of a disinfectant to materials and surfaces to destroy pathogenic microorganisms.

   terminal d. Disinfection of the room and infected materials at the end of the infectious stage of a disease.

disinfection, high-level The inactivation of all bacteria, fungi, mycobacteria, and viruses on an instrument or surface used in patient care. The elimination of all spores is a separate process.

disinfestation (dĭs″ĭn-fĕs-tā′shŭn) [L.

Method of Transmission of Some Common Communicable Diseases

Disease	How Agent Leaves the Body	How Organisms May Be Transmitted	Method of Entry into the Body
Acquired immuno-deficiency syndrome (AIDS)	Blood, semen, or other body fluids, including breast milk	Sexual contact Contact with blood or mucous membranes or by way of contaminated syringes Placental transmission	Reproductive tract Contact with blood Placental transmission Breastfeeding
Cholera	Feces	Water or food contaminated with feces	Mouth to intestine
Diphtheria	Sputum and discharges from nose and throat Skin lesions (rare)	Droplet infection from patient coughing	Through mouth or nose to throat
Gonococcal disease	Discharges from infected mucous membranes	Sexual activity	Reproductive tract or any mucous membrane
Hepatitis A, viral	Feces	Food or water contaminated with feces	Mouth to intestine
Hepatitis B, viral and Hepatitis D	Blood and serum-derived fluids, including semen and vaginal fluids	Contact with blood and body fluids	Exposure to body fluids including during sexual activity, injection drug abuse, or surgery Contact with blood
Hepatitis C	Blood and other body fluids	Parenteral drug use Laboratory exposure to blood Health care workers exposed to blood (e.g., dentists and their assistants and clinical and laboratory staff)	Infected blood Contaminated needles Cuts; mucosal exposures
Hookworm	Feces	Cutaneous contact with soil polluted with feces Eggs in feces hatch in sandy soil	Larvae enter through skin (esp. of feet), migrate through the body, and settle in small intestine
Influenza	As in pneumonia	Respiratory droplets or objects contaminated with discharges	As in pneumonia
Leprosy	Cutaneous or mucosal lesions that contain bacilli Respiratory droplets	Cutaneous contact or nasal discharges of untreated patients	Nose or broken skin
Measles (rubeola)	Discharges from nose and throat	Respiratory droplets	Through mouth and nose
Meningitis, meningococcal	Discharges from nose and throat	Respiratory droplets	Mouth and nose

Table continued on following page

Method of Transmission of Some Common Communicable Diseases
(Continued)

Disease	How Agent Leaves the Body	How Organisms May Be Transmitted	Method of Entry into the Body
Mumps	Discharges from infected glands and mouth	Respiratory droplets and saliva	Mouth and nose
Ophthalmia neonatorum (gonococcal infection of eyes of newborn)	Vaginal secretions of infected mother	Contact with infected areas of vagina of infected mother during birth	Directly on conjunctivae
Pertussis	Discharges from respiratory tract	Respiratory droplets	Mouth and nose
Pneumonia	Sputum and discharges from nose and throat	Respiratory droplets	Through mouth and nose to lungs
Poliomyelitis	Discharges from nose and throat and via feces	Respiratory droplets; contaminated water	Through mouth and nose
Rubella	Discharges from nose and throat	Respiratory droplets	Through mouth and nose
Streptococcal pharyngitis	Discharges from nose and throat	Respiratory droplets	Through mouth and nose
Syphilis	Lesions	Sexual intercourse; contact with skin or mucous membrane lesions	Directly into blood and tissues through breaks in skin or membrane
	Blood	Contaminated needles and syringes	Contaminated needles and syringes
		Transfer through placenta to fetus	
Trachoma	Discharges from infected eyes	Cutaneous contact Hands, towels, handkerchiefs	Directly on conjunctivae
Tuberculosis, bovine		Milk from infected cow	Mouth to intestine
Tuberculosis, human	Sputum	Droplet infection from person coughing with mouth uncovered	Through nose to lungs or intestines
Typhoid fever	Feces and urine	Food or water contaminated with feces or urine from patients	Through mouth via infected food or water and thence to intestinal tract

dis, apart, + *infestare,* to strike at] The process of killing infesting insects or parasites.

disinhibition (dĭs″ĭn-hĭ-bĭsh′ŭn) **1.** Abolition or countering of inhibition. **2.** In psychiatry, freedom to act in accordance with one's drives with a decrease in social or cultural constraint. **3.** Loss of typical behavioral or social restraints.

disinsertion (dĭs″ĭn-sĕr′shŭn) Retinodialysis.

disintegration [″ + *integer,* entire] **1.** The product of catabolism; the falling apart of the constituents of a substance. **2.** Disorganization of the psyche.

disintegrative disorder A personality disorder of children marked by regression in many areas of functioning after at least 2 yr of normal development. Individuals exhibit social, communicative, and behavioral characteristics similar to those of autistic disorder. Also called *Heller's syndrome, dementia infantalis,* or *disintegrative psychosis.* SYN: *childhood disintegrative disorder.*

disjoint To disarticulate or to separate

Inherited Diseases and Conditions: A Brief List

Name	How is it inherited?	What is the problem?	When does it become symptomatic or apparent?	How common is it?*
Alpha₁-antitrypsin deficiency	Autosomal dominant	Deficiency of enzyme that protects liver and lungs from enzymatic injury. Results in early onset of chronic obstructive pulmonary disease (COPD) or liver disease. There are more than 70 genetic variants.	Childhood: Liver disease; Adulthood: Lung disease	Homozygotes: 1:3000
Autosomal dominant polycystic kidney disease	Autosomal dominant	Abnormal cell membrane protein predisposes to cyst formation in epithelial organs, esp. the kidney. Causes about 5% of all end-stage renal disease in the U.S.	Renal failure usually by ages 55 to 60	1:1000 (Europeans)
Chronic granulomatous disease	X-linked or autosomal recessive	Defect in phagocytic cells results in susceptibility to recurrent severe infections	Infancy/ Early childhood	1: 300,000
Color blindness (red-green)	X-linked recessive	Abnormalities of visual pigment expression in retinal cone cells	Childhood	1:12-20 males 1:200 females
Cystic fibrosis	Autosomal recessive	Abnormality in cellular sodium and chloride management. Infant may have meconium ileus at birth; later, azoospermia, biliary, lung, pancreatic, and sinus disease	Early childhood	Heterozygotes: 1:2000 (United Kingdom); 1:3500 (U.S.); 1:350,000 (Japan)
Diabetes mellitus, type 2	Polygenic	Resistance to the action of insulin in muscles and other peripheral tissues; insufficient insulin production by the pancreas. Hyperglycemia, with metabolic damage to eyes, kidneys, nerves, and blood vessels	Often at onset of inactivity; patient is overweight or obese, usually in adulthood	1-30:1000 per year; highest incidence in some ethnic groups (Africans, Hispanics, Native Americans, Polynesians)
Duchenne muscular dystrophy	X-linked recessive	Missing protein within myocyte membranes results in weakness of proximal muscles, with difficulty walking, frequent falling, and pseudohypertrophy of muscle groups	Early childhood	1:3000-5000 (Europeans)
Familial adenomatous polyposis	Autosomal dominant	Faulty gene results in growth of hundreds of polyps within the large bowel, with the potential for malignant transformation	Adolescence/ early adulthood	1-2:1,000,000

Table continued on following page

Inherited Diseases and Conditions: A Brief List (Continued)

Name	How is it inherited?	What is the problem?	When does it become symptomatic or apparent?	How common is it?*
Familial hyper-cholester-olemia	Autosomal dominant	Excessively high levels of LDL and total cholesterol, resulting in premature atherosclerosis	Homozygotes may have heart attacks in their 20s	Heterozygotes: 1:500 Homozygotes: 1:3,000,000
Hemophilia A	X-linked	Insufficient production of clotting factor VIII. Produces bleeding, esp. into injured joints or after surgery	Early childhood	1:5000 to 10,000 males
Hemophilia B	X-linked	Insufficient production of clotting factor IX. Produces bleeding, esp. into injured joints and after surgery	Early childhood	1:30,000 males
Hereditary hemochromatosis	Autosomal recessive	Increased iron absorption from the gastrointestinal tract. Iron deposits gradually accumulate in and damage joints, pancreas, liver, heart, testes	Middle age	Heterozygotes: 1:8; Homozygotes: 1:200
Huntington disease	Autosomal dominant	Degeneration of the caudate nucleus of the brain, with early onset dementia, schizophreniform illnesses, and movement disorders (chorea)	Middle age	1:115,000
Long QT syndrome	Autosomal recessive; autosomal dominant	Abnormalities in management of sodium by myocytes results in prolonged action potentials and cardiac depolarization, producing life-threatening heart rhythm disturbances. Recessive form (very rare) associated with deafness	Childhood and adolescence	Not well quantified
Marfan syndrome	Autosomal dominant	Mutations in a gene that produces extracellular matrix protein result in tall body type, with elongated fingers; flat feet; hernias; hyperextensible joints; sternal deformities; and potential for aortic dissection	Risk of aortic dissection highest after age 50	1:10,000
Neurofibromatosis I and II	Autosomal dominant	Absence of a tumor-suppressing gene results in growth of multiple skin and nerve tumors	Infancy	1:3000

Table continued on following page

Inherited Diseases and Conditions: A Brief List (Continued)

Name	How is it inherited?	What is the problem?	When does it become symptomatic or apparent?	How common is it?*
Phenylketonuria (hyperphenylalanemia)	Autosomal recessive	Inability to convert phenylalanine to tyrosine. Results in eczema and hypopigmentation, hyperactivity, mental retardation, and seizures	Infancy	1:16,000 (general U.S. population) to 1:200,000 (lower incidence in African Americans and Jews)
Porphyria, acute intermittent	Autosomal dominant	Attacks of abdominal pain, sometimes associated with autonomic dysfunction, muscle weakness, seizures	Adolescence	1:10,000 (Most common in Northern Europeans)
Rett syndrome	X-linked dominant	After a brief period of normal development, young girls regress neurologically, developing speech disturbances, loss of normal hand movements, seizures, ataxia, and autism	Six to 18 months old	1:10-15,000
Sickle cell anemia	Autosomal recessive	Abnormal amino acid in hemoglobin molecule results in deformed red blood cells that may cause infarcts in bones and other internal organs. High risk of pneumococcal infections and painful crises	Early childhood	Heterozygotes: (African-Americans) 8-13:100; (Brazilians) 5-6:100
Tay-Sachs disease	Autosomal recessive	Deficiency of enzyme results in accumulation of sphingolipids in the brain, causing mental retardation, blindness, paralysis	Early childhood	Heterozygotes (Eastern European Jews) 1:25

*Approximate number of affected persons per number of births; ethnic predominance in parentheses where known.

bones from their natural positions in a joint.

disjunction (dĭs-jŭnk′shŭn) Separation of the homologous pairs of chromosomes during anaphase of the first meiotic division.

disk (disk) [Gr. *diskos*, a dish, quoit] A flat, round, platelike structure. SYN: *disc*.

    anisotropic d. A band.

    articular d. The biconcave oval disk of fibrous connective tissue that separates the two joint cavities of the temporomandibular joint on each side.

    choked d. Papilledema.

    embryonic d. An oval disk of cells in the blastocyst of a mammal from which the embryo proper develops. Its lower layer, the endoderm, forms the roof of the yolk sac. Its upper layer, the ectoderm, forms the floor of the amniotic cavity. The primitive streak develops on the upper surface of the disk. SEE: *embryo* for illus.

    herniated d. Rupture of the soft tissue that separates two vertebral bones into the spinal canal or adjacent spinal nerve roots. Herniation of intervertebral disks can cause back pain and, occasionally, loss of neurological function in the distribution of affected nerves. SYN: *herniated intervertebral d.*; *lumbar disk* **prolapse**; *slipped d.* SEE: *herniation* of *nucleus pulposus* for illus.

    herniated intervertebral d. herniated **d.**

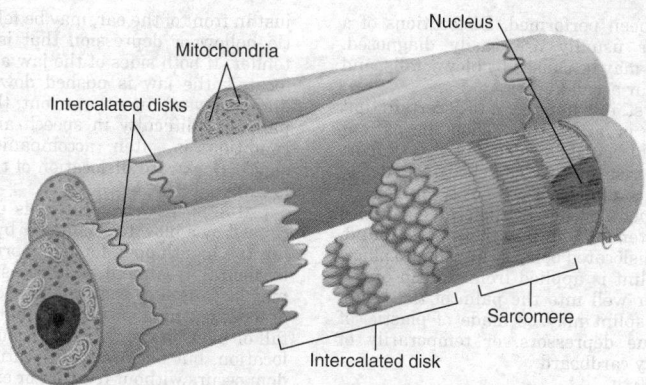

INTERCALATED DISK

Intercalated disk at the ends of adjacent cardiac muscle cells

intercalated d. A modification of the cell membrane of adjacent cardiac muscle cells; it consists of extensive folds and intercellular junctions for electrical and mechanical linkage of contiguous cells. SEE: illus.

intervertebral d. The fibrocartilaginous tissue between the vertebral bodies. The outer portion is the anulus fibrosus; the inner portion is the nucleus pulposus. The disk is a shock absorber, or cushion, and permits movement.

M d. M **line.**

optic d. The area of the retina where the optic nerve enters. SYN: *blind* **spot** *(1).*

slipped d. Colloquial term for herniated disk.

Z d. A thin, dark disk that transversely bisects the I band (isotropic band) of a striated muscle fiber. The thin filaments, made primarily of actin, are attached to the Z disk; the area between the two Z disks is a sarcomere, the unit of contraction.

diskectomy, discectomy (dĭs-kĕk′tō-mē) Surgical removal of a herniated intervertebral disk.

diskography, discography (dis-kog′ră-fē) [*disk* + *-graphy*] Use of a contrast medium injected into an intervertebral disk so that it can be examined radiographically.

⚠ Diskography may increase the risk of disk degeneration and herniation.

dislocation (dis″lō-kā′shŏn) [¹*dis-* + *location*] The displacement of any part, esp. the temporary displacement of a bone from its normal position in a joint.

ankle d. Traumatic displacement of the talocrural joint with or without con-

current fracture of the tibial or fibular malleoli, or both.

anterior hip d. A dislocation of the hip through the obturator foramen, on the pubis, in the perineum, or through a fractured acetabulum.

SYMPTOMS: Pain, tenderness, and immobility accompany the dislocation. Shortening is present in the pubic and suprapubic forms, lengthening in the obturator and perineal forms.

TREATMENT: Hyperextension and direct traction are used to treat this condition, followed by flexion, abduction with inward rotations, and adduction.

closed d. A dislocation in which the skin overlying the joint remains intact. SYN: *simple* **d.**

complete d. A dislocation that separates the surfaces of a joint completely.

complicated d. A dislocation associated with other major injuries.

compound d. A dislocation in which separation of the joint causes disruption of the overlying skin. SYN: *open* **d.**

d. of clavicle Traumatic displacement of the clavicle at either the sternoclavicular or the acromioclavicular joint.

TREATMENT: Open or closed reduction is the treatment.

congenital d. A dislocation existing from or before birth.

congenital d. of the hip A congenital defect of the hip joint, probably caused by multifactorial effects of several abnormal genes. SYN: *developmental* **d.** *of the hip; developmental* **dysplasia** *of the hip.*

developmental d. of the hip ABBR: DDH. Congenital **d.** of the hip.

d. of finger Displacement of a finger bone. This occurs only at a joint. If there has been a crushing injury, it should be treated as a fracture until radiography has been performed. Dislocations of a finger usually are easily diagnosed. They may be caused by blows, falls, and similar accidents.

First, it is important to ascertain that there is no fracture. Then the patient should be asked to steady and support the wrist (or have somebody else do so) for countertraction. The finger is grasped beyond the dislocated muscles and tendons and, with the free hand, the dislocated bone is slipped into place. A splint is applied from the tip of the finger well into the palm of the hand. The splint may be made of plastic, of tongue depressors, or temporarily of heavy cardboard.

⚠️ No attempt should be made to reduce a dislocation of any finger joint until radiography has ruled out the possibility of fracture.

fracture d. A fracture near a dislocated joint.

habitual d. Recurrent joint dislocation resulting during normal motion. The patella and the hip are the most commonly affected joints.

d. of the hip A dislocation of the head of the femur from its normal location in the acetabulum. It is very often accompanied by a fracture.

SYMPTOMS: The dislocation is characterized by pain, rigidity, and loss of function. The dislocation may be obvious by the abnormal position in which the leg is held, seen, or felt.

DIAGNOSIS: The person has great difficulty in straightening the hip and leg. The knee on the injured side resists being pointed inward toward the other knee and typically appears in a position of flexion, adduction, and internal rotation.

FIRST AID: The patient should be placed on a large frame, gurney, or support, such as that used for a fractured back. A large pad or pillow should be placed under the knee of the affected side. The patient should be treated for shock if required.

incomplete d. A slight displacement of opposing surfaces. SYN: *partial d.* SEE: *subluxation (1).*

inferior hip d. A rare type of hip dislocation in which the femoral head is displaced below the acetabulum. Inferior hip dislocations are treated with traction in the flexed position, followed by external rotation and extension.

d. of jaw Traumatic or spontaneous displacement of the mandible. Jaw dislocations are uncomfortable and may be psychologically distressing. They may occur on either side, in which instance the tip of the jaw is pointed away from the dislocation. On the unaffected side,

just in front of the ear, may be felt a little hollow or depression that is often tender. If both sides of the jaw are dislocated, the jaw is pushed downward and backward. In either event, there is pain and difficulty in speech and the condition is often accompanied by shock. Backward dislocation of the jaw is rare.

CAUSES: Jaw dislocation is usually caused by a blow to the face or by keeping the mouth open for long periods as in dental treatment, but occasionally may be caused by chewing large chunks of food, yawning, or hearty laughing. A fall or blow on the chin could cause dislocation, but backward dislocation seldom occurs without fracture or extreme trauma.

REDUCTION: These dislocations are reduced by placing well-padded thumbs inside of the mouth on the lower molar (back) teeth with the fingers running along the outside of the jaw as a lever. The thumbs should press the jaw downward and backward. The jaw will glide posteriorly over the ridge of bone (articular eminence), which can be felt, and just as this occurs the jaw usually snaps into place. When this motion is noted, the thumbs should be moved laterally toward the cheeks to keep them from being crushed between the molars.

This snapping into place is due to an involuntary spasm of the muscles, which pulls the jaw as though an overstretched rubber band were attached to it. Following the reduction, an immobilizing bandage or double cravat should be applied.

⚠️ It is important that the hands be protected by heavy gloves to prevent trauma by the teeth. SEE: *Standard Precautions Appendix.*

d. of knee Displacement of the knee (tibiofemoral joint), an uncommon injury, universally complicated by tearing of the cruciate ligaments, and often associated with peroneal nerve or popliteal artery damage. In a knee dislocation at least three of the four major ligaments, anterior cruciate, posterior cruciate, medical collateral, lateral collateral, are torn. Dislocations should be reduced by an orthopedic surgeon as soon as is feasible to preserve circulation to the lower extremity.

mandibular d. SEE: *subluxation.*

old d. A dislocation in which no reduction has been accomplished even after many days, weeks, or months.

open d. Compound **d.**

partial d. Incomplete **d.**

pathological d. A dislocation resulting from paralysis or disease of the joint or supporting tissues.

posterior hip d. A dislocation of the hip onto the dorsum ilii or sciatic notch. Most such dislocations occur when the hip is flexed and adducted and a violent longitudinal force is applied to the femur that forces the femoral head posterior relative to the acetabulum. This dislocation is often seen in automobile accidents.

SYMPTOMS: The condition is characterized by an inward rotation of the thigh, with flexion, inversion, adduction, and shortening; pain and tenderness; and a loss of function and immobility.

TREATMENT: The patient should first be anesthetized and then laid on his back with the leg flexed on the thigh and the thigh on the abdomen. The thigh is adducted and rotated outward. Circumduction is performed outwardly across the abdomen and then back to the straight position. Traction may be required.

recent d. A dislocation seen shortly after it occurred.

d. of shoulder Displacement of the head of the humerus beyond the boundaries of the glenoid fossa. SEE: *Bankart lesion; Hill-Sachs lesion.*

ETIOLOGY: The most common cause is from trauma with the arm in external rotation with abduction, causing the head of the humerus to sublux anteriorly; a posterior subluxation may occur from a fall on an outstretched arm. An inferior dislocation may occur from poor muscle tone as with hemiplegia and from the weight of the arm pulling the humerus downward. Anterior glenohumeral dislocations are common among athletes, esp. football players.

SIGNS: A patient with a dislocated shoulder usually has a hollow in place of the normal bulge of the shoulder, as well as a slight depression at the outer end of the clavicle. Glenohumeral range of motion is restricted and such patients often cannot touch their opposite shoulder with the hand of the involved arm. Both shoulders should always be compared for symmetry. Vital signs are assessed to provide baseline data. The patient is assessed for pain, and analgesia prescribed and provided as needed.

TREATMENT/FIRST AID: Radiographs and/or MRI are needed to determine the type of dislocation and the presence of any fracture. If no fractures are present, one of several maneuvers can be used to reduce the humerus into the glenoid.

PATIENT CARE: Because of the potential damage to neurovascular structures as they cross the glenohumeral joint line, the vascular and neurological status of the arm and hand must be assessed. A decreased or diminished ulnar or radial pulse warrants immediate intervention and reduction of the dislocation. For example, an anterior dislocation of the shoulder can be reduced, with passive traction on the arm or by placing the patient in a supine position and medially displacing the scapula. A sling or other shoulder support is provided after reduction to limit shoulder mobility for the prescribed time, and activity is gradually resumed using a guided rehabilitation protocol.

simple d. Closed **d.**

d. of the toe Traumatic displacement of bones of a toe. This condition is treated essentially the same as dislocation of the finger. SEE: *d. of finger.*

traumatic d. A dislocation due to injury or violence.

dislodgement, dislodgment (dis-loj'mĕnt) [Fr. *desloger,* to dislodge] Displacement of a device (such as a catheter or tracheal tube) thought to be securely in position. Dislodgment of catheters, endotracheal tubes, or other devices may sometimes occur when patients are agitated, when they are moved, or when equipment is checked or adjusted. It may result in patient injury or failure in administration of required treatments. **dislodge,** *v.*

dismember (dĭs-mĕm'bĕr) To remove an extremity or a portion of it.

dismiss (dis-mis') [L. *dimissus, dismissus,* sent away] In law, to end a legal dispute without a trial, e.g., because the judge rules that the accusation does not merit consideration. **dismissal** (-mis'ăl), *n.*

dismutase (dĭs-mū'tās) An enzyme that acts on two molecules of the same substance. One of these is oxidized and the other reduced; two new compounds are thus produced.

disobliteration (dis″ŏ-blit″ĕ-rā'shŏn) [¹*dis-* + *obliteration*] Removal of a blood clot or atherosclerotic plaque from an obstructed blood vessel.

disocclusion (dĭs″ŏ-kloo'zhŭn) Loss of contact between opposing teeth.

disorder (dis-ord'ĕr) A pathological condition of the mind or body. Particular disorders are listed under the first word. SEE: e.g., *acute stress disorder; bipolar disorder; learning disorder.* SEE: *disease.*

disorder of sex development ABBR: DSD. The technical, preferred term for hermaphroditism or pseudohermaphroditism.

disorder of written expression An inability to draft grammatically correct phrases, sentences, or paragraphs, a disability that may impair advancement in school or work. This communication disorder is said to be present only when

1. it cannot be attributed to sensory, medical, or neurological deficits (e.g., hearing impairment); and

2. it is an isolated deficit, out of proportion to one's age and measured intelligence.

disorganization [L. *dis*, apart, + Gr. *organon*, a unified organ] **1.** Alteration in an organic part, causing it to lose most or all of its distinctive characteristics. **2.** In psychology and psychiatry, affective and/or cognitive chaos.

disorientation (dis″ōr-ē-ĕn-tā′shŏn) [¹*dis- + orientation*] Inability to estimate direction or location or to be cognizant of time or of persons.

spatial d. In aerospace medicine, a term used to describe a variety of incidents occurring in flight, when the pilot fails to sense correctly the position, motion, or attitude of the aircraft or himself or herself within the coordinate system provided by the surface of the earth and gravitation.

disparate (dĭs′pă-răt) [L. *disparitas*, unequal] Dissimilar, not equally paired.

dispensary (dĭs-pĕn′să-rē) [L. *dispensare*, to give out] **1.** A clinic or similar place for obtaining medical care. **2.** An outpatient pharmacy.

dispensatory (dĭs-pĕn′să-tō-rē) [L. *dispensatorium*] A publication, in book form, of the description and composition of medicines.

dispense (dĭs-pĕns′) To prepare or deliver medicines.

dispersant (dis-pĕr′sănt) [*disperse*] A chemical that prevents organic substances from concentrating as sludge in a particular location. Such agents are used to break up oil spills or other substances but may have their own toxic effects.

disperse (dĭs-pĕrs′) [L. *dis*, apart, + *spargere*, to scatter] **1.** To scatter, esp. applied to light rays. **2.** To dissipate or cause to disappear, as a tumor or the particles of a colloidal system.

disperse dye A textile pigment used to color polyester fabrics. It is a cause of allergic contact dermatitis, esp. seen in skin folds, where clothes may chafe against the skin. Allergies to disperse dyes can be avoided by wearing natural-fiber clothing.

dispersion (dis-pĕr′zhŏn) [L. *dispersio*, scattering] **1.** The act of dispersing. **2.** That which is dispersed. **3.** In statistics, the degree to which data are distributed widely (or closely) to a central point, such as the mean or mode.

coarse d. Suspension (3).

colloidal d. A mixture containing colloid particles that fail to settle out and are held in suspension. They are common in animal and plant tissues; the protoplasm of cells is an example. Particles of colloidal dispersions are too large to pass through cell membranes. Such dispersions usually appear cloudy.

molecular d. A true solution.

Q-T d. The difference between the longest and the shortest Q-T interval recorded by electrocardiography. High levels of Q-T dispersion (e.g., greater than 100 msec) may be a risk factor for life-threatening ventricular arrhythmias.

QTc d. In electrocardiography, variation in the corrected QT interval in different leads. This has been correlated with an increased incidence of ventricular arrhythmias and sudden death.

dispersoid (dĭs-pĕr′soyd) A colloid with very finely divided particles.

displaced person (dis′plăst′) ABBR: DP. One who leaves his or her home or homeland because of war, disease, famine, political conflicts, economic pressure, or persecution. Displacement increases the likelihood of malnutrition, detachment from family and social networks, and exposure to abuse and violence.

displacement (dĭs″plăs′mĕnt) [Fr. *deplacer*, to lay aside] **1.** Removal from the normal or usual position or place. **2.** Addition to a fluid of another more dense, causing the first fluid to be dispersed. **3.** Transference of emotion from the original idea with which it was associated to a different idea, thus allowing the patient to avoid acknowledging the original source.

disposable (di-spō′ză-bĕl) Designed to be used once and discarded and not reused or recycled.

disposition [L. *disponere*, to arrange] **1.** A natural tendency or aptitude exhibited by an individual or group. It may be manifested by acquiring a certain disease, presumably due to hereditary factors. **2.** The sum of a person's behavior as determined by his or her mood. SEE: *diathesis*.

disproportion (dis″prŏ-por′shŏn) [¹*dis- + proportion*] A size different from that considered to be normal.

cephalopelvic d. ABBR: CPD. Disparity between the dimensions of the fetal head and those of the maternal pelvis. When the fetal head is larger than the pelvic diameters through which it must pass, or when the head is extended as in a face or brow presentation and cannot rotate to accommodate to the size and shape of the birth canal, fetal descent and delivery are not possible. SYN: *fetopelvic d.*

fetopelvic d. Cephalopelvic **d.**

disruptive [″ + *ruptura*, breaking] Socially or professionally unacceptable. Said of behaviors that adversely impact others, e.g., angry or intimidating outbursts, demeaning comments, or unwarranted criticisms.

disruptive behavior disorder Attention-deficit hyperactivity disorder.

dissect (dĭ-sĕkt′, dī-sĕkt′) [L. *dissecare*, to cut up] To separate tissues and parts of a cadaver for anatomical study.

dissecting cellulitis of the scalp (dis-ekt′ing) SEE: under *cellulitis*.

dissection (dis-ek′shŏn, dī-) [′*dis-* + *section*] **1.** Separation of tissues by use of sharp instruments (sharp dissection) or blunt instruments (blunt dissection) along tissue planes during surgery or autopsy. **2.** A surgical procedure to expose and excise certain tissues, e.g., regional lymph node dissection. **3.** The ripping or tearing of a vascular structure, e.g., at a site of trauma or within an aneurysm.

   aortic d. A disruption of the aortic wall that causes blood to leave the true arterial lumen, either to enter a false lumen between the intima and the deeper layers of the vessel, or to hemorrhage into the chest or abdomen. Aortic dissection usually occurs in patients with aneurysmal dilation of the aorta, but it may sometimes occur as a result of trauma. It causes severe chest pain, which may sometimes be described by patients as a ripping or tearing. It may sometimes be associated with lower blood pressure in the left arm than in the right. It often results in sudden death. Some patients may be able to be stabilized with antihypertensive agents such as beta blockers with intravenous nitroprusside. Surgical repair is usually recommended for patients with dissection of the proximal aorta or for patients with distal disease and complications.

   blunt d. In surgical procedures, separation of tissues with a rounded rather than a pointed or sharpened tip. This provides minimal damage to the part being dissected if anatomical planes are observed. In various pathological states, sharp dissection may be less traumatic.

   carotid artery d. Longitudinal tearing of the carotid artery, a rare cause of stroke, occurring esp. in patients who have suffered trauma or twisting of the head and neck.

   SYMPTOMS: Patients may report the sudden onset of unilateral neck pain that radiates toward the head, along with new neurological deficits.

   radical neck d. The removal of the sternocleidomastoid muscle, internal jugular vein, spinal accessory nerve, and lymph nodes of the neck. The surgery is used primarily for the treatment of head and neck cancers.

   selective neck d. One of several operations used for staging and treatment of neck cancers. In the most commonly used approach, the tissues above the omohyoid, including the submandibular gland and lymphatics, are removed.

   sharp d. In surgical procedures, gaining access to tissues by incising them with some sort of sharp instrument, such as a scalpel.

dissemble (dĭ-sĕm′bl) To mislead, to give a false impression, or to conceal the truth.

disseminated (dis-em′ĭ-nāt″ĕd) [′*dis-* + L. *seminare*, to sow] **1.** Scattered throughout an organ or the body. Of cancers or microorganisms, scattered or distributed over a considerable area.

dissemination (-em″ĭ-nā′shŏn), *n.*

disseminated intravascular coagulation SEE: under *coagulation*.

dissipation (dĭs-ĭ-pā′shŭn) [L. *dissipare*, to scatter] **1.** Dispersion of matter. **2.** The act of living a wasteful and dissolute life, esp. drinking alcoholic beverages to excess.

dissociation (dis-ō″sē-ā′shŏn, shē-) [L. *dissociatio*, separation] **1.** In chemistry, the separation of ions when a salt is dissolved. **2.** The ability to move one body segment independently of another. **3.** In psychiatry, the separation of identity, memory, and cognition from affect; the splitting of ideas and memory about oneself from their emotional and historical underpinnings. SYN: *dissociative reaction*.

   albuminocytologic d. An increase in the protein concentration of cerebrospinal fluid without an accompanying increase in the number of cells.

   atrioventricular d. Dissociation that occurs when the independent pacemakers of the atria and ventricles of the heart are not synchronized. This is a hallmark of third-degree heart block.

   microbic d. A change in the morphology of a cultured microbial colony due to mutation or selection.

   d. of personality A split in consciousness resulting in two different phases of personality, neither being aware of the words, acts, and feelings of the other. SEE: *dissociative identity disorder; multiple personality; vigilambulism; Nursing Diagnoses Appendix*.

   psychological d. A disunion of mind of which the person is not aware (e.g., dual personality, fugue, somnambulism, selective amnesia).

dissociative identity disorder A rare but increasingly reported psychiatric illness in which a person has two (or more) distinct personalities. It was formerly known as "multiple personality disorder." The patient's personalities may vary broadly with respect to interests, communication styles, aggression, and gender. Amnesia for differing personalities is characteristic.

   ETIOLOGY: Patients often report a history of abuse in childhood, but whether this causes the syndrome is unknown. SYN: *alternating personality; multiple personality; double personality*.

dissociative reaction Dissociation (3).

dissolution (dĭs″sō-lū′shŭn) [L. *dissolvere*, to dissolve] **1.** Death. **2.** A pathological resolution or breaking up of the integrity of an anatomical entity.

dissolve (diz-o lv′) [L. *dissolvere,* to dissolve] To cause a homogeneous dispersion of a solid, gas, or liquid in a liquid.

dissonance (dĭs′ō-năns) **1.** Discord or disagreement. **2.** Unpleasant sounds, particularly musical ones.

    cognitive d. Incongruity of thought, philosophy, or action.

distad (dĭs′tăd) [L. *distare,* to be distant] Away from the center.

distal (dĭs′tăl) [L. *distare,* to be distant] **1.** Farthest from the center, from a medial line, or from the trunk; opposed to proximal. **2.** In dentistry, the tooth surface farthest from the midline of the arch.

distal intestinal obstruction syndrome ABBR: DIOS. A form of intestinal obstruction uniquely found in children with cystic fibrosis, formerly known as meconium ileus equivalent.

distal muscular dystrophy SEE: under *dystrophy.*

distance (dis′tăns) [L. *distantia,* remoteness] The space between two objects.

    focal d. In ophthalmology, the distance from the optical center of a lens to the focal point.

    hearing i. The distance at which a given sound can be heard.

    infinite d. **1.** A distance without limits. **2.** In ophthalmology, the assumption that the light rays coming from a point of a distance beyond 20 ft (6.1 m) are practically parallel and accommodation is unnecessary.

    interocclusal d. The distance between the occlusal surfaces of opposed teeth when the mandible is at rest.

    interocular d. In ophthalmology, the distance between the eyes. SEE: *hypertelorism.*

    interpupillary d. In ophthalmology, the distance between the centers of the pupils of the eyes.

    margin crease d. In ophthalmology, the height that the crease of the eyelid sits above the upper eyelid margin when the eye is positioned in primary gaze.

    object-film d. ABBR: OFD. In radiography, an obsolete term for object-image receptor distance.

    source-object d. ABBR: SOD. In radiography, the distance between a source of radiation and the object that it images or radiates.

    source-skin d. In radiography, the distance from a radiation source to a patient's skin.

    target-skin d. ABBR: TSD. **1.** In radiography, the distance from the source of radiation to the point where the beam enters the patient. **2.** In radiation therapy, a common value used for determination of the depth at which the treatment time is calculated.

distemper (dĭs-tĕm′pĕr) In veterinary medicine, one of several viral infections of animals that cause fever, anorexia, and nerve disease.

distend (dĭ-stĕnd′) [L. *distendere,* to stretch out] **1.** To stretch out. **2.** To become inflated.

distensibility (dĭs-tĕn″sĭ-bĭl′ĭ-tē) The ability to become distended.

distention, distension (dis-ten′shŏn) The state of being distended.

distichiasis (dĭs″tĭ-kī′ă-sĭs) [Gr. *distichia,* a double row] A condition in which there are two rows of eyelashes, one or both being directed inward toward the eye.

distill (dĭs-tĭl′) [L. *destillare,* to drop from] To vaporize by heat and condense and collect the volatilized products.

distillate (dĭs′tĭl-āt, dĭs-tĭl′āt) That which has been derived from the distillation process.

distillation (dĭs″tĭ-lā′shŏn) [*distill*] Condensation of a vapor that has been obtained from a liquid heated to the volatilization point, as the condensation of steam from boiling water. Distillation is used to purify water and for other purposes. Distilled water should be stored in covered containers because it readily takes up impurities from the atmosphere.

    destructive d. The process of decomposing complex organic compounds by heat in the absence of air and condensing the vapor of the liquid products.

    fractional d. Separation of liquids based on the difference in their boiling points.

distinct part Any section of a nursing home specifically designated for the care of Medicare or Medicaid patients. The admissions, discharges, census, expenses, provisioning, and staffing of the distinct part are accounted for separately from the rest of the institution.

distobuccal (dĭs″tō-bŭk′ăl) [L. *distare,* to be distant, + *bucca,* cheek] Pert. to the distal and buccal walls of bicuspid and molar teeth; also pert. to the distal or buccal walls of a cavity preparation.

distoclusion (dĭs″tō-kloo′zhŭn) A condition in which the lower teeth meet the upper teeth behind the normal position.

distolingual (dĭs″tō-lĭng′gwăl) [″ + *lingua,* tongue] Pert. to the distal and lingual surfaces of a tooth.

distome (dĭs-tōm′) A fluke with two suckers, an oral and a ventral sucker, or acetabulum.

distomer (dis′tō-mĕr) Of two enantiomeric compounds, the one with the weaker chemical activity. SEE: *eutomer.*

disto-occlusal (dĭs″tō-ŏ-kloo′zăl) Concerning the distal and occlusal surfaces of a tooth or the distal and occlusal walls of a cavity preparation.

distortion (dĭs-tŏr′shŭn) [L. *distortio,* twist, writhe] **1.** A twisting or bending out of regular shape. **2.** A writhing or twisting movement as of the muscles of the face. **3.** A deformity in which the part or structure is altered in shape. **4.** In ophthalmology, visual perception of an image that does not provide a true picture, due to astigmatism or to retinal abnormalities. **5.** In psychiatry, the process of modifying unconscious mental elements so that they can enter consciousness without being censored. **6.** In radiology, the difference in size and shape of a radiographic image as compared with the actual part examined. **7.** Variation in the amplitude or frequency of a signal that may be caused by overdriving the amplifier in the circuit.

distractibility (dĭs-trăk″tĭ-bĭl′ĭ-tē) Inability to focus one's attention; loss of the ability to concentrate.

distraction (dis-trak′shŏn) [L. *distractio*, a pulling apart, separation] **1.** A state of mental confusion or derangement. **2.** An attempt to redirect a patient's attention from a painful or noxious stimulus to another, more pleasant one. **3.** Separation of joint surfaces by extension without injury or dislocation of the parts. **4.** A joint mobilization technique causing separation of opposing joint surfaces. It is used to inhibit pain, move synovial fluid, or stretch a tight joint capsule.

   music d. Audioanalgesia.

distraction therapy The use of pleasing sensory stimuli (such as aromas, images of nature, massage, or music) to divert the attention of a patient from an unpleasant clinical experience. Distraction therapy can reduce the pain experienced by patients during, e.g., reduction of fractures, placement of catheters, or wound debridement.

distraught (dĭs-trawt′) [L. *distrahere*, to perplex] In doubt, deeply troubled, and having conflicting thoughts.

distress (dĭs-trĕs′) [L. *distringere*, to draw apart] Physical or mental pain or suffering.

   fetal d. A nonspecific clinical diagnosis indicating pathology in the fetus. The distress, which may be due to lack of oxygen, is judged by fetal heart rate or biochemical changes in the amniotic fluid or fetal blood.

distress, moral Response to the inability to carry out one's chosen ethical/moral decision/action. SEE: *Nursing Diagnoses Appendix.*

distressed personality SEE: under *personality.*

distribution (dis″trĭ-bū′shŏn) [L. *distributio*, division] **1.** In anatomy, the dividing and spreading of anything (esp. blood vessels and nerves) among tissues. **2.** The presence of entities (e.g., hair, fat, or nutrients) at various sites or in particular patterns throughout the body. **3.** In demography or statistics, the pattern of events or locations.

   frequency d. In statistics, the assignment of continuous data points into arbitrarily chosen, mathematically useful clusters; a list of the number of times different ranges of values appear in a given data set. When a frequency distribution is graphed, it forms a histogram.

   Gaussian d. Normal distribution.

   normal d. In statistics, the theoretical, smooth, continuous, symmetrical bell-shaped curve made by tallying the frequency distribution of random data points. The mean, median, and mode of the data coincide. SYN: *bell curve; Gaussian curve; Gaussian d.; normal curve.*

distributive justice (dis-trib′yŭ-tiv) The ethical concept that favors the value of doing some good for a community, as opposed to doing great good for an individual. It may be illustrated by the dilemma of providing a costly organ transplant to save the life of one person versus providing vaccination against polio to thousands of others. When monetary resources are limited, health care planners, providers, and patients compete for those resources and must decide whether to concentrate them on a single major task or distribute them broadly to the population at large.

disturbance (dis-tŭr′băns) **1.** Interruption of the normal sequence of continuity. **2.** A departure from the considered norm. **3.** In traditional Chinese medicine, an imbalance of energy.

   emotional d. Mental disorder.

disulfate (dī-sŭl′fāt) A compound containing two sulfate radicals.

disulfiram (dī-sŭl′fĭ-răm) Antabuse.

disulfiram poisoning SEE: *Antabuse in Poisons and Poisoning Appendix.*

disuse syndrome, risk for A state in which an individual is at risk for deterioration of body systems as the result of prescribed or unavoidable musculoskeletal inactivity. SEE: *Nursing Diagnoses Appendix.*

diurese (dī″ū-rēs′) To cause diuresis.

diuresis (dī″yŭ-rē′sĭs) [Gr. *diourein*, to urinate + *-sis*] The secretion and passage of large amounts of urine. Diuresis occurs as a complication of metabolic disorders such as diabetes mellitus, diabetes insipidus, and hypercalcemia, among others. It also occurs when obstruction to urinary flow is suddenly relieved ("post-obstructive diuresis"), after childbirth, and after supraventricular tachycardias.

   Diuretic drugs are used to manage conditions marked by fluid overload, (e.g., cerebral edema, cirrhosis, congestive heart failure, cirrhosis with ascites, hyperkalemia, and nephrotic syndrome). SEE: *diuretic.*

diuretic (dī″yŭ-ret′ik) [L. *diureticus,* fr Gr. *diourētikos,* [ert. to urination] **1.** Increasing urine secretion. SEE: *diuresis.* **2.** An agent that increases urine output. Diuretics are used to treat hypertension, congestive heart failure, and edema. Common side effects of these agents are potassium depletion, low blood pressure, dehydration, and hyponatremia.

   loop d. A diuretic agent that acts on the ascending limb of Henle's loop in the kidney to produce sodium and fluid excretion. An example is furosemide. Loop diuretics are used to treat conditions such as edema, heart failure, hyperkalemia, and hypertension.

   potassium-sparing d. An agent that stimulates the kidneys to excrete water and sodium while retaining potassium. Drugs from this therapeutic class are used to treat hypertension, fluid retention in cirrhosis, and congestive heart failure.

diurnal (dī-ŭrn′ăl) [L. *diurnalis,* belonging to the day, daily] **1.** Occurring every day; daily. **2.** Pert. to or occurring in the daytime. SEE: *circadian; biological clock; jet lag; nocturnal.*

divagation (dī-vă-gā′shŭn) [L. *divagatus,* to wander off] **1.** Wandering astray. **2.** Rambling or incoherent speech.

divalent (dī-vā′lĕnt) In a molecule, having an electric charge of two.

divergence (dĭ-vĕr′jĕns, dī-) [L. *divergentia,* a bending aside] Separation from a common center, e.g., from a source of radiation or, of the eyes, a turning outward from a fixed point.

divergent (dī-vĕr′jĕnt) Radiating in different directions.

diversion (dĭ-vĕr′zhŭn) **1.** In hospital management, the routing of patients away from one facility to others, usually because the first institution is inaccessible, overcrowded, or understaffed. **2.** In surgery, the redirection of the normal flow of body contents from one organ to another. **3.** The illicit use of a controlled substance for a purpose other than that which was intended by its prescriber.

diversional activity, deficient The state in which an individual experiences a decreased stimulation from or interest or engagement in recreational or leisure activities (because of internal/external factors that may or may not be beyond the individual's control). SEE: *Nursing Diagnoses Appendix.*

diverticulectomy (dī″vĕr-tĭk″ū-lĕk′tō-mē) [″ + Gr. *ektome,* excision] Surgical removal of a diverticulum.

diverticulitis (dī″vĕr-tĭk″ū-lī′tĭs) [″ + Gr. *itis,* inflammation] Inflammation of a diverticulum or diverticula in the intestinal tract, esp. in the colon, causing pain, anorexia, fevers, and rarely intestinal perforation, hemorrhage, abscess formation, peritonitis, fistula formation, or death. SEE: *Nursing Diagnoses Appendix.*

   PATIENT CARE: During an acute episode, prescribed treatment with fluid and electrolyte replacement; antibiotic, antispasmodic, analgesic, and stool softener therapy; and nasogastric suction, if required, is initiated. The patient is observed for increasing or decreasing distress and for any adverse reactions to the therapy. Stools are inspected for mucus, blood, and consistency, and the frequency of bowel movements is noted. The patient is assessed for fever, increasing abdominal pain, blood in the stools, and leukocytosis, and for indications of perforation, such as rebound tenderness. Rest is prescribed, and the patient is instructed not to lift, strain, bend, cough, or perform other actions that increase intra-abdominal pressure. When the patient resumes a normal diet, stool softeners may be employed.

   Patients need to be educated about the disease and its symptoms. A well-balanced diet that provides dietary roughage in the form of fruit, vegetable, and cereal fiber, but that is nonirritating to the bowel, is recommended, and fluid intake should be increased to 2 to 3 L daily (unless otherwise restricted). Constipation and straining at stool should be avoided, and the patient is advised to relieve constipation with stool softeners and bulk cathartics, taken with plenty of water. The importance of regular medical evaluation is emphasized. If medical treatment is not effective, a colon resection may be necessary to remove the affected area. Perforation, peritonitis, obstruction, or fistula formation may necessitate a temporary colostomy (so that abscesses may drain and the colon can rest), followed in 6 weeks to 3 months by reanastomosis.

   acute d. Diverticulitis in which the symptoms are similar to those of appendicitis but usually located in the left rather than the right lower quadrant of the abdomen: inflammation of the peritoneum, formation of an abscess, and in untreated patients, intestinal gangrene accompanied by perforation.

   chronic d. Diverticulitis marked by worsening constipation, mucus in the stools, and intermittent left lower quadrant abdominal pains. The walls of the bowels may thicken, which may produce stricture formation and chronic intestinal obstruction.

diverticulosis (dī″vĕr-tĭk″ū-lō′sĭs) [″ + Gr. *osis,* condition] Diverticula in the colon without inflammation or symptoms. Only a small percentage of persons with diverticulosis develop diverticulitis. SEE: illus.

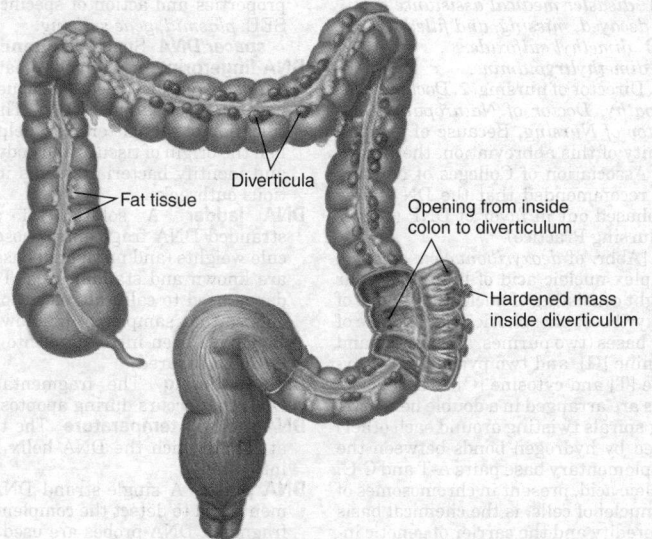

DIVERTICULA OF THE COLON

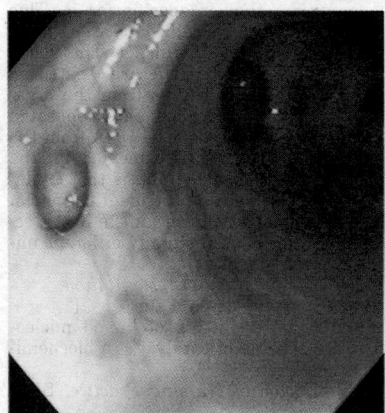

**DIVERTICULOSIS, SEEN
ENDOSCOPICALLY**

diverticulum (dĭ″vĕr-tĭk′ū-lŭm) *pl.* **diverticula** [L. *devertere*, to turn aside] An outpouching of the walls of a canal or organ. SEE: illus.

   d. of the colon An outpocketing of the colon. These may be asymptomatic until they become inflamed.

   d. of the duodenum A diverticulum commonly located near the entrance of the common bile or pancreatic duct.

   false d. A diverticulum without a muscular coat in the wall or pouch. This type of diverticulum is acquired.

   gastric d. A pulsion-type diverticulum usually on the lesser curvature of the esophagogastric junction.

   Meckel's d. SEE: *Meckel's diverticulum.*

   true d. A diverticulum involving all the coats of muscle in the pouch wall. It is usually congenital.

   Zenker's d. SEE: *Zenker's diverticulum.*

divulsion (dĭ-vŭl′shŭn) [L. *dis*, apart, + *vellere*, to pluck] A forcible pulling apart.

divulsor (dĭ-vŭl′sor) [L. *dis*, apart, + *vellere*, to pluck] A device for dilatation of a part, esp. the urethra.

Dix, Dorothea Lynde (dĭks) A Massachusetts schoolteacher (1802–1887) who crusaded for prison reform and for care of the mentally ill. She was responsible for founding many hospitals in the U.S., Canada, and several other countries. During the Civil War, she organized the nursing service of the Union armies.

dizziness [AS. *dysig*, foolish] **1.** Lightheadedness, unsteadiness, loss of spatial orientation, or loss of balance. **2.** Generalized weakness, faintness, or presyncope. **3.** Mental uncertainty; difficulty concentrating; feeling disconnected from one's normal sense of clarity or focus. SYN: *giddiness.* SEE: *vertigo.*

DJD *degenerative joint disease.*

DKA *Diabetic* **ketoacidosis**.

DL *Down low.*

dl *deciliter.*

DLCO *diffusion capacity of the lung.*

DM *diabetes mellitus; myotonic* **dystrophy**.

DMARD *disease-modifying antirheumatic drug.*

DMAT *disaster medical assistance team.*

DMF *decayed, missing, and filled* (teeth).

DMSO *dimethyl sulfoxide.*

DMT *dimethyltryptamine.*

DN 1. Director of nursing. **2.** *Doctor of Naprapathy, Doctor of Naturopathy,* and *Doctor of Nursing.* Because of the ambiguity of this abbreviation, the American Association of Colleges of Nursing has recommended that the DN degree be phased out in favor of DNP (Doctor of Nursing Practice).

DNA [Abbr. of *deoxyribonucleic acid*] A complex nucleic acid of high molecular weight consisting of nucleotides made of deoxyribose, phosphoric acid, and one of four bases (two purines, adenine [A] and guanine [G], and two pyrimidines, thymine [T] and cytosine [C]). The nucleotides are arranged in a double helix (two long spirals twisting around each other) joined by hydrogen bonds between the complementary base pairs A-T and C-G. Nucleic acid, present in chromosomes of the nuclei of cells, is the chemical basis of heredity and the carrier of genetic information for all organisms except the RNA viruses. SEE: *chromosome; gene; RNA; virus.*

   complementary DNA A double-stranded copy of a single-stranded RNA molecule, made by reverse transcriptase, an enzyme used by retroviruses such as HIV-1.

   covalently closed circular DNA ABBR: cccDNA. SEE: *cccDNA.*

   fecal D. Traces of nucleic acids found in the stool of people with colorectal cancers and polyps. Detection of DNA in stool has been proposed as an alternative to testing samples of stool for occult blood loss. Testing stool for traces of malignant DNA is a more sensitive screening test for intestinal cancer than screening stool samples for occult blood, but the test is expensive and is not as accurate a screening tool as colonoscopy. SYN: *stool DNA testing.*

   mitochondrial DNA ABBR: mtDNA. DNA found in mitochondria. It differs from nuclear DNA in its nucleotide sequences, its size (about 16.5 kb), and its source (it is derived solely from the egg, not the sperm). Variations in mtDNA point to the ways in which members of a related population differ from each other genetically.

   naked DNA DNA that has been modified to remove the proteins that normally surround it. It is used for genetic transfers and vaccine manufacture.

   recombinant DNA Segments of DNA from one organism artificially manipulated or inserted into the DNA of another organism through gene splicing. When the host's genetic material is reproduced, the transplanted genetic material is also copied. Gene splicing permits isolation and examination of the

properties and action of specific genes. SEE: *plasmid; gene splicing.*

   spacer DNA Spacer **sequence**.

DNA fingerprint A distinctive pattern of bands formed by repeating sequences of base pairs of satellite DNA. The identification of the pattern can help establish the origin of tissues and body fluids, and identify bacterial strains in infectious outbreaks.

DNA ladder A solution of double-stranded DNA fragments whose molecule weights (and number of base pairs) are known and standardized. The ladder is used to calibrate electrophoresis gels so that samples of unknown DNA that have been introduced into the gel can be measured.

DNA laddering The fragmentation of DNA that occurs during apoptosis.

DNA melting temperature The temperature at which the DNA helix loosens into a coil.

DNA probe A single-strand DNA fragment used to detect the complementary fragment. DNA probes are used widely in bacteriology. Recombinant DNA techniques are used to isolate, reproduce, and label a portion of the genetic material, DNA, from the nucleus of a microorganism that is specific for it. This fragment can be added to a specimen containing the organisms. The specimen and known DNA are treated so that the DNA strands from the organisms in the specimen are separated into single strands. The DNA from the specimen rejoins (is annealed to) the known labeled DNA and is thereby labeled. This permits the identification of a single pathogenic organism in a specimen that contains many different microorganisms.

DNAR *do not attempt resuscitation.*

DNAzyme (dē-ĕn-ā′zīm″) [″ + (en)zyme] A string of linked nucleotides capable of catalyzing a biochemical reaction.

DNP *Doctor of Nursing Practice.* SEE: *DN.*

DNR *Do not resuscitate.*

DNSc, DNS *Doctor of Nursing Science.*

DO *Doctor of Osteopathy; Doctor of Optometry.*

DOA *dead on arrival* (at a hospital).

dobutamine hydrochloride (dō-būt′ă-mēn) A synthetic beta-agonist whose primary effect is to increase cardiac contractility, with little effect on systemic vascular resistance. It produces less tachycardia than dopamine and has no effect on renal blood flow. It is of use in congestive heart failure and cardiogenic shock.

doctor [L. *docere,* to teach] **1.** The recipient of an advanced degree, such as doctor of medicine (MD), doctor of osteopathy (or DO), doctor of philosophy (Ph.D.), doctor of science (D.Sc.), doctor of nursing science (DNS), doctor of dental medicine (D.M.D.), doctor of education (Ed.D.), or doctor of divinity (DD). **2.** One who, after graduating from a medical, veterinary, or dental school, successfully passes an examination and is licensed by a state government to practice medicine, veterinary medicine, or dentistry. SEE: *optometry; osteopathy*. Because of the great variety of doctoral degrees, the use of the word *doctor* is sometimes confusing. This may be remedied by using the word *physician* when writing or speaking of those who possess an MD or DO (doctor of osteopathy) degree.

   barefoot d. A practitioner of traditional or native medicine in the People's Republic of China. Although barefoot doctors have not attended medical school, they are trained in the use of traditional Chinese therapies (e.g., the use of acupuncture and herbs), and in some Western medicines, such as first aid.

doctorally prepared Pert. to someone who possesses the highest academic degree, e.g., PhD., EdD. Such a degree is usually regarded by an institution of higher education as necessary for promotion and tenure.

Doctor of Nursing Practice ABBR: DNP. A practice-focused doctoral program designed to prepare experts in specialized advanced nursing practice. Such programs focus heavily on practice that is innovative and evidence-based, reflecting the application of credible research findings.

doctor-patient relationship All the interactions between a patient and a health care professional. These interactions establish the basis for interpersonal communication, trust, compliance, and satisfaction.

doctor shopping A colloquial term for the unethical and illegal practice of seeking care from multiple health care providers for an illicit purpose (often, but not solely, to obtain prescriptions for controlled substances).

doctrine (dok'trin) [Fr. *doctrine,* fr L. *doctrina,* teaching] A system of principles taught or advocated.

   borrowed servant d. The legal doctrine, a form of vicarious liability, that a patient care supervisor (e.g., an attending physician who oversees the work of a resident physician) may be held responsible for the negligent acts of a subordinate. SEE: *Captain of the Ship d.; vicarious liability.*

   Captain of the Ship d. The legal doctrine, a form of vicarious liability, that the legal responsibility for errors in a medical setting falls on the most highly trained or senior health care provider present at the time. This doctrine has been used to hold attending physicians or surgeons responsible for the negli-

gent acts of the surgical or anesthesia team. SEE: *borrowed servant d.; vicarious liability.*

   learned intermediary d. The legal doctrine that a pharmaceutical manufacturer need only advise or warn physicians, and not the public at large, of the potential hazards of the drugs it produces. Under this doctrine physicians act as agents for the public when they prescribe medications. Their education and clinical experience help them decide when to use a medication and when, because of safety concerns, to avoid its use. Exceptions to the doctrine are illustrated by direct-to-consumer drug advertising (e.g., on television or the Internet) in which pharmaceutical companies present their products directly to patients without the physician acting as intermediary. SYN: *learned intermediary rule.*

documentation (dŏk″ū-mĕn-tā′shŭn) **1.** Manuals, instruction books, and programs or help menus that provide guidance to a user. **2.** Recording pertinent medical information in a patient's medical record. The information may be handwritten on the patient's chart or keyboarded into an electronic medical record. SEE: *charting.*

DoD *Department of Defense.*

dog-ear (dog′ēr″) A colloquial term for an uneven wound edge, e.g., one created by faulty wound closure.

dogmatic (dog-mă′tĭk) **1.** Pert. to dogma or doctrine, e.g., of a religion. **2.** Pert. to the expression of opinions in an uncompromising, arrogant manner.

Döhle bodies (dē′lĕ) [Paul Döhle, Ger. pathologist, 1855–1928] A leukocyte inclusion in the periphery of a neutrophil. It is composed of liquefied endoplasmic reticulum and is frequently accompanied by toxic granulations. Döhle bodies are present in association with burns, severe or systemic infections, exposure to cytotoxic agents, uncomplicated pregnancy, trauma, and neoplastic diseases.

dol The unit of pain intensity registered on a dolorimeter.

dolicho-, dolich- [Gr. *dolichos,* long] Prefixes meaning *long.*

dolichocephalic (dŏl″ĭ-kō-sĭ-făl′ĭk) [Gr. *dolichos,* long, + *kephale,* head] Having a skull with a long anteroposterior diameter.

dolichocolon (dŏl″ĭ-kō-kō′lŏn) [″ + *kolon,* colon] An abnormally long colon.

dolichoectasia (dŏl″ĭ-kō-ek-tā′zh(ē-)ă) [*dolicho-* + *ectasia*] Abnormal lengthening and twisting of an artery or vein.

dolichofacial (dŏl″ĭ-kō-fā′shăl) Having a long face.

dolichohieric (dŏl″ĭ-kō-hī-ĕr′ĭk) [″ + *hieron,* sacred] Having a long, slender sacrum.

dolichomorphic (dŏl″ĭ-kō-mor′fĭk) [″ +

morphe, form] Pert. to a body type that is long and slender. SEE: *ectomorph.*

dolichopellic (dol″ĭ-kō-pel′ik) [Gr. *dolichos,* long + Gr. *pella,* wooden bowl, pelvis + *-ic*] Having an abnormally long or narrow pelvis in which the anteroposterior diameter is greater than the transverse diameter.

dolichosigmoid (dŏl″ĭ-kō-sĭg′moyd) [″ + *sigmoeides,* sigmoid] Having an abnormally long sigmoid colon.

dolor (dō′lor) *pl.* **dolores** [L.] Pain. This is one of the principal indications of inflammation. The others are rubor (redness), tumor (swelling), functio laesa (loss of function), and calor (heat).

dolorimeter (dō″lor-ĭm′ĭ-tĕr) [″ + Gr. *metron,* measure] A device that applies pressure evenly and reproducibly to a body part; it can be used to measure a patient's pain tolerance (e.g., in arthritis or fibromyalgia).

dolorogenic (dō″lor-ō-jĕn′ĭk) [″ + Gr. *gennan,* to produce] Causing pain.

domain (dō-mān″) In immunology, the portion of a protein, such as an immunoglobulin, that has a functional role independent of the remainder of the protein.

   lipid d. Lipid raft.

dome (dōm) [L *domus,* house] A semicircular or balloon-shaped weakness in the wall of an aneurysm.

domiciliary (dŏm″ĭ-sĭl′ē-ār″ē) [L. *domus,* house] Pert. to or conducted in a house.

domiciliary care facility A home providing mainly custodial and personal care for persons who do not require medical or nursing supervision, but may need assistance with activities of daily living because of a physical or mental disability. This may also be referred to as a sheltered living environment. SEE: *adult foster care.*

dominance (dom′ĭ-năns) [L. *dominans,* ruling] **1.** A genetic pattern of inheritance in which one of an allelic pair of genes has the capacity to suppress the expression of the other so that the first prevails in the heterozygote. **2.** Often, the preferred hand or side of the body, as in right-hand dominance. **3.** In psychiatry, the tendency to be commanding or controlling of others.

   cerebral d. The control of speech and handedness by one hemisphere of the brain. In 90% to 95% of human beings, the left cerebral hemisphere is functionally dominant; as a result most people are right-handed. A lesion (such as a stroke or tumor) to the left cerebral hemisphere of such people will produce aphasia and right-sided paralysis. Aphasia rarely occurs in right-handed people from a right cerebral lesion. In 60% of left-handed people with aphasia from a cerebral lesion, the left side is affected. In some left-handed patients, it is possible that language function is controlled partially by both the left and right cerebal hemispheres. SEE: *stroke.*

   ocular d. The use of one eye by choice for particular tasks such as aiming a gun. This may or may not be related to right-hand or left-hand dominance.

   strong d. In health care management, any strategy that provides a more effective and less costly solution to a problem.

   weak d. In health care management, a strategy that provides a more effective but also a more costly solution to a problem than an alternative.

dominant (dom′ĭ-nănt) [L. *dominari,* to be master, rule] **1.** In genetics, pert. to a trait or characteristic that is expressed in the offspring although it is carried on only one of the homologous chromosomes. **2.** Pert. to the preferred hand or side of the body, as in right-handed or left-handed. **3.** In psychiatry, pert. to the tendency to exercise command over or control others. SEE: *recessive.*

dominant hand SEE: under *hand.*

dominate (dom′ĭnāt″) [L. *dominari,* to master, control] **1.** In behavioral health, to control, govern, or wield authority over others. **2.** In health care administration or public health, to provide an option superior to others.

domoic acid (dŏ-mō′ik) SEE: under *acid.*

DON *Director of nursing.*

Donath-Landsteiner antibody (dō′nath″ land′stīn″ĕr) [Julius Donath, Austrian physician, 1870–1950; Karl L. Landsteiner, Austrian-born U.S. biologist, 1868–1943] A test for paroxysmal hemoglobinuria. Blood from the patient is cooled to 5°C, and a cold hemolysin in the plasma combines with the red blood cells if the patient has the disease. On warming, the sensitized red cells are hemolyzed by the complement normally present.

donation rate In organ transplantation the number of potential organ donors in a community divided by the number of actual donors.

donation service area In U.S. organ donation, a region of the country usually specified as containing certain counties from which all organs received from non-excluded donors may be obtained by an organ procurement organization.

dong quai, dang gui (dŏng kwī) [Chinese] An herbal remedy from the East Asian perennial herb *Angelica sinensis,* promoted for its palliative effects on the symptoms of menopause. Formal studies of the herb show that it is ineffective in relieving hot flashes.

Donnan equilibrium (don′ăn) [Frederick G. Donnan, Brit. chemist, 1871–1956] A condition in which an equilibrium is established between two solutions separated by a semipermeable membrane so that the sum of the anions and cations on one side is equal to that on the other side.

donor (dō′nŏr) [Fr. *doneur* fr L. *donator, giver, donor*] **1.** A person or animal that furnishes blood, tissue, or an organ to be used in another person. **2.** In chemistry, a compound that frees part of itself to unite with another compound called an acceptor.

artificial insemination d. ABBR: AID. A male who provides sperm to be used to fertilize a woman seeking to become pregnant.

blood d. One who gives blood (or its components) to be used for transfusion.

cadaveric d. One who donates an organ or tissue after his or her death.

directed d. A family member, friend, or significant other who gives blood, an organ, or tissue to another person to support a vital function or prevent death.

HLA-mismatched related d. Mismatched related **d.**

human leukocyte antigen matched unrelated d. Matched unrelated **d.**

hydrogen d. In oxidation-reduction reactions, a substance that gives up hydrogen atoms to another substance, the acceptor. SEE: *hydrogen acceptor*.

living d. One who donates an organ or tissue while he or she is still living. Living donors must be healthy and antigenically matched to the recipient.

matched unrelated d. ABBR: MUD. One who donates an organ or tissue (such as bone marrow stem cells) to another person with human leukocyte antigens identical to those of the organ recipient. SYN: *human leukocyte antigen matched unrelated d.*

mismatched related d. ABBR: MMRD. An organ or tissue donor who is a family member of the organ recipient but whose human leukocyte antigens are not identical to those of the recipient. In general, in organ transplantation, organ and recipient survival are highest when the donor and the recipient share the same HLA antigens. SYN: *HLA-mismatched related d.*

nondirected d. A person who donates blood, an organ, or tissue to the community at large and is unknown to the recipient.

related HLA-identical d. Related identical **d.**

related identical d. ABBR: RID. A family member who donates an organ or tissue (such as a kidney or bone marrow stem cells) to another family member who shares perfectly matched human leukocyte antigens. Organ transplantations from RIDs have higher success rates than transplants obtained from mismatched related donors (MMRDs) or from matched unrelated donors (MUDs). SYN: *related HLA-identical d.*

universal d. A person who has group O red blood cells. In a life-threatening emergency this person's cells can be transfused into any patient in need of red blood cells.

donor card A document used by a person who wishes to make an anatomical gift, at the time of his or her death, of an organ or other body part needed for transplantation. SEE: illus.; *transplantation*.

donor deferral registry SEE: under *registry*.

donor deferral tracking Donor deferral **registry**.

do not attempt resuscitation ABBR: DNAR. An order somewhat more precise than "do not resuscitate" (DNR). DNR implies that, if a resuscitation attempt is made, the patient can be revived. DNAR indicates that resuscitation efforts should not be attempted regardless of their expected outcome. SEE: *allow natural death; do not resuscitate*.

do not hospitalize ABBR: DNH. An advance directive that explicitly limits the

---

✂   **Fold Here** ↙

UNIFORM DONOR CARD Carry with your driver's license

Name:_____

In the hope that I may help others, I hereby make this anatomical gift, if medically acceptable, to take effect upon my death. The words and marks below indicate my desire:

I Give: (a)____any needed organ or tissues
(b)____only the following organs or tissues:

_____
specify organ(s) or tissue(s):
for the purpose of transplantation, therapy, medical research or education.

Limitations or special wishes, if any:_____

Signed by the donor and the following witnesses in the presence of each other:

Signature of the Donor _____ Date of Birth

City/State _____ Date Signed

Witness:_____

Witness:_____

This is a legal document under the uniform Anatomical Gift Act or similar laws.

NOTE: If you are under 19 years of age, please have your signature witnessed by a parent or guardian.

TO NEXT OF KIN: Please notify physician that I am a donor.

UNIFORM DONOR CARD

transfer of patients from the community to hospitals. Patients or their surrogate decision makers may choose DNH status when they hope to die in familiar surroundings or when they perceive further hospital care to be futile.

do not resuscitate ABBR: DNR. An order stating that a patient should not be revived. It may be written by a physician at the patient's request. If the patient is not competent or is unable to make such a decision, the family, legal guardian, or health care proxy may request and give consent for such an order to be written on the patient's chart and followed by the health care providers. The hospital or physician should have policies regarding time limits and reordering. SEE: *allow natural death; do not attempt resuscitation.*

Donovan body (don'ŏ-văn) [Charles Donovan, Irish physician, 1863–1951] The intracytoplasmic inclusion present in the microphages of a patient having granuloma inguinale caused by *Klebsiella granulomatis.*

donovanosis (dŏn"ŏ-vă-nō'sĭs) SEE: *granuloma inguinale.*

donut sign, doughnut sign One of several radiologic findings in which a halo surrounding an apparently empty space is present. It is seen, e.g., (a) on chest x-rays of hilar lymphadenopathy, when lymph nodes surround a bronchus; (b) in abdominal imaging, when a thickened bowel wall surrounds the intestinal lumen or an intussusception; and (c) in bone scans, when a rim of tracer uptake surrounds a "cold" center.

DOOR syndrome An acronym for an autosomal recessive syndrome characterized by congenital Deafness, Onychodystrophy (abnormal development of the nails), Osteodystrophy (abnormal development of bones), and mental Retardation.

dopa, DOPA (dōp'ă) A chemical substance, 3,4-dihydroxyphenylalanine, produced by the oxidation of tyrosine to tyrosinase. It is a precursor of catecholamines and melanin.

dopamine (dō'pă-mēn) A catecholamine synthesized by the adrenal gland. Synthetic dopamine (d. hydrochloride) is used to treat cardiogenic and septic shock. Dopamine affects nerves and blood vessels, among other tissues. In the brain, it works as a neurotransmitter, affecting cells that influence body movement, emotional states, and pleasure/reward. Its effects on receptors in the kidneys, blood vessels, and heart vary with the dose of the drug that is given. At low doses, about 2.0 to 10.0 μg/kg/min, it increases the force of heart muscle contraction, improves cardiac output, and increases heart rate. High doses (more than 10.0 μg/kg/min) ele-

vate blood pressure by causing vasoconstriction.

⚠ Dopamine hydrochloride should not be administered as a bolus or by intravenous push. The access used to infuse dopamine should be monitored frequently for evidence of extravasation. Other drugs should not be coadministered through the same tubing. Frequent monitoring of blood pressure, pulse, and renal function are required during the infusion.

dopaminergic (dō"pă-mēn-ĕr'jĭk) **1.** Caused by dopamine. **2.** Concerning tissues that are influenced by dopamine.

dopa-oxidase (dō"pă-ŏk'sĭ-dās) An enzyme in some epithelial cells that converts dopa to melanin.

dope A slang term used to describe almost any drug of abuse. SEE: *doping; blood doping.*

doping (dō'pĭng) In sports, the illicit use of a drug or blood product by an athlete in an effort to improve performance.

    blood d. The illicit technique of increasing one's hematocrit prior to athletic competition either by surreptitiously injecting erythropoietin or by autologous transfusion.

Doppler, Christian Andreas (dop'lĕr) Austrian mathematician and physicist, 1803–1853.

    D. echocardiography The use of ultrasound technology to determine the velocity of blood flow in different locations in the heart but esp. across the heart valves.

    D. effect The variation of the apparent frequency of waves, e.g., sound, light, and radio waves, with a change in distance between the source and the receiver. The frequency seems to increase as the distance decreases and to decrease as the distance increases.

    D. measurement of blood pressure and fetal heart rate The use of Doppler sound waves to determine fetal systolic blood pressure or the fetal heart rate.

    D. velocimetry The use of Doppler ultrasound to determine the speed of blood flow through arteries and veins. During pregnancy Doppler ultrasonography can determine whether blood flow rates are adequate in the uterine artery, placenta, and umbilical cord vessels. SEE: *uteroplacental insufficiency.*

Dorendorf sign (dor'ĕn-dorf") [Hans Dorendorf, Ger. physician, 1866–1953] A filling or fullness of the supraclavicular groove in an aneurysm of the aortic arch.

dormancy (dor'măn-sē) Temporary inactivity; e.g., a state of transiently reduced metabolic activity. **dormant,** *adj.*

dornase (dor'nās) Short for deoxyribonuclease.

d. alfa An enzyme that lessens the viscosity of sputum by cleaving DNA deposited in it. It is used to treat patients with cystic fibrosis, who have exceptionally thick pulmonary secretions that are hard to expectorate.

pancreatic d. Dornase prepared from beef pancreas, used to loosen thick pulmonary secretions.

dorsad (dōr′săd) [″ + *ad,* toward] Toward the back.

dorsal (dor′săl) [L. *dorsalis,* fr. L. *dorsum,* back] **1.** Pert. to the dorsum (back). **2.** Lying on the back with the face upward; supine. **3..** Toward the back of an organism.

dorsal cord stimulation SEE: under *stimulation.*

dorsal hump An enlargement or lump on the nasal bridge. In rhinoplasty a rasp is used to reduce it.

dorsalis (dor-sā′lĭs) [L.] Dorsal (i.e., pert. to the back).

dorsal reduction SEE: under *reduction.*

dorsal slit SEE: under *slit.*

dorsiduct (dor′sĭ-dŭkt″) [L. *dorsum,* back, + *ducere,* to lead] To draw toward the back or backward.

dorsiduction (dor″sĭ-dŭk′shŭn) Drawing toward the back.

dorsiflect (dor′sĭ-flĕkt) [″ + *flectere,* to bend] To bend backward.

dorsiflexion (dor″sĭ-flĕk′shŭn) Movement of a part at a joint to bend the part toward the dorsum, or posterior aspect of the body. Thus, dorsiflexion of the foot indicates movement backward, in which the foot moves toward its top, or dorsum; the opposite of plantar flexion. Dorsiflexion of the toes indicates a movement of the toes away from the sole of the foot. When the hand is extended, or bent backward at the wrist, it is dorsiflexed; this is the opposite of palmar flexion, or volar flexion of the wrist.

dorso-, dorsi-, dors- Prefixes meaning the *back* or *dorsum.*

dorsolateral (dor″sō-lăt′ĕr-ăl) Pert. to the back and side. SEE: *posterolateral.*

dorsoplantar (dor″sō-plăn′tăr) [″ + *planta,* sole of the foot] From the top to the bottom of the foot.

dorsoventral (dor″sō-vĕn′trăl) Concerning the back and frontal surfaces of the body.

dorsum (dor′sŭm) [L.] The back or posterior surface of a part; in the foot, the top of the foot.

dosage (dō′sĭj) [Gr. *dosis,* a giving] **1.** A specified or prescribed quantity of any therapeutic intervention. **2.** The determination of the prescribed quantity of a therapeutic agent.

stress d. A larger dosage of a medication (esp. a hormone) than is usually given to a patient to help that patient survive an acute or life-threatening illness. SYN: *stress dose.*

dose (dōs) [Gr. *dōsis,* a giving] **1.** The amount of medicine or radiation administered. **2.** The measurable exposure to an agent, e.g., to a poison, a quantity of radiation, or an irritant in the environment.

absorbed d. **1.** Radiation absorbed **d.** **2.** The amount of a substance ingested, inhaled, or taken up through any protective surface into the body.

air d. The intensity of radiation measured in air at the target.

birth d. Any dose, e.g., of a vaccine, administered to a neonate. The term is commonly used to describe a neonatal injection of hepatitis B vaccine.

bolus d. A quantity of fluid or medicine given intravenously at a controlled, rapid rate.

booster d. SEE: *booster.*

collective d. SEE: *cumulative d.*

cumulative d. **1.** The total medication or radiation dose to which an organism is exposed after repeated treatments. **2.** The total ionizing radiation dose resulting from repeated exposures to an occupationally exposed individual over a period of time. This dose can be calculated for whole-body acute exposure or for specific organs or body parts, e.g., the hands. **3.** The amount of a drug present in the body after repeated doses.

curative d. ABBR: CD. The dose required to heal an illness or disease.

depth d. The actual amount of radiation exposure at a specific point below the surface of the body.

dialysis d. The percentage by which blood urea nitrogen (BUN) is reduced during renal dialysis. Inadequate BUN reductions have been linked to increases in patient care costs, hospitalizations, and increased risk of death in patients with chronic renal failure. SEE: *blood* urea *nitrogen.*

divided d. Fractional portions of a dose administered at specified intervals. For example, a patient may be given 2 g of cephalexin daily, divided as 500 mg orally every 6 hr.

equianalgesic d. A dose of one form of analgesic drug equivalent in pain-relieving effect to another analgesic. In pain control, this equivalence permits substitution of one analgesic to avoid undesired side effects from another.

equivalent d. ABBR: HT. The biologically active dose of radiation damage that a particular absorbed radiation dose will have on living cells and tissues.

erythema d. Minimal erythema **d.**

fatal d. A dose that kills. SEE: *median lethal d.*

infective d. The number of infectious organisms, esp. bacteria or viruses, that will cause disease in a healthy organism.

lethal d. The dose of a substance that

results in the death of cells, tissues, or the organism.

lethal d. low ABBR: LDlo. The lowest dose of a substance that will kill at least one exposed organism.

maintenance d. The dose required to sustain a desired effect.

maximum d. The largest dose that is safe to administer.

maximum permissible d. ABBR: MPD. The highest dose of radiation to which a person may be exposed over 1 year.

⚠️ Each U.S. state sets limits on exposure to ionizing radiation. For example, for an adult over 18, the MPD is typically 5 rem (50 mSv). For a pregnant female, the MPD is limited to 0.5 rem (5 mSv).

maximum tolerated d. ABBR: MTD. The most extensive exposure to a treatment that a patient may receive before he or she experiences unbearable side effects.

median infective d. ABBR: ID_{50}. An infective dose that causes disease in half the subjects exposed to it.

median lethal d. ABBR: LD_{50}. The amount of a substance, bacterium, or toxin that will kill 50% of the animals exposed to it. Dose is usually calculated on amount of material given per gram or kilogram of body weight or amount per unit of body surface area. SEE: *minimum lethal d.*

minimal erythema d., minimum erythema dose ABBR: MED. The shortest exposure to ultraviolet radiation that produces reddening of the skin within 1 to 6 hr and disappears in 24 hr. The minimal erythemal dose is used to calculate the duration of therapeutic exposure to ultraviolet light. For treatment using a "hot" ultraviolet lamp (UV-A or UV-B), the dose is calculated at a distance of 30 in. The minimal erythemal dose for "cold" ultraviolet (UV-C) is standardized at 30 to 38 sec at a distance of 1 in. SYN: *erythema d.; threshold d.* SEE: table.

⚠️ Burning, edema, and peeling occur at doses at or above the second degree erythemal dose.

minimum d. The smallest effective dose.

minimum lethal d. The smallest amount of a substance capable of producing death. SEE: *median lethal d.*

nursing d. 1. The number of nurses in the work force divided by the population of the community at large. 2. The number of nurses available for clinical

Ultraviolet Treatment Dosages

Dose	Description
Suberythemal dose (SED)	No erythema
Minimal erythemal dose (MED)	Smallest dose that produces erythema within 1 to 6 hr and disappears within 24 hr
First degree erythemal dose (E_1)	Erythema lasts for 1 to 3 days. Some scaling of the skin is present. E_1 is approximately 2.5 times the MED.
Second degree erythemal dose (E_2)	Erythema with associated edema, peeling, and pigmentation. E_2 is approximately 5 times the MED.
Third degree erythemal dose (E_3)	Severe erythema and burning with associated blistering, peeling, and edema. E_3 is approximately 10 times the MED.

responsibilities, divided by the quantity of those duties.

percentage depth d. In radiation therapy, the ratio of the absorbed dose at a given depth to the absorbed dose at a fixed reference depth. It is dependent on four factors: energy, depth, field size, and source-to-skin distance.

primary d. An initial, large dose given to provide a high blood level as soon as possible.

radiation d. 1. Energy (joules) deposited by radiation in 1 kg of body tissue. 2. The exposure of a biological system to radiation, measured in rems or sieverts. 3. Radioactivity, measured in curies or becquerels. 4. SEE: *radiation absorbed d.*

radiation absorbed d. ABBR: rad. The quantity of ionizing radiation, measured in rad or gray (Gy), absorbed by any material, e.g., a person, per unit mass of matter. One Gy equals 100 rad. SYN: *absorbed d.*

shock d. In cardioversion and defibrillation, the energy in joules selected to terminate an abnormal heart rhythm.

skin d. A radiation dose to the skin including secondary radiation from backscatter.

stress dose Stress **dosage.**

sublethal d. A dose containing not quite enough of a toxin or noxious substance to cause death.

test d. 1. A low dose of a medication given to assess its safety or tolerability.

2. A small dose given to determine its precise effect on living tissues.

therapeutic d. The dose required to produce the desired effect.

threshold d. SEE: *minimal erythema d.*

tissue culture infective d. ABBR: $TCID_{50}$. The dose that will produce a cytopathic effect in 50% of the cultures inoculated.

tolerance d. The dose of a drug or physical agent, e.g., radiation, that will not cause perceptible or immediate injury. This dose will vary among individuals.

toxic d. A poisonous dose.

unit d. A dose of medicine prepared in an individual packet for convenience, safety, or monitoring. SYN: *monodose*.

dose area product ABBR: DAP. In nuclear medicine and radiology, the dose of radiation delivered to a patient or area of tissue multiplied by the area of skin exposed. The DAP gives an estimate of the likelihood of skin damage from a specific dose of radiation. It is measured in gray square centimeters.

dose escalation A progressive increase in the strength of any treatment (e.g., a drug or a radiation dose), to improve its tolerability or maximize its effect.

dose length product ABBR: DLP. The sum of the radiation to which a patient or area of tissue is exposed during the taking of a series of images.

dose-ranging study SEE: under *study*.

dose reconstruction SEE: under *reconstruction*.

dose response SEE: under *response*.

dosha (dō′shă) [Sanskrit, *dosha*, fault, disease, bodily humor] In ayurvedic medicine, one of three bodily humors or energies that link the body, its elemental liquids, and the mind. SEE: *kapha*.

dosimeter (dō-sĭm′ĭ-tĕr) [″ + *metron*, measure] A device for measuring the output of any ionizing radiation.

dosimetric (dō″sĭ-mĕt′rĭk) Pert. to dosimetry.

dosimetrist (dō-sĭm′ĕ-trĭst″) In radiation oncology, an allied health professional who designs a treatment plan based on the prescribed radiation dose and the field to which the treatment will be administered. The work involves mathematical precision, knowledge of physics, and technical expertise with radiation-generating equipment.

dosimetry (dō-sĭm′ĕ-trē) [″ + *metron*, measure] Measurement of doses.

dosing weight SEE: under *weight*.

DOT *directly observed therapy*.

dotage (dōt′ij) [ME. *doten*, to be silly] A pejorative term for cognitive impairment.

double (dŭb′l) [L. *duplus*, twofold] Duplicate, or combining two qualities.

double balloon endoscopy SEE: under *endoscopy*.

double-blind, double-blinded (dŭb′ĕl-blīnd′) Pert. to a method, study, or clinical trial in which neither the subjects nor the investigators know the identities of the subjects nor what treatment or medication, if any, the subjects receive. A double-blind study attempts to eliminate observer and subject bias. SEE: *blind* (2); *single-blind*.

double diabetes SEE: under *diabetes*.

double effect In ethics, the doctrine or principle explaining under what conditions one may perform an act that has both good and bad consequences. In medicine, an example of the double effect is that the medications used in palliative care may have the side effect of hastening death even though the intent of the practitioner is to achieve relief of symptoms and not euthanasia.

double personality SEE: under *personality*.

double reading Evaluation of the results of an examination, especially a mammogram, by two individuals. SEE: *mammography*.

double uterus SEE: under *uterus*.

douche (doosh) [Fr. douche fr Italian *doccia*, water pipe] A current of vapor or a stream of water directed against a body part. A douche may be plain water or a medicated solution. It may be for personal hygiene or treatment of a local condition.

air d. An air current directed onto the body for therapeutic purposes, usually directed to the tympanum for opening the eustachian tube.

nasal d. An injection of fluid into the nostril with fluid escaping through the nasopharynx out of the mouth. The patient should keep the mouth open and the glottis closed to prevent fluid from entering the throat and bronchus, and should not blow his or her nose during the treatment. The force of the douche must be moderate. The container should not be suspended more than 6 in (9.2 cm) above the patient. An atomized spray works more quickly.

vaginal d. Gentle, low-pressure irrigation of the vagina. Common protocols for antiseptic irrigations require preparing and administering 1000 to 2000 mL of 105°F (40.5°C) povidone-iodine solution while maintaining standard precautions. For hemostasis, solution temperature is increased to 118°F or 120°F (47.8° to 48.9°C). The container should be elevated up to 2 ft (61 cm) above the woman's pelvis to allow slow, low-pressure flow of the solution.

NOTE: The vagina, like many other areas of the body, can cleanse itself. Thus there is very little reason for a normal, healthy woman to use a vaginal douche. Douching can upset the balance of the vaginal flora and change the vaginal pH, thus predisposing the woman to vaginitis. There is no evidence that a postcoital vaginal douche is effective as a contraceptive.

In at least one investigation, vaginal douching has been shown to be a risk factor for pelvic inflammatory disease (PID). The more frequently the subjects douched, the more likely they were to have PID.

Douglas, James (dŭg′lăs) Scottish anatomist, 1675–1742

D. cul-de-sac The peritoneal space or pouch that lies behind the uterus and in front of the rectum. SYN: *cul-de-sac* (2); *Douglas pouch; rectouterine pouch*.

D. line A crescent-shaped line at the lower limit of the posterior sheath of the rectus abdominis muscle. It is sometimes indistinct.

D. pouch   Douglas cul-de-sac.

Douglas bag (dŭg′lăs) [Claude G. Douglas, Brit. physiologist, 1882–1963] A container, usually a bag made of flexible material, for collecting expired air. It is used in investigating respiratory function and physiology.

doula (doo′lä) **1.** A woman trained to provide emotional support, guidance, and comfort measures during childbirth. **2.** Highest ranking ancient Greek female servant who assisted women during childbirth.

dowager's hump (dow′ă-jerz) Cervical lordosis with dorsal kyphosis due to slow loss of bone (i.e., osteoporosis). This may occur at any age but is seen most commonly in elderly women.

dowel (dow′ĭl) [ME. *dowle*, peg] A fastening pin, used, e.g., in orthopedic surgery or in dental casting.

down 1. Lanugo, the fine hairs of the skin of the newborn. **2.** The fine soft feathers of the young of some birds and the small feathers underneath the large feathers of adult birds, particularly waterfowl. It is used in clothing to give protection from the cold.

downcode (down′kōd″) To assign a lower billing code than usual to a patient visit.

down low, downlow (down′lō″) [Slang, short for *on the down low,* to keep a secret, in secret] ABBR: DL. **1.** Keeping an act, a plan, or some information secret. **2.** Leading a double life, esp. with respect to sexual preferences. It usually refers to men who represent themselves publicly as strictly heterosexual but secretly have sex with men.

downregulate (down-rĕg′ū-lāt″) To inhibit or suppress the normal response of an organ or system (e.g., the immune system or the central nervous system).

downsizing (down′sīz″ing) Downstaging.

downstaging (down′stāj″ing) Decreasing the size, extent of metastases, and/or lymph node involvement of a tumor

by means of anticancer therapy. SYN: *downsizing.* SEE: *debulking.*

downstream (down′strēm″) **1.** In descriptions of genetic material, pert. to codons or base pairs that are on the 3′ side of a specific gene. **2.** In health care economics, pert. to the consequences of an action, e.g., an increase in the risk of stroke as the consequent cost of not treating hypertension.

Down syndrome (down) [J. Langdon Down, Brit. physician, 1828–1896] The clinical consequences of having three copies of chromosome 21. The condition is marked by mild to moderate mental retardation and physical characteristics that include a sloping forehead, low-set ears with small canals, and short broad hands with a single palmar crease ("simian" crease). Cardiac valvular disease and a tendency to develop Alzheimer-like changes in the brain are common consequences of the syndrome. The syndrome is present in about 1 in 700 births in the U.S. and is more common in women over age 34 or when the father is older than 42. In women who conceive after age 45, the incidence rises dramatically. SYN: *trisomy 21.* SEE: *amniocentesis; chorionic villus sampling; mosaicism; Nursing Diagnoses Appendix.*

Women at high risk of giving birth to a child with Down syndrome are those over 34, those who have had a previous child with the syndrome (1%-2%), and those who themselves have Down syndrome (pregnancy is rare in this condition, although females may menstruate and be fertile). In addition, there is a high risk of having a child with Down syndrome when there is parental mosaicism with a 21 trisomic cell population.

ETIOLOGY: Patients with Down syndrome have an extra chromosome, usually number 21 or 22.

DIAGNOSIS: Amniocentesis or chorionic villus sampling can be used to diagnose the syndrome early in pregnancy.

GENETIC MOSAICISM: The possibility of mosaicism should be explored when children who exhibit classic physical characteristics of Down syndrome later demonstrate normal or near-normal developmental cognitive abilities.

PATIENT CARE: The importance of amniocentesis in detecting the syndrome is explained to the at-risk pregnant woman and her partner or support person. Amniocentesis is recommended for women over age 34 even with a negative family history, as well as for a pregnant woman of any age when she or the father carries a translocated chromosome. Procedural and sensation information to communicate includes that the test can be conducted anytime after the 14th week of pregnancy (when sufficient amniotic fluid is present), only a small amount of fluid will be removed, and the potential for complications to the fetus or woman is less than 1%.

Throughout the procedure, emotional support is provided, and explanations are reinforced. Following the procedure, fetal heart rate is monitored for 30 min., and the woman is assessed for uterine contractions. If test results are positive, the patient is referred for genetic counseling. If she elects to have a therapeutic abortion, physical and emotional support are provided throughout and after the procedure, and postprocedure care is explained.

If the pregnancy continues, the patient and her partner must understand the multisystem anomalies that may occur. After delivery, the infant is assessed for the major clinical manifestations, including physical characteristics and congenital anomalies. Health care professionals establish a trusting relationship with the parents, and parental responses, including grief, are anticipated, and support is provided. Encouraging the parents to hold and nurture their child is of great importance. The family is taught about management of the infant, beginning with possible feeding problems related to poor sucking ability and the risk for upper respiratory infections. A social worker may explore with the family available support systems and social and financial resources, making referrals to community agencies as appropriate.

The child with Down syndrome requires ongoing assessment for mental retardation, social development, sensory problems, physical growth, sexual development, and congenital anomalies. IQ ranges are usually between 30 and 70, but with social performance above the expected level. Early and maximal environmental stimulation positively affects intellectual function. Genitalia may be poorly developed, with delayed puberty; males are infertile, have low serum testosterone, and may have undescended testicles. The parents are advised that surgery may be indicated for correction of serious congenital anomalies. Such surgeries, and the use of antibiotics for recurring infections, have improved life expectancy for these children.

Most children with Down syndrome are cared for at home and attend special education classes with occasional mainstreaming. Balanced nutrition and exercise are increasingly important to prevent obesity. All Down syndrome children should be checked for atlantoaxial (first cervical vertebra or atlas and second cervical vertebra or axis) instability. The child's participation in self-care, recreational, vocational, educational, and social opportunities to his or her maximum capabilities is encouraged. Other children in the family require emotional support from parents and trusted teachers and counselors. Adult patients may live in a group home facility or work in a sheltered workshop. The family also is encouraged and assisted to investigate opportunities for and with the child, such as Special Olympics, sheltered workshops, and residential care settings, and to use available supportive services and organizations, such as the National Down Syndrome Congress or the National Down Syndrome Society (800-221-4602; www.ndss.org).

doxazosin (dŏk″să′z-ă-sīn) A peripherally acting antiadrenergic administered orally to treat hypertension and to manage the symptoms of benign prostatic hyperplasia.

DP *Digital pathology.*

2,3-D.P.G. *2,3-diphosphoglycerate.*

DR *reaction of degeneration; digital radiography.*

dr *drachm; dram.*

Dr. *Doctor.*

dracotoxin (drā′kō-tŏk-sĭn) [Gr. *Draco,* an ancient Athenian who promulgated laws, + *toxikon,* poison] A 105-kilodalton protein isolated from the glands of the weever fish, a common bottom-dwelling poisonous fish. The protein destroys blood cells and is damaging to nerves.

dracunculiasis (dră-kŭng″kyŭ-lī′ă-sĭs, -sēz″) *pl.* **dracunculiases** [*Dracunculus* + *-iasis*] Infestation with the nematode *Dracunculus medinensis.* SEE: *guinea worm.*

dracunculosis (dră-kŭng″kū-lō′sĭs) Dracunculiasis.

Dracunculus (dră-kŭng′kyŭ-lŭs) [L. *dracunculus,* small dragon] A genus of parasitic nematodes of the family Dracunculidae.

D. medinensis SEE: *guinea worm.*

draft, draught A dose of liquid medicine intended to be taken all at once.

drain (drān) **1.** An exit opening or a tube in a body space, used to evacuate unwanted blood, cellular debris, fluids, or pus. **2.** To draw off a fluid.

cigarette d. A drain made by covering a small strip of gauze with rubber.

Jackson-Pratt d. Jackson-Pratt drain.

Penrose d. SEE: *Penrose drain.*

surgical d. A drain that withdraws blood, pus, or other fluids from an operative site. It may be placed in an abscess, e.g., to speed recovery from a localized infection, or in a cyst or seroma, to remove collected fluids and cells. Drains may also be inserted into obstructed organs to relieve pressure resulting from fluid buildup within the organs. Surgical drains are composed of a variety of substances, such as latex or plastic.

drainage (drān′ĭj) The flow or withdrawal of fluids, such as blood, infused saline, pus, and collected debris, from a cavity, organ, surgical site, or wound. SEE: *autodrainage; drain.*

active d. Drainage in which negative pressure is maintained in the drainage tube. It is used in treating pneumothorax and in certain types of drains or catheters in the intestinal tract, body cavity, or surgical wound. SYN: *negative pressure d.; suction d.*

autogenic d. A diaphragmatic breathing pattern used by patients with respiratory illnesses (e.g., cystic fibrosis, bronchiectasis) to clear the lungs of mucus and other secretions. Various techniques are used, all of which combine positive reinforcement of deep breathing and voluntary cough suppression for as long as possible before evacuating the airways of mucus.

capillary d. Drainage by means of capillary attraction.

chest d. Placement of a drainage tube in the chest cavity, usually in the pleural space. The tube is used to drain air, fluid, or blood from the pleural space so the compressed and collapsed lung can expand. The tube is connected to a system that produces suction. This helps to remove the material from the pleural space and also prevents air from being sucked into the space.

closed d. Drainage of a wound or body space into a self-contained, sealed collecting system.

lymphatic d. Manual lymphatic **d.**

manual lymphatic d. ABBR: MLD. Gentle massage techniques used to correct localized lymphedema, e.g., in patients who have swelling of an arm after mastectomy with lymph node dissection. The therapist assists lymphatic flow from the extremity toward the heart. SYN: *lymphatic d.*

negative pressure d. Active **d.**

open d. Drainage of a wound or body cavity using absorbent materials or catheters that are in contact with the ambient conditions outside the patient.

postural d. A passive airway clearance technique in which patients are positioned so that gravity will assist the removal of secretions from specific lobes of the lung, bronchi, or lung cavities. It can be used for patients with pneumonia, chronic bronchitis, cystic fibrosis, bronchiectasis, inhaled foreign bodies, before surgery for lobectomy, or in any patient having difficulty with retained secretions. A side effect of the treatment in some patients is gastroesophageal reflux. SEE: illus.

PATIENT CARE: Physical tolerance to the procedure is evaluated. The respiratory therapist teaches and assists the patient in the procedure, as ordered, by positioning the patient for effective drainage of the affected lung region(s). The patient is encouraged to remove secretions with an effective cough. To decrease the risk of aspiration, the patient should not perform the procedure after meals. Chest vibration and percussion are often performed at the same time to assist movement of retained secretions in the lung.

suction d. Active **d.**

tidal d. A method, controlled mechanically, of filling the bladder with solution by gravity and periodically emptying the bladder with a catheter. It is usually used when the patient lacks bladder control as in injuries or lesions of the spinal cord.

drainage tube A tube that, when inserted into a cavity, facilitates removal of fluids.

drained weight SEE: under *weight.*

dram (dram) [L. *drachma,* fr Gr. *drachmē,* a Gr. unit of weight] ABBR: dr. SYMB: ℨ. A unit of weight in the apothecaries', avoirdupois, and troy weights. SYN: *drachm.*

drape (drāp) [F. *drap,* cloth] A covering, usually of cloth, plastic, or sterile paper, used to cover body parts (e.g., during surgical operations or the examination of patients).

drapetomania (drăp″ĕt-ō-mā′nē-ă) [Gr. *drapetes,* runaway, + *mania,* madness] Wandering behavior; an uncontrollable urge to travel.

drastic [Gr. *drastikos,* effective] **1.** Excessively vigorous; said in the past of some medications. **2.** A very active cathartic, usually producing many explosive bowel movements accompanied by pain and tenesmus. The use of this type of cathartic is not advisable.

draught (drăft) [ME. *draught,* a pulling] **1.** A drink. **2.** Liquid drawn into the mouth. **3.** A breeze produced by wind or a fan. **4.** Draft.

Dravet syndrome (dra-vā′) [Charlotte Dravet, Fr. psychiatrist and epileptologist, b. 1936] A severe form of childhood epilepsy, often beginning in the first year of life as a febrile seizure. As the affected children grow up, they develop myoclonic jerking, and their seizures may become refractory to treatment. SYN: *severe myoclonic epilepsy of infancy.*

Draw-a-Person test A nonverbal test used to assess intelligence and to screen for emotional and behavioral disorders. It was developed in 1967 by Karen Machover. The test subject is asked to draw an image of a man, a woman, and oneself. The images drawn are assessed according to several criteria for their complexity, completeness, and other qualities. SYN: *Machover test.*

drawer sign Drawer test.

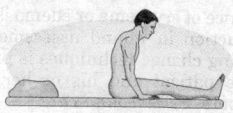

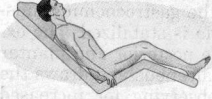

POSTURAL DRAINAGE OF LUNGS

posterior apical segments of the right and left upper lobes

anterior apical segments of the right and left upper lobes

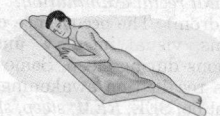

anterior apical segments of the right and left upper lobes

anterior segments of the right and left upper lobes

posterior segment of the left upper lobe

posterior segment of the right upper lobes

left lingula

right middle lobe

anterior basal segments of the right and left lung

posterior basal segments of the right and left lung

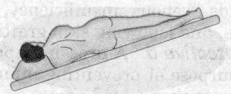

left lateral segment of the lower lobes

superior segment of the right and left lower lobes

drawer test (dro'(ĕ)r) Determination of the instability of ligaments by forcibly displacing one bone or structure relative to another.

1. Assessment of the cruciate ligament(s) of the knee. The knee is flexed to 90° with the foot stabilized on the examination table. The examiner applies an anterior, then a posterior, force against the upper tibia, perpendicular to the long axis of the leg. An increased glide, anterior or posterior, of the tibia is caused by rupture of the anterior or posterior cruciate ligament, respectively.

2. Assessment of the anterior talofibular ligament of the ankle. The foot is placed in its neutral position, the knee

is flexed to a minimum of 20° to release the tension of the gastrocnemius muscle, and the tibia is stabilized. The examiner cups the posterior and plantar surface of the calcaneus and draws the foot forward, observing for increased displacement of the lateral foot and talus relative to the opposite extremity. These findings suggest rupture of the ligament. SYN: *drawer sign*.

DRE *digital rectal examination.*

dream (drēm) The occurrence of ideas, emotions, visual imagery, and other sensations during sleep. Some dreams may be recalled on awakening; others may not be. SEE: *REM; sleep; sleep disorder; wet dream.*

Interpretation of the meaning of dreams has been of interest to humans for millennia and to psychoanalysts for the past century. The idea that a dream conceals a meaning buried deep in the subconscious is probably mistaken and is difficult to confirm scientifically although it is still accepted by many psychoanalysts. Less controversial are the research results correlating changes in the electroencephalogram and rapid eye movements (REM) during sleep with dream activity.

lucid d. A dream or nightmare in which a person becomes aware that he or she is dreaming.

wet d. Nocturnal **emission.**

dream enactment Making purposeful or semipurposeful movements in sleep, such as punching, flailing, or fighting with one's bed partner. It typically occurs during REM sleep and is characteristically found in some dementia patients or sometimes as a side effect of a psychically directed medication.

dream state The state of diminished consciousness in which the surroundings are perceived as if in a dream.

drench A dose of medicine that is administered to an animal by pouring it into its mouth.

DRESS *Drug rash with eosinophilia and systemic symptoms.*

dressing [O.Fr. *dresser,* to prepare] A covering, protective or supportive, for diseased or injured parts.

PATIENT CARE: The procedure and expected sensations are explained to the patient. His or her privacy is ensured, and necessary supplies are assembled. Strict aseptic technique is followed during dressing changes, and dressings are properly disposed of in biohazard containers. Personnel must wash their hands before and after the procedure. The wound or incision and dressing are assessed for the presence and character of any drainage. The mnemonic COCA (color, odor, consistency, amount) is useful in assessing and documenting drainage. The condition of the wound or suture line is also checked, and the presence of erythema or edema is noted. Instruction in wound assessment and dressing change techniques is provided to the patient and his or her family members. SEE: *wound care.*

absorbent d. A dressing of cotton gauze or other absorbent material.

antiseptic d. A dressing consisting of gauze permeated with an antiseptic solution.

dry d. A dressing consisting of dry gauze, absorbent cotton, or other dry material.

film d. A transparent wound covering, made of polyurethane, that enables health care providers to visually inspect an injured part as it heals. The dressing allows water vapor to escape from the wound but does not permit liquids or bacteria to enter.

foam d. An opaque polyurethane dressing that is permeable to vapors but partially occlusive to liquids. It is typically used to cover wounds over bony ridges or near inflamed skin.

hydrocolloid d. A flexible dressing made of an adhesive, gumlike (hydrocolloid) material such as karaya or pectin covered with a water-resistant film. The dressing keeps the wound surface moist, but, because it excludes air, it may promote anaerobic bacterial growth. It should not be used on wounds that are, or are suspected to be, infected. The directions that come with the dressing should be followed.

nonadherent d. A dressing that has little or no tendency to stick to dried secretions from the wound.

occlusive d. A dressing that seals a wound completely to prevent infection from outside and to prevent inner moisture from escaping through the dressing.

periodontal d. Periodontal pack.

pressure d. A dressing used to apply pressure to the wound. It may be used for arterial and venous punctures and wounds, venous insufficiency, venous ulcers, and following skin grafting.

protective d. A dressing applied for the purpose of preventing injury or infection to the treated part.

water d. A dressing consisting of gauze, cotton, or similar material that is kept wet by the application of sterilized water.

wet-to-dry d. A dressing consisting of gauze moistened with prescribed solution (e.g., sterile saline) applied directly and conforming to the wound and covered with dry gauze pads and a bandage. Gentle removal of the dressing after it has dried provides some degree of débridement of the wound; the process is then repeated at intervals.

dressing stick An assistive device designed to permit independent dressing by persons with limited range of motion. SYN: *dressing wand.*

dressing wand Dressing stick.

Dressler syndrome (dres'lĕr) [William Dressler, U.S. physician, 1890–1960] Postmyocardial infarction syndrome, characterized by pleuritic chest pain, pericarditis, fever, and leukocytosis.

DRG *diagnosis-related group.*

drift (drift) Aimless movement, or movement that falls away from an established norm.

    antigenic d. A minor change in the protein marker or antigen on an organism. Small changes in the antigenic surface markers of some microorganisms (such as the influenza virus) occur from year to year. Vaccinations against the virus are adapted annually to combat these changes and prevent epidemic infection. SEE: *antigenic* **shift**.

    genetic d. The chance variation of genetic frequency, seen most often in a small population.

    mesial d. The natural tendency for teeth to move in a mesial direction within the dental arch to maintain tight interproximal contacts between adjacent teeth. SYN: *physiological tooth* **movement**. SEE: *pathological tooth* **migration**; *physiological tooth* **migration**; *tooth* **movement**.

    pronator d. Inability to hold an arm up against the effects of gravity. It is a common finding in patients with motor weakness, as from a stroke.

    ulnar d. A joint abnormality at the metacarpophalangeal joints, resulting from chronic synovitis, and frequently seen in rheumatoid arthritis. In this condition, the long axis of the fingers deviates in an ulnar direction with respect to the metacarpals.

drill A device for rotating a sharp and shaped cutting instrument, used for preparing teeth for restoration and in orthopedics. SEE: *bur.*

Drinker respirator (drĭng'kĕr) [Philip Drinker, U.S. engineer in industrial hygiene, 1894–1972] An obsolete apparatus in which alternating positive and negative air pressure on the patient's thoracic area was used to produce artificial respiration by allowing the air in the otherwise immobile lung to be alternately filled with air and emptied. This device is commonly called an *iron lung.*

drip [ME. *drippen,* to drip] **1.** To fall in drops. **2.** To instill a liquid slowly, drop by drop.

    gravity d. Infusion of an intravenous solution by hanging the source of the solution above the patient and controlling the rate of flow with a manually operated clamp.

    intravenous d. Slow injection of a solution into a vein a drop at a time.

    Murphy d. Slow rectal instillation of a fluid drop by drop.

    nasal d. A method of administering fluid slowly to dehydrated babies by means of a catheter with one end placed through the nose into the esophagus.

    postnasal d. A condition due to rhinitis or sinusitis in which a discharge flows from the nasopharynx region into the oropharynx.

drive (drīv) [AS. *drifan*] The force or impulse to act.

drive control One of various devices and adapted equipment, including hand or foot controls, for modifying a motor vehicle for use by persons with physical disability.

driver rehabilitation therapist A specialist who evaluates and provides training to increase driving independence in persons with physical, cognitive, or perceptual deficits. A trained expert in driver rehabilitation is known as a *certified driver rehabilitation specialist* (CDRS).

driving while intoxicated ABBR: DWI. A crime defined as the operation of a motor vehicle after the use of any substance, including alcohol or illicit drugs, that may impair one's judgment, cognition, coordination, reflexes, or ability to react appropriately in traffic. Most states rely on a standard test that includes both observable impairment in motor function, speech, and balance and an elevated blood alcohol level or a positive screening test for other intoxicants. Also called *driving under the influence.*

dromomania (drŏ″mō-mā′nē-ă) [Gr. *dromos,* a running, + *mania,* madness] An uncontrolled impulse to wander.

dromotropic (drŏ″mō-trŏp′ĭk) [″ + *tropikos,* a turning] Affecting the conductivity of nerve or muscle fibers. SEE: *inotropic.*

dronabinol (drō-năb′ĭ-nol) The principal psychoactive substance present in *Cannabis sativa* (marijuana). SEE: *marijuana.*

-dronate A suffix used in pharmacology to designate a drug that alters the metabolism of calcium.

drooling Ptyalism.

droop (droop) The sagging of an organ or tissue; ptosis.

drop (drop) **1.** A minute spherical mass of liquid. **2.** Failure of a part to maintain its normal position, usually due to paralysis or injury.

    culture d. A bacterial culture in a drop of culture medium.

    falling d. **1.** In physical diagnosis, a metallic tinkle heard over the normal stomach and bowel when they are inflated. **2.** A metallic tinkle heard over large cavities containing fluid and air, as in hydropneumothorax.

    hanging d. Application of a drop of solution to a small glass coverslip. This is then inverted over a glass slide with a depression in it. The contents of the suspended solution can be examined microscopically.

   head d. Dropped head syndrome.

   nose d. Medication instilled in or sprayed into the nasal cavity.

   toe d. Inability to lift the toes.

   wrist d. A condition in which the hand is flexed at the wrist and cannot be extended. It may be due to injury of the radial nerve or paralysis of the extensor muscles of the wrist and hand. SYN: *drop hand*.

drop arm test A test used to identify tears of the rotator cuff muscle group, esp. supraspinatus. With the patient sitting or standing, the painful shoulder is fully abducted by the examiner and released. The patient actively lowers the arm without support from the examiner. In the presence of rotator cuff tears, the arm will fall uncontrollably to the side from a position of about 90 degrees of abduction. SEE: illus.

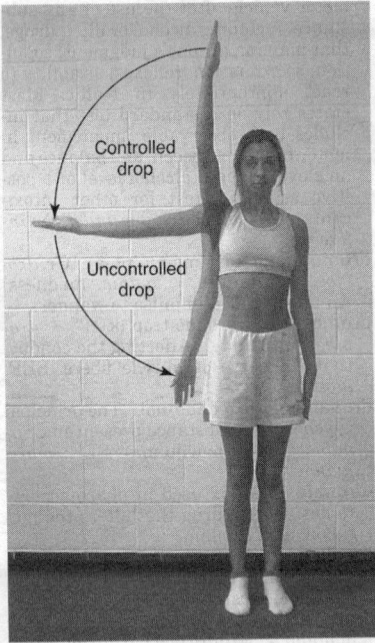

DROP ARM TEST

drop attack SEE: under *attack*.
drop factor SEE: under *factor*.
droplet A very small drop.
droplet nuclei Spray or mist in which infectious particles are suspended in air (e.g., from the cough or sneeze of an infected person). Many common contagious pathogens are spread by droplets, including adenovirus, corona virus, and influenza virus.

   PATIENT CARE: Patients who present to urgent care facilities with cough or other respiratory symptoms are given masks to prevent the spread of droplet nuclei to other waiting patients or to staff. Standard precautions are also followed. Patients admitted to hospital who are suspected of harboring respiratory contagions may be placed in respiratory isolation (airborne isolation—special air handling and ventilation and the use of a respirator in addition to standard precautions when entering the patient's room) until the cause of their illness is identified.

dropout (drŏp′out″) **1.** An individual who matriculates in, but does not complete a course of study sponsored by an academic institution. **2.** One who, after enrollment, chooses not to participate in a research investigation. In health care jargon, those who stop participating in a study and do not maintain contact with the investigators are said to be "lost to follow-up."

dropped head syndrome Profound weakness of the extensor muscles of the neck, resulting in the chin being positioned on the chest, which the patient cannot correct voluntarily. SYN: *head drop*.

dropper A tube, usually narrowed at one end, for dispensing drops of liquid. If water is so dispensed, about 20 drops equals 1 mL. SEE: *medicine dropper*.

   medicine d. According to *USP XXII*, a tube made of glass or other suitable transparent material that generally is fitted with a collapsible bulb and, while varying in capacity, is constricted at the delivery end to a round opening having an external diameter of 3 mm. When held vertically, it delivers water in drops each weighing between 45 mg and 55 mg.

   In using a medicine dropper, one should keep in mind that few medicinal liquids have the same surface and flow characteristics as water, and therefore the size of drops may vary considerably from one preparation to another.

   When accurate dosing is important, one should use a dropper that has been calibrated for and supplied with the preparation. The volume error incurred in measuring any liquid by means of a calibrated dropper should not exceed 15% under normal use conditions.

dropsy (drop′sē) [Ult. fr Gr. *hydrōps*, dropsy] Edema (no longer in technical use).

Drosophila (drō-sŏf′ĭ-lă) A genus of flies belonging to the order Diptera. It includes the common fruit flies.

   D. melanogaster A genus of fruit flies used extensively in the study of genetics. The development of the chromosome theory of heredity was largely the outcome of research on this species.

drowning Death resulting from immersion and suffocation in a liquid.

near d. Survival after immersion in water. About 330,000 persons, most of whom are children, adolescents, or young adults, survive an immersion injury in the U.S. each year, and of these, about 10% receive professional attention. Many who suffer near drowning do so because of preventable or avoidable conditions, such as the use of alcohol or drugs in aquatic settings or the inadequate supervision of children by adults. Water sports (e.g., diving, swimming, surfing, or skiing) and boating or fishing accidents also are common causes of near drowning. A small percentage of near drowning episodes occur when patients with known seizure disorders convulse while swimming or boating.

ETIOLOGY: The injuries suffered result from breath holding ("dry drowning"), the aspiration of water into the lungs ("wet drowning"), and/or hypothermia.

SYMPTOMS: Common symptoms of near drowning result from oxygen deprivation, retention of carbon dioxide, or direct damage to the lungs by water. These include cough, dyspnea, coma, and seizures. Additional complications of prolonged immersion may include aspiration pneumonitis, noncardiogenic pulmonary edema, electrolyte disorders, hemolysis, disseminated intravascular coagulation, and arrhythmias.

TREATMENT: In unconscious patients rescued from water, the airway is secured, ventilation is provided, and cardiopulmonary resuscitation is begun. Oxygen, cardiac, and blood pressure monitoring, rewarming techniques, and other forms of support are provided (e.g., anticonvulsants are given for seizures; electrolyte and acid-base disorders are corrected).

PROGNOSIS: Most patients who are rapidly resuscitated from a dry drowning episode recover fully. The recovery of near drowning victims who have inhaled water into the lungs depends on the underlying health of the victim, the duration of immersion, and the speed and efficiency with which oxygenation, ventilation, and perfusion are restored.

drownproofing A method of staying afloat by using a minimum amount of energy. It may be kept up for hours even by nonswimmers, whereas only the most fit and expert could swim for more than 30 min. Details of the drownproofing technique may be obtained from local chapters of the American Red Cross. SEE: illus.

TECHNIQUE: 1. *Rest:* The person takes a deep breath and sinks vertically beneath the surface, relaxes the arms and legs, keeps the chin down, and allows the fingertips to brush against the knees. The neck is relaxed and the back of the head is above the surface. 2. *Get set:* The arms are raised gently to a crossed position with the back of the wrists touching the forehead. At the same time, the person steps forward with one leg and backward with the other. 3. *Lift head, exhale:* With the arms and legs in the previous position, the head is raised quickly but smoothly to the vertical position and the person exhales through the nose. 4. *Stroke and kick, inhale:* To support the head above the surface while inhaling through the mouth, the arms sweep gently outward and downward and both feet step downward. 5. *Head down, press:* As the person drops beneath the surface, the head goes down and the arms and hands press downward to arrest descent. 6. *Rest:* It is important to relax completely as in the first step for 6 to 10 sec.

drowsiness A decreased level of consciousness that often precedes or follows sleep.

daytime d. Drowsiness occurring during the day rather than just before normal bedtime. It may have many causes, including insomnia and other

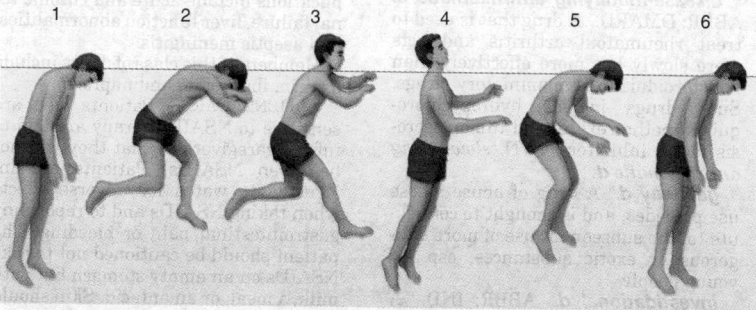

1	2	3	4	5	6
Rest	Get set	Lift head, exhale	Stroke and kick, inhale	Head down, press	Rest

DROWNPROOFING TECHNIQUE

sleep disturbances, anxiety, overwork, or the effects of prescribed or abused drugs.

DRSP *Drug-resistant Streptococcus pneumoniae.*

Dr. Strangelove syndrome Alien limb phenomenon.

drug (drŭg) [Fr. *drogue*, chemical material] Any substance that, when taken into a living organism, may modify one or more of its functions.

    d. of abuse Any agent that impairs behavior, health, social interactions, or thought and lends itself to compulsive use. Many of these agents, including ecstasy, lysergic acid (LSD), methamphetamines, the opiates, and phencyclidine, are considered controlled substances in the U.S. Alcohol and tobacco products are not traditionally considered to be drugs of abuse although they are addictive and harm many people.

    antimicrobial d. A drug that either kills microorganisms or prevents their growth.

    antisense d. Antisense **compound**.

    club d. A colloquial term for a drug used for its euphoric or intoxicating effects at a party, rave, nightclub, or bar. Such drugs include ecstasy, gamma hydroxybutyrate, ketamine, and rohypnol.

    code d. A drug to treat acute, life-threatening emergencies including dysrhythmias, cardiac arrest, pulmonary edema, and shock. Code drugs include atropine, epinephrine, morphine, and vasopressin. SEE: *basic life support; code* (3); *code cart.*

    counterfeit d. **1.** Any drug that has been adulterated, contaminated, diluted, or falsely labeled. **2.** Any drug marketed under false pretenses.

    designer d. An illicitly produced drug of abuse. Designer drugs include methamphetamine, fentanyl and its analogues, and phencyclidine hydrochloride (PCP). They have serious side effects or are addictive; deaths and injury from overdose are common.

    disease-modifying antirheumatic d. ABBR: DMARD. A drug that is used to treat rheumatoid arthritis and acts more slowly but more effectively than nonsteroidal anti-inflammatory drugs. Such drugs include hydroxychloroquine, methotrexate, and tumor necrosis factor inhibitors. SYN: *slow-acting antirheumatic d.*

    gateway d. A drug of abuse whose use precedes, and is thought to contribute to, the subsequent use of more dangerous or exotic substances, esp. by young people.

    investigational d. ABBR: IND. A drug available only for experimental purposes because its safety and effectiveness have not been proven. SYN: *investigational new d.*

    investigational new d. Investigational **d.**

    legend d. A medication that cannot be obtained legally without a prescription from a licensed health care provider.

    neuromuscular blocking d. A type of drug used during the administration of anesthesia to allow surgical access to body cavities, esp. in particular the abdomen and thorax, by preventing voluntary or reflex muscle movement. These drugs are also used to facilitate compliance in critically ill patients undergoing intensive therapy such as mechanical ventilation.

    new d. A drug for which premarketing approval is required by the Food, Drug and Cosmetic Act (a U.S. law granting authority to the FDA to oversee the safety of food, drugs, and cosmetics).

    nonprescription d. An over-the-counter medication.

    nonsteroidal anti-inflammatory d. ABBR: NSAID. A drug that has analgesic, anti-inflammatory, and antipyretic actions. NSAIDs are used to treat acute and chronic pain, e.g., of injuries, arthritis, and dysmenorrhea, to reduce inflammation, and to prevent complications in serious illness such as sepsis.

⚠️ All NSAIDS increase the risk of gastrointestinal bleeding and ulceration and, to some extent, the risk of renal failure, abnormalities in liver function, myocardial infarction, and stroke. These side effects occur most often in older patients, e.g., those with multiple risk factors for atherosclerotic vascular disease.

Many patients experience side effects of these medications, including upper gastrointestinal inflammation or bleeding. These side effects occur most often in the elderly, tobacco users, and those who drink alcohol. Other potential complications include acute and chronic renal failure, liver function abnormalities, and aseptic meningitis.

Members of this class of drugs include aspirin, ibuprofen, and naproxen.

PATIENT CARE: Patients who are sensitive to NSAID therapy are told to inform caregivers so that they will not be given NSAIDs. Patients are instructed to watch for adverse effects when taking NSAIDs and to report any gastrointestinal pain or bleeding. The patient should be cautioned not to take NSAIDs on an empty stomach but with milk, a meal, or an antacid. Skin should be protected from the sun. Pregnant women should avoid NSAIDs during their last trimester.

    orphan d. A drug effective for a certain illness but not profitable for manufacturers to produce.

performance-enhancing d. Any drug used to gain an advantage in sports. Such drugs may improve endurance or strength or accelerate healing after injury.

pioneer d. The brand-name or patented version of a drug, later copied to make generic drugs after the patent expires.

psychotherapeutic d. A drug to improve the principal symptoms, e.g., anxiety, depression, and psychosis, in the mentally disturbed.

psychotropic d. A drug that affects psychic function, behavior, or experience. Many drugs can be classed as intentionally psychotropic, but many other drugs also occasionally may produce undesired psychotropic side effects.

radioprotective d. A drug that protects humans against the damaging or lethal effects of ionizing radiation. For example, Lugol's solution blocks the uptake of inhaled or ingested radioactive iodine by the thyroid.

recreational d. A drug used for enjoyment rather than for a medical purpose.

scheduled d. SEE: *Controlled Substance Act.*

soft d. **1.** A drug that is easily metabolized by the body to inactive, nontoxic metabolites. **2.** An illicit drug that has fewer psychoactive, addictive, or other adverse effects than a *street* drug or *hard* drug. **3.** A drug that dissolves in the mouth and is quickly absorbed.

specialty d. A drug that has unusually complex requirements for development, manufacturing, storage, transportation, administration, or monitoring. Most drugs in this category are extraordinarily expensive.

street d. A drug obtained illegally, usually a drug of abuse.

sulfa d. Any drug of the sulfonamide group possessing bacteriostatic properties.

drug abuse SEE: under *abuse.*

Drug Abuse Warning Network ABBR: DAWN. A national system of surveillance that records the number of deaths and emergency department visits caused by illicit drugs. It was renamed "New DAWN" in 2003.

drug addiction SEE: under *addiction.*

drug administration The giving of a therapeutic agent to a patient, e.g. by infusion, inhalation, injection, paste, suppository or tablet.

drug approval The formal process through which drugs are tested before they are permitted to be sold. In the U.S., the process involves a series of studies on small groups of patients affected by diseases for which the drug may prove beneficial. These trials include:

1. studies of the drug's safety;
2. studies of the drug's efficacy;
3. studies of the drug's comparative efficacy relative to other agents that treat the same or similar problems.

drug companion A medication whose efficacy depends on its use with a second agent. The same drug may have little effect when used alone.

drug compatibility SEE: *compatible (2).*

drug contract A common colloquial term for an agreement between a patient and a health care provider about the prescription and use of narcotic medications. The provider agrees to furnish the patient with pain-relieving medications as long as the patient agrees to use them safely, without abusing them, diverting them, or obtaining similar prescriptions from other practitioners. It is formally known as an *opiate treatment agreement.* SYN: *pain agreement.*

drug delivery, new methods of Several methods of drug delivery have been used experimentally. Included are chemical modification of a drug to enable it to penetrate membranes such as the blood-brain barrier; incorporation of microparticles in colloidal carriers made of proteins, carbohydrates, lipids, or synthetic polymers; controlled-release systems that permit a drug to be delivered for very long periods; and transdermal controlled-release systems (e.g., those currently in use for administration of scopolamine or nitroglycerin). In addition to the use of various carriers for drugs, cell transplantation could be used to provide therapeutic agents, and the possibility of inserting genes into cells to produce desired effects is being explored. SEE: *liposome.*

drug dependence A psychic (and sometimes physical) state resulting from interaction of a living organism and a drug. Characteristic behavioral and other responses include a compulsion to take the drug on a continuous or periodic basis to experience its psychic effects or to avoid the discomfort of its absence. Tolerance may be present. A person may become dependent on more than one drug.

drug development, computer-assisted ABBR: CADD. The automated design and testing of new chemical compounds for therapeutic use. Commonly, CADD involves using computerized algorithms to build molecules with specific sizes, shapes, or combining characteristics and assessing the biological activity of the molecules in various solutions.

Drug Enforcement Administration number ABBR: DEA number. A number assigned by the DEA to health care providers indicating that the person or facility is registered with the DEA to prescribe controlled substances.

drug-fast Drug-resistant.

druggable, drugable (drŭg′ă-bĕl) **1.** Amenable to treatment with drugs or susceptible to alteration or manipulation with drugs. **2.** In genetics, pert. to the ability of a molecule to regulate the function of an endogenous protein for the benefit of the organism. **druggability,** n. **drugability** (-bil′ĭt-ē), n.

druggist (drŭg′ĭst) Pharmacist.

drug handling The manipulation of medications in order to administer them. It is important to carefully read the label or other printed instruction issued with medications. The ordered doses (quantities) should be measured accurately and never estimated. A measuring glass or spoon marked in milliliters, ounces, or both should be used. In giving a dose of medicine, it is necessary to know to whom it is to be given, what has to be given, when it has to be given, and the prescribed amount. If medicine is to be taken orally, the patient should be observed until he or she has actually swallowed it.

NOTE: The cover must never be left off the container because a necessary property may evaporate, the drug may become dangerously concentrated, or it may absorb moisture from the air and become difficult to handle or dilute. The drug storage compartment must be kept locked.

drug holiday A planned interruption in the use of a medication, usually to minimize its costs, limit side effects, or to preserve its effectiveness for later use.

drug-in-adhesive patch ABBR: DIA. A transdermal medication delivery system in which the active drug that is administered to the patient is combined with the agent that holds or adheres the delivery system to the skin. DIA patches are thinner than patches in which the adhesive and active drug layers are separated. They fit the skin more closely and with less bulk than alternative transdermal delivery systems.

drug-induced hypersensitivity syndrome Drug rash with eosinophilia and systemic and systemic symptoms.

drug-induced liver injury (drŭg′in-doost′, -dūst′) SEE: under *injury.*

drug interaction SEE: under *interaction.*

drug latentiation (lā-ten″shē-ā′shŏn) The modification of a drug so that it can be taken up by the body (for example, for oral administration) but neither digested nor metabolized until it is delivered to its target organ. The drug is designed to convert to its active form only after it arrives in the tissues where it will prove useful.

druglikeness The structural or functional similarity of a chemical to a known therapeutic agent. It includes

several components, including the size and shape of the molecule, its ability to bind hydrogen, or its ability to be taken up by lipids or water.

drug overdose The clinical consequence of any excess dose of a drug, e.g., of a self-administered, potentially lethal dose of a drug of abuse, an antidepressant, a nonnarcotic pain reliever, or other medication. Drug overdose may be unintentional or deliberate. When such a dose results in coma or death, the person is said to have *OD'd* (overdosed).

PATIENT CARE: Emergency department personnel assess the patient's airway, breathing, circulation, level of consciousness, and vital signs, and try to ascertain (from the patient or significant others) what drug was taken, how much, when, and by what route. Blood and urine (and when it becomes available, emesis) are sent to the laboratory for toxicology screening to aid in identifying specific substances.

If the drug was administered by inhalation or parenterally, or if time lapse has allowed for absorption, an intravenous site is established, and fluid is administered as prescribed. If the patient is unconscious on admission, he will be given a narcotic antagonist, a bolus of 50% dextrose in water, and 50 to 100 mg of thiamine routinely to reverse rapidly the potential effects of opiates or low blood sugar. Depending on the patient's response to the drug's actions (such as central nervous system depression or stimulation, respiratory depression, cardiac arrhythmias, or renal failure), emergency department personnel provide necessary supportive therapies (such as airway intubation and ventilation), activated charcoal, or bowel irrigation. Because absorption rates vary and may fluctuate, the patient requires frequent reassessment with immediate intervention as appropriate.

The possibility of attempted suicide should be considered in any case of drug overdose. A psychiatric history is obtained, with any history of depression noted. Suicide precautions are established to protect the patient from further self-injury. Psychological or psychiatric follow-up is initiated for overdose resulting from depression or suicidal ideation. Drug counseling and rehabilitation may also be needed. SEE: *Nursing Diagnoses Appendix.*

drug product A medication in its marketed form, including its fillers, coloring agents, and other active or inactive agents.

Drug Product Problem Reporting Program A program managed by the U.S. Pharmacopeial Convention, Inc., that informs the product manufacturer, the labeler, and the Food and Drug Administration (FDA) of potential health hazards and defective drug products. The reports may be submitted by any health professional.

drug rash with eosinophilia and systemic symptoms ABBR: DRESS. A potentially fatal allergic reaction to an administered drug in which a nonblistering skin eruption is accompanied by fever, markedly elevated serum eosinophil levels, and, often, bone marrow, kidney or liver injury. Common causes include allopurinol, and anticonvulsant drugs (such as carbamazepine and phenytoin). SYN: *drug-induced hypersensitivity syndrome.*

drug reaction Adverse and undesired reaction to a substance taken for its pharmacological effects. An estimated 15% of hospitalized patients develop toxic or allergic drug reactions. SEE: table.

drug-resistant 1. Unaffected by chemotherapy. **2.** Unable to be killed or eradicated with antibiotics, said of certain bacteria. SYN: *pharmacoresistant; drug-fast.*

drug screen SEE: under *screen.*

drug substitution 1. In pharmacy dispensing, the replacement of one drug by another. Typically a generic drug, or a drug available in a restricted formulary, is substituted for a brand-name drug. **2.** A treatment for addiction in which a drug with limited potential for abuse is used to replace a more hazardous agent that the addict craves.

drug testing, mandated The enforced testing of individuals for evidence of drug or alcohol use or abuse. Some state or federal regulatory or licensing agencies require random drug testing of employees in specific industries to ensure public safety and to prevent on-the-job injuries. In addition, some health care professionals who have a history of drug or alcohol abuse may be required to participate in such testing as a means of monitoring compliance with abstinence.

drug withdrawal The removal from the market of a therapeutic agent that had been previously approved for use in patient care. Drug withdrawals affect millions of patients annually. They usually result from the aftermarket recognition of adverse drug reactions that were not noted during the drug approval process. Prominent examples of drug withdrawals include: Bextra, Fen/Phen, and Vioxx.

drum Tympanic **membrane**.

drunkalogue (drŭngk′ŭ-lŏg) [Fm *drunk* + *(di)alogue*] A colloquial term for a personal history of one's addiction to alcohol and its consequences, often recited at a meeting with other alcoholics. The recital is often used for therapeutic purposes, e.g., it defines the speaker as an alcoholic and details the ways in which alcoholism has harmed or continues to harm the person seeking freedom from its effects.

drunkenness [AS. *drinean,* to drink] Alcoholic intoxication. In legal medicine, intoxication or being "under the influence" of alcohol is defined according to the concentration of alcohol in the blood or exhaled air. The precise concentration used to define legal intoxication varies among states. Drivers are considered intoxicated with alcohol (in many states) when the blood level is 0.08% or more. A blood alcohol level over 0.5% is sufficient to cause alcoholic coma in most people.

drusen (droo′zĕn) [Ger. *Druse,* weathered ore] Small, yellowish deposits found between the retinal pigment epithelium and Bruch's membrane.

   optic nerve head d. Calcified bodies located on the optic nerve head, which can give the mistaken appearance of optic nerve edema

dry (drī) **1.** Containing little or no moisture; not wet. **2.** A colloquial term for dehydrated.

dry measure A measure of volume for dry commodities. SEE: *Weights and Measures Appendix.*

dry mouth Xerostomia.

dry orgasm The experience of male sexual climax without ejaculation or the emission of semen. Dry orgasm may be experienced by boys before puberty and by adult males with neurological or prostatic diseases.

dry powder inhaler ABBR: DPI. An inhaler that administers tiny particles of medication to the airways. Dry powder inhalers are used to treat diseases such

Comparison of Toxic and Allergic Drug Reactions

	Toxic	Allergic
Incidence	May occur with any drug	Occurs infrequently
Dosage	Usually high	Therapeutic
Reaction time	May occur with first dose, or may be due to cumulative effect	Usually only upon re-exposure, but some drugs cross-react with chemicals of similar structure
Symptoms	May be similar to pharmacological action of drug	Not related to pharmacological action of drug
Associated disorders	None	Asthma, hay fever

as asthma and chronic obstructive lung disease.

Dryvax (drī'vaks″) A smallpox vaccine derived from the New York City Board of Health vaccinia virus strain, grown in calf lymph culture.

dry weight SEE: under *weight*.

DS *double strength.*

DSA *digital subtraction angiography.*

DSAEK *Descemet stripping automated endothelial keratoplasty.*

DSMB *data safety monitoring board.*

DSM-IV *Diagnostic and Statistical Manual of Mental Disorders (Fourth Edition).*

dsRNA *double-stranded ribonucleic acid.*

DT *delirium tremens.*

D-test (dē'tĕst″) A method of assessing erythromycin-resistant strains of *Staphylococcus aureus* for their susceptibility to the antibiotic clindamycin. Erythromycin-impregnated disks are placed near clindamycin, or lincomycin-impregnated disks on a growth medium, and the effect of inducible erythromycin resistance on the inhibition of bacterial growth around the clindamycin disk is assessed. A flattening of the zone of inhibition around the clindamycin disk is indicative of clindamycin drug resistance.

DU *Duodenal ulcer.*

dual eligibility In the U.S. health care system, meeting the qualifications that grant a person access to both Medicare and Medicaid insurance.

dualism (doo'ă-lizm, dū'ă) [L. *dualis,* containing two +-*ism*] **1.** The condition of being double or twofold. **2.** The theory that human beings consist of two entities, mind and matter, that are independent of each other. SYN: *mind-body duality.* **3.** The theory that various blood cells arise from two types of stem cells: myeloblasts, giving rise to the myeloid elements, and lymphoblasts, giving rise to the lymphoid elements.

dual protection In obstetrics and reproductive health, a method of contraception, e.g., the use of condoms, that also provides some protection against sexually transmitted diseases.

dual reuptake inhibitor SEE: under *inhibitor*.

Duane syndrome (dwān) [Alexander Duane, U.S. ophthalmologist, 1858–1926] A disorder of eye movement in which the affected eye does not move centrally or temporally in a normal manner and pulls into the orbit on adduction.

DUB *dysfunctional uterine bleeding.*

Dubini disease (doo-bē'nē) [Angelo Dubini, It. physician, 1813–1902] Rapid rhythmic contractions of a group or groups of muscles. SYN: *electric chorea; spasmus Dubini.*

Dubin-Johnson syndrome (dū'bĭn-jŏn'sŏn) [Isadore Nathan Dubin, U.S.

pathologist, 1913–1980; Frank B. Johnson, U.S. pathologist, b. 1919] An inherited defect of bile metabolism that causes retention of conjugated bilirubin in hepatic cells. The patient is asymptomatic except for mild intermittent jaundice. No treatment is required.

dubnium (doob'nē-ŭm, dŭb') [*Dubna,* Russia] ABBR: Db. A synthetic radioactive element; atomic mass 268; atomic number 105.

Dubowitz tool, Dubowitz score (doo'bŏ-wĭts) [Lilly and Victor Dubowitz, contemporary South African physicians] A method of estimating the gestational age of an infant based on 21 strictly defined physical and neurological signs. This method provides the correct gestational age ±2 weeks in 95% of infants.

Duchenne, Guillaume B. A. (doo-shen', dŭ-) Fr. neurologist, 1806–1875.

   D. disease Degeneration of the posterior roots and column of the spinal cord and of the brainstem. It is marked by attacks of pain; progressive ataxia; loss of reflexes, functional disorders of the bladder, larynx, and gastrointestinal system; and impotence. This disorder develops in conjunction with syphilis and most frequently affects middle-aged men. SYN: *tabes dorsalis.*

   D. muscular dystrophy Pseudohypertrophic muscular dystrophy marked by weakness and pseudohypertrophy of the affected muscles. It is caused by mutation of the gene responsible for producing the protein dystrophin. The disease begins in childhood, is progressive, and affects the shoulder and pelvic girdle muscles. The disease, mostly affecting males, is transmitted as a sex-linked recessive trait. SYN: *pseudohypertrophic muscular* **dystrophy***; dystrophinopathy.* SEE: *Nursing Diagnoses Appendix.*

Duchenne-Aran disease (dū-shĕn'ăr-ăn') [Duchenne; Francois Amilcar Aran, Fr. physician, 1817–1861] Spinal muscular atrophy.

Duchenne-Erb paralysis (dū-shĕn'ayrb) [Duchenne; Wilhelm Heinrich Erb, Ger. neurologist, 1840–1921] Paralysis of the muscles of the upper arm due to injury of the fifth and sixth cervical roots, of the brachial plexus. The hand muscles are unaffected. SYN: *Erb's palsy; Erb's paralysis.*

duckwalk, duck walk (dŭk'wok″) To ambulate in a crouched position with the buttocks just above the heels.

duct (dŭkt) [L. *ductus,* conveyance (for water)] **1.** A narrow tubular vessel or channel, esp. one that conveys secretions from a gland. **2.** A narrow enclosed channel containing a fluid, e.g., the semicircular duct of the ear.

   accessory pancreatic d. A duct of the pancreas leading into the pancreatic duct or the duodenum near the mouth of the common bile duct. SYN: *d. of San-torini.*

alveolar d. A branch of a respiratory bronchiole that leads directly to the alveolar sacs of the lungs. SEE: *alveolus* for illus.

Bartholin d. SEE: under *Bartholin, Caspar (the younger).*

bile d. Any of the intercellular passages that convey bile from the liver to the hepatic duct, which joins the duct from the gallbladder (cystic duct) to form the common bile duct (ductus choledochus), and which enters the duodenum about 3 in (7.6 cm) below the pylorus. SYN: *biliary d.* SEE: illus.

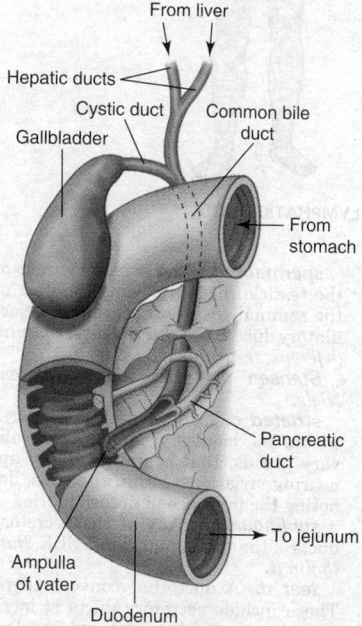

From liver

Hepatic ducts

Cystic duct

Common bile duct

Gallbladder

From stomach

Pancreatic duct

To jejunum

Ampulla of vater

Duodenum

BILE DUCTS

biliary d. Bile **d.**

Botallo d. Ductus arteriosus.

cochlear d. Cochlear spiral **canal.**

common bile d. The duct that carries bile and pancreatic juice to the duodenum. It is formed by the union of the cystic duct of the gallbladder and the hepatic duct of the liver and is joined by the main pancreatic duct. SYN: *ductus choledochus.* SEE: *biliary tract* for illus.

cystic d. The secretory duct of the gallbladder. It unites with the hepatic duct from the liver to form the common bile duct. SEE: *biliary tract* for illus.

efferent d. Any of a group of 12 to 14 small tubes that constitute the efferent ducts of the testis. They lie within the epididymis and connect the rete testis with the ductus epididymidis. Their

coiled portions constitute the lobuli epididymidis.

ejaculatory d. The duct that conveys sperm from the vas deferens and secretions from the seminal vesicle to the urethra.

endolymphatic d. In the embryo, a tubular projection of the otocyst ending in a blind extremity, the endolymphatic sac. In the adult, it connects the endolymphatic sac with the utricle and saccule of the inner ear.

d. of the epoophoron Gartner's duct.

excretory d. Any duct that conveys a waste product from an organ, such as the collecting duct of the renal tubule.

Gartner d. SEE: under *Gartner, Hermann.*

hepatic d. Either of the ducts that receive bile from the right or left lobe of the liver and carries it to the common bile duct. SYN: *ductus hepaticus dexter; ductus hepaticus sinister.*

intercalated d. Any of several short, narrow ducts that lie between the secretory ducts and the terminal alveoli in the parotid and submandibular glands and in the pancreas.

interlobular d. A duct passing between lobules within a gland, e.g., one of the ducts carrying bile.

lacrimal d. Any of the small excretory ducts of the lacrimal glands.

lactiferous d. Any of 15 to 20 ducts that drain the lobes of the mammary gland. Each opens in a slight depression in the tip of the nipple. SYN: *milk d.*

lymphatic d. Either of two main ducts conveying lymph to the bloodstream: the left lymphatic (thoracic) and the right lymphatic duct, which drains lymph from the right side of the body above the diaphragm. It discharges into the right subclavian vein. It is smaller than the left lymphatic duct. SEE: *thoracic d.;* illus.

mesonephric d. Wolffian duct.

milk d. Lactiferous **d.**

müllerian d. Either of the bilateral embryonic tubes in the embryo from which the oviducts, uterus, and vagina develop in the female; in the male, they atrophy. SYN: *Müller duct.*

nasolacrimal d. A membranous tube that runs in the nasolacrimal canal and drains tears from the lacrimal sac to the nasal cavity. It opens beneath the inferior nasal concha.

omphalomesenteric d. Yolk stalk.

pancreatic d. The duct that conveys pancreatic juice to the common bile duct and duodenum. SYN: *duct of Wirsung.*

papillary d. Any of the large ducts formed by the uniting of the collecting tubules of the kidney; it empties into the renal pelvis.

paramesonephric d. The genital canal in the embryo. In females it develops into the oviducts, uterus, and vagina; in

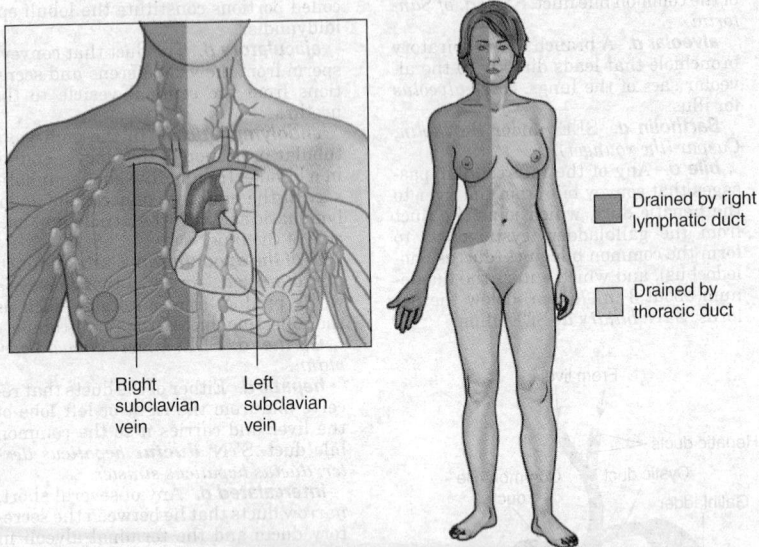

Right subclavian vein   Left subclavian vein

■ Drained by right lymphatic duct

□ Drained by thoracic duct

DRAINAGE AREAS FOR LYMPHATIC DUCTS

males it degenerates to form the appendix testis.

paraurethral d. Skene duct.

parotid d. Stensen duct.

prostatic d. One of about 20 ducts that discharge prostatic secretion into the urethra. SYN: *d. prostaticus*.

d. of Rivinus SEE: under *Rivinus, August.*

salivary d. Any of the ducts that drain a salivary gland.

d. of Santorini Accessory pancreatic d.

secretory d. Any of the smaller canals of a gland.

semicircular d. One of three membranous tubes forming a part of the vestibular labyrinth of the inner ear. They lie within the semicircular canals and bear corresponding names: anterior, posterior, and lateral. The semicircular ducts originate from the utricle as a single common tube (crus communale). The three ducts then branch, and each follows the course of a different bony semicircular canal. At their far ends the ducts widen into an ampulla that contains a specialized endothelium that is sensitive to motion of the endolymph. Axons from receptor cells in these sensory epithelia transmit motion information to the brain via the vestibular division of the vestibulocochlear nerve (CN VIII). SEE: *labyrinth* for illus.

seminal d. Any of the ducts that convey sperm, specifically the ductus deferens and the ejaculatory duct.

Skene d. SEE: under *Skene, Alexander.*

spermatic d. The secretory duct of the testicle that later joins the duct of the seminal vesicle to become the ejaculatory duct. SYN: **ductus** *deferens; vas deferens; testicular d.*

Stensen d. SEE: under *Stensen, Niels.*

striated d. Any of a class of ducts within the lobules of glands, esp. salivary glands, that contain radially appearing striations within the cells, denoting the presence of mitochondria.

sublingual d. Any of the secretory ducts of the sublingual gland. SEE: *Bartholin d.*

tear d. A duct that conveys tears. These include secretory ducts of lacrimal glands, and lacrimal and nasolacrimal ducts.

thoracic d. The main lymphatic duct, originating at the cisterna chyli. It passes upward through the diaphragm into the thorax and continues upward along the aorta and esophagus to the neck, where it turns to the left and enters the left subclavian vein near its junction with the left internal jugular vein. It receives lymph from all parts of the body except the right side of the head, neck, thorax, and upper extremity. SEE: *lymphatic system* for illus.

thyroglossal d. In the embryo, a duct that connects the thyroid diverticulum with the tongue. It eventually disappears, its point of origin being indicated as a pit, the foramen cecum. It sometimes persists as an anomaly.

utriculosaccular d. A narrow tube emanating from the utricle, connecting it to the saccule, and opening into the endolymphatic duct of the inner ear.

vitelline d. Yolk **stalk**.

wolffian d. In the embryo, the duct leading from the mesonephros to the cloaca. From it develop the ductus epididymis, ductus deferens, seminal vesicle, ejaculatory duct, ureter, and pelvis of the kidney. SYN: *mesonephric d.*

duct-, ducto- [L. *ductus*, fr. *ducere*, to lead] Prefixes meaning *to lead, carry, or convey*.

ductal carcinoma in situ of breast ABBR: DCIS. A cluster of malignant cells in the mammary ducts that has not spread to surrounding breast tissue. It is the most common noninvasive breast cancer and accounts for 25% of all breast cancer diagnoses. If left untreated, as many as 50% of patients with DCIS will develop invasive cancer. Because these cells grow in the ducts, they develop without forming a palpable mass. In its early stage this condition can be diagnosed through the use of mammography.

TREATMENT: Lumpectomy is the most common treatment, followed by radiation. Mastectomy may be recommended if multiple areas are found or if there is a strong family history of breast cancer. SYN: *comedocarcinoma*. SEE: *breast cancer; mammography*.

duct ectasia SEE: under *ectasia*.

ductile (dŭk′tĭl) [L. *ductilis*, fr. *ducere*, to lead] Capable of being elongated without breaking.

duction (dŭk′shŭn) In ophthalmology, the rotation of an eye about an axis. This movement is controlled by the action of the extraocular muscles.

ductogram (dŭk′tō-grăm) Injection of radiographic contrast into a duct of the breast, to determine the cause of nipple discharge.

duct of Rivinus SEE: under *Rivinus, August*.

duct of Santorini Accessory pancreatic **duct**.

ductule (dŭk′tūl) A very small duct.

ductus (dŭk′tŭs) *pl.* **ductus** Duct.

d. arteriosus In the fetus, a blood vessel connecting the main pulmonary artery and the aortic arch. In the fetal circulation, it permits most of the blood to bypass the fetal lungs. Normally, the ductus arteriosus closes soon after birth. SYN: *Botallo's duct*.

d. deferens Vas deferens.

patent d. arteriosus SEE: *patent ductus arteriosus*.

d. venosus The smaller, shorter, and posterior of two branches into which the umbilical vein divides after entering the abdomen of the fetus. It empties into the inferior vena cava.

due care SEE: under *care*.

due process SEE: under *process*.

duet reading (doo-ĕt′ rēd′ĭng, dū-) Reading aloud simultaneously by two people, one of whom is learning or relearning to read, and the other who is the teacher or role model.

Duffy system (dŭf′ē) [Named after the family in whom the blood group was first discovered.] A blood group consisting of two antigens determined by allelic genes. SEE: *blood group*.

DUI *driving under the influence* (of alcohol or drugs).

Duke method (dook, dūk) [William Waddell Duke, U.S. pathologist, 1883–1945.] SEE: *bleeding time*.

Dukes classification (dooks, dūks) [Cuthbert E. Dukes, Brit. pathologist, 1890–1977] A system of classifying the extent of spread of adenocarcinoma of the colon or rectum.

dull [ME. *dul*] **1.** Not resonant on percussion. **2.** Not mentally alert.

dullness **1.** The state of being dull. **2.** Lack of normal resonance on percussion.

shifting d. A mobile area of decreased resonance found during percussion of a body part as the body changes position. The finding suggests that fluid is contained within a body cavity and that it moves with gravity.

dumb [AS.] Lacking the power or faculty to speak; mute.

dumbness Muteness.

dumping **1.** In medical care, the practice of transferring a patient who is unable to pay for care to a hospital that accepts such patients. **2.** The abandonment of infirm patients in health care facilities.

dumping syndrome A syndrome marked by sweating and weakness after eating, occurring in patients who have had gastric resections. The exact cause is unknown but rapid emptying (dumping) of the stomach contents into the small intestine is associated with the symptoms. This syndrome consists of weakness, nausea, sweating, palpitations, diarrhea, and occasionally, syncope. Eating small meals or lying down after eating may afford some relief.

duodenal (dū-ō-dē′năl, dū-ŏd′ĕ-năl) [L. *duodeni*, twelve] Pert. to the duodenum.

duodenal delay Delay in the movement of food through the duodenum due to conditions such as inflammation of the lower portion of the intestine, which reflexly inhibits duodenal movements.

duodenectasis (dū″ō-dĕn-ĕk′tă-sĭs) [″ + Gr. *ektasis*, expansion] Chronic dilatation of the duodenum.

duodenectomy (dū″ō-dĕn-ĕk′tō-mē) [″ + Gr. *ektome*, excision] Excision of part or all of the duodenum.

duodenitis (dū″ŏd-ĕ-nī′tĭs) [″ + Gr. *itis*, inflammation] Inflammation of the duodenum, usually resulting from *Helicobacter pylori* or the use of alcohol, tobacco, or nonsteroidal anti-inflammatory drugs.

duodeno-, duoden- [L. *duodeni,* twelve-inch-long intestine] Prefixes meaning *duodenum.*

duodenocholecystostomy (dū″ō-dē″nō-kō-lĭ-sĭs-tŏs′tō-mē) [″ + Gr. *chole,* bile, + *kystis,* bladder, + *stoma,* mouth] Surgical formation of a passage between the duodenum and the gallbladder. SYN: *duodenocystostomy.*

duodenocholedochotomy (doo-od″ĕn-ō-kō-led″ō-kot′ō-mē, dū-) [*duodeno- + choledochotomy*] Surgical incision of the duodenum and the common bile duct.

duodenocystostomy (dū″ō-dē″nō-sĭs-tŏs′tō-mē) Duodenocholecystostomy.

duodenoenterostomy (doo-od″ĕn-ō-ent″ĕ-ros′tō-mē, dū-) [*duodeno- + enterostomy*] The formation of a passage between the duodenum and the more distal small intestine.

duodenogram (dū-ŏd′ĕ-nō-grăm) [″ + Gr. *gramma,* something written] A radiograph of the duodenum after it has been filled with a contrast medium.

duodenography (dū″ō-dē-nŏg′ră-fē) [″ + Gr. *graphein,* to write] Radiographic examination of the duodenum.

   hypotonic d. Radiographic examination of the duodenum after medication has been administered to halt the peristaltic action of the gastrointestinal tract.

duodenohepatic (dū-ŏd″ĕ-nō″hĕ-păt′ĭk) [″ + Gr. *hepatos,* liver] Pert. to the duodenum and liver.

duodenoileostomy (dū″ō-dē″nō-ĭl″ē-ŏs′tō-mē) Surgical formation of a passage between the duodenum and the ileum when the jejunum has been surgically excised.

duodenojejunostomy (dū″ō-dē″nō-jĕ-joo-nŏs′tō-mē) [″ + *jejunum,* empty, + Gr. *stoma,* mouth] Surgical creation of a passage between the duodenum and the jejunum.

duodenorrhaphy (dū″ō-dē-nor′ă-fē) [″ + Gr. *rhaphe,* seam, ridge] Suturing of the duodenum.

duodenoscopy (dū″ŏd-ĕ-nŏs′kō-pē) [″ + Gr. *skopein,* to examine] Inspection of the duodenum with an endoscope.

duodenostomy (doo-od″ĕn-ō-stō-mē, dū-) [*duodeno- + -stomy*] Surgical creation of a permanent opening into the duodenum through the wall of the abdomen.

duodenotomy (dū″ŏd-ĕ-nŏt′ō-mē) [″ + Gr. *tome,* incision] An incision into the duodenum.

duodenum (dū″ō-dē′nŭm, dū-ŏd′ĕ-nŭm) [L. *duodeni,* twelve] The first part of the small intestine, between the pylorus and the jejunum; it is 8 to 11 in (20 to 28 cm) long. The duodenum receives hepatic and pancreatic secretions through the common bile duct. SEE: *liver; pancreas; digestive system* for illus.

   ANATOMY: The wall of the duodenum contains circular folds (plicae circulares) and villi, both of which increase the surface area. The microvilli of the epithelial cells are called the *brush border,* which also increases surface area for absorption. Intestinal glands (of Lieberkühn) between the bases of the villi secrete digestive enzymes, and Brunner's glands in the submucosa secrete mucus. The common bile duct opens at the ampulla of Vater. The nerve supply is both sympathetic (the celiac plexus) and parasympathetic (the vagus nerves). Blood is supplied by branches of the hepatic and superior mesenteric arteries. SEE: *digestive system* for illus.

   FUNCTION: Acid chyme enters the duodenum from the stomach, as do bile from the liver via the gallbladder and pancreatic juice from the pancreas. Bile salts emulsify fats; bile and pancreatic bicarbonate juice neutralize the acidity of the chyme. Pancreatic enzymes are lipase, which digests emulsified fats to fatty acids and glycerol; amylase, which digests starch to maltose; and trypsin, chymotrypsin, and carboxypeptidase, which continue the protein digestion begun in the stomach by pepsin. Intestinal enzymes are peptidases, which complete protein digestion to amino acids, and sucrase, maltase, and lactase, which digest disaccharides to monosaccharides. Some of these enzymes are in the brush border of the intestinal epithelium and are not secreted into the lumen. Three hormones are secreted by the duodenum when chyme enters. Gastric inhibitory peptide decreases gastric motility and secretions. Secretin stimulates the pancreas to secrete sodium bicarbonate and the liver to produce bile. Cholecystokinin stimulates secretion of enzymes from the pancreas and contraction of the gallbladder to propel bile into the common bile duct.

   The end products of digestion (amino acids, monosaccharides, fatty acids, glycerol, vitamins, minerals, and water) are absorbed into the capillaries or lacteals within the villi. Blood from the small intestine passes through the liver by way of the portal vein before returning to the heart.

duplex Having two components or two functions.

duplication, duplicature [L. *duplicare,* to double] Doubling or folding of a part or an organ; the state of being folded.

duplicitas (dū-plĭs′ĭ-tăs) A fetal abnormality in which an organ or a part is doubled or apparently doubled.

dupp (dŭp) In cardiac auscultation, the expression for the second heart sound heard over the apex. This sound is shorter and of higher pitch than *lubb,* the first heart sound. SEE: *auscultation; heart.*

Dupuytren, Baron Guillaume (dŭ-pwē-tran′) French surgeon, 1777–1835.

   D. contracture Contracture of palmar fascia usually causing the ring and little fingers to bend into the palm so that they cannot be extended. This condition tends to occur in families, after middle age, and more frequently in men. There is no correlation between occupation and development of this condition. It is associated with liver disease and long-term use of phenytoin. SEE: illus.

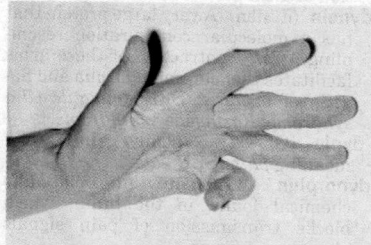

DUPUYTREN CONTRACTURE

ETIOLOGY: The cause is unknown.
TREATMENT: The tissue causing the contracture is removed surgically.

   D. fracture Fracture of the fibula occurring near the distal tibiofibular syndesmosis. Although the exact definition is unclear, this fracture is often accompanied by concurrent rupture of the distal tibiofibular ligaments, medial deltoid ligament, and dislocation of the talus. The medial malleolus may also be fractured.

   D. splint A splint used to prevent eversion in Pott fracture.

dura (door′ă, dū′ră) [L. *durus,* hard] SEE: under *mater.*

durable medical equipment (door′ă-bĕl, dūr′) ABBR: DME. Assistive devices used by patients, e.g., walkers, electric beds, and bedside commodes.

durable power of attorney for health care Health care proxy.

dural (dū′răl) [L. *durus,* hard] Pert. to the dura.

Durand-Nicolas-Favre disease (dū-răn′nĭk′ō-lăs-făv′r) Lymphogranuloma venereum.

duraplasty (dū″ră-plăs′tē) [″ + Gr. *plassein,* to form] Plastic repair of the dura mater.

duration 1. The period of time something has been present. 2. In obstetrics, the time between the beginning and the end of one uterine contraction.

duration of response In cancer care, the time between the initial response to therapy and subsequent disease progression or relapse.

durematoma (dū″rĕm-ă-tō′mă) [″ +

Gr. *haima,* blood, + *oma,* tumor] Accumulation of blood between the arachnoid and the dura.

Durham rule (of criminal responsibility) (dŭr′ăm, dur′) [From *Durham v. United States* (1954)] SEE: under *rule.*

duritis (dū-rī′tĭs) [″ + Gr. *itis,* inflammation] Inflammation of the dura. SYN: *pachymeningitis.*

Durkan test (dŭrk′ăn) Compression of the carpal canal at the wrist to see if this action elicits symptoms of carpal tunnel syndrome.

duroarachnitis (dū″rō-ăr″ăk-nī′tĭs) [″ + Gr. *arachne,* spider, + *itis,* inflammation] Inflammation of the dura and the arachnoid membrane.

Duroziez murmur (du-rō″zē-ā′) [Paul Louis Duroziez, Fr. physician, 1826–1897] The systolic and diastolic murmur heard over peripheral arteries in patients with aortic insufficiency. The murmur is audible when pressure is applied to the area just distal to the stethoscope.

dust Minute, fine particles of earth; any powder, esp. something that has settled from the air.

   blood d. Hemoconia.

   house d. The total of particles present in the air in a house. Materials included are mites, hairs, fibers, pollens, and smoke particles.

dust cell SEE: under *cell.*

dusting powder Any fine powder for dusting on skin.

duty (doo′tē, dū′) A social, professional, legal, or ethical expectation that compels a standard of performance; an obligation or requirement.

duty of care The legal and moral obligation to act responsibly and prudently, e.g., to avoid taking actions that one may foresee as being potentially hazardous to others.

duty cycle SEE: under *cycle.*

duty hour Time spent at work in a health care institution providing direct patient care, performing administrative functions, or attending meetings and conferences.

duty to warn 1. An obligation to advise a patient about potential risks of a treatment or procedure. 2. The obligation of health care providers to advise people of the potential risks that others may pose to them.

Duverney, Joseph G. (doo-ver-nā′, dŭ-, -ne′) Fr. anatomist, 1648–1730.

   D. fracture A fracture of the ilium just below the anterosuperior spine.

DVT *deep vein thrombosis; deep venous thrombosis.*

dwarf (dwarf) A person of abnormally short stature and esp. of abnormal proportions. SEE: *achondroplasia; cretinism.* **dwarfism** (dwarf′izm), *n.*

   achondroplastic d. SEE: *achondroplasia.*

hypopituitary d. A dwarf whose short stature results from insufficient production of growth hormone.

pituitary d. Hypophyseal **d.**

dwarfism The condition of being abnormally small. It may be hereditary or a result of endocrine dysfunction, nutritional deficiency, renal insufficiency, diseases of the skeleton, or other causes.

Names of specific diseases and bone and connective tissue disorders causing dwarfism are listed under the first word. SEE: e.g., *Bloom's syndrome; Cockayne syndrome; thanatophoric dysplasia.*

DWI *driving while intoxicated* (by alcohol or drugs).

dwindles (dwĭn′dĭlz) [AS *dwinan,* to waste away] A colloquial term for *failure to thrive.*

Dwyer instrumentation (dwī′ĕr) [Allan Frederick Dwyer, Australian orthopedic surgeon, 1920–1975] A surgical procedure for stabilization of scoliosis. The spine is approached from the front, and bolts are inserted transversely through each vertebra. A cable attached to the bolts is applied to the convexity of the curve, and the vertebrae are pulled together.

dx *Diagnosis.*

DXA *Dual energy x-ray absorptiometry*

Dy Symbol for the element dysprosium.

dyad (dī′ăd) [Gr. *duas,* pair] **1.** A pair. SYN: *couple.* **2.** A pair of chromosomes formed by the division of a tetrad in meiosis. A dyad is a single chromosome that has already replicated for a subsequent division. **3.** In chemistry, a bivalent element or radical. **4.** In psychiatry, two people interacting. SYN: *couple.*

dyadic (dī-ăd′ĭk) Pert. to the social interaction between two people.

dye Any substance that is of itself colored or that is used to impart color to another material, such as a thin slice of tissue prepared for microscopic examination. Dyes may also be employed in manufacturing test reagents used in medical laboratories.

dying **1.** The end of life and the transition to death. **2.** Degenerating (e.g., "dying back").

dynamic (dī-năm′ĭk) [Gr. *dynamis,* power] Pert. to vital force or inherent power; opposed to static.

dynamics The science of bodies in motion and their forces.

group d. **1.** In politics, sociology, and psychology, the study of the interactions of people who are members of a common class or community. **2.** The interactions of the people who share a common class, status, task, or community.

dynamo- [Gr. *dynamis,* power] Prefix meaning *power, energy,* or *strength.*

dynamogenic (dī″nă-mō-jĕn′ĭk) [″ + *gennan,* to produce] Pert. to or caused by an increase of energy.

dynamometer (dī″nă-mŏm′ĕ-tĕr) [″ + *metron,* measure] **1.** A device for measuring muscular strength. **2.** A device for determining the magnifying power of a lens.

dynamometry (dī″nă-mŏm′ē-trē) The process of obtaining quantifiable measurements of muscular strength, power, and/or endurance. SEE: *dynamometer.*

dynamoscopy (dī-năm-ŏs′kō-pē) **1.** Auscultation of muscles. **2.** Visual evaluation of the function of an organ or system.

dyne (dīn) [Gr. *dynamis,* power] The force needed for imparting an acceleration of 1 cm per second to a 1-g mass.

dynein (dī′nēn) A very large protein that has a molecular configuration resembling arms. Contraction of these arms facilitates the movement of cilia and flagella of bacteria. SEE: *immotile cilia syndrome; Kartagener's syndrome.*

-dynia [Gr. *odynē,* bodily pain] Suffix meaning *pain.* SEE: *-algia.*

dynorphin (dī-nŏr′fĭn) An opiate-like chemical found in the brain, which blocks transmission of pain signals along nerve fibers.

dys- [Gr. *dys-,* ill-, bad-, "un-," "mis-"] Prefix meaning *abnormal, bad, difficult, painful.* "Dys-" must not be confused with "dis-."

dysacusis, dysacousia, dysacousma (dĭs″ă-koo′sĭs, dĭs″ă-koo′zh(ē-)ă, dĭs″ă-kooz′mă) [Gr. *dys,* bad, + *akousis,* hearing] **1.** Discomfort caused by loud noises. **2.** Difficulty in hearing.

dysantigraphia (dĭs″ăn-tĭ-grăf′ē-ă) [″ + *anti,* against, + *graphein,* to write] Inability to copy writing or printed letters.

dysaphia (dĭs-ă′fē-ă) [″ + *haphe,* touch] Dullness of the sense of touch.

dysaptation, dysadaptation (dis-ap″tā′shŏn, dis-ad″ap″tā′shŏn) Impaired ability of the iris of the eye to accommodate to varying intensities of light.

dysarthria (dĭs-ăr′thrē-ă) [″ + *arthroun,* to utter distinctly] Impairments or clumsiness in the uttering of words due to diseases that affect the oral, lingual, or pharyngeal muscles. The patient's speech may be difficult to understand, but there is no evidence of aphasia.

dysarthrosis (dĭs″ăr-thrō′sĭs) [″ + *arthrosis,* joint] Joint malformation or deformity.

dysautonomia (dĭs″aw-tō-nō′mē-ă) [″ + *autonomia,* freedom to use one's own laws] A rare hereditary disease involving the autonomic nervous system and characterized by mental retardation, motor incoordination, vomiting, frequent infections, and convulsions. It is seen almost exclusively in Ashkenazi Jews. SEE: *Mecholyl test.*

dysbarism (dĭs′băr-ĭzm) [″ + *barys,*

heavy, + -ismos, condition] Decompression illness.

dysbasia (dĭs-bā′zē-ă) [″ + basis, a step] Difficulty in walking, esp. when due to disease of the brain or spinal cord.

dysbiosis (dĭs″bī-ō′sĭs) [″ + Gr. biosis, living] An unhealthy change in the normal bacterial ecology of a part of body, e.g., of the intestines or the oral cavity.

dyscalculia (dĭs″kăl-kū′lē-ă) [″ + L. calculare, to compute] An inability to make calculations. It may be found in childhood as a learning disability or may result from a stroke.

dyscephaly (dĭs-sĕf′ă-lē) Malformation of the head and facial bones.

dyschezia (dĭs-kē′zē-ă) [″ + chezein, to defecate] Painful or difficult bowel movements.

dyschiria (dĭs-kī′rē-ă) [″ + cheir, hand] Inability to tell which side of the body has been touched. If the sensation is referred to the wrong side, it is called allochiria, or allesthesia. If referred to both sides, it is called synchiria. SYN: acheiria.

dyschondroplasia (dĭs″kŏn-drō-plā′zē-ă) Chondrodysplasia.

dyschromatopsia (dĭs″krō-mă-tŏp′sē-ă) [″ + chroma, color, + opsis, vision] Imperfect color vision.

dyschromia (dĭs″krō′mē-ă) Discoloration, as of the skin.

dyschronism (dĭs-krō′nĭzm) [″ + chronos, time] A disturbed sense of time esp. that occurring after transportation from one time zone to another that is 5 to 10 hr ahead or behind. This leads to disturbances of sleep/wake cycles. SYN: jet lag.

dyscompetence Poor professional performance in a limited number of crucial or expected skills.

dyscontrol syndrome (dĭs″kŏn-trōl′) [″ + ″] A condition marked by sudden outbursts of violence or rage, associated with abnormal electrical discharges in the amygdaloid nuclear complex of the brain.

dyscoria (dĭs-kō′rē-ă) [″ + kore, pupil] Abnormal form or shape of the pupil.

dyscrasia (dĭs-krā′zē-ă) [Gr. dyskrasia, bad temperament] An old term meaning abnormal mixture of the four humors. The word is now used as a synonym for disease, esp. hematologic disease.

dysdiadochokinesia, dysdiadokokinesia (dĭs″dī″ad″ō-kō″kī-nē′zh(ē-)ă) [dys- + Gr. diadochos, succeeding + -kinesia] An impairment in making smooth and rapid alternating movements, e.g., tapping two objects separated by 30.5 cm (12 in.) 32 times in 15 seconds. This indicates ataxia (impaired cerebellar function). SYN: rapid alternating movement test.

dyseidesia (dĭs″ī-dē′zē-ŭ) [″ + Gr. ei-

dos, form, shape + ″] Difficulty in reading caused by an inability to recognize printed words.

dysembryoplasia (dis-em″brē-ō-plā′zh(ē-)ă) [dys- + embryo + -plasia] Fetal malformation occurring during growth of the embryo.

dysenteric (dĭs″ĕn-tĕr′ĭk) Pert. to dysentery.

dysentery (dĭs′ĕn-tĕr′ē) [″ + enteron, intestine] Diarrhea containing blood and mucus, resulting from inflammation of the walls of the gastrointestinal tract, esp. the colon. Abdominal pain, rectal urgency, and sometimes fever are present. Dysentery is caused by bacterial, viral, protozoan, or parasitic infections and is most common in places with inadequate sanitation, where food and water become contaminated with pathogens. SEE: diarrhea; Escherichia coli; Shigella.

TREATMENT: Prevention of infection is the major emphasis of health care providers, by improving the handling of waste products in the community and teaching proper techniques for handling, cooking, and storing food. Patients, particularly infants, may become severely dehydrated, develop metabolic acidosis, and require rehydration and, on occasion, antibiotic therapy.

PATIENT CARE: The basic principles of food handling should be taught to all those in the home: the need to wash hands frequently, particularly after using the toilet; using a meat thermometer to check that meat and dishes containing eggs are adequately cooked; refrigerating foods (below 40°F) until just before cooking and within 1 hr after cooking (esp. in warm weather); and separating raw and cooked food and not using the same utensils or dishes for raw and cooked foods.

amebic d. Amebiasis.

bacillary d. Diarrheal illness caused by bacterial infections of the colon, esp. strains of Shigella, Salmonella, Campylobacter, and Escherichia coli. It can be relatively mild or severe, endemic or epidemic in presentation. Virulent strains (e.g., Shigella dysenteriae and 0157:H7 E. coli) release exotoxins that can cause systemic infection and damage to the glomeruli of the kidney (hemolytic-uremic syndrome). SEE: Campylobacter jejuni; Escherichia coli; hemolytic uremic syndrome; Salmonella; Shigella.

dysesthesia (dĭs″es-thē′zh(ē-)ă) [dys- + esthesia] An abnormal and unpleasant sensation, e.g., as of burning, cutting, numbness, prickling, stinging, or tingling of the skin. SEE: paresthesia.

dysexecutive syndrome (dĭs″eg-zek′yŭ-tiv) [dys- + L. executivus, carried out] The consequences of diseases of the frontal lobe of the brain, in which people have cognitive difficulties, e.g., paying attention, organizing time and tasks, making plans, and solving problems, as well as psychological and emotional problems.

dysferlin (dĭs-fĕr′lĭn) A skeletal muscle cell membrane protein. Deficiency or absence of this protein results in several forms of muscular dystrophy.

dysferlinopathy (dĭs-fĕr″lĭn-ŏp′ă-thē) [″ + ″] Any form of muscular dystrophy caused by deficient expression of dysferlin. Dysferlinopathies tend to weaken proximal and distal muscles.

dysfibrinogenemia (dĭs″fī-brĭn″ō-gĕ-nē′mē-ă) [Gr. *dys,* bad, + L. *fibra,* fiber, + Gr. *gennan,* to produce, + Gr. *haima,* blood] Any anomaly in the molecular architecture of fibrinogen. It may cause abnormal bleeding, abnormal blood clotting, or both.

dysfluency (dĭs-flū′ĕn-sē) Hesitant or halting verbal or written language use. Examples of dysfluencies are cluttering and stuttering. This lack of linguistic fluency may be normal during the early phases of language acquisition (e.g., in childhood).

dysfunction (dis-fŭngk′shŏn) [*dys-* + *function*] Abnormal, inadequate, or impaired action of an organ or part.

   constitutional hepatic d. Gilbert syndrome.

   coronary microvascular d. Coronary microvascular disease.

   erectile d. ABBR: ED. The inability to achieve or sustain a penile erection for sexual intercourse. It is a common disorder that affects millions of men worldwide. Although about half of all men between ages 40 and 70 experience some degree of ED, it is not an inevitable part of aging. The many causes of erectile dysfunction include tension or anxiety, vascular diseases of the pelvis, spinal cord injuries, autonomic nervous system disorders, testosterone deficiencies, pelvic injuries resulting from surgery, pelvic radiation, stroke, and side effects from intoxicants such as alcohol or medications (some antihypertensives, sedatives, opiates, and antidepressants). SYN: *impotence.* SEE: table.

   PATIENT CARE: Lack of information and emotional barriers such as embarrassment, fear, and anxiety can worsen ED. Because some patients with ED may be reluctant to discuss it, primary practitioners should include questions about sexual function as a routine part of history-taking. Physical examination should cover examination of the abdomen and genitalia, assessment of secondary sex characteristics and of peripheral pulses and blood pressure, and a digital rectal examination to evaluate prostate size. Laboratory testing to rule out underlying causes should include serum chemistries, fasting glucose and

Risk Factors for Erectile Dysfunction

Age > 60
Depression (or treatment with antidepressant medications)
Diabetes mellitus
Heart disease
Hypertension (or treatment with some antihypertensive medications)
Obesity or increased body mass index
Prostate cancer or its treatment
Sedentary lifestyle
Stroke
Tobacco use

lipid levels, thyroid function tests, and testosterone levels. In some patients, ultrasonography or arteriography may be helpful. Healthy males have involuntary erections during sleep. The presence of these erections helps to focus care away from an emphasis on purely physical causes. Psychological assessment may be indicated to rule out depression or other mental conditions.

Commonly prescribed drugs to treat ED may have serious side effects and drug interactions. Drugs like sildenafil (Viagra) or tadalafil (Cialis) should never be given to patients who use nitrates to control angina pectoris. The combination can cause severe and even fatal hypotension. Colorful visual disturbances while taking erectile aids may precipitate loss of vision. Other common side effects of these ED medications include headache, upset stomach, and priapism (an erection that does not go away after several hours).

Nonmedical treatments for ED include vacuum constriction devices (a plastic tube placed around the penis). Such devices are available without prescription. Pumping the air out of the tube creates a vacuum that draws blood into the penis, producing an erection, which then is maintained by placing one or more tension bands around the base of the penis for up to 30 minutes. These devices are often not well tolerated.

Surgical therapies include the implantation of devices in the penis that can be manipulated to create an erection. All patients being treated for ED should be taught that sexual problems can be reduced by avoiding recreational drugs and excessive alcohol, getting treatment for hypertension (and medication dosage adjustment as related to ED), and for patients with diabetes, maintaining glucose control. Exercising regularly, avoiding tobacco, maintaining low cholesterol levels and ideal body weight, and good communications between sexual partners can help men to manage ED.

hypertonic uterine d. Polysystole.

minimal brain d. ABBR: MBD. Former term for *attention-deficit hyperactivity disorder.*

pursuit d. Inability of the eyes to follow or track a moving object.

respiratory pump d. Any disease or condition that impairs ventilation due to failure of the nerves, muscles, or skeleton of the abdomen and thorax to function properly. It may be caused by a variety of purely neurological diseases, e.g., the polyneuropathy that paralyzes respiration in Guillain-Barré syndrome. Alternatively it may be caused by skeletal conditions, e.g., multiple rib fractures or ankylosing spondylitis; by excessive adipose tissue, as in obesity/hypoventilation; or by diaphragmatic paralysis from surgical injury to the phrenic nerves.

sexual d. A state in which a person experiences a change in sexual function during the sexual response phases of desire, excitation, and/or orgasm that is viewed as unsatisfying, unrewarding, or inadequate. There may be multiple causes, including lack of sexual interest or desire; impairments in sexual arousal, e.g., erectile function in men or vaginal lubrication or clitoral enlargement in women; inability to achieve or delay orgasm until one's partner is satisfied; pain during intercourse; medical or hormonal conditions that impair sexual function; and problems with substance abuse or prescription drugs. A careful history and physical examination will help determine the possible pathological aspects of the various phases. Is desire absent, overactive, or is there aversion? Is arousal sufficient to maintain desire and, in men, to attain erection? Does orgasm occur, and, if so, is it delayed or premature? Do the partners experience satisfaction at the completion of orgasm? Is pain present at any stage of the sexual activity?

The physical or mental factors that are involved should be treated and, when medications are responsible, alternative drugs should be substituted for those that appear to cause the disorder. SEE: *Nursing Diagnoses Appendix.*

vocal cord d. A disorder that mimics asthma in that it causes episodic wheezing and often inspiratory stridor. It is caused by closure of the vocal cords during inspiration. Unlike asthma it does not improve with bronchodilating drugs such as albuterol or ipratropium. It is primarily treated with patient education, biofeedback, and speech therapy. SYN: *paradoxical vocal cord **motion**.*

dysgammaglobulinemia (dĭs″găm″ă-glŏb″ū-lĭ-nē′mē-ă) Disproportion in the concentration of immunoglobulins in the blood. It may be congenital or acquired.

dysgenesis (dis-jen′ĕ-sĭs) [*dys-* + *genesis*] Defective or abnormal development, esp. in the embryo.

gonadal d. A congenital endocrine disorder caused by failure of the ovaries to respond to pituitary hormone (gonadotropin) stimulation. Clinically there is amenorrhea, failure of sexual maturation, and usually short stature. About one third of these patients have webbing of the neck and may have cubitus valgus. Intelligence may be impaired. Affected patients have a 45–chromosome XO karyotype. SYN: *Turner's syndrome.*

ETIOLOGY: The cause is a defect in or absence of the second sex chromosome.

reticular d. Severe combined immunodeficiency disease.

dysgenic (dĭs-jĕn′ĭk) [″ + *gennan,* to produce] Pert. to dysgenesis.

dysgenitalism (dĭs-jĕn′ĭ-tăl-ĭzm) [″ + L. *genitalia,* organs of reproduction, + Gr. *-ismos,* condition] A condition caused by abnormal genital development.

dysgerminoma (dĭs″jĕr-mĭn-ō′mă) [″ + L. *germen,* a sprout, + Gr. *oma,* tumor] A malignant neoplasm of the ovary.

dysgeusia (dĭs-gū′zē-ă) [″ + *geusis,* taste] Impairment or perversion of the gustatory sense in which normal tastes are interpreted as being unpleasant or completely different from the characteristic taste of a particular food or chemical compound.

dysglobulinemia (dĭs-glŏb″ū-lĭn-ē′mē-ă) [″ + L. *globulus,* globule, + Gr. *haima,* blood] Abnormality of the amount or quality of blood globulins.

dysglycemia (dis″glī-sē′mē-ă) [*dys-* + *-glycemia*] An abnormal level of blood sugars, whether high (hyperglycemia) or low (hypoglycemia).

dysgnathia (dĭs-nā′thē-ă) [″ + *gnathos,* jaw] Abnormality of the mandible and maxilla.

dysgonesis (dĭs″gō-nē′sĭs) [Gr. *dys,* bad, + *gone,* seed] 1. A functional disorder of the genital organs. 2. Poor growth of bacterial culture.

dysgonic (dĭs-gŏn′ĭk) Pert. to a bacterial culture of sparse growth.

dysgraphia (dĭs-grăf′ē-ă) [″ + *graphein,* to write] 1. A persistent deficit in handwriting, usually the result of developmental diseases (in children) and of brain injury, dementia, or stroke (in adults). 2. An infrequently used term for "writer's cramp."

dyshemoglobin (dĭs-hĕm″ō-glō′bĭn) ABBR: dysHb. A hemoglobin derivative that is incapable of reversibly associating with oxygen, and so is unable to carry oxygen from the lungs to the cells. The primary defect in dyshemoglobins is a chemical (or stereochemical) alteration of the heme prosthetic group. Two common dyshemoglobins are carboxyhemoglobin (COHb) in which carbon monoxide is covalently bonded to the hemoglobin molecule, and methemoglobin (metHb) in which the ferrous iron is oxidized to the ferric form. Other, indeterminate dyshemoglobins exist in minute amounts in circulating blood.

dyshidrosis, dysidrosis (dĭs-hĭ-drō'sĭs) [″ + ″ + *osis*, condition] **1.** A disorder of the sweating apparatus. **2.** A recurrent vesicular eruption on the skin of the hands and feet marked by intense itching. SEE: *pompholyx.*

TREATMENT: The control of sweating or proper absorption of perspiration is beneficial. For the feet, wearing absorbent socks and well-ventilated shoes and applying substances that reduce sweating help to control symptoms. Individuals who do not wear shoes are rarely found to have this disorder. Acute attacks respond to treatment with a corticosteroid in an ointment combined with iodoquinol. This is applied at night with an occlusive dressing.

dyskaryosis (dĭs-kăr″ē-ō'sĭs) Abnormality of the nucleus of a cell.

dyskeratosis (dĭs″kĕr-ă-tō'sĭs) [″ + *keras*, horn, + *osis*, condition] **1.** Epithelial alterations in which certain isolated malpighian cells become differentiated. **2.** Any alteration in the keratinization of the epithelial cells of the epidermis. This is characteristic of many skin disorders.

dyskeratosis congenita A rare X-linked or autosomal dominant disease characterized by dystrophic formation of the nails, oral leukoplakia, and hyperpigmentation of the skin. Affected patients may also suffer bone marrow failure, resulting in aplastic anemia or pulmonary fibrosis.

dyskinesia (dĭs″kĭ-nē′zh(ē-)ă) [*dys-* + *-kinesia*] **1.** A defect in the ability to perform voluntary movement. **2.** Any disorder characterized by uncontrolled or involuntary movements.

   biliary d. Symptoms of recurrent biliary colic in patients without gallstones, who nonetheless have an abnormal gallbladder ejection fraction on cholecystokinin-stimulated studies of the gallbladder.

   d. intermittens Periodic or intermittent inability to execute voluntary limb movements.

   primary ciliary d. Immotile cilia syndrome.

   tardive d. A neurological syndrome marked by slow, rhythmical, stereotyped movements, either generalized or in single muscle groups. These occur as an undesired effect of therapy with certain psychotropic drugs, esp. the phenothiazines. SYN: *tardive dystonia.*

   uterine d. Painful or spasmodic contractions of the uterus.

dyskinetic (dĭs″kĭ-nĕt′ĭk) Concerning dyskinesia.

dyslalia (dĭs-lā′lē-ă) [″ + *lalein*, to talk] Impairment of speech due to a defect of the speech organs.

dyslexia (dis-lek′sē-ă) [*dys-* + Gr. *lexis*, diction + *-ia*] Difficulty using and interpreting written forms of communication by a person whose vision and general intelligence are otherwise unimpaired. The condition is usually noticed in schoolchildren by the third grade. They can see and recognize letters but have difficulty spelling and writing words. They have no difficulty recognizing the meaning of objects and pictures and typically have no other learning disorders. SYN: *reading disability.* SEE: *learning disorder.*

ETIOLOGY: Although the exact cause is unknown, evidence suggests that dyslexia may be caused by an inability to break words into sounds and assemble word sounds from written language.

dyslipidemia (dĭs″lip″ĭ-dē′mē-ă) [*dys-* + *lipidemia*] Any disorder of fat metabolism, e.g., hypercholesterolemia or hypertriglyceridemia.

dyslogia (dĭs-lō′jē-ă) [″ + *logos*, word, reason] Difficulty in expressing ideas.

dysmaturity (dĭs″mă-choor-ĭt-ē) A condition in which newborns weigh less than established normal parameters for the estimated gestational age. SEE: *intrauterine growth retardation; postmaturity.*

dysmegalopsia (dĭs″mĕg-ă-lŏp′sē-ă) [″ + *megas*, big, + *opsis*, vision] Inability to visualize correctly the size of objects; they appear larger than they really are.

dysmelia (dĭs-mē′lē-ă) [″ + *melos*, limb] Congenital deformity or absence of a portion of one or more limbs.

dysmenorrhea (dĭs″men″ŏ-rē′ă) [*dys-* + *meno-* + *-rrhea*] Pain associated with menstruation. It is one of the most frequent gynecological disorders and is classified as primary or secondary. An estimated 50% of menstruating women experience this disorder, and about 10% of these are incapacitated for several days during each menstrual period. This disorder is the greatest single cause of absence from school and work among menstrual-age women. In the U.S. this illness causes the loss of an estimated 140 million work hours each year. SEE: *premenstrual tension syndrome; Nursing Diagnoses Appendix.*

ETIOLOGY: Primary dysmenorrhea has multiple possible causes, including hormonal imbalances, psychogenic factors, and increased prostaglandin secretion in menstrual flow, which intensifies uterine contractions, resulting in increased uterine hypoxia and pain. Above age 20, dysmenorrhea usually has a secondary cause. Secondary dysmenorrhea may be related to gynecologic disorders such as endometriosis, cervical stenosis, uterine leiomyomas (fibroids), uterine malposition, pelvic inflammatory disease, pelvic tumors, or adenomyosis. Dysmenorrhea may be associated with premenstrual syndrome symptoms such as frequent urination, nausea, vomiting, diarrhea, headache, backache, abdominal bloating, painful breasts, chills, irritability, and depression. Prostaglandins and their metabolites also can cause headache, syncope, and GI disturbances.

PATIENT CARE: Young women experiencing discomfort or pain during menstruation are encouraged to seek medical evaluation to attempt to determine the cause. Dysmenorrheal pain usually begins just before or at the start of menstrual flow and peaks within 24 hr. Pain is described as sharp, intermittent, cramping, radiating to the lower back, thighs, groin, or vulva. Relieving the pain should be the initial concern. Patients are taught to evaluate pain severity using a 1 to 10 scale. Pharmacological therapies include analgesics (aspirin, NSAIDs) for mild to moderate pain. These are most effective if taken 24 to 48 hr before the onset of menses, and are effective because they are anti-inflammatory and inhibit prostaglandin synthesis (by inhibiting the enzyme cyclooxygenase), decreasing the strength and severity of uterine contractions. Opioids or acetaminophen/opioid combinations may be prescribed for severe pain, to be used infrequently (when pain is at its worst). In primary dysmenorrhea, hormonal contraceptives relieve symptoms by suppressing ovulation (dysmenorrhea is associated with ovulatory cycles). Patients who would like to become pregnant should use antiprostaglandins rather than hormonal therapies for their dysmenorrhea.

Support and assistance are offered to help the patient to deal with the problem. Appropriate patient teaching should be provided, including explanations of normal female anatomy and physiology and the pathophysiology of dysmenorrhea. This is esp. important for adolescents and should include determining the patient's understanding of conception and pregnancy, and provision of information on contraception as appropriate. Application of mild heat to the abdomen may be helpful, but care must be taken in young adolescents because appendicitis may mimic dysmenorrhea. A well-balanced diet and moderate exercise are encouraged. Noninvasive pain relief measures (e.g.,

relaxation, distraction, and guided imagery) are employed, and the patient may be referred for biofeedback training to control pain and to support and self-help groups. Treatment in secondary dysmenorrhea focuses on identifying and, if possible, correcting the underlying cause. Conservative therapies are tried initially, but in some cases surgical treatment may be required.

primary d. Painful menses.

SYMPTOMS: The pain usually begins just before or at menarche. The pain is spasmodic and located in the lower abdomen, but it may also radiate to the back and thighs. Some individuals also experience nausea, vomiting, diarrhea, low back pain, headache, dizziness, and in severe cases, syncope and collapse. These symptoms may last from a few hours to several days but seldom persist for more than 3 days. They tend to decrease or disappear after the individual has experienced childbirth the first time, and to decrease with age. Primary dysmenorrhea is much more common than secondary dysmenorrhea.

ETIOLOGY: The exact cause is unknown, but uterine ischemia due to increased production of prostaglandins with increased contractility of the muscles of the uterus (i.e., the myometrium) is thought to be the principal mechanism. As in any disease or symptom, the individual's reaction to and tolerance of pain influences the extent of the disability experienced. Primary dysmenorrhea is not a behavioral or psychological disorder.

One study revealed that prevalence and severity of dysmenorrhea might have been reduced in those who used oral contraceptives and that severity was increased in those who had long duration of menstrual flow, who smoked, and who had had early menarche. Exercise did not influence the prevalence or severity of dysmenorrhea.

DIAGNOSIS: Cramping, labor-like pains that start just before or at onset of menstruation are characteristic of dysmenorrhea.

TREATMENT: Effective drugs are oral contraceptives and nonsteroidal anti-inflammatory drugs including aspirin. These medicines should be taken in the appropriate dose 3 to 4 times a day and with milk to lessen the chance of gastric irritation.

secondary d. Painful menses that manifest some years after menarche and result from identifiable pelvic disorders or diseases. Common causes include a history or finding of use of an intrauterine device, pelvic inflammatory disease, endometriosis, uterine leiomyomas, adenomyosis, fertility problems related to imperforate hymen, cervical stenosis, ovarian cysts, or pronounced uterine retroflexion and/or retroversion.

TREATMENT: Nonsteroidal anti-inflammatory drugs are recommended for pain management. Medical or surgical management is directed toward resolving the underlying problem.

dysmetabolic syndrome (dis-met″ă-bol′ik) [*dys-* + *metabolic*] Metabolic syndrome.

dysmetria (dĭs-mē′trē-ă) [Gr. *dys*, bad, + *metron*, measure] An inability to control the range of movement (e.g., on trying to touch an object with an index finger).

dysmetropsia (dĭs″mĕ-trŏp′sē-ă) [″ + ″ + *opsis*, vision] Inability to visualize correctly the size and shape of things.

dysmimia (dĭs-mĭm′ē-ă) [″ + *mimos*, imitation] **1.** Inability to express oneself by gestures or signs. **2.** Inability to imitate.

dysmnesia (dĭs-nē′zē-ă) [″ + *mneme*, memory] Any impairment of memory.

dysmorphic (dĭs-mor′fĭk) Misshapen.

dysmorphophobia (dĭs″mor-fō-fō′bē-ă) [″ + *morphe*, formed, + *phobos*, fear] Irrational fear of being deformed or the illusion that one is deformed.

dysmotility (dĭs′mō-tĭl″ĭ-tī) Any abnormality of smooth muscle function in the gastrointestinal tract, such as gastroparesis, gastric atony, intestinal pseudo-obstruction, or biliary dyskinesia.

dysmyotonia (dĭs″mī-ō-tō′nē-ă) [″ + *mys*, muscle, + *tonos*, tone] Muscle atony; abnormal muscle tonicity.

dysnomia (dĭs-nō′mē-ă) An aphasia in which the patient forgets words or has difficulty finding words for written or oral expression.

dysodontiasis (dĭs″ō-dŏn-tī′ă-sĭs) [″ + *odous*, tooth, + *-iasis*, process] Painful or difficult dentition.

dysontogenesis (dĭs″ŏn-tō-jĕn′ĕ-sĭs) [″ + *ontos*, being, + *gennan*, to produce] Defective development of an organism, esp. of an embryo. **dysontogenetic** (dĭs″ŏn-tō-jĕ-nĕt′ik), *adj*.

dysopia, dysopsia (dis-ō′pē-ă, dis-op′sē-ă) [″ + *opsis*, vision] Defective vision.

dysosmia (dĭs-ŏz′mē-ă) [″ + *osme*, smell] Distortion of normal smell perception.

dysostosis (dĭs″os-tō′sĭs) [*dys-*, + *ostosis*] Defective ossification.

    cleidocranial d. A congenital anomaly of bone and connective tissue characterized by cranial and facial malformation and incomplete development of the clavicles.

    mandibulofacial d. A condition marked by hypoplasia of the facial bones, downward sloping of the palpebral tissues, and malformation of the ears. It occurs in two forms thought to be autosomal dominants.

    maxillofacial d. Hypoplasia of the maxillae and nasal bones resulting in a flattened face, elongated nose, and small maxillary arch with crowding or malocclusion of teeth. SYN: *Binder syndrome; maxillofacial syndrome.* SEE: *Ellis-van Creveld syndrome; Weyers acrofacial dysostosis.*

dyspareunia (dĭs″pă-roo′nē-ă) [*dys-* + *pareunos*, lying beside + *-ia*] Pain in the labia, vagina, or pelvis during or after sexual intercourse.

ETIOLOGY: Causes are infections in the reproductive tract, inadequate vaginal lubrication, uterine myomata, endometriosis, atrophy of the vaginal mucosa, psychosomatic disorders, and vaginal foreign bodies.

TREATMENT: Specific therapy is for primary disease; counseling is given with respect to appropriate water soluble vaginal and vulvar lubrication. Petroleum jelly is of no benefit.

dyspepsia (dis-pep′shă, sē-ă) [*dys-* + Gr. *pepsis*, digestion + *-ia*] Upper abdominal discomfort, often chronic or persistent; indigestion. It is sometimes related to the ingestion of food and may be a side effect of many medications. It may include such symptoms as fullness, eructation, bloating, nausea, loss of appetite, or upper abdominal pain. SYN: *indigestion*.

    acid d. A dated term for *gastroesophageal reflux*.

    functional d. A term for functional digestive diseases.

    nonulcer d. Upper abdominal discomfort, often chronic, in which endoscopy reveals nondiagnostic, or normal, findings.

dyspeptic (dĭs-pĕp′tĭk) **1.** Affected with or pert. to dyspepsia. **2.** One afflicted with dyspepsia.

dyspermasia (dĭs″pĕr-mā′zē-ă) [″ + *sperma*, seed] Dyspermia.

dyspermia (dĭ-spĕrm′ē-ă) Difficult or painful emission of sperm during coitus.

dysphagia (dis-fā′j(ē-)ă) [*dys-* + *-phagia*] Inability to swallow or difficulty in swallowing. SEE: *achalasia; cardiospasm*.

PATIENT CARE: Nurses are often in the room with patients while they are eating and are therefore the health care professionals most likely to identify swallowing disorders in adults and children. When a swallowing problem is suspected, consultation with a speech therapist or trained nurse will often identify the need for further testing. Screening examinations include assessing patients for an intact gag reflex, testing how they respond to swallowing water, or modifying their diet to specified consistencies and thicknesses. Patients who appear to be aspirating should be kept from eating (made NPO) until they complete a modified barium swallow or other more formal testing.

Instructing patients in tucking in the chin while swallowing or turning the head to the side may be helpful for many with dysphagia after stroke. Other causes of dysphagia have other disease-specific remedies.

d. lusoria Dysphagia caused by pressure exerted on the esophagus by an anomaly of the right subclavian artery. SYN: *vascular d.*

oropharyngeal d. Difficulty in propelling food or liquid from the oral cavity into the esophagus. SYN: *transfer d.*

pharyngeal d. Aspiration of food into the trachea during the act of swallowing.

vascular d. Dysphagia lusoria.

dysphasia (dĭs-fā′zē-ă) [″ + *phasis,* speech] Impairment of speech resulting from a brain lesion or neurodevelopmental disorder. The speech impairment in dysphasia is less marked than the severe or global language loss found in aphasia. SYN: *dysphrasia.*

dysphonesia (dĭs″fō-nē′zē-ŭ) Difficulty in reading caused by an inability to sound out printed words.

dysphonia (dĭs-fō′nē-ă) [″ + *phone,* voice] Difficulty in speaking; hoarseness.

spasmodic d. A strained, strangled, or abnormally breathy voice in a patient with normal laryngeal anatomy. Flexible laryngoscopy reveals laryngeal tremor or spasm during respiration or vocalization. Adductor or abductor muscle spasms may cause the dysfunction. Adductor spasms respond to the injection of botulinum toxin into the thyroarytenoid muscles. Usually, the response lasts several months but provides only partial symptomatic relief.

dysphoria (dis-fōr′ē-ă) [*dys-* + *-phoria*] A long-lasting mood disorder marked by depression and unrest without apparent cause; a mood of general dissatisfaction, restlessness, anxiety, discomfort, and unhappiness.

gender d. Dissatisfaction or discomfort with one's phenotypic gender.

dysphrasia (dĭs-frā′zē-ă) [Gr. *dys,* bad, + *phrasis,* speech] Dysphasia.

dyspigmentation (dĭs″pĭg-měn-tā′shŭn) Abnormality of the skin or hair pigment.

dysplasia (dis-plā′zh(ē-)ă) [*dys-* + *-plasia*] Abnormal development of tissue. SYN: *alloplasia; heteroplasia.*

anal d. Anal intraepithelial **neoplasia.**

arrhythmogenic right ventricular d. ABBR: ARVD. A rare degenerative disease of desmosomes within heart muscle that may produce life-threatening cardiac arrhythmias. It is a cause of sudden death or ventricular tachycardia in athletes. The dysplasia is diagnosed by a combination of tests (specific angiographic, electrocardiographic, echocardiographic, MRI, and biopsy or necropsy criteria). Some forms of the disease are autosomal dominantly inherited. SYN: *arrhythmogenic right ventricular* **cardiomyopathy;** *arrhythmogenic right ventricular dysplasia / cardiomyopathy.*

bronchopulmonary d. The need for supplemental oxygen in an infant born prematurely, esp. when that need is present after 36 weeks' gestation. SYN: *chronic lung disease of the newborn.*

PATIENT CARE: A team approach is necessary to provide optimal inpatient and outpatient care to infants and their families. Educating the family about the disease, its treatment, and its prognosis are critical to providing optimal care to affected infants. Inpatient care emphasizes respiratory support for the infant, appropriate nutrition to support growth and development, and regular physical contact with parents to encourage bonding esp. during long, and emotionally taxing hospital stays. Enrolling the family in a follow-up program with supportive care for the infant is important to help the parents in the early months after hospital discharge. Educating the family about continuing care about follow-up appointments and therapies is essential. The care team addresses the nutritional, developmental, general medical and social services each infant and family need to promote optimal long-term development of the infant.

cervical d. Precancerous changes in the cells of the uterine cervix, typically obtained for cytological examination by brushing or scraping cells from the cervix during a Pap test or colposcopy. Changes found on the Papanicolaou test (Pap test) are called a *squamous intraepithelial lesion* (SIL) and are classified as low grade (LSIL), high grade (HSIL), or possibly malignant. When a biopsy of the cervix is performed, the dysplasia is called a *cervical intraepithelial neoplasia* (CIN) and is classified as CIN I-mild, CIN II-moderate, and CIN III-severe to carcinoma in situ.

chondroectodermal d. Ellis–van Creveld syndrome.

developmental d. of the hip Congenital **dislocation** of the hip.

ectodermal d. Any of a group of rare inherited disorders in which there are defects in the function or development of glands, hair, nails, or teeth, i.e., organs that originate embryologically in the ectoderm.

fibromuscular d. A dysplasia of the fibrous and muscular walls of an artery, resulting in impaired blood flow or stenosis. It is most often found in the renal arteries, esp. in young women as a cause of hypertension, or in the carotid arteries of adults.

fibrous d. A rare, nonheritable congenital bone disease characterized by disorganized alignment of collagen within bone and weak bone formation. Symptoms include bone pain, bone deformities, fractures, and neurological deficits. Some patients are also affected by endocrine disorders, such as diabetes mellitus, acromegaly, or hyperprolactinemia. There are two forms of the disease: monostotic fibrous dysplasia is a variant of the disease in which a single bony lesion is found; in polyostotic fibrous dysplasia, lesions are found in multiple bones, including long bones, facial and cranial bones, or other locations.

hereditary ectodermal d. A form of anhidrotic dysplasia marked by few or absent sweat glands and hair follicles, smooth shiny skin, abnormal or absent teeth, nail deformities, cataracts or corneal alterations, absence of mammary glands, a concave face, prominent eyebrows, conjunctivitis, deficient hair growth, and mental retardation.

Kniest d. SEE: *Kniest dysplasia.*

McCusick metaphyseal d. SEE: *McCusick metaphyseal dysplasia.*

monostotic fibrous d. Fibrous dysplasia that affects a single bone.

neuronal intestinal d. ABBR: NID. A disorder of bowel motility in which the innervation of the intestines is ectopic (the ganglions that provide nervous control of intestinal musculature being misplaced).

oculoauricular vertebral D. Hemifacial microsomia.

osteofibrous d. An extremely rare, benign bone tumor occurring in children under 10. The primary symptoms are painless swelling or bowing of bone. It usually develops in the tibia or fibula.

periapical cemento-osseous d. A benign, asymptomatic fibro-osseous lesion that develops at the apex of the anterior mandibular teeth. No treatment is necessary.

polyostotic fibrous d. Fibrous dysplasia affecting multiple bones, including, in some children, long bones as well as facial or cranial bones. SEE: *McCune-Albright syndrome.*

septo-optic d. A rare developmental disorder of the brain and eye in which the optic disk and septum pellucidum do not develop normally, resulting in blindness, hormonal deficiencies, learning disabilities, decreased muscular tone, and, occasionally, seizures. SYN: *Morsier syndrome.*

thanatophoric d. ABBR: TD. An often lethal form of osteochondrodysplasia in which abnormalities of bone and cartilage development are accompanied by underdevelopment of the lungs. It is detectable in utero with prenatal ultrasound.

dysplasminogen (dĭs″plăz-mĭn′ă-jĕn) [″

+ ″] Any of several varieties of abnormal plasminogen. Their presence in the bloodstream causes excessive blood clotting.

dyspnea (dis(p)-nē′ă) [*dys-* + *-pnea*] Shortage of air resulting in labored or difficult breathing, sometimes accompanied by pain. It is normal when it is due to vigorous work or athletic activity and should quickly return to normal when the activity ceases. SYN: *air hunger; breathlessness.* **dyspneic** (-nē-ik), *adj.*

SYMPTOMS: The patient reports that the work of breathing is excessive. Signs of dyspnea include audibly labored breathing, hyperpnea and/or tachypnea, retraction of intercostal spaces, a distressed facial expression, dilated nostrils, paradoxical movements of the chest and abdomen, gasping, and occasionally cyanosis.

PATIENT CARE: The patient is assessed for airway patency, and a complete respiratory assessment is performed to identify additional signs and symptoms of respiratory distress and alleviating and aggravating factors. Arterial blood gas values are obtained if indicated, and oxygen saturation is monitored. The patient is placed in a high Fowler, orthopneic, or other comfortable position. Oxygen and medications are administered as prescribed, and the patient's response is evaluated and documented. The nurse or respiratory therapist remains with the patient until breathing becomes less labored and anxiety has decreased. Blood work, pulmonary function studies, chest x-ray, ECG, CT-pulmonary angiography, or other studies may be used as part of the diagnostic workup, depending on findings of the history and physical examination.

cardiac d. Dyspnea due to inadequate cardiac output, i.e., from heart failure.

expiratory d. Dyspnea associated with obstructive lung diseases such as asthma or chronic bronchitis. Wheezing is often present.

inspiratory d. Dyspnea due to interference with the passage of air to the lungs. SEE: *stridor.*

paroxysmal-nocturnal d. ABBR: PND. Sudden attacks of dyspnea that usually occur when patients are asleep in bed. The affected patient awakens gasping for air and tries to sit up (often near a window) to relieve the symptom. PND is one of the classic symptoms of left ventricular failure, although it may also occasionally be caused by sleep apnea or by nocturnal cardiac ischemia.

dyspoiesis (dis″poy-ē′sĭs, -ē′sēz″) *pl.* **dyspoieses** [*dys-* + *-poiesis*] Abnormal formation of blood cells. **dyspoietic** (-et′ik), *adj.*

dyspraxia (dis-prak'sē-ă, 'sh(ē-)ă) [*dys- + -praxis + -ia*] A disturbance in the programming, control, and execution of volitional movements. It cannot be explained by absence of comprehension, inadequate attention, or lack of cooperation. It is usually associated with a stroke, head injury, or other condition affecting the cerebral hemispheres.

speech d. In people with normal muscle tone and speech muscle coordination, partial loss of the ability to pronounce words consistently, resulting from injury to the central nervous system or stroke.

dysprosium (dis-prō'zē-ŭm, -zh(ē-)ŭm) [Gr. *dyspros(itos),* hard to get to + *-ium* (1)] SYMB: Dy. A metallic element of the yttrium group of rare earths, atomic number 66, atomic mass 162.50. It has a metallic, bright silver luster, is relatively stable in air at room temperature, but dissolves in dilute or concentrated mineral acids. Dysprosium is used with vanadium and other elements to make laser materials.

dysprosody (dĭs-prŏs'ă-dē) Lack of the normal rhythm, melody, and articulation of speech. This condition may be present in patients with parkinsonism and in other disorders.

dysraphism, dysraphia (dis"rā'fizm, dis"rā'fē-ă) [" + *rhaphe,* seam, ridge] In the embryo, failure of raphe formation or failure of fusion of parts that normally fuse. SEE: *neural tube defect.*

spinal d. A general term applied to failure of fusion of parts along the dorsal midline that may involve any of the following structures: skin, vertebrae, skull, meninges, brain, and spinal cord.

dysreflexia (dĭs"rē'flĕks-ē-ă) The state in which an individual with a spinal cord injury at T-7 or above experiences a life-threatening uninhibited sympathetic response of the nervous system to a noxious stimulus.

dysrhythmia (dis-rith'mē-ă) [*dys-rhythm + -ia*] Abnormal, disordered, or disturbed rhythm. SEE: *arrhythmia.*

cardiac d. arrhythmia. SEE: *Nursing Diagnoses Appendix.*

ventricular d. Ventricular **arrhythmia.**

dyssomnia (dĭ-sŏm'nē-ă) Sleep disorders characterized by a disturbance in the amount, quality, or timing of sleep. Disorders include primary insomnia, primary hypersomnia, narcolepsy, breathing-related sleep disorders, altitude insomnia, food allergy insomnia, environmental sleep disorder, and circadian rhythm sleep disorders. SEE: *sleep; sleep disorder.*

dysstasia (dĭ-stā'zē-ă) [" + *stasis,* standing] Difficulty in standing.

dyssynchrony (dis-sing'krŏ-nē) [*dys- + synchrony*] Any disorder in the normal or expected coordination of timed events.

auditory d. Auditory neuropathy.

neuromechanical d. Any difference between the respiratory support provided to a patient by a mechanical ventilator and the patient's breathing. In neuromechanical dyssynchrony, the inspiration of the ventilator is typically longer than the patient's. This difference is referred to colloquially as "fighting the ventilator."

patient-ventilator d. Failure of synchronous interaction between a patient's neurally controlled breathing and the timing of a mechanical ventilator. SEE: *patient-ventilator interaction.*

dyssynergy (dĭs-sĭn'ĕr-jē) **1.** Uncoordinated contractions of muscle fibers (e.g., of the myocardium or of the urinary bladder when the external urinary sphincter is closed). **2.** The tendency of one addiction to predispose a person to another.

dystaxia (dĭs-tăk'sē-ă) [" + *taxis,* arrangement] Partial ataxia.

dysthymia (dĭs-thī'mē-ă) [" + *thymos,* mind] Dysthymic disorder. SEE: *Nursing Diagnoses Appendix.*

dysthymic disorder (dĭs-thī'mĭk) A chronically depressed or dysphoric mood that is present more than 50% of the time for at least 2 years in adults or as an irritable mood for 1 year for children or adolescents. Affected people describe themselves as being chronically sad and "down in the dumps." SYN: *dysthymia; dysthymic mood disorder.*

SYMPTOMS: The symptoms include: poor appetite or overeating; insomnia or hypersomnia; low energy or fatigue; low self-esteem; poor concentration or difficulty making decisions; and feelings of hopelessness. The diagnosis of this disorder is not made if the patient has ever had a manic, hypomanic, or mixed manic and hypomanic episode. Often beginning in childhood or adolescence (where it occurs equally in both sexes), in adults the disorder is more common in women and may cause social or occupational impairment.

TREATMENT: Treatment traditionally has included tricyclic antidepressants, monoamine oxidase inhibitors, or second-generation antidepressants such as citalopram, fluoxetine, bupropion, paroxetine, sertraline, or venlafaxine. The latter drugs have the advantage of having no anticholinergic side effects, nor causing weight gain, nor altering cardiac conduction. They may, however, cause nausea, weight loss, or insomnia.

PATIENT CARE: All professional care providers teach the patient about depression, emphasizing available methods to relieve symptoms. As the patient learns to recognize depressive thought patterns, he can begin to consciously substitute self-affirming thoughts. The patient is encouraged to talk about and write down feelings. Health care providers listen attentively and share their observations of the patient's behavior but avoid feigning cheerfulness and judgmental responses. A structured routine with noncompetitive and group activities may help build the patient's self-confidence and ability to socialize. The patient is assessed for suicidal thoughts and ideation, and suicide precautions are instituted for patients at risk.

If antidepressant drug therapy has been prescribed, the patient is taught about the medications and is monitored for desired, adverse, and side effects. For drugs that produce anticholinergic effects, sugarless gum or hard candy may relieve dry mouth. For sedative drugs the patient should avoid activities that require alertness until the degree of such effects is known. The patient taking a tricyclic antidepressant should avoid alcohol and other central nervous system depressants. The patient taking a monoamine oxidase inhibitor should avoid foods that contain tyramine (ingestion may result in a hypertensive crisis). Patients prescribed serotonin reuptake inhibitors should avoid tryptans because of the risk of inducing a serotonergic crisis. The patient is reminded that most antidepressants take several weeks to work.

dysthyroid (dĭs-thī′-rŏyd) A state of abnormal thyroid functioning.

dysthyroidism (dĭs-thī′roy-dĭzm) [″ + ″ + *eidos*, form, shape, + *-ismos*, condition] Imperfect development and function of the thyroid gland. SYN: *dysthyreosis*.

dysthyroid optic neuropathy SEE: under *neuropathy*.

dystocia (dis-tō′sh(ē-)ă) [*dys-* + *toco-* + *-ia*] Difficult labor. It may be produced by either the size of the fetus or the small size of the pelvic outlet.

FETAL CAUSES: Large fetal size (macrosomia) usually causes this condition. Other factors are malpositions of the fetus (transverse, face, brow, breech, or compound presentation), abnormalities of the fetus (hydrocephalus, tumors of the neck or abdomen, hydrops), and multiple pregnancy (interlocked twins).

MATERNAL CAUSES: *Uterus:* Causes include uterine inertia, congenital anomalies (bicornuate uterus), tumors (fibroids, carcinoma of the cervix), and abnormal fixation of the uterus by previous operation. *Bony pelvis:* Causes include flat or generally contracted pelvis, funnel pelvis, exostoses of the pelvic bones, and tumors of the pelvic bones. *Cervix uteri:* Causes include Bandl ring, a rigid cervix that will not dilate, and stenosis and stricture preventing dilatation. *Ovary:* Ovarian cysts may block the pelvis. *Vagina and vulva:* Causes include cysts, tumors, atresias, and stenoses. *Pelvic soft tissues:* A distended bladder or colon may interfere.

DIAGNOSIS: Dystocia generally can be detected by vaginal examination, ultrasound, and external pelvimetry before the patient goes into labor.

TREATMENT: Treatment varies according to the condition that causes the dystocia. The goal is correction of the abnormality in order to allow the fetus to pass. If this is not possible, operative delivery is necessary. SEE: *cesarean section*.

dystonia (dĭs-tō′nē-ă) [*dys-* + *tono-* + *-ia*] Prolonged involuntary muscular contractions that may cause twisting (torsion) of body parts, repetitive movements, and increased muscular tone. These movements may be in the form of rhythmic jerks. The condition may progress in childhood, but progression is rare in adults. In children the legs are usually affected first. **dystonic** (-ton′ik), *adj*.

ETIOLOGY: Many childhood dystonias are genetically inherited. Drugs used to treat psychosis, Parkinson disease, strokes, brain tumors, toxic levels of manganese or carbon dioxide, and viral encephalitis may produce dystonia.

TREATMENT: Offending drugs are withdrawn, and the patient may be treated with diphenhydramine. Focal dystonias, such as blepharospasm or torticollis, may be treated with injected botulinum toxin, which paralyzes hypertonic muscle groups. Physiotherapy may also be helpful. Other treatments include physical therapy, deep brain stimulation, and pallidotomy.

cervical d. Spasmodic **torticollis**.

focal d. Prolonged contraction affecting a single body part or a group of muscles, e.g., in the neck or hand. The most common focal dystonias are blepharospasm, torticollis, and writer's (musician's) cramp.

idiopathic torsion d. A relatively uncommon, progressive neurological syndrome beginning in childhood and marked by twisting postures of the neck, limbs, and/or pelvis. The condition is an autosomal dominant trait. SYN: *d. musculorum deformans*.

d. musculorum deformans Idiopathic torsion **d.**

tardive d. Tardive **dyskinesia**.

dystopia (dĭs-tō′pē-ă) [″ + *topos*, place] Malposition (1); displacement of any organ.

d. canthorum Lateral displacement of the inner canthi of the eyes. **dystopic** (-tŏp′ik), *adj*.

dystrophia (dĭs-trō′fē-ă) Dystrophy.

dystrophin (dĭs-trŏf′ĭn) A protein of skeletal and cardiac muscle; it attaches the thin filaments of the sarcomeres to the proteins of the sarcolemma. Production of dystrophin is impaired in Duchenne's muscular dystrophy.

dystrophinopathy (dĭs-trŏf″ĭn-ŏp′ă-thē) [″ + ″] Diseases of muscle, such as Duchenne or Becker muscular dystrophy, that result from deficiencies or abnormalities of dystrophin.

dystrophoneurosis (dĭs-trŏf″ō-nū-rō′sĭs) [″ + *trephein*, to nourish, + *neuron*, nerve, + *osis*, condition] Defective nutrition caused by disease of the nervous system.

dystrophy (dĭs′trŏ-fē) [*dys-* + *-trophy*] A disorder caused by defective nutrition or metabolism. **dystrophic** (dĭs-trŏ′fĭk), *adj.*

    adiposogenital d. Fröhlich syndrome.

    asphyxiating thoracic d. Jeune syndrome.

    Becker muscular d. SEE: *Becker muscular dystrophy*.

    Bietti crystalline d. SEE: *Bietti crystalline dystrophy*.

    cone-rod d. A form of retinitis pigmentosa in which central visual loss occurs first. Common symptoms include progressive visual loss followed by the loss of color perception, and eventually peripheral visual loss and night blindness. The visual loss is not correctable with standard lenses. SEE: *retinitis pigmentosa*.

    congenital hereditary endothelial d. ABBR: CHED. An eye disorder in which the corneal endothelium becomes cloudy, resulting in myopia.

    corneal d. Any of several inherited disorders in which the cornea becomes cloudy, hazy, or speckled, resulting in variable degrees of visual loss.

    distal muscular d. ABBR: DD. One of several rare forms of muscular dystrophy in which the forearm, hand, calf, and foot muscles are primarily affected as opposed to the muscles of the shoulders or pelvic girdle. Its onset is usually in adults between the ages of 40 and 60. SYN: *distal myopathy*.

    Duchenne muscular d. SEE: under *Duchenne, Guillaume B. A.*

    Emery-Dreifuss muscular d. SEE: *Emery-Dreifuss muscular dystrophy*.

    facioscapulohumeral muscular d. A hereditary, progressive muscular dystrophy with onset in childhood or adolescence. It is marked by atrophic changes in the muscles of the shoulder girdle and face, inability to raise the arms above the head, myopathic facies, eyelids that remain partly open in sleep, and inability to whistle or purse the lips.

TREATMENT: Therapy is supportive; e.g., orthopedic devices can be used to prevent functional losses at the shoulder girdle. The patient should be encouraged to maintain as full and normal a life as possible and to avoid prolonged bed rest.

    macular d. Any inherited, progressive degeneration of the macula lutea retinae marked by progressive central visual loss beginning in childhood or adolescence. Representative forms of macular dystrophy include Best disease and Stargardt disease. SEE: *macula lutea retinae*.

    muscular d. Any of nine distinct genetic syndromes that affect muscular strength and action, some of which first become obvious in infancy, whereas others manifest in adolescence or young adulthood. The syndromes are marked by either generalized or localized muscle weakness, difficulties with walking or maintaining posture, muscle spasms, and sometimes neurological, behavioral, cardiac, or other functional limitations. Detailed information about the disease can be obtained from the Muscular Dystrophy Association website at www.mdausa.org.

    myotonic d. ABBR: DM. An autosomal dominant disorder caused by the repeated expansion of the trinucleotide sequence cytosine-thymidine-guanine (CTG)) in the DNA of chromosome 19. It is the most commonly inherited of the muscular dystrophies.

    oculopharyngeal muscular d. ABBR: OPMD. A rare form of muscular dystrophy in which muscles that control the eyelids and swallowing are primarily affected. Ptosis and dysphagia beginning in the patient's late 40s or early 50s are characteristic symptoms. Weakness in the limbs often follows. The disease occurs most often in French-Canadian or Hispanic kindreds.

    progressive muscular d. Spinal muscular **atrophy**.

    pseudohypertrophic muscular d. Duchenne muscular dystrophy.

    reflex sympathetic d. An abnormal response of the nerves of the face or of an extremity, marked by pain, autonomic dysfunction, vasomotor instability, and tissue swelling. Although the precise cause of the syndrome is unknown, it often follows trauma, stroke, neuropathy, or radiculopathy. In about one third of all patients, the onset is insidious. Affected patients often complain of burning pain with any movement of an affected body part, excessive sensitivity to light touch or minor stimulation, temperature changes (heat or cold) in the affected limb, localized sweating, localized changes of skin color, or atrophic changes in the skin, nails, or musculature. SYN: *algodystrophy; complex regional pain syndrome, type 1; shoulder-hand syndrome; Sudeck disease*. SEE: *Nursing Diagnoses Appendix*.

TREATMENT: Early mobilization of the body part with multimodality therapy may improve the symptoms of reflex sympathetic dystrophy. Drug therapies often include prednisone or other corticosteroids and narcotic analgesics; trancutaneous electrical stimulation, physical therapy, or nerve blocks may also prove helpful.

rod-cone d. A form of retinitis pigmentosa in which rod degeneration precedes cone degeneration. Night blindness is usually the first symptom, followed by peripheral visual loss.

Schnyder crystalline d. SEE: *Schnyder crystalline dystrophy.*

twenty-nail d. Longitudinal ridging and fragmentation of all the fingernails and toenails. It is a characteristic finding in lichen planus.

vitelliform d. Vitelliform macular **d.**

vitelliform macular d. An autosomal dominant retinal disease in which central visual acuity is diminished when lipofuscin accumulates under the macula. When the disease occurs in childhood, it is called Best disease.

vulvar d. Lichen sclerosus et atrophicus.

dysuria (dīs-ū′rē-ă) [″ + *ouron*, urine] Painful or difficult urination, symptomatic of numerous conditions. Dysuria may indicate cystitis; urethritis; infection anywhere in the urinary tract; urethral stricture; hypertrophied, cancerous, or ulcerated prostate in men; prolapse of the uterus in women; pelvic peritonitis and abscess; metritis; cancer of the cervix; dysmenorrhea; or psychological abnormalities. The condition may also be caused by certain medications, esp. opiates and medicines used to prevent motion sickness as well as bladder irritants such as caffeine, artificial sweeteners, nicotine, and acidic foods. Pain and burning may be caused by concentrated acid urine.

PATIENT CARE: The patient with dysuria should be taught how to obtain a midstream, clean-catch urine specimen for culture and sensitivity. Additional diagnostic testing (e.g., urethral swabs or pelvic examinations) may be required based on patient history and physical examination. Unless fluids are restricted as a result of heart or kidney failure, the patient with dysuria may benefit from drinking fluids liberally to dilute the urine and reduce irritation. If phenazopyridine HCl is prescribed as a urinary analgesic/antiseptic, the patient should be advised to take the drug with meals to minimize gastric distress and be reminded that the drug colors urine, saliva, and tears red or orange and may stain fabrics and contact lenses. If urinary tract or sexually transmitted infections are suspected or isolated, the patient may be prescribed an antibiotic. Patients found to have vaginal yeast infections may need antifungal treatment. SEE: *urinary tract infection.*

dyszoospermia (dĭs″zō-ō-spĕrm′ē-ă) [″ + ″ + *sperma,* seed] Imperfect formation of spermatozoa.

¹E *emmetropia; energy; Escherichia; eye.*

²E In echocardiography, the initial velocity of blood flow through the opening mitral valve.

e *electric charge; electron;* L. *ex,* out of.

E₁ *estrone.*

E₂ *estradiol.*

E₃ *estriol.*

Eₕ The symbol for the oxidation-reduction (redox) potential. The redox potential is the electric potential energy needed to transfer a mole of electrons from an oxidant to a reductant. The use of catalysts to remove contaminants from water supplies during water treatment relies on measurements of the redox potential. It is usually referenced to the potential of a standard electrolytic cell.

ea *each.*

EACA *epsilon-aminocaproic acid.*

ead L. *eadem,* the same.

EAFUS *Everything added to food in the United States.*

eAG *Estimated average* **glucose.**

EaggEC Enteroaggregative *Escherichia coli.*

EAH *Exercise-associated* **hyponatremia.**

Eales disease (ēlz) [Henry Eales, Brit. physician, 1852–1913] Recurrent hemorrhage into the retina and vitreous, most commonly seen in men in the second and third decades of life. The cause is unknown.

ear (ēr) The organ of hearing and equilibrium. It consists of outer, middle, and inner portions, and is innervated by the eighth cranial nerve. SEE: illus.

The pathway of hearing is as follows: the auricle funnels sound waves from the environment through the external auditory canal to the tympanic membrane, which makes this thin epithelial structure vibrate. The vibrations are transmitted to the auditory ossicles and then to the perilymph and endolymph. The receptors are part of the organ of Corti and generate impulses transmitted by the cochlear branch of the eighth cranial nerve to the spiral ganglion and auditory tracts of the brain. The auditory areas are in the temporal lobes.

The healthy human ear responds to a variety of sounds, with frequencies ranging from about 20 to 20,000 Hz. It is most sensitive, however, to sounds whose frequencies fall in the 1500- to 3000-Hz range, the frequency range of most human speech. SEE: *hearing.*

The receptors for equilibrium are in the utricle, saccule, and semicircular ducts, which are innervated by the vestibular branch of the eighth cranial nerve. Impulses from the utricle and saccule provide information about the position of the head, those from the semicircular ducts about the speed and direction of three-dimensional movement.

cauliflower e. A colloquial term for a thickening of the external ear resulting from trauma. It is commonly seen in boxers. Plastic surgery may restore the ear to a normal shape.

external e. The portion of the ear consisting of the auricle and external auditory canal, and separated from the middle ear by the tympanic membrane or eardrum. SYN: *auris externa; outer* **e.**

foreign bodies in e. Objects that enter the ear accidentally or are inserted deliberately. These are usually insects, pebbles, beans or peas, cotton swabs, or coins.

SYMPTOMS: Foreign objects cause pain, ringing, or buzzing in the ear. A live insect usually causes a noise.

TREATMENT: Water must not introduced if any vegetable matter is in the ear because the water may push the foreign body further into the ear or cause the matter to swell and become firmly embedded.

To remove insects from the ear, a few drops of lidocaine should be instilled. Inorganic foreign bodies can be removed with small forceps by a health care provider.

glue e. The chronic accumulation of a viscous exudate in the middle ear, occurring mostly in children between 5 and 8. It causes deafness, which can be treated by removal of the exudate.

inner e. The portion of the ear consisting of the cochlea, the vestibule, and the bony semicircular canals, which contain the receptors for static and dynamic equilibrium. The receptors are innervated by the vestibulocochlear nerve. SYN: *auris interna; Internal* **e.** SEE: illus.

internal e. Inner ear.

lop e. A cosmetic deformity of the earlobe in which the upper portion of the earlobe bows out laterally from the head.

middle e. The air-filled expansion of the auditory tube separating the external auditory canal from the inner ear. Sound is transmitted through the middle ear as vibrations along a chain of three tiny bones, the auditory ossicles.

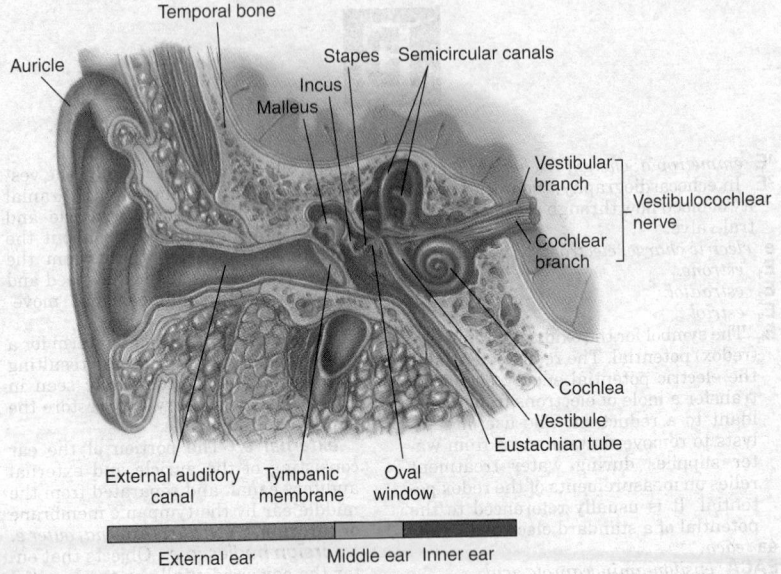

Temporal bone
Auricle
Stapes
Incus
Malleus
Semicircular canals
Vestibular branch
Vestibulocochlear nerve
Cochlear branch
Cochlea
Vestibule
Eustachian tube
External auditory canal
Tympanic membrane
Oval window

External ear   Middle ear   Inner ear

STRUCTURE OF THE EAR

SYN: *tympanic cavity.* SEE: *eardrum; tympanum.*

nerve supply of e. *External:* The branches of the facial, vagus, and mandibular nerves and the nerves from the cervical plexus. *Middle:* The tympanic plexus and the branches of the mandibular, vagus, and facial nerves. *Internal:* The vestibulocochlear nerve (eighth cranial).

outer e. External e.

pierced e. An earlobe that has been pierced with a needle so that a perma-

nent channel will remain, permitting the wearing of an earring attached to the ear by a connector that passes through the channel.

surfer's e. The formation of an exostosis in the external auditory canal of surfers, esp. those who habitually surf in colder waters.

swimmer's e. A type of external otitis seen in swimmers, usually during the summer. It is typically caused by *Staphylococcus aureus* or *Pseudomonas aeruginosa* and is treated with a sus-

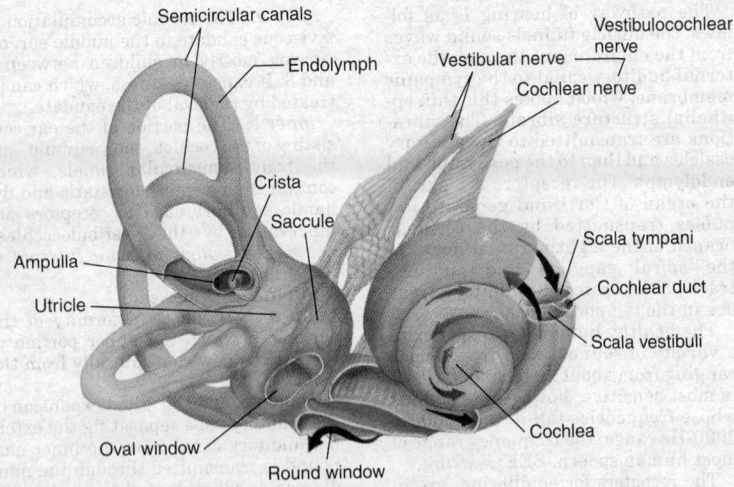

Semicircular canals
Endolymph
Vestibular nerve
Vestibulocochlear nerve
Cochlear nerve
Crista
Saccule
Scala tympani
Ampulla
Cochlear duct
Utricle
Scala vestibuli
Oval window
Cochlea
Round window

STRUCTURE OF THE INNER EAR

pension of neomycin, polymyxin B sulfate, and hydrocortisone.

earache Pain in the ear. SYN: *otalgia; otodynia.*

ear candling, ear coning An alternative medicine practice in which a cone of waxed paper is placed in the patient's external auditory canal and then set on fire. It is promoted as a treatment for cerumen impaction and for removal of unspecified toxins from the body. The practice is dangerous; it occasionally results in burns or perforation of the eardrum. In Canada and the U.S., it is considered an unregulated medical practice because it is unproven, untested, and illegal to use.

eardrops A medication in liquid form for instillation into the external ear canal, usually to treat infections or loosen cerumen.

⚠ Eardrops should not be used if the tympanic membrane is damaged or broken.

eardrum (ēr'drŭm) Tympanic **membrane**.

earlobe, ear lobe The soft bottom edge of the outer ear containing no cartilage.

early intervention In rehabilitative medicine, a system of coordinated, community-based services for infants and toddlers from birth to 3 years of age who are at risk for developmental delay. Services are designed to identify, prevent, or remediate existing problems and enhance development through individual and family intervention strategies. SEE: *developmental delay.*

early neonatal death SEE: under *death.*

early supported discharge SEE: under *discharge.*

ear pinning A colloquial term for *otoplasty.*

ear plug SEE: under *plug.*

earth eating Eating of clay or dirt, sometimes by children as a form of pica.

ear thermometry Determination of the temperature of the tympanic membrane by use of a device for rapidly sensing infrared radiation from the membrane. Commercially available devices do this in 3 sec. The convenience of assessing body temperature using this method is obvious, but if the probe is left in the ear canal for more than a few seconds, the reading may be abnormally low. In general, the accuracy and reproducibility of ear thermometry is poor. SEE: *temperature.*

ear tube Grommet.

earwax (ēr'wăks) Cerumen.

Eastern Cooperative Oncology Group ABBR: ECOG. An association of cancer centers in the eastern United States that jointly study the effects of cancer and the efficacy of cancer treatments.

eat [AS. *etan*] **1.** To devour, as food. **2.** To take solid food. **3.** To corrode.

eating disorder (ēt'ing) Any pattern of eating that results in compromises or potential compromises to one's health. Anorexia nervosa, bulimia, pica, and rumination disorder of infancy are included.

Eaton agent (ēt'ŏn) [Monroe D. Eaton, U.S. neurologist, 1905–1958] *Mycoplasma pneumoniae,* one of the causes of atypical pneumonia. SEE: *Mycoplasma.*

Eaton-Lambert syndrome (ēt'ĭn-lăm'bĕrt sĭn'drōm") Lambert-Eaton myasthenic syndrome.

Eberthella (eb"ĕr-thel'ă) [Karl Joseph Eberth, Ger. pathologist, 1835–1926] The former name for the genus of bacteria now classified as *Salmonella.*

Ebola virus hemorrhagic fever (ē"bō'lă) [*Ebola,* Democratic Republic of the Congo (formerly Zaire)] SEE: under *fever.*

EBP Evidence-based practice SEE: under *practice.*

Ebstein anomaly (eb'stīn", ep') [Wilhelm Ebstein, Ger. physician, 1836–1912] A congenital heart condition resulting from downward displacement of the tricuspid valve from the anulus fibrosus. It causes fatigue, palpitations, and dyspnea.

eburnation (eb"ŭr-nā'shŭn) [L. *eburnus,* made of ivory] Changes in bone that cause it to become dense, hard, and smooth like ivory; often seen at sites of active arthritis. **eburnated** (-nāt'ĕd), *adj.*

EBV *Epstein-Barr virus.* SEE: *mononucleosis, infectious.*

EC *Enteric-coated; Enzyme Commission; extracranial.*

ecarin (ē'kă-rĭn) [Gr. *echis,* viper] A prothrombin activator purified from the venom of the Indian saw-scaled viper. It is used in laboratory assays of anticoagulation by prothrombin inhibitors such as hirudin.

ecbolic (ĕk-bŏl'ĭk) [Gr. *ekbolikos,* throwing out] **1.** Hastening uterine evacuation by causing contractions of the uterine muscles. **2.** Any agent producing or hastening labor or abortion. SYN: *oxytocic.*

ECC *emergency cardiac care; external cardiac compression; emergency cardiovascular care.*

ECCE *Extracapsular cataract **extraction.***

eccentric (ĕk-sĕn'trĭk) [Gr. *ek,* out, + kentron,* center] **1.** Proceeding away from a center. **2.** Peripheral. **3.** Departing from the usual, as in dress or conduct.

eccentric muscle contraction SEE: under *contraction.*

eccentric viewing A method of scanning peripheral visual fields to optimize vision in patients with diseases that cause central visual loss, such as macular degeneration.

eccentro-osteochondrodysplasia (ĕk-sĕn″trō-ŏs″tē-ō-kŏn″drō-dĭs-plā′zhē-ă) [Gr. *ekkentros*, from the center, + *osteon*, bone, + *chondros*, cartilage, + *dys*, bad, + *plassein*, to form] A pathological condition of bones caused by imperfect bone formation. Ossification occurs in several different centers instead of in one common center.

ecchymosis (ĕk-ĭ-mō′sĭs) *pl.* **ecchymoses** [″ + ″ + *osis*, condition] Superficial bleeding under the skin or a mucous membrane; a bruise. SEE: illus. **ecchymotic** (-mŏt′ĭk), *adj.*

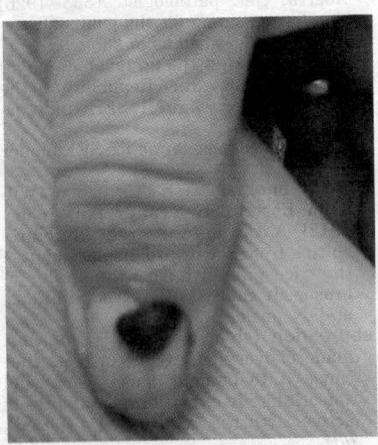

TRAUMATIC ECCHYMOSIS

ECCO2R *Extracorporeal carbon dioxide removal.*

eccrine (ĕk′rĭn) [Gr. *ekkrinein*, to secrete] Pert. to secretion, esp. of sweat. SEE: *apocrine; endocrine; exocrine.*

eccritic (ĕk-krĭt′ĭk) [Gr. *ekkritikos*] **1.** Promoting excretion. **2.** An agent that promotes excretion.

ecdysis (ĕk′dĭ-sĭs) *pl.* **ecdyses** [Gr. *ekdysis*, getting out] **1.** The shedding or sloughing off of the epidermis of the skin. SYN: *desquamation.* **2.** The shedding (molting) of the outer covering of the body as occurs in certain animals such as insects, crustaceans, and snakes.

ECF *extracellular fluid.*

ECG, ecg *electrocardiogram.*

Echidnophaga (ĕk″ĭd-nŏf′ă-gă) A genus of fleas belonging to the family Pulicidae.

E. gallinacea The sticktight flea, an important pest of poultry. It collects in clusters on the heads of poultry and in the ears of mammals. It may infest humans, esp. children.

Echinacea angustifolia, blacksamson echinacea (ĕk-ĭ-nā′sē-ă ahng-gŭs″tĭ-

fōl′ē-ă) A native American perennial herb of the family Compositae. Its extracts have been promoted as a means of treating or preventing upper respiratory infections. Many studies of Echinacea show conflicting results based on timing of administration, dosage, and varying plant preparation. Those allergic to ragweed should not take Echinacea as there is a cross allergen sensitivity.

Echinacea purpurea (pŭr-pūr′ēă, poor′) A native American perennial herb (purple coneflower) of the family Compositae. Its root and leaf extracts are promoted both for their effects on wound healing and for their impact on the treatment and prevention of respiratory infections.

echinate (ĕk′ĭ-nāt) [Gr. *echinos*, hedgehog] **1.** Spiny. **2.** In agar streak, a bacterial growth with pitted or toothed margins along the inoculation line; in stab cultures, coiled growth with pointed outgrowths. SYN: *echinulate.*

echinocandin (ē-kī″nō-kan′din) [Gr. *echinos*, hedgehog, sea urchin, + *Cand(ida albicans)* + *-in*] Any of a class of antifungal drugs that block the synthesis of the fungal cell wall.

echinococcosis (ĕ-kī″nŏ-kok-ō′sĭs, -ō′sēz″) *pl.* **echinococcoses** [*Echinococcus* + *-osis*] Infestation with *Echinococcus.*

alveolar e. Infection with the larval stage of *Echinococcus multilocularis*, a tapeworm that primarily colonizes foxes, coyotes, voles, and sometimes domestic cats and dogs. It is primarily a disease of the northern hemisphere and is transmitted by the consumption of tapeworm eggs. The larvae grow in a cyst, usually within the liver, but sometimes in adjacent organs, such as the lungs. The tumor in the liver may be initially mistaken for liver cancer. SYN: *human alveolar e.; alveolar hydatid disease.*

human alveolar e. Alveolar **e.**

echinococcotomy (ĕ-kī″nō-kŏk-ŏt′ō-mē) [″ + ″ + *tome*, incision] An operation for evacuation of an echinococcal cyst.

Echinococcus (ĕ-kī″nō-kok′ŭs) [L. *echinus*, fr Gr *echinos*, hedgehog, sea urchin + *coccus*] A genus of very short tapeworms.

E. granulosus A species that infests dogs and other carnivores. Its hydatid (larva) develops in other mammals, including humans, and causes the formation of hydatid cysts in the liver or lungs. SYN: *dog tapeworm.* SEE: illus.; *hydatid.*

E. hydatidosus A species characterized by development of daughter cysts from the mother cyst. SEE: *hydatid.*

E. multilocularis A species that primarily infests foxes and moles. It is the cause of alveolar hydatid disease in hu-

ECHINOCOCCUS GRANULOSUS CYSTS

mans, one of the deadliest helminthic infections.

E. vogeli A species that causes polycystic hydatid disease (a neotropical parasitic infection).

echinococcus (ĕ-kī″nŏ-kok′ŭs, ĕ-kī″nŏ-kok′sī″) *pl.* **echinococci** A tapeworm of the genus *Echinococcus*.

echinocyte (ĕ-kī′nō-sīt) An abnormal erythrocyte with multiple, regular, spiny projections from the surface.

Echinostoma (ĕk″ĭ-nŏs′tō-mă) [″ + *stoma,* mouth] A genus of flukes characterized by a spiny body and the presence of a collar of spines near the anterior end. They are found in the intestines of many vertebrates, esp. aquatic birds. They occasionally occur as accidental parasites in humans.

echinulate (ĕ-kĭn′ū-lāt) Echinate.

Echis carinatus (ĕ′kĭs kă-rĭ-nā′tŭs) [Gr. *echis,* viper + L *carina,* keel] The Indian saw-scaled viper. Its venom contains a prothrombin activator, a potent anticoagulant.

echo (ek′ō″) [Gr. *ēkhō*] A reverberating sound produced when sound waves are reflected back to their source.

echocardiogram (ĕk″ō-kăr′dē-ō-grăm″) The graphic record produced by echocardiography.

echocardiography (ek″ō-kard″ē-og′ră-fē) [*echo* + *cardiography*] A noninvasive test that uses ultrasound to visualize cardiac structures. The heart's chambers, ejection fraction, valves, and wall motion can be evaluated, and intracardiac masses or clots can often be seen. **echocardiographic** (ē-ō-graf′ik), *adj.*

dobutamine stress e. ABBR: DSE. Echocardiography for coronary artery disease in which dobutamine is given to patients to increase the workload of the heart, and then the heart is evaluated with ultrasonic imaging. Regions of the heart that do not receive adequate blood flow (ischemic regions) contract poorly during the stress of the test but normally when the patient is at rest. Heart muscle that does not contract normally either at rest or with stimulation has been injured previously by myocardial infarction.

Doppler e. SEE: *Doppler echocardiography.*

multidimensional visualization e. An experimental echocardiographic technique using computer technology for three-dimensional visualization of cardiac structures. This becomes four-dimensional when time is used to impart the cinematic perception of motion.

stress e. Echocardiography of segments of heart muscle that do not move properly when a patient with coronary artery disease exercises or takes a vasodilating drug (e.g., adenosine or dipyridamole). Stress-induced impairments in regional heart muscle activity are used as markers of obstructions in specific coronary arteries.

transesophageal e. ABBR: TEE. A technique for obtaining echocardiographic images in which the ultrasonographic transducer is introduced into the esophagus. TEE is useful in detecting cardiac sources of emboli, prosthetic heart valve malfunction, endocarditis, aortic dissection, cardiac tumors, and valvular and congenital heart disease. SEE: illus.

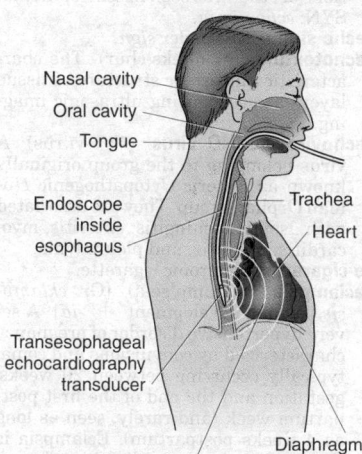

Nasal cavity
Oral cavity
Tongue
Endoscope inside esophagus
Trachea
Heart
Transesophageal echocardiography transducer
Diaphragm
Sound waves are analyzed and recorded

TRANSESOPHAGEAL ECHOCARDIOGRAPHY

transthoracic e. ABBR: TTE. Echocardiography of the heart and great vessels by means of an ultrasonic transducer placed on the chest wall. Sound waves are transmitted to the underlying organs (e.g., the heart or aorta), and an image is constructed from those that rebound toward the transducer.

echoendoscope (ek″ō-en″dŏ-skōp″) [*echo* + *endoscope*] An endoscope fitted with an ultrasound probe. It is used to visualize both the lumen of the gastrointestinal tract and abnormalities (such as enlarged lymph nodes or tumor masses) that are present in or near the wall of the intubated organ.

echogenic (ek″ō-jen′ik) [*echo* + *-genic*] Capable of producing echoes, i.e., of intensely reflecting sound waves rather than transmitting them. **echogenicity** (-jĕ-nis′ĭt-ē), *n.*

echogram (ĕk′ō-grăm) Sonogram

echography (ĕk-ŏg′ră-fē) [″ + *graphein*, to write] The use of ultrasound to image the echo produced when sound waves are reflected from tissues of different density. SEE: *ultrasonography.*

echoic (ĕ-kō′ik) [*echo* + *-ic*] **1.** Pert. to an echo. **2.** Pert. to the imitation of a natural sound; onomatopoeic

echolalia (ĕk-ō-lā′lē-ă) [″ + *lalia*, talk, babble] Involuntary repetition of words spoken by others.

echomimia (ĕk″ō-mĭm′ē-ă) [″ + *mimesis*, imitation] Echopraxia.

echopathy (ĕ-kŏp′ă-thē) [″ + *pathos*, disease, suffering] Pathological repetition of another's actions and words.

echo planar imaging SEE: under *imaging.*

echopraxia (ĕk″ō-prăk′sē-ă) [″ + *prassein*, to perform] Imitation of the actions of others, as seen in schizophrenia. SYN: *echomimia.*

echo sign SEE: under *sign.*

echotexture (ĕk′ō-tĕks-chŭr) The characteristic pattern or structure of tissue layers as seen during ultrasonic imaging.

echovirus, ECHO virus (ĕk′ō-vī′rŭs) A virus belonging to the group originally known as *E*nteric *C*ytopathogenic *H*uman *O*rphan group. They are associated with aseptic meningitis, enteritis, myocarditis, myositis, and pleurodynia.

e-cigarette Electronic cigarette.

eclampsia (e-klamp′sē-ă) [Gr. *eklampsis,* sudden development + *-ia*] A severe hypertensive disorder of pregnancy characterized by convulsions and coma, typically occurring between 20 weeks' gestation and the end of the first postpartum week (and rarely, as long as 4 weeks postpartum). Eclampsia is the most serious complication of pregnancy-induced hypertension (PIH). It occurs in 0.5% to 4.0% of all deliveries; roughly 25% of seizures occur within the first 72 hr of delivery. Perinatal maternal mortality is about 1%. Neonatal mortality (about 12%) usually occurs because of fetal hypoxia, complications of premature birth, inadequate intrauterine growth, or abrupt separation of the placenta. SEE: *pregnancy-induced hypertension.*

ETIOLOGY: Although the cause is unknown, vasospasm is one of the underlying mechanisms. Risk factors for the disorder include nulliparity, advanced maternal age, maternal hypertension or renal disease, diabetes mellitus, collagen-vascular disorder, molar pregnancy, and multifetal pregnancies. SEE: *preeclampsia.*

SYMPTOMS: The woman suffers a seizure, often without warning, but usually preceded by high blood pressure. Other symptoms include severe headache, changes in vision, nausea and vomiting, abdominal pain, edema, and, possibly, multiorgan dysfunction. Without treatment seizures may recur within minutes.

TREATMENT: Immediate and effective seizure management is vital. The mother's airway should be secured, and oxygenation and ventilation provided. The patient should be turned onto her left side. In order to abort subsequent seizures, an intravenous bolus and a continuous infusion of magnesium sulfate are administered. Intravenous drugs are used to control maternal blood pressure. Oxygen is administered at 8 to 10 L/m and the fetus is electronically monitored. An indwelling catheter is inserted and hourly output is measured; oliguria is an ominous sign that may indicate renal failure or magnesium toxicity. The mother should be assessed for these signs of placental abruption: vaginal bleeding, tachycardia and hypotension, abdominal or uterine tenderness or contractions, and decreased fetal heart tones. Once the mother's condition is stabilized, induction of labor or cesarean delivery is indicated in pregnancies of 24-28 weeks duration. It is better to give regional anesthesia rather than general anesthesia to assist delivery.

PATIENT CARE: Emergency care is provided during convulsions, and prescribed medications are administered as directed. After a seizure a quiet, darkened environment is provided until the patient is stabilized. The patient is maintained in a left-lateral position to increase venous return, cardiac output, renal blood flow, and placental perfusion. Because of the risk of aspiration, the eclamptic mother is given nothing by mouth. There should be elevated, padded side rails to protect the patient from injury during any further seizures. Both fetal and maternal response to magnesium sulfate must be monitored closely because of the risk of toxicity. Signs of maternal magnesium toxicity include absence of patellar reflexes, respiratory rate less than 12 breaths/min, urinary output less than 30 mL/hr, serum magnesium level greater than 8 mg/dL, flushing and muscle flaccidity, fetal bradycardia, or severe maternal hypotension. Calcium gluconate must be immediately available at bedside to counteract the effects of magnesium therapy. Stress and nonstress tests are used to monitor for fetal hypoxemia. The health care provider also must be particularly alert to signs of impending labor and abruptio placentae. Emergency resuscitative equipment and drugs should be readily available in case of seizure or cardiac or respiratory arrest.

Emotional support and information are given to the woman and her family. Postdelivery assessments vary in frequency depending on the woman's condition, eventually decreasing to every 4 hr for 48 hr postpartum. If the patient received magnesium sulfate before delivery, the infusion should be continued for 24 hr after delivery, with antihypertensive drugs administered as prescribed. Infants of eclamptic mothers may be small for gestational age and will require close monitoring for this condition. SEE: *Patient Care* under *pregnancy-induced* **hypertension**.

eclamptic Rel. to, or of the nature of, eclampsia.

eclamptogenic (ĕk-lămp″tō-jĕn′ĭk) [Gr. *ek*, out, + *lampein*, to shine, + *gennan*, to produce] Causing eclampsia.

eclectic (ĕk-lĕk′tĭk) [Gr. *eklektikos*, selecting] Selecting what elements seem best from various sources.

eclecticism (ĕk-lĕk′tĭ-sĭzm) [″ + *-ismos*, state of] A system of herbal medical practice popularized in the late 19th and early 20th centuries by Finley Ellingwood.

eclipse (ĕ-klĭps′) [Gr. *ekleipein*, to leave out, omit] To make or become dark or obscure. **eclipse**, *n*.

eclipse black bean (i-klĭps′) [Gr. *ekleipsis*, failure to appear] *Phaseolus vulgaris L.*, a darkly pigmented kidney bean that has a higher content of phenolic acids than related species. Like other beans, it is a good source of amino acids and dietary fiber.

eclipse nevus SEE: under *nevus*.

eclipse phase SEE: under *phase*.

eclipse retinopathy SEE: under *retinopathy*.

ECM *erythema chronicum migrans*.

ecmnesia (ĕk-nē′zē-ă) [Gr. *ek*, out, + *mnesis*, memory] A term formerly used to indicate impaired recall of recent events.

ECMO *extracorporeal membrane oxygenator*.

EC-Naprosyn SEE: *naproxen*.

eco- [Gr. *oikos*, house, household] Prefix meaning *habitat, environment*.

ecocide (ĕk″ō-sīd′) [Gr. *oikos*, house, + L. *caedere*, to kill] Willful destruction of some portion of the environment.

ECOG *Eastern Cooperative Oncology Group*.

E. coli. *Escherichia coli*.

ecological fallacy In epidemiology, the erroneous attempt to determine an individual's specific risk of developing a disease from an analysis of the risk found in the study of a community or population.

ecological terrorism The threat to use violent acts that would harm the quality of the environment in order to blackmail a group or society.

ecology (ē-kol′ō-jē) [Gr. *oikos*, house + *-logy*] The science of the relationship of organisms to their environment, including the interactions among organisms. **ecologic, ecological** (ē″kŏ-loj′ĭk, ĭ-kăl), *adj.* SEE: *food chain*.

e. of human performance ABBR: EHP. A conceptual framework for occupational therapy practice aimed at improving task performance by considering the person's skills and experiences, the context of the situation in which a task is performed, and the nature of the task. Interventions include altering the context of task performance to make it more supportive or a better match for the person's skills and remediating a person's skill deficits, among others.

ecomap (ĕk′ō-măp″) A family interview and assessment tool that delineates the needs, patterns, and relationships among family members and the environment.

economic credentialing (e″kŏ-nom′ik, ē″) The use of data about a health care provider's asset generation or resource utilization to determine whether that provider should be given clinical privileges in a hospital or health maintenance organization.

Economo disease (ĕ-kon′ŏ-mō) Encephalitis lethargica.

economy of movement [Gr. *oikos*, house, + *nomos*, law] The efficient, energy-sparing motion or activity of the system or body.

écorché (ā″kor-shā′) [Fr.] A representation of an animal or human form without skin so that the muscles are clearly seen.

ecosphere (ĕk′ō-sfēr″) [Gr. *oikos*, house, + L. *sphera*, ball] The portions of the earth habitable by microorganisms, plants, and animals.

ecostate (ē-kŏs′tāt) [L. *e*, without, + *costa*, rib] Without ribs.

ecosystem (ĕk′ō-sĭs″tĕm) A defined portion of the environment (e.g. lake, tundra, desert), including all its living organisms.

écouvillonage (ā-koo″vē-yŏ-năzh′) [Fr. *ecouvillon*, a stiff brush or swab] The cleansing and application of remedies to a cavity by means of a brush or swab.

écrasement (ā-krăz-mŏn′) [Fr.] Excision by means of an écraseur.

écraseur (ā-kră-zěr′) [Fr., crusher] A wire loop used for excisions.

ecstasy (ek′stă-sē) [Gr. *ekstasis*, a standing out] **1.** An exhilarated, trance-like condition or state of exalted delight. **2.** A synthetic, psychoactive, amphetamine-like drug, 3,4-methylene-dioxymethamphetamine (MDMA). Known colloquially as "lemon drops." In the U.S. 15% of teenagers have used the drug illicitly. It is most often used as a euphoric agent (e.g., at dance parties called "raves"). The powder is snorted or dissolved in water or alcohol for ingestion or injection; the crystals are usually smoked. It was prescribed in the 1970s in some forms of psychotherapy. Use of the drug has been associated with hyperthermia, disseminated intravascular coagulation, liver damage, hallucinations, convulsions, coma, and death.

TREATMENT: The priorities of emergency care are to control agitation, prevent or treat convulsions, measure the core temperature, and reverse hyperthermia by rapid rehydration and active cooling measures.

PATIENT CARE: The patient who has overdosed on ecstasy may be brought to the ER by a friend, usually with symptoms such as nausea and vomiting, dry mouth, bruxism, muscle ache or stiffness, ataxia, sweating, dilated pupils, hypertension, or tachycardia. Nystagmus, hypotension, paranoia, hallucinations, and seizures may also be present. Fever is a serious finding: severely hyperthermic patients (i.e., with a body temperature above 103°F [39°C]) should be cooled with cooling blankets, rehydration, iced saline gastric lavage, convection evaporation, or other means. Neuromuscular blocking agents and muscle relaxants are often used to minimize muscle contraction, esp. shivering, which causes additional heat production. Agitation and seizures should be treated with prescribed benzodiazepines (e.g., diazepam), haloperidol, and long-acting anticonvulsants. Hypertension may be treated with drugs such as labetolol, which may be titrated intravenously until blood pressure (BP) is controlled. Urine and blood toxicology screening should be performed as quickly as possible. Blood cultures, electrolyte levels, blood urea nitrogen (BUN), creatinine, liver profile, troponin-I, and creatinine kinase levels can help assess the patient for complications of drug overdose (e.g., rhabdomyolysis or acute coronary syndromes) and assist in the differential diagnosis. The overdosed patient should be treated as gently as possible and be kept in quiet surroundings. While the patient may initially appear lethargic, he may suddenly become combative and require sedation. Seizure pads may be used to protect the patient from injury; mechanical restraints are used only if absolutely necessary because they may exacerbate combativeness. The patient should also be frequently reoriented to allay his fears, and necessary procedures should be explained to him. Severely ill patients must be admitted to intensive care units for monitoring and support. Before the patient is discharged, he should be taught the risks of abusing stimulants and hallucinogens and be encouraged to seek appropriate substance-abuse counseling. Testing for hepatitis and HIV should be carried out if IV drug use places the patient at risk for these diseases.

ECT *electroconvulsive therapy.*

ectasia, ectasis (ek-tā′zh(ē-)ă, ek′tă-sĭs) [Gr. *ektasis,* stretching, tension] Dilatation of any tubular vessel.

    duct e. An inflammatory condition of the lactiferous ducts of the breast. There may be a discharge from the nipple, inversion of the nipple, and periareolar sepsis. The ectasia may occur at any age following menarche. Even though it resembles carcinoma of the breast, it is not malignant.

    ETIOLOGY: The cause is unknown, but in some cases it may be associated with hyperprolactinemia due to a pituitary tumor.

    TREATMENT: Duct ectasia is treated with surgical drainage of the abscess and antibiotics.

    dural e. A dilation of the membranes that line the lumbosacral spine, typically seen in patients with Marfan syndrome.

    hypostatic e. Dilatation of a blood vessel from the pooling of blood in dependent parts, esp. the legs.

    e. iridis Small size of the pupil of the eye caused by displacement of the iris.

-ectasis [L. fr. Gr. *ektasis,* extension] Suffix meaning *dilation* or *expansion.*

ectatic (ĕk-tăt′ĭk) Distensible or capable of being stretched.

ecthyma (ek-thī′mă) [Gr. *ekthyma,* pimple] A crusting skin infection caused by pyogenic streptococci. It is similar to impetigo but extends more fully into the epidermis. Typically lesions are found on the shins or the dorsum of the feet.

    TREATMENT: Topical skin cleansing, mupirocin ointment, and/or oral antibiotics (such as clindamycin) are needed to eradicate the infection.

    e. gangrenosum ABBR: EG. Ecthyma in patients with *Pseudomonas aeruginosa,* bacteremia, or sepsis. The disease consists of pustules, localized skin infarcts, or necrotic ulcers surrounded by inflamed, reddened skin. It can be diagnosed by culturing the lesions.

ecto- [Gr. *ektos,* outside] Prefix meaning *outside.*

ectoantigen (ek″tō-ant′ĭ-gĕn) [*-ecto-* + *antigen*] A surface antigen of bacteria that may be separated from them by agitation.

ectoblast (ĕk′tō-blăst) [″ + *blastos,* germ] **1.** The outer layer of cells (the "epithelium") of an embryo. **2.** The ectoderm.

ectocardia (ĕk'tō-kăr'dē-ă) [" + *kardia,* heart] Displacement of the heart.

ectocervix (ĕk"tō-sĕr'vĭks) The portion of the canal of the uterine cervix that is lined with squamous epithelium. **ectocervical** (-sĕr'vĭ-kăl), *adj.*

ectocondyle (ĕk"tō-kŏn'dĭl) [" + *kondylos,* knuckle] The outer condyle of a bone.

ectocornea (ĕk-tō-kor'nē-ă) [" + L. *corneus,* horny] The external layer of the cornea.

ectocuneiform (ĕk-tō-kū'nē-ĭ-form) [" + L. *cuneus,* wedge, + *forma,* form] The most lateral of the three cuneiform bones.

ectodactylism (ĕk"tō-dăk'tĭl-ĭzm) [Gr. *ektrosis,* miscarriage, + *daktylos,* finger, + *ismos,* state of] Lack of a digit or digits.

ectoderm (ĕk'tō-dĕrm") [Gr. *ektos,* outside, + *derma,* skin] The outer layer of cells in an embryo. SYN: *epiblast.* SEE: *endoderm; mesoderm.* **ectodermal, ectodermic** (ĕk"tō-dĕrm'ăl, ĕk"tō-dĕrm'ĭk), *adj.*

ectomorph (ĕk'tō-morf") [*ecto- + -morph*] A person with a body build marked by predominance of tissues derived from the ectoderm. The body is linear with sparse muscular development. SEE: *endomorph; mesomorph; somatotype.*

-ectomy [Gr. *ektomē,* a cutting out + -ia] Suffix meaning *surgical excision* of an anatomical structure.

ectoparasite (ĕk"tō-păr'ă-sīt") [" + Gr. *parasitos,* parasite] Any parasite that thrives in or on the skin; such as fleas, lice, maggots, mites, ticks.

ectoperitonitis (ĕk"tō-pĕr"ĭ-tō-nī'tĭs) [*ecto- + peritonaion,* peritoneum, + *itis,* inflammation] Inflammation of the parietal layer of the peritoneum (the layer lining the abdominal wall).

ectophyte (ĕk'tō-fīt) [" + *phyton,* plant] A plant parasite that grows on the surface of a host.

ectopia (ek-tō'pē-ă) [Gr. *ektopos,* displaced + -ia] Malposition or displacement, esp. congenital, of an organ or structure. SYN: *ectopy.*

cervical e. The presence of glandular cells (normally found within the cervical canal) on the surface of the cervix. It is a benign condition found in young women, during pregnancy, and in some women taking contraceptive pills.

e. cordis A malposition of the heart in which it lies outside the thoracic cavity.

e. lentis Displacement of the crystalline lens of the eye.

e. pupillae congenita Congenital displacement of the pupil.

e. renis Displacement of the kidney.

e. testis Displacement of the testis.

e. vesicae Displacement, esp. exstrophy, of the bladder.

visceral e. Umbilical hernia.

ectopic (ek-top'ik) [*ex- + topo- + -ic*] **1.** In an abnormal position; out of place. **2.** Emanating from some source in the body other than the usual or expected tissue. SEE: *entopic.*

ectopic corticotropin production (ek-top'ik) The production of corticotropin by nonendocrine tissue. This is usually but not always associated with a cancer such as a small-cell cancer of the lung. In some cases, the production site may not be found. SEE: *dexamethasone suppression test.*

ectopic fat (ek-top'ik) SEE: under *fat.*

ectopic hormone production (ek-top'ik) The secretion of hormones by nonendocrine tissue. Ectopically produced hormones may arise from both benign and malignant tissues. SYN: *ectopic hormone secretion.*

ectopic hormone secretion (ek-top'ik) Ectopic hormone production.

ectopic lymph node (ek-top'ik) SEE: under *node.*

ectoplasm (ek'tō-plăzm) [Gr. *ektos,* outside, + L. *plasma,* form, mold] The outermost layer of cell protoplasm. **ectoplasmic, ectoplastic** (ĕk"tō-plaz'mĭk, ĕk"tō-plas'tĭk), *adj.*

ectopotomy (ĕk-tō-pŏt'ō-mē) [Gr. *ektopos,* displaced, + *tome,* incision] Removal of the fetus in ectopic pregnancy.

ectopy (ek'tō-pē) Ectopia.

ectoretina (ĕk"tō-rĕt'ĭ-nă) [*ecto- + retina*] The outer layer of the retina.

ectostosis (ĕk-tŏs-tō'sĭs) [" + *osteon,* bone, + *osis,* condition] Formation of bone beneath the periosteum.

ectotherm (ek'tō-thĕrm") [*ecto- therm-*] Cold-blooded animal. **ectothermic** (ĕk"tō-thĕr'mĭk), *adj.*

ectothrix (ĕk'tō-thrĭks) [" + *thrix,* hair] Any fungus that produces arthrospores on the hair shafts.

Ectotrichophyton (ĕk"ō-trī-kŏf'ĭ-tŏn) [" + *thrix,* hair, + *phyton,* plant] A former name for *Trichophyton megalosporon ectothrix.*

ectozoon (ĕk-tō-zō'ŏn) [" + *zoon,* animal] A parasitic animal that lives on the outside of another animal.

ectro- [Gr. *ektrōsis,* miscarriage] Prefix meaning *congenital absence.*

ectrodactylism (ĕk"trō-dăk'tĭl-ĭzm) [" + *daktylos,* finger, + *-ismos,* state of] Congenital absence of all or part of a digit.

ectromelia (ĕk"trō-mē'lē-ă) [" + *melos,* limb] Hypoplasia of the long bones of the limbs.

ectromelus (ĕk-trŏm'ĕ-lŭs) [" + *melos,* limb] An individual with ectromelia.

ectropic (ĕk-trō'pĭk) [Gr. *ek,* out, + *trope,* turning] Pert. to complete or partial eversion of a part, generally the eyelid.

ectropion (ĕk-trō′pē-ŏn) Eversion of an edge or margin, as the edge of an eyelid.
ETIOLOGY: Causes include aging or loss of tone of the skin, scarring, infection, and palsy of the facial nerve.

ectrosyndactyly (ĕk″trō-sĭn-dăk′tĭ-lē) [″ + *syn*, together, + *dactylos*, finger] Congenital absence of one or more fingers; the remaining fingers are fused together.

eczema (eg-zē″mă, eg′zĕ-, ĕk′sĕ-) [L. *eczema*, fr. Gr. *ekzema*, fr. *ekzein*, to boil out] A general term for an itchy red rash that initially weeps or oozes serum and may become crusted, thickened, or scaly. Eczematous rash may result from various causes, including allergies, irritating chemicals, drugs, scratching or rubbing the skin, or sun exposure. It may be acute or chronic. The rash may become secondarily infected. SEE: *dermatitis*.
TREATMENT: Avoiding the cause of the rash (such as a sun-sensitizing drug; the leaves of the poison oak plant; an irritating soap or perfume, wool clothing, etc) prevents recurrences and allows the skin to heal. Locally applied astringent solutions (such as Burow's solution), antihistamines, or corticosteroid ointments, tablets, or injections may relieve the inflammation.
PATIENT CARE: Patients are helped to identify and avoid allergens in their diet or environment. Clothing should be soft textured, preferably cotton, and washed in a mild detergent and rinsed thoroughly. Fingernails should be kept short to decrease damage from scratching. Antihistamines may help to reduce itching at night. Maintaining a room temperature below 72°F (22°C), using humidifiers during the winter, and bathing in tepid water help keep the skin hydrated and decrease itching. SEE: *Nursing Diagnoses Appendix; Standard Precautions Appendix*.

asteatotic e. Winter **itch**.

dyshidrotic e. Pompholyx.

erythematous e. Dry, pinkish, ill-defined patches with itching and burning; slight swelling with tendency to spread and coalesce; branny scaling; roughness and dryness of skin. This type may become generalized.

e. fissum Eczema marked by a thick, dry, inelastic skin with cracks and fissures.

e. herpeticum Massive crops of vesicles that become pustular, occurring when herpes simplex virus infection occurs in a person, usually an infant, with pre-existing eczema. SYN: **Kaposi** *varicelliform eruption*.

lichenoid e. Eczema with thickening of the skin.

e. madidans Eczema marked by a raw, red surface covered with moisture.

nummular e. Eczema with coin-shaped or oval lesions. It is often associated with dry skin and worsens in dry weather. SEE: illus.

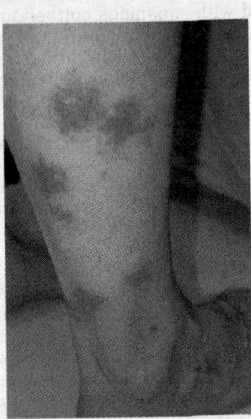

NUMMULAR ECZEMA

pustular e. Follicular, impetiginous, or consecutive eczema including eczema rubrum, eczema madidans, eczema fissum, and squamous eczema.

e. rubrum Eczema marked by a red, glazed surface with little oozing.

seborrheic e. Eczema marked by excessive secretion from the sebaceous glands. SYN: *seborrhea*.

squamous e. Chronic eczema on the soles, legs, and scalp; marked by multiple circumscribed, infiltrated patches with thin, dry scales

e. vaccinatum The spreading of vaccinia virus to localized areas of skin, or to the entire body, in patients recently vaccinated against smallpox. This reaction is a rare complication of smallpox vaccination, occurring in about 40 per million of newly vaccinated individuals. It usually occurs in people with pre-existing eczema and is occasionally fatal.

vesicular e. Eczema accompanied by the formation of vesicles occurring on the hands or feet.

eczematous (ĕk-zĕm′ă-tŭs) Marked by or resembling eczema.

ED *effective dose; Emergency Department; erythema dose.*

ED$_{50}$ The median effective dose, producing the desired effect in 50% of subjects tested.

EDC *expected date of confinement.*

EDD *expected date of delivery.*

edema (ĕ-dē′mă, -dē′măt-ă) *pl.* **edemas**, **edemata** [Gr. *oidēma*, swelling, tumor] A local or generalized condition in which body tissues contain an excessive amount of tissue fluid in the interstitial spaces. SYN: *hydrops*. SEE: *anasarca; ascites; dropsy; hydrothorax; pericardial* *effusion*. SEE: illus. **edematous** (ĕ-dē'măt-ŭs), *adj.*

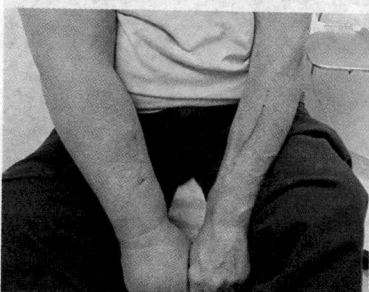

EDEMA

Edematous arm caused by subclavian vein stenosis

ETIOLOGY: Edema may result from increased permeability of the capillary walls; increased capillary pressure due to venous obstruction or heart failure; lymphatic obstruction; disturbances in renal function; reduction of plasma proteins; inflammatory conditions; fluid and electrolyte disturbances, esp. those causing sodium retention; malnutrition; starvation; or chemical substances such as bacterial toxins, venoms, caustics, and histamine. Diagnostic studies (thorough history, physical examination, urinalysis, serum chemistries and liver functions, thyroid function, and chest x-ray) help determine the cause and guide treatment.

TREATMENT: Bed rest helps relieve lower extremity edema. Sitting with the feet and legs elevated may also reduce edema in the lower extremities. Dietary salt should be restricted to less than 2 g/day. Fluid intake may be restricted to about 1500 mL in 24 hr. This prescription may be relaxed when free diuresis has been attained. Diuretics relieve swelling when renal function is good and when any underlying abnormality of cardiac function, capillary pressure, or salt retention is being corrected simultaneously. Any effective diuretic may be used. Diuretics are contraindicated in preeclampsia and when serum potassium levels are very low (<3.0 mEq/dL). They may be ineffective in edema associated with advanced renal insufficiency. The diet in edema should be adequate in protein, high in calories, and rich in vitamins. Patients with significant edema should weigh themselves daily to gauge fluid loss or retention.

PATIENT CARE: Edema is documented according to type (pitting, nonpitting, or brawny), extent, location, symmetry, and degree of pitting. Areas over bony prominences are palpated for edema by pressing with the fingertip for 5 sec, then releasing. Normally, the tissue should immediately rebound to its original contour; therefore the depth of indentation is measured and recorded. The patient is questioned about increased tightness of rings, shoes, waistlines of garments, and belts. Periorbital edema is assessed; abdominal girth and ankle circumference are measured; and the patient's weight and fluid intake and output are monitored. Fragile edematous tissues are protected from damage by careful handling and positioning and by providing and teaching about special skin care. Edematous extremities are mobilized and elevated to promote venous return, and lung sounds auscultated for evidence of increasing pulmonary congestion. Prescribed therapies, including sodium restriction, diuretics, ACE inhibitors, protein replacement, and elastic stockings are provided, and the patient is instructed in their use.

angioneurotic e. Angioedema.

Berlin e. Commotio retinae.

brain e. Swelling of the brain. It may be caused by increased permeability of brain capillary endothelial cells, focal strokes, swelling of brain cells associated with hypoxia or water intoxication, trauma to the skull, or interstitial edema due to obstructive hydrocephalus. SYN: *brain* **swelling**; *cerebral* **e.**

cardiac e. Edema due to congestive heart failure. It is most apparent in the dependent portion of the body and/or the lungs.

cerebral e. Brain **e.**

dependent e. Edema of the lower extremities or, if the patient is lying down, of the sacrum.

diabetic macular e. Swelling of the retina resulting from leakage of fluids from damaged blood vessels in the eye. It is a major cause of visual loss in diabetics, and is related to poor control of blood glucose.

e. of the glottis Pathological edema in the tissues lining the vocal structures of the larynx. It may result from improper use of the voice, excessive use of tobacco or alcohol, chemical fumes, or viral, bacterial, or fungal infections. Clinically, the patient often presents with hoarseness or, in severe cases, with respiratory distress and stridor. SEE: *epiglottitis*.

SYMPTOMS: Initially, hoarseness and, later, complete aphonia characterize this condition. Other symptoms are extreme dyspnea, at first on inspiration only, but later also on expiration; stridor; and a barking cough when the epiglottis is involved.

inflammatory e. Edema associated with inflammation. The cause is assumed to be damage to the capillary endothelium. It is usually nonpitting and localized, red, tender, and warm.

laryngeal e. Edema of the larynx, usually resulting from allergic reaction and causing airway obstruction unless treated. Therapy consists of intravenous or intratracheal epinephrine, emergency tracheostomy, or both.

malignant e. Rapid destruction of tissue by cutaneous or subcutaneous infections, such as anthrax or clostridial species.

negative pressure pulmonary e. Pulmonary edema occurring in a patient with upper airway obstruction and negative intrapleural pressures, e.g., in a child with epiglottitis.

pitting e. Evidence of fluid in soft tissues, esp. those of dependent body parts like the lower extremities. When pressed firmly with a finger, tissues that are swollen with extravascular fluid retain the shape of the depression produced by the finger. SEE: illus.

post-traumatic e. Traumatic **e.**

pretibial e. Edema of the lower leg anterior to the shin (the tibia).

pulmonary e. A potentially life-threatening edema in the interstitium and alveoli of the lungs. The collected fluid may block the exchange of oxygen and carbon dioxide and produce respiratory failure. SEE: *Nursing Diagnoses Appendix.*

ETIOLOGY: Fluid may seep out of the alveolar capillaries if these blood vessels are damaged and become excessively permeable to liquids (noncardiogenic pulmonary edema) or if hydrostatic pressures within blood vessels exceed the strength of the normal alveolar capillary wall (cardiogenic pulmonary edema). Cardiogenic pulmonary edema can result from any condition that compromises left ventricular function, causing elevations in pulmonary venous and capillary hydrostatic pressures (congestive heart failure), including myocardial infarction, ischemia, or myocardial stunning; severe valvular heart disease; arrhythmias; excessive intravenous fluid administration; and diastolic dysfunction.

Noncardiogenic pulmonary edema usually results from blood vessel injury, as happens in the adult respiratory distress syndrome (sepsis, shock, aspiration pneumonia, airway obstruction). Occasionally, protein-rich fluid floods the lungs from drug exposure (such as heroin overdose), hypoalbuminemia, high-altitude exposure (mountain sickness), fresh water aspiration in near drowning, hemorrhage in or around the brain, or other conditions. Pulmonary edema can occur as a chronic or acute condition.

SYMPTOMS: Chronic symptoms include dyspnea or exertion, nocturnal

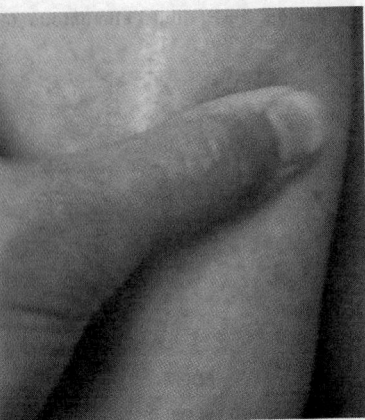

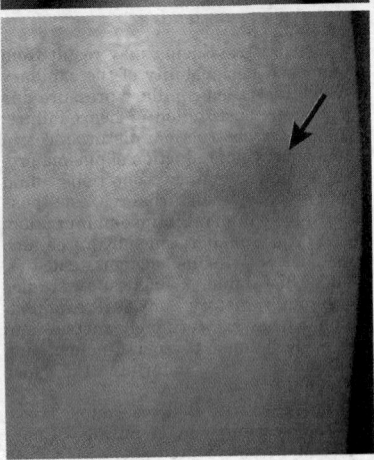

PITTING EDEMA

Demonstration of pitting edema

dyspnea, orthopnea, and cough. When pulmonary edema develops rapidly, patients experience a rapid onset of shortness of breath and suffocation and often demonstrate labored, noisy breathing; cough producing frothy, bloody sputum; gasping; anxiety; palpitations; and altered mental status caused by inadequate oxygenation. Signs of the condition include a rapid respiratory rate, heaving of the chest and abdomen, intercostal muscle retractions, diffuse crackles on lung exam, and, often, cold, clammy skin with diaphoresis and cyanosis. Tachycardia, jugular vein distension, and a diastolic (S3) gallop occur. As cardiac output decreases, the pulse becomes thready, and blood pressure falls. Pulmonary artery catheterization helps identify left-sided failure (elevated pulmonary wedge pressures), and arterial blood gases show hypoxia. Profound respiratory alkalosis occurs when patients hyperventilate when trying to increase their oxygenation; acidosis may occur with respiratory fatigue and failure. To improve the movement of air into and out of the chest, the patient will often sit upright to breathe and resist lying down.

TREATMENT: Oxygen (in high concentrations by cannula, face mask, or nonrebreather mask) should be administered immediately. Assisted ventilation (continuous positive airway pressure or intubation with mechanical ventilation) may be needed to reach acceptable levels of PaO2 and improve acid-base balance. Morphine sulfate, nitrate vasodilators (IV nitroglycerin or nitroprusside) and loop diuretics are typically given to patients with cardiogenic pulmonary edema to improve dyspnea, alter preload and afterload on the heart, and promote diuresis. Angiotensin-converting enzyme inhibitors, inotropic drugs (digoxin), antiarrhythmic agents, beta-adrenergic blockers, human B-type natriuretic peptide, and phosphodiesterase inhibitors may be used in selected circumstances. Bronchodilators may also be administered. Depending on the underlying cause, invasive interventions may occasionally include coronary angiography, intraaortic balloon pump therapy, or surgical interventions such as coronary artery revascularization or valve repair, or ventricular assist device therapy.

PROGNOSIS: The outlook is good if the condition is stabilized or reversed with treatment.

PATIENT CARE: The patient's head is elevated; respirations and ventilatory effort are assessed. Oxygen is administered as prescribed, with care taken to limit the flow rate in patients whose respiratory drive is compromised. The lungs are auscultated for adventitious breath sounds such as crackles, gurgles, and wheezes, and the heart is assessed for apical rate and gallops. The patient is monitored for a cough productive of pink, frothy sputum. The skin is checked for diaphoresis and pallor or cyanosis. A medication history is collected, esp. for cardiac or respiratory drugs and use of recreational drugs. The patient's cardiac rate and rhythm, blood pressure, and oxygen saturation levels are monitored continuously. An intravenous (IV) line administering normal saline solution (NSS) is inserted at a keep-vein-open rate to provide access for medication administration. Prescribed first-line drug therapy is administered, and the patient's response to the drugs is evaluated. IV morphine slows respirations, improves hemodynamics, and reduces anxiety. It should be administered before initiating continuous positive air pressure (CPAP). CPAP improves oxygenation and decreases cardiac workload, thus decreasing the need for intubation and ventilation with positive end-expiratory pressure (PEEP). An indwelling urinary catheter is inserted to monitor the patient's fluid status; diuresis should begin within 30 min of administration of an IV loop diuretic. Pulmonary edema is a life-threatening respiratory emergency. Everyone involved with the patient must remain calm and quiet, provide ongoing reassurance, and validate everything occurring through basic and simply understood explanations. After the crisis resolves, health care providers should discuss with the patient his or her feelings about the episode and give thorough explanations of what occurred. The at-risk patient is taught early warning signs to act on immediately (such as weight gain or increasing peripheral edema), in an effort to recognize and prevent future episodes. Medications and dietary and lifestyle restrictions are explained (low-sodium diet, losing weight, smoking cessation), and written information provided for home review. The patient should be encouraged to enroll in a cardiac rehabilitation program (as applicable) for regular exercise tailored to his condition.

reexpansion pulmonary e. ABBR: RPE, REPE. Alveolar flooding that occurs after a collapsed or trapped lung reinflates, e.g., after the draining of a pleural effusion or the evacuation of a pneumothorax.

Reinke e. SEE: *Reinke edema.*

traumatic e. Tissue swelling occuring after blunt or penetrating injury. SYN: *post-traumatic e.*

edema factor SEE: under *factor.*

edematogenic (ĕ-dĕm″ă-tō-jĕn′ĭk) Causing edema.

Eden Alternative (ēd′ĕn) An international nonprofit organization that advocates the creation of long-term care environments for the elderly that emphasize aging as a period of development rather than a period of decline through the use of facility design, staff training, and a core philosophy of care.

edentulous (ē-dĕnt′ū-lŭs) Without teeth.

edetate calcium disodium (ĕd′ĕ-tāt) The disodium salt of ethylenediaminetetra-acetic acid. A chelating agent, it is used in diagnosing and treating lead poisoning. Trade names are Calcium Disodium Versenate and Versene CA.

edetate disodium (ĕd′ĕ-tāt dī-sō′dē-ŭm) A chelating agent, disodium dihydrogen ethylenediaminetetra-acetate dihydrate. It is used to treat hypercalcemia.

edge A margin or border.

bevel e. A tooth edge produced by beveling.

cutting e. An angled or sharpened edge for cutting, as an incisor tooth or the blade of a knife.

denture e. The margin or border of a denture.

incisal e. The sharpened edge of a tooth produced by occlusal wear; the labiolingual margin.

EDI *Estimated daily intake.*

edible (ĕd'ĭ-bl) [L. *edere,* to eat] Suitable for food; fit to eat; nonpoisonous.

Edinger-Westphal nucleus, Westphal-Edinger nucleus (ed'ĭng-ĕr-west'fal") [Karl Westphal, Ger. neurologist, 1833–1890; Ludwig Edinger, Ger. neurologist, 1855–1918] A nucleus of the visceral motor column in the hindbrain. It lies in the midbrain tegmentum, just beneath the cerebral aqueduct and lateral to the oculomotor nucleus. The Edinger-Westphal nucleus is the origin of preganglionic parasympathetic axons in the oculomotor nerve (CN III) and it innervates the ciliary and pupillary constrictor muscles of the eye.

editosome (ē-dĭt'ŏ-sōm") [Fr. *editer,* to edit + Gr. *soma,* body] An intracellular protein complex that processes RNA, altering it from its original form into its final, mature form.

edrophonium chloride (ĕd"rō-fō'nē-ŭm) A cholinergic drug. SEE: *edrophonium test.*

edrophonium test The use of edrophonium chloride to test for the presence of myasthenia gravis. The appropriate dose is injected intravenously; if there is no effect, a larger dose is given within 45 sec. A positive test demonstrates brief improvement in strength unaccompanied by lingual fasciculation. The test may also be used to determine an overdose of a cholinergic drug. An excessive dose of cholinergic drug produces weakness that closely resembles myasthenia. A very small dose of edrophonium chloride given intravenously worsens the weakness if it is due to cholinergic drug overdose and improves it if it is due to myasthenia gravis.

⚠ The test should not be performed unless facilities and staff for respiratory resuscitation are immediately available.

EDTA *ethylenediaminetetraacetic acid*

education (e"jŭ-kā'shŏn) [L. *educatio,* bringing up, training] Imparting, receiving, or acquiring knowledge.

clinical e. Health care education conducted in health care facilities, outpatient clinics, emergency centers, hospitals, or private offices, under the supervision of a qualified practitioner or teaching staff.

continuing e. ABBR: CE. Postgraduate education in the health professions. Its purpose is to enhance or expand a person's knowledge or skills through coursework; home study; live, audio, or video conferences; electronic media; or clinical practice. Postgraduate courses may be required for continued certification or licensure requirements in a practice such as medicine, nursing, physical therapy, respiratory therapy, and social work. The time spent in CE by health care professionals is usually recorded in hours, each one of which reflects one continuing education unit. SYN: *continuing medical e.*

continuing medical e. ABBR: CME. Continuing education.

cross e. Contralateral facilitation or changes resulting from exercise.

distance e. A formalized teaching system to disseminate knowledge between teachers and students who are separated in space (location), time, or both. SYN: *distance learning.*

e-nursing e. Nursing education aided or wholly provided via online resources, texts, clips, and discussion groups, among other Web-based technologies.

health e. An educational program directed to the general public rather than health educators or professionals.

patient e. Health information and instruction to help patients learn about specific or general medical topics. Topics include the need for preventive services, the adoption of healthy lifestyles, the correct use of medications, and the care of diseases or injuries at home.

educational audiologist An audiologist who works in a school and who screens pupils for evidence of hearing loss that may affect their ability to learn.

educator (ĕj'oo-kā"tĕr) A person who demonstrates, instructs, leads, or teaches clients, families, patients, or students.

eduction (ē-dŭk'shŭn) [L. *e,* out, + *ducere,* to lead] Emergence from a particular state or condition (e.g., coming out of the effects of general anesthesia). SEE: *induction* (4).

Edwards syndrome (ed'wărdz) [James H. Edwards, U.S. geneticist, b. 1928] Trisomy 18.

EE *coefficient of elastic expansion.*

EEE *eastern equine encephalitis.*

EEG *electroencephalogram.*

EENT *eyes, ears, nose, and throat.*

EEOC *Equal Employment Opportunity Commission.*

EF *Ejection fraction.*

EFA *essential fatty acid.*

effacement (ĕ-fās'mĕnt) In obstetrics, the thinning of the cervix as the internal os is slowly pulled up into the lower uterine segment.

effect (i-fekt') [L. *effectus,* outcome, result] The result of an action or force. Particular effects are listed under the first word. SEE: *cumulative effect; Doppler effect; side effect.*

effectiveness (ĕ-fĕk'tĭv-nĕs) The ability to cause the expected or intended effect or result.

effective radiating area ABBR: ERA. The area of a therapeutic ultrasound head that produces useful ultrasonic energy, measured in square centimeters (cm²). The effective radiating area is calculated by identifying all points where the ultrasonic energy is at least 5% of the maximum measured intensity at the transducer's surface.

effector (ĕ-fĕk'tor) A cell, tissue, or organ that produces the final result of a stimulus. SYN: *effector organ.*

effector cell SEE: under *cell.*

effector organ Effector.

effeminate (ĕ-fĕm'-ĭ-nătt) **1.** Pert. to a male who has the appearance or mannerisms traditionally considered feminine. **2.** Excessively soft, delicate, or self-indulgent.

effemination (ĕ-fĕm"ĭ-nā'shŭn) [L. *effeminare*, to make feminine] The production of female physical characteristics in a male. SYN: *feminization.*

efferent (ef'ĕ-rĕnt) [Fr. fr. L. *efferre*, to carry out] Transporting away from a central organ or section. It applies, for example, to nerves that conduct impulses from the brain or spinal cord to the periphery; to lymph vessels that convey lymph from lymph nodes; and to arterioles that carry blood from glomeruli of the kidney. SEE: *afferent.*

effervesce (ef"ĕr-ves') [L. *effervescere*, to boil up] To form bubbles; to become fizzy, foamy, or frothy.

effervescence (ĕf-ĕr-vĕs'ĕns) Formation of gas bubbles that rise to the surface of a fluid.

effervescent Bubbling; rising in little bubbles of gas.

efficacy The ability to produce a desired effect.

efficiency (ĭ-fĭsh'ĭn-sē) [L. *efficentia*] The optimal use of resources, e.g., chemical reagents in a laboratory, human resources in an institution, or health care dollars in a governmentally administered public health program.

effleurage (ef"lĕ-rozh') [Fr. *effleurer*, to stroke lightly] A massage technique that employs gliding movements that follow the contours of the body. SYN: *stroking* (1).

   abdominal e. Light stroking with the fingertips in a circular pattern from the symphysis pubis to the iliac crests, a Lamaze technique for coping with uterine contractions during the first stage of labor.

efflorescence (ĕf-flor-ĕs'ĕns) [L. *efflorescere*, to bloom] **1.** A rash; a redness of the skin. SYN: *exanthem.* **2.** The for-

mation of a powder on the surface of a compound as it gives up water and becomes anhydrous.

efflorescent (ĕf"floo-rĕs'ĕnt) Becoming powdery or dry from loss of water in crystallization.

effluent (ĕf'loo-ĕnt) [L. *effluere*, to flow out] **1.** A flowing out. **2.** Fluid material discharged from a sewage treatment or industrial plant.

effluvium (ĕf-loo'vē-ŭm) *pl.* **effluvia** A malodorous outflow of vapor or gas, particularly one that is toxic.

efflux (ĕf'lŭks) [" + "] Outward flow, i.e., the movement of chemicals or other fluids from within a structure, such as a cell, to the outside.

effort Expenditure of physical or mental energy.

effort-independent test A test whose accuracy or success does not depend on patient compliance.

effort syndrome Unusual or unexpected fatigue with exertion. The fatigue is increased by mild exertion and may be more pronounced in the morning. SEE: *chronic fatigue syndrome.*

effuse (ĕ-fūs') [L. *effusio*, pour out] Thin, widely spreading; applied to a bacterial growth that forms a very delicate film over a surface.

effusion (ĕ-fū'zhŭn) [L. *effusio*, a pouring out, shedding] Escape of fluid into a part, as the pleural cavity, such as pyothorax (pus), hydrothorax (serum), hemothorax (blood), chylothorax (lymph), pneumothorax (air), hydropneumothorax (serum and air), and pyopneumothorax (pus and air).

   joint e. Increased fluid within a joint cavity. There may be increased production of synovial fluid following trauma, with some arthritic disease processes, or blood accumulating in the joint following trauma or surgery or due to hemophilia. Excessive amounts of synovial fluid, pus, or blood accumulate in many arthritic diseases (such as gout or rheumatoid arthritis), after trauma, in joint infections, following joint surgery, or in hemophilia.

   pericardial e. Edema marked by excess serous fluid in the pericardial cavity, between the visceral and the parietal pericardium. This condition may produce symptoms of cardiac tamponade, such as difficulty in breathing, chest pain, dizziness, anxiety and rapid heart rate.

   pleural e. Fluid in the thoracic cavity between the visceral and parietal pleura. It may be seen on a chest radiograph if it exceeds 300 ml.

EGCg, EGCG *Epigallocatechin gallate.*

egesta (ē-jĕs'tă) [L. *egere*, to cast forth] Waste matter eliminated from the body, esp. excrement.

eGFR *estimated glomerular filtration rate.*

egg (eg) **1.** The female sex cell or ovum, applied esp. to a fertilized ovum that is passed from the body and develops outside, as in fowls. **2.** The mammalian ovum.

  raw e. An egg in its fresh, uncooked state, esp. one intended for food. Human consumption of raw or inadequately cooked eggs has caused *Salmonella* infections. To kill *Salmonella* organisms, if present, eggs should be boiled for 7 min, fried for 3 min per side, or poached for 5 min. It is unsafe to use sauces or dressings made with raw eggs. Fresh eggs should be refrigerated; cracked eggs should be discarded. SEE: *salmonellosis*.

egg freezing A colloquial term for cryopreservation of oocytes. It is a technique to preserve female fertility.

eglandulous (ē-glănd′ū-lŭs) [*ex-* + *glandula*] Without glands.

ego (ē′gō, ĕg′ō) [L. *ego*, I] In psychoanalytic theory, one of the three major divisions in the model of the psychic apparatus. The others are the id and superego. The ego is involved with consciousness and memory and mediates among primitive instinctual or animal drives (the id), internal social prohibitions (the superego), and reality. The psychoanalytic use of the term should not be confused with its common usage in the sense of self-love or selfishness. SEE: *id; superego*.

egocentric (ē″gō-sĕn′trĭk) [L. *ego*, I, + Gr. *kentron*, center] Pert. to a withdrawal from the external world with concentration on the self.

egocentricity (ē″gōsĕn-trĭs′ĭ-tē) The stage of cognitive development in which perception is almost exclusively from the child's own viewpoint and in the child's own way. This stage is characteristic of toddlers and early preschool children.

ego-dystonic (ē″gō-dĭs-tŏn′ĭk) [″ + Gr. *dys*, bad, + *tonos*, tension] Pert. to something repulsive to the individual's self-image.

ego-integrity (ē′gō-ĭn-tĕg′rĭ-tē) The eighth stage in Erik Erikson's developmental theory; the opposite of despair. It is the major psychic task of the mature elderly and is marked by a healthy unifying philosophy and the wisdom learned from experience. The individual feels vital, balanced, and whole in relation to the self and the world.

egoism (ē′gō-ĭzm) An inflated estimate of one's value or effectiveness.

egomania (ē″gō-mā′nē-ă) [″ + Gr. *mania*, madness] Abnormal self-esteem and self-interest.

egophony (ē-gŏf′ō-nē) [Gr. *aix*, goat, + *phone*, voice] An abnormal change in tone, somewhat like the bleat of a goat, heard in auscultation of the chest when the subject speaks normally. It is associated with bronchophony and may be heard over the lungs of persons with pleural effusion, or occasionally pneumonia.

ego-syntonic (ē″gō-sĭn-tŏn′ĭk) [″ + Gr. *syn*, together, + *tonos*, tension] Pert. to something that is consistent with the individual's self-image.

egotism (ē′gō-tĭzm) **1.** The tendency to regard oneself more highly than is warranted by the facts, and to boast of one's abilities or achievements. **2.** An inflated sense of self-importance; conceit. SEE: *egoism*.

egotropic (ē″gō-trŏp′ĭk) [L. *ego*, I, + Gr. *tropos*, a turning] Interested chiefly in one's self; self-centered.

e-health The application of electronic information technology to health care by using websites providing a common set of standards across operating systems.

EHEC Enterohemorrhagic *Escherichia coli*.

Ehlers-Danlos syndrome (ā′lĕrz-dăn′lŏs) [Edvard Ehlers, Danish dermatologist, 1863–1937; H. A. Danlos, Fr. dermatologist, 1844–1912] Any of six inherited disorders of connective tissue (collagen and collagen-related proteins). Characteristic findings in most Ehler-Danlos patients include: joint hypermobility with dislocations (e.g., during childbirth) and velvety, loose and easily bruised skin. The syndrome is relatively rare. It affects about 1 child per 5000 births.

EHR *Electronic health* **record**.

Ehrlichia (er-lik′ē-ă) [*Ehrlich* + *-ia*] A genus of gram-negative bacteria that use the adenosine triphosphate (ATP) of other cells to survive. They are the pathogenic agents responsible for influenza-like illnesses in humans and canines.

  Ehrlichia chaffeensis An obligate intracellular gram-negative bacterium that causes human monocytic ehrlichiosis in humans.

  Ehrlichia phagocytophila The former name of the bacterium now known as *Anaplasma phagocytophilum*. SEE: *Anaplasma phagocytophilum*.

  Ehrlichia ewingii An ehrlichial species that causes human granulocytic ehrlichiosis in Tennessee and neighboring states.

  Ehrlichia sennetsu An ehrlichial species that causes a mononucleosis-like syndrome in Japan known as Sennetsu fever.

ehrlichiosis (ār″lĭk-ē-ō′sĭs) [Paul Ehrlich, Ger. physician, 1854–1915. Awarded Nobel Prize in medicine in 1908] One of several forms of an infectious disease of monocytes and granulocytes transmitted by exposure to species of *Ehrlichia* (small, gram-negative, obligate intracellular cocci of the Rickettsiaceae family). It was first reported in humans in the U.S. in 1987 and is considered an emerging disease.

ETIOLOGY: There are three causes of ehrlichiosis:

1. *E. chaffeensis*, carried by the Lone Star tick, causes human monocytic ehrlichiosis (HME);

2. *Anaplasma phagocytophila* (formerly named *E. phagocytophila*), carried by *Ixodes* (e.g., the Western black-legged tick [*I. Pacificus*]), causes human granulocytic ehrlichiosis (HGE);

3. *E. ewingii* causes a related syndrome.

Thirty states have reported cases, but HME is found mostly in the southern U.S., and HGE in the northern U.S. In Japan, *E. sennetsu* causes a mononucleosis-like illness (Sennetsu fever).

SYMPTOMS: Both HME and HGE are marked by nonspecific influenza-like symptoms. A high fever with rigors, headache, malaise, myalgia, leukopenia, and thrombocytopenia are most common; a rash may be present in HME. The symptoms last for approx. 3 weeks; it is unclear if a latent infection remains. Complications of renal failure, cardiomegaly, coagulopathies, or coma occur in 16% of patients, mostly in the older adults. Most patients are men over 40.

TREATMENT: Doxycycline (or other tetracyclines) is the recommended treatment.

DIAGNOSIS: Serological tests are used; a polymerase chain reaction (PCR) applied to whole blood samples can confirm the diagnosis in 24 to 48 hr.

PREVENTION: Ticks should be avoided by avoiding grassy areas where they reside, by wearing long pants and light-colored clothing, and by applying tick repellents to clothing before entering grasslands or woodlands. After leaving these areas, exposed clothing should be immediately laundered, and the skin bathed and inspected for the presence of adult ticks and tiny nymphs. Any attached ticks should be promptly removed with tweezers, making certain to remove the entire insect.

EIA *Enzyme immunoassay.*

eicosa- [Gr. *eikosi,* twenty] Prefix used in chemistry to indicate *twenty.*

eicosanoid (ī-kō′să-noyd″) Any of several autocrine or paracrine cytokines formed from the metabolism of arachidonic acid. They include prostaglandins, thromboxanes, and leukotrienes.

eICU *Electronic intensive care unit.*

EID *Electroimmunodiffusion; electronic infusion device; esophageal intubation detector device.*

eidetic (ī-dĕt′ĭk) [Gr. *eidos,* form, shape] Rel. to or having the ability of total visual recall of anything previously seen.

EIEC Enteroinvasive *Escherichia coli.*

EIEE *Early infantile epileptic encephalopathy with suppression bursts.*

Eikenella corrodens (ī″kĕn-ĕl′ă) A gram-negative bacillus that is part of normal oral flora. It can cause serious human infections, including abscesses, empyema, and endocarditis, among others.

Eimeria (ī-mē′rē-ă) A genus of sporozoan parasites belonging to the class Conoidasida, order Eucoccidiorida. They are intracellular parasites living in the epithelial cells of vertebrates and invertebrates. They rarely are parasitic to humans.

E. hominis A species that has been found in empyema in humans.

EIP *electrical impedance plethysmography; end-inspiratory pause; end-inspiratory pressure.*

Eisenmenger syndrome, Eisenmenger complex (ī′zĕn-meng″ĕr, ′sĕn-) [Victor Eisenmenger, Austrian physician, 1864–1932] A congenital cyanotic heart defect that may include atrial septal defects, ventricular septal defects, dextroposition of the aorta, pulmonary hypertension with pulmonary artery enlargement, hypertrophy of the right ventricle, and patent ductus arteriosus.

E & IT *electronic and information technology.*

ejaculate (i-jak′yŭ-lāt″, -lăt) [L. *ejaculari,* to throw out] **1.** To eject or discharge suddenly, esp. semen. **2.** The semen released during ejaculation.

split e. In sperm analysis, the separation of the first drops of ejaculated semen from the rest of the ejaculate. The earliest ejaculated fluid contains the highest concentration of spermatozoa. Latter ejaculate contains relatively more seminal fluid.

ejaculatio (ē-jăk″ū-lā′shē-ō) [L.] Sudden expelling; ejaculation.

e. praecox Premature ejaculation.

ejaculation (i-jak″yŭ-lā′shŏn) Ejection of the seminal fluid from the male urethra.

PHYSIOLOGY: Ejaculation consists of two phases: (1) the passage of semen and the secretions of the accessory organs (bulbourethral and prostate glands and seminal vesicles) into the urethra and (2) the expulsion of the seminal fluid from the urethra. The former is brought about by contraction of the smooth muscle of the ductus deferens and the increased secretory activity of the glands, the latter by the rhythmical contractions of the bulbocavernosus and ischiocavernosus muscles and the levator ani. The prostate discharges its secretions before those of the seminal vesicle. The sensations associated with ejaculation constitute the male orgasm. Ejaculation occurs without ejection of the seminal fluid from the male urethra in patients who have had a prostatectomy. In that case, the ejaculate is in the bladder.

Ejaculation is a reflex phenomenon. Afferent impulses arising principally from stimulation of the glans penis pass to the spinal cord by way of the internal pudendal nerves. Efferent impulses arising from a reflex center located in the upper lumbar region of the cord pass through sympathetic fibers in the hypogastric nerves and plexus to the ductus deferens and seminal vesicles. Other impulses arising from the third and fourth sacral segments pass through the internal pudendal nerves to the ischiocavernosus and bulbocavernosus muscles. Erection of the penis usually precedes ejaculation. Ejaculation occurs normally during copulation or masturbation or as a nocturnal emission. The seminal fluid normally contains 60 million to 150 million sperm/mL. The volume of the ejaculation is from 2 to 5 mL. SEE: *orgasm; semen.*

premature e. An imprecise term that usually indicates ejaculation occurring very shortly after the onset of sexual excitement, or ejaculation occurring before copulation or before the partner's orgasm. This disorder is usually accompanied by feelings of guilt or relationship difficulties.

retarded e. Inability of a male to achieve orgasm despite sexual arousal and stimulation, often after 30 min of sexual activity.

retrograde e. Ejaculation in which the seminal fluid is discharged into the bladder rather than through the urethra. Retrograde ejaculation can occur as a consequence of some psychotropic drugs or radical prostatectomy.

ejaculatory (ē-jăk′ū-lă-tōr″ē) Pert. to ejaculation.

ejecta (ē-jĕk′tă) [L. *ejectus,* thrown out, ejected] Material, especially waste material, excreted by the body. SYN: *dejecta; egesta.*

ejection (ē-jĕk′shŭn) Removal, esp. sudden, of something.

ventricular e. Forceful expulsion of blood from the ventricles of the heart.

ejection fraction SEE: under *fraction.*

Ekbom syndrome (ek′bōm″, āk′) [Karl A. Ekbom, Swedish neurologist, 1907–1977] The delusion that one is infested with parasites, esp. those that burrow under the skin.

EKG Abbreviation for the German *elektrokardiogramm.* SEE: *electrocardiogram.*

ekphorize (ĕk′fō-rīz) [Gr. *ek,* out, + *phorein,* to bear] In psychiatry, to bring to mind a psychological experience so as to repeat the experience in memory. SEE: *engram.*

elaboration (ē-lăb″ō-rā′shŭn) In body metabolism, the formation of complex compounds from simpler substances (e.g., formation of proteins from amino acids).

elapse (i-laps′) [L. *elapsus,* slipped by] Of time, to pass.

elastase (ē-lăs′tās) A pancreatic enzyme that cleaves amino acids from proteins in the presence of trypsin.

elastic (ē-lăs′tĭk) [Gr. *elastikos,* driven on, set in motion] Capable of being stretched and then returning to its original state.

intermaxillary e. An elastic band used between the maxillary and mandibular teeth in orthodontic therapy; also called a maxillomandibular elastic.

intramaxillary e. An elastic band used in a horizontal space closure by attachments within the same arch.

vertical e. An elastic band applied to arch brackets perpendicularly to the occlusal plane for approximating teeth.

elasticity (ē″lăs-tĭs′ĭ-tē) The quality of returning to original size and shape after compression or stretching.

elastic shoelaces A type of assistive device that makes shoes with laces easier to wear by eliminating the movements needed to tie and untie them.

elastic stocking A stocking worn to apply pressure to the extremity, aiding the return of blood from the extremity to the heart through the deep veins. SEE: *thrombosis, deep venous.*

elastin (ē-lăs′tĭn) An extracellular connective tissue protein that is the principal component of elastic fibers in the middle layer of arteries and around the alveoli of the lungs.

elastinase (ē-lăs′tĭn-ās) An enzyme that dissolves elastin.

elasto-, elast- [Gr. *elastos,* beaten (of metal), ductile] Prefixes meaning *elastic, elasticity.*

elastofibroma (ē-lăs″tō-fĭ-brō′mă) [″ + L. *fibra,* fiber, + Gr. *oma,* tumor] A benign soft tissue tumor that contains elastic and fibrous elements.

elastography (i-las″tog′ră-fē) A procedure to diagnose malignant tissue by imaging with ultrasonography. Since healthy tissue is significantly less stiff than malignant tissue, the imaged tissue may be distorted to differing degrees, and thus it may be possible to distinguish a malignancy in the ultrasound image, e.g., in the diagnosis of breast cancers.

elastoid (ē-lăs′toyd) [″ + *eidos,* form, shape] Pert. to a substance formed by hyaline degeneration.

elastoma (ē″lăs-tō′mă) [″ + *oma,* tumor] A yellow nodular or papular lesion of the skin composed of elastic fibers. Elastomas are seen in the genetic disease pseudoxanthoma elasticum.

elastometer (ē″lăs-tŏm′ĕ-tĕr) [″ + Gr. *metron,* measure] A device for measuring elasticity.

elastometry (ē″lăs-tŏm′-ĕ-trē) The measurement of tissue elasticity.

elastorrhexis (ē-lăs″tō-rĕk′sĭs) [*elasto-*

+ *-rrhexis*] Rupture of elastic tissue.

elastose (ē-lăs′tōs) A peptone resulting from gastric digestion of elastin.

elastosis (ĕ-las″tō′sĭs) [*elasto-* + *-osis*] Loss of elasticity in the skin.

    nodular e. A severe form of elastosis caused by prolonged exposure to the sun. Elastotic material accumulates in the skin and forms cysts and comedones around the face. This condition occurs almost exclusively in middle-aged or older adult white men.

    TREATMENT: Treatment consists of removal of cysts and comedones, followed by nightly application of retinoic acid cream to the area for 6 to 8 weeks. The patient should avoid sun exposure to prevent recurrence.

    e. perforans serpiginosa SEE: *perforating disorder.*

elation (ē-lā′shŭn) [L. *elatus,* exalted] Joyful emotion. It is pathological when out of accord with the patient's actual circumstances.

elbow (el′bō″) [Old English. *eln,* forearm + *boga,* bend] The joint between the arm and forearm. SEE: illus.

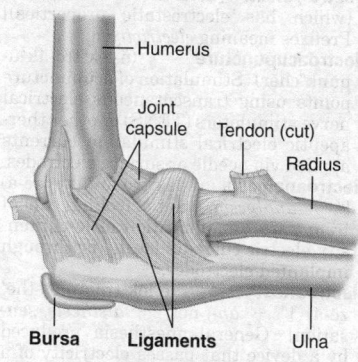

- Humerus
- Joint capsule
- Tendon (cut)
- Radius
- **Bursa**
- **Ligaments**
- Ulna

ELBOW JOINT

    little league e. A form of overuse syndrome marked by tension being placed on the medial structures of the elbow and, possibly, compression forces being placed on the lateral structures. Long-term consequences include abnormal growth of the medial epicondyle and avulsion of the medial epicondyle. It is seen in adolescent baseball players, esp. in pitchers. In order to help prevent this condition, Little League Baseball regulations limit the number of pitches a player can throw per week.

    nursemaid's e. Subluxation of the head of the radius with entrapment of the annular ligament in the radiohumeral joint, esp. in a young child after being lifted by the hand or wrist. The condition is acutely painful, and the child will not willingly use the affected arm.

    TREATMENT: The subluxation can be readily reduced with closed manipulation. SYN: *radial head* **subluxation**.

    tennis e. SEE: *tennis elbow.*

elbow unit A component of the upper-extremity prosthesis that permits the arm to bend at the elbow.

ELBW *extremely low birth* **weight.**

elder (ĕl′dĕr) A person over 65 years old.

elderberry (el′dĕr-ber″ē) A flowering shrub (*Sambucus nigra*) that produces dark blue or black berries that contain antioxidants. Studies suggest an extract derived from the berries may treat symptoms of influenza or help patients in weight loss.

eldercare Providing health care and assistance with activities of daily living for older adults, either at home or in care facilities. Family members usually provide most of the needed assistance, although friends, professional agencies, or volunteers often participate.

    PATIENT CARE: Although all patients benefit from respectful, dignified, and professional care, and generalizations about older patients' needs may not apply to every patient, some special needs of some older patients are addressed here. Sensory problems (self-reported) are fairly prevalent in older adults. For example hearing impairments are present in about a third of 65 to 74 year olds and half those 75 and older, and vision problems are present in a seventh of those age 65 to 74, and in a fifth age 75 and older. Tooth loss, which influences both chewing and clarity of speech, occurs in more than a fifth of individuals over the age of 65. Age-related changes in heart and kidney function make older adults more vulnerable to shifts in water balance that can result in dehydration, e.g., in hot weather, when left alone, or while waiting for medical or surgical procedures. In older adults, adequate fluid intake is associated with fewer falls, less constipation, lower rates of laxative use, and better rehabilitation outcomes in orthopedic patients. In older adults dehydration can precipitate emergency hospitalization and increase mortality. The decline in renal function that occurs with aging means that the kidneys are less able to concentrate urine, so more water is lost in an older person than would be in a younger individual. Institutionalized adults should be ensured of access to something to drink at all times, with fluid offered regularly since thirst may not prompt older individuals to drink. Fasting should be minimized. Ambulatory adults should be reminded to increase their fluid intake during exercise, hot weather, and illness, and healthy older adults should be taught to monitor urine color as one indicator of dehydration: darker urine often represents incipient dehydration; clear, watery urine is seen in well-hydrated adults. Individuals with urinary incontinence should be advised not to limit their intake in an effort to prevent incontinence episodes; 1500 to 2000 mL (1½ to 2 quarts) of fluid daily is required to maintain hydration for most individuals.

When communicating with the elderly, caregivers in all settings should remember to encourage the patient's use of hearing aids and/or eyeglasses; use the patient's name, make eye contact, and use touch as appropriate; enunciate clearly; allow time for the patient to respond; ask only one question at a time, develop a signaling system for "yes" and "no" answers, and post it clearly for all caregivers and visitors to see and use; use gestures that relate to the information being conveyed verbally; and write questions/options so that the patient can see them as they are read aloud for the patient to hear. Other critical elements of the care of the elderly include providing physical therapy to improve balance and prevent falls; limiting the use of medications that may contribute to cognitive dysfunction, confusion or delirium; ensuring adequate nutrition; screening for cancers, dementia, depression, and other diseases that become more common with advancing age; remaining aware of "atypical" presentations of illnesses and infections; protecting the skin from ulceration; and maintaining healthful participation in the community.

elder mistreatment Elder **abuse**.

elder neglect Elder abuse.

e-learning Any technique that facilitates and enhances learning through both computer and communications technology. It can include only the text portion of a computer or it can include Internet-based distance learning using a multimedia-capable computer.

elective therapy A treatment or surgical procedure not requiring immediate attention and therefore planned for the patient's or provider's convenience.

Electra complex (ē-lĕk′trä) [Gr. Elektra, Agamemnon's daughter, who helped assassinate her mother because of love for her father, whom the former had slain] In psychoanalysis, a group of symptoms due to suppressed sexual love of a daughter for her father. SEE: *Jocasta complex; Oedipus complex.*

electric, electrical [Gr. *elektron,* amber] Pert. to, caused by, or resembling electricity.

electrical alternans Beat-to-beat changes in one or more portions of the electrocardiogram.

electrical leakage (ĭ-lĕk′trĭ-kĭl lĕk′ĭj) The presence of unwanted current from an electrical device, such as a patient monitoring or treatment device.

electrical stimulation SEE: under *stimulation.*

electricity A form of energy that is generated by the interactions of positive and negative charges and that exhibits magnetic, chemical, mechanical, and thermal effects.

   frictional e. Static electricity generated by rubbing two objects together.

   galvanic e. Electricity generated by chemical action.

   induced e. Electricity generated in a body from another body nearby without contact between them.

   magnetic e. Electricity induced by a magnetic device.

   negative e. An electric charge caused by an excess of negatively charged electrons.

   positive e. An electric charge caused by loss of negatively charged electrons.

   static e. Electricity generated by friction of certain materials.

electric shock treatment Electroconvulsive therapy.

electro-, electr- [L. fr. Gr. *ēlektron,* amber (which has electrostatic properties)] Prefixes meaning *electricity.*

electroacupuncture (ē-lĕk″trō-ăk′ū-pŭnk″chĕr) Stimulation of acupuncture points using transcutaneous electrical nerve stimulators (TENS) or other therapeutic electrical stimulation currents applied via needle or surface electrodes.

electroanalgesia (ē-lĕk″trō-ăn″ăl-jē′zē-ă) [″ + *analgesia,* want of feeling] Relief from pain by application of low-intensity electric currents locally or through implanted electrodes.

electroanesthesia (ē-lĕk″trō-ăn″ĕs-thē′zē-ă) [″ + *an-,* not, + *aisthesis,* sensation] General anesthesia produced by a device that passes electricity of a certain frequency, amplitude, and wave form through the brain.

electrobiology (ē-lĕk″trō-bī-ŏl′ō-jē) [″ + *bios,* life, + *logos,* word, reason] The science of electrical phenomena in the living body.

electrocardiogram (ē-lĕk″trō-kăr′dē-ō-grăm″) [″ + *kardia,* heart, + *gramma,* something written] ABBR: ECG. A record of the electrical activity of the heart, consisting of waves called P, Q, R, S, T, and sometimes U. The first, or P, wave is caused by the depolarization of the atria, whose electrical changes in turn cause atrial contraction. The Q, R, and S waves (QRS complex) correspond to depolarization of ventricular muscle. The T wave corresponds to ventricular repolarization. The electrocardiogram gives important information concerning the spread of electricity to the different parts of the heart and is used to diagnose rhythm and conduction disturbances, myocardial infarction or ischemia, chamber enlargement, and metabolic disorders, among others.

exercise e. A record of the electrical activity of the heart taken during graded increases in the rate of exercise. SEE: *stress test.*

signal-averaged e. ABBR: SAECG. An electrocardiographic study, usually performed on patients with unexplained loss of consciousness or suspected dysrhythmias, in which hundreds of QRS complexes are collected, filtered, and analyzed to discover the presence or absence of certain abnormalities in the conducting system of the ventricle. These abnormalities, called late potentials, point to an increased risk of ventricular tachycardia or ventricular fibrillation. SAECG allows late potentials to be examined free from random electrical discharges ("noise"), which often are present when only a small number of QRS complexes are evaluated.

electrocardiograph (ē-lěk″trō-kăr′dē-ŏ-grăf) [″ + ″ + *graphein,* to write] A device for recording changes in the electrical energy produced by the action of heart muscles.

electrocardiographical technician A technician who operates and maintains electrocardiographic machines, records the heart's electrical activity, and provides data for diagnosis and treatment of heart ailments.

electrocardiography (ē-lěk″trō-kăr″dē-ŏg′ră-fē) The creation and study of graphic records (electrocardiograms) produced by electric currents originating in the heart.

electrocautery (ē-lěk″trō-kaw′těr-ē) [*electro-* + *cautery*] Cauterization using a variety of electrical modalities to create thermal energy, including a directly heated metallic applicator, or bipolar or monopolar electrodes.

electrocerebral silence (ě-lěk″trō-sǎ-rē′ brǐl, sěr′ǐ) In electroencephalography (EEG), the absence of detectable electrical activity in the cortex of the brain. The EEG tracing shows no deflections from its baseline. This finding is diagnostic of brain death.

electrochemiluminescence, electrochemoluminescence (ē-lek″trō-kēm″ĭ-loo″mĭ-nes′ěns, ē-lek″trō-kēm″ō-loo″mĭ-nes′ěns) The production of visible light by an electrochemical reaction in which molecules, after becoming electronically excited, release visible electromagnetic energy when they return to their relaxed state. Electrochemiluminescence is used in laboratory science as a means of measuring the concentration of specific chemicals in solution. Light-emitting molecules that commonly bind to the chemical of interest are introduced into the solution, and the amount of light given off by the "labeled" or "tagged" chemical is measured.

electrochemistry (ē-lěk″trō-kěm′ĭ-strē) [″ + *chemeia,* chemistry] The science of chemical changes produced by or resulting in electricity.

electrochromatography (ě-lek″trō-krō″mă-tog′ră-fē) [*electro-* + *chromatography*] The separation of large organic chemicals (such as proteins) from mixtures or solutions with the combined use of filtration (to separate molecules on the basis of their size) and electricity (which separates them based on their electrical polarity).

electrocision (ē-lek′trō-sizhŏn) [*electro-* + *(ex)cision*] Excision by electric current.

electrocoagulation (ē-lěk″trō-kō-ǎg″ū-lā′shŭn) [″ + L. *coagulare,* to thicken] Coagulation of tissue by means of a high-frequency electric current. SEE: *electrocautery.*

electrocochleography (ē-lek″trō-kok-lē-og′ră-fē) [*electro-* + *cochlea* + *-graphy*] ABBR: EcochG. Measurement of electrical activity produced when the cochlea is stimulated. A needle electrode is passed through the eardrum and placed on the cochlea. The electrical activity is then recorded.

electroconvulsive therapy (ě-lek″trō-kŏn-vǔl′siv) ABBR: ECT. The use of an electric shock to produce convulsions and thereby treat drug-resistant or esp. severe psychiatric disorders (major depression, bipolar disorder, suicidal ideation, schizophrenia).

PATIENT CARE: Before ECT, the patient should sign an informed consent form for the procedure, which may be withdrawn orally at any time. ECT may only be administered involuntarily if the patient has been judged mentally incompetent and a court order has been obtained. In preparation for the procedure, the patient must have nothing by mouth (NPO) from midnight before the procedure and remove all jewelry and dentures and have an empty bladder. Resuscitation equipment and staff should be on hand during the procedure. The patient receives anesthetic and a neuromuscular blocker to relax skeletal muscles and is mechanically ventilated with 100% oxygen while unable to breathe unassisted. As soon as the patient is unconscious and paralyzed, the psychiatrist applies unilateral or bilateral electrodes to the head and delivers an electrical stimulus of 70 to 150 volts to the brain for 0.1 to 1 second. This produces a generalized seizure lasting 30 to 60 sec. Neuromuscular blockades minimize muscular contractions and the risk of vertebral fractures or other complications. Application of electrical current only to the nondominant hemisphere may cause fewer cognitive adverse reactions, but some psychiatrists believe that bilateral ECT is more effective. The patient typically becomes responsive about 15 min after the treatment and fully recovered 1 to 2 hr later. Staff monitors vital signs, assesses the patient's orientation and alertness, notes any signs of confusion, constantly reorients and reassures the patient, and frequently checks blood pressure and pulse until the patient's vital signs are stable. Postural hypotension is a common response to ECT. Confusion and short-term memory loss are the most common adverse reactions to ECT; the confusion usually resolves within an hour. Short-term memory further deteriorates during a treatment course, but it, too, usually resolves within a few weeks after the final treatment. Other complications include delayed short-term memory loss, heart arrhythmias, and seizures. An ECT treatment course usually involves 6 to 12 treatments: 3 treatments each week for 2 to 6 weeks. Many patients show improvement after only a few treatments. Benefit 30 days after treatment has not been established. ECT usually begins during inpatient care to treat severe depression, where the patient's response can be closely evaluated and adverse effects noted. Treatment may continue on an outpatient basis as the patient improves. After a full course of therapy, the patient may require intermittent ECT as maintenance therapy. Antidepressant drug therapy usually is instituted even if previously unsuccessful, and individual or group psychotherapy and psychoeducation are instituted, as a combination of therapies generally provides the most successful treatment. SYN: *electric shock treatment; electroshock therapy; shock therapy.*

electrocorticography (ē-lek″trō-kort″ĭ-kog′ră-fē) [*electro-* + *cortex* + *-graphy*] Recording of the electrical impulses from the brain by electrodes placed directly on the cerebral cortex. It is used in neurosurgery to determine whether a tumor or an epileptic focus has been completely resected.

electrocution (ē-lĕk″trō-kū′shŭn) [″ + L. *acutus,* sharpened] Destruction of life by electric current. In the U.S. about 1000 people die of electrical shocks each year; about a fourth of these die of lightning strikes. SEE: *electric shock; lightning safety rules.*

electrode (i-lek′trōd″) [*electro-* + Gr. *hodos,* a way] **1.** An electrical terminal or lead. **2.** A conductive medium. **3.** In electrotherapy, an instrument with a point or surface from which to discharge current to a patient's body. **4.** An electrical terminal or lead that is adapted to sense current or voltage in response to

specific analytes, for purposes of quantifying the particular analyte.

active e. An electrode that is smaller than a dispersive electrode and produces stimulation in a concentrated area.

calomel e. An electrode that develops a standard electric potential and is used to provide a reference voltage in the circuit for sensing electrodes. It is composed of an amalgam of mercury and mercury (I) chloride. It is used as a standard in determining the pH of fluids.

carbon dioxide e. A blood gas electrode used to measure the carbon dioxide tension (symbolized as P_{CO_2}) in blood. Its operation is based on the diffusion of carbon dioxide from the blood sample through a semipermeable membrane into a buffer solution with a subsequent change in the pH of the buffer. SYN: *Severinghaus electrode.*

Clark e. Oxygen electrode.

coated wire e. ABBR: CWE. A chemical sensor in some clinical laboratory analyzers that functions similarly to a pH electrode. SEE: *hydrogen e.; saturated calomel e.*

dispersive e. Indifferent electrode.

gas-sensing e. An electrode in which a gas-permeable membrane separates the test solution fluid from an aqueous electrode solution in contact with an ion-selective electrode. Gas permeation of the membrane changes the chemical equilibrium within the electrolyte, and the ion-sensitive electrode detects this change.

glass e. In chemistry, a chemical sensor that uses a glass membrane as the sensing surface, as opposed to one that uses an organic or solid-state membrane. The glass contains materials in its structure that are sensitive to a material that is to be measured. In the case of a pH glass electrode, lithium ions are commonly used

hydrogen e. An electrode that absorbs and measures hydrogen gas; used as the reference for pH measurement in research laboratories.

immobilized enzyme e. A chemical sensor that is highly selective due to a specific enzyme incorporated into its structure.

indifferent e. An electrode larger than an active electrode. It produces electrical stimulation over a large area. SYN: *dispersive e.*

internal reference e. The metal electrode inside all chemical-sensing potentiometric electrodes. The two most common internal reference electrodes are the calomel and the silver/silver chloride.

ion-selective e. A chemical transducer that yields a response to variations in the concentration of a given ion in solution.

liquid membrane e. An electrode in which the sensing membrane is made up of a hydrophobic ion-exchange neutral carrier (ionophore) dissolved in a viscous, water-insoluble solvent. The liquid membrane is physically supported by an inert porous matrix such as cellulose acetate.

multiple point e. Several sets of terminals providing for the use of several electrodes. SEE: *multiterminal.*

negative e. A cathode; the pole by which electric current leaves the generating source.

oxygen e. An electrode used to measure the partial pressure of oxygen (PO_2) or the blood glucose concentration of a fluid sample. SYN: *Clark electrode; PO_2e.; polarographic e.*

PO_2e. Oxygen **e.**

point e. An electrode with an insulating handle at one end and a small metallic terminal at the other for use in applying static sparks.

polarographic e. Oxygen **e.**

polymer membrane e. An electrode in which the sensing membrane is an organic polymer containing a hydrophobic ion-exchange neutral carrier (ionophore).

positive e. An anode; the pole opposite a cathode.

reference e. A chemical electrode whose cell potential remains fixed and against which an indicator electrode is compared. The most common reference electrode is the silver/silver chloride (Ag/AgCl) electrode.

saturated calomel e. ABBR: SCE. One of two practical reference electrodes, used with a mercurous chloride (calomel) paste in pH and other potentiometric instruments. The other is the silver/silver chloride electrode. The calomel electrode has been the standard secondary reference electrode used in the laboratory since the introduction of the pH electrode.

Severinghaus e. Carbon dioxide electrode.

solid-state membrane e. An electrode in which the sensing membrane is made of a single crystal or pressed pellet containing the salt of the ion to be sensed.

standard hydrogen e. ABBR: SHE. The standard reference electrode against which all others are measured. Its assigned electrode potential is 0.000 V.

subcutaneous e. An electrode placed beneath the skin.

surface e. An electrode placed on the surface of the skin or exposed organ.

therapeutic e. An electrode used for introduction of medicines through the skin by ionization. SEE: *iontophoresis.*

electrodesiccation (ē-lĕk″trō-des″ĭ-kā′ shŏn) [Gr. *electro-* + *desiccation*] The destructive drying (dehydration) of cells with electrical energy of lower intensity than what is used in electrocoagulation. Electrodesiccation is used for hemostasis of very small capillaries or veins that have been severed during surgery.

electrodiagnosis (ĕ-lĕk″trō-dī″ăg-nō′sĭs, ĕ-lĕk″trō-dī″ăg-nō′sēz″) *pl.* **electrodiagnoses** [*electro-* + *diagnosis*] The use of electrical and electronic devices for diagnostic purposes. This technique, which includes electroencephalography, electromyography, polysomnography, and evoked potentials, is helpful in almost all branches of medicine, but particularly in investigating the function of the heart, nerves, and muscles. **electrodiagnostic** (ĕ-lĕk″trō-dī″ăg-nos′tĭk), *adj.*

electrodialysis (ē-lĕk″trō-dī-ăl′ĭ-sĭs) *pl.* **electrodialyses** [″ + *dia-,* apart, + *lysis,* dissolution] A method of separating electrolytes from colloids by passing a current through a solution containing both. A semipermeable membrane is usually used to aid in the separation, with one electrode on each side.

electroejaculation (ĭ-lĕk″trō-ē-jăk″ū-lā′ shŭn) [″ + L. *ejaculare,* to throw out] The retrieval of semen by electrical stimulation of the prostate. Electroejaculation is used to obtain sperm from men who are unable to ejaculate, e.g., because of spinal cord injury. It has also been used in veterinary medicine.

electroencephalogram (ē-lĕk″trō-ĕn-sĕf′ ă-lō-grăm) [″ + *enkephalos,* brain, + *gramma,* something written] ABBR: EEG. A tracing on an electroencephalograph. SEE: *electroencephalography.*

electroencephalograph (ē-lĕk-trō-ĕn-sĕf′ ă-lō-grăf) [″ + ″ + *graphein,* to write] An instrument for recording the electrical activity of the brain. SEE: *electroencephalography.*

electroencephalographic technologist (ĕ-lĕk″trō-ĕn-sĕf″ă-lō-grăf′ĭk) A technologist who operates and maintains electroencephalographic machines.

electroencephalography (ē-lĕk″trō-ĕn-sĕf″ă-lŏg′ră-fē) Amplification, recording, and analysis of the electrical activity of the brain. The record obtained is called an electroencephalogram (EEG).

Electrodes are placed on the scalp in various locations. The difference between the electric potential of two sites is recorded. The difference between one pair or among many pairs at a time can be obtained. The most frequently seen pattern in the normal adult under resting conditions is the alpha rhythm of 8½ to 12 waves per sec. A characteristic change in the wave occurs during sleep, on opening the eyes, and during periods of concentration. Some persons who have intracranial disease will have a normal EEG and others with no otherwise demonstrable disease will have an abnormal EEG. Nevertheless, the use of this diagnostic technique has proved to be very helpful in studying epilepsy and convulsive disorders and in localizing lesions in the cerebrum. SEE: *rhythm, alpha; rhythm, beta; wave, theta.*

electrogoniometer (ē-lĕk″trō-gō″nē-ŏm′ĕ-tĕr) An electrical device for measuring angles of joints and their range of motion.

electrogram (i-lek′trŏ-gram″) [*electro- + -gram*] A recording of the electrical activity of any organ of the body.

electrohydraulic (ĕ-lĕk″trō-hī-drŏl′ĭk) Pert. to the electrical generation of shock waves in a fluid; said of a device or system.

electroimmunodiffusion (i-lek″trō-im″yū-nō-dif-ū′zhŏn, i-im-ū′-nō-) [*electro- + immunodiffusion*] ABBR: EID. A laboratory method of identifying antigens in the blood by creating an artificial antigen-antibody reaction.

electrolarynx (ē-lĕk′trō-lăr″ĭnks) A voice-restoring device used by some patients after surgical removal of the larynx. The device works by amplifying breath sounds.

electrolysis (ē″lĕk-trŏl′ĭ-sĭs) [″ + *lysis,* dissolution] The decomposition of a substance by passage of an electric current through it. Hair follicles may be destroyed by this method. SEE: *depilatory technique.*

electrolyte (ē-lĕk′trō-līt) [″ + *lytos,* soluble] **1.** A solution that conducts electricity. **2.** A substance that, in solution, conducts an electric current and is decomposed by its passage. Acids, bases, and salts are common electrolytes. **3.** An ionized salt in blood, tissue fluids, and cells. These salts include sodium, potassium, and chlorine. SEE: table.

    amphoteric e. A solution that produces both hydrogen (H^+) and hydroxyl (OH^-) ions.

    fecal e.'s Osmotically and electrically active ions present in stool. They are measured in the evaluation of chronic diarrhea, to determine whether the diarrhea is secretory or osmotic. SEE: *osmotic diarrhea; secretory diarrhea.*

electrolytes, direct measurement of Measurement of serum-plasma ions, such as sodium, chloride, and potassium, without prior dilution of the sample. Direct measurement of electrolytes is considered more physiologically accurate than indirect measurement.

electrolytes, indirect measurement of Measurement of serum ions, such as sodium, chloride, and potassium, using a sample diluted before analysis. The method is prone to physiological error in patients with hyperlipidemia, myeloma,

and other disturbances of plasma water concentration.

electrolytic (ē-lĕk″trō-lĭt′ĭk) Caused by or rel. to electrolysis.

electrolytic conduction The passage of a direct current between metallic electrodes immersed in an ionized solution. In metals, the electric charges are carried by the electrons of inappreciable mass. In solutions, the electric charges are carried by electrolytic ions, each having a mass several thousand times as great as the electron. The positive ions move to the cathode and the negative ions to the anode.

electromagnet (ē-lĕk″trō-măg′nĕt) [″ + *magnes,* magnet] A magnet consisting of a length of insulated wire wound around a soft iron core. When an electrical current flows through the wire, a magnet is produced. **electromagnetic,** *adj.*

electromagnetic field SEE: under *field.*

electromagnetic induction SEE: under *induction.*

electromagnetic spectrum The complete range of wavelengths of electromagnetic radiation. SEE: table.

electromagnetism (ē-lĕk″trō-măg′nĕ-tĭzm) Magnetism produced by an electric current.

electromotive (ē-lĕk″trō-mō′tĭv) [″ + L. *motor,* mover] Pert. to the passage of electricity in a current or motion produced by it.

electromyogram (ē-lĕk″trō-mī′ō-grăm) [″ + *mys,* muscle, + *gramma,* something written] The graphic record of resting and voluntary muscle activity as a result of electrical stimulation.

electromyographical technician A technician who assists the neurologist in recording and analyzing bioelectric potentials that originate in muscle tissue. This includes the operation of various electronic devices, maintenance of electronic equipment, assisting with patient care during testing, and record keeping.

electromyography, electroneuromyography (ē-lĕk″trō-mī-ŏg″ră-fē) [″ + ″ + *graphein,* to write] ABBR: EMG. The preparation, study, and interpretation of electromyograms that record the electrical activity of selected skeletal muscle groups while at rest and during voluntary contraction.

    PATIENT CARE: The test determines whether a person's perceived muscle weakness is caused by a disease within the muscle or by a problem in a nerve supplying the muscle. It aids in differentiating between primary muscle disorders (e.g. muscular dystrophies) and secondary muscle disorders, helps assess diseases characterized by central neuronal degeneration (e.g. amyotrophic lateral sclerosis or ALS), and aids in diagnosis of neuromuscular disorders (e.g. myasthenia gravis) and rad-

Major Electrolytes

Electrolyte mEq/L*	Plasma Level mEq/L	ICF Level	Functions
Sodium (Na⁺) • Essential for electrical activity of neurons and muscle cells	136–142	10	• Creates much of the osmotic pressure of ECF; the most abundant cation in ECF
Potassium (K⁺) • Essential for electrical activity of neurons and muscle cells	3.8–5.0	141	• Creates much of the osmotic pressure in ICF; the most abundant cation in ICF
Calcium (Ca⁺²) • Maintains normal excitability of neurons and muscle cells • Essential for blood clotting	4.6–5.5	1	• Most (98%) is found in bones and teeth.
Magnesium (Mg⁺²) • More abundant in ICF than in ECF • Essential for ATP production and activity of neurons and muscle cells	1.3–2.1	58	• Most (50%) is found in bone
Chloride (Cl⁻) • Part of hydrochloric acid (HCl) in gastric juice	95–103	4	• Most abundant anion in ECF; diffuses easily into and out of cells; helps regulate osmotic pressure
Bicarbonate (HCO₃⁻)	28	10	• Part of the bicarbonate buffer system
Phosphate (HPO₄⁻²) • Primarily an ICF anion • Part of DNA, RNA, ATP, phospholipids • Part of phosphate buffer system	1.7–2.6	75	• Most (85%) is found in bones and teeth
Sulfate (SO₄⁻²)	1	2	• Part of some amino acids and proteins

*The concentration of an ion is often expressed in milliequivalents per liter (mEq/L), which is the number of electrical charges per liter of solution.
Key: (ICF) intracellular fluid; (ECF) extracellular fluid; (ATP) adenosine triphosphate; (DNA) deoxyribonucleic acid; (RNA) ribonucleic acid.
SOURCE: Scanlon, VC and Sanders, T: Essentials of Anatomy and Physiology, ed 6. FA Davis, Philadelphia, 2011.

iculopathies. It is an invasive test: it is performed by inserting needles percutaneously into muscles and measuring their responsiveness to electrical stimulation. The conduction velocity of nerves is often measured simultaneously. Risks include pain during needle insertion, bleeding, or infection. Bleeding or infection occurs infrequently. The patient will feel electrical shocks in the muscles tested during the EMG. If the patient understands the test and wants to proceed, he or she should complete a consent form. The patient's history should be checked for medications that may interfere with test results (e.g. cholinergics, anticholinergics, and skeletal muscle relaxants). EMG is contraindicated in patients with bleeding disorders.

Electromagnetic Spectrum

Fre-quency (Hz)	Type of Radiation	Wave-length (cm)
10^{22}		10^{-12}
	Gamma rays	
10^{19}		10^{-9}
	X-rays	
10^{16}		10^{-6}
	Ultraviolet radiation	
10^{15}		10^{-5}
	Visible light	
10^{14}		10^{-4}
	Infrared radiation	
10^{13}		10^{-2}
	Submillimeter waves	
10^{12}		10^{-1}
	Microwaves	
10^{9}		10
	Television and radio waves	
10^{4}		10^{6}

Prohibited medications are withheld before testing, as necessary. In some cases, cigarettes, coffee, tea, and cola drinks may be restricted for 2 to 3 hours before the test, but usually no food or fluid restrictions are imposed.

A typical EMG lasts between 15 and 90 min. The patient is positioned on an examination table or in a chair, wearing a hospital gown or comfortable clothing that permits access to the muscles being tested, with the muscles to be tested at rest. Next, an antiseptic is used to cleanse the skin at the planned needle insertion points, and a metal plate to serve as a reference electrode is positioned under the muscle(s) being tested. Several needle electrodes are then quickly inserted through the skin and into the muscle. The muscle's electrical activity will be measured at rest and with voluntary contraction. The electrical activity (motor unit potential) will be amplified 1 million times to be audible over an audio amplifier. It is also visible on an oscilloscope or computer monitor and recorded on graph paper. At rest the normal muscle shows minimal electrical activity, which increases markedly during voluntary contraction. After the test the patient may take a mild analgesic and/or apply warm compresses to the muscles for soreness. Needle insertion sites should be observed and the patient's primary health care provider notified if bleeding, a hematoma, or signs of infection are noted. The patient may resume any prescribed medications withheld for the test.

electron (i-lek'tron″) An extremely minute particle with a negative electrical charge that revolves about the central core or nucleus of an atom. Its mass is about $\frac{1}{1840}$ that of a hydrogen atom, or 9.11×10^{-28} g. The negative electrical charge is 1.602×10^{-19} coulombs. When emitted from radioactive substances, electrons are known as negative beta particles.

electron boost An adjunct to external beam radiation therapy in which small focused fields of radiation are applied to a tumor in an attempt to destroy it. Electron boost radiation is used to treat some breast cancers.

electron cryomicroscopy ABBR: cryo-EM. Electron microscopic imaging of rapidly frozen molecules and crystals in solution.

electron-dense In electron microscopy, having a density that prevents penetration by electrons.

electronegative (i-lek″trō-neg′ă-tiv) [*electro-* + *negative*] **1.** The tendency of one element to attract electrons to it from the outer energy level of another element. Using the periodic table, the most electronegative atom is fluorine (upper right), with decreasing electronegativity as one traverses the table down or to the left. **2.** Charged with negative electricity, which results in the attraction of positively charged bodies and the repulsion of negatively charged bodies. SEE: *electropositive*.

electroneurolysis (ē-lĕk″trō-nū-rŏl′ĭ-sĭs) Electrical destruction of a nerve.

electronic (i-lek″tron′ik) [*electron* + *-ic*] Pert. to electrons or electronics.

electronic cigarette (sig″ă-ret′, sig′ă-ret″) A cylindrical device shaped like a cigarette, which releases smokeless nicotine, heated vapor, flavorings, and other chemicals into the mouth and lungs when it is inhaled. Although the device is smokeless, it is nonetheless a health hazard. SYN: *e-cigarette*.

electronic fetal monitoring ABBR: EFM. The use of an electronic device to monitor vital signs of the fetus.

electronic health record ABBR: EHR. SEE: under *record*.

electronic ICU *Electronic intensive care unit.*

electronic intensive care unit ABBR: eICU, electronic ICU. A method of delivering care to critically ill patients in several remote hospitals by a staff of critical care specialists who work in a central supervisory location. Data on patients (including historical information, physical exam findings, hemodynamics, laboratory test results, and radiologic images) sent from the satellite hospitals are transmitted to and from the bedside to the supervisory staff, who select and adjust the drugs used for patient treatment, alter ventilator settings, and generate other care plans.

electronic portfolio E-portfolio.

electronics (i-lek″tron′iks) [*electron* + *-ics*] The science of the systems involving the use of electrical devices used for communication, information processing, and control.

electron transport chain SEE: under *chain*.

electron volt SYMB: eV. The energy acquired by an electron as it passes through a potential of 1 V.

electronystagmography (ĭ-lek″trō-nis″tag-mog′rǎ-fē) [*electro-* + *nystagmus* + *-graphy*] ABBR: ENG. A method of recording the electrical activity of the extraocular muscles. ENG is used to distinguish conditions such as peripheral vertigo from central vertigo. SEE: *nystagmus*.

electro-oculogram (ē-lĕk″trō-ŏk′u-lō-grăm″) Recording of the electric currents produced by eye movements. SEE: *electro-retinogram*.

electropathology (ē-lĕk″trō-pǎ-thŏl′ō-jē) [″ + *pathos*, disease, suffering, + *logos*, word, reason] Determination of the electrical reaction of muscles and nerves as a means of diagnosis.

electrophobia (ē-lĕk″trō-fō′bē-ǎ) Irrational fear of electricity.

electrophoresis (i-lek″trŏ-fŏ-rē′sĭs) [*electro-* + Gr. *phorēsis*, being carried] The movement of charged colloidal particles through the medium in which they are dispersed as a result of changes in electrical potential. Electrophoretic methods are useful in the analysis of protein mixtures because protein particles move with different velocities depending on their mass and charge. **electrophoretic** (-ret′ik), *adj*.

   gel e. The separation of whole or fragmented molecules, such as nucleic acids, through an electrically charged gel. The smaller the molecule, the faster its migration through the gel.

electrophrenic (ē-lĕk″trō-frĕn′ĭk) Pert. to stimulation of the phrenic nerve by electricity.

electrophysiology (ě-lek″trō-fiz″ē-ol′ŏ-jē) [*electro-* + *physiology*] **1.** Study of the relationships of body functions to electrical phenomena (e.g., the effects of electrical stimulation on tissues, the production of electric currents by organs and tissues, and the therapeutic use of electric currents). **2.** The study and treatment of cardiac arrhythmias. **electrophysiologist** (ě-lek″trō-fiz″ē-ol′ŏ-jĭst), *n*.

electrophysiology study SEE: under *study*.

electroporation (ē-lĕk″trō-po-rā′shŭn) **1.** An electrical device for delivering medications transdermally. **2.** The opening of pores in cellular or nuclear membranes with electrical current. It

has been used as a treatment for some solid tumors.

electropositive (i-lek″trō-poz′ĭt-iv) [*electro-* + L. *positive*] **1.** . Charged with positive electricity, which results in the repulsion of bodies electrified positively and the attraction of bodies electrified negatively. **2.** Pert. to the lesser tendency of some elements to attract electrons from another element or complex. For example, boron is more electropositive than fluorine. SEE: *electronegative*.

electroresection (ē-lĕk″trō-rē-sĕk′shŭn) Removal of tissue by use of an electric device such as an electrocautery.

electroretinogram (ē-lĕk″trō-rĕt′ĭ-nō-grăm) ABBR: ERG. A record of the electrical responses of the retina to stimulation by light.

electroscission (ē-lĕk″trō-sĭ′zhŭn) [″ + L. *scindere,* to cut] Division of tissues by electrocautery.

electroscope (ē-lĕk′trō-skōp) [″ + *skopein,* to examine] An instrument that detects radiation intensity.

electroshock (ē-lĕk′trō-shŏk″) Shock produced by an electric current, used in psychiatry to treat depression.

electroshock therapy Electroconvulsive therapy.

electrosleep (ē-lĕk′trō-slēp″) Sleep produced by the passage of mild electrical impulses through parts of the brain.

electrostatic (ē-lĕk″trō-stăt′ĭk) [″ + *statikos,* causing to stand] Pert. to static electricity.

electrostatic unit ABBR: ESU or ESE (from the German *elektrostatische Einheit*). Any electrical unit of measure based on the attraction or repulsion of a static charge, as distinguished from an electromagnetic unit, which is defined in terms of the attraction or repulsion of magnetic poles.

electrostimulation (ē-lek″trō-stim″yŭ-lā′shŏn) Electrical **stimulation**.

electrosurgery (ĭ-lek″trō-sŭr′jĕ-rē) An operative procedure performed with an instrument that converts electricity to heat, used for cutting, cautery, coagulation, or coaptation of tissues. **electrosurgical** (-sŭr′ji-kăl), *adj*.

⚠️ Potential (but rare) complications of electrosurgery include unanticipated burns, interference with implanted electronic devices (such as pacemakers, defibrillators), operating room fires, and exposure to noxious fumes.

electrosurgical unit ABBR: ESU. A device used to cut and coagulate tissues during surgery, using alternating current that changes direction at a frequency of between 500,000 and 3,000,000 hertz. An ESU is an alternative to other cutting tools, such as surgical blades or lasers.

electrotaxis (ē-lĕk″trō-tăks′ĭs) The movement of cells, tissues, or organisms under the influence of an electromagnetic stimulus.

electrotherapy (ĭ-lek″trō-ther′ă-pē) [*electro-* + *therapy*] The use of electricity in treating musculoskeletal or neuromuscular dysfunction, pain, or disease.

electrothermal (ĭ-lĕk″trō-thĕr′mĭl) Pert. to the heat generated by electricity and its uses (e.g., in surgery).

electrotonus (ē-lĕk-trŏt′ō-nŭs) The change in the irritability of a nerve or muscle during the passage of an electric current.

electrovalence (ĭ-lek″trō-vā′lĕns) [*electro-* + *valence*] The ionic bond between atoms in which each accepts or donates electrons so that each atom ends up with a completed orbital.

electrovaporization (ĭ-lĕk″trō-vā″pĕr-ĭ-zā′shŭn) Cutting of tissues with an instrument that uses electricity to convert solid tissues into gas.

electuary (ē-lĕk′tū-ă-rē) [Gr. *ekleikhein*, to lick up] A medicinal substance mixed with honey or sugar to form a paste suitable for oral consumption.

eleidin (ĕ-lē′ĭ-dĭn) [Gr. *elaion*, oil] A translucent protein present in the stratum lucidum of the epidermis of the palms and soles.

element (el′ĕ-mĕnt) [L. *elementum*, a rudiment] In chemistry, a pure substance consisting of only one type of atom. Further breakdown by nonchemical means of an element results in subatomic particles (protons, neutrons and electrons), which are indistinguishable from those from other elements. Elements exist in free and combined states. There are 110 named elements and others yet to be fully characterized and named. SEE: illus.

Oxygen, carbon, hydrogen, nitrogen, phosphorus, and sulfur are found in all living organisms. These six elements and calcium make up 99% of the human body mass. Sodium, potassium, magne-

Name	Symbol	Percentage of Body Weight
Major elements		
Oxygen	O	65.0
Carbon	C	18.0
Hydrogen	H	10.0
Nitrogen	N	3.0
Calcium	Ca	1.5
Phosphorus	P	1.0
Lesser elements		
Sulfur	S	0.25
Potassium	K	0.20
Sodium	Na	0.15
Chlorine	Cl	0.15
Magnesium	Mg	0.05
Iron	Fe	0.006

Trace elements			
Chromium	Cr	Molybdenum	Mo
Cobalt	Co	Selenium	Se
Copper	Cu	Silicon	Si
Fluorine	F	Tin	Sn
Iodine	I	Vanadium	V
Manganese	Mn	Zinc	Zn

TABLE OF ELEMENTS IN THE BODY

sium, chlorine, iodine, and iron form 0.9% of the body mass.

movable genetic e. Transposon.

rare earth element One of a series of metallic elements that follow lanthanum (at. no. 57) in the periodic table of elements and that have oxides with similar properties. The series comprises the 14-element lanthanide series (at. nos. 58-71 and includes praseodymium, promethium, and ytterbium.

trace e. An element needed by the body in very small amounts; many are essential for enzyme functioning. Trace elements include chromium, copper, fluoride, iodine, iron, manganese, molybdenum, selenium, and zinc.

elemental (ĕl″ĕ-mĕn′tĭl) Pert. to diets that are easy to digest or predigested; rudimentary or simple.

elephantiasis (ĕl″ĕ-făn-tī′ă-sĭs) [Gr. *elephas*, elephant, + *-iasis*, condition] Massive swelling, esp. of the genitalia and lower extremities, resulting from obstruction of lymphatic vessels, for example by filarial parasites, malignancies, neurofibromatosis, or a familial congenital disease (Milroy's disease). Prolonged swelling can cause an increase in interstitial fibrous tissue and skin puckering or breakdown. In patients with parasitic elephantiasis (i.e., the filarial diseases, which are common in the tropics), single-dose therapy with ivermectin or ivermectin plus albendazole destroys immature but not adult worms. SEE: *lymphedema*.

scrotal e. Swelling of the scrotum, usually as a result of infection of the pelvic lymphatics by filaria. SYN: *chyloderma*.

elephant man disease Colloquial name for Recklinghausen's disease.

Eleutherococcus senticosus (ĕ-loo″thĕ-rō″kok′ŭs sen″tĭ-kō′sŭs) SEE: *Siberian ginseng*.

elevation (ĕl″ĕ-vā′shŭn) **1.** A raised area that protrudes above the surrounding area. **2.** The measured distance above a fixed object, e.g., the distance above sea level, or above a fixed anatomic structure. **3.** The rise of a physiological variable above normal, e.g., in ophthalmology, the rise in intraocular pressure above what is healthy or normal; in serology, an increase in the level of an electrolyte or other blood test result.

S-T segment e. The height of the ST segment of an electrocardiogram relative to a level line that can be drawn between the preceding P-R interval and the subsequent T-P interval. S-T segment elevation in two or more contiguous leads of the electrocardiogram is one of the diagnostic criteria for acute myocardial infarction.

tactile e. A small raised area of the palm and sole that contains a cluster of nerve endings.

elevator [L. *elevare*, to lift up] **1.** A curved retractor for holding the lid away from the globe of the eye. **2.** A retractor for raising depressed bones by levers or screws. **3.** Instrument used for soft tissue; e.g., periosteal elevator. **4.** An instrument of varying design for extracting teeth or removing root or bone fragments.

periosteal e. A surgical instrument for separating the periosteum from the bone.

elevator talk A colloquial term for inappropriate public discussion of the private details of a person's medical record.

eleventh cranial nerve The motor nerve, made up of a cranial and a spinal part, that supplies the trapezius and sternomastoid muscles and the pharynx. The accessory portion joins the vagus to supply motor fibers to the pharynx, larynx, and heart.

elfin Having the facial appearance of an elf. The term is used to describe the facial structure of children with Williams syndrome.

eligible (el′ĭ-jĭ-bĭl) [L. *eligibilis*] Qualified to be considered a candidate for a role, e.g., membership in a professional society or enrollment in an insurance program or a research study. **eligibility** (el″ĭ-jĭ-bil′ĭt-ē), *n.*

eligible for organ donation Any person who is expected to die in the near future, is under 70 years old, and is free of excluded medical conditions for organ donation such as Creutzfeldt-Jakob disease, human immunodeficiency virus infection, or leukemia.

eliminant (ē-lĭm′ĭ-nănt) [L. *e*, out, + *limen*, threshold] **1.** Effecting evacuation. **2.** An agent aiding in elimination.

eliminate (ē-lĭm′ĭ-nāt) To expel; to rid the body of waste material.

elimination 1. Excretion of waste products by the skin, kidneys, lungs, and intestines. **2.** Leaving out, omitting, removing.

ELISA *Enzyme-linked immunosorbent assay.*

elixir (i-lik′sĕr) [L. from Arabic *al-iksir*, (a)chemical preparation, fr. Gr. *xērion*, drying powder (for wounds)] A sweetened, aromatic, hydroalcoholic liquid used in the compounding of oral medicines. Elixirs constitute one of the most common types of medicinal preparation taken orally in liquid form.

aromatic e. A flavoring agent used in preparing medicines.

Elizabethkingia meningoseptica (i-liz″ă-bĕth-king′ē-ă mĕ-ning″gō-sep′tĭ-kă) [Elizabeth O. King, 20th-cent. U.S. microbiologist] An aerobic, gram-negative, nonmotile, yellow rod-shaped bacterium found extensively in nature. It sometimes causes opportunistic infections in immunocompromised hosts.

-ella [L. *-ella*, feminine adj. suffix] Suffix

used for taxonomic names, esp. of genera of bacteria, e.g., *Bartonella, Legionella, Shigella.*

ellagic acid An antioxidant and anticancer polyphenol found in strawberries, raspberries, and pecans, among other foods.

ellipse (i-lips′) [L. *ellipsis,* fr Gr. *elleipsis,* a falling short] In geometry, an oval or egg-shaped figure. In surgery, incisions of such shape are commonly made to remove lesions from the skin. **elliptic** (-lip′tik), *adj.* **elliptical** (′ti-kăl), *adj.* **elliptically** (′ti-k(ă-)lē), *adv.*

ellipsis (ē-lĭp′sĭs) [L. *ellīpsis* fr. Gr., a falling short, defective] In psychoanalysis, omission by the patient of important words or ideas during treatment.

ellipsoid (ē-lĭp′soyd) Spindle-shaped.

elliptocyte (ē-lĭp′tō-sīt) An oval-shaped red blood cell. About 11% to 15% of red blood cells are normally oval, but in anemia and hereditary elliptocytosis, the percentage is increased to 25% to 100%. In birds, reptiles, and some other animals, the red cells are normally elliptocytes.

elliptocytosis (ē-lĭp″tō-sī-tō′sĭs) A condition in which the number of elliptocytes is increased. It occurs in some forms of anemia.

   hereditary e. An inherited condition in which the red blood cells are oval or elliptical. This anomaly occurs in about 1 in every 2000 births.

Ellis–van Creveld syndrome (ĕl′ĭs-văn-krĕ′vĕld) [Richard W. B. Ellis, Scot. physician, 1902–1966; Simon Creveld, Dutch physician, 1894–1977] A congenital syndrome consisting of polydactyly, chondrodysplasia with acromelic dwarfism, hydrotic ectodermal dysplasia, and congenital heart defects. It is thought to be transmitted as an autosomal trait. SYN: *chondroectodermal dysplasia.*

Elocon SEE: *mometasone.*

elongation (ē″lŏng-gā′shŭn) The condition of being extended or lengthened, or the process of extending.

elope **1.** To run away secretly with a lover, esp. to marry. **2.** To leave a hospital, esp. a psychiatric hospital, without permission.

eloquent brain Those parts of the brain that control speech, movement, and sensation, i.e., whose functions are readily felt, heard, and observed.

eluate (ĕl′ū-āt) The material washed out by elution.

eluent (ē-lū′ĕnt) The solvent or dissolving substance used in elution.

elution (ē-lū′shŭn) [L. *e,* out, + *luere,* to wash] In chemistry, separation of one material from another by washing. If a material contains water-soluble and water-insoluble materials, the passage of water (the eluent) through the mixture will remove the portion that is wa-

ter soluble (the eluate) and leave the water-insoluble residue.

elutriation (ē-loo″trē-ā′shŏn) [L. *elutriare,* to cleanse] The separation of larger insoluble particles from smaller, finer ones.

EM *Erythema multiforme.*

emaciate (ē-mā′shē-āt″) [L. *emaciare,* to make thin, waste away] To cause to become excessively lean.

emaciated (ē-mā′shē-āt-ĕd) [L. *emaciare,* to make thin, waste away] Excessively thin; having a body mass index below 16 kg/m^2.

emaciation (ē-mā″shē-ā′shŏn) [L. *emaciare,* to make thin, waste away] The state of being extremely lean. SYN: *wasting.* SEE: *cachexia.*

emailloid (ā-mī′loyd) [Fr. *email,* enamel, + Gr. *eidos,* form, shape] A tumor having its origin in tooth enamel.

emanation (ĕm-ă-nā′shŭn) [L. *e,* out, + *manare,* to flow] **1.** Something given off; radiation; emission. **2.** A gaseous product of radioactive disintegration.

   actinium e. The radioactive gas given off by actinium; a radioactive isotope of actinium. SYN: *actinon.*

   radium e. The radioactive gas given off by radium. SYN: *radon.*

   thorium e. The radioactive gas given off by thorium. SYN: *thoron.*

emancipatory teaching (i-man′sĭ-pă-tor″ē) [L. *emancipare,* to declare free and independent] **1.** A model of teaching in which coaching, dialogue, and encouragement are more important than the dissemination of information from teacher to student. Teachers show and allow students to take control of their lives and learning **2.** Online teaching.

emasculation (ē-măs″kū-lā′shŭn) [L. *emasculare,* to castrate] **1.** Castration. **2.** Excision of the entire male genitalia. **3.** Figuratively, the act of making another person powerless or ineffective.

embalming (ĕm-băm′ĭng) [L. *im-,* on, + *balsamum,* balsam] Preparing a body or part of a body for burial by injecting it with a preservative such as a 4% formaldehyde solution. This is usually done within 48 hr of death. SEE: *Standard Precautions Appendix.*

embarrass (ĕm-băr′ăs) To interfere with or compromise function.

EMBASE (ĕm′bās′) [Fm. *Excerpta Medica* + *base*] An electronic database of biomedical and pharmacological information administered by Excerpta Medica. It contains citations and abstracts of journal articles culled from about 4600 scientific journals published since 1974 in 70 countries.

Embden-Meyerhof pathway (ĕm′dĕn-mī′ĕr-hof) [Gustav G. Embden, Ger. biochemist, 1874–1933; Otto Fritz Meyerhof, Ger. biochemist, 1884–1951] A series of metabolic and enzymatic changes that occur in many plants and animals when glucose, glycogen, or starch is metabolized anaerobically to produce acetic acid. The process produces energy in the form of adenosine triphosphate (ATP).

embedding (ĕm-bĕd'ĭng) [" + AS. *bedd,* to bed] In histology, the process by which a piece of tissue is placed in a firm medium such as paraffin to support it and keep it intact during the subsequent cutting into thin sections for microscopic examination.

embole (ĕm'bō-lē) [Gr. *emballein,* to throw in] **1.** Reduction of a dislocation. **2.** Formation of the gastrula by invagination.

embolectomy (ĕm"bō-lĕk'tō-mē) [" + *ektome,* excision] Removal of an embolus from a vessel. It may be done surgically or by the use of enzymes that dissolve the clot. The latter method is used in treating acute myocardial infarction and in other areas where blood flow is obstructed by a blood clot. SEE: *tissue plasminogen activator.*

embolia cutis medicamentosa (em-bō'lē-ă kūt'ĭs mĕ-dik"ă-mĕn-tō'să) Nicolau syndrome.

embolic (ĕm-bŏl'ĭk) Pert. to or caused by embolism.

embolic protection filter In interventional vascular procedures, a net or umbrella placed distal to the site of an angioplasty to capture debris that has been released by the procedure and that might occlude downstream vessels.

emboliform (ĕm-bŏl'ĭ-fŏrm") [" + L. *forma,* form] **1.** Resembling an embolus. **2.** Wedge-shaped, as the nucleus emboliformis.

embolism (em'bŏ-lĭzm) [*embolus* + *-ism*] Sudden obstruction of a blood vessel by debris. Blood clots, cholesterol-containing plaques, masses of bacteria, cancer cells, amniotic fluid, fat from the marrow of broken bones, and injected substances (e.g., air bubbles or particulate matter) all may lodge in blood vessels and obstruct the circulation.

air e. Obstruction of a blood vessel caused by an air bubble.

ETIOLOGY: Air may enter a vessel postoperatively, during intravenous injections, after failure to purge intravenous lines, or as a result of rupture of a central line balloon. NOTE: A very small amount of air in a vessel or intravenous tubing is not hazardous.

SYMPTOMS: Symptoms include sudden onset of dyspnea, unequal breath sounds, hypotension, weak pulse, elevated central venous pressure, cyanosis, sharp chest pains, hemoptysis, a churning murmur over the precordium, and decreasing level of consciousness.

PATIENT CARE: When an air or gas embolism is suspected in the systemic venous circulation, echocardiography

should be used to confirm its presence. The suspected site of gas entry should be secured and flooded with normal saline to prevent entry of more gas into the circulation. One hundred percent oxygen should be administered to the patient by nonrebreather mask. The patient should be immediately repositioned with the right atrium above the gas entry site, so that air will be trapped there and not move into the pulmonary circulation or the right heart. A central venous catheter should be placed into the central venous circulation and any gas bubbles and air aspirated from the catheter. Intravenous fluids and inotropic medications may be needed to support blood pressure and pulse.

Prevention: All air should be purged from the tubing of all IV administration sets before hookup and when solution bags or bottles are changed; air elimination filters should be used close to the patient; infusion devices with air detection capability should be used, as well as locking tubing, locking connection devices, or taped connections. For central lines, to increase peripheral resistance and prevent air from entering the superior vena cava, the patient should be instructed to perform a Valsalva maneuver as the stylet is removed from the catheter, during attachment of the IV tubing, and when adapters or caps are changed on ports.

amniotic fluid e. The entry of amniotic fluid through a tear in the placental membranes into the maternal circulation. This rare event may occur at any gestational age, but most commonly during labor, delivery or in the immediate postpartum period. The contents of the fluid (e.g., shed fetal cells, meconium, lanugo, vernix) may produce pulmonary or cerebral emboli. Cardiac arrest and disseminated intravascular coagulation (DIC) commonly occur. Maternal death is a frequent complication

SYMPTOMS: Chest pain, dyspnea, cyanosis, tachycardia, hemorrhage, hypotension, or shock are potential symptoms. Amniotic fluid embolism is frequently fatal.

drug e. Embolism due to injected drugs, debris, or talc, often resulting in pulmonary infarction.

fat e. ABBR: FE. Embolism caused by globules of fat obstructing small blood vessels in the brain, lungs, and skin. It frequently occurs after fracture of long and pelvic bones or after orthopedic surgery and has been linked to episodes of acute pancreatitis, sickle-cell crisis, diabetes mellitus, osteomyelitis, and liposuction. Effects may be mild and undetected but can be severe, leading to acute respiratory distress syndrome, multiple organ dysfunction syndrome, or disseminated intravascular coagulation. Those most at risk for FE are males age 20 to 40 injured in serious motor vehicle accidents and elderly adults after hip fracture.

SYMPTOMS: Findings often include agitation, restlessness, delirium, convulsions, coma, tachycardia, tachypnea, dyspnea, wheezing, blood-tinged sputum, and fever, esp. during the first 12 to 72 hr after injury or insult, when fat emboli are most likely to occur. Petechiae may appear on the buccal membranes, conjunctival sacs, and the chest and axillae in a vestlike distribution. Retinal hemorrhages may be seen on fundoscopic examination. If fat globules lodge in the kidneys, renal failure may occur. Laboratory values are nonspecific but may show hypoxemia, suddenly decreased hemoglobin and hematocrit levels, leukocytosis, thrombocytopenia, increased serum lipase, and fat globules in urine and/or sputum.

PATIENT CARE: There is evidence that FE can be prevented when long bone fractures are immobilized immediately. Limited movement and gentle handling of any fractures before fixation may help prevent fat globule release. Patients at risk, i.e., those with fractures of long bones, severe soft tissue bruising, or fatty liver injury, are assessed for symptoms of fat embolism. Chest radiograph reports are reviewed for evidence of mottled lung fields and right ventricular dilation, and the patient's electrocardiogram is checked for large S waves in lead I, large Q waves in lead III, and right axis deviation.

The patient's respiratory and neurological status are monitored frequently for signs of hypoxemia. The treatment for the syndrome is nonspecific: good general supportive care of fluid balance, vital signs, oxygenation, electrolytes, and hemodynamics. The patient is placed in the high Fowler's, orthopneic, or other comfortable position to improve ventilation; high-concentration oxygen is administered, and endotracheal intubation and mechanical ventilation are initiated if the patient cannot maintain a PaO_2 of 60 mm Hg on 40% oxygen by face mask. Positive and end-expiratory pressure may be used to keep functional alveoli inflated to improve functional reserve capacity. IV fluid administration helps prevent shock. Deep breathing exercises and incentive spirometry to open and stabilize atelectatic lung areas may improve lung capacity and ventilation. Prescribed pharmacological agents are administered; these may include steroids, heparin, and anxiolytic agents such as diazepam.

paradoxical e. Embolism arising from the venous circulation that enters the arterial circulation by crossing from the right side of the heart to the left side through a patent foramen ovale or septal defect. It may occasionally cause stroke in a patient with a deep venous thrombosis.

pulmonary e. ABBR: PE. Embolism of the pulmonary artery or one of its branches, usually caused by a blood clot in a lower extremity. Roughly 10% to 15% of patients with the disease will die. Risks for it include genetic predisposition, recent limb or pelvic fracture, burns, surgery (esp. hip or knee replacement), long-term immobility, enforced immobilization (long car or plane trips or hospitalization), pregnancy, use of estrogen-containing hormonal contraceptives, postmenopausal hormones, atrial fibrillation, vascular injury, IV drug abuse, polycythemia vera, heart failure, autoimmune hemolytic anemia, sickle cell anemia, thrombocytosis, dehydration,, advanced age, cancer, and obesity. Diagnosis is challenging because symptoms are nonspecific and often misinterpreted and may mimic other diseases of the limbs, abdomen, or chest. It is often assumed that a sudden, unexpected death occurring after a hospitalization was caused by an unsuspected PE, which is the third most common cause of death in the U.S. When a pulmonary embolism is suspected, evaluation includes oximetry, chest x-ray, blood tests for D-dimer, and, depending on local hospital practices, duplex venous ultrasonography of the legs, ventilation/perfusion scanning, or multidetector CT angiography of the chest. Pulmonary angiography was formerly the standard test but is now rarely performed because it is invasive, poses risk to the patient, and requires angiographic skill and excellent radiographic equipment. Treatment includes the administration of anticoagulants (low molecular weight heparins or unfractionated heparins, followed by oral warfarin). Oxygen is administered as prescribed by nasal cannula or mask. In critically ill patients, intubation and mechanical ventilation may be required. Thrombolytic drugs may be needed for massive emboli, i.e., those that cause shock or that impair the filling of the right atrium and ventricle with blood. Thrombolectomy may be attempted in critically ill patients when a competent surgical team is available. SEE: illus.; *thrombosis, deep venous.*

PATIENT CARE: In the hospitalized patient, early mobilization, administration of prophylactic anticoagulants, and compression stockings (elastic or pneumatic) may prevent deep venous thrombosis (DVT). Vital signs, oxygen saturation, respiratory effort, breath sounds, cardiac rhythm, and urinary output are monitored closely in affected patients. Signs of deterioration are

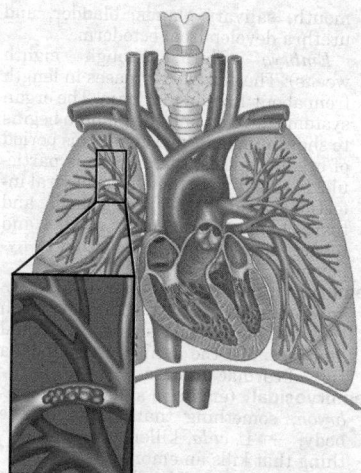

Pulmonary embolism

PULMONARY EMBOLISM

promptly reported. The nurse assists with diagnostic studies and medical treatment and provides explanations of procedures and treatments, analgesics for pain, prescribed medications, supplemental oxygen, patient education, and emotional support. Once the pain is stable, the patient is encouraged to resume normal activities. After a pulmonary embolism most patients remain on anticoagulant therapy for at least 6 months. The patient is taught about taking the medication dosage precisely as prescribed, bleeding signs to be reported, avoidance of over-the-counter and prescription drugs that may influence anticoagulation, regulation of foods high in vitamins, and the need for frequent blood tests to ensure appropriate levels of anticoagulation. SEE: *International Normalized Ratio*.

In patients who cannot use anticoagulants, a filtering device may be inserted transvenously into the vena cava to try to prevent blood clots from embolizing from the legs to the heart and lungs. SEE: *Nursing Diagnoses Appendix*.

   pyemic e. Septic embolism.

   septic e. An embolism made up of purulent matter that arises from the site of an infection caused by a pyogenic (pus-forming) organism. It can result in the spread of infection to a distant site. SYN: *pyemic e.*

embolization (em″bŏ-lĭ-zā′shŏn) Obstruction of a blood vessel by intentionally injected material or by physiologic migration of loosened intravascular plaque or thrombi.

   arterial e. **1.** Pathological migration of an embolus into an artery. **2.** Embolotherapy.

   therapeutic e. Embolotherapy.

   uterine artery e. The injection of particles into the uterine artery to block its blood supply. Uterine artery embolization is used as an alternative to hysterectomy in the management of uterine fibroids and, occasionally, postpartum bleeding. Complications from the procedure include pelvic pain, cramping, fever, nausea, vomiting, or occasionally uterine injury that necessitates surgical removal of the uterus. SEE: *embolotherapy*.

   varicocele e. A treatment for varicocele in which a catheter is inserted into the femoral vein and advanced to the testicular vein, obstructing blood flow from the incompetent vessel. The radiologist may use one of several injected materials to block the responsible vein. The procedure is an alternative to surgical varicocele repair and is used principally to treat cases of male infertility.

embolotherapy (em″bŏ-lō-ther′ă-pē) [*embolus* + *therapy*] The use of any type of embolic material (autologous thrombus, muscle fragment, or foreign body) for therapeutic occlusion of a blood vessel. This technique is used to control bleeding, close fistulae or arteriovenous malformations, devascularize organs, and reduce tumors or varicoceles. Generally a catheter is threaded through the vascular system to the origin of the vessel to be occluded, and an agent is injected under radiographic control. SYN: *arterial* **embolization** (2).

embolus (ĕm′bō-lŭs) *pl.* **emboli** [Gr. *embolos,* stopper] A mass of undissolved matter present in a blood or lymphatic vessel and brought there by the blood or lymph. Emboli may be solid, liquid, or gaseous. Occlusion of vessels from emboli usually results in the development of infarcts. SEE: *thrombosis; thrombus*.

   air e. Air embolism.

   coronary e. An embolus in one of the coronary arteries. It may be a complication of arteriosclerosis and may cause angina pectoris.

   pulmonary e. An embolus in the pulmonary artery or one of its branches. SEE: *pulmonary embolism*.

embolysis (ĕm-bŏl′ĭ-sĭs) The dissolution of an embolus, esp. one due to a blood clot.

embrasure (em-brā′zhŭr) [Fr. *embrasure,* a window opening from within] The spillway (space) formed by the contour and position of adjacent teeth.

   buccal e. The embrasure spreading toward the cheek between the molar and premolar teeth.

   labial e. The embrasure opening

toward the lips between the canine and incisor teeth.

lingual e. The embrasure opening to the lingual sides of the teeth.

occlusal e. The embrasure marked by the marginal ridge on the distal side of one tooth and that on the mesial side of the adjacent tooth, and the contact points.

embryectomy (ĕm″brē-ĕk′tō-mē) [Gr. *embryon*, something that swells in the body, + *ektome*, excision] Removal of an extrauterine embryo.

embryo (em′brē-ō″) [Gr. *embryon*, growing inside] 1. The young of any organism in an early stage of development. 2. In mammals, the stage of prenatal development between fertilized ovum and fetus. SEE: table; illus.

DEVELOPMENT: First week after fertilization: The zygote begins a series of mitotic divisions called cleavage and forms a morula, a solid sphere of cells. The morula develops into a blastocyst, which has an outer trophoblast and an inner cell mass. The trophoblast gives rise to the chorion, and after implantation in the uterus, becomes the fetal placenta. Second week: The amniotic cavity and yolk sac form within the inner cell mass; they are separated by the embryonic disk, which at this time consists of ectoderm and endoderm. Third week: Mesoderm develops between ectoderm and endoderm; all three germ layers are established.

The epithelium of the alimentary canal, liver, pancreas, and lungs develops from endoderm. Muscle, all connective tissues, blood, lymphatic tissue, and the epithelium of blood vessels, body cavities, kidneys, gonads, and suprarenal cortex develop from mesoderm. The epidermis, nervous tissue, hypophysis, and the epithelium of the nasal cavity,

mouth, salivary glands, bladder, and urethra develop from ectoderm.

Embryo (Third through eighth weeks): The embryo increases in length from about 1.5 mm to 23 mm. The organ systems develop and the embryo begins to show human form. During this period of organogenesis, the embryo is particularly sensitive to the effects of viral infections of the mother, e.g., rubella, and toxic chemicals, including alcohol and tobacco smoke, and is sensitive to hypoxemia.

embryocardia (ĕm″brē-ō-kăr′dē-ă) [″ + *kardia*, heart] Heart action in which the first and second sounds are equal and resemble the fetal heart sounds; a sign of cardiac distress.

embryocidal (ĕm″brē-ō-sī′dăl) [Gr. *embryon*, something that swells in the body, + L. *cida*, killer] Pert. to anything that kills an embryo.

embryoctony (ĕm″brē-ŏk′tō-nē) [″ + *kteinein*, to kill] Destruction of the fetus in utero, as when delivery is impossible or during abortion. SEE: *craniotomy*.

embryogenetic, embryogenic (ĕm″brē-ō-jĕ-nĕt′ĭk, ĕm″brē-ō-jĕn′ĭk) [″ + *gennan*, to produce] Giving rise to an embryo.

embryogeny (ĕm″brē-ŏj′ĕ-nē) The growth and development of an embryo.

embryology (ĕm″brē-ŏl′ŏ-jē) [″ + *logos*, word, reason] The science that deals with the origin and development of an organism in the womb.

embryoma (ĕm-brē-ō′mă) [″ + *oma*, tumor] A tumor, such as Wilms' tumor of the kidney, neuroblastoma, or teratomas, consisting of derivatives of the embryonic germ layers but lacking in organization.

embryonal (em-brī′ŏ-năl) [*embryo* + *-al*] Embryonic (1).

Derivatives of Embryonic Tissues

Ectoderm	Mesoderm	Endoderm
Nervous tissue	Bone, cartilage, and other connective tissues	Epithelium of respiratory tract except nose; digestive tract except mouth and anal canal; bladder except trigone
Sense organs		
Epidermis, nails, and hair follicles	Male and female reproductive tracts	
		Proximal portion of male urethra
Epithelium of external and internal ear, nasal cavity and sinuses, mouth, anal canal	Heart, blood vessels, and lymphatics	Female urethra
	Kidneys, ureters, trigone of bladder	Liver
Distal portion of male urethra	Pleura, peritoneum, and pericardium	Pancreas
	Skeletal muscle	

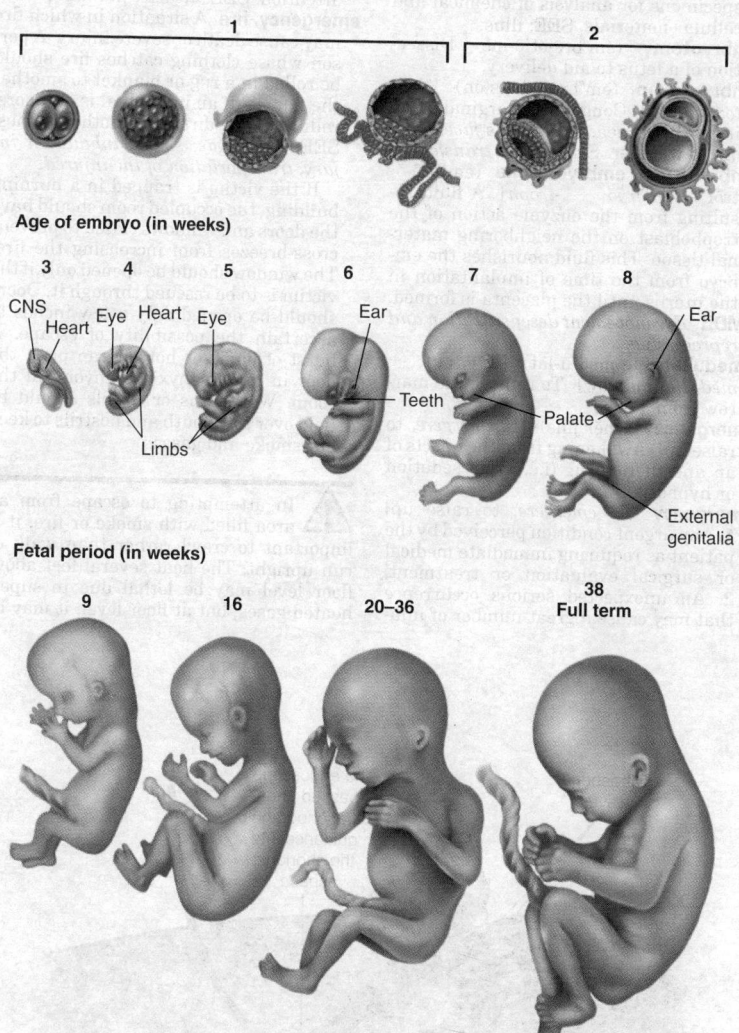

Period of dividing zygote, implantation, and bilaminar embryo (in weeks)

1   2

Age of embryo (in weeks)

3   4   5   6   7   8

CNS   Heart   Eye   Heart   Eye   Ear

Teeth   Palate   Ear

Limbs   External genitalia

Fetal period (in weeks)

9   16   20–36   38 Full term

STAGES OF DEVELOPMENT OF HUMAN EMBRYO INCLUDING MATURE FETUS

embryonated (em′brē-ŏ-nāt″ĕd) Fertilized.

embryonated chicken eggs Fertilized chicken eggs, in which vaccines for diseases such as influenza are produced.

embryonic (em″brē-on′ik) [embryo + -ic] **1.** Pert. to or in the condition of an embryo. SYN: embryonal. **2.** In human gestation, pert. to the stage of prenatal development between the fourth day after fertilization and the end of the eighth week.

embryopathy (em″brē-ŏp′ă-thē) [″ + pathos, disease, suffering] Any acquired or genetic disease of a developing embryo.

embryoplastic (em″brē-ō-plăs′tĭk) [″ + plassein, to form] Having a part in the formation of an embryo; said of cells.

embryoscopy (em″brē-ŏs′kŏ-pē) Direct visualization of the fetus or embryo in the uterus by insertion of the light source and image-detecting portion of a fetoscope into the amniotic cavity through a small incision in the abdominal wall. This technique permits visualization and photography, surgical correction of certain types of congenital defects, and collection of amniotic fluid specimens for analysis of chemical and cellular materials. SEE: illus.

embryotomy (ĕm″brē-ŏt′ō-mē) Dissection of a fetus to aid delivery.

embryotoxon (ĕm″brē-ō-tŏks′ŏn) [″ + *toxon,* bow] Congenital marginal opacity of the cornea. SYN: *arcus juvenilis.*

embryo transfer SEE: under *transfer.*

embryotroph, embryotrophe (em′brē-ŏ-trŏf″) [*embryo* + *-troph*] A fluid resulting from the enzyme action of the trophoblast on the neighboring maternal tissue. This fluid nourishes the embryo from the time of implantation in the uterus until the placenta is formed.

EMDR *Eye movement desensitization and reprocessing.*

emedullate (ē-mĕd′ū-lāt) [L. *e,* out, + *medulla,* marrow] To remove the marrow from a bone.

emergence (ĭ-mĕr′jĭns) [L. *emergere,* to raise up] Awakening from the effects of an anesthetic drug (i.e., from sedation or hypnosis).

emergency [L. *emergere,* to raise up] **1.** Any urgent condition perceived by the patient as requiring immediate medical or surgical evaluation or treatment. **2.** An unexpected serious occurrence that may cause a great number of injuries, which usually require immediate attention. SEE: *disaster planning.*

emergency, fire A situation in which fire may cause death or severe injury. A person whose clothing catches fire should be rolled in a rug or blanket to smother the flames. If an individual is outdoors, rolling in the dirt will smother flames. SEE: *burn; gas; smoke inhalation injury; transportation of the injured.*

If the victim is trapped in a burning building, the occupied room should have the doors and windows closed to prevent cross-breezes from increasing the fire. The window should be opened only if the victim is to be rescued through it. Doors should be opened only a few inches to ascertain the possibility of escape. A burst of flame or hot air can push the door in and asphyxiate anyone in the room. Wet cloths or towels should be held over the mouth and nostrils to keep out smoke and gases.

⚠ In attempting to escape from an area filled with smoke or fire, it is important to crawl rather than walk or run upright. The heat several feet above floor level may be lethal due to superheated gases, but at floor level, it may be

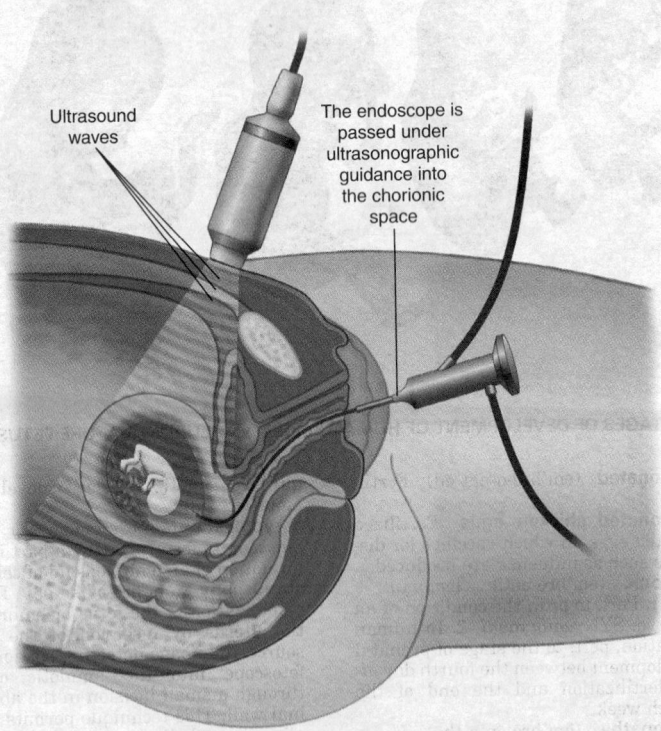

Ultrasound waves

The endoscope is passed under ultrasonographic guidance into the chorionic space

EMBRYOSCOPY

cool enough to tolerate. Even when crawling, it is important to proceed as quickly as possible. Carbon monoxide is present in higher concentration at floor level because it is heavier than air.

---

emergency cardiac care SEE: under *care*.

Emergency Department ABBR: E.D. The unit of a hospital in which acute, severe, or urgent illnesses and/or injuries are treated.

emergency kit A box or bag containing the equipment, supplies, and medications needed to provide an initial assessment and to manage life-threatening conditions. The kit typically includes tools for managing the airway and breathing, supporting circulation, providing basic or advanced life support, inserting intravenous access, and measuring vital signs.

emergency medical dispatch A communications system that uses the telephone to interview witnesses to an emergency, make triage decisions, and provide protocol-based advice so that first-aid treatment may be initiated before emergency services providers arrive at the scene.

emergency medical identification SEE: *Medic Alert®*.

emergency medical responder ABBR: EMR. Any person who has taken courses to acquire skills in the management of patients with acute illnesses or injuries. EMRs include those who have learned how to manage minor injuries (i.e., to use first aid), those who have mastered basic life support, and those with more advanced skills involving the management of cardiac or respiratory arrest or major trauma.

emergency medical services medical director The physician responsible for the patient care and clinical components of an EMS system.

Emergency Medical Service System ABBR: EMSS. A comprehensive approach to providing emergency medical services, including the following components: manpower, training, communications, transportation facilities, critical care units, public safety agencies, consumer participation, access to care, patient transfer, coordinated patient record keeping, public information and education, review and evaluation, and disaster planning. SEE: *disaster planning*.

emergency medical technician ABBR: EMT. An individual trained to administer emergency care in a variety of conditions, but esp. to patients who have suffered illnesses such as cardiac arrest, chest pain, stroke, or trauma. EMTs function in an EMS system, are certified by the state after completing instruction, and work under the authority of a supervising medical control physician, using treatment protocols approved by a medical advisory committee. SEE: *Emergency Medical Service System; EMS medical control; EMS treatment protocol; paramedic.*

   e.m.t.-basic ABBR: EMT-B. An individual who has become state certified or nationally registered after completion of the U.S. Department of Transportation EMT-B standard curriculum.

   e.m.t.-defibrillation ABBR: EMT-D. During the transition from the 1985 to the 1994 U.S. Department of Transportation standard curriculum, the title given in many states to individuals who became certified EMTs in the skill of defibrillation.

   e.m.t.-intermediate ABBR: EMT-I. An individual who has become state certified or nationally registered after completion of the U.S. Department of Transportation EMT-I standard curriculum. This curriculum emphasizes basic life support skills as well as advanced life support procedures such as assessment, intravenous fluid administration, advanced airway procedures (i.e., endotracheal intubation), defibrillation, trauma management, and a limited number of medications given in medical emergencies.

   e.m.t.-paramedic ABBR: EMT-P. An EMS provider who has completed the U.S. DOT EMT-Paramedic curriculum and is licensed or certified to provide assessment and management of patients in the field. Paramedics work under treatment protocols that are developed by the medical control physicians and require either standing orders or direct online medical control. SEE: *medic; paramedic.*

Emergency Medical Treatment and Active Labor Act ABBR: EMTALA. An American federal statute that prohibits a hospital from failing to treat or stabilize indigent medical patients simply because of their low-income status. The statute mandates that the hospital where a patient comes for care 1. perform a screening medical examination and 2. stabilize any emergent condition the patient has. The hospital must not transfer the patient to another facility without receiving explicit permission to do so from an attending physician at the receiving facility.

Emergency Nurses Association A professional organization representing and certifying nurses who are proficient in emergency care.

emergency preparation of safe drinking water The purification of water when only unclean water is available or when the available drinking water is believed to be contaminated. Any one of the following methods may be used: 1. Water is strained through a filter and boiled vigorously for 30 min. 2. Three drops of alcoholic solution of iodine are added to each qt (approx. 1 L) of water. The water is then mixed well and left to stand for 30 min before using. 3. Ten drops of 1% chlorine bleach, 2 drops of 4% to 6% chlorine bleach, or 1 drop of 7% to 10% chlorine bleach is added to each qt (L) of water. The water is then mixed well and left to stand for 30 min. If the water is cloudy to begin with, the amount of chlorine is doubled.

When the water is contaminated by *Giardia* organisms, heating to 55°C (131°F) kills the protozoa (method 1). Methods 2 and 3 also kill the cysts, but more time is required. Bacteria and viruses are killed by water kept at 60°C (140°F) for 30 min.

emergency readiness Planning in advance for an unexpected crisis, esp. a natural disaster such as a flood or hurricane. The home should be inspected for potential hazards, and those discovered should be corrected. Flammable materials such as paints, oils, and fuels should be isolated. Utility shut-off valves should be located and pointed out to all members of the household. It is important to know the location of the nearest public shelter and the time required to go there on foot and by car. Family members should be trained in basic life support techniques. Emergency telephone numbers, including names and telephone numbers of neighbors, should be posted and easily accessible. A first-aid kit should be available and restocked when supplies have been used. Fire extinguishers and flashlights should be in working condition. Supplies of food and water for least 3 days and protective clothing and blankets should be available. It is important to provide for the special needs of infants, the elderly, and the ill. Emergency drills should be practiced, including evacuation from the home by various routes in case the usual exits are blocked or surrounded by flames. SEE: *emergency, fire*.

emergency responder The preferred term for those individuals previously known as "first responders" who are trained to assist victims of injury or ill health at the scene of the emergency.

Emergency Room ABBR: E.R. The term that was previously used for the room in the hospital where patients with emergencies were taken. Today most hospitals that receive emergency patients have an emergency department or E.D.

emergent (ĕ-mĕr′jĕnt) [L. *emergere*, to raise up] **1.** Making an appearance or coming into view. **2.** Growing from a cavity or other part. **3.** Needing immediate action or treatment.

emergent literacy **1.** The attitudes and learning that lead to the ability to ma-

nipulate graphic symbols (e.g., the letters of the alphabet), form sounds, and develop vocabulary. **2.** Attainment of mastery in reading and writing.

emergi-center (ĕ-mĕr′jĭ-sent″ĕr) [*emerge(ncy) + center*] A free-standing health care clinic that treats walk-in or scheduled patients who have urgent health care needs, e.g., minor traumas, allergies, or upper respiratory illnesses. SYN: *urgi-center*.

emerging adulthood (i-mĕrj′ing ă-dŭlt′hud″) A period of personal development in which young adults (between about 18 and 25 years old) become less dependent on their parents but have not yet completed their education, established a durable relationship with another person, formed a family, or entered the work force. SYN: *prolonged adolescence*. **emerging adult**, *n.*

emerging infectious disease Any previously unknown communicable illness or any previously controlled contagion whose incidence and prevalence are suddenly rising. In recent years, some emerging (and re-emerging) infections have been bovine spongiform encephalopathy (mad cow disease), Ebola hemorrhagic fever, cholera, plague, hemolytic uremic syndrome caused by *Escherichia coli* 0157:H7, drug-resistant strains of enterococcus, the human immunodeficiency virus, SARS, and antibiotic-resistant organisms, among many others.

emery (ĕm′ĕ-rē) A granular mineral substance used as an abrasive.

Emery-Dreifuss muscular dystrophy (em′ĕ-rē-drī′fŭs) [Alan E. H. Emery, British geneticist, b. 1928; Fritz Emanuel Dreifuss, German-born Brit. neurologist, 1926–1997] ABBR: EDMD. One of several rare forms of muscular dystrophy, characterized by muscular degeneration principally in the shoulders, arms, and calves. Cardiac conduction abnormalities resulting in heart block and joint contractures are common complications.

emesis (ĕm′ĕ-sĭs) [Gr. *emein*, to vomit] Vomiting. It may be of gastric, systemic, or neurological origin. SEE: *antiemetic; aspiration; emetic; vomit*.

PATIENT CARE: The relationship of emesis to meals, administered drugs, or other environmental stimuli should be noted. The presence of any aggravating factors, e.g., pain, anxiety, nauseating medications, pregnancy, neurological conditions (e.g., head trauma, hemorrhage, or tumors); the type of foods eaten; and noxious environmental stimuli; as well as the type of vomiting, amount, color, and characteristics of the emesis are documented. Assistance is provided with oral hygiene, and antiemetics are administered, if prescribed, to control vomiting. If vomiting leaves the patient weak, dysphagic, or with an impaired sensorium, or if the patient is comatose or has an impaired cough mechanism and is receiving enteral feedings, safety measures are instituted to prevent aspiration of vomitus into the lungs; these include placing the patient in a side-lying position with the head lowered or in a high-Fowler's position after feeding and having suction and emergency tracheostomy equipment readily available.

    chemotherapy-induced e. Vomiting associated with or caused by drug treatments for cancer. Even though this side effect is usually self-limiting and seldom life-threatening, the prospect of it may produce anxiety and depression in many patients. Treatments may include drugs such as dronabinol, granisetron, lorazepam, prochlorperazine, and steroids, among others.

    gastric e. Vomiting present in gastric ulcer, gastric carcinoma, acute gastritis, chronic gastritis, hyperacidity and hypersecretion, and pressure on the stomach.

    e. gravidarum Vomiting of pregnancy. SEE: *hyperemesis gravidarum.*

emetic (ĕ-mĕt′ĭk) [Gr. *emein,* to vomit] An agent that promotes vomiting. An emetic may induce vomiting by irritating the gastrointestinal tract or by stimulating the chemoreceptor trigger zone of the central nervous system. Some drugs, such as narcotic pain relievers and chemotherapeutic agents used to treat cancer, have emetic properties as unwanted side effects of their administration. SEE: *vomiting.; vomitus.*

    TREATMENT OF DRUG OVERDOSES: Drugs that promote vomiting (such as syrup of ipecac and apomorphine hydrochloride) are given occasionally to treat toxic ingestions. Gastric lavage or the oral administration of activated charcoal usually is preferred for the management of patients who have overdosed on medications, because these methods are generally safer, better tolerated, and more effective than are emetics. Emetics are particularly hazardous in patients with altered mental status or patients who have ingested petroleum distillates, because of the risk of aspiration, and in patients who have ingested corrosive agents, because the emetic drug may worsen the injury to the esophagus and oropharynx. Emetics are also contraindicated in patients with known cardiac or epileptic disorders because they occasionally trigger seizures or arrhythmias. SEE: *Poisons and Poisoning Appendix.* SYN: *emetogenic.*

    direct e. An emetic that acts by its presence in the stomach (e.g., mustard).

    indirect e. An emetic that acts on the vomiting center of the brain (e.g., apomorphine).

emetine (ĕm′ĕ-tēn) [Gr. *emein,* to vomit] A powdered white alkaloid emetic obtained from ipecac.

    bismuth iodide e. A combination of emetine and bismuth containing about 20% emetine and 20% bismuth.

    e. hydrochloride The hydrated hydrochloride of an alkaloid obtained from ipecac. It is used for the treatment of both intestinal and extraintestinal amebiasis. It should be used cautiously in elderly or debilitated patients. Children, pregnant women, and patients with serious organic disease should not receive emetine.

emetism (ĕm′ĕ-tĭzm) [″ + *-ismos,* condition of] Poisoning from an overdose of ipecac.

    SYMPTOMS: Symptoms are acute inflammation of the pylorus, hyperemesis, diarrhea, and sometimes aspiration and suffocation.

emetocathartic (ĕm″ĕ-tō-kă-thăr′tĭk) [″ + *katharsis,* a purging] Producing both emesis and catharsis.

emetogenic (ĕ-mĕt″ō-jĕn′ĭk) Emetic.

emetogenicity (em″ĕ-tō-jĕ-nis′ĭt-ē) [Gr. *emetos,* vomiting + *-genic*] The likelihood that a drug or toxin will stimulate a person to vomit.

emetology (ĕm″ĕ-tŏl′ō-jē) [″ + *logos,* word, reason] The study of the anatomy and physiology of vomiting.

E.M.F. *electromotive force; erythrocyte maturation factor.*

EMG *electromyogram.*

-emia [Gr. *haima,* blood + *-ia*] Suffix meaning *blood condition.* The variant *-aemia* is used outside the U.S.

EMIC *emergency maternal and infant care.*

emic (ē′mĭk) In anthropology and transcultural nursing, rel. to a type of disease analysis that focuses on the culture of the patient. The emic perspective emphasizes the subjective experience and cultural beliefs pertinent to the illness experience. For example, in psychiatric settings in the southeastern U.S., many patients believe that their illness is caused by a spell or curse from evil spirits. In these cases, a health care worker using an emic perspective would ask an indigenous health care provider to consult with the patient in addition to providing care within the traditional health care system. SEE: *etic.*

emigration [L. *e,* out, + *migrare,* to move] The passage of white blood cells through the walls of capillaries and into surrounding tissue during inflammation. SEE: *inflammation.*

eminence (em′ĭ-nĕns) [L. *eminere,* to stand out] A prominence, bump, bulge, or projection, esp. of a bone.

articular e. of the mandibular fossa
A rounded eminence forming the anterior boundary of the glenoid fossa.

Doyère's e. SEE: *Doyère's eminence.*

frontal e. A gently rounded prominence on either side of the median line and a little below the center of the frontal bone.

hypothenar e. Hypothenar.

parietal e. A marked convexity on the outer surface of the parietal bone.

pyramidal e. An elevation on the mastoid wall of the tympanic cavity. It contains a cavity through which the stapedius muscle passes. SYN: *pyramid of the tympanum.*

thenar e. An prominence formed by muscles on the palm below the thumb.

eminentia (ĕm″ĭn-ĕn′shē-ă) *pl.* **eminentiae** [L.] Eminence.

emiocytosis (ē″mē-ō-sī-tō′sĭs) [L. *emitto,* to send forth, + Gr. *kytos,* cell, + *osis,* condition] The process of movement of intracellular material to the outside. Granules join the cell membrane, which ruptures to allow the substance to be free in the intercellular fluid. SYN: *exocytosis.* SEE: *endocytosis; pinocytosis.*

emissary (ĕm′ĭ-să-rē) [L. *e,* out, + *mittere,* to send] **1.** Providing an outlet. **2.** An outlet.

emissary vein SEE: under *vein.*

emission (ē-mĭsh′ŭn) [L. *e,* out, + *mittere,* to send] An issuance or discharge; the sending forth or discharge of, for example, an atomic particle, an exhalation, or a light or heat wave.

nocturnal e. The involuntary discharge of semen during sleep, usually occurring in conjunction with an erotic dream. SYN: *wet dream.*

thermionic e. The process by which electrons are released from an x-ray filament after a current has been passed through it.

emissivity (ĕm″ĭ-sĭv′ĭ-tē) The ability of a substance or surface to emit radiant energy.

EMIT *enzyme-multiplied immunoassay technique.*

emit To produce or release something (e.g., light, heat, or sound waves).

EMLA *eutectic mixture of local anesthetics.*

emmenagogue (ĕ-men′ă-gog″) [Gr. *emmena,* menses + *-agogue*] A substance that promotes or assists the flow of menstrual fluid. SEE: *ecbolic.*

direct e. An agent, such as a hormone or a natural herb, that induces menstruation by a direct effect on the reproductive tract.

indirect e. An agent that alters menstrual function as a side effect of the treatment of another illness.

emmeniopathy (ĕ-mē″nē-ŏp′ă-thē) [″ + *pathos,* disease, suffering] Any disorder of menstruation.

Emmet operation (em′ĕt) [Thomas A. Emmet, U.S. gynecologist, 1828–1919] **1.** Uterine trachelorrhaphy (i.e., suturing of a torn uterine cervix). **2.** Suturing of a lacerated perineum. **3.** Conversion of a sessile submucous tumor of the uterus into a pedunculated one.

Additional procedures attributed to Emmet, such as repair of prolapsed uterus and creation of a vesicovaginal fistula, have been superseded by more modern procedures.

emmetrope (ĕm′ĕ-trōp) [Gr. *emmetros,* in measure, + *opsis,* sight] One endowed with normal vision. **emmetropic** (-trŏp′ĭk), *adj.*

emmetropia (ĕm″ĕ-trō′pē-ă) The normal condition of the eye in refraction in which, when the eye is at rest, parallel rays focus exactly on the retina. SEE: illus.; *astigmatism; myopia.*

Emmetropia

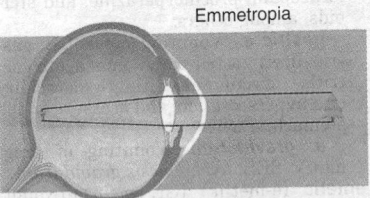

Myopia

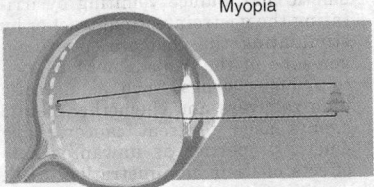

Hyperopia

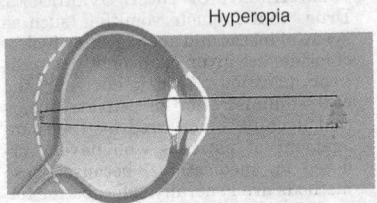

EMMETROPIA, MYOPIA, HYPEROPIA

emollient (i-mol′yĕnt) [L. *emollire,* to soften] An agent that moisturizes, softens, and soothes the surface to which it is applied, usually the skin. SEE: *demulcent.*

emotion (ē-mō′shŭn) [L. *emovere,* to stir up] A mental state or feeling such as fear, hate, love, anger, grief, or joy arising as a subjective experience rather than as a conscious thought. Physiological changes invariably accompany emotions, but such change may not be apparent to either the person experiencing the emotion or an observer. **emotional** (-ăl), *adj.*

DISORDERS: See names of specific mood disorders for more information, e.g., depression, bipolar mood disorders.

emotivity (ē″mō-tĭv′ĭ-tē) One's capability for emotional response.

empacho (ĕm-pă′chō) [Sp., surfeit, impacted stomach] A culture-based syndrome of gastrointestinal distress in infants and children ascribed to intestinal blockage, whose symptoms may include bloating, diarrhea, vomiting, and lethargy. In some Latin American cultures, empacho is treated by a folk practitioner, who may use external massage or internal treatments, including herbal teas, commercial laxatives, or olive or castor oil. Some traditional treatments use mercury compounds or lead salts, which may poison affected infants. SEE: *curanderismo.*

empathy (ĕm′pă-thē) Awareness of and insight into the feelings, emotions, and behavior of another person and their meaning and significance. It is not the same as sympathy, which is usually nonobjective and noncritical.

empathic (-pă′thĭk), *adj.*

emperipolesis (ĕm-pĕr″ĭ-pĕ-lē′sĭs) [Gr. *en,* in + *peri,* around + *poleisthai,* to wander] The presence of cells of one type within the cytoplasm of cells of another lineage. One example of emperipolesis is erythrophagocytosis.

emperor of pruritus The intense itching that accompanies poison ivy dermatitis affecting the anal area.

emphysema (em″fĭ-zē′mă, ĭ-sē′) [L. *emphysema,* fr Gr. *emphysēma,* inflation] **1.** Pathological distention of interstitial tissues by gas or air. The distention can be palpated or seen radiographically. Causes include leaking tracheostomy tubes or open pneumothoraces. **2.** A chronic obstructive pulmonary disease marked by an abnormal increase in the size of air spaces distal to the terminal bronchiole, with destruction of the alveolar walls. These changes result in a loss of the normal elastic properties of the lungs and difficulty exhaling air. Alveolar septa are destroyed, and portions of the capillary bed are eliminated. Residual volume increases. **emphysematous** (em″fĭ-zē′măt-ŭs, ĭ-sē′), *adj.*

ETIOLOGY: Tobacco smoking is the most common cause of the tissue destruction found in emphysema. Exposure to environmental dust, smoke, or particulate pollution may also contribute to the disease. A small number of people with emphysema may have developed it as a result of alpha-1-antitrypsin deficiencies, a group of genetic illnesses in which there is inadequate protection against destructive enzyme activity in the lung. Complications include cor pulmonale, recurrent respiratory infections, and respiratory failure.

SYMPTOMS: Symptoms include difficulty breathing, esp. during exertion. Weight loss, chronic cough, and wheezing are also characteristic. Physical findings include prolongation of expiration, diminished breath sounds, a decrease in the measured distance between the thyroid cartilage and the chin, and heart tones that are audible only in the subxiphoid region of the chest.

TREATMENT: Smoking cessation helps preserve remaining alveoli. Inhaled bronchodilators and anticholinergics, such as ipratropium, tiotropium, albuterol, or salmeterol may improve respiratory function. Aerosolized corticosteroids reduce inflammaton, and mucolytics thin inspissated secretions and aid mucus expectoration. Antibiotics are only used when bacterial infections are identified. Oxygen therapy prevents right heart failure. The respiratory therapist administers oxygen at low-flow settings to maintain adequate oxygenation (PaO2 60/80 mm/Hg). Lung volume reduction surgery can eliminate hyperinflated (nonfunctional) portions of the lungs, allowing the healthier lung tissue that is left behind to expand and contract with improved efficiency. The patient is protected from environmental bronchial irritants, such as smoke, automobile exhaust, aerosol sprays, and industrial pollutants. SEE: *chronic obstructive pulmonary disease* for further treatment recommendations.

PATIENT CARE: The patient's oxygenation, weight, and the results of electrolyte and complete blood count measurements are monitored. The patient is evaluated for infection and other complications, and the effects of the disease on functional capabilities. Prescribed medications are administered by parenteral or oral route or by inhalation.

The patient is encouraged to intersperse normal activities with rest periods. Respiratory infections may be devastating to the emphysema patient; some of them can be prevented by avoiding crowds and contact with infectious persons; by using correct pulmonary hygiene procedures, including thorough hand hygiene; and by obtaining influenza and pneumococcal immunizations. Patients are taught breathing techniques to control dyspnea. Frequent small meals of easy-to-chew, easy-to-digest, high-calorie, high-protein foods and food supplements are encouraged. Small meals conserve patient energy, prevent fatigue, and also reduce intraabdominal pressure on the diaphragm and reduce dyspnea.

When patients with emphysema are hospitalized, the respiratory therapist and physician monitor the results of arterial blood gas assays, pulmonary function studies, and breath sounds. Once stabilized, the patient often benefits from participation in a pulmonary rehabilitation program to promote improved lung function and more efficient breathing techniques. SEE: *Nursing Diagnoses Appendix*.

congenital lobar e. A rare cystic lesion of a lobe of the lung that may cause infantile respiratory distress. The affected lobe is distended and appears excessively lucent on plain radiographs of the chest.

TREATMENT: Surgical excision of the lobe is used to treat infants with severe symptoms.

interlobular e. The presence of air between the lobes of the lung.

pulmonary interstitial e. ABBR: PIE. The presence of air in the connective tissues of the lung; seen, e.g., in neonates treated with high-pressure mechanical ventilation. This condition can cause insufficient oxygenation and cystic lung damage.

subcutaneous e. The presence of air in subcutaneous tissue.

empiric (ĕm-pĭr′ĭk) [Gr. *empeirikos*, skilled, experienced] **1.** Empirical. **2.** A practitioner whose skill or art is based on what has been learned through experience.

empirical (em-pir′ĭ-kăl) Based on experience or observations rather than on scientific or theoretical principles.

empirical therapy Use of antibiotics to treat an infection before the specific causative organism has been identified with laboratory tests.

empiricism (ĕm-pĭr′ĭs-ĭzm) [Gr. *empeirikos*, skilled, experienced, + *-ismos*, condition of] Experience, not theory, as the basis of medical science.

empiric treatment Empirical therapy.

employee benefit program A group of economically useful goods or services that workers receive from their employer in addition to salary. These often provide protection against unpleasant or catastrophic events. Examples include medical and dental insurance, disability income, retirement income, and life insurance.

Employee Retirement Income Security Act of 1974 ABBR: ERISA. A federal law that protects individuals covered by voluntarily administered health insurance and pension plans. Important amendments to ERISA are the Consolidated Omnibus Budget Reconciliation Act of 1985 (COBRA), the Health Insurance Portability and Accountability Act (HIPAA), Newborns' and Mothers' Health Protection Act, Mental Health Parity Act, and the Women's Health and Cancer Rights Act.

empowerment 1. Investing power in another person or group by sharing leadership roles, or helping others to engage fully in a process. **2.** Participating actively and autonomously in policies or events that affect one's health or well-being.

empty can test An orthopedic test of the shoulder, used to determine the integrity of the supraspinatus muscle. With the patient sitting or standing, the shoulder is fully internally rotated, abducted to 90 degrees, and placed in 30 degrees of forward flexion, as if emptying a beverage can. The patient then attempts to maintain this position against resistance. Inability to hold this position, or pain while holding it, suggests pathology of the supraspinatus muscle. SYN: *Jobe test*.

empty follicle syndrome In in vitro fertilization investigations, the absence of oocytes in the stimulated follicle of the ovary. This may be a cause of infertility in some individuals.

empty-sella syndrome A condition, shown by radiography of the skull, in which the sella turcica, which normally contains the pituitary gland, is found to be empty. Clinically, patients may show no endocrine abnormality or may have signs of decreased pituitary function. Hormonal replacement is given to patients with hypopituitarism. In autopsy studies, empty-sella syndrome has been found in about 5% of presumably normal persons. SEE: *pituitary gland*.

empyema (ĕm″pī-ē′mă) [Gr.] A collection of pus in a body cavity, esp. the pleural space. SEE: *thoracentesis*.

ETIOLOGY: It is usually caused by the local spread of infection from a pneumonia or lung abscess but may be caused by organisms brought to the pleural space via the blood or lymphatic system or an abscess extending upward from below the diaphragm. *Streptococcus pneumoniae, Staphylococcus aureus,* and *Klebsiella pneumoniae* are the most common pathogens, but anaerobic organisms also can cause empyema.

SYMPTOMS: Patients are usually quite ill, with high fevers and sweats, malaise, anorexia, and fatigue. They frequently present with tachycardia, pleurisy, cough, and dyspnea. Depending on the amount of pus and fluid present, physical examination may reveal unequal chest expansion, dullness to percussion, and decreased or absent breath sounds over the involved area. Fibrinous adhesions may fill the pleural space and inhibit lung expansion.

DIAGNOSIS: Empyema may be diagnosed indirectly by chest x-rays, computerized tomography, magnetic resonance imaging, or definitively by thoracentesis (insertion of a large-bore needle into the pleural space). Withdrawal of fluid from the pleural space provides material for a culture and sensitivity test of the organism and helps the infection resolve.

TREATMENT: The purulent exudate and fluid are drained via thoracentesis and insertion of one or more chest tubes to underwater-seal chest drainage with suction. Surgical removal of the thick coating over the lung (decortication) or rib resection may be required to allow open drainage and lung expansion. Standard dressing precautions are used if the patient has open drainage. Medications such as urokinase may be injected into the pleural space to minimize fibrous adhesions and to help keep the chest tube patent; surgical drainage may be necessary. Intravenous antibiotic therapy is administered based on pathogen sensitivity. Oxygen is administered to treat associated hypoxia.

PATIENT CARE: The patient should be prepared for the procedure and its associated sensations, and urged to breathe normally and avoid coughing, sighing, or sudden movement. Vital signs are assessed before, during, and after the procedure, and the patient observed for syncope, respiratory distress, or pneumothorax. Sterile preparation of the chest before insertion of a needle, or any incision, is mandatory. After the fluid is definitively located (e.g., by ultrasonography), the skin on the chest wall is anesthetized, e.g., with an injection of lidocaine through a small gauge (29 or 30 g) needle. A larger needle is inserted deeper into the soft tissues and guided just above a rib (not below it, where the rib's neurovascular bundle is found). The patient will experience a sudden, intense pain when the needle penetrates the parietal pleura. Another needle with a very wide bore (12 or 14 gauge) is then used to withdraw fluid from the pleural space. Samples should be labeled immediately with unique patient identifiers and sent to the lab for analysis (pH, cell count, cultures, chemistries, fungal, and AFB stains). After the procedure is completed, the patient's vital signs, oxygen saturation, and symptoms are monitored for evidence of pneumothorax. Patency of any indwelling drainage system is maintained; drainage volume, color, and characteristics are documented; and the patient is protected from accidental dislodgement of the drainage tube. Increased fluid and protein are provided, and adequate pain relief is ensured. Breathing exercises and the use of incentive spirometry are encouraged. The patient may be discharged to home or rehabilitative care with a drainage tube still in place. Home health care is arranged as necessary.

interlobular e. A form of empyema with pus between the lobes of the lung.

empyesis (em″pī″ē′sĭs) [Gr. *empyēsis*, suppuration] **1.** Any skin eruption marked by pustules. **2.** Any accumulation of pus. **3.** Hypopyon (accumulation of pus in the anterior chamber of the eye).

EMR *electronic medical record; emergency medical responder.*

EMS *emergency medical service.*

EMS communication SEE: under *communication.*

EMS medical advisory committee Representatives of medical groups that provide medical direction to the EMS system.

EMS medical control Direction of life support procedures by a physician and carried out by emergency medical technicians (EMT) and paramedics in prehospital care, including online and offline supervision. *Online:* The physician provides instruction via radio or telephone to an EMS crew. *Off-line:* The EMS crews receive direction and supervision via treatment protocols, case review, in-service training, and standing orders for treatment.

Medical control is also divided into prospective, immediate, and retrospective forms. *Prospective form:* Treatment protocols for EMTs are developed under a license from the medical director or medical advisory committee. *Immediate form:* Direct medical orders or consultation is given by radio or telephone (defined above as online control). *Retrospective form:* Call reports are reviewed to determine whether protocols have been followed. SEE: *medical direction.*

EMS medical director The physician responsible for ensuring and evaluating the appropriate level of quality of care throughout an EMS system.

EMS standing orders Instructions preapproved by the medical advisory committee directing EMS crews to perform specific advanced life support measures *before* contacting a medical control physician. These orders are implemented in cases in which a delay in treatment could harm the patient (e.g., cardiac arrest).

EMS treatment protocol Written procedures for assessment, treatment, patient transportation, or patient transfer between hospitals. These procedures are part of the official policy of the EMS system and are approved by representatives of the medical advisory committee. The EMS treatment protocols may either be implemented as standing orders or require prior approval of a medical control physician.

EMT *emergency medical technician.*

EMTALA *emergency medical treatment and active labor act.*

EMT-B *emergency medical technician-basic.*

EMT-D *emergency medical technician-defibrillation.*

EMT-I *emergency medical technician-intermediate.*

EMT-P *emergency medical technician-paramedic.*

emulsification (ē-mŭl″sĭ-fĭ-kā′shŭn) [L. *emulsio,* emulsion, + *facere,* to make] **1.** The process of making an emulsion, allowing fat and water to mix. **2.** The breaking down of large fat globules in the intestine into smaller, uniformly distributed particles, largely accomplished through the action of bile acids, which lower surface tension.

emulsifier (ē-mŭl′sĭ-fĭ-ĕr) Anything used to make an emulsion.

emulsify (ē-mŭl′sĭ-fī) To form into an emulsion.

emulsion [L. *emulsio*] **1.** A mixture of two liquids not mutually soluble. If they are thoroughly shaken, one divides into globules in what is called the discontinuous or dispersed phase; the other is then the continuous phase. Milk is an emulsion in which butterfat is the discontinuous phase. **2.** In radiology, the part of the radiographic film sensitive to radiation and containing the image after development.

    fat e. A combination of liquid, lipid, and an emulsifying system suitable for intravenous use because the lipid has been broken into small droplets that can be suspended in water. Such a solution should not be mixed with other fluids prior to intravenous administration.

ENA *Emergency Nurses Association; extractable nuclear antigen.*

enablement (ĕn-ā′bĭl-mĕnt) Creation of the opportunity to participate in life tasks and occupations despite physical or mental limitations and environmental barriers.

enalapril (ĕn-ăl′-ă-prĭl) An angiotensin-converting enzyme inhibitor used to treat hypertension and congestive heart failure.

enamel (i-nam′ĕl) [Fr. *émail, esmail,* enamel] The hard, white, dense, inorganic substance covering the crown of the teeth. Enamel is composed of hydroxyapatite crystal, a salt that contains calcium. The crystals are arranged to form a rod. The enamel rods are organized to form the enamel. Enamel is the hardest substance in the body. Demineralization may result in a carious lesion (cavity).

    aprismatic e. A thin surface layer of the tooth, thought to be solid without individual enamel rods or prisms.

    cervical e. In a healthy dentition, before any gingival disease, the enamel at the neck of the crown of the tooth where the tooth meets the gum line.

    gnarled e. Enamel under the cusp of a tooth characterized by twisting, intertwining groups of enamel rods, thought to resist shearing forces.

    mottled e. Discoloration and defective calcification of teeth caused by malfunctioning of ameloblasts. The defects range from minor surface irregularities to areas where no enamel forms. It may be caused by exposure to drugs, esp. fluoride, during tooth formation. SEE: *fluorosis.*

enamel stripping In dentistry and orthodontics, the narrowing of a tooth by grinding away some of its enamel. It is used to create room for overcrowded teeth.

enanthem, enanthema (en-an′thĕm, en″a″-thē′mă) [Gr. *en,* in, + *anthema,* blossoming] An eruption on a mucous membrane. SEE: *exanthem; Koplik's spots; rash.* **enanthematous** (-thĕm′ă-tŭs), *adj.*

enantio- [Gr. *enantios,* face to face, opposite] Prefix meaning *opposite.*

enantiobiosis (ĕn-ăn″tē-ō-bī-ō′sĭs) [Gr. *enantios,* opposite, + *bios,* life] The condition in which associated organisms are antagonistic to each other. SEE: *symbiosis.*

enantiomer (ĕn-ăn′tē-ō-mĕr) [″ + Gr. *meros,* part] Enantiomorph.

enantiomorph (ĕn-ăn′tē-ō-mŏrf″) One of a pair of isomers, each of which is a mirror image of the other. They may be identical in chemical characteristics, but in solution one rotates a beam of polarized light in one direction and the other in the opposite direction. Isomers are called dextro if they rotate light to the right, and levo if they rotate light to the left. SYN: *enantiomer.*

enarthrosis (ĕn″ăr-thrō′sĭs) *pl.* **enarthroses** [Gr. *en,* in, + *arthron,* joint, + *osis,* condition] Ball-and-socket joint.

en bloc (ĕn blŏk) [Fr., as a whole] As a whole or as en masse; used to refer to surgical excision.

encanthis (ĕn-kăn′thĭs) [Gr. *en,* in, + *kanthos,* angle of the eye] An excrescence or new growth at the inner angle of the eye.

encapsidate (in-kap′sĭ-dāt″) To enclose within a capsid. **encapsidation** (-kap″sĭ-dā′shŏn), *n.*

encapsulated Confined; surrounded by an envelope, capsule, or membrane. Said of certain tumors, abscesses, and medications.

encapsulation (ĕn-kăp′sŭ-lā′shŭn) [″ + *capsula,* a little box] **1.** Enclosure in a sheath not normal to the part. **2.** Formation of a capsule or a sheath about a structure.

encatarrhaphy (ĕn″kăt-ăr′ă-fē) [Gr. *enkatarrhaptein,* to sew in] Insertion of an organ or tissue into a part where it is not normally found.

encephalalgia (ĕn-sĕf″ăl-ăl′jē-ă) [Gr. *enkephalos,* brain, + *algos,* pain] Deep-seated head pain. SYN: *cephalalgia.*

encephalatrophy (ĕn-sĕf″ă-lăt′rō-fē) ["
+ *a-*, not, + *trophe*, nourishment]
Cerebral atrophy.

encephalic (ĕn″sĕf-ăl′ĭk) [Gr. *enkephalos*, brain] Pert. to the brain or its cavity.

encephalitis (en-sef″ă-līt′ĭs) [*encephalo- + -itis*] Inflammation of the white and gray matter of the brain. It is almost always associated with meningoencephalitis and may involve the spinal cord (encephalomyelitis). In the U.S. 20,000 cases are reported annually. SEE: *arbovirus; herpesviruses; rabies.*

ETIOLOGY: Most cases are caused by viruses: there are about 100 different viral agents that may infect the brain. The disease occurs more often in the very young, the very old, and patients with immune-suppressing illnesses. Mosquito-borne equine arboviruses (or, in some cases, a tick-borne virus) are the most common cause of encephalitis in the U.S. Mosquitoes are infected by feeding on infected birds, which then transmit the virus to humans and animals. Viruses may also be transmitted by inhalation (and passed person to person) or by ingestion of infected goat milk. The West Nile virus (WNV) can cause encephalitis and is related to St. Louis encephalitis (SLE). Encephalitis also occurs as a component of rabies, AIDS, and an aftereffect of systemic viral diseases, e.g., herpesvirus, influenza, measles, German measles, and chickenpox. Central nervous system (CNS) involvement occurs in 15% to 20% of patients with AIDS who develop cytomegalovirus infections. Other organisms causing encephalitis in immunosuppressed patients include fungi (such as *Candida, Aspergillus,* and *Cryptococcus*) and protozoa (such as *Toxoplasma gondii*).

SYMPTOMS: Patients present with a wide variety of neurological symptoms, depending on the infected region of the brain and the type and amount of damage the organism has caused. Sudden onset of fever with headache and vomiting may be the first symptoms. These progress to stiff neck and back (meningeal irritation) and to signs of neuronal damage: drowsiness, seizures, tremors, ataxia, cranial nerve paralysis, abnormal reflexes, and muscle weakness and paralysis are common. Personality changes and confusion usually appear before the patient becomes stuporous or comatose. Coma may persist for weeks after the acute phase of illness.

DIAGNOSIS: The diagnosis is based on clinical presentation, culture and examination of blood and cerebrospinal fluid, and computerized tomography (CT) scan or magnetic resonance imaging (MRI) results.

TREATMENT: Acyclovir is given for herpes simplex virus infection, the only common viral pathogen for which there is effective treatment. Survival and residual neurological deficits appear to be tied to mental status changes before acyclovir therapy begins. Rabies is treated with rabies immune globulin and vaccine. If the infection is bacterial, antibiotics are used. For other viruses, treatment focuses on supportive care and control of increased intracranial pressure (ICP) using osmotic diuretics, e.g., mannitol), corticosteroids, and drainage.

PATIENT CARE: The acutely ill patient's mental status, level of consciousness, orientation, and motor function are assessed for indications of increasing ICP and documented to monitor changes. The head of the bed is raised slightly to promote venous return; neck flexion is contraindicated. Sedatives help to control restlessness; aspirin or acetaminophen reduces fever and relieves headache. Measures to prevent stimuli that increase ICP are implemented, e.g., preoxygenating with 100% oxygen before suctioning, preventing isometric muscle contraction, using diet and stool softeners to minimize straining at stool, and using turning sheets and head support when turning the patient. Fluid intake should be adequate to prevent dehydration, but overload must be avoided to prevent further cerebral edema. Fluid balance and weight are monitored daily. Adequate nutrition should be maintained with small, frequent meals or enteral or parenteral feeding as necessary. Frequent oral care should be provided. Passive and/or active range-of-motion exercises and resistive exercises to prevent contractures and maintain joint mobility and muscle tone are used as long as they do not increase ICP.

Normal supportive care is provided in a quiet environment, with lights dimmed to ease photophobia, with no shadows, which increase the potential for hallucinations. Emotional support and reassurance should be provided and the patient reoriented if delirium or confusion is present. Behavioral changes that occur with encephalitis usually fade as the acute phase passes, but rehabilitation programs are necessary for the treatment of residual neurological deficits. Public health preventive measures include controlling standing water that provides mosquito breeding sites and insecticide spraying to kill larvae and adult mosquitoes. Public education should focus on reducing outdoor time during early morning and early evening hours, wearing appropriate covering clothing when exposure is unavoidable, and use of insect repellents containing DEET. SEE: *Nursing Diagnoses Appendix*.

acute disseminated e. Postinfectious **e.**

Australian e. Murray Valley **e.**

California (La Crosse) virus e. A viral encephalitis that is the most common mosquito-borne illness in the U.S. It typically affects children in summer or early fall, largely in the Middle Atlantic or midwestern states, causing fever, headache, seizures, and localized muscle paralysis. The primary vector is *Aedes triseriatus*. A full recovery usually follows the illness.

cortical e. Encephalitis of only the brain cortex.

eastern equine e. Encephalitis caused by the eastern equine arbovirus, which is transmitted from horses to humans by mosquitoes; the incubation period is 1 to 2 weeks. Although this is the least common of the arboviruses, mortality is approx. 25%, and those who survive often have neurological problems. In the U.S. it occurs on the East Coast, Gulf Coast, and in the Great Lakes region during the mosquito season from midsummer to early fall.

epidemic e. Any form of encephalitis that occurs as an epidemic.

equine e. Encephalitis caused by either the western or the eastern equine arbovirus, which is carried by mosquitoes from horses. The disease ranges from mild to fatal.

hemorrhagic e. Herpes encephalitis in which there is hemorrhage with brain inflammation.

herpetic e. Encephalitis caused by infection of the brain with herpes simplex virus-1 (or, less often, herpes simplex virus-2). This relatively common form of encephalitis typically involves the inferior surfaces of the temporal lobes and may cause hemorrhagic necrosis of brain tissue. It is fatal in at least one third of all cases. Acyclovir (or an analog) is used to treat the infection.

infantile e. Encephalitis that occurs in infants. The most common agents are arboviruses and herpes simplex virus.

Japanese (B type) e. ABBR: JE. Encephalitis caused by the Japanese B type arbovirus, an infection carried by swine. It occurs sporadically in Japan, Taiwan, China, and Korea and is controlled by vaccine.

lead e. Encephalitis due to lead poisoning.

e. lethargica A form of encephalitis that occurred frequently after the influenza pandemic of 1917–1918, but rarely since. Its hallmarks include paralysis of oculomotor function and marked sleepiness or coma. Survivors developed a parkinsonism-like illness. SYN: *Economo disease*.

Murray Valley e. An epidemic viral encephalitis originating in Murray Valley, Australia. SYN: *Australian e.*

neonatal e. A form of encephalitis occurring within the first several weeks of life.

paraneoplastic limbic e. ABBR: PNLE. A brain disorder occurring in some patients with cancer, characterized by the rapid onset of memory loss, often with temporal lobe disease, seizures, delirium, or disturbances of mood. Patients with PNLE often have antibodies against tumor antigens that also react with nerve cell antigens. In some patients the neurological disorder improves after treatment of the responsible tumor.

e. periaxialis Inflammation of the white matter of the cerebrum, occurring mainly in the young.

postinfectious e. Encephalitis that follows a systemic viral infection (such as mumps or measles) or a reactivation to varicella-zoster in adults. SYN: *acute disseminated e.*

postvaccinal e. Acute encephalitis after vaccination.

purulent e. Encephalitis characterized by abscesses in the brain.

raccoon roundworm e. Encephalitis characterized by inflammation of the meninges, eosinophilia, prolonged encephalopathy, retinitis, and delayed recovery with profound neurological deficits. It is transmitted to children (or others) who eat soil contaminated by raccoon feces.

Rasmussen e. SEE: *Rasmussen encephalitis*.

Russian spring-summer e. Encephalitis due to a tick-borne virus. Humans may also contract it by drinking goat milk.

St. Louis e. Encephalitis caused by the St. Louis arbovirus and carried by mosquitoes. It emerged during an epidemic in the summer of 1933 in and around St. Louis, Missouri. Now endemic in the U.S. (esp. Florida), Trinidad, Jamaica, Panama, and Brazil, it occurs most frequently during summer and early fall.

tick-borne e. A flaviviral infection of the brain transmitted by *Ixodes* ticks.

toxic e. Encephalitis resulting from metal poisonings, e.g., lead poisoning.

western equine e. A mild type of viral encephalitis that has occurred in the western U.S. and Canada.

Encephalitozoon (ĕn-sĕf″ă-lĭt″-ŏ-zō′ŏn) A genus of the order Microsporidia. SEE: *microsporidiosis*.

encephalo-, encephal- [Gr. *enkephalos*, brain] Prefixes meaning *brain*.

encephalocele (ĕn-sĕf′ă-lō-sēl) [Gr. *enkephalos*, brain, + *kele*, hernia] A protrusion of the brain through a cranial fissure.

encephalocystocele (ĕn-sĕf″ă-lō-sĭs′tō-sēl) [" + *kystis,* sac, + *kele,* tumor, swelling] A hernia through a defect in the skull that contains brain and cerebrospinal fluid.

encephalogram (ĕn-sĕf'ă-lō-grăm) [" + *gramma,* something written] A radiograph of the brain, usually performed with air in the ventricles as a contrast medium. This procedure has been replaced by computed tomography and magnetic resonance imaging.

encephalography (ĕn-sĕf"ă-lŏg'ră-fē) [" + *graphein,* to write] Radiography of the head, esp. examination following the introduction of air into the ventricles through a lumbar or cisternal puncture. This procedure is no longer performed. SEE: *encephalogram.*

encephaloid (ĕn-sĕf'ă-loyd) [" + *eidos,* form, shape] **1.** Resembling the cerebral substance. **2.** A malignant neoplasm of brainlike texture.

encephalolith (ĕn-sĕf'ă-lō-lĭth) [" + *lithos,* stone] A calculus of the brain.

encephaloma (ĕn-sĕf'ă-lō-mă) [" + *oma,* tumor] A tumor of the brain.

encephalomalacia (en-sĕf"ă-lō-mă-lā'sh(ē-)ă) [*encephalo-* + *-malacia*] Paresis with progressive dementia.

　　multicystic e. A rare disorder of childhood in which multiple fluid-filled cavities replace brain tissue deprived of oxygen or blood.

encephalomeningitis (ĕn-sef'ă-lō-men"ĭn-jīt'ĭs) [*encephalo-* + *meningitis*] Meningoencephalitis.

encephalomeningocele (ĕn-sĕf"ă-lō-mĕ-nĭng'gŏ-sēl) [" + " + *kele,* tumor, swelling] A protrusion of membranes and brain substance through the cranium.

encephalomere (ĕn-sĕf'ă-lō-mēr") [" + *meros,* part] A primitive segment of the embryonic brain. SYN: *neuromere.*

encephalometer (ĕn-sĕf'ă-lŏm'ĕ-tĕr) [" + *metron,* measure] An instrument for measuring the cranium and locating brain regions.

encephalomyelitis (en-sef'ă-lō-mī"ĕ-līt'ĭs) [*encephalo-* + *myelitis*] Encephalitis accompanied by infection and inflammation of the spinal cord. It may follow a viral infection or, in rare instances, a vaccination with a live, weakened virus.

　　acute disseminated e. An uncommon demyelinating, inflammatory brain disease that may occur after some viral infections or some vaccinations. SYN: *postinfectious e.*

　　benign myalgic e. An epidemic disease of unknown cause marked by influenza-like symptoms, severe pain, and muscular weakness. SYN: *Iceland disease.*

　　herpesvirus simian e. A severe, almost always fatal encephalomyelitis caused by the herpesvirus simiae (also called B virus). It occurs among veterinarians, laboratory workers, and others who come in contact with infected monkeys.

　　equine e. A viral disease of horses that may be communicated to humans. It includes eastern and western equine encephalitis.

　　paraneoplastic encephalomyelitis ABBR: PEM. An inflammatory disorder of the central nervous system that occurs in the setting of a cancer found in another part of the body and probably results from the remote effects of some antigen or hormone released by the tumor.

　　postinfectious e. Acute disseminated encephalomyelitis.

　　postvaccinal e. Encephalomyelitis following smallpox vaccination.

encephalomyeloneuropathy (ĕn-sĕf"ă-lō-mī"ĕ-lō-nū-rŏp'ă-thē) Any disease involving the brain, spinal cord, and nerves.

encephalomyelopathy (ĕn-sĕf"ă-lō-mī"ĕl-ŏp'ă-thē) [" + " + *pathos,* disease, suffering] Any disease of the brain and spinal cord.

　　subacute necrotizing e. Leigh disease.

encephalomyeloradiculitis (ĕn-sĕf"ă-lō-mī"ĕ-lō-ră-dĭk"ū-lī'tĭs) Inflammation of the brain, spinal cord, and nerve roots.

encephalomyocarditis (ĕn-sĕf"ă-lō-mī"ō-kär-dī'tĭs) Any disease involving the brain and cardiac muscle.

encephalon (ĕn-sĕf'ă-lŏn) [Gr. *enkephalos,* brain] The brain, including the cerebrum, cerebellum, medulla oblongata, pons, diencephalon, and midbrain.

encephalopathy (en-sef'ă-lŏp'ă-thē) [*encephalo-* + *-pathy*] Generalized brain dysfunction marked by varying degrees of impairment of speech, cognition, orientation, and arousal. In mild instances, brain dysfunction may be evident only during specialized neuropsychiatric testing. In severe instances, e.g., the last stages of hepatic encephalopathy, the patient may be unresponsive even to unpleasant stimuli.

　　acute lead e. A syndrome seen mostly in children who have absorbed a large amount of lead. Initially there are clumsiness, vertigo, ataxia, headache, insomnia, restlessness, and irritability. As the syndrome progresses, vomiting, agitation, confusion, convulsions, and coma will occur. A sudden, marked increase in intracranial pressure accompanies these symptoms. Sequelae include permanent damage to the central nervous system, causing mental retardation, electroencephalogram abnormalities, cerebral palsy, and optic atrophy.

TREATMENT: Exposure to lead must be discontinued. Corticosteroids and intravenous mannitol (20% solution) will relieve increased intracranial pressure.

Lead can be removed from the body by giving dimercaprol (BAL) and calcium disodium edetate in a carefully administered doses. Convulsions may be controlled with phenobarbital, hydantoin, or diazepam. Hydration should be maintained with intravenous administration of fluids; solutions containing sodium should be avoided. Oral fluids or food should not be given for at least 3 days.

bovine spongiform e. ABBR: BSE. A progressive neurological disease of cattle, marked by spongelike changes in the brain and spinal cord and associated with rapid and fatal deterioration. SYN: *mad cow disease*. SEE: *Creutzfeldt-Jakob disease; transmissible spongiform e.*

ETIOLOGY: BSE is found in cattle that have been fed offal. A prion is thought to be the cause.

PREVENTION: Because of the possible link between BSE and rapidly fatal neurological diseases in humans, many countries have banned the use of ruminant proteins in the preparation of cattle feed.

early infantile epileptic e. with suppression bursts ABBR: EIEE. Ohtahara syndrome.

hepatic e. Portal-systemic **e.**

HIV e. AIDS-dementia **complex.**

hypertensive e. The abrupt onset of headache and altered mental status that may occur with sudden and extreme elevations in blood pressure (usually diastolic pressures greater than 125 mm Hg). The altered mental states include irritability, confusion, convulsions, and/or coma. Nausea, vomiting, and visual disturbances are common. The symptoms resolve as the blood pressure is brought under control. Hypertensive encephalopathy is an emergency requiring immediate treatment, usually with intravenous medications. SYN: *posthypoxia syndrome*.

hypoxic e. Neurological damage due to deprivation of oxygen or blood or of both to the brain for several minutes. The damage may range from a transient loss of short-term memory to persistent vegetative coma. Many conditions can result in an oxygen deficiency in the brain, including carbon monoxide inhalation, cardiac arrest, hypotensive episodes of any kind, e.g., any form of shock, near-drowning, and suffocation. If patients are not rapidly revived and oxygenation restored, the hippocampus, and later the other cerebral structures, may be permanently injured and the patient may suffer irreversible brain damage. SYN: *hypoxic-ischemic e.*

hypoxic-ischemic e. Hypoxic **e.**

metabolic e. An alteration of brain function or consciousness due to failure of other internal organs. In the hospital, metabolic encephalopathy is among the most common causes of altered mental status. Renal failure, liver injury, electrolyte or acid-base abnormalities, hypoxia, hypercarbia, and inadequate brain perfusion caused by a failing heart are but some of the medical conditions that may produce treatable encephalopathies.

SYMPTOMS: Confusion, irritability, seizures, and coma are common findings.

perinatal asphyxial e. Brain damage to newborn infants due to insufficient oxygenation and blood flow during delivery. Affected newborns have persistently low Apgar scores and need prolonged resuscitation; they are also affected by coma, lethargy, floppy musculature, seizures, acidosis, and/or absent reflexes. The long-term effects of asphyxia on the child can include impaired cognition, motor function, vision, and altered behavior.

portal-systemic e. ABBR: PSE. Brain dysfunction in patients with chronic liver disease and portal hypertension, in which chemicals that the liver normally detoxifies are shunted past it and left to circulate in the blood. Some patients are asymptomatic; others have mild impairments in memory, calculation, speech, affect, or judgment. Severely affected patients may lapse into coma. SYN: *hepatic e.* SEE: *asterixis.*

subcortical arteriosclerotic e. Binswanger disease.

transmissible spongiform e. Encephalopathy marked by rapidly developing dementia or the sudden onset of psychiatric illnesses, often with myoclonus, ataxia, and aphasia. Death may occur within months of onset. These illnesses are believed to be caused by prions. Examples include kuru, mad cow disease (bovine spongiform encephalopathy), and Creutzfeldt-Jakob disease.

Wernicke e. SEE: under *Wernicke, Carl.*

encephalopyosis (ĕn-sĕf″ă-lō-pī-ō′sĭs) [″ + *pyosis*, suppuration] An abscess of the brain.

encephalospinal (ĕn-sĕf″ă-lō-spī′năl) [″ + L. *spina*, thorn, spine] Pert. to the brain and spinal cord.

encephalotomy (ĕn-sĕf″ă-lŏt′ō-mē) **1.** Brain dissection. **2.** Surgical destruction of the brain of a fetus to facilitate delivery.

-encephalus, -encephali [L. *encephalus* fr. Gr. *enkephalos,* brain] Suffixes meaning (*a fetus) having such a head.*

enchondroma (ĕn″kŏn-drō′mă) [Gr. *en,* in, + *chondros,* cartilage, + *oma,* tumor] A benign cartilaginous tumor occurring generally where cartilage is absent, or within a bone, where it expands the diaphysis. SYN: *enchondrosis.*

enchondrosarcoma (ĕn-kŏn″drō-săr-kō′mă) [″ + ″ + *sarx,* flesh, + *oma,* tumor] A sarcoma made up of cartilaginous tissue or growing within an enchondroma.

enchondrosis (ĕn-kŏn-drō′sĭs) [″ + ″ + *osis,* condition] A benign cartilaginous outgrowth from bone or cartilaginous tissue. SYN: *enchondroma.*

enclave (ĕn′klāv) [Fr. *enclaver,* to enclose] A mass of tissue that becomes enclosed by tissue of another kind.

encode 1. To express or represent in genetic code, i.e., in a string of nucleotide bases that can be translated into the amino acids that make up a protein. **2.** To program or represent computer instructions in software.

encopresis (ĕn-kō-prē′sĭs) [″ + *kopros,* excrement] A condition associated with constipation and fecal retention in which watery colonic contents bypass the hard fecal masses and pass through the rectum. This condition is often confused with diarrhea.

encrust, incrust (in-krŭst′) [L. *incrustare,* to cover with a rind or crust] To coat with a crust of debris, e.g., of lipids, proteins, salts, slime, or sugars.

encrustation (ĕn-krŭs-tā′shŭn) Obstruction of a body part or of a stent placed in the body with granulation tissue or calcified debris. The term is used in particular to refer to blockage of urethral stents.

encrypt (ĕn-krĭpt′) [″ + Gr. *kryptos,* hidden] To disguise; to shield from view by representing one symbolic character with another.

enculturation (ĕn-kŭl′tū-rā′shŭn) The adjustment of a person to the norms and values of his community.

encysted (ĕn-sĭst′ĕd) [″ + *kystis,* bladder, pouch] Surrounded by membrane; encapsulated. SYN: *saccate.*

end [AS. *ende*] A termination; an extremity.

endadelphos (ĕnd″ă-dĕl′fŏs) [Gr. *endon,* within, + *adelphos,* brother] A congenitally deformed fetus whose twin is enclosed in the body or in a cyst on the fetus.

Endamoeba (ĕn″dă-mē′bă) Entamoeba.

endangiitis, endangeitis (ĕnd″ăn-jē-ī′tĭs) [Gr. *endon,* within, + *angeion,* vessel, + *itis,* inflammation] Inflammation of the endothelium, the innermost layer of a blood vessel. SYN: *endoangiitis; endarteritis; endophlebitis.*

endangium (ĕn-dăn′jē-ŭm) [″ + *angeion,* vessel] The innermost layer, or intima, of a blood vessel.

endaortitis (ĕnd″ā-or-tī′tĭs) [″ + *aorte,* aorta, + *itis,* inflammation] Inflammation of the inner layer of the aorta.

endarterectomy (ĕnd″ăr-tĕr-ĕk′tō-mē) Surgical removal of the lining of an artery. It can be performed on almost any major artery that is diseased or blocked,

such as the carotid, femoral, or popliteal artery.

    carotid e. A surgical technique for removing intra-arterial obstructions (plaque) from an artery, especially the internal carotid artery. When performed on a significantly narrowed carotid artery, this operation can reduce the risk of stroke. An alternative to the procedure for patients who have a higher operative risk is carotid artery stenting, which is usually performed in an angiography suite under local anesthesia. SEE: *transient ischemic attack.*

    PATIENT CARE: *Preoperative:* To reduce anxiety, the procedure and expected sensations are explained to the patient and family, and their questions answered. Expected postoperative pain and discomfort are explained, and the patient is instructed in pain assessment and administration of pain relief medications and other noninvasive pain relief measures. The procedure requires informed consent. Not proceeding with surgery markedly increases the patient's risk of stroke or death, even with optimal medical treatment; however, the risk of heart attack, stroke, wound infection, or death with the procedure is not insignificant.

    Postoperative: Vital signs are monitored every 15 min for several hours, then hourly for 24 to 48 hr (or according to protocol) until the patient is stable. (Alterations in blood pressure and heart rate and respirations could indicate cerebral ischemia, intracerebral hemorrhage, or other complications). Neurological assessments are performed for the first 24 to 48 hr (or according to protocol) evaluating cranial nerve function, extremity strength, speech, level of consciousness, pupillary dilation, and orientation. Intake and output are monitored hourly for the first 24 hr (or according to protocol) and IV fluids administered at a controlled rate and volume to help prevent ICP increases. Continuous cardiac and hemodynamic monitoring is performed for the first 24 hr (or according to protocol). Prescribed analgesic medication is administered, and other noninvasive pain relief measures are offered.

    The surgical wound is assessed for hematoma development, dehiscence, or infection. Wound care is provided and taught to the patient and family, and the signs and symptoms of infection to be reported to the surgeon (redness, swelling, or drainage from the incision, fever, or sore throat) are reviewed. Patients who smoke cigarettes are encouraged to stop. Smoking almost doubles the risk for ischemic stroke. Smokers should be referred to a smoking cessation program. Modification of other risk factors (such as high lipid levels, hypertension, diabetes mellitus, obesity) is critical to disease prevention. Prescribed medications are administered, and the patient is instructed in their use and adverse reactions to report to the physician.

The patient who has had a cerebrovascular accident and needs follow-up care is referred to a rehabilitation or home health care agency. Instruction is given in the management of postsurgical neurological, sensory, or motor deficits, and the importance of regular checkups explained. The surgeon or neurologist should be contacted immediately if any new neurological symptoms occur. The patient should wear or carry a medical identification tag to alert others to the condition and treatments in case of an emergency.

endarterial (ĕnd″ăr-tē′rē-ăl) [″ + *arteria,* artery] **1.** Pert. to the inner portion of an artery. **2.** Within an artery.

endarteritis, endoarteritis (en″dart″ĕ-rīt′ĭs, en″dō-art″ĕ-rīt′ĭs) [*endo-* + *arteritis*] Infection or inflammation of the lining of a blood vessel.

   e. deformans A condition in which the intima is thickened or replaced with atheromatous or calcium-containing deposits.

   e. obliterans Chronic progressive thickening of the intima leading to stenosis or obstruction of a lumen. SYN: *arteritis obliterans; Friedländer disease.*

   syphilitic e. Endarteritis caused by syphilis.

endbrain (ĕnd′brān″) Telencephalon.

end-bulb The enlarged tip of the end of an axon.

endemic (ĕn-dĕm′ĭk) [Gr. *en,* in, + *demos,* people] Found in a specific population or particular region of the world. The term is usually used to refer to a disease that occurs continuously or with a stable baseline incidence within a locale or a group of people.

endemic pemphigus foliaceus Fogo selvagem.

endemoepidemic (ĕn-dĕm″ō-ĕp-ĭ-dĕm′ĭk) [″ + ″ + *epi,* on, among, + *demos,* people] Endemic, but becoming epidemic periodically.

endergonic (ĕnd″ĕr-gŏn′ĭk) [Gr. *endon,* within, + *ergon,* work] Pert. to chemical reactions that require energy in order to occur.

end feel In physical therapy and rehabilitation, the feeling experienced by an evaluator when overpressure is applied to tissue at the end of the available passive range of motion. It is interpreted as abnormal when the quality of the feel is different from normal response at that joint. The feeling may be soft as when two muscle groups are compressed or soft tissues are stretched, firm as when a normal joint or ligament is stretched, or hard as when two bones block motion.

Abnormal end feels may include a springy sensation when cartilage is torn within a joint, muscle guarding when a muscle involuntarily responds to acute pain, or muscle spasticity when there is increased tone due to an upper motor neuron lesion or when the feeling is different from that normally experienced for the joint being tested.

end-foot A terminal button; the enlarged end of a nerve fiber that terminates adjacent to the dendrite of another nerve cell.

ending The terminal or final portion of a tissue or cell.

end-inspiratory pause SEE: under *pause.*

endo-, end- Prefixes meaning *within.*

endoaneurysmorrhaphy (ĕn″dō-ăn″ū-rĭs-mor′ăf-ē) [Gr. *endon,* within, + *aneurysma,* aneurysm, + *rhaphe,* seam, ridge] Surgical opening of an aneurysmal sac and suturing of its orifice.

endoangiitis (ĕn″dō-ăn-jē-ī′tĭs) [″ + *angeion,* vessel, + *itis,* inflammation] Endangiitis.

endoauscultation (ĕn″dō-ăws″kŭl-tā′shŭn) [″ + L. *auscultare,* to listen to] Auscultation by an esophageal tube passed into the stomach or by a tube passed into the heart.

endobiotic (ĕn″dō-bī-ŏt′ĭk) [″ + *bios,* life] Pert. to an organism living parasitically in the host.

endoblast (ĕn′dō-blăst) [″ + *blastos,* germ] The endoderm.

endobronchial (ĕn″dō-brŏng′kē-ăl) Within a bronchus.

endobronchial tube A double-lumen tube used in anesthesia. One tube may be used to aerate a portion of the lung, while the other is occluded to deflate the other lung or a portion of it.

endobronchial ultrasonography SEE: under *ultrasonography.*

endocannabinoid (ĕn″dō-kŭ-năb′ĭn-oid, -kăn′ŭ-bĭn) Any chemical produced by the body that stimulates receptors for *Cannabis sativa* in the central nervous system.

endocardiac, endocardial (en″dō-kard′ē-ak, en″dō-kard′ē-ăl) [″ + *kardia,* heart] Within the heart or arising from the endocardium.

endocarditis (ĕn″dō-kăr-dī′tĭs) [″ + ″ + *itis,* inflammation] Infection or inflammation of the heart valves or of the lining of the heart. In casual clinical speech, this word is often used to mean "infective endocarditis." SEE: *infective e.*

   acute bacterial e. ABBR: ABE. Infective endocarditis with a rapid onset, usually a few days to 2 weeks. The infection is typically caused by virulent organisms such as *Staphylococcus aureus,* which may rapidly invade and destroy heart valvular tissue and also metastasize to other organs or tissues. SEE: *ulcerative e.*

atypical verrucous e. An infrequently used term for nonbacterial thrombotic endocarditis.

culture-negative e. Infective endocarditis produced by organisms that do not quickly or readily grow in blood cultures, usually because their growth is masked by the previous use of antibiotics or because the causative organisms require special culture media or grow slowly in the laboratory. *Mycoplasma, Ricksettsia,* HACEK (an acronym for *Haemophilus, Actinobacillus, Cardiobacterium, Eikenella, Kingella*) organisms, and some fungi produce culture-negative endocarditis. SEE: *infective e.*

infective e. ABBR: IE. Endocarditis caused by any microorganism, esp. any species of streptococci or staphylococci, and less often by *Haemophilus* spp. or other HACEK bacteria (e.g., *Actinobacillus actinomycetem comitans, Cardiobacterium hominis, Eikenella corrodens,* or *Kingella kingae*), enteric bacteria, ricksettsiae, chlamydiae, or fungi. Traditionally, IE can be categorized as *acute* if the illness has a fulminant onset; *catheter-related* if the causative microorganism gains access to the heart from an indwelling line; *culture-negative* if echocardiograms reveal vegetations and other criteria for the disease are present, but the causative microbes have not been isolated in the laboratory; *left-sided* if it develops on the mitral or aortic valves; *nosocomial* if it occurs after 48 hr of hospitalization or an invasive surgical procedure; *pacemaker-related* if the disease occurs on an implanted pacemaker or cardioverter-defibrillator; *prosthetic* if it occurs on a surgically implanted heart valve; *right-sided* if it develops on the tricuspid or pulmonary valves; and *subacute* if it develops after several weeks or months of anorexia, low-grade fevers, and malaise. The incidence in the U.S. is about 2 to 4 cases per 100,000. Patients who are elderly or have a history of injection drug abuse, diabetes mellitus, immunosuppressing illnesses, aortic stenosis, mitral valve prolapse, or rheumatic heart disease are more likely than others to become infected.

SYMPTOMS: Patients with *subacute* IE may have vague symptoms, including low-grade fevers, loss of appetite, malaise, and muscle aches. *Acutely* infected patients often present with high fevers, prostration, chills and sweats, stiff joints or back pain, symptoms of heart failure (esp. if the infection has completely disrupted a heart valve or its tethers), heart block (if the infection erodes into the conducting system of the heart), symptoms caused by the spread-

ing of the infection to lungs or meninges (e.g., cough, headache, stiff neck, or confusion), stroke symptoms, symptoms of renal failure, rashes (including petechiae), or other findings. Signs of the illness typically include documented fevers, cardiac murmurs, or (more rarely) nodular eruptions on the hands and feet (Osler's nodes or Janeway lesions). Cottonwool spots may be seen on the retinas of some affected persons. SEE: illus.

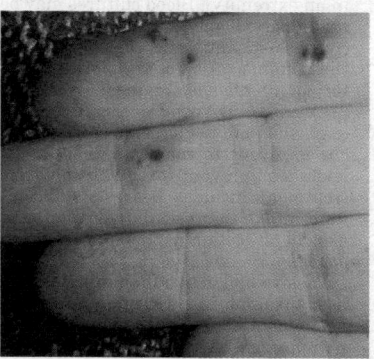

JANEWAY LESIONS

DIAGNOSIS: Blood cultures, esp. if persistently positive, form the basis for the diagnosis of endocarditis. Contemporary criteria for diagnosis also include visual confirmation of endocardial infection (vegetations) by echocardiography, the presence of several other suggestive anomalies (e.g., persistent fevers in a patient who is known to inject drugs or a patient with an artificial heart valve), infective emboli in the lungs or other organs; and characteristic skin findings. Occasionally, a patient who dies of a febrile illness may be found to have infective vegetations on the heart valves at autopsy.

PROGNOSIS: Endocarditis is deadly in about 10% to 25% of patients. Death is most likely to occur in patients who suffer strokes resulting from infected fragments embolizing to the brain and in patients who suffer congestive heart failure. Patients with right-sided endocarditis have a better prognosis than patients with other forms of the disease.

TREATMENT: Many patients recover after treatment with prolonged courses of parenteral antibiotics. Some (e.g., those with heart failure or severely injured hearts) may not respond without surgery to replace damaged valves or débride abscesses within the myocardium.

PATIENT CARE: During the acute phase of treatment, patients are monitored for signs and symptoms of heart failure (e.g., dyspnea, orthopnea, crackles, dependent edema, changes in the heart murmur, and a postsystolic gallop), cerebral emboli (e.g., paralysis, aphasias, changes in mental status), and embolization to the kidney (e.g., decreased urine output, hematuria); lung involvement (e.g., dyspnea, cough, egophony, hemoptysis, pleuritic pain, or friction rub) or spleen involvement (e.g., left upper quadrant abdominal pain radiating to the left shoulder, abdominal rigidity); and peripheral vascular occlusion (e.g., numbness or tingling, changes in pulses, pallor, and coolness in an extremity). Blood cultures may be taken periodically to monitor the effectiveness of antibiotic therapy. Before the administration of antibiotics, a history of allergies is obtained. Treatment peak and trough drug levels are checked (e.g. when aminoglycoside or vancomycin is given) to maintain therapeutic levels and prevent toxicity. Supportive treatment includes bedrest, sufficient fluid intake to preserve hydration, and aspirin or acetaminophen for fever and aches.

Passive and active limb exercises are used to maintain muscle tone and quiet, diversional activities to prevent excessive physical exertion until a slow, progressive activity program that limits cardiac workload can be established.

PROPHYLAXIS: The American Heart Association recommends that patients at high risk for endocarditis should receive prophylactic antibiotics prior to many procedures, including dental and periodontal cleanings and extractions, intraligamentary local anesthetic injections, tonsillectomy, adenoidectomy, bronchoscopy with rigid instrument, sclerotherapy for esophageal varices, esophageal stricture dilation, biliary tract procedures, barium enema or colonoscopy, surgery involving the respiratory or intestinal mucosa, prostate surgery, cystoscopy, and urethral dilation.

Libman-Sacks e. SEE: *Libman-Sacks endocarditis*.

Löffler's endocarditis SEE: *Löffler's endocarditis*.

malignant e. 1. An old term for endocarditis that is rapidly fatal. **2.** Valvular vegetations composed of tumor cells.

mural e. Endocarditis of the lining of the heart but not the heart valves.

native valve e. Infective endocarditis occurring on a patient's own heart valve(s), rather than on a prosthetic (surgically implanted) valve(s).

nonbacterial thrombotic e. ABBR: NBTE. The presence on the heart valves of vegetations that are produced not by bacteria but by sterile collections of platelets in fibrin. NBTE is characteristically found in severe cases of systemic lupus erythematosus, tuberculosis, or malignancy. The vegetations of NBTE readily embolize, causing infarctions in other organs. SYN: *verrucous e.*

prosthetic valve e. Bacterial infection of a surgically implanted artificial heart valve.

rheumatic e. Valvular inflammation and dysfunction (esp. mitral insufficiency) occurring during acute rheumatic fever.

right-sided e. Endocarditis affecting the tricuspid or pulmonary valve. It is usually the result of a percutaneous infection and is most often seen in injection drug users.

subacute bacterial e. ABBR: SBE. A heart valve infection that becomes clinically evident after weeks or months. It usually results from infection with streptococcal species that have relatively low virulence (e.g., viridans group streptococci). The infection often develops on a previously abnormal heart valve. SYN: *e. viridans*.

syphilitic e. Endocarditis due to syphilis having extended from the aorta to the aortic valves.

tuberculous e. Endocarditis caused by *Mycobacterium tuberculosis*.

ulcerative e. A rapidly destructive form of acute bacterial endocarditis characterized by necrosis or ulceration of the valves.

valvular e. Endocarditis affecting the heart valves and not the inner lining of the heart.

vegetative e. Endocarditis associated with fibrinous clots on ulcerated valvular surfaces.

verrucous e. Nonbacterial thrombotic e.

e. viridans Subacute bacterial e.

endocardium (ĕn″dō-kăr′dē-ŭm) [Gr. *endon*, within, + *kardia*, heart] The endothelial membrane that lines the chambers of the heart and is continuous with the lining (intima) of the arteries and veins. It is a single layer of cells under which lie nerves, Purkinje cells, and veins.

endocervical (ĕn″dō-sĕr′vĭ-kăl) [″ + L. *cervix*, neck] Pert. to the endocervix.

endocervicitis (ĕn″dō-sĕr″vĭ-sī′tĭs) [″ + ″ + Gr. *itis*, inflammation] Inflammation of the mucous membranes that line the uterine cervix. It is usually caused by chlamydia, gonorrhea, or malignancy.

endocervix (ĕn″dō-sĕr′vĭks) [″ + L. *cervix*, neck] The mucous membrane that lines the opening into the uterine cervix.

endochondral (ĕn″dō-kŏn′drăl) [″ + *chondros*, cartilage] Within a cartilage.

endochondral bone formation One of the two types of bone formation in skeletal development. Each long bone is formed as a cartilage model before bone is laid down, replacing the cartilage.

endoclip (en′dō-klip″) [*endo(scopy)* +

clip] A two- or three-pronged device employed during endoscopy to suture two surfaces together.

endocoagulation (ĕn″dō-kō-ăg″ū-lā′shŭn) Thermocoagulation.

Endocodone (ĕn″dō-kō′dōn″) Oxycodone.

endocolitis (ĕn″dō-kō-lī′tĭs) [″ + *kolon,* colon, + *itis,* inflammation] Inflammation of the mucosa of the colon. SEE: *colitis.*

endocorpuscular (ĕn″dō-kor-pŭs′kū-lăr) [″ + L. *corpusculum,* small body (corpuscle)] Within a cell.

endocranial (ĕn″dō-krā′nē-ăl) [″ + *kranion,* cranium] **1.** Intracranial or within the cranium. **2.** Pert. to the endocranium.

endocranium (ĕn″dō-krā′nē-ŭm) The dura mater of the brain, which forms the lining membrane of the cranium.

endocrine (ĕn′dō-krĭn, -krĭn, -krēn) [″ + *krinein,* to secrete] Secreting macromolecules into the bloodstream to influence distant cells. One of three general mechanisms (the others being autocrine and paracrine) by which ductless glands regulate or control the activities of cells. SEE: *endocrine* **gland.**

e. regulation, **endocrine regulation** The secretion of macromolecules, such as insulin, into the blood stream to regulate the activities of distant cells.

endocrine disruptor (dĭs-rŭp′tĕr) A chemical that may imitate or block the function of natural hormones if it is absorbed by the body. Many pesticides and plasticizing compounds, e.g., phthalates, are thought to disrupt endocrine pathways, esp. if they are absorbed by pregnant women during embryonic and fetal development.

endocrine-inactive tumor SEE: under *tumor.*

endocrine system The ductless glands or the glands of internal secretion. SEE: illus.; *endocrine* **gland.**

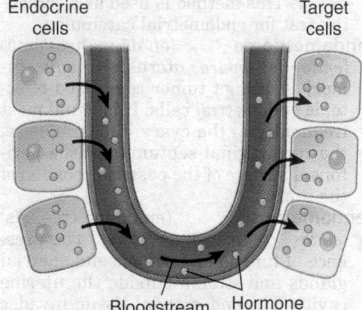

Endocrine cells — Target cells

Bloodstream — Hormone

ENDOCRINE (HORMONAL) COMMUNICATION

endocrino- [Gr. *endon,* within + *krinein,* to secrete] Prefix meaning *endocrine.*

endocrinologist (ĕn″dō-krĭ-nŏl′ŏ-jĭst) A specialist who diagnoses, prevents, or treats hormonal disease.

endocrinology (ĕn″dō-krĭn-ŏl′ō-jē) [″ + ″ + *logos,* word, reason] The scientific study of hormones and of the glands that secrete them.

endocrinopathy (ĕn″dō-krĭn-ŏp′ă-thē) [″ + ″ + *pathos,* disease, suffering] Any disease resulting from a disorder of an endocrine gland or glands. **endocrinopathic** (-krĭn″-ō-pă′thĭk), *adj.*

endocrinotherapy (ĕn″dō-krĭn″ō-thĕr′ă-pē) [″ + ″ + *therapeia,* treatment] Hormonotherapy.

endocurietherapy (en″dō-kūr″ē-ther′ă-pē) [*endo-* + *curietherapy*] Brachytherapy.

endocyst (ĕn′dō-sĭst) [″ + *kystis,* bladder, pouch] The innermost layer of any hydatid cyst.

endocystitis (ĕn″dō-sĭs-tī′tĭs) [″ + ″ + *itis,* inflammation] Inflammation of the mucous membrane of the bladder. SEE: *cystitis.*

endocytoscopy (en″dō-sī-tos′kŏ-pē) [*endo-* + *cytoscopy*] Direct visualization of the epithelial cells of an organ with an extremely high magnification endoscope.

endocytosis (ĕn″dō-sī-tō′sĭs) A method of ingestion of a foreign substance by a cell. The cell membrane invaginates to form a space for the material and then the opening closes to trap the material inside the cell. SEE: *emiocytosis; exocytosis; phagocytosis; pinocytosis.*

endoderm (ĕn′dō-dĕrm) [″ + *derma,* skin] The innermost of the three primary germ layers of a developing embryo. It gives rise to the epithelium of the digestive tract and its associated glands, the respiratory organs, bladder, vagina, and urethra. SYN: *hypoblast.* **endodermal** (-dĕrm′ăl), *adj.*

endodontia (ĕn″dō-dŏn′shē-ă) [″ + *odous,* tooth] Endodontics.

endodontics (ĕn″dō-dŏn′tĭks) The branch of dentistry concerned with diagnosis, treatment, and prevention of diseases of the dental pulp and its surrounding tissues.

endodontist (ĕn″dō-dŏn′tĭst) A specialist in endodontics.

endodontitis (ĕn″dō-dŏn-tī′tĭs) [″ + *odous,* tooth, + *itis,* inflammation] Inflammation of the dental pulp. SYN: *pulpitis.*

endoectothrix (ĕn″dō-ĕk′tō-thrĭks) [″ + *ektos,* outside, + *thrix,* hair] Any fungus growth on and in the hair.

End-of-Life Nursing Education Consortium ABBR: ELNEC. An educational initiative for U.S. nurses to improve core clinical competencies in the care of dying patients.

endogamy (ĕn-dŏg′ă-mē) [″ + *gamos,* marriage] **1.** The custom or tribal restriction of marriage within a tribe or group. **2.** In biology, reproduction by joining together gametes descended from the same ancestral cell.

endogastritis (ĕn″dō-găs-trī′tĭs) Gastritis.

endogenic (ĕn″dō-jĕn′ĭk) [″ + *gennan,* to produce] Endogenous.

endogenous (ĕn-dŏj′ĕ-nŭs) **1.** Produced or originating from within a cell or organism. **2.** Concerning spore formation within the bacterial cell. SYN: *endogenic.*

endogenous opiate-like substance SEE: *endorphin; enkephalin; opiate receptor.*

endoglobar, endoglobular (ĕn″dō-glŏb′ăr, ĕn″dō-glŏb′ū-lăr) [Gr. *endon,* within, + L. *globulus,* a globule] Within blood cells.

endointoxication (ĕn″dō-ĭn-tŏk″sĭ-kā′shŭn) [″ + L. *in,* into, + Gr. *toxikon,* poison] Poisoning due to an endogenous toxin (e.g., by hepatotoxins in liver failure, or urea compounds in renal failure).

endolabyrinthitis (ĕn″dō-lăb″ĭ-rĭn-thī′tĭs) [″ + *labyrinthos,* labyrinth, + *itis,* inflammation] Inflammation of the membranous labyrinth.

endoleak (ĕn′dō-lēk″) [″ + *leak*] Seepage of blood from a graft placed in a diseased blood vessel. The blood leaks out of the graft into the aneurysm that the graft was used to repair.

Endolimax nana (ĕn″dō-lī′măks nă′nă) [″ + *leimax,* meadow] A species of ameba inhabiting the intestines of humans, monkeys, and other mammals. Although it is often found in stool specimens, it is usually thought to be a commensal or nonpathogenic inhabitant of the gut.

endoluminal (en″dō-loo′mĭn-ăl) [*endo- + luminal*] Within a tubular organ or structure (e.g., a blood vessel, duct, or the gastrointestinal tract); within a lumen.

endoluminal sleeve ABBR: ELS. A flexible tube attached to the inside of the duodenum to block the absorption of nutrients by the proximal small intestine. It prevents the modification of consumed foods by bile and pancreatic enzymes (a process that normally takes place in the duodenum) and delivers unprocessed nutrients to the jejunum. It is used in bariatric surgery.

endolymph (ĕn′dō-lĭmf) [″ + L. *lympha,* clear fluid] A pale transparent fluid within the vestibular labyrinth of the inner ear. Endolymph differs in composition from the perilymph that is outside the vestibular labyrinth: endolymph is similar to intracellular fluid; perilymph, to extracellular cerebrospinal fluid. **endolymphatic** (-lĭm-făt′ĭk), *adj.*

endolysin (ĕn-dŏl′ĭ-sĭn) [″ + *lysis,* dissolution] A bacteriocidal substance within a leukocyte that destroys bacteria.

endomastoiditis (ĕn″dō-măs″toy-dī′tĭs) [″ + *mastos,* breast, + *eidos,* form, shape, + *itis,* inflammation] Inflammation of the mucosa lining the mastoid cavity and cells.

endometrial (ĕn″dō-mē′trē-ăl) [″ + *metra,* uterus] Pert. to the lining of the uterus (the endometrium).

endometrial ablation Removal or destruction of the whole thickness of the endometrium and of some superficial myometrium. It is used to remove all of the endometrial glandular material to treat benign disturbances of menstrual bleeding in women who do not wish to preserve fertility. Ablation may be done by laser or electrosurgery. The laser method employs an yttrium aluminum garnet (YAG) laser or high-powered "rollerball" electrocoagulation to destroy the uterine endometrium and 2/3 cm of myometrium. The thermal means uses a balloon catheter containing a heating element that delivers temperatures to 188° F (87° C) and a controller that monitors, displays, and regulates pressure, time, and temperature.

endometrial dating Microscopic examination of a suitable, stained specimen from the endometrium to establish the number of days to the next menstrual period. The dating is based on an ideal 28-day cycle. Thus, day 8 indicates menstruation is 20 days away, and day 23 that it is 5 days away. This system was devised by the late Dr. John Rock, a physician at Harvard Medical School, to enable gynecologists to visualize endometria being discussed without having to provide detailed descriptions of the material studied.

endometrial jet washing Collection of fluid that has been used to irrigate the uterine cavity. Cells present in the fluid are examined for evidence of malignancy. This method is used as a screening test for endometrial carcinoma.

endometrioma (ĕn″dō-mē″trē-ō′mă) [*endo- + metra,* uterus, + *oma,* tumor] A benign tumor comprised of ectopic endometrial cells. It is found most frequently in the ovary, the cul-de-sac, the rectovaginal septum, and the peritoneal surface of the posterior portion of the uterus.

endometriosis (en″dō-mē″trē-ō′sĭs) [*endo- + ¹metro- + osis*] The presence of functioning ectopic endometrial glands and stroma outside the uterine cavity. The endometrial tissue invades other tissues and spreads by local extension, intraperitoneal seeding, and lymphatic and vascular routes. The endometrial implants may be present in almost any area of the body although generally they are confined to the pelvic area. In the U.S. this condition is estimated to occur in 10% to 15% of actively menstruating women between the ages of 25 and 44. Estimates are that 25% to 35% of infertile women are affected. Women whose mothers or sisters have endometriosis are 6 times more likely to develop the condition than those with no family history. Postmenopausal women on estrogen replacement therapy also can develop endometriosis. If a woman has had a history of endometriosis, she may develop it when treated with menopausal estrogen replacement. The fallopian tubes are common sites of ectopic implantation. Ectopic endometrial cells respond to the same hormonal stimuli as does the uterine endometrium. The cyclic bleeding and local inflammation surrounding the implants may cause fibrosis, adhesions, and tubal occlusion. Infertility may result. SYN: *endomyometritis.* SEE: illus.

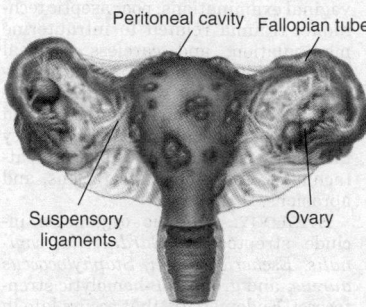

Peritoneal cavity   Fallopian tube

Suspensory ligaments   Ovary

SITES OF OCCURRENCE OF ENDOMETRIOSIS

ETIOLOGY: Although the cause is unknown, hypotheses are that either endometrial cell migration occurs during fetal development, or the cells shed during menstruation are expelled through the fallopian tubes to the peritoneal cavity.

SYMPTOMS: No single symptom is diagnostic. Patients often complain of dysmenorrhea with pelvic pain, premenstrual dyspareunia, sacral backache during menses, and infertility. Dysuria may indicate involvement of the urinary bladder. Cyclic pelvic pain, usually in the lower abdomen, vagina, posterior pelvis, and back, begins 5 to 7 days before menses, reaches a peak, and lasts 2 to 3 days. Premenstrual tenesmus and diarrhea may indicate lower bowel involvement. Dyspareunia may indicate involvement of the cul-de-sac or ovaries. No correlation exists between the degree of pain and the extent of involvement; many patients are asymptomatic.

DIAGNOSIS: Although history and findings of physical examination may suggest endometriosis, and imaging studies (transvaginal ultrasound) may

be helpful, definitive diagnosis of endometriosis and staging requires laparoscopy, a procedure that allows direct visualization of ectopic lesions and biopsy.

TREATMENT: Medical and surgical approaches may be used to preserve fertility and to increase the woman's potential for achieving pregnancy. Pharmacological management includes the use of hormonal agents to induce endometrial atrophy by maintaining a chronic state of anovulation.

Surgical management includes laparotomy, lysis of adhesions, laparoscopy with laser vaporization of implants, laparotomy with excision of ovarian masses, or total hysterectomy with bilateral salpingo-oophorectomy and removal of aberrant endometrial cysts and implants to encourage fertility. The definitive treatment for endometriosis ends a woman's potential for pregnancy by removal of the uterus, tubes, and ovaries.

PATIENT CARE: Providing emotional support and meeting informational needs are major concerns. The patient is encouraged to verbalize feelings and concerns.

The woman is prepared physically and emotionally for any surgical procedure.

Adolescent girls with a narrow vagina or small vaginal meatus are advised to use sanitary napkins rather than tampons to help prevent retrograde flow. Because infertility is a possible complication of endometriosis, a patient who wants children is advised not to postpone childbearing. An annual pelvic examination and Papanicolaou test are recommended. SEE: *Nursing Diagnoses Appendix.*

peritoneal e. Endometrial tissue found throughout the pelvis.

thoracic e. Presence of uterine lining in the thorax. Ectopic endometrioses resulting from an ectopic location can cause catamenial hemorrhage or catamenial air leaks.

transplantation e. Endometriosis occurring within an abdominal incision scar following pelvic surgery.

endometritis (en″dō-mĕ-trīt′is) [*endo-* + *metritis*] Inflammation of the lining of the uterus. Organisms may migrate through the cervical canal along mucosal surfaces, piggyback on sperm, or be carried on tampons or intrauterine devices. The inflammation may be acute, subacute, or chronic. The disorder is most common among females of childbearing age. The woman is at highest risk for endometritis during the immediate postpartum period. Endometritis that is not associated with pregnancy may result from pelvic inflammatory disease or invasive gynecologic procedures. SEE: *puerperal e.*

ETIOLOGY: Endometritis usually results from an ascending bacterial invasion of the uterine cavity. Common offenders include *Staphylococcus aureus* and group B streptococcus, both of which are present in normal vaginal flora. SEE: *pelvic inflammatory disease; toxic shock syndrome.*

SYMPTOMS: The woman usually presents with low, cramping abdominal pain, low back pain, dysmenorrhea, dyspareunia, and fever. Depending on the causative organism, a purulent, mucopurulent, or serosanguinous cervical discharge is seen on vaginal examination. In postpartum endometritis, lochia is foul-smelling. Bimanual palpation finds a tender, boggy uterus. SEE: *cervix uteri; endometrium; uterus.*

DIAGNOSIS: Culturing the causative organisms from lochia, cesarean or episiotomy incisional exudate, cervical swab or aspirated materials establishes the diagnosis.

TREATMENT: Antibiotic regimens that treat a broad spectrum of organisms (anaerobes, aerobes, sexually transmitted microorganisms) are used empirically.

PATIENT CARE: The patient should be made aware that the infectious process may spread beyond the endometrium, into the fallopian tubes, ovaries, pelvic perineum, pelvic veins, or pelvic connective tissue. SEE: *pelvic inflammatory disease.*

Standard precautions are used when caring for the patient. The patient is assessed for changes in the amount, color, odor, and consistency of vaginal discharge. Pain also is assessed and treated as prescribed. The patient is taught about the drugs used for treatment, their desired effects, and any adverse effects. In acute cases, the patient may be febrile; fever is treated with antipyretic drugs if it exceeds 101°F and with PO or intravenous (IV) fluids for hydration as required. The patient may be placed on bedrest in a semi-Fowler's position to facilitate dependent drainage. Vital signs should be monitored every 4 hours, and fluid intake and output recorded. Heat may be applied to the abdomen to improve circulation.

The varied consequences of endometritis are explained. They can include the need for surgery to relieve chronic pain or to manage acute infections that are unresponsive to antibiotic therapy, adhesions, tubal scarring, and infertility. The potential or actual loss of reproductive capabilities can devastate the woman's self-concept. All professional care providers must assist the patient to adjust her self-concept to fit reality and to accept any alterations in a way that promotes future health. The patient should abstain from sexual contact until treatment is complete, the sexual partner has also received treatment as appropriate, and follow-up testing has been done. Sterile technique should be maintained throughout all vaginal examinations. Some states require that chlamydial infections be reported to local public health authorities. All female patients should be taught correct perineal and hand hygiene to help prevent endometritis.

decidual e. Inflammation of the mucous membrane of a gravid uterus.

e. dissecans Endometritis accompanied by development of ulcers and shedding of the mucous membrane.

puerperal e. Acute endometritis following childbirth. Risk factors for development of this condition include premature or prolonged rupture of membranes, dystocia with multiple vaginal examinations, poor aseptic technique, trauma related to intrauterine manipulation, and careless perineal care. Constitutional factors that predispose the parturient woman to endometritis include anemia, malnutrition, and hemorrhage. Portals of bacterial entry include the site of previous placental attachment, episiotomy, lacerations, and abrasions.

ETIOLOGY: Aerobic organisms include streptococci, *Gardnerella vaginalis, Escherichia coli, Staphylococcus aureus,* and group A β-hemolytic streptococci. Endometritis that occurs late in the postpartal period is most commonly caused by *Chlamydia trachomatis.*

SYMPTOMS: Abdominal tenderness is common. Severe endometritis may cause fever, chills, tachycardia, extreme uterine tenderness, and subinvolution. Although a moderate-to-profuse foul-smelling vaginal discharge usually is seen, the lochia of women infected by β-hemolytic streptococci is scant, odorless, and serosanguineous to serous.

TREATMENT: Antibiotics that treat aerobic and anaerobic bacteria are administered, usually for a 4- or 5-day course. Supportive therapy includes bedrest, analgesics, and oral and IV fluids.

endometrium (en″dŏ-mē′trē-ŭm) [*endo-* + ¹*metro-* + -*ium*] The mucous membrane that lines the uterus. It consists of two highly vascular layers of areolar connective tissue; the basilar layer is adjacent to the myometrium, and the functional layer is adjacent to the uterine cavity. Simple columnar epithelium forms the surface of the functional layer and the simple tubular uterine glands. Straight arteries supply blood to the basilar layer; spiral arteries supply the functional layer. Both estrogen and progesterone stimulate the growth of endometrial blood vessels.

Beginning with menarche and ending at menopause, the uterine endometrium passes through cyclical changes that constitute the menstrual cycle. These changes are related to the development and maturation of the graafian follicle in the ovary, the discharge of the ovum, and the subsequent development of the corpus luteum in the ovary.

If the ovum is not fertilized or the zygote not implanted, the functional layer of the endometrium is shed in menstruation.

The cycle then begins again, with the functional layer regenerated by the basilar layer.

Following implantation of the zygote, the endometrium becomes the maternal portion of the placenta; it fuses with the chorion of the embryo. After birth, the uterine lining is shed. SEE: *fertilization* for illus.

proliferative e. Endometrial hypertrophy due to estrogen stimulation during the preovulatory phase of the menstrual cycle. This condition is detected through endometrial biopsy.

secretory e. Histological changes in the endometrium due to the effects of postovulatory progesterone secretion by the corpus luteum. SEE: *luteal phase defect; menstrual cycle.*

endomorph (en′dŏ-morf″) [*endo-* + *-morph*] A person with a body build marked by predominance of tissues derived from the endoderm. The body is pear shaped, often with significant adipose tissues in the upper arms, abdomen, and thighs. SEE: *ectomorph; mesomorph; somatotype.*

endomyocarditis (ĕn″dō-mī-ō-kăr-dī′tĭs) [″ + *mys*, muscle, + *kardia*, heart, + *itis*, inflammation] Inflammation of the endocardium and myocardium.

endomyometritis (en″dō-mī″ŏ-mē″trīt′ĭs) [*endo-* + *myometritis*] Endometriosis.

endomysium (ĕn″dō-mīs′ē-ŭm) [″ + *mys*, muscle] A thin sheath of connective tissue, consisting principally of reticular fibers, that invests each striated muscle fiber and binds the fibers together within a fasciculus.

endonasal (ĕn′dō-nāz′ăl) Inside the nose.

endoneuritis (ĕn″dō-nū-rī′tĭs) [″ + *neuron*, nerve, + *itis*, inflammation] Inflammation of the endoneurium.

endoneurium (en″dō-noor′ē-ŭm) [*endo-* + *neur-* + *-ium*] A delicate connective tissue sheath that surrounds nerve fibers within a fasciculus. SYN: *Henle′s sheath.*

endonuclease (en″dō-noo′klē-ās″, -nū′) [*endo-* + *onuclease*] An enzyme that cleaves the ends of polynucleotides.

restriction e. Restriction enzyme.

endoparasite (ĕn″dō-păr′ă-sīt) [″ + *para*, beside, + *sitos*, food] Internal **parasite**.

endopelvic (ĕn″dō-pĕl′vĭk) [″ + L. *pelvis*, basin] Within the pelvis.

endopelvic fasciae The downward continuation of the parietal peritoneum of the abdomen to form the pelvic fasciae, which contribute to the support of the pelvic viscera.

endopeptidase (ĕn″dō-pĕp′tĭ-dās) A proteolytic enzyme that cleaves peptides in their centers rather than from their ends.

endopericarditis (ĕn″dō-pĕr″ĭ-kăr-dī′tĭs) [″ + *peri*, around, + *kardia*, heart, + *itis*, inflammation] Endocarditis complicated by pericarditis.

endoperimyocarditis (ĕn″dō-pĕr″ĭ-mī″ō-kăr-dī′tĭs) [″ + ″ + *mys*, muscle, + *kardia*, heart, + *itis*, inflammation] Inflammation of the pericardium, myocardium, and endocardium.

endoperitonitis (ĕn″dō-pĕr″ĭ-tō-nī′tĭs) [″ + *peritonaion*, peritoneum, + *itis*, inflammation] Inflammation of the peritoneum.

endophlebitis (ĕn″dō-flĕ-bī′tĭs) [″ + *phleps*, vein, + *itis*, inflammation] Inflammation of the inner layer or membrane of a vein. SYN: *endangiitis.*

e. obliterans Endophlebitis causing obliteration of a vein.

e. portalis Inflammation of the portal vein.

endophthalmitis (ĕn″dŏf-thăl-mī′tĭs) [″ + *ophthalmos*, eye, + *itis*, inflammation] Inflammation of the inside of the eye that may or may not be limited to a particular chamber (i.e., anterior or posterior).

endoplasm (en′dō-plăzm) [″ + LL. *plasma*, form, mold] The central, more fluid portion of the cytoplasm of a cell. Opposed to ectoplasm.

endopyelotomy (ĕn″dō-pī″ĕ-lŏt′ŏ-mē) [*endo-* + *pyelo-* + *-otomy*] An endoscopic incision of the renal pelvis or the ureteropelvic junction.

endorectal (en″dō-rek′tăl) [*endo-* + *rectal*] Within the rectum. An endorectal ultrasound, e.g., is one in which the ultrasound transducer is placed inside the rectum so that it can be used to examine the last portion of the large intestine or the prostate gland.

endorectal coil (en″dō-rek′tăl) [*endo-* + *rectal*] A magnetic resonance imaging enhancement device placed inside the rectum, and used to evaluate pelvic and perirectal masses and malignancies.

endorectal ultrasound SEE: under *ultrasound.*

endorphin (ĕn-dor′fĭn, ĕn′dor-fĭn) A polypeptide produced in the brain that acts as an opiate and produces analgesia by binding to opiate receptor sites involved in pain perception. The threshold for pain is therefore increased by this action. The most active of these compounds is beta-endorphin. SEE: *enkephalin; opiate receptor; substance P.*

endosalpingitis (ĕn″dō-săl″pĭn-jī′tĭs) [″ + *salpinx,* tube, + *itis,* inflammation] Inflammation of the lining of the fallopian tubes.

endosalpingoma (ĕn″dō-săl″pĭn-gō′mă) An adenomyoma of the uterine tube.

endosalpinx (en″dō-sal′pingks″) [*endo-* + *salpinx*] The mucous membrane lining the uterine (fallopian) tube.

endoscope (en′dŏ-skōp) [*endo-* + *-scope*] A device consisting of a tube and optical system for observing the inside of a hollow organ, cavity, or tissue plane. This observation may be done through a natural body opening or a small incision. SYN: *enteroscope.*

    mother-baby endoscope Mother-baby scope.

endoscopic (en″dŏ-skop′ik) Pert. to endoscopy or an endoscope.

endoscopic air pulse stimulation A test of the integrity of the sensory nerves of the larynx used in patients suspected of having swallowing disorders. It consists of delivering incrementally more powerful blasts of air to the hypopharynx to measure how much stimulation is required to trigger reflex movement of the laryngeal adductor muscle, closing the vocal folds. The test is used during fiberoptic endoscopic evaluation of swallowing with sensory testing (FEESST).

endoscopic laser cholecystectomy SEE: under *laparoscopic laser **cholecystectomy.***

endoscopic mucosectomy SEE: under *mucosectomy.*

endoscopic positioning Precise placement of an endoscope so that it can be used to extract biopsy specimens or perform other surgical functions. The procedure may be carried out manually or under robotic control.

endoscopic retrograde cholangiopancreatography SEE: under *cholangiopancreatography.*

endoscopic transthoracic sympathectomy SEE: under *sympathectomy.*

endoscopy (en-dos′kŏ-pē) [*endo-* + *-scopy*] Inspection of body organs or cavities by use of an endoscope. Although endoscopy is well tolerated by nearly all patients, major complications, e.g., perforation of the organ being examined, bleeding, difficulty with breathing, chest pain, or adverse anesthetic reactions occur rarely.

    autofluorescence e. An enhanced form of endoscopic examination of the lining of an organ in which the organ is examined with light with specific limited wavelengths. This monochromatic light helps distinguish normal tissues from precancerous or malignant tissues and may increase the likelihood of ob-

taining a useful biopsy specimen during endoscopy.

    capsule e. ABBR: CE. Endoscopy of the gastrointestinal tract with a pill that contains a miniature camera. The pill is swallowed by the patient and travels through the gut unaided. CE is used to examine the small intestine, which is difficult to reach with standard upper endoscopy or with colonoscopy. CE can be used to identify otherwise occult sources of gastrointestinal bleeding.

⚠️ In patients with gastrointestinal strictures the camera may become lodged in the narrows and occasionally may need to be removed surgically.

SYN: *video e.; wireless capsule e.*

    double balloon e. Endoscopy to evaluate and treat sources of gastrointestinal bleeding within the small bowel. It allows visualization of successively deeper segments of the small bowel by catching the bowel wall with one balloon (located on an overtube that surrounds the endoscope) and then advancing the endoscope ahead of it. When the endoscope reaches a new section of bowel, a new balloon is inflated, fixing the bowel in place. The overtube balloon is deflated, and the overtube is advanced until its balloon is reinflated. The process is repeated until the scope has been successively moved through the entire small intestine, visualizing it fully. SYN: *push-and-pull e.*

    magnification e. The use of digital and optical magnification to enhance the visualization of small lesions within an organ during endoscopy. It is used to identify changes in the esophagus suggestive of Barrett esophagus and may be combined with other imaging techniques (e.g., the spraying of the lining of the examined organ with acetic acid or methylene blue or the illumination of the organ with fluorescent chemicals).

    push-and-pull e. Double balloon endoscopy.

    video e. Capsule endoscopy.

    wireless capsule e. Capsule endoscopy.

endoskeleton (ĕn″dō-skĕl′ĕt-ŏn) [″ + *skeleton,* skeleton] The internal bony framework of the body. Opposite of exoskeleton.

endosome (ĕn′dō-sōm) [″ + L. *soma,* body] The vacuole formed when material is absorbed in the cell by endocytosis. The vacuole fuses with lysosomes. SYN: *receptosome.*

endosonography [″ + L. *sonus,* sound, + Gr. *gramma,* something written] Endoscopic ultrasonography, i.e., the imaging of an internal body part by attaching an ultrasonographic transducer to an endoscope or laparoscope.

endospore (ĕn'dō-spor) [" + *sporos,* a seed] A thick-walled spore produced by a bacterium to enable it to survive unfavorable environmental conditions.

endosseous (ĕn-dŏs'ē-ŭs) [" + "] Within bone.

endostatin (ĕn'dŏ-stăt'ĭn) A protein fragment of collagen that contributes to the regulation of blood vessel growth. It is being investigated for its potential to shrink malignant tumors by decreasing their blood supply.

endosteoma (ĕn-dŏs"tē-ō'mă) [" + " + *oma,* tumor] A tumor in the medullary cavity of a bone.

endosteum (en-dos'tē-ŭm) [*endo-* + Gr. *osteon,* bone] The membrane lining the marrow cavity of a bone. **endosteal** (en"dos'tē-ăl), *adj.*

endostoma (ĕn-dŏs-tō'mă) [" + " + *oma,* tumor] An osseous tumor within a bone.

endostosis (ĕn"dŏs-tō'sĭs) [" + " + *osis,* condition] The development of an endostoma.

endosurgery (en"dō-sŭrj'ĕ-rē) [*endo-* + *surgery*] Any form of minimally invasive surgery in which a small video endoscope is inserted into the body. Commonly performed endosurgeries include appendectomies, bowel resections, gallbladder surgeries, hernia repairs, splenectomies, and cancer staging operations.

endosymbiont, endosymbiote (en"dō-sim'bē"ont, en"dō-sim'bē"ōt) [*endo-* + *symbiont* or *symbiote*] An organism that lives inside the body of another, benefiting both organisms. In some cases of endosymbiosis, neither organism would survive without the other.

endothelial (ĕn'dŏ-thē'lē-ăl) [Gr. *endon,* within, + *thele,* nipple] Pert. to or consisting of endothelium.

endothelin (ĕn'dō-thē'lĭn) A peptide released from the lining of blood vessels that causes blood vessels to constrict and blood pressure to increase. Endothelins are one of several agents involved in raising blood pressure and contributing to congestive heart failure.

endotheliocyte (ĕn'dŏ-thē'lē-ō-sīt") [" + " + *kytos,* cell] An endothelial cell.

endotheliocytosis (ĕn'dŏ-thē"lē-ō-sī-tō'sĭs) [" + " + " + *osis,* condition] An abnormal increase in endothelial cells.

endotheliolysin (ĕn'dŏ-thē-lē-ŏl'ĭ-sĭn) [" + *thele,* nipple, + *lysis,* dissolution] An antibody found in snake venom that dissolves endothelial cells.

endotheliolytic (ĕn'dŏ-thē-lē-ō-lĭt'ĭk) Capable of destroying endothelial tissue.

endothelioma (ĕn'dŏ-thē-lē-ō'mă) [" + *thele,* nipple, + *oma,* tumor] A malig-

nant growth of lining cells of the blood vessels.

endotheliomyoma (ĕn'dŏ-thē"lē-ō-mī-ō'mă) [" + " + *mys,* muscle, + *oma,* tumor] A muscular tumor with elements of endothelium.

endotheliomyxoma (ĕn'dŏ-thē"lē-ō-mĭks-ō'mă) [" + " + *myxa,* mucus, + *oma,* tumor] A myxoma with elements of endothelium.

endotheliosis (ĕn'dō-thē"lē-ō'sĭs) Increased growth of endothelium.

endotheliotoxin (ĕn'dō-thē-lē-ō-tŏks'ĭn) [" + " + *toxikon,* poison] A toxin that acts on endothelial capillary cells and causes bleeding.

endothelium (ĕn'dō-thē'lē-ŭm) [" + *thele,* nipple] A form of squamous epithelia-like tissue consisting of flat cells that line the blood and lymphatic vessels, the heart, and various other body cavities. Endothelia differ from epithelia in that the former is derived from mesoderm while the later is derived from ectoderm or endoderm. Taken together, the endothelium throughout the body has a surface area more than twice that of the skin. Endothelial cells are metabolically active and produce a number of compounds that affect the vascular lumen and platelets. Included are endothelium-derived relaxing factor (EDRF), prostacyclin, endothelium-derived contracting factors 1 and 2 (EDCF1, EDCF2), endothelium-derived hyperpolarizing factor (EDHF), and thrombomodulin. SEE: *intima.*

endothelium-derived hyperpolarizing factor SEE: under *factor.*

endothelium-derived relaxing factor SEE: under *factor.*

endotherapy (en"dō-ther'ă-pē) [*endo(scope)* + *therapy*] Any treatment, e.g., sclerotherapy, esophageal varix banding, or radiofrequency ablation, that can be performed with an endoscope.

endotherm (en'dō-thĕrm") [*endo-* + *thermo-*] Warm-blooded animal.

endothermal, endothermic (en"dō-thĕr'măl, en"dō-thĕr'mik) [*endo-* + *thermal*] **1.** Storing up potential energy or heat. **2.** Absorbing heat. **3.** Pert. to absorption of heat during chemical reactions. **4.** Pert. to a warm-blooded animal.

endothermy (en'dō-thĕr"mē) [*endo-* + *thermo-*] **1.** Diathermy. **2.** Regulation of body temperature by internal, metabolic means; warm-bloodedness.

endothrix (ĕn'dō-thrĭks) [" + *thrix,* hair] Any fungus growing inside the hair shaft.

endotoscope (ĕn-dō'tō-skōp) [" + *ous,* ear, + *skopein,* to examine] An ear speculum. SYN: *otoscope.*

endotoxemia (ĕn'dō-tŏks-ē'mē-ă) Toxemia due to the presence of endotoxins in the blood.

endotoxicosis (ĕn″dŏ-tŏk″sĭ-kō′sĭs) [Gr. *endon,* within, + *toxikon,* poison, + *osis,* condition] Poisoning due to an endotoxin.

endotoxin (ĕn″dō-tŏks′ĭn) A lipopolysaccharide that is part of the cell wall of gram-negative bacteria. It binds with CD14 receptors on leukocytes.The linkage stimulates the release of interleukin-1, tumor necrosis factor, and other cytokines, affecting inflammation, the specific immune response, vascular tone, hematopoiesis, and wound healing. When large amounts of lipopolysaccharides are present, the clinical state of sepsis or systemic inflammatory response syndrome occurs. Endotoxins are still active even after bacteria are destroyed; thus, in treating some infections, the positive effects of antibiotics may be delayed or absent. SEE: *bacterium; inflammation; sepsis; systemic inflammatory response syndrome.*

endotracheal tube (ĕn″dō-trā′kē-ăl) [″ + ″] ABBR: ET. A catheter inserted into the trachea to provide or protect an airway. SEE: illus. SYN: *tracheal tube; intubation tube.*

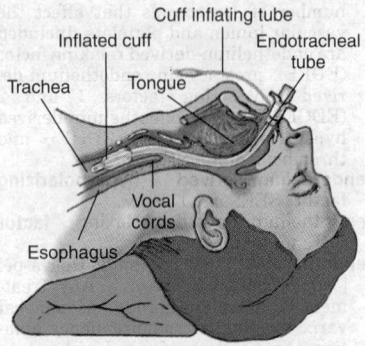

CUFFED ENDOTRACHEAL TUBE

⚠️ Although an ET is often thought to be the most secure and definitive airway, its use in emergencies may be complicated by misplacement (e.g., in the esophagus instead of in the trachea), displacement (e.g., during patient transport), or injury to the airway.

endotracheitis (ĕn″dō-trā-kē-ī′tĭs) [″ + *tracheia,* trachea, + *itis,* inflammation] Inflammation of the tracheal mucosa.

endoureterotomy (ĕn″dō-ūr-ē″tĕr-ŏt′ă-mē) [″ + ″] Endoscopic surgery to open a stricture in a ureter.

endovaginal (ĕn″dō-văj′ĭ-năl) [″ + ″] Within the vagina.

endovasculitis (ĕn″dō-văs″kū-lī′tĭs) [″ + L. *vasculum,* vessel, + Gr. *itis,* inflammation] Endangiitis.

endovenous (en″dō-vēn′ŭs) [*endo- + venous*] Within a vein.

end-plate (end′plāt″) **1.** Either of the upper and lower cushions on each vertebral body. They are made of cartilage, and are adjacent to the intervertebral disks. **2.** The distal part of a motor nerve. It stimulates muscle contraction by releasing neurotransmitters into the synapse with its adjacent muscle fiber.

end product The final material or substance left at the completion of a series of reactions, either chemical or physical.

end-stage The final phase of a disease process.

end-stage renal disease ABBR: ESRD. The stage of chronic kidney disease in which the clearance of creatinine has decreased so much that the patient will not long survive without renal replacement therapies, e.g., dialysis or kidney transplantation. This stage of renal failure occurs when the creatinine clearance is about 10% of normal, or the glomerular filtration rate is 5 to 10 mL/min. Renal replacement therapies are required to prevent fatal fluid overload, hyperkalemia, and other uremic complications. In the U.S., approximately 400,000 people are actively treated for ESRD with dialysis or kidney transplantation.

ETIOLOGY: End-stage renal disease may occur as a consequence of many other illnesses, including diabetes mellitus, hypertension, glomerulonephritis, recurrent or chronic renal infections, congenital kidney anomalies, vasculitis, multiple myeloma, analgesic overuse, or any of the causes of acute renal failure, e.g., shock, dehydration, post obstructive nephropathy; or exposure to nephrotoxins such as aminoglycosides, lead; or radiocontrast media.

SYMPTOMS: All body systems experience major changes as a result of chronic and end-stage renal failure. Patients may complain of fatigue (such as from anemia), difficulty concentrating, irritability, personality changes, increased sleepiness, muscle cramping and twitching, nausea, vomiting, anorexia, edema, breathlessness (if fluid retention results in pulmonary edema), or decreased urination. Some patients who become frankly uremic may develop uremic frost or become stuporous or comatose; others may develop uremic pericarditis.

TREATMENT: Hemodialysis, peritoneal dialysis, or kidney transplantation are used to restore renal function to patients with end-stage renal disease. Other therapies include the administration of water-soluble vitamins, phosphate-binding medications, erythropoietin, iron and folic acid (to treat anemia), and bicarbonate buffers (to prevent acidemia). The diet of patients with ESRD is restricted to limited quantities of fluids, and small concentrations of sodium, potassium, and protein, to prevent complications like fluid retention and hyperkalemia. Tight control of blood pressure and blood sugars in patients with hypertension or diabetes, respectively, will prolong kidney function and prevent deterioration.

PATIENT CARE: Patients with ESRD should avoid medications that may damage the kidneys (such as nonsteroidal anti-inflammatory drugs) or drugs that may accumulate in toxic concentrations as a result of renal failure, i.e., drugs that are normally excreted by the kidneys, such as aspirin, magnesium, or metformin. Serum potassium levels must be closely monitored.

Because donor organs are in relatively short supply, most patients should be prepared for dialysis with educational materials and ample opportunities to discuss the procedure and learn from professional staff. For most patients a fistula should be surgically constructed using a natural artery and vein in one of the upper extremities. Once this fistula has matured, it can be used for hemodialysis, typically in a dialysis center. SEE: *hemodialysis.*

Peritoneal dialysis (PD) is an alternative in which an access is surgically constructed through the patient's abdomen, and dialysis fluid is used to fill and drain the peritoneal cavity several times a day to remove accumulated toxins. PD requires greater effort on the part of the patient or caregivers to manage since it is administered at home but may have a greater degree of patient acceptance by competent patients than hemodialysis. However, some evidence suggests that it is associated with increased mortality. Whichever method of renal replacement is chosen, the patient will require close monitoring by a nephrologist (and other medical professionals) to optimize renal function and to maintain general health. Patients with ESRD and the professionals who care for them should familiarize themselves with information provided by the National Institute of Diabetes, Digestive and Kidney Diseases, the American Kidney Fund, and the National Kidney Foundation.

Good oral hygiene, skin care, and respiratory hygiene are encouraged. When the patient is hospitalized, all patient care concerns apply. Patients and their families will benefit from referral to agencies that provide counseling to assist them in coping. If the patient in ESRD decides that dialysis and ongoing therapies limit the quality of life, his or her decision should be supported and

family assisted to understand. The patient is referred for hospice care.

end-tidal (end′tīd′ăl) Pert. to or occurring at the end of exhalation.

endurance The ability to withstand extraordinary mental or physical stress for a prolonged period.

endurance training SEE: under *training.*

-ene [Gr. *-ēnē,* feminine adj. suffix] Suffix in chemistry used in naming *unsaturated hydrocarbons,* e.g., *benzene,* and esp. a *compound with one double bond,* e.g., *ethylene.*

enema (en′ĕ-mă) [Gr. *enema,* injection] **1.** The introduction of a solution into the rectum and colon to stimulate bowel activity and cause emptying of the lower intestine, for feeding or therapeutic purposes, to give anesthesia, or to aid in radiographic studies. **2.** A solution introduced into the rectum.

   air contrast e. An enema in which two contrast agents, thick barium sulfate and air, are introduced simultaneously under fluoroscopic control, followed by multiple radiographs of the colon. This technique produces better visualization of mucosal lining lesions, such as polyps or diverticula, than barium enemas performed without air.

   barium e.

   lubricating e. An enema to soften and ease the passage of feces through the anal canal. SYN: *emollient e.*

   nutrient e. An enema containing predigested foods to nourish a patient unable to be fed otherwise. SYN: *nutritive e.*

   retention e. An enema that may be used to provide nourishment, medication, or anesthetic. It should be made from fluids that will not stimulate peristalsis. A small amount of solution (e.g., 100 to 250 mL) is typically used in adults.

PATIENT CARE: The procedure and expected sensations are explained to the patient. Necessary equipment is assembled; the patient is draped for warmth and privacy and assisted into a left side-lying position with the right knee flexed (Sim's position). The tubing is cleared of air, and the small lubricated tube is inserted 3 to 4 in (7.5 to 10.0 cm) into the rectum and is not removed (unless absolutely necessary) until the procedure is completed. The fluid is allowed to flow very slowly, with stops made at intervals to aid retention. If the patient experiences an urge to defecate, the fluid flow is stopped until the urge passes. When the entire volume has been instilled, the tube is quickly withdrawn, the patient's buttocks are compressed together for a few minutes to prevent evacuation, and the patient is encouraged to retain the enema for at least 30 min. The type and amount of fluid instilled, the patient's ability to retain it, and the amount, type, and consistency of the returned fluid and stool are documented. SYN: *medicinal e.*

    saline e. Physiological salt solution enema.

    soapsuds e. An enema consisting of prepared soapsuds or, if liquid soap is used, 30 mL of liquid soap to (1000 mL of water. Strong soapsuds should not be used because of the danger of injuring intestinal mucosa. Mild white soaps, such as castile, are best.

energetic (ĕn-ĕr-gĕt'ĭk) **1.** Rel. to energy. **2.** Full of energy or vigor.

energetics (ĕn″ĕr-jĕt'ĭks) The study of energy, esp. in relation to human use of energy in the form of food and the expenditure of energy in work or athletic exercise.

energy (en'ĕr-jē) [Gr. *energeia,* activity] In physics, the capacity to do work, effect change. Energy is manifested in motion (kinetic energy) or position or chemical bonding (potential energy).

    Changes in energy may be physical, chemical, or both. Movement of a part of the body shortens and thickens the muscles involved and temporarily changes the position and size of cells, but intake of oxygen in the blood combined with glucose and fat creates a chemical change and produces heat (energy) and waste products within the cells; fatigue is produced in turn. SEE: *calorie; energy expenditure, basal.*

    conservation of e. The principle according to which energy cannot be created or destroyed, but is transformed into other forms.

    kinetic e. The energy of motion. It consists of the mass of an object and its velocity.

    latent e. Potential energy.

    phosphate-bond e. Energy derived from phosphorylated compounds such as adenosine triphosphate (ATP) and creatine phosphate.

    potential e. Energy stored but not actively used. It includes, for example, the energy stored in chemical bonds or in objects based on their position in space. SYN: *latent e.*

    radiant e. A form of energy transmitted through space. Radio waves, infrared waves, visible rays, ultraviolet waves, x-rays, gamma rays, and cosmic rays are examples of energy in this form. SEE: *electromagnetic spectrum* for table.

energy conservation In rehabilitation, a process for managing fatigue by prioritizing goals and time use, simplifying tasks, and organizing the environment to make necessary work more efficient.

energy drink A usually caffeinated soft drink supplemented with vitamins, minerals, and/or herbs, used to stimu-

late concentration, memory, or reaction time, or to reduce sleepiness.

energy expenditure, basal ABBR: BEE. The energy used by an individual who is at rest but not asleep. The BEE (expressed as calories) may be calculated by using the Harris-Benedict equations. These account for sex, age, height, and weight. If the individual is sedentary, moderately active, or engaged in strenuous activity, 30%, 40%, or 50%, respectively, are added to the BEE. SEE: *diet; dietetics; food.*

    The Harris-Benedict equation involves W (weight in kg), H (height in cm), and A (age in years). The formulae are:

    For women: BEE = $6.55 + (9.6 \times W) + (1.8 \times H) - (4.7 \times A)$

    For men: BEE = $6.6 + (13.7 \times W) + (5 \times H) - (6.8 \times A)$

    Hospitalized patients who are nonstressed require 20% more calories than for basal needs.

    Energy expended is increased by about 13% over basal needs for each degree centigrade of fever; burn and trauma patients require 40% to 100% more calories than for basal requirements.

energy field disturbance A hypothetical disruption of the flow of energy surrounding a person's being that results in a disharmony of the body, mind, and/or spirit. SEE: *Nursing Diagnoses Appendix.*

enervate (ĕn'ĕr-vāt) To make weak or to lessen the vitality of.

enervation (ĕn″ĕr-vā'shŭn) [L. *enervatio*] **1.** Deficiency in nervous strength; weakness. **2.** Resection or removal of a nerve.

enforcement (en-fors'mĕnt) Ensuring public compliance with a law, regulation, or ruling by the appropriate authorities.

enfranchisement (en-fran″chĭz'mĕnt) [Fr. *enfranchir,* to free] A recognized freedom to participate fully in society, such as the right to citizenship and the right to vote. SEE: *disenfranchisement.*

ENG *electronystagmography.*

engagement (in-gāj'mĕnt) **1.** In obstetrics, the entry of the largest diameter of the fetal presenting part into the pelvic inlet. SYN: *lightening.* SEE: *labor.* **2.** In the behavioral sciences, active involvement in meaningful everyday activities with other people. The involvement includes participation in family life, community activities, clubs, and organizations; maintenance of friendships; and attendance at religious services. Research has shown that people with higher levels of social engagement are more likely to maintain cognitive and physical capacity as they age.

Engerix-B (ĕn'jĕr-ĭks-bē′) Hepatitis B (recombinant) vaccine.

engine A device for converting energy into mechanical motion.

    dental e. A machine that rotates dental instruments.

    high-speed e. A machine that rotates a dental instrument in excess of 12,000 rpm.

    ultraspeed e. A machine that rotates a dental instrument at speeds from 100,000 to 300,000 rpm.

engineering In medical science, the practical application of principles of science and technology to problems posed by health or disease. Branches of this science include human, dental, genetic, and biomechanical.

English as a Second Language ABBR: ESL. A curriculum designed to teach English diction, fluency, grammar, idioms, pronunciation, and vocabulary to people who want to attain English language mastery after a primary education in another language.

    PATIENT CARE: Poor English language skills may be barriers to the achievement of good health or the use of health services in nations where English is spoken as the primary language (e.g., Australia, Britain, Canada, New Zealand, and the U.S.). Illiteracy may result in the misuse of medications, nonadherence to medical regimens, or obstacles to achieving access to health care. Translators skilled in the patient's native language should be employed to enhance understanding whenever the patient's English language skills are in question.

engorged (ĕn-gorjd′) [O. Fr. *engorgier,* to obstruct, to devour] Distended, as with blood or fluids.

engorgement (ĕn-gorj′mĕnt) **1.** Vascular congestion; distention. **2.** Filling of a breast with milk.

engram (ĕn′grăm) [Gr. *engramm*] The physiological basis of a memory in the central nervous system.

engrossment (ĕn-grōs′mĕnt) An attitude of total focus on something or someone. In obstetrics, the term denotes attachment behavior exhibited by new parents during initial contacts with their newborns.

enhancement (ĕn-hăns′mĕnt) An increase in the effect of ionizing radiation on tissues, produced by the use of oxygen or other chemicals.

enhancer (ĕn-hăn′sĕr) **1.** A nucleic acid sequence that increases the transcription or utilization of a gene. **2.** In neurophysiology any chemical that increases the propagation of impulses between neurons.

enissophobia (ĕn-ĭs″ō-fō′bē-ă) [Gr. *enissein,* to reproach, + *phobos,* fear] Fear of criticism, esp. for having committed a sin.

enkephalin (ĕn-kĕf′ă-lĭn) A pentapeptide produced in the brain. It acts as an opiate and produces analgesia by binding to opiate receptor sites involved in pain perception. The threshold for pain is therefore increased by this action. Enkephalins may have a role in explaining the withdrawal signs of narcotic addiction. SYN: *endogenous opiate-like substance.* SEE: *endorphin; opiate receptor.*

enlargement (ĕn-lărj′mĕnt) An increase in size of anything, esp. of an organ or tissue.

enol (ē′nŏl) A form that a ketone may take by tautomerism. A substance changes from an enol to a ketone by the oscillation of a hydrogen atom from the enol form to the ketone form.

enolase (ē′nō-lās) An enzyme present in muscle tissue that converts phosphoglyceric acid to phosphopyruvic acid.

enology (ē-nŏl′ō-jē) [Gr. *oinos,* wine, + *logos,* word, reason] The science of producing and evaluating wine. Also spelled *oenology.*

enophthalmos (ĕn″ŏf-thăl′mŭs) [Gr. *en,* in, + *ophthalmos,* eye] Recession of the eyeball into the orbit. Opposite of exophthalmos.

enosimania (ĕn″ōs-ĭ-mā′nē-ă) [Gr. *enosis,* a quaking, + *mania,* madness] A mental state marked by excessive and irrational terror.

enostosis (ĕn″ōs-tō′sĭs) [Gr. *en,* in, + *osteon,* bone, + *osis,* condition] An osseous tumor within the cavity of a bone.

enriched Having something extra added. For example, vitamins or minerals may be added to a food in order to *enrich* it.

enroll, enrol (en-rōl′) To register or be registered as a participant in a clinical trial, course of study, or insurance plan.

    enrollee (-rō-lē′), *n.* **enroller** (-rōl′ĕr), *n.* **enrollment** (-rōl′mĕnt), *n.*

enrollee (en-rō-lē′) A person who is registered in and receives health care from a commercial or governmentally administered health plan. SYN: *subscriber.*

ensiform (ĕn′sĭ-form) [L. *ensis,* sword, + *forma,* form] Xiphoid.

enstrophe (ĕn′strō-fē) [Gr. *en,* in, + *strephein,* to turn] Entropion.

ENT *ear, nose, and throat.*

ental (ĕn′tăl) [Gr. *entos,* within] Pert. to the interior; inside; central.

entamebiasis (ĕn″tă-mē-bī′ă-sĭs) [" + *amoibe,* change] Infestation with *Entamoeba.*

Entamoeba (ĕn″tă-mē′bă) A genus of ameba, some of which are found in the human intestine or oral cavity.

    E. buccalis E. gingivalis.

    E. coli A species of ameba normally found in the human intestinal tract. This species is nonpathogenic to humans.

    E. gingivalis A nonpathogenic species of ameba that inhabits the mouth. SYN: *E. buccalis.*

    E. hartmanni A commensal species

(one that does not cause disease). It lives in the colon.

E. histolytica A pathogenic species of ameba, the cause of amebic dysentery and tropical liver abscess.

enteral (ĕn'tĕr-ăl) [Gr. *enteron*, intestine] Within or by way of the intestine.

enteralgia (ĕn"tĕr-ăl'jē-ă) [" + *algos*, pain] Pain in the intestines; intestinal cramps or colic. SYN: *enterodynia*.

enteral tube feeding SEE: under *feeding*.

enterectomy (ĕn"tĕr-ĕk'tō-mē) [" + *ektome*, excision] Excision of a portion of the intestines.

enteric (ĕn-tĕr'ĭk) [Gr. *enteron*, intestine] Pert. to the small intestine.

enteric bacilli A broad term for bacilli present in the intestinal tract. Included are gram-negative non−spore-forming facultatively anaerobic bacilli such as *Escherichia, Shigella, Salmonella, Klebsiella,* and *Yersinia.* They may be present in the intestines of vertebrates as normal flora or pathogens.

enteric-coated ABBR: EC. Pert. to a drug formulation in which tablets or capsules are coated with a compound that does not dissolve until the pill is exposed to the fluids in the small intestine.

enteric cytopathogenic human orphan virus ABBR: echovirus. SEE: under *virus*.

enteric nervous system ABBR: ENS. A division of the autonomic nervous system (ANS) arising from its own line of neural crest cells and composed of the tens of millions of neurons and their supporting cells inside the walls of the gastrointestinal tract, pancreas, and gallbladder. Although the enteric nervous system is innervated (and modulated) by sympathetic and parasympathetic axons from the other divisions of the ANS, the enteric nervous system also acts independently. Reflex activities (e.g., maintaining gut wall tension and producing peristalsis) are initiated and coordinated via networks entirely inside the gut walls and organized via complex intrinsic ganglionated neural networks of two kinds: Auerbach's plexus and the submucous (Meissner's and Henle's) plexus lying between the circular and muscularis mucosae muscle layers.

enteritis (ent"ĕ-rīt'ĭs) [*entero-* + *-itis*] Inflammation of the intestines, particularly of the mucosa and submucosa of the small intestine. SEE: *Nursing Diagnoses Appendix.*

  infectious e. Enteritis caused by bacteria, fungi, parasites, or viruses.

  lupus e. Vasculitis of the gastrointestinal tract.

  radiation e. Enteritis from exposure to ionizing radiation (e.g., after radiation therapy for cancers of the gastrointestinal or pelvic organs).

  regional e. Crohn's disease.

entero-, enter- [Gr. *enteron*, intestine] Prefixes meaning *intestines*.

enteroanastomosis (ĕn"tĕr-ō-ăn-ăs"tō-mō'sĭs) [" + *anastomosis*, opening] An intestinal anastomosis.

enteroantigen (ĕn"tĕr-ō-ăn'tĭ-jĕn) [" + *anti*, against, + *gennan*, to produce] An antigen derived from the intestines.

Enterobacter (ĕn"tĕr-ō-băk'tĕr) A genus of gram-negative bacilli of the family Enterobacteriaceae that occurs in water, soil, and in the intestines of humans and animals. Species of enterobacter are an important cause of opportunistic infections and hospital-acquired infections, many of which may be resistant to multiple antibiotics.

  E. aerogenes A species that occurs normally in the intestines of humans and other animals and is found in decayed matter, on grains, and in plants. It causes opportunistic infections of the urinary tract and of the intestine when antibiotic therapy diminishes other microorganisms.

  E. agglomerans A species that has been associated with serious systemic infections, particularly septicemia from contaminated intravenous fluids.

  E. cloacae A species that, along with *E. agglomerans,* accounts for most nosocomial infections caused by this genus, esp. those due to intravenous line contamination.

Enterobacteriaceae (ĕn"tĕr-ō-băk-tē"rē-ā'sē-ē) A family of gram-negative, non−spore-forming, facultatively anaerobic bacilli. Some are intestinal pathogens, others are usually normal colonizers of the human intestinal tract. Included in the family are *Shigella, Salmonella, Escherichia, Klebsiella, Proteus, Enterobacter,* and *Yersinia.*

enterobiasis (ĕn"tĕr-ō-bī'ă-sĭs) [Gr. *enteron,* intestine, + *bios,* life] Infestation with pinworms (*Enterobius vermicularis*). SYN: *oxyuriasis.*

enterobiliary (ĕn"tĕr-ō-bĭl'ē-ār-ē) [" + L. *bilis,* bile] Pert. to the intestines and the bile passages.

Enterobius (ĕn"tĕr-ō'bē-ŭs) [" + *bios,* life] A genus of parasitic nematode worms, formerly *Oxyuris.*

  E. vermicularis The species commonly known as "pinworms," which causes enterobiasis, a parasitic infestation of the large intestine. The small, white adult worms live in the cecum and adjacent portions of the colon; at night the females migrate to the anus and lay their eggs on the perianal skin. The eggs hatch by morning. Infestations cause irritation of the anal region and allergic reaction of the neighboring skin, accompanied by intense itching, which may result in loss of sleep, excessive irritability, and a secondary infection of the area around the anus as a result of the scratching. Distribution is worldwide. The infection is most prevalent among preschool and school-age children. It is estimated that in temperate climates 20% of children have this condition. According to the Center for Disease Control and Prevention (CDC), pinworms infect 40 million children and adults in the U.S. Female worms average 8 to 13 mm in length and males 2 to 5 mm. SYN: *pinworm*.

DIAGNOSIS: The presence of adult worms in feces or on the anus confirms the diagnosis. Transparent, pressure-sensitive tape or an adhesive pinworm paddle may be applied to the perianal area and then examined microscopically for eggs. This latter test is more likely to be positive in the morning before bathing, urinating, or defecating.

TREATMENT: Pyrantel pamoate, albendazole, or mebendazole is effective.

PATIENT CARE: Family members and other close contacts of infected persons should be assessed and treated as necessary. During treatment tight-fitting sleepwear should be used to prevent the eggs from contaminating bedding. The house, bedding, and night clothes must be thoroughly cleaned for several days during treatment. Infected individuals should trim their nails short and bathe every morning on arising, using a clean washcloth and towel each time. An infected child can return to school or daycare once he/she has received one dose of medication, been bathed, and had fingernails trimmed. To eradicate pinworms and prevent reinfection, children, parents, teachers, and other close contacts should be taught how to perform hand hygiene correctly, and to perform this throughout the day, esp. before food preparation or eating and after toileting or diaper changes, handling underwear or bed linens, or touching any potentially contaminated objects.

enterocele (ĕn'tĕr-ō-sēl) [" + *keke*, hernia] **1.** A hernia of the intestine through the vagina. **2.** A posterior vaginal hernia.

enterocentesis (ĕn"tĕr-ō-sĕn-tē'sĭs) [" + *kentesis*, puncture] Puncture of the intestine to withdraw gas or fluids.

enterocholecystostomy (ĕn"tĕr-ō-kō"lē-sĭs-tŏs'tō-mē) [" + *chole*, bile, + *kystis*, bladder, + *stoma*, mouth] A surgically created opening between the gallbladder and small intestine. SYN: *cholecystenterostomy*.

enterocholecystotomy (ĕn"tĕr-ō-kō"lē-sĭs-tŏt'ō-mē) [" + " + " + *tome*, incision] Incision of both the gallbladder and the intestine.

enteroclysis (ĕn"tĕr-ŏk'lĭ-sĭs) [" + *klysis*, a washing out] **1.** Injection of a nutrient or medicinal liquid into the bowel. **2.** Irrigation of the colon with a large amount of fluid intended to fill the colon completely and flush it. SEE: *enema*. **3.** Radiography of the small bowel. A tube is advanced into the duodenum under fluoroscopic guidance and barium is given, followed by insufflation of the bowel with air.

Enterococcus (ĕn"tĕr-ō-kŏk'ŭs) A genus of gram-positive cocci of the family Enterococcaceae, formerly classified as part of the genus *Streptococcus*, but now classified as a separate genus. Of the 12 or more species, *E. faecalis* and *E. faecium* are found normally in the human gastrointestinal tract. They may cause urinary tract infections or other serious infections that are resistant to many antibiotics.

vancomycin-resistant e. ABBR: VRE. A strain of *Enterococcus faecium* resistant to antibiotics, including penicillins, aminoglycosides, and vancomycin. Infection with VRE presents a major threat to infected patients; although it can be treated with linezolid, its antibiotic resistance can be transferred to other gram-positive organisms, such as *Staphylococcus aureus*, making these bacteria also more difficult to eradicate.

To prevent the spread of VRE, the organism is identified by culture and sensitivity testing as soon as the infection is recognized. Contact precautions and cohorting of infected patients are used to control nosocomial spread. All persons entering the patient's room don gloves; hands are washed carefully both before they are donned and after they are removed. Gloves are removed just before leaving the room. Charts and flow sheets should not be taken into the room. Hospitals should heed the guidelines that have been developed for the use of vancomycin, to minimize the spread of vancomycin resistance to other organisms. SEE: *antibiotic resistance; multidrug resistance; Standard Precautions Appendix*.

enterocolectomy (ĕn"tĕr-ō-kō-lĕk'tō-mē) [" + *kolon*, colon, + *ektome*, excision] Surgical removal of a portion of the small intestine and colon.

enterocolitis (ĕn"tĕr-ō-lī'tĭs) [" + " + *itis*, inflammation] Inflammation of the small or large bowel, usually as a result of an infectious disease. The most common causative organisms include rotaviruses and other enteric viruses, *Salmonella, Escherichia coli, Shigella, Campylobacter,* and *Yersinia* species. A potentially severe presentation, pseudomembranous enterocolitis, may be induced by prolonged use of antibiotics allowing the overgrowth of *Clostridium difficile*. SEE: *diarrhea; gastroenteritis*.

necrotizing e. ABBR: NEC. Severe damage to the intestinal mucosa of the preterm infant due to ischemia resulting from asphyxia or prolonged hypoxemia.

enterocolostomy (ĕn″tĕr-ō-kō-lŏs′tō-mē) [″ + ″ + *stoma*, mouth] A surgical joining of the small intestine to the colon.

enterocutaneous (ĕn″tĕr-ō-kū-tā′nē-ŭs) Pert. to communication between the skin and intestine.

enterocyst (ĕn′tĕr-ō-sĭst) [Gr. *enteron*, intestine, + *kystis*, bladder] A benign cyst of the intestinal wall.

enterocystocele (ĕn″tĕr-ō-sĭs′tō-sēl) [″+ *kele*, tumor, swelling] A hernia of the bladder wall and intestine.

enterocystoma (ĕn″tĕr-ō-sĭs-tō′mă) [″ + ″ + *oma*, tumor] A cystic tumor of the intestinal wall.

enterocystoplasty (ĕn″tĕr-ō-sĭs′tō-plăs″tē) [″ + ″ + *plastos*, formed] A plastic surgical procedure involving the use of a portion of intestine to enlarge the bladder.

enterocyte (ĕn′tĕr-ō-sīt″) [″ + ″] A nutrient-absorbing cell located on the surface of the small intestinal villus. Its free surface cell membrane is folded into microvilli that increase the surface area available for absorption.

Enterocytozoon (ĕn″tĕr-ō-sī″tō-zō′on) A genus of protozoa of the order Microsporidia. *E. bieneusi* is a cause of chronic diarrhea in AIDS patients. SEE: *microsporidiosis*.

enterodynia (ĕn″tĕr-ō-dĭn′ē-ă) [″ + *odyne*, pain] Enteralgia.

enteroenterostomy (ĕn″tĕr-ō-ĕn″tĕr-ŏs′tō-mē) [″ + *enteron*, intestine, + *stoma*, mouth] Surgical creation of a communication between two intestinal segments.

enteroepiplocele (ĕn″tĕr-ō-ē-pĭp′lō-sēl) [″ + *epiploon*, omentum, + *kele*, tumor, swelling] A hernia of the small intestine and omentum.

enterogastritis (ĕn″tĕr-ō-găs-trī′tĭs) [″ + *gaster*, belly, + *itis*, inflammation] Inflammation of the stomach (gastritis) and the intestines (enteritis).

enterogastrone (ĕn″tĕr-ō-găs′trōn) A hormone such as secretin that is released by the intestinal mucosa and controls the release of food from the stomach into the duodenum by depressing gastric motility and secretion. A fatty meal causes greater secretion of this hormone than a normal meal does.

enterogenous (ĕn″tĕr-ŏj′ĕ-nŭs) [″ + *gennan*, to produce] Originating in the small intestine.

enterohepatic (ĕn″tĕr-ō-hĕ-păt′ĭk) [″ + *hepar*, liver] Pert. to the intestines and liver.

enterohepatitis (ĕn″tĕr-ō-hĕp-ă-tī′tĭs) [″ + ″ + *itis*, inflammation] Inflammation of the intestine and liver.

enterohydrocele (ĕn″tĕr-ō-hī′drō-sēl) [″ + *hydor*, water, + *kele*, tumor, swelling] A hydrocele with a loop of intestine in the sac.

enterokinase (ĕn″tĕr-ō-kī′nās) [″ + *kinesis*, movement] Previous term for enteropeptidase.

enterology (ĕn″tĕr-ŏl′ŏ-jē) [″ + *logos*, word, reason] The study of the intestinal tract.

enterolysis (ĕn″tĕr-ŏl′ĭ-sĭs) [″ + *lysis*, dissolution] Surgical division of intestinal adhesions.

enteromegalia, enteromegaly (ĕn″tĕr-ō-mĕ-gā′lē-ă, ĕn″tĕr-ō-mĕg′ă-lē) [″ + *megas*, large] Abnormal enlargement of the intestines. SYN: *megacolon*.

Enteromonas hominis (ĕn″tĕr-ŏm′ō-năs hŏm′ĭn-ĭs) A flagellated protozoan that lives in the intestine of humans. It is rare and considered nonpathogenic.

enteromycosis (ĕn″tĕr-ō-mī-kō′sĭs) [″ + *mykes*, fungus, + *osis*, diseased condition] A disease of the intestine resulting from bacteria or fungi.

enteromyiasis (ĕn″tĕr-ō-mī-ī′ă-sĭs) [″ + *myia*, fly] A disease caused by the presence of maggots (the larvae of flies) in the intestines.

enteron (ĕn′tĕr-ŏn) [Gr.] Alimentary canal.

enteroneuritis (ĕn″tĕr-ō-nū-rī′tĭs) [″ + *neuron*, nerve, + *itis*, inflammation] Inflammation of the intestinal nerves.

entero-oxyntin (ĕn″tĕr-ō-ŏk-sĭn′tĭn) A hormone found in animals but not humans believed to be released by the small intestine in response to the presence of chyme. It is thought to cause the parietal cells of the gastric mucosa to release hydrochloric acid. SEE: *gastrin*.

enteroparesis (ĕn″tĕr-ō-păr′ē-sĭs) [″ + *paresis*, relaxation] Reduced peristalsis of the intestines; an old term for ileus.

enteropathogen (ĕn″tĕr-ō-păth′ō-jĕn) [″ + *pathos*, disease, suffering, + *gennan*, to produce] Any microorganism that causes intestinal disease.

enteropathy (ent″ĕ-rop′ă-thē) [*entero-* + *-pathy*] Any intestinal disease.

    gluten-induced e. Celiac sprue.

    protein-losing e. The abnormal loss of protein into the gastrointestinal (GI) tract or a failure of the GI tract to absorb consumed proteins. It may be caused by a wide variety of diseases and conditions, including inflammatory bowel disease, lymphoma, and right-sided heart failure.

    radiation e. Damage to the intestines due to radiation.

enteropeptidase (ĕn″tĕr-ō-pĕp′tĭ-dās) An enzyme of the duodenal mucosa that converts pancreatic trypsinogen to active trypsin. Formerly called *enterokinase*.

enteropexy (ĕn′tĕr-ō-pĕks″ē) [″ + *pexis*, fixation] Fixation of the intestine to the abdominal wall or to another portion of the intestine.

enteroplegia (ĕn″tĕr-ō-plē′jē-ă) [″ + *plege,* stroke] Paralysis of the intestines. SEE: *paralytic ileus.*

enteroplexy (ĕn″tĕr-ō-plĕk′sē) Surgical union of divided parts of the intestine. SYN: *enteroanastomosis.*

enteroptosis (ĕn″tĕr-ŏp-tō′sĭs) [″ + *ptosis,* a falling or dropping] Prolapse of the intestine or abdominal organs.

enterorrhaphy (ĕn″tĕr-or′ă-fē) [″ + *rhaphe,* seam, ridge] Stitching of an intestinal wound, or of the intestine to some other structure.

enterorrhexis (ĕn″tĕr-ō-rĕks′ĭs) [″ + *rhexis,* rupture] Rupture of the intestine.

enteroscope (ĕn′tĕr-ō-skōp″) [″ + *skopein,* to examine] Endoscope.

enterosepsis (ĕn″tĕr-ō-sĕp′sĭs) [″ + *sepsis,* decay] A condition in which bacteria in the intestines produce intestinal sepsis. SEE: *enterotoxemia.*

enterospasm (ĕn′tĕr-ō-spăzm) [Gr. *enteron,* intestine, + *spasmos,* spasm] Intermittent painful contractions of the intestines.

enterostasis (ĕn″tĕr-ō-stā′sĭs) [″ + *stasis,* a standing] Cessation of or delay in the passage of food through the intestine; an old term for ileus.

enterostenosis (ĕn″tĕr-ō-stĕ-nō′sĭs) [″ + *stenosis,* a narrowing] Narrowing or stricture of the intestine.

enterostomal therapist (ĕn″tĕr-ŏs′tă-măl) ABBR: ET. An individual trained to teach patients proper methods of caring for an ostomy. The certification title is *certified enterostomal therapy nurse* (CETN).

enterostomy (ĕn″tĕr-ŏs′tō-mē) [″ + *stoma,* mouth] A surgically created opening into a portion of the gastrointestinal tract.

enterotoxemia (ĕn″tĕr-ō-tŏk-sē′mē-ă) A condition in which bacterial toxins are absorbed from the intestine and circulate in the blood.

enterotoxigenic (ĕn″tĕr-ō-tŏk″sĭ-jĕn′ĭk) Producing enterotoxins, as in some strains of bacteria.

enterotoxin (ĕn″tĕr-ō-tŏk′sĭn) [″ + *toxikon,* poison] **1.** A toxin produced in or originating in the intestinal contents. **2.** An exotoxin specific for the cells of the intestinal mucosa. **3.** An exotoxin produced by certain species of bacteria that causes various diseases, including food poisoning and toxic shock syndrome.

enterovirus (ent′ĕ-rō-vī′rŭs) [*entero-* + *virus*] Any of a group of viruses that originally included poliovirus, coxsackievirus, and ECHO virus, which infect the human gastrointestinal tract. Enteroviruses are now classed as a genus of picornaviruses. SEE: *picornavirus.*

   e. **71** ABBR: EV71. The virus that causes hand-foot-and-mouth disease. In about 30% of infected people, it causes

neurological disease, e.g., encephalitis, viral meningitis, or flaccid paralysis.

enterozoic (ĕn″tĕr-ō-zō′ĭk) [″ + *zoon,* animal] Pert. to parasites inhabiting the intestine.

enterprise computing A computer network system that seamlessly connects all the computers in a single organization or institution, even if those computers are housed in different locations.

enthalpy (en′thal″pĭ, en-thal′) [Gr. *enthalpein,* to heat] SYMB: H. The heat content of a system. The heat content is the internal energy of the system plus the product of its pressure and volume. This content can be harnessed to do work. It may be represented symbolically by the equation $H = U + PV$, where U is the internal energy, P is the pressure, and V is the volume.

enthesis An attachment to a bone of a tendon or ligament.

enthesitis (en″thĕ-sīt′ĭs) Inflammation at the site of attachment of bone to a tendon, ligament, or joint capsule.

enthesopathy (en″thĕ-sŏ′pă-thē) [Gr. *en,* in, into, + *thesis,* placing, + *pathos,* illness, suffering] Any disease that affects the attachment of tendons or ligaments to bone. Enthesopathies can result from inflammation associated with conditions including Reiter's syndrome, psoriatic arthritis, ankylosing spondylitis, and rheumatoid arthritis.

enthlasis (ĕn′thlă-sĭs) [Gr., dent caused by pressure] A depressed fracture of the skull.

entire (ĕn-tīr′) In bacteriology, the smooth, regular border of a bacterial colony.

entitlement **1.** A right or benefit. **2.** A form of compensation granted to an individual because of a special status under the law (e.g., an entitlement to health insurance under the Medicare program).

entity (ĕn′tĭ-tē) [L. *ens,* being] **1.** A thing existing independently, containing in itself all the conditions necessary to individuality. **2.** Something that forms a complete whole, denoting a distinct condition or disease.

ento-, ent- [Gr. *entos,* within] Prefixes meaning *within, inside.*

entocele (ĕn′tō-sēl) [″ + *kele,* tumor, swelling] Internal hernia.

entochondrostosis (ĕn″tō-kŏn″drŏs-tō′sĭs) [″ + *chondros,* cartilage, + *osis,* condition] The development of bone within cartilage.

entome (ĕn′tōm) [Gr. *en,* in, + *tome,* incision] A knife for division of urethral strictures.

entomology (ĕn″tō-mŏl′ō-jē) [Gr. *entomon,* insect, + *logos,* word, reason] The study of insects.

   forensic e. The use of evidence provided by insect infestations to determine the condition of cadavers, esp. the time of death of a body left outdoors.

medical e. The branch of entomology that deals with insects and their relationship to disease, esp. of humans.

entomophthoramycosis (ĕn-tō-mŏf'thō-ră-mĭ-kō'sĭs) A disease caused by fungi of the class Zygomycetes, which includes two genera (*Conidiobolus* and *Basidiobolus*) responsible for human disease. *Conidiobolus* causes infections of the heart and face; *Basidiobolus* produces infections in other parts of the body.

SYMPTOMS: Clinically, there is swelling of the nose, perinasal tissues, and mouth. Nodular subcutaneous masses are palpable in the skin.

TREATMENT: Antifungal drugs such as amphotericin B, terbinafine, or ketoconazole are used, often as part of a regimen that includes surgery to remove infected tissues.

entopic (en-top'ĭk) [Gr. *en,* in + *topo-* + *-ic*] Normally situated; in a normal place. SEE: *ectopic.*

entoptic (ĕn-tŏp'tĭk) [Gr. *entos,* within, + *optikos,* seeing] Pert. to the interior of the eye.

entoptic phenomenon A visual phenomenon arising from within the eye, marked by the perception of floating bodies, circles of light, black spots, and transient flashes of light. It may be due to the individual's own blood cells moving through the retinal vessels, or to floaters, which are small specks of tissue floating in the vitreous fluid. SEE: *Moore lightning streaks; muscae volitantes; photopsia.*

Individuals may see imperfections of their own cornea, lens, and vitreous by looking at a white background through a pinhole held about 17 mm (4.3 in) from the eye. The person sees a patch of light the size of which varies with the diameter of the pupil. The abnormalities are seen as shadows or bright areas. This method can be used also to see early discrete lens opacities.

entozoon (ĕn″tō-zō′ŏn) *pl.* **entozoa** [″ + *zoon,* animal] Any animal parasite living within the body of another animal.

entrails (ĕn′trālz) The intestines of an animal.

entrain (ĕn-trān′) To alter the biological rhythm of an organism so that it assumes a cycle different from a 24-hour one.

entrainment (ĕn-trān′mĕnt) **1.** Gaining control of a heart rhythm (esp. a tachycardic rhythm) with an external stimulus such as a cardiac pacemaker. **2.** The drawing of a second fluid into a stream of gas or fluid by the Bernoulli effect.

entrance skin exposure SEE: under *exposure.*

entrapment (en-trap′mĕnt) In medicine, compression, as of a peripheral nerve or vessel.

entropion (ĕn-trō′pē-ŏn) [Gr. *en,* in, + *trepein,* to turn] An inversion or turning inward of an edge, esp. the margin of the lower eyelid. SYN: *enstrophe.*

cicatricial e. An inversion resulting from scar tissue on the inner surface of the lid.

spastic e. An inversion resulting from a spasm of the orbicularis oculi muscles.

entropy (ĕn′trŏ-pē) [Gr. *en,* in, + *trope,* a turning] **1.** The portion of energy within a system that cannot be used for mechanical work but is available for internal use. **2.** The quantity or degree of randomness, disorder, or chaos in a system.

entry **1.** The passage of extracellular chemicals or organisms into cells. **2.** The inputting of data into a computer, e.g., for recording or ordering drugs or treatments.

entry criterion SEE: under *criterion.*

enucleate (ē-nū′klē-āt) [L. *enucleare,* to remove the kernel of] **1.** To remove a part or a mass in its entirety. **2.** To destroy or take out the nucleus of a cell. **3.** To remove the eyeball surgically. **4.** To remove a cataract surgically.

enucleation (ē-nū″klē-ā′shŭn) Removal of the entire eyeball after cutting the extraocular muscles and optic nerve.

enucleator (ĕ-nū′klē-ā-tor) An instrument for evacuating tissue intact, such as the ocular globe.

enuresis (en″ū-rē′sĭs, ′sēz″) *pl.* **enureses** [Gr. *enourein,* to void urine] Involuntary discharge of urine after the age at which bladder control should have been established. In children, voluntary control of urination is usually present by 5 years of age. Nevertheless, nocturnal enuresis is present in about 10% of otherwise healthy 5-year-old children and in 1% of normal 15-year-old children. Enuresis is slightly more common in boys than in girls and occurs more frequently in first-born children. This condition has a distinct family tendency. SEE: *nocturnal e.; bladder drill.*

TREATMENT: When no organic disease is present, the use of imipramine as a temporary adjunct may be helpful. This is usually given in a dose of 10 to 50 mg orally at bedtime, but the effectiveness may decrease with continued administration. The bladder may be trained to hold larger amounts of urine. This procedure has decreased the occurrence rate of enuresis. No matter what the cause, the child should not be made to feel guilty or ashamed, and the family and the child should regard enuresis as they would any other condition that lends itself to appropriate therapy. If the child tries too hard to control the condition, it may worsen. Conditioning devices that sound an alarm when bed-wetting occurs should not be used unless prescribed by a health care professional familiar with the treatment of enuresis.

⚠️ Imipramine is not recommended for children under 6 years of age. Blood counts should be taken at least monthly during therapy to detect the possible onset of agranulocytosis.

diurnal e. Urinary incontinence during the day. Its cause is usually pathological. It may be caused by muscular contractions brought about by laughing, coughing, or crying. SEE: *stress urinary incontinence.*

It often persists for long periods, esp. after protracted illness. It occurs more commonly in women and girls.

monosymptomatic e. Isolated bed-wetting, without any daytime urinary signs or symptoms.

nocturnal e. Urinary incontinence during the night; bed-wetting. It is irregular and unaccompanied by urgency or frequency. It is more common in boys than in girls.

PATIENT CARE: The two primary approaches to bed-wetting are behavioral or drug-based. Fluid should be restricted late in the day, and daytime voidings should be spaced to try to build bladder control. The child may be awakened once or twice in the night and, when fully awake, robed and walked to the bathroom. Children who maintain a dry bed may be given rewards for continence. Alarm therapy may be used to awaken a sleeping child who wets his or her bed clothes. As improvement is noticed, the number of awakenings may be lessened. Desmopressin acetate (oral) at bedtime has been successful in preventing bed-wetting. Tricyclic antidepressant drugs, such as imipramine are also moderately effective, but their risk-benefit ratio limits their use. Adults who experience nocturnal enuresis should be evaluated for neurological disorders. SEE: *enuresis.*

nonmonosymptomatic e. Bed-wetting accompanied by urinary frequency, urinary incontinence, or urinary urgency during the day.

primary e. Enuresis in a child who has never been dependably continent.

secondary e. Enuresis in a child with no history of incontinence for 6 months or more.

envelope (ĕn'vĕ-lōp) A covering or container.

nuclear e. Two parallel membranes containing a narrow perinuclear space and enveloping the nucleus of a cell. SEE: *nuclear membrane.*

envenomation (ĕn-vĕn″ō-mā'shŭn) The

introduction of venoms into the body by means of a bite or sting.

environment (en-vī'rŏn-mĕnt, vī'ĕrn-) [Fr. *environ,* around] The surroundings, conditions, or influences that affect an organism or the cells within it.

built e. The physical structure of cities, homes, and workplaces. How humans interact with the structures they design and construct influences a variety of health concerns, including accessibility, childhood and geriatric safety, the likelihood of injuries or illnesses, the mental health of the population, and the quality of shared environmental resources, e.g., air and water.

hostile work e. Place of employment in which a reasonable person would find conditions that are abusive or intolerable. Prohibited conduct may take place repeatedly and may include physical intimidation; sexual harassment; or political, racial, religious, or sex-based discrimination.

least restrictive e. 1. An environment that enables an adult to function with as much choice and self-direction as safely appropriate. 2. An educational environment that enables a child to learn without constraining opportunities for normal interaction or social development.

neutral thermal e. In the care of newborn infants, maintenance of ambient temperatures in an incubator within 0.5° C of the newborn's body temperature, to avoid heat or cold stress, and to optimize energy use and oxygen consumption. SYN: *neutrothermal e.; thermoneutral e.*

neutrothermal e. Neutral thermal e.

protective e. 1. Any setting in which vulnerable people (such as adolescents, the elderly, or those with a history of mental illness or drug dependence) are cloistered for therapeutic reasons. 2. A room or unit in a hospital with positive atmospheric pressure relative to its surroundings.

thermoneutral e. Neutral thermal e.

virtual learning e. A form of computer-assisted education in which students participate in their studies by accessing recorded lectures, case-based tutorials, weblinks, audio and video clips, and e-mail, instead of gathering in a single geographically limited location for group lectures and laboratory study.

environmental control 1. In occupational health and safety, a design feature, e.g., in a hospital or workplace, that limits the risk of on-the-job injury. 2. In the practice of allergy and immunology, a process or design that limits the exposure of the patient to particular antigens.

environmental control unit ABBR: ECU. An electronic device that remotely controls home climate (e.g., heating, air conditioning), security (e.g., lighting, door locks, drapes), and communication devices (telephone, television). ECUs are often, but not exclusively, used by persons with functional limitations.

environmental health SEE: under *health*.

environmental interpretation syndrome, impaired Consistent lack of orientation to person, place, time, or circumstances over more than 3 to 6 months, necessitating a protective environment. SEE: *Nursing Diagnoses Appendix*.

environmental sleep disorder Sleep disturbances resulting from excessive noise, light, heat, cold, movements of one's bed partner, or unfamiliar surroundings (e.g., sleeping in hospitals, hotels, planes, trains).

envy Unhappiness about or the wish to possess qualities, physical attributes, or belongings of someone else.

enzootic (ĕn″zō-ŏt′ĭk) [Gr. *en*, in, + *zoon*, animal] An endemic disease limited to a small number of animals.

enzymatic, enzymic (en″zĭ-mat′ik, en-zī′mik) Pert. to an enzyme. **enzymatically** (en″zĭ-mat′ĭ-k(ă-)lē), *adv*. **enzymically** (en-zī′mi-k(ă-)lē), *adv*.

enzymatic cleaning, enzymatic cleansing Any method of disinfection that relies on biological catalysts to remove proteins or biofilms from an instrument to be used in the body, e.g., an endoscope, or a device that is placed on the body, e.g., a contact lens.

enzyme (en′zīm″) [Gr. *en*, in + *-zyme*] An organic catalyst produced by living cells but capable of acting outside cells or even in vitro. Most enzymes are proteins (some RNAs are enzymes) that change the rate of chemical reactions without needing an external energy source or being changed themselves; an enzyme may catalyze a reaction many times. Enzymes are reaction specific in that they act only on certain substances (called substrates). The enzyme and its substrate or substrates form a temporary configuration, called an enzyme-substrate complex, that involves both physical shape and chemical bonding. The enzyme promotes the formation of bonds between separate substrates, or induces the breaking of bonds in a single substrate to form the product or products of the reaction. The human body contains thousands of enzymes, each catalyzing one of the many reactions that take place as part of metabolism.

Each enzyme has an optimum temperature and pH at which it functions most efficiently. For most human enzymes, these would be body temperature and the pH of cells, tissue fluid, or blood. Enzyme activity can be impaired by extremes of temperature or pH, the presence of heavy metals (lead or mercury), dehydration, or ultraviolet radi-

ation. Some enzymes require coenzymes (nonprotein molecules such as vitamins) to function properly; still others require certain minerals (iron, copper, zinc). Certain enzymes are produced in an inactive form (a proenzyme) and must be activated (e.g., inactive pepsinogen is converted to active pepsin by the hydrochloric acid in gastric juice).

ACTION: Of the many human enzymes, the digestive enzymes are probably the most familiar. These are hydrolytic enzymes that catalyze the addition of water molecules to large food molecules to split them into simpler chemicals. Often the name of the enzyme indicates the substrate with the addition of the suffix *-ase*. A lipase splits fats to fatty acids and glycerol; a peptidase splits peptides to amino acids. Some enzymes such as pepsin and trypsin do not end in *-ase;* they were named before this method of nomenclature was instituted.

Enzymes are also needed for synthesis reactions. The synthesis of proteins, nucleic acids, phospholipids for cell membranes, hormones, and glycogen all require one if not many enzymes. DNA polymerase, for example, is needed for DNA replication, which precedes mitosis. Energy production also requires many enzymes. Each step in cell respiration (glycolysis, Krebs cycle, cytochrome transport system) requires a specific enzyme. Deaminases remove the amino groups from excess amino acids so that they may be used for energy. Long-chain fatty acids are split by enzymes into smaller compounds to be used in cell respiration. Blood clotting, the formation of angiotensin II to raise blood pressure, and the transport of carbon dioxide in the blood all require specific enzymes.

  activating e. An enzyme that catalyzes the attaching of an amino acid to the appropriate transfer ribonucleic acid.

  allosteric e. An enzyme whose activity can change when certain types of effectors, called allosteric effectors, bind to a nonactive site on the enzyme.

  amylolytic e. An enzyme that catalyzes the conversion of starch to sugar.

  angiotensin-converting e. ABBR: ACE. An enzyme normally found in the capillary endothelium throughout the vascular system. It converts angiotensin I (a part of the renin-angiotensin-aldosterone mechanism of the kidney) to angiotensin II, the final step in the renin-angiotensin mechanism. The latter stimulates aldosterone secretion and sodium retention.

  autolytic e. An enzyme that produces autolysis, or cell digestion.

  bacterial e. An enzyme produced by bacteria; many have specific, toxic effects on humans.

branching e. An enzyme, called a glycosyltransferase, that transfers a carbohydrate unit from one molecule to another.

brush border e. An enzyme produced by the cells of the villi and microvilli (brush border) lining the small intestine.

coagulating e. An enzyme that catalyzes the conversion of soluble proteins into insoluble ones. SYN: *coagulase*.

deamidizing e. An enzyme that splits amine off amino acid compounds.

debranching e. An enzyme, dextrin-1-6-glucosidase, that removes a carbohydrate unit from molecules that contain short carbohydrate units attached as side chains.

decarboxylating e. An enzyme, such as carboxylase, that separates carbon dioxide from organic acids.

digestive e. Any enzyme involved in digestive processes in the alimentary canal.

extracellular e. An enzyme that acts outside the cell that produces it.

fermenting e. An enzyme produced by bacteria or yeasts that brings about fermentation, esp. of carbohydrates.

glycolytic e. An enzyme that catalyzes the oxidation of glucose.

hydrolytic e. An enzyme that catalyzes hydrolysis.

inhibitory e. An enzyme that blocks a chemical reaction.

intracellular e. An enzyme that acts within the cell that produces it.

inverting e. An enzyme that catalyzes the hydrolysis of sucrose.

lipolytic e. An enzyme that catalyzes the hydrolysis of fats. SYN: *lipase*.

mucolytic e. An enzyme that depolymerizes mucus by splitting mucoproteins. Examples are lysozyme and hyaluronidase. SYN: *mucinase*.

oxidizing e. An enzyme that catalyzes oxidative reactions. SYN: *oxidase*.

proteolytic e. An enzyme that catalyzes the conversion of proteins into peptides.

redox e. An enzyme that catalyzes oxidation-reduction reactions.

reducing e. An enzyme that removes oxygen. SYN: *reductase*.

respiratory e. An enzyme, such as a cytochrome or a flavoprotein, that acts within tissue cells to catalyze oxidative reactions by releasing energy.

restriction e. Any of numerous bacterial enzymes that inactivate foreign DNA but do not interfere with the cell's DNA. This type of enzyme is used to cleave strands of DNA at specific sites. SEE: *restriction endonuclease*.

splitting e. An enzyme that facilitates removal of part of a molecule.

transferring e. An enzyme that facilitates the moving of one molecule to another compound. SYN: *transferase*.

uricolytic e. An enzyme that catalyzes the conversion of uric acid into urea.

yellow e. One of a group of flavoproteins involved in cellular oxidation.

Enzyme Commission ABBR: EC. An organization created in 1956 by the International Union of Biochemistry to standardize enzyme nomenclature.

enzyme immunoassay SEE: under *immunoassay*.

enzyme induction SEE: under *induction*.

enzyme-linked immunosorbent assay ABBR: ELISA. The former name for *enzyme immunoassay*.

enzyme modulator A chemical that modifies the allosteric binding site of an enzyme, changing its catalytic kinetics.

enzyme replacement therapy Administration of enzymes to patients with congenital or acquired enzyme deficiency diseases, e.g., oral pancreatic enzymes to patients with chronic pancreatitis, or infused enzymes to patients with genetic disorders in which a single enzyme is lacking, such as galactosidase to patients with Fabry disease.

enzymology (ĕn″zī-mŏl′ō-jē) The study of enzymes and their actions.

enzymolysis (ĕn-zī-mŏl′ĭ-sĭs) [Gr. *en*, in, + *zyme*, leaven, + *lysis*, dissolution] Chemical change or disintegration due to an enzyme.

enzymopathy (ĕn″zī-mŏp′ă-thē) Any disease involving an enzyme abnormality (can be due to sufficient quantities but defective structure, for example, 2° to mutation).

enzymopenia (ĕn-zī″mō-pē′nē-ă) Deficiency of an enzyme.

enzymuria (ĕn″zī-mū′rē-ă) [″ + ″ + *ouron*, urine] The presence of enzymes in the urine.

EO *Eosinophil;* (clinical laboratory).

EOM *extraocular muscles.*

eosin, eosine (ē′ŏ-sin, ē′ŏ-sēn″) [Gr. *ēōs*, dawn + *-in*] Any of several red dyes used in histology, often in conjunction with hematoxylin. It has an affinity for cytoplasm, which stains pink.

eosinopenia (ē″ŏ-sĭn-ō-pē′nē-ă) [″ + *penia*, poverty] An abnormally small number of eosinophilic cells in the peripheral blood.

eosinophil, eosinophile (ē″ŏ-sin′ŏ-fil, ē″ŏ-sin′ŏ-fīl″) [*eosin* + *-phile*] ABBR: EO. A white blood cell with a lobed nucleus and cytoplasmic granules that stain red with Wright's stain. Eosinophils make up 1% to 3% of the white cell count. They contribute to the destruction of parasites and to allergic reactions by releasing chemical mediators such as histamine. SYN: *acidophilic* **leukocyte;** *eosinophilic* **leukocyte.** SEE: *blood* for illus.; *leukocyte*.

eosinophil chemotactic factor SEE: under *factor*.

eosinophil colony-stimulating factor Interleukin-5.

eosinophil differentiation factor Interleukin-5.

eosinophilia (ē″ŏ-sin″ŏ-fil′ē-ă) [*eosin* + *-philia*] **1.** An unusually large number of eosinophils in the blood, usually in response to allergies, infections, or some forms of cancer. **2.** The characteristic of staining readily with eosin.

   urinary e. An abnormal amount of eosinophils in the urine, a finding that sometimes indicates an allergic interstitial nephritis.

eosinophilia-myalgia syndrome, tryptophan-induced Eosinophilia and severe muscle pain and joint stiffness seen in patients with a history of taking oral preparations of the amino acid L-tryptophan.

   SYMPTOMS: There is abrupt onset, within a week or so, of pain, edema, and induration of the extremities, esp. the legs. Skin involvement includes alopecia, transient rash, and subjective weakness. The disease is disabling and chronic. To establish the diagnosis, it is necessary to exclude other diseases (e.g., infections or neoplasia) that could cause these findings.

   TREATMENT: Treatment is supportive; tryptophan should be discontinued.

eosinophilic (ē″ŏ-sĭn-ŏ-fil′ĭk) Readily stainable with eosin.

eosinophilic pustular folliculitis ABBR: EPF. An itchy papular, plaquelike, or pustular rash of uncertain cause, often occurring on the face. It is found in patients of Asian descent, in those with HIV/AIDS, after exposure to some drugs, and after parasitic infestations. SYN: *Ofuji's disease*.

eosinophilous (ē″ŏ-sĭn-ŏf′ĭ-lŭs) [″ + *philein*, to love] **1.** Easily stainable with eosin. **2.** Having eosinophilia.

eosinotactic (ē″ŏ-sĭn-ō-tăk′tĭk) [″ + *taktikos*, arranged] Attracting or repulsing eosinophilic cells.

eotaxin (ē-ō-tŏks′ĭn) [Gr. *eos*, dawn (rose-colored) + (chemo)taxin] A chemokine that specifically attracts eosinophils to particular tissues (e.g., to bronchial tissues in asthma or to the skin in contact dermatitis). Tumor necrosis factor alpha stimulates its release. SEE: *chemotaxis; cytokine*.

EPAP *Expiratory positive airway* ***pressure***.

epaxial (ĕp-ăk′sē-ăl) [″ + L. *axis*, axis] Situated above or behind an axis.

EPEC Enteropathogenic *Escherichia coli.*

ependyma (ĕp-ĕn′dĭ-mă) [Gr. *ependyma*, an upper garment, wrap] The epithelial lining of the cerebral ventricles and the central canal of the spinal cord. The lining is composed of a single cell layer. Most of the cells have microvilli and motile cilia on their outer surface. SEE: illus. **ependymal**, *adj.*

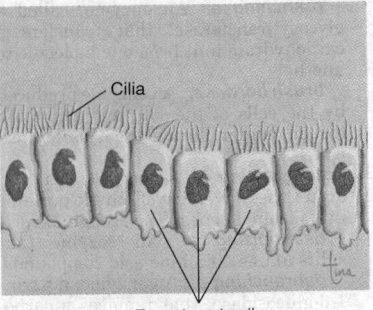

Cilia

Ependymal cells

EPENDYMA

ependymitis (ĕp″ĕn-dĭ-mī′tĭs) [″ + *itis*, inflammation] Inflammation of the ependyma.

ependymoblast (ĕp-ĕn′dĭ-mō-blăst) [″ + *blastos*, germ] An embryonic ependymal cell, or ependymocyte.

ependymocyte (ĕp-ĕn′dĭ-mō-sīt) [″ + *kytos*, cell] Ependymal cell.

ependymoma (ĕp-ĕn″dĭ-mō′mă) [″ + *oma*, tumor] A tumor arising from fetal inclusion of ependymal elements.

ephebiatrics (ĕ-fē-bē-ăt′rĭks) [Gr. *epi*, at, + *hebe*, youth, + *iatrikos*, healing] A branch of medicine dealing with adolescents.

ephedra (ĕf-ĕd′ră) An herbal remedy (*Ephedra sinica*) promoted as a dietary aid, energy booster, and asthma treatment. SYN: *ma huang.*

⚠ Its use has been associated in some patients with heart attack, stroke, arrhythmias, and emergency room visits for chest pain. The sale and use of ephedra has been banned in the U.S.

ephedrine (ĕ-fed′rĭn, ef′ĕ-drĭn) [*Ephedra*, a genus name + *-ine*] A synthetic sympathomimetic alkaloid originally obtained from species of *Ephedra*; first isolated in 1887. In ancient Chinese medicine it was used as a diaphoretic and antipyretic. Its action is similar to that of epinephrine. Its effects, although less powerful, are more prolonged, and it exerts action when given orally, whereas epinephrine is effective only by injection. Ephedrine dilates the bronchial muscles, contracts the nasal mucosa, and raises the blood pressure. It is used chiefly for its bronchodilating effect in asthma, and for its constricting effect on the nasal mucosa in hay fever.

   INCOMPATIBILITY: Calcium chloride, iodine, and tannic acid are incompatible with ephedrine.

⚠ Ephedrine and ephedra may produce hypertensive crises, myocar-

dial ischemia, and cardiac rhythm disturbances.

ephelis (ĕf-ē′lĭs) *pl.* **ephelides** [Gr.
ephelis, freckle] A freckle.

ephemeral (ĕ-fĕm′ĕr-ăl) [Gr. *epi*, on, +
hemera, day] Of brief duration.

e-PHI (ē′fī′) Confidential patient care
data that are transmitted or stored electronically.

epi-, ep- [Gr. *epi*, on, upon, towards] Prefixes meaning *upon, over, at, in addition
to, after.*

epiandrosterone (ĕp″ē-ăn-drŏs′tĕr-ōn)
An androgenic hormone normally present in the urine.

epiblast (ĕp′ĭ-blăst) [Gr. *epi*, upon, +
blastos, germ] The outer layer of cells
of the blastoderm. SYN: *ectoderm*. **epi-
blastic** (-blăst′ik), *adj.*

epiblepharon (ĕp″ĭ-blĕf′ă-rŏn) [″ + Gr.
blepharon, eyelid] A fold of skin that
passes across the margin of either the
upper or lower eyelid so that the eyelashes are pressed against the eye.

epibulbar (ĕp″ĭ-bŭl′băr) Lying on the
bulb of any structure; more specifically,
located on the eyeball.

epibulbar dermoid A benign whitish/
pink tumor of the eye. It is a hallmark
of Goldenhar sequence, a variant of
hemifacial microsomia.

epicanthus (ĕp″ĭ-kăn′thŭs) [Gr. *epi*,
upon, + *kanthos*, canthus] A vertical
fold of skin extending from the root of
the nose to the median end of the eyebrow, covering the inner canthus and
caruncle. It is a characteristic of certain
races and may occur as a congenital
anomaly in others.

epicardia (ĕp″ĭ-kărd′ē-ă) [″ + *kardia*,
heart] The abdominal portion of the
esophagus extending from the diaphragm to the stomach, about 2 cm in
length.

epicardium (ĕp″ĭ-kăr′dē-ŭm) The serous
membrane on the surface of the myocardium; the visceral layer of the pair of
serous pericardial membranes. The fat
that normally surrounds the heart is
just under the epicardium.

epichordal (ĕp″ĭ-kord′ăl) [″ + *khorde*,
cord] Located dorsad to the notochord.

epichorion (ĕp″ĭ-kō′rē-ŏn) [″ + *chorion*]
The portion of the endometrium that
covers the implanted early embryo.

epicondylalgia (ĕp″ĭ-kŏn-dĭ-lăl′jē-ă) [″
+ *kondylos*, condyle, + *algos*, pain]
Pain in the elbow joint in the region of
the epicondyles.

epicondyle (ĕp-ĭ-kŏn′dīl) [″ + *kondylos*, condyle] The eminence at the articular end of a bone above a condyle.

epicondylitis (ĕp″ĭ-kŏn″dĭ-lī′tĭs) [″ + ″
+ *itis*, inflammation] Inflammation of
the epicondyle of the humerus and surrounding tissues.

    lateral humeral e. **Tennis** elbow.

    medial humeral e. Tendonitis occur-

ring at the medial epicondyle. This injury is commonly seen as a result of
overuse of the elbow or repetitive wrist
flexion. SYN: *golfer's elbow*. SEE: *tennis
elbow.*

epicranium (ĕp″ĭ-krā′nē-ŭm) [″ +
kranion, cranium] The soft tissue covering the cranium.

epicranius (ĕp″ĭ-krā′nē-ŭs) The occipitofrontal muscle and scalp.

epicrisis (ĕp′ĭ-krī″sĭs) [″ + *krisis*, crisis]
A secondary turning point following the
initial critical stage of a disease.

epicritic (ĕp-ĭ-krĭt′ĭk) [Gr. *epikritikos*,
judging] **1.** Pert. to acute sensibility,
such as that of the skin when it discrim-
inates among degrees of sensation
caused by touch or temperature. **2.** Pert.
to an epicrisis. **3.** Something such as
pain or itching that is well localized.

epicutaneous (ep″ĭ-kū-tā′nē-ŭs) [*epi-* +
cutaneous] Located upon or applied to
the skin.

epicutaneous test In allergy testing, a
test administered by applying a patch or
plaster containing an antigen to the
skin or by pricking or scratching the
skin with an antigen-loaded needle,
scalpel, or other sharp object.

epicystotomy (ĕp″ĭ-sĭs-tŏt′ō-mē) [″ + ″
+ *tome*, incision] A surgically created
opening above the symphysis pubis into
the bladder.

epidemic (ep″ĭ-dem′ik) [*epi-* + Gr. *dēmos*, people] **1.** Pert. to a disease affecting an exceptionally high percentage of people in a community or larger
area at one time. SEE: *endemic; epizootic; pandemic*. **2.** Such a disease.

Epidemic Intelligence Service ABBR:
EIS. An epidemiology field training
program for postdoctoral fellows at the
Centers for Disease Control and Prevention. It provides epidemiological assistance in the investigation and prevention of public health problems and a
source of trained field epidemiologists
for federal, state, and local health departments around the U.S.

epidemiologist (ĕp″ĭ-dē-mē-ŏl′ō-jĭst) A
specialist in the field of epidemiology.

epidemiology (ep″ĭ-dē-mē-ol′ō-jē) [*epi-*
+ Gr. *dēmos*, people + *-logy*] The
study of the distribution and determinants of health-related states and
events in populations and the application of this study to the control of health
problems. Epidemiology is concerned
with the study of epidemic diseases
caused by infectious agents and with
health-related phenomena including accidents, suicide, climate, toxic agents
(e.g., lead, air pollution), and catastrophes due to ionizing radiation. SEE:
pharmacoepidemiology. **epidemiologic,
epidemiological** (ĕp″ĭ-dē-mē-ŏ-loj′ik,
ep″ĭ-dē-mē-ŏ-loj′ĭ-kăl), *adj.*

epidermal growth factor SEE: under *factor.*

epidermal nevus syndrome The association of multiple cutaneous abnormalities, including multiple nevi, hemangiomas, and/or skin cancers, with scattered skeletal, neurological, urological, ophthalmic, and vascular malformations. The syndrome is sometimes transmitted to offspring by autosomal dominant inheritance.

epidermatoplasty (ĕp″ĭ-dĕr-măt′ō-plăs-tē) [″ + ″ + plassein, to mold] A surgical procedure grafting pieces of epidermis with the underlying layer of the corium.

epidermis (ĕp″ĭ-dĕr′mĭs) [″ + derma, skin] The outermost layer of the skin. SEE: skin. **epidermal, epidermic,** adj.

epidermitis (ĕp″ĭ-dĕr-mī′tĭs) [″ + ″ + itis, inflammation] Inflammation of the superficial layers of the skin.

epidermization (ĕp″ĭ-dĕr″mĭ-zā′shŭn) **1.** Skin grafting. **2.** Conversion of the deeper germinative layer of cells into the outer layer of the epidermis.

epidermodysplasia verruciformis (ĕp″ĭ-dĕr″mō-dis-plā′z(hē-)ă) [epiderm(is) + dysplasia] ABBR: EV. A rare skin condition characterized by the eruption of multiple wartlike lesions on the skin, often in association with human papillomavirus (HPV) infection. The lesions of EV are sometimes confused with or insinuated into other skin lesions, such as seborrheic keratoses. EV often occurs in childhood as an autosomal recessive disease. Its expression is most severe in the immunocompromised. EV lesions sometimes transform into carcinomas.

epidermoid (ĕp″ĭ-dĕr′moyd) [Gr. epi, upon, + derma, skin, + eidos, form, shape] **1.** Resembling or pert. to the epidermis. **2.** A tumor arising from aberrant epidermal cells. SYN: cholesteatoma.

epidermolysis (ĕp″ĭ-dĕr-mol′ĭ-sĭs) [epidermis + -lysis] Loosening of the epidermis.

   e. bullosa One of several inherited forms of epidermolysis marked by blistering and erosion of the skin after chafing or rubbing.

epidermomycosis (ĕp-ĭ-dĕr″mō-mī-kō′sĭs) [″ + ″ + mykes, fungus, + osis, condition] A skin disease caused by a fungus.

Epidermophyton (ĕp″ĭ-dĕr-mŏf′ĭ-tŏn) [″ + ″ + phyton, plant] A genus of fungi, similar to Trichophyton but affecting the skin and nails instead of the hair.

   E. floccosum The causative agent of certain types of tinea, esp. tinea pedis (athlete's foot), tinea cruris, tinea unguium, and tinea corporis.

epidermophytosis (ĕp″ĭ-dĕr-mō-fī-tō′sĭs) [″ + ″ + ″ + osis, condition] Infection by a species of Epidermophyton.

epididymectomy (ĕp″ĭ-dĭd″ĭ-mĕk′tō-mē)

[″ + didymos, testis, + ektome, excision] Removal of the epididymis.

epididymis (ĕp″ĭ-dĭd′ĭ-mĭs) pl. **epididymides** A small oblong organ resting on and beside the posterior surface of a testis, consisting of a convoluted tube 13 to 20 ft (3.97 to 6.1 m) long, enveloped in the tunica vaginalis, ending in the ductus deferens. It consists of the head (caput or globus major), which contains 12 to 14 efferent ducts of the testis, the body, and the tail (cauda or globus minor). It is the first part of the secretory duct of each testis. The epididymis is supplied by the internal spermatic, deferential, and external spermatic arteries; it is drained by corresponding veins. SEE: illus.

epididymitis (ĕp″ĭ-dĭd″ĭ-mī′tĭs) [″ + didymos, testis, + itis, inflammation] Inflammation of the epididymis, usually as a result of infection, and rarely as a result of trauma or urinary reflux from the urethra. SEE: Nursing Diagnoses Appendix.

   ETIOLOGY: The causes of epididymitis are age- and activity-dependent. Children may have epididymal infection as a result of congenital malformations of the genitourinary tract. In sexually active young men, chlamydia and gonorrhea are the most common causes. Middle-aged and older men typically have infections caused by gram-negative urinary pathogens, such as Escherichia coli or other enteric bacteria. Syphilis, tuberculosis, mumps, and other microorganisms are also occasionally responsible for epididymal infection.

   SYMPTOMS: The primary symptom in adults is pain and mild to moderate tenderness, redness, and swelling in the scrotum that is usually localized to the superior pole of one of the testicles. Urethral discharge, fever, and chills are also common. In an attempt to protect the groin and scrotum while walking, the patient may walk with a waddling gait.

   DIAGNOSIS: Urinalysis, urine culture and sensitivity, gram staining of urethal discharge, and white blood cell count above 10,000 aid diagnosis. Scrotal ultrasonography helps to differentiate this condition from testicular torsion, which is a urological surgical emergency.

   TREATMENT: Treatment is aimed at combating the infection and reducing pain and swelling. Antibiotic therapy (such as a tetracycline for sexually active men) and nonsteroidal anti-inflammatory drugs (for pain and fever) are effective. Drug therapy usually begins to relieve symptoms in 2 or 3 days and eradicates infection in about a week.

   PATIENT CARE: The patient is encouraged to rest in bed with his legs

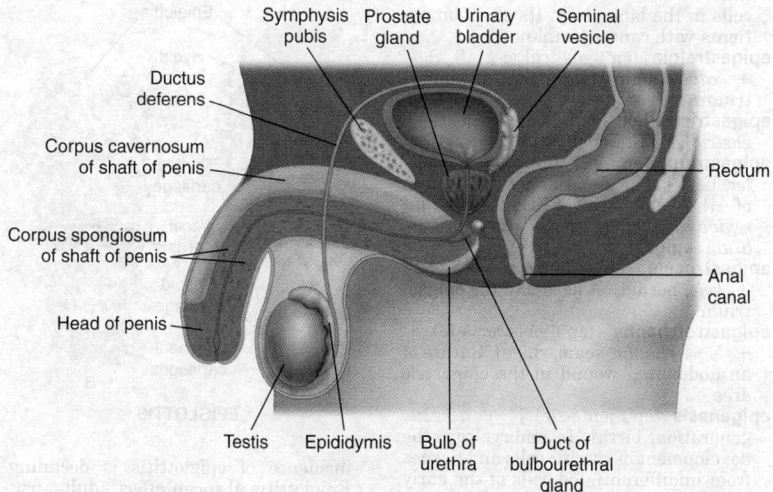

Symphysis pubis — Prostate gland — Urinary bladder — Seminal vesicle
Ductus deferens
Corpus cavernosum of shaft of penis
Rectum
Corpus spongiosum of shaft of penis
Anal canal
Head of penis
Testis — Epididymis — Bulb of urethra — Duct of bulbourethral gland

EPIDIDYMIS

slightly apart and with the testes elevated on a towel roll or adhesive strapping to promote venous return, reduce edema, and relieve pain. Local intermittent application of an ice bag also helps to relieve pain and swelling. Heat is contraindicated, as it may cause damage to germinal cells. The patient should wear nonconstrictive, lightweight clothing until the swelling subsides. Straining at stool is minimized through the use of stool softeners. The patient should wear a scrotal support when he sits, stands, or walks. Lifting more than 20 pounds is discouraged. The patient is observed for signs of abscess formation (a localized hot, red, tender area) or extension of the infection into the testes. The importance of adhering to the prescribed antibiotic regimen for the full course of therapy is emphasized.

If epididymitis is secondary to a sexually transmitted disease, the patient is educated regarding preventing transmission, encouraged to use a condom during sexual intercourse, and to notify sexual partners so that they can be treated for the infection. The patient should abstain from sexual activity until he and his partner have completed treatment regimens and follow-up cultures are negative.

epididymodeferentectomy (ĕp″ĭ-dĭd″ĭ-mō-dĕf″ĕr-ĕn-tĕk′tō-mē) [″ + ″ + L. *deferens,* carrying away, + Gr. *ektome,* excision] Excision of the epididymis and ductus deferens.

epididymodeferential (ĕp″ĭ-dĭd″ĭ-mō-dĕf″ĕr-ĕn′shăl) Concerning both the epididymis and ductus deferens.

epididymography (ĕp″ĭ-dĭd″ĭ-mŏg′ră-fē) [″ + ″ + *graphein,* to write] Radi-

ography of the epididymis after the introduction of a contrast medium.

epididymo-orchitis (ĕp″ĭ-dĭd″ĭm-ō-or-kī′tĭs) [″ + *didymos,* testis, + *orchis,* testis, + *itis,* inflammation] Epididymitis with orchitis.

epididymotomy (ĕp″ĭ-dĭd″ĭ-mŏt′ō-mē) [″ + ″ + *tome,* incision] An incision into the epididymis.

epididymovasostomy (ĕp-ĭ-dĭd″ĭ-mō-văs-ŏs′tō-mē) [″ + ″ + L. *vas,* vessel, + Gr. *stoma,* mouth] A surgical anastomosis between the epididymis and the vas.

epididymovesiculography (ĕp″ĭ-dĭd″ĭ-mō-vĕ-sĭk″ū-lŏg′ră-fē) Radiography of the epididymis and seminal vesicle after introduction of a contrast medium.

epidural (ep″ĭ-door′ăl, -dūr′) [*epi-* + *dura (mater)* + *-al*] **1.** Located over or on the dura. **2.** An injection of anesthetic into the peridural space to produce epidural anesthesia.

epidurogram (ĕp″ĭ-dūr′ō-grăm) A spinal x-ray examination that uses injected contrast to provide an outline of compressed nerve roots. This study is sometimes used in the evaluation of back pain.

epiduroscopy (ep″ĭ-door-os′kŏ-pē, -dūr-) [*epidur(al)* + *-scopy*] The insertion of a fiber-optic scope into the epidural space that surrounds the spinal cord to diagnose and treat chronic back pain.

epifolliculitis (ĕp″ĭ-fŏl-lĭk″ū-lī′tĭs) [″ + L. *folliculus,* follicle, + Gr. *itis,* inflammation] Inflammation of the hair follicles of the scalp.

epigallocatechin gallate (ĕp″ĭ-găl′ō-kăt-ĕ-chĭn găl′lăt) ABBR: EGCg, EGCG. A polyphenol compound present in green tea that inhibits the growth of cancer cells in the laboratory. Its effect on patients with cancer is unknown.

epigastralgia (ĕp″ĭ-găs-trăl′jē-ă) [″ + ″ + *algos*, pain] Pain in the epigastrium.

epigastric reflex (ep″ĭ-gas′trĭk) [*epi-* + *gastric*] SEE: under *reflex*.

epigastrium (ĕp″ĭ-găs′trē-ŭm) [″ + *gaster*, belly] The superior central portion of the abdomen. SEE: *abdominal regions; Auenbrugger's sign; precordium*. **epigastric** (-găs′trĭk), *adj*.

epigastrocele (ĕp″ĭ-găs′trō-sēl) [″ + ″ + *kele*, hernia] A hernia in the epigastrium.

epigastrorrhaphy (ĕp″ĭ-găs-tror′ă-fē) [″ + ″ + *rhaphe*, seam, ridge] Suture of an abdominal wound in the epigastric area.

epigenesis (ĕp″ĭ-jĕn′ĕ-sĭs) [″ + *genesis*, generation, birth] In embryology, the development of specific cells and tissues from undifferentiated cells of the early embryo.

epigenetic (ep″ĭ-jĕ-net′ik) [*epi-* + *genetic*] Pert. to changes in the way genes are expressed by a cell or an organism; altering the phenotype without changing the genotype.

epigenetics (ĕp″ĭ-jĕ-nĕt′ĭks) Changes in the way genes are expressed that occur without changes in the sequence of nucleic acids. In mammals the most common form of epigenetic change results from methylation (the addition of methyl [-CH3] moieties) to the promoter regions of genes. Although epigenetic changes do not alter the sequence of nucleotides, they are inheritable.

epiglottidectomy (ĕp″ĭ-glŏt″ĭd-ĕk′tō-mē) [″ + ″ + *ektome*, excision] Excision of the epiglottis.

epiglottiditis (ĕp″glŏt-ĭd-īt′ĭs) Epiglottitis.

epiglottis (ĕp″ĭ-glŏt′ĭs) *pl*. **epiglottides** [Gr.] The uppermost cartilage of the larynx, located immediately posterior to the root of the tongue. It covers the entrance of the larynx when the individual swallows, thus preventing food or liquids from entering the airway. **epiglottidean** (-glō-tĭd′ē-ăn), *adj*. SEE: illus.

epiglottitis (ĕp″ĭ-glŏt-ī′tĭs) [″ + *itis*, inflammation] Inflammation of the epiglottis as the result of infection. The severe swelling above the epiglottis may obstruct air flow and can cause death. Epiglottitis is an emergency and must be treated immediately. SYN: *epiglottiditis; supraglottitis*. SEE: *croup; laryngotracheobronchitis*.

ETIOLOGY: It usually occurs in children, esp. from ages 2 to 5, as a result of infection with bacteria such as *Haemophilus influenzae*, Type B (Hib), streptococci, and staphylococci. Since most children born in the U.S. are immunized against Hib (which previously was the primary causative agent) the

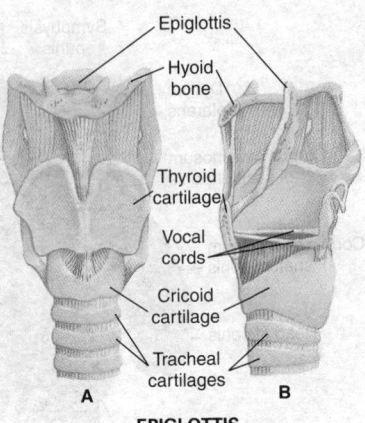

Epiglottis
Hyoid bone
Thyroid cartilage
Vocal cords
Cricoid cartilage
Tracheal cartilages
A   B

EPIGLOTTIS

incidence of epiglottitis is declining. Epiglottitis also can affect adults, usually resulting from group A streptococcal infection.

SYMPTOMS: Children abruptly develop a sore throat, dysphagia, and high fever, usually at night. They are agitated and frightened and want to sit in a tripod position (upright, leaning forward, mouth open). Drooling, muffled voice, dyspnea with substernal and suprasternal retractions, and stridor are common. Severe respiratory distress and cyanosis may develop suddenly. Unlike children with croup, those with epiglottitis have no cough or hoarseness.

TREATMENT: Epiglottitis is treated with intravenous second- or third-generation cephalosporins, or ampicillin with sulbactam. A specialist in otorhinolaryngology or critical care medicine may need to provide an artificial airway, mechanical ventilation, and care in a pediatric critical care facility. Intubation is continued until epiglottal swelling has decreased. Blood and throat cultures are obtained to support the antibiotic treatment choice, and IV fluid and sedation are provided while the child is intubated. Close observation is essential even after antibiotic therapy begins. Corticosteroids may be given prior to extubation to decrease laryngeal swelling. If a child with epiglottitis is observed but not intubated, a tracheostomy set should be kept nearby for 24 to 48 hr, in the event of complete airway occlusion. If siblings have not been immunized, they should be given antibiotic prophylaxis and immunized as soon as possible.

epilate (ĕp′ĭ-lāt) [L. *e*, out, + *pilus*, hair] To extract the hair by the roots.

epilating (ĕp″ĭ-lāt′ĭng) Depilating; extracting a hair.

epilation (ĕp-ĭ-lā′shŭn) **1.** Extraction of hair. SYN: *depilation; electrolysis*.

2. Loss of hair due to exposure to ionizing radiation.

epilemma (ĕp-ĭ-lĕm′ă) [Gr. *epi*, upon, + *lemma*, husk] The neurilemma of small branches of nerve filaments.

epilepsy (ep′ĭ-lep′sē) [L. *epilepsia* fr. Gr. *epilēpsia*, (epileptic) seizure] A disease marked by recurrent seizures, i.e., by repetitive abnormal electrical discharges within the brain. Epilepsy is found in about 2% or 3% of the population. Its incidence is highest in children under 10 and in the elderly (over 70); adolescents and adults are affected less frequently.

The International League Against Epilepsy categorizes epilepsy as partial, generalized, drug-resistant, or unclassified. Partial seizures typically begin with focal or local discharges in one part of the brain (and body); sometimes they may become generalized. When a patient remains awake during a seizure, the seizure is said to be simple and partial. If loss of consciousness occurs after a focal seizure, the seizure is said to be partial and complex. Drug-resistant epilepsy is a failure to control seizures despite adequate trials of two appropriately chosen and dosed antiepileptic drugs.

Patients who suffer recurrent episodes of alcohol withdrawal or frequent severe hypoglycemia, hypercalcemia, or similar metabolic illnesses may have repetitive seizures but are not considered to have epilepsy if the seizures stop after their underlying illnesses are treated.

ETIOLOGY: Epilepsy may result from congenital or acquired brain disease. Infants born with lipid storage diseases, tuberous sclerosis, or cortical dysplasia, e.g., may have recurrent seizures, as may children born with intracranial hemorrhage or anoxic brain injury. Adults may develop epilepsy as a result of strokes, tumors, abscesses, brain trauma, encephalitis, meningitis, uremia, or other illnesses. In many instances the underlying cause is undetermined.

SYMPTOMS: Symptoms may vary from the almost imperceptible alteration in consciousness, as in absence seizures, to dramatic loss of consciousness, tonic-clonic convulsions of all extremities, urinary and fecal incontinence, and amnesia for the event. Some attacks are preceded by an aura; others provide no warning. Other forms are limited to muscular contractions of a localized area or only one side of the body. SEE: *postical* **confusion**.

DIAGNOSIS: The diagnosis of epilepsy is made by a careful assessment of the patient's history, augmented by diagnostic studies. Typically, these include blood tests to assess for metabolic disarray, brain imaging using magnetic resonance imaging or computed tomography, and electroencephalography. The differential diagnosis of epilepsy includes many other illnesses marked by episodes of loss of consciousness, including pseudoseizures, syncope, transient ischemic attacks, orthostatic hypotension, and narcolepsy.

TREATMENT: Therapy is available for the prevention and control of recurrent seizures. Antiepileptic agents include phenytoin or carbamazepine for partial seizures, valproic acid for absence seizures, and any of these agents or phenobarbital, with or without newer drugs, e.g., gabapentin or lamotrigine, for generalized seizures. All these agents may have significant side effects, and many of them have a range of drug-drug interactions.

Surgical therapy to remove an epileptic focus within the brain is used occasionally to manage seizures that have been difficult to control medically. In specialized neurosurgical centers, this may cure or reduce the impact of epilepsy in about 75% of patients.

   benign partial e. of childhood Benign rolandic **e.**

   benign rolandic e. Repetitive seizures usually perceived as facial or oral movements or paresthesias, typically affecting children at night. The seizures sometimes generalize (cause tonic/clonic convulsions). Affected children usually outgrow the disease by the end of adolescence. SYN: *benign partial e. of childhood.*

   catamenial e. Menstrual **e.**

   familial myoclonic e. Lafora disease.

   intractible e. Epilepsy that cannot be controlled by two or more anticonvulsant drugs. SYN: *medically intractable e.*

   juvenile myoclonic e. A form of epilepsy typically noticed in teenagers, characterized by early morning jerking movements of the extremities, and during stress or sleep deprivation, generalized tonic/clonic or absence seizures. SYN: *Janz syndrome.*

   Lennox-Gastaut syndrome e. SEE: *Lennox-Gastaut syndrome.*

   medically intractable e. Intractible **e.**

   menstrual e. Seizures that occur preferentially during particular portions of the menstrual cycle, e.g., during ovulation or menses. SYN: *catamenial e.*

   musicogenic e. Epilepsy in which the convulsive attacks are induced by music.

   photogenic e. Epilepsy that occurs as a result of intermittent light stimulus.

   psychomotor e. Temporal lobe **e.**

   reflex e. Recurrent epileptic seizures

that occur in reaction to a specific stimulus, e.g., photic stimulation while looking at flashing lights or television, auditory stimulation while listening to specific musical compositions, tactile stimulation, or reading.

refractory e. Epilepsy that cannot be controlled with two anticonvulsant drugs. Refractory epilepsy is found in about a third of all patients who have seizures.

sensory e. Disturbances of sensation without convulsions.

severe myoclonic e. of infancy Dravet syndrome.

sleep e. A term formerly and improperly used for narcolepsy.

temporal lobe e. Epilepsy originating in a temporal lobe of the brain. SEE: *psychomotor e.*

SYMPTOMS: Temporal lobe seizures produce one of two typical findings: (1) complex partial seizures (loss of consciousness with abnormal gesturing or automatic movements); and (2) simple partial seizures (preserved consciousness with the sense of unusual smell, taste, thought, or altered body function)

TREATMENT: Surgery to remove the irritable focus in the brain appears more effective than treatment with anticonvulsant drugs.

traumatic e. Epilepsy caused by trauma to the brain.

vasomotor e. Epilepsy with vasomotor changes in the skin.

epileptic (ĕp″ĭ-lĕp′tĭk) [Gr. *epileptikos*] **1.** Concerning epilepsy. **2.** An individual suffering from attacks of epilepsy.

epileptiform (ĕp″ĭ-lĕp′tĭ-form) [Gr. *epilepsia*, to seize, + L. *forma*, form] Having the form or appearance of epilepsy.

epileptogenic, epileptogenous (ep″ĭ-lep-tŏ-jen′ĭk, ep″ĭ-lep-toj′ĕ-nŭs) [″ + *gennan*, to produce] Predisposed to or giving rise to seizures. SEE: table.

epileptoid (ĕp″ĭ-lĕp′toyd) [″ + *eidos*, form, shape] Resembling epilepsy. SEE: *epileptiform.*

epileptologist (ĕp″ĭ-lĕp-tŏl′ŏ-jĭst) [Gr. *epilepsia*, seizure, + *logos*, word, reason] A specialist in the diagnosis and treatment of seizures.

epileptology (ĕp″ĭ-lĕp-tŏl′ŏ-jē) [″ + *logos*, word, reason] The study of epilepsy.

epiloia (ĕp″ĭ-lŏy′ă) Tuberous sclerosis.

epimandibular (ĕp″ĭ-măn-dĭb′ū-lăr) [Gr. *epi*, upon, above, + L. *mandibulum*, jaw] Located on the lower jaw.

epimer (ĕp′ĭ-mĕr) One of a pair of isomers that differ only in the position of the hydrogen atom and the hydroxyl group attached to one asymmetrical carbon atom.

epimerite (ĕp″ĭ-mĕr′ĭt) [″ + *meros*, part] An organelle of certain protozoa by which they attach themselves to epithelial cells.

epimorphosis (ĕp″ĭ-mor′fŏ-sĭs) [″ + *morphoun*, to give shape, + *osis*, condition] Regeneration of a part of an organism by growth at the cut surface.

epimysium (ĕp″ĭ-mĭz′ē-ŭm) [″ + *mys*, muscle] The outermost sheath of connective tissue that surrounds a skeletal muscle. It consists of irregularly distributed collagenous, reticular, and elastic fibers; connective tissue cells; and fat cells.

epinephrine (ep″ĭ-nef′rin) [*epi-* + *nephr-*

Common Causes of Seizures

Cause	Examples
Degenerative brain diseases	Alzheimer's dementia, amyloidosis, and amyloid angiopathy
Developmental brain defects	Cortical dysgenesis and vascular malformations of the brain
Drug overdose	Antihistamines, cholinesterase inhibitors, cocaine, methylxanthines, muscarinic agonists, and tricyclic antidepressants
Drug withdrawal	Alcohol; benzodiazepines
Electrolyte disorders	Profound hyponatremia, hypernatremia, hypoglycemia, and hypomagnesemia
Head trauma	Accidental or athletic injuries; complications of childbirth
Hyperthermia	Heatstroke; febrile seizures in childhood
Inborn errors of metabolism	Phenylketonuria
Infections	Brain abscesses; encephalitis; meningitis (bacterial or viral); parasitic infestations (neurocysticercosis)
Pregnancy complications	Eclampsia
Stroke	Embolic, hemorrhagic, or ischemic cerebrovascular accidents
Tumors	Metastatic cancers or primary brain tumors (astrocytoma and glioblastoma)

+ *-in*] $C_9H_{13}NO_3$; a catecholamine produced by the adrenal gland, secreted
when the sympathetic nervous system
is stimulated. In the physiological response to stress, it is responsible for
maintaining blood pressure and cardiac
output, keeping airways open wide, and
raising blood sugar levels. All these
functions are useful to frightened, traumatized, injured, or sick humans and
animals. The therapeutic uses of epinephrine are diverse. As one of the key
agents used in advanced cardiac life
support, it is helpful in treating asystole, ventricular arrhythmias, and other
forms of cardiac arrest. It counteracts
the effects of systemic allergic reactions
and is an effective bronchodilator. It
helps control local hemorrhage by constricting blood vessels; because of this
action, it prolongs the effects of local anesthesia. SEE: *catecholamine*.
   INCOMPATIBILITY: Epinephrine is
incompatible with light, heat, air, iron
salts, and alkalies. SYN: *adrenaline*.
   racemic e. A mixture of dextro and
levo-isomers of epinephrine that, when
nebulized, can be used in the treatment
of croup and bronchiolitis. The drug is
usually given with parenteral dexamethasone.

⚠ Some infants and children who initially respond to this treatment will
relapse. Patients treated with racemic epinephrine should be observed for several
hours to determine if they should be admitted to the hospital or are stable enough
for discharge to home.

epinephritis (ĕp″ĭ-nĕf-rī′tĭs) [″ + *nephros,* kidney, + *itis,* inflammation] Inflammation of an adrenal gland.
epineural (ĕp″ĭ-nū′răl) [″ + *neuron,*
nerve] Located on a neural arch of a
vertebra.
epineurium (ĕp″ĭ-nū′rē-ŭm) The connective tissue sheath of a nerve. SEE:
nerve.
epiotic (ĕp″ē-ŏt′ĭk) [″ + *ous,* ear] Located above the ear.
epipastic (ĕp″ĭ-păs′tĭk) [″ + *passein,* to
sprinkle] Resembling a dusting pow-
der.
epipharynx (ĕp″ĭ-făr′ĭnks) [″ + *pharynx,* throat] Nasopharynx.
epiphenomenon (ĕp″ĭ-fĕ-nŏm′ĕ-nŏn) [″
+ *phainomenon,* phenomenon] An exceptional symptom or occurrence in a
disease that is not related to the usual
course of the disease.
epiphora (ĕ-pĭf′ō-ră) [Gr., downpour]
An abnormal overflow of tears down the
cheek due to excess secretion of tears or
obstruction of the lacrimal duct.
epiphyseolysis (ĕp″ĭ-fĭz″ē-ŏl′ĭ-sĭs) [″ +
″ + *lysis,* dissolution] Separation of

an epiphysis. Also spelled *epiphysi-
olysis.*
epiphyseopathy (ĕp″ĭ-fĭz-ē-ŏp′ă-thē) [″
+ ″ + *pathos,* disease, suffering]
1. Any disease of the pineal gland.
2. Any disease of the epiphysis of a bone.
Also spelled *epiphysiopathy.*
epiphysiodesis (ĕ-pē-fĭz″ē-ō-dē′sĭs) [″ +
Gr. *dein,* to bind] The scraping and surgical obliteration of the growth plate of
a bone.
epiphysis (ĕ-pĭf′ĭ-sĭs) *pl.* **epiphyses** [Gr.,
a growing upon] **1.** In the developing
infant and child, a secondary bone-forming (ossification) center separated from
a parent bone in early life by cartilage.
As growth proceeds (at a different time
for each epiphysis), it becomes a part of
the larger, or parent, bone. It is possible
to judge the biological age of a child from
the development of these ossification
centers as shown radiographically. **2.** A
center for ossification at each extremity
of long bones. SEE: *diaphysis.* **3.** The
end of a long bone. **epiphyseal, epiphys-
ial** (ĕp″ĭ-fĭz′ē-ăl), *adj.*
epiphysitis (ĕ-pĭf″ĭ-sī′tĭs) [″ + *itis,* in-
flammation] Inflammation of an epiphysis, esp. that at the hip, knee, or shoulder in an infant.
epiplocele (ĕ-pĭp′lō-sēl) [Gr. *epiploon,*
omentum, + *kele,* tumor, swelling] A
hernia containing omentum.
epiploenterocele (ĕ-pĭp″lō-ĕn′tĕr-ō-sēl)
[″ + *enteron,* intestine, + *kele,* tumor, swelling] A hernia consisting of
omentum and intestine.
epiploic (ĕp″ĭ-plō′ĭk) [Gr. *epiploon,*
omentum] Pert. to the omentum.
epiploitis (ĕ-pĭp″lō-ī′tĭs) [″ + *itis,* in-
flammation] Inflammation of the
omentum.
epiplomerocele (ĕ-pĭp″lō-mē′rō-sēl) [″
+ *meros,* thigh, + *kele,* tumor, swell-
ing] A femoral hernia containing omentum.
epiplomphalocele (ĕ-pĭp″lŏm-făl′ō-sēl) [″
+ *omphalos,* navel, + *kele,* hernia]
An umbilical hernia with omentum protruding.
epiploon (ĕ-pĭp′lō-ŏn) [Gr., omentum]
The omentum, esp. the greater omentum. SYN: *omentum.*
epiplopexy (ĕ-pĭp′lō-pĕks″ē) [″ + *pexis,*
fixation] Suturing of omentum to the
anterior abdominal wall.
epiplosarcomphalocele (ĕ-pĭp″lō-săr″kŏm-
făl′ō-sēl) [″ + *sarx,* flesh, + *omphalos,* navel, + *kele,* tumor, swelling] An
umbilical hernia with omentum protruding. SYN: *epiplomphalocele.*
epiploscheocele (ĕ-pĭp″lŏs-kē′ō-sēl) [″
+ *oscheon,* scrotum, + *kele,* tumor,
swelling] An omental hernia into the
scrotum.
epiretinal (ĕ″pĭ-rĕt′ĭn-ĭl) [Gr. *on, over,* +
L. *rete,* net] On the surface of the retina.

episclera (ĕp″ĭ-sklē′ră) [″ + *skleros,* hard] The outermost superficial layer of the sclera of the eye.

episcleral (ĕp″ĭ-sklē′răl) **1.** Pert. to the episclera. **2.** Overlying the sclera of the eye.

episcleritis (ĕp″ĭ-sklē-rī′tĭs) [″ + *skleros,* hard, + *itis,* inflammation] Inflammation of the subconjunctival layers of the sclera.

episio- [Gr. *episeion, epision,* the pubic region] Prefix meaning *loins, perineum,* or *vulva.*

episioperineoplasty (i-piz″ē-ō-per″ĭ-nē′ō-plas″tē) [*episio-* + *perineo-* + *-plasty*] Plastic surgery of the perineum and vulva.

episioperineorrhaphy (i-piz″ē-ō-per″ĭ-nē-or′ă-fē) [*episio-* + *perineo-* + *-rrhaphy*] Repair of a lacerated perineum and vulva or repair of a surgical incision of the vulva and perineum.

PATIENT CARE: The perineum is inspected at intervals to assess healing and to observe for indications of formation of hematomas or of infection. Throughout hospitalization, general patient care concerns apply. Perineal care is provided as needed, and the patient is taught correct perineal hygiene (wiping from front to back). To relieve pain, anesthetic sprays or creams are applied as prescribed. Other pain relief measures include local heat using a heat lamp, warm soaks, or sitz baths as prescribed. The patient is taught to apply these therapies.

episioplasty (i-piz′ē-ŏ-plas″tē) [*episio-* + *-plasty*] Plastic surgery of the vulva.

episiostenosis (i-piz″ē-ō-stĕ-nō′sĭs) [*episio-* + *stenosis*] Narrowing of the vulvar opening.

episiotomy (i-piz″ē-ot′ŏ-mē, -pēz″) [*episio-* + *-tomy*] Incision of the perineum at the end of the second stage of labor to avoid spontaneous laceration of the perineum and to facilitate delivery. In the U.S. episiotomy is done in about 40% of all vaginal deliveries, making the procedure one of the most common forms of surgery performed on women. Perineal massage in the weeks before delivery can reduce the use of episiotomy.

episode (ep′ĭ-sōd″) [Gr. *epeisodion,* addition, episode] One occurrence in a sequence of events. **episodic** (ep″ĭ-sod′ik), *adj.*

episode of care A discrete unit of health care, from the first time a patient comes to a practitioner for help in managing a problem, until the services provided for that condition come to an end.

episodic dyscontrol A personality disorder marked by episodes of impulsive aggressiveness disproportionate to precipitating events. Intermittent explosive disorder is a pattern of behavior that

may result in serious assaults or destruction of property. SEE: *amok* (1).

In recent years the disorder has gained media attention after several instances of aggressive, violent, or homicidal behavior by previously normal high school students resulted in the deaths of classmates, teachers, or family members. The disorder is more common in young men than in women. It is only diagnosable when other causes of violent behavior (such as conduct disorder, cognitive impairment, delirium, hallucinations) or other psychiatric illnesses have been excluded. SYN: *intermittent explosive disorder.*

episome (ĕp′ĭ-sōm) Plasmid.

epispadias (ep″ĭ-spā′dē-ăs) [*epi-* + Gr. *spadōn,* a eunuch] **1.** A congenital opening of the urethra on the dorsum of the penis. **2.** An opening caused by separation of the labia minora and a fissure of the clitoris. SYN: *anaspadias.*

episplenitis (ĕp″ĭ-splē-nī′tĭs) [″ + *splen,* spleen, + *itis,* inflammation] Inflammation of the splenic capsule.

epistasis (ĕ-pis′tă-sĭs) [Gr. *epistasis,* stoppage] **1.** In genetics, the interference or suppression in the expression of one gene by another. **2.** The suppression of any discharge. SEE: *hypostasis.*

epistaxis (ĕp″ĭ-stăk′sĭs) [Gr.] Hemorrhage from the nose; nosebleed. SEE: *Kiesselbach's area.*

ETIOLOGY: Epistaxis may occur spontaneously or secondary to local infections (vestibulitis, rhinitis, sinusitis), systemic infections (scarlet fever, typhoid), drying of nasal mucous membranes, trauma (including picking the nose), chemical inhalation (esp. tobacco smoke), tumors of the paranasal sinus or nasopharynx, septal perforation, arteriosclerosis, hypertension, and bleeding tendencies associated with anticoagulant drug use, anemia, antiplatelet agents (aspirin, nonsteroidal anti-inflammatory drugs), leukemia, hemophilia, thrombocytopenia, or liver disease.

TREATMENT: Epistaxis from the anterior nasal septum is usually mild and easily controlled with firm continuous pressure on the nose and nasal septum for five to ten minutes; bleeding from the posterior nasal cavity cannot usually be controlled with first aid measures at home, often drips into the throat or larynx, and requires professional management. Any bleeding that lasts more than 10 min despite firmly applied pressure to the bleeding source should receive professional care.

In the emergency room, the patient should lean forward slightly and expectorate to avoid swallowing blood and becoming nauseated, and breathe through the mouth while the pressure is maintained for an additional 5 min. Vital signs, a complete blood count, bleeding time, coagulation studies, and type and crossmatch are obtained. Patients who are bleeding vigorously, or those who are hypotensive require intravenous access and fluids. The anterior nasal cavity is examined with a nasal speculum to identify anterior bleeding. Anesthetic/vasoconstricting drugs such as topical cocaine or epinephrine are applied to shrink blood vessels. Cauterization using a silver nitrate stick, electrocautery or petroleum gauze nasal packing may be used for anterior bleeding if a bleeding site is clearly identified. The patient should then lie quietly, propped up at a 45° angle in bed and limit talking. Oral hygiene is provided to remove the taste of blood. The patient and family should be reassured that epistaxis usually looks much worse than it actually is. SEE: *nosebleed* for illus.

If the bleeding is in the posterior nasal cavity or bleeding from the anterior nasal cavity cannot be controlled, nasal packing, nasal sponges, or inflatable balloons are inserted to tamponade the responsible blood vessels.

PATIENT CARE: Airway clearance and level of discomfort and anxiety are determined. The patient is assured that he or she may breathe through the mouth, with oxygen administered by mask if oximetry demonstrates a need. Antibiotics are typically prescribed if packing is to remain more than 24 hr. Vitamin K or frozen plasma may be used in cases of over-anticoagulation or bleeding disorders. If an artery is bleeding, surgical ligation or embolization and blood transfusion may be required.

After emergent care, the patient should avoid blowing or picking at the nose, removing nasal packing, or bending or lifting weights of more than 5 lb. until the site has healed. All procedures and expected sensations and outcomes are explained to the patient and caregivers. The need for follow-up, usually with an otorhinolaryngologist, to remove packing and inspect the nasal cavity is stressed. Future bleeding episodes may sometimes be prevented by controlling hypertension, carefully monitoring anticoagulation, humidifying ambient air, or avoiding digital trauma to the nose. The patient is shown how to apply anterior pressure to the nostrils to control anterior hemorrhage.

apple packer's e. Nosebleed due to handling packing trays containing certain dyes.

episternum (ĕp″ĭ-stĕr′nŭm) Manubrium. **episternal** (ĕp″ĭ-stĕr′năl), *adj.*

epitenon (ĕp″ĭ-ten′ŏn) [*epi-* + Gr *tenōn*, tendon] The fibrous sheath enveloping a tendon.

epithalamus (ĕp″ĭ-thăl′ă-mŭs) [″ + *thalamos*, chamber] The uppermost portion of the diencephalon of the brain. It includes the pineal body, trigonum habenulae, habenula, and habenular commissure.

epithelia (ĕp″ĭ-thē′lē-ă) Pl. of *epithelium*.

epithelialization (ĕp″ĭ-thē″lē-ăl-ĭ-zā′shŭn) The growth of skin over a wound.

epithelial tissue Epithelium.

epitheliitis (ĕp″ĭ-thē″lē-ī′tĭs) Overgrowth and inflammation of the mucosal epithelium following injury such as is caused by ionizing radiation.

epithelioblastoma (ĕp″ĭ-thē″lē-ō-blăs-tō′mă) [″ + *thele*, nipple, + *blastos*, germ, + *oma*, tumor] An epithelial cell tumor.

epithelioglandular (ĕp″ĭ-thē″lē-ō-glăn′dū-lăr) Concerning the epithelial cells of a gland.

epithelioid (ĕp″ĭ-thē′lē-oyd) [″ + ″ + *eidos*, form, shape] Resembling epithelium.

epitheliolysin (ĕp″ĭ-thē-lē-ō-lĭ′ĭ-sĭn) [″ + ″ + *lysis*, dissolution] A specific lysin formed in blood serum of an animal into which epithelial cells of an animal of a different species were injected. The epitheliolysin destroys the cells of an animal of the same species as that from which the epithelial cells were derived.

epitheliolysis (ĕp″ĭ-thē-lē-ōl′ĭ-sĭs) Death of epithelial tissue. Destruction or dissolving of epithelial cells by an epitheliolysin.

epithelioma (ĕp″ĭ-thē-lē-ō′mă) [″ + *thele*, nipple, + *oma*, tumor] A malignant tumor consisting principally of epithelial cells; a carcinoma. A tumor originating in the epidermis of the skin or in a mucous membrane. **epitheliomatous** (-mă-tŭs), *adj.*

e. adamantinum An epithelioma of the jaw arising from the enamel organ. It may be solid or partly cystic. SYN: *adamantinoma*.

e. adenoides cysticum A basal cell carcinoma occurring on the surface of the body, esp. the face, and characterized by formation of cysts. SYN: *acanthoma adenoides cysticum; trichoepithelioma.*

basal cell e. Basal cell carcinoma.

deep-seated e. An epithelioma that invades and destroys tissue, forming irregular rounded ulcers. SYN: *rodent ulcer.*

epitheliopathy (ep″ĭ-thēl″ē-op′ă-thē) [*epithelium* + *-pathy*] Any disease that affects the layer of cells that surrounds or lines another tissue.

epitheliosis (ĕp″ĭ-thē″lē-ō′sĭs) [″ + *thele*, nipple, + *osis*, condition] Trachomatous proliferation of the conjunctival epithelium.

epithelium (ep″ĭ-thē′lē-ŭm, ′lē-ă) *pl.* **epithelia** [*epi-* + Gr. *thēlē*, nipple, teat + *-ium (2)*] The layer of cells forming the epidermis of the skin and the surface layer of mucous and serous membranes. The cells rest on a basement membrane and lie in close approximation with little intercellular material between them. They are devoid of blood vessels. The epithelium may be simple, consisting of a single layer, or stratified, consisting of several layers. Cells making up the epithelium may be flat (squamous), cube-shaped (cuboidal), or cylindrical (columnar). Modified forms of epithelium include ciliated, pseudostratified, glandular, and neuroepithelium. The epithelium may include goblet cells, which secrete mucus. Stratified squamous epithelium may be keratinized for a protective function or abnormally keratinized in pathological response. Squamous epithelium is classified as endothelium, which lines the blood vessels and the heart, and mesothelium, which lines the serous cavities. Epithelium serves the general functions of protection, absorption, and secretion, and specialized functions such as movement of substances through ducts, production of germ cells, and reception of stimuli. Its ability to regenerate is excellent; it may replace itself as frequently as every 24 hr. SEE: illus.; *skin*. **epithelial** (-ăl), *adj.*

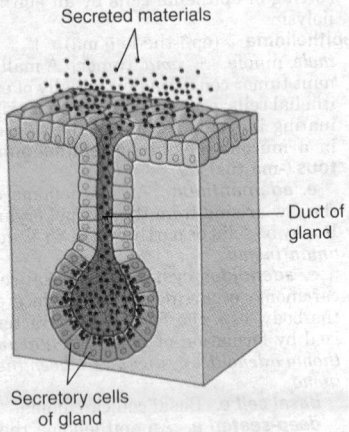

Secreted materials

Duct of gland

Secretory cells of gland

GLANDULAR EPITHELIUM

(Orig. mag. ×430)

ciliated e. Epithelium with hairlike processes on the surface that wave actively only in one direction. This type is present in the respiratory tract and fallopian tubes.

columnar e. Epithelium composed of cylindrical cells.

cuboidal e. Epithelium consisting of cube-shaped or prismatic cells with height about equal to their width.

germinal e. 1. Epithelium that covers the surface of the genital ridge of the urogenital folds of an embryo. It gives rise to the seminiferous tubules of the testes and the surface layer of the ovary. It was once thought to produce the germ cells (spermatozoa and ova). **2.** The epithelium that covers the surface of a mature mammalian ovary.

glandular e. Epithelium consisting of secretory cells.

junctional e. A band of nonkeratinized stratified squamous epithelium that attaches both to the gingiva (on one side) and the crown of the tooth (on the other). SYN: *epithelial attachment; gingival cuff.*

laminated e. Stratified **e.**

mesenchymal e. Squamous epithelium that lines the subarachnoid and subdural cavities, the chambers of the eye, and the perilymphatic spaces of the ear.

pavement e. Epithelium consisting of flat, platelike cells in a single layer.

pigmented e. Epithelium containing pigment granules.

pseudostratified e. Epithelium in which the bases of cells rest on the basement membrane but the distal ends of some do not reach the surface. Their nuclei lie at different levels, giving the appearance of stratification.

reduced enamel e. Combined epithelial layers of the enamel organ, which form a protective layer over the enamel crown as it erupts and then become the primary epithelial attachment surrounding the tooth.

squamous e. The flat form of epithelial cells.

stratified e. Epithelium with the cells in layers; mitosis takes place in the lowest layer. SYN: *laminated e.*

sulcular e. The nonkeratinized epithelium that lines the gingival sulcus.

transitional e. A form of stratified epithelium in which the cuboidal cells adjust to mechanical changes such as stretching and recoiling. This type of tissue is found only in the urinary system (renal pelvis, ureter, bladder, and a part of the urethra).

epitope (ĕp'ĭ-tōp") [*epi-* + Gr. *topos*, a place] Any component of an antigen to which an antibody binds. SYN: *antigenic determinant*. SEE: *paratope*.

immunodominant e. Immunodominant **peptide.**

epitrichium (ĕp"ĭ-trĭk'ē-ŭm) [Gr. *epi*, upon, + *trichion*, hair] The superficial layers of the epidermis of the fetus. SYN: *epitrichial layer; periderm.*

epitrochlea (ĕp"ĭ-trŏk'lē-ă) [" + *trochalia*, pulley] The inner condyle of the humerus. **epitrochlear**, *adj.*

epizoon (ĕp"ĭ-zō'ŏn) *pl.* **epizoa** [" + *zoon*, animal] An animal organism living as a parasite on the exterior of the host animal. **epizoic** (-zō'ĭk), *adj.*

epizootic (ĕp"ĭ-zō-ŏt'ĭk) **1.** Any disease of

animals that becomes epidemic. **2.** Widely disseminated in a group of animals; said of diseases and conditions.

Epley maneuver (ĕp′lē) Canalith repositioning maneuver.

epoch (ĕp′ŏk) A measurable amount of time; e.g., the length of time used in standardized sleep studies (usually 30 sec to 1 min), or the duration of a particular geological or biological event, as indicated in earth sciences.

epoetin alfa (ĕ″pō-ĕt′ĭn) Synthetic human erythropoietin. SEE: *erythropoietin.*

eponychium (ĕp″ō-nĭk′ē-ŭm) [″ + *onyx,* nail] **1.** The horny embryonic structure from which the nail develops. **2.** The perionychium.

eponym (ĕp′ō-nĭm) [Gr. *eponymos,* named after] A name for anything (disease, organ, function, place) adapted from the name of a particular person or sometimes a geographical location (e.g., Haverhill fever, Lyme disease).

epoophorectomy (ep″ō-of″ŏ-rek′tŏ-mē) [*epoophoron* + *-ectomy*] Removal of the parovarium (in the broad ligament between the ovary and fallopian tube).

epoophoron (ĕp″ō-ŏf′ō-rŏn) A rudimentary structure located in the mesosalpinx. Consisting of a longitudinal duct (duct of Gartner) and 10 to 15 transverse ducts, it is the remains of the upper portion of the mesonephros and is the homologue of the head of the epididymis in males. SYN: *parovarium; Rosenmüller's body.*

e-portfolio (ē′pŏrt-fō′lē-ō) An electronic resume on a personalized website with links to one's personal data, philosophical perspectives, and academic, avocational, creative, and professional accomplishments. SYN: *digital portfolio; electronic portfolio.*

epoxide (ĕ-pŏk′sīd) Any chemical compound that contains two carbon atoms joined to a single oxygen atom.

epoxy (ĕ-pŏk′sē) A general term for a polymer that contains molecules in which oxygen is attached to two different carbon atoms. These compounds are widely used as adhesives.

e-prescribing The use of the Internet and e-mail for prescribing and acquiring medical orders for patients.

EPS *Electrophysiology study; extrapyramidal syndrome.*

EPSP *excitatory postsynaptic potential.*

Epstein-Barr virus (ep′stīn′bar′) [Michael Anthony Epstein, Brit. physician, b. 1921; Yvonne M. Barr, Brit. physician, b. 1932] ABBR: EBV. A member of the herpesvirus family, discovered in 1964. It is one of the causes of infectious mononucleosis. In South African children, it is associated with Burkitt's lymphoma; in Asian populations, with nasopharyngeal carcinoma. SYN: *human herpesvirus 4.*

Epstein pearls (ep′stīn″) [Alois Epstein, Czech. pediatrician, 1849–1918] In infants, benign retention cysts resembling small pearls, which are sometimes present in the palate. They disappear in 1 to 2 months.

EPT *expedited partner therapy.*

epulis (ĕp-ū′lĭs) *pl.* **epulides** [Gr. *epoulis,* a gumboil] **1.** A fibrous sarcomatous tumor having its origin in the periosteum of the lower jaw. **2.** A nonpathological softening and swelling of the gums due to hyperemia that begins during midtrimester pregnancy and subsides after delivery. In susceptible women, this condition tends to recur during subsequent pregnancies. **epuloid,** *adj.*

epulosis (ĕp″ū-lō′sĭs) [Gr. *epoulosis*] Cicatrization. **epulotic,** *adj.*

epulotic (ĕp″ū-lŏt′ĭk) [Gr. *epoulotikos*] Promoting cicatrization.

EQA *external quality assessment.*

Equal Employment Opportunity Commission ABBR: EEOC. A federal agency that enacts and enforces regulations that protect against discrimination in the workplace, esp. on the basis of age, gender, race, religious preference, or functional impairment.

equation (ĕ-kwā′zhŏn) [L. *aequare,* to make equal] **1.** The state of being equal. **2.** In chemistry, a symbolic representation of a chemical reaction. The equation includes symbols for the involved elements and/or compounds, and their molar ratios. By convention, the input (reactants) are listed on the left, and the products of the reaction are placed on the right. **3.** A description of a mathematical relation between two or more constants or variables.

   Arrhenius e. SEE: *Arrhenius equation.*

   e. of motion A statement of the variables of pressure, volume, compliance, resistance, and flow for respiratory system mechanics.

   Henderson-Hasselbalch e. SEE: *Henderson-Hasselbalch equation.*

   personal e. A personal bias or peculiarity that may explain a difference in approach or interpretation.

equator [L. *aequator*] A line encircling a round body and equidistant from both poles. **equatorial,** *adj.*

   e. of cell The boundary of a plane through which the division of a cell occurs.

   e. of crystalline lens The line that marks the junction of the anterior and posterior surfaces of the crystalline lens. The fibers of the suspensory ligament are attached to it.

   e. oculi An imaginary line encircling the eyeball midway between the anterior and posterior poles.

equi- [L. *aequus,* equal] Prefix meaning *equal.*

equilibrating (i-kwil′ĭ-brāt″ing) [L. *ae-*

quilibrare, be in balance] Coming into a state of equilibrium.

equilibration (ē-kwĭl″ĭ-brā′shŭn) The modification of masticatory forces or occlusal surfaces of teeth to produce simultaneous occlusal contacts between upper and lower teeth, and to equalize the stress of occlusal forces of the supporting tissues of the teeth. SYN: *occlusal equilibration.*

    occlusal e. Equilibration.

equilibrium (ē″kwĭ-lib′rē-ŭm, ek″wĭ-) [*aequilibrium* level or horizontal position] A state of balance; a condition in which contending forces are equal.

    Donnan e. SEE: *Donnan equilibrium.*

    dynamic e. **1.** The sense of balance while the body or head is in motion. This is maintained by coordinating data from postural (stretch) receptors in the limbs with data from the inner ear and cerebellum. **2.** Homeostasis.

    nitrogen e. Nitrogen **balance.**

    nitrogenous e. Nitrogen **balance.**

    physiological e. In nutritional theory, a state in which the body's intake and excretion of nutrients are perfectly matched.

    static e. The ability to maintain a steady position of the head and body in relation to gravity. It is integrated with the equilibrium of movement, or dynamic equilibrium. SYN: *static balance.*

    thermal e. A condition in which two substances exist at the same temperature and in which heat transfer is therefore in a steady state.

equilin (ĕk′wĭl-ĭn) [L. *equus,* horse] Crystalline estrogenic hormone derived from the urine of pregnant mares.

equimolar (ē″kwī-mō′-lăr) In the quantitative comparison of chemical substances, having the same molar concentration.

equine (ē′kwīn) [L. *equus,* horse] Concerning or originating from a horse.

equinovarus (ē-kwī″nō-vā′rŭs) [L. *equinus,* equine, + *varus*] A form of clubfoot with a combinination of pes equinus and pes varus (i.e., walking without touching the heel to the ground and with the sole turned inward).

equipoise (ē′kwĭ-poyz″, ĕk′wĭ-) In the design of clinical trials, a state in which the risks and benefits of alternative treatments offered during the trial are balanced, so that no pre-existing advantage is known to exist for one treatment arm over the other. This is a required ethical consideration in clinical research.

equipotential (ē″kwĭ-pō-tĕn′shăl) [L. *aequus,* equal, + *potentia,* ability] Having the same electric charge or physical strength.

equivalence (ē-kwĭv′ă-lĕns) [″ + *val-*

ere, to be worth] The quality of being equal in power, potency, force, value, or clinical effectiveness.

equivalence trial A randomized clinical trial in which two distinct agents are compared head-to-head against each other, and sometimes, but not always, against an inert agent (a placebo) as well. If two agents work equally well, the treatment that is less expensive, better tolerated, or more easily administered, may be preferable to use.

equivalent (i-kwĭv′ă-lĕnt) [L. *aequivalere,* to have equal force or power] **1.** Equal in power, force, or value. **2.** The amount of weight of any element needed to replace a fixed weight of another body. **3.** Bioequivalent (1).

    anginal e. The occasional idiosyncratic signs and symptoms that patients may experience during coronary ischemia or myocardial infarction. The most common signs are breathlessness, isolated pain in the arm, neck, jaw, or shoulder, sweating, syncope, or nausea and vomiting. Patients may also be anxious and an elevated heart rate or palpitations. Older patients may show changes in mental status. Older patients and women are more likely than men to have atypical signs and symptoms of coronary ischemia.

    dose e. In radiology, the product of the absorbed dose and the quality factor. Expressed in rems or sieverts, it measures the effects of absorbing different types of radiation. SEE: *quality factor.*

    human skin e. Graft made of living human skin grown in a laboratory and used, e.g., to treat leg ulcers in patients with peripheral vascular disease or diabetes mellitus. The graft bonds with healthy tissue in a wound from which necrotic tissue has been removed, improving healing. It is grown from foreskin removed from neonates but also contains bovine (cow) proteins, limiting its use to those with no allergy to these proteins. SYN: *artificial skin; tissue-engineered skin.*

    mechanical e. of heat The value of heat units in terms of work units. One Calorie (kilocalorie) is equal to 4.1855×10^4 joules.

    metabolic e. ABBR: MET. A unit used to estimate the metabolic cost of physical activity. One MET equals the uptake of 3.5 ml of oxygen per kilogram of body weight per minute. Approximate MET values of common physical activities range from sleeping (0.9), light housework (2-4), golf (4-5), and lap swimming (more than 6).

    therapeutic e. A drug that has the same pharmacological effects and actions in the treatment of illnesses as another drug even though the drugs may not be chemically equivalent.

toxicity e. ABBR: TEQ. **1.** The toxicity of a component of a toxic mixture to the toxicity of all the materials in the mixture. **2.** The toxicity of a substance relative to a pure sample of a known toxin, such as dioxin.

equivalent dose SEE: under *dose.*

ER *Emergency Room; external resistance; external rotation.*

Er Symbol for the element erbium.

eradication (ē-rad″ĭ-kā′shŏn) [L. *eradicatio,* pulling up by the roots] **1.** Complete elimination of a disease from a population, esp. an epidemic or endemic disease. **2.** Complete elimination of a pathogen or a tumor from the body.

Erb, Wilhelm (ĕrb, erp) Wilhelm Heinrich Erb, Ger. neurologist, 1840–1921.

   E.'s paralysis Duchenne-Erb paralysis.

   E.'s point The point on the side of the neck 2 to 3 cm above the clavicle and in front of the transverse process of the sixth cervical vertebra. Electrical stimulation over this area causes various arm muscles to contract.

***erb*-B2** (ĕrb′bē′too′) A member of the *erb*-B family of oncogenes. This oncogene is overexpressed in some cancers and is associated with progression of breast cancer. Its protein product contains part of the epidermal growth factor (EGF) receptor. SYN: *HER2.* SEE: *oncogene; epidermal growth factor; breast cancer.*

Erben reflex (erb′ĕn, ĕrb′) [Siegmund Erben, Austrian physician, b. 1863] The slowing of the pulse when the head and trunk are forcibly bent forward.

erbium (ĕr′bē-ŭm) [*Erbium,* L. name of Ytterby, Sweden + *-ium* (1)] SYMB: Er. A rare metallic chemical element, atomic weight (mass) 167.26, specific gravity 9.051, atomic number 68.

ERCP *endoscopic retrograde cholangiopancreatography.*

erectile (ē-rĕk′tĭl) [L. *erigere,* to erect] Able to assume an upright position.

erectile dysfunction ABBR: ED. SEE: under *dysfunction.*

erection (ē-rĕk′shŭn) The state of swelling, hardness, and stiffness observed in the penis and to a lesser extent in the clitoris, generally due to sexual excitement. It is caused by engorgement with blood of the corpora cavernosa and the corpus spongiosum of the penis in men and the corpus cavernosa clitoridis in women.

   Erection is necessary in men for the natural intromission of the penis into the vagina but not for the emission of semen. The blood withdraws from the penis after ejaculation and the erection is reduced. Erection of the penis may occur as the result of sexual excitement, during sleep, or due to physical stimulation of the penis. Abnormal persistent erection of the penis due not to sexual excitement but to certain disease states is called priapism. SEE: *nocturnal emission; penile prosthesis; priapism.*

erector (ē-rĕk′tor) [L. *erigere,* to erect] A muscle that raises a body part.

erector spinae reflex SEE: under *reflex.*

eremophobia (ĕr″ĕm-ō-fō′bē-ă) [Gr. *eremos,* solitary, + *phobos,* fear] Dread of being alone.

erethism (er′ĕ-thizm) [Gr. *erethismos,* irritation] **1.** Unusual or excessive response or irritability of tissue or an organ to a stimulus. SEE: *apathism.* **2.** Erethism mercurialis.

   e. mercurialis, erethismus mercurialis A group of psychological signs and symptoms associated with acute mercury poisoning. Included are restlessness, irritability, insomnia, difficulty in concentrating, and impaired memory. In severe cases, delirium and toxic psychosis may develop. SEE: *mercury poisoning.*

erethismic (ĕr″ĕ-thĭz′mĭk) Pert. to or causing erethism.

erethisophrenia (ĕr″ĕ-thĭ-zō-frē′nē-ă) [″ + *phren,* mind] Unusual mental excitability.

ereuthrophobia (ĕr″ū-thrō-fō′bē-ă) [Gr. *erythros,* red, + *phobos,* fear] Pathological fear of blushing. SYN: *erythrophobia.*

ERG *electroretinogram.*

erg (ĕrg) [Gr. *ergon,* work] In physics, the amount of work done when a force of 1 dyne acts through a distance of 1 cm. One erg is roughly ¹⁄₉₈₀ gram-centimeter. That is, raising a load of 1 g against gravity the distance of 1 cm requires that a force of 980 dynes operate through a distance of 1 cm, and hence that 980 ergs of work be done.

ergastic (ĕr-găs′tĭk) [Gr. *ergastikos*] Possessing potential energy.

ergo-, erg- [Gr. *ergon,* work] Prefixes meaning *work.*

ergocalciferol (ĕr-gō-kăl-sĭf′ĕr-ŏl) Vitamin D_2, an activated product of ergosterol. It is used primarily in prophylaxis and treatment of vitamin D deficiency.

ergogenic (ĕr″gō-jĕn′ĭk) [Gr. *ergon,* work, + *gennan,* to produce] Having the ability to increase work, esp. to increase the potential for work output.

ergogenic aid SEE: under *aid.*

ergometer (ĕr-gŏm′ĕ-tĕr) [″ + *metron,* measure] An apparatus for measuring the amount of work done by a human or animal subject.

   arm e. A hand-driven crank used instead of a bicycle or treadmill to measure cardiopulmonary conditioning or health.

   bicycle e. A stationary bicycle used in determining the amount of work performed by the rider.

ergonomic aid SEE: under *aid.*

ergonomics (ĕr″gō-nŏm′ĭks) [″ + *nomikos,* law] The science concerned with fitting a job to a person's anatomical, physiological, and psychological characteristics in a way that enhances human efficiency and well-being.

ergophobia (ĕr″gō-fō′bē-ă) [″ + *phobos*, fear] Morbid dread of working.

ergoreceptor (ĕr″gŏ-rĕ-sep′tŏr) Any of the sensory receptors in muscle that detect chemical by-products of skeletal muscle contraction and relaxation.

ergoreflex (ĕr″gŏ-rē′fleks) In respiratory physiology, the difference between ventilation at rest and ventilation just after exercise.

ergosterol (ĕr-gŏs′tĕr-ŏl) The primary steroid found in the cell membrane of some fungi; it stabilizes the membrane, as does cholesterol in human cells. Many antifungal drugs act on ergosterol to increase permeability of the cell membrane of the fungus, promoting its destruction.

ergot (ĕr′gŏt) A drug obtained from *Claviceps purpurea*, a fungus that grows parasitically on rye. Several valuable alkaloids, such as ergotamine, are obtained from ergot.

ergotherapy (ĕr″gō-thĕr′ă-pē) [*ergo-* + *therapy*] The use of an appropriate amount of physical exertion as a treatment for disease (e.g., in the treatment of type 2 diabetes mellitus or hyperlipidemia).

ergothioneine (ĕr-gō-thī′ō-nēn) $C_9H_{15}N_3O_2S \cdot 2H_2O$; thiolhistidine-betaine. A compound containing crystalline sulfur, it is found in ergot and red blood cells.

ergotism (ĕr′gŏ-tĭzm) Ergot poisoning.

ergotope, ergotype (ĕr′gō-tōp″, ĕr′gō-tīp″) [Gr. *ergon*, work + ″] An activation marker on a T cell.

ergot poisoning SEE: under *poisoning*.

Erickson, Helen Cook (er′ĭk-sŏn) A U.S. nursing theorist. With Evelyn Tomlin and Mary Ann Swain, she developed and published the grand nursing theory of Modeling and Role-Modeling in 1983. SEE: *Nursing Theory Appendix*.

Erikson, Erik H. (ĕr′ĭk-sŏn) [Ger.-born U.S. psychoanalyst, 1902–1993] A psychological theorist who proposed eight developmental stages from birth to late adulthood. In each stage, there is a conflict between a specific psychosocial task and an opposing ego threat that must be resolved:

Birth to 1 year: Trust/mistrust

2 to 3 year: Autonomy/shame and doubt

4 to 5 year: Initiative/guilt

6 to 12 year: Industry/inferiority

13 to 18 year: Identity/role confusion

Young adult: Intimacy/isolation

Middle-aged adult: Generativity/self-absorption

Old adult: Ego integrity/despair

ERISA Employee Retirement Income Security Act.

Eristalis (ĕ-ris′tă-lĭs) A genus of flies belonging to the family Syrphidae. The larva of the species *E. tenax*, called the rat-tailed maggot, may cause intestinal myiasis in humans. SEE: *myiasis*.

erm gene (ŭrm) [Acronym fm. *erythromycin ribosomal methylase*] A gene that promotes methylation of ribosomal RNA and other intracellular molecules. It is responsible for bacterial resistance to antibiotics such as the macrolides, lincosamides, and streptogramins.

erode (ē-rōd′) [L. *erodere*] 1. To wear away. 2. To eat away by ulceration.

erogenous (ĕr-ŏj′ĕ-nŭs) [Gr. *eros*, love, + *gennan*, to produce] Causing sexual excitement. SYN: *erotogenic*.

eros (ĕr′ŏs) 1. In psychoanalysis, the collective instincts for self-preservation. 2. The Greek god of love.

E rosette test A laboratory test performed to identify human T lymphocytes. When T lymphocytes combine with sheep red blood cells in a culture, a cluster of cells called a rosette forms. This test is often replaced by the use of monoclonal antibodies that identify the CD4 receptor specific for T cells.

erosion (ē-rō′shŭn) [L. *erodere*, to gnaw away] 1. An eating away of tissue. 2. External or internal destruction of a surface layer by physical or inflammatory processes.

e. of cervix uteri The alteration of the epithelium on a portion of the cervix as a result of irritation or infection.

SYMPTOMS: In the early stages, the epithelium shows necrosis; in healing, there is a downgrowth of epithelium from the endocervical canal. If the growth is a single layer of tissue with a grossly granular appearance, it is called a simple granular erosion. If the growth is excessive and shows papillary tufts, it is called a papillary erosion. Histologically, the papillary erosion shows many branching racemose glands; their epithelium is the mucus-bearing cell with the nucleus at the base. In the healing process, squamous epithelium grows over the eroded area with one of the following results: the squamous cells replace the tissue beneath them completely, giving complete healing; the glands fill with squamous plugs and remain in that state; or the mouths of the glands are occluded by the squamous cells and nabothian cysts form. In the congenital type of erosion, the portio is covered by high columnar epithelium. SEE: *carcinoma in situ; Papanicolaou test*.

TREATMENT: Treatment consists of proper care of the cervix following delivery. Electrocauterization of the early erosion is usually curative. Cryotherapy may be used.

dental e. The wearing away of the

surface layer (enamel) of a tooth. SEE: *abrasion; attrition; bruxism*.

marginal e. Bony destruction that occurs at the outer borders of a joint space in inflammatory arthritis such as rheumatoid arthritis. It is visible on radiographic images of joints, e.g., plain films or magnetic resonance imaging.

erosive (ē-rō′sĭv) **1.** Able to produce erosion. **2.** An agent that erodes tissues or structures.

erotic (ĕ-rŏt′ĭk) [Gr. *erotikos*] **1.** Stimulating sexual desire. **2.** Pert. to sexual love. **3.** Pert. to sexuality. **4.** Marked by or subject to sexual desire.

eroticism (ĕ-rŏt′ĭ-sĭzm) [″ + *-ismos,* condition] Sexual desire.

anal e. 1. Sensations of pleasure experienced through defecation during a stage in the development of children. **2.** In psychiatry, fixation of the libido at the anal-erotic developmental stage. Personality traits associated with anal eroticism include cleanliness, frugality, and neatness, and an unusual interest in regularity of bowel movements. SYN: *anal erotism.* SEE: *anal stage.*

oral e. 1. Sexual pleasure derived from use of the mouth. **2.** In psychiatry, fixation of the libido to the oral phase of development.

erotogenic (ĕ-rŏ″tō-jĕn′ĭk) [Gr. *eros,* love, + *gennan,* to produce] Producing sexual excitement. SEE: *erogenous zone.*

erotomania (ĕ-rō″tŏ-, ĕ-rŏt″ŏ-mā′nē-ă) [″ + *mania,* madness] The delusion that one is loved by another person, esp. a person of high economic, social, or political status. The delusion is more one of romantic or spiritual love, rather than physical. The object is usually someone of higher status or fame, but may be a complete stranger.

erratic (ĭ-răt′ĭk) [L. *errare,* to wander] Having an unpredictable or fluctuating course or pattern; wandering.

error (er′ŏr) [L. *errare,* to wander] A mistake or miscalculation.

active e. A mistake that immediately injures a patient. Active errors result directly from the actions of health care professionals. SEE: *latent e.*

anchoring e. A mistake made in reasoning in which a judgment is made that depends excessively on preconceptions, bias, or an initial point of reference. For example, a patient on a hospital neurology service is found unconscious. The caregivers assume or are committed to the idea that, like many other patients cared for on the neurology service, the patient may have suffered a stroke. The patient is sent for an imaging study of the brain to rule out stroke. Other common and potentially deadly causes of coma, e.g., a dangerously low blood glucose level, are overlooked during the initial assessment.

connection e. The linking of incompatible devices, drug delivery systems, or power sources with one another. It is a potential cause of patient injury.

PATIENT CARE: Systems approaches to equipment engineering in which devices used for different purposes are made physically incompatible with each other (as by designing links between structures so that physiologically incompatible tubes cannot be fastened to each other) can prevent connection errors. Careful labeling of devices and drug delivery systems by nurses, with cross-checking of labels by staff, may also be helpful.

inborn e. of metabolism Any inherited metabolic disease caused by the absence or deficiency of specific enzymes necessary to the metabolism of basic substances such as amino acids, carbohydrates, vitamins, or essential trace elements. SEE: *metabolism.*

latent e. A flaw in the design or organization of health care delivery systems that may allow, on occasion, injuries to occur to patients.

measurement e. The difference between the true value of something being measured and the value obtained by measurement. Measurement error can be the result of one or more of several different factors, including operational blunders, random error, and systematic error. SEE: *bias; proportional e.; random e.*

medication e. Administering the wrong medicine, administering an incorrect dose of a medicine, failing to administer a prescribed medicine, or administering the medicine either at the incorrect time or via the incorrect route. Every effort should be made to prevent errors in medication, many of which are detailed in the table. If an error occurs, it should be reported immediately (following agency protocols). Appropriate patient protection procedures should be implemented. SEE: table; *drug handling.*

misconnection e. The linking of two sets of wires or tubes that share a common fitting and therefore seem to work with each other even though they may carry incompatible or dangerous substances that should not be administered to a patient.

PATIENT CARE: Misconnection errors can be prevented by carefully tracing each tube to its source and verifying its contents; or systematically by manufacturing unique fittings or connectors that cannot link incompatible agents.

no-fault e. A mistake made during the provision of health care that could not be foreseen and was impossible to prevent even by the most careful practitioner.

prescribing e. An error in the choice

Common Medication Errors

Error	Explanation
Expired medication given	The correct medication and dose are given, but the medication is no longer potent
Incorrect dose	The correct medication is given to the correct patient, but the dose (e.g., 75 mg instead of 75 mcg) is improperly identified and administered
Incorrect labeling	The medication is given with improper identification, inadequate warnings about side effects or interactions, or with the wrong patient's name
Inadequate monitoring for side effects	The medication is given properly, but prudent assessment of vital signs or heart rhythms (e.g., antiarrhythmic drugs) is not performed
Incorrect quantity	The patient receives medications in the correct dosage, but the wrong number of pills of that dosage are administered
Mixing error	The correct medication is given, but it is given in the wrong diluent or with an incompatible intravenous fluid
Patient allergy not recognized	The patient is given an agent (a drug or vaccine, for example) to which he or she has reacted adversely in the past
Self-administration of drugs	A patient takes a medication without supervision, and then receives additional or conflicting medications under provider supervision
Stocking errors	Medications are dispensed to satellite dispensaries or pharmacies in a facility and given to patients without oversight from a coordinating center, where important patient-centered information is stored
Timing error	A medication is given too often or not often enough
Wrong patient	A medication is given to one patient in a room, when another should have been treated; a medication is mistakenly given to a patient whose name resembles the name of the intended patient
Wrong route of administration	A medication intended for oral use is given intravenously, or by another inappropriate or potentially hazardous route.

or administration of drugs for patients. Included are incorrect dose or medicine, duplicate therapy, incorrect route of administration, or wrong patient. In one extensive study of prescriptions written by physicians in a tertiary-care teaching hospital, 0.3% were erroneous, and more than half of these were rated as having the potential for adverse consequences. Monitoring of medications and patients is thought to be helpful in limiting these errors.

proportional e. Systematic error that varies directly with the concentration or activity of the analyte.

random e. The patternless differences observed between successive analytical results or statistical trials. Even though the individual results are patternless and unpredictable, the range of random error can be predicted with a given probability once sufficient experience has been gained. The random error is then quantified by the standard deviation, the coefficient of variation, and other statistics. SEE: *measurement e.; systematic e.*

e. of refraction Ametropia.

standard e. ABBR: S.E. A measure of variability that could be expected of a statistical constant following the taking of random samples of a given size in a particular set of observations. An important standard error is that of the difference between the means of two samples.

systematic e. Residual error after random error has been subtracted from total error. SEE: *bias; proportional e.*

type I e. In statistics, experimental medicine, and epidemiology, erroneous rejection of a hypothesis.

type II e. In statistics, experimental medicine and epidemiology, erroneous acceptance of a hypothesis.

error chain Linked events that ultimately result in an adverse patient outcome.

error disclosure Reporting to a patient that a mistake was made in the provision of his or her health care. It is a practice that is widely advocated by bioethicists but generally eschewed by practitioners because of fears of litigation or investigation. When surveyed, patients report wanting full disclosure of any errors made during their treatment. They prefer to hear how the error occurred, and how similar errors can be prevented. Finally, most patients want their practitioners to apologize or express regret about their errors.

Laws to encourage health care providers to disclose errors are known colloquially as "apology laws." These laws encourage expressions of regret by exempting statements made in apology from legal action or liability.

ERT *estrogen replacement therapy.*

eructation (ĕ-rŭk-tā′shŭn) [L. *eructare*] Producing gas from the stomach, usually with a characteristic sound; belching.

eruption (e-rŭp′shŏn) [L. *eruptio*, outbreak] **1.** A visible breaking out, esp. of a skin lesion or rash accompanying a disease such as measles or scarlet fever. **2.** The appearance of a lesion such as redness or spotting on the skin or mucous membrane. **3.** The breaking of a tooth through the gum; the cutting of a tooth. **eruptive** (-tiv), *adj.*

   active e. Movement of the tooth toward the occlusal plane.

   creeping e. A skin lesion marked by a tortuous elevated red line that progresses at one end while fading out at the other. It is caused by the migration into the skin of the larvae of certain nematodes, esp. *Ancylostoma braziliense* and *A. caninum*, which are present in ground exposed to dog or cat feces. SYN: *cutaneous larva migrans.*

   delayed e. The most common variation in the tooth eruption pattern. It may be due to crowding or to various genetic, endocrine, or physiological factors.

   drug e. Dermatitis produced in some patients by application or ingestion of drugs. Drug rashes usually appear on the trunk (chest and back). SEE: illus.

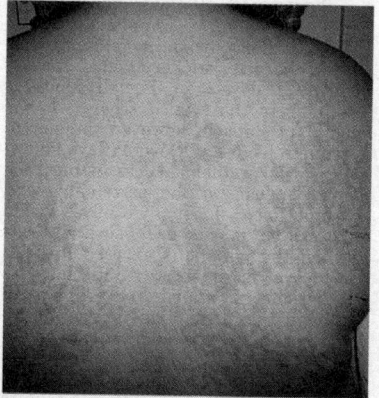

DRUG ERUPTION

   fixed drug e. A localized red rash with a sharp border, which follows exposure to a drug. The rash usually burns, occurs on the face or the genitals, and, if the offending agent is given again, recurs in the same location.

   passive e. Increased size of the clinical crown of a tooth by apical migration of the attachment epithelium and periodontium.

   polymorphous light e., polymorphic light eruption ABBR: PMLE. A rash occurring after exposure to sunlight, typically consisting of papules, plaques, or papulovesicles on sun-exposed skin. It is more common in fair-skinned patients and in women than in men or people with darker skin color. The rash is usually itchy but may produce a burning or stinging sensation. Avoiding sun exposure with protective clothing and sunblock helps prevent PMLE. Immune-modulating drugs are available for refractory cases.

   seabather's e. Itching red papules that may appear on the skin within a few hours of swimming in saltwater. The rash is caused by the sting of the larval forms of the thimble jellyfish or the sea anemone. The rash is usually more prominent under swimsuits than on exposed skin because the pressure of clothing on the skin releases the stinging barbs of the larvae. The swimsuit should be washed before it is worn again. Treatment is symptomatic, with oral antihistamines or topical corticosteroids.

   serum e. An eruption that occurs following the injection of serous fluid. It may be accompanied by chills, fever, and arthritic symptoms.

ERUS *Endorectal **ultrasound**.*

eRx *Electronic prescribing.*

erysipelas (ĕr′ĭ-sĭp′ĕ-lăs) [Gr. *erythros,* red, + *pella,* skin] An infection of the skin (usually caused by group A streptococci) that is marked by a bright red, swollen, sharply defined rash (that stings or itches) on the face, scalp, arms, legs, or trunk. Systemic symptoms such as fevers, chills, sweats, or vomiting may occur; local tissue swelling and tenderness and blistering of the rash are common. A toxin released into the skin by *Streptococcus pyogenes* creates many of the signs and symptoms of the infection. Erysipelas occurs primarily in children, adults over age 60, people with immunocompromising illnesses, and individuals with prior lymphatic or venous obstruction or surgery. SEE: illus; *cellulitis.*

   TREATMENT: Oral or IV penicillins or erythromycin, or first-generation cephalosporins, vancomycin, or clindamycin may effectively eradicate the responsible bacteria. Analgesic and antipyretic drugs, such as acetaminophen or

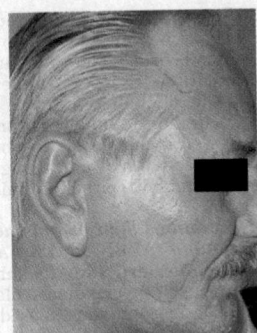

ERYSIPELAS

ibuprofen, cold packs and topical anesthetics, and elevation of the affected area provide comfort. Standard and barrier precautions are employed.

PROGNOSIS: The prognosis is excellent with treatment. Without treatment, the infection may spread, or cause nephritis, abscesses, septicemia and death.

PATIENT CARE: Patients and family members are taught to use thorough handwashing before and after touching the affected area to prevent the spread of infection and how to safely clean or dispose of drainage-contaminated articles. The application of cool compresses and elevating the affected parts may reduce discomfort. SEE: *Standard Precautions Appendix*.

erysipelatous (ĕr″ĭ-sĭ-pĕl′ă-tŭs) Of the nature of or pert. to erysipelas.

erysipeloid (ĕr-ĭ-sĭp′ĕ-loyd) [″ + ″ + *eidos*, form, shape] Inflammation of the skin, primarily the hands and fingers, caused by the bacteria *Erysipelothrix rhusiopathiae*. It occurs in butchers, fishermen, and others who handle raw fish and poultry. The infected areas are warm, swollen, and reddish-purple. The infection rarely moves to the bloodstream and is treated with penicillin G or ampicillin, which resolves the infection in approx. 3 weeks. Erysipeloid-like rashes of the hands are sometimes caused by other infectious agents, such as *Leishmania* or fungi.

Erysipelothrix rhusiopathiae (ĕr″ĭ-sĭ-pĕl′ŏ-thrĭks) [″ + ″ + *thrix*, hair] A species of gram-positive, filamentous bacilli that causes erysipeloid.

erysipelotoxin (ĕr″ĭ-sĭp″ĕ-lō-tŏk′sĭn) The poisonous substance produced by *Streptococcus pyogenes*, the causative agent of erysipelas.

erysiphake (ĕr-ĭs′ĭ-fāk) A small spoon-shaped device used in cataract surgery to remove the lens by suction.

erythema (er″ĭ-thē′mă) [Gr. *erythēma*, redness] Reddening of the skin. Erythema is a common but nonspecific sign

of skin irritation, injury, or inflammation. It is caused by dilation of superficial blood vessels in the skin. **erythematic, erythematous** (er″ĭ-thĕ-mat′ĭk, er″ĭ-them′ăt-ŭs), *adj*.

e. ab igne Localized erythema due to exposure to heat. SYN: *toasted skin syndrome*.

e. annulare A red, ring-shaped rash. SEE: illus.

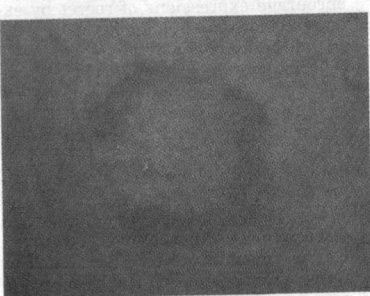

ERYTHEMA ANNULARE

e. chronicum migrans ABBR: ECM. **Erythema** migrans.

e. elevatum diutinum A form of vasculitis that affects the skin on the extensor surfaces of the forearms or legs. Iit is often seen in those infected with HIV.

e. induratum Chronic vasculitis of the skin occurring in young women. Hard cutaneous nodules break down to form necrotic ulcers and leave atrophic scars. SYN: *Bazin disease*.

e. infectiosum A mild, moderately contagious disease seen most commonly in school-age children. SYN: *fifth disease*.

ETIOLOGY: The causative agent is human parvovirus B-19. Transmission is thought to be via respiratory secretions from infected patients; however, maternal-fetal transmission can occur and hemolytic disease of the newborn may result.

SYMPTOMS: Patients experience a mild, brief illness; complaints include fever, malaise, headache, and pruritus. The characteristic erythema appears about 10 days later. Facial redness is similar to that which occurs when a child is slapped; however, circumoral redness is absent. Several days following initial erythema, a less distinct rash may appear on the extremities and trunk. The rash usually resolves within 1 week but may occur for several weeks when the patient is exposed to heat, cold, exercise, or stress. Adults may also experience arthralgia and arthritis although these symptoms are less common in children. In addition, mild transient anemia, thrombocytopenia, and leukopenia may develop.

TREATMENT: Most patients require no specific therapy. Patients with chronic hemolytic anemia may experience transient aplastic crisis (TAC). These patients should be warned of the danger of exposure to parvovirus B-19 infection, informed of the early signs and symptoms, and instructed to seek medical consultation promptly if exposure is suspected. Patients with TAC may develop a life-threatening anemia that requires immediate blood transfusion or partial exchange transfusion.

e. intertrigo Chafing.

linear gingival e. A band of inflammation of the periodontium, appearing as a reddish gingival band about 2 to 3 mm in width. It is often associated with HIV/AIDS. SYN: *red band gingivitis*.

e. marginatum A form of erythema multiforme in which the center of the area fades, leaving elevated edges.

e. migrans ABBR: EM. The hallmark of acute infection with Lyme disease. EM is an expanding red rash with a sharply defined border and (typically) central clearing. The rash usually appears within 3–32 days after a tick bite. The center of the rash is the site of inoculation. The causative agent is *Borrelia burgdorferi,* a spirochete that may later invade the joints, the central nervous system, or the conducting system of the heart. SYN: *e. chronicum migrans*. SEE: *Lyme disease* for illus.

e. multiforme ABBR: EM. A rash usually caused by an immune response to drugs or to an infection, esp. herpes simplex virus. It may express itself on the skin in multiform ways, including macules, papules, blisters, hives, and, characteristically, iris or target lesions. It may involve the palms and soles, the mucous membranes, the face, and the extremities. The disease is usually self-limited. The most severe (and occasionally fatal) variant of the illness, in which the eyes, mouth, and internal organs are involved, is called Stevens-Johnson syndrome, or toxic epidermal necrolysis. SYN: *Hebra disease* (1.). SEE: illus.

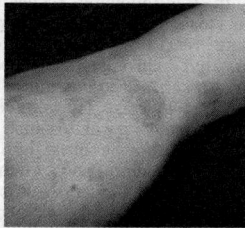

ERYTHEMA MULTIFORME

necrolytic migratory e. ABBR: NME. Red, blistering or crusting patches that appear on the skin of the buttocks, groin, lower extremities, or perineum. The lesions are itchy and painful. NME is often associated with glucagonomas.

e. nodosum A tender, red, nodular rash on the shins that typically arises in conjunction with another illness, e.g., such as a streptococcal, fungal, or tubercular infection; inflammatory bowel disease; occult cancer; or sarcoidosis. Biopsies of the rash reveal inflammation of subcutaneous fat (panniculitis). Because the disease is often associated with other serious illnesses, a diagnostic search for an underlying cause usually is undertaken. In some patients, no cause is identified.

TREATMENT: Therapy is directed at the cause, when it is known. Nonsteroidal anti-inflammatory drugs provide symptomatic relief for many patients.

e. nodosum leprosum ABBR: ENL. A red, nodular vasculitic rash, which may be a complication of the treatment for leprosy. SEE: *lepra*.

TREATMENT: Treatment consists of withdrawing therapy against leprosy (clofazimine, steroids, thalidomide).

punctate e. Erythema occurring in minute points, such as scarlet fever rash.

toxic e. Redness of the skin or a rash resulting from toxic agents such as drugs.

e. toxicum neonatorum A benign, self-limited rash marked by firm, yellow-white papules or pustules from 1 to 2 mm in size present in about 50% of full-term infants. The cause is unknown, and the lesions disappear without need for treatment.

e. venenatum Erythema caused by contact with a toxic substance.

erythemogenic (ĕr″ĭ-thē″mō-jĕn′ĭk) [″ + *gennan,* to produce] Producing erythema.

erythralgia (ĕr″ĭ-thrăl′jē-ă) [″ + *algos,* pain] Erythromelalgia.

erythrasma (ĕr″ĭ-thrăz′mă) A red-brown eruption in patches in the axillae and groin caused by *Corynebacterium minutissimum*.

erythremia (ĕr″ĭ-thrē′mē-ă) [″ + *haima,* blood] Polycythemia vera.

erythrism (ĕr′ĭ-thrĭzm) [″ + *-ismos,* condition of] Red hair and beard with a ruddy complexion. **erythristic** (-thrĭs′tĭk), *adj.*

erythro-, erythr- [Gr. *erythros*] Prefixes meaning *red.*

erythroblast (ĕ-rĭth′rō-blăst) [″ + *blastos,* germ] Normoblast. **erythroblastic** (-blăs′tĭk), *adj.*

erythroblastemia (ĕ-rĭth″rō-blăs-tē′mē-ă) [″ + ″ + *haima,* blood] An excessive number of erythroblasts in the blood.

erythroblastoma (ĕ-rĭth″rō-blăs-tō′mă) [″ + *blastos,* germ, + *oma,* tumor] A tumor (myeloma) with cells resembling megaloblasts.

erythroblastosis (ĕ-rǐth″rō-blăs-tō′sǐs) [″ + ″ + *osis*, condition] A condition marked by erythroblasts in the blood.

   e. fetalis A hemolytic disease of the newborn marked by anemia, jaundice, enlargement of the liver and spleen, and generalized edema (hydrops fetalis). SYN: *hemolytic disease of the newborn.*

erythrochloropia (ĕ-rǐth″rō-klor-ō′pē-ă) [Gr. *erythros*, red, + *chloros*, green, + *ops*, eye] Partial color blindness with ability to see red and green, but not blue and yellow.

erythrochromia (ĕ-rǐth″rō-krō′mē-ă) [″ + *chroma*, color] Hemorrhagic red pigmentation of the spinal column.

erythroclastic (ĕ-rǐth-rō-klăs′tǐk) [″ + *klasis*, a breaking] Destructive to red blood cells.

erythrocyanosis (ĕ-rǐth-rō-sī″ă-nō′sǐs) [″ + *kyanos*, blue, + *osis*, condition] Red or bluish discoloration on the skin with swelling, itching, and burning.

erythrocyte (ĕ-rǐth′rŏ-sīt″) [*erythro-* + *-cyte*] A blood cell (i.e., a circulating cell that contains hemoglobin and carries oxygen to tissue). Each erythrocyte is a nonnucleated, biconcave disk averaging 7.7 μm in diameter. An erythrocyte has a typical cell membrane and an internal stroma made of lipids and proteins to which more than 200 million molecules of hemoglobin are attached. The total surface area of the erythrocytes of an average adult is 3820 sq m, or about 2000 times more than the external total body surface area. SYN: *red blood cell; red blood corpuscle; red cell; red corpuscle.* SEE: illus.

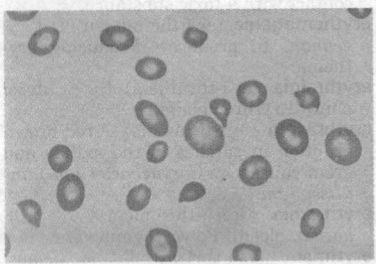

ERYTHROCYTES

Note the different size and shape of the red blood cells

NUMBER: In a normal person, the number of erythrocytes averages about 5,000,000/μL (5,500,000 for men and 4,500,000 for women). The total number in an average-sized person is about 35 trillion. The number per μL varies with age (higher in infants), time of day (lower during sleep), activity and environmental temperature (increasing with both), and altitude. People living at altitudes of 10,000 ft (3048 m) or more may have an erythrocyte count of 8,000,000/μL or more.

If a person has a normal blood volume of 5 L (70 mL/ kg of body weight) and 5,000,000 erythrocytes per μL of blood, and the erythrocytes live 120 days, the red bone marrow must produce 2,400,000 erythrocytes per second to maintain this erythrocyte count.

PHYSIOLOGY: The primary function of erythrocytes is to carry oxygen. The hemoglobin also contributes to the acid-base balance of the blood by acting as a buffer for the transport of carbon dioxide in the plasma as bicarbonate ions.

DEVELOPMENT: Erythrocyte formation (erythropoiesis) in adults takes place in the bone marrow, principally in the vertebrae, ribs, sternum, hip bone, diploë of cranial bones, and proximal ends of the humerus and femur. erythrocytes arise from large nucleated stem cells (promegaloblasts), which give rise to pronormoblasts, in which hemoglobin appears. These become normoblasts, which extrude their nuclei. erythrocytes at this stage possess a fine reticular network and are known as reticulocytes. This reticular structure is usually lost before the cells enter circulation as mature erythrocytes. The proper formation of erythrocytes depends primarily on nutrition, with protein, iron, and copper essential for the formation of hemoglobin, and vitamin B_{12} and folic acid necessary for DNA synthesis in stem cells of the red bone marrow.

As erythrocytes age and become fragile, they are removed from circulation by macrophages in the liver, spleen, and red bone marrow. The protein and iron of hemoglobin are reused; iron may be stored in the liver until needed for the production of new erythrocytes in the bone marrow. The heme portion of the hemoglobin is converted to bilirubin, which is excreted in bile as one of the bile pigments.

VARIETIES: On microscopic examination, erythrocytes may reveal variations in the following respects: size (anisocytosis), shape (poikilocytosis), staining reaction (achromia, hypochromia, hyperchromia, polychromatophilia), structure (possession of bodies such as Cabot's rings, Howell-Jolly bodies, Heinz bodies; parasites such as malaria; a reticular network; or nuclei), and number (anemia, polycythemia).

   achromatic e. An erythrocyte from which the hemoglobin has been dissolved; a colorless cell.

   basophilic e. An erythrocyte in which cytoplasm stains blue. The staining may be diffuse (material uniformly distributed) or punctate (material appearing as pinpoint dots).

   crenated e. An erythrocyte with a serrated or indented edge, usually the result of withdrawal of water from the cell, as occurs when cells are placed in hypertonic solutions.

immature e. Any incompletely developed erythrocyte.

orthochromatic e. An erythrocyte that stains with acid stains only, the cytoplasm appearing pink.

polychromatic e. An erythrocyte that does not stain uniformly.

erythrocyte reinfusion 1. Infusion of blood into the person who donated it.

PATIENT CARE: This is usually done by obtaining one or two units of blood, separating the red blood cells, and infusing them at a later date. It may also be performed by capturing blood lost during an operation with a cell saver and returning it to the patient intraoperatively.

2. Infusion with his or her own blood by a healthy person in an attempt to enhance athletic performance. SYN: *blood doping.*

erythrocythemia (ĕ-rĭth″rō-sī-thē′mē-ă) [Gr. *erythros,* red, + *kytos,* cell, + *haima,* blood] An obsolete term for polycythemia vera.

erythrocytometer (ĕ-rĭth″rō-sī-tŏm′ĕ-tĕr) [″ + ″ + *metron,* measure] An instrument for counting red blood cells.

erythrocyto-opsonin (ĕ-rĭth″rō-sī″tō-ŏp-sō′nĭn) [″ + ″ + *opsonein,* to buy food] A substance opsonic for red blood cells.

erythrocytopenia (ĕ-rĭth″rō-sī″tō-pē′nē-ă) [″ + ″ + *penia,* poverty] A deficiency in the number of red blood cells in the body. SYN: *erythropenia.*

erythrocytopoiesis (ĕ-rĭth″rō-sī″tō-poy-ē′sĭs) Erythropoiesis.

erythrocytorrhexis (ĕ-rĭth″rō-sī″tō-rĕk′sĭs) [″ + ″ + *rhexis,* rupture] The breaking up of red blood cells with particles or fragments of the cells escaping into the plasma.

erythrocytosis (ĕ-rĭth″rō-sī-tō′sĭs) [″ + ″ + *osis,* increasing condition] An abnormal increase in the number of red blood cells in circulation, found, for example, in hypoxemic patients or patients with polycythemia vera.

spurious e. Gaisböck's syndrome.

stress e. Gaisböck's syndrome.

erythroderma, erythrodermia (ĕ-rĭth″rō-dĕr′mă, ĕ-rĭth″rō-dĕr′mē-ă) [″ + *derma,* skin] Abnormally widespread redness and scaling of the skin, sometimes involving the entire body. This condition may be seen in patients with extensive psoriasis, cutaneous T-cell lymphoma, drug reactions, seborrheic or atopic dermatitis, or other conditions. SEE: illus. SYN: *erythrodermia; exfoliative dermatitis.*

e. desquamativum A disease of breast-fed infants. Resembling seborrhea, it is characterized by redness of the skin and development of scales.

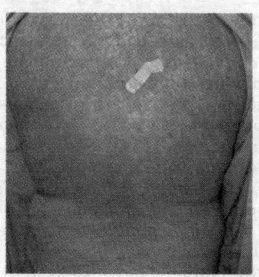

ERYTHRODERMA

e. ichthyosiforme congenitum The Latin name for congenital ichthyosiform erythroderma.

erythrodermia (ĕ-rĭth″rō-dĕr′mē-ă) Erythroderma.

erythrogenesis (ĕ-rĭth″rō-jĕn′ĕ-sĭs) [″ + *genesis,* generation, birth] The development of red blood cells.

erythroid (ĕr′ĭ-throyd) [″ + *eidos,* form, shape] **1.** Reddish. **2.** Concerning the red blood cells.

erythrokeratodermia (ĕ-rĭth″rō-kĕr″ă-tō-dĕr′mē-ă) [″ + *keras,* horn, + *derma,* skin] Reddening and hardening of the skin.

erythrokinetics (ĕ-rĭth″rō-kĭ-net′ĭks) [*erythro-* + *kinetics*] The study of the production rate of red blood cells and their life span.

erythroleukemia (ĕ-rĭth″rō-loo-kē′mē-ă) [Gr. *erythros,* red, + *leukos,* white, + *haima,* blood] ABBR: AEL. A variant of acute myelogenous leukemia with anemia, bizarre red blood cell morphology, erythroid hyperplasia in the bone marrow, and occasionally hepatosplenomegaly. The leukocyte count may be extremely high or quite low.

erythromelalgia (ĕ-rĭth″rō-mĕl-ăl′jē-ă) [″ + *melos,* limb, + *algos,* pain] Episodic burning, throbbing, and redness of the extremities caused by local dilation of blood vessels. The affected areas (typically the feet or lower legs) become flushed and warm. This condition is a symptom of myeloproliferative diseases, such as polycythemia vera, and of neuritis, multiple sclerosis, and systemic lupus erythematosus. It may also occur as a drug reaction. SYN: *acromelalgia; erythralgia.*

erythromelia (ĕ-rĭth″rō-mē′lē-ă) [″ + *melos,* limb] Painless erythema of the extensor surfaces of the extremities.

erythromycin (ĕ-rĭth″rō-mī′sĭn) [″ + *mykes,* fungus] An antibiotic derived from *Streptomyces erythraeus,* used primarily to treat gram-positive and atypical microorganisms, such as streptococci, mycoplasma, and legionella. Its primary side effects are nausea, vomiting, abdominal pain, bloating, and diarrhea.

erythron (ĕr'ĭ-thrŏn) [Gr. *erythros*, red] The blood as a body system including the circulating red cells and the tissue from which they originate.

erythroparasite (ĕ-rĭth″rō-păr'ă-sīt) [″ + *parasitos*, parasite] A red blood cell parasite.

erythropenia (ĕ-rĭth″rō-pē'nē-ă) [″ + *penia*, poverty] Erythrocytopenia.

erythrophage (ĕ-rĭth'rō-fāj) [″ + *phagein*, to eat] A phagocyte that destroys red blood cells.

erythrophagia (ĕ-rĭth″rō-fā'jē-ă) Destruction of red blood cells by phagocytes.

erythrophile (ĕ-rĭth'rō-fī) [″ + *philein* to love] An agent that readily stains red. **erythrophilous** (ĕr″ĭ-thrŏf'ĭ-lŭs), *adj.*

erythrophobia (ĕ-rĭth″rō-fō'bē-ă) [″ + *phobos*, fear] **1.** Abnormal dread of blushing or fear of being diffident or embarrassed. **2.** Morbid fear of, or aversion to, anything red.

erythropia, erythropsia (er″ĭ-thrō'pē-ă, er″ĭ-throp'sē-ă) [″ + *opsis*, vision] A condition in which objects appear to be red.

erythroplasia (ĕ-rĭth″rō-plā'zē-ă) [″ + *plasis*, molding, forming] A condition characterized by erythematous lesions of the mucous membranes.

   e. of Queyrat [Louis A. Queyrat, Fr. physician, 1856–1953] A precancerous lesion or invasive squamous cell carcinoma of the glans penis. It usually appears moist or velvety, and typically arises in uncircumcised middle-aged men.

erythropoiesis (ĕ-rĭth″rō-poy-ē'sĭs) [*erythro-* + *poiesis*] The formation of red blood cells. **erythropoietic** (-et'ik), *adj.*

   e. with morphologic dysplasia Stress e.

      stress e. Increased red blood cell production associated with malformation of red blood cells in illnesses in which erythropoietin levels are increased. SYN: **e. with morphologic dysplasia.**

erythropoietin (ĕ-rĭth″rō-poy'ĕ-tĭn) A cytokine made by the kidneys that stimulates the proliferation of red blood cells. Synthetic erythropoietin (epoetin alfa) is used to treat anemia, esp. in patients with renal or bone marrow failure. Hypertension is a common side effect of the drug. SEE: *blood doping; cytokine; epoetin alfa.*

⚠️ Athletes have used erythropoietin in an attempt to enhance performance. When the hormone is used without medical supervision and in large doses, it can cause an abnormal increase in red blood cell mass and may lead to death.

erythropoietin independence A characteristic of red blood cell colonies in poly-

cythemia rubra vera. Normal red blood cell progenitors do not multiply without stimulation by erythropoietin; cells from patients with polycythemia vera can replicate independently of this cytokine because of the intracellular derangement of other growth-promoting proteins.

erythropsin (ĕ-rĭth-rŏp'sĭn) [″ + *opsis*, vision] A term formerly used to indicate rhodopsin, or visual purple. SYN: *rhodopsin.*

erythrosine sodium (ĕ-rĭth'ră-sĭn, sĭn″) A dye used as a dental disclosing agent. It is applied to the teeth in a 2% solution or in soluble tablets, which are chewed. SEE: *disclosing agent.*

erythrosis (ĕr-ĭ-thrō'sĭs) [″ + *osis*, condition] A reddish-purple discoloration of the skin and mucous membranes in polycythemia.

erythrostasis (ē-rĭth″rō-stā'sĭs) [″ + *stasis*, standing still] Accumulation of red blood cells in vessels due to cessation of the blood flow. SEE: *sludged blood.*

erythrovirus B19 (ĕ-rĭth″rō-vī'rŭs) A type of parvovirus that causes erythema infectiosum (fifth disease), a usually benign, nonfebrile disease. However, intrauterine infection may produce fetal anemia with hydrops fetalis and death. Infection of immunocompromised patients or patients with sickle cell anemia may cause aplastic anemia, and complications may lead to death. It was formerly known as *parvovirus B19.*

Es Symbol for the element einsteinium.

escalate (ĕs'kă-lāt) [L. *scala*, staircase] **1.** To increase, esp. the dosage of a medication. **2.** To become more angry, dangerous, or intense, as in an interpersonal crisis.

escape (es-kāp') [Fr. *escaper*] **1.** To break out of confinement; to leak or seep out. **2.** The act of attaining freedom.

   mutational e. Escape mutation.

   vagal e. An ectopic heartbeat that occurs when the normal rhythm of the heart has been stopped or inhibited by stimulation of the vagus nerve.

   ventricular e. Single or repeated ventricular beats that arise from pacemakers in the ventricular muscle when beats from pacemakers in the sinoatrial or atrioventricular nodes fail to appear.

escape phenomenon The development of resistance to the effects of a continuously present stimulus.

eschar (es'kar″) [Gr. *eschara*, hearth, brazier, burning coal, burn, scab] Dead matter that is cast off from the surface of the skin, esp. after a burn. The tissue is hard, black or brown, and leathery in texture. SEE: illus.; *escharotic.*

escharotic (ĕs-kăr-ŏt'ĭk) [Gr. *escharotikos*] A caustic agent, such as a strong acid or base, that is used to destroy tissue and cause sloughing. Escharotics

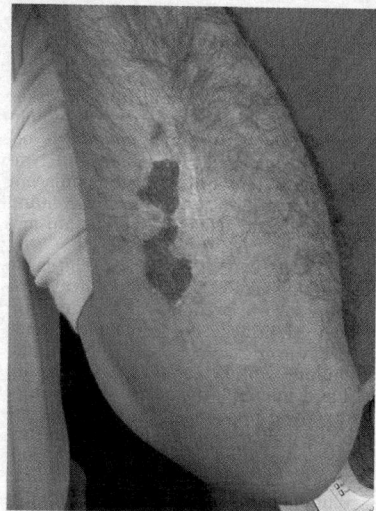

ESCHAR

may be acids, alkalies, metallic salts, phenol or carbolic acid, carbon dioxide, or electric cautery.

escharotomy (ĕs-kăr-ŏt′ō-mē) [Gr. *eschara*, scab, + *tome*, incision] **1.** Removal of the eschar formed on the skin and underlying tissue of severely burned areas. This procedure can be life-saving when used to allow expansion of the chest and is also used to restore circulation to the extremities of patients in which the eschar forms a tight swollen band around the circumference of the limb. **2.** Excision of dense necrotic skin about a decubitus or ischemic ulcer.

Escherichia (ĕsh-ĕr-ĭk′ē-ă) A genus of gram-negative, motile, facultatively anaerobic, non–spore-forming bacilli of the family Enterobacteriaceae. These bacteria are part of the normal flora of the intestines of humans and animals.

Escherichia coli ABBR: *E. coli.* A gram-negative bacillus in the human colon. These small, plump, bacilli are normally nonpathogenic in the intestinal tract, but some serotypes may cause diarrheal illnesses, urinary tract infections, sepsis, or hemolytic uremic syndrome. Certain enterotoxigenic strains are a principal cause of travelers' diarrhea.

TREATMENT: *E. coli* are sensitive to many antibiotics, including sulfa drugs and quinolones. Diarrhea caused by *E. coli* should also be treated with aggressive fluid and electrolyte replacement to prevent dehydration.

    E.c. 0157:H7 A strain of *E. coli* that may cause bloody diarrhea (and other more serious illnesses) as a result of its production of a potent toxin. Outbreaks of diarrheal illnesses caused by 0157:H7 have occurred in day care centers, families, farms, fast-food restaurants, nursing homes, petting zoos, and schools. The organism may contaminate undercooked meat, esp. hamburger; unpreserved apple cider; vegetables grown in manure; or contaminated water supplies. The infection caused by this bacillus may spread from animal-to-person, person-to-person, or through contamination of food or water.

SYMPTOMS: Asymptomatic infection is common. In other cases, after the 3- to 8-day incubation period, an afebrile and self-limiting diarrhea occurs; however, the infection may progress to hemorrhagic colitis with bloody diarrhea, severe abdominal pain, and low-grade fever. Resolution usually occurs in 1 week. In about 15% of cases, patients develop hemolytic uremic syndrome (HUS); the mortality among patients who develop HUS ranges from 3 to 5%. The highest incidence of HUS is found among children and older adults.

DIAGNOSIS: Without a high index of suspicion, diagnosis in either a lone case or an outbreak may be delayed. To prevent unnecessary diagnostic or therapeutic intervention, such as colonoscopy or colectomy, diagnosis should be made as quickly as possible.

PREVENTION: Ground meat should be cooked until it reaches a temperature of 160°F (71.1°C) and the meat should not be pink in the center. Leftovers should be reheated to 165°F (73.3°C). Individuals who change a baby's diapers should thoroughly wash their hands immediately afterward. Food handlers must wash their hands after using the toilet.

    enteroaggregative E.c. ABBR: EAggEC. A type of *E. coli* that causes persistent diarrhea, esp. in the immunosuppressed.

    enterohemorrhagic E.c. ABBR: EHEC. The strain of *E. coli* that causes colitis with copious bloody diarrhea.

    enteroinvasive E.c. ABBR: EIEC. A type of *E. coli* that invades and multiplies in the epithelial cells of the distal ileum and colon causing dysentery, principally in infants and children.

    enteropathogenic E.c. ABBR: EPEC. A type of *E. coli* that produces infantile diarrhea, esp. in developing countries.

    enterotoxigenic E.c. ABBR: ETEC. A type of *E. coli* that can cause diarrhea in infants and travelers to developing nations. Fluid loss and abdominal cramping may be severe. The diarrhea results from the ingestion of tainted food or water and is produced by a heat stable toxin (ST) or a heat labile toxin (LT).

Escherich reflex (esh′ĕ-rik) [Theodor Escherich, Ger. physician, 1857–1911] A pursing or muscular contraction of the lips resulting from irritation of the mucosa of the lips.

escorcin (ĕs-kor′sĭn) A stain derived from escalin. It is used to stain and identify defects or injury of the cornea.

escutcheon (ĕs-kŭch′ăn) [L. *scutum*, a shield] The pattern of pubic hair growth. It is different in males and females.

eserine (ĕs′ĕr-ĭn) [*esere*, African name for the Calabar bean] The salicylate of an alkaloid usually obtained from the dried ripe seed of the Calabar bean, the seed of a poisonous legume *Physostigma venenosum* of tropical Africa.

ACTION/USES: The substance is a cholinergic; it inactivates cholinesterase, prolonging and intensifying the action of acetylcholine. It improves the tone and action of skeletal muscle, increases intestinal peristalsis through its effects on the parasympathetic nervous system, and acts as a miotic in the eye. It is used to treat tetanus, strychnine poisoning, and myasthenia gravis. SYN: *physostigmine salicylate*.

ESF *erythropoietic stimulating factor.* SEE: *erythropoietin.*

-esis [Gr. *-esis*, fr. *-sis*] Suffix meaning *action* or *process*. SEE: *-sis.*

ESL *English as a Second Language.*

Esmarch bandage (es′mark″) [Johannes Friedrich August von Esmarch, Ger. surgeon, 1823–1908] A rubber bandage used to minimize bleeding.

⚠ If the bandage is applied too tightly or too long, tissue damage may occur because of decreased blood supply.

PATIENT CARE: Before any incisions are made, the bandage is applied tightly to the limb, starting at the distal end and reaching above the site of operation. A pneumatic tourniquet is firmly applied proximally. The bandage makes the surgical area virtually bloodless and is then removed.

eso- [Gr. *esō*, within] Prefix meaning *inward*.

esoethmoiditis (ĕs″ō-ĕth″moy-dī′tĭs) [Gr. *eso*, inward, + *ethmos*, sieve, + *eidos*, form, shape, + *itis*, inflammation] Inflammation of the membrane of ethmoid cells.

esogastritis (ĕs″ō-găs-trī′tĭs) [″ + *gaster*, belly, + *itis*, inflammation] Inflammation of the gastric mucous membrane.

esophagalgia (ē-sŏf-ă-găl′jē-ă) [Gr. *oisophagos*, esophagus, + *algos*, pain] Pain in the esophagus.

esophageal apoplexy SEE: under *apoplexy.*

esophageal cancer An adenocarcinoma or squamous cell carcinoma of the esophagus. The disease causes more than 10,000 deaths each year in the U.S. It occurs most often in men over 60.

Esophageal tumors are usually fungating and infiltrating; in most cases the tumor partially constricts the esophageal lumen. Regional metastasis occurs early by way of submucosal lymphatics, often fatally invading adjacent vital intrathoracic organs. The liver and lungs are the usual sites of distant metastases.

PREDISPOSING FACTORS: The cause of esophageal cancer is unknown; however, several predisposing factors have been identified. These include chronic smoking or excessive use of alcohol; consumption of hot beverages; stasis-induced inflammation, as in achalasia or stricture; previous head and neck tumors; gastroesophageal reflux and Barrett esophagus, and nutritional deficiency, as in untreated sprue and Plummer-Vinson syndrome. The disease is more commonly found in Asia and in the Middle East than elsewhere.

COMPLICATIONS: Direct invasion of adjoining structures may lead to severe complications, such as mediastinitis, tracheoesophageal or bronchoesophageal fistula (causing an overwhelming cough when swallowing liquids), and aortic perforation with sudden exsanguination. Obstruction of the esophagus by the tumor often results in an inability to control secretions, malnutrition, and loss of lower esophageal sphincter control, which can result in aspiration pneumonia.

SIGNS AND SYMPTOMS: Early in the disease, the patient may report a feeling of fullness, pressure, indigestion, or substernal burning and may report using antacids to relieve gastrointestinal upset. Later, the patient may complain of dysphagia and weight loss. The degree of dysphagia varies, depending on the extent of the disease, ranging from mild dysphagia occurring only after eating solid foods (esp. meat) to difficulty in swallowing soft foods and even liquids. The patient may complain of hoarseness (from laryngeal nerve involvement), chronic cough (possibly from aspiration), anorexia, vomiting, and regurgitation of food.

DIAGNOSTIC TESTS: Radiography of the esophagus, with barium swallow and motility studies; chest radiography or esophagography; esophagoscopy; punch and brush biopsies; and exfoliative cytological tests; bronchoscopy; endoscopic ultrasonography of the esophagus; computed tomography scan; magnetic resonance imaging; liver function studies; a liver scan; and mediastinal tomography may be performed to delineate the tumor, confirm its type, reveal growth into adjacent structures, and reveal distant metastatic lesions. These studies determine disease staging and possible treatments.

TREATMENT: Because esophageal cancer usually is advanced when diagnosed, treatment is often palliative rather than curative. Treatment to keep the esophagus open includes esophageal dilation, laser therapy, external beam radiation therapy, bipolar electrocoagulation, and insertion of stents or prosthetic tubes to bridge the tumor. Radical surgery can excise the tumor and resect either the esophagus alone or the stomach and esophagus with jejunal or colonic bypass grafts. Chemotherapy (5-flourouracil or cisplatin) and radiation therapy can slow the growth of the tumor. Gastrostomy or jejunostomy can help provide adequate nutrition. A prosthesis can be used to seal fistulae. Analgesics provide pain control.

PROGNOSIS: Regardless of cell type, the prognosis for esophageal cancer is grim: 5-year survival rates are about 10%, and most patients die within 6 months of diagnosis.

PATIENT CARE: During hospitalization, food and fluid intake and body weight are monitored. All procedures and expected sensations are explained; the patient is prepared physically and emotionally for surgery and postsurgical care.

A high-calorie, high-protein diet is provided. Pureed or liquefied foods and commercially available nutritional supplements are offered if needed. Supplemental parenteral nutrition is administered as prescribed. The patient is placed in Fowler's position for meals and is allowed plenty of time to eat to prevent aspiration. Any regurgitation is documented, and oral hygiene is provided. Prescribed analgesics and noninvasive pain relief measures are provided and the patient's response noted.

When a gastrostomy tube is used, feedings are administered slowly by gravity in prescribed amounts (usually 200 to 500 ml), and the patient may be given something to chew before and during each feeding to stimulate gastric secretions and promote some semblance of normal eating. The patient and family are taught about nutritional concerns (care of any feeding tubes, checking patency; administering the feeding; providing skin care at the insertion site; and keeping the patient upright during and immediately after feedings).

After surgery, vital signs and fluid and electrolyte balance are monitored. The patient is observed for complications (infection, fistula formation, pneumonia, empyema, and malnutrition). If surgical resection with an esophageal anastomosis was performed, the patient is observed for signs of an anastomotic leak and kept supine to prevent suture-line tension. If a prosthetic tube was inserted, the patient is monitored for signs of blockage or dislodgement, which can perforate the mediastinum or precipitate tumor erosion.

If chemotherapy is prescribed, the patient is monitored for complications such as bone marrow suppression and gastrointestinal reactions. Adverse oral reactions are minimized by use of a soft toothbrush (brushing twice a day), flossing once a day and saline/bicarbonate mouthwashes (1 tsp salt and 1 tsp baking soda dissolved in 1 pint water, swished for 20 seconds 4 times a day). Extra periods of rest are encouraged; medications (antiemetics, analgesics, bone marrow stimulants, antidepressants) are administered, and the patient evaluated for desired and adverse affects. If radiation therapy is used, the patient is monitored for complications such as esophageal perforation, pneumonitis, pulmonary fibrosis, and myelitis.

Expected outcomes of the prescribed therapies are explained to the patient and family. Additional rest is encouraged. Assurance is provided that pain will be managed, and the health care providers stay with the patient during periods of anxiety or distress. The patient is encouraged to participate in decisions about care.

The patient should resume as normal a routine as possible during recovery to maintain a sense of control and to reduce complications associated with immobility. Referral to a home health care agency provides ongoing physical care, assessment for complications, and psychological support. Both patient and family are referred to appropriate organizations for information and support. Because of the generally poor prognosis, patient and family should be encouraged to discuss end-of-life concerns, and referral should be made to local hospice for home or inpatient palliative care as desired and needed.

esophageal tube A tube inserted in the esophagus.

esophagectasia, esophagectasis (ē-sŏf″ă-jĕk-tā′sē-ă, ē-sŏf″ă-jĕk′tă-sĭs) [″ + *ektasis,* distention] Dilatation of the esophagus.

esophagectomy (ē-sŏf″ă-jĕk′tō-mē) [″ + *ektome,* excision] Surgical removal of all or a portion of the esophagus.

esophagismus (ē-sŏf-ă-jĭs′mŭs) [″ + -*ismos,* condition] Spasm of the esophagus.

esophagitis (ē″sof-ă-jīt′ĭs) [*esophago-* + -*itis*] Inflammation of the esophagus. SEE: *acid reflux test.*

    eosinophilic e. Dysphagia and heartburn resulting from allergy to inhaled or consumed antigens. Biopsies of the esophagus reveals infiltration of the mucosa by eosinophils. It is treated with corticosteroids.

   medication-induced e. Pill-induced e.

   necrotizing e. Severe injury to the cells that line the esophagus, with cellular death and eventual desquamation. SYN: *acute esophageal* **necrosis**; *black* **esophagus**.

   pill-induced e. Inflammation of the esophageal mucosa by caustic medications, e.g., bisphosphonates, tetracyclines, or nonsteroidal anti-inflammatory drugs. SYN: *medication-induced e.*

   reflux e. SEE: *gastroesophageal reflux; reflux disease.*

esophago-, esophag- [Gr. *oisophagos*, esophagus] Prefixes meaning *esophagus*. The variant *oesophago-* is used outside the U.S.

esophagocele (ē-sŏf″ă-gō-sēl) [″ + *kele*, tumor, swelling] A hernia of the esophagus.

esophagodynia (ē-sŏf″ă-gō-dīn′ē-ă) [Gr. *oisophagos*, esophagus, + *odyne*, pain] Pain in the esophagus.

esophagogastrectomy (ē-sŏf″ă-gō-găs-trĕk′tō-mē) [″ + *gaster*, belly, + *ektome*, excision] Surgical removal of all or part of the stomach and esophagus.

esophagogastroanastomosis (ĕ-sŏf″ă-gō-găs″trō-ă-năs″tō-mō′sĭs) [″ + ″ + *anastomosis*, opening] A joining of the esophagus to the stomach.

esophagogastroduodenoscopy, esophagealgastroduodenoscopy (ē-sŏf″ă-gō-gas″trō-doo″ŏ-dē-nos′kŏ-pē, -dū″ŏ, ē-sof ″ă-jē″ăl-gas″trō-doo″ŏ-dē-nos′kŏ-pē, -dū″ŏ) [*esophago-* + *gastroduodenoscopy*] ABBR: EGD. Examination of the upper gastrointestinal tract with a flexible fiber-optic endoscope. EGD is often performed to identify the cause of or to treat bleeding, pain, or difficulty with swallowing.

esophagogastroplasty (ē-sŏf′ă-gō-găs′trō-plăs″tē) [″ + ″ + *plassein*, to form] Plastic repair of the esophagus and stomach.

esophagogastroscopy (ē-sŏf″ă-gō-găs-trŏs′kă-pē) [″ + ″ + ″] Inspection of the esophagus and stomach with an endoscope.

esophagogastrostomy (ē-sŏf″ă-gō-găs-trŏs′tō-mē) [″ + ″ + *stoma*, mouth] Formation of an opening or anastomosis between the esophagus and stomach.

esophagography (ĕ-sŏf″ă-gog′ră-fē) [*esophago-* + *-graphy*] Radiological evaluation of the lumen of the esophagus, usually performed with an oral contrast agent such as barium.

esophagojejunostomy (ē-sof″ă-gō-je″jŭ-nos′tō-mē) [*esophago-* + *jejunostomy*] The surgical anastomosis of an end of the divided jejunum to the esophagus or of the side of the jejunum to the esophagus. It provides a bypass for food in cases of esophageal stricture.

esophagomalacia (ē-sŏf″ă-gō-mă-lā′shă) [Gr. *oisophagos*, esophagus, + *malakia*, softness] Softening of the esophageal walls.

esophagomycosis (ē-sŏf″ă-gō-mī-kō′sĭs) [″ + *mykes*, fungus, + *osis*, condition] A fungal disease of the esophagus, typically esophageal candidiasis.

esophagomyotomy (ē-sŏf″ă-gō-mī-ŏt′ă-mē) [″ + ″ + ″] Cutting of the muscular coat of the esophagus, used to treat stenosis of the lower esophagus. SEE: *achalasia.*

esophagoplasty (ē-sŏf″ă-gō-plăs″tē) [″ + *plassein*, to form] Repair of the esophagus by plastic surgery.

esophagoplication (ē-sŏf″ă-gō-plī-kā′shŏn) [*esophago-* + *plication*] The surgical narrowing of the esophagus by creating longitudinal folds in the esophageal wall. The operation is rarely performed. SYN: *esophageal plication.*

esophagoptosia, esophagoptosis (ē-sof″ă-gop-tō′sē-ă, ē-sof″ă-gop-tō′sĭs) [″ + *ptosis*, a dropping] Relaxation and prolapse of the esophagus.

esophagoscope (ē-sŏf″ă-gō-skōp) [″ + *skopein*, to examine] An endoscope for examination of the esophagus.

esophagospasm (ē-sŏf′ă-gō-spăzm) [″ + ″] A painful muscular contraction of the esophagus.

esophagostenosis (ē-sŏf″ă-gō-stĕn-ō′sĭs) [″ + *stenosis*, act of narrowing] Stricture or narrowing of the esophagus.

esophagostomiasis Variant spelling of oesophagostomiasis.

esophagostomy (ē-sŏf-ă-gŏs′tō-mē) [″ + *stoma*, mouth] Surgical formation of an opening into the esophagus.

esophagotomy (ē-sŏf-ă-gŏt′ō-mē) A surgical incision into the esophagus. SEE: *achalasia; cardiospasm; dysphagia.*

esophagotracheal (ē-sŏf″ă-gō-trā′kē-ăl) Concerning the esophagus and the trachea, or a communication between them.

esophagram (ĕ-sof′ă-gram″) [*esophagus* + *-gram*] A radiographic study of the lumen (interior space) of the esophagus after the patient drinks a solution (typically of barium or water-soluble contrast) to outline its features.

esophagus (ē-sof′ă-gŭs, -gī″, -jī″) *pl.* **esophagi** [Gr. *oisophagos*] The muscular tube, about 10 to 12 in (25 to 30 cm) long, that carries swallowed foods and liquids from the pharynx to the stomach. In the upper third of the esophagus, the muscle is striated; in the middle third, striated and smooth; and in the lower third, entirely smooth. Peristalsis is regulated by the autonomic nervous system. At the junction with the stomach is the lower esophageal sphincter, which relaxes to permit passage of food, then contracts to prevent backup of stomach contents. **esophageal** (ē-sof″ă-jē′ăl), *adj.* SEE: illus.

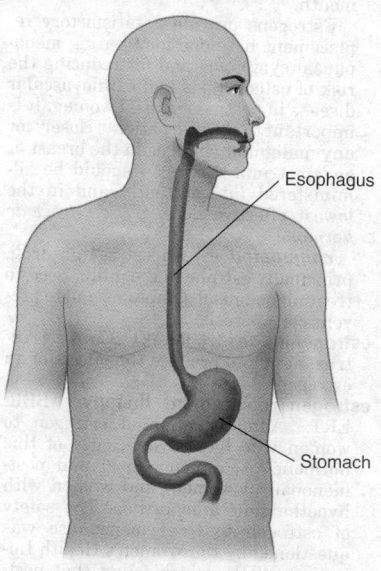

ESOPHAGUS

Barrett e. SEE: *Barrett esophagus.*
black e. Necrotizing **esophagitis**.
foreign bodies in the e. Items trapped in the esophagus (typically fishbones, coins, or large unchewed pieces of food). Parenteral glucagon may help the material pass through the esophageal sphincter to the stomach, but endoscopic retrieval of the material is usually necessary. SEE: illus.

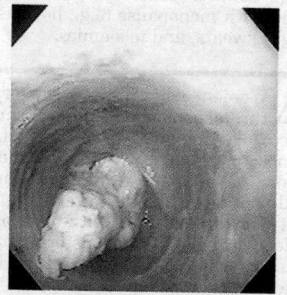

FOREIGN BODY IN ESOPHAGUS

Meat impaction in the lower esophageal sphincter (as seen through an endoscope)

esophoria (ĕs-ō-fō′rē-ă) [Gr. *eso,* inward, + *phorein,* to bear] **1.** The tendency of visual lines to converge. **2.** An inward turning, or the amount of inward turning, of the eye. Opposite of exophoria. SEE: *heterotropia.*

esosphenoiditis (ĕs″ō-sfē-noyd-ī′tĭs) [″ + *sphen,* wedge, + *eidos,* form, shape, + *itis,* inflammation] Osteomyelitis of the sphenoid bone.

esotropia (es-ŏ-trō′pē-ă) [Gr. *esō,* within + Gr. *tropē,* turning] Marked turning inward of the eye; crossed eyes. SYN: *adtorsion.*

ESP *extrasensory perception.*

ESR *electron spin resonance; erythrocyte sedimentation rate.* SEE: under *rate.*

ESRD *end-stage renal disease.*

essence [L. *essentia,* being or quality] **1.** The spirit or principle of anything. **2.** An alcoholic solution of volatile oil.

essential [L. *essentialis*] **1.** Pert. to an essence. **2.** Indispensable. **3.** Independent of a local abnormal condition; having no obvious external cause. SEE: *idiopathic.*

essential medicine SEE: under *medicine.*

Essiac A tea containing anti-inflammatory, antioxidant, and immunostimulatory chemicals; it has been promoted as a treatment for cancer but has not been scientifically studied. Essiac was first used in the 1920s. Trials of its usefulness have not shown any evidence of efficacy; it is not approved for use in the U.S. by the Food and Drug Administration.

EST *electroshock therapy.* SEE: *electroconvulsive therapy.*

established customary standard of care Standard of care.

Estelle v. Gamble (es-tel′ gam′bĕl) A 1976 U.S. Supreme Court case in which the court decided that federal, state, and local correctional facilities must provide inmates with medical care. The court decided that "deliberate indifference" to the medical needs of the incarcerated is a violation of the Eighth Amendment of the Bill of Rights because it constitutes "cruel and unusual punishment."

ester (ĕs′tĕr) [L. *aether,* ether] In organic chemistry, a fragrant compound formed by the combination of an organic acid with an alcohol. This reaction removes water from the compound.

esterase (ĕs′tĕr-ās) Generic term for an enzyme that catalyzes the hydrolysis of esters.

esterification (ĕs-tĕr″ĭ-fĭ-kā′shŭn) The combination of an organic acid with an alcohol to form an ester.

esthesi- [Gr. *aisthēsis,* feeling, sensation] Prefix meaning *sensation, feeling.* The variant *aesthesi-* is used outside the U.S.

esthesia (es-thē′zh(ē-)ă) [Gr. *aisthesis,* sensation + *-ia*] **1.** Perception; feeling; sensation. **2.** Any disease that affects sensation or perception.

esthesiology (ĕs-thē″zē-ŏl′ō-jē) [″ + *logos,* word, reason] The science of sensory phenomena.

esthesiometer, aesthesiometer (ĕs-thē-zē-ŏm′ĕ-tĕr) [″ + *metron,* measure] A device for measuring tactile sensibility.

esthesioneuroblastoma (ĕs-thēz″ē-ō-nūr″ō-blăs-tōm′ă) A malignant glioma of the nasal passages. The tumor is occasionally partially responsive to surgical removal, chemotherapy, or radiotherapy.

esthesioneurosis (ĕs-thē″zē-ō-nū-rō′sĭs) [″ + *neuron,* nerve, + *osis,* condition] Any sensory impairment.

esthesioscopy (ĕs-thē″zē-ŏs′kō-pē) [″ + *skopein,* to examine] The testing of tactile and other forms of sensibility.

esthetics (ĕs-thĕt′ĭks) Aesthetics.

estimated daily intake ABBR: EDI. The presumed daily exposure to or consumption of an nutrient or chemical residue.

estimated fetal weight An estimate of the weight of a fetus based on ultrasonographic measurement and the use of standard reference tables incorporating fetal growth parameters, i.e., biparietal diameter, circumference of the head, and circumference of the abdomen.

estival (ĕs′tĭ-văl) [L. *aestivus*] Pert. to or occurring in summer.

estradiol (ĕs-tră-dī′ŏl) $C_{18}H_{24}O_2$, a steroid produced by the ovary and possessing estrogenic properties. Large quantities are found in the urine of pregnant women and of mares and stallions, the latter two serving as sources of the commercial product that is used to treat estrogen deficiencies, e.g. menopause. Estradiol is effective when given subcutaneously or intramuscularly but not when given orally. It is converted to estrone in the body. SEE: *diethylstilbestrol; estrogen.*

estrin (ĕs′trĭn) Estrogen.

estrinization (ĕs″trĭn-ĭ-zā′shŭn) The production of vaginal epithelial changes characteristic of estrogen stimulation.

estriol (es′trī″ol″, e-strī′, ōl″) $C_{18}H_{24}O_3$, an estrogenic hormone considered to be the metabolic product of estrone and estradiol. It is found in the urine of women, esp. during pregnancy, and is used as a marker of fetal health.

estrogen (ĕs′trō-jĕn) [Gr. *oistros,* mad desire + *gennan,* to produce] Any natural or artificial substance that induces estrus and the development of female sex characteristics; more specifically, the estrogenic hormones produced by the ovary; the female sex hormones. Estrogens are secreted by the ovaries and the placenta in women and by the adrenal cortex in both sexes. Estrogens are responsible for cyclic changes in the vaginal epithelium and endometrium of the uterus. Natural estrogens include estradiol, estrone, and their metabolic product, estriol. When used therapeutically, estrogens are usually given in the form of a conjugate such as ethinyl estradiol, conjugated estrogens, or the synthetic estrogenic substance diethylstilbestrol. These preparations are effective when given by mouth.

Estrogens provide a satisfactory replacement hormone for treating menopausal symptoms and for reducing the risk of osteoporosis and cardiovascular disease in postmenopausal women. It is important to observe patients closely for any malignant changes in the breast or endometrium. Estrogen should be administered intermittently and in the lowest effective dose. SYN: *estrogenic hormone.*

   conjugated e. An estrogenic drug, principally estrone and equilin, used to treat menopausal symptoms and to prevent osteoporosis.

estrogenic (ĕs-trō-jĕn′ĭk) Causing estrus; acting to produce the effects of an estrogen.

estrogen replacement therapy ABBR: ERT. Administration of estrogen to women who have a deficiency of this hormone (e.g., menopausal and postmenopausal women) and women with hypothalamic amenorrhea. The safety of estrogen to treat menopause was questioned by the Women's Health Initiative (WHI), which found that postmenopausal women who took estrogen and progesterone had an increased risk of breast cancer, heart attack, stroke, and venous thromboembolism relative to controls. Estrogen and estrogen-like compounds can be used in men to treat prostate cancer. SEE: *conjugated estrogen; hormone replacement therapy.*

   Reported health benefits are vigorously debated. ERT is credited with retarding bone loss and lowering the risk of osteoporotic fractures. In addition, ERT relieves some symptoms associated with menopause (e.g., hot flashes, night sweats, and insomnia).

> ⚠ Women who have a history of thromboembolic disorders, current tobacco use, impaired liver function, undiagnosed vaginal bleeding, endometrial cancer, or estrogen-stimulated tumors should not receive ERT. Estrogen replacement should be used with caution in women who have a family history of breast cancer or who have diseases of the liver, kidney, or gallbladder.

estrone (ĕs′trōn) $C_{18}H_{22}O_2$, an estrogenic hormone found in the urine of pregnant women and mares. Also prepared synthetically, it is used in the treatment of estrogen deficiencies. It is less active than estradiol but more active than estriol.

estropipate (ĕs-trō-pī′pāt) Estrogen manufactured synthetically from plant sources.

estrual (ĕs′troo-ăl) [Gr. *oistros,* mad desire] Pert. to the estrus of animals.

estruation (ĕs″troo-ā′shŭn) The sexually fertile period in female mammals. In lay terminology, the period of heat.

estrus, oestrus (es′trŭs) [Gr. *oistros,* mad desire] The cyclic period of sexual activity in nonhuman female mammals, marked by congestion of and secretion by the uterine mucosa, proliferation of vaginal epithelium, swelling of the vulva, ovulation, and acceptance of the male by the female. During estrus, the animal is said to be "in heat."

estrus cycle SEE: under *cycle.*

ESU *electrosurgical unit.*

e.s.u. *electrostatic unit.*

état criblé (ā-tă′ krēb-lā′) [Fr., sievelike state] Multiple irregular perforations of Peyer's patches of the intestines. These patches are characteristic of typhoid fever.

etching (ĕch′ĭng) [Ger. *ätzen,* to feed] Application of a corrosive or abrasive material to a glass or metal surface to create a pattern or design.

   acid e. A dental procedure used to prepare the surface of tooth enamel for better retention in bonding material to the tooth structure. Phosphoric acid is placed on the enamel surface. The acid removes the organic portion of the enamel, leaving microscopic pores (micropores) in the enamel approx. 5 μm in length. The micropores allow for improved retention of dental restorations.

ETEC Enterotoxigenic *Escherichia coli.*

e-text, electronic text book (ē′tĕkst′) Any online instructional resource that organizes knowledge and guides learning.

ethanol (eth′ă-nol″) ABBR: ETOH. Ethyl **alcohol**.

   diluted e. Diluted **alcohol**.

ethene (ĕth-ēn′) Ethylene.

ethenylbenzene, ethenyl benzene (eth′ĕ-nil-ben′zēn″, -ben-zēn′) Styrene.

ether (ĕth′ĕr) [Gr. *aither,* air] Any organic compound in which an oxygen atom links with carbon chains. The ether used for anesthesia is diethyl ether, $C_4H_{10}O$. As an anesthetic it causes postoperative nausea and profuse salivation. **ethereal** (ĕ-thē′rē-ăl), *adj.*

⚠️ Ether is highly flammable and should be handled with great care. Also, it should not be stored once its container has been opened because toxic products form when ether is exposed to light.

ethical reasoning (ĕth′ĭ-kĭl) Reasoning about what one ought to do as a guide for what one actually does; moral reasoning.

ethical review A formal evaluation of the moral grounding of a proposed academic or research project before it is begun. The review is an attempt to ensure that the research will treat its subjects fairly and safely, without exposing them or society at large to undue risk.

ethical will A formal but not legally binding document in which individuals relay their blessings, concerns, feelings, regrets, thoughts, moral guidance, or life instructions to others.

ethics (eth′iks) [Gr. *ēthikos,* pert. to morals] A system of moral principles or standards governing conduct.

   applied e. The use of moral principles and reasoning to solve problems that arise in practical fields, such as health care, law, or management.

   biomedical e. Moral inquiry into issues raised by health care education, practice, and research.

   dental e. A system of principles governing dental practice; a moral obligation to render the best possible quality of dental service to the patient and to maintain an honest relationship with other members of the profession and society at large.

   environmental e. The application of moral principles to human (especially commercial or industrial) interactions with nature. It is an important principle of occupational safety and public health because of the potential threats posed to health when biological agents, pollutants, toxins, or other commercial waste products are not carefully managed.

   medical e. A system of principles governing medical conduct. It deals with the relationship of a physician to the patient, the patient's family, fellow physicians, and society at large. SEE: *advance directive; do not attempt resuscitation; euthanasia; Hippocratic oath; living will.*

   nursing e. A system of principles governing the conduct of a nurse. Nursing ethics deals with the relationship of a nurse to the patient, the patient's family, associates and fellow nurses, and society at large. SEE: *Nightingale Pledge.*

ethics committee Committee, patient care advisory

Ethics in Patient Referrals Act ABBR: EPRA. An American federal law that makes it illegal for a physician to refer a patient to a health care facility in which the physician (or a family member) has a financial interest. Also known as the *Stark Act.*

ethidium bromide (e-thid′ē-ŭm) A fluorescent dye used to highlight nucleic acids.

ethinyl estradiol (ĕth′ĭ-nĭl) SEE: *estradiol.*

ethionine (ĕ-thī′ō-nĭn) A progestational agent used in some oral contraceptives.

ethmoid (ĕth′moyd) [Gr. *ēthmos,* sieve, + *eidos,* form, shape] Cribriform.

ethmoidal (ĕth-moy′-dl) Pert. to the ethmoid bone or its air cells.

ethmoidectomy (ĕth-moy-dĕk′tō-mē) [″ + *eidos,* form, shape, + *ektome,* excision] Excision of the ethmoid sinuses that open into the nasal cavity.

ethmoiditis (ĕth″moy-dī′tĭs) [″ + ″ + *itis,* inflammation] Inflammation of the ethmoidal sinuses. This may be acute or chronic.

SYMPTOMS: Symptoms include headache, acute pain between the eyes, and a nasal discharge.

ethmoid sinus An air cavity or space within the ethmoid bone, opening into the nasal cavity.

ethnic (ĕth′nĭk) [Gr. *ethnikos,* of a nation] Concerning groups of people within a cultural system who desire or are given a distinct classification based on traits such as religion, culture, language, or appearance.

ethnobiology (ĕth″nō-bī-ŏl′ō-jē) [Gr. *ethnos,* race, + *bios,* life, + *logos,* word, reason] The study of the biological characteristics of various races.

ethnocentrism (ĕth″nō-sĕn′trĭzm) **1.** A belief that one's own way of viewing and experiencing the world is superior to other perspectives; a mindset that judges the actions and beliefs of others according to one's own cultural rules. **2.** In health care, a perspective that supports the worldview of the caretaker, rather than considering the patient's perspective of health and illness. **ethnocentric,** *adj.*

ethnogerontology (ĕth″nō-jĕ-rŏn-tŏl′ō-jē) The study of aging and population groups in reference to race, national origin, and cultural practices. Ethnogerontology addresses the causes, processes, heritage, and consequences specific to these groups.

ethnography (ĕth-nŏg′rǎ-fē) [″ + *graphein,* to write] The study of the culture of a single society. Data are gathered by direct observation during a period of residence with the group. SEE: *anthropology.*

ethnology (ĕth-nŏl′ō-jē) [″ + *logos,* word, reason] The comparative study of cultures using ethnographic data. SEE: *anthropology.*

ethology (ĕ-, ē-thŏl′ō-jē) [Gr. *ethos,* manners, habits, + *logos,* word, reason] The scientific study of the behavior of animals in their natural habitat and in captivity.

ethyl (eth′ĭl) [Ger. *Ethyl*] In organic chemistry, the radical $C_2H_5^-$, present in many compounds, including ethyl ether, ethyl alcohol, and ethyl acetate.

ethylamine (ĕth″ĭl-ăm′ĭn) An amine, $CH_3CH_2NH_2$, formed in the decomposition of certain proteins.

ethylcellulose (ĕth″ĭl-sĕl′ū-lōs) An ether of cellulose, used in preparing drugs.

ethylene (eth′ĭ-lēn″) [*ethyl* + *-ene*] A flammable, explosive, colorless gas, CH_2CH_2, prepared from alcohol by dehydration. It is present in illuminating gas. It is colorless and has a sweetish taste but a pungent, foul odor. It is lighter than air and diffuses when liberated.

e. glycol The simplest glycol, $C_2H_6O_2$; a colorless alcohol used as an antifreeze. Fomepizole is a specific antidote for intoxications with ethylene glycol. SEE: *Poisons and Poisoning Appendix.*

e. oxide ABBR: ETO. A chemical, C_2H_4O, that in its gaseous state is used to sterilize materials that cannot withstand heat or steam. It is also used as a fumigant.

ethynyl (ĕth′ĭ-nĭl) An organic radical, $HC≡C-$.

etic (ē′tĭk) In anthropology and transcultural nursing, related to a kind of analysis that relies on objective criteria; the description of an illness by an observer of a phenomenon rather than by someone experiencing that phenomenon. SEE: *emic.*

etio- [Gr. *aitia,* cause] Prefix meaning *causation.* The variant *aetio-* is used outside the U.S.

etiocholanolone (ē″tē-ō-kō-lăn′ō-lōn) A steroid produced by testosterone catabolism. It is excreted in the urine.

etiology (ēt″ē-ol′ŏ-jē) [Gr. *aitia,* cause, + *logos,* word, reason] **1.** The study of the causes of disease. **2.** The cause of a disease.

etiologic, etiological (ēt″ē-ŏ-loj′ik, ēt″ē-ŏ-loj′ĭ-kăl), *adj.*

etiotropic (ē″tē-ō-trŏp′ĭk) [Gr. *aita,* cause, + *tropos,* turning] Directed against the cause of a disease; used of a drug or treatment that destroys or inactivates the causal agent of a disease. Opposite of nosotropic.

ETO *ethylene oxide.*

etodolac (ĕt′ō-dō′lăk) A nonsteroidal anti-inflammatory agent.

ETOH *ethanol.*

etretinate (ĕ-trĕt′ĭn-āt) A tretinoin drug formerly used to treat severe recalcitrant psoriasis.

⚠ Etretinate must not be used by women who are pregnant or who intend to become pregnant. It should be prescribed only by physicians knowledgeable in the systemic use of retinoids.

etymology (ĕt″ĭ-mŏl′ō-jē) [L. *etymon,* origin of a word, + *logos,* word, reason] The science of the origin and development of words. Most medical words are derived from Latin and Greek, but many of those from Greek have come through Latin and have been modified by it. Generally, when two Greek words are used to form one word, they are connected by the letter "o." Many medical words have been formed from one or more roots—forms used or adapted from Latin or Greek—and many are modified by a prefix, a suffix, or both. A knowledge of important Latin and Greek roots and prefixes will reveal the meanings of many other words. SEE: Abbreviations Appendix; Prefixes and Suffixes Appendix.

Eu Symbol for the element europium.

eu- [Gr. *eus,* good] Prefix meaning *healthy; normal; good; well.*

Eubacteria (ū″băk-tēr′ē-ă) A group of single-celled organisms without a defined cell nucleus or organelles. They contain peptidoglycans in their cell walls. Eubacteria are prokaryotes and include many familiar microorganisms, (e.g., *Escherichia, Helicobacter, Legionella,* nitrogen-fixing bacteria, *Spirochetes,* and staphylococci.) In some classification systems the other prokaryotes also include the archaebacteria and cyanobacteria. In other taxonomic systems the archaebacteria are considered to be a separate kingdom or domain.

Eubacterium (ū″băk-tē′rē-ŭm) A genus of gram-positive, anaerobic bacilli, part of the resident flora of the human colon and skin. They are opportunists in necrotic tissue.

eubiotics (ū″bī-ŏt′ĭks) [″ + *bios,* life] The science of healthy and hygienic living.

eucalyptol, eucalyptole (ū″kă-lip′tōl″, tōl″) [*eucalyptus* + *-ol*] An aromatic substance derived from eucalyptus leaves, occasionally used as an expectorant. SYN: *eucalyptus oil.*

Eucalyptus (ū″kă-lip′tŭs) [Gr. *eukalyptos,* well hidden, well covered] A genus, *Eucalyptus,* of giant flowering trees in the myrtle family, native to Australia and neighboring islands. They produce a variety of herbal, medicinal, and industrial oils. The diluted oil is used for infections, fevers, upset stomach, and esp. for breathing problems. It is also used against inflammation.

eucapnia (ū-kăp′nē-ă) [″ + *kapnos,* smoke] The presence of normal amounts of carbon dioxide in the blood.

euchromatin (ū-krō′mă-tĭn) [″ + *chroma,* color] Unfolded or uncondensed portions of chromosomes during interphase. Transcription of DNA by messenger RNA occurs, and proteins are synthesized. SEE: *heterochromatin.*

eucrasia (ū-krā′sē-ă) [″ + *krasis,* mixture] Normal health; the state of the body in which all activities are in normal balance.

eudaimonia (ū″dī-mōn′ē-ă, dī) [Gr. *eudaimonia,* good fortune, happiness] A sense of fulfillment that arises from achieving one's full potential as a human being.

eudiaphoresis (ū″dī-ă-fō-rē′sĭs) [″ + *dia,* through, + *pherein,* to carry] Normal perspiration.

eugenics (ū-jĕn′ĭks) [″ + *gennan,* to produce] The study of improving a population by selective breeding in the belief that desirable traits will become more common and undesirable traits will be eliminated. Ths practice may have some utility in controlled animal populations, but it is unethical in humans.

eugenol (ū′jĕn-ŏl) A material obtained from clove oil and other sources. It is used as a topical analgesic in dentistry. It is also mixed with zinc oxide to form a material that hardens sufficiently to be used as a temporary dental filling.

euglobulin (ū-glŏb′ū-lĭn) A true globulin, or one that is insoluble in distilled water and soluble in dilute salt solution. SEE: *pseudoglobulin.*

euglobulin lysis time SEE: under *time.*

euglycemia (ū″glī″sē′mē-ă) [*eu-* + *glycemia*] A normal concentration of glucose in the blood.

eugonic (ū-gŏn′ĭk) [″ + ″ + ″] Growing rapidly in culture; said of some bacteria.

euhydration (ū-hī-drā′shŭn) A normal amount of water in the body.

eukaryon (ū-kăr′ē-ŏn) [″ + *karyon,* nucleus] The nucleus of a eukaryote cell.

eukaryote (ū-kăr′ē-ōt) An organism in which the cell nucleus is surrounded by a membrane. SEE: *prokaryote.*

Eulenburg disease (oyl′ĕn-bŭrg″) [Albert Eulenburg, Ger. neurologist, 1840–1917] Paramyotonia congenita.

Eumycetes (ū″mī″sēt′ēz) [*eu-* + *mycetes*] A subkingdom of the kingdom Fungi that includes the Ascomycetes (Ascomycotina), Basidiomycetes (Basidiomycotina), and Zygomycetes (Zygomycotina). SYN: *Eumycota; true fungi.*

eumycetoma (ū″mī-sĕ-tō′mă) [*eu-* + *mycetoma*] Mycetoma caused by Eumycetes or Eumycota (true fungi). SEE: *mycetoma.*

Eumycota (ū″mī″kōt′ă) Eumycetes.

eunuch (ū′nŭk) [Gr. *eune,* bed, + *echein,* to guard] A castrated man; one who has had his testicles removed, esp. before puberty so that secondary sexual characteristics do not develop. Absence of the male hormones produces a high-pitched voice and loss of hair on the face. In Middle Eastern and some Asian countries, eunuchs were employed to guard the women of a harem.

eunuchism (ū′nŭk-ĭzm) [*eunuch* + *-ism*] A condition resulting from complete lack of male hormones. It may be due to atrophy or removal of the testicles.

eunuchoid (ū′nŭ-koyd) [″ + ″ + *eidos,* form, shape] Having the characteristics of a eunuch, such as retarded development of sex organs, absence of beard and bodily hair, high-pitched voice, and striking lack of muscular development.

eunuchoidism (ū'nŭk-oyd-ĭzm) [" + " + " + -*ismos*, condition] Deficient male hormone production by the testes.

euphonia (ū-fōn'ē-ă) [" + *phone,* voice] The condition of having a normal clear voice.

euphoria (ū-for'ē-ă) [" + *phoros,* bearing] 1. A condition of good health. 2. An exaggerated feeling of well-being or elation.

euphoriant (ū-for'ē-ănt) Any agent or drug that induces an extraordinary sense of well-being.

Euphrasia (ū"frā'zh(ē)ă) SEE: *eyebright.*

euplastic (ū-plăs'tĭk) [" + *plastikos,* formed] Healing quickly and well.

euploidy (ū-ploy'dē) [" + *ploos,* fold, + *eidos,* form, shape] In genetics, the state of having complete sets of chromosomes.

eupnea (ūp-nē'ă) Normal, unimpaired respiration.

Euroglyphus (ūr"o-glī'fŭs) [L. *Europa,* Europe + Gr. *glyphein,* to carve] A genus of common house dust mite that causes allergic rhinitis and contact dermatitis in sensitized people. It inhabits beds, linens, carpets, and other places in the home.

  E. maynei A species that is an important, widespread source of indoor allergens.

europium (ū-rō'pē-ŭm) [*Europe* + -*ium* (1)] SYMB: Eu. A chemical element of the lanthanide series, atomic weight (mass) 151.96, atomic weight 151.96; atomic number 63.

EuroSCORE (ūr'ō-skor") *European System for Cardiac Operative Risk Evaluation* (an algorithm to estimate the likelihood of death from cardiac surgery, based on patient history, cardiac physiology, and the nature of the surgery).

Eurotium (ū-rō'shē-ŭm) [Gr. *euros,* mold] A genus of molds that rarely causes disease.

eury- [Gr. *eurys,* wide] Prefix meaning *broad.*

EUS An abbreviation for endoscopic ultrasound.

eustachian (ū-stā'kē-ăn, -shěn) [Bartolomeo Eustachio (Eustachi), It. anatomist, 1520–1574] Pert. to the auditory tube. SEE: *ear; eustachian tube.*

eustachianography (ū-stā"shē-ăn-ŏg'ră-fē, stā"kē-) Radiography of the eustachian tube and middle ear after the introduction of a contrast medium.

eustachian tube The auditory tube, extending from the middle ear to the nasopharynx, 3 to 4 cm long and lined with mucous membrane. Occlusion of the tube leads to the development of otitis media. SYN: *auditory tube; .* SEE: *politzerization.*

eustachian valve SEE: under *valve.*

eustachitis (ū"stă-kī'tĭs) Inflammation of the eustachian tube.

eustress (ū'stres") [*eu-* + *stress,* by analogy with *distress*] Psychological stress that affects performance in a positive way, e.g., by making a person more alert, more aware of his or her surroundings, or more enthusiastic.

eutectic mixture of local anesthetics ABBR: EMLA. A topical anesthetic cream composed of a mixture of lidocaine and prilocaine. A thick layer is applied to the skin to be anesthetized, covered with an occlusive bandage, and left in place for 1–2 hr. This anesthetizes the skin to a depth of about 5 mm so that superficial skin lesions can be removed or needle penetrations or minor surgeries can be performed, esp. in pediatric patients. Patients will not be aware of a needle piercing the skin; however, they will feel any tissue irritation caused by the fluid injected.

euthanasia (ū-thă-nā'zē-ă) [Gr. *eus,* good, + *thanatos,* death] 1. An easy, quiet, and painless death. 2. The deliberate ending of the life of people (or in veterinary practice, animals) with incurable or terminal illnesses or unbearable suffering. The ethical ramifications are actively debated and unresolved: Should patients have the right to choose death? When is death imminent, or suffering intolerable? Does participation by a health care provider (e.g., a doctor, nurse, or pharmacist) violate personal, professional, religious, or social mores? SEE: *advance directive; death, assisted; suicide, assisted; death; death with dignity; do not attempt resuscitation; dying; living will.*

  PATIENT CARE: Active euthanasia (sometimes called "mercy killing") occurs when a person, usually a physician or nurse, performs an act (e.g., administering a lethal injection) to end a patient's life. Additional descriptors for euthanasia include "voluntary" (i.e., the patient requests euthanasia), "involuntary" (i.e., the patient specifically refuses euthanasia), and "nonvoluntary" (i.e., the patient is not able to inform others of his wishes concerning euthanasia). Currently euthanasia is illegal in most countries except for the Netherlands, which allows limited, voluntary euthanasia. The general terms "assisted death" and "aid in dying" apply to actions intended to hasten death and include both assisted suicide (AS) and active euthanasia. "Withdrawing or withholding life-sustaining therapy" (WWLST) is the discontinuance or foregoing of therapies that may keep someone alive (e.g., cardiopulmonary resuscitation [CPR], mechanical ventilation, artificially provided nutrition and hydration, and antibiotics or other drug therapies). Most patients who die in acute care settings, particularly in intensive care units, do so after the withholding or withdrawing of CPR or other life-prolonging therapies. The U.S. Supreme Court has consistently upheld the right of patients to refuse such therapies via living wills or advanced medical directives. Euthanasia, however, is illegal and may be treated by the courts as an act of murder.

involuntary e. Euthanasia performed without a competent person's consent.

nonvoluntary e. Euthanasia provided to an incompetent person according to a surrogate's decision.

euthenics (ū-then'iks) [Gr. *euthēnein*, to prosper + *-ics*] The science of improvement of a population through modification of the environment.

Eutheria (ū-thēr'ē-ă) A subclass of mammals with a true placenta.

euthyroid (ū"thī'royd") [*eu- + thyroid*] Having a normally functioning thyroid gland and normal levels of circulating thyroid hormone.

euthyroid sick syndrome Any derangement in thyroid hormone blood levels in patients affected by another (usually critical) illness. The altered levels of thyroid hormones are not caused by primary thyroid dysfunction; they return to normal when the underlying illness is successfully treated.

eutomer (ūt'ŏ-měr) Of two enantiomeric compounds, the one with the stronger chemical activity. It causes beneficial effects when it is administered. SEE: *distomer.*

Eutrombicula (ū"trŏm-bĭk'ū-lă) A genus of mites.

eutrophication (ū-trŏf"ĭ-kā'shŭn) [Gr. *eutrophein*, to thrive] Alteration of the environment by increasing the nutrients required by one species to the disadvantage of other species in the ecosystem, esp. in an aquatic environment.

euvolemic (ū-vŏ-lēm'ik) [*eu- + vol(ume) + -emia*] Having appropriate hydration. **euvolemia** (-lēm'ē-ă), *n.* SYN: *normovolemic.*

ev, eV, EV electron volt.

EVA enlargement of the vestibular aqueduct.

evacuant (ē-văk'ū-ănt) [L. *evacuans*, making empty] A drug that stimulates the bowels to move. A laxative.

evacuate (ĭ-văk'ū-āt") [L. *evacuatio*, emptying] 1. To discharge, esp. from the bowels; to empty the uterus. 2. To move patients from the site of an accident or catastrophe to a hospital or shelter.

evacuation (ē-văk"ū-ā'shŭn) 1. The act of emptying (e.g., the bowels). In obstetrics, the term refers to emptying the uterus of the products of conception, as in abortion or removal of retained placental fragments. 2. The material discharged from the bowels; stool. 3. Removal of air from a closed container; production of a vacuum. 4. The act of moving people to a safe place, esp. from a disaster or a war-torn area.

air e. Transport of patients from one location to another by specially equipped helicopters or other aircraft. Indications for air transport include severe trauma, burns, and other conditions requiring immediate skilled care and treatment.

evacuator (ē-văk'ū-ā-tor) A device for emptying, as the bowels, or for irrigating the bladder and removing calculi.

evagination (ē-văj-ĭ-nā'shŭn) 1. Emergence from a sheath. 2. Protrusion of an organ or part. SEE: *invagination.* **evaginate** (-nāt), *adj.*

evaluation (ĕ-val"ū-ā'shŏn) [Fr *évaluation*] 1. A rating or assessment, e.g., of the accuracy of a diagnosis, the effectiveness of a plan of care, or the quality of care. 2. An appraisal of the health or status of an individual, based on specific criteria. 3. A clinical judgment. SEE: *nursing assessment; nursing intervention; nursing process; planning; problem-oriented medical record.*

evanescent (ĕv"ă-něs'ĕnt) [L. *evanescere*, to vanish] Not permanent; of brief duration.

Evans blue (ĕv'ănz) [Herbert M. Evans, U.S. anatomist, 1882–1971] A diazo dye occurring as a blue-green powder, very soluble in water. It is used intravenously as a diagnostic agent.

Evans syndrome [Robert S. Evans, U.S. physician, b. 1912] An autoimmune disease characterized by thrombocytopenia and hemolytic anemia.

evaporation (i-vap"ō-rā'shŏn) [L. *evaporare*, to disperse in steam] 1. Change from liquid to vapor. 2. Loss in volume due to conversion of a liquid into a vapor. **evaporate** (i-vap'ŏ-rāt"), *v.* **evaporative** (i-vap'ŏ-rāt"ĭv), *adj.*

evaporative cooling (ĕ-vap'ŏ-rā"tiv, -ŏ-rā-tiv) Reducing the body temperature of a patient with fever or heat stroke by spraying his or her skin with mist and then fanning the patient.

evenomation (ē-věn"ō-mā'shŭn) [L. *ex,* from, + *venenum*, poison] Removal of venom from a biting insect or reptile; removal of venom from the victim of a bite.

eventration (ē"věn-trā'shŭn) [L. *e,* out, + *venter*, belly] 1. Partial protrusion of the abdominal contents through an opening in the abdominal wall. 2. Removal of the contents of the abdominal cavity.

event recorder A portable heart rhythm monitor worn by a patient who suffers intermittent palpitations or loss of consciousness of unclear cause. The device transmits the patient's heart rhythms by telephone to a central laboratory, where symptomatic and asymptomatic dysrhythmias (such as atrial fibrillation and atrioventricular nodal re-entrant tachycardias) or heart blocks can be detected.

events odds ratio Odds ratio.

eversion (ē-vĕr′zhŭn) [″ + *vertere*, to turn] Turning outward. SEE: *cheilectropion.*

evert To turn outward.

Everything Added to Food in the United States ABBR: EAFUS. An inventory of the more than 3000 food additives included in human food in the U.S.

evidement (ā-vēd-mŏn′) [Fr., a scooping out] Scraping away of diseased tissue.

evidence In forensic medicine, all the tangible items and record materials pertinent to the legal considerations.

    anecdotal e. Evidence based on anecdotes arising from the analysis of individual clinical cases, rather than the study of scientifically randomized groups of patients. Such evidence may be true or false, but it is always unreliable because it is based on hearsay, faulty reasoning, or other cause.

    material e. In medicolegal considerations, such things as facts, medical records, documents, or expert testimony that are important to proving or disproving matters of dispute.

evidence-practice gap, evidence/practice gap SEE: under *gap.*

evil [AS. *yfel*] An infrequently used term for disease or illness.

evil eye Mal de ojo.

eviration (ē″vī-rā′shŭn) [L. *e*, out, + *vir*, man] 1. Castration. 2. In psychiatry, delusion in a man who thinks he has become a woman.

evisceration (ē-vĭs″ĕr-ā′shŭn) [″ + *viscera*, viscera] 1. Removal of the viscera or of the contents of a cavity. 2. Spilling out of abdominal contents resulting from wound dehiscence.

    PATIENT CARE: The patient's surgeon should be contacted immediately. The wound is covered with a sterile towel moistened with warm sterile physiological saline solution. Tension on the abdomen is decreased by placing the patient in the low Fowler's position and raising the knees or by instructing the patient to flex the knees and support them with a pillow. Vital signs are monitored, and fluid therapy is initiated via IV line. The patient is reassured and prepared for surgical repair.

Evista Raloxifene.

evocation (ĕv″ō-kā′shŭn) [″ + *vocare*, to call] 1. Re-creation by recollection or by imagination. 2. In the embryo, the induction or formation of a tissue in response to an evocator.

evocator (ĕv′ō-kāt″or) A chemical produced by one part of an embryo that stimulates organ and tissue development in another part.

evoked potential SEE: under *potential.*

evolution (ev″ŏ-loo′shŏn) [L. *evolutio*, unrolling] The accumulation over time of sufficient heritable changes within the germ cells of organisms to significantly change their adult forms. More generally, any orderly and gradual process of modification whereby a system, whether physical, chemical, social, or intellectual, becomes more highly organized.

    theory of n SEE: under *theory.*

evolution of infarction The normal healing process after myocardial infarction. It is seen on an electrocardiogram as a series of progressive changes in the QRS complex and S-T segment.

evulsion (ē-vŭl′shŭn) Avulsion.

Ewing tumor (ū′ing) [James Ewing, U.S. pathologist, 1866–1943] An aggressive bone cancer, occurring principally in childhood or adolescence, and often involving the pelvis, femur, lower leg, arms, or ribs. It occurs more commonly in boys than girls. Treatments include local surgery, radiation, and systemic chemotherapy.

ex- [L., Gr. *ex*, out, out of] Prefix meaning *out; away from; completely.*

exa- [Fr. *hexa-*, representing the sixth power of a thousand] In the International System of Units (SI), a prefix meaning 10^{18}.

exacerbation (ĕks-ăs″ĕr-bā′shŭn) [″ + *acerbus*, harsh] Aggravation of symptoms or increase in the severity of a disease.

exaltation (ĕks-ăl-tā′shŭn) [L. *exaltare*, to lift up] A mental state characterized by feelings of grandeur, excessive joy, elation, and optimism; an abnormal feeling of personal well-being or self-importance.

examination (eg-zam″ĭ-nā′shŏn) [L. *examinatio*, equipoise, balance, examination] Inspection of the body to determine the presence or absence of disease. *Examination* has been proposed as an international replacement for *test, testing,* and *analysis* although each of these words is more common in professional literature.

    e. under anesthesia ABBR: EUA. Any operative or invasive procedure done while the patient is sedated, in order to improve patient tolerance, alleviate pain or anxiety, or improve the quality of the exam.

    bimanual e. SEE: *pelvic e.*

    dental e. The visual, digital, and radiographic inspection of the teeth and surrounding structures, including the head and neck. The depth of the gingival sulcus is also probed and measured around each tooth to assess the state of health of the periodontium. The examination is completed with a mirror, explorer, periodontal probe, and dental radiographs.

    digital rectal e. ABBR: DRE. Palpation of the anus, rectum, and prostate gland with a gloved finger, used in the diagnosis of intestinal bleeding, anorectal pain, and both benign and malignant diseases of the prostate.

PATIENT CARE: The patient should be positioned for comfort, e.g., in Sims position (lying on the left side with knees and hips comfortably flexed). A chaperone and/or a drape should be provided for patient safety, comfort, and dignity. After an explanation of the procedure to the patient, several mL of surgical lubricant are placed on the examiner's glove, usually on the index finger. The examiner visually inspects the anus and perineum, then places the gloved finger on the anal opening while asking the patient to bear down gently. After the finger enters the anus, it is used to sweep circumferentially around the interior of the distal intestine. It is then directed anteriorly (when examining a male patient) to evaluate the consistency, size, and nodularity of the prostate gland. Samples of stool obtained during the exam may be sent to the lab to test them for the presence of occult blood.

double-contrast e. A radiographic examination in which a radiopaque and a radiolucent contrast medium are used simultaneously to visualize internal anatomy.

endoscopic e. Direct visualization of an internal organ with a fiber-optic tube, often accompanied by biopsy of suspicious lesions.

Folstein Mini Mental Status E. SEE: *Folstein Mini Mental Status Exam.*

laboratory e. Examination by urinalysis, blood tests, microbiological cultures, and other tests of body fluids.

Mini-Mental State E. ABBR: MMSE. A common test to quantify a person's cognitive ability. It assesses orientation, registration, attention, calculation, and language. Scoring is from 0 to 30, with 30 indicating intact cognition.

multilingual aphasia e. ABBR: MAE. A battery of tests to measure language abilities in patients with speech disturbances. It consists of 11 components, including the abilities to repeat a sentence, spell, read, understand spoken directions, identify objects depicted in drawings, and articulate clearly.

pelvic e. Physical examination of the vagina and adjacent organs. A speculum is used first to visualize anatomical structures. During speculum examination, cultures and Pap test specimens may be obtained. After the speculum is removed, the pelvic organs and rectum are examined manually by the examiner. SEE: illus.

periodic health e. A health screening examination performed on a scheduled or routine basis. The appropriate fea-

tures of this examination depend on the patient's age, gender, and sometimes health history, family history, or employment status. Adult women should have periodic examinations that include Pap smears and mammography; professional pilots and truckers are screened periodically for visual impairment and hypertension. All adults over age 45 should be screened for diabetes mellitus. Patients with a personal history of cancer may be screened periodically for evidence of disease recurrence. For many patients, the periodic examination may include blood tests (e.g., to check levels of cholesterol and other lipids), immunological tests (e.g., health care workers are periodically screened for tuberculosis), or invasive examinations (e.g., sigmoidoscopy or colonoscopy to look for colon cancer). SYN: *annual exam; periodic medicale.* SEE: *mammography; Papanicolaou test;* table under *cancer.*

periodic medical e. Periodic health examination.

physical e. ABBR: PEx. Examination of the body by auscultation, palpation, percussion, inspection, and olfaction.

radiological e. Examination by various means of visualizing body spaces and organs and their functions, e.g., by computed tomography, fluoroscopy, magnetic resonance imaging, ultrasonography, or related techniques.

rapid trauma e. Rapid trauma assessment.

rectoabdominal e. Physical examination of the abdomen and rectum, e.g., to determine the cause of abdominal pain, or to identify guarding, internal bleeding or organ enlargement, masses, or tenderness.

Examinations, National Board Examinations administered to test the qualifications of medical, dental, and other professional students. Successful completion of the basic science and clinical parts of the examinations is required for licensure in most states.

exanthem, exanthema (eks-an′thĕm, ek″san″thē′mă) *pl.* **exanthemas, -mata, exanthems** [Gr. *exanthema,* eruption] Any eruption or rash that appears on the skin, as opposed to one that appears on the mucous membranes (enanthem). The term is often used to describe childhood or infectious rashes (e.g., measles or scarlet fever) but it also applies to other rashes. **exanthematous** (-ăn-thĕm′ă-tŭs), *adj.*

e. subitum Sixth disease.

exarticulation (ĕks″ăr-tĭk-ū-lā′shŭn) [L. *ex,* out, + *articulus,* joint] **1.** Amputation of a limb through a joint. **2.** Excision of a part of a joint.

excavation (ĕks″kă-vā′shŭn) [″ + *ca-*

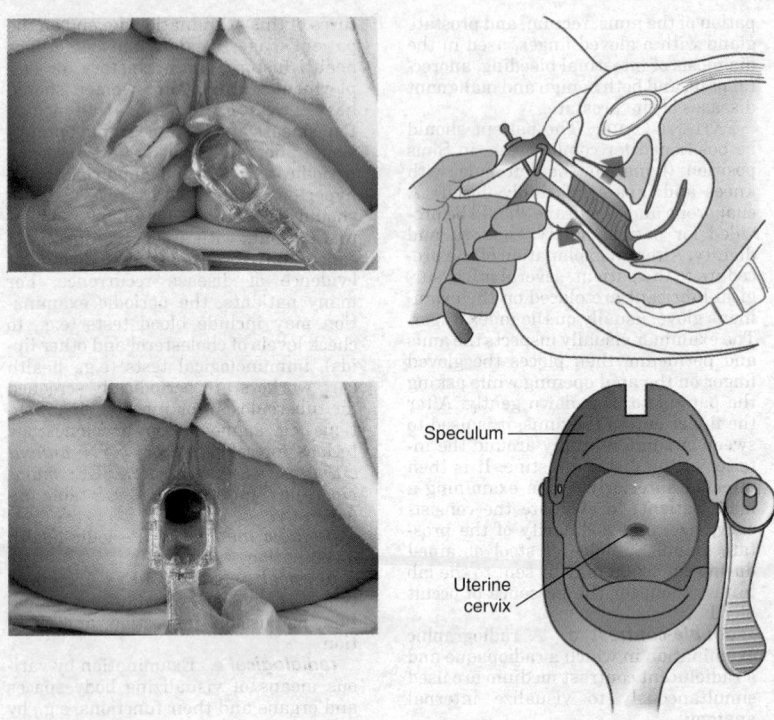

Speculum

Uterine cervix

PELVIC EXAMINATION WITH SPECULUM

vus, hollow] **1.** A hollow or depression. **2.** Formation of a cavity.

   atrophic e. A cupped appearance of the optic nerve due to atrophy of the nerve fibers.

   caries e. The removal of the diseased portion of a tooth, before it is filled. It may be accomplished with air, burs, chemicals, drills, lasers, ultrasound, and other means.

   dental e. Caries excavation.

   rectouterine e. The rectouterine pouch or pouch of Douglas.

excavator (ĕks′kă-vā″tor) An instrument for removing tissue or bone. It may be spoon-shaped if used on soft tissue and spoon-shaped with sharp edges if used in dentistry.

excerebration (ĕk″sĕr-ĕ-brā′shŭn) [″ + *cerebrum,* brain] Removal of the brain, esp. that of the dead fetus to facilitate delivery.

exchange (eks-chānj′) **1.** To give up or substitute something for something else. **2.** In dietetics, the substitution of an equivalent amount of one food substance for another so that the caloric intake remains the same. Exchange diets are used frequently to help manage diabetes mellitus, and they have been adapted for use in proprietary weight

loss programs. **3.** In peritoneal dialysis, to drain fluid from the peritoneal cavity and replace it with fresh dialysate.

   anion e. SEE: *resin, ion-exchange.*

   cation e. The transfer of cations between those in a liquid medium and those in a solid polymer. The polymer is termed the cation exchanger. Cation exchange is used in ion-exchange chromatography and in certain water purifiers.

   food e. A grouping of commonly consumed foods according to similarities in composition so that the foods may be used interchangeably in diet planning.

   sister chromatid e. The exchange of corresponding parts of homologous maternal and paternal chromosomes during the first meiotic division. This contributes to genetic diversity in the offspring. SYN: *crossing over.*

exchange list A grouping of foods to assist people on special diets. In each group, foods are listed in serving sizes that are interchangeable with respect to carbohydrates, fats, protein, and calories. The groups are starches and bread; meat; vegetables and fruit; milk; and fats. This approach is esp. useful in managing diets for diabetics. The exchange list has been adapted in the

My Pyramid eating plan (website: www.mypyramid.gov).

excipient (ĕk-sĭp′ē-ĕnt) [L. *excipiens,* excepting] Any substance added to a medicine so that it can be formed into the proper shape and consistency; the vehicle for the drug.

excise (ĕk-sīz′) [L. *ex,* out, + *caedere,* to cut] To cut out or remove surgically.

excise tax (ek′sīz″) [Dutch *excijs,* fr L. *accisa,* tax] A graduated tax charged by a city, state, or national government on the use of a commodity or service. The greater the use, the higher the tax. Excise taxes are used to discourage the purchase of hazardous but legal substances, such as cigarettes or alcohol. The added cost to these products makes them less appealing to those with limited incomes and deters their consumption by adolescents. Excise taxes have also been used to pay for the costs of health care that societies incur because of the use of hazardous agents.

excision (ek-sizh′ŏn) [L. *excisio*] The act of cutting away or taking out. SEE: illus.

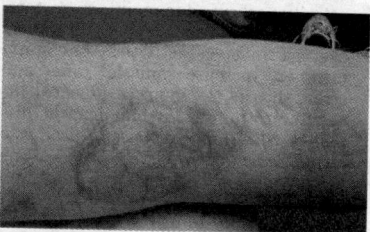

WIDE AND DEEP EXCISION OF SKIN AND SUBCUTANEOUS TISSUES

A treatment for melanoma

   tangential e. In burn management or surgery, removal of the outer layer of devitalized tissue by shaving it off at an angle. Blood loss can be a significant complication.

   total mesorectal e. Removal of the mesentery of the rectum, including its lymphoid and vascular tissue, during surgery for rectal adenocarcinoma.

excitability (ĕk-sīt″ă-bĭl′ĭ-tē) [L. *excitare,* to arouse] The property of a cell to generate an electrical impulse. This is a function of the permeability of the cell membrane.

   muscle e. In a muscle fiber, the inducibility to contract. This is a function of the chemical and electrical state of the sarcolemma and the time since a previous stimulus was applied.

   reflex e. Sensitivity to reflex irritation.

excitant (ĕk-sīt′ănt) A stimulant.

excitation (ĕk″sī-tā′shŭn) [L. *excitatio*] 1. The act of exciting. 2. The condition of being stimulated or excited.

   direct e. Stimulation of a muscle physically or by placement of an electrode in it.

   indirect e. Stimulation of a muscle via its nerve.

excited skin syndrome The eruption of inflammatory rashes far from an initial exposure to an allergen or irritant. The syndrome can cause false-positive reactions during allergy patch testing.

excited state The new state produced when energy is added to a nucleus, atom, or molecule. The energy is added by the absorption of photons or by collisions with other particles.

exciting Causing excitement.

excitomotor (ĕk-sīt″ō-mō′tor) [″ + *motor,* moving] Causing or capable of causing muscular activity.

excitor (ĕk-sī′tor) [L. *excitare,* to arouse] Something that incites to greater activity. SYN: *stimulant.*

excitotoxin (ĕk-sī′tō-tŏks′ĭn) A neurotransmitter (e.g., glutamate or aspartate) that can cause brain cell injury or death if its action is unabated. Brain damage is mediated by excitotoxins during prolonged seizure activity and stroke.

exclusion (ĕks-kloo′zhŭn) [L. *exclusio,* fr. *ex,* out, + *claudere,* to shut] 1. Shutting off or removing from the main part. 2. In medical insurance programs, a list of specific hazards, perils, or conditions for which the policy will not provide benefits or coverage payments. Common exclusions include preexisting conditions such as cancer, heart disease, diabetes, hypertension, a pregnancy that began before the effective date of the policy, self-inflicted injuries, combat injuries, plastic surgery for cosmetic reasons, and on-the-job injuries covered by workers' compensation.

exclusivity (ĕks″kloo-sĭv′ĭ-tē) [Med. L.] In the pharmaceutical industry, patent protection for drug manufacturers who may produce a therapeutic agent without competition from other drug suppliers.

excoriation (ĕks-kō-rē-ă′shŭn) [″ + *corium,* skin] An abrasion of the skin or of the surface of other organs by scratching, traumatic injury, chemicals, burns, or other causes. On the skin, the lesion is typically linear and scaly.

excrement (ĕks′krē-mĕnt) [L. *excrementum*] Waste material passed out of the body, esp. feces. SEE: *excretion.* **excrementitious** (ĕks″krē-mĕn-tĭsh′ŭs), *adj.*

excrescence (ĕks-krĕs′ĕns) [L. *ex,* out, + *crescere,* to grow] Any abnormal growth from the surface of a part.

excreta (ĕks-krē′tă) [L.] Waste matter excreted from the body, including feces, urine, and perspiration. SYN: *excre-*

tion. SEE: *Standard Precautions Appendix.*

excrete (ĕks-krēt′) [L. *excretus,* sifted out] To expel or eliminate waste material from the body, blood, or organs.

excretion (ĕks-krē′shŭn) [L. *excretio*] 1. Excreta. 2. The elimination of waste products from the body.

excretory (ĕks′krē-tō-rē) [L. *excretus,* sifted out] Pert. to or bringing about excretion.

excretory urography An occasionally used synonym for intravenous pyelography (IVP).

exculpatory (ĕks-kŭl′p-ŭ-tŏr″ē) [″ + L. *culpare,* to blame] Granting a waiver or yielding a legal right. Exculpatory language that asks human subjects in research projects to waive their rights in informed consent agreements is unethical and illegal.

excursion (ek-skŭr′zhŏn) [L. *excursio,* a running out, attack] 1. Wandering from the usual course. 2. The extent of movement of a part such as the extremities or eyes. 3. In diabetes, an increase in blood glucose levels above normal or typical values, esp. after a meal.

  diaphragmatic e. In respiration, the movement of the diaphragm from its level during full exhalation to its level during full inhalation. Normal diaphragmatic excursion is 5 to 7 cm bilaterally in adults. It may be seen during fluoroscopic or ultrasonographic examinations of the chest, or percussed during physical examination of the chest wall.

excuse of infancy A legal standard that limits the culpability of minors. It states that an unlawful act may not be criminal if it is committed by a minor who, by virtue of age alone, may not have enough understanding of right and wrong to act with criminal intent.

excystation (ĕk″sĭs-tā′shŭn) [″ + *kystis,* cyst] The escape of certain organisms (parasitic worms or protozoa) from an enclosing cyst wall or envelope. This process occurs in the life cycle of an intestinal parasite after the encysted form is ingested.

exempt (ĕg-zĕmpt′, ĭg-) [L. *eximere,* to take out, release, free] Free from oversight or supervision by any regulation or authority.

exemption (ĕg-zĕmp′shŭn) [L. *exemptio,* removal] Legal relief from an obligation, e.g., from the requirement that children be vaccinated before attending school, or that certain medications or devices be tested according to standard protocols before they are released to consumers.

exempt research SEE: under *research.*

exencephalia (ĕks″ĕn-sĕf-ā′lē-ă) [″ + *enkephalos,* brain] A congenital anomaly in which the brain is located outside the skull; a term for encephalocele, hydrencephalocele, and meningocele.

exenteration (ĕks-ĕn″tĕr-ā′shŭn) [″ + *enteron,* intestine] Evisceration.

exercise (ek′sĕr-sīz″) [L. *exercitus,* trained, drilled] A physical or mental activity performed to maintain, restore, or increase normal capacity. Physical exercise involves activities that maintain or increase muscle tone and strength, esp. to improve physical fitness or to manage a handicap or disability. SEE: table; *physical fitness; risk factor; sedentary lifestyle.*

  Daily physical activity for a minimum of 35 min will increase exercise capacity and the ability to use oxygen to derive energy for work, decrease myocardial oxygen demands for the same level of work, favorably alter lipid and carbohydrate metabolism, prevent cardiovas-

Exercise: Energy Required*

Calories Required per Hour of Exercise	Activity†
80	Sitting quietly, reading
200	Golf with use of powered cart
250	Walking 3 miles/hr (4.83 km/hr); housework; light industry; cycling 6 miles/hr (9.7 km/hr)
330	Heavy housework; walking 3.5 miles/hr (5.6 km/hr); golf, carrying own bag; tennis, doubles; ballet exercises
400	Walking 5 miles/hr (8 km/hr); cycling 10 miles/hr (16.1 km/hr); tennis, singles; water skiing
500	Manual labor; gardening; shoveling
660	Running 5.5 miles/hr (8.9 km/hr); cycling 13 miles/hr (20.9 km/hr); climbing stairs; heavy manual labor
1020	Running 8 miles/hr (12.9 km/hr); climbing stairs with 30-lb (13.61-kg) load

* These estimates are approximate and can serve only as a general guide. They are based on an average person who weighs 160 lb (72.58 kg).

† Energy requirements for swimming are not provided because of variables such as water temperature, whether the water is fresh or salt, buoyancy of the individual, and whether the water is calm or not.

cular disease, and help to control body weight and body composition. An exercise program should include developing joint flexibility and muscle strength, esp. in the trunk and limbs. This is of particular importance as people age. Exercise can have a beneficial effect in patients with depression or anxiety. It is thought to have a positive effect on balance, endurance, attitude, and outlook.

An exercise program should be neither begun nor continued if the individual or the person prescribing the exercise program has evidence that the activity is painful or harmful. Persons have died while exercising, and heavy physical exertion may precede acute myocardial infarction, particularly in people who are habitually sedentary. SEE: *exercise prescription.*

Mental exercise involves activities that maintain or increase cognitive faculties. Daily intellectual stimulation improves concentration, integration, and application of concepts and principles; enhances problem-solving abilities; promotes self-esteem; facilitates self-actualization; counteracts depression associated with social isolation and boredom; and enhances the quality of one's life. This is particularly important during aging. SEE: *reminiscence therapy.*

Most of the negative aspects of aging can be either altered or diminished by a lifelong healthy lifestyle. For example, the loss of physical fitness and strength, an inevitable consequence of aging, can be altered by an individualized fitness and strength program. Progressive loss of bone mass due to osteoporosis may be either prevented or slowed by a program of regular exercise. Loss of cardiac fitness can be forestalled by an ongoing aerobic fitness program. Many cases of type 2 diabetes can be controlled by exercise and an appropriate diet. Arthritic stiffness and loss of flexibility can be influenced favorably by exercise, e.g., by walking and jogging; for patients who experience joint pain with impact exercise, swimming is an alternative. Obesity and loss of muscle mass can be prevented or minimized.

Exercise stimulates release of endorphins, and people who participate in regular exercise programs express positive feelings toward living. Exercise programs can be adapted for patients who are confined to wheelchairs. An important consideration for any exercise program is that it be enjoyable. No matter how beneficial the program may be, if it is not enjoyable or rewarding, it will not be continued.

active e. A type of bodily movement performed by voluntary contraction and relaxation of muscles.

aerobic e. Exercise during which oxygen is metabolized to produce energy. Aerobic exercise is required for sustained periods of physical exertion and vigorous athletic activity. SEE: *anaerobic e.*

anaerobic e. High-intensity exercise, such as sprinting or weight lifting, that places more demand on muscles than oxygen delivery can match. When this occurs, glucose is metabolized for its stored energy without using oxygen as a reactant. Adenosine triphosphate (ATP) is produced rapidly, as well as the byproduct, lactic acid. SEE: *aerobic e..*

aquatic e. The use of a pool or an immersion tank filled with water for exercise. Such exercises may be used to improve balance and gait, enhance physical endurance, mobilize joints, and/or strengthen or stretch muscles. SEE: *hydrotherapy.*

assistive e. A type of bodily movement performed by voluntary muscle contractions that are augmented by an extrinsic force such as a clinician or mechanical device.

Bates e. SEE: *Bates exercises.*

breathing e. Exercise that enhances the respiratory system by improving ventilation, strengthening respiratory muscles, and increasing endurance. It is used in pulmonary rehabilitation

Buerger postural e. SEE: under *Buerger, Leo.*

Codman e. SEE: *Codman exercise.*

concentric e. A form of isotonic exercise in which the muscle fibers shorten as tension develops. SEE: *concentric muscle* **contraction***; eccentric muscle* **contraction.**

corrective e. Use of specific exercises to correct deficiencies caused by trauma, inactivity, muscular imbalances, poor flexibility, or biomechanical inadequacies.

dynamic stabilization e. Stabilization e.

eccentric e. An exercise in which there is overall lengthening of the muscle in response to an external resistance. SEE: *concentric muscle* **contraction***; eccentric muscle* **contraction.**

flexibility e. An activity, e.g., stretching, designed to increase joint range of motion and extensibility of muscle.

free e. An exercise carried through with no external assistance.

isokinetic e. An exercise with equipment that uses variable resistance to maintain a constant velocity of joint motion during muscle contraction, so that the force generated by the muscle is maximal through the full range of motion.

isometric e. Contraction and relaxation of a skeletal muscle or group of muscles in which the force generated by the muscle is equal to the resistance.

There is no change in muscle length, and no movement results. SEE: illus. SYN: *muscle-setting e.; static e.*

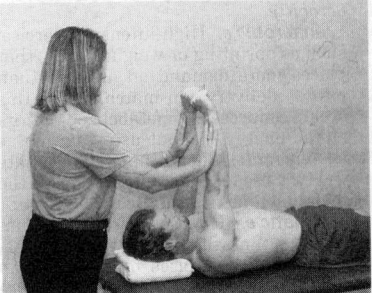

ISOMETRIC EXERCISE

Isometric exercise of the upper extremities

isotonic e. An active muscle contraction in which the force exerted remains constant and muscle length changes.

Kegel e. SEE: *Kegel exercise.*

kinetic chain e. An exercise that requires the foot (or hand) to apply pressure against a plate, pedal, or ground. This rehabilitation concept was determined by the anatomical functional relationship in the lower extremities. It also applies to the upper extremities. Kinetic chain describes how forces occur during human motion and how segments of the body are linked together. Kinetic chain exercises can either be open or closed. Open kinetic chain exercises are unrestricted movements in space of a peripheral segment of the body. Closed kinetic chain exercises are movements in which the distal segment meets with external resistance and remains fixed. Closed kinetic chain exercises are more functionally based than open chain exercises.

Kinetic chain exercises can either be open or closed. Kinetic chain describes how forces occur during human motion and how segments of the body are linked together. Open kinetic chain applies to unrestricted movement in space of a peripheral segment of the body. In closed kinetic chain exercises, the distal segment meets with external resistance, and remains fixed.

muscle-setting e. Isometric **e.**

neurobic e. Brainteasers, association tasks, calculations, puzzles, and other mental and physical exercises designed to stimulate thinking, problem solving, and other cerebral functions.

passive e. Passive **motion**.

pelvic floor e. Kegel exercise.

pendulum e. Codman exercise.

progressive resistive e. ABBR: PRE. A form of active resistive exercise based on a principle of gradual increase in the amount of resistance in order to achieve maximum strength.

range-of-motion e. Movement of a joint through its available range of motion. It can be used to prevent loss of motion. SEE: illus.

regressive resistive e. ABBR: RRE. A form of active resistive exercise that advocates gradual reduction in the amount of resistance as muscles fatigue.

relaxation e. An exercise (such as yoga, tai chi, dance, prayer, or meditation) that induces a relaxation response.

resistance e. Exercise in which a muscle contraction is opposed by force to increase strength or endurance. If the resistance is applied by using weights, it is mechanical resistance; if applied by a clinician, it is manual resistance. SYN: *resistive e.*

resistive e. Resistance **e.**

stabilization e. The application of fluctuating resistance loads while the patient stabilizes the part being trained in a symptom-free position. Exercises begin easily so that control is maintained, and progress in duration, intensity, speed, and variety. SYN: *dynamic stabilization e.*

static e. Isometric **e.**

stretching e. A therapeutic exercise maneuver, using physiological principles, designed to increase joint range of motion or extensibility of pathologically shortened connective tissue structures.

therapeutic e. The use of physical activity or training as a means of improving flexibility, health, strength, or well being; fostering recovery from injury or surgery; preventing complications of injury or illness; or improving or maintaining functional performance. Therapeutic exercise interventions may include techniques to improve motion, strength, motor control, muscle and cardiopulmonary endurance, and efficiency, posture, balance, and coordination.

exercise accumulation Physical exertion that is divided into several short periods of exercise scattered throughout the day instead of a single longer daily workout.

exercise addiction SEE: under *addiction.*

exercise-associated hyponatremia SEE: under *hyponatremia.*

exercise capacity The ability of a person to increase oxygen uptake above his or her oxygen uptake at rest. While lying comfortably in bed each individual's body uses a basal (resting) level of oxygen to perform basic metabolic functions. This level of oxygen usage is referred to as one metabolic equivalent, or informally, as 1 MET. While walking on level ground the average person doubles his oxygen uptake, that is, his oxygen uptake increases to 2 MET. Higher levels of exercise (such as jogging) can only be achieved by individuals with greater

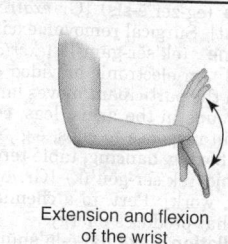

Extension and flexion of the wrist

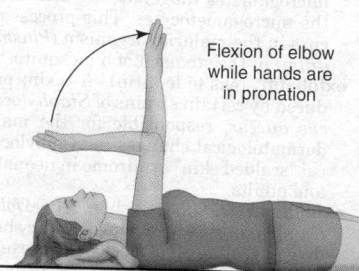

Flexion of elbow while hands are in pronation

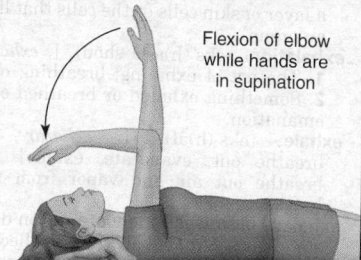

Flexion of elbow while hands are in supination

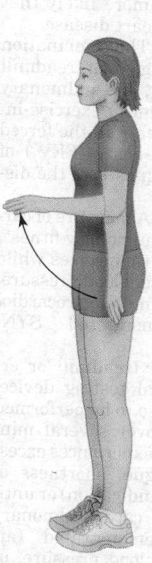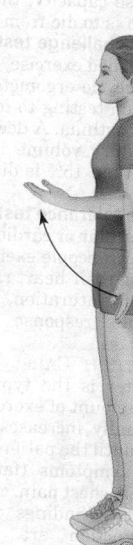

Flexion against gravity of arm with hands pronated

Flexion against gravity of arm with hands in supination

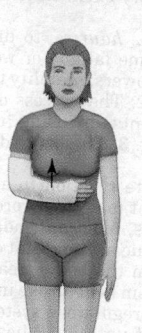

Flexion of shoulder against gravity when elbow is immobilized

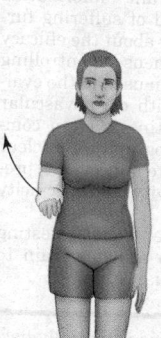

Abduction and external rotation of arm against gravity when elbow is immobilized

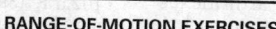

RANGE-OF-MOTION EXERCISES

exercise capacity; jogging at 6 miles per hour requires 6 MET. Highly trained athletes can achieve 15 MET or more. Studies have shown that the lower one's exercise capacity, the more likely that person is to die from heart disease.

exercise challenge test The combination of a graded exercise, e.g., on a treadmill or a bicycle ergometer, and pulmonary function testing to identify exercise-induced asthma. A decrease in the forced expiratory volume in 1 sec (FEV_1) of more than 15% is diagnostic of the disease.

exercise tolerance test A measure of cardiovascular or cardiopulmonary fitness, in which people exert themselves while having their heart rate, blood pressure, oxygen saturation, and electrocardiographic response monitored. SYN: *stress test*.

PATIENT CARE: A treadmill or ergometer is the typical testing device. The amount of exercise to be performed gradually increases over several minutes until the patient experiences excessive symptoms (fatigue, shortness of breath, chest pain, claudication) or until objective findings of cardiopulmonary malfunction are demonstrated (arrhythmias, lowered blood pressure, or ST-segment changes on the electrocardiogram).

Exercise tests are used most often to help diagnose symptoms or signs suggestive of coronary ischemia. They also are frequently used after patients have suffered a myocardial infarction or an exercise-induced arrhythmia. In these situations, the test may provide patients with important information about their likelihood of suffering further cardiac events or about the efficacy of their medical regimens in controlling their symptoms. When used in the evaluation of patients with cardiovascular disease, exercise testing is often combined with echocardiography or nuclear imaging of the heart to improve the predictive value, sensitivity, and specificity of the assessment.

In sports medicine, exercise testing can be used to help athletes train to achieve peak performance.

⚠ Exercise testing is potentially hazardous to patients with unstable angina pectoris, myocardial infarction within the last 48 hours, uncontrolled heart failure, aortic dissection, pulmonary embolism, ataxia or severe arthritic disease. In patients with conditions such as these in which exercise testing could be dangerous, pharmacological stress testing may sometimes be considered instead of exercise testing.

exeresis (eg-zer'ĕ-sĭs) [Gr. *exairesis,* taking out] Surgical removal; excision.

exergame (ek'sĕr-gām″) [*exer(cise)* + *game*] An electronic or video game in which the participant moves large muscle groups in the arms, legs, core, and neck in response to cues, e.g., in simulated boxing, dancing, table tennis, etc.

exergonic (ĕk″sĕr-gŏn'ĭk) [Gr. *ex,* out, + *ergon,* work] Pert. to a chemical reaction that produces energy.

exflagellation (ĕks″flăj-ĕ-lā'shŭn) [″ + L. *flagellum,* whip] The formation of microgametes (flagellated bodies) from the microgametocytes. This process occurs in the malarial organism (*Plasmodium*) in the stomach of a mosquito.

exfoliatin (ĕks'fō-lē-ă-tĭn) A toxin, produced by certain strains of *Staphylococcus aureus,* responsible for the major dermatological changes in staphylococcal "scalded skin" syndrome in neonates and adults.

exfoliation (eks-fō″lē-ā'shŏn) [L. *exfoliatio,* stripping away of leaves] The shedding or casting off of a body surface (e.g., the outer table of bone or the primary set of teeth) or an epithelial lining (e.g., a layer of skin cells or the cells that line an organ).

exhalation (eks″(h)ă-lā'shŏn) [. *exhale*] **1.** The act of exhaling; breathing out. **2.** Something exhaled or breathed out; emanation.

exhale (eks-(h)āl) [L. *exhalare,* to breathe out, evaporate, exhale] To breathe out air and vapor from the lungs.

exhaled breath condensate (kon'dĕn-sāt″, den″) Exhaled air that is collected and analyzed, particularly for the presence of inflammatory chemicals or toxins.

exhaustion [″ + L. *haurire,* to drain] **1.** A state of extreme fatigue or weariness; loss of vital powers; inability to respond to stimuli. **2.** The process of removing the contents or using up a supply of anything. **3.** The act of drawing or letting out.

heat e. An acute reaction to a hot, humid environment marked by profuse sweating, dizziness, nausea, headache, and profound fatigue as the result of excess fluid loss from the body. Heat exhaustion differs from heat stroke in that the body's thermoregulatory system is still functioning; if untreated, heat exhaustion can progress to heat stroke. SYN: *heat **prostration***. SEE: table.

SYMPTOMS: The patient's rectal temperature will be elevated to about 102.5°F (39.0°C). The patient's pulse may be rapid but weak; blood pressure is decreased. The patient may appear disoriented and complain of thirst. Nausea and vomiting may also be noted.

PREVENTION: See heat stroke for preventive measures.

Comparison of Heatstroke and Heat Exhaustion

Heat Exhaustion	Heatstroke
Definition A state of weakness produced by exposure to heat, humidity, and excessive loss of fluids and electrolytes	**Definition** A derangement of thermoregulation with altered mental status and high body temperature

History
Nonexertional
  Same as for heatstroke
  Use of medications that increase heat production or inhibit perspiration
  Absence of fans or air conditioners
  Demographics: urban poor, elderly, obese
Exertional
  Same as for heatstroke
  Demographics: outdoor laborers, athletes, military recruits
	History
	Nonexertional
	  Exposure to high temperatures and high humidity
	
	Exertional
	  Excessive exercise under tropical conditions

Physical Exam *Rectal temperature:* <104°F *Pulse:* weak, thready, and rapid *Blood pressure:* usually normotensive *Skin:* Exertional—Signs of profuse sweating may be present *Neurological:* Normal mental status	**Physical Exam** *Rectal temperature:* usually >104°F *Pulse:* tachycardic *Blood pressure:* variable *Skin:* Nonexertional—Absence of sweating is common *Neurological:* Altered mental status, possible convulsions or coma
Treatment Rest Removal of patient from hot environment Administration of fluids and electrolytes by mouth or by vein Administration of fluids and electrolytes Cease cooling when rectal temperature returns to the upper limits of normal.Avoidance of alcohol bath (risk of intoxication); and of antipyretics (ineffective)	**Treatment** Rest Removal of patient from hot environment Active cooling by any available means, often by bathing or spraying skin with water, then fanning the patient
Mortality Rare	**Mortality** Common

TREATMENT: The patient should be removed from the hot, humid environment to a cooler, well-ventilated location (e.g., indoors, under a shade tree) and placed in a head-low position. Clothing should be loosened and the patient's body cooled by placing cold packs in the axilla, on the neck, groin, and behind the knees. Fluid consumption, in the form of water or electrolyte drinks, should be administered to conscious patients. Intravenous infusion of isotonic saline may be required. Prognosis is favorable if the patient is properly treated in the acute stages. SYN: *heat prostration*.

exhibitionism [" + Gr. *-ismos,* condition] **1.** A tendency to attract attention to oneself by any means. **2.** A sexual identity disorder manifesting itself in an abnormal impulse that causes one to expose one's genitals to a stranger.

exhibitionist 1. A person with an abnormal desire to attract attention. **2.** A person who yields to an impulse to expose the genitals to a stranger.

exhilarant (ĕg-zĭl'ăr-ănt) [L. *exhilarare,* to gladden] Something that is mentally stimulating.

exhumation (ĕks"hū-mā'shŭn) [L. *ex,* out, + *humus,* earth] Removal of a dead body from the grave after it has been buried.

exigency (ĕk'sĭ-jĭn-sē, ĕg-zĭj'ĭn-) [L. *exigere,* to drive out, demand] A situation requiring immediate management. SEE: *emergency*.

exitus (ĕk'sĭ-tŭs) [L., going out] Death.

exo- [Gr. *exō,* outside] Prefix meaning *without; outside of*.

exoantigen (ĕks"ō-ăn'tĭ-jĕn) [" + "] A soluble antigen found on the surface of a microorganism, identified in the supernatant of a culture of that organism.

exobiology (ĕk"sō-bī-ŏl'ō-jē) The biological science of the universe, exclusive of our planet.

exocardia (ĕk″sō-kăr′dē-ă) [″ + *kardia*, heart] A congenitally abnormal position of the heart.

exocardial (ĕk″sō-kăr′dē-ăl) Occurring outside the heart.

exocrine (ĕks′ō-krĭn) [″ + *krinein*, to separate] 1. A term applied to the external secretion of a gland. Opposite of endocrine. 2. A term applied to glands whose secretion reaches an epithelial surface either directly or through a duct.

exocytosis (ĕks″ō-sī-tō′sĭs) [″ + *kytos*, cell, + *osis*, condition] The discharge of particles from a cell. They are too large to pass through the cell membrane by diffusion. SEE: *pinocytosis*.

exodeviation (ĕk″sō-dē″vē-ā′shŭn) A turning outward. When this condition occurs in the eyes, it is termed exotropia.

exodontia (ĕks-ō-dŏn′shē-ă) [″ + *odous*, tooth] Dental extraction of teeth.

exodontology (ĕks″ō-dŏn-tŏl′ō-jē) [″ + ″ + *logos*, word, reason] The branch of dentistry concerned with extraction of teeth.

exoenzyme (ĕk-sō-ĕn′zīm) [″ + *en*, in, + *zyme*, leaven] An enzyme that does not function within the cells that secrete it.

exoerythrocytic (ĕk″sō-ĕ-rĭth″rō-sī′tĭk) [″ + *erythros*, red, + *kytos*, cell] Occurring outside the red blood cells. Most of the life cycle of the malaria parasite in a human host is inside the red blood cell, where it causes symptoms; the rest is outside the red blood cell, and latent (i.e., exoerythrocytic).

exogamy (ĕks-ŏg′ă-mē) [″ + *gamos*, marriage] 1. Marriage outside a particular group. 2. In biology, conjugation between protozoan gametes of different ancestry.

exogastritis (ĕks″ō-găs-trī′tĭs) [″ + *gaster*, belly, + *itis*, inflammation] Inflammation of the peritoneal coat of the stomach.

exogenous (ek-sŏj′ĕ-nŭs) [*exo-* + *-genous*] Originating outside an organ or an organism.

exome (ek′sōm″) [*ex(on)* + *-ome*] All of the exons in the DNA of an organism. It is all of the DNA sequences that are transcribed into proteins, not including introns.

exomphalos (ĕks-ŏm′fă-lŭs) [Gr. *ex*, out, + *omphalos*, navel] 1. An umbilical protrusion. 2. An umbilical hernia.

exon (ĕk′sŏn) One of the coding regions of the DNA of genes. SEE: *intron*.

Exophiala (ĕk″sō-fī-ā′lă) [NL.] A widespread genus of dematiaceous fungi that have brown hyphae and two-celled blastoconidia. Exophiala species may cause skin, heart, and brain infections in humans, esp. in those with immunosuppressive illnesses. Exophiala species are among the fungi causing infections referred to as phaeohyphomycosis. Subcutaneous infections such as mycetoma and chromoblastomycosis can also be due to Exophiala infection.

E. dermatitidis A species of the imperfect fungi that is usually a soil saprophyte but has caused meningitis following steroid therapy.

exophoria (ĕks″ō-fō′rē-ă) [″ + *phoros*, bearing] A tendency of the visual axes to diverge outward. Opposite of esophoria.

exophthalmometer (ĕk″sŏf-thăl-mŏm′ĕ-tĕr) A device for measuring the degree of protrusion of the eyeballs.

exophthalmos, exophthalmia, exophthalmus (ĕks″ŏf-thăl′mōs, -mŭs) Abnormal anterior protrusion of the eyeball. This may be due to thyrotoxicosis, tumor of the orbit, orbital cellulitis, leukemia, aneurysm, or vascular malformation. **exophthalmic** (-mĭk), *adj*.

pulsating e. Exophthalmos accompanied by pulsation and bruit due to an aneurysm behind the eye.

exoplasm (ĕk′sō-plăzm) [″ + LL. *plasma*, form, mold] Ectoplasm.

exoserosis (ĕks″ō-sĕr-ō′sĭs) [″ + *serum*, whey, + Gr. *osis*, condition] An oozing of serum or discharge of an exudate from the skin.

exoskeleton (ĕk″sō-skĕl′ĕ-tŏn) [″ + *skeleton*, a dried-up body] The hard outer covering of certain invertebrates such as the mollusks and arthropods. It is composed of chitin, calcareous material, or both.

exosome (ĕks′ō-sōm″) [″ + Gr. *soma*, body] An intracellular complex that degrades and processes messenger RNA molecules.

exostosis (ĕk″sos-tō′sĭs, -tō′sēz) *pl.* **exostoses** [*ex-* + *ostosis*] A bony growth that arises from the surface of a bone, often involving the ossification of muscular attachments. SYN: *bone spur*; *hyperostosis*; *osteoma*.

e. bursata An exostosis arising from the epiphysis of a bone and covered with cartilage and a synovial sac.

e. cartilaginea An exostosis consisting of cartilage underlying the periosteum.

multiple osteocartilaginous e. A hereditary growth disorder marked by the development of multiple exostoses, usually on the diaphyses of long bones near the epiphyseal lines. It causes irregular growth of the epiphyses and often secondary deformities.

retrocalcaneal e. Abnormal bone growth over the Achilles tendon's attachment on the calcaneus. The colloquial term "pump bumps" is derived from this condition's association with the wearing of tight-fitting, high-heeled shoes. SYN: *Haglund deformity*.

SYMPTOMS: A hard nodule is present

over the Achilles tendon attachment. The area appears inflamed and is sensitive to the touch. Patients often demonstrate hindfoot rigidity and decreased foot pronation. The patient may complain of pain during resisted plantar flexion (e.g., during the toe-off phase of gait). Symptoms may increase when wearing tight-fitting shoes.

TREATMENT: Physical agents and anti-inflammatory medications are used to minimize the inflammatory response. The patient should be instructed to wear loose-fitting shoes or open-backed shoes such as sandals, whenever practical. Improper foot biomechanics should be corrected, if applicable.

exothermal, exothermic (ek″sō-thĕr′măl, -thĕr′mik) [exo- + thermo-] Pert. to a chemical reaction that produces heat. **exothermally** (mă-lē), adv. **exothermically** (mik(ă-)lē), adv.

exotic (ĕg-zŏt′ĭk) [Gr. exotikos] Not native; originating in another part of the world.

exotoxin (ĕks″ō-tŏks′ĭn) [Gr. exo, outside, + toxikon, poison] A poisonous substance produced by bacteria, including staphylococci, streptococci, *Vibrio cholerae, Pseudomonas* species, and *Escherichia coli*. The actions of specific exotoxins vary with the organism. Staphylococcal exotoxins stimulate release of gamma interferon and can cause systemic inflammatory response syndrome. Inactivated exotoxins are used as the basis for diphtheria and tetanus vaccines. SEE: *bacterium; sepsis; systemic inflammatory response syndrome; toxoid.*

exotropia (ĕks″ō-trō′pē-ă) [″ + tropos, turning] Divergent strabismus; abnormal turning outward of one or both eyes.

expanded access Any of several methods used by the FDA to make experimental treatments available to patients who have failed conventional treatments and are not participating in formal clinical trials.

expander (ek-span′dĕr) [L.expandere, to spread out] **1.** A device that increases the size or volume of a structure. **2.** An agent, e.g. plasma or dextran, that expands blood volume.

expansion of morbidity Increase in the number of years of life and the proportion of disability by the elimination of a fatal disorder, such as cancer or heart disease.

expectant (ĕk-spek′tănt) [L. exspectare, to look out for, await] **1.** In the final trimester of pregnancy. **2.** Anticipated in the very near future; soon to emerge or happen.

expectant treatment (ĕk-spek′tĭnt) Relief of symptoms as they arise (i.e., not directed at the specific cause).

expected date of confinement ABBR: EDC. The predicted date of childbirth. SEE: *Naegele's rule; pregnancy* for table.

expectorant (ĕk-spĕk′tō-rănt) [Gr. ex, out, + L. pectus, breast] An agent, such as guaifenesin, that promotes the clearance of mucus from the respiratory tract.

expectoration (ĕk-spĕk″tō-rā′shŭn) **1.** The act or process of spitting out saliva or coughing up materials from the air passageways leading to the lungs. **2.** The expulsion of mucus or phlegm from the throat or lungs. It may be mucoid, mucopurulent, serous, or frothy. In pneumonia, it is viscid and tenacious, sticks to anything, appears rusty, and contains blood. In bronchitis, it is mucoid, often streaked with blood, and greenish-yellow from pus. In advanced tuberculosis, it varies from small amounts of frothy fluid to abundant, offensive greenish-yellow sputum often streaked with blood. SEE: *sputum.*

expedite (ĕk′spĕ-dīt″) [L. expeditus, unencumbered] To facilitate or speed up any process, e.g., to review and publish the results of important research rapidly.

expedited partner therapy ABBR: EPT. Patient-delivered partner treatment.

expel (ĕks-pĕl′) [L.expellere] To drive or push out.

experience 1. To encounter something personally or undergo an event. **2.** The knowledge or wisdom obtained from one's own observations.

experience rating 1. A projection of the cost of an insurance policy (e.g., of a malpractice insurance policy) based on the claims history of the person or party seeking to be insured. **2.** A calculation of future insurance payments based on historical data.

experiment [L. experimentum, to test] A scientific procedure used to test the validity of a hypothesis, gain further evidence or knowledge, or test the usefulness of a drug or type of therapy that has not been tried previously.

experimental gerontology Life extension.

expert consensus An agreed-upon set of principles for the care of a particular disease or condition, established after a review of contemporary knowledge by specialists in the field.

expert system A computer program using a set of rules that analyzes information and simulates the judgment and behavior of a specialist in a particular field to provide analysis and to possibly recommend a course of action.

expiration (ĕks″pĭ-rā′shŭn) [Gr. ex, out, + L. spirare, to breathe] **1.** Expulsion of air from the lungs in breathing. Normally the ratio of the duration of inspiration to expiration is 1:3. Exhalation takes longer than inspiration because exhalation occurs passively. SEE: *diaphragm* for illus.; *inspiration; respiration*. **2.** Death.

active e. Expiration accomplished as a result of muscular activity, as in forced respiration. The muscles used in forced expiration are those of the abdominal wall (external and internal oblique, rectus, and transversus abdominis), the internal intercostalis, serratus posterior inferior, platysma, and quadratus lumborum.

passive e. Expiration, performed during quiet respiration, that requires no muscular effort. It is brought about by the elasticity of the lungs, and by the ascent of the diaphragm and the weight of the descending chest wall, which compress the lungs.

expiration date The last day on which a drug or other therapeutic agent is still considered potent.

expiratory (ĕks-pī'ră-tor"ē) Pert. to expiration of air from the lungs.

expiratory pause time ABBR: TEP. The interval between the end of one exhalation and the beginning of the next.

expiratory positive airway pressure SEE: under *pressure*.

expiratory trigger sensitivity The adjustment of a pressure-support breath to the neurally mediated end of expiration. This machine adaptation to the patient's respiratory efforts is a refinement of mechanical ventilation that decreases patient discomfort and the work of breathing.

expire (ĕk-spī'ĕr) **1.** To breathe out or exhale. **2.** To die.

explant (ĕks-plănt') [" + L. *planta*, sprout] **1.** To remove a piece of living tissue from the body and transfer it to an artificial culture medium for growth, as in tissue culture. Opposite of implant. **2.** To remove a donor organ for transplantation. **3.** An organ removed for transplantation.

explicit (ĕk-splĭs'ĭt) [L. *explicare*, to unfold, set forth] **1.** Clearly and definitively stated. **2.** Unequivocal.

explode (eks-plōd') [L. *explodere*, to drive away by clapping the hands] **1.** To release energy suddenly, as when a bomb detonates. **2.** In epidemiology, to appear suddenly or have rapid onset. **3.** To display a powerful emotion in words or deeds

exploration [L. *explorare*, to search out] Examination of an organ or part by various means. **exploratory,** *adj.*

explorer (ĕks-plor'ĕr) An instrument used in exploration, esp. a device used to locate foreign bodies or to define passageways in body sinuses or cavities.

dental e. A sharp-pointed instrument used to detect unsound enamel, carious lesions, or imperfect margins of restorations in teeth.

exponent (ĕks'pō-nĕnt) In mathematics, the number that indicates the power to which another number is to be raised. It is written as a superscript (e.g., 10^2 or x^2 indicates that 10 and x are to be squared, or multiplied by themselves). The exponent can have any numerical value and may be positive or negative; it does not have to be a whole number. SEE: Scientific Notation in Units of Measurement Appendix.

expose 1. To open, as in surgically opening the abdominal cavity. **2.** To cause someone or something to lack heat or shelter. **3.** To place in contact with an infected person or agent. **4.** To display one's genitals publicly, esp. when members of the opposite sex are present. **5.** To deliver an amount of radiation.

ex post facto (eks pōst fak'tō) [L., from (what was) done afterwards] After the fact; retrospectively.

exposure (ek-spō'zhŭr) **1.** The amount of radiation delivered or received over a given area or to the entire body or object. **2.** Contact with an agent able to cause disease or injury, such as a bacterium or other contagious microbe; a chemical; an infected animal or person; or a physical agent, such as a radioactive source. **3.** The making visible of a body part, e.g., in a surgical procedure. **4.** The placing of an object or person in a particular environment, e.g., in warm or cold water. **5.** The physical consequences of being outdoors for a long time, including lowered body temperature; damage to skin, muscles, or nerves; altered judgment; coma; or, in some instances, death.

acute e. Exposure to radiation that is of short duration and usually of high intensity.

chronic e. Repeated exposure to a toxic agent or radiation over an extended period of time.

double e. Two exposures on one photographic or radiographic film or image.

entrance skin e. ABBR: ESE. The dose of radiation to which the surface of the body is exposed during a radiographic procedure.

image receptor e. ABBR: IR exposure. The quantity of ionizing radiation received by a radiologic device and used to produce a viewable image. The term is used in digital imaging in place of the older term *image density* (used in the past for the same concept when radiologic images were captured directly on exposed film).

pulp e. An opening through the wall of a tooth, produced by pathologic processes or accidentally, thereby exposing the dental pulp. SYN: *tooth perforation*.

exposure assessment A formal study of the impact of a hazardous substance on people, places, or things. It includes determination of the source(s) of the substance, its diffusion through the environment, its concentration, its duration and half-life, and the populations or media that are vulnerable to its effects.

exposure limit SEE: under *limit*.

exposure pathway SEE: under *pathway*.

exposure response prevention therapy A treatment for obsessive-compulsive disorder in which a person is repeatedly exposed to something that would normally trigger a stereotyped or ritualistic response but is prevented from engaging in the ritual.

exposure therapy A form of cognitive behavioral therapy for treating symptoms of post-traumatic stress disorder, in which the patient identifies the emotional, cognitive, and physiological responses to a fearful event in an attempt to gain psychological control over them. The goal is to reduce the vulnerability of the patient to his or her memories of a fearful event; to help a victim cope with the anxiety, fear, guilt, or humiliation that the original exposure produced; and to prevent those feelings from being triggered in the patient by new exposures that revive painful memories.

express (ek-spres′) [L. *expressare*, to keep pressing out] **1.** To force out by applying pressure. **2.** To speak; to use language or symbols to communicate with others. **3.** To translate a gene into a protein.

expression 1. Expulsion by pressure. **2.** Facial disclosure of feeling or a physical state. SYN: *facies*. SEE: *face*.

   differential gene e. The biochemical processes that determine which genes are actively transcribed and translated into mRNA and proteins in a cell and under what conditions.

expressive arts therapy The use of plastic arts, e.g., painting, sculpting, drawing, or the performing arts, e.g., dance, music, drama, for psychotherapeutic purposes.

expressive language delay Speech delay.

expressive language disorder Failure of a child to learn how to speak, write, or use sign language properly, despite having normal understanding of language and otherwise normal cognitive functions. The impairment in language use is apparent in the child's abnormal composition of sentences, frequent grammatical errors, limited word choices, and difficulty in learning new vocabulary.

expressivity The extent to which a heritable trait is manifest in the individual carrying the gene.

expulsion rate In gynecology, the rate of spontaneous rejection of intrauterine contraceptive devices in the group of women who use them. It is usually expressed with respect to the time elapsed following implantation.

expulsive (ĕks-pŭl′sĭv) [L. *expellere*, to drive out] Having a tendency to expel.

exsanguinate (ĕks-săn′gwĭn-āt) [Gr. *ex*, out, + *sanguis*, blood] To lose blood to the point at which life can no longer be sustained.

exsanguination (ĕk-săn″gwĭn-ā′shŭn) Massive bleeding.

exsanguine (ĕks-săn′gwĭn) Anemic; bloodless.

exsiccation (ĕk″sĭ-kā′shŭn) **1.** The process of drying up. **2.** In chemistry, removing the water from compounds or solutions. SYN: *desiccation*.

exsorption (ĕk-sorp′shŭn) Movement of material including cells and electrolytes from the blood to the lumen of the intestines. In pathological conditions such as intestinal obstruction, this process may greatly increase pressure inside the affected area of the intestinal tract.

exstrophy (ek′strŏ-fē) [Gr. *ekstrophē*, a turning inside out, (uterine) inversion] Congenital turning inside out of an organ. SEE: *eversion*.

   e. of bladder Congenital eversion of the urinary bladder. The abdominal wall fails to close, and the inside of the bladder may protrude through the abdominal wall.

exsufflation (ĕk″sŭ-flā′shŭn) [″ + *sufflatio*, blown up] Forceful expulsion of air from a cavity by artificial means, such as use of a mechanical exsufflator. Exsufflation is often used to simulate a cough and remove secretions from the airway.

ext [L. *extractum*] extract.

extein (ĕk′stē-ĭn) [″ + *(pro)tein*] Fragments of a protein that link to form a new protein after an internal sequence (an intein) of the larger molecule is removed by post-translational splicing.

extemporaneous (ĕks-tĕm″po-rān′ē-ŭs) [LL. *extemporaneus*] Not prepared according to formula but devised for the occasion.

extend (ĕk-stĕnd′) [Gr. *ex*, out, + L. *tendere*, to stretch] **1.** To straighten a joint such as the knee or elbow by increasing the angle formed by the proximal and distal bones. **2.** To move forward. **3.** To increase the angle between the bones forming a joint.

extended care facility A health care institution for patients who require long-term custodial, nursing, or medical care, esp. for a chronic disease or prolonged rehabilitation.

extended-field radiation therapy ABBR: EFRT. A treatment for lymphoma and leukemias in which therapeutic radiation is delivered not only to detectable areas involved by tumor but more extensively.

extender (ĕk-stĕn′dĕr) Something that increases duration or effect. The time required for absorption of some medicines given intramuscularly may be increased by injecting them with a substance such as an oil, which slows absorption.

leg e. A device added to lengthen the legs of furniture (e.g., beds, tables, chairs) to accommodate the needs of persons with functional limitations.

extension (ek-sten'shŏn) [L. *extensio,* a stretching out] **1.** A movement that pulls apart both ends of any part. **2.** A movement that brings the members of a limb into or toward a straight position. Opposite of flexion. **3.** The application of a pull (traction) to a fractured or dislocated limb. **4.** In the polymerase chain reaction, the synthesis of a desired strand of nucleic acid. Particular extensions are listed under the first word. SEE: e.g., *Buck's extension; extracapsular extension; shelf-life extension.*

extension of infarction An increase in the size of a myocardial infarction, occurring after the initial infarction and usually accompanied by a return of acute symptoms, such as angina that is not relieved by medication.

extensive (ĕk-sten'siv) [L. *extendere,* to stretch out] Widespread. In cancer, widely metastatic.

extensive limb swelling SEE: under *swelling.*

extensor (ĕks-tĕn'sor) [L.] A muscle that extends a part of the body.

exterior [L.] Outside of; external; opposite of interior or internal.

exteriorize (ĕks-tĕr'ē-o-rīz) **1.** To mobilize without the body, a part temporarily in surgery. SEE: *marsupialization.* **2.** In psychiatry, to turn one's interests outward.

extern (eks'tĕrn") [L. *externus,* outside] A nonresident physician or medical student who assists in the medical and surgical care of patients. **externship,** *n.* SEE: *intern.*

external Exterior; the opposite of interior or internal.

external fixator A device for holding fractured bones in place by use of external rather than internal fixation. SEE: illus.

externalize (ĕks-tĕr'nă-līz) **1.** In surgery, to provide exposure to the outside. **2.** In psychiatry, to direct one's inner conflicts to the outside rather than keeping them hidden inside.

exteroceptive (ĕks"tĕr-ō-sĕp'tĭv) [L. *externus,* outside, + *receptus,* having received] Pert. to receptors detecting external (environmental) stimuli.

exteroceptor (ĕks"tĕr-ō-sĕp'tor) A sense organ (e.g., in the eye, ear, or skin) adapted for the reception of stimuli from outside the body.

extinction [L. *exstinctus,* having extinguished] **1.** The process of extinguishing or putting out. **2.** The complete inhibition of a conditioned reflex through failure to reinforce it.

extinguish (ĕks-tĭng'gwĭsh) [L. *extingu-*

ere, to render extinct] To abolish, esp. to remove a reflex, by surgical, psychological, or pharmacological means, depending on the type of reflex involved.

extirpation (ek"stĭr-pā'shŏn) [L. *exstirpatio,* uprooting] Complete removal of a part.

pulp e. Pulpectomy.

extorsion (ĕks-tor'shŭn) [Gr. *ex,* out, + L. *torsio,* twisting] Rotation of an organ or limb outward.

extra- [L. *extra,* outside] Prefix meaning *outside of; in addition to; beyond.*

extra-adrenal catecholamine-secreting paraganglioma (ek"stră-ă-drē'năl kat"ĕ-kōl'ă-mēn-sĕ-krēt'ing) SEE: under *paraganglioma.*

extra-articular (ĕks"tră-ăr-tĭk'ū-lăr) [" + *articulus,* joint] Outside a joint.

extracapsular (ĕks"tră-kăp'sū-lăr) Outside a capsule (e.g., a joint capsule or the capsule of the lens of the eye).

extracapsular extension The spread of a tumor outside the organ in which it arose, specifically, outside the tissue that separates the organ from neighboring anatomical structures.

extracellular (ĕks"tră-sĕl'ū-lăr) Outside the cell.

extrachromosomal (ĕks"tră-krō"mŏ-sō'măl) Not connected to the chromosomes; exerting an effect other than through chromosomal action.

extracorporeal (ĕks"tră-kor-por'ē-ăl) [" + *corpus,* body] Outside the body.

extracorporeal carbon dioxide removal ABBR: ECCO2R. An infrequently used treatment for severe hypercapnic respiratory failure (high carbon dioxide blood levels with accompanying respiratory acidosis), in which carbon dioxide is swept from venous blood and replaced, typically with oxygen.

extracorporeal membrane oxygenator SEE: under *oxygenator.*

extracorporeal shock wave lithotripsy, extracorporeal shock wave therapy ABBR: ESWL. The fragmentation of kidney stones with an extracorporeal shock wave lithotriptor. In addition to breaking up gallstones and kidney stones, shock wave lithotripsy may be used in some orthopedic applications (orthotripsy), e.g., in the treatment of nonunion of fractures and bone spurs.

> ⚠ ESWL for gallstones or kidney stones is contraindicated during pregnancy.

extracorporeal shock-wave lithotriptor A device used to fragment calcified objects within the body, such as kidney stones. After the patient is given analgesics and anesthetic drugs, electrically generated shock waves are focused on the object in an attempt to disrupt it. In the case of kidney stones and gallstones,

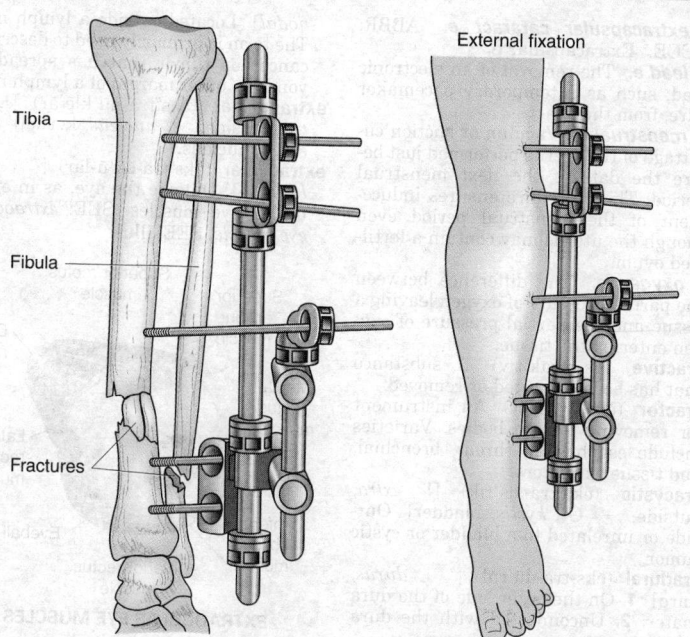

Tibia

Fibula

Fractures

External fixation

EXTERNAL FIXATION OF FRACTURES OF THE TIBIA AND FIBULA

the stone fragments may subsequently pass either into the urine or the bile. SEE: *percutaneous ultrasonic lithotriptor.*

extracranial (eks″tră-krā′nē-ăl) [*extra- + cranial*] ABBR: EC. Located or happening outside the skull.

extract (eks-trakt′, eks′trakt″) [L. *extractum,* drawn out] **1.** To remove by surgery or by force. **2.** A solid or semisolid preparation made by removing the soluble portion of a compound by using water or alcohol as the solvent and evaporating the solution. **3.** The active principle of a drug obtained by distillation or chemical processes.

   citrus seed e. Grapefruit seed **e.**

   compound e. An extract prepared from more than one drug or substance.

   fluid e. An extract of a vegetable drug made into a solution. It contains medicinal components.

   grapefruit seed e. ABBR: GFSE, GSE. An extract from grapefruit seed and grapefruit pulp that contains polyphenols. The extract is used in alternative and complementary medicine for a wide variety of diseases and conditions, esp. for the treatment of bacterial or viral illness. SYN: *citrus seed e.*

   liver e. A dry brown powder obtained from mammalian livers that was once used as a crude source of vitamin B_{12} and other vitamins.

   pine bark e. SEE: *pycnogenol.*

   red yeast rice e. A dietary herbal

supplement derived from the mold *Monascus purpureus.* It contains 3-hydroxy-3-methylglutaryl coenzyme A (HMG-CoA) reductase inhibitors, is similar to the prescription drug lovastatin, has similar effects and side effects (including muscle injury with elevation of serum creatine kinase levels), and is promoted for its effect in lowering serum cholesterol and triglyceride. SYN: *Chinese red rice.*

⚠ Side effects can include dizziness, gastritis, heartburn, flatulence, and elevated hepatic enzymes. It is chemically related to the statin class of cholesterol-lowering medications.

   solid e. An extract made by evaporating the fluid part of a solution.

extraction (eks-trak′shŏn) [L. *extractio,* a drawing out] **1.** Surgical removal, as of a tooth. **2.** The removal of the active portion of a drug from its vehicle.

   breech e. SEE: *breech delivery.*

   extracapsular e. A surgical technique for cataract removal. The nucleus, cortex, and anterior capsule are removed; the posterior capsule is left intact. This is often done by phacoemulsification under local anesthesia using a microscope. SYN: *extracapsular cataract e.* SEE: *cataract; phacoemulsification.*

extracapsular cataract e. ABBR: ECCE. Extracapsular **e.**

lead e. The removal of an electronic lead, such as a temporary pacemaker wire, from the heart.

menstrual e. Vacuum or suction curettage of the uterus performed just before the date of the next menstrual period. The procedure ensures inducement of the menstrual period even though the uterus may contain a fertilized ovum.

oxygen e. The difference between the partial pressure of oxygen leaving a tissue and the partial pressure of oxygen entering the tissue.

extractive (ek-strak'tiv) A substance that has been extracted or removed.

extractor (ĕks-trăk'tor) An instrument for removing foreign bodies. Varieties include esophageal, throat, bronchial, and tissue extractors.

extracystic (ĕks″tră-sĭs′tĭk) [L. *extra,* outside, + Gr. *kystis,* bladder] Outside or unrelated to a bladder or cystic tumor.

extradural (ĕks-tră-dū′răl) [″ + *durus,* hard] **1.** On the outer side of the dura mater. **2.** Unconnected with the dura mater.

extraembryonic (ĕks″tră-ĕm″brē-ŏn′ĭk) [″ + Gr. *embryon,* something that swells in the body] Apart from and outside the embryo (e.g., concerning the amnion).

extrafusal fibers (ek″stră-fū′zăl) SEE: under *fiber.*

extragenital (ĕks″tră-jĕn′ĭ-tăl) [″ + *genitalis,* genital] Outside or unrelated to the genital organs.

extrahepatic (ĕks″tră-hĕ-păt′ĭk) [L. *extra,* outside, + Gr. *hepatos,* liver] Outside or unrelated to the liver.

extramarginal (ĕks″tră-măr′jĭ-năl) [″ + *margo,* margin] Pert. to subliminal consciousness.

extramastoiditis (ĕks″tră-măs″toyd-ī′tĭs) [″ + Gr. *mastos,* breast, + *eidos,* form, shape, + *itis,* inflammation] Inflammation of tissues contiguous to the mastoid process.

extramedullary (ĕks″tră-mĕd″ū-lă-rē) [″ + *medulla,* marrow] Outside the medulla or the bone marrow.

extramural (ĕks″tră-mū′răl) [″ + *murus,* wall] Outside the wall of an organ or vessel.

extraneous (ĕks-trā′nē-ŭs) [L. *extraneus,* external] Outside and unrelated to an organism.

extranet A private network that uses Internet technology and the public telecommunication system to secure a business's information or operations with suppliers, vendors, partners, customers, or other businesses. It is an extension of an intranet with added security features.

extranodal (ek″stră-nōd′ăl) [*extra-* + *nodal*] Located outside a lymph node. The term is primarily used to describe a cancerous tumor that has spread beyond the outer margin of a lymph node.

extranuclear (ĕks″tră-nū′klē-ăr) [L. *extra,* outside, + *nucleus,* kernel] Outside a nucleus.

extraocular (ĕks″tră-ŏk′ū-lăr) [″ + *oculus,* eye] Outside the eye, as in extraocular eye muscles. SEE: *extraocular eye muscle.* SEE: illus.

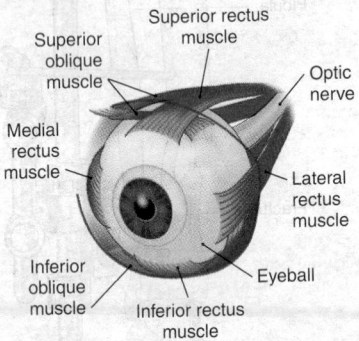

EXTRAOCULAR EYE MUSCLES

Eye globe with attachment of extraocular eye muscles

extraperitoneal 1. Outside the peritoneum. **2.** Not completely enveloped by the peritoneum.

extrapolar (ĕks″tră-pō′lăr) [″ + *polus,* pole] Outside instead of between poles, as the electrodes of a battery.

extrapolate (ĕks″tră′pō-lāt′) To infer a point between two given, or known, points on a graph or progression. Thus, if an infant weighed 20 lb at a certain age and 4 months later weighed 23 lb, it could be inferred that at a point halfway between the two time periods, the infant might have weighed 21.5 lb.

extrapyramidal (ĕks″tră-pī-răm′ĭ-dăl) Pert. to the extrapyramidal motor system.

extrapyramidal disease Any of several degenerative diseases of the nervous system that involve the extrapyramidal system and the basal ganglion of the brain. Symptoms include tremors, chorea, athetosis, and dystonia. Parkinsonism is a form of extrapyramidal disease.

extrapyramidal side effects of medications ABBR: EPS. Muscular rigidity, tremor, bradykinesia, and difficulty walking induced by neuroleptic medications; drug-induced parkinsonism.

extrapyramidal syndrome ABBR: EPS. Any of several degenerative nervous system diseases that involve the extrapyramidal system and the basal ganglion of the brain. The symptoms include tremors, chorea, athetosis, and dystonia. Parkinsonism is an extrapyramidal syndrome.

extrapyramidal system 1. All the central nervous system (CNS) nuclei and axon tracts that generate and transmit motor programs outside the corticospinal tracts. The major extrapyramidal nuclei include the basal ganglia and the red nucleus, including the ansa lenticularis and the rubrospinal tract. **2.** Certain CNS nuclei and axon tracts in the brain that control and modulate movement but do not directly synapse on motor neurons. The main extrapyramidal nuclei are the basal ganglia. The main extrapyramidal tracts form a loop: axons from the motor cortices of the cerebral hemisphere synapse in the basal ganglia, axons from the basal ganglia (via the ansa lenticularis) synapse in the ventral anterior (VA) and ventral lateral (VL) nuclei of the thalamus, and axons from the VA and VL nuclei synapse back in the motor cortices.

extrasensory (ĕks″tră-sĕn′sō-rē) Pert. to forms of perception, such as thought transference, that are not dependent on the five primary senses.

extrasystole (ĕks″tră-sĭs′tō-lē) [″ + Gr. *systole*, contraction] Premature contraction of the heart. It may occur in the presence or absence of organic heart disease. It may be of reflex origin or may be triggered by stimulants (e.g., caffeine, cocaine, or theophylline), hypoxia, psychological stress, electrolyte abnormalities, thyroid disorders, or myocardial infarction.

  atrial e. Premature contraction of the atrium.

  junctional e. Nodal e.

  nodal e. Extrasystole occurring as a result of an impulse originating in the atrioventricular node. SYN: *junctional e.*

  ventricular e. Premature ventricular beat.

extrathoracic (ĕks″tră-thō-răs′ĭk) Outside the thorax.

extratubal (ĕks″tră-tū′băl) Outside a tube, esp. the uterine tube.

extrauterine (ĕks″tră-ū′tĕr-ĭn) [″ + *uterus*, womb] Outside the uterus.

extravaginal (ĕks″tră-văj′ĭ-năl) [″ + *vagina*, sheath] Outside the vagina.

extravasate (ĕks-trăv′ă-sāt) [″ + *vas*, vessel] **1.** To escape from a vessel into the tissues, said of serum, blood, or lymph. **2.** Fluid escaping from vessels into surrounding tissue.

extravasation (ĕks-trăv″ă-sā′shŭn) The escape of fluid from its physiologic contained space, e.g., bile, blood, cerebrospinal fluid (CSF), into the surrounding tissue. SEE: illus. SYN: *suffusion.*

extravascular (ĕks″tră-văs′kū-lăr) [″ + *vasculum*, vessel] Outside a vessel.

extraventricular (ĕks″tră-vĕn-trĭk′ū-lăr) [″ + *ventriculus*, little belly] Outside any ventricle, esp. one of the heart.

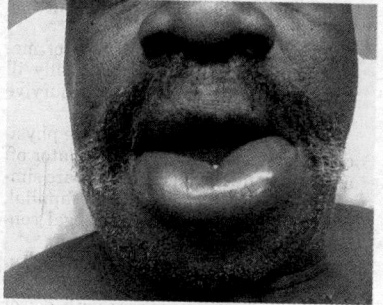

EXTRAVASATION
Massive release of fluid into the tissues of the lower lips of a patient with angiodema

extremely low birth weight ABBR: ELBW. SEE: under *birth weight.*

extremital (ĕks-trĕm′ĭ-tăl) [L. *extremus*, outermost] Pert. to an extremity. SYN: *distal.*

extremity (ĕks-trĕm′ĭ-tē) **1.** The terminal part of anything. **2.** An arm or leg.

  lower e. The lower limb, including the hip, thigh, leg, ankle, and foot.

  upper e. The upper limb, including the shoulder, arm, forearm, wrist, and hand.

extricate (eks′trĭ-kāt″) [L. *extricare*, to disentangle, clear] To free from entrapment, as a person from a fallen building or a crushed automobile. **extrication** (eks″trĭ-kā′shŏn), *n.*

extrinsic (ek-strin′zik, ′sik) [L. *extrinsecus*, from outside, outer] **1.** External. **2.** Originating or coming from outside. **3.** Directed inward from the outside of a structure. **4.** Nonessential.

extrinsic factor SEE: under *factor.*

extroversion (ĕks″trō-vĕr′zhŭn) [″ + *vertere*, to turn] **1.** Eversion; turning inside out. **2.** The direction of attention and energy outward from the self. SEE: *introversion.*

extrovert (ĕks′trō-vĕrt″) An outgoing or extremely sociable person interested mainly in external objects and actions.

extrude (ĕks-trūd′) [L. *extrudere*, to squeeze out] To push or force out.

extrusion (ĕks-troo′zhŭn) **1.** Something occupying an abnormal external position. **2.** In dentistry, the overeruption or migration of a tooth beyond its natural occlusal plane. This condition often follows the removal of an opposing tooth. **3.** A herniated nucleus pulposus in which the nuclear material ruptures through the outer fibers of the annulus fibrosis and is present in the spinal canal but still partially within the disk and still attached to it.

extrusion reflex SEE: under *reflex.*

extubation (eks″too″bā′shŏn, ″tū″) [*ex-*

+ *tubus*] Removal of a tube, such as an endotracheal tube.

terminal e. The withdrawal of mechanical ventilation from critically ill patients who are not expected to survive without respiratory support.

PATIENT CARE: Although the physical process of switching a ventilator off and removing the tracheal tube are simple, there are serious ethical, familial, psychological, religious, and legal considerations of terminal extubation.

In most jurisdictions terminal extubation is not allowed unless patients or surrogate decision makers with power of attorney have explicitly specified that, if care is futile and death imminent, they would want life-support measures withdrawn. If these conditions are met, the patient's family and the health care team may meet to discuss withdrawal of support. Negotiations are made for the timing of extubation and the use of medications or other means to alleviate breathlessness, pain, suffering, and other conditions for withdrawal. Arrangements are made for the funeral and the advisability of or need for autopsy or organ donation. Time is set aside for the family and staff to prepare for death and grieving. Terminal extubation differs from terminal weaning in that the withdrawal of support is sudden. The patient may survive either method of withdrawal for minutes, hours, or, occasionally, days.

unplanned endotracheal e. The inadvertent removal of an endotracheal tube (ET) by patients who are either not responsible for or not aware of their actions. To prevent a recurrence, the health care provider must be skilled in securing the ET. The tube must be firmly secured, tube-related discomfort minimized, and the patient's delirium and agitation controlled. This may require careful patient monitoring, or, occasionally, sedation, paralysis, or the application of physical restraints. Immediate reintubation may be indicated in a patient unable to oxygenate or ventilate on his own.

extubation failure SEE: under *failure*.

exuberant (eg-zoo″bĕ-rănt) [L. *exuberare*, to be (very) fruitful] **1.** Excessive, as in the increased and excessive growth of granulation tissue or a bacterial culture. **2.** Joyful, happy.

exudate (ĕks′ū-dāt) [L. *exsudare*, to sweat out] Any fluid released from the body with a high concentration of protein, cells, or solid debris.

Exudates are classified as fibrinous, hemorrhagic, diphtheritic, purulent, and serous. A fibrinous exudate may wall off a cavity, resulting in adhesions after surgery, or in restrictive lung disease, after an empyema. SEE: *empy-*

ema; infection; inflammation; pus; resorption; transudate.

exudation (ĕks″ū-dā′shŭn) Pathological oozing of fluids, usually the result of inflammation. SEE: *exudate*. **exudative** (ĕks″ū-dā″tĭv), *adj.*

exude (ĕg-zūd′) [L. *exsudare*, to sweat out] To ooze out of tissues; said of a semisolid or fluid.

ex-utero-intrapartum procedure (eks″ūt′ ĕ-rō-in″tră-part′ŭm) SEE: under *procedure*.

Eyach virus (ī′akh) [*Eyach*, Germany]

eye (ī) The organ of vision. SEE: illus.

ANATOMY: The eyeball has three layers: the inner retina, which contains the photoreceptors; the middle uvea (choroid, ciliary body, and iris); and the outer sclera, which includes the transparent cornea. The eyeball contains two cavities: the anterior cavity and the posterior cavity. The smaller anterior cavity is in front of the lens and is further divided by the iris into an anterior chamber, filled with aqueous humor, and a posterior chamber, filled with the vitreous. Behind the lens is the larger posterior cavity, which contains the vitreous. The lens is behind the iris, held in place by the ciliary body and suspensory ligaments called zonules. The visible portion of the sclera is covered by the conjunctiva. Six extrinsic muscles move the eyeball: the superior, inferior, medial, and lateral rectus muscles, and the superior and inferior oblique muscles.

Nerve supply: The optic (second cranial) nerve contains the fibers from the retina. The eye muscles are supplied by the oculomotor, trochlear, and abducens (third, fourth, and sixth cranial) nerves. The lid muscles are supplied by the facial nerve to the orbicularis oculi and the oculomotor nerve to the levator palpebrae. Sensory fibers to the orbit are furnished by ophthalmic and maxillary fibers of the fifth cranial (trigeminal) nerve. Sympathetic postganglionic fibers originate in the carotid plexus, their cell bodies lying in the superior cervical ganglion. They supply the dilator muscle of the iris. Parasympathetic fibers from the ciliary ganglion pass to the lacrimal gland, ciliary muscle, and constrictor muscles of the iris.

PHYSIOLOGY: Light entering the eye passes through the cornea, then through the pupil, and on through the crystalline lens and the vitreous to the retina. The cornea, aqueous humor, lens, and vitreous are the refracting media of the eye. Changes in the curvature of the lens are brought about by its elasticity and by contraction of the ciliary muscle. These changes focus light rays on the retina, thereby stimulating the rods and cones. The rods

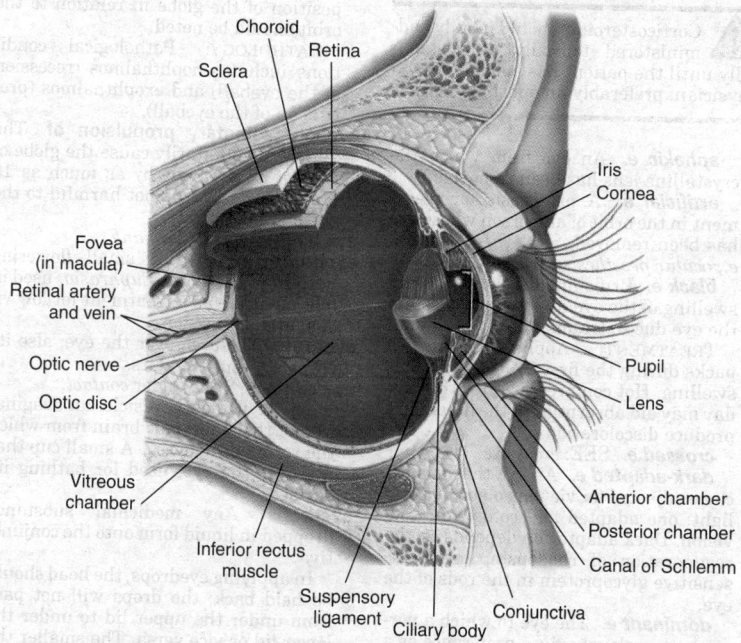

ANATOMY OF THE EYE

Labels on figure: Choroid, Retina, Sclera, Iris, Cornea, Fovea (in macula), Retinal artery and vein, Optic nerve, Optic disc, Pupil, Lens, Vitreous chamber, Anterior chamber, Posterior chamber, Canal of Schlemm, Inferior rectus muscle, Suspensory ligament, Ciliary body, Conjunctiva

detect light, and the cones detect colors in the visible spectrum. The visual area of the cerebral cortex, located in the occipital lobe, registers them as visual sensations. The amount of light entering the eye is regulated by the iris; its constrictor and dilator muscles change the size of the pupil in response to varying amounts of light. The eye can distinguish nearly 8 million differences in color. As the eye ages, objects appear greener. The principal aspects of vision are color sense, light sense, movement, and form sense.

PATIENT CARE: When injury to the eye occurs, visual acuity is assessed immediately. If the globe has been penetrated, a suitable eye shield, not an eye patch, is applied. A penetrating foreign body should not be removed. All medications, esp. corticosteroids, are withheld until the patient has been seen by an ophthalmologist.

The patient is assessed for pain and tenderness, redness and discharge, itching, photophobia, increased tearing, blinking, and visual blurring. When any prescribed topical eye medications (drops, ointments, or solutions) are administered, the health care provider should wash his or her hands thoroughly before administering the agent. The patient's head is turned slightly toward the affected eye; his or her cooperation is necessary to keep the eye wide open. Drops are instilled in the conjunctival sac (not on the orb), and pressure is applied to the lacrimal apparatus in the inner canthus if it is necessary to prevent systemic absorption. Ointments are applied along the palpebral border from the inner to the outer canthus, and solutions are instilled from the inner to the outer canthus. Touching the dropper or tip of the medication container to the eye should be avoided, and hands should be washed immediately after the procedure.

Both patient and family are taught correct methods for instilling prescribed medications. Patients with visual defects are protected from injury, and family members are taught safety measures. Patients with insufficient tearing or the inability to blink or close their eyes are protected from corneal injury by applying artificial tears and by gently patching the eyes closed. The importance of periodic eye examinations is emphasized. Persons at risk should protect their eyes from trauma by wearing safety goggles when working with or near dangerous tools or substances. Tinted lenses should be worn to protect the eyes from excessive exposure to bright light. Patients should avoid rubbing their eyes to prevent irritation or possibly infection. SEE: *eyedrops*; *artificial tears*.

⚠️ Corticosteroids should not be administered topically or systemically until the patient has been seen by a physician, preferably an ophthalmologist.

aphakic e. An eye from which the crystalline lens has been removed.

artificial e. A prosthesis for placement in the orbit of an person whose eye has been removed. SYN: *false e.; glass e.; ocular prosthesis.* SEE: *ocularist.*

black e. Bruising, discoloration, and swelling of the eyelid and tissue around the eye due to trauma.

TREATMENT: Application of ice packs during the first 24 hr will inhibit swelling. Hot compresses after the first day may aid absorption of the fluids that produce discoloration.

crossed e. SEE: *cross-eye.*

dark-adapted e. An eye that has become adjusted for viewing objects in dim light; one adapted for scotopic, or rod, vision. Dark adaptation depends on the regeneration of rhodopsin, the light-sensitive glycoprotein in the rods of the eye.

dominant e. The eye to which a person unconsciously gives preference as a source of stimuli for visual sensations. The dominant eye is usually used in sighting down a gun or looking through a monocular microscope.

dry e. Insufficient quantity and/or quality of tears caused by aging, the environment, hormonal changes, or disease. This condition produces pain and discomfort in the eyes. Dry eye may occur in any disorder that scars the cornea (such as erythema multiforme), Sjögren syndrome, lagophthalmos, Riley-Day syndrome, absence of one or both of the lacrimal glands, paralysis of the facial or trigeminal nerves, medication with atropine, and deep anesthesia. Suitably prepared water-soluble polymers are effective in treating this condition. SYN: *alacrima..* SEE: *Sjögren syndrome.*

exciting e. In sympathetic ophthalmia, the damaged eye, the source of sympathogenic influences.

fixating e. In strabismus, the eye directed toward the object of vision.

Klieg e. SEE: *Klieg eye.*

lazy e. Amblyopia.

light-adapted e. An eye that has become adjusted to viewing objects in bright light; one adapted for phototic, or cone, vision. In this type of eye, most rhodopsin has broken down.

squinting e. An eye that deviates from the object of fixation in strabismus.

sympathizing e. In sympathetic ophthalmia, the uninjured eye, which reacts to the pathological process in the injured eye.

eyeball The globe of the eye. Tension and position of the globe in relation to the orbit should be noted.

PATHOLOGY: Pathological conditions include enophthalmos (recession of the eyeball) and exophthalmos (protrusion of the eyeball).

eyeball, voluntary propulsion of The ability to voluntarily cause the globe of the eye to protrude by as much as 10 mm (0.4 in). This is not harmful to the eye or visual acuity.

eye bank SEE: under *bank.*

eyebright (ī′brīt″) A small flowering herb from the genus *Euphrasia,* used in folk medicine as a treatment for low vision and depression.

eyebrow The arch over the eye; also its covering, esp. the hairs.

eye contact SEE: under *contact.*

eyecup 1. The optic vesicle, an evagination of the embryonic brain from which the retina develops. **2.** A small cup that fits over the eye, used for bathing its surface.

eyedrops Any medicinal substance dropped in liquid form onto the conjunctiva.

In applying eyedrops, the head should be held back; the drops will not pass from under the upper lid to under the lower lid or vice versa. The smaller the eyedrops, the better. Too much liquid in the eye causes the patient to blink, and the medication is then washed away by the increased lacrimal secretion.

⚠️ Many medicines are not absorbed from the conjunctiva; they may be readily absorbed from the nasolacrimal duct. For this reason, esp. in children, it is advisable to close off the duct by applying pressure to the inner canthus of the eye for a few minutes after each instillation.

eyeglass A glass lens used to correct a defect in visual acuity or to prevent exposure to bright light if the lens is tinted. SEE: *glasses.*

eyeground The fundus of the eye, seen with an ophthalmoscope.

eye-hand coordination (ī′hand′) The ability to identify objects by sight and touch, and to grasp, push, pull, or direct their movement with the hand. is the coordinated control of eye movement with hand movement, and the processing of visual input to guide reaching and grasping along with the use of proprioception of the hands to guide the eyes.

Hand-eye coordination is the ability of the vision system to coordinate the information received through the eyes to control, guide, and direct the hands in the accomplishment of a given task, such as handwriting or catching a ball. SYN: *hand-eye coordination.*

eyelash A stiff hair on the margin of the eyelid. SYN: *cilium.*

eyelid One of two movable protective folds that cover the anterior surface of the eyeball when closed. They are separated by the palpebral fissure. The upper (palpebra superior) is the larger and more movable. It is raised by contraction of the levator palpebrae superioris muscle. Angles formed at the inner and outer ends of the lids are known as the canthi. The cilia, or eyelashes, arise from the edges of the eyelids. The posterior surface is lined by the conjunctiva, a mucous membrane.

   drooping e. Ptosis of the eyelid.

   fused e. A congenital anomaly resulting from failure of the fetal eyelids to separate.

eye movement desensitization and reprocessing ABBR: EMDR. A treatment for post-traumatic stress disorder and other conditions in which a person recalls a disturbing memory while looking to the left or right (or listening to sounds or attending to tactile stimulation of one hand and then the other).

eye muscle imbalance SEE: under *imbalance.*

eyepiece (ī′pēs) The portion of an optical device closest to the viewer's eye.

eye protection Goggles, face masks, or shatterproof glasses worn to prevent injury to the eye.

⚠️ Protective eye wear should be worn in surgery (and other health care settings where splashes or splatters are common), in many sports, and in most vocations or occupations where splinters, cinders, hooks, or other small objects may injure the cornea, lens, or ocular bulb.

eyestrain, eye strain (ī′strān″) Asthenopia.

eyetooth (ī′tooth″, ′tēth″) *pl.* **eyeteeth**- Canine (2).

eyewash Any suitable liquid used to rinse the eyes (e.g., sterile physiological saline or sterile water).

eyeworm Colloquial term for *Loa loa.*

F **1.** *Fahrenheit; femto-; field of vision; folic acid; formula; function.* **2.** Symbol for the element fluorine. **3.** Symbol for filial generation. The symbol is usually used with a following subscript number, e.g., F_1, the first filial generation, for the offspring of a cross between two unrelated individuals, F_2, the second filial generation, for the offspring of a cross between two individuals of the F_1 generation; etc.

FA *fatty acid; filterable agent; first aid; fluorescent antibody.*

FAAN *Fellow of the American Academy of Nursing.*

FAARC *Fellow of the American Association of Respiratory Care.*

Fab *fragment antigen binding.*

fabella (fă-bel′ă, fă-bel′ē″) *pl.* **fabellae** [L. *fabella,* little bean] Fibrocartilage or bone that sometimes develops in the head of the gastrocnemius muscle.

FABERE maneuver [Flexion, ABduction, External, Rotation, and Extension] Patrick test.

FABERE test, FABER test Acronym for *flexion, abduction, external rotation,* and *extension* of the hip. The FABERE test is used to identify hip arthritis or sacroiliac dysfunction. SEE: *Patrick's test.*

fabrication (fab″rĭ-kā′shŏn) [L. *fabricare,* to make] **1.** Deliberate falsification in order to deceive, e.g., the faking of research results; a lie. **2.** Confabulation.

Fabry disease (fob′rē) [Johannes Fabry, Ger. physician, 1860–1930] An X-linked disease in which there is a galactosidase deficiency, which leads to accumulation of glycosphingolipids throughout the body. Paresthesias in the hands and feet are common early symptoms. As affected patients age, glycolipid deposition in the kidneys, heart, and brain may produce a variety of organ dysfunctions.

FACCP *Fellow of the American College of Chest Physicians.*

FACD *Fellow of the American College of Dentists.*

face (fās) [Fr. *face* fr. L. *facies,* form, figure, face] **1.** The front part of the head from the forehead to the chin, extending laterally to but not including the ears. SEE: illus.

ANATOMY: There are 14 bones in the face. The blood supply is bilateral from the facial, maxillary, and superficial temporal branches of the external carotid artery and the ophthalmic branch of the internal carotid artery. The veins include the external and internal jugular veins.

2. The visage or countenance.

moon f. A full, round face seen in Cushing's syndrome or, more often, as a side effect of corticosteroid therapy.

faceblind (fās′blīnd″) Pert. to the inability to recognize the facial features of a familiar person when that person's face is seen in a new context, in different lighting, or at an unusual angle.

facebow (fās′bō″) [″ + AS *boga*] In orthodontics, an appliance that maintains the position of the posterior molars or moves the molars distally. A metal archwire (a metal wire fitting the dental or alveolar arch) is attached to a molar tooth in each arch. External attachments connect to an elastic strap that fits behind the head. The force for this active appliance is supplied by the neck strap.

face-lift (fās′lift″) The common term for plastic surgery of the face. SEE: *rhytidectomy.*

face mask (fās mask) SEE: under *mask.*

FACEP *Fellow of the American College of Emergency Physicians.*

face sheet SEE: under *sheet.*

facet (fās′ĕt) [Fr. *facette,* small face] A small, smooth area on a bone or other hard surface.

wear f. A line or plane worn on a tooth surface by attrition.

facetectomy (fās″ĕ-tĕk′tō-mē) [″ + Gr. *ektome,* excision] Surgical removal of the articular facet of a vertebra.

facial (fā′shăl) [L. *facialis,* pert. to the face] Pert. to the face.

facial bones Any of the 14 cranial bones that make up the face: maxillae (2); nasal (2); palatine (2); inferior nasal conchae (2); mandible (1); zygoma (2); lacrimal (2); vomer (1).

facial droop Loss of motor control on one side of the face, resulting in weakness of the muscles on one side of the mouth, with an inability to smile symmetrically. A common finding in acute stroke and Bell's palsy. In stroke, the weakness is limited to the lower half of the face.

facial lipoatrophy syndrome The loss of subcutaneous fat from the face, arms, and legs, and its redistribution to the abdomen, back, and visceral organs. It gives the face an unusually defined or drawn appearance. The syndrome occurs in about half of all patients treated with highly active antiretroviral therapy (HAART) for HIV/AIDs. SYN: *facial lipodystrophy syndrome.*

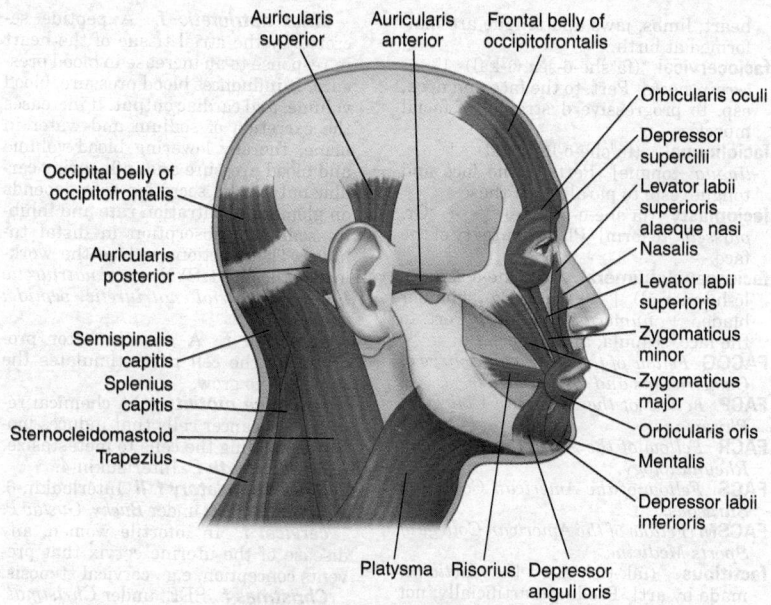

Auricularis superior — Auricularis anterior — Frontal belly of occipitofrontalis

Orbicularis oculi

Depressor supercilii

Levator labii superioris alaeque nasi

Nasalis

Levator labii superioris

Zygomaticus minor

Zygomaticus major

Orbicularis oris

Mentalis

Depressor labii inferioris

Occipital belly of occipitofrontalis

Auricularis posterior

Semispinalis capitis

Splenius capitis

Sternocleidomastoid

Trapezius

Platysma   Risorius   Depressor anguli oris

MUSCLES OF FACE AND SCALP

facial lipodystrophy syndrome Facial lipoatrophy syndrome.

facial reflex SEE: under *reflex*.

facial spasm SEE: under *spasm*.

-facient [L. *faciens*, stem *facient-*, participle of *facere*, to do, make] Suffix meaning *to make happen; to cause*.

facies (fā′sh(ē-)ēz) *pl.* **facies** [L. face] **1.** The face or the surface of any structure. **2.** The expression or appearance of the face.

   adenoid f. A dull, lethargic appearance with open mouth, which may be due to hypertrophy of adenoids or to chronic mouth breathing.

   masklike f., masked facies An expressionless face with little or no animation, seen in parkinsonism.

   myopathic f. The facies due to muscular relaxation. The lids drop and the lips protrude.

   parkinsonian f. A masklike facies with infrequent eye blinking and decreased facial expressiveness.

   thalassemic f. Enlargement of the cheek bones and forehead in people with thalassemia major. In thalassemic patients the bone marrow cavity expands, and the cortex of bone is thinner than normal.

facilitation (fă-sil″ĭ-tā′shŏn) [L. *facilis*, easy] **1.** The hastening of an action or process; esp., addition of the energy of a nerve impulse to that of other impulses activated at the same time. **2.** In neuromuscular rehabilitation, a generic term referring to various techniques that elicit muscular contraction through reflex activation.

   autogenic f. The process of inhibiting the muscle that generated a stimulus while providing an excitatory impulse to the antagonist muscle.

   proprioceptive neuromuscular f. ABBR: PNF. An approach to therapeutic exercise directed at relaxing muscles, increasing joint range of motion, and regaining function by using rotational-diagonal patterns of movement. These patterns replicate normal patterns of movement and are more functional than exercises limited to the cardinal planes. The principles and techniques were created and refined in the 1940s by Dr. Herman Kabat and two physical therapists, Maggie Knott and Dorothy Voss. PNF uses a developmental sequence of mobility, stability, controlled mobility, and skill; it emphasizes precision in patient position, manual contacts, verbal cueing, and timing.

facing [L. *facies*, face] A veneer of restorative material used on a tooth or on a prosthesis to simulate a natural tooth.

facio-auriculo vertebral syndrome Hemifacial microsomia.

faciobrachial (fā″shē-ō-brā′kē-ăl) [″ + Gr. *brachion*, arm] Pert. to the face and arm, esp. to juvenile muscular dystrophy.

faciocardiomelic syndrome (fā″sh(ē-)ō-kar″dē-ō-mē′lik) [*facies* +*cardio-* + ¹*melo-*] A rare, usually lethal autosomal recessive disorder in which the heart, limbs, jaws and tongue are malformed at birth.

faciocervical (fā″shē-ō-sĕr′vĭ-kăl) [″ + *cervix,* neck] Pert. to the face and neck, esp. to progressive dystrophy of facial muscles.

faciolingual (fā″shē-ō-lĭn′gwăl) [″ + *lingua,* tongue] Pert. to the face and tongue, esp. to paralysis of these.

facioplasty (fā″shē-ō-plăs′tē) [″ + Gr. *plassein,* to form] Plastic surgery of the face.

facioscapulohumeral (fā″shē-ō-skăp″ū-lō-hū′mĕr-ăl) [″ + *scapula,* shoulder blade, + *humerus,* shoulder] Pert. to the face, scapula, and upper arm.

FACOG *Fellow of the American College of Obstetricians and Gynecologists.*

FACP *Fellow of the American College of Physicians.*

FACR *Fellow of the American College of Rheumatology.*

FACS *Fellow of the American College of Surgeons.*

FACSM *Fellow of the American College of Sports Medicine.*

factitious (făk-tĭsh′ŭs) [L. *facticius,* made by art] Produced artificially; not natural.

factitious disorder A disorder that is not real, genuine, or natural. The symptoms, physical and psychological, are produced by the individual and are under voluntary control. These symptoms and the behavior are used to pursue a goal, i.e., to assume the role of patient and to stay in a hospital. This is attained by various means, such as taking anticoagulants or other drugs when they are not needed, or feigning pain with nausea and vomiting, dizziness, fainting, fever of unknown origin, or other illnesses. Psychological symptoms may include feigned memory loss, hallucinations, and uncooperativeness. Affected patients have a severe personality disturbance. SEE: *malinger; Munchausen syndrome.*

factor (făk′tŏr) [L. *factor,* maker] **1.** A contributing cause in an action. **2.** In genetics, a gene. **3.** An essential chemical such as a vitamin or immunoglobulin.

angiogenic growth f. Any of a group of polypeptides that stimulate the formation of new blood vessels. They include agents like vascular endothelial growth factor (VEGF) and blood vessel fibroblastic growth factor (bFGF). These factors are active in healing wounds, chronic inflammatory conditions, retrolental fibroplasia, and malignant tumors, which require new blood vessels for continued growth.

antihemophilic f. ABBR: AHF. Coagulation factor VIII, a glycoprotein clotting factor essential for the formation of blood thromboplastin. A deficiency results in hemophilia A. SEE: *blood coagulation; coagulation f.*

atrial natriuretic f. A peptide secreted by the atrial tissue of the heart in response to an increase in blood pressure. It influences blood pressure, blood volume, and cardiac output. It increases the excretion of sodium and water in urine, thereby lowering blood volume and blood pressure and influencing cardiac output. Its secretion rate depends on glomerular filtration rate and inhibits sodium reabsorption in distal tubules. These actions reduce the workload of the heart. SYN: *atrial natriuretic hormone; atrial natriuretic peptide; atriopeptin.*

autocrine f. A growth factor produced by the cell that stimulates the same cell to grow.

autocrine motility f. A chemical released by cancer cells that induces motility, enabling the cells to metastasize.

B cell growth f. Interleukin-4.

B cell stimulatory f. II Interleukin-6.

Bucky f. SEE: under *Bucky, Gustav P.*

cervical f. In infertile women, any disease of the uterine cervix that prevents conception, e.g., cervical stenosis.

Christmas f. SEE: under *Christmas, Stephen.*

citrovorum f. Leucovorin.

clotting f. Coagulation **f.**

coagulation f. Any of the factors involved in blood clotting. The generally accepted terms for the factors and their Roman numeral designations are as follows:

factor I, fibrinogen; *factor II,* prothrombin; *factor III,* thromboplastin; *factor IV,* calcium (ions); *factor V,* proaccelerin; *factor VII,* serum prothrombin conversion accelerator; *factor VIII,* antihemophilic factor; *factor IX,* plasma thromboplastin component; *factor X,* Stuart-Prower factor; *factor XI,* plasma thromboplastin antecedent; *factor XII,* Hageman factor; *factor XIII,* fibrin-stabilizing factor; prekallikrein; and high-molecular-weight kininogen, also called *Fitzgerald, Flaujeac,* or *Williams factor,* or *contact activation cofactor.* Factor VI, once called accelerin, is no longer used. SYN: *clotting f.* SEE: *blood coagulation.*

colony-stimulating f.–1 ABBR: CSF-1. A protein in human serum that promotes monocyte differentiation. SEE: *granulocyte-macrophage colony-stimulating f.*

contact f. Hageman **f.**

correction f. A number by which a measured value is multiplied to correct for systematic measurement error.

corticotropin-releasing f. Corticotropin-releasing **hormone.**

drop f. The number of drops of an infusion that add to a volume equal to 1 milliliter.

edema f. An enzyme made by *Bacil-*

lus anthracis. It causes the cellular and tissue swelling characteristic of anthrax infection.

endothelium-derived hyperpolarizing f. ABBR: EDHF. A vasodilating substance released by the vascular endothelium. SEE: *endothelium.*

endothelium-derived relaxing f. ABBR: EDRF. An active vasodilator released by the vascular endothelium. It facilitates relaxation of vascular smooth muscle and inhibition of adhesion and aggregation of platelets. When the normal function of the endothelium is disrupted by mechanical trauma, hypertension, hypercholesterolemia, or atherosclerosis, less EDRF is released, and the inhibition of platelet aggregation is decreased. In addition, the damaged vessels constrict, which favors the formation of thrombi. SEE: *endothelium.*

eosinophil chemotactic f. A mediator released in response to inflammation when mast cells are injured.

eosinophil colony-stimulating f. Interleukin-5.

eosinophil differentiation f. Interleukin-5.

epidermal growth f. ABBR: EGF. A polypeptide that stimulates growth of several different cells, including keratinocytes. A receptor for EGF is located on the surface of many cancer cells. It has been used experimentally to promote wound healing.

extrinsic f. 1. Serum prothrombin conversion accelerator. **2.** An obsolete term for vitamin B_{12}. SEE: *pernicious anemia.*

fibrin-stabilizing f. ABBR: FSF. Coagulation factor XIII, a clotting factor that is active in the intrinsic, extrinsic, and common pathways of coagulation and, when activated by thrombin, transforms monomeric fibrin to stable fibrin polymers. SYN: *plasma transglutaminase.* SEE: *blood* **coagulation**; *coagulation f.*

fibroblast growth f. Any of a group of polypeptides that stimulate the growth of tissues rich in fibroblasts, including blood vessels, connective tissues, and skin. Overactivity of these factors has been associated with neoplasia.

general intelligence f. ABBR: g. The hypothetical common feature identified by all intelligence (IQ) tests. The concept of general intelligence was developed by Charles Spearman, a British psychologist and statistician, who noticed that students who do well in one subject tend to do well in all school subjects and that students who do poorly in one field of study also lag behind in others. He proposed that the general ability to master academic material was due to superior general intelligence and that specific cognitive talents correlated with overall intellectual superiority. This concept, like many others in the field of psychometrics and intelligence testing, is controversial.

granulocyte colony-stimulating f. ABBR: G-CSF. A naturally occurring cytokine glycoprotein that stimulates the proliferation and functional activity of neutrophils. It is effective in treating bone marrow deficiency after cancer chemotherapy or bone marrow transplantation. The generic name is filgrastim. SEE: *colony-stimulating f.-1.*

granulocyte-macrophage colony-stimulating f. ABBR: GM-CSF. A naturally occurring cytokine glycoprotein that stimulates the production of neutrophils, monocytes, and macrophages. It is effective in treating bone marrow deficiency following cancer chemotherapy or bone marrow transplantation. The generic name is sargramostim; trade names are Leukine and Prokine. SEE: *colony-stimulating f.-1.*

growth f. ABBR: GF. A substance (generally a protein, polypeptide, or peptide) that stimulates the differentiation, division, development, and maintenance of cells and the tissues they make up. Growth factors are signaling molecules released by certain groups of cells, e.g., lymphocytes, to influence the activities of other cells. Growth factors can be divided into families, e.g., platelet-derived GFs, transforming GFs, and angiogenic GFs. They are released normally during fetal and embryonic development, wound healing, and tissue maturation. Massive releases of GFs are characteristic of some types of cancer cells. Artificial GFs, e.g., granulocyte colony-stimulating factor, are used in health care to restore depressed levels of cells to normal values, e.g., in patients who have received chemotherapy. SEE: *cytokine.*

Hageman f. Coagulation factor XII, a serine protease, not vitamin-K–dependent, involved in the intrinsic pathway of coagulation. SYN: *contact f.* SEE: *blood* **coagulation**; *coagulation f.*

hematopoietic growth f. Any of a group of at least seventeen substances involved in the production of blood cells, including several interleukins and erythropoietin.

heparin-binding epidermal growth f. ABBR: HB-EGF. A cytokine monokine involved in immune and inflammatory responses. It is produced by macrophages and stimulates production of smooth muscle cells and fibroblasts.

hepatocyte growth f. A cytokine monokine involved in immune and inflammatory responses. It is produced by platelets, fibroblasts, macrophages, endothelial cells, and smooth muscle cells. It stimulates growth of hepatocytes and increases migration and motility of various epithelial and endothelial cells.

hepatocyte stimulatory f. Interleukin-6.

human f. A general term for several areas of research that include human performance, technology, design, and human-computer interaction. It focuses on human abilities, limitations, and characteristics as they relate to their environment.

hypoxia-inducible f. A factor within aerobic cells that helps them adapt to abnormally low oxygen concentrations.

insulin sensitivity f. The decrease in blood sugar produced by each unit of injected insulin.

insulin-like growth f. ABBR: IGF. Any of a group of related peptides, synthesized by the liver as a result of human growth hormone secretion. The IGF family of polypeptides is structurally similar to insulin in that it is composed of two subunits that are short polypeptides. IGF-1 and IGF-2, e.g., each contain about 70 amino acids. They have a wide variety of functions, including the stimulation of cell growth and proliferation (as in the developing embryo and neonate), DNA synthesis, bone growth, and the replication of cancer cells. Drugs that block IGF have been tested for use in cancer chemotherapy.

intrinsic f. A glycoprotein secreted by the parietal cells of the gastric mucosa. It is necessary for the absorption of ingested vitamin B_{12}. The absence of this factor leads to vitamin B_{12} deficiency and pernicious anemia. SYN: *Castle intrinsic factor*.

labile f. Proaccelerin.

lethal f. **1.** A gene or an abnormality in genetic composition that causes death of a zygote or of an individual before reproductive age. **2.** A protein made by *Bacillus anthracis*. It splits signal transduction proteins within infected cells, resulting in cellular dysfunction and death.

leukemia inhibitory f. ABBR: LIF. A cytokine that regulates the growth and differentiation of many cells throughout the body, including endothelial cells, fat cells, embryonic stem cells, germ cells, osteoblasts, and peripheral nerve cells.

leukocyte inhibitory f. Leukocyte migration inhibition **f.**

leukocyte migration inhibition f. ABBR: LMIF. A lymphokine that inhibits movement of neutrophils. SYN: *leukocyte inhibitory f.*

lymphocyte mitogenic f. ABBR: LMF. A lymphokine that stimulates production of lymphocytes and other lymphokines.

lipotropic f. Any of the compounds that promote the transportation and use of fats and help to prevent accumulation of fat in the liver.

macrophage activating f. ABBR: MAF. A lymphokine that stimulates macrophages to become more effective killers of certain microbial cells. Macrophages stimulated by MAF can kill tumor cells.

macrophage chemotactic f. ABBR: MCF. A lymphokine released by T and B cell lymphocytes in response to an antigen. It attracts macrophages to the site of the invading antigen.

macrophage colony stimulating f. ABBR: M-CSF. A hematopoietic growth factor that stimulates monocytes to form colonies.

magnification f. ABBR: MF. A quantitative expression of the degree of enlargement of an image in which the image size is divided by object size. In radiography, it is the ratio of the source-to-image-receptor distance to the source-to-object distance.

male f. Any cause for a couple's difficulty in conceiving a child that results from diseases of the male reproductive organs, e.g., a low sperm count or inadequate sperm motility.

mast cell growth f. Interleukin-3.

mast cell growth f. II Interleukin-4.

maturation-promoting f. ABBR: MPF. A complex cellular protein that stimulates cell division in eukaryotic cells. Part of MPF is the protein cyclin, which accumulates during interphase and triggers mitosis or meiosis. SYN: *M-phase promoting f.*

milk f. A substance present in certain strains of mammary cancer-prone mice that is transferred to offspring through milk from the mammary glands. It can induce the development of mammary cancer in suckling mice exposed to the factor.

M-phase promoting f. Maturation-promoting **f.**

multi-colony stimulating f. Interleukin-3.

natural killer cell stimulating f. Interleukin-12.

neutrophil chemotactic f. A lymphokine that attracts neutrophils, but not other white blood cells, and causes proteolytic damage in sepsis and trauma.

nerve growth f. ABBR: NGF. A protein necessary for the growth and maintenance of sympathetic and certain sensory neurons.

osteoclast-activating f. ABBR: OAF. A lymphokine produced in certain conditions associated with resorption of bone, including periodontal disease and lymphoid malignancies such as multiple myeloma and malignant lymphoma. Interleukin-1 and other substances produced by T lymphocytes and prostaglandins are OAFs.

osteoclastogenesis inhibitory f.

ABBR: OCIF. A protein produced by activated T cells that inhibits the proliferation of osteoclasts. SYN: *osteoprotegerin.*

ovarian f. Any cause of female infertility that results from failure of egg production by the ovaries

ovulatory f. 1. In women who are infertile, any disease or condition that interferes with the monthly release of an unfertilized egg from the ovaries. **2.** In ovarian cancer, the carcinogenic effect of ovulation on the surface epithelium of an ovary.

plasmacytoma simulating f. Interleukin-11.

platelet-activating f. ABBR: PAF. A phospholipid that affects the signaling between cells in important body processes such as inflammation, sepsis, and thrombosis. It is released by mast cells, basophils, and activated eosinophils.

platelet-derived growth f. A polypeptide that stimulates collagen synthesis, smooth muscle formation, tissue repair, and the proliferation of fibroblasts and microglia.

platelet tissue f. Thromboplastin.

pre-B cell growth f. A polypeptide that stimulates collagen synthesis, smooth muscle formation, tissue repair, and the proliferation of fibroblasts and microglia.

predictive f. A characteristic of a patient that indicates a greater or lesser likelihood of responding to a specific treatment regimen.

procoagulant f. A lymphokine that can assume the role of factor VIII (antihemophilic factor) in coagulation cascade.

prognostic f. Any feature of a disease or of a patient's presentation that suggests that he or she will be affected for better or worse by an illness.

quality f. ABBR: Q. In radiology, a scale used to account for the biological effects of different radiations. Factors include beta, electron, and gamma x-radiation (Q = 1), thermal neutrons (Q = 5), and alpha neutrons and protons (Q = 20).

R f. Resistance transfer **f.**

resistance transfer f. ABBR: RTF. A genetic factor in bacteria that controls resistance to certain antibiotic drugs. The factor may be passed from one bacterium to another. This makes it possible for nonpathogenic bacteria to become resistant to antibiotics and to transfer that resistance to pathogens, thereby establishing a potential source for an epidemic. SYN: *R f.* SEE: *plasmid.*

Rh f. An antigen found on the membranes of the red blood cells. It was discovered in 1940 by Karl Landsteiner and Alexander S. Wiener, who prepared anti-Rh serum by injecting red cells from Rhesus monkeys into rabbits and other animals. They found that the red cells of 85% of Caucasians agglutinates in contact with anti-Rh serum. These people are called *Rh-positive.* The remaining 15%, whose red cells are not agglutinated by anti-Rh serum, are called *Rh-negative.* More than 25 blood factors are known to belong to the Rh system. Rh incompatibility between mother and fetus is the cause of hemolytic disease of the newborn.

rheumatoid f. Antibodies raised by the body against immunoglobulins. They are present in roughly 80% of patients with rheumatoid arthritis and in many patients with other rheumatological and infectious illnesses. This factor is used, with other clinical indicators, in the diagnosis and management of rheumatoid arthritis.

risk f. An environmental, chemical, psychological, physiological, or genetic element that predisposes someone to the development of a disease. Risk factors for coronary artery disease include hypertension, high circulating blood lipids and cholesterol, obesity, cigarette smoking, diabetes mellitus, physical inactivity, microalbuminuria, chronic kidney disease, and an early family history of atherosclerosis. SYN: *risk marker.*

spreading f. The hyaluronidase made by *Bacillus anthracis.* SEE: *hyaluronidase.*

stable f. Serum prothrombin conversion accelerator.

susceptibility f. A condition that increases a person's likelihood of acquiring a disease. The propensity to develop disease is often the result of a genetic mutation in a single base DNA base pair.

stem cell f. ABBR: SCF. A cytokine glycoprotein that influences the development of sperm and egg cells, the production of melanin, and mast cell development.

Stuart-Prower f. Coagulation factor X, a vitamin-K–dependent protease, synthesized by the liver, that, when activated to factor Xa, is the first coagulation factor in the common final pathway of blood coagulation that generates thrombin from prothrombin. The factors that lead to it are limited to the extrinsic or intrinsic coagulation pathways. The Stuart-Prower factor was formerly called "thrombokinase." SEE: *blood coagulation; coagulation f.*

T-cell growth f. Interleukin-2.

T-cell growth f. II Interleukin-4.

thyroid-stimulating hormone-releasing f. ABBR: TSH-RF. An obsolete term for Thyrotropin-releasing **hormone.**

tissue f. ABBR: TF. Thromboplastin.

transfer f. Any of the low-molecular-weight chemicals extracted from immune cells activated to respond to specific antigens. These products can be taken from a sensitized person and given to another. The recipient will react to the same antigen originally used to sensitize the lymphocytes of the donor. The factor can be transferred by injecting the recipient with either intact lymphocytes or extracts of disrupted cells. It has been studied as adjunctive therapy to modulate the immune system in several clinical trials.

transforming growth f. ABBR: TGF. A polypeptide growth factor that competitively binds to epidermal growth factor (EGF) receptors. This molecule can promote growth of fibroblasts in cell cultures, thus transforming normal cells into those with the abnormal properties of malignant cells.

tubal f. Any abnormality of the fallopian tubes that produces infertility.

tumor angiogenesis f. ABBR: TAF. A protein in animal and human cancer tissue that in experimental studies appears to be essential to growth of the cancer. This factor is thought to act by stimulating the growth of new blood capillaries that supply the tumor with nutrients and remove waste products.

tumor necrosis f. ABBR: TNF. A polypeptide protein mediator or cytokine released primarily by macrophages and T lymphocytes. It helps regulate the metabolism of fats, the immune response, and some hematopoietic functions. There are two factors: alpha (TNFα), also called *cachectin,* produced by macrophages; and beta (TNFβ), called *lymphotoxin,* produced by activated CD4+ T cells. The functions of TNF are similar to those of interleukin-1. A monoclonal antibody against TNFα, infliximab, is used to treat rheumatoid arthritis and other diseases in which TNFα causes inflammatory damage. Antagonists to tumor necrosis factor, e.g., adalimumab, etanercept, and infliximab, are used to treat diseases affected by TNF, such as rheumatoid arthritis or Crohn's disease. SEE: *cytokine; interleukin-1.*

uterine f. Any abnormality of the uterus that produces infertility.

V f. Nicotinamide adenine dinucleotide.

vascular endothelial growth f. ABBR: VEGF. A growth factor produced by endothelial cells that promotes angiogenesis and increases microvascular permeability Inhibitors of VEGF are used to treat a variety of cancers. Their use is associated with hypertension, which sometimes may be severe.

virulence f. A substance released by a microorganism that allows it to evade host defenses or cause serious injury to its host. Although most virulence factors are released by bacteria for their own benefit, sometimes factors released by one microorganism foster another disease-causing organism.

windchill f. Loss of heat from exposure of skin to wind. Heat loss is proportional to the speed of the wind. Thus, skin exposed to a wind velocity of 20 mph (32 km/hr) when the temperature is 0°F (−17.8°C) is cooled at the same rate as in still air at −46°F (−43.3°C). Similarly, when the temperature is 20°F (−6.7°C) and the wind is 10, 20, or 35 mph (16.1, 32.2, or 56.3 km/hr), the equivalent skin temperature is −4°, −18°, or −28°F (−20°, −27.8°, or −33.3°C), respectively.

The windchill factor is calculated for dry skin; skin that is wet from any cause and exposed to wind loses heat at a much higher rate. Wind blowing over wet skin can cause frostbite, even on a comfortably warm day as judged by the thermometer.

X f. A growth factor, identified as hemin, that is needed to grow *Haemophilus influenzae* in culture. SEE: *hemin.*

facultative (făk″ŭl-tā″tĭv) [L. *facultas,* capability] **1.** Having the ability to do something that is not compulsory. **2.** In biology and particularly bacteriology, having the ability to live under certain conditions. Thus a microorganism may be facultative with respect to oxygen and be able to live with or without oxygen.

faculty 1. A normal mental attribute or sense; ability to function. **2.** Persons employed as teachers at a college or university.

FAD *flavin adenine dinucleotide.*

fading (fād′ing) **1.** In electronics, signal attenuation. **2.** Gradual loss of strength or intensity; degeneration. **3.** In education, the stepwise withdrawal of instructional prompts to determine whether a student can perform a new skill on his own.

FADS *Fetal akinesia deformation sequence.*

Faecalibacterium (fē″kă-lē-bak″tēr′ē-ŭm) [L. *faex,* sediment, dregs + *bacterium*] A genus of gram-negative rod-shaped commensal bacteria that live in the gastrointestinal tract.

Fagales (fŏg-ā′lēs) [L. *fagus,* beech] The order of trees and shrubs that includes alder, birch, and hazel. The pollen from such trees causes hay fever, principally in the early spring.

Fahr, Karl Theodor (far) [Ger. pathologist, 1877–1945]

F.'s disease Idiopathic basal ganglia calcification.

F.'s syndrome A rare autosomal dominant movement disorder caused by the abnormal accumulation of calcium in the basal ganglia and the cerebral cortex. SYN: *familial idiopathic basal ganglia calcification*.

Fahrenheit, Daniel Gabriel (far′ĕn-hīt″) Daniel Gabriel Fahrenheit, Ger.-Dutch physicist, 1686–1736.

    F. scale ABBR: F. A temperature scale with the freezing point of water at 32° and the boiling point at 212°. SEE: table; ***Celsius***[1]***scale; Kelvin***[1]***scale***.

    F. thermometer A thermometric scale used in many English-speaking countries in which the boiling point is 212°F and the freezing point is 32°F. SEE: tables at *Celsius thermometer* under **Celsius, Anders**).

failed back surgery syndrome Persistent or recurring low back pain (with or without sciatic symptoms) in patients who have undergone one or more surgeries on a lumbar disk.

fail-first requirement A method of drug plan formulary control in which a patient must try a less expensive drug before being prescribed a more expensive one.

fail-safe (fāl′sāf″) Free of problems; infallible. It is used of a device, system, or program manufactured or conceived not to malfunction or to compensate automatically for a malfunction.

failure (fāl′yĕr) [Fr. *faillir*, fr L. *fallere*, to deceive] Inability to function, esp. loss of what was once present, as in failing eyesight or hearing.

    acute kidney f. Acute renal **f.**

    acute liver f. The development of severe liver damage with encephalopathy and jaundice within eight weeks of the onset of liver disease. Coagulopathy, electrolyte imbalance, and cerebral edema are common. Death is likely without liver transplantation. SYN: *fulminant hepatic f.; fulminant hepatitis*.

    ETIOLOGY: The most common causes of acute liver failure are viral hepatitis, acetaminophen overdose (and other drug reactions), trauma, ischemia, acute fatty liver of pregnancy, and autoimmune disorders.

    SYMPTOMS: Early symptoms are often nonspecific and may include nausea, vomiting, dizziness, lightheadedness, or drowsiness. As liver injury becomes more obvious, bile permeates the skin, producing jaundice. Alterations in mental status (lethargy or coma) and bleeding caused by coagulopathy may develop.

    DIAGNOSIS: The diagnosis is suggested by jaundice and altered mental status in addition to elevations in liver function tests and prolongation of the protime and international normalized ratio (INR).

    PATIENT CARE: Affected patients should be hospitalized, usually in intensive care under very close monitoring. General patient care concerns apply. Airway support and mechanical ventilation are often needed. Fluids and/or pressors, such as dopamine, may be needed to maintain blood pressure and cardiac output. Nutritional support with a low salt, protein-restricted diet, and most calories supplied by carbohydrates, blood product infusions (fresh frozen plasma and platelets), and lactulose are usually administered. Potassium supplements help to reverse the affects of high aldosterone levels; potassium-sparing diuretics increase urine volume. Ascitic fluid is removed by par-

Fahrenheit and Celsius Scales*

F	C	F	C	F	C
500°	260°	203°	95°	98°	36.67°
401	205	194	90	97	36.11
392	200	176	80	96	35.56
383	195	167	75	95	35
374	190	140	60	86	30
356	180	122	50	77	25
347	175	113	45	68	20
338	170	110	43.3	50	10
329	165	109	42.8	41	5
320	160	108	42.2	32	0
311	155	107	41.7	23	−5
302	150	106	41.1	14	−10
284	140	105	40.6	5	−15
275	135	104	40.0	−4	−20
266	130	103	39.4	−13	−25
248	120	102	38.9	−22	−30
239	115	101	38.3	−40	−40
230	110	100	37.8	−76	−60
212	100	99	37.2		

* To convert a Fahrenheit temperature to degrees Celsius, subtract 32 and multiply by 5/9. To convert a Celsius temperature to degrees Fahrenheit, multiply by 9/5 and add 32.

acentesis or shunt placement to relieve abdominal discomfort and aid respiratory effort. Portal hypertension requires shunt placement to divert blood flow, and variceal bleeding is treated with vasoconstrictor drugs, balloon tamponade, vitamin K administration, and perhaps surgery (to ligate bleeding portal vein collateral vessels).

Medications that are normally metabolized by the liver and medications that may injure the liver further should be avoided. Patients who have overdosed on acetaminophen may benefit from the administration of acetylcysteine if it can be administered within 12 hr of a single ingestion.

Liver transplantation is the definitive treatment for acute liver failure. Early transplant evaluation should be carried out for every patient for whom there is a donated organ available. Without transplantation, the mortality from acute liver injury may reach 80%.

The patient's level of consciousness should be assessed frequently, with ongoing orientation to time and place. Girth should be measured daily. Signs of anemia, infection, alkalosis, and GI bleeding should be documented and reported immediately. A quiet atmosphere is provided. Physical restraints are applied as minimally as possible, with chemical restraint prohibited. If the patient is comatose, the eyes are protected from corneal injury using artificial tears and/or eye patches.

The prognosis for the illness should be discussed in a sensitive but forthright fashion and emotional support provided to family members. Agency social workers, the hospital chaplain, and other support personnel should be involved in the patient's care as appropriate to individual needs.

acute renal f. ABBR: ARF. A sudden, significant decrease in the filtration capabilities of the kidneys and, within hours or days, an increase in the levels of creatinine and other waste products in the systemic circulation. ARF occurs in approximately 5% of all patients admitted to hospitals. It often results from accidents, e.g., severe burns and trauma, that cause large losses in body fluid. A number of drugs can cause ARF. Hospital procedures can also cause ARF, and ARF affects more than 25% of surgical patients who require cardiopulmonary bypass and almost 30% of patients in ICU. When ARF is the result of a decrease in blood volume without kidney damage, the condition can often be quickly and completely reversed. When the kidneys have been injured, however, they must heal if the ARF is to resolve. SYN: *acute kidney f.; acute kidney injury.* SEE: *dialysis;* table; *Nursing Diagnoses Appendix.*

ETIOLOGY: *Prerenal:* Most ARF is caused by low perfusion of the kidneys due to problems that do not at first directly damage the kidneys: hypovolemia (such as burns, cirrhosis with portal hypertension and ascites, dehydration, diarrhea, excess diuresis hemorrhage, vomiting); low cardiac output (such as arrhythmias, cardiac tamponade, massive pulmonary embolus, mechanical ventilation, myocardial diseases, pulmonary hypertension); systemic vasodilation (such as anaphylaxis, anesthesia, antihypertensives, sepsis); or bilateral renal vascular blockage (such as emboli, stenosis, thrombi).

Intrarenal: A less common ARF is caused from direct damage to the kidneys. Ninety percent of these cases are caused either by ischemia (from prolonged prerenal ARF or from diseases of blood vessel walls, glomerulonephritis, hyperviscosity syndromes, malignant hypertension, thrombotic microangiopathies, or vasculitis) or by nephrotoxins.

Postrenal: The least common ARF (less than 5% of cases) is caused by urinary obstruction that leads to increased back-pressure in the kidney tubules, which, in turn, decreases the glomerular filtration rate (GFR). Urinary obstruction most often occurs at the bladder neck due to anticholinergic drug therapy, neurogenic bladder, or prostatic disease.

TREATMENT: Acute renal failure caused by urinary outlet obstruction (postrenal failure) often completely resolves when urinary flow is restored, i.e., after a urinary catheter is placed or a prostatectomy performed. Renal fail-

Causes of Acute Renal Failure

Where	What's Responsible	Examples
Prerenal	Inadequate blood flow to the kidney	Severe dehydration; prolonged hypotension; renal ischemia or emboli; septic or cardiogenic shock
Renal	Injury to kidney glomeruli or tubules	Glomerulonephritis; toxic injury to the kidneys, e.g., by drugs or poisons
Postrenal	Obstruction to urinary outflow	Prostatic hyperplasia; bladder outlet obstruction

ure caused by prerenal conditions, i.e., from reduced blood flow to the kidneys (as in dehydration or shock), sometimes improves with fluid and pressor support but may require other therapies, including dialysis. The resolution of ARF caused by intrarenal diseases (as in acute tubular necrosis) and kidney toxins depends on the underlying cause and the duration of the exposure. For example, immunosuppressant drugs may reverse ARF due to glomerulonephritis or renal vasculitis whereas forced diuresis is the treatment for those whose disease is caused by rhabdomyolysis.

PATIENT CARE: Patients with ARF may stop making urine, have a sudden rise in BUN and creatinine levels, and develop metabolic acidosis and electrolyte imbalances, esp. hyperkalemia. Other complications may follow as uremia develops, e.g., altered mental status, anorexia, arrhythmias, and fluid overload. The specific cause is identified and removed if possible. The nurse instructs the patient about dietary and fluid restrictions and implements these restrictions, promotes infection prevention, and advises the patient about activity restrictions due to metabolic alterations.

Neurological status is assessed, and safety measures are instituted. Intake and output and daily weights (measures of fluid status) are monitored. Daily blood tests determine acid-base and electrolyte balance. Hyperkalemia is treated with dialysis, intravenous hypertonic glucose solutions, insulin infusion, sodium bicarbonate, or potassium exchange resins administered orally or by enema, depending on its severity. The nurse should assess the patient for edema in the legs and feet, hands and sacrum, and around the eyes. It is also usual to record urine color and clarity. The patient is assessed for gastrointestinal (GI) and cutaneous bleeding and anemia; blood components are replaced, or erythropoietin therapy is administered as prescribed. Blood pressure, pulse, respiratory rate, and heart and lung sounds are regularly assessed for evidence of pericarditis or fluid overload. Cardiac monitoring is used to detect changes in cardiac conduction related to hyperkalemia. Anorexia, nausea, and vomiting result from uremia and lead to poor nutrition with loss of body muscle and mass. Nutritional support is critical to combat malnutrition, infection, and to limit electrolyte imbalances. Protein calorie malnutrition is prevalent in ARF. Renal failure diet requires careful management of total calories, protein, electrolytes, minerals, vitamins, and fluid volume. It should provide enough calories (30–35

kcal/kg) through fats and carbohydrates to limit muscle breakdown. At the same time, protein intake should be restricted to about 1.2 to 1.3 g/kg to minimize azotemia. Sodium intake should be limited to 2 to 4 g a day to limit water retention and hypertension. Potassium intake is restricted because, in renal failure, potassium is not excreted by the kidneys, and hyperkalemia may produce muscle weakness and cardiac rhythm disturbances. Oral intake of phosphorus must also be limited as prescribed; alternately, phosphorus-binding medications are taken with meals to prevent hyperphosphatemia. Oral calcium supplements are often used for this purpose. Vitamins B, C, and folate supplements are often given. Fluids are usually limited to the amount of the patient's urine output plus 500 to 700 ml for metabolic needs. Oral hygiene and misting provide relief for dry mucous membranes and help to prevent inflammation and infection. All stools are tested to monitor for GI bleeding. Aseptic technique is used in caring for this patient, who is extremely susceptible to infection. Other therapies include incentive spirometry, coughing, passive range-of-motion exercises, antiembolism stockings or pneumatic leg dressings, and ambulation. Acute renal failure often results in a protracted illness. Many patients with ARF requiring intensive care will die. As a result, the patient and family require continuous emotional support, and education about the treatment regimen (including dialysis if it is employed), nutritional restrictions, and the use of medications. Because some patients will eventually need to have arteriovenous fistula constructed for dialysis, intravenous access should be limited to the dorsal aspects of the hands whenever possible.

If ARF is not reversed but progresses to chronic (end-stage) renal failure, follow-up care with a nephrologist is arranged, and evaluation and teaching are provided for maintenance dialysis and/or possible kidney transplant. Referral is made for vocational or other counseling as needed.

acute respiratory f. Any impairment in oxygenation or ventilation in which the arterial oxygen tension falls below 60 mm Hg, and/or the carbon dioxide tension rises above 50 mm Hg, and the pH drops below 7.35.

TREATMENT: In most cases the patient will need supplemental oxygen therapy. Intubation and mechanical ventilation may be needed if the patient cannot oxygenate and ventilate adequately, i.e., if carbon dioxide retention occurs. Treatment depends on the underlying cause of the respiratory failure, e.g., bronchodilators for asthma, antibiotics for pneumonia, diuretics or vasodilators for congestive heart failure.

PATIENT CARE: Patients with acute respiratory failure are usually admitted to an acute care unit. The patient is positioned for optimal gas exchange, as well as for comfort. Supplemental oxygen is provided, but patients with chronic obstructive lung disease who retain carbon dioxide are closely monitored for adverse effects. A normothermic state is maintained to reduce the patient's oxygen demand. The patient is monitored closely for signs of respiratory arrest; lung sounds are auscultated and any deterioration in oxygen saturation immediately reported. The patient is also watched for adverse drug effects and treatment complications such as oxygen toxicity and acute respiratory distress syndrome. Vital signs are assessed frequently, and fever, tachycardia, tachypnea or bradypnea, and hypotension are reported. The electrocardiogram is monitored for arrhythmias. Serum electrolyte levels and fluid balance are monitored and steps are taken to correct and prevent imbalances. If mechanical ventilation or non-invasive support is needed, ventilator settings and inspired oxygen concentrations are adjusted based on arterial blood gas results. SEE: *ventilation.*

To maintain a patent airway, the trachea is suctioned after oxygenation as necessary, and humidification is provided to help loosen and liquefy secretions. Secretions are collected as needed for culture and sensitivity testing. Sterile technique during suctioning and change of ventilator tubing helps to prevent infection. Use of the minimal leak technique for endotracheal tube cuff inflation helps prevent tracheal erosion. Positioning the nasoendotracheal tube midline within the nostril, avoiding excessive tube movement, and providing adequate support for ventilator tubing all help to prevent nasal and endotracheal tissue necrosis. Periodically loosening the securing tapes and supports prevents skin irritation and breakdown. The patient is assessed for complications of mechanical ventilation, including reduced cardiac output, pneumothorax or other barotrauma, increased pulmonary vascular resistance, diminished urine output, increased intracranial pressure, and gastrointestinal bleeding.

All tests, procedures, and treatments should be explained to the patient and family to improve understanding and help reduce anxiety. Rationales for such measures should be presented, and concerns elicited and answered. If the patient is intubated (or has had a tracheostomy), the patient should be told why speech is not possible and should be taught how to use alternative methods to communicate needs, wishes, and concerns to health care staff and family members.

adult f. to thrive A progressive functional deterioration of a physical and cognitive nature. The individual's ability to live with multisystem diseases, cope with ensuing problems, and care for himself are markedly diminished. SEE: *Nursing Diagnoses Appendix.*

backward heart f. Heart failure in which blood congests the lungs, and often the right ventricle, liver, and lower extremities.

cardiac f. Heart **f.**

chronic respiratory f. Chronic inability of the respiratory system to maintain the function of oxygenating blood and remove carbon dioxide from the lungs. Many diseases can cause chronic pulmonary insufficiency, including asthmatic airway obstruction, emphysema, chronic bronchitis, and cystic fibrosis; and chronic pulmonary interstitial tissue diseases such as sarcoidosis, pneumoconiosis, idiopathic pulmonary fibrosis, disseminated carcinoma, radiation injury, and leukemia.

PATIENT CARE: The focus of patient care is to relieve respiratory symptoms, manage hypoxia, conserve energy, and avoid respiratory irritants and infections. The nurse, respiratory therapist, primary care physician, and pulmonologist carry out the prescribed treatment regimen and teach the patient and family to manage care at home.

Patients may require supplemental oxygen. The patient is taught how to use the equipment and the importance of maintaining an appropriate flow rate. Low flow rates (1–2 L/min) are often best for patients with chronic obstructive lung disease. Drug therapy can include inhaled bronchodilators (if bronchospasm is reversible), oral or inhaled corticosteroids, oral or inhaled sympathomimetics, inhaled mucolytic therapy, and prompt use of oral antibiotics in the presence of respiratory infection. The patient and family are taught the order and spacing for administering these drugs, as well as how to use a metered-dose inhaler (with spacer if necessary). They are taught the desired effects, serious adverse reactions to report, and minor adverse effects and how to deal with them. Patients are taught care of inhalers and other respiratory equipment and are advised to rinse the mouth after using these devices to help limit bad tastes, dryness, and *Candida* infections.

Unless otherwise restricted, the patient will benefit from increased fluid intake (to 3 L/day) to help liquefy secretions and aid in their expectoration. Deep-breathing and coughing techniques are taught to promote ventilation and remove secretions. The patient also may be taught postural drainage and chest physiotherapy to help mobilize secretions and clear airways. Such therapy is to be carried out at least 1 hr before or after meals. Incentive spirometry may help to promote optimal lung expansion. A high-calorie, high-protein diet, offered as small, frequent meals, helps the patient maintain needed nutrition, while conserving energy and reducing fatigue.

Daily activity is encouraged, alternating with rest to prevent fatigue. Patients may benefit from a planned respiratory rehabilitation program to teach breathing techniques, provide conditioning, and help increase exercise tolerance. Diversional activities also should be provided, based on the patient's interests.

The patient is assessed for changes in baseline respiratory function; restlessness, changes in breath sounds, and tachypnea may signal an exacerbation. Any changes in sputum quality or quantity are noted. The patient is taught to be aware of these changes.

Patients need help in adjusting to lifestyle changes necessitated by this chronic illness. Patients and their families are encouraged to ask questions and voice concerns; answers are provided when possible, and support is given throughout. The patient and family should be included in all care planning and related decisions. The patient also is taught to avoid air pollutants such as automobile exhaust fumes and aerosol sprays, as well as crowds and people with respiratory infections. Patients should obtain influenza immunization annually and pneumonia immunization every 6 years. The patient also may benefit from avoiding exposure to cold air and covering the nose and mouth with a scarf or mask when outdoors in cold, windy weather. Patients who smoke tobacco are advised to abstain, using nicotine replacement therapy, hypnotism, support groups, or other methods.

circulatory f. Failure of the cardiovascular system to provide body tissues with enough blood for proper functioning. It may be caused by cardiac failure or peripheral circulatory failure, as occurs in shock, in which there is general peripheral vasodilation with pooling of blood in the expanded vascular space, resulting in decreased venous return.

f. of compensation The inability of the heart muscle or other diseased organs to meet the body's needs. In cardiac failure, this results in pulmonary congestion, difficult breathing, and sometimes hypotension or lower extremity swelling. Causes of cardiac compensatory failure may occur in patients with ischemic heart disease, valvular heart disease, or cardiomyopathies.

congestive heart f. ABBR: CHF. Heart f. SEE: *Nursing Diagnoses Appendix.*

extubation f. Respiratory failure after discontinuation of mechanical ventilation, accompanied by the need to reintubate the patient.

forward heart f. Heart failure in which forward flow of blood to the tissues is inadequate because the left ventricle is unable to pump blood with enough force to the systemic circulation (such as a result of cardiomyopathy, muscular stunning, or infarction) or because outflow from the left ventricle is obstructed as in aortic stenosis).

fulminant hepatic f. Acute liver **f.**

heart f. Inability of the heart to circulate blood effectively enough to meet the body's metabolic needs. Heart failure may affect the left ventricle, right ventricle, or both. It may result from impaired ejection of blood from the heart during systole or from impaired relaxation of the heart during diastole. In the U.S., about 400,000 people are diagnosed with heart failure each year, and about 10% to 20% of affected persons die of the disease annually. Heart failure is one of the most common causes of hospitalization and rehospitalization in the U.S. The prognosis for patients with heart failure depends on the ejection fraction, that is, the proportion of blood in the ventricle that is propelled from the heart during each contraction. In healthy patients, the ejection fraction equals about 55% to 78%. SYN: *cardiac f.; congestive heart f.* SEE: *ejection fraction; pulmonary edema.*

DIAGNOSIS: Heart failure is easily diagnosed in a patient with typical symptoms and signs, esp. when these findings are accompanied by a chest x-ray that shows an enlarged heart and pulmonary edema. In patients with an uncertain presentation, elevated levels of B-type natriuretic peptide (BNP) may aid in the diagnosis.

SYMPTOMS: Difficulty breathing is the predominant symptom of heart failure. In patients with mild impairments of ejection fraction (45% to 50%), breathing is normal at rest but labored after climbing a flight of stairs or lifting lightweight objects. Patients with advanced heart failure (ejection fraction 20%) may have such difficulty breathing that getting out of bed or taking a few steps is very tiring.

Difficulty breathing while lying flat (orthopnea) or awakening at night with shortness of breath (paroxysmal nocturnal dyspnea) are also hallmarks of heart failure, as are exertional fatigue and lower extremity swelling (edema).

ETIOLOGY: Heart failure may result from myocardial infarction, myocardial ischemia, arrhythmias, heart valve lesions, congenital malformation of the heart or great vessels, constrictive pericarditis, cardiomyopathies, or conditions that affect the heart indirectly, including renal failure, fluid overload, thyrotoxicosis, severe anemia, and sepsis. Of the many causes of heart failure, ischemia and infarction are the most common.

TREATMENT: Diuretics (including furosemide and bumetanide), neurohormonal agents (such as angiotensin-converting enzyme inhibitors or angiotension receptor blockers), beta blockers (such as carvedilol or bisoprolol) are often combined in the acute and chronic treatment of heart failure. Other drugs that have been shown to be effective are nitrates with hydralazine, and aldosterone (a potassium-sparing diuretic). All of these medications must be monitored closely for side effects. In patients with heart failure caused by valvular heart disease, valve replacement surgery may be effective. Cardiac transplantation can be used in advanced heart failure when donor organs are available.

PATIENT CARE: In the patient who presents for medical attention in heart failure, signs and symptoms are assessed, and vital signs, cardiac rhythm, and neurological status are closely monitored. A 12-lead ECG is examined for evidence of acute coronary syndromes and cardiac monitoring is instituted. Hemodynamic monitoring is initiated based on the severity of patient symptoms. The chest is auscultated for abnormal heart sounds and for lung crackles or gurgles. Daily weights are obtained to detect fluid retention, and the extremities are inspected for evidence of peripheral edema. If the patient is confined to a bed, the sacral area of the spine is assessed for edema. Fluid intake and output are monitored esp. if the patient is receiving diuretics. Blood urea nitrogen and serum creatinine, potassium, sodium, chloride, and bicarbonate levels are monitored frequently. The complete blood count, liver function tests, thyroid function tests, and kidney functions should be evaluated to determine whether any comorbid conditions such as anemia, nephrotic syndrome, cirrhosis, or hyperthyroidism are contributing to or worsening heart failure. Echocardiography helps measure ejection fraction, a key component in distinguishing between systolic heart failure and diastolic dysfunction. It is also used to estimate ventricular dysfunction, measure intracardiac pressures and wall motion, assess ventricular relaxation and compliance, and demonstrate abnormal chamber sizes, valve deformities, pericardial effusions, and ventricular thrombi. Multiple gated acquisition (MUGA) scans may be used as an alternative. Cardiac catheterization, recommended for patients with angina or large ischemic areas, can exclude coronary artery disease as a cause of HF. Cardiopulmonary exercise testing, employing computers and gas analyzers to determine maximal oxygen consumption, evaluates ventricular performance during exercise. Acceptable total oxygen uptake is 20 ml/kg/m or higher. A result of less than 12 indicates severe HF. Continuous ECG monitoring is provided during acute and advanced disease stages to identify and manage dysrhythmias promptly. The patient's blood pressure and pulse are assessed while the patient is supine, sitting, and standing to detect orthostasis, esp. during diuretic therapy. The legs are assessed for symmetrical pitting edema, a common finding. The patient is placed in high Fowler's position and on prescribed bedrest, and high concentration oxygen is administered as prescribed to ease the patient's breathing. Prescribed medications, such as carvedilol, candesartan, digoxin, furosemide, lisinopril, spironolactone, and potassium, are administered and evaluated for desired responses and any adverse reactions. All patient activities are organized to maximize rest periods. To prevent deep venous thrombosis due to vascular congestion, the caregiver assists with range-of-motion exercises and applies antiembolism stockings or uses heparins or warfarin. Any deterioration in the patient's condition is documented and reported immediately. To help curb fluid overload, the patient should avoid foods high in sodium content, such as canned and commercially prepared foods and dairy products, restricting dietary sodium to 2 to 3 grams a day and fluid intake to 2 liters a day. The importance of regular medical checkups is emphasized, and the patient is advised to notify the health care practitioner if the pulse rate is unusually irregular, falls below 60, or increases above 120, or if the patient experiences palpitations, dizziness, blurred vision, shortness of breath, persistent dry cough, increased fatigue, paroxysmal nocturnal dyspnea, swollen ankles, decreased urine output, or a weight gain of 3 to 5 lb (1.4 to 2.3 kg) in 1 week. Patients and their families and other care givers must understand the action of each of the medications prescribed, along with their possible adverse reactions and actions to be taken if a dose is missed. The importance of renewing prescriptions in a timely manner so that doses are available when needed should be stressed.

Patient activity as tolerated is encouraged with tasks divided into small segments to avoid shortness of breath.

Annual influenza vaccines and a pneumococcal vaccine (repeated every 5 years) help patients minimize the risk of systemic infections. Smokers are encouraged to quit. Frequent rehospitalizations are the rule rather than the exception in heart failure. Effective treatment may depend on a multidisciplinary approach that includes active participation by the patient, the primary care provider and nurse educator, case managers, pharmacists, dietitians, and social workers, among others. Evidence-based clinical pathways for managing heart failure are available from the American Heart Association and other agencies.

high output heart f. Heart failure that occurs in spite of high cardiac output, for example, in severe anemia, thyrotoxicosis, arteriovenous fistulae, or other diseases.

intestinal f. An inability to meet the nutritional requirements of the body for growth, development, and homeostasis that results from either a poorly functioning or a surgically-resected intestine. People with intestinal failure require parenteral or enteral nutritional support.

kidney f. Renal **f.**

left ventricular heart f. Failure of the heart to maintain left ventricular output.

liver f. The inability of the liver to function due to liver disease or demands beyond the capabilities of the liver. SEE: *acute liver f.*

low output heart f. Heart failure in which cardiac output low (as in most kinds of heart disease).

metabolic f. Rapid failure of physical and mental functions ending in death.

multiple systems organ f. Multiple organ dysfunction syndrome.

multisystem organ f. Multiple organ dysfunction syndrome.

organ f. Inability of one or more of the body's organ systems to perform the tasks of preserving health or homeostasis. The failure may be acute or chronic. Examples include blindness, chronic kidney disease, cirrhosis, dementia, fulminant hepatic failure, hearing loss, heart failure, hypothyroidism, menopause, respiratory failure, and shock.

ovarian f. Cessation of normal ovarian function, the ability to produce fertilizable eggs when stimulated by gonadotropins.

pump f. A colloquial term for cardiac failure. SEE: *cardiac f.*

renal f. Inability of the kidneys to function adequately. It may be partial, temporary, chronic, acute, or complete. SYN: *kidney f.* SEE: *end-stage renal disease.*

respiratory f. SEE: *acute respiratory f.; chronic respiratory f.*

right ventricular heart f. Failure of the heart to maintain right ventricular output.

f. to thrive ABBR: FTT. A condition in which infants and children not only fail to gain weight but also may lose it, or in which older persons lose the physiological or psychosocial reserves needed to care for themselves. The causes include almost any chronic and debilitating condition.

failure to progress In pregnancy, a stall during labor. It may be due to slow cervical dilation, a delay in the descent of the fetal head through the birth canal, or ineffective uterine contractions.

failure-to-rescue (fāl'yĕr-too-rĕs'kū) ABBR: FTR. Loss of life among hospitalized patients resulting from inadequate recognition and treatment of life-threatening complications. FTR is correlated with high ratios of patients to nurses and with psychological variables, e.g., burnout. It has been used, along with complication rates of surgery and other criteria, as an indicator of the quality of hospital care.

faint [O. Fr. *faindre,* to feign] **1.** To feel weak as though about to lose consciousness. **2.** Weak. **3.** Loss of consciousness resulting from vasovagal or vasodepressor mechanisms. SEE: *syncope.*

faintness 1. A sensation of impending loss of consciousness. SYN: *presyncope.* **2.** A sensation of weakness due to lack of food.

faith healing SEE: under *healing.*

falces (fal'sēz") [L.] Pl. of falx.

falcial (fāl'shăl) Pert. to a falx.

falciform (fāl'sĭ-form) [L. *falx,* sickle, + *forma,* form] Sickle-shaped.

fall 1. To drop accidentally to the floor, ground, or lower level, e.g., into a chair. **2.** Any unexplained event that results in the patient's inadvertently coming to rest on the floor, ground, or lower level, e.g., into a chair. In older adults, falls are a leading cause of non-fatal injuries, and injuries sustained during falls are a leading cause of death. Lacerations, head injuries, and fractures of the arm, wrist, hip, ribs, and spine are caused by falls. Falls also may have long-term psychological sequelae, e.g., loss of independence, social isolation, anxiety, and depression. About 35%–40% of people 65 years of age or older fall each year; by age 80 that figure increases to 50%. Women are somewhat more likely to fall than men and also are more likely to sustain significant injuries. It is important for health care providers to search for the cause or causes of the fall. The single biggest predictor of a fall is a history of falls. Other proven risk factors for falls include reduced visual acuity and hearing, vestibular dysfunction, peripheral neuropathy, and musculoskeletal disorders, e.g., physical weakness, inability to get up from a chair without using one's arms, Parkinson's disease, a history of stroke, postural hypotension, increased body sway when standing, inability to perform a tandem walk, the use of medicines, e.g., antihypertensives, antidepressants, sedatives, or benzodiazepines, daily use of four or more prescription drugs, inability to transfer from bed or chair to bathtub or toilet, and environmental hazards. With careful clinical investigation the cause of falls can sometimes be determined and appropriate steps taken to prevent them.

PATIENT CARE: Hazards in the home that increase the chances of falling are improper footwear, scatter rugs that are not secure or slip resistant, uneven flooring, out-of-the-way light switches or electrical outlets, cluttered access to paths through a room or entrance, poorly lighted steps and stairways, lack of handrails along the entire length of a stairway, and tubs and showers that are not fitted with sturdy grab bars and have slippery floors.

The Joint Commission on the Accreditation of Hospital Organizations (JCAHO) mandates that hospitalized and nursing-home patients be assessed for fall risk, with periodic reevaluation, according to a standard assessment tool, e.g., the Morse Fall Scale, Tinetti Balance & Gait Evaluation or St. Thomas's Risk Assessment Tool in Falling Elderly Inpatients (STRATIFY). A complete health history should be obtained and lab test results evaluated for changes that could lead to falls. Vital signs should also be monitored, with attention paid to orthostatic hypotension. During hospitalizations, care providers need to be observant to detect motor, sensory, or cognitive deficits that could lead to falls; to respond promptly to the patient's call lights; to make sure the patient is kept oriented; to avoid the use of side rails (which may provoke injuries); to use low bed positions and bed alarms as necessary; and to provide time for procedures, moves, etc. Balanced food and fluid intake and the correction of fluid, electrolyte, or nutritional imbalances may decrease fall risk, as may careful, systematic reviews of patient medication usage.

After hospital discharge, a home visit should be made to assess the environment for safety hazards, and patient and family assisted in revising any hazards. The patient should be encouraged to remain mobile, to wear walking shoes rather than slippers, to wear glasses, and to use assistive devices (canes, walkers) to help gait and balance. Physical therapy and occupational therapy consultations help the patient with muscle strengthening and balance training (e.g., with exercise regimens such as tai ch'i).

fall and injury prevention Techniques, such as exercise and balance training, the use of bed alarms, warnings posted at the bedside, and video surveillance, that reduce the incidence and severity of falls in health care facilities. Falls occur most often in older or infirm patients, in people undergoing rehabilitation from injury or surgery, and in patients with altered mental status or neuromuscular diseases.

fallen bladder SEE: under *bladder*.

fallen lung sign SEE: under *sign*.

falling drop SEE: under *drop*.

fallophobia (făl″ō-fō′bē-ă) A colloquial term for the fear of falling and of what it may mean for one's future health and prospects for independent living.

fallopian tube The hollow, cylindrical structure that extends laterally from the lateral angle of the fundal end of the uterus and terminates near the ovary. It conveys the ovum from the ovary to the uterus and spermatozoa from the uterus toward the ovary. Each lies in the superior border of the broad ligament of the uterus. SYN: *oviduct; uterine tube*. SEE: *female genitalia* for illus; *uterus*.

ANATOMY: The narrow region near the uterus, the isthmus, continues laterally as a wider ampulla. The latter expands to form the terminal funnel-shaped infundibulum, at the bottom of which lies a small opening, the ostium, through which the ovum enters the tube. Surrounding each ostium are several finger-like processes called fimbriae extending toward the ovary. Each tube averages about $4\frac{1}{2}$ in (11.4 cm) in length and $\frac{1}{4}$ in (6 mm) in diameter. Its wall consists of three layers: mucosa, muscular layer, and serosa. The epithelium of the mucosa consists of ciliated and nonciliated cells. The muscular layer has an inner circular and an outer longitudinal layer of smooth muscle. Ciliary action and peristalsis move the ovum or zygote toward the uterus. The serosa is connective tissue underlying the peritoneum.

falloposcopy (făl-lō-pos′kŏ-pē) [*fallop(ian tube)* + *-scopy*] Imaging the interior of the fallopian tube (the endosalpinx) with a flexible fiber-optic endoscope. The procedure is used in the diagnosis and treatment of tubal infertility.

fallotomy (făl-ŏt′ō-mē) Salpingotomy.

fallout Settling of radioactive molecules from the atmosphere after their release into the air following an explosion or radiation accident.

falls, risk for Increased susceptibility to

falling that may cause physical harm. SEE: *Nursing Diagnoses Appendix.*

false imprisonment An intentional tort; unlawful intentional confinement of another within fixed boundaries so that the confined person is conscious of the confinement or harmed by it.

false-negative (făwls′něg′ă-tĭv) A test result that falsely indicates that a condition is not present when in fact it is. SEE: *Bayes' theorem; false-positive.*

false-negative ratio ABBR: FNR. The ratio of subjects affected by an illness whose test results wrongly suggest they are disease-free to all those subjects who have the disease. The false-negative ratio of a test is useful in determining the test's reliability, i.e., the higher the ratio, the less reliable the test.

A high FNR may be biological or analytical in origin. Biological false-negative test results may occur when a test is performed at the wrong stage of an illness, e.g., before an antibody or antigen is found in the blood. Analytical false negatives may result when a test lacks adequate sensitivity or specificity to detect an agent that is already present.

false-negative reaction SEE: *false-negative.*

false-positive (făwls′pŏs′ĭ-tĭv) A result in a test or procedure that falsely indicates that a condition is present when in fact it is not. It may result from faulty laboratory technique or from the presence of another disease or condition that mimics the one sought. SEE: *Bayes' theorem; false-negative.*

false-positive ratio ABBR: FPR. The ratio of patients who are disease-free but test positive for an illness, as a result of error, to all patients who do not have the disease.

false-positive reaction SEE: *false-positive.*

falsification (făwl″sĭ-fĭ-kā′shŭn) The act of writing or stating what is not true.

    retrospective f. Deliberate or unconscious alteration of memory for past events or situations, a mental mechanism for ego preservation.

falx (fălks, făl′sēz) *pl.* **falces** [L.] Any sickle-shaped structure.

    f. cerebelli A fold of the dura mater that forms a vertical partition between the hemispheres of the cerebellum.

    f. cerebri A fold of the dura mater that lies in the longitudinal fissure and separates the two cerebral hemispheres.

famciclovir (făm-sī′klō-vēr) An antiviral drug used to treat herpes simplex and herpes zoster.

familial [L. *familia,* family] Pert. to or common to the same family, e.g., a disease occurring more frequently in a family than would be expected by chance.

familial adenomatous polyposis ABBR:

FAP. A rare autosomal dominant syndrome that predisposes patients to colorectal cancers. FAP is characterized by the growth of hundreds of polyps in the colonic mucosa. Polyps may also proliferate in the stomach and small bowel, and patients may have congenital hypertrophy of the retinal pigment epithelium; desmoid tumors; osteomas; and facial or dental anomalies. Prophylactic colectomy protects affected persons from developing colon cancer. Because of the dominant inheritance of the disease, screening of family members with endoscopy or virtual colonoscopy is strongly recommended. FAP is found in about 0.12% of the population. SYN: *Gardner's syndrome; multiple intestinal polyposis.* SEE: *Turcot syndrome.*

familial cancer syndrome Any genetic predisposition to cancer that is found in several generations of a kindred. Some recognized cancer syndromes that recur in families include the multiple endocrine neoplasias, retinoblastoma, familial polyposis of the colon, and Fanconi's anemia, among others.

familial disease A disease that occurs in several members of the same family.

familial Hibernian fever SEE: under *fever.*

familial Mediterranean fever SEE: under *fever.*

familial medullary thyroid cancer SEE: under *cancer.*

familial periodic paralysis SEE: under *paralysis.*

family (fam′(ĭ-)lē) [L. *familia,* household] **1.** A group of individuals descended from a common ancestor. **2.** In biological classification, the division between an order and a genus. **3.** A group of people living in a household who share common attachments, such as mutual caring, emotional bonds, regular interactions, and common goals, which include the health of the individuals in the family.

    blended f. A common contemporary family group including children from previous and current relationships.

    extended f. The basic or nuclear family plus close relatives.

    nuclear f. The basic family unit consisting of parents and their children.

    single-parent f. A family in which only one of the parents is living with the child or children.

Family and Medical Leave Act ABBR: FMLA. A federal law, enacted in 1993, that requires large employers to grant up to 12 weeks of unpaid leave during any 12-month period to long-standing employees for compelling medical or family reasons. Reasons include care of spouse, child, or parent of employee who has a serious health problem; birth of child of employee and care of the child; adoption or foster care-placement of a child with employee; and serious employee health problems that do not allow person to perform essential functions of job position.

family balancing Choosing to have a child of a particular sex according to the parents' preferences; prenatal gender selection.

family care leave Permission to be absent from work to care for a family member who is pregnant, ill, disabled, or incapacitated.

family of origin The family into which one is born and to whom one is related.

family planning The spacing of conception of children according to the wishes of the parents rather than to chance. It is accomplished by practicing some form of birth control.

> *natural f.p.* **1.** Fertility **awareness**. **2.** A kind of fertility awareness in which a woman plots on a graph her daily basal body temperature, cervical mucus characteristics, and common subjective complaints associated with ovulation, e.g., mittelschmerz, to identify the days of the menstrual cycle during which there is the highest potential for conception. The validity of this method is controversial.

family practice SEE: under *practice*.

family processes, dysfunctional: alcoholism The state in which the psychosocial, spiritual, and physiological functions of the family unit are chronically disorganized, leading to conflict, denial of problems, resistance to change, ineffective problem solving, and a series of self-perpetuating crises. SEE: *Nursing Diagnoses Appendix*.

family processes, interrupted A change in family relationships and/or functioning. SEE: *Nursing Diagnoses Appendix*.

family processes, readiness for enhanced A pattern of family functioning that is sufficient to support the well-being of family members and can be strengthened. SEE: *Nursing Diagnoses Appendix*.

family therapy Treatment of the members of a family together, rather than as individual patients. The family unit is viewed as a social system important to all of its members.

famine Pronounced scarcity of food in a broad geographical area, causing widespread starvation, disease, and/or death in a population.

Fanconi syndrome (fan-kō'nē) [Guido Fanconi, Swiss pediatrician, 1892–1979] **1.** Diamond-Blackfan anemia. **2.** Any of several diseases marked by abnormal functioning of the proximal tubules of the kidney in which amino acids, glucose, phosphates and urates are lost in abnormal concentrations in the urine. Polyuria, osteomalacia, and growth failure are common consequences.

fang [AS., to plunder] A sharp hollow tooth through which some animals inject toxins into their prey.

fango (făn'gō) [Italian, mud] Mud obtained from thermal springs in Battaglia, Italy, used to treat rheumatism and gout.

Fannia (făn'ē-ă) A genus of small houseflies.

fanning of toes (fan'ing) Spreading of toes, esp. when the sole is stroked; plantar reflex.

fantasy (făn'tă-sē) [Gr. *phantasia*, imagination] An imaginary (mental) image; a daydream.

FAOTA *Fellow of the American Occupational Therapy Association.*

FAP familial adenomatous polyposis.

FAPTA *Fellow of the American Physical Therapy Association.*

farad (făr'ăd) [Michael Faraday, Brit. physicist, 1791–1867] A unit of electrical capacity. The capacity of a condenser that, charged with 1 coulomb, gives a difference of potential of 1 V. This unit is so large that 1 millionth of it has been adopted as a practical unit called a microfarad.

faraday (făr'ă-dā) The amount of electric charge associated with 1 g equivalent of an electrochemical reaction. It is equal to approx. 96,000 coulombs. SEE: *coulomb; farad*.

faradic (fă-răd'ĭk) Pert. to induced electricity.

faradism (făr'ă-dĭzm) Therapeutic use of a faradic (induced) current to stimulate muscles and nerves. Such a current is derived from the secondary, or induction, coil.

faradization (făr"ă-dĭ-zā'shŭn) **1.** The treatment of nerves or muscles with faradic current. **2.** The condition of nerves or muscles so treated.

Farber disease (far'bĕr) [Sidney Farber, U.S. pediatric pathologist, 1903–1973] A rare autosomal recessive lysosomal storage disease in which abnormal byproducts of lipid metabolism accumulate in the brain. It is one of the lipid storage diseases, which include Gaucher's disease and Niemann-Pick disease. SYN: *ceramidase deficiency*.

farcy (far'sē) [L. *farcire*, to stuff] A chronic form of glanders.

farina (fă-rē'nă) [L.] Finely ground meal commonly made from wheat or other grain, used as cereal and flour.

farinaceous (făr"ĭ-nā'shŭs) **1.** Starchy. **2.** Pert. to flour.

farmer's lung SEE: under *lung*.

farpoint (far'poynt) The greatest distance at which objects can be seen distinctly with the eyes in complete relaxation.

farsightedness (far'sīt'ĕd-nĕs) An error of refraction in which, with accommodation completely relaxed, parallel rays come to a focus behind the retina. Affected individuals can see distant objects clearly, but cannot see near objects in proper focus. SYN: *hyperopia*. **farsighted,** *adj.*

fas (făs) A receptor for tumor necrosis factor that induces apoptosis (cell death). SYN: *CD95*.

fasci-, fascio- [L. *fascia*, band, bandage] Prefixes meaning *band or fascia (fibrous membrane).*

fascia (făsh'(ē-)ă, făsh'ē-ē) *pl.* **fasciae** [L. *fascia*, a band] A fibrous membrane covering, supporting, and separating tissue. There are two kinds of fascia: deep fasciae for muscles, and superficial fasciae for connecting the skin to the muscles. **fascial** (făsh'sh(ē-)ăl), *adj.*

   Abernethy f. SEE: *Abernethy fascia.*

   anal f. A fascia covering the levator ani muscle from the perineal aspect.

   aponeurotic f. A tendinous fascia that provides attachment for a muscle.

   Buck f. The fascial covering of the penis, derived from Colles fascia.

   Cloquet f. SEE: under *Cloquet, Jules G.*

   Colles f. SEE: under *Colles, Abraham.*

   cremasteric f. The fascia covering the cremaster muscle.

   cribriform f. The fascia of the thigh covering the saphenous opening.

   crural f. The deep fascia of the leg.

   deep f. Fascia that covers structures below the skin and lined by superficial fascia.

   deep cervical f. The fascia of the neck covering the muscles, vessels, and nerves.

   f. dentata, dentate fascia Dentate gyrus.

   endothoracic f. The fascia that separates the pleura of the lung from the inside of the thoracic cavity and the diaphragm. SYN: *extrapleural f.*

   extrapleural f. Endothoracic fascia.

   iliac f. Transversalis fascia over the anterior surface of the iliopsoas muscle.

   lumbodorsal f. Thoracolumbar fascia.

   pectineal f. The pubic section of the fascia lata.

   pelvic f. The fascia within the pelvic cavity. It is extremely important in maintaining normal strength in the pelvic floor. SEE: *diaphragm, pelvic.*

   perineal f. Three layers of tissue between the muscles of the perineum comprising the urogenital diaphragm.

   pharyngobasilar f. The fascia lying between the mucosal and muscular layers of the pharyngeal wall. SYN: *pharyngeal aponeurosis.*

   plantar f. The fascia investing the muscles of the sole of the foot. SYN: *plantar aponeurosis.*

   Scarpa f. SEE: under *Scarpa, Antonio.*

   subcutaneous f. Superficial fascia.

   superficial f. The areolar connective tissue and adipose tissue below the dermis of the skin. SYN: *hypodermis; subcutaneous f.; subcutaneous tissue.*

   superficial cervical f. The fascia of the neck just inside the skin. It includes cutaneous blood vessels, nerves, lymphatics, lymph nodes, and some fat. In the front it also contains the platysmus muscle.

   thoracolumbar f. The fascia and aponeuroses of the latissimus dorsi, serratus posterior inferior, internal oblique, and transverse abdominis muscles. They provide support and stability for the lumbar spine in postural and lifting activities. The fascia attaches medially to the spinous processes of the vertebral column and inferiorly to the iliac crest and sacrum. SYN: *lumbodorsal f.*

   f. transversalis The fascia located between the perineum and the transversalis muscle. It lines the abdominal cavity.

fascial reflex (făsh'sh(ē-)ăl) SEE: under *reflex.*

fasciaplasty (făsh'ē-ă-plăs"tē) [" + Gr. *plassein*, to form] Plastic surgery of a fascia.

fascicle (făs'ĭ-kl) [L. *fasciculus*, little bundle] A fasciculus.

fascicular (fă-sĭk'ū-lăr) **1.** Arranged like a bundle of rods. **2.** Pert. to a fasciculus.

fasciculation (fă-sĭk"ū-lā'shŭn) **1.** Formation of fascicles. **2.** Involuntary contraction or twitching of muscle fibers, visible under the skin. **3.** Spontaneous contractions of muscle fibers that do not cause movement at a joint.

fasciculus (fă-sĭk'yŭ-lŭs, fă-sĭk'yŭ-lī") *pl.* **fasciculi** [L. *fasciculus*, a small bundle] **1.** A small bundle of longitudinal elements, e.g., muscle fibers. **2.** A bundle of axons. Peripheral nerves can contain one or more axonal fasciculi. In the brain and spinal cord, many of the fasciculi are named, and 'fasciculus' is synonymous with 'tract.'

   arcuate f. A myelinated axon tract lying under the cerebral cortex. It is a long association tract that interconnects the superior and middle gyri of the frontal lobe with the ipsilateral temporal lobe.

   cingulate f. Cingulum (1).

   f. cuneatus The more lateral of the two large ascending axon tracts that fill the dorsal funiculus of the spinal cord. The fasciculus cuneatus contains dorsal root ganglion cell axons transmitting discriminative sensations from the ipsilateral arm, shoulder, and neck.

   dorsal longitudinal f. An axon tract that interconnects the brainstem reticular formation and the hypothalamus.

   dorsolateral f. Lissauer's tract.

   fronto-occipital f. A myelinated axon tract lying under the cerebral cortex. It is a long association tract that interconnects the frontal lobe with the ipsilateral temporal and occipital lobes.

f. gracilis The more medial of the two large ascending axon tracts that fill the dorsal funiculus of the spinal cord. The fasciculus gracilis contains dorsal root ganglion cell axons transmitting discriminative sensations from the legs and trunk.

inferior longitudinal f. A myelinated axon tract lying under the cerebral cortex. It is a long association tract interconnecting the occipital lobe with the ipsilateral temporal lobe.

medial longitudinal f. ABBR: MLF. A long discrete tract running ventrally, close to the midline, through the brainstem and upper spinal cord. With contributions from the vestibulospinal tracts, the medial longitudinal fasciculus is the main pathway by which equilibrium and balance information reaches lower motor neuron circuits to automatically adjust eye, neck, and limb movements to match sensory signals from the semicircular canals. SYN: *medial longitudinal bundle.*

f. retroflexus The main output tract from the habenular nuclei, which lie above the thalamus. It innervates the interpeduncular nuclei, which then send axons to the median raphe nuclei of the midbrain SYN: *habenulo-interpeduncular tract.*

f. solitarius Tractus solitarius.

superior longitudinal f. A myelinated axon tract lying under the cerebral cortex. It is a long association tract that interconnects the superior and middle gyri of the frontal lobe with the ipsilateral parietal and occipital lobes.

thalamic f. A heterogeneous bundle of axons heading dorsally into the ventral anterior and ventral lateral thalamic nuclei. Axons in this fasciculus include part of the ansa lenticularis (from the globus pallidus) and axons from the contralateral deep cerebellar nuclei.

uncinate f. A compact, myelinated axon tract lying under the cerebral cortex. It is a long association tract that interconnects the frontal association cortex of the frontal lobe with the inferior temporal association cortex of the ipsilateral temporal lobe.

fasciectomy (făsh″ē-ĕk′tō-mē) [L. *fascia*, band, + Gr. *ektome*, excision] Excision of strips of fascia.

fasciitis (fash″ē-īt′ĭs, fas″) [*fascia* + -*it is*] Inflammation of a fascia.

eosinophilic f. Inflammation of muscle fascia, associated with eosinophilia, pain, and swelling.

necrotizing f. A severe bacterial infection that spreads rapidly through the body along superficial or deep fascial planes, resulting in necrosis of subcutaneous tissue and extensive undermining. SYN: *hospital* **gangrene**.

SYMPTOMS: The onset of illness is usually acute and progression is rapid. Initially there is severe pain (out of proportion to the injury), swelling at the injury site, fever, chills, and flulike symptoms or malaise. These symptoms worsen as the infection spreads. If extensive surgical débridement, drainage, and antibiotics are not instituted early, the patient may die.

ETIOLOGY: Bacteria most commonly responsible are invasive group A hemolytic streptococci, *Staphylococcus aureus, Clostridium perfringens,* oral flora (as after a bite), enteric flora, coliforms, proteus, pseudomonas, klebsiella, and *Vibrio vulnificus* (particularly in alcoholics, diabetics, and the immunocompromised). The size of the wound that gives these bacteria access to the subcutaneous tissue is not related to the severity of infection. Predisposing factors include surgical or traumatic wounds (including those with foreign bodies), drug injections (particularly contaminated drugs of abuse), burns, frostbite, insect bites, and other skin lesions (open sores or varicella). Those with diabetes, cancer, alcoholism, obesity, or malnutrition are at increased risk.

TREATMENT: Emergency surgical débridement is required.

PATIENT CARE: Health care professionals should maintain contact and standard precautions, administer oxygen, establish an IV access (avoiding use of the infected extremity), obtain specimens for blood studies (complete blood count and differential, electrolytes, glucose, blood urea nitrogen, creatinine, and arterial blood gas specimens), urinalysis, and cultures (wound tissue specimens are collected during debridement). IV fluids and antibiotics and analgesics are administered as prescribed. Cardiac monitoring is initiated, and an indwelling urinary catheter inserted (unless the infection involved the perineal area). The patient also may require imaging studies (x-rays, CT, MRI) to assess for gas and necrosis in subcutaneous facial planes. Hyperbaric oxygen therapy, when combined with antibiotic and surgical débridement, helps to promote healing by encouraging growth of epithelial tissue and blood vessels.

Patient care also includes frequent assessment of the patient and lab values for indications of life-threatening complications (sepsis, gangrene, coagulation disorders, multiple organ dysfunction). The infection site should be monitored continually for changes such as edema, color changes, and increased or decreased pain (anesthesia). The patient's pain should be documented using a standard pain-rating scale. Opioids or opiates should be provided as indicated, particularly during painful dressing changes. Patient-controlled analgesia with added drugs for break-through pain may be appropriate. A nutritionist should ensure that the patient's caloric and nutrient intake is sufficient to support wound healing. Enteral feeding may be needed. Ongoing emotional support should be provided to the patient and family, as they confront the possibility of death, and the threat of amputation or disfigurement, knowing that further surgery and extensive skin grafting may be required in the future. The patient should be assessed for depression and anxiety, given information about rehabilitation, and encouraged to seek additional counseling to deal with role changes and body image issues. SEE: *Fournier gangrene*.

plantar f. Painful inflammation of the heel and bottom surface of the foot caused by excessive stretching of the fibrous tissue (fascia) that attaches the heel to the forefoot. It can be caused or exacerbated by excessive physical activity, improper footwear, obesity, or pregnancy.

fasciodesis (făsh″ē-ŏd′ĕ-sĭs) [″ + Gr. *desis,* binding] Surgical attachment of a fascia to a tendon or another fascia.

Fasciola (fă-sī′ō-lă) [L. *fasciola,* a band] A genus of flukes belonging to the class Trematoda.

F. hepatica A species that infests the liver and bile ducts of cattle, sheep, and other herbivores; the common liver fluke. Infested aquatic plants are the source of human infection. SEE: illus.

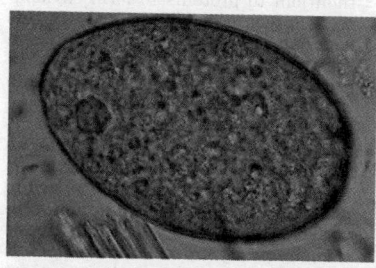

FASCIOLA HEPATICA EGG

fasciolopsiasis (făs″ē-ō-lŏp-sī′ă-sĭs) Infection with *Fasciolopsis buski.* It is contracted by ingestion of plants grown in water infested by the intermediate host, snails.

SYMPTOMS: The symptoms are diarrhea, abdominal pain, anasarca, and eosinophilia.

TREATMENT: Praziquantel.

Fasciolopsis buski (făs″ē-ō-lŏp′sĭs) A trematode (fluke) that infests the intestinal tract of certain mammals includ-

ing humans. Symptoms include vomiting, anorexia, and diarrhea alternating with constipation. The number of flukes present may be sufficient to cause intestinal obstruction. The disease occurs in Asia, including central and southern China. SEE: illus.; *fasciolopsiasis.*

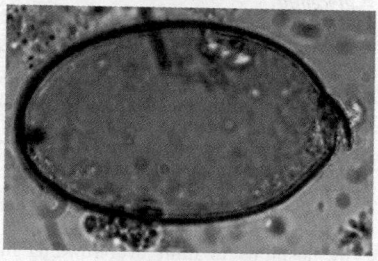

FASCIOLOPSIS BUSKI EGG

(Orig. mag. ×400)

fascioplasty (făsh′ē-ō-plăs″tē) [L. *fasciola,* a band, + Gr. *plassein,* to form] Plastic operation on a fascia.

fasciorrhaphy (făsh-ē-or′ă-fē) [″ + Gr. *rhaphe,* seam, ridge] Suturing of a fascia.

fasciotomy (făsh-ē-ŏt′ō-mē) [″ + Gr. *tome,* incision] Surgical incision and division of a fascia.

FASRT *Fellow of the American Society of Radiologic Technologists.*

¹fast [AS. *faest,* fixed] Resistant to the effects or action of a chemical substance.

²fast [AS. *faestan,* to hold fast] Abstention from food, usually voluntary.

fastidious In microbiology, concerning an organism that has precise nutritional and environmental requirements for growth and survival.

fastigium (făs-tĭj′ē-ŭm) [L., ridge] **1.** The highest point. **2.** The fullest point of development of acute, infectious diseases when the temperature reaches the maximum. **3.** The most posterior portion of the fourth ventricle, formed by the junction of the anterior and posterior medullary vela projecting into the medullary substance of the cerebellum of the brain.

fasting [AS. *faestan,* to hold fast] Going without food or other nutritional support. This forces the body to catabolize its own glycogen, fat, and protein reserves in order to produce glucose. The products of incomplete fat metabolism (fatty acids, diacetic acid and acetic acid) produce ketosis and mild acidosis. Since glycogen reserves are depleted quickly in children, fasting can be esp. hazardous to their health.

⚠ Unsupervised fasting to lose weight can cause severe health hazards, including cholecystitis, electrolyte disturbances, cardiac dysrhythmias, and occasionally death.

---

fasting blood draw Fasting blood **sample**.

fasting blood test Fasting blood **sample**.

fasting hypoglycemia SEE: under *hypoglycemia*.

fastness [AS. *faest,* fixed] The ability of cells to resist stains or destructive agents.

fast-track (fast'trak") **1.** A colloquial term for a clinic in which patients seeking care for nonacute conditions in the emergency department are triaged for medical or surgical attention; an urgent-care clinic affiliated with an emergency department.

PATIENT CARE: Fast-tracks are used by hospitals to limit overcrowding in emergency departments and reduce patients' waiting times. Patients with upper respiratory illnesses and minor trauma are commonly referred to fast-tracks, which permits emergency departments to focus on the critically or acutely ill.

2. A colloquial term for a more rapid evaluation and approval of a new or investigational agent than is allowed for most other new drugs.

fat (fat) **1.** Body tissue that serves as an energy reserve and as a source of inflammatory cytokines. Excessive amounts of fat in the body are found in obesity. SEE: *heart; obesity.* **fatty** (fat'ē), *adj.* **2.** In chemistry, a triglyceride ester of fatty acids; any of a group of organic compounds closely associated in nature with the phosphatides, cerebrosides, and sterols. The term *lipid* is applied in general to a fat or fatlike substance. Fats are insoluble in water but soluble in ether, chloroform, benzene, and other fat solvents. During hydrolysis, fats break down into fatty acids and glycerol (an alcohol). Fats are hydrolyzed by the action of acids, alkalies, lipases (fat-splitting enzymes), and superheated steam.

CHEMICAL STRUCTURE: In the fat molecule, one molecule of glycerol is combined with three of fatty acids. Three fatty acids, oleic acid ($C_{18}H_{34}O_2$), stearic acid ($C_{18}H_{36}O_2$), and palmitic acid ($C_{16}H_{32}O_2$), constitute the bulk of fatty acids in neutral fats found in body tissues. According to the fatty acid with which the glycerol is combined, corresponding fats are triolein, tristearin, and tripalmitin. These three fats are the principal fats present in foods.

PHYSIOLOGY: The most important function of fats is as a form of stored or potential energy. In conjunction with carbohydrates, fats are protein sparers: dietary or body protein need not be used for energy production. Glycogen storage is sufficient to supply energy needs for about 12 hr, but in a 70-kg man of average build, 12 kg of stored fat (as triglycerides) can supply energy needs for as long as 8 weeks. Subcutaneous fat provides a small amount of insulation against heat loss, and some organs such as the eyes and kidneys are cushioned by fat. The diglyceride phospholipids are part of all cell membranes. Dietary fat provides the essential fatty acids needed for normal growth.

Because certain fatty acids (linoleic, D-linolenic, and arachidonic) are necessary for formation of other products and because the body does not synthesize these fatty acids, they are classed as *essential fatty acids.* Linolenic acid can be converted into other fatty acids including arachidonic acid.

Animals fed a fat-free diet develop dermatitis and fail to grow; the liver becomes fatty, and there are neurological disturbances. These changes can be prevented or reversed by the addition of linoleic and linolenic acids to the diet. The human diet should consist of about 4% of the calories from linoleic and 1% from linolenic acids.

DIGESTION AND ABSORPTION: In the stomach, emulsified fats such as cream or egg yolk are acted on by gastric lipase. Most fats undergo digestion in the intestine, where a pancreatic lipase hydrolyzes them to fatty acids and glycerol. The salts in bile are not enzymes; they emulsify fats and permit pancreatic lipase to digest them. Bile salts then make fatty acids soluble in water so that they may be readily absorbed. In the intestinal mucosa, fatty acids and glycerol combine to form neutral fats, then join to proteins to form chylomicrons, which enter the lacteals. In this form, they are carried in the lymph through the lymph vessels to the thoracic duct, which empties lymph into the blood.

METABOLISM: Absorbed fats are oxidized to carbon dioxide and water to produce energy; stored in adipose tissue for energy production later; changed to phospholipids for cell membranes; converted to acetyl groups for the synthesis of cholesterol, from which other steroids are made; and used to make secretions such as sebum.

Intermediary metabolism: In the oxidation of fat to carbon dioxide and water, several ketones are formed, esp. acetoacetic acid, betahydroxybutyric acid, and acetone. Excessive production of ketone bodies, when fats are incompletely oxidized, is called ketosis.

SOURCES: In addition to fat being absorbed from the intestine, body fat may arise from the conversion of carbohydrates (glucose) or excess amino acids into fat. Fatty acids cannot be converted directly to glucose, but they are split into two-carbon acetyl groups that enter the Krebs cycle and thereby have the same energy-producing function as carbohydrates.

NUTRITION: Fats have a high caloric value, yielding about 9 kcal per gram as compared with about 4 kcal per gram for carbohydrates and proteins. The average American diet of 3000 kcal may derive 40% of the caloric value from fats. Nutritionists and epidemiologists believe that decreasing dietary fat to 30% would decrease the risk of developing cancer, esp. of the colon, breast, and prostate.

Fats improve the taste and smell of foods, provide a feeling of satiety, and, because of their high caloric content, are important in high-calorie diets. Fat-free fat substitutes that have been termed "designer fats" have been investigated for several decades. Whether they will play a major role in providing foods with fewer calories from fat has not been determined. SEE: table.

CONTRAINDICATIONS: Fat intake should be reduced in certain diseases such as hepatitis and in low-calorie diets.

body f. The portion of the human body that consists of fat. This is estimated in several ways: by hydrodensitometry, by calculating the ratio of weight in kilograms to height in meters squared (Quetelet index), and more recently, by estimating bioelectrical impedance of the body. None of these methods provides a precise indicator of body composition, but bioelectrical impedance is the simplest, least expensive, and most nearly accurate.

brown f. Adipose tissue occurring primarily in the full-term newborn. It is located near major vessels. The fat produces heat metabolically and is therefore an important factor in temperature regulation. As the infant matures, shivering is established as a means of controlling body temperature. In inactive individuals, brown fat largely disap-

pears after infancy, although stores of metabolically active brown fat increase with exercise. SEE: *tissue, brown adipose.*

ectopic f. Fat that collects in abnormal locations in the body and adversely affects health. These locations include: the liver (steatohepatitis), muscle (marbling), and around the intraperitoneal organs (visceral fat).

neutral f. Compounds of the higher fatty acids (palmitic, stearic, and oleic) with glycerol. They are the common fats of animal and plant tissues.

subcutaneous f. A layer of fat that lies just beneath the skin. It differs from visceral fat in that it has fewer adverse effects on glucose metabolism.

trans f. A fat derived from the partial hydrogenation of vegetable oils. Examples include vegetable shortening and margarine. Studies have associated trans-fat consumption with an increased risk for coronary artery disease.

visceral f. Fat that accumulates around internal organs, esp.organs within the peritoneum, pleura, or pericardium. It is more common in men than in women. It contributes to insulin resistance and other aspects of the metabolic syndrome.

wool f. A fatty substance obtained from sheep's wool and containing not more than 0.25% water. It is used as an ointment base that has the ability to absorb water and can produce contact dermatitis in susceptible people. SYN: *anhydrous lanolin.* SEE: *trans-fatty acid.*

fatal (fāt′l) [L. *fatalis*] **1.** Inevitable. **2.** Causing death.

fatalism (fāt′ăl-izm) [*fatal* + *-ism*] **1.** A person's belief that events will occur regardless of one's efforts. **2.** The philosophical doctrine that events are predestined or preordained. **fatalistic** (fāt″ă-lis′tik), *adj.*

fatality A death, esp. one caused by an accident, injury, occupational illness, or catastrophe.

fat client A computer within a network

Food Sources of Saturated and Trans Fats

Meat products	Visible fat and marbling in beef, pork, and lamb, esp.in prime-grade and ground meats, lard, suet, salt pork
Processed meats	Frankfurters, luncheon meats such as bologna, corned beef, liverwurst, pastrami, and salami
	Bacon and sausage
Poultry and fowl	Chicken and turkey (mostly beneath the skin), cornish hens, duck, and goose
Whole milk and whole-milk products	Cheeses made with whole milk or cream, condensed milk, ice cream, whole-milk yogurt, all creams (sour, half-and-half, whipped)
Plant products	Coconut oil, palm-kernel oil, cocoa butter
Miscellaneous	Fully hydrogenated shortening and margarine, many cakes, pies, cookies, and mixes

SOURCE: Lutz, CA and Przytulski, KR: Nutrition and Diet Therapy. FA Davis, Philadelphia, 2001.

that has its own disc drive and relies little on the central server. SEE: *thin client*.

fate map SEE: under *map*.

father, biological The male who contributes the ovum-fertilizing sperm that subsequently becomes a fetus.

fatigability (făt″ĭ-gă-bĭl′ĭ-tē) The condition of becoming easily tired or exhausted.

fatigue (fă-tēg′) [Fr. fr L. *fatigare*, to tire] **1.** An overwhelming sustained feeling of exhaustion and diminished capacity for physical and mental work. SEE: *Nursing Diagnoses Appendix*. **2.** The condition of an organ or tissue in which its response to stimulation is reduced or lost as a result of overactivity. **3.** To cause fatigue. Fatigue may be the result of excessive activity, which causes the accumulation of metabolic waste products such as lactic acid; malnutrition (deficiency of carbohydrates, proteins, minerals, or vitamins); circulatory disturbances such as heart disease or anemia, which interfere with the supply of oxygen and energy materials to tissues; respiratory disturbances, which interfere with the supply of oxygen to tissues; infectious diseases, which produce toxic products or alter body metabolism; endocrine disturbances such as occur in diabetes, hyperinsulinism, and menopause; psychogenic factors such as emotional conflicts, frustration, anxiety, neurosis, and boredom; or physical factors such as disability. Environmental noise and vibration contribute to the development of fatigue. SEE: *chronic fatigue syndrome*.

   accommodative f. The inability of the eye to sustain accommodation over time. It is usually due to repeated or sustained visual effort.

   acute f. Fatigue with sudden onset. It may occur after excessive exertion and is relieved by rest.

   alert f. The tendency of health care professionals to ignore prompts given to them by clinical decision support systems in electronic health records because of the excessive number or limited clinical significance of these records.

   chronic f. Long-continued fatigue not relieved by rest. It is indicative of disease such as tuberculosis, diabetes, or other conditions of altered body metabolism. SEE: *chronic fatigue syndrome*.

   compassion f. Cynicism, emotional exhaustion, or self-centeredness occurring in a health care professional previously dedicated to his or her work and clients.

   muscle f. The reduced capacity of a muscle to perform work as a result of repeated contractions and accumulation of lactic acid in anaerobic cell respira-

tion. The fatigue may be partial or complete.

fatigue state Exhaustion.

fat maldistribution (mal″dĭs″trĭ-bū′shŏn) Lipodystrophy.

fat overload syndrome A rare complication of intravenous administration of fat emulsion. Findings include sudden elevation of the serum triglyceride level, fever, hepatosplenomegaly, coagulopathy, and dysfunction of other organs. Specific therapy is not available, but plasma exchange has been used experimentally.

fat replacement Any substance developed to provide the physical characteristics of fats with relatively few or no calories. Fat replacements may be carbohydrate polymers, protein or fat-based materials that are either not absorbed or not digested in human metabolism.

   Simplesse is the trade name for a fat replacement made of milk and egg white and provides only 1 to 2 kcal/gram as opposed to the 9 kcal/gram supplied by fat. Olestra is a calorie-free fat replacement made from sucrose and vegetable oil and is suitable for cooking. Overconsumption of Olestra may result in fat-soluble vitamin deficiency. SYN: *fat substitute*.

fat replacer A substance that tastes like fat or acts like fat in food preparation, but has fewer calories.

fat suppression SEE: under *suppression*.

fatty change Any abnormal accumulation of fat within parenchymal cells. It may occur in the heart or other organs. When seen in the liver, it often is a result of excessive and prolonged alcohol intake or obesity.

fatty streak (fat′ē) SEE: under *streak*.

fauces (fŏ′sēz) [L.] The constricted opening leading from the oral cavity to the oropharynx. It is bounded by the soft palate, the base of the tongue, and the palatine arches. The anterior pillars of the fauces are known as the glossopalatine arch, and the posterior pillars as the pharyngopalatine arch. SEE: *fossa*. **faucial** (-shăl), *adj.*

fault In legal medicine, failing to meet an obligation; a legal responsibility for a failed outcome.

fauna (faw′nă) [L. *Faunus*, mythical deity of herdsmen] **1.** Animal life as distinguished from plant life. **2.** All the animals, including microscopic forms, in a specified area. SEE: *flora*.

faveolate (fă-vē′ŏ-lāt) [L. *faveolus*, little honeycomb] Honeycombed. SYN: *alveolate*.

faveolus (fă-vē′ŏ-lŭs) [L., little honeycomb] A depression or small pit, esp. on the skin. SYN: *foveola*.

favism (fā′vĭzm) [It. *fava*, bean, + Gr. *-ismos*, condition] A hereditary condition common in Sicily and Sardinia resulting from sensitivity to a species of bean, *Vicia faba*. It is marked by fever, acute hemolytic anemia, vomiting, and diarrhea, and may lead to prostration and coma. It is caused by ingestion of the beans or inhalation of the pollen of the plant by persons who have an inherited deficiency of the enzyme glucose-6-phosphate dehydrogenase.

favus (fā′vŭs) [L. *favus*, honeycomb] A skin disease caused by the fungus *Trichophyton schoenleinii*. It is marked by pinhead- to pea-sized, cup-shaped, yellowish crusts (scutulum) over the hair follicles of the scalp and is accompanied by musty odor and itching. It may spread all over the body.

FBCT *full body computed tomography*.

FCAP *Fellow of the College of American Pathologists*.

Fc fragment A small piece of an immunoglobulin (an antibody) used by macrophages in processing and presenting foreign antigens to T lymphocytes. SEE: *immune response; macrophage processing*.

Fc receptor SEE: under *receptor*.

F.D. *fatal dose; focal distance*.

FDA *Food and Drug Administration*.

FDG *Fluorodeoxyglucose*.

FDG imaging A type of positron emission tomography using the contrast agent fluorodeoxyglucose (FDG). This technique is esp. useful in detecting melanomas, lymphomas, and cancers of the head, neck, lung, and breast and of the colorectal and genitourinary systems.

FDP *fibrin degradation products*.

Fe [L. *ferrum*, iron] Symbol for the element iron.

fear [AS. *faer*] Anxiety caused by a perceived threat, real or imagined. Focussed apprehension and fright. SEE: *emotion; Nursing Diagnoses Appendix; Phobias Appendix*.

features Any part of the face.

febrifacient (fĕb-rĭ-fā′shĕnt) [L. *febris*, fever, + *facere*, to make] Producing fever.

febrifuge (fĕb′rĭ-fūj) Something that reduces fever. SYN: *antipyretic*. **febrifugal**, *adj*.

febrile (fē′brĭl, fē′brīl, fĕb′rĭl) [L. *febris*, fever] Pert. to fever; feverish.

febrile state A term used to describe constitutional symptoms that accompany a rise in temperature. The pulse and respiration rate usually increase, with headache, pains, malaise, loss of appetite, concentrated and diminished urine, chills or sweating, restlessness, insomnia, and irritability.

fecal (fē′kăl) [*fec(es)* + *-al*] Pert. to feces. **fecally** (fē′kă-lē), *adv*.

fecal DNA (fē′kăl) SEE: under *DNA*.

fecal fat test (fē′kăl) The measurement of the total quantity of lipids in a timed stool specimen, as a part of the evaluation of chronic diarrhea, esp. when fat

malabsorption is suspected. The collected feces must not be contaminated by urine or by chemicals used in toilets. High levels of fecal fat (e.g., more than 14 g/day) suggest biliary, pancreatic, or small bowel disorders.

fecal impaction (fē′kăl) SEE: under *impaction*.

fecalith (fē′kă-lĭth) [″ + Gr. *lithos*, stone] A fecal concretion. SYN: *coprolith*.

fecal occult blood test (fē′kăl) A screening test for disorders of the gastrointestinal tract, including anemias that may be caused by gastrointestinal blood loss, e.g., cancer of the colon. Traditionally, a small amount of feces is collected on cards accompanying several consecutive bowel movements. These cards are submitted to a lab for analysis. Alternatively, a flushable pad is dropped into the toilet bowl after a bowel movement. A change in color (to blue or green) in the pad reveals occult blood if present.

PATIENT CARE: Patients should be taught how to collect and protect card specimens submitted to the laboratory. They should avoid taking nonsteroidal anti-inflammatory drugs (NSAIDs) such as ibuprofen or aspirin and should not take more than one adult aspirin (325 mg) per day for several days before and during specimen collection. They should also avoid red meats (including cold cuts) for 3 days before and during the testing period (since the test detects animal as well as human blood), and limit vitamin C intake to less than 250 mg/day. The patient should avoid contaminating the stool sample by not allowing it to touch the toilet or the water. The bowel movement should be made into a clean, dry container or onto the flushable collection tissue supplied with the kit. A wooden stick or swab transfers a small quantity of the specimen to the collection card. Specimens should be protected from heat, light, and chemicals. When developing the test, the manufacturer's instructions should be followed precisely. Gloves should be worn and standard precautions followed. If the specimen is fresh, 3 to 5 min should elapse before adding developer to make sure the stool has penetrated the paper. For all guaiac tests, a blue color indicates the presence of blood. Blue-green also may indicate blood, while green alone is considered negative. After reading the results, the positive and negative controls should be tested to verify test accuracy. The results are then documented. Care should be taken to be sure that a test kit is not used after its expiration date. Specimens should not be collected or the test run if blood can be seen in the stool or urine, if the patient is menstruating, or if a urinary tract infection is present.

⚠️ The developer bottle should be stored in a lab area and not in a patient area because it could be mistaken for a liquid medication or a toy.

fecaloid (fē'kă-loyd) [" + Gr. *eidos,* form, shape] Resembling feces.

fecaluria (fē"kăl-ū'rē-ă) [" + Gr. *ouron,* urine] Feces in the urine. It may arise when a fistula forms between the lower gastrointestinal tract and the urinary bladder.

fecal vomit (fē'kăl) SEE: under *vomit.*

feces (fē'sēz") [L. *faex,* sediment, dregs] Bodily waste such as food residue, bacteria, epithelium, and mucus, discharged from the bowels by way of the anus.

Fe(C₃H₅O₃)₂ Ferrous lactate; lactate of iron.

FeCl₂ Ferrous chloride.

FeCl₃ Ferric chloride.

FeCO₃ Ferrous carbonate.

fecula (fĕk'ū-lă) [L. *faecula,* dregs] 1. Sediment. 2. Starch.

feculent (fĕk'ū-lĕnt) [L. *faeculentus*] Having sediment.

fecund (fek'ŭnd, fĕk') [L. *fecundus,* fruitful, fertile] 1. Having produced or reproduced rapidly and abundantly; prolific. 2. Able to produce or reproduce rapidly and abundantly.

fecundability (fē-kŭn"dă-bil'ĭt-ē) The probability of pregnancy during a single menstrual cycle.

fecundate (fē'kŭn-dāt) [L. *fecundare,* to bear fruit] To fertilize, impregnate, or render fertile.

fecundation (fek"ŭn-dā'shŏn, fē"kŭn-) [*fecundate*] Impregnation; fertilization.
   artificial f. Artificial insemination.

fecundity (fē-kŭn'dĭ-tē) Ability to produce offspring; fertility.

Federal Emergency Management Agency ABBR: FEMA. The agency of the federal government that supervises civil defense, disaster planning, and emergency medical services in communities that have suffered floods, tornados, hurricanes, and other catastrophes.

Federal False Claims Act An American federal law that makes the submission of a falsified bill to a federal agency, such as Medicare, illegal.

Federal Register A publication that makes available to the public proposed and final government rules, legal notices, orders, and documents having general applicability and legal effect. It contains published material from all federal agencies.

Federal Torts Claims Act ABBR: FTCA. A statute enacted by Congress in 1946 that specifies how and when private parties may sue the U.S. in federal court for torts committed by those acting on behalf of the U.S. It controls the legal liability of health care professionals employed at government clinics, e.g., in the Indian Health Service, military clinics, and federally funded clinics for underserved communities.

feedback 1. The influence of the output or result of a system on the input or stimulus. Feedback may be positive or negative. In positive feedback, the result of the process intensifies the stimulus, e.g., uterine contraction stimulates oxytocin secretion, which brings about increased contractions and increased oxytocin. In negative feedback, the result of the process reverses or shuts off the stimulus, e.g., a high blood glucose level stimulates insulin secretion, which lowers blood glucose, which in turn decreases insulin secretion. 2. In psychiatry, the expressed verbal reaction or physical reaction, i.e., body language of one person to another person's actions or behaviors. 3. In motor learning, the use of sensory information from contracting muscles to influence subsequent muscular contractions.

feeder A device used to introduce nutrition into the mouth of an infant who has difficulty eating, sucking, or swallowing, e.g., a child with a cleft lip or palate.

feeder layer SEE: under *layer.*

feedforward (fēd"for'wĭrd) Anticipatory motor impulses sent before movement to prepare the musculoskeletal system for postural adjustments. The feedforward mechanism is thought to help prepare muscles to perform required tasks.

feeding (fēd'ing) Taking or giving nourishment.
   artificial f. 1. Providing a liquid food preparation through a tube passed into the stomach, duodenum, jejunum, or rarely, the rectum or intravenously. This is also done through gastrostomy or duodenostomy. SEE: *hyperalimentation.* 2. Feeding of an infant with food other than mother's milk.
   cup f. A method of augmenting the diet of a newborn child who is unable to breast-feed by having the infant sip milk from a cup rather than suck it from a bottle.
   enteral tube f. A means of providing nutrition for a patient unable to consume food normally. The patient may have difficulty with chewing or swallowing or an oral, pharyngeal, or esophageal deformity. The patient is fed an appropriate nutritional formula through a tube passed into the stomach or duodenum from the nasal passage (nasogastric or nasoduodenal tube) or by a gastrostomy tube, gastrostomy button, or gastrojejunostomy tube. SYN: *total enteral nutrition.*
   PATIENT CARE: Short-term feeding (less than 4 weeks' duration) can usually be managed with a nasogastric tube. Longer-term feeding requires a surgically implanted feeding tube. The

choice of tube is determined by a number of factors, including the expected duration of feeding, the condition necessitating the feeding, concomitant conditions, and clinician preference. The percutaneous endoscopic gastrostomy tube (PEG) is the most common method for tube insertion. The tube is placed using direct endoscopic visualization through an abdominal incision, and anchored in place with an outer flange and an inner bump or balloon. It enters through the abdominal wall into the stomach. The gastrojejunostomy tube is a smaller-bore tube advanced through the stomach into the jejunum tube. It delivers contents into the jejunum and is used for patients with recurrent aspiration, upper gastrointestinal obstruction or fistula, gastroparesis, and gastroesophageal reflux. It cannot be used in patients with small bowel disease because it can cause enterocutaneous fistulae. The smaller bore increases the probability of clogging, which requires more frequent tube flushing and replacement. The gastrostomy button prevents some of the chronic complications of gastrostomy tubes (clogging, leaking, and skin irritation). The button is skin level and out of sight when the patient is clothed. It usually replaces a gastrostomy tube 4 weeks after the initial PEG to ensure development of a mature tract. Tube placement is confirmed by X-ray. Health care professionals need to assess the patient (and teach the patient and other care providers how to assess) for leakage (recognizing that high abdominal pressure, as occurs with sneezing or coughing, often causes some normal leakage), skin irritation, infection, and formation of granulation tissue. Nutrition and hydration status and signs and symptoms of aspiration, pneumonia, or GI complications (such as bleeding or peritonitis) also need to be assessed. The professional care provider should use the time with the patient while flushing and assessing tube concerns to teach the patient and family caregivers how to care for the tube and to offer support as the patient and significant others adjust to body image changes and the loss of eating pleasures. Flushing enteral tubes to keep them free from build-up is essential, because unclogging a tube wastes time, effort, and resources. The best method of tube flushing is a matter of active research; local protocols apply. Tubes that cannot be unclogged must be replaced.

There are four types of nutrient formulas: *intact nutrient, hydrolyzed nutrient, elemental (defined),* and *modular. Intact nutrient* formulas are called *standard* because the nutrients are whole and therefore are appropriate for use whenever normal digestion takes place. They usually provide 1 kcal/ml and can be used orally. In *hydrolyzed nutrient* formulas the nutrients are predigested and are suitable for use whenever malabsorption is present or when the jejunum is the feeding site. These formulas are not appropriate for oral use because of their taste. They are more expensive than intact nutrient formulas. In *elemental (defined)* formulas the nutrients are in the simplest, most basic, form and are rapidly absorbed from the gut. These formulas are not appropriate for oral use. This type of formula is the most expensive. Formulas designed for specific diseases are available. In *modular* formulas, commercially produced nutritional products may be used as supplements to standard formulas. For example, the addition of a protein module would convert a standard formula to a high-protein formula.

There are four kinds of delivery: *bolus, intermittent infusion, cyclic infusion,* and *continuous drip.* In *bolus administration* the formula is delivered in four to six daily feedings by a large syringe attached to the feeding tube in the stomach. This type of delivery is the least well tolerated. In *intermittent infusion* the formula is delivered four to six times daily over 30 to 60 minutes using a pump or gravity flow. In *cyclic infusion* an infusion pump delivers the nutrient solution for specified hours of the day and is turned off during other hours. In *continuous drip* an infusion pump delivers nutrition all day long.

forced f. Tube feeding to an individual who does not want to eat or to be fed by this means. It is accomplished by passing a feeding tube through the nasal passage or mouth into the esophagus.

intravenous f. The provision of total or partial nutritional requirements intravenously; essential in treating some diseases. It is accomplished by carefully controlling the composition of fluid given with respect to total calories derived from protein hydrolysates, dextrose, and fat emulsions, and the electrolytes, minerals, and vitamins. Patients unable to safely eat have been completely maintained for extended periods via intravenous nutritional support, usually through a major vein, such as the subclavian or the jugular. SEE: *total parenteral nutrition.*

postpyloric f. The provision of nutrients directly to the duodenum or jejunum via a small-bore catheter advanced through the nose, nasopharynx, esophagus, and stomach into the small bowel. It can be used to manage conditions such as acute pancreatitis, gastric outlet obstruction, or gastroparesis.

rectal f. The introduction of fluid nutrients into the colon through the rectum, a mode of feeding rarely used because little nourishment other than water is absorbed through the colon. SYN: *nutritive* **enema**.

    supplemental f. Any dietary additive provided to patients to enhance their nutritional status.

fee-for-service Payment for specific health care services provided to a patient (as opposed to payments received for the number of patients seen, the number of hours worked, or the number of patients enrolled in a health care panel). The individual or an insurance carrier may make the payment.

feeling [AS. *felan*, to feel] **1.** The conscious experience of emotion. **2.** A sensory perception.

Feer disease (fār) [Emil Feer, Swiss pediatrician, 1864–1955] Acrodynia.

fee splitting The unethical practice of returning to the referring health care provider a portion of the fee received from a patient who is seen in consultation.

FEESST *Fiberoptic endoscopic evaluation of swallowing with sensory testing.*

feet (fēt) Pl. of foot.

Feingold diet (fīn'gōld″) [Benjamin Feingold, U.S. pediatrician, 1900–1982] A diet from which all artificial colors, artificial flavors, preservatives, and salicylates have been eliminated. It had been used in treating hyperactive children.

Feiss line [Henry Feiss, 20th-century U.S. orthopedic surgeon] A line that extends from the first metatarsophalangeal joint, over the navicular tubercle, to the apex of the medial malleolus. Changes in the angle formed by this line before and during the application of weight can be used to determine excessive pronation of the foot. If the angle formed by the Feiss line is between 30° and 90° while the foot is bearing weight, the foot may be considered hyperpronated. SEE: illus.

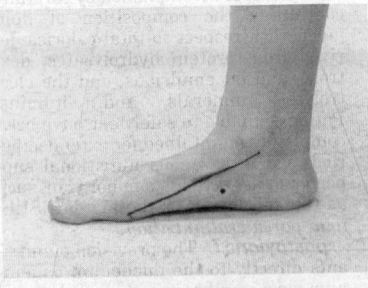

FEISS LINE

Fel d 1 *feline uteroglobin* (the major allergen found in cat dander). It is produced in the sweat glands and epithelial cells of the domestic cat and is transferred to the cat's fur during self-grooming.

Feldenkrais method [Dr. Moshe Feldenkrais, Ukrainian physicist, 1904–1984] A form of therapy devoted to improving limitations of range of motion, improving poor posture, and relieving stress.

feline (fē'līn) [L. *feles*, cat] Concerning cats.

Felis domesticus (fē'lĭs dŏm-ĕs'tĭ-kŭs) [L., house cat] The scientific name for the domestic cat whose dander is a source of allergenic protein. Cat-related allergens are abbreviated Fel by the World Health Organization.

fellatio (fĕl-ā'shē-ō) [L. *fellare*, to suck] Oral stimulation of the penis. SYN: *oral sex*. SEE: *cunnilingus*.

fellow (fĕl'ō) [ME. *felowe*] **1.** A physician who has received primary training in a medical specialty and is pursuing further specialized training. SEE: *fellowship*.

    2. A member of a professional, scholarly, or scientific society.

fellowship (fĕl'ō-shĭp″) [ME. *felaweshipe*] An awarded or sponsored educational experience leading to specialized training. SEE: *fellow*.

felon (fĕl'ŏn) [ME. *feloun*, malignant] An infection or abscess of the soft tissue of the terminal joint of a finger. SYN: *whitlow*.

felony A more serious crime than a misdemeanor with punishment greater than that for misdemeanors; can be grounds for license denial, revocation, suspension, or probation of a health care provider. It is punishable by imprisonment or death, depending on state law and the type of crime.

feltwork (fĕlt'wŭrk) **1.** A fibrous network. **2.** A plexus of nerve fibrils.

Felty syndrome (fĕl'tē) [Augustus Roi Felty, U.S. physician, 1895–1963] Rheumatoid arthritis associated with splenomegaly and neutropenia.

FEMA *Federal Emergency Management Agency.*

female [L. *femella*, little woman] **1.** An individual of the sex that produces ova or bears young. **2.** Characteristic of this sex or gender. SEE: *female* **genitalia**.

female genital cutting Partial or complete surgical removal of the clitoris, a traditional practice in some African, Middle Eastern, and Southeast Asian cultures. The cutting usually is performed between the ages of 1 week and 14 years. The procedure is performed by nonmedical personnel without benefit of anesthesia or sterile conditions. The most common procedures are removal of the clitoral prepuce, excision of the clitoris, removal of the labia minora and sometimes most of the labia majora. The two sides may be sutured together to occlude the vagina. Possible immediate complications include infection, tetanus, shock, hemorrhage, and death.

The possible long-term physical and mental disabilities include chronic pelvic infection, keloids, vulvar abscesses, sterility, incontinence, depression, anxiety, sexual dysfunction, and obstetric complications. SYN: *female **circumcision**; female genital mutilation; infibulation* (2).

female genital mutilation Female genital cutting.

female sexual arousal disorder According to the DSM-IV, the essential feature of this condition is a persistent or recurrent inability to attain, or to maintain until completion of the sexual activity, an adequate vaginal lubrication-swelling response of sexual excitement. In order to establish this diagnosis, the disturbance must cause marked distress or interpersonal difficulty, and the difficulty cannot be attributed to a medical condition, substance abuse, or medications. SEE: *male erectile disorder.*

feminine (fĕm'ĭ-nĭn) Concerning or being of the female sex.

feminism [L. *femininus*] **1.** The development of female secondary sexual characteristics in a man. **2.** A political philosophy whose aim is to advance the standing of women in society. SEE: *gynecomastia.*

feminization (fem″ĭ-nĭ-zā'shŏn) The normal development of female secondary sexual characteristics or the pathological development of these in a man.

    testicular f. Androgen insensitivity syndrome.

femoral (fĕm'or-ăl) [L. *femoralis*] Pert. to the femur.

femoral compression device SEE: under *device.*

femoral length femur length.

    fetal f.l.femoral length femur length measurement.

femoral reflex SEE: under *reflex.*

femoral vein SEE: under *vein.*

femto- [Danish *femten*, fifteen] ABBR: f. In the International System of Units (SI), a prefix meaning *one quadrillionth* (10^{-15}).

femur (fē'mŭr) *pl.* **femora** [L.] The thigh bone. It extends from the hip to the knee and is the longest and strongest bone in the skeleton. SEE: illus.

femur length The distance from the head of the femur to its distal end. SYN: *femoral length.*

femur length measurement An assessment made during a fetal ultrasound that uses the length of the femur (from the head to the distal end) to estimate the gestational age and growth of the fetus, especially to see if there is evidence of intrauterine growth retardation (IUGR). SYN: *fetal femoral length.*

fenestra (fē-nĕs'tră) *pl.* **fenestrae** [L., window] **1.** An aperture frequently closed by a membrane. **2.** An open area,

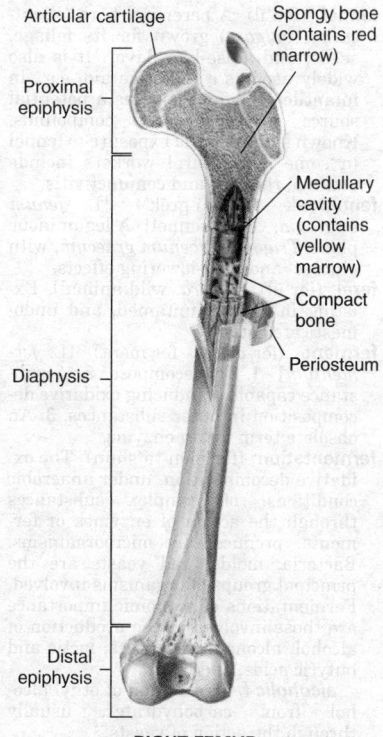

Articular cartilage

Spongy bone (contains red marrow)

Proximal epiphysis

Medullary cavity (contains yellow marrow)

Compact bone

Periosteum

Diaphysis

Distal epiphysis

RIGHT FEMUR

as in the blade of an obstetrical forceps.

fenestral (-trăl), *adj.*

    f. cochleae Round window.

    f. vestibuli Oval window.

fenestrated (fĕn'ĕ-strāt-ĕd) Having openings.

fenestrated tracheostomy tube A double-cannulated tracheostomy tube that allows patients to breathe through the mouth or nose when the inner cannula is removed. The tube has an opening in the posterior wall of the outer cannula above the inflatable cuff. It allows the patient to exhale through his natural airway without impeding speech.

fenestration (fĕn″ĕ-strā'shŭn) **1.** The condition of having a fenestra. **2.** An operation in which an artificial opening is made into the labyrinth of the ear. This procedure is performed to treat deafness associated with otosclerosis. **3.** An operation to open the mucoperiosteum and alveolar plate of bone over the root of an infected tooth to remove the inflammatory exudate and relieve pain.

feng shui (fŭng shwä) [Chinese *fĕng shui*, wind (and) water] An ancient Chinese art of interior and architectural design, the object of which is to create a soothing and healthful living environment, one that is in accord with the qi (energy or life force).

fennel (fĕn'ĭl) A perennial herb (*Foeniculum vulgare*) grown for its foliage, seeds, and anise-like flavor. It is also widely used as a digestive aid, e.g., in infantile colic, and used as a potential source of estrogen-like compounds. Known side effects of exposure to fennel in some agricultural workers include asthma, rhinitis, and conjunctivitis.

fenugreek (fen'yŭ-grēk″) [L. *fenum Graecum,* Greek fennel] A leguminous plant, *Trigonella foenum graecum,* with glucose- and lipid-lowering effects.

feral (fĕr'ŭl) [L. *fera,* wild animal] Existing in a wild, untamed, and undomesticated state.

ferment (fĕr-mĕnt', fĕr'mĕnt) [L. *fermentum*] **1.** To decompose. **2.** A substance capable of inducing oxidative decomposition in other substances. **3.** An obsolete term for an enzyme.

fermentation (fĕr″mĕn-tā'shŭn) The oxidative decomposition, under anaerobic conditions, of complex substances through the action of enzymes or ferments, produced by microorganisms. Bacteria, molds, and yeasts are the principal groups of organisms involved. Fermentations of economic importance are those involved in the production of alcohol, alcoholic beverages, lactic and butyric acids, and bread.

   alcoholic f. Production of ethyl alcohol from carbohydrates, usually through the action of yeasts.

   butyric f. Formation of butyric acid from bacterial action on carbohydrates under anaerobic conditions.

   citric acid f. Formation of citric acid from the action of molds on carbohydrates.

   lactic f. Formation of lactic acid from carbohydrates by bacterial action. The genera *Streptococcus* and *Lactobacillus* are the forms usually involved. Bacterial action is responsible for the souring of milk.

   propionic acid f. Formation of propionic acid from carbohydrates by the action of certain bacteria.

   viscous f. Production of gelatinous material by different forms of bacilli.

fermentation tube A U-shaped culture tube open at one end. If gas is produced by the bacteria cultured, the level of fluid decreases in the side of the tube with the closed end.

fermium (fĕr'mē-ŭm) [Enrico *Fermi,* Italian-born U.S. physicist and Nobel Prize winner, 1901–1954 + *-ium*] SYMB: Fm. A radioactive chemical element, atomic weight (mass) (most stable isotope) 257, half life 100.5 days, atomic weight 257; atomic number 100.

ferning, fern pattern (fĕrn'ĭng) **1.** The palm leaf (arborization) pattern that mid-cycle cervical mucus assumes when it is placed in a thin layer on a glass slide and allowed to dry. The pattern, caused by crystallization of the mucus as it dries, depends on the concentration of electrolytes, esp. sodium chloride, which in turn depends on the amount of estrogen in the mucus. Smears of cervical mucus may be helpful in determining when a woman has ovulated. The mucus has a beaded pattern at other times in the menstrual cycle. SYN: *cervical mucus.* **2.** Arborization found on microscopic examination of a sample of dried vaginal fluid at term; it confirms the rupture of membranes.

-ferous [L. *ferre,* to bear] Suffix meaning *producing.*

ferri- [L. *ferrum,* iron] In chemistry, a prefix meaning *iron* in its *ferric* (trivalent) state.

ferric (fĕr'ĭk) [ferri- + -ic] **1.** Pert. to iron. SYN: *ferruginous.* **2.** Pert. to a compound containing iron in its trivalent form.

   f. chloride $FeCl_3$, used principally in tincture form as an astringent.

ferric subsulfate (sŭb″sŭl'fāt″) $H_2Fe_4O_{22}S_5$, used in solution as a topical hemostatic liquid. SYN: *Monsel solution.*

ferritin (fĕr'ĭ-tĭn) An iron-phosphorus-protein complex containing about 23% iron. It is formed in the intestinal mucosa by the union of ferric iron with a protein, apoferritin. Tissues store iron in this form, principally in the reticuloendothelial cells of the liver, spleen, and bone marrow.

ferro- [L. *ferrum,* iron] In chemistry, a prefix meaning *iron* in its *ferrous* (bivalent) state.

ferrochelatase (fĕr″ō-kē'lă-tās) Heme synthetase.

ferrokinetics (fĕr″rō-kĭ-nĕt'ĭks) [″ + Gr. *kinesis,* movement] The study of the absorption, use, storage, and excretion of iron.

ferromagnetic (fer″ō-mag-net'ik) [*ferro- + magnetic*] Pert. to a metal, e.g., cobalt, iron, nickel, and some alloys capable of being magnetized when placed in a magnetic field.

> ⚠ Ferromagnetic materials are unsafe in magnetic resonance imaging environments.

ferromagnet (fer″ō-mag'nĕt), *n.* **ferromagnetism** (fer″ō-mag'nĕ-tizm), *n.*

ferroportin (fĕr″ō-pŏr'tĭn) [″ + L. *portare,* to carry] An iron-transporting molecule that spans cell membranes in the upper gastrointestinal tract and many other organs. Excessive expression of ferroportin by cells can result in iron overload.

ferroprotein (fĕr″ō-prō'tē-ĭn) A protein combined with an iron-containing radical. Ferroproteins are important oxygen-transferring enzymes, e.g., nicotinamide adenine dinucleotide dehydrogenase, cytochrome oxidase.

ferrotherapy (fĕr″ō-thĕr′ă-pē) [″ + Gr. *therapeia*, treatment] The use of iron in treating anemia.

ferrous (fer′ŭs) [*ferr(um)* + *-ous*] **1.** Pert. to iron. SYN: *ferruginous.* **2.** Pert. to a compound containing bivalent iron.

    f. fumarate $C_4H_2FeO_4$, an iron preparation used to treat anemias.

    f. gluconate $C_{12}H_{22}FeO_{14}$, an iron preparation occurring as a yellowish powder or granules. It is used to treat iron deficiency anemia.

    f. sulfate An iron compound used to treat iron-deficiency anemia. SYN: *iron (II) sulfate*. SEE: *copperas; copper salts in Poisons and Poisoning Appendix.*

ferruginous (fĕr-ū′jĭ-nŭs) [L. *ferrugo*, iron rust] **1.** Pert. to or containing iron. **2.** Having the color of iron rust.

ferrule (fĕr′ūl) [L. *viriola*, little bracelet] A band or ring of metal applied to the end of the root or crown of a tooth to strengthen it.

ferrum (fer′ŭm) [L. *ferrum*, iron] SYMB: Fe. Iron.

fertile (fĕrt′ĭl) [L. *fertilis*, fruitful] **1.** Capable of breeding or reproduction. **2.** Capable of growth or development. **3.** Pert. to the period in the female reproductive cycle that begins a few days before ovulation and ends with ovulation, during which the woman is most likely to conceive.

fertile period The time during the menstrual cycle when the ovum can be fertilized.

fertility (fĕr-tĭl′ĭ-tē) The quality of being productive or fertile.

fertility preservation In cancer care, the storing of the patient's embryos or sperm prior to the administration of chemotherapy. The stored reproductive cells can be used when the patient achieves remission for conception.

fertilization (fĕrt″ĭl-ĭ-zā′shŏn) [L. *fertilis*, reproductive] The process that begins with the penetration of the secondary oocyte by the spermatozoon and is completed with the fusion of the male and female pronuclei. This usually takes place in the fallopian tube. Viable spermatozoa have been found in the tube 48 hr after the last coitus. After the ovum is fertilized and the diploid chromosome number is restored in the zygote, cell division begins. The blastocyst then enters the uterus, where it may implant for continued nurture and development. SEE: illus.

    heterologous f. Assisted fertilization of a woman's ova with donor sperm. SEE: *in vitro f.; artificial insemination.*

    homologous f. Artificial fertilization of a woman's ovum by her husband's sperm. The ovum and sperm are united while both are outside the body and then are placed in the uterus during the optimum time for fertilization.

    in vitro f. ABBR: IVF. Laboratory-produced conception, used to enable pregnancy in infertile women when sperm access to ova is prevented by structural defects in the fallopian tubes or other factors, or in combination with her partner's sterility. After drug-induced follicle maturation, a sample of ova and follicular fluid is removed surgically and mixed with a specimen of the partner's sperm for incubation. The resulting zygote is introduced into the woman's uterus for implantation. SEE: *embryo transfer; GIFT; ZIFT.*

FESS *functional endoscopic sinus surgery.*

fester (fĕs′tĕr) [L. *fistula*, ulcer] To become inflamed and suppurate.

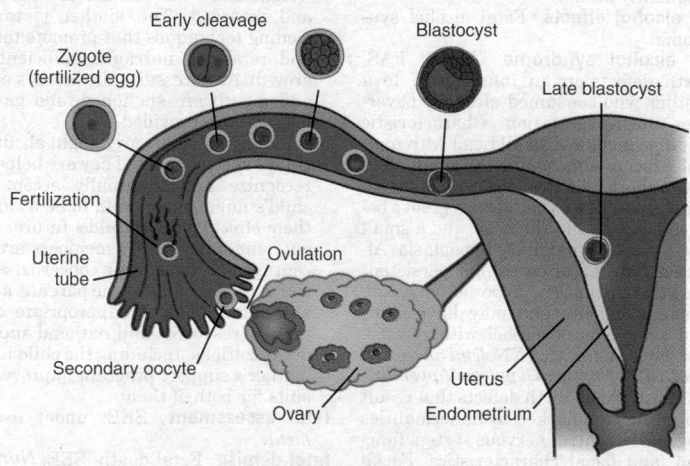

FERTILIZATION

festinant (fĕs'tĭ-nănt) Increasing in speed; accelerating.

festination (fĕs"tĭ-nā'shŭn) [L. *festinatio*] Festinating gait.

festoon (fĕs-toon') [L. *festus*, festal] **1.** A carving that resembles scalloping or festooning in the base material of a denture and simulates the natural indentations of the gums. **2.** To carve or reproduce the natural shape or architecture of the gums around teeth or dentures.

festooned (-toond'), *adj.*

FET *Forced expiratory* **technique**; *forced expiratory* **time**.

fetal (fē'ăl) [*fet(us)* + *-al*] Pert. to a fetus.

fetal abdominal circumference The ultrasonographic measurement of the circumference of the abdomen of a fetus at the level of the stomach, the left portal vein, and the left umbilical vein. The measurement is used to estimate fetal weight and gestational age.

fetal activity diary A periodic record used to count and compare fetal movements at different times. The woman may record the number of fetal movements in a given time, e.g., 1 hr, the average number of movements occurring during the same length of time at different times during the day, or the amount of time needed for a specified number of movements to occur, e.g., 10. SEE: *Cardiff Count-to-Ten*.

fetal akinesia deformation sequence ABBR: FADS. A rare, autosomal recessive syndrome of unknown cause in which the developing fetus does not move normally and suffers severe developmental consequences. FADS is characterized by intrauterine growth retardation, underdevelopment of the lungs, contractures of joints, and malformation of the face. The condition is frequently fatal.

fetal alcohol effects Fetal alcohol syndrome.

fetal alcohol syndrome ABBR: FAS. Birth defects in an infant born to a mother who consumed alcoholic beverages during gestation. Characteristic findings include a small head with multiple facial abnormalities: small eyes with short slits, a wide, flat nasal bridge, a midface that lacks a groove between the lip and the nose, and a small jaw related to maxillary hypoplasia. Affected children often exhibit persistent growth retardation, hyperactivity, and learning deficits and may have signs and symptoms of alcohol withdrawal a few days after birth. SYN: *fetal alcohol effects*. SEE: *Nursing Diagnoses Appendix*.

SYMPTOMS: Birth defects that result from FAS are marked by abnormalities in growth, central nervous system function, and facial characteristics. Facial abnormalities detected at birth may become less obvious as the child continues to grow. Even more serious, however, are the developmental delays that affect the child's behaviors, social skills, and learning. Included are hyperactivity, poor social skills and judgment, impulsiveness, poor ego or self-image, sensory processing problems, and high levels of anxiety. Mental retardation due to the abnormal migration of neural and glial cells during cell differentiation may be the cause of an IQ below 79 at age 7. It may seriously impair the child's potential. Poor fine motor function (weak grasp and poor hand-to-mouth coordination) adds to the child's functional defects.

PREVENTION: The patient should be taught that when she drinks, her baby also drinks, as alcohol crosses into the baby's bloodstream and affects its developing organs and tissues. No amount of alcohol is known to be safe for the developing fetus; thus, all health care providers should make ongoing efforts to educate women who are planning pregnancy or are pregnant to abstain completely from alcohol. They should suggest effective contraception and referral to abstinence treatment programs to individuals with known alcohol problems. The father's drinking does not directly affect his unborn child; however, his drinking may influence his partner to drink.

PATIENT CARE: Initial infant care is related to clinical problems that include increased respiratory effort, poor sucking ability, irritability, and hypotonia. A patent airway is maintained, and the infant's respiratory effort is monitored, with ventilatory assistance provided if required. Seizure activity must be assessed, treated, and prevented with medical management. The infant's weight and fluid balance are assessed and recorded. The mother is taught feeding techniques that promote taking and retaining nutrients sufficient for growth. As necessary, the infant's nares and mouth are suctioned, and gavage feedings are provided.

Family members are taught about the child's special needs. They are helped to recognize and eventually accept the child's impairments and to be aware of their effects on the child's future. Parents and other family members are encouraged to voice their concerns. A social worker evaluates the parents' needs and refers them to appropriate community resources and national support organizations. Including the child in the mother's support program improves results for both of them.

fetal assessment SEE: under *assessment*.

fetal demise Fetal death. SEE: *Nursing Diagnoses Appendix*.

fetal development The growth and maturation of the fetus in utero. This is divided into three periods: the preembryonic period begins with conception and ends on gestational day 14; the embryonic period encompasses gestational weeks 3 through 8; and the remainder of the pregnancy is known as the fetal period. Body organs and systems arise from three primary germ layers (ectoderm, mesoderm, and endoderm) and rudimentary formation of all organ systems is completed by gestational week 16. Systems maturation essential to extrauterine survival begins during week 24 with the formation of pulmonary surfactant. Two critical events occur between weeks 26 and 29: the pulmonary vasculature becomes capable of gas exchange and the central nervous system becomes capable of controlling respiration. SYN: *fetal **maturation***. SEE: *preterm **birth***.

fetal echogenic bowel An abnormality of the fetal bowel, sometimes seen on prenatal ultrasound, in which the bowel has a brightness similar to that seen in bone. Most instances of echogenic bowel are not associated with any fetal or neonatal disease, but some are seen in diseases and conditions such as aneuploidy, cystic fibrosis, cytomegalovirus infection, and intrauterine growth retardation.

fetal growth restriction ABBR: FGR. Intrauterine growth retardation.

fetal heart rate monitoring The techniques used to determine the heart rate of the fetus. They include auscultation, use of an electronic device, or Doppler ultrasound. SEE: *deceleration; Doppler echocardiography; fetal assessment*.

fetal origins hypothesis The controversial hypothesis that chronic adult diseases, e.g., hypertension, result from undernutrition of the fetus.

fetal overgrowth The excessive enlargement of fetal fat mass in expectant mothers with gestational diabetes mellitus.

fetal scalp blood sampling SEE: under *sampling*.

fetal viability The ability of a fetus to survive outside of the womb. Historically, a fetus was considered to be capable of living at the end of gestational week 20 when the mother had felt fetal movement (quickening) and the fetal heart tones could be auscultated with a fetoscope. In actuality, even with prompt and intensive neonatal support, a preterm fetus of less than 23 weeks' gestation has little chance of surviving outside of the womb. SEE: *viable*.

feticide (fē'tĭ-sīd) [″ + *cidus*, kill] Killing of a fetus. SEE: *infanticide*.

fetid (fē'tĭd) [L. *fetidus*, stink] Rank or foul in odor.

fetish (fē'tĭsh) [Portug. *feitico*, charm, sorcery] **1.** An object, such as an idol or charm, that is thought to have mysterious, magical, and supernatural power. **2.** In psychiatry, the love object of a person who suffers from fetishism.

fetishism (fē'tĭsh-, fĕt'ĭsh-ĭzm) [″ + Gr. *-ismos*, condition] **1.** Belief in some object as possessing power or capable of being a stimulus. **2.** Erotic stimulation or sexually arousing fantasies involving contact with nonliving objects, such as an article of dress or a braid of hair.

fetochorionic (fē″tō-kor-ē-ŏn'ĭk) [L. *fetus* + Gr. *chorion*, membrane] Pert. to the fetus and the chorion, or chorionic membrane, of the placenta.

fetoglobulin (fē″tō-glŏb'ū-lĭn) Fetoprotein.

fetography (fē-tŏg'ră-fē) Radiography of the fetus in utero. This procedure has been virtually replaced by ultrasound.

fetology (fē-tŏl'ō-jē) [″ + Gr. *logos*, word, reason] Study of the fetus.

fetomaternal hemorrhage (fĕt'ō-mă-tĕr'năl) SEE: under *hemorrhage*.

fetometry (fē-tŏm'ĕ-trē) [L. *fetus* + Gr. *metron*, measure] Estimation of fetal size, e.g., biparietal diameter and crown-rump length, age, and growth, typically using ultrasonography.

fetoplacental (fē″tō-plă-sĕn'tăl) [″ + *placenta*, a flat cake] Pert. to the fetus and its placenta.

fetoprotein (fē″tō-prō'tēn) An antigen present in the human fetus and in certain pathological conditions in adults. The amniotic fluid level can be used to evaluate fetal development. Elevated serum levels are found in adults with certain kinds of liver diseases. SYN: *fetoglobulin*. SEE: *alpha-fetoprotein*.

fetor (fē'tor) [L.] Stench; an offensive odor.
  f. hepaticus A mousy odor in the breath of persons with severe liver impairment. SEE: *hepatic coma*.
  f. oris Halitosis.

fetoscope (fĕt'ō-skōp″) [*fetus* + -*scope*] **1.** An optical device, usually flexible and made of fiber-optic materials, used for direct visualization of the fetus in the uterus. SEE: *embryoscopy*. **2.** Historical name for stethoscope for auscultating fetal heart sounds.

fetoscopy (fē-tŏs'kŏ-pē) Direct visualization of the fetus in the uterus through a fetoscope. SEE: *embryoscopy*.

fetotoxic (fē″tō-tŏk'sĭk) [L. *fetus*, fetus, + Gr. *toxikon*, poison] Poisonous to the fetus. Materials considered potentially fetotoxic include alcohol, morphine, cocaine, salicylates, coumarin anticoagulants, sedatives, tetracyclines, thiazides, tobacco smoke, and large doses of vitamin K. SEE: *teratogenic; thalidomide*.

fetotoxin [+ Gr. *toxikon*, poison] An infrequently used synonym for a teratogen, i.e., a substance that damages a developing fetus.

fetus (fē'ŭs) [L. *fetus,* bearing young, fetus, offspring] **1.** An unborn animal in its later stages of development. **2.** The unborn human from the beginning of the ninth week, i.e., the third month, of gestation until birth. (Before nine weeks, the developing zygote is called an embryo.) During the fetal period, the organ systems mature and grow. At nine weeks, a human fetus weighs about 14 g (1/2 oz); in the subsequent approx. 29 weeks, the fetus becomes 250 times heavier, so a typical newborn weighs about 3500 g (7 3/4 lb). A human fetus gets all its nutrition through the placenta, which increases in size with the fetus. SEE: *dermoid cyst.*

   harlequin f. A newborn with abnormal skin resembling a thick horny armor and divided into areas by deep red fissures. Infants may suffer from limited movement, severe dehydration, and infection. In the past this condition was always fatal, but present therapies and support allow some children to survive past adolescence. SYN: *ichthyosis* congenita; *ichthyosis* fetalis.

   mummified f. A dead fetus that has become dried and shriveled after resorption has failed to occur.

   f. papyraceus In a twin pregnancy, a dead fetus pressed flat by the development of the living twin.

Feulgen stain (foyl'gĕn) [Robert Joachim Feulgen, Ger. chemist, 1884–1955] A histological stain used to identify chromosomal banding and DNA.

FEV *forced expiratory volume.*

FEV₁ *forced expiratory volume in 1 sec.*

fever (fē'vĕr) [L. *febris*] **1.** Abnormal elevation of temperature. The normal temperature taken orally ranges from about 97.6° to 99.6°F (36.3°C to 37.6°C). Rectal temperature is 0.5° to 1.0°F higher than oral temperature. Normal temperature fluctuates during the day and is lowest in the morning and highest in the late afternoon; these variations are maintained during a fever. The expended basal energy is estimated to be increased about 12% for each degree centigrade of fever. SYN: *pyrexia.* SEE: *basal energy expenditure; temperature.*

   ETIOLOGY: Fever is caused by the release of interleukin-1 (IL-1), interleukin-2 (IL-2), and tumor necrosis factor from white blood cells (esp. macrophages), secretion of acute phase proteins, and redistribution of the blood away from the skin by the autonomic nervous system. The body cools itself and returns its temperature to normal range by diaphoresis (sweating). Elevated temperature caused by inadequate thermoregulatory responses during exercise in very hot weather is called hyperthermia; the set point is not increased. Infections, drugs, tumors, breakdown of necrotic tissue, CNS damage, and collagen diseases are the underlying causes of fevers. Despite common beliefs, fever is not harmful except in patients who cannot tolerate its hypermetabolic effects, some older patients in whom it can cause delirium, and children with a history of febrile seizures.

   PATIENT CARE: Patients with fever frequently seek professional medical attention. Fever is often an important indicator of infections or inflammations that may cause significant injury if left untreated. Diagnosing the cause of a fever may lead to specific therapies that limit the duration of an illness, prevent secondary organ damage or even death. The suppression of fever, however, is controversial. Some believe that fever helps to eradicate infecting organisms that cannot survive in a hot environment. Nonetheless, medications such as acetaminophen, aspirin, and other nonsteroidal anti-inflammatory drugs (NSAIDs) can lower body temperatures in febrile patients and are commonly used esp. if the body temperature exceeds 101°F (38.3°C). It is unknown whether using antipyretics results in improvements in survival or decreases in morbidity. In some settings (e.g., the care of the hospice patient with a fever) withholding an antipyretic drug is considered to be inadequate symptom management by most health care providers. In other settings, e.g., in patients with malignant hyperthermia or heatstroke, giving antipyretics represents a standard of care. To date, however, controlled trials of withholding antipyretics in many illnesses have not been performed.

   Suppression of fever (by induced hypothermia) is recommended for those who have suffered sudden death, stroke, or persistent seizures; however, proof of the effectiveness of lowering the body temperature of stroke victims is based on laboratory data rather than clinical effectiveness. Suppression of fever in young children with viral and bacterial infections is often a comfort for them; yet some researchers have speculated about adverse effects of this common practice, e.g., whether there is a link suppression of fever and autistic disorders. When the choice is made to suppress a fever, it is probably most comfortable to give antipyretics on a regular basis (every 4 or 6 hr) rather than intermittently. Intermittent dosing of antipyretics may produce alternating bouts of chills and sweats, which most patients find unpleasant. Some patients may never mount a fever; this is particularly true of those over 65, who may have serious treatable infections without elevations of body temperature. In older patients, the first indication of inflammatory or infectious illnesses may be a cough, lethargy, anorexia, or alterations in mental status.

⚠️ Aspirin and other salicylates are contraindicated as antipyretics or analgesics in children because of their association with an increased risk of Reye's syndrome. Public and parental education should be provided to make certain this knowledge is widely disseminated.

2. A disease characterized by fever.

African tick bite f. A disease transmitted to humans by ticks of the genus *Amblyomma* infected with *Rickettsia africae*. The disease is found in sub-Saharan Africa and the French West Indies and is characterized by fevers, headache, scabs that form at the site of tick inoculation, and localized lymph node swelling.

biphasic f. An illness characterized by an early elevation in body temperature followed by a later one. It is often caused by systemic bacterial infection.

blackwater f. Bloody urine (hemoglobinuria) that occurs as a complication of falciparum malaria infection. It is the result of red blood cell destruction and the release of hemoglobin. It occurs most commonly in patients who have been treated with drugs derived from quinine. SEE: *falciparum malaria*.

SYMPTOMS: The illness is marked by high fevers, dark urine, epigastric pain, vomiting, jaundice, and shock. Physical findings include enlargement of the liver and spleen. Laboratory hallmarks include severe anemia and, occasionally, renal failure.

boutonneuse f. Mediterranean spotted **f.**

brain f. Meningitis.

childbed f. Puerperal **sepsis**.

Canefield f. Leptospirosis.

Congo-Crimean viral hemorrhagic f. A frequently fatal viral infection found in the Middle East, Africa, and southwestern Asia, characterized by bleeding, diarrhea, hepatitis, high fevers, throat pain, and vomiting. The cause is the Congo-Crimean hemorrhagic fever virus, which is transmitted to humans by ticks or exposure to the blood of infected animals or patients. Ribavirin has been used to treat the disease in some patients.

continuous f. A sustained fever, as in scarlet fever, typhus, or pneumonia, with a slight diurnal variation.

dengue f. Dengue.

dengue hemorrhagic f. ABBR: DHF. A grave sequela of dengue, marked by

fever, headache, myalgia, arthralgias, rash, spontaneous bleeding, increased blood vessel permeability to proteins, and low platelet counts ($<100,000/mm^3$).

drug f. Fever caused by the administration of a drug. Because fevers are more often caused by infections, rheumatological illnesses, or malignancies, the diagnosis of drug fever may be overlooked initially.

Ebola virus hemorrhagic f. An often fatal viral disease that appears in sporadic outbreaks in Africa. The clinical presentation of widespread bleeding into many organs and fever is similar to that seen in Lassa, Marburg, and Congo-Crimean viral hemorrhagic fevers.

ETIOLOGY: The disease is caused by one of three species of Ebola virus, a Filoviridae virus distinguished by long threadlike strands of RNA. The animal host has not been identified, which limits its study of the disease. In each outbreak, the first human infection is believed to be caused by a bite from an infected animal. Subsequent cases are the result of contact with blood or body secretions from an infected person or the reuse of contaminated needles and syringes.

PATIENT CARE: The use of standard barrier precautions prevents transmission, with the addition of leg and shoe covers if large amounts of blood, vomit, or diarrhea are present; negative-pressure isolation rooms are used if available. The spread of Ebola virus between humans by airborne droplets has not been documented, but face masks are recommended if the patient has respiratory symptoms. All equipment must be sterilized before reuse.

SYMPTOMS: The incubation period of 2–3 weeks is followed by sudden onset of high fever, myalgia, diarrhea, headache, fatigue, and abdominal pain; a rash, sore throat, and conjunctivitis may be present. Within 7 days, shock develops, usually associated with hemorrhage; more than 50% of patients die. The patient is infectious after fever appears.

enteric f. Typhoid **f.**

epidemic hemorrhagic f. Hemorrhagic **nephrosonephritis**.

factitious f. Fever produced artificially by a patient. This is done by artificially heating the thermometer or by self-administered pyrogenic substances. An artificial fever may be suspected if the pulse rate is much less than expected for the degree of fever noted. This diagnosis should be considered in all patients in whom there is no other plausible explanation for the fever. Patients who pretend to have fevers may have serious psychiatric problems. SEE: *facti-*

tious disorder; malinger; Munchausen syndrome.

familial Hibernian f. A rare autosomal dominant syndrome characterized by intermittent elevations of body temperature, muscle pains, abdominal pain, inguinal hernias, and rash. SYN: *TNF receptor associated periodic syndrome.*

familial Mediterranean f. An autosomal recessive disorder in which patients suffer repeated febrile illnesses without evidence of infection. It occurs most often in people of Middle Eastern or Italian descent. Symptomatic attacks typically begin in children between 5 and 15 and often consist of fever, joint pains, abdominal pain resembling peritonitis, pleurisy or pericarditis, and rashes (although individual symptoms may vary). Duration and frequency of the attacks can be unpredictable. About 40% of patients ultimately develop amyloidosis. SYN: *periodic f.; recurrent polyserositis.*

Flinders island spotted f. ABBR: FISF. A spotted fever transmitted to humans by the bite of *Ixodes* ticks infected with *Ricksettsia honei.* It is found primarily in Victoria and Tasmania, Australia, and is similar to Rocky Mountain Spotted Fever in the U.S.

Fort Bragg f. Pretibial **f.**

Haverhill f. Rat-bite **f.**

hay f. A seasonal illness, marked by sneezing, sniffling, runny nose, and itchy or watery eyes. This condition, which affects 10% to 20% of the U.S. population, results from a type I hypersensitivity reaction involving the mucous membranes of the nose and upper air passages. It is the most common manifestation of atopic (inherited) allergy. SYN: *allergic rhinitis; pollinosis.* SEE: *allergen; desensitization; hypersensitivity reaction; Nursing Diagnoses Appendix.*

ETIOLOGY: Airborne pollens, fungal spores, dust, and animal dander cause hay fever. It is most commonly triggered in the spring by pollen from trees, in the summer by grass pollen, and in the fall by pollen from wildflowers, e.g., ragweed. Nonseasonal rhinitis may result from inhalation of animal dander, dust from hay or straw, or house dust mites.

TREATMENT: Seasonal usage of antihistamines, cromolyn, and corticosteroid nasal sprays are the usual therapy in the U.S. Prophylaxis through desensitization is also useful but is less convenient and usually more expensive. Avoiding allergens is also effective but not always possible.

⚠ Overuse of corticosteroids may damage the nasal mucosa, and absorption of the drug can cause adverse side effects.

humidifier f. Allergic alveolitis caused by exposure to inhaled antigens and marked by flulike symptoms. SEE: *alveolitis.* SYN: *humidifier lung.*

induced f. Fever produced artificially to treat certain diseases such as central nervous system syphilis. Sustained fever of 105°F (40.5°C), or even higher, maintained for 6 to 8 or 10 hr may be induced by medical diathermy or injection of malarial parasites.

intermittent f. Fever in which symptoms disappear completely between paroxysms. SEE: *malaria; undulant f.*

Japanese spotted f. A spotted fever transmitted to humans by the bite of *Ixodes* ticks infected with *Rickettsia japonica.* The disease has been identified mostly in Japan and Korea.

Karelian f. An infectious disease caused by the Sindbis virus and marked by influenza-like symptoms and rashes, esp. blistering rashes on the hands and feet. A postinfectious arthritis sometimes follows.

Katayama f. A systemic allergic reaction to invasion of the body by *Schistosoma* larvae. It is marked by fevers, an urticarial rash, cough, enlargement of the lymph nodes and viscera, and eosinophilia.

Korean hemorrhagic f. Hemorrhagic **nephrosonephritis.**

Lassa f. A potentially lethal viral illness marked by hemorrhage, extreme muscle pain, and, in some cases, shock. It is contracted only in Africa. The responsible agent, an arenavirus, is spread to people after contact with infected rodents or their urine or feces. Each year, approx. 300,000 people are infected.

SYMPTOMS: Patients have abrupt onset of high fever that is continuous or intermittent and spiking, with generalized myalgia, chest and abdominal pain, headache, sore throat, cough, dizziness with flushing of the face, conjunctival injection, nausea, diarrhea, and vomiting. Hemorrhagic areas of the skin and mucous membranes may appear on the fourth day. Mortality of those in Africa with this disease varies from 16% to 45%.

TREATMENT: Ribavirin given in the first week of illness and continued for 10 days has been very effective in reducing the death rate. This medicine should also be given orally for 10 days prophylactically to those who have been percutaneously exposed to the virus. Patients are isolated in special isolation units that filter the air leaving the room and maintain negative pressure. All sputum, blood, excreta, and objects that the patient has handled are disinfected. SEE: *Standard Precautions Appendix.*

Malta f. Brucellosis.

Mediterranean f. Brucellosis.

Mediterranean spotted f. An infectious, occasionally fatal illness transmitted to humans by ticks infected with *Rickettsia conorii.* The disease is clinically similar to Rocky Mountain spotted fever. SYN: *boutonneuse f.*

metal fume f. A syndrome resembling influenza, produced by inhalation of excessive concentrations of metallic oxide fumes such as zinc oxide or antimony, arsenic, brass, cadmium, cobalt, copper, iron, lead, magnesium, manganese, mercury, nickel, or tin. It occurs in those whose occupations lead to exposure to these metals. SEE: *polymer fume f.*

SYMPTOMS: The onset of symptoms is usually delayed. There are chills, weakness, lassitude, and profound thirst, followed some hours later by sweating and anorexia. Occasionally, there is mild inflammation of the eyes and respiratory tract. The symptoms are more acute at the beginning of the work week than at the end. This is felt to be due to the individual's adapting to the fumes as exposure continues.

FIRST AID: Therapy includes analgesics, antipyretics, and rest.

neutropenic f. Fever associated with an abnormally low neutrophil level, usually caused by infection. This condition is treated with empirical antibiotic therapy pending the results of cultures. Neutropenia has many causes, including chemotherapy, radiation exposure, aplastic anemia, bone marrow infiltration from malignancy, and complications of bone marrow transplantation. The risk of potentially life-threatening infection is substantial when the absolute neutrophil count is below $500/\text{mm}^3$.

Oroya f. A clinical form of bartonellosis. It is an acute, potentially life-threatening disease endemic in Peru and other South American countries, characterized by high intermittent fever, lymphadenopathy, severe anemia, and pains in the joints and long bones. If untreated, the fever has a 10% to 90% fatality rate. SEE: *bartonellosis.*

paratyphoid f. A rare form of febrile gastroenteritis in Western societies, marked by fevers, abdominal pain, diarrhea, headache, and occasionally intestinal perforation. It is caused by *Salmonella paratyphi* (A and B strains) and related *Salmonella* species, typically contracted by travelers who have visited tropical countries. Antibiotic treatments include ciprofloxacin or chloramphenicol.

Pel-Ebstein f. SEE: *Pel-Ebstein fever.*

periodic f. Familial Mediterranean fever.

phlebotomus f. Sandfly **f.**

Pontiac f. An infection with Legionella species that causes fevers, chills, headache, muscle aches, gastrointestinal upset, and prostration but not pneumonia.

puerperal f. Puerperal **sepsis**.

Q f. An acute infectious disease characterized by headache, fever, severe sweating, malaise, myalgia, and anorexia. Q fever is caused by rickettsia, *Coxiella burnetii,* an intracellular, gram-negative bacterium, and is contracted by inhaling infected dust, drinking unpasteurized milk from infected animals, or handling infected animals such as goats, cows, or sheep. Transmission by human contact is rare but has occurred. An effective vaccine is available for the prevention of infection for those who have a good chance of being exposed to the disease. Tetracyclines are used to treat the infection. SYN: *Query f.*

Query f. Q **f.**

rabbit f. Tularemia.

rat-bite f. Either of two infectious diseases transmitted by the bite of a rat. One is caused by *Streptobacillus moniliformis* and is marked by skin inflammation, fever, chills, headache, vomiting, and back and joint pain. The other is caused by *Spirillum minus* and is associated with ulceration, rash, and recurrent fever. The latter disease is rare in the U.S. SYN: *Haverhill f.; sodokosis; sodoku.*

TREATMENT: Both diseases are treated with penicillin. Therapy is most effective when penicillin is given intravenously for 1 week, then orally for 1 week. Tetanus prophylaxis is also administered.

relapsing f. Borreliosis.

remittent f. A pattern of fever that varies over a 24-hr period but does not return to normal. SEE: *malaria.*

rheumatic f. A multisystem, febrile inflammatory disease that is a delayed complication of untreated group A streptococcal pharyngitis (strep throat). It is believed to be caused by an autoimmune response to bacterial antigens in the streptococci although the precise mechanism responsible for the illness has not been identified. Primarily seen in children between ages 5 and 15, the disease is now uncommon in Western societies because of effective and prompt treatment for strep throat, but it remains a major cause of morbidity in the developing world. SEE: *Nursing Diagnoses Appendix.*

SYMPTOMS: After a pharyngeal infection with group A streptococci, some patients experience sudden fever and joint pain. Other symptoms include migratory joint pains, pain on motion, abdominal pain, chorea, and cardiac involvement (pericarditis, myocarditis, and endocarditis). Precordial discomfort and heart murmurs develop suddenly. Skin manifestations include erythema marginatum or circinatum and the development of subcutaneous nodules.

Rheumatic fever may occur without any sign or symptom of joint involvement. Two major manifestations (carditis, polyarthritis, chorea, erythema marginatum, subcutaneous nodules) or one major and two minor criteria (fever of at least 100.4°F [38°C], arthralgia, previous rheumatic fever, elevated erythrocyte sedimentation rate or positive C-reactive protein, prolonged P-R interval) are required to establish the diagnosis of acute rheumatic fever.

PROPHYLAXIS: Prompt and adequate treatment of streptococcal infections with oral penicillin or cephalosporin is given for at least 10 days. Erythromycin or sulfa drugs are substituted in patients with penicillin allergy.

To prevent recurrence of rheumatic fever in a patient who has already been affected by the disease, benzathine benzylpenicillin is given intramuscularly every 3 or 4 weeks. Low-dose oral penicillin, erythromycin, or sulfa drugs are alternatives for compliant patients.

TREATMENT: Salicylates, acetaminophen, and NSAIDs are used to lower fever, reduce inflammation, and alleviate pain. Corticosteroids may be needed if the salicylates, acetaminophen, and NSAIDs do not relieve inflammation in patients with carditis. Diuretics and other cardiac medications are prescribed as necessary to treat heart failure. Severe heart valve dysfunction requires surgical correction but usually not until late adolescence or adulthood. Patients known to have carditis who must undergo dental or surgical procedures, esp. those involving instrumentation of the urinary tract, rectum, or colon, should receive additional antibiotic coverage on the day of the procedure and for several days thereafter.

PATIENT CARE: During the acute phase, diversional activities that are not physically demanding are offered; family and friends are encouraged to visit; a tutor ought to be provided to help the child stay current with school work. The child and family are taught about the disease and treatment, and all diagnostic measures are described. The child and family are also taught about signs of recurrent streptococcal infection and of heart failure, which require immediate reporting and treatment. Health care professionals advise the patient about lifestyle and activity modifications, as well as the importance of taking prescribed antibiotics for the full course of treatment and prophylaxis. The child and family are informed about symptoms of hypersensitivity reaction to the antibiotic and are advised to stop the drug and immediately and to notify the primary care provider if a rash, fever, chills, or other signs of allergy develop anytime during the course of therapy. The importance of maintaining a salt-restricted diet and of adhering to treatment with diuretics, digoxin, or afterload-reducing drugs is emphasized for patients with congestive heart failure. The American Heart Association provides educational materials and current protocol for prevention of bacterial endocarditis, which is different from the RF regimen used to prevent recurrence. (800-AHA-USA1; www.americanheartr.org).

Rocky Mountain spotted f. An infectious disease caused by the bacterium *Rickettsia ricketsii* and transmitted by the wood tick *Dermacentor andersoni* or *D. variabilis*. Originally thought to exist only in the western U.S., it can occur anywhere that the tick vector is present.

The organism causes fever, headache, myalgia, and a characteristic vasculitic rash. The rash appears several days after the other symptoms, first erupting on the wrists and ankles, then on the palms and soles. It is nonpruritic and macular and spreads to the legs, arms, trunk, and face. Disseminated intravascular coagulation or pneumonia may be serious complications. Tetracyclines are the drug of choice for treating this disease, but their use in pregnant women is not advised. Chloramphenicol may be substituted.

People living in areas with wood ticks should wear clothing that covers much of their bodies, including the neck, to prevent ticks from attaching to the skin. People who live in or travel to areas where ticks flourish should examine their scalps, skin, and clothing daily. Ticks should be grasped close to the mouthparts (not on the tick's body), as close to their point of attachment to their human host as possible. Pets should be examined regularly for ticks.

rose f. Hay fever of early summer attributed to inhaling rose pollen. SEE: *hay f.*

sandfly f. A mild viral disease that clinically resembles influenza. The causative organism is any of several species of Bunyaviridae viruses and is transmitted by the common sandfly *Phlebotomus papatasi*. The disease occurs in tropical and subtropical areas that have long periods of hot, dry weather. Several antiviral drugs (e.g., alpha interferon and ribavirin) have some effect against the disease. SYN: *pappataci f.; phlebotomus f.; three-day f.*

San Joaquin valley f. Coccidioidomycosis.

scarlet f. An acute, contagious disease characterized by pharyngitis and a pimply red rash. It is caused by group A beta-hemolytic streptococcus and usually affects children between 3 and 15.

SYN: *scarlatina; second disease.* SEE: *Nursing Diagnoses Appendix.*

ETIOLOGY: The disease is caused by more than 40 strains of group A, beta-hemolytic streptococci that elaborate an erythrogenic toxin.

SYMPTOMS: After an incubation period of 1 to 7 days, children develop a fever, chills, vomiting, abdominal pain, and malaise. The pharynx and tonsils are swollen and red, and an exudate is present. Initially the tongue is white, with red, swollen papilla (*white strawberry tongue*); within 5 days, the white disappears, creating a red strawberry tongue. A red pinpoint rash that blanches on pressure with a sandpapery texture appears on the trunk (chest to neck, abdomen, legs and arms, sparing soles and palms) within 12 hr after the onset of fever. Cheeks are flushed, with pallor surrounding the mouth. Faint lines in the elbow creases, called Pastia's lines, are characteristic findings in full-blown disease. Over several days, sloughing of the skin begins, which lasts approx. 3 weeks.

INCUBATION: The incubation period is probably never less than 24 hr. It may be 1 to 3 days, and rarely longer.

TREATMENT: Scarlet fever is treated with 10 days of penicillin (or erythromycin for those allergic to penicillin). A full course of therapy is vital to decrease the risk of rheumatic fever or glomerulonephritis. In general, patients are taught to isolate the infected child from siblings until they have received penicillin for 24 hr.

PATIENT CARE: Good hand hygiene techniques and proper disposal of tissues with purulent discharge are emphasized. The parents also are advised about the importance of administering the prescribed antibiotic as directed for the entire course of treatment even if the child looks and feels better. Because the child may be irritable and restless, the parents are taught how to encourage the child rest and relax. The child should be kept occupied with age-appropriate books, games, toys, and television.

Sennetsu f. A form of ehrlichiosis first identified in Japan, transmitted to humans by tick bite or, possibly, consumption of infected raw fish, and caused by *Ehrlichia sennetsu*. Symptoms include fever, malaise, backache, and lymphadenopathy.

snail f. Schistosomiasis.

spotted f. A general, imprecise name for a variety of infectious diseases (including typhus and rickettsial illnesses) characterized by fever and rash. SEE: *Rocky Mountain spotted f.*

spring f. A feeling of rejuvenation or increased sex drive that affects some people in the spring.

three-day f. Sandfly fever.

trench f. A disease characterized by fever, headache, malaise, pain, tenderness (esp. in the shins), splenomegaly, and, often, a transient macular rash. The causative agent is *Bartonella quintana*. The disease is rarely encountered in industrialized nations, except among the homeless; it is prevalent in many developing nations. The disease is treated with doxycycline 100 mg administered orally, twice a day. SYN: *Wolhynia f.*

typhoid f. A severe infectious disease marked by fever and septicemia, caused by *Salmonella typhi*. The CDC reports 400 cases per year in the U.S., mostly among travelers. An estimated 21 million cases of typhoid fever and 200,000 deaths occur worldwide because it is endemic in areas of poor sanitation. SYN: *enteric f.* SEE: *typhoid* **vaccine**.

SYMPTOMS: Gastrointestinal symptoms may develop within 1 hr of ingestion of *S.,* but they usually subside before the onset of the typhoid fever symptoms. The disease is marked initially by a gradually increasing fever up to 104°F (40°C), anorexia, malaise, myalgia, headache, and slow pulse for about 7 days, followed by remittent fever up to 104°F (40°C) that usually occurs in the evening, a flat, rose-colored, fleeting rash (primarily on the abdomen), chills and sweating, increasing abdominal pain and distention, diarrhea or constipation, generalized lymphadenopathy, abdominal pain, anorexia, weakness, and exhaustion, cough and moist crackles, a tender abdomen with enlarged spleen, and delirium as the bacteria spread through the bloodstream. About 14 days after the infection begins, persistent fever and increased weakness and fatigue are present but usually subside by about 21 days into the illness although relapses may occur. Internal bleeding usually develops due to gastrointestinal ulcers, abscesses, and intestinal perforation; this may lead to hypovolemic shock. Damage to the liver and spleen is common. In approx. 10% of patients, typhoid fever is complicated by pneumonia, thrombophlebitis, osteomyelitis, septic arthritis, cerebral thrombosis, meningitis, myocarditis, or acute circulatory failure, which account for most of the deaths.

ETIOLOGY: The *Salmonella* enters the gastrointestinal tract, infects the biliary tract, invades the lymphoid tissues and walls of the ileum and colon, seeds the intestinal tract with millions of bacilli, and then gains access to the bloodstream. The disease is most commonly transmitted via the fecal-oral route through water or food contaminated by human feces, but it can be spread also by vomitus and oral secretions during the acute stage. Unlike *S. enteritidis*, it lives only in humans. A small percentage of people become carriers after recovering from infection.

DIFFERENTIAL DIAGNOSIS: Paratyphoid, pneumonia, dysentery, meningitis, smallpox, and appendicitis are among the differential diagnoses. Diagnostic points of value are the presence of rose spots, splenomegaly, leukopenia, the Widal serological test result, blood culture, and examination of feces for the presence of the causative organism. The best means of providing bacterial confirmation is through bone marrow culture. This method is successful even after patients have received antibiotics. SEE: *paratyphoid f.*

TREATMENT: The disease is treated with ciprofloxacin or other antimicrobials based on organism sensitivity testing for 10 days. Dexamethasone is administered a few minutes before antibiotics are given in patients with shock or decreased levels of consciousness. Travelers should be aware that the most important safeguards are good food handling and water sanitation. The CDC recommends vaccination with typhoid vaccine, which is available in a live attenuated oral and parenteral form and intramuscular form for people traveling to developing countries in Africa, Asia, the Indian subcontinent, Central and South America, and the Caribbean. The oral vaccine is taken in multiple doses, with adults and children over 6 prescribed one capsule every other day for a total of four doses. Each dose should be taken 1 hr before a meal with cool water, and the capsules kept in the refrigerator. The one-dose parenteral vaccine may be used as an option for children 2 to 6, for the immunocompromised, and for those who might not adhere to the oral regimen. Vaccination protects only 50% to 80% of those vaccinated; therefore all travelers should protect themselves by following the adage, "boil it, cook it, peel it, or forget it." The vaccinations should be completed at least 1 week before the trip; boosters are required every 2 to 5 yrs, depending on the type of vaccine. The vaccinations should not be given to patients who are taking mefloquine for malaria prophylaxis. SEE: *Standard Precautions Appendix.*

PATIENT CARE: Contact precautions (handwashing, patient handwashing, glove and gown for disposal of feces or fecally contaminated objects) are followed until three consecutive stool cultures at 24-hr intervals are negative. Drugs are administered as prescribed, and the patient is observed for signs of complications, e.g., bacteremia, intestinal bleeding, and bowel perforation. During the acute phase, the temperature is monitored, but antipyretics are usually not administered because these mask the fever and can result in hypothermia; tepid sponge baths are also provided to promote vasodilation without shivering. The incontinent patient is cleansed, and high fluid intake (oral or intravenous) is encouraged to maintain adequate hydration. Fluid and electrolyte balance is monitored. Adequate nutrition is maintained. Rest is encouraged and oral hygiene and skin care provided. Abscesses may have to be drained surgically. The caregiver explains the importance of follow-up care and examination to ensure that the patient is not a carrier.

If the patient's stool cultures are still positive at the time of discharge, he should be careful to use good hand hygiene, esp. after defecating, and should avoid preparation of uncooked foods, e.g., salads, for family members. Those who retain positive cultures (asymptomatic carrier state) should not be employed as food handlers. All cases of typhoid fever should be reported to the state health department. While traveling in endemic areas, people should be careful to buy bottled water or boil tap water for 5 min before drinking, cooking, or brushing teeth with it; they should avoid ice in beverages and desserts and treats containing ice; eat well-cooked foods that are still steaming hot; avoid raw food, including garden or fruit salads. Before eating fresh fruit, people should wash their hands vigorously, wash the outside of the fruit, then peel the fruit, and they should avoid food sold by street vendors.

undulant f. Brucellosis.

f. of unknown origin ABBR: FUO. An illness of at least 3 weeks' duration with fever exceeding 100.9°F (38.3°C) on several occasions and diagnosis not established after 1 week of hospital investigation. The main causes are systemic and localized infections, neoplasms, or collagen-vascular diseases, e.g., rheumatoid arthritis, disseminated lupus erythematosus, and polyarteritis nodosa. Less common causes are granulomatous disease, inflammatory disease of the bowel, pulmonary embolization, drug fever, cirrhosis, and rare conditions such as Whipple's disease. Diseases such as AIDS, chronic fatigue syndrome, or Lyme disease are occasionally the cause of FUO. Some cases remain undiagnosed.

valley f. Coccidioidomycosis.

viral hemorrhagic f. ABBR: VHF. Any of a group of diseases caused by arthropod-borne viruses, esp. the Bunyaviridae group, including Alkhurma, Congo-Crimean, Ebola, Lassa, Marburg, and Rift Valley hemorrhagic fever viruses.

Wolhynia f. Trench **f.**

yellow f. Either of two forms of an acute, infectious disease caused by a flavivirus and transmitted by species of the *Aedes* mosquito. It is endemic in Western Africa, Brazil, and the Amazon region of South America but is no longer present in the U.S.

There are two forms of yellow fever: *urban,* in which the transmission cycle is mosquito to human to mosquito; and *sylvan,* in which the reservoir is wild primates.

According to the World Health Organization, yellow fever afflicts about 200,000 people a year in Africa and South America, about 30,000 of whom die.

ETIOLOGY: The virus is carried most commonly by the *Aedes aegypti* mosquito, but the *A. vittatus* and *A. taylori* mosquitoes also are important vectors.

SYMPTOMS: After an incubation period of 3 to 6 days, patients develop high fever, headache, muscle aches, nausea and vomiting, and gastrointestinal disturbances such as diarrhea or constipation. In most patients, the disease resolves in 2 or 3 days, but in about 20% the fever returns after a 1 to 2 day remission and is accompanied by abdominal pain, severe diarrhea, gastrointestinal bleeding (producing a characteristic black vomit), anuria, and jaundice (hence the name *yellow fever*) caused by liver infection. Rarely, there is progressive liver failure, renal failure, and death.

Yellow fever can be distinguished from dengue by the presence of jaundice, and from malaria by the absence of splenomegaly and low serum transaminase levels. Blood tests can identify the virus and its antigens, to which antibodies are formed in 5 to 7 days. A liver biopsy to isolate the virus is contraindicated because of the risk of bleeding.

LABORATORY FINDINGS: As in many viral infections, the white blood cell count and platelet count may be suppressed. The erythrocyte sedimentation rate is rarely elevated. In severely ill patients with jaundice or renal failure, the serum bilirubin and creatinine levels are elevated.

DIAGNOSIS: Diagnosis on clinical grounds alone is almost impossible during the period of infection or in atypical mild forms. Yellow fever viral antigen or antibodies may be detected during the acute phase of the illness.

PROPHYLAXIS: Preventive measures include mosquito control by screening, spraying with nontoxic insecticides, and destruction of breeding areas. Yellow fever vaccine prepared from the 17D strain is available for those who plan to travel or live in areas where the disease is endemic. The vaccine is contraindicated in infants under 4 months old and in women in the first trimester of pregnancy.

TREATMENT: No antiviral agents are effective against the yellow fever virus. Fluids are given to maintain fluid and electrolyte balance, acetaminophen to reduce fever, and histamine blockers, e.g., ranitidine or gastric acid pump inhibitors, e.g., omeprazole to decrease the risk of gastrointestinal bleeding. Vitamin K is given if there is decreased production of prothrombin by the liver.

A live virus vaccine, which can be obtained only at designated vaccination centers, may be given to adults and children over 9 months old who are traveling to countries where yellow fever is endemic; the vaccine is effective for 10 years, after which a booster is required. Those who are immunosuppressed, pregnant, or allergic to eggs should not receive the vaccine. Travelers must determine if the country they are visiting has regulations about vaccination.

PROGNOSIS: The prognosis is grave. Mortality is 5% in an area where the disease is endemic.

fever blister SEE: under *blister*.

feverfew (fee'věr-fū) A perennial herb (*Tanacetum parthenium*) grown as an ornamental plant and promoted to treat rheumatologic illnesses and to prevent migraines.

fexofenadine (fĕk″sō-fĕn'ĭ-dēn) A piperidine, administered orally to treat colds and coughs, relieve symptoms of seasonal allergic rhinitis, and to manage chronic idiopathic urticaria. Its therapeutic classes are allergy, cold, and cough remedies and antihistamines.

FFB *flexible fiber-optic bronchoscope.*

fFN *Fetal fibronectin.*

ffNA *Free fetal nucleic **acid**.*

FFPE *formalin-fixed, paraffin-embedded.*

FFR *Fractional flow **reserve**.*

FGR *Fetal growth restriction.*

FH₄ *5,6,7,8-tetrahydrofolic acid* (folacin).

FHPE *Focused history and physical examination.*

FHx *Family **history**.*

fiat (fī'ăt) [L.] Let there be made, a term used in writing prescriptions.

fiber (fī'běr) [L. *fibra,* filament, fiber] **1.** A threadlike or filmlike structure, e.g., a nerve fiber. **2.** A neuron or its axonal portion. **3.** An elongated threadlike structure. It may be cellular as nerve fiber or muscle fiber, or may be a cellular product, as collagen, elastic, oxytalan, or reticular fiber. **4.** A slender cellulosic structure derived from plants such as cotton. SEE: *rayon, purified*.

A f. A heavily myelinated, fast-conducting nerve fiber.

afferent f. A nerve fiber that carries sensory impulses to the central nervous system from receptors in the periphery.

cholinergic f. Any preganglionic,

postganglionic parasympathetic, postganglionic sympathetic fiber to a sweat gland, or efferent fiber to skeletal muscle.

circular f. Collagen bundles in the gingiva that surround a tooth.

climbing f. An excitatory axon from the inferior olivary nucleus that synapses with dendrites of Purkinje cells in the cerebellar cortex

dietary f. The components of food that resist chemical digestion, including cellulose, hemicellulose, lignin, gums, mucilages, and pectin. Dietary fibers are classified according to their solubility in water.

Water-insoluble fibers include cellulose, lignin, and some hemicelluloses. These substances can soften and increase the bulk of the bowel movement. Natural gel-forming fibers found in fruits and vegetables such as gums, mucilages, and some hemicelluloses are water soluble. Most foods of plant origin contain both soluble and insoluble dietary fiber. Many disease processes including constipation, diabetes mellitus, gallstones, hemorrhoids, high blood pressure, irritable bowel syndrome, and obesity have been shown to be ameliorated by a high-fiber diet. There are epidemiological data supporting the existence of an inverse relationship between the disease and dietary fiber consumption. The relation between fiber intake and colorectal cancer is complex; some studies suggest that fiber intake is protective, while others suggest that it is not.

Foods rich in fiber include wholegrain foods, bran flakes, beans, fruits, leafy vegetables, nuts, root vegetables and their skins.

efferent f. A nerve fiber that carries motor impulses from the central nervous system to effector organs.

extrafusal f.s The muscle fibers surrounding a muscle spindle.

fermentable f. Soluble **f.**

gingival f. Collagen fibers that support the marginal or interdental gingiva and are adapted to the tooth surface.

inhibitory f. A nerve fiber that carries impulses to decrease heart rate.

insoluble f. Any dietary fiber that does not dissolve in water. Insoluble dietary fiber includes hemicellulose, cellulose, and lignin. An example is wheat bran.

intercolumnar f. An intercrural fiber, part of the superficial inguinal ring.

interradicular f. The collagen fibers of the periodontal ligament in the interradicular area, attaching the tooth to alveolar bone.

intrafusal muscle f. The structural component of the muscle spindle, made up of small skeletal muscle fibers at either end and a central noncontracile region where the sensory receptors are located.

James f.s SEE: *James* *fibers*.

Mahaim f.s SEE: *Mahaim* *fibers*.

man-made f. A synthetic fiber made from chemicals, e.g., rayon or polyester. SYN: *synthetic* **f.**

Müller fibers SEE: under *Müller, Heinrich.*

mossy f. An excitatory axon from outside the cerebellum that synapses in the granular layer of the cerebellar cortex. Mossy fiber terminals are the central elements in complex synaptic formations that include dendrites of granular neurons and neurites of Golgi cells.

motor f. Any of the axons of motor neurons that innervate skeletal muscles.

muscle f. A muscle cell in striated, smooth, or cardiac muscle.

myelinated f. A nerve fiber whose axon (dendrite) is wrapped in a myelin sheath.

nerve f. SEE: *nerve fiber*.

nigrostriatal f.s Nigrostriate **bundle.**

nonmedullated f. Unmyelinated **f.**

oxytalan f. Bundles of thin, acid-resistant fibrils found in the periodontium.

preganglionic f. The axon of a preganglionic neuron.

principal f. The major fiber groups of the functioning periodontium. They attach the tooth to the bone and adjacent teeth.

propriospinal f. Axons that connect regions of the spinal cord.

Purkinje f. SEE: under *Purkinje, Johannes E. von.*

reticular f. Any of the extremely fine argyrophilic (silver-staining) fibers found in reticular tissue.

soluble f. Any dietary fiber that dissolves in water. Soluble fiber is metabolized by bacteria in the gastrointestinal tract into short chain fatty acids, which in turn nourish commensal bacteria in the gut. Examples include most fruit and vegetable fibers, e.g., pectins, barley, cereal grains, cornmeal, and oats. SEE: *fermentable* **f.**

transseptal f. Any of the collagenous fibers that extend between the teeth and are embedded in the cementum of adjacent teeth.

unmyelinated f. A nerve fiber that lacks a myelin sheath, although a neurilemma may be present in the peripheral nervous system. SYN: *nonmedullated* **f.**

zonular f. Any of the interlacing fibers of the zonula ciliaris.

fiberglass, fiber glass (fī'bĕr-glas″) Material made from fine fibers of glass and having many industrial uses, e.g., as insulation. The fibers are irritating and potentially damaging to the skin and lungs. Fiberglass is used in health care in the construction of orthopedic casts and splints. SYN: *fibrous glass*.

fiber illumination SEE: under *illumination*.

fiberoptic endoscopic evaluation of swallowing ABBR: FEES. A bedside diagnostic test to evaluate dysphagia. In the procedure a small endoscope is advanced through the nasal passages to the back of the throat, where it can directly visualize the movement of foods through the esophagus (or, in cases of aspiration, into the larynx or lower airways). The test is esp. useful in debilitated or intensive care patients who may not be able to swallow barium in the radiology suite for videofluoroscopy.

fiberoptic endoscopic evaluation of swallowing with sensory testing ABBR: FEESST. A fiberoptic endoscopic evaluation of swallowing (FEES) test in which pulses of air are used to assess the responsiveness of the laryngeal muscles to stimulation.

fiberoptics (fī″bĕr-op′tiks) [*fiber* + *optics*] SEE: *fiber* **optics**. **fiber-optic** (fī″bĕr-op′tik), *adj*.

fiberscope (fī′bĕr-skōp) A flexible endoscope that uses fiberoptics for visualization.

fibrate (fī′brāt″) Any of a class of carboxylic acid compounds commonly used as lipid-lowering medications, including gemfibrozil and fenofibrate, that primarily reduce levels of triglycerides. Medications of this class have a minor impact on low-density and high-density lipoprotein cholesterol. SYN: *fibric acid derivative*.

fibremia (fī-brē′mē-ă) [″ + Gr. *haima*, blood] Fibrin formed in the blood, causing embolism or thrombosis. SYN: *inosemia*.

fibric acid derivative (fī′brik) Fibrate.

fibril (fī′brĭl) [L. *fibrilla*] **1.** A small fiber. **2.** A very small filamentous structure, often the component of a cell or a fiber.
   muscle f. Myofibril.
   nerve f. Neurofibril.

fibrilla (fī-brĭl′ă) *pl*. **fibrillae** [L.] A fibril or small fiber.

fibrillar, fibrillary (fĭb′rĭ-lăr, fĭb′rĭ-ler″ē) Pert. to or consisting of fibrils.

fibrillated (fī′brĭ-lāt′d) [L. *fibrilla*, little fiber] Composed of minute fibers.

fibrillation (fīb″rĭ-lā′shŏn, fīb″) [*fibrilla*] **1.** Formation of fibrils. **2.** Quivering or spontaneous contraction of individual muscle fibers. **3.** An abnormal bioelectric potential occurring in neuropathies and myopathies.
   atrial f. ABBR: AF. The most common cardiac dysrhythmia, affecting as many as 5 to 10% of people age 70 and over. It is marked by rapid, irregular electrical activity in the atria, resulting in ineffective ejection of blood into the ventricles and an irregular ventricular

response (apical pulse rate). Blood that eddies in the atria may occasionally form clots that may embolize, esp. to the brain, but also to other organs. As a result, AF is an important risk factor for stroke. In the U.S., about 75,000 strokes occur each year in patients with AF. AF may also contribute to other diseases and conditions, including congestive heart failure, dyspnea on exertion, and syncope.

ETIOLOGY: AF may occur in otherwise healthy persons with no structural heart disease (*lone* AF), e.g., during stress or exercise. It may also develop *secondary to* alcohol withdrawal; in patients with underlying arrhythmias (such as tachybrady syndrome or Wolff-Parkinson-White syndrome); after cardiac surgery; during cocaine intoxication; in hypertensive urgencies, hypoxia, or hypercarbia (carbon dioxide retention); during myocardial infarction; in pericarditis and pulmonary embolism; or as a consequence of congestive heart failure, chronic obstructive pulmonary disease, sepsis, or thyrotoxicosis or other metabolic disorders. Chronic AF, also known as persistent, permanent, or sustained AF, usually occurs in patients with structural abnormalities of the heart, such as cardiomyopathies; enlargement of the left atrium; mitral valve disease; or rheumatic heart disease. Paroxysmal AF is AF that occurs intermittently and resolves spontaneously. Recurrent AF is a term used to describe two or more episodes of AF occurring in the same person.

SYMPTOMS: Some patients may not notice rapid or irregular beating of their heart even though the ventricular rate rises to 200 bpm. Most patients, however, report some of the following symptoms at slower heart rates (100 bpm or greater): dizziness, dyspnea, palpitations, presyncope, or syncope.

DIAGNOSIS: Patients who present with their first episode of atrial fibrillation are typically evaluated with thyroid function tests, cardiac enzymes, a complete blood count, and blood chemistries. In patients with a cardiac murmur or evidence of congestive heart failure, echocardiography is typically performed.

TREATMENT: The acutely ill (unstable) patient with a rapid ventricular response (>150/m) and signs or symptoms of angina pectoris, congestive heart failure, hypotension, or hypoxia should be prepared for immediate cardioversion. Patients who are stable and tolerate the rhythm disturbance without these signs or symptoms are typically treated first with drugs to slow the heart rhythm, e.g., calcium-channel blockers, beta blockers, or digoxin. For most patients with atrial fibrillation with a rapid ventricular response, controlling the rapid heart rate alleviates symptoms. Electrical or chemical cardioversion of initial episodes of atrial fibrillation may successfully restore sinus rhythm, often for a period of several months to as long as a year but does not affect morbidity or mortality. Anticoagulation (as with warfarin, which requires frequent dosage adjustments and close monitoring, or with factor Xa inhibitors, which do not) markedly reduces the risk of stroke in atrial fibrillation. Warfarin or related vitamin K antagonists should be given for several weeks before, and about a week after, elective cardioversion, and to patients in chronic AF who do not return to sinus rhythm with treatment. Patients who elect not to use anticoagulants or factor Xa inhibitors for chronic AF, or for whom these agents pose too great a risk of bleeding, are usually given 325 mg of aspirin daily. AF can also be treated with radiofrequency catheter ablation, or with surgical techniques to isolate the source of the rhythm disturbance in the atria or pulmonary veins. SEE: *ablation*.

PATIENT CARE: The acutely ill patient is placed on bedrest and monitored closely, with frequent assessments of vital signs, oxygen saturation, heart rate and rhythm, and 12-lead electrocardiography. Supplemental oxygen is supplied and intravenous access established. Preparations for cardioversion (if necessary) and the medications prescribed for the patient are explained. Patients should be carefully introduced to the risks, benefits, and alternatives to stroke prevention with anticoagulation. Stroke is one of the most serious complications for patients with atrial fibrillation. The risk of embolic stroke in AF is about 5% annually without anticoagulation but lower with it. However, the use of anticoagulants increases the risk of bleeding. Patients treated with anticoagulants should maintain an International Normalized Ratio (INR) in the 2.0 to 3.0 range. Regular assessment of the INR reduces the hazard of serious bleeding.

lone atrial f. Atrial fibrillation that is not caused by or associated with underlying disease of the heart muscle, heart valves, coronary arteries, pulmonary circulation, or thyroid gland. Prognosis seems better for this type of atrial fibrillation than for that which results from anatomical or metabolic abnormalities.

paroxysmal atrial f. Intermittent episodes of atrial fibrillation.

ventricular f. ABBR: VFIB. A treatable but lethal dysrhythmia present in nearly half of all cases of cardiac arrest. It is marked on the electrocardiogram by rapid, chaotic nonrepetitive waveforms; and clinically by the absence of effective circulation of blood (pulselessness). Rapid defibrillation (applying unsynchronized electrical shocks to the heart) is the key to treatment. Basic measures, such as opening the airway and providing rescue breaths and chest compressions, should be undertaken until the defibrillator is available. SEE: *defibrillation; advanced cardiac life support*.

fibrillin (fĭ′brĭl-ĭn) A protein constituent of connective tissue. It is present in skin, ligaments, tendons, and in the aorta. In Marfan syndrome, there is reduced content of microfibrils that contain fibrillin. SEE: *elastin*.

fibrillogenesis (fĭ-brĭl″ō-jĕn′ĕ-sĭs) Formation of fibrils.

fibrin (fĭ′brĭn) [L. *fibra*, fiber + *-in*] A whitish, filamentous protein formed by the action of thrombin on fibrinogen. The conversion of fibrinogen to fibrin is the third and final stage of blood clotting. The fibrin is deposited as fine interlacing filaments which entangle red and white blood cells and platelets, the whole forming a coagulum, or clot. SEE: *blood* **coagulation**. **fibrinous,** *adj.*

fibrin-fibrinogen degradation products A group of soluble protein fragments produced by the proteolytic action of plasmin on fibrin or fibrinogen. These products impair the hemostatic process and are a major cause of hemorrhage in intravascular coagulation and fibrinogenolysis.

fibrin glue Fibrin sealant.

fibrinocellular (fĭ″brĭ-nō-sĕl′ū-lăr) Composed of fibrin and cells, as in certain exudates.

fibrinogen (fĭ-brĭn′ŏ-jĕn) [*fibrin* + *-gen*] Coagulation factor I, a plasma protein, synthesized by the liver, and converted into fibrin through the action of thrombin in the presence of calcium ions. Fibrin forms the clot.

PATIENT CARE: Low plasma fibrinogen levels can be replenished with transfusions of cryoprecipitate. SEE: *blood* **coagulation**; *coagulation* **factor**.

fibrinogenic, fibrinogenous (fĭ″brĭn-ŏ-jĕn′ĭk, fĭ″brĭ-noj′ĕ-nŭs) Producing fibrin.

fibrinogenolysis (fĭ″brĭ-nō-jĕ-nŏl′ĭ-sĭs) [″ + ″ + *lysis,* dissolution] Decomposition or dissolution of fibrin.

fibrinogenopenia (fĭ-brĭn″ō-jĕn″ō-pē′nē-ă) [″ + Gr. *gennan,* to produce, + *penia,* poverty] Reduction in the amount of fibrinogen in the blood, usually the result of a liver or coagulation disorder.

fibrinoid (fĭ′brĭ-noyd) [″ + Gr. *eidos,* form, shape] Resembling fibrin.

fibrinoid change Alteration in connective tissues in response to immune reactions. The tissue becomes swollen, homogeneous, and bandlike.

fibrinoid material A fibrinous substance that develops in the placenta, increasing in quantity as the placenta develops. Its origin is attributed to the degenerating decidua and trophoblast. It forms an incomplete layer in the chorion and decidua basalis and also occurs as small irregular patches on the surface of the chorionic villi. In late pregnancy it may have a striated, or canalized, appearance and is then termed *canalized fibrinoid.*

fibrinolysin (fī″brĭn-ŏ-līs′ĭn) [*fibrin* + *lysin*] Any proteolytic enzyme, esp. plasmin, that causes fibrinolysis.

fibrinolysis (fī″brĭn-ŏl′ĭ-sĭs) The breakdown of fibrin in blood clots, and the prevention of the polymerization of fibrin into new clots. The principal physiological activator of the fibrinolytic system is tissue plasminogen activator. It converts plasminogen in a fibrin-containing clot to plasmin. The fibrin polymer is degraded by plasmin into fragments that are then scavenged by monocytes and macrophages. This process begins immediately after a clot forms. It can be stimulated by administering fibrinolytic drugs, such as recombinant tissue plasminogen activator. **fibrinolytic** (-ō-lĭt′ĭk), *adj.*

fibrinopenia (fī″brĭn-ō-pē′nē-ă) [″ + Gr. *penia,* poverty] Fibrin and fibrinogen deficiency in the blood.

fibrinopeptide (fī″brĭ-nŏ-pep′tīd″) [*fibrin* + *peptide*] Any of the short chains of linked amino acids released when fibrinogen is cleaved by thrombin to form fibrin. Excess levels of fibrinopeptides are present in the blood in certain diseases, e.g., disseminated intravascular coagulation.

fibrinosis (fī-brĭ-nō′sĭs) [″ + Gr. *osis,* condition] Excess of fibrin in the blood.

fibrin sealant A biological agent used to help control bleeding in those injuries or surgeries in which cautery, ligation, or suturing do not provide adequate hemostasis. SYN: *fibrin glue.*

fibrin split products The materials released into the bloodstream when the crosslinked fibrin in a blood clot is digested by plasmin.

fibrin-stabilizing factor (fī′brĭn-stā′bĭ-līz″ing) ABBR: FSF. Clotting factor XIII.

fibrinuria (fī-brĭn-ū′rē-ă) [″ + Gr. *ouron,* urine] Passage of fibrin in the urine.

fibro-, fibr- [L. *fibra,* fiber] Prefix meaning *fiber; fibrous tissues.*

fibroadenia (fī″brō-ă-dē′nē-ă) [L. *fibra,* fiber, + Gr. *aden,* gland] Fibrous degeneration of glandular tissue.

fibroadenoma (fī″brō-ăd″ĕ-nō′mă) [″ + ″ + *oma,* tumor] An adenoma with fibrous tissue forming a dense stroma.

fibroadipose (fī″brō-ăd′ĭ-pōs) [″ + *adeps,* fat] Containing fibrous and fatty tissue.

fibroangioma (fī″brō-ăn″jē-ō′mă) [″ + Gr. *angeion,* vessel, + *oma,* tumor] A fibrous tissue angioma.

fibroareolar (fī″brō-ă-rē′ō-lă) Fibrocellular.

fibroblast (fī′brō-blăst) [″ + Gr. *blastos,* germ] Any cell from which connective tissue develops; it produces collagen, elastin, and reticular protein fibers.
fibroblast growth factor SEE: under *factor.*

fibroblastoma (fī″brō-blăs-tō′mă) [″ + ″ + *oma,* tumor] A tumor of connective tissue, or fibroblastic, cells.

fibrocalcific (fī″brō-kăl-sĭf′ĭk) Fibrous and partially calcified.

fibrocarcinoma (fī″brō-kăr″sĭ-nō′mă) [″ + Gr. *karkinos,* cancer, + *oma,* tumor] A carcinoma in which the trabeculae are resistant and thickened with granular degeneration of the cells.

fibrocartilage (fī″brō-kăr′tĭ-lĭj) [″ + *cartilago,* gristle] A type of cartilage in which the matrix contains thick bundles of white or collagenous fibers. It is found in the intervertebral disks.

fibrocellular (fī″brō-sĕl′ū-lăr) [″ + *cellula,* little cell] Containing fibrous and cellular tissue. SYN: *fibroareolar.*

fibrochondritis (fī″brō-kŏn-drī′tĭs) [″ + Gr. *chondros,* cartilage, + *itis,* inflammation] Inflammation of fibrocartilage.

fibrochondroma (fī″brō-kŏn-drō′mă) [″ + ″ + *oma,* tumor] A tumor of fibrous tissue and cartilage.

fibrocyst (fī′brō-sĭst″, fĭb′rŏ-) [*fibro-* + *cyst*] A fibrous tumor that has undergone cystic degeneration or has accumulated fluid in the interspaces. **fibrocystic** (fī″brō-sĭs′tĭk, , fĭb″rŏ-), *adj.*

fibrocystic (fī″brō-sĭs′tĭk) **1.** Consisting of fibrocysts. **2.** Fibrous with cystic degeneration.

fibrocystic breast change A nonspecific diagnosis for a benign condition characterized by palpable lumps in the breasts, usually associated with pain and tenderness. At least 50% of women of reproductive age have palpably irregular breasts caused by this condition. This benign condition was formerly known as *fibrocystic disease of the breast* SEE: *breast self-examination.*

Women with marked lumpiness in one or both breasts have a two to five times greater risk of developing breast cancer. If hyperplasia is present in the lesion, or if there is a family history of breast cancer, the risk of developing breast cancer is greatly increased. Women should practice breast self-examination once a month, about a week after the menstrual period, have a clinician breast exam every 6 months, and, if indicated, a mammography once a year or other screening tests as recommended by their health care providers. Any palpable, distinct, or dominant mass requires immediate evaluation

TREATMENT: Some women obtain relief by reducing fat intake in the diet to less than 25%, limiting salt intake premenstrually, eliminating caffeine, foods containing methylxanthines, tobacco products, and alcohol, or by taking complementary remedies such as vitamin E supplements. Occasionally providers may prescribe danazol, an androgenic (male) hormone. Patients with benign symptomatic nodularity or mastalgia often respond well to low-dose oral contraceptives.

PATIENT CARE: Emotional support is provided for women who have a heightened awareness or fear of developing breast cancer. Instructing the patient includes discussion and demonstration of breast self-examination, with emphasis placed on the importance of monthly self-exams, periodic mammography, and annual examinations by a health care professional. The accuracy of the patient's self-exam is evaluated by asking her to locate any currently palpable lumps and to describe the present contour and texture (feel) of her breasts (mapping).

If pain and tenderness are bothersome, suggestions include taking aspirin or other nonsteroidal anti-inflammatory over-the-counter drugs and wearing a well-fitting brassiere day and night.

fibrocystic disease of the breast SEE: *fibrocystic breast change*.

fibrocystic disease of the pancreas Cystic fibrosis.

fibrocystoma (fī″brō-sĭs-tō′mă) [″ + Gr. *kystis*, cyst, + *oma*, tumor] A fibroma combined with a cystoma.

fibrocyte (fī′brō-sīt) [″ + Gr. *kytos*, cell] A mature, older fibroblast.

fibrodysplasia (fī″brō-dĭs-plā′sē-ă) [″ + Gr. *dys*, bad, + *plassein*, to form] Abnormal development of fibrous tissue.

fibroelastic (fī″brō-ē-lăs′tĭk) [″ + Gr. *elastikos*, elastic] Pert. to connective tissue containing both white nonelastic collagenous fibers and yellow elastic fibers.

fibroelastosis (fī″brō-ē″lăs-tō′sĭs) Overgrowth of fibroelastic tissue.

   endocardial f. Fibroelastosis of the endocardium. It leads to cardiac failure.

fibroenchondroma (fī″brō-ĕn″kŏn-drō′mă) [″ + Gr. *en*, in, + *chondros*, cartilage, + *oma*, tumor] A benign cartilaginous tumor containing fibrous elements.

fibroepithelioma (fī″brō-ĕp″ĭ-thē″lē-ō′mă) [″ + Gr. *epi*, upon, + *thele*, nipple, + *oma*, tumor] A benign tumor containing fibrous and epithelial elements.

fibroid (fĭb′royd, fib′) [*fibro-* + *-oid*] **1.** Pert. to, containing, or resembling fi-

bers. SEE: *degeneration*. **2.** A benign tumor of the uterine myometrium. SEE: *uterine* **leiomyoma**.

   f.s of uterus Uterine **leiomyoma**.

fibroidectomy (fī-broyd-ĕk′tō-mē) [″ + ″ + *ektome*, excision] Surgical removal of a fibroid tumor.

fibrolipoma (fī″brō-lĭ-pō′mă) [″ + Gr. *lipos*, fat, + *oma*, tumor] Lipofibroma.

fibroma (fī-brō′mă, ′mă-tă) *pl.* **fibromata** [*fibro-* + *-oma*] A fibrous, encapsulated connective tissue tumor. It is irregular in shape, slow in growth, and has a firm consistency. Pressure or cystic degeneration may cause pain. It may affect the periosteum, jaws, occiput, pelvis, vertebrae, ribs, long bones, or sternum. **fibromatous** (-mă-tŭs), *adj.*

   f. of breast A benign, nonulcerative, painless breast tumor.

   interstitial f. A tumor in the muscular wall of the uterus that may grow inward and form a polypoid fibroid, or outward and become a subperitoneal fibroid. SEE: *uterine* **leiomyoma**.

   intramural f. A tumor in the muscle tissue of the uterus between the peritoneal coat and endometrium.

   submucous f. A fibroma encroaching on the endometrial cavity. It may be sessile or pedunculated.

   subserous f. A fibroma, often pedunculated, lying beneath the peritoneal coat of the uterus.

   uterine f. Uterine **leiomyoma**.

fibromatosis (fī″brō-mă-tō′sĭs) [L. *fibra*, fiber, + Gr. *oma*, tumor, + *osis*, condition] The simultaneous development of many fibromata.

   f. colli Congenital muscular torticollis.

   gingival f. An inherited condition marked by hypertrophy of the gums before the eruption of the teeth. Hypertrichosis is usually present.

   palmar f. Dupuytren's contracture.

fibromectomy (fī″brō-mĕk′tō-mē) [″ + Gr. *oma*, tumor, + *ektome*, excision] Removal of a fibroma.

fibromembranous (fī″brō-mĕm′bră-nŭs) [″ + *membrana*, web] Having both fibrous and membranous tissue.

fibromuscular (fī″brō-mŭs′kū-lăr) [″ + *musculus*, muscle] Consisting of muscle and connective tissue.

fibromyalgia (fī″brō-mī-ăl′jē-ă) [″ + Gr. *mys*, muscle, + *algos*, pain] Chronic and frequently difficult to manage pain in muscles and soft tissues surrounding joints. It is more common in women than men and affects about six million Americans. Symptoms sometimes include fatigue and mood and sleep disturbances. Efforts to classify this condition resulted in the American College of Rheumatology criteria for classification of fibromyalgia, published in 1990.

SYN: *fibromyositis; fibrositis.* SEE: illus.; table.

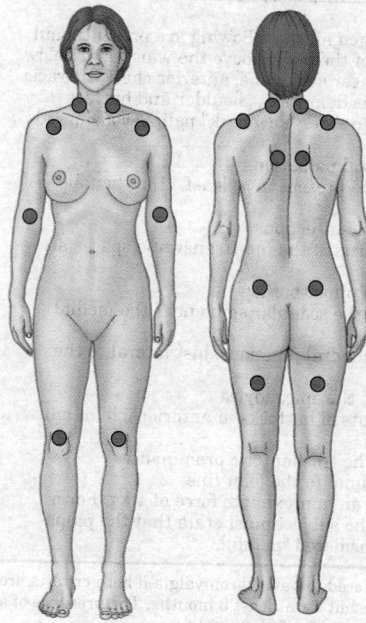

FIBROMYALGIA

Fibromyalgia tender points

PATIENT CARE: Fibromyalgia is a condition in which objective findings are limited, but subjective fatigue, pain, and distress are often significant. Essential to its management are reassurance that it does not cause harm, cognitive behavioral therapy, and reasonable participation in physical activities or physical therapy to prevent deconditioning. Muscle aches may be eased by massage, and stretching and yoga help to maintain range of motion. Drug therapies include oral pregabalin, topical capsaicin, anti-inflammatories, antidepressants, muscle relaxants, trigger point injections, and/or narcotic analgesics. Referral to a rheumatologist, physiatrist, psychologist, psychiatrist, or pain management therapist is sometimes necessary.

fibromyalgia impact questionnaire ABBR: FIQ. A 21-item self-reported questionnaire used to assess the current health status of women diagnosed with fibromyalgia syndrome.

fibromyoma (fĭ″brō-mī″ō′mă, ″ō′mă-tă) *pl.* **fibromyomasfibromyomata** [*fibro- + myoma*] **1.** A fibrous tissue myoma. **2.** Uterine **leiomyoma**.

fibromyomectomy (fĭ″brō-mī″ō-měk′tō-mē) [″ + ″ + *ektome,* excision] Removal of a fibromyoma from the uterus, leaving that organ in place.

fibromyositis Fibromyalgia.

fibromyotomy (fĭ″brō-mī-ŏt′ō-mē) [″ + ″ + *tome,* incision] Surgical incision of a fibroid tumor.

fibromyxoma (fĭ″brō-mĭk-sō′mă) [″ + Gr. *myxa,* mucus, + *oma,* tumor] An encapsulated fibrous tumor composed of large fibroblasts in loose connective tissue.

fibromyxosarcoma (fĭ″brō-mĭk″sō-săr-kō′mă) [″ + ″ + *sarkos,* flesh, + *oma,* tumor] **1.** A sarcoma containing fibrous and myxoid tissue. **2.** A sarcoma that has undergone mucoid degeneration.

fibronectin (fī″brō-něk′tĭn) Any of a group of opsonic proteins present in blood plasma and extracellular matrix that are involved in wound healing and cell adhesion. The presence of fetal fibronectin in the cervical and vaginal secretions may be a marker for subsequent development of preterm labor. SEE: *fetal fibronectin assay.*

fibroneuroma (fĭ″brō-nū-rō′mă) [″ + Gr. *neuron,* nerve, + *oma,* tumor] Neurofibroma.

fibro-odontoma (fĭ″brō-ō″dŏn-tō′mă) A rare benign tumor of the oral cavity, typically found in the posterior mandible of children.

fibro-osteoma (fĭ″brō-ŏs-tē-ō′mă) [″ + Gr. *osteon,* bone, + *oma,* tumor] A tumor containing bony and fibrous elements. SYN: *osteofibroma.*

fibropapilloma (fĭ″brō-păp-ĭ-lō′mă) [″ + *papilla,* nipple, + Gr. *oma,* tumor] A mixed fibroma and papilloma sometimes occurring in the bladder.

fibroplasia (fī″brō-plā′sē-ă) [″ + Gr. *plasis,* a molding] The development of fibrous tissue, as in wound healing or by other stimulating factors, e.g., as retrolental fibroplasia in the neonate due to the administration of excessive oxygen.

   retrolental f. ABBR: RLF. Retinopathy of prematurity.

fibroplastic (fī″brō-plăs′tĭk) [″ + Gr. *plassein,* to form] Giving formation to fibrous tissue.

fibropurulent (fī″brō-pūr′ū-lěnt) [″ + *purulentus,* festering] Pert. to pus that contains flakes of fibrous tissue.

fibrosarcoma (fī″brō-săr-kō′mă) [L. *fibra,* fiber, + Gr. *sarkos,* flesh, + *oma,* tumor] A spindle-celled sarcoma containing a large amount of connective tissue.

fibrose (fī′brōs) To form or produce fibrous tissue (e.g., a scar).

fibroserous (fī″brō-sē′rŭs) [″ + *serosus,* serous] Containing fibrous and serous parts, such as the pericardium.

fibrosis (fi-brō′sĭs) [*fibro-* + *-sis*] The repair and replacement of inflamed tissues or organs by connective tissues. The process results in the replacement of normal cells by fibroblasts (and even-

The American College of Rheumatology 1990 Criteria for Classification of Fibromyalgia*

1. History of widespread pain

Definition: Pain is considered widespread when all the following are present: pain in the left side of the body, the right side of the body, above the waist, and below the waist. In addition, axial skeletal pain (cervical spine, anterior chest, thoracic spine, or low back) must be present. In this definition, shoulder and buttock pain is considered as pain for each involved side. "Low back" pain is considered lower segment pain.

2. Pain in 11 of 18 tender point sites on digital palpation

Definition: On digital palpation, pain must be present in at least 11 of the following 18 tender point sites:

Occiput—bilateral, at the suboccipital muscle insertions

Low cervical—bilateral, at the anterior aspects of the intertransverse spaces at C5–7

Trapezius—bilateral, at the midpoint of the upper border

Supraspinatus—bilateral, at origins, above the scapular spine near the medial border

Second rib—bilateral, at the second costochondral junctions, just lateral to the junctions on upper surfaces

Lateral epicondyle—bilateral, 2 cm distal to the epicondyles

Gluteal—bilateral, in upper outer quadrants of buttocks in anterior fold of muscle

Greater trochanter—bilateral, posterior to the trochanteric prominence

Knee—bilateral, at the medial fat pad proximal to the joint line

Digital palpation should be performed with an approximate force of 4 kg. For a tender point to be considered "positive," the subject must state that the palpation was painful. "Tender" is not to be considered "painful."

* For classification purposes, patients are considered to have fibromyalgia if both criteria are satisfied. Widespread pain must have been present for at least 3 months. The presence of a second clinical disorder does not exclude the diagnosis of fibromyalgia.

SOURCE: American College of Rheumatology, Multicenter Criteria Committee, Arthritis Rheum 1990; 33(2):160–172, with permission.

tually, the replacement of normal organ tissue by scar tissue).

arteriocapillary f. Arteriolar and capillary fibroid degeneration. SYN: *arteriofibrosis.*

cystic f. ABBR: CF. A potentially fatal autosomal recessive disease that manifests itself in multiple body systems, including the lungs, the pancreas, the urogenital system, the skeleton, and the skin. It causes chronic obstructive pulmonary disease, frequent lung infections, deficient elaboration of pancreatic enzymes, osteoporosis, and an abnormally high electrolyte concentration in the sweat. The name is derived from the characteristic histologic changes in the pancreas. CF usually begins in infancy and is the major cause of severe chronic lung disease in children. In the U.S., CF occurs in 1 in 2500 white live births and 1 in 17,000 black live births and is the most common fatal genetic disease in European-American children SYN: *fibrocystic disease of the pancreas; mucoviscidosis.*

SYMPTOMS: A great variety of clinical manifestations may be present, including nasal polyposis; lung changes related to thick, tenacious secretions leading to bronchiectasis; bronchitis; pneumonia; atelectasis, emphysema and respiratory failure; gallbladder diseases; intussusception; meconium ileus; salt depletion; pancreatic exocrine deficiency causing intestinal malabsorption of fats, proteins, and, to a lesser extent, carbohydrates; pancreatitis; peptic ulcer; rectal prolapse; diabetes; nutritional deficiencies; arthritis; absent vas deferens with consequent aspermia and absence of fructose in the ejaculate; failure to thrive; and delayed puberty. The child exhibits a nonproductive, paroxysmal cough, barrel chest, cyanosis, clubbed fingers and toes, malabsorption leading to poor weight gain and growth, fat-soluble vitamin deficiency (A, D, E, K) leading to clotting abnormalities, and excretion of frequent pale stools that are bulky, foul-smelling and have a high fat content.

TREATMENT: Therapy must be individualized, carefully monitored, and continued throughout life. Pulmonary infection is controlled with antibiotics. It is essential that secretions be cleared from the airway by intermittent aerosol therapy. A mucolytic agent may be helpful as well as postural drainage, mist inhalation, and bronchodilator therapy. Bronchoalveolar lavage has been of use in some patients. In addition, bronchial drainage may be improved by use of aerosolized recombinant human DNase (rhDNase). Use of a Flutter device for airway mucus clearance is considerably more effective in increasing sputum expectoration than traditional postural drainage and clapping the chest. Lung transplantation may also be used to treat CF. High doses of ibuprofen taken consistently for years may slow progression of the disease by limiting airway inflammation. SEE: *bronchoalveolar lavage; Flutter device.*

PROGNOSIS: Median cumulative survival is approximately 30 years, with males surviving much longer than females for unknown reasons.

GENETIC SCREENING: In 2001 The American College of Obstetricians and Gynecologists and the American College of Medical Genetics recommended that all prospective parents undergo screening to see if they are carriers of cystic fibrosis genes.

PATIENT CARE: Both patient and family are taught to perform pulmonary chest physiotherapy and postural drainage followed by deep breathing and coughing to help mobilize secretions. Fluid intake is encouraged to thin inspissated secretions. Humidified air, with intermittent positive-pressure breathing therapy if prescribed, is provided. Dornase alfa is also administered by nebulizer as prescribed. A DNA enzyme produced by recombinant gene therapy, the drug is used to reduce the frequency of respiratory infections, to decrease sputum thickness (viscosity), and to improve pulmonary functioning in patients with cystic fibrosis.

The patient should take precautions, e.g., annual influenza immunization and at least one pneumococcal vaccination to prevent respiratory infections and should learn to recognize and report signs and symptoms and to initiate prescribed antibiotic prophylaxis promptly. Oral pancreatic enzymes are given with meals and snacks to replace deficiencies, and foods are well-salted or a sodium supplement prescribed to combat electrolyte losses in sweat. A well-balanced high-calorie, high-protein diet is recommended, including replacement of fat-soluble vitamins if laboratory analysis indicates any deficiencies. Aerobic exercise and physical activity within permitted limits are encouraged; breathing exercises should be performed during activity to improve ventilatory capacity and activity tolerance. The child is encouraged in age-appropriate developmental tasks, and acceptable activities are substituted for those in which the child is unable to participate.

Caregivers involve the child in care by offering valid choices and encouraging decision making. The family is encouraged to discuss their feelings and concerns. Genetic testing is explained. Realistic reassurance is offered regarding expectations after an exacerbation, and emotional support is provided to help both patient and family work through feelings of anticipatory grief. Referral is made to available local chapters of support groups such as the Cystic Fibrosis Foundation. SEE: *Nursing Diagnoses Appendix.*

diffuse interstitial pulmonary f. Idiopathic pulmonary **f.**

idiopathic pulmonary f. The formation of scar tissue in the parenchyma of the lungs, following inflammation of the alveoli. The disease results in difficulty breathing caused by impaired gas exchange. SYN: *diffuse interstitial pulmonary f.; pulmonary f.; Hamman's syndrome.*

SYMPTOMS: Dyspnea, cough, exertional fatigue, and generalized weakness are common. Signs of the illness include pulmonary crackles, finger clubbing, cyanosis, and evidence of right ventricular failure (such as lower-extremity swelling). The disease typically progresses to end-stage lung disease and death within 7 years of diagnosis.

DIAGNOSIS: A biopsy of the lung is needed to make the diagnosis.

TREATMENT: Corticosteroids (such as prednisone) may be helpful in 10% to 20% of patients. Lung transplantation can be curative if a donor organ is available.

pleural f. A condition occurring in pulmonary tuberculosis, asbestosis, and other lung diseases in which the pleura becomes thickened and the pleural space may be obliterated.

postfibrinosis f. Development of fibrosis in a tissue in which fibrin has been deposited.

premacular f. Macular pucker.

proliferative f. Formation of new fibrous tissue from connective tissue cells.

pulmonary f. Idiopathic pulmonary fibrosis.

retroperitoneal f. Development of a mass of scar tissue in the retroperitoneal space. This may lead to physical compression of the ureters, vena cava, or aorta. This disease may be associated with taking methysergide for migraine, and with other drugs. SYN: *Ormond's disease.*

fibrositis (fī-brō-sī'tĭs) [" + Gr. *itis*, inflammation] Fibromyalgia.

fibrotic (fī-brŏt'ĭk) Marked by or pert. to fibrosis.

fibrous Composed of, containing, resembling, or separable into fibers.

fibula (fĭb'ū-lă) [L., pin] The outer and smaller bone of the leg from the ankle to the knee, articulating above with the tibia and below with the tibia and talus. It is one of the longest and thinnest bones of the body. **fibular,** *adj.*

FIC *John E. Fogarty International Center* (of the National Institutes of Health)

ficin (fĭ'sĭn) [L. *ficus*, fig] Sap from the fig tree. It contains an enzyme capable of hydrolyzing proteins.

Fick, Adolf Eugen (fik) Ger. physiologist, 1829–1901.

F. equation Fick principle.

F.'s halo A colored halo around light observed by some persons as a result of wearing contact lenses.

F's. law Diffusion through a tissue membrane is directly proportional to the cross-sectional area, driving pressure, and gas coefficient and inversely proportional to tissue thickness.

F. method Determination of cardiac output by calculation of the difference in oxygen content of mixed venous and arterial blood. This figure is then divided into the total oxygen consumption.

F. principle In respiratory physiology, blood flow equals the amount of a substance absorbed in an organ divided by the difference in the amount of the substance entering and leaving the organ. Usually the substance is oxygen or a dye. SYN: *Fick equation.*

FICS *Fellow of the International College of Surgeons.*

fictive kin (fik'tiv) A group of individuals chosen as a surrogate family by a genetically unrelated person; an adopted family.

FID *flame ionization detector.*

fiduciary abuse (fĭ-doo'shē-ĕr"ē, dŭ') [L. *fiduciarius*, held in trust] SEE: under *abuse.*

field (fēld) **1.** An open expanse of land. **2.** A discipline or an area of study. **3.** A region of space in which a given force operates or a given condition exists. **4.** A place of natural conditions, as opposed to a controlled environment, such as a laboratory or a hospital.

auditory f. The spatial region in which a given person can hear sounds.

cortical f. A segment of the cerebral cortex that carries out a given function. For example, the front of the parietal lobe -- the postcentral gyrus -- can be called a primary somatosensory field, and the parietal cortex farther back can be called an association field.

electric n The region in space in which the attractive or repulsive effects of a given electric charge have an effect.

electromagnetic f. ABBR: EMF. The region in space in which the photons produced by moving electric charges have an effect. EMFs can be produced by power lines, radio waves, and microwaves. The energy produced in an EMF increases as the frequency of the photons increases, and EMFs produced by very high frequency photons (e.g., xrays and gamma rays) are sufficiently energetic to induce cancer.

eye n Any region of the cortex concerned with sensation from or movement of an eye.

f. of fixation The widest limits of vision in all directions within which the eyes can fixate.

f. of Forel One the layers of axons -- many originating in the globus pallidus -- that form the lower (inferior) border of the thalamus in the brain. Together, the axons and neighboring neuronss are called the subthalamic reticular nucleus.Forel's field, prerubral field.

gravitational f. The region in space in which the attractive effects of a given mass have an effect.

hand f. Any region of the cortex concerned with sensation from or movement of a hand.

heart f. The region of the embryo destined to produce the heart.

high-power f. The portion of an object seen when the high-magnification lenses of a microscope are used.

hippocampal f. Any of the three contiguous, but histologically distinguishable, sheets of cells that form the cortex of the hippocampus; the fields are usually called CA1, CA2, and CA3.

low-power f. The portion of an object seen when the low-magnification lenses of a microscope are used.

lung f. The region in the body containing a lung. Often,'lung field' refers to the section of a medical image (e.g., chest xray) that shows a lung.

magnetic f. The space permeated by the magnetic lines of force surrounding a permanent magnet or coil of wire carrying electric current.

prerubral f. F. of Forel.

pulsing electromagnetic f. ABBR: PEMF. An alternating electrical current used to produce an electromagnetic field. This may induce healing when applied to a fractured bone. The field is applied noninvasively to the affected limb. It may be moderately helpful in treating bony nonunion. SEE: *diathermy.*

receptive f. A description of the effective stimuli of a given neuron. For sensory receptor neurons, the receptive field is the type of effective stimulation (e.g., light, sound, mechanical pressure) and the range of sensitive locations (e.g., center of visual field, left auditory field, tip of right thumb).

sterile f. A body surface, along with surrounding drapes or towels, within which an operation may safely take place without introducing potentially hazardous microorganisms into a patient.

PATIENT CARE: The field is prepared by meticulously washing and scrubbing the patient on whom an operation will be performed with disinfectant solution. Sterile drapes and towels are placed over the patient to cover any unprepared skin or clothing with sterilized fabric. All surgical instruments that enter the operative theatre are cleansed according to decontamination and sterilization practices. Finally, all surgical personnel scrub for prescribed time periods with disinfectants before entering the operating room. They must wear sterile gloves, gowns, masks and shoe covers and replace these if any of them contact nonprepared items during surgery.

surgical f. The area in which an operation is performed. This field is prepared and covered to maintain sterility during operations.

useful f. of view ABBR: UFOV. A test of visual attention that measures the space in which an individual can receive information rapidly from two separate sources. It is a strong predictor of accidents in older drivers. Training can expand the useful field of view and increase the visual processing speed of an elderly person.

f. of vision Visual **f.**

visual f. The area within which objects may be seen when the eye is fixed. SYN: **f. of vision.** SEE: illus.; *perimetry.*

field effect Field **carcinogenesis.**

fieldwork (fēld′wŏrk) Studies and practical experience gained during the direct observation and care of patients. It is used to supplement and broaden the education of students, usually in addition to academic study performed in the classroom, home, or library. Fieldwork is also used in ethnographic nursing research.

fifth cranial nerve Trigeminal nerve.

fifth disease Erythema infectiosum.

fight-or-flight reaction of Cannon SEE: under *Cannon, Walter B.*

FIGO staging system The staging system for cancer of the cervix uteri developed by the International Federation of Gynecology and Obstetrics.

figurate (fĭg′ū-rāt) [L. *figuratum*, figured] Having a rounded, curved, circular, or ringed shape. The term is used to describe rashes that leave elaborately embroidered markings on the skin.

figure [L. *figura*] **1.** A body, form, shape, or outline. **2.** A number.

figure-ground The perceptual difference between an object and its surroundings.

filament (fĭl′ă-mĕnt) [L. *filamentum*, threading] **1.** A fine thread. **2.** A threadlike coil of tungsten found in the x-ray tube that is the source of electrons.

axial f. A filament forming the central axis of the flagellum of a spermatozoon.

intermediate f. ABBR: IF. Slender proteins found in all eukaryotic cells, measuring about 8 to 12 mm in diameter. Intermediate filaments are composed of proteins including desmin, keratins, lamins, and vimentin and

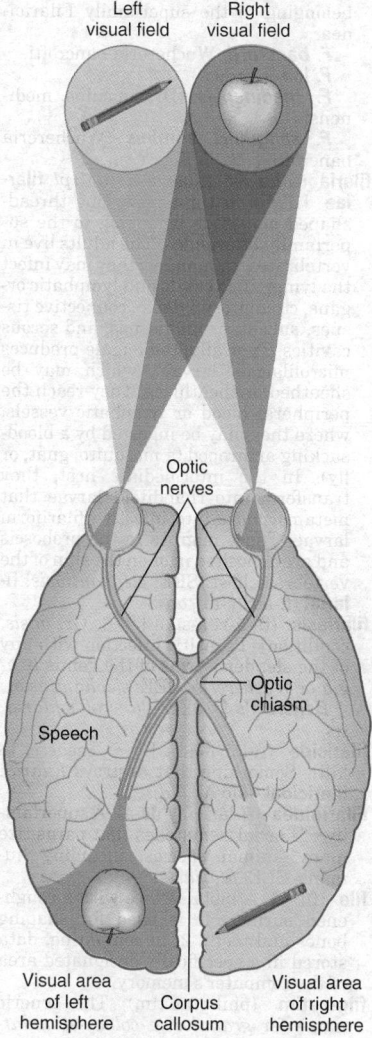

Left visual field

Right visual field

Optic nerves

Optic chiasm

Speech

Visual area of left hemisphere

Corpus callosum

Visual area of right hemisphere

VISUAL FIELD

together with microtubules and microfilaments form the cytoskeleton. Some malignant cells can be identified by the specific proteins in their intermediate filaments.

thick f.'s Myosin, seen microscopically.

thin filaments Actin, seen microscopically.

filamentous (fĭl″ă-mĕn′tŭs) Made up of long, interwoven or irregularly placed threadlike structures.

filar (fī′lăr) [L. *filum*, thread] Filamentous.

Filaria (fĭ-lar′ē-ă) [L. *filum*, thread] The former name for a genus of nematodes belonging to the superfamily Filarioidea.

F. bancrofti Wuchereria bancrofti.

F. loa Loa loa.

F. medinensis Dracunculus medinensis.

F. sanguinis hominis Wuchereria bancrofti.

filaria (fĭ-lar′ē-ă, fĭ-lar′′ē-ē′′, ′ē-ī′′) *pl.* **filariae** [L. *filum,* thread] A long thread-shaped nematode belonging to the superfamily Filarioidea. The adults live in vertebrates. In humans, they may infect the lymphatic vessels and lymphatic organs, circulatory system, connective tissues, subcutaneous tissues, and serous cavities. Typically, the female produces microfilariae (larvae), which may be sheathed or sheathless. They reach the peripheral blood or lymphatic vessels, where they may be ingested by a blood-sucking arthropod (a mosquito, gnat, or fly). In the intermediate host, they transform into rhabditoid larvae that metamorphose into infective filariform larvae. These migrate to the proboscis and are deposited in or on the skin of the vertebrate host. SEE: *elephantiasis.* **filarial** (fĭ-lar′′ē-ăl), *adj.*

filariasis (fĭl-ă-rī′ă-sĭs) [″ + Gr. *-iasis,* condition] Parasitic infection with any of the slender worms of the genus *Brugia* or *Wuchereria.* SEE: *elephantiasis.*

Bancroft's f. SEE: *Bancroft's filariasis.*

filaricide (fĭ-lăr′ĭ-sīd) [″ + *caedere,* to kill] Something that destroys *Filaria.* **filaricidal** (-sīd′ăl), *adj.*

Filarioidea (fĭ-lăr′′ē-oy′dē-ă) A superfamily of filarial nematodes that parasitize many animal species, including humans. SEE: *filariasis.*

file (fĭl) **1.** A metal device with a roughened surface. It is used for shaping bones and teeth. **2.** In computing, data stored in a specifically designated area of the computer's memory.

filgrastim (phil-gras′tĭm) The generic name for *granulocyte colony-stimulating factor.*

filiform (fĭl′ĭ-form) [″ + *forma,* form] **1.** In biology, pert. to a growth that is uniform along the inoculation line in stab or streak cultures. **2.** Hairlike; filamentous.

filler (fĭl′ĕr)
1. In plastic surgery, any substance inserted into another to give it a plumper shape or contour. **2.** In dentistry and orthopedics, a porous material used in bone cements, resins, or other bonding materials to improve their performance, e.g., bonding strength, elution rates, or resistance to wear in the body. **3.** Inert ingredient. SYN: *filling agent.*

fillet (fĭl′ĕt) [Fr. *filet,* a band] **1.** A loop of thread, cord, or tape used to provide traction or suspension of tissue during surgery or obstetrical delivery. **2.** Lemniscus.

filling (fĭl′ing) **1.** A material inserted into a cavity preparation. Common materials include amalgam, acrylics, resins, and glass ionomers. **2.** The operation of filling tooth cavities. SEE: *dental amalgam, restoration.*

film (film) [Old English *filmen,* membrane] **1.** A thin skin, membrane, or covering. **2.** A thin sheet of material, usually cellulose and coated with a light-sensitive emulsion, used in taking photographs and radiographs. **3.** In microscopy, a thin layer of blood or other material spread on a slide or coverslip.

base f. A layer of polyester or other suitable material that supports the radiographical film emulsion.

laser f. A single emulsion material used in dry imaging systems to reproduce images through electronic control of a laser light directly onto the film.

plain f. A simple x-ray image of a body part, taken from an anterior, posterior, lateral, or oblique projection.

spot f. A radiograph of a small anatomical area.

x-ray f. A special photographic film with a sensitive emulsion layer that blackens in response to the light from intensifying screens. The emulsion has silver halide crystals immersed in gelatin. *Single-emulsion film* has the emulsion on one side of the cellulose base. It is used for digital, mammographic, and extremity imaging, in which high detail is necessary. *Duplitized film* has the emulsion on both sides of the cellulose base. It is used for general-purpose radiological studies.

film badge A badge containing film that is sensitive to x-rays. It is used to determine the cumulative occupational exposure to ionizing radiation.

film speed The sensitivity of a photographic medium, e.g., a radiograph to light or radiation. The film speed is determined by the size of its silver halide crystals; the thickness of the emulsion; and the presence of radiosensitive dyes. Films are described as "fast" if the film requires little radiation to produce an image and "slow" if more radiation is needed.

filopodia Bundles of actin filaments that project from the cell surface.

filovaricosis (fī′′lō-văr-ĭ-kō′sĭs) [″ + *varix,* a dilated vein, + Gr. *osis,* condition] Dilation or thickening of the axis of a nerve.

Filovirus (fĭl′ă-vī′rŭs, fĭl′) A family of encased, negative-stranded RNA viruses that can cause fatal hemorrhagic fevers. They include Marburg and Ebola viruses. SEE: *Ebola virus hemorrhagic fever; Marburg virus disease.*

filter (fĭl′tĕr) [L. *filtrum,* felt (for straining)] **1.** To pass a liquid through any porous substance that prevents particles larger than a certain size from passing through. **2.** A device for filtering liquids, light rays, or radiations. SEE: *absorption; osmosis.* **3.** Material, such as aluminum or molybdenum, inserted between the radiation source and the patient to absorb low-level radiation that would increase the dose.

Berkefeld f. SEE: *Berkefeld filter.*

compensating f. In radiography, a filter that shields less dense areas to produce a more nearly uniform radiographic image.

high efficiency particulate air f. ABBR: HEPA filter. An air filter capable of removing 99.7% of particles greater than 0.3 μm in diameter.

infrared f. A filter that permits passage of only infrared waves of a certain wavelength.

membrane f. A filter made from biologically inert cellulose esters, polyethylene, or other porous materials.

Millipore f. Trademark name of a filter usually composed of cellulose acetate with controlled pore size that separates particles above specific sizes from the solutions that flow through.

optical f. A device that passes only a portion of the visible light spectrum. Absorption filters absorb the unwanted wavelengths. Interference filters employ the wave effects of constructive and destructive superposition to pass or inhibit appropriate wavelengths.

Pasteur-Chamberland f. An unglazed porcelain filter capable of retaining bacteria and some viruses. Either pressure or suction is required to force or draw the liquid through the filter.

umbrella f. A filter placed in a blood vessel to prevent emboli from passing that point. It has been used in the vena cava to prevent emboli reaching the lungs via the chambers of the right heart and pulmonary arteries.

⚠️ Complications of filter use include perforation of the vein, migration of the filter, or fragmentation and embolization of its parts.

vena cava f. A wire apparatus inserted through a catheter into the inferior vena cava to prevent pulmonary emboli.

wedge f. A filter used in radiography and radiation therapy to vary the intensity of the x-ray beam. This compensates for differences in the thicknesses of the parts being exposed to radiation.

Wood's f. An ultraviolet light source used to diagnose some fungal and bacterial skin diseases.

filterable [L. *filtrare*, to strain through] Capable of passing through the pores of a filter.

filtering In neuropsychology, devoting selective focus to certain stimuli while ignoring or minimizing others.

filtrate (fĭl'trāt) The fluid that has been passed through a filter. The residue is the precipitate.

glomerular f. The fluid that passes from the blood through the capillary walls of the glomeruli of the kidney. It is similar to plasma but with far less protein; urine is formed from it.

filtration (fĭl-trā'shŭn) The process of removing particles from a solution by allowing the liquid portion to pass through a membrane or other partial barrier. This contains holes or spaces that allow the liquid to pass but are too small to permit passage of the solid particles. SEE: *filter.*

membrane differential f. ABBR: MDF. The removal of high-molecular-weight plasma proteins and lipoproteins from circulating blood to increase the flow to microcirculatory blood vessels. SYN: *rheophoresis.*

f. of x-ray photons The absorption of some longer-wavelength, low-energy x-ray photons by an absorbing medium placed in the path of the beam. Materials used for x-ray absorption include aluminum, copper, molybdenum, and zinc.

filtration slits The spaces between the pedicels on the glomerular basement membrane through which water, glucose, amino acids, and other chemicals pass as they become renal filtrate.

filum (fī'lŭm) *pl.* **fila** [L.] A threadlike structure.

f. terminale A long, slender filament of connective tissue at the end of the spinal cord.

fimbria (fĭm'brē-ă, brē-ē", -ī") *pl.* **fimbriae** [L. *fimbria*, a fringe] **1.** Any structure resembling a fringe or border, such as the ones found in the fallopian tubes. **2.** A pilus.

f. tubae The fringelike portion at the abdominal end of a fallopian tube.

fimbriate, fimbriated (fĭm'brē-āt", fĭm'brē-āt"ĕd) **1.** Having finger-like projections. **2.** Fringed.

fimbriocele (fĭm'brē-ō-sēl") [" + Gr. *kele*, tumor, swelling] A hernia including the fimbriated portion of the oviduct.

fimbrioplasty (fĭm'brē-ŏ-plas"tē) [*fimbria* + *-plasty*] Surgical treatment of diseases of the fimbriae of the fallopian tubes.

finasteride (fĭ-năs'tĕr-īd) A 5-alpha-reductase inhibitor used to treat benign prostatic hypertrophy and male hair loss. Trade name is Proscar.

Finegoldia magna (fĭn'gōld'ē-ă măg'nă) The preferred name for the species of anaerobic gram-positive cocci formerly known as *Peptostreptococcus magna.* It is a potential cause of soft tissue abscess, endocarditis, or joint or wound infection.

fine motor skill Any of the motor skills that require greater control of the small muscles than large ones, esp. for hand-eye coordination or for precise hand and finger movement. Fine motor skills include handwriting, sewing, and fastening buttons. Most movements require both large and small muscle groups, and there is considerable overlap between fine and gross motor skills, but distinguishing between the two is useful in rehabilitation settings, special education, adapted physical education tests, motor development tests, and aptitude tests in industry and in the military.

fineness The proportion of pure gold in a gold alloy.

finger (fing´gĕr) Any of the five digits of the hand.

    baseball f. Mallet **f.**

    clubbed f. Clubbing.

    coach's f. Dorsal dislocation of any of the proximal interphalangeal joints of the hands. This common dislocation, which may occur when catching a rapidly moving ball, is often associated with a middle phalangeal avulsion.

    dislocation of f. SEE: under *dislocation.*

    hammer f. Mallet **f.**

    hippocratic f. Clubbing.

    jersey f. A traumatic avulsion of the insertion of the flexor digitorum profundus, caused by a forceful extension motion during an active muscular contraction. It is commonly seen in football players: a tackler grabs an opponent's jersey, and the opponent pulls the jersey out of the tackler's hand.

    mallet f. A flexion deformity of the distal joint of a finger, caused by avulsion of the extensor tendon. SYN: *baseball f.; hammer f.*

    seal f. A painful cellulitic infection of a finger caused by a species of mycoplasma, sometimes occurring in arctic hunters or fishers. It is treated with tetracycline antibiotics.

    trigger f. A state in which flexion or extension of a digit is arrested temporarily but is finally completed with a jerk. Any finger may be involved, but the ring or middle finger is most often affected.

    TREATMENT: A finger splint or cortisone injection may be used to treat this condition. Surgery may be required.

    webbed f. A congenital condition in which some or all of the fingers are fused; syndactylism.

finger cot A protective covering for a finger. It is usually made of plastic, rubber, metal, or leather. The injured finger is protected from trauma during the healing process.

fingernail SEE: *nail.*

fingerprint **1.** A smudge made when oils

from the distal portions of the finger come into contact with an object. Fingerprints are used in forensics for personal identification. **2.** A unique sequence of nucleotides in a gene, used to identify specific organisms or individuals. SEE: illus.

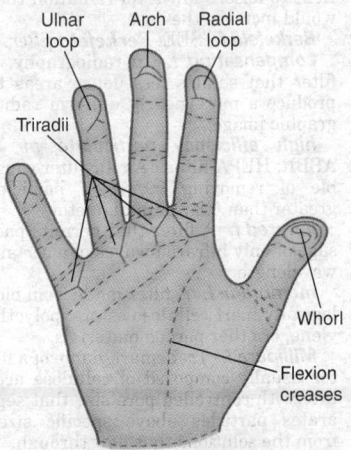

FINGERPRINT

finger rolling test A test for subtle hemiparesis in which the patient is asked to rapidly tap a hard surface with both index fingers at the same time. A finger that taps more slowly than its companion suggests a lesion in the corticospinal tract on the opposite side. SEE: *forearm rolling test.*

finger separator Finger **spreader.**

finger spelling A method of communication used by persons with hearing or visual impairment in which words are spelled out letter by letter rather than depicted with single signs as in American Sign Language. Finger spelling can be done visually as well as tactually.

finger spreader SEE: under *spreader.*

finger spring A device for assisting extension or flexion of finger joints.

finger sweep Placing a finger in the mouth or pharynx of a person with an obstructed upper airway in an attempt to clear a visible foreign body from the airway. Blind finger sweeps, that is, using the hand to clear objects that are not seen, are not recommended.

⚠️ The examiner should wear a glove and use a crossed-fingers technique while attempting to clear foreign bodies from the upper airway because of the risk of injury to the hand from accidental biting by the patient.

fingertip The most dorsal segment of the finger, beyond the nailbed.

finger-to-finger test A test for coordination of the movements of the upper extremities. The patient is asked to touch the tips of the fingers of one hand to the opposite fingertips.

finger-to-nose test A test of cerebellar function wherein the patient is asked, while keeping the eyes open, to touch the nose with the finger and remove the finger, and repeat this rapidly. The test is done by using a finger of each hand successively or in concert. How fast and well this is done is recorded. This test assesses the function of the cerebellum.

finger trapping Using an adjacent digit to provide passive range of motion to an affected (injured, paralyzed) digit.

finite Having limits or boundaries.

Finkelstein test (fing′kĕl-stīn″) [H. Finkelstein, U.S. Surgeon, 1865–1939] A test to assist in the diagnosis of de Quervain disease. The patient tucks the thumb in a closed fist, and the examiner deviates the fist ulnarly. Pain indicates a positive result.

Finney pyloroplasty (fin′ē) [John M. T. Finney, U.S. surgeon, 1865–1939] A side-to-side pyloroplasty in which a single incision opens the pyloric antrum and the proximal duodenum. The two organs are then connected via a U-shaped anastomosis. The procedure is used to treat gastric outlet obstruction.

FIO₂ *fractional concentration of inspired oxygen.*

fire [AS. *fyr*] **1.** Flame that produces heat. **2.** Fever.
  St. Anthony's f. Former term for erysipelas.

firearm (fīr′ärm″) A small, portable gun, e.g., a pistol or a rifle or handheld weapon that uses explosive materials to propel an object toward a person, place, or target at high speed. More firearm-related injuries and deaths occur in the U.S. than in any other industrialized nation. Most of these are among young males, esp. those between 15 and 24 years old.

fire-damp Methane, CH_4, found in coal mines.

firewall A set of programs that protects the resources of a private computer network from users of other networks. It screens the messages that attempt to enter or leave the network and permits or denies access to outside users based on pre-programmed rules.

first aid SEE: under *aid.*

first cranial nerves The nerves supplying the nasal olfactory mucosa. They consist of delicate bundles of unmyelinated fibers, the fila olfactoria, which pass through the cribriform plate and terminate in the olfactory bulb. The fila are the central processes of bipolar receptor neurons of the olfactory mucous membrane. SYN: *olfactory* **nerves.**

first-degree relative One's mother, father, or biologically related sister(s) or brother(s). People are more likely to share potentially inherited conditions with first-degree relatives than with other more distantly related family members.

first disease Measles.

first-dollar coverage (fŭrst′dŏl′ĭr kŏvĭ′r-ĭj) A type of medical insurance in which all costs of care are reimbursed by the insurer, without copayments, deductibles, or other out-of-pocket payments by the insured.

first-in-man study SEE: under *study.*

first intention healing, first-intention healing SEE: *healing* by *first intention.*

first language Native language.

first-line therapy First-line treatment.

first-line treatment The initial, preferred, or best treatment for a disease. It is often the therapy that combines the best efficacy with the best safety profile and/or the lowest cost. SYN: *first-line therapy.*

first responder **1.** The first individual to arrive at the scene of an emergency. Many communities have made an effort to train public safety personnel, e.g., police and fire department or other volunteers to respond to trauma and medical emergencies and provide CPR and first aid. SEE: *emergency medical responder.* **2.** The U.S. Department of Transportation training curriculum designed for the first arriving personnel on the scene of a medical emergency or traumatic event. The focus of this training is to assess and manage life-threatening emergencies.

Fishberg concentration test (fish′bĕrg) [A. M. Fishberg, U.S. physician, 1898–1992] An obsolete test of the ability of the kidneys to produce urine of high specific gravity.

Fisher exact test [R. A. Fisher, Brit. mathematician, 1890–1962] A test used to determine the statistical significance of findings generated from small sets of data.

fish oil SEE: under *oil.*

fish poisoning SEE: under *poisoning.*

fishskin disease A skin disease characterized by increase of the horny layer with scaling and dryness. SYN: *ichthyosis.*

fission (fish′ŭn) [L. *fissio*] **1.** Splitting into two or more parts. **2.** Bombardment or splitting of the nucleus of a heavy atom to release energy and neutrons.
  binary f. Asexual reproduction, or cell division, in prokaryotic cells. The cell enlarges, duplicates its chromosome, and produces a transverse septum to form two identical daughter cells.

fissiparous (fĭ-sĭp′ă-rŭs) [L. *fissus,* cleft, + *parere,* to bring forth] Reproducing by fission.

fissura (fĭs-ū'ră) *pl.* **fissurae** [L.] Fissure.

fissure (fish'ŭr) [L. *fissura,* cleft] **1.** A groove, natural division, cleft, slit, or deep furrow in the brain, liver, spinal cord, and other organs. SYN: *fissura; sulcus.* **2.** An ulcer or cracklike sore. **3.** A break in the enamel of a tooth. **fissural,** *adj.*

anal f. A painful linear ulcer on the margin of the anus. It is a common problem in infancy and fairly common in constipated adults.

PATIENT CARE: Conservative, nonoperative care heals most anal fissures. Patients should be advised to drink a lot of water to lubricate stools, adopt a high-fiber diet, and take a stool softener to ease the passage of stool. Sitting in a warm bath several times a day may help relax the anal sphincters. Medicated creams or ointments may provide topical anesthesia to the anus.

Patients who do not improve with medical therapies may require local injection of botulinum toxin to relax the sphincters or surgery to repair chronic fissures.

anterior median f. In the spinal cord, the groove that runs along the ventral midline.

calcarine f. The fissure extending from the occipital end of the cerebrum to the occipitoparietal fissure.

central f. Rolando fissure.

cerebellar f. A fissure that consists of five deep horizontal (transverse) grooves that separate the cerebellum into its lobes and lobules.

Henle f. SEE: under *Henle, Friedrich J.*

hippocampal f. The fissure extending from the posterior part of the corpus callosum to the tip of the temporal lobe of the brain.

horizontal f. Transverse **f.** (3).

inferior orbital f. The fissure at the apex of the orbit through which the infraorbital blood vessels and maxillary branch of the trigeminal nerve pass.

interparietal f. Intraparietal sulcus.

lateral f. Fissure of Sylvius.

occipitoparietal f. The fissure between the occipital and parietal lobes of the brain.

palpebral f. The opening separating the upper and lower eyelids.

portal f. The opening into the undersurface of the liver. It continues into the liver as the portal canal.

Rolando f. SEE: under *Rolando, Luigi.*

sylvian f. SEE: *Sylvius, Franciscus.*

f. of Sylvius SEE: under *Sylvius, Franciscus.*

transverse f. **1.** The fissure between the cerebellum and cerebrum. **2.** The fissure on the lower surface of the liver that serves as the hilum transmitting

vessels and ducts to the liver. **3.** The fissure that divides the upper right lobe of the lung from the middle right lobe. SYN: *horizontal f.*

umbilical f. The anterior portion of the longitudinal fissure of the liver. It contains the round ligament, the obliterated umbilical vein.

fistula (fis'chŭ-lă) [L. *fistula,* pipe] An abnormal tubelike passage from a normal cavity or tube to a free surface or to another cavity. It may result from a congenital failure of organs to develop properly, or from abscesses, injuries, radiation, malignancies, or inflammatory processes that erode into neighboring organs. **fistulous** (-lŭs), *adj.*

anal f. A fistula near the anus.

arteriovenous f. A fistula between an artery and a vein.

biliary f. A fistula through which bile is discharged after a biliary operation.

blind f. A fistula open at only one end.

branchial f. An open branchial cleft.

bronchopleural f. An abnormal opening between the pleural space and an airway in the lung.

cervical f. **1.** An abnormal opening into the cervix uteri. **2.** An opening in the neck leading to the pharynx, resulting from incomplete closure of the branchial clefts.

complete f. A fistula with both external and internal openings.

congenital pulmonary arteriovenous f. A direct communication of a pulmonary artery with a pulmonary vein within the lung. This congenital condition allows blood to bypass the oxygenation process in the lungs.

craniosinus f. A fistula between the intracranial space and a paranasal sinus.

enterovaginal f. An abnormal canal between the bowel and vagina.

fecal f. A fistula in which there is a discharge of feces through the opening.

gastric f. A tract from the stomach to the abdominal wall or another internal organ, such as the small or large bowel.

horseshoe f. A perianal fistula in which the tract goes around the rectum and communicates with the skin at one or more points.

incomplete f. A fistula with only one opening, which leads to the skin (i.e., it does not communicate with an internal cavity or organ).

metroperitoneal f. An abnormal connection between the uterine and peritoneal cavities.

obstetric f. A complication of excessively prolonged labor and childbirth in which the blood supply to the vagina is interrupted, leading to tissue death and the development of a tract between the vagina and the large bowel or the urinary bladder.

oroantral f. A communicating tract between the oral cavity and the maxillary sinus, occasionally resulting from the extraction of the first or second molar. It may become infected. Treatment varies with the size of the defect. Small lesions heal spontaneously; larger ones may be repaired with flap surgery or with prostheses.

parotid f. A fistula from the parotid gland to the skin surface.

perilymphatic f. A canal through which inner ear fluid may leak into the middle ear that may produce sudden hearing loss, tinnitus, or vertigo. The lesion, which can arise congenitally, after trauma, or by erosion, is one of the few examples of sensorineural hearing loss that can be repaired with surgery to the cochlear aqueduct.

perineovaginal f. An opening from the vagina through the perineum.

pilonidal f. A sinus tract related to a pilonidal cyst.

rectovaginal f. An opening between the rectum and the vagina.

thyroglossal f. A midline fistula just above the thyroid that connects the openings in the skin to a persistent embryonic thyroglossal duct.

tracheoesophageal f. A congenital defect linking the trachea and the esophagus, resulting from failure of the lungs to separate from the gastrointestinal tract during embryological development. Surgery is needed to prevent recurring episodes of aspiration pneumonia in the newborn.

umbilical f. An abnormal congenital passageway between the umbilicus and the gut. It is usually due to nonclosure of the urachal duct.

ureterovaginal f. A fistula between the ureter and the vagina.

vesicouterine f. An abnormal connection between the urinary bladder and the uterus.

vesicovaginal f. An abnormal connection between the urinary bladder and the vagina, usually resulting from surgical trauma, irradiation, or malignancy.

fistulectomy (fĭs″tū-lĕk′tō-mē) [″ + Gr. ektome, excision] Excision of a fistula.

fistulization (fĭsh′chŭ-lĭ-zā′shŏn, -lī-) [fistula] Formation of a fistula by an extension of an inflammatory process from the tissue of origin to an adjacent structure.

fistuloenterostomy (fĭs″tū-lō-ĕn-tĕr-ŏs′tō-mē) [″ + Gr. enteron, intestine, + stoma, mouth] A surgical connection of a fistula into the intestine (e.g., biliary fistula).

fistulogram (fĭs′chŭ-lă-gram″) [fistula + -gram] A radiographical image of any abnormal tunnel found on the surface or inside the body. Images of fluids injected into the fistula reveal the dimensions of the fistula and show the organs in which it originates and ends.

fistulotomy (fĭs″chŭ-lot′ŏ-mē, fĭsh″) [fistula + -tomy] Surgical treatment of a fistula typically originating in the gastrointestinal tract, e.g., an anal fistula or a fistula resulting from Crohn disease.

fit (fĭt) [AS. fitt] **1.** A sudden attack, convulsion, or paroxysm. SEE: convulsion. **2.** Modification of one structure to that of another, as in dental restoration.

fitness (fĭt′nĕs) **1.** Biological fitness. **2.** Physical fitness.

biological f. The ability of an individual to produce offspring that survive to adult life and are themselves able to reproduce.

physical f. The ability to carry out daily tasks with vigor and alertness, without undue fatigue, and with enough energy to enjoy leisure-time pursuits and meet unforeseen emergencies. It is the ability to withstand stress and persevere under difficult circumstances in which an unfit person would quit. Fitness is more than absence of illness; it is a positive quality that everyone has to some degree. It is minimal in the severely ill and maximal in the highly trained athlete. People who maintain a high level of fitness may have increased longevity as compared to those who are sedentary. In addition, the quality of life is enhanced for those who are fit.

fit test A test to determine how effectively a mask or respirator will protect the wearer from inhaled dusts, gases, or pathogens.

PATIENT CARE: The tester places the mask on the wearer's face, making certain that it covers the nose and mouth when the wearer is stationary, moves the head and neck, or speaks. Then the tester sprays an aromatic aerosol into the air around the wearer, who is asked if he or she can taste or smell it. A mask that fits properly prevents detection of odor or taste. SYN: respirator fit testing.

Fitzpatrick skin type (fĭts-pa′trĭk) [T. B. Fitzpatrick, U.S. Dermatologist, 1919–2003] A classification system for determining how reactive a person's skin is to ultraviolet light. The system divides people into six phototypes, numbered I to VI. Type I skin type is the fairest, most freckled, and most susceptible to photodamage or damage by laser treatments. Type VI is the darkest skin type and the most resistant to sunburn and photodamage.

fix 1. To treat tissues chemically so that the components and products of the cells are preserved for staining and microscopic examination. **2.** Slang for a dose of a drug of abuse. **3.** In film processing, the step that stops the development action, removes the undeveloped silver halide crystals, and makes the image permanent.

fixation (fĭk-sā'shŏn) [L. *fixatio,* fixed state] **1.** The act of holding or fastening in a rigid position. The act of immobilizing or making rigid. **2.** Rigidity or immobility. **3.** A phase of Freudian psychosexual development in which the libido is arrested at an early or presexual level. **4.** Staining of microscopic specimens for examination. **5.** The process of making a film-recorded image permanent.

   binocular f. Focusing of both eyes on an object.

   complement f. A common blood assay used to determine if antigen-antibody reactions have occurred. Complement that combines with the antigen-antibody complex becomes inactive and is unable to lyse (kill) red blood cells in vitro. The degree of complement fixation is determined by the number of red blood cells destroyed, which indicates the amount of free complement not bound to the antigen-antibody complexes. Complement fixation can measure the severity of an infection because it helps indicate the extent and effectiveness of antigen-antibody reactions occurring in the body. SEE: *complement.*

   external f. The placement of devices (such as metallic pins) through the skin and soft tissues into fractured bone segments to hold the fragments in place while they heal.

   f. of eyes Movement of the eyes so that the visual axes meet and the image of an object falls on corresponding points of each retina. This provides the most acute visualization of the object.

   internal f. The use of internal wires, screws, or pins applied directly to fractured bone segments to keep them temporarily or permanently in place.

   nitrogen f. The conversion of atmospheric nitrogen into nitrates through the action of bacteria in the soil.

fixative (fĭk'să-tĭv) [L. *fixus,* fastened] **1.** A substance that firms or makes rigid. **2.** A substance used to preserve normal and pathological specimens for gross examination or for the sectioning and preparation of microscope slides.

fixed-dose combination A combination of two or more drugs in one capsule, injection, or tablet to simplify drug regimens and improve compliance.

fixer (fĭk'sĕr) A reagent that stops the development of a radiographic image, removes undeveloped silver halide crystals, and hardens the emulsion. The typical fixer consists of a clearing agent, preservative, hardener, and acidifier.

Fl *fluid.*

FLACC behavioral pain assessment scale [*Face, Legs, Activity, Cry, and Consolability of the patient*] A method of assessing postoperative pain levels in young children or in those with cognitive impairments that prevent them from expressing themselves clearly.

flaccid (flăk'sĭd) [L. *flaccidus,* flabby] Relaxed; flabby; having defective or absent muscular tone.

flagella (flă-jĕl'ă) [L.] Pl. of flagellum.

flagellant (flăj'ĕ-lănt) [L. *flagellum,* whip] **1.** Pert. to a flagellum. **2.** Pert. to stroking in massage. **3.** One who practices flagellation.

flagellate (flăj'ĕ-lāt) **1.** Having one or more flagella. **2.** A protozoon with one or more flagella.

flagellation (flăj'ĕ-lā'shŭn) **1.** Whipping. **2.** Massage by strokes. **3.** A form of sexual behavior in which the libido is stimulated by whipping oneself, being whipped, or whipping someone else. **4.** The arrangement of flagella on the surface of a microorganism.

flagelliform (flă-jĕl'ĭ-form) [" + *forma,* shape] Shaped like a flagellum.

flagellum (flă-jĕl'ŭm) *pl.* **flagella** [L., whip] A threadlike structure that provides motility for certain bacteria and protozoa (one, few, or many per cell) and for spermatozoa (one per cell).

flag sign SEE: under *sign.*

flammable Burning easily.

flange (flănj) **1.** A border that projects above the main structure. **2.** In dentistry, the part of an artificial denture that extends from the embedded teeth to the border of the denture.

flank [O. Fr. *flanc*] The part of the body between the ribs and the upper border of the ilium. The term also refers loosely to the outer side of the thigh, hip, and buttock. SEE: *latus.*

flap (flap) **1.** A mass of partially detached tissue. **2.** A mass of partially detached tissued incurred by accidental trauma used in plastic surgery of an adjacent area or in covering the end of a bone after resection. **3.** An uncontrolled movement seen in some diseases. SEE: *asterixis.*

   flip-flop f. In plastic surgery, the turning of a partially detached flap or island of tissue in a new direction to cover a defect or to reconstruct a missing structure.

   island f. A skin flap or myocutaneous tissue in which the edges are free but the center is attached and contains the vascular supply.

   liver f. Asterixis.

   mucoperiosteal f. A flap of mucosal tissue, including the underlying periosteum, reflected from the bone during oral surgery.

   pedicle f. A partially detached piece of tissue that is attached on one end to a source of blood. The other end may be surgically connected to a site from which a new blood supply may develop. SYN: *pedicle graft.*

periodontal f. A section of soft tissue surgically separated from underlying bone and removed or repositioned to eliminate periodontal pockets or to correct mucogingival defects.

skin f. A flap containing only skin.

sliding f. Horizontal movement of a flap to cover a nearby denuded area.

tube f. A variety of pedicle flap which is fashioned into a tubular configuration. SEE: *pedicle f.*

flare **1.** A flush or spreading area of redness that surrounds a line made by drawing a pointed instrument across the skin. It is the second reaction in the triple response of skin to injury and is due to dilatation of the arterioles. SEE: *triple response.* **2.** An exacerbation of any inflammatory condition or disease, such as the sudden worsening of rheumatoid arthritis or systemic lupus erythematosis (SLE).

flaring, nasal Dilation of the nostrils during inspiration; a sign of respiratory distress.

flash **1.** A hot flash. A flush accompanied by a sensation of heat. It is common during menopause. SYN: *hot flush.* SEE: *menopause.* **2.** Excess material from a mold.

flashback The return of imagery and/or hallucinations after the immediate effects of a traumatic or hallucinogenic experience.

flash method SEE: under *method.*

flask [LL. *flasco*] A small bottle with a narrow neck.

flat (flat) **1.** Level and smooth. **2.** Of a line on a chart, horizontal. **3.** In psychology, lacking in expressive range. **4.** In electrocardiography, isoelectric.

flatfoot Abnormal flatness of the sole and the arch of the foot. This condition may exist without causing symptoms or interfering with normal function of the foot. The inner longitudinal and anterior transverse metatarsal arches may be depressed. This condition may be acute, subacute, or chronic. SYN: *pes planus; splayfoot.* SEE: illus.

spasmodic f. Flatfoot in which the foot is held everted by spasmodic contraction of the peroneal muscle.

flatness Resonance heard on percussion over solid organs or when there is fluid in the thoracic cavity.

flatplate (flăt′plāt) A radiograph requiring a frontal projection of the abdomen or other body part with the patient supine.

flat screen, flat screen display, flat screen monitor A thin viewing monitor that utilizes a plasma or liquid display.

flatulence (flăt′ū-lĕns) [L. *flatulentus*] Excessive gas in the stomach and intestines. SEE: *distention; gastrointestinal decompression; paralytic ileus.* **flatulent** (flăch′ŭ-lĕnt), *adj.*

PATIENT CARE: Initial assessment

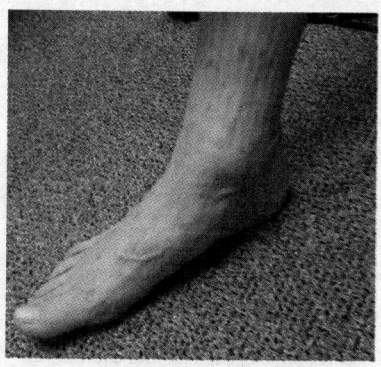

FLATFOOT (PES PLANUS)

should include auscultation of bowel sounds, percussion, and observation and measurement of abdominal girth. The patient is questioned about the presence and location of any pain or cramping and the passage of flatus. Bowel sounds are assessed and abdominal girth measured. If the situation is acute in onset or associated with severe pain or altered vital signs, x-rays or other investigative studies may be ordered. If the condition is deemed functional, ambulation is encouraged to increase peristalsis. If the patient cannot ambulate or if ambulation is ineffective, the patient is turned from side to side (or as permitted by activity restrictions). If the gaseous accumulation is thought to be intracolonic, laxative suppositories or enemas may be given to help the patient expel flatus and to relieve gaseous distention. If the patient is able to eat, medications containing simethicone may provide some degree of relief. If bowel sounds decrease or abdominal distention increases (as demonstrated by percussion, abdominal girth measurement, and increasing patient discomfort) and flatus is not passed, a diagnosis of ileus is suggested.

flatus (flā′tŭs) [L. *flatus,* a blowing] **1.** Gas in the digestive tract. **2.** Expulsion of gas from a body orifice, esp. the anus. The average person excretes 400 to 1200 cc of gas each day. The gas passages may average a dozen a day in some persons and up to a hundred in others. Flatus from the lower intestinal tract contains hydrogen, methane, skatoles, indoles, carbon dioxide, and small amounts of oxygen and nitrogen. SEE: *borborygmus; eructation.*

Foods known for their ability to cause excess intestinal gas include beans, peas, lentils, cabbage, onions, Brussels sprouts, bananas, apples, raisins, apricots, high-fiber cereals, whole wheat products, milk and milk products, and sorbitol present in some dietetic foods.

TREATMENT: Some persons can control excess intestinal gas by avoiding foods they have found to be flatulogenic. Simethicone, an ingredient in many over the counter anti-gas medications, is also effective.

Administration of the enzyme alpha-D-galactosidase derived from *Aspergillus niger* may be effective in treating intestinal gas or bloating due to eating a variety of grains, cereals, nuts, and seeds of vegetables containing sugars such as raffinose or verbacose. This includes oats, wheat, beans, peas, lentils, foods containing soy, pistachios, broccoli, Brussels sprouts, cabbage, carrots, corn, onions, squash, and cauliflower.

vaginal f. Expulsion of air from the vagina. Air can enter the vagina during sexual intercourse.

flatus tube A rectal tube to facilitate expulsion of flatus. It formerly was used in cases of severe distention or before a saline enema.

flatworm (flăt'worm) A worm belonging to the phylum Platyhelminthes.

flavescent (flă-vĕs'ĕnt) Yellowish.

Flavimonas oryzihabitans (flă''vĭ-mō'năs, vĭm'ŏ, ō-rī''zĭ-hăb'ĭ-tăns) [L. *flavus,* tawny, yellow + Gr. *monas,* unit; L. fm. Gr. *oryza,* rice + L. *habitare,* to inhabit] SEE: *Pseudomonas oryzihabitans.*

flavin (flā'vĭn) One of a group of natural water-soluble pigments occurring in milk, yeasts, bacteria, and some plants. All contain the flavin or isoalloxazine nucleus and are yellow. Flavin is present in riboflavin and nicotinamide adenine dinucleotide dehydrogenase.

flavin adenine dinucleotide ABBR: FAD. A hydrogen carrier in the citric acid cycle of cell respiration; it is a derivative of riboflavin.

flavism (flā'vĭzm) [L. *flavus,* yellow, + Gr. *-ismos,* condition] Having a yellow tinge.

Flavivirus (flā''vē-vī'rŭs) A genus of RNA viruses of the family Flaviviridae, previously called arboviruses. In this genus are the agents of yellow fever, West Nile and St. Louis encephalitis, and dengue fever. The vectors are usually mosquitoes.

Flavobacterium (flā''vō-băk-tē'rē-ŭm) A genus of gram-negative, rod-shaped bacteria found in soil and water. In culture the bacteria produce an orange-yellow pigment. Members of the genus rarely cause human infections. When they do, they typically infect immune-suppressed or critically ill patients. One species, *Flavobacterium meningosepticum* is esp. virulent for premature infants, in whom it causes a potentially fatal meningitis.

flavone (flā'vōn) $C_{15}H_{10}O_2$; the chemical from which the natural colors of many vegetables are derived.

flavonoid (flā'vŏ-noyd'') Any of a large group of pigmented compounds found in fruits and vegetables. They are antioxidants SYN: *bioflavonoid.*

flavoprotein (flā''vō-prō'tēn) One of a group of conjugated proteins that contain nicotinamide adenine dinucleotide (NAD) phosphate and NAD dehydrogenase, enzymes that are essential in cellular respiration.

flavor (flā'vor) **1.** The quality of a substance that affects the sense of taste. It may also stimulate the sense of smell. **2.** A material added to a food or medicine to improve its taste.

flaxseed (flăks'sēd) The seed of *Linum usitatissimum.* SYN: *linseed.*

flaxseed oil (flăks'sēd'') SEE: under *oil.*

fl. dr. *fluidram.*

flea (flē) An insect of the order Siphonaptera. Fleas are wingless, suck blood, and have legs adapted for jumping. Usually they are parasitic on warm-blooded animals, including humans. Fleas of the genus *Xenopsylla* transmit the plague bacillus *(Yersinia pestis)* from rats to humans. Fleas may transmit other diseases such as tularemia, endemic typhus, and brucellosis. They are intermediate hosts for cat and dog tapeworms.

cat f. SEE: *Ctenocephalides.*

chigger f. **Tunga** penetrans.

dog f. SEE: *Ctenocephalides.*

human f. **Pulex** irritans

rat f. **Xenopsylla** cheopis

flea infestation The harboring of fleas, esp. in a home with dogs or cats. It is possible to kill the flea population by treating the house for 24 hr by using naphthalene, permethrins, and other substances.

⚠ Any plants, pets, or humans could suffer adverse effects if they remain in the house during the treatment period. The house should be thoroughly ventilated afterwards to remove the fumes.

fleece of Stilling A meshwork of white fibers that surrounds the dentate nucleus of the cerebellum.

Fleming, Sir Alexander (flĕm'ĭng) A Scottish physician, 1881–1955, who in 1945, along with Ernst B. Chain and Sir Howard W. Florey, was awarded the Nobel Prize in medicine and physiology for the discovery of penicillin.

flesh (flesh) The soft tissues of the animal body, esp. the muscles. SEE: *carnivorous; meat.*

goose f. Cutis anserina.

proud f. SEE: *lobular capillary hemangioma* under hemangioma.

Fletcher factor (flech'ĕr) [*Fletcher,* name of a family in Kentucky in whom the factor was first described] Prekallikrein.

flex (fleks) [L. *flexus,* bent] **1.** To contract, as a muscle; to decrease the angle of a joint. **2.** To fold the bones and soft tissues of a joint from a more or less straightened condition into a V-shaped position.

Flexeril SEE: *cyclobenzaprine.*

flexibilitas cerea (flĕks″ĭ-bĭl′ĭ-tăs sē′rē-ă) [L.] Waxy flexibility.

flexibility [L. *flexus,* bent] **1.** Adaptability. **2.** The quality of bending without breaking;. SYN: *pliability.*

relative f. Increased mobility or frequency of movement in a joint adjacent to a body part with restricted mobility, such as an injured muscle, bone, capsule, tendon, or ligament. This can be a normal relationship between segments, but it can cause pathology and impairments. Relative flexibility can account for overuse, sprain, or strain of a joint due to stiffness in an adjacent joint. For example, lumbar spine strain due to short hamstrings limits hip motion.

waxy f. A cataleptic state in which limbs retain any position in which they are placed. It is characteristic of catatonic patients. SYN: *flexibilitas cerea.* **flexible,** *adj.*

flexicurve (fleks′ĭ-kŭrv″) [*flexible* + *curve*] A flexible ruler consisting of a length of lead covered with synthetic rubber and applied to the skin to estimate degree of spinal contour. It has been used to measure kyphosis and lordosis, but its measurements do not always match those found radiographically. SYN: *surveyor's flexicurve.*

flexile (flĕks′ĭl) [L. *flexus,* bent] Pliant, flexible.

flexion (flĕk′shŭn) [L. *flexio*] **1.** The act of bending or condition of being bent in contrast to extension. SEE: *antecurvature.* **2.** Decrease in the angle between the bones forming a joint.

flexor (flĕks′or) [L.] A muscle that brings two bones closer together, causing flexion of the part or a decreased angle of the joint. Opposed to extensor.

flexure (flek′shŭr) [L. *flexura,* bending, winding] **1.** A bend. **2.** The state or quality of being flexed or bent. **3.** Something flexed or bent.

anorectal f. The sharp forward bend at the anorectal junction as the rectum passes through the pelvic diaphragm muscles. This acute bend, which is normally maintained by the puborectalis sling muscles, helps to keep feces in the rectum. During defecation the pelvic diaphragm muscles relax (so the puborectalis sling relaxes) and the sharp bend between rectum and anus straightens; this makes the passage of feces from rectum to anus easier.

duodenojejunal f. A sharp curve at the meeting point of the jejunum and duodenum. The duodenojejunal flexure hangs from the diaphragm by a thin

muscle, the suspensory muscle of the diaphragm.

hepatic f. The bend of the colon under the liver; the junction of the ascending and transverse colon. SYN: *right colic f.*

left colic f. Splenic **f.**

right colic f. Hepatic **f.**

sigmoid f. An S-like curve (in the left iliac fossa) of the descending colon as it joins the rectum. Former name for sigmoid colon. SEE: *colon* for illus.

splenic f. The bend of the colon near the spleen; the junction of the transverse and descending colon. The splenic fixture is suspended from the diaphragm by the phrenocolic ligament, which passes over the lower part of the left kidney. SYN: *left colic f.* **flexural** ('shŭr-ăl), *adj.*

flicker The visual sensation of alternating intervals of brightness caused by rhythmic interruption of light stimuli.

flicker phenomenon A sensation of continuous light caused by an intermittent light stimulus produced at a certain rate.

flight of ideas Continuous but fragmented use of language. It is a hallmark of psychosis or mania. The general train of thought can be followed, but direction is frequently changed, often by chance stimuli from the environment.

Flinders island spotted fever (flin′dĕrz) [Name of an island off northeast Tasmania] SEE: under *fever.*

flip-flop A condition in which the reduction in fraction of inspired oxygen to reduce hypoxemia in infants causes a persistent and greater-than-expected decrease in oxygen tension (PaO_2).

floater (flō′tĕr) [AS. *flotian,* float] A translucent speck that passes across the visual field. Floaters vary in size and shape. They are due to small bits of protein or cells floating in the vitreous. Most people have these benign materials in their eyes. They can also be associated with posterior vitreous detachments, retinal hemorrhages, inflammation, or detachment SEE: *muscae volitantes.*

floating [AS *flota,* a raft] **1.** Moving about; out of normal location. **2.** A staffing arrangement in which one may be asked to work on any of several hospital wards or units, depending on the immediate needs of the health care institution. **3.** In anatomy, free; unattached.

floating ribs The 11th and 12th ribs, which do not articulate with the sternum.

floccillation, floccitation (flok″sĭ-lā′shŏn, flok″sĭ-tā′shŏn) [L. *floccilatio*] Semiconscious picking at bedclothes in association with fever, stupor, and delirium. SYN: *carphology.*

floccose (flŏk′ōs) [L. *floccosus,* full of

wool tufts] In biology, pert. to a growth consisting of short and densely but irregularly interwoven filaments.

flocculence (flŏk′ū-lĕns″) Resemblance to shreds or tufts of cotton.

flocculent (flŏk′ū-lĕnt) **1.** Resembling tufts or shreds of cotton. **2.** Pert. to a fluid or culture containing whitish shreds of mucus.

flocculus (flŏk′ū-lŭs) *pl.* **flocculi** [L., little tuft] **1.** A small tuft of woollike fibers. **2.** A lobe below and behind the middle peduncle of the cerebrum on each side of the median fissure. **floccular,** *adj.*

Flonase SEE: *fluticasone.*

flood (flŭd) **1.** A pathological uterine hemorrhage. **2.** Excessive menstrual bleeding. **3.** To fill or overflow with fluid.

flooding (flŭd′ĭng) **1.** A colloquial term for excessive menstrual flow. **2.** In treating phobias, repeated exposure to the disturbing ideas, situations, or conditions until these no longer produce anxiety.

floor (flor) The surface that forms the lower limit of a cavity or space, as of the cranial cavity, fourth ventricle, mouth, nasal fossa, pelvis, or a cavity preparation in a tooth.

    pelvic f. The connective tissues and muscles (including the coccygeus and the levator ani muscles) that lie beneath and support the perineum and pelvis. Weakening of the tissues of the pelvic floor can occur during childbirth or after radiation, surgery, or trauma to the pelvis, resulting in pelvic floor disorders such as organ prolapse or urinary or fecal incontinence. SYN: *pelvic dia-phragm; pelvic support.*

floor effect A statistical error in which very low data points are not registered or counted because of an artificial limitation that prevents them from being appropriately noted and recorded. In research on certain variables, e.g., body temperature, data are meaningless below levels incompatible with life.

floppy infant syndrome An umbrella term for a variety of disorders appearing in childhood in which the child's muscular tone is reduced. SYN: *infantile hypotonia.*

floppy-valve syndrome Mitral valve prolapse.

flora [L. *flos*, flower] **1.** Plant life as distinguished from animal life. **2.** Microbial life occurring or adapted for living in a specific environment, such as the intestinal, vaginal, oral, or skin flora. SEE: *fauna.*

    intestinal f. Bacteria present in the intestines. The colon of the fetus is sterile, but bacteria are acquired during vaginal birth and subsequently from people and the environment. These bacteria produce vitamins, esp. vitamin K, and inhibit the growth of pathogens.

Certain antibiotics may reduce the number and kinds of bacteria present. SEE: *Clostridium difficile.*

    normal f. Microorganisms including bacteria, protozoa, and fungi that are found on or in specific areas of the body. The skin and mucous membranes of the oral cavity, intestines, upper respiratory tract, and vagina have specific, permanent flora. They are harmless, even beneficial, in their usual sites, and they inhibit the growth of pathogens, but they can cause infection if they are introduced into unusual sites. If the proportions of the various microorganisms are disrupted, one species may overgrow, as does *Candida* when bacterial flora are diminished by antibiotics. SYN: *resident f.* SEE: *colitis, pseudomembranous; infection; microorganism.*

    The largest concentration of bacteria in humans is in the colon, where more than 400 genera may coexist. In the colon, anaerobic bacteria outnumber aerobic bacteria 1000:1, and there may be 10^{11} per g of fecal material. The anaerobic gram-positive lactobacilli may be concentrated in the vagina at the 10^5 to 10^8/ml level, but 20% of women have no detectable anaerobes in the vagina. In dental plaque and gingival sulci, the bacteria may reach a concentration of 10^{12}/ml.

    resident f. Normal flora.

    transient f. Microbes inhabiting a body surface or cavity for a brief period of time, usually as a result of their promotion and selection by antibiotic therapy, chemotherapy, hospitalization, illness, or surgery.

Flor-Essence A tea containing anti-inflammatory, antioxidant, and immunostimulatory chemicals. It is not approved as a treatment for cancer by the U.S. Food and Drug Administration.

florid (flor′ĭd) [L. *floridus*, blossoming] **1.** Bright deep-red. The term describes skin coloration. **2.** Complete or full-bodied, as in an illness that is in full flower.

floss **1.** A waxed or unwaxed tape or thread used to clean and remove plaque between teeth and below the gumline. SYN: *dental f.* **2.** To use dental floss or tape to remove plaque and calculus from the otherwise inaccessible dental surfaces between teeth.

    dental f. Floss (1).

flour [L. *flos*, flower] Finely ground meal obtained from wheat or other grain; any soft fine powder.

Flovent SEE: *fluticasone.*

flow [AS. *flowan*, to flow] **1.** Movement of a gas or liquid. **2.** The act of moving or running freely.

    laminar f. Laminar air flow.

    peak f. The maximum volume of air that can be expelled from the lungs during a vigorous exhalation. Its measurement is used to determine the degree of respiratory impairment in patients with obstructive lung diseases.

turbulent f. A movement of gas in disorderly currents, associated with high velocity and high density with increased tubing diameter.

flow cell SEE: under *cell*.

flowmeter (flō′mēt″ĕr) [*flow* + *-meter*] A device for measuring the movement of a gas or liquid. It is used esp. in monitoring the use of anesthetic gases. **flowmetry,** *n.*

flow-sensitive alternating inversion recovery magnetic resonance imaging ABBR: FAIR-MRI. Magnetic resonance imaging of an organ of the body, e.g., the heart or the brain, that allows visualization not only of the organ but also of the movement of body fluids such as blood or cerebrovascular fluid through it.

flow state An altered state of consciousness in which the mind functions at its peak, time may seem distorted, and a sense of happiness prevails. In such a state the individual feels truly alive and fully attentive to what is being done. This state is distinguished from strained attention, in which the person forces himself to perform a task in which he has little interest.

floxuridine (flōks-ŭr′ĭ-dēn) An antimetabolite used to treat solid cancers (e.g., adenocarcinomas).

fl. oz. *fluid ounce.*

flu (floo) [(*in*)*flu*(*enza*)] **1.** Influenza. **2.** An imprecise term for any respiratory or gastrointestinal illness, but esp. influenza.

avian f. Avian **influenza**.
bird f. Avian **influenza**.
swine f. Swine **influenza**.

Fluarix (floo′ă-rĭks) Influenza virus vaccine, trivalent, types A and B.

fluconazole (floo-kŏn′ĭ-zōl″) A systemic antifungal administered orally or intravenously to treat fungal infections caused by susceptible organisms. Such conditions include oropharyngeal and esophageal candidiasis, serious systemic candidal infections, urinary tract infections, peritonitis, and cryptococcal meningitis. SYN: *Diflucan*.

fluctuant (flŭk′chū-ănt) Varying or unstable. SEE: *fluctuation*.

fluctuation (flŭk″chū-ā′shŭn) [L. *fluctuatio*] **1.** A variation from one course to another. **2.** A wavy impulse felt during palpation. It is produced by vibration of body fluid, e.g., the contents of an abscess.

flucytosine (flū-sī′tō-sēn″) An antifungal drug used to treat candida, cryptococci, and other fungi. It is used with amphotericin B to improve the efficacy of therapy against cryptococcal meningitis.

fludeoxyglucose (floo″dē-ok″sē-gloo′kōs″) Fluorodeoxyglucose.

fluence (floo′ĕns) [L. *fluere*, to flow] In radiation oncology, the number of photons per unit area, measured in J/m^2 (joules/square meter). Fluence is one of several modifiable factors in the treatment of diseased tissues with radiation.

fluency (floo′ĕn-sē) The ease and efficiency of speech; the production of speech without pauses, lapses, or hesitation. **fluent,** *adj.*

fluid (floo′id) [L. *fluidus,* flowing] A nonsolid, liquid, or gaseous substance. SEE: *secretion*.

allantoic f. Fluid found in the fetal membrane that develops from the yolk sac.

amniotic f. A clear fluid that surrounds the fetus in the amniotic sac. Its primary functions are to suspend and protect the growing fetus, allow freedom of movement, maintain even constant temperature, and aid normal development of the fetal lungs. Volume increases from about 50 ml at 12 gestational weeks to around 800 ml at 38 weeks. The fluid is constantly being circulated by the fetus swallowing fluid, urinating, and inhaling/exhaling fluid during fetal respiration. Samples of amniotic fluid may be collected by amniocentesis to identify fetal chromosomal abnormalities, state of health, and maturity. SYN: *liquor amnii*. SEE: *amniocentesis; oligohydramnios; polyhydramnios*.

ascitic f. Clear, pale, straw-colored fluid occurring in ascites. The fluid is normally sterile; its specific gravity is normally 1.005 to 1.015; the cellular content is less than 250 white blood cells per cubic millimeter, and its protein content is low. Cancer, heart failure, liver failure, peritonitis, and tuberculosis may alter the amount or character of ascites.

body f. A fluid found in one of the fluid compartments of the body. The principal fluid compartments are intracellular and extracellular. A much smaller segment, the transcellular, includes fluid in the tracheobronchial tree, the gastrointestinal tract, and the bladder; cerebrospinal fluid; and the aqueous humor of the eye. The chemical composition of fluids in the various compartments is carefully regulated. In a normal 154 lb (70 kg) adult human male, 60% of total body weight, i.e., 42 L is water; in a normal adult female is 55% of total body weight is water (39 L). SEE: *acid-base balance; fluid replacement; fluid balance*.

Bouin f. SEE: *Bouin fluid*.

cerebrospinal f. ABBR: CSF. The sodium-rich, potassium-poor tissue fluid of the brain and spinal cord. The fluid supplies nutrients and removes waste products; it is also a watery cushion that absorbs mechanical shock to the central nervous system. SYN: *spinal f.* SEE: *lumbar puncture*.

FORMATION: The fluid is formed by the choroid plexuses of the lateral and third ventricles. That of the lateral ventricles passes through the foramen of Monro to the third ventricle, and through the aqueduct of Sylvius to the fourth ventricle. There it may escape through the central foramen of Magendie or the lateral foramina of Luschke into the cisterna magna and to the cranial and spinal subarachnoid spaces. It is reabsorbed through the arachnoid villi into the blood in the cranial venous sinuses, and through the perineural lymph spaces of both the brain and the cord. SEE: illus.

CHARACTERISTICS: The fluid is normally watery, clear, colorless, and almost entirely free of cells. The initial pressure of spinal fluid in a side-lying adult is about 100 to 180 mm of water. On average, the total protein is about 15 to 50 mg/dL, and the concentration of glucose is about twothirds the concentration of glucose in the patient's serum. Its pH, which is rarely measured clinically, is slightly more acidic than the pH of blood. Its concentration and alkaline reserve are similar to those of blood. It does not clot on standing. Turbidity suggests an excessively high number of cells in the fluid, typically white blood cells in infections such as meningitis or red blood cells in intracerebral hemorrhage.

CSF may appear red following a recent subarachnoid hemorrhage or when the lumbar puncture that obtained the CSF caused traumatic injury to the dura that surround the fluid. Centrifugation of the fluid can distinguish between these two sources of blood in the spinal fluid: the supernatant is usually stained yellow (xanthochromic) only when there has been a recent subarachnoid hemorrhage.

Many conditions may cause increases in CSF total protein: infections, such as acute or chronic meningitis; multiple sclerosis (when oligoclonal protein bands are present); Guillain-Barré syndrome; and chronic medical conditions like cirrhosis and hypothyroidism (when diffuse hypergammaglobulinemia is present). The concentration of glucose in the CSF rises in uncontrolled diabetes mellitus and drops precipitously in meningitis, sarcoidosis, and some other illnesses. Malignant cells in the CSF, demonstrated after centrifugation or filtering, are hallmarks of carcinomatous meningitis.

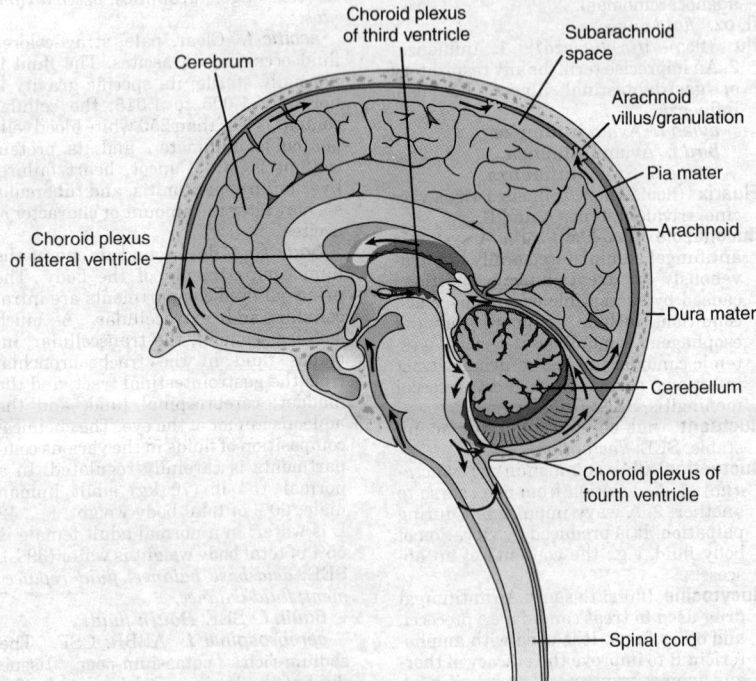

FLOW OF CEREBROSPINAL FLUID THROUGH THE BRAIN AND SPINAL COLUMN
Formation, circulation, and reabsorption of CSF

MICROORGANISMS: The CSF is normally sterile. Meningococci, streptococci, *Haemophilus influenzae, Listeria monocytogenes,* and gram-negative bacilli are recovered from the CSF only in cases of meningitis. Syphilitic meningitis is usually diagnosed with serological tests for the disease, such as the venereal disease research laboratory (VDRL) test, the rapid plasma reagin (RPR) test, or the fluorescent treponemal antibody test. Cryptococcal infection of the CSF may be demonstrated by India ink preparations, or by latex agglutination tests. Tuberculous meningitis may sometimes be diagnosed with Ziehl-Neelsen stains, but more often this is done with cultures. These last three infections (syphilis, cryptococcosis, and tuberculosis) are much more common in patients who have acquired immunodeficiency syndrome (AIDS) than in the general population.

crevicular f. Gingival sulcular **f.**

extracellular f. The body fluid outside of cells. It includes the interstitial, intravascular, and cerebrospinal fluids. Water is the common solvent of all these fluids. Approximately 36% of an adult's body fluids and 47% of and infant's body fluids are extracellular.

extravascular f. Interstitial **f.**

follicular f. The liquid rich in heparin sulfate, hyaluronic acid, anti-müllerian hormone, defensins, and other chemicals that surrounds developing oocytes as they mature in the ovary.

gingival f. Gingival sulcular **f.**

gingival sulcular f. ABBR: GSF. In dentistry, the fluid that seeps through the gingival epithelium. It increases with gingival inflammation. Cellular elements within GSF include bacteria, desquamated epithelial cells, and leukocytes. Electrolytes and some organic compounds are also present. SYN: *crevicular f.; gingival f.*

interstitial f. Water and dissolved substances inside tissues but outside of cells and vessels. Interstitial fluid is largely the ultrafiltrate of arterial blood, having been pushed through capillary walls by hydrostatic force; therefore it has a salt concentration similar to blood serum. Normally, approximately 29% of an adult's body fluids and 40% of an infant's body fluids are interstitial fluids. Excess interstitial fluid is returned to the circulation by the lymphatics. An accumulation of excess interstitial fluid is called edema. SYN: *extravascular f.*

intracellular f. ABBR: ICF. The potassium-rich, sodium-poor watery solution inside cells. Approx. 55 to 75% of total body water is intracellular.

intraocular f. Fluid within the anterior and posterior chambers of the eye. SYN: *aqueous humor.*

intravascular f. That portion of the total body fluid contained within blood and lymphatic vessels.

peritoneal f. The clear straw-colored serous fluid secreted by the cells of the peritoneum. The few milliliters present in the peritoneal cavity moisten the surfaces of the two peritoneal layers and allow them to glide over each other as the intestinal tract changes shape during the process of digestion and absorption. In certain diseases (such as right-sided heart failure, cirrhosis, or ovarian malignancy) the amount of peritoneal fluid increases, and its appearance may become bloody or cloudy. SEE: *ascites.*

pleural f. Fluid secreted by serous membranes in the pleurae that reduces friction during respiratory movements of the lungs. When excessive pleural fluid is secreted and not absorbed, a pleural effusion accumulates.

seminal f. Semen.

serous f. Fluid secreted by serous membranes that reduces friction in the serous cavities (pleural, pericardial, and peritoneal).

spinal f. Cerebrospinal **f.**

synovial f. Clear viscid lubricating fluid of the joint, bursae, and tendon sheaths, secreted by the synovial membrane of a joint. It contains mucin, albumin, fat, and electrolytes. SYN: *synovia.* SEE: *synovial joint.*

transcellular f. The extracellular fluid that lubricates the potential spaces of the body, such as the pleura and pericardium.

Zenker f. SEE: under *Zenker, Friedrich Albert von.*

fluid ability SEE: under *ability.*

fluid balance SEE: under *balance.*

fluid balance, readiness for enhanced A pattern of equilibrium between fluid volume and chemical composition of body fluids that is sufficient for meeting physical needs and can be strengthened. SEE: *Nursing Diagnoses Appendix.*

fluidextract, fluid extract (floo″ĭd-ek′strakt″\) [*fluid + extract*] A solution of the soluble constituents of vegetable drugs in which each cubic centimeter or milliliter represents 1 g of the drug. Fluidextracts contain alcohol as a solvent or preservative. Many of them form precipitates when water is added.

fluidized therapy (floo′ĭd-īzd″) The use of small solid particles suspended within moving air to treat pain, decrease hypersensitivity in extremities, or prevent or treat pressure sores.

fluidotherapy (floo″ĭd-ō-thĕr′ă-pē) [″ + ″] The application of warmed cellulose particles suspended in forced dry air to heat an injured or painful body part, esp. prior to muscle strengthening or range-of-motion exercises.

fluid ounce (floo″ĭd-owns′) ABBR: fl. oz.

An apothecaries' measure of fluid volume, equal to 8 fluidrams or 29.57 ml.

fluidram (floo″ĭ-drăm′) An apothecaries' measure of fluid volume, equal to 3.697 ml.

fluid replacement Administration of liquids to a patient by any route to correct volume and electrolyte deficits. The deficit may be physiological, as when a ballplayer sweats excessively without rehydrating on a hot day. It may be pathological, as in traumatic or septic shock, acute respiratory distress syndrome, severe vomiting or diarrhea or both. It may be metabolic, as in diabetic ketosis or adrenal insufficiency. SEE: *intravenous infusion* for illus; *central venous catheter; central line; intravenous infusion; oral rehydration therapy; solution.*

The goal of fluid replacement is to correct electrolyte, fluid, and acid-base imbalances. The oral route of replacement is used if possible. The intravenous, intraperitoneal, or subcutaneous routes are also used, with the intravenous route being used most frequently. Fluids may be isotonic, hypotonic, or hypertonic; may contain certain crystalloids, e.g., sodium, potassium, chloride, or calcium; or may contain osmotically active substances, e.g., glucose, protein, starch, or a synthetic plasma volume expander such as dextran or hetastarch. The composition, rate of administration, and route depend on the clinical condition being treated.

⚠ A critically ill patient receiving fluid replacement should be monitored frequently to be certain that fluid overload is prevented and that the solution is flowing and not extravasating. This is esp. important in treating infants, small children, and the elderly.

fluid retention Failure to eliminate fluid from the body because of renal, cardiac, or metabolic disease, or combinations of these disorders. Excess dietary salt can contribute to fluid retention. A low-sodium diet is a helpful adjunct to treatment. The advisability of using diuretics, angiotensin-converting enzyme inhibitors, and/or other drug therapies depends on the functional state of the kidneys, heart, and liver.

fluid volume, deficient [hyper/hypotonic] Decreased intravascular, interstitial, and/or intracellular fluid. This refers to dehydration with changes in sodium. SEE: *Nursing Diagnoses Appendix.*

fluid volume, deficient [isotonic] Decreased intravascular, interstitial and/or intracellular fluid. This refers to dehydration, water loss alone without change in sodium. SEE: *Nursing Diagnoses Appendix.*

fluid volume, excess The state in which an individual experiences increased isotonic fluid retention. SEE: *Nursing Diagnoses Appendix.*

fluid volume, risk for deficient At risk for experiencing vascular, cellular, or intracellular dehydration. SEE: *Nursing Diagnoses Appendix.*

fluid volume, risk for imbalance A risk of a decrease, increase, or rapid shift from one to the other of intravascular, interstitial, and/or intracellular fluid. This refers to the loss, gain, or both of body fluids. SEE: *Nursing Diagnoses Appendix.*

fluke (flook) [Old English *flōc,* flatfish] A parasitic worm belonging to the class Trematoda, phylum Platyhelminthes. Those parasitic in humans belong to the order Digenea. Most flukes have complex life cycles including asexual reproductive forms that live in a mollusc (snail or bivalve). Stages of a typical fluke include adult, egg, miracidium, sporocyst, redia, cercaria, and metacercaria.

   blood f. A fluke of the genus *Schistosoma,* including *S. haematobium, S. mansoni,* and *S. japonicum.* Adults live principally in the mesenteric and pelvic veins. They cause schistosomiasis.

   intestinal f. Any of several species of flukes infesting the intestine in humans. They include *Gastrodiscoides hominis, Fasciolopsis buski, Heterophyes heterophyes,* and *Metagonimus yokogawai.*

   lancet f. Liver **f.**

   liver f. Any of several species of fluke infesting the liver and bile ducts. Those infesting humans include *Clonorchis sinensis, Fasciola hepatica, Dicrocoelium dendriticum, Metorchis conjunctus,* and *Opisthorchis felineus.* Adult liver flukes infest biliary and pancreatic ducts. The eggs pass from the body with the feces and continue their development in snails of the subfamily Buliminae (family Hydrobiidae). Cercariae emerge and infest numerous species of freshwater fishes in which they encyst. Infestation results from eating raw fish containing encysted metacercariae. SYN: *lancet f.*

   lung f. A fluke that infests lung tissue. Only one species, *Paragonimus westermani,* is common in humans.

flumina pilorum (floo′mĭ-nă pī-lō′rŭm) [L., rivers of hair] **1.** The curved lines along which the hairs of the body are arranged, esp. in the fetus. **2.** Hairs lying in the same direction.

FluMist Influenza vaccine, live, intranasal.

fluor-, fluoro-, fluo- [L. *fluor,* flowing, a flow] **1.** A prefix used in chemistry for *fluorine, fluoride* **2.** A prefix meaning *fluorescence.*

fluorapatite, fluoroapatite (floo(-ŏ)-rap′ă-tīt″, floo″(-ŏ-)rō-ap′ă-tīt″) A compound formed when tooth enamel is treated with appropriate concentrations of the fluoride ion. The modified hydroxyapatite is less acid soluble and therefore resistant to caries. Fluorapatite is formed in bone and in enamel and dentin of teeth when fluoride is taken systemically. SYN: *fluorhydroxyapatite*.

fluorescein sodium (floor″es′ē-ĭn, floo″ŏr-) [*fluoresce* + *-in*] An orange-colored vegetable dye used to examine the eye. Topically, it is used to make visible defects in the corneal epithelium, such as those seen in dry eyes and corneal abrasions and ulcers. Intravenously injected fluorescein is used in retinal angiography to diagnose vascular leakage in the retina.

fluorescence (floo″ō-rĕs′ĕnts) The emission of a longer wavelength light by a material exposed to a shorter wavelength light. Fluorescent materials, such as fluorspar, the first material found to have this property, emit light only while a light is shining on them.

fluorescence in situ hybridization ABBR: FISH. A process in which a small section of fluorescently labeled DNA (a DNA probe) is linked with (hybridized to) the DNA from a chromosome of interest. This technique is used to identify the location of specific genes on chromosomes or areas in which chromosomes have been damaged or duplicated. FISH is used in amniocentesis to analyze retrieved fetal cells for evidence of specific genetic anomalies such as trisomy.

fluorescence polarization immunoassay SEE: under *immunoassay*.

fluorescent (floo-ō-rĕs′ĕnt) **1.** In biology, having one color by transmitted light and another by reflected light. **2.** Luminous when exposed to other light rays.

fluorescent polarization immunoassay SEE: under *immunoassay*.

fluorescent screen SEE: under *screen*.

fluorescent treponemal antibody-absorption test ABBR: FTA, FTA-ABS. A test for syphilis using the fluorescent antibody technique that is used to confirm a positive rapid plasma reagin, or Venereal Disease Research Laboratory test.

fluorhydroxyapatite (floor-hī″drŏk-sē-ăp′ĭ-tīt″, floor-ă-hī″) Fluorapatite.

fluoridation (floo″or-ĭ-dā′shŭn) The addition of fluorides to a water supply to prevent dental caries. The development of dental caries in the deciduous and permanent teeth can be decreased by providing fluoride as a supplement in the drinking water, as a topical application to the teeth, or as a daily medication. There are several important considerations. Fluoride that exceeds the daily dose discolors the teeth if a child ingests fluoride while the teeth are de-

veloping, i.e., from birth to 8 or 10 years. If a woman consumes fluoridated water during pregnancy, the deciduous teeth of the fetus, which begin to mineralize during the fourth or fifth month in utero, incorporate that compound and become more resistant to caries. In the adult tooth, when enamel has lost mineral (white spot lesion), fluoride greatly enhances the remineralization, because it leads to the precipitation of calcium phosphate.

The most commonly used method of administering fluoride is by providing drinking water that contains between 0.7 and 1.2 parts per million, depending on the climate. In rural areas without a central water supply, fluoridation of the school's water supply is an alternative to community water fluoridation. Because children spend only 5 to 7 hours a day in school, the advisable concentration of fluoride in the school water supply should be 4.5 times the optimal level recommended for the community water fluoridation for that locale. Persons exposed to chronically high levels of fluoride may develop fluorosis. Acute intoxication with extremely high doses of fluoride may be fatal.

⚠ Children drinking fluoridated water should not receive supplemental fluoride medication.

fluoride (floo′(ŏ)-rīd″) [*fluor-* + *-ide*] A compound of fluorine, usually with a radical; a salt of hydrofluoric acid. Considerable evidence shows that some fluoride compounds prevent dental caries (tooth decay).

⚠ Topical fluoride applications are toxic if swallowed. Seek medical care immediately.

   acidulated phosphate f. ABBR: APF. A fluoride compound applied topically to the teeth to prevent dental caries (tooth decay).
   hydrogen f. HF, a colorless corrosive gas used in industry as a source of fluorine and of hydrofluoric acid. SEE: *fluorine; hydrofluoric* ***acid***.
   sodium f. SEE: under *sodium*.
   stannous f. SnF_2, a fluoride compound applied topically to the teeth to prevent dental caries (tooth decay).

fluoride dental treatment The application of a fluoride solution or gel to the teeth as a means of controlling or preventing caries. SEE: *dental sealant*.

fluorine (floor′ēn″, floo′ō-rēn″) SYMB: F. A gaseous chemical element, a member of the halogen family, atomic weight (mass) 18.9984, atomic number 9. It is found in the soil in combination with calcium. SEE: *fluoridation.*

fluoroacetate (floo″or-ō-ăs′ĕ-tāt) A salt of fluoroacetic acid. SEE: *Poisons and Poisoning Appendix.*

fluorocarbon (floor′ō-kar″bŏn) [*fluor-* + *carbon*] A general term for a hydrocarbon in which some of the hydrogen atoms have been replaced with fluorine. The use of chlorofluorocarbons (CFCs) is discouraged because of their adverse effect on the ozone layer of the earth's atmosphere.

fluorochrome (floo′ŏr-ō-krōm″) A coloring agent that adds a fluorescent glow to an object, e.g., in the staining of microscopic specimens for analysis. A common use of fluorescent stains is to identify acid-fast bacteria, such as *Mycobacterium tuberculosis.*

fluorodeoxyglucose, fluorine-18 fluorodeoxyglucose (floo″(ŏ-)rō-dē-ok″sē-gloo′kōs″, floor′ēn″dē-ok″sē-gloo′kōs″, floo′ŏ-rēn″dē-ok″sē-gloo′kōs″) ABBR: FDG; fluorine-18 FDG. A fluorinated radiographically visible glucose molecule that serves as a contrast agent. SYN: *fludeoxyglucose.*

fluorometer (floo-or-ŏm′ĕ-tĕr) **1.** A device for determining the amount of radiation produced by x-rays. **2.** A device for adjusting a fluoroscope to establish the location of the target more accurately and to produce an undistorted image or shadow. **3.** A clinical laboratory instrument used in many types of immunochemistry assays, e.g., fluorescent polarization immunoassay.

fluorophores (floor′ă-fŏr, floo′ă-rä) A substance that tends to fluoresce, such as fluorescein.

fluoroquinolone (flŏr-ō-kwĭn′ō-lōn) A class of antimicrobial agents that kill bacteria by inhibiting their DNA gyrase and topoisomerase enzymes. Antibiotics of this class include ciprofloxacin, levofloxacin and moxifloxacin.

⚠️ Pregnant women should not take these antibiotics because of their adverse effects on the developing fetus. Fluoroquinolone use is associated with tendon rupture.

fluoroscope (floor′ŏ-skōp″) [*fluoro-* + *-scope*] A device consisting of a fluorescent screen, mounted separately or with an x-ray tube, that shows the images of objects set between the tube and the screen. It has been replaced by the image intensifier.

fluoroscopy (floo(-ŏ)r″os′kŏ-pē″) [*fluoro-* + *-scopy*] Examination of the body with a fluoroscope. Fluoroscopy is used in clinical medicine to provide real-time images of moving objects, e.g. to evaluate the motion of the diaphragm in a patient suspected of having phrenic nerve

paralysis, or to visualize the movement of needles or catheters when they are placed inside the body, e.g., during cannulation of vessels or lumbar puncture.

fluorosis (floor-ō-sĭs, floo″ră-) [″ + ″] Chronic fluorine poisoning, sometimes marked by mottling of tooth enamel. It may result from excessive exposure to fluorides from dietary, waterborne, and supplemental sources.

fluoxetine hydrochloride (floo-ŏks′ĭ-tēn″) A drug used in the treatment of depression, bulimia, and obsessive-compulsive disorder. It is an inhibitor of serotonin reuptake in the central nervous system.

flush, flushing (flush, flush′ing) **1.** Sudden redness of the skin. **2.** Irrigation of a cavity, or a device such as a feeding tube, with water.

   hot f. Flash (1).

   malar f. A bright-colored flush over the malar area and cheekbones. It may be associated with any febrile disease.

fluticasone (floo-tĭ′kă-sōn″) A corticosteroid administered in an aerosol inhaler to treat and prevent asthma. It is also used as a nasal spray to treat seasonal allergic rhinitis, nasal polyps, and other chronic inflammatory conditions; and topically to manage allergic and immunological skin problems. Its therapeutic classes are antiasthmatics, corticosteroids, and allergy, cold, and cough remedies.

flutter [AS. *floterian,* to fly about] A tremulous movement, esp. of the heart, as in atrial and ventricular flutter.

   atrial f. ABBR: AF. A cardiac dysrhythmia marked by rapid (about 300 beats per minute) regular atrial beating, and usually a regular ventricular response (whose rate may vary depending on the conduction of electrical impulses from the atria through the atrioventricular node). On the electrocardiogram, the fluttering of the atria is best seen in leads II, III, and F as "sawtooth" deflections between the QRS complexes. Atrial flutter usually converts to sinus rhythm with low-voltage direct current (DC) cardioversion or atrial pacing.

   SYMPTOMS: Patients may be asymptomatic, esp. when ventricular rates are less than 100 bpm. During tachycardic episodes, patients often report palpitations, dizziness, presyncope, or syncope.

   TREATMENT: Radiofrequency catheter ablation of the responsible circuit eliminates the arrhythmia about 90% of the time.

   diaphragmatic f. Rapid contractions of the diaphragm. They may occur intermittently or be present for an extended period. The cause is unknown.

   mediastinal f. Abnormal side-to-side motion of the mediastinum during respiration.

   ventricular f. Ventricular contractions of the heart at 250 beats per minute, creating a high-amplitude, sawtooth pattern on the surface electrocardiogram. The rhythm is lethal unless immediate life support and resuscitation are provided.

Flutter device (flŭt'ĕr) A handheld device to facilitate clearance of mucus in hypersecretory lung disorders. Exhalation through the Flutter causes oscillations of expiratory pressure and airflow, which vibrate the airway walls, loosen mucus, decrease the collapsibility of the airways, and accelerate airflow. This facilitates movement of mucus up the airways. SEE: *cystic fibrosis*.

flutter-fibrillation Cardiac dysrhythmia alternating between atrial fibrillation and atrial flutter, or showing a pattern that is difficult to distinguish during routine cardiac monitoring.

Fluvirin Influenza virus vaccine, trivalent, types A and B.

flux [L. *fluxus,* a flow] **1.** An excessive flow or discharge from an organ or cavity of the body. **2.** In physics, the flow rate of liquids, particles, or energy. **3.** In dentistry, an agent that lowers the fusion temperature of porcelain and metals. **4.** In metallurgy, a substance used to increase the fluidity of a molten metal and to prevent or reduce its oxidation. **5.** A substance that deoxidizes, cleans, and promotes the union of surfaces to be brazed, soldered, or welded together.

Fluzone (floo'zōn") Influenza virus vaccine, trivalent, types A and B.

fly (flī) An insect belonging to the order Diptera, characterized by sucking mouth parts, one pair of wings, and complete metamorphosis, such as the housefly, horsefly, or deerfly. The term is sometimes applied to insects belonging to other orders. SEE: *Diptera*.

   black f. A fly of the genus *Simulium* whose bites often cause local bleeding and pain.

   bluebottle f. A fly of the Calliphoridae family that delivers a painful and venomous sting. It breeds in dung or the flesh of dead animals.

   deer f. A biting fly, *Chrysops discalis,* that transmits the causative organism of tularemia (deer fly fever).

   flesh f. SEE: *Sarcophagidae.*

   screwworm f. A fly belonging to the families Calliphoridae and Sarcophagidae.

   Spanish f. Cantharides.

   tsetse f. One of several species of bloodsucking flies of the genus *Glossina,* order Diptera, confined to Africa south of the Sahara Desert. It is an important transmitter of trypanosomes, the causative agents of African sleeping sicknesses in humans, and of nagana and other diseases in cattle and game animals. SEE: *Trypanosoma; trypanosomiasis.*

   tumbu f. A species of fly belonging to the genus *Cordylobia* in Africa and the genus *Dermatobia* in tropical America. Their larvae develop in the skin of wild domesticated animals, and humans are frequently attacked.

   warble f. Dermatobia.

Fm Symbol for the element fermium.

f.m. L. *fiat mistura,* let a mixture be made. This abbreviation is used in prescription writing.

fMRI *Functional magnetic resonance imaging.*

FNR *False-negative ratio.*

foam (fōm) [AS. *fam*] A mixture of finely divided gas bubbles interspersed in a liquid.

foam stability test Shake test.

FOBT *Fecal occult blood test.*

focal (fō'kăl) Pert. to a focus.

focal disease A disease located at a specific and distinct area such as the tonsils, adenoids, or a boil.

focal infection SEE: under *infection.*

focal neuropathy SEE: under *neuropathy.*

focal spot SEE: under *spot.*

foci (fō'sī) [L.] Pl. of focus.

focus , foci [L.*focus,* hearth] **1.** The point of convergence of light rays or sound waves. **2.** The starting point of a disease process.

   real f. The point at which convergent rays intersect.

   virtual f. The point at which divergent rays would intersect if extended backward.

focused abdominal sonography for trauma ABBR: FAST. Focused assessment in the bedside sonographic imaging examination of the trauma patient to identify potentially serious internal injuries.

focused assessment with sonography for trauma ABBR: FAST. The use of rapid ultrasound screening of the injured patient to identify major internal injuries, such as free fluid in the peritoneum or pericardium or pneumothorax.

focused history and physical examination ABBR: FHPE. In emergency medicine, a combination of appropriate questions (SAMPLE, History, and OPQRST) and physical examination directed to the specific body system (cardiopulmonary, neurological, musculoskeletal) that an EMS provider suspects may be causing a patient's presenting problem. The assessment is conducted after the primary assessment has been completed and differs for medical or trauma patients.

FOD *focus-object distance.* The distance from the target of an x-ray tube to the surface being radiographed.

fog Droplets suspended in a gas, as minute water droplets in air.

fogging (fog'ing) **1.** A method of testing vision, used particularly in testing myopia and in postcycloplegic examination, in which accommodation is relaxed by overcorrection. **2.** A method of intense application of an insecticide. The solution is nebulized and appears in the air as a mist. **3.** Unwanted density on radiographic film resulting from exposure to secondary radiation, light, chemicals, or heat. **4.** The loss of intensity of the radiologic appearance of a cerebral infarct on magnetic resonance imaging (MRI) of the brain several weeks after the stroke occurs.

fogging effect Transient difficulty in visualizing an ischemic stroke with computed tomography (CT) or magnetic resonance (MR) imaging, typically occurring about 10 days after the stroke.

fogo selvagem (fō′gō, goo sĕl-vă′zhĕm) [Portuguese, literally "wild fire"] ABBR: FS. An autoimmune disease that causes blistering of the skin of the head, neck or trunk, esp. when the skin is rubbed (Nikolsky's sign). It often causes a burning dysesthesia, from which its popular name is derived. The disease is typically found in Brazil or Colombia and has been associated with chronic or recurrent exposure to black flies. SYN: *endemic pemphigus foliaceus.*

foil A thin, pliable sheet of metal. In dentistry, various types of gold foil are used for restoring teeth.

folacin (fŏl′ă-sĭn) Folic **acid.**

folate (fō′lāt″) Folic **acid.**

fold (fōld) **1.** A ridge or a crevice formed when a flexible surface doubles back on itself. SYN: *plica.* **2.** A bend, e.g., one of the bends in a polypeptide that determines its in situ three-dimensional structure. **3.** A particular three-dimensional folded shape assumed by a polymer, such as a protein. **4.** A thin, doubled sheet extending from a tissue or a cell.

amniotic f. In the gastrula stage of the embryo, a small bulge of embryonic ectoderm and mesoderm that begins extending into the proamniotic cavity; it eventually gives rise to the amnion and the chorion.

aryepiglottic f. Each of the two lateral rims of the inlet to the larynx, which are the top edges of the quadrate membranes.

axillary f. Two ridges of skin-covered muscle along the sides of the chest where the under side of each arm meets the shoulder. The anterior axillary fold is formed by the lateral edge of the pectoralis major muscle; the posterior axillary fold is formed by the lateral edges of the latissimus dorsi and teres major muscles.

circular f. Transverse ruffles that ring the inner wall of the small intestine. The circular folds (plicae) are soft ridges of mucosa that protrude into the intestinal lumen. These folds are largest and closest together in the duodenum distal to the major duodenal papilla, they decrease in height and number through the distal jejunum, and they disappear in the distal ileum. SEE: *circular* **plica.**

epicanthal f. Epicanthus.

gastric f. Any of the mostly longitudinal folds of mucosa found in the empty stomach. SEE: *ruga.*

genital f. A fold of skin in the embryo on each side of the genital tubercle that develops into the labia minora in females.

gluteal f. The linear crease in the skin that separates the buttocks from the thighs. This fold marks the lower limits of the gluteus maximus muscle.

inframammary f. The lower border of the breast where it meets the chest wall. SYN: *submammary* **f.**

mucobuccal f. Along the back wall of the mouth, the ridge of oral mucosa that runs from the maxilla (superiorly) or the mandible (inferiorly) to the cheek.

mucosal f. A fold of mucosal tissue.

nail f. A groove in the skin surrounding the margins and proximal edges of the nail.

neural f. In the early embryo, the raised lateral edges of the neural plate. The neural folds are thickened ridges of epithelium that are pushed up and that meet in the midline as the neural plate curls into a longitudinal tube. These folds, transition zones between the neural tissue in the neural plate and the surrounding surface ectoderm, give rise to the neural crest cells and to ectodermal placodes.

semilunar f. of conjunctiva The fold of conjunctiva at the inner angle (inner canthus) of the eye.

skin f., skinfold A doubling of skin and its underlying adherent subcutaneous tissue. To assess a person's body fat, a skin fold is pinched at a standard site, and the thickness of the doubled skin is measured, using skin fold calipers; a body fat estimate is then calculated using a table or a computer program. There are 6-12 standard locations for measuring skin fold thickness, including over the triceps muscle along the back of the arm and just above the iliac crest of the hip.

submammary f. Inframammary **f.**

transverse f. of rectum Any of the three permanent folds projecting into the lumen of the rectum. SYN: *Houston valve.*

urogenital f. SEE: *urogenital ridge.*

ventricular f. of the larynx The upper pair of ridges that project into the midsection of the larynx; these define the upper boundary of the laryngeal vestibule. Each fold is composed of pinkish mucosa covering a thin ligament (the vestibular ligament), which runs from the thyroid cartilage anteriorly to the arytenoid cartilage posteriorly, roughly parallel to the vocal ligament below it. The ventricular vocal folds contribute to certain types of sound production. SYN: *false* **vocal cord**; *vestibular* **f.**

vestibular f. Ventricular **f.** of the larynx.

vocal f. The lower pair of ridges that project into the midsection of the larynx; these define the lower boundary of the laryngeal vestibule, a disk shaped subcavity of the laryngeal cavity. The protruding vocal folds create the narrowest cross-section of the larynx, and they are the edges of the glottis, i.e., rima glottidis, where phonation is produced.

Each vocal fold is composed of whitish, stratified squamous epithelium covering a thin ligament (the vocal ligament), which runs from the thyroid cartilage anteriorly to the arytenoid cartilage posteriorly. The vocal ligament is the medial edge of the vocalis muscle.

During a strong inspiration, the vocal folds are pulled farther apart to widen the opening into the trachea. During swallowing, the vocal folds are pulled together to protect the trachea. During phonation, the vocal folds are pulled together and airflow causes them to vibrate and make a sound; the pitch of this sound can be changed by varying the tension on the vocal ligaments. SYN: *true* **vocal cord**.

Foley catheter (fō'lē) [Frederic W. B. Foley, U.S. urologist, 1891–1966] A urinary tract catheter with a balloon attachment at one end. After the catheter is inserted, the balloon is inflated. Thus the catheter is prevented from leaving the bladder until the balloon is emptied.

⚠️ Indwelling urinary catheters are the most important cause of hospital-acquired infections in the U.S.

FOLFIRI Leucovorin, irinotecan, and fluorouracil, chemotherapeutic agents used to treat solid tumors, such as those arising in the colon or pancreas.

FOLFOX Oxaliplatin, leucovorin, and fluorouracil, chemotherapeutic drugs used to treat cancers of the intestine, pancreas, and stomach, among other organs.

folia (fō'lē-ă) [L.] Pl. of folium.

folie (fŏ-lē') [Fr.] Psychosis.

folinic acid (fō-lin'ik) SEE: under *acid*.

folium (fō'lē-ŭm) *pl.* **folia** [L., leaf] A thin, broad, leaflike structure.

follicle (fŏl'ĭ-kl) [L. *folliculus*, little bag] A small secretory sac or cavity. **follicular,** *adj.*

atretic f. An ovarian follicle that has undergone degeneration or involution.

dental f. 1. The connective tissue structure that encloses the developing tooth within the substance of the jaw before tooth eruption. **2.** The dental sac and its contents.

graafian f. SEE: *graafian follicle*.

hair f. An invagination of the epidermis that forms a cylindrical depression, penetrating the corium into the connective tissue that holds the hair root. Sebaceous glands, which secrete sebum, and tiny muscles (arrectores pili), which cause the hair to stand, are attached to these follicles.

lymphoid f. A densely-packed, spherical or ovoid aggregation of B lymphocytes that forms a lymphocyte proliferation and maturing zone in a lymphoid tissue, such as a lymph node.lymph follicle.

maturing f. SEE: *graafian follicle*.

nabothian f. A dilated cyst of the glands of the cervix uteri.

ovarian f. A spherical structure in the cortex of the ovary consisting of an oogonium or an oocyte and its surrounding epithelial (follicular) cells. The follicles are of three types. The first type, or primary follicle, consists of an oogonium and a single layer of follicular cells. In the second type, or growing follicle, cells proliferate, forming several layers, and the first maturation division occurs. The third type, the vesicular (graafian) follicle, possesses a cavity (antrum) containing the follicular fluid (liquor folliculi). The oocyte lies in the cumulus oophorus, a mass of cells on the inner surface. The cells lining the follicle constitute the stratum granulosum. The follicle is a secretory structure producing estrogen and progesterone. SEE: *corpus luteum*.

primordial f. An ovarian follicle consisting of the ovum enclosed in a single layer of cells.

sebaceous f. Sebaceous gland.

thyroid f. A spherical or oval subunit of the thyroid gland, made of cuboidal epithelium, which contains colloid and the thyroglobulin and iodine from which thyroxine and triiodothyronine are synthesized.

vesicular f. A follicle containing a cavity; a mature ovarian (graafian) follicle.

follicular (fŏ-lĭk'ū-lăr) Pert. to a follicle or follicles.

follicular occlusion triad SEE: under *triad*.

folliculitis (fŏ-lik″yŭ-līt'ĭs) [*folliculus,* + *-itis*] Inflammation of a follicle or follicles.

hot tub f. An inflammation of the hair follicles caused by *Pseudomonas aeruginosa,* occurring after exposure to contaminated bath, spa, or swimming pool water. The infection resolves without treatment in about 14 days. SYN: *Pseudomonas* **f.**; *splash rash*.

keloidal f. Chronic dermatitis with production of hard papules that join together to form hypertrophied scars.

Pseudomonas f. Hot tub **f.**

folliculoma (fŏ-lĭk″ū-lō′mă) [″ + Gr. *oma,* tumor] A tumor of the ovary originating in a graafian follicle in which the cells resemble those of the stratum granulosum.

folliculose (fŏ-lĭk′ū-lōs) Composed of follicles.

folliculosis (fŏ-lĭk″ū-lō′sĭs) [″ + Gr. *osis,* condition] The presence of an abnormal number of lymph follicles.

folliculostatin (fŏ-lĭk″yŭ-lō-stat′ĭn) [*follicle* + *statin*] A hormone produced by granulosa cells in the ovary. It reduces the release of follicle stimulating hormone by the anterior pituitary gland.

folliculus (fŏ-lĭk′ū-lŭs) *pl.* **folliculi** [L.] A follicle.

Folling disease Phenylketonuria.

follistatin (fŏl″ĭs-tă′tĭn) [*folli(cle)* + ″] A protein that regulates the actions of activins in the body. It antagonizes the effects of many members of the transforming growth factor family of cytokines. One function of follistatin is to decrease the secretion of FSH.

follow-up (fŏl′ō-ŭp) The continued care or monitoring of a patient after the initial visit or examination.

Folstein Mini Mental Status Exam, Folstein Mini Mental State Exam A screening test to assess cognitive function in people suspected of delirium or dementia. The test assesses orientation, registration, recall, speech, and language. A perfect score is 30 correct answers. Scores below 24 are generally considered to indicate cognitive impairment. However, since scores are affected by age and education level, normed scores provide more accurate assessment.

fomentation (fō″měn-tā′shŭn) [L. *fomentatio*] A hot, wet application for the relief of pain or inflammation. It is used primarily in complementary and alternative health care.

fomepizole 4-methylpyrazole A drug used as an antidote for ethylene glycol (antifreeze) poisoning.

fomes, fomite (fō′mēz, fō′mīt″) *pl.* **fomites** [L., tinder] Any substance that adheres to and transmits infectious material.

fomites (fō′mĭ-tēz) Pl. of fomes.

Fontana spaces (fon-tan′ă) [Felice Fontana, Italian scientist, 1730–1805] The spaces between the processes of the ligamentum pectinatum of the iris. These convey the aqueous humor.

fontanel, fontanelle (fŏn″tă-něl′) [Fr. *fontanelle,* little fountain] Any of the tough, fibrous membranes lying between the bones of the cranial vault of a fetus or infant. Fontanels, colloquially known as soft spots, allow an infant's skull to be compressed during passage through the birth canal. The fontanels ossify generally by age two. SEE: illus.

anterior f. The diamond-shaped junction of the coronal, frontal, and sagittal sutures; it becomes ossified within 18 to 24 months.

posterior f. The triangular fontanel at the junction of the sagittal and lambdoid sutures; ossified generally by age one.

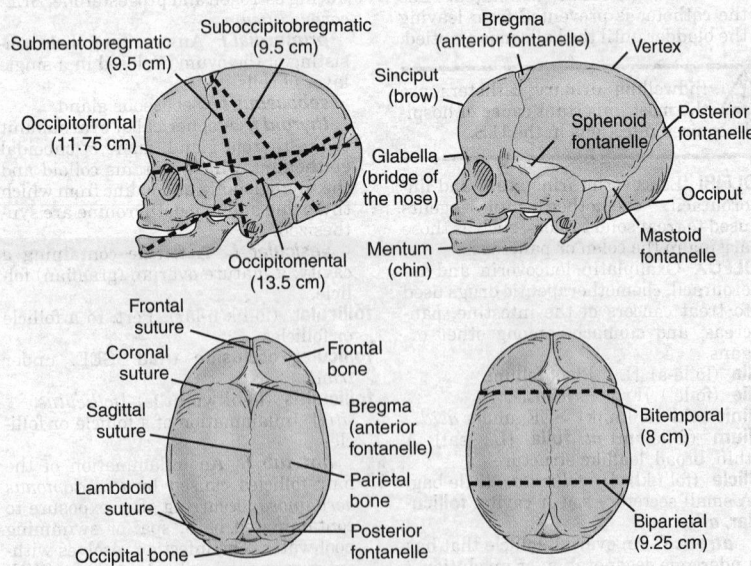

FONTANELS OF INFANT SKULL

Fontan procedure (fon-tan') [Francois Maurice Fontan, Fr. surgeon, b. 1929] A procedure to repair complex congenital heart defects, e.g., tricuspid atresia associated with a single ventricle, that interferes with blood being oxygenated. The superior vena cava (SVC) is divided adjacent to its entry to the right atrium; the pulmonary trunk is divided close to the pulmonic valve, and both ends are closed. The distal and cardiac ends of the divided SVC are anastomosed to the right pulmonary artery. The inferior vena cava is connected to the atrial orifice of the SVC, usually by a vascular prosthesis. This procedure may be modified.

food Any material, including water, that provides the nutritive requirements of an organism to maintain growth and physical well-being. For humans, food includes carbohydrates, fats, proteins, vitamins, and minerals. SEE: *carbohydrate; digestion; fat*(2); *nutrition; protein; stomach*.

   bioengineered f. Genetically modified **f.**

   f. chain SEE: under *chain*.

   contamination of f. The presence, introduction, or development of infectious or toxic material in food. Food may be contaminated by chemical residues (such as pesticides), bacteria (*Salmonella, Escherichia coli, Listeria*), viruses (hepatitis A, Norwalk), protozoa (*Giardia*), worms (tapeworms and roundworms), molds (*Aspergillus*), or toxins (botulinum, staphylococcal enterotoxin).

   convenience f. Food in which one or more steps in preparation have been completed before the product is offered for retail sale. Examples include frozen vegetables, bake mixes, heat-and-serve foods, and ready-to-eat foods.

   dietetic f. Food in which the nutrient content has been modified for use in special diets, esp. for diabetics.

   enriched f. A processed food that has lost nutrients during milling, grinding, pasteurization, or other processes and then had those nutrients added back to the marketed product. Two examples of vitamins commonly used in food enrichment are vitamins B_1 and B_2, thiamine and riboflavin, respectively.

   fast f. Commercially available, ready-to-eat meals (such as hamburgers, hot dogs, pizza, fried chicken, french fries) with a high fat content, little fiber, and minimal quantities of vitamins or calcium.

   functional f. **1.** Food products with additives for which, following FDA approval, health claims can be made. **2.** A food that has a defined health benefit for the person who consumes it.

   genetically modified f. Any crop or agricultural product altered by biological engineering for drought resistance, increased growth, resistance to pests or pesticides, prolonged shelf-life, altered textures or flavors, or other economically or commercially desirable characteristics. Promoters of genetically modified foods point to their improved yields (which may have a beneficial impact on agricultural profits or world hunger). Opponents of genetic modification have raised concerns about its effects on ecosystems, human food allergies, and religious dietary laws. SYN: *bioengineered f.*

   junk f. A colloquial term for food that has limited nutritional value. Typically it refers to foods high in salt, sugar, fat, or calories with low nutrient content. These include most salted snack foods, candy, gum, most sweet desserts, fried fast food, and carbonated beverages.

   medical f. A food formulated by the selective use of nutrients and manufactured for the dietary treatment of a specific condition or disease.

   novel f. A nutritional source that has not been used in the past or one that has been made by a new manufacturing process, including, e.g., genetic modification.

   organic f. A crop or animal product cultivated with specific guidelines that limit the use of petrochemicals, radiation, or genetically engineered technologies in its agriculture.

   processed f. Raw food that has been adulterated or modified to increase its nutritional content or make it more palatable and easier to ship, to store, or to sell.

   ready-to-use therapeutic f. ABBR: RUTF. A nutritional supplement consisting of a roasted, ground cereal and a roasted, ground legume, fortified with vitamins, minerals, and micronutrients. The cereal provides a source of carbohydrates; the legume, a source of protein. RUTFs are used to treat and prevent malnutrition in impoverished populations, esp. undernourished children.

   risky f. Any food that is contaminated or more likely than most other foods to be contaminated with bacteria, carcinogens, or toxins.

   textured f. Food products manufactured from various nutritional components made to resemble conventional protein-source foods in texture such as meat, seafood, or poultry.

food adulterant A substance that makes food impure or inferior, such as toxins, organisms, pesticide residues, radioactive fallout, any poisonous or deleterious substance, or any substance added to increase bulk or weight.

Food and Drug Administration ABBR: FDA. In the U.S., an official regulatory body for foods, drugs, cosmetics, and medical devices. It is a part of the U.S. Department of Health and Human Services.

food and drug interactions SEE: under *interaction*.

food-borne disease ABBR: FBD. Illnesses caused by the ingestion of contaminated or toxic nutrients. Among the food-borne diseases are infectious diarrheas, e.g., those caused by *Salmonella, Shigella, Vibrio cholerae, Escherichia coli, Campylobacter*; helminth diseases, e.g., those caused by beef, pork, or pike tapeworms; protozoan infections, e.g., giardiasis; food poisoning, e.g., those caused by *Bacillus cereus, Staphylococcus aureus, Clostridium botulinum,* mushrooms, or ciguatera; and viral illnesses, esp. hepatitis A.

Proper selection, collection, preparation, and serving of food can reduce the risk of food-borne disease, esp. if combined with regular inspections of food-service facilities and periodic evaluations of food-service workers.

DISEASE TRENDS: An increase in food-borne illnesses has been seen in recent decades, probably as a result of increases in foreign trade and travel and the increased consumption of raw foods.

food efficiency The relative ability of a food source to contribute to weight gain, weight maintenance, or growth and development.

food exchange SEE: under *exchange*.

food frequency questionnaire ABBR: FFQ. A tool used in clinical and research nutrition designed to identify the types and quantities of nutrients contained in the foods ingested by a subject.

Food Guide Pyramid Recommendations developed by the U.S. Department of Agriculture for planning a balanced diet, subsequently replaced by MyPlate. Foods are divided into six groups: bread, cereal, rice, and pasta; fruits; vegetables; milk, yogurt, and cheese; meat, poultry, fish, dry beans, eggs, and nuts; and fats, oils, and sweets. The guide recommends the number of servings for each food group, and suggests that regular physical activity is an important part of nutritional health. SEE: *Nutrition Appendix.*

Food Guide Pyramid for the Elderly A modification of the original Food Guide Pyramid, for those over age 70. At its base is eight servings of water, and at its peak is the recommendation for supplements of calcium, vitamin D, and vitamin B_{12}. SEE: *Nutrition Appendix.*

Food Guide Pyramid for Young Children A modification of the original Food Guide Pyramid intended to provide guidance to adults about nutritional choices for children aged 2 to 6. The pyramid illustrates the importance of eating balanced meals with a variety of food choices including daily consumption of grains and vegetables; moderate

intake of fruits, dairy products, and meats; and limited use of fatty foods and sweets. Images placed around the pyramid show children running and playing ball, thus emphasizing the importance of regular physical activity as a component of a healthy lifestyle. SEE: *Nutrition Appendix.*

food hypersensitivity reaction SEE: *food allergy.*

food intolerance An abnormal, nonimmunological response to ingested food. The basis for the intolerance may be pharmacological, enzymatic, metabolic, or toxic. Pharmacological intolerance is the body's reaction to a component of the food that produces druglike effects; enzymatic intolerance results in an inability to digest a food because of an inadequate production or the absence of an enzyme necessary for its digestion; metabolic intolerance is due to the effect of the food on the person's metabolism; and food toxicity is due to toxins in the food or released by microorganisms contaminating the food.

food label The information provided on a food package indicating the various nutrients, calories, and additives present in the food. U.S. Food and Drug Administration regulations mandate the listing of total fats, calories from fat, cholesterol, saturated fats, total carbohydrates, sugars, sodium, potassium, protein, vitamin and minerals, among other nutritional components.

food poisoning SEE: under *poisoning*.

food rendering The conversion of the waste products of animal butchery into feeds, bone meal, tallows, oils, and fertilizer. Consumption of rendered feed products sometimes results in animal and human infections, such as bovine spongiform encephalopathy (mad cow disease).

food requirements The need for various amounts and types of food according to a person's use of energy. It is calculated that an average healthy man (154 lb or 70 kg) performing light to moderate muscular work requires 2700 kcal/day, while an average healthy woman (128 lb or 58 kg) requires 2000 kcal/day. These needs are met through the intake of carbohydrate, protein, and fat. An estimation of the protein requirement for the average adult is 1 g of protein per day for each kilogram of their ideal weight. Generally, a woman requires fewer calories per day than a comparably active man because of her smaller build. Sedentary individuals generally require fewer calories. On a body weight basis, children and pregnant women require more calories than predicted to support growth and development. Febrile patients have an increased basal energy expenditure of about 12% for each degree centigrade of fever. It is generally agreed that a diet that is rich in fruits, vegetables, legumes, and whole grains and has adequate minerals (including calcium) and vitamins is superior to diets that are rich in fats and sugars. SEE: *calorie; diet; energy expenditure, basal; nutrition; Recommended Daily Dietary Allowances Appendix.*

foot (fut, fĕt) *pl.* **feet** ABBR: ft. The terminal part of the leg below the ankle. The bones of the foot include the tarsals, metatarsals, and phalanges. SEE: illus.; *leg* for illus.; *skeleton.*

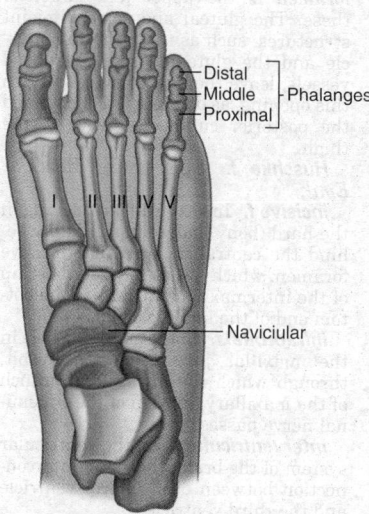

BONES OF FOOT AND ANKLE

Left foot, lateral view

    athlete's f. A scaling, cracked, or macerated rash, typically found between the toes and usually caused by a fungal skin infection (such as tinea) although bacteria may also be involved. The rash is usually mildly itchy. SYN: *dermatophytosis; tinea pedis.* SEE: illus.; *Nursing Diagnoses Appendix.*

    TREATMENT: The feet, esp. the webbing between the toes, should be carefully dried after bathing. Well-ventilated shoes and absorbent socks should be worn. Topically applied antifungal drugs, such as terbinafine, effectively treat the condition except when maceration is prominent and bacterial infection is also present. In these instances, oral antibiotics are needed.

    immersion f. A condition of the feet, resulting from prolonged immersion in cold water, in which pain and inflammation are followed by swelling, discoloration, and numbness. SYN: *tropical immersion* **foot.**

    jogger's f. A colloquial term for tarsal tunnel syndrome.

    Madura f. SEE: **Madura** *foot.*

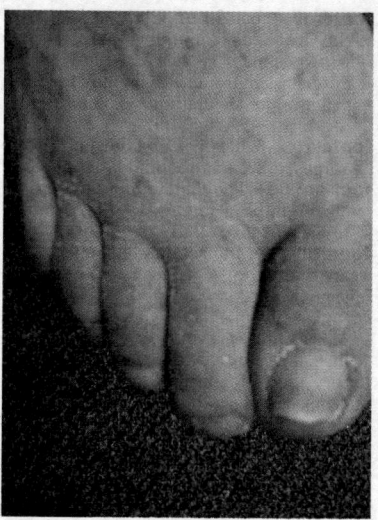

ATHLETE'S FOOT

    mossy f. Non-filarial lymphatic obstruction of the legs, commonly found in volcanic regions of Africa, where it occurs primarily in those who walk barefoot on alkaline, mineral-rich soil. SYN: *podoconiosis.*

    Seattle f. An artificial foot designed to absorb the impact of foot-to-floor contact with a dynamic elastic structure.

    trench f. Degeneration of the skin of the feet due to prolonged exposure to moisture. The condition, which resembles frostbite, may be prevented by ensuring that clean, dry socks are worn at all times. The feet do not have to be exposed to cold to develop this condition.

    SACH f. *Solid ankle cushion heel* foot; a prosthetic foot that has no definite ankle joint but is designed to absorb shock and allow movement of the shank over the foot during ambulation.

    tropical immersion f. Immersion foot.

foot and mouth disease A viral disease of cattle and horses that is rarely transmitted to humans. Because of a similarity in name, it is occasionally confused with hand-foot-and-mouth disease, a common viral infection of children.

    SYMPTOMS: In humans, symptoms include fever, headache, and malaise with dryness and burning sensation of the mouth. Vesicles develop on the lips, tongue, mouth, palms, and soles.

    TREATMENT: Therapy is symptomatic. Full recovery occurs in 2 to 3 weeks. Several preventive vaccines are available.

foot board SEE: under *board.*

foot-candle An amount of light equivalent to 1 lumen per square foot.

footdrop (foot′drŏp) Plantar flexion of the foot due to injury, paralysis, or weakness of the nerves supplying the anterior tibial muscles. It may result in dragging of the foot or toes while walking.

footplate (foot′plāt) The flat part of the stapes, a bone in the middle ear.

foot-pound The amount of energy required to lift 1 lb of mass a vertical distance of 1 ft.

footprint An impression of the foot, esp. an ink impression used for identification of infants.

forage (for′ăj) [Fr., *fourrage*, fodder] **1.** Creation of a channel through an enlarged prostate by use of an electric cautery. This technique may be used in other tissues. **2.** Fodder for cattle or horses or cattle. **3.** A search for food of any kind.

foramen (fŏ-rā′měn, -ram′ĭ-nă) *pl.* **foramina** [L.] A passage; an opening; an orifice; a communication between two cavities; a hole in a bone, often for the passage of vessels or nerves.

   alveolar foramina In the skull, the tiny holes on the outer surface of the maxillary tuberosity of the maxilla through which nerves and vessels pass to reach the upper molars.

   anterior condyloid f. Hypoglossal canal.

   anterior sacral f. One of the four paired openings on the anterior (ventral or pelvic) surface of the sacrum through which the first four pairs of ventral rami of the sacral nerve roots pass. (The fifth pair of sacral ventral rami pass between the sacrum and the coccyx.) The anterior sacral foramina connect to the sacral canal via the sacral interventricular foramina.ventral sacral foramen.

   apical f. The opening in the end of the root of a tooth through which the blood, lymphatic, and nerve supplies pass to reach the dental pulp.

   f. of Bochdalek SEE: under *Bochdalek, Vincent.*

   f. cecum (caecum) of the skull A small round depression in the midline of the floor of the anterior fossa of the skull between the base of the frontal crest and the crista galli of the ethmoid bone.

   f. cecum (caecum) of the tongue The small midline depression at the border between the anterior (oral) and the posterior (pharyngeal) portions of the tongue. It is the point from which the thyroid diverticulum (the tubular duct destined to form the thyroid gland) descended in the embryo.

   emissary f. A generic term for small holes in the bones of the skull through which blood vessels pass.

   epiploic f. The foramen of Winslow.

   ethmoidal f. A space in the suture between the frontal and ethmoid bones in the medial wall of the orbit of the skull through which the ethmoidal nerve and artery pass.

   greater sciatic f. The larger of two posterior openings into the bony pelvis. Along the back edge of the ilium and ischium bones, there are two semicircular indentations, the greater and lesser sciatic notches. Two crossed ligaments (the sacrotuberous and sacrospinous ligaments) make these notches into enclosed ovals, the greater and lesser sciatic foramena. The greater sciatic foramen is the upper and larger of these. The gluteal and some hip-joint structures, such as the piriformis muscle and the gluteal nerves and blood vessels, leave the pelvic cavity through this opening, as do the sciatic nerve and the posterior cutaneous nerve of the thigh.

   Huschke f. SEE: under *Huschke, Emil.*

   incisive f. In the skull, an opening in the hard (bony) palate immediately behind the central incisors. The incisive foramen, which lies at the frontmost tip of the intermaxillary suture, is the bottom end of the incisive canal.

   infraorbital f. In the skull, the hole in the maxilla, just below the orbit, through which the infraorbital branch of the maxillary division of the trigeminal nerve passes.

   interventricular f. In the ventricular system of the brain, the small interconnection between each lateral ventricle and the third ventricle.

   intervertebral f. The opening between adjacent vertebrae through which spinal nerves pass.

   jugular f. A large irregular space between the occipital bone and the petrous portion of the temporal bone on either side of the base of the skull. The internal jugular vein emerges from the cranial cavity through this foramen, along with the glossopharyngeal (CN IX), vagus (CN X), and accessory (CN XI) nerves.

   f. lacerum An opening in the base of the middle fossa of the skull medial to the foramen ovale and just below the anterior end of the carotid canal at the point where it turns upward to form the carotid groove (carotid sulcus) along the lateral side of the sella turcica. The foramen lacerum has a fibrous covering pierced by a few small vessels.

   lesser sciatic f. The opening bounded by the hip bone, sacrum, and sacrospinous ligament.greater sciatic foramen.

   lingual f. A small midline opening on the lingual (internal) surface of the mandible above the pair of small bony protuberances called the genial tubercles. A single artery, the anastomoses of two branches of the lingual artery, passes into this foramen.genial foramen.

f. of Luschka Each of the two lateral apertures through which cerebrospinal fluid can leave the fourth ventricle of the brain and flow into the subarachnoid space.

f. of Magendie The unpaired median aperture through which cerebrospinal fluid can leave the fourth ventricle of the brain and flow into the subarachnoid space.

f. magnum The large opening in the base of the occipital bones between the posterior cranial fossa of the skull and the vertebral canal through which the spinal cord passes as it becomes the hindbrain.

mandibular f. The opening on the medial (interior) surface of the ramus of the mandible through which the inferior alveolar vessels and nerve enter the mandibular canal. A thin pointed lip, the lingula, shelters the medial edge of the foramen.

mastoid f. A small opening, usually found on the outer surface of the mastoid part of the temporal bone of the skull, through which a small vein and artery pass.

mental f. An opening, on the outer surface of each side of the body of the mandible below the premolars, through which the mental nerve (a terminal branch of the inferior alveolar nerve) and blood vessels exit. SYN: *intraventricular f.*

f. of Monro The interventricular foramen. SYN: *intraventricular f.*

nutrient f. A hole in the surface of a bone through which vessels and nerves enter and exit. SEE: *nutrient canal*.

obturator f. The large oval (in males) or triangular (in females) space, in each hip bone, formed by the inner edges of the pubis and the ischium. This foramen is almost entirely covered by the attached obturator membrane.

optic f. Optic canal.

f. ovale 1. The opening, in the septum between the two atria of the fetal heart, that permits blood to bypass the lungs by flowing directly from the right to the left atrium. This opening usually closes shortly after birth as a result of hemodynamic changes related to respiration, leaving an oval depression (fossa ovalis) on the right side of the interatrial septum. Incomplete closure of the foramen ovale can lead to cardiac symptoms later in life, in which case surgical or transcatheter repair is usually recommended. SEE: *fetal circulation*. 2. Along the base of the middle fossa of the skull, an oval opening in the lower margin of the greater wing of the sphenoid bone -- just anterior and medial to the foramen spinosum. The mandibular division of the trigeminal nerve (CN V), the accessory meningeal artery, and sometimes the lesser petrosal nerve pass through this foramen.

palatine (greater and lesser) f. In the posterior corners of the hard palate, the single large (anterior) and two small (posterior) openings at the lateral edge of the horizontal plate of each palatine bone. The greater and lesser palatine nerves and vessels pass through their respective foramina.

parietal f. A hole near the superior (sagittal) edge of the parietal bone of the skull through which a vein and sometimes an artery passes. This foramen is not always present.

posterior sacral f. One of the four pairs of openings on the posterior (dorsal) surface of the sacrum through which dorsal rami of the sacral roots pass. The posterior sacral foramina, which connect to the sacral canal via the sacral interventricular foramina, are smaller than the anterior sacral foramina.dorsal sacral foramen.

f. rotundum A round opening in anterior medial edge of the greater wing of the sphenoid bone, just below the superior orbital fissure, through which the maxillary division of the trigeminal nerve (CN V) passes. The foramen rotundum is anterior to the foramen ovale in the middle fossa of the skull.

sphenopalatine f. A rounded space in the suture between the sphenoid bone and the top (superior) edge of the palatine bone; it is located behind the orbit and connects the nasal cavity with the pterygopalatine fossa. The sphenopalatine branch of the maxillary artery and the nasopalatine nerve pass through this foramen. sphenopalatine notch.

f. spinosum The hole in the outer edge of the greater wing of the sphenoid bone through which the middle meningeal artery passes as it enters the middle cranial fossa. It is just lateral to the foramen ovale.

stylomastoid f. A hole in the base of the skull between the mastoid process and the styloid process. The motor root of the facial nerve (CN VII) and the stylomastoid artery pass through this foramen.

supraorbital f. An opening in the bony supraorbital margin along the outer superior border of the orbit of each eye. The supraorbital branch of the ophthalmic division of the trigeminal nerve (CN V) and the supraorbital vessels pass through this foramen.supraorbital notch.

transverse f. An oval hole in the transverse processes of each cervical vertebra; found only in cervical vertebrae. The vertebral arteries pass consecutively through all these foramina except the foramina in cervical vertebra C7.

vertebral f. The large opening between the neural arch and the body of the vertebra that contains the spinal cord.

f. of Winslow The narrow opening between the greater and the lesser sacs of the peritoneal cavity. Its upper border is formed by the hepatoduodenal ligament, the mesenteric sleeve that encloses the portal triad.epiploic foramen.

Forbes disease (forbz) [Gilbert B. Forbes, U.S. pediatrician, 1916–2003] Glycogen storage disease type III.

force (fors) [Fr. *force*, fr L. *fortia*] A push or pull exerted on an object, changing its speed or direction. The metric unit for force is the newton, which equals 0.225 lb of force.

catabolic f. Energy produced by metabolism of food.

centrifugal f. The force that impels a thing, or parts of it, outward from the center of rotation. SEE: *centrifuge*.

electromotive f. ABBR: EMF. Energy that causes flow of electricity in a conductor. The energy is measured in volts.

G f. The gravitational constant. In aerospace medicine, the term indicates the forces acting on the human body during acceleration in certain flight maneuvers. Thus a force of 2 positive G means that the aviator is being subjected to a force twice that of gravity with a doubling of weight in that condition, i.e., the force against the seat is 2 G. G force may be in any axis and may be negative or positive.

maximum inspiratory f. ABBR: MIF. The output of the inspiratory muscles measured in negative centimeters of water pressure. It is measured by having the subject inhale from a tube connected to a manometer under conditions of no flow. SYN: *maximum inspiratory pressure; negative inspiratory f.*

negative inspiratory f. Maximum inspiratory f.

psychic f. Force generated apart from physical energy.

reserve f. The energy available above that required for normal functioning of the heart.

force couple Biomechanical principle whereby two or more muscles acting in different directions influence the rotation of a joint in a specific direction. When the forces are of equal magnitude and in opposite directions, the limb will rotate about its long axis. SEE: *biomechanics*.

forced duction test A test used in ophthalmology to assess whether eye elevation or movements of the inferior muscles of the eye are restricted as a result of an injury, e.g., of an orbital floor fracture. Used to determine if an ocular deviation is mechanically restricted versus paretic.

forced expiratory technique SEE: under *technique*.

forced expiratory time SEE: under *time*.

forced expiratory volume SEE: under *volume*.

force plate SEE: under *plate*.

forceps (for'sĕps, 'seps″) *pl.* **forceps** [L. *forceps*, pincers, tongs] A two-bladed hinged or spring-loaded instrument for holding and manipulating tissues.

alligator f. A straight or angled forceps with jawlike movement at its end.

Allis f. SEE: under *Allis, Oscar Huntington*.

artery f. An atraumatic forceps with teeth that will not injure the vessel; used for temporary occlusion of a vessel.

axis-traction f. An obstetrical forceps fitted with a handle that makes it possible to provide traction in line with the direction in which the head must be moved.

bone f. A heavy-duty forceps for cutting bone and removing bone fragments.

brain f. Obstetrical **f.**

capsule f. A forceps for making an opening in the anterior capsule of the lens during cataract surgery.

Chamberlen f. SEE: *Chamberlen forceps*.

clamp f. Any forceps with an automatic lock.

dental f. Any of several forceps of varying shapes for grasping teeth during extraction procedures.

dressing f. A smooth forceps for dressing wounds or inserting drainage tubes.

Graefe f. SEE: under *Graefe, Albrecht von*.

grasping f. A forceps with a strong beaked end, used for seizing body tissues, foreign bodies, or removing objects such as stones from organs.

Halsted f. SEE: under *Halsted, William Stewart*.

intestinal f. A forceps used in abdominal surgeries to temporarily block the large or small bowel without crushing them.

Knapp f. SEE: *Knapp forceps*.

Magill f. SEE: *Magill forceps*.

mosquito f. A smaller variety of Halsted's forceps with a finely pointed tip.

needle f. A forceps for grasping and holding a needle.

obstetrical f. A forceps for extracting the fetal head from the pelvis during delivery. In obstetrics, forceps application is classified according to the position of the fetal head when the forceps are applied, i.e., outlet forceps, low forceps, and midforceps. The forceps allows withdrawal force to be applied to the fetal head and protects the head during the passage. SYN: **brain f.** SEE: *station*.

Piper f. SEE: *Piper forceps*.

rongeur f. A forceps for cutting bone.

Russian f. A forceps with serrated, spoon-shaped tips.

splinter f. A fine-tipped forceps, used in first aid, to remove tiny foreign bodies from tissues, and in other applications, e.g., to handle sutures.

sponge f., sponge-holding forceps A blunt-tipped forceps used to grasp tissues, esp. in gynecological procedures, without damaging tissue. They are often used to hold the uterine cervix, for example.

thumb f. A forceps used to hold tissues, esp. while suturing them.

tissue f. A pincer-like toothed forceps for grasping delicate tissues.

towel f. A sharply pointed forceps for holding a surgical drape on the body without damaging the tissue that it grasps.

tubing f. A forceps with a hollow beak, used to place catheters or other instruments inside cylindrical body structures.

forcing function Any management device or tool used to limit user errors by prohibiting specific actions without prior use of necessary safety procedures. In nursing a device that stores and dispenses medications and that may prevent the withdrawal of those medications unless the patient's vital signs or allergy list is recorded by the nurse and found to meet specified criteria for safe use.

forcipate (for'sĭ-pāt) [L. *forceps*, tongs] Shaped like forceps.

Fordyce disease, Fordyce spots (for'dīs") [John Fordyce, U.S. dermatologist, 1858–1925] Enlarged ectopic sebaceous glands in the mucosa of the mouth and genitals. They appear as small yellow spots. They are asymptomatic and are present in most people.

Fordyce-Fox disease (for'dīs-fōks') [George Henry Fox, U.S. dermatologist, 1846–1937] SEE: *Fox-Fordyce disease*.

forearm (for'ärm) [AS. *fore*, in front, + *arm*, arm] The portion of the arm between the elbow and wrist.

forearm rolling test A test for subtle hemiparesis in which the patient is asked to roll his or her forearms around each other. If one arm moves more slowly than the other, it is evidence of a lesion in the corticospinal tract on the opposite side. SEE: *finger rolling test*.

forebrain (for'brān) [" + *bregen*, brain] Prosencephalon.

forecast (for'kast") To make an informed prediction about a future event based on history, data, and personal experiences and professional judgments.

forefinger (for'fin"gĕr) The index finger; the second digit of the hand (the thumb is the first).

forefoot (for'foot) The part of the foot in front of the tarsometatarsal joint.

foregut (for'gŭt) [" + *gut*, a pouring] The most rostral part of the embryonic gut tube. The foregut gives rise to the caudal part of the buccal cavity, the pharynx, the esophagus, the stomach, and the initial segment of the duodenum. In addition, the liver, the gallbladder, the biliary ducts, the pancreas, and the respiratory system develop from the foregut.

forehead [AS *forheafod*] The anterior part of the head below the hairline and above the eyes.

foreign body SEE: under *body*.

foreign body reaction A localized inflammatory response elicited by any material, e.g., a splinter or a suture that would not normally be found within the body.

forelock (for'lŏk) A lock of hair that grows on the forehead.

white f. A white tuft of hair that grows on the forehead. It is associated with Waardenburg syndrome, and is seen in vitiligo.

forensic (for-ĕn'sĭk) [L. *forensis*, public] Pert. to the law; legal.

foreplay Fondling of the sex partner to produce mutual sexual arousal and pleasure prior to intercourse.

foreskin (for'skĭn) [AS. *fore*, in front, + O. Norse *skinn*, skin] The prepuce, the loose skin at and covering the end of the penis or clitoris like a hood. Excision of the prepuce constitutes circumcision. Smegma praeputii is secreted by Tyson's glands and collects under the foreskin.

forest plot A tool used in meta-analysis to show how different studies that have evaluated a specific condition or treatment have produced independent results. The plot graphs the results of each study and how far those results vary from zero. It also includes a point that shows the sum of all the findings in the studies, suggesting what conclusions might be drawn if all the results from each study were combined.

forewaters (for'wăt-ĕrz) A pocket of amniotic fluid that precedes the presenting part of the fetus into the cervical canal. Expulsion or dissolution of the mucus plug (cervical operculum) allows the pocket to descend into the canal during the first stage of labor. SEE: *operculum*.

forgetting Inability to remember something previously known or learned. SEE: *memory*.

fork An elongated instrument that splits at the end to form two or more prongs.

tuning f. SEE: ***tuning fork***.

form (form) [Fr. *forme*, fr L. *forma*, form, contour, figure] The distinctive size, shape, and external appearance of an object.

arch f. The shape of the dental arch when viewed in the horizontal plane.

consent f. A legal document, dated and signed by a patient and his or her health care provider, designating that the patient has been advised about the care about to be received.

PATIENT CARE: The document should specify the nature of the care and its proposed merits and hazards. If the care involves an invasive procedure, the document should provide enough detail about the procedure so that a reasonable person can decide whether it is in his or her interest to proceed. The material risks of the procedure, and consequences of not undergoing the procedure, should be listed. Alternatives to the procedure should be enumerated. Any special terms or conditions should be explicitly stated in the document. The form should include the name and title of the practitioner who provides the information to the patient. The document becomes valid when it is dated and signed by all parties.

-form [L. *forma*, shape, form] Suffix meaning *in the form of* or *in the shape of*.

formaldehyde (for-mal′dĕ-hīd″) [*form(ic)* + *aldehyde*] A colorless, pungent, irritant gas (HCOH) commonly made by oxidation of methyl alcohol, the simplest member of the aldehyde group. It dissolves in water and is toxic and carcinogenic.

formalin (for′mă-lĭn) [*Formalin*, formerly a trademaRK] An aqueous solution of 37% formaldehyde, used as a tissue preservative. It is toxic and carcinogenic.

formate (for′māt) A salt of formic acid.

formation 1. A particular structure. 2. An arrangement. 3. The giving of form or shape to, or the development of, a structure.

hippocampal f. Hippocampus.

reticular f. A diffuse complex of nuclei, axons, and dendrites extending rostrocaudally through the entire core of the brainstem. Some of the reticular nuclei are sufficiently distinct to have names and functional descriptions. In the midbrain, the reticular formation (which is found in the tegmentum, dorsal and lateral to the red nucleus) includes the pedunculopontine and the cuneiform nuclei. In the rostral hindbrain, the formation includes the caudal and the oral pontine reticular nuclei and the reticulotegmental and superior central nuclei. In the caudal hindbrain, it includes the lateral, gigantocellular, and paramedian reticular nuclei. The inputs to the reticular formation come from the sensory, cerebellar, cortical, striatal, and limbic systems; the outputs of the formation are carried by reticular axons throughout the nervous system from the forebrain to the caudal spinal cord. Signals from the midbrain and rostral hindbrain reticular formation control the level of the brain's alertness; signals from the hindbrain reticular formation help to control body posture; and signals from other parts of the reticular formation control homeostatic processes, e.g., the rate and rhythm of respiration.

form constancy The ability to identify an object even when it is rotated, reversed, or displaced spatially. In reading, for example, it is the ability to identify the similarities and differences between the letters "p" and "q" or the letters "b" and "d."

forme fruste (form froost) *pl.* **formes frustes** [Fr., defaced] An aborted or incomplete form of disease arrested before running its course; an atypical and indefinite manifestation of an illness.

formic (for′mĭk) [L. *formica*, ant] Pert. to ants or to formic acid.

formic aldehyde Formaldehyde.

formication (for″mĭ-kā′shŭn) The profoundly disturbing sensation that insects are crawling on one's skin. This is one of the more troublesome side effects of alcohol and cocaine withdrawal.

formiciasis (for″mĭs-ĭ′ă-sĭs) [L. *formica*, ant, + Gr. *-iasis*, condition] Irritation caused by ant bites.

Formicidae (for-mis′ĭ-dē″) [L. *formica*, ant + *-idae*] The family of insects (order Hymenoptera) that includes ants.

formilase (for′mĭ-lās) An enzyme that catalyzes conversion of acetic acid to formic acid.

formol (for′mŏl) Formaldehyde solution. SEE: *formalin*.

formula (for′myŭ-lă) [L. *formula*, a register] 1. A rule prescribing ingredients and proportions for the preparation of a compound. 2. In chemistry, a symbolic expression of the constitution of a molecule. It consists of the symbols of its component elements, each denoting one atom, with subscripted numbers denoting the number of atoms present. Water, or H_2O, consists of two molecules of the element hydrogen and one of oxygen. It may also be written HOH.

Collections of atoms that constitute a group by themselves (radical) are often separated by periods or parentheses. In this case, figures prefixed or appended to the parentheses, or prefixed to an expression contained within periods, apply to all the symbols embraced by the parentheses or periods. In all other cases, a figure prefixed to a symbolic expression for a molecule, such as a coefficient in an algebraic formula, is a multiplier of all the symbols following.

3. Any liquid diet containing variable amounts of protein, fat, carbohydrate, vitamins, and minerals administered to infants as an alternative or a supplement to breast milk.

chemical f. SEE: *formula* (2).

dental f. A brief method of expressing the dentition of mammals in which the numbers of the teeth are given in the form of a fraction, each portion representing one quadrant; the numbers of the upper teeth form the numerator, and those of the lower teeth the denominator.

The first number listed represents the incisors; the second, the canines; the third, the premolars; and the fourth, the molars. The dental formula of the upper and lower right half of the mouth in humans is

$$\frac{2 - 1 - 2 - 3 \text{ (right upper jaw)}}{2 - 1 - 2 - 3 \text{ (right lower jaw)}}$$

   empirical f. A chemical formula that indicates the simplest numerical ratio of the elements within a molecule, without demonstrating the molecule's chemical bonds or structure. For example, the empirical formula for water is H_2O. SYN: *molecular f.*

   molecular f. Empirical **f.**

   official f. A formula in a pharmacopeia.

   spatial f. Stereochemical **f.**

   stereochemical f. A method of depicting chemical formulas so that the elements and their number are depicted as well as their position in space in relation to each other. SYN: *spatial f.*

   structural f. A formula of a compound that shows the relationship of the atoms in a molecule. The atoms are shown joined by valence bonds (e.g., H—O—H) as opposed to the empirical formula (H_2O).

formulary (for′myŭ-ler″ē) **1.** A book of formulas. **2.** A list of drugs available for routine use at a health care facility.

formulate (for′myŭ-lāt″) **1.** To construct or prepare a recipe or formula. **2.** In pharmacology, to make a medication according to a recipe or formula. **formulation** (for″myŭ-lā′shŏn), *n.*

formyl (for′mĭl) The radical of formic acid, HCO.

¹fornicate (for′nĭ-kăt, -kāt″) [L. *fornicatus*, arched, vaulted, fr *fornix*, vault] Shaped like a fornix; arched; vaulted.

²fornicate (for′nĭ-kāt″) [L. *fornicari* fr *fornix*, arch (because brothels were located in vaulted basements)] To commit fornication.

fornication (for″nĭ-kā′shŏn) [² *fornicate*] Voluntary sexual intercourse between unmarried people.

fornices (for′nĭ-sēz) [L.] Pl. of fornix.

fornix (for′niks, for′nĭ-sēz) *pl.* **fornices** [L. *fornix*, vault, arch] **1.** A thick axon tract that originates in the hippocampus and synapses in the septum and the hypothalamus, esp., in the mammillary bodies. The fornix, a major component of the limbic circuit, receives its name from the broad arch that it makes along the hidden inner edge of the cerebral cortex, under the corpus callosum. SEE:

limbic system for illus. **2.** Any vaultlike or arched body.

fortification spectrum (fŏr″tĭ-fĭ-kā′shŭn spĕk′trŭm) The appearance of a dark patch with a zigzag outline in the visual field, causing a temporary blindness there. SYN: *teichopsia.*

fortify (for′tĭ-fī) In food science technology, to add one or more substances to a food to increase its nutrient density. **fortifier** (-fī″ĕr), *n.*

forward surgical team ABBR: FST. A small mobile military unit consisting of surgeons, anesthetists, nurses, and support personnel. It is used in or near a battlefield to rescue and stabilize injured soldiers. The seriously injured are transported from FSTs to larger military hospitals for definitive care of their wounds.

fos (făs) A family of cancer-causing genes, first identified in viruses, that function within cells as transcription factors. Members of this family can transform normal cells, e.g., fibroblasts, into cancer cells, e.g., osteosarcomas, chondrosarcomas. SEE: *oncogene; transformation.*

   ETIOLOGY: The name is derived from "FBJ osteosarcoma virus," in which these oncogenes were first identified.

Fosamax (fŏs′ă-măks″) SEE: *alendronate.*

fossa (fos′ă) *pl.* **fossae** [L. *fossa*, ditch] A furrow, recess, or shallow depression.

   acetabular f. The rough-surfaced depression in the center of the acetabulum (femoral socket) of the hipbone. The fossa is deeper than the actual joint articulation and does not directly contact the head of the femur.

   antecubital f. The triangular region in the forearm on the anterior (flexor) surface of the elbow. Bounded laterally by the brachioradialis muscle and medially by the pronator teres muscle, the fossa contains the tendon of the biceps brachialis muscle and the brachial artery. Two large superficial veins, the cephalic and its branch, the median cubital, are common sites for blood drawing. SYN: *cubital f.*

   anterior cranial f. The anterior one-third of the floor of the cranial cavity; the fossa is formed from the orbital part of the frontal bones, the cribriform plates of the ethmoid bone, and one third of the anterior sphenoid bones (the anterior body and lesser wings). The olfactory lobes and the inferior surfaces of the cerebral hemispheres lie in this fossa.

   articular f. of mandible Mandibular **f.**

   articular f. of temporal bone Mandibular **f.**

   axillary f. The armpit; axilla.

   canine f. On the skull, the vertical

furrow along the surface of the maxilla beginning between the upper canine tooth and the first premolar tooth and extending up toward the orbit.

central f. of tooth The front-to-back (anterior-posterior) midline groove along the upper (occlusal) surface of a postcanine tooth. SEE: *central fissure*.

cerebral f. Cranial **f.**

condylar f.of occipital bone On the base of the occipital bone of the skull along the lateral edge of the foramen magnum, a prominent depression behind the occipital epicondyle.

coronoid f. On the anterior surface of the lower end of the humerus, a depression proximal to the trochlea and between the lateral and medial epicondyles; it is analogous to the olecranon fossa on the opposite side of the humerus. During full flexion of the forearm, the coronoid process of the ulna fits into the coronoid fossa of the humerus.

cranial f. One of the three floor "levels" (anterior, middle, and posterior cranial fossae) of the interior surface of the cranial cavity. Each level contains the impressions of surface features of corresponding brain regions. SYN: *cerebral f.; hypophyseal f.*

cubital f. Antecubital **f.**

digastric f. A small depression in the mandible behind its lower margin at either side of the midline (symphysis menti). The anterior belly of the digastric muscle attaches in this fossa.

glenoid f. 1. The shallow ovoid depression on the top of the lateral side of the scapula that articulates with the head of the humerus. The acromion of the scapula overhangs the glenoid fossa. SYN: *glenoid cavity*. 2. Mandibular **f.**

hypophyseal f. Cranial **f.**

iliac f. On each hip bone, the smooth, concave upper surface of the ilium, which makes a shelf that gently slopes downward and inward from the iliac crest.

implantation f. of sperm On a spermatozoon, the small segment behind the head to which the internal filaments of the tail attach.

incisive f. The vertical furrow along the surface of the maxilla beginning between the lateral upper incisor and the canine tooth and extending up toward the anterior nasal aperture.

f. incudis In the tympanic cavity of the middle ear, a small depression inside the epitympanic recess, in which the short process of the incus fits and is attached by tiny ligaments.

infraspinous f. On the dorsal (posterior) surface of the scapula, the broad, shallow, triangular-shaped depression filling the area below the scapular spine. The infraspinatus muscle is attached to and covers most of this fossa.

infratemporal f. On the lateral surface of the skull, an irregular pocket formed largely by the concave outer surface of the greater wing of the sphenoid bone as it curves into the lateral pterygoid plate of the sphenoid. This fossa is deep (medial) to the zygomatic arch and is continuous with the bottoms of both the temporal fossa and the inferior orbital fissure. The medial wall of the infratemporal fossa is split vertically by the pterygomaxillary fissure, which leads into the pterygopalatine fossa.

inguinal f. One of two vertical valleys in the peritoneum along each side of the anterior abdominal wall. The medial inguinal fossa is the depression between the medial and lateral umbilical folds; direct inguinal hernias typically protrude through the abdominal wall in the lower end of this fossa. The lateral inguinal fossa is the depression lateral to the lateral umbilical fold; the lower end of this fossa becomes the deep inguinal ring, the internal end of the inguinal canal.

interpeduncular f. On the anterior (ventral) surface of the midbrain, a trapezoidal depression behind the mammillary bodies and between the cerebral peduncles. The oculomotor nerve (CN III) leaves the midbrain through this fossa, and a number of separate branches of the posterior cerebral arteries enter the midbrain through the base of the fossa, in an area called the perforated substance.

ischioanal f. Ischiorectal **f.**

ischiorectal f. A wedge-shaped region just under the skin on either side of the lower end of the rectum and anal canal. The fossa is bounded laterally by the obturator internus muscle and the tuberosity of the ischium, medially by the levator ani and coccygeus muscles, and posteriorly by the gluteus maximus muscle. The ischiorectal fossa contains fat, connective tissue, blood vessels, and nerves. SYN: *ischioanal f.*

jugular f. On the base of the skull, a kidney bean-shaped depression in the undersurface of petrous portion of the temporal bone. The fossa is behind the carotid canal, from which it is separated by a ridge of bone, and it forms a pocket for the superior bulb of the jugular vein, just after the vein has exited the skull through the jugular foramen.

lacrimal f. A shallow depression in the lateral side of the roof of the orbit, just inside the upper orbital margin, into which the lacrimal gland fits.

mandibular f. In the skull, the depression in the temporal bone into which the condyle of the head (condylar process) of the mandible fits; the condyle of the mandible sits on an interposed articular disc when the mandible is fully elevated (teeth clenched). The fossa, a part of the temporomandibular joint, is a horizontal furrow lying underneath and behind the zygomatic process of the temporal bone. SYN: *articular f. of mandible; glenoid f. (2)*.

middle cranial f. The middle one-third of the floor of the cranial cavity; it is deeper and wider than the anterior cranial fossa. The middle cranial fossa is formed from the posterior two thirds of the sphenoid bones (the greater wings, the dorsum sella, and the clinoid processes) and the petrous and squamous portions of the temporal bones. The middle cranial fossa contains the superior orbital fissures, optic canals, foramina rotundum, foramina ovale, foramina spinosum, and foramina lacerum. The temporal lobes of the cerebral hemispheres, the optic chiasm, the hypophysis (pituitary), internal carotid arteries, circle of Willis, and cavernous sinuses lie in the middle cranial fossa.

navicular f. In the female perineum, the recess at the posterior end of the vaginal vestibule. This fossa is posterior to the vaginal opening and anterior to the fourchette, i.e., the frenulum, where the labia minora join posteriorly. SYN: *f. of the vaginal vestibule*.

olecranon f. On the posterior surface of the lower end of the humerus, a depression proximal to the trochlea and between the medial and lateral epicondyles; it is analogous to the coronoid fossa on the opposite side of the humerus. During full extension of the forearm, the olecranon process of the ulna fits into the olecranon fossa of the humerus

f. ovalis of heart An oval depression in the septal wall of the right atrium; it has a raised rim along its top and front edges. In the embryo, the floor of the fossa ovalis is a flap valve (the primary atrial septum or septum primum) that lets blood flow from the right atrium to the left atrium, bypassing the lungs. If the flap valve fails to seal after birth, the heart can have an atrial septal defect.

ovarian f. A shallow depression in the wall of the pelvis behind the lateral ends of the broad ligament; the ovary lies in this fossa covered by the parietal peritoneum.

pituitary f. Sella turcica.

popliteal f. A rhomboid space, just below the skin, behind the knee. Its edges are defined by muscles — laterally, the biceps femoris and the lateral head of the gastrocnemius; medially, the semitendinosus, the semimembranosus, and the medial head of the gastrocnemius. This fossa contains the popliteal vessels and the tibial and common fibular nerves.

posterior cranial f. The posterior third of the floor of the cranial cavity; it is larger and deeper than the anterior and middle cranial fossae. The posterior cranial fossa is formed from the posterior surface of the body of the sphenoid bone (the dorsum sella), the posterior surfaces of the petrous and mastoid portions of the temporal bones, and the inner surfaces of the occipital bones. The posterior cranial fossa contains the internal auditory canals, the foramen magnum, and the jugular foramina. The brainstem, the cerebellum, and the transverse and sigmoid sinuses lie in the posterior cranial fossa.

pterygoid f. The vertical trough between the medial and lateral pterygoid plates of the pterygoid process of the sphenoid bone. This fossa is on the deep, basal surface of the skull, just outside (lateral to) the nasopharynx.

pterygopalatine f. A thin wedge-shaped space behind the nasal cavity and below the deep apex of the orbit; laterally, it opens into the infratemporal fossa (via the pterygomaxillary fissure). The pterygopalatine fossa contains the pterygopalatine ganglion. The maxillary branch of the trigeminal nerve (CN V) enters the fossa from behind, through the foramen rotundum, and the pterygoid nerve enters the fossa via the pterygoid canal. SYN: *sphenomaxillary f.*

radial f. of humerus A small depression in the distal humerus on its anterior surface proximal to the capitulum. When the elbow is in complete flexion, the proximal end (the head) of the radius slides up along the capitulum and one edge of the head of the radius fits into the radial fossa.

rhomboid f. In the brainstem, the floor of the fourth ventricle, which runs along the dorsal surface of the pons and part of the medulla.

scaphoid f. of auricle (pinna) In the auricle of the ear, the C-shaped groove between the helix and the antihelix.

sphenomaxillary f. Pterygopalatine **f.**

subarcuate f. In the posterior cranial fossa, a variably shaped small depression in the petrous portion of the tympanic bone superior and lateral to the internal acoustic foramen. The subarcuate fossa leads into the subarcuate canal, which contains the subarcuate artery, a main blood supplier to the bony labyrinth, facial canal, and mucosa of the mastoid antrum.

supraclavicular f. The depression that can be felt below the skin at the base of the neck behind the clavicle and extending from the attachment of the sternal head of the sternocleidomastoid muscle medially to the medial edge of the deltoid muscle laterally.

supraspinous f. The sloping, triangular concave surface above the spine on the dorsal (posterior) side of the scapula. The supraspinatus muscle attaches to and fills most of this fossa.

supratonsillar f. A slit-like recess extending into the upper part of the palatine tonsil. This fossa is a remnant of the embryological second pharyngeal pouch. SYN: *intratonsillar* **cleft**.

supravesical f. On the internal surface of the anterior abdominal wall, a depression in the parietal peritoneum between the middle (median) and medial umbilical folds.

temporal f. On the side of the skull, a large fan-shaped depression containing the temporalis muscle. The fossa's upper edge forms a broad crescent (the temporal lines) along the frontal, parietal, and temporal bones, from the upper outer edge of the orbit to the most posterior edge of the zygomatic arch. From the crescent, the fossa gradually deepens toward the "handle" of the fan, which lies inside the zygomatic arch.

tonsillar f. A valley between the glossopalatine and pharyngopalatine arches along the lateral wall of the oropharynx and containing the palatine tonsil. SYN: *tonsillar* **recess**.

trochanteric f. At the proximal end of the femur, an irregular recess along the upper inner (proximal medial) surface of the great trochanter, where the medial edge of the greater trochanter overhangs the neck of the femur.

f. of the vaginal vestibule Navicular **f.**

fossae (fŏs'ē) [L.] Pl. of fossa.

fossette (fŏ-sĕt') [Fr.] **1.** A small depression or fossa. **2.** A small but deep corneal ulcer.

foster care SEE: under *care*.

Fothergill disease (foth'ĕr-gil) [John Fothergill, Brit. physician, 1712–1780] **1.** Scarlatina anginosa, an ulcerative sore throat present in severe scarlet fever. **2.** Trigeminal neuralgia.

Fountain syndrome A rare autosomal recessive syndrome characterized by mental retardation, short and stubby fingers and toes, a swollen appearance of the cheeks and lips, and, frequently, seizures, short stature, and a large cranial circumference.

four-chamber view An echocardiographic view that transects the heart approximately parallel with the anterior and posterior surfaces of the body, thus providing an image of all four chambers of the heart.

fourchette, fourchet (foor-shĕt') [Fr. *fourchette*, a fork] A tense band or transverse fold of mucous membrane at the posterior commissure of the vagina, connecting the posterior ends of the labia minora. The fossa navicularis, a cul-de-sac anterior to the fourchette, separates it from the hymen. It disappears after defloration or parturition, leaving a more open vulva below and behind.

four-dimensional, 4D (for"dĭ-men"shŏn-ăl) Of or pert. to four dimensions. A technique that measures three spatial dimensions plus time is four-dimensional.

four-dimensional ultrasonography SEE: under *ultrasonography*.

Fournier gangrene, Fournier disease (fŏr-nē'ā) [Jean Alfred Fournier, French dermatologist, 1832–1915] Necrotizing fasciitis of the genitalia that may spread to the thighs or abdomen. This aggressive and life-threatening form of cellulitis typically occurs in patients who have had local trauma to the perineum and patients with diabetes mellitus.

ETIOLOGY: Multiple aerobic and anaerobic bacteria cause the infection.

TREATMENT: Treatment consists of broad-spectrum antibiotics and wide surgical débridement.

fourth cranial nerve A small mixed nerve exiting from the dorsal surface of the midbrain. It contains efferent motor fibers to the superior oblique muscle of the eye and afferent sensory fibers conveying proprioceptive impulses from the same muscle. SYN: *trochlear nerve*.

fovea (fō'vē-ă) *pl.* **foveae** [L.] A pit or cuplike depression. SEE: *fossa*.

foveate (fō'vē-āt) [L. *foveatus*] Pitted.

foveation (fō"vē-ā'shŭn) Pitting, as in smallpox.

foveola (fō-vē'ō-lă) *pl.* **foveolae** [L., little pit] **1.** A minute pit or depression. **2.** The thinnest part of the retina, where vision is most acute. Unlike other regions of the retina, it has no layer of ganglion cells between it and the retinal pigment epithelium.

Fowler position (fowl'ĕr) [George R. Fowler, U.S. surgeon, 1848–1906] A semi-sitting position. The head of an adjustable bed can be elevated to the desired height to produce angulation of the body, usually 45° to 60°. The knees may or may not be bent. A wedge support can be used to elevate the patient's head and back if an adjustable bed is not available. The position is used to facilitate breathing and drainage and for the comfort of the bedridden patient while eating or talking.

NOTE: Fowler's position has three variations: high (sitting upright in bed), regular (head or torso elevated 45° or more), and low or semi-low (head and torso elevated to 30°). SEE: illus.; *dorsal recumbent position* for illus.

Fox-Fordyce disease (fŏks'for'dīs) [George Henry Fox, U.S. dermatologist, 1846–1937; John Fordyce, U.S. dermatologist, 1858–1925] A chronic pruritic papular eruption of areas of the skin that contain apocrine sweat glands. The intraepidermal ducts of the apocrine glands become obstructed and eventually rupture. The disease occurs mostly

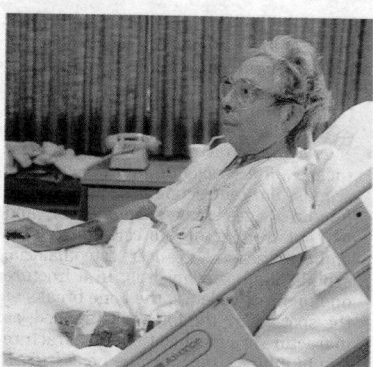

HIGH FOWLER'S POSITION

in persons 13 to 35 years of age and about 10 times more frequently in women than men. It does not occur before puberty.

TREATMENT: Several agents, including estrogens, corticosteroids, and topical tretinoin cream, have been used, but with little benefit. SYN: *Fordyce-Fox disease.*

foxglove (fŏks'glŏv) The common name for the flowering plant *Digitalis purpurea*, from which digitalis is obtained. SEE: illus.

FOXGLOVE

Springtime appearance before the plant flowers

FP24 Plasma collected and frozen within 24 hr of its collection from a donor. It differs from fresh frozen plasma (frozen within 8 hr of its donation) by having lower levels of several coagulation factors, esp. factor VIII.

FPIA *Fluorescence polarization immunoassay.*

FPR *False-positive ratio.*

FQHC *federally qualified health center.*

Fr Symbol for the element francium.

fraction (frak'shŏn) [L. *fractio*, act of breaking] **1.** In biological chemistry, the separable part of a substance such as blood or plasma. **2.** The ratio of a component to the total, e.g., the substance fraction of carboxyhemoglobin (relative to the total hemoglobin).

attributable f. The percentage of instances of an illness that can be accounted for by a particular risk factor. For example, people exposed to asbestos have a certain risk of developing lung cancer, and if they also smoke tobacco, they are also at risk from that factor. These risks may be estimated from cohort studies. SYN: *additional risk; attributable risk.*

carboxyhemoglobin f. The percentage of total hemoglobin in a blood sample that is covalently bonded to carbon monoxide.

ejection f. ABBR: EF. In cardiac physiology, the percentage of the blood emptied from the ventricle during systole. The left ventricular ejection fraction averages 60% to 70% in healthy hearts but can be markedly reduced if part of the heart muscle dies (as after myocardial infarction) or in cardiomyopathy or valvular heart disease.

immature platelet f. ABBR: IPF. The percent of platelets found in the circulating blood that still retains RNA. It is elevated (greater than 12%) in diseases in which platelets are rapidly destroyed after their release from the bone marrow, e.g., disseminated intravascular coagulation (DIC), idiopathic thrombocytopenic purpura (ITP), and thrombotic thrombocytopenic purpura (TTP). These diseases can be distinguished from other thrombocytopenic conditions in which platelet regeneration is slower, e.g., aplastic anemia, liver failure, or kidney failure, because the IPF is usually less than 12% in diseases characterized by bone marrow inactivity or suppression. The IPF is determined using flow cytometry.

f. of inspired oxygen ABBR: FIO_2. The concentration of oxygen in the inspired air, esp. that supplied as supplemental oxygen by mask or catheter.

mass f. The ratio of the mass of a constituent to the total mass of the system in which the constituent is contained.

oxyhemoglobin f. SYMB: F O2Hb. That portion of hemoglobin present in a sample of blood that is reversibly bound to oxygen.

plasma protein f. A standard sterile preparation of serum albumin and globulin obtained by fractionating blood, serum, or plasma from healthy human donors and testing for absence of hepatitis B surface antigen. It is used as a blood volume expander.

substance f. The ratio of the amount (number of moles or entities) of a constituent of a mixture to the total of constituents of the system. SEE: *mass f.*

volume f. The ratio of the volume of a constituent to the volume of the whole. In practice, it may be difficult to determine the volume fraction because differences in the molecular sizes of the constituents may produce a total volume that differs from the sum of the individual volumes of the mixture. When materials of similar physicochemical characteristics (such as multiple aqueous solutions) are combined, this is not a problem.

fractional (frak′shŏn-ăl) [*fraction + -al*] **1.** Made of equal parts of a whole; partial. **2.** Pert. to a fraction.

fractional ablation Fractional photothermolysis.

fractional excretion of sodium The urinary sodium concentration multiplied by the plasma creatinine concentration multiplied by 100, all divided by the product of the plasma sodium concentration and the urinary creatinine concentration.

fractional flow reserve SEE: under *reserve.*

fractional shortening The reduction of the length of the end-diastolic diameter that occurs by the end of systole. Like the ejection fraction, this is a measure of the heart's muscular contractility. If the diameter fails to shorten by at least 28%, the efficiency of the heart in ejecting blood is impaired.

fractional test meal Extended examination of the stomach contents. First the residual contents are removed and then the test meal is given. After the meal, assessments of gastric emptying, gastric acidity, pancreatic secretion, or nutrient absorption may be undertaken.

fractional urine SEE: under *urine.*

fractionate (frak′shŏ-nāt″) To separate or divide a mixture, usually by means of the differing physical or chemical properties of its components.

fractionation (frak″shŏ-nā′shŏn) [*fractionate*] **1.** In radiation therapy, the process of spreading the total required treatment dose over an extended period. **2.** In chemistry, the separation of a mixture into its components, usually to isolate a particular substance for use or study.

acceleration f. The treatment of a tumor with radiation doses given over a shorter period than usual, e.g., over a 5-week period as opposed to a 7-week period. Accelerated fractionation may provide clinical and survival benefits to some patients with inoperable tumors.

size f. The separation of substances in a mixture on the basis of their molecular size, e.g., the separation of DNA strands based on their number of nucleotides.

fracture (frak′chŭr) [L. *fractura,* a break] **1.** An injury that upon assessment is painful, swollen, and deformed. **2.** A break of a bone. SEE: illus.

CAUSES: Fractures may be due to pathology, direct violence, indirect violence, or muscular contraction. In a pathological fracture, bones break, spontaneously and without trauma, due to certain diseases and conditions like cancer, osteomalacia, syphilis, and osteomyelitis, In a fracture due to direct violence, the bone breaks at the spot where the force was applied, as in fracture of a crushed tibia. In a fracture due to indirect violence, the bone is fractured by a force applied at a distance from the site of fracture and transmitted to the fractured bone, as a fracture of the clavicle by a fall on an outstretched hand. In a fracture due to muscular contraction, the bone breaks from a sudden, violent contraction of the muscles.

SIGNS: Signs include loss of the power of movement, pain with acute tenderness over the site of fracture, swelling and bruising, deformity and possible shortening, unnatural mobility, and crepitus or grating heard when the ends of the bone rub together.

TREATMENT: Immediate first aid includes splinting of the fracture site and joints above and below it to limit further movement and displacement. Applying a cold pack to the fracture site and elevating it above the level of the heart may limit pain and swelling. Radiography should be used to identify the fracture and the exact position of the bone fragments.

The physician reduces the fracture. The bone is kept in position by a cast or splint until union has taken place. Afterwards the limb is restored to complete function by physical therapy and exercise.

In open or compound fractures, bleeding must be arrested before the fracture is treated. Initially, the open fracture should be covered with a clean or sterile dressing and the fracture site immobilized. Open reduction may be required. The wound is then washed and cleaned with sterile saline. If the area is grossly contaminated, mild soap solution may be used provided it is thoroughly washed away with generous amounts of sterile saline. When the wound is clean, a sterile dressing is secured by a bandage. The bone may then be immobilized by external fixation until the wound heals.

Skeletal traction may be used instead of a cast or external fixator for certain fractures, such as femoral shaft fractures. Pins are placed in the bone, and the bone ends are held in place by pulleys and weights until union occurs.

If the bone does not heal, a weak electric current applied to the bone ends (bone stimulation) may promote heal-

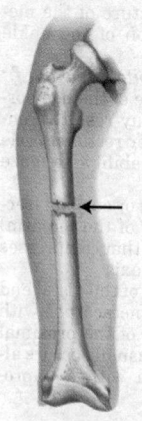

Closed

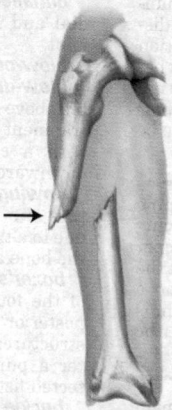

Open

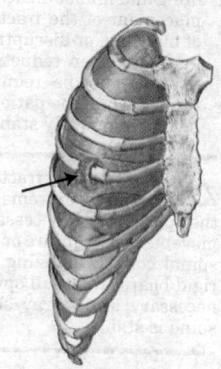

Complicated

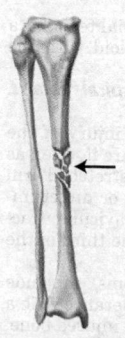

Comminuted

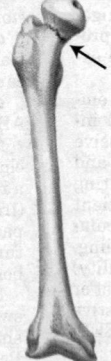

Impacted

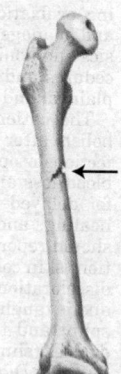

Incomplete

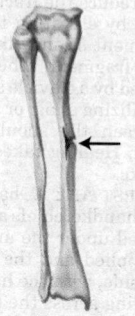

Greenstick

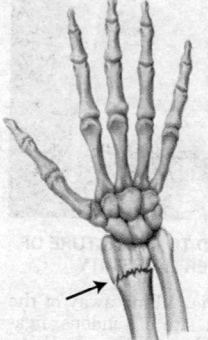

Colles fracture

TYPES OF FRACTURES

ing. Hip fractures require gentle handling and immobilization to prevent displacement of the fracture, aggravation of bleeding, or disruption of a pelvic hematoma. Open reduction with internal fixation may be required and is performed when the patient is judged to be hemodynamically stable.

⚠ First aid for fractures of the spine requires extreme care in moving the patient. Unnecessary or improper movement may injure or even transect the spinal cord. Stabilizing the patient on a rigid board, with full spinal protection, is necessary until x-ray studies reveal the spine is stable.

PATIENT CARE: Vascular and neurological status of the limb distal to the fracture site are monitored before and after immobilization with traction, casting, or fixation devices. Pain is assessed and managed with prescribed analgesics and noninvasive measures. All procedures and related sensations are explained, and reassurance given.

The patient is evaluated for fat embolism after long bone fractures, for infection in open fractures, for excessive blood loss and hypovolemic shock, and for delayed union or nonunion during healing and follow-up. The patient should report signs of impaired circulation (skin coldness, numbness, tingling, discoloration, and changes in mobility) and is taught how to care for the cast or splint and the correct use of assistive devices (slings, crutches, walker). SEE: *Nursing Diagnoses Appendix; illus.*

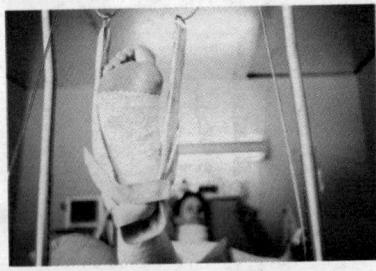

TRACTION APPLIED TO A FRACTURE OF THE LOWER EXTREMITY

avulsion f. The pulling away of the bony attachment site of tendons, ligament, joint capsule, or fascia. Avulsion fractures of tendons are usually caused by a forceful contraction of the muscle. Ligamentous avulsions are caused by forcing the joint beyond its normal range of motion and are often associated with sprains or dislocations.

bend f. Plastic deformation of bone.

Bennett f. SEE: *Bennett fracture.*

bimalleolar f. A fracture of the medial and lateral malleoli of the ankle joint.

blow-out f. SEE: *orbital blow-out f.*

blow-up f. A fracture of the bony orbit above the eye. It may result in entrapment of the superior rectus muscle with a consequent inability to gaze downward.

bowing f. A bending or curving fracture of a bone (usually of the forearm) due to a traumatic load that compresses the bone along its long axis.

boxer's f. A fracture of the distal end of the fourth or fifth metacarpal with posterior displacement of the proximal structures. The injury usually occurs after a punch is thrown with a unprotected fist.

buckle f. Torus **f.**

burst f. A vertebral fracture similar to a compression fracture but typically more severe and involving displacement of the bony fragments. SEE: *compression f.*

chauffeur's f. A colloquial term for a fracture of the radial styloid with the carpal joint.

childhood accidental spiral tibial f. ABBR: CAST. Toddler's **f.**

f. of clavicle Physical injury of the clavicle sufficient to fracture it, often as a result of a fall on an outstretched arm (from a ladder or bicycle) or direct impact to the bone. Most clavicular fractures involve the distal one third of the bone.

SYMPTOMS: Symptoms include swelling, pain, and protuberance with a sharp depression over the injured bone. Palpable deformity and crepitus are commonly present.

TREATMENT: If indicated, an emergency care physician or an orthopedist will reduce the fracture. This usually is done by elevating the arm and lateral fragment so they line up with the medial fragment. The position is maintained by a clavicle strap, spica cast, immobilizing sling, or figure-of-eight wrap between the shoulders and over the back. Healing takes from about 6 to 8 weeks.

FIRST AID: A ball of cloth or one or two handkerchiefs are tightly rolled and placed under the armpit. An arm sling is applied and the elbow bandaged to the side, with the hand and forearm extending across the chest. Alternatively, the patient may lie on his or her back on the floor with a rolled-up blanket under the shoulders until medical aid arrives. This position keeps the shoulders back and prevents the broken ends of the bone from rubbing.

clay shoveler's f. A colloquial term for a fracture of the base of the spinous process of the lower cervical spine associated with sudden flexion of the neck. It may also be caused by direct trauma.

closed f. A fracture of the bone with no skin wound.

Colle f. SEE: under *Colles, Abraham*.

comminuted f. A fracture in which the bone is broken or splintered into pieces.

complete f. A fracture in which the bone is completely broken (i.e., neither fragment is connected to the other).

complicated f. A fracture in which the bone is broken and has injured some internal organ, such as a broken rib piercing a lung.

compound f. A fracture in which fragments of bone protrude through the skin or in which there is a break in the skin or soft tissue at the fracture site. Such a fracture exposes the wound to possible infection. SYN: *open f.*

compression f. A fracture of a vertebra by pressure along the long axis of the vertebral column. Such fractures, which may occur traumatically or as a result of osteoporosis, are marked by loss of bone height.

depressed f. A fracture in which a piece of bone (as of the skull or ribs) is broken and driven inward.

diastatic f. A fracture that follows a cranial suture and causes it to separate.

direct f. A fracture at a site where force was applied.

dislocation f. A fracture near a dislocated joint. SEE: *dislocation*.

double f. Two fractures of the same bone.

Dupuytren f. SEE: under *Dupuytren, Baron Guillaume*.

Duverney f. SEE: under *Duverney, Joseph G.*

epiphyseal f. A separation of the epiphysis from the bone between the shaft of the bone and its growing end. It occurs only in skeletally immature patients. SEE: *Salter-Harris fracture*.

fatigue f. Stress **f.**

fissured f. A narrow split in the bone that does not go through to the other side of the bone.

flexion-teardrop f. An unstable fracture of the cervical spine in which a small fragment of the anteroinferior corner of a vertebral body avulses from the rest of the vertebra due to massive flexion applied to the cervical spine. Patients with this fracture have sustained injuries to all the spinal ligaments and usually severe spinal cord injury and quadriplegia.

fragility f. A fracture that occurs in a bone weakened by osteoporosis.

greenstick f. A fracture in which the bone is partially bent and partially broken, as when a green stick breaks. It occurs in children, esp. those with rickets. There is a compression fracture on the concave side of the bend and a tension fracture on the convex side.

hairline f. A minor fracture in which all the portions of the bone are in perfect alignment. The fracture is seen on a radiograph as a very thin line lying between the two segments and not extending through the bone.

hangman's f. A bipedicular fracture of the second cervical vertebra, often with a concomitant dislocation of the vertebra. The term originates from properly performed judicial hangings. At the moment when the dropped criminal fully extends the rope, the hangman's knot causes fracture dislocation of the upper cervical spine and transection of the spinal cord or medulla. If the knot is not made or applied properly, death is usually due to asphyxia. Contemporary hangman's fractures occur mostly in automobile accidents or athletic competitions.

hip f. A fracture of the proximal portion of the femur, i.e., of either the head, neck, intertrochanteric or subtrochanteric regions of the hip. Hip fracture occurs each year in approximately 225,000 Americans over 50. It is more common in women than in men due to osteoporosis and is esp. common in slender, elderly women. Mortality rates after hip fracture are influenced by the patient's age, general physical health, and the type of fracture.

ETIOLOGY: Osteoporosis predisposes an elderly person to hip fracture.

SYMPTOMS: Pain in the knee or groin is the classic presenting sign of a hip fracture. If the femur is displaced, shortening and rotation of the leg may be present.

TREATMENT: Preoperatively, Buck's traction may be used in the short term to alleviate muscle spasms. An open reduction is the preferred surgical treatment. A femoral prosthesis may be used for femoral neck or head fractures. The bone takes 6 to 12 weeks to heal in an elderly patient.

PATIENT CARE: During hospitalization, general patient care concerns apply. The patient is prepared physically and emotionally for surgery according to the orthopedic surgeon's protocol, and postsurgical care and pain control (epidural or intravenous patient-controlled analgesia [PCA]) is discussed. Neurovascular status of the affected limb is assessed according to protocol and compared to the unaffected limb. The patient is referred for physical and occupational therapy and uses a walker until the bone is completely healed. Prevention and relief of pain and monitoring of postoperative complications, including infection, hip dislocation, and deep venous thrombosis or pulmonary embolism, are primary concerns. Use of an incentive spirometer is encouraged to prevent atelectasis and respiratory complications. Prophylactic antibiotics and anticoagulants are administered as prescribed, and hip precautions are implemented to prevent dislocation. These precautions include having the patient avoid hip adduction (usually by an abductor wedge), rotation, and flexion greater than 90° during transfer and ambulation activities, and by using a raised toilet seat and semi-reclining chair. The patient is typically hospitalized for 2 to 4 days and then discharged to a nursing home, subacute unit, transitional care unit, rehabilitation center, or home for rehabilitation for several weeks.

f. of humerus Disruption of the bony cortex of the upper arm. If the fracture is of the upper end of the humerus, the arm is abducted and splinted for about 4 weeks. Movements of the elbow and wrist are started early, and active movements of the shoulder are begun in about 3 weeks. SEE: illus.; *acromiohumeral; capitellum; cubitus; glenoid cavity.*

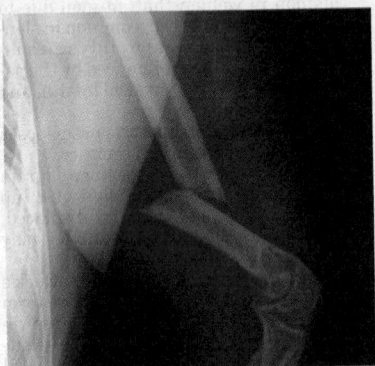

FRACTURE OF THE HUMERUS
Radiographic image of a fracture of the humerus (COURTESY of W. Robert Strauss, Jr.)

In a fracture of the shaft and lower end of the humerus, the limb is put in a cast in a position midway between pronation and supination with the humerus at right angles to the forearm. Movement of the shoulder, wrist, and finger is allowed.

impacted f. A fracture in which the bone is broken and one end is wedged into the interior of the opposing end.

incomplete f. A fracture in which the line of fracture does not transverse the bone.

indirect f. A fracture distant from the place where the force was applied.

insufficiency f. A stress fracture oc-

curring in abnormal bone (e.g., osteoporotic bone) subjected to normal forces.

intracapsular f. A fracture occurring within the capsule of a joint.

intrauterine f. A broken fetal bone.

Jefferson f. SEE: *Jefferson fracture.*

Jones f. SEE: *Jones fracture.*

lead pipe f. A fracture in which the bone is compressed and bent so that one side of the fracture bulges and the other side shows a slight fracture line.

LeFort f. A fracture usually involving more than one of the facial bones: maxillary, nasal, orbital, and/or zygomatic. SYN: *mid-face f.*

lover's f. A colloquial term for a fracture of the calcaneus, due to jumping from a height, e.g., a balcony or second-story window.

march f. A fracture of the metatarsals as a result of overuse.

mid-face f. LeFort **f.**

Monteggia f. SEE: *Monteggia fracture.*

nightstick f. A nondisplaced transverse fracture of the ulna resulting from a direct blow.

nonunion of f. SEE: *nonunion.*

occult f. A fracture that is suspected based on clinical grounds (e.g., guarding, pain, and swelling) but not seen on x-rays. The fracture may be seen with bone scans or magnetic resonance imaging.

open f. Compound **f.**

orbital blow-out f. A fracture of the bony floor beneath the eye. It typically results in entrapment of the inferior rectus muscle, with a consequent inability to look upward with the affected eye, which causes double vision during vertical gaze.

overriding f. Overriding.

pathological f. A fracture of a diseased or weakened bone caused by a force that would not have fractured a healthy bone. The underlying disease may be a metastasized cancer, primary cancer of the bone, or osteoporosis.

PATIENT CARE: The limbs and joints of at-risk patients are gently and carefully supported when repositioning, exercising, or mobilizing. If such patients fall or are injured, and report limb, pelvic, or back pain or inability to bear weight, the patient and the affected limb should be stabilized and - diagnostic imaging obtained.

pelvic f. Fracture of one of more of the bones of the pelvis, i.e. of the ilium, ischium, or pubis. Pelvic fractures occur after falls, esp. in the elderly, in whom the pelvic bones may be weakened by osteoporosis, and after high-impact trauma, e.g., motor vehicle crashes. Some pelvic fractures are accompanied by internal organ damage, esp. to the genitourinary organs. Regaining the ability to walk after pelvic fracture sometimes requires months of rehabilitation.

penile f. Sudden trauma to the tunica albuginea of the penis, resulting in a rupture of the corpus cavernosum and sometimes a tearing of the urethra. The injury typically occurs during sexual intercourse (or, less often, during masturbation) and may be accompanied by bleeding into the penis.

ping-pong f. A depressed skull fracture in a newborn or very young infant in which the bone bends inward (like a dented ping-pong ball) without breaking. It may occur during strenuous labor and delivery, or in trauma to the pliant skull in the first weeks of life.

Pott f. SEE: under *Pott, John Percival*.

pretrochanteric f. A fracture that passes through the greater trochanter of the femur.

Rolando f. SEE: *Rolando fracture*.

simple f. A fracture without rupture of ligaments and skin.

f. of skull, fractured skull Loss of the integrity of one or more bones of the cranium. A fracture is classified according to whether it is in the vault or the base but, from the point of view of treatment, a more useful classification is differentiating between a *simple fracture* (uncommon) and a *compound fracture*. When a compound fracture occurs in the vault of the skull, the bone is depressed and driven inward, possibly damaging the brain. Treatment is operative.

sleeve f. An avulsion fracture of the patella that typically occurs as a result of a sudden strong contraction of the quadriceps muscle group.

Smith f. SEE: *Smith fracture*.

snowboarder's f. A fracture of the lateral border of the talus caused by inversion and rotation of the talus within the mortise. Signs and symptoms often mimic those of an inversion (lateral) ankle sprain.

f. of the spine Fracture of a vertebral body or its bony prominences. SYN: *vertebral f.* SEE: *burst f.; compression f.; hangman's f.; Jefferson fracture*.

TREATMENT: The patient is carefully assessed for evidence of neuromuscular compromise and other internal injuries. To prevent complications and promote healing, vests, casts, or halo devices may be used, depending on the location of the fracture. A program of supervised physical therapy may be needed during recovery.

PROGNOSIS: Prognosis depends on the type of spinal fracture and associated spinal cord involvement.

spiral f. A fracture that follows a helical line along and around the course of a long bone.

stellate f. A fracture with numerous

fissures radiating from the central point of injury.

straddle f. A traumatic fracture of all four pubic rami, often associated with injury to the urethra.

stress f. A microfracture that appears without evidence of a single traumatic onset. This type of fracture is difficult to diagnose by standard radiography and may not become visible until 3 to 4 weeks after the onset of symptoms. Scintigraphy, CT, and/or MRI may lead to earlier identification of the fracture lines. Stress fractures occur from repetitive microtraumas (from running, aerobic dancing, or marching or other cyclical actions), from improper shoes on hard surfaces, or from inadequate healing time after stress. Stress fractures are classified as fatigue fractures or insufficiency fractures based on their etiology. Undiagnosed and untreated stress fractures may progress to frank fractures. SYN: *fatigue f.* SEE: *insufficiency f.*

T f. A fracture in which bone splits both longitudinally and transversely.

toddler's f. A fracture of the distal third of the tibia, sustained in a child typically aged 2 to 4. The child may limp or refuse to walk because of pain. The fracture may not be easily seen on plain radiographs. SYN: *childhood accidental spiral tibial f.*

torus f. A fracture where the structure of one side of the bone is compressed, while the opposite side deflects from the growth plate, leaving the cortex intact. SYN: *buckle f.*

transcervical f. A fracture through the neck of the femur.

transverse f. A fracture in which the fracture line is at right angles to the long axis of the bone.

trimalleolar f. A fracture of the lateral and medial malleoli of the ankle joint with an additional fracture of the posterior edge of the distal tibia.

tripod f. A fracture in which the zygoma is separated from its attachment to the maxilla and the temporal and frontal bones.

vertebral f. F. of the spine.

Wagstaffe f. SEE: *Wagstaffe fracture*.

fracture dislocation SEE: under *dislocation*.

fragile X syndrome A chromosomal disease, often associated with mental retardation, in which the tip of the long arm of the X chromosome can separate from the rest of the genetic material. This is the most common of the X-linked mental retardation syndromes. Most males and 30% of females with this syndrome are mentally retarded. Males also develop greatly enlarged testicles (macro-orchidism), enlarged ears, and a prominent jaw.

fragilitas (frǎ-jǐl′ǐ-tǎs) [L.] Fragility.

fragility (frǎ-jǐl′ǐ-tē) Brittleness; having the property of being readily broken, injured, or damaged.

   capillary f. A breakdown of capillaries with hemorrhage into almost any site but most noticeably in the skin.

   f. of red blood cells The tendency of red blood cells to rupture. This is determined by subjecting the cells to different concentrations of saline in laboratory tests.

   If red blood cells are placed in distilled water, they swell rapidly and burst because they normally are suspended in a solution of much greater osmotic pressure. This phenomenon is called hemolysis. If they are suspended in a solution of normal saline, the cells retain their normal shape and do not burst. If they are placed in successively weaker solutions of saline, a point is reached at which some of the cells burst and liberate their hemoglobin within a given length of time. Finally, at a given dilution, all the cells have burst within the allotted time, which is usually 2 hr. Normal blood cells begin to hemolyze in about 0.44% saline solution, and complete hemolysis occurs in about 0.35% solution.

fragility fracture SEE: under *fracture.*

fragment (frǎg′mĕnt) A part broken off a larger entity.

   Fab f. Area on an immunoglobulin (antibody) to which antigens bind. The enzyme papain splits antibodies into three fragments, two Fab fragments, each of which is antigen-specific, and an Fc or crystallizable fragment, which is involved in secondary antibody activities such as activating complement.

   immunoglobulin f. The portion of the IgG molecule that contains an antibody-combining site. Specific fragments are obtained by treating the molecule with the enzyme papain under specified conditions. The resultant fragments are designated "F(zz) Fragment," where zz represents the specific fragment. SYN: *immunoglobulin isotype.*

fragment antigen binding ABBR: Fab. Area on an immunoglobulin (antibody) to which antigens bind.

fragmentation (frǎg″mĕn-tā′shŭn) [L. *fragmentum,* detached part] Breaking up into pieces.

   sleep f. Arousals and awakenings that disrupt the normal stages and architecture of sleep. These events, which occur commonly in patients who have sleep apnea or chronic pain, contribute to daytime sleepiness and other health problems. SYN: *sleep interruption.*

frail elderly Older persons with medical, nutritional, cognitive, emotional, or activity impairments. These deficits may limit their ability to live independently and predispose them to illnesses and the side effects of treatment.

frailty Weakness, fragility, lack of balance or endurance, sarcopenia, immobility, and wasting.

frambesia (frǎm-bē′zē-ǎ) [Fr. *framboise,* raspberry] Yaws.

frambesioma (frǎm-bē-zē-ō′mǎ) [″ + Gr. *oma,* tumor] The primary lesion of yaws in the form of a protruding nodule. This mother yaw appears at the site of inoculation of the causative agent, *Treponema pertenue.*

frame (frām) A supporting structure.

   Balkan f. A framework that fits over a bed. Weights suspended from the frame and connected through ropes and pulleys are used to produce continuous traction while permitting freedom of motion, thus maintaining desired immobilization of the part being treated.

   Bradford f. SEE: *Bradford frame.*

   quadriplegic standing f. A device for supporting a patient with all four extremities paralyzed.

   Stryker f. SEE: under *Stryker, Homer H.*

   trial f. An eyeglass frame for holding trial lenses while a person is being fitted for glasses.

Framingham Heart Study, Framingham Study [named for Framingham, MA, the town where the investigation took place] A study of the risk factors that contribute to the development of coronary artery disease and stroke, performed with a group of about 5000 residents of a small New England town under the auspices of the National Institutes of Health (National Heart, Lung, and Blood Institute). The study began shortly after World War II and has followed a cohort of individuals, aged 30-62, for signs and symptoms of atherosclerotic vascular disease and those physical findings and lifestyle choices that contribute to the development of the disease. In 1971, 5124 children of the original cohort were enrolled in the study, and in 2002, a third generation of townspeople were enrolled in an attempt to further understand genetic factors that contribute to the development of heart attack and stroke. The Framingham study identified the major acknowledged risk factors for vascular disease: diabetes, high blood pressure, hyperlipidemia, obesity, a sedentary lifestyle, and smoking. The Framingham database has also been used to explore illnesses other than heart disease, including arthritis, dementia, lung disease, osteoporosis, and a wide variety of genetic illnesses.

Franceschetti syndrome (fran″chesket′ē) [Adolphe Franceschetti, Swiss ophthalmologist, 1896–1968] Mandibulofacial dysostosis with hypoplasia of the facial bones, downward angulation of the palpebral fissures, macrostomia, ear defects, and defectively formed extremities. SYN: *Treacher Collins syndrome.*

Francisella tularensis (frăn″sĭ-sĕl′ă too″lă-rĕn′sĭs) [Edward Francis, Tulare County, California] A gram-negative, aerobic, non–spore-forming bacillus that causes tularemia in humans and animals.

francium (fran′sē-ŭm) [*France*, where it was discovered + -*ium* (1)] SYMB: Fr. A radioactive chemical element, occurring as a natural isotope, atomic weight (mass) (most stable isotope) 223, half-life 22 min, atomic number 87.

frank Obvious, esp. in reference to a clinical sign or condition such as blood in the urine, sputum, or feces.

Frankfort horizontal plane (frănk′fort) A cephalometric plane joining the anthropometric landmarks of porion and orbitale; the reproducible position of the head when the upper margin of the ear openings and lower margin of the orbit of the eye are horizontal.

Franklin glasses (frănk′lĭn) [Benjamin Franklin, U.S. statesman and inventor, 1706–1790] Bifocal spectacles.

Frank sign (frangk) [Sanders T. Frank, U.S. pulmonologist, b. 1938] A crease that extends diagonally across both ear lobes. It has been linked as a marker in some studies with coronary artery disease or diabetic vascular disease.

Frank-Starling law (frănk′stär′lĭng) In cardiac physiology, the rule stating that cardiac output increases in proportion to the diastolic stretch of heart muscle fibers.

fratricide (frăt′rĭ-sīd″) [L. *fratricidium*] Murder of one's brother or sister.

fraud (frod) [L. *fraus*, deceit] SEE: *health care fraud.*

FRC *functional residual capacity.*

FRCP *Fellow of the Royal College of Physicians.*

FRCP(C) *Fellow of the Royal College of Physicians of Canada.*

FRCS *Fellow of the Royal College of Surgeons.*

FRCS(C) *Fellow of the Royal College of Surgeons of Canada.*

freckle (frek′ĕl) A small stained or pigmented spot on skin exposed to the sun. SYN: *ephelis; lentigo.*

   Hutchinson f. SEE: under *Hutchinson, Sir Jonathan.*

free (frē) **1.** Devoid of, as in *cell-free, gluten-free,* or *sugar-free.* **2.** Natural, wild, or unrestrained, as in *freerange* or *freespirit.* **3.** Available at no cost; gratis. **4.** Unbound by proteins in the plasma, and therefore biologically active.

free base A highly addictive form of cocaine consumed by smoking. It is prepared by alkalinizing the hydrochloride salt, extracting it with an organic solvent such as ether, and then heating the

extract to 90°C. The inhaled material is rapidly absorbed from the lung. SEE: *cocaine hydrochloride; crack; freebasing.*

freebasing (frē′bās-ĭng) The inhalation of a form of cocaine called free base. SEE: *cocaine hydrochloride; crack.*

Freeman-Sheldon syndrome (frē′măn-shĕl′dŏn) A congenital malformation with muscle dysfunction that produces a masklike "whistling face," hypoplastic nasal bones, and clubfeet. The genetic transmission may be autosomal recessive. SYN: *Whistling face syndrome.*

free medical clinic SEE: under *clinic.*

free-tissue transfer SEE: under *transfer.*

freeway space The gap between the upper and lower teeth when the mandible is in a comfortably resting position.

freeze (frēz) **1.** In health care economics, to limit expenditures to current levels. **2.** In health care economics, to block increases in reimbursement.

freeze-drying (frēz′drī-ĭng) Preservation of tissue by rapidly freezing the specimen and then dehydrating it in a high vacuum. SYN: *lyophilization.*

freezing (frēz′ing) **1.** Passing from a liquid to a solid state due to heat loss. **2.** Damaging or being damaged by exposure to cold temperatures. SEE: *frostbite; hypothermia.*

Fregoli's delusion [L. Fregoli, 19th century Italian actor, known for his many characters and rapid costume changes] The delusion that someone is assuming a variety of disguises to pursue one (the patient) with craft and cunning.

Freiberg infraction (frī′bĕrg) [Albert Henry Freiberg, U.S. surgeon, 1868–1940] Osteochondritis of the head of the second metatarsal bone of the foot.

fremitus (frem′ĭ-tŭs) [L. *fremitus*, murmuring] Vibratory tremors, esp. those felt through the chest wall by palpation. Varieties include vocal or tactile, friction, hydatid, rhonchal or bronchial, cavernous on succussion, pleural, pericardial, tussive, and thrills. SEE: *palpation.*

   tactile f., tactile vocal f. The vibration or thrill felt while the patient is speaking and the hand is held against the chest.

   vocal f. Vibrations of the voice transmitted to the ear during auscultation of the chest of a person speaking. In determining vocal fremitus, the examiner should take care to assess symmetric parts of the chest and to apply the same pressure to the stethoscope on each side. Fremitus is decreased in pleural effusions (air, pus, blood, serum, or lymph), emphysema, pulmonary collapse from an obstructed bronchus, pulmonary edema, and cancers of the lung.

Frenchay Activities Index (fren′chā) [*Frenchay Hospital*, near Bristol, England] SEE: under *index.*

frenectomy (frē-něk′tō-mē) [L. *fraenum,* bridle, + Gr. *ektome,* excision] Surgical cutting of any frenum, usually of the tongue.

frenotomy (frē-nŏt′ō-mē) [″ + Gr. *tome,* incision] Division of any frenum, esp. for tongue-tie.

frenuloplasty (frěn′ū-lō-plăs″tē) [″ + Gr. *plassein,* to form] Surgical correction of an abnormally attached frenulum.

frenulum (frěn′ū-lŭm) *pl.* **frenula** [L., a little bridle] **1.** A small frenum. SYN: *vinculum.* **2.** A small fold of white matter on the upper surface of the anterior medullary velum extending to the corpora quadrigemina of the brain.

    f. of the tongue A thin fold of mucosa in the middle of the floor of the mouth that runs from the gums behind the lower central incisors to the middle of the underside of the tongue. It divides the space between the tongue in half and can easily be seen when the tongue is raised. At birth this fold of mucosa may be tight, a condition called tongue-tie.

frenum (frē′nŭm) *pl.* **frena** [L. *fraenum,* bridle] A fold of mucous membrane that connects two parts, one more or less movable, and checks the movement of this part. SEE: *frenulum.* **frenal,** *adj.*

frenzy (frěn′zē) [ME. *frenesie*] A state of violent mental agitation; maniacal excitement. SEE: *panic.*

frequency [L. *frequens,* often] **1.** The number of repetitions of a phenomenon in a certain period or within a distinct population, such as the frequency of heartbeat, sound vibrations, or a disease. SEE: *incidence.* **2.** The rate of oscillation or alternation in an alternating current circuit, in contradistinction to periodicity in the interruptions or regular variations of current in a direct current circuit. Frequency is computed on the basis of a complete cycle, in which the current rises from zero to a positive maximum, returns to zero, descends to an opposite negative minimum, and returns to zero. **3.** The rate at which uterine contractions occur, measured by the time elapsed between the beginning of one contraction and the beginning of the next.

frequency of breathing ABBR: fb. The number of spontaneous or machine-generated breaths per unit time.

Fresnel lenses (frä-něl′) [A. J. Fresnel, Fr. physicist 1788–1827] A magnifying glass that distorts vision, preventing the eye from fixating. Under its influence spontaneous and gaze-specific nystagmus can be precisely evaluated.

Fresnel membrane prism A prism that can be applied to an eyeglass lens to correct double vision, e.g., in patients with ocular nerve palsies or difficulties with ocular convergence.

F response SEE: under *response.*

fretum (frē′tŭm) [L.] A constriction.

Freud, Sigmund (froyd) An Austrian neurologist and psychoanalyst (1856–1939) whose teachings involved analysis of resistance and transference, and a procedure for investigating mental function by use of free association and dream interpretation. Freud did not consider psychoanalysis to be scientific. He believed that its purpose was to elucidate the darkest recesses of the mind and to enable individuals to integrate the emotional and intellectual sides of their nature, i.e., the forces of love and death and to develop better knowledge of self and a level of maturity and peace of mind that would help the individual and others have better lives.

    Freudian Pert. to Sigmund Freud's theories of unconscious or repressed libido, or past sex experiences or desires, as the cause of various neuroses, the cure for which he believed to be the restoration of such conditions to consciousness through psychoanalysis.

    F. slip A mistake in speaking or writing that is thought to provide insight into the individual's unconscious thoughts, motives, or wishes.

Freudian (froy′dē-ăn) SEE: under *Freud, Sigmund.*

Freudian slip (froyd′ē-ăn) SEE: under *Freud, Sigmund.*

Freund, Jules Thomas (froynd) Hungarian-born U.S. immunologist, 1890–1960.

    F. adjuvant A mixture of killed microorganisms, usually mycobacteria, in an oil and water emulsion. The material is administered to induce antibody formation. Because the oil retards absorption of the mixture, the antibody response is much greater than if the killed microorganisms were administered alone.

    F. complete adjuvant A water-in-oil emulsion in which an antigen solution is emulsified in mineral oil with killed mycobacteria to enhance antigenicity. The intense inflammatory response produced by this emulsion makes it unsuitable for use in humans.

    F. incomplete adjuvant A water-in-oil emulsion in which an antigen solution without mycobacteria is emulsified in mineral oil. On injection, this mixture induces a strong persistent antibody formation.

Frey syndrome (frī) [Lucja Frey, Polish neurologist, 1899–1944] Sweating and/or flushing of the skin overlying the parotid gland that occurs after chewing or eating a meal. It is seen most often after parotid gland surgery but may also accompany traumatic injuries to the face and other conditions. SYN: *auriculotemporal syndrome.*

friable (frī'ă-b'l) [L. *friabilis*] Easily broken or pulverized.

fricative (frik'ă-tiv) [L. *fricare*, to rub] A vibrating sound made when air passes through a tight space in the mouth. Consonants with this characteristic sound include "f" and "v," "s" and "z," and the "th" in "thin" and "then."

Fricke bandage A special bandage for supporting and immobilizing the scrotum.

friction (frik'shŏn) [L. *fricare*, to rub] **1.** Rubbing. **2.** A massage technique in which one surface is rubbed over another, e.g., the skin over muscle. Both compressive and shearing forces are involved. Types of friction include warming, rolling, wringing, linear, stripping, cross-fiber, chucking, and circular. Most types of friction are performed with little or no lubricant. **3.** Any force resisting motion that is generated when two surfaces move with respect to each other.

    dry f. Friction using no liquid or other lubricant.

friction blister SEE: under *blister.*

friction rub The distinct sound heard when two dry surfaces are rubbed together. If the sound is loud enough, the condition producing the sound can also be felt.

    pericardial f. rub SEE: under *rub.*

    pleural f. rub SEE: under *rub.*

Friedländer, Carl (frēt'len"dĕr, frēd') Ger. pathologist, 1847–1887.

    F. bacillus Klebsiella pneumoniae.

    F. disease Endarteritis obliterans.

    F. pneumonia Lobar pneumonia caused by infection with *Klebsiella pneumoniae,* characterized by fevers, chills, sweats, cough, pleuritic pain, bloody sputum, and bulging interlobar fissures on chest x-ray.

Friedreich, Nikolaus (frēt'rīk", frēd') Ger. neurologist, 1825–1882.

    F. ataxia An inherited degenerative disease with sclerosis of the dorsal and lateral columns of the spinal cord. It is accompanied by muscular uncoordination, speech impairment, lateral curvature of the spinal column, with muscle paralysis, esp. of the lower extremities. The onset is in childhood or early adolescence. SYN: *heredoataxia.*

    F. sign **1.** Sudden collapse of the cervical veins that were previously distended at each diastole. The cause is an adherent pericardium. **2.** Lowering of the pitch of the percussion note that occurs over an area of cavitation during inspiration.

fright [AS. *fryhto*] Extreme sudden fear.

frigid (frij'id) [L. *frigidus*] **1.** Cold. **2.** Unresponsive to emotion, applied esp. to the inability of a person to feel sexual desire. SEE: *impotence.*

frigidity (frĭ-jĭd'ĭ-tē) A state of sexual dysfunction marked by the inability to respond to erotic stimuli. SEE: *female sexual arousal disorder; male erectile disorder.*

frigolabile (frĭg"ō-lā'bĭl) [L. *frigor*, cold, + *labilis*, unstable] Capable of being destroyed by low temperature.

frigostabile (frĭg"ō-stā'b'l) [" + *stabilis*, firm] Incapable of being destroyed by low temperature.

frit (frĭt) [It. *fritta*, fry] **1.** The material from which glass or the glazed portion of pottery is made. **2.** A similar material for making the glaze of artificial teeth.

frog face Flatness of the face resulting from intranasal disease.

Fröhlich syndrome (frā'lik) [Alfred Fröhlich, Austrian neurologist, 1871–1953] A condition characterized by obesity and sexual infantilism, atrophy or hypoplasia of the gonads, and altered secondary sex characteristics. It is caused by disturbance of the hypothalamus and hypophysis, usually secondary to a neoplasm. SYN: *adiposogenital dystrophy; adiposogenital syndrome.*

Froin syndrome (frwon) [Georges Froin, Fr. physician, 1874–1932] The presence of yellow cerebrospinal fluid that coagulates rapidly. This is associated with any condition in which the fluid in the spinal canal is prevented from mixing with the cerebrospinal fluid in the ventricles.

Froment sign (frō-mon') [Jules Froment, Fr. physician, 1878–1946] Flexion of the distal phalanx of the thumb when a sheet of paper is held between the thumb and index finger. It indicates ulnar nerve palsy.

Frommann lines (from'ăn) [Carl Frommann, Ger. anatomist, 1831–1892] Transverse lines on the axon of a myelinated nerve fiber; they stain with silver nitrate.

frontal [L. *frontalis*] **1.** In anatomy, pert. to or located in the front; anterior. **2.** Pert. to the forehead bone.

front-line medicine SEE: under *medicine.*

fronto- [L. *frons*, brow] Combining form meaning *anterior; forehead.*

frontomalar (frŏn"tō-mā'lăr) [" + *mala*, cheek] Pert. to the frontal and malar bones.

frontomaxillary (frŏn"tō-măx'ĭ-lār"ē) [" + *maxilla*, jawbone] Pert. to the frontal and maxillary bones.

frontotemporal (frŭn"tō-tĕm'por-ăl) [" + *tempora*, the temples] Pert. to the frontal and temporal bones.

front-tap reflex SEE: under *reflex.*

FROPVD *Flow-restricted oxygen-powered ventilation device.*

frost [AS.] A frozen vapor deposit.

    uremic f. A deposit of urea crystals on the skin from evaporation of sweat in a patient whose kidneys are severely impaired, as in uremia.

frostbite (fröst'bīt) Severe tissue and cell damage caused by freezing a body part. The injury occurs both because intracellular water turns to ice and because extremely cold temperatures damage and block the blood supply to exposed parts. Exposed areas (e.g., ears, cheeks, nose, fingers, and toes) are most often affected. SEE: *freezing; frostnip; Nursing Diagnoses Appendix.*

SYMPTOMS: The frozen tissue is usually numb until it is rewarmed, when it may become extremely painful. Hands, feet, noses, and ears are typically affected first. Signs of frostbite depend on the depth of tissue damage: there may be swelling and hyperemia of the skin (superficial frostbite); blistering or hemorrhagic blistering and pain (second- and third-degree frostbite); or gangrene of muscles and necrosis of other subcutaneous tissues (deep or fourth-degree frostbite).

TREATMENT: After the patient's airway, breathing, and circulation are stabilized, he or she is warmed and rehydrated to prevent systemic effects of hypothermia (low body temperature). Wet and constrictive clothing and jewelry are removed; the patient is kept dry and placed in a warm area, and warm fluids are given by mouth. If the patient's core temperature exceeds 89.6°F (32°C), external warming is used. The frozen body part is immersed in a tepid to warm water bath (100° to 104°F [37.8° to 42.2°C]) or a warming blanket is applied to cover the trunk and limbs. If the patient's core temperature is less than 89.6°F (32°C), internal and external warming should be used concurrently to gradually warm the body core and surface, as rewarming the surface first could result in ventricular fibrillation (rewarming shock). Internal rewarming involves using warmed oxygen inhalation, warmed saline gastric lavage, and sometimes warmed peritoneal lavage. Rewarming often produces uncomfortable tingling, or frankly painful sensations in the frostbitten body part. Tetanus prophylaxis, analgesics, and nonsteroidal anti-inflammatory drugs are given. If tissue sloughing occurs, minimal débridement is performed, unless the patient is septic or otherwise systemically compromised by the injury. Because tissue that appears severely damaged often heals spontaneously, surgery is sometimes delayed for weeks or months. SEE: *freezing* for treatment of frozen parts.

⚠ Rubbing or using frozen limbs should be avoided, to minimize injury to the skin and soft tissues.

PATIENT CARE: Emergency department personnel assess for frostbite in any patient who has been exposed to cold and complains of a cold, numb extremity or body part. The elderly, patients taking beta blockers, malnourished patients, alcoholics, diabetics, smokers, and people with peripheral vascular disease are at the highest risk for damage due to frostbite. They should be advised to take special precautions when outdoors. While the extent of tissue damage depends on the degree of cold and the duration of exposure, the degree of injury may be difficult to determine on initial assessment, and requires ongoing monitoring. Neurovascular status is monitored closely, along with arterial blood gas levels, cardiac rhythm and central venous pressure, and fluid and electrolyte balance. A complete blood count, blood urea nitrogen, partial thromboplastin time, prothrombin time, and an international normalized ratio are also assessed. Preventing infection is an important consideration, and the patient may be placed in protective (reverse) isolation to minimize contact with infectious agents. During rewarming, the patient is assessed frequently for complications, e.g., compartment syndrome.

Depending on the extent of débridement and the necessity for amputation, the physical therapist and occupational therapist work with the patient to manage activities of daily living. Outpatient rehabilitation may be required for an extended period. The patient may require assistance to deal with the emotional stress of the injury. Needs are determined, supportive care is provided, and the patient is referred for further psychological care as necessary. If the frostbite developed because of inadequate clothing or shelter, a community social service referral may be appropriate. To prevent frostbite, patients should avoid prolonged cold exposure and get adequate food, warmth and rest when outdoors. Teach individuals to wear mittens rather than gloves, to clothe themselves in waterproof, windproof multilayers, to wear two pairs of socks (cotton next to the skin and wool outside), and to wear a scarf and hat covering the ears to reduce loss of heat through the head (highest area of loss). Shelter should be sought or physical activity increased when exposed to cold (as in a snowstorm). Advise individuals that alcohol draws blood out of body organs and into capillary beds, and that smoking interferes with circulation, so both should be avoided when cold exposure is unavoidable.

frost itch SEE: under *itch.*

frostnip A mild form of cold injury, consisting of reversible blanching of the skin, usually on the earlobes, cheeks, nose, fingers, and toes. SEE: *frostbite.*

frotteurism (frō-tūr′ĭzm) Recurrent intense sexual urges and fantasies involving touching and rubbing against a non-consenting person. These acts are usually performed in crowded places where arrest is unlikely. The perpetrators are usually young men. Persons who have acted on these urges are usually distressed about them.

frozen watchfulness The hopeless reproachful stare of battered children.

FRS *Fellow of the Royal Society.*

FRSC *Fellow of the Royal Society (Canada).*

fructofuranose (frŭk″tō-fū′ră-nōs) The furanose form of fructose.

fructokinase (frŭk″tō-kī′nās) An enzyme that catalyzes transfer of high-energy phosphate from a donor to fructose.

fructosamine (frŭk-tōs′ă-mēn″, fruk-) [*fructose* + *amine*] A protein-carbohydrate complex found in elevated concentrations in the plasma of patients who have consistently high blood glucose levels, e.g., people with diabetes mellitus.

fructose (frŭk′tōs″, fruk′, frook′) [L. *fructus,* fruit + *²-ose*] A monosaccharide and a hexose, having the same empirical formula as glucose, $C_6H_{12}O_6$. It is found in corn syrup, honey, fruit juices, and as part of the disaccharide sucrose. In the liver, fructose is changed to glucose to be used for energy production or to be stored as glycogen.

⚠ Increased consumption of fructose (as in sweetened beverages) has been associated with a higher than average risk of gout.

SYN: *fruit **sugar**; levulose.* SEE: *disaccharide.*

fructose intolerance Inability to metabolize the carbohydrate fructose due to a hereditary absence or deficiency of the enzyme 1,6-biphosphate aldolase B. Clinical signs develop early in life. They include hypoglycemia, jaundice, hepatomegaly, vomiting, lethargy, irritability, and convulsions. Fructose can be identified in the urine. The fructose tolerance test should not be used because it can induce irreversible coma.

TREATMENT: Acute attacks are treated by glucose administration. For long-term therapy, all foods containing fructose (present in sweet fruits and sugar cane) and sucrose and sorbitol (the latter used as a sweetening agent in foods and drugs) must be eliminated from the diet.

fructosemia (frŭk″tō-sē′mē-ă) [″ + Gr. *haima,* blood] Fructose in the blood.

fructoside (frŭk′tō-sīd) A carbohydrate that yields fructose on hydrolysis.

fructosuria (frŭk″tō-sū′rē-ă) [″ + Gr. *ouron,* urine] Fructose in the urine.

fruit [L. *fructus,* fruit] **1.** The ripened ovary of a seed-bearing plant and the surrounding tissue, such as the pod of a bean, nut, grain, or berry. **2.** The edible product of a plant consisting of ripened seeds and the enveloping tissue. Fruits add vitamins, minerals, and fiber to the diet. They help prevent constipation and vitamin deficiency syndromes. Most people should eat 2 to 3 servings of fruit every day, although people with impaired glucose tolerance or diabetes mellitus should consume just 1 to 2 servings.

COMPOSITION: Carbohydrates in the form of fruit sugars are the chief calorie component of fruits. Seventy-five percent of the calories in most fruit is a mixture of dextrose and fructose. Fruits are a good source of vitamins and minerals.

Pectose bodies: Pectose, the principle in fruits that causes them to jell, is found in unripe fruit; pectin is found in ripe fruit or fruit that has been cooked in a weak acid solution.

Fruit acids: Acetic acid is found in wine and vinegar. Citric acid is found in lemons, oranges, limes, and citrons. Malic acid is found in apples, pears, apricots, peaches, and currants. Oxalic acid is found in rhubarb, sorrel, and cranberries. Tartaric acid is found in grapes, pineapples, and tamarinds. Salicylic acid is found in currants, cranberries, cherries, plums, grapes, and crabapples.

Combined acids: Citric and malic acid are found in raspberries, strawberries, gooseberries, and cherries. Citric, malic, and oxalic acid are found in cranberries.

fruitarian (froo-tăr′ē-ăn) Someone who eliminates all foods from the diet except fruits, vegetable oils, nuts, and honey. SEE: *vegan.*

frumentaceous (froo-měn-tā′shŭs) [L. *frumentum,* grain] Resembling or pert. to grain.

frustration (frŭs-trā′shŏn) [L. *frustrari,* to deceive, disappoint] **1.** Lack of an adequate outlet for the libido. **2.** The condition that results from the thwarting or prevention of acts that would satisfy or gratify physical or personal needs.

Frye's standard (frī) [Fm. *Frye v. U.S. 1923*] One of several standards governing the admissibility of scientific or expert testimony in courts of law. To gain acceptance the proposed evidence or testimony must agree with generally accepted scientific methods or thinking.

Fryns syndrome A rare autosomal dominant disorder characterized by diaphragmatic hernia and facial, limb, cardiac, lung, and brain anomalies. The disease is often fatal in infancy; survivors may have cognitive deficits.

FSBG *finger stick blood **glucose**.*

FSE *fetal scalp electrode* (a device to measure the health of the fetus during complicated or protracted labor and delivery).

FSF *fibrin-stabilizing factor*.

FSH *follicle-stimulating hormone*.

FSH/LHRH *follicle-stimulating hormone and luteinizing hormone–releasing hormone*.

FSH-RF *follicle-stimulating hormone–releasing factor*.

FSH-RH *follicle-stimulating hormone–releasing hormone*.

ft L. *fiat* or *fiant*, let there be made; *florentium*, former name for promethium; *foot*.

FTA-ABS *fluorescent treponemal antibody-absorption test for syphilis*.

FTT *failure to thrive*.

Fuchs heterochromic iridocyclitis (fūks, fuks) [Ernst Fuchs, Austrian ophthalmologist, 1851–1930.] Heterochromic iridocyclitis.

fuchsin, fuchsine (fūk´sĭn, sēn″) [Leonhard *Fuchs*, Ger. botanist 1501–1566 + *-ine*] Rosaniline.

fucose (fū´kōs) A mucopolysaccharide present in blood group substances and in human milk.

fucosidosis (fū″kō-sī-dō´sĭs) An autosomal recessive disease resulting from absence of the enzyme required to metabolize fucosidase. Clinically, neurological deterioration begins shortly after a period of normal early development. Heart disease, thick skin, and hyperhidrosis develop and are followed by death at an early age.

Fucus vesiculosus (fū´kŭs vĕ-sĭk-ū-lō´sŭs, foo´) [L., "vesicular lichen"] Bladderwrack.

fuel source (fū´ĕl) [ME. *feuel*] A flammable substance that provides energy.

-fuge [L. *fugare*, to put to flight] Suffix meaning *something that expels or drives away*.

fugetaxis (fū″jĭ-tăk´sĭs) [L. *fugere*, to flee + ″] The movement of white blood cells away from signaling chemicals, such as chemokines. chemorepulsion.

fugitive (fū´jĭ-tĭv) [L. *fugitivus*]. **1.** Temporary, transient. **2.** Wandering; pert. to inconstant symptoms.

fugue (fūg) [L. *fuga*, flight] A dissociative disorder in which the person acts normally but has almost complete amnesia for what happened when recovery occurs.

    psychogenic f. Sudden, unexpected travel away from one's home or place of work with inability to recall one's past. The individual may assume a partial or complete new identity. The condition is not due to organic brain disease. It may follow severe mental stress such as marital quarrels or a natural disaster. It is usually of short duration but can last for

months. Recovery is the usual outcome without recurrences.

Fukuyama disease (foo-koo-yah´mă) A rare autosomal recessive muscular dystrophy found almost exclusively in people of Japanese descent, in which muscular weakness, inability to walk, micropolygyria, and mental retardation are common.

fulcrum (fŭl´krŭm) The object or point on which a lever moves.

fulgurant (fŭl´gū-rănt) [L. *fulgurare*, to lighten] Coming and going intensely like a flash of light, or a shooting pain. SYN: *fulminant*.

fulgurate (fŭl´gū-rāt) To destroy or remove tissue by means of fulguration.

fulguration (fŭl″g(y)ŭ-rā´shŏn) [L. *fulgurare*, to flash, glitter] Destruction of tissue by heat-producing long high-frequency electric sparks. SEE: *electrodesiccation*.

full body CT scanning Whole body CT scanning.

fuller's earth (ful´ĕrz) [Ult. fr. L. *fullo*, a cleaner of cloth, a fuller] Clay that is similar to kaolin. It is used as an absorbent, as a filler in textiles, and in cosmetics.

fulling (ful´ing) A form of massage in which the hands move along a muscle, widening outward as they move away from the masseur's body, and then lifting the muscle as they return.

full-term (ful´tĕrm´) In obstetrics, pert. to an infant born between the beginning of the 38th and the end of the 41st week of gestation.

full-thickness (ful´thik´nĕss) Pert. to a burn, flap, or graft consisting of the epidermis and the entire depth of the dermis.

full width half maximum ABBR: FWHM. The width of a peak or the bandpass of an emission or absorption spectrum in a laboratory photometer or spectrophotometer. When combined with other characteristics of the device, this can be used to predict suitability of the photometer or spectrophotometer for specific applications and measurements.

fulminant (fool´mĭ-nănt, fŭl´) [L. *fulminare*, to hurl lightning] **1.** Having a rapid and severe onset. **2.** Coming in lightning-like flashes of pain, as in tabes dorsalis. SYN: *fulgurant*.

fulminate To occur suddenly; to have a rapid or explosive onset. Said of some diseases.

fumagillin (fū″mă-jĭl´ĭn) A molecule produced by fungi that prevents new blood vessel formation ("angiogenesis"), and may be useful in treating cancers.

fumarase (fū´mă-rās) An enzyme present in many plants and animals. It catalyzes the production of L-malic acid from fumaric acid.

fumaric acid (fū-mar´ik) SEE: under *acid*.

fume hood An enclosed, ventilated space used in a laboratory to contain and exhaust aerosols, chemicals, dusts, microbes, powders, vapors, and other inhalational hazards.

fumes [L. *fumus,* smoke] Vapors, esp. those with irritating qualities.

  nitric acid f. The vapors of nitric acid (HNO_3). They are used in various chemical processes. Poisoning is produced by the action of the corrosive fumes on the respiratory tract.

  SYMPTOMS: Findings include choking, gasping, swelling of mucous membranes, tightness in the chest, pulmonary edema, cough, and shock. Symptoms may last for 1 week or more. TREATMENT: The patient must be removed immediately from the fumes and good ventilation of the lungs maintained. Therapy is given for shock and pulmonary edema. Administration of oxygen under pressure using a mask may be required along with analgesics and anxiolytics as needed. Clothes must be removed if they are contaminated. Steroids may help diminish the inflammatory response of the lungs.

fumigant (fū″mĭ-gănt) [L. *fumigare,* to make smoke] An agent used in disinfecting a room. The substance produces fumes that are lethal to insects and rodents. Chemicals used include hydrogen cyanide gas, acrylonitrile, carbon tetrachloride, ethylene oxide, and methyl bromide.

⚠ All of these chemicals are highly toxic, potentially lethal, and in some cases explosive. They should be used only by persons skilled in their application.

fumigation (fū″mĭ-gā′shŭn) **1.** The use of poisonous fumes or gases to destroy living organisms, esp. rats, mice, insects, and other vermin. Fumigants are relatively ineffective against bacteria and viruses; consequently, terminal disinfection of the sickroom, formerly a common practice, has been discontinued. **2.** The disinfection of rooms by gases.

fuming (fū′mĭng) [L. *fumus,* smoke] Having a visible vapor.

function (fŭngk′shŏn) [L. *functio,* performance] **1.** The action performed by a structure. In a living organism this may pertain to a cell or a part of a cell, tissue, organ, or system of organs. **2.** The act of carrying on or performing a special activity. Normal function is the normal action of an organ. Abnormal activity or the failure of an organ to perform its activity is the basis of disease or disease processes. Structural changes in an organ are pathological and are common causes of malfunction, although an organ may function abnormally without observable structural changes. In humans, function can pertain to the manner in which the individual can perform successfully the tasks and roles required for everyday living.

  discriminant f. Any algorithm or assessment tool to evaluate disease severity or guide clinical or administrative decisions in health care. In gastroenterology, e.g., a discriminant function is commonly used to gauge the severity of alcoholic hepatitis. It uses two variables, the patient's measured protime (PT) and total serum bilirubin level. The difference between the patient's PT and the control PT is multiplied by 4.6 and added to the bilirubin level. If the derived number is greater than 32, the patient may benefit from treatment with corticosteroids or pentoxifylline.

  executive f. Any of the abilities to make plans and carry them out, including the organization of tasks and one's use of time, to set goals and priorities, and assess the progress one makes in meeting them. The loss of executive function (called executive dysfunction) is a common finding in patients with dementia.

  hazard f. A formula used to estimate the prognosis of a person who has already survived an illness for a specific time.

  visual f. Vision.

functional (fŭngk′shŏn-ăl) [L. *functio,* performance] **1.** Pert. to a function. **2.** Pert. to a symptom that has not been found to be caused by an organic disease. **3.** In endocrinology, pert. to an active secretion of hormones. **functionally** (-ă-lē), *adv.*

functional cortex SEE: under *cortex.*

functional disease A general term for inorganic disease or a disease in which organic changes are not evident; a disturbance of the function of any organ. SYN: *functional disorder; functional illness.* SEE: *organic disease; somatoform disorder.*

functional disorder Functional disease.

functional endoscopic sinus surgery ABBR: FESS. Any surgical procedure performed during direct inspection of the sinuses with fiber-optic endoscopes. FESS is frequently used to treat chronic sinusitis that has not responded to treatment with medications. It can also be used to remove nasal polyps or foreign bodies in the nose, to excise some tumors, and to control nosebleeds.

functional health pattern Collective features of an individual's health history used to assess, plan, diagnose, intervene, and evaluate appropriate nursing care. The term is associated with Margery Gordon. SEE: *Nursing Diagnoses Appendix.*

Functional Independence Measure ABBR: FIM. A clinical tool used to assess the ability of persons needing rehabilitative services to cope independently and perform activities of daily living. These activities include self-care, sphincter control, mobility, locomotion, communication, and social cognition. Data derived from FIM correlate with some outcome measures in rehabilitation, such as the length of time a patient may need to stay in care or the resources the patient will use. The version of FIM for children is called WeeFIM. SEE: *WeeFIM*.

functional limitation SEE: under *limitation*.

functional mapping SEE: under *mapping*.

functional mobility SEE: under *mobility*.

functional neurosurgery SEE: under *neurosurgery*.

functional overlay SEE: under *overlay*.

functional reach The furthest distance in front of the body that a person, standing in a fixed position with arms fully extended, can touch without falling. The *functional reach test,* as originally devised by Duncan et al, is a measure of frailty in addition to an assessment of balance, flexibility, and fall risk. Norms for this test are: reach < 6 inches = high risk of falls/frailty; reach > 6 inches and < 10 inches = moderate risk for falls/frailty; reach > 10 inches = low risk for falls/frailty. A variation of the test, called the *multidimensional reach test,* assesses a subject's ability to reach both forward and side-to-side.

functional reach test SEE: *functional reach*.

functional residual capacity ABBR: FRC. The amount of air remaining in the lungs after a normal resting expiration.

functional somatic syndrome Any of several poorly understood conditions in the group that includes multiple chemical sensitivity syndrome, sick building syndrome, repetition stress injury, chronic whiplash, chronic fatigue syndrome, irritable bowel syndrome, and fibromyalgia syndrome.

functional vision SEE: under *vision*.

funda (fŭn′dă) [L., sling] A four-tailed bandage.

fundal, *adj.*

fundectomy (fŭn-dĕk′tō-mē) [L. *fundus,* base, + Gr. *ektome,* excision] Removal of the fundus of any organ.

fundic (fŭn′dĭk) Pert. to a fundus.

fundiform (fŭn′dĭ-form) [L. *funda,* sling, + *forma,* shape] Sling-shaped or looped.

fund of knowledge Information that a person has stored in memory about people, places, and things. The fund of stored memories increases with education and decreases in dementia.

fundoplication (fŭn″dō-plĭ-kā′shŭn) Procedure used to treat gastroesophageal reflux and/or hiatal hernia by reestablishing a gastroesophageal angle and creating a barrier to intrathoracic gastric displacement. Most of this is accomplished by the Nissen technique by wrapping the fundus about the gastric cardia. This procedure may be performed laparoscopically as well as by open surgery in adults, children, or infants.

Nissen f. The surgical correction of an esophageal hiatal hernia or gastroesophageal reflux, by wrapping the gastric cardia with adjacent portions of the gastric fundus. This procedure, which is frequently performed laparoscopically, reestablishes the gastroesophageal angle, enhances the lower esophageal sphincter, and prevents intrathoracic displacement of the stomach.

PATIENT CARE: The patient is prepared physically and psychologically for surgery, and postsurgical procedures to be expected are explained. Vital signs and fluid intake and output, including wound and nasogastric tube drainage (if used) should be checked and recorded. Postoperative care includes attention to oral hygiene; care of chest tube thoracostomy (if a thoracic approach was employed); pain assessment and management; and incentive spirometry, deep breathing and coughing to prevent atelectasis or pneumonia. Before hospital discharge, dietary restrictions should be reviewed with the patient, and small, frequent meals recommended. Lifting, straining, and other activities that would increase intra-abdominal pressure should be avoided for about 5 weeks. Follow-up care should be scheduled.

fundus (fŭn′dŭs) [L. *fundus,* bottom] **1.** The larger part, base, or body of a hollow organ. **2.** The portion of an organ most remote from its opening. **fundic** (fŭn′dik), *adj.*

   f. flavimaculatus Stargardt disease.

   ocular f. The posterior part of the eye including the retina and optic nerve.

   f. uteri F. of the uterus.

   f. of the uterus The area of the uterus above the openings of the fallopian tubes. SYN: **f. uteri.** SEE: illus.

fundus albipunctatus An autosomal recessive form of night blindness in which the retina is flecked or pigmented, and resynthesis of rhodopsin is delayed.

funduscope, fundoscope (fŭn′dŭ-skōp″) [*fundus* + *-scope*] A device for examining the fundus of the eye. **funduscopic, fundoscopic** (fŭn″dŭ-skop′ik), *adj.*

funduscopy, fundoscopy (fŭn″dŭs′kŏ-pē) [*fundus* + *-scopy*] Examination, esp. visual, of the fundus of any organ. In ophthalmology, visual examination of the fundus of the eye. SYN: *ophthalmoscopy.*

fundusectomy (fŭn″dŭs-ĕk′tō-mē) [″ +

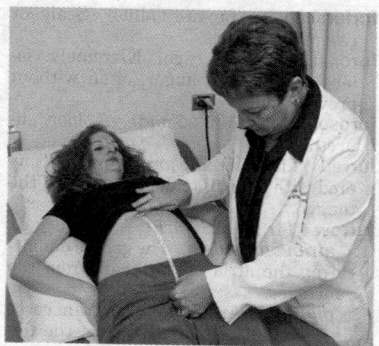

FUNDUS OF THE UTERUS

Measuring the size of the fundus

Gr. *ektome*, excision] Excision of the fundus of the stomach. SYN: *cardiectomy*.

fungal septicemia Fungemia.

fungate (fŭn′gāt) [L. *fungus*, mushroom] To grow like a fungus.

fungating (fŭn′gāt-ĭng) Growing rapidly like a fungus; said of certain tumors.

fungemia (fŭn-jē′mē-ă) [″ + Gr. *haima*, blood] The presence of fungi in the blood, most commonly *Candida* or *Aspergillus*. It can be life-threatening, esp. in immunocompromised patients. SYN: *fungal septicemia*. SEE: *sepsis*.

Fungi (fŭn′jī) [L. *fungus*, mushroom] The kingdom of organisms that includes yeasts, molds, and mushrooms. Fungi grow as single cells, as in yeast, or as multicellular filamentous colonies, as in molds and mushrooms. They do not contain chlorophyll, so they are saprophytic (obtain food from dead organic matter) or parasitic (obtain nourishment from living organisms). Most fungi are not pathogenic, and the body's normal flora contains many fungi. SEE: illus.

Fungi that cause disease come from a group called fungi imperfecti. In immunocompetent humans they cause minor infections of the hair, nails, mucous membranes, or skin. In a person with a compromised immune system due to AIDS or immunosuppressive drug therapy, fungi are a source of opportunistic infections that can cause death.

fungicide (fŭn′jĭ-sīd) [L. *fungi*, mushrooms, + *cidus*, killing] An agent that kills fungi and their spores.

fungiform (fŭn′jĭ-form) [″ + *forma*, shape] Mushroom-shaped.

-fungin A suffix used in pharmacology to designate an *antifungal drug*.

fungistasis (fŭn-jĭ-stā′sĭs) [″ + Gr. *stasis*, a halting] A condition in which the growth of fungi is inhibited.

fungistat (fŭn′jĭ-stăt) [″ + Gr. *statikos*, standing] An agent that inhibits the growth of fungi. **fungistatic** (-stăt′ĭk), *adj.*

fungitoxic (fŭn″jĭ-tŏk′sĭk) Poisonous to fungi.

fungoid (fŭn′goyd) [″ + Gr. *eidos*, form, shape] Having the appearance of a fungus.

fungosity (fŭn-gŏs′ĭ-tē) A soft, spongy fungus-like growth.

fungus (fŭng′gŭs, fŭn′jī, fŭng′gī″) *pl.* **fungi** [L. *fungus*, mushroom] **1.** An organism belonging to the kingdom Fungi; a yeast, mold, or mushroom. SEE: *Fungi*. **2.** A spongelike morbid growth

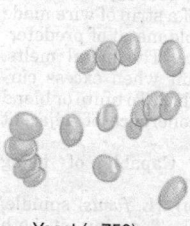

Yeast (x 750)

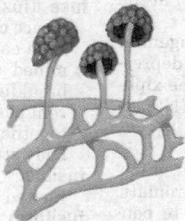

Rhizopus (x 40)

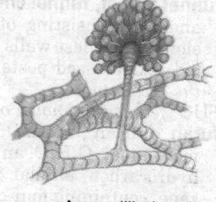

Aspergillis (x 40)

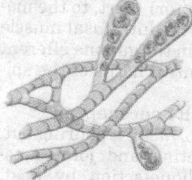

Ringworm (x 750)

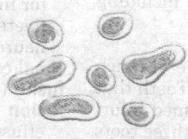

Cryptococcus (x 500)

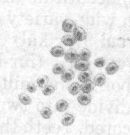

Pneumocystis jiroveci (x 1200)

FUNGI

on the body that resembles fungi. SEE: *actinomycosis*. **fungal, fungous,** (fung'găl, fung'gŭs), *adj.*

dematiaceous f. Dematiaceae.

filamentous f. Mold (2).

true fungi Eumycetes.

fungus ball SEE: under *ball*.

funic (fū'nĭk) [L. *funis*, cord] Pert. to the umbilical cord.

funicular (fū-nĭk'ū-lăr) Pert. to the spermatic or umbilical cord.

funiculitis (fū-nĭk″ū-lī'tĭs) [″ + Gr. *itis*, inflammation] Inflammation of the spermatic cord.

funiculopexy (fū-nĭk'ū-lō-pĕks″ē) [″ + Gr. *pexis*, fixation] Suturing of the spermatic cord to the tissues in cases of undescended testicle.

funiculus (fū-nĭk'yŭ-lŭs, fū-nĭk'yŭ-lī″, -lē″) *pl.* **funiculi** [L. *funiculus*, slender rope, cord] **1.** A cord-like structure. **2.** One of the three main divisions of the white matter in the right or left half of the spinal cord. The funiculi lie peripherally and are separated by the dorsal and ventral horns of the gray matter.

dorsal f. Dorsal column.

lateral f. 2 Lateral column.

ventral f. Ventral column.

funipuncture (fū″nĭ-pŭnk'chūr) [L. *funis*, a cord, + *punctura*, to prick] Puncture of the umbilical vein in utero, to obtain a sample of fetal blood. The needle is inserted under ultrasonic guidance.

funis (fū'nĭs) [L., cord] A cordlike structure, such as the spermatic cord or the umbilical cord.

funisitis (fū″nĭ-sī'tĭs) Infection of the umbilical cord.

funnel (fŭn'ĕl) [L. *fundere*, to pour] A conical device open at both ends used to direct a fluid from the larger opening (at one end of the cone) to the smaller at the other.

funnel breast, funnel chest A congenital anomaly consisting of sternal depression of the chest walls so that the xiphoid is depressed posteriorly. SYN: *pectus excavatum*.

FUO *fever of unknown origin.*

furan (fūr'an″, fū-ran') [*furfuran*, a former name] C_4H_4O, an organic aromatic hydrocarbon, similar in shape to benzene, containing four carbon atoms and one oxygen atom. It is the structural source from which many useful pharmaceuticals are synthesized, including a wide variety of antibiotics.

furcal (fūr'kăl) Forked.

furcation (fūr-kā'shŭn) The branch point of a multirooted tooth. Teeth that divide into two roots are termed bifurcated. Teeth that divide into three roots are termed trifurcated. SYN: *bifurcation* (2).

furfur (fūr'fŭr) [L., bran] Dandruff scales.

furfuraceous (fūr-fū-rā'shŭs) Scaly or resembling scales.

furor (fūr'ŏr) [L., rage] Extremely violent outbursts of anger, often without provocation.

furosemide (fū-rō'sĕ-mīd) A loop diuretic.

furred (fŭrd) [O. Fr. *forre*, lining] Covered with a dustlike deposit; used of the tongue.

furrow (fŭr'ō) [AS. *furh*] A groove.

atrioventricular f. The groove demarcating the atria of the heart from the ventricles.

digital f. Any of several transverse lines on the palmar surface of the fingers across the joints.

gluteal f. The vertical groove on the skin between the buttocks.

furuncle (fū'rŭng-k'l) [L. *furunculus*] Boil.

furunculoid (fū-rŭng'kū-loyd) [L. *furunculus*, a boil, + Gr. *eidos*, form, shape] Resembling a furuncle or boil. SEE: *furunculous*.

furunculosis (fū-rŭng″kū-lō'sĭs) [″ + Gr. *osis*, condition] A condition resulting from furuncles or boils.

furunculous (fū-rŭng'kū-lŭs) Pert. to or of the nature of a furuncle or boil.

furunculus (fū-rŭng'kū-lŭs) *pl.* **furunculi** [L., a boil] Boil.

fusariosis (fū-zār″ē-ō'sĭs) [Fusarium + ″] Infection or intoxication by species of the genus *Fusarium*. It typically affects immunocompromised patients.

Fusarium (fū-zā'rē-ŭm) [L. *fusus*, spindle] A genus of fungi, most of which are plant pathogens, and a few of which may be opportunistic in humans.

fuscin (fŭs'ĭn) [L. *fuscus*, dark brown] A brown pigment, a melanin, present in the outermost layer (pigmented epithelium) of the retina.

fuse (fūz) [L. *fusus*, poured] **1.** A safety device consisting of a strip of wire made from easily meltable metal of predetermined conductance. The metal melts, breaking the circuit when excess current passes through. **2.** To unite or blend together, as the coherence of adjacent body structures.

fusible (fū'zĭ-b'l) Capable of being melted or joined.

fusiform (fū'zĭ-form) [L. *fusus*, spindle, + *forma*, shape] Tapering at both ends; spindle-shaped.

fusimotor (fū″sĭ-mō'tor) Pert. to the motor innervation of the intrafusal muscle fibers originating in the gamma efferent neurons of the ventral horns of the spinal cord.

fusin (fū'zin) CXCR4 **coreceptor**.

fusion (fū'zhŏn) [L. *fusio*, a pouring out, effusion] **1.** Meeting and joining together through liquefaction by heat. **2.** The process of fusing or uniting. **3.** The union of adjacent tooth germs to form an oversize tooth of abnormal configuration or two teeth partially fused at the crown or root. **4.** The blending of genetic material of two distinct cells or species.

nuclear f. Joining of the nucleus of small atoms to form larger atoms. It occurs when temperatures reach millions of degrees. An example is the nuclear reaction joining hydrogen together to form helium and resulting in the significant release of energy.

spinal f. Surgical immobilization of adjacent vertebrae. This procedure may be done for several conditions, including herniated disk.

fusion imaging SEE: under *imaging*.

Fusobacterium (fū″zō-băk-tē′rē-ŭm) A genus of long, slender, gram-negative, non–spore-forming bacilli that is part of the resident flora of the intestines and oral cavity, esp. the gingival sulci. They are strict anaerobes and may infect necrotic tissue. *F. nucleatum* has been cultured from lesions of gangrenous stomatitis.

F. necrophorum A species that causes sore throat, and sometimes, life-threatening infections such as septic thrombophlebitis of the jugular veins (Lemierre's syndrome) in humans.

fusocellular (fū″sō-sĕl′ū-lăr) [L. *fusus,* spindle, + *cellulus,* little cell] Spindle-celled.

fusogen (fūz′ō-jĕn″) [Fm. *fus(ion)* + ″] A substance that can cause cellular membranes to merge.

fusospirochetal (fū″sō-spī-rō-kē′tăl) [″ + Gr. *speira,* coil, + *chaite,* hair] Pert. to fusiform bacilli and spirochetes.

fusospirochetosis (fū″sō-spī″rō-kē-tō′sĭs) [″ + ″ + ″ + *osis,* condition] Infection with fusiform bacilli and spirochetes, such as necrotizing gingivitis.

futile care SEE: under *care*.

FVC *forced vital capacity.*

FWB *full weight bearing.*

γ SEE: *gamma*.

G 1. The newtonian constant of gravitation. **2.** Symbol for giga, 10⁹, in SI units.

g 1. Symbol for the standard force of attraction of gravity, 980.665 m/sec², or about 32.17 ft/sec². **2.** *gingival; gram; gender.*

Ga Symbol for the element gallium.

GABA *gamma-aminobutyric acid.*

gabapentin (gă-bă-pĕn′tĭn) A gamma-aminobutyric acid (GABA) administered orally in adjunct with other treatment of adults with partial seizures with and without secondary generalization. Its U.S. Food and Drug Administration–approved therapeutic class is anticonvulsant.

gadfly (gad′flī″) A fly belonging to the family Tabanidae that lays eggs under the skin of its victim, causing swelling simulating a boil. Multiple furuncles appear with hatching of larvae. SEE: *botfly; warble.*

gadolinium (gad″ŏl-in′ē-ŭm) [Johan *Gadolin,* Finnish chemist, 1760–1852 + *-ium*] SYMB: Gd. A chemical element of the lanthanide series, atomic weight (mass) 157.25, atomic number 64. It is used as a contrast agent in magnetic resonance imaging, as a gamma ray source in bone densitometry, and in quality assurance tests of nuclear medicine imaging devices.

Gaenslen test, Gaenslen sign (gĕns′lĕnz) [Frederick J. Gaenslen, U.S. orthopedist, 1877–1937] A procedure used to identify the presence of sacroiliac dysfunction. The patient lies supine close to the edge of the examination table or is placed in a side-lying position with both legs pulled to the chest. The examiner extends the patient's leg and forces it into hyperextension while the other leg remains held against the chest. A positive test result produces pain in the sacroiliac region. SEE: illus.

GAF *Global Assessment of Functioning.*

gag 1. A device for keeping the jaws open during surgery. **2.** To retch or cause to retch. SEE: *gag reflex.* **3.** To restrict free speech or expression.

gag clause Any item in a contract that restricts free speech or personal expression.

gain (gān) **1.** To increase in weight, strength, or health. **2.** In electronics, the amplification factor for a given circuit or device. **3.** The real or imagined positive effect of an action or situation. For example, an illness might allow a person to put off going to school or meeting some other obligation such as a court appearance.

  brightness g. The increase in the intensity of a fluoroscopic image by the use of an image intensifier.

  primary g. In psychiatry, the relief of symptoms when the patient converts emotional anxiety to what he or she perceives as an organic illness, e.g., hysterical paralysis or blindness.

  secondary g. The advantage gained by the patient indirectly from illness, such as attention, care, and release from responsibility.

gait (gāt) [ME. *gait,* passage] A manner of walking.

  PATIENT CARE: Patients with gait problems should be evaluated by an interdisciplinary team, often including a neurologist, physiatrist, physical therapist, occupational therapist, and home health nurse. The home or care setting should be assessed for hazards that may increase the risk of falling; it should be altered to enhance its safety. Care providers should be taught how to safely assist an individual who has fallen, without compounding any injuries that may have occurred. Fall protection (hip pads, stair rails and tub rails, low bed position, appropriate kinds of chairs) should be provided to safeguard the patient from injury, and patients should be encouraged to practice and use techniques that specifically address their strengths and weaknesses so that their mobility is optimized.

  antalgic g. A gait in which the patient experiences pain during the stance phase and thus remains on the painful leg for as short a time as possible.

  ataxic g. An unsteady, staggering gait pattern. If related to cerebellar pathology, the gait is unsteady, irregular, and generally characterized by use of a wide base of support. The deviation is equally severe if the individual walks with eyes open or closed. If the cerebellar lesion is localized to one hemisphere, the individual will sway toward the affected side. Ataxic gait patterns related to spinal ataxia are characterized by a wide base of support, with the feet thrown out. There is a characteristic double tapping sound, as the individual steps on heels first, then on toes. This gait pattern occurs in such conditions as tabes dorsalis and multiple sclerosis and is believed to result from the disruption of the sensory pathways in the central nervous system. SEE: *ataxia* and its subentries.

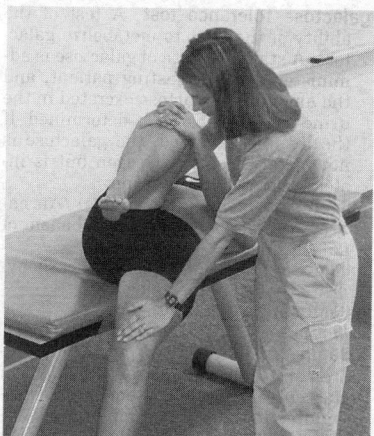

GAENSLEN TEST

cerebellar g. An ataxic gait resulting, e.g., from a cerebellar stroke or tumor.

crouch g. A gait seen in cerebral palsy in which the hamstrings and psoas muscles are shorter than normal and the affected person walks with a stooped posture.

festinating g. A gait in which short, shuffling steps are initially taken, with the feet barely clearing the floor. After several steps the walking pace becomes quicker and quicker. The upper body is flexed forward, and the head is bent toward the floor. The arms, elbows, hips, and knees are bent. This gait is typical of parkinsonism and related brain disorders.

hemiplegic g. A gait in which the patient abducts the paralyzed limb, swings it around, and brings it forward so that the foot comes to the ground in front. During the stance phase the patient bears very little weight on the involved leg.

Parkinson's g. In patients with Parkinson's disease, a gait marked by short steps with the feet barely clearing the floor in a shuffling and scraping manner. As the steps continue, they may become successively more rapid. The posture is marked by flexion of the upper body with the spine bent forward, head down, and arms, elbows, hips, and knees bent. SEE: *festination.*

spastic g. A stiff movement of the legs while walking, usually the result of an upper motor neuron lesion and spasticity in the muscles of the lower extremity. There are several variations. Spasticity in the ankle plantar flexors results in the toes dragging or walking on the toes; spasticity in the hip adductors results in a scissoring or crossing of the legs; spasticity in the quadriceps femoris results in the knee being held rigid. If the upper extremities are involved, the arms do not swing rhythmically but are usually held still with the elbows and wrists flexed.

steppage g. A gait in which the foot is lifted high to clear the toes, there is no heel strike, and the toes hit the ground first. It is seen in anterior tibialis paralysis, peripheral neuritis, late stages of diabetic neuropathy, alcoholism, and chronic arsenic poisoning.

swing-through g. A gait in which the crutches are advanced and the legs are swung between and ahead of the crutches.

three-point g. A gait in which the crutches and the affected leg are advanced first, then the other leg.

waddling g. A gait in which the feet are wide apart and the walk resembles that of a duck. It occurs in coxa vara and double congenital hip displacement when lordosis is present. In late pregnancy, hormone-induced softening allows some pelvic movement at the sacroiliac and pubic symphysis articulations on ambulation. Compensatory widening of the stance results in the characteristic waddle.

gait analysis SEE: *gait assessment.*

gait assessment SEE: under *assessment.*

gait speed The time it takes to walk a specified distance, usually 6 m or less. Slower speeds correlate with an increased risk of mortality in geriatric patients.

galactagogue (gă-lăk'tă-gŏg) [″ + *agogos,* leading] An agent that promotes the flow of milk.

galactase (gă-lăk'tās) An enzyme of milk.

galactic (gă-lăk'tĭk) Pert. to the flow of milk.

galacto-, galact- [Gr. *gala,* stem *galakt-,* milk] Prefixes meaning *milk.*

galactocele (gă-lăk'tō-sēl) [″ + *kele,* tumor, swelling] **1.** A cystic tumor of the female breast caused by occlusion of a milk duct. Fully emptying the breasts during feedings and cleaning the nipples to avoid nipple caking help the cyst resolve. **2.** A hydrocele containing a milk-like liquid.

galactogogue (gă-lăk'tō-gŏg″) [″ + ″] Any substance that increases milk secretion.

galactography Radiological imaging of breast ducts in women who have spontaneous nipple discharge without an obvious breast mass. A radiological contrast medium is injected into the nipple to highlight tissue distortion, ductal obstruction, or other abnormalities. The image obtained by galactography is called a "galactogram."

galactokinase (gă-lăk″tō-kī′nās) An enzyme that catalyzes the transfer of high-energy phosphate groups from a donor to D-galactose. D-galactose-1-phosphate is produced by this reaction.

galactolipin (gă-lăk″tō-lĭp′ĭn) [″ + *lipos*, fat] A phosphorus-free lipid combined with galactose; a cerebroside.

galactomannan (gă-lăk″tō-măn′ĭn) [″ + *mann(ose)*] A polysaccharide composed of a skeleton made of the sugar mannose to which galactose side groups are attached. Detection of galactomannan in blood is used to diagnose invasive aspergillosis infections in humans.

galactophore (găl-ăk′tō-for) [″ + *pherein*, to bear] A lactiferous duct.

galactopoiesis (gă-lăk″tō-poy-ē′sĭs) [″ + *poiesis*, forming] Milk production.

galactopoietic (gă-lăk″tō-poy-ĕt′ĭk) [″ + *poiein*, to make] **1.** Pert. to milk production. **2.** A substance that promotes galactopoiesis.

galactorrhea (gă-lak″tŏ-rē′ă) [*galacto-* + *-rrhea*,] **1.** The continuation of milk secretion at intervals after nursing has ceased. **2.** Excessive or abnormal secretion of milk.

galactosamine (gă-lăk″tō-săm′ĭn) A derivative of galactose containing an amine group on the second carbon of the compound.

galactose (gă-lăk′tōs) A dextrorotatory monosaccharide or simple hexose sugar, $C_6H_{12}O_6$. Galactose is an isomer of glucose and is formed, along with glucose, in the hydrolysis of lactose. It is a component of cerebrosides. Galactose is readily absorbed in the digestive tract; in the liver it is converted to glucose and may be stored as glycogen.

galactosemia (gă-lăk″tō-sē′mē-ă) An autosomal recessive disorder marked by an inability to metabolize galactose because of a congenital absence of one of two enzymes needed to convert galactose to glucose. The diagnosis is confirmed by testing the newborn's urine for noncarbohydrate reducing substances or more accurately by tests for the missing enzymes in blood cells. The infant with galactosemia will fail to thrive within a week after birth due to anorexia, vomiting, and diarrhea unless galactose and lactose are removed from the diet. If untreated, the disease may progress to starvation and death. Untreated children who do survive usually fail to grow, are mentally retarded, and have cataracts. If galactose is excluded from the diet early in life, the child may live to adulthood but suffer reproductive and brain disorders. Galactosemia can be diagnosed in utero by amniocentesis. If a pregnant woman is a known carrier, it is advisable that she exclude lactose and galactose from her diet.

galactose tolerance test A test of the ability of the liver to metabolize galactose. A standard dose of galactose is administered to the fasting patient, and the amount of galactose excreted in the urine in the next 5 hr is determined. If the liver is damaged, the galactose is not metabolized to glycogen but is instead excreted in the urine.

galactosidase (gă-lăk″tō-sī′dās) An enzyme that catalyzes the metabolism of galactosides.

galactoside (gă-lăk′tō-sīd) A carbohydrate that contains galactose.

galactosuria (găl-ăk″tō-sū′rē-ă) [″ + *ouron*, urine] Galactose in the urine.

galanin (găl′ăn-ĭn) A peptide neurotransmitter with numerous functions in the central nervous system and the gastrointestinal tract. It stimulates gastrointestinal smooth muscle contraction and inhibits insulin secretion.

galea (gāl′ē-ă) [L. *galea*, helmet] **1.** A helmet-like structure. **2.** A type of head bandage. **3.** Galea aponeurotica.
  g. aponeurotica Epicranial aponeurosis.

galectin (gă-lek′tĭn) Any of a family of galactosidase-binding proteins. Galectin-3 is a potential biomarker of myocardial fibrosis in patients with heart failure.

GALEN Global Allergy and Asthma European Network, a European effort to create reusable terminological classification services using a concept-oriented approach. GALEN supplements the development of nursing terminology, allowing comparisons among present nursing terminologies and making them available for describing day-to-day nursing care.

Galen, Claudius (gā′lĕn) A noted Greek physician and medical writer, circa A.D. 129–199. He lived in Rome and was physician to the Emperor Marcus Aurelius. He is called the father of experimental physiology.
  great vein of G. Vein of **G.**
  vein of G. A short midline unpaired vein between the cerebral hemispheres of the brain. It forms as the merger of the right and the left internal cerebral veins, and it bends upward (around the splenium of the corpus callosum) to empty into the straight sinus. SYN: *great vein of G.; great cerebral vein.*

galenic (gă-lĕn′ĭk) Pert. to Galen or his teachings.

galenicals, galenics (gă-lĕn′ĭ-kăls, -ĭks) **1.** Herb and vegetable medicines. **2.** Crude drugs and medicinals as distinguished from the pure active principles contained in them. **3.** Medicines prepared according to an official formula.

Galium aparine (gal′ē-ŭm) An invasive weed native to Eurasia and North America from which a tea is made that is used in herbal medicine as a diuretic and to promote healing. SYN: *catch-weed; cleavers; goosegrass.*

gall (gol) [AS. *gealla,* sore place] **1.** An excoriation. **2.** The bitter liver secretion stored in the gallbladder; bile. It has no enzymes, but emulsifies fats to permit digestion by pancreatic lipase, and stimulates peristalsis. Gall is discharged through the cystic duct into the duodenum.

gallate (găl'lāt) A salt of gallic acid.

gallbladder (gol'blăd″ĕr) [AS. *gealla,* sore place, + *blaedre,* bladder] A pear-shaped gray-blue sac that lies attached to the underside of the liver in a shallow depression between the right and quadrate lobes. The gallbladder has a capacity of approx. 50 mL and stores bile from the liver; while in the gallbladder, the bile is concentrated by the removal of water. Fat or acid in the duodenum stimulates the release of the hormone cholecystokinin (CCK), which then causes the gallbladder to contract and push its bile out through the 4-cm (1.5 in) long cystic duct. This duct joins the common hepatic duct to form the bile duct. Variations in the extra hepatic ducts and the arterial supply of the organ are common.

gallium (gal'ē-ŭm) [L. *Gallus,* rooster, cock, a punning translation of Paul E. *Lecoq,* Fr. chemist, who discovered the element + -*ium*] SYMB: Ga. A rare metallic chemical element, atomic weight (mass) 69.72, atomic number 31. Small amounts of gallium are found in bauxite and zinc blends. Gallium-67 (^{67}Ga) is used in nuclear medicine to provide images of tumors (such as lymphomas) and of inflamed tissues (such as are found in sarcoidosis, osteomyelitis, and abscesses).

gallon [Med. L. *galleta,* jug] Four liquid measure quarts; 231 cu in or 3.79 L. In England the Imperial liquid gallon is 277.4 cu in or 4.55 L.

gallop (gal'ŏp) An extra heart sound (i.e., a third or fourth heart sound), typically heard during diastole. SYN: *gallop rhythm.*

gallstone (gol'stōn) A concretion formed in the gallbladder or bile ducts. Gallstones are found in about 15% of men and 30% of women in the U.S., i.e. in about 20 million Americans. They may cause pain in the right upper quadrant of the abdomen (biliary colic) or they may be clinically silent. Gallstones typically are made either of crystallized cholesterol deposits or calcium crystals ionized with bilirubin. Cholesterol stones are about four times as common as calcium-containing stones (also known as pigment stones). Either type of stone may cause biliary symptoms such as pain or inflammation of the gallbladder; the two types of stones differ in that cholesterol stones are nonradiopaque and may on occasion be dissolved by medication, whereas calcium-containing radiopaque stones are not amenable to chemical dissolution and are therefore visible on plain x-rays of the abdomen. SEE: illus.; *Nursing Diagnoses Appendix.* SYN: *biliary calculus.*

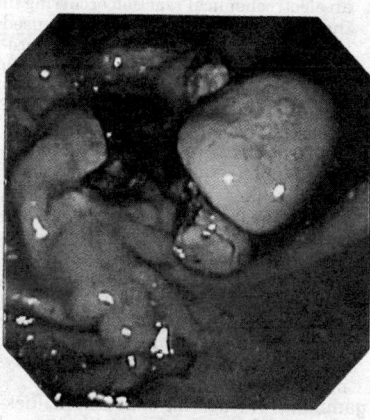

GALLSTONES
Seen endoscopically (orig. mag. ×3)

SYMPTOMS: Intense pain in the right upper quadrant of the abdomen that may radiate to the right flank, back, or shoulder is typical of biliary colic due to gallstones. The symptoms may occur after a fatty meal and may be associated with nausea or vomiting or fever. Jaundice may be present on physical examination.

TREATMENT: Asymptomatic gallstones are neither removed nor treated. Symptomatic gallstone disease is treated primarily in the U.S. by laparoscopic cholecystectomy which, when successful, avoids prolonged hospitalization. Drug therapy for gallstones may include the use of ursodiol. Stones found in the extrahepatic bile ducts are treated surgically according to the presentation. Cholecystotomy is reserved for patients who are judged to be too ill to tolerate cholecystectomy, usually as a temporizing procedure. Gallstone lithotripsy is infrequently used because it is technically more complex than laparoscopic cholecystectomy (and relatively equipment and labor is intensive, and less universally effective).

⚠️ Ursodiol (ursodeoxycholic acid), taken orally, is sometimes effective in treating cholesterol gallstones. Treatment may need to be continued for 1 year. A similar agent, chenodiol, is no longer available as it caused unacceptable incidence of hepatotoxicity.

GALT *gut-associated lymphoid tissue.*

galvanic (gal-van′ik) [Luigi Galvani, Italian physiologist, 1737–1798] Pert. to galvanism.

galvanic battery A series of cells giving a combined effect of all the units and generating electricity by chemical reaction.

galvanism (găl′vă-nĭzm) **1.** In dentistry, an electrochemical reaction occurring in the mouth when dissimilar metals used to restore teeth come into contact, producing a direct electric current that may cause pain. **2.** Electricity caused by chemical reaction. **3.** The application of a direct current to the body.

Gambierdiscus toxicus (găm″bē-ĕr-dĭs′kŭs tŏk′sĭ-kŭs) [NL.] A species of dinoflagellate that produces ciguatoxin, a neurotoxin that is the cause of ciguatera poisoning acquired from fish. SEE: *ciguatera poisoning.*

Gamblers Anonymous (gam′blĕrz) A self-help group for gamblers. It uses a 12-step program to encourage abstinence from gambling, similar to the work pioneered by Alcoholics Anonymous.

gambling 1. Wagering or betting. **2.** Risking something of value in the hope of winning something even more valuable or rare in exchange.

gambling, pathological Frequent, compulsive, uncontrolled, or addictive wagering or betting.

SYMPTOMS: The person may exhibit a constant preoccupation with gambling, resulting in impairment of social functioning or job performance; tolerance for very high levels of risk; denial of involvement in wagering activity; and anxiety, depression, irritability, or other withdrawal symptoms when unable to gamble.

⚠ Some drugs used to treat Parkinson's disease have been associated with the sudden onset of pathological gambling.

gamete (găm′ēt) [Gr. *gamein*, to marry] A mature male or female reproductive cell; the spermatozoon or ovum. **gametic** (-ĕt′ĭk), *adj.*

gamete intrafallopian transfer SEE: under *transfer.*

gametocide (găm′ĕ-tō-sīd″) [″ + L. *caedere*, to kill] An agent destructive to gametes or gametocytes, particularly those of malaria.

gametocyte (gă-mē′tō-sīt) [″ + *kytos*, cell] **1.** A cell of the ovary or testis that will divide to produce an ovum or spermatozoa. **2.** A stage in the life cycle of the malarial protozoon (*Plasmodium*). Ingested human blood cells taken up by the *Anopheles* mosquito release gametocytes, which develop into mature sex cells called gametes.

gametogenesis (găm″ĕt-ō-jĕn′ĕ-sĭs) [″ + *genesis*, generation, birth] Development of gametes; oogenesis or spermatogenesis.

gametogony (găm″ĕ-tŏg′ō-nē) The phase in the life cycle of the malarial parasite (*Plasmodium*) in which male and female gametocytes, which infect the mosquito, are formed.

gametophyte (găm′ĕ-tō-fīt) [″ + *phyton*, plant] In plants, the sexual (gamete-producing) generation that alternates with the asexual (spore-producing) generation.

gamic (găm′ĭk) [Gr. *gamein*, to marry] Sexual, esp. as applied to eggs that develop only after fertilization in contrast to those that develop without fertilization. SEE: *parthenogenesis.*

gamma (gam′ă) **1.** Γ or γ, the uppercase and lowercase symbols, respectively, for the fourth letter of the Greek alphabet. **2.** In chemistry, the third of a series (e.g., the third carbon atom in an aliphatic chain). **3.** Symbol for *microgram; immunoglobulin.*

gamma-aminobutyric acid (gam″ă-ă-mē″nō-bū-tir′ik, gam″ă-am″ĭ-nō-) SEE: under *acid.*

gamma benzene hexachloride (găm′ă bĕn′zēn hĕk″să-klor′īd) A miticide used to treat scabies. Trade names are Kwell and Scabene. SYN: *lindane.* SEE: *scabies.*

gamma camera A scintillation detector used in nuclear medical imaging to detect the release of radioisotopes taken up by diseased and healthy body tissues.

gamma-glutamyl transpeptidase, γ-glutamyl transpeptidase (gam′ă-gloot′ă-mil″ trans-pep′tĭ-dās″, -gloo-tam′ĭl) SEE: *gamma-glutamyl transpeptidase.*

gamma-hydroxybutyrate, gamma-hydroxy butyrate (gam″ă-hī-drok″sē-būt′ĭ-rāt″) ABBR: GHB. A central nervous system depressant used in some countries as an anesthetic agent. It has no approved use in the U.S., where it is sometimes abused as an illicit drug. Its street names include grievous bodily harm, liquid ecstasy, and organic quaalude.

gamma knife surgery SEE: under *surgery.*

gamma scan SEE: under *scan.*

gammopathy (găm-ŏp′ă-thē) Any disease in which serum immunoglobulins are increased, such as multiple myeloma, benign monoclonal gammopathy, and cirrhosis.

gamo-, gam- [Gr. *gamos*, marriage] Prefixes meaning *sexual union* or *union, joining.*

gamont (găm′ŏnt) [″ + *on*, being] A sexual form of certain protozoa. SEE: *gametocyte* (2).

gangli-, ganglio- [L. *ganglion* frGr. *ganglion*, tumor, cystic tumor] Prefixes meaning *ganglion*.

ganglia (găng′glē-ă) Pl. of ganglion.

gangliectomy (găng″glē-ĕk′tō-mē) [″ + *ektome*, excision] Excision of a ganglion.

gangliocytoma (găng″glē-ō-sī-tō′mă) [″ + ″ + *oma*, tumor] Ganglioneuroma.

ganglioglioma (găng″glē-ō-glī-ō′mă) [″ + *glia*, glue, + *oma*, tumor] A ganglion-cell glioma.

ganglioma (găng-lē-ō′mă) [″ + *oma*, tumor] **1.** A tumor of neural or neuroectodermal origin. **2.** A swelling of lymphoid tissue.

ganglion (gang′glē-ŏn, gang′glē-ă) *pl.* **ganglia, ganglions** [Gr *ganglion*, tumor, cystic tumor.] **1.** An autonomic ganglion. **2.** A dorsal root ganglion or spinal ganglion. **3.** A cystic tumor developing on a tendon or aponeurosis. It sometimes occurs on the back of the wrist. SEE: illus.

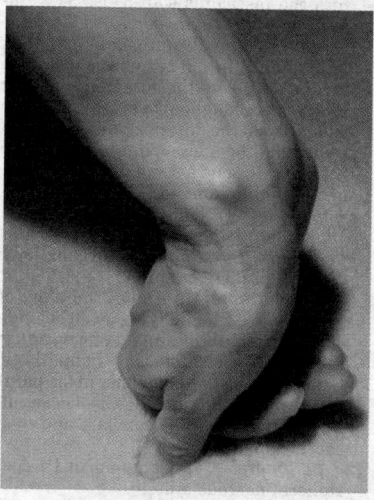

GANGLION CYST

Proximal to the radial surface of the wrist

acoustic g. Spiral **g.**

aorticorenal g. Either of the paired prevertebral autonomic ganglia in the nerve plexus that surrounds the aortic roots of the renal arteries. It receives preganglionic sympathetic axons via the major splanchnic nerves.

auditory g. Spiral **g.**

autonomic g. A collection of postganglionic autonomic neurons in the peripheral nervous system that are surrounded by a loose connective tissue capsule. Dendrites of the neurons can be limited to the neuropil inside the ganglion, or they can pierce the capsule and extend into the surrounding regions.

Each preganglionic autonomic axon usually synapses on the dendrites of many ganglionic neurons. During development, the autonomic ganglia are derived from the neural crest.

basal ganglia Large central nervous system nuclei lying deep in the cerebral hemispheres below the cortex. The core nuclei that compose the basal ganglia include the caudate nucleus and putamen (together, called the striatum), the globus pallidus (the pallidum), and the amygdaloid complex. The putamen and globus pallidus are adjacent and are sometimes grouped together as the lentiform nucleus. Other nearby nuclei are key controllers and modulators of the basal ganglia; these include the substantia nigra, the ventral tegmental area, and the subthalamic nucleus. The basal ganglia, which are central players in the extrapyramidal motor system, are involved in initiating motor programs, and diseases of the basal ganglia, eg, tremor, athetosis, hemiballismus, chorea, and Parkinsonism, are associated with movement problems.

cardiac ganglia Collections of autonomic (mainly postganglionic parasympathetic) neurons clumped in the superficial and deep cardiac plexuses. These plexuses are a meshwork of visceral afferent, sympathetic, and parasympathetic axons that coat the lower part of the trachea, its bifurcation, the aorta, the pulmonary trunk, and the coronary arteries.

celiac g. Either of a pair of interconnected prevertebral autonomic ganglia in the celiac plexus, a meshwork of autonomic axons that wrap around the celiac trunk and the root of the superior mesenteric artery. The celiac ganglia are the largest of the prevertebral ganglia and receive preganglionic sympathetic axons via the major splanchnic nerves.

cervical g. Any of the three pairs of ganglia (superior, middle, inferior) in the cervical portion of the sympathetic trunk.

cervicothoracic g. Stellate **g.**

ciliary g. A small autonomic ganglion lying on the outside of the optic nerve in the rear portion of the orbit. This ganglion receives preganglionic parasympathetic axons from the midbrain via the oculomotor nerve (CN III). It sends postganglionic parasympathetic axons into the eye, via the short ciliary axons, to innervate the ciliary muscle, the sphincter of the iris, the smooth muscles of local blood vessels, and the cornea.

cochlear g. Spiral **g.**

dorsal root g. A roughly spherical collection of unipolar neuronal cell bodies in the dorsal roots of each spinal nerve near the intervertebral foramina.

Dorsal root ganglia are enclosed in a capsule that is a continuation of the epineurium of the spinal nerve. Besides neuronal cell bodies, these ganglia contain satellite cells, Schwann cells, axonal processes, and blood vessels. The ganglion's neurons are part of the primary visceral or somatic sensory pathways; their peripheral processes extend into the peripheral nerve and terminate in sensory endings, and their central processes follow the dorsal roots into the central nervous system and synapse in sensory areas. Microscopically, the peripheral processes of dorsal root ganglion neurons look identical to axons. During development, dorsal root ganglia develop from neural crest cells. SYN: *intervertebral g.; spinal g.*

g. of the facial nerve Geniculate **g.**

gasserian g. Trigeminal **g.**

geniculate g. The sensory ganglion of the facial nerve (CN VII). The ganglion lies inside a bend in the facial canal (at the geniculum of the facial nerve) where the preganglionic parasympathetic axons leave the facial nerve and form the greater petrosal nerve. The geniculate ganglion contains the cell bodies of the bipolar neurons that receive taste information from the palate and the anterior two-thirds of the tongue via the chorda tympani. The axons of the neurons of the ganglion run in the nervus intermedius component of the facial nerve and synapse in the nucleus of the fasciculus solitarius. SYN: **g.** *of the facial nerve.*

inferior cervical g. The lowest (most caudal) of the cervical ganglia. It is adjacent to vertebra C7 or T1. Postganglionic sympathetic axons from the inferior cervical ganglion join spinal nerves C7–T1 and the pulmonary nerves. SEE: *stellate g.*

inferior g. of the glossopharyngeal nerve Petrosal **g.**

inferior g. of the vagus nerve Nodose **g.**

inferior mesenteric g. A prevertebral sympathetic ganglion located in the inferior mesenteric plexus, a meshwork of autonomic axons on and near the origin of the inferior mesenteric artery.

jugular g. The smaller of the two sensory ganglia of the vagus nerve (CN X). The jugular ganglion lies in the jugular foramen of the skull. Neurons in the ganglion send somatic sensory fibers to the dura of the posterior cranial fossa, the skin behind the ear, and the skin along the inferior portion of the tympanic membrane and the adjacent floor of the external auditory canal; the axons of these neurons follow the vagus nerve into the brainstem where they join the spinal trigeminal tract. SYN: *superior* **g.** *of the vagus nerve.*

lumbar g. Any of the three or four pairs of paravertebral ganglia in the lumbar section of the sympathetic trunk. The lumbar ganglia send postganglionic sympathetic axons, via lumbar splanchnic nerves, to the superior hypogastric plexus; from there the axons are distributed to the pelvic viscera.

middle cervical g. The central and smallest of the cervical ganglia. It is adjacent to vertebra C6. Approximately 40% of people lack this ganglion. In some people, it merges with the superior cervical ganglion, forming one elongated ganglion. Postganglionic sympathetic axons from the middle cervical ganglion join cervical nerves C5–C6.

nodose g. The larger of the two sensory ganglia of the vagus nerve; it is located in the nerve below the jugular foramen. The ganglion contains a mix of somatic and visceral sensory neurons; somatic neurons send their axons into the spinal trigeminal tract in the brainstem; visceral neurons send their axons into the fasciculus solitarius. SYN: *inferior g. of the vagus nerve.*

otic g. A small autonomic ganglion located deep in the zygomatic fossa immediately below the foramen ovale. It receives preganglionic parasympathetic axons from the inferior salivatory nucleus via the glossopharyngeal nerve (CN IX); it sends postganglionic parasympathetic axons to innervate the parotid gland. SYN: *auricular g.*

parasympathetic g. An autonomic ganglion containing postganglionic parasympathetic neurons.

paravertebral g. Any of the pairs of sympathetic ganglia lying on either side of the vertebral column and forming the thickened nodes of the sympathetic trunk. The usual complement of paravertebral ganglia includes 2–3 cervical, 11–12 thoracic, 3–4 lumbar, and 4–5 sacral ganglia.

peripheral g. A ganglion in the peripheral nervous system.

petrosal g. The larger of the two sensory ganglia in the glossopharyngeal nerve (IX). The ganglion lies on the outer surface of the base of the skull in a groove in the petrous portion of the temporal bone just outside the jugular foramen. The petrosal ganglion contains cell bodies of unipolar neurons that receive taste and tactile sensation from the posterior third of the tongue and the oropharynx. Axons of these neurons follow the glossopharyngeal nerve into the hindbrain. SYN: *inferior g. of the glossopharyngeal nerve.*

prevertebral g. An irregular and sometimes fragmented sympathetic ganglia in one of the nerve plexuses along the abdominal aorta or its major branches. The major prevertebral ganglia (the celiac, aorticorenal, phrenic, and superior and inferior mesenteric ganglia) are interconnected by autonomic nerves.

pterygopalatine g. Sphenopalatine **g.**

semilunar g. Trigeminal **g.**

sensory g. Any ganglion (e.g., trigeminal ganglion or dorsal root ganglion) containing neurons that receive afferent (sensory) signals.

simple g. A cystic tumor in a tendon sheath. SYN: *wrist* **g.**

sphenopalatine g. An autonomic ganglion found in the pterygopalatine fossa. It receives preganglionic axons from the superior salivatory nucleus via the facial nerve (CN VII). It sends postganglionic parasympathetic axons to innervate the lacrimal glands and the blood vessels and glands of the mucosa of the nose and palate. SYN: *pterygopalatine* **g.**

spinal g. Dorsal root **g.**

spiral g. A chain of tiny sensory ganglia that winds through the cochlea of the inner ear. These ganglia contain the cell bodies of the neurons that receive auditory signals from the organ of Corti. The axons of these neurons form the cochlear component of the vestibulocochlear nerve and synapse in the cochlear nuclei in the brainstem. SYN: *acoustic* **g.**; *auditory* **g.**; *cochlear* **g.**

stellate g. The merger of the inferior cervical ganglion and the first thoracic ganglion, which occurs in many people. SYN: *cervicothoracic* **g.**

submandibular g. An autonomic ganglion suspended from the lingual nerve between the mylohyoid and hyoglossus muscles. It receives preganglionic parasympathetic axons from the superior salivatory nucleus via the facial nerve (CN VII). It sends postganglionic parasympathetic axons to innervate the submandibular and sublingual salivary glands and the mucosa of the floor of the mouth.

superior cervical g. The uppermost cervical ganglion and the largest paravertebral autonomic ganglion. It is adjacent to vertebra C2 or C3. It sends postganglionic sympathetic axons into cranial nerves CN VIII–XII, cervical nerves C1–C4, and the pharyngeal, carotid, and cardiac nerves.

superior g. of the vagus nerve Jugular ganglion.

superior mesenteric g. Either of the paired prevertebral autonomic sympathetic ganglia in the lower celiac plexus and adjacent to the superior mesenteric artery. It receives preganglionic sympathetic axons via the major splanchnic nerves.

sympathetic g. Any of the paravertebral or prevertebral autonomic ganglia that are innervated by preganglionic axons from the intermediolateral

column of neurons in spinal cord segments T1–L2.

thoracic g. Any of 11 or 12 pairs of paravertebral ganglia in the thoracic section the sympathetic trunk. The first four or five thoracic ganglia send postganglionic sympathetic axons to the cardiac nerves. Three major splanchnic nerves (greater, lesser, and least splanchnic nerves) appear to emerge from the thoracic ganglia. They then run through the diaphragm and end in the celiac, mesenteric, and aorticorenal prevertebral ganglia. These nerves are actually bundles of preganglionic sympathetic axons that originate in the spinal cord and pass through the thoracic paravertebral ganglia without synapsing on their way to synapse in the abdominal prevertebral ganglia.

trigeminal g. The somatic sensory ganglion of the trigeminal nerve (CN V). It is semilunar in shape and flattened along the front and medial surfaces of the floor of the middle cranial fossa. The ophthalmic, the maxillary, and the sensory portion of the mandibular nerves emerge from the front of the ganglion, while the motor portion of the mandibular nerve runs under the ganglion. SYN: *gasserian* **g.**; *semilunar* **g.**

vestibular g. A two-part ganglion in the vestibular branches of the vestibulocochlear nerve (CN VIII) inside the internal auditory meatus. The ganglion contains the cell bodies of bipolar neurons that receive equillibrium information from the membranous labyrinth of the semicircular canals in the inner ear. The axons of these neurons form the vestibular component of the vestibulocochlear nerve and synapse in the vestibular nuclei in the brainstem. SYN: *Scarpa ganglion.*

wrist g. Simple **g.**

ganglionated (găng′lē-ŏ-nāt″ĕd) Having or consisting of ganglia.

ganglionectomy (găng″lē-ō-nĕk′tō-mē) [Gr. *ganglion,* knot, + *ektome,* excision] Excision of a ganglion.

ganglioneuroma (găng″lē-ō-nū-rō′mă) [″ + *neuron,* nerve, + *oma,* tumor] A neuroma containing ganglion cells. SYN: *gangliocytoma.*

ganglionic (găng-lē-ŏn′ĭk) Pert. to or of the nature of a ganglion.

ganglionic blockade SEE: under *blockade.*

ganglionitis (găng″lē-ŏn-ī′tĭs) [″ + *itis,* inflammation] Inflammation of a ganglion.

ganglioplegic (găng″lē-ō-plē′jĭk) Any drug that prevents transmission of nervous impulses 'through sympathetic or parasympathetic ganglia. Such drugs have limited therapeutic applicability because of undesired side effects. They are useful in treating hypertensive crises. Because they decrease blood pressure, they are used to limit bleeding during certain surgical procedures.

ganglioside (găng′glē-ō-sīd) A particular class of glycosphingolipid present in nerve tissue and in the spleen.

gangliosidosis (găng″glē-ō-sī-dō′sĭs) *pl.* **gangliosidoses** An accumulation of abnormal amounts of specific gangliosides in the nervous system.

   adult-onset g. A rare, slowly progressing dementing illness caused by the gradual accumulation of the GM ganglioside in neurons. It is marked clinically by impaired learning and social interactions, altered emotional expressions, psychosis, muscle atrophy, and clumsiness. SEE: *sphingolipidosis.*

gangrene (gang′grēn″, gan′) [Gr. *gangraina,* an eating sore] Necrosis or death of tissue, usually resulting from deficient or absent blood supply. SEE: illus.; *necrosis.*

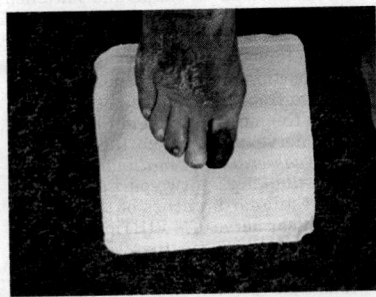

GANGRENE

ETIOLOGY: Gangrene is usually caused by obstruction of the blood supply to an organ or tissue, e.g., from inflammation, injury, or degenerative changes such as arteriosclerosis. It is commonly a sequela of infections, frostbite, crushing injuries, or diseases such as diabetes mellitus and Raynaud disease. Emboli in large arteries in almost any part of the body can cause gangrene of the area distal to that point. The part that dies is known as a slough (for soft tissues) or a sequestrum (for bone). The dead matter must be removed before healing can take place.

PATIENT CARE: The older or diabetic patient is assessed for arterial insufficiency related to decreases in the strength and elasticity of blood vessels. Capillary refill is also assessed. The presence and strength of distal pulses and the patient's normal sensation response to light and deep palpation are checked. Symmetry, color, temperature, and quantitative and qualitative changes in fingernails or toenails, skin texture, and hair patterns are assessed. Any unusual areas of pigmentation indicating new skin lesions or scarring from past injury or ulceration are ob-

served and documented, with description given of the extent and nature of gangrene that is present.

If prescribed, vasodilating and thrombolytic agents are administered, and the patient's response is evaluated. If surgical intervention is required, the patient's understanding of the procedure, its desired effects, and possible complications are evaluated. Health care professionals collaborate with the surgeon to instruct and prepare the patient for surgery and the postoperative period. Care required will depend on the particular procedure. If amputation is required, the patient must understand that the level of amputation depends on determining the presence of viable tissues to ensure healing and the requirements for fitting a prosthesis. The entire health care team must understand the patient's perception of the amputation in order to assist with resolution of grief and adjustment to a permanent change in body image. Physical and occupational therapists help the patient deal with changes in mobility and ability to perform activities of daily living. The multidisciplinary rehabilitation team involves the patient, nurse, physician, social worker, psychologist, prosthetist, and physical and occupational therapists. The patient's age and presence of other body system dysfunctions affect immediate and long-term responses to treatment. The at-risk patient should be taught preventive measures such as avoiding exposure to cold; keeping the extremities covered with gloves, clean, dry socks, and well-insulated footwear; and promptly treating any breaks in skin integrity.

   diabetic g. Gangrene, esp. of the lower extremities, occurring in some diabetics as a result of vascular insufficiency, neuropathy, and infection.

   dry g. Gangrene that results when the necrotic part has a progressive reduction in its blood supply but does not typically become infected. This occurs when arterial blood flow to a tissue is obstructed. The tissue gradually dries, the process continuing for weeks or months. SEE: *Nursing Diagnoses Appendix.*

   SYMPTOMS: Dry gangrene causes pain in the early stages. The affected part is cold and black and begins to atrophy. The most distal parts (the fingers or toes) are generally affected first. Dry gangrene is often seen in arteriosclerosis associated with diabetes mellitus.

   PATIENT CARE: Patient care concerns for dry gangrene are similar to those of moist gangrene. Necrotic matter must be removed and circulation to the remaining tissues ensured before healing can occur. The older diabetic patient with microvascular and macrovascular disease may experience very little pain because of a reduction in feeling produced by peripheral neuropathy. The condition may come to light only upon inspection. For this reason, all patients with diabetes mellitus or peripheral vascular disease should avoid cigarette smoking, be taught proper foot inspection and care, and show their feet to their caregivers at every office and/or home visit.

The recommended plan of care may include amputation of gangrenous tissue or observation while the tissue sloughs on its own. The gangrenous limb should be kept clean and dry and protected as much as possible from trauma or infection. Psychological needs resulting from the loss of a body part may require a psychiatric nurse practitioner, a psychologist, or a spiritual counselor of the patient's choice.

Fournier g. SEE: *Fournier gangrene*.

gas g. Gangrene in a wound infected by a gas-forming microorganism, the most common causative agent being *Clostridium perfringens*.

TREATMENT: Gas gangrene is treated with débridement of the wound site, antibiotics, and clostridial antitoxin.

hospital g. Necrotizing **fasciitis**.

moist g. Gangrene that is wet as a result of tissue necrosis and bacterial infection. The condition is marked by serous exudation and rapid decomposition.

SYMPTOMS: At first the affected part is hot and red; later it is cold and bluish, starting to slough. Moist gangrene spreads rapidly and carries a significant risk of local or systemic infection and occasionally death. SYN: *wet* **g.**

symmetrical g. Gangrene on opposite sides of the body in corresponding parts, usually the result of vasomotor disturbances. It is characteristic of Raynaud disease and Buerger disease.

wet g. Moist **g.**

white g. Gangrene caused by local impairments of blood flow.

gangrenous (găng′grĭ-nĭs) Pert. to gangrene.

gantry (găn′trē) [Gr. *kanthēlios*, pack ass] **1.** The housing for the imaging source and detectors into which the patient is placed for computed tomography and magnetic resonance imaging. **2.** The portion of the radiation therapy machine (linear accelerator, cobalt unit) that houses the source of therapeutic particles.

gap (gap) **1.** An opening or a break; an interruption in continuity. **2.** The difference between the expected and the measured concentration of solute in the plasma.

anion g. The difference between the measured cations sodium (Na^+) and potassium (K^+) and the measured anions chloride (Cl^-) and bicarbonate (HCO_{3-}). In accordance with the principle of electroneutrality, in any body fluid the number of net positive charges contributed by cations must equal the number of net negative charges contributed by anions. The unmeasured anions include lactate, sulfates, phosphates, proteins, ketones, and other organic acids. In general an anion gap of 10 to 14 mmol/L is normal. An increased value is present in metabolic acidosis.

auscultatory g. A period of silence that sometimes occurs in the determination of blood pressure by auscultation. It may occur in patients with hypertension or aortic stenosis. SEE: *blood pressure; pulsus paradoxus.*

evidence-practice g. The failure of clinicians to adopt proven practices that enhance outcomes for patients. The disparity between usual professional practice and evidenced-based guidelines.

health care g. A disparity between health care needs and health care services, esp. as it applies to the medically indigent.

osmolal g. The difference between the measured osmolality of the plasma, and the calculated osmolality of the plasma (plasma glucose/18 + blood urea nitrogen/2.8 + sodium*2). A gap is present when the difference exceeds 10 mmol/kg of water. Osmolal gaps are present when unmeasured osmotically active solutes, such as toxins, e.g., methanol or ethylene glycol, are present in the plasma.

urine anion g. ABBR: UAG. The sum of the concentrations of sodium and potassium in a specimen of urine, minus the urine chloride concentration. The UAG is used to assess the source of a metabolic acidosis. A positive value indicates the kidney is responsible for the acidosis. A large negative value indicates the kidneys are compensating for a metabolic acidosis caused by other organs.

gap junction Minute pores between cells that provide pathways for intercellular communication. Originally described in muscle tissue, they are known to be present in most animal cells.

Garcinia cambogia (găr-sĭn′ē-ă kăm-bō′jă, jē-ă) [NL] An herbal agent promoted for the treatment of obesity. Evidence is insufficient to recommend its usage for this purpose.

Gardasil (găr′dă-sĭl) Quadrivalent human papillomavirus (types 6, 11, 16, 18) recombinant vaccine.

Gardnerella vaginalis (gard-ně-rel′ă vaj-ĭ-nā′lĭs, nal′ĭs) [Herman L. Gardner, 20th-cent. U.S. physician] One of several bacteria implicated in bacterial vaginosis in women. The bacilli are usually gram-negative, but in older cultures the bacilli may stain variably (some gram-negative and some falsely gram-positive). *G. vaginalis* was formerly called *Corynebacterium vaginale* and *Haemophilus vaginalis*. SEE: *bacterial vaginosis*.

Gardner syndrome (gard′nĕr) [Eldon J. Gardner, U.S. geneticist, 1909–1989] Familial adenomatous polyposis.

Gardos channel A cell membrane pore that regulates intracellular volume with a pump that forces potassium ions out of the cell. The pump is activated by calcium ions.

gargle [Fr. *gargouille*, throat; but may be onomatopoeia for gargle] **1.** A throat wash. **2.** To wash out the mouth and throat by tipping the head back and allowing the fluid to accumulate in the back of the throat, while agitating it by the forceful expiration of air.

gargoylism (gär′goyl-ĭsm) Hurler's syndrome.

Garland triad (gar′lănd) [George M. Garland, U.S. physician, 1848–1926] Radiologic findings in the chest suggestive of sarcoidosis. The findings consist of right- and left-sided hilar lymph node enlargement and isolated right-sided paratracheal adenopathy.

garlic An edible, strongly flavored bulb, *Allium sativa*, used mainly for seasoning foods. Garlic is said to have beneficial effects on heart disease; however there is little scientific evidence to support this claim.

GART *genotypic antiretroviral resistance testing*.

Gartner, Hermann (gart′nĕr) Hermann Treschow Gartner, Danish surgeon and anatomist, 1785–1827.

    G. cyst A cyst developing from Gartner's duct in a female.

    G. duct A small duct lying parallel to the uterine tube. It is a vestigial structure representing the persistent mesonephric duct. SYN: *duct of the epoophoron; ductus epoophori longitudinalis*.

GAS 1. *general adaptation syndrome*. **2.** *Group A streptococci*.

gas (gas) **1.** One of the basic forms or states of matter. Gas molecules are free and move swiftly in all directions. Their motion and energy are directly proportional to the temperature. A gas not only takes the shape of the containing vessel but expands and fills the vessel no matter what its volume. Among the common important gases are oxygen; nitrogen; hydrogen; helium; sewer gas, which contains carbon monoxide; carbon dioxide; the anesthetic gases; ammonia; and the poisonous war gases. Liquids and solids may release toxic fumes or gases when heated. SEE: *war g.; anesthesia*. **2.** A colloquial term for an *anesthetic*.

arterial blood g. ABBR: ABG. Any of the gases present in blood. Operationally and clinically, ABGs include the determination of levels of pH, oxygen (O_2), and carbon dioxide (CO_2) in the blood. ABGs are important in the diagnosis and treatment of disturbances of acid-base balance, pulmonary disease, electrolyte balance, and oxygen delivery. Values of the gases themselves are usually expressed as the partial pressure of carbon dioxide or oxygen although derived values are reported in other units. Several other blood chemistry values are important in managing acid-base disturbances, including the levels of the bicarbonate ion (HCO_3), blood pH, sodium, potassium, and chloride.

binary g. Any gas made of two gaseous components mixed with each other. Some chemical warfare agents are chemically benign when separate but are damaging to living organisms when combined. SEE: *war g.*

blood g. The content of dissolved carbon dioxide and oxygen in plasma. Levels of these gases vary in response to many diseases that affect respiration, e.g., asthma, chronic obstructive lung disease, congestive heart failure, and ketoacidosis. SEE: *acidosis; alkalosis; arterial blood g.; blood gas analysis*.

coal g. A flammable, explosive, toxic gas produced from the distillation of coal. It is used for heating and lighting. Its principal constituents are methane, carbon monoxide, and hydrogen.

illuminating g. A mixture of various combustible gases including hydrogen and carbon monoxide. Its poisonous effects are largely due to carbon monoxide.

inert g. Noble **g.**

intestinal g. Any of several gaseous compounds (including carbon dioxide, oxygen, nitrogen, hydrogen, methane, methylmercaptan, and hydrogen sulfide) present in the intestinal tract. They are produced by digestive processes and intestinal bacteria. SYN: *digestive tract*. SEE: *digestion; flatus*.

laughing g. An informal term for nitrous oxide. SEE: *nitrous oxide*.

mustard g. Dichlorethyl sulfide, a poisonous gas used in warfare. SEE: *vesicant g.; war g.*

nerve g. Any of several gaseous materials used in chemical warfare. The agents may be stored in liquid form but are aerosolized at the time of use. These chemicals are readily absorbed through the skin. Some forms, i.e., organophosphates that inhibit acetylcholinesterase cause copious secretions from the nose, eyes, mouth, lungs, and intestines. Muscle fasiculations, twitching, and miosis will result from exposure. A large dose may cause sudden unconsciousness, convulsions, flaccid paralysis, apnea, and death. With some agents, only a few breaths of the vapor may cause death.

PROTECTION: Charcoal-lined suits offer barrier protection. The agents will penetrate ordinary clothing worn with a gas mask.

TREATMENT: Pretreatment with pyridostigmine and concurrent treatment at the time of exposure with atropine, pralidoxime, and diazepam may be life-saving. Artificial respiration is mandatory. The skin should be decontaminated with household bleach diluted with water at a ratio of 1:10, or with soap and water, and the eyes should be irrigated with plain water. Military personnel carry small towels impregnated with chloramine, hydroxide, and phenol.

⚠️ Gas masks should cover face and eyes and be proven to be adequately effective. People treating patients must protect themselves from contact with toxic chemicals on clothing, hair, and skin.

SEE: *war g.*

nitric oxide g. A toxic gas administered in very small concentrations during mechanical ventilation to treat persistent pulmonary hypertension. SEE: *nitric oxide.*

noble g. Any of the six colorless, odorless, minimally chemically reactive gaseous elements found in group 18 of the periodic table. The gases are argon, helium, krypton, neon, radon, and xenon. SYN: *inert g.*

sewer g. A gas that is produced by decaying matter in sewage and contains methane and hydrogen sulfide. It is toxic, usually flammable, explosive, and may be used for fuel.

tear g. SEE: *riot control **agent**.*

war g's. Any chemical substance, whether solid, liquid, or vapor, used to produce poisonous gas with irritant effects. The agents can be classified as lacrimators, sternutators (sneeze-causing), lung irritants, vesicants, and systemic poisons, such as nerve gas. Some gases have multiple effects.

War gases are known as nonpersistent (diffusing and dispersing fairly rapidly) or persistent (lingering and evaporating slowly).

FIRST AID: When giving first aid, the rescuer avoids becoming a casualty by taking appropriate precautions. All gas masks are checked to ensure that they are in working order. The rescuer first puts on his or her own mask, then fits masks to patients. The rescuer's skin is covered, and exposed skin of persons at risk is flooded with water to flush off suspected chemical contaminants.

PATIENT CARE: Decontamination

centers are essential to the rescue effort. Thorough decontamination of patients, clothing, foot coverings, equipment, and even ambulances precedes admitting patients to emergency care areas to prevent unaffected people in the area from becoming casualties. Pulmonary and neurological functions are closely monitored, and specific or supportive therapies instituted as necessary.

gas chromatography SEE: under *chromatography*.

gas distention Accumulation of excessive gas within the lumen of the gastrointestinal tract, the peritoneum, or the bowel wall. Treatment may be surgical or nonsurgical, depending on the etiology.

gaseous (găs′sē-ŭs) Having the nature or form of gas.

gas exchange, impaired The state in which the individual experiences a deficit in oxygenation and/or carbon dioxide elimination at the alveolar-capillary membrane, often producing subjective fatigue or anxiety. SEE: *Nursing Diagnoses Appendix.*

GASH (găsh) An acronym for *g*lare, *a*rc, *s*tarburst, and *h*alo, four potential complications of refractive eye surgery.

gasoline, gasolene (ga′sŏ-lēn″, ga″sŏ-lēn′) [*gas* + *-ol* + *-ine*] A product of the destructive distillation of petroleum, a liquid mixture of hydrocarbons, with chain length between 4 and 12 C atoms, frequently containing additives to improve combustion. Commercial gasoline may contain toxic additives.

⚠️ Using the mouth to produce suction on a tube for siphoning gasoline from a tank is dangerous because the gasoline may be inhaled or swallowed.

gasoline poisoning SEE: under *poisoning.*

gasometric (găs″ō-mĕt′rĭk) Pert. to the measurement of gases.

gasometry (ga-som′ĕ-trē) [*gas* + *-metry*] Estimation or measurement of the amount of gas in a mixture.

gasp [Old Norse *geispa*] To catch the breath; to inhale and exhale with quick, difficult breaths; the act of gasping.

gastero-, gaster- [Gr. *gastēr*, stem *gastr-*, stomach] Prefixes meaning *stomach* or *ventral.*

Gasterophilus (găs″tĕr-ŏf′ĭ-lŭs) A genus of botflies belonging to the family Oestridae, order Diptera. The larvae infest horses.

G. intestinalis A species that infests the stomachs of horses.

gastralgia (găs-trăl′jē-ă) [″ + *algos*, pain] Pain in the stomach from any cause.

gastrectomy (ga-strek′tŏ-mē) [*gastro-* + *-ectomy*] The surgical removal of part or all of the stomach.

laparoscopic vertical g. Sleeve **g.**

sleeve g. A bariatric surgical treatment in which a large portion of the stomach is removed, leaving a 60 to 80-ml gastric tube. The greater curvature of the stomach is removed during the procedure. The small residual stomach tube prevents overeating by creating a feeling that the stomach is full after a small meal. (The operation may also affect serum levels of hormones like ghrelin, which influence hunger and satiety.) The operation is purely restrictive and does not produce malabsorption of nutrients. It is relatively easy to perform compared with other forms of bariatric surgery. Complications of the procedure include nausea, vomiting, and gastric leaks. SYN: *laparoscopic vertical* **g.**

gastric (găs′trĭk) [Gr. *gaster,* stomach] Pert. to the stomach. SEE: *digestion; stomach.*

gastric analysis Analysis of stomach contents to determine the stomach's basal acid secretion and maximal acidity after stimulation. The analysis is used to diagnose diseases such as pernicious anemia and Zollinger-Ellison syndrome.

gastric-inhibitory polypeptide ABBR: GIP. A polypeptide hormone secreted by the duodenum and jejunum that inhibits motility and the secretion of gastric hydrochloric acid and pepsin and that stimulates insulin secretion. SEE: *enterogastrone.*

gastric intramucosal pH An experimental procedure to measure the pH of gastric mucosa to determine the adequacy of its oxygenation. The goal is to obtain an index of tissue oxygenation in general.

gastric lavage SEE: under *lavage.*

gastrin (găs′trĭn) A hormone secreted by the mucosa of the pyloric area of the stomach and duodenum in various species of animals, including humans. The hormone is released into gastric venous blood, from which it flows into the liver and into the general circulation. When the hormone reaches the stomach, it stimulates gastric acid secretion. Gastrin causes the lower esophageal sphincter to contract and the ileocecal valve to relax. Also, it has a mild effect on small-intestine and gallbladder motility. Gastrin is released in response to partially digested protein, ethyl alcohol in about 10% concentration, and distention of the antrum of the stomach. SEE: *Zollinger-Ellison syndrome.*

gastrinoma (găs″trĭn-ō′mă) The gastrin-secreting tumor associated with Zollinger-Ellison syndrome. SEE: *Zollinger-Ellison syndrome.*

gastritis (găs-trī′tĭs) [″ + ″] Acute or chronic inflammation of the lining of the stomach. Worldwide, the most common cause is infection with *Helicobacter py-lori.* Other relatively common causes of gastric inflammation include use of alcohol and tobacco products and injury to the lining of the stomach by nonsteroidal anti-inflammatory drugs (NSAIDs). Autoimmune diseases (e.g., pernicious anemia); duodenal reflux; and gastric ischemia are sometimes responsible. Acute gastritis may develop in hospitalized patients (e.g., those with major traumatic injuries, burns, severe infections, organ failure, or major surgery). SYN: *endogastritis.* SEE: *Helicobacter pylori.*

SYMPTOMS: The inflammation may be asymptomatic or evidenced only by mild upper abdominal discomfort (typically "burning"), or it may present with epigastric pain, nausea, vomiting, and hematemesis.

TREATMENT: When *H. pylori* is responsible, antibiotics and a potent acid-suppressing agent cure most patients. Abstaining from alcohol, tobacco, and NSAIDs improves gastritis caused by these agents. Antacids, an H2 blocking drug (e.g., famotidine), or proton pump inhibitors (e.g., esomeprazole) are also given to promote healing.

PATIENT CARE: If the patient requires hospitalization, general patient care concerns apply. If bleeding occurs, the patient is monitored for anemia, and appropriate treatment is instituted. In severe hemorrhage blood transfusion, vasopressin infusion, and (less frequently) surgery may be required. The patient is educated about the disorder. Compliance with multidrug antibiotic regimens is encouraged when the patient is found to have gastritis caused by *H. pylori.* If gastritis is caused by smoking, alcohol, or NSAIDs, abstinence from these substances is encouraged. Patients are advised that, if they are unable to take foods or liquids by mouth or begin to vomit blood, they should seek medical attention promptly.

acute g. Acute, sudden irritation of the gastric mucosa. It may be caused by ingestion of toxic substances such as alcohol or poisons or overuse of NSAIDs. Symptoms include anorexia, nausea, epigastric pain, vomiting, thirst, and, whenever patients become dehydrated, prostration. Therapy includes antacids, H_2 receptor blockers, or proton pump inhibitors (all of which reduce gastric acidity). Antibiotics treat bacterial and endotoxic infections. SEE: *Nursing Diagnoses Appendix.*

PATIENT CARE: A thorough patient history is conducted to assist in determining the cause. Vital signs, fluid intake and output, appearance, and gastric symptoms are monitored. Symptomatic and supportive therapy is given as prescribed (e.g., antiemetics, IV fluids). Prescribed histamine antagonists and proton pump inhibitors such as pantoprazole are administered, and the patient is instructed in their use. Antibiotic therapy for *Helicobacter pylori* is also discussed if appropriate. The patient is advised to avoid aspirin-containing over-the-counter (OTC) compounds and other NSAIDs. Antiemetics and analgesics may be provided before meals to manage associated nausea and pain. The patient is assisted to identify foods that contribute to symptoms and to eliminate them from the diet. The nurse can provide an initial diet that is bland and contains frequent small servings; referral to a dietitian enables further instruction. Emotional support is given to help the patient manage symptoms and to deal with lifestyle changes (e.g., stress reduction, smoking cessation, alcohol elimination) that may be required.

atrophic g. Chronic gastritis with atrophied mucosa and glands. The most common causes are autoimmune destruction of gastric glandular cells (a cause of pernicious anemia) or infection of the upper gastrointestinal tract with *H. pylori*.

chronic g. Prolonged continual or intermittent inflammation of the gastric mucosa. *H. pylori* is the most common cause. It typically produces superficial changes in the lining of the antrum of the stomach and is often also associated with peptic ulcers. Prolonged *H. pylori*-induced gastritis disposes patients to gastric adenocarcinoma and gastric lymphoma. SEE: *Helicobacter pylori; Nursing Diagnoses Appendix.*

PATIENT CARE: *H. pylori* infections are diagnosed and treated. Other common causes include pernicious anemia. A careful history helps determine the cause. Symptoms may be vague or, in the case of atrophic gastritis, absent. The patient is prepared for diagnostic testing. He or she is instructed to avoid spicy foods and other foods noted to exacerbate symptoms and is also warned to avoid aspirin. If symptoms persist, the patient may take antacids. When pernicious anemia is the underlying cause, the patient (or significant other who provides care) is taught to administer vitamin B$_{12}$ parenterally or orally.

giant hypertrophic g. Gastritis in which the mucosal folds of the stomach become abnormally thick. It is sometimes a precursor to gastric malignancy. SYN: *Ménétrier's disease.*

gastro-, gastr-, gastri- [Gr. *gastēr*, stem *gastr-*, stomach] Prefixes meaning *stomach* or *ventral.*

gastrocnemius (găs″trŏk-nē′mē-ŭs) [″ + *kneme,* leg] The large muscle of the posterior portion of the lower leg. It is the most superficial of the calf muscles. It plantar flexes the foot and flexes the knee.

gastrocolic (găs″trō-kŏl′ĭk) [″ + *kolon,* colon] Pert. to the stomach and colon.

gastrocutaneous (găs″trō-kū-tā′nē-ŭs) [″ + L. *cutis,* skin] A communication between the stomach and the skin.

gastroduodenal (găs″trō-dū″ō-dēn′ăl) [Gr. *gaster,* stomach, + L. *duodeni,* twelve] Rel. to the stomach and duodenum.

gastroduodenitis (găs″trō-dū-ŏd″ĕn-ī′tĭs) [″ + ″ + Gr. *itis,* inflammation] Inflammation of the stomach and duodenum.

gastroduodenoscopy (găs″trō-dū″ō-dĕnŏs′kă-pē) [″ + ″ + ″] The visual examination of the stomach and duodenum.

gastroduodenostomy (găs″trō-dū″ō-dĕnŏs′tă-mē) [″ + ″ + Gr. *stoma,* mouth] **1.** Excision of the pylorus of the stomach with anastomosis of the upper portion of the stomach to the duodenum. **2.** Any other opening formed between the stomach and the duodenum.

gastroenteric (găs″trō-ĕn-tĕr′ĭk) Pert. to the stomach and intestines or to a condition involving both.

gastroenteritis (gas″trō-ent-ĕ-rīt′ĭs) [*gastro-* + *entero-* + *-itis*] Inflammation of the stomach and intestinal tract that causes vomiting, diarrhea, or both. The most common causes are viruses (such as rotavirus) and bacteria (such as *Salmonella*) in food and water. SEE: *diarrhea; enterocolitis; Nursing Diagnoses Appendix.*

SYMPTOMS: The patient typically suffers episodes of vomiting and diarrhea and may develop symptoms of dehydration (such as thirst and dizziness when standing up), as well as malaise, abdominal cramps, or fever.

TREATMENT: Rehydration, usually with liquids taken by mouth, is the key to avoiding dehydration or electrolyte imbalance. Symptomatic remedies that reduce the frequency or volume of diarrhea (such as kaolin/pectin or loperamide) often are helpful.

PREVENTION: Prevention is emphasized by teaching children and adults correct handwashing techniques, water purification methods, and proper care of food. The basic principles of food handling should be taught to all those in the home, including the following topics: the need to wash hands frequently, particularly after using the toilet; use of a meat thermometer to check that meat and dishes containing eggs are adequately cooked; refrigeration of foods (below 40°F) until just before cooking and again within 1 hr after cooking, esp. in warm weather; separation of raw and cooked foods; and use of different utensils and dishes for raw and cooked meats. Travelers, esp. to developing countries, should not eat raw seafood, raw vegetables, or salads and should peel all fruit themselves. Campers should determine if they are in a location where streams are known to be contaminated with protozoa, e.g., New Hampshire, upstate New York, and Oregon.

viral g. Gastroenteritis caused by ingested viruses. The median incubation period is 24 to 48 hr and the median duration of the symptoms is 12 to 60 hr. Most patients will experience diarrhea, nausea, abdominal cramps, and vomiting and many become dehydrated. There is no specific treatment other than supportive therapy and fluid replacement.

ETIOLOGY: The rotavirus, which causes more than 100 million cases and approx. 1 million deaths each year worldwide, most frequently strikes children 6 to 24 months of age, causing 3 to 8 days of diarrhea and vomiting. The Norwalk virus causes most foodborne infections in older children and adults and may cause epidemics in schools and institutions. Diarrhea, accompanied by vomiting and abdominal pain, lasts 1 to 3 days.

PATIENT CARE: Adequate fluid and electrolyte replacement through oral rehydration therapy (ORT) solutions or, when severe, intravenous fluids are the basis for treatment. Prevention is emphasized by teaching children and adults correct handwashing techniques and proper care of food.

PATIENT CARE: Because rotavirus is more prevalent in children under age 2, parents, day care personnel, and other caregivers require teaching about methods to prevent the spread of infection (which is primarily fecal-oral transmission). Caregivers also must learn proper handling and disposal of diapers. They must understand that, while the illness usually is mild and self-limited (seldom lasting more than 3 days), infected children are at risk for dehydration. Caregivers are taught early indicators of dehydration that necessitate bringing the child to a physician or pediatric nurse practitioner; hospitalization may be required in severe cases.

If the child is hospitalized, he or she is isolated from children without diarrhea, and parents are taught necessary isolation procedures. Intravenous (IV) fluids are administered as prescribed for rehydration; fluid and electrolyte balance, body weight, and other indicators are monitored throughout. If the child is able to ingest oral fluids, an oral rehydration formula is used, with fluids given at room temperature for better tolerance. Age-appropriate foods are reintroduced gradually, once liquids are well tolerated. Protective mouth and skin care to relieve dryness and prevent breakdown is provided and taught to caregivers. Comfort measures are an important part of the child's care, including age-appropriate sensory stimulation and diversion. Additionally, the family requires support and reassurance, with explanations of therapeutic measures and diet. Good hygiene and sanitary measures are emphasized.

In older children or adults, antidiarrheal agents may be used, although antiemetics should be avoided. The patient is encouraged to rest, which relieves symptoms and conserves strength, and to avoid sudden movements, which can increase the severity of nausea. Warm sitz baths, witch hazel compresses, and petroleum jelly as a barrier may help to ease anal irritation. The patient is taught about prescribed treatments, preventive measures, and careful handwashing. Worldwide, waterborne gastroenteritis is a leading cause of death in at-risk populations. Children, the elderly, and the debilitated are at greater risk for death because of their intolerance to fluid and electrolyte losses. Developing and safeguarding community water supplies, providing information on water testing protocols and interpretation, and encouraging use of point-of-use water purification systems are important public health education issues.

gastroenteroanastomosis (găs″trō-ĕn″tĕr-ō-ă-năs″tō-mō′sĭs) The formation of a passage between the stomach and small intestine.

gastroenterocolitis (găs″trō-ĕn″tĕr-ō-kŏl-ī′tĭs) [″ + ″ + *kolon,* colon, + *itis,* inflammation] Inflammation of the stomach, small intestine, and colon.

gastroenterology (găs″trō-ĕn″tĕr-ŏl′ă-jē) [″ + ″ + ″] The branch of medical science concerned with the study of the anatomy, physiology, and diseases of the digestive organs and their treatment. The digestive organs include the stomach, intestines, and related structures (e.g., esophagus, liver, gallbladder, and pancreas).

gastroenterostomy (găs″trō-ĕn-tĕr-ŏs′tō-mē) [″ + *enteron,* intestine, + *stoma,* mouth] Surgical anastomosis between the stomach and small bowel. This operation may be employed for a variety of malignant and benign gastroduodenal diseases.

gastroepiploic (găs″trō-ĕp″ĭ-plō′ĭk) [″ + *epiploon,* omentum] Pert. to the stomach and greater omentum.

gastroesophageal (găs″trō-ĕ-sŏf″ă-jē′ăl) [″ + *oisophagos,* esophagus] Concerning the stomach and esophagus.

gastroesophageal reflux disease ABBR: GERD. A common condition in which acid from the stomach (gastric and/or duodenal) flows back into the esophagus, causing discomfort and, in some instances, damage to the esophageal lining. The condition is thought to affect nearly half of all adults at least once a month.

ETIOLOGY: GERD occurs when the lower esophageal sphincter (LES) fails to keep gastric acid out of the esophagus. Predisposing factors include use of any agent that reduces LES pressure, hiatal hernia with incompetent sphincter, any condition that raises intra-abdominal pressure, history of nasogastric intubation lasting more than 4 days, or pyloric surgery.

SYMPTOMS: Common symptoms include heartburn, indigestion, and noncardiac chest pain (which may mimic angina pectoris by radiating to the neck, jaw, and/or arms). Patients occasionally experience asthma, cough, hoarseness, difficulty in swallowing, or nocturnal regurgitation. Patients are taught to avoid factors that decrease LES, cause esophageal irritation, or increase intra-abdominal pressure.

PATIENT CARE: Patients should avoid eating meals late in the evening or for several hours before lying down. Elevating the head of the bed 6 to 8 in (15 to 20 cm) on blocks may help in some cases. All affected patients should avoid food and beverages that worsen reflux, including alcohol, caffeine, chocolate, mints, and fatty and spicy foods. Patients should sit upright while eating rather than reclining and eat small, frequent meals. Tight clothing, bending, coughing, vigorous exercise, and straining should be avoided after eating. Smokers should be encouraged to quit. Many patients benefit from antacids (taken 1 hr before or 3 hr after meals and at bedtime) or over-the-counter histamine-2-receptor antagonists, e.g., ranitidine. Patients who do not respond to these therapies are usually treated with proton pump inhibitors to reduce gastric acidity. Relatively uncommon but worrying conditions caused by GERD include Barrett's esophagus and esophageal cancer. When patients do not respond to empirical treatment, they should undergo endoscopy after being educated about the procedure, its objectives, techniques, and potential complications.

gastrogastrostomy (găs″trō-găs-trŏs′tō-mē) [″ + *gaster,* stomach, + *stoma,* mouth] Surgical anastomosis between one portion of the stomach and another.

gastrogavage (găs″trō-gă-văzh′) [″ + Fr. *gavage,* cramming] Artificial feeding through an opening into the stomach or a tube passed into the stomach.

gastrogenic (găs″trō-jĕn′ĭk) [″ + *gennan,* to produce] Originating in the stomach.

gastrografin, gastrographin (gas″trō-graf′ĭn) A liquid radiologic contrast medium that absorbs x-rays because of its iodine content. It can be administered orally or rectally to highlight the internal structure of the gastrointestinal tract.

gastrohepatic (găs″trō-hĕ-păt′ĭk) Pert. to the stomach and liver.

gastroileostomy (gas″trō-il″ē-os′tŏ-mē) [*gastro-* + *ileostomy*] A surgical anastomosis between the stomach and ileum performed only by surgical error unless the jejunum is surgically unavailable.

gastrointestinal (găs″trō-ĭn-tĕs′tĭn-ăl) [″ + L. *intestinalis,* intestine] Pertaining to the entire digestive tract, from the mouth to the anus.

gastrointestinal decompression The removal of contents of the intestinal tract by use of suction through a tube inserted into the upper gastrointestinal tract. The tube may be inserted through the nasopharynx or oropharynx, or via gastrostomy. SEE: *Salem sump tube; Levin tube.* SEE: *Wangensteen tube.*

gastrojejunostomy (găs-trō-jĕ-jū-nŏs′tō-mē) [″ + L. *jejunum,* empty, + Gr. *stoma,* mouth] A connection, usually constructed surgically, between the stomach and the jejunum.

gastrology (găs-trŏl′ō-jē) [″ + *logos,* word, reason] The study of function and diseases of the stomach.

gastroparesis (găs″trō-pă-rē′sĭs) Delayed emptying of food from the stomach into the small bowel. Gastroparesis occurs acutely in patients receiving parenteral nutrition. It may also be a chronic complication of diseases marked by autonomic failure, such as diabetes mellitus, chronic renal failure, and amyloidosis. It may occur during pregnancy, as a result of elevated levels of progesterone.

gastropathy (găs-trŏp′ă-thē) [″ + *pathos,* disease, suffering] Any disorder of the stomach.

   hypertrophic g. An uncommon disorder marked by protein loss from the upper gastrointestinal tract and enlarged gastric rugal folds.

gastropexy, gastropexis (găs′trō-pĕk″sē, -sĭs) [″ + *pexis,* fixation] Suturing of the stomach to the abdominal walls for correction of displacement.

gastroplasty (găs′trō-plăs″tē) [″ + *plassein,* to form] Plastic surgery of the stomach. This procedure has been used in several ways to decrease the size of the stomach to treat morbid obesity; its success is variable.

gastroplication (gas″trō-plĭ-kā′shŏn) [*gastro-* + *plication*] Stitching of the walls of the stomach to treat gastroesophageal reflux.

gastroptosis (găs″trŏp-tō′sĭs) [″ + ″] Downward displacement of the stomach, a condition that rarely causes symptoms or illness.

gastropulmonary (găs″trō-pŭl′mō-năr-ē)

[" + L. *pulmo,* lung] Concerning the stomach and lungs.

gastropyloric (găs″trō-pī-lor′ĭk) Rel. to the stomach and pylorus.

gastroschisis (găs-trŏs′kĭ-sĭs) [" + *schisis,* a splitting] A congenital fissure that remains open in the wall of the abdomen.

gastroscope (gas′trŏ-skōp″) [*gastro-* + *-scope*] A rigid endoscope for inspecting the interior of the stomach. This instrument has been replaced by flexible, fiber-optic endoscopes.

gastroscopy (gas-tros′kŏ-pē) [*gastro-* + *-scopy*] Examination of the upper gastrointestinal tract with a gastroscope. It is usually performed with a flexible scope as an esophagogastroduodenoscopy (EGD).

gastrosplenic (găs″trō-splĕn′ĭk) [" + *splen,* spleen] Of or pert. to the stomach and spleen.

gastrostomy (găs-trŏs′tō-mē) Surgical creation of a gastric fistula through the abdominal wall, used, e.g., for introducing food into the stomach. SEE: illus.

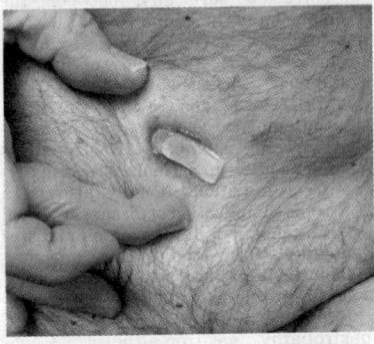

GASTROSTOMY BUTTON

PATIENT CARE: The skin around the tube is inspected for signs of irritation or excoriation and kept clean, dry, and protected from excoriating gastric secretions. Tension on the tube that may cause the incision to widen and allow spillage of gastric secretions on the skin or into surrounding tissues is prevented.

Before the patient is fed, tube patency and position are assessed, and the volume of the remaining stomach contents is measured by aspirating the stomach. If the volume is greater than the amount permitted by protocol or the physician's direction, feeding is withheld. The patient should be placed in high Fowler's position during feedings, and the blenderized food or formula administered slowly by gravity in the prescribed amount (200 to 500 ml). Encouraging the patient to chew prior to enteral feeding promotes gastric secretions to aid digestion. After feedings and after introduction of medications, the tube is flushed with an adequate amount of water (at least 60 ml). Fluid intake and output (which includes aspirated feeding) should be monitored and recorded.

Assistance is provided with oral hygiene at intervals throughout the day to prevent dryness and parotitis. Both patient and family are taught correct techniques for tube and skin care and for feeding through the gastrostomy tube, for keeping track of intake and output, and concerns to be reported to the primary care provider.

   percutaneous endoscopic g. ABBR: PEG. A feeding ostomy. PEG tubes are inserted transorally into the stomach with the aid of an endoscope and then pulled through a stab wound made in the abdominal wall.

gastrostomy tube A tube placed directly into the stomach for long-term enteral feeding or gastric decompression. This may be done laparoscopically, surgically, or by percutaneous endoscopic gastrostomy tube technique.

gastrotomy (gas-trot′ŏ-mē) [*gastro-* + *-tomy*] An incision into the stomach.

gastrula (găs′troo-lă) [L., little belly] The stage in embryonic development following the blastula in which the embryo assumes a two-layered condition. The outer layer is the ectoderm or epiblast; the inner layer, the endoderm or hypoblast. The latter lines a cavity, the gastrocoele or archenteron, that opens to the outside through an opening, the blastopore.

gastrulation (găs″troo-lā′shŭn) The development of the gastrula in the embryo.

gated blood pool study Gated blood pool imaging.

gatekeeper (gāt′kē″pĕr) A person who decides whether further medical assistance or care should be sought or allowed.

gatekeeping (gāt′kē″pĭng) In medical care, deciding the allocation, limitation, or rationing of services. Decisions are based on a variety of factors including need; cost; the potential for success of the proposed therapy; and the availability of facilities, staff, and equipment. SEE: *triage.*

gate theory SEE: under *theory.*

gating (gāt′ĭng) In radiology, a procedure used to reduce image artifacts caused by involuntary motion.

   cardiac g. Medical image information consistently collected during a specific phase of the cardiac cycle.

   respiratory g. Medical image information consistently collected during a specific phase of respiration. It is used in radiation oncology to minimize the exposure of tissues around a tumor to radiation, while maximizing the dosage given directly to the tumor.

Gaucher, Philippe C. E. (gō-shā') Fr. physician, 1854–1918.

   G. cell A large reticuloendothelial cell seen in Gaucher disease, which contains a small, eccentrically placed nucleus and kerasin.

   G. disease Any of several autosomal recessive disorders of lipid metabolism caused by a deficiency of the enzyme beta-glucocerebrosidase,in which glycosphingolipids accumulate in the reticuloendothelial cells. The severe form is rare, but milder forms frequently occur, esp. in those of Jewish descent. SYN: *cerebroside lipoidosis.*

   Three clinical subtypes of the disease exist. Type 1, comprising 99% of cases, is associated with an enlarged liver and spleen, increased skin pigmentation, and painful bone marrow lesions. Enzyme replacement therapy is effective in this type but may be prohibitively expensive. Type 2 is characterized by neurological symptoms including oculomotor apraxia, strabismus, and hypertonicity. These symptoms usually occur in the first year of life, with death following by age 18 months. Therapy is symptomatic. Type 3 is similar to type 2, but the onset of symptoms is much later and the course is longer. Therapy is symptomatic.

gauge, gage (gāj) **1.** A device for measuring the size, capacity, amount, or power of an object or substance. **2.** A standard of measurement, e.g., of the diameter of a wire. **3.** To judge or estimate a condition.

gauntlet (gawnt'lĕt) [Fr. *gant*, glove] A glovelike bandage that fits the hand and fingers.

gauss (gows) [Johann Carl Friedrich Gauss, Ger. mathematician and physical scientist, 1777–1855] The unit of intensity of a magnetic field (B). One gauss is one maxwell cm^2, equal to 1×10^{-4} tesla.

gauze (gawz) [O.Fr. *gaze*, gauze] Thin, loosely woven muslin or similar material used for bandages and surgical sponges.

   antiseptic g. Gauze containing any chemical that kills or retards the growth of microorganisms.

   aseptic g. Sterilized **g.**

   petrolatum g. Sterilized absorbent gauze saturated with petrolatum. It is used to cover wounds without adhering to them.

gavage (gă-väzh') [Fr. *gaver*, to stuff] Feeding a patient via a tube passed through the nostrils, oropharynx, and esophagus into the stomach or duodenum. The food is typically infused in liquid or semiliquid form at room temperature.

G$_{AW}$ *Airway conductance.*

gay Homosexual.

gay bowel syndrome Infectious diarrhea, condyloma acuminatum, hemorrhoids, anal fissures, and/or sexually transmitted proctitis in men who have receptive anal intercourse, esp. those infected with HIV.

gaze (gāz) **1.** To look or stare intently in one direction. **2.** The act of looking or staring intently in one direction.

   conjugate g. The paired movements of the eyes as they track moving objects.

   disconjugate g. Unpaired movements of the eyes. SEE: *ophthalmoplegia.*

   ETIOLOGY: Uncoupling of eye movements may occur in many diseases and conditions, including injuries to the oculomotor nerves; fractures of the orbit; strokes affecting the brainstem, frontal lobes, or cerebrum; multiple sclerosis; some nutritional deficiencies (e.g., Wernicke-Korsakoff's syndrome); and Bell's palsy.

GB *gallbladder.*

GBS *group B streptococci.*

GCS *Glasgow Coma Scale.*

Gd Symbol for the element gadolinium.

Gd-DTPA *Gadolinium-diethylenetriamine pentaacetic **acid**.*

Ge Symbol for the element germanium.

gegenhalten (gā"gĕn-hălt'ĕn) [Ger.] In cerebrocortical disease, involuntary resistance to passive movement.

Geiger counter (gī'gĕr) [Hans Geiger, Ger. physicist in England, 1882–1945] An instrument for detecting ionizing radiation.

gel (jel) [Abbr. of *gel(atin)*] A semisolid precipitated or coagulated colloid; a jelly-like colloid; jelly. It contains a large amount of water.

   conductive g. A gel applied to the body to reduce its impedance, thereby facilitating the delivery of an electric shock.

   coupling g. A thin colloidal suspension placed on the patient's skin, used as a conductive medium for the sound waves generated by an ultrasonic transducer.

gelate (jĕl'āt) To cause formation of a gel.

gelatin (jĕl'ă-tĭn) [L. *gelatina*, gelatin] **1.** A derived protein obtained by the hydrolysis of collagen present in the connective tissues of the skin, bones, and joints of animals. It is used as a food, in the preparation of pharmaceuticals, and as a medium for culture of bacteria. It is unusual as an animal protein in that it is not a good source of essential amino acids. **2.** The substance on an x-ray film in which the silver halide crystals are suspended in the radiographic emulsion.

   nutrient g. A bacterial culture medium composed of broth and gelatin.

gelatinase (jĕl'ă-tĭn-ās) ABBR: MMP-2;

MMP-9. Metalloproteinases that cleave gelatin, or nondenatured collagen. Two forms of gelatinase, A and B, have been identified. Gelatinase A (MMP-2) has a molecular weight of about 72,000, and gelatinase B (MMP-9) has a molecular weight of about 92,000. Both are involved in cancer angiogenesis and metastasis and are blocked by a variety of naturally occurring and synthetic inhibitors.

gelatinize (jĕl-ăt′ĭn-īz) [L. *gelatina*, gelatin] To convert into gelatin.

gelatinous (jĕl-ăt′ĭn-ŭs) Containing or of the consistency of gelatin.

gelation (jĕl-ā′shŭn) The transformation of a colloid from a sol into a gel.

gelling (jĕl′ĭng) In arthritis, becoming stiff and fixed in any position in which movement does not occur for a prolonged period.

gelose (jĕ′lōs) [L. *gelare*, to congeal] **1.** The gelatinous component of agar $(C_6H_{10}O_5)_n$. **2.** A bacterial culture medium.

Gemella morbillorum (jĕ-mĕl′ă mŏr-bĭ-lŏr′ŭm) [NL] A gram-positive coccus formerly classified in the genus *Streptococcus;* it is a cause of septic arthritis, endocarditis, oral abscesses, and peritonitis.

gemellus (jĕm-ĕl′ŭs) *pl.* **gemelli** [L., twin] Either of two muscles inserted in the obturator internus tendon.

geminate (jĕm′ĭ-nāt) [L. *geminatus,* paired] In pairs.

gemination (jĕm-ĭ-nā′shŭn) **1.** The development of two teeth or two crowns within a single root. **2.** A doubling.

gemma (jĕm′mă) [L., bud] **1.** A small budlike reproductive structure produced by some invertebrates. **2.** Any small budlike structure such as a taste bud or endbulb. SYN: *gemmule* (1).

gemmation (jĕm-mā′shŭn) [L. *gemmare*, to bud] Cell reproduction by budding. Budlike processes or daughter cells, each containing chromatin, separate from the mother cell from which the bud is projected.

gemmule (jĕm′ŭl) [L. *gemmula*, little bud] **1.** Gemma (2). **2.** One of numerous minute processes present on the dendrites of a neuron.

gen-, geno- [Gr. *genos*, kind, race, descent] Prefixes meaning *gene, generation* or *sex, race* or *ethnicity, genus* or *kind.*

-gen, -gene [Fr. *-gène* fr. Gr. *-genēs,* born] Suffixes meaning *producer,* e.g., *androgen,* or *produced,* e.g., *hydrogen.*

gena (jē′nă) [L.] The side of the face; the cheek.

gender [L. *genus,* kind] The sex of an individual (i.e., male or female).

gender-based (jen′dĕr-bāst′) Pert. to individuals of only one sex, i.e., only to women or only to men, but not to both.

gender identification Assignment of gender to a newborn. Genetic or chromosomal anomalies may create ambiguous genitalia, as may exposure of a female fetus to an androgenic hormone, or inhibition of androgen production or metabolism in a male fetus. In such cases, it is important to delay the final disposition until the chromosomal studies and endocrinological evaluation have been completed. These studies should be done as soon as possible. SEE: *gender identity.*

gender identity One's self-concept with respect to being male or female; a person's sense of his or her true sexual identity.

gender identity disorder A disorder marked by a strong cross-gender identification and a persistent discomfort with one's biologically assigned sex. Generally, adults with the disorder are preoccupied with the wish to live as a member of the other sex. This often impairs social, occupational, or other types of functioning. SEE: *Nursing Diagnoses Appendix.*

gene (jēn) [Ger. *Gen,* ult. fr Gr. *genos,* kind, race, descent] The basic unit of heredity, made of DNA, the code for a specific protein. Each gene occupies a certain location on a chromosome. Genes are self-replicating sequences of DNA nucleotides, subject to random structural changes (mutations). Hereditary traits are controlled by pairs of genes in the same position on a pair of chromosomes. These alleles may be either dominant or recessive. When both pairs of an allele are either dominant or recessive, the individual is said to be homozygous for the traits coded by the gene. If the alleles differ (one dominant and one recessive), the individual is heterozygous. SEE: illus.; *chromosome; DNA; RNA.*

    autosomal dominant g. A dominant

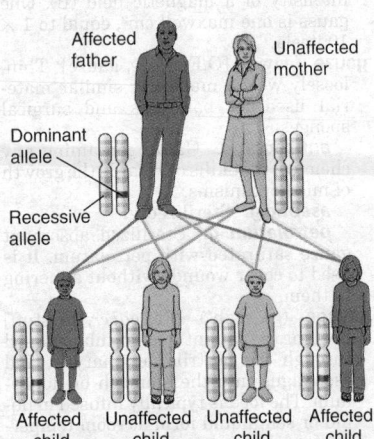

Affected father — Unaffected mother

Dominant allele

Recessive allele

Affected child — Unaffected child — Unaffected child — Affected child

AUTOSOMAL DOMINANT INHERITANCE

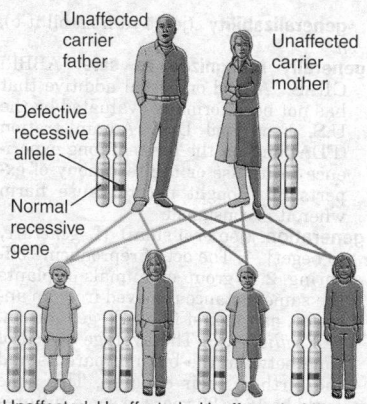

Unaffected carrier father

Unaffected carrier mother

Defective recessive allele

Normal recessive gene

Unaffected child   Unaffected carrier child   Unaffected carrier child   Affected child

AUTOSOMAL RECESSIVE INHERITANCE

gene that is found on any chromosome other than the X or Y chromosome.

autosomal recessive g. A recessive gene that is found on any chromosome other than the X or Y chromosome.

BRCA1 g. A breast cancer gene found in a small percentage of patients with this malignancy, and carried by some individuals who will develop breast cancer later in life.

PATIENT CARE: **BRCA1 Gene Mutation**: Patient care focuses on determining the family history of the patient and referral to a genetic counselor with expertise in this mutation when appropriate.

BRCA2 g. A breast cancer gene found in a small number of patients with breast and ovarian cancers, and carried by some individuals who will develop breast cancer later in life.

complementary g. Nonallelic, independently located genes, neither of which will be expressed in the absence of the other.

cystic fibrosis transmembrane conductance regulator g. The gene that codes for a protein that regulates the movement of ions, esp. chloride, across cell membranes.

dominant g. SEE: *dominant*.

histocompatibility g. One of the genes composing the HLA complex that determines the histocompatibility antigenic markers on all nucleated cells. These genes create the antigens by which the immune system recognizes "self" and determines the "nonself" nature of pathogens and other foreign antigens. These antigens are crucial determinants of the success or failure of organ transplantation. SEE: *histocompatibility locus antigen*.

homeobox g. Any transcription factor that regulates the growth, differentiation, replication, and movement of cells in the body. These genes influence both normal and abnormal embyological development and the development or suppression of malignant tumors.

housekeeping g. A gene expressed in nearly every cell and every tissue of an organism, i.e., one that encodes a protein fundamental to cellular activity throughout the organism.

immune response g. One of the many genes that control the ability of leukocytes to respond to specific antigens. SEE: *antigen; B cell; HLA complex; T cell*.

inhibiting g. A gene that prevents the expression of another gene.

lethal g. A gene that creates a condition incompatible with life and usually results in the death of the fetus.

modifying g. A gene that influences or alters the expression of other genes.

mutant g. An altered gene that permanently functions differently than it did before its alteration.

operator g. A gene that controls the expression of other genes. SEE: *operon*.

g. p53 A gene thought to be important in controlling the cell cycle, DNA repair and synthesis, and programmed cell death (apoptosis). Mutations of p53 have occurred in almost half of all types of cancer, arising from a variety of tissues. Mutant types may promote cancer. The normal, wild-type gene produces a protein important in tumor suppression.

pleiotropic g. A gene that has multiple effects.

posttranscriptional g. silencing RNA interference.

presenilin g. Rare traits responsible for early-onset Alzheimer's disease.

RB g. Tumor suppressor gene encoding for the retinoblastoma (RB) protein, mutations of which are associated with various human tumors, including retinoblastoma, osteosarcoma, some leukemias, and some adenocarcinomas. SEE: *tumor suppressor g.; retinoblastoma*.

recessive g. A trait that is not expressed unless it is present in the genes received from both parents. A recessive trait may be apparent in the phenotype only if both alleles are recessive. SYN: *recessive characteristic*.

regulator g. A gene that can control some specific activity of another gene.

sex-linked g. Sex-linked characteristic.

structural g. A gene that determines the structure of polypeptide chains by controlling the sequence of amino acids.

susceptibility g. A gene that increases a person's likelihood of contracting a heritable illness.

tumor suppressor g. A gene that suppresses the growth of malignant cells. SEE: *cancer*.

X-linked g. A gene on the X chromosome for which there is no corresponding gene on the Y chromosome. X-linked genes (e.g., the gene for red-green color blindness) are expressed but in males even these genes are recessive because there is no correponding gene to dominate them.

genealogy The study of the ancestry of an individual or group. Such investigations are particularly important in tracing the inheritance of genetically transmitted conditions or traits. One of the most important collections of genealogical information is in the archives of the Church of Jesus Christ of Latter Day Saints (i.e., the Mormon Church) in Salt Lake City, Utah.

gene amplification The duplication of regions of DNA to form multiple copies of a specific portion of the original region. This method of gene enhancement is important in increasing a tumor cell's resistance to cytotoxic drugs, and in allowing multiple drug resistance to a wide range of unrelated drugs after resistance to a single agent has developed.

gene chip Microarray.

gene expression The process by which genetic information from the DNA is carried to the RNA and translated into proteins.

gene family A group of genes that codes for related proteins.

gene flow The movement of genes from one group of organisms to another.

gene gun A device used to inject DNA into cells, membrane-bound organelles, or tissues.

gene knockout SEE: *knockout.*

gene mapping SEE: under *mapping.*

gene probe The technique of matching a short segment of DNA or RNA with the matching sequence of bases on a chromosome. Use of this method permits identification of the precise area on a chromosome responsible for the genetic abnormality being investigated. SEE: *gene splicing.*

genera (jĕn'ĕr-ă) Pl. of genus.

generalization (jen"ĕ-răl-ĭ-zā'shŏn) **1.** An act, process, or instance of generalizing. **2.** The principle or general idea resulting from that act or process. **3.** The progression of a seizure from one with focal motor, psychic, or sensory characteristics, to one in which there is complete loss of consciousness with tonic-clonic motor activity. **4.** The ability to apply a skill or strategy to a task in an environment that differs from the one in which the task was learned. **5.** In research, the ability to project results of a study to a larger percentage of a similar population. SEE: *intelligence.*

generalize (jen'ĕ-ră-līz") [L. *generalis*] **1.** To become or render nonspecific. **2.** To become systemic, as a local disease.

generalizable (jen"ĕ-ră-lī'ză-bl), *adj.*

generalizability (jen"ĕ-ră-lī"ză-bil'ĭt-ē), *n.*

generally recognized as safe ABBR: GRAS. A food or herbal additive that has not been formally evaluated by the U.S. Food and Drug Administration (FDA) but, on the basis of long experience in its use or the testimony of experts, is thought not to cause harm when it is consumed.

generation (jĕn"ĕr-ā'shŭn) [L. *generare,* to beget] **1.** The act of reproducing offspring. **2.** A group of animals or plants the same distance removed from an ancestor, as the first filial (F_1) generation. SEE: *filial g.* **3.** The average period of time between the birth of parents and the birth of their children. This time could be 16 to 20 years in some cultures and 20 to 25 years in others. The time would also be different if only mothers were considered in computing this average, unless all marriages occurred between persons of the same age. **4.** The production of an electric current.

alternation of g. Reproduction in which a sexual generation alternates with an asexual generation, characteristic of some fungi and protozoa.

asexual g. Asexual reproduction.

filial g. SYMB: F. In genetics, the first offspring of a specific mating or crossmating. This is abbreviated F_1. Descendants resulting from F_1 matings are known as the F_2, or second, filial generation.

parental g. In genetics, the generation that precedes the first filial generation.

sexual g. Sexual reproduction.

generative (jĕn'ĕr-ă-tĭv) Concerned with reproduction of, or affecting, the species.

generator (gĕn'ĕr-ā"tor) That which produces something, esp. a device that produces heat, electricity, or impulses.

aerosol g. A device that produces minute particles suspended in air from liquid materials such as medicines in solution. These particles may be used in inhalation therapy.

electric g. A device that changes mechanical energy into electrical energy.

flow g. A pneumatic engine that powers life-support equipment and uses a gauge of 5 to 50 lb/sq in to supply gas to a ventilator circuit, allowing for a constant flow pattern.

pressure g. A pneumatic engine that powers a life-support ventilator and incorporates a proportional meter, a motor-driven piston, or a blower. Pressure generators can adjust flow according to the patient's condition.

pulse g. A device that produces intermittent electrical discharges (e.g., in a cardiac pacemaker).

generic (jĕ-ner'ik) [L. *genus,* stem, *gener-,* kind] **1.** Pert. to all the members of a type, kind, or group; general. **2.** In biology, pert. to a genus. **3.** In law, not protected by a patent registration or trademark; nonproprietary. In pharmaceuticals, for example, it applies to a drug that does not have a brand name and is not sold under one but is identified and sold only by its chemical name. Likewise, the word is applied to a food, cosmetic, or other product ordinarily sold under a brand name but now sold in a package without a brand name. SEE: *proprietary (3)* . **4.** A generic food, drug, cosmetic, or other product. In the U.S., a generic drug must be bioequivalent to its brand-name alternative. In 2010, nearly 80% of all drugs prescribed in the U.S. were generics. SEE: *nonproprietary name.*

genesis (jĕn′ĕ-sĭs) **1.** The act of reproducing; generation. **2.** The origin of anything.

gene splicing The insertion of a portion of a gene from one chromosome or one species into a gene from another. This allows the altered gene to function in a new context. Gene splicing can be used to alter the expression of gene products or to produce new proteins in cells. SEE: *recombinant DNA.*

gene testing Genetic testing.

gene therapy The treatment of genetic illnesses, metabolic diseases, cancers, and some infections by introducing nucleic acid sequences into the chromosomes of diseased cells. The goal of gene therapy is to modify the genetic instructions of the diseased cells, so that the cells will express a protein or enzyme that modifies or treats the disease.

   somatic g.t. An experimental method of cloning genes and reintroducing them into cells for the purpose of correcting inherited disease. As this form of therapy develops so do ethical questions concerning its use: what diseases should be treated, and whether an individual could be treated to enhance his or her normal condition (e.g., to become a stronger or faster athlete).

genetic (jĕn-ĕt′ĭk) **1.** Pert. to genetics. **2.** Pert. to reproduction.

genetically conserved Pert. to a pattern found in numerous species that are biologically related to one other because they share common DNA sequences.

genetic association SEE: under *association.*

genetic burden **1.** The number of diseases and deaths that occur as a result of inherited traits. **2.** The cost to the genome of mutations or selection pressure that eliminate alleles from it.

genetic counseling The education of patients and families about prenatal diagnosis of illnesses; diagnosis and management of children with birth defects or developmental delay; or diagnosis and management of adult-onset syndromes and their potential effects on disability, employment, health, and longevity.

genetic counselor A health care professional who specializes in the education and support of patients, families, or prospective parents about inherited diseases to which they or their offspring may be susceptible.

genetic discrimination SEE: under *discrimination.*

genetic engineering The synthesis, alteration, replacement, or repair of the genetic material of an organism.

genetic enhancement The use of genetics to improve selected characteristics or traits of an organism. It is a practice common in agriculture, e.g., in the engineering of supersweet corn or pesticide-resistant soybeans and is both welcomed and feared in human affairs.

   In general human enhancements differ from genetic therapies in that they concern the alteration of inherited traits that do not cause disease.

   Nongenetic enhancements are common in contemporary medical practice: many middle-aged people undergo surgery to reduce facial wrinkles or replace lost hair; men with erectile dysfunction use drugs to facilitate sexual intercourse; and some parents obtain human growth hormone to administer to their children in order to increase their children's height.

   Ethicists and the general public hold varying opinions on whether it is advisable or desirable to use genetic technology to enhance human qualities, e.g., the selection of the sex of their offspring, or the enhancement of their children's musculature, intelligence, or behavior. Some genetic enhancements may have dual functions: genetic alterations that treat muscular dystrophies might also be used to enhance the athletic abilities of healthy individuals. These intersections between health and cosmetics provoke the thorniest ethical questions: Should humans try to optimize selected characteristics of their species through genetics? Who will pay for such enhancements? Will they be available only to those with the wealth to purchase them? Will they be restricted in some nations because of religious or social concerns and available in others where these considerations are not shared? These and other problems remain to be addressed by ethicists, scientists, families, and society at large.

geneticist (jĕn-ĕt′ĭ-sĭst) [Gr. *gennan,* to produce] One who specializes in genetics.

genetic marker SEE: under *marker.*

genetics (jĕ-net′iks) The study of heredity and its variations.

   behavioral g. The study of the inherited basis for animal behavior and the impact that environment has on behavioral phenotypes. The field inquires into the influence of genes on addiction, aggression, intelligence, personality, sexuality, and sociability, among other realms of animal and human experience.

biochemical g. The study of the impact of genes on enzymes and the cellular reactions they catalyze.

clinical g. The study and use of genetics in health and disease.

molecular g. The study of the molecular structure of genes and their cellular and subcellular functions. SEE: *gene splicing*.

genetic screening Testing individuals or communities for the presence of specific genetic traits.

genetic signature A pattern of specific, detectable nucleic acids that identify a particular cell, tissue, disease, or malignancy.

genetic testing An assessment of a person's sex or somatic cells for evidence of specific genetic and chromosomal abnormalities and disease-causing genes. SYN: *gene testing*.

gene transfer SEE: under *transfer*.

Geneva Convention (jĕ-nē′vă) Regulations concerning the status of those wounded in military action on land, established in 1864 by military powers meeting in Geneva, Switzerland. The sick and wounded and all those involved in their care, including physicians, nurses, corpsmen, ambulance drivers, and chaplains, were declared to be neutral and, therefore, would not be the target of military action. These provisions were expanded in 1868 to include naval military action. Much evidence indicates that warring nations have not always abided by the provisions of the Convention.

genial (jē′nē-ăl) [Gr. *geneion*, chin] Pert. to the chin.

genic (jĕn′ĭk) [Gr. *gennan*, to produce] Relating to or caused by genes.

-genic [-*gen* + -*ic*] Suffix meaning *generation* or *production*.

genicular (jĕ-nĭk′ū-lăr) Concerning the knee.

geniculate (jĕ-nĭk′ū-lāt) [L. *geniculare*, to bend the knee] **1.** Bent, like a knee. **2.** Pert. to the ganglion or geniculum of the facial nerve.

geniculum (jĕn-ĭk′ū-lŭm) [L. *geniculum*, little knee] A structure resembling a knot or a knee, indicating an abrupt bend or angle in a small structure.

genioplasty (jē′nē-ō-plăs″tē) [″ + *plassein*, to form] Plastic surgery of the chin or cheek.

genistein (jĕ-nĭs′tēn, tē-ĭn) A soy isoflavone that has been found to inhibit the activity of enzymes involved in the control of cell proliferation. It is a phytoestrogen with weak estrogenic and antiestrogenic effects.

genital (jĕn′ĭ-tăl) [L. *genitalis,* belonging to birth] Pert. to the genitals.

genital cutting SEE: *female genital cutting*.

genitalia, genitals (jĕn-ĭ-tāl′ē-ă, jĕn′ĭ-tăls) Organs of generation; reproductive organs.

ambiguous g. External reproductive organs that are not easily identified as male or female.

female g. Reproductive organs of the female sex. The external genitalia collectively are termed the vulva or pudendum and include the mons veneris, labia majora, labia minora, clitoris, fourchet, fossa navicularis, vestibule, vestibular bulb, Skene's glands, glands of Bartholin, hymen and vaginal introitus, and perineum. The internal genitalia are the two ovaries, two fallopian tubes, uterus, and vagina. SEE: illus.

male g. Reproductive organs of the male sex, including two bulbourethral (Cowper's) glands, two ejaculatory ducts, two glands producing spermatozoa (the testes or gonads), the penis with urethra, two seminal ducts (vasa deferentes or ducti deferentes), two seminal vesicles, two spermatic cords, the scrotum, and the prostate gland. SEE: illus.; *penis; prostate*.

genital system Reproductive **system**.

genital ulcer disease Any sexually transmitted illness that manifests with eroded sores on the penis, vulva, scrotum, or other genital areas. The most common causes are herpes simplex infection, syphilis, and chancroid.

genito- [L. *genitivus,* pert. to birth, generation] Prefix meaning *genital, reproduction*.

genitocrural (jĕn″ĭ-tō-kroo′răl) Concerning the genitalia and leg. SYN: *genitofemoral*.

genitofemoral (jĕn″ĭ-tō-fĕm′or-ăl) Genitocrural.

genitoplasty (jĕn′ĭ-tō-plas″tē) [*genito-* + -*plasty*] Reparative surgery on the genital organs.

feminizing g. Surgical reduction in the size of the clitoris, along with construction of a vagina and labia, used to treat female children born with ambiguous genitalia, e.g., those with congenital adrenal hyperplasia or intersex.

genitourinary (jĕn″ĭ-tō-ūr′ĭ-nār-ē) [″ + Gr. *ouron*, urine] Pert. to the genitals and urinary organs; urogenital.

genitourinary system The urinary and reproductive systems, which are anatomically adjacent in the adult and develop from the same mesodermal ridge in the embryo. In men, the urethra is part of both systems. In women, the systems are entirely separate, but infections and other diseases in one may affect the other. SYN: *urogenital system*. SEE: *genitalia* for illus.

genius (jēn′yŭs) **1.** The distinctive or in-

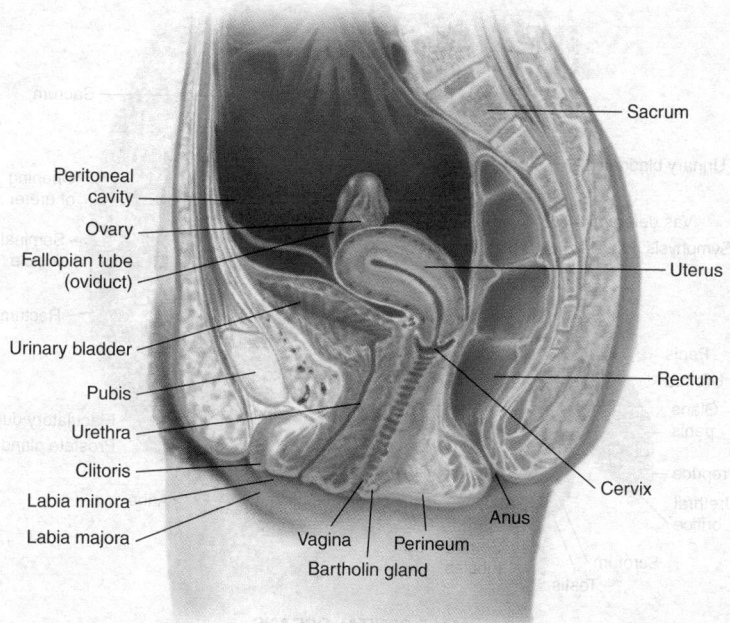

FEMALE GENITAL ORGANS

Sagittal section showing organs within the pelvic cavity

herent character of a disease. **2.** An individual with exceptional physical, mental, or creative power.

genocide (jĕn′ō-sīd″) [Gr. *genos,* race, + L. *caedere,* to kill] The willful and planned murder of a particular social or ethnic group.

genodermatosis (jē″nō-dĕr″mă-tō′sĭs, -tō′sēz″) *pl.* **genodermatoses** [*geno-* + *dermatosis*] Any of a group of hereditary skin diseases such as hereditary angioedema, hereditary coproporphyria, hereditary telangiectasia, tuberous sclerosis, Recklinghausen disease, and Peutz-Jeghers syndrome.

genogram (jē′nō-grăm″) A family map of three or more generations that records relationships, deaths, occupations, and health and illness history.

genome (jē′nōm″) [*gen(e)* + *(chromos)ome*] The complete set of genetic information present in a cell, an organism, or a species. **genomic** (jē-nō′mik, -nom′ik), *adj.*

genome mapping SEE: under *mapping.*

genome-wide association study A research study that compares all of the DNA of people affected by an illness with the DNA of matched healthy individuals. Its aim is to identify specific genetic variations that make some people more likely than others to become sick.

These variations (mutations) are often minor, consisting of as little as a change in a single nucleotide in a DNA strand.

genophore [Gr. *gennan,* to produce + *phoresis,* being born] A prokaryotic chromosome.

genotoxic (jĕn″ŏ-tok′sik) [*gen-* + *toxic*] Toxic to the genetic material in cells (i.e., their DNA or RNA).

genotoxic damage Injury to the chromosomes of the cells. This may be determined by noting the number of micronuclei in the target tissues. When a cell with damaged genetic material divides, fragments of chromosomes and micronuclei remain in the cytoplasm.

genotype (jĕn′ō-tīp) [″ + *typos,* type] **1.** The total of the hereditary information present in an organism. **2.** The pair of genes present for a particular characteristic or protein. **3.** A type species of a genus. SEE: *phenotype.*

APOE g. A genetic variant with some use in the diagnosis of Alzheimer's disease and other dementias.

genotypic antiretroviral resistance testing ABBR: GART. Analysis of HIV samples to see if they will respond to treatment with antiretroviral drugs.

-genous [*-gen* + *-ous*] Suffix meaning *producing, yielding, arising from,* or *produced by,* added to nouns ending in -gen.

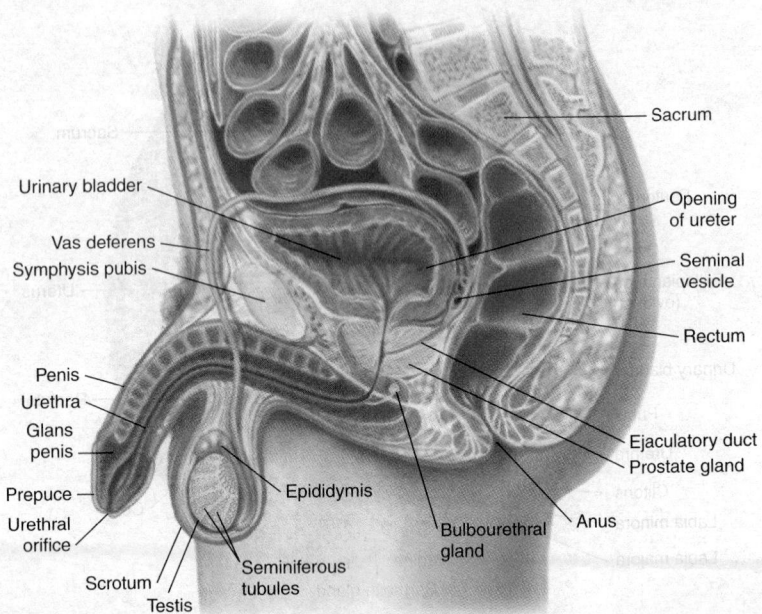

MALE GENITAL ORGANS

Midsagittal section of male reproductive structures shown through the pelvic cavity

gentian (jĕn′shŭn) Dried rhizome and roots of the plant *Gentiana lutea*.

gentian violet $C_{25}H_{30}ClN_3$, a dye derived from coal tar occurring primarily as a dark green powder that is widely used as a stain in histology, cytology, and bacteriology. It has also been used therapeutically as a topical anti-infective in the treatment of the skin and mucous membranes.

genu (jē′nū) *pl.* **genua** [L.] **1.** The knee. **2.** Any structure of angular form resembling a bent knee.

    g. recurvatum Hyperextension at the knee joint. SEE: illus.

    g. valgum Valgus **knee**.

    g. varum Varus **knee**.

genupectoral (jē″noo″pek′tŏ-răl, jen″ū jen″oo-) [*genu* + *pectoral*] Pert. to the chest and knees (as in the knee-chest position).

genus (jē′nŭs, jen′ŭs, jen′ĕ-ră) *pl.* **genera** [L. *genus*, type, kind, race] **1.** In taxonomy, the classification between the family and the species. **2.** A type or kind.

Geobacillus (jē″ō-bă-sĭl′ŭs) [Gr. *ge*, earth + ″] A genus of heat- and pressure-resistant motile gram-positive aerobic or facultatively anaerobic spore-forming rod-shaped bacteria. The bacteria thrive at temperatures from 35° to 75°C. The ability of this genus to survive at high temperatures is used as a biological indicator of the effectiveness of sterilizers used in medicine and dentistry.

geobiology (jē″ō-bī-ŏl′ō-jē) [Gr. *geo,* earth, + *bios,* life, + *logos,* word, reason] The study of terrestrial life.

geochemical disease (jē″ō-kem′ĭ-kăl) A disease that primarily affects people who live where they are exposed to unusually high concentrations of specific

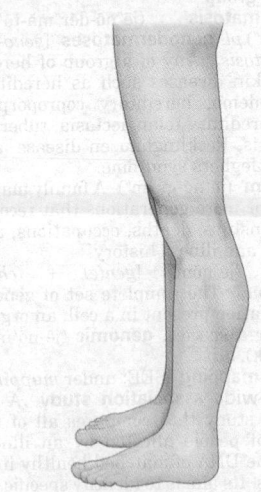

GENU RECURVATUM

minerals in the air, soil, or water that are not found in high concentrations elsewhere. Examples include fluorosis (in Sri Lanka) and iodine deficiency (in many tropical countries and in the north central U.S.).

geode (jē″ōd) [Gr. *geodes,* earthlike] A subchondral (bony) cyst occasionally found in patients with rheumatological illnesses.

geographical bias (jē″ō-grăf′ĭ-kăl) The tendency of a scientist or educator to refer only to those journal articles published in his or her own country or native language. As a result of this bias, American health care educators are more likely to cite studies reported in the *New England Journal of Medicine* than in the (British) journal *Lancet.*

geographical distribution of disease The relationship between the prevalence of a disease and specific geographical-environmental conditions. For example, goiter occurs in inland iodine-deficient areas of the U.S., and pulmonary hypertension occurs in those who reside at high altitude. Certain infectious diseases, such as leprosy, leishmaniasis, and Chagas disease, are endemic in specific tropical or subtropical areas.

geohelminth (jē″ō-hĕl′mĭnth) [Gr., geo, earth + ″] Any of the tropical soil worms, including ascaris, hookworm, and *Trichuris trichiura* (whipworm), that may parasitize human beings and other organisms.

geophagia, geophagism, geophagy (jē-ō-fā′jē-ă, -ŏf′ă-jĭzm, -ŏf′ă-jē) [″ + *phagein,* to eat] A condition in which the patient eats inedible substances such as chalk, clay, or earth. SEE: *pica.*

geotaxis (jē″ō-tăk′sĭs) [″ + *taxis,* arrangement] Geotropism.

geotrichosis (jē″ō-trĭ-kō′sĭs) Infection by the fungus *Geotrichum,* which usually attacks the lungs, causing symptoms resembling those of chronic bronchitis or tuberculosis. This infection may also affect the mouth or intestine.

Geotrichum (jē-ŏt′rĭ-kŭm) A genus of fungi belonging to the family Endomycetaceae; the causative agent of geotrichosis. Geotrichosis is usually acquired by ingestion or inhalation, and occasionally after trauma. Bronchial, pulmonary, and systemic infections occur.

geotropism (jē″ŏt′rō-pĭzm) [″ + *tropos,* a turning] The influence of gravity on living organisms. SYN: *geotaxis.*

GERD *gastroesophageal reflux disease.*

Gerdy, Pierre Nicholas (zher-dē′, gĕr′dē) Fr. physician, 1797–1856.

   G. fibers The superficial transverse ligament of the palm.

   G. tubercle A bony prominence on the tibia that is the attachment site for the iliotibial band. It is located on the anterolateral portion of the proximal tibia just lateral to the superior tibial tuberosity.

geriatric day hospital SEE: under *hospital.*

Geriatric Depression Scale SEE: under *scale.*

geriatric dosing In a person older than 65, any adjustment in the strength and/or the frequency of drug administration designed to minimize the risk of adverse drug reactions. Older patients should typically begin a new drug regimen by taking a smaller dose of a pharmaceutical agent than younger individuals.

⚠️ In general, older people metabolize drugs more slowly than younger ones. Slower metabolism may produce higher drug concentrations or longer half-lives. In addition older people often excrete drugs more slowly than the young. Subtle impairments in kidney or liver function that occur with aging often combine to increase the risk of drug toxicity. Drugs that frequently impair thinking in the elderly include sedatives, hypnotics, analgesics, anticholinergics, and psychotropic medications. NSAIDs and anticoagulants are more likely to cause bleeding in older people than younger ones; NSAIDs also pose an increased risk of kidney failure in the elderly. This brief list of potential pharmaceutical problems in the elderly is not meant to be comprehensive. Before administering any drug to an older patient, it is prudent to assess the proposed benefits of the treatment relative to known risks.

geriatric evaluation and management unit, geriatric evaluation unit ABBR: GEM. An inpatient unit or program devoted to the assessment of the needs of the older patient.

geriatrician (jĕr″ē-ă-trĭsh′ŭn) A clinician who specializes in the care of older people.

geriatrics (jer″ē-a′trĭks) [Gr. *geras,* old age + *-iatric* + *-ics*] The branch of health care concerned with the care of the aged, including physiological, pathological, psychological, economic, and sociological problems. As life expectancy in society as a whole increases, geriatrics takes on ever greater importance in health care. SYN: *geriatric medicine.* **geriatric,** *adj.* SEE: *aging; gerontology;* table.

   dental g. The study and treatment of dental conditions of the elderly, including the detection and prevention of caries and the management of periodontal disease and dentures. SYN: *geriatric dentistry.*

geriatric syndrome Any symptom or group of symptoms that is more common in the elderly than in other populations. Examples include falls, sleep

Some Important Issues in Geriatric Health Care

The prevention and treatment of avoidable infectious diseases

The prevention and treatment of delirium

The prevention and treatment of dementia

The prevention of falls; the treatment of gait disturbances

The preservation of functional independence

The prevention and treatment of atherosclerotic vascular disease and heart failure

The treatment of hypertension and the prevention of stroke

The optimization of long-term care

The maintenance of optimal nutrition

The prevention of osteoporotic fractures

The optimal use of palliation and end-of-life care

The optimal use of physical or chemical restraints

The optimal use of pharmaceutical agents

The prevention and treatment of urinary incontinence

---

disturbances, incontinence, pressure ulcers, and weight loss.

germ [L. *germen*, sprout, fetus] **1.** A colloquial term for a microorganism, esp. one that causes disease. **2.** The first rudiment of a developing organ or part.

hair g. The rudimentary structure from which a hair develops. It consists of an ingrowth of epidermal cells called *hair peg*, which pushes into the corium.

wheat g. SEE: *wheat germ.*

German chamomile SEE: under *chamomile.*

germanium (jĕr-mā'nē-ŭm) [L. *Germania,* Germany + *-ium*] SYMB: Ge. A grayish-white metalloid element of the silicon group, atomic weight 72.59, atomic weight (mass) 72.64, specific gravity 5.323 (25°C), atomic number 32.

germ cell aplasia, germinal cell aplasia SEE: under *aplasia.*

germicidal (jĕrm″ĭ-sī'dăl) [L. *germen,* sprout, + *caedere,* to kill] **1.** Destructive to germs. **2.** Pert. to an agent destructive to germs.

germicide (jĕr'mĭ-sīd) A substance that destroys microorganisms. SEE: *antiseptic; disinfectant.*

germinal (jĕr'mĭ-năl) [L. *germen,* sprout] Pert. to a germination, or to a reproductive cell such as egg or sperm.

germination (jĕr″mĭ-nā'shŭn) [L. *germinare,* to sprout] **1.** The sprouting of the spore or seed of a plant. **2.** The development of a fertilized ovum into an embryo.

germinoma (jĕr″mĭ-nō'mă) A neoplasm usually arising from germ cells in the testis, ovary, or mediastinum.

germ line, germline The cells from which the gametes (the ova and sperm) originate.

germling (jĕrm'ling) A germinating fungal spore.

germ theory SEE: under *theory.*

germ tube test A screening test used for the rapid identification and specification of candidiasis caused by *Candida albicans,* a common fungal infection in immunosuppressed hosts. A clinical specimen is added to serum. If *Candida* germ tubes appear in the specimen within 2 hr, the test is presumed to be positive, pending confirmation by other laboratory assays.

geronto-, geront- [Gr. *gerōn,* stem *geront-,* old man] Prefixes meaning *old age.*

Gerontological Society of America (jĕ-rŏn″tŏ-lŏ'jĭ-kăl) ABBR: GSA. An organization established in 1945 for the main purpose of promoting scientific study of aging. Researchers, practitioners, and educators are members. The society publishes *The Journal of Gerontology* and *The Gerontologist.* Website: www.geron.org

gerontology (jer″ŏn-tol'ŏ-jē) [*geronto-* + *-logy*] The scientific study of the processes and effects of aging and of age-related diseases on humans. SEE: *geriatrics.*

geropsychiatry (jĕr″ō-sī-kī'ĕ-trē) A subspecialty of psychiatry dealing with mental illness in the elderly.

Gerstmann syndrome (gĕrst'măn) [Josef Gerstmann, Austrian neurologist, 1887–1969] A neurological disorder resulting from a lesion in the left (or dominant) parietal area. Patients are unable to point or name different fingers, have confusion of the right and left sides of the body, and are unable to calculate or write. In addition, they may have word blindness and homonymous hemianopia.

Gerstmann-Sträussler-Scheinker syndrome (shtroys'lĕr-shīng'kĕr) ABBR: GSS syndrome. A rare autosomal dominant neurodegenerative disorder that may also be transmitted from person to person by infectious proteins (called prions). Clinically, the onset of symptoms and signs in midlife are related to progressive cerebellar dysfunction with ataxia, unsteadiness, incoordination, and progressive gait difficulty. The prognosis is poor and there is no specific therapy. SEE: *prion disease.*

-gest [Fr. *(pro)gest(in)*] A suffix used in pharmacology to designate a *progestin.*

gestagen (jĕs'tă-jĕn) Something that produces progestational effects. This general term is usually applied to natural or synthetic steroid hormones used to alter reproductive physiology.

gestalt (gĕs-tawlt') [Ger. *Gestalt*, form] The understanding of an experience in its entirety, rather than through an analysis of its components.

g. therapy A form of therapy that emphasizes the treatment of the person as a whole, with a focus on the reality of the present time and place and with an emphasis on personal growth and enhanced self-awareness.

gestation (jes-tā'shŏn) [L. *gestare*, to carry around] In mammals, the length of time from conception to birth. The average gestation time is a species-specific trait. In humans, the average length, as calculated from the first day of the last normal menstrual period, is 280 days, with a normal range of 259 days (37 weeks) to 287 days (41 weeks). Infants born prior to the 37th week are considered premature and those born after the 41st week, postmature. SEE: *pregnancy*. **gestational**, *adj*.

ectopic g. Pregnancy in which the fetus develops outside the uterus.

multiple g. The presence of two or more embryos in the uterus. Twin and higher gestations have greatly increased in the past two decades due to the increased use of ovulation induction agents and assisted reproduction technologies. Currently 3% of all births are multiple gestations. When twins are diagnosed by ultrasound early in the first trimester, in about half of these cases one twin will silently abort, and this may or may not be accompanied by bleeding. This phenomenon has been termed the vanishing twin. The incidence of birth defects in each fetus of a twin pregnancy is twice that in singular pregnancies. Triplet, quadruplet, and higher gestation pregnancies are usually a result of commonly used fertility drugs. Multiple gestations are associated with an increased risk of perinatal morbidity and mortality.

prolonged g. Pregnancy that continues past 41 weeks.

secondary abdominal g. Extrauterine pregnancy in which the embryo, originally situated in the oviduct or elsewhere, has developed in the abdominal cavity.

tubal g. Ectopic pregnancy in which the embryo grows in the fallopian tube.

gestational transient thyrotoxicosis A brief increase in thyroid hormone levels during pregnancy resulting from stimulation of thyroid hormone receptors by human chorionic gonadotropin. It is often associated with hyperemesis gravidarum.

gestational trophoblastic disease ABBR: GTD. Any of several neoplastic diseases of the fetal chorion, including complete and partial hydatidiform mole, chorioadenoma destruens, and choriocarcinoma. The disease is an abnormal growth of cells that would normally develop into the placenta. Villi form and grow into the endometrium; and, while most are benign, some are cancerous. Sudden rapid uterine enlargement and early second-trimester vaginal bleeding characterize all forms of GTD. Other common signs include hyperemesis gravidarum, pregnancy-induced hypertension before 24 weeks' gestation, vaginal discharge of hydropic vesicles, and an absence of fetal heart tones.

TREATMENT: Aggressive forms of GTD, e.g., choriocarcinoma, which can metastasize throughout the body, are treated with chemotherapy, radiation therapy, and surgery. Moles and chorioadenoma destruens are treated with prompt evacuation of the uterus.

PATIENT CARE: Close follow-up care of patients with GTD is needed to detect recurrent disease before it has a chance to spread. Quantitative serum human chorionic gonadotropin (hCG) levels should be drawn every 2 weeks until normal, then monthly for 1 year to assess for tumor recurrence. Affected women should avoid pregnancy during the year-long follow-up period.

gestation period SEE: under *period*.

gestation sac The amnion and its contents.

gestation time SEE: under *time*.

gestosis (jĕs-tō'sĭs) [L. *gestare*, to bear, + Gr. *osis*, condition] Any disorder of pregnancy.

gesture 1. A body movement that helps to express or conceal thoughts or emphasize speech. SEE: *body language*. **2.** An act, written or spoken, to indicate a feeling.

get-up-and-go test Timed up-and-go test.

GFR *glomerular filtration rate*.

GFSE *grapefruit seed **extract***.

GH *growth hormone*. SEE: under *hormone*.

Ghent nosology Formal criteria for the diagnosis of Marfan syndrome, including cardiovascular (aortic root aneurysm), musculoskeletal (pectus excavatum), and ophthalmological findings (ectopia lentis). Definitive diagnosis of Marfan syndrome is made by combining physical findings with detection of a point mutation in one of the fibrillin genes.

Ghon, Anton (gon) Czech pathologist, 1866–1936.

G. complex A small, sharply defined shadow in radiographs of the lung seen in certain cases of pulmonary tuberculosis. It represents the necrotic, calcified remains of the primary lesion of tuberculosis. The mycobacteria within the lesion may remain viable and be the source of endogenous and generalized reinfection with tuberculosis.

ghost riding, ghost riding the whip Exiting an automobile while it is moving, either walking or dancing alongside it, or balancing on top of it. It is an activity that has been associated with serious and sometimes fatal trauma.

ghrelin (grĕ'lĭn) A polypeptide made in the stomach that stimulates the release of growth hormone by the pituitary gland. It regulates appetite and body weight.

GH-RH *growth hormone–releasing hormone*. SEE: under *hormone*.

GI *gastrointestinal*.

Giannuzzi, Giuseppe (jă-noot'sē) Italian anatomist, 1839–1876.

    crescents of G. A crescent-shaped group of serous cells lying at the base of or along the side of a mucous alveolus of a salivary gland. SYN: *Heidenhain demilunes*.

giant [Gr. *gigas,* giant] An individual or structure much larger than normal.

giantism (jī'ăn-tĭzm) Gigantism.

Giardia (jē-ăr'dē-ă) [Alfred Giard, Fr. biologist, 1846–1908] A genus of protozoa possessing flagella. They inhabit the small intestine of humans and other animals, are pear shaped, and have two nuclei and four pairs of flagella. They attach themselves to the cells of the intestinal mucosa, from which they absorb nourishment. Cysts can survive in water for up to 3 months. The concentration of chlorine routinely used in treating domestic water supplies does not kill *Giardia* cysts, but boiling water inactivates them.

    G. lamblia A species of *Giardia* found in humans, transmitted by ingestion of cysts in fecally contaminated water or food. In current usage, the preferred name for *G. lamblia* is *G. duodenalis*. These organisms are found worldwide. The most common symptoms of *G. duodenalis* infection are diarrhea, fever, cramps, anorexia, nausea, weakness, weight loss, abdominal distention, flatulence, greasy stools, belching, and vomiting. Onset of symptoms begins about 2 weeks after exposure; the disease may persist for up to 2 to 3 months.

    There is no effective chemoprophylaxis for this disease. Metronidazole, quinacrine, or tinidazole are preferred treatments. SEE: *water, emergency preparation of safe drinking*.

    DIAGNOSIS: Cysts or trophozoites can be identified in feces. Three consecutive negative tests are required before the feces are considered to be negative. Duodenal contents also can be examined by aspiration or string test, in which an ordinary string is swallowed and allowed to remain in the duodenum long enough for the protozoa to attach.

On removal, it is examined for the presence of cysts or trophozoites. A stool antigen assay test detects *Giardia*. This involves either immunofluorescence or enzyme-linked immunosorbent assay.

giardiasis (jī"ăr-dī'ă-sĭs) Infection of the small intestine with the flagellate protozoan *duodenalis* (also known as *G. lamblia* and *G. intestinalis*). It occurs when cysts are ingested and parasitize the small bowel.

    PATIENT CARE: Health care providers should suspect giardiasis in travelers with intestinal symptoms (such as bloating, diarrhea, weight loss, or abdominal pain) returning from endemic areas (developing countries, and other areas, e.g., parts of the world with poor sanitation and hygiene) and/or in campers who have been drinking unpurified water from contaminated streams. To help prevent giardiasis, travelers should be educated about the dangers of consuming uncooked or unpeeled fruits or vegetables, which may be contaminated. During travel, the consumption of bottled water is preferable to the consumption of tap water. Bottled water should be used for toothbrushing and for making ice or diluting drinks. During outdoor recreation, water should be purified or boiled before it is consumed. Antibiotics cannot prevent giardiasis or other intestinal infections, but should be considered at the onset of symptoms. Most patients with giardiasis have mild to moderately severe diarrhea with some measure of fluid and electrolyte losses. Oral rehydration therapy and oral antibiotics (such as metronidazole) typically provide effective relief. While the patient is symptomatic, he or she should be excluded from work or school. Careful handwashing after defecation may limit transmission of cysts from the infected to those individuals with whom they have contact. Hospitalization may be necessary for a patient with severe diarrhea or one with severe hypokalemia or hyponatremia. In these severely affected patients, careful attention to intravenous hydration, serum electrolyte levels, and renal function is an essential element of supportive care. The hospitalized patient with giardiasis or other infectious diarrheas should be placed on enteric precautions to limit the spread of infection to others. Fecal material should be quickly disposed of, using the normal sewage system. Potential contacts of infected persons should have stool examinations for *Giardia*. Cases should be reported to public health authorities as required.

giardins (gē-ăr'dĭnz) Proteins of the sucker disks of *Giardia lamblia* (*G. duodenalis*) that help the parasite adhere to the lining of the small intestine.

gibbosity (gĭ-bŏs'ĭ-tē) [LL. *gebbosus,* humped] **1.** The condition of having a humpback. **2.** A hump or gibbus, as the deformity of Pott's disease.

gibbous (gĭb'bŭs) Humped; protuberant or hunchbacked.

gibbus (gĭb'ŭs) [L. *gibbosus*] Hump; protuberance. SEE: *protuberance.*

giddiness Dizziness.

Giemsa stain (gē-em'ză) [Gustav Giemsa, Ger. chemist, 1867–1948] A stain for blood smears, containing azure II–eosin and azure II and used for differential leukocyte counts and for detecting parasitic microorganisms.

Gierke disease (gēr'kĕ) [Edgar von Gierke, Ger. pathologist, 1877–1945] Glycogen storage disease type 1a.

GIFT *gamete intrafallopian transfer.*

giga- [Gr. *gigas,* giant] In the International System of Units (SI), a prefix meaning a *billion* (10⁹).

gigant-, giganto- [Gr. *gigas,* stem *gigant-,* giant] Prefixes meaning *giant,* e.g., *gigantism, gigantoblast.*

gigantiform cementoma (jī"gan'tĭ-form" sē"men"tō'mă, 'măt-ă) *pl.* **cementomas, cementomata** [*cementum + -oma*] A benign fibrous connective tissue growth containing small masses of cementum, usually found in the periodontal ligament near the apex of the tooth.

gigantism (jī'găn-tĭzm) [Gr. *gigas,* giant, + *-ismos,* state of] The excessive development of the body or a body part. SYN: *giantism.*

Gigli saw (jēl'yē) [Leonardo Gigli, Italian gynecologist, 1863–1908] A flexible wire saw with specialized teeth used for cutting bony structures. It is operated manually by pulling its handles back and forth. It was first used to section the symphysis pubis as a way of making difficult deliveries easier.

Gilbert syndrome (zhĕl-bār') [Nicolas A. Gilbert, Fr. physician, 1858–1927] A benign, hereditary form of jaundice secondary to glucuronyl-transferase deficiency, resulting in elevated unconjugated bilirubin. There are no hemolytic changes. No treatment is necessary. The presence of jaundice may not be noticed by the patient until it is detected by a laboratory test for bilirubin. Food deprivation increases serum bilirubin in these patients. SYN: *constitutional hepatic* **dysfunction**; *familial nonhemolytic* **jaundice***.*

Gilles de la Tourette syndrome SEE: *de la* **Tourette** *syndrome.*

Gilmer wiring (gil'mĕr) [Thomas Lewis Gilmer, U.S. oral surgeon, 1849–1931] Wiring of single opposed teeth by use of wire passed circumferentially around the two teeth and the ends twisted together. The twisted ends are placed where they will not irritate adjacent soft tissues. This procedure is used to produce intermaxillary fixation.

GINA *Genetic Information Nondiscrimination Act.*

ginger A pungent, spicy material obtained from the root (rhizome) of the plant *Zingiber officinale* and used to flavor medicines and foods. It may prevent nausea, vomiting, and motion sickness in patients affected by these conditions.

gingiva (jin'jĭ-vă, jin-jī'vă) [L. *gingiva,* gum] The tissue that surrounds the necks of the teeth and covers the alveolar processes of the maxilla and mandible; the gums. The gingiva can be divided into three regions: the gingival margin, free gingiva, and attached gingiva. Normal gingival tissue is pale coral pink, firm, and resilient. The attached gingiva is stippled, the gingival margin and free gingiva are not. SEE: ² *gum.* **gingival** (jin'jĭ-văl), *adj.*

    attached g. Gingiva lying between the free gingival groove and the mucogingival line. It is firmly attached by lamina propria to underlying periosteum, bone, and tooth.

    free g. The unattached portion of the gingiva. It forms part of the wall of the fissure surrounding the anatomical crown of a tooth.

    labial g. Gingiva covering the labial surfaces of the teeth.

    lingual g. Gingiva covering the lingual surfaces of the teeth.

    marginal g. The crest of the free gingiva surrounding the tooth like a collar. It is about 1 mm wide and forms the soft tissue portion of the gingival sulcus.

gingivally (jĭn'jĭ-văl"lē) Toward the gums.

gingivectomy (jĭn"jĭ-vĕk'tō-mē) [" + Gr. *ektome,* excision] Excision of diseased gingival tissue. It reduces the periodontal pocket depth to keep the pocket free of dental plaque.

gingivitis (jin-jĭ-vī'ĭs) [*gingiva + -itis*] Inflammation of the gums characterized by redness, swelling, and tendency to bleed. SYN: *ulitis.*

    ETIOLOGY: Gingivitis may be local due to improper dental hygiene, poorly fitting dentures or appliances, or poor occlusion. It may accompany generalized stomatitis associated with mouth and upper respiratory infections. It may also occur in deficiency diseases such as scurvy, blood dyscrasias, or metallic poisoning.

    hyperplastic g. Overgrowth of the gums, associated with an increase in the number of the gingival component cells, usually in response to inflammation. Its causes include dental plaque; local irritants; long-term use of phenytoin, nifedipine, or cyclosporine; puberty; use of hormonal contraceptives; and leukemia.

    SYMPTOMS: The primary lesion starts as a painless enlargement of the gingiva. This lesion may develop into tissue masses that cover the crowns of the teeth and produce periodontitis.

TREATMENT: Treatment includes avoiding causative factors and surgical removal of enlarged tissue.

PATIENT CARE: The presence of the enlarged gingiva makes plaque removal difficult. Patients should schedule regular dental appointments for dental prophylaxis and oral hygiene instruction.

necrotizing ulcerative g. ABBR: NUG. A relatively rare and severe form of periodontal disease, marked by destruction of the gingiva and ulcerations of the epithelium of the mouth. It is associated with infection with multiple oral microbes. SYN: *trench mouth; Vincent angina*.

TREATMENT: This condition is treated by débriding the teeth, and rinsing the mouth with saline or a dilute hydrogen peroxide solution. Chlorhexidine (2%) rinses are also effective. Chemical or physical trauma to the mucosa must be avoided. Fluids should be forced and proper nutrition and dental hygiene provided. Antibiotic therapy with penicillin or metronidazole is effective.

pregnancy g. Gingivitis of pregnancy, a form of hyperplastic gingivitis.

SYMPTOMS: The clinical picture varies considerably. The gingival tissue tends to be bright red or magenta, soft, and friable, with a smooth, shiny surface. Bleeding occurs spontaneously or with little provocation. Lesions are typically generalized and more prominent at interproximal areas.

PATIENT CARE: A dental professional must remove the local irritants. Patients should be referred for a dental prophylaxis and instructed about effective oral hygiene using a very soft toothbrush or sponge stick.

red band g. Linear gingival **erythema**.

gingivo-, gingiv- [L. *gingiva,* gum (of the mouth)] Prefixes meaning *gums* (of the mouth).

gingivolabial (jĭn″jĭ-vō-lā′bē-ăl) Concerning the gums and lips.

gingivoplasty (jĭn″jĭ-vō-plăs″tē) [″ + Gr. *plassein,* to form] Surgical repair of the gums. It may be performed to close a cleft in the gums to correct the gingival margin.

gingivostomatitis (jĭn″jĭ-vō-stō″mă-tī′tĭs) [″ + Gr. *stoma,* mouth, + *itis,* inflammation] Inflammation of the gingival tissue and the mucosa of the mouth due to herpesvirus types 1 or 2.

ginglymus (jĭng′lĭ-mŭs) [Gr. *ginglymos,* hinge] Ginglymoid **joint**.

Ginkgo biloba, gingko (ging′kō bĭ″lō′bă) [Japanese (fr Chinese) *ginkyō,* silver apricot + L. *bilobus,* two-lobed] An herbal remedy extracted from a decid-

uous tree of the genus *Ginkgo,* native to China, which has fan-shaped leaves and spherical cones. *G. biloba* is promoted as a treatment for memory loss and dementia, for tinnitus, and has been proven to be an effective treatment for intermittent claudication. Occasional side effects of its use include bleeding and augmentation of the anticoagulant effect of warfarin.

⚠ Ginkgo should be avoided by pregnant or breast-feeding women. It should never be used by people with bleeding disorders. It should be used only under medical supervision by people taking warfarin or other anticoagulants.

ginseng (jĭn′seng″) [Chinese *rén-shēn,* man-image (fr the shape of the root)] **1.** An aromatic herb of various species of *Panax,* esp. *P. ginseng.* **2.** An herbal remedy used as a stimulant, a tonic, an immune booster, and for sexual potency. Scientific studies supporting these indications are limited. SEE: *Panax.*

American g. A species of ginseng (*Panax quinquefolius*) used in alternative medicine as an adaptogen, aphrodisiac, stimulant, for the treatment of type II diabetes and for sexual dysfunction in men,

Asian g. **Panax** ginseng.

Chinese g. **Panax** ginseng.

Japanese g. A Japanese species of ginseng (*Panax japonicus*) purported to have similar effects as American ginseng.

Korean g. **Panax** ginseng.

Russian g. Siberian **g.**

Siberian g. A species of small, woody shrubs (*Eleutherococcus senticosus*) native to northeastern Asia, used as an adaptogen in traditional Chinese and alternative medicine. SYN: *Russian g.*

girdle **1.** A zone or belt. **2.** A structure that resembles a circular belt or band.

pelvic g. The bones that attach the lower limbs to the axial skeleton; the two innominate or hip bones.

shoulder g. The bones that attach the upper limbs to the axial skeleton; the two clavicles and two scapulae.

girth (gĭrth) **1.** A measurement around a body; circumference. **2.** A measurement around a person's waist.

GIST *gastrointestinal stromal tumor.*

glabella (glă-bĕl′ă) [L. *glaber,* smooth] The smooth surface of the frontal bone lying between the superciliary arches; the portion directly above the root of the nose.

glabrate, glabrous (glăb′rāt, glăb′rŭs) [L. *glaber,* smooth] **1.** Bald. **2.** Smooth.

glacial (glā′shĭl) [L. *glacialis,* icy] **1.** Glassy; resembling ice. **2.** Highly purified. **3.** Very slow, like the movement of a glacier.

glairy (glăr'ē) Viscous; albuminous; mucoid.

gland (gland) [L. *glans*, acorn] **1.** An epithelial tissue that is specialized for the manufacture and export of particular molecules. Glands can be unicellular or multicellular. The multicellular glands are classified according to their architectures, e.g., multicellular glands are categorized as ducted or ductless. The cells of ductless glands secrete specific molecules into the adjacent interstitial space (paracrine glands) or into the bloodstream (endocrine glands), while the cells of ducted glands (exocrine glands) secrete into a cylindrical sac (tubular glands) or into a flask-shaped sac (alveolar glands). The ducted glands are further divided into those in which there is only a single sac (simple tubular glands or simple alveolar glands) and those in which the sacs are connected by branching ducts (branched or compound glands). Glands can also be classified according to the secretory mechanisms of their cells. The most common secretory mechanism is merocrine, in which secretion-filled intracellular vesicles release their contents by fusing with the cell membrane. Other secretory mechanisms include holocrine (in which the gland cell membrane disintegrates to release its secretion), apocrine (in which the ends of the gland cells pinch off, carrying the secretion), and direct active transport of particular molecules across the gland cell membrane. Gland cells and their intertwined vascular beds can be controlled by autonomic innervation and by hormones from other glands. **2.** An obsolete term for lymph node.

    accessory g. **1.** An additional (usually smaller) gland that secretes the same substances as a primary gland. **2.** A gland secreting substances that enhance the function of another gland or organ; e.g., in the male reproductive tract, the prostate, which secretes fluids that improve the viability of sperm, is an accessory gland to the testis.

    acinar g. Alveolar **g.**

    adrenal g. Either of two triangular glands covering the superior surface of each kidney. SYN: *suprarenal* **g.** SEE: illus.

    EMBRYOLOGY: Each adrenal gland is a two-part organ composed of an outer cortex and an inner medulla. The cortex arises in the embryo from a region of the mesoderm that also gives rise to the gonads. The medulla arises from ectoderm, which also gives rise to the sympathetic nervous system.

    ANATOMY: The entire gland is enclosed in a tough connective tissue capsule from which trabeculae extend into the cortex. The cortex consists of cells

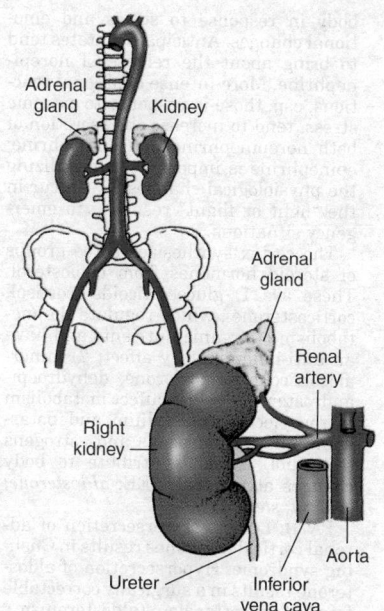

ADRENAL GLANDS

arranged into three zones: the outer zona glomerulosa, the middle zona fasciculata, and the inner zona reticularis. The cells are arranged in cords. The medulla consists of chromaffin cells arranged in groups or in anastomosing cords. The two adrenal glands are retroperitoneal, each embedded in perirenal fat above its respective kidney. In an adult, the average weight of an adrenal gland is 5 g (range: 4 to 14 g).

    PHYSIOLOGY: The adrenal medulla synthesizes and stores three catecholamines: dopamine, norepinephrine, and epinephrine. The chief effects of dopamine are the dilation of systemic arteries, increased cardiac output, and increased flow of blood to the kidneys. The primary action of norepinephrine is constriction of the arterioles and venules, resulting in increased resistance to blood flow, elevated blood pressure, and slowing of the heart. Epinephrine constricts vessels in the skin and viscera, dilates vessels in skeletal muscle, increases heart rate, dilates the bronchi by relaxing bronchial smooth muscle, increases the conversion of glycogen to glucose in the liver to increase the blood glucose level, and diminishes activity of the gastrointestinal system. The three catecholamines are also produced in other parts of the body.

    The adrenal medulla is controlled by the sympathetic nervous system and functions in conjunction with it. It is intimately related to adjustments of the body in response to stress and emotional changes. Anticipatory states tend to bring about the release of norepinephrine. More intense emotional reactions, esp. those in response to extreme stress, tend to increase the secretion of both norepinephrine and epinephrine; epinephrine is important in mobilizing the physiological changes that occur in the "fight or flight" response to emergency situations.

The cortex synthesizes three groups of steroid hormones from cholesterol. These are 1) glucocorticoids (cortisol, corticosterone), which regulate the metabolism of organic nutrients and have an anti-inflammatory effect; 2) mineralocorticoids (aldosterone, dehydroepiandrosterone), which affect metabolism of the electrolytes sodium and potassium; and 3) androgens and estrogens (estradiol), which contribute to body changes at puberty. SEE: *aldosterone; cortisol; steroid.*

PATHOLOGY: Hypersecretion of adrenal cortical hormones results in Cushing syndrome. Hypersecretion of aldosterone results in a surgically correctable form of hypertension (aldosteronism). Adrenocortical insufficiency may be acute or chronic; acute insufficiency of adrenal hormones produces circulatory shock, while chronic insufficiency results in Addison disease. SEE: *Addison disease; aldosteronism; Cushing syndrome; pheochromocytoma.*

alveolar g. A multicellular gland in which the cells secrete specific molecules into an oval or flask-shaped sac. SYN: *acinar g.; acinous g.*

anal g. Any of the glands in the region of the anus. SYN: *circumanal g.*

apocrine g. Any of the glands, e.g., the mammary glands, whose cells lose some of their cytoplasmic contents in the formation of secretion.

apocrine sweat g. Any of the sweat glands in the axillae and pubic region that open into hair follicles rather than directly onto the surface of the skin as do eccrine sweat glands. They appear after puberty and are more developed in women than in men. The characteristic odor of perspiration is produced by the action of bacteria on the material secreted by the apocrine sweat glands. SEE: *sweat g.'s*

Bartholin g.'s SEE: under *Bartholin, Caspar (the younger).*

Blandin g.'s SEE: *Blandin glands.*

Bowman g. SEE: under *Bowman, Sir William.*

bronchial g. Any of the mixed glands lying in the submucosa of the bronchi and bronchial tubes.

Brunner g.'s SEE: *Brunner glands.*

buccal g. Any of the alveolar glands in the mucosa of the cheek.

bulbourethral g. Cowper gland.

cardiac g. A gastric gland in the cardiac region of the stomach.

carotid g. A rare term for the carotid body.

ceruminous g. Any of the glands in the external auditory canal that secrete cerumen.

cervical g. Any of the lymph nodes in the neck.

circumanal g. Anal **g.**

compound g. A multicellular gland containing branching ducts.

Cowper g. SEE: *Cowper gland.*

cutaneous g. Any of the glands of the skin, esp. the sebaceous and sudoriferous glands. These include modified forms such as the ciliary, ceruminous, anal, preputial, areolar, and meibomian glands.

ductless g. A gland with cells that secrete specific molecules into the adjacent interstitial space (paracrine glands) or into the blood stream (endocrine glands).

duodenal g. SEE: *Brunner glands.*

eccrine g. A simple tubular sweat gland of the skin. SEE: *apocrine g.; eccrine sweat g.*

eccrine sweat g. Any of the skin glands that regulate body heat by secreting sweat. The number of glands ranges from 2 million to 5 million. There are over 400 per square centimeter on the palms and about 80 per square centimeter on the thighs. SEE: *sweat gland* for illus.

endocrine g. One of two broad categories of glands; exocrine glands are the complementary category. Endocrine glands, e.g., the thyroid gland, are ductless glands that secrete macromolecules, called hormones, directly into the bloodstream, and such glands are richly supplied by blood capillaries. The endocrine glands include the adrenals, the parathyroids, the pineal, the pituitary, and the thyroid. Major clusters of endocrine tissue are also found in the gastrointestinal tract, the hypothalamus, the ovaries, the pancreas, the testes, and the placenta. In addition, chromaffin and other neuroendocrine cells are found individually and in small clusters throughout the body. SEE: illus.; table.

The hormones produced by endocrine cells regulate the body's salt, water, mineral, and glucose levels; they adjust the body's metabolic balances, growth rates, and reproductive cycles; and they maintain the body's stress responses. Like exocrine and paracrine cells, endocrine cells are stimulated and inhibited by autonomic axons; the activities of endocrine cells are also modulated by circulating hormones, especially pituitary hormones. Both the neural and the hormonal signals to the endocrine system are ultimately regulated by the hypothalamus of the brain, which is the in-

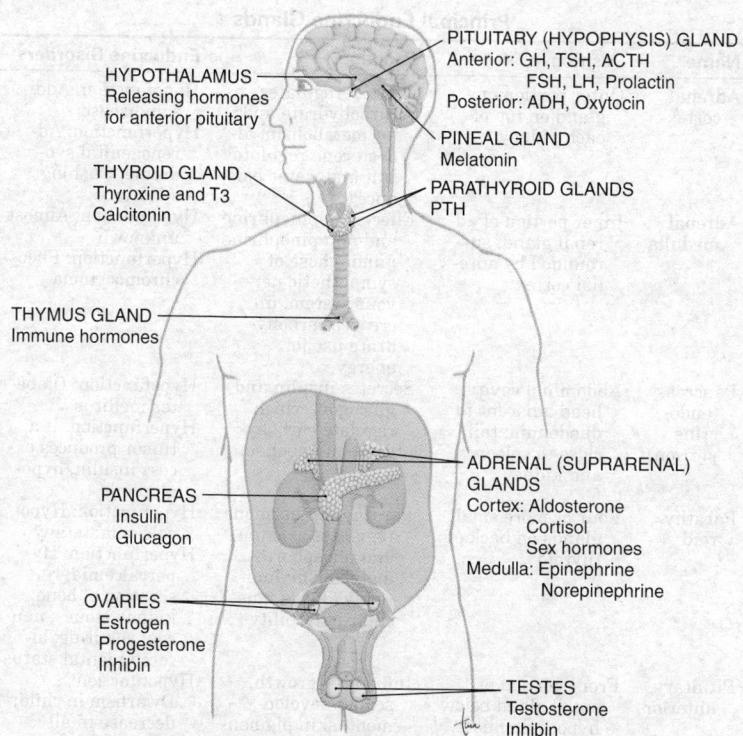

HYPOTHALAMUS
Releasing hormones
for anterior pituitary

PITUITARY (HYPOPHYSIS) GLAND
Anterior: GH, TSH, ACTH
             FSH, LH, Prolactin
Posterior: ADH, Oxytocin

PINEAL GLAND
Melatonin

THYROID GLAND
Thyroxine and T3
Calcitonin

PARATHYROID GLANDS
PTH

THYMUS GLAND
Immune hormones

PANCREAS
Insulin
Glucagon

ADRENAL (SUPRARENAL)
GLANDS
Cortex: Aldosterone
          Cortisol
          Sex hormones
Medulla: Epinephrine
            Norepinephrine

OVARIES
Estrogen
Progesterone
Inhibin

TESTES
Testosterone
Inhibin

ENDOCRINE SYSTEM

tegration center for the body's visceral homeostasis. SEE: *hormone.*

Endocrine health disorders usually result from the production of either too much or too little of a hormone.

esophageal g. Any of the small scattered mucus-secreting exocrine glands in the submucosa of the esophagus.

exocrine g. One of two broad categories of glands; endocrine glands are the complementary category. Exocrine glands, e.g., the salivary glands, secrete specific molecules either onto the outer surface of the body or into a duct that empties onto surfaces that connect to the outer surface of the body. Most exocrine glands are multicellular: goblet cells are examples of unicellular exocrine glands.

fundic g. A gastric gland in the fundus of the stomach.

gastric g. Any of the mixed exocrine glands that form the epithelial pockets (pits) in the lining of the stomach; the glands are named for their location, e.g., cardiac glands, fundic glands, pyloric glands. Typically, the neck of the gland secretes mucus, the body of the gland secretes hydrochloric acid, and the base of the gland secretes enzymes and hormones. SYN: *peptic g.; stomach g.*

genital g. The ovary or the testis.

holocrine g. A gland, such as a sebaceous gland of the skin, in which the secretory cells release intracellular macromolecules by disintegration of their cell membranes; these cells then die.

inguinal g. A rarely used synonym for inguinal lymph node.

interstitial g. Leydig cell.

intestinal g. Lieberkühn crypt.

g. of Krause SEE: under *Krause, Karl.*

labial g. Any of the alveolar glands of the mucosa of the lips.

lacrimal g. The gland that secretes tears. It is a tubuloalveolar gland located in the orbit, superior and lateral to the eyeball, and consists of a large superior portion (pars orbitalis) and a smaller inferior portion (pars palpebralis).

laryngeal g. Any of the mixed serous and mucus glands in the submucosa of the laryngeal section of the respiratory tract.

lingual g. Any of the glands of the tongue, including the anterior lingual glands, Ebner glands, and mucous glands at the root of the tongue.

lymph g. A rarely used term for lymph node.

Principal Endocrine Glands

Name	Position	Function	Endocrine Disorders
Adrenal cortex	Outer portion of gland on top of each kidney	Cortisol regulates carbohydrate and fat metabolism; aldosterone regulates salt and water balance	Hypofunction: Addison disease Hyperfunction: Adrenogenital syndrome; Cushing syndrome
Adrenal medulla	Inner portion of adrenal gland; surrounded by adrenal cortex	Effects of epinephrine and norepinephrine mimic those of sympathetic nervous system; increases carbohydrate use for energy	Hypofunction: Almost unknown Hyperfunction: Pheochromocytoma
Pancreas (endocrine portion)	Abdominal cavity; head adjacent to duodenum; tail close to spleen and kidney	Secretes insulin and glucagon, which regulate carbohydrate metabolism	Hypofunction: Diabetes mellitus Hyperfunction: If a tumor produces excess insulin, hypoglycemia
Parathyroid	Four or more small glands on back of thyroid	Parathyroid hormone regulates calcium and phosphorus metabolism; indirectly affects muscular irritability	Hypofunction: Hypocalcemia; tetany Hyperfunction: Hypercalcemia; resorption of bone; kidney stones; nausea; vomiting; altered mental status
Pituitary, anterior	Front portion of small gland below hypothalamus	Influences growth, sexual development, skin pigmentation, thyroid function, adrenocortical function through effects on other endocrine glands (except for growth hormone, which acts directly on cells)	Hypofunction: Dwarfism in child; decrease in all other endocrine gland functions except parathyroids Hyperfunction: Acromegaly in adult; giantism in child
Pituitary, posterior	Back portion of small gland below hypothalamus	Oxytocin increases uterine contraction Antidiuretic hormone increases absorption of water by kidney tubule	Hypofunction: Diabetes insipidus Hyperfunction: Unknown
Testes and ovaries	Testes—in the scrotum Ovaries—in the pelvic cavity	Testosterone and estrogen regulate sexual maturation and development of secondary sex characteristics; some effects on growth	Hypofunction: Lack of sex development or regression in adult Hyperfunction: Abnormal sex development
Thyroid	Two lobes in anterior portion of neck	Thyroxine and T_3 increase metabolic rate; influence growth and maturation; calcitonin regulates calcium and phosphorus metabolism	Hypofunction: Cretinism in young; myxedema in adult; goiter Hyperfunction: Goiter; thyrotoxicosis

major salivary g. Any of the six large salivary glands; the two parotids, the two sublinguals, and the two submandibulars.

mammary g. A compound alveolar gland that secretes milk. In women, these glands are made up of lobes and lobules bound together by areolar tissue. Each of the 15 to 20 main ducts, known as lactiferous ducts, discharges through a separate orifice on the surface of the nipple. The dilatations of the ducts form reservoirs for the milk during lactation. SYN: *lactiferous* **g.**

meibomian g. Long thin sebaceous glands aligned in parallel in a single row in the tarsal plates of the eyelids. They open along the inner free margin of the eyelid, and their lipid-rich secretion mixes with aqueous secretions of lacrimal glands to form the tear film that coats the surface of the eye. SYN: *tarsal* **g.**

minor salivary g. Any of the hundreds of 1- to 2-mm diameter mucus-secreting salivary glands distributed throughout the oral submucosa. These small glands are named by their locations, e.g., buccal salivary glands, lingual glands, although some glands are also known by the name of their original describers, and von Ebner glands, which are lingual salivary glands found in the circumvallate papillae of the tongue.

mixed g. 1. A gland that secretes in two different fashions, e.g., endocrine and exocrine, such as the pancreas. **2.** A gland that contains two different secretory cell types, e.g., mucous and serous cells, such as in the salivary glands.

g.'s of Moll Small secretory and apocrine glands adjacent to follicles of eyelashes. Their secretions are thought to be antibacterial. SEE: *ciliary* **g.**

Morgagni g. SEE: *Littré gland.*

muciparous g. Any of the glands that secrete mucus.

odoriferous g. Any of the glands exuding odoriferous materials, as those around the prepuce or anus.

olfactory g. Any of the glands in the olfactory mucous membranes.

oxyntic g. Any of the gastric glands found in the fundus and body of the gastric mucosa.

palatine g. Any of the mucous glands in the tissue of the palate.

parathyroid g. Any of four small endocrine glands about 6 mm long by 3 to 4 mm broad on the back of and at the lower edge of the thyroid gland or embedded within it. These glands secrete parathormone.

ABNORMALITIES: An excess of parathormone results in hyperparathyroidism. A deficiency of parathormone results in hypoparathyroidism, with neuromuscular hyperexcitability mani-

fested by carpopedal spasm, wheezing, muscle cramps, urinary frequency, mood changes, and lassitude. Blood calcium falls and blood phosphorus rises. Other symptoms include blurring of vision caused by cataracts, poorly formed teeth if onset was in childhood, maldevelopment of hair and nails, and dry and scaly skin. Hyperparathyroidism or hypersecretion results in a rise in blood calcium and fall in blood phosphorus. Calcium is removed from bones, resulting in increased fragility. Muscular weakness, reduced muscular tone, and general neuromuscular hypoexcitability occur. Osteitis fibrosa cystica is associated with hyperplasia and resulting hypersecretion of the parathyroids.

paraurethral g. SEE: *Skene g.*

parotid g. The largest of the salivary glands, located below the ear and inside the ramus of the mandible. It is a compound tubuloalveolar serous gland. Its secreting tubules and acini are long and branched, and it is enclosed in a sheath, the parotid fascia. Saliva lubricates food and makes it easier to taste, chew, and swallow. SEE: *mumps.*

peptic g. Gastric **g.**

pineal g. An endocrine gland in the brain, shaped like a pine cone and located in a pocket near the splenium of the corpus callosum. It is the site of melatonin synthesis, which is inhibited by light striking the retina. SYN: *pineal body.*; SEE: *melatonin.*

pituitary g. A small, gray, rounded gland that develops from ingrown oral epithelium (Rathke pouch) and is attached to the lower surface of the hypothalamus by the infundibular stalk. The Rathke pouch portion forms the anterior lobe and an intermediate area; the neural tissue of the infundibular stalk forms the posterior lobe. The pituitary gland averages $1.3 \times 1.0 \times 0.5$ cm in size and weighs 0.55 to 0.6 g. SYN: *hypophysis; hypophysis cerebri.* SEE: illus.

FUNCTION: The pituitary is an endocrine gland secreting a number of hormones that regulate many bodily processes including growth, reproduction, and other metabolic activities. It is often referred to as the "master gland of the body."

Hormones are secreted in the following lobes: *Intermediate lobe:* In cold-blooded animals, intermedin is secreted, influencing the activity of pigment cells (chromatophores) of fishes, amphibians, and reptiles. In warm-blooded animals, no effects are known.

Anterior lobe: Secretions here are the somatotropic, or growth hormone (STH or GH), which regulates cell division and protein synthesis for growth; adrenocorticotropic hormone (ACTH), which

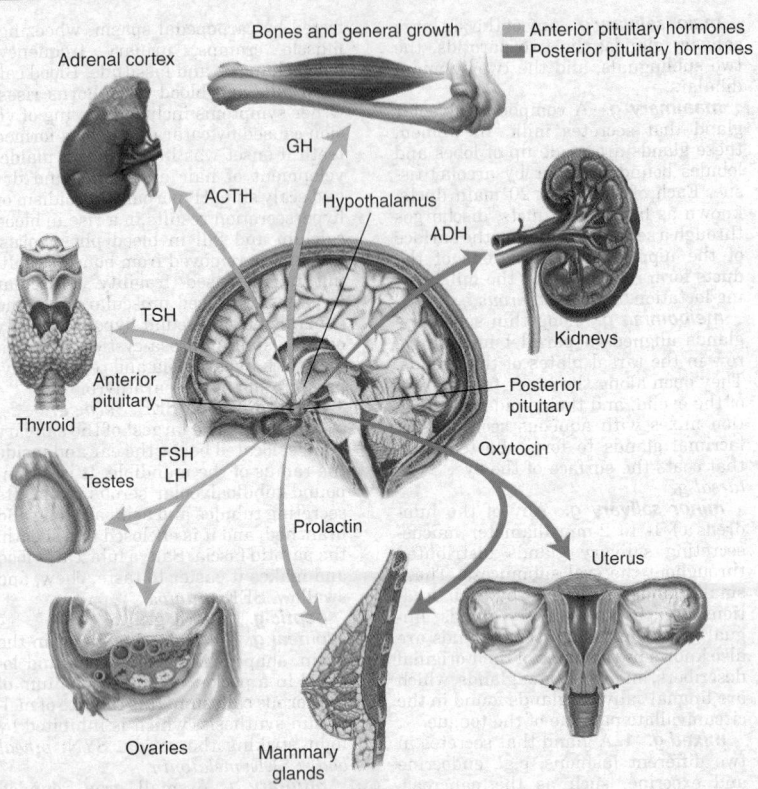

PITUITARY GLAND

Hormones secreted by the anterior and posterior pituitary gland, along with target organs

regulates functional activity of the adrenal cortex; thyrotropic hormone (TTH or TSH), which regulates functional activity of the thyroid gland; and prolactin, also called lactogenic hormone, which induces secretion of milk in the adult female. The gonadotropic hormones are as follows: in women, follicle-stimulating hormone (FSH) stimulates development of ovarian follicles and their secretion of estrogen; in men, it stimulates spermatogenesis in the testes. In women, luteinizing hormone (LH) stimulates ovulation and formation of the corpus luteum and its secretion of estrogen and progesterone. In men, LH also called interstitial cell-stimulation hormone (ICSH), stimulates testosterone secretion.

Posterior lobe: Hormones are secreted by the neurosecretory cells of the hypothalamus and pass through fibers in the supraopticohypophyseal tracts in the infundibular stalk to the neurohypophysis, where they are stored. Secretions here are oxytocin, which acts specifically on smooth muscle of the uterus, increasing tone and contractility, and antidiuretic hormone (ADH), which increases reabsorption of water by the kidney tubules. In large amounts, ADH also causes vasoconstriction, and is also called vasopressin.

DISORDERS: *Hypersecretion of anterior lobe* causes gigantism, acromegaly, and pituitary basophilism (Cushing disease). *Hyposecretion of anterior lobe* causes dwarfism, pituitary cachexia (Simmonds disease), Sheehan syndrome, acromicria, eunuchoidism, or hypogonadism. *Posterior lobe deficiency or hypothalamic lesion* causes diabetes insipidus. *Anterior and posterior lobe deficiency* and *hypothalamic lesion* cause Fröhlich syndrome (adiposogenital dystrophy) and pituitary obesity.

preputial g. A modified sebaceous gland located on the neck of the penis and the inner surface of the prepuce; its secretion is a component of smegma. SYN: *Tyson g.*

prostate g. The gland in the male that surrounds the neck of the bladder and the urethra. It is partly glandular, with ducts opening into the prostatic portion of the urethra, and partly muscular. It secretes a thin, opalescent, slightly alkaline fluid that forms part of the semen. The prostate consists of a median lobe and two lateral lobes measuring about $2 \times 4 \times 3$ cm and weighing about 20 g; it is enclosed in a fibrous capsule containing smooth muscle fiber in its inner layer. The nerve supply is from the inferior hypogastric plexus.

pyloric g. A gastric gland in the pyloric region of the stomach.

racemose g. Acinar **g.**

Rivinus g. SEE: under *Rivinus, August Quirinus.*

salivary g. Any of the glands near the oral cavity that secrete saliva. The major glands are paired and include the parotid, the sublingual, and the submandibular. There are numerous minor salivary glands in the oral cavity, named according to their locations: lingual, sublingual, palatal, buccal, labial, and glossopharyngeal. SEE: illus.

Salivary secretion is under nervous control, reflexly initiated by mechanical, chemical, or radiant stimuli acting on taste buds in the mouth, olfactory receptors, or the eyes. Secretion may also be due to conditioned reflexes as when one thinks about food or hears a dinner bell. The nerve supply of the salivary glands is from the facial and glossopharyngeal nerves, which increase secretion, and from the sympathetic nerves, which decrease secretion. The blood supply is from branches of the external carotid artery.

sebaceous g. An oil-secreting gland of the skin. The glands are simple or branched alveolar glands, most of which open into hair follicles. They are holocrine glands whose secretion arises from the disintegration of cells filling the alveoli. Some aberrant glands are found in the cheeks or lips of the oral cavity, well separated from hair follicles. SEE: *Fordyce disease.*

seromucous g. A mixed serous and mucous gland.

serous g. An exocrine gland with a relatively watery secretion, isotonic with blood plasma, and containing enzymes, glycoproteins, lysozymes, and bactericides. Serous glands are most common in the gastrointestinal tract, notably in the salivary glands.

sex g. An ovary or testis.

simple g. A gland shaped like a single unbranched sac. When the sac is cylindrical, the gland is called simple tubular; when the sac is flask-shaped, the gland is called simple alveolar.

Skene g. SEE: under *Skene, Alexander.*

stomach g. Gastric **g.**

sublingual g. The smallest of the major salivary glands, located in the tissue in the floor of the mouth between the tongue and mandible on each side. It is a mixed seromucous gland. Its main duct opens into or near the submandibular duct, but several smaller ducts may open to the oral cavity independently along the sublingual fold. Numerous minor sublingual glands are scattered throughout the mucosa under the tongue, each with its own duct to the oral surface.

submandibular g. A mixed tubuloalveolar salivary gland about the size of a walnut that lies below the posterior

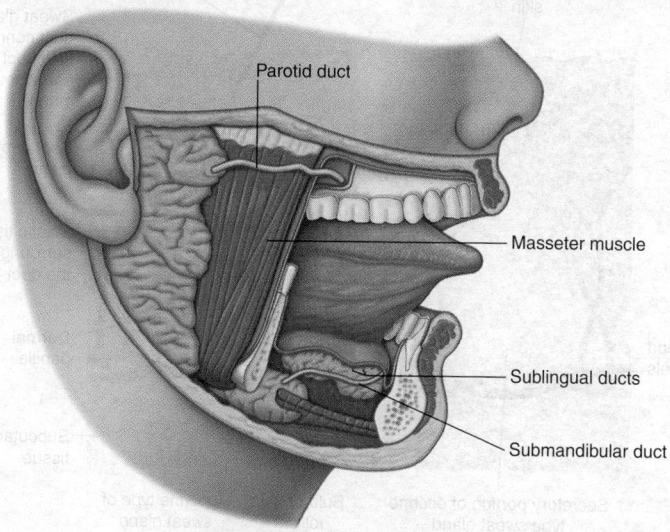

Parotid duct

Masseter muscle

Sublingual ducts

Submandibular duct

SALIVARY GLANDS

floor of the mouth, medial to the body of the mandible. Its main duct (Wharton duct) opens at the side of the frenulum linguae.

suprarenal g. Adrenal **g.**

sweat g. Any of the simple, coiled, tubular glands found on all body surfaces except the margin of the lips, glans penis, and inner surface of the prepuce. The coiled secreting portion lies in the corium or subcutaneous portion of skin; the secretory duct follows a straight or oblique course through the dermis but becomes spiral in passing through the epidermis to its opening, a sweat pore. Most sweat glands are merocrine; those of the axilla, areola, mammary gland, labia majora, and circumanal region are apocrine. Sweat glands are most numerous on the palms of the hands and soles of the feet. SEE: illus.; *apocrine g.; eccrine g.*

target g. Any gland affected by the action or secretion of another gland, e.g., the thyroid is a target gland of the pituitary.

tarsal g. Meibomian **g.**

thymus g. SEE: *thymus.*

thyroid g. A large endocrine gland located in the center of the base of the neck. The gland is composed of two lobes, one on each side of the trachea, and an isthmus of tissue connecting the lower two thirds of each lobe. The isthmus is usually located at the level of the second to third tracheal rings. The whole gland is surrounded by a thin fibrous capsule attached in back to the cricoid cartilage and the first few tracheal rings. The lobes of the thyroid lie under the sternothyroid and sternohyoid muscles. The thyroid is filled with capillary networks (supplied by the superior and inferior thyroid arteries) that surround the many spherical units (follicles) packed inside the gland. Thyroid follicles consist of a ring of follicular cells surrounding a space filled with a clear colloid (a mixture of thyroglobulin proteins and iodine), from which the thyroid hormones (thyroxine and related molecules) are synthesized. These hormones regulate the rate of cellular metabolism throughout the body. All the steps in synthesizing and releasing thyroid hormones are stimulated by thyroid-stimulating hormone (TSH) secreted by the pituitary gland. Another class of thyroid cells, the parafollicular or C cells, is found outside the follicles; C cells secrete calcitonin, a calcium-lowering hormone. SEE: illus.

tracheal g. Any of the acinar glands of the tracheal mucosa.

tubular g. A multicellular gland in which the cells secrete specific molecules into a cylindrical sac.

unicellular g. A lone secretory epithelial cell, often found in the midst of nonsecretory cells. A common example

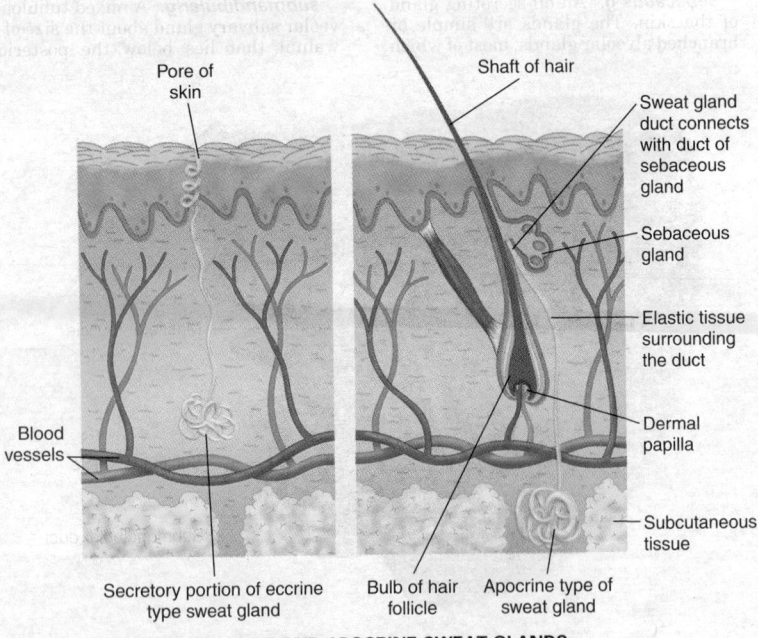

Pore of skin

Shaft of hair

Sweat gland duct connects with duct of sebaceous gland

Sebaceous gland

Elastic tissue surrounding the duct

Dermal papilla

Subcutaneous tissue

Blood vessels

Secretory portion of eccrine type sweat gland

Bulb of hair follicle

Apocrine type of sweat gland

ECCRINE AND APOCRINE SWEAT GLANDS

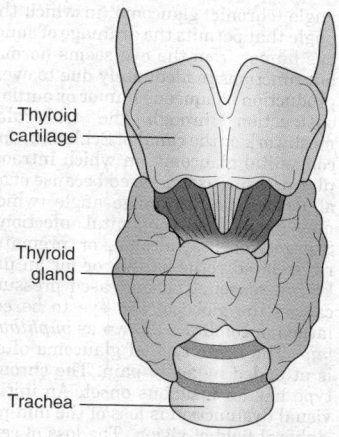

THYROID GLAND

is the goblet (chalice, calceiform) cell, a unicellular mucous-secreting gland found in the columnar epithelium of the intestinal tract.

urethral g. Littré gland.

uterine g. Any of the tubular glands in the endometrium.

vaginal g. Any of the alveolar glands found in the uppermost portion of the vaginal mucosa near the cervix, most of the vaginal mucosa being devoid of glands.

vestibular g. Any of the glands of the vaginal vestibule. They include the minor vestibular glands and the major vestibular glands (Bartholin glands).

von Ebner g. Any of the lingual salivary glands in the circumvallate papillae.

g. of Zeis Small sebaceous glands surrounding the follicles of eyelashes. Their lipid-rich secretions coat the shafts of lashes.

glanders (glăn′dĕrz) A contagious infection caused by *Burkholderia mallei* in horses, donkeys, mules, and other animals. It is communicable to humans, but no cases have occurred in the Western Hemisphere since 1938. Experience with the disease is limited, but sulfa drugs are the recommended therapy.

SYMPTOMS: Patients develop fever, inflammation of the skin and mucous membranes (esp. in the nasal cavity), with formation of ulcers and abscesses. Small subcutaneous nodules develop, break down, and give rise to ulcers. Beginning as small areas, these tend to spread and coalesce and finally involve large areas that exude a viscid, mucopurulent discharge with a foul odor. The infection may occur in an acute or chronic form. In the acute septicemic form, prognosis is grave and the disease is almost invariably fatal.

glands of Moll (mol) [Jacob Anthoni-

Moll, Dutch ophthalmologist, 1832–1914] The combined apocrine and secretory gland on the margin of the eyelid next to eyelash follicles. Products of the gland coat the eyelashes and the eye surfaces and are thought to be antibacterial.

glandula (glăn′dū-lă) *pl.* **glandulae**-Glandule.

glandular (glăn′dū-lăr) [L. *glandula*, little acorn] Pert. to or of the nature of a gland.

glandular therapy Hormonotherapy.

glandule (glăn′dūl) A small gland. SYN: *glandula*.

gland of Zeis (tsīs) [Eduard Zeis, Ger. ophthalmologist, 1807–1868] One of the sebaceous glands of the eyelid, close to the free edge of the lid. Each gland is associated with an eyelash.

glans (glănz) [L. *glans*, acorn] A gland.

g. penis The cone-shape expanded end of the corpus cavernosa of the penis. The urethral orifice is at the tip of the glans, and the foreskin (prepuce) covers the glans (to a variable extent) in uncircumcised males. SEE: *penis*.

Glanzmann thrombasthenia (glanz′man″) [Edward Glanzmann, Swiss pediatrician, 1887–1959] A rare autosomal recessive abnormality of platelet glycoprotein IIb-IIIa, characterized by easy bruising and epistaxis that sometimes requires blood transfusions. Bleeding is prolonged, clot retraction is diminished, and platelets do not aggregate during blood coagulation or after addition of adenosine diphosphate. Treatments include platelet transfusions, progestational agents, and iron replacement, among others.

glare [ME. *glaren*, to gleam] A condition causing temporary blurring of vision with possible permanent injury to the retina. The condition is caused by intense light (visible radiation) emanating from highly reflective objects (such as sunlight reflected on water or snow), or projected by an automobile headlight or by a therapeutic lamp. SEE: *dazzle*.

Glasgow Coma Scale (glas′kō, ′gō) [*Glasgow*, Scotland] SEE: under ¹ *scale*.

Glasgow Outcome Scale (glas′kō, ′gō) [*Glasgow*, Scotland] SEE: under ¹ *scale*.

glass (glas) A hard, brittle, amorphous, transparent material composed of silica and various bases.

cover g. Coverslip.

fiber g. SEE: *fiberglass*.

fibrous g. Fiberglass.

ground g. Abnormal shadowing seen radiographically. In chest x-ray films, it may indicate interstitial fibrosis of the lung; in abdominal films, it suggests ascites.

leaded g. Safety glass that contains lead, used in radiology to help protect personnel from x-rays.

photochromic g. Glass that is manufactured to appear clear until light strikes it. When used in sunglasses, the lens becomes dark and reduces the amount of light transmitted, becoming clear again when no longer exposed to bright light.

safety g. A type of laminated glass that meets specific requirements concerning the force necessary to break it and is designed to break without shattering. Its use in automobiles reduces the risk of injury from broken glass.

tempered g. Glass that has been heat-treated to increase the force required to break it.

ultraviolet transmitting g. Glass designed to admit ultraviolet radiation through it. It transmits about half of the solar radiation, between the wavelengths of 290 and 320 nm.

vita g. Window glass containing quartz for transmitting the ultraviolet rays of sunlight.

watch g. A shallow, saucer-like glass dish, resembling the glass cover widely used to cover the face of a large pocket watch.

glasses [AS. *glaes,* glass] **1.** A transparent refractive device worn to correct refraction errors in the patient's eyes. **2.** A device worn to protect eyes from glare or particles in the air. SYN: *eyeglass; spectacles.*

prism g. An optical device, used by persons who must lie supine for extended periods, to allow them to view objects in their environment without eye or neck strain. Prisms mounted on spectacle frames bend the image to make the feet visible while the person is looking straight ahead.

safety g. Glasses using heat-treated glass or impact-resistant plastic lenses. Their use serves to protect the eyes from dangerous slivers of glass that are produced when ordinary lenses are broken in an accident. Use of safety glass in manufacturing eyeglass lenses is mandatory in the U.S.

glassy Hyaline; vitreous; glasslike, smooth, and shiny.

glaucoma (glaw-kō′mǎ) [L., cataract] A group of eye diseases characterized by increased intraocular pressure, resulting in atrophy of the optic nerve. Glaucoma causes gradual loss of peripheral vision, and, ultimately, blindness. Glaucoma is the third most prevalent cause of visual impairment and blindness in the U.S, although the incidence of blindness is decreasing due to early detection and treatment. An estimated 15 million residents of the U.S. have glaucoma; of these, 150,000 have bilateral blindness. The three major categories of glaucoma are narrow-angle or closed-angle (acute) glaucoma, which occurs in persons whose eyes are anatomically predisposed to develop the condition; open-

angle (chronic) glaucoma, in which the angle that permits the drainage of aqueous humor from the eye seems normal but functions inadequately due to overproduction of aqueous humor or outflow obstruction through the trabecular meshwork or the canal of Schlemm; and congenital glaucoma, in which intraocular pressure is increased because of an abnormal fluid drainage angle (which may result from congenital infections, Sturge-Weber syndrome, or prematurity-related retinopathy), or for an unknown reason. The increased pressure causes the globe of the eye to be enlarged, a condition known as *buphthalmia.* The acute type of glaucoma often is attended by acute pain. The chronic type has an insidious onset. An initial visual dysfunction is loss of the mid-peripheral field of vision. The loss of central visual acuity occurs later in the disease. SEE: *visual field* for illus.

ETIOLOGY: Glaucoma occurs when the aqueous humor drains from the eye too slowly to keep up with its production in the anterior chamber. Thus, narrowing or closure of the filtration angle that interferes with drainage through the canal of Schlemm causes intraocular fluid to accumulate, after which intraocular pressure increases. Glaucoma may develop, however, even if the filtration angle is normal and the canal of Schlemm appears to be functioning; the cause of this form of glaucoma is not known.

DIAGNOSIS: Glaucoma may not cause symptoms. It is best detected early by measurements of elevated intraocular pressure (IOP), often made by adjusting the raw values that are obtained for changes in corneal thickness (as demonstrated with a pachymeter or with optical coherence tomography). A normal tonometer reading ranges from 13 to 22. The frequent need to change eyeglass prescriptions, vague visual disturbances, mild headache, and impaired dark adaptation may also be present. The standard for determining visual loss in glaucoma is the visual-field test.

Open-angle glaucoma causes mild aching in the eyes, loss of peripheral vision, haloes around lights, and reduced visual acuity (esp. at night) that is uncorrected by prescription lenses. Acute angle-closure glaucoma (an ophthalmic emergency) causes excruciating unilateral pain and pressure, blurred vision, decreased visual acuity, haloes around lights, diplopia, lacrimation, and nausea and vomiting due to increased IOP. The eyes may show unilateral circumcorneal injection, conjunctival edema, a cloudy cornea, and a moderately dilated pupil that is nonreactive to light. It requires immediate treatment to reduce IOP.

TREATMENT: Nonoperative treatment includes the use of miotics (eserine, pilocarpine), timolol maleate, intravenous mannitol, and parenteral acetazolamide. Experimental studies indicate that marijuana alleviates the symptoms of severe glaucoma. Control of associated disorders such as diabetes mellitus should be maintained. Operative treatment includes laser trabiculoplasty, trabiculectomy, paracentesis of the cornea, iridectomy (broad peripheral), cyclodialysis, anterior sclerotomy, sclerotomy with inclusion of the iris, as iridotasis or iridencleisis; sclerectomy. SEE: illus.; *ciliarotomy; trabeculoplasty.*

⚠ Acute glaucoma may be precipitated in patients with closed-angle glaucoma by dilating the pupils. In glaucoma patients, cycloplegic drops are given only after trabeculectomy and only in the eye that had the procedure. Administering drops in an eye affected with glaucoma can precipitate an acute attack in an eye already compromised by elevated IOP.

PATIENT CARE: Health care providers should wash their hands thoroughly before touching the patient's eye. Prescribed topical and systemic medications are administered and evaluated.

The patient is prepared physically and psychologically for diagnostic studies and surgery as indicated. If the patient has a trabeculectomy, prescribed cycloplegic drugs are administered to relax the ciliary muscle and decrease iris action, thus reducing inflammation and preventing development of adhesions.

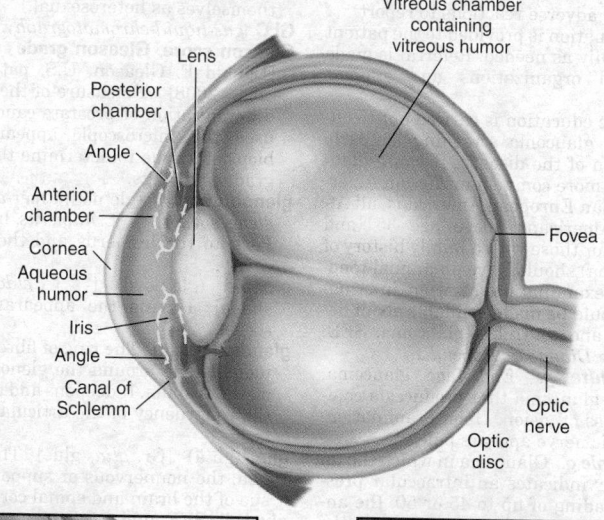

Vitreous chamber containing vitreous humor

Lens

Posterior chamber

Angle

Anterior chamber

Cornea

Aqueous humor

Iris

Angle

Canal of Schlemm

Fovea

Optic nerve

Optic disc

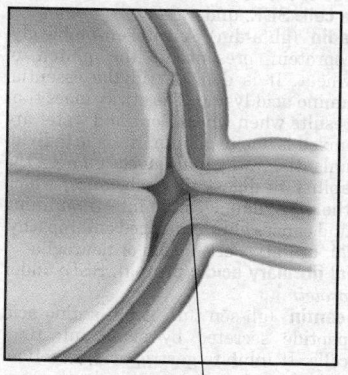

Normal optic disc

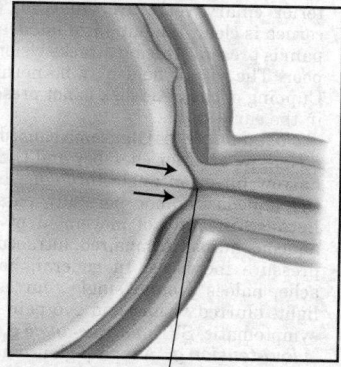

Increased pressure on head of optic disc causing destruction of the nerve fiber

GLAUCOMA

After any surgery, an eye patch and shield are applied to protect the eye, the patient is positioned with the head slightly elevated, and general safety measures geared to the patient's level of sensory alteration are instituted. Usually, the patient is encouraged to ambulate as soon as possible following surgery.

Patients with glaucoma need to know that the disease can be controlled, but not cured. Fatigue, emotional upsets, excessive fluid intake, and use of antihistamines may increase IOP. Signs and symptoms such as vision changes or eye pain should be reported immediately. Both the patient and family are instructed in correct techniques for hand hygiene and eyedrop administration; the importance of adherence to the prescribed regimen; the need for regular follow-up care with an ophthalmologist; and any adverse reactions to report.

Information is provided to the patient and family as needed. Referral is made to local organizations and support groups.

Public education is carried out to encourage glaucoma screening for early detection of the disease. Because glaucoma is more common in African Americans than European Americans, all African Americans above age 35 (and earlier for those with a family history of glaucoma) should have an annual tonometric examination. Written information should be made available about detection and control of glaucoma. SEE: *Nursing Diagnoses Appendix.*

   absolute g. End-stage glaucoma, that is, glaucoma that produces a complete loss of vision. Upon examination, the optic nerve appears pale.

   chronic g. Glaucoma in which the tonometer indicates an intraocular pressure reading of up to 45 or 50, the anterior ciliary veins are enlarged, the cornea is clear, the pupil is dilated, and pain is present. During attacks vision is poor. The visual field may be normal. Cupping of the optic disk is not present in the early stages.

   closed-angle g. Glaucoma caused by a shallow anterior chamber and thus a narrow filtration angle through which the aqueous humor normally passes. Because the rate of movement of the aqueous humor is impaired, intraocular pressure increases. In general, headache, haloes around single sources of light, blurred vision, and eye pain are symptomatic. SYN: *narrow-angle* **g.**

   low-tension g. A type of glaucoma in which intraocular pressures are normal (less than 22 mm Hg).

   narrow-angle g. Closed-angle **g.**

   pigmentary g. Glaucoma produced by the dispersion of organic pigment from the zonula ciliaris to the trabecular meshwork of the eye.

   primary open-angle g. The most common type of glaucoma. It usually affects both eyes, and there is a characteristic change in the appearance of the optic disk. The cup (the depression in the center of the disk) is enlarged. Visual loss is determined by the visual-field test. Many patients with glaucoma have increased intraocular pressure but this is not considered essential to the diagnosis because some patients have normal intraocular pressure.

   secondary g. Glaucoma caused by ocular trauma or an underlying disease that affects the eye.

glaucomatous (glaw-kō′mă-tŭs) Pert. to glaucoma.

GLBTQI *gay, lesbian, bisexual, transgendered, questioning, intersex* (an abbreviation for those who do not identify themselves as heterosexual.)

GLC *gas-liquid chromatography.*

Gleason score, Gleason grade (glē′sŏn) [Donald F. Gleason, U.S. pathologist, 1920–2008] A measure of the cellular differentiation of prostate cancers that uses the microscopic appearance of biopsied tissue to determine the tumor grade and stage.

glenohumeral (glē″nō-hū′mĕr-ăl) [Gr. *glene*, socket, + L. *humerus*, humerus] Pert. to the humerus and the glenoid cavity.

glenoid (glē′noyd) [″ + *eidos*, form, shape] Having the appearance of a socket.

glenoid labrum The ring of fibrocartilaginous tissue around the glenoid cavity on the scapula. It deepens and increases the congruency of the articulating surface.

glia (glī′ă) [Gr. *glia*, glue] The neuroglia; the nonnervous or supporting tissue of the brain and spinal cord.

glia cell SEE: under *cell.*

gliadin (glī′ă-dĭn) A water-insoluble glycoprotein present in the gluten of wheat. It is deficient in the essential amino acid lysine. The sticky mass that results when wheat flour and water are mixed is due to gliadin. In some individuals the intestinal mucosa lacks the ability to digest this substance, which therefore damages the intestinal lining and causes gluten-induced enteropathy.

glial (glī′ăl) Pert. to glia or neuroglia.

glial fibrillary acidic protein SEE: under *protein.*

glicentin (glī-sĕn′tĭn) A 69–amino acid peptide secreted by small intestinal cells. It inhibits gastric acid secretion, stimulates insulin secretion by the pancreas, regulates intestinal motility, and fosters the growth of intestinal mucosal cells.

glide 1. To move in a smooth, virtually

frictionless manner. **2.** Movement in a smooth, virtually frictionless manner. **3.** A joint mobilization technique in which the clinician applies a force to move bones in a direction parallel to the treatment plane. This technique is used to maintain or increase joint play. **4.** The smooth movement of acoustic frequencies, e.g., in audible speech.

mandibular g. The movement of the mandible in any direction as the teeth come into contact.

glinide Meglitinide.

glioblastoma (glī″ō-blăs-tō′mă) [″ + *blastos*, germ, + *oma*, tumor] A neuroglial cell tumor. SYN: *glioma*.

g. multiforme A type of astrocytoma marked pathologically by the presence of extremely abnormal malignant brain cells. Clinically, this tumor is among the most aggressive of the primary brain tumors. Survival 1 to 2 years after diagnosis is rare. Treatments include radiation therapy and chemotherapy.

glioma (glī-ō′mă) *pl.* **gliomata** [glia + -oma] **1.** A sarcoma of neuroglial origin. **2.** A neoplasm or tumor composed of neuroglial cells, (i.e., cells that provide the supportive structure for neurons). Examples of gliomas include astrocytomas, ependymomas, and oligodendrogliomas. SYN: *glioblastoma; neuroglioma.* **gliomatous** (glī-ō′mă-tŭs), *adj.*

mixed g. A glioma composed of several different types of cells, including astrocytes, ependymal cells, and/or oligodendrocytes.

g. retinae A malignant tumor of the retina that occurs in children and metastasizes late. SEE: *pseudoglioma.*

gliomatosis (glī″ō-mă-tō′sĭs) [″ + ″ + *osis*, condition] The formation of a large glioma or of multiple gliomas.

glioneuroma (glī″ō-nū-rō′mă) [″ + *neuron*, nerve, + *oma*, tumor] A tumor having the characteristics of glioma and neuroma.

gliosarcoma (glī″ō-săr-kō′mă) [″ + *sarx*, flesh, + *oma*, tumor] A glioma combined with fusiform sarcoma cells.

gliosis (glī-ō′sĭs) [″ + *osis*, condition] The proliferation of astrocytes in the central nervous system after an injury to the brain or spinal cord.

glipizide (glĭp′ĭ-zīd) An oral drug from the class of medications called sulfonylureas used to lower blood sugar levels in type 2 diabetes mellitus. It is used as part of a regimen that includes regular exercise and a calorically restricted diet. Its side effects may include weight gain and hypoglycemia.

gliptin Any of a class of drugs that are inhibitors of the enzyme dipeptidyl peptidase-4 (DPP-4). Members of this class include sitagliptin and saxagliptin and are used to treat type 2 diabetes mellitus. SYN: *dipeptidyl peptidase-4 **inhibitor**.*

Glisson, Francis (glĭs′ŏn) Brit. physician and anatomist, 1597–1677.

G.'s capsule The fibrous connective tissue membrane that covers the liver and the bases of the hepatic duct, hepatic artery, and portal vein. SYN: *fibrous capsule of the liver.*

global (glō′bĭl) [L.] **1.** Encompassing; complete; overall. **2.** Pertaining to the earth in its entirety. **3.** Spherical.

Global Assessment of Functioning Scale SEE: under ¹ *scale.*

Global Assessment of Relational Functioning Scale SEE: under ¹ *scale.*

Global Public Health Intelligence Network ABBR: GPHIN. An Internet-based information resource that gathers and disseminates data about disease outbreaks, natural disasters, and other potential sources of epidemic illness. The network is a collaboration of the World Health Organization (WHO) and the Public Health Agency of Canada.

global warming The effect of increasing levels of greenhouse gases, esp. carbon dioxide, on the temperature of the earth, causing it to rise. Global warming can adversely affect many biological systems, including that of human health (e.g., by allowing tropical disease vectors to spread to temperate climates). SEE: *greenhouse effect; ozone.*

globe (glōb) [Fr. *globe*, fr L. *globus*, ball, sphere, globe] **1.** A ball or sphere. **2.** The eyeball.

globi (glō′bī) [L.] Pl. of globus.

globin (glō′bĭn) [L. *globus*, globe] **1.** A protein constituent of hemoglobin. **2.** One of a particular group of proteins.

globoid (glō′boyd) [″ + Gr. *eidos*, form, shape] Resembling a globe. SYN: *spheroid.*

globular (glŏb′ū-lăr) [L. *globus*, a globe] Resembling a globe or globule; spherical.

globule (glŏb′ūl) [L. *globulus*, globule] Any small, rounded body.

globulin (glŏb′ū-lĭn) [L. *globulus*, globule + -*in*] Any of the group of plasma proteins that controls colloidal osmotic pressure (oncotic pressure) within capillaries, participates in the immune response, and binds with substances to transport them in blood. Globulins make up approx. 38% of all plasma proteins. Alpha globulins transport bilirubin and steroids; beta globulins carry copper and iron. Gamma globulins, the most common, are immunoglobulins (antibodies). SEE: *antibody; immunoglobulin; oncotic **pressure**.*

Ac g. Accelerator globulin; a globulin present in blood serum that speeds up the conversion of prothrombin to thrombin in the presence of thromboplastin and calcium ions.

antihemophilic g. Antihemophilic **factor**.

antilymphocyte g. ABBR: ALG. A solution containing polyclonal antibodies, created by injecting animals with human lymphocytes, which is used as a nonspecific immunosuppressant in the treatment of transplant rejection. Because it is polyclonal, ALG is active against many antigens; in contrast, monoclonal antibodies act against one specific antigen only. SEE: *polyclonal* **antibody**.

antithymocyte g. An agent used for immunosuppression in organ transplantation.

cytomegalovirus immune g. intravenous An immune globulin preparation containing cytomegalovirus (CMV)–specific antibodies used to treat or prevent CMV infection after organ or tissue transplantation. Antiviral drugs like ganciclovir may be used for the same purpose.

gamma g. The name commonly used for immune globulin, a solution containing antibodies (immunoglobulins) to specific organisms that are obtained from human blood plasma of donors; most of these antibodies are gamma class (IgG). Preparations of gamma globulins are used to provide immediate, short-term protection against specific infectious diseases (e.g., measles, diphtheria, hepatitis A and B, varicella, and respiratory syncytial virus [RSV]) if antibody-specific immune globulins are unavailable. They are also used to treat autoimmune illnesses (e.g., idiopathic thrombocytopenic purpura and Guillain-Barré syndrome). Intravenous immune globulin (IVIG) is also called immunoglobulin. SEE: *antibody; globulin; immunoglobulin.*

hepatitis B immune g. ABBR: HBIG. A sterilized solution of antibodies against hepatitis B surface antigen obtained from plasma of human donors who have high titers of antibodies. It provides passive immunity against infection for those who have not been vaccinated and are exposed to HBV. SEE: ***hepatitis B; hepatitis B virus vaccine.***

immune g. A drug created from serum containing antibodies (immunoglobulins). It is used to supply necessary antibodies to patients with immunoglobulin deficiencies and to provide passive immunization against common viral infections, e.g., hepatitis A, and measles. It also has been used successfully to treat patients with idiopathic thrombocytopenic purpura because it seems to inhibit phagocytosis of platelets coated with autoantibodies, although the exact mechanism of its action is unknown. SYN: *immunoglobulin* (2).

intramuscular immune g. A preparation of immune globulin that is injected directly into a muscle. It can be used to provide passive immunity to a wide variety of infections, e.g., hepatitis A.

intravenous immune g. ABBR: IVIG, IGIV. An immune globulin preparation used intravenously in patients with immunodeficiency syndromes and in immunosuppressed recipients of bone marrow transplants. Together with aspirin, it is the standard of care for children during the first 10 days of Kawasaki disease to prevent the development of coronary aneurysms.

IVIG is also used to treat idiopathic thrombocytopenic purpura and Guillain-Barré syndrome as well as to prevent bacterial infections in patients with hypogammaglobulinemia or recurrent infections associated with B-cell chronic lymphocytic leukemia.

⚠️ The administration of sucrose-containing IVIGs has been associated with acute renal failure, which in about 10% of patients has proved fatal. Patients should be hydrated before being treated with IVIG.

Rh immune g. A solution of gamma globulin containing anti-Rh; it is given to Rh-negative women at 28 weeks' gestation to minimize the potential for sensitization secondary to transplacental bleeding. The injection is repeated within 72 hr after delivery of an Rh-positive newborn if the mother's indirect and the newborn's direct Coombs tests are negative. The globulin also should be given to Rh-negative women after spontaneous or induced abortion. Previously called $Rh_0(D)$ *immune globulin.*

Rh₀(D) immune g. SEE: under *immune globulin.*

serum g. Any of the globulins present in blood plasma or serum. By electrophoresis, they can be separated into alpha, beta, and gamma globulins, which differ in their isoelectric points. SEE: *oncotic pressure.*

sex hormone-binding g. A plasma glycoprotein that binds androgens or estrogens, leaving small concentrations of free hormones to circulate in the blood.

tetanus immune g. A solution containing antibodies to *Clostridium tetani.* It is obtained from human blood and is used to provide passive immunity to prevent and treat tetanus infection. The average prophylactic dose for children and adults is 250 to 500 units injected intramuscularly.

thyroxine-binding g. An acidic plasma glycoprotein; the principal carrier of thyroxine from the thyroid gland to cell membrane receptors on target tissue cells. It bonds more weakly to triiodothyronine.

varicella-zoster immune g. ABBR: VZIG. An immune globulin used for passive immunization of susceptible immunodeficient individuals after significant exposure to varicella. VZIG does not modify established varicella-zoster infections.

⚠️ VZIG should not be injected intravenously.

globus (glō′bŭs) [L.] A globe or sphere.

   g. hystericus A lump in the throat felt as a choking sensation in anxiety, hypertension, or panic attacks.

   g. pallidus One of the core nuclei of the basal ganglia; it is the main target of axons originating in the other core nucleus, the striatum. The globus pallidus is composed of an internal and external segment. The internal pallidal segment sends most of its axons to the ventral nucleus of the ipsilateral thalamus via the ansa lenticularis; the external segment sends axons to and receives axons from the subthalamic nucleus, a satellite nucleus of the globus pallidus. SYN: *pallidum.* SEE: *basal **ganglia**.*

glomangioma (glōm″an″jē-ō′mă) [L. *glomus,* a ball, + *angioma*] A benign tumor that develops from an arteriovenous glomus of the skin. SYN: *angiomyoneuroma; angioneuromyoma.*

glomectomy (glō-měk′tō-mē) The surgical removal of a glomus.

glomerate (glŏm′ĕr-āt) [L. *glomerare,* to wind into a ball] Conglomerate, clustered, grouped.

glomerul-, glomerulo- [L. *glomus,* stem *glomer-,* ball (of yarn) + *-ule,* a diminutive suffix] Prefixes meaning *glomerulus.*

glomerular (glō-měr′ū-lăr) [L. *glomerulus,* little ball] Pert. to a glomerulus; clustered.

glomerular disease Any of a large group of diseases that affect the glomerulus of the kidneys. They may be classified by clinical severity, by histological changes in the kidney, or by etiology. Etiological factors include *primary glomerular disease;* disease secondary to *systemic disease,* such as lupus erythematosus or polyarteritis; *infectious disease* such as streptococcal infection, malaria, syphilis, or schistosomiasis; *metabolic disease* such as diabetes or amyloidosis; *toxins* such as mercury, gold, or snake venom; *serum sickness;* and drug *hypersensitivity.*

   Glomerular disease may also be associated with hereditary disorders (e.g., Alport's syndrome, Fabry's disease). SEE: *glomerulonephritis; kidney; nephritis; nephrotic syndrome.*

   The clinical consequences of glomerular diseases are associated both with the causes and with the extent of glo-

merular damage and typically include edema, proteinuria and hypertension.

glomerular filtration rate ABBR: GFR. The rate of urine formation as plasma passes through the glomeruli of the kidneys. A normal GFR is between 90 and 120 mL/min.

glomerulitis (glō-měr″ū-lī′tĭs) [″ + Gr. *itis,* inflammation] An inflammation of glomeruli, esp. of the renal glomeruli.

glomerulonephritis (glō-měr″ū-lō-nĕ-frī′tĭs) [″ + Gr. *nephros,* kidney, + *itis,* inflammation] A form of nephritis in which the lesions involve primarily the glomeruli. It may be acute, subacute, or chronic. Acute glomerulonephritis, also known as acute nephritic syndrome, frequently follows infections, esp. those of the upper respiratory tract caused by particular strains of streptococci. It may also be caused by systemic lupus erythematosus, subacute bacterial endocarditis, cryoglobulinemia, various forms of vasculitis including polyarteritis nodosa, Henoch-Schönlein purpura, and visceral abscess. The condition is characterized by the presence of blood in the urine (hematuria), protein in the urine (proteinuria), and red cell casts; oliguria, edema, pruritus, nausea, constipation, and hypertension. Investigation of serum complement levels and renal biopsy facilitates diagnosis and helps to establish the prognosis. SEE: *glomerular disease; glomerulonephritis, rapidly progressive; Nursing Diagnoses Appendix.*

   PATIENT CARE: The primary causative condition must be treated. Serum creatinine, blood urea nitrogen, and urine creatinine clearance levels are monitored to assess renal function, and the patient is assessed for electrolyte and acid-base imbalance. Fluid balance is monitored, and changes in the amount of edema, daily weight, and fluid intake and output are documented. Vital signs are monitored every 4 hr or as necessary, and skin is inspected for signs of breakdown. Skin care and frequent repositioning are provided. General patient care concerns apply during hospitalization.

   The patient is instructed to limit activities while at home during acute periods of hematuria, azotemia, gross edema, and hypertension; but self-care is encouraged as acute symptoms subside, depending on fatigue levels and changes in blood pressure. Appropriate activities are encouraged. Instruction is provided in dietary and fluid restrictions; the importance of low-sodium, high-calorie meals with adequate (though at times restricted) protein content is stressed. Prescribed medications should be taken as scheduled and the patient made aware of desired effects, as well as adverse effects, that should be reported.

The patient should avoid individuals with communicable illnesses, practice good handwashing, and should report signs of infection, particularly respiratory and urinary tract infections, immediately. The importance of keeping follow-up appointments during and following convalescence to detect any recurrence is stressed. Pregnant women with a history of glomerulonephritis should be encouraged to have frequent medical evaluations because of the added stress placed on the kidneys by the pregnancy (increasing the risk for real failure). The patient should be encouraged to express feelings and concerns. Staff should provide honest but empathic answers to questions, explaining all procedures and treatments. The patient's response is monitored, and the patient with severe renal dysfunction is prepared for dialysis or kidney transplant.

membranoproliferative g. A condition in which kidney biopsy shows subendothelial deposits and proliferating mesangial cells in the glomerulus. Some patients have progressive renal impairment.

SYMPTOMS: Edema and hypertension are frequently noted. Laboratory findings typically show proteinuria and hematuria.

TREATMENT: Patients with hypertension are medicated to lower their blood pressure. If creatinine levels rise, steroids or other immunosuppressive agents are used.

rapidly progressive g. ABBR: RPGN. Any glomerular disease in which there is rapid loss of renal function, usually with crescent-shaped lesions in more than 50% of the glomeruli.

glomerulopathy (glō-mĕr″ū-lŏp′ă-thē) Any disease of the renal glomeruli. SEE: *glomerular disease.*

glomerulosclerosis (glō-mĕr″ū-lō-sklē-rō′sĭs) Fibrosis of renal glomeruli associated with protein loss in the urine; the loss of protein may be massive.

diabetic g. A type of glomerulosclerosis seen in some cases of diabetes mellitus. Eosinophilic material is present in various parts of the glomerulus. SYN: *intercapillary g.*

focal segmental g. An irreversible form of glomerular injury often seen in patients with a history of injection drug use or AIDS.

intercapillary g. Diabetic **g.**

glomerulus (glō-mĕr″ū-lŭs) *pl.* **glomeruli** [L.] **1.** One of the capillary networks that are part of the renal corpuscles in the nephrons of the kidney. Each is surrounded by a Bowman's capsule, the site of renal (glomerular) filtration, which is the first step in the formation of urine. SEE: illus. **2.** A group of twisted capillaries or nerve fibers.

olfactory g. A neural network found in the olfactory bulb, formed by the dendrites of mitral cells intertwined with the axons of olfactory receptor cells.

glomus (glō′mŭs) [L. *glomus,* a ball] A small, round swelling made of tiny blood vessels and found in stromata containing many nerve fibers. **glomoid,** *adj.* (glō′moyd″)

glossa (glŏs′ă) [Gr. *glossa,* tongue] The tongue.

glossal (glŏs′ăl) Rel. to the tongue.

glossectomy (glŏs-ĕk′tō-mē) [″ + *ektome,* excision] Surgical excision of the tongue.

-glossia [Gr. *glōssa,* tongue + *-ia*] Suffix meaning *tongue* (of a specific kind, e.g., *diglossia, microglossia*).

Glossina (glŏs-sī′nă) A genus consisting of the tsetse flies, which includes 23 bloodsucking species that live principally in central and southern Africa. They transmit the trypanosomes (*Trypanosoma gambiense, T. rhodesiense*),

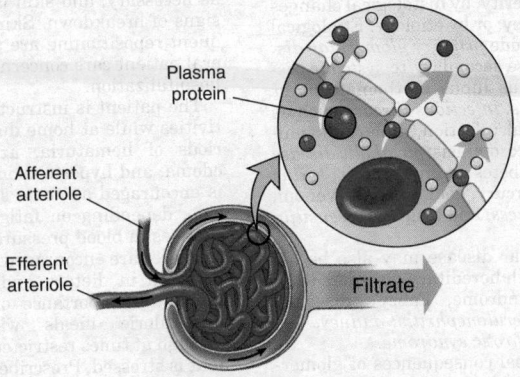

Plasma protein

Afferent arteriole

Efferent arteriole

Filtrate

FILTRATION IN GLOMERULUS

the causative agents of sleeping sickness in humans, and other trypanosomes that infect wild and domestic animals. SEE: *sleeping* **sickness;** *Trypanosoma.*

glossitis (glo-sīt′ĭs) [*glosso-* + *-itis*] An inflammation of the tongue.

   median rhomboid g. An inflammatory area, somewhat diamond-shaped, found on the dorsum of the tongue anterior to the vallate papillae.

glosso-, gloss- [Gr. *glōssa,* tongue] Prefixes meaning *tongue.*

glossodynia (glŏs″ō-dĭn′ē-ă) [″ + *odyne,* pain] Pain in the tongue. SEE: *burning mouth syndrome.*

glossoptosis (glŏs″ŏp-tō′sĭs) [″ + *ptosis,* a dropping] A dropping of the tongue downward from its normal position. It is a common, potentially life-threatening finding in Pierre Robin syndrome.

glossy Smooth and shining.

glottic (glŏt′ĭk) [Gr. *glottis,* back of tongue] Of or pert. to the tongue or glottis.

glottis (glot′ĭs) *pl.* **glottises, glottides** [Gr. *glōttis,* (back of the) tongue] The sound-producing apparatus of the larynx consisting of the two vocal cords and the intervening space, the rima glottidis. A leaf-shaped lid of cartilage (the epiglottis) protects this opening.

glove (glŏv) A protective covering for the hand. In medical care the glove is made of a flexible impervious material that permits full movement of the hand and fingers. Gloves are used to protect both the operative site from contamination with organisms from the health care worker and the health care worker from contamination with pathogens from the patient. SEE: *Standard Precautions Appendix.*

⚠ It is not advisable to wash gloves and wear them again while treating another patient.

   double g. The wearing of two pairs of gloves during invasive procedures to decrease the likelihood of direct contact between the surgeon and the patient. Similarly: "triple glove."

   surgical g. A sterile glove worn to prevent contamination of the patient during invasive procedures and to protect the hand from exposure to potentially infectious materials.

   thermally insulated g. A glove that provides protection against frostnip and frostbite.

glove barrier value The relative resistance of a glove to puncture or perforation.

glove box An anaerobic chamber used to support the growth of anaerobic bacteria that thrive in the absence of oxygen.

gloving Placing of gloves on the hands. During physical examination and invasive procedures, such as phlebotomy or surgery, this is done to protect both caregiver and patient from transmissible diseases.

GLP-1 *glucagon-like peptide-1.*

glucagon (gloo′kă-gŏn) A polypeptide hormone secreted by the alpha cells of the pancreas that increases the blood glucose level by stimulating the liver to change stored glycogen to glucose. Glucagon opposes the action of insulin, and it is used as an injection in diabetes to reverse hypoglycemic reactions and insulin shock. It also increases the use of fats and excess amino acids for energy production. It is obtained from pork and beef pancreas glands. Parenteral administration of glucagon relaxes the smooth muscle of the stomach, duodenum, small bowel, and colon.

glucagon-like peptide-1 ABBR: GLP-1. An incretin released by the gastrointestinal tract in response to consumed sugars. Analogs of GLP-1 such as exenetide and liraglutide are used to treat type 2 diabetes mellitus.

glucagonoma (glū″kă-gŏn-ō′mă) A malignant tumor of the alpha cells of the pancreatic islets of Langerhans. The principal signs and symptoms include weight loss, diabetes mellitus, skin rash, glossitis, elevated serum glucagon levels, and anemia. The treatment is surgical excision or octreotide.

gluco-, gluc- [Fr. *gluco(se)*] Prefixes meaning *sugar* or *glucose* and its derivatives. SEE: *glyco-.*

glucocerebroside (gloo″kō-sĕr′ĕ-brō-sīd″) A cerebroside with the carbohydrate glucose contained in the molecule; accumulates in tissues in individuals with Gaucher's disease.

glucocorticoid (gloo″kō-kort′ĭ-koyd) [*gluco-* + *cortex* + *-oid*] Any of the adrenal cortical (steroid) hormones that have anti-inflammatory and immunosuppressive effects. They affect the metabolism of carbohydrates, fats, and proteins by binding to and activating receptors on cells. The most important glucocorticoid is cortisol (hydrocortisone). SEE: *mineralocorticoid.*

glucofuranose (gloo″kō-fū′ră-nōs) The form of glucose containing the furanose ring.

glucogenesis (gloo″kō-jĕn′ĕ-sĭs) The formation of glucose.

glucokinase (gloo″kō-kī′nās) An enzyme in liver cells that, in the presence of adenosine triphosphate, catalyzes the conversion of glucose to glucose-6-phosphate. This is the first step in glycolysis, the breakdown of glucose to two molecules of pyruvic acid.

glucomannan (gloo″kō-man′an) A polysaccharide gel obtained from the Japanese konjac plant, used as a source of nutritional fiber and to treat constipation and hyperlipidemia.

glucometer (gloo-kom′ĕt-ĕr) [*glucose* + *-meter*] A device that measures the level of blood glucose from a few drops of blood obtained subcutaneously.

PATIENT CARE: All glucometers measure the level of glucose in whole blood, but different meters offer different features. Discussing the various features with a diabetes educator can help patients decide which one best suits their needs, personal preferences, abilities, and finances. Patients should answer the following questions to guide their choice: Have you ever used a blood glucose meter? If so, what features did you find helpful, and what features were not important to you? Is cost a concern? Do you have insurance to cover the meter itself, lancets, and strips? Do you have vision problems? Do you have difficulty in using your hands to do small tasks? Would you like to use sites other than your fingertips to obtain blood? Are you interested in electronically tracking your blood glucose results, insulin dosages, and food intake? Health insurance plans commonly cover the cost of blood glucose monitoring, but patients should ask their carriers about specific coverage for the meter and needed supplies. Some plans cover only specific meters and accessories. Medicare pays for meters and supplies for all recipients regardless of their treatment regimen. The cost of test strips, lancets, and cartridges used to monitor blood glucose may be prohibitive for some people. Before choosing a meter, patients should know, in order to help calculate expenses, how many times each day the levels will need to be checked. A written prescription from a health care provider indicates how many times each day monitoring is required and may help patients to get needed insurance coverage. Ease of use is an important concern. Larger meters may be easier to handle if manual dexterity is a problem, and meters with large digital readouts are helpful for patients with visual impairments. Some meters feature an electronic voice (available in several languages) to guide the user through the process and announce results. Most meters have a memory that automatically records reading. All blood glucose meters require calibration to maintain accuracy (monthly or according to manufacturer recommendations). Patients who use a blood glucose monitor and suspect technical malfunctions should have a clinician review the user's technique and draw blood for a lab assessment and comparison of results. SYN: *blood glucose* **monitor**; *glucose* **monitor**; *glucose meter*.

gluconeogenesis (gloo″kō-nē″ō-jĕn′ĕ-sĭs)

[″ + *neos,* new, + *genesis,* generation, birth] The formation of glucose from excess amino acids, fats, or other noncarbohydrate sources.

glucopenia, glycopenia (gloo″kō-pē′nē-ă) [″ + Gr. *penia,* lack] Hypoglycemia.

Glucophage (gloo′kō-fāj″) [″ + ″] SEE: *metformin.*

glucoprotein (gloo″kō-prō′tē-ĭn) Glycoprotein.

glucopyranose (gloo″kō-pī′ră-nōs) The form of glucose containing the six-carbon pyran ring.

glucosamine, glucosamine sulfate (gloo″kō-să-mēn″, -ză) A health food supplement used to treat pain caused by osteoarthritis. Studies show that it has limited, if any, effectiveness, e.g., in treating osteoarthritic pain in the knees.

glucose (gloo′kōs″) [Fr., fr Gr. *gleukos,* sweet (new wine)] A simple sugar or monosaccharide, $C_6H_{12}O_6$, that is the end product of carbohydrate digestion. Its right-handed (dextrorotatory) isomer (D-glucose) serves as a primary energy source for living organisms. Glucose is found naturally in fruits and other plants. It is also formed during digestion from the hydrolysis of disaccharides and polysaccharides. After absorption by the small intestine, glucose is carried by the portal vein, where it may be stored as glycogen. Within cells, glucose is used to synthesize the pentose sugars, ribose and deoxyribose, for RNA and DNA, respectively. SYN: *dextrose.* SEE: *carbohydrate.*

In healthy people, normal fasting blood glucose levels are maintained at about 70 to 100 mg/dL. (To convert glucose measurements from mg/dL to SI units, multiply by 0.0555.) Lower blood glucose levels (hypoglycemia) may cause confusion, anxiety, or other neurological complications. Higher blood glucose levels (hyperglycemia) may result in the glycosylation (sugarcoating) of body tissues. Hyperglycemia is characteristic of diabetes mellitus (diagnosed when a fasting patient has two blood glucose measurements exceeding 126 mg/dL); and of prediabetes (in which the fasting blood sugar levels are 100 to 125 mg/dL). Hypoglycemia may result from starvation, the treatment of diabetes mellitus, or, rarely, insulin-secreting tumors of the pancreas.

GLUCOSE METABOLISM: Within most cells, glucose is the primary energy source and is oxidized in cell respiration to carbon dioxide and water to produce energy in the form of adenosine triphosphate. There are three stages of cellular respiration: glycolysis, the Krebs (citric acid) cycle, and the electron transport chain. Stage 1 (glycolysis) takes place in the cytoplasm; stages

2 and 3 (the Krebs cycle and the electron transport chain) take place in the mitochondria. Insulin facilitates the entry of glucose into cells, fueling cellular respiration. Excess glucose may be converted to glycogen and stored in the liver and muscles; insulin and cortisol facilitate this process. The hormone glucagon (and epinephrine in stress situations) stimulates the liver to change glycogen back to glucose when the blood glucose level decreases. Any further excess glucose is converted to fat and stored in adipose tissue.

When the glucose level is below normal, fat stores are metabolized. Incomplete metabolism of fats leads to the formation of ketone bodies, a finding in poorly controlled diabetes. Blood glucose acts as a protein sparer. Neurons are esp. dependent on glucose as their source of energy; the brain oxidizes glucose directly.

PATIENT CARE: Blood glucose monitoring is used by patients with diabetes mellitus to provide immediate glucose readings that guide decisions on dietary intake, medications, and exercise. Self-monitoring data (along with hemoglobin A_{1C} values) give the patient and the health care providers information on the effectiveness of treatment.

capillary blood g. ABBR: CBG. The level of circulating blood glucose as measured by glucometer analysis of a fingerstick sample. Regular measurements of CBG allow diabetic patients to make frequent adjustments in their caloric intake, exercise levels, and use of antidiabetic medications, esp. insulin. SYN: *finger stick blood* **g.**

estimated average g. ABBR: eAG. An average glucose value derived from and based upon the hemoglobin A1c value.

PATIENT CARE: Like the A1c, the eAG provides an estimate of blood glucose levels during the two to three months preceding the test. It is used to help patients understand how their A1c levels, measured as the percent of hemoglobin molecules that are sugar-coated, would translate into daily capillary blood glucose values. An A1c of 7%, for example, translates into an eAG of 154 mg/dL; an A1c of 9% suggests that a patient's average blood glucose in the past few months was 212 mg/dL. Because the eAG value matches the units that patients see when they test their own glycemic levels, it may be more readily understandable and a better tool for communicating to patients how to control their blood sugar levels than the A1c test.

finger stick blood g. ABBR: FSBG. Capillary blood **g.**

impaired fasting g. ABBR: IFG. Abnormal glucose metabolism demonstrated by the presence of a fasting blood sugar that is greater than 100 mg/dL, but less than 126 mg/dL.

liquid g. A thick, syrupy, sweet liquid obtained from the incomplete hydrolysis of starch, containing D-glucose (dextrose), dextrins, and other carbohydrates. It is used for nutritive purposes and in various pharmaceutical and food preparations.

glucose, risk for unstable blood Risk for variation of blood glucose/sugar levels from the normal range. SEE: *Nursing Diagnoses Appendix.*

glucose meter Glucometer.

glucose-6-phosphate dehydrogenase ABBR: G6PD. An enzyme that dehydrogenates glucose-6-phosphate to form 6-phospho-D-glucono-δ-lactone. This is the initial step in the pentose phosphate pathway of glucose catabolism.

glucose-6-phosphate dehydrogenase deficiency SEE: under *deficiency.*

glucose polymer A glucose saccharide mixture of 3% glucose, 7% maltose, 5% maltotriose, and 85% polysaccharides of 4 to 15 glucose units, used in oral glucose tolerance tests. SEE: *oral glucose tolerance test.*

glucose ratio The concentration of the glucose level in the cerebrospinal fluid divided by its concentration in the blood. A ratio of less than 0:3 suggests acute bacterial meningitis rather than viral or aseptic meningitis. SYN: *cerebrospinal fluid-to-blood glucose ratio.*

glucose toxicity SEE: under *toxicity.*

glucosidase (gloo-kō′sĭ-dās) An enzyme that catalyzes the hydrolysis of a glucoside.

glucoside (gloo′kō-sīd) A glycoside that on hydrolysis yields a sugar, glucose, and one or two additional products. Glucosides are numerous and widely distributed in plants. Many glucosides have medicinal properties (e.g., digitalin, present in digitalis, the purple foxglove used for centuries to treat dysrhythmia and heart failure). SEE: *glycoside.*

glucosuria (gloo″kō-sū′rē-ă) [″ + *ouron*, urine] Glycosuria.

glucotoxicity (gloo″kō-tok-sis′ĭt-ē) [*gluco*- + *toxicity*] Glucose **toxicity** (2).

Glucotrol XL (gloo′cŏ-trōl″) [″ + (*con*)*trol*] SEE: *glipizide.*

glucuronide (gloo-kū′rŏn-īd) The combination of glucuronic acid with phenol, alcohol, or any acid containing the carboxyl, ⁻COOH, group.

glucuronyl transferase (gloo-kūr′ă-nĭl) An enzyme that converts unconjugated or indirect bilirubin to conjugated or direct bilirubin.

glue-sniffing (gloo′snif′ing) The inhalation of vapor from types of glue or solvents that contain toxic chemicals such as benzene, toluene, or xylene. This may produce an altered state of consciousness and occasionally death.

GLUT (gloot) Abbreviation for *glucose transporter,* a family of six closely related cell membrane proteins that carry glucose from the blood into cells. Slightly different GLUTs are found in different organs (e.g., in brain, muscle) and are designated GLUT 1, GLUT 2, up to GLUT 6.

glutamate (gloo'tă-māt) A salt of glutamic acid that functions as the brain's main excitatory neurotransmitter.

glutamic acid decarboxylase (glootam'ĭk) SEE: under *decarboxylase.*

glutamic acid decarboxylase antibody (gloo-tam'ĭk) SEE: under *antibody.*

glutaminase (gloot'ă-mĭ-nās″, ″glootam'ĭ-, -nāz″) [*glutamine* + *-ase*] An enzyme that catalyzes the breakdown of glutamine into glutamic acid and ammonia.

glutamine (gloo'tă-mĭn, -mēn″) ABBR: Q, or, Gln. A nonessential amino acid thought to play a major role in maintaining the integrity of the gastrointestinal mucosa, esp. during the hypermetabolic phase of the stress response. By enhancing cellular proliferation, it may reduce the incidence of bacterial translocation from the gut and improve absorption from the mucosa.

glutaral (gloot'ă-ral″) A solution of glutaraldehyde in sterile water. It is used as a disinfectant, has been used in pulpotomy, and is a component of some cosmetics.

glutaraldehyde (gloo″tă-răl'dĕ-hīd) **1.** A sterilizing agent effective against all microorganisms including viruses and spores. **2.** A fixative, usually followed by osmium, when preparing tissue specimens for transmission electron microscopy.

glutathione (gloo-tă-thī'ōn) [″ + Gr. *theion,* sulfur] ABBR: GSH. $C_{10}H_{17}N_3O_6S$; a tripeptide of glutamic acid, cysteine, and glycine. Found in small quantities in active animal tissues, it takes up and gives off hydrogen and is a powerful antioxidant important in cellular respiration.

PATIENT CARE: Overdose with acetaminophen depletes glutathione resources in the liver, resulting in hepatic failure. This toxic effect can be reversed by giving acetylcysteine (a biochemical precursor of cysteine and glutathione) to the intoxicated patient, if treatment can be initiated within 12 hr of dosing.

reduced g. The redox form of glutathione present in red blood cells.

glutathione peroxidase An antioxidant enzyme found in many mammalian cells, including red blood cells. Deficiencies of the enzyme have been linked to an increased risk of acute coronary syndrome.

gluteal (gloo'tē-ăl) [Gr. *gloutos,* buttock] Pert. to the buttocks.

gluten (gloot'ĕn) [L., glue] A group of proteins, found in barley, oats, rye, and wheat, that give flour its stickiness. Immunological intolerance to gluten causes celiac sprue.

gluten-free Containing little or no barley, oat, rye, or wheat proteins. The phrase is used to certify that particular foods or nutritional products are safe to eat for people with celiac disease.

glutenin (gloot'ĭn-ĭn) A protein, along with gliadin, that makes up gluten. One of its' properties is giving elasticity to bread doughs.

gluten-sensitive enteropathy Celiac sprue.

glutinous (gloo'tĭn-ŭs) [L. *glutinosus,* glue] Adhesive; sticky.

gly *glycine.*

glyburide (glī'bū-rīd) An oral drug, from the class of medications called sulfonylureas, used to lower blood glucose in type 2 diabetes mellitus. Glyburide should be used as part of a coordinated care plan that includes regular exercise and a diabetic diet. Its side effects include weight gain and excessively low blood glucose.

glycan (glī'kăn) Polysaccharide.

glycation (glī-kā'shŏn) The binding of a sugar molecule to an amino acid. In hyperglycemia and poorly controlled diabetes mellitus, sugar molecules become attached to cell surface proteins throughout the body; this sugar coating leads to microvascular damage in nerves, nephrons, and the retina. **glycated,** *adj.*

glycemia (glī-sē'mē-ă) [″ + *haima,* blood] The level of sugar (glucose) in the blood. **glycemic,** *adj.*

DL-glyceraldehyde (glĭs″ĕr-ăl'dĕ-hīd) An aldose, $CHOCH(OH)CH_2OH$, produced by the metabolism of fructose in the liver.

glyceride (glĭs'ĕr-īd) [Gr. *glykys,* sweet] An ester of glycerin compounded with an acid.

glycerin, glycerine (glĭs'ĕ-rĭn, ĕ-rēn″) [Gr. *glykeros,* sweet + *-ine*] $C_3H_8O_3$; a trihydric alcohol, trihydroxy-propane, present in chemical combination in all fats. It is a syrupy colorless liquid, soluble in all proportions in water and alcohol. It is made commercially by the hydrolysis of fats, esp. during the manufacture of soap, and is used extensively as a solvent, a preservative, and an emollient in various skin diseases. SYN: *glycerol.*

glycero-, glycer- [*glycer(in)*] Prefixes meaning *glycerol* or*glyceric acid.*

glycerol (glĭs'ĕ-rol″, röl″) [*glycero-* + *-ol*] Glycerin.

glycerolipid (glĭs″ĕ-rō-lĭp'ĭd) [*glycero-* + *lipid*] A fatty molecule composed of glycerol linked esterically to a fatty acid.

Glycerolipids include triglycerides and diglycerides.

glycerophosphocholine ABBR: GPC. A metabolite of lecithin. It is a phospholipid precursor.

glyceryl (glĭs′ĕr-ĭl) The trivalent radical C_3H_5 of glycerol.

glycine (glī′sēn, -sĭn) [Gr. *glykys*, sweet] ABBR: gly. NH_2CH_2COOH; a nonessential amino acid. SYN: *aminoacetic acid*.

Glycine max (glī′sēn măks) The scientific name for soybean.

glyco-, glyc- [Gr. *glykys*, sweet] Prefixes meaning *sugar, glucose*, or the presence of glycerol or a similar substance. SEE: also *gluco-*.

glycocalyx (glī″kō-kăl′ĭks) **1.** A thin layer of glycoprotein and oligosaccharides on the outer surface of cell membranes that contributes to cell adhesion and forms antigens involved in the recognition of "self." **2.** An adhesive substance secreted by microorganisms such as *Staphylococcus epidermidis* that helps them to adhere to prosthetic material in the body and prevents their phagocytosis by white blood cells.

glycocholate (glī″kō-kōl′āt) A salt of glycocholic acid.

glycogen (glī′kŏ-jĕn) [″ + *gennan*, to produce] A polysaccharide, $(C_6H_{10}O_5)$ *n*, commonly called animal starch, which is the storage form for glucose in the liver and muscles. Formation of glycogen from carbohydrate sources is called glycogenesis; from noncarbohydrate sources, glyconeogenesis. The conversion of glycogen to glucose is called glycogenolysis. SEE: *glycogen storage disease; glyconeogenesis*.

Glycogen is the form in which excess carbohydrate is stored in the liver and muscles; the hormones insulin and cortisol facilitate this process. When the blood glucose level decreases, the liver converts glycogen to glucose; this process is facilitated by the hormone glucagon or, in stressful situations, by epinephrine. In cells, glucose is oxidized to carbon dioxide and water with the release of energy in the forms of ATP and heat. In muscle cells under anaerobic conditions, glucose is metabolized only to lactic acid, and oxygen is needed to convert lactic acid back to glucose, primarily in the liver.

glycogenesis (glī″kō-jen′ĕ-sĭs) [″ + *genesis*, generation, birth] The formation of glycogen from glucose. SEE: *glyconeogenesis*. **glycogenetic** (glī″kŏ-jĕ-net′ik), *adj*.

glycogenic (glī′kō-jĕn′ĭk) Rel. to glycogen.

glycogenolysis (glī″kŏ-jĕ-nol′ĭ-sĭs) [″ + *gennan*, to produce, + *lysis*, dissolution] Conversion of glycogen into glucose in the liver and muscles. **glycogenolytic** (glī″kŏ-jĕn-ŏ-lit′ik), *adj*.

glycogenosis (glī″kō-jĕ-nō′sĭs) [*glycogen* + *-osis*] Glycogen storage disease.

glycogen storage disease Any of several heritable diseases characterized by the abnormal storage and accumulation of glycogen in the tissues, esp. in the liver. These diseases are grouped into various types according to the enzyme deficiency responsible. SYN: *glycogenosis*.

    g.s.d. type Ia A glycogen storage disease with onset usually in the first year of life. This autosomal recessive genetic disorder is due to a glucose-6-phosphatase deficiency. SYN: *Gierke disease*.

    g.s.d. type Ib A glycogen storage disease similar to type Ia but occurring at only one tenth its frequency. The disorder is due to a deficiency of glucose-6-phosphatase microsomal translocase.

    g.s.d. type II A glycogen storage disease caused by a deficiency of lysosomal α-glucosidase. SYN: *Pompe disease*.

    g.s.d. type III A glycogen storage disease caused by a deficiency of two debranching enzymes in liver and muscle tissues. SYN: *Forbes disease*.

    g.s.d. type IV A glycogen storage disease marked by liver failure, muscular weakness, muscular contractures, and death in the first few years of life. SYN: *Andersen disease; branching enzyme deficiency*.

    g.s.d. type V McArdle disease

glycogen supercompensation Carbohydrate **loading**.

glycohemoglobin (glī″kō-hēm′ă-glō-bĭn) *Hemoglobin* A_{1c}.

glycol (glī′kŏl, -kōl) [″ + *alcohol*] Any one of the dihydric alcohols related to ethylene glycol, $C_2H_6O_2$.

PATIENT CARE: The glycols, including ethylene and propylene glycol, are found in many antifreezes, solvents, detergents, and lacquers, and their ingestion is a common cause of accidental poisoning in the U.S. The intoxicated patient should be treated by decontaminating the stomach in order to decrease uptake of the chemical. Sodium bicarbonate is also given if metabolic acidosis develops. Seizures, brain damage, ophthalmic injury, and renal failure are common complications of exposure. Support of the patient often includes parenteral administration of thiamine and other vitamins, as well as of alcohol dehydrogenase inhibitors.

glycolipid(e) (glī″kō-lĭp′ĭd) [″ + *lipos*, fat] A compound of fatty acids with a carbohydrate, containing nitrogen but not phosphoric acid. It is found in the myelin sheath of nerves.

glycolysis (glī-kol′ĭ-sĭs) [″ + *lysis*, dissolution] The first stage of cell respiration, the series of reactions that convert a molecule of glucose to two molecules of pyruvic acid with the formation of a small amount of ATP. **glycolytic** (glī″kŏ-lit′ik), *adj*.

glycometabolism (glī″kō-mĕ-tăb′ō-lĭzm) Use of glucose by the body. SEE: *metabolism*.

glyconeogenesis (glī″kō-nē″ō-jĕn′ĕ-sĭs) [″ + *neos,* new, + *genesis,* generation, birth] The formation of glycogen from amino acids. It occurs in the liver when there are excess amino acids and decreased carbohydrate intake.

glycopeptide (glī-kō″pĕp′tĭd″) [″ + ″] A chemical compound in which carbohydrate molecules are linked covalently to a short amino acid chain.

glycopeptide antibiotic SEE: under *antibiotic*.

glycophorin (glī″kō-fō′rĭn) A glycoprotein that spans the bilipid layer of the red blood cell membrane. The extracellular end attaches to oligosaccharide blood group antigens. This protein provides the conduit through which anions pass in and out of the red blood cell.

glycoprotein (glī″kŏ-prō′tēn″, prōt′ē-ĭn) [*glyco-* + *protein*] A compound consisting of a carbohydrate and protein. SYN: *glucoprotein.*

    P-g. A cell membrane pump that influences cellular uptake and release of chemicals. It affects the relative resistance or susceptibility of cells to drug therapy.

    pregnancy-specific beta₁ glycoprotein A protein found in 97% of women who have been pregnant for 6 to 8 weeks and in 100% of those at later stages of pregnancy. The function of this protein is not known, but it may be useful in estimating the quality of placental function.

    variable surface g. ABBR: VSG. An antigen expressed on the surface of an microorganism that changes over time and helps the organism evade host antibodies.

glycosaminoglycan (glī″kōs-ăme-nō-glī′kăn) A complex polysaccharide found in cartilage, intercellular material, and the basement membranes of epithelial tissues; also called mucopolysaccharide.

glycoside (glī′kō-sīd) A substance derived from plants that, on hydrolysis, yields a sugar and one or more additional products. Depending on the sugar formed, glycosides are designated glucosides or galactosides. Digitalis is a cardiac glycoside. SEE: *glucoside*.

glycosphingolipids (glī″kō-sfĭng″ō-lĭp′ĭds) A group of carbohydrate-containing fatty acid derivatives of ceramide. Three classes of these lipids are cerebrosides, gangliosides, and ceramide oligosaccharides. When the enzymes essential to the metabolism of these compounds are absent, the glycosphingolipids accumulate, particularly in the nervous system. Death is the usual outcome.

glycosuria (glī″kō-shoor′ē-ă) [*glyco-* + *-uria*] An abnormal amount of glucose in the urine. Traces of sugar, particularly glucose, may occur in normal urine but are not detected by ordinary qualitative methods. The presence of a reducing sugar found during routine urinalysis is suggestive but not diagnostic of diabetes mellitus. It is found when the blood glucose level exceeds the renal threshold (about 170 mg/dL of blood). The fasting level of blood glucose is normally between 70 and 99 mg/dL of blood. SYN: *glucosuria.* SEE: *diabetes mellitus.*

    renal g. Glycosuria occurring when glucose is persistent and not accompanied by hyperglycemia and when the renal threshold for glucose is decreased.

glycosylation (glī″kōs-ī-lā′shŭn) The chemical linkage of sugar molecules to proteins. In diabetes mellitus and some other diseases, excessive levels of glucose in the blood may gradually sugarcoat tissues and cells, causing them to function improperly. Glycosylation may injure cytokines, cell receptors, the extracellular matrix, retinas, kidneys, nerves, and arteries. SYN: *protein g.*

    protein g. Glycosylation.

glycosylphosphatidylinositol (glī″kō-sĭl-fŏs″fă-tī-dĭl-ĭn-ŏs′ī-tŏl″) ABBR: GPI. A lipid in the plasma membrane of cells that anchors proteins on the cell's surface. Some of the proteins held on the cell surface protect cells against attack by serum complement. Mutations that decrease or eliminate GPI are responsible for the destruction of blood cells by the complement system, which characterizes the disease called paroxysmal nocturnal hemoglobinuria.

glycyltryptophan (glĭs″ĭl-trĭp′tō-făn) A dipeptide of glycine and tryptophan.

glycyrrhiza (glĭs-ĭ-rī′ză) [L. *glycyrrhiza* fr Gr. *glykyrrhiza,* sweet root] The dried root of *Glycyrrhiza glabra,* known commercially as Spanish licorice, used as an ingredient of glycyrrhiza fluid extract and glycyrrhiza syrup, both of which are used as flavoring agents in compounding medicine. This substance has a weak aldosterone-like effect and may therefore increase blood pressure. SEE: *licorice.*

Glycyrrhiza glabra (glĭs-ĭ-rī′ză gla′bră) Licorice.

glyoxalase (glē-ōk′să-lās) An enzyme that catalyzes the conversion of methylglyoxal to lactic acid by the addition of water.

glyoxylic acid (glī″ok-sil′ik) SEE: under *acid.*

glyphosate (glī-fŏs′āt) [gly(cine) + phos(ph)ate] A water-soluble, broad-spectrum herbicide commonly used in American agriculture. It is the active ingredient of several brand-name weed killers.

CAS Number: 1071-83-6. It is a suspected human health hazard.

GNA *geriatric nursing assistant.*

gnashing (năsh'ing) Grinding, as of the teeth. SEE: *bruxism.*

gnat (năt) Any of a number of small insects belonging to the order Diptera, suborder Orthorrhapha, including black flies, midges, and sandflies. The term applies generally to insects smaller than mosquitoes.

gnathic (năth'ĭk) [Gr. *gnathos,* jaw] Pert. to an alveolar process or to the jaw.

gnathion (năth'ē-ŏn) The lowest point of the middle line of the lower jaw; a craniometric point.

gnatho-, gnath- [Gr. *gnathos,* jaw] Prefixes meaning *jaw* or *cheek.*

Gnathostoma (nă-thos'tŏ-mă) [*gnatho- + stoma*] A genus of nematodes (worms) that infest the intestines of cats, dogs, and other animals. They are endemic to Asia and occasionally are acquired by humans, in whom they cause eosinophilic meningoencephalitis.

gnathostomiasis (năth″ŏ-stō-mī'ă-sĭs) A form of visceral larva migrans infection of human tissues caused by the nematode parasite of dogs and cats, *Gnathostoma spinigerum.* Acquisition is by ingestion of undercooked fish and poultry containing the larvae. The parasite migrates through various body tissues and causes a transient inflammatory response and possibly abscess formation. If the brain is invaded, eosinophilic meningoencephalitis may develop and can be fatal. Travelers to Asia should avoid eating raw or undercooked fish or poultry.

TREATMENT: Therapy consists of surgical removal of lesions and administration of albendazole.

gnotobiotics (nō″tō-bī-ŏt'ĭks) [Gr. *gnotos,* known, + *bios,* life] The study of

animals that have been raised in germ-controlled or germ-free surroundings.

Gn-RH *gonadotropin-releasing hormone.* SEE: *hormone.*

goal The desired outcome of actions to alter status or behavior. SEE: *nursing goal.*

Godfrey test (god'frē″) A test to identify a tear of the posterior cruciate ligament. With the patient lying supine and the hips and knees flexed to 90°, the examiner lifts both of the patient's lower legs and holds them parallel to the table. The relative position of the lower legs is then observed. Inferior displacement (a downward sagging) of the involved knee can indicate a tear of the posterior cruciate ligament.

goiter (goyt'ĕr) [Fr. *goitre* fr L. *guttur,* throat] Enlargement of the thyroid gland. An enlarged thyroid gland may be caused by thyroiditis, benign thyroid nodules, malignancy, iodine deficiency, or any condition that causes hyperfunction or hypofunction of the gland. SYN: *struma.* SEE: illus.

   adenomatous g. An outdated term for multinodular goiter.

   colloid g. A goiter in which there is a great increase of the follicular contents.

   congenital g. A goiter present at birth.

   diffuse g. A goiter in which the thyroid tissue is diffuse, in contrast to its nodular form as in adenomatous goiter.

   diving g. A movable goiter, located either below or above the sternal notch.

   endemic g. Goiter development in certain geographic localities, esp. where the iodine content in food and water is deficient. Goiters are more prevalent in freshwater and lake areas and less so on the seacoast, owing to the lack of iodine in freshwater. The treatment con-

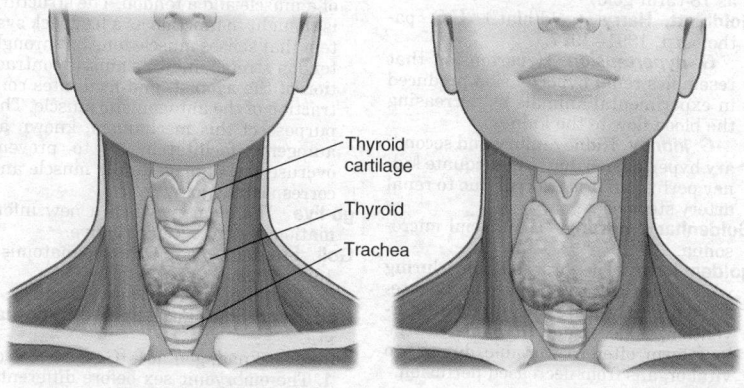

Thyroid cartilage

Thyroid

Trachea

Normal thyroid   **Goiter**

GOITER

sists of iodine taken orally or in iodized salt.

exophthalmic g. Goiter associated with exopthalmos, as in Graves ophthalmopathy. SYN: *thyroid **cachexia***.

intrathoracic g. A goiter in which a portion of the thyroid tissue lies within the thoracic cavity.

multinodular g. A goiter having many circumscribed nodules.

nodular g. A goiter that contains nodules.

simple g. A goiter unaccompanied by constitutional symptoms.

substernal g. An enlargement of the lower part of the thyroid isthmus.

toxic g. An exophthalmic goiter or a goiter in which there is an excessive production of the thyroid hormone.

goitrogen (goy′trō-jĕn) [L. *guttur*, throat, + *gennan*, to produce] A substance that produces massive enlargement of the thyroid by inhibiting iodide metabolism and thyroid hormone synthesis. Goitrogens are found naturally in cabbage, cassava, rutabagas, soy, and raw turnips. They are inactivated by cooking.

gold (gōld) SYMB: Au. A yellow metallic chemical element, atomic weight (mass) 196.967, specific gravity 19.32, atomic number 79. Its salts have been used to treat early rheumatoid arthritis not adequately controlled by other anti-inflammatory agents or conservative therapy. Injection of radioactive gold, [198]Au, is used to treat certain types of cancer and to help outline certain organs, as in liver scanning. SYN: *aurum*. SEE: *scanning*.

g. alloy An alloy of gold with copper, silver, platinum, or other metals added for strength or hardness. Pure gold is rated 24 carats. A gold alloy that contains other metals is less than 24 carats. Thus, 18 parts of gold mixed with 6 parts of another metal would be rated as 18-carat gold.

Goldblatt, Harry (gōld′blat″) U.S. pathologist, 1891–1977.

G. hypertension Hypertension that resembles renal hypertension produced in experimental animals by decreasing the blood flow to the kidney.

G. kidney Kidney injury and secondary hypertension due to inadequate kidney perfusion. It may occur due to renal artery stenosis.

Goldenhar syndrome Hemifacial microsomia.

golden hour The first 60 min during which a critical trauma patient must receive definitive care and surgical intervention, as necessary, to counteract the long-term, often irreversible, damage to vital organs from decreased perfusion.

⚠ The concept of a "golden hour" is a rough approximation. It has not been determined whether critically injured patients on average do best when their care is provided in 60 min versus, say, 30 min or 75 min.

goldenseal (gōld′ĕn-sēl) An herbal remedy used as an eyewash and as a treatment for irritated mucous membranes. Some illicit-drug users believe the herb will mask the results of drug-screening tests; this use has not been validated. It is also purported to enhance immunity. Although goldenseal is one of the top-selling herbal remedies, many commonly marketed products advertised as goldenseal contain adulterants (ingredients other than those in the natural herb). Goldenseal is an endangered plant species.

gold standard In medical care and experimental medicine, a therapeutic action, drug, or procedure that is the best available. This standard is the one to which other therapeutic actions, drugs, or procedures are compared in order to determine their efficacy.

Golgi, Camillo (gol′jē) Italian pathologist, 1843–1926.

G. apparatus A lamellar membranous organelle in almost all cells, best viewed by electron microscopy. It consists of curved parallel series of flattened sacs that are often expanded at their ends. In secretory cells, the apparatus concentrates and packages the secretory product. Its function in other cells, although apparently important, is poorly understood. SYN: ***Golgi*** *complex*.

G. cell A multipolar nerve cell in the cerebral cortex and posterior horns of the spinal cord. Type I possesses long axons; type II, short axons. SYN: ***Golgi*** *neuron*.

G. complex G. apparatus.

G. neuron G. cell.

G. tendon organ ABBR: GTO. A spindle-shaped structure at the junction of a muscle and a tendon. The structure is thought to function as a feedback system that senses muscle tension through tendon stretch, inhibits muscle contraction of the agonist, and facilitates contraction of the antagonistic muscle. The purpose of this mechanism, known as autogenic facilitation, is to prevent overuse and damage to the muscle and corresponding joint.

go-live The moment when a new information system becomes active.

Goll, Friedrich (gol) Swiss anatomist, 1829–1903.

column of G. Fasciculus gracilis.

Goltz syndrome Focal dermal **hypoplasia**.

gonad (gō′năd, gŏn′ăd) [Gr. *gone*, seed] **1.** The embryonic sex before differentiation into definitive testis or ovary. **2.** A generic term referring to the female ovaries and the male testes. Each forms the cells necessary for human reproduction: spermatozoa from the testes, ova from the ovaries. SEE: *estrogen; ovary; testicle; testosterone.*

HORMONES: *Female:* The follicles of the ovaries secrete estrogen, which helps regulate the menstrual cycle and the development of the secondary sex characteristics. The corpus luteum also produces progesterone, which stimulates growth of blood vessels in the endometrium for the implantation of a fertilized egg. *Male:* The interstitial cells of the testes secrete testosterone, which is essential for maturation of sperm and for development of the secondary sex characteristics.

Hormones from both sexes have been isolated and standardized and are used to treat conditions arising from an insufficiency of these hormones. **gonadal,** *adj.*

gonadarche (gō″nă-dar′kē) [*gonado-* + Gr. *archē,* beginning] The maturation of the gonads, i.e., of the ovaries in young females or the testes in young males.

gonadectomy (gŏn-ă-dĕk′tō-mē) [Gr. *gonos,* genitals, + *ektome,* excision] The excision of a testis or ovary.

gonadoblastoma (gŏn″ă-dō-blăs-tōm′ă) A benign germ cell tumor typically found in children with gonadal dysgenesis or intersex disorders. It is associated with pseudohermaphroditism (the external development of masculine sexual organs coupled with the internal development of a uterus). Untreated patients may occasionally develop malignant germ cell tumors. Surgical removal is the preferred treatment.

gonadotrophic, gonadotropic (gŏn″ă-dō-trŏf′ĭk) [″ + *trophe,* nourishment] Rel. to stimulation of the gonads.

gonadotropin, gonadotrophin (gō-nad″ŏ-trō′pĭn, gō-nad″ŏ-trō′fĭn) [*gonado-* + *-tropin*] A gonad-stimulating hormone, such as luteinizing hormone (LH) or follicle-stimulating hormone (FSH). SYN: *gonadotropic hormone.*

    human chorionic g. ABBR: hCG. A hormone, secreted in early pregnancy by the trophoblasts of the fertilized ovum, that maintains the corpus luteum during early pregnancy, stimulating it to secrete both estrogen and progesterone. Laboratory tests for hCG in maternal blood or urine are used as pregnancy tests and in follow-up assessments after treatment for hydatid mole and choriocarcinoma.

    human menopausal g. ABBR: hMG. A purified form of the pituitary gonadotropins follicle-stimulating hormone and luteinizing hormone; it may be used therapeutically to treat infertility, hypogonadotropic hypogonadism, polycystic ovary disease, and other conditions. In the management of infertility, it is particu-

larly used for women with ovulatory difficulties, in whom it stimulates follicular growth and maturation, ovulation, and development of the corpus luteum.

gonadotropin-releasing hormone analog SEE: under *analogue.*

gonarthritis (gŏn″ăr-thrī′tĭs) [Gr. *gony,* knee, + *arthron,* joint, + *itis,* inflammation] Inflammation of the knee joint.

Gongylonema (gon″jĭ-lō-nē′mă) [Gr. *gongylos,* round, + *nēma,* thread, yarn] A genus of nematode worms belonging to the suborder Spirurata, usually parasitic in the wall of the esophagus and stomach of domestic animals. Occasionally, they are parasitic in humans. *G. pulchrum* is the species most frequently involved.

gonio lens, gonioscopy lens SEE: under *lens.*

goniometer (gō″nē-om′ĕt-er) [Gr. *gōnia,* angle + *-meter*] An instrument to measure joint movements and angles. Various sizes and types of goniometers are available, including finger goniometers, bubble goniometers, gravity goniometers, and recording electrogoniometers. SYN: *arthrometer.* SEE: illus.

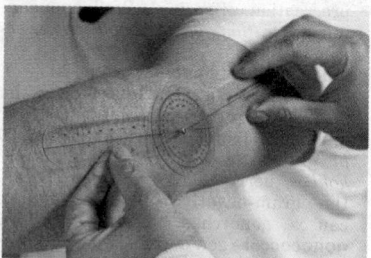

Extension

Flexion

GONIOMETER

These goniometers are measuring a patient's elbow at extension and flexion.

    bubble g. Inclinometer (2).

gonion (gō′nē-ŏn) [Gr. *gonia,* angle] The lowest and most lateral point of the angle of the mandible or lower jaw.

gonio photography (gōn′ē-ō) [*gonio-*

(scope)] Photography of the anterior chamber of the eye with a gonioscope.

goniopuncture (gō″nē-ō-pŭnk′tūr) A surgical procedure for allowing aqueous humor to drain from the eye, used in treating glaucoma.

gonioscope (gō′nē-ō-skōp) [″ + *skopein*, to examine] An instrument for inspecting the angle of the anterior chamber of the eye and for determining ocular motility and rotation.

gonioscopy Inspection of the anterior chamber of the eye using a gonioscope.

   indentation g. A means of examining the anterior chamber of the eye in proven or suspected glaucoma, in which a small lens is pressed on the cornea, moving fluid from the anterior chamber toward the periphery of the iris and trabecular meshwork. The displacement of fluid toward the margins of the anterior chamber allows the examiner to see if the iris is stuck to the meshwork or just resting upon it.

goniotomy (gō″nē-ŏt′ō-mē) [″ + *tome*, incision] A surgical procedure for removing obstructions to the free flow of aqueous humor into the canal of Schlemm of the eye.

gono-, gon- [L. fr. Gr. *gonos*, genitals, procreation, offspring] Prefixes meaning *generation, genitals, offspring, semen.*

gonococcemia (gŏn″ō-kŏk-sē′mē-ă) [″ + ″ + *haima*, blood] Gonococci in the blood; gonococcal septicemia.

gonococcus (gŏn″ō-kok′ŭs, gŏn″ō-kok′sī″) *pl.* **gonococci** [Gr. *gonos*, genitals, + *kokkos*, berry] *Neisseria gonorrhoeae*, the gram-negative diplococcus that causes gonorrhea. SEE: *gonorrhea.* **gonococcal** (gŏn″ō-kok′ăl), *adj.* **gonococcic** (gŏn″ō-kok′sik), *adj.*

gonorrhea (gŏn″ō-rē′ă) [*gono- + -rrhea*] A sexually transmitted infection caused by the gram-negative diplococcus *Neisseria gonorrhoeae*. The disease often causes inflammation of the urethra, prostate, cervix, fallopian tubes, rectum, and/or pharynx. Bloodborne infection may spread to the joints and skin, and congenitally transmitted infection to the eyes of a newborn during vaginal birth may cause neonatal conjunctivitis. Infection around the liver may result from peritoneal spread of the disease. Although members of either sex with urogenital gonorrhea may be asymptomatic, women are much less likely to notice burning with urination, urethral discharge, or perineal pain than men, in whom these symptoms are present 98% of the time. Coinfection with *Chlamydia trachomatis* is common in both sexes: some studies have shown simultaneous infection with both organisms to be as high as 30%. Even though syphilis rarely accompanies gonorrheal infection, patients with gonorrhea are routinely tested for this disease. Young, sexually active teenagers and young adults with multiple partners are at highest risk for contracting gonorrhea. In 2009 301,174 cases of gonorrhea were reported in the U.S., a rate of 99.1 cases per 100,000 population. Source: www.cdc.gov/std/tats09/gonorrhea.htm SEE: *safe sex; Nursing Diagnoses Appendix; Standard Precautions Appendix.*

SYMPTOMS: Urethral symptoms in men typically include discomfort with urination (dysuria) accompanied by a yellow, mucopurulent penile discharge. Painful induration of the penis may occur in some cases. Women may have urethral or vaginal, greenish yellow discharge, dysuria, urinary frequency, lower abdominal pain, tender Skene and Bartholin glands, or fever, dyspareunia, and other symptoms of pelvic inflammatory disease. Most women are asymptomatic.

DIAGNOSIS: In men, Gram stain of the urethral discharge is very accurate in diagnosing gonorrhea. In both men and women, urethral, cervical, or anal swabs, or urinary specimes are typically tested with nucleic acid testing that detects genetic sequences unique to the bacteria. Single specimens can be used to identify infections with gonorrhea and/or *Chlamydia* simultaneously.

PROPHYLAXIS: Safe sexual practices limit the spread of gonorrhea and have decreased the incidence of the disease. To prevent gonorrhea in newborns, all babies are treated with a thin ribbon of either erythromycin or tetracycline ointment in the conjunctival sac of each eye. SEE: *ophthalmia neonatorum.*

TREATMENT: Gonorrhea can be treated with cephalosporins (such as ceftriaxone, cefixime, or cefpodoxime) or fluoroquinolones, although bacteria have evolved that are resistant to many of these antibiotics. *Chlamydia* coinfection is typical and is usually treated with doxycycline. For pregnant women and for those allergic to penicillin, a single dose of ceftriaxone and erythromycin is recommended (doxycycline is contraindicated in pregnancy). Patients should return for a follow-up visit 1 week after treatment for recheck of cultures to confirm that a cure has been effective. Updates on the treatment of gonorrhea and other sexually transmitted infections are available at www.cdc.gov/std.

PATIENT CARE: Antibiotics should be taken as prescribed and, if more than one dose is needed, the full course of therapy completed. Moist heat or sitz baths should be taken as directed to relieve discomfort. The patient should avoid contact with his or her genitourinary discharges and wash hands carefully so that the eyes do not become contaminated. Until a course of treatment and follow-up cultures are completed, the patient should abstain from sexual intercourse because he or she may still be infectious and able to transmit the infection.

The patient is taught to recognize and report adverse drug reactions. The need for testing for other sexually transmitted diseases is discussed, as well as prevention of future infections (using condoms, washing genitalia with soap and water preintercourse and postintercourse, avoiding sharing washcloths) and the importance of follow-up testing. All persons with whom the patient has had sexual contact should be tested and receive treatment, even if a culture is negative. The patient and known sexual contacts are reported to the local and public health department for appropriate follow-up. **gonorrheal,** *adj.*

Gonyaulax (go″nē-ō′laks″) [Gr. *gony,* knee + Gr. *aulax,* furrow] A genus of dinoflagellates that causes certain shellfish that eat them to become toxic. It is one of the causes of red tides.

Goodpasture syndrome (gud′pas″chŭr) [Ernest William Goodpasture, U.S. pathologist, 1886–1960] A rare autoimmune illness characterized by progressive glomerulonephritis, hemoptysis, and hemosiderosis. Death is usually due to renal failure.

Good Samaritan Law SEE: under *law.*

gooseflesh (goos′flĕsh) Piloerection.

goosegrass (goos′gras″) Galium aparine.

Gossypium (gŏ-sĭp′ē-ŭm) [L.] A genus of perennial shrubs of the Malvaceae family, widely grown because of the cotton fiber derived from its seed covering. The bark of some species is diuretic, emmenagogic, and oxytocic. SEE: *cotton; gossypol.*

gossypol (gŏs′ē-pōl) A toxic chemical present in cottonseed, which has been used experimentally as an infertility agent in men.

Gottron's papules [Gottron, H.A., Ger. dermatologist, 1890–1974] Faint red or violet papules occurring over the knuckles and sometimes the interphalangeal joints in patients with dermatomyositis. This sign is diagnostic of the illness.

gotu kola (gōt′oo kō′lă) Centella asiatica.

gouge (gowj) An instrument used for cutting away the hard tissue of bone.

gout (gowt) [Fr. *goute,* fr L. *gutta,* a drop] A form of arthritis marked by the deposition of monosodium urate crystals in joints and other tissues. Any joint may be affected, but gout usually begins in the knee or the first metatarsophalangeal joint of the foot. SYN: *monosodium urate deposition disease.* SEE: *tophus; Nursing Diagnoses Appendix.*

SYMPTOMS: Most hyperuricemic people are asymptomatic between acute attacks. When an attack of acute gouty arthritis develops, it usually begins at night with moderate pain that increases in intensity to the point where no body position provides relief. Low-grade fever and joint inflammation (hot, exquisitely tender, dusky-red or cyanotic joints) may be present. SEE: illus.

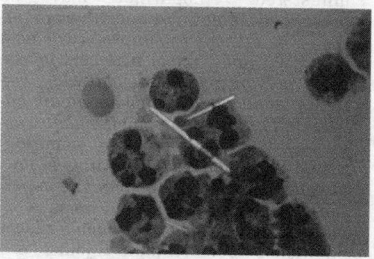

GOUT

Uric acid crystals and white blood cells in synovial fluid (orig. mag. ×500)

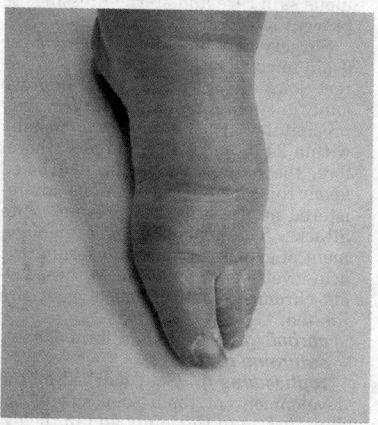

ACUTE GOUT

The entire foot of this patient is inflamed and swollen.

TREATMENT: Colchicine, nonsteroidal anti-inflammatory agents, or corticosteroids are used to treat acute gouty attacks. Long-term therapy aims at preventing hyperuricemia by giving uricosuric drugs such as probenecid, or xanthine oxidase inhibitors such as allopurinol. Patients with gout have a tendency to form uric acid kidney stones. The diet should be well balanced and devoid of purine-rich foods, e.g., anchovies, sardines, liver, kidneys, sweetbreads, lentils, beer, wine, and other alcoholic beverages, because these raise urate levels. Fluid intake should be encouraged.

PATIENT CARE: During the acute

phase, bedrest is prescribed for at least the first 24 hr, and affected joints are elevated, immobilized, and protected by a bed cradle. Analgesics are administered, and hot or cold packs applied, depending on which the patient finds most helpful. The patient is taught about these measures. Colchicine, nonsteroidal anti-inflammatory agents, prednisone, or other prescribed drugs are administered. Allopurinol may be prescribed as maintenance therapy after acute attacks to suppress uric acid formation and control uric acid levels, thus preventing future attacks. Patients should be warned to report adverse effects of allopurinol, e.g., drowsiness, dizziness, nausea, vomiting, urinary frequency, dermatitis. A low-purine diet is recommended. The importance of gradual weight reduction is explained if obesity, which places additional stress on painful joints, is a factor. If soft-tissue tophi are present, e.g., near joints in fingers, knees, or feet, the patient should wear soft clothing to cover these areas and should use meticulous skin care and sterile dressings to prevent infection of open lesions.

Surgery may be required to excise or drain infected or ulcerated tophi, to correct joint deformities, or to improve joint function. Even minor surgery may precipitate attacks of gout, usually within 24 to 96 hr after surgery; therefore, the patient should be instructed about this risk and medications administered as prescribed to prevent acute attacks. The goal of chronic management of gout is to maintain serum uric acid levels below 6 mg/dL. At these levels chronic complications of gout are limited.

chronic g. A persistent form of gout.

saturnine g. Lead **g.**

tophaceous g. Gout marked by the development of tophi (deposits of sodium urate) in the joints and in the external ear.

gouty (gowt′ē) Of the nature of or rel. to gout.

governor vessel SEE: under *vessel*.

Gowers, Sir William Richard (gow′ĕrz) Brit. neurologist, 1845–1915.

G. maneuver G. sign.

G. sign A clinical sign of muscular dystrophy in childhood, indicative of weakness of the hip and knee extensors.

G. tract A bundle of fibers from the posterior roots of the lateral tract of the spinal cord, reaching the cerebellum by way of the superior peduncle.

GP *general practitioner.*

gp120 A glycoprotein found on the outer surface of the HIV virus. It facilitates binding of the virus to CD4+ lymphocytes. Its molecular weight is 120 kD.

G6PD *glucose-6-phosphate dehydrogenase.*

GPT *glutamic-pyruvic* **transaminase**.

gr *grain.*

graafian follicle (gräf′ē-ăn) [Regnier de Graaf, Dutch physician and anatomist, 1641–1673] A mature vesicular follicle of the ovary. Beginning with puberty and continuing until the menopause, except during pregnancy, a graafian follicle develops at approx. monthly intervals. Each follicle contains a nearly mature ovum (an oocyte) that, on rupture of the follicle, is discharged from the ovary, a process called ovulation. Ovulation usually occurs 12 to 16 days before the first day of the next menstrual period. Within the ruptured graafian follicle, the corpus luteum develops. Both the follicle and the corpus luteum are endocrine glands, the former secreting estrogens, and the latter, estrogen and progesterone. SEE: *ovum* for illus.

gracile (grăs′ĭl) [L. *gracilis,* slender] Slender; slight.

gracile nucleus SEE: under *nucleus*.

gracilis (grăs′ĭ-lĭs) [L., slender] A long slender muscle on the medial aspect of the thigh.

grade (grād) A standard measurement or assessment.

Gradenigo syndrome (gra-dĕn-ē′gō) [Giuseppe Gradenigo, Italian physician, 1859–1926] Suppurative otitis media, pain in the distribution of the trigeminal nerve, and abducens palsy, typically associated with infection or cancer at the base of the skull.

gradient (grād′ē-ĕnt) [L. *gradi,* to step, walk] **1.** A slope or grade. **2.** An increase or decrease of varying degrees or the curve that represents such.

alveolar/arterial g. ABBR: A/a gradient. The difference between the calculated oxygen pressure available in the alveolus and the arterial oxygen tension. It measures the efficiency of gas exchange. SYN: *respiratory* **index**.

The formula for measuring the gradient is known as the partial pressure of oxygen dissolved in arterial blood and is shown below.

$$PaO_2 = FIO_2(P_B - P_{H2O}) - PaCO_2/0.8,$$

where FIO_2 is the inspired oxygen concentration; P_B, barometric pressure; P_{H2O}, partial pressure of water vapor (47 mm Hg); $PaCO_2$, partial pressure of carbon dioxide dissolved in arterial blood; and PaO_2, partial pressure of oxygen dissolved in arterial blood.

authority g. The perceived difference in status between different members of an organization. It is a barrier to effective communication and a potential source of interpersonal resentment and organizational error. Authority gradients exist in health care organizations when one member of a team, e.g., a medical assistant, feels he or she cannot broach an important safety issue with another member on a higher level.

average g. In sensitometry, a measure of the contrast of the film or film-screen system by determination of the slope of the sensitometric curve.

axial g. A gradient of physiological or metabolic activity exhibited by embryos and many adult animals. The principal gradient follows the main axis of the body, being highest at the anterior end and lowest at the posterior end.

concentration g. The difference in the amounts of a substance on either side of a membrane or in two areas of a biological system. Substances diffuse down a concentration gradient, from the area of higher concentration to lower concentration.

hepatic venous pressure g. The venous pressures differences in the portal vein and the inferior vena cava distal to the liver. Large pressure gradients are found in patients with liver diseases such as cirrhosis. Cirrhosis causes portal hypertension and the development of esophageal and gastric varices.

metabolic g. A gradient in metabolic activity that exists in certain structures, such as the small intestine from duodenum to ileum or in embryos from animal to vegetal poles, in which metabolic activity is highest in one region and becomes progressively lower away from this region.

pressure g. The difference in hydrostatic pressure on either side of a membrane. As the difference in pressures rises, filtration increases from the area of high pressure to the area of low pressure.

graduate (graj′ū-āt″, -ăt) [L. *graduari*, to take a degree] **1.** A vessel, usually a cylinder with one end closed, and marked by scribed lines for measuring liquids. **2.** One who has been awarded an academic or professional degree from a college or university. **3.** One who has completed a course of treatment, esp. a complex or intensive treatment. The term is used colloquially, e.g., a graduate of the neonatal intensive care unit or a graduate of the hematologic stem cell transplantation program.

graduated (grăj-oo-ā′tĭd) Marked by a series of lines indicating degrees of measurement, weight, or volume.

Graefe, Albrecht von (grāf′ĕ) Ger. ophthalmologist, 1828–1870.

   G. forceps Serrated ophthalmologic forceps, straight or curved.

   G. sign Failure of the upper lid to follow a downward movement of the eyeball when the patient changes his or her vision from looking up to looking down. This finding, referred to colloquially as "lid lag," is seen in Graves' disease (hyperthyroidism) with exophthalmos.

graft (graft) [L. *graphium*, hunting knife] **1.** Tissue transplanted or implanted in a part of the body to repair a defect. A homograft (or allograft) is a graft of material from another individual of the same species. A heterograft (or xenograft) is a graft of material from an individual of another species. **2.** The process of placing tissue from one site to another to repair a defect.

allogeneic g. Allograft.

autologous g. A graft taken from another part of the patient's body.

axillofemoral bypass g. The surgical establishment of a connector between the axillary artery and the common femoral arteries. A synthetic artery graft is used and implanted subcutaneously. This technique is used in treating patients with insufficient blood flow to the legs (peripheral vascular disease).

bone g. A piece of bone taken from one location (such as the ilium or fibula) and inserted to replace or restore another osseous structure. Bone storage banks have been established.

bypass g. A surgical conduit inserted into the vascular system that routes blood around an obstructed vessel. SEE: *coronary artery bypass*.

cable g. A nerve graft made up of bundles of segments from an unimportant nerve. SYN: *rope g.*

cadaver g. Grafting tissue, including skin, cornea, or bone, obtained from a body immediately after death.

delayed g. A skin graft that is partially elevated and then replaced so that it may be moved later to another site.

dermal g. A split-thickness or full-thickness skin graft. The graft will grow hair and have active sweat and sebum glands.

endovascular g. A graft implanted within an existing blood vessel.

fascia g. A graft using fascia, usually removed from the fascia lata, for repairing defects in other tissues.

free g. A graft that is completely separated from its original site and then transferred.

full-thickness g. A graft of the entire layer of skin without the subcutaneous fat.

gingival g. A sliding graft employing the gingival papilla as the graft material.

heterotopic g. SEE: *heterotopic transplantation*.

homologous g. A graft taken from a donor of the same species as the recipient.

lamellar g. A very thin corneal graft used to replace the surface layer of opaque corneal tissue.

mesh g. A split-thickness graft that contains multiple perforations or slits, which allow the graft to be expanded so that a much larger area is covered. The holes in the graft are covered by new tissue as the graft spreads. A mesh graft heals with a less smooth cosmetic result than a sheet graft but is able to cover a larger defect.

nerve g. The transplantation of a healthy nerve to replace a segment of a damaged nerve.

omental g. The use of a portion of the omentum to cover or repair a defect in a hollow viscus or to cover a suture line in an abdominal organ.

ovarian g. The implantation of a section of an ovary into the muscles of the abdominal wall.

pedicle g. Pedicle **flap**.

punch g. A full-thickness graft, usually circular, for transplanting skin containing hair follicles to a bald area.

sheet g. A skin graft, typically removed from a donor site on the thigh, that is placed directly over a burn wound to promote healing.

skin g. The use of small sections of skin harvested from a donor site and transplanted to an injured area of skin to repair a defect, such as a large full-thickness burn. Commonly used grafts include split-thickness, full-thickness, and xenografts. Biosynthetic grafts (collagen and synthetics) also are used to minimize fluid and protein loss from burn injuries, prevent infection, and reduce pain. The skin surface at the receiving site should be clean and raw.

PATIENT CARE: Before surgery, assessments are made of the patient's general health. Confirmation is needed that appropriate laboratory parameters, including hemoglobin and coagulation studies, are acceptable as they may affect the surgical result. The donor and recipient sites are prepared according to protocol. The postsurgical appearance of the wound and dressing and, if applicable, the need to immobilize the part after surgery are explained. Both patient and family receive support and encouragement. The graft is observed at regular intervals postoperatively for swelling or for development of hematoma and signs of purulent drainage. Aseptic technique is followed in applying dressings and compresses to prevent infection. Prophylactic antibiotics are administered as prescribed, and the graft site is immobilized to allow healing. Analgesics are administered as necessary to relieve pain. Before discharge, the patient learns about wound care and the need to keep the graft site clean, well lubricated, and away from sunlight according to the health care provider's instructions. Elastic support garments, reconstructive surgery, physical and occupational therapy, and psychological counseling may be required.

split-skin g. Split-thickness **g.**

split-thickness g. A graft of a part of the epidermis and part of the dermis. SYN: *split-skin g.*

grafting (grăft′ing) The act of applying a graft of skin or tissue from a healthy site to an injured site.

graft-versus-host disease ABBR: GVH. Immunological injury suffered by an immunosuppressed recipient of a bone marrow transplant. The donated lymphoid cells (the "graft") attack the recipient (the "host"), causing damage, esp. to the skin, liver, and gastrointestinal tract. GVH occurs in about 50% of allogeneic bone marrow transplants. It may develop in the first 60 days after transplantation ("acute" GVH) or many months later ("chronic" GVH).

graft versus leukemia effect In allogeneic bone marrow transplantation, the killing of the recipient's leukemic clone by lymphocytes in the donated marrow. SYN: *graft versus tumor effect.*

graft versus tumor effect Graft versus leukemia effect.

grain [L. *granum*] ABBR: gr. **1.** A weight; 0.065 of a gram. **2.** The seed or seedlike fruit of many members of the grass family, esp. corn, wheat, oats, and other cereals. **3.** Direction of fibers or layers. SYN: *granum.*

gram ABBR: g. A unit of weight (mass) of the metric system. It equals approx. the weight of a cubic centimeter or a milliliter of water. One gram is equal to 15.432 gr or 0.03527 oz (avoirdupois), 1000 g are equal to 1 kg. SEE: *kilogram;* table.

fat g. A standard measure of fat and the calories (9 kcal/g) contained. Counting and limiting fat grams is a method used in weight-reduction diets.

-gram [Gr. *gramma*, letter, piece of writing] Suffix meaning a *record, writing.*

gram molecular mass SEE: under *mass.*

gram molecule The weight (mass) in grams of a substance equal to its molecular weight (mass).

gram-negative Losing the crystal violet stain and taking the color of the red counterstain in the Gram method of staining, a primary characteristic of certain microorganisms. SEE: *Gram stain.*

gram-positive Retaining the color of the crystal violet stain in the Gram method of staining. SEE: *Gram stain.*

Gram stain (gram) [Hans C. J. Gram, Danish physician, 1853–1938] A method of staining bacteria, which is important in their identification.

PROCEDURE: A film on a slide is prepared, dried, and fixed with heat. The film is stained with crystal violet for 1 min; rinsed in water, then immersed in Gram iodine solution for 1 min. The iodine solution is rinsed off and the slide decolorized in 95% ethyl alcohol. The slide is then counterstained with dilute

Gram Conversion into Ounces (Avoirdupois)*

g	Oz	g	Oz	g	Oz	g	Oz
1	0.03	30	1.06	59	2.08	88	3.10
2	0.07	31	1.09	60	2.12	89	3.14
3	0.11	32	1.13	61	2.15	90	3.17
4	0.14	33	1.16	62	2.18	91	3.21
5	0.18	34	1.20	63	2.22	92	3.24
6	0.21	35	1.23	64	2.26	93	3.28
7	0.25	36	1.27	65	2.29	94	3.31
8	0.28	37	1.30	66	2.33	95	3.35
9	0.32	38	1.34	67	2.36	96	3.38
10	0.35	39	1.37	68	2.40	97	3.42
11	0.39	40	1.41	69	2.43	98	3.46
12	0.42	41	1.44	70	2.47	99	3.49
13	0.45	42	1.48	71	2.50	100	3.53
14	0.49	43	1.51	72	2.54	125	4.41
15	0.53	44	1.55	73	2.57	150	5.30
16	0.56	45	1.59	74	2.61	175	6.18
17	0.60	46	1.62	75	2.64	200	7.05
18	0.63	47	1.65	76	2.68	250	8.82
19	0.67	48	1.69	77	2.71	300	10.58
20	0.70	49	1.73	78	2.75	350	12.34
21	0.74	50	1.76	79	2.79	400	14.11
22	0.77	51	1.80	80	2.82	450	15.87
23	0.81	52	1.83	81	2.85	454	16.00
24	0.84	53	1.87	82	2.89	500	17.64
25	0.88	54	1.90	83	2.93	600	21.16
26	0.91	55	1.94	84	2.96	700	24.69
27	0.95	56	1.97	85	3.00	800	28.22
28	0.99	57	2.01	86	3.03	900	30.75
29	1.02	58	2.04	87	3.07	1000	35.27

* 1 g is equal to 0.03527 oz (avoirdupois).

carbolfuchsin or safranin for 30 sec, after which it is rinsed with water, blotted dry, and examined. Gram-positive bacteria retain the violet stain and gram-negative bacteria adopt the red counterstain. SEE: illus.

NOTE: As a simple means of checking on the accuracy of the staining materials, a small amount of material from between one's teeth can be placed on the slide at the opposite end from that of the specimen being examined. As gram-negative and gram-positive organisms are always present in the mouth, that end of the slide should be examined first. If both types of organisms are seen, the specimen may then be examined.

grandiose (grăn'dē-ōs″, grăn″dē-ōs′) In psychiatry, pert. to one's unrealistic and exaggerated concept of self-worth, importance, wealth, and ability. **grandiosity** (grăn″dē-os′ĭt-ē), n.

grand mal (grănd măl) SEE: under *epilepsy*.

grant (grănt) [ME.] A financial award given to an academic or professional investigator to support his or her research.

grant writing The drafting of a written proposal seeking financial support for a demonstration or research project in the health sciences.

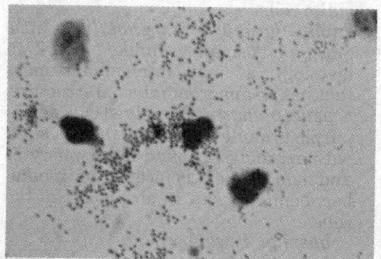
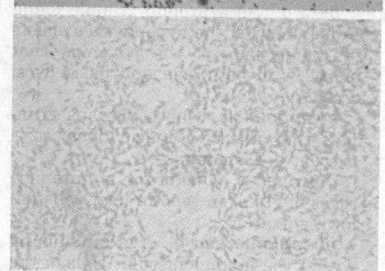

GRAM STAIN

(*Top*) Gram-positive *Staphylococcus aureus* in a pus smear (orig. mag. ×500) (*Bottom*) Gram-negative *Campylobacter jejuni* bacilli (orig. mag. ×500)

granul-, granuli-, granulo- [L. *granulum*, diminutive of *granum*, grain] Prefixes meaning *granule*.

granular (grăn'ū-lăr) [L. *granulum*, little grain] **1.** Of the nature of granules. **2.** Roughened by prominences like those of seeds.

granulation (grăn"ū-lā'shŭn) **1.** The formation of granules or the condition of being granular. **2.** Fleshy projections formed on the surface of a gaping wound that is not healing by first intention or indirect union. Each granulation represents the outgrowth of new capillaries by budding from the existing capillaries and then joining up into capillary loops supported by cells that will later become fibrous scar tissue. Granulations bring a rich blood supply to the healing surface.

arachnoid g. Folds of the arachnoid layer of the cranial meninges that project through the inner layer of dura mater into the superior sagittal sinus and other venous sinuses of the brain. Through them, cerebrospinal fluid reenters the bloodstream. SYN: *arachnoid villus; pacchionian body.*

exuberant g. An excessive mass of granulation tissue formed in the healing of a wound or ulcer; proud flesh.

toxic g. The abnormal appearance of white blood cells in patients with serious infectious diseases. The intracytoplasmic granules in the white blood cells show increased staining caused by the increased acid mucoprotein content of the cells.

granule (grăn'ūl) [L. *granulum*, little grain] **1.** A small, grainlike mass. **2.** In histology, a small intracellular mass that has no apparent internal structure.

azurophilic g. A small red or reddish-purple granule that easily takes a stain with azure dyes. Found in lymphocytes and monocytes, it is inconstant in number, being present in about 30% of the cells.

basal g. Basal body.

beta g. An azurophil granule found in beta cells of the hypophysis or islets of Langerhans of the pancreas that stains with both acid and basic dyes. SYN: *amphophil g.*

eosinophil g. One of various granules that react with acid dyes. It is present in eosinophils.

glycogen g. One of the minute particles of glycogen seen in liver cells following fixation.

juxtaglomerular g. A granule found within the juxtaglomerular cells of the kidneys. Juxtaglomerular cells secrete renin.

neutrophil g. Any of the cytoplasmic granules of a neutrophil that often stain a pale blue.

pigment g. A granule seen in pigment cells.

protein g. A minute protein particle found in cells.

secretory g. Zymogen **g.**

zymogen g. A granule present in gland cells, esp. the secretory cells of the pancreas, the chief cells of the gastric glands, and the serous cells of the salivary glands. It is the precursor of the enzyme secreted. SYN: *secretory g.*

Granulicatella (grăn"ū-lĭk-ă-tĕl'ă) A genus of disease-causing organisms, formerly referred to as "nutritionally variant streptococci." Species within the genus may cause infections of bones and joints, the central nervous system, heart valves, and other body parts.

granulocyte (gran'yŭ-lō-sīt") [*granule* + *-cyte*] A polymorphonuclear leukocyte (neutrophil, eosinophil, or basophil) whose cytoplasm contains granules. Informally, granulocytes are often referred to as "polys" because of their polymorphonuclear nuclei. SYN: *agranular leukocyte; lymphoid leukocyte; nongranular leukocyte.*

granulocyte colony-stimulating factor SEE: under *factor*.

granulocyte-macrophage colony-stimulating factor SEE: under *factor*.

granulocytopenia (grăn"ū-lō-sī"tō-pē'nē-ă) [" + " + *penia*, poverty] An abnormal reduction of granulocytes in the blood. SYN: *granulopenia.*

granulocytopoiesis (grăn"ū-lō-sī"tō-poy-ē'sĭs) [" + " + *poiein*, to form] The formation of granulocytes.

granulocytosis (grăn"ū-lō-sī-tō'sĭs) [" + " + *osis*, condition] An abnormal increase in the number of granulocytes in the blood.

granuloma (gran"yŭ-lō'mă, gran"yŭ-lō'mă-tă) *pl.* **granulomas, granulomata** [*granulo-* + *-oma*] An inflammatory response that results when macrophages are unable to destroy foreign substances that have entered or invaded body tissues. Large numbers of macrophages are drawn to the affected area over 7 to 10 days, surround the target, and enclose it. They in turn are surrounded by polymorphonuclear leukocytes, other immune cells, and fibroblasts. Granulomas are common in many conditions, including leprosy, tuberculosis, cat scratch disease, some fungal infections, and foreign body reactions, e.g., reactions to sutures. **granulomatous** (gran"yŭ-lō'mă-tŭs), *adj.* SEE: *giant cell; tuberculosis; Wegener granulomatosis.*

g. annulare A circular rash with a raised red border, usually found on the hands, knuckles, or arms of young patients. The cause is unknown. The rash often lasts 1 or 2 years and then may disappear spontaneously. SEE: illus.

benign g. of the thyroid A lymphadenoma of the thyroid.

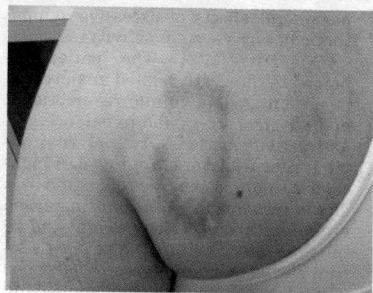

GRANULOMA ANNULARE

(On the back, near the left shoulder)

coccidioidal g. A chronic, generalized granuloma caused by the fungus *Coccidioides immitis.* SEE: *coccidioidomycosis.*

eosinophilic g. A form of xanthomatosis accompanied by eosinophilia and the formation of cysts on bone.

foreign body g. Chronic inflammation around foreign bodies such as sutures, talc, splinters, or gravel. SYN: *foreign body reaction.*

infectious g. Any infectious disease in which granulomas are formed, e.g., tuberculosis or syphilis. Granulomas are also formed in mycoses and protozoan infections.

g. inguinale A granulomatous ulcerative disease in which the initial lesion commonly appears in the genital area as a painless nodule.

ETIOLOGY: This type of granuloma is caused by a short, gram-negative bacillus, *Calymmatobacterium granulomatis* (Donovan body).

TREATMENT: Erythromycin, trimethoprim-sulfamethoxazole, or tetracyclines are used in treating this disease. Single-dose therapy with intramuscular ceftriaxone or oral ciprofloxacin may be effective.

malignant g. **Hodgkin** disease.

pyogenic g. SEE: *lobular capillary hemangioma.*

pyrogenic g. SEE: *lobular capillary hemangioma.*

swimming pool g. A chronic skin infection caused by *Mycobacterium marinum.*

g. telangiectaticum A very vascular granuloma at any site, but esp. in the nasal mucosa or pharynx.

trichophytic g. Majocchi disease.

granulomatosis (grăn″ū-lō″mă-tō′sĭs) [L. *granulum,* little grain, + Gr. *oma,* tumor, + *osis,* condition] The development of multiple granulomas.

Wegener's g. SEE: *Wegener's granulomatosis.*

granulopenia (grăn″ū-lō-pē′nē-ă) [″ + Gr. *penia,* poverty] Granulocytopenia.

granulopoiesis (grăn″ū-lō-poy-ē′sĭs) [″

+ Gr. *poiein,* to make] The formation of granulocytes.

granulosa (grăn″ū-lō′să) A layer of cells in the theca of the graafian follicle.

granulosis (grăn″ū-lō′sĭs) [″ + Gr. *osis,* condition] A mass of minute granules.

g. rubra nasi A disease of the skin of the nose, characterized by a moist erythematous patch on numerous macules. The disease is caused by an inflammatory infiltration about the nose, with slightly elevated papules and dilated sweat glands.

granum (grā′nŭm) [L.] Grain.

granzyme (grăn′zīm) Any of a family of proteases stored in the granules of cytotoxic T lymphocytes. They are involved in cytolytic functions.

grapefruit A tropical tree (*Citrus paradisi*) that produces a large, yellow, tart (acidic) fruit, rich in flavonoids, lycopene, and vitamin C.

⚠ The consumption of the fruit alters the metabolism of a wide variety of medications, including 3-hydroxy-3-methylglutaryl coenzyme A (HMG-CoA) reductase inhibitors (statins), calcium channel blockers, and immunosuppressive drugs, e.g., cyclosporine, among others, by inhibiting cytochrome CYPA34 enzymes in the liver.

grapefruit seed extract SEE: under *extract.*

graph (grăf) [Abbr. of *graphic formula*] **1.** A visual presentation of statistical, clinical, or experimental data represented by a relationship between two sets of numbers or variables on the ordinate (y, or vertical) axis and the abscissa (x, or horizontal) axis. **2.** Any visual representation of a numerical relationship.

-graph [Gr. *graphos,* written, writing] Suffix meaning *an instrument used to make a drawing or written record or the record itself.*

grapheme (grăf′ēm) **1.** A letter of an alphabet. **2.** The smallest element in a writing system. **3.** A written symbol or group of symbols used to represent a single sound.

graphesthesia (grăf″ĕs-thē′zē-ă) [″ + *aisthesis,* sensation] The ability to recognize outlines, numbers, words, or symbols traced or written on the skin.

graphite (grăf′īt) [*grapho-* + *-ite*] One of the allotropes of carbon. It has been used as a dry lubricant and as an erasable lead in pencils.

grapho-, graph- [Gr. *graphos,* something written] Prefix meaning *writing.*

graphomotor (grăf″ō-mō′tor) [″ + L. *motor,* mover] Pert. to movements involved in writing.

-graphy [Gr. *-graphia* fr. *graphein,* to

write] Suffix meaning *process or form of writing or recording.*

GRAS *generally recognized as safe.*

GRAS List A list of food additives *generally recognized as safe* by the U.S. Food and Drug Administration. SEE: *food additive.*

grasp (grasp) Holding or clasping objects with the fingers, the palm, or both.

    pincher g. The apposition of the thumb and index finger to pick up small objects. This fine motor skill is a developmental milestone usually attained by 10 months of age.

    plantar g. A type of prehension involving the toes, which curl forward in response to pressure from the examiner's finger across their base. This normal newborn reflex usually disappears by age 8 to 9 months. The reflex reappears in adults with frontal lobe diseases or dementia.

grasper (gräsp'ĕr) A device used to grab and hold tissue (e.g., during laparoscopic surgery).

grating (grāt'ing) In spectrophotometry, the element used in a monochromator that disperses white light into the visible spectrum. It is composed of finely etched lines in the reflecting material.

grattage (grä-täzh') [Fr., a scraping] The removal of epithelial lesions by rubbing with a brush or harsh sponge.

grave [L. *gravis,* heavy] Serious; dangerous; severe.

gravel (grăv'ĭl) [Fr. *gravelle,* coarse sand] Crystalline dust or concretions of crystals from the kidneys; generally made up of phosphates, calcium, oxalate, and uric acid.

Graves, Robert James (grāvz) Robert James Graves, Irish physician, 1796–1853.

    G. disease Hyperthyroidism caused by an autoimmune destruction of the thyroid gland. It typically increases thyroxine (T_4) production, produces enlargement of the thyroid gland, and also may cause ocular findings (proptosis, lid lag, and stare).

    SYMPTOMS: Other findings include palpitations, nervousness, heat intolerance, sweating, frequent defecation, insomnia, menstrual irregularities, tremor, and weight loss despite increased appetite.

    DIAGNOSIS: The clinical signs of goiter and proptosis, elevated levels of thyroxine and a suppressed thyroid-stimulating hormone are diagnostic.

    TREATMENT: Drugs that limit the thyroid gland's output of thyroid hormone are effective. The thyroid gland may be removed surgically, or it may be inactivated with radioactive iodine (^{131}I) therapy. Beta-adrenergic blockers are prescribed to manage tachycardia and peripheral effects of excessive sympathetic nervous system activity.

    PATIENT CARE: The patient is helped to cope with related anxiety and is encouraged to minimize emotional and physical stress and to balance rest and activity periods. A quiet environment is provided or encouraged. A high-calorie, high-protein diet of six meals a day is recommended to treat increased protein catabolism. Body weight and vital signs are monitored, along with serum electrolyte and glucose levels. The patient is taught comfort measures to deal with elevated body temperature and GI complaints (abdominal cramping, frequent bowel movements); safety measures to protect the eyes from injury, including moistening the conjunctiva frequently with isotonic eye drops and wearing sunglasses to protect the eyes from light; and appropriate administration and safety procedures for iodide therapy, beta-blocker therapy, and propylthiouracil and methimazole therapy, as prescribed. If the patient is being maintained on propylthiouracil or methimazole, potential side effects of the medications are reviewed with the patient, including the importance of having blood counts done periodically to detect blood dyscrasias. Special instructions are provided for therapeutic use of radioactive iodide (pretherapy and posttherapy medication restrictions; care with and disposal of expectorated saliva and of urine that remain slightly radioactive for 24 hr, vomitus for 6 to 8 hr; need to drink fluids in large quantities for 48 hr after therapy; and, if discharged less than 7 days after therapy, avoiding close contact with children and sleeping in the same room with others until 7 days after therapy).

    The patient is prepared physically and psychologically for surgery if planned; postoperative care specific to thyroidectomy is provided. Regular medical follow-up is needed to detect and treat hypothyroidism, which may develop 2 to 4 weeks after surgery and after radioactive iodine therapy. The patient is advised of the possible need for lifelong thyroid hormone replacement therapy and should wear or carry a medical identification tag and keep a supply of medication with him or her at all times.

    G. ophthalmopathy Ophthalmopathy associated with hyperthyroidism with the clinical characteristics of exophthalmos, periorbital edema, periorbital and conjunctival inflammation, decreased extraocular muscle mobility, and corneal injury. Accompanying these may be lacrimation, eye pain, blurring of vision, photophobia, diplopia, and loss of vision.

    TREATMENT: The underlying hyperthyroidism must be treated. The patient should sleep with the head of the bed elevated. Methylcellulose eyedrops and diuretics will help to relieve eye discomfort. If the condition is severe and progressive, surgical decompression of the orbit will be required to treat impaired retinal function and exposure keratopathy.

gravid (grăv′ĭd) [L. *gravida*, pregnant] Pregnant; heavy with child.

gravida (grăv′ĭ-dă) [L.] A pregnant woman.

gravidity (gră-vĭd′ĭ-tē) [L. *gravida*, pregnant] The total number of a woman's pregnancies.

gravimetric (grav″ĭ-me′trĭk) [L. *gravis*, heavy + *metric*] Determined by mass or weight.

gravitation (grăv″ĭ-tā′shŭn) [L. *gravitas*, weight] The force and movement tending to draw every particle of matter together, esp. the attraction of the earth for bodies at a distance from its center.

gravity **1.** The property of possessing weight. **2.** The force of the earth's gravitational attraction.

   specific g. SEE: *specific gravity.*

gray [L. Harold Gray, Brit. physician, 1905–1965] ABBR: Gy. The SI unit for the quantity of ionizing radiation absorbed by any material per unit mass of matter (radiation absorbed dose). 1 Gy = the absorption of 1 J of ionizing radiation per kg of matter. 1 Gy equals 100 rad. 1 μGy (microgray) = 10^{-6} Gy. SEE: *radiation absorbed dose.*

grayanotoxin (grā″ăn′ŭ-tŏk′sĭn) [Fr. NL *grayana*, species name + ″.] A diterpene cyclic hydrocarbon found in honey produced by bees that feed on rhododendrons. Consumption of tainted honey or rhododendrons results in nausea, vomiting, and numbness and tingling around the mouth and in the arms and legs. Weakness, loss of coordination, and heart rhythm disturbances rarely occur, and only after massive ingestion. The poisoning typically resolves on its own within 24 hr.

gray literature Any information not commercially published and therefore difficult to retrieve with standard bibliographical techniques or electronic search engines. It includes information contained in reports of congressional committees or subcommittees, bulletins issued by private interest groups or government agencies (e.g., the Food and Drug Administration), summaries of conference proceedings, dissertations and theses, documentation of data closely held for internal use by commercial interests, scientific weblogs, and working papers.

gray platelet syndrome Alpha granule deficiency syndrome.

green A color intermediate between blue and yellow, afforded by rays of wavelength between 492 and 575 nm. words beginning with *chloro-*.

   brilliant g. A derivative of malachite green, used in staining bacteria.

   indocyanine g. SEE: *indocyanine green.*

   malachite g. A dye used as a stain and antiseptic.

green bottlefly Sheep **blowfly.**

greenhouse effect Planetary warming as a result of the trapping of solar energy beneath atmospheric gases. The composition and concentration of the gases in the atmosphere influence the earth's surface temperature because some gases more effectively retain heat than others. Fossil fuel combustion has increased at a rapid rate since the 1950s and has deposited increasing amounts of carbon dioxide in the upper atmosphere. This is thought to be a contributory factor in global warming, a phenomenon suspected of having widespread effects on all ecosystems. SEE: *global warming; ozone.*

green nail syndrome Paronychia caused by infection of the nails with *Pseudomonas aeruginosa*. SYN: *chloronychia.*

greifer (grīf′ĕr) [Ger. *greifer*, gripper, claw] An electrically powered hook-shaped prosthesis used to grip, grasp, or hold objects.

Grey Turner sign (grā′tŭr′nĕr) [George Grey Turner, Brit. surgeon, 1877–1951] A blue discoloration of the skin around the flanks in a patient with hemorrhagic pancreatitis.

grid (grĭd) **1.** A chart with an abscissa (x) (horizontal) axis and an ordinate (y) (vertical) axis on which to plot graphs. **2.** A device made of parallel lead strips, used to absorb scattered radiation during radiography of larger body parts.

grid ratio In a radiographical grid, the ratio of the height of the lead strips to the distance of the interspace. High ratios indicate increased ability of the grid to remove scatter.

grief (grēf) [Fr. *gref*, fr. L. *gravis*, heavy, burdensome] The sadness or sorrow following the loss of a loved person or thing. Symptoms include fatigue, depressed mood, insomnia, anorexia, feelings of regret or guilt, or a variety of physical discomforts.

   anticipatory g. Mental anguish caused by the impending loss of a body part, a function, or a loved one.

   chronic g. Unresolved denial of the reality of a personal loss.

grieving (grē′vĭng) A normal process that includes emotional, physical, spiritual, social, and intellectual responses and behaviors by which individuals, families, and communities incorporate an actual, anticipated, or perceived loss into their daily lives. This diagnosis was previously titled, "grieving, anticipatory". SEE: *Nursing Diagnoses Appendix.*

grieving, anticipatory (grē′vĭng) Intellectual and emotional responses and behaviors by which individuals (families, communities) work through the process of modifying self-concept based on the perception of potential loss. SEE: *Nursing Diagnoses Appendix.*

grieving, complicated A disorder that occurs after the death of a significant other, in which the experience of distress accompanying bereavement fails to follow normative expectations and manifests in functional impairment. This diagnosis was previously titled, "grieving, dysfunctional". SEE: *Nursing Diagnoses Appendix.*

grieving, dysfunctional Extended, unsuccessful use of intellectual and emotional responses by which individuals (families, communities) attempt to work through the process of modifying self-concept based upon the perception of potential loss. SEE: *Nursing Diagnoses Appendix.*

grieving, risk for complicated At risk for a disorder that occurs after the death of a significant other, in which the experience of distress accompanying bereavement fails to follow normative expectations and manifests in functional impairment. This diagnosis was previously titled, "grieving, risk for dysfunctional". SEE: *Nursing Diagnoses Appendix.*

Grifola frondosa (grĭ′fō-lă frŏn-dō′să, grĭf′) Maitake.

Grignard reaction (grē-nyar′) [François AugusteVictor Grignard, French chemist and Nobel laureate, 1871–1935] A classical organic-chemical process that forms carbon-carbon bonds. It is used to build carbon chains in compounds including drugs, food additives, toxins, and pesticides.

grinder (grīn′dĕr) A colloquial term for a molar tooth.

grinding A forceful rubbing together, as in chewing. SEE: *bruxism.*

   selective g. Altering and correcting the dental occlusion by grinding in accordance with what is required.

gripes (grīps) Intermittent severe pains in the bowels. SYN: *intestinal colic.*

griping (grī′pĭng) An acute intermittent cramplike pain, esp. in the abdomen.

grippe (grip) [Fr. *grippe,* seizure] Influenza.

groin (groyn) The depression between the thigh and trunk; the region of the hip creases below the abdomen and lateral to the perineum. SYN: *inguinal region.*

groin disruption Athletic pubalgia.

groin pull A colloquial term for a strained thigh adductor muscle.

grommet (grŏm′ĭt) A device, also known as a ventilation tube, placed in an artificial opening in the tympanic membrane to permit air to flow freely between the inner ear and the external auditory canal. The prosthesis is used as a treatment adjunct in managing chronic otitis media with effusion. The routine use of grommets as part of the initial therapy for otitis media is not advised. Their use should be reserved for persistent or recurrent infections that have failed to respond to appropriate antibiotic therapy.

groove (groov) A narrow channel, depression, or furrow. SYN: *sulcus.*

   anal g. An indented ring that is palpable just inside the anus along a circumferential line called the white line. The groove is caused by a space between the end of the internal anal sphincter (above) and the subcutaneous part of the external sphincter (below). SYN: *intersphincteric **g.***

   atrioventricular g. A furrow running circumferentially around the heart's surface and separating the atria from the ventricles; it is approximately perpendicular to the interventricular groove The atrioventricular groove is obscured on the anterior (front) surface of the heart by the pulmonary trunk and the aorta as they emerge from the heart. For parts of their courses, the major epicardial blood vessels run in the atrioventricular groove. SYN: *atrioventricular **sulcus**, coronary **g.**, coronary **sulcus**.*

   bicipital g. A valley on the proximal anterior surface of the humerus between the greater and lesser trochanters. The long tendon of the biceps slides along the bicipital groove. SYN: *intertubercular **g.**, intertubercular **sulcus**.*

   branchial g. Branchial arch.

   coronary g. Atrioventricular groove.

   costal g. A furrow along the lower internal border of a rib; the intercostal vessels and nerve run in this groove.

   deltopectoral g. A depression (palpable through the skin) at the boundary of the deltoid, pectoralis major, and biceps brachii muscles. The cephalic vein, running superficially up the arm, dives beneath the muscles through this groove to empty into the axillary vein.

   infraorbital g. The groove on the orbital surface of the maxilla that runs forward to become the infraorbital canal. The infraorbital nerve runs in the groove and canal to exit through the infraorbital foramen on the front of the skull just below the orbit.

   interatrial g. A shallow furrow on the posterior surface of the heart that marks the boundary between the right and left atria. It runs approximately perpendicular to the atrioventricular groove, which it meets at the same point as does the posterior interventricular groove.

intersphincteric g. Anal **g.**

intertubercular g. Bicipital **g.**

interventricular g. A furrow on the anterior and posterior surfaces of the heart that marks the boundary between the right and left ventricles; it runs approximately perpendicular to the atrioventricular groove. The left anterior descending artery and the great cardiac vein run in the anterior interventricular groove; the posterior descending artery and the middle cardiac vein run in the posterior interventricular groove. SYN: *interventricular sulcus*.

labial g. A furrow that develops in each of the embryonic jaws and that will give rise to the vestibule separating the lips from the gums.

lacrimal g. A vertical groove along the upper front edge of the medial wall of the orbit. The groove, formed by matching furrows on the maxillary and lacrimal bones, holds the lacrimal sac and leads into the lacrimal canal.

laryngotracheal g. A furrow along the inside ventral surface of the anterior portion of the embryonic gut tube; this groove will give rise to the lower part of the larynx and the trachea, bronchi, and lungs.

mylohyoid g. The groove on the inner surface of the mandible that runs obliquely forward and downward and contains the mylohyoid nerve and artery. In the embryo it lodges Meckel's cartilage.

nail g. The indentation between the edges of the nail plate and the skin.

nasolabial g. The furrow on either side of the face that runs down and laterally from the nostril and that marks the outer edge of the upper lip. SYN: *nasolabial sulcus*.

neural g. In the embryo, a longitudinal indentation along the midline of the neural plate; it overlies the forming notocord. The neural plate rolls up around the indentation, transforming the neural groove into the neural tube.

olfactory g. In the anterior cranial fossa, a longitudinal depression on the superior surface of the ethmoid bone on each side of the crista galli; the cribriform plate forms the floor of the olfactory groove. The olfactory bulb fits in the olfactory groove.

patellar g. A deep V-shaped groove on the anterior surface of the distal humeral condyle; the posterior surface of the patella slides in this groove.

peroneal g. Grooves in the leg and ankle bones for the tendons of the peroneus longus and peroneus brevis muscles. These grooves are found on the posterior surface of the lateral malleolus (the distal end of the fibula), on the lateral surface of the calcaneus bone, and

on the plantar (inferior) surface of the cuboid bone.

primitive g. In the embryo, a shallow longitudinal midline groove in primitive streak of the blastoderm. The rostralmost end of the primitive groove becomes the primitive pit, a circular depression through which surface cells descend during gastrulation.

radial g. Spiral groove.

sagittal g. A single shallow longitudinal groove that runs along the superior inner surface of the cranial cavity where the left and right parietal bones meet in the midline. The superior sagittal venous sinus fits in the sagittal groove.

spiral g. A broad, shallow groove that spirals down the posterior surface of the humerus and marks the route of the radial nerve and the deep brachial artery. SYN: *radial g.*

urethral g. In the embryo, a midline furrow between the developing genital folds. In the male, the genital folds fuse over the urethral groove, which then becomes incorporated into the distal urethra. In the female, the genital folds remain apart and become the labia minora; the open space between them is the remnant of the urethral groove.

gross (grōs) [L. *grossus*, thick] **1.** Visible to the naked eye. **2.** Consisting of large particles or components; coarse or large.

gross motor skills The group of motor skills (including walking, running, and throwing) that require large muscle groups to produce the major action, and require less precision than that exerted by small muscles. Most motor activities combine some elements of both fine and gross motor function.

gross tumor volume SEE: under *volume*.

ground **1.** Basic substance or foundation. **2.** Reduced to a powder; pulverized. **3.** In electronics, the negative or earth pole that has zero electrical potential.

ground state The state of the lowest energy of a system such as an atom or molecule.

ground transportation In medical services, the use of ambulances to convey patients to health care facilities.

group (groop) A number of similar objects or structures considered together, e.g., bacteria with similar metabolic characteristics. Atomic molecules and compounds with similar structures or properties are classified with certain groups.

alcohol g. The hydroxyl, —OH, which imparts alcoholic characteristics to organic compounds. These exist in three forms: primary, —CH_2OH; secondary, =CHOH; and tertiary, ≡COH.

amino acid g. The NH_2 group that characterizes the amines.

azo g. In organic chemistry, the group —N=N—.

blood g. SEE: *blood group*.

clinical cooperative g. A network of clinicians and scientists who work together from widely separated locations to study and treat relatively rare diseases, e.g., certain forms of cancer. In cancer care, prominent clinical cooperative groups include the Children's Oncology Group (COG), the Gynecology Oncology Group (GOG), and the Eastern Cooperative Oncology Group (ECOG).

coli-aerogenes g. Coliform bacteria. SEE: *coliform* (2).

colon-typhoid-dysentery g. The collective term for *Escherichia, Salmonella,* and *Shigella* bacteria.

control g. Control (4).

diagnosis-related g. ABBR: DRG. An indexing or classification system for standardizing prospective payment for medical care. Diseases and conditions are assigned to a single DRG when they are felt to share similar clinical and health care utilization features. The reimbursement for treating all individuals within the same DRG is the same regardless of actual cost to the health care facility. SEE: table.

focus g. An assembly of individuals affected by a specific subject (as by disease, health care delivery system, marketed service, professional or management issue) to solicit and study their opinions, identify interests, and make strategic plans to meet expressed needs.

Hh blood g. SEE: under *blood group*.

historical control g. In a research study, a person or group of persons who were treated in the past and who pro-

Top Diagnosis-Related Groups (DRGs) in the U.S.

DRG Numerical Designation	Diagnosis
371, 372, 373, 374,388, 389, 390, 391	Childbirth with or without operative obstetrics; with or without complications
359	Uterine and adnexal procedures for nonmalignant diseases
430	Psychoses
498, 500, 243	Spinal fusion and other back and neck procedures; medical back pain
143, 125, 112	Chest pain; circulatory disorders other than acute myocardial infarction with cardiac catheterization
116	Permanent pacemaker placement or percutaneous transluminal coronary angioplasty with coronary artery stent
182, 183	Esophagitis, gastritis, and miscellaneous digestive disorders
89, 91	Simple pneumonia and pleurisy
494	Laparoscopic cholecystectomy
127, 87	Heart failure and shock; pulmonary edema
294	Diabetes mellitus
106	Coronary bypass graft surgery with cardiac catheterization
209	Major joint and limb reattachment procedures (esp. hip and knee replacement)
25	Seizures and headache
462	Rehabilitation
14	Specific cerebrovascular disorders, excluding transient ischemic attack
79, 97, 98	Complicated respiratory infections; bronchitis and asthma
174	Gastrointestinal hemorrhage
167	Appendectomy
148	Major small and large bowel procedures
483	Tracheostomy
475	Respiratory system diagnosis with ventilator support
416	Septicemia
320	Kidney and urinary tract infections
297	Nutritional and miscellaneous metabolic disorders
128	Deep vein thrombosis
130	Peripheral vascular disorders
277	Cellulitis
294	Renal failure
489	HIV disease with major related conditions

vide contrast and comparison to participants currently being studied. Because a wide variety of variables may change over time, the use of historical controls as opposed to a contemporary control group is often an indication that an investigation has less methodological rigor.

isogenous g. A cluster of cells that have come from one cell, e.g., the clusters of chondrocytes in cartilage.

Kell blood g. SEE: under *blood group.*

Leapfrog G. SEE: *Leapfrog Group.*

mutual help g. Support **g.**

peptide g. The CONH radical.

prosthetic g. The nonamino acid component of a conjugated protein. It is usually the portion of an enzyme that is not an amino acid. SEE: *apoenzyme; holoenzyme.*

rabies virus g. A genus of viruses whose official designation is *Lyssavirus.* The group includes the causative agent of rabies in humans.

reference g. Control (3).

support g. A group of patients or families of patients with similar problems such as breast cancer, multiple sclerosis, or alcoholism, who meet to assist one another in coping with their problems and seeking solutions. The composition and focus of support groups vary. Some groups comprise patients who have or have had the same disorder. Discussions often center on current treatments, resources available for assistance, and what individuals can do to improve or maintain their health. Other groups involve those who have had the same psychological and emotional trauma, such as rape or the death of a loved one. Benefits expressed by members include the knowledge that they are not alone and that others have experienced the same or similar problems and have learned to cope effectively. SYN: *mutual help* **g.**

grouping The classification of individual traits according to a shared characteristic.

blood g. Classification of blood of different individuals according to agglutinating and hemolyzing qualities before making a blood transfusion. SEE: *blood group; blood transfusion.*

perceptual g. The processing of information derived from nerves in the eyes, ears, nose, tongue, skin, and any other sensory structures. This function helps in understanding the environment and forming a coherent image of what is perceived.

group therapy A form of psychiatric treatment in which six to eight patients meet a specific number of times with a therapist. The value of this type of therapy is the opportunity for gaining insight from others into one's life experience.

group transfer An oxidation-reduction chemical reaction involving the exchange of chemical groups. A transferase enzyme is required.

Grover disease (grōv'ĕr) [R. W. Grover, contemporary U.S. dermatologist] A common itchy (pruritic) condition of sudden onset, characterized by a few or numerous smooth or warty papules, vesicles, eczematous plaques, or shiny translucent nodules. The pruritus may be mild or severe and is aggravated by heat. Even though the condition is self-limiting, it may last months or years.

TREATMENT: The patient should be treated symptomatically. Heat and sweat-inducing activities should be avoided. Retinoic acid may be helpful.

growth (grōth) Development, maturation, or expansion of physical structures or cognitive and psychosocial abilities. The process may be normal, as in the development of a fetus or a child, or pathological, as in a cyst or malignant tumor.

GROWTH OF INTERNAL ORGANS: General body growth is seen in the increase in bodily size and in the total weight of the muscles and of the internal organs. Growth is usually slow and steady but has a marked acceleration just after birth and at the time of puberty (the growth spurt).

Lymphoid organs (such as the thymus and the lymph nodes) grow fastest early in life, reach their peak of development at about the age of 12, and then stop growing or regress.

The brain, spinal cord, eye, and meninges grow in childhood but reach adult size by the age of 8. This size is maintained without regression.

The testes, ovaries, and other genitourinary structures grow slowly in infancy, but at puberty they develop rapidly and cause the striking changes in appearance that make up the secondary sex characteristics.

catch-up g. The accelerated growth of a malnourished, premature, or small neonate during the first two years of life. This growth enables the child to attain a normal size.

cognitive g. Growth shown by the progressive maturation of thought, reasoning, and intellect, esp. in school-aged children.

fetal g. The development of body cells, tissues, organs, and functions while the fetus is supported by the maternal placenta and uterus.

linear g. An increase in the length (height) of a child.

psychosocial g. Development of personality, judgment, and temperament. It evolves throughout life as experience in work, play, and emotional interactions with others broaden.

growth and development, delayed Deviations from age growth norms. SEE: illus. ; *Nursing Diagnoses Appendix.*

growth attenuation A decrease in the rate of growth of a child or adolescent from a previously observed pattern of increasing height and weight. Growth attenuation may be caused by many factors such as genetics, malnutrition, hormone deficiencies, toxins, or medications.

growth delay A disruption or cessation in the normal linear growth rate of a child,

usually as a result of illness or malnutrition.

growth factor SEE: under *factor.*

growth hormone, human synthetic SEE: ***hormone,*** *synthetic human growth.*

growth hormone insensitivity syndrome ABBR: GHIS. Laron syndrome.

growth hormone receptor antagonist SEE: under *antagonist.*

growth plate SEE: under *plate.*

gruel (groo'ăl) [L. *grutum,* meal] Cereal that is boiled in water or milk.

grumose, grumous (groo'mōs, -mŭs) [L. *grumus,* heap] **1.** Made up of coarse

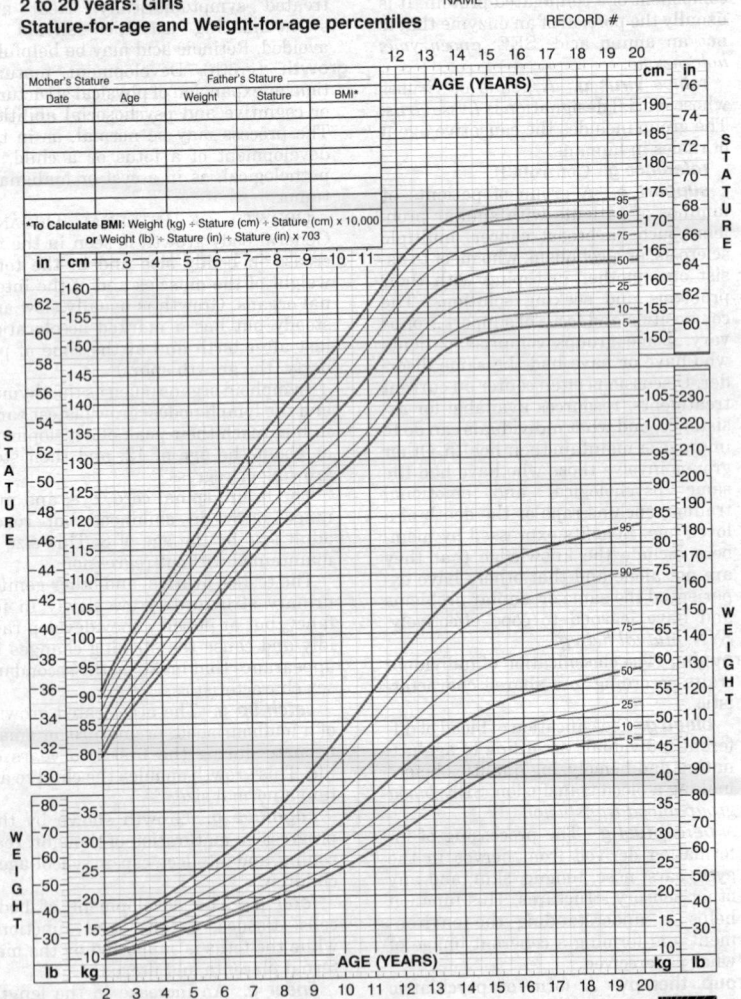

2 to 20 years: Girls
Stature-for-age and Weight-for-age percentiles

Published May 30, 2000 (modified 11/21/00).
SOURCE: Developed by the National Center for Health Statistics in collaboration with
the National Center for Chronic Disease Prevention and Health Promotion (2000).
http://www.cdc.gov/growthcharts

SAFER · HEALTHIER · PEOPLE™

GROWTH CHART GIRLS

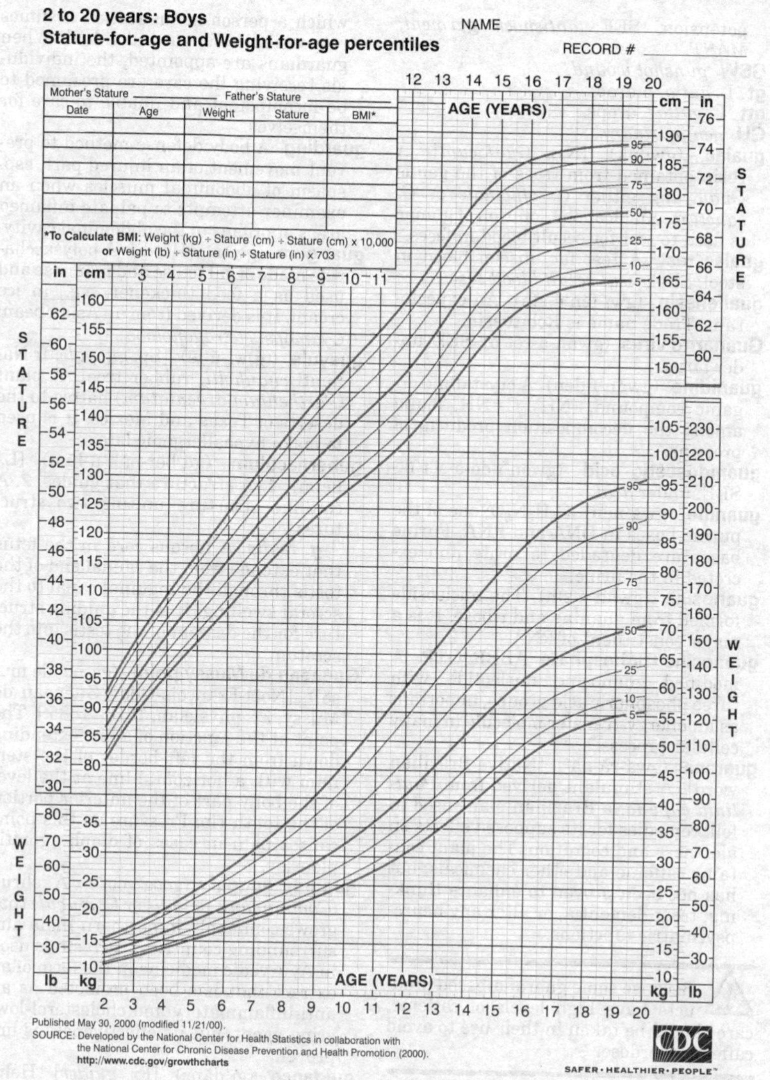

2 to 20 years: Boys
Stature-for-age and Weight-for-age percentiles
NAME
RECORD #
Mother's Stature
Father's Stature
Date
Age
Weight
Stature
BMI*
*To Calculate BMI: Weight (kg) ÷ Stature (cm) ÷ Stature (cm) x 10,000
or Weight (lb) ÷ Stature (in) ÷ Stature (in) x 703
AGE (YEARS)
STATURE
WEIGHT
in
cm
lb
kg
95
90
75
50
25
10
5
Published May 30, 2000 (modified 11/21/00).
SOURCE: Developed by the National Center for Health Statistics in collaboration with
the National Center for Chronic Disease Prevention and Health Promotion (2000).
http://www.cdc.gov/growthcharts
CDC
SAFER·HEALTHIER·PEOPLE™

GROWTH CHART BOYS

granular bodies in the center. **2.** Lumpy, clotted.

grunt (grŭnt) [ME. grunten] An abnormal sound heard during labored exhalation that indicates a need for high chest pressures to keep the airways open. It is caused by closing of the glottis at the end of expiration.

PATIENT CARE: A grunting patient is laboring to breathe and may soon suffer respiratory failure without intervention to improve respiratory status.

gryposis (grĭ-pō′sĭs) [G. *gryposis,* a crooking] Abnormal curvature of any part of the body, esp. the nails.

GSA *Gerontological Society of America.*

GSE *grapefruit* SEE: ***extract;*** *grape seed* ***extract.***

GSF *gingival sulcular fluid.*

GSR *galvanic skin response.*

G-suit (jē-sŭt) A coverall-type garment designed for use by aviators. It contains compartments that inflate and bring pressure on the legs and abdomen to prevent blood from pooling there. In aviators this helps to prevent unconsciousness caused by positive acceleration with resulting pooling of blood in the lower extremities. The suit has been used in medicine to treat postural hy-

potension. SEE: *antishock garment; MAST.*

GSW *gunshot wound.*

gt L. *gutta*, a drop.

gtt L. *guttae*, drops.

GU *genitourinary.*

guaiac (gwī'ăk) [NL. *Guaiacum*] A resin obtained from trees of the genus *Guaiacum*, either *G. officinale* or *G. sanctum*. An alcoholic solution of guaiac is used to test for occult blood in feces.

guaiac test A test for unseen blood in stool. SEE: *fecal occult blood test.*

guaifenesin (gwī-fĕn'ĕ-sĭn) An expectorant. Trade name is Robitussin.

Guanarito virus (gwan-ă-rēt'ō) SEE: under *virus*.

guanidine (gwăn'ĭ-dēn) A crystalline organic compound, $(NH_2)_2C=NH$, found among the decomposition products of proteins.

guanidoacetic acid (gwon"ĭ-dō-ă-sēt'ĭk) SEE: under *acid*.

guanine (gwă'nēn) $C_5H_5N_5O$; one of the purine bases in DNA and RNA. Purine bases are degraded to urate and excreted in the urine.

guanosine (gwăn'ō-sĭn) The nucleoside formed from guanine and ribose. It is a major constituent of RNA.

guanosine triphosphate ABBR: GTP. A modified guanosine nucleotide with three phosphoric acid groups, important as an energy-transfer molecule in many cellular processes.

guarana (gwă-ră-nă') [Native Brazilian word] A stimulant derived from *Paullinia cupana*, a Brazilian plant used in folk remedies for its supposed effects on alertness and cognition. The plant contains caffeine and other chemicals, but has not been proven to enhance thinking, treat dementia, or alter any neuropsychiatric functions.

⚠️ Because some guarana-based products have high levels of caffeine, care should be taken in their use to avoid caffeine overdose.

guard A device for protecting something (e.g., a mouth guard or a face guard).

    occlusal g. A removable dental appliance that covers one or both arches and is designed to minimize the damaging effects of bruxism, jaw and head trauma during contact sports, or any detrimental occlusal habits. SEE: *mouth guard; nightguard.*

guarded knife SEE: under *knife.*

guarded prognosis A prognosis given by a physician when the outcome of a patient's illness is in doubt.

guardian ad litem (gār'dē-ăn) [L.] In cases of child abuse, a guardian for the child appointed by the court to protect the best interests of the child.

guardianship A legal arrangement by which a person or institution assumes responsibility for an individual. When guardians are appointed, the individuals receiving the care are presumed to be incompetent and unable to care for themselves.

guarding A body defense method to prevent movement of an injured part, esp. spasm of abdominal muscles when an examiner attempts to palpate inflamed areas or organs in the abdominal cavity.

guar gum (gwär) [Hindi] A polysaccharide made of galactose and mannose and used as a food thickener, e.g., in ice cream. It is derived from an Asian bean, *Cyamopsis tetragonoloba.*

guayule ((g)wī-ū'lē) [Sp. *guayule*, fr Nahuatl *cuauholli*, rubber tree] A plant (*Parthenium argentatum*) native to the deserts of Texas and Mexico. It is used to make hypoallergenic latex.

gubernaculum (gū"bĕr-năk'ū-lŭm) [L., helm] **1.** A structure that guides. **2.** A cordlike structure uniting two structures.

    g. testis A fibrous cord in the fetus that extends from the caudal end of the testis through the inguinal canal to the scrotal swelling. It is the guiding structure for the descent of the testis into the scrotum.

Guéneau de Mussy point (gā-nō' dĕ mu-sē') [Noël-François-Odon Guéneau de Mussy, Fr. physician, 1813–1885.] The point at the junction of a line extending down from the left border of the sternum with a horizontal line at the level of the bony part of the anterior portion of the tenth rib. Pressure on this point causes pain in cases of diaphragmatic pleurisy.

guggul, guggal (goog'gool") A shrub (*Commiphora wightii* or *C. mukul*) that grows commonly in northern India and surrounding countries. Its resin is used in Ayurvedic medicine in the form of an extract that has been promoted as an anti-inflammatory and cholesterol-lowering agent, but its effectiveness is unproven.

guidance (gī'dăns) [Fr. *guider*] Helping, instructing, coaching, or counseling (e.g., of a patient).

    anticipatory g. Information about normal expectations of an age group (or of a disease) to provide support for coping with problems before they arise. It is a component of many health care encounters, e.g., well-child checkups in infancy.

    manual g. Physical cueing or prompting by a therapist, to facilitate the mastery of movements needed to perform a specific task or to extinguish or suppress undesired movements.

    vocational g. Helping people find jobs or careers that match their skills, needs, and interests.

guide A mechanical aid or device that assists in setting a course or directing the motion either of one's hand or of an instrument one holds.

guide catheter   SEE: under *catheter*.

guide dog   A dog specifically trained to assist blind or partially sighted persons with mobility.

guideline   An instructional guide or reference to indicate a course of action in a specified situation (e.g., critical care guideline).

guidewire, guide wire (gīd′wī″ĕr)   A device used to enter tight spaces, e.g., obstructed valves or channels, within the body, or to assist in inserting, positioning, and moving a catheter. Guidewires vary in size, length, stiffness, composition, and shape of the tip. SEE: illus.

guiding   In osteopathic medicine the movement of a body part gently along its normal axis through its normal range of motion.

guile   The use of deception or cunning in order to accomplish something.

Guillain-Barré syndrome (gē-yan′bar-ā′) [Georges Guillain, Fr. neurologist, 1876–1961; J. A. Barré, Fr. neurologist, 1880–1967] ABBR: GBS. A rare autoimmune illness, affecting 1 to 2 persons per 100,000 in the U.S., marked by progressive, potentially fatal ascending paralysis, with loss of motor reflexes, ataxia, and paresthesias. Loss of motor function begins in the extremities and moves upward through the body; when it includes the diaphragm, it may result in respiratory failure. The loss of motor function can occur in a few days to 2 to 3 weeks. Uncomfortable sensations (paresthesias and dysesthesias) in the hips, thighs, and back are commonly experienced. Recovery is spontaneous and complete in the vast majority of patients, but may take more than a year. The syndrome may produce only limited muscle weakness or complete paralysis, followed by general recovery or partial recovery with residual weakness in the extremities. SYN: *acute inflammatory demyelinating polyneuropathy*.

ETIOLOGY: The syndrome often follows an acute infection or vaccination. Antibodies react with antigens on the surface of peripheral myelinated nerves, causing demyelination.

TREATMENT: Treatment is aimed at supporting the patient until motor function returns and preventing complications. Approximately one third of patients need intubation and mechanical ventilation until they can breathe on their own. Total enteral or parenteral nutrition as necessary, physical therapy, cardiac monitoring, and close observation for infection are important to reduce complications. Plasmapheresis and use of intravenous immune globulin (IVIG) is most beneficial in treating patients with rapidly progressing paralysis.

PATIENT CARE: The patient is carefully assessed for evidence of impending respiratory failure, through the use of bedside spirometry. If the inspiratory force, vital capacity, or arterial blood gases deteriorate respiratory support is provided. Testing for thoracic sensation and monitoring and marking the level of diminished sensation as it ascends helps to predict impairment of intercostal muscle function.

Noninvasive interventions such as passive ROM exercises, massage, distraction, imagery, ice, heat, cutaneous stimulation, and transcutaneous electrical nerve stimulation should be offered and added to the patient's plan of care, depending upon his or her response. Range-of-motion exercises are provided three to four times daily within the patient's limits. As the patient's condition stabilizes, gentle stretching and active-assisted exercises are provided.

The GBS patient may be anxious, frightened, or depressed. Questions or

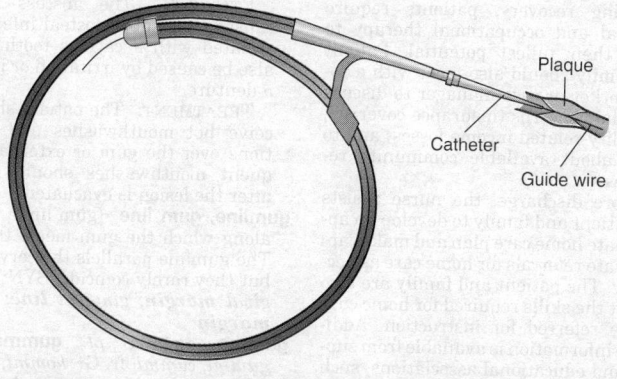

Plaque

Catheter

Guide wire

GUIDEWIRE

misconceptions about the illness and the procedures used to address it should be answered thoughtfully and compassionately. Feelings of isolation and fear can be reduced by family visits, patient education, or the assistance of former GBS patients who can share feelings and offer hope and information on coping. Routine care of the paralyzed patient is implemented including range of motion exercises, turning and positioning every 2 hr, and scrupulous skin care.

Fluid and electrolyte balance is maintained. To prevent aspiration, the head of the bed is elevated and the gag reflex tested before oral intake. If the gag reflex is impaired, nasogastric enteral feedings are provided until the reflex returns. The nurse encourages adequate fluid intake (2000 ml/day) orally, enterally, or if necessary, parenterally unless contraindicated. The bladder should be palpated and percussed to assess for urine retention. Either urinal or bedpan is offered every 3 to 4 hr. Intermittent urinary catheterization is instituted if necessary. To prevent or relieve constipation, prune juice and a high-bulk diet, stool softeners and laxatives, glycerin or bisacodyl suppositories, or enemas (as prescribed) are provided daily or on alternate days.

If the patient has facial paralysis, the nurse provides oral hygiene and eye care every 4 hr, protecting the corneas with shields and isotonic eye drops. If the patient cannot vocalize, establishing alternative methods of communication, such as eye blink or letter boards, is essential to ensure that patient needs are met. If the patient cannot use the regular call light to signal for assistance, a pressure-sensitive cell device activated with minimal pressure is placed near the hand or head; or a sip-and-puff call system should be used. The patient's legs are inspected regularly for signs of thrombophlebitis, and antiembolism devices are applied and anticoagulants given if prescribed.

During recovery, patients require physical and occupational therapy to reach their fullest potential. Patient and family should also meet with a social worker or case manager to discuss financial concerns (insurance coverage, disability-related income losses) and to learn about available community resources.

Before discharge, the nurse assists the patient and family to develop an appropriate home care plan and makes appropriate referrals for home care as necessary. The patient and family are also taught the skills required for home care or are referred for instruction. Additional information is available from support and educational associations, such as the GBS/CIPD Foundation International (www.gbs-cidp.org/). SEE: *Nursing Diagnoses Appendix.*

guillotine (gĭl′ŏ-tēn) [Fr., instrument for beheading] An instrument for excising tonsils and laryngeal growths.

guilt (gĭlt) [AS *gylt*, offense] **1.** The state or feeling of remorse or self-reproach for having committed a wrong or crime. **2.** Voluntary confession or conviction in a trial of commission of a crime.

guinea pig (gĭn′ē pĭg) **1.** A small rodent used in laboratory research. **2.** A colloquial term for persons used in medical experiments.

guinea worm SEE: under *worm.*

gullet (gŭl′ĕt) [L. *gula*, throat] The esophagus.

¹ **gum** (gŭm) [L. *gumma, gummi, cummi* fr Gr. *kommi*, resin, gum] A resinous substance given off by or extracted from certain plants. It is sticky when moist but hardens while drying. Roughly, gum is any resin-like substance produced by plants.

² **gum** (gŭm) [Old English *gōma*, palate] The mucosal tissue covering the alveolar processes of the mandible and maxilla. SEE: *gingiva.*

DIAGNOSIS: *Bleeding:* If the gums bleed easily, gingivitis, scurvy, acute necrotizing ulcerative gingivitis (trench mouth), or anticoagulation may be present. Silver poisoning causes the gums to turn *blue;* mercurial stomatitis or lead poisoning turns the gums *bluish red,* with a bluish line at the edge of the teeth. A *greenish line* at the edge of the teeth may indicate copper poisoning. A *purplish line or color* indicates scurvy. In youth, gingivitis, pyorrhea, or scurvy may cause a *red line. Spongy gums and ulceration* may indicate gingivitis, scurvy, stomatitis, leukemia, tuberculosis, or diabetes.

gumboil (gŭm′boyl″) A gum abscess. SYN: *parulis.*

SYMPTOMS: The gum is red, swollen, and tender. A fluctuating swelling containing pus may appear, which may point and break or require incision.

ETIOLOGY: The abscess may be caused by a subperiosteal infection associated with a carious tooth. It may also be caused by irritation or injury by a denture.

TREATMENT: The patient should receive hot mouthwashes and applications over the gum or externally. Frequent mouthwashes should continue after the lesion is evacuated.

gumline, gum line (gŭm′līn″) The line along which the gum meets the tooth. The gumline parallels the cervical line, but they rarely coincide. SYN: *free gingival* **margin**; *gingival* **line**; *gingival* **margin**.

gumma (gŭm′ă) *pl.* **gummata** [L. *gummi, cummi,* fr. Gr. *kommi*, gum] A soft granulomatous tumor characteristic of the tertiary stage of syphilis. It consists of a central necrotic mass surrounded by a zone of inflammation and fibrosis. Spirochetes may be present in the mass. Gummas vary in diameter from a millimeter or a centimeter or more and tend to occur in the liver, brain, testes, heart, and elsewhere. SEE: *syphilis.*

SYMPTOMS: Symptoms vary depending on the gumma location. Bursting of a gumma leads to a gummatous ulcer that is painless but slow to heal. The base is formed by a slough somewhat resembling a chamois cloth, but surrounding tissues are healthy.

gummatous (gŭm′ă-tŭs) Having the character of a gumma.

gummy [L. *gummi,* gum] Sticky, swollen, puffy.

Gunn, Robert Marcus (gŭn) Brit. ophthalmologist, 1850–1909.

G. dots White spots occurring on the retina of the eye, close to the macula.

G. pupil, Marcus Gunn pupil Diminished pupillary reaction to direct light; the symptom is secondary to optic nerve disease. SEE: *swinging flashlight test.*

gurmarin A polypeptide produced by the Indian vine (*Gymneva sylvestre*), which suppresses the taste of sweet foods.

gurney (gĕr′nē) Stretcher.

gustation (gŭs-tā′shŭn) [L. *gustare,* to taste] The sense of taste.

gustatory (gŭs′tă-tō-rē) Pert. to the sense of taste.

gut [AS.] **1.** The bowel or intestine. **2.** The primitive gut or embryonic digestive tube, which includes the foregut, midgut, and hindgut. **3.** Short term for catgut.

gut-associated lymphoid tissue ABBR: GALT. A term used for all lymphoid tissue associated with the gastrointestinal tract, including the tonsils, appendix, and Peyer's patches. GALT contains lymphocytes, primarily B cells, and is responsible for controlling microorganisms entering the body via the digestive system. SEE: *mucosal immune system.*

Guthrie test (gŭth′rē) [Robert Guthrie, U.S. microbiologist, 1916–1995] A blood test used to detect hyperphenylalaninemia and to diagnose phenylketonuria (PKU) in the newborn.

PATIENT CARE: The blood for the test is obtained by pricking a newborn's heel. The drop of blood obtained is placed on filter paper and allowed to dry. It can then be analyzed for evidence of particular sequences of DNA. The dried blood on the filter paper is often referred to as a "Guthrie spot." SEE: *phenylketonuria.*

gutta (gŭt′ă) [L., a drop] ABBR: gt. (pl. *gtt.*) A drop. The amount in a drop varies with the nature of the liquid and its temperature. It is therefore not advisable to use the number of drops per minute of a solution as anything more than a general guide to the amount of material being administered intravenously.

gutta-percha (gŭt″ă-pĕr′chă) The purified dried latex of certain trees, used in dentistry.

guttate (gŭt′āt) [L. *gutta,* drop] Resembling a drop, said of certain cutaneous lesions.

guttering (gŭt′ĕr-ĭng) Cutting a channel or groove in a bone.

guttural (gŭt′ŭ-răl) Pert. to the throat.

Guyon, Felix J.C. (gē-yōn′) Fr. surgeon, 1831–1920.

G. canal A tunnel on the ulnar side of the wrist formed by the hook of the hamate and pisiform bones. The ulnar nerve may be compressed at this site in long-distance bicyclists, by falling on the wrist, or by repetitive wrist actions.

G. sign Ballottement of the kidney.

GV *Governor* **vessel.**

GVHD *graft-versus-host disease.*

Gy *gray* (unit of measurement of radiation).

gymnastics [Gr. *gymnastikos,* pert. to nakedness] Systematic body exercise with or without special apparatus.

Gymnema (jĭm-nē′mă) An herbal remedy extract from the leaves of a vine, *Gymnema sylvestre,* native to tropical India, and promoted for its effect on high blood glucose levels.

Gymnema sylvestre (jim-nē′mă sil-ves′trē) A climbing herb native to the tropical forests of India. It has been used in Ayurvedic medicine as a treatment for diabetes mellitus. It is sometimes referred to locally as gurmar.

gynaeco- SEE: *gyneco-.*

gyneco-, gynec- [Gr. *gynē,* stem *gynaik-,* woman] Prefixes meaning *woman, female, female reproduction.* The variant *gynaeco-* is used outside the U.S.

gynecoid (jĭn′ĕ-koyd) [″ + *eidos,* form, shape] Resembling the female of the species.

gynecologic, gynecological (gī″nĕ-kŏ-loj′ĭk, jī″, jĭn″ĕ-, gī″nĕ-kŏ-loj′ĭ-kăl, jī″, jĭn″ĕ-) [*gyneco-* + *-logy*] Pert. to gynecology.

gynecologist (gī″nĕ-kŏl′ō-jĭst, jī″, jĭn″ĕ-) A physician who specializes in gynecology.

gynecology (gī″nĕ-kŏl′ō-jē, jī″, jĭn″ĕ-) [″ + *logos,* word, reason] The study of women's health care, esp. diseases and conditions that affect reproduction and the female reproductive organs. **gynecologic,** *adj.*

gynecomastia (jī″nĕ-kō-mas′tē-ă, gī″, jĭn″ĕ-) [*gyneco-* + *masto-* + *-ia*] Enlargement of breast tissue in the male. This may occur during three distinct age periods: transiently at birth, again beginning with puberty and declining during the late teenage years, and finally in adults over age 50 years. In the newborn, it is caused by stimulation from maternal hormones. A milky secretion ("witch's milk") may be produced; the condition disappears within a few weeks. During middle adolescence, as many as 60% of boys may develop some degree of gynecomastia, either unilateral or bilateral and, if bilateral, often with varying degrees of growth between the two sides. It may be produced by the use of alcohol, marijuana, and heroin, but it is often a normal, nonpathological condition and usually disappears within 18 months. Hormonal assays should be performed only if the condition appears before puberty, persists longer than 2 years, or is associated with other signs of endocrine disorders. In older men, the condition can be caused by pituitary or testicular tumors, medications such as spironolactone or antiandrogens, or cirrhosis of the liver causing enhanced activity (due to delayed liver catabolism) of naturally produced estrogens. SEE: illus.

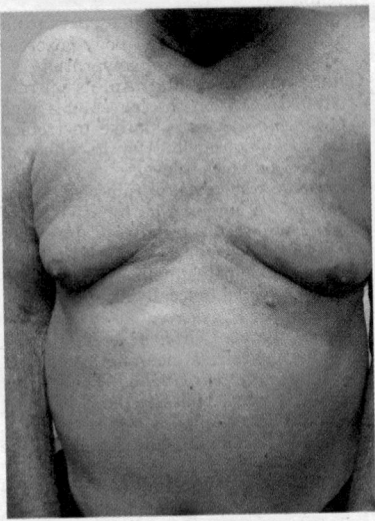

GYNECOMASTIA

TREATMENT: Therapy depends on the cause. Because gynecomastia has a high rate of spontaneous regression, medical therapies are most effective during the active proliferative phase. To help alleviate the acute embarrassment from the condition adolescent boys may suffer, they should be reassured that the problem will go away. Tender breasts should be treated with analgesics.

gyno-, gyn- [Gr. *gynē,* woman] Prefixes meaning *woman, female, female reproduction.*

gypsum (jĭp′sŭm) [L.; G. *gypsos,* chalk] **1.** A natural form of hydrated calcium sulfate. When heated to 130°C, it loses its water and becomes plaster of Paris. **2.** A hemihydrate of gypsum resulting from heating gypsum and allowing it to dehydrate in the presence of sodium succinate or calcium hydrochloride. This form is used as a dental stone in preparing investments for dental casting.

gyrate (jī′rāt) [Gr. *gyros,* circle] **1.** Ring-shaped, convoluted. **2.** To revolve.

gyration (jī-rā′shŭn) A rotary movement.

gyre (jīr) [Gr. *gyros,* circle] Gyrus.

gyrectomy (jī-rĕk′tō-mē) [″ + *ektome,* excision] Surgical removal of a cerebral gyrus.

gyri (jī′rī) Pl. of gyrus.

gyro-, gyr- [Gr *gyros,* ring, round.] Prefix meaning *circle, spiral, ring.*

gyrus (jī′rŭs) *pl.* **gyri** [L. *gyrus* fr. Gr. *gyros,* ring, circle] Any of the surface convolutions or rounded ridges that are packed along the cerebral hemispheres of the brain. Each gyrus is separated from its neighbor by a furrow called a sulcus. Details of the shape of gyri vary from individual to individual. SYN: *convolution; gyre.* SEE: illus.

    angular g. A gyrus of the ventral region of the parietal lobe; it caps the posterior (ascending) end of the superior temporal sulcus, and it is just ventral to the supramarginal gyrus. The cortex of the angular gyrus plays a role in the association of the visual and tactile perceptions of forms and shapes. SYN: *g. angularis.*

    g. angularis Angular g.

    cingulate g. A long curving gyrus on the medial surface of each cerebral hemisphere; it follows the arch of the corpus callosum, from which it is separated by a deep fissure, the callosal sulcus. The cortex of the cingulate gyrus and the underlying axon tract, the cingulum, are parts of the main circuitry of the limbic system. SYN: *callosal convolution.*

    dentate g. A curved gyrus hidden along the medial surface of the temporal lobe of each cerebral hemisphere. It contains a cortex of three layers, with a single cell layer, that is part of the hippocampal formation, and it is folded inside the hippocampal sulcus, where it lies against the subicular edge of the parahippocampal gyrus. The surface of the dentate gyrus has regularly-spaced transverse grooves, which make the gyrus resemble a row of teeth. SYN: *fascia dentata.* SEE: *limbic system* for illus.

    g. fornicatus The ring along the medial surface of each cerebral hemisphere that forms a large segment of the limbic circuitry. The gyrus fornicatus comprises the subcallosal gyrus, the cingulate gyrus, the retrosplenial area, the parahippocampal gyrus, and the uncus.

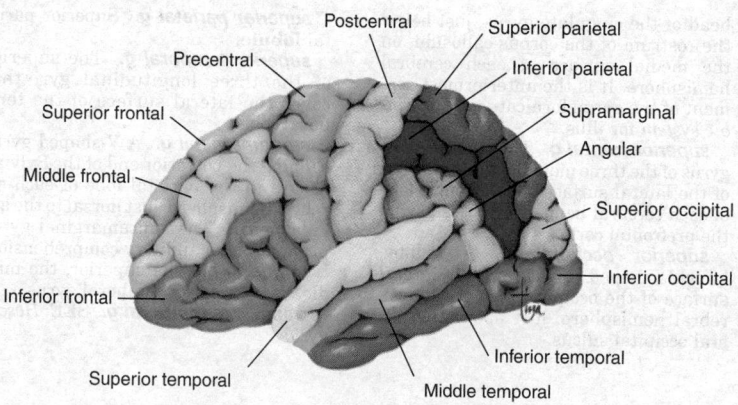

CEREBRAL GYRI

Heschl g. SEE: *Heschl gyrus.*

hippocampal g. Parahippocampal **g.**

inferior frontal g. The inferior-most of the three major longitudinal gyri of the lateral surface of the frontal lobe of each cerebral hemisphere; it is part of the prefrontal cortex. In the dominant hemisphere, the posterior two-thirds of the inferior frontal gyrus are the Broca speech area, which is involved in activating the muscle groups used when speaking

inferior occipital g. A stubby, knuckle-shaped gyrus on the lateral surface of the occipital lobe of each cerebral hemisphere, just below the lateral occipital sulcus.

inferior temporal g. The inferior-most of the three longitudinal gyri that cover the lateral surface of the temporal lobe.

lingual g. A tongue-shaped gyrus that, at its anterior end (tip), abuts the parahippocampal gyrus on the under surface (ventral) of the occipital lobe. The calcarine fissure (calcarine sulcus) forms the medial (upper) edge of the lingual gyrus, and the collateral sulcus forms the lateral (lower) edge. Part of the primary visual cortex is found along the wall of the lingual gyrus inside the calcarine fissure.

medial frontal g. The major anterior gyrus of the medial surface of the frontal lobe of each cerebral hemisphere; it is part of the prefrontal cortex. The medial frontal gyrus curves over the cingulate gyrus, separated from it by the cingulate sulcus.

middle frontal g. The middle of the three major longitudinal gyri of the lateral surface of the frontal lobe of each cerebral hemisphere; it is part of the prefrontal cortex.

middle temporal g. The middle the three longitudinal gyri that cover the lateral surface of the temporal lobe.

occipital g. The inferior or the superior occipital gyrus.

occipitotemporal g. The lateral or the medial occipitotemporal gyrus, both of which run longitudinally along the bottom (ventral surface) of the temporal lobe of each cerebral hemisphere.

orbital g. Any of the gyri forming the inferior, concave surface of the frontal lobe, which lies along the orbital surface of the frontal bone.

paracentral g. Paracentral **lobule.**

parahippocampal g. A gyrus along the medial (inner) edge of the temporal lobe of each cerebral hemisphere; it is bounded by the hippocampal fissure medially and the collateral sulcus laterally. The medial edge of the parahippocampal gyrus is called the subiculum; the remainder of the gyrus is called the entorhinal cortex. Together, the ventricular side of the subiculum and dentate gyrus form the hippocampus. SYN: *hippocampal g.* SEE: *limbic system* for illus.

parietal g. The inferior or the superior parietal lobule.

postcentral g. A major dorsoventral gyrus in the parietal lobe of each cerebral hemisphere; its anterior border is the central sulcus, and its posterior border is the postcentral sulcus. This gyrus contains the primary somatosensory cortex. SYN: *ascending parietal* **convolution.**

precentral g. A major dorsoventral gyrus in the parietal lobe of each cerebral hemisphere; its anterior border is the precentral sulcus, and its posterior border is the central sulcus. This gyrus contains the primary motor cortex. SYN: *ascending frontal* **convolution.**

g. rectus A longitudinal gyrus on the medial edge of the orbital (ventral) surface of the frontal lobe of each cerebral hemisphere; the lateral edge of the gyrus rectus is the olfactory sulcus.

subcallosal g. The short gyrus at the

head of the cingulate gyrus, just below the rostrum of the corpus callosum, on the medial surface of each cerebral hemisphere. It is the anteriormost segment of the gyrus fornicatus. SYN: *limbic system* for illus.

superior frontal g. The superiormost gyrus of the three major longitudinal gyri of the lateral surface of the frontal lobe of each cerebral hemisphere; it is part of the prefrontal cortex.

superior occipital g. A stubby, knuckle-shaped gyrus on the lateral surface of the occipital lobe of each cerebral hemisphere, just above the lateral occipital sulcus.

superior parietal g. Superior parietal **lobule**.

superior temporal g. The superior of the three longitudinal gyri that cover the lateral surface of the temporal lobe.

supramarginal g. A V-shaped gyrus capping the posterior end of the Sylvian fissure in the parietal lobe of each cerebral hemisphere, just dorsal to the angular gyrus. The supramarginal gyrus plays a role in auditory comprehension.

temporal g. The superior, the middle, or the inferior temporal gyrus.

transverse temporal g. SEE: *Heschl gyrus*.

H, h *haustus,* a draft of medicine; *height; henry; hora; hour; horizontal; hypermetropia; hemagglutinin.*

h Symbol for hecto, a term used in SI units.

ℏ Symbol for Planck's constant (the amount of energy in a photon). The constant, $\hbar$, = 6.626068 x 10^{-34} m^2 kg/s.

H Symbol for the element hydrogen.

¹H Symbol for protium.

²H Symbol for deuterium.

³H Symbol for tritium, a radioactive isotope of hydrogen.

[H⁺], cH⁺ Symbol for molar hydrogen ion concentration.

HA *hospital-acquired.*

HAAg *hepatitis A antigen.*

HAART *Highly active antiretroviral therapy.*

HAART attack A colloquial term for IRIS (the immune reconstitution inflammatory syndrome).

habenula (hă-ben′yŭ-lă) *pl.* **habenulae** [L. *habenula,* little rein, strap] **1.** A frenum or any reinlike or whiplike structure. **2.** A peduncle or stalk attached to the pineal body of the brain. Fibers that travel posteriorly along the dorsomedial border of the thalamus to the habenular ganglia (epithalamus) resemble reins. **3.** A narrow bandlike stricture. **habenular** (-lăr), *adj.*

Haber-Weiss reaction (hob′ĕr-vīs′) [Fritz Haber, Ger. physical chemist, 1868–1934; Joseph Weiss, Haber's student] The generation of toxic oxygen and hydroxyl radicals from hydrogen peroxide and superoxide. These radicals contribute to cell injury in many diseases, e.g., in the brain or heart after a stroke or heart attack.

habilitation (hă-bĭl″ĭ-tā′shŭn) **1.** The process of educating or training persons with functional limitation to improve their ability to function in society. **2.** Qualification for office. **3.** Academic accreditation. SEE: *rehabilitation.*

habit [L. *habere, habitus,* to have, hold] **1.** A motor pattern executed with facility following constant or frequent repetition; an act performed at first in a voluntary manner but after sufficient repetition as a reflex action. Habits result from the passing of impulses through a particular set of neurons and synapses many times. **2.** A particular type of dress or garb. **3.** Mental or moral constitution or disposition. **4.** Bodily appearance or constitution, esp. as related to a disease or predisposition to a disease. SYN: *habitus.* **5.** Addiction to the use of drugs or alcohol.

habituation (hă″bĭch′oo-ā′shŭn) **1.** The process of becoming accustomed to a stimulus as a result of frequent exposure or use. **2.** The newborn's unconscious suppression or extinction of automatic physiological responses to selective levels of commonly experienced stimuli, such as environmental noise.

habitus (hăb′ĭ-tŭs) [L., habit] A physical appearance, body build, or constitution.

HACCP *hazard analysis and critical control point.*

HACEK An acronym for *Haemophilus, Actinobacillus, Cardiobacterium, Eikenella, Kingella* (a group of slow-growing, gram-negative bacilli that occasionally causes endocarditis in humans).

HAD *HIV-associated dementia.*

hadron (ha′dron″) A member of a group of subatomic particles including the proton and the neutron. Tightly focused beams of hadrons are used in radiation therapy to destroy cancerous tissue.

haem- SEE: *hem-.*

Haemagogus (hē″mă-gŏg′ŭs) [″ + *agogos,* leading] A genus of mosquitoes that includes species that are vectors of yellow fever.

Haemaphysalis (hĕm″ă-fĭs′ă-lĭs) [″ + *physallis,* bubble] A genus of ticks that includes species that are vectors for tick-borne viral diseases including hemorrhagic fever.

haemato-, haemat- SEE: *hemat-.*

Haemophilus (hē-mof′ĭ-lŭs) [L. *haemophilus*] A genus of gram-negative, nonmotile bacilli; some are normal flora of the upper respiratory tract, and others cause serious illness.

  H. aegyptius A causative species of bacterial conjunctivitis and Brazilian purpuric fever (a potentially life-threatening pediatric infection).

  H. aphrophilus A species that often colonizes the upper respiratory tract but may occasionally cause endocarditis, brain abscesses, meningitis, or osteomyelitis.

  H. ducreyi The causative species of chancroid or soft chancre. SEE: *chancroid.*

  H. influenzae A causative species of acute respiratory infections and meningitis, esp. in children. Encapsulated type b is the form most commonly seen, but nonencapsulated forms also cause infections. Infections may be mild (such as, pharyngitis, tonsillitis, otitis media) or severe and life-threatening (such as epiglottitis, septicemia, meningitis, postviral pneumonia, endocarditis). SEE: *epiglottitis; meningitis.*

H. influenzae type b ABBR: HIB. A species that is an important, vaccine-preventable cause of meningitis. In children, this organism also causes acute epiglottitis, pneumonia, septic arthritis, and cellulitis.

TREATMENT: A cephalosporin that penetrates into the cerebrospinal fluid, such as cefotaxime or ceftriaxone, should be used.

PREVENTION: Administer the HIB vaccine three or four doses beginning at 2 months of age. Because the various forms of HIB vaccine are administered on different schedules, it is important to check the package insert for the appropriate information. Booster doses may be required. SEE: *Recommended Immunization Schedules Appendix.*

H. parainfluenzae A species that normally colonizes the human respiratory tract and sometimes causes serious infections, including abscesses, endocarditis, and sepsis.

H. vaginalis A former name for Gardnerella vaginalis.

hafnium (haf'nē-ŭm) [*Hafnia,* L. name for *København,* Copenhagen + *-ium*] SYMB: Hf. A rare radioactive chemical element, atomic weight (mass) (standard) 178.49, specific gravity 13.31, atomic number 72.

Haglund deformity (hag'lund″) [S.E. Haglund, Swedish orthopedist, 1870–1937.] A bone spur at the upper outer border of the calcaneus. It can cause pain felt behind the heel or in the Achilles tendon.

Hahnemann, Samuel (hon'ĕ-măn) [Ger. physician, 1755–1843] The founder of homeopathy. SEE: *homeopathy.*

HAI *Health-care associated **infection**.*

Hailey-Hailey disease (hāl'ē-hāl'ē) [William Howard Hailey, 1898–1967; and his brother Hugh Edward Hailey, b. 1909, U.S. dermatologists] A rare autosomal dominant skin disease in which plaques form in intertriginous areas. SYN: *familial benign chronic **pemphigus**.*

hair (har) **1.** A keratinized, threadlike outgrowth from the skin of mammals. **2.** Collectively, the threadlike outgrowths that form the fur of animals or that grow on the human body.

A hair is a thin, flexible shaft of cornified cells that develops from a cylindrical invagination of the epidermis, the hair follicle. Each consists of a free portion or shaft (scapus pili) and a root (radix pili) embedded within the follicle. The shaft consists of three layers of cells: the cuticle or outermost layer; the cortex, forming the main horny portion of the hair; and the medulla, the central axis. Hair color is due to pigment in the cortex. SEE: illus.

Hair in each part of the body has a definite period of growth, after which it is shed. In the adult human there is a constant gradual loss and replacement of hair. Hair of the eyebrows lasts only 3 to 5 months; that of the scalp lasts 2 to 5 years. Baldness or alopecia results when replacement fails to keep up with hair loss. It may be hereditary or due to pathologic conditions, e.g., infections or irradiation injury. Cytotoxic agents

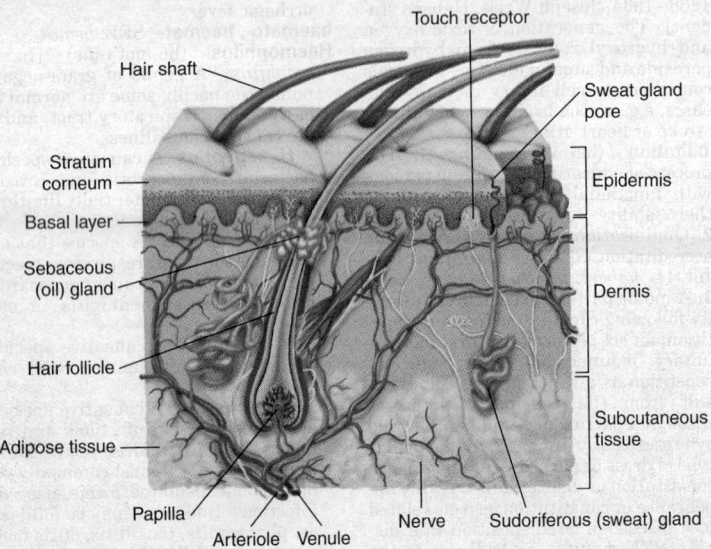

HAIR AND ADJACENT STRUCTURES OF CROSS-SECTION OF SKIN

used in cancer chemotherapy may cause temporary loss of hair. SEE: *alopecia*.

auditory h. The stereocilia of a specialized epithelial cell. These are present in the ear in the spiral organ of Corti, concerned with hearing; and in the crista ampullaris, macula utriculi, and macula sacculi, concerned with equilibrium.

kinky h. Short, sparse, tightly twisted hair that may be poorly pigmented.

lanugo h. SEE: *lanugo*.

moniliform h. Monilethrix.

pubic h. Hair over the pubes, which appears at onset of sexual maturity. The distribution is somewhat different in men than in women. SEE: **mons** *veneris;* **mons** *pubis*.

sensory h. Specialized epithelial cells with hairlike processes.

tactile h. Hair that is receptive to touch or contact.

terminal h. The long, coarse, pigmented hair of the adult.

hair analysis, hair specimen analysis Investigation of the chemical composition of hair. It is used in studying exposure to toxic chemicals in the environment, in poisoning investigations, in nutritional studies, and in monitoring the course of certain diseases. The sample should be obtained from new-growth hair within 5 cm of the scalp to reduce the chance of contamination of the hair by air pollutants. The technique of hair analysis has not been scientifically validated.

hairball, hair ball (har′bal″) A concrete mass of hair in the stomach. SYN: *trichobezoar*.

halal (hă-lăl′) Pert. to food prepared and served according to Muslim dietary laws.

halation (hăl-ā′shŭn) [Gr. *alos,* a halo] A blurring of vision caused by light being scattered to the side of the source.

Haldane effect (hăl′dān) The oxygenation of hemoglobin, which lowers its affinity for carbon dioxide. SEE: *Bohr effect*.

half-life (haf′līf″) **1.** The time required for half the nuclei of a radioactive substance to lose their activity by undergoing radioactive decay. **2.** In biology and pharmacology, the time required by the body, tissue, or organ to metabolize or inactivate half the amount of a substance taken in. This is an important consideration in determining the proper amount and frequency of drug administration. **3.** The time required for radioactivity of material taken in by a living organism to be reduced to half its initial value by a combination of radioactive decay and biological elimination.

biologic h. The time required to reduce the concentration of a drug in the blood, plasma, or serum by 50%. This is a measure of the rate of drug distribution and elimination. SEE: *half-life; pharmacokinetics*.

half-value thickness, half-value layer The thickness of a substance that, when placed in the path of a given beam of radiation, will lower its intensity to one half of the initial value. Half-value layers are stated in millimeters of aluminum equivalency (mm/AlEq).

halfway house (hălf′wā) A facility to house psychiatric patients who no longer need hospitalization but are not yet ready for independent living.

halide (hăl′īd) A compound containing a halogen (i.e., bromine, chlorine, fluorine, or iodine) combined with a metal or some other radical.

halitosis (hăl-ĭ-tō′sĭs) [L. *halitus,* breath, + Gr. *osis,* condition] Offensive odor of the breath. Its origin may be in the mouth or nose, lungs, blood, or digestive tract. Many individuals have halitosis due to drying of the oral mucosa. On awakening, those who snore or sleep with their mouths open may have particularly noticeable bad breath. Bad breath may also be due to an ingested food, such as onions or garlic. Other causes are respiratory infections such as bronchiectasis or lung abscess, acute necrotizing gingivitis, herpetic gingivostomatitis, periodontal disease, dental caries, cigarette smoking, hepatic failure, or diabetic ketoacidosis.

Halle point (al) [Adrien Joseph Marie Noël Halle, Fr. physician, 1859–1947] The point at the intersection of a horizontal line drawn from the anterior superior iliac spine and an angled line extending up from the pubic spine. At that point, the ureter is palpable as it crosses the pelvic brim.

Hallervorden-Spatz disease, H.-S. syndrome (hăl′ar-vor″dĕn-spăts′) [Julius Hallervorden, 1882–1965; H. Spatz, 1888–1969, Ger. neurologists] An inherited or sporadically appearing neurological disease, beginning in childhood and affecting the globus pallidus, red nucleus, and reticular part of the substantia nigra of the brain. Clinical characteristics include progressive rigidity; retinal degeneration; athetotic movements; and mental and, late in the disease, emotional retardation. There is no effective therapy. SYN: *neurodegeneration with brain iron accumulation*.

hallex (hăl′ĕks) *pl.* **hallices** [L.] Hallux.

Hallpike maneuver, Hallpike-Dix maneuver (hol′pīk) [Charles Skinner Hallpike, Brit. neurologist, 1900–1979] A test performed to diagnose benign positional vertigo. The patient is moved from a sitting position to recumbency with the head tilted down over the end of the bed and turned toward either shoulder. If vertigo develops after a delay of several seconds, the test is subjectively positive. If vertigo is associated with visible nystagmus, it is objectively positive. Vertigo and nystagmus that occur immediately, rather than after a delay, are suggestive of intracranial, rather than labyrinthine, disease. SEE: *benign positional vertigo.*

hallucination (hă-loo-ĭ-nā′shŏn) [L. *hallucinari*, to wander in one's mind] A false perception having no relation to reality and not accounted for by any exterior stimulus. It is a dreamlike (or nightmarish) perception occurring while awake. It may be visual, esp. in medical illnesses or drug withdrawal syndromes; auditory, esp. in psychoses; tactile; gustatory; or olfactory. Affected patients typically appear confused and agitated and are unable to distinguish between the real and the imaginary. SEE: *delusion; illusion.*

   auditory h. A hallucination of sounds, usually voices. Auditory hallucinations are a hallmark of psychotic illnesses but are also heard by patients with acquired hearing impairments and by some persons with temporal lobe seizures.

   microptic h. A hallucination in which things seem smaller than they are.

   visual h. The sensation of seeing objects that are not really there. This is a hallmark of alcohol and drug withdrawal and of other medical illnesses that adversely affect the brain.

hallucinogen (hă-loo′sĭ-nō-jĕn) [″ + Gr. *gennan*, to produce] A drug that produces hallucinations (e.g., LSD, peyote, mescaline, PCP, and sometimes ethyl alcohol).

hallucinosis (hă-loos″ĭ-nō′sĭs) [*hallucin(ate)* + *-osis*] The state of having hallucinations more or less persistently. SEE: *hallucination.*

hallux, hallus (hal′ŭks, hal′ŭs, hal′ŭ-sēz″) *pl.* **halluces** [L.] The great toe.

   h. limitus Limitation of range of motion of the first metatarsophalangeal joint, usually with arthritic degeneration of the joint and pain. SEE: *h. rigidus.*

   h. rigidus The most advanced form of hallux limitus.

   h. valgus Displacement of the great toe toward the other toes. SEE: *valgus.*

   h. varus Displacement of the great toe away from the other toes. SEE: *varus.*

halo [Gr. *halos*, a halo] **1.** The areola, esp. of the nipple. **2.** A ring surrounding the macula lutea in ophthalmoscopic images. **3.** A circle of light surrounding a shining body.

   h. symptom The perception of one or more colored circles around lights, seen by patients with glaucoma or cataract.

halo effect 1. The giving of an inflated performance appraisal or grade to an employee or student because of the appraiser's tendency to regard all subordinates fondly. **2.** The rating of any object or person more highly than merited because of an established bias.

halogen (hal′ŏ-jĕn) [Gr. *hals,* salt + *-gen*] Any of the elements (chlorine, bromine, iodine, fluorine, and astatine) forming Group 7 (VII) of the periodic table. These elements have very similar chemical properties, combining with hydrogen to form acids and with metals to form salts.

haloperidol (hă″lō-pĕr′ĭ-dŏl) A neuroleptic drug used to treat patients with psychotic illnesses, extreme agitation, or Tourette's syndrome.

halophilic (hăl″ō-fĭl′ĭk) [″ + *philein,* to love] Concerning or having an affinity for salt or any halogen.

halothane (hăl′ō-thān) A fluorinated hydrocarbon used as a general anesthetic.

halo vest (hā′lō″) A device used to immobilize the head and cervical spine following vertebral injury or surgery. It is designed to provide in-line traction of the cervical spine while allowing for a moderate amount of functional independence. The halo vest consists of three parts: (1) the halo, secured into the skull through the use of four pins or screws; (2) the vest, worn over the shoulders and trunk to support the weight of the halo, skull, and cervical spine; and (3) four metal bars connecting the halo to the vest.

   PATIENT CARE: The screws attaching the halo to the skull must be kept clean to reduce the risk of infection. Hygiene consists of cleaning each pin two to three times a day as prescribed by a physician. The patient should be instructed on how to use a mirror to inspect the sites for signs of infection, e.g., redness of the skin, or purulent drainage from around the pins. If the vest becomes wet, it should be dried with a hairdryer set on its lowest temperature setting. The shoulders and thorax should be inspected for signs of irritation from the vest. Additional padding may be required around pressure-sensitive areas.

   ⚠ Complications reported with the halo vest include: (1) incomplete cervical fracture healing (in about 10% to 15% of patients); (2) impairments in balance, vision, and some activities of daily living; (3) infection; (4) loosening of pins; and (5) scarring of skin at pin insertion sites.

   SYN: *halo vest* **orthosis.**

Halsted, William Stewart (hal′sted″) U.S. surgeon, 1852–1922.

   H. forceps A small curved or straight hemostatic forceps.

H. operation **1.** An operation for inguinal hernia. **2.** A radical mastectomy for breast.

H. suture An interrupted suture for intestinal or cutaneous wounds.

hamartoma (hăm-ăr-tō′mă) [Gr. *hamartia*, defect, + *oma*, tumor] A tumor resulting from new growth of normal tissues. The cells grow spontaneously, reach maturity, and then do not reproduce. Thus, the growth is self-limiting and benign.

multiple h. A congenital malformation that presents a slowly growing mass of abnormal tissue in multiple sites. The tissues are appropriate to the organ in which the hamartomas are located but are not normally organized. They may appear in blood vessels as hemangiomata, and in the lung and kidney. They are not malignant but cause symptoms because of the space they occupy.

hamate (hăm′āt) **1.** Hooked; unciform. SYN: *hamular*. **2.** Hamate bone.

hamatum (hă-mā′tŭm) [L. *hamatus*, hooked] Hamate bone.

Hamman, Louis (hăm′ăn) U.S. physician, 1877–1946.

hammer (ham′ĕr) **1.** An instrument with a head attached crosswise to the handle for striking blows. **2.** Malleus.

percussion h. A hammer with a rubber head used for tapping surfaces of the body in order to produce sounds for diagnostic purposes. SEE: *plexor*.

reflex h. A hammer used for tapping body parts such as a muscle, tendon, or nerve in order to test nerve function.

hammertoe, hammer toe (hăm′ĕr-tō″) A toe posture characterized by hyperextension of the metatarsophalangeal and distal interphalangeal joints and flexion of the proximal interphalangeal joint.

HAMRSA Hospital-acquired methicillin-resistant *Staphylococcus aureus*.

hamstring (hăm′strĭng) [AS. *haum*, haunch] **1.** One of the tendons that form the medial and lateral boundaries of the popliteal space. **2.** Any one of three muscles on the posterior aspect of the thigh, the semitendinosus, semimembranosus, and biceps femoris. They flex the leg and adduct and extend the thigh.

Ham test A test for diagnosing paroxysmal nocturnal hemoglobinuria, in which red cells are assessed for resistance to lysis during incubation with acidified serum. SEE: *acid hemolysin test*.

hamular (hăm′ū-lăr) [L. *hamulus*, a small hook] Hamate.

hamulus (hăm′ū-lŭs) *pl.* **hamuli** [L., a small hook] **1.** Any hook-shaped structure. **2.** The hooklike process on the hamate bone.

hand (hand) The body part attached to the forearm at the wrist. It includes the wrist (carpus) with its eight bones, the metacarpus or body of the hand (ossa

metacarpalia) having five bones, and the fingers (phalanges) with their 14 bones. In some occupations and recreational endeavors, workers use their hands as hammers, which may damage the ulnar nerve and artery, with consequent signs of ischemia and neuropathy. SYN: *manus*. SEE: illus.

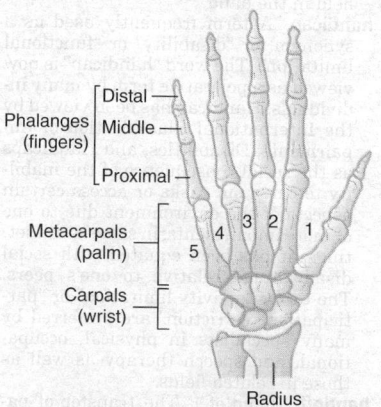

BONES OF HAND

cleft h. A bipartite hand resulting from failure of a digit and its corresponding metacarpal to develop. SYN: *lobster-claw h.*; *split h.*

diabetic h. Stiffness and fibrotic contractures of the metacarpophalangeal (MCP) and proximal interphalangeal (PIP) joints in patients with advanced diabetes mellitus.

dominant h. In American Sign Language, the hand that moves during the formation of a sign. SYN: *preferred h.*

preferred h. Dominant hand.

split h. Cleft hand.

hand-arm vibration syndrome (hănd′ărm′) ABBR: HAVS. Injury to the nerves, muscles, and tendons of the wrist and hand due to the repetitive use of vibrating hand tools. SYN: *vibration-induced neuropathy*.

SYMPTOMS: Patients may report intolerance of cold, muscular weakness, tingling sensations, or changes of color in the hand, fingers, or wrist.

H and E *hematoxylin* and *eosin*, a stain used in histology.

handedness The tendency to use one hand in preference to the other. Preferential use of the left hand is called sinistrality and of the right hand dextrality.

More than 90% of people are right-handed. Being left-handed may be hereditary or due to disease of the left cerebral hemisphere in early life.

hand-eye coordination (hand′ī′) Eye-hand coordination.

hand-foot-and-mouth disease An infectious disease characterized by painful oral ulcers and vesicles, papules, or pustules on the hands and feet. It is caused by enterovirus 71 and typically affects children. The disease usually begins with a fever, followed by the appearance of a distinctive rash, which resolves spontaneously in about a week.

handheld, hand-held (hand′held′) To be held in the hand, esp. to be used while held in the hand.

handicap A term frequently used as a synonym for "disability" or "functional limitation." The word "handicap" is now viewed as a pejorative term by many individuals. Handicap has been viewed by the International Classification of Impairments, Disabilities, and Handicaps as the social consequence of the inability to carry out tasks or access certain aspects of the environment due to one or more impairments; in some social settings, it has been equated with social disadvantage relative to one's peers. The terms "activity limitation" or "participation restriction" are preferred by many specialists in physical, occupational, and speech therapy as well as those in related fields.

handoff (hand′of″) The transfer of patient care from one health care provider to another or from one health care facility to another. SYN: *handover; sign-out*.

handover (hand′ō″vĕr) Handoff.

handrub (hănd′rŭb″) A rapidly drying solution that contains ethanol or propanol and is applied to the hands after contact with patients. It is used as a topical disinfectant.

Hand-Schüller-Christian disease [Alfred Hand, Jr., U.S. pediatrician, 1868–1949; Artur Schüller, Austrian neurologist, b. 1874; Henry A. Christian, U.S. physician, 1876–1951] Histiocytosis.

hands-only CPR CC-CPR.

handwashing Hand **hygiene**. SEE: *precautions, standard; Standard Precautions Appendix.*

handwriting (hand′rīt″ing) **1.** The writing of letters, numbers, words, or symbols with a handheld pen or pencil. **2.** Penmanship. Flawed penmanship is characteristic of several childhood learning disorders and of some adult illnesses, such as the micrographia of Parkinson's disease.

hangnail [AS. *ang-*, tight, painful, + *naegel*, nail] Partly detached piece of skin at the root or lateral edge of the finger or toenail.

hangover A nontechnical term for the malaise that may be present after ingesting a considerable amount of an alcoholic beverage or other central nervous system depressant. Symptoms usually present upon awakening from a sleep include some if not all of the following: mental depression, headache, thirst, nausea, irritability, and fatigue. Symptoms and their severity will vary with the individual. The presence of congeners in alcoholic beverages is thought to be related to the development of a hangover. There is no specific therapy. SEE: *alcoholism, acute; delirium tremens.*

Hansen, Gerhard Henrik Armauer (han′sĕn, hon′) Norwegian physician, 1841–1912. He studied leprosy (also known as Hansen disease) and identified its causative bacillus in 1873.

   H. disease Leprosy.

Hantavirus (han′tă-vī″rŭs) [*Hantaan River*, in Republic of Korea (South Korea), where the disease was first identified] A genus of viruses of the family Bunyaviridae and the cause of hemorrhagic nephrosonephritis and hantavirus pulmonary syndrome. The natural reservoir is rodents. In the U.S., identified species of *Hantavirus* include the Bayou virus, Black creek virus, New York virus, and Sin Nombre virus. On other continents, epidemic hantaviruses include the Dobrava, Hantaan, Puumala, and Seoul viruses.

hantavirus cardiopulmonary syndrome Hantavirus pulmonary syndrome.

hantavirus pulmonary syndrome ABBR: HPS. An acute respiratory illness, characterized by acute noncardiogenic pulmonary edema. It first appeared in the southwestern U.S. in 1993 and is caused by several strains of hantaviruses. The Sin Nombre virus is the most common in the U.S., but other pathogenic strains have been identified throughout the world. SYN: *hantavirus cardiopulmonary syndrome.*

   ETIOLOGY: Hantaviruses are single-stranded RNA viruses. They are carried by rodents, of which the deer mouse is the most common in the U.S. Infection usually is the result of inhalation of aerosolized excreta from rodents infected with the virus, but person-to-person transmission was documented in Argentina with infection from the Andes hantavirus. As of 2004, less than 400 cases of HPS have been identified in the U.S. The disease has had a mortality of about 35%. The incidence rises after warm, wet winters during which few rodents die. All cases originated in rural areas in people who were involved in rodent control activities, or camped or hiked in rodent-infested areas.

   SYMPTOMS: After an incubation period of about 5 to 33 days (median 18), patients usually report myalgia, fever, headache, nausea, vomiting, and diarrhea. The abrupt onset of dyspnea and nonproductive cough follows, which rapidly progresses to noncardiogenic pulmonary edema and shock. Disseminated intravascular coagulation and renal failure are common.

   DIAGNOSIS: HPS is diagnosed by clinical presentation, the presence of IgM antibodies to the virus in the blood, and Western blot enzyme-linked immunosorbent assays, among other tests.

TREATMENT: No effective antiviral drug therapy has been identified. Patients are given supportive care in the intensive care unit, with oxygen, mechanical ventilation, intravenous fluids, and vasopressors. Arterial blood gases, pulmonary status, neurological status, serum electrolytes and renal function, and hemodynamics are monitored closely, and airway patency maintained by careful suctioning. Fluid replacement should be based on hemodynamic monitoring. Vaccines against the virus provide a possible source of protection for persons at risk of exposure.

PATIENT CARE: People living in or visiting areas where the disease has been reported need to be educated about being careful under porches, in basements, and in attics or storage areas, where mouse droppings may be present. Mouse droppings should not be vacuumed or swept with a broom; these practices increase the risk of inhalation. Instead, individuals should cover infestations with a 10% solution of household bleach, wipe them up while wearing protective clothing and a HEPA filter mask, and place them in a bag for disposal. Dead rodents should be sprayed with a disinfectant, then double-bagged along with the cleaning material and disposed of according to local statutes. Health care providers should promptly report to state or federal public health agencies (e.g., the Centers for Disease Control and Prevention [CDC]) any disease outbreak to protect public health. Consider the possibility of bioterrorism if the disease occurs outside an endemic area, at an unusual time of year, or in an unusual pattern. Vacation cottages should be aired before anyone enters. Campers should avoid burrows and sleep on cots or mattresses rather than the bare ground. Children must be taught not to try to catch or play with deer mice, chipmunks, moles, or other rodents. A safety pamphlet is available from the Centers for Disease Control, Atlanta, Georgia. www.cdc.gov.

haplo-compatible (hap′lō-kŏm-pat′ĭ-bĕl) [Gr. *haploos,* simple, single + *compatible*] Having half of the same human leukocyte antigens (HLA-antigens) as another person. Typically a parent is haplo-compatible with each of his or her children, because each child inherits half of its HLA genes from each parent. In immunology and transplant medicine, this means that a parent and child are only halfmatched with respect to these crucial tissue markers. When a haplo-compatible donor gives an organ, e.g., bone marrow, to his or her child, T lymphocytes must be removed from the donated marrow to limit the risk of graft-versus-host disease.

haploid (ha′ployd″) [Gr. *haploos,* simple, + *-oid*] Of germ cells, possessing half (23 chromosomes in humans) the diploid number of chromosomes found in somatic cells. **haploidy** (-ploy′dē), *n.* SEE: *chromosome.*

haploinsufficient (hăp″lō-ĭn″sŭ-fĭsh′ĭnt) [Fr. Gr. *haploos,* simple + *insufficient*] Having only one copy of a wild-type allele at a genetic locus. This results in an abnormal phenotype.

haplo-transplant An organ transplantation between a donor and a recipient who have 50% of their human leukocyte antigens in common.

haplotype (hăp′lō-tīp) The combination of several alleles in a gene cluster.

HapMap (hap′map″) [*hap(lotype) map*] A record of the presence of single nucleotide polymorphisms (alleles) on the chromosomes of some individuals but not others. It is used to identify the inheritance of diseases that do not follow simple mendelian genetics.

happiness (hăp′ē-nĕs) [ME.] A subjective sense of well-being. A bright and positive outlook toward life.

hapten, haptene, haptin (hap′ten″, hap′tĭn, hap″tēn) [Gr. *haptein,* to seize] A substance that does not act as an antigen or stimulate an immune response on its own but can do so when combined with an immunogenic carrier molecule.

haptic (hăp′tĭk) [Gr. *haptein,* to touch] Tactile.

haptics (hăp′tĭks) The techniques and technology of using the sense of touch to drive computer or mechanical applications. Haptics has been applied to the rehabilitation of victims of stroke and sensory loss and to clinician education (e.g., in telemedicine).

haptoglobin (hăp″tō-glō′bĭn) A mucoprotein to which hemoglobin released from lysed red cells into plasma is bound. It is increased in certain inflammatory conditions and decreased in hemolytic disorders.

hardening (hard′ĕn-ing, ′ning) **1.** Rendering a pathological or histological specimen firm or compact, for making thin sections for microscopic study. **2.** The development of increased resistance to extremes of environmental temperature. SEE: *acclimation.*

　h. of the arteries A colloquial term for arteriosclerosis.

　work h. A series of conditioning exercises that an injured worker performs in a rehabilitation program. Programs address psychological and vocational needs in addition to simulating the functional tasks encountered on the job to which the individual will return. SYN: work **conditioning.**

hardiness (hăr′dē-nĕs) [ME.] Those physical and/or psychological characteristics that contribute to resiliency or the ability to withstand stress.

hard metal disease A respiratory disorder caused by the inhalation of cobalt and metal carbides, esp. tungsten carbide. Its primary symptoms are cough and breathlessness during exertion. Lung biopsies show markedly abnormal giant cells in the interstitium of the lung. The disease is occasionally fatal if untreated.

hardness 1. A quality of water containing certain substances, esp. soluble salts of calcium and magnesium. These react with soaps, forming insoluble compounds that are precipitated out of solution, thus interfering with their cleansing action. **2.** The quality or penetrating power of x-rays. Hardness increases as wavelengths become shorter. **3.** The quality of firmness or density of a material imparted by the cohesion of the particles that compose it.

hardness test A test designed to determine the relative hardness of materials by correlating the size or depth of an indent produced by a particular instrument with a known amount of compressive force. SEE: *hardness number.*

hardy Resourceful and resilient.

harelip (hār′lĭp) [AS. *hara,* hare, + *lippa,* lip] Cleft lip.

harm Anything that impairs or adversely affects the safety of patients in clinical care, drug therapy, research investigations, or public health. Harms include adverse drug reactions, side effects of treatments, and other undesirable consequences of health care products and services.

harmful algal bloom Red **tide.**

harmful drinking Any level of alcohol consumption that results in physical, psychological, or social complications or injury; e.g., drinking during pregnancy.

Harmonia axyridis (har-mōn′ē-ă ak-sir′ĭd-ĭs) The scientific name for a small multicolored beetle that may take up residence indoors, esp. during cooler weather. It is an important source of indoor allergies. It is found in the southern U.S. and in many other parts of the world. SYN: *Asian lady beetle; multicolored Asian lady beetle.*

harmonic In physics, concerning wave forms, an oscillation or frequency that is a whole number multiple of the basic frequency.

harmony (hăr′mō-nē) Agreement, balance, or compatibility.

harness (har′nĕs) In postamputation rehabilitation, the part of an upper extremity prosthesis that fits around the shoulder and back to permit mechanical control of the terminal device and hold the socket firmly around the stump.

harpoon (hăr-poon′) [Gr. *harpazein,* to seize] A device with a hook on one end

for obtaining small pieces of tissue such as muscle for examination.

Harrison Narcotic Act A law enacted in 1914 that classified certain drugs as habit forming and restricted their sale and distribution.

Hartmann procedure (hart′man″, ar-mon′) [Henri Hartmann, Fr. surgeon, 1860–1952] The surgical removal of a diseased portion of the distal colon or proximal rectum with formation of an end colostomy, accompanied by oversewing of the distal colonic or rectal remnant. This procedure may be the first stage of a two-part operation, in which at a later date, the colostomy and the oversewn remnant are reconnected. The Hartmann procedure is most often employed in debilitated patients or in emergent circumstances in which primary anastomosis or complete distal segment excision would not be appropriate.

Hartmann solution (hart′man) [Alexis F. Hartmann, U.S. pediatrician, 1849–1931] Lactated Ringer's injection used for fluid and electrolyte replacement. A sterile solution of 0.6 g of sodium chloride, 0.03 g of potassium chloride, 0.02 g of calcium chloride, and 0.31 g of sodium lactate is diluted with water for injection to make 100 mL.

Hartnup disease (hărt′nŭp) [*Hartnup,* the family name of the first reported case] A rare autosomal recessive metabolic disease in which absorption, excretion, and kidney resorption of amino acids, esp. tryptophan, is abnormal. Clinical signs resemble pellagra, with a rash that is worsened by exposure to sunlight.

harvest 1. To obtain samples or remove bacteria or other microorganisms from a culture. **2.** Removal of donor organs for transplantation.

Harvey, William (hăr′vē) British physician, 1578–1657, who described the circulation of the blood.

Hashimoto thyroiditis (ha″shē-mōt′ō) [Hakaru Hashimoto, Japanese surgeon, 1881–1934] An autoimmune illness in which there is inflammation, followed by destruction and fibrosis of the thyroid gland, and ultimately resulting in hypothyroidism. Autoantibodies against thyroglobulin and receptors for thyroid-stimulating hormone cause the progressive destruction. Hashimoto thyroiditis is the most common cause of hypothyroidism where there are inadequate levels of iodine. It affects people of all ages but is most common in older women and in those with a family history of autoimmune diseases. Thyroid hormone replacement is required. SYN: *chronic lymphocytic* **thyroiditis.** SEE: *thyroid* **gland.**

hashish (hash′ēsh, ha-shēsh′) [Arabic, *hashīsh,* hemp, dried grass, hay] A more or less purified, gummy extract prepared from the flowers, stalks, and leaves of the hemp plant *Cannabis sativa*. It is smoked or chewed for its euphoric effects. Its psychoactive effects are usually stronger than those of marijuana. SEE: *Cannabis sativa; marijuana; tetrahydrocannabinol*.

Hassall corpuscle (has'ăl) [Arthur H. Hassall, Brit. chemist and physician, 1817–1894] A spherical or oval body present in the medulla of the thymus. It consists of a central area of degenerated cells surrounded by concentrically arranged flattened or polygonal cells. SYN: *Gierke corpuscle*.

hatching In embryology, the separation of the blastocyst from the zona pellucida.

haunch (hawnsh) [Fr. *hanche*] The hips and buttocks.

haustration (hos-trā'shŏn) [*haustrum*] The presence of a segment or recess, esp. in the bowel. SEE: illus.

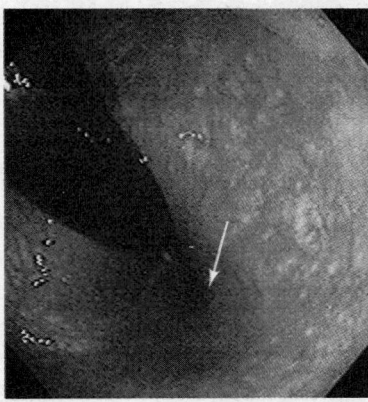

HAUSTRATION, SEEN ENDOSCOPICALLY

haustrum (haw'strŭm) *pl.* **haustra** [L. *haurire*, to draw, drink] One of the sacculations of the colon caused by longitudinal bands of smooth muscle (taeniae coli) that are shorter than the gut. **haustral** (haw'străl), *adj.*

HAV *hepatitis A virus*.

haversian canal (hă-vĕr'zhăn) SEE: under *canal*.

haversian system The structural unit of compact bone; it consists of a central haversian canal surrounded by concentric cylinders of osteocytes within the calcium matrix. SEE: *bone* for illus; *osteon*.

Havrix (hăv'rĭks) Hepatitis A vaccine, inactivated.

Hawkins test (hok'ĭnz) A clinical assessment of rotator cuff tendonitis or subacromial impingement. The patient's arm is raised in front of the body to 90°, and then the examiner forces it into internal rotation. The test is positive

when the patient complains the movement is painful. SEE: illus.

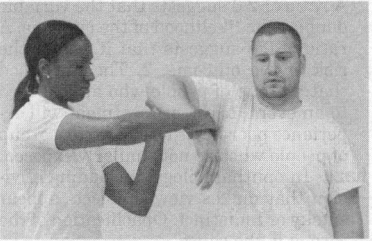

HAWKINS TEST

hawthorn (haw'thawrn") [AS. hagut-horn] An herbal remedy from the berries and leaves of the hawthorn tree (*Crataegus laevigata*), also known as hagthorn, haw, hazel, May, Mayblossom, and whitethorn. Hawthorn is promoted for its effect in treating cardiovascular conditions, including hypertension and congestive heart failure. SYN: *Crataegus laevigata*.

Hawthorne effect (haw'thawrn") [The Hawthorne plant of the Western Electric Company] The tendency of research outcomes to be altered by virtue of their being studied.

hay fever SEE: under *fever*.

hazard analysis and critical control point ABBR: HACCP. A food safety program designed initially for astronauts and adopted by the U.S. Food and Drug Administration and other international agencies. It consists of seven principles: 1. identify potential hazards to a nutrient or the food supply; 2. find the critical control points in food production where interventions can block the hazard; 3. establish protocols for preventing each identified hazard at the control points; 4. establish monitoring standards to identify problems arising at those control points; 5. develop policies to correct monitoring failures; 6. develop procedures to verify that the system functions well; 7. establish and implement policies for record keeping.

hazardous material ABBR: hazmat. A toxic material that may cause personal injury or property damage. The hazard of any material is determined by its chemical, physical, and biological properties and by the possibility of exposure to that material. SEE: *health hazard; permissible exposure limits; right-to-know law*.

hazard ratio (haz'ărd) ABBR: HR. **1.** In biostatistics, the calculated likelihood that a particular intervention will make a study outcome more or less likely to occur. A hazard ratio of 1.0 indicates that the variable has no impact on the outcome. A hazard ratio of less than 1.0 indicates that the variable decreases the likelihood of the outcome. A ratio exceeding 1.0 indicates that the variable increases the likelihood of the outcome. A ratio of 2.0 suggests that the variable doubles the likelihood of the outcome. A ratio of 0.5 suggests that it halves the risk of the outcome. **2.** The likelihood that a group of people who are exposed to an event, toxin, or treatment will experience poor health, relative to a group of people who are not similarly exposed.

haze In ophthalmology, a clouding of vision that makes viewed objects appear smoky or indistinct. Opacification of the cornea is the cause.

hazmat (hăz'măt) Contraction for hazardous material.

Hb *hemoglobin.*

HB Ag An obsolete term for any one of the hepatitis B antigens. SEE: *hepatitis B.*

HbCo *Carboxyhemoglobin.*

Hbg *hemoglobin.*

H2 blocker SEE: under *blocker.*

HBV *hepatitis B virus.*

HCFA *Health Care Financing Administration.*

HCG, hCG *human chorionic gonadotropin.*

HCl *hydrochloric acid.*

H₂CO₃ Formula for carbonic acid.

HCO₃⁻ Chemical formula for bicarbonate ion.

HCT *Hematopoietic cell* **transplantation.**

Hct *Hematocrit.*

HCV *hepatitis C virus.*

HCW *health care worker.*

hcy *homocystine.*

H.D. *hearing distance.*

HDAg *hepatitis D virus antigen.*

HDCV *human diploid cell vaccine* (for rabies).

HDFN *hemolytic disease of the fetus and newborn* or *hemolytic disease of the newborn.*

H disease *Hartnup disease.*

HDL *high-density lipoprotein.*

He Symbol for the element helium.

head [AS. *heafod*] **1.** The upper segment of the body, which is shaped by the skeletal structure called the skull, which contains the brain and the specialized sense organs (of the eyes, ears, nose, and tongue), and through which external matter (eg, food and air) is internalized. SEE: illus. **2.** The larger extremity of any organ.

ABNORMALITIES: *An abnormal fixation* of the head may be caused by postpharyngeal abscess, arthritis deformans, swollen cervical glands, rheumatism, traumatism of the neck, sprains of cervical muscles, congenital spasmodic torticollis, caries of a molar tooth, burn scars, or eye muscle imbalance (hyperphoria). An inability to move the head may be due to caries of the cervical vertebrae and diseases of articulation between the occiput and atlas or paralysis of neck muscles.

Abnormal movements of the head include habit spasms such as nodding. Rhythmical nodding is seen in aortic regurgitation, chorea, and torticollis. A retracted head is seen in acute meningitis, cerebral abscess, tumor, thrombosis of the superior longitudinal sinus, acute encephalitis, laryngeal obstruction, tetanus, hydrophobia, epilepsy, spasmodic torticollis, strychnine poisoning, hysteria, rachitic conditions, and painful neck lesions at the back.

after-coming h. Childbirth with the head delivered last.

articular h. A projection on bone that articulates with another bone.

headache (hed'āk") ABBR: HA. Pain felt in the forehead, eyes, jaws, temples, scalp, skull, occiput, or neck. Headache is exceptionally common; it affects almost everyone at some time. From a clinical perspective, benign HA must be distinguished from a potentially life-threatening HA. Types of benign HA include tension, migraine, cluster, sinus, and environmentally induced (e.g., "ice cream" HA or "caffeine-withdrawal" HA). A life-threatening HA may be caused by rupture of an intracranial aneurysm, subarachnoid hemorrhage, hemorrhagic stroke, cranial trauma, encephalitis, meningitis, brain tumors, or brain abscesses. SYN: *cephalalgia.* SEE: *migraine.*

Typically, benign HAs have a recurrent or chronic history with which the patient is familiar. The tension HA sufferer, for example, develops bandlike pressure around the head at the end of a difficult or stressful day. The onset of the HA is gradual and progressively worsens but is usually not severe or intense.

The migraine HA sufferer also typically has a history of recurrent HA, often dating back to childhood. Migraine HA is often of rapid onset, unilateral, throbbing, or beating in character. It may be preceded by scotoma and be associated with nausea, vomiting, or even transient neurological deficits, such as hemibody weakness. The HA may be triggered by eating chocolate, monosodium glutamate, or some cheeses, drinking alcohol, or taking certain medications, such as the hormone estrogen. By contrast, an HA that is life-threatening may have some of the following hallmarks: (1) first, or the worst, HA a patient has ever suffered (i.e., subarachnoid hemorrhage should be suspected); (2) first occurrence in a patient with a history of cancer (metastatic tumor); (3) accompanying fever, stiff neck, or photophobia (meningitis, intracranial hemorrhage); (4) associated loss of consciousness or severely altered mental

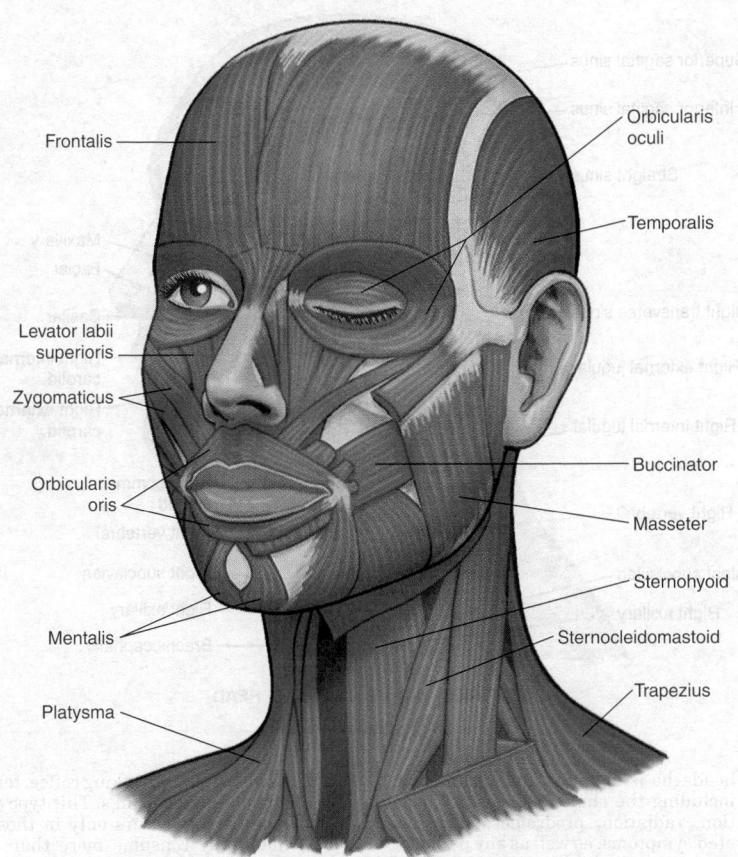

MUSCLES OF THE FACE AND NECK

(Anterior view)

status (intracerebral hemorrhage, brain embolism, encephalitis, meningitis); (5) associated neurological deficits that do not quickly resolve (intracerebral hemorrhage, brain embolism, brain abscesses); (6) occurrence in a patient with recent head trauma (hemorrhage, carotid artery dissection) or a history of recent foreign travel (neurocysticercosis; falciparum malaria); and (7) occurrence in a patient with acquired immunodeficiency syndrome (cryptococcal meningitis, *Toxoplasma gondii*, central nervous system lymphoma).

Only a few examples are given here. Almost any disturbance of body function may cause HA, including sunstroke, motion sickness, insomnia, altitude sickness, spinal puncture, alcohol withdrawal, prolonged fasting, exposure to loud noise, menstruation, psychological stressors, or new medications (e.g., nitrates).

TREATMENT: Mild HA often responds to rest, massage, acetaminophen, or listening to relaxing music. Moderate HA typically requires nonsteroidal anti-inflammatory drug (NSAID) therapy. Caffeine helps ameliorate many mild to moderate HAs. Antiemetics (e.g., prochlorperazine, metoclopramide) help relieve moderate to severe HAs, esp. those accompanied by nausea; ergotamines and the triptan drugs are particularly suited to treating migraines. Cluster HAs often resolve after treatment with corticosteroids or high-flow oxygen. The HA of temporal arteritis also responds to high-dose steroids, but these agents must be continued for months or years until the syndrome remits. Narcotic analgesics relieve HA pain, but habitual use may diminish their effectiveness or result in dependence.

PATIENT CARE: A description of the

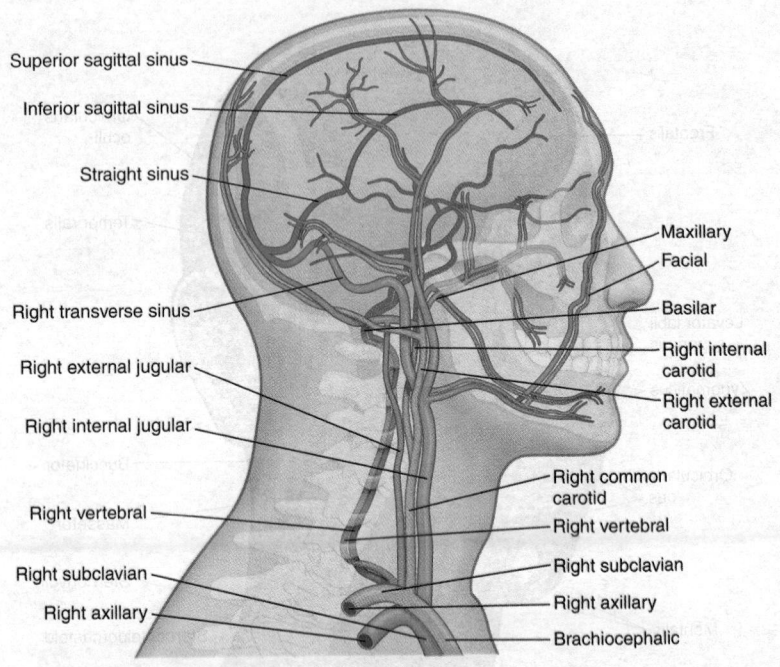

ARTERIES AND VEINS OF THE HEAD

(Right lateral view)

headache is obtained and documented, including the character, severity, location, radiation, prodromes, or associated symptoms, as well as any palliative measures that have brought relief. Temporal factors and any relationship of recurring headaches to other activities are also documented. The patient is taught to avoid precipitating or exacerbating factors. Noninvasive comfort measures (lying down in a quiet, darkened room with an ice pack on the forehead or cool compresses on the eyes) and prescribed drug therapy are instituted, and the patient is taught about these and evaluated for desired responses and any adverse reactions. If nausea and vomiting precede or accompany HA, the patient is taught to use antiemetics, and to drink fluids for rehydration once the medication has taken effect.

analgesic-rebound h. A headache that occurs when a patient who has chronic or recurring headaches and overuses medications to control them stops using pain relievers. Analgesic rebound is a common cause of daily headache pain; it may respond to treatment with antidepressant medications and withdrawal of the offending analgesics. SYN: *medication overuse h.*

caffeine withdrawal h. Headache, usually mild to moderate, that begins after someone stops drinking coffee, tea, or other caffeinated drinks. This type of headache usually occurs only in those who habitually consume more than 4 cups of caffeine daily and is often accompanied by fatigue and malaise.

cervicogenic h. A headache that begins in the superior segments of the cervical spine and radiates to one side of the neck, forehead, and/or shoulder. It typically is worsened by movements or postures of the head or neck, or by pressure applied directly to the neck. It may be relieved by massage, manipulation, or occipital nerve blocks.

cluster h. A series of headaches, typically occurring in men, that are intense; recurring; felt near one eye; and often associated with nasal congestion, rhinorrhea, and watering of the affected eye. They typically occur 1 or 2 hr after the patient has fallen asleep, last for about 45 min, and recur daily for several weeks before spontaneous resolution. The cause of the headaches is unknown, but their recurrence during certain seasons of the year and certain times of day may suggest a circadian or chronobiological mechanism.

TREATMENT: Medications that alleviate cluster headaches include corticosteroids, ergotamines, gabapentin, lithium, melatonin, NSAIDs, sumatriptan and other "-triptan" drugs, and high-flow oxygen. Surgery is sometimes used to cut affected nerves.

   coital h. A headache that begins suddenly during coitus or immediately after orgasm. These are uncommon, occur more frequently in men than in women, and may last for minutes or hours.

   exertional h. An acute headache of short duration that appears after strenuous physical activity. Usually benign, it is relieved by aspirin and prevented by changing to a less strenuous exercise.

   histamine h. A headache resulting from ingestion of histamine (found in some wines), injection of histamine, or excessive histamine in circulating blood. This type of headache is due to dilatation of branches of the carotid artery. SEE: *cluster h.*

   hypnic h. A headache that awakens a patient from sleep. Hypnic headaches are typically bilateral, and are experienced more often by the elderly than by other patients. Unlike cluster headaches, which also occur during rest or sleep, the hypnic headache is not felt on one side of the face, and not associated with tearing of the eye or painful congestion of the sinuses.

   idiopathic stabbing h. Stabbing headache.

   medication overuse h. Analgesic-rebound headache.

   migraine h. Migraine.

   mixed h. Headache that may have features of some combination of migraine headache, tension headache, and analgesic withdrawal.

   postdural puncture h. Postlumbar puncture headache.

   postlumbar puncture h. A headache occurring after a spinal tap, felt mostly in the front and the back of the head. It is markedly worse when the patient sits up and better when the patient lies down. The headache is sometimes associated with double vision.

   ETIOLOGY: It is caused by the leakage of spinal fluid through a hole that fails to close when the spinal needle is removed from the dura mater. It is less likely to occur when pencil-point needles are used for lumbar puncture and when the spinal needle has a small diameter (e.g., 25 gauge).

   TREATMENT: Bedrest in a completely flat and prone position (without a pillow), forced oral and intravenous fluids, and administration of cortical steroids are useful in treating the headache. If the headache persists in spite of therapy, it may be possible to stop the leakage of spinal fluid by injecting 10 ml of the patient's blood in the epidural space at the site of the lumbar puncture. The blood may "patch" the hole in the dura. SYN: *postdural puncture h.*

   primary stabbing h. Stabbing headache.

   stabbing h. A headache of very brief duration, consisting of jabbing or stabbing pain that lasts only a few seconds and then recurs. It often improves when treated with indomethacin. SYN: *idiopathic stabbing h.; primary stabbing h.*

   tension h. **1.** A headache associated with chronic contraction of the muscles of the neck and scalp. **2.** A headache associated with emotional or physical strain.

   thunderclap h. A sudden, severe headache that reaches maximal intensity within seconds. Common causes include subarachnoid hemorrhage, cerebral aneurysm, arterial dissection, and cerebral venous sinus thrombosis. Its absence does not rule out intracranial hemorrhage.

   weight-lifter's h. A form of exertional headache that occurs after straining during workouts with free weights or weight-training machines.

head banging, head-banging In children, a rhythmic movement of the neck muscles in which the head is repeatedly shaken against other objects. It may be done for a variety of reasons, including anxiety, boredom, frustration, or anger. It is more common in boys than girls, and usually persists for months or a few years before and then ceases.

head control 1. The ability to maintain the head and the cervical spine in an upright position. **2.** The placement of the head in an erect position so that it can be more easily or precisely examined or treated.

headgear 1. A covering for the head, esp. a protective one, such as a helmet used by soldiers and those who participate in contact sports, auto racing, bicycle riding, or aviation. **2.** Extraoral traction and anchorage used to apply force to the teeth and jaws.

headrest (hĕd′rĕst) **1.** A pad made of soft material placed beneath the occiput, around the neck or lower face or both, designed to limit head movement during surgery or to prevent neck pain in cervical arthritis. **2.** A padded device used in cars, airplanes, or boats to prevent neck trauma during accidents. **3.** A padded device used in some types of wheelchairs to support the head and neck of patients with flaccid muscles or other neurological conditions. SEE: *assistive technology.*

head upright tilt test ABBR: HUT. A test in which the patient lies flat on a table in order to identify the reason for fainting spells. The table has adjustable head and foot positions so that the effect of different positions on the patient's blood pressure, pulse, and heart rhythm can be assessed for abnormal responses, such as a marked slowing of the heart rate.

heal (hēl) [AS. *hael*, whole] To cure; to make whole or healthy.

healer An individual who cures diseases, eases discomfort, or relieves the suffering of others.

healing (hēl′ing) The restoration to a normal mental or physical condition, esp. of an inflammation or a wound. Tissue healing usually occurs in predictable stages: formation of blood clots at the wound; inflammatory phase, during which plasma proteins enter the injured part; cellular repair, with an influx of fibroblasts and mesenchymal cells; regrowth of blood vessels (angiogenesis); and synthesis and revision of collagen fibers (scar formation).

In skin lesions, regrowth of epithelial tissues also occurs. The many processes involved in the healing of a wound take 3 weeks or more to complete. Many factors may delay tissue healing, including malnutrition, wound infection, and coexisting conditions, e.g., diabetes mellitus, advanced age, tobacco abuse, can-

cer; as well as the use of several drugs, including corticosteroids. SEE: illus.

COMPLICATIONS: These may result from the formation of a scar that interferes with the functioning of a part and possible deformity; the formation of a keloid, the result of overgrowth of connective tissue forming a tumor in the surface of a scar; necrosis of the skin and mucous membrane that produces a raw surface, which results in an ulcer; a sinus or fistula, which may be due to bacteria or some foreign substance remaining in the wound; proud flesh, which represents excessive growth of granulation tissue.

   aboriginal h. **1.** Shamanism (2). **2.** Health practices of native or indigenous peoples within a geographic region, which often include folk and spiritual elements. In Canada, the term pertains to specific governmental efforts to address health issues of indigenous or First Nations peoples.

   faith h. Healing from illness attributed to the agency of a divine being or power, usually through a variety of spir-

---

Healing by first intention

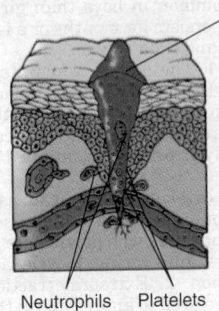
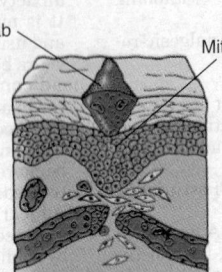
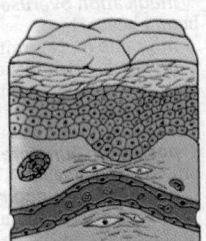

Scab

Mitoses

Neutrophils   Platelets clot

Granulation tissue: macrophages, fibroblasts 3–7 days

Fibrous union, remodeled tissue Weeks

Healing by second intention
Healing by third intention

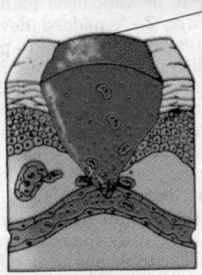
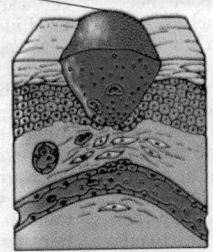
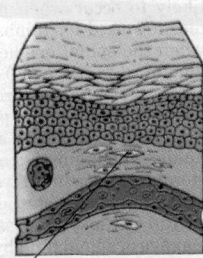

Scab

Platelets clot

Granulation tissue 3–7 days

Wound contraction Weeks

WOUND HEALING

itual practices such as prayer, laying on of hands, or anointing with oil.

h. by first intention A process that closes the edge of a wound with little or no inflammatory reaction and in such a manner that little or no scar is left to reveal the site of the injury. New cells are formed to take the place of dead ones, and the capillary walls stretch across the wound to join themselves to each other in a smooth surface. New connective tissue may form an almost imperceptible but temporary scar. In repairing lacerations and surgical wounds, the goal is to produce a repaired area that will heal by first intention.

h. by second intention Healing by granulation or indirect union. Granulation tissue is formed to fill the gap between the edges of the wound with a thin layer of fibrinous exudate. Granulation tissue also excludes bacteria from the wound and brings new blood vessels to the injured part. Healing by second intention takes longer than healing by primary intention and typically results in the formation of a prominent scar; wounds that heal by second intention show signs of failure if the wound loses the normal red-gray appearance of granulation tissue and becomes pale, dry, or insubstantial. When granulations first form at the top instead of the bottom of the wound, the base of the wound may have to be kept open with wicks or drains to promote healthy tissue repair.

h. by third intention Delayed wound healing that occurs in the base of ulcerated or cavitary wounds, esp. those that have become infected. The wound fills very slowly with granulation tissue and often forms a large scar. Wound revision surgery, including use of grafting, may be needed.

holistic h. Holism.

health (helth) A condition in which all functions of the body and mind are normally active. The World Health Organization defines health as a state of complete physical, mental, or social well-being and not merely the absence of disease or infirmity.

environmental h. The theory and practice of assessing, correcting, controlling, and preventing environmental factors that can adversely affect the health of present and future generations.

industrial h. The health of employees.

mental h. Psychological adjustment to one's circumstance or environment; the ability to cope with or make the best of changing stresses and stimuli. Individuals are considered mentally healthy if they have adjusted to life in such a way that they are comfortable with themselves and, at the same time, are able to live so that their behavior does not conflict with their associates or the rest of society. Inherent in this, for most individuals, are feelings of self-worth and accomplishment and the ability to be gainfully employed with sufficient reward for that employment to satisfy economic needs.

public h. The discipline concerned with measures that affect the health of communities. It includes the study and practice of techniques that protect communities from epidemics or toxic exposures, predict environmental disasters, and enforce the laws that provide a safe supply of water and food. In the U.S. various government agencies (such as the Centers for Disease Control and Prevention, Food and Drug Administration, and National Institutes of Health) are active in maintaining public health. Each of the 50 states has a health department in which at least one physician is the public health official. SEE: table; *preventive medicine; preventive nursing.*

Major Public Health Achievements of the 20th Century

Vaccination
Enhanced motor vehicle safety
Improvements in sanitation and clean water
Discovery of antibiotics
Risk factor modification to reduce heart attack and stroke
Improvements in food safety and nutrition
Maternal/child care innovations
Family planning
Fluoridation of drinking water
Antismoking campaigns

SOURCE: Adapted from the Centers for Disease Control and Prevention. *MMWR* 1999; 48:241–243.

wholistic h. Holistic **medicine**.

Health Belief Model ABBR: HBM. A theory used to explain health-seeking or health-avoiding behavior that is based on the assumption that attitude and belief motivate action. The model proposes that an individual facing health-related decisions weighs: 1. the likelihood that she may be at risk for a disease; 2. the gravity of the disease, were she to succumb to it; 3. the value of making choices that will prevent the illness; 4. the costs or challenges of making those choices. Health-benefiting actions will be taken when: cues/reminders to take that action are delivered to her and she believes that she has the capability to make her efforts count.

Health Canada The Canadian federal agency that oversees and regulates the Canadian Institutes of Health Research, the pricing and safety of patent medicines marketed in Canada, the safety of Canadian health and food products, the health care provided to First Nations and Inuit peoples, and the Canadian Public Health Agency.

health care SEE: under *care.*

health care-associated pneumonia SEE: under *pneumonia.*

Healthcare Common Procedure Coding System ABBR: HCPCS. A standardized coding system used to process claims for insurance payments by the Centers for Medicare and Medicaid Services. It consists of two parts: a coding system devised by the American Medical Association called the Current Procedural Terminology, which describes procedures and services provided by health care professionals; and a system that identifies health-related products and services that are not provided by physicians, e.g., emergency medical services, durable medical equipment, supplies, and orthotics.

Health Care Financing Administration ABBR: HCFA. The former name of the Centers for Medicare and Medicaid Services, the U.S. government agency responsible for funding and supervising health care provided under Medicare and Medicaid.

health care fraud Deceptive, dishonest, and unlawful misrepresentations to a health insurer (such as Medicare) made by a provider or a patient in order to obtain money or services to which one is not entitled.

health care proxy A legal document that allows individuals to name a person they know and trust to act as a proxy, that is, to make health care decisions for them if, for any reason and at any time, they become unable to make or communicate those decisions. The document goes into effect when it is signed. It also lists medical treatments that the person would not want to receive. Some states limit the age at which such a proxy may be established and prohibit certain persons (e.g., an estate administrator or an employee of a health care facility in which the person becoming the proxy is a resident) from being appointed to make health care decisions unless he or she is related to the person by blood, marriage, or adoption. **2.** An agent legally designated by a proxy. SYN: *durable power of attorney for health care.* SEE: *advance directive; do not attempt resuscitation; living will; donor card* for illus.

health care system An organization that manages and provides treatments and preventive services for the healthy, the sick, and the injured. The system includes physicians and their assistants, dentists and their assistants, nurses and their surrogates, the various levels

of diagnostic and care facilities, voluntary organizations, medical administrators in hospitals and government agencies, the medical insurance industry, and the pharmaceutical and medical device manufacturers. An ideal health care system emphasizes preventive medicine and encourages preventive self-care; enables access to primary care for assessment of and assistance with health problems; provides secondary or acute care involving emergency medical services and complex medical and surgical services; facilitates tertiary care for patients who need referral to facilities that provide rehabilitative services; offers respite care to allow families temporary relief from the daily tasks of caring for individuals for whom they are responsible; provides continuing supportive services for those whose mental or physical illness or disability is such that they need assistance with everyday tasks of living (e.g., home health and nursing home care); and provides hospice care for those with terminal illnesses, all at a reasonable cost.

health certificate An official statement signed by a physician attesting to the state of health of a particular individual.

health disparity A difference in health status between two or more groups of people that results from differences in their socioeconomic status.

health educator An individual professionally trained to instruct clients, families, or students about health-related topics, such as the diagnosis or the care of people with specific diseases or conditions.

health-enhancing physical activity and exercise Any exercise program designed to improve the functional abilities and quality of life of an individual by increasing strength, flexibility, or balance; preventing falls; increasing mobility; reducing blood glucose or serum lipid levels; or improving self-image and mood.

healthful Conducive to good health.

health hazard Any organism, chemical, condition, or circumstance that may cause injury or illness. Regarding chemicals, a substance is considered a health hazard if at least one study, conducted in accordance with established scientific principles, documents that acute or chronic effects may occur in connection with use of or exposure to that chemical. SEE: *hazardous material; permissible exposure limits; right-to-know law; health indicator* for table.

health indicator A limited but measurable element of the health of a community that is used to gauge public health as a whole. SEE: table.

health information technology SEE: under *technology.*

Some Public Health Indicators

Environmental	General	Maternal-Child	Prevention and Screening	Treatment
Air quality advisories	Birth rate	Infant mortality rate	Mammography use	Access to care
Motor vehicle emissions	Life expectancy	Birth weight of infants	Pap testing	Availability of primary care providers
Pesticide levels in foods	Obesity	Maternal mortality rate	Tobacco counseling	Waiting times for diagnostic services
Source (drinking) water contaminants	Self-reported health levels	Prenatal visits	Vaccination rates	Waiting times for therapeutic services

Health Information Technology for Economic and Clinical Health Act of 2009 ABBR: HITECH. A U.S. law that provides financial incentives to health care providers and institutions that invest in electronic health records that are used meaningfully (i.e., they incorporate electronic drug prescribing, links between clinics and hospitals, and quality reporting tools).

health insurance Indemnification to cover some or all of the costs of treating an injury or a disease.

Health Insurance Portability and Accountability Act of 1996 ABBR: HIPAA. A group of federal laws that establish rights, protections, and other standards of care for working people with pre-existing medical conditions. These laws affect obstetrical and neonatal care, the health care of women in general, the treatment of people with psychiatric illnesses, the confidentiality of medical records, and other aspects of health care.

health literacy 1. The ability to understand the causes, prevention, and treatment of disease. 2. The degree of communication that enhances the public's ability to obtain, understand, and act on health-related information.

PATIENT CARE: Patient teaching specific to the individual's needs is vital to health literacy. Low health literacy is a common, serious problem in health care. SEE: table.

health maintenance, ineffective Inability to identify, manage, and/or seek out help to maintain health. SEE: *Nursing Diagnoses Appendix.*

Health Maintenance Organization ABBR: HMO. A prepaid health care program of group practice that provides comprehensive medical care, esp. preventive care, while aiming to control health care expenditures.

Health On the Net Foundation ABBR: HON. A not-for-profit organization based in Switzerland, which in 1995 developed a Code of Conduct to guide the reader of health care information available on the Internet. The set of rules allows the reader to know the source and the purpose of the data being read.

health physics The scientific discipline devoted to the establishment and promotion of radiation safety. See the website of the Health Physics Society, http://www.hps.org.

Health Plan Employer Data and Information Set ABBR: HEDIS. A set of benchmarks used to assess the quality of care provided to patients by managed-care organizations. Included in these benchmarks are the numbers of immunizations administered by the plans and the extent of health screening tests provided by them.

health promotion Any process that fosters improvements in an individual's or a community's health and well-being. It may include formal education for patients, behavior modeling by influential people or community leaders, and mass media/communications. In the U.S. major health promotion goals include eliminating vaccine-preventable illnesses; improving the early treatment of stroke; decreasing cardiovascular risk factors related to inappropriate diet, high blood pressure, obesity, and use of tobacco; and reducing high-risk behavior that may contribute to the spread of acquired immunodeficiency syndrome (AIDS), hepatitis, and other illnesses.

Health Promotion Model A theory of nursing developed by Nola J. Pender that focuses on health promotion and disease prevention. The HPM can be used to structure nursing protocols and interventions that will help clients to develop skill and confidence in caring for themselves and their dependents and ultimately to live healthier and more productive lives. SEE: *Nursing Theory Appendix.*

Misconceptions About Health Care

Misconception	Explanation
Oral contraceptives decrease the risk of sexually transmitted diseases (STDs)	Oral contraceptives prevent pregnancy, but they do not provide any protection against STDs, e.g., AIDS, chlamydia, gonorrhea, genital herpes, or syphilis
Vaccines cause autism	Vaccines cause occasional injection-site reactions, allergic reactions, fevers, and rare episodes of febrile seizures or encephalopathy. However, multiple detailed investigations of large populations of vaccinated patients have failed to substantiate the fear that autism or autism-spectrum disorders are more prevalent in vaccinated than unvaccinated populations
Pneumococcal vaccine prevents pneumonia	Pneumococcal vaccine has been clearly shown to prevent pneumococcal bacteremia (a relatively rare form of sepsis). It has not been convincingly shown to prevent pneumonia, the reason most people receive it
More aggressive health care is better health care	Appropriate levels of health care combined with prudent behaviors and habits can optimize health. However, more medications or vitamin supplements than are needed, more operations than are required for normal healing, and many disease screening tests are prominent contributors to health care complications rather than better health
A person who is injured should get an MRI immediately	Most minor injuries, e.g., sprains, strains, bumps, and bruises, can be diagnosed and managed by patient history and hands-on physical examination. While professional athletes often undergo MRI testing when they are injured, the reasons for this practice relate more to the economics of the sport franchise than the health of the athlete
Prescription drugs are better than generic medications	Despite years of testing, many newly marketed prescription medications are withdrawn from the market soon after they are released for general use. Many generic medications, which have been in use by millions of patients for decades, are not only less expensive, but are also among the safest and most effective agents available
Personalized medicine has evolved far enough that one should get genetic testing followed by genetic counseling	While the field of personalized diagnosis is rapidly evolving, it has not yet achieved adequate predictive power to ensure that it can help most people to prevent or evade disease.
Breast implants cause rheumatological disease	Even though some court cases have ruled in favor of patients who have been diagnosed with rheumatological diseases and having received breast implants, there is little scientific data to support a causal association
Antibiotics cure the common cold	The cure for the common cold remains elusive
Patients treated by hospice services always die within a short time	Over 200,000 patients treated in hospice are discharged alive from hospice services each year

health risk appraisal An analysis of all that is known about a person's life and health, including personal and family medical history, occupation, and social environment, in order to estimate his or her risk of disability or death as compared with statistical averages. The data used for comparison vary with the patient's age, sex, ethnic background, and income. Also integral to the analysis are the skill of the evaluator and the sensitivity and specificity of the tests used in the evaluation.

Actions that could modify health risks include: 1) talking with the patient about alcohol or drug use; obesity; regular exercise, and the use of seat belts while driving; 2) assessing patient blood glucose, blood pressure, and lipid status; and 3) performing screening tests in appropriate populations, such as mammography in women over the age of 40 or colon cancer screening tests in patients over 50.

health-seeking behaviors Alterations in personal health habits or the environment in order to move toward a higher level of health. Stable health status is defined as age-appropriate illness prevention measures achieved, client reports good or excellent health, and signs and symptoms of disease, if present, are controlled. SEE: *Nursing Diagnoses Appendix.*

healthy Being in a state of good health.

Healthy People 2020 An initiative of the United States Department of Health and Human Services created to promote healthy behaviors. The plan identifies ten targets for health improvement in the U.S.: physical activity, overweight and obesity, tobacco use, mental health, responsible sexual behavior, injury and violence, substance abuse, environmental quality, immunization, and access to health care services. Private agencies have joined state and local governments in promoting and establishing educational and interventional programs to

reduce acute and chronic disease in these areas.

healthy worker effect The observation that the health of employed people is generally better than that of the unemployed population. Conversely, the health of people who stop working is generally worse than the health of a similar group of people who continue to work.

hearing (hēr′ing) The sense or perception of sound. The normal human ear can detect sounds with frequencies ranging from about 20 Hz to 20,000 Hz but is most sensitive to sounds in the 1500-Hz to 3000-Hz frequency range, which is the range most often used in speech. Hearing deficits occur when sound waves are not conducted properly to the cochlea, when lesions interrupt the workings of the cochlear nerve, or when central nervous system pathways involved in the processing of auditory stimuli are injured. SEE: illus.

FUNCTION TESTS: Hearing acuity can be determined by measuring the distance at which a person can hear a certain sound, such as a water tick, by using audiometers, and by bone conduction. In audiometers, electrically produced sounds are conveyed by wires to a receiver applied to the subject's ear. Intensity and pitch of sound can be altered and are indicated on the dials. Results are plotted on a graph known as an audiogram. In bone conduction tests, a device such as a tuning fork or an apparatus that converts an electric current into mechanical vibrations is applied to the skull. This is of value in distinguishing between perceptive and

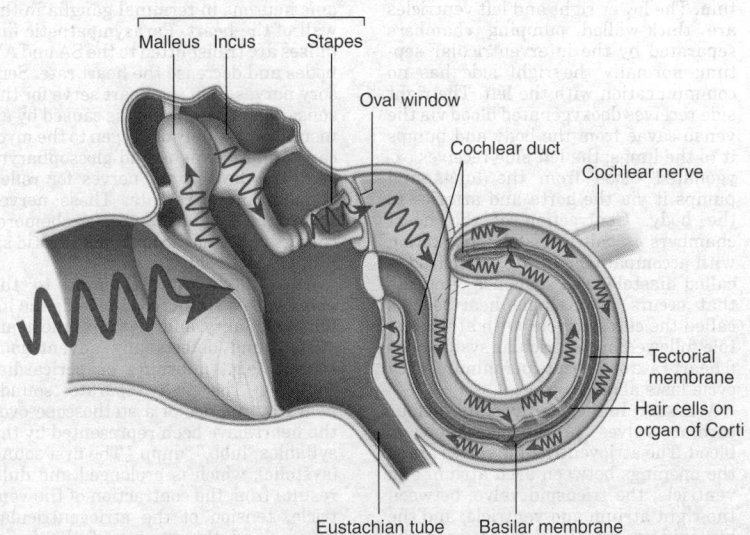

Malleus   Incus   Stapes

Oval window

Cochlear duct

Cochlear nerve

Tectorial membrane

Hair cells on organ of Corti

Eustachian tube   Basilar membrane

HOW HEARING OCCURS

conductive deafness. Conductive hearing loss may be diagnosed with the Weber test. Having the patient hum produces no difference in the sound heard if hearing is normal. The sound is perceived as louder in the ear with conductive hearing loss.

    residual h. Hearing acuity that remains after hearing loss.

hearing aid SEE: under *aid*.

hearing impaired Having a degree of hearing loss that interferes with communication, development, learning, or interpersonal interactions.

hearing threshold level The intensity of sound at which it is first perceived. More formally, it is the sound intensity of a pure tone that elicits a response from a test subject more than 50% of the time.

hearsay Statements overheard and repeated, rather than personally witnessed.

heart (hart) A hollow, muscular organ, the pump of the circulatory system. Its wall has three layers: the outer epicardium, a serous membrane; the middle myocardium, made of cardiac muscle; and the inner endocardium, endothelium that lines the chambers and covers the valves. The heart is enclosed in the pericardium, a fibroserous sac; the potential space between the parietal pericardium and the epicardium is called the pericardial cavity, which contains serous fluid to prevent friction as the heart beats. SEE: illus.; *circulation, coronary* for illus.; *cardiomyopathy, hypertrophic*.

    CHAMBERS: The upper right and left atria are thin-walled receiving chambers separated by the interatrial septum. The lower right and left ventricles are thick-walled pumping chambers separated by the interventricular septum; normally the right side has no communication with the left. The right side receives deoxygenated blood via the venae cavae from the body and pumps it to the lungs; the left side receives oxygenated blood from the lungs and pumps it via the aorta and arteries to the body. Contraction of the heart chambers is called systole; relaxation with accompanying filling with blood is called diastole. The sequence of events that occurs in a single heartbeat is called the cardiac cycle, with atrial systole followed by ventricular systole. For a heart rate of 70 beats per minute, each cycle lasts about 0.85 sec.

    VALVES: In the healthy state, all four cardiac valves prevent backflow of blood. The atrioventricular valves are at the openings between each atrium and ventricle; the tricuspid valve, between the right atrium and ventricle; and the bicuspid or mitral valve, between the left atrium and ventricle. The pulmo-

nary semilunar valve is at the opening of the right ventricle into the pulmonary artery; the aortic semilunar valve is at the opening of the left ventricle into the aorta.

    FUNCTION: In adults, the cardiac output varies from 5 L/min at rest to as much as 20 L/min during vigorous exercise. At the rate of 72 times each minute, the adult human heart beats 104,000 times a day, 38,000,000 times a year. Every stroke forces approx. 5 cu in (82 ml) of blood out into the body, amounting to 500,000 cu in (8193 L) a day. In terms of work, this is the equivalent of raising 1 ton (907 kg) to a height of 41 ft (12.5 m) every 24 hr.

    BLOOD SUPPLY: The myocardium receives its blood supply from the coronary arteries that arise from the ascending aorta. Blood from the myocardium drains into several cardiac veins.

    NERVE SUPPLY: The heart initiates its own beat, usually from 60 to 80 beats per minute, but the rate may be changed by impulses from the cardiac centers in the medulla oblongata. Accelerator impulses are carried by sympathetic nerves. Preganglionic neurons in the thoracic spinal cord synapse with postganglionic neurons in the cervical ganglia of the sympathetic trunk; their axons continue to the heart. Sympathetic impulses are transmitted to the sinoatrial (SA) node, atrioventricular (AV) node, bundle of His, and myocardium of the ventricles and increase heart rate and force of contraction. Inhibitory impulses are carried by the vagus nerves (parasympathetic). Preganglionic neurons (vagus) originating in the medulla synapse with postganglionic neurons in terminal ganglia in the wall of the heart. Parasympathetic impulses are transmitted to the SA and AV nodes and decrease the heart rate. Sensory nerves from the heart serve for the sensation of pain, which is caused by an insufficient supply of oxygen to the myocardium. The vagus and glossopharyngeal are the sensory nerves for reflex changes in heart rate. These nerves arise from pressoreceptors or chemoreceptors in the aortic arch and carotid sinus, respectively.

    AUSCULTATION: Listening to the heart with a stethoscope reveals the intensity, quality, and rhythm of the heart sounds and detects any adventitious sounds (e.g., murmurs or pericardial friction). The two separate sounds heard by the use of a stethoscope over the heart have been represented by the syllables "lubb," "dupp." The first sound (systolic), which is prolonged and dull, results from the contraction of the ventricle, tension of the atrioventricular valves, and the impact of the heart against the chest wall and is synchro-

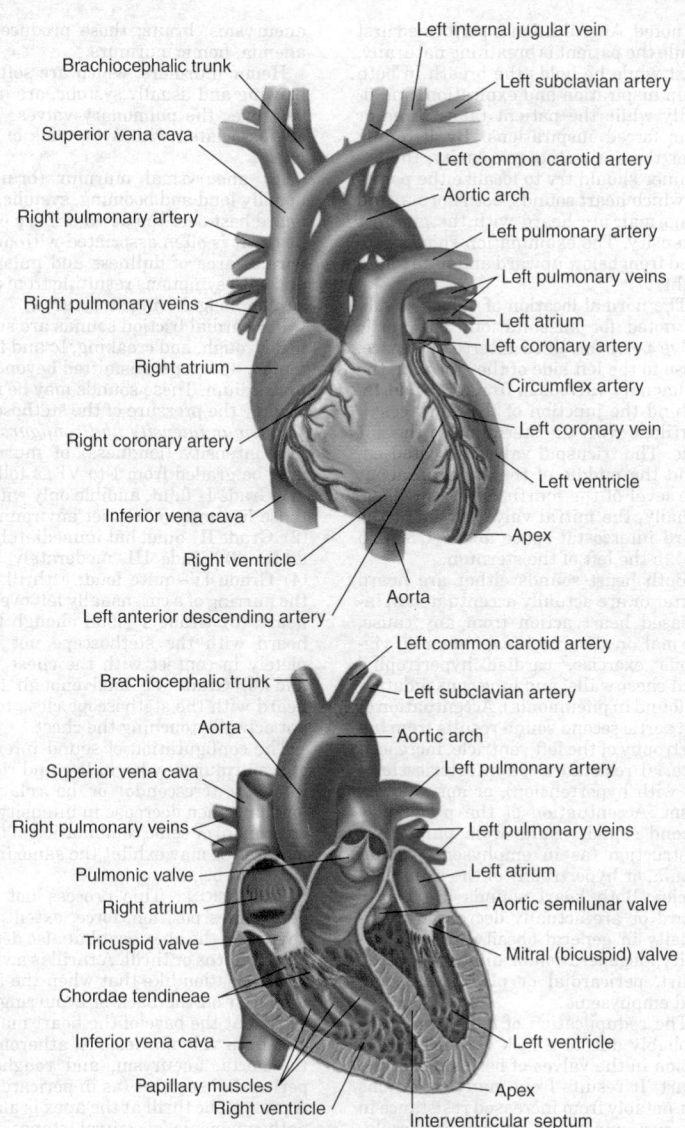

STRUCTURES OF THE HEART

(A) Anterior view of the heart; (B) frontal section of the heart

nous with the apex beat and carotid pulse. The first sound is followed by a short pause, and then the second sound (diastolic) is heard, resulting from the closure of the aortic and pulmonary valves. This sound is short and high pitched. After the second sound there is a longer pause before the first is heard again. A very useful technique for listening to the variation in sounds be-

tween one area and another is to move the stethoscope in small steps from site to site.

PROCEDURE: The patient should be recumbent when the examination begins. After all possible signs have been elicited, the examination should be repeated with the patient sitting, standing, or leaning forward, and any variations from this change of position should be noted. Auscultation is performed first while the patient is breathing naturally, next while he holds the breath in both deep inspiration and expiration, and finally while the patient takes three or four forced inspirations. By listening over the entire thoracic cavity, the examiner should try to localize the points at which heart sounds, both normal and abnormal, are heard with the greatest intensity. The examination should proceed from below upward and from left to right.

The normal location of valves should be noted for auscultation. The aortic valve is in the third intercostal space, close to the left side of the sternum; the pulmonary valve is in front of the aorta, behind the junction of the third costal cartilage with the sternum, on the left side. The tricuspid valve is located behind the middle of the sternum about the level of the fourth costal cartilage. Finally, the mitral valve is behind the third intercostal space about 1 in (2.5 cm) to the left of the sternum.

Both heart sounds either are heard better or are actually accentuated in increased heart action from any cause, normal or abnormal (e.g., anemia, vigorous exercise, cardiac hypertrophy, thin chest walls, and lung consolidation as found in pneumonia). Accentuation of the aortic second sound results from hypertrophy of the left ventricle, increased arterial resistance (as in arteriosclerosis with hypertension), or aortic aneurysm. Accentuation of the pulmonary second sound results from pulmonary obstruction (as in emphysema, pneumonia, or hypertrophy of the right ventricle). Both heart sounds are poorly heard or are actually decreased in intensity in general obesity, general debility, degeneration or dilatation of the heart, pericardial or pleural effusion, and emphysema.

The reduplication of heart sounds is probably due to a lack of synchronous action in the valves of both sides of the heart. It results from many conditions but notably from increased resistance in the systemic or the pulmonary circulation (as in arteriosclerosis and emphysema). It is also frequently noted in mitral stenosis and pericarditis.

A murmur (an abnormal sound heard over the heart or blood vessels) may result from obstruction or regurgitation at the valves following endocarditis; dilatation of the ventricle or relaxation of its walls rendering the valves relatively insufficient; aneurysm; a change in the blood constituents (as in anemia); roughening of the pericardial surfaces (as in pericarditis); and irregular action of the heart. Murmurs produced within the heart are called endocardial; those outside, exocardial; those produced in

aneurysms, bruits; those produced by anemia, hemic murmurs.

Hemic murmurs, which are soft and blowing and usually systolic, are heard best over the pulmonary valves. They are associated with symptoms of anemia.

An aneurysmal murmur (bruit) is usually loud and booming, systolic, and heard best over the aorta or base of the heart. It is often associated with an abnormal area of dullness and pulsation and with symptoms resulting from pressure on neighboring structures.

Pericardial friction sounds are superficial, rough, and creaking, to and fro in tempo, and not transmitted beyond the precordium. These sounds may be modified by the pressure of the stethoscope.

Murmur intensity and configuration: The intensity (loudness) of murmurs may be graded from I to VI as follows: (1) Grade I—faint, audible only with intense listening in a quiet environment; (2) Grade II—quiet but immediately audible; (3) Grade III—moderately loud; (4) Grade IV—quite loud; a thrill (like the purring of a cat) usually felt over the heart; (5) Grade V—loud enough to be heard with the stethoscope not completely in contact with the chest wall; and (6) Grade VI—loud enough to be heard with the stethoscope close to but not actually touching the chest.

The configuration of sound intensity of a murmur may begin low and rise in intensity (crescendo) or be relatively loud and then decrease in intensity (decrescendo) or some combination of those features or may exhibit the same intensity from beginning to end.

PALPATION: This process not only determines position, force, extent, and rhythm of the apex beat but also detects any fremitus or thrill. A thrill is a vibratory sensation like that when the hand is placed on the back of a purring cat. Thrills at the base of the heart may result from valvular lesions, atheroma of the aorta, aneurysm, and roughened pericardial surfaces (as in pericarditis). A presystolic thrill at the apex is almost pathognomonic of mitral stenosis. In children especially, a precordial bulge, substernal thrust, or apical heave suggests cardiac enlargement.

PERCUSSION: This procedure determines the shape and extent of cardiac dullness. The normal area of superficial or absolute percussion dullness (the part uncovered by the lung) is detected by light percussion and extends from the fourth left costosternal junction to the apex beat; from the apex beat to the juncture of the xiphoid cartilage with the sternum; and thence up the left border of the sternum. The normal area of deep percussion dullness (the heart projected on the chest wall) is detected by firm percussion and extends from the third left costosternal articulation to the apex beat; from the apex beat to the junction of the xiphoid cartilage with the sternum; and thence up the right border of sternum to the third rib. The lower level of cardiac dullness fuses with the liver dullness and can rarely be determined. The area of cardiac dullness is increased in hypertrophy and dilation of the heart and in pericardial effusion; it is diminished in emphysema, pneumothorax, and pneumocardium.

abdominal h. A heart displaced into the abdominal cavity.

artificial h. A mechanical device that pumps blood to augment or replace a failing heart. It may be located inside the body (intracorporeally) or outside it (extracorporeally). SEE: *heart-lung machine*.

athlete's h. Enlargement of the heart (cardiomegaly), with slowing of the heart rate (bradycardia) as a result of prolonged physical training, e.g., the aerobic exercise of running. This is not known to be a predisposing factor for any form of heart disease. SYN: *athletic bradycardia*.

beriberi h. Heart failure caused by thiamine (vitamin B_1) deficiency (e.g., in patients with chronic alcoholism or malnutrition).

boatshaped h. A heart in which one ventricle is dilated and hypertrophied as a result of aortic regurgitation.

cervical h. A heart displaced into the neck.

fibroid h. An obsolete term for scarring of the myocardium (e.g., after myocardial infarction).

left h. The left atrium and ventricle. The left atrium receives oxygenated blood from the lungs; the left ventricle pumps this blood into the systemic circulation.

right h. The right atrium and ventricle. The right atrium receives deoxygenated blood from the body; the right ventricle pumps this blood to the lungs.

heart attack SEE: under *attack*.

heartbeat The rhythmic contraction of the heart.

heart block Interference with the normal transmission of electrical impulses through the conducting system of the heart. The condition is seen on electrocardiogram as a prolongation of the P-R interval, a widening of the QRS complex, a delay in the appearance of an expected beat, the loss of synchrony of atrial and ventricular beats, or dropped (missing) beats.

ETIOLOGY: Heart block may be produced by temporary changes in vagal tone, drugs or toxins (such as some antiarrhythmics or antihypertensives), infections (such as infective endocarditis or Lyme disease), fibrosis or other de-generative diseases of the conducting system, ischemia or infarction, or other mechanisms.

atrioventricular h.b. SEE: *atrioventricular block*.

bilateral bundle branch h.b. SEE: *atrioventricular block*.

bundle branch h.b. Bundle branch block.

complete h.b. A condition in which there is a complete dissociation between atrial and ventricular systoles. Ventricles may beat from their own pacemakers at a rate of 30 to 40 beats per minute while atria beat independently. SYN: *third-degree h.b.*

congenital h.b. Heart block present at birth, caused by faulty cardiac development in the womb, autoimmune diseases, or other causes.

fascicular h.b. A conduction defect in either or both of the subdivisions of the left bundle branch.

first-degree h.b. First-degree atrioventricular **block**.

interventricular h.b. Bundle branch block.

second-degree h.b. A form of atrioventricular block in which only some atrial impulses are conducted to the ventricles. Two variants exist: Mobitz I (Wenckebach) and Mobitz II. In Mobitz I, the P-R intervals become progressively longer until a QRS complex is dropped. Because of the dropped beats, the QRS complexes appear to be clustered (*grouped beating*) on the electrocardiogram. In Mobitz II, P-R intervals have a constant length, but QRS complexes are dropped periodically, usually every second, third, or fourth beat.

sinoatrial h.b. A partial or complete heart block characterized by interference in the passage of impulses from the sinoatrial node. SYN: *sinoatrial block*. SEE: *sick sinus syndrome*.

third-degree h.b. Complete **h.b.**

heartburn A burning sensation felt in the mid-epigastrium, behind the sternum, or in the throat caused by reflux of the acid contents of the stomach into the esophagus and usually related to reduced lower esophageal sphincter action, hiatal hernia, or increased abdominal pressure. SYN: *brash; pyrosis*. SEE: *gastroesophageal reflux disease*.

TREATMENT: Antacids, H_2-receptor antagonists (e.g., famotidine), and proton pump inhibitors (e.g., esomeprazole) are potentially effective remedies.

PATIENT CARE: Patients are helped to identify the time of occurrence in relation to food intake, if position changes exaggerate discomfort, precipitating factors (such as type and amount of food), and factors that aggravate the discomfort. For many people mints, chocolates, alcohol, late meals, and anti-inflammatory drugs all worsen the symptom. If antacids are used to treat heartburn, their ability to limit the effect of other oral medications is explained and a schedule established to prevent interactions. Sitting upright during and after eating and elevating the head of the bed 6 to 8 in for sleep often reduces the problem. Patients should be advised that further diagnostic studies may be required if heartburn persists despite therapy. Persistent, untreated heartburn can lead to esophageal damage and cancer.

heart disease Any pathological condition of the coronary arteries, heart valves, myocardium, or electrical conduction system of the heart.

    ischemic h.d. A lack of oxygen supply to the heart altering cardiac function. The most common cause of myocardial ischemia is atherosclerosis of the coronary arteries. Depending upon several factors, including oxygen demand of the myocardium, degree of narrowing of the lumen of the arteries, and duration of the ischemia, the end result is temporary or permanent damage to the heart. SEE: *risk factors for h.d.; coronary artery; coronary artery disease.*

    risk factors for ischemic h.d. Conditions that predispose people to ischemic heart disease (coronary artery disease). These may be divided into those that are not reversible (aging, male gender, menopause, genetic factors) and those that are potentially reversible (tobacco use, hypertension, hyperlipidemia, diabetes mellitus, left ventricular hypertrophy, obesity, and sedentary lifestyle).

heart failure SEE: under *failure.*

heart failure with preserved ejection fraction Signs and symptoms of heart failure, including dyspnea, orthopnea or nocturnal dyspnea, and radiological evidence of pulmonary congestion, but an ejection fraction that exceeds 40%.

heart fatty acid-binding protein SEE: under *protein.*

heart-lung machine A device that maintains the functions of the heart and lungs while either or both are unable to continue to function adequately. The device pumps, oxygenates, and removes carbon dioxide from the blood. In animal studies and in open heart surgery, these machines take over the function of the heart and lungs while these organs are being treated or possibly replaced. The function of the heart-lung machine is also called heart-lung bypass. SEE: illus.

heart rate recovery ABBR: HRR. The decrease in heart rate that occurs 1 min after maximal exercise. Normal people decrease their heart rates by at least 12 beats per minute (bpm) 1 min after stopping maximal exercise. People whose heart rate does not decrease by 12 bpm have an increased risk of cardiac-related death.

heart size The dimensions of the cardiac image as seen on radiographs, echocardiographs, computed tomography, angiography, or magnetic resonance imaging of the thorax.

heart valve, prosthetic SEE: *valve, prosthetic heart.*

heat (hēt) **1.** The condition or sensation of being hot; opposite of cold. **2.** Higher than normal body temperature; generalized fever or localized warmth caused by an infection. Calor (fever), dolor (pain), rubor (redness), and tumor (swelling) are the four classic signs of inflammation. SEE: *febrile convulsion; fever.* **3.** Estrus. **4.** Energy that increases the temperature of surrounding tissues

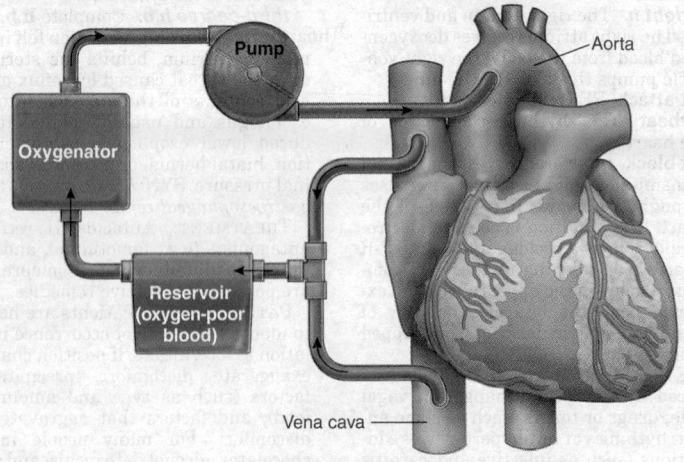

HEART-LUNG MACHINE

Elimination of Body Heat

Mode of Elimination	Percentage of Heat Lost
Radiation	55%*
Convection and conduction	15%*
Evaporation through skin	25%*
Warming inspired air	3%*
Warming ingested food and water, and loss through feces and urine	2%*

* Figures are approximate and vary with physiological activity of the body, type of clothing worn, relative humidity, and degree of acclimatization to a particular environment.

or objects by conduction, convection, or radiation. SEE: table.

conductive h. Heat transferred by conduction from a heat source to a colder object when the two materials are in contact with each other.

convective h. The flow of heat to an object or part of the body by passage of heated particles, gas, or liquid from the heat source to the colder body.

deep h. The application or direction of radiant energy to organs beneath the skin and subcutaneous tissue, e.g., muscles and tendons.

diathermy h. Diathermy.

dry h. Heat that has no moisture. It may take the form of a hot dry pack, hot water bottle, electric light bath, heliotherapy, hot bricks, resistance coil, electric pad or blanket, hot air bath, or therapeutic lamp.

h. of evaporation The heat absorbed per unit of mass when a substance is converted from a liquid to a gas, such as the change of water to steam when it is heated sufficiently. For water, the amount of heat required to transform water into steam is 540 cal/g of water.

initial h. Muscular heat produced during contraction when tension is increasing, during maintenance of tension, and during relaxation when tension is diminishing.

latent h. The caloric or heat energy absorbed by matter changing from solid to liquid or from liquid to vapor with no change in temperature.

latent h. of fusion The heat required to convert 1 g of a solid to a liquid at the same temperature. For example, the process of converting 1 g of ice at 0°C to water at 0°C requires 80 cal, and, until it is completed, there will be no rise in the temperature.

latent h. of vaporization The heat required to change 1 g of a liquid at its boiling point to vapor at the same temperature.

luminous h. Heat derived from light. This form may be tolerated better than other forms of radiation. Light may be converted into heat. Short infrared rays penetrate subcutaneous tissues to a greater extent than long invisible rays.

moist h. Heat that has moisture content. It may be applied as hot bath pack, hot wet pack, hot foot bath, or vapor bath. The patient should be observed for dizziness, headache, or weakness.

h. of passion In forensic medicine, a state of mind that might influence one's propensity to commit violent or aggressive acts.

prickly h. An inflamed papular or vesicular rash that results when the flow of sweat from sweat glands is blocked. It often affects athletes and military personnel. SYN: *heat **rash**; **lichen** tropicus; **miliaria** rubra; tropical **lichen**.*

radiant h. The heat given off as waves through the air from a heated body.

specific h. The heat needed to raise the temperature of 1 g of a substance 1°C.

superficial h. The application of heat to the skin and subcutaneous tissues.

heat and moisture exchanger A device that retains some warmth and moisture from expired air and returns it to the intubated or laryngectomized patient during the following inspiration. The device prevents the patient from inhaling excessively cool, dry air that may damage the lower airways.

heat gun A device used in splint fabrication that produces heated air to render thermoplastic splinting materials malleable for fitting.

heat-labile (hēt′lā′bīl″, ′bĭl) Easily changed or destroyed by heat; unstable. SYN: *thermolabile.*

heatstroke A condition caused by failure of the body's heat-regulating mechanisms during or after exposure to heat and high relative humidity (normally air temperatures of greater than 79°F (26.1°C) and relative humidity greater than 70%). In the U.S., 250 people die of heatstroke each year. In young, healthy people it most often follows strenuous physical activity; in inactive individuals or the elderly it commonly is related to cardiovascular disease or use of drugs that influence temperature regulation. SYN: *sunstroke.* SEE: *Nursing Diagnoses Appendix.*

SYMPTOMS: Heatstroke is marked by high body temperature, usually above 105°F (40.6°C); headache; numbness and tingling; confusion preceding sudden onset of seizures, delirium, or coma; tachycardia; rapid respiratory rate; and increased blood pressure followed by hypotension. Patients with an insidious (non–activity-related) onset of heatstroke may have hot, dry, red skin; the skin of active people may still be damp from perspiration, but sweating will cease as the condition worsens.

TREATMENT: Effective, immediate treatment in an inpatient setting to lower the body's core temperature can save the patient's life. Airway, breathing, and circulation should be monitored and maintained. The patient's clothes should be removed immediately and the patient actively cooled with ice packs on arterial pressure points and a hypothermia blanket. For several days the patient should be observed for signs of fluid and electrolyte imbalance and renal failure.

PATIENT CARE: The patient suspected of heatstroke is assessed for airway patency, breathing adequacy, circulation, mental status using AVPU, and other associated signs and symptoms such as: shock, weakness, dizziness, nausea, vomiting, blurred vision, infection, and skin findings. Vital signs are obtained and, using a rectal or core probe, the caregiver monitors the patient's temperature; initially it may be extremely elevated. In the hospital setting, laboratory studies, including blood chemistry, arterial blood gases, urinalysis, complete blood count, and appropriate cultures are obtained to aid in treatment management. Cooling procedures are promptly instituted in the field and continued in the hospital. Intravenous therapy is begun to replace fluids in the dehydrated patient and high-concentration oxygen is administered. Fluid intake and urinary output are monitored. A nasogastric tube is inserted to prevent aspiration, and an indwelling urinary catheter may also be required. Seizure activity is controlled or prevented with diazepam. Dobutamine is used to correct cardiogenic shock. Invasive hemodynamic monitoring, endotracheal intubation and ventilation, or emergency dialysis may be needed in severe instances.

PREVENTION: Heat-related illnesses (heat cramps, heat exhaustion, heatstroke) are preventable through education of the public. Athletes, soldiers, and laborers are taught to recognize the signs and symptoms of heat problems and the importance of prevention (e.g., by avoiding prolonged exposure to heat, and by increasing their electrolyte and water intake) and prompt treatment of symptoms. High-risk patients (those who are elderly, obese, diabetic, or alcoholic, those with cardiac disease and other chronic debilitating illnesses, and those taking phenothiazines or anticholinergics) are advised to take the following precautions: wear loose-fitting, lightweight clothing; take frequent rest breaks, esp. during strenuous activities; ingest adequate amounts of fluids, including electrolyte drinks; avoid hot, humid environments if possible; use proper room cooling (fans and open windows) or an air conditioner and seek air-conditioned areas for relief. As necessary, the patient is referred to a social service agency for assistance with home cooling. Patients who have experienced heatstroke should be warned that they may experience hypersensitivity to high temperatures for several months.

heat unit ABBR: HU. The amount of heat created at the anode during the production of x-ray photons. It is the product of the milliamperage times the seconds of exposure times the kilovoltage peak.

heaves (hēvs) Vomiting.

heavy chain disease ABBR: HCD. Any one of several abnormalities of immunoglobulins in which excessive quantities of alpha, gamma, delta, epsilon, or mu chains are produced. The immunoglobulins formed are incomplete, causing, in some cases, distinct clinical signs and symptoms including weakness, recurrent fever, susceptibility to bacterial infections, lymphadenopathy, hepatosplenomegaly, nephrotic syndrome and renal failure, anemia, leukopenia, thrombocytopenia, and eosinophilia. The disease may be diagnosed with immunoelectrophoresis or biopsy of affected organs.

    alpha h.c.d. A form of heavy chain disease that is related to Mediterranean lymphoma and celiac sprue. The principal organ involved is the small intestine, although respiratory tissues are occasionally affected. The symptoms and signs may include malabsorption, diarrhea, abdominal pains, and weight loss. In some patients there is peripheral adenopathy and splenomegaly with no signs of intestinal or respiratory tract changes. Diagnosis is made through tests for the abnormal immunoglobulins. Chemotherapy may produce long-term remissions. SYN: *Seligmann's disease.*

    gamma h.c.d. A rare disease whose hallmark is the production of abnormal immunoglobulins (made of gamma heavy chains) by malignant B-lymphocytes. Clinical findings may include lymphadenopathy, hepatosplenomegaly, arthritis, edema of the uvula, and infiltration of the skin and thyroid gland. Treatment includes therapy for the underlying disorders, including the particular type of lymphoma present. SEE: *heavy chain disease.*

    mu h.c.d. A heavy chain disease with presenting symptoms of a lymphoproliferative malignancy, especially chronic lymphocytic leukemia. Treatment focuses on the underlying disorders.

heavy metals Metals such as mercury, lead, chromium, cadmium, and arsenic that have known toxic effects on internal organs, such as the kidneys, brain, bone, or retina. SEE: *Poisons and Poisoning Appendix.*

Heberden nodes Hard nodules or enlargements of the distal interphalangeal joints of the fingers; seen in osteoarthritis.

hebetude (hĕb′ĕ-tŭd) [L. *hebet,* dull] Dullness or lethargy.

Hebra disease (heb′rä) [Ferdinand Ritter von Hebra, Austrian dermatologist, 1816–1880] **1. Erythema** mulitforme. **2. Impetigo** herpetiformis.

hecto- [Gr. *hekaton,* hundred] In the International System of Units (SI), a prefix meaning 100 times (10^2).

hectogram (hĕk′tō-grăm″) [″ + *gramma,* small weight] One hundred grams, or 3.527 avoirdupois ounces.

hectoliter (hĕk′tō-lē″tĕr) [″ + *litra,* a pound] One hundred liters.

hectometer (hĕk-tōm′ĕ-tĕr) [″ + *metron,* measure] One hundred meters.

HEDIS Health Plan Employer Data and Information Set.

hedonic (hē-dŏn′ĭk) [Gr. *hedonikos,* pleasurable] Pertaining to pleasure and its perception.

hedonism (hēd′ŏn-ĭzm) [Gr. *hedone,* pleasure, + *-ismos,* condition] **1.** The pursuit of pleasure or the gratification of the senses as a primary goal of ethical living. **2.** Self-indulgence.

heel (hēl) The rounded posterior portion of the foot under and behind the ankle. SYN: *calx.*

heel pad syndrome Pain and tenderness on palpation experienced directly beneath the calcaneus and not in the plantar fascia. It typically affects avid runners and other active athletes.

HEENT *head, eyes, ears, nose, throat.*

Heidelberg retinal tomography SEE: under *tomography.*

Heidenhain, Rudolph P. (hīd′ĕn-hīn″) Ger. physiologist and histologist, 1834–1897.

   H. pouch A small, surgically constructed pouch of the stomach that is denervated and separated from the stomach and drained to the outside of the body. It is used to study the physiology of the stomach.

height (hīt) The vertical distance from the bottom to the top of an organ or structure.

   h. of contour A line encircling a structure, designating its greatest diameter in a specified plane. In dentistry, the term refers to the largest circumferential measurement around a tooth. The height of contour must be maintained during restoration of a tooth to maintain the normal flow of food over the tooth.

   fundal h. The distance (in centimeters) from the portion of the uterus above the insertion of the fallopian tubes to the symphysis pubis. *Antepartum:* The standard fundal height at 20 weeks gestation is at the maternal umbilicus. Thereafter, measurement from the pubic symphysis to the top of the fundus (in centimeters) should equal the number of weeks of gestation.

height velocity The vertical growth of a child during a specified unit of time, e.g., per month or per year.

Heimlich, Henry Jay (hīm′lĭk) U.S. surgeon, b. 1920

   H. flutter valve Flutter **valve.**

   H. valve Flutter **valve.**

   H. maneuver A technique for removing a foreign body, such as a food bolus, from the throat, trachea, or pharynx of a choking victim, where it is preventing air flow to and from the lungs. SYN: *abdominal thrust maneuver.*

   For a conscious victim, the maneuver consists of the rescuer applying subdiaphragmatic pressure by wrapping his or her arms around the victim's waist from behind, making a fist with one hand, placing it against the patient's abdomen between the navel and the rib cage, and then clasping the fist with the free hand and pressing in with a quick, forceful upward thrust. This procedure should be repeated several times if necessary. If one is alone and experiences airway obstruction caused by a foreign body, this technique may be self-applied.

   For the unconscious victim, starting CPR is now the recommended procedure because chest compressions are often effective for removing a foreign body. It is a simple method that can be taught to the general public.

   When the patient is a child and can speak, breathe, or cough, the maneuver is unnecessary. If the maneuver is done, it should be applied as gently as possible but still forcibly enough to dislodge the obstruction (the abdominal viscera of children are more easily damaged than those of adults).

   This treatment is quite effective in dislodging the obstruction by forcing air against the mass, much as pressure from a carbonated beverage forcibly removes a cork or cap from a bottle. The average air flow produced is 225 L/min.

⚠ The Heimlich maneuver should not be performed unless complete airway obstruction is present. If the patient can cough, this maneuver should not be performed. In infants, extremely obese patients, and obviously pregnant patients, chest thrusts are used instead of abdominal thrusts to facilitate removal of the obstruction.

SEE: illus; *choking.*

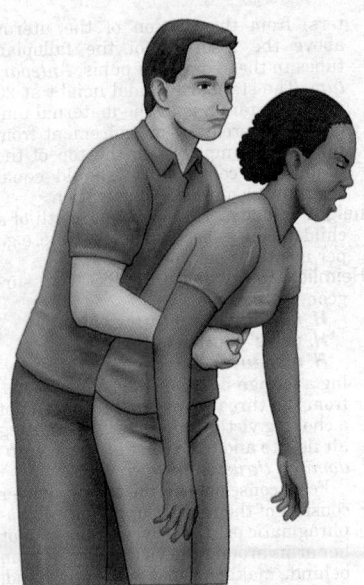

HEIMLICH MANEUVER

(for removal of a foreign body blocking the airway)

Heinz, Robert (hīns, hīnz) German pathologist, 1865–1924.

 H. bodies Granules in red blood cells usually attached to the red blood cell membrane, seen in blood smears of persons with hemoglobinopathies, thalassemias, and after splenectomy. The bodies are best seen when the blood is stained with a special stain.

 H. body anemia Hemolytic anemia associated with the finding of Heinz bodies in red blood cells.

HeLa cells (hē′lă) SEE: *cell, HeLa.*

helical (hĕl′ĭ-kăl) In the shape of a helix.

helicase (hĕl′ĭ-kās″) A donut-shaped enzyme that uncoils double-stranded DNA, allowing it to replicate. Syndromes in humans in which helicase is deficient predispose these people to premature aging or cancer.

helices (hel′ĭ-sēz″, hē′lĭ-) [Gr.] Plural of helix.

helicine (hĕl′ĭ-sĭn) [Gr. *helix,* coil] **1.** Spiral. **2.** Pert. to a helix or coil.

 h. arteries Tortuous arteries in the cavernous tissue of the penis, clitoris, and uterus.

Helicobacter pylori (hĕl″ĭ-kō-băk-tĕr) [Gr. *helix,* a twist + NL *bacter,* from *bacterium*] ABBR: H. pylori. A motile, spiral, gram-negative bacterium that causes 90% of peptic ulcers, 80% of gastric ulcers, and, in some patients, gastric cancer or mucosal-associated lymphoid-type lymphomas. Treatment consists of the suppression of gastric acidity in additon to combined antibiotics.

 DIAGNOSIS: Noninvasive diagnostic tests for *H. pylori* include stool antigen tests, urea breath tests, and serum antibody levels. Invasive tests include endoscopy, gastric biopsy, and biopsy with bacterial culture for *H. pylori.*

helicoid (hĕl′ĭ-koyd) [″ + *eidos,* form, shape] Resembling a helix or spiral.

helicotrema (hĕl″ĭ-kō-trē′mă) [″ + *trema,* a hole] The opening at the tip of the cochlear canal where the scala tympani and scala vestibuli unite.

heliotherapy (hē″lē-ō-thĕr′ă-pē) [″ + *therapeia,* treatment] Exposure to sunlight for therapeutic purposes.

heliotrope A faint purple or pink-purple skin color; e.g., the color of rashes seen in patients with dermatomyositis.

heliotropism (hē″lē-ŏt′rō-pĭzm) [″ + *trepein,* to turn, + *-ismos,* condition] The tendency of living organisms to turn or grow toward the sun.

heliox (hē′lē-oks″) A therapeutic mixture of helium and oxygen, usually >60% helium. The mixture is used to decrease airway resistance in conditions such as airway obstruction by tumors and acute respiratory distress syndrome.

helipad (hĕl′ĭ-păd″) [Fr. *heli(copter)* + *(landing) pad*] A designated landing site for helicopters. Helipads are used at hospitals for the emergent transport of critically ill and injured patients.

helium (hē′lē-ŭm) [Gr. *hēlios,* the sun + *-ium* (1)] SYMB: He. A chemical element, one of the noble gases, atomic weight (mass) 4.0026, atomic number 2. A liter of the gas at sea level pressure and 0°C weighs 0.1785 g. The second lightest element known, it is given off by radium and other radioactive elements in the form of charged helium ions known as alpha rays. Because of its low density, it is mixed with air or oxygen and used in the treatment of various respiratory disorders. Because of its low solubility, it is mixed with air supplied to workers laboring under high atmospheric pressure, as in caissons. When so used, it reduces the time required to adjust to increasing or decreasing air pressure and reduces the danger of bends. SEE: *noble gas.*

 h. 3 SYMB: ³He. A stable isotope of helium whose nucleus contains two protons and a single neutron. The isotope is polarizable, making it suitable as a gaseous contrast agent for use in magnetic resonance imaging.

helix (hē′liks, hel′ĭ-sēz″, hē′lĭ-, hē′lik-sĕz″) *pl.* **helices, helixes** [Gr., *helix,* (something shaped like a) spiral, coil] **1.** A coil or spiral. **2.** The margin of the external ear.

Heller procedure (hel′ĕr) [Ernst Heller, Ger. surgeon, 1877–1964] Surgical esophagomyotomy, an operation for gastroesophageal reflux.

HELLP An acronym derived from the first letters of the terms that describe the following laboratory findings: Hemolysis, Elevated Liver enzymes, and Low Platelet count.

HELLP syndrome A laboratory diagnosis of a combination of events signaling a variation of severe preeclampsia, marked by *h*emolytic anemia, *e*levated *l*iver enzymes, and *l*ow *p*latelet count. This potentially life-threatening condition usually arises in the last trimester of pregnancy. Initially, the affected women may complain of nausea, vomiting, epigastric pain, headache, and vision problems. Complications include acute renal failure, disseminated intravascular coagulation, liver failure, respiratory failure, or multiple organ system failure. SEE: *preeclampsia*.

TREATMENT: Treatment includes management of coagulation disorders and hypertension, and preventing seizures. Corticosteroids may be given to increase maturity of the fetal lung. If the health of the mother or the fetus is endangered, early delivery will be necessary.

helminth (hĕl′mĭnth) [Gr. *helmins*, worm] **1.** A wormlike animal. **2.** Any animal, either free-living or parasitic, belonging to the phyla Platyhelminthes (flatworms), Acanthocephala (spiny-headed worms), Nemathelminthes (threadworms or roundworms), or Annelida (segmented worms). SEE: illus.

helminthiasis (hĕl-mĭn-thī′ă-sĭs) [″ + *iasis*, condition] Infestation with worms.

helminthic (hĕl-mĭn′thĭk) **1.** Pert. to worms. **2.** Pert. to that which expels worms. SYN: *anthelmintic; vermifugal*.

helminthology (hĕl″mĭn-thŏl′ō-jē) [″ + *logos*, word, reason] The study of worms.

heloderma (hē″lō-dĕr′mă) Fibromas that form on the extensor surfaces of the proximal interphalangeal joints of the hands.

HELP *Heat escape lessening position*.

helper T cells SEE: *cell, helper T.*

helplessness A feeling of dependence, powerlessness, defenselessness, or depression, e.g., in the face of crisis or overwhelming circumstances. SEE: *hopelessness; powerlessness*.

learned h. A passive fatalistic behavior that one cannot influence one's environment, or alter one's existence. This condition may sometimes arise in persons who have chronic illnesses, depression, phobias, or loss of functional independence.

hem-, hema-, hemo- [Gr. *haima*, blood] Prefixes meaning *blood*. The variant "haem-" is used outside the U.S. SEE: *hemat-*.

hemad (hē′măd) [Gr. *haima*, blood, + L. *ad*, toward] Hemal (2).

hemadsorption (hĕm″ăd-sorp′shŭn) The adherence of red blood cells to other cells or surfaces.

hemagglutination, hemoagglutination (hē″mă-gloot″ĭn-ā′shŏn, hē″mō-ă-gloot″ĭn-ā′shŏn) [*hem-* + *agglutination*] The clumping of red blood cells. SEE: *agglutination*.

hemagglutinin (hē″mă-gloot′ĭn-ĭn) [*hem-* + *agglutinin*] ABBR: H. **1.** An antibody that induces clumping of red blood cells. SEE: *agglutination; agglutinin*. **2.** An influenza virus protein that helps viral particles attach themselves to cells in the respiratory tract and enter these cells through their cellular membranes.

This protein mutates regularly, changing the pathogenicity of the influenza virus. Vaccines that are manufactured each year to prevent influenza are formulated by trying to anticipate the hemagglutinin (H) and the neuraminidase (N) antigens of novel influenza viruses that will circulate around the world in that particular year.

hemal (hē′măl) **1.** Pert. to the blood or blood vessels. **2.** Pert. to the ventral side of the body, in which the heart is located, as opposed to the neural or dorsal side. SYN: *hemad; hemic*.

hemangioblast (hĕ-măn′jē-ō-blăst) [″ + ″ + *blastos*, germ] A mesodermal cell that can form either vascular endothelial cells or hemocytoblasts.

hemangioblastoma (hĕ-măn″jē-ō-blăs-tō′mă) [″ + ″ + *oma*, tumor] A hemangioma of the brain, usually in the cerebellum. SYN: *angioblastoma*.

hemangioendothelioblastoma (hĕ-măn″jē-ō-ĕn″dō-thē″lē-ō-blăs-tō′mă) [″ + ″ + *endon*, within, + *thele*, nipple, + *blastos*, germ, + *oma*, tumor] A neoplasm of the epithelial cells that line the blood vessels.

hemangioendothelioma (hē″man-jē-ō-ĕn″dō-thē-lē-ō′mă) [*hem-* + *angioendothelioma*] A tumor of the endothelium of the minute capillary vessels. It varies in size and is commonly seen in the capillary net of the meninges.

Kaposiform h. ABBR: KHE. A rare vascular tumor, resembling a hemangioma. Like the hemangiomas in Kasabach-Merritt syndrome, it can cause coagulopathy associated with severe reductions in circulating levels of platelets.

hemangioma (hē-man″jē-ō′mă, -ō′mă-tă) *pl.* **hemangiomas, -mata** [*hem-* + *angioma*] A benign tumor found on the skin or in an internal organ, composed of dilated blood vessels, and often encapsulated within a fibrous shell. SYN: *cavernous **h.*** SEE: illus.

cavernous h. Hemangioma.

infantile h. A dull red benign lesion,

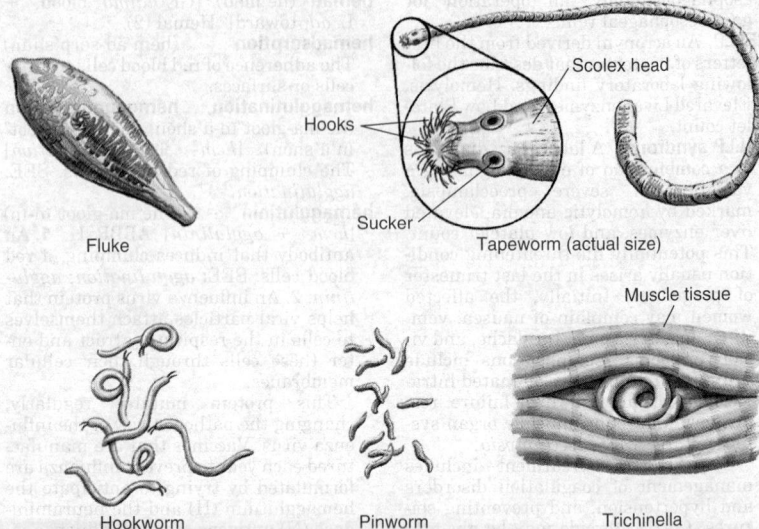

Fluke

Hooks

Scolex head

Sucker

Tapeworm (actual size)

Muscle tissue

Hookworm Pinworm Trichinella

REPRESENTATIVE HELMINTHS

usually present at birth or appearing within 2 to 3 months thereafter. This type of birthmark is usually found on the face or neck and is well demarcated from the surrounding skin. It grows rapidly and then regresses. It is caused by a proliferation of immature capillary vessels in active stroma. SYN: *strawberry h.; strawberry **mark**; strawberry **nevus** (2).*

TREATMENT: If removal is necessary, plastic surgical excision using the carbon dioxide, argon, or potassium titanium oxide phosphate laser is effective in ablating this lesion.

⚠ The use of laser treatment necessitates observance of all laser safety precautions.

lobular capillary h. A fleshy, polyp-shaped hemangioma that may develop

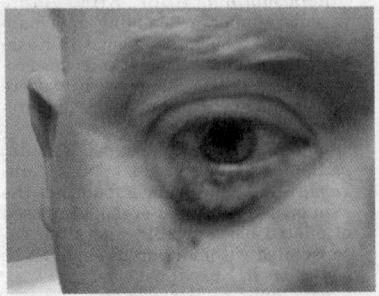

HEMANGIOMA BENEATH THE RIGHT EYE

at the site of a wound. It bleeds easily and is usually tender.

📖 *strawberry h.* Infantile **h.**

hemangiomatosis (hē-măn″jē-ō-mă-tō′sĭs) [″ + ″ + ″ + *osis*, condition] Multiple angiomata of the blood vessels.

hemangiopericytoma (hĕ-măn″jē-ō-pĕr″ĕ-sī-tō′mă) A tumor arising in the capillaries, composed of pericytes.

hemangiosarcoma (hĕ″man″jē-ō-sar-kō′mă) [*hemangio(ma)* + *sarcoma*] Angiosarcoma.

hemapheresis (hĕm″ă-fĕ-rē′sĭs) Plasma exchange therapy.

hemarthros, hemarthrosis (hĕm-ăr′thrōs, hĕm-ăr-thrō′sĭs) [″ + *arthron*, joint] A bloody effusion within a joint.

hemat-, hemato- [Gr. *haima*, stem *haimat-*, blood] Prefixes meaning *blood*. The variant "haemato-" is used outside the U.S. SEE: *hem-*.

hematemesis (hĕm″ă-tĕm′ĕ-sĭs) [″ + ″] The vomiting of blood. SEE: *hemoptysis* for table; *hemorrhage*.

ETIOLOGY: The lesions most likely to cause vomiting of blood are duodenal or gastric ulcers, esophageal varices, esophagitis, gastritis, duodenitis, Mallory-Weiss tears in the esophagus, arteriovenous malformations, or, rarely, fistulae between the aorta and the upper gastrointestinal tract. Typically, the vomiting of blood implies that the responsible lesion is located in the upper gastrointestinal tract (i.e., above the ligament of Treitz).

SYMPTOMS: The blood may be clotted, fluid, or mixed with food. Subsequent stools may be black and tarry (melanic). If blood loss is severe enough, shock and collapse may occur.

TREATMENT: The patient should be resuscitated with intravenous fluids. Transfusions are given when blood loss is massive, prolonged, or life-threatening. Endoscopy of the upper gastrointestinal tract may reveal a lesion susceptible to coagulation, sclerosis, ligation, or surgical excision. H_2-receptor antagonists (e.g., famotidine) or proton pump inhibitors (e.g., omeprazole, pantoprazole) may be given when bleeding results from peptic disease.

PATIENT CARE: Vital signs and mental status are monitored, often in an intensive care unit. Vomitus is inspected and its character and quantity documented, along with associated signs and symptoms. Management is focused at determining the underlying cause of bleeding. The patient is supported in an upright position (or turned to the left side) to prevent aspiration. Oral hygiene is provided after episodes of vomiting and as needed while the patient is not taking anything by mouth. Hematemesis can be very frightening to both the patient and family. A calm quiet environment should be provided, and realistic reassurance given. All diagnostic and treatment procedures should be briefly explained, questions answered as honestly and completely as possible, and continued emotional support provided.

hematic (hē-măt′ĭk) Hematinic.

hematin (hĕm′ă-tĭn) The nonprotein portion of the hemoglobin molecule wherein the iron is in the ferric (Fe^{3+}) rather than the ferrous (Fe^{2+}) state. SEE: *ferritin; heme.*

hematinic (hē-mă-tĭn′ĭk) [Gr. *haima,* blood] 1. Pert. to blood. 2. An agent that facilitates blood formation, used in treating anemia. SYN: *hematic.*

hemato- SEE: *hemat-.*

hematobilia (hĕm″ă-tō-bĭl′ē-ă) [″ + L. *bilis,* bile] Blood in the bile or bile ducts.

hematobium (hē″mă-, hĕm″ă-tō′bē-ŭm) [″ + *bios,* life] Hemocytozoon.

hematocele (hē′mă-, hĕm′ă-tō-sēl) [″ + *kele,* tumor, swelling] 1. A blood cyst. 2. The effusion of blood into a cavity. 3. A swelling due to effusion of blood into the tunica vaginalis testis.
    parametric h. A tumor formed by blood in the cul-de-sac of Douglas walled off by adhesions.
    pudendal h. A blood-filled swollen area of the labium.

hematochezia (hē″mă-tŏ-kē′zē-ă, hĕm″ă-) [*hemato-* + Gr. *chezein,* to defecate] The passage of bright red blood in the stool. SEE: *melena.*

hematocolpos (hē″mă-, hĕm″ă-tō-kŏl′pŏs) Retention of menstrual blood in the vagina, caused by an imperforate hymen.

hematocrit (hē-mat′ŏ-krĭt) [*hemat-* + *-crit*] ABBR: Hct. 1. The volume of erythrocytes packed by centrifugation in a given volume of blood. The hematocrit is expressed as the percentage of total blood volume that consists of erythrocytes or as the volume in cubic centimeters of erythrocytes packed by centrifugation of blood. Approximate normal values at sea level: men, average 47%, range 40% to 54%; women, average 42%, range 37% to 47%; children, varies with age from 35% to 49%; newborn, 49% to 54%. SEE: *blood.* 2. An obsolete term for a centrifuge for separating solids from plasma in the blood.

hematocytometer (hē″mă-, hĕm″ă-tō-sī-tŏm′ě-ter) [″ + ″ + *metron,* measure] SEE: *hemocytometer.*

hematogenesis (hē″mă-, hĕm″ă-tō-jĕn′ě-sĭs) [″ + *genesis,* generation, birth] Hematopoiesis.

hematogenic, hematogenous (hē″măt-ŏ-jen′ĭk, hem″ă-, hē″mă-toj′ě-nŭs, hem″) [″ + *gennan,* to produce] 1. Hematopoietic. 2. Pert. to or originating in the blood.

hematoidin (hē″mă-, hĕm-ă-toy′din) The yellow crystalline substance, biliverdin, that remains when red blood cells are destroyed in bruised tissue.

hematologist (hē″mă-, hĕm″ă-tŏl′ō-jĭst) [″ + *logos,* word, reason] A physician who specializes in the diagnosis and treatment of disorders of blood and blood-forming tissues.

hematology (hē″mă-, hĕm″ă-tŏl′ō-jē) The science concerned with blood and the blood-forming tissues.

hematoma (hē″mă-, hĕm-ă-tō′mă) [Gr. *haimatos,* blood, + *oma,* tumor] A swelling comprising a mass of extravasated blood (usually clotted) confined to an organ, tissue, or space and caused by a break in a blood vessel.
    h. auris An effusion of blood, causing a hard swelling between perichondrium and the cartilage of the pinna of the ear. it is common in fighters and wrestlers. SYN: *othematoma.* SEE: *cauliflower ear.*
    epidural h. A hematoma above the dura mater, usually arterial, except in posterior fossa.
    intracerebral h. A hemorrhage localized in one area of the brain.
    pelvic h. A hematoma present in the cellular tissue of the pelvis.
    subarachnoid h. A hemorrhage between the arachnoid membrane and the pia mater; usually caused by the rupture of a congenital intracranial aneurysm or berry aneurysm, hypertension, or trauma.
    subdural h. Bleeding into the space between the dura mater and arachnoid layer, usually the result of a head in-

jury. Symptoms may be delayed in appearing, but include severe headaches, forgetfulness, disorientation, and confusion. History of a fall, older age, and use of oral anticoagulants all increase the risk for bleeding.

PATIENT CARE: Health care professionals who suspect a patient has suffered intracranial bleeding should initiate cardiac monitoring and obtain a 12-lead ECG; provide supplemental oxygen; establish an IV access; obtain blood samples for CBC, electrolytes, cardiac markers, and coagulation studies; and prepare the patient for a noncontrast CT of the head. The patient with a confirmed bleed may then undergo a craniotomy to evacuate the clot. Recovery should be in a neurosurgery intensive care unit, with close monitoring for complications such as increased intracranial pressure, recurrent hematoma, seizures, and infection. After recovery discharge teaching should review any medications the patient takes, and educate the patient and family about safety measures and fall prevention. A home health care practitioner should carry out an evaluation of home safety issues, and assist the family in making appropriate changes based on any new neurological deficits suffered as a result of the injury.

vulvar h. Extravasation of blood into the soft tissues of the external female genitalia. The bleeding may occur after childbirth or as a result of trauma (e.g., rape trauma). Postpartum bleeding usually is due to the shearing of submucosal tissues during a difficult or forceps-assisted delivery.

PATIENT CARE: The woman usually complains of severe vulvar pain. Inspection may reveal a unilateral firm area of the labia majora that is extremely painful to the touch. Prompt application of an ice pack may limit further bleeding; however, large or enlarging hematomas may require surgical intervention (i.e., ligation and evacuation).

hematometra (hē″mă-, hĕm″ă-tō-mē′tră) [″ + *metra*, uterus] **1.** Hemorrhage in the uterus. **2.** An accumulation of menstrual blood in the uterus. SEE: *hematocolpos; hydrometra; pyometra.*

hematomyelia (hē″mă-, hĕm″ă-tō-mī-ē′lē-ă) [″ + *myelos*, marrow] Hemorrhage into the spinal cord.

hematopathology (hē″mă-, hĕm″ă-tō-păth-ŏl′ŏ-jē) [″ + *pathos*, disease, suffering, + *logos*, word, reason] The study of pathologic conditions of the blood.

hematophagous (hē-mă-tof′ă-gŭs) [*hemato-* + Gr. *-phagos*, fr. *phagein*, to eat] Of mosquitoes, ticks, and some bats, feeding on blood; bloodsucking.

hematopoiesis (hē″mă-, hē-mat″ŏ-poy-ē′sĭs, hē″măt-ō-) [*hemat-* + *-poiesis*] The production and development of blood cells, normally in the bone marrow.

extramedullary h. The production of blood cells in tissues other than bone marrow, e.g., in the liver or spleen. It occurs in severe or chronic anemias and other diseases that affect blood cell formation. SYN: *myeloid **metaplasia**.*

hematopoietic (hē-mat″ŏ-poy-et′ik, hē″măt-ō-) **1.** Pert. to the production and development of blood cells. **2.** A substance that assists in or stimulates the production of blood cells. SYN: *hematogenic; hematoplastic.*

hematopoietic malignancy Any of the cancers that arise from unregulated clonal proliferation of hematopoietic stem cells, such as leukemia and lymphoma. In these disorders, genetically abnormal blood-forming cells (derived from precursors of granulocytes, lymphocytes, platelets, or red blood cells) reproduce in an unchecked fashion, consume nutrients, infiltrate various tissues, and replace the body's normally functioning cells. SEE: *leukemia; lymphoma.*

hematopoietic system The blood-forming tissues and organs of the body. It includes the bone marrow, spleen, and lymphatic tissue.

hematopoietin (hē″mă-tō-poy′ĕ-tĭn, hĕm″) [″ + Gr. *poiein*, to make] Any growth factor that influences the development of blood cells.

hematoporphyrin (hē″mă-, hĕm″ă-tō-por″fĭ-rĭn) [″ + *porphyra*, purple] Iron-free heme, a decomposition product of hemoglobin present in the urine in certain conditions.

hematosalpinx (hē″măt-ŏ-sal′pingks″, hem″ăt-) [*hemato-* + *salpinx*] Accumulation of blood in the fallopian tube. It is most commonly caused by tubal pregnancy or, occasionally, endometriosis. SYN: *hemosalpinx.*

hematospermia (hĕm″ă-tō-spĕr′mē-ă) Semen that contains blood. SYN: *hemospermia.*

h. spuria Hematospermia coming from the prostatic urethra.

h. vera Hematospermia coming from the seminal vesicles.

hematothorax (hĕm″ă-tō-thō′răks) [″ + *thorax*, chest] Hemothorax.

hematoxylin (hĕm″ă-tŏk′sĭ-lĭn) $C_{16}H_{14}O_6$; a dye widely used in histology, often in conjunction with eosin. It has an affinity for cell nuclei, which stain a deep blue.

hematuria (hē″mă-, hĕm″ă-tū′rē-ă) [″ + *ouron*, urine] Blood in the urine.

ETIOLOGY: Blood may appear in the urine as a result of a wide variety of conditions, including contamination during menstruation or the puerperium; internal trauma or kidney stones; vigorous exercise; urinary tract infections or systemic infections with renal involvement; some cases of glomerulonephritis; vascular anomalies of the urinary tract; or cancers of the urethra, bladder, prostate, ureters, or kidneys.

FINDINGS: The urine may appear tea-colored, slightly smoky, reddish, or frankly bloody.

DIAGNOSIS: The clinical history may help determine the cause of bleeding in the urine. Kidney stones often cause hematuria associated with intense flank pain that radiates into the groin. Hematuria in a child with recent sore throat, new edema, and hypertension may reflect a poststreptococcal glomerulonephritis. Urinary bleeding in a patient with abdominal pain and an enlarged or prosthetic aorta may have a fistulous connection to a ureter—a true surgical emergency. In the laboratory, microscopic examination of the urine also provides clues to the cause of bleeding. Red blood cells from the upper urinary tract often are deformed or misshapen, whereas those from the urethra or bladder have a normal microscopic appearance.

benign familial h. An inherited structural abnormality of the kidneys in which small numbers of red blood cells are found in the urine. On biopsy the glomeruli of affected patients are found to have thin basement membranes. The condition is not associated with progressive kidney failure or other progressive renal diseases. SYN: *thin basement membrane disease.*

glomerular h. Blood loss in the urine resulting from inflammation of the renal glomeruli. Its hallmark is the finding of misshapen or shattered red blood cells on urine microscopy

microscopic h. Red blood cells that are not grossly obvious but are found instead on microscopic examination of a urine specimen. They may be found in patients with tumors of the urinary tract (kidneys, ureters, or bladder); glomerular diseases; kidney or ureteral stones; urinary tract infections; trauma; or in patients without obvious or demonstrable pathology. SYN: *microhematuria.*

nonglomerular h. Blood in the urine that has a normal appearance on microscopic examination. The most common causes are urinary tract infections, urinary stones, or cancers of the genitourinary tract.

renal h. Hematuria in which the blood comes from the upper urinary tract. On gross examination, the urine is often smoky, red, or cola-colored. Causes include glomerular diseases, kidney tumors, and kidney stones.

urethral h. Urinary bleeding that may result from urethral trauma, surgery, adenomas, or other lesions of the lower urinary tract. The voided urine usually is bright red at the onset of urination and more dilute in appearance as the stream continues.

vesical h. Urinary bleeding typically produced by bladder malignancies, stones, or cystitis.

heme (hēm) An iron-containing nonprotein portion of the hemoglobin molecule wherein the iron is in the ferrous (Fe^{2+}) state. Disorders of heme synthesis are known as the *porphyrias.* SEE: *ferritin; hematin.*

heme oxygenase ABBR: HO. An enzyme that cleaves the ring structure of heme, releasing biliverdin, carbon monoxide, and iron. It is present in humans in two active forms: HO-1 and HO-2.

hemeralopia (hĕm″ē-ră-lō′pē-ă) [Gr. *hēmera,* day + Gr. *alaos,* blind + *opia,* eye] Diminished vision in bright light. In hemeralopia, vision is poor in sunlight and in good illumination; it is good at dusk, at twilight, and in poor illumination. This is noted in albinism, retinitis with central scotoma, toxic amblyopia, coloboma of the iris and choroid, opacity of the crystalline lens or cornea, and in conjunctivitis with photophobia.

The term was formerly erroneously applied to nyctalopia (night blindness). SEE: *nyctalopia.* SYN: *day blindness.*

heme synthetase The enzyme that catalyzes the chelation of iron (Fe^{++}) to porphyrin, a crucial step in the synthesis of heme. SYN: *ferrochelatase.*

hemi- [Gr. *hēmi-,* half] Prefix meaning *half.*

hemianalgesia (hĕm″ē-ăn-ăl-jē′zē-ă) [″ + ″ + *algos,* pain] Lack of sensibility to pain (analgesia) on one side of the body.

hemianesthesia (hĕm″ē-ăn-ĕs-thē′zē-ă) [″ + ″ + *aisthesis,* sensation] Anesthesia of half of the body.

hemianopia, hemianopsia (hem″ē-ă-nōp′ē-ă, -nop′sē-ă) [] Blindness in one half of the visual field. SYN: *half vision; hemiamaurosis; hemiamblyopia.* **hemianoptic** (-ă-nop′tik), *adj.*

altitudinal h. Blindness in upper or lower half of the visual field of one or both eyes.

binasal h. Blindness in the nasal half of the visual field in each eye.

bitemporal h. Blindness in the temporal half of the visual field in each eye.

complete h. Blindness in half the visual field.

crossed h. Either bitemporal or binasal hemianopsia. SYN: *heteronymous h.*

heteronymous h. Crossed hemianopia.

homonymous h. Blindness of the nasal half of the visual field of one eye and of the temporal half of the other, or right-sided or left-sided hemianopsia of corresponding sides in both eyes.

incomplete h. Blindness in less than half of the visual field of each eye.

quadrant h. Blindness of a symmetrical quadrant of the field of vision in each eye.

unilateral h. Hemianopsia affecting only one eye.

hemiataxia (hĕm″ē-ă-tăks′ē-ă) [″ + *ataxia*, lack of order] Impaired muscular coordination causing awkward movements of the affected side of the body.

hemiatrophy (hĕm-ē-ăt′rō-fē) [″ + *atrophia*, atrophy] Impaired nutrition resulting in atrophy of one side of the body or of an organ or part.

hemiballism (hĕm-ē-băl′ĭzm) [″ + *balismos*, jumping] Jerking and twitching movements of one side of the body.

hemiblock (hĕm′ĭ-blŏk) In heart block, a failure of conduction in one of the two main divisions of the left bundle branch.

hemic (hē′mĭk, hĕm′ĭk) [Gr. *haima*, blood] Pert. to blood. SYN: *hemal* (1).

hemicastration (hĕm″ē-kăs-trā′shŭn) [″ + L. *castrare*, to prune] The removal of one ovary or testicle. At one time, removal of the left testicle was done on the erroneous assumption that sperm from the right testicle produced only sons.

hemicellulose (hĕm-ē-sĕl′ū-lōs) One of a group of polysaccharides that differ from cellulose in that they may be hydrolyzed by dilute mineral acids, and from other polysaccharides in that they are not readily digested by amylases. The group includes pentosans, galactosans (agar-agar), and pectins.

hemichorea (hĕm-ē-kō-rē′ă) [″ + *choreia*, dance] Chorea affecting only one side of the body.

hemicolectomy (hĕm″ē-kō-lĕk′tō-mē) [″ + *kolon*, colon, + *ektome*, excision] Surgical removal of half (either left or right) or less of the colon.

hemicrania (hĕm-ē-krā′nē-ă) [″ + *kranion*, skull] **1.** Unilateral head pain, usually migraine. **2.** A malformation in which only one half of the skull is developed.

h. continua A long-lasting, one-sided headache of moderate to severe intensity. It responds to treatment with nonsteroidal anti-inflammatory drugs, such as indomethacin.

paroxysmal h. A relatively rare form of headache, more common in women than in men, characterized by multiple daily episodes of unilateral facial or ocular pain that may be precipitated by movements of the head or neck. It is related to trigeminal neuralgia, and often is effectively treated with nonsteroidal antiinflammatory agents, such as indomethacin.

hemicraniectomy (hĕm″ē-krā-nē-ĕk′tō-mē) [″ + ″ + *ektome*, excision] The surgical division of the cranial vault from front backward, exposing half of the brain.

hemidesmosome (hĕm″ē-dĕs′mō-sōm) The half of a desmosome produced by epithelial cells for attachment of the basal surface of the cell to the underlying basement membrane or the enamel or cementum tooth surface in the case of junctional epithelium.

Hemidesmus indicus (hem″ē-dez′mŭs in′dik-ŭs) An herb widely used in Ayurvedic and alternative medicine as an antioxidant and as a protector of kidney function. SYN: *Indian sarsaparilla*.

hemidiaphragm (hĕm″ē-dī′ă-frăm) [″ + ″ + *phragma*, wall] Half of the diaphragm.

hemifacial (hĕm″ē-fā′shăl) [″ + L. *facies*, face] Pert. to one side of the face.

hemifacial microsomia (mī″krō-sō′mē-ă) ABBR: HFM. A rare congenital anomaly, usually inherited sporadically, in which one side of the body, usually the right, fails to develop equally with the left. The ear, nose, and maxilla on the affected side are hypoplastic. In addition the right lung and kidney may be smaller than normal, and affected children often have ventriculoseptal defects. Surgical treatment of facial defects associated with HFM is often undertaken by combined teams of oral and maxillofacial surgeons. SYN: *facioauriculo vertebral syndrome; Goldenhar syndrome; oculoauricular vertebral dysplasia*.

hemigastrectomy (hĕm″ē-găs-trĕk′tō-mē) [″ + *gaster*, belly, + *ektome*, excision] Excision of half of the stomach.

hemiglossectomy (hĕm″ē-glŏs-sĕk′tō-mē) [″ + ″ + *ektome*, excision] The surgical removal of one side of the tongue.

hemihepatectomy (hĕm″ē-hĕp″ă-tĕk′tō-mē) [″ + *hepatos*, liver, + *ektome*, excision] The surgical removal of half of the liver.

hemihydrate (hĕm″ē-hī′drāt) A chemical compound with one molecule of water for every two molecules of the other substance. In dentistry, calcium sulfate hemihydrate is mixed with water to produce a hardened plaster or stone (calcium sulfate dihydrate), which, in turn, is commonly used to produce dental models.

hemihyperesthesia (hĕm″ē-hī-pĕr-ĕs-thē′zē-ă) [″ + *hyper*, over, + *aisthesis*, sensation] Abnormal sensitivity to touch or pain on one side of the body.

hemihyperplasia (hĕm″ē-hī″pĕr-plā′zē-ă) [″ + ″ + *plassein*, to form] The excessive development of one side or one half of the body or of an organ.

hemihypesthesia, hemihypoesthesia (hĕm″ē-hī″pĕs-thē′zē-ă, -pō-ĕs-thē′zē-a) [Gr. *hemi-*, half, + *hypo*, under, +

aisthesis, sensation] Diminished sensibility on one side of the body.

hemi-inattention (hĕm″ē-ĭn-ă-tĕn′shŭn) Unilateral inattention.

hemilaminectomy (hĕm″ē-lăm″ĭ-nĕk′tō-mē) [″ + L. *lamina,* thin plate, + Gr. *ektome,* excision] The surgical removal of the lamina of the vertebral arch on one side.

hemilaryngectomy (hĕm″ē-lăr″in-jĕk′tō-mē) [″ + *larynx,* larynx, + *ektome,* excision] The surgical removal of the lateral half of the larynx.

hemilateral (hĕm″ē-lăt′ĕr-ăl) [″ + L. *latus,* side] Relating to one side only.

hemimandibulectomy (hĕm″ē-măn-dĭb-ū-lĕk′tō-mē) [″ + L. *mandibula,* lower jawbone, + Gr. *ektome,* excision] The surgical removal of half of the mandible.

hemin (hē′mĭn) [*hem-* + *-in*] A brownish-red crystalline salt of heme formed when hemoglobin is heated with glacial acetic acid and sodium chloride. The iron is present in the ferric (Fe^{3+}) state. Hemin is used in testing for presence of blood. SYN: ***crystal*** *of hemin.* SEE: *heme; X* ***factor.***

heminephrectomy (hĕm″ē-nĕ-frĕk′tō-mē) [Gr. *hemi-,* half, + *nephros,* kidney, + *ektome,* excision] The excision or removal of a portion of a kidney.

hemiopia (hĕm-ē-ō′pē-ă) [″ + *ops,* eye] Hemianopia.

hemiparalysis (hĕm″ē-pă-răl′ĭ-sĭs) [″ + *paralyein,* to disable] Hemiplegia.

hemiparesis (hĕm″ē-păr′ĕ-sĭs, hĕm-ē-păr-ē′sĭs) [″ + *paresis,* paralysis] Hemiplegia.

hemiparesthesia (hĕm″ē-păr-ĕs-thē′zē-ă) [″ + ″] Numbness, tingling, or other unpleasant sensations affecting one half of the body.

hemipelvectomy (hĕm″ē-pĕl″vĕk′tō-mē) [″ + L. *pelvis,* basin, + Gr. *ektome,* excision] The surgical removal of half of the pelvis, and the corresponding lower extremity.

hemiplegia (hĕm-ē-plē′jē-ă) [″ + *plege,* a stroke] Paralysis of one side of the body, usually resulting from damage to the corticospinal tracts of the central nervous system. SYN: *hemiamyosthenia; hemiparalysis; hemiparesis.* SEE: *Benedikt's syndrome; paralysis; thalamic syndrome.*

ETIOLOGY: The most common cause of hemiplegia is stroke caused by thrombosis, brain hemorrhage, or cerebral embolism. Tumors and spinal cord injuries are responsible for hemiplegia in a smaller number of patients.

SYMPTOMS: The patient will be unable to move the arm and/or leg or facial muscles on one side of the body. Usually the paralysis is more complete in the proximal muscles (e.g., at the shoulder or hip muscles) than it is in the more distal muscles of the hands or feet. If the nondominant parietal lobe of the brain is injured (e.g., after an occlusion of the middle cerebral artery on that side), the patient may neglect the paralyzed side of the body. He or she may deny neurological deficits on that side and may be unable to see or feel stimuli presented to the affected hemibody or visual field. SEE: *visual anosognosia.*

PATIENT CARE: Depending upon which part of the central nervous system is affected, the patient may also have other neurological deficits (e.g., visual field disturbances, aphasia, dysphagia, vertigo, sensory changes and/or personality changes), which may impact rehabilitation. Assistance is provided with active range-of-motion exercises to unaffected limbs and passive exercises to affected limbs. Correct body positioning and alignment of extremities are maintained, and measures are taken to prevent foot drop, contractures, and pressure ulcers. The patient is assessed for dysphagia, and a nutritional plan developed to provide adequate calories and fluids. Active participation in rehabilitation through physical therapy and occupational therapy is encouraged. The patient is taught to use the unaffected limbs to move and exercise the affected limbs to maintain joint mobility and prevent contractures and to maintain muscle tone and strength. The patient is protected from injury through the use of supportive devices to prevent subluxation or dislocation of affected joints. The patient and the family are taught how to use assistive devices (e.g., slings, splints, walkers), and the goals and processes involved in rehabilitation are explained. Accurate information, realistic reassurance, and emotional support are provided to assist with coping. Both patient and family may benefit from referral to local support groups and the National Stroke Association (800-787-6537; www.stroke.org).

capsular h. Hemiplegia resulting from a lesion of the internal capsule of the brain.

cerebral h. Hemiplegia caused by a brain lesion.

facial h. Paralysis of the muscles on one side of the face.

hypoglossal alternating h. Medulla lesion paralyzing the tongue by involving the 12th nerve fibers as they course through the uncrossed pyramid. The pathology may extend across the midline or dorsally, involving the medial fillet, causing contralateral anesthesia.

pontile h. Hemiplegia due to a lesion of the pons. The arm and leg on one side and the face on the opposite side are affected.

spastic h. Increased muscular tone occurring in half of the body. It results from an upper motor neuron lesion, such as a stroke, central nervous system trauma, or tumor.

spinal h. Hemiplegia resulting from a lesion of the spinal cord. SEE: *Brown-Séquard's syndrome.*

hemiplegic (hĕm-ē-plē'jĭk) **1.** Pert. to hemiplegia. **2.** A colloquial reference to a patient having hemiplegia.

Hemiptera (hĕm-ĭp'tĕr-ă) [Gr. *hemi-,* half, + *pteron,* wing] The true bugs; an order of insects characterized by piercing and sucking mouth parts. The first pair of wings is leathery at the base and membranous at the tip; the second pair is membranous. Metamorphosis is incomplete. The order includes bedbugs, kissing bugs, and several other species that are pests or vectors of pathogenic organisms.

hemisection (hĕm″ē-sĕk'shŭn) [″ + L. *sectio,* a cutting] Bisection.

hemispasm (hĕm'ē-spăzm) [″ + *spasmos,* a convulsion] A spasm of only one side of the body or face.

hemisphere (hĕm'ĭ-sfēr) [″ + *sphaira,* sphere] Either half of the cerebrum or cerebellum.

dominant h. The cerebral hemisphere (usually the left hemisphere of the brain) that controls both language use and the hand a person uses for most fine motor functions.

nondominant h. In neurology, the hemisphere of the brain that does not control speech or the predominantly used hand.

hemispherectomy (hĕm″ĭ-sfēr-ĕk'tō-mē) Surgical removal of one hemisphere of the brain; an operation sometimes used to treat severe brain diseases such as refractory epilepsy.

hemispheric specialization (hĕm″ĭ-sfēr'ĭk) The control of distinct neurological functions by the right and left hemispheres of the brain. In most people, the left hemisphere controls language use, analytical thought, and abstract thinking, while the right manages visual and spatial relations, musical abilities, and other functions.

hemisyndrome (hĕm″ē-sĭn'drōm) [″ + *syndrome,* a running with] A syndrome indicating a unilateral lesion of the spinal cord.

hemithorax (hĕm″ē-thō'răks) [″ + *thorax,* chest] One half of the chest.

hemithyroidectomy (hĕm″ē-thī″royd-ĕk'tō-mē) [″ + *thyreos,* shield, + *eidos,* form, shape, + *ektome,* excision] The surgical removal of one half of the thyroid gland tissue.

hemivertebra (hĕm″ē-vĕr'tĕ-bră) The congenital absence of or the failure to develop half of a vertebra.

hemizygosity (hĕm″ē-zī-gŏs'ĭ-tē) [″ + *zygotos,* yoked] Possessing only one of the gene pair that determines a particular genetic trait.

hemlock (hĕm'lŏk) [AS. *hemleac*] **1.** A species of evergreen plant. **2.** The volatile oil from either *Conium maculatum* or *Cicuta maculata* containing cicutoxin. Ingestion of these hemlock plants, esp. their roots, may cause fatal poisoning.

Hemlock Society (hĕm'lŏk″) An organization that publishes information about physician-assisted suicide, and decisions by patients regarding end-of-life choices. Address: P.O. Box 101810, Denver, CO 80250. Telephone: 800-247-7421. Website: www.hemlock.org

hemoagglutination (hē″mō-ă-gloo″tĭ-nā'shŭn) [Gr. *haima,* blood, + L. *agglutinans,* gluing] The clumping of red blood corpuscles.

hemoagglutinin (hē″mō-ă-gloo'tĭ-nĭn) An agglutinin that clumps the red blood corpuscles.

hemobilia (hē″mō-bĭl'ē-ă) Blood in the bile or bile ducts.

hemochromatosis (hē″mō-krō″mă-tō'sĭs) [″ + *chroma,* color, + *osis,* condition] A genetic disease marked by excessive absorption and accumulation of iron in the body. The disease is caused by one of several recessive mutations that result in excessive absorption of iron from the gastrointestinal tract. It is not caused by secondary iron overload, as may occur in patients who have received multiple transfusions or who have hemolytic anemia. The disease is often diagnosed before it causes symptoms. SYN: *bronze diabetes.*

SYMPTOMS: At the time of diagnosis, the patient may be asymptomatic. Symptomatic patients may experience weakness, fatigue, arthralgias, abdominal pain, liver failure (cirrhosis), symptoms of diabetes mellitus or heart failure, thyroid disorders, or impotence. These symptoms are caused by the deposition of excess iron into multiple organ systems.

DIAGNOSIS: Physical findings include gray or bronzed skin pigmentation changes, enlarged liver, arthritis, signs of congestive heart failure, and in males, testicular atrophy. Laboratory studies used to screen for the disease include transferrin saturation or ferritin tests. Liver biopsies from affected persons show excessive stainable iron. Genetic testing is available to identify patients with the most common forms of hemochromatosis. SEE: illus.

TREATMENT: Treatment includes phlebotomy (blood drawing) done at regular intervals until the patient's iron stores drop to below normal. Typically, the ferritin level is monitored to ensure that this has occurred. Initially, approximately 1 unit of blood is removed each week until the desired ferritin level is reached. Maintenance therapy consists of removal of blood at 1- to 4-month intervals. Iron chelators such as deferox-

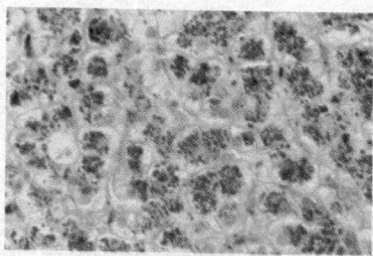

HEMOCHROMATOSIS
With excessive quantities of iron found in liver cells

amine are used if phlebotomy is not possible, but they are much less effective at decreasing iron stores than is blood drawing.

⚠ Blood removed from patients with iron overload cannot be used for transfusion.

PATIENT CARE: The need for phlebotomy and its role in the removal of excess iron are explained to the patient. To prevent dizziness or hypotension, the patient is encouraged to drink plenty of fluids and to abstain from vigorous exercise for the first 24 hr after the procedure.

hemochromogen (hē″mō-krō′mō-jěn) [″ + *chroma*, color, + *gennan*, to produce] A compound, such as hemoglobin, in which heme is combined with a nitrogen-containing molecule; e.g., protein.

hemoclip (hē′mō-klĭp) A metal or absorbable clip used to ligate blood vessels.

hemoconcentration (hē″mō-kŏn-sĕn-trā′shŭn) A relative increase in the number of red blood cells resulting from a decrease in the volume of plasma (e.g., in dehydration).

hemoculture (hē′mŏ-kŭl″chŭr) [*hem-* + *culture*] The isolation of bacterial or parasitic infectious agents from blood incubated in the laboratory on special nutrients, such as glucose or nitrates.

hemocuprein (hē″mō-kū′prē-ĭn) A blue copper-containing compound present in red blood cells.

hemocyte (hē′mō-sīt) [″ + *kytos*, cell] 1. Any blood cell. 2. A red blood cell.

hemocytoblast (hē″mō-sī′tō-blăst) [″ + ″ + *blastos*, germ] An undifferentiated stem cell found in mesenchymal tissues that may give rise to any type of blood cell. SEE: illus.

hemocytometer, hemacytometer, hematocytometer (hē″mŏ-sī-tom′ĕt-ĕr, hē″mă-tō-sī-tom′ĕt-ĕr) [*hemocyte* + *-meter*, measure] A device for determining the number of cells in a stated volume of blood.

hemodiafiltration (hē″mō-dī″ŏ-fĭl-trā′

shŭn) [″ + Gk. *dia*, through + ″] A method of ultrafiltration in which a patient's blood is directed through a hemofilter and then dialyzed by a countercurrent solution before it is returned to the patient. Volume, electrolytes, metabolites, or toxins are removed from the blood before it re-enters the body.

hemodialysis (hē″mō-dī-al′ĭ-sĭs, ′ĭ-sēz″) *pl.* **hemodialyses** [*hemo-* + *dialysis*] The clearing of urea, metabolic waste products, toxins, and excess fluid from the blood by use of an artificial kidney. This procedure is used to treat end-stage renal failure, transient renal failure, and some cases of poisoning or drug overdose. In the U.S., more than 345,000 patients undergo hemodialysis regularly for end-stage renal disease. The primary use of hemodialysis is to manage renal failure, a disorder in which fluids, acids, electrolytes, and many drugs are ineffectively eliminated in the urine. Hyperkalemia, uremia, fluid overload, acidosis, and uremic pericarditis are other indications for hemodialysis. SEE: table; *hemoperfusion; Nursing Diagnoses Appendix.*

Hemodialysis separates solutes by differential diffusion through a cellophane membrane placed between the blood and the dialysate solution, and involves the following: 1) establishing access to the circulation, e.g., via an arteriovenous fistula, cannula, or via a synthetic or bovine graft or temporary catheter; 2) anticoagulating the patient's blood to prevent extracorporeal clotting; 3) pumping the blood to a dialysis membrane; 4) adjusting the diffusion of solutes from the blood into a buffered dialysate solution; 5) returning the cleansed and buffered blood to the patient.

Adequacy of hemodialysis is determined by the amount of fluid and solute, esp. urea, removed from the body. Typically, hemodialysis lasts about 3 or 4 hr per treatment and is repeated several times a week.

Even with regular hemodialysis sessions, patients with end-stage renal disease have high mortality rates. In the U.S., about 25% of all patients receiving hemodialysis die each year, usually because of heart disease, stroke, or pre-existing diabetes mellitus. SYN: *renal dialysis*. SEE: *dialysis; hemofiltration; uremia.*

⚠ Hemodialysis has many potential complications, including hypotension, infection of the site of access, sepsis, air embolism, hypersensitivity reactions, dialysis disequilibrium, muscle cramping, anemia, and bleeding.

PATIENT CARE: *Preprocedure:* If this is the patient's first hemodialysis ses-

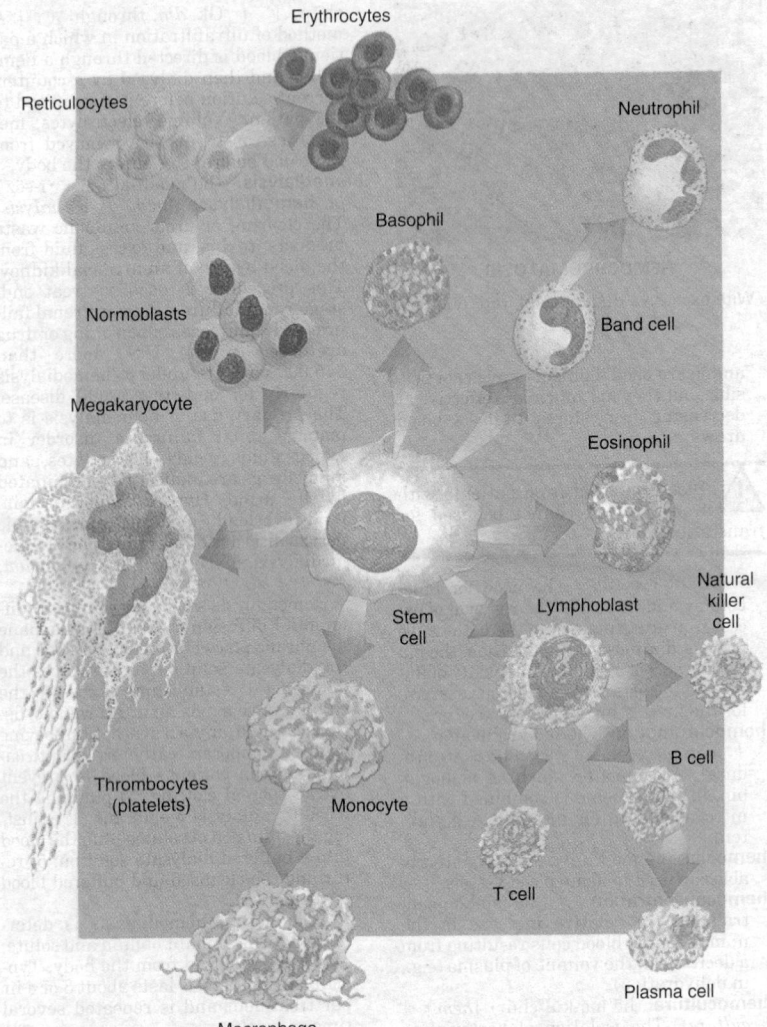

Erythrocytes

Reticulocytes

Neutrophil

Basophil

Normoblasts

Band cell

Megakaryocyte

Eosinophil

Natural
killer
cell

Stem
cell

Lymphoblast

B cell

Thrombocytes
(platelets)

Monocyte

T cell

Plasma cell

Macrophage

HEMOCYTOBLAST (STEM CELL) AND BLOOD CELLS

sion, the purpose of the treatment and expected results are explained. First, the patient undergoes a surgical procedure to create a vascular access. After the access site has been created and matured, the patient is readied for dialysis. The patient's weight is obtained and vital signs are checked; blood pressure is measured in the arm that does not have the vascular access with the patient in both supine and standing positions. The hemodialysis equipment is prepared according to the manufacturer's guidelines and the institution's protocol. Strict aseptic technique is maintained to avoid introducing pathogens into the

patient's bloodstream during treatment. The patient is placed in a supine or low Fowler position and made as comfortable as possible, with the venous access site well supported and resting on a sterile drape or sterile barrier shield.

During the procedure: Health care providers follow standard precautions by wearing appropriate gloves and protective eye shields throughout the procedure. The patient is monitored continually throughout dialysis. Vital signs are checked and documented every 30 min to detect possible complications. Fever may indicate infection from pathogens in the dialysate or equipment and

Routine Precautions for the Care of All Hemodialysis Patients

Patients should have specific stations assigned to them, and their chairs and beds should be cleaned after each use.
Ancillary supplies, e.g., trays, blood pressure cuffs, clamps, scissors, and nondisposable items, should not be shared by patients.
Nondisposable items should be cleaned or disinfected appropriately after each use.
Medications and supplies should not be shared among patients, and medication carts should not be used.
Medications should be prepared and distributed from a centralized area.
Clean areas and contaminated areas should be separated, e.g., handwashing, handling of blood samples, and equipment cleaning should be kept distinct from areas for preparation of food, drink, and medications.

Adapted from Recommendations for prevention and control of hepatitis C virus (HCV) infection and HCV-related chronic disease. Morbidity and Mortality Weekly Report 47(N0. RR-19), Centers for Disease Control and Prevention.

should be reported to the physician. Hypotension may indicate hypovolemia, sepsis, or a decreased hematocrit level, e.g., from bleeding; IV fluid supplements or blood should be administered as prescribed. Rapid respirations may signal hypervolemia or hypoxemia; supplemental oxygen should be administered as prescribed. A blood sample is drawn approx. every hour for analysis of clotting time. The patient is weighed regularly on the dialyzing unit's bed scale or a portable scale to ensure adequate ultrafiltration during treatment. The dialyzer's blood lines also are checked periodically to ensure that all connections are secure, and the lines are monitored for clotting. The patient is assessed for headache, muscle twitching, backache, nausea or vomiting, and agitation or seizures, which may indicate disequilibrium syndrome caused by rapid fluid removal and electrolyte changes. If this syndrome occurs, the physician should be notified immediately; he or she may reduce the blood flow rate or stop the dialysis. Muscle cramps also may result from rapid fluid and electrolyte shifts. Cramps may be relieved by injecting prescribed 0.9% sodium chloride solution into the venous line. Health care providers are esp. alert for signs of air embolism, a potentially fatal complication characterized by sudden hypotension; dyspnea; chest pain; cyanosis; and a weak, rapid pulse. If these signs occur, the patient is turned onto the left side, the head of the bed lowered (to help keep air bubbles on the right side of the heart, where they can be absorbed from the pulmonary vasculature), and the physician notified immediately.

Postprocedure: The venous access site is monitored for bleeding. If bleeding is excessive, pressure is maintained on the site and the physician notified. To prevent clotting and other blood flow prob-lems, the arm used for venous access is not used for any other procedures, including IV line insertion, blood pressure monitoring, and venipuncture. At least four times daily, circulation at the access site is assessed by auscultating for a bruit and by palpating for a thrill. The patient is instructed in these assessment techniques and in the care of the venous access site, cleaning the incision daily and keeping it dry until healing is complete (usually 10 to 14 days). Any pain, swelling, redness, or drainage in the accessed arm should be reported immediately. The patient also should avoid putting excessive pressure on the arm, such as sleeping on it, wearing constricting clothing, or lifting heavy objects. He or she should avoid showering, bathing, or swimming for several hours after dialysis. The patient is instructed to use exercises to promote venous dilation and to enhance blood flow in the affected arm.

If the patient is to perform hemodialysis at home, both the patient and a family member must thoroughly understand all aspects of the procedure. They are provided with the phone number of the dialysis center and encouraged to call if any questions or concerns arise. The patient also is advised to arrange for another (trained) person to be present during dialysis in case any problems occur and to contact the National Association of Patients on Hemodialysis and Transplantation or the National Kidney Foundation for information and support.

hemodialyzer (hē″mō-dī′ă-līz″ĕr) [*hem- + dialyzer*] Dialyzer.

hemodilution (hē″mō-dī-lū′shŭn) A relative increase in the volume of blood plasma, resulting in a decrease in the measured concentration (but not in the absolute number) of red blood cells.

hemodynamic monitoring (hē″mō-dī-năm′ĭk) A general term for determining the functional status of the cardiovascular system as it responds to acute stress such as myocardial infarction and cardiogenic or septic shock. This may include frequent assessments of blood pressure, pulse, mental status, urinary output, intracardiac pressure changes, and cardiac output. The data obtained permit the critical care team to follow the patient's course closely. SEE: table.

hemodynamics (hē″mō-dī-nam′iks) [hemo- + dynamics] A study of the forces involved in circulating blood through the body. **hemodynamic,** adj. **hemodynamically** (-nam′i-k(ă-)lē), adv.

hemofiltration (hē″mō-fĭl-trā′shŭn) An ultrafiltration technique to remove excess metabolic products from the blood. The technical aspects are similar to those of hemodialysis in that the blood flows from the patient to the hemofilter and is then returned.

⚠ Depending on the type of filter membrane used, essential materials may be removed from the blood. It is important to replace the excess crystalloids removed.

 continuous arteriovenous h. ABBR: CAVH. Continuous renal replacement therapy.

 continuous venovenous h. Continuous renal replacement therapy.

hemoflagellate (hē″mō-flăj′ĕ-lāt″) [″ + L. flagellum, whip] Any flagellate protozoan of the blood. Two important genera are Trypanosoma and Leishmania.

hemoglobin (hē′mŏ-glō″bĭn) [hem- + globin] ABBR: Hb, Hbg, Hgb. The iron-containing pigment of red blood cells (RBCs) that carries oxygen from the lungs to the tissues. The amount of hemoglobin in the blood averages 12 to 16 g/100 ml in women, 14 to 18 g/100 ml in men, and somewhat less in children. Hemoglobin is a crystallizable, conjugated protein consisting of heme and globin. In the lungs, 1 g of hemoglobin combines readily with 1.36 cc of oxygen by oxygenation to form oxyhemoglobin. In the tissues where oxygen concentration is low and carbon dioxide (CO_2) concentration is high (low pH), hemoglobin releases its oxygen. Hemoglobin also acts as a buffer for the hydrogen ions produced in RBCs when (CO_2) is converted to bicarbonate ions for transport in the plasma.

When old RBCs are phagocytized by macrophages in the liver, spleen, and red bone marrow, the iron of hemoglobin is reused immediately to produce new RBCs or is stored in the liver until needed. The globin is converted to amino acids for the synthesis of other proteins. The heme portion is of no further use and is converted to bilirubin.

Hemoglobin combines with carbon

Hemodynamic Parameters Frequently Measured in Critical Care

Parameter	Formula	Normal Values
cardiac index (CI)	cardiac output/body surface area	2.5-4 L/min
cardiac output (CO)	heart rate x stroke volume	4-8 L/min
central venous pressure (CVP)		2-8 mm Hg
cerebral perfusion pressure (CPP)	mean arterial pressure − intracranial pressure	80-100 mm Hg
ejection fraction (EF)	(ventricular end systolic volume/end diastolic volume) x 100	55-70%
heart rate (HR)		60-100 beats/min
left atrial pressure		8-12 mm Hg
mean arterial pressure (MAP)	systolic blood pressure + (diastolic blood pressure x 2)/3	70-110 mm Hg
pulmonary artery pressure (PAP)		systolic: 15-30 mm Hg; diastolic: 5-12 mm Hg
pulmonary artery wedge pressure (PAWP)		8-12 mm Hg
right atrial pressure		2-8 mm Hg
stroke volume (SV)	(cardiac output/heart rate) x 1000	60-120 ml/beat
systemic vascular resistance (SVR)	[(mean arterial pressure − right atrial pressure)/cardiac output] x 100	800-1200 dynes/sec/cm^2
urinary output (UO)		>0.5 ml/hr/kg

monoxide (in carbon monoxide poisoning) to form the stable compound carboxyhemoglobin, which renders hemoglobin unable to bond with oxygen and results in hypoxia of tissues. Oxidation of the ferrous iron of hemoglobin to the ferric state produces methemoglobin.

Hundreds of different types of hemoglobin have been discovered. SEE: *blood.*

h. A A hemoglobin molecule composed of two alpha and two beta chains. SEE: illus.

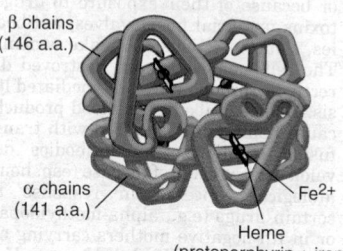

β chains
(146 a.a.)

α chains
(141 a.a.)   Fe^{2+}

Heme
(protoporphyrin + iron)

HEMOGLOBIN A MOLECULE

h. A$_{1c}$ ABBR: Hb A$_{1c}$. Hemoglobin A that contains a glucose group linked to the terminal amino acid of the beta chains of the molecule. Levels of hemoglobin A$_{1c}$ can be used to determine both the presence of diabetes mellitus (in previously undiagnosed patients) and the degree of glycemic control of known diabetics. The amount of glucose bound to the hemoglobin depends on the average concentration of glucose in the blood over time. In patients with diabetes mellitus, when the blood glucose level is optimally and carefully regulated over 8 to 12 weeks, the Hb A$_{1c}$ level is normal or slightly elevated. If the blood glucose level has not been controlled (and has been abnormally elevated) in the preceding 8 to 12 weeks, the Hb A$_{1c}$ blood level is increased. Hb A$_{1c}$ is a good indicator of long-term glycemic control. The blood test for it may be performed when the patient is not fasting. SYN: *glycohemoglobin; glycated h.; glycosylated h.*

Barts h. SEE: *Barts hemoglobin.*

h. C A hemoglobin molecule in which lysine is substituted for glutamic acid at the sixth position of the beta chain. This substitution decreases the solubility of the hemoglobin molecule and increases the rigidity of the red blood cell membrane.

h. E A hemoglobin molecule in which lysine is substituted for glutamic acid at the 26th position of the beta chain. This variation is found most often in those of Southeast Asian ancestry.

fetal h. The type of hemoglobin found in the erythrocytes of the normal fetus. It has better oxygen-binding capacity than adult hemoglobin and is able to extract oxygen from the placenta to meet the needs of the fetus.

PATIENT CARE: The induction of fetal hemoglobin (with drugs such as hydroxyurea) in patients with sickle cell anemia often improves their clinical status because fetal hemoglobin does not deform or "sickle" in the circulation. It is capable of taking up and giving off oxygen at lower oxygen tensions than the hemoglobin in adult erythrocytes.

glycated h. Hemoglobin A$_{1c}$.

glycosylated h. Hemoglobin A$_{1c}$.

h. Lepore A variant hemoglobin formed by an unequal crossover and fusion of the beta and delta genes. A single copy of the variant gene causes thalassemia minor. Homozygotes have thalassemia intermedia.

mean cell h. The hemoglobin content of the average RBC, usually expressed in picograms per red cell and calculated by multiplying the number of grams of hemoglobin/100 ml by 10 and dividing by the red cell count. SYN: *mean corpuscular h.*

mean corpuscular h. ABBR: MCH. Mean cell **h.**

plasma h. Hemoglobin released from red blood cells when they are destroyed (lyzed). It circulates in the blood and extravascular tissues. SYN: *free plasma h.*

hemoglobin C disease Chronic hemolytic anemia with splenomegaly, arthralgias, and abdominal pain, caused by a genetic variant of the hemoglobin molecule.

hemoglobin E disease A mild form of hemolytic anemia caused by a genetic variant of hemoglobin molecule. It is found primarily in people of Southeast Asian origin, in whom it may provide protection against falciparum malaria.

hemoglobinemia (hē″mō-glō-bin-ē′mē-ă) [Gr. *haima*, blood, + L. *globus*, globe, + Gr. *haima*, blood] The presence of hemoglobin in the blood plasma.

hemoglobin H disease Thalassemia intermedia.

hemoglobin M disorder Methemoglobinemia and cyanosis caused by a genetic variant of hemoglobin. The iron in this type of hemoglobin is in the ferric state and cannot combine with oxygen.

hemoglobinometer (hē″mō-glō-bin-ŏm′ĕ-ter) [″ + ″ + Gr. *metron*, measure] A device for determining the amount of hemoglobin in the blood.

hemoglobinopathy (hē″mō-glō″bĭ-nŏp′ă-thē) Any one of a group of genetic diseases caused by or associated with the presence of one of several forms of abnormal hemoglobin in the blood. SEE: *hemoglobin.*

hemoglobin SC disease A disease of those who have inherited two abnormal forms of hemoglobin, S and C. The affected may have vaso-occlusive crises similar to those seen in sickle cell anemia, with bony and visceral infarcts.

hemoglobin S disease A genetic variant of hemoglobin that causes sickle cell trait in heterozygotes and sickle cell disease in homozygotes. It is esp. common in people of African ancestry, in whom sickle cell trait is found in 8% to 10% of the population. SEE: *sickle cell **anemia***.

hemoglobinuria (hē″mŏ-glō-bĭn-ūr′ē-ă) [*hemoglobin* + *-uria*] The presence in urine of hemoglobin free from red blood cells. It occurs when the amount of hemoglobin from disintegrating red blood cells or from rapid hemolysis of red cells exceeds the ability of the blood proteins to combine with the hemoglobin. **hemoglobinuric** (-bĭn-ūr′ik), *adj.*

ETIOLOGY: Causes include hemolytic anemia, scurvy, purpura, exposure to or ingestion of certain chemicals, such as arsenic and phosphorus, typhoid fever, and septicemia.

   cold h. Hemoglobinuria following local or general exposure to cold. SYN: *paroxysmal **h.***

   epidemic h. Hemoglobinuria of the newborn characterized by jaundice, cyanosis, and fatty degeneration of heart and liver. SYN: *Winckel disease.*

   intermittent h. Paroxysmal nocturnal **h.**

   malarial h. Blackwater fever.

   march h. Urinary bleeding that occurs following strenuous exercise, e.g., running a marathon.

   paroxysmal h. Intermittent, recurring attacks of bloody urine following exposure to cold (cold hemoglobinuria) or strenuous exercise (march hemoglobinuria). It results from increased fragility of red blood cells or presence of a thermolabile autohemolysin.

   paroxysmal nocturnal h. ABBR: PNH. A rare form of an acquired hemolytic anemia that results from a defect in membrane-anchored proteins of red blood cells.

SYMPTOMS: The syndrome is characterized by acute onset of fevers and chills, back and extremity pain, and abdominal cramps. Hemoglobinuria occurs if enough red blood cells have been destroyed.

TREATMENT: Erythropoietin may be used to treat the anemia of PNH. SYN: *intermittent **h.***

   toxic h. Hemoglobinuria resulting from toxic substances such as muscarine or snake venom; toxic products of infectious diseases such as yellow fever, typhoid fever, syphilis, and certain forms of hemolytic jaundice; organisms such as *Plasmodium malariae*, which destroy red blood cells; and foreign protein in blood, e.g., following blood transfusion.

hemolysate (hē-mŏl′ĭ-sāt) The product of hemolysis.

hemolysin (hē-mŏl′ĭ-sĭn) [″ + *lysis*, dissolution] A toxic agent or condition that destroys red blood cells. SYN: *hemotoxin.*

hemolysin BL ABBR: HBL. An enterotoxin produced by *Bacillus cereus,* which causes epithelial necrosis, invasion of blood vessels, and destruction of blood cells.

hemolysis (hē-mŏl′ĭ-sĭs) [″ + *lysis,* dissolution] The destruction of red blood cells (RBCs) because of RBC diseases (e.g., spherocytosis or sickle cell disease) or because of their exposure to drugs, toxins, artificial heart valves, antibodies, some infections, or snake venoms. The cell membranes are destroyed directly or through antibody-mediated lysis. Donor antibodies in blood products cause hemolysis associated with transfusion reactions. Autoantibodies develop as the result of disease (esp. hematological cancers), in response to certain drugs (e.g., alpha-methyldopa), or in Rh-negative mothers carrying an Rh-positive fetus. Viral and bacterial infections are frequent causes of hemolysis in children, whose RBC membranes are very fragile. Organisms causing hemolysis include certain streptococci, staphylococci, and the tetanus bacillus. It also occurs in smallpox and diphtheria and following severe burns.

When the RBCs are destroyed, hemoglobin is released into the surrounding plasma and lost through the kidneys, turning the urine red, a condition called hemoglobinuria.

When hemolysis is gradual, patients compensate for the resulting anemia, reporting only fatigue and a slight tachycardia with physical exertion. Laboratory tests show decreased RBC count, hemoglobin, haptoglobin, and hematocrit, as well as elevated levels of lactate dehydrogenase and unconjugated bilirubin. Fragments of RBCs may sometimes be seen under the microscope. SEE: *autoantibody; fragility of red blood cells; hemolytic anemia.*

   colloid osmotic h. The swelling and rupture of red blood cells when they become excessively permeable to sodium and fill with water.

hemolytic (hē″mŏ-lit′ik) [*hem-* + *-lytic*] Pert. to the breaking down of red blood cells.

hemolytic disease of the newborn A neonatal disease characterized by anemia, jaundice, liver and spleen enlargement, and generalized edema (hydrops fetalis). SYN: *erythroblastosis fetalis.* SEE: *Rh blood group.*

ETIOLOGY: This disease is caused by transplacental transmission of maternal antibody, usually evoked by maternal and fetal blood group incompatibility. Incompatibilities of the ABO system are common but are not severe because maternal antibodies are too large to cross the placenta readily. Rh incompatibility, however, can result in profound fetal anemia, causing death in utero.

Rh incompatibility may develop when an Rh-negative woman carries an Rh-positive fetus. At the time of delivery, fetal red blood cells may enter maternal circulation, stimulating antibody production against the Rh factor. In a subsequent pregnancy, these antibodies cross the placenta to the fetal circulation and destroy fetal red blood cells.

TREATMENT: In cases of Rh incompatibility, the condition can be controlled during pregnancy by following the anti-Rh titer of the mother's blood and the bilirubin level of the fetus by amniocentesis. These indices show whether the pregnancy should be allowed to go to full term and if intrauterine transfusion is indicated; or if labor should be induced earlier. Delivery should be as free of trauma as possible and the placenta should not be manually removed. The infant with hemolytic disease should be immediately seen by a physician who is capable of and has the facilities and blood supplies available for exchange transfusion. The use of Rh (D) immune globulin after abortion, at 28 weeks' gestation, and within 72 hr of delivery has been beneficial.

hemolytic transfusion reaction The destruction of donated and infused red blood cells by antibodies in the person receiving the transfusion. SEE: under *transfusion reaction.*

hemolytic unit The amount of inactivated immune serum that causes complete hemolysis of 1 ml of a 5% emulsion of washed red blood cells in the presence of complement.

hemolytic uremic syndrome ABBR: HUS. An acute condition consisting of microangiopathic hemolytic anemia, thrombocytopenia, and acute nephropathy. *Escherichia coli* 0157:H7 (and *E. Coli* 0111) are causative agents that may be acquired from eating contaminated raw or rare hamburger or other meats. Children are most often affected. Onset may initially involve gastroenteritis and diarrhea or an upper respiratory tract infection. Hallmarks of the acute phase are a purpuric rash, irritability, and lethargy. Findings include oliguria, splenomegaly, mild jaundice, seizures (in some patients), hepatomegaly, pulmonary edema, and renal failure. The acute phase may last from 1 to 2 weeks in mild cases and much longer in severe cases.

TREATMENT: The treatment of this syndrome is management of the renal failure and anemia. Antibiotics are ineffective.

PROGNOSIS: The usual outcome is complete recovery, but about 5% of affected persons die, and 10% develop end-stage renal disease and require lifelong hemodialysis.

PATIENT CARE: If the child has been anuric for 24 hr or demonstrates oliguria with seizures and hypertension, the physician places a peritoneal catheter and the nurse institutes peritoneal dialysis as prescribed, with fluid replacement based on estimated sensible and insensible losses. Fluid and electrolyte balance, complete blood count, body weight, sensorium, and vital signs are carefully monitored, and blood urea nitrogen and azotemia levels are followed to evaluate therapy. Hypertension is reported and controlled with antihypertensive drugs. Severe anemia is treated with fresh, washed packed red blood cells; careful assessment is required throughout the transfusion to prevent circulatory overload, hypertension, and hyperkalemia. Seizures are managed by treating specific causes when known (hypertension, hyponatremia, hypocalcemia), and with anticonvulsant drugs as required. The patient is protected from injury during seizure activity, with the airway guarded. Heart and breath sounds are auscultated periodically, as cardiac failure with pulmonary edema can occur in association with hypervolemia. Prevention and treatment include water and sodium restriction and diuretic therapy, if prescribed. Meeting the child's nutritional needs can be difficult, as concentrated foods must be ingested without fluids and the child may be nauseated. The dietitian should be consulted for nutrition management. The child who is quite ill also may be irritable, restless, anxious, and frightened by frequent painful and stress-producing tests and treatments. Comfort and stability are provided in this threatening environment. Whenever possible, arrangements are made for one or both parents to remain with their child at all times. Support and reassurance are given to the parents and significant others, who are stressed by the severity of the illness and who may experience a degree of guilt if the illness resulted from ingestion of contaminated or raw foods. The family benefits not only from explanations about tests and treatments and information about their child's progress but also from sympathetic listening.

hemolyze (hē″mō-līz) To destroy red blood cells.

hemomediastinum (hē″mō-mē″dē-ă-stī′nŭm) [Gr. *haima*, blood, + L. *mediastinus*, in the middle] Effusion of blood into mediastinal spaces. SYN: *hematomediastinum.*

hemoperfusion (hē″mō-pĕr-fū′zhŭn) The perfusion of blood through substances, such as activated charcoal or ion-exchange resins, to remove toxic materials. The blood is then returned to the patient. This technique differs from hemodialysis in that the blood is not separated from the chemicals or solutions by a semipermeable dialysis membrane. SEE: *hemodialysis.*

hemopericardium (hē″mō-pĕr′ĭ-kăr′dē-ŭm) [″ + *peri,* around, + *kardia,* heart] Accumulation of blood in the pericardium.

hemoperitoneum (hē″mō-pĕr′ĭ-tō-nē′ŭm) [″ + *peritonaion,* peritoneum] Bleeding into the peritoneal cavity.

hemopexin (hē″mō-pek′sĭn) [*hem-* + *pexin*] A beta globulin that binds circulating hemoglobin in hemolytic diseases transporting it to the liver where it is recycled for its iron content.

hemophagocyte (hē″mō-făg′ō-sīt) [″ + ″ + *kytos,* cell] A phagocyte that ingests red blood cells.

hemophagocytosis (hē″mō-făg″ō-sī-tō′sĭs) [″ + ″ + ″ + *osis,* condition] The ingestion of red blood cells by phagocytes.

hemophil (hē′mŏ-fĭl) [″ + *philein,* to love] A type of bacteria that grows very well on agar that contains blood.

hemophilia (hē″mō-, hĕm″ō-fĭl′ē-ă) [″ + *philein,* to love] A group of hereditary bleeding disorders marked by deficiencies of blood-clotting proteins. Hemophilias are rare. Hemophilia A affects 1 in 5,000 to 10,000 boys; hemophilia B is present in about 1 in 30,000 boys. SEE: *blood; Nursing Diagnoses Appendix.*

ETIOLOGY: There are two principal types: hemophilia A (in which blood clotting factor VIII: C is either missing from the bloodstream or defective) and hemophilia B (in which blood clotting factor IX is deficient or defective). Both of these disorders are sex-linked (i.e., caused by X chromosome mutations) and occur in boys only.

SYMPTOMS: Bleeding after minor trauma is the hallmark of the hemophilias. Typically, bleeding occurs in the joints (hemarthrosis), in soft tissues, and in the urinary tract. Bleeding may also occur during dental procedures and surgery. Intracranial bleeding and bleeding into deep body sites may be life-threatening.

TREATMENT: Deficient clotting factors can be replaced intravenously, but doing so has carried significant risks. In the 1980s, for example, the injection of contaminated clotting factors spread hepatitis C and human immunodeficiency virus to many patients with hemophilia. Before these epidemics, these patients had life expectancies of about 65 years. Acquired immunodeficiency syndrome and other bloodborne infections decreased the average lifespan of patients with hemophilia to about 50 years. Today, the purification of clotting factors has resulted in safer treatment for patients with hemophilia.

Genetic counseling: Females are the carriers of sex-linked hemophilias and have a 50% chance of transmitting the affected X gene to each daughter (who would then also be a carrier) and a 50% chance of transmitting the affected X gene to each son, who would be born with hemophilia.

Expression of the disease: The severity of hemophilia is determined by the degree of factor deficiency: mild–factor levels 5% to 40% of normal; moderate–factor levels 1% to 5% of normal; severe–factor levels less than 1% of normal. Mild hemophilia may not be diagnosed until adulthood if the patient does not bleed spontaneously or after minor trauma.

Replacement of clotting factors: Factor replacement products include cryoprecipitate, lyophilized factor VIII or IX, and fresh frozen plasma. Other agents that aid blood clotting, such as desmopressin DDAVP (administered intravenously or intranasally) and epsilon-aminocaproic acid, are also helpful in managing or preventing bleeding episodes. The goal of treatment is to limit bleeding and prevent the irreversible destructive arthritis that results from repeated hemarthrosis and synovial hypertrophy.

⚠ Patients with hemophilia should avoid drugs that interfere with anticoagulation and should avoid sports or other activities in which there is a high likelihood of traumatic injury. In addition, they should wear bracelets identifying their illness to medical personnel.

PATIENT CARE: In the bleeding patient, vital signs are monitored, and the patient is observed for signs and symptoms of decreased tissue perfusion (i.e., restlessness, anxiety, confusion, pallor, cool and clammy skin, chest pain, decreased urine output, hypotension, tachycardia). Clotting factors are administered as prescribed. Repeat infusions will be required until bleeding stops, as the body uses up these factors in 48 to 72 hr. The skin, mucous membranes, and wounds are inspected for bleeding. Emergency care is provided for external bleeding; wounds are cleaned; and gentle, consistent pressure is applied to stop the bleeding. The injured part is elevated, and cold compresses or ice bags are applied to the site. Oral analgesics are provided as prescribed to manage pain (IM or SC administration could result in hematoma formation), and the patient and family are taught to avoid aspirin, aspirin-containing drugs, and NSAIDs because they decrease platelet adherence and thus may increase bleeding. Safety measures are instituted to prevent injury, and the patient and family are instructed in these measures. The patient is assessed for development of hemarthrosis, and appropriate care is provided, which includes elevating the affected part, immobilizing the joint in a slightly flexed position, and applying ice intermittently. Replacement of the deficient factor will be needed pre- and post-surgery, and possibly even for dental extractions or other dental care, although DDAVP may be used for dental concerns. The patient is monitored for adverse reactions to blood products, such as flushing, headache, tingling, fever, chills, urticaria, and anaphylaxis. Movement of the injured part is restricted, and exercise and weight bearing are prohibited for 48 hours until bleeding has stopped and swelling has subsided. Gentle passive range-of-motion exercises are then provided, with gradual progression to active-assisted and then active exercise. Intracranial, muscle, subcutaneous, renal, and cardiac bleeding are monitored and managed according to protocols or as prescribed by the hematologist. Fluid balance is monitored throughout emergencies, and adequate fluid replacement is instituted as needed.

Both the patient and family are encouraged to verbalize their fears and concerns, and accurate information, realistic reassurance, and emotional support are provided. Health care providers remain with the anxious or fearful patient or family. Gentle, careful, but thorough oral care is provided with a soft toothbrush or sponge-stick (toothette) to prevent inflamed and bleeding gums, and the patient is instructed in this method. Regular dental examinations are recommended. Regular isometric exercise is encouraged to strengthen muscles, which in turn protects joints by reducing the incidence of hemarthrosis. Use of safety measures to protect the patient from injury is encouraged, while unnecessary restrictions that impair normal development are discouraged. The patient should remain independent and self-sufficient; assistance is provided to both the patient and family to identify safe activities. Techniques are taught for managing bleeding episodes at home. The use of transfusion therapy is explained, and information is provided on all available methods of obtaining such therapy (including how to administer cryoprecipitate at home if appropriate). The seriousness of head injuries and the need for their immediate treatment are explained. Diversional activities and private time with family and friends are provided to help the patient overcome feelings of isolation. The patient's and family's knowledge of the disease and its treatment, as well as the impact on the patient, siblings, and parents' marital relationship, are continually assessed. The patient and family are encouraged to talk with others in similar circumstances through local support groups and services, and they are referred for genetic counseling and for information and support to the National Hemophilia Foundation (800-42-HANDI; www.hemophilia.org).

_h. A_ Hemophilia due to a deficiency of blood coagulation factor VIII C.

_h. B_ Hemophilia due to a deficiency of blood coagulation factor IX (plasma thromboplastin component). This condition can be treated with a lyophilized product that contains concentrated factor IX. SYN: _Christmas disease._

_h. C_ Hemophilia due to a deficiency of blood coagulation factor XI.

hemophiliac (hē″mō-fĭl′ē-ăk) One afflicted with hemophilia.

hemophilic (hē″mō-fĭl′ĭk) **1.** Fond of blood; said of bacteria that grow well in culture media containing hemoglobin. **2.** Pert. to hemophilia or hemophiliacs.

Hemophilus (hē-mŏf′ĭ-lŭs) _Haemophilus._

hemopneumothorax (hē″mō-nū-mō-thō′răks) [″ + ″ + _thorax,_ chest] Hemorrhage and the release of air into the chest, often as a result of trauma, but occasionally occurring spontaneously.

hemopoiesis (hē″mō-poy-ē′sĭs) [″ + _poiesis,_ formation] Hematopoiesis.

hemoprotein (hē″mō-prō′tē-ĭn) Any protein combined with the heme blood pigment.

hemoptysis (hē-mŏp′tĭ-sĭs) [″ + _ptyein,_ to spit] The expectoration of blood that arises from the larynx, trachea, bronchi, or lungs. Massive hemoptysis, which occurs rarely, should be managed by a pulmonary specialist experienced in bronchoscopy. Small amounts of hemoptysis may occur in many illnesses, including acute bronchitis, pneumonia, pulmonary tuberculosis, and cancers of the lung. Management depends on the underlying disorder. A careful history and physical examination, along with chest x-ray examination and laboratory studies, often help identify the underlying cause. SEE: table; _bleeding; hematemesis; hemorrhage; Nursing Diagnoses Appendix._

PATIENT CARE: Vital signs are monitored to determine the patient's stability; special emphasis is placed on evaluations of respiration and hemodynamics. Standard precautions are used when blood and secretions are handled and when the patient is cleansed. Expectorated blood is in-

Comparison of Hemoptysis and Hematemesis

Hemoptysis	Hematemesis
Blood is coughed up.	Blood is vomited.
Blood is frothy, bright red, and alkaline.	Blood is either dark or bright red, usually not frothy, and acid. It may have a coffee-ground appearance.
Blood may be mixed with sputum.	Blood may be mixed with food or bile.
Dyspnea, pleuritic pain, or other chest discomfort is common.	Nausea or abdominal pain is common.
Underlying diagnoses commonly include bronchitis, pneumonia, tuberculosis, nosebleed, lung cancer, pulmonary embolism or infarct, foreign bodies, and, rarely, autoimmune illnesses.	Underlying diagnoses commonly include peptic ulcers, gastritis, esophagitis, duodenitis, esophageal varices, upper GI tumors, vascular malformations, nosebleed, and tears in the esophagus.

spected to assist in determining the site of bleeding. Blood and secretions are saved for the physician's inspection and possible laboratory analysis. A quiet, calm, and reassuring environment is maintained. The patient is placed on bedrest with the head slightly elevated and turned to keep the bleeding side, if known, down. Oral care is provided and fluids are administered as ordered. Excessive coughing is discouraged. Anticoagulants are withheld.

hemorrhage (hem′(ŏ-)rǎj) [*hem-* + *-rrhage*] Blood loss. The term is usually used for episodes of bleeding that last more than a few minutes, compromise organ or tissue perfusion, or threaten life. The most hazardous forms of blood loss result from arterial bleeding, internal bleeding, or bleeding into the cranium. The risk of uncontrolled bleeding is greatest in patients who have coagulation disorders or take anticoagulant drugs. **hemorrhagic** (hem-ŏ-raj′ĭk), *adj.* SEE: table.

SYMPTOMS: Orthostatic dizziness, weakness, fatigue, shortness of breath, and palpitations are common symptoms of hemorrhage. Signs of hemorrhage include tachycardia, hypotension, pallor, and cold moist skin.

TREATMENT: Pressure should be applied directly to any obviously bleeding body part, and the part should be elevated. Cautery may be used to stop bleeding from visible vessels. Ligation of blood vessels, surgical removal of hemorrhaging organs, or the instillation of sclerosants is often effective in managing internal hemorrhage. Procoagulants (such as vitamin K, fresh frozen plasma, cryoprecipitate, desmopressin) may be administered to patients with primary or drug-induced bleeding disorders. Transfusions of red blood cells may be given if bleeding compromises heart or lung function or threatens to do so because of its pace or volume.

For trauma patients with massive bleeding, the experienced nurse or emergency care provider may apply pneumatic splints or antishock garments during patient transportation to the hospital. These devices may prevent hemorrhagic shock.

⚠ Standard precautions should be used for all procedures involving contact with blood or wounds.

antepartum h. Excessive blood loss during the prenatal period, most commonly associated with spontaneous or induced abortion, ruptured ectopic pregnancy, placenta previa, or abruptio placentae.

arterial h. A hemorrhage from an artery. In arterial bleeding, which is bright red, the blood ordinarily flows in waves or spurts; however, the flow may be steady if the torn artery is deep or buried.

FIRST AID: Almost all arterial bleeding can be controlled with direct pressure to the wound. If it cannot be controlled with applied pressure, the responsible artery may need to be surgically ligated. SEE: *arterial* **bleeding** for table; *pressure point*.

capillary h. Bleeding from minute blood vessels, present in all bleeding.

Common Sites of Bleeding

Location	Descriptive Term
Biliary tract	Hemobilia
Fallopian tubes	Hemosalpinx
Lower GI tract	Hematochezia; melena
Upper GI tract	Hematemesis
Joints	Hemarthosis
Lungs/Bronchi (coughed up)	Hemoptysis
Nasal passages	Epistaxis
Skin	Ecchymosis
Urinary tract	Hematuria

When large vessels are not injured, capillary bleeding may be controlled by simple elevation and pressure with a sterile dry compress.

   carotid artery h. Bleeding from the carotid artery. This type of hemorrhage can be rapidly fatal because it may be profuse and may deprive the brain of oxygen.

   FIRST AID: The wound should be compressed with the thumbs placed transversely across the neck, both above and below the wound, and the fingers directed around the back of the neck to aid in compression. Urgent surgical consultation is required.

   cerebral h. Bleeding into the brain, a common cause of stroke. SEE: *stroke*.

   ETIOLOGY: It usually results from rupture of aneurysm, extremely high blood pressure, brain trauma, or brain tumors.

   SYMPTOMS: Most people with intracerebral bleeding experience headache. This type of hemorrhage may cause symptoms of stroke (such as unconsciousness, apnea, vomiting, hemiplegia) and death. There may be speech disturbance, incontinence of the bladder and rectum, or other findings, depending on the area of brain damage.

   TREATMENT: Supportive therapy is needed to maintain airway and oxygenation. Neurosurgical consultation should be promptly obtained. Hydration and fluid and electrolyte balance should be maintained. Rehabilitation may include physical therapy, speech therapy, and counseling.

   choroidal h. Bleeding into the choroid of the eye, a complication of systemic anticoagulation, hypertension, macular degeneration, some ocular surgeries, and ocular metastases of malignant tumors. Visual impairment resulting from the bleeding is usually significant.

   eight-ball h. A hyphema in which the anterior chamber of the eye fills completely with blood.

   fetomaternal h. ABBR: FMH. The transfer of fetal blood cells through the placenta into the maternal circulation, usually at the time of delivery. Less than 1 ml is considered normal, but greater than 30 ml, as in trauma or placental abruption, is a major cause of fetal morbidity and death. The condition often occurs during pregnancy and may result in the immunization of the mother against Rh antigens in the fetus, esp. when the mother is Rh-negative and the child is Rh-positive. SEE: *Kleihauer-Betke test*.

   fibrinolytic h. A hemorrhage due to a defect in the fibrin component in blood coagulation.

   gastrointestinal h. Gastrointestinal **bleeding**.

   internal h. Occult **bleeding**.

   intracranial h. ABBR: ICH. Bleeding into the cranium. It is a devastating form of stroke with a high rate of mortality.

   PATIENT CARE: Patients with ICH should be treated emergently with infusions of recombinant factor VIIa in an intensive care unit, where minute-to-minute monitoring of intracranial pressures, blood glucose levels, neurological status, and hemodynamics can be carried out. Patients should initially be kept at bedrest with the head of the bed elevated. Fever should be suppressed and seizures prevented with the administration of anticonvulsant drugs. As the patient stabilizes, rehabilitation supervised by occupational therapists, physical therapists, and speech therapists should be initiated.

   h. of the knee Bleeding from the knee.

   TREATMENT: If the bleeding is at the knee or below, a pad should be applied with pressure. If the bleeding is behind the knee, a pad should be applied at the site and the leg bandaged firmly. The bandage should be loosened at 12-min to 15-min intervals to prevent arterial obstruction.

   lung h. Hemorrhage from the lung, with bright red and frothy blood, frequently coughed up.

   nasal h. Epistaxis.

   petechial h. Hemorrhage in the form of small rounded spots or petechiae occurring in the skin or mucous membranes.

   postmenopausal h. Bleeding from the uterus after menopause.

   postpartum h. ABBR: PPH. Hemorrhage that occurs after childbirth. It is a major cause of maternal morbidity and mortality in childbirth. *Early postpartum hemorrhage* is defined as a blood loss of more than 500 ml of blood during the first 24 hr after delivery. The most common cause is loss of uterine tone caused by overdistention. Other causes include prolonged or precipitate labor; uterine overstimulation; trauma, rupture, or inversion; lacerations of the lower genital tract; or blood coagulation disorders. *Late postpartum hemorrhage* occurs after the first 24 hr have passed. It usually is caused by retained placental fragments.

   PATIENT CARE: Many instances of PPH can be prevented with the administration of oxytocin, misoprostol, or other uterotonic medications. The woman's prenatal, labor, and delivery records are reviewed. The presence of risk factors is noted, and the woman's pulse, blood pressure, fundal and bladder status, and vaginal discharge are assessed every 15 min. If the fundus is boggy, it is massaged to stimulate uterine contractions, and then the status of the woman's bladder is assessed. If the bladder is distended, the patient is encouraged to void and then postvoiding fundal status is assessed; if the fundus remains firm after massage, the fundus and vaginal flow are reassessed in 5 min. SEE: *fundal massage*.

If bleeding does not respond to the above measures or if the fundus remains firm and the patient exhibits bright red vaginal discharge, retained placental fragments or cervical or vaginal laceration should be suspected; the practitioner who delivered the baby should be notified. Continued massage at this point is contraindicated; the physician or nurse midwife may order uterotonic agents to stimulate uterine contractions. Vital signs should be closely monitored. Common findings in hemorrhage include an increase in pulse rate, often associated with a drop in blood pressure. Pharmacological agents such as methylergonovine or prostaglandin F2 analogs may be administered intramuscularly or intravenously. If blood loss has been extensive, intravenous infusions or blood transfusion may be needed to combat hypovolemic shock. If the patient exhibits signs of a clotting defect, prompt life-saving treatment is imperative. SEE: *disseminated intravascular coagulation*.

The patient is prepared for and the primary caregiver is assisted with examination of the uterine cavity, removal of any placental fragments, or repair of any lacerations. To reduce the patient's anxiety, all procedures are explained, support and comfort are provided, and the mother is assured that her newborn is receiving good care.

primary h. A hemorrhage immediately following any trauma.

retroperitoneal h. Bleeding into the retroperitoneal space.

secondary h. **1.** A hemorrhage occurring some time after primary hemorrhage, usually caused by sepsis and septic ulceration into a blood vessel. It may occur after 24 hr or when a ligature separates, usually between the 7th and 10th days. **2.** Bleeding from the mother's uterus or the infant's umbilicus, resulting from a septic infection.

splinter h. A small linear hemorrhage under the fingernails or toenails. It may be due to subacute bacterial endocarditis.

subarachnoid h. ABBR: SAH. Bleeding into the subarachnoid space of the brain, usually because of the rupture of an intracranial aneurysm or arteriovenous malformation, and occasionally because of hypertensive vascular disease. The bleeding causes intense headache pain, often with nausea and vomiting, loss of consciousness,

paralysis, and, in some cases, coma, decerebrate posturing, and brain death. About 30,000 Americans are affected annually. Prompt diagnosis is facilitated by neuroimaging or lumbar puncture. A neurosurgical consultation should be obtained.

subconjunctival h. Rupture of the superficial capillaries with associated hemorrhage into the subconjunctival space.

ETIOLOGY: Subconjunctival hemorrhage can result from blunt trauma to the eye or from increased intracranial or intraocular pressure.

SYMPTOMS: Patients have visible bleeding between the sclera and the conjunctiva.

TREATMENT: A subconjunctival hemorrhage normally resolves within 1 to 7 days.

thigh h. Bleeding at the upper part of the thigh, near the groin.

TREATMENT: A pad or gauze should be inserted into the wound and pressure applied. Failure of the bleeding to stop requires surgical consultation.

typhoid h. Gastrointestinal (GI) bleeding due to ulceration of the upper GI tract, typically during the second or third week of untreated typhoid.

uterine h. Hemorrhage into the cavity of the uterus. The three types of pathologic uterine hemorrhage are essential uterine hemorrhage (metropathia haemorrhagica), which occurs with pelvic, uterine, or cervical diseases; intrapartum hemorrhage, which occurs during labor; and postpartum hemorrhage, which occurs after the third stage of labor. The last may be caused by rupture, lacerations, relaxation of the uterus, hematoma, or retained products of conception, including the placenta or membrane fragments.

ETIOLOGY: Common causes are trauma; congenital abnormalities; pathologic processes (such as tumors; infections, esp. of the alimentary, respiratory, and genitourinary tracts); and generalized vascular disorders such as purpuras and coagulation defects. Hemorrhage may also result from premature separation of the placenta, particularly with extravasation into the uterine musculature, and from retained products of conception after abortion or delivery. SEE: *abruptio placentae; Couvelaire uterus*.

TREATMENT: An umbrella pack will apply pressure to the uterine arterial supply. When ultrasonography reveals that retained placental fragments are the source of hemorrhage, they are usually removed by suction or surgical curettage. If the uterus is flaccid, it can usually be stimulated to contract by administering intravenous oxytocin. The patient may need transfusion and, in some cases, surgery to prevent fatal hemorrhage.

variceal h. SEE: *esophageal varix.*

venous h. Hemorrhage from a vein, characterized by steady, profuse bleeding of rather dark blood.

PATIENT CARE: The patient should be reassured while direct pressure to the wound is applied and the affected body part is elevated. If bleeding does not stop after 15 min of direct pressure, evaluation by a health care provider is advisable. Vital signs should be monitored whenever bleeding does not stop with direct pressure, and IV fluids should be initiated as necessary to prevent hypovolemic shock.

vicarious h. Hemorrhage from one part as a result of suppression of bleeding in another part. SEE: *vicarious menstruation.*

hemorrhagic disease of the newborn
Hemorrhaging in the newborn caused by an inadequate supply of prothrombin received from the mother or a delay in the establishment of the bacterial intestinal flora that produces vitamin K. Parenteral vitamin K given to the infant within 6 hr of birth prevents this condition.

hemorrhagic fever with renal syndrome
An arthropod-borne viral disease caused by the *Hantavirus* or related viruses. SEE: *hantavirus pulmonary syndrome.*

hemorrhoid (hĕm′ō-royd) [Gr. *haimorrhois*] Veins of the internal or external hemorrhoidal plexuses and the immediately surrounding tissues. Hemorrhoids are most often referred to only when diseased (i.e., enlarged, painful, bleeding). Other anorectal conditions (e.g., anal fissure, condylomata, anal cancers) may produce similar symptoms and must be distinguished from hemorrhoids by appropriate examination. SYN: *piles.* SEE: illus.; *Nursing Diagnoses Appendix.*

TREATMENT: Therapy depends on the severity of the symptoms, not the extent of the hemorrhoids. In many instances, the only therapy required is improvement in anal care, adherence to appropriate fluid intake and diet if necessary, and administration of stool softeners to prevent straining to have a bowel movement. Measures to reduce local pain and congestion include the temporary use of local anesthetic agents, lubrication, cold compresses, warm sitz baths, and thermal packs. The necessity of surgery or other modalities of direct intervention (e.g., latex band ligation, sclerotherapy, cryosurgery, infrared photocoagulation, laser surgery) need not be applied until the acute process resolves except in cases of significant bleeding, intractable pain, recurrent episodes, and various individ-

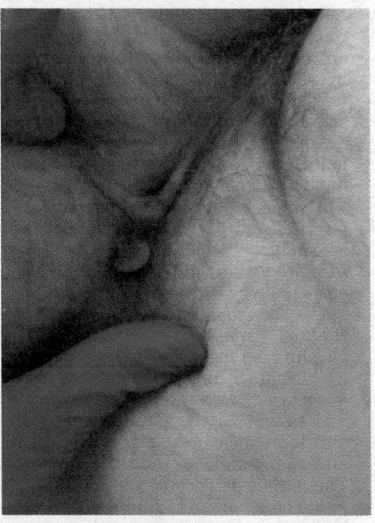

HEMORRHOID

ualized considerations. SEE: *hemorrhoidectomy.*

external h. Hemorrhoid located at or distal to the pectinate line (dentate margin), covered by anodermal epithelium or skin and extremely sensitive to most stimuli. SEE: *hemorrhoid* for illus.

internal h. Hemorrhoid located proximal to the pectinate line, covered by mucous membrane and relatively insensitive to direct noxious stimuli. SEE: *hemorrhoid* for illus.

mixed (or combined) h. Hemorrhoid that incorporates both internal and external components.

prolapsed h. The protrusion of an internal hemorrhoid through the anus.

strangulated h. A prolapsed hemorrhoid that is trapped by the anal sphincter, thus compromising blood flow to the vein in the hemorrhoid.

hemorrhoidal (hĕm-ō-roy′dăl) **1.** Relating to hemorrhoids. **2.** Pert. to anal structures, e.g., inferior hemorrhoidal nerve, hemorrhoidal venous plexuses, and inferior hemorrhoidal arteries, etc.

hemorrhoidectomy (hĕm″ō-royd-ĕk′tō-mē) [Gr. *haimorrhois,* vein liable to bleed, + *ektome,* excision] The excision or destruction of hemorrhoids by one of several techniques, including traditional surgery, cryosurgery, laser surgery, infrared photocoagulation, latex band ligation, and sclerotherapy. The latter three modalities are used exclusively for internal hemorrhoids. SEE: *Nursing Diagnoses Appendix.*

PATIENT CARE: Preparation for diagnostic testing is explained. The patient is taught about the use of stool softeners and is encouraged to increase fluid and fiber intake (unless otherwise restricted) and to exercise to prevent constipation. The patient should not sit on the toilet for longer than necessary in order to avoid venous congestion. The need for good anal hygiene is emphasized, and the patient is cautioned against vigorous wiping and the use of harsh soaps and toilet tissues containing dyes or perfumes.

If hemorrhoidectomy is indicated, physical and psychological preparation is conducted; details of postoperative care are explained to the patient. Postoperatively, vital signs and fluid balance are monitored, dressings are checked, and excessive drainage or bleeding is reported. The patient's ability to void within the designated period is ensured. Perianal care is provided and taught to the patient; analgesics and local measures (sitz baths) to reduce pain and swelling are provided. The patient is encouraged to assume a prone position for 15 minutes every few hours to reduce edema at the surgical site. When oral intake is tolerated, a bulk-forming or stool-softening laxative is administered as prescribed to ease defecation. Before discharge the patient is instructed to report increased rectal bleeding, purulent drainage, fever, constipation, or rectal spasm. The patient also is cautioned against overuse of laxatives.

hemosiderin (hē″mō-sĭd′ĕr-ĭn) [″ + *sideros,* iron] An iron-containing pigment derived from hemoglobin from disintegration of red blood cells. It is one form in which iron is stored until it is needed for making hemoglobin.

hemosiderosis (hē″mō-sĭd-ĕr-ō′sĭs) [″ + ″ + *osis,* condition] A condition characterized by the deposition, esp. in the liver and spleen, of hemosiderin. It occurs in diseases associated with excess iron accumulation in the body (e.g., the iron storage diseases) and hemolytic anemias and after multiple transfusions. SEE: *hemochromatosis.*

hemospermia (hē″mō-spĕr′mē-ă) [″ + *sperma,* seed] Hematospermia.

hemostasis (hē″mŏ′stā′sĭs) [*hemo-* + *stasis*] **1.** The cessation of bleeding. **2.** Stagnation of blood.

hemostat (hē′mō-stăt) [″ + *statikos,* standing] **1.** A device or medicine that arrests the flow of blood. **2.** A compressor for controlling hemorrhage of a bleeding vessel.

hemostatic (hē″mō-stat′ĭk) **1.** Pert. to or caused by hemostasis. **2.** Arresting hemorrhage. **3.** Any drug, medicine, surgical device, or blood component that serves to stop bleeding. Such agents include vasopressin, gamma-aminobutyric acid, vitamin K, whole blood, fibrin sealant, or epinephrine applied locally.

hemostyptic (hē-mō-stĭp′tĭk) [″ + *styp-*

tikos, astringent] An astringent that stops bleeding; a chemical hemostatic.

hemosuccus pancreaticus (hē″mō-sŭk′ŭs pang″krē-at′ĭ-kŭs, pan″) Bleeding from the pancreatic duct. A rare cause of upper gastrointestinal bleeding most often seen in patients with necrotic pancreatitis, it occurs when the inflamed pancreatic mass erodes into a local artery, such as the splenic artery.

hemotherapy (hē″mŏ-ther′ă-pē) [*hem-* + *therapy*] The transfusion of blood cells, serum, plasma, or their components.

hemothorax (hē″mŏ-thōr′aks″) [*hem-* + *thorax*] Blood or bloody fluid in the pleural cavity caused by rupture of blood vessels resulting from inflammation of the lungs in pneumonia or pulmonary tuberculosis, lung cancer, or trauma. SEE: *Nursing Diagnoses Appendix.*

hemotoxin (hē″mō-tŏks′ĭn) [″ + *toxikon,* poison] Hemolysin.

hemotrophic (hē-mŏ-trŏf′ik) [*hemo-* + *trophic*] Pert. to nutrients carried in the blood.

hemotropic (hē-mō-trŏp′ĭk) [″ + *tropos,* turning] Attracted to or having an affinity for blood or blood cells.

hemotympanum (hē″mō-tĭm′pă-nŭm) [″ + *tympanon,* drum] Blood in the middle ear, a finding sometimes identified in serious traumatic brain injury. SYN: *hematotympanum.*

hemovigilance (hē″mō-vij′ĭ-lăns) [*hemo-* + *vigilance*] Monitoring of possible adverse effects associated with blood transfusion therapy. It is directed at improving blood transfusion safety.

Henderson, Virginia (hĕn′dĕr-sŏn) A U.S. nursing educator, 1897–1996, who developed a definition of nursing that was adopted by the International Council of Nurses. SEE: *Nursing Theory Appendix.*

H. definition of nursing A definition, adopted by the International Council of Nurses, stating that the unique function of the nurse is to help sick or well individuals to perform activities that contribute to health, recovery, or a peaceful death. SEE: *Nursing Theory Appendix.*

Henderson-Hasselbalch equation (hen′dĕr-sŏn-has′ĕl-balk″) [Lawrence Joseph Henderson, U.S. biochemist, 1878–1942; K. A. Hasselbalch, Danish physician, 1874–1962] An equation that describes the dissociation constant of an acid. In fluid and electrolyte balance, this important equation may be expressed in terms of the bicarbonate (HCO_3^-) system as: $pH = 6.095 + \log HCO_3^-/\alpha$ ($PaCO_2$), where $\alpha = 0.0307$ mM/L/mm Hg at 37°C. At the normal pH of the blood, 7.4, the ratio of HCO_3^- to α ($PaCO_2$) is 20 to 1.

Henle, Friedrich G. J. (hen′lē) Friedrich

Gustav Jacob, Ger. anatomist, 1809–1885.

H. layer The outer layer of cells of the inner root sheath of the hair follicle.

H. loop The U-shaped portion of a renal tubule lying between the proximal and distal convoluted portions. It consists of a thin descending limb and a thicker ascending limb.

H. tubules The portion of the nephron following the proximal tubule. SEE: *nephron*.

Henoch-Schönlein disease Idiopathic thrombocytopenic purpura.

Henoch-Schönlein purpura (hĕn′ōk-shän′lĭn) [Eduard H. Henoch, Ger. pediatrician, 1820–1910; Johann Lukas Schönlein, Ger. physician, 1793–1864] A form of small vessel vasculitis of unknown cause that affects children, esp. between the ages of 3 and 5, more often than adults. It is marked by a purpuric rash on the buttocks and legs, and, in some patients, abdominal pain or gastrointestinal bleeding, polyarticular joint disease, and renal involvement (e.g., glomerulonephritis). The illness usually lasts about 2 weeks before resolving spontaneously. In some instances (more commonly in adults than in children) renal failure can complicate the illness. SYN: *anaphylactoid **purpura***. SEE: illus.

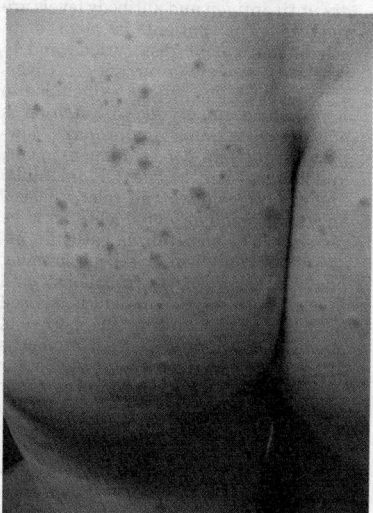

HENOCH-SCHÖNLEIN PURPURA
Characteristic rash on the buttocks

TREATMENT: Joint symptoms respond to rest and administration of nonsteroidal anti-inflammatory drugs. Corticosteroid drugs, such as prednisone, are used to treat patients with severe gastrointestinal or renal involvement.

Hemodialysis is used to support patients who develop chronic renal failure.

henry (hĕn′rē) [Joseph Henry, U.S. physicist, 1797–1878] A unit designating electrical inductance.

Henry law (hen′rē) [William Henry, Brit. chemist, 1774–1836] The weight of a gas dissolved by a given volume of liquid at a constant temperature is directly proportional to the pressure.

Hensen, Christian Andreas Victor (hen′sĕn) Ger. zoologist and physiologist, 1835–1924.

H. body A modified Golgi net found in the hair cells of the organ of Corti.

H. cell Any of the tall columnar cells that form the outer border cells of the organ of Corti of the cochlea.

H. node A mass of rapidly proliferating cells at the anterior end of the primitive streak of the embryo.

H. stripe A dark band on the undersurface of the tectorial membrane of the inner ear.

hepacivirus (hĕ-pă-sē′ĭ-vī″rŭs) A genus of flaviviruses that includes the hepatitis C virus.

hepadnavirus Hepatitis DNA virus. The hepatitis DNA virus that infects humans is hepatitis B.

HEPA filter *high efficiency particulate air filter.*

hepar (hē′par″) [Gr. *hēpar*, stem *hēpat-*, liver] The liver.

heparan sulfate (hep′ă-răn) ABBR: HS. A macromolecule of the proteoglycan family found on cell walls and in basement membranes. It is instrumental in embryonic organ development, blood vessel development, and cell adhesion. It also regulates blood coagulation and growth factor–cytokine action.

heparin (hep′ă-rĭn) [*hepar* + *-in*] A parenteral anticoagulant drug with a faster onset than warfarin or its derivatives. It is composed of polysaccharides that inhibit coagulation by forming an antithrombin that prevents conversion of prothrombin to thrombin and by preventing liberation of thromboplastin from platelets. Because heparin is poorly absorbed from the gastrointestinal tract, it is usually administered intravenously or subcutaneously as a sodium or calcium salt.

USES: Heparin is used as an anticoagulant to prevent and treat thrombosis and embolism. It is an important agent in the management of acute coronary syndromes (e.g., unstable angina pectoris or acute myocardial infarction). Because heparin compounds are too large to cross the placental barrier, they are the preferred anticoagulants in pregnant women. The antagonist for an overdose is protamine sulfate. The most common side effect of heparin is abnormal bleeding.

h. lock A device attached to an intravenous catheter to prevent it from clotting. It is used for intermittent administration of fluids or medication. SEE: *heparin lock flush solution; venous access device.*

low molecular weight h. ABBR: LMWH. The most bioavailable fraction of heparin. It has a more precise anticoagulant effect than unfractionated heparins and is used to prevent and treat deep venous thrombosis, pulmonary embolism, and acute coronary syndromes.

⚠️ It should be used selectively, if at all, in patients with reduced kidney function.

h. sulfate A sulfurated mucopolysaccharide that accumulates in the connective tissue in abnormal amounts in some mucopolysaccharidoses. SEE: *mucopolysaccharidosis.*

heparinize (hĕp′ă-rĭ-nīz″) To inhibit blood coagulation with heparin.

heparinoid (hĕp′ă-rĭ-noyd″) A substance that prevents or treats blood clots. Heparinoids have a lower risk for bleeding and thrombocytopenia than heparin.

hepatectomy (hĕp″ă-tĕk′tō-mē) [″ + *ektome,* excision] Excision of part or all of the liver.

hepatic (hĕ-păt′ĭk) [Gr. *hepatikos*] Pert. to the liver.

h. vein The vein that takes blood from the liver to the inferior vena cava.

hepaticoduodenostomy (hĕ-păt″ĭ-kō-dū″ō-dĕ-nŏs′tō-mē) [″ + L. *duodeni,* duodenum, + Gr. *stoma,* mouth] The establishment of an opening from the hepatic bile duct into the duodenum.

hepaticoenterostomy (hĕ-păt″ĭ-kō-ĕn-tĕr-ŏs′tō-mē) [″ + *enteron,* intestine, + *stoma,* mouth] An operation to create an artificial opening between the hepatic duct and intestine.

hepaticojejunostomy (hĕ-păt′ĭ-kō-jē″jū-nŏs′tō-mē) [″ + L. *jejunum,* empty, + Gr. *stoma,* mouth] The surgical joining of the hepatic duct and the jejunum. SEE: *hepaticoenterostomy.*

hepaticotomy (hĕ-păt″ĭ-kŏt′ō-mē) [″ + *tome,* incision] An incision into the hepatic duct.

hepatic venous pressure gradient SEE: under *gradient.*

hepatitis (hep″ă-tīt′ĭs) [*hepato-* + *-itis*] Inflammation of the liver, usually caused by exposure to an infectious agent (such as a hepatitis virus), a toxin (such as alcohol), or a drug (such as acetaminophen). The illness may be mild or life-threatening, chronic or acute. Chronic cases may be detected only by the discovery of elevated liver enzymes in the blood. Acute cases are marked by jaundice, hepatic enlargement, and occasional bleeding, altered mental status, and multiple organ system failure. Usually, a history of any type of hepatitis (esp. after age 10), is a contraindication to being a blood donor.

PATHOLOGY: Damage to liver cells is caused by direct injury from the causative agent or indirectly as a result of inflammatory or autoimmune responses. During acute inflammation, the swollen hepatocytes are less able to detoxify drugs; to produce clotting factors, cholesterol, plasma proteins, bile, and glycogen; to store fat-soluble vitamins; or to perform other functions. All of the hepatitis viruses may cause fulminant hepatitis, but hepatitis B and D are the most common causes. Drug overdoses, ingestion of toxins, and shock are also responsible for rapid liver deterioration.

PATIENT CARE: Patients are not generally hospitalized unless they experience significant liver damage or complications; the more severely affected need supportive medical and psychological care. Patients at home should be instructed about the nature and course of the illness, its care and treatment, and signs and symptoms of complications. When hepatitis is food-borne, thorough washing of the hands, food handling, and cleaning of dishes and silverware are necessary to prevent transmission to household members. The patient should avoid intimate contact with others until antigen and antibody levels are reduced. The patient is advised to schedule frequent rest periods and to rest between major activities. Diversionary activities should be included to help reduce anxiety. Good nutrition is encouraged (small, high-calorie, low-protein, nutrient-dense, frequent meals, and fluids to 4 qt (4 L)/day). Fluid intake and output, and weight, color, consistency, and frequency of stools should be recorded. The hospitalized patient is assessed for complications (hepatic coma, pneumonia, vascular problems, and pressure ulcers). The patient is advised to avoid alcohol during the period of acute illness and for at least 6 months after recovery. Depression may occur because of the patient's concerns about the illness, but the depression may also be linked to changes in body chemistry or adverse drug reactions. Hepatitis is the primary reason for liver transplants, and the concerns of potential need and treatment should be explained to the patient. Emotional support and reassurance should be offered to the patient because there may be considerable interference with the patient's habits and lifestyle. SEE: *Nursing Diagnoses Appendix; Standard Precautions Appendix; hepatitis A; autoimmune hepatitis; hepatitis E; fulminant hepatitis.*

h. A Hepatitis caused by hepatitis A virus (HAV), an RNA virus without an envelope. Because hepatitis A can be contracted through contaminated water or food, young adults and children in institutional settings and travelers in areas with minimal sanitation are at greatest risk for infection; small epidemics have been seen among people eating at restaurants that served contaminated shellfish. The course of the illness is usually mild, although it can be severe; the incubation period is 2 to 6 weeks, the acute stage lasts 2 to 12 weeks, and complete recovery takes weeks to months. The infection affects about 90,000 people every year, about half of whom develop clinically obvious infection. Hepatitis A does not produce a carrier state and does not cause chronic hepatitis. The two antibodies produced in response to hepatitis A antigen serve as markers for infection; one of these, IgG anti-HAV, provides immunity against reinfection. Hepatitis A previously was called *infectious hepatitis*.

TREATMENT: No drugs specifically treat hepatitis A. Immune globulin containing IgG anti-HAV antibodies may be prescribed for family members; it provides passive immunity for 6 to 8 weeks. Preventive education focuses on good personal hygiene, esp. washing of the hands; use of good judgment in choice of food and eating places; and, in some areas of the world, basic sanitation. Hepatitis A vaccine prevents infection either before or immediately after exposure to the virus and is recommended for health care workers, travelers to developing countries, day care workers, people with liver disease, and others at high risk.

⚠️ Hepatitis A is transmitted by fecal-oral contact. To prevent the spread of the disease, those infected should not be involved in food preparation.

---

acute anicteric h. Hepatitis marked by slight fever, gastrointestinal upset, and anorexia but without jaundice.

alcoholic h. Destruction of large numbers of hepatocytes due to excessive ingestion of alcohol. Fever, jaundice, altered mental status, and enlargement of the liver are common findings. It can be treated with abstinence, corticosteroids, pentoxifylline, and supportive therapy.

amebic h. A syndrome marked by a tender, enlarged liver; pain over the liver; fever; and leukocytosis in a patient with amebic colitis. This term is a misnomer because the liver changes are not due to an infestation of that organ with amebae but are a part of the non-specific reaction to the infection in the intestinal tract. Nevertheless, a liver abscess will occasionally develop, and the walls of the abscess will contain amebae.

TREATMENT: Metronidazole plus iodoquinol, or chloroquine phosphate plus either emetine or dehydroemetine are used to treat amebic hepatitis. These latter two drugs are toxic and should be given only if their course can be carefully observed with a cardiac monitor. The drugs should not be given to a patient who has cardiac disease or is pregnant. Needle aspiration of the abscess may be needed.

autoimmune h. Persistent hepatic inflammation and necrosis, in the setting of hypergammaglobulinemia and autoantibodies and in the absence of other common causes of liver injury.

h. B Injury to liver cells caused by hepatitis B virus (HBV), a double-stranded DNA virus. It may appear as an asymptomatic, acute, chronic, or fulminant infection. Acute infection often is marked by jaundice, nausea and vomiting, joint pains, rashes, and marked elevations in serum liver function tests. Chronic infection typically is asymptomatic and may be detected only by blood tests until it causes late complications (cirrhosis, portal hypertension, or hepatocellular carcinoma). Fulminant hepatitis B infection occurs when the patient suffers hepatic encephalopathy within 8 weeks of the onset of the disease.

The virus is transmitted by exposure to the blood or body fluids of an infected person. The incubation period is approximately 2 to 6 months. Acute infection usually resolves in less than 6 months. When HBV surface antigen does not clear from the blood within 6 months, chronic hepatitis is said to have developed. Each year in the U.S., about 300,000 people are infected with HBV. Worldwide, chronic hepatitis affects about 300 million people.

Those at greatest risk for infection include intravenous drug abusers, people with multiple sex partners, men who have sex with men, infants born of HBV-infected mothers, and health care workers. Blood banks now routinely screen for HBV antigens, which has greatly reduced the transmission of infection by transfusion.

⚠️ People who have not been vaccinated against HBV and receive a needlestick or have mucous membrane contact with blood or other body secretions should contact their occupational health department. Hepatitis B virus immune globulin (HBIg) can be given to provide temporary protection.

ANTIGENS AND ANTIBODIES: The primary antigenic markers used to diagnose hepatitis B infection include the following: 1. hepatitis B surface antigen (HBsAg), the first marker to appear in the blood. It is sometimes detected before serum levels of hepatic enzymes rise; 2. hepatitis Be antigen (HBeAg) and hepatitis B DNA, markers of active viral replication and high infectivity; and 3. Hepatitis B core antibodies (antibodies against the core antigen of hepatitis B), which indicate infection of a patient with HBV. IgM antibodies against the core antigen (IgM anti-HBc) are present early in the course of infection and may sometimes be the only detectable evidence of an acute infection. IgG antibodies against the core antigen (anti-HBc) are present in any patient infected with the virus, either acutely or at some time in the past.

Protective IgG antibodies to the HB surface antigen (HBsAB), which develop late in the disease, persist for life and protect against reinfection. As hepatitis B surface antibody levels rise, HBsAg levels fall, indicating resolution of acute infection. Antibodies against hepatitis B core antigen and hepatitis Be antigen are not protective. Approx. 5% to 10% of patients develop chronic infection.

PREVENTION: Hepatitis B vaccine, which contains the HB surface antigen, provides active immunity and is recommended for those at increased risk (children, health care workers, hemodialysis patients, intravenous drug abusers). All pregnant women should be screened for infection. Hepatitis B immune globulin, which contains antibodies against hepatitis HBV, provides passive immunity to those who have not been vaccinated and are exposed to the virus.

TREATMENT: No drug therapy is available that controls acute HBV infection, and treatment for this phase of the illness is supportive. Interferon-alfa has been effective in some patients with chronic infection. Antiviral drugs such as adefovir, entecavir, and lamivudine are used to treat chronic hepatitis B infections.

h. C A chronic blood-borne infection believed to affect roughly 3,200,000 people in the U.S. Hepatitis C (formerly known as non-A, non-B hepatitis) is caused by a single-stranded RNA virus transmitted from person to person by exposure to blood or body fluids. In the past it was the most common form of hepatitis transmitted by transfusions of blood or blood products and by organ transplantation.

About 30,000 to 40,000 new cases occur each year in the U.S., most of which result from needle sharing during intravenous drug abuse. A smaller number of infections are acquired as a result of ex-

posure to tainted blood at work, e.g., in health care. About 6% of cases are the result of the transmission of the virus from mother to child during childbirth. Tattooing, body piercing, and cocaine snorting are associated with some cases. Sexual transmission of the virus seems rare. Long-term infection develops in 55% to 85% of those infected, and 5% to 20% develop cirrhosis over 20 to 30 years. Chronic hepatitis C infection has become the preeminent cause of cirrhosis, liver cancer, and death from liver failure in the U.S. The incubation period is usually 6 to 12 weeks, although it can be longer, and the acute phase lasts approx. 4 weeks. Signs and symptoms of acute infection are often milder than those of hepatitis A and B.

Infection with hepatitis C virus (HCV) is usually identified (often years after exposure) when an asymptomatic person is found to have repeatedly elevated liver enzymes on routine blood tests. Antibodies to HCV or HCV RNA in the blood confirm the infection. Antibody production is stimulated by HCV RNA, but antibodies against HCV do not destroy the virus or provide immunity.

PATIENT CARE: Antiviral agents such as pegylated alpha interferon in combination with ribavirin and boceprevir may cure hepatitis C if given for prolonged courses (about 24 to 48 weeks, depending on the viral genotype). Genotype 1, the type most often found in the U.S., responds to treatment about 30–85% of the time. Genotypes 2 and 3 respond to combination therapy more than 60% of the time. The treatment can cause significant side effects, including high fevers, chills, malaise, muscle aches, and other flulike symptoms. Prevention of hepatitis C in health care professionals stresses using safely engineered sharps, providing safe sharps disposal, limiting contact with blood and body fluids, and properly sterilizing instruments. Public health teaching regarding prevention for the general public includes use of properly sterilized instruments for body piercing, single-use needles for tattooing, and avoiding needle sharing and taking advantage of needle-replacement programs (for intravenous drug users). Health care providers can provide invaluable education to affected patients by giving them written and verbal information on high-risk behavior, including the need to avoid needle sharing by users of intravenous drugs, having unprotected sex, or drinking alcohol. Regular consumption of alcohol increases the risk of liver cancer dramatically for a person with HCV.

Other recommendations for people infected with hepatitis C are summarized in the following list: 1. do not donate blood, blood products, tissue, or semen; 2. avoid sharing cosmetic items or personal grooming items that may be contaminated by blood, e.g., toothbrushes or razors; 3. do not use over-the-counter, herbal, or prescription medications unless they have been approved by a knowledgeable health care provider; and 4. get vaccinations for hepatitis A and B to avoid additional viral insults to the liver.

Community support groups and Internet-based resources may help those infected to learn more about disease management, e.g., www.liverfoundation.org. Regular professional care may help optimize health and well-being.

chronic h. Hepatic inflammatory and necrotic changes that continue for more than 6 months. The most common causes are hepatitis B, C, and D viruses. Chronic liver inflammation may also result from abuse of alcohol or other drugs, exposure to toxic chemicals, fatty infiltration of the liver, or autoimmune processes. Patients may be asymptomatic or present with only elevated serum transaminase levels, fatigue, anorexia, malaise, or mild jaundice. In other patients, the disease actively progresses, eventually leading to cirrhosis and death. Depending on the underlying cause, corticosteroids, interferons, or antiviral agents such as ribavirin may be used to manage chronic hepatitis. In alcoholic patients, abstinence from alcohol may allow the liver to heal.

h. D A form of hepatitis caused by the hepatitis delta virus (HDV). It is considered a defective virus because it can produce infection only when hepatitis B virus (HBV) is present and therefore can be prevented through hepatitis B vaccination. It is rare in the U.S. In healthy people, coinfection with HDV and HBV usually causes acute disease and recovery with immunity. In patients with chronic hepatitis B, it may produce severe acute disease or, more commonly, chronic progressive disease that may lead to cirrhosis. Mortality is approx. 10%. Hepatitis D antigens (HDV RNA) are found in the blood and liver and stimulate production of an antibody that is present only briefly during early acute infection. HDV is also sometimes referred to as delta hepatitis. SEE: *hepatitis B.*

PREVENTION: Because hepatitis D only occurs in people already infected with hepatitis B, vaccination against hepatitis B helps prevent the spread of this virus.

h. E A form of hepatitis similar to hepatitis A, occurring primarily in regions with contaminated water supplies or in travelers returning from abroad. It is caused by an RNA virus that produces acute infection only.

fulminant h. Acute liver **failure.**

hypoxic h. Ischemic **h.**

infectious h. A term formerly used for hepatitis A virus infection.

ischemic h. Acute, severe liver injury that results from an episode of hypotension, typically in someone with underlying heart or lung disease. This type of hepatitis may result in bleeding, encephalopathy, coma, or death. SYN: *hypoxic h.*

serum h. A term formerly used for HBV infection.

toxic h. Inflammation of the liver caused by the ingestion or absorption of toxins or drugs into the body. Included in the great number of agents known to be able to cause this type of hepatitis are common drugs and chemicals (such as halothane, isoniazid, anabolic steroids, carbon tetrachloride, trichlorethylene) used in either the treatment of disease or in the workplace.

hepatitis G virus SEE: under *virus.*

hepatization (hĕp″ă-tĭ-zā′shŭn) The second and third stages in consolidation in lobar pneumonia, in which the lung's surface looks solid, like the liver.

hepato-, hepat- [Gr. *hēpar,* stem *hēpat-,* liver] Prefixes meaning *liver.*

hepatoblastoma (hĕp″ă-tō-blăs-tō′mă) [″ + ″] A rare, aggressive malignant tumor of the liver, typically found in children age 3 or younger. It may consist of epithelial cells, fetal cells, or mesenchymal tissues.

hepatocarcinogen (hĕp″ă-tō-kăr-sin′ŏ-jĕn) Anything that causes cancer of the liver.

hepatocarcinoma (hĕp″ă-tō-kăr″sĭn-ō′mă) [″ + *karkinos,* crab, + *oma,* tumor] Carcinoma of the liver.

hepatocellular (hĕp″ă-tō-sĕl′ū-lăr) Concerning the cells of the liver.

hepatocholangiogastrostomy (hĕp″ă-tō-kō-lăn″jē-ō-găs-trŏs′tō-mē) [″ + ″ + ″ + *gaster,* belly, + *stoma,* mouth] The establishment of drainage of bile ducts into the stomach.

hepatocyte (hĕp′ă-tō-sīt) A parenchymal liver cell.

hepatoenteric (hĕp″ă-tō-ĕn-tĕr′ĭk) [″ + *enteron,* intestine] Relating to the liver and intestines.

hepatogastric (hĕp″ă-tō-găs′trĭk) [Gr. *hepatikos,* liver, + *gaster,* belly] Relating to the liver and stomach.

hepatogenous (hĕp″ă-tŏj′ĕ-nŭs) Originating in the liver.

hepatography (hĕp″ă-tŏg′ră-fē) [″ + *graphein,* to write] Radiography of the liver, usually after injection of a radiographic contrast medium.

hepatojugular (hĕp″ă-tō-jŭg′ū-lăr) Concerning the liver and jugular vein.

hepatolenticular (hĕp″ă-tō-lĕn-tĭk′ū-lăr) [″ + L. *lenticula,* lentil, lens] Relating to the liver and lenticular nucleus of the eye.

hepatolithiasis (hĕp″ă-tō-lĭ-thī′ă-sĭs) [″ + ″ + -iasis, disease condition] A condition characterized by stones in the intrahepatic ducts.

hepatologist (hĕp″ă-tŏl′ō-jĭst) [″ + logos, word, reason] A specialist in diseases of the liver.

hepatology (hĕp″ă-tŏl′ō-jē) [″ + logos, word, reason] The study of the liver.

hepatoma (hĕp″ă-tō′mă) [″ + oma, tumor] Any liver tumor, benign or malignant. The term is usually used to describe a hepatocellular carcinoma.

hepatomegaly (hep″ăt-ō-meg′ă-lē) [hepato- + -megaly] Enlargement of the liver (e.g., in alcoholic hepatitis, passive congestion of the liver, or liver cancer).

hepatopulmonary syndrome (hĕp″ă-tō-pŭl′mō-năr″ē) [″ + L. pulmo, lung] A combination of liver disease, decreased arterial oxygen concentration, and dilatation of the blood vessels of the lung. Clinically the patient may have signs and symptoms of liver disease, including gastrointestinal bleeding, esophageal varices, ascites, palmar erythema, and splenomegaly. Pulmonary signs include clubbing of the fingers, cyanosis, dyspnea, and decreased arterial oxygen concentration while in an upright position (orthodeoxia).

hepatorenal (hĕp″ă-tō-rē′năl) [″ + L. renalis, kidney] Pert. to the liver and kidneys.

hepatorenal syndrome (hep″ăt-ō-pul′mŏner″ē, -pŭl′) ABBR: HRS. Renal failure resulting from abnormal kidney perfusion in patients with cirrhosis and ascites. Patients with HRS are typically critically ill and have a very poor prognosis. Liver transplantation or portosystemic shunts are occasionally effective treatments.

hepatorrhaphy (hĕp-ă-tor′ă-fē) [″ + rhaphe, seam, ridge] The suturing of a wound of the liver.

hepatosplenomegaly (hĕp″ă-tō-splē″nō-mĕg′ă-lē) [″ + ″ + ″] Enlargement of the liver and spleen.

hepatotomy (hĕp″ă-tŏt′ō-mē) [″ + tome, incision] An incision into the liver.

hepatotoxic (hĕp″ă-tō-tŏks′ĭk) Toxic to the liver.

hepatotoxin (hĕp″ă-tō-tŏk′sĭn) A cytotoxin specific for liver cells.

hepcidin (hĕp′sĭd-ĭn) A protein secreted by the liver that acts as a regulatory hormone that controls the amount of iron in the body. Elevated levels of hepcidin in the blood prevent iron from being taken up by red blood cells. Hepcidin levels rise in many chronic illnesses and infections, causing the anemia of chronic disease. Proteins that block the action of hepcidin result, by contrast, in iron overload diseases such as hemochromatosis.

hept-, hepta- [Gr. hepta, seven] Prefixes meaning seven.

heptapeptide (hĕp″tă-pĕp′tīd) [″ + peptein, to digest] A polypeptide containing seven amino acids.

heptose (hĕp′tōs) A sugar containing seven carbon atoms in its molecule.

HER2 erbB-2.

herb (ĕrb) [L. herba, grass] An annual, biennial, or perennial plant with a soft stem containing no wood, esp. an aromatic plant used in medicine or seasoning. The plant usually produces seeds and then dies back at the end of the growing season.

herbal (ĕr′băl) [L. herbalis, pert. to grass or herbs] **1.** Pert. to an herb or herbs. **2.** A book dealing with the medicinal properties of plants. **3.** A botanical substance used for preventive or therapeutic purposes. The substances include leaves, roots, seeds, or extracts. They may be prescribed individually or in combination with dietary supplements or medicinal preparations. Some may be chewed or ingested directly; others are prepared in capsules or pills or are brewed, extracted, and administered as lozenges, ointments, compresses, liniments, or put into baths.

    PATIENT CARE: Patients should be advised to inform their health care providers about all herbal supplements they take. Herbal products can cause health problems in some instances (such as high doses of vitamin E) or when they are combined with over-the-counter drugs or such prescribed drugs as warfarin sodium. Pregnant or breast-feeding women should discuss herbal supplements with their health care providers before taking them because some herbals may harm the fetus or infant. Herbal products should never be taken for a serious medical condition in place of or concurrently with proven therapies without first discussing them with a health care provider or licensed pharmacist.

herbalist (ĕrb′ă-lĭst) A practitioner who has studied the use of herbs to promote healing, wellness, and disease prevention.

herbicide (ĕrb′ĭ-sīd) A chemical that kills plants or inhibits their growth.

herbivorous (hĕr-bĭv′ō-rŭs) [″ + vorare, to eat] Vegetarian.

herbology (ĕr-bŏl′ō-jē) [″ + ″] The study of the uses and effects of herbs.

herd [AS. heord] Any large aggregation of people or animals.

hereditary (hĕ-rĕd′ĭ-tĕr-ē) [L. hereditarius, an heir] Pert. to a genetic characteristic transmitted from parent to offspring. SEE: chromosome; gene.

hereditary thrombophilia Antithrombin-III **deficiency**.

heredity (hĕ-rĕd′ĭ-tē) [L. *hereditas,* heir] The transmission of genetic characteristics from parent to offspring.

heredo- [L. *heres,* stem *hered-,* heir] Prefix meaning *heredity.*

heredodegeneration (hĕr″ĕ-dō-dē-jĕn″ĕr-ā′shŭn) Any genetically inherited disorder marked by progressive decline in neurological structure and function. Some examples include: Leber's disease, Marie's ataxia, and Machado-Joseph disease.

heredofamilial (hĕr″ĕ-dō-fă-mĭl′ē-ăl) Referring to any disease that occurs in families owing to an inherited defect.

heritable (hĕr′ĭ-tă-bl) Able to be inherited.

heritage The genetic and other characteristics transmitted to offspring.

hermaphrodism (hĕr-măf′rō-dĭzm) Hermaphroditism.

hermaphrodite (hĕr-măf′rō-dīt) [Gr. *Hermaphroditos,* mythical son of Hermes and Aphrodite, who was man and woman combined] An individual possessing genital and sexual characteristics of both sexes. The clitoris is usually enlarged, resembling the male penis. SYN: *androgyne.*

hermaphroditism (hĕr″maf′rŏ-dīt″izm) [*hermaphrodite* + *-ism*] A condition in which both ovarian and testicular tissue exist in the same individual, occurring rarely in humans. SYN: *disorder of sex development; hermaphrodism.* SEE: *intersex.*

    bilateral h. A condition in which an ovary and testicle are present on both sides.

    complex h. A form of hermaphroditism in which the person has internal and external organs of both sexes.

    dimidiate h. Lateral **h.**

    false h. Pseudohermaphroditism.

    lateral h. A condition in which a testis is present on one side and an ovary on the other. SYN: *dimidiate h.*

    transverse h. Hermaphroditism characterized by having the outward organs of one sex and the internal organs of the other.

    true h. Hermaphroditism in which the individual possesses functional ovarian and testicular glands. SYN: *ovotesticular disorder of sex development.*

    unilateral h. Hermaphroditism in which an ovary and a testis or an ovotestis is present on one side and either an ovary or a testis is present on the other side.

hermetic (hĕr-mĕt′ĭk) [L. *hermeticus*] Airtight.

hernia (hĕr′nē-ă) [L. *hernia,* rupture] The protrusion of an anatomical structure through the wall that normally contains it. SYN: *rupture* (2). SEE: illus.; *herniotomy.* **hernial, hernioid,** *adj.*
    ETIOLOGY: Hernias may be caused

by congenital defects in the formation of body structures, defects in collagen synthesis and repair, trauma, or surgery. Conditions that increase intra-abdominal pressures, e.g., pregnancy, obesity, weight lifting, straining (the Valsalva maneuver), and abdominal tumors, may also contribute to hernia formation.
    TREATMENT: Surgical or mechanical reduction is the treatment of choice.

    abdominal h. A hernia through the abdominal wall. SEE: illus.

    acquired h. A hernia that develops any time after birth in contrast to one that is present at birth (congenital hernia).

    bladder h. The protrusion of the bladder or part of the bladder through a normal or abnormal orifice. SYN: *cystic* **h.**

    Cloquet h. SEE: under *Cloquet, Jules G.*

    complete h. A hernia in which the sac and its contents have passed through the aperture.

    concealed h. A hernia that is not easily palpated.

    congenital h. A hernia existing from birth.

    crural h. A hernia that protrudes behind the femoral sheath. SYN: *femoral* **h.**

    cystic h. Bladder **h.**

    direct inguinal h. Inguinal **h.**

    diverticular h. The protrusion of an intestinal congenital diverticulum.

    encysted h. A scrotal protrusion that, enveloped in its own sac, passes into the tunica vaginalis.

    epigastric h. A hernia through a defect in the linea alba above the umbilicus.

    fascial h. Protrusion of muscular tissue through its fascial covering.

    femoral h. Crural **h.**

    hiatal h. The protrusion of the stomach into the chest through the esophageal hiatus of the diaphragm. SEE: *Nursing Diagnoses Appendix.*

    incarcerated h. A hernia in which the presenting content cannot be returned to its site of origin, e.g., a hernia in which a segment of intestine cannot be returned to the abdominal cavity. It may produce pain or intestinal obstruction. If left untreated, an incarcerated hernia may cause strangulation of the bowel.

    incisional h. A hernia through a surgical scar.

    incomplete h. A hernia that has not gone completely through the aperture.

    indirect inguinal h. Inguinal **h.**

    inguinal h. The protrusion of a hernial sac containing intraperitoneal contents (e.g., intestine, omentum, or ovary) at the superficial inguinal ring. In an indirect inguinal hernia, the sac protrudes lateral to the inferior epigas-

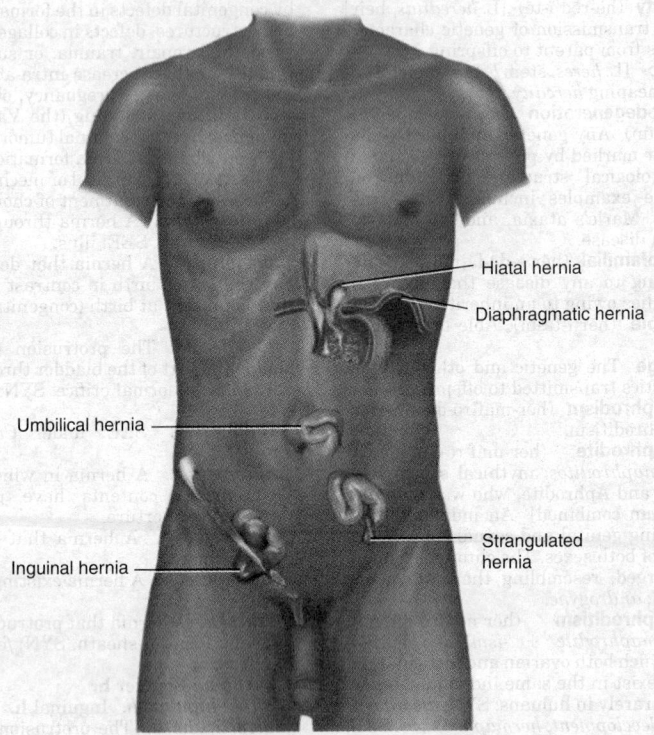

COMMON LOCATIONS OF HERNIAS

tric artery through the internal inguinal ring into the inguinal canal, often descending into the scrotum (in males) or labia (in females). In a direct inguinal hernia, the sac protrudes through the abdominal wall within Hesselbach's triangle, a region bounded by the rectus abdominis muscle, inguinal ligament, and inferior epigastric vessels. The sliding hernia is a kind of indirect inguinal hernia, in which a portion of the wall of the protruding cecum or sigmoid colon is part of the sac, the rest composed of parietal peritoneum. Femoral hernias

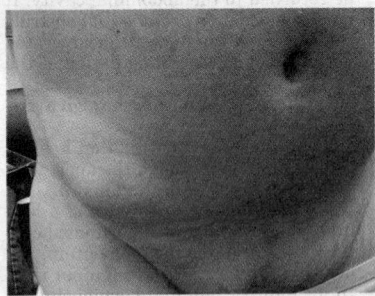

ABDOMINAL WALL HERNIA

occur where the femoral artery passes into the femoral canal. Indirect and direct inguinal hernias and femoral hernias are collectively referred to as groin hernias. Inguinal hernias account for about 80% of all hernias. SYN: *direct inguinal h.; indirect inguinal h.; h. inguinalis; lateral h.; medial h.; oblique h.*

PATIENT CARE: *Preoperative:* The surgical procedure and expected postoperative course are explained to the patient. The patient should understand that the surgery will repair the defect caused by the hernia but that surgical failures can occur. If the patient is undergoing elective surgery, recovery usually is rapid; if no complications occur, the patient probably will return home the same day as surgery and usually can resume normal activity within 4 to 6 weeks. Patients who undergo emergency surgery for a strangulated or incarcerated hernia may remain hospitalized longer commensurate with the degree of intestinal involvement. The patient is prepared for surgery.

Postoperative: Vital signs are monitored. The patient is instructed on the changing of position to avoid undue stress on the wound area. Stool softeners may be administered to prevent straining during defecation, and the patient is instructed in their use. Early ambulation is encouraged, but other physical activities are modified according to the surgeon's instructions. The patient should void prior to discharge and be able to tolerate oral fluids. The patient is taught to check the incision and dressing for drainage, inflammation, and swelling and to monitor his/her temperature for fever, any of which should be reported to the surgeon. Analgesics are administered as prescribed, and the patient is taught about their use and supplied with a prescription for home use. Male patients are advised that scrotal swelling can be reduced by supporting the scrotum on a rolled towel and applying an ice bag. The patient is warned to avoid lifting heavy objects or straining during bowel movements. Drinking plenty of fluids should help the patient prevent constipation and maintain hydration. The patient is advised to make and keep a postoperative surgical visit and to resume normal activity and return to work only as permitted by the surgeon.

h. inguinalis Inguinal **h.**

inguinocrural h. A hernia that is both femoral and inguinal.

internal h. A hernia that occurs within the abdominal cavity. It may be intraperitoneal or retroperitoneal.

interstitial h. A form of inguinal hernia in which the hernial sac lies between the layers of the abdominal muscles.

irreducible h. A hernia that cannot be returned to its original position out of its sac by manual methods. SEE: *incarcerated h.*

labial h. The protrusion of a loop of bowel or other intraperitoneal organ into the labia majora.

lateral h. Inguinal **h.**

lumbar h. A hernia through the inferior lumbar triangle (Petit) or the superior lumbar triangle (Grynfelt). It occurs most often in association with surgery on the kidneys or ureters.

mesocolic h. A hernia between the layers of the mesocolon.

Nuckian h. A hernia into the canal of Nuck.

oblique h. Inguinal **h.**

obturator h. A hernia through the obturator foramen.

omental h. A hernia containing a portion of the omentum.

ovarian h. The presence of an ovary in a hernial sac.

parastomal h. A hernia in the abdominal wall adjacent to a constructed stoma, e.g., a colostomy or iliostomy.

perineal h. Perineocele.

phrenic h. A hernia projecting through the diaphragm into one of the pleural cavities.

posterior vaginal h. A hernia of Douglas' sac downward between the rectum and posterior vaginal wall. SYN: *enterocele* (2).

properitoneal h. A hernia located between the parietal peritoneum and the transversalis fascia.

reducible h. A hernia whose contents can be restored to its normal position by manipulation. SEE: illus.

retroperitoneal h. A hernia protruding into the retroperitoneal space, e.g., duodenojejunal hernia, Treitz's hernia.

Richter's h. A hernia in which only a portion of intestinal wall protrudes, the main portion of the intestine being excluded from the hernial sac and the lumen remaining open. The patient may present with groin swelling and vague abdominal complaints; when incarcerated the hernia may produce bowel ischemia and related complications.

scrotal h. A hernia that descends into the scrotum.

sliding h. A hernia in which a portion of the wall of the herniated structure

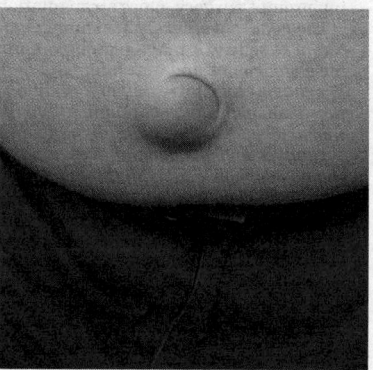

REDUCIBLE HERNIA
Umbilical hernia

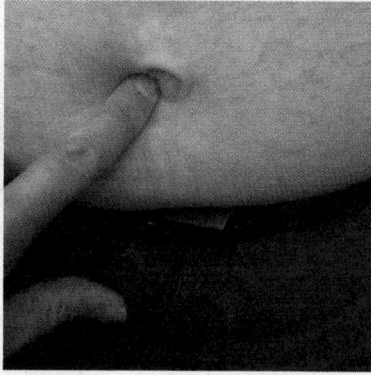

Hernia reduces with digital pressure

forms part of the hernia sac, e.g. an inguinal hernia in which a wall of the cecum or sigmoid colon forms a portion of the sac, the remainder of the sac being parietal peritoneum.

Spigelian h. A defect that occurs at or below the linea semicircularis but above the point at which the inferior epigastric vessels cross the lateral border of the rectus abdominis muscle. This type of hernia may contain preperitoneal fat or may be a peritoneal sac containing intraperitoneal contents. It is rare and difficult to diagnose unless large, because it is typically not palpable when small. Large Spigelian hernias may be mistaken for sarcomas of the abdominal wall. Ultrasonography or computed tomography scans are often used in diagnosis.

TREATMENT: Small Spigelian hernias are easily repaired; larger ones may require a prosthesis.

sports h. Athletic pubalgia.

strangulated h. A hernia in which the protruding viscus is so tightly trapped that gangrene results, requiring prompt surgery. Once strangulation of the contents occurs, a nonsurgical attempt to reduce it may severely compromise treatment and outcome.

synovial h. Protrusion of a portion of synovial membrane through a tear in the stratum fibrosum of a joint capsule.

umbilical h. A hernia occurring at the navel, seen mostly in children. Usually it requires no therapy if small and asymptomatic. An umbilical hernia usually resolves when the child begins to walk (and muscles strengthen).

uterine h. The presence of the uterus in the hernial sac.

vaginal h. Pelvic organ **prolapse**.

vaginolabial h. A hernia of a viscus into the posterior end of the labia majora.

ventral h. A hernia through the abdominal wall. SEE: *incisional h.*

herniated (hĕr'nē-āt″ĕd) Enclosed in or protruding like a hernia.

herniation (hĕr-nē-ā'shŭn) The displacement of body tissue through an opening or defect.

cerebral h. Downward displacement of the brain (usually as a result of cerebral edema, hematoma, or tumor) into the brainstem. The resulting injury to brainstem functions rapidly leads to coma, nerve palsies, and death if treatment is ineffective.

h. of nucleus pulposus Prolapse of the nucleus pulposus of a ruptured intervertebral disk into the spinal canal. This often results in pressure on a spinal nerve, which causes lower back pain that may radiate down the leg, a condition known as sciatica. SEE: illus.; *Nursing Diagnoses Appendix.*

PATIENT CARE: A history is obtained of any unilateral low back pain that radiates to the buttocks, legs, and feet. Almost all herniations occur in the lumbar and lumbosacral region; 8% in the cervical region and only 1% to 2% in the thoracic region. When herniation follows trauma, the patient may report sudden pain, subsiding in a few days, then a dull, aching sciatic pain in the buttocks that increases with Valsalva's maneuver, coughing, sneezing, or bending. The patient may also complain of muscle spasms accompanied by pain that subsides with rest. The health care professional inspects for a limited ability to bend forward, a posture favoring the affected side, and decreased deep tendon reflexes in the lower extremity. In some patients, muscle weakness and atrophy may be observed. Palpation may disclose tenderness over the affected region. Tissue tension assessment may reveal radicular pain from straight leg raising (with lumbar herniation) and increased pain from neck movement (with cervical herniation). Thorough assessment of the patient's

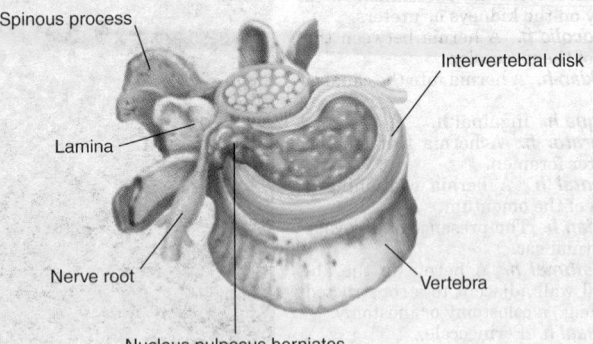

Spinous process

Intervertebral disk

Lamina

Nerve root

Vertebra

Nucleus pulposus herniates
and compresses nerve root

HERNIATED DISK

peripheral vascular status, including posterior tibial and dorsalis pedis pulses and skin temperature of the arms and legs, may help to rule out ischemic disease as the cause of leg numbness or pain.

The patient is prepared for diagnostic testing by explaining all procedures and expected sensations. Tests may include radiographic studies of the spine (to show degenerative changes and rule out other abnormalities), myelography (to pinpoint the level of herniation), computed tomography scanning (to detect bone and soft tissue abnormalities and possibly show spinal compression resulting from the herniation), magnetic resonance imaging (to define tissues in areas otherwise obscured by bone), electromyography (to confirm nerve involvement by measuring the electrical activity of muscles innervated by the affected nerves), and neuromuscular testing (to detect sensory and motor loss as well as leg muscle weakness).

Pain and its management are often crucial elements of care; levels of pain are monitored, prescribed analgesics are administered, the patient is taught about noninvasive pain relief measures (such as relaxation, transcutaneous nerve stimulation, distraction, heat or ice application, traction, bracing, or positioning), and the patient's response to the treatment regimen is evaluated. During conservative treatment, neurological status is monitored (esp. in the first 2 to 3 weeks after beginning treatment) for signs of deterioration, which may indicate a need for surgery. Neurovascular assessments of the patient's affected and unaffected extremities (both legs or both arms) are performed to check color, motion, temperature, sensation, and pulses. Vital signs are monitored, bowel sounds are auscultated, and the abdomen is inspected for distention. The disorder and the various treatment options are explained to the patient, including bedrest and pelvic (or cervical) traction, local heat application, a physical therapy designed exercise program, muscle-relaxing and anti-inflammatory drug therapy, injection of local anesthetic and steroid drugs, acupuncture, and surgery.

Both the patient and family are encouraged to express their concerns about the disorder; questions are answered honestly, and support and encouragement are offered to assist the patient and family to cope with the frustration of impaired mobility and the discomfort of chronic back pain. The patient is encouraged to perform self-care to the extent that immobility and pain allow, to take analgesics before activities, and to allow adequate time to perform activities at a comfortable pace.

Walking and gentle stretching are encouraged as part of daily exercise during conservative therapy. If the patient is restricted to bedrest (or in traction), the patient should increase fluid intake and use incentive spirometry to avoid pulmonary complications. Skin care and a fracture bedpan are provided if the patient is not permitted bathroom or commode privileges.

For patients who require surgery, the patient is prepared physically and psychologically for the specific procedure (laminectomy, spinal fusion, microdiskectomy) and postoperative care regimen, and informed consent is obtained. The patient may donate blood prior to surgery for later autotransfusion as needed.

Postoperative Care: Bedrest is enforced for the prescribed period, the blood drainage system in use is managed, and the amount and color of drainage are documented. Any colorless moisture or excessive drainage should be reported; the former may indicate cerebrospinal fluid leakage. A log-rolling technique is used to turn the patient from side to side, and the patient is taught how to turn in this manner when moving about or getting up from bed at home. Analgesics are administered as prescribed, esp. 30 min before early attempts at mobilization. The health care professional assists the patient with prescribed mobilization. Depending on the surgery required, the patient may require a back brace (individually fitted) for a period of time after surgery, and this is carefully fitted and the patient taught about its use.

Before discharge, proper body mechanics are reviewed with the patient: bending at the knees and hips (never the waist), standing straight, and carrying objects close to the body. The patient is advised to lie down when tired and to sleep on the side or back (never on the abdomen) on an extra-firm mattress or a bed board. All prescribed medications are reviewed, including dosage schedules, desired actions, and adverse reactions to be reported. Referral for home health care or physical/occupational therapy may be necessary to help the patient manage activities of daily living.

tonsillar h. The protrusion of the cerebellar tonsils through the foramen magnum. It causes pressure on the medulla oblongata and may be fatal.

transtentorial h. A herniation of the uncus and adjacent structures into the incisure of the tentorium of the brain. It is caused by increased pressure in the cranium. SYN: *uncal h.*

uncal h. Transtentorial **h.**

hernioenterotomy (hĕr″nē-ō-ĕn″tĕr-ŏt′ō-mē) [″ + Gr. *enteron*, intestine, +

tome, incision] Herniotomy and enterotomy done during the same surgical procedure.

herniography (hĕr″nē-ŏg′ră-fē) [″ + Gr. *graphein,* to write] The radiographical examination of a hernia after the introduction of a contrast medium.

hernioplasty (hĕr′nē-ō-plăs″tē) [″ + Gr. *plassein,* to form] Surgical repair of a hernia.

herniorrhaphy (hĕr-nē-or′ă-fē) [″ + Gr. *rhaphe,* seam, ridge] A surgical procedure for repair of a hernia.

herniotomy (hĕr-nē-ŏt′ō-mē) [″ + Gr. *tome,* incision] Surgery for the relief of a hernia; an operation for the correction of irreducible hernia, esp. strangulated hernia.

heroic measures In medical practice, the undertaking of a procedure or therapy in an attempt to save or sustain the life of a patient with life-threatening injuries or illness.

heroin (hĕr′ō-ĭn) An opioid derived from morphine, whose importation, sale, and use are illegal in the U.S. SYN: *diacetylmorphine.* SEE: *drug addiction; endorphin.*

    black tar h. A form of illicitly manufactured diacetylmorphine known for its tarry appearance and increased potency relative to "white" heroin.

    h. toxicity Poisoning by heroin. SEE: *opiate poisoning.*

herpangina (hĕrp-ăn-jī′nă, -ăn′jī-nă) [Gr. *herpes,* creeping skin disease, + L. *angina,* a choking] A benign infectious disease of children and, less commonly, of young adults, caused by one of several strains of group A coxsackievirus and rarely other enteroviruses. Epidemics occur worldwide, most often in summer and early fall.

    SYMPTOMS: This disease is marked by sudden onset of fever, severe sore throat, nausea, vomiting, excess salivation, and malaise. The throat and posterior area of the mouth are covered with vesicles 1 to 2 mm in diameter that rupture and form ulcers.

    TREATMENT: The treatment is symptomatic and supportive. There is no specific therapy, but recovery is prompt, usually within 3 to 6 days.

herpes (hĕr′pēz″) [Gr. *herpēs,* creeping] Vesicular eruption caused by a virus, esp. herpes simplex virus or herpes zoster. SEE: *Nursing Diagnoses Appendix.*

    h. corneae Inflammation of the cornea caused by herpesvirus.

    h. facialis A form of herpes simplex that occurs on the face.

    h. febrilis Herpes simplex of the lips and nasal mucosa.

    genital h. A persistent, recurring eruption of the genital or anorectal skin or mucous membranes, caused by herpes simplex virus (usually herpes simplex virus type II). It usually affects adolescents and young adults, is spread by intimate contact, and is classified as a sexually transmitted disease. Worldwide about 85 to 90 million people are infected. SEE: illus.

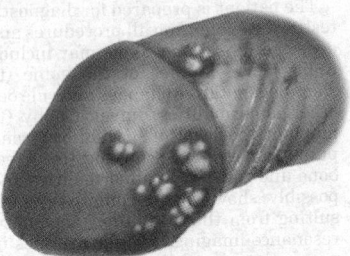

GENITAL HERPES

SYMPTOMS: Patients often experience local pain, itching, burning, dysuria, or other uncomfortable sensations that sometimes begin before a rash or lesion(s) appears on the skin. The skin lesion consists of a reddened patch or small blisters (vesicles) or pustules that ulcerate before healing. These typically take about 10 days to heal. Regional lymph nodes often enlarge and become tender. Systemic symptoms (e.g., fever and malaise) sometimes accompany the initial outbreak or recurrences. However, asymptomatic shedding of the virus is common and may represent the most common way in which the virus is transmitted from person to person.

POTENTIAL COMPLICATIONS: Genital herpes may be transmitted to the newborn during childbirth and may cause serious complications, including respiratory illnesses, retinal infection, liver infection, encephalitis, mental retardation, blindness, deafness, seizures, microcephaly, and diabetes insipidus. Cesarean delivery or maternal suppression of the virus with acyclovir are two methods used to prevent newborn infection. Poor hand hygiene may transmit the virus to the eye(s), resulting in herpetic keratoconjunctivitis.

TREATMENT: Oral acyclovir or its derivatives can treat both the initial outbreak and subsequent recurrences and diminish asymptomatic viral shedding.

⚠ Herpetic lesions are contagious, and those caring for the patient must avoid contact with the exudates. Wearing gloves when in contact with mucous membranes followed by good hand hygiene helps health care professionals prevent herpetic whitlow (finger infections). SEE: *Standard Precautions Appendix.*

PATIENT CARE: The patient should be taught to avoid all skin-to-skin contact when lesions are present and to practice safe sex. Patients should not share towels or other personal care items. Patients with genital herpes often experience anger, self-doubt, fear, or guilt, esp. at the time of initial diagnosis or during recurrences. Counseling and support may help the patient address these issues. Patient education improves understanding of the prevalence of the disease in the general population, the recurring nature of the eruption, safe sexual practices, medication use, and psychosocial and relationship issues.

h. gestationis An autoimmune rash usually occurring in pregnancy or trophoblastic disease, characterized by red, itchy, blistering, or papular lesions. The lesions stain positive for the third component of complement on immunofluorescent microscopy.

h. labialis A form of herpes simplex that occurs on the lips. SEE: *cold sore; fever blister;* illus.

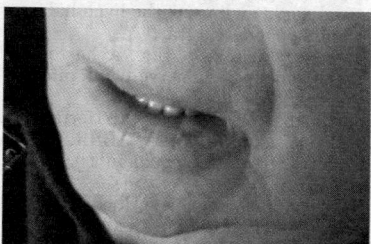

HERPES LABIALIS

h. menstrualis Herpetic lesions appearing at the time of the menstrual period.

ocular h. Herpes of the eye.

h. simplex An acute infection caused by herpes simplex viruses 1 and 2. The infections are categorized by the site of infection, e.g., herpes corneae, herpes facialis, genital herpes, etc. SEE: *herpes simplex virus* under virus.

traumatic h. Herpes at a wound site.

h. zoster Reactivation of varicella virus years after the initial infection with chickenpox. It is marked by inflammation of the posterior root ganglia of only a few segments of the spinal or cranial peripheral nerves. A painful vesicular eruption occurs along the course of the nerve (called a dermatome) and almost always is unilateral. The trunk is the region most often affected, but the face, the groin, or the limbs may also be affected. The virus may cause meningitis or affect the optic nerve or hearing. Chickenpox (varicella zoster) virus incorporates itself into nerve cells and lies dormant there after patients recover from the initial infection. Normally, immunity is boosted by exposure to infected children; as more children are

vaccinated against chickenpox, adult immunity against herpes zoster is decreased.

The incubation period is from 7 to 21 days. The total duration of the disease from onset to complete recovery varies from 10 days to 5 weeks. If all the vesicles appear within 24 hr, the total duration is usually short. In general, the disease lasts longer in adults than in children. It is estimated that about 50% of people who live to age 80 will have an attack of herpes zoster. This infection is more common in persons with a compromised immune system: older adults, those with AIDS or illnesses such as Hodgkin's disease and diabetes, those taking corticosteroids, or those undergoing cancer chemotherapy.

Pain often develops along affected skin and persists for months after resolution of the rash. This discomfort, which may be severe in patients older than 50, is known as postherpetic neuralgia. It may intensify at night or worsen when clothes rub against the skin. SYN: *shingles.* SEE: illus; ***h. zoster ophthalmicus; Nursing Diagnoses Appendix.***

DIAGNOSIS: Diagnosis is usually made based on clinical assessment. If further studies are required, the CDC recommends direct fluorescent antibody testing of specimens collected by rubbing a swab on the base of an open lesion.

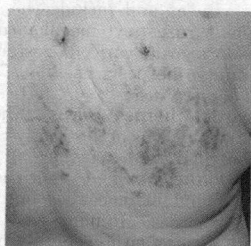

HERPES ZOSTER

TREATMENT: In healthy adults, acyclovir, famciclovir, and valacyclovir are effective in reducing viral shedding and nerve pain damage if administered within 3 days of onset of the rash. Corticosteroids, gabapentin, pregabalin, nonsteroidal anti-inflammatory drugs, some antidepressants, and narcotics may decrease the pain of postherpetic neuralgia. Itching may be reduced with colloidal oatmeal or other topical treatments. Capsaicin cream (an extract of hot chili peppers) may be applied topically for pain relief, but this should be done only after active lesions have subsided.

PATIENT CARE: The prescribed antiviral agent is administered and explained to the patient, along with information about desired and adverse effects. Skin lesions are inspected daily for signs of healing or secondary infection; the patient's response to treatment is evaluated regularly, and he is monitored for associated complications. Prescribed analgesics are given on a schedule to minimize neuralgic pain. Patients experiencing neuralgia following the acute stage of the disease should be referred for ongoing therapy. He is reassured that HSV pain will subside eventually, that the prognosis for complete recovery is good, and that the infection seldom recurs.

PREVENTION: Reactivation of varicella zoster virus (VZV) may be prevented with a vaccine. VZV vaccination is approved for use in the U.S. in adults at age 60.

    h. zoster ophthalmicus Herpes zoster affecting the first division of the fifth cranial nerve. The area of the face, eye, and nose supplied by this nerve is affected. Ocular complications may threaten sight. It is important that the eye be treated early with antiviral agents and that therapy be supervised by an ophthalmologist.

Herpesviridae (hĕr″pēz″vī′rĭ-dē) [*herpes* + *virus* + *-idae*] A large family of structurally similar DNA viruses, all of which produce chronic infections and some of which can transform normal cells into malignant ones. Members of the Herpesviridae family are known as herpesviruses and include the herpes simplex viruses, cytomegalovirus, Epstein-Barr virus, varicella-zoster virus, and human herpesviruses 6, 7, and 8. SEE: *herpesvirus.*

herpesvirus, herpes virus (hĕr′pēz-vī″rŭs) Any virus of the family Herpesviridae. SEE: *Herpesviridae.*

    cercopithecine h. 1 A virus commonly found in macaques but not in other primates. Humans who handle macaques may be infected by bites or exposure to animal blood or body fluids. Although in macaques the virus causes a herpetic rash, in humans it often produces deadly infections of the brain and meninges. SYN: *B virus; cercopithecine virus 1.*

    h. hominis Herpes simplex **virus.**

    human h. 1 ABBR: HHV1. Herpes simplex virus 1. SEE: *herpes simplex virus.*

    human h. 2 ABBR: HHV2. Herpes simplex virus 2. SEE: *herpes simplex virus.*

    human h. 3 ABBR: HHV3. Varicella-zoster **virus.**

    human h. 4 ABBR: HHV4. Epstein-Barr virus.

    human h. 5 ABBR: HHV5. Cytomegalovirus.

    human h. 6 A herpesvirus that causes sixth disease and childhood feb-

rile seizures. It causes infections in immunocompromised patients (e.g., patients who have received organ transplants and patients with human immunodeficiency virus infection). Among children, infants between 6 months and 2 years of age are at highest risk for this infection, and asymptomatic or unrecognized infection is probably common. The incubation period is about 5 to 15 days.

    human h. 8 A herpesvirus thought to cause Kaposi's sarcoma. It has also been implicated in the pathogenesis of some lymphomas and lymphomatoid illnesses. SYN: ***Kaposi*** *sarcoma–associated herpesvirus;* ***Kaposi*** *sarcoma herpesvirus.*

herpetic (hĕr-pet′ik) [*herpes* + *-ic*] Pert. to herpes.

herpetiform (hĕr-pĕt′ĭ-form) [″ + L. *forma,* form] Resembling herpes.

Herring bodies (hĕr′ĭng) [Percy T. Herring, Brit. physiologist, 1872–1967] Secretory granules found in the terminal nerve endings of the hypothalamus and hypophyseal tract.

hersage (ār-săzh′) [Fr., a harrowing] The splitting of a nerve trunk into separate fibers.

hertz (hĕrtz) [Heinrich R. Hertz, Ger. physicist, 1857–1894] ABBR: Hz. A unit of frequency equal to 1 cycle/sec. (CPS)

Heschl gyrus (hesh′ĕl) [Richard Ladislaus Heschl, Austrian anatomist, 1824–1881] One of a set of short transverse gyri in the temporal lobe along the lateral sulcus. The gyri of Heschl include the primary auditory cortex. SYN: *transverse temporal* ***gyrus.***

hesitancy (he′zĭ-tăn-sē) Involuntary delay in initiating urination. This symptom may be caused by drugs, such as tricyclic antidepressants, by abnormal relaxation of the detrusor muscle of the bladder, by prostatic hyperplasia, urethral stricture, and other urinary tract disorders.

hesperidin (hĕs-pĕr′ĭ-dĭn) A citrus bioflavonoid found in the membranes and peel of lemons and oranges.

Hesselbach, Franz (hes′ĕl-bok″) Ger. surgeon, 1759–1816.

    H. hernia A lobated hernia that passes through the cribriform fascia of the anterior thigh.

    H. triangle The interval in the groin bounded by the Poupart ligament, the edge of the rectus muscle, and the inferior epigastric artery (IEA). SEE: illus.

hetastarch (hĕt′ă-stärch″) A synthetic polymer plasma volume expander composed of >90% amylopectin molecules. It has an average molecular weight of 450,000. SEE: *fluid replacement.*

hetero-, heter- [Gr. *heteros,* other, the

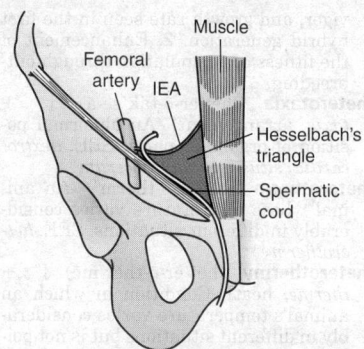

Muscle

Femoral artery   IEA

Hesselbach's triangle

Spermatic cord

HESSELBACH TRIANGLE

other] Prefixes meaning *different, other.*

heteroagglutinin (hĕt″ĕr-ō-ă-glū′tĭ-nĭn)
1. Agglutinin formed as the result of an injection of an antigen from an animal of a different species. **2.** Agglutinin capable of agglutinating blood cells of other species of animals.

heteroantibody (hĕt″ĕr-ō-ăn″tĭ-bŏd′ē)
An antibody corresponding to an antigen from another species.

heteroblastic (hĕt″ĕr-ō-blăs′tĭk) [″ + *blastos,* germ] Developing from several kinds of tissue.

heterocellular (hĕt″ĕr-ō-sĕl′ū-lăr) Composed of different kinds of cells.

heterocephalus (hĕt″ĕr-ō-sĕf′ă-lŭs) [″ + *kephale,* head] Congenitally deformed fetus with two heads of unequal size.

heterochromatin (hĕt″ĕr-ō-krō′mă-tĭn) [″ + *chroma,* color] Highly condensed or folded portions of chromosomes during interphase. They stain less distinctly than euchromatin. There is apparently no transcription of the DNA by messenger RNA (mRNA); these portions may be inactive genes. SEE: *euchromatin.*

heterochromia (hĕt″ĕr-ō-krō′mē-ă) A difference in color. SYN: *heterochromatosis* (2).

    h. iridis Different colors of the iris or sector of the iris in the two eyes. It may occur naturally or as a result of previous disease in the lighter-colored eye. Rarely it is associated with Waardenberg syndrome.

heterochromosome (hĕt″ĕr-ō-krō′mō-sōm) **1.** The X and Y or sex chromosomes. **2.** A chromosome containing material, heterochromatin, that stains differently from the remainder of the chromatin material.

heterochronic (hĕt″ĕr-ō-krŏn′ĭk) Occurring at different or at abnormal times.

heterocyclic (hĕt″ĕr-ō-sīk′lĭk) [″ + *kyklos,* circle] Pert. to ring compounds that contain one or more elements other than carbon in the ring.

heterodont (hĕt″ĕr-ō-dŏnt) [″ + *odous,* tooth] SEE: under *dentition.*

heterogametic (hĕt″ĕr-ō-gă-mĕt′ĭk) [″ + *gamos,* marriage] Pert. to the production of unlike gametes, applied esp. to a male that produces two types of sperm, one containing the X chromosome, the other the Y chromosome. SEE: *homogametic.*

heterogamy (hĕt″ĕr-ŏg′ă-mē) The union of gametes that are dissimilar in size and structure. This union occurs in higher plants and animals. SEE: *isogamy.*

heterogeneity (hĕt″ĕr-ō-jĕ-nē′ĭ-tē) The quality of being heterogeneous.

heterogeneous (hĕt″ĕr-ō-jē′nē-ŭs) [″ + *genos,* type] Of unlike natures; composed of unlike substances; the opposite of homogeneous.

heterogeneous system Any system whose components may be separated mechanically.

heterogenesis (hĕt″ĕ-rō-jĕn′ĕ-sĭs) [″ + *genesis,* generation, birth] The production of offspring that have different characteristics in alternate generations, as in the regular alternation of asexual with sexual reproduction. This characteristic is found in some fungi. SYN: *metagenesis.* SEE: *homogenesis.*

heterogenetic (hĕt″ĕ-rō-jĕ-nĕt′ĭk) Relative to heterogenesis.

heterograft (het′ĕ-rō-graft″) [*hetero-* + *graft*] Xenotransplant.

heteroimmunity (hĕt″ĕr-ō-ĭm-mū′nĭ-tē) Having immunity to an antigen from another species.

heterologous (hĕt″ĕr-ŏl′ō-gŭs) [″ + *logos,* word, reason] **1.** Containing tissue not usually found, e.g., in an organ. **2.** Obtained from a different individual or species with respect to tissue, cells, or blood. SEE: *autologous; homologous.*

heteromeric (hĕt″ĕr-ō-mĕr′ĭk) [″ + *meros,* a part] **1.** Pert. to spinal neurons with processes extending to the opposite side of the spinal cord. **2.** Possessing a different chemical composition.

heteromorphosis (hĕt″ĕr-ō-mawr′fă-sĭs) [″ + *morphe,* form, + *osis,* condition] The regeneration of an organ different from the one that it replaced.

heteromorphous (hĕt″ĕr-ō-mor′fŭs) [″ + *morphe,* form] Deviating from the normal type.

heteronomous (hĕt″ĕr-ŏn′ō-mŭs) [″ + *nomos,* law] Abnormal; differing from type.

heterophil(e) (hĕt′ĕr-ō-fĭl, -fīl) [″ + *philein,* to love] **1.** Pert. to an antibody reacting with other than the specific antigen. **2.** Pert. to a tissue or microorganism that takes a stain other than the ordinary one. **3.** Pert. to antigens that occur in more than one species of animal and that may be immunologically related to plant or microbe antigens.

heterophile antibody test A laboratory test for infectious mononucleosis.

heterophilic (hĕt″ĕr-ō-fĭl′ĭk) [Gr. *heteros*, other, + *philein*, to love] **1.** Having an affinity for something abnormal. **2.** Having an antibody response to an antigen other than the specific one.

heterophoria (hĕt″ĕ-rō-for′ē-ă) [″ + *phoros*, bearing] A tendency of the eyes to deviate from their normal position for visual alignment, esp. when one eye is covered; latent deviation or squint. This tendency is caused by an imbalance or weakness of the ocular muscles. SEE: *phoria*.

Heterophyes (hĕt″ĕr-ō-fī′ēz) [″ + *phye*, stature] A genus of flukes belonging to the family Heterophyidae.

   H. heterophyes A species of intestinal fluke commonly infesting humans. In heavy infestations, it may cause diarrhea, nausea, and abdominal discomfort.

heteroplasia (het″ĕr-ō-plā′zh(ē-)ă) [hetero- + -plasia] The development of tissue at a location where that type of tissue would not normally occur. SYN: *alloplasia*.

heteroplasmy (hĕt′ĕr-ō-plăz″mē) Having two or more mitochondrial DNA sources within a person, cell, or mitochondrion.

heteroplastic (hĕt″ĕr-ō-plăs′tĭk) Relating to heteroplasia.

heteroploid (hĕt′ĕr-ō-ployd) [″ + *ploos*, fold] Possessing a chromosome number that is not a multiple of the haploid number common for the species.

heteropyknosis (hĕt″ĕr-ō-pĭk-nō′sĭs) [″ + *pyknos*, dense, + *osis*, condition] The property whereby various parts of a chromosome stain with varying degrees of intensity. This is thought to be due to variations in the concentration of nucleic acid.

heteroreceptor A cellular receptor that influences how the cell manufactures and releases neurotransmitters different from the agent that stimulated the receptor.

heteroresistance (hĕt″ĕr-ō-rĭ-zĭs′tĭns) [″ + ″] The presence within a population of a pathogen of some organisms that are susceptible to an antimicrobial drug and some that are not. Heteroresistance may explain why failure to eradicate an infection occurs in some patients treated with a seemingly appropriate antibiotic. **heteroresistant,** *adj.*

heterosexual (hĕt″ĕr-ō-sĕk′shū-ăl) [″ + L. *sexus*, sex] **1.** Pert. to the opposite sex. **2.** A person who has sexual interest in or sexual intercourse exclusively with partners of the opposite sex.

heterosexuality (hĕt″ĕr-ō-sĕk″shū-ăl′ĭ-tē) Sexual attraction for one of the opposite sex.

heterosis (het-ĕ-rō′sĭs) [Gr. *heterōsis*, alteration] **1.** The greater strength, size,

vigor, and growth rate seen in the first hybrid generation. **2.** Enhancement of the fitness of a population through outbreeding.

heterotaxia (hĕt″ĕr-ō-tăk′sē-ă) [″ + *taxis*, arrangement] An abnormal position of organs or parts. SEE: *dextrocardia; situs inversus viscerum*.

heterotherm (hĕt′ĕr-ō-thĕrm″) An animal whose temperature varies considerably in different situations. SEE: *heterothermy*.

heterothermy (hĕt′ĕr-ō-thĕr″mē) [″ + *therme*, heat] Condition in which an animal's temperature varies considerably in different situations but is not poikilothermic.

heterotopia (hĕt″ĕr-ō-tō′pē-ă) [″ + *topos*, place] **1.** The appearance of a cluster of normal cells in an abnormal location (e.g., of a cluster of cells from the adrenal glands found in a tissue specimen taken from the ovaries). **2.** The displacement of an organ or body part from its normal location. **heterotopic,** *adj.*

heterotopy (hĕt″ĕr-ŏt′ō-pē) [″ + *topos*, place] Heterotopia (2).

heterotransplant (het′ĕ-rō-trans′plant″) [*hetero-* + *transplant*] Xenotransplant. **heterotransplantation** (het″ĕ-rō-trans″plan″tā′shŏn), *n.*

heterotroph (hĕt′ĕr-ō-trōf) [″ + *trophe*, food] An organism such as a human requiring complex organic food in order to grow and develop, in contrast to plants, which can synthesize food from inorganic materials.

heterotropia (hĕt″ĕr-ō-trō′pē-ă) [″ + *tropos*, a turning] A manifest deviation of the eyes resulting from the absence of binocular equilibrium. SEE: *strabismus*.

heterotypic (hĕt″ĕr-ō-tĭp′ĭk) Concerning something of a different type than that which is being discussed or examined, esp. a tissue.

heteroxenous (hĕt″ĕr-ŏk′sē-nŭs) [″ + *xenos*, stranger] The property of a parasite that requires two different hosts in order to complete its life cycle.

heterozygosis (hĕt″ĕr-ō-zī-gō′sĭs) [″ + *zygone*, yoke, pair, + *osis*, condition] The state of having different alleles at a specific locus. SEE: *homozygosis*.

heterozygote (hĕt″ĕr-ō-zī′gōt) An individual with different alleles for a given characteristic. SEE: *allele*.

heterozygous (hĕt″ĕr-ō-zī′gŭs) Possessing different alleles at a given locus. SEE: *homozygous*.

Heubner, Johann Otto L. (hoyb′nĕr) German pediatrician, 1843–1926.

   H.-Herter disease Nontropical sprue in infants.

heuristic (hū-rĭs′tĭk) [Gr. *heuriskein*, to find out, discover] A rule or model used to simplify problem solving or the interpretation of complex sets of data.

hevein (hē′vē-ĭn) A protein allergen

found in natural rubber latex that stimulates neutrophils to release oxygen radicals. Hevein is a lectin responsible for the IgE-mediated hypersensitivity response to latex products.

HEW U.S. Department of Health, Education and Welfare. This agency is now the U.S. Department of Health and Human Services.

hex-, hexa- [Gr. *hex,* six] Prefixes meaning *six.*

hexacanth (hěk′să-kănth) [Gr. *hex,* six, + *akantha,* hook, thorn] The embryonic stage in the life cycle of the tapeworm that has six hooklets to penetrate the intestinal mucosa. SYN: *oncosphere.*

hexachlorophene (hěks″ă-klō′rō-fēn) An antibacterial compound typically used in soaps and scrubs and experimentally used as a cholinesterase inhibitor.

hexad (hěk′săd) **1.** Six similar things. **2.** An element with a valence of six.

hexadecimal (hěks″ă-děs′ĭ-măl) [″ + L. *decimus,* tenth] In computers, a number system using base 16 rather than base 2 (binary) or 10 (decimal).

hexaploidy (hěk′să-ploy″dē) [″ + *ploos,* fold] A condition of having six sets of chromosomes.

Hexapoda (hěks-ăp′ō-dă) [″ + *pous,* foot] Insecta.

hexavalent (hěks″ă-vā′lěnt) [″ + L. *valere,* to have power] Having a chemical valence of six.

hexokinase (hěks″ō-kī′nās) [″ + *kinein,* to move, + *-ase,* enzyme] An enzyme in cells that in the presence of ATP catalyzes the conversion of glucose to glucose-6-phosphate, the first step in glycolysis.

hexosamine (hěk′sŏs″ă-mēn″) A sugar containing an amino group in place of a hydroxyl group (e.g., glucosamine).

hexose (hěk′sōs) Any monosaccharide of the general formula $C_6H_{12}O_6$; the group includes glucose, fructose, and galactose.

hexosephosphate (hěks″ōs-fŏs′fāt) [Gr. *hex,* six, + *phosphoros,* phosphorus] A phosphoric acid ester of glucose; one of several esters formed in the muscles and other tissues in the metabolism of carbohydrates.

HF *Hageman factor; heart failure; high frequency (high-frequency, adj.); hydrofluoric acid.*

Hf Symbol for the element hafnium.

H-FABP *Heart fatty acid-binding **protein.***

HFE protein SEE: under *protein.*

HFJV *high-frequency jet ventilation.*

HFOV *High-frequency oscillatory **ventilation.***

Hg [L. *hydrargyrum, hydrargyrus* fr Gr. *hydrargyros,* liquid silver] Symbol for the element mercury.

Hgb *hemoglobin.*

HgCl₂ Formula for mercury (II) chloride (mercuric chloride).

Hg₂Cl₂ Formula for mercury (I) chloride (mercurous chloride).

HGE *human granulocytic ehrlichiosis.*

HGF 1. *human growth factor.* **2.** *hyperglycemic-glycogenolytic factor* (glucagon).

HGH *Human growth **hormone.***

HGSIL *high-grade squamous intraepithelial lesion.*

HHb *reduced hemoglobin (deoxyhemoglobin).*

HHS U.S. Department of Health and Human Services.

5-HIAA *5-hydroxyindoleacetic acid.*

hiatus (hī-āt′ŭs) [L. *hiatus,* an opening] An opening or aperture; a foramen.

   h. aorticus An opening in the diaphragm through which pass the aorta and the thoracic duct.

   h. canalis facialis A hiatus of the canal for the greater petrosal nerve. SYN: ***h.*** *canalis facialis.*

   h. esophageus The opening in the diaphragm through which the esophagus passes.

   h. maxillaris The opening of the maxillary sinus into the nasal cavity, located on the nasal surface of the maxillary bone.

   sacral h. The opening on the inferoposterior surface of the sacrum into the sacral canal.

   h. semilunaris The groove in the external wall of the middle meatus of the nasal fossa into which the frontal sinus, maxillary sinus, and anterior ethmoid sinuses drain. The opening may be blocked in patients with acute or chronic sinusitis.

Hib *Haemophilus influenzae type b.*

hibernation (hī″běr-nā′shŭn) [L. *hiberna,* winter] The condition of spending the winter asleep and in an almost comatose state. Some animals adapt to winter by this method.

   artificial h. A state of hibernation produced therapeutically by use of drugs alone or drugs and hypothermia. This greatly reduces the metabolic rate during procedures such as open heart surgery.

hibernoma (hī″běr-nō′mă) A rare multilobular encapsulated tumor that contains fetal fat tissue closely resembling the fat stored in the foot pads of hibernating animals.

hiccup, hiccough (hĭk′ŭp) [probably of imitative origin] A spasmodic periodic closure of the glottis following spasmodic lowering of the diaphragm, causing a short, sharp, inspiratory cough. Hiccups may occur transiently or may occasionally be intractable, lasting days, weeks, or longer. SYN: *singultus.*

   ETIOLOGY: Phrenic nerve or diaphragmatic irritation, distention of the stomach, chest or abdominal surgery, metabolic disorders (e.g., hyponatremia), and intracerebral lesions (e.g., tumors, infections) commonly cause prolonged hiccuping.

TREATMENT: Hiccups may be treated by antiemetic drugs, rebreathing in a paper bag, briefly applying ice cubes to both sides of the neck at the level of the larynx, or inhalation of carbon dioxide. Stimulation of the nasopharynx with a soft rubber tube or placement of a thin coating of dry granulated sugar in the hypopharynx may also be tried. If these are not effective, anesthetization of the phrenic nerve may be helpful.

Hickman catheter (hĭk′măn) A tunneled central venous catheter commonly used to administer solutions by central intravenous therapy for a prolonged period. Applications include total parenteral nutrition, antibiotic therapy, or blood transfusion.

HIDA scan SEE: under *scan.*

hidr-, hidro- [Gr. *hidrōs,* sweat] Prefixes meaning *sweat.*

hidradenitis (hī-drăd-ĕ-nī′tĭs) [Gr. *hidros,* sweat, + *aden,* gland, + *itis,* inflammation] An inflammation of the sweat glands.

hidradenoma (hī″drăd-ĕ-nō′mă) [″ + ″ + *oma,* tumor] Adenoma of the sweat glands.

hidrocystoma (hī″drō-sĭs-tō′mă) [″ + *kystis,* cyst, + *oma,* tumor] Hydrocystoma.

hidrosadenitis (hī″drŏs-ăd″ĕ-nī′tĭs) [″ + *aden,* gland, + *itis,* inflammation] Hidradenitis.

hidrosis (hī-drō′sĭs) [″ + *osis,* condition] **1.** The formation and secretion of sweat. **2.** Excessive sweating.

hidrotic (hī-drŏt′ĭk) **1.** Causing the secretion of sweat. SYN: *diaphoretic; sudorific.* **2.** Any drug or medicine that induces sweating.

hierarchy (hī′ĕ-rar-kē) [Gr. *hierarchia,* power or rule of the (high) priest] The ordering or classification of things in ascending or descending order of importance or value. For example, the needs of a human being might be listed in order of theoretical importance, e.g., air, water, food, health, protection from the elements and predators, security, esteem, and love.

HIFU *High-intensity focused ultrasound.*

high colonic (hī kō-lŏn′ĭk) Irrigation of the bowel with large volumes of fluid. It is promoted as a form of internal cleansing and detoxification.

⚠️ Colonic irrigation poses a potential risk of bowel perforation and electrolyte disturbances, among other potential injuries to the patient.

high-dose-rate remote brachytherapy Radiation treatment for an internal cancer, e.g., cancer of the prostate, in which a powerful source of radiation is placed inside the body for a specified time and then removed. It may be replaced several times over the course of a treatment to achieve the desired effect on the tumor.

high endothelial venule ABBR: HEV. A postcapillary venule found in gut-associated lymphoid tissue, e.g., Peyer's patches, and in lymph nodes. It regulates the movement of lymphocytes in and out of the blood.

higher order aberration SEE: under *aberration.*

high-frequency chest compressions During emergency cardiac care, chest compressions that are given at a rate of more than 100 per minute.

high-grade squamous intraepithelial lesion SEE: under *lesion.*

high-intensity focused ultrasound SEE: under *ultrasound.*

highly active antiretroviral therapy ABBR: HAART. The combination of antiviral agents from three or more classes of drugs to treat patients with HIV infection. HAART reduces the number of viruses circulating in the blood (viral load) and prolongs life and disease-free survival. Reverse transcriptase inhibitors, nonnucleoside reverse transcriptase inhibitors, and protease inhibitors are used in HAART. SYN: *combination antiretroviral therapy.* SEE: *HIV/AIDS.*

highly pathogenic avian influenza SEE: under *influenza.*

highly reliable organization ABBR: HRO. An institution that consistently makes fewer mistakes than others working in the same field despite conditions that are stressful, fast-paced, or full of risk. Health care institutions strive to be HROs, i.e., to copy the performance achieved by other industries such as airlines, power plants, and utilities. Becoming an HRO requires a commitment to quality as well as productivity, to open communication, and a culture that encourages self-driven improvement.

high mobility group box chromosomal protein 1 SEE: under *protein.*

high-molecular-weight kininogen ABBR: HWMK. A protein kininogen that is one of the early participants of the intrinsic pathway of coagulation and functions as a cofactor for activating kallikrein and the Hageman factor. SEE: *coagulation factor* under factor.

Highmore, Nathaniel (hī′mor″) Brit. surgeon, 1613–1685.

    antrum of H. Maxillary **antrum.**

high-resolution anoscopy Visual inspection of the anus after a 3% solution of acetic acid has been applied to it. The acetic acid enhances the appearance and detection of premalignant lesions of the anal squamous epithelium.

hila (hī′lă) [L.] Pl. of hilum.

Hilgenreiner epiphyseal angle (hil′gĕn-rīn″ĕr) [Heinrich Hilgenreiner, Austrian orthopedist and surgeon, 1870–1954.] The angle formed by a line drawn through the triradiate and a line drawn through the physes of the femoral head. This angle is normally 25°. Coxa vara is marked by angles greater than 25°; coxa valga by angles less than 25°.

hillock (hĭl′ŏk) [ME. *hilloc*] A small eminence or projection.

    axon h. A small conical elevation on the cell body of a neuron from which the axon arises.

Hill-Sachs lesion (hil′saks′) [Harold A. Hill, U.S. radiologist, b. 1901; Maurice Sachs, U.S. radiologist, b. 1909] An osteochondral fracture of the posterolateral humeral head that occurs following an anterior dislocation of the glenohumeral joint. The lesion involves the cartilage of the humeral head, causing instability that may predispose the individual to subsequent anterior glenohumeral dislocations.

    ETIOLOGY: A Hill-Sachs lesion occurs in about 40% of all first-time anterior dislocations and up to 80% of recurrent dislocations. The relative size of the lesion, as determined through an arthroscope or diagnostic imaging, can be used to ascertain the relative magnitude of the original dislocation.

    SYMPTOMS: Although many Hill-Sachs lesions are asymptomatic, pain may arise from the posterolateral humeral head when the glenohumeral joint is abducted to 90°, and passive external rotation is applied.

    TREATMENT: Surgical repair may be needed to increase anterior stability of the glenohumeral joint.

Hilton, John (hil′tŏn) Brit. surgeon, 1804–1878.

    H.'s law The trunk of a nerve sends branches not only to a particular muscle but also to the joint moved by that muscle and to the skin overlying the insertion of that muscle.

hilum (hī′lŭm, ′lă) pl. **hila** [L. *hilum*, a little thing, trifle] **1.** A depression or recess at the exit or entrance of a duct into a gland or of nerves and vessels into an organ. **2.** The root of the lungs at the level of the fourth and fifth dorsal vertebrae. The hilum, on the medial side of each lung, is where the main bronchus, pulmonary arteries, bronchial arteries, and nerves enter the lung and where the pulmonary veins, bronchial veins, and lymphatic vessels leave the lung. SYN: *hilus*. **hilar** (hī′lăr), adj.

hilus (hī′lŭs, ′lī″) pl. **hili**Hilum.

hilus cell SEE: under *cell*.

HIMSS   *Healthcare Information and Management Systems Society.*

hindbrain (hīnd′brān) [AS. *hindan*, behind, + *bragen*, brain] The most caudal of the three divisions of the embryonic brain. It differentiates into the metencephalon, which gives rise to the cerebellum and pons; and the myelencephalon, which develops into the medulla oblongata. SYN: *rhombencephalon*.

hindfoot (hīnd′foot) The posterior part of the foot consisting of the talus and calcaneus.

hindgut (hīnd′gŭt) The caudal portion of the embryonic gut tube; the caudal segment of the transverse colon, the descending colon, the sigmoid colon, the rectum, and the rostral segment of the anal canal (to the region of the anal valves) develop from the hindgut. A ventral outpouching from the caudal hindgut separates to form the allantois, which develops into parts of the bladder and urethra.

hindsight The ability to look backwards in time and feel comfortable with one's ability to predict an event that has occurred even if one may have predicted the outcome differently before the event.

Hinman syndrome, Hinman-Allen syndrome (hin′măn) [Frank Hinman, Jr., U.S. urologist, b. 1915] A habitual dyscoordination between contraction of the detrusor muscles and relaxation of the urethra. It is a cause of urinary incontinence that is sometimes called non-neurogenic neurogenic bladder. It can be treated with bladder training or medications.

hip (hip) The region lateral to the ilium of the pelvic bone.

HIPAA   *Health Insurance Portability and Accountability Act.*

HIPEC   *Hyperthermic intraperitoneal chemotherapy.*

Hippel disease, von Hippel-Lindau disease (hip′ĕl, von hip′ĕl-lin′dow″) [Eugen von Hippel, Ger. ophthalmologist, 1867–1939; Arvid Lindau, Swedish pathologist, 1892–1958] Angiomatosis of the retina and various areas of the body including the central nervous system, spinal cord, and visceral organs.

hippocampal (hĭp″ō-kăm′păl) [Gr. *hippokampos*, seahorse] Pert. to the hippocampus.

    h. formation Olfactory structures lying along the medial margin of the pallium. They include the hippocampus, dentate gyrus, supracallosal gyrus, longitudinal striae, subcallosal gyrus, diagonal band of Broca, and hippocampal commissure.

hippocampus (hĭp″ō-kăm′pŭs) An elevation of the floor of the inferior horn of the lateral ventricle of the brain, occupying nearly all of it. The hippocampus seems to be important in establishing new memories.

Hippocrates (hi-pok′ră-tēz″) [ca. 460–375 B.C.] A Greek physician referred to as the Father of Medicine because he was the first healer to attempt to record medical experiences for future reference. By so doing he established the foundation for the scientific basis of medical practice. SEE: *Hippocratic oath*.

Hippocratic oath [*Hippocrates*] An oath traditionally attributed to Hippocrates of Cos and sworn by physicians and other health care professionals to practice medicine according to a code of ethics. It precludes the use of surgery, euthanasia, or abortion by medical practitioners; requires that practitioners give professional courtesy to their instructors (and their children); recommends the use of diet as a primary therapeutic tool; and specifies that medical practitioners always maintain the confidentiality of patient information.

hip protector A padded garment worn around the buttocks, iliac crest, and proximal femur designed to absorb the shock of a fall and decrease the likelihood of a hip fracture, esp. in athletes, older adults, or persons with osteoporosis.

hippuric acid (hip-ūr′ik) SEE: under *acid*.

hippuricase (hĭ-pūr′ĭ-kās) An enzyme found in the liver, kidney, and other tissues that catalyzes the synthesis of hippuric acid from benzoic acid and glycine. SYN: *hippurase*.

hippus (hĭp′ūs) [Gr. *hippos,* horse] The rhythmic, spasmodic dilation and contraction of the pupil in response to light. It is usually normal and is often more evident in younger people.

    respiratory h. A dilatation of the pupil during inspiration and contraction on expiration.

hircus (hĭr′kŭs) *pl.* **hirci** [L., goat] An axillary hair.

Hirschsprung disease (hĭrsh′sprŭngz) [Harald Hirschsprung, Danish physician, 1830–1916] The most common cause of lower gastrointestinal obstruction in neonates. Patients with this disease exhibit signs of an extremely dilated colon and accompanying chronic constipation, fecal impaction, and overflow diarrhea. It occurs in 1 in 5000 children, with a male-to-female ratio of 4:1. About 15% of cases are diagnosed in the first month of life, 64% by the third month, and 80% by age 1 year. Only 8% remain undiagnosed by 3 years of age. SYN: *aganglionic* **megacolon**. SEE: *megacolon*.

ETIOLOGY: The condition is caused by congenital absence of some or all the normal bowel parasympathetic ganglion cells, beginning at the anus and extending variable lengths proximally, though 75% of cases are limited to the immediate rectosigmoid area. The aganglionic bowel segment contracts but there is no reciprocal relaxation, so feces cannot be propelled onward through the bowel. Unless diagnosed and treated quickly, the colonic obstruction caused by Hirschsprung may result in fecal stagnation, bacterial overgrowth with toxin production, enterocolitis, overflow diarrhea, hypovolemic shock, and infant death.

DIAGNOSIS: Barium contrast enema (BE) is usually used for diagnosis, but for mild cases when the BE result is negative, rectal biopsy is the diagnostic standard.

TREATMENT: Treatment is surgical excision of the affected segment and reanastomosis of healthy bowel, by any of several procedures.

PATIENT CARE: In the neonatal period, health care providers assist the parents to adjust to their child's congenital defect and foster infant-parent bonding. They prepare the parents intellectually and emotionally for medical-surgical intervention and teach them about care of the infant's colostomy (if complete obstruction necessitates this) after discharge.

Preoperative patient care focuses on ensuring adequate nutrition to withstand surgery and aid healing. Surgical preparation in any baby other than a newborn (whose bowel is sterile) requires bowel cleansing and sterilization, using saline enemas and antibiotic therapy. A nasogastric tube may be inserted to manage or prevent abdominal distention. Progressive abdominal distention signals worsening bowel obstruction; the abdominal circumference is measured at the umbilicus each time that vital signs are checked. Psychological preparation for surgery is dictated by the child's age; spacing explanations appropriately can prevent anxiety and confusion. Parents and older children should be reminded that the colostomy (if needed) will be temporary.

Postoperative care is similar to that for any infant or child experiencing abdominal surgery in which colostomies are required. Appropriate analgesics are prescribed and provided, and the parents are assured that the infant's pain will be managed and comfort maintained. Fluid and electrolyte balance is monitored, as are cardiac and ventilatory status. If a nasogastric tube was placed, it may be clamped periodically for brief periods when drainage decreases, assessing for abdominal distention. Once bowel sounds return and distention is absent, oral intake is initiated in a stepwise fashion. Parents are instructed to secure diapers below the area of incision to prevent urine contamination of the wound. Before discharge, the ability of parents to carry out colostomy care and skin protection is evaluated; children from preschool age up should be involved in self-care as appropriate. Follow-up care includes attention to the child's nutrition and well-being. After a variable duration of healing, the colostomy is taken down and reconnected to the remnant bowel. For continuity of care, the child and family are referred to a home health care agency. The community nurse also assists in preparing the family for subsequent surgery. The family may be referred to a social worker, psychologist, or other service agency as appropriate if financial assistance or further psychological support is required.

hirsute (hŭr'sūt) [L. *hirsutus,* shaggy] Hairy.

hirsuties (hŭr-sū'shē-ēz) Hirsutism.

hirsutism (hŭr'sŭ-tizzm) [*hirsute* + *-ism*] Excessive growth of hair or the presence of hair in unusual places, esp. in women. Hirsutism in women is usually caused by abnormalities of androgen production or metabolism, or it may be a side effect of medication or hormonal therapies. In patients who do not have an adrenal tumor, this condition may be treated symptomatically by shaving, depilatories, or electrolysis, in combination with spironolactone, and, if pregnancy is not desired, an oral contraceptive.

hirudin (hĭ-rū'dĭn) A substance present in the secretion of the buccal glands of the leech that prevents coagulation of the blood by inactivating thrombin. Hirudin can be used to treat acute myocardial infarction and unstable angina pectoris.

Hirudinea (hĭr″ū-dĭn'ē-ă) A class of Annelida. This group is hermaphroditic, lacks setae or appendages, usually has two suckers, and includes the blood-sucking leeches. SEE: *hirudin; leech.*

Hirudo (hĭ-roo'dō) [L., leech] A genus of leeches belonging to the family Gnathobdellidae.

His, Wilhelm Jr. (hĭs) German physician, 1863–1934.

   bundle of H. The atrioventricular (AV) bundle, a group of modified muscle fibers, the Purkinje fibers, forming a part of the impulse-conducting system of the heart. It arises in the AV node and continues in the interventricular septum as a single bundle, the crus commune, which divides into two trunks that pass respectively to the right and left ventricles, fine branches passing to all parts of the ventricles. It conducts impulses from the atria to the ventricles, which initiates ventricular contraction.

   H. disease Trench fever.

histaminase (hĭs-tăm'ĭ-nās) An enzyme widely distributed in the body that inactivates histamine.

histamine (hĭs'tă-mĭn, -mēn) $C_5H_9N_3$; a substance produced from the amino acid histidine, which causes dilation of blood vessels, increased secretion of acid by the stomach, smooth muscle constriction (e.g., in the bronchi), and mucus production, tissue swelling, and itching (during allergic reactions). The release of histamine from mast cells is a major component of type I hypersensitivity reactions, including asthma.

   h. blocking agent Antihistamine.

histaminemia (hĭs-tăm″ĭ-nē'mĕ-ă) [*histamine* + Gr. *haima,* blood] Histamine in the blood.

histamine test **1.** Injection of histamine subcutaneously to stimulate gastric secretion of hydrochloric acid. **2.** A test for vasomotor headache; a histamine injection precipitates the onset of a headache in persons with this disease.

histidase (hĭs'tĭ-dās) Histidine ammonia-lyase.

histidine (hĭs'tĭ-dĭn, -dēn) An essential amino acid, $C_6H_9N_3O_2$, that is, one that must be consumed in the diet.

   h. ammonia-lyase A liver enzyme that catalyzes L-histidine with the resultant formation of urocanic acid and ammonia. Deficiency of this enzyme causes histidinemia.

histidinemia (hĭs″tĭ-dĭ-nē'mē-ă) A hereditary metabolic disease caused by lack of the enzyme histidine ammonia-lyase, which is normally present in the urine.

histio-, histi- [Gr. *histion,* web, cloth, sail] Prefixes meaning *tissue.* SEE: *histo-.*

histiocyte (hĭs'tē-ō-sīt″) [Gr. *histion,* little web, + *kytos,* cell] A monocyte that enters and remains within a particular tissue. SYN: *histocyte; macrophage.*

histiocytoma (hĭs″tē-ō-sī-tō'mă) [″ + ″ + *oma,* tumor] A tumor containing histiocytes.

histiocytosis (hĭs″tē-ō-sī-tō'sĭs) [*histiocyte* + *-osis*] An abnormal number of histiocytes in the blood.

   Langerhans cell h. Any of a number of clinical conditions, most commonly seen in infants and children, caused by disease of Langerhans cell histiocytes. These cells, which are characteristic of all of the variants of the disease, cause granulomas. The great variation in the signs and symptoms produced depends upon their location and how widely spread they are. Almost any organ system including the skeleton may be involved. These diseases were previously given names such as histiocytosis X, Hand-Schüller-Christian disease, Letterer-Siwe disease, and eosinophilic granuloma. Treatment may consist of surgical removal of bone lesions and radiation therapy for lesions threatening vital functions such as sight and hearing. Corticosteroids or cytotoxic agents are useful in controlling soft-tissue disease and multiple skeletal lesions. Bone marrow transplantation has been used in recurrent and progressive Langerhans cell histiocytosis.

histo-, hist- [Gr. *histos,* mast, beam (of a ship)] Prefixes meaning *tissue.* SEE: *histio-.*

histoblast (hĭs'tō-blăst) [" + *blastos,* germ] A tissue-forming cell.

histochemistry (hĭs"tō-kĕm'ĭs-trē) The study of chemistry of the cells and tissues. It involves use of both light and electron microscopy and special chemical tests and stains.

histocompatibility (hĭs"tō-kŏm-păt"ĭ-bĭl'ĭ-tē) Cell-mediated immunological similarity or compatibility.

histocyte (hĭs'tō-sīt) [" + *kytos,* cell] Histiocyte.

histodiagnosis (hĭs"tō-dī"ăg-nō'sĭs) [" + *dia,* through, + *gnosis,* knowledge] A diagnosis made from examination of the tissues, esp. by use of microscopy.

histodifferentiation (hĭs"tō-dĭf"ĕr-ĕn"shē-ā'shŭn) The process of tissue maturation during which cells become specialized.

histogenesis (hĭs-tō-jĕn'ĕ-sĭs) [" + *genesis,* generation, birth] The development into differentiated tissues of a germ layer; the origin and development of tissue. **histogenetic** (hĭs"tō-jĕ-nĕt'ĭk), *adj.*

histogram (hĭs'tō-gram) [L. *historia,* observation, + Gr. *gramma,* something written] A graph showing frequency distributions.

histoincompatible (hĭs"tō-ĭn"kŏm-pă'tĭ-bl) Immunologically incompatible (e.g., for tissue transplantation).

histological technologist (hĭs"tō-lŏj'ĭk) A technologist who performs all the functions of the histological technician, as well as more complex procedures for processing tissues, such as identifying tissue structures, cell components, their staining characteristics, and their relation to physiology. He or she may also implement and test new techniques and procedures.

histologist (hĭs-tŏl'ō-jĭst) [" + *logos,* word, reason] A specialist in the microscopic study of cells and tissues.

histology (hĭs-tŏl'ō-jē) The study of the microscopic structure of tissue. **histological** (hĭs"tō-lŏj'ĭ-kăl), *adj.*
    normal h. The microscopic study of healthy tissue.
    pathologic h. Histopathology.

histolysis (hĭs-tŏl'ĭ-sĭs) [" + *lysis,* dissolution] Disintegration of the tissues. **histolytic** (hĭs-tō-lĭt'ĭk), *adj.*

histomorphometry (hĭs"tō-mŏr-fŏm'ĕ-trē) The quantitative analysis of tissue structure (e.g., its components, its strength, or its deterioration in stress or illness).

histone (hĭs'tŏn, -tōn) [Gr. *histos,* web, tissue] One of the five kinds of proteins that are part of chromatin in eukaryotic cells. Their positive charge attracts the negatively charged DNA that is folded around them into units called nucleosomes. Histones also regulate some of the further folding of DNA in chromosomes about to undergo mitosis.

histopathology (hĭs"tō-pă-thŏl'ō-jē) [" + *pathos,* disease, suffering, + *logos,* word, reason] The microscopic study of diseased tissues. SYN: *pathologic histology.*

histophysiology (hĭs"tō-fĭz"ē-ŏl'ō-jē) [" + *physis,* nature, + *logos,* word, reason] The study of the functions of cells and tissues.

Histoplasma (hĭs"tō-plaz'mă) [*histo-* + *plasma*] A genus of parasitic fungi.
    H. capsulatum The causative agent of histoplasmosis and endemic in the Ohio and Mississippi river valleys.

histoplasmin (hĭs"tō-plăz'mĭn) An antigen prepared from cultures of *Histoplasma capsulatum* and used as a skin test for the diagnosis of histoplasmosis.

histoplasmosis (hĭs"tō-plăz-mō'sĭs) [" + " + Gr. *osis,* condition] A systemic fungal respiratory disease caused by *Histoplasma capsulatum.* The reservoir for this fungus is in soil with a high organic content and undisturbed bird droppings, esp. around old chicken houses; caves harboring bats; and starling, blackbird, and pigeon roosts. In the U.S., the infection is endemic in the Ohio River valley. Disseminated histoplasmosis is a common opportunistic infection in patients with acquired immunodeficiency syndrome (AIDS) and other immunosuppressing illnesses.

SYMPTOMS: The signs and symptoms vary from those of a mild self-limited infection (in primary acute histoplasmosis) to a severe or fatal disease (in disseminated disease). Immunocompromised persons are esp. susceptible. In disseminated disease fever, anemia, enlargment of the spleen and liver, leukopenia, pneumonia, adrenal necrosis, and gastrointestinal tract ulcers occur. Chronic pulmonary histoplasmosis produces lung cavitations similar to those in tuberculosis.

DIAGNOSIS: Diagnosis is based on a history of exposure, a positive histoplasmin skin test or urine antigen test, and rising complement fixation and agglutination titers. It is confirmed by stained tissue biopsy or culture of *H. capsulatum* from sputum, blood, lymph nodes, or bone marrow.

TREATMENT: The treatment is high-dose or long-term intravenous amphotericin B or other potent antifungal agents (azoles). Patients with acquired immunodeficiencies require lifelong treatment using fluconazole.

PATIENT CARE: In patients with severe pneumonia, respiratory status is monitored every 8 hr (or more frequently as necessary) to assess for diminished breath sounds, pleural friction rub, or effusion; cardiovascular status every 8 hr (or more frequently as necessary) to document and immediately report any muffling of heart sounds, jugular vein distention, pulsus paradoxus, or other signs of cardiac tamponade; and neurological status every 8 hr (or more frequently as necessary) to document and report any changes in level of consciousness or any nuchal rigidity (either of which may be evidence of fungal meningitis). The patient is assessed for signs and symptoms of hypoglycemia and hyperglycemia, indicating adrenal dysfunction. All stools are tested for occult blood, and its presence is documented and reported. Prescribed antifungal therapy (amphotericin B, itraconazole, or ketaconazole) is administered and evaluated for desired effects and any adverse reactions. If needed, oxygen therapy is administered. Glucocorticoids are administered if adrenal insufficiency occurs. A dietitian is consulted to construct an appetizing and nutritious diet incorporating the patient's food preferences. If the patient has oropharyngeal ulceration, soothing oral hygiene and soft, bland foods are provided. (Parenteral nutrition may be required if ulcerations are severe, resulting in dysphagia.) Emotional support is offered to the patient with chronic or disseminated histoplasmosis, and referral to a social worker, psychologist, or occupational therapist for further counseling and support may be necessary to help the patient cope with long-term therapy. The nurse assists parents of a child with this disease to arrange for home-bound instruction. The patient is advised that follow-up care on a regular basis will be required for at least a year. Cardiac and pulmonary signs and symptoms that may indicate effusions should be reported to the health care provider immediately. To help prevent disseminated histoplasmosis, persons in endemic areas are taught to watch for early signs of this infection and to seek treatment promptly. Persons who risk occupational exposure to contaminated soil are instructed to wear face masks.

historical control group (his-tor-ĭ-kăl) SEE: under *group*.

history (his'tō-rē) [Gr. *historia*, inquiry] ABBR: Hx. In the health care professions, a systematic record of past events as they relate to a person and his medical background. A carefully taken medical, surgical, and occupational history will enable diagnosis in about 80% of patients. SYN: *medical h.*

TECHNIQUE: The patient should be given the opportunity to describe his symptoms in his own words, fully, completely, and without interruption. The examiner encourages the patient to speak by maintaining a sympathetic and nonjudgmental attitude. After the patient finishes his explanations, the examiner usually asks carefully chosen questions to elicit details about an illness and to gain deeper insights. SEE: *nursing assessment*.

case h. The complete medical, family, social, and psychiatric history of a patient up to the time of admission for the present illness.

dental h. A record of all aspects of a person's oral health, previous evaluations and treatments, and the state of general physical and mental health. SEE: *oral diagnosis*.

family h. ABBR: FHx. A record of the state of health and medical history of members of the patient's immediate family, which may be of interest to the physician or other health care provider because of genetic or familial tendencies noted.

medical h. History.

natural h. (of disease) The expected or predictable course of an untreated illness. The knowledge of the expected course of a disease is usually based on prior study of the effects of the illness on a large group of patients over time. SEE: *disease progression*.

nursing h. The first step of the assessment stage of the nursing process that leads to development of a nursing care plan. Valuable information can be obtained from this history, and reactions to previous hospitalization can be recorded and utilized in managing the patient's care during the current stay.

occupational h. A semistructured interview process used by occupational therapists to determine a person's roles, approach to tasks, and sense of identity.

sexual h. A medical history of a person's sexual practices, concerns, illnesses, partners, preventive activities, and risk factors for sexually transmitted diseases.

histotoxic (hĭs″tō-tŏk'sĭk) [″ + *toxikon,* poison] Toxic to tissue.

histotropic (hĭs″tō-trŏp'ĭk) [″ + *trope,* a turning] Having attraction for tissue cells, as certain parasites, stains, or chemicals.

histozoic (hĭs″tō-zō'ĭk) [″ + *zoe,* life] Living within or on tissues, said of certain protozoan parasites.

HIT *Health information technology.*

hit (hit) In toxicology and medicine, exposure to a substance that causes an injury to a function or structure. For example, a *one-hit* model of toxicity would propose that a single exposure to a poison might injure an organism. A *multi-hit* model of carcinogenesis would propose that several exposures to a variety of toxins are required for a cancer to form.

hitting bottom A colloquial term for reaching the lowest limits of depression or depravity. The term is often used by addicts in support groups to describe the depths to which their addiction has taken them.

HIV *human immunodeficiency virus.* SEE: *HIV/AIDS.*

HIV/AIDS The spectrum of infection caused by the human immunodeficiency virus (HIV). SEE: *AIDS.*

HIVAN An abbreviation for HIV-associated nephropathy (kidney disease resulting from infection with the human immunodeficiency virus.

HIV-associated dementia AIDS-dementia **complex**.

HIV-associated nephropathy SEE: under *nephropathy.*

hives (hīvz) [origin uncertain] Urticaria.

HIV positive SEE: *Nursing Diagnoses Appendix.*

HIV-related fat redistribution syndrome The atrophy of subcutaneous fat from the arms, legs, and face of some patients treated with highly active antiretroviral therapy for HIV/AIDS, accompanied by increased fat accumulation in the abdomen, the trunk, and near the intra-peritoneal organs. SYN: *antiretroviral treatment-related lipodystrophy syndrome.*

hL *hectoliter.*

HLA *histocompatibility locus antigen; human lymphocyte antigen.*

HLA complex SEE: under *complex.*

HLA mismatch, human leukocyte antigen mismatch The number of human leukocyte antigens (HLAs) found on the cells of a donor organ but not found on the cells of the organ recipient. The greater the disparity between the antigens, the lower the probability of a successful transplantation.

HMD *hyaline membrane disease.*

HMG *human menopausal gonadotropin.*

HMO *health maintenance organization.*

HNC *Certified Holistic Nurse.*

hnRNA Long RNA molecules (heterogeneous nuclear) found in the cell nucleus. They are fashioned into mature RNA by splicing introns.

Ho Symbol for the element holmium.

h/o *history of.*

H_2O Formula for water.

H_2O_2 Formula for hydrogen peroxide.

hoarseness [AS. *has,* harsh] A rough quality of the voice.

ETIOLOGY: Hoarseness may be caused by simple chronic inflammations secondary to chronic nasopharyngitis,

chemical irritants, tobacco, or alcohol. Specific causes of chronic laryngitis include syphilis, tuberculosis, leprosy, neoplasms, papilloma, angioma, fibroma, singer's nodes, carcinoma, paralyses, overuse of the vocal cords, and prolapse of the ventricle of the larynx. Female virilization also usually causes hoarseness.

Hodge, Hugh Lennox (hoj) U.S. gynecologist, 1796–1873.

    H.'s pessary A pessary used to correct retrodeviations of the uterus.

    H.'s plane A plane running parallel to the pelvic inlet and passing through the second sacral vertebra and the upper border of the os pubis.

Hodgkin, Thomas (hoj'kĭn) Brit. physician, 1798–1866.

    H.'s disease ABBR: HD. A malignant lymphoma whose pathological hallmark is the Reed-Sternberg (RS) cell. The disease may affect persons of any age but occurs most often in adults in their early 30s. Its incidence is higher in males than in females. It is slightly more common in Caucasians than in other racial groups. The disease has a bimodal age distribution: it is common in people between the ages of 15 and 35 and in another group of patients older than 50. About 7500 new cases of the disease are diagnosed annually in the U.S. This lymphoma typically begins in a single lymph node (esp. in the neck, axilla, groin, or near the aorta) and spreads to adjacent nodes if it is not recognized and treated early. It may metastasize gradually to lymphatic tissue on both sides of the diaphragm or disseminate widely to tissues outside the lymph nodes. The degree of metastasis defines the stage of the disease; early disease (stage I or II) is present in one or a few lymph nodes, whereas widespread disease has disseminated to both sides of the diaphragm (stage III) or throughout the body (stage IV). The lower the stage of the disease, the better the prognosis. Patients with stage I Hodgkin lymphoma have a 90% survival rate 5 years after diagnosis. SYN: *Hodgkin lymphoma.* SEE: *non-Hodgkin lymphoma; Reed-Sternberg cell; Nursing Diagnoses Appendix.*

    ETIOLOGY: Epstein-Barr virus has been found in the cells of nearly half of all patients with Hodgkin disease.

    SYMPTOMS: Early stage patients may have no symptoms other than a painless lump or enlarged gland in the armpit or neck. Others may develop fevers, night sweats, loss of appetite, and weight loss.

    DIAGNOSIS: The presence of the giant, multinucleated RS cell in tissue obtained for biopsy is diagnostic.

    TREATMENT: The goal of therapy is cure, not only palliation of symptoms.

Treatment depends on accurate staging. Combinations of radiation therapy with chemotherapy have been traditionally used (radiation alone for stages I and II, radiation and chemotherapy for stage III, and chemotherapy for stage IV), although chemotherapies that rely on multiple agents may be as effective. Autologous bone marrow transplant or autologous peripheral blood stem cell transfusion (along with high-dose chemotherapy) also has been used in treatment, esp. among younger patients. Antiemetics, sedatives, antidiarrheals, and antipyretic drugs are given for patient comfort.

PATIENT CARE: All procedures and treatments associated with the plan of care are explained. The patient is assessed for nutritional deficiencies and malnutrition by obtaining regular weight readings, checking anthropomorphic measurements, and monitoring appropriate laboratory studies (e.g., serum protein levels, transferrin levels) and, as necessary, using anergy panels. A well-balanced, high-calorie, high-protein diet is provided. The patient is observed for complications during chemotherapy, including anorexia, nausea, vomiting, mouth ulcers, alopecia, fatigue, and bone marrow depression as well as for adverse reactions to radiation therapy, such as hair loss, anorexia, nausea, vomiting, and fatigue. Supportive care is given as indicated for adverse reactions to chemotherapy or radiation therapy. Comfort measures are provided to promote relaxation, and periods of rest are planned because the patient tires easily. Hematological studies are followed closely during treatment, and colony-stimulating factors are administered as necessary to stimulate red and white blood cell production. Antiemetic drugs are administered as prescribed. The importance of gentle but thorough oral hygiene to prevent stomatitis is stressed. To control pain and bleeding, a soft toothbrush or spongestick (toothette), cotton swabs, and a soothing or anesthetic mouthwash, such as a sodium bicarbonate mixture or viscous lidocaine, are used as prescribed. The patient can apply petroleum jelly to the lips and should avoid astringent mouthwashes. He or she is advised to pace activities to counteract therapy-induced fatigue and is taught relaxation techniques to promote comfort and rest and reduce anxiety. The patient should avoid crowds and any person with a known infection and notify the health care provider if any signs or symptoms of infection develop. Health care providers should stay with the patient during periods of stress and anxiety and provide emotional support to the patient and family. Referral to local support groups may be helpful. Women of childbearing age should delay pregnancy until long-term remission occurs. Follow-up care includes regular examinations with an oncologist and blood tests or radiographic studies to assess for disease recurrence. As necessary, both patient and family are referred for respite or hospice care. The American Cancer Society (through local chapters) provides information and counseling and can assist in obtaining financial assistance if needed. (800-ACS-2345; www.cancer.org)

H.'s lymphoma Hodgkin disease.

Hohmann retractor (hō′măn, ′mon″) [Georg Hohmann, 19th-cent. Ger. surgeon] A handheld retractor used in orthopedic surgery to pull soft tissues away from the operative field and expose the bony tissues being operated upon.

hol-, holo- [Gr. *holos,* entire] Prefixes meaning *complete, entire,* or *homogeneous.*

holding area An Emergency Department area in which patients are kept temporarily before being transferred to an intensive care unit.

holiday heart syndrome The association of cardiac arrhythmias, esp. atrial fibrillation, with binge drinking.

holism (hō′lizm) [*hol-* + *-ism*] The philosophy based on the belief that, in nature, individual entities function as complete units that cannot be reduced to the sum of their parts. The view of the person in holism encompasses the person's body, mind, spirit, and the environment and the society in which he or she lives. SEE: *holistic medicine.* **holistic** (hō-lis′tik), *adj.*

Hollenhorst plaques, Hollenhorst bodies (hŏl′ĕn-horst″) [R. W. Hollenhorst, U.S. ophthalmologist, 1913–2008] Atheromatous plaques that have lodged in the retinal vessels after having been broken off from the lining of other vessels. They appear as shiny irregular patches in the vessels of the retina.

hollow (hŏl′ō) **1.** Having a cavity or space inside. **2.** A depressed area, lower than the surrounding tissue.

Sebileau's h. A depression in the floor of the mouth between the tongue and the sublingual glands.

holmium (hol′mē-ŭm) [*Holmia,* L. name for Stockholm + *-ium* (1)] SYMB: Ho. A rare-earth metal, atomic weight (mass) 164.930, atomic number 67.

holocrine (hŏl′ō-krīn) [″ + *krinein,* to secrete] Pert. to a secretory gland or its secretions consisting of altered cells of the same gland, the opposite of merocrine. SEE: *apocrine.*

holodiastolic (hŏl″ō-dī″ă-stŏl′ĭk) [″ + *diastellein,* to expand] Relating to the entire diastole, esp. a murmur that occurs during all of diastole.

holoenzyme (hŏl″ō-ĕn′zīm) [″ + *en,* in, + *zyme,* leaven] A type of enzyme consisting of a protein portion (apoenzyme) and a non–amino acid portion or prosthetic group. SEE: *apoenzyme; prosthetic group.*

holography (hŏl-ŏg′ră-fē) [″ + *graphein,* to write] A method of producing pictures in which the image appears as a three-dimensional representation of the original object. The picture obtained is called a hologram (i.e., whole message).

holoprosencephaly (hŏl″ō-prŏs″ĕn-sĕf′ă-lē) [″ + *proso,* before, + *enkephalos,* brain] A congenital defect caused by an extra chromosome, either trisomy 13–15 or trisomy 18, which causes deficiency in the forebrain.

holosystolic (hō″lō-sis-tol′ik, hol″ō-) [*hol-* + *systolic*] Pert. to the entire duration of systole. The term is typically used to describe a murmur heard throughout systole, i.e. the murmur of mitral regurgitation.

holotrichous (hōl-ŏt′rĭ-kŭs) [″ + *thrix,* hair] Covered entirely with flagella, said of certain protozoa and bacteria.

holozoic (hŏl″ō-zō′ĭk) [″ + *zoion,* animal] Resembling an animal with respect to the ingestion of food.

Holter monitor (hŏl′tĕr) [Norman Jefferis Holter, U.S. biophysicist, 1914–1983] A portable device small enough to be worn by a patient during normal activity. It consists of an electrocardiograph and a recording system capable of storing up to 24 hr of the individual's ECG record. It is particularly useful in obtaining a record of cardiac arrhythmias that would not be discovered by means of an ECG of only a few minutes' duration. Ambulatory electrocardiographic monitoring also can be used to diagnose losses of consciousness or palpitations of unclear etiology, to assess episodes of unrecognized myocardial ischemia, and to evaluate how well therapeutic interventions against such illnesses are working.

PATIENT CARE: The chest wall of the patient is cleansed and, when necessary, shaved to allow the monitoring electrodes to adhere to the skin. After attachment of electrodes, the patient is advised to wear a loose-fitting garment to avoid friction on the electrodes and their disconnection. The patient is advised to engage in normal physical activities during the day the monitor is worn and to keep a record of his activities (e.g. "3 pm--office meeting with boss; 6 pm--ate dinner; 6:45 pm rode bicycle to supermarket...felt irregular heart beat," etc.) so that any symptoms he experiences can be correlated with monitored heart rhythms. The device is returned typically after 24 hours of use, and the patient's heart rhythms are analyzed for irregularities.

Holt-Oram syndrome (hōlt-ŏr′ăm) [Mary Clayton Holt, contemporary Brit. physician; Samuel Oram, contemporary Brit. physician] An inherited disorder, transmitted as an autosomal trait, that is marked by anomalies of the upper limbs and heart. Clinical manifestations vary from minimal radiographic changes to overt structural changes in the hands and arms and single or multiple atrial and ventricular defects that may be life-threatening.

holy basil (hōl′ē ba′zĭl, bā′) An herb from the mint family, *Ocimum sanctum,* native to the tropics. It is used in Hindu gardens as an aromatic plant that focuses the mind during meditation and in Ayurvedic medicine as an adaptogen and a promoter of a long life. SYN: *tulasi.*

Homans sign (hō′mănz) [John Homans, U.S. surgeon, 1877–1954] Pain in the calf when the foot is passively dorsiflexed. This is a physical finding suggestive of venous thrombosis of the deep veins of the calf; however, diagnostic reliability is limited, that is, elicited calf pain may be associated with conditions other than thrombosis, and an absence of calf pain does not rule out thrombosis.

home A residence where individuals return regularly to eat, live, recreate, rest, and sleep.

home assessment An evaluation of the home environment of older persons and of persons with functional impairments, usually by an occupational therapist or home care specialist, in order to prevent falls and injuries, identify architectural barriers and safety hazards, and recommend modifications or devices for improving mobility, safety, and independent function. SYN: *home evaluation.*

home evaluation Home assessment.

home health care The provision for the medical, nursing, and social needs of a person in his or her own residence or in the residence of a family member.

homeless (hōm′lĕs) Having no permanent or usual domicile. People who are homeless are often economically disadvantaged, socially isolated, unemployed, and/or uninsured. They may have limited access to preventive and acute health care and may suffer from untreated acute, chronic, or infectious illnesses. Homelessness is associated with a marked increase in mortality. The incidence of homelessness in the U.S. population is estimated to be nearly 1%. Internet resources on homelessness include the webpage of the National Coalition for the Homeless (www.nationalhomeless.org/factsheets/).
homelessness (hōm′lĕs-nĕs), n.

home maintenance, impaired Inability to independently maintain a safe, growth-promoting immediate environment. SEE: *Nursing Diagnoses Appendix.*

home modification Any physical modification to a residence that increases its usage, safety, security, and independence, esp. for those with motor or sensory limitations.

homeo- [Gr. *homoios,* like, similar] Prefix meaning *likeness; resemblance; constant unchanging state.* The variant *homoeo-* is used outside the US. The less common variant *homoio-* is used inside and outside the U.S.

homeodynamics (hō″mē-ō-dī-năm′ĭks) Three principles proposed by nursing theorist, Martha Rogers, which suggest that human nature is dynamic, everchanging, and holistic. Rogers calls the homeodynamic principles "helicy," "resonancy," and "integrality." She asserts that human beings are an integral part of their environment rather than creatures that merely adapt to their environment. Nursing assessment should therefore focus on a person's experiences, expressions, and perceptions, rather than on his or her coping mechanisms, modes of adaptation, or reactions to illness.

homeopath, homeopathist (hō′mē-ō-păth″, hō-mē-ŏp′ă-thĭst) One who practices homeopathy.

homeopathy (hō-mē-op′ă-thē) [*homeo-* + *-pathy*] A school of healing founded in Germany by Dr. Samuel Christian Friedrich Hahnemann (1755–1843) in the late 18th century and introduced into the U.S. in the early 19th century. It is based on the proposal that very dilute doses of extracts, medicines, or other substances that produce symptoms of a disease in healthy people will cure that disease in affected patients, i.e., "like cures like." Homeopathy differs from traditional (allopathic) medicine in that it emphasizes stimulating the body to heal itself. SYN: *homeotherapy.* SEE: *allopathy; theory of infinitesimals, theory of psora* under theory. **homeopathic** (hō″mē-ō-path′ik), *adj.*

homeostasis (hō″mē-ō-stā′sĭs) [*homeo-* + *stasis,*] The state of dynamic equilibrium of the internal environment of the body that is maintained by the everchanging processes of feedback and regulation in response to external or internal changes. SYN: *dynamic equilibrium.* **homeostatic** (-stat′ik), *adj.*

homeotherapy (hō″mē-ō-thĕr′ă-pē) [″ + *therapeia,* treatment] **1.** Any treatment employed in homeopathy. **2.** A synonym for the discipline known as homeopathy.

homeotherm (hō″mē-ŏ-thĕrm″) [*homeo-* + *thermo-*] An organism that maintains a constant body temperature despite fluctuating environmental temperatures; a warm-blooded animal.

SYN: *homotherm.* SEE: *ectotherm.*

homeothermal, homeothermic (-thĕr′măl, -thĕr′mik), *adj.*

home safety checklist A documentation tool to evaluate, anticipate, and prevent injuries (usually caused by accidental falls) to an impaired individual in his or her own home.

homesharing (hōm′shar″ing) The occupation of a residence by two or more unrelated people. Rent-free living may be provided to one of the people, typically in exchange for services, e.g., housekeeping or meal preparation, for the other.

homesickness [AS. *ham,* home, + *seoc,* ill] Sadness, depression, and anxiety related to being away from home or loved ones.

home visitation The practice by a health care professional of going to a patient's residence to provide care.

homework A task assigned by a mental health counselor for a patient to complete between-therapy sessions.

homicide (hŏm′ĭ-sīd) [L. *homo,* man, + *caedere,* to kill] **1.** Murder. **2.** A murderer. **homicidal,** *adj.*

homing (hōm′ĭng) Movement of a cell toward specific tissues, cytokines, or antigens.

hominid (hŏm′ĭ-nĭd) [″ + *eidos,* form, shape] A primate of the Hominidae family. Humans are the only surviving species.

Hominidae (hō-mŏn′ĭ-dē) [L. *homo,* man, + Gr. *ideos,* pert. to] A family of primates that includes ancient and modern humans.

Homo (hō′mō) [L., man] A genus of primates of the family Hominidae. The sole existing species is humankind, *Homo sapiens.* Evidence from fossils indicates extinct species (e.g., *H. habilis, H. erectus, H. australopithecus.*)

homo-, hom- [Gr. *homos,* same] Prefixes meaning *the same* or *a likeness.*

homocysteine (hō″mō-sis′-tĕ′ēn″) ABBR: hcy. $HSCH_2CH_2CH(NH_2)COOH$; amino acid produced by the catabolism of methionine. With serine, it forms a complex that eventually produces cysteine and homoserine. There is evidence that a high level of homocysteine in the blood may be associated with an increased risk of developing atherosclerosis. Although blood homocysteine levels may be lowered by eating foods rich in folic acid, e.g., green leafy vegetables and fruits, and by vitamin pills containing folic acid and vitamin B6 or B12, research has failed to show that any of these causes a significant reduction in cardiovascular disease.

homocystine (hō″mō-sīs′tĭn) $H_{16}N_2O_4S_2$; a homologue of cystine formed by condensation of two molecules of homocysteine.

homocystinuria (hō″mō-sīs-tĭn-ū′rē-ă)

An inherited disease caused by the absence of the enzyme essential to the metabolism of homocystine. Patients are mentally retarded and have subluxated lenses, a tendency toward seizures, liver disease, an increased risk of atherosclerosis and blood clotting disorders, and growth retardation (short stature).

homocytotropic (hō″mō-sī″tō-trŏp′ĭk) [″ + *kytos*, cell, + *tropos*, a turning] Having an affinity for cells of the same species.

homoeo- SEE: *homeo-*.

homoerotic (hō″mō-ĕ-rŏt′ĭk) Homosexual.

homogametic (hō″mō-gă-mĕt′ĭk) [″ + *gamos*, marriage] Pert. to the production of one kind of gamete with regard to the sex chromosome. In humans, the XX female is the homogametic sex, as all ova produced contain the X chromosome. SEE: *heterogametic*.

homogenate (hō-mŏj′ĕ-nāt) The material obtained when something is homogenized.

homogeneous (hō″mŏ-jē′nē-ŭs) [″ + *genos*, kind] Uniform in structure, composition, or nature; the opposite of heterogeneous.

homogeneous system Any system whose components cannot be separated mechanically.

homogenize (hō-mŏj′ĕ-nīz) To make homogeneous; to produce a uniform emulsion or suspension of two substances normally immiscible.

homograft (hō′mŏ-graft″) Allograft.

homoio- SEE: *homeo-*.

homolateral (hō″mō-lăt′ĕr-ăl) [Gr. *homos*, same, + L. *latus*, side] Ipsilateral.

homologous (hŏ-mol′ŏ-gŭs) [Gr. *homologos*, agreeing, of one mind] **1.** In biology, similar in origin and structure but different in function, such as the forelegs of a quadruped, the arms of a human, and the wings of a bird; or a penis and a clitoris. SEE: *analogous*. **2.** In genetics, having the same genes or alleles with loci usually in the same order.

homologue, homolog (hom′ŏ-log″) [Gr. *homologos*, agreeing, of one mind] **1.** An organ or part common to several species. **2.** One that corresponds to a part or organ in another structure. **3.** In chemistry, any member of a series that resembles the other members in action and general structure but has a constant compositional difference such as a methyl, CH_3, group.

homology (hŏ-mol′ŏ-jē) [Gr. *homologos*, agreeing, of one mind] In biology, similarity in structure or origin but difference in function. SEE: *analogy*.

homonomous (hō-mŏn′ŏ-mŭs) [″ + *nomos*, law] Pert. to parts arranged in a series that are similar in form and structure, as metameres of a segmented animal or the fingers and toes of a mammal.

homonymous (hō-mŏn′ĭ-mŭs) [″ + *onyma*, name] Having the same name.

homophobe (hō′mă-fōb″) One who fears or dislikes homosexuals.

homophobia (hō″mă-fō′bē-ă) An abnormal fear of homosexuals.

homoplastic (hō″mō-plăs′tĭk) [″ + *plassein*, to form] Having a similar form and structure.

Homo sapiens (hō′mō sā′pē-ĕnz) [L. *homo*, man, + *sapiens*, wise, sapient] The species to which modern humans belong. SEE: *Homo*.

homoserine lactone (hō″mō-sĕr′ēn lăk′tō″n) A signaling chemical used by gram-negative bacteria in quorum sensing.

homosexual (hō″mō-sĕks′ū-ăl) [Gr. *homos*, same, + L. *sexus*, sex] A person who has sexual interest in or sexual intercourse exclusively with members of his or her own sex.

homosexuality (hō″mō-sĕks″ū-ăl′ĭ-tē) A condition in which the libido is directed toward one of the same sex.

homotetramer (hō″mō-te′tră-mĕr) [*homo-* + *tetramer*] A structure such as a molecule or a polymer made of four identical parts.

homotopic (hōm″ō-tŏp′ĭk) [″ + *topos*, place] Occurring at the same site on the body.

homotransplantation (hō″mō-trăns″plăn-tā′shŭn) [″ + L. *trans*, across, + *plantare*, to plant] Allotransplantation.

homotype (hō′mō-tīp) [″ + *typos*, type] One organ or part similar in form and function to another, as one of two paired parts or organs.

homotypic (hō′mō-tīp′ĭk) Of the same form and type.

homovanillic acid (hō-mō-vă-nĭl′ĭk) ABBR: HVA. A catecholamine that is a metabolite of dopamine. It is found in excessive quantities in patients with neuroendocrine tumors, such as pheochromocytoma or neuroblastoma.

homozygosis (hōm″ō-zī-gō′sĭs) [″ + *zygon*, yoke, pair, + *osis*, condition] The formation of a zygote by the union of gametes that have one or more identical alleles. SEE: *heterozygosis*.

homozygote (hōm″ō-zī′gōt) A homozygous individual; an individual developing from gametes with similar alleles and thus possessing like pairs of genes for a given hereditary characteristic.

homozygous (hōm″ō-zī′gŭs) **1.** Produced by similar alleles. **2.** Said of an organism when germ cells transmit nearly identical alleles as a result of inbreeding.

homunculus (hō-mŭn′kū-lŭs) [L. diminutive of *homo*, man] **1.** A dwarf in whom the body parts develop in their normal proportions. **2.** An anatomic device for representing the innervation of body parts in the central nervous system.

HON *Health on the Net Foundation.*

honey [AS. *hunig*] A sweet thick liquid substance produced by bees via the enzymatic digestion of the sucrose in nectar into fructose and glucose. The honey's color and flavor are determined by the flowers from which the nectar was obtained. Honey has been used by humans as a food since ancient times. Honey is composed of mostly fructose and glucose with a typical moisture content of about 17%. It is unsafe for human infants to consume honey because it can contain *Clostridium botulinum* spores. This is usually not an issue for older individuals, as their stomach acid is sufficient to inhibit the growth of this organism.

honeymoon 1. A disease remission, used esp. to describe the brief period after the diagnosis of type 1 diabetes mellitus during which no insulin therapy is required. **2.** A period of celebration, travel, or increased sexual activity after a wedding.

honorific [L. *honorificus,* honor-making] To convey honor upon a person, esp. while writing or speaking about an individual. SEE: *pejorative.*

hook (hook) [AS. *hok,* an angle] **1.** A curved instrument. **2.** The terminal device in an upper extremity orthosis.

hookah (hoo′kă) [Arabic, box, bowl (for a pipe)] Water pipe.

Hooke law (huk) The stress used to stretch or compress a body is proportional to the strain as long as the elastic limits of the body have not been exceeded.

hookworm A parasitic nematode belonging to the superfamily Strongyloidea, esp. *Ancylostoma duodenale* and *Necator americanus.* SEE: illus.

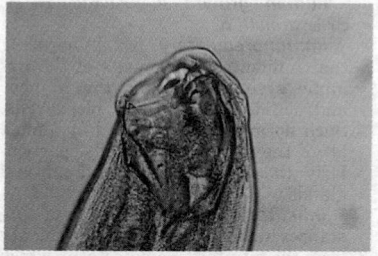

OLD WORLD HOOKWORM

The anterior end of an adult worm

HOOKWORM DISEASE: Hookworm eggs deposited on the soil in feces mature into larvae capable of penetrating the skin, esp. the bare skin of the foot. An allergic or inflamed rash may develop at the entry site. The larvae pass from the skin into the venous circulation and travel to the alveolar capillaries of the lungs, up the bronchi and trachea and into the gastrointestinal tract. There they mature, attach to the mucous membrane of the intestine, and begin feeding on host blood. The adults secrete an anticoagulant, which promotes additional bleeding. Eventually, the host develops iron-deficiency anemia. Patients sometimes report nausea, colicky abdominal pain, bloating, and pica. Affected children may suffer growth retardation. The adult worms produce eggs that are excreted in the feces, perpetuating the cycle of infection. The detection of these eggs in the stool provides the basis for diagnosis of the disease.

TREATMENT: Mebendazole and pyrantel pamoate are used to eradicate the infection. Iron supplements are needed to treat the anemia.

hope The expectation that something desired will occur. One of the bases of professional health care is encouraging and supporting the presence of hope while providing accurate information and realistic reassurance.

hope, readiness for enhanced A pattern of expectations and desires that is sufficient for mobilizing energy on one's own behalf and can be strengthened. SEE: *Nursing Diagnoses Appendix.*

hopelessness Despair; loss of faith in the possibility of a positive outcome. Loss of trust in one's prospects may give rise to depression, desperation, or antisocial behaviors. SEE: *grief reaction; helplessness; Nursing Diagnoses Appendix.*

Hopmann, Carl Melchior (hop′măn, man″) Ger. rhinologist, 1849–1925.

H. papilloma A papillomatous overgrowth of the nasal mucosa.

H. polyp A papillary growth of the nasal mucosa.

horizontal [L. *horizontalis*] **1.** Parallel to or in the plane of the horizon. **2.** A transverse plane of the body that is at right angles to the vertical axis of the body.

hormesis (hor-mē′sĭs) [Gr. *hormesis,* rapid motion] **1.** The stimulating effect of a low dose of a substance that is toxic in higher doses. **2.** The controversial hypothesis that very low doses of ionizing radiation may not be harmful and may even have beneficial effects.

hormone (hor′mōn″) [Gr. *horman,* to excite, urge on] **1.** A substance originating in an organ, gland, or body part, conveyed through the blood to another body part, and chemically stimulating that part to increase or decrease functional activity or to increase or decrease secretion of another hormone. **2.** The secretion of the ductless glands, e.g., insulin from the pancreas. SEE: *endocrine gland.* **hormonal** (hŏr-mōn′ăl), *adj.*

adrenocortical h. ABBR: ACH. A hormone (such as aldosterone or cortisol) secreted by the cortex of the adrenal gland. SYN: *cortical **h***. SEE: *adrenal gland*.

adrenocorticotropic h. ABBR: ACTH. A hormone that is secreted by the anterior lobe of the pituitary gland and controls the development and functioning of the adrenal cortex, including its secretion of glucocorticoids and androgens. SYN: *corticotropin*.

adrenomedullary h. Any of several hormones (such as epinephrine and norepinephrine) produced by the adrenal medulla.

androgenic h. Androgen.

anterior pituitary h. Any of several hormones secreted by the anterior lobe of the pituitary, including corticotropin, follicle-stimulating hormone, gonadotropin, growth hormone, luteinizing hormone, melanocyte-stimulating hormone, prolactin, and thyrotropin.

antidiuretic h. ABBR: ADH. A peptide hormone that plays a crucial role in limiting the amount of water excreted by the kidneys. Deficiency of ADH causes central diabetes insipidus, excess causes water retention and hyponatremia. SYN: *vasopressin*.

ADH is produced by the hypothalamus and stored in the posterior pituitary gland; it is secreted when the osmolarity of plasma rises. Secretion of ADH increases the concentration of the urine by preventing water losses from the renal tubules. ADH also causes constriction of arterioles (raising blood pressure) and increases levels of clotting factor VIII. ADH can be administered to patients in cardiac arrest as an alternative to epinephrine.

atrial natriuretic hormone Atrial natriuretic **factor**.

bioidentical natural h. Bioidentical synthetic **h.**

bioidentical synthetic h. ABBR: BSH. A compound extracted from plants or formulated in the laboratory and used to replace or increase concentrations of hormones found in the body. The most commonly manufactured and marketed BSHs are the sex steroid hormones (estrogen, progesterone, and testosterone). SYN: *bioidentical natural **h**.*

corpus luteum h. Progesterone.

cortical h. Adrenocortical **h.**

corticotropin-releasing h. ABBR: CRH. A hormone that is released from the hypothalamus and acts on the anterior pituitary to increase secretion of adrenal corticotropin hormone. In response to stress, CRH causes hyperglycemia, increased oxygen consumption, increased cardiac output, and decreased sexual activity; suppresses release of growth hormone; diminishes gastrointestinal function; stimulates respiration; and causes behavioral changes. SYN: *corticotropin-releasing **factor***.

counterregulatory h. Any of the hor-

mones that oppose the effects of insulin. They include glucagon, epinephrine, norepinephrine, cortisol, and growth hormone.

digestive h. Any of a group of hormones produced by the stomach or small intestinal mucosa and stimulating various tissues to release enzymes, produce fluids, or affect gastrointestinal motility. They include gastrin, motilin, secretin, cholecystokinin, and vasoactive intestinal peptide.

estrogenic h. Estrogen.

follicle-stimulating h. ABBR: FSH. A hormone that is secreted by the anterior lobe of the pituitary and stimulates maturation of the ovarian follicles in women. In men, the hormone is important in maintaining spermatogenesis.

follicle-stimulating h. releasing hormone ABBR: FSH-RH. A hormone from the hypothalamus that regulates release of follicle-stimulating hormone.

gonadotropic h., gonadotrophic hormone Gonadotropin.

gonadotropin-releasing h. ABBR: Gn-RH. The hormone produced in the hypothalamus that causes the pituitary to release luteinizing hormone and follicle-stimulating hormone. This hormone is used in treating endometriosis. SYN: *luteinizing hormone-releasing **h**.*

growth h. ABBR: GH. A hormone secreted by the anterior pituitary and regulating the cell division and protein synthesis necessary for normal growth. It is a protein made from a single chain of amino acids; molecular weight 22 kDa. SYN: *somatotropin*.

growth hormone-releasing h. ABBR: GH-RH. A hormone from the hypothalamus that stimulates the release of growth hormone. SYN: *somatotropin-releasing **h**.*

human growth h. ABBR: HGH. SEE: *growth **h**.*

immunoregulatory h. A hormone that influences components of the immune system, including the number and activity of the white blood cells. Such hormones are secreted by almost all of the glands in the body, particularly the hypothalamus and adrenal glands.

inhibitory h. Any of a group of substances limiting the release of hormones from the pituitary. Somatostatin, which inhibits the release of growth hormone, is included in this group.

interstitial cell-stimulating h. ABBR: ICSH. An obsolete term for luteinizing hormone.

intestinal h. Any of several hormones produced by the mucosa of the intestine. They include cholecystokinin, motilin, secretin, and vasoactive inhibitory peptide.

lipolytic h. Any hormone (such as epinephrine, glucagon, and cortisol) that promotes release of free fatty acids from fat tissue.

luteal h. Progesterone.

luteinizing h. ABBR: LH. A hormone produced by the anterior lobe of the pituitary, in females stimulating the development of the corpus luteum and helping in the secretion of progesterone, and in males stimulating the development of interstitial cells of the testes to produce testosterone. SYN: *luteotropic* **h.**

luteinizing hormone-releasing h. ABBR: LH-RH. Gonadotropin-releasing **h.**

luteotropic h. ABBR: LTH. Luteinizing **h.**

melanocyte-stimulating h. ABBR: MSH. A hormone of the anterior pituitary gland that causes pigmentation of the skin in humans. SYN: *intermedin*.

ovarian h. A hormone produced by the ovary. SEE: *estradiol; estriol; estrogen; estrone; progesterone.*

pancreatic h. A hormone produced by the islets of Langerhans of the pancreas. SEE: *glucagon; insulin.*

parathyroid h. ABBR: PTH. A hormone secreted by the parathyroid glands that regulates blood levels of calcium and phosphorus. A deficiency results in hypoparathyroidism and hypocalcemia; in excess, it causes hyperparathyroidism and hypercalcemia. SYN: *parathormone*.

placental h. Any of the hormones secreted by the placenta, including estrogen, progesterone, and human chorionic gonadotropin.

posterior pituitary h. Any of the hormones secreted by the posterior lobe of the pituitary (such as vasopressin and oxytocin). SEE: *antidiuretic* **h.**

progestational h. Progesterone.

releasing h. ABBR: RH. Any of a group of substances secreted by the hypothalamus that control or inhibit the release of various hormones. They include thyrotropin-releasing hormone, gonadotropin-releasing hormone, dopamine, growth hormone-releasing hormone, corticotropin-releasing hormone, and somatostatin. Dopamine and somatostatin act to inhibit release of the hormones they act upon.

sex h. An androgen or an estrogen.

somatotropic h. ABBR: STH. Somatotropin.

somatotropin-releasing h. Growth hormone-releasing **h.**

steroid h. One of the sex hormones and hormones of the adrenal cortex.

synthetic human growth h. A growth hormone made with recombinant DNA techniques.

testicular h. A hormone produced by the interstitial tissue of the testis (such as testosterone and inhibin).

thymic h. Any of the hormones produced by the thymus that may help attract lymphoid stem cells to the thymus and stimulate their development into mature T lymphocytes. They include thymulin, thymopoietin, and thymosin.

thyroid h. Either of two hormones, thyroxine (T_4) or triiodothyronine (T_3), secreted by the follicles of the thyroid gland. They act on receptors in tissues throughout the body to increase the production of cellular proteins, the metabolic rate, and the activities of the sympathetic nervous system. Deficiency of thyroid hormone produces clinical hypothyroidism; excess causes hyperthyroidism.

thyroid-stimulating h. ABBR: TSH. Thyrotropin.

thyrotropic h. Thyrotropin.

thyrotropin-releasing h. ABBR: TRH. A hormone secreted by the hypothalamus that stimulates the anterior pituitary to release thyrotropin. It was formerly called thyroid-stimulating hormone-releasing factor.

tropic h. A hormone secreted by one gland (e.g. the pituitary gland) that stimulates another gland to secrete its hormone or hormones.

hormone replacement therapy ABBR: HRT. The administration of supplemental conjugated estrogen and progestin to treat hormonal deficiency states, relieve menopausal vasomotor symptoms, and manage postmenopausal atrophic vaginitis. It may also be used, with caution, as adjunctive therapy for osteoporosis. HRT may increase a woman's risk of dying from heart disease, pulmonary embolism, stroke, and breast and endometrial cancers.

hormonogenesis (hor″mō-nō-jĕn′ĕ-sĭs) [″ + *genesis*, generation, birth] The production of hormones. **hormonogenic** (-jĕn′ĭk), adj.

hormonotherapy (hor″mō-nō-thĕr′ă-pē) The therapeutic use of hormones. SYN: *cytotherapy* (1); *endocrinotherapy; glandular therapy; organotherapy.*

horn (horn) A cutaneous outgrowth composed chiefly of keratin; a hornlike projection. SYN: *cornu.*

h. of Ammon Hippocampus.

anterior h. The main column of neuron cell bodies and unmyelinated cell processes (gray matter) running through the ventral quadrant of each half of the spinal cord. In stained cross-sections of spinal cord, the gray matter forms the rough shape of a butterfly; the anterior horns are the lower wings. SYN: *ventral* **h.** SEE: *spinal cord.*

cicatricial h. A cutaneous horn originating in scar tissue.

cutaneous h. A hard, horny outgrowth from the skin. It is slow-growing, benign, and may be small or large, 10 to 12 cm, in diameter.

dorsal h. The main column of neuron cell bodies and unmyelinated cell processes (ie, gray matter) running through the dorsal quadrant of each half of the spinal cord. In stained cross-sections of spinal cord, the gray matter forms the rough shape of a butterfly; the dorsal horns are the upper wings. SYN: *posterior horn.* SEE: *spinal cord.*

intermediolateral h. Lateral horn.

lateral horn A column of neuron cell bodies and unmyelinated cell processes (ie, gray matter) running through the lateral quadrant of spinal cord segments C8–L2 In stained cross-sections of spinal cord, the lateral horns form a small bulge of gray matter between the dorsal and ventral horns. The lateral horns contain the preganglionic cell bodies of the sympathetic nervous system. SYN: *intermediolateral h.; intermediolateral cell column; zona intermedia.* SEE: *spinal cord.*

posterior h. Dorsal horn.

sebaceous h. A hard protrusion from a sebaceous gland.

uterine h. Either of the two upper corners of the uterus into which the uterine tubes enter.

ventral h. Anterior horn.

warty h. A hard outgrowth from a wart.

Horner syndrome (hor′nĕr) [Johann F. Horner, Swiss ophthalmologist, 1831–1886] A syndrome characterized by contraction of the pupil, partial ptosis of the eyelid, enophthalmos, and sometimes loss of sweating over one side of the face. The syndrome is caused by paralysis of the cervical sympathetic nerve trunk, often as a result of an anesthetic mishap or a tumor in the superior sulcus of the lung.

horopter (hō-rŏp′tĕr) [Gr. *horos,* limit, + *opter,* observer] The sum of all points in space that have a corresponding point on the retina of the eye.

horror Intense fear, revulsion, or dread caused by seeing or hearing something that is terrifying, shocking, or perceived to be life-threatening to the individual or to others.

horse chestnut (hors ches′nŭt″) [translation of L. *Castanea equina*] A large deciduous tree (*Aesculus hippocastanum*) native to the Balkans and cultivated in temperate regions worldwide. An herbal remedy from this tree is promoted as a dietary supplement for venous insufficiency, nocturnal leg cramps, and edema in the lower extremities as well as a topical agent for hemorrhoids, skin ulcers, and sports injuries.

horsepower A unit of power equal to 745.7 watts or 550 foot pounds per second.

horseshoe crab (hŏrs′shoo″, hŏrsh′oo krăb) *Limulus polyphemus,* a species of saltwater arthropod that is a member of the Chelicerates, the subphylum containing scorpions and spiders, rather than the Crustaceans, the subphylum containing true crabs. The Limulus body structure has remained nearly unchanged for 450 million years, longer than almost any other living animal. Its blood is blue rather than red because oxygen is carried by a copper-based compound rather than hemoglobin, which is an iron-based compound; Limulus blood is used in testing drugs for bacterial contamination.

Hortaea werneckii A yeast that is the causative agent of the fungal skin infection known as tinea nigra. The lesions are brown or black and occur primarily on the hands.

hospice (hos′pĭs) [Fr. *hospice,* fr L. *hospitium,* entertainment, place of entertainment] An interdisciplinary program of palliative care and supportive services that addresses the physical, spiritual, social, and economic needs of terminally ill patients and their families. This care may be provided in the home or a hospice center. In 2008 more than 35% of Americans who died received hospice program support. To obtain information about locating a hospice program, contact the National Hospice and Palliative Care Organization (NHPCO) (www.nhpco.org/), telephone 800-658-8898; Hospice Foundation of America (www.hospicefoundation.org), telephone 202-638-5419; or the Hospice Association of America (www.hospice-america.org).

PATIENT CARE: Health care providers who care for the terminally ill should focus first and foremost on the comfort of the patient. They may provide counselling services, help patients with physical needs (such as bathing, dressing, or toileting), give respite to fatigued loved ones, and assist in the use of devices and medications that alleviate breathlessness, insomnia, pain, or suffering. The care is usually provided in the patient's home, but may periodically require hospitalization or skilled care, and is insured by many health care payers, such as Medicaid, Medicare, or commercial insurers. As death approaches, nurses, physicians, social workers, and/or volunteers marshal their efforts to support the patient and significant others. The members of the care team provide interpersonal, practical, and spiritual assistance to prepare for the patient's end of life respecting the patient's wishes for a religious service, a memorial service, care of the deceased, and/or burial arrangements. Follow up visits after death with family and intimate partners may help ease their acceptance of loss, and help them navigate a challenging life transition.

hospital (hos'pit"ăl) [L. *hospitalis,* pert. to a guest] An institution in which the sick and injured are confined during acute treatment.

    base h. **1.** A hospital unit within the lines of an army that receives wounded and sick patients from the front line. **2.** The medical control hospital for a paramedic unit.

    camp h. An immobile military unit for the care of the sick and wounded.

    charity h. A hospital that provides care to the poor and the uninsured.

    combat support h. ABBR: CSH. A large mobile military hospital that accepts seriously injured military personnel whose condition has been stabilized near the battlefield by a mobile surgical team. A CSH provides intensive care unit support for the critically injured. Some patients with battlefield injuries are stabilized at the CSH; others are transported to major medical centers for long-term care.

    critical access h. A hospital in a rural area that has a limited capacity and provides a limited number of services.

    evacuation h. A mobile advance hospital unit that replaces field hospitals and supplements base hospitals.

    field h. A portable military hospital beyond the zone of conflict and the dressing stations.

    geriatric day h. A form of adult day care providing rehabilitative, medical, and personal care services as well as social and recreational services for older adults. SEE: *respite **care***.

    magnet h. A hospital officially recognized for its leadership and policies that increase the recruitment and retention of registered professional nurses. The Magnet Recognition Program was developed by the American Nurses Credentialing Center (ANCC) to recognize health care organizations that provide nursing excellence. The program also provides a vehicle for disseminating successful nursing practices and strategies.

    nonprofit h. A hospital that is exempt from paying income and property taxes. In such a facility, funds earned are reinvested in the hospital and its services instead of being paid as dividends to shareholders.

    shuttered h. A hospital that has been closed and is no longer in active, daily use. It may be reopened in times of crisis to care for the homeless, injured, or sick, esp. after a mass casualty incident.

    specialty h. **1.** A hospital that provides a limited range of services (e.g., orthopedic surgery, ophthalmology, or obstetrics). 2. A hospital in which two thirds of Medicare patients receive care for just two Diagnosis-Related Groups (DRGs). **2.** A hospital in which two thirds of Medicare patients receive care for just two Diagnosis-Related Groups (DRGs). **3.** A hospital in which two thirds of patients are assigned for outpatient surgical procedures.

    teaching h. A hospital concerned with instructing medical students, house officers (residents), and allied health personnel in addition to providing medical care. The teaching programs may or may not be part of degree-granting programs, but most provide practical and didactic training that is needed to gain licensure in the health professions.

hospital-at-home care   SEE: under *care*.

hospital bed entrapment   Injury to a patient as a result of getting stuck within or pinned down by components of a hospital bed, e.g., between the bed rails and bed frame, or the mattress and head board. SYN: *bed entrapment*.

hospital cost-to-charge ratio   The total amount of money required to operate a hospital, divided by the sum of the revenues received from patient care and all other operating revenues.

hospital discharge   An official release from hospital care or from a medical care facility by a physician or other medical care worker.

hospital information system   ABBR: HIS. A large computerized database management system that processes patient data in order to support patient care. The system is used by health care clinicians to access patient data and to plan, implement, and evaluate care. SYN: *clinical information system; patient information system*.

hospitalism   [L. *hospitalis,* pert. to a guest, + Gr. *-ismos,* condition] **1.** The air of depression and apathy that often surrounds a group of seriously ill patients, esp. if they are in an overcrowded ward. **2.** A neurotic tendency to seek hospitalization and, once hospitalized, to resist being discharged.

hospitalist   A physician in charge of caring for hospitalized patients. These practitioners are rarely involved in outpatient care; they concentrate their efforts on caring for emergency patients, critical care patients, and patients confined to wards.

hospitalization   The confinement of a patient in a hospital.

Hospital Quality Alliance   ABBR: HQA. An alliance formed in 2002 by hospitals, health insurers, health care professional organizations, and public agencies interested in health care quality.

    It develops and publishes information for the general public on health-related quality, cost, and value on its website, www.hospitalcompare.hhs.gov.

hospital twinning   The sharing of resources between two or more hospitals, typically one in an urban, industrialized area and another in a less developed country or region. Twinning is a practice designed to make the technical expertise, infrastructure, and human resources of industrialized health care available to areas with extensive health care needs but relatively limited assets.

host (hōst) [L. *hospes,* stranger, guest, host] **1.** The organism from which a parasite obtains its nourishment. **2.** In embryology, the larger and more relatively normal of conjoined twins. **3.** In transplantation of tissue, the one who receives the graft.

> **accidental h.** A host other than the usual or normal one.

> **alternate h.** Intermediate **h.** (1).

> **compromised h.** A person who lacks resistance to infection due to to a deficiency in any of the host defenses. SEE: *AIDS; host defense mechanisms; immunocompromised.*

> **dead-end h.** An infected organism that does not have the ability to transmit infection to the definitive host. SYN: *incidental h.*

> **definitive h. 1.** The final host or the host in which the parasite reaches sexual maturity. SYN: *final h.* **2.** The vertebrate, when the intermediate host is an invertebrate.

> **final h.** Definitive **h.** (1).

> **immunocompromised h.** SEE: *immunocompromised.*

> **incidental h.** Dead-end **h.**

> **intermediate h. 1.** The host in which a parasite passes through its larval or asexual stages of development. SYN: *alternate h.* **2.** The invertebrate host, when the final host is a vertebrate.

> **paratenic h.** A parasitic organism in which the parasite thrives but does not undergo development.

> **h. of predilection** The host preferred by a parasite.

> **reservoir h.** A host other than the usual or normal one, in which a parasite is capable of living. The reservoir host is a source of infestation.

> **transfer h.** An interim host that is not essential for the completion of the life cycle of the parasite.

hostility (hŏ-stĭl´ĭ-tē) The manifestation of anger, animosity, or antagonism in a situation in which such a reaction is unwarranted. Hostility may be directed toward oneself, others, or inanimate objects. It is almost always a symptom of depression.

host range SEE: under *range.*

hot (hot) **1.** Having a high temperature. **2.** Actively conducting an electric current. **3.** A colloquial term for radioactive.

hot-cathode tube A vacuum tube in which the cathode is electrically heated to incandescence and in which the sup-

ply of electrons depends on the temperature of the cathode.

hot flash In women, a common but not universal symptom of declining ovarian function, falling estradiol levels, and impending menopause, marked by the sensation of sudden, brief flares of heat, followed by sweating. During the event, the face and anterior chest wall flush and radiate warmth. These symptoms may occur during the day, or they may interrupt sleep. In men, these same symptoms often occur during androgen ablation therapy for prostate cancer. SYN: *hot flush.*

> TREATMENT: For women, discriminant use of hormone replacement therapy may be effective in eliminating symptoms within 1 month; herbal remedies or soy protein have also been suggested but not unequivocally substantiated by research; however, in the absence of supplemental estrogen, spontaneous resolution occurs in about 2 to 3 years. Men with hot flashes during treatment for prostate cancer may respond to antidepressant medications, such as venlafaxine. SEE: *menopause; estrogen replacement therapy; hormone replacement therapy.*

hot knife SEE: under *knife.*

hotline A continuously managed telephone line for communicating with professionals who can help people experiencing crises, such as abuse or neglect, illicit drug distribution, impending suicide, intoxications and poisoning, domestic violence, or rape.

hot spot SEE: under *spot.*

hot water bag SEE: under *bag.*

hot water bottle A rubber or plastic bottle or bag for applying dry heat to circumscribed areas and for keeping moist applications warm. SYN: *hot water bag.*

Hounsfield unit (hownz´fēld) In computed tomography (CT), a number or value that represents the attenuation of x-rays through a voxel (volume element) in the body and is assigned to the corresponding pixel (picture element) on the image. This number is relative to the standard, which is the absorption of x-rays in water on a scale of +1,000 to −1,000. It is also known as a CT unit.

housefly *Musca domestica,* a fly belonging to the order Diptera. It may be a mechanical carrier of pathogenic microorganisms.

household system of measurement Any of the volumes represented by commonly used items, esp. kitchen utensils, as they are applied to administering medicines. In this system a teaspoon is considered to be roughly equivalent to 5 mL; a tablespoon, to 15 mL; and a cup, to 240 mL. Common utensils such as these are often used when giving liquid medications to children and others who have difficulty swallowing capsules or tablets.

Howell-Jolly bodies (howl-zhō-lē) [William H. Howell, U.S. physiologist, 1860–1945; Justin Jolly, Fr. histologist, 1870–1953] Spherical granules (the remnants of nuclear chromatin) seen in erythrocytes in red blood cells of persons who are asplenic and in hemolytic and pernicious anemias.

Hp *haptoglobin.*

HPAI *Highly pathogenic avian influenza.*

HPG *human pituitary gonadotropin.*

HPL *human placental lactogen.*

HPLC *high-pressure* or *high-performance liquid chromatography.*

H⁺ Symbol for hydrogen ion.

HpSA *Helicobacter pylori stool antigen.*

HPV *Human papillomavirus.*

HPV4 A vaccine that provides protection against infection with four types of human papillomavirus (HPV), specifically, types 6, 11, 16, and 18.

HPV DNA test A test to determine whether cancer-causing variants of human papillomavirus (HPV) are present in the endocervix or ectocervix of women undergoing Papanicolaou (Pap) testing.
PATIENT CARE: The test is performed by swabbing the cervix and endocervix carefully and then submitting the specimen for laboratory analysis. The test detects the most common types of HPV that may, in some patients, cause cervical cancer. It may be used to follow up abnormal Pap test results, e.g., atypical squamous cells of uncertain significance, or it may be employed in conjunction with Pap testing. Women whose Pap test results are normal and who have a negative HPV test have a very low risk for cervical cancer. Routine HPV screening should be performed for sexually active woman over the age of 30, but not before. SYN: *hybrid capture test.*

HQ *hazard quotient.*

hr *hour.*

H₃ receptor, histamine H₃ receptor A presynaptic receptor in the CNS that controls the release of histamine and other neurotransmitters, including acetylcholine, dopamine, and norepinephrine. It influences arousal and sleep, cognition, attention, and other body functions.

H₂-receptor antagonist SEE: under *antagonist.*

H₃ receptor antagonists Drugs that block H₃ receptors in the central nervous system. Such drugs may be used to treat disorders of sleep and arousal, wakefulness, and attention.

H reflex [after Johann *Hoffmann,* who described it in 1918] SEE: under *reflex.*

HRT *hormone replacement therapy.*

H₂S Formula for hydrogen sulfide.

H.S. *house surgeon.*

h.s. *hora somni,* at bedtime.

HSA *human serum albumin.*

H₂SO₃ Formula for sulfurous acid.

H₂SO₄ Formula for sulfuric acid.

HSV *herpes simplex virus.*

HT *Equivalent* **dose**; *histotechnician.*

ht *height.*

5-HT Serotonin.

HTL *histotechnologist.*

HTLV-I *human T-cell lymphotropic virus type I.*

HTLV-II *human T-cell lymphotropic virus type II.*

HTLV-III *human T-cell lymphotropic virus type III.*

HTN *Hypertension.*

hub (hŭb) A central structure into which other structures are anchored, attached, or stabilized.

Hubbard tank (hŭb′ărd) A tank of suitable size and shape for use in active or passive underwater exercises. It is also used for débridement of burn and other wounds.

huff (hŭf) **1.** A forced expiration to clear the airways of mucus and other secretions. Taken after a deep breath, a huff clears the upper airways. After a smaller or normal breath, a huff clears secretions from the lower airways. **2.** A slang term for inhaling the vapors of glue or solvents; glue-sniffing.

huffing (hŭf′ing) A colloquial term for the intentional inhaling of volatile chemical vapors of certain drugs or substances of abuse.

Huhner test (hoon′ĕr) [Max Huhner, U.S. urologist, 1873–1947] Postcoital examination of cervical mucus. Assessments include characteristics of the mucus as correlated with the phase of the woman's menstrual cycle, and the number, morphology, motility, and ability of the sperm to cross the cervical mucus. To maximize potential for coincidental conception, the test may be scheduled 1 to 2 days before the expected date of ovulation and within 2 to 3 hr after intercourse. SYN: *postcoital test.* SEE: *infertility.*

hum A soft continuous sound.
    venous h. SEE: *venous hum.*

human [L. *humanus,* human] **1.** An offspring of humans. **2.** Pert. to or characterizing people.

human alveolar echinococcosis Alveolar echinococcosis.

human astrovirus ABBR: HAstV. *astrovirus.*

human bocavirus ABBR: HBoV. A single-stranded DNA parvovirus that has been isolated from the respiratory tract of patients with bronchitis, pneumonia, and tonsillitis.

human chorionic somatomammotropin ABBR: HCS. human placental lactogen.

human factor SEE: under *factor.*

Human Genome Project An international research effort to map each human gene and to sequence the 3.1 billion chemical bases that make up human DNA. The U.S. National Human Genome Research Institute and Celera Genomics announced the initial deciphering of the genetic code in June 2000. This scientific milestone is expected to improve the way diseases are diagnosed, treated, and prevented, but it presents ethical, legal, and social issues regarding the use of genetic information.

humanism The concept that human interests, values, and dignity are of utmost importance. This is integral to the actions and thoughts of those who care for the sick.

humanitarian device exemption (hū-man″ĭ-ter′ē-ăn) ABBR: HDE. Legal permission from the FDA to a manufacturer of a new medical device granting it a waiver from some of the usual requirements in order to expedite introduction of the device into clinical use. HDEs are granted for devices that treat rare diseases for which it would be impractical or economically unfeasible to test the device thoroughly before use. SYN: *humanitarian use* **device**.

humanized (hū′mă-nīzd″) Chemically altered to resemble natural human amino acid sequences. It applies to proteins or polypeptides derived from animals, e.g., mice, that are altered to reduce their antigenic potential. **humanize,** *v.*

human milk fortifier A dietary supplement added to mother's milk to increase its caloric, mineral, protein, or vitamin content. It is used to enhance the nutritional status of premature babies and babies with very low birth weights.

human T-cell lymphotropic virus type I SEE: under *virus*.

human T-cell lymphotropic virus type II SEE: under *virus*.

human T-cell lymphotropic virus type III SEE: under *virus*.

human trafficking The illegal enslavement, kidnapping, rental, or sale of human beings for their labor, esp. as sex workers or low-level workers.

humectant (hū-mĕk′tănt) [L. *humectus,* moist] A moistening agent.

humeral (hū′mĕr-ăl) [*humerus* + -*al* (1)] Pert. to the humerus.

humeroradial (hū″mĕr-ō-rā′dē-ăl) [″ + *radius,* wheel spoke, ray] Pert. to the humerus and radius, esp. in comparison of their lengths.

humeroulnar (hū″mĕr-ō-ŭl′năr) [″ + *ulna,* elbow] Pert. to the humerus and ulna, esp. in comparison of their lengths.

humerus (hū′mĕr-ŭs) [L. *humerus,* upper arm, shoulder] The bone of the upper arm; it articulates with the scapula at the shoulder and with the ulna and radius at the elbow. SEE: illus.

   anatomical neck of h. The constricted segment of the humerus between the head and the greater tubercle.

   fracture of h. SEE: under *fracture*.

humid [L. *humidus,* moist] Moist, damp, esp. when pert. to air.

humidifier (hū-mĭd′ĭ-fī″ĕr) An apparatus to increase or regulate the moisture content of air in a room or ventilator circuit.

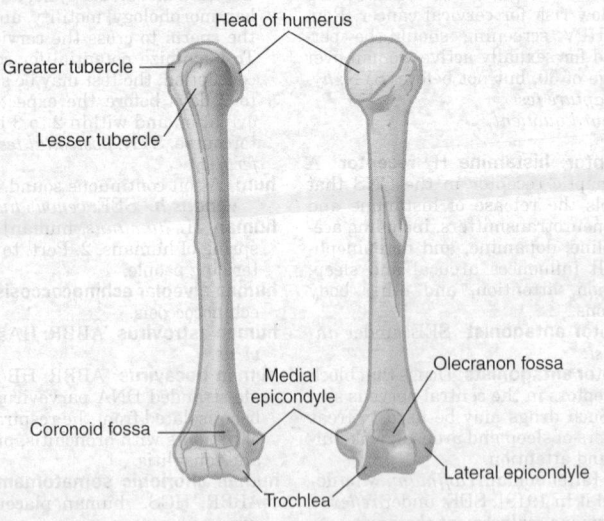

Head of humerus

Greater tubercle

Lesser tubercle

Medial epicondyle

Coronoid fossa

Trochlea

Olecranon fossa

Lateral epicondyle

Anterior   Posterior

HUMERUS

passover h. A device that passively adds moisture to a CPAP device. It works best at a water temperature of at least 30°C. It is used to reduce drying of the nasal passages.

wick h. An active humidification system in which gas flow is exposed to a material saturated with water.

humidifier fever SEE: under *fever*.

humidity [L. *humiditas*] Moisture in the atmosphere.

The moisture content of air usually is expressed as relative humidity. This indicates the amount of water vapor in the air compared with the maximum amount of moisture the air could contain at that temperature and atmospheric pressure. Air that is fully saturated with moisture has 100% relative humidity. When air that is fully saturated is cooled, the excess moisture condenses, as in the case of dew or moisture on a cold glass in the summer.

absolute h. The actual mass of water vapor in a volume of gas, expressed as grams per cubic meter or milligrams per liter. It usually refers to ambient air or gas in the mechanical ventilator circuit.

relative h. The ratio of the amount of water vapor present in an air sample to the amount that could be present if the sample were saturated with water vapor. This value depends on the temperature of the air sample.

humor (hū′mŏr) [L. *humor,* fluid] Any fluid or semifluid in the body. **humoral** (-ăl), *adj.*

aqueous h. The clear tissue fluid that circulates through the anterior cavity of the eye. It is produced by the ciliary processes and passes from the posterior to the anterior chamber and then to the venous system by way of the canal of Schlemm.

crystalline h. The fluid-like substance of the crystalline lens of the eye.

ocular h. Either of the humors of the eye (aqueous and vitreous).

vitreous h. Vitreous (2).

humpback SEE: *kyphosis*.

Humulin 70/30 Human insulin consisting of 70% NPH and 30% regular insulin. SEE: *human insulin*.

hunchback SEE: *kyphosis*.

hunger [AS. *hungur*] **1.** A sensation resulting from lack of food, characterized by a dull or acute pain referred to the epigastrium or lower part of chest. It is usually accompanied by weakness and an overwhelming desire to eat. Hunger pains coincide with powerful contractions of the stomach. Hunger is distinguished from appetite in that hunger is the physical drive to eat, while appetite is the psychological drive to eat. Hunger is affected by the physiological interaction of hormones and hormone-like factors, while appetite is affected by habits,

culture, taste, and many other factors. SEE: illus. **2.** To have a strong desire.

air h. Dyspnea; breathlessness.

hungry bone syndrome Hypocalcemia that develops in hyperparathyroid patients treated with parathyroidectomy or in patients with end-stage renal disease treated with calcimimetic drugs. It is caused by a sudden decrease in serum parathyroid hormone levels, which in turn increase the uptake of calcium, magnesium, and phosphate by bone. Clinical consequences include tetany (repetitive muscle twitching) esp. in patients whose calcium deficiency is severe.

Hunner ulcer (hŭn′ĕr) [Guy LeRoy Hunner, U.S. surgeon, 1868–1957] Interstitial cystitis.

Hunter canal (hŭn′tĕr) [John Hunter, Scottish anatomist and surgeon, 1728–1793] Adductor canal.

Hunter disease [Charles H. Hunter, Canadian physician, 1873–1955] Mucopolysaccharidosis II.

Huntington chorea, Huntington disease (hŭnt′ing-tŏn) [George Huntington, U.S. physician, 1850–1916] A dominantly inherited disease of the central nervous system, marked by choreoathetosis, gradually worsening emotional and behavioral disturbances, and eventual dementia. This rare disease affects about 5 persons in 100,000. Symptoms usually become obvious in adulthood, often after individuals who carry the causative gene have already transmitted it to their offspring. The hallmarks of the illness may take decades to come into being fully. Death usually occurs more than 15 yr after diagnosis. Postmortem examination reveals atrophy of the putamen and caudate nucleus.

DIAGNOSIS: The diagnosis is straightforward when typical symptoms develop in a son or daughter of a parent known to have the disease. Genetic testing for the illness is available although its use presents difficult ethical questions for couples who want to start a family.

TREATMENT: Dopamine agonist drugs (haloperidol, risperidone) can help control chorea, as can tetrabenazine. There is no known treatment to stop the degeneration of the affected portions of the brain.

Huperzia (hoo-pĕr′zē-ă) A genus of mossy ferns.

H. serrata The species from which huperzine is obtained.

huperzine (hoop′ĕr-zēn″) ABBR: Hup. An alkaloid present in the Asian herb *Huperzia serrata*. This alkaloid inhibits cholinesterases. It has been proposed as a treatment for dementia resulting from Alzheimer disease.

Hurler syndrome (hŭrl′ĕr) [Gertrud

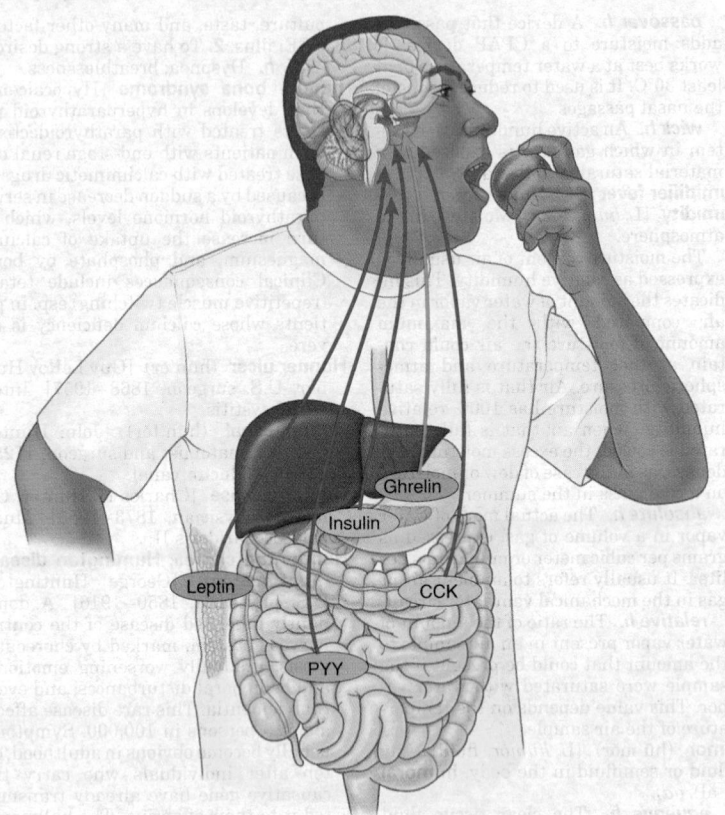

HORMONES AFFECTING HUNGER

Hurler, Ger. pediatrician, 1889–1965]
Mucopolysaccharidosis IH.

Hürthle, Karl W. (hürt′lē, hürt′lĕ) Ger. physiologist and neurologist, 1860–1945.

    H. cell A large granular cell found in pathological sections in some thyroid diseases.

    H. cell adenoma An adenoma of the thyroid that contains mostly eosinophil-staining cells. It is occasionally found in Hashimoto thyroiditis.

    H. cell tumor A benign or malignant tumor of the thyroid gland. The cells are large and acidophilic.

Hutchinson, Sir Jonathan (hŭtch′ĭn-sŏn) Brit. surgeon and pathologist, 1828–1913.

    H.'s incisors Hutchinson teeth.

    H.'s freckle A noninvasive malignant melanoma.

    H.'s mask A feeling of compression over the face, as though one were wearing a mask.

    H.'s patch A salmon-colored area of the cornea seen in interstitial keratitis caused by syphilis.

    H.'s pupil A condition in which one pupil is dilated and the other is not. The pupil on the side where a lesion exists is dilated and the other side is contracted. This condition is usually due to compression of the third cranial nerve occurring in meningitis.

    H. sign The presence of vesicles on the tip of the nose in patients with facial herpes zoster. The sign strongly suggests corneal involvement by zoster and therefore the need for treatment to prevent corneal scarring and loss of vision.

    H.'s teeth A congenital condition marked by pegged, lateral incisors and notched central incisors along the cutting edge. It is a sign of congenital syphilis. SYN: *Hutchinson incisors.*

    H.'s triad A syndrome characteristic of congenital syphilis consisting of notched teeth, interstitial keratitis, and eighth-nerve deafness due to meningeal involvement.

Hutchinson-Gilford disease (hŭtch′ĭn-sŏn-gil′fŏrd) [Sir Jonathan Hutchinson; Hastings Gilford, Brit. physician, 1861–1941.] Progeria.

Huxley, Thomas H. (hŭks'lē) Brit. biologist, 1825–1895.

   H. layer The inner layer of nucleated cells forming the inner root sheath of a hair follicle. SYN: *Huxley membrane.*

HVA *homovanillic acid.*

Hx *History.*

hyalin (hī'ă-lĭn) [Gr. *hyalos,* glass] **1.** A proteinaceous substance present in tissues that have undergone amyloid degeneration. **2.** Material deposited in the glomerulus in certain forms of glomerulonephritis.

hyaline (hī'ă-lĭn) **1.** A normal glassy appearance, such as hyaline cartilage. **2.** A glassy appearance acquired as the result of tissue injury or degeneration. SYN: *hyaloid.*

hyaline body SEE: under *body.*

hyaline membrane disease Respiratory distress syndrome of the newborn.

hyalinization (hī''ă-lĭn''ĭ-zā'shŭn) Transformation of a tissue to a glassy appearance.

hyalinosis (hī''ă-lĭn-ō'sĭs) [Gr. *hyalos,* glass, + *osis,* condition] Waxy or hyaline degeneration.

hyalitis (hī''ă-līt'ĭs) [*hyalo-* + *-itis*] Inflammation in the vitreous, often accompanied by uveitis (vitritis). SYN: *hyaloiditis; vitreocapsulitis.*

   asteroid h. One of the spherical or star-shaped bodies in the vitreous of the eye, caused by inflammation.

   h. punctata A form of hyalitis marked by minute opacities in the vitreous humor.

   h. suppurativa A purulent inflammation of the vitreous humor.

hyalo-, hyal- [Gr. *hyalos,* glass] Prefixes meaning *glass* or *resembling glass.*

hyalohyphomycosis (hī''ă-lō-hī''fō-mī-kō'sĭs) [" + Gr. *hyphos, hyphe,* web, net + "] A cutaneous or subcutaneous infection caused by a fungus that does not produce dark pigments. SEE: *phaeohyphomycosis.*

hyaloid (hī'ă-loyd) [" + *eidos,* form, shape] Hyaline.

hyalomere (hī'ă-lō-mēr") The peripherally located region of a platelet that stains light blue.

hyalosis (hī''ă-lō'sĭs) [*hyalo-* + *-sis*] Pathological changes in the vitreous humor of the eye.

   asteroid h. A benign condition in which small opaque bodies are dispersed in the vitreous humor. Patients rarely complain of decreased vision, but deposits can be so numerous as to make view of the ocular fundus difficult on examination.

hyaluronan (hī''ăl-ū-rōn'ĕn) Hyaluronic **acid**.

hyaluronidase (hī''ă-lūr-ŏn'ĭ-dās) An enzyme that disrupts or destroys the extracellular framework of body tissues. It is found in many animal tissues and can be synthesized for therapeutic use. In the testes and the acrosomes of spermatozoa, along with other acrosomal enzymes, it degrades the hyaluronic acid in the corona radiata, facilitating the entry of sperm. In malignant tumors, it participates in the invasion of cancer cells through the basement membranes of blood vessels. It is also a component of the venoms of several animals (including vipers, stonefish, and bees and wasps) and contributes to the tissue destruction that may follow bites or stings from these animals. Some infectious bacteria that invade fascial planes (e.g., *Clostridia*) release it as an exotoxin.

   USES: Synthetic hyaluronidase can be used to facilitate diffusion of injected local anesthetics (e.g., in cataract surgery).

hybrid (hī'brĭd) [L. *hybrida,* mongrel] The offspring of parents that are different, such as different species.

hybrid capture test HPV DNA test.

hybrid coronary artery revascularization SEE: under *revascularization.*

hybridization (hī'brĭd-ī-zā'shŭn) The production of hybrids by crossbreeding.

hybridoma (hī''brĭ-dō'mă) A cell produced by the fusion of a spleen cell from a mouse immunized with a specific antigen and a human multiple myeloma cell (a cancerous plasma B cell that makes antibodies). After the fusion, cells are screened to identify those capable of producing a continuous supply of monoclonal antibodies to the specific antigen. SEE: *monoclonal antibody.*

hydantoin (hī-dăn'tō-ĭn) A colorless base, glycolyl urea, $C_3H_4N_2O_2$, derived from urea or allantoin.

hydatid (hīd'ă-tĭd) [Gr. *hydatis,* watery vesicle] **1.** A cyst formed in the tissues, esp. the liver, from the development of the larval stage of *Echinococcus granulosus* (one of the species of the dog tapeworm). The cyst develops slowly, forming a hollow bladder from the inner surface of which hollow brood capsules are formed. These may be attached to the mother cyst by slender stalks or may fall free into the fluid-filled cavity of the mother cyst. Scolices form on the inner surface of the older brood capsules. Older cysts have a granular deposit of brood capsules and scolices called hydatid sand. Hydatids may grow for years, sometimes to an enormous size. lbendazole, mebendazole, and praziquantel have been used to treat the disease. The cyst should be removed surgically or percutaneously drained. SEE: illus.; *echinococcosis.* **2.** A small cystic remnant of an embryonic structure. SEE: *choriocarcinoma; hydatid mole.*

   h. of Morgagni A cystlike remnant of the müllerian duct attached to the fallopian tube.

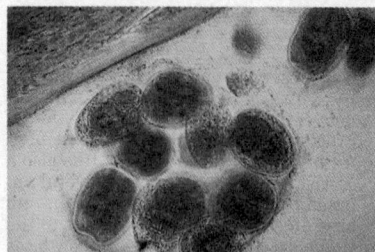

HYDATID CYST

(orig. mag. ×500)

sessile h. Morgagnian hydatid connected with a testicle.

stalked h. Morgagnian hydatid connected with a fallopian tube.

hydatid disease The disease produced by the cysts of the larval stage of the tapeworm *Echinococcus*. SYN: *echinococcosis*.

hydatidosis (hī″dă-tĭd-ō′sĭs) [Gr. *hydatis*, watery vesicle, + *osis*, condition] A condition caused by hydatid infestation.

hydradenitis (hī′drăd-ĕn-ī′tĭs) [Gr. *hydros*, sweat, + *aden*, gland, + *itis*, inflammation] Inflammation of a sweat gland.

hydramnion, hydramnios (hī-drăm′nē-ŏn, -ŏs) [″ + *amnion*, a caul on a lamb] An excess of amniotic fluid in the uterus.

hydranencephaly (hī″drăn-ĕn-sĕf′ă-lē) [″ + *an-*, not, + *enkephalos*, brain] Internal hydrocephalus caused by congenital absence of the cerebral hemispheres.

hydrargyrum (hī-dror′jĭ-rŭm) [L. *hydrargyrum, hydrargyrus* fr Gr. *hydrargyros*, liquid silver] Mercury.

hydrarthrosis (hī″drăr-thrō′sĭs) [″ + *arthron*, joint, + *osis*, condition] A joint effusion.

intermittent h. Recurring attacks of swelling of the large joints, lasting 2 to 5 days and then remitting spontaneously. The condition affects men and women equally. The period between attacks is commonly 2 to 4 weeks, during which time the joint is normal. The knee is usually involved, but the elbow, hip, and ankle also may be affected.

hydrase (hī′drās) An enzyme that catalyzes the addition or withdrawal of water from a compound without hydrolysis occurring.

hydrate (hī′drāt″) [*hydro-* + -*ate*] A crystalline substance formed by water combining with various compounds in specific molar ratios.

hydrated (hī′drā-tĕd) [L. *hydratus*] **1.** Combined chemically with water, forming a hydrate. **2.** Replete with fluids.

hydration (hī-drā′shŭn) **1.** The chemical combination of a substance with water. **2.** The addition of water to a substance, tissue, or patient.

hydraulics (hī-draw′lĭks) [Gr. *hydor*, water, + *aulos*, pipe] The science of fluids.

hydrazine (hī′dră-zēn″) H_4N_2, a colorless gas, with a peculiar odor; soluble in water.

h. sulfate A chemical promoted for the treatment of cancer. There are no evidence-based studies supporting the efficacy of hydrazine sulfate for cancer.

hydremia (hī-drē′mē-ă) [Gr. *hydor*, water, + *haima*, blood] An excess of watery fluid in the blood.

hydride (hī′drīd) A chemical compound containing hydrogen and an element or radical.

hydro-, hydr- [L. *hydr(o)-*, fr. Gr. *hydōr*, water] Prefixes meaning *water, liquid,* or *hydrogen.*

hydroa (hī-drō′ă) [L. *hydroa*, fr Gr. *hidrōia*, prickly heat] Any bullous skin eruption.

h. vacciniforme ABBR: HV. A vesicular rash that heals with crusting and scarring of sun-exposed regions of the skin. HV is a rare disease, typically occurring in children under 10. The rash heals with scars that resemble skin vaccination scars. HV may be prevented by wearing protective clothing or by using sunscreens.

hydrobromate (hī″drō-brō′māt) [″ + *bromos*, stench] A salt of hydrobromic acid.

hydrocarbon (hī″drō-kăr′bŏn) [″ + L. *carbo*, coal] A compound made up primarily of hydrogen and carbon.

alicyclic h. A hydrocarbon that contains cyclic and straight-chain components.

aliphatic h. A straight-chain hydrocarbon that contains no cyclic component.

aromatic h. A hydrocarbon in which the carbon atoms are in a ring, or cyclic, configuration.

cyclic h. A ring-shaped hydrocarbon.

saturated h. A hydrocarbon in which the carbon atoms are linked by a single electron pair and in which all valences are satisfied.

unsaturated h. A hydrocarbon in which carbon atoms share two or three pairs of electrons.

hydrocele (hī′drŏ-sēl″) [*hydro-* + -*cele*] The accumulation of serous fluid in a saclike cavity, esp. in the tunica vaginalis testis. It may be caused by infection or trauma.

acute h. The most common hydrocele. The majority of cases occur suddenly between the second and fifth years, usually the result of inflammation of the epididymis or testis.

cervical h. A hydrocele in the neck

resulting from the accumulation of serous fluid in the persistent cervical duct or cleft.

congenital h. A hydrocele present at birth, resulting from failure of closure of the vaginal process.

encysted h. A hydrocele in the vaginal process in which openings to the scrotal and peritoneal cavities are closed.

h. feminae A cystlike sac of serous fluid in the labia majora or canal of Nuck. SYN: **h.** *muliebris.*

h. hernialis A condition in which a hernia accompanies infantile or congenital hydrocele and peritoneal fluid accumulates in a hernial sac.

infantile h. Peritoneal fluid in the tunica vaginalis and vaginal process with the latter closed at the abdominal ring.

h. muliebris Hydrocele feminae.

spermatic h. Spermatic fluid in the tunica vaginalis of the testes.

h. spinalis Spina bifida cystica.

hydrocelectomy (hī″drō-sē-lĕk′tō-mē) [″ + ″ + *ektome,* excision] Surgical removal of a hydrocele.

hydrocephalus (hī-drō-sĕf′ă-lŭs) [″ + *kephale,* head] The accumulation of excessive amounts of cerebrospinal fluid (CSF) within the ventricles of the brain, resulting from blockage or destruction of the normal channels for CSF drainage. Common causes include congenital lesions (e.g., spina bifida or aqueductal stenosis), traumatic lesions, neoplastic lesions, and infections such as meningoencephalitis. Sometimes the accumulated fluid leads to increased intracranial pressure (ICP). SYN: *hydrencephalus.* SEE: *Nursing Diagnoses Appendix.* **hydrocephalic** (hī″drō-sē-făl-ĭk), *adj.*

TREATMENT: Several neurosurgical procedures are used to treat hydrocephalus. The most commonly used procedure has been to establish a conduit for CSF (called a "shunt") from the ventricles of the brain to the peritoneal cavity or the right atrium.

PROGNOSIS: The prognosis for an uncomplicated course is excellent when hydrocephalus is promptly treated by use of a surgically instituted shunt.

PATIENT CARE: Vital signs and neurological status are monitored hourly or as necessary according to institutional protocol or the surgeon's directions. The infant's anterior fontanel is inspected for bulging and the head circumference measured (an indelible ink mark on the forehead ensures that all measurements are at the same location). The patient is positioned as directed by the surgeon, usually on the nonoperative side with the head level with the body. Fluid intake and output are monitored, and IV fluids are administered as prescribed. The patient is assessed for vomiting (an early sign of increased ICP and shunt malfunction). The patient is monitored for signs of infection (esp. meningitis) such as fever, stiff neck, irritability, or tense fontanels. The area over the shunt tract also is inspected for redness, swelling, and other signs of local infection. Dressings are checked for drainage and the wound redressed as necessary using aseptic technique. The patient also is observed for other signs and symptoms of postoperative complications, such as adhesions, paralytic ileus, peritonitis, migration of the shunt, intestinal perforation (with peritoneal shunt), and dehydration and septicemia. The infant's head, neck, and shoulders are moved as a unit with the rest of the body to prevent neck strain during position changes. The family is taught postoperative care measures, including watching for signs of shunt malfunction, infection, and paralytic ileus. Maternal bonding is encouraged. The parents are assisted to set goals consistent with the patient's ability and potential; the family should focus on the child's strengths rather than weaknesses. They should be made aware that shunts will need to be surgically lengthened periodically as the child grows, and that surgery also may be required to correct shunt malfunctions. Special education programs also are discussed with the parents; the infant's need for sensory stimulation appropriate to age is emphasized.

communicating h. Hydrocephalus that maintains normal communication between the fourth ventricle and subarachnoid space.

congenital h. Hydrocephalus occurring in newborns, typically caused by birth defects such as spina bifida, aqueductal stenosis, or birth trauma with ventricular hemorrhage.

In congenital hydrocephalus, the faulty drainage of CSF from the ventricles of the brain often results in rapidly increasing head circumference, malformation of the skull (thin bone with widened fontanels and separated sutures), distended scalp veins, thin, shiny scalp skin, weak neck muscles incapable of supporting the head, and abnormal development of psychomotor and cognitive or language skills. In untreated cases of congenital hydrocephalus, the outcome is fatal in about half of the patients due to infection, malnutrition, or increased intracranial pressure. The parents of infants treated neurosurgically for congenital hydrocephalus are instructed in signs and symptoms that may indicate surgical complications: fever and headache, irritability, poor feeding, inconsolability.

external h. An accumulation of fluid in subdural spaces.

h. ex vacuo The appearance on brain imaging of enlarged lateral ventricles, caused by atrophy of the brain.

internal h. An accumulation of fluid within ventricles of the brain.

noncommunicating h. Hydrocephalus in which a blockage at any location in the ventricular system prevents flow of cerebrospinal fluid to the subarachnoid space.

normal pressure h. A type of hydrocephalus with enlarged ventricles of the brain with no increase in the spinal fluid pressure or no demonstrable block to the outflow of spinal fluid. Shunting fluids from the dilated ventricles to the peritoneal cavity may be helpful. The classic triad of symptoms includes disturbances of gait, progressive dementia, and urinary incontinence.

secondary h. Hydrocephalus following injury or infections such as meningitis or syphilis.

hydrochlorate (hī″drō-klō′rāt) [Gr. *hydor,* water, + *chloros,* green] Any salt of hydrochloric acid.

hydrochloride (hī″drō-klō′rīd) An alkaloid or other base combined with hydrochloric acid.

hydrochlorothiazide (hī″drō-klō″rō-thī′ă-zīd) ABBR: HCTZ. A thiazide diuretic used to treat high blood pressure. A common side effect is hypokalemia.

hydrocirsocele (hī″drō-sĭr′sō-sēl) [″ + *kirsos,* varix, + *kele,* tumor, swelling] A hydrocele combined with varicose veins of the spermatic cord.

hydrocolloid (hī″drō-kŏl′loyd) [″ + *kollodes,* glutinous] A colloidal suspension in which water is the liquid.

irreversible h. A hydrosol of alginic acid whose physical state is changed by an irreversible chemical reaction, forming insoluble calcium alginate. This substance is called alginate or dental alginate. Alginate is used in dentistry as a primary impression material. SYN: *alginate.*

 Care should be taken not to inhale the dust created by alginate.

hydrocolpos (hī″drō-kŏl′pŏs) [″ + *kolpos,* vagina] Retention cyst of the vagina containing watery, nonsanguineous fluid or mucus.

hydrocortisone (hī″drō-kor′tĭ-sōn″, -zōn″) [*hydro-* + *cortisone*] Cortisol.

hydrocystoma (hī″drō-sĭs-tō′mă) [″ + ″ + *oma,* tumor] A benign cystic lesion developing from apocrine glands, typically found on the eyelids or other facial structures. SYN: *hidrocystoma.*

hydrodensitometry (hī″drō-děn″sĭ-tŏm′ĕ-trē) The weighing of an object immersed in water and subsequent measurement of the water displaced. The specific gravity of the body can be esti-

mated from that information, and the percentage of the body fat can be estimated. SEE: *lean body mass.*

hydrodissection (hī″drō-dī-sĕk′shŭn) Technique employing a pressurized fine stream of water (jet) to develop tissue planes or to divide certain soft tissues less traumatically than ordinary sharp dissection. Examples of its use include division of brain and hepatic tissue without destroying smaller blood vessels and other tubular structures. In abdominal surgery, open or laparoscopic hydrodissection is used to develop tissue planes and separate adhesions. It facilitates dissection of diseased parietal pleura in order to treat malignant pleural effusion. A modification is used in ophthalmological surgery (e.g., phacoemulsification).

hydrodynamics (hī″drō-dī-năm′ĭks) The study of fluids in motion.

hydrogel (hī′drō-jĕl) [″ + L. *gelare,* to congeal] A colloid containing hydrophilic polymers. Hydrogels are used in numerous applications, including glucose sensors, breast implants, soft contact lenses, and sterile dressings.

hydrogen (hī′drō-jĕn) [*hydro-* + *-gen*] SYMB: H. A colorless, odorless, tasteless, gaseous chemical element, possessing one valence electron, atomic weight (mass) 1.0079, specific gravity 0.069, atomic number 1. A liter of the gas at sea level and at 0°C weighs 0.08988 g. There are three isotopes of hydrogen (protium, deuterium, and tritium), having atomic weights of approx. 1, 2, and 3, respectively.

OCCURRENCE: Hydrogen is present in the sun and stars. Even though it is the most abundant element in the known universe, its concentration in the earth's atmosphere is only 0.00005%. Hydrogen occurs in its free state (in natural gases and volcanic eruptions) only in minute quantities. It occurs principally on the earth as water (hydrogen oxide, H_2O) and is a constituent of all hydrocarbons. Hydrogen is present in all acids and in ionic form is responsible for the properties characteristic of acids. Hydrogen is present in nearly all organic compounds and is a component of all carbohydrates, proteins, and fats.

USES: It is highly flammable and used in the oxyhydrogen flame in welding, in hydrogenation of oils for solidifying purposes, as a reducing agent, and in many syntheses.

h. cyanide Hydrocyanic **acid.**

h. dioxide **Hydrogen** peroxide.

heavy p. Deuterium.

h. peroxide H_2O_2, a colorless syrupy liquid with an irritating odor and acrid taste. It decomposes readily, liberating oxygen. Because light is particularly effective in decomposing H_2O_2, it must be stored in tightly sealed glass jars in a dark place. SYN: *h. dioxide.*

USES: It is used as a commercial bleaching agent; as an oxidizing and reducing agent; and, in a 3% aqueous solution, as a mild antiseptic, germicide, and cleansing agent.

h. sulfide H_2S, a poisonous, flammable, colorless compound with a characteristic odor of rotten eggs. SYN: *sulfurated h.* SEE: *Poisons and Poisoning Appendix.*

hydrogenase (hī'drō-jĕn-ās) An enzyme that catalyzes reduction by molecular hydrogen.

hydrogenate (hī'drō-jĕn-āt″) To combine with hydrogen.

hydrogenation (hī″drō-jĕn-ā′shŭn) A process of changing an unsaturated fat to a solid saturated fat by the addition of hydrogen in the presence of a catalyst.

hydrokinetics (hī″drō-kī-nĕt′ĭks) [″ + *kinesis,* movement] The science of fluids in motion.

hydrolase (hī′drō-lās) An enzyme that causes hydrolysis.

hydrology (hī-drŏl′ō-jē) [″ + *logos,* word, reason] The scientific study of water. It is considered one of the earth sciences.

hydrolysate (hī-drŏl′ĭ-sāt) That which is produced as a result of hydrolysis.

protein h. The amino acids obtained from splitting proteins by hydrolysis; used as a source of amino acids in certain diets.

hydrolysis (hī-drŏl′ĭ-sĭs) [″ + *lysis,* dissolution] Any reaction in which water is one of the reactants, more specifically the combination of water with a salt to produce an acid and a base, one of which is more dissociated than the other. It involves a chemical decomposition in which a substance is split into simpler compounds by the addition or the taking up of the elements of water. This kind of reaction occurs extremely frequently in life processes. The conversion of starch to maltose, of fat to glycerol and fatty acid, and of protein to amino acids are examples of hydrolysis, as are other reactions involved in digestion. A simple example is the reaction in which the hydrolysis of ethyl acetate yields acetic acid and ethyl alcohol: $C_2H_5C_2H_3O_2 + H_2O = CH_3COOH + C_2H_5OH$. Usually such reactions are reversible; the reversed reaction is called esterification, condensation, or dehydration synthesis. SEE: *assimilation; enzyme.*

hydrolytic (-drō-lĭt′ĭk), *adj.*

hydrolyze (hī′drō-līz) To cause to undergo hydrolysis.

hydroma (hī-drō′mă) [Gr. *hydor,* water, + *oma,* tumor] Hygroma.

hydromassage (hī″drō-mă-săzh′) Massage that is performed either underwater or with water pressure applied to the body.

hydromeiosis (hī″drō-mī-ō′sĭs) [″ + *meiosis,* diminution] The swelling of the epidermis after it is exposed to water, with consequent blockage of the sweat ducts. This phenomenon limits fluid loss from sweating when the body is immersed in water.

hydromeningitis (hī″drō-mĕn″ĭn-jī′tĭs) [″ + *meninx,* membrane, + *itis,* inflammation] **1.** An inflammation of membranes of the brain with serous effusion. **2.** An inflammation of Descemet's membrane.

hydromeningocele (hī″drō-mĕn-ĭn′gō-sēl) [″ + ″ + *kele,* tumor, swelling] Protrusion of the meninges or spinal cord in a sac of fluid.

hydrometer (hī-drŏm′ĕ-tĕr) [″ + *metron,* measure] An instrument that measures the density of a liquid by the depth to which a graduated scale sinks into the liquid. SEE: *urinometer.*

hydrometra (hī″drō-mē′tră) [″ + *metra,* uterus] The collection of watery fluid or mucus in the uterus.

hydrometrocolpos (hī″drō-mē″trō-kŏl′pŏs) [″ + *metra,* uterus, + *kolpos,* vagina] The distention of the uterus and vagina by a collection of watery fluid.

hydromicrocephaly (hī″drō-mī″krō-sĕf′ă-lē) [″ + *mikros,* small, + *kephale,* head] A condition in which the head is abnormally small and contains an increased amount of cerebrospinal fluid.

hydromorphone hydrochloride (hī″drō-mor′fōn) An opioid pain reliever.

hydromphalus (hī-drŏm′fă-lŭs) [″ + *omphalos,* navel] Edematous enlargement of the umbilicus.

hydromyelia (hī″drō-mī-ē′lē-ă) [″ + *myelos,* marrow] Increased fluid in the central canal of the spinal cord. SYN: *hydrorrhachis.*

hydromyelocele (hī″drō-mī-ĕl′ō-sēl) [″ + ″ + *kele,* tumor, swelling] The protrusion of a sac with cerebrospinal fluid through a defect in a wall of the spinal canal.

hydromyelomeningocele (hī″drō-mī″ĕ-lō-mĕ-nĭng′gō-sēl) [″ + *myelos,* marrow, + *meninx,* membrane, + *kele,* tumor, swelling] Spinal deformity in which a fluid-filled sac containing spinal cord and surrounding membranes protrudes through the spine.

hydromyoma (hī″drō-mī-ō′mă) [″ + *mys,* muscle, + *oma,* tumor] An encapsulated, benign, cystic tumor of the uterine myometrium. SEE: *intramural fibroma.*

hydronephrosis (hī″drō-nĕf-rō′sĭs) [″ + *nephros,* kidney, + *osis,* condition] Stretching of the renal pelvis as a result of obstruction to urinary outflow. SYN: *nephydrosis.* SEE: illus.

ETIOLOGY: Anything that obstructs

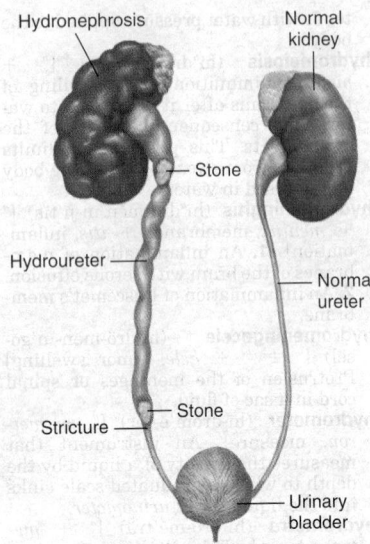

Hydronephrosis

Normal kidney

Stone

Hydroureter

Normal ureter

Stone

Stricture

Urinary bladder

HYDRONEPHROSIS

the ureter or bladder may cause hydronephrosis. Lodged kidney stones are a common cause of unilateral hydronephrosis; bilateral hydronephrosis often results from bladder outlet obstruction (e.g., in men who have hyperplasia of the prostate). Neurogenic bladder dysfunction, pregnancy, urogenital cancer, urinary tract inflammation, congenital malformations, ureteral strictures, and even parasites (schistosomiasis) may cause hydronephrosis. If urinary flow is not restored, the kidney tissue dilates and atrophies, and chronic renal failure may occur.

SYMPTOMS: Hydronephrosis often causes no localizing symptoms, except when it is associated with kidney stones (when the primary symptom is severe flank and abdominal pain that radiates to the groin).

DIAGNOSIS: Ultrasonography of the urinary tract, excretory urography, abdominal CT scan or MRI imaging are used to confirm the diagnosis.

TREATMENT: Unilateral hydronephrosis caused by a kidney stone resolves spontaneously if the stone passes. If the stone does not pass, procedures such as shock wave lithotripsy, surgical removal of the stone, nephrotomy, or nephrostomy tube drainage of the kidney or placement of a ureteral stent may be needed. Bilateral hydronephrosis caused by prostatic hyperplasia may be relieved if a catheter can be inserted through the obstructed urethra into the bladder, a cystotomy tube is inserted, or the enlarged prostate gland is surgically treated. Hydronephrosis

caused by other diseases (e.g., tumors) is often treated with surgical debulking, radiation, or chemotherapy.

PATIENT CARE: Renal function studies (e.g., blood urea nitrogen, serum creatinine, and serum potassium levels) are monitored daily. The condition, planned diagnostic procedures, and expected sensations are explained to the patient and family; if the patient is scheduled for a surgical procedure, the surgeon's explanations of the planned procedure are reinforced.

Postoperatively, intake and output, vital signs, and fluid and electrolyte balance are monitored (a rising pulse rate and cool, clammy skin may signal impending hypovolemia or hemorrhage and shock). Prescribed analgesics and noninvasive measures are used to relieve pain as necessary. Postobstructive diuresis may cause the patient to lose great volumes of dilute urine over hours or days along with excessive electrolyte loss. If this occurs, IV fluids are administered at a prescribed constant rate plus an amount equal to a given percentage of the patient's hourly urine output to safely replace intravascular volume. A dietitian can provide assistance to plan a diet consistent with the treatment plan while including foods that the patient enjoys and will eat. If a nephrostomy tube has been inserted, the tube is irrigated as specifically prescribed, checked for patency, and never clamped or allowed to kink. Meticulous skin care is provided to the tube entry site; if urine leaks around the tube, a protective skin barrier is provided to prevent excoriation, and the wound area is bagged to preserve the patient's dignity and to help prevent infection.

If the patient will be discharged with the nephrostomy tube in place, proper care of the tube and skin at the insertion site is taught. Prescribed drug therapies, such as antibiotics, are administered, and the patient is taught about expected outcomes, adverse effects to report, and the necessity to complete the prescribed course of therapy even if feeling better.

hydronium ion (hī-drō'nē-ŭm) [G. *Hydronium,* abbr. of *Hydroxonium*] SEE: under *ion.*

hydropenia (hī″drō-pē'nē-ă) [″ + *penia,* poverty] A deficiency of water in the body.

hydropericarditis (hī″drō-pĕr-ĭ-kăr-dī'tĭs) [″ + *peri,* around, + *kardia,* heart, + *itis,* inflammation] A serous effusion accompanying pericarditis.

hydropericardium (hī″drō-pĕr″ĭ-kăr'dē-ŭm) A dated term for a pericardial effusion.

hydroperitoneum (hī″drŏ-per″ĭt-ŏn-ē'ŭm) [*hydro-* + *peritoneum*] Ascites.

hydrophilia, hydrophilism (hī-drō-fĭl′ē-ă, -drŏf′ĭ-lĭzm) [″ + *philein*, to love] Attracting water molecules, as do molecules with many polar covalent bonds. **hydrophilic**, *adj.*

hydrophilous (hī-drŏf′ĭ-lŭs) Taking up moisture. SYN: *bibulous; hygroscopic.*

hydrophobia (hī-drō-fō′bē-ă) [*hydro-* + *-phobia*] **1.** Rabies. **2.** Aquaphobia. **3.** The repelling of water molecules, as do molecules with few or no polar covalent bonds. **hydrophobic** (-fō′bĭk), *adj.*

hydrophthalmos (hī″drŏf-thăl′mŏs) [″ + *ophthalmos*, eye] Distention of the eyeball owing to an accumulation of fluid within it. SEE: *glaucoma.*

hydropic (hī-drŏp′ĭk) [Gr. *hydropikos*] Edematous, or pert. to edema.

hydropneumoperitoneum (hī″drō-nū″mō-pĕr″ĭ-tō-nē′ŭm) [″ + ″ + *peritonaion*, peritoneum] Gas and serous fluid in the peritoneal cavity.

hydropneumothorax (hī″drō-nū″mō-thō′răks) [″ + ″ + *thorax*, chest] Gas and serous effusion in the pleural cavity. SYN: *pneumohydrothorax.*

hydrops, hydropsy (hī′drŏps″, -drŏp′sē) [Gr. *hydrōps*, dropsy] Edema.

   h. abdominis Ascites.

   delayed endolymphatic h. ABBR: DEH. A disease that resembles Ménière disease, typically developing a year or more after an episode of unilateral deafness. It can occur either in the ear affected by the hearing loss or in the contralateral ear.

   endolymphatic h. Labyrinthine **h.**

   h. fetalis Generalized edema in infants, marked by cardiac decompensation, hepatosplenomegaly, and respiratory and circulatory distress. It may be caused by erythroblastosis fetalis; infections; tumors; pulmonary, hepatic, or renal disease; diabetes mellitus; Gaucher disease; or multiple congenital anomalies. SEE: *erythema* infectiosum; *erythroblastosis* fetalis.

   labyrinthine h. Excessive fluid in the organ of balance in the inner ear. It may cause pressure or a sense of fullness in the ears, hearing loss, and vertigo. It often is found in Ménière's disease. SYN: *endolymphatic h.*

hydroquinone (hī″drō-kwĭn′ōn) A metabolite of benzene, sometimes topically applied to the skin.

hydrorrhea (hī″drō-rē′ă) [″ + *rhoia*, flow] Copious watery discharge from any part, as from the nose.

   h. gravidarum The discharge of a watery fluid from the vagina during pregnancy.

hydrosalpinx (hī″drō-săl′pĭnks) [″ + *salpinx*, tube] Distention of the fallopian tube by clear fluid. SYN: *hydrops tubae.*

   intermittent h. Edema of the fallopian tube in which the distention is so great that the tube is forced by the pres-

sure to empty itself via the uterus. SYN: *hydrops tubae profluens.*

hydrosol (hī′drō-sŏl) The fluid state of a colloidal solution (sol) in which the colloid particles, separated by water in a continuous phase, are free to move about. SEE: *hydrogel.*

hydrostat (hī′drō-stăt) [″ + *statikos*, standing] A device that maintains the water level in a container at a predetermined level.

hydrostatic (hī″drō-stăt′ĭk) [″ + *statikos*, standing] Pert. to the pressures on and exerted by fluids when they are in equilibrium, i.e., not moving.

   h. densitometry An underwater weighing technique for the determination of an individual's specific gravity. The amount of water displaced by the body is corrected for the air contained in the lungs. This technique can be used to estimate the percentage of body fat. SYN: *h. weighing.*

   h. test A test to determine if an infant breathed prior to its death. The infant's lungs are put in water; if they float, prior breathing is proven.

   h. weighing Hydrostatic densitometry.

hydrostatics (hī″drō-stăt′ĭks) The science of the properties of fluids in equilibrium.

hydrosurgery (hī″drō-sŭrj′ĕ-rē) [*hydro-* + *surgery*] Removal of tissue with a jet of water used as a dissecting tool.

hydrotherapist (hī″drō-thĕr′ă-pĭst) One who specializes in hydrotherapy.

hydrotherapy (hī-drō-thĕr′ă-pē) [″ + *therapeia*, treatment] The use of water (in baths, jetted, as a douche, packed as ice, heated, etc.) for irrigation, massage, relaxation, or as an anti-inflammatory.

hydrothorax (hī″drŏ-thōr′aks″, -thōr′ă-sēz″) *pl.* **hydrothoraces** [*hydro-* + *thorax*] Edema marked by excess serous fluid in the pleural cavities.

   hepatic h. A pleural effusion associated with cirrhosis of the liver, typically on the right side of the chest, above the liver.

hydrotropism (hī″drō-trō′pĭzm) [″ + *trope*, a turning] The response of plants toward moisture (positive hydrotropism) or away from it (negative hydrotropism).

hydrotubation (hī″drō-tū-bā′shŭn) Injection of saline solution or liquid medication into the uterus and fallopian tubes to dilate or treat them.

hydroureter (hī″drō-ū-rē′tĕr) [″ + *oureter*, ureter] The distention of the ureter with fluid owing to obstruction.

hydrous (hī′drŭs) Containing water. SEE: *anhydrous.*

hydroxide (hī-drŏk′sīd) [″ + *oxys*, sour] A compound that contains the OH⁻ group, such as NaOH (sodium hydroxide, or caustic soda).

hydroxocobalamin (hī-drŏk″sō-kō-băl′ămǐn) A naturally occurring form of vitamin B_{12} used to treat B_{12} deficiency.

hydroxy (hī-drok'sē) Pertaining to the hydroxyl (OH) moiety.

hydroxyapatite, hydroxylapatite (hī-drok"sē-ap'ă-tīt", "sǐ-lap'ă-tīt") [*hydro-* + *²oxy-* + *apatite*] $Ca_{10}(PO_4)_6(OH)_2$; the calcium- and phosphorus-containing compound that constitutes the bulk of the mineral structure of bones and teeth. In teeth it is soluble in the acids of soft drinks or carbohydrate fermentation, but it becomes decay-resistant fluoroapatite after combining with fluoride ions present in fluoridated water or fluoride toothpastes. Under some circumstances, it can deposit in and around joints, producing periarthritis or calcific tendinitis.

hydroxybenzene (hī-drok"sē-běn'zēn) Phenol.

25-hydroxycholecalciferol (hī-drok"sē-kō"lě-kal-sif'ě-rol", -rōl") [*hydroxy* + *cholecalciferol*] $C_{27}H_{44}O_2$, a vitamin D derivative.

hydroxyethyl starch ABBR: HES. Any one of several modified starches with differing molecular weights, used as plasma volume expanders because of their colloidal properties. Examples include hetastarch and pentastarch.

hydroxyl (hī-drok'sil) ABBR: OH. The chemical moiety made up of a single atom of hydrogen and a single atom of oxygen.

hydroxylase (hī-drŏk'sǐ-lās) Any enzyme that catalyzes the introduction of hydrogen into a substrate.

hydroxylysine (hī"drŏk-sǐl'ǐ-sǐn) An amino acid found in collagen.

hydroxyproline (hī-drŏk"sē-prō'lǐn) An amino acid found in collagen.

hydroxypropyl methylcellulose Cellulose hydroxypropyl methyl ester; a substance used to increase the viscosity of solutions.

5-hydroxytryptamine (hī-drok"sē-trip'tă-mēn") [*hydroxy* + *tryptamine*] Serotonin.

5-hydroxytryptophan (hī-drok"sē-trip'tŏ-fan") ABBR: 5HTP. An amine that is a precursor of serotonin. It is marketed as a dietary supplement for depression, insomnia, and weight loss.

hygiene (hī'jēn") [Gr. *hygieinē(technē)*, healthful (art)] **1.** Sanitation. **2.** Healthfulness. **3.** The study of health and observance of health rules.

bronchial h. Any of several techniques to help patients clear mucus from their airways and improve respiration. It is used in patients who have copious, tenacious, or thick sputum, e.g., those affected by bronchiectasis, cystic fibrosis, occluded endotracheal tubes, or some pneumonias. Techniques employed include chest percussion, coughing and huffing, flutter valves, positive expiratory pressure therapy, and postural drainage.

community h. A term sometimes used as a synonym for *public health*.

dental h. Oral **h.**

hand h. Any of several techniques to clean the hands, including handwashing with plain and antimicrobial soaps and the use of alcohol-based hand rubs. Hand hygiene is the single most effective method of decreasing nosocomial infections. The U.S. Centers for Disease Control and Prevention states that if hands are not visibly soiled, alcohol preparations containing between 60% and 90% ethanol or isopropanol kill microorganisms more effectively than plain or antimicrobial soap and are not as harsh. After the hand rub is applied to the palm of one hand, the hands and fingers should be rubbed together, covering all surfaces, until they are entirely dry. Hands that are visibly dirty or contaminated should still be washed with soap and water for at least 15 seconds. The need for hand hygiene is not eliminated by the use of gloves. Contact dermatitis caused by alcohol hand rubs is very uncommon. However, with increasing use of such products by health care personnel, true allergic reactions will occasionally be encountered. Hospital computers can serve as a reservoir for drug-resistant bacteria such as vancomycin-resistant *Enterococcus faecium* (VRE), methicillin-resistant *Staphylococcus aureus* (MRSA), and *Pseudomonas aeruginosa*.

⚠ Health care personnel should avoid wearing artificial nails and should keep nails less than a quarter of an inch long if they care for patients at high risk of acquiring infections (e.g., patients in ICUs, transplant units, or protective isolation).

industrial h. That branch of hygiene that deals primarily with health of industrial workers, esp. study, treatment, and prevention of occupational diseases.

mental h. The science of developing and maintaining mental health and preventing mental illness.

oral h. Any of several preventive techniques to avoid pathological conditions of the teeth and oral cavity. These include discontinuing the use of tobacco products, including smokeless tobacco (snuff); brushing the teeth and using dental floss daily; and removal of impacted food debris. Oral hygiene may be performed with manual or mechanical devices such as toothbrushes, floss, and mechanical toothbrushes. Edentulous people with partial restorations or false teeth should be sure that their appliances fit properly and are kept clean.

Removal of plaque by a dental hygienist at least twice each year is also important for prevention of periodontal disease. SYN: *dental h.* SEE: *mouth care; dental hygienist; toothbrushing.*

sleep h. The influence of behavioral patterns or sleeping environment on the quality and quantity of sleep. Persons with insomnia not caused by a known disease may find that the following may assist in obtaining a good night's sleep: establishing a routine time to go to bed; avoiding trying to sleep; using practices that assist in going to sleep such as reading, watching television, or listening to music; sleeping in a dark room, free of noise; and avoiding caffeine and excessive food or drink before bedtime.

hygienic (hī″jē-ĕn′ĭk) **1.** Pert. to health or its preservation. **2.** In a healthy condition.

hygienist (hī-jē′nĭst, hī′jē-ĕn-ĭst) A specialist in hygiene.

dental h. A licensed primary oral health care professional. The dental hygienist is educated to provide dental services that include education, prevention, and therapeutic services. The most common services provided are patient education, oral prophylaxis, dental radiographs, and fluoride applications. The goals of the dental hygienist include the control of oral diseases and the promotion of health. The practice of dental hygiene is regulated by laws called dental practice acts. The laws vary with each licensing jurisdiction.

industrial h. A scientist or engineer engaged in the study, control, and prevention of health risks in the workplace.

hygro-, hygr- [Gr. *hygros*, wet, moist] Prefixes meaning *moist* or *wet.*

hygroma (hī-grō′mă) *pl.* **hygromas or hygromata** [″ + *oma*, tumor] A sac or bursa containing fluid.

cystic h. A rapidly growing hygroma of lymphatic origin. It is usually located in the neck but may be in the thorax.

hygrometer (hī-grŏm′ĕ-tĕr) [″ + *metron*, measure] An instrument for measuring the amount of moisture in the air.

hygroscopic (hī-grō-skŏp′ĭk) [″ + *skopein*, to examine] **1.** Pert. to hygroscopy. **2.** Absorbing moisture readily. SYN: *bibulous; hydrophilous.*

hymen (hī′mĕn) [Gr.] A fold of mucous membrane that partially covers the entrance to the vagina. Contrary to folklore, the presence or absence (or rupture) of the hymen cannot be used to prove or disprove virginity or history of sexual intercourse. Pregnancy has been known to occur even when the hymen is intact. **hymenal** (-ăl), *adj.*

annular h. A hymen with a ring-shaped opening in the center.

h. biforis A vaginal membrane with two openings separated by a thick septum; the structure partially covers the os.

cribriform h. A hymen with many small perforations. SYN: *fenestrated h.*

h. denticulatus A hymen with an opening with serrated edges.

fenestrated h. Cribriform **h.**

imperforate h. A hymen without an opening. Menstruation occurs, but the blood cannot escape from the vagina because of the obstruction of the hymen. The treatment is surgical incision of the hymen. SYN: *unruptured h.*

lunar h. A hymen shaped like a crescent moon.

ruptured h. A hymen that has been torn by coitus, injury, or surgery.

septate h. A hymen in which the opening is separated by a thin septum.

unruptured h. Imperforate **h.**

Hymenolepis (hī″mĕ-nol′ĕ-pĭs) [*hymen* + Gr. *lepis*, scale] A genus of tapeworm parasitic in birds and mammals.

H. nana A species parasitic in the intestine of rats and mice and common in humans, esp. children. It averages about 1 in (2.51 cm) in length and differs from other tapeworms in that it is capable of completing its life cycle within a single host. The parasite in humans lives in the proximal ileum and can cause severe toxic symptoms, esp. in children, including diarrhea, abdominal pain, irritability, and convulsions that resemble epilepsy. The detection of eggs and gravid segments in the feces confirms the diagnosis of infestation with this parasite. Treatment is with praziquantel. SYN: *dwarf tapeworm; mouse tapeworm; rat tapeworm.*

Hymenoptera (hī″mĕn-ŏp′tur-ă) [Gr. *hymenopteros,* membrane-winged] An order of insects that includes ants, bees, hornets, and wasps. SEE: *bite, insect; sting.*

hyo-, hy- [L. fr. Gr. *hyo-,* fr. *hy,* the ancient Gr. name for upsilon (Y)] Prefixes meaning *hyoid* arch or bone.

hyoepiglottic, hyoepiglottidean (hī″ō-ĕp″ĭ-glŏt′ĭk, hī″ō-ĕp″ĭ-glŏt-ĭd′ē-ăn) [″ + *epiglottis,* epiglottis] Relating to the hyoid bone and epiglottis.

hyoglossal (hī″ō-glŏs′ăl) [″ + *glossa,* tongue] **1.** Pert. to the hyoglossus. **2.** Extending to the tongue from the hyoid bone.

hyoglossus (hī″ō-glŏs′ŭs) A muscle arising from the body and greater cornu of the hyoid bone and inserted into the dorsum of the tongue. It draws the sides of the tongue down and retracts it.

hyoid (hī′oyd) [Gr. *hyoeides,* U-shaped] **1.** Shaped like the Gr. letter upsilon (*v*). **2.** Pert. to the hyoid bone.

hyoscyamus (hī″ō-sī′ă-mŭs) [Gr. *hys,* a pig, + *kyamos,* bean] The dried leaves of the plant *Hyoscyamus niger;* a narcotic that also acts as an antispasmodic. A relative of atropine, hyoscyamus is also known as henbane.

hypalgesia (hī-păl-jē′zē-ă) [″ + *algesis,* sense of pain] A lessened sensitivity to pain; the opposite of hyperalgesia.

hyper- [Gr. *hyper,* over, above, excessive] Prefix meaning *above, excessive,* or *beyond.* SEE: *super-*.

hyperabduction (soo″pĕr-ăb-dŭk′shŭn) [L. *super,* over, above, + *abducens,* drawing away] Pronounced or extreme abduction.

hyperacid (hī″pĕr-ăs′ĭd) [″ + L. *acidus,* sour] Containing too much acid.

hyperacidity (hī″pĕr-ă-sĭd′ĭ-tē) [″ + L. *acidus,* sour] **1.** An excess of acid. **2.** An excess of acid in the stomach, as may occur in Zollinger-Ellison syndrome. SEE: *hyperchlorhydria.*

hyperactive child syndrome SEE: *attention-deficit hyperactivity disorder; hyperactivity.*

hyperactivity (hī″pĕr-ăk-tīv′ĭ-tē) **1.** Increased or excessive activity of any cell, organ, tissue, or organism. **2.** Excessive muscular activity. **3.** Manifestations of disturbed behavior in children or adolescents characterized by constant overactivity, distractibility, impulsiveness, inability to concentrate, and aggressiveness. Hyperkinetic behavior may lessen as a child grows older. SEE: *attention-deficit hyperactivity disorder.*

Hyperactivity may be caused by emotional disorders, central nervous system dysfunction, mental retardation, or an exaggeration of a normal personality trait.

hyperacuity (hī″pĕr-ă-kū′ĭ-tē) [Gr. *hyper,* over, above, excessive, + L. *acuitas,* sharpness] Abnormal sensitivity to sensory stimulation.

hyperacusis (hī″pĕr-ă-kū′sĭs) [″ + *akousis,* hearing] An abnormal sensitivity to sound. SYN: *oxyacusis.*

hyperacute (hī″pĕr-ă-kūt′) Extremely or excessively acute.

hyperadrenalism (hī″pĕr-ă-drē′năl-ĭzm) Increased hormonal secretion from the adrenal gland.

hyperalbuminemia (hī″pĕr-ăl-bū″mĭ-nē′mē-ă) [″ + L. *albumen,* white of egg, + Gr. *haima,* blood] Increased albumin in the blood.

hyperaldosteronism (hī″pĕ-ral″dos-tĕ′rō-nĭzm) [*hyper-* + *aldosteronism*] The excessive production of aldosterone by the adrenal gland. This can cause high blood pressure that is difficult to treat. Unprovoked hypokalemia and excessive secretion of potassium in the urine are commonly present. SEE: *aldosteronism.*

hyperalgesia (hī″pĕr-ăl-jē′zē-ă) [″ + *algesis,* sense of pain] An excessive sensitivity to pain; the opposite of hypalgesia. SYN: *hyperalgia.*

hyperalgia (hī-pĕr-ăl′jē-ă) [″ + *algos,* pain] Hyperalgesia.

hyperalimentation (hī″pĕr-ăl″ĭ-mĕn-tā′shŭn) The enteral and parenteral infusion of a solution that contains sufficient amino acids, glucose, fatty acids, electrolytes, vitamins, and minerals to sustain life, maintain normal growth and development, and provide for needed tissue repair. The gastrointestinal tract is the route of choice if it is functional. Intravenous hyperalimentation must utilize less concentrated formulations because of the potential for chemical phlebitis that may result from osmotic stress. Infusion through a central line catheter into the superior vena cava provides a sufficient blood volume to dilute more hypertonic solutions. One crucial drawback of a central line is the potential for the line to become infected with either bacteria or fungi.

PATIENT CARE: Vital signs, electrolyte values, and fluid balance (intake, output, and daily weight) are monitored for indications of fluid overload or dehydration. Urine specific gravity is measured, and the patient's urine is checked for the presence of glucose and acetone every 6 hours. If the hyperalimentation is enteral, the nurse is aware of the placement of the distal end of the tube (above or below the pyloric sphincter); auscultates for bowel sounds; inspects, percusses, and measures for abdominal distention; and assesses for, documents, reports, and treats nausea, vomiting, or diarrhea. As appropriate, stomach contents are monitored for residual volume. Tube patency as well as volume, rate, and type of feeding are maintained; comfort measures are provided (oral misting, oral hygiene, and analgesic throat sprays); and any indications of infections due to long-term nasal tube placement, such as sinusitis, aspiration reflux chemical pneumonia, and other infections, are assessed. For example, sinusitis can occur because the tube impedes sinus drainage, allowing organisms to colonize the sinuses and resulting in fever and nasopurulent drainage. Chemical aspiration pneumonias often occur because of silent reflux regurgitation, resulting in acidic stomach contents and gram-negative organisms entering the respiratory tract. If hyperalimentation is via peripheral blood vessels, the insertion site is checked frequently for evidence of phlebitis; if via a central line, the site is monitored for signs of inflammation or infection, and the patient is assessed for signs and symptoms of sepsis. The insertion site is redressed and administration sets and connectors are changed according to institutional protocol; strict asepsis is maintained throughout these procedures. For all parenteral hyperalimentation, the flow rate should never be sped up if an infusion is behind unless this action is specifically prescribed by the physician. The physician is notified if the line becomes occluded or if fluids are stopped or slowed for any reason. The patient is assessed for hypoglycemia or fluid deficit. For all hyperalimentation, the patient is mobilized as possible. Nutritional status is monitored weekly; weight gain or loss, serum protein levels, transferrin levels, and anthropomorphic measurements are documented and reported as directed. Strict asepsis is maintained in handling fluids and equipment, with special vigilance maintained for immobile or paralyzed patients.

hyperaminoacidemia (hī″pĕr-ăm″ĭ-nō-ăs″ĭ-dē′mē-ă) An abnormal concentration of amino acids in the blood.

hyperaminoaciduria (hī′pĕr-am′ĭ-nō-as-ĭ-doo′rē-ă) [″ + ″ + *amine* + Gr. *ouron,* urine] The presence of an excess of amino acids in the urine. SYN: *acidaminuria.*

hyperammonemia (hī″pĕr-ăm″mō-nē′mē-ă) An excess concentration of ammonia in the blood. SEE: *ammonia toxicity.*

  congenital h. An accumulation of an excess of ammonia in the body due to a congenital deficiency of enzymes, either carbamyl phosphate synthetase or ornithine transcarbamylase, essential to the metabolism of ammonia. Clinical signs of ammonia toxicity are present, including vomiting, lethargy, coma, and, eventually, death.

hyperamylasemia (hī″pĕr-ăm″ĭl-ās-ē′mē-ă) Increased blood amylase. It is often found in pancreatitis and/or diseases of the salivary glands, but may occasionally be present in healthy people.

hyperandrogenism (hī″pĕr-an″droj′ĕ-nizm) [*hyper-* + *androgen* + *-ism*] Excessive concentrations of male hormones and their physiological consequences, e.g., in conditions such as polycystic ovarian syndrome or congenital adrenal hyperplasia. SYN: *androgen excess; androgenism.* **hyperandrogenic** (-an″drŏ-jen′ik), *adj.*

  adrenal h. Excessive production of dehydroepiandrosterone (DHEA) and DHEA sulfate by the adrenal glands.

hyperarousal (hī″pĕr-ă-rowz′ăl) Excessive responsiveness to sensory stimulation. It is found in alcohol withdrawal, post-traumatic stress disorder, and other conditions.

hyperazotemia (hī″pĕr-ăz″ō-tē′mē-ă) [″ + L. *azotum,* nitrogen, + Gr. *haima,* blood] An increased amount of nitrogenous substances such as urea in the blood.

hyperbaric Having an increased pressure or density when compared with a standard gas or liquid. Hyperbaric oxygen, e.g., has a greater oxygen concentration than air at sea level, and hyperbaric anesthetics have a greater concentration of dextrose than does the cerebrospinal fluid.

hyperbetalipoproteinemia (hī″pĕr-bā″tă-lĭp″ō-prō″tē-ĭn-ē′mē-ă) An excessive amount of β-lipoproteins in the blood. SEE: *hyperlipoproteinemia.*

hyperbilirubinemia (hī″pĕr-bil″ĭ-roo-bĭ-nē′mē-ă) [*hyper-* + *bilirubinemia*] An excessive amount of bilirubin in the blood. It is seen in any illness causing jaundice, including diseases in which the biliary tree is obstructed, blood formation is ineffective, or severe hemolysis is present. SEE: *jaundice.*

hypercalcemia (hī″pĕr-kal-sē′mē-ă) [*hyper-* + *calci-* + *-emia*] An excessive amount of calcium in the blood. Causes include primary hyperparathyroidism, lithium therapy, malignancies (such as solid tumors and hematological malignancies), vitamin D intoxication, hyperthyroidism, vitamin A intoxication, aluminum intoxication, and milk-alkali syndrome.

  SYMPTOMS: Clinically, fatigue, depression, confusion, nausea, vomiting, constipation, renal stones, increased urination, and occasional cardiac arrhythmias are present. A short Q-T interval is present.

  TREATMENT: Patients initially should be given hydration with saline, followed by diuretics after dehydration has been resolved. Bisphosphonates, glucocorticoids, and other drugs may be administered to lower serum calcium levels. Therapy is also directed at the underlying cause of the high serum calcium levels, e.g., by treating underlying malignancies or by excising overactive parathyroid glands.

  idiopathic h. A type of hypercalcemia seen in infants, caused by vitamin D intoxication. SEE: *bends.*

hypercalciuria (hī″pĕr-kăl″sē-ū′rē-ă) [″ + ″ + Gr. *ouron,* urine] An excessive concentration of calcium in the urine.

hypercapnia (hī″pĕr-kap′nē-ă) [*hyper-* + Gr. *kapnos,* smoke + *-ia*] An increase in the partial pressure of carbon dioxide in the blood, typically to levels greater than 45 or 50 mm Hg. Elevated levels of carbon dioxide in the blood result from inadequate ventilation or from massive mismatches between ventilation and perfusion of the blood. When CO_2 levels are greater than 45 mm Hg, cerebral vasodilation can occur. Some of the common symptoms of hypercapnia include dizziness, drowsiness, confusion, tremors, and twitching. **hypercapnic** (-nik), *adj.*; SYN: *hypercarbia.*

  permissive h. Intentional limiting of airway pressures and tidal volumes during mechanical ventilation, thereby allowing $PaCO_2$ to rise above normal, in order to minimize the risk of lung injury.

⚠️ Permissive hypercapnia should be avoided in patients who may not tolerate high carbon dioxide levels or acidosis, e.g., patients with sickle cell anemia or those with high intracranial pressures.

hypercarbia (hī″pĕr-kăr′bē-ă) Hypercapnia.

hypercellularity (hī″pĕr-sĕl″ū-lăr′ĭ-tē) An increased number of cells in any location, but esp. in the bone marrow.

hypercementosis (hī″pĕr-sē″mĕn-tō′sĭs) [″ + L. *cementum,* cement, + Gr. *osis,* condition] An overgrowth of tooth cement (cementum).

hyperchloremia (hī″pĕr-klō-rē′mē-ă) [″ + *chloros,* green, + *haima,* blood] An increase in the chloride content of the blood.

hyperchlorhydria (hī″pĕr-klor-hī′drē-ă) [″ + ″ + *hydor,* water] An excess of hydrochloric acid in the stomach. SEE: *achlorhydria; gastrin; gastritis;* H_2-receptor antagonist; *hydrochloric acid; hypochlorhydria; peptic ulcer; Zollinger-Ellison syndrome.*

hypercholesterolemia (hī″pĕr-kō-lĕs″tĕr-ŏl-ē′mē-ă) [″ + *chole,* bile, + *stereos,* solid, + *haima,* blood] An excessive amount of cholesterol in the blood.
   familial h. A type of hyperlipoproteinemia in which low-density lipoproteins are not removed from the bloodstream in normal amounts by lipoprotein receptors in the liver. Affected persons have massively elevated serum lipid levels. SEE: *hyperlipoproteinemia.*

hyperchromatic (hī″pĕr-krō-măt′ĭk) [″ + *chroma,* color] Overpigmented.

hyperchromatism (hī″pĕr-krō′mă-tĭzm) [″ + ″ + *-ismos,* condition] **1.** Excessive pigmentation. **2.** The increased staining capacity of any structure.

hyperchromia (hī″pĕr-krō′mē-ă) Hyperchromatism.

hyperchromic (hī-pĕr-krō′mĭk) **1.** Pert. to excessive pigmentation. **2.** Intensely colored.

hyperchylomicronemia (hī″pĕr-kī″lō-mī″krō-nē′mē-ă) The excessive concentration of chylomicrons in the blood.
   familial h. An inherited disorder of lipoprotein metabolism characterized by elevated plasma chylomicrons and triglycerides. It is usually caused by a deficiency of lipoprotein lipase or its cofactor apolipoprotein C-II. Clinical findings include repeated episodes of pancreatitis. The blood of affected patients has a creamy or milky appearance.

hyperCKemia (hī″pĕr-sē″kā″ē′mē-ă) Persistent elevations in the serum levels of creatine kinase ("CK"), a muscle enzyme. The condition is sometimes found in persons with congenital muscle diseases, such as muscular dystrophies or other myopathies.

hypercoagulability (hī″pĕr-kō-ag″yŭ-lă-bil′ĭt-ē) [*hyper-* + *coagulability*] An increased ability of anything to coagulate, but esp. the blood. **hypercoagulable** (-kō-ag′yŭ-lă-bĕl), *adj.*

hypercortisolism (hī″pĕr-kort″ĭ-sol″izm) [*hyper-* + *cortisol* + *-ism*] Excess levels of cortisol in the blood, caused by administered corticosteroid drugs, an adrenocorticotropic hormone–secreting tumor, or adrenal overproduction of cortisol.

hypercupremia (hī″pĕr-kū-prē′mē-ă) An increased level of copper in the blood. SEE: *Wilson's disease.*

hypercyanotic (hī″pĕr-sī″ă-nŏt′ĭk) Severely cyanotic.

hyperdynamic (hī″pĕr-dī-năm′ĭk) Overactive or overstimulated; said, for example, of the circulation in cirrhosis, sepsis, and other diseases.

hyperechoic (hī′pĕr-ĕ-kō′ik) [*hypere-* + *echoic*] Pert. to a sonographic echo texture that is more echogenic than surrounding tissue. Hyperechoic masses in the breast are nearly always benign. SEE: *echogenic.*

hyperekplexia, hyperexplexia (hī″pĕr-ĕk-plĕk′sē-ă, -ĕks-) [Gr. *hyper,* over, above, excessive, + *ekplexia,* sudden shock] Excessive startling in response to sound or physical contact. Extreme reflex reaction to neurological stimulation is often an autosomal (dominant or recessive) disorder. It may also occur in some degenerative neurological disorders (e.g., multiple sclerosis).

hyperemesis (hī″pĕr-em′ĕ-sĭs, -ĕ-mē′sĭs, -sēz″) *pl.* **hyperemeses** [*hyper-* + *emesis*] Excessive vomiting.
   h. gravidarum Persistent, continuous, severe, pregnancy-related nausea and vomiting, often accompanied by dry retching. The condition can cause systemic effects such as dehydration, weight loss, fluid-electrolyte and acid-base imbalance leading to metabolic acidosis, and rarely, death. About 2 out of 1000 pregnant women require hospitalization for medical management of the disorder. SYN: *pernicious* **vomiting.** SEE: *morning* **sickness***; Nursing Diagnoses Appendix.*
   SYMPTOMS: This condition of unknown etiology may start as a simple vomiting of early pregnancy, but if it persists, dehydration, protein, chloride, sodium and potassium depletion, dehydration, and contraction alkalosis occur.
   TREATMENT: Early management includes bedrest; small, frequent, high-carbohydrate feedings; moderate fluid restriction; and mild sedation. In severe cases, the patient is hospitalized for complete bedrest and rehydration. Vitamin and electrolyte-enhanced parenteral fluids are administered. An antiemetic safe for use in early pregnancy may be used to control vomiting. Feed-

ing via total parenteral nutrition is rarely necessary.

When the patient improves, food taken by mouth should consist of a light solid diet given in frequent small feedings, with fruit juice or milk between feedings and a mid-night snack to help stabilize blood glucose levels. Vitamin B may be prescribed intramuscularly or intranasally to begin correction of vitamin deficiencies. Sitting upright during and for 30 to 45 min after meals helps to reduce gastric reflux. Termination of the pregnancy is indicated only when the woman fails to respond to medical measures and is approaching serious physiological jeopardy.

⚠ During therapy the patient's retinas should be monitored for evidence of hemorrhagic retinitis. If it occurs, the pregnancy should be terminated without delay.

PATIENT CARE: The patient's emotional state is assessed. Environmental stimuli are minimized, with rest, relaxation, and verbalization of concerns encouraged. Prescribed treatments are explained and implemented, and psychological support is provided. Ongoing assessments include vital signs and fetal heart rate; the time, amount, and character of any emesis; fluid intake and output; and the woman's response to treatment. Aspects of complementary medicine may be incorporated by using and teaching techniques that induce the relaxation response.

hyperemia (hī″pĕr-ē′mē-ă) [*hyper-* + *-emia*] **1.** An unusual amount of blood in a part; congestion. **2.** A form of macula; red areas on the skin that disappear on pressure. **3.** In physical therapy, an increase in the quantity of blood flowing through any part of the body, shown by redness of the skin caused by the application of heat.

    active h. Hyperemia caused by increased blood inflow. SYN: *arterial **h.***

    arterial h. Active **h.**

    artificial h. Bringing of blood to the superficial tissues by means of counterirritation, such as may be produced by coining, cupping, or acupuncture.

    Bier h. SEE: under *Bier, August Karl Gustav.*

    constriction h. Bier hyperemia.

    leptomeningeal h. Pia-arachnoid congestion.

    passive h. Hyperemia caused by decreased drainage of blood. SYN: *venous **h.***

    reactive h. The increased flow of blood into an ischemic tissue area after restoration of blood flow.

    venous h. Passive **h.**

hyperenzymemia (hī″pĕr-ĕn″zī-mē′mē-ă)

[″ + ″ + ″] Excessive secretion of enzymes, esp. the digestive enzymes manufactured by the pancreas.

hypereosinophilia (hī″pĕr-ē″ŏ-sin″ŏ-fil′ē-ă) [*hyper-* + *eosinophilia*] An abnormally high level of eosinophils in the blood; typically more than 1500 cells/mL of blood and sometimes > 5000.

hyperesthesia (hī″pĕr-ĕs-thē′zē-ă) [″ + *aisthesis*, sensation] An increased sensitivity to sensory stimuli, such as pain or touch. SYN: *algesia; oxyesthesia.* **hyperesthetic** (-ĕs-thĕt′ĭk), *adj.*

    acoustic h. An abnormal sensitivity to sound.

    cerebral h. Hyperesthesia caused by a cerebral lesion.

    gustatory h. An oversensitivity of taste.

    muscular h. Muscular sensitivity to pain and fatigue.

    optic h. An abnormal sensitivity to light.

    h. sexualis An abnormal increase in libido.

    tactile h. An abnormal sensitivity to touch.

hyperextension (hī″pĕr-ĕks-tĕn′shŭn) [″ + L. *extendere*, to stretch out] Extreme or abnormal extension of a joint, usually the result of trauma, increased muscle tone, joint adhesions, or congenital formation.

hyperfibrinogenemia (hī″pĕr-fī-brĭn″ō-jĕ-nē′mē-ă) An increased amount of fibrinogen in the blood; a possible but unproven risk factor for cardiovascular disease.

hyperflexion (hī″pĕr-flĕk′shŭn) Increased flexion of a joint, usually the result of trauma, decreased muscle tone, or joint laxity.

hyperfractionation (hī″pĕr-frăk-shŭn-ā′shŭn) The treatment of a tumor with radiation applied in several small doses several hours apart on the same day instead of in a once-a-day dose. Hyperfractionation decreases the side effects of delivery and may permit a tumor to be treated with a greater total radiation dose than traditional fractionation.

hyperfunction (hī″pĕr-fŭnk′shŭn) [Gr. *hyper*, over, above, excessive, + L. *functio*, performance] Excessive activity. **hyperfunctional,** *adj.*

hypergammaglobulinemia (hī″pĕr-găm″ă-glŏb″u-lĭ-nē′mē-ă) An excessive amount of immunoglobulin G (IgG) in the blood. It may occur in patients with monoclonal gammopathy, multiple myeloma, and in some chronic infections.

hyperglobulinemia (hī″pĕr-glŏb″u-lĭn-ē′mē-ă) [″ + L. *globulus,* a globule, + Gr. *haima,* blood] Excessive globulin in the blood.

hyperglycemia (hī″pĕr-glī-sē′mē-ă) [*hyper-* + *glycemia*] Abnormally high blood sugar levels. Hyperglycemia can cause numerous unwanted effects. It can impair wound healing; decrease the body's ability to fight infections; worsen the neurological deficits found in stroke; increase the risk of death in critically ill patients; and damage the kidneys, peripheral nerves, retinae, blood vessels, and heart. SEE: *diabetes*.

ETIOLOGY: Hyperglycemia may result from damage to the insulin secreting cells of the pancreas; infusions of dextrose; insulin resistance; obesity; overeating; a sedentary lifestyle; the stress of heart attack or other critical illnesses; or treatment with some drugs such as steroids or protease inhibitors.

PATIENT CARE: In patients with diabetes mellitus, controlling blood glucose levels reduces many complications of the disease. In pregnancy management of elevated blood sugars reduces the likelihood of overnutrition of the fetus (macrosomia). In the acutely ill patient, maintaining plasma glucose levels below 150 mg/dl reduces the length of hospital stay, helps prevent infection, improves wound healing, and reduces health care costs. Elevated blood sugars in the hospitalized patient can be managed with adjustments in nutrition, intravenous (IV) hydration, and IV insulin. When insulin is infused IV, blood glucose levels should be monitored hourly and insulin doses titrated to achieve levels as close to normal as possible without producing hypoglycemia.

Among outpatients, high blood sugar levels can be reduced with caloric restriction (dieting), regular exercise, oral hypoglycemic agents, insulin, and/or withholding offending drugs. Self–blood glucose monitoring and the keeping of a blood sugar log helps patients and their health care providers to recognize and manage hyperglycemic trends. Patients with diabetes mellitus need to understand the role maintaining glycemic control plays in preventing complications of their disease. Consultation with a diabetic nurse educator can provide the necessary information (and impetus) for good management of diet, medication regimens, and exercise.

stress-induced h. A transient rise in blood glucose to abnormally high concentrations during acute illness, such as infection or myocardial infarction; trauma, such as burns; or stroke. SYN: *stress h.*

　stress h. Stress-induced hyperglycemia.

hyperglycemic (hī″pĕr-glī-sē′mĭk) [Gr. *hyper-*, above, excessive, + *glykys*, sweet, + *haima*, blood] **1.** Pert. to an elevated blood glucose concentration. **2.** An agent that produces an elevated blood glucose level.

hyperglyceridemia (hī″pĕr-glĭs″ĕr-ĭ-dē′mē-ă) Hypertriglyceridemia.

hyperglycinemia (hī″pĕr-glī″sĭ-nē′mē-ă)

An accumulation of glycine in the blood. It is caused by a congenital defect in the ability to metabolize the amino acid glycine. There are at least six forms of this disease, all of which are associated with mental and growth retardation.

hypergonadism (hī″pĕr-gō′năd-ĭzm) [″ + *gone*, seed, + *-ismos*, state of] Excessive hormonal secretion of the sex glands.

hypergraphia (hī″pĕr-grăf′ē-ă) A compulsion to write. It is found in persons with temporal lobe epilepsy and right hemispheric strokes and tumors, among other brain disorders.

hyperhidrosis (hī″pĕr-hī-drō′sĭs) [″ + *hidros*, sweat, + *osis*, condition] Sweating greater than would be expected considering the temperature of the environment. SEE: *bromidrosis; sweat.*

ETIOLOGY: This symptom may be caused by stimulants, sepsis, hyperthyroidism, menopausal hot flashes, obesity, intense activation of the sympathetic nervous system, and other conditions.

TREATMENT: If the sweating is due to a systemic disease, appropriate therapy for that condition is indicated. If localized, application of a 20% solution of aluminum chloride hexahydrate in absolute alcohol at night using occlusive dressings is beneficial. The dressed sites must be dried before application and the salt washed away in the morning.

hyperhomocysteinemia (hī″pĕr-hō″mō-sĭs-tē″ĭn-ēm′ē-ă) [″ + ″] Elevated levels of homocysteine in the bloodstream. High levels of homocysteine are found in the blood of patients with homocystinuria. Mildly elevated levels are found in many persons who consume a Western diet.

hyperhydration (hī″pĕr-hī-drā′shŭn) [″ + ″] Excessive fluid intake, e.g., before athletic events or in some psychiatric illnesses. SEE: *water intoxication.*

Hypericum perforatum (hī-pĕr′ĭ-kŭm pĕr-fō-rā′-tŭm) [L., perforated Saint John's wort] The scientific name for Saint John's wort. SEE: *Saint John's wort* for illus.

hyperimmune (hī″pĕr-ĭm-mūn′) A state of greater than normal immunity.

hyperimmunoglobulinemia E syndrome (hī″pĕr-ĭm″ū-nō-glŏb″ū-lĭn-ēm′ē-ă, -mū″) An autosomal dominant disorder marked by high serum levels of IgE; eczema, mucosal candidiasis, and other cutaneous infections; pulmonary infections; retained primary dentition; scoliosis; and increased frequency of fractures.

hyperinflation (hī″pĕr-ĭn-flā′shŭn) An excess of air in anything, esp. the lungs.

hyperinsulinemia (hī″pĕr-in-sŭ-lĭ-nē′mē-ă) [*hyper-* + *insulin* + *-emia*] In patients with type 2 diabetes mellitus

(DM) or impaired fasting glucose, a condition in which hyperglycemia is present despite high levels of insulin in the bloodstream. Insulin resistance and hyperinsulinemia have been linked to hypertension, obesity, hyperlipidemia, and increased cardiovascular mortality in patients with type 2 DM.

TREATMENT: Diet, exercise, and some oral antidiabetic drugs (e.g., metformin) increase the sensitivity of body tissues to the effects of insulin and decrease hyperinsulinemia.

hyperinsulinism (hī″pĕr-ĭn′sū-lĭn-ĭzm) [″ + L. *insula,* island, + Gr. *-ismos,* condition] A relative or absolute excess of insulin in the blood. The condition is commonly found in insulin-resistant patients with type 2 diabetes mellitus and rarely found in patients with insulin secreting tumors of the pancreas. In type 2 diabetes, the condition is marked by hyperglycemia, weight gain, hypertension, and atherosclerosis. The resistance of such patients to the effect of insulin prevents hypoglycemia. By contrast, in patients with insulin-secreting tumors, severe hypoglycemia may be present.

congenital h. Persistent infant hyperinsulinemic hypoglycemia.

hyperirritability (hī″pĕr-ĭr″ĭ-tă-bĭl′ĭ-tē) An increased response to a stimulus.

hyperkalemia (hī″pĕr-kā-lē′mē-ă) [*hyper-* + L. *kalium,* potassium + *-emia*] An abnormally high concentration of potassium in the blood (> 5 meq/L). SEE: *hypokalemia.*

ETIOLOGY: It is usually caused by inadequate excretion of potassium or by the shift of potassium from tissues. Causes of inadequate secretion include acute renal failure, severe chronic renal failure, renal tubular disorders, hypoaldosteronism, and decreased renin secretion due to kidney disease or drugs (e.g., nonsteroidal anti-inflammatory agents, ACE inhibitors, or angiotensin receptor blockers) that inhibit potassium excretion. The shift of potassium from tissues occurs in tissue damage due to trauma, hemolysis, digitalis poisoning, acidosis, and insulin deficiency.

SYMPTOMS: Hyperkalemia is often a symptomless condition until very high levels of potassium are present in the blood. The precise level at which cardiac or skeletal muscle toxicities arise varies greatly from patient to patient. Eventually, muscular weakness, electrocardiographic abnormalities (such as peaked T waves, widened QRS complex, prolonged P-R interval, flattened or absent P waves, depressed ST segment), and intractable cardiac rhythm disturbances leading to cardiac arrest may result.

PREVENTION: To help prevent hyperkalemia, patients who use salt substitutes containing potassium should be advised to discontinue them if urine output decreases. Predisposed patients, esp. those with poor urinary output or taking oral or intravenous potassium supplements, require regular laboratory testing to assess their serum potassium levels.

TREATMENT: Mild hyperkalemia can be treated by eliminating its cause, often a medication or a potassium source in the diet or dietary supplement (e.g., potassium chloride taken as a salt substitute). Severe or progressive hyperkalemia can be treated with infusions of calcium gluconate, sodium bicarbonate, or insulin and glucose, or by the administration of potassium-binding resins orally or rectally. Hemodialysis is also effective.

PATIENT CARE: Cardiac rhythm, serum potassium, and other electrolyte levels are monitored. Intake and output are recorded. Prescribed drugs are given and their effects on potassium levels are promptly evaluated. A dietitian is consulted to recommend optimal quantities of potassium in foods and fluids. Safety measures are implemented for the patient with muscle weakness. If the patient requires transfused blood, only fresh blood may be used, since older blood contains potassium released by hemolysis.

hyperkeratinization (hī″pĕr-kĕr″ă-tĭn″ĭ-zā′shŭn) [″ + *keras,* horn] A thickening of the horny layers of the skin, esp. of the palms and soles. It may be caused by vitamin A deficiency or chronic arsenic toxicity.

hyperkeratosis (hī″pĕr-ker″ă-tō′sĭs, -tō′sēz″) *pl.* **hyperkeratoses** [*hyper-* + *keratosis*] **1.** An overgrowth of the cornea. **2.** An overgrowth of the horny layer of the epidermis. **hyperkeratotic** (″ă-tot′ik), *adj.*

h. congenitalis Hyperkeratosis in the harlequin fetus.

epidermolytic h. A congenital disorder characterized by hyperkeratosis, erythema, and blisters.

follicular h. Toad skin.

hyperketonemia (hī″pĕr-kē″tō-nē′mē-ă) Accumulation of an excess of ketone bodies in the blood.

hyperkinesia, hyperkinesis (hī″pĕr-kĭ-nē′zh(ē-)ă, -nē′sĭs) [*hyper-* + *-kinesia*] Increased muscular movement and physical activity. In children it may be due to attention-deficit hyperactivity disorder (ADHD) or cerebral palsy. SEE: *hyperactivity.*

hyperkinetic disorder **1.** A brain-based motor system disorder characterized by excessive involuntary movements and some amount of hypotonia. The classic hyperkinetic disorder is Huntington's disease. **2.** The British term for attention deficit and hyperactivity disorder.

hyperlactatemia, hyperlactemia (hī″pĕr-lak″tă-tē′mē-ă) [*hyper-* + *lactate* + *-emia*] Increased levels of lactate in the blood, without evidence of lactic acidosis or shock.

hyperleptinemia (hī″pĕr-lĕp″tĭn-ē′mē-ă) [″ + ″ + ″] Excess levels of leptin in the blood. Hyperleptinemia increases body fat content and stimulates appetite.

hyperleukocytosis (hī″pĕr-loo″kō-sī-tō′sĭs) A concentration of white blood cells that exceeds 100×10^9 cells/mm³. Extremely elevated white blood cell counts can cause blood clotting, heart attack, or stroke due to abnormal blood viscosity.

hyperlipemia (hī″pĕr-lĭp-ē′mē-ă) [″ + *lipos,* fat, + *haima,* blood] An excessive quantity of fat in the blood.

hyperlipidemia (hī″pĕr-lĭp″ĭ-dē′mē-ă) An increase of lipids in the blood.

hyperlipoproteinemia (hī″pĕr-lĭp″ō-prō″tē-ĭn-ē′mē-ă) Increased lipids in the blood resulting either from an increased rate of synthesis or from a decreased lipoprotein breakdown rate. The lipoproteins transport triglycerides and cholesterol in the plasma. Clinically, an increased lipoprotein level may cause atherosclerosis and pancreatitis. Hyperlipoproteinemias can develop as a result of a primary and inheritable biochemical defect of either lipoprotein lipase activity or one of the cofactors essential to the function of that enzyme. They may also develop secondary to certain endocrine and metabolic disorders, such as diabetes mellitus; glycogen storage disease, type I; Cushing's syndrome; acromegaly; hypothyroidism; anorexia; use of drugs such as alcohol, oral contraceptives, and glucocorticoids; renal disease; liver disease; immunological disorders; and stress. The hyperlipoproteinemias have been divided into five different lipoprotein patterns describing the changes found in the plasma. Types I and III are autosomal recessive traits; types II, IV, and V are autosomal dominant. These patterns are not descriptive of specific diseases. SEE: *cholesterol; lipoprotein.*

PATIENT CARE: The patient should receive instruction about and support for a high-fiber, calorically restricted diet that is low in saturated fats and total cholesterol. A formal consultation with a nutritionist facilitates this process. Regular exercise lasting at least 35 to 60 min a day also helps the patient to metabolize lipids and raise protective levels of high-density lipoproteins (HDLs) while decreasing levels of low-density lipoproteins (LDLs). Patient education also should include information about serum lipid-lowering drugs, such as niacin, statins, or bile acid sequestrants and about their side effects and potential drug interactions and the need for follow-up blood work (esp. liver function tests). Other lifestyle and medical interventions may be indicated for patients with hyperlipoproteinemia and other risk factors for coronary artery disease, such as tobacco abuse, obesity, or diabetes mellitus.

hyperlucency (hī″pĕr-loo′sĕn-sē) In radiology, increased radiolucency.

hypermagnesemia (hī″pĕr-mag″ni-sē′mē-ă) [*hyper-* +*magnesium* + *-emia*] An excess of magnesium in the blood serum levels. SYN: *magnesemia.* SEE: *magnesium.*

hypermature (hī″pĕr-mă-tūr′) [″ + L. *maturus,* ripe] **1.** Pert. to anything that has passed the stage of maturity. **2.** Overripe, as a cataract or abscess that has gone past the optimum time for removal or incision.

hypermelanosis (hī″pĕr-mĕl-ă-nō′sĭs) One of several disorders of melanin pigmentation resulting in increased melanin in either the epidermis (melanoderma), in which case the coloration is brown, or in the dermis, in which case it is blue or slate gray (ceruloderma). This disorder may be caused by a number of diseases and conditions, including pregnancy, ACTH-producing tumors, Wilson's disease, porphyria, biliary cirrhosis, chronic renal failure, certain drugs, suntanning, and chronic pruritus. SEE: *hypomelanosis.*

hypermenorrhea (hī″pĕr-mĕn″ō-rē′ă) [″ + *men,* month, + *rhoia,* flow] Menorrhagia.

hypermetabolic state (hī″pĕr-met″ă-bol′ik) [*hyper-* + *metabolic*] Hypermetabolism.

hypermetabolism (hī″pĕr-mĕ-tab′ŏ-lizm) [*hyper-* + *metabolism*] An increased rate of metabolism (e.g., as in fever, salicylate overdose, and other physiological or toxic stresses). It may be caused by sepsis and severe burn injuries. SYN: *hypermetabolic state.* SEE: *response, stress.* **hypermetabolic** (hī″pĕr-met″ă-bol′ik), *adj.*

 extrathyroidal h. An increased rate of metabolism not related to thyroid disease.

hypermetria (hī″pĕr-mē′trē-ă) [Gr. *hyper,* over, above, excessive, + *metron,* measure] An unusual range of movement; motor incoordination in which muscular movement causes a person to overreach the objective.

hypermetrope (hī″pĕr-mĕt′rōp) [″ + ″ + *ops,* eye] Hyperope.

hypermetropia (hī″pĕr-mē-trō′pē-ă) Hyperopia. **hypermetropic** (-trŏp′ĭk), *adj.*

hypermobility (hī″pĕr-mō-bil′ĭt-ē) [*hyper-* + *mobility*] Excessive joint play (movement) evidenced by the ability to place both hands on the floor, while bending the spine forward, but not bending the knees; the ability to pull the thumb so that it touches the radial surface of the forearm; or the ability to hyperextend the elbow or knee 10% beyond a straightened (neutral) position. It is present in some connective tissue diseases such as Marfan or Ehlers-Danlos syndromes.

hypermorph (hī″pĕr-mŏrf) [″ + *morphe,* form] **1.** A person with disproportionately long limbs whose standing height is high in proportion to the sitting height. **2.** A mutant gene that expresses more than the usual amount of gene product expressed by the wild type. SEE: *hypomorph; somatotype.*

hypermotility (hī″pĕr-mō-tĭl′ĭ-tē) [″ + L. *motio,* motion] Unusual or excessive movement. SYN: *hyperkinesia.*

hypernatremia (hī″pĕr-nă-trē′mē-ă) [*hyper-* + *natremia*] An elevated concentration of sodium in the bloodstream. Hypernatremia is present when the sodium concentration exceeds about 145 mmol/L. It is almost always the result of free water deficits (dehydration) and not an excess of salt and is treated with intravenous or oral replacement of water. Rarely, hypernatremia may develop after intravenous infusions of solutions with high concentrations of sodium. Symptoms of hypernatremia include thirst, orthostatic dizziness, altered mental status, and neuromuscular dysfunction.

hypernephroma (hī″pĕr-nĕ-frō′mă) [*hyper-* + *nephroma*] Renal cell carcinoma.

hypernutrition (hī″pĕr-nū-trĭsh′ŭn) [″ + L. *nutrire,* to nourish] Overfeeding.

hyperope (hī′pĕr-ōp) [″ + *ops,* eye] One who is farsighted. SYN: *hypermetrope.*

hyperopia (hī″pĕr-ō′pē-ă) [″ + *ops,* eye] Farsightedness; a defect in vision in which parallel rays come to a focus behind the retina as a result of flattening of the globe of the eye or of an error in refraction. Symptoms include ocular fatigue and poor vision. SYN: *hypermetropia.* SEE: *emmetropia* for illus.

   axial h. Hyperopia caused by shortness of the eye's anteroposterior axis.

   facultative h. Hyperopia that can be corrected by accommodation.

   latent h. Hyperopia in which the error of refraction is overcome and disguised by ciliary muscle action.

   manifest h. Total amount of hyperopia that can be neutralized by a convex lens without interfering with clarity of vision.

   relative h. Hyperopia in which vision is clear only when excessive convergence is made.

   total h. Complete hyperopia combining both latent and manifest types; the amount of hyperopia present when accommodation is completely suspended

by paralyzing the ciliary muscle, which is done by use of a cycloplegic drug.

hyperorality (hī″pĕr-ŏ-răl′ĭ-tē) [″ + ″] Excessive chewing, sucking, lip smacking, or food craving. It is seen in some neurological disorders (e.g., Klüver-Bucy syndrome and Pick's disease).

hyperosmia (hī″pĕr-ŏz′mē-ă) [″ + *osme,* smell] An abnormal sensitivity to odors.

   general h. Total **h.**

   partial h. Increased sensitivity to some odors.

   total h. Increased sensitivity to all odors. SYN: *general h.*

hyperosmolarity (hī″pĕr-ŏz″mō-lăr′ĭ-tē) Increased osmolarity of the blood.

hyperostosis (hī″pĕr-ŏs-tō′sĭs) [″ + *osteon,* bone, + *osis,* condition] An abnormal growth of osseous tissue. SYN: *exostosis; torus.*

   frontal internal h. An osteoma, usually multiple or arising from the internal area of the frontal bone.

   infantile cortical h. An increased growth of subperiosteal bone occurring most frequently in the mandible and clavicles, accompanied by fever and irritability. SYN: *Caffey's disease.*

hyperoxaluria (hī″pĕr-ŏk″să-lū′rē-ă) Increased oxalic acid in the urine.

   enteric h. Hyperoxaluria caused by disease or surgical removal of the ileum.

   primary h. An inherited metabolic disease caused by a defect in glyoxalate metabolism. This causes an increased secretion of oxalate in the urine, renal calculi, renal failure, and generalized deficit of oxalate crystals in tissues.

hyperoxemia (hī″pĕr-ŏk-sē′mē-ă) [″ + *oxys,* sharp, + *haima,* blood] Increased oxygen content of the blood.

hyperoxia (hī″pĕr-ŏk′sē-ă) Increased oxygen in the blood.

hyperoxia test The administration of 100% oxygen to a patient (typically a neonate) to determine the cause of respiratory distress, hypoxemia, cyanosis, and/or shock. The resolution of cyanosis with treatment usually indicates that the cause of the hypoxia is a lung disease, e.g., pneumonia. If the PaO_2 at the conclusion of the test is > 150 torr, cardiac disease can usually be excluded. Failure of neonates to respond to 100% oxygen is usually an indication of severe congenital heart disease.

hyperoxygenation (hī″pĕr-ŏk″sĭ-jĕn-ā′shŭn) The temporary administration of excess oxygen to a patient to prevent hypoxemia during subsequent therapeutic procedures.

hyperparasitism (hī″pĕr-păr′ă-sī″tĭzm) A condition in which a parasite lives in or upon another parasite.

hyperparathyroidism (hī″pĕr-par″ă-thī′royd-ĭzm) [*hyper-* + *parathyroid* + *-ism*] A condition caused by excessive levels of parathyroid hormone in the body. Hyperparathyroidism is usually caused by benign tumors of the parathyroid glands (primary hyperparathyroidism), although occasionally it occurs secondary to renal failure or other systemic illnesses. The consequences of excess parathyroid hormone may include symptomatic or unnoticed hypercalcemia, hypophosphatemia, hyperchlorhydria, kidney stone formation, and bone resorption. Hyperparathyroidism is the most common cause of hypercalcemia, which can lead to central nervous system, musculoskeletal, metabolic, gastrointestinal, and cardiovascular problems when the concentration of calcium in the blood rises to very high levels. SEE: *hypercalcemia; parathyroid glands; osteitis fibrosa cystica.*

PATIENT CARE: The majority of patients with hyperparathyroidism are older women. Mild hyperparathyroidism may initially be managed expectantly without harm to the patient. In most patients a single adenoma produces the excess parathyroid hormone; in only about 15% of patients is hyperparathyroidism caused by generalized hyperplasia of all four parathyroid glands. Severe primary hyperparathyroidism may require surgical removal of the parathyroid gland or glands to prevent potential complications of hyperparathyroidism, including kidney stone disease, degeneration of bone, neuromuscular and neuropsychiatric illnesses, and pancreatitis, among others. In some cancer patients, malignant tumors release a parathyroid-like hormone with hypercalcemia, which mimics hyperparathyroidism.

primary h. Hyperparathyroidism caused by a parathyroid adenoma. Its laboratory hallmark is a high (or normal) parathyroid hormone level despite elevated concentrations of calcium in the serum.

secondary h. Excessive levels of parathyroid hormone (PTH) released in response to a low serum calcium, or a high serum phosphate level. It may be due to vitamin D deficiency or chronic kidney disease.

hyperpathia (hī″pĕr-păth′ē-ă) [″ + *pathos,* disease, suffering] Hypersensitivity to sensory stimuli. Includes hyperesthesia, allodynia, and hyperalgesia.

hyperphagia (hī″pĕr-fā′jē-ă) [″ + Gr. *phagein,* to eat] Eating more food than is required; gluttony or binge eating.

hyperphenylalaninemia (hī″pĕr-fĕn″ĭl-ăl″ă-nĭ-nē′mē-ă) An increased amount of phenylalanine in the blood. SEE: *phenylketonuria.*

hyperphoria (hī″pĕr-fŏr′ē-ă) [*hyper-* + *-phoria*] A tendency of one eye to turn upward. SYN: *anophoria; anopsia* (1).

hyperphosphatasemia (hī″pĕr-fŏs″fă-tă-sē′mē-ă) Increased alkaline phosphatase in the blood.

hyperphosphatemia (hī″pĕr-fŏs″fă-tē′mē-ă) [″ + L. *phosphas,* phosphate, + Gr. *haima,* blood] An abnormal amount of phosphorus in the blood. SYN: *hyperphospheremia.*

Hyperphosphatemia is caused by increased absorption of phosphorus from the gut, decreased excretion in the urine (seen in renal failure), or increased production. Increased intake can occur as a result of excessive intravenous administration (e.g., in hyperalimentation solutions), or oral ingestion, or excessive vitamin D intake.

hyperphosphaturia (hī″pĕr-fŏs-fă-tū′rē-ă) [″ + ″ + Gr. *ouron,* urine] An increased amount of phosphates in the urine.

hyperpigmentation (hī″pĕr-pĭg″mĕn-tā′shŭn) Increased pigmentation, esp. of the skin.

hyperpituitarism (hī″pĕr-pĭ-tū′ĭ-tăr-ĭsm) [″ + L. *pituita,* mucus, + Gr. *-ismos,* condition] A condition resulting from overactivity of the anterior lobe of the pituitary. SEE: *acromegaly; gigantism.*

hyperplasia (hī″pĕr-plā′zh(ē-)ă) [*hyper-* + *-plasia*] An abnormal increase in the number of normal cells in an organ or tissue with no evidence of cancer. SYN: *hypergenesis.* **hyperplastic** (-plas′tik), *adj.*

angiofollicular lymph node h. Castleman disease.

atypical ductal h. ABBR: ADH. A premalignant lesion of the breast. It is often found in biopsy specimens of patients with breast cancer. It is characterized by a small number of breast ducts with abnormal cellular and glandular structures. It is hypothesized that atypical ductal hyperplasia is one of several breast lesions that can develop into ductal carcinoma in situ and, ultimately, into an invasive cancer.

benign prostatic h. ABBR: BPH. A nonmalignant enlargement of the prostate gland caused by excessive growth of prostatic nodules. It is the most common benign neoplasm of aging men, found on microscopic examination of the prostate in about 70% of men by age 60, and 90% of men by age 70. More than 440,000 men in the U.S. have surgery to correct the problem each year. SYN: *benign prostatic hypertrophy; enlarged prostate.* SEE: *Nursing Diagnoses Appendix; prostate; prostate cancer; transurethral resection of the prostate.*

ETIOLOGY: The prostate gland grows as a result of stimulation of the gland by sex hormones. Dihydrotestosterone directly stimulates the growth of the gland's epithelial and stromal cells; estrogens, found in increasing concentrations in aging men, increase the number of hormone receptors in the prostate, making the gland more susceptible to stimulation by male hormones. Under these influences prostate nodules enlarge around the urethra and may compress the urinary outlet limiting the flow of urine from the bladder.

DIAGNOSIS: The diagnosis of BPH is made based on a description of typical symptoms, digital rectal examination, prostate-specific antigen testing, and/or ultrasonography. The American Urological Association (AUA) has developed a self-administered screening tool (The AUA Symptom Index) to determine the frequency and severity of urinary symptoms.

SYMPTOMS: Patients often complain of difficulty starting or stopping their urinary stream, frequent urination, a reduced urinary stream, urinary hesitancy and/or urgency, and frequent awakenings at night to urinate. They may also develop urinary tract infections and sudden obstruction of all urinary flow (acute urinary retention). Urinary retention increases the risk for development of urinary tract infection, pyelonephritis, or renal atrophy. Bladder hypertrophy, hydronephrosis, kidney damage, or sepsis may also develop.

TREATMENT: Men with mild to moderate symptoms often get symptomatic relief from medicines such as alpha-1 adrenergic antagonists (e.g., terazosin) and/or 5-alpha reductase inhibitors (such as finasteride), which block the effect of testosterone on prostatic growth and may reduce the need for prostate surgery. Two herbal remedies are also commonly employed: saw palmetto and pygeum. When patients have recurrent urinary infections, unmanageable urinary symptoms, urinary retention, or damage to the bladder or kidneys, surgery is performed. Transurethral resection of the prostate (TURP) is the most common procedure. Alternatives to TURP include transurethral incision of the prostate (TUIP), laser reduction in the size of the gland, transurethral microwave heat treatment, transurethral needle ablation, urethral stent placement, or open prostatectomy.

PATIENT CARE: The patient is evaluated for his ability to effectively empty his bladder, the caliber and force of his urinary stream, reduction in urinary hesitancy, difficulty initiating his stream, dribbling, incontinence, and nocturia.

A midstream urine specimen is collected for culture and sensitivity. Antibiotics are prescribed if the patient is to undergo urethral procedures involving instrumentation.

If urinary retention develops, a urinary catheter is inserted by the nurse or urologist. Sometimes the catheter is inserted with guides. Suprapubic cysto-

tomy is used if a catheter cannot be passed transurethrally. The patient is monitored for rapid bladder decompression and for signs of postobstruction diuresis (increased urine output, hypotension), which may lead to serious dehydration, lowered blood volume, shock, electrolyte losses, and anuria.

The patient with BPH is taught to avoid prescription and over-the-counter drugs that can worsen obstruction, e.g., decongestants, alcohol, caffeine, anticholinergics, tranquilizers, or antidepressants.

Postoperative Care: After excision, continuous bladder irrigation and an indwelling catheter with a large balloon may be used to control bleeding. If an open prostatectomy is needed, the patient should receive routine prophylaxis for venous thromboembolism using low-dose unfractionated heparin two or three times a day for a few days after surgery. The patient is taught to recognize and report signs of infection, which can worsen obstruction, and to seek medical care immediately if he is unable to void. The patient is advised that regular sexual intercourse will help to relieve prostatic congestion. Men over age 50 (and younger men with a family history of the disease) should be encouraged to have regular prostate checkups.

congenital adrenal h. ABBR: CAH. Any of a group of rare autosomal recessive disorders characterized by deficiencies of one or more enzymes essential for the synthesis of hormones made from cholesterol (cortisol, aldosterone, progesterone, and/or dihydrotestosterone). These enzyme deficiencies produce a variety of clinical syndromes resulting from the excessive concentration of precursor hormones. The most common of these is 21-hydroxylase deficiency.

fibrous h. An increase in connective tissue cells after inflammation.

neointimal h. An increase in the thickness of the lining of a blood vessel in response to injury or vascular reconstruction. It is an important cause of vein graft obstruction after coronary artery bypass surgery and in the premature closure of other vascular conduits, e.g., in dialysis access devices. It is characterized by the migration of smooth muscle cells into the graft, followed by the release of cytokines that damage the vessel wall and contribute to its degradation by inflammation.

hyperploidy (hī″pĕr-ploy′dē) A condition of having one extra chromosome and thus not balanced sets of chromosomes. SEE: *Down syndrome; trisomy 21.*

hyperpnea (hī″pĕrp-nē′ă) [″ + *pnoia,* breath] An increased respiratory rate, or breathing that is deeper than that usually experienced during normal activity. A certain degree of hyperpnea is normal after exercise; it may also be caused by pain, a variety of respiratory diseases, fever, heart failure, certain drugs, panic attacks, or atmospheric conditions experienced at high altitude.

hyperpolarization (hī-pĕr-pōl″ăr-ĭ-zā′shŭn) An increase in the resting potential of a cell membrane (e.g., a cell membrane of a neuron), causing the inside of the cell to become more negative. This change raises the threshold level for depolarization, thus making the cell relatively less sensitive to stimuli.

hyperprolactinemia (hī″pĕr-prō-lak″tĭ-nē′mē-ă) [*hyper-* + *prolactin* + *-emia*] Excessive concentrations of prolactin in serum. It may be caused by a prolactinoma, or by the administration of drugs that increase serum prolactin levels (e.g., neuroleptic agents).

hyperprolinemia (hī″pĕr-prō″lĭ-nē′mē-ă) One of two metabolic diseases of amino acid metabolism that result in an excess of proline in the body.

hyperproteinemia (hī″pĕr-prō″tē-ĭn-ē′mē-ă) [″ + *protos,* first, + *haima,* blood] An excess of protein in the blood.

hyperpyrexia (hī″pĕr-pī-rek′sē-ă) [*hyper-* + *pyrexia*] Hyperthermia.
  malignant h. Malignant hyperthermia.

hyperreactio luteinalis (hī″pĕr-rē-ak′sh(ē-)ō loot″ē-ĭn-ā′lis) Theca-lutein **cyst.**

hyperreactive (hī″pĕr-rē-ăk′tĭv) Pert. to an increased response to stimuli.

hyperreflexia (hī″pĕr-rē-flĕk′sē-ă) [″ + L. *reflexus,* bent back] An increased action of the reflexes.
  autonomic h. A serious (emergency) medical condition commonly seen in patients with injury to the upper spinal cord (above T6). It is caused by massive sympathetic discharge of stimuli from the autonomic nervous system. It may be triggered by distention of the bladder or colon, a skin lesion (pressure sore), catheterization or irrigation of the bladder, cystoscopy, or transurethral resection. Symptoms include sudden hypertension, bradycardia, sweating, severe headache, and cold gooseflesh below the trauma lesion level. The stimulus must be quickly identified and eliminated. SEE: *autonomic dysreflexia.*
  PATIENT CARE: Vital signs and symptoms are assessed with the patient seated (to decrease blood pressure) and are monitored until the episode resolves. The urinary bladder is assessed for distention (palpation, bladder ultrasound), and (as necessary) drained by catheterization. The indwelling catheter is checked for kinking or other obstruction and irrigated with no more than 30 ml of sterile normal saline solution if necessary. If the catheter remains obstructed, it is removed and a new catheter is inserted immediately.

The patient's rectum is checked for impaction; a local anesthetic ointment is used for lubrication and for anesthesia if removal of an impaction is necessary. Any other stimuli that may be triggering the response are also removed. A urine specimen is obtained for culture because infection may be a cause. If the cause cannot be rapidly removed, prescribed medications to reduce blood pressure and headache are administered, and the patient's response is evaluated. A calm atmosphere is created, and emotional support is offered throughout the episode. The patient is educated about this complication, and actions are explained to prevent and alleviate it.

hyperresonance (hī″pĕr-rĕz′ō-năns) [″ + L. *resonare,* to resound] An increased resonance produced when an area is percussed.

hypersalivation (hī″pĕr-săl″ĭ-vā′shŭn) [″ + L. *salivatio,* salivation] Ptyalism.

hypersecretion (hī″pĕr-si-krē′shŏn) [*hyper-* + *secretion*] The excessive release of a substance by a cell, gland, tissue, or organism.

hypersensibility (hī″pĕr-sĕn″sĭ-bĭl′ĭ-tē) [″ + L. *sensibilitas,* sensibility] Hypersensitivity.

hypersensitive (hī″pĕr-sĕn′sĭ-tĭv) [″ + ″] Excessively and abnormally susceptible to a stimulus (e.g., an antigen like pollen). SYN: *supersensitive.* SEE: *allergy; anaphylaxis; hay fever.*

hypersensitivity (hī″pĕr-sĕn″sĭ-tĭv′ĭ-tē) An abnormal sensitivity to a stimulus of any kind.
  visceral h. An abnormally low tolerance for painful stimuli in the internal organs. It is seen, e.g., in patients with irritable bowel syndrome.

hypersensitivity reaction Allergy.

hypersensitization (hī″pĕr-sĕn″sĭ-tĭ-zā′shŭn) **1.** Producing or inducing increased sensitivity to an organism or drug. **2.** The condition of being highly sensitive to something.

hypersomnia (hī″pĕr-sŏm′nē-ă) [″ + L. *somnus,* sleep] **1.** Excessive daytime sleepiness resulting from any cause (e.g., inadequate sleep hygiene, the use of intoxicating drugs, or obstructive sleep apnea). **2.** Excessive daytime sleepiness lasting more than 1 hr every day for several months; the inability to feel refreshed after sleeping; excessively long periods of sleep (total sleep time of more than 10 hr a day); no evidence of cataplexy or narcolepsy. SYN: *idiopathic h.*
  idiopathic h. Hypersomnia.
  recurrent h. Excessive sleepiness that occurs periodically (e.g., every few weeks or months).
  traumatic h. Excessive sleepiness in patients with traumatic brain injury.

hypersplenism (hī″pĕr-splĕn′ĭzm) Increased sequestration of blood cells by the spleen.

hypersthenic (hī″pĕr-sthĕn′ĭk) **1.** Denoting excessive strength or tension. **2.** Denoting a body habitus characterized by a broad, deep thorax; short thoracic cavity; and a large abdominal cavity; a massive build.

hypersusceptibility (hī″pĕr-sŭ-sĕp″tĭ-bĭl′ĭ-tē) [″ + ″] An exaggerated susceptibility to an antigen, chemical, disease, or other stimulus.

hypertelorism (hī″pĕr-tĕl′or-ĭzm) [″ + telouros, distant] Abnormal distance between two paired organs, esp. the eyes.

hypertension (hī″pĕr-ten′shŏn) [hyper- + tension] ABBR: HTN. In adults, a condition in which the blood pressure (BP) is higher than 140 mm Hg systolic or 90 mm Hg diastolic on three separate readings recorded several weeks apart. Hypertension is one of the major risk factors for coronary artery disease, heart failure, stroke, peripheral vascular disease, kidney failure, and retinopathy. It affects about 50 million people in the U.S. Considerable research has shown that controlling HTN increases longevity and helps prevent cardiovascular illnesses. SYN: *high blood pressure*. SEE: *blood pressure*. **hypertensive** (hī″pĕr-ten′siv), adj.

All systems for categorizing high BP are somewhat arbitrary, but the current consensus is that normal BPs are < 120 mm Hg systolic and < 80 mm Hg diastolic. Borderline high BPs (prehypertension) are between 120 and 139 mm Hg systolic and 80 to 89 mm Hg diastolic. Patients with BP readings between 140/90 and 160/100 mm Hg are said to have stage 1 HTN.

Stage 2 HTN is a pressure from 160/100 to 179/109 mm Hg. Stage 3 HTN begins at 180/110 mm Hg and has no upper limit. At each stage of HTN, from prehypertensive levels through the three stages of HTN, the risks of strokes, heart attacks, and kidney failure increase. SEE: table.

Hypertension in children has been defined as BP above the 95th percentile for age, height, and weight. As many as 28% of children have secondary HTN compared to 1% to 5% in adults.

ETIOLOGY: Hypertension results from many different conditions, some curable and others treatable. Curable forms of HTN (secondary HTN), which are relatively rare, may be caused by coarctation of the aorta, pheochromocytoma, renal artery stenosis, primary aldosteronism, and Cushing's syndrome. Excess alcohol consumption (more than two drinks daily) is a common cause of high BP; abstinence or drinking in moderation effectively lowers BP in these cases. Aortic valve stenosis, pregnancy, obesity, and the use of certain drugs (such as cocaine, amphetamines, steroids, or erythropoietin) also may lead to hypertension. Usually, however, the cause is unknown; then high BP is categorized as *primary, essential,* or *idiopathic.* Primary hypertension may result from the body's resistance to the action of insulin, hyperactivity of the sympathetic nervous system, hyperactivity of the renin-angiotensin-aldosterone system, or endothelial dysfunction.

SYMPTOMS: Hypertension is usually

Classification of Blood Pressure for Adults Age 18 and Older*

Category	Systolic (mm Hg)		Diastolic (mm Hg)
Optimal†	120	and	80
Prehypertension	120–139	or	80–89
Hypertension‡			
Stage 1	140–159	or	90–99
Stage 2	160–179	or	100–109
Stage 3	≥ 180	or	≥ 110

*Not taking antihypertensive drugs and not acutely ill. When systolic and diastolic BPs fall into different categories, the higher category should be selected to classify the person's BP status. For example, 160/92 mm Hg should be classified as stage 2 HTN, and 174/120 mm Hg should be classified as stage 3 HTN. Isolated systolic HTN is defined as systolic BP of 140 mm Hg or greater and diastolic BP below 90 mm Hg and staged appropriately (e.g., 170/82 mm Hg is defined as stage 2 isolated systolic HTN). In addition to classifying stages of HTN on the basis of average BP levels, clinicians should specify presence or absence of target organ disease and additional risk factors. This specificity is important for risk classification and treatment.

† Optimal blood pressure with respect to cardiovascular risk is below 120/80 mm Hg. However, unusually low readings should be evaluated for clinical significance.

‡ Based on the average of two or more readings taken after a period of rest and using the correct techniques at each of two or more visits after an initial screening.

SOURCE: Adapted from the Sixth Report of the Joint National Committee on Prevention, Detection, Evaluation, and Treatment of High BP, NIH publication No. 98-4080, November 1997, and other sources.

a silent (asymptomatic) disease in the first few decades of its course. Because most patients are symptom-free until complications arise, they may have difficulty taking seriously a condition from which they perceive no immediate danger. Occasionally, patients with HTN report headache. When complications result from high BPs, patients mention symptoms referable to the affected organs.

TREATMENT: If HTN is newly diagnosed, routine studies should be done on the patient to establish a baseline for treatment. In addition to a thorough patient history, assessment for risk factors, and physical examination, these studies include an ECG, urinalysis, serum potassium and calcium levels, blood urea nitrogen, fasting glucose level, and cholesterol profile, including triglycerides. The Joint National Committee on Prevention, Detection, Evaluation and Treatment of High Blood Pressure (JNC) guidelines to reduce cardiovascular disease complications recommends a target blood pressure of less than 140/90; 130/80 for patients with diabetes mellitus or renal disease. Because HTN has been identified as a growing concern among children, the JNC recommends regular BP checks beginning at age 3. Lifestyle modifications that lower BP include dietary sodium restriction to about 2 g/day, made possible by avoiding salted food such as ham, potato chips, and processed foods and by not adding salt to food at the table; maintaining a healthy weight (a body mass index above 24.9 can elevate BP); eating lower-calorie foods; restricting total cholesterol and saturated fat intake; quitting smoking; limiting alcohol intake (to about one drink daily); and participating in a program of regular exercise. When lifestyle modifications fail over the course of several months to control BP naturally, medications should be used. Drug therapy for stage 1 HTN includes low-dose thiazide diuretics for most patients, although angiotensin converting enzyme (ACE) inhibitors, beta blockers, calcium channel blockers or a combination of these may be prescribed. For stage 2 HTN, two-drug combinations are prescribed for most patients, usually a thiazide-type diuretic along with a beta blocker, ACE inhibitors, angiotensin receptor blockers, alpha blockers, or centrally active alpha blocking agents. If a woman develops HTN during pregnancy, treatment should be with methyldopa, a beta blocker, or a vasodilator, as these drugs provide the least risk to the fetus. SEE: table; *pregnancy-induced h.*

PATIENT CARE: Blood pressure should be checked at every health care visit, and patients should be informed of

Methods to Reduce Blood Pressure without Medication

Intervention	Approximate Decrease (in mm Hg)
Weight loss (20 lb)	5–10
Dietary approaches to stop hypertension (DASH) diet	8–14
Regular exercise	4–9
Reducing sodium intake	2–8
Limiting alcohol intake to one or two drinks a day	2–4

their BP reading and its meaning. Positive lifestyle changes should be encouraged. Adherence to medical regimens is also emphasized, and patients are advised to inform their health care providers of any side effects of therapy that they experience because these can often be managed with dosage adjustment or a change in medication. The technique of home BP monitoring is taught to receptive patients. Pressures should be measured and recorded for both arms, unless there is a medical prohibition for one arm, indicating which arm was used for each reading. SEE: *Nursing Diagnoses Appendix.*

accelerated h. A significant increase in BP, with some evidence of vascular damage on funduscopic examination of the retina. Prompt treatment is indicated to prevent organ damage. SEE: *malignant h.*

benign intracranial h. Pseudotumor cerebri.

chronic thromboembolic pulmonary h. ABBR: CTEPH. Pulmonary HTN that results from the migration of blood clots (usually from the lower extremities) into the lungs. Elevated BP in the lungs gradually overloads the right ventricle and causes right-sided heart failure.

SYMPTOMS: Symptoms usually include shortness of breath, esp. during exercise.

TREATMENT: The disease, when identified, may be treated with surgical removal of blood clots.

cuff-inflation h. A marked increase in BP in association with inflation of the sphygmomanometer cuff. This does not represent true hypertension.

drug-resistant h. Resistant **h.**

essential h. Hypertension that develops without apparent cause. SYN: *primary h.*

gestational h. High BP developing after 20 weeks of pregnancy. It may be mild; it often resolves after delivery, and it usually does not produce proteinuria or other features of preeclampsia.

Goldblatt h. SEE: under *Goldblatt, Harry.*

idiopathic intracranial h. Pseudotumor cerebri.

intra-abdominal h. ABBR: IAH. An increase in measured abdominal pressures, from a normal of 0 mm Hg to levels between 15 and 20 mm Hg. It may occur in patients with multiple traumatic injuries to the abdomen or with intraperitoneal diseases, e.g., severe pancreatitis. It is associated with the development of abdominal compartment syndrome, shock, and multiple organ failure.

intracranial h. ABBR: ICH. An increase in the pressure inside the skull from any cause such as a tumor, hydrocephalus, intracranial hemorrhage, trauma, infection, or interference with the venous flow from the brain. SEE: *hydrocephalus.*

⚠️ Patients with intracranial HTN should not undergo a lumbar puncture or any other procedure that decreases the cerebrospinal fluid pressure in the vertebral canal.

malignant h. A form of HTN that progresses rapidly, accompanied by severe vascular damage. It may be life-threatening or cause stroke, encephalopathy, cardiac ischemia, or renal failure.

masked h. Elevated BP that is not identified during professional evaluations in the office but only during ambulatory home blood pressure monitoring.

ocular h. Increased intraocular pressure, typically exceeding 21 mm Hg. This condition, present in glaucoma, may predispose affected persons to optic nerve damage and visual field loss.

portal h. Hypertension in the portal vein caused by an obstruction of the flow of blood through the liver. It is found in diseases such as cirrhosis, in which it is responsible for ascites, splenomegaly, and the formation of varices.

pregnancy-induced h. ABBR: PIH. High blood pressure, proteinuria, and edema occurring during pregnancy. Diagnostic criteria include an increase of 30 mm Hg systolic or 15 mm Hg diastolic over the baseline pressure for the individual woman (or readings of 140/90) on two assessments with at least a 6-hr interval between measures; and proteinuria of at least 300 mg/24 hr. PIH occurs most commonly in the late second trimester or last trimester, but it may manifest earlier in women with molar pregnancies. It is potentially life-threatening and may worsen rapidly and, if untreated, develop into eclampsia. SEE: *eclampsia; HELLP syndrome; preeclampsia.*

ETIOLOGY: The cause of PIH is unknown, but there are several major contributing theories: vasoconstriction and vasospasm, and a possible imbalance between prostaglandins, prostacyclin, and thromboxane A^2. The incidence is higher among adolescent and older primigravidas, diabetics, and women with pre-exisitng vascular problems or multiple pregnancies. Geographical, ethnic, racial, familial, low socioeconomic, nutritional, and immunological factors may contribute to PIH. Characteristic complaints include sudden weight gain, severe frontal headaches, and visual disturbances. Indications of increasing severity include complaints of epigastric or abdominal pain; generalized, presacral, and facial edema; oliguria; and hyperreflexia.

The treatment consists of bedrest, a high-protein diet, and medications including mild sedatives, antihypertensives, and intravenous anticoagulants if indicated. Complications are HELLP syndrome (hemolysis, elevated liver enzymes and low platelets) and eclampsia (the convulsive form of PIH).

PATIENT CARE: To enable the woman to actively participate in her health maintenance, reduce the potential for development of PIH, and facilitate early diagnosis and treatment, the health care provider should emphasize the importance of regular prenatal visits and good prenatal nutrition. Signs to report promptly are identified with the patient: sudden weight gain, swelling of the hands and face, headache, pitting edema of the ankles and legs, and reduced urine output.

At each prenatal visit, the pregnant woman's BP is monitored. The patient also is assessed for albuminuria; weekly weight gain of more than 3 lb (1.36 kg) in the second trimester or more than 1 lb (0.45 kg) in the third trimester; and generalized edema, esp. of the face and hands, and pitting edema of the ankles and legs. Protein intake is monitored to ensure adequate maternal serum protein levels, normal oncotic pressure, limitation of edema formation, and normal fetal development.

As preeclampsia progresses, the woman may complain of headaches, blurred vision or other visual disturbances, epigastric pain or heartburn, chest pressure, irritability, emotional tension, and decreased fetal activity. The patient is assessed for hyperreflexia of the deep tendon reflexes and clonus and, if preeclampsia worsens, for oliguria. The goals of treatment are to stop progress of the condition and to ensure survival of the fetus and the mother's health.

Hospitalization may be necessary if the patient exhibits signs of moderate to severe preeclampsia and has failed to respond to home management. Intravenous magnesium sulfate may be given, first as a bolus and continued as a maintenance dose, until the severity of the disease decreases. If magnesium sulfate is used, the patient must be assessed frequently for the presence of deep tendon reflexes, respirations over 12 per minute, hourly urine output, and signs and symptoms of magnesium toxicity. Calcium gluconate, if needed, is the antidote for magnesium sulfate.

The clinical status of mother and fetus is continually evaluated; maternal vital signs and fetal heart rate are monitored. The patient is assessed for impending labor, and fetal and maternal responses to labor contractions are evaluated. The obstetrician is notified of any change in the patient's or the fetus' condition. Emergency care is provided during convulsions; prescribed medications are administered as directed, and patient and fetal response are evaluated. Careful monitoring of the administration of magnesium sulfate, intake and output, and the woman's response to the medication are necessary. Health care providers should be esp. alert for signs of toxicity, e.g., an absence of patellar reflexes (hyporeflexia), flushing, and muscle flaccidity.

Psychological support and assistance to develop effective coping strategies are provided to both patient and family, who are to be prepared for possible premature delivery. Cesarean birth or oxytocin induction may be required. Although infants of mothers with PIH are usually small for gestational age, they sometimes fare better than other premature infants of similar weight because they have developed adaptive ventilatory and other responses to intrauterine stress. SEE: *Nursing Diagnoses Appendix.*

primary h. Essential **h.**

pulmonary h. Hypertension in the pulmonary arteries (above 25 to 30 mm Hg). *Primary pulmonary hypertension* is a rare familial illness in which small pulmonary arteries become blocked as a result of abnormalities in the structure of blood vessels in the lung. *Secondary pulmonary hypertension* is an elevation in pulmonary artery pressure as a result of left ventricular failure, blood clots in the pulmonary arteries, or chronic lung diseases.

rebound h. Hypertension after withdrawal of an antihypertensive drug.

renal h. **1.** Hypertension produced by kidney disease. It is caused by alter-ation in the renal regulation of sodium and fluids or by alteration in renal secretion of vasoconstrictors, which alter the tone of systemic or local arterioles. **2.** Hypertension produced experimentally by constriction of renal arteries. It is due to a humoral substance (renin) produced in an ischemic kidney.

renovascular h. Hypertension that is caused by decreased blood flow through one or both renal arteries and that normalizes after angioplasty or surgery to open the affected artery. It is an uncommon but surgically treatable form of high blood pressure.

resistant h. Hypertension that does not normalize with the use of a diuretic medication plus optimal doses of two additional antihypertensive drugs. SYN: *drug-resistant* **h.**

venous h. Hypertension in the legs of patients with venous insufficiency. Its hallmark is pain in the legs when the patient is standing or sitting and dangling his legs but not when lying down.

white coat h. A colloquial term for an episode of hypertension when the reading is taken by a health care professional. It is attributed to anxiety over medical examination procedures or fear of possible findings.

hypertensive (hī″pĕr-tĕn′sĭv) Marked by a rise in blood pressure.

hyperthecosis (hī″pĕr-thē-kō′sĭs) Hyperplasia of the theca interna of the ovary. Hirsutism, amenorrhea, and an enlarged clitoris may be present.

hyperthermia (hī″pĕr-thĕr′mē-ă) [*hyper-* + *thermo-* + *-ia*] **1.** Artificial elevation of body temperature for therapeutic reasons. **2.** An unusually high fever. SYN: *hyperpyrexia.*

ETIOLOGY: Hyperthermia may be caused by heat stroke; central nervous system diseases; thyroid storm; and infections including encephalitis, malaria, meningitis, or sepsis, esp. due to gram-negative organisms.

PATIENT CARE: To treat hyperthermia, the patient is placed in a cool environment; tepid water baths may be used to promote reduction in surface temperature by convection and evaporation. Hypothermia blankets may be used if hyperthermia is the result of neurologic dysfunction or initial therapy is ineffective. Fluid intake is increased to at least 3 liters per day (unless otherwise restricted by cardiac or renal disorders) to replace fluids lost through diaphoresis, rapid respirations, and increased metabolic activity. Frequent oral hygiene is provided because dehydration dries the oral mucosa. Shivering is prevented through administration of diazepam.

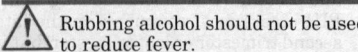 Rubbing alcohol should not be used to reduce fever.

malignant h. An autosomal dominant disease marked by skeletal muscle dysfunction after exposure to some anesthetics or other stressors. Body temperatures may climb above 105° F (40.5°C). The condition may be fatal. SYN: *malignant hyperpyrexia.*

hyperthermia treatment The use of microwave or radiofrequency energy to increase body temperature. This type of therapy, which is usually combined with chemotherapy or radiation, has been used in treating some malignancies and infectious diseases.

hyperthymia (hī″pĕr-thī′mē-ă) [″ + *thymos,* mind] Pathological sensitivity or excitability.

hyperthyroidism (hī″pĕr-thī′royd-ĭzm) [″ + *thyreos,* shield, + *eidos,* form, shape, + *-ismos,* state of] A disease caused by excessive levels of thyroid hormone in the body. SEE: *Nursing Diagnoses Appendix.*

ETIOLOGY: The condition may result from various disorders such as nodular goiter and toxic adenomas, hyperemesis gravidarum, excessive thyroid hormone replacement, excessive iodine ingestion, or pituitary adenoma; however, the most common cause is Graves's disease. SYN: *thyrotoxicosis.* SEE: *Graves' disease.*

SYMPTOMS: In general, the signs and symptoms of hyperthyroidism are divided into two categories—those secondary to excessive stimulation of the sympathetic nervous system and those due to excessive levels of circulating thyroxine (T_4). The symptoms caused by sympathetic (adrenergic) stimulation include tachycardia, tremor, increased systolic blood pressure, hyperreflexia, eyelid lag (lagophthalmos), staring, palpitations, depression, nervousness, and anxiety. Symptoms caused by increased circulating thyroxine include increased metabolism, hyperphagia, weight loss, and some psychological disturbances. In elderly persons, symptoms of hyperthyroidism are often blunted. SEE: *apathetic h.*

TREATMENT: Definitive therapies include surgical removal of the thyroid gland, radioactive iodine ablation of the gland, or antithyroid drugs. The choice of treatment is individualized for each patient, depending on the size of the goiter, the cause, patient's age, and parity.

PATIENT CARE: Vital signs, fluid balance, and weight are monitored, and activity patterns are documented. Serum electrolyte levels are monitored, blood glucose levels are checked for evidence of hyperglycemia and urine for glycosuria, and the ECG is evaluated for arrhythmias and ST-segment changes. The patient is assessed for classic signs and symptoms (as above) and for indications of thyrotoxic crisis or heart failure. The patient's knowledge of the disorder is determined, misconceptions are corrected, and information on the condition, related problems, and symptom management is provided. Medical treatments, including radioactive iodine, are administered and evaluated for desired response and adverse reactions, and the patient is instructed about these treatments (esp. regarding ^{131}I precautions). If the patient has exophthalmos, isotonic eyedrops are instilled to moisten the conjunctivae, and sunglasses or eye patches are recommended to protect the eyes from light. A high-caloric, high-vitamin, high-mineral diet, including between-meal snacks and avoidance of caffeinated beverages, is encouraged. Frequency and characteristics of the patient's stools are checked, and related skin care is provided as needed. The patient should minimize physical and emotional stress, balance rest and activity periods, and wear loose-fitting cotton clothing. A cool, dim, quiet environment also is recommended. The patient is prepared physically and emotionally for surgery if needed. Both patient and family are reassured that mood swings and nervousness will subside with treatment. The patient is encouraged to verbalize feelings about changes in body image. Assistance is provided to help the patient to identify and develop positive coping strategies. Emotional support is offered, and referral for further counseling is arranged as necessary. Life-long thyroid hormone replacement therapy will be necessary after surgical removal or radioactive iodine ablation treatment. The patient should wear or carry a medical identification device describing the condition and treatment and carry medication with him or her at all times.

apathetic h. Overactivity of the thyroid gland, presenting as heart failure, arrhythmias (such as atrial fibrillation), weight loss, or psychological withdrawal. This is more often a presentation of hyperthyroidism in older than in younger patients. Diagnosis is usually easier in the latter group because they present with the classic symptoms of hyperthyroidism. SYN: *subclinical h.*

subclinical h. Apathetic hyperthyroidism.

hyperthyroxinemia (hī″pĕr-thī-rŏk″sĭ-nē′mē-ă) An excess of thyroxine in the blood.

hypertonia (hī″pĕr-tō′nē-ă) [″ + *tonos,* tension] Hypertonicity.

hypertonic (hī″pĕr-tŏn′ĭk) **1.** Pert. to a solution of higher osmotic pressure than another. **2.** In a state of greater than normal tension or of incomplete relaxation, said of muscles; the opposite of hypotonic.

hypertonicity (hī″pĕr-tŏn-ĭ′sĭ-tē) An excess of muscular or arterial tone or intraocular pressure. SYN: *hypertonia*.

hypertonus (hī″pĕr-tō′nŭs) Increased tension, as muscular tension in spasm.

hypertrichosis (hī″pĕr-trĭ-kō′sĭs) [″ + ″ + *osis*, condition] An excessive growth of hair, possibly caused by endocrine disease, esp. of the adrenal gland, and in women, disease of the ovary. SYN: *polytrichia; polytrichosis*.

hypertriglyceridemia (hī″pĕr-trī-glĭs″ĕr-ĭ-dē′mē-ă) An increased blood triglyceride level; a possible risk factor for cardiovascular disease.

hypertrophia (hī″pĕr-trō′fē-ă) [Gr. *hyper*, over, above, excessive, + *trophe*, nourishment] Hypertrophy.

hypertrophic scar A keloidal scar that develops with excessive or exuberant fibrous tissue, is easily visible, is raised above the surrounding skin, and sometimes causes contracture.

hypertrophy (hī-pĕr′trŏ-fē) [*hyper-* + *-trophy*] **1.** An increase in the size of an organ, structure, or the body due to growth rather than tumor formation. This term is generally restricted to an increase in size or bulk that results not from an increase in the number of cells but from an increase in a cellular component, e.g., proteins. It applies to any increase in size as a result of functional activity. SYN: *hypertrophia*. SEE: *hyperplasia*. **hypertrophic** (hī″pĕr-trō′fĭk), *adj.* **2.** To cause or experience hypertrophy.

   adaptive h. Hypertrophy in which an organ increases in size to meet increased functional demands, as of the heart in valvular disorders.

   adenoid h. Hypertrophy of the pharyngeal tonsil. It occurs commonly in children and may be congenital or result from infection of Waldeyer ring.

   benign prostatic h. Benign prostatic **hyperplasia**.

   cardiac h. A regional or generalized hypertrophy in myocardial mass. It may be caused by exercise, chronic hypertension, genetic illnesses, or valvular dysfunction. SYN: *h. of the heart*.

   compensatory h. Hypertrophy due to increased function of an organ because of a defect or impaired function of the opposite of a paired organ.

   concentric h. Hypertrophy in which the walls of an organ become thickened without enlargement but with diminished capacity.

   congenital h. of the retinal pigment epithelium SEE: *congenital hypertrophy of the retinal pigment epithelium*.

   eccentric h. Hypertrophy of an organ with dilatation.

   false h. Hypertrophy with degeneration of one constituent of an organ and its replacement by another.

   gingival h. Hypertrophy of the gums,

sometimes associated with prolonged treatment with medications such as cyclosporine, nifedipine, or phenytoin. Thorough professional cleaning of the teeth, electrosurgical, laser, or conventional surgical treatments can remove the excess tissue.

   h. of the heart Cardiac **h.**

   left ventricular h. ABBR: LVH. Hypertrophy of the left ventricle of the heart to greater than 100 g/m² in women or 131 g/m² in men. Hypertrophy of the left ventricle is associated with an increased risk of death due to cardiovascular disease, stroke, and other causes. The size of the left ventricle can be reduced through regular exercise, weight loss, and by drugs that control high blood pressure. LVH can be detected noninvasively by its appearance on the 12-lead electrocardiogram or by echocardiography.

   Marie h. SEE: under *Marie, Pierre Marie*.

   numerical h. Hypertrophy caused by an increase in structural elements.

   physiological h. Hypertrophy due to natural rather than pathological factors.

   pseudomuscular h. A disease, usually of childhood, characterized by paralysis, depending on degeneration of the muscles, which paradoxically become enlarged from a deposition of fat and connective tissue.

   SYMPTOMS: The disease causes muscle weakness. The patient is awkward and often seeks support while walking to prevent falls. As the disease progresses, the muscles, particularly those of the calf, thigh, buttocks, and back, enlarge. The upper extremities are less frequently affected. When the patient stands erect, the feet are wide apart, the abdomen protrudes, and the spinal column shows a marked curvature with convexity forward. Rising from the recumbent position is accomplished by grasping the knees or by resting the hands on the floor in front, extending the legs and pushing the body backward. The gait is characterized by waddling. In a few years the paralysis becomes so marked that the patient is unable to leave the bed, which leads to further generalized muscular atrophy.

   TREATMENT: Physical therapy helps to prevent contractures, but there is no effective therapy. The prognosis for this disease is unfavorable.

   simple h. Hypertrophy due to an increase in the size of structural parts.

   true h. Hypertrophy caused by an increase in the size of all the different tissues composing a part.

   ventricular h. Left or right ventricular hypertrophy.

   vicarious h. Hypertrophy of an organ

when another organ of allied function is disabled or destroyed.

hypertropia (hī″pĕr-trō′pē-ă) [Gr. *hyper,* over, above, excessive, + *tropos,* turning] Vertical strabismus upward.

hyperuricemia (hī″pĕr-ū″rĭs-ē′mē-ă) [″ + *ouron,* urine, + *haima,* blood] An excessive amount of uric acid in the blood.

hyperuricuria (hī″pĕr-ū″rĭk-ū′rē-ă) [″ + ″ + *ouron,* urine] An excessive amount of uric acid in the urine.

hypervascular (hī″pĕr-văs′kū-lăr) [″ + L. *vasculus,* vessel] Excessively vascular.

hyperventilation (hī″pĕr-vent″ĭ-lā′shŏn) [*hyper-* + *ventilation*] Increased minute volume ventilation, which results in a lowered carbon dioxide (CO_2) level (hypocapnia). It is a frequent finding in many disease processes such as asthma, metabolic acidosis, pulmonary embolism, and pulmonary edema, and also in anxiety-induced states.

TREATMENT: Treatment is directed at the underlying cause. Immediate therapy for panic attacks consists of coaching the patient to slow down the breathing process to decrease the rate of blowing off CO_2. One way to do this is to have the patient breathe through only one nostril, with the mouth closed. Having the patient breathe in and out of a paper bag is discouraged, as it leads to hypoxemia. After the acute phase of the hyperventilation has been managed, the underlying cause of the problem must be determined.

therapeutic h. The use of carefully controlled but exaggerated ventilation to lower carbon dioxide (CO_2) levels in the blood and reduce cerebral blood flow. It is used to treat cerebral edema (e.g., after head injury), but its use remains controversial despite decades of research. Typically, the partial pressure of CO_2 is lowered to about 28 to 32 mm Hg. Lower levels of CO_2 produce reductions in cerebral blood flow that may damage the brain.

⚠️ Having the patient breathe in and out of a paper bag is to be discouraged because it leads to hypoxia.

hypervigilance (hī″pĕr-vĭj′ĭ-lăns) Excessive attentiveness to stimuli.

hypervirulent (hī″pĕr-vir′(y)ŭ-lĕnt) [*hyper-* + *virulent*] Exceptionally capable of producing severe illness; said of certain strains of bacteria, fungi, and viruses.

hyperviscosity (hī″pĕr-vĭs-kŏs′ĭ-tē) [″ + L. *viscosus,* gummy] Excessive resistance to the flow of liquids. Impaired hydraulic behavior, esp. of the plasma. Hyperviscous plasma is found in several hematological illnesses, including mul-

tiple myeloma and Waldenström's macroglobulinemia. In the latter illness, it can be treated with plasma exchange therapy.

hypervitaminosis (hī″pĕr-vī″tă-mĭn-ō′sĭs) [″ + L. *vita,* life, + *amine* + Gr. *osis,* condition] A condition caused by an excessive intake of vitamins in the diet or through the consumption of supplements; most commonly due to excessive consumption of fat-soluble vitamins.

hypervolemia (hī″pĕr-vol-ē′mē-ă) [*hyper-* + *vol(ume)* +*-emia*] Volume **overload**.

hypesthesia (hī″pĕs-thē′zē-ă) [Gr. *hypo,* under, beneath, below, + *aisthesis,* sensation] A reduced sensibility to touch; variant of hypoesthesia.

hypha (hī′fă) *pl.* **hyphae** [Gr. *hyphe,* web] A filament of mold or part of a mold mycelium.

hyphema (hī-fē′mă) [Gr. *hyphaimos,* suffused with blood] Layer or clot of red blood cells in the anterior chamber of the eye, in front of the iris; usually grossly visible. A total hyphema may be red or black. It is often caused by a contusion from a fast-moving object but may sometimes occur spontaneously, e.g., in patients with diabetes mellitus or intraocular tumors.

PATIENT CARE: Hyphema may be accompanied by an acute rise in intraocular pressure (IOP). When this occurs, urgent treatment is needed. The patient with a small hemorrhage ("microhyphema") can often be treated expectantly at home; patients with a larger hemorrhage should be referred to an eye care specialist. After acute treatment the patient should be encouraged to keep follow-up appointments with the eye care specialist.

Hyphomycetes (hī″fō-mī-sē′tēz) [Gr. *hyphe,* web, + *mykes,* fungus] In one system of taxonomy, a class of the fungi imperfecti; it includes the genera *Aspergillus, Blastomyces,* and *Histoplasma.* This class is equivalent to the phylum Deuteromycotina in another system of taxonomy.

hypnagogic (hĭp″nă-goj′ik, -gō′jik) [*hypno-* + Gr. *agōgē,* course + *-ic*] **1.** Inducing sleep or induced by sleep. SYN: *hypnotic.* SEE: *zone, hypnogenic.* **2.** In psychology, pert. to hallucinations or dreams occurring just before loss of consciousness.

hypnagogic state A transitional state between sleeping and waking and the delusions that may result therefrom.

hypno-, hypn- [Gr. *hypnos,* sleep] Prefixes meaning *sleep.*

hypnoanalysis (hĭp″nō-ă-năl′ĭ-sĭs) [″ + *analysis,* a dissolving] Combined psychoanalytic therapy and hypnosis.

hypnogenic (hĭp″nŏ-jĕn′ĭk) [″ + *gennan,* to produce] Producing sleep.

hypnogram (hĭp′nō-grăm) [Gr. *hypnos,* sleep, + *gramma,* drawing] A chart representing the different stages of sleep in a person studied in a sleep laboratory.

hypnopompic (hĭp″nŏ-pŏm′pĭk) [″ + *pompe,* procession] Pert. to dreams or visual images persisting after sleep and before complete awakening.

hypnosis (hĭp-nō′sĭs) [″ + *osis,* condition] A condition resembling sleep in which the objective manifestations of the mind are more or less inactive, accompanied by an increased susceptibility to suggestions. SEE: *autohypnosis; hypnotism; sleepwalking; somnambulism.*

hypnotherapy (hĭp″nō-thĕr′ă-pē) [″ + *therapeia,* treatment] Therapeutic use of hypnotism. It has been used to treat phobias and anxiety, to manage pain, and to extinguish habits and addictions.

hypnotic (hĭp-nŏt′ĭk) [Gr. *hypnos,* sleep] **1.** Pert. to sleep or hypnosis. **2.** An agent that causes an insensitivity to pain by inhibiting afferent impulses or by inhibiting the reception of sensory impressions in the cortical centers of the brain, thus causing partial or complete unconsciousness. Hypnotics include sedatives, analgesics, anesthetics, and intoxicants and are sometimes called somnifacients and soporifics when used to induce sleep.

hypnotism (hĭp′nŏ-tizm) [*hypnotic* + *-ism*] The act of inducing hypnosis.

    self-induced h. The use of hypnotism by those who seek to achieve specific goals for themselves, e.g., controlling pain, promoting health, improving relaxation, or quitting tobacco use. SYN: *autohypnosis; self-hypnosis.*

hypnotist (hĭp′nō-tĭst) [Gr. *hypnos,* sleep] One who practices hypnotism.

hypnotize (hĭp′nō-tīz) To put under hypnosis.

hypo (hī′pō) [Gr. *hypo,* under, beneath, below] Popular name for hypodermic syringe or injection.

hypo-, hyp- [Gr. *hypo,* under, beneath, below] Prefixes meaning *below, under, beneath,* or *deficient.* SEE: *sub-.*

hypoacidity (hī″pō-ă-sĭd′ĭ-tē) [″ + L. *acidus,* sour] A condition of decreased acid in the stomach caused by lowered hydrochloric acid secretion. This condition may occur secondary to other disorders, such as stomach cancer, pernicious anemia, infection with *Helicobacter pylori,* or treatment with acid-suppressing medications or surgeries.

  ⚠ Gastric hypoacidity may alter the uptake and metabolism of many commonly used drugs.

hypoactive sexual desire disorder (hī″pō-ak′tiv) [*hypo-* + *active*] ABBR:

HSDD. Loss of interest in sexual intercourse; a decrease in libido.

hypoacusis (hī″pō-ă-kū′sĭs) [″ + *akousis,* hearing] Decreased sensitivity to sound stimuli.

hypoadrenalism (hī″pō-ăd-rē′năl-ĭzm) [″ + L. *ad,* to, + *renalis,* pert. to kidney, + Gr. *-ismos,* state of] Adrenal insufficiency.

hypoadrenocorticism (hī″pō-ă-drē″nō-kor′tĭ-sĭzm) Decreased secretion, or the effect of adrenal cortical hormones.

hypoalbuminemia (hī″pō-ăl-bū″mĭn-ē′mē-ă) Decreased albumin in the blood. It is found in people who are malnourished or cachectic, and in individuals with chronic kidney, liver, and pancreatic diseases, among others.

hypoaldosteronism (hī″pō-ăl″dō-stēr′ōn-ĭzm) A condition characterized by decreased aldosterone in the blood associated with hypotension and increased salt excretion.

hypoallergenic (hī″pō-ăl″ĕr-jĕn′ĭk) [″ + ″] Having diminished potential for causing an allergic reaction.

hypobaric (hī″pō-băr′ĭk) [″ + *baros,* weight] Decreased atmospheric pressure or density when compared with a standard or reference gas or liquid. SEE: *bends; edema, high-altitude pulmonary.*

hypoblast (hī′pŏ-blast″) [*hypo-* + *-blast*] The inner cell layer between the cell mass and cavity of the blastocyst. This layer becomes the endoderm, which develops into the respiratory and digestive tracts. **hypoblastic** (hī″pŏ-blas′tik), *adj.*

hypocalcemia (hī″pō-kal-sē′mē-ă) [*hypo-* + *calci-* + *-emia*] An abnormally low amount of calcium in the blood. It occurs transiently in patients with severe sepsis, severe pancreatitis, burns, and acute renal failure. It also may result from multiple transfusions with citrated blood, parathyroidectomy, malabsorption, and medications such as protamine, heparin, and glucagon. Chronic hypocalcemia may be caused by chronic renal failure, hypoalbuminemia, and malnutrition. Clinical manifestations in chronic hypocalcemia include muscle spasm, carpopedal spasm, grimacing, possible convulsions, and mental changes such as irritability, depression, and psychosis. Treatment consists of calcium infusions and appropriate therapy for the causative disease.

    newborn h. Low serum calcium levels present in the first days of life, caused by maternal disease (such as gestational diabetes or parathyroid disorders), by the child's diseases and conditions (such as congenital hypoparathyroidism), or by treatments administered to the newborn (transfusion therapy or phototherapy). Tremors or seizures are common symptoms of low calcium in newborns.

hypocalcemic (hī″pō-kăl-sē′mĭk) [Gr. *hypo-*, less than, deficient, + L. *calx*, lime, + Gr. *haima*, blood] **1.** Pert. to a low concentration of calcium in the blood. **2.** An agent that lowers blood calcium levels.

hypocalciuria (hī″pō-kăl″sē-ū′rē-ă) Decreased calcium in the urine.

hypocaloric (hī″pō-kăl′ūr-ĭk) **1.** Having few calories (e.g., a hypocaloric meal). **2.** Calorically restricted (e.g., a hypocaloric diet).

hypocapnia (hī″pō-kăp′nē-ă) [Gr. *hypo*, under, beneath, below, + *kapnos*, smoke] A decreased amount of carbon dioxide in the blood. An excessively rapid rate of respiration ("hyperventilation") is usually responsible.

hypocarbia (hī″pō-kăr′bē-ă) Hypocapnia.

hypocellularity (hī″pō-sĕl″ū-lăr′ĭ-tē) Decreased cell content of any tissue.

hypochloremia (hī″pō-klō-rē′mē-ă) [″ + *chloros*, green, + *haima*, blood] Deficiency of the chloride content of the blood. SYN: *chloropenia*.

hypochlorhydria (hī″pō-klor-hī′drē-ă) [″ + ″ + *hydor*, water] Hypoacidity. SEE: *achlorhydria; hyperchlorhydria*.

hypochlorite (hī″pŏ-klōr′īt″) [*hypo-* + *chlorite*] A salt or ester of hypochlorous acid, esp. sodium hypochlorite (household bleach). SEE: *sodium hypochlorite*.

hypocholesteremia (hī″pō-kō-lĕs-tĕr-ē′mē-ă) [″ + *chole*, bile, + *stereos*, solid, + *haima*, blood] Decreased blood cholesterol. As cholesterol has some important functions in the body, excessively low cholesterol levels are not desirable.

hypochondria (hī″pō-kŏn′drē-ă) [″ + *chondros*, cartilage] An abnormal concern about one's health, with the false belief of suffering from some disease, despite medical reassurance to the contrary. This is a common symptom among depressed patients. SYN: *hypochondriasis*. SEE: *somatization*.

hypochondriac (hī″pŏ-kon′drē-ak″) [L. *hypochondriacus* fr. Gr *hypochondriakos*, below the cartilage (of the ribs), affected in the upper abdomen] **1.** Pert. to the region of the hypochondrium or the upper lateral region on each side of the body and below the thorax; beneath the ribs. **2.** A person with a heightened response to physical stimuli who believes his or her physical sensations are indicative of disease. **hypochondriacal** (-kŏn-drī′ă-kăl), *adj.*

hypochondriasis (hī″pō-kŏn-drī′ă-sĭs) [″ + *chondros*, cartilage, + *-iasis*, diseased condition] Hypochondria.

hypochondrium (hī″pō-kŏn′drē-ŭm) The part of the abdomen beneath the lower ribs on each side of the epigastrium.

hypochromasia (hī″pō-krō-mā′sē-ă) [″ + *chroma*, color] Hypochromia.

hypochromia (hī″pŏ-krō′mē-ă) [*hypo-* + *chrom-* + *-ia*] Decreased hemoglobin concentration in red blood cells. SYN: *hypochromasia*.

hypochromic (-krōm′ĭk), *adj.*

hypocitraturia (hī″pō-sī″trāt-ūr′ē-ă, -sī″) A decrease in urinary citrate excretion. It increases the likelihood that calcium-containing salts will crystallize in urine and produce obstruction to urinary flow by stones.

hypocomplementemia (hī″pō-kŏm″plē-mĕn-tē′mē-ă) Decreased complement in the blood.

hypocone (hī″pō-kŏn) [″ + *konos*, cone] The distolingual cusp of an upper molar tooth.

hypocontractile (hī″pō-kŏn-trak′til, tīl″) [*hypo-* + *contractile*] Incapable of shortening effectively. It is said of weak muscle fibers, such as those in the heart or the urinary bladder.

hypocorticism (hī″pō-kor′tĭ-sĭzm) Decreased adrenal cortical hormone.

hypocretin (hī″pō-krēt′ĭn) [hypo(thalamus) + (se)cretin] Orexins.

hypocupremia (hī″pō-kū-prē′mē-ă) Decreased copper in the blood.

Hypoderma (hī″pŏ-dĕr′mă) [*hypo-* + *derma*] A genus of warble flies of the family Oestridae. The maggots (larvae) of some species attack cattle and, rarely, humans. They cause a subcutaneous channel of inflammation as they burrow under the skin. SEE: *cutaneous **larva** migrans; myiasis; warble*.

hypodermic (hī″pō-dĕr′mĭk) [″ + *derma*, skin] Under or inserted under the skin, as a hypodermic injection. A hypodermic injection may be given subcutaneously (under the skin), intracutaneously (into the skin), intramuscularly (into a muscle), intraspinally (into the spinal canal), or intravascularly (into a vein or artery). It is given to secure prompt action of a drug when the drug cannot be taken by mouth, when it may not be readily absorbed in the stomach or intestines or when it might be changed by the action of the gastric secretions, or it acts as an anesthetic about the site of injection. SEE: *anesthesia, local*.

⚠ When the injected substance is not intended for intravascular injection, the syringe plunger should be pulled back after the needle is inserted to determine if the needle is in a vein or artery. If blood is obtained, the needle must be repositioned and the procedure repeated. It may be necessary to use a fresh needle and syringe. Because medicines not intended for intravenous injection produce serious undesired effects when given by this route, do not inject the medicine if the needle is in a vessel. If the medicine is to be injected into an artery or vein, it must not be administered unless pulling back on the plunger permits blood to freely enter the syringe.

intracutaneous h. Injection into the skin. SEE: *injection*.

intramuscular h. Injection given in the gluteal or lumbar muscular region. This route is used when a drug is not easily absorbed, when it is irritating, or when a large quantity of liquid is to be used.

intraspinal h. Injection into the spinal canal.

intravenous h. Injection into a vein, the usual site being the median basilic or median cephalic vein of the arm.

subcutaneous h. Injection given just under the skin, usually in the outer surface of the arm and forearm.

hypodermis (hī″pŏ-dĕr′mĭs) [*hypo-* + *dermis*] Superficial fascia.

hypodermoclysis (hī″pō-dĕr-mŏk′lĭ-sĭs) [Gr. *hypo,* under, beneath, below, + *derma,* skin, + *klysis,* a washing out] The treatment of dehydration by injecting fluids into the subcutaneous tissues (e.g., of the thighs, buttocks, or below the breasts or scapulae). This practice is used, rarely, as a palliative measure to treat dehydration or cachexia when other methods of rehydration (oral or intravenous) are not available. Common complications include fluid overload, electrolyte disturbances, and wound infections, among others.

hypodontia (hī″pō-dŏn′shē-ă) The developmental absence of one or more teeth.

hypodynamia (hī″pō-dī-nā′mē-ă) [″ + *dynamis,* power] Diminished muscular power or energy. SEE: *adynamia*.

hypodysplasia (hī″pō-dis-plā′zh(ē-)ă) [*hypo-* + *dysplasia*] A condition in which an organ, most often the kidneys, is abnormally small and malformed. **hypodysplastic** (-plas′tik), *adj*.

hypoechoic (hī″pō-ĕ-kō′ik) [*hypo-* + *echoic*] Pert. to a sonographic echo texture that is less echogenic than surrounding tissue. Most solid breast masses (including carcinoma) are hypoechoic. SEE: *echogenic*.

hypoesthesia (hī″pō-ĕs-thē′zē-ă) [″ + *aisthesis,* sensation] A dulled sensitivity to touch.

hypoferremia (hī″pō-fĕ-rē′mē-ă) Iron deficiency as indicated by diminished iron in the blood.

hypofibrinogenemia (hī″pō-fī-brĭn″ō-jĕ-nē′mē-ă) Decreased fibrinogen in the blood.

hypofunction (hī″pō-fŭnk′shŭn) Decreased function.

hypogalactia (hī″pō-gă-lăk′shē-ă) [″ + *gala,* milk] Deficient milk production.

hypogammaglobulinemia (hī″pō-gam″ă-glob″yŭ-lĭ-nē′mē-ă) [*hypo-* + *gamma*

globulin + *-emia*] A deficiency of one or more of the five classes of immunoglobulins. It is caused by defective functioning of B lymphocytes. People who manufacture insufficient quantities of immunoglobulins become susceptible to infections from pyogenic organisms, e.g., staphylococci, streptococci, and pseudomonas species.

acquired h. Immunoglobulin deficiency caused by another illness, such as the loss of immunoglobulins in the urine in nephrotic syndrome, or in the stool, in patients with malabsorption.

congenital h. Total immunoglobulin levels that are below 250 mg/dl. Chronic bacterial infections are common. Administration of intravenous immune globulin (beginning at 200 mg/kg per month) is usually effective.

transient h. of infancy ABBR: THI. A reduction in circulating immunoglobulin levels that begins around the third month of life and typically resolves by 2 to 3 years. It is due to a delay in the normal synthesis of immunoglobulins, esp. IgG, and occasionally IgA and IgM. Affected children occasionally suffer infectious diseases (sometimes recurring or serious), allergies, and autoimmune illnesses.

hypogastric (hī″pŏ-gas′trik) [*hypo-* + *gastric*] Pert. to the lower middle of the abdomen or to the hypogastrium.

hypogastrium (hī″pŏ-gas′trē-ŭm) [*hypo-* + *gastro-* + *-ium (2)*] The region below the umbilicus or navel, between the right and left inguinal regions. SYN: *hypogastric region*.

hypogenesis (hī″pō-jĕn′ĕ-sĭs) [Gr. *hypo,* under, beneath, below, + *genesis,* generation, birth] Cessation of growth or development at an early stage, causing defective structure. SEE: *ateliosis*.

hypogenitalism (hī″pō-jĕn′ĭ-tăl-ĭzm) [″ + L. *genitalis,* a genital, + Gr. *-ismos,* condition] A condition in which the genital organs are underdeveloped. It is characterized by reduced size of genital organs, failure of testes to descend in some cases, and incomplete development of secondary sex characteristics. SEE: *hypogonadism*.

hypogeusia (hī″pō-gū′sē-ă) [″ + *geusis,* taste] A blunting of the sense of taste. SEE: *dysgeusia*.

hypoglossal (hī″pō-glŏs′ăl) [″ + *glossa,* tongue] **1.** Situated under the tongue. **2.** The hypoglossal nerve.

hypoglottis (hī″pō-glŏt′ĭs) The undersurface of the tongue.

hypoglycemia (hī″pō-glī-sē′mē-ă) [*hypo-* + *glycemia*] An abnormally low level of glucose in the blood, often associated with neurological side effects and arousal of the sympathetic nervous system. Medication-induced hypoglycemia is a common occurrence during the treatment of diabetes mellitus. SYN:

glucopenia. SEE: *brittle* **diabetes***; hypoglycemic* **coma***;* **diabetes** *mellitus* for table; *hyperglycemia; neuroglycopenia; Nursing Diagnoses Appendix.* **hypoglycemic** (-sē′mik), *adj.*

ETIOLOGY: Hypoglycemia may be caused by insulin or oral antidiabetic drug overdoses; failure to eat an adequate number of calories despite diabetic treatments; unusual levels of exercise (usually among treated diabetics); extreme starvation (fasting hypoglycemia); alcoholic depletion of carbohydrate reserves from the liver; salicylate overdoses; and, rarely, an insulin-secreting tumor of the pancreas.

SYMPTOMS: A patient with moderately low blood sugar may feel fatigued, dizzy, restless, hungry, or unusually irritable; have difficulty concentrating; or have spontaneous episodes of sweating, palpitations, tremor, or nausea. Severely low blood sugar produces delirium, violent behaviors, obtundation, seizures, coma, and, occasionally, death. Some patients who have treated their diabetes mellitus with insulin for many years may lose the normal ability to recognize symptoms of low blood sugar.

DIAGNOSIS: The condition is demonstrated when a symptomatic patient has a capillary blood glucose or plasma glucose level that is less than (54 mg/dl).

TREATMENT: The acute treatment for hypoglycemia is glucose by mouth or per rectum, dextrose (D50) intravenously, or glucagon intramuscularly or subcutaneously. Treated patients who remain relatively hypoglycemic may require continuous infusions of dextrose during in-hospital observation.

⚠ Oral glucose supplements, e.g., juice or candy, should never be given to patients with a severely impaired level of consciousness because of the risk of aspiration. In an emergency setting, all comatose patients are routinely assumed to be hypoglycemic and are treated immediately with dextrose infusions.

After a hypoglycemic episode resolves, diabetic management regimens often need adjustment. Patients should be educated to recognize the symptoms that low blood sugar causes and to intervene quickly to reverse it in the future. Patients who follow strenuously restricted diets are often encouraged to increase their calorie intake. They may need to reduce doses of insulin or antidiabetic drugs. A patient who suffers repeated hypoglycemic episodes should perform self-monitoring of blood glucose before meals, at bedtime, in the middle of the night, and whenever dietary, exercise, or work routines change.

PATIENT CARE: Hypoglycemic epi-sodes must be prevented or treated promptly when they occur to avoid severe complications. The caregiver ensures that the patient understands the signs and symptoms and key dangers of hypoglycemia and the importance of reporting episodes to the health care provider. If the hypoglycemic patient is conscious and has an intact gag reflex, he should consume a readily available source of glucose, such as five to six pieces of hard candy; 4 to 6 oz of apple juice, orange juice, cola, or other soft drink; or 1 tbsp of honey or grape jelly. Commercially prepared sugar cake icing may be placed in the buccal cavity for absorption via mucous membranes (1 tbsp). If the patient is unconscious, EMS should be alerted immediately and then the patient should receive a subcutaneous injection of glucagon; the patient's family should also be taught how to administer glucagon injections. The diabetic patient should follow prescribed diets (without skipping meals or scheduled snacks) to prevent a rapid drop in blood glucose levels. Diabetic patients should wear or carry a medical identification device describing the condition and emergency treatment measures. Awareness of hypoglycemia may be reduced in patients taking beta blocking drugs or who have been diabetic for many years. These patients should monitor their blood sugars frequently, esp. when their daily regimen changes, to avoid low blood sugars.

POSTPRANDIAL "HYPOGLYCEMIA": Many people mistakenly believe that they are hypoglycemic if they become drowsy or fatigued after meals. There is no evidence to support this belief.

fasting h. A blood glucose level less than 50 mg/dl (3.3 mmol/L) that occurs before or between meals. Its most common cause in diabetic patients is an excessive dose of insulin or of another medication used to control high blood glucose. It may also be caused by some other medications, e.g., pentamidine or quinine, or by alcohol consumption, critical illnesses, prolonged exercise, or, rarely, insulin-secreting tumors.

idiopathic h. 1. Hypoglycemia of unclear origin. 2. Reactive **h.**

newborn h. Blood glucose levels less than 40 mg/dl in infants during the first hours of life.

ETIOLOGY: A high metabolic rate, low glycogen and fat reserves, and limited capacity for gluconeogenesis contribute to the normal newborn's post-birth risk of hypoglycemia. Approximately 8% of normal term infants who were born vaginally and nearly 16% of those born by cesarean delivery experience one or more episodes of hypoglycemia, usually within the 24 to 72 hr period following birth.

Premature and small-for-gestational-age infants experience an earlier onset (6 hr or so after birth) because of reduced glycogen production by their smaller, immature livers. Infants of diabetic mothers and those who are small for gestational age exhibit a higher incidence of low blood sugar. Other maternal risk factors for newborn hypoglycemia include erythroblastosis fetalis, glycogen storage diseases, and toxemia. Newborn risk factors include postmaturity, macrosomia, cold stress, perinatal asphyxia, sepsis, and respiratory distress syndrome.

PATIENT CARE: Newborns are monitored closely for muscle twitching, tremors, seizures, lethargy, poor feeding, vomiting, sweating, limpness, weak or high-pitched cry, apnea, and cyanosis. For high-risk infants, glucose levels are assessed every 2 hr for 6 hr, then at 12, 24, and 48 hr after delivery. Prompt treatment is provided with oral breast milk or a 5% to 10% glucose solution or intravenous glucose as necessary. IV infusions must be closely monitored to avoid hyperglycemia, circulatory overload, and cellular dehydration. Solutions should be terminated gradually to prevent hypoglycemia due to hyperinsulinemia.

nocturnal h. A low blood glucose level (<50 mg/dl or 3.3 mmol/L) that occurs after bedtime. It may be asymptomatic, or it may cause nightmares, night sweats, other sleep disturbances, tachycardia, convulsions, or, rarely, death. It typically results from relatively high levels of insulin in insulin-treated diabetic patients. It may be prevented by consuming a bedtime snack or by adjusting evening doses of insulin based on bedtime blood glucose levels.

persistent infant hyperinsulinemic h. ABBR: PHHI. The most common cause of recurring low blood glucose levels in newborns. PHHI is typically caused either by diffuse overgrowth of insulin-secreting cells (beta cells) throughout the pancreas or by a single beta cell adenoma. It is characterized by the abnormal secretion of insulin despite low blood glucose levels. Neonates affected by PHHI may suffer brain injury caused by low blood glucose levels. SYN: *congenital hyperinsulinism.*

reactive h. A postprandial blood glucose reading less than 70 mg/dl in a patient who is not being treated for diabetes mellitus. It sometimes can occur in patients who have undergone gastric bypass surgery and in a few other conditions. SYN: *idiopathic hypoglycemia* (2).

hypoglycemia unawareness The absence of symptoms of hypoglycemia (anxiety, confusion, palpitations, or sweating) in a patient with diabetes mellitus treated with insulin or oral antidiabetic drugs.

hypoglycorrhachia (hī″pō-glī″kō-rā′kē-ă) [″ + ″ + *rhachis,* spine] A decreased concentration of glucose in the cerebrospinal fluid, such as is found in meningitis.

hypognathous (hī-pŏg′nă-thŭs) [″ + *gnathos,* jaw] Having a lower jaw smaller than the upper jaw.

hypogonadism (hī″pō-gō′năd-izm) [″ + *gone,* semen, + *-ismos,* condition] Inadequate production of sex hormones.

hypogonadotropism (hī″pō-gŏn″ă-dō-trŏp′ism) Low serum levels of gonadotropins. **hypogonadotropic,** *adj.*

hypohidrosis (hī″pō-hī-drō′sĭs) [″ + *hidros,* sweat, + *osis,* condition] Diminished perspiration.

hypohydration (hī″pō-hī-drā′shŭn) [″ + ″] The provision of less than the normal amount of water to the body to meet its metabolic demands. SEE: *hyperhydration; euhydration; dehydration.*

hypoinsulinism (hī″pō-ĭn′sū-lĭn-izm) [″ + L. *insula,* island, + Gr. *-ismos,* condition] **1.** Type 1 diabetes mellitus. **2.** Relative deficiency in insulin secretion or insulin dosing.

hypokalemia (hī″pō-kā-lē′mē-ă) [*hypo-* + L. *kalium,* potash + *-emia*] An abnormally low concentration of potassium in the blood (less than 3.5 meq/L). SYN: *hypopotassemia.* SEE: *hyperkalemia.* **hypokalemic** (-lē′mĭk), *adj.*

ETIOLOGY: Causes include deficient potassium intake or excess loss of potassium due to vomiting, diarrhea, or fistulas; metabolic acidosis; diuretic therapy; aldosteronism; excess adrenocortical secretion; renal tubule disease; and alkalosis.

SYMPTOMS: Common manifestations of mild to moderate potassium depletion include muscle aches, fatigue, or mild weakness. As potassium concentrations drop significantly below 3.0 mmol/L, ileus, paralysis, or cardiac conduction and rhythm disturbances may arise. Arrhythmias are particularly likely to affect those patients taking digoxin who become hypokalemic.

PREVENTION: To prevent hypokalemia, patients taking cardiac glycosides or potassium-wasting diuretics are instructed to include potassium supplements in their medical regimens. Potassium-rich foods (such as oranges, bananas, and tomatoes) are not an adequate source of the potassium that is lost by diuresis.

TREATMENT: Therapy consists of oral, intravenous, or combined potassium replacement.

⚠ Severely hypokalemic patients may require close electrocardiographic monitoring and frequent assessment of plasma potassium levels.

PATIENT CARE: Potassium and other electrolyte levels are monitored frequently during replacement therapy to avoid overcorrection leading to hyperkalemia. Fluid balance is monitored. A physician must be notified if the patient's urine output is less than 600 ml/day because 80% to 90% of potassium is excreted through the kidneys. Cardiac rhythm is monitored, and arrhythmias are reported immediately. Additional care is taken if the patient takes a cardiac glycoside because hypokalemia enhances its action. The patient is assessed for indications of digitalis toxicity (anorexia, nausea, vomiting, blurred vision, arrhythmias). Other signs to watch for include decreased bowel sounds, abdominal distention, and constipation.

Prescribed IV potassium replacement is administered slowly with a volumetric device if the concentration exceeds 40 mEg/L. The rate should not exceed 200-250 mEg/24 hr, and the drug should never be given as a bolus because it may precipitate cardiac arrest. If the patient is prescribed a liquid oral potassium supplement, he or she is advised to dilute it in a full glass of water or fruit juice and to sip it slowly to prevent gastric irritation. Safety measures are implemented for the patient experiencing muscle weakness due to postural hypotension. The importance of taking potassium supplements as prescribed is emphasized, particularly if the patient also is prescribed a diuretic or digitalis preparation. The patient is taught signs of potassium imbalance to report, including weakness and pulse irregularities.

hypokinesia (hī″pō-kĭ-nē′zē-ă) [″ + *kinesis,* movement] Decreased motor reaction to stimulus. **hypokinetic** (-nĕt′ĭk), *adj.*

hypokinetic disease SEE: under *disease.*

hypolactasia (hī″pō-lăk-tāz′ē-ă) Lactase deficiency. The absence of enzymes that break down dietary lactose is common in adults, esp. those of Northern European heritage, in whom it is a common cause of abdominal gas or indigestion.

hypolipidemic (hī″pō-lĭp″ĭ-dē′mĭk) Decreasing the lipid concentration of the blood.

hypomagnesemia (hī″pŏ-mag″nĕ-sē′mē-ă) [*hypo-* + *magnesium* + *-emia*] A deficiency of magnesium in blood serum. SEE: *magnesium.*

hypomania (hī″pō-mā′nē-ă) [″ + *mania,* madness] Mild mania and excitement, with a moderate change in behavior.

hypomastia (hī-pō-măs′tē-ă) [″ + *mastos,* breast] A condition of having abnormally small breasts.

hypomelanosis (hī″pō-mĕl-ăn-ō′sĭs) One of several disorders of melanin pigmentation in which melanin in the epidermis is decreased or absent. It may be caused by albinism, chronic protein deficiency, burns, trauma, or vitiligo. SEE: *hypermelanosis.*

hypomenorrhea (hī″pō-mĕn-ō-rē′ă) [″ + *men,* month, + *rhoia,* flow] A deficient amount of menstrual flow, but with regular periods. SEE: *oligomenorrhea.*

hypometabolism (hī″pō-mĕ-tab′ŏ-lizm) [*hypo-,* + *metabolism*] A decreased metabolic rate, such as one evidenced by diminished uptake of a biomarker. For example, decreased metabolism in the parietal and temporal regions of the brain for fluorodeoxyglucose characterizes Alzheimer disease.

hypometria (hī″pō-mē′trē-ă) [″ + *metron,* measure] A shortened range of movement. SEE: *dysmetria.*

hypomimia (hī″pō-mĭm′ē-ă) A reduction in the expressiveness of the face, as occurs in patients with Parkinson's disease. It is marked by diminished animation and movement of the facial muscles.

hypomobility (hī″pō-mō-bĭl′ĭ-tē) Restricted joint movement (play) that limits normal range of motion; the opposite of hypermobility.

hypomorph (hī′pō-mŏrf) [″ + *morphe,* form] 1. A person with disproportionately short limbs with respect to the length of the trunk; the opposite of hypermorph. 2. A mutant gene that has a loss of function or expresses much less gene product than the wild type. SEE: *somatotype.*

hypomotility (hī″pō-mō-tĭl′ĭ-tē) [″ + L. *motus,* moved] Hypokinesia.

hyponatremia (hī″pō-nā-trē′mē-ă) [*hypo-* + *natremia*] A decreased concentration of sodium in the bloodstream. Hyponatremia is extremely common in clinical medicine and is caused by one of the following conditions: congestive heart failure, renal failure, cirrhosis; syndrome of inappropriate antidiuretic hormone (SIADH); dehydration; thyroid or adrenal hormone dysfunction; side effects of drugs; psychogenic polydipsia; or laboratory error, i.e., pseudohyponatremia. Symptoms of hyponatremia include weakness, confusion, and anorexia. If serum sodium levels drop rapidly, seizures may occur. Treatment of hyponatremia depends on the underlying cause. **hyponatremic** (′mĭk), *adj.*

acute h. Hyponatremia that develops in 48 hr or less. It may be corrected rapidly without concern for neurological dysfunction.

chronic h. Hyponatremia of gradual onset, present for 48 hr or more. It should be corrected slowly to avoid neurological complications, e.g., by about 10–12 meq/L per day.

hypoparathyroidism (hī″pō-păr-ă-thī′royd-ĭzm) [″ + ″ + ″ + *eidos,* form, shape, + *-ismos,* condition] A condition caused by an insufficient or absent secretion of the parathyroid glands. SEE: *Nursing Diagnoses Appendix.*

hypoperfusion (hī″pō-pĕr-fū′zhŏn) [*hypo-* + *perfusion*] Inadequate blood flow to a single organ or through the entire circulatory system. SYN: *circulatory collapse.*

hypoperistalsis (hī″pō-pĕr″ĭ-stăl′sĭs) Diminished peristalsis. SEE: *paralytic ileus.*

hypopharynx (hī″pō-făr′ĭnks) [″ + *pharynx,* throat] The lower portion of the pharynx that opens into the larynx anteriorly and the esophagus posteriorly. SYN: *laryngopharynx.*

hypophonia (hī″pō-fō′nē-ă) An abnormally weak voice resulting from incoordination of speech muscles, including weakness of muscles of respiration.

hypophosphatasia (hī″pō-fŏs″fă-tā′zē-ă) A rare inherited disorder of bony mineralization with a deficiency of alkaline phosphatase. There are four forms of this condition: lethal perinatal, infantile, childhood, and adult. The perinatal and infantile forms are inherited as autosomal recessive traits. The inheritance pattern of the childhood and adult forms is unknown. In the adult form, signs and symptoms may not become apparent until middle age, but there may be a history of early loss of either deciduous or permanent teeth and short stature.

hypophosphatemia (hī″pō-fos″fă-tē′mē-ă) [*hypo-* + *phosphate* + *-emia*] An abnormally low concentration of phosphate in the blood (< 3 mg/dL).

hypophosphatemic (hī″pō-fŏs″fă-tē′mĭk) [Gr. *hypo-,* less than, deficient, + L. *phosphas,* phosphate, + Gr. *haima,* blood] **1.** Having an abnormally low blood phosphate concentration. **2.** An agent that lowers the blood phosphate concentration, e.g., in renal failure.

hypophosphaturia (hī″pō-fŏs″fă-tū′rē-ă) [″ + ″ + Gr. *ouron,* urine] Decreased excretion of phosphate in the urine.

hypophyseal, hypophysial (hī″pof″ĭ-sē′ăl, hī″pō-fĭ-sē′ăl, hī″pō-fiz′ē-ăl) [*hypophysis* + *-al*] Pert. to the hypophysis or pituitary.

hypophysectomy (hī-pof″ĭ-sek′tŏ-mē) [*hypophysis* + *-ectomy*] Excision of the hypophysis cerebri (pituitary gland).

hypophysis (hī-pof′ĭ-sĭs) *pl.* **hypophyses** [Gr., *hypophysis,* outgrowth, undergrowth] **1.** An undergrowth. **2.** Pituitary gland.

    h. cerebri Pituitary gland.

    pharyngeal h. A small structure anterior to the pharyngeal bursa. It is derived from the lower portion of Rathke's pouch and occasionally gives rise to a cyst or tumor.

hypophysitis (hī-pof″ĭ-sīt′ĭs) [*hypophysis,* + *-itis*] Inflammation of the pituitary gland.

    autoimmune h. Lymphocytic **h.**

    lymphocytic h. A relatively rare autoimmune disease in which the pituitary gland is infiltrated and damaged by lymphocytes, esp. during pregnancy or the postpartum period. Imaging studies of the pituitary gland show massive enlargement. Hormone deficiencies, or in some cases, hyperprolactinemia, can occur. SYN: *autoimmune h.*

hypopigmentation (hī″pō-pĭg″mĕn-tā′shŭn) Diminished pigment in a tissue.

hypopituitarism (hī″pō-pĭ-tū′ĭt-ă-rizm) [*hypo-* + *pituitar(y)* + *-ism*] A condition resulting from diminished secretion of pituitary hormones, esp. those of the anterior lobe.

hypoplasia (hī″pō-plā′zh(ē-)ă) [*hypo-* + *-plasia*] Underdevelopment of a tissue organ or body. **hypoplastic** (-plas′tik), *adj.* SEE: *tissue.*

    enamel h. Incomplete formation of tooth enamel, caused by local trauma to the tooth, infections such as syphilis, exposure to fluoride during dental development, or genetic and metabolic diseases.

    focal dermal h. A rare, usually X-linked syndrome characterized by underdevelopment of the ectodermis, mesodermis, and neurodermis, and abnormal development of the eyes and hands. SYN: *Goltz syndrome.*

hypopnea (hī″pō-nē′ă) [″ + *pnoia,* breath] Decreased rate and depth of breathing. SEE: *apnea.*

hypopotassemia (hī″pō-pō″tăs-sē′mē-ă) [″ + *potassium* + Gr. *haima,* blood] Hypokalemia.

hypoproteinemia (hī″pō-prō″tē-ĭn-ē′mē-ă) [″ + *protos,* first, + *haima,* blood] An abnormally decreased concentration of protein in the blood. It is one of many causes of edema, esp. in the lower extremities.

hypoprothrombinemia (hī″pō-prō-thrŏm″bĭn-ē′mē-ă) [″ + L. *pro,* for, + Gr. *thrombos,* clot, + *haima,* blood] A deficiency of blood clotting factor II (prothrombin) in the blood.

hypopyon (hī-pō′pē-on″) [*hypo-* + Gr. *pyon,* pus] Pus in the anterior chamber of the eye. The pus consists of layered white blood cells and may be infectious or inflammatory (sterile).

hyporeactive (hī″pō-rē-ăk′tĭv) A decreased response to stimuli.

hyporeflexia (hī″pō-rē-flĕk′sē-ă) [″ + L. *reflexus,* bent back] A diminished function of the reflexes.

hyporeninemic (hī″pō-rē″nĭn-ē′mik,

-ren″ĭn-) [*hypo-* + *renin* + *-emia*] Characterized by a low serum level of renin. **hyporeninemia** (hī″pō-rē″nĭn-ē′mē-ă, -ren″ĭn-), *n.*

hyposalivation (hī″pō-săl″ĭ-vā′shŭn) An abnormal decrease in flow of saliva.

hyposecretion (hī″pō-sē-krē′shŭn) Lowered amount of secretion.

hyposensitive (hī″pō-sĕn′sĭ-tĭv) [″ + L. *sentire*, to feel] Having a reduced ability to respond to stimuli.

hyposensitization (hī″pō-sen″sĭt-ĭ-zā′shŏn) [*hypo-* + *sensitization*] Desensitization.

hyposmia (hī-pŏz′mē-ă) [″ + *osme*, smell] Decreased sensitivity to odors.

hyposmolarity (hī-pŏz″mō-lăr′ĭ-tē) Decreased osmolar concentration, esp. of the blood or urine.

hyposomnia (hī″pō-sŏm′nē-ă) A decreased ability to sleep.

hypospadia, hypospadias (hī″pō-spā′dē-ă, -ăs) [″ + *span*, to draw] **1.** An abnormal congenital opening of the male urethra upon the undersurface of the penis. **2.** A urethral opening into the vagina.

hypospermatogenesis A lower than normal sperm count.

hypostasis (hī″pŏs′tă-sĭs) [″ + *stasis*, a standing] **1.** A diminished blood flow or circulation. **2.** A deposit of sediment owing to decreased flow of a body fluid such as blood or urine.

hypostatic (hī″pō-stăt′ĭk) [″ + *statikos*, standing] **1.** Of or pert. to hypostasis. **2.** In genetics, hidden or suppressed; said of a gene whose effect is suppressed by the presence of another gene.

hyposthenuria (hī″pŏs-thĕn-ū′rē-ă) [″ + *sthenos*, strength, + *ouron*, urine] The secretion of urine of low specific gravity, chiefly in chronic nephritis.

   tubular h. Hyposthenuria resulting from disease of the renal tubule epithelial cells.

hypostosis (hĭp″ŏs-tō′sĭs) [″ + *osteon*, bone, + *osis*, condition] Deficient bone development.

hypotelorism (hī″pō-tĕl′ō-rĭzm) [″ + *telouros*, distant] Abnormally decreased distance between paired organs, esp. the eyes.

hypotension (hī″pō-ten′shŏn) [*hypo-* + *tension*] **1.** A deficiency in tone or tension. **2.** A decrease of the systolic and diastolic blood pressure to below normal. This occurs, for example, in shock, hemorrhage, dehydration, sepsis, Addison's disease, and in many other diseases and conditions. SEE: *blood pressure, chronic low.*

   orthostatic h. Hypotension occurring when a person assumes an upright position after getting up from a bed or chair. SYN: *Bradbury-Eggleston syndrome; postural h.* SEE: *orthostatic vital signs determination.*

   postprandial h. A decrease in systolic blood pressure of 20 mm Hg or more within 2 hr of the start of a meal. This may cause syncope, falls, dizziness, weakness, angina pectoris, or stroke. This condition occurs most often in older adults and in persons with autonomic failure. Although postural changes may increase the severity of the condition, postprandial hypotension is a different entity from postural hypotension.

   postural h. Orthostatic hypotension.

   spontaneous intracranial h. A chronically recurring headache caused by leakage of cerebrospinal fluid (CSF) into the epidural space; it worsens when a person stands and improves on lying down It is typically found in those with connective tissue disorders. The leakage of CSF limits the quantity of fluid in which the brain floats, drawing the brain toward the foramen magnum and base of the skull. Applying a blood patch to alleviate the leakage resolves the symptoms in most patients.

   supine h. syndrome A drop in blood pressure that occurs when a person, esp. a pregnant woman in the last trimester, lies on her back.

   ETIOLOGY: Compression of the vena cava or the abdominal aorta by the developing fetus results in decreased return of blood to the heart.

   PATIENT CARE: Most pregnant women regain a normal blood pressure if they shift to their left side.

hypotensive (hī″pō-tĕn′sĭv) **1.** Characterized by or causing low blood pressure. **2.** An agent that lowers blood pressure.

hypothalamus (hī″pō-thăl′ă-mŭs) [″ + *thalamos*, chamber] The bottom (ventral) half of the diencephalon of the brain. It is the regulator of the essential homeostatic balance of body fluids, salt concentrations, temperature, and energy metabolism as well as the governor of reproductive cycles and certain emotional responses. The hypothalamus is a single structure, but it comprises two mirror-image walls of neural tissue on the left and the right sides of the ventral half of the third ventricle. In the embryo, these walls are at the front end of the neural tube; in the adult, the hypothalamus begins at the lamina terminalis (at the base of the frontal lobes) and just below the lamina terminalis; the optic chiasm lies in front of the hypothalamus. The base of the hypothalamus ends in a stalk (the infundibulum) from which hangs the pituitary gland (the hypohysis); farther caudally, two mammillary bodies bulge from the bottom of the hypothalamus. At the top of the hypothalamus, the lateral ventricles empty into the third ventricle via a left and a right interventricular foramen, and behind (caudal to) the foramina are the right and left thalami. The hypothalamus is the central controller of the preganglionic sympathetic and parasympathetic nervous systems; it is also the central regulator of the pituitary gland. The hypothalamus is a collecting zone for input from the cerebral cortex, the hippocampus, the amygdala, the retina, and the brainstem; it sends output to the cerebral cortex, the thalamus, the brainstem, and the pituitary gland. Besides the pituitary gland and the mammillary bodies, the hypothalamus contains many discrete CNS nuclei in its walls, and these nuclei are categorized according to their regional locations. The anterior region (which is subdivided into the preoptic and supraoptic areas) contains nuclei involved in the regulation of gonadal hormones, body fluid levels, body temperature, and circadian rhythm; the middle (infundibular or tuberal) region contains nuclei involved in regulating levels of adrenocortical, thyroid, growth, and gonadal hormones; and the posterior (mammillary) region is a central part of the midbrain-mammillary-thalamic-midbrain circuit of the limbic system. SEE: *hormone, releasing.*

temperature regulation in the h.
Control of body temperature, locally in the periphery and centrally in the hypothalamus. Neurons in the preoptic area of the hypothalamus respond to the temperature of the blood in that region. The same or adjacent neurons also react to pyrogens (e.g., from bacteria).

hypothenar (hī-pŏth′ĕ-năr) [″ + *thenar,* palm] The fleshy prominence on the inner side of the palm next to the little finger. SYN: *hypothenar eminence.*

hypothenar hammer syndrome Damage to the ulnar artery from sports or occupations in which a person uses the side of the hand as a pounding tool, resulting in recurrent blunt trauma to the hand. It occasionally causes Raynaud phenomenon or other forms of digital ischemia.

hypothermal (hī″pō-thĕr′măl) [″ + *therme,* heat] **1.** Tepid. **2.** Subnormal temperature.

hypothermia (hī″pō-thĕr′mē-ă) [*hypo-* + *therm-* + *-ia*] A core body temperature below 35°C (95°F). It may be further classified as mild (93.2°–96.8°F [34°–36°C]); moderate (86°–93°F [30°–34°C]); or severe (<86°F [30°C]). It should be confirmed by temperature readings at two separate core locations (e.g., esophagus and rectum). Low body temperatures are most likely to affect newborns, older adults, demented individuals, individuals exposed to wet and cold conditions outdoors, alcoholics, septic patients, trauma patients, and patients with endocrine disorders such as severe hypothyroidism. Phenothiazines and benzodiazepines may contribute to

hypothermia by decreasing centrally mediated vasoconstriction; anesthetics by blocking shivering. Hypothermia can be life-threatening, impairing neurological, cardiovascular, respiratory, and gastrointestinal systems. SYN: *cold stress.*

PREVENTION: To help prevent hypothermia, patients with multiple traumas receiving treatment in emergency facilities should be maintained under radiant warmers. Individuals who anticipate prolonged exposure to cold should be advised not to smoke or drink alcohol. They should wear layered clothing, two pairs of socks, mittens (not gloves), and a scarf or hat that covers ears and head (to avoid loss of heat through the head). They also need adequate food and rest. If caught in severe cold weather, the individual should find warmth and shelter as soon as possible and increase physical activity to maintain body warmth.

PATIENT CARE: Emergency care of the hypothermic patient: Emergency department personnel first assess airway, breathing, and circulation. If breathing or pulse is not detected, cardiopulmonary resuscitation (CPR) begins immediately and continues until the patient's core body temperature reaches at least 89.6°F (32°C). Wet clothing should be removed and the patient protected against further heat loss. The patient is treated gently to avoid triggering cardiac dysrhythmias. If the patient has a core temperature of 93.2° to 96.8°F (34°–36°C) (mild hypothermia) and is breathing spontaneously, passive warming and active external warming are initiated. Passive warming involves covering the patient in dry insulating materials. Active external rewarming uses forced warm air, radiant heat sources, a fluid-circulating heat blanket, or heating pads to rewarm the body. If the patient's core temperature is 86° to 93°F (30°–34°C) (moderate hyperthermia), the patient is dried and covered and external rewarming is begun immediately. If the patient's core temperature is less than 86°F (30°C) (severe hypothermia), invasive core rewarming is initiated, e.g., with infusions of warmed IV, gastric, and/or peritoneal fluids, warmed humidified oxygen, esophageal warming tubes, and extracorporeal hemodialysis. SEE: *Nursing Diagnoses Appendix.*

 Oral thermometers are likely to be inaccurate outdoors.

Hypothermia in newborns is prevented by maintaining the dry but unclothed infant under a radiant warmer with thermistor probe until temperature is stabilized. The initial bath is postponed until skin temperature stabilizes between 97.6° and 99°F (36.5°–37.2°C). Once stabilized, the infant's temperature is maintained by keeping him or her dry and wrapped in warm blankets, with the head covered, in a nursery unit with an ambient temperature of 75°F (24°C). If the infant has become hypothermic (cold delivery room, birth in a car on the way to the birth center, inadequate drying and wrapping after birth), rewarming is accomplished with great care over a period of 2 to 4 hr, as rapid warming or cooling may result in apneic spells or acidosis.

accidental h. Hypothermia due to exposure to wet and cold conditions (as with skiers, hunters, sailors, swimmers, climbers, the indigent, homeless persons in winter, and alcoholics) rather than diseases (as in sepsis or hypothyroidism).

induced h. Any technique in which body temperature is lowered to reduce metabolic rates, oxygen demand, or organ damage. Induced hypothermia has been used to manage stroke and traumatic brain injury, to alleviate fever or pain, and to improve outcomes in surgery or after cardiac arrest. Informally known as *chill therapy.* SYN: *hypothermia therapy; targeted temperature management; therapeutic* **h.**

⚠️ Potential complications include cardiac dysrhythmias, disorders of blood coagulation, infections, and injuries to or burns of the skin.

PATIENT CARE: In adults, the body temperature should be lowered between 90°F to 93°F (32°C to 34° C); in children, 91°F to 96°F (33°C to 35.5°C).

therapeutic h. Induced **h.**

hypothermia blanket A specially designed blanket used either to reduce the body temperature of patients with hyperthermia or to induce an artificially low body temperature, e.g., in patients who have suffered hypoxic-ischemic brain injury. It has flexible tubing between the layers of cloth through which cold water is circulated. SYN: *cooling blanket.*

hypothermia therapy Induced **hypothermia.**

hypothesis (hī-poth′ĕ-sĭs, ′ĕ-sēz″) *pl.* **hypotheses** [Gr. *hypothesis,* basis, supposition] **1.** An empirically testable assertion about one or more concepts. It is assumed in order to test its soundness or to facilitate investigation of a class of phenomena. **2.** A conclusion drawn before all the facts are established and tentatively accepted as a basis for further investigation. Particular hypothe-

ses are listed under the first word. SEE: e.g., *baby lung hypothesis; Lyon hypothesis; null hypothesis.*

hypothyroid (hī″pō-thī′royd) [″ + *thyreos,* shield, + *eidos,* form, shape] Marked by insufficient thyroid secretion.

hypothyroidism (hī″pō-thī′royd″izm) [*hypo- + thyroid + -ism*] The clinical consequences of inadequate levels of thyroid hormone in the body. When thyroid deficiency is long-standing or severe, it results in diminished basal metabolism, intolerance of the cold temperatures, fatigue, mental apathy, physical sluggishness, constipation, muscle aches, dry skin and hair, and coarsening of features. Collectively, these symptoms are called *myxedema.* In infancy, inadequate levels of thyroid hormone cause *cretinism.* SEE: *thyroid function test; Nursing Diagnoses Appendix.*

ETIOLOGY: Most patients with hypothyroidism have either Hashimoto (autoimmune) thyroiditis or have undergone treatment for hyperthyroidism with thyroidectomy or radioactive iodine. Occasionally, hypothyroidism is drug-induced, e.g., in patients treated with antithyroid drugs (propylthiouracil) or the antiarrhythmic agent amiodarone. In areas where salt is not iodized, hypothyroidism may result from dietary iodine deficiency. Rarely, hypothyroidism results from inadequate stimulation of the thyroid gland by the anterior pituitary or inadequate release of thyrotropin-releasing hormone by the hypothalamus.

DIAGNOSIS: Long before the symptoms of hypothyroidism become obvious, the condition can be diagnosed with thyroid function tests. The plasma thyroid-stimulating hormone (TSH) test is used to screen for the disease; if it is high, hypothyroidism is likely to be present. Other tests, including a low serum free T_4 index, confirm the diagnosis.

TREATMENT: For most patients, the lifelong administration of thyroid hormone at a dose of approx. 1.6 mcg/kg/day of oral levothyroxine restores normal metabolism and well-being. Failure to treat hypothyroidism inevitably results in myxedema, eventual coma, or death. Drug-induced hypothyroidism sometimes requires no treatment other than discontinuation of the offending agent or adjustment of its dose.

PATIENT CARE: The patient is assessed for indications of decreased metabolic rate; easy fatigability; cool, dry, and scaly skin; hypercarotenemia; hair and eyebrow loss; brittle nails, facial puffiness, and periorbital edema; paresthesias; ataxias; cold intolerance; bradycardia; reduced cardiac output;

slow pulse rate, poor peripheral circulation, aching muscles and joint stiffness; changes in bowel habits; irregular menses; and decreased libido. Reflexes, esp. in the Achilles tendon, show delayed relaxation time. In acute hypothyroid crisis (myxedema coma) vital signs, fluid intake, urine output, weight, and neurological status are monitored.

Chronic management includes the prescription of long-term hormone replacement. The patient's activity level is increased gradually as treatment proceeds; adequate rest is a continual priority to limit fatigue and to decrease myocardial oxygen demand. The patient should wear or carry a medical identification device describing the condition and its treatment and carry medications at all times. Desired outcomes include understanding of and cooperation with treatment regimen, restoration of normal activity level, absence of complications, and restoration of psychological well-being.

central h. Hypothyroidism due to inadequate secretion of thyroid stimulating hormone (TSH) by the pituitary or of thyrotropin-releasing hormone (TRH) by the hypothalamus or by a malfunction in blood flow between the hypothalamus and the pituitary gland.

iatrogenic h. Inadequate secretion of thyroid hormone by the thyroid gland due to treatments that include medications (such as amiodarone), radioactive iodine ablation of the gland, or surgical excision of the thyroid.

primary h. Hypothyroidism due to failure of the thyroid gland to produce metabolically adequate amounts of thyroid hormones. It is the most common form of hypothyroidism.

subclinical h. A mild elevation of serum thyrotropin level without overt symptoms or signs of thyroid insufficiency. It occurs in 5% to 20% of women over 60 and about the same percentage of men over 75.

hypotonia (hī″pŏ-tō′nē-ă, pō-) [*hypo-* + *tono-* + *-ia*] **1.** In physiology, an abnormally low intrinsic resting tension, i.e., low tone in muscles or arteries. **2.** In chemistry, an osmotic pressure lower than a reference or isotonic solution. **hypotonic** (hī″pŏ-ton′ik, pō-), *adj.*

infantile h. Floppy infant syndrome.

hypotrichosis (hī″pō-trĭ-kō′sĭs) [″ + *thrix*, hair, + *osis*, condition] An abnormal deficiency of hair.

hypotrophy (hī-pŏt′rŏ-fē) [″ + *trophe*, nourishment] Atrophy.

hypotropia (hī″pō-trō′pē-ă) [″ + *trope*, a turning] Vertical strabismus downward.

hypotympanum (hī″pō-tĭm′pă-nŭm) The part of the middle ear beneath the level of the tympanic membrane.

hypoventilation (hī″pō-věn″tĭ-lā′shŭn) [″

+ L. *ventilatio*, ventilation] Reduced rate and depth of breathing that causes an increase in carbon dioxide.

hypovolemia (hī″pō-vō-lē′mē-ă) [″ + L. *volumen*, volume] A decreased blood volume that may be caused by internal or external bleeding, fluid losses, or inadequate fluid intake.

hypoxanthine (hī″pō-zăn′thĭn, -thēn) [″ + *xanthos*, yellow] A purine derivative, $C_5H_4N_4O$, in muscles and tissues in a stage of uric acid formation. It is formed during protein decomposition. Hypoxanthine is normal in urine in small amounts.

hypoxemia (hip″ok″sē′mē-ă, hī-pok″) [*hypo-* + *²oxy-* + *-emia*] Decreased oxygen tension (oxygen concentration) of arterial blood, measured by arterial oxygen partial pressures (PaO₂) values. It is sometimes associated with decreased oxygen content. **hypoxemic** (′mik), *adj.* SEE: *hypoxia; respiration*.

hypoxia (hī″poks′ē-ă, hip-ok′) [*hypo-* + *²oxy-* + *-ia*] **1.** An oxygen deficiency in body tissues. **2.** A decreased concentration of oxygen in inspired air. SEE: *anoxia; hypoxemia; posthypoxia syndrome*.

altitude h. Hypoxia due to insufficient oxygen content of inspired air at high altitudes.

anemic h. Hypoxia due to a decrease in hemoglobin concentration or in the number of erythrocytes in the blood.

anoxic h. Hypoxia due to disordered pulmonary mechanisms of oxygenation; may be due to reduced oxygen supply, respiratory obstruction, reduced pulmonary function, or inadequate ventilation.

autoerotic h. Cerebral oxygen deprivation that a person self-induces (such as by hanging oneself or by tying a constricting device around the neck) during masturbation. The practice of limiting cerebral blood flow during masturbation has been thought to intensify pleasure during orgasm. It has occasionally resulted in brain damage or death from hypoxia. SYN: *autoerotic* **asphyxia**; *sexual* **asphyxia**. SEE: *asphyxiophilia*.

cerebral h. Lack of oxygen supply to the brain, usually as a result of either diminished blood flow (such as in traumatic childbirth or cardiopulmonary arrest) or diminished oxygenation of the blood (such as in high-altitude exposures or patients with advanced cardiopulmonary disease). If nothing is done to treat this condition, irreversible anoxic damage to the brain begins after 4 to 6 min and sooner in some cases. If basic resuscitation measures are begun before the end of this period, the onset of cerebral death may be postponed. SEE: *cardiopulmonary* **resuscitation**.

fetal h. Low levels of oxygen in the fetus, commonly as a result of diminished placental perfusion, uteroplacental insufficiency, or compression of the umbilical cord. The condition is often accompanied by acidosis and is life-threatening unless prompt interventions are undertaken to restore well-oxygenated blood to the fetus. Signs of early fetal hypoxia include tachycardia and increased variability of the fetal heart rate; profound fetal hypoxia is characterized by bradycardia and a sinusoidal fetal heart rate pattern.

histotoxic h. Hypoxia due to inability of the tissues to use oxygen. SEE: *cyanide*.

hypokinetic h. Stagnant **h.**

post-traumatic h. Secondary hypoxic **injury**.

soft lens associated corneal h., soft lens-associated corneal hypoxia ABBR: SLACH. Damage to the epithelial surface of the cornea by a soft contact lens, which may deprive the outer surface of the cornea of oxygen.

stagnant h. Hypoxia due to insufficient peripheral circulation, as occurs in cardiac failure, shock, arterial spasm, and thrombosis. SYN: *hypokinetic h.*

hypoxia-inducible factor SEE: under *factor*.

hypoxia inhalation test An assessment of a person's ability to tolerate air travel (in which the oxygen concentration in the cabin at cruising altitude is reduced relative to that at sealevel).

PATIENT CARE: The prospective flier is exposed to an ambient oxygen saturation of 15% (normal = 21%) for a minimum of 15 min while undergoing electrocardiographic monitoring and continuous pulse oximetry. The test is imperfect but can provide some information about the supplemental oxygen needs of special patients, such as those with chronic obstructive lung disease, during commercial air travel.

hypsarrhythmia (hĭp″săr-ĭth′mē-ă) [Gr. *hypsi,* high, + *a-,* not, + *rhythmos,* rhythm] An abnormal electroencephalographic pattern of persistent generalized slow waves and very high voltage. Clinically it is often associated with infantile spasm and progressive mental deterioration.

hysterectomy (his″tĕ-rek′tŏ-mē) [*hystero-* + *-ectomy*] Surgical removal of the uterus. Each year, about 500,000 women undergo hysterectomies. Indications for the surgery include benign or malignant changes in the uterine wall or cavity and cervical abnormalities (including endometrial cancer, cervical cancer, severe dysfunctional bleeding, large or bleeding fibroid tumors (leiomyomas), prolapse of the uterus, intractable postpartum hemorrhage due to placenta accreta or uterine rupture, or severe endometriosis). The approach to excision may be either abdominal or vaginal. The abdominal approach is used most commonly to remove large tumors; when the ovaries and fallopian tubes also will be removed; and when there is need to examine adjacent pelvic structures, such as the regional lymph nodes. Vaginal hysterectomy is appropriate when uterine size is less than that in 12 week gestation; when no other abdominal pathology is suspected; and when surgical plans include cystocele, enterocele, or rectocele repair. SEE: illus.; Nursing Diagnoses Appendix.

In preparation for abdominal hysterectomy, the patient is placed in the dorsal position. The table is ready to be tipped into the Trendelenburg position. As soon as the incision is made through the peritoneum, the table should be put into the Trendelenburg position. This

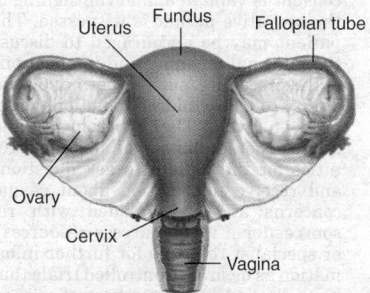

Subtotal hysterectomy (cervix not removed)

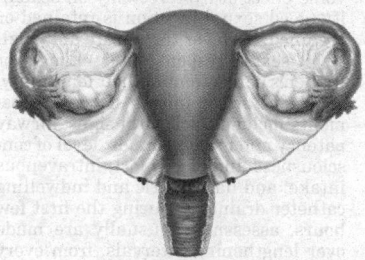

Total hysterectomy
(cervix removed)

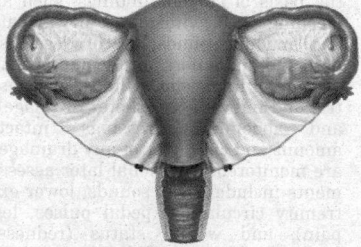

Total hysterectomy
plus bilateral salpingooopherectomy

HYSTERECTOMY

procedure is the same for all abdominopelvic surgery, as the Trendelenburg
position allows the abdominal organs to
fall away from the pelvis so that they
may be easily packed off and isolated
from the surgical field with large pads
or a large roll of packing.

PATIENT CARE: *Preoperative:* In general, preparations for an abdominal hysterectomy are similar to protocols for
any abdominopelvic surgery (e.g., abdominal skin preparation, insertion of
an intravenous line and, depending on
surgical protocol, an indwelling urinary
catheter). Vaginal irrigation with antibacterial solution also may be ordered.
All procedures are explained to the patient, who is provided with anticipatory
guidance for the postoperative period.
Misconceptions are clarified, informed
consent is validated, and the signing of
the operative permit is witnessed. The
patient may be encouraged to discuss
the personal meaning and implications
of the procedure, such as permanent inability to bear children; emotional support is given. The gynecologist and
nurses should make available opportunities for the patient to ask questions
and receive information about sexual
concerns and be provided with resources (or a way to access resources),
or specialist referrals for further information as desired. Controlled trials that
have studied large numbers of women
have not shown, in aggregate, any adverse effect of hysterectomy on sexuality (good sexual function is retained or
regained; however the nature and quality of sexual response may change) or
women's perceptions of their femininity.

Postoperative: Initial status assessments include color; vital signs; airway
patency and breath sounds; level of consciousness and discomfort; intravenous
intake; and nasogastric and indwelling
catheter drainage. During the first few
hours, assessments usually are made
over lengthening intervals, from every
10 to 15 min during the first hour to
every 30 min to hourly. Intervals and
assessment priorities may be altered on
the basis of current findings, such as
bleeding. Color; vital signs; airway patency and lung sounds; level of consciousness and discomfort; intake and output
(including intravenous fluids, nasogastric and indwelling catheter drainage);
and abdominal dressings (intact,
amount and character of any drainage)
are monitored. Additional later assessments include bowel sounds; lower extremity circulation (pedal pulses, leg
pain); and wound status (redness,
edema, ecchymosis, discharge, and approximation). The patient is encouraged
to splint the incision, turn from side to
side, use incentive spirometry, deep
breathe and cough every 2 hr, and use

incentive spirometry. Prescribed intravenous fluids and analgesics are administered. The woman is assisted in
self-administering patient-controlled
analgesia. Antithromboembolitic devices (pneumatic dressings or elastic
stockings) are applied as needed. The
patient is encouraged and assisted with
early ambulation. The patient is encouraged to splint the incision, turn
from side to side, deep breathe and
cough every 2 hr, and use incentive
spirometry.

If the patient's ovaries have been removed, the reasons for hormone therapy
are explained to her. Effective coping
strategies related to anticipated radiation and/or chemotherapy are targeted.
Desired outcomes include evidence of
incisional healing; absence of complications; return of normal GI and bladder
function; and understanding of and
compliance with the prescribed treatment regimen.

abdominal h. The removal of the
uterus through an abdominal incision.
SYN: *abdominohysterectomy.*

cesarean h. The surgical removal of
the uterus at the time of cesarean section.

pan h. Removal of the uterus, fallopian tubes, and ovaries.

radical h. The surgical removal of
the uterus, tubes, ovaries, adjacent lymph
nodes, and part of the vagina.

subtotal h. A procedure in which the
cervix is left intact after the uterus has
been removed. The cervix, which acts as
an anchor, and upper vagina are preserved, resulting in better support of the
remaining structures. Most women experience less discomfort and faster recovery with this procedure than with a
total hysterectomy. Routine pap screening following this procedure is recommended. Any woman with a history of
abnormal pap tests or cervical cancer is
not a candidate for subtotal hysterectomy. SYN: *supracervical h.; supravaginal h.*

supracervical h. Subtotal hysterectomy.

supravaginal h. Subtotal hysterectomy.

total abdominal h. Removal of the
uterus, including the cervix, through an
abdominal incision.

vaginal h. The surgical removal of
the uterus through the vagina.

hysteresis (hĭs″tĕr-ē′sĭs) [Gr., a coming
too late] **1.** The failure of related phenomena to keep pace with each other.
2. The failure of the manifestation of an
effect to keep up with its cause. **3.** The
difference between inflation and deflation of the lung, shown as a pressure
volume difference.

hysteria (hĭs-tĕ′rē-ă) [Gr. *hystera,*
uterus] A pejorative term used in pop-

ular speech to mean a conversion reaction or a widely fluctuating expression of emotions.

NOTE: Currently accepted nomenclature for mental disorders does not include the term *hysteria;* it is included here for historical reasons. SEE: *mass psychogenic illness; somatization disorder.*

SYMPTOMS: Symptoms include emotional instability, sensory disturbances, loss of motor function, or other disorders.

ETIOLOGY: It may be related to emotional or physical stress.

TREATMENT: Rest and reassurance are cornerstones of management.

anxiety h. Hysteria combined with an anxiety neurosis.

conversion h. Conversion disorder.

epidemic h. Mass sociogenic illness.

major h. Agitated behavior, sometimes accompanied by pseudoseizures.

mass h. Mass sociogenic illness.

hysteric, hysterical (hǐ-stěr′ĭk) Pert. to hysteria.

hystero-, hyster- [Gr. *hystera,* womb] Prefixes meaning *uterus* or *hysteria.* SEE: *metro-; utero-.*

hysterogram (hǐs′tĕr-ō-grăm) A radiograph of the uterus after injection of a contrast medium. It has been replaced by ultrasound.

hysterography (hǐs″tĕ-rŏg′ră-fē) [″ + *graphein,* to write] A recording of the frequency and intensity of contractions of the uterus.

hysteroid (hǐs′tĕr-oyd) [″ + *eidos,* form, shape] Resembling or pert. to hysteria.

hysterometry (hǐs″tĕ-rŏm′ĕ-trē) Measurement of the size of the uterus.

hysteromyoma (hǐs″tĕr-ō-mī-ō′mǎ) [Gr. *hystera,* womb, + *mys,* muscle, + *oma,* tumor] A myoma or fibromyoma of the uterus.

hysterosalpingography (hǐs″tĕ-rō-sal″pin″gog′ră-fē, -ping″) [*hystero-* + *salpingography*] ABBR: HSG. Radiography of the uterus and oviducts after injection of a contrast medium. This procedure is sometimes used to clear the fallopian tubes, but ultrasound provides superior imaging. SYN: *metrosalpingography; uterosalpingography.*

hysteroscope (hǐs′tĕr-ō-skōp) [″ + *skopein,* to examine] An instrument for examining the uterine cavity.

hysteroscopy (hǐs″tĕr-ŏs′kŏ-pē) Inspection of the uterus by use of a special endoscope. SEE: *hysteroscope.*

hysterotomy (hǐs-tĕr-ŏt′ō-mē) **1.** Incision of the uterus. **2.** Cesarean section.

abdominal h. Incision of the uterus through a surgical opening in the abdomen. SYN: *abdominohysterotomy.*

hysterotrachelorrhaphy (hǐs″tĕr-ō-trā″kĕl-or′ă-fē) [″ + ″ + *rhaphe,* seam, ridge] Plastic surgery of a lacerated cervix by paring the edges and suturing them together.

Hz *hertz.*

HZV *herpes zoster virus.*

I

I **1.** Symbol for the element iodine. **2.** Symbol for the quantity of electricity (electric current) expressed in amperes.

i *optically inactive.*

131I A radioactive isotope of iodine, mass number of 131, atomic mass (weight) 131.

132I A radioactive isotope of iodine, mass number of 132, atomic mass (weight) 132.

-ia [L., Gr. *-ia,* noun and adj. suffix] Suffix meaning *condition,* esp. an abnormal state, and taxonomyic *names of genera classes or orders.*

IA-2 autoantibody An autoantibody against islet cells, found in patients with type 1 diabetes mellitus and, frequently, in their close relatives.

IABC *intra-aortic balloon counterpulsation.*

IABP *intra-aortic balloon pump.*

IADR *International Association for Dental Research.*

IAET *International Association for Enterostomal Therapy.*

I and O *intake and output.*

-iasis [L. fr. Gr. *-iasis,* fr. *-ia* + *-sis*] Suffix meaning *disease characterized by or produced by* (something specified). SEE: *-sis.*

-iatric [Gr. *iatrikos,* medical] Suffix meaning *medicine, the medical profession,* or *physicians.*

iatro- [Gr. *iatros,* physician] Prefix *medicine, healing,* or *a physician.*

iatrogenesis (ī″a-trō-jen′ĕ-sĭs) [*iatro-* + *genesis*] Any injury or illness that occurs because of medical care. Some examples: chemotherapy used to treat cancer may cause nausea, vomiting, hair loss, or depressed white blood cell counts. The use of a Foley catheter for incontinence can create a urinary tract infection and urinary sepsis. In the U.S., 0.67% of patients admitted to a hospital die because of health care associated error. **iatrogenic** (-jen′ĭk), *adj.*

iatrogenic disease A disease caused by or arising as a complication of medical or surgical intervention.

iatrology (ī″ă-trŏl′ō-jē) [″ + *logos,* word, reason] Medical science.

IBC *iron-binding capacity.*

IBD *inflammatory bowel disease.*

IBS *irritable bowel syndrome.*

ibuprofen (ī″bū-prō′fĕn) A nonsteroidal anti-inflammatory agent with antipyretic and analgesic properties. It inhibits the synthesis of prostaglandins, which may be responsible for its effects. It is used in treating chronic symptomatic rheumatoid arthritis and osteoarthritis, dysmenorrhea, athletic injuries, and many other conditions.

> ⚠ All nonsteroidal anti-inflammatory agents may cause bleeding from the gastrointestinal tract and kidney failure.

IBW *ideal body **weight**.*

IC *inspiratory capacity.*

-ic [L. *-icus,* Gr. *-ikos,* adj. suffix] **1.** Suffix meaning *characteristic of* or *pertaining to.* **2.** Suffix used in chemistry meaning *the higher of two valencies.* SEE: *-ous.* **-ical,** *adj.*

ICAM *intercellular adhesion molecule.*

ICD *implanted cardioverter defibrillator; International Classification of Diseases.*

ice (īs) The solid form of water. Water becomes ice at a temperature of 32°F (0°C).

> **dry i.** Carbon dioxide cooled to the point at which it becomes solid, which occurs at −110°F (−78.9°C). It is used as a commercial refrigerant and for therapeutic refrigeration in the treatment of certain skin conditions, including warts.

iceberg phenomenon The recognition of gross conditions and diseases and failure to recognize the great majority of conditions that are mild and not clinically obvious.

Iceland disease Benign myalgic encephalomyelitis.

Iceland moss SEE: under *moss.*

I cell disease *mucolipidosis* type II.

ice slush *ice immersion.*

ice treatment The use of ice applied either directly or in a suitable container to cool an injured area. Ice therapy, at least in the first 24 to 48 hr after injury, is beneficial in treating musculoskeletal conditions such as contusions, strains, sprains, and localized burns. The application of cold in immediate treatment of these conditions helps to reduce the extent of inflammation and pain and reduce secondary cell death caused by hypoxia or enzymatic function. Ice therapy may also be used intermittently to prevent swelling and to reduce or control incisional, muscular, or joint pain.

ICF *intracellular fluid; International Classification of Functioning, Disability, and Health.*

ICF-CY *International Classification of Functioning, Disability, and Health for Children and Youth.*

ICH *intracranial **hemorrhage**.*

ichorous (ī′kor-ŭs) [Gr. *ichor,* serum] Resembling ichor or watery pus.

ichthyo-, ichthy- [Gr. *ichthys,* fish] Prefixes meaning *fish.*

ichthyoid (ĭk'thē-oyd) [" + *eidos,* form, shape] Fishlike.

ichthyology (ĭk"thē-ŏl'ō-jē) [" + *logos,* word, reason] The study of fish.

ichthyosis (ĭk"thē-ō'sĭs) [" + *osis,* condition] A condition in which the skin is dry and scaly, resembling fish skin. Because ichthyosis is so easily recognized, a variety of diseases have been called by this name.

A mild nonhereditary form is called winter itch. This is often seen on the legs of older patients, esp. during dry weather during the winter months. It may be more prevalent in those who bathe frequently, thus causing excessive dryness of the skin.

TREATMENT: The application of lotions or ointments that soften and soothe the skin provide symptomatic relief for all forms of ichthyosis. Dry scales can be removed by applying a combination of 6% salicylic acid in a gel containing propylene glycol, ethyl alcohol, hydroxy propylene cellulose, and water. This is most effective when applied to moistened skin at night and covered with an occlusive dressing. Soaps should be used sparingly.

i. congenita Harlequin **fetus**.

i. fetalis Harlequin **fetus**.

i. hystrix Linear nevus. The skin contains bands or lines of rough, thick, warty, hypertrophic papillary growths.

lamellar i. of newborn A rare form of inherited ichthyosis with lamellar desquamation.

i. vulgaris A hereditary form of ichthyosis that includes two genetically distinct types. Dominant ichthyosis vulgaris is produced by an autosomal dominant gene. Characterized by dry, rough, scaly skin, it is not present at birth and is usually noticed between the ages of one and four. Many cases improve in later life.

The second type is sex-linked ichthyosis vulgaris. It is present only in males and is transmitted by the female as a recessive gene. Onset of scattered large brown scales is seen in early infancy. The scalp may be involved, but the face is spared except for the sides and in front of the ear. There is little tendency for this condition to improve with age.

ichthyotic (ĭk"thē-ŏt'ĭk) [Gr. *ichthys,* fish] Relating to ichthyosis.

ichthyotoxin (ĭk"thē-ō-tŏk'sĭn) [" + *toxikon,* poison] A toxin present in the roe, spine, or muscle of fish or marine invertebrates.

ICIDH *International Classification of Impairment, Disability and Handicap.*

icing 1. A technique of cutaneous stimulation using cold agents (12°–17°C) to evoke or facilitate reflex muscular responses in patients with central nervous system dysfunction. **2.** Application of ice to a recently traumatized area in order to reduce pain, tissue damage, and swelling. SEE: *cryotherapy.*

ICN *International Council of Nurses.*

ICNP *International Classification of Nursing Practice.*

icosahedron (ī-kō"să-hē'drŏn, kŏs") [Gr. *eikosaedron*] A nearly spherical structure made of 20 identical subunits linked at 12 symmetrical corners. Each subunit is an equilateral triangle. Several viruses, including the human immunodeficiency virus (HIV), are icosahedral.

ICP *intracranial pressure.*

ICS *incident command system; intercostal space; inhaled corticosteroid; International College of Surgeons.*

-ics [Eng. pl. of L. *-ica,* Gr. *-ika,* pl. adj. ending] Suffix meaning *organized body of knowledge.*

ICSH *interstitial cell-stimulating hormone.*

ictal (ĭk'tăl) [L. *ictus,* a blow or stroke] Pert. to or caused by a sudden attack or stroke such as epilepsy. SEE: *postictal.*

icteric (ĭk-tĕr'ĭk) [Gr. *ikteros,* jaundice] Pert. to jaundice.

icterogenic, icterogenous (ĭk"tĕr-ō-jĕn'ĭk, -ŏj'ĕn-ŭs) [" + *gennan,* to produce] Causing jaundice.

icterohemoglobinuria (ĭk"tĕr-ō-hē"mō-glō"bĭ-nū'rē-ă) [" + *haima,* blood, + L. *globus,* globe, + Gr. *ouron,* urine] Concerning icterus and hemoglobinuria.

icteroid (ĭk'tĕr-oyd) [" + *eidos,* form, shape] Resembling jaundice; yellow-hued.

icterus (ĭk'tĕr-ŭs) [Gr. *ikteros,* jaundice] Jaundice.

i. gravis neonatorum Hemolytic disease of the newborn. SEE: *erythroblastosis fetalis; exchange transfusion; kernicterus; phototherapy.*

hemolytic i. Hemolytic **jaundice**.

i. neonatorum Neonatal **jaundice**.

nonobstructive i. Hemolytic **jaundice**.

obstructive i. Obstructive jaundice.

ictus (ĭk'tŭs) [L., stroke] Pert. to or caused by a sudden symptomatic attack—esp. the new onset of neurological symptoms such as those seen in seizures or strokes.

ICU *intensive care unit.*

electronic ICU *electronic intensive care unit.*

ID *identification; infective dose; infectious disease; inside diameter; intradermal.*

ID₅₀ The infective dose of microorganisms that will cause 50% of exposed individuals to become ill.

¹ **id** [L. *id,* it; later translators of Freud's writings believed that the word *es* should have been translated to *it* and not to *id*] In Freudian psychiatry, one of the three divisions of the psyche, the

others being the ego and superego. The id, the obscure, inaccessible part of personality, serves as a repository of instinctual drives continually striving for satisfaction.

² **-id** [Fr. Fr. *-ide*, fr. L. *-id-*, fem. suffix] Suffix indicating certain secondary skin eruptions that appear some distance from the site of primary infection. If the etiological agent of primary infection is known, the secondary lesion is designated by adding -id, as in tuberculid and trichophytid.

³ **-id** SEE: *-ide.*

IDA *Iron-deficiency* **anemia.**

-ida [L. neuter plural suffix fr. Gr. *-idēs*, offspring of] Suffix used for taxonomic orders and classes, e.g., *Arachnida.*

-idae [L. fr. Gr. *-idai*, pl. of *-idēs*, offspring of] Suffix used for naming zoological families, e.g., *Ancylostomatidae*

IDDM *insulin-dependent diabetes mellitus.*

-ide, -id [Fr. Fr. *(ox)ide*] Suffix in chemistry used in naming binary and other compounds, e.g., *anhydride, bromide, cyanide.*

IDEA *Individuals with Disability Education Act.*

idea (ī-dē′ă) [L. *idea*, fr Gr. *idea*, form, pattern] A mental image or concept.

    autochthonous i. A thought that comes into the mind independent of a train of thoughts, in an unaccountable way.

    dominant i. An idea that controls all one's actions and thoughts.

    fixed i. An idea that completely dominates the mind despite evidence to the contrary; a delusion. SYN: *idée fixe.*

    overvalued i. An unreasonable, strongly held belief or idea. Such a belief is beyond the norm of beliefs held or accepted by other members of the person's culture or subculture.

    i. of reference The mistaken idea that the conversation or actions of others allude to oneself.

ideal [L. *idea*, model] A goal or endeavor regarded as a standard of perfection.

ideation (ī-dē-ā′shŭn) The process of thinking; the formation of ideas. Ideation is impaired in dementias, depression, organic brain diseases, and some drug overdoses but speeds up in the early stage of some types of mild intoxication. It is esp. active in manic states.

idée fixe (ē-dā′ fēks′) [Fr.] Fixed idea.

identical [L. *identicus*, the same] Exactly alike.

identification (ī-dent″ĭ-fĭ-kā′shŏn) [*identify*] **1.** The classification of an object within a category. **2.** Pattern matching, e.g., in diagnosis or laboratory analysis; speciation. **3.** The patterning of one's behavior and attitudes on the perceived qualities demonstrated by others. This plays a major role in personality development.

Particular identifications are listed under the first word. SEE: e.g., *dental identification; gender identification; radiofrequency identification.*

identifier (ī-dĕn′tĭ-fī″ĕr) A unique fact, finding, number, symbol, or word that specifies a person, place, or thing, esp. in a hospital.

identity (ī-dĕn′tĭ-tē) The characteristics by which an individual, organism, specimen, or finding is known and recognized.

    ego i. The sense of self that provides a unity of personality.

    gender i. SEE: *gender identity.*

    i. testing SEE: *paternity test.*

identity, disturbed personal Inability to distinguish between self and nonself. SEE: *Nursing Diagnoses Appendix.*

ideo- [Gr. *idea*, form] Prefix meaning *idea* or *mental image.*

ideology (ī″dē-ŏl′ŏ-jē) [″ + *logos*, word, reason] **1.** The study of ideas or thought. **2.** A system or schema of ideas; a philosophy.

-ides [Gr. *idēs*, a patronymic suffix] Suffix for naming zoological genera, e.g., *Ctenocephalides.*

idio- [Gr. *idios*, own, private] Prefix meaning *individual, distinct, self-produced,* or *unknown.*

idiocy [Gr. *idiotes*, ignorant person] Any severe mental deficiency apparent in early childhood. The cause, which occurs either in utero or in the first years after birth, may be genetic or traumatic or due to severe insults to the brain. SEE: *mental retardation.*

idioglossia (ĭd″ē-ō-glŏs′ē-ă) [″ + *glossa*, tongue] **1.** An inability to articulate properly, so that the sounds emitted are like those of an unknown language. **2.** A unique form of speech that a child with congenital word deafness may utter. It simulates fluent language but does not share its vocabulary, diction, or syntax.

idiogram (ĭd′ē-ō-grăm″) [″ + *gramma*, something written] The graphic representation of the karyotype, or chromosome complement of a cell.

idioisolysin (ĭd″ē-ō-ī-sŏl′ĭ-sĭn) [″ + *isos*, equal, + *lysis*, dissolution] A hemolysin active against the cells of an individual of the same species.

idiolysin (ĭd″ē-ŏl′ĭ-sĭn) [″ + *lysis*, dissolution] A lysin normally present in the blood.

idiopathic (ĭd″ē-ŏ-path′ik) [*idio-* + *-pathic*] Pert. to an illness whose cause is uncertain or undetermined. SYN: *agnogenic.*

idiopathic disease A disease for which no causative factor can be recognized.

idiopathic hypereosinophilic syndrome (hī″pĕ-rē″ŏ-sin″ŏ-fil′ik) [*hyper-* + *eosinophilic*] Multisystem injury and organ damage caused by excessive numbers of eosinophils in the body. The disease is one of the myelodysplastic disorders. Almost any organ can be affected, but most patients have bone marrow, cardiac, and central nervous system involvement.

TREATMENT: Corticosteroids are given. Additional therapies include immune-suppressing agents, (e.g., cyclosporine or interferon) or cancer chemotherapy.

idiopathic hyperkinetic heart syndrome Hyperactivity of the heart not due to a disease process. Its cause is unknown. In the past, this syndrome was referred to as neurocirculatory asthenia.

idiopathic polypoidal choroidal vasculopathy SEE: under *vasculopathy*.

idiosyncrasy (ĭd″ē-ō-sĭn′kră-sē) [″ + *syn*, together, + *krasis*, mixture] **1.** Special characteristics by which persons differ from each other. **2.** That which makes one react differently from others; a peculiar or individual reaction to an idea, action, drug, food, or some other substance through unusual susceptibility. **idiosyncratic** (-sĭn-krăt′ĭk), *adj.*

drug i. An unusual response to a drug. It can manifest as an accelerated, toxic, or inappropriate response to the usual therapeutic dose of a drug. SYN: *i. of effect*.

i. of effect Drug **i.**

idiotope (ĭd′ē-ō-tōp) A single antigenic determinant on a variable region of an antibody or T-cell receptor. A set of idiotopes make up the idiotype.

idiot-savant (ēd-jō′să-vănt) [Fr., learned idiot] An individual who is generally mentally retarded, but has the ability to do complicated tasks such as play instruments, recall dates, or accurately and rapidly perform mathematical calculations. SEE: *autism*.

idiotype (ĭd″ē-ō-tīp′) [″ + ″] In immunology, the set of antigenic determinants (idiotopes) on an antibody that make that antibody unique. It is determined by the amino acids of immunoglobulin light and heavy chains. **idiotypic** (-tīp′ĭk), *adj.*

idiovariation (ĭd″ē-ō-văr″ē-ā′shŭn) [″ + L. *variare*, to vary] A mutation that occurs without known cause.

idioventricular (ĭd″ē-ō-věn-trĭk′ū-lăr) [″ + L. *ventriculus*, little belly] Pert. to the cardiac ventricle alone when dissociated from the atrium. A heart rhythm that arises in the ventricle is an idioventricular rhythm.

IDM *infant of diabetic mother*.

-id reaction A generalized or wide-spread rash appearing at a location distant from the original skin irritation site. SEE: *-id*.

IDU *idoxuridine; injection drug use; 5-iodo-2′deoxyuridine*.

IE *infective endocarditis*.

IED *improvised explosive device*.

IEP *Individualized Education Program*.

IFG *Impaired fasting glucose*.

-ify [F. *-ifier*, fr. L. *-ificare*, to make] Suffix meaning to *make, become, be made*.

Ig *immunoglobulin*.

IgA *immunoglobulin A*.

IgA nephropathy *immunoglobulin A nephropathy*.

IgD *immunoglobulin D*.

IgE *immunoglobulin E*.

IgG *immunoglobulin G*.

IgM *immunoglobulin M*.

IH *infectious hepatitis*.

IHC *immunohistochemistry*.

IHS *Indian Health Service*.

IL (ī′ĕl′) *interleukin*.

ILD *interstitial lung disorder*.

ile *isoleucine*.

ileac (ĭl′ē-ăk) **1.** Pert. to the ileum. **2.** Pert. to the ileus.

ileal conduit SEE: under *conduit*.

ileal pouch anal anastomosis A reservoir constructed in the terminal ileum of patients who have undergone colectomy, designed to create fecal continence. The pouch may be sewn or stapled together in a J-, W-, or S-shape. The procedure is complicated by inflammation ("pouchitis") in about 50% or by stricture formation in about 10% of patients.

ileectomy (ĭl″ē-ĕk′tō-mē) [L. *ileum*, ileum, + Gr. *ektome*, excision] Excision of the ileum.

ileitis (ĭl″ē-īt′ĭs) [*ileum* + *-itis*] Inflammation of the ileum. The most common cause is Crohn disease. SEE: *Crohn disease; inflammatory bowel disease*.

SYMPTOMS: Patients may have pain in the right lower quadrant of the abdomen, often with diarrhea, nausea, vomiting, weight loss, and fevers. The stool may contain pus, blood, or mucus.

backwash i. Inflammation of the ileum when the contents of the colon flow backward into the last segment of the small intestine. It is a risk factor for colon cancer.

regional i. Crohn disease.

ileo-, ile- [L. *ile, ileum, ilium*, pl. *ilia*, area of the abdomen from the lowest rib to the pubes; flank, groin] Prefixes meaning *ileum*. SEE: *ilio-*.

ileocecal (ĭl′ē-ō-sē′kăl) [″ + *caecus*, blind] Relating to the ileum and cecum.

ileocecostomy (ĭl″ē-ō-sē-kŏs′tō-mē) [″ + ″ + Gr. *stoma*, opening] The surgical formation of an opening between the ileum and cecum.

ileocolic (ĭl″ē-ō-kŏl′ĭk) [″ + Gr. *kolon*, colon] Pert. to the ileum and colon.

ileocolitis (ĭl″ē-ō-kō-lī′tĭs) [″ + ″ + *itis*, inflammation] Inflammatory bowel disease.

ileocolonoscopy (ĭl″ē-ō-kō″lŏn-ŏs′kō-pē) [″ + ″] Endoscopic examination of the distal gastrointestinal tract, including the rectum, colon, and terminal ileum.

ileocolostomy (ĭl″ē-ō-kō-lŏs′tō-mē) [″ + ″ + *stoma*, mouth] An anastomosis between the ileum and the colon.

ileocolotomy (ĭl″ē-ō-kō-lŏt′ō-mē) [″ + ″ + *tome*, incision] An incision of the ileum and colon.

ileocystoplasty (ĭl″ē-ō-sĭst′ō-plăs″tē) [″ + Gr. *kystis*, bladder, + *plassein*, to form] The use of an isolated ileal segment to increase the size of the bladder.

ileocystostomy (ĭl″ē-ō-sĭs-tŏs′tō-mē) [″ + ″ + *stoma*, mouth] The use of an isolated segment of ileum to replace an absent, diseased, or obstructed ureter. The distal portion is implanted into the bladder.

ileoileostomy (ĭl″ē-ō-ĭl″ē-ŏs′tō-mē) [″ + *ileum*, small intestine, + Gr. *stoma*, mouth] The surgical formation of an opening between two parts of the ileum.

ileoproctostomy (ĭl″ē-ō-prŏk-tŏs′tō-mē) [″ + Gr. *proktos*, rectum, + *stoma*, mouth] The establishment of an opening between the ileum and rectum. SYN: *ileorectostomy*.

ileorectal (ĭl″ē-ō-rĕk′tăl) [″ + *rectum*, rectum] Concerning the ileum and rectum.

ileorectostomy (ĭl″ē-ō-rĕk-tŏs′tō-mē) [″ + ″ + Gr. *stoma*, mouth] Ileoproctostomy.

ileorrhaphy (ĭl″ē-or′ă-fē) [″ + Gr. *rhaphe*, seam, ridge] Surgical repair of the ileum.

ileosigmoidostomy (ĭl″ē-ō-sĭg″moyd-ŏs′tō-mē) [″ + Gr. *sigma*, letter S, + *eidos*, form, shape, + *stoma*, mouth] A surgical opening between the ileum and sigmoid flexure.

ileostomy (ĭl′ē-os′tŏ-mē) [*ileo-* + *-stomy*] A surgical passage through the abdominal wall, through which a segment of ileum is exteriorized. An end stoma or loop stoma may be created. Feces drain into a pouch worn on the abdomen. SEE: *Nursing Diagnoses Appendix.*

   urinary i. The surgical formation of an opening from the urinary tract to an isolated segment of the ileum, most often by implanting the ureters into an ileal segment fashioned into a continent ileal conduit (e.g., Kock pouch).

ileotomy (ĭl″ē-ŏt′ō-mē) [″ + Gr. *tome*, incision] An incision into the ileum.

ileum (ĭl′ē-ŭm, ĭl′ē-ă) *pl.* **ilea** [L. *ile, ileum, ilium*, pl. *ilia*, area of the abdomen from the lowest rib to the pubes; flank, groin] The third and last part of the small intestine, which ends at the ileocecal orifice, the opening to the large intestine. The jejunum grades imperceptibly into the ileum, but as a whole the ileum has a narrower diameter (an average of 2.5 cm) than the jejunum. The ileum has many lymphoid nodules (Peyer's patches), but only a few low circular folds (plicae circulares), and the end of the ileum has no villi. The ileum is approx. 4 m (12.5 ft) long. (ĭl-ē-ăl), *adj.* SEE: *abdominal regions* and *digestive system* for illus.

duplex i. A congenital doubling of the ileum.

ileus (ĭl′ē-ŭs) [L. *ileus*, colic fr Gr. *eileos*, a twisting] Loss of bowel motility, occasionally resulting in intestinal obstruction. It is characterized by loss of the forward flow of intestinal contents, often accompanied by cramps in the abdomen, increasing abdominal distention, obstipation or constipation, vomiting, electrolyte disturbances, and dehydration. SEE: *Nursing Diagnoses Appendix.* SYN: *adynamic i.; paralytic i.*

   Ileus usually occurs after abdominal surgery but may also occur in response to trauma, toxemia, or peritonitis or because of electrolyte deficiencies (esp. hypokalemia) or from use of drugs (e.g., anticholinergics and ganglionic blocking agents).

   PREVENTION: Prevention of ileus in postoperative patients can sometimes be achieved by encouraging early ambulation and gradually increasing activity. The patient should receive analgesics so that pain does not interfere with mobilization; opioids, however, slow gastrointestinal (GI) motility.

   PATIENT CARE: The patient is assessed for abdominal distention (abdominal girth is measured and the site marked to ensure the accuracy of future assessments). In the absence of evidence of mechanical obstruction, oral intake may begin even before bowel sounds return. (Bowel sounds are an indication of bowel motility, not absorption; even when bowel sounds are absent, the small bowel is capable of absorbing nutrients.) Ambulation is encouraged, and when nausea, vomiting and obstipation are present, a nasogastric (NG) or weighted nasointestinal (Miller-Abbott) tube is inserted as prescribed. Characteristics and quantity of drainage from the NG tube are documented. The tube is attached to continuous low suction for decompression, and the pH of drainage from an intestinal tube is measured to help determine its placement level. Oral hygiene and misting are provided to manage dryness and prevent cracking of the lips, sordes, and obstruction of the salivary glands. Lemon and glycerin preparations may etch tooth enamel and add to drying and are not used. Intravenous fluids are given, renal function is assessed, and fluid and electrolyte balance is monitored to maintain normal hydration. Vital signs also are monitored: a drop in blood pressure may indicate dehydration or shock. If colonoscopy or a rectal tube is used to aid decompression, the treatment is explained. Cholinergic agents may sometimes be prescribed. When ileus develops secondary to another illness (e.g., severe infection or electrolyte imbalance), the primary problem is treated.

adynamic i. Ileus.

dynamic i. Ileus caused by intestinal muscle spasm. SYN: *spastic i.*

gallstone i. An obstruction of the small bowel, occurring typically but not exclusively in elderly female patients and caused by the trapping of a large gallstone at or near the ileocecal valve. Most gallstones responsible for ileus are greater than 2.5 cm in diameter.

mechanical i. Ileus produced by a physical obstruction (e.g., hernia, adhesion, or tumor).

meconium i. Ileus due to impacted meconium in the intestines. It is usually associated with newborn children with cystic fibrosis. It is only rarely seen in newborns with other diseases that affect pancreatic exocrine secretion.

PATIENT CARE: All newborns are observed for passage of meconium. Meconium ileus occurs in about 10% of infants with cystic fibrosis and is characterized clinically by constipation, bilious vomiting, and progressive abdominal distention. Dehydration and electrolyte imbalance follow. The newborn with meconium ileus can be treated with gastrografin enemas, intravenous hydration, and general supportive care in mild presentations; when ileus is severe, laparotomy is required to relieve the obstruction. In such a case, the infant is prepared for surgery, and the parents are given psychological and emotional support.

paralytic ileus Ileus.

postoperative i. Ileus resulting from handling the bowel during surgery, anesthesia, electrolyte imbalance, or intraperitoneal infection.

spastic i. Dynamic **i.**

ilia (il′ē-ă) Pl. of ilium.

iliac (il′ē-ak″) [L. *iliacus,* pert. to the ilium] Pert. to the ilium.

-ilide A suffix used in pharmacology to designate any Vaughan-Williams class III antiarrhythmic drug that blocks potassium channels.

ilio- [L. *ile, ileum, ilium* , pl. *ilia,* area of the abdomen from the lowest rib to the pubes; flank, groin] Prefix meaning *ilium* or *flank.* SEE: *ileo-.*

iliococcygeal (il″ē-ō-kŏk-sĭj′ē-ăl) [″ + Gr. *kokkyx,* coccyx] Concerning the ilium and coccyx.

iliocostal (il″ē-ō-kŏs′tăl) [″ + *costa,* rib] Joining or concerning the ilium and ribs.

iliofemoral (il″ē-ō-fĕm′or-ăl) [″ + *femoralis,* pert. to femur] Pert. to the ilium and femur.

iliohypogastric (il″ē-ō-hī″pō-găs′trĭk) [″ + Gr. *hypo,* under, + *gaster,* stomach] Concerning the ilium and hypogastrium.

ilioinguinal (il″ē-ō-ĭn′gwĭ-năl) [″ + *inguinalis,* pert. to groin] Pert. to the groin and iliac regions.

iliolumbar (il″ē-ō-lŭm′bar) [″ + *lumbus,* loin] Pert. to the iliac and lumbar regions.

iliopagus (il″ē-ŏp′ă-gŭs) [″ + Gr. *pagos,* thing fixed] Twins joined in the iliac region.

iliopectineal (il″ē-ō-pĕk-tĭn′ē-ăl) [L. *ilium,* flank, + *pecten,* a comb] Concerning the ilium and pubic bone.

iliopelvic (il″ē-ō-pĕl′vĭk) [″ + *pelvis,* basin] Concerning the iliac area and pelvis.

iliopsoas (il″ē-ō-sō′ăs) [″ + Gr. *psoa,* loin] The compound iliacus and psoas magnus muscles.

iliosacral (il″ē-ō-sā′krăl) [″ + *sacralis,* pert. to the sacrum] Concerning the sacrum and ilium.

iliosciatic (il″ē-ō-sī-ăt′ĭk) [″ + *sciaticus,* pert. to the ischium] Concerning the ilium and ischium.

iliospinal (il″ē-ō-spī′năl) [″ + *spinalis,* pert. to the spine] Concerning the ilium and spinal column.

iliotibial band syndrome, iliotibial band friction syndrome (il″ē-ō-tĭb′ē-ăl) ABBR: ITB or IT band. An inflammatory overuse syndrome caused by mechanical friction between the iliotibial band and the lateral femoral condyle. It is commonly seen in distance runners and cyclists. Pain is manifested over the lateral aspect of the knee along the iliotibial band often with no visible swelling.

ilioxiphopagus (il″ē-ō-zī-fŏp′ă-gŭs) [″ + Gr. *xiphos,* sword, + *eidos,* form, shape, + *pagos,* thing fixed] Twins joined from the pelvis to the xiphoid process.

ilium (il′ē-ŭm) *pl.* **ilia** [L. *ile, ileum, ilium,* pl. *ilia,* area of the abdomen from the lowest rib to the pubes; flank, groin] **1.** One of the bones of each half of the pelvis. It is the superior and widest part and serves to support the flank. In the child, before fusion with adjacent pelvic bones, it is a separate bone. SYN: *os ilium.* **2.** The flank. SEE: *sacroiliac.*

ill (ĭl) [Old Norse *illr,* bad] Sick; not healthy; diseased.

illiterate Being unable to read and write or to use written language to interpret graphs, charts, tables, maps, symbols, and formulas.

illness (il′nĭs) **1.** Sickness; disease. **2.** An ailment.

catabolic i. Rapid weight loss with loss of body fat and muscle mass that frequently accompanies short-term, self-limiting conditions such as infection or injury. This condition may be associated with diabetic ketoacidosis, multiple organ system failure, and chemotherapy or radiation therapy for cancer.

TREATMENT: Inflammation should

be reduced and appropriate nutrients provided.

catastrophic i. An unusually prolonged or complex illness, esp. one that causes severe organ dysfunction or threatens life. Catastrophic illnesses often make exceptional demands on patients, caregivers, families, and health care resources.

decompression i. Aeroembolism due to an excessively rapid ascent to the surface by a deep-sea diver. SYN: *bends; caisson disease.* SEE: *aeroembolism.*

TREATMENT: Affected patients should be transported to specialized treatment centers where recompression or hyperbaric chambers are available.

folk i. A disease or condition found only in specific societies, ethnic groups, or cultures. Often the culture has causal explanations for these illnesses, as well as preventive and treatment measures. Well-known examples are present in the Hispanic American culture (e.g., *empacho, caida de mollera, mal de ojo, susto*). These are diagnosed and treated by folk healers called *curanderos.* Some other examples of folk illnesses include *amok* and *piblokto,* though numerous other examples exist within multiple cultures. SEE: *amok; piblokto.*

functional i. Functional disease.

heat i. A general term used to describe the harmful effects on the human body of being exposed to high temperature and/or humidity. SEE: table; *heat cramp; heat* **exhaustion** for table; *heatstroke; syncope.*

influenza-like i. ABBR: ILI. Any disease of the respiratory tract that causes cough, fever, malaise, headache, sore throat, and fatigue. ILI can be caused by rhinoviruses, respiratory syncytial virus, coronaviruses, adenoviruses, rickettsia, and other infectious microorganisms.

mass psychogenic i. Mass sociogenic i.

mass sociogenic i. ABBR: MSI. An unexplained, self-limiting illness characterized by nonspecific symptoms among people in a social setting such as a school, workplace, church, or military group. The onset is usually rapid and may occur after an unusual or peculiar odor is detected. Symptoms may include dizziness, weakness, headache, abdominal pain, rash, itching, blurred vision, nausea and vomiting, and fainting. There are no laboratory studies to confirm an etiologic agent. Resolution of the mass illness may occur when those affected are reassured that it is not due to a toxic substance or disease. SYN: *mass psychogenic i.*

mental i. Any disorder that affects mood or behavior.

occupational i. Any acute or chronic disorder associated with or caused by an individual's occupation. SEE: table; *chronic lead poisoning.*

psychosomatic i. SEE: *somatoform disorder.*

terminal i. A final, fatal illness.

PATIENT CARE: The health care professional supports the patient and family by anticipating their loss and grief and helps the patient to deal with fear, pain and suffering, hopelessness, dependency, disability, loss of self-esteem, and loss of pleasure. Hospice care is provided if desired and available. The patient receives caring comfort and help in adjusting to decreased quality of life to ensure that death occurs with dignity.

illumination (il-oo″-mĭ-nā′shŏn) [L. *illuminare,* to light up] The lighting up of a part for examination or of an object under a microscope.

axial i. Light transmitted along the axis of a microscope. SYN: *central i.*

central i. Axial **i.**

dark-field i. The illumination of an object under a microscope in which the central or axial light rays are stopped and the object is illuminated by light rays coming from the sides, which causes the object to appear light against a dark background. This technique is used to observe extremely small objects such as spirochetes or colloid particles.

direct i. The illumination of an object under a microscope by directing light rays upon its upper surface.

fiber i. The transmission of light to an object through fiber-optic cables.

focal i. Concentration of light on an object by a mirror or a system of lenses.

oblique i. Illumination of an object from one side.

transmitted light i. Illumination in which the light is directed through the object. Light may come directly from a light source or be reflected by a mirror.

illusion (il-oo′zhŏn) [L. *illusio,* jeering, mockery] An inaccurate perception; a misinterpretation of sensory impressions, as opposed to a hallucination, which is a perception formed without an external stimulus. Vague stimuli are conducive to the production of illusions. If an illusion becomes fixed, it is said to be a delusion. SEE: *delusion; hallucination.*

clustering i. The mistaken belief that a pattern is present in a random cluster of data. For example, if three out of the four patients with chest pain admitted to a hospital in February had red hair, a naive observer might incorrectly conclude that having red hair increases the likelihood of having a heart attack during the winter.

optical i. A visual impression that is inaccurately perceived.

illusional Pert. to, or of the nature of, an illusion.

illusory (i-loo′sŏ-rē) [L. *illusorius,* mock-

Examination Findings of Heat Illnesses

Evaluation Finding	Heat Cramps	Heat Syncope	Heat Exhaustion	Heat Stroke
Hydration Status		Dehydrated	Dehydrated	Dehydrated
Core Temperature*	Within normal limits**	Within normal limits	102°–104°F (38.9°–40°C)	Greater than 104°F (40°C)
Skin Color and Temperature	Within normal limits	Within normal limits	Cool/clammy Pale	Hot Red
Pulse	Within normal limits	Decreased	Rapid and weak	Increased
Blood Pressure	Within normal limits	A sudden, imperceptible drop in blood pressure, which rapidly returns to normal	Low	High
Respiration	Within normal limits	Within normal limits	Hyperventilation	Rapid hyperventilation
Mental State	Within normal limits Possible fatigue	Fatigue Dizziness Fainting	Dizziness Fatigue Slight confusion	Dizziness Drowsiness Confusion/ disorientation Emotional instability Violent Behavior Weakness
Neuromuscular Changes	Cramping in one or more muscles		Muscle cramps	Decerebrate posture
Gastrointestinal and Urinary Changes			Weakness Intestinal Cramping Nausea Vomiting Diarrhea Decreased Urinary output	Nausea Vomiting Diarrhea
Central Nervous System			Syncope Headache	Headache Unconsciousness Seizures Coma Dilated pupils Loss of appetite (anorexia) Chills
Other Findings	Thirst	"Tunnel vision" may be reported	Thirst	

SOURCE: Starkey, C, Brown, S, and Ryan, J: Examination of Orthopedic and Athletic Injuries, ed 3, FA Davis, Philadelphia, 2010.
*As determined by the rectal temperature
** Within normal limits for an exercising athlete

Representative Occupational Illnesses

Condition	Exposed Workers
Anemia	Lead (battery reclaimers, shipyard workers)
Asbestosis	Shipyard workers and others exposed to asbestos fibers
Asthma	Meat wrappers, woodworkers, those exposed to platinum, nickel, solder, ammonia, cotton dust, formaldehyde, pesticides
Byssinosis	Cotton textile workers
Cancer	People who work with radioactive materials (health care, lab workers), x-ray workers (industrial and health care), miners
Carpal tunnel syndrome	Typists, computer programmers, and other people who work with their hands
Contact dermatitis	Health care workers using latex gloves, and florists
Decompression sickness	Divers, marine salvage workers
Hearing impairment	People who work in noisy environments without adequate ear protection
Leptospirosis	Veterinarians
Pneumoconiosis	Coal miners
Pneumonitis	Wood workers (esp. red cedar), mushroom growers, cheese handlers, and farmers
Silicosis	Miners, foundry workers
Skin granulomas	Beryllium workers (e.g., in auto or aircraft industries)
Tennis or golfer's elbow	Carpenters, plumbers, and athletes
Vibration syndrome, including Raynaud's phenomenon	Truck drivers, hand-vibrating drill operators, jackhammer workers

ing, ironic] Pert. to or causing an illusion; misleading; deceptive.

IM *internal* **medicine;** *intramuscular(ly).*

IMA *internal mammary* **artery.**

ima (ī′mă) [L.] Lowest.

image (im′ij) [Fr. *image* fr. L. *imago*, copy, likeness] **1.** A mental picture representing a real object. **2.** A more or less accurate likeness of a thing or person. **3.** A picture of an object as produced by a lens or mirror. **4.** In radiology, a representation of structures within the body as a result of examination by various physical phenomena (e.g., x-rays, gamma rays, sound, or radio).

body i. 1. The subjective image or picture people have of their physical appearance based on their own observations and the reaction of others. **2.** The conscious and unconscious perception of one's body at any particular time.

direct i. An image produced from radiation without secondary image receptors. SYN: *virtual i.*

double i. A perceived image that occurs in strabismus when the visual axes of the eyes are not directed toward the same object. SYN: *false i.* SEE: *diplopia.*

false i. Double **i.**

inverted i. An image that is turned upside down.

latent i. 1. An unprocessed image physically present within an image receptor but not yet visible. **2.** In radiology, the image within the emulsion of an exposed radiograph that is invisible because it has not been developed.

mirror i. An image of an object in which right and left are reversed. The term is also used to indicate the similarity of chemical substances or persons with quite similar personalities and looks (e.g., identical twins).

Purkinje-Sanson i.s SEE: under *Purkinje, Johannes E. von.*

radiographic i. Radiograph.

real i. The image formed by convergence of rays of light from an object.

virtual i. Direct **i.**

image intensifier A special vacuum tube used during fluoroscopic imaging that increases the brightness of an image. This increased brightness is controlled by image minification and electron acceleration. The minified image can be viewed directly, coupled with a television camera, or imaged by serial or digital radiography. The quality of the image is better than that of an unintensified fluoroscopic image.

imagery (im′ăj-rē) [L. *imago*, a copy, likeness] Imagination; the calling up of events or mental pictures. Mental imagery may be of various types.

active i. The direction of attention toward desired feelings, outcomes, or thoughts and away from unpleasant or unwanted feelings or thoughts. Also known as guided imagery or rehearsal imagery. SYN: *evocative i.; guided i.; rehearsal i.*

auditory i. A mental image of sounds that can be recalled, as thunder or wind.

guided i. Active **i.**

rehearsal i. Active **i.**

smell i. A mental concept of odor previously experienced.

tactile i. A mental image of the way an object feels.

taste i. A mental concept of taste sensations previously experienced.

visual i. A mental concept of an object seen previously. SEE: *afterimage.*

imagination [L. *imago,* likeness] The formation of mental images of things, persons, or situations that are wholly or partially different from those previously known or experienced.

imaging (im′ă-jing) The production of a picture, image, or shadow that represents the object being investigated. In diagnostic medicine the classic technique for imaging is radiographic or x-ray examination. Techniques using computer-generated images produced by x-ray, ultrasound, or magnetic resonance are also available.

black blood magnetic resonance i. ABBR: BB-MR. Imaging of arterial walls with magnetic resonance for evidence of atherosclerosis. Blood flow normally gives off a bright signal during magnetic resonance imaging but can be made to appear dark to distinguish it from the walls of the surrounding blood vessels. This enhancement in magnetic resonance imaging can be used noninvasively to show where arteries are obstructed and to determine the components of the plaque in those arteries.

cerebral blood pool i. Radionuclide brain imaging performed after a tracer molecule is injected angiographically into a blood vessel that supplies the brain and the tracer allowed to equilibrate (achieve a steady state) in the brain's arteries and veins.

diffusion tensor i. ABBR: DTI. An imaging technique in magnetic resonance imaging to identify the unique directional movement of molecules, esp. water molecules, along muscle and neural tracts. One of its uses is to identify the linkages and structures of white matter tracts in the brain.

diffusion weighted i. In magnetic resonance imaging, the use of changes in the movement of water through tissues as a contrast medium. Diffusion weighted imaging has been used in the diagnosis of strokes and other neurological diseases as well as abdominal and musculoskeletal injuries and diseases.

digital i. The capture and production of an image of an object, either on film or on a computerized display, where it can be reformatted and analyzed. Commonly used imaging modalities include x-rays, ultrasound, and magnetic resonance.

digital subtraction i. In radiology, the use of electronic means to subtract portions of the radiographic image in order to better visualize the object.

duplex i. A form of ultrasonography that incorporates both gray-scale imaging for the architecture of the tissue and a color Doppler signal for flow or movement within the tissue.

echo planar i. ABBR: EPI. A fast magnetic resonance imaging technique in which an image is acquired after a single radiofrequency excitation.

electrical source i. ABBR: ESI. A means of mapping the electrical activity of organs such as the brain or heart to diagnose or treat diseases such as seizures or dysrhythmias. ESI relies on the collection via external sensors of the electrical activity generated by multiple tissue sites within an organ, and the mathematical manipulation of that data to localize areas where patterns of electrical conduction are blocked or excessively active.

functional magnetic resonance h. ABBR: fMRI. The identification of metabolic activities during MRI studies of the brain. During an fMRI, magnetic resonance images of the brain are made while the subject performs specific tasks, e.g. using certain fingers or saying particular words. The study helps identify changes in blood flow during these activities, as well as changes in brain chemistry or the movement of water molecules in neural tissues. It is used to study brain injuries caused by cancer, multiple sclerosis, strokes, and trauma.

fusion i. Any combination of radiological technologies for generating images of body structures. Fusion imaging includes positron emission tomography-computed tomographic (PET-CT) scanning, CT–magnetic resonance fusion imaging, and single photon emissions computed tomographic (SPECT) fusion imaging.

gated blood pool i. Radioisotopic imaging of the heart, esp. of the muscular contraction of its walls and of its ejection fraction. Red blood cells are withdrawn and labeled with an isotope of technetium. A sequence of images is taken immediately after the radiolabeled blood is reinjected into a peripheral vein and allowed to circulate. The images are timed to begin with each ventricular depolarization (with each R wave of the electrocardiogram). Normally the ejection of blood from the heart occurs at the same time and with the same strength from all muscle segments. Areas of the heart affected by infarction may not move normally (they may be *akinetic* or *hypokinetic*) or they may move paradoxically (they may be *dyskinetic,* as when a ventricular aneurysm is present). SYN: *gated blood pool study*.

magnetic resonance i. ABBR: MRI. Imaging that uses the characteristic behavior of protons when placed in powerful magnetic fields to make images of tissues and organs. Certain atomic nuclei with an odd number of neutrons, protons, or both are subjected to a radiofrequency pulse, causing them to absorb and release energy. The resulting current passes through a radiofrequency receiver and is then transformed into an image. This technique is valuable in providing soft-tissue images of the central nervous and musculoskeletal systems. Imaging techniques allow visualization of the vascular system without the use of contrast agents. Agents such as gadolinium are available for contrast enhancement but must be used with caution in patients with renal insufficiency.

⚠️ Magnetic resonance imaging is contraindicated in patients with cardiac pacemakers or ferromagnetic aneurysmal clips in place. Metal may become damaged during testing; therefore, health care providers must establish whether the patient has magnetizable metal anywhere on or in the body. Patients should not wear metal objects, e.g., jewelry, hair ornaments, or watches. Patients who have had surgical procedures after which magnetizable metal clips, pins, or other hardware remain in the body should not have this imaging. Some patients with tattoos or permanent cosmetics should also avoid MRI because of the risk of burns.

PATIENT CARE: During imaging, the patient lies on a flat surface that is moved inside a tube encompassed by a magnet (the bore of the gantry). The patient must lie as still as possible. No discomfort occurs as a result of the MRI. Sounds heard during the imaging come from the pulsing of the magnetic field as it scans the body. Confinement during the 30 to 90 min required for scanning may frighten the patient, but the patient can talk to staff by microphone. Relaxation techniques may help claustrophobic patients endure MRI. Comfort measures and analgesics (as necessary and prescribed) should be provided before beginning the scan to offset the discomfort related to prolonged positioning in the scanner. Claustrophobic patients may require a mild sedative, or be better managed in an open MRI scanner which is less confining, however open MRI devices, which use weaker magnetic fields than closed systems may take longer to obtain images and may reveal less detail. Right angle eyeglasses, which divert the patient's gaze outside the bore of the MRI gantry, provide a helpful diversion for some patients. Most patients, however, are able to tolerate the close confinement of the gantry. A nurse or MRI technologist should maintain verbal contact with the patient throughout the procedure. An IV line with no metal components should be in place if the patient's condition is unstable. SEE: illus.; *brain* for illus.; *positron emission tomography*.

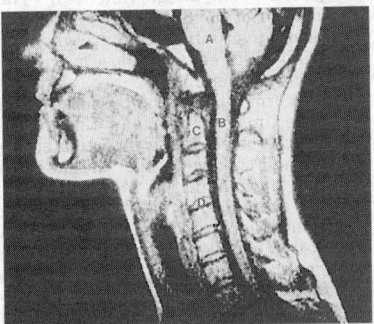

MAGNETIC RESONANCE IMAGING

MRI of the cervical spine, sagittal view.

myocardial perfusion i. ABBR: MPI. The use of radioactive isotopes, such as ^{201}Tl or ^{99}mTc sestamibi, to gauge the blood supply and viability of the regions or walls of the heart. MPI is frequently used to assess patients with coronary artery disease, often in conjunction with exercise tolerance tests. A patient with a coronary artery that is almost totally blocked may take up only a small quantity of radioisotope during exercise but much more of the tracer after several hours of rest. By contrast, heart muscle that is fed by a completely blocked artery will take up no radioisotope either during or after exercise.

near-infrared fluorescence i. ABBR: NIRI. Imaging of tissues within the body after they are bound by fluorescent molecules and stimulated with light in the 700/900 nm wavelength range. NIRI is used to provide images of solid cancers, bone and joint inflammation, and blood flow to tissues.

nuclear magnetic resonance i. ABBR: NMRI. SEE: *magnetic resonance i.*

perfusion weighted i. In radioisotopic imaging, the use of differences in blood flow through organs as a means of diagnosing diseases such as strokes or malignancies.

physiological i. Imaging of the functions of an organ, i.e., of its blood flow, electrical activity, metabolism, oxygen uptake, or working receptors.

polarized helium imaging A means

of assessing asthma in which a magnetic resonance image is made of the lungs after a patient inhales polarized helium gas. Asthmatics have ventilation defects in the lungs that are not present in nonasthmatics.

radionuclide reflux i. Imaging to determine whether an infant has gastroesophageal reflux. Radioactively labeled milk is given to the child orally, and the progress of the milk through the upper gastrointestinal tract (and in reflux, into the lungs) is monitored. The scan is typically used if an infant has had more than one episode of aspiration pneumonia.

retinal vascular i. Measurement of the caliber of the blood vessels in the retina as risk markers for coronary and cerebrovascular disease. Narrowing of retinal arterioles has been correlated with an increased risk of diabetes mellitus and coronary artery disease. Dilation of retinal venules has been associated with an increased risk of stroke.

volumetric brain i. Measurement of the size of specific structures within the brain with magnetic resonance imaging or other devices. It is used to diagnose and identify brain diseases noninvasively. Atrophy of certain anterior brain structures is found in patients with frontotemporal dementia. In schizophrenia, the hippocampus and amygdala are reduced. Other findings have been demonstrated in depression, fragile X syndrome, Rett disease, Tourette syndrome, and other neurological disorders. SYN: *volumetric neuroimaging.*

imago (ĭ-mā′gō) [L., likeness] **1.** An image or shadow. **2.** A memory, esp. of a loved one, developed during childhood that has become clouded by idealism and imagination. **3.** The adult, sexually mature form of an insect.

imbalance (im-bal′ăns) [*'in-* + L. *bilanx,* pair of scales] Lack of balance; the state of inequality in power between opposing forces.

autonomic i. An imbalance between sympathetic and parasympathetic divisions of the autonomic nervous system, esp. as pertains to vasomotor reactions.

eye muscle i. A pathological condition of the extraocular muscles of one or both eyes. It causes the eyes to be misaligned in one or more axes. SEE: *crossed eye; esophoria; exophoria; squint; strabismus.*

occupational i. A configuration of activities within a person's lifestyle that does not meet physiological, psychological, or social needs in a manner that is healthful and satisfactory to the individual.

sympathetic i. Vagotonia.

vasomotor i. Excessive vasoconstriction or vasodilation.

imbed (ĭm-bĕd′) [L. *in,* in, (put) into, + AS. *bedd,* bed] In histology, to surround with a firm substance, such as paraffin, preparatory to cutting sections. SEE: *embedding.*

imbibition (ĭm″bĭ-bĭsh′ŭn) [″ + *bibere,* to drink] The absorption of fluid by a solid body or gel.

imbricated, imbrication (ĭm′brĭ-kāt-ĕd, ĭm″brĭ-kā′shŭn) [L. *imbricare,* to tile] **1.** Overlapping, as tiles. **2.** The overlapping of aponeurotic layers in abdominal surgery.

Imerslund syndrome [Olga Imerslund, Norwegian pediatrician, 1907–1987] A rare, autosomal recessive form of vitamin B12 deficiency, also known as *juvenile-type pernicious anemia.*

imidazole (ĭm-ĭd-ăz′ōl) An organic compound, $C_3H_4N_2$, characterized structurally by the presence of the heterocyclic ring that occurs in histidine and histamine.

imide (ĭm′īd) A compound with the bivalent atom group (—NH).

IMIG *intramuscular immune globulin.*

immature (ĭm″mă-tūr′) [L. *in-,* not, + *maturus,* ripe] Not fully developed or ripened.

immature platelet Reticulated platelet.

immature platelet fraction SEE: under *fraction.*

immediate [″ + *mediare,* to be in middle] Direct; without intervening steps.

immediately dangerous to life and health air concentration value ABBR: IDLH. The presence in the atmosphere of any inhalable agent capable of causing severe injury or death after a brief exposure to it. In operational terms, the presence in any airborne contaminant that people should avoid unless they have access to respiratory protection.

immersion (i-měr′zhŏn, shŏn) [L. *immersio,* a dip into] **1.** Placing a body under water or other fluid. **2.** In microscopy, the act of immersing the objective (then called an immersion lens) in water or oil, preventing total reflection of rays falling obliquely upon peripheral portions of the objective.

homogeneous i. Immersion in which the stratum of air between objective and cover glass is replaced by a medium that deflects as little as possible the rays of light passing through the cover glass.

ice i. A technique for administering therapeutic cold treatments to the distal extremities (e.g., the ankle or hand) with a mixture of water and crushed, flaked, or cubed ice with a temperature range of 50° to 60°F (10°–15°C). The liquid medium allows for equal cooling of irregularly shaped body parts. To reduce the amount of discomfort initially experienced during this treatment, the fingers or toes can be covered with an insulating material.

Because ice immersion treatments

place the body part in a position that does not promote venous return, the treated limb may swell. It should be elevated and a compression wrap applied following the treatment to encourage venous and lymphatic drainage. SYN: *ice slush*. SEE: *cryotherapy*.

⚠ This treatment should not be used in patients with cold intolerance or in those for whom cold application is contraindicated.

immiscible (ĭ-mĭs′ĭ-bl) [L. *in-*, not, + *miscere*, to mix] Pert. to that which cannot be mixed, as oil and water.

immobilization (ĭ-mō″bĭ-lĭ-zā′shŭn) [″ + *mobilis*, movable] **1.** The making of a part or limb immovable. **2.** Restricting a patient to a bed or chair.

PATIENT CARE: The patient is assessed for development of any of the complications of immobilization, such as hypercalcemia, atelectasis, pneumonia, deep vein thrombosis (DVT), urinary tract infections, constipation, pressure ulcers, and contracture formation. Lung and heart sounds are auscultated, fluid balance and nutritional and dietary fiber intake monitored, and bowel and bladder function are assessed. Long-term immobilization will result in the atrophy of skeletal muscle and deconditioning.

Techniques to prevent complications include having the patient breathe deeply and cough every 2 hr, using incentive spirometry if prescribed; changing position completely every 2 hr, with lesser position changes in between; wearing antithromboembolic devices; doing quadriceps setting, gluteal muscle setting, and range-of-motion exercises regularly. Maintenance of hygiene and adequate nutrition and fluid intake may also be helpful. A bowel program is initiated to prevent constipation (fluid, fiber, stool softeners, bulk laxatives). Skin care is provided to keep the skin clean, dry, well lubricated, and intact, and low-pressure foam or flotation pads or mattresses are applied as needed. Footboards or right-angle foam heel and ankle supports are employed to prevent foot drop and prevent heel breakdown. Low-molecular-weight heparin may be prescribed to prevent DVT. Whenever possible, the patient is taught to use a trapeze (on a Balkan frame) to move about in bed. The health care professional should ensure that blood supply to the extremities is not restricted by any appliance or by tight bedcovers. Limbs should be evaluated regularly for distal neurovascular status, noting changes in the size, color, temperature, or pain of the limbs. Physical and occupational therapy as well as social and

psychological support may be used to restore independence or aid the adjustment to the immobilization. Family members are taught to provide care, often with the assistance of home-health aides. Assisted living or other long-term care facilities may be needed after hospital discharge for those immobilized patients who cannot return home.

immortality (ĭm″or-ăl′ĭ-tē) The ability of some cells, particularly cancer cells, to reproduce indefinitely. Normal human cells have a finite life expectancy. They may divide for a few dozen generations, but eventually stop reproducing and die.

immotile cilia syndrome (ĭ-mōt′ĭl, -mō′tīl″) An autosomal recessive condition characterized by severely impaired movement of the cilia or flagella of respiratory tract epithelial cells, sperm cells, and others. Affected cells lack the protein dynein, which is essential for effective ciliary motion. SYN: *primary ciliary dyskinesia*. SEE: *dynein; Kartagener's syndrome*.

immune (i-mūn′) [L. *immunis*, exempt, free from, safe] Protected from or resistant to a disease or infection by a pathogenic organism as a result of the development of antibodies or cell-mediated immunity.

immune globulin SEE: under *globulin*.

immune-mediated inflammatory reaction The process by which the immune system destroys, dilutes, or walls off injurious agents and injured tissue. Small blood vessels dilate and become permeable. This increases blood flow and permits exudation of plasma and leukocytes. The cells arriving from the blood include monocytes, neutrophils, basophils, and lymphocytes; those of local origin include endothelial cells, mast cells, tissue fibroblasts, and macrophages. Other mediators of inflammation include cytokines, interleukins, and neuropathies.

immune reaction 1. A demonstrated antigenic response to a specific antibody. **2.** The specific reaction of host cells to antigenic stimulation. SEE: *immune response*.

immune reconstitution The restoration of normal or improved immune function in a person with congenital or acquired immunodeficiency syndrome. Bone marrow transplantation or drug therapies may be used, depending on the underlying cause of the immune failure.

immune system The lymphatic tissues, organs, and physiological processes that identify an antigen as abnormal or foreign and prevent it from harming the body. The body is protected from pathogen invasion by the skin, mucosa, and normal flora of the gastrointestinal tract and skin; chemicals contained in tears; the sebaceous glands; gastric acid; and pancreatic enzymes. The bone marrow produces white blood cells (WBCs), the body's primary internal defense. Lymphoid tissues, including the thymus gland, spleen, and lymph nodes, influence the growth, maturation, and activation of WBCs; lymphoid tissue in the gastrointestinal and respiratory tracts and mucous membranes contain WBCs for site-specific protection. Finally, physiologically active protein mediators, called cytokines, help regulate the growth and function of immunologically active cells.

Effects of stress: Investigations of the influence of stress on susceptibility to disease have shown that in some but not all people who suffered stressful events, the possibility of onset of illness increased. A decrease in the usual number of pleasant events was a stronger predictor of susceptibility to illness than was an increase in unpleasant ones. Negative experiences included criticism, frustration, irritating encounters with fellow workers, deadlines, heavy workload, and burdensome or unpleasant chores or errands. Even though the concept that stress lowers resistance to disease appears to apply only to some people, the explanation of this mechanism has not been established.

immunifacient (ĭ-mū″nĭ-fā′shĕnt) [″ + *facere,* to make] Making immune.

immunity (im-ū′nĭt-ē) [L. *immunitas,* exemption] Protection from diseases, esp. from infectious diseases. SEE: *immune response; immune system; immunization; vaccine.*

   acquired i. Immunity owing to exposure to an antigen or to the passive injection of immunoglobulins.

   active i. Immunity resulting from the development within the body of antibodies or sensitized T lymphocytes that neutralize or destroy the infective agent. This may result from the immune response to an invading organism or from inoculation with a vaccine containing a foreign antigen. SEE: *immune response; vaccination.*

   B-cell–mediated i. Humoral **i.**

   cell-mediated i. ABBR: CMI. The regulatory and cytotoxic activities of T cells during the specific immune response. This process requires about 36 hr to reach its full effect. SYN: *T-cell–mediated i.* SEE: illus.; *humoral immunity.*

   Unlike B cells, T cells cannot recognize foreign antigens on their own. Foreign antigens are recognized by antigen-presenting cells (APCs) such as macrophages, which engulf them and display part of the antigens on the APC's surface next to a histocompatibility or "self-" antigen (macrophage processing). The presence of these two markers, plus the cytokine interleukin-1 (IL-1) secreted by the APCs activates CD4 helper T cells (T_H cells), which regulate the activities of other cells involved in the immune response.

   CMI includes direct lysis of target cells by cytotoxic T cells, creation of memory cells that trigger a rapid response when a foreign antigen is encountered for the second time, and delayed hypersensitivity to tissue and organ transplants. T cells also stimulate the activity of macrophages, B cells, and natural killer cells. These functions are controlled largely by the secretion of lymphokines such as the interleukins, interferons, and colony-stimulating factors. Lymphokines facilitate communication and proliferation of the cells in the immune system.

   cellular i. T-cell–mediated immune functions requiring cell interactions, e.g., graft rejection or destruction of infected cells.

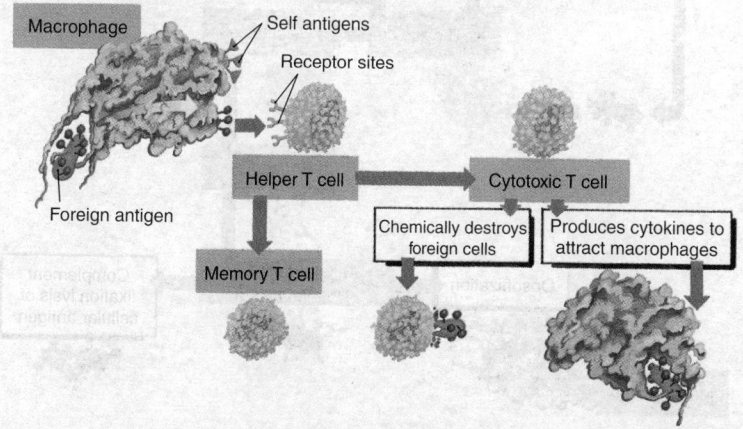

CELL-MEDIATED IMMUNITY

cocoon i. Vaccination of all the household contacts of an infant against those infectious diseases that he or she might contract. It is designed to protect disease-naive newborns from potentially fatal contagious illnesses. SYN: *cocoon strategy*.

community i. Herd **i.**

congenital i. Immunity present at birth. It may be natural or acquired, the latter depending on antibodies received from the mother's blood.

herd i. The ability of a community to resist epidemic disease. Herd immunity may develop naturally in a society as a result of widespread exposure to disease, or it may be stimulated artificially by mass vaccination programs.

PATIENT CARE: Members of every region or community should be alerted to local or widespread communicable diseases for which vaccination is available. Offering public immunization sessions through local health departments, schools, colleges and places of business, as well as public and private health care agencies will increase the percentage of persons who are vaccinated and will decrease risk of communicable disease epidemics. SYN: *community **i.***

humoral i. The protective activities of antibodies against infection or reinfection by common organisms, e.g., streptococci and staphylococci. B lymphocytes with receptors to a specific antigen react when they encounter that antigen by producing plasma cells (which produce antigen-specific antibodies) and memory cells (which enable the body to produce these antibodies quickly in the event that the same antigen appears later). B-cell differentiation also is stimulated by interleukin-2 (IL-2) secreted by CD4+ T cells and foreign antigens processed by macrophages.

Antibodies produced by plasma B cells, found mainly in the blood, spleen, and lymph nodes, neutralize or destroy antigens in several ways. They kill organisms by activating the complement system; neutralize viruses and toxins released by bacteria; coat the antigen (opsonization) or form an antigen-antibody complex to stimulate phagocytosis; promote antigen clumping (agglutination); and prevent the antigen from adhering to host cells. SYN: *B-cell–mediated **i.*** SEE: illus.; *cell-mediated **i.**; immunoglobulin*.

innate i. Those immune defenses against infection and cancer that are not determined by the specific responses of B or T lymphocytes. Innate immunity is not pathogen-specific and does not create immunological memory. It includes the actions of adhesion molecules; cellular chemotaxis; the secretion of cytokines; cytotoxicity; the activities of dendritic and natural killer cells; inflammation; and phagocytosis. SYN: *innate immune system*.

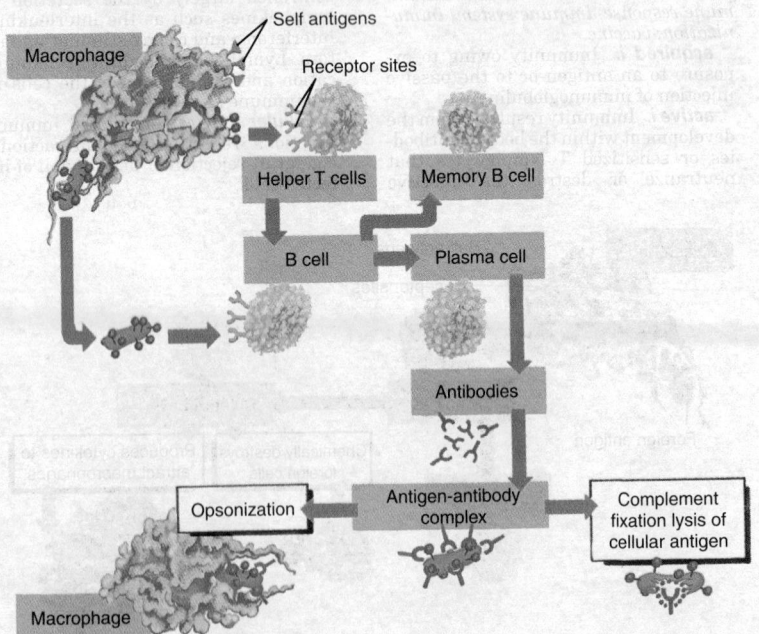

HUMORAL IMMUNITY

local i. Immunity limited to a given area or tissue of the body.

natural i. Immunity that is genetically determined in specific species, populations, or families. Some pathogens cannot infect certain species because the cells do not provide suitable environments. For example, the measles virus cannot reproduce in canine cells and therefore dogs have natural immunity to measles.

passive i. Immunity acquired by the introduction of preformed antibodies into an unprotected individual. This can occur through intravenous infusion of immune globulin or from antibodies that pass from the mother to the fetus through the placenta in utero. Newborns also may acquire immunity through breastfeeding.

T-cell–mediated i. Cell-mediated **i.**

waning i. The progressive loss of protective antibodies against an antigen or disease that occurs with the passage of time. It is a crucial factor in vaccination. Booster doses of a vaccine are given when the immune response to an antigen drops below protective levels.

immunization (im″yŭ-nĭ-zā′shŏn) [L. *immunitas,* immunity] The protection of individuals or groups from specific diseases by vaccination or the injection of immune globulins. SEE: *vaccination; vaccine* for table.

catch-up i. Catch-up **vaccination**.

immunization requirement Any of the compulsory vaccinations against those contagious diseases that are considered a threat to public health, established as a prerequisite for employment, enrollment in school, or travel abroad.

immunization status, readiness for enhanced A pattern of conforming to local, national, and/or international standards of immunization to prevent infectious disease(s) that is sufficient to protect a person, family, or community and can be strengthened. SEE: *Nursing Diagnoses Appendix.*

immuno- [L. *immunis,* exempt, free from] Prefix meaning *immune, immunity.*

immunoablation (ĭm-ū″-nō-ă-blā′shŭn) The systematic destruction of a patient's immune competence. Immunoablation is used to prepare patients for organ transplantation and to treat refractory autoimmune diseases, esp. when followed by immunoreconstruction (usually with autologous stem cell transplantation).

PATIENT CARE: Patients who have undergone immunoablation may be easily infected by caregivers. Careful handwashing and infection control techniques (such as "reverse isolation") should be used to limit exposing these patients to harmful pathogens.

immunoabsorbent, immunoabsorbant
(im″yŭ-nō-ăb-sor′bĕnt, im-ū″nō-) [*immuno-* + *absorbent*] Immunosorbent.

immunoabsorption (im″yŭ-nō-ăb-sorp′shŏn, i-mū″) Immunoadsorption.

immunoadhesin (ĭm″ū-nō-ăd-hē′sĭn) [L. *immunis,* safe, + *adhaerēre,* to stick to] A genetically engineered, antibody-like protein that fuses the Fc region of an immunoglobulin and the ligand-binding region of a receptor or adhesion molecule. Immunoadhesins can be used to direct the immune-responsive effect of cytokines to tumor cells and to stimulate the destruction of such cells.

immunoadsorbent (im″yŭ-nō-ad-sor′bĕnt, im-ū″nō-) [*immuno-* + *adsorbent*] Immunosorbent.

immunoadsorption (im″yŭ-nō-ad-sorp′shŏn, i-mū″) [*immuno-* + *adsorption*] The selective removal of a desired compound from a solution or a mixture, using an antibody or antigen that has been bound to a large, insoluble molecule. It is an immunological means of obtaining a pure sample of an antigenically unique substance from a disorderly specimen. SYN: *immunoabsorption.*

immunoaffinity purification (ĭ-mū″nō-ă-fĭn″ĭ-tē, ĭ-mū″) Exposure to monoclonal antibodies in order to isolate specific analytes. Immunoaffinity purification is used during the preparation of blood products to reduce their likelihood of contamination by specific disease-causing microorganisms.

immunoassay (im″yŭ-nō-as′ā″, im-ū″nō-) [*immuno-* + *assay*] Any of several laboratory techniques that detect or measure molecules involved in immunological reactions. SEE: *immunoelectrophoresis; immunofluorescence; radioimmunoassay.*

cloned enzyme donor i. ABBR: CEDIA. A homogeneous enzyme immunoassay (EIA), based on the modulation of enzyme activity by bound fragments of beta-galactosidase.

end point i. An immunoassay in which the signal is measured as the antigen-antibody complex reaches equilibrium.

enzyme i. ABBR: EIA. A rapid enzyme immunochemical method for determining the presence of an antigen, antibody, or hapten in the blood. In EIA an antigen or antibody is bound to an enzyme, e.g., horseradish peroxidase or alkaline phosphatase. The resulting molecule can bind specific immunological targets in body fluid samples and highlight their presence enzymatically. EIA, formerly known as enzyme-linked immunosorbent assay (ELISA), is used as one of the primary diagnostic tests for many infectious diseases, including treponema pallidum (the spirochete that causes syphilis) and HIV.

fluorescence polarization i., fluores-

cent polarization immunoassay ABBR: FPIA. A means of identifying and quantifying the amount of an antigen in a specimen in which a fluorescently labeled antibody is mixed with a sample thought to contain the antigen is exposed to polarized light. Bound fluorescently labeled antibody reacts to polarized light in a characteristic fashion not demonstrated by unbound antibody, allowing for identification and measurement of the ligand.

    sandwich i. An immunoassay in which the analyte is bound to a solid phase and a labeled reagent subsequently bound immunochemically to the analyte.

    tanned red cell hemagglutination inhibition i. ABBR: TRCHII. An assay for fibrinogen degradation products.

immunobiological (ĭm″ū-nō-bī″ō-lŏj′ĭ-kŭl) [L. immunis, safe, + Gr. bios, life] Any substance derived from a pathogen that can immunize a person or a community against disease; e.g., a vaccine. SYN: *immunobiological agent*.

immunobiology (ĭm″ū-nō-bī-ŏl′ō-jē) [″ + Gr. bios, life, + logos, word, reason] The study of immune phenomena in biological systems, including the immune response to infectious diseases, transplantation of organs, allergy, autoimmunity, and cancer.

immunochemistry (ĭm″ū-nō-kĕm′ĭs-trē) [″ + ″] The chemistry of antigens, antibodies, receptors, and other molecules involved in immunological reactions.

immunocompetence (ĭm″ū-nō-kŏm′pĕ-tĕns) The ability of the body's immune system to respond to pathogenic organisms and tissue damage. This ability may be diminished by drugs specifically developed to inhibit immune cell function (e.g., chemotherapeutic agents used to treat leukemia and drugs used to prevent organ transplant rejections), by diseases that attack elements of the immune system, or overwhelming infections. SEE: *immunocompromised*.

immunocompetent (i-mū″nō-kom′pĕt-ĕnt, im″yŭ-nō) [immuno- competent] Having an effective or intact immune response or immune system. **immunocompetence** (i-mū″nō-kom′pĕt-ĕns, im′yŭ-nō), *n*.

immunocompromised (ĭm″ū-nō-kŏm′prō-mīzd″) Having an immune system that is incapable of a normal, full reaction to pathogens or tissue damage, as the result of a disease (e.g., diabetes mellitus, overwhelming sepsis, or the acquired immunodeficiency syndrome) or drug therapy with agents that inhibit components of the immune system.

⚠ Live virus vaccinations should never be administered to immunocompromised persons.

SYN: *immunodeficient*. SEE: *immune system*.

immunoconglutinin (ĭm″ū-nō-kŏn-gloo′tĭ-nĭn) [″ + conglutinare, to glue together] A protein used in the laboratory to assess the number of immune complexes in blood, which may be related to immunological activity. It acts by binding with complement factor 3, a significant part of an antigen-antibody immune complex.

immunocontraception (im″yŭ-nō-kon″tră-sep′shŏn, i-mū″) [immuno- + contraception] The development of antibodies to bind with gamete-specific antigens, i.e., antigens on eggs, sperm, or sex hormones, as a means of preventing conception. It is used primarily in veterinary applications.

immunocytoadherence (ĭm″ū-nō-sī″tō-ăd-hēr′ĕns) A laboratory test used to identify antibody-bearing cells by the formation of rosettes composed of red blood cells and those cells bearing antibodies.

immunodeficiency (im″yŭ-nō-dĕ-fish′ĕn-sē, im-ū″) Decreased or compromised ability to respond to antigenic stimuli with an appropriate immune response, as the result of one or more disorders in B-cell−mediated immunity, T-cell−mediated immunity, phagocytic cells, or complement. This state may be genetic or acquired following infections, drug abuse, multiple transfusions, immunosuppressive therapy, or malnutrition. Affected patients develop chronic infections that are difficult to treat and recur frequently; these infections frequently are caused by opportunistic organisms. Other findings related to the type and degree of deficiency in the immune system include failure to thrive, thrombocytopenia, and hepatosplenomegaly. Treatments vary depending on the underlying cause. They may include combinations of antiviral agents in the acquired immunodeficiency syndrome; infusions of intravenous immune globulin (IVIG) in disorders of humoral immunity; bone marrow transplantation in patients with malignancies; and antibiotics that specifically treat active infections. Cytokine therapy and gene therapy may play a role in the treatment of patients with defined genetic defects. SYN: *immune deficiency*. SEE: *acquired immunodeficiency syndrome; agammaglobulinemia*. **immunodeficient,** *adj*.

immunodeficiency disease, severe combined ABBR: SCID. Any of a group of inherited autosomal or X-linked recessive disorders in which there is partial or complete dysfunction of the immune system. Defects are present in both B- and T-cell−mediated immunity responses and frequently include defective cytokine function. Within 6 months after birth, babies develop infections from bacterial, viral, fungal, or protozoan organisms. Intravenous immune globulin (IVIG) is given to provide antibodies, but a successful bone marrow transplant is required to prevent death. The efficacy of gene therapy is under investigation. SEE: *cytokine; cell-mediated immunity; humoral immunity.*

immunodeficient (ĭm″ū-nō-dĕ-físh′ĕnt) Immunocompromised.

immunodiagnosis (ĭm″ū-nō-dī″ăg-nō′sĭs) The use of antibody assays, immunocytochemistry, detection of lymphocyte markers, and other strategies to diagnose autoimmune diseases, immunodeficiencies, infections, or malignancies.

immunodiffusion (ĭm″ū-nō-dĭ-fū′zhŭn) [*immuno-* + *diffusion*] A test method in which an antigen and antibody are placed in a gel, where they diffuse toward each other. When they meet, a precipitate is formed.

immunodominant (ĭm″ū-nō-dŏm′ă-nĭnt) Pert. to the ability of a specific antigen or epitope to induce a measurable or clinically meaningful immune response when other structurally related antigens do not. **immunodominance,** *n.*

immunoelectrophoresis (im″yū-nō-ĕ-lek″trŏ-fŏ-rē′sĭs, im-ū″nō-) [*immuno-* + *electrophoresis*] A method of investigating the concentrations of proteins and antibodies (immunoglobulins) in body fluids using their movement in an electrophoretic gel.

immunofluorescence (ĭm″ū-nō-floo″ō-rĕs′ĕns) The detection of antibodies with fluorescein-labeled proteins. Bound antibodies glow when illuminated.

immunogen (ĭ-mū′nō-jĕn) [″ + Gr. *gennan,* to produce] A substance capable of producing an immune response. Proteins and some polysaccharides tend to be strong immunogens; some lipids and nucleic acids are as well. SEE: *antigen.*

immunogenetics (ĭm″ū-nō-jĕ-nĕt′ĭks) [″ + Gr. *gennan,* to produce] The study of the influence of genetic factors on one's susceptibility to infectious diseases (e.g., malaria) and autoimmune illnesses (e.g., rheumatoid arthritis) or on one's suitability for organ transplantation. SEE: *histocompatibility* and its subentries.

immunogenic (ĭm″ū-nō-jĕn′ĭk) Capable of inducing an immune response.

immunogenicity (ĭm″ū-nō-jĕ-nĭs′ĭ-tē) The capacity to induce a detectable immune response.

immunoglobulin (im″yŭ-nō-glob′yŭ-lĭn, im-ū″nō-) [*immuno-* + *globulin*] ABBR: Ig. **1.** Any of a diverse group of plasma polypeptides that bind antigenic proteins and serve as one of the body's primary defenses against disease. Two different forms exist. The first group of immunoglobulins lies on the surface of

mature B cells, enabling them to bind to thousands of antigens. When the antigens are bound, the B plasma cells secrete the second type of immunoglobulins, antigen-specific antibodies, which circulate in the blood and accumulate in lymphoid tissue, esp. the spleen and lymph nodes, binding and destroying specific foreign antigens and stimulating other immune activity. Antibodies also activate the complement cascade, neutralize bacterial toxins and viruses, and function as opsonins, stimulating phagocytosis.

Immunoglobulins are formed by light and heavy (depending on molecular weight) chains of polypeptides made up of about 100 amino acids. These chains determine the structure of antigen-binding sites and, therefore, the specificity of the antibody to one antigen. The five types of immunoglobulins (IgA, IgD, IgE, IgG, IgM) account for approximately 30% of all plasma proteins. Antibodies are one of the three classes of globulins (plasma proteins) in the blood that contribute to maintaining colloidal oncotic pressure. SYN: *antibody.* SEE: *antigen; B cell.* **2.** Immune globulin.

i. A ABBR: IgA. The principal immunoglobulin in exocrine secretions such as milk, respiratory and intestinal mucin, saliva, and tears. It prevents pathogenic bacteria and viruses from invading the body through the mucosa of the gastrointestinal, pulmonary, and genitourinary tracts. Its presence in colostrum and breast milk helps prevent infection in breast-feeding infants.

i. D ABBR: IgD. An immunoglobulin that is present on the surface of B lymphocytes and acts as an antigen receptor.

i. E ABBR: IgE. An immunoglobulin that attaches to mast cells in the respiratory and intestinal tracts and plays a major role in allergic reactions. About 50% of patients with allergies have increased IgE levels. IgE is also important in the formation of reagin, a type of immunoglobulin gamma E (IgGE), found in the blood of individuals with an atopic hypersensitivity.

i. G ABBR: IgG. The principal immunoglobulin in human serum. Because IgG moves across the placental barrier, it is important in producing immunity in the infant before birth. It is the major antibody for antitoxins, viruses, and bacteria. It also activates complement and serves as an opsonin. As gamma globulin, IgG may be given to provide temporary resistance to hepatitis or other diseases.

intravenous i. ABBR: IVIG. A solution containing concentrated human immunoglobulins (antibodies), primarily IgG. IVIG has numerous uses in health care, including as replacement therapy for patients with primary immune deficiencies; as a treatment for those with Kawasaki disease, bullous pemphigoid, Guillain-Barré syndrome, idiopathic thrombocytopenic purpura, chronic inflammatory demyelinating polyneuropathy, and other immune-mediated illnesses; and as a means of providing patients with passive immunity against infectious diseases.

    i. M ABBR: IgM. An immunoglobulin formed in almost every immune response during the early period of the reaction. IgM controls the A, B, O blood group antibody responses and is the most efficient antibody in stimulating complement activity. Its size prevents it from moving across the placenta to the fetus.

immunohematology (ĭ-mū-nō-hēm″ă-tŏl′ō-jē) [L. *immunis,* safe, + Gr. *haima,* blood, + *logos,* word, reason] The study of the immunology and genetics of blood groups, blood cell antigens and antibodies, and specific blood proteins (such as complement); esp. important in blood banking and transfusion medicine.

immunohistochemistry ABBR: IHC. The identification of antigens in tissues using antibodies that are linked to enzymes, fluorescent dyes, or radioactive labels. IHC is used to diagnose and track specific cellular anomalies, such as cancers, by identifying those antigens that are specifically found in affected cells.

immunoincompetency (ĭm″ū-nō-ĭn-kŏm′pĕ-tĕn-sē) An inability to produce an immune response. SEE: *immunodeficiency.*

immunoinfertility (ĭm″ū-nō-ĭn″fĕr-tĭl′ĭ-tē, ĭ-mū″) Inability to conceive offspring as a result of the production of antigamete antibodies that destroy sperm, esp. antisperm antibodies. It is a rare cause of infertility in humans.

immunological priming [im″yŭ-nŏ-loj′ĭ-kăl prīm′ĭng] Stimulation of the differentiation of memory B cells with an antigen exposure, so that subsequent exposures to that antigen will produce a rapid proliferation of plasma cells and a vigorous antibody response.

immunological therapy (im″yŭ-nŏ-loj′ĭ-kăl) Immunotherapy.

immunologic unresponsiveness (im″yŭ-nŏ-loj′ĭk ŭn″rē-spon′sĭv-nĕs) Tolerance to antigens that normally stimulate antibody production or cellular immunity.

immunologist (ĭm″ū-nŏl′ō-jĭst) An individual whose special training and experience is in immunology.

immunology (im″yŭ-nol′ō-jē) [″ + Gr. *logos,* word, reason] The study of the components of the immune system and their function. SEE: *immune system.*

    immunologic (im″yŭ-nŏ-loj′ik), *adj.*

immunomagnetic (ĭm″ū-nō-măg-nĕt′ĭk,

ĭ-mū″) Of, pertaining to, or using magnetic beads or spheres that have been coated with antibodies.

immunomagnetic technique SEE: under *technique.*

immunomics (ĭ-mū-nŏm′ĭks) [L. *immunis,* safe + Gr. *ome,* complete] The study of all the antigens present in particular biological specimens and the approaches that can be used to identify them or use them as potential targets for treatment.

immunomodulation (im″yŭ-nō-moj″ŭ-lā′shŏn, i-mū″nō-) [*immuno-* + *modulation*] **1.** The alteration of immune responses with monoclonal antibodies, cytokines, glucocorticoids, immunoglobulins, ultraviolet light, plasmapheresis, or related agents known to alter cellular or humoral immunity. SEE: *immunotherapy; biological response modifier.* **2.** In alternative medicine, the use of vitamins, minerals, natural foods, or other nutrients to promote health or prevent degenerative or malignant diseases. SEE: *biotherapy.*

    transfusion-related i. ABBR: TRIM. Alterations in the immune status of an individual who receives an allogeneic blood transfusion.

immunonutrient (ĭm″ū-nō-noo′trē-ĭnt, ĭ-mū″, nū′) [″ + ″] A nutritional supplement (e.g., arginine) that when added to a clinical diet is thought to improve resistance to infectious disease.

immunonutrition (ĭm″ū-nō-nū-trĭ′shŭn) The study of the effects of nutrients, including macronutrients, vitamins, minerals, and trace elements on inflammation, the actions of white blood cells, the formation of antibodies, and the resistance to disease.

immunopathology (ĭm″ū-nō-pă-thŏl′ō-jē) The study of tissue alterations that result from immune or allergic reactions.

immunophenotyping (ĭm″ū-nō-fēn′ă-tīp″ĭng, ĭ-mū″) Differentiation among subsets of lymphocytes, using antibodies that select for identifying molecules on their cell membranes.

immunoprecipitation (ĭm″ū-nō-prē-sĭp″ĭ-tā′shŭn) The formation of a precipitate when an antigen and antibody interact.

immunoprecipitin analysis (ĭm″ū-nō-prē-sĭp′ĭ-tĭn, ĭ-mū″) An immunoassay in which the antibody-antigen reaction forms a visible substance that drops out of solution. This is most commonly represented by turbidity in a liquid matrix or a band of turbidity in a gel matrix. The amount of turbidity or the size of the band allows quantification.

immunoproliferative (ĭm″ū-nō-prō-lĭf′ĕr-ă-tĭv) Pert. to the rapid growth and dissemination of cells and tissues involved in producing antibodies.

immunoprophylaxis (ĭm″ū-nō-prō″fĭ-lăk′sĭs) Prevention of disease with agents (e.g., vaccines) that affect the immune system.

immunoprotein (ĭm″ū-nō-prō′tē-ĭn) [″ + Gr. *protos,* first] An immunologically active protein, esp. one that is used as a target for immunological probes or therapies.

immunoreactant (ĭ-mū″nō-rē-ăk′tănt) Any of the substances involved in immunological reactions, including immunoglobulins, complement components, and specific antigens.

immunoreaction (ĭ-mū″nō-rē-ăk′shŭn) The reaction of an antibody to an antigen, exploited in some laboratory tests that stain, isolate, or purify cells that express specific markers on their cell membranes.

immunoscintigraphy (ĭm″ū-nō-sĭn-tĭg′ră-fē) The imaging of specific tissues by means of their binding to radioactively labeled monoclonal antibodies; used to detect metastatic cancer. The release of radiation from the antibodies is detected and quantified. SYN: *radioimmunoimaging.*

immunoselection (ĭm″ū-nō-sĕ-lĕk′shŭn) The enhanced survival of cells or organisms that have favorable cell surface markers. The antigens allow the cells organisms to escape destruction by humoral or cell-mediated immunity.

immunosenescence (ĭm″ū-nō-sĭ-nĕs′ĕns) The age-associated decline of the immune system and host defense mechanisms. Elderly individuals frequently have a decline in cell-mediated immunity and secondary declines in humoral immunity. The clinician caring for an older patient can assume that the individual has defective host defenses, is at greater risk for developing an infectious disease, and has an increased risk of morbidity and mortality from infectious diseases.

immunosorbent (ĭm″yŭ-nō-sor′bĕnt, ĭm-ū″nō-) [Shortening of *immunoadsorbent*] **1.** Pert. to an antibody or antigen used in immunoadsorption. SEE: *immunoadsorption.* **2.** An immunosorbent substance. SYN: *immunoabsorbent; immunoadsorbent.*

immunostimulator (ĭm″ū-nō-stĭm′ū-lā-tŏr) SEE: *immunotherapy.*

immunosuppressant (ĭm″yŭ-nō-sŭ-pres′ănt, ĭ-mū″nō-) [*immuno-* + *suppress*] An agent that decreases or inactivates the immune response to antigens. SYN: *immunosuppressive agent.*

immunosuppression (ĭm″yŭ-nō-sŭ-presh′ŏn, ĭ-mū″nō-) **1.** Prevention of immune responses (e.g., with drugs like mycophenolate or cyclosporine). **2.** Deterioration in the immune response resulting from certain diseases (e.g., alcoholism, diabetes mellitus, or infection HIV virus).

immunosuppressive therapy (ĭm″yŭ-nō-

sŭ-pres′ĭv, ĭ-mū″nō-) Treatment with drugs (such as cyclosporine, mycophenolate, or tumor necrosis factor inhibitors) that impair immune responses. SEE: *immunotherapy.*

⚠ CAUTION: Live vaccines should not be given to patients who are actively treated with immune-suppressing drugs.

immunosurveillance (ĭm″ū-nō-sĕr-vā′lĕns) The recognition and destruction of malignant cells by immune cells that travel through and scan the body for foreign or mutant antigens.

immunotherapy (im″yū-nō-thĕr′ă-pē, im-ū″nō-) [*immuno-* + *therapy*] The use of natural and synthetic substances to stimulate or suppress the immune response (as in patients with anaphylaxis or severe allergies), to treat deficits, or to interfere with the growth of malignant neoplasms. Therapeutic agents are either antigen-specific or non–antigen-specific. Immunological therapies include cytokines (such as alpha interferon and interleukin-2), monoclonal antibodies, intravenous immune globulin, heat shock proteins, and cancer vaccines. SYN: *immunological therapy.*

   adoptive i. The treatment of malignancies with T cells that are taken from patients with cancer, grown and activated in a culture where they are stimulated to react to specific tumor antigens, and then returned to patients by infusion. The adopted T cells invade the cancer and immunologically reject it. Side effects of the treatment include fever and nausea.

   allergen-specific i. Antigen-specific **i.**

   antigen-specific i. Immunotherapy in which individual antigens are used in gradually increasing concentrations to stimulate an immune response, e.g., against particular allergic diseases or tumors. SYN: *allergen-specific* ***i.***; *specific* ***i.***

   PATIENT CARE: Anyone who has suffered severe allergic reactions to an antigen (such as angioedema or anaphylaxis), should be considered for treatment with antigen-specific immunotherapy. After the administration of the antigen, (as in patients with allergies to the venom of stinging insects), the patient should be closely monitored for evidence of difficulty in breathing, palpitations, urticaria or angioedema, changes in blood pressure, dizziness or faintness, or changes in mental status. Periodic monitoring of vital signs, oximetry, and breath sounds is required to ensure stability. Patients can usually be discharged if they have experienced no untoward effects 30 min after administration. Epinephrine should be available for immediate injection if the patient develops an anaphylactic reaction.

nonspecific i. Induction of a general immune response with adjuvants, drugs, or vaccines that stimulate the release of interferons or other immune cytokines. Nonspecific immunotherapy differs from specific immunotherapy in that the agents used (such as BCG vaccine, Freund's adjuvant) do not stimulate antibody production for or against (or tolerance to) individual antigens.

passive i. The prevention of disease by administering antibodies in the form of a gamma globulin infusion or injection. Preparations enriched with specific antibodies can be used to prevent hepatitis B (HBIG), tetanus (Hyper-Tet), and chickenpox (VZIG).

rush i. Immunotherapy administered rapidly, e.g., over several days (with several injections of antigen daily) or even a single day.

specific i. Antigen-specific **i.**

stimulation i. The therapeutic use of agents that stimulate immune function (immunostimulants). These agents include cytokines and cytokine antagonists, monoclonal antibodies, compounds obtained from bacteria, and hormones from the thymus. The most successful immunostimulants have been laboratory-prepared cytokines, the protein mediators of immune responses. Granulocyte colony-stimulating factor (G-CSF) and granulocyte-macrophage colony-stimulating factor (GM-CSF) are used widely to increase white blood cell production in the bone marrow after cancer therapy, bone marrow transplantation, and AIDS. Erythropoietin is effective in treating anemia in patients with chronic renal failure, AIDS, and bone marrow depression following cancer therapy. Transforming growth factor beta seems to enhance healing of wounds and reduce fibrotic changes following inflammation. Interleukins and interferons are being studied for their beneficial effects in patients with certain leukemias and other malignant tumors. Lymphocyte-activated killer (LAK) cells and tumor-infiltrating lymphocytes (TILs), which are lymphocytes that have been removed from the patient and stimulated with interleukin-2, also show promise in treating malignant tumors. Monoclonal antibodies against mediators of inflammation have been created in the laboratory from hybridomas and are being studied for clinical use.

Bacteria-based compounds, which produce nonspecific stimulation, have been used the longest. Attenuated (weak) solutions of *Mycobacterium bovis* (bacille Calmette-Guérin) and endotoxins from *Staphylococcus aureus* and OK432, prepared from *Streptococcus pyogenes,* are being used as adjunct cancer therapy because of their ability to activate natural killer cells, T cells, and macrophages. New techniques have enabled researchers to isolate hormones from the thymus gland, where T lymphocytes mature, to treat viral infections and cancers. Their clinical effectiveness has not been established. SEE: *cytokine; monoclonal antibody.*

sublingual i. ABBR: SLIT. Allergen desensitization in which the antigen is administered in droplet form under the tongue instead of being injected subcutaneously. SLIT is a relatively safe form of immunotherapy and is often used at home instead of in a medical office, several times a week.

PATIENT CARE: Adverse effects include oral itching or swelling and gastrointestinal upset. The incidence of systemic side effects may be reduced with SLIT as opposed to immunotherapy by subcutaneous injection.

suppressive i. Any treatment used to block abnormal or excessive immune responses.

Corticosteroids, the most widely known anti-inflammatory agents, increase the number of neutrophils in the blood but decrease their aggregation at inflammatory sites, decrease the number and function of other white blood cells, and inhibit cytokine production. They are most effective during an acute flareup of a chronic autoimmune disease and in conjunction with other agents because they do not adequately block autoantibodies when used alone.

Cytotoxic drugs kill all white blood cells and their precursors and were originally developed as anticancer agents. However, low-dose methotrexate is now known to be effective in reducing the symptoms and the need for corticosteroids in chronic inflammatory diseases such as rheumatoid arthritis, Crohn disease, psoriasis, and asthma.

Cyclosporine and *tacrolimus* are related to the cytotoxic drugs, but these drugs selectively inhibit helper T-cell production of interleukin-2, effectively preventing replication rather than killing them. They are used extensively to prevent rejection of transplanted tissue and graft-versus-host disease.

Intravenous gamma globulin (IVIG) is used routinely to replace antibodies in patients with immunodeficiency disorders. It also can be used as an immunosuppressive. IVIG inhibits phagocytosis of platelets in idiopathic thrombocytopenic purpura; it has been most successful in the treatment of children but also can produce a short-term remission in adults. Because it seems to inhibit natural killer cells and augment suppressor T cells, it also has been used to treat other autoimmune diseases, but its clinical effectiveness has not been determined.

Antilymphocyte antibodies inhibit the T-cell–mediated immune response. The two types are monoclonal antibodies, which react with one specific antigen, and polyclonal antibodies, which target several different antigens. Polyclonal antibodies are created by injecting animals (usually mice) with human lymphocytes. The animals' B cells are harvested from lymphoid tissue or peripheral blood and used to create antilymphocyte serum (ALS); isolated antibodies from these B cells are the active agents in antilymphocyte globulin (ALG). Both ALS and ALG are used routinely to treat transplant rejection and graft-versus-host reactions. Because they come from animals, however, they can cause serum sickness. In addition, they are not specific to T cells and also can destroy platelets.

Monoclonal antibodies are laboratory-created antibodies developed from a single cell line that block the receptor molecules that bind and transfer cytokine signals on T cells. OKT3, a monoclonal antibody obtained from mice, is a strong immunosuppressant used in the primary treatment of acute transplant rejection; it also may be effective in preventing rejection. It frequently causes a massive release of cytokines whose effects must be controlled, usually by corticosteroids, after the first or second dose. In addition, over time it stimulates the production of antimouse antibodies that block its effectiveness. Monoclonal antibodies provide disease or tumor-specific therapy for various autoimmune illnesses and cancers by selectively binding to tumor cell surfaces. Interleukin's effects are exerted on the T lymphocytes. Interferons have antiviral, antiproliferative and immunomodulary effects. SEE: *hybridoma*.

Plasmapheresis, the separation and removal of plasma containing autoantibodies (AAb), is most effective against disorders in which the AAbs are tissue-specific, such as myasthenia gravis, and those in which more AAbs are found in the blood than in extravascular spaces.

⚠ Many immunosuppressant drugs increase patients' susceptibility to infections (e.g., the reactivation of tuberculosis) or the new acquisition of opportunistic infections. Some also increase the risk of developing malignant tumors, because of the loss of immunosurveillance.

PATIENT CARE: Patients need to learn to minimize their exposure to infectious organisms and consistently to use good hand and oral hygiene measures. The medication regimen may be rigorous and should be accompanied by intensive teaching about desired effects and side effects of the drugs and the need for frequent bloodwork; written as well as verbal instructions about the treatment regimen is often provided to the patient.

immunotoxin (ĭm″ū-nō-tŏk′sĭn) [″ + Gr. *toxikon*, poison] Any medication or poison chemically linked to antibodies, used to target and destroy cells with specific receptors, esp. cancerous cells. Immunotoxins have been used to eliminate malignant tumors in the bone marrow.

Imovax (ī′mō-văks″) Rabies vaccine.

impacted (ĭm-păk′tĕd) [L. *impactus*, pressed on] Pressed firmly together so as to be immovable. This term may be applied to a fracture in which the ends of the bones are wedged together, a tooth so placed in the jaw bone that eruption is impossible, a fetus wedged in the birth canal, cerumen, calculi, or accumulation of feces in the rectum.

impaction (ĭm-pak′shŏn) [L. *impactio*, concussion, impact] A condition of being tightly wedged into a part, as when the eruption of a tooth is blocked by other teeth or when an organ is overloaded, as the bowels by feces.

fecal i. Constipation caused by a firm mass of feces in the distal colon or rectum. The size or firmness of the mass prevents its passage.

ETIOLOGY: Fecal impaction is relatively common in the elderly, esp. in immobilized residents of nursing homes, and in children with encopresis. It may also result from painful anal conditions that inhibit the patient's desire to defecate; drugs such as narcotics, calcium-channel blockers, retained barium, or anticholinergics that retard bowel movements; neurological diseases such as spinal cord injury; complications of intestinal or obstetrical surgery; dehydration; rectoceles, colon cancers, or other pathological lesions; and functional (psychogenic) disorders.

SYMPTOMS: Abdominal colic and a sensation of fullness, anorexia, and rectal pain are common.

PATIENT CARE: Impaction of stool may be prevented by following a high-fiber, fluid-rich diet; getting regular exercise; limiting intake of constipating drugs; routinely using stool softeners or laxatives; and learning biofeedback and habit-training.

A trial of laxatives or enemas may relieve the obstructing feces. If this is unsuccessful, manual extraction is indicated. This may require local anesthesia. The impaction is fragmented by using a scissoring action of the fingers. After the impaction is fragmented, use of mild laxatives, such as mineral oil instilled into the rectum, provides lubrication and assists in passage of the fragments. Surgery is rarely required.

   food i. The forcing of food into the interproximal spaces of teeth by chewing (vertical impaction) or by tongue and cheek pressure (horizontal impaction).

impaired (im-pard′) [Fr. *empeirer,* to make worse] Not functioning or behaving appropriately because of damage, illness, or weakness. In the health care professions, it refers to a physician, nurse, or other professional too ill or incapacitated to carry out his or her professional duties. Neurological diseases, e.g., strokes or dementia, are prominent causes, as are behavioral health disorders, e.g., alcohol or drug dependency.

impaired fasting glucose SEE: under *glucose.*

impairment (im-par′měnt) [Fr. *empeirer* fr L. *(im)pejorare,* to make worse] Any loss or abnormality of psychological, physiological, or anatomical structure or function. Impairments represent a deviation from generally accepted benchmarks in biomedical or psychosocial functioning.

   age-associated memory i. ABBR: AAMI. Mild cognitive **i.**

   cerebral visual i. Cortical **blindness**.

   cognitive i. The loss of intellectual function, i.e., of thinking effectively. It may occur briefly after drug overdose or alcohol use, during sepsis, or after severe head injury. Permanent cognitive impairment may occur in older adults. Approximately half of the population over 85 show permanently impaired thinking when tested with standard assessment tools.

   cognitive i., not dementia Mild cognitive **i.**

   correctable visual i. ABBR: CVI. Any visual deficiency that can be improved with the use of eyeglasses.

   mild cognitive i. ABBR: MCI. A subjectively sensed, objectively verifiable loss of memory that may result in difficulties with word finding, naming, or complex skill execution. It does not generally impair a person's ability to carry out normal activities of daily living. About 15% of patients with MCI develop dementia within a year. SYN: *age-associated memory i.; cognitive i., not dementia.*

   nonsyndromic hereditary hearing i. Hearing loss, or deafness, that is inherited and is not associated with other inherited characteristics.

   specific language i. ABBR: SLI. A common impairment in language development affecting about 4% to 6% of children in which nonverbal intelligence is normal but skills such as the ability to name objects or to understand word meanings lags.

   subjective memory i. A person's perception that his or her memory is failing, as opposed to other external or objective forms of evidence of dementia. It is usually associated with normal performance when memory is tested. SYN: *subjective memory **complaint**.*

   syndromic hereditary hearing i. Hearing loss or deafness that is genetically transmitted and associated with other inherited diseases or deficits.

impairment evaluation A means of measuring an employee's suitability for a particular job, esp. one in which the employee's performance may affect the health or safety of the employee or others. Some employers prefer using impairment testing rather than random drug screening to assess the fitness of workers for employment in safety-conscious work environments, e.g., hospitals. SYN: *impairment testing.*

impairment testing Impairment evaluation.

impaled object A foreign body that penetrates the skin and remains embedded in tissue. Such objects should be stabilized to prevent movement and allowed to remain in place while the patient is transported to receive professional care. EMS providers are taught that an impaled object to the cheek may be removed if it is causing a compromise to the airway.

impalpable (ĭm-păl′pă-b′l) [L. *in-,* not, + *palpare,* to touch] Felt with difficulty, if at all; hardly perceptible to the touch.

impartial (im-par′shĭl) [²in- + *partial*] Unbiased and nonjudgmental.

impatent (ĭm-pă′těnt) [″ + *patere,* to be open] Closed; not patent.

impedance (im-pēd′ăns) [L. *impedire,* to hinder] Resistance met by alternating currents in passing through a conductor; consists of resistance, reactance, inductance, or capacitance. The resistance due to the inductive and condenser characteristics of a circuit is called reactance.

   acoustic i. Resistance to the transmission of sound waves.

   bioelectrical i. ABBR: BIA. Resistance to electrical current as it travels through body fluids and tissues. Its measurement is used in body composition analysis to determine total water, lean mass, and other body components. The results may vary with ambient temperature and humidity, the subject's hydration, and other variables. SEE: *body composition; body fat; fluid, body; lean body mass.*

   thoracic i. A measure of the electrical activity in the chest that varies with changes in body size and composition, fluid volume, ventilatory status, and other variables.

imperative (im-per′ăt-ĭv) [L. *imperati-*

vus, commanding] **1.** Required, necessary, or obligatory. **2.** Pert. to a sentence or tone of voice expressing a command.

imperception (ĭm″pĕr-sĕp′shŭn) [L. *in-,* not, + *percipere,* to perceive] The inability to form a mental picture; lack of perception.

imperforate (ĭm-pĕr′fō-rāt) [″ + *per,* through, + *forare,* to bore] Without an opening.

imperforation (ĭm-pĕr″fō-rā′shŭn) Atresia.

impermeable (ĭm-pĕr′mē-ă-bl) [L. *in-,* not, + *permeare,* to pass through] Not allowing passage, as of fluids; impenetrable.

impervious (ĭm-pĕr′vē-ŭs) [L. *impervius*] Unable to be penetrated.

impetiginous (ĭm″pĕ-tĭj′ĭ-nŭs) [L. *impetiginosus*] Relating to or resembling impetigo.

impetigo, impetigo contagiosa (ĭm″pĕ-tē′gō, -tī′gō) [L. *impetigo,* scabby eruption on the skin] A bacterial infection of the skin, caused by streptococci or staphylococci and marked by yellow to red, weeping and crusted or pustular lesions, esp. around the nose, mouth, and cheeks or on the extremities. Associated symptoms include itching, burning, and regional lymphadenopathy; glomerulonephritis is a rare but serious complication. The disease is common in children and adults and may develop after trauma or irritation to the skin. SEE: illus..; *Nursing Diagnoses Appendix.* **impetiginous** (-tĭj′ĭ-nŭs), *adj.*

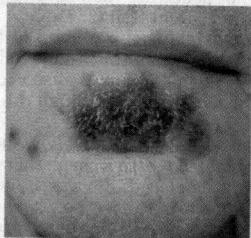

IMPETIGO

TREATMENT: The infection is highly contagious and spreads easily among infants, children, and the elderly, with outbreaks related to such predisposing factors as poor hygiene, crowded and unclean living conditions, warm climate, malnutrition, and anemia. Topically applied mupirocin ointment, related drugs, or oral agents effective against staphylococcus and streptococcus are used to treat the infection. Mupirocin also eliminates nasal carriage of the offending organisms.

PATIENT CARE: The appearance, location, and distribution of lesions are documented, along with any associated symptoms (pruritus, pain). Family members are taught to keep the skin clean and dry, removing exudate 2 to 3 times daily by washing the lesions with soap and water; warm saline soaks or compresses may be applied to remove stubborn crusts. Patients and families are taught the importance of not sharing washcloths, towels, or bed linens; the need for thorough handwashing and frequent bathing with a bactericidal soap; and the urgency for early treatment of any purulent eruption to limit spread to others.

Prescribed treatment must be continued for 7 to 10 days even if lesions have healed. Nonprescription antihistamines may be used to reduce itching. The fingernails should be cut and, if necessary, mittens applied to prevent further injury if the patient is unable to avoid scratching. Diversional activities appropriate to the patient's developmental stage are encouraged to distract from local discomforts. Black patients may develop deeper inflammation than whites and should be informed that this may result in hypopigmentation or hyperpigmentation changes after the inflammation has subsided. The school nurse or employer is notified of the infection, and family members are checked for evidence of impetigo. The patient can return to school or work when all lesions have healed.

    bullous i. A rare infection, usually occurring in infants, caused by a strain of *Staphylococcus aureus* that produces a toxin that splits the epidermis.

    i. herpetiformis A rare and occasionally life-threatening eruption that typically occurs in the third trimester of pregnancy. It is pathologically indistinguishable from pustular psoriasis. SYN: *Hebra disesae.*

impingement (ĭm-pĭnj′mĕnt) **1.** Degenerative alteration in a joint in which there is excessive friction between joint tissues. This typically causes limitations in range of motion and the perception of joint pain. **2.** An area of periodontal tissue traumatized by the occlusal force of a tooth. **3.** The unwanted compression of soft tissue between two or more harder, unyielding structures.

impingement syndrome The compromise of soft tissues in the subacromial space, esp. the rotator cuff, causing pain with overhead motions or rotational motions with an abducted arm, e.g., throwing. This syndrome is seen in repetitive overhead activities. It is treated with rotator cuff strengthening exercises, anti-inflammatory medications, and subacromial steroid injection. If conservative management fails, subacromial decompression (acromioplasty) is used.

implant (ĭm′plant″) [¹*in-* + *plant*] An object inserted into the body, e.g., a piece of tissue, a tooth, a pellet of medicine, a tube or needle containing a radioactive substance, liquid and solid plastic materials used to augment tissues or to fill in areas traumatically or surgically removed, artificial joints, and/or for other therapeutic purposes. SEE: *mammaplasty, augmentation.*

bone i. An implant to repair bone or to cover implanted objects such as artificial hips or tooth implants.

brain i. Any substance, tissue, or object placed surgically in the brain.

brainstem i. Auditory brainstem **i.**

breast i. A surgically inserted object used to change the size and/or contour of the breast or chest wall, either using the patient's own tissue, e.g., a pedicle graft, or a prosthesis.

cochlear i. An electrical device that receives sound and transmits the resulting signal to electrodes implanted in the cochlea. That signal stimulates the cochlea so that hearing-impaired persons can perceive sound.

> ⚠ Cochlear implants increase the likelihood of meningitis. Patients with cochlear implants should be vaccinated against pneumococcus and *Haemophilus influenzae* type b (Hib).

dental i. In dentistry, a prosthetic device in any of several shapes. It is implanted into oral tissues beneath the mucosa or the periosteal layer, or within the bone to support or hold a fixed or removable prosthesis. SYN: *tooth i.* SEE: illus.

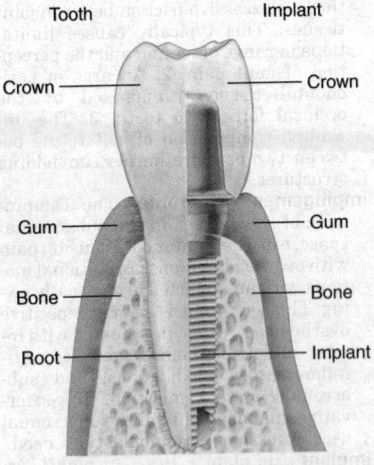

Tooth	Implant
Crown	Crown
Gum	Gum
Bone	Bone
Root	Implant

DENTAL IMPLANT

> ⚠ Ultrasonic devices should not be used on dental implants.

endosteal i. A dental prosthesis that is partially submerged and anchored within the bone. The blade form and the cylinder form are the two types of endosteal implants used. The cylinder form, which is most common, consists of a screw, a small titanium cylinder, and an abutment surgically inserted into the bone. The blade form consists of one or more abutments. In both forms, the prosthetic device is placed on the abutment(s).

interstitial i. An implant consisting of an applicator containing a radioactive source directly into a tumor to deliver a high radiation dose while sparing the surrounding tissues.

intracavitary i. An implant consisting of an applicator containing a radioactive source directly into a hollow organ to deliver a high radiation dose to the organ while sparing the surrounding tissues.

radioactive i. SEE: *brachytherapy; interstitial i.; intracavitary i.*

staple i. Transosteal **i.**

subperiosteal i. A prosthesis for edentulous patients who cannot wear dentures (e.g., because of mandibular atrophy). The implant consists of a metal framework that rests on the residual ridge beneath the periosteum but does not penetrate the mandible.

tooth i. Dental implant.

transosteal i. A rarely used type of dental prosthesis that completely penetrates the mandible. Its use is complicated by infection and a high rate of implant failure. SYN: *staple i.*

wafer i. A slowly dissolving polymer impregnated with chemotherapeutic drugs. It is placed into the tissue space from which a cancer has been removed to deliver a strong dose of chemotherapy to any residual cancer cells that escaped the resection.

implantation (im″plan″tā′shŏn) **1.** The grafting of tissue or the insertion of an organ such as tooth, skin, or tendon into a new location in the body. **2.** Embedding of the developing blastocyst in the uterine mucosa 6 or 7 days after fertilization. SYN: *nidation.*

autologous chondrocyte i. ABBR: ACI. The surgical collection of cartilage from a healthy joint, followed by the culturing of its cells and the return of those cells to a damaged or arthritic joint in another part of the body. SYN: *autologous chondrocyte transplantation.*

hypodermic i. The introduction of an implant under the skin; usually a solid substance placed by forcing a small amount out of a hypodermic needle.

teratic i. The union of an abnormal fetus with a nearly normal fetus.

transkaryotic i. The insertion into a cell nucleus of genetic information not normally present in the cell's DNA. This technique is used, e.g., to treat genetic illnesses in which a protein is absent or inadequately expressed by the cells of the patient.

implant radiation therapy Brachytherapy.

implicit (ĭm-plĭ′sĭt) [L. *implicare,* to enfold, to involve] **1.** Implied. **2.** Contained inside something.

implicit association test A test used to assess the attitudes or biases of the subject toward particular words or ideas. The examiner presents the subject with two words (e.g., the names of two different medical treatments) and two concepts (e.g., "safe" and "hazardous"). The subject is asked to choose which of the concepts best matches the offered words.

implosion (ĭm-plō′zhŭn) A violent collapse inward.

i. flooding A method of treating a phobia by systematically exposing the affected person to his greatest fear. The phobic situation is imagined first and, after the person becomes partly desensitized to it, experienced in reality. The fear is experienced at maximum intensity for up to an hour until the patient is no longer capable of experiencing further fear. SEE: *phobic desensitization.*

imponderable (ĭm-pŏn′dĕr-ă-bl) [L. *in-,* not, + *pondus,* weight] Incapable of being weighed or measured.

impotence, impotency (ĭm′pō-tĕns, ĭm′pō-tĕn-sē) [″ + *potentia,* power] A weakness, esp. pert. to the inability of a man to achieve or maintain an erection. SYN: *erectile dysfunction.* SEE: *penile prosthesis; sex therapy; sexual dysfunction; sexual stimulant.*

TREATMENT: Sildenafil, alprostadil, and several other drugs are used to treat erectile dysfunction. Penile vacuum pumps and penile prostheses are among the nonpharmacological alternatives.

anatomical i. Impotence caused by a genital defect.

atonic i. Impotence resulting from paralysis of nerves supplying the penis.

functional i. Impotence not due to an organic or anatomical defect; usually of psychogenic origin. The individual may experience impotence with one or more sexual partners, but not with others.

neurogenic i. Impotence due to central nervous system lesions, paraplegia, or diabetic neuropathy.

pharmacological i. Erectile dysfunction due to the side effects of certain drugs and medications (e.g., alcohol, cytotoxic agents, barbiturates, beta blockers, marijuana, cimetidine, clonidine,

guanethidine, immunosuppressives, lithium, opiates, phenothiazine, some antihypertensive agents, some diuretics, antidepressants, and anticholinergics).

psychic i. Psychogenic **i.**

psychogenic i. Impotence caused by emotional factors rather than organic disease. SYN: *psychic i.*

vasculogenic i. Impotence due to an inadequate supply of arterial blood to the corpora cavernosa of the penis.

impotent (ĭm′pō-tĕnt) **1.** Unable to copulate. **2.** Sterile; barren. **3.** Lacking effectiveness.

imprecision (ĭm-prē-sĭ′shŭn) The amount or degree of random error in an assay, research study, or calculation, usually represented by the standard deviation, coefficient of variation, or range.

impregnate (ĭm-prĕg′nāt) [L. *impregnare,* to make pregnant] **1.** To render pregnant; to fertilize an ovum. **2.** To saturate.

impregnation (ĭm″preg-nā′shŏn) [*impregnate*] **1.** Fertilization of an ovum. SYN: *fecundation.* **2.** Saturation.

impression (im-presh′ŏn) [L. *impressio,* a pressing into] **1.** A hollow or depression in a surface. **2.** An effect produced upon the mind by external stimuli. **3.** The imprint of all or part of the dental arch, individual teeth, or cavity preparations, made with appropriate dental materials and used to make records or dental protection devices, or to prepare for restorative procedures.

complete dental i. A negative impression of the entire edentulous area (e.g., the area that originally provided the base for the normal teeth).

final i. An impression used for making the master cast for a dental prosthesis.

partial dental i. A negative impression of a portion of the maxilla or mandible where teeth were previously present.

impression material Any of a variety of deformable materials for making a negative reproduction of oral structures. Some common impression materials are waxes, polymers, elastomers, reversible hydrocolloids, and irreversible hydrocolloids.

imprint (im-print′, im′print) [L. *imprimere,* to press into] **1.** To leave a pressure mark on an object. **2.** To guide or restrict the development or expression of a genetic, behavioral, or personal characteristic. **imprint** (im′print), *n.*; **imprinting,** *n.*

genomic i. The inactivation of a gene by its allele.

imprint cytology SEE: under *cytology.*

improvised explosive device SEE: under *device.*

impulse (ĭm′pŭls) [L. *impulsus*] **1.** The

act of driving onward with sudden force. SEE: *conation*. **2.** An incitement of the mind, prompting an unpremeditated act (e.g., impulse buying). **3.** In physiology, a change transmitted through certain tissues, esp. nerve fibers and muscles, resulting in physiological activity or inhibition.

   cardiac i. 1. The heartbeat felt through the chest wall overlying the apex of the heart. **2.** The electrical impulse transmitted over the conducting pathway of the heart that is responsible for the contraction of the muscular tissue of the heart. SEE: *heart*.

   ectopic i. A cardiac impulse arising in some part of the heart other than the sinoatrial node.

   enteroceptive i. An afferent nerve impulse arising from stimuli originating in receptors located in internal organs.

   excitatory i. A nerve signal that increases the activity of target cells, organs, or tissues.

   inhibitory i. A nerve signal that diminishes the activity of the target it acts upon.

   nerve i. A self-propagated electrical signal transmitted along the membrane of a nerve. At the end of the axon of the nerve, the electrical impulse stimulates the release of a neurotransmitter, which may stimulate or inhibit another electrical impulse in another nerve fiber, cause muscle contraction or glandular secretion, or produce a sensation in the brain. The velocity varies according to the diameter of the fiber and the presence or absence of a myelin sheath. The most rapid conducting mammalian neurons (50 to 80 m/sec) are large, myelinated neurons.

   proprioceptive i. An afferent nerve impulse arising from stimuli originating in joints, muscles, tendons, or other sensory endings that respond to pressure or stretch.

impulse-control disorder A disorder marked by failure to resist impulses, drives, or temptations that may potentially cause harm. Impulse-control disorders include kleptomania, pyromania, pathological gambling, trichotillomania, and intermittent explosive disorder.

impulsion (ĭm-pŭl'shŭn) A persistent psychic drive to act that is not relieved until the action is taken. Clear consciousness of the proposed act followed by an agonizing struggle, defeat, and sense of relief following the act are characteristics of impulsions, obsessions, and inhibitions. Impulsions may include folie du doute or doubting mania (e.g., repeatedly checking to determine whether something has been done); obsessive fears of contact or delirium of touch; agoraphobia; dipsomania; pyro-

mania; kleptomania; homicidal or suicidal impulsion; onomatomania; arithmomania; exhibitionism.

imputed negligence (ĭm-pūt'ĕd) [L. *putare*, to think] The liability of the manager, owner, or leader of an enterprise for faulty behavior or injuries committed by his or her employees or subordinates.

IMRT *intensity-modulated radiation therapy.*

IMS *incident management system.*

IMV *intermittent mandatory ventilation; intermittent mechanical ventilation.*

In Symbol for the element indium.

¹in-, il-, im-, ir- [L. *in*, in, into; rel. to Gr. *en*, Eng. *in*] Prefix meaning *in, inside, within;*, as in *incorporated;* also used as a *transitive* or *intensive* prefix, as in *inflammable*. In- remains in- before vowels and c, f, g, h, n, q, s, t, v; it becomes il- before l; im- before b, m, and p; and ir- before r.

²in-, il-, im-, ir- [L. *in-*, not; rel. to Gr. *a-, an-*, Eng. *un-*] Prefixes meaning a *negative.*, as in *inactive*. In- remains in- before vowels and c, f, g, h, n, q, s, t, v; it becomes il- before l; im- before b, m, and p; and ir- before r.

-in [L. *-ina*, adj. suffix] Suffix in chemistry used in naming certain compounds, including *enzymes*, e.g., *pepsin; hormones*, e.g., *insulin; tissue and cell components*, e.g., *myosin; antibodies*, e.g., *agglutinin;* and *pharmaceuticals*, e.g., *streptomycin*. SEE: *-ine*.

inaccuracy (ĭn-ăk'ūr-ăsē) Inexactness as a result of measurement error.

inaccurate (ĭn-ăk'ūr-ăt) **1.** Mistaken or incorrect; in error. **2.** In quantitative analysis, not in agreement with an accepted value.

inaction (ĭn-ăk'shŭn) [L. *in-*, not, + *actio*, act] Failure of or decreased response to a stimulus.

inactivate (ĭn-ăk'tĭ-vāt") [" + *activus*, acting] To render inactive, esp. the alteration or destruction of an enzyme system or a biologically active agent such as a microorganism or antigen.

inactivation (ĭn-ăk"tĭ-vā'shŭn) Rendering anything inert by using heat or other means.

inactive cirrhosis SEE: under *cirrhosis*.

inanimate (ĭn-ăn'ĭ-măt) [" + *animatus*, alive] **1.** Not alive; not animate. **2.** Dull, lifeless.

inanition (ĭn"ă-nĭsh'ŭn) [L. *inanis*, empty] A debilitated condition caused by a lack of sufficient food material essential to the body, such as in starvation or malabsorption syndrome. This condition may also be due to causes other than the food supply, such as malabsorption, or to other diseases of the gastrointestinal system that prevent absorption of food.

inappetence (ĭn-ăp'ĕ-tĕns) [" + *appe-*

tere, to long for] A lack of craving or desire, esp. for food.

inarticulate (ĭn″ăr-tĭk′ū-lāt) [″ + *articulus,* joined] **1.** Not jointed; without joints. **2.** Unable to pronounce distinct syllables or express oneself intelligibly. **3.** Not given to expressing oneself verbally.

in articulo mortis (in ar-tĭk′yŭ-lō mort′ĭs) [L. *in articulo mortis,* at the moment of death] At the very moment of death.

inassimilable (ĭn″ă-sĭm′ĭ-lă-b′l) [″ + *assimilis,* to make similar] Not capable of being used by the body for nutrition.

inattention 1. Neglect, e.g., of sensory stimuli. **2.** Distractibility.

   unilateral i. An inability to recognize stimulation provided to the side of the body or the visual field damaged by a stroke in the nondominant hemisphere of the brain. Sometimes called visual inattention or visual unilateral inattention. SYN: *neglect, altitudinal; neglect, hemispatial.* SEE: *hemi-inattention; unilateral spatial agnosia.*

inborn (ĭn′born″) **1.** Innate or inherent; said of structural and functional characteristics inherited or acquired during uterine development. **2.** A premature infant delivered at a tertiary care medical center. SEE: *outborn.*

inbreeding (ĭn′brēd″ĭng) The mating of closely related individuals. It increases offspring homozygosity. SEE: *outbreeding.*

incandescent (ĭn″kăn-dĕs′ĕnt) [L. *incandescere,* to glow] Glowing with light; white hot.

incapacitate (ĭn″kă-păs′ĭ-tāt) Being made incapable of some function, act or strength. This may be purely physical or intellectual or both.

incarcerated (ĭn″kăr′sĕ-rāt-ĕd) [L. *incarcerare*] Imprisoned, constricted, and confined of blood flow, as an irreducible hernia.

incarceration (ĭn″kăr″sĕ-rā′shŭn) **1.** Legal confinement. **2.** The imprisonment of a part; constriction, as in a hernia.

incasement (ĭn-kās′mĕnt) Becoming surrounded by a structure or wall.

incentive (ĭn-sĕn′tĭv) Any stimulus that encourages a desired response. Incentives may be provided to patients (e.g., to ensure adherence to treatment plans), to practitioners (e.g., to improve productivity or job performance), or to students (e.g., to improve grades).

   financial i. A cash payment made to a patient who achieves a health-related goal such as sustaining a weight loss over a 6-month period or maintaining abstinence from a toxic substance.

inception (ĭn-sĕp′shŭn) [L. *inceptio,* taking in, beginning] **1.** The beginning of anything. **2.** Ingestion. **3.** Intussusception.

incest (ĭn′sĕst) [L. *incestus,* unchaste, in-

cest] Coitus between close blood relatives.

incidence (ĭn′sĭd-ĕns) [L. *incidens,* falling upon] The frequency of new cases of a disease or condition in a specific population or group. SEE: *prevalence.*

incidence proportion The cumulative incidence or rate of occurrence of a disease in a community.

incident (ĭn′sĭd-ĕnt) [L. *incidere,* to befall, happen] **1.** A happening, event, or occurrence. **2.** Falling or striking, as a ray of light.

   critical i. Medical jargon for a crisis.

   medical i. In legal medicine, any action or failure to act that adversely affects a patient.

   multiple casualty i. ABBR: MCI. Medical or traumatic emergencies that involve more than one patient (e.g., in automobile or plane crashes, bombings, fires, hazardous materials spills, or acts of terrorism).

incidental host SEE: under *host.*

incidentaloma (ĭn″sĭd-ent″ăl-ō′mă) [*incidental* + *-oma*] A colloquial term for a glandular tumor discovered by chance during an imaging study performed to evaluate another organ, symptom, or disease.

incident command system ABBR: ICS. Incident management system.

incident management system ABBR: IMS. A system designed to assist in the management and command of emergency operations such as natural disasters, civil disturbances, multiple casualty incidents, hazardous materials incidents, fires, and acts of terrorism. The key components to the system include finance, logistics, operations, and planning. SYN: *incident command system.*

incident pain SEE: under *pain.*

incident screening The scheduling of follow-up screening examinations (e.g., mammograms) at predetermined intervals after an initial study.

incineration (ĭn-sĭn″ĕr-ā′shŭn) [L. *in,* into, + *cineres,* ashes] Destruction by fire; cremation.

incipient (ĭn-sĭp′ē-ĕnt) [L. *incipere,* to begin] Beginning; coming into existence.

incisal (ĭn-sī′zăl) Relating to or involving cutting.

incise (ĭn-sīz′) [L. *incisus*] To cut, as with a sharp instrument.

incised (ĭn-sīzd′) Cut cleanly, as with a knife.

incision (in-sizh′ŏn) [L. *incisio,* a cut] A cut made with a knife, electrosurgical unit, or laser, esp. for surgical purposes.

   coronal i. **1.** An incision made across the scalp in a plane that separates the front (anterior portion) of the head from the back (posterior portion). **2.** A crown-shaped incision.

   limbal relaxing i. ABBR: LRI. A surgical treatment for astigmatism in which the cornea is reshaped by placing small cuts in its periphery (the limbus of the cornea). These incisions make the misshapen cornea more spherical, which improves visual clarity.

McBurney i. SEE: under *McBurney, Charles.*

paramedian i. A surgical incision, esp. of the abdominal wall, close to the midline.

Pfannenstiel i. SEE: *Pfannenstiel incision.*

relaxing i. A second incision made during surgery to promote drainage, relieve the tension on a wound as it is sutured, or facilitate mobilization of a sliding tissue flap. SYN: *counterincision; counteropening.*

transurethral laser i. of the prostate ABBR: TULIP. The treatment of prostatic hyperplasia with a laser used as a cutting instrument. The laser is inserted into the penile urethra and directed at the diseased portion of the gland.

incisive (ĭn-sī′sĭv) [L. *incisivus*] **1.** Cutting; having the power of cutting. **2.** Relating to the incisor teeth.

incisor (ĭn-sī′zor) [L., a cutter] **1.** That which cuts. **2.** That which applies to the incisor teeth. **3.** One of the cutting teeth; the four front teeth in each jaw of the adult. SEE: *dentition.*

central i. One of two upper and lower incisors adjacent to the midsagittal plane.

incisura (ĭn″sī′-zhoor′ă) *pl.* **incisurae** [L.] **1.** An incision. **2.** Incisure; notch; emargination; indentation at the edge of any structure.

i. angularis gastrica A fold or notch on the distal end of the lesser curvature of the stomach.

incisure (ĭn-sī′zhĕr) [L. *incisura,* a cutting into] A notch or slit.

i. of Schmidt-Lanterman Channels of cytoplasm found in myelinated nerve fibers that were once thought to represent breaks in the myelin sheath.

incitant (ĭn-sīt′ănt) [L. *incitare,* to set in motion] The stimulus that sets off a reaction, disease, or incident.

inclination (ĭn″klĭ-nā′shŭn) [L. *inclinere,* to slope] Leaning from the normal or from the vertical, as a tooth or the pelvis.

inclinometer (ĭn″klĭ-nom′ĕt-ĕr) [*incline* + -*meter*] **1.** A device for measuring ocular diameter from vertical and horizontal lines. **2.** A device for measuring angles among different body parts, e.g., specific bones or joints. It can be used to determine the relative motion of these structures during active or passive bending. SYN: *bubble goniometer.*

inclusion (ĭn-kloo-zhŭn) [L. *inclusus,* enclosed] Being enclosed or included.

i. body Microscopic structures (made of a dense, occasionally infective core surrounded by an envelope) seen in the cytoplasm and nuclei of cells infected with some intracellular pathogens. Inclusion bodies are seen in cells infected with herpesviruses (esp. cytomegalovirus), smallpox, lymphogranuloma venereum, psittacosis, and other organisms. SYN: *cell i.*; SEE: *Negri bodies.*

cell i. Inclusion body.

fetal i. Malformed twins in which one, the parasite, is completely enclosed within the other, its host or autosite. SEE: *teratoma.*

incoagulability (ĭn″kō-ăg″ū-lă-bĭl′ĭ-tē) [L. *in-,* not, + *coagulare,* to congeal] Not coagulable.

incoherence (ĭn″kō-hēr′ĕns) [″ + *cohairens,* adhering] An inability to express oneself coherently or to present ideas in a related order.

incoherent (ĭn″kō-hē′rĕnt) Not coherent or understandable.

incombustible (ĭn″kŏm-bŭs′tĭ-bl) [″ + *combustus,* burned] Incapable of being burned.

incompatibility (ĭn″kŏm-pă″tĭ-bĭl′ĭ-tē) [L. *incompatibilis*] **1.** The quality of not being suitable for mixture. It can be applied to a state that renders admixture of medicines unsuitable through chemical action or interaction, insolubility, formation of poisonous or explosive compounds, difference in solubility, or antagonistic action. **2.** The quality of not being mixed without chemical changes, or without countering the action of other ingredients in a compound. **3.** The condition of not being in harmony with one's surroundings or associates, esp. a spouse or friend.

ABO i. An antigen-antibody immune response to infusion of another's red blood cells. Transfusion reactions occur most commonly in people with type O blood, which carries no antigens on the red blood cells and contains both anti-A and anti-B antibodies. People with type A blood carry A antigens on their red cells and anti-B antibodies; those with type B blood carry B antigens and anti-A antibodies; those with type AB blood carry both A and B antigens but no antibodies to A or B. The antibodies are called natural antibodies because their formation does not require sensitization by A and B antigens. The antibodies recognize the antigens on the donor cells as foreign and destroy them by agglutination and lysis. ABO incompatibilities are different from Rh incompatibilities, which are most commonly related to the D antigen in the Rh blood group. SEE: table; *blood group.*

Obstetrics: Transplacental fetal-maternal transfusion occurs when fetal blood cells escape into the maternal circulation, eliciting antibody formation. Maternal antibodies then cross the placenta into the fetal circulation, attack,

Blood Type Compatibility

Donor Blood Type	Compatibility with Recipient Blood Type			
	Type A Blood	Type B Blood	Type AB Blood	Type O Blood
A	yes	no	yes	no
B	no	yes	yes	no
AB	no	no	yes	no
O	yes	yes	yes	yes

and destroy red blood cells, as evidenced by neonatal hyperbilirubinemia and jaundice.

physiological i. A condition in which one or more substances in a mixture oppose or counteract one of the other compounds being administered.

incompatible (ĭn″kŏm-pă′tĭ-bl) **1.** Not capable of uniting. **2.** Antagonistic in action, said of some drugs. **3.** Not being in harmony with one's environment, situation, or associates, esp. a spouse or friend.

incompetence, incompetency (ĭn″kom′pĕt-ĕns, ĭn″kom′pĕt-ĕn-sē) [L. *incompetens* insufficient] Inadequate ability to perform the function or action normal to an organ or part.

aortic i. Aortic **insufficiency**.

cervical i. Structural inability of the cervical os to remain closed and support a growing fetus. This problem has commonly been associated with recurrent spontaneous second-trimester abortions. A higher incidence of this structural abnormality is noted after cervical trauma, e.g., previous vaginal or cesarean births, cervical laceration, conization of the cervix. It also has been reported among daughters whose mothers were treated with diethylstilbestrol (DES) during their pregnancies. Traditionally, cerclage has been used for treatment even though controlled trials of its effectiveness have not been uniformly successful. SEE: *cerclage; Shirodkar operation*.

chronotropic i. An inappropriate response of the heart rate to stimulation, e.g., a slow heart rate during an exercise stress test.

ileocecal i. Inability of the ileocecal valve to stop the return of the feces from the colon to the ileum.

mental i. Legal disqualification to execute a contract or perform normal activities and tasks.

muscular i. Imperfect closure of one of the atrioventricular valves due to weak action of papillary muscles.

pyloric i. A weakness of the pyloric sphincter, which permits undigested food to leave the stomach and enter the duodenum.

relative i. Excessive dilatation of a cardiac cavity, rendering it impossible for the cardiac valves leading in and out of the chamber to close perfectly.

valvular i. Backward flow of blood through a valve, e.g., a cardiac valve during the stage of the cardiac cycle when the valve leaflets should be closed. SYN: *valvular insufficiency*.

velopharyngeal i. Velopharyngeal **insufficiency**.

venous i. Inability of a vein to prevent the backward flow of blood because of valve diseases or complications of deep venous thrombosis.

incompetent palatal syndrome (ĭn-kŏm′pĭ-tĭnt păl′ă-tĭl sĭn′drŏm″) Incomplete or ineffective separation by the soft palate of the nasopharynx from the oropharynx, characterized by hypernasality and distortion of speech called whinolalia. This syndrome may be due to congenital or acquired defects of the palate.

incompressible (ĭn″kŏm-prĕs′ĭ-bl) [″ + *compressus*, pressed together] Compact; not compressible.

inconsolable (ĭn″kŏn-sō′lŏ-bĭl) [L. *inconsolabilis*] Said of an infant or child who is extremely irritable and cannot be comforted despite its parents' best efforts. In pediatrics inconsolability is a clinical indicator of severe illness.

incontinence (in-kont′ĭn-ĕns) [L. *incontinentia,* inability to retain] **1.** Loss of self-control, esp. of urine, feces, or semen. **2.** Loss of neurological or psychological control, e.g., of habits, speech, or of the appetites for food or sex.

anal i. fecal **i.**

fecal i. Failure of the anal sphincter to prevent involuntary expulsion of gas, liquid, or solids from the lower bowel. SYN: *anal i.* SEE: *encopresis*.

functional urinary i. Inability of a usually continent person to reach the toilet in time to avoid unintentional loss of urine. Urinary incontinence (UI) affects about 30% of older adults living at home and about 50% of those in nursing care facilities. Women are more likely than men to develop UI. UI can result in physical problems such as skin breakdown, but it also causes emotional problems such as embarrassment, frustration, depression, and loss of self-esteem, which may lead to social isolation, loss of independence, and even institutionalization. SEE: *Nursing Diagnoses Appendix.*

PATIENT CARE: Health care professionals should make questions about incontinence a routine part of taking a patient's history because the patient may be too embarrassed to report the problem without prompting. The type of episodes experienced should be documented and how long the problem has been present. Many factors may be involved, including neurologic disorders, urinary tract infection, adverse drug effects, irritants such as artificial sweeteners, caffeine, certain foods, and decreased muscle tone. Physical examination should follow up on the problem, and a urologic consultation may be warranted.

Functional UI may afflict older adults who have normal bladder control but have a difficult time getting to the toilet because of problems that interfere with mobility, e.g., arthritis, Parkinson disease, or stroke. Environmental factors (such as clutter, lack of ready access to facilities, distance to the toilet) may also play a part. Health care professionals should assess the patient's fluid intake to be sure he or she is drinking enough and should review his or her medication regimen to determine if any of the drugs affect continence. The patient should be encouraged to use the toilet on a planned schedule (upon arising, before and after each meal and at bedtime, and as adjusted to his or her needs). For patients living independently, walkways should be kept free of clutter, and, if necessary, a commode placed closer to the person's living space.

    giggle i. Involuntary passage of urine induced by laughter. The condition occurs commonly in young girls and women but tends to improve in the second or third decade of life. It is distinct from stress urinary incontinence, which usually begins after menopause. SEE: *stress urinary i.*

    intermittent i. Loss of control of the bladder upon sudden pressure or movement.

    i. of milk Galactorrhea.

    overflow i. Incontinence characterized by small frequent voidings due to leakage of small amounts of urine spilling from an overfilled bladder, or to a bladder with pathologically decreased volume. SEE: *Nursing Diagnoses Appendix.*

PATIENT CARE: Overflow incontinence is more common in men than in women and requires further evaluation because it may be triggered by diabetes mellitus, multiple sclerosis, spinal injury, or benign prostatic hypertrophy. Sterile intermittent catheterization or an indwelling urinary catheter may be prescribed because retained urine can

lead to infection and other complications. Male patients may benefit from alpha-adrenergic antagonists such as prazosin and terazosin, which decrease bladder outlet resistance and improve emptying. Patient, family, home health aides, and long-term-care health care assistants involved with the patient's care should be taught about adverse reactions to these drugs, which need to be observed for and reported and include postural hypotension, palpitations, headache, nausea, and dizziness. If the patient feels dizzy while taking medications for incontinence, he or she should be advised to sit or lie down and taught to change position slowly. The patient should not drive or operate machinery of any kind until he or she knows how the drug affects his or her safety and mental alertness.

Coping strategies for overflow incontinence include allowing enough time for toileting and providing external collection devices such as a urinal or external (condom) catheter at night. Teaching the patient to perform a Credé method (applying gentle pressure above the symphysis pubis in a downward direction with the blade of the hand) may increase emptying. Assessing residual urine with a portable noninvasive bladder ultrasound scanner, and following with intermittent catheterization if the residual amount is above specified limits, can assist the patient in learning to empty the bladder.

    overflow urinary i. Involuntary loss of urine associated with overdistention of the bladder. SEE: *Nursing Diagnoses Appendix.* SEE: *overflow i.*

    paralytic i. The constant voiding of small amounts of urine and feces owing to stroke or other central nervous system disorders.

    passive i. A form of urinary incontinence in which a full bladder allows urine to drip away upon pressure instead of emptying normally.

    reflex urinary i. An involuntary loss of urine at somewhat predictable intervals when a specific bladder volume is reached. SEE: *Nursing Diagnoses Appendix.*

    risk for urinary urge i. Risk for involuntary loss of urine associated with a sudden, strong sensation or urinary urgency. SEE: *Nursing Diagnoses Appendix.*

    stress urinary i. ABBR: SUI. Sudden leakage of urine with activities that increase intra-abdominal pressure. SEE: *Nursing Diagnoses Appendix.*

DIAGNOSIS: Direct observation of urine loss while coughing is a reliable method of establishing this diagnosis. Laughing, sneezing, lifting a heavy object, and exercising are other triggers. The urine should be cultured to rule out urinary tract infection. Ultrasound of the bladder after the patient voids establishes the residual urine volume and helps rule out retention with overflow. Stress urinary incontinence should be investigated to ensure that it is not caused by a structural abnormality.

TREATMENT: In addition to using devices to absorb urine that escapes, therapy consists of behavioral modification, pharmacological treatment, and surgical management. Behavioral therapy includes bladder training, timed voiding, prompted voiding, and pelvic muscle (Kegel) exercises. Pharmacotherapy includes oxybutynin hydrochloride, propantheline bromide, and imipramine hydrochloride. Surgery may restore anatomic support of the urethra or compensate for a poorly functioning urethral sphincter. The American Urological Association considers sling procedures and retropubic suspensions the most effective surgeries long term. The transvaginal tape (TVT) sling procedure is performed as outpatient surgery under local anesthesia with a small vaginal incision and two small suprapubic incisions. The sling supports the urethra during stress and the increases in intra-abdominal pressure that occur during routine activities. SEE: *bladder drill; Kegel exercise.*

PATIENT CARE: The patient learns Kegel exercises to strengthen pubococcygeal muscles and encouraged to practice the exercises at frequent intervals throughout the day, as well as during urination (by stopping and starting the urinary stream intermittently). The vulva and introitus should be kept clean and dry and free from free. Commercial barrier products should be used to protect clothing. To avoid the social isolation and depression that may result from this condition, the patient should be encouraged to continue or resume usual activities while using protective barriers. The patient's response to the exercise regimen is periodically evaluated. If conservative therapies are ineffective, surgery may be recommended to improve not only the urinary problem but also the patient's quality of life. Postoperative precautions include: avoid lifting objects weighing 15 lb (6.8 kg) or more for 3 months; avoid driving for 1 to 2 weeks; avoid strenuous exercise (running, cycling) for 4 to 6 weeks; avoid tub baths for 4 weeks (may shower immediately); refrain from sexual intercourse for 4 weeks. Oral analgesics are prescribed for discomfort expected during the first 24 to 48 hr. Continued or increasing pain, blood in the urine, or painful or difficult urination should be reported.

total urinary i. Continuous and un-predictable loss of urine. SEE: *Nursing Diagnoses Appendix.*

urge urinary i. Involuntary passage of urine occurring soon after a strong sense of urgency to void. Drugs that inhibit the detrusor muscle of the bladder, such as oxybutynin, can be used as treatment. SEE: *Nursing Diagnoses Appendix.*

PATIENT CARE: Healthy older adults may develop urge incontinence, but it also can affect those who have suffered a stroke or who have Alzheimer disease, Parkinson disease, multiple sclerosis, or diabetes mellitus. Bladder retraining and Kegel exercises should be the first therapies for urge incontinence. The patient should maintain a regular toileting schedule, beginning with every 1 to 2 hr, then gradually increasing the time between voiding. Keeping a diary of fluid intake, urine output, and any episodes of incontinence helps the patient and the primary health care provider recognize patterns and revise the regimen as needed. The patient should carry out Kegel exercises when the urge to void starts because these exercises help strengthen perineal muscles, which may provide the patient more time to reach the toilet. Anticholinergic drugs, such as oxybutynin and tolterodine, that inhibit the detrusor muscle of the bladder can be prescribed. Patients should be aware of potential adverse effects, which include confusion, dry mouth, dry eyes, urinary retention, constipation, and blurred vision.

urinary i. ABBR: UI. Intermittent or complete absence of ability to control loss of urine from the bladder. It is a problem that affects about 25% of women over 60 and may have significant impact on social, occupational, and psychological functioning.

TREATMENT: Therapy will depend upon the cause. Information on this subject may be obtained from Health for Incontinent People at 800-251-3337. SYN: ***i. of urine.*** SEE: *Kegel exercise.*

i. of urine Urinary **i.**

incontinence, overflow urinary Involuntary loss of urine associated with overdistention of the bladder. SEE: *overflow **incontinence**; Nursing Diagnoses Appendix.*

incontinentia pigmenti (in-kont″ĭn-en′sh(ē-)ă pig-ment′ī″) [L. *incontinentia pigmenti,* inability to retain pigment] An X-linked neurocutaneous disorder marked by excessive accumulation of melanin in the skin, cerebral atrophy, mental retardation and seizures, and defective development of bones and teeth. Affected males often die in early childhood. SYN: *Bloch-Sulzberger syndrome.*

in control Within an acceptable predetermined range. The limits that define the acceptable range may be set using one or more criteria, depending on the intent. A typical analytical "in-control" limit is based on the calculation of the dispersion of the data measured as standard deviation (SD). Subsequent multiplication of the SD by 2 and then by 3 results in what frequently are used as "warning" and "action" limits, respectively. Other statistical or clinical criteria also can be used to set the limits. SEE: *standard deviation*.

incoordinate (ĭn″kō-or′dĭ-nāt″) [L. *in-*, not, + *coordinare*, to arrange] **1.** Not able to make coordinated muscular movements. **2.** Unable to adjust one's work harmoniously with others.

incoordinate uterine contraction SEE: under *contraction*.

incoordination (ĭn″kō-or″dĭ-nā′shŭn) An inability to produce harmonious, rhythmic, muscular action that is not due to weakness. The condition is typically caused by a lesion on the cerebellum. SYN: *asynergia*.

incorporation [L. *in*, into, + *corporare*, to form into a body] Combining two ingredients to form a homogeneous mass.

increment (ĭn′krĕ-mĕnt) [L. *incrementum*] **1.** An increase or addition in number, size, or extent; an enlargement. **2.** Something added or gained. **3.** The beginning portion of a uterine contraction between baseline and acme. Increasing strength of contraction is shown by the upslope record recorded by the fetal monitor.

incretin (in-krēt′ĭn) One of several peptide hormones produced by the small intestine or colon in response to glucose. Incretins stimulate the secretion of insulin and inhibit the secretion of glucagon.

incrustation (ĭn″krŭs″tā′shŭn) [L. *in*, on, + *crusta*, crust] The formation of crusts or scabs.

incubation (ing″kyŭ-bā′shŏn, in′) [L. *incubare*, to lie down on] **1.** The interval between exposure to infection and the appearance of the first symptom. SYN: *incubation period; latent period* (2). SEE: table. **incubational** (′shŏn-ăl), *adj.* **2.** In bacteriology, the period of culture development. **3.** The development of a fertilized ovum. **4.** The care of a premature infant in an incubator.

incubation period SEE: under *period*.

incubator (ing′kyŭ-bāt″ŏr, in′) [L. *incubare*, to lie down on] **1.** An enclosed crib, in which the temperature and humidity may be regulated, for care of premature babies. SYN: *isolette*. **2.** An apparatus for providing suitable atmospheric conditions for culturing bacteria or for maintaining eggs until they hatch.

incubus (ĭn′kū-bŭs) [L. *incubare*, to lie upon] A nightmare.

incudectomy (ĭng″kū-dĕk′tō-mē) [″ +

Gr. *ektome*, excision] The surgical removal of all or part of the incus of the middle ear.

incurable (ĭn-kūr′ă-bl) [L. *in-*, not, + *curare*, to care for] Not capable of being cured.

incurvation (ĭn″kŭr-vā′shŭn) [L. *incurvare*, to bend in] State of being bent or curved in.

incus (ing′kŭs, ing-kūd′ēz″, ing′kyŭ-dēz″) *pl.* **incudes** [L. *incus*, anvil] The second of the three auditory ossicles, which form a chain that conducts vibrations through the middle ear from the tympanic membrane to the oval window of the inner ear. The incus has the shape of a bicycle saddle (the body) with its post (the long limb or lenticular process). The body articulates with the malleus, and the lenticular process articulates with the stapes. SYN: *anvil*. SEE: *ear* for illus.

incyclophoria (ĭn-sī″klō-for′ē-ă) [L. *in-*, not, + Gr. *kyklos*, circle, + *phoros*, bearing] Median or negative cyclophoria in which the affected eye, when covered, turns inward about its anteroposterior axis.

indemnify (ĭn-dĕm′nĭ-fī″) [L. *indemnis*, without loss] **1.** To protect the interests of another party against losses. **2.** To compensate another party for expenses incurred, as when a policy holder is indemnified by an insurance company.

indentation (ĭn″dĕn-tā′shŭn) [L. *in*, in, + *dens*, tooth] A depression or hollow.

indentation gonioscopy SEE: under *gonioscopy*.

independent living In rehabilitation, thriving on one's own; living autonomously and actively in one's own home and community.

independent living center SEE: under *center*.

independent living skills Skills such as shopping, cooking, cleaning, and child care that are necessary for maintaining the home environment.

independent practice association ABBR: IPA. An integrated group of health care professionals who share patients, premiums, and practices to jointly manage costs, risks, and health care delivery.

index (in′deks″, in′dĭ-sēz″) *pl.* **indexes, indices** [L. *index*, pointer] **1.** The forefinger. **2.** The ratio of the measurement of a given substance to that of a fixed standard.

 addiction severity i. A structured assessment tool that evaluates the impact of addictive behavior on seven areas of living: alcohol use, drug use, employment, family relationships, illegal activities, physical health, and psychological health.

 alveolar i. Gnathic **i.**

 ankle-brachial i. ABBR: ABI. A measure of the adequacy of blood flow to

Incubation and Isolation Periods in Common Infections*

Infection	Incubation Period	Isolation of Patient†
AIDS	Unclear; antibodies appear within 1–3 months of infection	Protective isolation if T-cell count is very low; private room only necessary with severe diarrhea, bleeding, copious blood-tinged sputum if patient has poor personal hygiene habits
Bloodstream (bacteremia, fungemia)	Variable; usually 2–5 days	
Brucellosis	Highly variable, usually 5–21 days; may be months	None
Chickenpox	2–3 weeks	1 week after vesicles appear or until vesicles become dry
Cholera	A few hours to 5 days	Enteric precautions
Common cold	12 hr–5 days	None
Dysentery, amebic	From a few days to several months, commonly 2–4 weeks	None
Dysentery, bacillary (e.g., shigellosis)	12–96 hr	As long as stools remain positive
Encephalitis, mosquito-borne	5–15 days	None
Giardiasis	3–25 days or longer; median 7–10 days	Enteric precautions
Gonorrhea	2–7 days; may be longer	No sexual contact until cured
Hepatitis A	15–50 days	Enteric (gloves with infected material; gowns as needed to protect clothing)
Hepatitis B	45–180 days	Blood and body fluid precautions (gloves and plastic gowns for contact with infective materials)
Hepatitis C	14–180 days	As for hepatitis B
Hepatitis D	2–8 weeks	As for hepatitis B
Hepatitis E	15–64 days	Enteric precautions
Influenza	1–3 days	As practical
Legionella	2–10 days	None
Lyme disease	3–32 days after tick bite	None
Malaria	7–10 days for *Plasmodium falciparum*; 8–14 days for *P. vivax, P. ovale*; 7–30 days for *P. malariae*	Protection from mosquitoes
Measles (rubeola)	8–13 days from exposure to onset of fever; 14 days until rash appears	From diagnosis to 7 days after appearance of rash; strict isolation from children under 3 years
Meningitis	2–10 days	Until 24 hr after start of chemotherapy
Mononucleosis, infectious	4–6 weeks	None; disinfection of articles soiled with nose and throat discharges
Mumps	12–25 days	Until the glands recede
Paratyphoid fevers	3 days–3 months; usually 1–3 weeks; 1–10 days for gastroenteritis	Until 3 stools are negative
Pneumonia, pneumococcal	Believed to be 1–3 days	Enteric precautions in hospital. Respiratory isolation may be required.

Table continued on following page

Incubation and Isolation Periods in Common Infections* (Continued)

Infection	Incubation Period	Isolation of Patient†
Puerperal fever, streptococcal	1–3 days	Transfer from maternity ward
Rabies	Usually 2–8 weeks; rarely as short as 9 days or as long as 7 years.	Strict for duration of illness; danger to attendants
Rubella (German measles)	16–18 days with range of 14–23 days	None; no contact with nonimmune pregnant women
Salmonellosis	6–72 hr, usually 12–36 hr	Until stool cultures are *Salmonella* free on two consecutive specimens collected in 24-hr period
Scabies	2–6 weeks before onset of itching in patients without previous infections; 1–4 days after re-exposed	Patient is excused from school or work until day after treatment
Trachoma	5–12 days	Until lesions disappear, but usually not practical
Tuberculosis	4–12 weeks to demonstrable primary lesion or significant tuberculin reactions	Variable, depending on conversion of sputum to negative after specific therapy and on ability of patient to understand and carry out personal hygiene methods

* SEE: *Standard Precautions Appendix.*
† Standard precautions and handwashing are assumed.

the arteries of the legs. It is used to gauge the severity of peripheral vascular disease.

PATIENT CARE: The index is obtained by measuring the systolic blood pressure in the upper and lower extremities after the patient has been lying on his or her back for about 5 min and then repeating the measurements after the patient walks for 5 min. There are several ways to obtain an ABI. The most accurate test results are obtained by measuring the blood pressure in both arms using a blood pressure cuff and Doppler ultrasound and recording the higher of these two pressures. The measurement is repeated in each leg, with measurement of blood pressures at both the posterior tibial and dorsalis pedis arteries. The pressure that should be recorded is the pressure found during the first return of a pulse to the cuffed limb. The blood pressure in each leg is divided by the blood pressure in the higher pressure of the two arms to obtain an ABI for each lower extremity. An ABI above 0.9 is normal, except when it exceeds 1.3 (an indicator of severe peripheral arterial obstruction). Severe obstruction is also indicated by an ABI of less than 0.5. Moderate peripheral arterial disease is suggested by an ABI of 0.8. A drop in the ABI after exercise also strongly suggests peripheral arterial disease. Patients with mild or moderately abnormal ABIs are usually treated with antiplatelet medica-

tions, an exercise regimen, and cholesterol-lowering drugs or diet. Those who smoke are encouraged to quit. Patients with severe disease may need angiography and, in some instances, arterial bypass surgery or stenting.

apnea-hypopnea i. ABBR: AHI. The number of times in an hour when a sleeping person either stops breathing completely or has limited airflow. Each episode must last at least 10 sec. The AHI is one indicator of obstructive sleep apnea, although it is recognized as an imperfect diagnostic tool. An AHI of 30 or more events in an hour indicates severe sleep apnea; 15 to 29 events suggests moderate apnea; and 5 to 14 events indicates mild apnea.

Barthel i. SEE: *Barthel index.*

bispectral i. ABBR: BIS. An electroencephalographic measure of the effect of sedative and hypnotic drugs on an anesthetized patient. It is used (along with clinical assessment of the patient) to determine the level of central nervous system depression. The index ranges from zero (completely unresponsive to stimulation) to 100 (awake and alert). At levels below 60, most patients are adequately sedated for surgery.

body mass i. ABBR: BMI. An index for estimating obesity. The BMI can be obtained by dividing weight in kilograms by height in meters squared, or according to the following formula: BMI = (Weight/2.205) / (Height/39.37)^2 . In adults, a BMI greater than 30 kg/m^2 indicates obesity; a BMI greater than 40 kg/m^2 indicates morbid obesity; and a BMI less than 18.5 kg/m^2 indicates a person is underweight. The lowest overall death rate is found in people with a BMI of 20 to 24.9 kg/m^2. SYN: *Quetelet i.* SEE: illus.

cardiac i. The cardiac output (expressed in liters per minute) divided by the body surface area (expressed in square meters).

cephalic i. The biparietal diameter of the skull divided by its occipitofrontal diameter, all multiplied by 100.

cerebral i. The ratio of greatest transverse diameter to the greatest anteroposterior diameter of the cranium.

chemotherapeutic i. The ratio of the toxicity of a drug, expressed as the maximum tolerated dose per kilogram of body weight to the minimal curative dose per kilogram of body weight. This index is used in judging the safety and effectiveness of drugs.

clinical risk i. for babies ABBR: CRIB. An index of the severity of illness, used to estimate the likelihood of mortality in very low birth weight infants who are cared for in a neonatal intensive care unit.

Cumulative I. to Nursing and Allied Health Literature SEE: *Cumulative Index to Nursing and Allied Health Literature*.

DMF i. The index of dental health and caries experience based on the number of decayed, missing, and filled (DMF) teeth or tooth surfaces.

dynamic gait i. ABBR: DGI. A semiquantitative tool used to evaluate a patient's ability to modify gait by changing task demands, esp. in patients with dizziness and balance deficits. This test is used to identify patients, esp. older adults, who are predisposed to falling. Patients are graded on their ability to vary speed, turn their heads, turn their bodies, step over and around obstacles, climb stairs, turn while walking, pick objects up from the floor, and perform alternate step-ups on a stool.

exposure i. A relative value indicating the quantity of ionizing radiation received by a digital radiographic image receptor. Although vendors currently use many kinds of exposure indices, e.g., Sensitivity Numbers, standardization is being developed by physicists' organizations.

fatigue i. The difference between the muscle power generated during peak exertion and the power that can be generated after repeated loading and unloading of the muscle.

Frenchay Activities I. A formal interview for patients who have suffered a stroke to compare their functional abilities preceding and following the stroke. The patient describes how employment, meal preparation and clean up, gardening, shopping, and other activities of daily living have been altered by the stroke.

gas exchange i. One of several measurements of the efficiency of respiration, esp. of the extent of intrapulmonary shunting in respiratory failure. Among the commonly used gas exchange indices is the alveolar-arterial oxygen tension difference (a measurement derived from an analysis of the oxygen tension of an arterial blood gas compared with the atmospheric oxygen content).

glycemic i. A ratio used to describe the ability of a food to increase blood glucose levels as compared with consumption of either glucose or white bread as the standard. Foods with a low

Federal health guidelines in the U.S. call for use of the Body Mass Index (BMI) to help assess overweight and obesity. A BMI of 25 or more is considered overweight. On the chart below your BMI is located at the intersection of your height and weight.

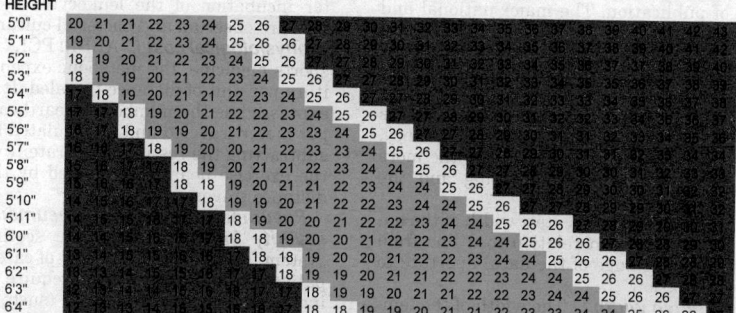

WEIGHT	100	105	110	115	120	125	130	135	140	145	150	155	160	165	170	175	180	185	190	195	200	205	210	215	220
HEIGHT																									
5'0"	20	21	21	22	23	24	25	26	27	28	29	30	31	32	33	34	35	36	37	38	39	40	41	42	43
5'1"	19	20	21	22	23	24	25	26	26	27	28	29	30	31	32	33	34	35	36	37	38	39	40	41	42
5'2"	18	19	20	21	22	23	24	25	26	27	27	28	29	30	31	32	33	34	35	36	37	37	38	39	40
5'3"	18	19	19	20	21	22	23	24	25	26	27	27	28	29	30	31	32	33	34	35	36	36	37	38	39
5'4"	17	18	19	20	21	21	22	23	24	25	26	27	27	28	29	30	31	32	33	33	34	35	36	37	38
5'5"		18	19	20	21	22	22	23	24	25	26	26	27	28	29	30	30	31	32	33	34	34	35	36	37
5'6"		18	19	19	20	21	22	23	23	24	25	26	27	27	28	29	30	30	31	32	33	34	34	35	36
5'7"			18	19	20	20	21	22	23	23	24	25	26	27	27	28	29	29	30	31	32	32	33	34	35
5'8"			18	19	20	21	21	22	23	24	24	25	26	26	27	28	29	29	30	31	31	32	33	34	34
5'9"			18	18	19	20	21	21	22	23	24	24	25	26	27	27	28	29	29	30	31	31	32	33	33
5'10"				18	19	19	20	21	22	22	23	24	24	25	26	27	27	28	29	29	30	31	31	32	33
5'11"					18	19	20	20	21	22	22	23	24	24	25	26	26	27	28	28	29	30	31	31	32
6'0"					18	18	19	20	20	21	22	22	23	24	24	25	26	26	27	28	28	29	30	30	31
6'1"						18	18	19	20	20	21	22	22	23	24	24	25	26	26	27	28	28	29	30	30
6'2"							18	19	19	20	21	21	22	23	23	24	24	25	26	26	27	28	28	29	29
6'3"								18	19	19	20	21	21	22	22	23	24	24	25	26	26	27	28	28	29
6'4"								18	18	19	19	20	21	21	22	23	23	24	24	25	26	26	27	27	28

SOURCES: Shape Up America; National Institutes of Health

BODY MASS INDEX

glycemic index result in a slower rise and lower maximum elevation of blood glucose levels than foods with a higher glycemic index. Consumption of low glycemic index foods can contribute to blood glucose regulation in patients with diabetes mellitus. Another use for the index is to identify the choice of food that will raise blood sugar levels after, e.g., endurance exercise.

gnathic i. A measure of the degree of projection of the upper jaw by finding the ratio of the distance from the nasion to the basion to that of the basion to the alveolar point and then multiplying by 100. SYN: *alveolar i.*

International Sensitivity I. ABBR: ISI. A laboratory standard for thromboplastins, the reagents used to determine the prothrombin time (PT). Because thromboplastin contents vary, PT results performed on the same sample of blood in different laboratories can be markedly different, even though the patient's actual level of anticoagulation is a constant. The ISI is used to calculate the international normalized ratio, a standardized measure of anticoagulation, thus enabling health care professionals working with different laboratories to compare results and adjust anticoagulant doses according to a single set of guidelines.

Karnofsky I. SEE: *Karnofsky Index.*

labeling i. The rate at which cells take up identifiable chemicals that they use in cell division. The index is a measure of the rate of the reproduction of the cells, as in fetal tissue development or the growth of cancers.

life satisfaction i. ABBR: LSI. A self-reporting instrument to measure personal fulfillment or contentment, esp. with one's social relationships, occupation, maturation, or aging. A total of five rating scales are used.

McMurtry I. SEE: *McMurtry index.*

I. Medicus A publication of the National Library of Medicine that lists biomedical and health sciences journal articles by title, subject, field, and country of publication. The major national and international medical and biological journals are indexed.

mitotic i. The number of mitoses seen in a biopsy specimen per square millimeter of tissue examined. Mitoses in tissue are indicative of malignancy. The higher the mitotic index, the more rapidly a tumor is dividing and the worse the prognosis.

nasal i. The greatest width of the nasal aperture in relation to a line from the lower edge of the nasal aperture to the nasion.

notch width i. The width of the femoral intercondylar notch divided by the width of the femoral condyles.

opsonic i. A ratio of the number of bacteria that are ingested by leukocytes contained in the serum of a normal individual compared with the number ingested by leukocytes in the study patient's blood serum.

oral hygiene i. ABBR: OHI. A popular indicator developed in 1960 to determine oral hygiene status in epidemiological studies. The index consists of an oral debris score and a calculus score. Six indicator teeth are examined for soft deposits and calculus. Numerical values are assigned to the six indicator teeth according to the extraneous deposits present. The scores are added and divided by the number of surfaces examined to calculate the average oral hygiene score.

Oswestry Disability I. ABBR: ODI. A questionnaire that requires a patient to rate the effect of back pain on 10 different activities, each having six levels of disability. The test was designed to assess patients with failed back surgery, but it is widely used for nonsurgical patients with other spinal conditions. SYN: *Oswestry disability score.*

oxygenation i. ABBR: OI. A measure of the efficiency of oxygen exchange by the lungs. The index is used in critical care medicine to assess the severity of acute lung injury and to gauge the effectiveness of ventilator management strategies. Mathematically it is represented as the product of the fractional concentration of inspired oxygen and the mean airway pressure, divided by the arterial oxygen concentration.

Pearl i. SEE: *Pearl index.*

pelvic i. The ratio of pelvic conjugate and transverse diameters multiplied by 100.

periodontal (Ramfjord) i. An extensive consideration of the periodontal status of six teeth by evaluating gingival condition, depth of gingival sulcus or pocket, appearance of plaque or calculus, attrition, tooth motility, and extent of tooth contact.

phagocytic i. The average number of bacteria ingested by each leukocyte after incubation of the leukocytes in a mixture of serum and bacterial culture.

physiological cost i. ABBR: PCI. In sports medicine, the metabolic expenditure per unit of distance traveled. It is expressed as the number of heartbeats per meter traveled and is calculated by subtracting the resting heart rate from the exercise heart rate divided by the distance traversed.

Pneumonia Severity I., pneumonia severity index A diagnostic scoring system for predicting the level of care a patient with pneumonia will require. It includes demographic factors (such as the patient's age, whether he or she resides in a nursing home); findings on physical examination (such as altered mental status, fever, tachycardia, and low blood pressure); laboratory data (including serum pH, glucose and sodium levels); and the presence of other illnesses (such as heart, lung, brain, liver, or kidney disease). SYN: *pneumonia PORT score.*

ponderal i. The ratio of an individual's height to the cube root of his or her weight; used to determine body mass. SEE: *body mass i.*

proliferative i. ABBR: PI. The proportion of cells within a tumor specimen that are actively reproducing. In general, as the number of replicating cells in a tumor increases, the cancer behaves more aggressively and the prognosis for the patient worsens.

i. of refraction 1. The ratio of the angle made by the incident ray with the perpendicular (angle of incidence) to that made by the emergent ray (angle of refraction). **2.** The ratio of the speed of light in a vacuum to its speed in another medium. The refractive index of water is 1.33; that of the crystalline lens of the eye is 1.413. SYN: *refractive i.*

refractive i. I. of refraction.

rapid shallow breathing i. ABBR: f/TV; RSBI. The ratio of the respiratory rate (f) and the tidal volume (TV) of a patient treated with mechanical ventilation while breathing on a T-piece (or at minimal levels of positive airway pressure or pressure support). Levels less than 105/min/L indicate that a patient may be able to be weaned successfully from the ventilator and breathe unassisted.

Reid i. SEE: *Reid index.*

respiratory i. ABBR: RI. Alveolar/arterial gradient.

respiratory disturbance i. A measurement of the number of disordered breathing cycles during sleep. Sleep disordered breathing, which includes both apneas and hypopneas, results in daytime fatigue. It is also associated with an increased prevalence of cardiovascular disease.

satiety i. The relative degree to which different foods of the same caloric value satisfy hunger.

saturation i. In hematology, the amount of hemoglobin present in a known volume of blood compared with the normal amount.

Science Citations I. ABBR: SCI. An electronic database of scientific journal articles published and referred to by other authors.

The Index is a proprietary product of the Thomson Corporation.

shock i. 1. The systolic blood pressure divided by the heart rate. **2.** The heart rate divided by the systolic blood pressure.

sulcus bleeding i. ABBR: SBI. A sensitive measure of gingival condition

that involves probing of all sulci. The score is based on six defined criteria. It is calculated by counting the number of sulci with bleeding, dividing by the total number of sulci, and multiplying by 100.

sunscreen protective factor i. In preparations for protecting the skin from the sun (using sunscreens), the ratio of the amount of exposure needed to produce a minimal erythematous response with the sunscreen in place divided by the amount of exposure required to produce the same reaction without the sunscreen. This index assesses the ability of sunscreens to block (short-wavelength) ultraviolet B rays but does not measure the protective effect of sunscreens against (long-wavelength) ultraviolet A radiation. SEE: *erythema dose.*

therapeutic i. The maximum tolerated dose of a drug divided by the minimum curative dose.

thoracic i. The ratio of the thoracic anteroposterior diameter to the transverse diameter.

ventilation i. ABBR: VI. **1.** A calculation used to determine the severity of respiratory illness (acute lung injury and/or respiratory distress syndrome) in critically ill patients. The VI is the partial pressure of arterial CO_2 multiplied by the peak airway pressure multiplied by the rate of ventilation, all divided by 1000.

Symbolically, the ventilation index is calculated as follows: $VI = [RR \times (PIP - PEEP) \times PaCo_2]/1000$. **2.** In environmental science, a measure of air pollution based on the speed of the wind and the height of the column of air in which smoke or other pollutants mix.

vital i. The ratio of the number of births to the number of deaths in a population over a stated period of time.

Western Ontario McMaster Osteoarthritis I. SEE: *Western Ontario McMaster Osteoarthritis Index.*

index of activities of daily living An assessment tool developed by American gerontologist S. Katz and his colleagues. It assesses self-maintenance in older adults and focuses on the unaided performance of six basic personal care activities: eating, toileting, dressing, bathing, transferring, and continence.

index case The first person whose condition leads to the investigation of a hereditary or infectious disease.

India ink (in'dē-ă) A black ink, commonly used in the past, made from lampblack. In clinical pathology, it is used to stain fungi, such as *Cryptococcus neoformans.*

Indian ginseng Winter cherry.

Indian Health Service ABBR: IHS. A bureau of the U.S. Department of Health and Human Services, responsible for providing public health and medical services to Native Americans.

indican (ĭn'dĭ-kăn") **1.** Potassium salt of indoxylsulfate, found in sweat and urine, and formed when intestinal bacteria convert tryptophan to indole. **2.** In plants, a yellow glycoside, the precursor of the dye indigo.

indicant (ĭn'dĭ-kănt) **1.** Something such as a sign or symptom that points to the presence of a disease. **2.** Something such as loss of a symptom or sign that indicates that the treatment of the disease is proper and effective.

indicanuria (ĭn"dĭ-kăn-ū'rē-ă) [" + Gr. *ouron,* urine] An excess of indoxylsulfate of potassium, a derivative of indole, in urine. It is found in small quantities in normal urine. SEE: *urocyanosis.*

indication (ĭn"dĭ-kā'shŏn) [L. *indicare,* a setting, valuation] **1.** A sign or circumstance that suggests the proper treatment of a disease. **2.** An approved use for any therapeutic intervention or drug, e.g., in the U.S., a use that has met the standards set by the U.S. Food and Drug Administration. SYN: *labeled use.*
   causal i. An indication provided by the knowledge of the cause of a disease.
   symptomatic i. An indication provided by the symptoms of a disease rather than because of precise knowledge of the actual disease process. For example, a patient may be given acetaminophen without knowing the cause of the symptoms of headache or fever

indicator (ĭn'dĭ-kāt'ŏr) [L. *indicare,* to show] In chemical analysis, a substance that can be used to determine pH. In a more general sense, any substance that can be used to determine the completeness of a chemical reaction, as in volumetric analysis. SEE: table.
   empirical i. An instrument, experimental condition, or clinical procedure that is used for observation, measurement, or protocol writing, esp. in clinical research.
   health i. SEE: *health indicator.*
   quality i. Any measure of the process, performance, or outcome of health care delivery. In general, quality indicators are chosen because they correlate with

greater patient safety and decreased mortality. In caring for patients with pneumonia, for example, the percentage of patients who have blood cultures drawn and antibiotics administered in the first hours of their arrival at a hospital was previously considered a marker of the quality of care that they receive.

indictment (ĭn-dīt'mĕnt) First step in criminal procedure; a written accusation or charge that identifies the alleged offense that must be proved at trial, beyond a reasonable doubt, in order to convict the defendant.

indifferent [L. *in-,* not, + *differre,* to differ] **1.** Neutral; tending in no specific direction. **2.** Not responsive to normal stimuli; apathetic. **3.** Pert. to cells that have not differentiated.

indigestible (ĭn"dĭ-jĕs'tĭ-bl) [L. *in-,* not, + *digerere,* to separate] Not digestible.

indigestion (ĭn"dĭ-jĕs'chĭn) [" + *digerere,* to separate] Incomplete or imperfect digestion, usually accompanied by one or more of the following symptoms: pain, nausea and vomiting, heartburn, acid regurgitation, accumulation of gas, and belching. SYN: *dyspepsia.*

indigitation (ĭn-dĭj"ĭ-tā'shŭn) [L. *in,* in, + *digitus,* finger] Intussusception.

indigo (ĭn'dĭ-gō) A blue dye obtained from plants or made synthetically.

indisposition (ĭn"dĭs-pō-zĭs'hŭn) [L. *in-,* not, + *dispositus,* arranged] A mild disorder; any slight or temporary illness.

indium (ĭn'dē-ŭm) [L. *indicum,* indigo + *-ium* (1)] SYMB: In. A rare metallic chemical element; atomic weight (mass) 114.82, atomic number 49, specific gravity 7.31. It is soft and malleable and used in electronics.
   i.-111 SYMB: [111]In. An isotope of indium with a half-life of 2.8 days; used in radioactive tracer studies.

Individualized Education Program ABBR: IEP. A documented program of intervention mandated for each child provided with education-related rehabilitation services under federal legislation. The program guarantees a free and appropriate public education for

Colors of Indicators of pH

	Color		
	Toward Acid	Toward Alkali	Range of pH
Methyl yellow	Red	Yellow	2.9–4.0
Congo red	Blue	Red	3.0–5.2
Methyl orange	Red	Yellow	3.1–4.4
Methyl red	Red	Yellow	4.2–6.2
Litmus	Red	Blue	4.5–8.3
Bromcresol purple	Yellow	Purple	5.2–6.8
Bromothymol blue	Yellow	Blue	6.0–7.6
Phenol red	Yellow	Red	6.8–8.4
Phenolphthalein	Colorless	Pink	8.2–10.0

children with disabilities. Decisions relating to IEPs must be approved in Admission, Review and Discharge conferences mandated by federal legislation. Participants in these conferences should include parents or guardians, special educators, rehabilitation providers, and others as appropriate.

Individuals with Disability Education Act ABBR: IDEA. A U.S. federal law that states that education from birth to age 21 should meet the unique learning needs of individuals with disabilities, including the preparation of students for further education, employment, and independent living.

individuation (ĭn″dĭ-vĭd″ū-ā′shŭn) **1.** During development, the emergence of specific and individual structures and functions. **2.** The process by which a healthy, integrated personality is developed.

indocyanine green (ĭn″dō-sī′ă-nēn″, -nĭn) A fluorescent contrast agent used for tests of liver function, blood volume, and retinal perfusion, e.g., during angiography.

indole (ĭn′dōl) C_8H_7N; a substance found in feces. It is the product of bacterial decomposition of tryptophan and is partially responsible for the odor of feces. In intestinal obstruction it is absorbed and eliminated in the urine in the form of indican.

Indole-3-carbinol ABBR: I3C. An aromatic hydrocarbon (C_9H_9NO)found in cruciferous vegetables such as broccoli and cauliflower. It has been suggested as a chemopreventive dietary agent that may help the liver detoxify poisonous chemicals or prevent the development of cancers.

indolent (ĭn′dō-lĕnt) [LL. indolens, painless] **1.** Indisposed to action. **2.** Inactive; slowly developing; sluggish.

indoxyl (ĭn-dŏk′sĭl) [Gr. indikon, indigo,+ oxys, sharp] C_8H_7NO; an oily substance sometimes found in the urine of apparently healthy individuals. It is formed from the decomposition of tryptophan by intestinal bacteria.

induce (ĭn-doos′, dūs′) [L. inducere, to lead in] **1.** To generate a product or bring about an effect. **2.** To produce a result by using a specific stimulus. SEE: induction.

inducible, adj.

induced (ĭn-dūsd′) [L. inducere, to lead in] Produced; caused.

induced pluripotent stem cell ABBR: iPS. A body cell that has been reprogrammed to behave like an embryonic stem cell, that is, to be able to differentiate into cells that could regenerate and repair many different kinds of damaged or diseased tissues.

inducer (ĭn-dūs′ĕr) In chemistry, a compound that increases the concentration of another molecule; in molecular biol-

ogy, something that facilitates the development of a gene. SEE: catalyst.

inductance (ĭn-dŭk′tăns) That property of an electrical circuit by virtue of which a varying current induces an electromotive force in that circuit or a neighboring circuit. The unit of inductance, or self-induction, is the henry.

induction (in-dŭk′shŏn) [L. inductio, leading in] **1.** The process of causing or producing, as induction of labor with oxytocic drugs in cases of uterine dysfunction. **2.** The generation of an electric current in a conductor by electricity in another conductor near it. **3.** In embryology, the production of a specific morphogenic effect by a chemical substance from one part of the embryo to another. SYN: evocation. **4.** In anesthesia, the period from the initial inhalation or injection of an anesthetic gas or drug until optimum level of anesthesia is reached. **5.** Reasoning from the particular to the general. SEE: deduction.

electromagnetic i. Generation of an electromotive force in an insulated conductor moving in an electromagnetic field or in a fixed conductor in a moving magnetic field.

enzyme i. The adaptive increase in the number of molecules of a specific enzyme secondary to either an increase in its synthesis rate or a decrease in its degradation rate.

i. of folliculogenesis Stimulation of the development of follicles with drugs, e.g., clomiphene, or hormones, e.g., gonadotropins. SEE: assisted reproductive technologies; clomiphene citrate; in vitro fertilization; gamete intrafallopian transfer.

i. of labor The use of pharmacological, mechanical, or operative interventions to initiate labor or to assist the progression of a previously dysfunctional labor. Induction may be considered when the risks of expectant management outweigh the benefits, placing the fetus and/or the mother in jeopardy. Among the more common indications are preeclampsia or eclampsia, premature rupture of membranes, fetal compromise, maternal medical diseases, chorioamnionitis, intrauterine fetal demise, postdate pregnancy, as well as some psychosocial factors. Contraindications include placenta previa, vasa previa, umbilical cord prolapse, history of classic uterine incision, and transverse fetal lie, as well as many relative contraindications. SYN: artificial labor; augmented labor. SEE: Nursing Diagnoses Appendix.

⚠ Oxytocin should be used only intravenously, using a device that permits precise control of flow rate. While oxytocin is being administered, the fetal heart rate and uterine contractions should be monitored electronically.

---

ovulation i. The stimulation of ovulation by drugs such as clomiphene citrate, bromocriptine, human menopausal gonadotropin, or gonadotropin-releasing hormone. SEE: *fertilization, in vitro; ovarian hyperstimulation syndrome.*
  rapid-sequence i. ABBR: RSI. Rapid-sequence **intubation.**

indulin (ĭn′dū-lĭn) Any one of a group of dyes used in histology.

indulinophil(e) (ĭn″dū-lĭn′ō-fĭl, -fīl) The state of being readily stained with indulin.

indurate (ĭn′dū-rāt) [L. *in,* in, + *durus,* hard] **1.** To harden. **2.** Hardened.

induration (ĭn″dū-rā″shun) **1.** The act of hardening. **2.** An area of hardened tissue. SEE: *sclerosis; skin.* **indurative** (-dūr-ā″tĭv), *adj.*
  black i. Anthracosis of the lung.
  brawny i. Pathological hardening and thickening of tissues, usually due to inflammation.
  brown i. Pigmentation and fibrosis of the lung as a result of chronic venous congestion of the lung.
  cyanotic i. Induration from long continued venous hyperemia, pressure on vessels causing transudation of blood and serum, and formation of a dark, hard mass. In the liver or spleen it leads to absorption of the parenchyma with formation of scar tissue.
  granular i. Fibrosis of an organ such as the liver or kidney in which small fibrotic granules are present.
  gray i. Unresolved pneumonia with fibrosis of the lung, and no pigmentation.
  red i. Chronic interstitial pneumonia with severe congestion.

industrial (ĭn-dŭs′trē-ĭl) Pert. to the workplace and the work done there.

indwelling (ĭn′dwĕl-ĭng) Inside the body; said of invasive diagnostic or therapeutic devices; pert. to a catheter, drainage tube, or other device that remains inside the body for a prolonged time.

-ine [L. *-ina,* adj. suffix; and Gr. *-inē,* adj. suffix] Suffix in chemistry used in naming basic substances, e.g., *aconitine, amine, nicotine.* SEE: *-in.*

inebriation (ĭn-ē″brē-ā′shŭn) Intoxication.

inelastic (ĭn″ē-lăs′tĭk) [L. *in-,* not, + Gr. *elastikos,* elastic] Not elastic.

inert (ĭn-ĕrt′) [L. *iners,* unskilled, idle] **1.** Not active; sluggish. **2.** In chemistry, having little or no tendency or ability to react with other chemicals.

inertia (in-ĕr′sh(ē-)ă) [L., *inertia,* inactivity] **1.** In physics, the tendency of a body to remain in its state (at rest or in motion) until acted upon by an outside force. **2.** Sluggishness; a lack of activity.

accommodative i. A rare disorder of accommodation in which the time between the application of an accommodative stimulus and the response of the eye is delayed. The delay is typically more than 0.7 sec.

clinical i. Inaction by a prescriber when guidelines or optimal care would recommend a more aggressive course. SYN: *therapeutic i.; watchful waiting.*

colonic i. A decreased rate or frequency of bowel activity, often associated with constipation.

secondary uterine i. Hypotonic uterine**dysfunction**.

sleep i. The normal impairment in thinking and motor performance that immediately follows awakening.

therapeutic i. Clinical **i.**

uterine i. An absence or weakness of uterine contractions in labor.

inert ingredient In pharmaceutical manufacturing, any nonreactive substance used to facilitate the manufacturing of pills and other forms of medication. SYN: *filler* (3).

in extremis (ĭn ĕks-trē′mĭs) [L.] At the point of death.

infancy The very early period of life from birth until age one year. SEE: *infant.*

Infanrix (ĭn′făn-rĭks) Diphtheria, tetanus toxoids, and acellular pertussis (Dtap) vaccine, adsorbed.

infant (ĭn′fănt) [L. *infans,* baby, infant, unspeaking] **1.** A child in the first year of life. SEE: *neonate.*
  Development: For 3 days after birth a baby loses weight; in the next 4 days, however, a baby should regain the loss and weigh as much as at birth.
  The average weekly weight gain in the first 3 months is 210 g for boys and 195 g for girls; from 3 to 6 months it is 150 g for both girls and boys; from 6 to 9 months, 90 g for boys and 105 g for girls; from 9 to 18 months 60 g for both sexes; and from 18 to 24 months 45 g, both sexes.
  The newborn is aware of shadow, movement, and voice. By the 4th week the infant lifts the head momentarily; by the 16th week, holds the head erect, coos, or laughs; walks with hands held by the 52nd week; and by the 15th month, toddles alone and may have a vocabulary of a few words. SEE: *psychomotor and physical development of infant.*
  Respiration: At birth, respirations are 40 to 50/min; during the first year, 20 to 40/min; during the fifth year, 20 to 25/min; during the 15th year, 15 to 20/min. SEE: *pulse; respiration; temperature.*
  Temperature: Normal (rectal) temperature may have a daily variation of 1° to 1.5°C (1.8° to 2.7°F). It is usually highest between 5 and 8 P.M. and lowest between 3 and 6 A.M. Therefore, there is

no specific normal temperature, but the values given should be regarded as ranging around the value of 37.6°C (99.7°F) when the temperature is taken rectally. Axillary temperatures in the normal newborn range from 36.4° to 37.2°C (97.5° to 99°F). Infants have poorly developed temperature-regulating mechanisms and need to be protected from chilling and overheating.

2. In the law, a person below the legal age; a minor. SEE: *minor* (2).

postterm i. An infant born after the beginning of the 42nd week of gestation (longer than 288 days).

premature i. Preterm **i.** SEE: *Nursing Diagnoses Appendix.*

preterm i. An infant born before the completion of 37 weeks (259 days) of gestation. SYN: *premature i.* SEE: *prematurity.*

i. of substance-abusing mother ABBR: ISAM. An all-inclusive term for a newborn whose birth mother used alcohol, cocaine, opiates, or other potentially hazardous chemicals during pregnancy. These babies are considered to be at high risk for complications during the neonatal period; many also exhibit related long-term disabilities that influence their potential for normal growth and development. *Perinatal complications* include intrauterine growth retardation, infection, asphyxia, congenital abnormalities, low birth weight, low Apgar score, withdrawal-related symptoms, jaundice, and behavioral problems. *Long-term complications* include behavioral problems such as short attention span, delayed development of language-related skills, and sudden infant death syndrome. SEE: *cocaine baby; fetal alcohol syndrome; heroin.*

term i. An infant born between the beginning of the 38th week through the 41st week of gestation (260 to 287 days).

infant behavior, disorganized Disintegrated physiological and neurobehavioral responses to the environment of the newborn. SEE: *Nursing Diagnoses Appendix.*

infant behavior, readiness for enhanced organized A pattern of modulation of the physiological and behavioral systems of functioning of an infant (i.e., autonomic, motor, state, organizational, self-regulatory, and attentional-interactional systems) that is satisfactory but that can be improved, resulting in higher levels of integration in response to environmental stimuli. SEE: *Nursing Diagnoses Appendix.*

infant behavior, risk for disorganized Risk for alteration in integration and modulation of the physiological and behavioral systems of functioning (i.e., autonomic, motor, state, organizational, self-regulatory, and attentional-inter-

actional systems). SEE: *Nursing Diagnoses Appendix.*

infant carrier SEE: under *carrier.*

infant feeding pattern, ineffective Impaired ability to suck or to coordinate the suck-swallow response resulting in inadequate oral nutrition for metabolic needs. SEE: *Nursing Diagnoses Appendix.*

infant heel warmer A contained source of chemically generated heat used to stimulate capillary circulation in the heel of a neonate, thus facilitating the collection of blood for laboratory analysis.

⚠️ The use of chemical heel warmers must be carefully monitored to avoid burning sensitive neonatal skin.

infanticide (ĭn-făn'tĭ-sīd) [LL. *infanticidium*] The killing of an infant.

infantile (ĭn'făn-tĭl) [Fr. *infantilis*] Pert. to infancy or an infant.

infantile acropustulosis (ak″rō-pŭs″tyŭ-lō'sĭs) [*acro-* + *pustulosis*] Cyclical eruption of pustules on the soles and feet of infants 2 to 10 months of age. The pustules become vesicopapular, crust over, and heal in 7 to 10 days. A new crop appears in 2 to 3 weeks, and they also heal. Periodic outbreaks occur for about 2 years and then cease. The cause is unknown; only symptomatic therapy is required.

infantile hemangioma SEE: under *hemangioma.*

infantile hypertrophic pyloric stenosis SEE: *pyloric stenosis.*

infantilism (in'făn-tĭl″izm, in-fan-tĭl-izm) [*infantile* + *-ism*] **1.** A condition in which the mind and body make slow development and the individual fails to attain adult characteristics. It is characterized by mental retardation, stunted growth, and sexual immaturity. **2.** Childishness.

intestinal i. Infantilism associated with a chronic intestinal disorder, causing poor growth.

infant relinquishment (ri-lingk'wish-mĕnt) The psychological process experienced by a birth mother during adoption of her child by others.

infarct (in'farkt″, in-farkt′) [L. *infarctus,* stuffed] An area of tissue in an organ or part that undergoes necrosis following cessation of the blood supply. This may result from occlusion or stenosis of the supplying artery or, more rarely, from occlusion of the vein that drains the tissue.

anemic i. An infarct in which blood pigment is lacking or decoloration has occurred. SYN: *pale i.; white i.*

bland i. An infarct in which infection is absent.

cerebral i. A stroke resulting from interrupted blood flow to one of the large or small arteries of the brain.

cicatrized i. An infarct that has been replaced or encapsulated by fibrous tissue.

hemorrhagic i. Red **i.**

infected i. Infarcted tissue that has been invaded by pathogenic organisms. SYN: *septic* **i.**

lateral medullary i. Wallenberg syndrome.

pale i. Anemic **i.**

red i. An infarct that is swollen and red as a result of hemorrhage. SYN: *hemorrhagic* **i.**

septic i. Infected **i.**

uric acid i. An infarct in the kidney caused by obstruction of the renal tubules by uric acid crystals.

white i. Anemic **i.**

infarct exclusion surgery SEE: under *surgery*.

infarction (in-fark'shŏn) [*infarct*] Death of tissue from deprivation of its blood supply.

aborted myocardial m.i. Reperfusion of an occluded coronary artery before damage is done to the muscle that receives blood from that artery.

cerebral i. SEE: *cerebral infarct*.

lacunar i. A small stroke deep within the brain (as in the internal capsule, basal ganglia, thalamus, or pons) caused by damage to or a blockage of a tiny penetrating artery. Lacunar infarctions are associated with a kind of vascular damage caused by chronic high blood pressure called lipohyalinosis. They may be asymptomatic, showing up only on brain imaging, or may produce pure motor, pure sensory, ataxic, or mixed motor and sensory symptoms. SYN: *lacunar* **stroke**.

malignant cerebral artery i. A massive stroke involving the middle cerebral artery, in which swelling of the brain leads either to herniation and death or to additional strokes in other arteries.

myocardial i. ABBR: MI. The loss of living heart muscle as a result of coronary artery occlusion. MI or its related syndromes (acute coronary syndrome or unstable angina) usually occurs when an atheromatous plaque in a coronary artery ruptures, and the resulting clot obstructs the injured blood vessel. Perfusion of the muscular tissue that lies downstream from the blocked artery is lost. If blood flow is not restored within a few hours, the heart muscle dies. SYN: *cardiac* **i.**

Acute MI affects 1.1 million people each year, and approx. 350,000 of them die. The probability of dying from MI is related to the patient's underlying health, whether arrhythmias such as ventricular fibrillation or ventricular tachycardia occur, and how rapidly the patient seeks medical attention and receives appropriate therapies (such as thrombolytic drugs, angioplasty, antiplatelet drugs, beta blockers, and intensive electrocardiographic monitoring). SEE: illus.; *advanced cardiac life support; atherosclerosis; cardiac arrest; sudden death*.

ETIOLOGY: Proven risk factors for MI are tobacco use, diabetes mellitus, abnormally high cholesterol levels, high blood pressure, gender, advanced age, obesity, physical inactivity, chronic kidney disease, a family history of MI at an early age, and loss of albumin in the urine. Some research suggests that high C reactive protein levels, and other conditions may also lead to increased risk.

SYMPTOMS: Classic symptoms of MI in men are a gradual onset of pain or pressure, felt most intensely in the center of the chest, radiating into the neck, jaw, shoulders, or arms, and lasting more than a half hour. Pain typically is dull or heavy rather than sharp or stabbing, and often is associated with difficult breathing, nausea, vomiting, and profuse sweating. Clinical presentations, however, vary considerably, and distinct presentations are seen in woman and the elderly, in whom, e.g., unexplained breathlessness is often the primary symptom. Many patients may mistake their symptoms for indigestion, intestinal gas, or muscular aches. About a third of all MIs are clinically silent, and almost half present with atypical symptoms. Often patients suffering MI have had angina pectoris for several weeks before and simply did not recognize it.

DIAGNOSIS: A compatible history associated either with segment elevation (on a 12-lead electrocardiogram) or with elevated blood levels of cardiac muscle enzymes such as troponins or creatine kinase can establish the diagnosis. An ST-segment elevation of more than 1 mm above baseline in at least two contiguous precordial leads or two adjacent limb leads suggests myocardial injury. Myocardial infarctions with this presentation are known as ST-segment elevation MI (STEMI). This finding usually indicates significant muscle damage in the infarct area, a poorer prognosis, and a higher incidence of complications (arrhythmias, cardiogenic shock) than in a non-ST-segment elevation MI. The differential diagnosis of chest pain must always be carefully considered because other serious illnesses, such as pulmonary embolism, pericarditis, aortic dissection, esophageal rupture, acute cholecystitis, esophagitis, or splenic rupture may mimic MI.

TREATMENT: Myocardial infarction is a medical emergency; diagnosis and treatment should not be delayed. People

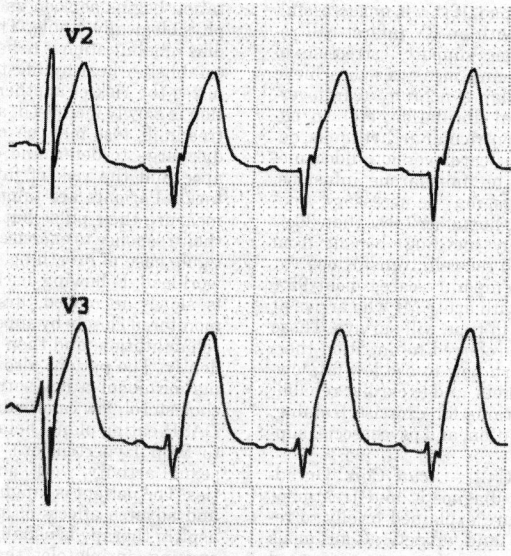

MYOCARDIAL INFARCTION

Myocardial infarction as seen on an electrocardiogram

who experience symptoms suggestive of MI should be taught to call 911 immediately and chew and swallow aspirin. Oxygen is administered at 4 L/min as soon as it is available. History is gathered throughout the first few minutes after admission even as a 12-lead ECG is being done and blood taken for biomarkers. Cardiac troponins may not become elevated until 4 or more hr after symptoms begin. If the patient is hypotensive or in cardiogenic shock, right-sided ECG leads are assessed for a right ventricular (RV) infarct. An intravenous access is established along with continuous cardiac monitoring, and medications (which may include chewed aspirin [162 to 325 mg], heparins, or other medications to inhibit platelet aggregation, nitroglycerin [given SL, sprayed or IV], IV morphine, and beta-blockers) are administered as prescribed. Pain is assessed on a 1 to 10 intensity scale, and morphine 2 to 10 mg administered IV, with incremental doses of 2 to 8 mg every 5 to 15 min until relief is obtained. Beta-blockers (such as metoprolol or atenolol) decrease myocardial oxygen demand, helping to limit the amount of heart muscle damaged. An IV beta-blocker should be given if the patient is hypertensive or has a tachyarrhythmia as long as no contraindications exist. Patients with STEMI who arrive at the hospital within 6 hr of the onset of symptoms are treated with fibrinolytic therapy or percutaneous coronary intervention (PCI). The goal for administra-

tion of fibrinolytic therapy is 30 min postsymptom onset (*door-to-needle*); for PCI 90 min (*door-to-balloon* inflation). Absolute contraindications of fibrinolytic therapy include previous intracranial hemorrhage or ischemic stroke within 3 months (*intracranial malignancy*), active bleeding, or bleeding disorders (except menses), significant closed head or facial trauma within 3 months (known structural cerebral vascular lesions), and suspected aortic dissection. Reperfusion is the immediate goal, usually best accomplished with balloon angioplasty and endovascular stent placement, although emergency coronary bypass surgery may be needed in cases when PCI fails. An angiotensin-converting enzyme (ACE) inhibitor is administered within 24 hr of a STEMI to suppress the renin-angiotensin-aldosterone system and prevent excess fluid retention. ACE inhibitors also prevent conversion of angiotensin I to angiotensin II (a potent vasoconstrictor), thus reducing afterload to help prevent heart failure.

In MI complicated by pulmonary edema, diuretics are administered, and dobutamine infusions may be necessary to increase cardiac output. Strict glucose control (maintaining blood sugars below 150 mg/dL, and preferably in the normal range) reduces mortality in acute MI. Hypotension and circulatory collapse frequently occur in patients with significant RV infarctions, and fluid challenge is administered to optimize RV preload. If this is unsuccessful, the patient with an RV infarct will require inotropic support, correction of bradycardia, and measures to achieve atrioventricular synchrony (cardioversion for atrial fibrillation, etc). In patients with ventricular arrhythmias, defibrillation, or cardioversion, lidocaine, vasopressin, or amiodarone infusions, or other drugs, may be necessary. Anemic patients (hematocrit less than 30 or those actively bleeding) benefit from blood (packed red cell) transfusions.

With contemporary care, about 95% of patients with acute MI who arrive at the hospital in time will survive. These patients are referred to nutrition therapists to learn how to use low-fat, low-cholesterol diets, and to cardiac rehabilitation programs for exercise training, tobacco cessation, and psychosocial support.

PATIENT CARE: *Acute Care:* On admission, all diagnostic and treatment procedures are explained briefly to reduce stress and anxiety. Continuous electrocardiographic monitoring is used to identify changes in heart rhythm, rate, and conduction. Location, radiation, quality, severity, and frequency of chest pain are documented and relieved with IV morphine. Bleeding is the most common complication of antiplatelet, anticoagulant, and fibrinolytic therapies. The complete blood count, prothrombin time, and activated partial thromboplastin time are monitored at daily intervals. IV sites are assessed for evidence of bleeding. Fluid balance and pulmonary status are closely monitored for signs of fluid retention and overload. Breath sounds are auscultated for crackles (which may resolve by having the patient cough when caused by atelectasis, or which may indicate pulmonary edema when they do not). Heart sounds are auscultated for S3 or S4 gallops or new heart murmurs. Patient care and other activities should be organized to allow for periods on uninterrupted rest. Stool softeners are prescribed to prevent straining during defecation, which can cause vagal stimulation and slow the heart rate. Antithrombotic stockings help prevent venostasis and deep vein thrombosis. Emotional support is provided to decrease stress and anxiety. Adjustment disorders and depression are often experienced by MI patients, and the patient and family are assisted to deal with these feelings. Stress tests, coronary angiography, cardiac imaging procedures, reperfusion techniques, and other interventions are explained. The patient receives assistance in coping with changes in health status and self-concept.

Ambulatory Care: Cardiac rehabilitation begins as soon as the patient is physiologically stable. The goal of cardiac rehabilitation is to have the patient establish a healthy lifestyle that minimizes the risk of another MI. Ambulation is slowly increased, and a low-level treadmill test may be ordered before discharge to determine exercise tolerance and the risk of future heart attacks. Patients are taught not only to measure their pulse but also to assess their response to exercise in terms of fatigue, ease of breathing, and perceived workload. Following discharge, exercise is slowly increased, first while being monitored closely by supervised cardiac rehabilitation, and then more independently. The patient also receives information about a low saturated fat, low cholesterol, low calorie diet, such as the DASH eating plan (Dietary Approaches to Stop Hypertension), resumption of sexual activity, work, and other activities. The patient is taught about desired and adverse affects of all medications: aspirin therapy is usually prescribed as ongoing antiplatelet therapy (with or without clopidogrel), but patients should be warned about the risk of bleeding and be advised to avoid products containing ibuprofen, which blocks aspirin's antiplatelet effects. Smoking cessation is an important preventive for future MIs. High blood pressure, obesity, adverse cholesterol levels, and diabetes mellitus also should be carefully managed to help prevent future MIs. Alcohol intake should be limited to 1 drink daily (women), 2 drinks daily (men). Opportunities are created for patients and families to share feelings and receive realistic reassurance about common fears.

placental i. A localized necrotic area caused by abruption. SEE: *abruptio placentae.*

pulmonary i. An infarction in the lung usually resulting from pulmonary embolism that may appear on x-rays as a wedge-shaped infiltrate near the pleura. Immediate therapy includes control of pain, oxygen administered continuously by mask, intravenous heparin (unless the patient has a known blood clotting defect), and treatment of shock or dysrhythmias, if present.

silent myocardial i. Unrecognized myocardial infarction. The patient may experience difficulty breathing, heartburn, nausea, arm pain, or other atypical symptoms.

infect [ME. *infecten*] To cause pathogenic organisms to be present in or upon, as to infect a wound.

infection (in-fek'shŏn) [L. *infectio*, discoloration, dye] A disease caused by microorganisms, esp. those that release toxins or invade body tissues. Worldwide, infectious diseases such as malaria, tuberculosis, hepatitis viruses, and diarrheal illnesses produce more disability and death than any other cause. Infection differs from colonization of the body by microorganisms in that during colonization, microbes reside harmlessly in the body or perform useful functions for it, e.g., bacteria in the gut that produce vitamin K. By contrast, infectious illnesses typically cause bodily harm.

ETIOLOGY: The most common pathogenic organisms are bacteria (including mycobacteria, mycoplasmas, spirochetes, chlamydiae, and rickettsiae), viruses, fungi, protozoa, and helminths. Life-threatening infectious disease usually occurs when immunity is weak or suppressed (such as during the first few months of life, in older or malnourished persons, in trauma or burn victims, in leukopenic patients, and in those with chronic illnesses such as diabetes mellitus, renal failure, cancer, asplenia, alcoholism, or heart, lung, or liver disease). Many disease-causing agents, however, may afflict vigorous persons, whether they are young or old, fit or weak. Some examples include sexually transmitted illnesses (such as herpes simplex or chlamydiosis), respiratory illnesses (influenza or varicella), and food or waterborne pathogens (cholera, schistosomiasis).

SYMPTOMS: Systemic infections cause fevers, chills, sweats, malaise, and occasionally, headache, muscle and joint pains, or changes in mental status. Localized infections produce tissue redness, swelling, tenderness, heat, and loss of function.

TRANSMISSION: Pathogens can be transmitted to their hosts by many mechanisms, namely, inhalation, ingestion, injection or the bite of a vector, direct (skin-to-skin) contact, contact with blood or body fluids, fetomaternal contact, contact with contaminated articles (fomites), or self-inoculation.

In health care settings, infections are often transmitted to patients by the hands of professional staff or other employees. Hand hygiene before and after patient contact prevents many of these infections.

DEFENSES: The body's defenses against infection begin with mechanisms that block entry of the organism into the skin or the respiratory, gastrointestinal, or genitourinary tract. These defenses include chemicals, e.g., lysozymes in tears, fatty acids in skin, gastric acid, and pancreatic enzymes in the bowel; mucus that traps the organism; clusters of antibody-producing B lymphocytes, e.g., tonsils, Peyer's patches; and bacteria and fungi (normal flora) on the skin and mucosal surfaces that destroy more dangerous organisms. In patients receiving immunosuppressive

drug therapy, the normal flora can become the source of opportunistic infections. Also, one organism can impair external defenses and permit another to enter; e.g., viruses can enhance bacterial invasion by damaging respiratory tract mucosa.

The body's second line of defense is the nonspecific immune response, inflammation. The third major defensive system, the specific immune response, depends on lymphocyte activation, during which B and T cells recognize specific antigenic markers on the organism. B cells produce immunoglobulins (antibodies), and T cells orchestrate a multifaceted attack by cytotoxic cells. SEE: *B cell*; *T cell*; *inflammation* for table.

SPREAD: Once pathogens have crossed cutaneous or mucosal barriers and gained entry into internal tissues, they may spread quickly along membranes such as the meninges, pleura, or peritoneum. Some pathogens produce enzymes that damage cell membranes, enabling them to move rapidly from cell to cell. Others enter the lymphatic channels; if they can overcome white blood cell defenses in the lymph nodes, they move into the bloodstream to multiply at other sites. This is frequently seen with pyogenic organisms, which create abscesses far from the initial entry site. Viruses or rickettsiae, which reproduce only inside cells, travel in the blood to cause systemic infections; viruses that damage a fetus during pregnancy (such as rubella and cytomegalovirus) travel via the blood.

DIAGNOSIS: Although many infections (such as those that cause characteristic rashes) are diagnosed clinically, definitive identification of infection usually occurs in the laboratory. Carefully collected and cultured specimens of blood, urine, stool, sputum, or other body fluids are used to identify pathogens and their susceptibilities to treatment.

TREATMENT: Many infections, like the common cold, are self-limited and require no specific treatment. Understanding this concept is crucial because the misuse of antibiotics does not help the affected patient and may damage society by fostering antimicrobial resistance, e.g., in microorganisms such as methicillin-resistant *Staphylococcus aureus*. Many common infections, such as urinary tract infections or impetigo, respond well to antimicrobial drugs. Others, like abscesses, may require incision and drainage.

acute i. An infection that appears suddenly and may be of brief or prolonged duration.

airborne i. An infection caused by inhalation of pathogenic organisms in droplet nuclei.

apical i. An infection located at the tip of the root of a tooth.

bacterial i. Any disease caused by bacteria. Bacteria exist in a variety of relationships with the human body. They colonize body surfaces and provide benefits, e.g., by limiting the growth of pathogens and by producing vitamins for absorption (in a symbiotic relationship). Bacteria can coexist with the human body without producing harmful or beneficial effects (in a commensal relationship). Bacteria may also invade tissues, damage cells, trigger systemic inflammatory responses, and release toxins (in a pathogenic or infectious relationship). SEE: *bacterium* for table.

bladder i. SEE: *urinary tract i.*

blood-borne i. An infection transmitted through contact with the blood (cells, serum, or plasma) of an infected individual. The contact may occur sexually, through injection, or via a medical or dental procedure in which a blood-contaminated instrument is inadvertently used after inadequate sterilization. Examples of blood-borne infections include hepatitis B and C and AIDS. SEE: *needle-stick injury; Standard Precautions Appendix.*

breakthrough i. An infection that occurs despite previous vaccination.

chronic i. An infection having a protracted course.

concurrent i. The existence of two or more infections at the same time. SEE: *superinfection.*

cross i. The transfer of an infectious organism or disease from one patient in a hospital to another.

cryptogenic i. An infection whose source is unknown.

cytomegalovirus i. ABBR: CMV infection. A persistent, latent infection of white blood cells caused by cytomegalovirus (CMV). Approx. 60% of people over 35 have been infected with CMV, usually during childhood or early adulthood; the incidence appears to be higher in those of low socioeconomic status. Primary infection is usually mild in people with normal immune function, but CMV can be reactivated and cause overt disease in pregnant women, AIDS patients, or those receiving immunosuppressive therapy following organ transplantation. CMV has been isolated from saliva, urine, semen, breast milk, feces, blood, and vaginal secretions of those infected; it is usually transmitted through contact with infected secretions that retain the virus for months to years. SEE: *Nursing Diagnoses Appendix.*

During pregnancy, the woman can transmit the virus transplacentally to the fetus with devastating results. Approx. 10% of infected infants develop CMV inclusion disease, marked by anemia, thrombocytopenia, purpura, hepatosplenomegaly, microcephaly, and abnormal mental or motor development; more than 50% of these infants die. Most fetal infections occur when the mother is infected with CMV for the first time during this pregnancy, but they may also occur following reinfection or reactivation of the virus. Patients with AIDS or organ transplants may develop disseminated infection that causes retinitis, esophagitis, colitis, meningoencephalitis, pneumonitis, and inflammation of the renal tubules.

ETIOLOGY: CMV is transmitted from person to person by sexual activity, during pregnancy or delivery, during organ transplantation, or by contaminated secretions; rarely, (5%) blood transfusions contain latent CMV. Health care workers caring for infected newborns or immunosuppressed patients are at no greater risk for acquiring CMV infection than are those who care for other groups of patients (approx. 3%). Pregnant women and all health care workers should strictly adhere to standard infection control precautions.

SYMPTOMS: Primary infection in the healthy is usually asymptomatic, but some people develop mononucleosis-type symptoms (fever, sore throat, swollen glands). Symptoms in immunosuppressed patients are related to the organ system infected by CMV and include blurred vision progressing to blindness; severe diarrhea; and cough, dyspnea, and hypoxemia. Antibodies seen in the blood identify infection but do not protect against reactivation of the virus.

TREATMENT: Antiviral agents such as ganciclovir and foscarnet are used to treat retinitis, colitis, and pneumonitis in immunosuppressed patients; chronic antiviral therapy has been used to suppress CMV, but this protocol has not been effective in preventing recurrence of CMV or development of meningoencephalitis. Ganciclovir has limited effect in congenital CMV. No vaccine is available.

PATIENT CARE: Health care providers can help prevent CMV infections by advising pregnant women and the immunocompromised to avoid exposure to contact with people who have confirmed and or suspected cases of CMV. The virus spreads from one person to another as a result of exposure to blood (as in transfusions) and other body fluids including feces, urine, and saliva. Contact with the diapers or drool of an infected child may result in infection of a person who has previously been unexposed to the infection. CMV is the most common congenital infection, affecting about 35,000 newborns each year. CMV infection that is newly acquired during the first trimester of pregnancy can be esp. hazardous to the developing fetus. As a result, young women who have no antibodies to CMV should avoid providing child care to infected youngsters. In the U.S., nurses who have failed to advise infected patients of the risk that CMV may pose to others have been judged to be negligent by the courts. Parents of children with severe congenital CMV require support and counseling. Although CMV infection in most nonpregnant adults is not harmful, it can cause serious illnesses or death in people with HIV/AIDS, organ transplants, and those who take immunosuppressive or cancer chemotherapeutic drugs. Infected immunosuppressed patients with CMV should be advised about the uses of prescribed drug therapies, the importance of completing the full course of therapy, and adverse effects to report for help in managing them. Family caregivers for infected people should be taught to observe standard precautions when handling body secretions. Since asymptomatic people may have and secrete the virus, standard precautions should be maintained by health care professionals at all times when such secretions are present or being handled.

deep neck i. An infection that enters the fascial planes of the neck after originating in the oral cavity, pharynx, or a regional lymph node. It may be life-threatening if the infection enters the carotid sheath, the paravertebral spaces, or the mediastinum. Death may also result from sepsis, asphyxiation, or hemorrhage. Aggressive surgical therapy is usually required because antibiotics alone infrequently control the disease.

diabetic foot i. A polymicrobial infection of the bones and soft tissues of the lower extremities of patients with diabetes mellitus, typically those patients who have vascular insufficiency or neuropathic foot disease. Eradication of the infection may require prolonged courses of antibiotics, surgical débridement or amputation, or reconstruction or bypass of occluded arteries. SYN: *diabetic foot ulcer*. SEE: illus.

droplet i. An infection acquired by the inhalation of a microorganism in the air, esp. one added to the air by sneezing or cough.

focal i. Infection occurring near a focus, such as the cavity of a tooth.

fungal i. Pathological invasion of the body by yeast or other fungi. Fungi are most likely to produce disease in patients whose immune defenses are compromised. SEE: table.

fungal i. of nail Infection of a nail by one of a number of fungi. Systemic ther-

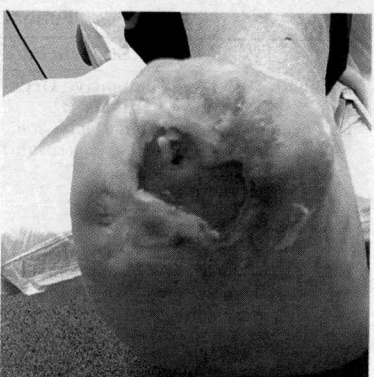

ULCER DUE TO DIABETIC FOOT INFECTION

apy with antifungal drugs may eradicate the infection.

health-care associated i. ABBR: HAI. Nosocomial **i.**

hospital-acquired i. Nosocomial **i.**

inapparent i. An infection that is asymptomatic or is not detected.

local i. An infection that has not spread but remains contained near the entry site.

low-grade i. A loosely used term for a subacute or chronic infection with only mild inflammation and without pus formation.

nosocomial i. An infection acquired in a hospital, nursing home, or other health care setting. Patients in burn units and surgical intensive care units have the highest rates of nosocomial infections. SYN: *health-care associated i.; hospital-acquired i.*

PATIENT CARE: Hospital-acquired infections result from the exposure of debilitated patients to the drug-altered environment of the hospital, where indwelling urinary catheters, intravenous lines, and endotracheal tubes enter normally sterile body sites and allow microbes to penetrate and multiply. Over 2 million nosocomial infections occur in the U.S. annually. Antibiotic-resistant organisms such as *Enterobacter* spp., *Pseudomonas* spp., staphylococci, enterococci, *Clostridium difficile*, and fungi often are responsible for the infectious outbreaks that result. Standard precautions and infection control procedures limit the incidence of nosocomial infections.

opportunistic i. ABBR: OI. **1.** Any infection that results from a defective immune system that cannot defend against pathogens normally found in the environment. Common types include bacterial (*Pseudomonas aeruginosa*), fungal (*Candida albicans*), protozoan (*Pneumocystis jirovecii*), and

Fungal Infections

Superficial Fungal Infections

Disease	Causative Organisms	Structures Infected	Microscopic Appearance
Epidermophytosis (e.g., dhobie itch)	*Epidermophyton,* (e.g., *floccosum*)	Inguinal, axillary, and interdigital folds; hairs not affected	Long, wavy, branched, and segmented hyphae and spindle-shaped cells in stratum corneum
Favus (tinea favosa)	*Trichophyton schoenleinii*	Epidermis around a hair; all parts of body; nails	Vertical hyphae and spores in epidermis; sinuous branching mycelium and chains in hairs
Ringworm (tinea, otomycosis)	*Microsporum* (e.g., *audouinii*)	Horny layer of epidermis and hairs, chiefly of scalp	Fine septate mycelium inside hairs and scales; spores in rows and mosaic plaques on hair surface
	Trichophyton (*e.g., tonsurans*)	Hairs of scalp, beard, and other parts; nails	Mycelium of chained cubical elements and threads in and on hairs; often pigmented
Thrush and other forms of candidiasis	*Candida albicans*	Tongue, mouth, throat, vagina, and skin	Yeastlike budding cells and oval thick-walled bodies in lesion

Systemic Fungal Infections

Aspergillosis	*Aspergillus fumigatus*	Lungs	Y-shaped branching of septate hyphae
Blastomycosis	*Blastomyces brasiliensis, B. dermatitidis*	Skin and lungs	Yeastlike cells demonstrated in lesion
Candidiasis	*Candida albicans*	Esophagus, lungs, peritoneum, mucous membranes	Small, thin-walled, ovoid cells
Coccidioidomycosis	*Coccidioides immitis*	Respiratory tract	Nonbudding spores containing many endospores, in sputum
Cryptococcosis	*Cryptococcus neoformans*	Meninges, lungs, bone, skin	Yeastlike fungus having gelatinous capsule; demonstrated in spinal fluid
Histoplasmosis	*Histoplasma capsulatum*	Lungs	Oval, budding, uninucleated cells

viral (cytomegalovirus). Opportunistic infections are seen in patients with impaired defenses against disease, such as those with cystic fibrosis, poorly controlled diabetes mellitus, acquired or congenital immune deficiencies, or organ transplants. **2.** An infection that results when resident flora proliferate and infect a body site in which they are normally present or at some other location. In healthy humans, the millions of bacteria in and on the body do not cause infection or disease. Host defenses and interaction with other microorganisms prevent excess growth of potential pathogens. A great number of factors, many poorly understood, may allow a normal bacterial resident to proliferate and cause disease.

pocket i. Infection of the tissues beneath the skin into which an implanted device, such as a pacemaker or defibrillator, has been surgically inserted.

protozoal i. An infection with a protozoon, e.g., malaria.

pyogenic i. An infection resulting from pus-forming organisms.

reproductive tract i. ABBR: RTI. Any infection of the reproductive organs. The most common causes are sexually transmitted diseases, but infections may also result from bacterial overgrowth or occasionally when instruments used in medical procedures introduce microorganisms. In women RTIs can cause pelvic pain, subfertility, infertility, or damage to the developing fetus. RTIs in men include epididymitis, prostatitis, and urethritis.

risk for i. An immunocompromised state. SEE: *Nursing Diagnoses Appendix.*

secondary i. An infection made possible by a primary infection that lowers the host's resistance, e.g., bacterial pneumonia following influenza.

slow virus i. An infection caused by a virus that remains dormant in the body for a prolonged period before causing signs and symptoms of illness. Such viruses may require years to incubate before causing diseases. Examples include progressive multifocal leukoencephalopathy and subacute sclerosing panencephalitis.

subacute i. An infection intermediate between acute and chronic.

subclinical i. An infection that is immunologically confirmed but does not produce obvious symptoms or signs.

surgical site i. An infection that occurs within thirty days of an operation, either at the suture line, just beneath it, or in internal organs and spaces that were operated upon. SYN: *surgical wound i.*

surgical wound i. Surgical site **i.**

systemic i. An infection in which the infecting agent or organisms circulate throughout the body.

terminal i. An often fatal infection appearing in the late stage of another disease.

transfusion-associated bacterial i. Transfusion-transmitted bacterial **i.**

transfusion-transmitted bacterial i. ABBR: TTBI. Illness in a transfusion recipient that develops after the infusion of contaminated blood or blood products, esp. platelets. It usually results from colonization of the blood product during handling or storage or, less frequently, from an unsuspected infection in the blood donor. Coagulase-negative staphylococci are often responsible. Other bacteria that sometimes cause TTBI include *Pseudomonas* species, *Anaplasma, Babesia,* and *Rickettsia.*

Viruses may also be transmitted from blood donors to transfusion recipients. They may include cytomegalovirus, encephalitis viruses, and, rarely, hepatitis viruses or human immunodeficiency virus. SYN: *transfusion-associated bacterial i.*

upper respiratory i. ABBR: URI. An imprecise term for any infection involving the nasal passages, pharynx, and bronchi. The cause is usually bacterial or viral, and, occasionally, fungal.

urinary tract i. ABBR: UTI. Infection of the kidneys, ureters, or bladder by microorganisms that either ascend from the urethra (95% of cases) or that spread to the kidney from the bloodstream (5%). About 7 million Americans visit health care providers each year because of UTIs. These infections commonly occur in otherwise healthy women, men with prostatic hypertrophy or bladder outlet obstruction, children with congenital anatomical abnormalities of the urinary tract, and patients with urinary stasis related to incomplete bladder emptying, neurogenic bladder or indwelling bladder catheters. SEE: clean-catch **method**; cystitis; pyelonephritis; urethritis.

ETIOLOGY: *Escherichia coli* causes about 80% of all UTIs. In young women, *Staphylococcus saprophyticus* is also common. In men with prostate disease, enterococci are often responsible. The small remaining percentage of infections may be caused by *Klebsiella* species, *Proteus mirabilis, Staphylococcus aureus, Pseudomonas aeruginosa,* or other virulent organisms.

SYMPTOMS: The presenting symptoms of UTI vary enormously. Young patients with bladder infections may have pain with urination; urinary frequency or urgency or both; pelvic or suprapubic discomfort; low-grade fevers; or a change in the appearance or odor of their urine (cloudy, malodorous, or rarely bloody). Older patients may present with fever, lethargy, confusion, delirium, or coma caused by urosepsis. Patients with pyelonephritis often complain of flank pain, prostration, nausea, vomiting, diarrhea, and high fevers with shaking chills. UTI may also be asymptomatic, esp. during pregnancy. Asymptomatic UTI during pregnancy is a contributing factor to maternal pyelonephritis, or fetal prematurity and stillbirth.

DIAGNOSIS: Urinalysis (obtained either as a clean catch or catheterized specimen) and subsequent urinary culture are used to determine the presence of UTI, the suspect microorganism, and the optimal antibiotic therapy. A dipstick test may identify leukocyte esterase and nitrite in a urinary specimen, strongly suggesting a UTI. The presence of more than 8 to 10 white blood cells per high-power field of spun urine also strongly suggests UTI, as does the presence of bacteria in an uncentrifuged urinary specimen.

TREATMENT: Sulfa drugs, nitrofurantoin, cephalosporins, or quinolones may be used for the outpatient treatment of UTIs while the results of cultures are pending. Patients sick enough to be hospitalized may also be treated with intravenous aminoglycosides, medicine to treat nausea and vomiting, and hydration. The duration of therapy and the precise antibiotics used depend on the responsible organism and the underlying condition of the patient. Patients with anatomical abnormalities of the urinary tract, e.g., children with ureteropelvic obstruction or older men with bladder outlet obstruction, may sometimes require urological surgery.

RISK FACTORS: The following conditions predispose sexually active women to development of UTI: the use of a contraceptive diaphragm, the method of sexual intercourse, (greatly prolonged or cunnilingus), and failure to void immediately following intercourse.

PREVENTION OF UTI IN YOUNG WOMEN: Fluid intake should be increased to and maintained at to six to eight glasses daily. Although cranberry and other fruit juices are often recommended for patients with UTI, there is little objective evidence to show they have an impact. The urinary tract anesthetic phenazopyridine and sitz baths may provide relief from perineal discomfort. The anal area should be wiped from front to back or wipe the front first to prevent carrying bacteria to the urethral area; the bladder should be emptied shortly before and after intercourse; the genital area should be washed before intercourse; if vaginal dryness is a problem, water-soluble vaginal lubricants should be used before intercourse; a contraceptive diaphragm, cap, shield, or sponge should not remain in the vagina longer than necessary. An alternative method of contraception should be considered.

PATIENT CARE: Instructing the patient should emphasize self-care and prevention of recurrences. The antibiotic regimen should be explained, and the patient should be aware of signs and symptoms and, when they occur, should report them promptly to the primary caregiver.

yeast i. A colloquial term for vulvovaginal candidiasis.

infection control In medical care, institutional procedures and policies for monitoring and attempting to control the transmission of communicable diseases. This includes establishing mandatory sanitation, sterilization, hand hygiene, and isolation procedures. SEE: table; *Standard Precautions Appendix.*

PATIENT CARE: Many individuals recover completely from their infections. Some, however, develop a terminal illness. Tertiary prevention means assisting those individuals whose infections lead to terminal illnesses. They should be assisted to achieve a peaceful death, while safety is maintained both for caregivers and the patients' significant others. Also contacts should be tracked and tested.

infectious (ĭn-fĕk'shŭs) [ME. *infecten,* infect] **1.** Capable of being transmitted with or without contact. **2.** Pert. to a disease caused by a microorganism. **3.** Producing infection.

infectious disease ABBR: ID. Any disease caused by growth of pathogenic microorganisms in the body. SEE: *incubation* for table.

infectivity (ĭn"fek"tiv'ĭt-ē) **1.** The capacity of a pathogen to cause infection. **2.** The number of people who are infected by a disease divided by the number of people who are exposed to it.

infecundity (ĭn-fē-kŭn'dĭ-tē) [L. *infecunditas,* sterility] Barrenness; an inability to conceive.

inference (ĭn'f(ĕ-)rĕns) A conclusion drawn by a logical analysis of the available evidence.

inferior (ĭn-fē'rē-or) [L. *inferus,* below] **1.** Beneath; lower. **2.** Used medically in reference to the undersurface of an organ or indicating a structure below another structure.

inferiority complex SEE: under *complex.*

infertility (ĭn"fer-til'ĭ-tē) [²*in-* + *fertility*] Inability to achieve pregnancy during a year or more of unprotected intercourse. The condition may be present in either or both partners and may be reversible. In the U.S., about 20% of all couples are infertile.

PATIENT CARE: In women, infertility may be primary (in women who have never conceived) or secondary (after previous conceptions or pregnancies). Causes of primary infertility in women include ovulatory failure, anatomical anomalies of the uterus, Turner's syndrome, and eating disorders, among many others. Common causes of secondary infertility in women include but are not limited to tubal scarring (as after sexually transmitted infections), endometriosis, cancers, and chemotherapy. In men, infertility usually is caused by failure to manufacture adequate

Basic Guidelines for Infection Control

Infection Control Recommendation	Summary of Useful Practices
Cleaning and disinfection	Disinfect or sterilize surfaces, such as bed rails, computer keyboards, nightstands, phones, and toilets.
Cough etiquette/respiratory courtesy	Wear masks; cover mouth and nose when coughing or sneezing. Maintain three feet distances from others when you have a cold or flu.
Drug formulary restrictions	Limit prescribing privileges for antibiotics to designated specialists.
Hand hygiene	Use alcohol-based rubs, or wash hands after contact with any blood, body fluids, or potentially contaminated items or patients.
Isolation procedures	Follow protocols for isolation of patients who are bleeding, coughing, giving off other excretions, secretions, or potentially hazardous body fluids. Segregate patients during outbreaks of infectious diseases. Separate immune-suppressed patients from others with potentially communicable diseases.
Laundry/linen and food service management	Gather patient clothing, eating utensils, gowns, sheets, and towels without contaminating other objects used in patient care. Gown and glove while collecting and washing laundry. Perform hand hygiene after laundry management procedures.
Personal protective equipment (PPE) use	Wear gloves, goggles, gowns, masks, and shoe covers while performing patient care procedures whenever exposure to blood, body fluids, aerosols, or splashes are possible. Dispose of PPEs in designated containers.
Resuscitation and invasive airway management	Avoid mouth-to-mouth contact with patients; wear personal protective equipment at all times, such as particulate respirators or masks. Disinfect or sterilize endoscopes, intubation equipment, nebulizers, face masks (e.g., for CPAP or supplemental oxygen), or other respiratory care devices.
Sharps (management of needles, wires, etc.)	Maintain sharps in open view, to avoid accidental injuries. Never recap or manipulate needles used in patient care. Dispose of sharp objects in puncture-proof solid waste containers.
Source control	Application of anti-infective rubs or soaps to patients to limit their colonization by disease-causing bacteria
Standard/universal precautions	Follow universal precautions during every patient encounter.

amounts of sperm (due to exposure to environmental toxins, viruses or bacteria, developmental or genetic diseases, varicoceles, or endocrine abnormalities).

Investigation begins with comprehensive histories from both partners, assessment of their usual timing of intercourse, and thorough physical examinations. The initial test for men is semen analysis to assess sperm morphology, motility, and number. This should be done after 2 to 3 days of sexual abstinence. At least two to three ejaculates, obtained at no less than 1-week intervals, should be examined because of the variability in sperm counts. Female assessment usually begins with evaluation of ovulation by a basal body temperature graph or home ovulation prediction kit. Additional special as-

sessments of the woman may be ordered to evaluate ovarian, tubal, uterine, and cervical factors.

The specific problems that testing identifies may be managed by either pharmacological or surgically assisted reproduction techniques. SEE: *embryo transfer; in vitro **fertilization**; gamete intrafallopian transfer; transcervical balloon tuboplasty.*

   secondary i. Infertility in which one or more pregnancies have occurred before the present condition of infertility.
infest (ĭn-fĕst′) [L. *infestare*, to attack] To invade or contaminate; said esp. of parasites.

infestation (ĭn″fĕs″tā′shŏn) [L. *infestatio*, disturbance] Invasion of the body by animal parasites, esp. by such macroscopic forms as worms, larvae, or nymphal forms of endoparasites or ectoparasites. Particular infestations are listed under the first word. SEE: e.g., *chigoe infestation; flea infestation*.

infibulation (ĭn-fĭb-ū-lā'shŭn) [L. *in*, in, + *fibula*, clasp] **1**. The process of fastening, as in joining the lips of wounds by clasps. **2**. Female genital cutting.

infiltrate (in-fil'trāt″, in'fil-) [*'in-* + L. *filtrare*, to strain through] **1**. To pass into or through a substance or a space. **2**. The material that has infiltrated. **3**. A shadow seen on a chest x-ray and assumed to represent blood, pus, or other body fluids in the lung.

   alveolar i. Opacification of air spaces, caused by the filling of alveoli with blood, pus, or fluid. Alveolar infiltrates are seen on the chest radiograph as patchy areas of increased density, often surrounding air bronchograms.

   lobar i. A well-defined site of lung consolidation, seen on the chest radiograph as an area of increased density confined within a specific lobe or segment. SYN: *lobar pneumonia*.

   ETIOLOGY: Lobar infiltrates are usually due to bacterial infection (pneumonia).

   TREATMENT: The patient will need antibiotics, oxygen, and bronchial hygiene.

   patchy i. A poorly defined area of lung consolidation seen on the chest radiograph as scattered opacification within normal lung tissue. It is usually caused by a mixture of normally aerated and infected lung lobules.

infiltration (in″fil-trā'shŏn) [*infiltrate*] The deposition and accumulation of an external substance within a cell, tissue, or organ, such as fat deposition within a damaged liver. **infiltrative** (in'fil-trāt″iv), *adj*.

   amyloid i. The infiltration of tissue or viscera with amyloid, a starchlike glycoprotein. SEE: *amyloid*.

   cellular i. An infiltration of cells, esp. blood cells, into tissues; invasion by cells of malignant tumors into adjacent tissue.

   fatty i. A deposit of fat in the tissues, or oil or fat globules in the cells.

   fatty i. of the heart An abnormal accumulation of triglycerides in the myocardium, seen on biopsy specimens as clear vacuoles or droplets. SYN: *fatty degeneration of the heart*.

   glycogenic i. Glycogen deposit in cells.

   lymphocytic i. An infiltration of tissue by lymphocytes.

   pulmonary i. with eosinophilia ABBR: PIE. Eosinophilic **pneumonia**.

   purulent i. Pus in tissue.

   serous i. An infiltration with lymph.

   waxy i. Amyloid **degeneration**.

infinite distance SEE: under *distance*.

infirm (ĭn-fĭrm') [L. *infirmis*] Weak or feeble, esp. from old age or disease.

infirmary (ĭn-fĭrm'ă-rē) [L. *infirmarium*] A small hospital; a place for the care of sick or infirm persons.

infirmity (ĭn-fĭr'mĭ-tē) **1**. Weakness. **2**. A sickness or illness.

inflammasome (in-flam'ă-sōm″) [*inflamma(tion)* + *-some*] A cytoplasmic complex that regulates the activation of caspase enzymes, which convert interleukins from their inactive forms to active forms.

inflammation (in″flă-mā'shŏn) [L. *inflammare*, to kindle] An immunological defense against injury, infection, or allergy, marked by increases in regional blood flow, immigration of white blood cells, and release of chemical toxins. Inflammation is one way the body uses to protect itself from invasion by foreign organisms and to repair wounds to tissue. Clinical hallmarks of inflammation are redness, heat, swelling, pain, and loss of function of a body part. Systemically, inflammation may produce fevers, joint and muscle pains, organ dysfunction, and malaise. SYN: *inflammatory response*. SEE: table; *autoimmune disease; infection*.

   THE INFLAMMATORY PROCESS: Local inflammatory responses begin when traumatized or infected tissues activate the humoral and cellular immune systems. Complement proteins and cytokines are manufactured. These signaling proteins start a cascade of chemical events that result in increases in local blood flow and the attraction of white blood cells to the damaged tissue. White blood cells in turn consume foreign or injured cells and release arachidonic acid metabolites, kinins, histamines, and more complement, thereby amplifying and perpetuating the immune response. The white blood cells also release toxic oxygen radicals, nitric oxide, and tissue-destroying enzymes in an attempt to kill any invading microorganisms. In healthy people, the process continues until all damaged tissues or invading pathogens are removed (usually about 5 days); an inpouring of fibroblasts, which repair the injury and form a healed scar, follows.

   Systemic inflammatory responses occur when foreign proteins are recognized, e.g., in the bloodstream, and immune complexes are formed or cytotoxic T cells are activated. If sepsis triggers the immune response, these agents may help clear microorganisms from the blood.

   Autoimmune illnesses occur when the chemical and cellular tools of inflammation are directed against the body's own tissues.

   DIAGNOSIS: Nonspecific test results that suggest inflammation include an elevated white blood cell count, eryth-

Mediating Factors in Inflammation

Factors	Source	Effect
Arachidonic acid metabolites (prostaglandins and leukotrienes)	Phospholipids of cell membranes, especially mast cells	Primary mediators of late-stage (>6 hr) inflammation; increase dilation and permeability of blood vessels; stimulate neutrophil adhesion to endothelial tissue; bronchoconstriction; anaphylaxis
Bradykinin	Kinin system of plasma proteins	Primary mediator of prolonged (>1 hr) inflammation; vasodilation and increased permeability of blood vessels; pain; release of leukotrienes and prostaglandins
Complement proteins	Macrophages; liver endothelium	Increase vasodilation and vascular permeability; coat antigens to enhance phagocytosis; attract neutrophils; destroy pathogens
Histamine and serotonin	Mast cells; basophils	Primary mediators of early (≤30 min) inflammation; rapid dilation and increase in permeability of venules; bronchoconstriction; stimulation of prostaglandin production
Interleukin 1 (IL-1)	Macrophages; B cells, dendritic cells, neutrophils, other nucleated cells	Increased production and activity of other chemical mediators, phagocytes and lymphocytes; promotes release of acute-phase proteins; causes fever
Interleukin 8 (IL-8)	T lymphocytes; monocytes	Attracts neutrophils and more T cells
Platelet-activating factor (PAF)	Platelets	Releases chemical mediators; activates neutrophils; dilates and increases permeability of vessels
Transforming growth factor β (TFGβ)	Activated macrophages and T lymphocytes	Attracts neutrophils and monocytes; stimulates growth of connective tissue; inhibits other mediators
Tumor necrosis factors (TFNα)	Activated macrophages and some lymphocytes	Increase synthesis of other cytokines; induce formation of new blood vessels; increase adhesion of neutrophils to endothelium; cause fever and cachexia

rocyte sedimentation rate, or C-reactive protein level.

TREATMENT: Mild inflammation (such as the inflammatory change from minor injuries) often resolves with the topical application of ice packs or cold water. Nonsteroidal anti-inflammatory drugs (such as ibuprofen) and steroids (such as prednisone) are useful in managing more severe inflammation, as are many disease-modifying antirheumatic drugs, such as methotrexate or azathioprine.

acute i. The early response to tissue injury, marked by the influx of white blood cells and inflammatory mediators into damaged tissues. Most of the response takes place in 12 to 24 hr.

adhesive i. Inflammation of the serous membrane, enhancing the likelihood of attachments.

chronic i. Inflammation that persists

weeks to months after tissue damage. Its pathological hallmarks include simultaneous tissue repair and destruction.

exudative i. Inflammation in which the fluid leaving the capillaries is rich in plasma proteins.

fibrinous i. Inflammation in which the exudate is rich in fibrin.

hyperplastic i. Inflammation characterized by excess production of young fibrous tissue. SYN: *proliferative* **i.**

i. of jejunum Jejunitis.

i. of liver Hepatitis.

interstitial i. Inflammation involving principally the noncellular or supporting elements of an organ.

lung i. Pneumonia.

productive i. An infrequently used term for any inflammatory process in which there is marked cellular proliferation, e.g., in proliferative retinopathy.

proliferative i. Hyperplastic **i.**

pseudomembranous i. Inflammation in which a shelf of fibrin and white blood cell debris forms on an epithelial lining, usually from a toxin that necroses tissue. This type of inflammation is most often seen in colitis caused by *Clostridium difficile.* Before there were vaccinations against diphtheria, this inflammation was frequently found in the oral cavities of those infected with that pathogen.

purulent i. Inflammation in which pus is formed. SYN: *suppurative* **i.**

serous i. Inflammation of a part with serous exudate, or inflammation of a serous membrane.

simple i. Inflammation without pus or other inflammatory exudates.

subacute i. Mild inflammation with minimal signs and symptoms. It may become chronic and gradually damage tissues.

suppurative i. Purulent **i.**

ulcerative i. The formation of an ulcer over an inflamed area.

inflammatory (ĭn-flăm′ă-tor″ē) [L. *inflammare,* to flame within] Pert. to or marked by inflammation.

inflammatory anemia SEE: under *anemia.*

inflammatory bowel disease ABBR: IBD. The term for a number of chronic, relapsing inflammatory diseases of the gastrointestinal tract of unknown etiology. The two most common types are ulcerative colitis and Crohn's disease.

PATHOLOGY: Ulcerative colitis is limited to the superficial layers of the wall of the colon, whereas Crohn's disease may involve all layers of the bowel wall, from the oropharynx to the anus. The inflammation of ulcerative colitis is continuous throughout the affected bowel, producing a raw, ulcerated, or effaced lumen. In contrast, Crohn's dis-

ease is characterized by patchy areas of granulomatous inflammation, creating a cobblestoned mucosal surface that may develop deep fissures or a thickened, rubbery texture. In Crohn's disease but not ulcerative colitis, fistulas to adjacent sections of the bowel, vagina, and bladder may develop.

DIAGNOSIS: Barium studies of the upper and lower gastrointestinal tract and endoscopic examinations are used to diagnose IBD.

inflation (ĭn-flā′shŭn) [L. *in,* into, + *flare,* to blow] The distention of a part by air, gas, or liquid.

inflator (in-flāt′ŏr) An apparatus for forcing air or other gas into an aperture.

inflection (ĭn″flĕk′shŭn) [″ + *flectere,* to bend] **1.** An inward bending. **2.** A change of tone or pitch of the voice; a nuance.

infliximab (ĭn-flĕx′ē-măb) A monoclonal antibody against tumor necrosis factor, used to treat patients used to treat inflammatory bowel disease and rheumatoid arthritis.

influenza (in″floo-en′ză) [Italian *influenza,* influence (of the stars)] An acute contagious respiratory infection marked by fevers, chills, muscle aches, headache, prostration, runny nose. watering eyes, cough, and sore throat. The disease usually strikes during the winter. In patients with serious pre-existing illnesses (such as diabetes, chronic obstructive lung disease, heart disease or renal failure) and people over 65, influenza frequently is fatal. The disease spreads primarily by inhalation of infectious aerosols, although spread by direct personal contact also is possible. Epidemics or pandemics arise intermittently around the world during periods of viral evolution; in the winter of 1918 to 1919, an influenza pandemic claimed 20 million victims. Sporadic cases occur each year in the U.S., where the disease is responsible for an average of 36,000 deaths annually. SYN: *flu; grippe.* SEE: *cold.* **influenzal** (-zăl), *adj.*

ETIOLOGY: The responsible virus is either influenza A (about 65% of cases) or influenza B (about 35% of cases). A negligible number of infections are caused by influenza C.

COURSE: The incubation period of influenza is about 1 to 3 days, and the acute course of the illness typically lasts less than a week. Bacterial superinfection may occur, causing secondary pneumonias, sinusitis, or otitis media. Many patients lack energy and feel fatigued during their recuperation from acute infection.

CLASSIFICATION: The classification and naming of Influenza viruses depends on several elements—the nucleoprotein of the virus; the geographic location from which it is first isolated, its surface antigens, the year when it was first isolated in a laboratory, the adaptation of the virus to animals other than humans (such as birds, pigs, or horses), and its strain number.

Whether an influenza virus is called *influenza A* or *influenza B* depends on its nucleoprotein. This is a protein within the nucleus of the virus, that packages the viral ribonucleic acid (RNA) and helps transcribe its genetic contents.

The location where the virus is first identified (the viral geographic source) is usually the name of a city, state, or country, e.g. Stockholm, Texas, Panama.

If the virus is first identified as a cause of disease in e.g., 2013, it is a 2013 virus. This identifier is the viral year.

The next feature in the naming system is linked to the two proteins that the virus uses to enter into and explode out of infected cells in the respiratory tract. These proteins are called hemagglutinin and neuraminidase, respectively; and are abbreviated H and N (or HA and NA). Fifteen hemagglutinins have been identified. Most of these infect water fowl, e.g., geese and ducks. Three of them are known to infect people. Several of them can infect both birds and people (and other animals like swine).

When an animal cell is infected with more than one influenza virus at the same time, reassortment of viral genes can occur, and new viruses with new mixtures of disease-causing proteins can emerge. The influenza virus has eight major components, and pieces of one virus may link with pieces of others to form novel, and occasionally deadly combinations. A virus that emerges from a pig (after it has been infected with an avian virus and a human virus) with parts that are mostly found in pigs is called a *swine flu* virus. Similarly, a virus that mutates on its own within a pig and becomes infectious to people is also called a swine flu virus.

Newly mutated and reassorted viruses appear fairly frequently around the world every year, and are carried (by migrating birds) rapidly from one place to another. People can also carry influenza viruses rapidly around the globe if they travel when they are actively infected.

Public health data clearly have shown that about 30,000 people die of infection with influenza each year.

PREVENTION: Worldwide surveillance for new influenza antigens is an ongoing public health project; each year, updated vaccines are developed to counteract new strains of the disease. In the U.S., about 70 million people are vaccinated each year. Vaccination is offered in the late autumn, prior to the start of flu season. The trivalent vaccine offered is based on the previous year's virus. Vaccination should be offered to people over 65 and individuals with underlying cardiac, pulmonary, renal, or hepatic disease, cancer, diabetes mellitus, and other chronic or debilitating illness, as well as all health care professionals. Vaccination of the general population prevents epidemic disease and prevents significant economic losses caused by employee absenteeism. Influenza vaccines are more than 70% effective in older adults and about 90% effective in younger recipients.

VACCINATION IN PREGNANCY: Women in the second and third trimesters of pregnancy are among the target groups for immunization: they, more than other members of the general population, should be recruited to receive influenza vaccination. Pregnant women with underlying heart, lung, or other chronic illnesses (such as diabetes mellitus) should receive influenza vaccination at *any* stage of pregnancy.

Recipients must be asked about hypersensitivity to eggs and egg products because the vaccine is made from chick embryos and must not be given to anyone with such allergies. Recipients also should be advised about possible adverse effects of the vaccine: local discomfort, low-grade fever, malaise, and the rare complication of Guillain-Barré syndrome, a form of ascending flaccid paralysis.

⚠️ Children with influenza-like illnesses should avoid aspirin products because of the risk of Reye syndrome. All patients receiving influenza vaccines should review federally mandated Vaccine Information Sheets carefully before getting their injections.

TREATMENT: Influenza A virus is treatable with antiviral drugs. These agents have an impact on the duration of infection with either influenza A or B virus. Symptom-based treatment with acetaminophen, NSAIDs, cough remedies (e.g., dextromethorphan, an antitussive; or guaifenesin, an expectorant), and other nonprescription remedies alleviate some of the misery the illness causes.

PATIENT CARE: Warm shower, baths, or heating pads help to relieve myalgias. All hospitalized patients should be protected from visitors who may have the flu (during flu season), and health care personnel should not provide patient care if they are ill or feel as if they may be coming down with flu. For the hospitalized patient, respiratory and blood and body fluid precautions are followed. Vital signs and fluid balance are monitored. Respiratory function is assessed for signs and symptoms of developing pneumonia, such as inspiratory crackles, increased fever, pleuritic chest pain, dyspnea, and coughing accompanied by purulent or bloody sputum. Prescribed analgesics, antipyretics, and decongestants are administered. Bedrest and increased oral fluid intake are encouraged, and intravenous fluids administered if prescribed. Oxygen therapy is administered if necessary. The patient is assisted to return to normal activities gradually. Nonalcoholic mouthwash or warm saline gargles are provided to ease throat soreness. The patient is taught proper cough etiquette and thorough hand hygiene to prevent spread of the virus. The patient treated at home is taught about all of the above supportive care measures as well as about signs and symptoms of serious complications to be reported.

Asian i. Influenza caused by a variant strain of influenza virus type A.

avian i. ABBR: AI. One of several influenza A viruses that primarily infects birds and poultry, and may occasionally cause a febrile illness in human beings. Symptoms in people include cough, muscle aches, sore throat and headache. Severe cases may cause viral pneumonia or acute respiratory distress syndrome. A pandemic of avian influenza (type H5N1) in the early 20th century killed millions of people worldwide. SYN: *bird flu*.

highly pathogenic avian i. ABBR: HPAI. Any genetic variant of avian influenza A that causes serious illness, or carries a high probability of death, in infected birds.

swine i. Any of several influenza A viruses that primarily infects cells that line the respiratory tracts of pigs. It can spread to humans or birds when a pig is infected with more than one strain of influenza at the same time and the nucleic acids from the separate species mix, forming a new, potentially dangerous combination. SYN: *swine flu*.

influenza-like illness SEE: under *illness*.

infolding (ĭn-fōld'ĭng) Process of enclosing within a fold; an operation formerly employed in the treatment of stomach ulcer in which the walls on either side of the lesion are sutured together.

informal care SEE: under *care*.

informatics (ĭn-fŏr-măt'ĭks) [Translation of Russian *informatika*] The theory, science, and practice of the use of computer and informational technologies to store, retrieve, transmit, and manipulate data.

health care i. The study of how health care data, information, knowledge, and wisdom are collected, stored,

processed, communicated, and used to support the process of health care delivery to clients, providers, administrators, and organizations involved in health care delivery. It is an interdisciplinary science developed from the integration of information science, computer science, cognitive science, and the health care sciences.

medical i. Informatics applied to medical knowledge, practice, management, education, and research. This process includes computer technology, internet access, and electronic applications and devices.

nursing i. Informatics applied to nursing science to manage, process, and analyze nursing data, information, and knowledge to support the practice of nursing and the delivery of patient care.

information (ĭn"fŏr-mā'shŏn) [L. *informatio*, idea, conception] 1. Data that are interpreted, organized, structured, and given meaning. 2. A message from a sender to one or more receivers.

information bias The mistaken use of information that has no value in making clinical decisions. It is based on the incorrect belief that more information, even irrelevant information, must always be acquired before making a decision.

information science SEE: under *science*.

information system 1. Any structure or device that converts data input from diverse systems into outputs such as reports and screen displays. 2. An automated or manual system that comprises people, machines, and/or methods organized to collect, process, transmit, and disseminate data that represent user information.

information technology SEE: under *technology*.

infra- [L. *infra*, below, underneath] Prefix meaning *below; under; beneath; inferior to; after*.

infra-axillary (ĭn"fră-ăks'ĭl-ă-rē) [" + *axilla*, little axis] Below the axilla.

infraclavicular (ĭn"fră-klă-vĭk'ū-lăr) [" + *clavicula*, little key] Below the clavicle.

infracostal (ĭn"fră-kŏs'tăl) [" + *costa*, rib] Below the rib.

infraction (ĭn-frăk'shŭn) [L. *infractus*, to destroy] An incomplete fracture of a bone in which parts do not become displaced.

infracture (ĭn"frăk'chĕr) [Abbrev. of *in(complete) fracture*] The removal of nasal bones medially (inward), e.g., to narrow a widened nose.

infradentale (ĭn"fră-děn-tā'lē) A craniometric landmark; it is the bony point between the mandibular central incisors. SEE: *cephalometry*.

infraglottic (ĭn"fră-glŏt'ĭk) [" + Gr. *glottis*, back of tongue] Below the glottis.

infrahyoid (ĭn″fră-hī′oyd) [″ + Gr. *hyoeides,* U-shaped] Below the hyoid bone.

inframammary (ĭn″fră-măm′ă-rē) [″ + *mamma,* breast] Below the mammary gland.

inframammary fold SEE: under *fold.*

inframandibular (ĭn″fră-măn-dĭb′ū-lăr) [″ + *mandibula,* lower jawbone] Below the lower jaw (mandible).

inframaxillary (ĭn″fră-măk′sĭ-lĕr″ē) [″ + *maxilla,* jawbone] Below the upper jaw (maxilla).

infraocclusion (ĭn″fră-ŏ-kloo′zhŭn) [″ + *occlusio,* a shutting up] Location of a tooth below the line of occlusion.

infraorbital (ĭn-fră-or′bĭ-tăl) [″ + *orbita,* track] Beneath the orbit.

infrapsychic (ĭn″fră-sī′kĭk) [″ + Gr. *psyche,* mind] Below the level of consciousness; automatic.

infrapubic (ĭn″fră-pū′bĭk) [″ + *pubes,* hair covering pubic area] Below the pubis.

infrared (ĭn″fră-rĕd′) Lying outside the red end of the visible spectrum.

infrascapular (ĭn″fră-skăp′ū-lăr) [″ + *scapula,* shoulder blade] Beneath the shoulder blade.

infrasonic (ĭn″fră-sŏn′ĭk) [L. *infra,* below, underneath, + *sonus,* sound] Sound wave frequency lower than those normally heard.

   i. recorder A device that can be used to determine blood pressure by detecting and recording the subaudible oscillations of the arterial wall under an occluding cuff. The resulting values are comparable to those determined by use of an intra-arterial catheter. SEE: *blood pressure, indirect measurement of; pseudohypertension.*

infrasound (ĭn″fră-sownd″) Sounds of low frequency used, e.g., in diagnostic and therapeutic technologies.

infraspinous (ĭn″fră-spī′nŭs) [″ + *spina,* thorn] Beneath the scapular spine.

infrastructure 1. The components of information technology, including computer hardware, software, networks, and peripheral devices that are used to connect and send signals to computers and users. 2. Those buildings, supplies, policies, procedures and other assets that support the human resources of an institution.

infratrochlear (ĭn″fră-trŏk′lē-ăr) [″ + *trochlea,* pulley] Beneath the trochlea.

infraversion (ĭn″fră-vĕr′zhŭn) [″ + *versio,* a turning] A downward deviation of the eye.

infundibulectomy (ĭn″fŭn-dĭb″yŭ-lek′tŏ-mē) [*infundibulum* + *-ectomy*] Surgical excision of the infundibulum of any structure or organ, e.g., the heart or a fallopian tube.

infundibulum (ĭn″fŭn-dĭb′ū-lŭm) [L.] 1. A funnel-shaped passage or structure. 2. The tube connecting the frontal sinus with the middle nasal meatus. 3. The stalk of the pituitary gland. 4. Any renal pelvis division. 5. The cavity formed by the fallopian fimbriae. 6. The terminus of a bronchiole. 7. The terminus at the upper end of the cochlear canal. 8. The conelike upper anterior angle of the right cardiac ventricle from which the pulmonary artery arises. SYN: *conus arteriosus.*

   ethmoidal i. The area in the middle meatus of the nose. The anterior ethmoid sinuses and the frontal sinus open into this area.

   i. of hypothalamus The stalk that extends from the hypothalamus to the posterior lobe of the pituitary gland.

   i. of the uterine tube The funnel-shaped opening at the lateral end of the uterine tube.

infusate (ĭn-fū′zāt) [L. *infusus,* poured into] Any liquid introduced into the body.

¹infusible (ĭn-fū′zĭ-bl) [L. *in-,* not, + *fusio,* fusion] Not capable of being fused or melted.

²infusible [L. *in,* into, + *fundere,* to pour] Capable of being made into an infusion.

infusion (ĭn-fū′zhŏn) [L. *infusio,* a pouring into, watering] 1. Any liquid substance (other than blood) introduced into the body for therapeutic purposes. 2. Steeping a substance in hot or cold water in order to obtain its active principle. 3. The product obtained from the process of steeping.

   continuous i. A controlled method of intravenous administration of drugs, fluids, or nutrients given without interruption, instead of by bolus. By adjusting the infusion rate, precise medication dosages or quantities of fluids can be given over time. Therapies administered continuously include some antibiotics, cancer chemotherapies, heparin, insulin, parenteral nutrition, and vasopressors, among others.

   continuous hepatic artery i. ABBR: CHAI. The use of an infusion pump to provide a continuous supply of chemotherapeutic agents to the hepatic artery to control metastases from cancers of the gastrointestinal tract.

   continuous subcutaneous insulin i. ABBR: CSII. Administration of insulin under the skin continuously with an infusion pump connected to a needle inserted beneath the epidermis. SEE: *insulin pump.*

   intraosseous i. A method of obtaining immediate access to the circulation by inserting a needle through the skin, subcutaneous tissues, and periosteum into the marrow cavity of a long bone, usually the proximal tibia. Once access is gained, substances may be injected into the bone marrow, where they are absorbed almost immediately into the general circulation. This avenue of access does not collapse in the presence of shock. SYN: *intraosseous injection*.

PATIENT CARE: Drugs infused intraosseously should be followed by a bolus of 5 mL or more of normal saline.

intravenous i. The injection into a vein of a solution, drugs, or blood components. SEE: illus.

SOLUTIONS: Many liquid preparations are given by intravenous (IV) infusion. Those commonly used include isotonic (normal) saline, lactated Ringer, dextrose 5% in water, and potassium chloride 0.2% in 5% dextrose. The type and quantity depend on the needs of the patient. The solution is usually given continuously at the rate of 1 to 2 or more liters per day. In shock, however, rapid infusion of larger volumes may be necessary to support the circulation.

SITE: Intravenous infusion is usually given in the arm through the median basilic or median cephalic vein, but veins at various other sites may be used. The vein must be exposed if a cannula is used. Introduction of solution should be at the rate required to deliver the needed amount of fluid and contained electrolytes, medicines, or nutrients in a prescribed time.

⚠ Intravenous infusions should be discontinued or infusion fluid replenished when the solution being administered is depleted. Clotting of blood in the catheter may occur when the infusion is not continuous.

PATIENT CARE: Using scrupulous aseptic technique and universal precautions, the nurse prepares the IV infusion, selects and prepares a venous site, disinfects the skin, inserts an IV catheter or cannula to initiate the infusion (if an IV access is not in place), and secures it in place, restraining joint motion near the insertion site as necessary. The amount of fluid to be infused per hour is calculated and the flow of the prescribed fluid (and additive as appropriate) initiated at the desired flow rate. A pump or controller is typically used to ensure desired volume delivery. After initiating the infusion, the nurse ensures that the correct fluid is being administered at the designated flow rate and observes the infusion site and the patient at least every hour for signs of infiltration or other complications, such as infection, thrombophlebitis, fluid or electrolyte overload, and air embolism. The site dressing and administration set are changed according to protocol. Central venous catheters and lines are associated with more infections and more serious infections and other complications

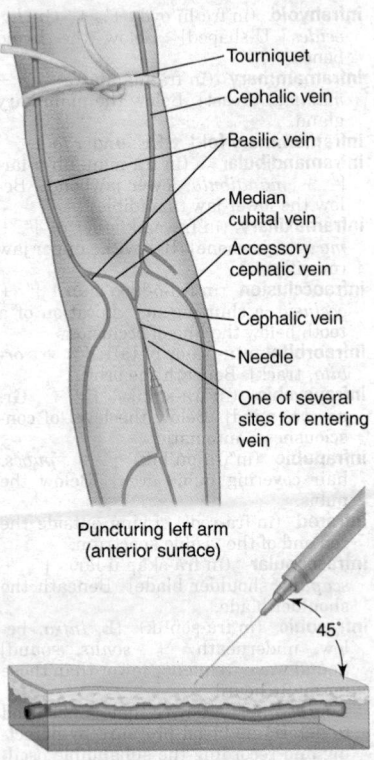

Puncturing left arm (anterior surface)

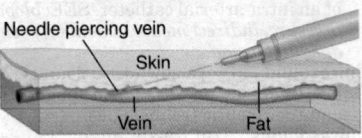

Technique in puncturing vein:
1. Pierce skin at a 45° angle

2. Decrease angle to 15° to puncture vein

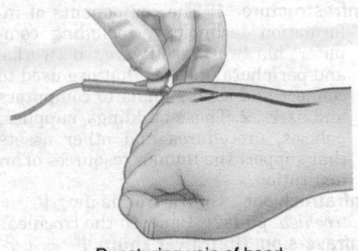

Puncturing vein of hand

INTRAVENOUS INFUSION TECHNIQUE

than peripheral catheters and lines. Strict protocols have been developed for their care.

lipid i. Hyperalimentation with a fat-containing solution administered intra-venously.

neuraxial i. An invasive approach to the relief of unremitting pain in which analgesic drugs are injected directly into the spinal fluid.

subcutaneous i. The infusion of so-lutions into the subcutaneous space.

infusion reaction Any adverse reaction to a constituent administered intra-venously, such as, an anaphylactic or anaphylactoid reaction to a monoclonal antibody. SEE: *transfusion reaction.*

ingesta (ĭn-jĕs′tă) [L. *in,* into, + *gerere,* to carry] Food and drink received into the body through the mouth.

ingestant (ĭn-jĕs′tănt) [″ + *gerere,* to carry] Any substance such as food and drink taken orally.

ingestion (ĭn-jĕs′shŭn) **1.** The process of taking material (particularly food) into the gastrointestinal tract. **2.** Phagocy-tosis.

caustic i. Exposure of the oral cavity, pharynx, larynx, or trachea to acids or alkalis, with resulting tissue damage. SEE: *burn of aerodigestive tract.*

ingredient (in-grēd′ē-ĕnt) [L. *ingredi,* to enter] Any part or component of a com-pound, a mixture, or a more complex substance.

ingrowing (ĭn′grō-ĭng) [L. *in,* into, + AS. *growan,* to grow] Growing inward so that a portion that is normally free becomes covered.

inguin-, inguino- [L. *inguen,* stem *inguin-,* groin] Prefixes meaning *groin.*

inguinal (ing′gwĭ-năl) [L. *inguinalis,* pert. to the groin] Pert. to the groin.

inguinal ring SEE: under *ring.*

INH *isoniazid.*

inhalant (ĭn-hā′lănt) [L. *inhalare,* to in-hale] A medication or compound suit-able for inhaling.

inhalant abuse SEE: under *abuse.*

inhalation (in″hă-lā′shŏn) [L. *inhalatio*] **1.** The act of drawing breath, vapor, or gas into the lungs; inspiration. **2.** The introduction of dry or moist air or vapor into the lungs for therapeutic purposes, such as metered-dose bronchodilators in the treatment of asthma.

inhalation therapy The administration of medicines, water vapor, gases (e.g., oxy-gen, carbon dioxide, or helium), or an-esthetics by inhalation. The medicines usually are nebulized by using an aero-sol or spray apparatus.

inhale (in-hāl′) [L. *inhalare*] To draw in the breath; to inspire.

inhaler (ĭn-hāl′ĕr) **1.** A device for admin-istering medicines by inhalation. **2.** One who inhales.

metered-dose i. ABBR: MDI. A de-vice used for self-administration of aero-solized drugs.

PATIENT CARE: When used cor-rectly, a metered-dose inhaler can de-liver accurate doses of medication to the respiratory tract. The MDI is a drug canister in an L-shaped mouthpiece, which can be used alone or with a "spacer" (a holding chamber designed to aerosolize medication so it can reach the lower respiratory tract). The health care professional teaching the patient proper MDI technique should gather the drug canister and mouthpiece, the package insert, and the spacer (if one is to be used). The MDI should be sprayed once or twice prior to initiating use, and the spacer inspected for foreign objects. The patient should wash his/her hands thor-oughly, and may either sit or stand. If a peak flow meter is being used, the pa-tient should take a reading prior to us-ing the MDI. The patient should then clear the throat and nasal passages. The patient should hold the inhaler upright and shake it as directed, then remove the cap and hold the inhaler with the canister on top and the mouthpiece fac-ing the patient's open mouth at the bot-tom. Tilting the head back slightly, the patient should breathe out slowly and completely. (When using an MDI with a spacer, the inhaler cap is removed and the mouthpiece is firmly inserted into the spacer, then the spacer and inhaler are held together upright and vigor-ously shaken 5 or 6 times. The space cap is then removed, the head tilted back, and the breath let out slowly and com-pletely.) The inhaler mouthpiece may be positioned in one of two ways: 1 to 2 inches (2.5 to 5 cm) in front of the open mouth, mouth open; or with the mouth-piece in the mouth and lips sealed around it. However, this latter tech-nique is less efficient in delivering med-ication and should never be used for steroids. While breathing in slowly, evenly, and deeply though the mouth, the patient should press once on the canister and continue inhaling for 3 to 5 sec. The breath should then be held for 10 sec (or as long as possible), allowing the medication to settle in the lungs. The inhaler should be removed from the mouth prior to exhaling. If a spacer is used, the patient should place the spacer mouthpiece in the mouth and seal the lips around it, then press on the canister to spray a puff of medication into the spacer and begin inhaling slowly through the mouth for 3 to 5 sec. The breath should then be held for 10 sec (or as long as possible). The spacer should be removed from the mouth prior to exhaling. If more than one puff is pre-scribed, the patient should wait 1 to 2 min between puffs to help the second puff to better penetrate the lungs. The patient should be taught to remember "B before C" when using an inhaled bronchodilator and corticosteroid; first inhaling the bronchodilator, waiting about 5 min, and then inhaling the corticosteroid. This helps to open the air passages for maximum absorption of the steroid. After inhaling a corticosteroid, the patient should rinse the mouth with water and expectorate it.

The spacer and the L-shaped mouthpiece and cap should be rinsed with warm, running water at least once each day, and washed with warm soapy water, then rinsed at least once each week. The equipment should always be allowed to air-dry. The patient can calculate how long a drug canister will last by reading the total number of doses on the label, counting the number of puffs used each day, and dividing the total doses by the number of daily puffs. (Thus if a canister contains 200 doses and the patient takes 8 to 10 each day, a new canister will be required in a month). The health care educator should provide the patient with written instructions and illustrations for proper MDI use. The patient also should be taught about (and provided with) information on the desired effects of each medication and the possible adverse reactions. The teaching session, the patient's demonstration of the method, and any questions raised should be documented in the patient's record. SEE: illus.

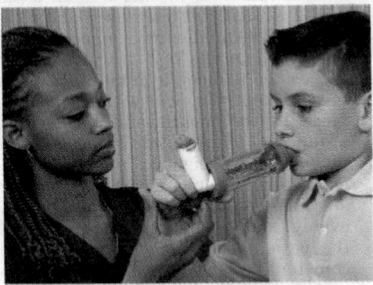

METERED-DOSE INHALER

Hand-held inhaler with spacer device.

inherent (ĭn-hĕr′ĕnt) [L. *inhaerens*, to inhere] Belonging to anything naturally, not as a result of circumstance. SEE: *innate* (1); *intrinsic* (1).

inheritance (in-her′ĭt-ăns) [L. *inhereditare*, to inherit] The sum total of all that is inherited, the result of genetic material (DNA) contained within the ovum and sperm.

   alternative i. The inheritance of a trait from one parent.

   extrachromosomal i. Inherited traits governed by mechanisms other than by chromosomes.

   holandric i. Inherited traits carried only by men; thus, the operative gene is on the Y chromosome.

   hologynic i. Transmission of traits from mothers only to daughters.

   multifactorial i. The inheritance of traits influenced by a number of genetic and nongenetic factors, none of which has a predominant effect.

   sex-influenced i. Inherited traits for which the genes are on autosomes, but their expression is influenced by the sex chromosomes (e.g., the reproductive organs).

   sex-limited i. A trait that can be expressed in only one sex.

   sex-linked i. The inheritance of traits regulated by either of the sex chromosomes, (X or Y) or contained in the genetic material of these chromosomes.

inherited Body traits and genetic makeup received as a result of genetic transmission rather than acquired.

inhibin (in-hib′ĭn) [inhib(in) + -in] A hormone secreted by the corpus luteum in females and by the testicle in males. It inhibits the secretion of gonadotropin-releasing hormone and human chorionic gonadotropin. In women, inhibin is secreted throughout the menstrual cycle and during pregnancy, but it normally is not present in postmenopausal women. It is, however, elevated in most postmenopausal women with granulosa or mucinous carcinomas of the ovary. In men, inhibin levels are elevated in prostatic hyperplasia and decreased in cancers of the prostate. SEE: *cancer, ovarian*.

inhibition (in″(h)ĭ-bish′ŏn) [L. *inhibitio*, restraint] **1.** The repression or restraint of a function. **2.** In physiology, a stopping of an action or function of an organ, as in the slowing or stopping of the heart produced by electrical stimulation of the vagus nerve. **3.** In psychiatry, restraint of one mental process almost simultaneously by another opposed mental process; an inner impediment to free thought and activity.

   arthrogenic muscle i. ABBR: AMI. A clinical impairment caused by an ongoing reflex inhibition of the musculature surrounding a joint following distention or damage to structures of that joint.

   competitive i. Inhibition of the function of an active material by competing for the cell receptor site. SYN: *selective i.*

   contact i. Inhibition of cell division due to the close contact of similar cells, a natural brake in the healing of wounds.

   hemagglutination i. A laboratory test in which the lack of agglutination (clumping) of red blood cells (RBCs) indicates that antibodies are present in the patient's blood. Certain viruses (e.g., mumps, measles, rubella, adenovirus) bind with RBCs and cause clumping. However, antibodies, if present, quickly bind with the virus, preventing viral binding to RBCs and the resulting agglutination. SEE: *agglutination.*

noncompetitive i. Inhibition of enzyme activity resulting only from the concentration of the inhibitor.

psychic i. The arrest of an impulse, thought, action, or speech.

reciprocal i. **1.** The inhibition of muscles antagonistic to those being facilitated. It is essential for coordinated movement. **2.** Inhibition of a complementary nerve center by the one being stimulated. For example, the inspiration center in the medulla generates impulses to the respiratory muscles to bring about inhalation and at the same time inhibits the expiration center.

i. of reflex The prevention of a reflex action, as inhibiting a sneeze by pressure on a facial nerve as it passes just under the upper lip.

selective i. Competitive inhibition.

inhibitor (in-hib′ĭt-ŏr) An agent that blocks a cellular receptor, stops a chemical reaction, prevents an enzyme from working, or suppresses a muscle or nerve.

acetylcholinesterase i. Cholinesterase **i.**

alpha–2 plasmin i. Alpha–2 antiplasmin.

alpha-glucosidase i. An oral drug that lowers blood sugars by preventing carbohydrate absorption from the gastrointestinal tract.

5-alpha reductase i. A medication to treat benign prostatic hyperplasia. It blocks the conversion of testosterone to dihydrotestosterone.

angiotensin-converting enzyme i. ABBR: ACE inhibitor. Any of the therapeutic agents that inhibit conversion of angiotensin I to angiotensin II. ACE inhibitors are used to treat hypertension and heart failure and to protect kidney function in patients with diabetes mellitus.

aromatase i. Any of a class of drugs that block the synthesis of estrogen in the body. A number of these agents have been developed to treat breast cancer, which is often a hormone-responsive malignancy.

attachment i. Entry **i.**

bone resorption i. A class of drugs that prevent or retard osteoporosis. Examples include the bisphosphonates.

cholesteryl ester transfer protein i. Any drug that inhibits the transfer of cholesteryl esters from high-density lipoproteins (HDLs) to other lipoproteins. Drugs from this class increase HDL levels, potentially improving the lipid profiles of patients and decreasing their risk of atherosclerosis.

cholinesterase i. ABBR: ChEI. Any of a class of drugs that prevent the degradation of the neurotransmitter acetylcholine, which is involved in memory and learning. Drugs from this class are used to treat Alzheimer's dementia. SYN: *acetylcholinesterase i.*

competitive i. **1.** A chemical that binds to or blocks another reagent from participating in a reaction. **2.** A medication, hormone, or other intercellular messenger that binds and blocks the cellular receptor or target enzyme of another agent. Drugs that act by competitive inhibition may treat or prevent disease by inactivating pathogenic enzymes or by blocking the effects of hormones or precursor molecules. For example, protease inhibitors interfere with production of human immunodeficiency virus (HIV) by binding and inactivating the protease enzyme; selective estrogen-receptor modulators limit the impact of estrogen by replacing this hormone on cells sensitive to its effects.

cyclooxygenase i. Any agent that suppresses inflammation by blocking the inflammatory effects of cyclooxygenase.

dipeptidyl peptidase-4 i. ABBR: DPP-4 inhibitor. Gliptin.

direct thrombin i. ABBR: DP. Any medication or substance that interferes with the coagulation of blood by blocking the action of thrombin. Unlike heparins, which are anticoagulants that require the presence of antithrombin to inactivate thrombin, DTIs exert their effects without an intermediary. DTIs can be used to treat and prevent clots in both arteries and veins (although heparin and warfarin are usually preferred for these uses). They are an alternative to heparin in patients with a history of heparin-induced thrombocytopenia. The primary side effect of DTIs is bleeding.

DPP-4 i. *dipeptidyl peptidase-4 i.*

dual reuptake i. An antidepressant medication that works by blocking the reuptake of both serotonin and norepinephrine.

entry i. Any agent that prevents a pathogen (e.g., human immunodeficiency virus) from binding to cell membranes and infecting cells. SYN: *attachment i.*

glycoprotein IIB/IIIa receptor i. Any of a class of drugs that block the fibrinogen receptor on the surface of platelets. Drugs from this class are used to treat acute myocardial infarction, unstable angina pectoris, and other acute coronary syndromes. The most common side effect of treatment with these drugs is bleeding.

HMG CoA enzyme i. Statin.

integrase i. Any agent that prevents the human immunodeficiency virus from inserting its viral DNA into host cell chromosomes.

matrix metalloproteinase i. An agent that inhibits cancer cells by blocking their abilities to invade tissues, demand new blood supply, and metastasize.

metalloprotease i. Metalloproteinase **i.**

metalloproteinase i. Any of numerous compounds that inhibit the activity of the metalloproteinase family of enzymes. These agents share the ability to suppress or eliminate the enzyme activity of the metalloproteinases. Agents identified in this group include the tetracycline antibiotics, numerous specially designed synthetic peptides and proteins, chemicals such as ethylenediaminetetra-acetic acid (EDTA), and a variety of agents used in cancer chemotherapy. SYN: *metalloprotease i.*

monoamine oxidase i. ABBR: MAOI. Any of a group of drugs that can be used to treat depression and Parkinson's disease. Nonselective versions of these medications produced hypertensive crises and other severe side effects when they were taken with tyramine-containing foods (some cheeses) and several other drugs. Newer members of this class of drugs do not have these effects, but should be used with caution, esp. by those taking selective serotonin reuptake inhibitors.

⚠️ MAOIs may have unfavorable drug-drug interactions with many anesthetics and should be discontinued approximately two weeks before surgery.

SEE: *tyramine.*

neuraminidase inhibitor Any of a class of antiviral drugs that block neuraminidase, which helps the influenza virus to bud from cells it has infected so that it can spread to other ciliated epithelial cells of the respiratory tract. Agents in this class include oseltamivir and zanamivir.

nonnucleoside analog reverse transcriptase i. ABBR: NNRTI. Any of a class of antiretroviral drugs used to treat those infected with HIV. NNRTIs bind with and inhibit the activity of reverse transcriptase, an enzyme needed to transcribe viral RNA into the host cell DNA. Examples include nevirapine, delavirdine, and efavirenz.

nucleoside reverse transcriptase i. ABBR: NRTI. Any of a class of antiretroviral drugs used to treat patients with HIV infection. NRTIs prevent transcription of viral RNA to host DNA by interfering with the action of the enzyme reverse transcriptase. Zidovudine, dideoxyinosine, zalcitabine, d4T, and abacavir are NRTIs. SEE: *reverse transcriptase inhibitor.*

phosphodiesterase i. ABBR: PDE inhibitor. Any agent that blocks phosphodiesterase, inhibiting the production of second messengers within cells, such as cyclic adenosine monophosphate or cyclic glucose monophosphate. Drugs that inhibit PDE include sildenafil, an agent used to treat erectile dysfunction, and other agents used as positive inotropes and vasodilators in heart failure.

prostaglandin i. A substance that inhibits the production of prostaglandins. Nonsteroidal and steroidal anti-inflammatory agents are two major categories of such inhibitors.

protease i. **1.** A substance that inhibits the action of enzymes. **2.** Any of a class of medications that prevent immature virions (as of hepatitis viruses or HIV) from assembling into structures capable of replication.

proton pump i. ABBR: PPI. Any of a class of medications that eliminate acid production in the stomach. Thes drugs are used to treat peptic ulcers, gastroesophageal reflux disease, *Heliobacter pylori* infection, and related disorders. Omeprazole and lansoprazole are members of this drug class.

reverse transcriptase i. ABBR: RTI. Any of a class of antiretroviral agents that competitively inhibit the reverse transcriptase enzyme of HIV and other viruses. SEE: *antiretroviral.*

selective serotonin reuptake i. ABBR: SSRI. Any of a class of drugs that interfere with serotonin transport, used in treating depression, obsessive-compulsive behaviors, eating disorders, and social phobias. Examples include fluoxetine (Prozac), paroxetine (Paxil), and sertraline.

⚠️ The use of SSRIs in the treatment of depression may sometimes be associated with an increased risk of suicide, esp. during the initiation of treatment. The risk is greatest among children and adolescents. All patients who begin treatment with SSRIs should be monitored closely for evidence that they intend to harm themselves.

serine protease i. ABBR: serpin. Any of the compounds that inhibit platelet function and coagulation. Serpins have been used to reduce deposition of microemboli in cases of disseminated intravascular coagulation associated with sepsis.

serotonin and norepinephrine reuptake i. ABBR: SNRI. An antidepressant medication (such as duloxetine or venlafaxine) that elevates mood by blocking neurons from taking up both norepinephrine and serotonin. Combined reuptake inhibitors differ from medications such as sertraline (Zoloft) or fluoxetine (Prozac), which are relatively selective serotonin reuptake inhibitors, and from tricyclic antidepressants, which primarily prevent the reuptake of norepinephrine by brain cells. SNRIs treat neuropathic pain as well as depression.

tumor necrosis factor alpha i. A drug that blocks the effects of tumor necrosis factor alpha (TNF-alpha), a biologically active cytokine that is a critical element of the inflammatory response. Such drugs, which include adalimumab, etanercept, and infliximab, are agents used to treat autoimmune illnesses such as rheumatoid arthritis.

⚠️ Because these drugs are immunologically active, patients with active infection or those with chronic infections such as tuberculosis should not use them. These agents also sometimes increase the risk of cancers and have rarely been associated with demyelinating diseases of the central nervous system such as multiple sclerosis.

vasopeptidase i. Any of a class of medications that blocks the actions of both angiotensin converting enzymes (ACE) and neural endopeptidase. Drugs from this class may be used to treat heart failure.

inhibitory (ĭn-hĭb′ĭ-tō-rē) Restraining, preventing.

inhibitory concentration SEE: under *concentration*.

in-home test A test done by patients rather than health care professionals to provide information about an individual's health status. Examples include tests to measure blood sugar (glucose), cholesterol, occult blood in feces, and blood pressure, as well as ovulation predictors and pregnancy tests. The materials and devices needed for in-home tests may be available over the counter (i.e., a prescription from a health care professional is not needed).

inion (ĭn′ē-on″) [Gr.] The center of the external occipital protuberance. **iniac, inial** (ĭn″ē-ak″, ĭn″ē-ăl), *adj.*

initial (ĭn-ĭsh′ăl) [L. *initium,* beginning] Relating to the beginning or commencement of a thing or process.

initiated cycle SEE: under *cycle*.

inject [L. *injicere,* to throw in] To introduce fluid into the body or its parts artificially.

injectable (ĭn-jĕk′tă-bl) Capable of being injected.

injected (ĭn-jĕkt′ĕd) [L. *injectus,* thrown in] **1.** Filled by injection of fluid. **2.** Congested.

injection (in-jek′shŏn) [*inject*] **1.** The forcing of a fluid into a vessel, tissue, or cavity.

PATIENT CARE: All supplies used in preparing and administering an injection should be sterile. The caregiver chooses the appropriate syringe size for the volume of fluid to be injected, the appropriate needle gauge for the type of fluid, and the appropriate needle length for the administration route and site, considering the amount of muscle and adipose tissue, mobility limitations, and other site-related factors. Hands should be thoroughly cleansed before and after the procedure, and gloves worn if preparing a chemotherapeutic agent. The prescribed dose is accurately measured. An appropriate site is identified by using anatomical landmarks, and the area is cleansed with an antiseptic swab (from the center outward) and time allowed for the antiseptic to evaporate. The needle is inserted at the appropriate angle, given the prescribed route. Intradermal injections use a short fine needle with the opening faced upward; the needle is placed nearly parallel to the surface of the skin and advanced far enough for the injected fluid to make a small bubble under the skin, then carefully removed; pressure that could cause the fluid to leak out onto the skin surface should be avoided. Subcutaneous injections should consist of no more than 1 ml. A short needle should be inserted at a 45° angle, without aspiration, and gentle pressure or no pressure applied to the site after needle removal. After insertion into muscle (the needle is inserted directed into the muscle, at a 90° angle), the syringe plunger is aspirated to ensure that no blood returns to prevent accidental injection into a blood vessel. The prescribed medication is injected slowly, then the needle is removed, and pressure is applied to the site with a dry sponge. A Z-track method helps to ensure that the medication remains in the muscle as desired and does not leak back into subcutaneous tissues. When administering an intravenous (IV) injection, the syringe is aspirated and blood obtained to be certain the needle is in the vein. When removing a needle after administering an IV injection directly into the vein, the caregiver lessens the chance of bleeding into soft tissue by applying firm pressure with a dry sponge while elevating the site above the heart for several minutes. However, the vast majority of intravenous injections are administered through an IV catheter or an IV fluid port with a needle or needleless device. Pressure is not applied when removing this device. The needle should not be recapped; both the needle and syringe should be disposed in a "sharps" container according to protocol. The injection time and site, any untoward responses to the injection, desired effects, and adverse reactions to the particular drug injected are recorded. **2.** A solution introduced in this manner. **3.** The state of being injected; congestion. SEE: *Standard Precautions Appendix*.

depot i. Parenteral administration of a long-acting medication or hormone.

epidural i. The injection of anesthetic solution or other medicines into the epidural space of the spinal cord.

fractional i. Injection of small amounts at a time until the total injection is complete.

hypodermic i. An obsolete term originally meaning the injection of a substance beneath the skin. It is preferable to specify the route of administration, e.g., intramuscular, subcutaneous, intracutaneous, or intravenous. SEE: *local anesthesia*.

intra-alveolar i. Introduction of anesthetic into the soft tissues adjacent to a tooth.

intracardial i. Injection into the heart.

intracytoplasmic sperm i. ABBR: ICSI. A commonly used assisted reproduction technique, in which spermatozoa, usually from a man with obstructive azoospermia or a low sperm count, are introduced directly into the ova of his partner. Some oocytes become fertilized and can then be transferred to the woman's uterus, where they mature.

intradermal i. Injection into the skin, used in giving serums and vaccines when a local reaction is desired.

intralingual i. The injection of medicines into the tongue, usually done as an emergency measure when a vein suitable for use is not available because of circulatory collapse.

intramuscular i. Injection into intramuscular tissue, usually the anterior thigh, deltoid, or buttocks. Intramuscular injections are used primarily in the administration of vaccines, immune globulins, long-acting corticosteroids, some antibiotics, some hormones, analgesics, and sedatives. In shock, medications given intramuscularly may not be rapidly absorbed. No more than 4 mL should be injected at one time into an adult with normal musculature; in children and adults with underdeveloped musculature, no more than 2 mL should be injected at one time. Patients should be advised that intramuscular injections, e.g., for vaccination, are painful.

⚠️ To avoid injury, newborn intramuscular injections should be administered in the middle third of the vastus lateralis muscle using a 5/8-in, 25-gauge needle.

intraosseous i. Intraosseous **infusion**.

intraperitoneal i. Injection into the peritoneal cavity.

intravenous i. The injection into a vein or, more commonly, into an intravenous catheter of drugs, electrolytes, or fluids. The insertion of a needle directly into a vein (rarely necessary) requires a degree of skill that is easily obtained if proper instruction is obtained. The vein may be distended by applying a tourniquet with sufficient pressure to stop venous return but not arterial flow. The tourniquet is applied several inches above the injection site. If the patient does not have vascular collapse, the arterial pulse can be palpated; if not, the tourniquet is too tight. Heat applied to the area for 15 min before starting the injection will also help distend the vessels. The use of a needle attached to a 5- or 10-mL syringe will greatly facilitate controlling the course of the needle. It is best to insert the needle into the vein with the bevel side facing out and then, after the needle is in the vein, to rotate it so that the bevel is face in. There should be resistance as the needle goes through one side of the vein wall. The vein should be entered with the needle making only a narrow angle with the long axis of the vein. This will help to prevent pushing the needle completely through the vein. SEE: *cutdown; intraosseous infusion; Standard Precautions Appendix*.

SOLUTIONS: Many liquid preparations are given by intravenous infusion. Those commonly used include isotonic saline, Ringer's lactate, dextrose 5% in sterile water, hyperalimentation fluids, lipids, vitamins, and numerous medications. The solution may be given continuously or by intermittent or bolus injection. The rate of infusion varies with the patient's needs.

SITE: Intravenous infusion usually is given through a vein in the hand or arm, but central veins or other peripheral veins may be used as indicated.

NOTE: In patients with collapsed veins, it may be possible to make the veins apparent by placing a tourniquet around the arm and leg and then inserting a 23- or 25-gauge catheter into a tiny superficial vein. Instillation of sterile intravenous fluid into the vein while the catheter is in place will distend the entire larger vein proximal to the small vein. A larger needle or catheter can then be inserted into the larger vein.

iodinated I 131 albumin i. A standardized preparation of albumin iodinated with the use of radioactive iodine, ^{131}I.

iodohippurate sodium I 131 i. A radioactive contrast medium used in testing renal function.

iron dextran i. A preparation of iron suitable for parenteral use.

⚠ Because of the risk of anaphylaxis, a test dose should be given before starting an infusion of iron.

jet i. The injection of medicines and vaccines through the skin or intramuscularly without a needle. A nozzle ejects a fine spray of liquid at such speed as to penetrate but not harm the skin. The procedure is harmless and is esp. useful in immunizing a great number of persons quickly and economically.

lethal injection A method of capital punishment by a combination of medications, typically, a sedative, a paralytic agent, an analgesic agent, and a fatal dose of potassium. Unlike other forms of execution (such as electrocution or the gas chamber), lethal injection is the only method that relies upon the direct participation of health care professionals. Some professional organizations (such as the American Medical Association) and several state boards with oversight over health care practic, have questioned whether the participation of health care professionals in lethal injection is appropriate, legal, or moral.

rectal i. An instillation (not an injection) into the rectum; an enema.

sclerosing i. The injection into a vessel or into a tissue of a substance that will bring about obliteration of the vessel or hardening of the tissues used, e.g., to manage esophageal varices or malignant pleural effusions.

spinal i. Introduction of fluids or medications into the spinal canal, i.e., the intrathecal space.

subcutaneous i. Injection beneath the skin. Typical sites include the abdomen, upper or outer arm, and the thigh. SEE: illus.

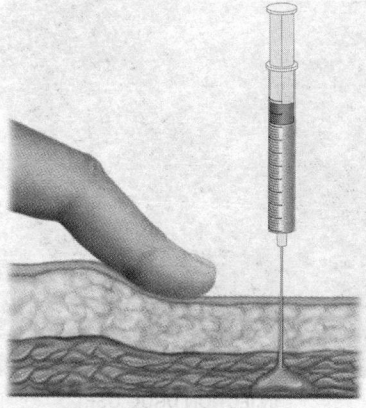

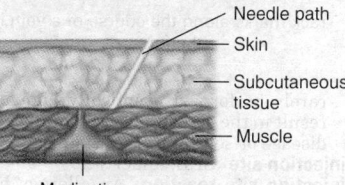

Needle path
Skin
Subcutaneous tissue
Muscle
Medication

Z-TRACK INJECTION

Z-track i. An injection technique in which the surface (skin and subcutaneous) tissues are pulled and held to one side before the needle is inserted deep into the muscle tissue in the identified site. The medication is injected slowly, followed by a 10-sec delay, at which time the needle is removed and the tissues are quickly permitted to resume their normal position. This provides a Z-shaped track, which makes it difficult for the injected drug to seep back into subcutaneous tissues. SEE: illus.

injection drug user A person who gives himself or herself drugs parenterally, usually to attain a euphoric or altered state of consciousness. The practice is

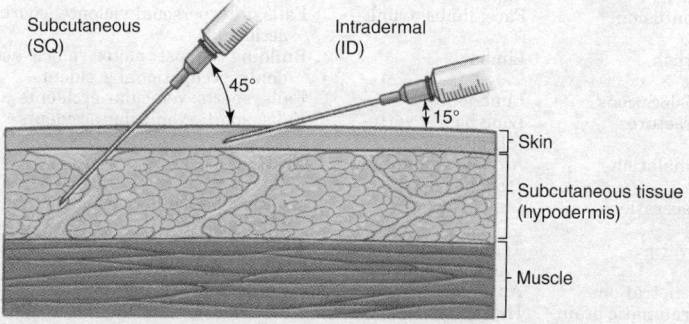

Subcutaneous (SQ)
Intradermal (ID)
45°
15°
Skin
Subcutaneous tissue (hypodermis)
Muscle

SUBCUTANEOUS INJECTION

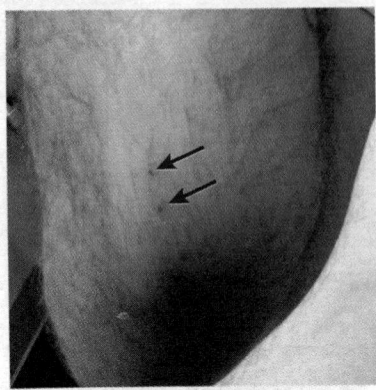

INJECTION DRUG USE

Track marks along the course of a vein in the forearm

rarely performed aseptically and may result in the spreading of communicable disease or self-injury. SEE: illus.

injection site   SEE: under *site*.

injection site reaction   An allergic, histaminic, or traumatic response of the skin and subcutaneous tissues to any substance introduced with a needle.

PATIENT CARE: The injection site should be carefully monitored for redness, swelling, necrosis, or purulence. The size of any injury should be measured and the patient's level of pain assessed. Management may depend on the nature of the introduced substance. In mild cases, topical application of a cold pack may alleviate symptoms. When a reaction occurs at the site of a vesicant injection (e.g., in patients receiving cancer chemotherapy), close monitoring by a physician or the injection of local antidotes may be required. Reactions that result in infection or necrosis may need to be treated with antibiotics or with surgical débridement.

injection site rotation   SEE: under *rotation*.

injector (ĭn-jĕk′tor)   A device for making injections.

   jet i.   SEE: *injection, jet.*

   pressure i.   A device that delivers a substance to be injected, often controlled by a timing mechanism, at a specified pressure.

injunction (ĭn-jŭnk′shŭn) [L. *injungere,* to fasten, join]   A court order prohibiting an individual from performing some act or demanding that a person begin to perform some act.

injury (ĭn′jŭ-rē) [L. *injuria,* injustice]   Blunt or penetrating trauma or damage to a part of the body. SEE: ***transportation*** *of the injured;* table.

SYMPTOMS: Various symptoms may occur, depending on the nature, extent, and severity of the damage. Mild injury produces pain, tissue swelling, redness, and temporary disruption of tissue function. Severe injury may result in irretrievable loss of the function of an organ, massive hemorrhage, or shock.

   acceleration i., impact-acceleration

Traumatic Injuries

Type of Injury	Parts of the Body Frequently Affected	Common Causes
Amputation	Limbs	Explosions; motor vehicle accidents; falls
Avulsion	Skin	Falls; scrapes
Bite	Hands; face	Pets (dogs and cats); humans (interpersonal violence)
Blast	Exposed body parts; hearing	Explosions
Burn	Limbs	Cooking; accidental fires
Contusion	Face; limbs; trunk	Falls; interpersonal violence; sports accidents
Crush	Limbs	Building collapse; motor vehicle accidents; occupational accidents
Dislocations	Limb joints	Falls; sports; vehicular accidents
Fractures	Long bones; vertebrae	Falls; sports; vehicular accidents
Inhalation	Airways; mouth, nasopharynx	Fires
Laceration	Limbs, face	Knives, glass, other sharp objects; falls; sports
Overuse	Tendons and muscles of the limbs	Repetitive use on the job or in sports
Penetration	Any	Gunshots; sharp objects
Traumatic brain injury	Head	Falls; sports; vehicular accidents

injury An injury that occurs when the head, cervical spine, or other body part is hit by a rapidly moving object.

acceleration-deceleration i. An injury caused when a rapidly moving body abruptly comes to a stop, causing internal injuries, e.g., whiplash, traumatic brain injury, or damage to the liver or spleen.

acquired brain i. Structural damage to the brain occurring after childbirth. It includes traumatic brain injury and insults to the brain resulting from strokes, tumors, or neurological diseases such as multiple sclerosis.

acute kidney i. ABBR: AKI. Acute renal failure.

acute lung i. ABBR: ALI. A clinically severe, sudden decline in lung function, marked by infiltrates in both lung fields and significantly diminished arterial oxygen saturation. There is no evidence that the condition is caused by left-sided heart failure. The disease is similar to adult respiratory distress syndrome (ARDS). Like ARDS, ALI may be life threatening. ALI is distinguished from ARDS by the severity of hypoxemia. ALI = PaO_2/FIO_2 ratio of < 300, ARDS = $PaO_2/FIO_2 < 200$.

acute spinal cord i. Acute traumatic injury of the spinal cord. Signs and symptoms depend upon the vertebral level injured and degree of injury. Damage may be due to the initial injury and to any inflammatory response or swelling that occurs in the next 48 to 72 hr. Therapy includes immobilization, high doses of corticosteroids, airway maintenance, cardiovascular resuscitation, and insertion of an indwelling catheter. The use of intravenous methylprednisolone given as a bolus dose of 30 mg/kg and then a maintenance dose of 5.4 mg/kg/hr for 24 to 48 hr during the acute phase improves neurological recovery and may reduce edema.

PATIENT CARE: Cooling the patient or the spinal cord has theoretical advantages, but clinical benefit has been difficult to document. Immediately after a spinal cord injury, the spine must be stabilized, adequate ventilation and circulation maintained, and problems with thermoregulation and urinary retention assessed and treated. After initial stabilization, all general patient care concerns apply. The patient is assessed for evidence of paralysis, loss of sensation or of reflexes, pneumonia, deep vein thrombosis, pulmonary embolism, decreased peristalsis, gastrointestinal bleeding, and problems associated with immobilization. Explanations of all procedures and support are provided to the patient and his or her supporters. Anxiolytics (if needed) should be administered as prescribed and their effects evaluated. The patient with serious trauma to the spinal cord may suddenly confront many challenges to body image and functional independence, including changes in mobility, urinary and fecal continence, erectile function, skin integrity, and mood. A sensitive and caring multidisciplinary approach to rehabilitation is needed to help the client.

birth i. Injury sustained by the neonate during birth.

blast i. An injury due to an explosion. The injury results from internal organ damage caused by a pressure wave in the atmosphere extending outward from the explosion. It can also produce secondary shrapnel injuries and burns.

blunt cardiac i. ABBR: BCI. Compression of the heart and/or great vessels, e.g., during motor vehicle crashes when the patient's thorax suddenly makes forceful contact with the steering wheel or instrument panel of a car or truck. BCI also encompasses myocardial contusion (bruising of the heart muscle), aortic dissection, and myocardial rupture. SYN: *blunt cardiac trauma*.

crush i. Trauma to body tissues resulting from an applied force that compresses or squeezes tissues, causing damage such as compartment syndrome, dislocation, fracture, laceration, or nerve damage. If there is no bleeding, cold should be applied; if the wound is bleeding, application of the dressing should be followed by cold packs until the patient can be given definitive surgical treatment. If the bone is fractured, a splint should be applied. SYN: *crushing wound*.

deceleration i. An injury in which a moving body hits a stationary object, as when a patient falls and hits the ground.

defensive i. An injury to the fingers, hands, wrists or extensor surfaces of the arms in an attempt to ward off an assault by another person. Such injuries include abrasions, bruises and other forms of blunt trauma, cuts, fractures, gun shot wounds, and lacerations.

drug-induced liver i. ABBR: DILI. Hepatic inflammation, hepatocellular necrosis, or jaundice due to exposure to a medication or toxin. The most common cause of DILI is an overdose of acetaminophen, but many other medications can damage liver cells and produce signs, symptoms, and laboratory findings suggestive of cholestasis or hepatitis.

glucopenic brain i. Neuroglycopenia.

immersion i. Drowning or near drowning.

inhalation i. Injury to the oropharynx, nasopharynx, trachea, bronchi, or lungs from exposure to smoke or heated gas. This injury is a potentially life-threatening complication of exposure to smoke and fire and is often present in those who have suffered facial burns; firefighters are esp. at risk. Early complications of inhalation injury include bronchospasm, airway edema, airway obstruction, and respiratory failure. Late complications include hospital-acquired pneumonias and other respiratory illnesses. Patients suspected of inhalation injury should be promptly and repeatedly assessed to make certain they have an open airway. Emergent tracheal intubation is used to prevent respiratory failure. SEE: *carbon monoxide*.

SYMPTOMS: Patients who have suffered smoke inhalation injury may complain of dyspnea, cough, and black sputum. Stridor may be present if the upper airway is narrowed as a result of inflammation. Confusion may occur if carbon monoxide poisoning is also present. SYN: *smoke inhalation i.*

internal i. Any injury to the organs occupying the thoracic, abdominal, or cranial cavities.

SYMPTOMS: Symptoms vary depending on the structures involved. Shock is often present, manifested by hypotension and tachycardia. The patient may be pale, cold, and perspiring freely and have an altered state of consciousness. In some internal injuries, pain may not be expressed.

PATIENT CARE: The patient's vital signs should be monitored carefully and frequently. Changes in level of consciousness should be noted. If the patient is in shock, the shoulders should be lowered and the lower extremities elevated. Intravenous infusions, oxygen, airway management, cardiac monitoring, control of hemorrhage, and bony stabilization are quickly begun pending definitive surgical management.

ionizing radiation i. Damage to cells and intracellular molecules by x-rays, gamma rays, radionuclides, or other sources of radioactive energy. In sufficient doses, radioactive energy can damage the cytoplasm and the genetic material of the cell, leading to organ dysfunction (esp. in rapidly dividing tissues such as the skin and the lining of the gastrointestinal tract), mutations, inhibition of cell division, cell death, or carcinogenesis. When the developing fetus is exposed to radiation in the womb, developmental malformations may result. SEE: *low-level **radiation**; radiation syndrome*.

local radiation i. Acute radiation exposure involving a limited part of the body, esp. the hands, after picking up an unshielded radioactive element. The exposure usually results in delayed skin damage and frequently in underlying tissue injury. It may require local wound care, débridement, or, in some instances, amputation.

needle-stick i. SEE: *sharps; needlestick*.

open head i. A head injury in which the integrity of the cranium is breached.

primary i. Cell death immediately associated with a traumatizing force and unrelated to subsequent hypoxic or enzymatic reactions.

primary brain i. Direct damage to the brain from blunt or penetrating force.

reperfusion i. Cellular damage that occurs after blood flow is restored to ischemic tissues.

repetitive motion i. Overuse syndrome.

repetitive strain i. Overuse syndrome.

risk for i. A state in which a person has the potential for being physically harmed due to environmental hazards and/or impairments in his adaptive and defensive resources. SEE: *Nursing Diagnoses Appendix*.

secondary brain i. Brain damage due to cellular disruption, electrolyte disarray, inflammation, insufficient oxygen, or vasospasm after head trauma.

secondary enzymatic i. Cell death resulting from an enzymatic reaction occurring after trauma that decreases cell membrane potential and produces hydropic swelling. Secondary enzymatic injury does not include cells damaged by the primary trauma.

secondary hypoxic i. Cell death caused by the lack of oxygen in tissues after trauma. It may sometimes be prevented by resting injured body parts and applying cold to them. SYN: *posttraumatic hypoxia*.

smoke inhalation i. Inhalation **i.**

spinal cord i. ABBR: SCI. Compression, contusion, or cutting of the spinal cord as a result of trauma. Depending on the type of lesion suffered, SCI may cause paralysis, loss of sensation, incontinence, or abnormal reflex activity.

steering wheel i. Blunt trauma to the chest sustained when an unrestrained driver hits the steering wheel or column. Typical injuries include rib fractures, inflamed cartilage, pneumothorax, hemothorax, or contusion of the heart. The trauma occasionally produces dissection of the thoracic aorta.

straddle i. Blunt trauma to the perineum, often with fractures of the pelvis and genital and internal injuries (e.g., to the vagina, penis, testes, bladder, or uterus).

transfusion-related acute lung i. ABBR: TRALI. A systemic immunological reaction to the transfusion of blood products marked by breathlessness, fever, hypotension, inadequate oxygenation, and noncardiogenic pulmonary edema. It is caused by antibodies in the donor's plasma reacting against the white blood cells of the transfusion recipient. Ventilatory support is commonly needed. The reaction is life-threatening in about 10% of patients.

traumatic brain i. ABBR: TBI. Any injury involving direct trauma to the head, accompanied by alterations in mental status or consciousness. TBI is one of the most common causes of neurological dysfunction in the U.S. Each year about 50,000 people die from brain trauma, and an additional 70,000 to 90,000 sustain persistent neurological impairment because of it. About 5.3 million Americans live with TBI disabilities. The most common causes of TBI are motor vehicle or bicycle collisions; falls; gunshot wounds; assaults and abuse; and sports-related injuries. Twice as many males as females suffer TBIs, with the incidence highest between ages 15 and 24. People over 75 are also frequently affected (because of falls).

PATIENT CARE: Many traumatic injuries to the head and brain are preventable if simple precautions are followed: motorists should never drive while intoxicated; cyclists and bicyclists should always wear helmets; frail, elderly people should wear supportive footwear and use sturdy devices to assist them while walking.

Symptoms of TBI may include problems with concentration, depressed mood, dizziness, headaches, impulsivity, irritability, post-traumatic stress, or, in severe injuries, focal motor, sensory or verbal deficits. Late effects of severe or repeated injuries can include dementia, Parkinsonism, or amyotrophic lateral sclerosis (Lou Gehrig's disease).

⚠ If an injury to the brain has occurred or is suspected, the victim should not be moved until spinal precautions are carefully implemented. Serial neurologic assessments are carried out to identify the severity of injury and any subsequent deterioration, using the Glasgow Coma Scale.

TBIs can produce intracranial hemorrhage (epidural hematoma [EDH]), subdural hematoma (SDH), intracerebral hemorrhage (ICH), and traumatic subarachnoid hemorrhage (SAH); cerebral contusions; concussion (with postconcussive syndrome); and diffuse axonal injury (DAI). Treatments vary depending upon the type of injury that occurred. SYN: *cerebral* **concussion**. SEE: table.

ventilator-induced lung i. ABBR: VILI. Injury to alveoli or alveolar capillaries caused by high airway pressures, excessive tidal volumes, or re-

Mechanisms of Brain Injury

Type of Injury	Examples
Penetrating injury	Gunshot wounds
Contact injury	Injuries during boxing or helmet-to-helmet collisions in football
Acceleration-deceleration injury	Automotive collisions
Rotational acceleration-deceleration injury	Falls from a height

peated expansion and collapse of the alveoli during mechanical ventilation. It can produce local inflammatory lung destruction and the release of inflammatory molecules throughout the systemic circulation.

whiplash i. An imprecise term for injury to the cervical vertebrae and adjacent soft tissues. It is produced by a sudden jerking or relative backward or forward acceleration of the head with respect to the vertebral column. This type of injury may occur in a vehicle that is suddenly and forcibly struck from the rear.

injury, risk for perioperative positioning At risk for inadvertent anatomical injury as a result of posture or equipment used during an invasive/surgical procedure, or during any procedure in which a patient is sedated or anesthetized. SEE: *Nursing Diagnoses Appendix.*

inlay (ĭn′lā) [L. *in*, in, + AS. *lecgan*, to lay] A solid filling made to the precise shape of a cavity of a tooth and cemented into it; usually the inlay is made of casting alloy, but it may be porcelain.

inlet A passage leading to a cavity.

in-line medication administration (ĭn′līn″) Administration of an inhaled medication into a ventilator circuit or any other positive airway pressure respiratory device (e.g., Bipap [bilevel positive airway pressure] or CPAP [continuous positive air pressure]).

inmate (ĭn′māt″) A person incarcerated in a detention center, jail, or prison. Such people have higher rates of certain illnesses, e.g., sexually transmitted diseases or chronic hepatitis, than the general population.

INN *International Nonproprietary Names,* a list of pharmaceuticals published periodically by the World Health Organization.

innate (ĭn-nāt′) [″ + *natus,* born]
1. Belonging to the essential nature of a living being. SYN: *inherent; intrinsic.*
2. Existing at birth.

innate immune system Innate **immunity**.

innervate (ĭn-nĕr′vāt, ĭn′ĕr-vāt) [″ + *nervus,* nerve] **1.** To send axons to synapse with another structure (as in, "a motor nerve innervates a muscle"). **2.** To send axons to receive signals from a structure (as in, "a sensory nerve innervates the skin").

innervation (ĭn″ĕr-vā′shŭn) **1.** The stimulation of a part through the action of nerves. **2.** The distribution and function of the nervous system. **3.** The nerve supply of a part.

    collateral i. Development of the nerve supply in a nerve tract adjacent to the original nerve supply that has been injured or destroyed.

    double i. Innervation of an organ with both sympathetic and parasympathetic fibers.

    reciprocal i. Innervation of muscles, as around a joint, in which contraction of one set of muscles leads to the relaxation of opposing muscles.

in network Contained within or supervised by a health maintenance organization or other managed care health provider. People insured by this kind of provider typically obtain better prices for services covered by their insurer than those insured by health care providers who have not agreed to the contractual obligations of the network.

innocent (ĭn′ō-sĕnt) [L. *innocens*] Harmless or benign; clinically unimportant; not pathological (as referring to a heart murmur). SYN: *innocuous.*

innocuous (ĭ-nŏk′ū-ŭs) [L. *innocuus*] Innocent.

innominate (ĭ-nŏm′ĭ-nĭt) [L. *innominatus,* unnamed] Nameless.

innovation in nursing education (ĭn″ō-vā′shŏn) [L. *innovatio,* renewal] Organized efforts to promote the education of new nursing students, including those that improve the recruiting of new students, improve the quality of nursing scholarship and didactics, and train nurse leaders for the future.

inoculable (ĭn-ŏk′ū-lă-bl) **1.** Transmissible by inoculation. **2.** Susceptible to a transmissible disease. **3.** Capable of being inoculated.

inoculate (ĭn-ŏk′ū-lāt″) To inject an antigen, antiserum, or antitoxin into an individual to produce immunity to a specific disease. SEE: *vaccine.*

inoculation (ĭn-ŏk″ū-lā′shŭn) **1.** The injection or introduction of an antigen or microbe into a person, animal, or organ or into a solution, growth medium, or other laboratory apparatus. **2.** Vaccination. This can be accomplished parenterally (through the skin), orally, or intranasally; by using an aerosol mist; or by scarification of the skin.

    animal i. The injection of serums, microorganisms, or viral organisms into laboratory animals for the purpose of immunizing them or of investigating the effects of the inoculated material on them.

inoculum (ĭn-ŏk′ū-lŭm) [L.] A substance introduced by inoculation.

inoculum effect In pharmacology, an increase in drug resistance that occurs with a larger burden of infecting organisms.

inoperable (ĭn-ŏp′ĕr-ă-bl) [L. *in-,* not, + *operari,* to work] Unsuitable for surgery. In the case of a tumor, the disease may have spread so extensively as to make surgery ineffective, or the patient's general condition may be so poor that surgery could result in the patient's death.

inorganic (ĭn″or-găn′ĭk) [L. *in-,* not, + Gr. *organon,* an organ] **1.** In chemistry, occurring in nature independently of living things; sometimes considered to indicate chemical compounds that do not contain carbon. **2.** Not pert. to living organisms.

inosculate (ĭn-ŏs′kū-lāt″) [L. *in,* in, + *osculum,* little mouth] Anastomose.

inosculation (ĭn-ŏs″kū-lā′shŭn) Anastomosis.

inose (ĭn′ōs) Inositol.

inosemia (ĭn-ō-sē′mē-ă) [Gr. *inos,* fiber, + *haima,* blood] **1.** An excessive amount of fibrin in the blood. **2.** The presence of inositol in the blood.

inosite (ĭn′ō-sīt) Inositol.

inositis (ĭn″ō-sī′tĭs) [″ + *itis,* inflammation] Inflammation of fibrous tissue.

inositol (ĭn-ŏs′ĭ-tŏl) Hexahydroxycyclohexane, $C_6H_6(OH)_6$; a sugar-like crystalline substance found in the liver, kidney, skeletal muscle, and heart muscle, as well as in the leaves and seeds of most plants. It is part of the vitamin B complex. Deficiency of inositol in experimental animals results in hair loss, eye defects, and growth retardation. Its significance in human nutrition has not been established. SYN: *inose; inosite.*

inositol-1,4,5-triphosphate (ĭn-ŏs′ĭ-tŏl) ABBR: IP3. An intracellular second messenger molecule that stimulates the endoplasmic reticulum of the cell to release calcium.

inosituria (ĭn″ō-sī-tū′rē-ă) [*inositol* + Gr. *ouron,* urine] Inosuria.

inosuria (ĭn-ō-sū′rē-ă) [*inositol* + Gr. *ouron,* urine] **1.** Inositol in the urine. SYN: *inosituria.* **2.** Fibrinous excess in urine.

inotropic (ē″nō″trō′pik, ī″nō-) [Gr. *inos,* fiber + *-tropic*] **1.** Influencing the force of muscular contractility. **2.** An agent that influences the force of muscular contraction. **inotrope** (ē′nō-trōp″, ī″nō), *n.* **inotropism** (ē″trō′pizm), *n.*

    negatively i. Pert. to an agent that weakens the force of muscular contraction.

    positively i. Pert. to an agent that

strengthens the force of muscular contraction.

inpatient (ĭn'pā"shĕnt) A patient who is hospitalized. SEE: *outpatient*.

inpatient rehabilitation facility ABBR: IRF. A hospital or institution devoted to the care of those who have suffered a stroke or other form of neurological trauma. It provides interdisciplinary care, including a minimum of three hours a day of occupational and physical therapy and close nursing and physician care at least five days a week.

in-person (ĭn'pĕr'sŏn) Pert. to direct contact between people rather than indirect contact by telephone, e-mail, text messaging, or voice messaging; person-to-person.

inquest (ĭn'kwĕst) [L. *in*, into, + *quaerere*, to seek] **1.** In legal medicine, an official examination and investigation into the cause, circumstance, and manner of sudden, unexpected, violent, or unexplained death. **2.** The act of inquiring.

INR *International normalized ratio.*

insalivation (ĭn-săl"ĭ-vā'shŭn) [" + *saliva*, spittle] The process of mixing saliva with food, as in chewing.

insane (ĭn-sān') [" + *sanus*, sound] Mentally deranged and, therefore, legally incompetent.

insanitary (ĭn-săn'ĭ-tăr-ē) Not conducive to health; unhealthful, unhygienic.

insanity (ĭn-săn'ĭt-ē) [L. *insanitas*, unhealthiness, disease] In legal medicine, the inability to manage one's own affairs or take responsibility for one's actions as a result of cognitive deficits, absence of self-control, or psychosis. The term is typically employed in courts of law or the popular press, but is not used in standard psychiatric or medical speech.

insanity defense In legal and forensic medicine, the premise that an insane person who commits a crime is not legally responsible for that act.

insatiable (ĭn-sā'shă-b'l) [L. *insatiabilis*] Incapable of being satisfied or appeased.

inscription (ĭn-skrĭp'shŭn) [L. *in*, upon, + *scribere*, to write] The body of a prescription, which gives the names of the drug(s) prescribed and the dosage.

insect [L. *insectum*] The common name for any of the class Insecta of the phylum Arthropoda. Insects of medical importance are flies, mosquitoes, lice, fleas, bees, hornets, and wasps. For more information, see entries for individual insects.

Insecta (ĭn-sĕk'tă) A class of the phylum Arthropoda characterized by three distinct body divisions (head, thorax, abdomen), three pairs of jointed legs, tracheae, and usually two pairs of wings. Insects are of medical significance in that some are parasitic, some are vectors of pathogenic organisms, and some

are annoying pests causing injury by their bites or stings. SYN: *Hexapoda*.

insecticide (ĭn-sĕk'tĭ-sīd) [L. *insectum*, insect, + *caedere*, to kill] **1.** An agent used to exterminate insects. **2.** Destructive to insects.

Insectivora (ĭn"sĕk-tĭv'ō-ră) [" + *vorare*, to devour] An order of small mammals, including moles and shrews.

insectivore (ĭn-sĕk'tĭ-vor) A member of the order Insectivora.

insecurity (ĭn"sĕ-kūr'ĭt-ē) **1.** Vulnerability (e.g., of a computer system to hackers). **2.** A subjective sense of vulnerability, esp. when confronted with particular challenges or social situations.

insemination (ĭn-sĕm"ĭ-nā'shŏn) [¹*in-* + *semination*] **1.** The discharge of semen from the penis into the vagina during coitus. **2.** The fertilization of an ovum.
    artificial i. ABBR: AI. Mechanical placement of semen containing viable spermatozoa into the female reproductive tract. SYN: *artificial **fecundation**; artificial **impregnation**; artificial **semination***.
    artificial i. by donor ABBR: AID. Donor artificial **i.**
    donor artificial i. ABBR: AID. Artificial insemination of a woman with sperm from an anonymous donor. The procedure is generally done in cases in which the husband is sterile. SYN: *therapeutic donor i.; artificial i. by donor*.
    heterologous artificial i. ABBR: AID. Artificial insemination in which the semen is obtained from a donor other than the husband or partner.
    homologous artificial i. ABBR: AIH. Husband artificial **i.**
    husband artificial i. ABBR: AIH. Use of a husband's sperm to artificially inseminate his wife. SYN: *Homologous artificial i.*
    therapeutic donor i. Donor artificial **i.** SEE: *Standard Precautions Appendix*.

insenescence (ĭn"sĕ-nĕs'ĕns) [" + *senescens*, growing old] The process of growing old or the approaching of old age.

insensible (ĭn-sĕn'sĭ-bl) [L. *in-*, not, + *sensibilis*, appreciable] **1.** Unconscious; without feeling or consciousness. **2.** Not perceptible. **3.** Not measurable.

insensible protein losses The loss of nitrogen-containing compounds in sweat and other body fluids exuded from the body through hair and skin.

insert (in-sĕrt', sense 1, in'sĕrt", sense 2) [L. *inserere*, to sow, plant in, implant] **1.** To place or put within. **2.** An object that is placed or put inside another.

insertion (in-sĕr'shŏn) [L. *insertio*, a putting in] **1.** The movable attachment of the distal end of a muscle, which produces shape changes or skeletal movement when the muscle contracts. **2.** The placement or implanting of something into something else (e.g., in dentistry, the process of placing a filling or inlay in a cavity preparation or placing dentures or other prostheses in the mouth).

blind i. The placement of a device into a body part or cavity without directly visualizing the organ in which the device will come to rest. Although the body part or cavity is not being directly visualized, anatomical landmarks may be used to help in obtaining proper placement.

chest tube i. Thoracostomy.

velamentous i. The attachment of the umbilical cord to the edge of the placenta.

insidious (ĭn-sĭd′ē-ŭs) [L. *insidiosus*, cunning] Of gradual, subtle, or indistinct onset; said of some slowly developing diseases.

insight **1.** Self-understanding; comprehension of one's circumstances; the opposite of denial. **2.** In psychiatry, the patient's comprehension that he is mentally ill and awareness of the character of the illness or of the unconscious factors responsible.

in silico (sĭ′lĭ-kō) [NL fm. L. *silex*, flint] The mimicking or modeling of biological processes within computer hardware and software.

in situ (ĭn sī′tū, sĭt′ū) [L.] **1.** In position, localized. **2.** In the normal place without disturbing or invading the surrounding tissue.

insolation (ĭn″sō′lā′shŏn) [L. *insolare*, to expose to the sun] **1.** Any exposure to the rays of the sun. **2.** Heatstroke or sunstroke. SEE: *heat; heat exhaustion; hyperthermia.*

In the past it was felt that exposure to the sunlight was therapeutic. It is now known that exposure to excess sunlight on either an acute or a chronic basis may be unwise. Acute overexposure leads to sunburn. Chronic exposure to the sun increases the likelihood of skin cancers.

insoluble (ĭn-sŏl′ū-b'l) [L. *insolubilis*] Incapable of solution or of being dissolved.

insomnia (in-som′nē-ă) [L. *insomnia*, sleeplessness] A disruption in the amount and quality of sleep that impairs functioning. **2.** The subjective experience of insufficient sleep or of sleep that is not refreshing. SEE: *sleep disorder;* table.

ETIOLOGY: Insomnia is called primary when it occurs in the absence of underlying diseases or conditions. It more often occurs as a secondary problem (e.g., from alcohol or drug dependence, mood disorders, restless leg syndrome, sleep apnea, or travel across time zones).

SYMPTOMS: People troubled by insomnia often report difficulty falling asleep, frequent nighttime awakenings,

Natural and Artificial Stimulants That May Contribute to Insomnia

Alcohol

Bright light; sunlight

Coffee, tea, and other caffeinated drinks (like carbonated cola beverages, guarana, and yerba maté, below)

Corticosteroids, such as prednisone

Ephedra sinica—an herbal stimulant

Ephedrine; pseudoephedrine

Guarana

Ma huang—Chinese name for ephedra

Methamphetamines, including methylphenidate

Modafinil—a drug used to treat narcolepsy

Nicotine, a psychoactive chemical found in tobacco smoke

Selective serotonin reuptake inhibitors (SSRIs), including fluoxetine, paroxetine, sertraline

Theophylline, a medication used to treat asthma

Venlafaxine, an antidepressant

Yerba maté

Yohimbine, an aphrodisiac and bodybuilding drug

or excessively early arousal in the morning. They also typically experience fatigue during the daytime, often with an inability to concentrate, to feel energetic, or to be productive.

PATIENT CARE: When poor-quality sleep affects daytime functioning, increasing exercise during the day and following sleep hygiene recommendations often improve sleep quality and duration. Cognitive behavioral therapies and relaxation techniques (e.g., listening to soothing music or closing the eyes and breathing deeply and quietly) also significantly improve sleep. Medications for sleep (e.g., the benzodiazepines [e.g., temazepam] or the nonbenzodiazepine sleep aids [e.g., zolpidem]) are generally thought to be safe and effective for acute insomnia. Melatonin may help some people improve sleep with jet lag or shift work. Patients with chronic insomnia may benefit from a variety of interventions. Few sleep medications are currently approved for long-term use by the Food and Drug Administration.

altitude i. A form of altitude sickness in which insomnia results from inadequate environmental oxygen. It occurs commonly in mountaineers and to a lesser extent in aviators. It is often accompanied by appetite disturbances, fatigue, headaches, and shortness of breath.

fatal familial i. ABBR: FFI. An inherited, rapidly progressive prion disease of middle or later life. Signs and symptoms include intractable insomnia, autonomic dysfunction, endocrine disturbances, dysarthria, myoclonus, coma, and death. There is no specific therapy. SEE: *prion disease*.

psychophysiological i. A sleep disturbance that occurs when a person worries excessively about not being able to fall asleep and stay asleep.

insomniac (ĭn-sŏm′nē-ăk) One who has insomnia.

insorption (ĭn-sorp′shŭn) [L. *in*, into, + *sorbere*, to suck in] The passage of material into the blood, as when substances move from the gastrointestinal tract into the bloodstream.

inspect [L. *inspectare*, to examine] To examine visually.

inspection Visual examination of the external surface of the body as well as of its movements and posture. SEE: *abdomen; chest; circulatory system*.

inspiration (ĭn″spĭr-ā′shŭn) [L. *in*, in, + *spirare*, to breathe] Inhalation; drawing air into the lungs; the opposite of expiration. The average rate is 12 to 18 respirations per minute in a normal adult at rest. SEE: *diaphragm* for illus.; *respiration*.

Inspiration may be costal or abdominal, the latter being deeper. The muscles involved in forceful inspiration are the external intercostals, diaphragm, levatores costarum, pectoralis minor, scaleni, serratus posterior, superior sternocleidomastoid, and sometimes the platysma.

crowing i. The peculiar noise heard in stridor or croup. SEE: *croup, spasmodic*.

forcible i. Inspiration in which the muscles of inspiration are assisted by accessory muscles of respiration, such as the sternocleidomastoids, intercostals, and serratus posterior. Forced inspiration is normal during vigorous exercise, but indicative of hypoxia, hypercarbia, or acidosis when it occurs at rest.

full i. Inspiration in which the lungs are filled as completely as possible (voluntarily, as in determining the vital capacity, or involuntarily, as in cardiac dyspnea).

sustained maximal i. A deep-breathing maneuver that mimics the normal physiological sigh mechanism. The patient inspires from a resting expiratory level up to maximum inspiratory capacity, with a pause at end inspiration.

inspiratory (ĭn-spīr′ă-tor″e) Pert. to inspiration.

inspiratory capacity The maximum amount of air a person can breathe in after a resting expiration.

inspiratory hold A ventilating maneuver in which the delivered volume of gas is held in the lung for a while before expiration.

inspiratory impedance threshold valve ABBR: ITV. A valve placed between a patient's airway and his or her source of respiratory gas, e.g., ambient air or, in the case of critically ill patients, a ventilator or bag-valve mask. It lowers tracheal and intrathoracic pressure and as a result increases blood pressure and blood flow to the brain and coronary arteries. It is used in cardiopulmonary resuscitation and advanced cardiac life support to support the circulation in the absence of volume resuscitation. It can also be used to prevent hypotension and syncope in patients with hypovolemia or reduced stroke volumes. The device works by allowing air to escape during chest compressions but not to re-enter the lungs until pressure is > -10 cm H_2O. This negative intrathoracic pressure increases venous return. SYN: *inspiratory impedance threshold **device***.

inspissate (ĭn-spĭs′āt) [L. *inspissatus*, thickened] To thicken by evaporation or absorption of fluid.

inspissated (ĭn-spĭs′ā-tĕd) Thickened by absorption, evaporation, or dehydration.

inspissation (ĭn-spĭ-sā′shŭn) 1. Thickening by evaporation or absorption of fluid. 2. Diminished fluidity or increased thickness.

instability (ĭn″stă-bil′ĭt-ē) The lack of ability to maintain alignment of bony segments, usually due to torn or lax ligaments and weak muscles.

detrusor i. A physiological mechanism in which contractions of the muscles of the urinary bladder during the filling phase of a urodynamic study or during coughing, sneezing, or other activities result in an increase of intra-abdominal pressures. Such a pressure increase may lead to urinary urges or to urinary incontinence, esp. in women. Some experts believe that detrusor instability is the most common cause of urinary incontinence in older adults. Underlying causes include urethral obstruction, cystitis, bladder carcinoma, stroke, Parkinson's disease, and multiple sclerosis. SYN: *detrusor hyperactivity with impaired contractility; detrusor overactivity*.

multidirectional i. Malfunction of the shoulder joint in more than one direction, resulting in a limited mobility or shoulder pain. Although the instability may be present from birth, it is often a result of injuries that occur in sports in which the arm is used overhead, as in gymnastics, swimming, or volleyball.

patellofemoral i. Laxity and/or tightness of the patellar restraints that results in abnormal tracking of the patella within the femoral trochlea. Patellofemoral instability causes pain during activity and may predispose the patient to recurring patellar subluxation or dislocation and to subsequently present with the clinical signs and symptoms of chondromalacia.

TREATMENT: Nonoperative treatment consists of strengthening weak muscles and/or stretching the tight soft tissue that leads to abnormal patellar tracking. Surgical intervention may be required to release overly taut tissue and shave the articular cartilage associated with chondromalacia.

 postural i. A tendency to fall or the inability to keep oneself from falling; imbalance.

instar (ĭn'stăr) Any one of the various stages of insect development during successive molts.

instep (ĭn'stĕp) The arched medial portion of the foot.

instillate (ĭn'stĭ-lāt″) [L. *instillare*, to drip into] A fluid infused into, dripped on, or injected into a body part.

instillation (ĭn″stĭl-ā'shŭn) [L. *in*, into, + *stillare*, to drop] Slowly pouring or dropping a liquid into a cavity or onto a surface. **instill**, *v.*

instillator (ĭn'stĭ-lāt″ŏr) [L. *instillare*, to drip into] An apparatus for introducing liquids into a cavity a drop at a time.

instinct (ĭn'stĭngkt) [L. *instinctus*, instigation] An inherited tendency to react to an environmental stimulus in a predictable but limited fashion.

 death i. In psychoanalytic theory, the unconscious will to destroy oneself.

 herd i. The desire to be associated with a group.

Institute of Electrical and Electronic Engineers ABBR: IEEE. An organization partially responsible for standards regulating electrical devices and equipment.

Institute for Safe Medication Practices ABBR: ISMP. A nonprofit organization devoted to the prevention of errors in medication and to the use of safe medications. It disseminates information about adverse drug events to health care professionals, institutions, and the public. It also operates the Medication Errors Reporting System. Website: www.ihi.org

Institute of Medicine ABBR: IOM. The branch of the National Academy of Sciences that seeks to provide "unbiased and authoritative advice" to Americans on matters relating to health and health care. Website: www.iom.edu

institutional ethics committee Patient care advisory committee.

institutionalization (ĭn″stĭ-too″shŭn-ăl-ĭ-zā'shŭn) **1.** Residence in or confinement to a nursing home or other long-term care setting for an extended period. **2.** Arranging for a person to be placed in a health care facility. **3.** The process in which people who live to-

gether gradually develop certain common patterns of behavior and thought (e.g., assumption of illness and depression apathy, behaviors frequently associated with nursing home residency). The current movement in medicine and nursing is away from institutionalism to a more homelike environment.

institutional review board SEE: under *board*.

instruction (in-strŭk'shŏn) [L. *instruere*, to draw up, train] **1.** A direction or command. **2.** The act of teaching or furnishing information. **instructional** (in-strŭk'shŏn-ăl), *adj.*

 computer-assisted i. ABBR: CAI. Computer-based instructional programs for individual learners. The term most often refers to drill and practice, tutorial, or simulation exercises used as stand-alone instruction or as supplementary materials. A more recent term is e-learning.

 dental hygiene i. A program in which patients are taught the methods of oral hygiene and the importance of plaque control through proper toothbrushing, flossing, and appropriate nutrition.

instructional cue SEE: *cue.*

instructional directive A form of advanced directive that specifies particular health care interventions that a patient anticipates he or she would accept or reject during treatment for a critical or life-threatening illness. A living will is an example of such a directive.

instrument (in'strŭ-mĕnt) [L. *instrumentum*, tool] **1.** A mechanical device. **2.** A special tool for accomplishing a specific task. Thus a reflex hammer, microscope, stethoscope, cystoscope, and surgeon's scalpel are all examples of instruments.

 counterpressure i. An instrument that provides counterretraction to offset that exerted by the exit of a needle.

 dental i. Any instrument used in the practice of dentistry including a variety of hand or machine-driven cutting instruments for soft and calcified tissues, forceps, elevators, clamps, reamers, wire pliers, pluggers, carvers, explorers, and other instruments unique to the dental specialties (oral surgery, endodontics, orthodontics, periodontics, prosthodontics, and restorative dentistry).

instrumental 1. Pert. to instruments. **2.** Important in achieving a result or goal.

instrumentarium (ĭn″stroo-mĕn-tā'rē-ŭm) Instruments required for a surgical or other procedure.

instrumentation (ĭn″strŭ-mĕn-tā'shŏn) **1.** The use of instruments and their care. **2.** The accomplishment of a task by use of instruments, e.g., removal of a foreign body from the bronchus with a bronchoscope.

biomedical i. The use of mechanical and electronic devices in medical diagnosis, therapy, or measurement.

Dwyer i. SEE: *Dwyer instrumentation.*

spinal i. 1. An imprecise term for any hardware used to stabilize or align the vertebrae, including hooks, rods, or screws. **2.** Any spinal surgery in which such hardware is inserted into the body.

insufficiency (in″sŭ-fish′ĕn-sē) [L. *insufficientia,* insufficiency] Inadequacy for a specific purpose.

active i. Loss of the ability to generate muscle tension because of muscle shortening.

acute adrenocortical i. Sudden deficiency of adrenocortical hormone brought on by sepsis, surgery, or Waterhouse-Friderichsen syndrome. A frequent cause is sudden withdrawal of adrenal corticosteroids from patients with adrenal atrophy secondary to chronic steroid administration. SYN: *addisonian* **crisis***; adrenal* **crisis***.*

adrenal i. Abnormally low production of cortisol. Primary adrenal insufficiency results from inadequate cortisol production by the adrenal glands, as in Addison disease. Secondary adrenal insufficiency results from a decrease in the production of adrenocorticotropic hormone (ACTH) or its release from the pituitary gland.

aortic i. ABBR: AI. An imperfect closure of the aortic semilunar valve at the junction of the left ventricle and the aorta, due to distortion of the valve leaflets or dilation of the aortic annulus. This causes blood that has been ejected into the aorta to fall back into the left ventricle. It may produce volume overload of the ventricle, leading to left ventricular dilation and hypertrophy, and congestive heart failure. Stroke volume and ejection fraction (EF) fall. SYN: *aortic* **incompetence***; aortic* **regurgitation***; aortic valve* **i***.*

Chronic aortic insufficiency produces a gradual volume overload of the heart and eventual congestive heart failure. It may occur in patients with poorly controlled hypertension, tertiary syphilis, Marfan's disease, or other disorders that affect aortic valve competence. Management often includes antihypertensive vasodilators such as nifedipine. If congestive heart failure becomes severe enough, valve replacement may be recommended for patients who are good operative candidates. Surgery usually is recommended to be done before EF falls below 55%.

SYMPTOMS: Chronic AI may be asymptomatic until heart failure (HF) occurs. With HF, patients often report difficulty breathing, e.g., during exercise or sleep, and lower extremity swelling. Patients may occasionally report palpitations or a subjective awareness of their heart beating.

PHYSICAL FINDINGS: The murmur of AI occurs in diastole, is high-pitched (best heard using the diaphragm of the stethoscope), and is usually described as "blowing" and "decrescendo." It is best heard at the left second to fourth intercostal spaces, radiating to the apex and sometimes the right sternal border, after the patient exhales and sits leaning forward, holding his or her breath. Patients with AI often have a widened pulse pressure with a waterhammer pulse and may have head bobbing, bobbing of the uvula, or visible movement of blood under the nails when the tips of the nails are gently compressed (Quincke pulse). The patient may experience dyspnea, orthopnea, paroxysmal nocturnal dyspnea, and fatigue.

PATIENT CARE: A history of related cardiac illnesses and symptoms is obtained. Fever and other signs of infection are noted. Vital signs, weight, and fluid intake and output are monitored for indications of fluid overload. Activity tolerance and degree of fatigue are assessed regularly, and the patient is taught to intersperse periods of activity with rest.

Desired outcomes include adequate cardiopulmonary tissue perfusion and cardiac output, reduced fatigue with exertion, and ability to manage the treatment regimen.

aortic valve i. Aortic **i.**

cardiac i. Heart **failure**.

coronary i. Obstruction to the flow of blood through the coronary arteries, resulting in an inadequate supply of blood relative to the metabolic demands of the heart muscle. SEE: *angina* pectoris; *coronary* artery disease.

gastric i. Inability of the stomach to empty itself.

hepatic i. Inability of the liver to produce albumin, bile, or proteins, or to detoxify xenobiotics that are taken up by the gastrointestinal tract.

ileocecal i. Ileocecal **incompetence**.

mitral i. Mitral **regurgitation**.

muscular i. A condition in which a muscle is unable to exert its normal force and bring about normal movement of the part to which it is attached.

i. of ocular muscles Absence of dynamic equilibrium of ocular muscles.

myocardial i. Inability of the heart to perform its usual function, eventually resulting in cardiac failure.

passive i. A restriction in the range of motion of multijoint muscles such as the extrinsic finger flexors and extensors, the hamstrings, and the quadriceps caused by inadequate extensibility of antagonist muscles, muscle groups or fascia. This limitation is a normal property of multijoint muscles and helps optimize the relation between muscle length and tension.

primary adrenal i. Addison disease.

pulmonary valvular i. Imperfect closure of the pulmonary semilunar valve at the junction of the right ventricle and the pulmonary artery. The clinical consequences may include right ventricular failure.

renal i. A less-preferred term for *chronic kidney disease.* SEE: *chronic kidney disease.*

respiratory i. Inadequate oxygen intake or carbon dioxide removal associated with abnormal breathing and signs and symptoms of distress.

secondary adrenal i. Insufficient stimulation of the adrenal glands caused by failure of the pituitary gland to secrete adrenocorticotropic hormone. In this disorder, cortisol levels are reduced, but aldosterone secretion, which is governed by the renin-angiotensin-aldosterone system, is preserved. This differs from primary adrenal insufficiency or Addison disease in which the adrenal glands secrete neither cortisol nor aldosterone.

tertiary adrenal i. Inadequate stimulation of the adrenal glands that results from a failure of the hypothalamus to secrete corticotropic-releasing hormone.

thyroid i. Hypothyroidism.

uteroplacental i. Inadequate blood flow through the placental intervillous spaces to enable sufficient transmission of nutrients, oxygen, and fetal wastes. It may be caused by diminished maternal cardiac output due to anemia, heart disease, regional anesthesia, or supine hypotension; vasoconstriction due to chronic or pregnancy-related hypertension or uterine overstimulation; vasospasm due to pregnancy-induced hypertension; vascular sclerosis due to maternal diabetes or collagen disease; or intrauterine infection. It increases the risk for intrauterine growth retardation.

valvular i. Valvular **incompetence**.

velopharyngeal i. Failure of the palatal sphincter to close, with inadequate separation of the nasopharynx from the oropharynx. This may result in snoring, nasal speech, or inhalation of food into the nasal passages SYN: *velopharygeal* **incompetence**. SEE: *cleft* **palate**.

venous i. A failure of the valves of the veins to function, which interferes with venous return to the heart, and may produce edema.

insufflate (ĭn-sŭf′-lāt) [L. *insufflare,* to blow into] **1.** To introduce a gas or air into the lungs. **2.** To blow a medicated powder or medicinal vapor into a cavity.

insufflation (in″sŭ-flā′shŏn) [*insufflate*] Blowing a gas, powder, or vapor into a cavity or an organ (such as the colon or the lungs).

CO_2 i. The introduction of carbon dioxide gas into a body cavity such as the peritoneum during laparoscopic surgery.

tracheal gas i. A ventilatory technique to reduce accumulated carbon dioxide in the central airways and improve alveolar ventilation while decreasing ventilatory pressures and tidal volumes. Gas may be injected either continuously or through a catheter into the airways during a specific phase of the respiratory cycle.

transtracheal i. The introduction of oxygen into the trachea during mechanical ventilation in order to decrease dead space. This technique can use a continuous flow or flow solely during the expiratory phase. Caution should be used when a continuous flow is chosen because delivered tidal volumes can rise to dangerous levels. Adequate humidification must be maintained because high flows can dry out the respiratory mucosa.

transtracheal jet i. The life-saving technique of ventilating a patient with a complete airway obstruction. A small catheter is placed via a cricothyroid puncture and attached to a pressure-controlled oxygen outlet via a one-way valve.

tubal i. Test for patency of the fallopian tubes. SEE: *Rubin test.*

insufflator (ĭn′sŭ-flā″tor) A device for blowing powders or a gas into a cavity.

insula (ĭn′sū-lă) [L.] **1.** A large oval or triangular region of cerebral cortex on the floor of the Sylvian fissure; the insula is hidden by the overlapping edges (the opercula) of the frontal, parietal, and temporal lobes. The insular cortex plays a role in the evaluation of and the attachment of emotional responses to pain, temperature, and other sensory perceptions within the body. SYN: *island of Reil.* **2.** Any structure resembling an island.

insular (ĭn′sū-lăr) [L. *insula,* island] Relating to any insula, e.g., the insular cortex of the brain.

insulation [L. *insulare,* to make into an island] **1.** The protection of a body or substance with a nonconducting medium to prevent the transfer of electricity, heat, or sound. **2.** The material or substance that insulates.

insulator That which insulates.

insulin (ĭn′sŭ-lĭn) [L. *insula,* island + *-in*] A hormone secreted by the beta cells of the pancreas. As a drug, insulin is used principally to control diabetes mellitus. Insulin therapy is required in the management of type 1 diabetes mellitus because patients with this illness do not make enough insulin on their own to survive. The drug also is used in the care of patients with gestational diabetes to prevent fetal complications caused by maternal hyperglycemia (insulin itself does not cross the placenta or enter breast milk). In type 2 diabetes mellitus, its use typically is reserved for those patients who have failed to control their blood sugars with diet, exercise, and oral drugs. SEE: illus.; *diabetes mellitus.*

Insulin preparations differ with respect to the speed with which they act and their duration and potency following subcutaneous injection. SEE: table.

In the past, insulin for injection was obtained from beef or swine pancreas. These peptides differed from human insulin by a few amino acids, causing some immune reactions and drug resistance. Most insulin now in use is made by recombinant DNA technology and from an immunological perspective is equivalent to human insulin.

PHYSIOLOGY: In health, the pancreas secretes insulin in response to elevations of blood glucose, such as occur after meals. It stimulates cells, esp. in muscular tissue, to take up sugar from the bloodstream. It also facilitates the storage of excess glucose as glycogen in the liver and prevents the breakdown of stored fats. In type 1 diabetes mellitus, failure of the beta cells to produce insulin results in hyperglycemia and ketoacidosis.

DOSAGE: The insulin dosage should always be expressed in units. There is no average dose of insulin for diabetics;

each patient must be assessed and treated individually Doses are titrated gradually to achieve near normal glucose levels, about 90 to 125 mg/dL.

STORAGE: The FDA requires that all preparations of insulin contain instructions *to keep in a cold place and to avoid freezing.*

⚠️ Those who use insulin should wear an easily seen bracelet or necklace stating that they have diabetes and use the drug. This helps to ensure that patients with hypoglycemic reactions will be diagnosed and treated promptly.

insulin a. SEE: under *analog.*

i. aspart A rapidly acting insulin administered subcutaneously, with action similar to that of insulin lispro. Aspartic acid replaces proline at a crucial position in the insulin molecule.

biphasic i. An insulin preparation that includes two components, typically a rapidly acting insulin, e.g., regular insulin, and an insulin that has a longer duration of action, e.g., NPH insulin.

i. glargine A form of insulin that provides basal insulin coverage throughout the day, with little variation in drug levels. It is typically administered as a single injection (often at bedtime) and is usually part of a regimen that includes multiple injections of short-acting insulins or multiple doses of metformin at meal time. It is made by changing the

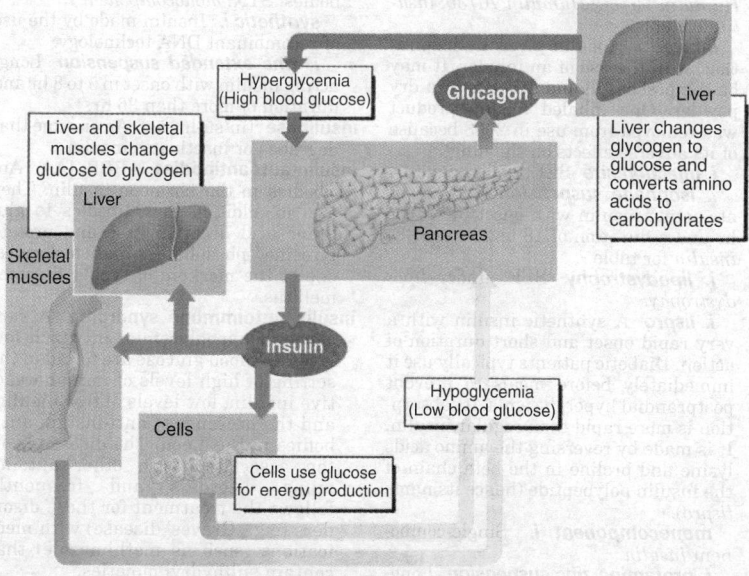

INSULIN AND GLUCAGON FUNCTIONS

Duration of Effect of Various Insulins When Given by Subcutaneous Injection*

Type of Insulin	Generic (Trade Names)	Onset (hr)	Maximum (hr)	Duration (hr)
Very rapid	Aspart (NovoLog)	0.2–0.5	1–3	3–5
Very rapid	Lispro (Humalog)	0.2–0.5	0.5–2.5	3–5
Very rapid	Glulisine (Apidra)	0.2–0.5	1.6–2.8	3–4
Rapid	Regular	0.5–1.0	2.5–5	4–6
Intermediate-acting	NPH (Humulin N, Novolin N)	2–4	4–12	10–18
Fixed-dose combination insulins **	70/30, 50/50, etc.	Variable, depending on mixture used		
Very long-acting	Glargine (Lantus)	2–4	none	11–32
Very long-acting	Detemir (Levemir)	3–4	3–9	6–23 Dose dependent
U 500 regular very concentrated (5 X U100)		0.5–1.0	2.5–5	up to 24 hr

* These times are estimates and may vary in individual patients.
** Contain NPH plus a rapid-acting insulin (Aspart, Lispro, or Regular); Novolog 70/30 contains 70% NPH, 30% Novolog

glycine and arginine content of the insulin polypeptide.

human i. Insulin prepared by recombinant DNA technology utilizing strains of *Escherichia coli.* In its effect it is similar to insulins secreted by the human pancreas. Trade names are Humulin and Novolin. SYN: *Novolin 70/30.* SEE: *Humulin 50/50; Humulin 70/30; insulin* for table.

inhaled i. Insulin given by inspiration, with the use of an inhaler. It may be composed of liquid droplets or a dry powder. One inhaled insulin product was removed from use in 2008 because of its adverse effects on the lungs.

i. injection site SEE: under *site.*

i. isophane suspension Intermediate-acting insulin with onset in ½ to 1 hr and a duration of 18 to 28 hr. SEE: *insulin* for table.

i. lipodystrophy SEE: under *lipodystrophy.*

i. lispro A synthetic insulin with a very rapid onset and short duration of action. Diabetic patients typically use it immediately before meals to prevent postprandial hyperglycemia. Its absorption is more rapid than regular insulin. It is made by reversing the amino acids lysine and proline in the beta chain of the insulin polypeptide (hence its name *lispro*).

monocomponent i. Single-component *insulin.*

i. protamine zinc suspension Long-acting insulin with onset in 6 to 8 hr and

a duration of 30 to 36 hr. SEE: *insulin* for table.

i. pump SEE: under *pump.*

i. shock Hypoglycemic **shock.**

single-component i. Highly purified insulin that contains less than 10 parts per million of proinsulin, capable of inducing formation of anti-insulin antibodies. SYN: *monocomponent i.*

synthetic i. Insulin made by the use of recombinant DNA technology.

i. zinc extended suspension Long-acting insulin with onset in 5 to 8 hr and duration of more than 36 hr.

insulinase (ĭn'sū-lĭn-ās) An enzyme that degrades or inactivates insulin.

insulin autoantibodies ABBR: IAA. Antibodies to the hormone insulin. They are, in addition to antibodies to glutamic acid decarboxylase and protein tyrosine phosphatase-like molecules, one of the markers of type 1 diabetes mellitus.

insulin autoimmune syndrome A rare cause of hypoglycemia, in which low levels of blood glucose are found in the setting of high levels of immunoreactive insulin, low levels of free insulin, and the presence of anti-insulin antibodies in the blood. The disease is often associated with other autoimmune disorders and frequently follows the treatment for those disorders (e.g., Graves' disease) with medications (such as methimazole) that contain sulfhydryl moieties.

insulinemia (ĭn-sū-lĭn-ē'mē-ă) [L. *in-*

sula, island, + Gr. *haima,* blood] Hyperinsulinemia.

insulin-like growth factor SEE: under *factor.*

insulinogenic (ĭn″sū-lĭn″ō-jĕn′ĭk) [″ + Gr. *gennan,* to produce] **1.** Caused by insulin whether administered therapeutically or produced naturally by the pancreas. **2.** Pert. to the production of insulin.

insulinoma (ĭn″sū-lĭn-ō′mă) [″ + Gr. *oma,* tumor] A tumor of the islets of Langerhans of the pancreas. These rare tumors secrete insulin and cause hypoglycemia. SEE: *hypoglycemia; neuroglycopenia.*

insulin pen An injector filled with insulin, used to administer specific doses of insulin subcutaneously.

insulin sensitivity factor SEE: under *factor.*

insulin sensitizer Any drug, such as pioglitazone or metformin, that improves the sensitivity of cells to the metabolic effects of insulin.

insulin-to-carbohydrate ratio ABBR: I:C ratio. The number of units of insulin that must be administered to a patient to prevent the carbohydrates consumed during a meal from elevating blood glucose levels. Typical I:C ratios for adults are 1:12. Children, who are usually more active than adults, may need only 1 unit of insulin for every 25 g of carbohydrates they eat.

insulin tolerance test ABBR: ITT. A test to determine a patient's hormonal responses to induced hypoglycemia. After 0.1 IU of insulin/kg is given intravenously, blood is drawn at regular intervals to measure serum cortisol in those patients with suspected adrenal insufficiency or growth hormone in suspected growth hormone deficiency. The goal of the test is to stress the body with low blood glucose levels (>40 mg/dL).

⚠ The test should be administered only by experienced professionals in order to reduce the risk of severe hypoglycemic reactions.

insulitis (ĭn″sū-lī′tĭs) [″ + Gr. *itis,* inflammation] Inflammation of the islets of Langerhans of the pancreas.

insult (ĭn′sŭlt) In medicine, an injury or trauma.

insure (in-shoor′) [ME. insuren, ensuren] **1.** To make sure or certain. **2.** To make safe or secure. **3.** To protect against injury, loss, or expense. **4.** To make a contract specifying the terms of such protection. **5.** To buy or sell insurance.

insusceptibility (ĭn″sŭ-sĕp″tĭ-bĭl′ĭ-tē) [L. *in,* not, + *suscipere,* to take up] **1.** Immunity or lack of susceptibility to infection or disease. **2.** The resistance of a microorganism to treatment.

intac (ĭn′tak″) A surgical treatment for nearsightedness in which small rings are inserted into the cornea to change its shape and improve its ability to focus. These intracorneal rings are removable and replaceable. They are an alternative to LASIK surgery for myopia.

intake (ĭn′tāk″) That which is taken in, esp. food and liquids.

   caloric i. The number of calories received orally and/or parenterally into the body.

intake and output ABBR: I and O. Measurement of a patient's fluid intake by mouth, feeding tubes, or intravenous catheters and output from kidneys, gastrointestinal tract, drainage tubes, and wounds. Accurate 24-hr measurement and recording is an essential part of patient assessment.

integrase (ĭn′tĕ-grās) A retroviral enzyme that incorporates DNA derived from the virus into host cell chromosomes. The enzyme is a target for experimental antiretroviral therapies.

integration (ĭn″tĕ-grā′shŭn) [L. *integrare,* to make whole] **1.** The bringing together of various parts or functions so that they function as a harmonious whole. **2.** The combining of peoples from diverse cultural, social, or ethnic backgrounds in communities, houses of worship, schools, workplaces, or other institutions.

   primary i. The early recognition of the body and its psyche as apart from one's environment.

   secondary i. The development of the adult personality so that the individual becomes fully socialized, engaged, and happy.

integrin (ĭnt′ĕ-grĭn) A polypeptide receptor of cell membranes that is involved in intercellular communication and adhesion. SEE: *cytokine; interleukin.*

integrity (in-teg′rĭt-ē) [L. *integritas,* wholeness] **1.** An undiminished or unimpaired state. **2.** Adherence to ethical standards.

   joint i. The soundness of the anatomical and kinematic properties of a joint. Joint integrity can be diminished by anatomical, congenital, infectious, pathological, or traumatic processes.

integument (ĭn-tĕg″ū-mĕnt) [L. *integumentum,* a covering] A covering; the skin, consisting of the corium, or dermis, and epidermis.

integumentary (ĭn-tĕg-ū-mĕn′tă-rē) Rel. to the integument.

integumentary system The skin and its derivatives (hair, nails) and the subcutaneous tissue.

intein (ĭn′tē-ĭn) [″ + *(pro)tein*] An internal sequence or segment of a protein that may be spliced out of the larger molecule after it is translated, leaving the remaining segments (the "exteins") to rejoin and form a new protein.

intellect [L. *intelligere,* to understand] The mind, or understanding; conscious brain function.

intellectual **1.** Pert. to the mind. **2.** Possessing intellect.

intellectual disability **1.** In childhood, any learning disability or form of mental retardation. **2.** In adulthood or old-age, any form of brain injury that impacts cognition; or any form of dementia.

intellectualization (ĭn″tĕ-lĕk″chū-ăl-ĭ-zā′shŭn) A coping mechanism that relies on purely cognitive solutions to problems, without engaging or incorporating one's emotional responses to them.

intelligence [L. *intelligere,* to understand] The capacity to comprehend relationships; the ability to think, solve problems, and adjust to new situations. The use of a single test to estimate the intelligence of persons from different social, racial, cultural, or economic backgrounds, however, is unreliable.

   artificial i. ABBR: AI. The ability of a computer to simulate intelligent thought or behavior.

intelligence quotient SEE: under *quotient.*

intelligence test A test to assess specific cognitive functions, including verbal abilities, visuospatial construction, mathematical skills, reasoning, and logic. Results obtained from intelligence testing are used to calculate the intelligence quotient (IQ). The most commonly used intelligence tests (e.g., Wechsler or Stanford-Binet) have been validated in broad population studies. Nonetheless, IQ tests have been criticized on a variety of grounds because they may in some cases assess achievement, experience, or sociocultural advantages rather than intelligence. SEE: *intelligence; quotient, intelligence.*

intensifying [L. *intensus,* intense, + *facere,* to make] Making intense; magnifying or amplifying.

   i. screen SEE: under *screen.*

intensity A state of increased force, muscle vigor, or energy.

   signal i. The relative brilliance of a radiographic image, radioactive tracer, or biological marker.

   spatial average i. ABBR: SAI. The measure of power per unit area of ultrasound application, expressed in watts per square centimeter (w/cm^2). The spatial average intensity is calculated by dividing the ultrasonic output, expressed in watts, by the effective radiating area of the sound head (e.g., 20 watts/10 cm^2 sound head = 2.0 w/cm^2 SAI).

   temporal average i. ABBR: TAI. The amount of therapeutic ultrasonic

energy delivered to tissues over a given time. The temporal average intensity is calculated by multiplying the spatial average intensity by the percent duty cycle (e.g., 20 w/cm^2 × 50% duty cycle = 1 w/cm^2 TAI). The temporal average intensity is meaningful only during the application of pulsed ultrasound.

intensity modulated radiation therapy Conformal radiation therapy.

intensive (ĭn-tĕn′sĭv) Rel. to or marked by intensity.

intensive care unit ABBR: ICU. A special hospital unit for patients who, because of the nature of their illness, injury, or surgical procedure, require almost continuous monitoring by specially trained staff. In large hospitals, units may be devoted to a single group of patients such as surgical cases, compromised newborns, or patients with burns, trauma, emergency cardiac care needs, or infectious diseases.

intensivist (ĭn-tĕn′sĭ-vĭst″) [*intensive* + *-ist*] A physician who specializes in the care of patients in intensive care units, e.g., those with acute respiratory failure, heart failure, kidney failure, liver failure, sepsis, and bleeding.

intent (ĭn-tĕnt′) A state of mind that reflects one's aims, goals, or objectives. Intent is the key element of and basis for lawsuits brought against plaintiffs in a court of law.

intention (ĭn-tĕn′chŏn) [L. *intentio,* purpose, aim] **1.** A natural process of healing. **2.** A goal or purpose.

   first i. SEE: *healing* by first intention.

   second i. SEE: *healing* by second intention.

   third i. SEE: *healing* by third intention.

intentional infliction of emotional distress ABBR: IIED. Deliberate destruction of a person's peace of mind; a common law tort. The conduct must be outrageous and beyond all bounds of decency; ordinary rude or insulting behavior is not enough. In those rare cases in which a health care provider inflicts intentional distress on a patient, he or she may be held liable for damages in a court of law.

intention to treat analysis, intent to treat analysis A clinical trial in which results from all randomized patients are included whether or not they actively participated in the complete study.

intention-to-treat analysis SEE: *as-treated analysis.*

inter- [L. *inter,* between, among] Prefix meaning *among* or *between.*

interacinar (ĭn″tĕr-ăs′ĭ-năr) [L. *inter,* between, + *acinus,* grape] Located between acini of a gland.

interaction (ĭnt″er-ak′shŏn) [*inter-* + *action*] Alternating, reciprocating, or mutual influence or effect.

dielectric i. Determination of the quantity of the electrical polarity or dipole moment of a molecule. SEE: *dipole.*

drug i., drug-drug interaction The combined effect of drugs taken concurrently. The result may be antagonism or synergism and may be lethal in some cases. It is important for the patient, pharmacist, physician, and nurse to be aware of the potential interaction of drugs that are prescribed as well as those that the patient may be self-administering.

Many patients, esp. the elderly, may take several medicines each day. The chances of developing an undesired drug interaction increase rapidly with the number of drugs used.

food and drug i. The effect of nutrients on the absorption, distribution, metabolism or excretion of medications. For example, alkaloids in potatoes may influence the effects of anesthetics; excess intake of vegetables rich in vitamin K may interfere with the action of anticoagulants; prolonged use of antacids may cause phosphate depletion; consumption of grapefruits or grapefruit juice may influence the half-life of some antiretroviral drugs.

patient-ventilator i. The complex link between a patient's neurologically mediated control of breathing (and the elasticity and resistance of his or her airways) and the pressures and volumes of gases injected into the patient by a mechanical ventilator. SEE: *patient-ventilator dyssynchrony.*

photoelectric i. The absorption of a photon by matter from its source of emission, producing a photoelectron and a K shell vacancy. The K shell vacancy is then filled by a cascade of electrons, each of which produces a characteristic photon. In clinical radiology, photoelectric absorption causes image contrast and increases the patient's exposure to scattered radiation.

interalveolar (ĭn″tĕr-ăl-vē′ō-lăr) [″ + *alveolus,* little tub] Between the alveoli, esp. the alveoli of the lungs.

interarticular (ĭn″tĕr-ăr-tĭk′ū-lăr) [″ + *articulus,* joint] **1.** Between two joints. **2.** Situated between two articulating surfaces.

interbody cage (ĭn′tĕr-bŏd″ē) A hollow, tube-shaped device placed between adjacent vertebral bodies in spinal fusion surgeries to improve or enhance bony fusion ("arthrodesis"). The cage is filled with either a bone graft or with bone graft substitutes.

intercalary (in-tĕr′kă-ler″ē) [*intercalate*] **1.** Inserted or interposed between. SYN: *extraneous.* **2.** Pert. to an upstroke or cardiac extrasystole that comes between two heartbeats.

intercalate (in-tĕr′kă-lāt″) [L. *interca-lare,* to insert (a day or month) into a (lunar) calendar] To insert between or among layers or components, e.g., between the bases of a DNA molecule. **intercalated** (-lāt″ĕd), *adj.*

intercanalicular (ĭn″tĕr-kăn″ă-lĭk′ū-lăr) [″ + *canalicularis,* pert. to a canaliculus] Between the canaliculi of a tissue.

intercellular (ĭn″tĕr-sĕl′ū-lăr) [″ + *cella,* compartment] Between the cells of a structure.

i. junctions The microscopic space between cells. These spaces are important in assisting the transfer of small molecules across capillary walls. These junctions may be widened by chemical or physical factors and are acted on by chemical mediators of inflammation to increase vascular permeability.

intercellular adhesion molecule ABBR: ICAM. Any of a group of immunoglobulin-like proteins on the surface of cells that help them bind to each other or to the extracellular matrix that surrounds them. These proteins also participate in cell-to-cell signaling, cytokine production, and cellular reproduction.

intercept (ĭn-tĕr-sĕpt′) The point at which the line representing a function intersects an axis.

intercerebral (ĭn″tĕr-sĕr′ĕ-brăl) [″ + *cerebrum,* brain] Between the two cerebral hemispheres.

interchange (ĭn-′tĕr-chănj″) In dispensing drugs, the use of a generic form of the drug in place of the proprietary form.

intercoccygeal (ĭn″tĕr-kŏk-sĭj′ē-ăl) [″ + Gr. *kokkyx,* coccyx] Between the segments of the coccyx.

intercostal (ĭn″tĕr-kŏs′tăl) [″ + *costa,* rib] Between the ribs.

intercostobrachial (ĭn″tĕr-kŏs″tō-brā′kē-ăl) [″ + ″ + *brachium,* arm] Pert. to the intercostal space and the arm, as the posterior lateral branch of the second intercostal nerve supplying the skin of the arm, or a similar branch of the third intercostal nerve; formerly called intercostohumeralis.

intercourse (ĭn-′tĕr-kors″) [L. *intercursus,* running between] The social interaction between individuals or groups; communication.

sexual i. SEE: *sexual intercourse.*

intercricothyrotomy (ĭn″tĕr-krī″kō-thī-rŏt′ō-mē) [L. *inter,* between, + Gr. *krikos,* ring, + *thyreos,* shield, + *tome,* incision] The surgical separation of the cricothyroid membrane in order to incise the larynx.

intercristal (ĭn″tĕr-krĭs′tăl) [″ + *crista,* crest] Between two crests of a bone, organ, or process.

intercurrent (ĭn″tĕr-kŭr′ĕnt) [″ + *currere,* to run] **1.** Intervening. **2.** Pert. to a disease attacking a patient with another disease.

intercurrent disease A disease occurring

during the course of an unrelated disease.

intercuspation (ĭn″tĕr-kŭs-pā′shŭn) [″ + *cuspis,* point] The cusp-to-fossa relation of the upper and lower posterior teeth in occlusion. SEE: *occlusion.*

interdental (ĭn″tĕr-dĕnt′ăl) [″ + *dens,* tooth] Between adjacent teeth in the same arch. SEE: *interproximal; interocclusal.*

interdentium (ĭn″tĕr-dĕn′shē-ŭm) The space between any two contiguous teeth.

interdialytic (int″ĕr-dī″ă-lit′ik) [*inter-* + *dialytic*] Pert. to the interval between treatments with hemodialysis or peritoneal dialysis.

interdigit (ĭn″tĕr-dĭ′jĭt) The area between any two contiguous toes or fingers or their associated metatarsals or metacarpals. SEE: *intermetacarpal; intermetatarsal.*

interdigitation (ĭn″tĕr-dĭj-ĭ-tā′shŭn) [″ + *digitus,* digit] 1. Interlocking of toothed or finger-like processes. 2. Processes so interlocked.

interdisciplinary (ĭn″tĕr-dĭ′sĭ-plĭ-năr″ē) Involving or overlapping of two or more health care professions in a collaborative manner or effort.

interest checklist Any assessment approach used to determine an individual's unique play, leisure, or work interests.

interface A connection between systems allowing access and exchange of information. An interface can occur between humans and devices (user interface), networks, or software components.

interference (int″ĕr-fēr′ĕns) [Fr. *s'entreferir,* to strike (one another)] 1. Clashing or colliding. 2. Dental malocclusion, esp. when it inhibits fluid mandibular movement. Particular interferences are listed under the first word. SEE: e.g., *bacterial interference; interference of impulses; semantic interference.*

interference of impulses A condition in which two excitation waves, upon approaching each other and meeting in any part of the heart, are mutually extinguished.

interferometer (ĭn″tĕr-fĕr-ŏm′ĕ-tĕr) An optical device that acts on the interference of two beams of light, permitting examination of the structure of spectral lines. It is also used in examining prisms of lenses for faults.

interferon (int″ĕr-fēr′on″) ABBR: IFN. Any of a group of glycoproteins with antiviral activity. The antiviral type I interferons (alpha and beta interferons) are produced by leukocytes and fibroblasts in response to invasion by a pathogen, particularly a virus. These interferons enable invaded cells to produce class I major histocompatibility complex surface antigens, increasing their ability to be recognized and killed by T lymphocytes. They also inhibit virus production within infected cells. Type I alpha interferon is used to treat condyloma acuminatum, chronic hepatitis B and C, and Kaposi's sarcoma. Type I beta interferon is used to treat multiple sclerosis.

Type II gamma interferon is distinctly different from and less antiviral than the other interferons. It is a lymphokine, excreted primarily by CD8+ T cells and the helper T subset of CD4+ cells that stimulates several types of antigen-presenting cells, particularly macrophages, to release class II MHC antigens that enhance CD4+ activity. It is used to treat chronic granulomatous disease. SEE: *cell, antigen-presenting; macrophage.*

interfibrillar, interfibrillary (ĭn″tĕr-fĭb′rĭ-lăr, -rĭ-lār″ē) [″ + *fibrilla,* a small fiber] Between fibrils.

interfilamentous (ĭn″tĕr-fĭl″ă-mĕn′tŭs) [″ + *filamentum,* filament] Between filaments.

intergenerational (int″ĕr-jen″ĕ-rā′shŏ-năl) Pert. to individuals of different generations, e.g., parents and children, or of different cohorts.

intergluteal (ĭn″tĕr-gloo′tē-ăl) [″ + Gr. *gloutos,* buttock] Between the buttocks.

interictal (ĭn″tĕr-ĭk′tăl) [″ + *ictus,* a blow] Between seizures.

interim (ĭn′tĕr-ĭm) [L. interim, in the meantime] 1. An intervening period. 2. Temporary, preliminary, or provisional.

interior [L. *internus,* within] The internal portion or area of something; situated within.

interkinesis (ĭn″tĕr-kĭ-nē′sĭs) [″ + Gr. *kinesis,* movement] The interval between the first and second meiotic divisions of cells.

interlabial (ĭn″tĕr-lā′bē-ăl) Between the lips or any two labia.

interleukin (ĭn″tĕr-loo′kĭn) ABBR: IL. A type of cytokine that enables communication among leukocytes and other cells active in inflammation or the specific immune response. The result is a maximized response to a microorganism or other foreign antigen. SEE: *cell-mediated immunity; cytokine; inflammation.*

i.-1 ABBR: IL-1. A cytokine released by almost all nucleated cells that activates the growth and function of neutrophils, lymphocytes, and macrophages; promotes the release of additional mediators that influence immune responses; enhances production of cerebrospinal fluid; and modulates certain adrenal, hepatic, bone, and vascular smooth muscle cell activity. Interleukin-1 and tumor necrosis factors, whose actions are almost identical to those of IL-1, are involved in fever production and other systemic effects of inflammation. SEE: *tumor necrosis factor*.

i.-1-beta ABBR: IL-1-β. A protein released by activated macrophages that stimulates B cells and thymocytes to proliferate and mature and increases the secretion of interleukin 2. It is found in high levels in the blood of patients with septic shock and in the cerebrospinal fluid of patients with meningitis. SYN: *catabolin*.

i.-2 ABBR: IL-2. A cytokine released primarily by activated CD4+ helper T lymphocytes. It is a major mediator of T cell proliferation, promotes production of other cytokines, enhances natural killer cell function, and is a cofactor for immunoglobulin secretion. SYN: *T-cell growth factor*.

i.-3 ABBR: IL-3. A cytokine produced by activated T cells that promotes proliferation of bone marrow stem cells. SYN: *mast cell growth factor; multi-colony stimulating factor*.

i.-4 ABBR: IL-4. A cytokine released by activated T cells and mast cells that stimulates B and T lymphocyte production and activity, prevents macrophages from releasing monokines, and promotes mast cell, immunoglobulin E, and eosinophil activity. SYN: *B cell growth factor; mast cell growth factor II; T-cell growth factor II*.

i.-5 ABBR: IL-5. A cytokine produced by T cells, eosinophils and mast cells that acts as the primary stimulant for eosinophil production. SYN: *eosinophil colony-stimulating factor; eosinophil differentiation factor*. SEE: *basophil(e); eosinophil*.

i.-6 ABBR: IL-6. A lymphokine produced by many cell types, including mononuclear phagocytes, T cells, and endothelial cells. It mediates the acute phase response, enhances B cell production and differentiation to immunoglobulin-secreting plasma cells, and stimulates megakaryocyte production. SYN: *B cell stimulatory factor II; hepatocyte stimulatory factor*. SEE: *acute phase reaction; lymphokine*.

i.-7 ABBR: IL-7. A cytokine produced by the thymus, spleen, and bone marrow stromal cells. It stimulates growth of B-cell precursors, development of thymocytes, and activity of cytotoxic T-cells. SYN: *lymphopoietin 1; pre-B cell growth factor*.

i.-8 ABBR: IL-8. A cytokine produced by many cell types. It acts as a neutrophil chemoattractant.

i.-9 ABBR: IL-9. A cytokine produced by T cells. Among other functions, it promotes the proliferation and multiplication of mast cells.

i.-10 ABBR: IL-10. A cytokine derived from mononuclear phagocytes, T cells, and keratinocytes. It inhibits cytokine synthesis by macrophages, T cells, and natural killer cells, and enhances B cell growth and secretion of immunoglobulin.

i.-11 ABBR: IL-11. A cytokine produced by bone marrow stromal cells. It mediates acute phase protein synthesis, enhances B cell growth and differentiation to plasma cells, and promotes megakaryocyte production. SYN: *plasmocytoma stimulating factor*.

i.-12 ABBR: IL-12. A cytokine produced by mononuclear phagocytes and B cells. It induces interferon gamma production from T cells and natural killer cells, and enhances T cell and natural killer cell cytotoxicity. SYN: *natural killer cell stimulating factor*.

i.-13 ABBR: IL-13. A cytokine produced by T cells. It induces major histocompatibility class II expression on mononuclear phagocytes and B cells, B cell proliferation, and immunoglobulin production.

i.-14 ABBR: IL-14. A cytokine produced by T lymphocytes and follicular dendritic cells. It stimulates proliferation of activated B lymphocytes and inhibits immunoglobulin secretion from activated B lymphocytes.

i.-15 ABBR: IL-15. A cytokine released by epithelial cells in the kidney, skeletal muscle, liver, lungs, heart, and bone marrow, which stimulates production of T cells, esp. cytotoxic T cells and natural killer cells. It can bind with interleukin-2 receptors and mimic IL-2's effects. SEE: *interleukin-2*.

i.-16 ABBR: IL-16. A cytokine produced by T lymphocytes that stimulates movement of monocytes, CD4+ T cells, and eosinophils to the area. It was previously known as lymphocyte chemoattractant factor.

i.-17 ABBR: IL-17. A cytokine produced by memory T lymphocytes that stimulates the proliferation of T cells and the differentiation of neutrophils.

i.-18 ABBR: IL-18. A cytokine produced by macrophages that stimulates the production of gamma interferon and other chemical mediators that enhance cell-mediated immune responses. It is similar in structure to IL-1.

interlobitis (ĭn″tĕr-lō-bī′tĭs) [″ + ″ + Gr. *itis*, inflammation] Inflammation of the pleura separating the pulmonary lobes.

interlock (int′ĕr-lok″) In biomedical engineering and computer science, a forcing function that prevents a user from undertaking certain actions while other potentially redundant or conflicting services are being used.

intermammary (ĭn″tĕr-măm′ă-rē) [″ + *mamma*, breast] Between the breasts.

intermaxillary (ĭn″tĕr-măk′sĭ-lĕr″ē) [″ + *maxilla*, jawbone] **1.** Between the two maxillae, as in an intermaxillary suture. **2.** Formerly meaning between the two jaws.

intermediary (ĭn″tĕr-mē′dē-ār-ē) [″ + *medius,* middle] **1.** Situated between two bodies. **2.** Occurring between two periods of time.

intermediate (ĭn″tĕr-mē′dē-ĭt) [″ + *medius,* middle] Between two extremes; sequentially, after the beginning and before the end.

intermediate allele SEE: under *allele.*

intermediate reaction The production of a compound during the synthesis of another compound. The first compound is ultimately converted to the final product.

intermediate vision SEE: under *vision.*

intermedin (ĭn″tĕr-mē′dĭn) Melanocyte-stimulating hormone.

intermediolateral (ĭn″tĕr-mē″dē-ō-lăt′ĕr-ăl) [″ + ″ + *latus,* side] Intermediate but not central.

intermedius (ĭn″tĕr-mē′dē-ŭs) [″ + *medius,* middle] The middle of three structures.

intermembranous (ĭn″tĕr-mĕm′bră-nŭs) [″ + *membrana,* membrane] Between membranes.

intermenstrual (ĭn″tĕr-mĕn′stroo-ăl) [″ + Gr. *men,* month] Between the menses or menstrual periods.

intermetacarpal (ĭn″tĕr-mĕt″ă-kăr′păl) [″ + Gr. *meta,* beyond, + *karpos,* wrist] Between any two contiguous metacarpals.

intermetatarsal (ĭn″tĕr-mĕt″ă-tăr′săl) Between any two contiguous metatarsals.

intermission [″ + *mittere,* to send] **1.** The interval between two paroxysms of a disease, e.g., the quiet period between two seizures or the comfortable period between two episodes of fever. **2.** A temporary cessation of symptoms.

intermittence (ĭn″tĕr-mĭt′ĕns) [″ + *mittere,* to send] **1.** A condition marked by intermissions in the course of a disease or of a process. **2.** A loss of one or more pulse beats.

intermittent (ĭn″tĕr-mit′ĕnt) [L. *intermittere,* to leave off] Happening at regular or irregular intervals.

intermittent explosive disorder (int″ĕr-mit′ĕnt) Episodic dyscontrol.

intermittent positive-pressure breathing SEE: under ***breathing.***

intern (ĭn′tĕrn) [Fr. fr. L. *internus,* within] A physician or surgeon on a hospital staff, usually a recent graduate receiving a year of postgraduate training before being eligible to be licensed to practice medicine. **intern,** *v.*; **internship** (ĭn′tĕrn″ship″), *n.* SEE: *extern.*

internal [L. *internus,* within] Within the body; within or on the inside; enclosed; inward; the opposite of external.

internal injury SEE: under *injury.*

internalization (ĭn-tĕr″năl-ĭ-zā′shŭn) In-corporation of the values and standards of family or community as one's own; acculturation

internal medicine SEE: under *medicine.*

internal radiation therapy Brachytherapy.

International Academic Nursing Alliance ABBR: IANA. An association of nursing educators who connect with one another on a website to share information, ideas, and resources for nursing education. Website: www.nursingalliance.org/portal/Main.aspx?PageID=2028, powered by Sigma Theta Tau.

International Association for Dental Research ABBR: IADR. An association founded in 1920 to provide research in dental science and application of research to develop dental treatment and oral health.

International Classification of Diseases ABBR: ICD. A codification of diseases, injuries, causes of death, and procedures including operations and diagnostic and nonsurgical procedures. The ICD's principal use is to standardize reporting of illness, death, and procedures. The publication is essential to the compilation of statistical information about diseases in a format that allows international comparison of those data.

International Classification of Functioning, Disability, and Health ABBR: ICF. An international framework published by the World Health Organization for describing and classifying factors that influence functioning, health, and disability. The ICF replaced the International Classification of Impairment, Disability, and Handicap. It specifies how people cope with health conditions and acknowledges the impact of environmental factors and body structure on levels of activity and social participation.

International Classification of Nursing Practice ABBR: ICNP. An international nursing vocabulary classification system standardizing nursing phenomena, nursing interventions, and nursing outcomes useful in both paper and electronic records.

International Conference on Harmonization of Technical Requirements for Registration of Pharmaceutics for Human Use ABBR: ICH. A global effort of pharmaceutical regulatory agencies in Asia, Europe, and the United States to standardize and streamline the approval of new drugs for use in human patients.

International Federation of Gynecology and Obstetrics ABBR: FIGO. A multinational organization that promotes the profession of obstetrics and gynecology and a wide variety of women's health issues.

international normalized ratio ABBR:

INR. The standard measurement of oral anticoagulation, introduced by the World Health Organization (WHO) in 1983 to replace the prothrombin time (PT). When a patient's blood is tested to determine its level of anticoagulation, the sample is treated with a thromboplastin, a laboratory reagent that may vary considerably depending on its chemical constituents. As a result, a single sample of blood tested in several different laboratories may give different PT results. To resolve the potential difficulties that this may create for patients who need to achieve a stable level of anticoagulation, the WHO has created the INR to be a rating scale for thromboplastins used around the world that standardizes the PT result. SEE: *International Sensitivity Index.*

PATIENT CARE: The INR is used in managing oral anticoagulant (warfarin) therapy. SEE: table.

Desirable Levels of Anticoagulation in Terms of INR

Disease or Condition	Optimal Anticoagulant Range (INR)
Deep venous thrombosis	2.0–3.0
Pulmonary embolism	2.0–3.0
Stroke prevention in atrial fibrillation	2.0–3.0
Prevention of clots in patients with mechanical heart valves	2.5–3.5
Hypercoagulable states	Variable, but often 3.0 or higher

International Nursing Minimum Data Set ABBR: i-NMDS. An international project under the auspices of the International Council of Nurses and the International Medical Informatics Association Nursing Informatics Special Interest Group to develop international standards. The project builds upon and supports data set work already done in individual countries as well as the work of the International Classification of Nursing Practice (ICNP).

International Psychogeriatric Association ABBR: IPA. An organization of health care professionals and scientists with an interest in the behavioral and biological aspects of mental health in the elderly.

International Sensitivity Index SEE: under *index.*

International Symbol of Access A symbol used to identify buildings and facilities that are barrier-free and therefore accessible to disabled persons with restricted mobility, including wheelchair users. SEE: illus.

INTERNATIONAL SYMBOL OF ACCESS

International System of Units ABBR: SI. An internationally standardized system of units. The basic quantity measured and the names of the units are meter (length), kilogram (mass), second (time), ampere (electric current), kelvin (temperature), candela (luminous intensity), and mole (amount of a substance). All other units of measurement are derived from these seven basic units. SEE: SI Units Appendix.

International Union of Pure and Applied Chemistry ABBR: IUPAC. An organization composed of experts from many countries whose charter is to standardize aspects of the basic science of chemistry, including nomenclature, structural formulae, and so forth.

international unit ABBR: I.U. An internationally accepted amount of a substance. Usually this form of expressing quantity is used for fat-soluble vitamins and some hormones, enzymes, and biologicals such as vaccines. These units are defined by the International Conference for Unification of Formulae.

⚠ The abbreviation "I.U." should not be used in the medical record. It is easily mistaken for other symbols or abbreviations; e.g., for the abbreviation for intravenous, "IV"

interneuron (ĭn″tĕr-nū′rŏn) [L. *inter*, between, + Gr. *neuron*, nerve] A neuron within the central nervous system (not directly connected to the periphery) that is neither sensory nor motor. There are two principal types: (a) those that convey information over short distances and are called local interneurons, internuncial neurons, local circuit neurons, or Golgi type II neurons, and (b) those that convey information from region to region and are called relay, principal, projection, or Golgi type I neurons.

internist (ĭn′tĕr″nĭst) A physician who specializes in internal medicine.

internode (ĭn′tĕr-nōd) [″ + *nodus*, knot] The space between adjacent nodes.

interocclusal (ĭn″tĕr-ŏ-kloo′zăl) [L. *inter*, between, + *occlusio*, a shutting up]

Between the occlusal surfaces or cusps of opposing teeth of the maxillary and mandibular arches. SEE: *interdental; interproximal.*

interoceptive (ĭn″tĕr-ō-sĕp′tĭv) [L. *internus,* within, + *capere,* to take] In nerve physiology, concerned with sensations arising within the body itself, as distinguished from those arising outside the body.

interoceptor Sensory receptor. SEE: under *receptor.*

interoperability (ĭn″tĕr-ŏp″ĕr-ŭ-bĭl′ĭ-tē) [″ + ″] The ability of different software programs, e.g., the ones that drive electronic medical records, to share information with each other.

interorbital (ĭn″tĕr-or′bĭt-ăl) [″ + *orbita,* orbit] Between the orbits.

interosseous (ĭn″tĕr-os′ē-ŭs) [*inter-* + *osseous*] ABBR: IO. Situated or occurring between bones, as muscles, ligaments, or vessels; specific muscles of the hands and feet.

interpalpebral (ĭn″tĕr-păl′pĕ-brăl) [″ + *palpebra,* eyelid] Between the eyelids.

interpandemic (ĭn″tĕr-pan-dem′ik) [*inter-* + *pandemic*] Occurring between outbreaks of a pandemic, such as influenza.

interparoxysmal (ĭn″tĕr-păr″ŏk-sĭz′măl) [″ + Gr. *paroxysmos,* spasm] Between paroxysms.

interpeduncular (ĭn″tĕr-pĕ-dŭnk′ū-lăr) [L. *inter,* between, + *pedunculus,* peduncle] Between peduncles.

interpersonal (ĭn″tĕr-pĕr′sŏn-ăl) Concerning the relations and interactions between persons.

interpersonal therapy A form of brief psychotherapy (typically lasting 20 sessions or less) in which patients explore the stresses of interpersonal relationships and how those stresses impact their attitudes and coping abilities.

interphalangeal (ĭn″tĕr-fă-lăn′jē-ăl) [″ + Gr. *phalanx,* closely knit row] In a joint between two phalanges.

interphase (ĭn′tĕr-fāz″) **1.** The stage of a cell between mitotic divisions during which DNA replication takes place. It consists of several gap or G phases and the S phase. **2.** The area or zone where two phases of a substance, such as a gas and a liquid, contact each other.

interphase cell death SEE: under *death.*

interpolation (ĭn-tĕr″pō-lā′shŭn) **1.** In surgery, the transfer of tissues from one site to another. **2.** In statistics, the estimation of an intermediate value from observed data that are larger and smaller.

interposed (ĭn′tĕr-pōzd) Inserted between.

interposition (int″ĕr-pŏ-zish′ŏn) **1.** The surgical placement of one body structure between two others. **2.** The ectopic migration of a body structure to an abnormal site between two others, e.g., of

the large intestine between the liver and the diaphragm.

interpretation (ĭn-tŭr″prĭ-tā′shŭn) **1.** In psychotherapy, the analysis of the meaning of what the patient says or does. It is explained to the patient to help provide insight. **2.** In dentistry or radiology, the analysis of a diagnostic radiograph and the integration of the findings with the case history and the laboratory and clinical evidence.

interpreter (in-tĕr′prĕt-ĕr) One who provides an oral translation for people who do not speak the same language, or a machine that performs the same function.

PATIENT CARE: The Joint Commission recommends that access to competent, culturally sensitive interpreters be a standard of care for everyone seeking health care. SYN: *translator* (2).

interproximal (ĭn″tĕr-prŏk′sĭ-măl) [″ + *proximus,* next] Between two adjoining surfaces. SEE: *interdental.*

interpubic (ĭn-tĕr-pū′bĭk) [″ + *pubes,* pubes] Between the pubic bones.

interradicular (ĭn″tĕr-ră-dĭk′ū-lăr) Between the roots of teeth; the furcation area.

interrater reliability SEE: under *reliability.*

interrogate (in-te′rŏ-gāt″) [L. *interrogare,* to ask, question, inquire] **1.** To question someone carefully and thoroughly, esp. someone involved in a legal proceeding. **2.** To extract data accumulated in the memory of a medical device, e.g., a pacemaker. **interrogation** (-ter″ŏ-gā′shŏn), *n.*

interrogatory (ĭn″tĕr-rŏg′ă-tor″ē) In law, a written question sent by one party to another requesting information about issues, facts, backgrounds, and witnesses surrounding the allegations in a lawsuit.

interscapular (ĭn″tĕr-skăp′ū-lăr) Between the shoulders or scapulae.

intersection (ĭn′tĕr-sĕk″shŭn) The site where one structure crosses another or joins a similar structure.

intersection syndrome Tendinitis (or tendinitis with synovitis) on the dorsal side of the wrist, usually from overuse during sports that require repeated extension of the wrist against a resisting force, e.g., canoeing, rowing, or weight lifting. It causes pain and swelling in the wrist when patients extend their wrists or move their arm in toward the ulna.

intersectoral collaboration (ĭn-tĕr-sĕk′tĕr-ĭl) [″ + *sector*] Cooperation among different social groups that enables them to solve common problems, e.g., a public health crisis.

intersegmental (ĭn″tĕr-sĕg-mĕn′tăl) [″ + *segmentum,* a portion] Between segments.

intersex (in'tĕr-seks") Hermaphroditism.

female i. A genetic female with external sexual characteristics of both
sexes.

male i. A genetic male with external
sexual characteristics of both sexes.

true i. An individual whose genetic
sex may be either male or female and
whose sexual characteristics are of both
sexes.

intersexuality (in"tĕr-sĕks"ū-ăl'ĭ-tē) The
varying expression of male and female
physical and sexual characteristics in
the same individual. SEE: *intersex.*

interspace (in'tĕr-spās) The space between two similar parts, as between two
ribs.

interspinal (in-tĕr-spī'năl) [" + *spinalis,* pert. to the spine] Between two spinous processes of the vertebral column.

interspinous (in"tĕr-spī'nŭs) [" + "]
Between the spines.

interstice (in-tĕr'stĭs) [L. *interstitium*]
The space or gap in a tissue or structure
of an organ. SYN: *interstitium.*

interstitial (in"tĕr-stish'ăl) [L. *interstitium,* a place between, interval]
1. Placed or lying between. **2.** Pert. to
interstices or spaces within an organ or
tissue.

interstitial lung disorder ABBR: ILD.
Any of a large group of diseases with different causes but with the same or similar clinical and pathological changes.
These are due to chronic, nonmalignant,
noninfectious diseases of the lower respiratory tract characterized by inflammation and disruption of the walls of
the alveoli. This manifests clinically as
a limitation in the ability of the lungs to
transfer oxygen from the alveoli to the
pulmonary capillary bed. Patients with
these disorders are dyspneic first in connection with exercise and, later, as the
disease progresses, even at rest.

Approximately 180 different types of
ILD exist, many of which are poorly understood. Known causes include inhalation of irritating or toxic environmental agents such as organic dusts, fumes,
vapors, aerosols, and inorganic dusts;
drugs; radiation; aspiration pneumonia;
and the consequences of acute respiratory distress syndrome. SEE: *idiopathic
pulmonary* **fibrosis**.

interstitium (in"tĕr-stĭsh'ē-ŭm) [L.] Interstice.

intertrigo (in"tĕr-trī'gō) [" + *terere,* to
rub] Skin chafing that occurs in or under folds of skin. The irritation and
trapped moisture often result in secondary bacterial or fungal infection. SEE:
illus.; *erythema intertrigo.* **intertriginous,** *adj.*

intertrochanteric (in"tĕr-trō"kăn-tĕr'ĭk)
[" + Gr. *trochanter,* trochanter] Situated between the greater and lesser trochanters of the femur.

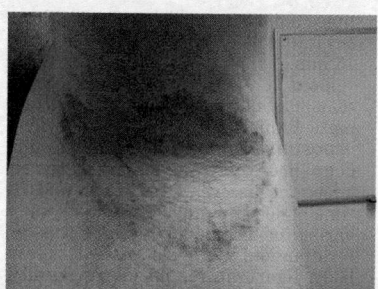

INTERTRIGO OCCURRING IN ARMPIT

interval (in'tĕr-văl) [L. *intervallum,* a
space between two palisades] **1.** A
space or time between two objects or periods. **2.** A break in the course of disease
or between paroxysms.

atriocarotid i. In a venous pulse tracing, the interval between the onset of
the presystolic wave (a) and that of the
systolic wave (c). It indicates the time
required for impulses to travel from the
sinoatrial node to the ventricle, normally about 0.2 sec.

atrioventricular (AV) i. An interval
between the beginning of atrial systole
and ventricular systole, measured by an
electrocardiogram, as the P-R interval.

birth i. The time elapsed between a
full-term pregnancy and the termination or completion of the next pregnancy. Parents manage the interval between births for personal, psychological,
or economic reasons. Intervals of less
than 17 months or more than 5 years
increase the risk of certain maternal
and child health problems, such as preeclampsia, eclampsia, low birth weight,
preterm birth, and maternal mortality.
SYN: *birth spacing; interpregnancy* **i.**

cardioarterial i. The time between
the apex beat and radial pulsation.

confidence i. ABBR: CI. The range
of values within which it is expected
(with a given probability) that the true
value of a parameter will lie. SEE:
confidence level.

contraction i. The period between
uterine contractions. Relaxation of the
uterine muscle replenishes the blood
flow to the muscle and to the intervillous spaces of the placenta.

fertile i. Safe **period**.

focal i. The distance between the anterior and posterior focal points of the
eyes.

interpregnancy i. Birth **i.**

isometric i. Presphygmic **i.**

lockout i. In patient-controlled analgesia (PCA), the number of minutes a
patient must wait between demanded
doses of pain relievers. During the lockout interval, no medications are delivered to the patient no matter how many

times a dose is requested. Typical lockout intervals in PCA are between 5 and 15 min.

lucid i. A brief remission of symptoms, e.g. in psychosis, stroke, or traumatic brain injury.

postmortem i. The estimated number of hours, days, weeks, or months between the discovery of a cadaver and the time of death. Forensic scientists use a variety of techniques to make this determination, e.g., evidence of changes in body temperature, muscular rigidity, blood pooling, and bodily decomposition. Infestation by insects with known larval or pupal developmental stages provides valuable information when forensic scientists are examining bodies that have been dead for a long time.

postsphygmic i. The interval between closure of the semilunar valves and opening of atrioventricular valves.

P-R i. In the electrocardiogram, the period between the onset of the P wave and the beginning of the QRS complex.

presphygmic i. The brief period between the beginning of ventricular systole and opening of the semilunar valves. SYN: *isometric i.*

Q-R i. In the electrocardiogram, the period between the onset of the QRS complex and the peak of the R wave.

QRS i. In the electrocardiogram, the interval that denotes depolarization of the ventricles, between the beginning of the Q wave and the end of the S wave. Its normal duration is 120–200 msec. Shorter durations are found, e.g., in preexcitation. Longer durations are indicative of first-degree heart block.

QRST i. The ventricular complex of the electrocardiogram. SEE: *electrocardiogram* for illus.

Q-T i. The representation on the electrocardiogram of ventricular depolarization and repolarization, beginning with the QRS complex and ending with the T wave. SYN: *Q-T segment.*

R-R i. In an electrocardiogram, the interval from the onset of one R wave to the onset of the next one, one complete cardiac cycle.

S-T i. In an electrocardiogram, the interval that represents ventricular repolarization. An elevation of the S-T segment may be seen in myocardial infarction, variant angina, and ventricular aneurysms; depression of the S-T segment is seen in conditions such as coronary ischemia, left ventricular hypertrophy, and digitalis use. SEE: *electrocardiogram* for illus.; *QRST complex.*

surveillance i. In screening patients at risk for the development of a disease, the time between the performance of successive tests.

TP i. The line drawn on an electrocardiogram that represents a period of electrical inactivity occurring after the end of the T wave and before the beginning of the P wave.

interval cancer SEE: under *cancer.*

intervention (int″ĕr-ven′shŏn) [L. *interventio*, a coming between, giving of security] **1.** An action taken to modify an effect. **2.** An invasive procedure, e.g., the insertion of catheters or other devices into the body. Particular interventions are listed under the first word. SEE: e.g., *early intervention; life-sustaining intervention; nursing intervention*. **interventional** (int″ĕr-ven′shŏn-ăl), *adj.*

interventional radiology (int″ĕr-ven′shŏn-ăl) A radiological subspecialty that makes use of imaging technologies to assist and guide invasive procedures, (e.g., the collection of tissue specimens from internal organs, or the placement of catheters, drugs, radioactive materials, or stents within body structures).

interventional ultrasound (int″ĕr-ven′shŏn-ăl) SEE: under *ultrasound.*

intervertebral (ĭn″tĕr-vĕrt′ĕ-brăl, -vĕr-tē″brĕl) [″ + *vertebra*, joint] Between two adjacent vertebrae.

interviewer bias (ĭn′tĕr-vū″ĕr) Distortion in a research investigation, introduced by the intentional or unrecognized behavior of the data collector, e.g., personal beliefs, cultural background, style of dress, use of language, or body language. The distortions may influence the person providing or interpreting the data.

intestinal (in-tes′tĭn-ăl) [*intestine + -al*] Pert. to the intestines. SEE: *digestion; intestine.*

intestinal spirochetosis, human intestinal spirochetosis ABBR: IS. Colonization or invasion of the bowel epithelium by spirochetes, most often by species of *Brachyspira*. Colonization without invasion of the epithelium is not thought to cause symptoms such as abdominal cramping or diarrhea.

intestinal tube A flexible tube, usually made of plastic or rubber, placed in the intestinal tract to aspirate gas, fluid, or solids from the stomach or intestines or to administer fluids, electrolytes, or nutrients to the patient. The tube may be passed through the nose, mouth, or anus, or through an abdominal opening (e.g., jejunostomy).

PATIENT CARE: When a long, weighted intestinal tube is inserted, the caregiver must assist its advancement into the intestinal tract. The patient is usually placed on the right side for 30 min, then the left side for 30 min, and then on the back as the tube is slowly advanced. These position changes, as well as ambulation, will facilitate movement of the tube into the intestinal tract. These maneuvers may be performed under radiographic control.

Frequent oral hygiene and oral misting is needed to prevent oral ulceration because the patient usually will not be taking fluids by mouth. While the tube is in, the patient should be taught not to mouth breathe or swallow air. Air swallowing enhances entry of air into the gastrointestinal tract opposing intestinal drainage. SYN: *Cantor tube.*

intestine (in-těs′tĭn) [L. *intestinum*] The portion of the alimentary canal that extends from the pylorus of the stomach to the anus. It includes the duodenum, jejunum, ileum (small intestine), and colon (large intestine) and is responsible for the completion of digestion and the absorption of nutrients and water. SYN: *bowel; gut (1).* SEE: *abdomen.*

large i. The large intestine extends from the ileum to the anus and is about 1.5 m (5 ft) in length. It absorbs water, minerals, and vitamins from the intestinal contents and eliminates undigested material during defecation. The mucosa has no villi but contains glands that secrete mucus. Hyperactivity of the colon may cause diarrhea. SEE: illus.

The first part of the large intestine is the cecum, a pouch on the right side into which the ileum empties. Attached to the cecum is the vermiform appendix, about 7.5 to 10.4 cm (3 to 4 in) long. The ascending colon extends from the cecum upward to the undersurface of the liver, where it turns left (hepatic flexure) and becomes the transverse colon, which continues toward the spleen and turns downward (splenic flexure) to become the descending colon. At the level of the pelvic brim, the descending colon turns inward in the shape of the letter S and is then called the sigmoid colon. The rectum, about 10.2 to 12.7 cm (4 to 5 in) long, is the straight part that continues downward; the last 2.5 cm (1 in) is called the anal canal, which surrounds the anus.

small i. The first part of the small intestine is the duodenum, approx. 8 to 11 in (20 to 28 cm) long, which receives chyme from the stomach through the pyloric orifice and, by way of the common bile duct, bile from the liver and gallbladder, and pancreatic juice from the pancreas. The second part is the jejunum, about 9 ft (2.8 m) long. The third part is the ileum, about 13 ft (4 m) long. The ileum opens into the cecum of the large intestine, and the ileocecal valve prevents backup of intestinal contents.

The wall of the small intestine has circular folds (plicae circulares), which are folds of the mucosa and submucosa that look like accordion pleats. The mucosa is further folded into villi, which look like small (0.5 to 1.5 mm long) projections. The free surfaces of the epithelial cells have microscopic folds called microvilli that are collectively called the brush border. All of the folds increase the surface area for absorption of the end products of digestion. Intestinal glands (of Lieberkühn) between the bases of the villi secrete enzymes. The duodenum has submucosal Brunner's glands that secrete mucus. Enzymes secreted by the small intestine are peptidases, which complete protein digestion, and sucrase, maltase, and lactase, which digest disaccharides to monosaccharides. Some of these enzymes function in the brush border rather than in the lumen of the intestine. Hormones secreted by the duodenum are gastric inhibitory peptide, secretin, and cholecystokinin; these influence secretions or motility of other parts of the digestive tract.

The end products of digestion (amino acids, monosaccharides, fatty acids, glycerol, vitamins, minerals, and water) are absorbed into the capillaries or lacteals within the villi. Blood from the small intestine passes through the liver by way of the portal vein before return-

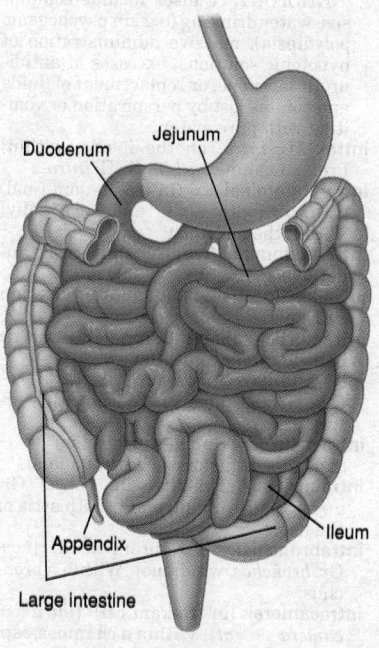

Duodenum

Jejunum

Appendix

Ileum

Large Intestine

INTESTINE

ing to the heart. SEE: *duodenum; liver; pancreas.*

intima (ĭn′tĭ-mă) [L.] The innermost layer of the wall of an artery or vein. It consists of a continuous layer of endothelial cells. Normally these cells are a semipermeable barrier that regulates the entry of substances from the lumen into the wall of the vessel. Materials may cross this barrier by means of transport systems. The endothelial cells are very smooth, which prevents abnormal clotting; they secrete chemicals that are important for normal blood coagulation and for controlling relaxation and contraction of the smooth muscle tissue in the middle layer of the vessel. As the normal artery ages, the intima thickens due to an increase in lipid material.

intimacy 1. A close familial, personal, or emotional relationship with another person. **2.** Sexual relations.

intimal (ĭn′tĭ-măl) Pert. to the inner layer of a blood vessel, the intima.

intima-media thickness ABBR: IMT. The depth in millimeters of the two inner layers of an arterial wall. IMT is a marker of generalized atherosclerosis. It increases with age, cholesterol intake, smoking, body mass index, and other established risk factors for cardiovascular disease. IMT is measured ultrasonographically, typically in the carotid arteries.

into-bed time SEE: under *time.*

intolerance (in-tol′ĕ-răns) [L. *intolerantia,* impatience] An inability to endure, or an incapacity for bearing, pain or the effects of a drug or other substance. Particular intolerances are listed under the first word. SEE: e.g., *activity intolerance; fructose intolerance; lactose intolerance.* **intolerant** (-rănt), *adj.*

intorsion (ĭn-tor′shŭn) [L. *in,* toward, + *torsio,* twisting] Rotation of the eye inward toward the nose on the anterioposterior axis of the eye. In this condition, twelve o'clock on the corneal margin would be closer to the nose than normal.

intoxicant (ĭn-tŏks′ĭ-kănt) An agent that produces intoxication.

intoxication (ĭn-tŏk″sĭ-kā′shŭn) [L. *in,* in, + Gr. *toxikon,* poison] **1.** Poisoning by a drug or toxic substance. **2.** Impaired cognitively by alcoholic beverages. Colloquially: drunk.

The determination of alcohol content of the blood (i.e., ethyl alcohol or the alcohol present in commercial beverages such as beer, wine, and whiskey) is sometimes of value in the diagnosis of alcohol intoxication, esp. in differentiating it from other disorders. Normally the alcohol content of body tissues and fluids is negligible. Upon ingestion, alcohols are absorbed slowly or quickly, depending upon the amount swallowed,

presence of food in the stomach, the drinker's gender (women become inebriated more easily with the same amount of alcohol consumption as men), and rate of gastric emptying. The amount of alcohol found in each milliliter of blood also depends on body size.

The amount of alcohol present in the blood does not provide valid information about the degree of intoxication because of the ability of the central nervous system, liver, and other organs to adapt to alcohol. SEE: *alcoholism.* SYN: *inebriation.*

    ammonia i. Ammonia toxicity.

    caffeine i. The reaction that follows the ingestion of excessive caffeine, usually more than 250 mg. At least five of the following side effects are experienced: restlessness, nervousness, excitement, insomnia, flushed face, gastrointestinal disturbance, muscle twitching, diuresis, rambling flow of thought and speech, tachycardia or arrhythmia, and psychomotor agitation. Other physical or mental disorders such as anxiety disorder must be ruled out. SYN: *caffeinism.*

    water i. Excess intake or undue retention of water, with symptomatic hyponatremia or hypo-osmolality or both. SEE: *brain edema; hyponatremia.*

    SYMPTOMS: Abdominal cramps, nausea, vomiting, dizziness, lethargy, or edema may be present. Severe water intoxication may produce convulsions or coma.

    ETIOLOGY: Causes include compulsive water drinking (e.g., in psychogenic polydipsia), massive administration of hypotonic solutions, excesses of antidiuretic hormone, or replacement of fluids and solutes lost by perspiration or vomiting with pure water.

intra- [L. *intra,* on the inside, within] Prefix meaning *within.* SEE: *intro-.*

intra-abdominal (ĭn″tră-ăb-dŏm′ĭ-năl) [L. *intra,* within, + *abdomen,* belly] Within the abdomen.

intra-abdominal hypertension SEE: under *hypertension.*

intra-aortic balloon counterpulsation SEE: under *counterpulsation.*

intra-aortic balloon pump Intra-aortic balloon counterpulsation.

intra-arterial (ĭn″tră-ăr-tē′rē-ăl) [″ + Gr. *arteria,* artery] Within the artery(ies).

intra-articular (ĭn″tră-ăr-tĭk′ū-lăr) [″ + *articulus,* little joint] Within a joint.

intra-atrial (ĭn″tră-ā′trē-ăl) [″ + Gr. *atrion,* hall] Within one or both atria of the heart.

intrabronchial (ĭn″tră-brŏng′kē-ăl) [″ + Gr. *bronchos,* windpipe] Within a bronchus.

intracameral (ĭn″tră-kam′răl) [*intra-* + *camera* + *-al*] Within a chamber, esp. a chamber of the eye or the heart.

intracapsular (ĭn″tră-kăp′sū-lăr) [″ + *capsula*, little box] Within a capsule.

   i. **extraction** The basic surgical technique for cataract removal, in which the nucleus, cortex, and capsule are removed as one unit. SEE: *cataract.*

intracardiac (ĭn″tră-kăr′dē-ăk) Within the heart.

intracarpal (ĭn″tră-kăr′păl) [″ + Gr. *karpalis*, pert. to the carpus] Within the wrist.

intracartilaginous (ĭn″tră-kăr″tĭ-lăj′ĭn-ŭs) [″ + *cartilago*, gristle] Within a cartilage or cartilaginous tissue.

intracellular (ĭn″tră-sĕl′ū-lăr) [″ + *cellula*, cell] Within the cell.

intracerebellar (ĭn″tră-sĕr″ĕ-bĕl′ăr) [″ + *cerebellum*, little brain] Within the cerebellum of the brain.

intracerebral (ĭn″tră-sĕr′ĕ-brăl) [″ + *cerebrum*, brain] Within the main portion of the brain, the cerebrum.

intracervical (ĭn″tră-sĕr′vĭ-kăl) [″ + *cervicalis*, pert. to the neck] Within the neck of the uterus.

intracoronary (ĭn-tră-kŏr′ō-nă-rē) Within the coronary arteries.

intracorporeal (ĭn″tră-kŏr-pŏr′ē-ăl) Within the body.

intracranial (ĭn″tră-krā′nē-ăl) [″ + Gr. *kranion*, skull] Within the cranium or skull.

intracranial adaptive capacity, decreased A clinical state in which intracranial fluid dynamic mechanisms that normally compensate for increases in intracranial volumes are compromised, resulting in repeated disproportionate increases in intracranial pressure in response to a variety of noxious and nonnoxious stimuli. SEE: *Nursing Diagnoses Appendix.*

intracranial pressure monitoring Assessment of the pressure of the cerebrospinal fluid in the head with a sensor inserted through the skull. Intracranial pressure monitoring is used in the management of critically ill patients, esp. those who have suffered severe brain injury or intracranial bleeding. In healthy people intracranial pressures range between 0 and 10 mm Hg. Pressures higher than 20 mm Hg increase the risk of compression or herniation of the brain or brainstem.

intractable (ĭn-trăk′tă-b'l) Incurable or resistant to therapy.

intracutaneous (ĭn″tră-kū-tā′nē-ŭs) [″ + *cutis*, skin] Within the skin. SEE: *intradermal.*

intracutaneous reaction A reaction following the injection of a substance into the skin. SYN: *intradermal reaction.* SEE: *skin test.*

intracutaneous test A test done by injecting an antigen into the skin and observing the response. SEE: *skin test.*

intracystic (ĭn″tră-sĭs′tĭk) [″ + Gr. *kystis*, bladder] Within a bladder or cyst.

intradermal (ĭn″tră-dĕr″măl) [″ + Gr. *derma*, skin] ABBR: ID. Intracutaneous or, more specifically, within the dermis.

intradermal reaction Intracutaneous reaction.

intradiscal electrothermal therapy, intradiskal electrothermal therapy (ĭn″tră-dĭsk′ăl) ABBR: IDET. A treatment for low back pain without sciatica that involves inserting a needle into the posterior annulus of a painful intravertebral disc and heating it to 90°C.

intradural (ĭn-tră-dū′răl) [″ + *durus*, hard] Within or enclosed by the dura mater.

intraepidermal (ĭn″tră-ĕp″ĭ-dĕr′măl) [L. *intra*, within, + Gr. *epi*, upon, + *derma*, skin] Within the epidermis.

intraepithelial (ĭn″tră-ĕp″ĭ-thē′lē-ăl) [″ + ″ *thele*, nipple] Within the epithelium or located between its cells.

intrafamilial (ĭn″tră-fă-mil′yăl) [*intra-* + *familial*] Within a family.

intrafebrile (ĭn″tră-fē′brĭl) [″ + *febris*, fever] During the febrile stage. SYN: *intrapyretic.*

intragyral (ĭn″tră-jī′răl) [″ + Gr. *gyros*, circle] Within a gyrus of the brain.

intrahepatic (ĭn″tră-hĕ-pat′ĭk) [*intra-* + *hepaticr*] Within the liver.

intrahepatic cholestasis of pregnancy (ĭn″tră-hĕ-pat′ĭk kō″lĕ-stā′sĭs) SEE: under *cholestasis.*

intralesional (ĭn″tră-lē′zhŭn-ăl) [″ + *laesio*, a wound] Within a lesion.

intraligamentary (ĭn″tră-lĭg″ă-mĕn′t-ă-rē) [″ + *ligamentum*, a binding] Within the folds of a ligament; usually used in referring to fibroid tumors or cysts of the ovary that have grown within the broad ligament.

intralocular (ĭn″tră-lŏk′ū-lăr) [″ + *loculus*, a cavity] Within the cavity of any structure.

intraluminal (ĭn″tră-lū′mĭ-năl) [″ + *lumen*, light] Intratubal.

intramastoiditis (ĭn″tră-măs″tŏyd-ī′tĭs) [″ + Gr. *mastos*, breast, + *eidos*, form, shape, + *itis*, inflammation] An inflammation of the antrum and mastoid process. SYN: *endomastoiditis.*

intramedullary (ĭn″tră-mĕd′ū-lăr″ē) [″ + *medullaris*, marrow] **1.** Within the medulla oblongata of the brain. **2.** Within the spinal cord. **3.** Within the marrow cavity of a bone.

intramural (ĭn″tră-mūr′ăl) [″ + *murus*, a wall] Within the walls of a hollow organ or cavity. SYN: *intraparietal* (2).

intramuscular (ĭn″tră-mŭs′kyŭ-lăr) [*intra-* + *muscular*] ABBR: IM. Within a muscle. **intramuscularly** (-lăr-lē), *adv.*

intramuscular stimulation ABBR: IMS. SEE: under *stimulation.*

intranasal (ĭn″tră-nā′zl) [″ + *nasus*, nose] Within the nasal cavity.

intranatal (ĭn″tră-nā′tăl) [″ + *natalis*, birth] Occurring during birth.

intranet (ĭn″trä-nĕt″) A network of computers exclusive to an enterprise that uses the World Wide Web and other Internet technologies to share company information and computing resources among employees.

intraocular (ĭn″trä-ŏk′ū-lĕr) [″ + *oculus*, eye] Within the eyeball.

intraoperative (ĭn″trä-op′(ĕ-)răt″ĭv) [*intra-* + *operative*] ABBR: IO. Occurring during surgery.

intraoperative neurophysiological monitoring ABBR: IONM. The moment-to-moment evaluation of brain or spinal cord activity during operations on or near those organs. It is used to identify and minimize the effects of hypoxia or ischemia on nerves. Technologies used in IONM include brainstem auditory evoked potentials, electromyography, muscle motor evoked potentials, and somatosensory evoked potentials. SYN: *surgical neurophysiology*.

intraoral (ĭn″trä-or′ăl) [″ + *oralis*, pert. to the mouth] Within the mouth.

intraorbital (ĭn″trä-or′bĭt-ăl) [″ + *orbita*, mark of a wheel] Within the orbit.

intraosseous (ĭn″trä-ŏs′ē-ŭs) [″ + *os*, bone] Within the bone matrix.

intraosseous infusion SEE: under *infusion*.

intraosseous injector A device that inserts a needle into the bone marrow. It is used in emergency resuscitation to gain access to the central circulation of a patient with severely low blood pressure caused by cardiogenic arrest, cardiogenic shock, diarrhea, hemorrhage, sepsis, or vomiting.

intraovarian (ĭn″trä-ō-vā′rē-ăn) [″ + *ovarium*, ovary] Within the ovary.

intraparietal (ĭn″trä-pă-rī′ĕ-tăl) [″ + *paries*, wall] 1. Within the parietal lobe of the cerebrum. 2. Intramural.

intrapartal (ĭn″trä-păr′tăl) The period from the onset of labor to its termination, marked by delivery of the placenta.

intrapartum (ĭn″trä-păr′tŭm) [″ + *partus*, birth] Happening during childbirth.

intrapelvic (ĭn″trä-pĕl′vĭk) [″ + *pelvis*, basin] Within the pelvis.

intraperitoneal (ĭn″trä-pĕr″ĭ-tō-nē′ăl) [″ + Gr. *peritonaion*, peritoneum] Within the peritoneal cavity.

intraplacental (ĭn″trä-plä-sĕn′tăl) [″ + *placenta*, a flat cake] Within the placenta.

intrapleural (ĭn″trä-ploo′răl) [″ + Gr. *pleura*, rib] Within the pleural cavity.

intrapsychic, intrapsychical (ĭn″trä-sī′kĭk, -kĭ-kăl) [″ + Gr. *psyche*, mind] Having a mental origin or basis, such as conflicts and complexes.

intrarenal (ĭn″trä-rē′năl) [″ + *renalis*, pert. to the kidney] Within the kidney.

intraretinal microvascular abnormalities ABBR: IRMA. Retinal vascular changes, including dilated tortuous retinal capillaries, dot and blot hemorrhages, microaneurysms, and capillary loss seen in diabetic retinopathy.

intraspinal (ĭn″trä-spī′năl) [L. *intra*, within, + *spina*, thorn] 1. Ensheathed; within a sheath. 2. Within the spinal canal.

intrathecal (ĭn″trä-thē′kăl) [″ + Gr. *theke*, sheath] 1. Within the spinal canal. 2. Within a sheath.

intrathoracic (ĭn″trä-thō-răs′ĭk) [″ + Gr. *thorax*, chest] Within the thorax.

intratracheal (ĭn″trä-trāk′ē-ăl) [″ + Gr. *tracheia*, trachea] Introduced into, or inside, the trachea.

intratubal (ĭn″trä-tū′băl) [″ + *tubus*, hollow tube] Within a tube, esp. the fallopian tube. SYN: *intraluminal*.

intratumoral (ĭn″trä-tū′mĕr-ĭl) Within or into a tumor.

intratympanic (ĭn″trä-tĭm-păn′ĭk) [″ + Gr. *tympanon*, drum] Within the tympanic cavity.

intrauterine (ĭn″trä-ūt′ĕ-rĭn, -rīn″) [*intra-* + *uterine*] Within the uterus.

intrauterine contraceptive device ABBR: IUCD, IUD. An artifact inserted into the uterine cavity to interfere with conception or implantation. Many such devices are impregnated with progestins or copper. IUDs block fertilization and implantation, although the actual mechanism by which IUDs function is unclear. The estimated pregnancy rate is between 0.5% and 3%.

Although once manufactured in several different shapes and materials, the incidence of uterine perforation, severe pelvic inflammatory disease, or both led to product liability lawsuits and the discontinuance of many models in the U.S. The two contemporary IUDs are T-shaped. The most commonly used device is the copper T380A, which may remain in place in the uterus for as long as 10 years; the levonorgestrol-releasing IUD may remain in place for 5 years. Common clinical criteria for insertion include primiparity (having given birth once) or multiparity (having given birth more than once); a monogamous relationship; and the absence of vaginal, cervical, or pelvic disease. The device is inserted during menstruation or on the first postpartum visit.

⚠ Because of the increased risk of sexually transmitted infections, the IUD is contraindicated for women who have multiple sexual partners.

PATIENT CARE: To help prospective users make informed decisions, patients should be taught the comparative advantages and disadvantages of IUDs. *Advantages:* Little maintenance is required, other than checking for the presence of the string each week during the first month after insertion and thereafter each month after menses and having an annual routine pelvic examination. Only 10% of users experience spontaneous expulsion of the device during the first year after insertion. Women using hormone-releasing IUDs may experience decreased menstrual flow, or, over time, no menses. *Disadvantages:* Transient cramping or bleeding for a few weeks after insertion is not uncommon; dysmenorrhea, menorrhagia, and/or metrorrhagia also may occur. An increased risk of ectopic pregnancy (10 times more common) may be related to the increased risk of pelvic inflammatory disease. Uterine perforation is rare. Health care professionals should instruct users to promptly inform their health care providers if they experience delayed menses, abnormal vaginal discharge, dyspareunia, abdominal pain, or signs of infection.

An IUD may be inserted into the uterus within five days of unprotected intercourse as a means of emergency contraception. SEE: illus.

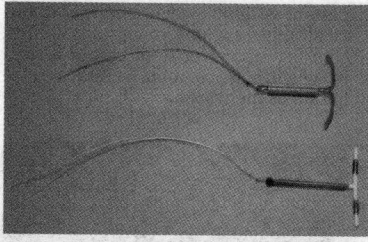

INTRAUTERINE CONTRACEPTIVE DEVICES

intrauterine growth retardation ABBR: IUGR. A decreased rate of fetal growth, most commonly related to inadequate placental perfusion resulting from pre-existing or coexisting maternal or placental factors. The infant's birth weight is below the 10th percentile on the intrauterine growth curve for the calculated gestation period. Although about 50% of cases of IUGR cannot be linked to any particular cause, certain characteristics are associated with increased fetal jeopardy: *Demographic factors*: Maternal age under 16 or over 40, primiparity or grand multiparity, low socioeconomic status, low weight gain, poor nutrition, and inadequate prenatal care. *Maternal medical disorders*: Common pre-existing and coexisting health problems, including heart disease, chronic or pregnancy-related hypertensive disease, advanced diabetes mellitus, hemoglobinopathies, asymptomatic pyelonephritis, substance abuse, drug addiction, and smoking. *Placental factors*: Placenta previa, small placenta, abnormal site of cord insertion, large or multiple infarcts, or thrombosis. *Fetal*

factors: Congenital infections such as rubella, cytomegalovirus, or toxoplasmosis, particularly when occurring during an early stage of fetal development; chromosomal abnormalities and fetal anomalies; and multiple gestation, i.e., two or more fetuses. SYN: *fetal growth restriction*.

SYMPTOMS: The first prenatal sign of abnormal fetal growth usually is noted during the second trimester, when the increase in fundal height is found to be less than expected for the number of weeks of gestation. Ultrasonography enables comparisons of measurements of the fetal head circumference, biparietal diameter, abdominal circumference, and femur length and the expected norms for the estimated gestational week. IUGR newborns evidence birth weights at or below the 10th percentile on the intrauterine growth curve for an equal number of weeks' gestation. SEE: *gestational age assessment*.

TYPES: *Asymmetric.* There may be a disproportional reduction in size of structures. For example, the biparietal diameter may be within normal limits for gestational age, while the abdominal circumference is less than expected. Asymmetry usually reflects episodic interference with uteroplacental circulation accompanying such events as placental infarction and pre-eclampsia. During the neonatal period, these infants are at high risk for asphyxia, aspiration syndrome, hypocalcemia, polycythemia, and pulmonary hemorrhage. *Symmetric.* A generalized proportional reduction in the size of all structures and organs, other than the brain and heart, reflects diminished cell numbers related to persistent, chronic nutritional deprivation, resulting from substance abuse, congenital anomalies, and early intrauterine infection. SEE: *cocaine baby; parabiosis*.

PROGNOSIS: Asymmetric IUGR infants usually exhibit normal weights within 3 to 6 months of birth. Symmetric IUGR infants exhibit an individual potential for growth; however, their growth usually does not equal that of their peers. Later, these children may exhibit learning disabilities associated with a lessened ability to concentrate and focus on tasks because of their hyperactivity and short attention spans, and they may become frustrated because of their poor fine motor coordination. SEE: *dysmaturity*.

intravasation (in-trav′ă-sā′shŏn) [*intra-* + *vas,* vessel] The penetration of a blood or lymphatic vessel by cells, fluids, or other materials that are not normally found there. Common forms of intravasation include the invasion of an artery or vein by cancer or the inadvertent injection of contrast material into an artery or vein.

intravascular (ĭn″tră-văs′kū-lăr) Within blood vessels.

intravenous (in″tră-vē′nŭs) [*intra-* + *venous*] ABBR: IV. Within or into a vein.

intravenous fluorescein angiography SEE: under *angiography*.

intravenous treatment Intravenous injection or infusion.

intraventricular (ĭn″tră-vĕn-trĭk′ū-lăr) [L. *intra*, within, + *ventriculus*, ventricle] Within a ventricle.

intraventricular conduction delay (ĭn″tră-vĕn-trĭk′ū-lĕr) ABBR: IVCD. Abnormally slow conduction of electricity through the ventricular walls of the heart, resulting in a QRS complex on the electrocardiogram that lasts longer than 0.12 sec but less than 0.16 sec. IVCD is sometimes referred to as an incomplete bundle branch block.

intravital (ĭn″tră-vī′tl) [″ + *vita*, life] During life. SYN: *intra vitam.*

intra vitam (ĭn′tră vī′tăm) [L.] Intravital.

intravitreal, intravitreous (ĭn″tră-vi′trē-ăl, ĭn″tră-vi′trē-ŭs) [*intra-* + L. *vitreus*, glassy] Within the vitreous body of the eye.

intrinsic (ĭn-trĭn′zĭk) [L. *intrinsicus*, on the inside] **1.** Belonging to the essential nature of a thing. It is both essential and natural, not merely apparent or accidental. SYN: *inherent; innate.* **2.** In anatomy, structures belonging solely to a certain body part, as intrinsic nerves or muscles. **3.** Due to causes or elements within the body, an organ, or a part.

intrinsic factor SEE: under *factor.*

intro- [L. *intro*, internally, on the inside] Prefix meaning *in* or *into.* SEE: *intra-.*

introducer (ĭn″trō-dūs′ĕr) [L. *intro*, into, + *ducere*, to lead] Intubator.

introflexion (ĭn″trō-flĕk′shŭn) [″ + *flexus*, bent] A bending inward.

introitus (ĭn-trō′ĭ-tŭs) [L.] An opening or entrance into a space or cavity.

   i. vaginae The exterior orifice of the vagina.

introjection (ĭn″trō-jĕk′shŭn) [″ + *jacere*, to throw] In psychoanalysis, identification of the self with another person or with some object, internalizing the perspective of the other, unconsciously or uncritically.

intromission (ĭn″trō-mĭsh′ŭn) [″ + *mittere*, to send] An insertion or placing of one part into another, esp. insertion of the penis into the vagina.

intromittent (ĭn-trō-mĭt′ĕnt) Conveying or injecting into a cavity or body.

intron (ĭn′trŏn) The noncoding space between the discrete coding regions (exons) of the DNA of the gene.

introspection (ĭn″trō-spĕk′shŭn) [″ + *spicere*, to look] Looking within, esp.

examination of one's own feelings and thoughts.

introversion (ĭn″trō-vĕr′shŭn) [″ + *versio*, a turning] **1.** Turning inside out of a part or organ. **2.** Preoccupation with oneself.

introvert (ĭn′trō-vĕrt) **1.** A personality-reaction type characterized by withdrawal from reality, fantasy formation, and stress on the subjective side of life adjustments, seen pathologically in extreme form in schizophrenia. **2.** To turn one's psychic energy inward upon oneself.

intubate (ĭn′too-bāt″, ′tū-, ′tŭ-) [*in* + L. *tuba*, a tube] To insert a tube into a body part, e.g., into the larynx or trachea.

intubation (ĭn″too-bā′shŏn, tū-) The insertion of a tube into any hollow organ. Intubation of the trachea provides an open airway and thus is an essential step in advanced life support. It also permits the instillation of certain critical care drugs, such as lidocaine, epinephrine, and atropine, which the lungs can absorb directly when other forms of internal access are unavailable. In the patient with no evidence of head or cervical spine trauma, using a head-tilt, chin-lift maneuver to place the patient in a "sniffing" position facilitates intubation of the trachea. SEE: illus.

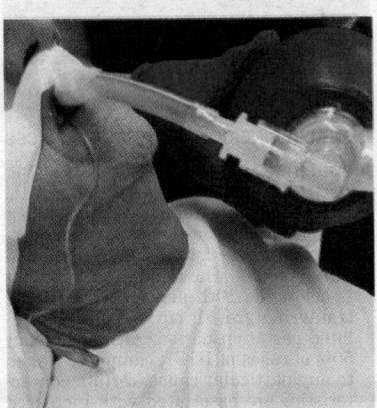

OROTRACHEAL INTUBATION

endotracheal tube with bag-mask ventilation

Intubation of other structures, such as the organs of the upper gastrointestinal tract, may permit enteral nutrition, the dilation of strictures, or the visualization of internal anatomy.

   endotracheal i. The insertion of an endotracheal tube through the nose or mouth into the trachea to maintain the airway, to administer an anesthetic gas or oxygen, or to aspirate secretions.

⚠️ Endotracheal intubation can be hazardous to patients with injuries to, or instability of, the cervical vertebra. In trauma patients suspected of cervical fracture, or in patients (such as those with advanced rheumatoid arthritis) who may have an unstable cervical spine, it is safer to use nasotracheal, rather than orotracheal intubation to control the airway.

esophageal i. The improper placement of an endotracheal tube, intended to provide a conduit for air to and from the lungs, into the esophagus. It is a common and potentially life-threatening occurrence during anesthesia and critical illnesses.

PATIENT CARE: Health care practitioners have several ways of recognizing esophageal intubation, including direct observation of the endotracheal tube, as it passes through the vocal cords, or capnography.

⚠️ Failure to recognize esophageal intubation can result in inadequate oxygenation of the patient.

nasogastric i. The insertion of a Levine or other gastrointestinal tube through the nose into the stomach. SEE: *gastric lavage; nasogastric tube.*

nasotracheal i. The insertion of an endotracheal tube through the nose and into the trachea. Unlike orotracheal intubation, the tube is passed "blindly" without using a laryngoscope to visualize the glottic opening. Because this technique may be used without hyperextension of the neck, it is used in patients suspected of having cervical spinal trauma or known to have oral lesions. Endotracheal tubes inserted nasally need to be of smaller diameter than those inserted orally.

⚠️ Endotracheal tubes frequently irritate the nasopharynx, and can cause both bleeding (on insertion), and sinusitis.

SEE: *endotracheal i.*
rapid sequence i. ABBR: RSI. An airway control technique that uses powerful sedatives and paralytic drugs to quickly gain control of the airway, e.g., in life-threatening emergencies.

stomach i. Passage of a tube into the stomach to obtain gastric contents for examination, for prophylaxis and treatment of ileus, to remove ingested poisons, or for feeding.
intubation tube Endotracheal tube.
intubator (ĭn′tū-bāt″or) A device for controlling, directing, and placing an intu-

bation tube within the trachea, blood vessel, or heart (as in Swan-Ganz catheter placement). SYN: *introducer.*
intuition (ĭn″too-ĭsh′ĭn, tū-) **1.** Assumed knowledge; guesswork; a hunch. **2.** Nonrational cognition.
intumesce (ĭn-tū-měs′) [L. *intumescere*] To enlarge or swell.
intumescence (ĭn″tū-měs′ĕns) **1.** A swelling. **2.** The process of enlarging. SYN: *tumefaction.*
intumescent (ĭn-tū-měs′ĕnt) Swelling or becoming enlarged.
intussusception (ĭn″tŭ-sŭ-sĕp′shŭn) [L. *intus*, within, + *suscipere*, to receive] The slipping of one part of an intestine into another part just below it; becoming ensheathed. Although it is an infrequent cause of bowel obstruction in adults, it is the most common cause in infants and usually occurs in the ileocecal region of the bowel. In some instances, the process may be reduced by low pressure contrast enema; ultimately, surgery may be necessary if the process recurs. Prognosis is good if surgery is performed immediately, but mortality is high if this condition is left untreated more than 24 hr.

PATIENT CARE: An early version of a rotavirus vaccine was linked to an increased frequency of intussusception in infants. This vaccine is no longer available in the U.S. SYN: *indigitation; introsusception; invagination.* SEE: *ileus.*
intussusceptum (ĭn″tŭ-sŭ-sĕp′tŭm) [L.] The inner segment of intestine that has been pushed into another segment.
intussuscipiens (ĭn″tŭ-sŭ-sĭp′ē-ĕns) [L.] The portion of intestine that receives the intussusceptum.
Inuit (ĭn′ū-ĭt) [Eskimo people] People native to Arctic America.
inulase (ĭn′ū-lās) An enzyme that converts inulin to levulose.
inulin (ĭn′ū-lĭn) A polysaccharide found in plants that yields fructose when hydrolyzed. It is used to study renal function.
inunction (ĭn-ŭngk′shŭn) [L. *in*, into, + *unguere*, to anoint] An ointment or medicated substance rubbed into the skin to secure a local or a more general systemic effect.
in utero (ĭn ū′tĕr-ō) [L.] Within the uterus.
in vacuo (ĭn văk′ū-ō) [L.] Within a cavity or a space from which air has been exhausted.
invaginate (ĭn-văj′ĭn-āt) [L. *invaginatio*] **1.** To ensheath. **2.** To insert one part of a structure within a part of the same structure. **3.** In embryology, to grow in or from an ingrowth or inpocketing, esp. the ingrowth of the wall of the blastula, which results in the formation of the gastrula.
invaginated (ĭn-văj′ĭ-nāt″ĕd) Enclosed in a sheath; ensheathed.

invagination (ĭn-văj″ĭ-nā′shŭn) Intussusception.

invalid (ĭn′vă-lĭd) [L. *in-*, not, + *validus*, strong] **1.** A former term for a person who is not well; weak. Use of the term is archaic. **2.** Based on false premises, reasonings, or justifications.

invasion [L. *in*, into, + *vadere*, to go] The penetration of body tissues by infectious organisms or malignant cells.

invasive (in-vā′siv, ′ziv) [L. *invasivus*] **1.** Tending to spread, esp. the tendency of a malignant process or growth to spread into healthy tissue. **2.** Pert. to an incision, penetration, or puncture of the body or one of its parts, e.g., during a procedure.

inventory (ĭn′vĭn-tŏr″ē) Any list of items, esp. items to describe an individual's personality.

invermination (ĭn-vĕr″mĭn-ā′shŭn) [″ + *vermis*, worm] Infestation by intestinal worms.

inversion (ĭn-vĕr′zhŭn) [L. *inversio*, to turn inward] **1.** The reversal of a normal relationship. **2.** A turning inside out of an organ (e.g., the uterus). **3.** In chemistry, the process of converting sucrose (which rotates the plane of polarized light to the right) into a mixture of dextrose and levulose (which rotates the plane to the left). The resulting mixture is called invert sugar, and the enzyme that catalyzes this conversion is called invertase. SEE: *enzyme*. **4.** Turning inward (e.g., medial distortion or injury of the ankle joint).

    T-wave i. In electrocardiography, the changing of the normal upright (convex) appearance of the ventricular repolarization to a concave tracing in which the concavity is depressed below the isoelectric line. T-wave inversion is often associated with ventricular hypertrophy, ventricular ectopic beats, and coronary ischemia, among other conditions.

    uterine i. A condition that may occur during the third stage of labor in which a relaxed uterus is turned inside out, causing the internal surface to protrude into the vagina. Uterine inversion most commonly is caused by traction on an umbilical cord attached to a yet-adherent placenta or to application of forceful fundal pressure to empty the uterus. It is accompanied by profound maternal blood loss if normal anatomical position is not restored immediately. Inversion also can occur during the fourth stage of labor if forceful fundal massage is applied to an uncontracted uterus without support of the lower uterine segment.

inversion injury of the ankle Injury to the ankle joint when weight is suddenly forced onto the lateral surface of the heel and foot.

invert (ĭn-vĕrt′) **1.** To turn inside out or upside down. **2.** To bend the foot in at

the ankle so that the sole is facing toward the inside of the leg.

invertase (ĭn-vĕr′tās) Sucrase.

invertebrate (ĭn-vĕr′tĕ-brāt) [L. *in-*, not, + *vertebratus*, vertebrate] **1.** Without a notochord. **2.** Species of animals that do not have a notochord, i.e., animals not of the phylum Chordata.

invertin (ĭn-vĕr′tĭn) Sucrase.

invertor (ĭn-vĕr′tor) A muscle that rotates a part inward.

investigational Undergoing active study in a clinical trial or another form of systematic research. The term is used to describe drugs, devices, vaccines, or other treatments that are currently being studied, but not yet approved for general clinical use.

investing [L. *in*, into, + *vestire*, to clothe] **1.** Ensheathing, encircling with a sheath or coating, as tissue; surrounding. **2.** In dentistry, the complete or partial covering of an object (e.g., a tooth, denture, wax form, or crown) with a suitable material before processing, soldering, or casting.

investment A covering or sheath.

    dental casting i. A material combining principally a form of silica and a bonding agent. The bonding substance may be gypsum or silica phosphate according to the casting temperature.

inveterate (ĭn-vĕt′ĕ-răt) [″ + *vetus*, old] Chronic; firmly seated, as a disease or a habit.

in vitro (ĭn vē′trō″) [L., in glass] In glass, i.e., a test tube. An in vitro test is one done in the laboratory, usually involving isolated tissue, organ, or cell preparations. SEE: *in vivo*.

in vivo (ĭn vē′vō) [L., in the living body] In the living body or organism. An in vivo test is one performed on a living organism. SEE: *in vitro*.

involucre, involucrum (ĭn′vō-lū″kĕr, ĭn″vō-lū′krŭm) [″ + *volvere*, to wrap] **1.** A sheath or covering. **2.** The covering of newly formed bone enveloping the sequestrum in infection of the bone.

involuntary (ĭn″vol′ŭn-ter″ē) [²*in-* + *voluntary*] **1.** Independent of or contrary to volition. **2.** Occurring as a result of a reflex. **involuntarily** (ĭn″vol-ŭn-ter′ĭ-lē), *adv.*

involution (ĭn″vŏ-loo′shŏn) [L. *involvere*, to roll up, wrap] **1.** A turning or rolling inward. **2.** The reduction in size of the uterus after childbirth. **3.** The retrogressive change in vital processes after their functions have been fulfilled, such as the change that follows the menopause. **4.** A backward change. **5.** The diminishing of an organ in vital power or in size. **6.** In bacteriology, digression from the usual morphological type such as occurs in certain bacteria, esp. when grown under unfavorable conditions; degeneration.

i. of uterus The return of the uterus to normal size after childbirth.

senile i. The atrophy of an organ as a result of the aging process.

involutional (ĭn-vō-lū'shŭn-ăl) Concerning involution or a turning inward.

involved-field radiation therapy SEE: under *radiation therapy*.

IO *Interosseous; intraoperative.*

Iodamoeba (ī'ō-dă-mē'bă) A genus of amebae that colonizes the colons of humans and animals such as monkeys and pigs. They are not considered pathogenic.

I. bütschlii The species that may be found in humans. Their cysts may be mistaken for those of pathogenic amebae but have only one nucleus.

iodide (ī'ō-dīd) A compound of iodine containing another radical or element, as potassium iodide.

cesium i. A phosphor used in radiographical image intensifiers that emits light when struck by radiation.

iodinate (ī'ŭ-dĭ-nāt') To combine with iodine.

iodinated I 131 albumin injection SEE: under *injection*.

iodine (ī'ō-dīn", -dēn") [Gr. *ioeidēs*, violet-colored + *-ine*] SYMB: I. A nonmetallic chemical element of the halogen group, atomic weight (mass) 126.904, atomic number 53, specific gravity (solid, 20°C) 4.93. It is a black crystalline substance with a melting point of 113.5°C; it boils at 184.4°C, giving off a characteristic violet vapor. Sources of iodine include vegetables, esp. those growing near the seacoast; iodized salt; and seafoods, esp. liver of halibut and cod, or fish liver oils.

FUNCTION: Iodine is part of the hormones triiodothyronine (T_3) and thyroxine (T_4), and prevents goiter by enabling the thyroid gland to function normally. The amount of iodine in the entire body averages 50 mg, of which 10 to 15 mg is found in the thyroid. The adult daily requirement for iodine is from 100 to 150 μg. Growing children, adolescents, pregnant women, and those under emotional strain need more than this amount of iodine.

DEFICIENCY SYMPTOMS: Iodine deficiency in the diet may lead to simple goiter characterized by thyroid enlargement and hypothyroidism. In young children, this deficiency may result in retardation of physical, sexual, and mental development, a condition called cretinism.

i.-131 SYMB: [131]I. SEE: *radioactive i.*

protein-bound i. ABBR: PBI. Iodine that is attached to serum protein. In the past, thyroid function was tested with a serum measurement of PBI.

radioactive i. Any of the radioactive isotopes of iodine, esp. iodine-131, used in diagnosis and treatment of thyroid

disorders and in the treatment of toxic goiter and thyroid carcinoma. SEE: *radioiodine*.

tincture of i. SEE: under *tincture*.

iodine poisoning SEE: under *poisoning*.

iodipamide sodium I 131 Radioactive chemical used in examining body organs and cavities.

iodize (ī'ō-dīz) To administer or impregnate with iodine, most commonly as a fortification of salt.

iododerma (ī-ō″dō-dĕr'mă) [″ + *derma*, skin] Dermatitis due to iodine.

iodoform (ī-ō'dō-form) [Gr. *ioeides*, violet colored, + L. *forma*, form] CHI$_3$; a yellow crystalline substance with a disagreeable odor, produced by the action of iodine on acetone in the presence of an alkali. Used topically, it has mild antibacterial action.

iodoglobulin (ī″ō-dō-glŏb'ū-lĭn) [″ + L. *globus*, globe] A globulin that contains iodine.

iodohippurate sodium I 131 injection (ī-ō″dō-hip'yŭ-rāt″) SEE: under *injection*.

iodophilia (ī-ōd″ă-fĭl'ē-ă) [″ + *philein*, to love] A condition in which certain cells, esp. polymorphonuclear leukocytes, when stained, show a pronounced affinity for iodine. These cells turn a brownish-red color. It is seen in pathologic conditions such as acute infections and anemia.

extracellular i. Iodophilia in which substances in the plasma outside the cells are colored.

intracellular i. Iodophilia in which color changes occur within the cells.

iodophor (ī-ō'dō-for) A combination of iodine and a solubilizing agent or carrier that liberates free iodine in solution. Some forms are used as general antiseptics; they are less irritating than elemental forms of iodine. SEE: *povidone-iodine*.

iodopsin (ī″ō-dŏp'sĭn) In cones of the retina, the photopsin molecule and retinal, the functional photopigment.

IOL *intraocular lens.*

IOM *Institute of Medicine.*

IOML *infraorbitomeatal line.*

ion (ī'on″) [Gr. *iōn, iont-*, going] An atom or group of atoms that has lost one or more electrons and has a positive charge, or has gained one or more electrons and has a negative charge. In aqueous solutions, ions are called electrolytes because they permit the solution to conduct electricity. Positive ions such as sodium, potassium, magnesium, and calcium are called cations; negative ions such as chloride, bicarbonate, and sulfate are called anions. In body fluids, ions are available for reactions (e.g., calcium ions from food may be combined with carbonate ions to form calcium carbonate, part of bone matrix). SEE: *electrolyte* for table.

Ions occur in gases, esp. at low pressures, under the influence of strong electrical discharges, x-rays, and radium; and in solutions of acids, bases, and salts.

dipolar i. An ion that contains both positive and negative charges.

hydrogen i. A hydrogen atom that has lost an electron. It has a positive charge, and its symbol is H^+. In aqueous solution (i.e., water) it represents an acid.

hydronium i. H_3O^+, a hydrated hydrogen ion. It is formed when an acid dissolves in water.

ion channel disease A group of diseases marked clinically by muscular weakness, absent muscle tone, or episodic muscular paralysis. The diseases are caused by congenital defects in the cell membrane proteins that move ions into and out of the cell. These defects alter the cells' resting potential, action potential, or both, and make them "fire" ineffectively.

ion-exchange resins SEE: under *resin.*

ionic (ī-ŏn′ĭk) [Gr. *ion,* going] Pert. to ions.

ionization (ī-ō-nĭ-zā′shŭn) The process of adding or subtracting an electron from an atom. In radiology, ionization is the most common cause of radiobiological damage.

ionize (ī′ŏ-nīz″) To separate into ions.

IONM *Intraoperative neurophysiological monitoring.*

ionogen (ī-ŏn′ō-jĕn) [Gr. *ion,* going, + *gennan,* to produce] Anything that can be ionized.

ionophore (ī-ŏn′ă-fawr″) A compound that binds and carries metallic ions across cellular membranes.

ionotropic (ī″ŏn-ŏ-trō′pĭk) [″ + ″] Having an influence on glutamate-gated cell surface receptors, i.e., on cell membrane channels that open or close in the presence of ions.

iontophoresis (ī″ont″ŏ-fĕ-rē′sĭs) [Gr. *īŏn, iont-,* going + *-phoresis*] **1.** The introduction of an electric current into a salt solution, causing migration of the metal (positive) ion to the negative pole and the radical (negative) ion to the positive pole. **2.** The introduction of various ions into tissues through the skin by means of electricity. SYN: *ionic medication; ionotherapy; iontotherapy.* SEE: *electrical patch.*

pilocarpine i. Sweat test.

IOP *intraocular pressure.*

iopanoic acid (ī″ō-pă-nō′ĭk) SEE: under *acid.*

iophendylate (ī″ō-fĕn′dĭ-lāt) A radiopaque contrast medium used in myelography.

IOQPTH *intraoperative quick assay of intact parathyroid hormone.*

iotacism (ī-ō′tă-sĭzm) [Gr. *iota,* letter i] An abnormal speech pattern marked by the constant substitution of an ē sound (Greek iota) for other vowels.

IP *intraperitoneal; isoelectric point.*

IPA *independent practice association.*

IPAP *inspiratory positive airway pressure.*

ipecac (ĭp′ē-kăk) A drug that induces vomiting. For many years, it was used to help empty the upper gastrointestinal tract after toxic ingestions and accidental overdoses. It no longer is used for this purpose in hospitals, where activated charcoal and whole bowel irrigation have proved to be more effective and better tolerated. The drug is derived from the dried root of ipecacuanha, a plant that is native to Brazil. It typically is given as a syrup. SEE: *Poisons and Poisoning Appendix.*

IPL *interpupillary line;* the line between the center of both pupils.

ipodate sodium A radiopaque contrast medium used in radiographical studies of the gallbladder.

IPPB *intermittent positive-pressure breathing.*

IPPV *intermittent positive-pressure ventilation.*

ipratropium bromide An anticholinergic bronchodilator used for bronchoconstriction associated with chronic bronchitis, chronic obstructive pulmonary disease, asthma, and emphysema. It is dispensed via a metered-dose inhaler or as a solution for nebulized use, and usually is combined with another bronchodilator such as albuterol. SEE: *asthma.*

ipriflavone (ī″prĭ-flā′vŏn) A dietary supplement, 7-isopropoxyisoflavone, synthesized from the soy protein isoflavone daidzein. It is promoted as a treatment for osteoporosis.

ipsi- [L. *ipse,* same] Prefix meaning *same* or *self.*

IPSID *immunoproliferative small intestinal disease.*

ipsilateral (ĭp″sĭ-lăt′ĕr-ăl) [″ + *latus,* side] On the same side; affecting the same side of the body; the opposite of contralateral. For example, when the right patellar tendon is tapped, an ipsilateral knee-jerk is observed on the same side. In paralysis, this term is used to describe findings appearing on same side of the body as the brain or spinal cord lesion producing them. SYN: *homolateral.*

IPSP *inhibitory postsynaptic potential.*

IPV *Intimate partner* **violence.**

IQ *intelligence quotient.*

IR *infrared; internal resistance; internal rotation.*

Ir Symbol for the element iridium.

irascible (ĭ-răs′ĭ-b′l) [LL. *irascibilis*] Marked by outbursts of temper or irritability; easily angered.

I : E ratio In respiratory therapy or mechanical ventilation, the ratio of a patient's inspiratory to expiratory time.

IRB *Institutional review board.*

irid-, irido- [Gr. *iris,* stem *irid-,* rainbow, iris] Prefixes meaning the *iris* (of the eye).

iridal (ĭr'ĭd-ăl) Iridic.

iridalgia (ĭr"ĭd-ăl'jă) [" + *algos,* pain] Pain felt in the iris.

iridectome (ĭr"ĭ-děk'tōm) [" + *tome,* incision] An instrument for cutting the iris in iridectomy.

iridectomize (ĭr"ĭd-ĕk'tō-mīz) [" + *ektome,* excision] To excise a portion of the iris.

iridectomy (ĭr"ĭ-dek'tŏ-mē) [*irid-* + *-ectomy*] The surgical removal of a portion of the iris. SYN: *corectomy.*

> **peripheral i.** Removal of peripheral tissue from the iris.

> **sector i.** The removal of a wedge-shaped section of the iris (e.g., as a treatment for a local melanoma or a vascular tumor).

iridectropium (ĭr-ĭ-děk-trō'pē-ŭm) [" + *ektrope,* a turning aside] Partial eversion of the iris.

iridemia (ĭr-ĭ-dē'mē-ă) [" + *haima,* blood] Bleeding from the iris.

iridencleisis (ĭr"ĭ-děn-klī'sĭs) [" + *enklein,* to lock in] An operation for relieving increased intraocular pressure, as in glaucoma, in which the iris and a portion of the limbus are excised to allow increased volume of the aqueous humor under the conjunctiva.

iridentropium (ĭr"ĭ-děn-trō'pē-ŭm) [" + *en,* in, + *tropein,* to turn] Partial inversion of the iris.

irides (ĭr'ĭ-dēz") [Gr.] Pl. of iris.

iridescence (ĭr"ĭ-děs'ĕns) [L. *iridescere,* to gleam like a rainbow] Having the capability to disperse light into the colors of the spectrum.

iridesis (ĭ-rĭd'ĕ-sĭs) [" + *desis,* a binding] Repositioning the pupil by bringing a portion of the iris through an incision in the cornea.

iridic (ĭ-rĭd'ĭk) [Gr. *iris,* colored circle] Relating to the iris. SYN: *iridal; iritic.*

iridium (ir-id'ē-ŭm) [Gr. *iris,* rainbow, halo, iris + *-ium*] SYMB: Ir. A white, hard metallic element, atomic weight (mass) 192.2, atomic number 77.

> **i.-192** SYMB: ¹⁹²Ir. A radioactive isotope of iridium, half-life 73.8 days. It is commonly used in brachytherapy oncology procedures.

iridocele (ĭ-rĭd'ō-sēl) [" + *kele,* tumor, swelling] Protrusion of a portion of the iris through a defect in the cornea.

iridocyclectomy (ĭr"ĭ-dō-sī-klĕk'tō-mē) [" + *kyklos,* circle, + *ektome,* excision] Surgical removal of the iris and ciliary body.

iridocyclitis (ĭr"ĭ-dō-sī-klīt'ĭs, ĭr") [*irid-* + *cyclo-* + *-itis*] An inflammation of the iris and ciliary body.

> **heterochromic i.** A low grade, unilateral inflammation of the ciliary body and iris, lighter in color than the unaffected eye. A secondary cataract and/or glaucoma may develop SYN: *Fuchs heterochromic i.*

iridocyclochoroiditis (ĭr"ĭ-dō-sī"klō-kō"roy-dī'tĭs) [" + " + *chorioeides,* skinlike, + *itis,* inflammation] An inflammation of the iris, ciliary body, and choroid of the eye.

iridocystectomy (ĭr"ĭ-dō-sĭs-tĕk'tō-mē) [" + *kystis,* bladder, + *ektome,* excision] Surgical removal of a cyst from the iris.

iridodenesis Wobbling of the iris during eye movement.

iridodesis (ĭr-ĭ-dŏd'ĕ-sĭs) [" + *desis,* a binding] Wobbling movements of the iris. SEE: *iridesis.*

iridodiagnosis (ĭr"ĭ-dō-dī"ăg-nō'sĭs) [" + *dia,* through, + *gnosis,* knowledge] Diagnosis of disease by examination of the iris.

iridodialysis (ĭr"ĭd-ō-dī-ăl'ĭ-sĭs) [" + *dialysis,* loosening] Separation of the outer margin of the iris from its ciliary attachment.

iridodilator (ĭr"ĭ-dō-dī-lā'tor) [" + L. *dilatare,* to dilate] A substance causing dilatation of the pupil.

iridodonesis (ĭr"ĭd-ō-dō-nē'sĭs) [" + *donesis,* tremor] Hippus.

iridokeratitis (ĭr"ĭ-dō-kĕr"ă-tī'tĭs) [" + *keras,* horn, + *itis,* inflammation] An inflammation of the iris and cornea.

iridoleptynsis (ĭr"ĭ-dō-lĕp-tĭn'sĭs) [" + *leptynsis,* attenuation] Thinning or atrophy of the iris.

iridology (ĭr"ĭ-dol'ŏ-jē) [*irid-* + *-logy*] In alternative medicine, a diagnostic method of indicating disease by the variations in the color, morphology, or other characteristics of the iris.

iridoparalysis (ĭr"ĭ-dō-pă-răl'ĭ-sĭs) [" + *paralyein,* to disable] Iridoplegia.

iridopathy (ĭr"ĭ-dŏp'ă-thē) [" + *pathos,* disease, suffering] Disease of the iris.

iridoperiphacitis, iridoperiphakitis (ĭr"ĭ-dō-pĕr"ĭ-fă-sī'tĭs, -pĕr"ĭ-fă-kī'tĭs) [" + *peri,* around, + *phakos,* lens, + *itis,* inflammation] An inflammation of the iris and anterior portion of the capsule of the lens.

iridoplegia (ĭr"ĭ-dō-plē'j(ē-)ă, ĭr") [*irid-* + *-plegia*] Paralysis of the sphincter of the iris. SYN: *iridoparalysis.*

> **accommodative i.** Noncontraction of the pupils during accommodation.

> **complete i.** Iridoplegia in which the iris fails to respond to any stimulation; seen in Adie's pupil.

> **reflex i.** The absence of light reflex, with retention of the accommodation reflex (Argyll Robertson pupil).

iridopupillary (ĭr"ĭ-dō-pū'pĭ-lĕr"ē) [" + L. *pupilla,* pupil] Concerning the iris and the pupil of the eye.

iridoschisis (ĭr"ĭ-dŏs'kĭ-sĭs) [" + *schisis,* a splitting] Separation of the stroma of the iris into two layers with disintegration of the anterior layer.

iridotomy (ĭr-ĭ-dŏt′ō-mē) [″ + *tome,* incision] A puncture made through the iris without removing any iris tissue, done for the purpose of making a new aperture in the iris when the pupil is closed. This allows free drainage of aqueous from the anterior to posterior chamber in narrow angles, chronic angle closure glaucoma, pupillary block, and aqueous misdirection syndrome SYN: *iritomy; irotomy.*

IRIS An abbreviation for *immune reconstitution inflammatory syndrome,* a temporary clinical deterioration of a patient with HIV/AIDS occurring after the initiation of effective treatment with highly active antiretroviral therapy (HAART).

iris (ī′rĭs) [Gr.] The opaque, pigmented continuation of the choroid layer of the eye that partly covers the lens, surrounding the pupil and regulating the amount of light that strikes the retina. The iris lies in the aqueous compartment of the eye. It divides the posterior chamber of the aqueous compartment (into which aqueous fluid is secreted) and the anterior chamber (from which aqueous fluid is absorbed). Muscles in the iris can expand or contract the pupil. SEE: *aniridia; choroidoiritis; heterochromia iridis; irid-; iris, chromatic asymmetry of; rubeosis iridis.*

ANATOMY: Its front surface is irregular, covered in grooves and ridges. The posterior surface contains radially oriented myofilaments, which together form the dilator pupillae muscle; this muscle widens the pupil in response to sympathetic stimulation. A separate set of concentric myofilaments forming circles around the pupil compose the sphincter pupillae muscle, which narrows the pupil in response to parasympathetic stimulation. The color of the iris is determined by the concentration of melanin-containing pigment cells: if the cells are few, the color will be blue, while increasing concentrations of pigment cells lead to darkening color on a spectrum from greenish-blue, to gray, to brown.

    i. bombé A condition seen in annular posterior synechia. The iris balloons forward from the posterior pressure, blocking the aqueous outflow through the anterior chamber angle.

    It can be caused by adhesions at the pupillary border and the anterior lens capsule, resulting in aqueous misdirection and significantly elevated intraocular pressure. Treatment is peripheral iridectomy.

    chromatic asymmetry of i. A difference in color between the two irides (heterochromia). For example, one may be blue or gray and the other brown. The asymmetry may occur in early iritis or cyclitis, or may be present without an associated pathological process.

    piebald i. A dark discoloration in an irregularly shaped area. It may be in one or both eyes.

iris prolapse SEE: under *prolapse.*

iritic (ī-rĭt′ĭk) [Gr. *iris,* colored circle] Iridic.

iritis (ī-rĭt′ĭs) [*iris* + *-itis*] An inflammation of the iris.

SYMPTOMS: In iritis, there is pain, photophobia, lacrimation, and diminution of vision. The iris appears swollen, dull, and muddy; the pupil contracted, irregular, and sluggish in reaction.

Iritis may be secondary to systemic disease such as ulcerative colitis, Crohn's disease, collagen vascular disease, sarcoid, infectious agents, or HLA-B27.

TREATMENT: Steroids are used topically and occasionally systemically. Mydriatic or cycloplegic drugs are used for symptomatic relief. Cortisone or hydrocortisone is used systemically as well as topically. If the primary disease causing the iritis is known, it should be treated; however, the etiological factor is usually not known.

  ⚠ Ophthalmic corticosteroids should be prescribed only by an ophthalmologist or other physician skilled in their use and side effects.

---

    plastic i. Iritis in which the fibrinous exudate forms new tissue.

    purulent i. Iritis with a purulent exudate.

    secondary i. Iritis in which the inflammation has spread from neighboring parts, as in diseases of the cornea and sclera.

    serous i. Iritis in which serum forms the exudate.

iron (ī′ĕrn) SYMB: Fe. A metallic chemical element widely distributed in nature, atomic weight (mass) 55.847, atomic number 26. Compounds (oxides, hydroxides, salts) exist in two forms: ferrous, in which iron has a valence of two (Fe^{++}), and ferric, in which it has a valence of three (Fe^{+++}). Iron is widely used to treat forms of anemia, is essential for the formation of chlorophyll in plants although it is not a constituent of chlorophyll, and is part of the hemoglobin and myoglobin molecules. SYN: *ferrum.* SEE: *ferritin.*

FUNCTION: Iron, as part of hemoglobin, is essential for the transport of oxygen in the blood; it is also part of some of the enzymes needed for cell respiration. Men's bodies have approx. 3.45 g of iron and women approx. 2.45 g, distributed as follows: 60% to 70% in hemoglobin; 10% to 12% in myoglobin and enzymes; and, as ferritin, 29% in men and

10% in women, stored in the liver, spleen, and bone marrow. Iron is stored in the tissues principally as ferritin. It is absorbed from the food in the small intestine and passes, in the blood, to the bone marrow. There it is used in making hemoglobin, which is incorporated into red blood cells. A red cell, after circulating in the blood for approx. 120 days, is destroyed, and its iron is used over again.

Men require from 0.5 to 1.0 mg of iron a day. A woman of menstrual age requires about twice this amount. During pregnancy and lactation from 2 to 4 mg of iron per day is required. Before puberty and after menopause, women require no more iron than men. Because only a fraction of the iron present in food is absorbed, it is necessary to provide from 15 to 30 mg of iron in the diet to be certain that 1 to 4 mg will be absorbed.

In the first few months of life, infants will use up most of their iron stores, and the typical diet or formula may not have sufficient iron to replenish those stores. It is therefore important to add iron-containing foods to an infant's diet by age 6 months.

Manganese, copper, and cobalt are necessary for the proper use of iron. Copper is stored in the body and reused repeatedly.

There are two broad types of dietary iron. About 90% of iron from food is in the form of iron salts and is called non-heme iron, which is poorly absorbed. The other 10% of dietary iron is in the form of heme iron, which is derived primarily from the hemoglobin and myoglobin of meat and is well absorbed. Iron absorption is influenced by other dietary factors. About 50% of iron from breast milk is absorbed but only about 10% of iron in whole cow's milk is absorbed. The reasons for the higher bioavailability of iron in breast milk are unknown. Ascorbic acid, meat, fish, and poultry enhance absorption of nonheme iron. Bran, oxalates, vegetable fiber, tannins in tea, and phosphates inhibit absorption of iron. Orange juice doubles the absorption of iron from the meal and tea decreases it by 75%.

DEFICIENCY SYMPTOMS: Iron deficiency is characterized by anemia, lowered vitality, exertional breathlessness, pale complexion, conjunctival pallor, retarded development, and a decreased amount of hemoglobin in each red cell.

NOTE: Sometimes a disturbance in iron metabolism occurs, in which an iron-containing pigment, hemosiderin, and hemofuscin are deposited in the tissues, leading to hemochromatosis. Excessive deposition of hemosiderin in the tissues, such as may occur as a result of excessive breakdown of red cells, is

called hemosiderosis. SEE: *hemochromatosis*.

SOURCES: The following foods provide iron in the diet: almonds, asparagus, bran, beans, Boston brown bread, cauliflower, celery, chard, dandelions, egg yolk, graham bread, kidney, lettuce, liver, oatmeal, oysters, soybeans, and whole wheat. Other good sources are apricots, beets, beef, cabbage, cornmeal, cucumbers, currants, dates, duck, goose, greens, lamb, molasses, mushrooms, oranges, parsnips, peanuts, peas, peppers, potatoes, prunes, radishes, raisins, rhubarb, pineapple, tomatoes, and turnips.

i. (II) sulfate Ferrous **sulfate**.

iron dextran injection SEE: under *injection*.

iron overload SEE: under *overload*.

iron poisoning SEE: under *poisoning*.

iron storage disease Hemochromatosis.

irradiate (ĭ-rā′dē-āt) [L. *in*, into, + *radiare*, to emit rays] **1.** To expose to radiation. **2.** To treat with high-energy x-rays or other forms of radiation. SEE: *irradiation*.

irradiating (ĭ-rā′dē-āt″ĭng) Diverging or spreading out from a common center.

irradiation (i-rād″ē-ā′shŏn) **1.** The diagnostic or therapeutic application of x-ray photons, nuclear particles, high-speed electrons, ultraviolet rays, or other forms of radiation to a patient. **2.** The application of a form of radiation to an object or substance to give it therapeutic value or increase that which it already has. **3.** A phenomenon in which a bright object on a dark background appears larger than a dark object of the same size on a bright background. **4.** The spreading in all directions from a common center, e.g., nerve impulses, the sensation of pain.

food i. The preservation of foods with ionizing radiation. Radiation extends the shelf life of foods by decreasing the number of germs and insects present in them. The process is expensive and has met with considerable resistance from consumers.

interstitial i. Therapeutic irradiation by insertion into the tissues of capillary tubes or beads containing radon (a radioactive isotope). It may be temporary or permanent.

lymphoid i. Exposure of an organ recipient's lymphocytes to ionizing radiation before organ transplantation, in an effort to decrease the likelihood of rejection of the donor graft.

prophylactic cranial i. ABBR: PCI. Radiation therapy used to prevent cancers, e.g., small cell carcinoma of the lung, from metastasizing to the brain.

i. of reflexes The spreading of reflexes through the central nervous system whereby impulses entering the cord in one segment activate motor neurons located in many segments.

irrational (ĭr-răsh′ŭn-ăl) Contrary to what is reasonable or logical; used to describe ideas that are unprovable, unsound, or unwise.

irreducible (ĭr″rē-dū′sĭ-bl) [L. *in-*, not, + *re,* back, + *ducere,* to lead] Not capable of being reduced or made smaller, as a fracture or dislocation.

irreversible (ĭr″ē-vĕr′sĭ-bl) Impossible to reverse.

irrigate (ĭr′ĭ-gāt) [L. *in,* into, + *rigare,* to carry water] To wash out with a fluid.

irrigation (ĭr″ĭ-gā′shŏn) [L. *irrigatio,* watering] The cleansing of a canal or cavity by flushing with water or other fluids; the washing of a wound. The solutions used for cleansing should be sterile and, for comfort, have an approximate temperature slightly warmer than body temperature (100° to 115°F [37.8° to 46.1°C]). When irrigation is performed for bleeding, cold or iced irrigant may be used. SYN: *lavage.* SEE: *gastric lavage.*

  bladder i. Washing out the bladder to treat inflammation or infection or to keep a urinary catheter flowing. The irrigation may be intermittent or continuous. Normal saline is commonly used.
  PATIENT CARE: The necessary sterile equipment and the prescribed irrigant are assembled. The patient is covered with draping to preserve privacy and maintain antisepsis, and provided with information about how the procedure is done and what sensations will be experienced. A triple-lumen indwelling catheter is inserted into the urinary bladder via the urethra; placement is confirmed by the flow of urine, and the anchoring balloon inflated via its lumen. The prescribed volume of irrigant is instilled via the irrigation lumen; the catheter is clamped to allow the solution to remain in the bladder for the prescribed period of time; then the catheter is unclamped to allow the irrigant to flow out of the bladder via the drainage lumen by gravity into a collecting basin or closed drainage system. The irrigation is repeated the prescribed number of times. The character of the irrigation solution returned and the presence of any mucus, blood, or other material visible in the drainage is noted. The catheter is removed as per practitioner order. The time of the procedure, the type and volume of irrigant instilled, the type and volume of return, and the patient's response to the procedure are documented. If intermittent or continuous bladder irrigation is required, the catheter remains in place. Two large bags of irrigating fluid on a Y tubing are hung for continuous irrigation, with flow-rate controlled to maintain clear

drainage. Urine output is determined by subtracting the amount of irrigant instilled from the total drainage obtained.

⚠ Patients who receive high volumes of dilute fluids may absorb these irrigants and develop fluid overload or hyponatremia. To ensure patient safety, careful measurement of inputs and outputs and regular assessments of electrolytes, BUN, Cr, and oxygenation should be performed.

  colonic i. Flushing of the colon with water; an enema. SYN: *colonic lavage.*
  continuous bladder i. ABBR: CBI. A constant flow of normal saline (or other bladder irrigant) through a three-way urinary catheter to keep the catheter patent. It is typically used postoperatively following a transurethral resection of the prostate gland.
  PATIENT CARE: During CBI the volume of fluid infused and the volume returned is monitored and recorded.
  high-pressure i. Irrigation of a wound with sterile fluid at a pressure of 7.0 pounds per sq. inch.
  joint i. The flushing of a joint space with fluids to remove particles such as crystals or fragments of bone or cartilage. It may be used as a treatment for osteoarthritic joint pain.
  low-pressure i. Irrigation of a wound with sterile fluid at a pressure of 0.5 pounds per sq. inch.
  nasal i. Nasal **lavage.**
  oral i. Flushing of the mouth, teeth, and gums with fluids. This is done to remove plaque and to treat or prevent periodontal disease.
  whole bowel i. The administration of large volumes of a nonabsorbable fluid to remove potentially hazardous contents from the gastrointestinal tract. It is used to prepare some patients for bowel surgery and to decontaminate the gut after overdose.

irrigator (ĭr′ĭ-gāt-or) A device used to flush or wash a part or cavity with fluids.

irritability (ĭr″ĭt-ă-bĭl′ĭ-tē) [L. *irritabilitas*] **1.** Excitability. **2.** An ability to respond in a specific way to a change in environment, a property of all living tissue. **3.** A condition in which a person, organ, or a part responds excessively to a stimulus. **4.** A quick response to annoyance; impatience.

  muscular i. The normal response of muscle to a stimulus.
  nervous i. The response of a nerve to a stimulus.
  paradoxical i. An increase in the fussiness of a sick child when comforted by a parent. It is considered to be a

physical sign of meningitis or of recent child abuse.

irritable 1. Capable of reacting to a stimulus. **2.** Sensitive to stimuli.

irritable bowel syndrome ABBR: IBS. A condition marked by abdominal pain (often relieved by the passage of stool or gas); disturbances of evacuation (constipation, diarrhea, or alternating episodes of both); bloating and abdominal distention; and the passage of mucus in stools. These symptoms must be present despite the absence of anatomical, biochemical, or clinical evidence of active intestinal disease. The condition is common and found in as many as 15 to 25% of women in Western societies. Its prognosis is benign. It is not associated with weight loss, fevers, or intestinal bleeding. Patients are symptomatic during the day, but they do not have pain, bloating, distention, diarrhea, or other abdominal symptoms while sleeping. Women are typically affected more often than men; in some studies the ratio of women to men is 3:1.

ETIOLOGY: The symptoms of irritable bowel occur more often in patients who have had a history of physical or sexual abuse in childhood than in patients without such a history. Many studies have found a relationship between irritable bowel syndrome and a history of anxiety, psychological stress, or personality disorders. Physiologically, patients with IBS may have an increased or decreased rate of bowel motility.

TREATMENT: Management of IBS should begin by establishing a therapeutic relationship between clinician and client. Educating the patient about the benign nature of the illness and the excellent long-term prognosis may be helpful. Avoiding poorly tolerated ("trigger") foods may lessen symptoms. Foods that the patient has found to cause difficulties are eliminated (dairy products, beans, and some vegetables may cause symptoms). Specific symptoms can be alleviated by taking bulk-forming agents (e.g., psyllium) by mouth, by increasing one's intake of fluids, and by engaging in increased levels of physical exercise. Low doses of antidepressant medications are sometimes helpful. Alternative therapy, including psychotherapy, hypnotherapy, imagery, and biofeedback, alone or in combination, may be effective in some patients.

DIAGNOSIS: Young patients suspected of having IBS should undergo testing to exclude other illnesses; tests should include a careful physical examination, complete blood count, metabolic panel, assessment of thyroid and liver functions; estimated sedimentation rate; and stool testing for occult blood. Patients over age 45 should also have sigmoidoscopy to rule out structural or anatomical lesions of the colon.

    postinfectious irritable bowel syndrome Prolonged daily, and disabling diarrhea that follows an episode of gastroenteritis. SYN: *irritable colon; spastic colon.*

irritant An agent that stimulates or inflames cells or tissues.

irritation [L. *irritatio*] **1.** A reaction to a noxious or unpleasant stimulus. It is important to distinguish between irritation and sensitization. A substance in contact with the skin may cause no irritation when initially applied but can cause allergic sensitization that will not become obvious until the material is applied again. SEE: *allergen; sensitization.* **2.** An extreme reaction to pain or disease. **3.** A normal response to stimulus of a nerve or muscle.

irritative (ĭr′ĭ-tāt″ĭv) Pert. to that which causes irritation.

IRV *Inverse ratio* ***ventilation.***

ischemia (ĭs-kē′mē-ă) [Gr. *ischein,* to hold back + *-emia*] A temporary deficiency of blood flow to an organ or tissue. The deficiency may be caused by diminished blood flow either through a regional artery or throughout the circulation.

    bowel i. Abdominal **angina**.

    demand-induced i. Insufficient blood flow to meet the needs of the heart produced by tachycardia and relative hypotension rather than by flow-limiting blockages within the coronary arteries. Demand ischemia may occur in atrial fibrillation with a rapid ventricular response; in hypotension or hypovolemia; or in sepsis or the systemic inflammatory response syndrome.

    intestinal i. SEE: *abdominal* ***angina***.

    lower limb i. Ischemia to one or both legs due either to chronic arterial obstruction caused by atherosclerosis or to acute obstruction caused by embolism.

TREATMENT: Treatment depends on the obstruction's cause, location, and size. Mild chronic disease may be managed using supportive measures such as smoking cessation, hypertension control, and increased exercise. Medications that improve blood flow such as aspirin, pentoxifylline and cilostazol may improve symptoms in patients with intermittent claudication. Surgeries for arterial insufficiency in the limbs include arterectomy, balloon angioplasty, bypass grafting, and combinations of the above. Embolectomy, laser angioplasty, lumbar sympathectomy, patch grafting, stents, thromboendarterectomy, and thrombolytic therapy also may be required. Amputation becomes necessary with failure of reconstructive surgery or development of gangrene, persistent infection, or intractable pain.

PATIENT CARE: Patients with lower limb ischemia related to acute obstruction suffer severe to excruciating pain in the limb, leg pallor and coolness, and absence of palpable pulses below the arterial obstruction. Emergency intervention is required, using thrombolytic therapy, thromboendarterectomy, embolectomy, or other surgical intervention to restore circulation to the affected area. More gradual arterial occlusive disorders may be evidenced by intermittent claudication of the calves on exertion, reduced pulses in the ankles and feet, gradually increasing pallor, hair loss, coolness, pretrophic pain (heralding necrosis and ulceration), and, in the worst circumstances, gangrene of the extremity. Diagnosis is based largely on the patient's history and physical examination, followed by supportive diagnostic studies such as Doppler ultrasonography and plethysmography, and arteriography.

Patient teaching should include explanations of diagnostic tests and procedures and prescribed exercise and medication regimens, proper foot care, and smoking cessation programs. For patients undergoing surgery, fluid and electrolyte balance is assessed and the patient prepared emotionally and physically. Postoperatively, vital signs and circulation are monitored, comparing the operative to the unoperated limb for color, temperature, and pulses, and the patient is closely observed for hemorrhage (hypotension and tachycardia), chest pain, or other vascular complications. Early ambulation is encouraged. When ischemic limbs or digits need amputation, the stump is checked for drainage and the amount and color recorded. The stump is elevated based on the surgeon's or agency's protocol, and pain is carefully assessed and relieved, with phantom limb pain explained to the patient. Discharge teaching should include plans for rehabilitation (in a rehabilitation center or as an outpatient), signs to report that could indicate graft occlusion or occlusion at another site, desired and adverse effects related to any medications prescribed, and the importance of scheduled follow-up visits.

myocardial i. An inadequate supply of blood and oxygen to meet the metabolic demands of the heart muscle. SEE: *angina* pectoris; *atherosclerosis; coronary artery disease.*

vertebrobasilar i. Inadequate blood flow through the arteries that supply nutrients and oxygen to the structures at the base of the brain, esp. the brain stem and cerebellum. This can cause difficulties with balance, swallowing, or vision and may be a source of vertigo in some individuals, esp. older adults or those with atherosclerosis.

warm i. The absence of blood flow to a body part or organ intended for transplantation before its removal from a cadaveric donor.

ischia (ĭs′kē-ă) [L.] Pl. of ischium.

ischial (ĭs′kē-ăl) [Gr. *ischion*, hip] Pert. to the ischium.

ischialgia (ĭs″kē-ăl′jē-ă) [″ + *algos,* pain] Sciatica.

ischiatic (ĭs″kē-ăt′ĭk) [Gr. *ischion*, hip] Sciatic.

ischiatitis (ĭs″kē-ă-tī′tĭs) [″ + *itis,* inflammation] Sciatic nerve inflammation.

ischidrosis (ĭs″kĭ-drō′sĭs) [Gr. *ischein*, to hold back, + *hidrosis*, sweat] The suppression of perspiration.

ischio- [Gr. *ischion*, hip, hip joint] Prefix meaning *ischium.*

ischioanal (ĭs″kē-ō-ā′năl) [″ + L. *anus,* anus] Concerning the ischium and anus.

ischiocavernosus (ĭs″kē-ō-kă″vĕr-nō′sŭs) [″ + L. *cavernosus,* cavernous] A muscle extending from the ischium to the penis or clitoris and assisting in their erection.

ischiocele (ĭs′kē-ō-sēl) [″ + *kele,* tumor, swelling] A hernia through the sciatic notch.

ischiococcygeus (ĭs″kē-ō-kŏk-sĭj′ē-ŭs) [″ + *kokkyx,* coccyx] **1.** The coccygeus muscle. **2.** The posterior portion of the levator ani.

ischiodynia (ĭs″kē-ō-dĭn′ē-ă) [″ + *odyne,* pain] Pain in the ischium.

ischiofemoral (ĭs″kē-ō-fĕm′or-ăl) [″ + L. *femur,* thigh] Rel. to the ischium and femur.

ischiofibular (ĭs″kē-ō-fĭb′ū-lăr) [″ + L. *fibula,* pin] Rel. to the ischium and fibula.

ischioneuralgia (ĭs″kē-ō-nū-răl′jē-ă) [″ + *neuron,* nerve, + *algos,* pain] Sciatica.

ischionitis (ĭs″kē-ō-nī′tĭs) [″ + *itis,* inflammation] Inflammation of the tuberosity of the ischium.

ischiopubic (ĭs″kē-ō-pū′bĭk) [″ + L. *pubes,* the pubes] Rel. to the ischium and pubes.

ischiorectal (ĭs″kē-ō-rĕk′tăl) [″ + L. *rectus,* straight] Pert. to the ischium and rectum.

ischiosacral (ĭs″kē-ō-sā′krăl) [″ + L. *sacralis,* pert. to the sacrum] Concerning the ischium and sacrum.

ischium (ĭs′kē-ŭm) *pl.* **ischia** [Gr. *ischion,* hip] The lower, posterior portion of the innominate or hip bone. It is a separate bone at birth; it begins to fuse with the pubis by age 8; and it is fully fused with the pubis and ilium by 16 to 18 years of age.

ISCLT *International Society of Clinical Laboratory Technologists.*

iseikonia (ī″sī-kō′nē-ă) [Gr. *isos,* equal, + *eikon,* image] Isoiconia.

island [AS. *igland,* island] A structure

detached from surrounding tissues or characterized by difference in structure; an islet.

    blood i. The early collections of cells in the embryo that give rise to blood and blood-forming organs later in life.

    i. of Reil Insula (1).

islet (ī′lĕt) A tiny isolated mass of one kind of tissue within another type.

    i. of Langerhans Clusters of cells in the pancreas. They are of three types: alpha, beta, and delta cells. The alpha cells secrete glucagon, which raises the blood glucose level; the beta cells secrete insulin, which lowers it; and the delta cells secrete somatostatin, an inhibitor of growth hormone secretion. Destruction or impairment of function of the islets of Langerhans may result in diabetes or hypoglycemia. SYN: *islands of Langerhans; pancreatic islands.*

islet amyloid polypeptide ABBR: AIPP. Amylin

islet autoantibodies, islet cell antibodies ABBR: ICA. Antibodies formed against insulin, glutamic acid decarboxylase, or protein tyrosine phosphatase-like molecules. They are serum markers for type 1 diabetes mellitus (DM). Children whose parents have type 1 DM and who have these markers present in their serum have a high risk of developing type 1 DM.

-ism [L. fr. Gr. *-ismos, -isma,* noun suffix] Suffix meaning *condition* or *theory of; principle* or *method.*

ISO *International Organization for Standardization.*

iso-, is- [Gr. *isos,* equal] Prefixes meaning *equal.*

isoagglutination (ī″sō-ă-gloo″tĭ-nā′shŭn) [″ + L. *agglutinare,* to glue to] Agglutination of red blood cells by agglutinins from the blood of another member of the same species. SYN: *isohemagglutination.*

isoagglutinin (ī″sō-ă-glū′tĭn-ĭn) [″ + L. *agglutinare,* to glue to] An antibody in a serum that agglutinates the blood cells of those of the same species from which it is derived. SEE: *agglutinin; blood group; isohemagglutinin.*

isoagglutinogen (ī″sō-ă-glū-tĭn′ō-jĕn) Agglutinin.

isoantibody (ī″sō-ăn′tĭ-bŏd″ē) An antibody produced in response to an isoantigen.

isoantigen (ī″sō-ăn′tĭ-jĕn) [″ + L. *anti,* against, + *gennan,* to produce] A substance present in certain individuals that stimulates antibody production in other members of the same species but not in the donor, e.g., blood group isoantigens that are harmless to the donor but may produce severe antibody response in a recipient of a different blood group or type. SYN: *alloantigen.*

isobar (ī′sō-băr) [″ + *baros,* weight] **1.** A locus of equal pressure. When pressures are unequal, fluids and gases will flow from a high- to a low-pressure region. **2.** In chemistry, one of two or more chemical bodies having the same atomic weight but different atomic numbers.

isobaric (ī″sō-băr′ĭk) **1.** Pressure equal to that with which it is being compared. **2.** Specific gravity equal to that with which it is being compared. For example, an anesthetic solution used in spinal anesthesia, if isobaric, would have the same specific gravity as the spinal fluid.

isocaloric (ī″sō-kă-lō′rĭk) [″ + L. *calor,* heat] Containing the same number of calories as the food or diet with which it is being compared.

isocellular (ī″sō-sĕl′ū-lăr) [″ + L. *cellula,* cell] Composed of equal and similar cells.

isocenter (ī″sō-sent′ĕr) [*iso-* + *center*] In radiation oncology, the point through which the central beam of the radiation passes. SYN: *radiation i.*

    mechanical i. The point at which optical beams intersect

    radiation i. Isocenter.

isochromatic (ī″sō-krō-măt′ĭk) [″ + *chroma,* color] **1.** Having the same color. **2.** Of uniform color.

isochromatophil(e) (ī″sō-krō-măt′ō-fīl, -fĭl) [″ + ″ + *philein,* to love] Having the same affinity for a dye.

isochromosome (ī″sō-krō′mō-sōm) [″ + ″ + *soma,* body] A chromosome with arms that are morphologically identical and contain the same genetic loci. This is the result of the transverse rather than the longitudinal splitting of a chromosome.

isochronal (ī-sŏk′rō-năl) [″ + *chronos,* time] Acting in uniform time, or taking place at regular intervals.

isochronia (ī″sō-krō′nē-ă) [Gr. *isos,* equal, + *chronos,* time] **1.** The correspondence of events with respect to time. **2.** Occurring at the same time, rate, or frequency.

isocitrate dehydrogenase (ī″sō-cĭt′rāt dē″hī-drŏj′ĕn-ās) An enzyme that catalyzes the conversion of isocitric acid to α-ketoglutaric acid.

isocolloid (ī-sō-kŏl′oyd) [″ + *kollodes,* glutinous] A colloid having the same composition in every transformation.

isocoria (ī″sō-kō′rē-ă) [″ + *kore,* pupil] Equality of pupillary size. SEE: *anisocoria.*

isocortex (ī″sō-kor′tĕks) [″ + L. *cortex,* bark] Neocortex.

isocytosis (ī″sō-sī-tō′sĭs) [″ + *kytos,* cell, + *osis,* condition] Cells of equal size.

isocytotoxin (ī″sō-sī″tō-tŏk′sĭn) [″ + ″ + *toxikon,* poison] Cytotoxin destructive to homologous cells of the same species.

isodactylism (ī-sō-dăk′tĭl-ĭzm) [″ +

daktylos, finger] A condition of having fingers or toes of equal length.

isodiametric (ī″sō-dī-ă-mĕt′rĭk) [″ + *dia,* across, + *metron,* measure] Having equal diameters.

isodisomy A rare chromosomal defect in which a chromosome pair has two identical segments from one parent and no corresponding segment from the other parent.

isodontic (ī″sō-dŏn′tĭk) [″ + *odous,* tooth] Having teeth of equal size.

isodose (ī′sō-dōs) In radiology, equal doses of radiation received by different areas of the body.

 i. curve In radiation therapy, a graph on which the points plot areas or levels of equal radiation dose.

isodynamic (ī″sō-dī-năm′ĭk) [″ + *dynamis,* power] Having equal power.

isoechoic (ī″sō-ĕ-kō′ĭk) Producing ultrasound echoes equal to those of neighboring or of normal tissues.

isoelectric (ī″sō-ē-lĕk′trĭk) [″ + *elektron,* amber] Having equal electric potentials.

isoelectric focusing A method for separating proteins according to their surface charge by placing them in a gel with a pH gradient and subjecting them to an electrical current. The proteins stop migrating through the gel when they meet ampholytes with similar charges.

isoenergetic (ī″sō-ĕn″ĕr-jĕt′ĭk) [Gr. *isos,* equal, + *energeia,* energy] Showing equal force or activity.

isoenzyme (ī″sō-ĕn′zīm) [″ + *en,* in, + *zyme,* leaven] One of several forms in which an enzyme may exist. Although isoenzymes have similar catalytic qualities, they may be readily separated from each other. SYN: *isozyme.* SEE: *lactic dehydrogenase.*

isoflavone (ī″sō-flā′vō′n) A relatively weak estrogen-like compound. SEE: *phytoestrogen.*

isoflurophate (ī-sō-floo′rō-fāt) An anticholinesterase drug used in treating glaucoma as well as atony of the smooth muscle of the intestinal tract and urinary bladder.

isoform One of two or more proteins coded independently by different genes, which have identical or nearly identical structures and functions.

isogamete (ī″sō-găm′ēt) [″ + *gamete,* wife, *gametes,* husband] **1.** A cell that reproduces through conjugation or fusion with a similar cell. **2.** A gamete of the same size as the one with which it fuses or unites.

isogamy (ī-sŏg′ă-mē) [″ + *gamos,* marriage] Reproduction resulting from the conjugation of isogametes or identical cells.

isogeneic (ī″sō-jĕ-nē′ik) [Formed fr. *isogenic*] Syngeneic.

isogeneric (ī″sō-jĕ-nĕr′ĭk) [″ + L. *ge-*

nus, kind] Of the same kind; concerning or obtained from members of the same genus.

isogenesis (ī″sō-jĕn′ĕ-sĭs) [″ + *genesis,* generation, birth] A similarity in morphological development.

isogenic (ī″sō-je′nik) [*iso-* + *-genic*] Isologous.

isogenous group (ī″soj′ĕ-nŭs) [*iso-* + *-genous*] SEE: under *group.*

isograft (ī′sō-grăft) [″ + L. *graphium,* grafting shoot] A graft taken from another individual or animal of the same genotype as the recipient. SEE: *autograft.*

isohemagglutination (ī″sō-hēm″ă-gloot″ĭ-nā′shŭn) [″ + *haima,* blood, + L. *agglutinare,* to glue to] Isoagglutination.

isohemagglutinin (ī″sō-hēm″ă-gloot′ĭn-ĭn) [″ + *haima,* blood, + L. *agglutinare,* to glue to] The naturally occurring anti-A and anti-B antibodies against the antigens present on red blood cells. If incompatible blood is transfused, these antibodies destroy the recipient's red blood cells through agglutination and hemolysis. Patients with type A blood cannot receive blood from a donor with type B or AB blood, because they have anti-B antibodies. Patients with type B blood cannot receive type A or AB blood, because they have anti-A antibodies. Patients with type O blood cannot receive type A, B, or AB blood, because they have anti-A and anti-B antibodies. Type O patients have no A or B antigens and are called universal donors because they can donate blood to any of the other groups. Type AB patients are universal recipients because they lack both anti-A and anti-B antibodies, and thus can receive blood from donors with any blood type. SEE: *agglutinin; agglutinogen.*

isohemolysis (ī″sō-hē-mŏl′ĭ-sĭs) The destruction of red blood cells produced by an isolysin; the action of an isohemolysin. SEE: *hemolysis.*

isoiconia (ī″sō-ī-kō′nē-ă) [Gr. *isos,* equal, + *eikon,* image] Equality of both retinal images. SYN: *iseikonia.*

isoiconic (ī″sō-ī-kŏn′ĭk) Having equal retinal images.

isoimmunization (ī″sō-ĭm″ū-nĭ-zā′shŭn) [″ + L. *immunis,* safe] Active immunization of an individual against blood from an individual of the same species, esp. the production of anti-Rh antibodies by Rh-negative mothers against red fetal blood cell antigens. During maternal trauma, loss of pregnancy (abortion), or delivery, some of the infant's blood is transferred to the mother, stimulating antibody production. If a second child is Rh-positive, the mother's anti-Rh antibodies will cross the placenta and cause hemolytic disease of the newborn. SEE: *erythroblastosis fetalis.*

isokinetic (ī″sō-kĭ-net′ĭk) [*iso-* + *ki-*

netic] Pert. to muscular contractile force exerted at a fixed velocity against variable resistance.

isolate (ī′sō-lāt) [It. *isolato,* isolated] **1.** To separate or quarantine from contact with other persons, as during an infectious disease. **2.** In chemistry, to obtain a substance in pure form from the mixture or solution that contains it. **3.** An organism identified in pure form in a microbial culture.

isolated limb perfusion SEE: under *perfusion.*

isolation (ī′sō-lā′shŏn) **1.** Solitude, or the psychological discomfort that accompanies it. SEE: *loneliness.* **2.** The physical separation of those with certain infections (such as anthrax or tuberculosis) from other people to prevent or limit the transmission of disease. In contrast, quarantine applies to restriction on healthy contacts of an infectious agent. SEE: *incubation* for table; *infectious i.; protective i.; quarantine; Standard Precautions Appendix.*

PATIENT CARE: Standard precautions are used to care for all patients to prevent nosocomial infections and apply to contact with blood, body fluids, secretions and excretions (except sweat), nonintact skin, and mucous membranes. Transmission-based precautions (second-tier precautions) are used for patients known to be or suspected of being infected with a highly transmissible infection. The rules to be followed for achieving isolation are based on the mode of transmission of the particular organism: airborne, droplet, and contact. Thus, if the organism is spread by droplet (such as tuberculosis), then all items that come in contact with the patient's upper respiratory tract are isolated and destroyed or disinfected. Those in contact with the patient are also protected from droplet transmission by wearing protective barriers such as special masks (and, if necessary, gowns, caps, boots, and gloves), by careful and thorough hand hygiene, and by keeping the hands away from the nose and mouth to prevent transmission of infections. Most agencies use disposable equipment as much as possible in the care of an isolated patient. Contaminated disposables are double-bagged for safe disposal, usually by incineration. Contaminated linens and other nondisposable equipment are also double-bagged and marked "isolation," so that they will be properly decontaminated or disinfected on receipt by the laundry or supply service. Laboratory specimens also are double-bagged and marked with the particular type of isolation, so that personnel handle them appropriately. CDC recommendations and institutional procedure are followed for the specific type of isolation that is in effect.

The purpose of the isolation precautions is explained to the patient and family to decrease their fears and to increase their cooperation, and the family and other visitors are taught how to use and discard the required barriers and esp. how to thoroughly cleanse their hands. When an at-risk patient (such as an immunosuppressed patient) requires protection from others (reverse isolation), equipment brought to the patient's room is disposable or sterilized, and human contacts wear barriers that must be clean or sterile depending on the circumstances and protocol. After use, these items are handled in the agency's usual manner, with no special care necessary beyond those specified for the care of every patient.

3. The identification of a cell, a chemical, or a microorganism in purified form.

    airborne i. Any of the techniques used in addition to standard precautions to decrease transmission of infectious agents less than 5 μ in size or those attached to dust particles. SYN: *airborne precaution.*

PATIENT CARE: Patients are placed in a private room, preferably one with negative air pressure and between 6 and 12 changes of air each hour. Hospital workers should wear respirator masks when in the room. If transport is necessary, the patient should wear a surgical mask. Patients with diseases such as active tuberculosis, SARS, varicella, and measles are placed on airborne precautions.

    contact i. Any of the techniques used in addition to standard precautions that decrease the likelihood of infection by microorganisms transmitted through direct or indirect contact with the patient or patient care items, e.g., methicillin-resistant *Staphylococcus aureus* and *Clostridium difficile.* Patients placed on contact isolation should preferably have a private room, but patients may be placed with others infected with the same organism (patient cohort). Hospital workers must wear gloves when entering the room for any reason and gowns if close patient contact is required, e.g., when bathing or turning the patient or caring for wounds. Masks and eye shields are required only if there is a potential for splash or splatter of body fluids onto the face. Stethoscopes and other noncritical patient care equipment should be dedicated to single-patient or patient-cohort use. SYN: *contact precaution.*

PATIENT CARE: Patients with diarrhea caused by *Clostridium difficile,* hepatitis A, rotavirus, or multidrug-resistant organisms, with wounds infected with vancomycin-resistant enterococcus, or children infected with respiratory syncytial or parainfluenza virus should be placed on contact precautions. Infection with some viruses, such as varicella or adenovirus, require droplet or airborne precautions in addition to contact precautions. Caregivers should remove gloves and gown before leaving the patient's room, avoid contact with potentially contaminated items or environmental surfaces, and wash hands immediately with an antimicrobial agent or waterless antiseptic agent after touching patients placed on contact isolation status.

    denial and i. SEE: *denial and isolation.*

    droplet i. Any of the techniques that decrease transmission of organisms larger than 5 μ that are generated when an infected patient coughs, sneezes, or spits. SYN: *droplet* **precaution.**

    infectious i. An isolation technique that protects both health care personnel and patients from anyone who has or is suspected of having an infectious disease.

    protective i. Isolation in which a vulnerable patient is protected from potentially harmful microorganisms in the environment. This is particularly important in caring for immunodeficient patients, e.g., those who have received chemotherapy or organ transplants. SYN: *reverse i.*

    reverse i. Protective **i.**

    social i. Isolation felt by a person and perceived as a negative or threatening state imposed by others. SEE: *Nursing Diagnoses Appendix.*

isolation unit A hospital unit in which patients suffering from communicable diseases may be separated from other patients.

isolette Incubator (1).

isoleucine (ī″sō-lū′sēn) ABBR: ile. $C_6H_{13}NO_2$; an amino acid formed during hydrolysis of fibrin and other proteins. It is essential in the diet.

isologous (ī-sŏl′ō-gŭs) Genetically identical. In transplantations, being isologous (or isogenic) indicates the absence of any tissue incompatibility between the recipient of tissue and the tissue or organ itself. SYN: *isogenic; syngeneic.*

isomer (ī′sō-mĕr) [Gr. *isos*, equal, + *meros*, part] One of two or more chemical substances that have the same molecular formula but different chemical and physical properties owing to a different arrangement of the atoms in the molecule. Dextrose is an isomer of levulose. SEE: *polymer.*

isomerase (ī-sŏm′ĕr-ās) Any enzyme that catalyzes the isomerization of its substrate. For example, phosphoglucose isomerase interconverts glucose and fructose-6-phosphate. SEE: *isomerism.*

isomeric (ī″sō-mĕr′ĭk) Pert. to isomerism.

isomerism (ī-sŏm′ĕr-ĭzm) The state of being composed of compounds of the same number of atoms but having different atomic arrangements in the molecule. SEE: *metamerism; polymerism.*

isomerization (ī-sŏm″ĕr-ī-zā′shŭn) The conversion of one chemical substance to an isomer. SEE: *isomer; isomerism.*

isometric (ī″sō-me′trĭk) [*iso-* + Gr. *metrikos*, pert. to meter, measuring] **1.** Having equal dimensions. SEE: *isotonic* (2). **2.** Muscle contraction without associated joint movement.

isometropia (ī″sō-mĕ-trō′pē-ă) [″ + ″ + *ops,* eye] Same refraction of the two eyes.

isomorphism (ī-sō-mor′fĭzm) [″ + *morphe,* form, + *-ismos,* state of] A condition marked by possession of the same form.

isomorphous (ī″sō-mor′fŭs) Possessing the same shape.

isoniazid (ī″sō-nī′ă-zĭd) ABBR: INH. $C_6H_7N_3O$. An odorless compound occurring as colorless or white crystals or as a white crystalline powder. It is an antibacterial, used principally in treating tuberculosis. Side effects of its use include hepatitis and peripheral neuropathy. The antidote for isoniazid overdose is pyridoxine.

isopia (ī-sō′pē-ă) [″ + *ops,* vision] Equal vision in the eyes.

isoprene (ī′sō-prēn″) 2-methyl-1,3 butadiene. A volatile hydrocarbon produced naturally by plants and animals and used in industry to make synthetic rubber and many copolymers. In humans it is involved in mevalonate and therefore cholesterol synthesis. Industrial exposures to high levels of isoprenes are toxic and potentially carcinogenic.

isopropanol (ī″sō-prō′pă-nŏl) Isopropyl alcohol.

isoprostane (ī-sō-prŏs′tān″) Any compound similar to prostaglandin that can be used as a marker for tissue damage caused by oxygen-derived free radicals. It is measured in human blood through the use of immunoassay technique and may enhance the study of diseases caused by oxidative stress.

isopters (ī-sŏp′tĕrz) [″ + *opter,* observer] Lines on a chart of the field of vision that connect points of equal visual acuity.

Isoptin SEE: *verapamil.*

isopyknosis (ī″sō-pĭk-nō′sĭs) [″ + *pyknosis,* condensation] Having uniform density, esp. being in a state of equal condensation, as in comparing different chromosomes.

isosexual (ī″sō-sĕks′ū-ăl) Concerning or characteristic of the same sex.

isosmotic (ī″sŏs-mŏt′ĭk) [″ + *osmos,* impulsion] Having the same total concentration of osmotically active molecules or ions in solution as the solution or body fluid to which it is being compared. SEE: *isotonic* (1).

Isospora (ī-sŏs′pō-ră) [″ + *sporos*, spore] A genus of Sporozoa belonging to the order Coccidia; found worldwide in warm climates as intestinal parasites of mammals, birds, and amphibians.

I. belli A species that causes acute, non-bloody diarrhea with crampy abdominal pain, which can last for weeks in immunocompromised patients, e.g., people with AIDS.

I. hominis SEE: under *Sarcocystis*.

isospore (ī′sō-spor) [Gr. *isos*, equal, + *sporos*, spore] A nonsexual spore from plants with only one kind of spore. It grows to maturity without conjugating.

isosporiasis (ī-sos″pŏ-rī′ă-sĭs) [*Isospora* + *-iasis*] Infection with *Isospora belli*, an intestinal parasite.

isosthenuria (ī-sŏs″thă-nūr′ē-ă) [″ + *sthenos*, strength, + *ouron*, urine] Having a uniform urinary specific gravity and osmolarity despite marked variations in plasma osmolarity; a sign of impaired renal tubular function.

isostimulation (ī″sō-stĭm″ū-lā′shŭn) [″ + L. *stimulare*, to goad] Stimulation of an animal by the use of antigenic material derived from another animal of the same species.

isosulfan blue dye (ī″sŏ-sŭl′fan″) A radioactive tracer used in sentinel lymph node biopsy to identify the lymphatic vessels and lymph nodes into which a tumor drains.

isothermal (ī″sō-thĕr′măl) [″ + *therme*, heat] Having equal temperature.

isothermognosis (ī″sō-thĕrm″ŏg-nō′sĭs) [″ + ″ + *gnosis*, knowledge] Abnormal perception in which pain, heat, and cold are all felt as heat.

isothiocyanate (ī″sō-thī″ō-sī′ă-nāt″) [″ + ″] ABBR: ITC. A member of a family of compounds found in some cruciferous vegetables, as well as horseradish and mustards. ITCs have cancer-preventing effects in animals.

isotone (ī′sō-tōnz) One of several nuclides with the same number of neutrons but a different number of protons.

isotonia (ī″sō-tō′nē-ă) [″ + *tonos*, tone] The state of equal osmotic pressure of two or more solutions or substances.

isotonic (ī″sō-tŏn′ĭk) **1.** Relating to the maintenance of a constant amount of resistive force during muscular contraction. **2.** Having equal pressure. SEE: *isometric*. **3.** Pert. to a solution with the same osmotic pressure as a reference solution.

isotonicity (ī″sō-tō-nĭs′ĭ-tē) The state or condition of being isotonic.

isotope (ī′sŏ-tōp″) [*iso-* + Gr. *topos*, place (chemical isotopes occupy the same place on the periodic table)] One of a series of chemical elements that have nearly identical chemical properties but different atomic weights and electric charges. Many isotopes are radioactive.

radioactive i. An isotope in which the nucleus is unstable and emits ionizing radiation such as gamma rays. SEE: table.

stable i. An isotope that does not undergo radioactive decay into another element.

isotretinoin (ī″sō-tret″ĭ-nō′ĭn) [*iso-* + *tretinoin*] A keratolytic agent used in treating acne.

⚠ This medicine should not be used by pregnant women or women who are sexually active and at risk of becoming pregnant.

isotropic (ī″sō-trŏp′ĭk) [″ + *tropos*, a turning] **1.** Possessing similar qualities in every direction. **2.** Having equal refraction.

isotropy (ī-sŏt′rō-pē) The state of being isotropic.

isotype (ī′sō-tīp) In immunology, one of the determinants on the immunoglobulin molecule that distinguish among the main classes of antibodies of a given species. They are the same for all normal individuals of that species. SEE: *idiotype*.

immunoglobulin i. Immunoglobulin fragment.

isotypical (ī-sō-tĭp′ĭ-kăl) [″ + *typos*, mark] Belonging to the same variety or classification.

isovaleric acidemia (ī″sō-vă-ler′ĭk) SEE: under *acidemia*.

isozyme (ī′sō-zīm) Isoenzyme.

issue (ĭsh′ū) [ME.] **1.** Offspring. **2.** A suppurating sore maintained by a foreign body in the tissue to act as a counterirritant. **3.** A discharge of pus or blood. **4.** A matter of conflict or dispute.

-ist [L. *-ista* fr. Gr. *-istēs*, noun suffix] An agent noun suffix, frequently used with verbs ending in *-ize* or with nouns ending in *-ism*.

isthmectomy (ĭs-mĕk′tō-mē) [Gr. *isthmos*, isthmus, + *ektome*, excision] Excision of an enlarged isthmus, esp. of the thyroid gland.

isthmitis (ĭs-mī′tĭs) [″ + *itis*, inflammation] An inflammation of the throat or fauces.

isthmus (ĭs′mŭs) *pl.* **isthmuses, isthmi** [Gr. *isthmos*, neck (of land), isthmus] **1.** A narrow passage connecting two cavities. **2.** A narrow structure connecting two larger parts. **3.** A constriction between two larger parts of an organ or structure.

cavotricuspid i. The electrically conductive tissue that separates the inferior vena cava from the tricuspid valve. It is the part of the atrium in which the re-entrant electrical activity of atrial flutter circulates.

Radioactive Isotopes Having Important Long-Term Health Effects

Element	Source	Primary Emission	Decay [half-life]	Organ	Potential Treatment	Potential Long-term Effects
Cesium 137	mining of ores	beta and gamma rays	30 years	soft tissues	Prussian blue	multiple soft-tissue cancers
Iodine 131	nuclear power plants; imaging in nuclear medicine	beta and gamma rays	8.04 days	thyroid	Potassium iodide	thyroid cancer
Plutonium 239	nuclear reactors and nuclear bombs	alpha, beta, and gamma rays	24,000 years	bone, bone marrow, liver, lungs	metal chelating agents	bone marrow cancers (e.g., leukemias & lymphomas), lung cancers
Radon 222	decay product of radium, thorium, and uranium	isotopes of polonium, into which the radon decays	3.8 days	lungs	mitigation by removal by means of fans and ventilation systems	lung cancer
Strontium 90	radioactive fallout	beta rays	29 years	bone	calcium phosphate or aluminum phosphate	bone cancers, bone marrow cancers

i. of eustachian tube The narrowest section of the auditory tube, where the bony canal meets the cartilaginous tube.

isthmus of the fauces A constriction connecting the posterior mouth cavity proper with the pharynx. The walls of the isthmus are the palatoglossal arches.

pharyngeal i. The passageway between the nasopharynx and oropharynx.

i. of thyroid gland A narrow band of thyroid tissue connecting the right and left lobes of the thyroid gland.

i. of uterine tube The thick-walled segment of the uterine (fallopian) tube just before it enters the wall of the uterus.

i. of uterus A narrowing of the body of the uterus just above the cervix.

IT *Information* **technology**.

itch (ich) A generally unpleasant sensation in the skin that creates the urge to rub or scratch it; pruritus. Itch is a frequent manifestation of many inflammatory, infectious, and allergic skin disorders (as in most forms of dermatitis); of dry or cracked skin (xerosis); and of systemic illnesses (such as jaundice, hyperbilirubinemia, and some leukemias and lymphomas).

baker's i. A rash that occurs on the hands and forearms of bakers. It may be due to mechanical or chemical factors.

barber's i. **Sycosis** barbae

dhobie i. **Tinea** cruris.

frost i. Winter **i.**

grain i. Dermatitis caused by mites in stored grain.

grocer's i. Dermatitis caused either by mites in grain or cheese or by sugar.

ground i. A local irritation produced by penetration of the skin of the foot by hookworm larvae, esp. *Necator americanus*. SYN: *ancylostomiasis*.

jock i. **Tinea** cruris.

seven-year i. Scabies.

straw i. A self-limiting skin condition accompanied by itching due to working in straw or sleeping on a straw mattress. The straw contains a mite that causes the pruritic eruption.

swimmer's i. The appearance of papules resembling insect bites on the skin of persons who swim in water containing the cercariae of certain schistosomes. It is usually present only on exposed surfaces of the skin. The papules appear from 4 to 13 days after exposure. The disease is self-limited; thus treatment is symptomatic. SYN: *cercarial* **dermatitis**; *schistosome* **dermatitis**; *water* **i.**

water i. Swimmer's **i.**

winter i. A mild form of eczematous dermatitis of the lower legs of the elderly during dry periods of the year. The skin contains fine cracks and there is no erythema. The skin should be rehydrated with a cream or emulsion of water in oil. SYN: *asteatosis* cutis; *asteatotic* **eczema**; *frost* **itch**; *pruritus* *hiemalis*.

-ite [Fr. *-ite* fr. L., *-ita* fr. Gr. *-itēs*, a noun suffix] **1.** Suffix meaning *of the nature of* or *resembling*. **2.** In chemistry, a salt of an acid having the termination *-ous*.

iter (ī′tĕr) [L.] A passageway between two parts. **iteral** (-ăl), *adj*.

iteroparity (ĭt″ĕr-ō-păr′ĭ-tē) [L. *iterare*, to repeat, + *parere*, to bear] The state of reproducing more than once in a lifetime. SEE: *multiparity*.

-itic [*-ite* + *-ic*] Suffix meaning *pertaining to* or *relating to*.

-itis, -itises, -itides [Gr. *-itis*, stem *-itid-*, inflammation] Suffixes meaning *inflammation (of)*.

-itol Suffix for names of alcohols with more than one hydroxyl group.

Ito nevus (ē′tō) A cutaneous lesion resembling the Mongolian spot over the shoulders, supraclavicular areas, sides of the neck, scapula areas, and upper arms. It is present at birth and tends to disappear with time, usually by age 4 or 5. Although cosmetically undesirable to some, the lesion is benign.

ITP **1.** *idiopathic thrombocytopenic purpura*. **2.** *immune thrombocytopenic purpura*.

IU *immunizing unit; international unit*.

IUCD *Intrauterine contraceptive* **device**.

IUD *Intrauterine contraceptive* **device**.

IUFD *intrauterine fetal death*.

IUGR *intrauterine growth retardation*.

-ium [L. *-ium*, neuter noun suffix] **1.** A suffix used in chemistry for names of *elements*, e.g., *einsteinium*. **2.** A suffix used as a Latinization of the Greek suffix-*ion*, e.g., *endoneurium*

IUPAC *International Union of Pure and Applied Chemistry*.

IUPC *Intrauterine pressure* **catheter**.

IV *intravenous(ly)*.

IVC *intravenous cholangiography*.

IVCD *intraventricular conduction defect*.

IVF *in vitro fertilization*.

IVIG, IGIV *intravenous immune globulin*.

IVP *intravenous pyelogram*.

IV push The administration of medicine intravenously by injection. The rate of injection is determined by the type of medication being administered and by the patient's response.

IVT *intravenous transfusion*.

IVU *intravenous urography*.

IVUS *Intravascular* **ultrasound**.

Ivy loop wiring (ī′vē) [Robert Henry Ivy, Brit.-born U.S. oral surgeon, 1881–1974] The placement of wire around adjacent teeth to provide an attachment site for rubber bands.

Ivy method (ī′vē) [Andrew Conway Ivy, U.S.physiologist, 1893–1978.] SEE: *bleeding time*.

Ixodes (ik″-sō′dēz″) [Gr. *ixōdēs*, like bird-lime] A genus of ticks of the family Ixodidae, many of which are parasitic on humans and animals. In the U.S., Ixodes ticks are vectors for several severe illnesses, including anaplasmosis, babesiosis, and Lyme disease.

ixodiasis (ĭks″ō-dī′ă-sĭs) **1.** Lesions of the skin caused by tick bites. **2.** Any disease caused by ticks, such as Rocky Mountain spotted fever.

ixodic (ĭks-ŏd′ĭk) Pert. to or caused by ticks.

Ixodidae (ĭks-ŏd′ĭ-dē) A family of ticks belonging to the order Acarina, class Arachnida, comprising the hard-bodied ticks including the genera *Amblyomma,*

Boophilus, Dermacentor, Haemaphysalis, Hyalomma, Ixodes, and *Rhipicephalus.* All are parasitic and of significance as pests or as transmitters of disease in domestic animals and humans. Among the diseases transmitted by ticks are Rocky Mountain spotted fever, relapsing fever, tularemia, and Lyme disease.

Ixodides (ĭks-ŏd′ĭ-dēz) Ticks.

Ixodoidea (ĭks″ō-doy′dē-ă) A superfamily of Acarina, the ticks, in which the adults have a thick cuticle.

Iyengar, B. K. S. A renowned Indian yogi and yoga educator, b. 1918.

J

J Symbol for joule.

Jaccoud syndrome (zha-koo′) [Francois Sigismond Jaccoud, Fr. physician, 1830–1913] A rare joint disease in which recurring bouts of arthritis affect multiple joints. The fingers show prominent ulnar deviation with subluxation of the metacarpals that can be reduced manually; typically there is no loss of cartilage or bone erosion. This syndrome has been associated with several diseases, including rheumatic fever, progressive systemic sclerosis, sarcoidosis, and systemic lupus erythematosus.

jacket [O.Fr. *jacquet*, jacket] A bandage usually applied to the trunk to immobilize the spine or correct deformities.

    porcelain j. A jacket crown tooth restoration made of porcelain.

jackscrew (jăk′skroo) A threaded screw used for expanding the dental arch or for positioning bone fragments after a fracture.

jacksonian seizure (jak-sō′nē-ăn) [John Hughlings Jackson, Brit. neurologist, 1835–1911] SEE: under *seizure*.

Jackson-Pratt drain (jak′sŏn-prat′) A soft tube placed in an operative site to drain blood and inflammatory fluid following surgery. The tube is connected to a small, compressed, plastic bulb. The compression creates suction; the bulb expands as it fills. The collected liquid is emptied and measured when the bulb is about 60% filled, and the bulb is recompressed. The drains are removed when only minimal drainage is observed. Fluid in a surgical wound interferes with healing, can place pressure on suture sites, and increases the risk of infection.

Jackson syndrome A dysfunction of cranial nerves X through XII caused by medullary lesions, resulting in unilateral muscle paralysis in the head, the mouth including the soft palate, and the vocal cords.

Jacob, Arthur (jā′kŏb) Irish ophthalmologist, 1790–1874.

    J. ulcer Rodent ulcer.

Jacquemier sign (zhak-mē-ā′) [Jean Jacquemier, Fr. obstetrician, 1806–1879] Blue or purple color of the vaginal mucosa; a presumptive sign of pregnancy.

jactatio (jăk-tā′shē-ō) [L., tossing] Restless tossing of the head and body; seen in acute illness. SYN: *jactitation*.

    j. capitis nocturna A form of sleep disturbance characterized by nocturnal head-banging.

jactitation (jăk″tĭ-tā′shŭn) [L. *jactitatio*, tossing] Jactatio.

Jadad score [A.R. Jadad, contemporary Brit. physician] A tabulation of the academic rigor and quality of a clinical trial, based on its randomization, blinding, and monitoring of patient withdrawals and dropouts.

JAK2 mutation SEE: under *mutation*.

jamais vu (zhăm′ă voo) [Fr., never seen] The subjective sense of being in a completely strange environment when in familiar surroundings. It may be associated with temporal lobe lesions. SEE: *déjà vu.*

James fibers (jāmz) [Thomas N. James, U.S. cardiologist and physiologist, b. 1925] A pathway for conduction of cardiac impulses so that they bypass the atrioventricular node. This alternate fiber pathway permits pre-excitation of the ventricle with resultant tachycardia.

Janeway lesion (jān′wā″) [Edward Gamaliel Janeway, U.S. physician, 1841–1911] A small, painless, red-blue macular lesion a few millimeters in diameter, found on the palms and soles in patients with subacute bacterial endocarditis. SEE: *Osler nodes; Roth spots.*

janiceps (jăn′ĭ-sĕps) [L. *Janus*, a two-faced god, + *caput*, head] A deformed embryo having a face on both the anterior and the posterior aspects of the single head.

Jansky-Bielschowsky syndrome (jăn′skē-bē-ăl-show′skē) [Jan Jansky, Czech physician, 1873–1921; Max Bielschowsky, Ger. neuropathologist, 1869–1940] ABBR: CLN2. A neuronal ceroid lipofuscinosis that first becomes evident in late infancy or early childhood, usually at age 2 to 4 years.

Janus family of protein kinases (jān′ĭs) ABBR: JAK. A group of enzymes that influence the growth and differentiation of cells through their impact on cytokine receptors. SEE: *protein kinase.*

Japanese spotted fever SEE: under *virus.*

¹jar (jar) [Fr. *jarre*, ult fr Arabic *jarrah*, earthen water vessel] A dome-topped container made of glass, plastic, or other sturdy material, used as a protective cover or as a pressurized container when the opening is properly sealed. It is usually taller than it is wide and may be cylindrical, square, or another shape.

    bell j. A glass vessel with an opening at only one end.

²jar (jar) [Imitative] To move suddenly, as in a jolt or shock.

heel j. The production of pain by having the patient stand on tiptoes and suddenly bring the heels to the floor. This physical finding may be suggestive of spinal disease, pelvic inflammatory disease in women, or kidney stones, among other ailments.

jargon (jăr′gŭn) [O.Fr., a chattering] **1.** Paraphasia. **2.** The technical language or specialized terminology used by those in a specific profession or group.

jar sign Jar **tenderness**.

jar tenderness SEE: under *tenderness*.

jaundice (jon′dĭs) [Fr. *jaunisse*, fr. *jaune*, yellow] Yellow staining of body tissues and fluids, due to excessive levels of bilirubin in the bloodstream. Jaundice is not usually visible until the total bilirubin level rises above 3 mg/dL. It is a symptom of many illnesses, including those marked by any of the following: obstruction of the biliary tract by gallstones, inflammatory masses, or tumors (such as cholecystitis, pancreatic carcinoma); slowing of the release of bile from hepatic portals (such as cholestasis); alteration of bile metabolism at the cellular level (such as in genetic diseases such as Gilbert's disease); release of bilirubin because of liver cell injury by toxins or viruses (such as acetaminophen overdose; hepatitis B virus infection); release of bile pigments as a result of the destruction or ineffective manufacturing of red blood cells (such as hemolysis; hereditary spherocytosis); or resorption of bile from hematomas within the body, esp. after trauma. SEE: illus. **jaundiced** (jon′dĭst), *adj*. SYN: *icterus*.

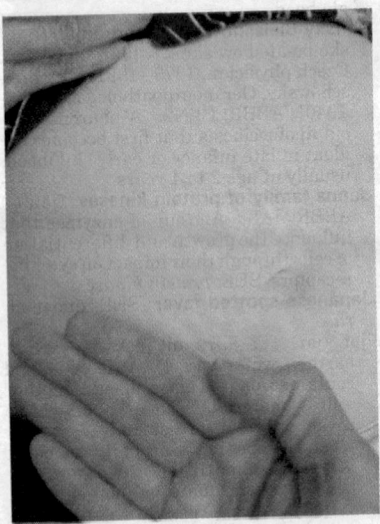

JAUNDICE

Skin of the abdomen

SYMPTOMS: Deposits of bilirubin in the skin often cause itching. Other symptoms of jaundice depend on whether the bilirubin is direct (conjugated [i.e., soluble in body fluids]) or indirect (unconjugated). Obstructive jaundice causes conjugated hyperbilirubinemia; in this disease, bile pigments dissolve in the urine, which turns bright green, and the stool appears gray or white owing to the deprivation of bile.

DIAGNOSIS: Tests to determine the cause of jaundice include a carefully performed history and physical exam, urinalysis (positive for bilirubin only in conjugated hyperbilirubinemia), liver function tests, blood tests for hepatitis, and abdominal ultrasonography. Invasive diagnostic testing with cholangiography, endoscopic retrograde cholangiopancreatography, or percutaneous trans-hepatic cholangiography is performed when occult biliary obstruction is suspected.

TREATMENT: The precise cause of jaundice must be determined in each patient to provide suitable therapies. For example, patients with gallstones obstructing the cystic duct need surgical treatment, and newborns with severe jaundice may require treatment with ultraviolet light to prevent kernicterus, but jaundiced patients with acute hepatitis A usually heal with symptomatic rather than specific remedies.

breast milk j., breast-feeding jaundice Hyperbilirubinemia resulting from pregnanediol or free fatty acids that inhibit bilirubin conjugation. Serum bilirubin level usually peaks above 20 ml/dl by 14 to 21 days of age. Some pediatricians recommend stopping breast-feeding for 24 to 36 hr if the level exceeds 20 ml/dl. If the infant's bilirubin level drops rapidly, the mother may resume nursing. It typically lasts for the first week of life or until the mother produces adequate milk.

cholestatic j. Jaundice produced by failure of bile to flow to the duodenum. It may be caused by intrahepatic bile duct obstruction (as in certain drug reactions), liver cell damage (as in viral hepatitis), or extrahepatic obstruction to the flow of bile (as in cholecystitis).

congenital j. Jaundice occurring at or shortly after birth.

familial nonhemolytic j. Gilbert syndrome.

hematogenous j. Hemolytic **j.**

hemolytic j. Jaundice caused by the fragmentation of red blood cells and the release of unconjugated bilirubin in the bloodstream. This finding is associated with hemolytic anemia (HA). Because the bilirubin is not conjugated by the liver, it is not soluble in water and does not discolor the urine. Many conditions may be responsible, including congenital HA; sickle cell anemia; autoimmune HA (as in infectious mononucleosis or *Mycoplasma pneumoniae* infections); microangiopathic HA (as in hemolytic uremic syndrome); or transfusion-associated HA. SYN: *hematogenous j.; hemolytic* **icterus**; nonobstructive **icterus**.

    hemorrhagic j. Leptospiral **j.**

    hepatocellular j. Jaundice resulting from disease of liver cells, e.g., in acute hepatitis. SYN: *parenchymatous j.*

    infectious j. Infectious **hepatitis**.

    leptospiral j. Jaundice caused by leptospirosis. SYN: *hemorrhagic j.*

    neonatal j. Nonpathological jaundice affecting newborns, usually resulting from the destruction of red blood cells by the immature liver at birth. The destruction of red blood cells causes unconjugated bilirubin to accumulate in the blood and skin. Benign neonatal jaundice manifests 48 to 72 hr after birth, lasts only a few days, and typically does not require therapy.

PATIENT CARE: Levels of bilirubin less than 2 in the first week of life are common, occurring in about 80% of premature babies and half of all full-term babies. They are typically not hazardous to the developing infant. When jaundice develops in the first 24 hr of life, however, or when bilirubin levels exceed published guidelines, kernicterus (neurotoxicity caused by bilirubin) may develop. Infants with potentially damaging levels of bilirubin in the blood are treated with phototherapy (bili lights). SYN: *icterus neonatorum; j. of newborn; physiologic j.* SEE: *hemolytic disease of the newborn; isoimmunization; kernicterus; phototherapy; Nursing Diagnoses Appendix.*

    j. of newborn Neonatal **j.**

    nonhemolytic j. Jaundice due to abnormal metabolism of bilirubin or to biliary tract obstruction, and not to excessive destruction of red blood cells.

    obstructive j. Jaundice caused by a mechanical impediment to the flow of bile from the liver to the duodenum. Gallstones are the most common cause. Cholangitis, obstructing cancers, cysts, parasites in the bile ducts, or hepatic abscesses are responsible less frequently. SYN: *obstructive* **icterus**; *postobstructive j.; regurgitation j.*

SYMPTOMS: The condition is marked by yellow staining of the skin, mucous membranes, sclera, and secretions. The patient may complain of pruritus caused by bile pigments in the skin. The urine is yellow or green, but the stools turn light or clay-colored because of absence of bile pigment in the intestinal tract. Acute obstruction to the flow of bile causes right upper quadrant pain and may be associated with biliary colic due to entrapment of gallstones.

TREATMENT: Cholecystectomy with common bile duct exploration (choledochostomy) is used to resolve obstructive jaundice caused by gallstones. Radical surgeries (as the Whipple procedure) or stenting of the biliary tract with or without external damage may temporarily relieve obstructive jaundice caused by cancer.

    parenchymatous j. Hepatocellular **j.**

    pathological j. of newborn Hemolytic disease of the newborn.

    physiologic j. Neonatal **j.**

    postobstructive j. Obstructive **j.**

    regurgitation j. Obstructive **j.**

    retention j. Jaundice resulting from the inability of liver cells to remove bile pigment from circulation.

    spirochetal j. Leptospirosis.

    toxic j. Jaundice resulting from chemical injury to the liver or sepsis.

jaw (jo) **1.** Either or both of the maxillary and mandibular bones, bearing the teeth and forming the mouth framework. SEE: illus. **2.** The grasping part of a surgical instrument. The word is usually used in the plural.

    cleft j. An early embryonic malformation resulting in lack of fusion of the right and left mandible into a single bone.

    crackling j. Noise in the normal or diseased temporomandibular joint during movement of the jaw. SYN: *crepitation.*

    lumpy j. Actinomycosis.

jawbone Unscientific term used to indicate the maxilla or mandible.

jaw thrust SEE: under *thrust.*

jaw winking Involuntary movements of the eyelid when the jaw is elevated or depressed. This may be seen in patients who have recovered from Bell's palsy.

jazz ballet bottom An abscess in the cleft between the buttocks, caused by excessive exertion combined with chafing of the skin.

JC *Joint Commission, The.*

JCAH *Joint Commission on the Accreditation of Hospitals.*

JCAHO *Joint Commission on Accreditation of Healthcare Organizations.* SEE: *Joint Commission, The.*

JE *Japanese (B type)* **encephalitis**.

Jebsen-Taylor Hand Function Test (jĕb′sĕn-tā′lŏr) A standardized battery of tasks used to measure upper extremity function.

Jefferson fracture (jĕf′ĕr-sŏn) [Geoffrey Jefferson, British neurologist and neurosurgeon, 1886–1961] A burst fracture of the first cervical vertebra (atlas), usually involving the anterior and posterior arches, that results from compression of the cervical spine. Jefferson fractures are classified as stable when the transverse ligament is intact and unstable when the ligament has been ruptured. The majority of Jefferson fractures are associated with other spi-

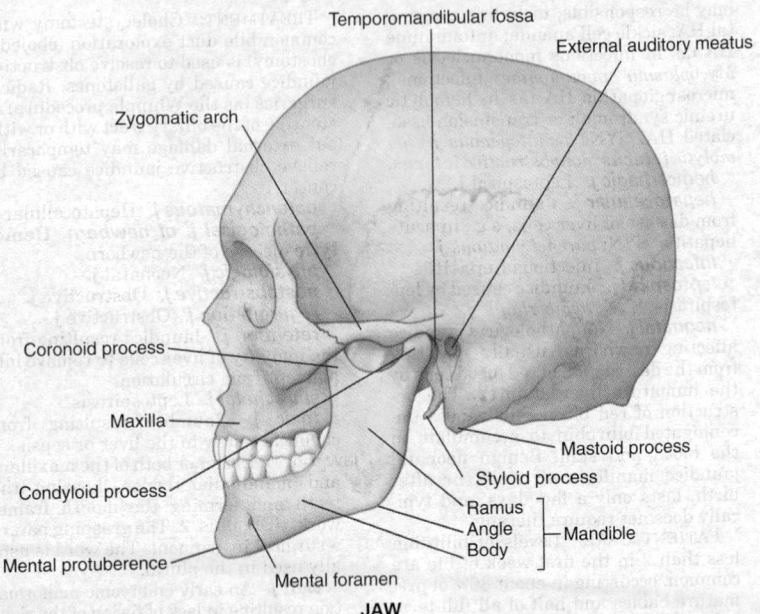

Temporomandibular fossa

External auditory meatus

Zygomatic arch

Coronoid process

Maxilla

Condyloid process

Mental protuberence

Mastoid process

Styloid process

Ramus
Angle   — Mandible
Body

Mental foramen

JAW

nal pathology, esp. fractures of the second cervical vertebra (axis). SEE: *halo vest.*

SYMPTOMS: The patient may complain of pain arising from the upper cervical spine but may not demonstrate signs or symptoms of neurological impairment. On x-ray examination, odontoid views may demonstrate displacement of the C1-C2 facets. Lateral and flexion-extension views are needed to ascertain the status of the transverse ligament.

TREATMENT: For unstable fracture, cranial traction, skeletal traction, and/or halo vest are applied for a total of 3 months. A nondisplaced stable fracture may be treated with the use of a soft cervical collar. Stable fractures with less than 7 mm displacement require the use of a rigid cervical collar. Follow-up evaluations should be performed regularly, to rule out insidious subluxation of the first cervical vertebra.

jejunal (jē-jū'năl) [L. *jejunum*, empty] Rel. to the jejunum.

jejunectomy (jē"jū-něk'tō-mē) [" + Gr. *ektome*, excision] Excision of part or all of the jejunum.

jejunitis (jē"jū-nī'tĭs) [" + Gr. *itis*, inflammation] Inflammation of the jejunum, caused by one of many possible diseases, including bacterial infections, celiac sprue, Crohn's disease, ischemia, radiation, injury, or vasculitis. SYN: *inflammation of jejunum.*

jejuno- [L. *jejunum*, empty, poor (the jejunum being thought to be empty after death)] Prefix meaning *jejunum.*

jejunocecostomy (jē-joo"nō-sē-kŏs'tō-mē) [" + *caecum*, blindness, + Gr. *stoma*, mouth] The formation of a passage between the cecum and jejunum.

jejunocolostomy (jē-jū'nō-kōl-ŏs'tō-mē) [" + Gr. *kolon*, colon, + *stoma*, mouth] The formation of an artificial passage between the jejunum and colon.

jejunoileal (jē-joo"nō-ĭl'ē-ăl) [" + *ileum*, small intestine] Concerning the jejunum and ileum.

jejunoileitis (jē-jū"nō-ĭl"ē-ī'tĭs) [" + " + Gr. *itis*, inflammation] Inflammation of the jejunum and ileum.

jejunoileostomy (jē-jū"nō-ĭl"ē-ŏs'tō-mē) [" + " + Gr. *stoma*, mouth] The formation of a passage between the jejunum and ileum.

jejunoileum (jē-joo"nō-il'ē-ŭm) [*jejuno-* + *ileum*] The jejunum and the ileum considered together. **jejunoileal** (jē-joo"nō-il'ē-ăl), *adj.*

jejunojejunostomy (jē-jū"nō-jē"jū-nŏs'tō-mē) [" + *jejunum*, empty, + Gr. *stoma*, mouth] The formation of a passage between two parts of the jejunum.

jejunorrhaphy (jē"joo-nor'ă-fē) [" + Gr. *rhaphe*, seam, ridge] Surgical repair of the jejunum.

jejunostomy (jē"jū-nŏs'tō-mē) [" + Gr. *stoma*, mouth] Surgical creation of an opening into the jejunum.

   needle catheter j. ABBR: NCJ. A jejunostomy created by using a needle to insert a catheter into the jejunum. It is intended exclusively for feeding, created by direct surgical approach or percutaneously. SEE: *percutaneous endoscopic j.*

percutaneous endoscopic j. ABBR: PEJ. A jejunostomy created for feeding purposes with the use of an endoscope and guide wire.

venting j. A jejunostomy constructed with a portal used either to facilitate sampling the contents of the jejunum or to inspect its interior with an endoscope.

jejunostomy tube A tube placed directly into the jejunum for long-term enteral feeding. This may be done laparoscopically, with a percutaneous endoscopic jejunostomy tube, or surgically. It is not as commonly used as the gastrostomy tube.

jejunotomy (jē″jū-nŏt′ŏ-mē) [″ + Gr. *tome,* incision] Surgical incision into the jejunum.

jejunum (ji-joo′nŭm) [L. *jejunus,* empty] The second part of the small intestine. It grades imperceptibly into the ileum, the final part of the small intestine. The jejunum has a wider diameter (avg. 3 cm) and larger, taller, and more closely packed internal circular folds (plicae circulares) than the ileum. It has few lymphoid nodules (Peyer's patches). The jejunum is about 2.5 m (8.5 feet) long.

jelly [L. *gelare,* to freeze] A thick, semi-solid, gelatinous mass.

contraceptive j. Water-soluble gel introduced into the vagina for the prevention of conception. It serves as a vehicle for spermicides. SEE: *contraceptive.*

mineral j. Petrolatum.

petroleum j. Petrolatum.

vaginal j. Water-soluble gel introduced into the vagina for therapeutic or contraceptive purposes.

Wharton's j. SEE: *Wharton's jelly.*

Jendrassik maneuver (yen-drä′sik) [Ernö Jendrassik, Hungarian physician, 1858–1921] A method used to facilitate elicitation of the deep tendon reflexes of the lower extremities. The patient hooks together the fingers of the hands and attempts to pull them apart. While this pressure is maintained, the patellar or Achilles tendon reflex is tested.

Jenner, Edward (jen′ĕr) Brit. physician, 1749–1823. Jenner observed that individuals exposed to cowpox, such as milkmaids, would develop a minor skin lesion and then be immune to smallpox. From this observation he developed a vaccine from cowpox lesions, which provides immunity to smallpox.

Jenner stain (jen′ĕr) [Louis Jenner, Brit. physician, 1866–1904] Eosin methylene blue stain, used for staining blood.

jerk (jĕrk) A colloquial term for reflex.

Achilles j. Achilles tendon reflex.

ankle j. SEE: *ankle clonus reflex.*

biceps j. SEE: *biceps reflex.*

elbow j. Triceps reflex.

jaw j. Chin reflex.

knee j. The extension of the lower leg upon striking the patellar tendon when the knee is flexed at a right angle. Knee jerk is absent in locomotor ataxia, infantile paralysis, meningitis, destructive lesions of the lower part of the spinal cord, and certain forms of paralysis. It is increased in lesions of pyramidal areas, brain tumors, spinal irritability, and cerebrospinal sclerosis. SEE: *knee-jerk reflex.*

tendon j. The contraction of a muscle after tapping its tendon.

triceps surae j. Achilles tendon reflex.

Jerusalem syndrome (jĕ-roo′să-lĕm) A temporary or permanent delusional disorder following a pilgrimage to Jerusalem, characterized by extreme religious preoccupations or the belief that the pilgrim has become the embodiment or incarnation of an important biblical character.

jet A sudden pulse or burst of gas or liquid. **jetted,** *adj.*

jet lag An upset of a person's internal biological clock, caused by the difference between the time at a person's present location and the time to which the person is accustomed, and occurring in people traveling across several time zones in a short period.

Jeune syndrome (zhen) [Mathis Jeune, Fr. pediatrician, b. 1910] A rare autosomal recessive form of dwarfism, accompanied by severe narrowing of the thoracic skeleton. SYN: *asphyxiating thoracic dystrophy.*

jig A mechanical device used to maintain a stable, correct relationship between a piece of work and a tool, or between components during assembly.

jigger (jig′ĕr) SEE: *chigger.*

Jimson weed (jĭm′sŏn) Stramonium.

Jin Bu Huan (jĭn-bū-whăn′) An herb (*Lycopocium seratum*) promoted as a sedative and hypnotic. Its use has been associated with acute hepatitis in some patients.

Jin shin do, Jin shin jyutsu (jin shin dō, joo′tsoo) [Japanese, way of the compassionate spirit] A form of acupressure used by practitioners of alternative medicine and conventional health care providers to treat selected health problems.

job aid SEE: under *aid.*

Jobe test Empty can test.

job satisfaction The extent to which people find that their employment meets their economic, personal, social, and intellectual needs. Job satisfaction and mental health are closely linked. Health care professionals associate their own job satisfaction with on-the-job autonomy, professional friendships, challenges, skill sets, task variety, workload, shift work, staffing ratios, opportunities for career development and advancement, and earnings.

Jobst pressure garment (jŏbst) An elastic garment fabricated to apply varying pressure gradients to an area. It may be worn over severely burned areas for the purpose of reducing hypertrophic scarring as wounds heal or may be used to prevent or control lymphedema in the arms or legs.

Job syndrome (jōb) [*Job,* biblical character] Recurrent staphylococcal infections of the skin related to impaired immune defenses.

Jocasta complex (jō-kăs′tă) [Jocasta, mythical character who was the wife and mother of Oedipus] The psychological or emotional fixation of a mother toward her son. SEE: *Oedipus complex.*

Joffroy reflex (zhof-rwhah′) [Alexis Joffroy, Fr. physician, 1844–1908] Twitching of the gluteal muscles when pressure is applied to the buttocks.

jogger's foot SEE: under *foot.*

jogger's heel An irritation of the fibrous and fatty tissue covering the heel. The condition is due to the type of running characteristic of jogging, in which the heel strikes the surface first, rather than that of sprinting, in which the toes strike first. Persons prone to develop this may diminish the risk by wearing pads on their heels and by running on surfaces softer than wood, concrete, or asphalt.

jogging Running for enjoyment or to maintain physical fitness. In contrast to running, jogging is not a competitive exercise and is performed at a submaximal intensity.

Johanson-Blizzard syndrome Blizzard syndrome.

John Doe, Jane Doe 1. In law, a fictitious name used when that of the actual defendant is unknown. 2. Name assigned to an unidentified patient (e.g., one admitted to a hospital in a coma) or to an unidentified corpse brought to the hospital for confirmation of death.

Johnson, Dorothy (jŏn′sŏn) A nursing educator (1919–1999) who developed the Behavioral System Model of Nursing. SEE: *Nursing Theory Appendix.*

joint (joynt) [Fr. *jointe,* fr L. *junctio,* a joining] The place where two or more bones meet. Some joints are fixed or immobile attachments of bones; other joints allow the bones to move along each other. A joint usually has a thin, smooth articular cartilage on each bony surface and is enclosed by a joint capsule of fibrous connective tissue. A joint is classified as immovable (synarthrodial), slightly movable (amphiarthrodial), or freely movable (diarthrodial). A synarthrodial joint is one in which the two bones are separated only by an in-

tervening membrane, such as the cranial sutures. An amphiarthrodial joint is one having a fibrocartilaginous disk between the bony surfaces (symphysis), such as the symphysis pubis; or one with a ligament uniting the two bones (syndesmosis), such as the tibiofibular articulation. A diarthrodial joint is one in which the adjoining bone ends are covered with a thin cartilaginous sheet and joined by a joint capsule lined by a synovial membrane, which secretes synovial fluid. SYN: *arthrosis*(1). SEE: illus.

MOVEMENT: Joints are also grouped according to their motion: ball and socket (enarthrodial); hinge (ginglymoid); condyloid; pivot (trochoid); gliding (arthrodial); and saddle joint.

Joints can move in four ways: *gliding,* in which one bony surface glides on another without angular or rotatory movement; *angulation,* occurring only between long bones, increasing or decreasing the angle between the bones; *circumduction,* occurring in joints composed of the head of a bone and an articular cavity, the long bone describing a series of circles, the whole forming a cone; and *rotation,* in which a bone moves about a central axis without moving from this axis. Angular movement, if it occurs forward or backward, is called flexion or extension, respectively; away from the body, abduction; and toward the median plane of the body, adduction.

Because of their location and constant use, joints are prone to stress, injury, and inflammation. The main diseases affecting the joints are rheumatic fever, rheumatoid arthritis, osteoarthritis, and gout. Injuries comprise contusions, sprains, dislocations, and penetrating wounds.

   acromioclavicular j. ABBR: AC joint. A gliding or plane joint between the acromion and the acromial end of the clavicle.

   amphidiarthrodial j. A joint that is both ginglymoid and arthrodial.

   ankle j. Ankle.

   arthrodial j. Diarthrosis permitting a gliding motion. SYN: *gliding j.*

   ball-and-socket j. A joint in which the round end of one bone fits into the cavity of another bone. SYN: *enarthrodial j.; multiaxial j.; polyaxial j.*

   biaxial j. A joint with two chief movement axes at right angles to each other.

   bilocular j. A joint separated into two sections by interarticular cartilage.

   bleeders' j. Hemorrhage into joint space in hemophiliacs. SYN: *hemophilic j.*

   cartilaginous j. A joint with cartilage between the bones.

   Charcot j. SEE: under *Charcot, Jean M.*

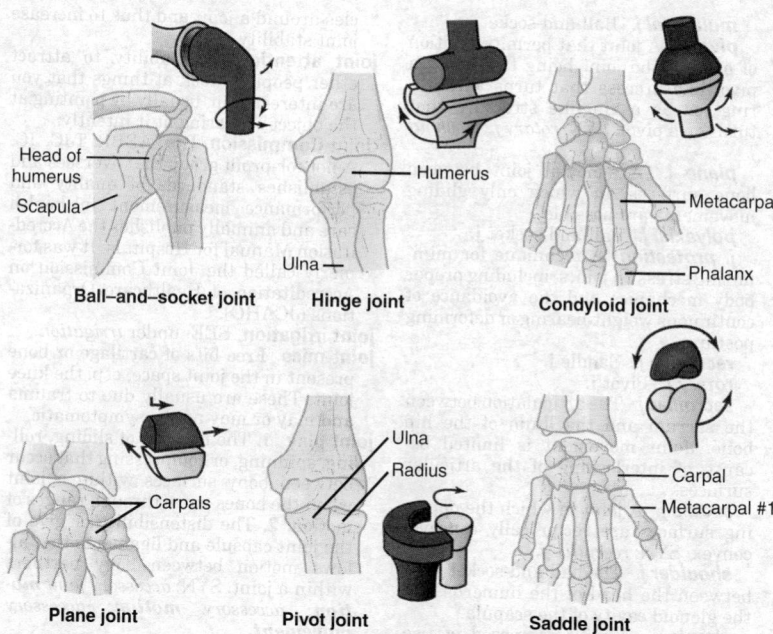

Ball–and–socket joint   Hinge joint   Condyloid joint

Plane joint   Pivot joint   Saddle joint

TYPES OF JOINTS

Chopart j. SEE: under *Chopart, François.*

Clutton j. SEE: *Clutton joint.*

compound j. A joint made up of several bones.

condylar j. Ellipsoid **j.**

condyloid j. A joint permitting all forms of angular movement except axial rotation.

cracking j. The sound produced by forcible movement of a joint by contracting the muscles that contract or extend a joint, esp. the metacarpophalangeal joints. The cause is not known. SEE: *crepitation.*

craniomandibular j. Either of the encapsulated, double synovial joints between the condylar processes of the mandible and the temporal bones of the cranium. The double synovial joints are separated by an articular disk and function as an upper gliding joint and a lower modified hinge or ginglymoid joint. SYN: *temporomandibular j.*

diarthrodial j. A joint characterized by the presence of a cavity within the capsule separating the bones, permitting considerable freedom of movement.

elbow j. The hinge joint between the humerus and the ulna.

ellipsoid j. A joint with two axes of motion through the same bone. SYN: *condylar j.*

enarthrodial j. Ball-and-socket **j.**

false j. A false joint formation after a fracture.

fibrous j. Any of the joints connected by fibrous tissue.

flail j. A joint that is extremely relaxed, the distal portion of the limb being almost beyond the control of the will.

ginglymoid j. A synovial joint having only forward and backward motion, as a hinge. SYN: *ginglymus.* SEE: *hinge j.*

gliding j. arthrodial **j.**

hemophilic j. Bleeders' **j.**

hinge j. A synovial joint in which two bones flex and extend in only one plane, usually because side (collateral) ligaments limit the direction of motion, e.g., elbow joint.

hip j. A synovial ball-and-socket joint in which the head of the femur fits into the acetabulum of the hip bone. More than seven separate ligaments hold the joint together and restrict its movements.

intercarpal j. Any of the articulations formed by the carpal bones in relation to one another.

knee j. The joint formed by the femur, patella, and tibia.

midcarpal j. A joint separating the navicular, lunate, and triangular bones from the distal row of carpal bones.

movable j. A slightly movable or freely movable joint, amphiarthrodial and diarthrodial, respectively.

multiaxial j. Ball-and-socket **j.**

pivot j. A joint that permits rotation of a bone, the joint being formed by a pivot-like process that turns within a ring, or by a ringlike structure that turns on a pivot. SYN: *rotary* **j.**; *trochoid* **j.**

plane j. A synovial joint between bone surfaces, in which only gliding movements are possible.

polyaxial j. Ball-and-socket **j.**

j. protection A technique for minimizing stress on joints, including proper body mechanics and the avoidance of continuous weight-bearing or deforming postures.

receptive j. Saddle **j.**

rotary j. Pivot **j.**

sacroiliac j. The articulation between the sacrum and the ilium of the hip bone. Joint movement is limited because of interlocking of the articular surfaces.

saddle j. A joint in which the opposing surfaces are reciprocally concavo-convex. SYN: *receptive* **j.**

shoulder j. The ball-and-socket joint between the head of the humerus and the glenoid cavity of the scapula.

simple j. A joint composed of two bones.

spheroid j. A multiaxial joint with spheroid surfaces.

sternoclavicular j. The joint space between the sternum and the medial extremity of the clavicle.

stiff j. A joint with reduced mobility.

subtalar j. Any of the three articular surfaces on the inferior surface of the talus.

sutural j. An articulation between two cranial or facial bones.

synarthrodial j. Synarthrosis.

synovial j. A joint in which the articulating surfaces are separated by synovial fluid. SEE: *joint* for illus.

talocrural joint Ankle.

tarsometatarsal j. A joint composed of three arthrodial joints, the bones of which articulate with the bases of the metatarsal bones.

temporomandibular j. Craniomandibular **j.**

trochoid j. Pivot **j.**

ulnomeniscal-triquetral j. The functional articulation of the distal ulna, articular disk, and triquetrum. The disk may subluxate following injury or with arthritis and block supination of the forearm.

uniaxial j. A joint moving on a single axis.

unilocular j. A joint with a single cavity.

joint approximation A rehabilitation technique whereby joint surfaces are pressed together, usually with the patient in a weight-bearing posture. It is used to facilitate cocontraction of muscles around a joint and thus to increase joint stability.

joint attention The ability to attract other people to look at things that you are interested in, usually by pointing at the object or staring at it intently.

Joint Commission, The ABBR: TJC, JC. A not-for-profit group that oversees and establishes standards of quality and performance measurement in health care and annually publishes the Accreditation Manual for Hospitals. It was formerly called the Joint Commission on Accreditation of Healthcare Organizations (JCAHO).

joint irrigation SEE: under *irrigation*.

joint mice Free bits of cartilage or bone present in the joint space, esp. the knee joint. These are usually due to trauma and may or may not be symptomatic.

joint play 1. The motions of sliding, rolling, spinning, or compressing that occur between bony surfaces within a joint when the bones move through ranges of motion. 2. The distensibility or give of the joint capsule and ligaments that allows motion between bony partners within a joint. SYN: *accessory joint* ***motion***; *accessory* ***motion***; *accessory* ***movement***.

joint-space narrowing The radiographic appearance of a joint that has lost its surface cartilage. The bones in the joint are not separated by the normal or usually observed distance. They appear to be too close to each other, and they are often eburnated or sclerotic.

jojoba (hŏ-hō'bă) [Mexican Span. fr the O'odham Indians] A shrub of the Mojave and Sonoran deserts of North America (*Simmondsia chinensis*), whose seeds produce an oil used as an emollient.

Jones criteria (jōnz) [T. D. Jones, U.S. physician, 1899–1954] The criteria for diagnosis of acute rheumatic fever. SEE: *rheumatic fever*.

Jones fracture A transverse fracture of the proximal diaphysis, approx. ¾ in from the base of the fifth metatarsal. This fracture is commonly confused with an avulsion fracture of the styloid process of the fifth metatarsal. The distinction is important because the true Jones fracture often results in a nonunion if the fracture is not properly identified and managed. It is usually repaired by internal fixation with a screw.

Joplin neuroma A compression neuropathy affecting the nerve that supplies sensation to the medial side of the great toe. The condition often occurs in runners or in people whose shoes are too tight at the metatarsophalangeal joint, where the medial plantar proper digital nerve is found.

Joubert syndrome (zhoo-běr') A rare, autosomal-recessive neurological disorder, marked by failure of development of the vermis cerebelli and by improper formation of the brainstem and medulla.

SYMPTOMS: Common symptoms include mental retardation, ataxia, disordered breathing, abnormal eye movements, and decreased muscle tone.

joule (jool) [James Prescott Joule, Brit. physicist, 1818–1889] ABBR: J. The work done in one second by a current of one ampere against a resistance of one ohm. One kilogram calorie (kcal or Calorie) is equal to 4185.5 J. One calorie (small calorie) equals 4.1855 J. Electrical current for defibrillation and cardioversion is delivered in joules.

journaling (jŭr′năl-ng) [O.Fr. *journal,* daily] Keeping a diary or journal as a means of self-exploration, stress reduction, or enlightenment.

joystick A pivoting electronic input device, used in assistive technology to register side-to-side, forward and backward, and diagonal movements, so that these can be processed. The stick may also include preprogrammed buttons that, when depressed, activate specific electronic commands or mechanical outputs.

JRA *juvenile rheumatoid arthritis.*

JRCDMS *Joint Review Committee for Diagnostic Medical Sonography.*

JRCERT *Joint Review Committee on Education in Radiologic Technology.*

JRCRTE *Joint Review Committee for Respiratory Therapy Education.*

judgment The use of available evidence or facts to formulate a rational opinion or to make socially acceptable choices or decisions. Judgment may be impaired by conditions such as mental illness, medications, delirium, fatigue, or bias.

substituted j. Instructions regarding patients' wishes from significant others, usually with respect to their preferences for life support, drug therapy, fluid infusions, or supplemental nutrition. Substituted judgments are relied upon when patients are unable to advocate for themselves, and are generally respected by health care workers, but their validity in representing the actual desires of patients has been questioned.

Judgment of Line Orientation Test ABBR: JLO. A neuropsychiatric test to assess visual/spatial orientation. The full test consists of 30 items (a shorter version consists of 15).

judgment sample SEE: under *sample.*

judicial (joo-dish′ăl) [L.*judicialis,* pert. to law courts, judicial] Pert. to a judgement at law, or to the administration of law or of justice, or to the judiciary or judges. **judicially** (′ă-lē), *adv.*

jugal (jū′găl) [L. *jugalis,* of a yoke] **1.** Connected or united as by a yoke. **2.** Pert. to the malar or zygomatic bone.

jugular (jŭg′ū-lăr) [L.*jugularis*] **1.** Pert.

to the throat. **2.** Pert. to a jugular vein. **3.** A jugular vein.

j. vein Any of the two pairs of bilateral veins that return blood to the heart from the head and neck. The external jugular vein receives the blood from the exterior of the cranium and the deep parts of the face. It lies superficial to the sternocleidomastoid muscle as it passes down the neck to join the subclavian vein. The internal jugular vein receives blood from the brain and superficial parts of the face and neck. It is directly continuous with the transverse sinus, accompanying the internal carotid artery as it passes down the neck, and joins with the subclavian vein to form the innominate vein. The jugular veins are more prominent during expiration than during inspiration and are also prominent during cardiac decompensation.

When the patient is sitting or in a semirecumbent position, the height of the jugular veins and their pulsations can provide an accurate estimation of central venous pressure and give important information about cardiac compensation.

jugular venous oximetry SEE: under *oximetry.*

jugulation (jŭg″ū-lā′shŭn) The sudden arrest of a disease by therapeutic means.

jugum (jū′gŭm) *pl.* **juga** [L., a yoke] **1.** A ridge or furrow connecting two points. **2.** A type of forceps.

j. penis A forceps for temporarily compressing the penis.

j. petrosum An eminence on the petrous section of the temporal bone showing the position of the superior semicircular canal. SEE: *arcuate eminence.*

juice (joos) [Fr.*jus,* fr L.*jus,* broth] Liquid excreted, secreted, or expressed from any part of an organism.

digestive j. Any of several secretions that aid digestion.

fruit j. The liquid expressed when fruit is compressed. Fruit juice contains water, vitamin C, sugars, pulp, minerals such as calcium, and varying amounts of acid and other biologically active chemicals.

gastric j. The digestive secretion of the gastric glands of the stomach. It is a thin, colorless fluid; is mostly water; and contains mucus, intrinsic factor, hydrochloric acid, the enzyme pepsin, and the enzyme lipase. The pH is 1–2, strongly acidic, which destroys pathogens and changes pepsinogen to the active pepsin. Pepsin begins the digestion of proteins. Gastric lipase has little effect on unemulsified fats; most fat digestion takes place in the small intestine. The amount of gastric juice secreted in 24 hr varies with food intake. SEE: *stomach.*

glove j. The bacteria, sweat, and skin cells that accumulate under a glove worn during an operation.

grapefruit j. A drink derived from a fruit rich in chemicals called flavonoids, which impair the metabolism of drugs processed by the liver's cytochrome P 450 system.

⚠️ Patients should be advised that the juice alters the metabolism of several important drugs, including warfarin, steroids, calcium channel blockers, statins, second-generation antihistamines, protease inhibitors, and others.

intestinal j. Alkaline secretion that contains peptidases and enzymes to complete the digestion of disaccharides. SEE: *digestion.*

pancreatic j. A clear, viscid, alkaline fluid (pH 8.4 to 8.9) whose secretion is stimulated by secretin and cholecystokinin and is produced by the duodenal mucosa. Pancreatic juice flows through the main pancreatic duct to the common bile duct to the duodenum, its site of action; 500 to 1200 mL is secreted every 24 hr. It contains sodium bicarbonate and trypsinogen, chymotrypsinogen, amylase, and lipase. Sodium bicarbonate neutralizes the acidity of the chyme entering the duodenum from the stomach and prevents irritation of the duodenal mucosa. Trypsinogen is converted to active trypsin by intestinal enteropeptidase (enterokinase); trypsin in turn converts chymotrypsinogen to active chymotrypsin. Both trypsin and chymotrypsin continue protein digestion, forming peptides. Amylase hydrolyzes starch to maltose, and lipase digests emulsified fats to fatty acids and glycerol. SEE: *enzyme; pancreas; secretion.*

juicing (joo'sĭng) The conversion of vegetables and fruits into consumable liquids.

Julian date (jool'yăn) [Julius Caesar, Roman general, ca 44 B.C., who devised the Julian calendar] In medical records, identifying a calendar date by using a code for the day of the year. Each day is numbered sequentially from 1 through 365, or 366 on leap years.

jun (joon) A family of oncogenes that can transform some normal cells (e.g., rat embryo cells) into cancer cells. All members of this family can bind to activating protein-1 (AP-1) sites and to specific DNA sequences. SEE: *oncogene; transformation.*

junction (jŭnk'shŭn) [L. *junctio*, a joining] The place of union or coming together of two parts or tissue layers.

     ameldentinal j. Dentinoenamel junction.

     atrioventricular j. The area of cardiac conduction pathway connecting the AV node with the atrioventricular bundle.

     cementodentinal j. The interface of dentin and cementum of the tooth. SYN: *dentinocemental j.*

     cementoenamel j. The line around the tooth that marks the boundary between the crown and root of the tooth; the interface between enamel and cementum.

     cervicomedullary j. The nexus between the most superior part of the spinal cord and the medulla oblongata of the brainstem.

     costochondral j. The articulation or meeting place of the bony rib and its costal cartilage.

     dentinocemental j. Cementodentinal junction.

     dentinoenamel j. The plane or interface between the dentin of the tooth and the enamel crown; histological sections show it to be a scalloped boundary at the site of the basement membrane which separated the cell layers that formed the calcified enamel and dentin. SYN: *ameledentinal j.*

     dentogingival j. The interface and zone of attachment between the gingiva and enamel or cementum of the tooth. It holds in place the junctional or attachment epithelium.

     liquid j. The point in a potentiometric reference electrode measurement system at which the reference solution makes contact with the test solution. An example is pH reference electrode.

     mucocutaneous j. The junction between the skin and a mucous membrane.

     mucogingival j. A scalloped, indistinct boundary between the gingiva and the oral mucosa on the alveolar process. The coral color of gingiva may be contrasted with the more vascular oral mucosa. Also called the mucogingival line.

     myoneural j. The axon terminal of a motor neuron, synaptic cleft, and sarcolemma of a muscle cell. SYN: *neuromuscular j.* SEE: illus.

     neuromuscular j. Myoneural junction.

     saphenofemoral j. The merging of the saphenous and femoral veins in the inguinal region.

     sclerocorneal j. The meeting point between the sclera and the cornea marked on the external surface of the eyeball by the outer scleral sulcus.

     squamocolumnar j. 1. The point in the cervical canal at which the squamous and columnar epithelia meet. As most cervical cancers begin in this area, it is important to obtain cells from this location for the Pap test. 2. The point above the lower esophageal sphincter where the squamous epithelium of the esophagus and the columnar epithelium

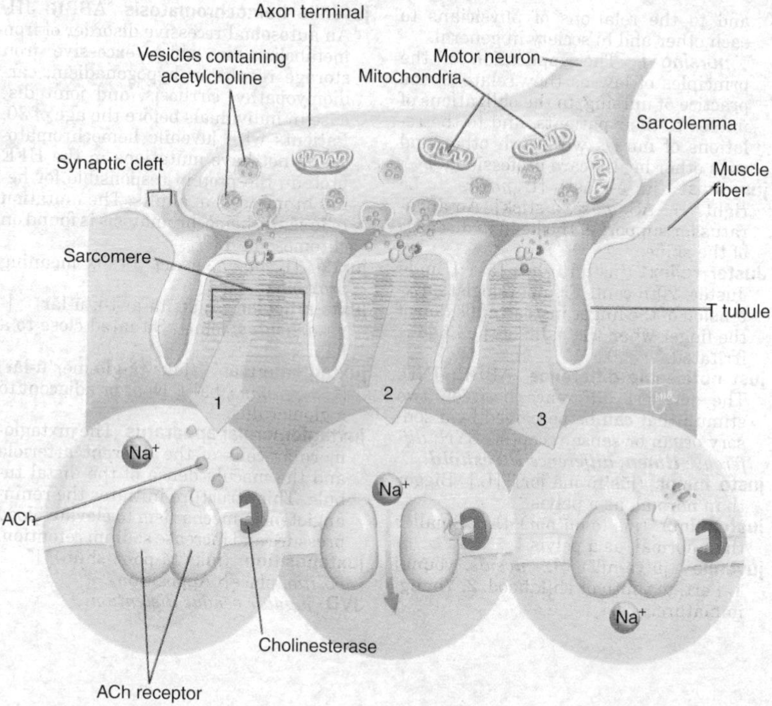

Axon terminal

Vesicles containing
acetylcholine

Motor neuron

Mitochondria

Sarcolemma

Synaptic cleft

Muscle
fiber

Sarcomere

T tubule

Na⁺

ACh

Na⁺

Na⁺

ACh receptor

Cholinesterase

MYONEURAL JUNCTION

of the stomach meet. SYN: *transition zone*. SEE: illus.

tight j. A part of the junctional complex at the lateral interface between epithelial cells; also called zonula occludens.

Jung, Carl Gustav (yŭng) [Swiss psychiatrist, 1875–1961] The founder of a school of analytic psychology. In his early career, Jung was associated with Sigmund Freud. Later he proposed his own theory of the unconscious mind, based on his belief that all human beings share common myths and symbols. This concept has not been objectively validated.

juniper tar (joo′nĭ-pĕr) SEE: under *tar*.

Juniperus oxycedrus (joo-nip′ĕ-rŭs ok″sē-se′drŭs) SEE: *juniper tar*.

junk DNA (jŭngk) A sequence of base pairs of DNA that does not code for a gene or have a recognizable function.

jurisdiction The authority and power of courts to hear and render judgments on the parties and subject matter of a case.

jurisprudence (joor″ĭs-proo′dĕns) [L. *juris prudentia,* knowledge of law] The scientific study or application of the principles of law and justice.

dental j. The application of the principles of law as they relate to the practice of dentistry, to the obligations of the practitioners to their patients, and to the relations of dentists to each other and to society in general. This term and forensic dentistry are sometimes used as synonyms, but some authorities consider the first as a branch of law and the second as a branch of dentistry.

medical j. The application of the principles of law as they relate to the practice of medicine, to the obligations of the practitioners to their patients,

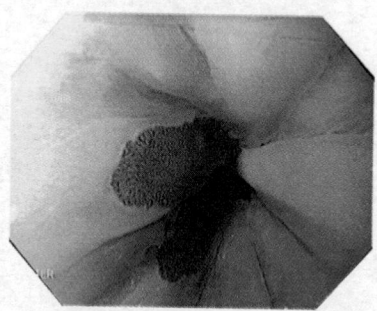

SQUAMOCOLUMNAR JUNCTION

Squamocolumnar junction of the distal esophagus (seen endoscopically)

and to the relations of physicians to each other and to society in general.

nursing j. The application of the principles of law as they relate to the practice of nursing, to the obligations of nurses to their patients, and to the relations of nurses with each other and with other health care professionals.

jury-mast (jūr′ē-măst) [L. *jurare*, to be right, + AS. *masc*, a stick] An apparatus for support of the head in diseases of the spine.

Juster reflex (jŭs′ter, zhüs-tā′) [Emile Juster, 20th-cent. Fr. neurologist] Extension of the finger instead of flexion of the finger when the palm of the hand is irritated.

just noticeable difference ABBR: JND. The smallest difference between two stimuli that can be perceived by a sensory organ or sense receptor. SYN: *difference limen; difference threshold*.

justo major (jŭs′tō mā′jor) [L.] Bigger than normal, as a pelvis.

justo minor (jŭs′tō mĭ′nor) [L.] Smaller than normal, as a pelvis.

juvenile (jū′vĕ-nīl″) [L. *juvenis*, young] **1.** Pert. to youth or childhood. **2.** Young; immature.

juvenile hemochromatosis ABBR: JH. An autosomal recessive disorder of iron metabolism in which excessive iron storage results in hypogonadism, cardiomyopathy, cirrhosis, and joint disease in individuals before the age of 30. Patients with juvenile hemochromatosis do not have mutations in the HFE protein, the protein responsible for hemochromatosis in adults. The mutation in juvenile hemochromatosis is found on chromosome 1.

juxta- [L., *juxta*, near] Prefix meaning *proximity*.

juxta-articular (jŭks″tă-ăr-tĭk′ū-lăr) [″ + *articulus*, joint] Situated close to a joint.

juxtaglomerular (jŭks″tă-glō-mĕr′ū-lăr) [″ + *glomus*, ball] Near or adjacent to a glomerulus.

juxtaglomerular apparatus The juxtaglomerular cells of the afferent arteriole and the macula densa of the distal tubule. This structure initiates the renin-angiotensin mechanism to elevate blood pressure and increase sodium retention.

juxtaposition (jŭks″tă-pō-zĭ′shŭn) [″ + *positio*, place] Apposition.

JVD *jugular venous distention*.

K

¹K 1. Symbol for the element potassium. The *K* derives from Latin *kalium,* from Arabic *al-qalyah,* plant ashes, alkali. **2.** Symbol for equilibrium constant (used in some formulas in chemistry and physics). **3.** Symbol for solubility.

²K *kelvin; kilo-; kilometer.*

k *kilo-.*

Kabuki syndrome, Kabuki make up syndrome (kă-boo′kē) [From the resemblance of patients to actors wearing the white makeup of Kabuki theater] An autosomal dominant disorder characterized by mild to moderate mental retardation, cranial and facial anomalies, poor muscle tone, and often cleft palate, seizures, heart defects, and other anomalies. SYN: *Niikawa-Kuroki syndrome.*

Kader operation (kod′ĕr) [Bronislaw Kader, Polish surgeon, 1863–1937] The surgical formation of a gastric fistula with the feeding tube inserted through a valvelike flap.

Kahler's disease [O. Kahler, Austrian physician, 1849–1893] multiple myeloma.

kahweol (kah′wē-ol″) [Turkish *kahve,* fr. Arabic *qahwah,* coffee] A lipid obtained by boiling coffee beans.

kaiserling (kī′zĕr-lĭng) [Karl Kaiserling, Ger. pathologist, 1869–1942] A solution used in preserving pathological specimens.

kala-azar (kă′lă ă-zăr′) [Hindi, black fever] An infectious disease caused by *Leishmania donovani,* an intracellular protozoan. It is marked by fevers, splenic enlargement, and decreased blood cell counts. The disease is common in the rural parts of tropical and subtropical areas of the world, where it is often fatal. SYN: *visceral leishmaniasis.*

kalium (kā′lē-ŭm) [L. *kalium,* fr Arabic *al-qalyah,* plant ashes, alkali] SYMB: K. Potassium.

kaliuresis (kă″lē-ū-rē′sĭs) [L. *kalium,* potassium, + Gr. *ouresis,* urination] The excretion of potassium in the urine.

kallidin (kăl′ĭ-dĭn) A plasma kinin. SEE: *kinin.*

kallikrein (kal″lĭ-krē′ĭn, kă-lik′rē-ĭn) [Gr. *kallikreas,* pancreas + *-in*] An enzyme normally present in plasma, urine, and body tissue in an inactive state. When activated, kallikrein has many actions: it dilates blood vessels, influences blood pressure, modulates salt and water excretion by the kidneys, and influences cardiac remodeling after myocardial infarction.

kallikreinogen (kăl″ĭ-krī′nō-jĕn) [″ +

gennan, to produce] The precursor of kallikrein in plasma.

Kallmann syndrome (kal′măn) [Franz Josef Kallman, U.S. psychiatrist, 1897–1965] A disorder whose hallmarks are congenital absence of the sense of smell and decreased functional activity of the sex organs, resulting from insufficient production of gonadotropin-releasing hormone. Affected individuals also may have hearing loss and other deficits caused by intracranial, sinus, or facial abnormalities.

Kampo (kŏm′pō′) [Japanese, Chinese medicine] Traditional Japanese medicine, a healing discipline adapted from ancient Chinese healing traditions. It includes the use of acupuncture, herbal remedies, and moxibustion, among others.

kangaroo care, kangaroo mothering The placing of a newborn infant, esp. a premature baby, in an upright position between the breasts of the mother for several hours a day.

Kanner syndrome (kăn′ĕr) [Leo Kanner, Austrian psychiatrist in the U.S., 1894–1981] Infantile autism.

kaolin (kā′ō-lĭn) [Fr., from Mandarin Chinese *kao,* high, + *ling,* mountain] A yellow-white or gray clay powder occurring in a natural state as a form of hydrated aluminum silicate. It is used internally as an absorbent, e.g., in treating diarrhea, externally as a protective by absorbing moisture. SYN: *China clay.*

kaolin cephalin time SEE: under *time.*

kaolinosis (kā″ō-lĭn-ō′sĭs) Pneumoconiosis caused by inhaling kaolin particles.

kapha (kaf′ă, kap′ă) [Sanskrit, *kapha,* mucus, phlegm] In ayurvedic medicine, the dosha responsible for the structure of the body. SEE: *dosha.*

Kaposi, Moritz K. (ko′pō-sē) Hungarian dermatologist, 1837–1902. His original name was Moritz Kohn.

    K. disease Xeroderma pigmentosum.

    K. sarcoma ABBR: KS. A lymphatic endothelial malignancy, rather than a true sarcoma, composed of multiple red or purple macules, papules, or nodules, that is first apparent on the skin or mucous membranes but may involve the internal organs. Once a rare disease seen primarily in elderly men of Mediterranean, African, or Ashkenazi descent (so-called classic KS), it is the most common cancer related to AIDS. In patients with AIDS, KS is believed to be sexually ac-

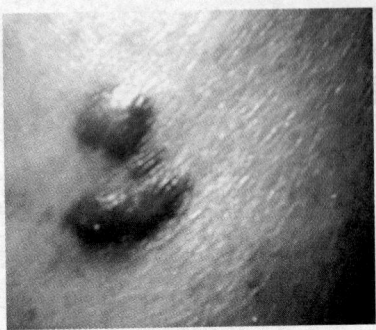

KAPOSI SARCOMA

on skin

quired due to acquisition of human herpesvirus 8. When KS is associated with AIDS, it progresses and disseminates rapidly to multiple skin sites, as well as the lymph nodes and visceral organs. SEE: illus.; *AIDS.*

SYMPTOMS: The lesions are typically painless but may be cosmetically disfiguring or may interfere with internal organ function. They are found most often on the dorsa of the feet and lower extremities in patients with classic KS, and on the face, trunk, oral cavity, and internal organs in immunosuppressed patients. KS is sometimes referred to as "epidemic" in patients with HIV infection; "endemic" in parts of Africa; and "acquired" in patients taking immune-suppressing drugs after organ transplantation. In advanced disease, the lesions may merge into large plaques, sometimes blocking lymphatics and causing localized edema. Involvement of internal organs, primarily the gastrointestinal tract or the lungs, may result in dyspepsia or dyspnea.

DIAGNOSIS: Characteristic tumors on the skin suggest the diagnosis, which should be confirmed by tissue biopsy.

TREATMENT: Treatment options include radiation therapy, cancer chemotherapies, cryotherapy, hormone therapies, and biotherapy (interferon alfa-2b).

PATIENT CARE: Epidemic KS may profoundly alter the patient's appearance. Emotional support for the patient and family may help them cope with the diagnosis and its effects on body image. Psychological counseling may be needed. Standard precautions should be followed when assessing or caring for the patient. The skin should be assessed for new lesions at each health care contact.

K. sarcoma-associated herpesvirus ABBR: KSHV. Human **herpesvirus** 8.

K. sarcoma herpesvirus Human **herpesvirus** 8.

K.'s varicelliform eruption Eczema herpeticum.

Kaposiform hemangioendothelioma SEE: under *hemangioendothelioma.*

karela (kă-rĕ′lă) [Sanskrit] Bitter melon.

Karelian fever (kă-rēl′ē-ăn) [*Karelia,* territory shared by Finland and Russia] SEE: under *fever.*

Karenia brevis (kă-ren′ē-ă brev′ĭs) A marine dinoflagellate commonly found in red tides. It produces a toxin that can be irritating to the respiratory tract of animals when inhaled, or neurotoxic to humans when contaminated shellfish are eaten.

Karnofsky Index (kar′nof-skē) [D. A. Karnofsky, U.S. oncologist, 1914–1969] A tool to estimate clinically a patient's physical state, performance, and prognosis. The scale is from 100%, perfectly well and active, to 0%, completely inactive, or dead. It has been used in studying cancer and chronic illness. Lower Karnofsky scores are generally associated with poorer treatment response and prognosis. SYN: *Karnofsky Scale.* SEE: table.

Kartagener syndrome (kar′tă-gān″ĕr) [Manes Kartagener, Swiss physician, 1897–1975] A hereditary syndrome consisting of abnormal ciliary movement, bronchiectasis, maldevelopment

Karnofsky Index

Score	Physical State, Performance, and Prognosis
100%	Normal, no complaints; no evidence of disease
90%	Able to carry on normal activity; minor signs or symptoms of disease
80%	Normal activity with effort, some signs or symptoms of disease
70%	Cares for self; unable to carry on normal activity or do active work
60%	Requires occasional assistance, but is able to care for most personal needs
50%	Requires considerable assistance and frequent medical care
40%	Disabled; requires special care and assistance
30%	Severely disabled; hospitalization is indicated, although death not imminent
20%	Very sick; hospitalization is necessary; active supportive treatment is required
10%	Terminally ill; fatal processes progressing rapidly
0%	Dead

of the sinuses, and transposition of the viscera. SEE: *immotile cilia syndrome*.

Karvonen formula (kăr-vōn′ĕn) A calculation of the optimal range of heart rate for achieving physical fitness during cardiovascular endurance exercise. The calculation is based on a percentage of predicted maximum heart rate of 220 minus the person's age (HR_{max}) and the resting heart rate (HR_{rest}). The formula that determines the best physical training range is: $HR = HR_{rest} + (HR_{max} - HR_{rest})$ (.60 to .80).

karyo-, kary-, cary-, caryo- [Gr. *karyon*, kernel] Prefixes meaning the *nucleus of a cell.*

karyochrome (kăr′ē-ō-krōm″) A neuron in which the nucleus stains readily but the cytoplasm does not.

karyocyte (kăr′ē-ō-sīt) [″ + *kytos*, cell] An immature normoblast.

karyogamy (kăr-ē-ŏg′ă-mē) [″ + *gamos*, marriage] The union of nuclei in cell conjugation.

karyogenesis (kăr″ē-ō-jĕn′ē-sĭs) [″ + *genesis*, generation, birth] The formation and development of a cell nucleus.

karyokinesis (kăr″ē-ō-kĭn-ē′sĭs) [″ + *kinesis*, movement] The equal division of nuclear material that occurs in cell division. SYN: *karyomitosis*. SEE: *cytokinesis; mitosis*.

karyokinetic (kăr″ē-ō-kĭ-nĕt′ĭk) **1.** Pert. to karyokinesis. **2.** Ameboid.

karyolysis (kăr-ē-ŏl′ĭ-sĭs) [″ + *lysis*, dissolution] Chromatolysis. **karyolytic** (-ō-lĭt′ĭk), *adj.*

karyomere (kăr′ē-ō-mēr″) [″ + *meros*, part] **1.** Chromomere. **2.** A vesicle containing only a small portion of the nucleus.

karyomicrosome (kăr″ē-ō-mī′krō-sōm) [″ + *mikros*, small, + *soma*, body] Any of the segments or portions of chromatin within the nucleus.

karyomitosis (kăr″ē-ō-mī-tō′sĭs) [″ + *mitos*, thread, + *osis*, condition] Karyokinesis.

karyomorphism (kăr-ē-ō-mor′fĭzm) [″ + *morphe*, form, + *-ismos*, state of] The form of a cell nucleus.

karyon (kăr′ē-ŏn) [Gr.] The nucleus of a cell.

karyophage (kăr′ē-ō-fāj) [Gr. *karyon*, kernel, + *phagein*, to eat] An intracellular protozoan parasite that destroys the nucleus of a cell.

karyopyknosis (kăr″ē-ō-pĭk-nō′sĭs) [″ + *pyknos*, thick, + *osis*, condition] Shrinkage of the nucleus of the cell with condensation of the chromatin.

karyorrhexis (kăr″ē-ō-rĕk′sĭs) [″ + *rhexis*, rupture] Fragmentation of the chromatin in nuclear disintegration.

karyosome (kăr′ē-ō-sōm) [″ + *soma*, body] Irregular clumps of nondividing chromatin material seen in the nuclei of cells. SYN: *chromocenter*.

karyostasis (kăr″ē-ŏs′tă-sĭs) [″ + *stasis*, standing] The resting stage of a cell nucleus.

karyotheca (kăr″ē-ō-thē′kă) [″ + *theke*, sheath] The enveloping membrane of a cell nucleus.

karyotype (kăr′ē-ō-tīp) [″ + *typos*, mark] A photomicrograph of the chromosomes of a single cell, taken during metaphase, when each chromosome is still a pair of chromatids. The chromosomes are then arranged in numerical order, in descending order of size.

karyozoic (kăr″ē-ō-zō′ĭk) [″ + *zoon*, animal] Living in the cell nucleus, as would occur with an intracellular protozoal parasite.

Kasabach-Merritt syndrome (kăs′ă-bŏk-mĕr′ĭt) [Haig H. Kasabach, U.S. pediatrician, 1898–1943; Katherine K. Merritt, U.S. physician, b. 1886] Capillary hemangioma associated with thrombocytopenic purpura.

Kasai procedure (kă-sī′) [Morio Kasai, Japanese surgeon] A procedure to treat biliary atresia in the newborn. SYN: *hepatic portoenterostomy*.

Kashin-Beck disease (ka-shin′-bek) [Nicolai Ivanovich Kashin, Russian military physician, 1825–1872; Evgeny Vladimirovich Beck (Bek), 20th-cent. Russian military physician] Endemic polyarthritis typically found in children in Tibet, China, and neighboring regions. Its cause is unknown, but it is associated with the consumption of grains contaminated with fungi, with selenium deficiency, and possibly with iodine deficiency.

kata-, kat- SEE: *cata-*.

katal ABBR: kat. A measure of the activity of an enzyme, specifically the quantity of an enzyme that catalyzes one mole of substrate production each second.

katathermometer (kăt″ă-thĕr-mŏm′ĕ-ter) [″ + *therme*, heat, + *metron*, measure] A device consisting of two thermometers, one a dry bulb and the other a wet bulb. Both are heated to 110°F (43.3°C) and the time required for each thermometer to fall from 100° to 90°F (37.8° to 32.2°C) is noted. The dry bulb gives the cooling power by radiation and convection, the wet bulb by radiation, convection, and evaporation.

Katayama fever (kot-ă-yom′ă) [*Katayama* River Valley in Japan, where the disease was first identified] SEE: under *fever*.

katzenjammer (kăts′ĕn-yăm′ĕr) [Ger. *katzen*, cats, + *jammer*, distress, misery] German word meaning hangover.

Katz hand diagram (kats) A drawing made by a patient of symptoms such as numbness, tingling, or pain affecting the hand and fingers. The drawing is a useful means of eliciting symptoms that suggest carpal tunnel syndrome.

Kaufman assessment battery for children (kowf'măn) [Alan and Nadeen Kaufman, U.S. educators] ABBR: K-ABC. A test consisting of 16 subtests, used to assess cognitive development in children ages 3 to 18. This intelligence test, consisting of both verbal and nonverbal subtests, asks children to place objects in order or logical sequence. It may be used alone or with other intelligence tests to gauge overall intelligence.

kava, kava kava (kav'ă) [Tongan (Polynesia) *kava(kava), bitter] *Piper methysticum,* a plant native to the Pacific islands, whose dried roots are used medicinally to treat anxiety and stress. It can produce stomach upset and side effects like those of alcohol.

⚠️ Kava should not be used by women who are pregnant or breast-feeding, or by children. Usage should be discontinued if the skin becomes dry, scaly, or yellowed. Cases of hepatotoxicity have been reported.

---

kavalactone (kă'vă-lăk-tōn) The active ingredient derived from kava; it has a sedative effect on the central nervous system. Its use has been banned in Canada and Western Europe as a result of idiosyncratic cases of severe liver injury.

Kawa Model [The title of a text by Michael Iwama.] A framework for viewing occupational therapy based on Eastern philosophical principles.

Kawasaki disease (ka"wă-sa'kē) [Tomisaku Kawasaki, Japanese pediatrician, b. 1925] An acute febrile vasculitis of children, marked acutely by fever, rashes, lymphadenopathy, and irritability and chronically by late cardiac complications, including coronary artery aneurysms and myocardial infarction. Fever is present on the first day of the illness and may last from 1 to 3 weeks. The child with Kawasaki disease is irritable, lethargic, and has bilateral congestion of the conjunctivae. The oral mucosa may turn deep red, and the lips often become dry and cracked. It is common for the affected child to have unilateral cervical lymphadenopathy. A strawberry tongue is a prominent sign, as is redness and peeling of the skin of the hands and feet. The disease is rarely fatal in the acute phase, but children may die suddenly from coronary artery disease some years later. This disease was previously called *mucocutaneous lymph node syndrome.* Cervical lymph nodes are most often the ones enlarged. SEE: *toxic shock syndrome; Nursing Diagnoses Appendix.*

EPIDEMIOLOGY: In 80% of the children, diagnosis takes place before age 5, and usually the younger the age at onset, the more severe the disease. The disease is rare after age 8. It occurs more commonly in Asian children than in other ethnic groups. In Japan, there are about 5000 to 6000 cases annually. By comparison, about 4000 cases occur annually in the U.S.

DIAGNOSIS: Because of the similarities of this disease to others (e.g., scarlet fever and toxic shock syndrome), diagnostic criteria are strict. There must be fever and at least four of the following five findings: conjunctivitis; oral lesions like those described above; redness, swelling, and peeling of the fingers and toes; rash similar to that described above; cervical lymphadenopathy. The erythrocyte sedimentation rate (ESR) is elevated.

ETIOLOGY: The cause is unknown, but both infectious and immune mechanisms have been proposed.

COMPLICATIONS: Formation of giant aneurysms of the coronary artery (esp. in infants and very young children) is the major complication and can lead to sudden death or myocardial infarction later in life. Mortality from the disease is about 1%. Other findings may include arthritis, otitis media, diarrhea, uveitis, pyuria (sterile), and hepatic dysfunction.

TREATMENT: If given within 10 days of onset of fever, high-dose intravenous immunoglobulin (IVIG) therapy over 12 to 24 hr can dramatically relieve the symptoms and prevent coronary artery dilation. Daily aspirin therapy has traditionally also been given to decrease the risk of coronary artery dilation, but its safety (given the risk of Reye's syndrome) and its effectiveness have been questioned. Neither antibiotics nor high-dose corticosteroids are effective. Frequent follow-up care, including repeat evaluations to detect or monitor heart disease, is essential.

PATIENT CARE: Medications are administered as prescribed, and the child is observed for salicylate toxicity. Both child and family benefit from psychological support during the acute period of illness and require continued support through the chronic phase. Parents learn about the importance of following the prescribed regimen and early signs of toxicity. The child requires careful monitoring during the acute phase and conscientious follow-up thereafter. The child's progress is monitored; parents must understand the importance of normal activity, sound nutrition, and good hygiene. Referral to a mental health practitioner, support groups such as the

Kawasaki Disease Foundation, or spiritual counselor may be helpful for patients and families.

Kayser-Fleischer ring (kī'zĕr-flī'shĕr) A pigmented ring seen within the limbus of patients with Wilson's disease and some other liver disorders. SEE: *Wilson's disease*.

KBr Formula for potassium bromide.

K-B test *Kleihauer-Betke test.*

kc *kilocycle.*

KCCT *Kaolin cephalin time.*

K cells A type of T lymphocyte activated by an antigen-antibody reaction that directly lyses (kills) infected cells.

KCl Formula for potassium chloride.

kc.p.s., kc/s *kilocycles per second.*

KCT *Kaolin cephalin time.*

kD, kDa *Kilodalton.*

KDIGO *Kidney Disease:Improving Global Outcomes.*

KED *Kendrick extrication device.*

K-edge In radiography, the sharp increase in characteristic x-ray production resulting when the incoming x-ray beam matches the K-shell-binding energy of an atom. K-edge production can cause problems in predicting radiation exposure; i.e., when kilovolts peak is decreased and the K-edge is matched by the incoming x-ray photons, image density may increase.

keepsake fetal ultrasound (kēp'sāk″) SEE: under *ultrasound*.

keep vein open ABBR: KVO. An order indicating that the patency of an intubated vessel be maintained so that subsequent intravenous solutions or medicines can be administered. This is done using the lowest possible infusion rate with a microdrop set or a volume controller.

kefir, kefyr (ke'fir, kē'fĕr) [Russian *kefir*] A preparation of curdled milk made originally in the Caucasus by adding grains of kefir (a probiotic combination of bacteria, yeasts, proteins, lipids, and sugars) to milk.

Kegel exercise (kā'gĕl) [Arnold H. Kegel, U.S. gynecologist, 1894–1981] An exercise for strengthening the pubococcygeal and levator ani muscles. The patient should repeatedly and rapidly alternate contracting and relaxing the muscles for 10 seconds; relax for 20 seconds, then sustain the contraction for 10 to 20 seconds; the patient should then rest for 10 seconds and repeat the routine until fatigued. The number of repetitions should be increased gradually to between 50 and 150 per day. SYN: *pelvic floor exercise*. SEE: *incontinence, stress urinary*.

Kehr sign (ker) [Hans Kehr, Ger. surgeon, 1862–1916] Pain that radiates into the shoulder during respiration. The sign points to a diaphragmatic or peridiaphragmatic lesion and, when it involves the left shoulder, is considered an indication of splenic rupture.

Keith-Wagener-Barker classification (kēth'wag'(ĕ-)nĕr-bark'ĕr) Classification of the funduscopic findings in hypertensive patients. Grades 1 to 4 indicate progressive pathological changes. Grade 1 is moderate narrowing of the retinal arterioles; grade 2 indicates retinal hemorrhages in addition to arteriolar narrowing; in grade 3 there are cotton-wool exudates; grade 4 shows papilledema, i.e., edema of the optic disk.

Kell blood group (kel) [Named after the family in whom the blood group was first discovered in 1946] One of the human blood groups. It is composed of three forms of antigens present on the surface of the red blood cells. SEE: *blood group*.

keloid (kē'lŏyd) [Gr. *kele*, tumor, + *eidos*, form, shape] An exuberant scar that forms at the site of an injury (or an incision) and spreads beyond the borders of the original lesion. The scar is made up of a swirling mass of collagen fibers and fibroblasts. Grossly it appears to have a shiny surface and a rubbery consistency. The most common locations for keloid formation are on the shoulders, chest, and back. SEE: illus.

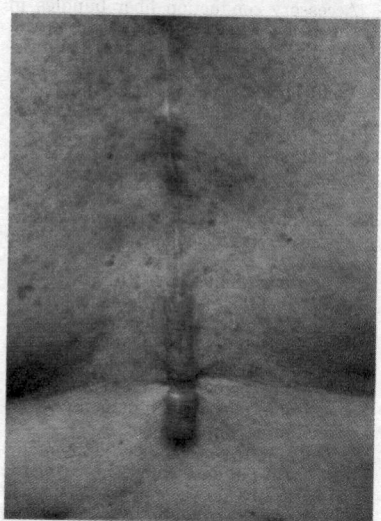

KELOID

TREATMENT: The injection of a corticosteroid sometimes helps the lesion regress. Freezing the tissue with liquid nitrogen, applying pressure dressings, treating it with lasers, excising it surgically, or a combination of these treatments may be used, but recurrences are frequent.

acne k. A keloid that develops at the site of an acne pustule.

keloidosis (kē″loy-dō′sĭs) [″ + ″ + *osis,* condition] The formation of keloids.

kelp (kĕlp) **1.** Any member of the brown seaweeds of the order Laminariales. **2.** The ash of seaweed from which potassium and iodine salts are prepared.

Kelvin, Lord (kel′vĭn) Sir William Thomson (First Baron Kelvin of Largs), Brit. physicist, 1824–1907.

   K. scale The temperature scale that uses the kelvin as the unit of measurement and in which absolute zero is equal to minus 273.15° on the Celsius scale. On the Kelvin scale the freezing point of water is 273.15°K, and the boiling point 373.15°K.

   K. thermometer A thermometric scale in which absolute zero is 0°K; the freezing point of water is 273.15°K; and the boiling point of water is 373.15°K. Thus 1°K on the Kelvin scale is exactly equivalent to 1°C.

Kendrick Extrication Device (kĕn′drĭk) ABBR: KED. A vest-type immobilizer designed to limit movement of the cervical and thoracic spine in seated patients with suspected spinal cord injuries.

Kent bundles (kent) [Albert Frank Stanley Kent, Brit. physiologist, 1863–1958] Accessory conduction fiber bundles in the heart which rapidly convey atrial impulses across the atrioventricular tissue. They are usually present in the Wolff-Parkinson-White syndrome.

kerasin (kĕr′ă-sĭn) A cerebroside isolated from brain tissue.

keratectasia (kĕr″ă-tĕk-tā′sē-ă) [″ + *ektasis,* extension] Conical protrusion of the cornea.

keratectomy (ker″ă-tek′tŏ-mē) [*kerato- + -ectomy*] Excision of a portion of the cornea.

   photorefractive k. ABBR: PRK. The removal of microscopic layers of corneal cells and the resculpting of the cornea with an excimer laser. The procedure is used to correct myopia. Its complications may include corneal haze, keratitis, retinal tears, and a delay in refractive stabilization.

   Only one eye is treated at a time. This allows the patient to function during the 24 to 48 hr that the corrected eye may be covered. Frequently, the treated patient does not need glasses after the procedure.

⚠ Potential complications include corneal swelling, double vision, shadow images, light sensitivity, tearing, and pupil enlargement. Possible long-term adverse effects are as follows: anterior stromal reticular haze, glare, halo, loss of previously corrected vision, im-

proper correction, induced astigmatism, increased intraocular pressure, and night vision difficulties.

SYN: *LASEK.*

keratic (kĕr-ăt′ĭk) **1.** Horny. **2.** Relating to the cornea.

   k. precipitates ABBR: KP. Inflammatory cells of the iris and ciliary body that enter the aqueous and adhere to the corneal endothelium. These precipitates are present in uveitis.

keratin (kĕr′ă-tĭn) A family of durable protein polymers that are found only in epithelial cells. They provide structural strength to skin, hair, and nails. The fibrous protein is produced by keratinocytes and may be hard or soft.

   hard k. Keratin found in the hair and nails.

   soft k. Keratin found in the epidermis of the skin as the flexible, tough stratum corneum in the form of flattened non-nucleated scales which slough continually.

keratinase (kĕr′ă-tĭ-nās) An enzyme that hydrolyzes the protein keratin.

keratinization (kĕr″ă-tĭn-ĭ-zā′shŭn) The process of keratin formation, that is, of maturation or hardening of the skin, hair, and nails.

keratinize (kĕr′ă-tĭn-īz) [Gr. *keras,* horn] To become hard or horny; usually said of tissue.

keratinocyte (kĕ-răt′ĭ-nō-sīt) [″ + *kytos,* cell] Any one of the cells in the skin that synthesize keratin.

   cultured k. Keratinocytes that are grown in the laboratory so that a small biopsy sample from uninjured skin may grow as a sheet and expand to have a surface area 1,000 to 10,000 times the area of the sample. The sheet can be used to cover wounds such as burns. The culture technique requires 2 to 3 weeks, and the regeneration of tissue below the sheet may not be complete for 5 to 6 months.

keratinous (kĕr-ăt′ĭ-nŭs) Pert. to or composed of keratin.

keratitis (ker-ă-tīt′ĭs) [*kerato- + -itis*] Inflammation of the cornea, usually associated with decreased visual acuity and, if untreated, sometimes resulting in blindness. Eye pain, tearing, light sensitivity, and low vision are the most common symptoms.

   ETIOLOGY: It is often caused by contact lenses, but it may also result from drugs, microorganisms, immunodeficiency, trauma, or vitamin A deficiency.

   TREATMENT: Therapy depends upon the underlying cause. Bacterial infections respond to antibacterial medications (typically administered in drops); herpes simplex viral infection requires antiviral agents; fungal keratitis is treated with antifungal agents; exposure keratitis, as in Bell's palsy, is preventable with topical lubricants.

PATIENT CARE: Because of the seriousness of keratitis, patients experiencing eye inflammation or pain should seek immediate medical attention. The patient is assessed for a history of recent upper respiratory infection accompanied by cold sores, pain, central vision loss, the sensation of a foreign body in the eye, contact lens use, photophobia, and blurred vision. The eye is inspected for loss of normal corneal luster and inflammation. A slit lamp examination is often used for optimal viewing of the eye to confirm the condition. Fluorescein staining helps determine the extent and depth of corneal ulcerations. The patient should refrain from rubbing the eye, which can cause complications. Prescribed therapies are administered, and the patient is instructed in their use. Warm compresses are applied as prescribed to relieve pain. If the patient complains of photophobia, the use of dim lighting or sunglasses is recommended. The patient should follow the prescribed treatment regimen carefully for the entire course and return for follow-up examination.

Patient education: the correct instillation of prescribed eye medications and the importance of thorough handwashing before and after touching the eye are emphasized. Contact lenses are removed and are not replaced until infectious forms of keratitis are cured. Any potentially contaminated lenses or lens solutions should be discarded. Stress, traumatic injury, fever, colds, and overexposure to the sun may trigger flare-ups. Both patient and family are taught about safety precautions pertaining to visual sensory or perceptual alterations. They are encouraged to verbalize their fears and concerns. Appropriate information and emotional support and reassurance are provided.

⚠️ Because many common forms of keratitis are infectious, examiners should use standard precautions during the evaluation of the eye.

chlamydial k. Corneal ulcerations that accompany chlamydial infection of the conjunctiva.

dendritic k. Superficial branching corneal ulcers.

k. disciformis A gray, disk-shaped opacity in the middle of the cornea.

exposure k. Epithelial defects of the cornea that result from inadequate protection of the eye by the eyelids, as in Bell's palsy.

fascicular k. A corneal ulcer resulting from phlyctenules that spread from limbus to the center of cornea accompanied by fascicle of blood vessels.

herpetic k. Dendritic keratitis in herpes zoster or herpes simplex infections.

hypopyon k. A serpent-like ulcer with pus in the anterior chamber of the eye.

interstitial k. A deep form of nonsuppurative keratitis with vascularization, occurring usually in syphilis and rarely in tuberculosis. It commonly occurs between ages 5 and 15. Symptoms include pain, photophobia, lacrimation, and loss of vision. SYN: *parenchymatous k.*

lagophthalmic k. Drying due to air exposure of the cornea resulting from a defective closure of the eyelids.

microbial k. Keratitis due to bacterial infection, often in patients who wear contaminated contact lenses.

mycotic k. Keratitis produced by fungi.

neuroparalytic k. The dull and slightly cloudy insensitive cornea seen in lesions of the fifth nerve. SYN: *neurotrophic k.*

neurotrophic k. Neuroparalytic **k.**

parenchymatous k. Interstitial **k.**

phlyctenular k. Circumscribed inflammation of the conjunctiva and cornea accompanied by the formation of small projections called phlyctenules, which consist of accumulations of lymphoid cells. The phlyctenules soften at the apices, forming ulcers. SEE: *phlyctenular **keratoconjunctivitis***.

punctate k. Punctate epithelial defects on the cornea epithelium, often seen in dry eye. SYN: *superficial punctate k.*

purulent k. Keratitis with the formation of pus.

reapers' k. Corneal inflammation caused by grain dust.

sclerosing k. A triangular opacity in the deeper layers of the cornea, associated with scleritis.

superficial punctate k. Punctate **k.** SEE: *Thygeson disease.*

thermal k. Damage to the cornea resulting from a burn.

trachomatous k. A form of chlamydial keratitis. SEE: *pannus.*

traumatic k. Keratitis caused by a wound of the cornea.

xerotic k. Softening, desiccation, and ulceration of cornea resulting from dryness of the conjunctiva.

kerato-, kerat-, cerat-, cerato- [Gr. *keras,* stem *kerat-,* horn] Prefixes meaning *horny substance* or *cornea.*

keratoacanthoma (kĕr″ă-tō-ăk″ăn-thō′mă) [″ + *akantha,* thorn, + *oma,* tumor] A common benign tumor that has a mound-shaped body with a central keratin-filled crater. The lesion clinically and histologically resembles squamous cell carcinoma of the skin, and may be related to this cancer. SEE: illus.

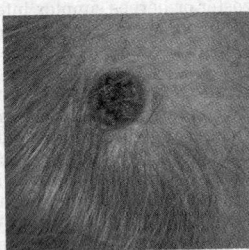

KERATOACANTHOMA

TREATMENT: Spontaneous healing of the tumor is common. Lesions that do not heal on their own can be surgically excised.

keratocele (kĕr-ăt′ō-sēl) [″ + *kele,* tumor, swelling] The protrusion or herniation of Descemet's membrane through a weakened or absent corneal stroma as a result of injury or ulcer.

keratoconjunctivitis (kĕr″ă-tō-kŏn-jŭnk″tĭ-vī′tĭs) Inflammation of the cornea and the conjunctiva.

epidemic k. An acute, self-limited keratoconjunctivitis caused by a highly infectious adenovirus. SYN: *acute contagious* **conjunctivitis.**

flash k. Painful keratoconjunctivitis resulting from exposure of the eyes to intense ultraviolet irradiation. Arc welders whose eyes are not properly protected will develop this acute condition.

phlyctenular k. A delayed hypersensitivity response (type IV) to antigens in the conjunctiva. The disease may be caused by *Chlamydia, Mycobacterium tuberculosis,* and *Staphylococcus aureus.* Symptoms include pain and photophobia; in severe cases, perforation of the cornea can occur. Treatment depends on the underlying cause.

k. sicca Dryness with hyperemia of the conjunctiva in Sjögren's syndrome owing to autoimmune-mediated decreased lacrimal function. The corneal epithelium may be thickened and visual acuity impaired. The condition is treated by use of artificial tears and other ocular lubricants. SYN: *dry eye; xerophthalmia.* SEE: *Schirmer's test; Sjögren's syndrome.*

keratoconus (kĕr-ă-tō-kō′nŭs) [″ + *konos,* cone] A hereditary, degenerative corneal disease resulting in a conical protrusion of the central cornea with thinning. It is often bilateral, occurring in the second decade of life. Initially, the disease is asymptomatic with a decrease in vision, correctable with glasses. Significant astigmatism is associated with progression of the disease.

Rigid contact lenses and eventually a corneal transplant may be needed to improve vision. Perforation of the thinned central cornea may result and is called hydrops, which can significantly decease visual acuity.

keratocyte (kĕr′ă-tō-sīt) **1.** A corneal connective tissue cell. **2.** A spiculated or spindle-shaped red blood cell, sometimes seen in peripheral blood smears in patients with hemolytic anemias.

keratoderma, keratodermia (kĕe″ăt-ō-dĕr′mă, -dĕr′mē-ă) [*kerato-* + *derma*] A disease, localized or disseminated, of the horny layer of the skin.

k. blennorrhagica Prominent hyperkeratotic scaling lesions of the palms, soles, and penis; around the nails; and occasionally in other areas. This condition is associated with Reiter syndrome.

k. climactericum Hyperkeratosis of the palms and soles of women, which may occur during menopause.

keratodermatitis (kĕr″ă-tō-dĕr″mă-tī′tĭs) [″ + ″ + *itis,* inflammation] Inflammation of the horny layer of the skin with proliferation.

keratogenous (kĕr-ă-tŏj′ĕ-nŭs) [″ + *gennan,* to produce] Causing horny tissue development.

keratoglobus (kĕr″ă-tō-glō′bŭs) [″ + L. *globus,* circle] A globular protrusion and enlargement of the cornea, seen in congenital glaucoma.

keratohelcosis (kĕr″ă-tō-hĕl-kō′sĭs) [″ + *helkosis,* ulceration] Corneal ulceration.

keratohyalin (kĕr″ă-tō-hī′ă-lĭn) The precursor of keratin, present in the form of granules in the cytoplasm of cells in the stratum granulosum of keratinized mucosa or epidermis of the skin.

keratoid (kĕr′ă-toyd) [″ + *eidos,* form, shape] Horny; resembling corneal tissue.

keratoiritis (kĕr″ă-tō-ī-rī′tĭs) [″ + *iris,* iris, + *itis,* inflammation] Inflammation of the cornea and iris.

keratoleptynsis (kĕr″ă-tō-lĕp-tĭn′sĭs) [″ + *leptynein,* to make thin] A cosmetic operation performed on a sightless eye. The procedure involves removing the corneal surface and covering the area with bulbar conjunctiva.

keratoleukoma (kĕr″ă-tō-lū-kō′mă) [″ + *leukos,* white, + *oma,* tumor] White corneal opacity.

keratolysis (kĕr-ă-tŏl′ĭ-sĭs) [″ + *lysis,* dissolution] **1.** A loosening of the horny layer of the skin. **2.** Shedding of the skin at regular intervals.

pitted k. Hyperkeratotic areas of the soles and palms with erosion and pitting. The etiology is unknown but may involve infection with *Corynebacterium* or *Actinomyces.* It occurs mostly in barefooted adults in the tropics.

keratolytic (kĕr″ă-tō-lĭt′ĭk) **1.** Rel. to or

causing keratolysis. SYN: *desquamative*. **2.** An agent that causes or promotes keratolysis.

keratoma (kĕr″ă-tō′mă) [″ + *oma*, tumor] Keratosis (2).

keratomalacia (kĕr″ă-tō-mă-lā′shē-ă) [″ + *malakia*, softness] Softening of the cornea seen in early childhood owing to deficiencies of vitamin A. SEE: *xerotic keratitis*.

keratome (kĕr′ă-tōm) [″ + *tome*, incision] A knife for incising the cornea. SYN: *keratotome*.

keratometer (kĕr-ă-tŏm′ĕ-ter) [″ + *metron*, measure] An instrument for measuring the curves of the cornea that is used to prepare contact lenses.

keratometry (kĕr″ă-tŏm′ĕ-trē) [″ + *metron*, measure] Measurement of the cornea.

keratomileusis (kĕr″ă-tō-mĭ-loo′sĭs) [″ + *smileusis*, carving] Plastic surgery of the cornea in which a portion is removed and frozen and its curvature reshaped; then it is reattached to the cornea.

   laser-assisted in-situ k. ABBR: LASIK. A surgical treatment for nearsightedness, farsightedness, and other refractive errors of vision. In this procedure, a microtome is used to cut a thin flap on the surface of the cornea and a laser is used to resculpt the deeper tissue and correct refractive errors. Many patients have a marked improvement in their visual acuity as a result of the procedure. Complications can include infections, hazy vision, double vision, visual halos, the need for reoperation, corneal burns requiring corneal transplant, and blindness.

keratomycosis (kĕr″ă-tō-mī-kō′sĭs) [″ + *mykes*, fungus, + *osis*, condition] Fungal infection of the cornea.

keratonosis (kĕr″ă-tō-nō′sĭs) [″ + *nosos*, disease] Any noninflammatory disease or deformity of the horny layer of the skin.

keratopathy (kĕr″ă-top′ă-thē) [*kerato-* + *-pathy*] A degenerative process with small blister-like lesions in a swollen corneal epithelial layer; vision is significantly decreased.

   band k. Band-shaped calcium deposits in the superficial layer of the cornea and Bowman's membrane. This occurs with chronic intraocular inflammation such as in juvenile rheumatoid arthritis, and with systemic diseases in which there is hypercalcemia.

   bullous k. Either of two corneal edemas in an eye in which the natural lens has been removed, aphakic (ABK) or pseudophakic (PBK).

   pseudophakic bullous k. Keratopathy occurring after cataract surgery; more common after placement of an anterior chamber lens.

keratoplasty (ker′ăt-ō-plas″tē) [*kerato-* + *-plasty*] Corneal grafting. The replacement of a cloudy cornea with a transparent one, typically derived from an organ donor. SEE: *lens, corneal contact*.

   deep lamellar endothelial k. ABBR: DLEK. Transplantation of the two innermost layers of the cornea, Descemet's membrane and the corneal endothelium, leaving the outer cornea layers intact.

   Descemet stripping automated endothelial k. ABBR: DSAEK. Transplantation of the layer of the cornea just anterior to the corneal endothelium with donor tissue after Descemet's membrane has been removed from the recipient's eye. It is used to treat corneal diseases such as Fuchs' corneal dystrophy which impact only the innermost layers of the cornea.

   lamellar k. Transplantation of donated corneal tissue into the middle layers of the cornea, leaving the corneal endothelium and inner layers of the cornea intact.

   optic k. The removal of a corneal scar and replacement with corneal tissue.

   refractive k. Treatment of myopia or hyperopia by removing a portion of the cornea, freezing it in order to reshape it surgically to correct refractive error, and then replacing it after it has thawed. SEE: *keratomileusis*.

   tectonic k. Use of corneal tissue to replace that lost because of trauma or disease.

   therapeutic penetrating k. A treatment for corneal ulceration with perforation or keratitis that has not responded to aggressive medical treatment in which a donated cornea is transplanted into the patient's diseased cornea after the cornea has been completely removed from the eye, the anterior chamber is cleansed, and the lens removed.

keratoprosthesis (kĕr″ă-tō-prŏs-thē′sĭs) A corneal implant, used to replace a clouded portion of the cornea.

keratoprotein (kĕr″ă-tō-prō′tē-ĭn) [″ + *protos*, first] The protein of the hair, nails, and epidermis. SEE: *keratin*.

keratorrhexis (kĕr″ă-tō-rĕks′ĭs) [″ + *rhexis*, rupture] Corneal rupture.

keratoscleritis (kĕr″ă-tō-sklĕr-ī′tĭs) [″ + *skleros*, hard, + *itis*, inflammation] Inflammation of both cornea and sclera.

keratoscope (kĕr′ăt-ō-skōp) [″ + *skopein*, to examine] An instrument for examination of the cornea.

keratoscopy (kĕr″ă-tŏs′kŏ-pē) Examination of the cornea and its reflection of light.

keratose (kĕr′ă-tōs) [Gr. *keras*, horn] Horny.

keratosis (ker″ă-tō′sĭs, -tō′sēz″) *pl.* **keratoses** [*kerato-* + *-osis*] **1.** Growth of the horny layer of the skin; a callus, callosity, or keratoma. **2.** Any condition of the skin characterized by the formation of horny growths or excessive development of the horny growth. **keratotic** (″ă-tot′ik), *adj.* SYN: *keratoma.*

actinic k. ABBR: AK. A rough, sandpaper-textured, premalignant macule or papule caused by excess exposure to ultraviolet light. AKs often appear on facial skin (such as near the eyes, on the nose, on the ears, or the lips) and the parts of the body that receive the most sunlight exposure. Prevention of AKs depends on limiting one's exposure to sunlight, beginning in childhood and continuing throughout life. SEE: illus.

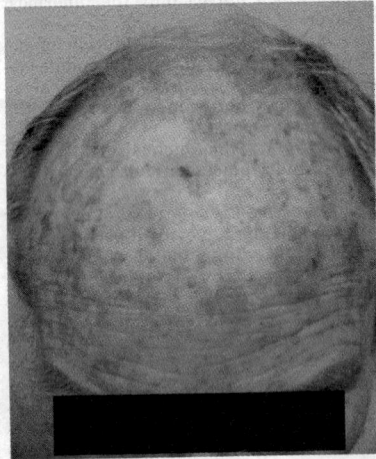

ACTINIC KERATOSIS

Actinic skin damage on forehead and scalp

TREATMENT: Liquid nitrogen destroys these lesions and prevents them from progressing to other cancers of the skin. SYN: *solar k.* SEE: *sunscreen.*

k. follicularis Darier's disease.

k. nigricans **Acanthosis** nigricans.

oral k. Keratinization of the mucosa of the mouth to an unusual extent, or in locations normally not keratinized, as a result of an inherited autosomal dominant gene or the more common effect of tobacco and other carcinogens.

k. palmaris et plantaris A congenital abnormality of the palms and soles, characterized by a dense thickening of the keratin layer in these regions.

k. pharyngis Horny projections from the pharyngeal tonsils and adjacent lymphoid tissue.

k. pilaris Chronic inflammatory disorder of area surrounding the hair follicles. It is often found in patients with

atopic dermatitis. SYN: *lichen pilaris; lichen spinulosus.*

SYMPTOMS: The disorder is characterized by an accumulation of horny material at follicular orifices of persons with rough, dry skin. It is most pronounced in winter on lateral aspects of thighs and upper arms with possible extension to legs, forearms, and scalp.

TREATMENT: There is no specific therapy, but keratolytic lotions may be of some value.

k. punctata Discrete horny projections from the sweat pores of the palms and soles.

seborrheic k. A benign skin tumor that may be pigmented. It is composed of immature epithelial cells and is quite common in older adults. Its etiology is unknown.

SYMPTOMS: Keratoid, nevoid, acanthoid, or verrucose types occur in older adults and in those with long-standing dry seborrhea, on the face, scalp, interscapular or sternal regions, and backs of the hands. The yellow, gray, or brown sharply circumscribed lesions are covered with a firmly adherent scale, greasy or velvety on the trunk or scalp but harsh, rough, and dry on the face or hands.

TREATMENT: Thorough curettage is effective. This leaves a flat surface that becomes covered with normal skin within about 1 week. Pedunculated lesions can be removed surgically. Cautery may produce scarring and should not be used. SYN: *wart, seborrheic.* SEE: illus.

SEBORRHEIC KERATOSES ON BACK

k. senilis An inaccurate synonym for actinic keratosis, which is caused by accumulated ultraviolet light exposure, not by aging.

solar k. Actinic **k.**

stucco k. Benign papules, typically found on the lower extremities, histologically related to seborrheic keratoses. SEE: illus.

keratotome (kĕr-ăt′ō-tōm) [″ + *tome,* incision] Keratome.

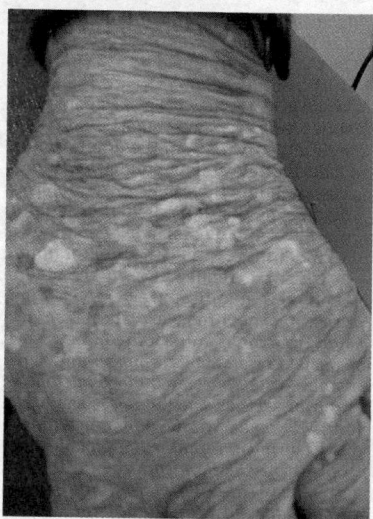

STUCCO KERATOSIS
White warty lesions of the dorsum of the
fist

keratotomy (ker-ă-tot′ŏ-mē) [*kerato-* +
-tomy] **1.** Incision of the cornea. **2.** Removal of the corneal epithelium, typically by scraping.
   radial k. Surgical therapy for nearsightedness. Very shallow, bloodless,
hairline, radial incisions are made, e.g.,
by a laser, in the outer perimeter of the
cornea where they will not interfere
with vision. This allows the cornea to
flatten and helps correct the nearsightedness. About two thirds of patients undergoing this procedure will be able to
eliminate the use of glasses or contact
lenses.
keratouveitis Inflammation of both the
cornea and the uveal tract (i.e., of both
the cornea and the iris, ciliary body, and
choroid). SYN: *cyclokeratitis.*
kerion (kē′rē-ŏn) [Gr., honeycomb] An
inflamed, boggy mass that appears on
the scalp of some patients with tinea
capitis. It is believed to represent a hypersensitivity reaction to fungal antigens. It may result in a localized area of
permanent hair loss.
Kerley lines (kĕr′lē) [P. J. Kerley, Brit.
radiologist, b. 1900] Lines present on
chest radiographs of patients with any
disease that causes thickening or infiltration of the interlobular septa. Those
in the costophrenic angle area are called
Kerley B lines, and those extending peripherally from the hilum are termed
Kerley A lines. Kerley C lines are fine
lines in the middle of pulmonary tissue.
kernicterus (kĕr-nĭk′tĕr-ŭs) [Ger.] A
form of jaundice occurring in newborns

during the second to eighth day after
birth. The basal ganglia and other areas
of the brain and spinal cord are infiltrated with bilirubin, a yellow substance produced by the breakdown of
hemoglobin. The disorder is treated by
phototherapy and exchange transfusion
to limit neurological damage. The prognosis is quite poor if the condition is left
untreated. SEE: *erythroblastosis fetalis;
hemolytic disease of the newborn; hyperbilirubinemia; icterus gravis neonatorum; phototherapy.*
Kernig sign (ker′nig) [Vladimir Mikhailovich Kernig, Russian physician, 1840–
1917] A sign of meningeal irritation evidenced by reflex contraction and pain
in the hamstring muscles, when attempting to extend the leg after flexing
the hip.
kerosene (kĕr′ō-sēn) A flammable liquid
fuel distilled from petroleum. It is used
as a solvent as well as a fuel source.
SEE: *Poisons and Poisoning Appendix.*
keto-, ket- [Formed fm *ketone*] Prefixes
meaning *containing a ketone group*, e.g.,
ketoacidosis, ketosis, ketolysis.
ketoacidosis (kēt″ō-as″ĭ-dō′sĭs) [*keto-* +
acidosis] Acidosis due to an excess of
ketone bodies. It occurs in individuals
who do not produce adequate insulin to
sustain normal fat metabolism.
   alcoholic k. Ketoacidosis that results
from the hypercatecholaminergic effects
of alcohol withdrawal, in addition to
starvation, and dehydration.
   diabetic a. ABBR: DKA. Acidosis
caused by an accumulation of ketone
bodies, in advanced stages of uncontrolled diabetes mellitus. SEE: *diabetic
coma; Nursing Diagnoses Appendix.*
ketoaciduria (kē″tō-ăs″ĭ-dū′rē-ă) [″ + ″
+ Gr. *ouron,* urine] The presence of
keto acids in the urine.
ketogenesis (kē-tō-jĕn′ĕ-sĭs) [″ + Gr.
genesis, generation, birth] The production of acetone or other ketones.
ketolide (kē′tō-līd″) A derivative of the
macrolide antibiotics, modified by the
addition of a ketone to the macrolide
structure. Telithromycin is a ketolide.
ketolysis (kē-tŏl′ĭ-sĭs) [″ + Gr. *lysis,*
dissolution] The dissolution of acetone
or ketone bodies. **ketolytic,** *adj.*
ketone (kē′tōn″) [Ger. *Keton,* fm Ger.
Aceton, acetone] A substance containing the carbonyl group (C=O) attached
to two carbon atoms. Acetone, C_3H_6O, is
a simple ketone.
ketone body SEE: under *body.*
ketonemia (kē″tō-nē′mē-ă) [″ + Gr.
haima, blood] The presence of acetone
bodies in the blood, which causes the
characteristic fruity breath odor in ketoacidosis.
ketonuria (kē-tō-nū′rē-ă) [″ + Gr.
ouron, urine] Acetone bodies in the
urine.

ketoplasia (kē-tō-plā′sē-ă) [″ + Gr. *plassein,* to form] The formation or excretion of ketones.

ketoplastic (kē″tō-plăs′tĭk) [″ + Gr. *plastikos,* formed] Pert. to ketoplasia or to the formation of ketones.

ketose (kē′tōs) A carbohydrate containing the ketones.

ketosis (kē-tō′sĭs) [*ketone* + *-osis*] The accumulation in the body of the ketone bodies. It is frequently associated with acidosis. Ketosis results from the incomplete metabolism of fatty acids, usually from carbohydrate deficiency or inadequate use, and is commonly observed in starvation, high-fat diet, and pregnancy; and most significantly in inadequately controlled diabetes mellitus. Large quantities of these ketone bodies may be eliminated in the urine (ketonuria). Ketosis is easily determined by testing for the presence of ketones in blood specimens. **ketotic,** *adj.*

17-ketosteroid (kē-tō-stĕr′oyd) One of a group of neutral steroids having a ketone group in carbon position 17. They are produced by the adrenal cortex and gonads and appear normally in the urine. Among them are androsterone, dehydroisoandrosterone, corticosterone, and 11-hydroxyisoandrosterone. A greater than normal or less than normal excretion in the urine is indicative of certain endocrine disorders such as adrenal adenomas or Cushing's syndrome.

ketosuria (kē″tō-sū′rē-ă) Presence of ketone bodies in the urine. SEE: *ketosis.*

keV *kiloelectron volts.*

keystone area ABBR: K area. The junction of the perpendicular portion of the ethmoid bones with the nasal septum.

kg *kilogram.*

kg-m *kilogram-meter.*

khat, kat, qat (kot) [Arabic *qāt*] A plant (*Catha edulis*) found in east Africa and the Arabian peninsula whose leaves are chewed for their stimulant properties.

The leaves contain norpseudoephedrine (a drug with amphetamine-like properties that can cause anxiety, insomnia, and, occasionally, psychosis).

KHE *Kaposiform* **hemangioendothelioma**.

kHz *kilohertz.*

KI Formula for potassium iodide.

kidney (kid′nē) One of a pair of purple-brown organs situated at the back (retroperitoneal area) of the abdominal cavity; each is lateral to the spinal column. The kidneys form urine from blood plasma. They are the major regulators of the water, electrolyte, and acid-base content of the blood and, indirectly, all body fluids.

ANATOMY: The top of each kidney is opposite the 12th thoracic vertebra; the bottom is opposite the third lumbar vertebra. The right kidney is slightly lower than the left one. Each kidney weighs 113 to 170 g (4 to 6 oz), and each is about 11.4 cm (4½ in) long, 5 to 7.5 cm (2 to 3 in) broad, and 2.5 cm (1 in) thick. The kidneys in the newborn are about three times as large in proportion to body weight as they are in the adult.

Each kidney is surrounded by adipose tissue and by the renal fascia, a fibrous membrane that helps hold the kidney in place. On the medial side of a kidney is an indentation called the hilus or hilum, at which the renal artery enters and the renal vein and ureter emerge. The microscopic nephrons are the structural and functional units of the kidney; each consists of a renal corpuscle and renal tubule with associated blood vessels. In frontal section, the kidney is composed of two areas of tissue and a medial cavity. The outer renal cortex is made of renal corpuscles and convoluted tubules. The renal medulla consists of 8 to 18 wedge-shaped areas called renal pyramids; they are made of loops of Henle and collecting tubules. Adjacent to the hilus is the renal pelvis, the expanded end of the ureter within the kidney. Urine formed in the nephrons is carried by a papillary duct to the tip (papilla) of a pyramid, which projects into a cuplike calyx, an extension of the renal pelvis. SEE: illus. (Kidney).

NEPHRON: The nephron consists of a renal corpuscle and renal tubule. The renal corpuscle is made of a capillary network called a glomerulus surrounded by Bowman's capsule. The renal tubule extends from Bowman's capsule. The parts, in order, are as follows: proximal convoluted tubule, loop of Henle, distal convoluted tubule, and collecting tubule, all of which are surrounded by peritubular capillaries. SEE: illus. (Nephron With Its Associated Blood Vessels).

FORMATION OF URINE: Urine is formed by filtration, reabsorption, and secretion. As blood passes through the glomerulus, water and dissolved substances are filtered through the capillary membranes and the inner or visceral layer of Bowman's capsule; this fluid is now called glomerular filtrate. Blood cells and large proteins are retained within the capillaries. Filtration is a continuous process; the rate varies with blood flow through the kidneys and daily fluid intake and loss. As the glomerular filtrate passes through the renal tubules, useful materials such as water, glucose, amino acids, vitamins, and minerals are reabsorbed into the peritubular capillaries. Most of these have a renal threshold level, i.e., a limit to how much can be reabsorbed, but this level is usually not exceeded unless the blood level of these materials is above

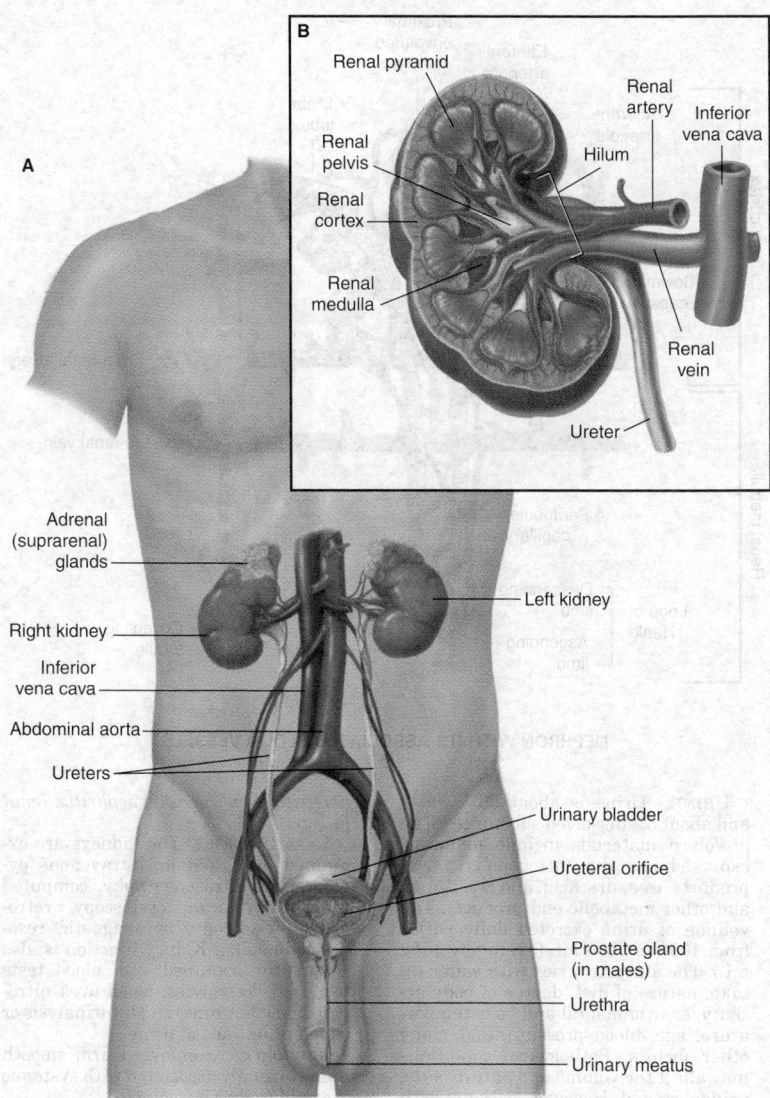

KIDNEY
A. Urinary Structures; B. Cross section of the kidney

normal. Reabsorption of water is regulated directly by antidiuretic hormone and indirectly by aldosterone. Most waste products remain in the filtrate and become part of the urine. Hydrogen ions, creatinine, and the metabolic products of medications may be actively secreted into the filtrate to become part of the urine. The collecting tubules unite to form papillary ducts that empty urine into the calyces of the renal pelvis, from

which it enters the ureter and is transported to the urinary bladder. Periodically the bladder is emptied (a reflex subject to voluntary control) by way of the urethra; this is called micturition, urination, or voiding. If a normally hydrated individual ingests a large volume of aqueous fluids, in about 45 min a sufficient quantity will have been excreted into the bladder to cause the urge to urinate.

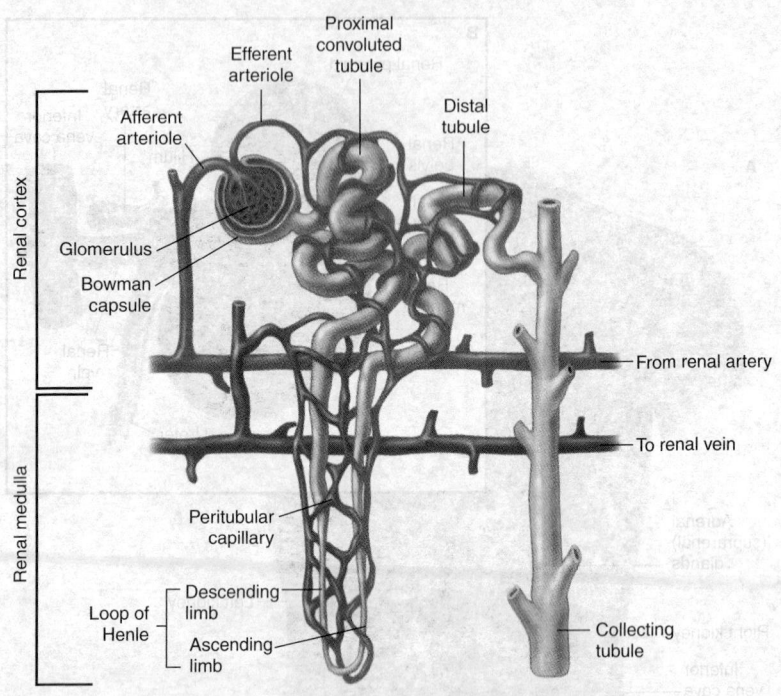

NEPHRON WITH ITS ASSOCIATED BLOOD VESSELS

URINE: Urine is about 95% water and about 5% dissolved substances. The dissolved materials include minerals, esp. sodium, the nitrogenous waste products urea, uric acid, and creatinine, and other metabolic end products. The volume of urine excreted daily varies from 1000 to 2000 mL (averaging 1500 mL). The amount varies with water intake, nature of diet, degree of body activity, environmental and body temperature, age, blood pressure, and many other factors. Pathological conditions may affect the volume and nature of the urine excreted. However, patients with only one kidney have been found to have normal renal function even after half of that kidney was removed because of cancer. There is no evidence that forcing fluids is detrimental to the kidneys.

NERVE SUPPLY: The nerve supply consists of sympathetic fibers to the renal blood vessels. These promote constriction or dilation, esp. of arteries and arterioles.

DISORDERS: Frequently encountered diseases of the kidney include infection (pyelonephritis), stone formation (nephrolithiasis), dilation (hydronephrosis), protein loss (nephrosis), cancer (hypernephroma), and acute or chronic renal failure. SEE: *dialysis; glomerulo-nephritis; nephropathy; nephritis; renal failure*.

EXAMINATION: The kidneys are examined by palpation, intravenous pyelography, ultrasonography, computed tomography scan, cystoscopy, retrograde cystoscopy, or magnetic resonance imaging. Kidney function is also frequently examined with blood tests (e.g., for electrolytes, blood urea nitrogen, and creatinine) and by urinalysis or timed collections of urine.

amyloid k. An enlarged, firm, smooth kidney usually associated with systemic amyloidosis. SYN: *waxy k.*

SYMPTOMS: Infected persons typically lose large quantities of protein in the urine and may present with edema or symptoms of fluid overload, nephrosis, or renal failure.

artificial k. Dialyzer.

cake k. Congenitally fused kidneys.

contracted k. The abnormally small kidney found in end-stage renal disease.

cystic k. A kidney that has undergone cystic degeneration. SEE: *polycystic kidney disease.*

embolic contracted k. A kidney in which embolic infarction of the renal arterioles produces degeneration of renal tissue and hyperplasia of fibrous tissues produces irregular contraction.

fatty k. A kidney with fatty infiltration or degeneration of tubular, glomerular, or capsular epithelium, or of vascular connective tissue.

flea-bitten k. A kidney with small petechiae covering the surface, a pathological finding in bacterial endocarditis and some other systemic illnesses.

floating k. A kidney that is displaced and movable.

fused k. A condition in which the kidneys are joined into one anomalous organ.

   Goldblatt k. SEE: under *Goldblatt, Harry.*

   horseshoe k. A congenital malformation in which the superior or inferior extremities are united by an isthmus of renal or fibrous tissue, forming a horseshoe shape.

   hypermobile k. A freely movable kidney. SYN: *wandering k.*

   medullary sponge k. A congenital condition characterized by the presence—seen best during urography—of spongy or porous appearing renal collecting tubules. The disease may be asymptomatic or may cause urinary bleeding, stone formation with renal colic, or recurrent urinary tract infections. SYN: *Cacchi-Ricci syndrome.*

   movable k. A kidney that is not firmly attached owing to lack of support of fatty tissue and perinephric fascia. SYN: *nephroptosis.*

   myeloma k. Cast nephropathy.

   polycystic k. A kidney bearing many cysts. SEE: *kidney disease, polycystic.*

   sacculated k. A condition in which the kidney has been absorbed and only the distended capsule remains.

   small indented calcified k. ABBR: SICK. The computed tomographic (CT) appearance of the kidneys in patients who develop chronic kidney disease from the overuse of analgesic medications like acetaminophen, aspirin, ibuprofen, or phenacetin.

   syphilitic k. Kidney with fibrous bands running across it, and caseating gummata, as a result of syphilis.

   wandering k. Hypermobile **k.**

   waxy k. Amyloid **k.**

kidney disease, polycystic ABBR: PKD. An inherited renal disorder transmitted as an autosomal recessive trait in infants and as an autosomal dominant trait in adults. PKD was previously termed *adult polycystic kidney disease.* It is characterized by cyst formation in ductal organs, particularly the kidney and liver, and by gastrointestinal and cardiovascular abnormalities. Included are colonic diverticula, cardiac valvular abnormalities, and intracranial and aortic aneurysms. Symptoms include hypertension, acute and chronic pain, and urinary tract infections. It is one of the most common hereditary disorders, occurring in about 1 in 400 to 1 in 1000 people. An estimated 500,000 persons have the disease in the U.S. It accounts for 10% of cases of end-stage renal disease. Treatment includes medical therapy for renal failure with eventual renal dialysis and renal transplantation.

Kidney Disease: Improving Global Outcomes ABBR: KDIGO. An international foundation administered by the National Kidney Foundation (U.S.) that aims to foster collaboration in the study of kidney diseases and the dissemination of the best treatment practices through the publication of clinical guidelines.

kidney stone Renal **calculus**.

Kienböck, Robert (kēn'bek″, bōk″) Austrian radiologist, 1871–1953.

   K. disease Osteochondrosis or slow degeneration of the lunate bone of the wrist, usually resulting from trauma. Radiographic evidence includes sclerosis and collapse of the lunate bone. Treatment goals are to reduce pain, maintain motion, and prevent carpal collapse and ultimately arthritis. Untreated, it may result in loss of ulnar deviation

   K. sign Paradoxical movement of the diaphragm upward during inspiration and downward during exhalation, a physical finding in diaphragmatic paralysis.

Kiesselbach area (kē'sěl-bok″) [Wilhelm Kiesselbach, Ger. laryngologist, 1839–1902] A rich network of veins on the anteroinferior portion of the nasal septum. Because of its abundant supply of capillaries, it is a common site of nosebleed.

Kikuchi lymphadenitis (kē-koo-chē) [Masahiro Kikuchi, contemporary Japanese pathologist] Necrotizing inflammation of lymph nodes, usually occurring in young adults. The disease typically affects lymph nodes in the neck, is often associated with a rash and fever, and remits without treatment.

kilo- [Fr. fr Gr. *chilioi*, a thousand] ABBR: k, K. In the Système International d'Unités (SI system), a prefix meaning *1000.*

kilobase (kǐl'ō-bās″) ABBR: kb. Unit indicating the length of a nucleic acid sequence. One kb is 1000 nucleotide sequences long.

kilocalorie (kǐl'ō-kǎl'ŏ-rē) ABBR: C, kcal. A unit of measure for heat. In nutrition, a kilocalorie is known as a large Calorie and is always written with a capital C. SEE: *calorie.*

kilocycle (kǐl'ō-sī″k'l) ABBR: kc. One thousand cycles; previous name for kilohertz.

kilodalton (kĭl'ŏ-dolt"ŏn) [*kilo-* + *dalton*] ABBR: kD, kDa. A unit of molecular mass consisting of 1000 daltons.

kilogram (kĭl'ō-grăm") [Fr. *kilo,* a thousand, + *gramme,* a weight] ABBR: kg. One thousand grams or 2.2 lb avoirdupois. A unit of mass. SEE: *newton; pascal;* SI Units.

kilogram-meter (kĭl'ō-grăm"-mē'tĕr) ABBR: kg-m. The work required to raise a mass of 1 kg by a height of 1 m.

kilohertz (kĭl'ō-hĕrtz") ABBR: kHz. In electricity, a unit of 1000 cycles; formerly called kilocycle.

kilojoule (kil'ŏ-jool") [*kilo-* + *joule*] ABBR: kJ. One thousand joules. Nutritionally, one kilojoule is equal to one calorie.

kiloliter (kĭl'ō-lē"tĕr) [Fr. *kilolitre*] ABBR: kl, kL. One thousand liters.

kilometer (kĭl'ō-mēt"ĕr, ki-lom'ĕt-ĕr) [Fr. *kilomètre*] ABBR: K, km. In the metric system, one thousand meters, or 3281 feet (roughly 0.62 mile).

kilopascal (kĭl"ō-păs-kăl') [Fr. *kilo,* a thousand, + *Pascal,* Fr. scientist] ABBR: kPa. In SI units, a unit of pressure equal to 1000 pascals. Attempts to have blood pressure expressed in kPa have not been accepted. SEE: *pascal.*

kilounit (kĭl'ŏ-ū'nĭt) One thousand units.

kilovolt (kĭl'ŏ-vōlt") ABBR: kV. One thousand volts.

kilovoltage peak (kĭl'ō-vōlt"ĭj) ABBR: kVp. The highest voltage occurring during an electrical cycle.

kilowatt (kĭl'ō-wăt") ABBR: kW. A unit of electrical energy equal to 1000 watts.

Kimmelstiel-Wilson syndrome (kĭm'ĕl-stēl-wĭl'sŏn) [Paul Kimmelstiel, Ger. physician, 1900–1970; Clifford Wilson, Brit. physician, 1906–1997] A syndrome that may develop in patients in whom diabetes mellitus has been present for several years. Hypertension, glomerulonephrosis, edema, and retinal lesions are present; arteriosclerosis of the renal artery is a common complication. SEE: *diabetes.*

kinanesthesia (kĭn-ăn-ĕs-thē'zē-ă) [Gr. *kinesis,* movement, + *an-,* not, + *aisthesis,* sensation] The inability to perceive the extent of a movement or direction, resulting in ataxia.

kinase (kĭn'ās) An enzyme that catalyzes the conversion of a proenzyme to a fully active enzyme.

cyclin-dependent k. ABBR: CDK. A family of enzymes involved in regulation of the cell cycle. They serve as targets for pharmacological manipulation of this cycle, particularly during the unregulated proliferation of tumor cells.

myosin light chain k. An enzyme in smooth muscle cells that catalyzes the transfer of a phosphate group from adenosine triphosphate to myosin, which initiates contraction.

protein k. SEE: *protein kinase.*

tyrosine k. Any of a group of enzymes that influence signaling between cells, esp. as relates to cell growth and death, cellular adhesion and movement, and cellular differentiation. Abnormalities in tyrosine kinases are found in some human diseases, including chronic myeloid (myelogenous) leukemia.

kindling (kĭnd'lĭng) The triggering of seizures as a result of repetitive low-amplitude electrical stimulation of the brain. This phenomenon is typical of seizures in persons suffering alcohol (and other forms of drug) withdrawal.

kinematics (kĭn"ē-măt'ĭks) [Gr. *kinematos,* movement] The branch of biomechanics concerned with description of the movements of segments of the body without regard to the forces that caused the movement to occur. SEE: *arthrokinematics; osteokinematics.*

kinescope (kĭn'ĕ-skōp) [" + *skopein,* to examine] A device for testing the refraction of the eye. A slit of variable width moves as the patient observes a fixed object.

-kinesia [Gr. *-kinēsia,* fr. *kinēsis,* movement] Suffix meaning *motion, movement,* or *sickness caused by motion.* SEE: *kinesis.*

kinesiatrics (kĭ-nē"sē-ăt'rĭks) [" + *iatrikos,* curative] Kinesiotherapy.

kinesics (kī-nē'sĭks) Systematic study of the body and the use of its static and dynamic position as a means of communication. SEE: *body language.*

kinesigenic (kĭ-nē"sĭ-jĕn'ĭk) [" + "] Said of certain involuntary body movements, triggered by voluntary muscular activity.

kinesimeter (kĭn"ĕ-sĭm'ĕ-tĕr) [" + *metron,* measure] An apparatus for determining the extent of movement of a part.

kinesiodic (kĭ-nē"sē-ŏd'ĭk) [" + *hodos,* path] Pert. to paths through which motor impulses pass.

kinesiology (kĭ-nē"sē-ol'ŏ-jē, kī-, "zē-) [*kinesis* + *-logy*] The study of muscles and body movement. SEE: *biomechanics.*

applied k. A technique used in chiropractic and other alternative medicine in which the strength and movement of muscle groups are purported to represent the functional abilities and weaknesses of other body systems.

kinesioneurosis (kĭ-nē"sē-ō-nū-rō'sĭs) [" + *neuron,* nerve, + *osis,* condition] A functional disorder marked by tics and spasms. SEE: *Tourette's syndrome.*

external k. Kinesioneurosis affecting external muscles.

vascular k. Kinesioneurosis of the vasomotor system.

visceral k. Kinesioneurosis affecting muscles of internal organs.

kinesiotherapy, kinesitherapy (kĭ-nē″sē-ō-thĕr′ă-pē, kĭ-nē″sē-thĕr′ă-pē) [″ + *therapeia,* treatment] A rehabilitative treatment that uses exercise or movement. It was formerly known as corrective therapy and was devised by the U.S. Armed Forces to help physical therapists with the large number of soldiers wounded during World War II. SYN: *kinesiatrics; motorpathy.*

kinesis (kĭ-nē′sĭs) [Gr. *kinēsis,* movement] Movement, esp. of an organism in reaction to a stimulus, as of a plant toward light. SEE: *-kinesia.*

kinesthesia (kĭn″ĕs-thē′zē-ă) [″ + *aisthesis,* sensation] The ability to perceive extent, direction, or weight of movement. **kinesthetic,** *adj.*

kinesthesiometer (kĭn″ĕs-thē-zē-ŏm′ĕ-tĕr) [″ + ″ + *metron,* measure] An instrument for testing the ability to determine the position of the muscles.

kinetic (kĭ-nĕt′ĭk) [Gr. *kinesis,* motion] Pert. to or consisting of motion.

kinetics (kĭ-net′iks, kī-) **1.** The branch of biomechanics that examines the forces acting on the body during movement and the motion with respect to time and forces. **2.** The turnover rate or rate of change of a factor, esp. a chemical process.

cell k. The study of cells and their growth and division. Study of these factors has led to understanding of cancer cells and has been useful in developing chemotherapeutic methods.

kinetochore (kĭ-nĕt′ō-kor″) A protein disk attached to the DNA of the centromere that connects a pair of chromatids during cell division. A spindle fiber is in turn attached to the kinetochore.

Kinetoplastida An order of flagellate protozoa. It contains several pathogenic genera including *Leishmania* and *Trypanosoma.*

kinetotherapy (kĭ-nĕt″ō-thĕr′ă-pē) [″ + *therapeia,* treatment] Kinesiotherapy.

King, Imogene (kĭng) [1923–2007] A nurse educator and theorist who developed King's Conceptual System (formerly called the General Systems Framework) and the Theory of Goal Attainment. SEE: *Nursing Theory Appendix.*

kingdom [AS. *cyningdom*] The largest category in the classification of living organisms. There are five kingdoms: Procaryotae (Monera), Protista, Fungi, Plantae, and Animalia. SEE: *taxonomy.*

Kingella (kĭng-ĕl′lăh) A genus of gram-negative bacilli of the family Neisseriaceae, normal flora of the oral cavity.

K. kingae A species that may cause bone or joint infections in children.

kinin (kī′nĭn) [Gr. *kinesis,* movement] A general term for a group of polypeptides

that have considerable biological activity. They are capable of influencing smooth muscle contraction, inducing hypotension, increasing the blood flow and permeability (vasodilation) of small blood capillaries, and inciting pain.

kininases, plasma (kī′nĭ-nās″ĕz) Plasma carboxypeptidases that inactivate plasma kinins.

kininogen (kī′nĭn-ō-jĕn) A substance that produces a kinin when acted on by certain enzymes.

kink [Low Ger. *kinke,* a twist in rope] An unnatural angle or bend in a duct or tube such as the intestine, umbilical cord, or ureter.

kinky hair disease A congenital syndrome caused by an autosomal recessive gene, consisting of short, sparse, often poorly pigmented, kinky hair and physical and mental retardation. The disease is due to a metabolic defect that causes an abnormality in the fatty acid composition of the gray matter of the brain. Death follows progressive severe degenerative changes in the central nervous system.

kino-, kin-, kine-, cino-, cin- [Gr. *kinein,* to move] Prefixes meaning *movement* or *action.*

kinocilium (kī″nō-sĭl′ē-ŭm) [″ + L. *cilium,* eyelash] Protoplasmic filament on the cell surface.

Kinsbourne syndrome (kinz′bŭrn″) [Marcel Kinsbourne, contemporary Austrian pediatric neurologist] Opsoclonus myoclonus syndrome.

kinship (kĭn′shĭp) The descendants of a common ancestor.

Kirschner wire (kĕrsh′nĕr) [Martin Kirschner, Ger. surgeon, 1879–1942] Steel wire placed through a long bone in order to apply traction to the bone.

Kisch reflex (kish) [Bruno Kisch, Ger. physiologist, 1890–1966] Closure of an eye resulting from stimulation by heat or some tactile irritant on the auditory meatus. SYN: *auriculopalpebral **reflex**.*

KJ *knee jerk.*

KK *knee kick* (knee jerk).

kL *kiloliter.*

Klatskin tumor (klat′skin) [Gerald Klatskin, U.S. physician, 1910–1986] A cholangiocarcinoma that arises in the large intrahepatic bile ducts.

Klebsiella (kleb″zē-el′ă) [*Klebs* + *-ella*] [T. A. Edwin Klebs, Ger. bacteriologist, 1834–1913] A genus of gram-negative, encapsulated bacilli of the family Enterobacteriaceae.

K. granulomatis A species that causes granuloma inguinale. It was formerly called *Calymmatobacterium granulomatis.*

K. ozaenae A species found in ozena.

K. pneumoniae A species that may cause sinusitis, bronchitis, or pneumonia. SYN: *Friedländer's bacillus.*

K. rhinoscleromatis A species that can cause rhinoscleroma, a destructive granuloma of the nose and pharynx.

Kleiger test (klīg′ĕr) A test used to determine stability of the distal tibiofibular syndesmosis and rotatory instability of the ankle mortise. With the patient sitting with the knee flexed over the table's edge, the examiner stabilizes the patient's lower leg, slightly dorsiflexes the ankle, and externally rotates the foot. Pain along the lateral ankle indicates a sprain of the distal tibiofibular syndesmosis or a fracture of the fibula. Medial ankle pain or a palpable subluxation of the talus within the ankle mortise is indicative of ankle rotatory instability.

Kleihauer-Betke test (klī′how″ĕr-bet′kē) ABBR: K-B test. A test to identify fetal red blood cells in the maternal circulation, an abnormal finding identified when fetomaternal hemorrhage has occurred.

PATIENT CARE: The test is used in several settings: 1. In Rh− mothers to determine if they have been exposed to Rh+ fetal blood. If they have, it is used to determine the dose of Rh immune globulin needed by the exposed mother to prevent future episodes of hydrops fetalis; 2. in pregnant women who have experienced traumatic injury, it is used to identify the presence of fetomaternal hemorrhage; 3. in amniocentesis, to determine whether any blood found to be present is maternal or fetal in origin. A sample of maternal blood is obtained from a vein and treated with acid. Maternal blood cells develop a pale, ghostly appearance when exposed to acid; fetal cells do not. The number of fetal cells identified microscopically per a specified number of low-power fields is used to estimate the mL of fetal bleeding into the maternal circulation.

Klein-Bell ADL Scale (klīn′bel′) In rehabilitation, an objectively scored measure of functional independence, which includes items related to self-care, mobility, and communication.

klepto- [Gr. *kleptein,* to steal] Prefix meaning *stealing, theft.*

kleptomania (klĕp-tō-mā′nē-ă) [″ + *mania,* madness] A compulsion to steal, often expressed by the repeated theft of meaningless or economically worthless objects.

kleptomaniac (klĕp″tō-mā′nē-ăk) **1.** Pert. to kleptomania. **2.** An individual who repeatedly steals objects that he or she does not need.

Klieg eye (klēg) [after John H. Kliegl, Ger. manufacturer, 1869–1959] Conjunctivitis, lacrimation, and photophobia from exposure to the intense lights used in making motion pictures or television films.

Klinefelter syndrome (klīn′felt″ĕr) [Harry F. Klinefelter, Jr., U.S. physician, 1912–1990] The most common sex chromosome syndrome, marked by primary testicular failure. The classic form is associated with the presence of an extra X chromosome. Those affected have small, firm testes, gynecomastia, abnormally long legs, minimal body and facial hair, and are infertile. The chromosomal abnormalities vary in different forms of the syndrome, and therefore the severity and number of abnormal findings are diversified. The syndrome is estimated to occur in one of 500 live male births. Diagnosis may be confirmed by chromosomal analysis of tissue culture, which usually demonstrates a 47, XXY genotype.

Klippel disease (klip′ĕl, kli-pel′) [Maurice Klippel, Fr. neurologist, 1858–1942] Weakness or pseudoparalysis due to generalized arthritis.

Klippel-Feil syndrome (fīl, fā) [Maurice Klippel; André Feil, Fr. physician, b. 1884] A congenital anomaly characterized by a short, wide neck; low hairline, esp. on the back of the neck; reduction in the number of cervical vertebrae; and fusion of the cervical spine. The central nervous system also may be affected.

Klumpke paralysis (kloomp′kē) [Augusta Déjérine-Klumpke, Fr. neurologist, 1859–1927] Atrophic paralysis of the forearm.

Klüver-Bucy syndrome (kloo′vĕr-bū′sē, klü′) [Heinrich Klüver, Ger.-born U.S. neurologist, 1897–1979; Paul C. Bucy, U. S. neurologist, b. 1904] Behavioral syndrome usually following bilateral temporal lobe removal. It is characterized by loss of recognition of people, loss of fear, rage reactions, hypersexuality, uncontrolled appetite, memory deficits, and overreaction to certain stimuli.

Kluyvera (klī′vĕr-ă) A genus of bacteria in the family Enterobacteriaceae whose members are all motile, gram-negative rods.

km *Kilometer.*

kMc *kilomegacycle.*

Knapp forceps (nap) [Herman J. Knapp, U.S. ophthalmologist, 1832–1911] A forceps with roller-like blades for expressing trachomatous granulations on the palpebral conjunctiva.

kneading (nēd′ĭng) Pétrissage.

knee (nē) **1.** The articulations formed by the distal femur, proximal tibia, and the patella. SEE: illus. **2.** Any structure shaped like a semiflexed knee. SYN: *geniculum.*

   Brodie k. SEE: under *Brodie, Sir Benjamin Collins.*

   carpetlayer's k. Prepatellar **bursitis.**

   game k. A colloquial term for internal derangement of the knee joint, char-

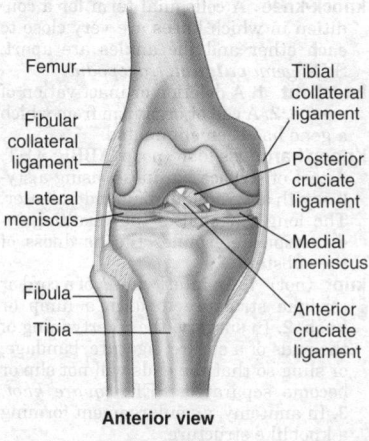

Anterior view
KNEE

acterized by pain or instability, locking, and weakness. It is usually the result of a torn internal cartilage, a fracture of the tibial spine, or an injury to the collateral or cruciate ligaments.

FIRST AID: The knee should be immobilized with a posterior splint.

DIAGNOSIS: Arthroscopy and/or magnetic resonance imaging may be necessary for a definitive diagnosis.

    housemaid's k. Prepatellar **bursitis**.

    jumper's k. A colloquial term for an overuse syndrome, marked by chronic inflammation and infrapatellar tendonitis, resulting from repetitive jumping or leg extension exercises. The usual treatment is nonsteroidal anti-inflammatory drugs, rest, and phonophoresis.

    locked k. A condition in which the leg cannot be extended. It is usually due to displacement of meniscal cartilage or dislocation of the patella.

    posterolateral corner k. The ligamentous, capsular, and muscular structures that stabilize the knee against varus, external rotation, and anterior/posterior forces. Disruption of these structures can result in posterolateral rotary instability of the knee.

    replacement of k. Orthopedic implantation of a prosthetic knee joint, particularly useful in treating patients with severe disabling arthritis of the knee. SEE: *arthroplasty*.

    roofer's k. Prepatellar **bursitis**.

    runner's k. A colloquial term for several overuse conditions resulting from excessive exercise of the lower extremities. These may involve the extensor mechanism and other musculotendinous insertions. Patellar tendonitis (jumper's knee), patellofemoral dysfunction, iliotibial band syndrome, and

pes anserinus tendonitis or bursitis have all been called by this term.

    valgus k. A medial alignment of the femur and tibia of less than 180°. SYN: *bandy leg; bowleg; genu valgum; tibia valga*. SEE: *valgus*.

    varus k. A lateral alignment of the femur and tibia of greater than 195°. SYN: *genu varum*. SEE: *varus*.

kneecap Patella.

kneeling chair An ergonomically designed chair in which most of the body weight is supported on the buttocks, but some of it is borne on the knees and shins. It creates a greater angle between the thigh and torso than a regular sitting chair to more closely approximate standing and promote maintenance of the lumbar lordosis. It is designed to alleviate or prevent low back pain.

Kneipp cure (nīp) [Sebastian Kneipp, Ger. priest, 1821–1897] The application of water in various forms and temperatures to treat disease. Treatments used in kneippism include walking barefoot in the morning dew, bathing in cool water, applying wet compresses, and hosing or spraying with water, among others. SYN: *kneippism*. SEE: *hydrotherapy*.

kneippism (nīp′izm) Kneipp cure.

knemometry (nē-mŏm′ĕt-rē) [Gr. *kneme*, shinbone, + *metron*, measure] A precise method of determining the length of a limb, esp. the lower leg. It has been used to assess infant and

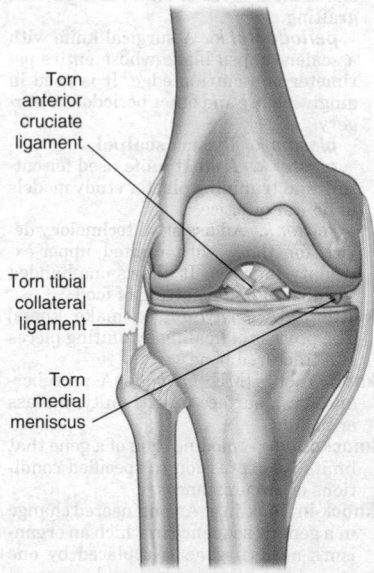

KNEE INJURIES

childhood growth and development (e.g., in premature infants or children treated with corticosteroids).

Kniest dysplasia ((k)nēst) [Wilhelm Kniest, 20th-cent. Ger. pediatrician] An autosomal-dominant collagen disorder that causes dwarfism. Findings include a short trunk, prominent and stiff joints, flattened face, eye abnormalities, deafness, inguinal hernias, hip dislocation, cleft palate, and talipes equinovarus. Patients develop severe dorsal kyphosis or kyphoscoliosis and lumbar lordosis. SYN: *Swiss cheese cartilage syndrome.*

knife (nīf) A cutting device.

> **diamond k.** A cutting instrument with a very thin, hard mineral edge, used to incise specimens or to perform delicate operations, e.g., on facial skin or the eyes.

> **electric k.** A knife that functions by a high-frequency cutting current.

> **gamma k.** A radiosurgical device that uses gamma rays from radioactive cobalt to cut or excise diseased tissue, esp. in the brain. The radioactive energy emitted by the knife is focused stereotactically to limit injury to healthy tissue.

> **gold k.** A contra-angle knife used to trim a gold filling in a tooth.

> **guarded k.** A cutting instrument in which the sharp point or edge is ensheathed rather than exposed.

> **hot k.** An electric, ultrasonic, or radiation-powered scalpel that cuts and coagulates tissues simultaneously

> **Humby k.** A cutting blade used to shave off a layer of skin, used in skin grafting.

> **periodontal k.** A surgical knife with a scaler-shaped blade whose entire perimeter is a cutting edge. It is used in gingivectomy and other periodontal surgery.

> **plasma k.** Plasma **scalpel**.

> **plaster k.** A stout knife used for cutting and trimming plaster study models in dental practice.

> **rocker k.** An assistive technology device for those with limited upper-extremity function. It allows one-handed stabilization and cutting of food.

knitting [AS. *cnyttan*, to make knots] The process of healing by uniting pieces of a fractured bone.

knob (nŏb) [ME. *knobbe*] A protuberance on a surface or extremity; a mass or nodule.

knockdown A modification of a gene that limits its expression to specified conditions or circumstances.

knock-in (nok′in″) An engineered change in a genetic sequence in which an organism's natural gene is replaced by one with a modified nucleic acid sequence that produces a functional protein.

knock-knee A colloquial term for a condition in which knees are very close to each other and the ankles are apart. SYN: *genu **valgum***; *tragopodia.*

knockout 1. A deletion or inactivation of a gene. 2. A cell or organism from which a gene has been eliminated.

Knoop hardness test (noop) ABBR: KHT. A test of surface hardness, using a stylus with a pyramidal diamond indenter. The long diagonal of the resulting indentation determines the hardness of the substance.

knot (not) 1. An intertwining of a cord or cordlike structure to form a lump or knob. 2. In surgery, the intertwining of the ends of a suture, ligature, bandage, or sling so that the ends will not slip or become separated. SEE: *square knot.* 3. In anatomy, an enlargement forming a knoblike structure.

> **false k.** An external bulging of the umbilical cord, resulting from the coiling of the umbilical blood vessels.

> **granny k.** A double knot in which the ends of the cord do not lie parallel, but alternate being over and under each other. This knot is not as secure as a square knot. SEE: *knot* for illus.

> **square k.** A double knot in which the ends of the second knot are in the same place as the ends of the first knot. SEE: *knot* for illus.; *square knot.*

> **surgeon's k.** A double knot in which the cord is passed through the first loop twice. SEE: *knot* for illus.

> **syncytial k.** A protuberance formed by many nuclei of the syntrophoblast and found on the surface of a chorionic villus.

> **true k.** A knot formed by the fetus slipping through a loop of the umbilical cord.

knowledge, deficient Lack of specific information necessary for the patient and significant other(s) to make informed choices regarding condition/therapies/treatment plan. SEE: *Nursing Diagnoses Appendix.*

knowledge (specify), readiness for enhanced The presence or acquisition of cognitive information related to a specific topic is sufficient for meeting health-related goals and can be strengthened. SEE: *Nursing Diagnoses Appendix.*

knowns (nōnz) In hypnotherapy those feelings, ideas, or images familiar to a person and therefore comfortably identifiable.

knuckle (nŭk′ĕl) [Middle Low Ger. *knokel*] Prominence of the dorsal aspect of any of the phalangeal joints, esp. of the distal heads of the metacarpals when the fist is clenched.

> **k. pad** A discrete fibromatous pad appearing over a finger joint. It usually appears between the ages of 15 and 30.

The etiology is unknown but trauma is not a significant factor.

Koch, Heinrich Herman Robert (kōk) German bacteriologist, 1843–1910.

    K.'s bacillus *Mycobacterium tuberculosis.*

    K.'s phenomenon A local inflammatory reaction resulting from injection of tuberculin into the skin of a person who has been previously exposed to the tubercle bacillus. The test represents the clinical application of a type IV (delayed-type) hypersensitivity reaction. In contemporary skin tests for tuberculosis, Koch's, or "old," tuberculin has been replaced by tuberculin purified protein derivative. SEE: *tuberculosis.*

    K.'s postulate The criterion used in proving an organism is the cause of a disease or lesion: the microorganism in question is regularly found in the lesions of the disease; pure cultures can be obtained from it. When inoculated into susceptible animals, pure cultures can reproduce the disease or pathological condition; and the organism can be obtained again in pure culture from the inoculated animal.

Koch, Walter (kōk) German surgeon, 1880–1962.

    K.'s node Atrioventricular **node.**

kocherization (kōk″ĕ-ri-zā′shŏn) [Emil Theodor *Kocher*] An operative maneuver to mobilize the duodenum before performing other procedures locally or before incising the duodenum, e.g., to expose the papilla of Vater.

Kocher reflex (kō′kĕr) [Emil Theodor Kocher, Swiss surgeon, 1841–1917] A contraction of abdominal muscles following moderate compression of the testicle.

Kock pouch, Koch pouch (kok) [Nils Kock, 20th-cent. Swedish surgeon] A continent ileostomy, constructed with a reservoir that holds intestinal waste until a catheter is used to empty it.

Koebner phenomenon (kĕb′nēr) [Heinrich Koebner, Ger. dermatologist, 1838–1904] The appearance of a skin lesion as a result of nonspecific trauma (e.g., sunlight, burn, operative wound). It will appear at the trauma site and may be of a type found elsewhere on the skin. It may be seen in lichen planus or eczema but is particularly characteristic of psoriasis. The lesion must be sufficient to act on the papillary and epidermal layers of the skin and will appear in 3 to 18 days following the trauma.

KOH Formula for potassium hydroxide.

Köhler disease (kōl′ĕr) [Alban Köhler, Ger. physician, 1874–1947] **1.** Aseptic necrosis of the navicular bone of the wrist. **2.** Osteochondrosis of the head of the second metatarsal bone of the foot.

Kohler syndrome (kōl′ĕr) Pain in the midfoot with accompanying point tenderness over the navicular bone, with increased density and narrowing of the tarsal navicular on radiographs. Most patients respond to 6 weeks' cast immobilization without long-term sequelae.

Kohlman Evaluation of Living Skills (kōl′măn) ABBR: KELS. A standard assessment for determining the ability of an individual to perform self-care and community living tasks. The assessment includes an interview and tasks that measure self-care, safety and health, money management, transportation and telephone use, and work and leisure behaviors.

koilocyte (koy′lŏ-sīt″) [Gr. *koilos*, hollow + *-cyte*] An abnormal cell of the squamous epithelium. It is characterized by a double nucleus with a perinuclear halo and is associated with an infection with the human papilloma virus.

koilocytotic atypia (koy″lŏ-sī-tŏt′ĭk ā-tĭp′ē-ă) [″ + ″ + *osis*, condition, + *a-*, not, + *typicalis*, typical] Abnormality of the top layers of the epithelium of the uterine cervix wherein the cells undergo vacuolization and enlargement. SEE: *koilocyte.*

koilonychia (koy-lŏ-nĭk′ē-ă) [″ + *onyx*, nail] Dystrophy of the fingernails in which they are thin and concave with raised edges. This condition is sometimes associated with iron-deficiency anemia. It is often called *spooning of nails.*

koilosternia (koy″lŏ-stĕr′nē-ă) [″ + Gr. *sternon*, sternum] Condition in which the chest has a funnel-like depression in the middle of the thoracic wall.

kombucha tea A folk remedy made by fermenting tea in the Kombucha "mushroom," a culture composed of yeast and other microorganisms mixed with brewed sweetened green or black tea. The tea is promoted for its healthful effects but has not been studied formally. Some outbreaks of illness and occasional deaths have been associated with its consumption.

Kondoleon operation (kon-dō′lē-on) [Emmanuel Kondoleon, Gr. surgeon, 1879–1939] The surgical removal of layers of subcutaneous tissue to relieve elephantiasis.

koniocellular (kŏn″ē-ō-sĕl′ū-lĭr) [Gr. *konis*, dust + ″] Having a granular appearance; said of cells, esp. those found in the lateral geniculate nucleus of the thalamus.

koniosis (kō-nē-ō′sĭs) [″ + *osis*, condition] Coniosis.

Koplik spot (kop′lik) [Henry Koplik, U.S. pediatrician, 1858–1927] Any of the small red spots with blue-white centers on the oral mucosa, particularly in the region opposite the molars; a diagnostic sign in measles before the rash appears. Not infrequently, the spots disappear as the rash develops.

koro (kō'rō) In China and Southeast Asia, a phobia that the penis will retract into the abdomen (or in females, that the nipples or vulva will retract into the chest or pelvis). The individual believes that once the sexual organ disappears completely, he or she will die.

Korotkoff sounds (ko-rot'kof) [Nikolai S. Korotkoff, Russian physician, 1874–1920] Sounds heard in auscultation over an artery (brachial). SEE: *blood pressure.*

Korsakoff syndrome (kor'să-kof") [Sergei S. Korsakoff, Russian neurologist, 1854–1900] Anterior superior polioencephalitis.

kosher (kō'shĕr) [Hebrew *kasher,* proper] Pert. to food prepared and served according to Jewish dietary laws.

Kostmann syndrome (kost'măn) [Rolf Kostmann, Swedish pediatrician, b. 1909] Congenital neutropenia.

koumiss, kumiss, kumyss (koo'mĭs) [Tartar *kumyz*] Fermented cow's milk or substance used for fermenting cow's milk. It is a drink traditionally consumed in Central Asia. Its alcoholic content is about 2%.

Kr Symbol for the element krypton.

Krabbe disease (krab'ē) [Knud H. Krabbe, Danish neurologist, 1885–1961] Globoid cell leukodystrophy due to the accumulation of galactocerebroside in the tissues, resulting from a deficiency of galactocerebrosidase. Clinically, affected infants develop seizures, deafness, blindness, cachexia, paralysis, and marked mental deficiency. Survival beyond 2 years is rare.

Kraepelin classification (krā'pĕ-lĭn) [Emil Kraepelin, Ger. psychiatrist, 1856–1926] An obsolete classification of mental illness into two groups: the manic-depressive and the schizophrenic.

krait (krāt) A small venomous snake of the genus *Bungarus,* indigenous to India.

kraurosis (krŏ-rō'sĭs) [Gr. *krauros,* dry] Atrophy and dryness of the skin and any mucous membrane, esp. of the vulva. The subcutaneous fat of the mons pubis and labia disappears, clitoris and prepuce atrophy, and stenosis of the vaginal orifice is common. Fissures may develop.
    k. penis Kraurosis in which the glans penis atrophies and becomes shriveled.
    k. vulvae Lichen sclerosis et atrophicus.

Krebs cycle (krebz) [Sir Hans Krebs, German-born Brit. biochemist, 1900–1981, cowinner of a Nobel prize in 1953.] A complicated series of reactions in the body involving the oxidative metabolism of pyruvic acid and liberation of energy. It is the main pathway of terminal oxidation in the process of which not only carbohydrates but proteins and fats are utilized. SYN: *citric acid cycle; tricarboxylic acid cycle.*

kringle (krĭng'gl) A subunit of plasminogen consisting of 80 amino acids in a loop structure.

kriya (krē'yă) [Sanskrit *kriya,* action] A yoga ceremony, practice, or ritual used for self-purification.

Krönig area (krā'nig) [Georg Krönig, Ger. physician, 1856–1911] Resonant region in the thorax over the apices of the lungs.

Krukenberg, Friedrich Ernst (kroo'kĕn-bĕrg) Ger. pathologist, 1871–1946.
    K. spindle Vertical pigment deposits seen on the corneal endothelium in pigment dispersion syndrome or pigmentary glaucoma.
    K. tumor A malignant metastasis to the ovary, usually bilateral and frequently secondary to malignancy of the gastrointestinal tract. Histologically, these tumors consist of myxomatous connective tissue and cells having a signet ring arrangement of their nuclei. The epithelial tissue resembles the malignancy of the original site.

krypton (krip'ton") [Gr. *krypton,* hidden] SYMB: Kr. A gaseous chemical element, one of the noble gases, atomic weight (mass) 83.80, atomic number 36. It is found in small amounts in the atmosphere. SEE: *noble **gas**.*

K-space In magnetic resonance imaging, the computer memory where frequency multiecho data can be stored prior to full reconstruction of the image.

Kt/V A mathematical formula representing a dose of dialysis. K represents the relative efficiency of the dialyzer in removing harmful solutes from the circulation; t, the duration of the treatment; and V, the volume of urea in the body.
    Increases in dialyzer efficiency and the duration of dialysis increase the dialysis dose, as do decreases in the total body volume of urea.

KUB *kidneys, ureters, bladder;* pert. to anteroposterior projection films of the abdomen.

kubisagari (koo-bĭs"ă-gă'rē) [Japanese, hang-head] Ptosis and bulbar weakness in nutritionally deficient children; endemic in Japan. A similar disorder was observed in prisoners of war in Japan. Parenteral administration of thiamine has been beneficial.

Kübler-Ross, Elisabeth (koob'lĕr-ros') [Swiss-born U.S. psychiatrist, 1926–2004] A pioneer in the understanding and treatment of dying patients and their families. She proposed that the experience of a terminal illness involves five stages: denial, anger, bargaining, depression, and acceptance.

Kufs disease (kufs) [H. Kufs, Ger. psychiatrist, 1871–1955] An adult-onset neuronal ceroid lipofuscinosis. The onset of symptoms is usually between 21 and 26 years and always before 40. The disease is characterized by the development of dementia, myoclonic jerks, blindness, and retinitis pigmentosa.

Kugelberg-Welander disease (koo′gĕl-bĕrg-vō′lăn-dĕr) [Eric Klaus Henrik Kugelberg, 1913–1983; L. Welander, b. 1909; Swedish neurologists] Juvenile spinal muscular atrophy.

Kümmell disease, Kümmell spondylitis (kim′ĕl) [Hermann Kümmell, Ger. surgeon, 1852–1937] Spondylitis following compression fracture of the vertebrae.

Kunjin virus (kŭn′jin) SEE: under *virus*.

Kupffer cell (koop′fĕr) [Karl W. von Kupffer, Ger. anatomist, 1829–1902] A macrophage of the liver. SEE: *liver*.

Kurtzke Expanded Disability Status Scale (kŭrts′kē) A widely used scale for measuring the functional status of people with multiple sclerosis. Ratings on eight systems (pyramidal, cerebellar, brainstem, sensory, bowel and bladder, visual, mental, and other) provide a combined disability score.

kuru (koo′roo) A rapidly progressive neurological disease that is invariably fatal. The disease affects mostly adult women and children of both sexes belonging to the Fore tribe of New Guinea. This disease is transmitted by consuming tissues that harbor infectious proteins (called "prions") from an individual who has died (ritual cannibalism) and rubbing infected tissues over the bodies of the women and children kin to the victim. With the decline of this practice, the incidence of kuru has decreased.

Kussmaul, Adolph (koos′mowl″) [Ger. physician, 1822–1902]
   K.'s breathing A very deep, repetitive, gasping respiratory pattern associated with profound acidosis (e.g., diabetic ketoacidosis). Kussmaul's respiration may be a sign of impending death. SYN: **Kussmaul's** *respiration*.
   K.'s disease An infrequently used eponym for polyarteritis nodosa.
   K.'s pulse Paradoxical pulse.
   K.'s respiration Kussmaul's breathing.
   K.'s sign Elevation of the neck veins (and of the central venous pressure) during inspiration, a visible indication of pericardial effusion or tamponade or of other disorders that affect the filling of the right side of the heart (e.g., severe obstructive lung disease).

kV *kilovolt.*

KVO *Keep vein open.*

kVp *kilovoltage peak.*

kwashiorkor (kwăsh-ē-or′kor) [Ghana, Africa, deposed child, i.e., child that is no longer suckled] A severe protein-deficiency type of malnutrition of children.

It occurs after the child is weaned. The clinical signs are, at first, a vague type of lethargy, apathy, or irritability and, later, failure to grow, mental deficiency, inanition, increased susceptibility to infections, edema, dermatitis, and liver enlargement. The hair may have a reddish color.
   TREATMENT: In addition to dietary therapy, the acute problems of infections, diarrhea, poor renal function, and shock need immediate attention. At first the diet must be carefully supervised to prevent overloading the system with calories or protein. In the first weeks of therapy, the child may lose weight owing to the loss of edema. If the disease has been severe and long-standing, the child may never attain full growth and mental development.

Kyasanur Forest disease (kya″să-noor′) A viral encephalitis transmitted to humans by tick bite, esp. in certain regions of India. The responsible virus is a flavivirus.

Kyasanur Forest virus (kya″să-noor′) [*Kyasanur* Forest, Karnataka, India] SEE: under *virus*.

kymatism (kī′mă-tĭzm) [Gr. *kyma*, wave, + *-ismos*, state of] Twitching of isolated segments of muscle. SYN: *myokymia*.

kymogram (kī′mō-grăm) A tracing or recording made by a kymograph.

kymograph (kī′mō-grăf) [Gr. *kyma*, wave, + *graphein*, to write] **1.** An apparatus for recording the movements of a writing pen, designed so that the pen moves in response to a force applied to it. The device consists of a drum rotated by a spring or electric motor. The drum is covered by a paper on which the record is made by the stylus of a pen. It is widely used in physiology to record activities such as blood pressure changes, muscle contractions, respiratory movements, and so on. **2.** An obsolete radiographical device for recording the range of motion of involuntary movements of the heart or diaphragm.

kymography (kī-mŏg′ră-fē) Radiographical examination to record the range of involuntary movements such as those of the heart or diaphragm.

kynocephalus (kī″nŏ-sef′ă-lŭs) [Gr. *kyon*, dog + Gr. *kephalē*, head] A deformed fetus in which the head resembles that of a dog.

kynurenine (kī″nū-rĕn′ĭn) [″ + L. *ren*, kidney] An intermediate compound in tryptophan metabolism.

kypho- [Gr. *kyphos*, bent, hunchback] Prefix meaning *humped*.

kyphoplasty (kī′fō-plas′tē) [*kypho-* + *-plasty*] A treatment for a vertebral compression fracture in which a collapsed vertebral body is restored to its normal size and shape with a balloon, followed by the injection of bone cement to maintain the bone's shape and strength.

kyphorachitis (kī″fō-răk-ī′tĭs) [″ + *rhachis,* spine, + *itis,* inflammation] A rachitic deformity involving the thorax and spinal column, which results in the development of an anteroposterior hump.

kyphos (kī′fŏs) [Gr., hump] A convex prominence of the spine.

kyphoscoliosis (kī″fō-skō″lē-ō′sĭs) [″ + *skoliosis,* curvation] Lateral curvature of the spine accompanying an anteroposterior hump. SYN: *scoliokyphosis.*

kyphosis (kī-fō′sĭs) [Gr., humpback] **1.** The normal posterior curvature of the thoracic and sacral spine. **2.** An exaggeration or angulation of the posterior curve of the thoracic spine, giving rise to the condition commonly known as humpback, hunchback, or Pott's curvature. It may be due to congenital anomaly, disease (tuberculosis, syphilis), malignancy, or compression fracture. This term also refers to excessive curvature of spine with convexity backward, which may result from osteoarthritis or rheumatoid arthritis, rickets, or other conditions. SYN: *humpback; spinal curvature.* SEE: illus. **kyphotic** (-fŏt′ĭk), *adj.*

kyuki-chouketsu-in (kū′kē-chō-ket′soo-in″) [Japanese] Xiong-gui-tiao-xue-yin.

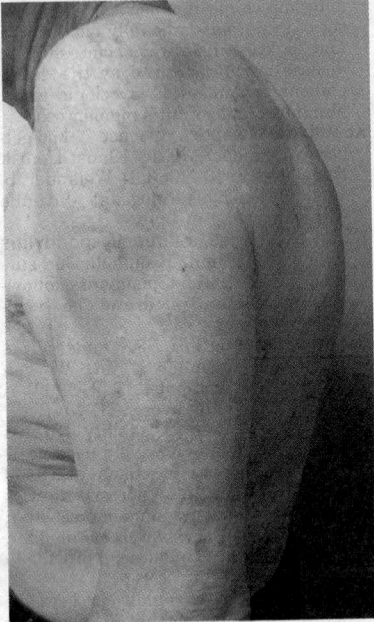

KYPHOSIS

L, l *Lactobacillus; Latin; left; left eye; length; lethal; light sense; liter.*

L- In biochemistry, a symbol used as a prefix to indicate that the carbon atom is symmetrical (or achiral) and that only three dissimilar groups attach to it. SEE: *D-*.

L1, L2, etc. *first lumbar nerve, second lumbar nerve,* and so forth.

LA *left atrium.*

La Symbol for the element lanthanum.

lab (lab) Colloquial for laboratory.

LABA *long-acting beta agonist.*

label (lā′bĕl) [Fr. *label,* strip of cloth, ribbon] The attachment of a radioactive marker or other chemical to a biologically active substance such as a drug or body chemical (such as glucose, protein, or fat). The metabolic fate of the labeled material may be investigated by detecting the presence of the label in various body sites or in excretions. The labeling material is chosen so that it does not alter the metabolism or action of the substance being investigated. SEE: *tracer.*

labeled line principle SEE: under *principle.*

labeled use (lā′bĕld) Indication (2).

labeling SEE: *radioactive tag; tagging.*

labeling index SEE: under *index.*

la belle indifference, la belle indifférence (la bel en-di-fā-rons′) [Fr., beautiful indifference] A disproportionate degree of indifference to, or complacency about, symptoms such as paralysis or loss of sensation in a part of the body. It is characteristic of conversion disorders.

labia (lā′bē-ă) [L.] Pl. of labium.

   l. majora The two folds of skin and adipose tissue on either side of the labia minora and vaginal opening; they form the lateral borders of the vulva. Their medial surfaces unite anteriorly above the clitoris to form the anterior commissure; posteriorly they are connected by a poorly defined posterior commissure. They are separated by a cleft, the rima pudendi, into which the urethra and vagina open. In young girls, their medial surfaces are in contact with each other, concealing the labia minora and vestibule. In older women, the labia minora may protrude between them.

   l. minora The two thin folds of integument that lie between the labia majora. They enclose the vestibule. Anteriorly each divides into two smaller folds that unite with similar folds from the other side and enclose the clitoris, the more anterior one forming the prepuce (preputium clitoridis) of the clitoris

and the posterior one the frenulum clitoridis. In young girls, they are hidden entirely by the labia majora.

labial (lā′bē-ăl) [L. *labialis*] Pert. to the lips.

labialism (lā′bē-ăl-ĭzm) [*labial* + *-ism*] A kind of stammering in which sounds made by the lips are prominent.

labile (lā′bīl″, -′bĭl) [L. *labilis,* slipping, gliding] Changeable; not fixed; unsteady.

lability (lă-bil′ĭt-ē) The state of being unstable or changeable.

   emotional l. Excessive emotional reactivity associated with frequent changes or swings in emotions and mood.

labio- [L. *labium,* lip] Prefix meaning *lip* or *labial.*

labioalveolar (lā″bē-ō-al-vē′ō-lăr) [*labio- + alveolar*] Pert. to the lips and tooth sockets.

labiocervical (lā″bē-ō-sĕr′vĭ-kăl) [*labio- + cervical*] Pert. to the buccal surface of the lips and the neck of a tooth.

labioclination (lā″bē-ō-kli-nā′shŏn) In dentistry, deviation of a tooth from the normal vertical toward the labial side.

labiodental (lā″bē-ō-dent′ăl) [*labio- + dental*] **1.** Pert. to the lips and teeth, esp. the labial surface of a tooth. **2.** Pert. to the pronunciation of certain sounds, like *f* and *v* in English, that require interaction of the teeth and lips.

labiogingival (lā″bē-ō-jin′jĭ-văl) [*labio- + gingival*] Pert. to the lips and gums or to the labial and gingival surfaces of a tooth.

labioglossolaryngeal (lā″bē-ō-glos″ō-lă-rin′j(ē-)ăl) [*labio- + glosso- + laryngeal*] Pert. to the lips, tongue, and larynx.

labioglossopharyngeal (lā″bē-ō-glŏs″ō-fă-rin′j(ē-)ăl) [*labio- + glosso- + pharyngeal*] Pert. to the lips, tongue, and pharynx.

labiomental (lā″bē-ŏ-ment′ăl) [*labio- + ²mental*] Pert. to the lower lip and chin.

labioplasty (lā′bē-ō-plas″tē) [*labio- + -plasty*] **1.** Cheiloplasty. **2.** Plastic surgery to reduce the size of the labia minora. SYN: *vaginal l.; vaginal rejuvenation.*

   vaginal l. Labioplasty (2).

labioversion (lā″bē-ō-vĕr′zhŏn) [*labio- + version*] The state of being twisted in a labial direction, esp. a tooth.

labium (lā′bē-ŭm, -ă) *pl.* **labia** [L. *labium,* lip] A lip or a structure like one; an edge or fleshy border.

   l. majus SEE: *labia majora.*

   l. minus SEE: *labia minora.*

l. uteri The thickened margin of the cervix uteri.

labor (lā′bŏr) [L., *labor*, hard work] In pregnancy, the process that begins with the onset of repetitive and forceful uterine contractions sufficient to cause dilation of the cervix and ends with delivery of the placenta. SYN: *childbirth; parturition*. SEE: illus.

Traditionally, labor is divided into three stages. The *first stage of labor*, progressive cervical dilation and effacement, is completed when the cervix is fully dilated, usually 10 cm. This stage is subdivided into the latent phase and the active phase.

First stage (stage of dilation): This is the period from the onset of regular uterine contractions to full dilation and effacement of the cervix. This stage averages 12 hr in primigravidas and 8 hr in multiparas.

The identification of this stage is particularly important to women having their first baby. Its diagnosis is complicated by the fact that many women experience false labor pains, which may begin as early as 3 to 4 weeks before the onset of true labor. False labor pains are quite irregular, are usually confined to the lower part of the abdomen and groin, and do not extend from the back around the abdomen as in true labor. False labor pains do not increase in frequency and duration with time and are not made more intense by walking. The conclusive distinction is made by determining the effect of the pains on the cervix. False labor pains do not cause effacement and dilation of the cervix as do true labor pains. SEE: *Braxton Hicks contractions*.

A reliable sign of impending labor is *show*. The appearance of a slight amount of vaginal blood-tinged mucus is a good indication that labor will begin within the next 24 hr. The loss of more than a few milliliters of blood at this

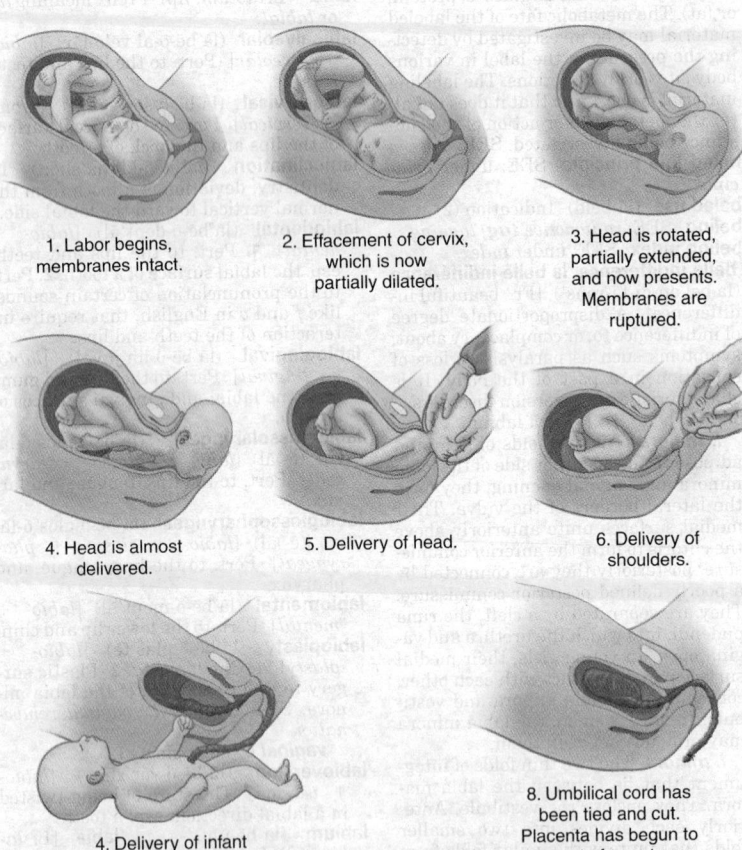

1. Labor begins, membranes intact.

2. Effacement of cervix, which is now partially dilated.

3. Head is rotated, partially extended, and now presents. Membranes are ruptured.

4. Head is almost delivered.

5. Delivery of head.

6. Delivery of shoulders.

4. Delivery of infant is complete. Uterus begins to contract.

8. Umbilical cord has been tied and cut. Placenta has begun to separate from uterus.

SEQUENCE OF LABOR AND CHILDBIRTH

time, however, must be regarded as being due to a pathological process. SEE: *placenta previa.*

Second stage (stage of expulsion): This period lasts from complete dilatation of the cervix through the birth of the fetus, averaging 50 min in primigravidas and 20 min in multiparas. Labor pains are severe, occur at 2- or 3-min intervals, and last from a little less than 1 min to a little more than 1½ min.

Rupture of the membranes (bag of water) usually occurs during the early part of this stage, accompanied by a gush of amniotic fluid from the vagina. The muscles of the abdomen contract involuntarily during this portion of labor. The patient directs all her strength to bearing down during the contractions. She may be quite flushed and perspire. As labor continues the perineum bulges and, in a head presentation, the scalp of the fetus appears through the vulvar opening. With cessation of each contraction, the fetus recedes from its position and then advances a little more when another contraction occurs. This continues until more of the head is visible and the vulvar ring encircles the head like a crown (therefore often called *crowning*).

At this time the decision is made concerning an incision in the perineum (episiotomy) to facilitate delivery. If done, it is most commonly a midline posterior episiotomy. When the head is completely removed out of the vagina it falls posteriorly; later the head rotates as the shoulders turn to come through the pelvis. There is usually a gush of amniotic fluid as the shoulders are delivered.

Third stage (placental stage): This is the period following the birth of the fetus through expulsion of the placenta and membranes. As soon as the fetus is delivered, the remainder of the amniotic fluid escapes. It will contain a small amount of blood. Uterine contractions return, and usually within 8 to 10 min the placenta and membranes are delivered. After this, there is some bleeding from the uterus. The amount may vary from 100 to 500 mL.

The amount of blood loss will vary with the size of the fetus, but the average is 200 mL. The probability that blood loss will exceed 500 mL is increased with a large fetus or multiple fetuses, as the placental attachment area on the uterine wall is larger and the uterus is more distended, meaning it does not contract as well after delivery of the fetus, placenta, and membranes. The above probability is less than 5% if the fetus weighs 5 lb (2268 g) or less. Other factors such as episiotomy or perineal laceration will also affect the amount of blood loss. SEE: *birthing*

chair; Credé method for assisting with the expulsion of the placenta.

PATIENT CARE: Often pregnant women and their partners or a labor coach who will be with them attend prenatal classes taught by obstetrical nurses to prepare the patient and family for labor, delivery, and care of the newborn. Such classes include exercises; breathing techniques; supportive care measures for labor, delivery, and the postpartum period; and neonatal care and feeding techniques. Expectant couples (or the pregnant woman and a support person) should attend classes together. The goals of expectant parent education are the birth of a healthy infant and a positive experience for the woman/couple. Labor and delivery may take place in a hospital, birthing center, or at home. Hospitals offer care in traditional labor and delivery rooms and, increasingly, in birthing rooms that simulate a homelike environment. Prenatal records are made available in order to review medical, surgical, and gynecological history; blood type and Rh; and esp. any prenatal problems in the pregnancy. If the mother is Rh negative and if the Rh status of the fetus is unknown or positive, the nurse will administer Rh immune globulin to the mother within 72 hr after delivery.

As part of the admission workup of the laboring woman, the nurse assesses vital signs, height and weight, fetal heart tone and activity, and labor status, i.e., condition of membranes, show, onset time of regular contractions, contraction frequency and duration, and patient anxiety, pain, or discomfort). Initial laboratory studies are carried out according to protocol. The obstetrician, resident physician or other house staff, nurse-midwife, lay midwife, or obstetrical nurse examines the patient, depending on the site and policy. The abdomen is palpated to determine fetal position and presentation (Leopold maneuvers), and a sterile vaginal examination determines cervical dilatation and effacement, fetal station, and position of the presenting part. The attending nurse or midwife monitors and assesses fetal heart rate and the frequency and duration of contractions, using palpation and a fetoscope or electronic monitoring. The frequency of assessment and repetition of vaginal examination are determined by the patient's labor stage and activity and by fetal response. In the past, admission to a labor suite usually included a perineal shave and enema in preparation for delivery, but these procedures have been largely discontinued and are currently done only if prescribed for a particular patient. The patient should urinate and have a bowel movement, if possible.

Bladder distention is to be avoided, but catheterization is carried out only if all other efforts to encourage voiding in a patient with a distended bladder fail. The perineum is cleansed (protecting the vaginal introitus from entry of cleansing solutions) and kept as clean as possible during labor. Special cleansing is performed before vaginal examination and delivery, as well as after expulsion of urine or feces.

First stage: The patient may be alert and ambulating, depending on membrane status, fetal position, and labor activity. Electrolyte-rich oral liquids may be prescribed, or intravenous therapy initiated. The nurse supports the patient and her partner or other support person and monitors the progress of the labor and the response of the fetus, notifying the obstetrician or midwife of any abnormal findings. When membranes rupture spontaneously or are ruptured artificially by the midwife or obstetrician, the color and volume of the fluid and the presence of meconium staining or unusual odor are noted. To distinguish it from a sudden spurt of urine having a slightly acid pH, the fluid may be tested for alkaline pH using nitrazine paper. The fetal heart rate, an indicator of fetal response to the membrane's rupture, is noted. Noninvasive pain relief measures are provided, prescribed analgesia is administered as required by the individual patient, and regional anesthetic use is monitored. Patient-controlled epidural anesthesia (PCEA) or continuous epidural anesthesia is frequently employed, based on patient satisfaction regarding its timeliness and effectiveness, and the patient's preference for having pain management under her control.

Second stage: The patient may deliver in any agreed-on position, including lithotomy or modified lithotomy, sitting, or side lying, in a birthing chair, in a birthing bed, or on a delivery table. The nurse, midwife, or physician continues to monitor the patient and fetus; prepares the patient for delivery (cleansing and draping); sets up delivery equipment; and supports the father or support person (positioned near the patient's head), positioning the mirror or TV monitor to permit viewing of delivery by the couple. The nurse also notes and documents the time of delivery, determines the infant's Apgar score, and provides initial infant care after delivery, including further suctioning of the nasopharynx and oropharynx as necessary (initial suctioning is done by the deliverer before delivering the infant's shoulders), drying and warming the infant (head covering, blanket wrap, or thermal warmer), application of cord clamp (after the deliverer double-

clamps the cord and cuts between the clamps), and positive identification (footprints of infant and thumb prints or fingerprints of mother, and application of numbered ankle and wrist band to the infant and wrist band to the mother). Eye prophylaxis for gonorrhea and *Chlamydia* may be delayed up to 2 hr to facilitate eye contact and to enhance maternal-infant bonding, or may be refused by the parents, on signing of an informed consent. An Apgar score of the infant's overall condition is obtained at 1 min and 5 min after the birth. The infant in good condition is placed on the mother's chest or abdomen for skin to skin contact. This position enhances bonding and maintains infant warmth. Alternatively, the infant is put to the breast, and the woman/couple is encouraged to inspect and interact with the infant. An infant in distress is hurried to the nursery, usually with the father or support person attending, so that specialized care can be provided by nursery and neonatal-nurse specialists, and a pediatrician. If the infant is critically ill, its birth may be attended by a chaplain, and photographs may be taken to assist the parents in dealing with the life, critical time, and possible death of the infant.

Third stage: The nurse continues to monitor the status of the patient and the fundus through delivery of the placenta and membranes (documenting the time), examination of the vagina and uterus for trauma or retained products, and repair of any laceration or surgical episiotomy. The placenta is examined to ascertain that no fragments remain in the uterus. The perineal area is cleansed and the mother is assisted to a comfortable position and covered with a warm blanket.

The nurse continues to observe the patient closely and is alert for hemorrhage or other complications through frequent assessment, including monitoring vital signs, palpating the fundus for firmness and position in relation to the umbilicus at intervals (determined by agency policy or patient condition), and massaging the fundus gently or administering prescribed oxytocic drugs to maintain or assist uterine contraction and to limit bleeding. The character (including presence, size, and number of clots) and volume of vaginal discharge or lochia are assessed periodically; the perineum is inspected and ice applied as prescribed, and the bladder is inspected, palpated, and percussed for distention. The patient is encouraged to void, and catheterization is performed only if absolutely necessary. The nurse notifies the obstetrician or midwife if any problems occur or persist. This period also is used for parent-infant bonding, because the infant is usually awake for the first hour or so after delivery. The mother can breast-feed if she wants to, and the immediate family couple can inspect the infant. The nurse supports the family's responses to the newborn, as well as to the labor and delivery experience. The infant is then taken to the nursery for initial infant care.

Early postpartum period: Once the infant's temperature has stabilized, measurements have been taken (length, head and chest circumference, weight), and other prescribed care carried out, the infant may be returned to the mother's side (in its crib carrier). The nurse continues to assess the mother's physical and psychological status after delivery, checking the fundus, vulva, and perineum according to policy; inspects the mother's breasts and assists her with feeding (whether by breast or bottle) and with measures to prevent lactation as desired; helps the mother to deal with other responsibilities of motherhood; and carries out the mandated maternal teaching program, including providing written information for later review by the patient. In hospitals or birthing centers, the nurse prepares the mother for early discharge to the home setting and arranges for follow-up care as needed and available. In many settings, the nurse makes follow-up calls or visits to the mother during the early postpartum period or encourages her to call in with concerns, or she may receive follow-up visits by a caregiver from her health maintenance organization. The mother may also be referred to support groups, such as the La Leche League, Nursing Mothers' Club, and others as available in the particular community.

active l. Regular uterine contractions that result in increasing cervical dilation and descent of the presenting part. This encompasses the active phase of stage 1, as well as stages 2 and 3 of labor.

arrested l. Failure of labor to proceed through the normal stages. This may be due to uterine inertia, obstruction of the pelvis, or systemic disease.

artificial l. Induction of labor.

augmented l. Induction of labor.

back l. Labor involving malposition of the fetal head with the occiput opposing the mother's sacrum. The laboring woman experiences severe back pain. SEE: *persistent* **occiput** *posterior.*

complicated l. Labor occurring with an accompanying abnormal condition such as hemorrhage or inertia.

dry l. A colloquial, imprecise term for labor associated with extensive loss of amniotic fluid related to premature rupture of membranes.

dysfunctional l. Abnormal progress

of dilation and/or descent of the presenting part.

false l. Uterine contractions that occur before the onset of labor. The contractions do not result in dilation of the cervix. They may resolve spontaneously or continue until effective contractions occur and labor begins. SYN: *missed l.* (1). SEE: *Braxton Hicks contractions.*

hypertonic l. A condition in which frequent, painful, but poor-quality contractions fail to accomplish effective cervical effacement and dilation. Hypertonicity usually occurs in the latent phase of labor and most often is related to fetal malpresentation and cephalopelvic disproportion.

hypotonic l. A condition during the active phase of labor in which contractions are inadequate in frequency, intensity, and duration and are ineffective in causing cervical dilation, effacement, or fetal descent. Hypotonicity usually occurs after the woman has entered the active phase of labor and most often is related to uterine overdistention, fetal macrosomia, multiple pregnancy, or grand multiparity.

instrumental l. Labor completed by mechanical means, e.g., the use of forceps or vacuum assist.

missed l. **1.** False **l.** **2.** Labor in which true labor pains begin but subside. This may be a sign of a dead fetus or extrauterine pregnancy.

normal l. Progressive dilation and effacement of the cervix with descent of the presenting part.

obstructed l. Interference with fetal descent related to malposition, malpresentation, and cephalopelvic disproportion.

precipitate l. Labor marked by sudden onset, rapid cervical effacement and dilation, and delivery within 3 hr of onset.

premature l. Preterm **l.**

preterm l. Labor that begins before completion of 37 weeks from the last menstrual period. The condition affects 7% to 10% of all live births and is one of the most important risk factors for preterm birth, the primary cause of perinatal and neonatal mortality. Although associated risk factors do exist, in most cases the cause is unknown. SYN: *premature l.* SEE: *premature rupture of membranes; prematurity; Nursing Diagnoses Appendix.*

Note: Treatment for active premature labor is best managed in a regional perinatal intensive care center, where staff members are prepared to handle the required care and treatment, and so that the neonate can remain in the same setting as the mother, rather than being transferred alone for neonatal intensive care after delivery.

PATIENT CARE: *In-hospital manage-*

ment: The patient is prepared for the use of cardiac, uterine, and fetal monitors along with intravenous therapy. Maternal vital signs and fetal heart rate (FHR) are monitored. If prescribed a tocolytic agent (beta-adrenergic drug) is administered intravenously; the infusion rate is increased every 10 to 30 min, depending on uterine response, but never exceeds a rate of 125 mL/hr. Uterine activity is monitored continuously; vital signs and FHR are checked every 15 min. Maternal pulse should not exceed 140/min; FHR should not exceed 180 bpm. When counting respiratory rate, breath sounds are noted, and the lungs are auscultated at least every 8 hr. The patient is assessed for desired response and adverse effects to treatment and is taught about symptoms she may expect and should report. If signs of drug toxicity occur, the medication is stopped. The intravenous line is kept open with a maintenance solution, and the prescribed beta-blocker as an antidote is prepared and administered. The patient is placed in high Fowler position, and oxygen is administered. Cardiac rate and rhythm, blood pressure, respiratory rate, auscultatory sounds, and FHRs are closely monitored to evaluate the patient's response to the antidote. If no complications are present, absolute bed rest is maintained throughout the infusion, with the patient in a left-lateral position or supine with a wedge under the right hip to prevent hypotension. Antiembolism stockings are applied, and passive leg exercises are performed. A daily fluid intake of 2 to 3 L is encouraged to maintain adequate hydration, and fluid intake and output are measured. The patient is weighed daily to assess for overhydration. The patient is instructed in methods to deal with stress. Health care providers should respond to parental concern for the fetus with empathy, but never with false reassurance. Fetal fibronectin enzyme immunoassay may be carried out on a sample of vaginal secretions taken from the posterior vaginal fornix; the patient should understand that this test can help assess the risk of preterm delivery within 7 days from the sampling date. As prescribed, a glucocorticoid is administered to stimulate fetal pulmonary surfactant production.

Patients who undergo in-house therapy often receive magnesium sulfate, which helps restore the patient's beta-2 receptor sensitivity (thus improving the effectiveness of terbutaline) and decrease uterine contractions. The patient may be discharged on oral or subcutaneous tocolytic therapy. Intravenous therapy may be employed using a portable micropump that can deliver a basal rate or programmed intermittent bolus doses at predetermined times when the patient's circadian rhythms are known to increase uterine activity.

Home management: The plan for at-home care must target individuals whom the woman can call upon to help with home management. A social service referral can help the family access available community and financial assistance. Home health care nurses assist the patient to carry out the plan, provide ongoing emotional support, and evaluate fetal and patient response to therapy.

The treatment regimen is reviewed with the family, and written instructions are provided to help those involved to cooperate. The patient is maintained on bed rest (left-side, supine, with head on small pillow, feet flat or elevated) to increase uterine perfusion and to keep fetal pressure off the cervix. The patient usually is allowed out of bed only to go to the bathroom. The women's physical and psychological rest are the highest priority, as anxiety is known to compromise uterine blood flow. Paid or voluntary helpers must care for other children and all household chores. The patient's tocolytic therapy (most frequently using terbutaline) is scheduled around the clock (with food if desired), and the patient is taught about its action and adverse effects. The patient must be able to count her pulse, and is instructed to report a rate above 120/min. The patient also is taught about symptoms to report (palpations, tremors, agitation, nervousness) and how to palpate for contractions twice each day. Home uterine activity monitoring may be employed, with the patient or home health care provider recording uterine activity for an hour twice daily. The perinatal nurse analyzes the results. If contractions exceed a predetermined threshold, the patient is advised to drink 8 to 12 oz of water, rest, then empty her bladder and monitor uterine activity for another hour. The process can reduce unnecessary visits to the medical setting, and increase the patient's peace of mind. The patient is encouraged to drink water throughout the day to prevent dehydration and reduce related uterine irritability. She also is warned not to take over the counter drugs without her obstetrician's approval. The patient is taught how to use sedation, if prescribed. Avoidance of activities that could stimulate labor is emphasized; these include sexual and nipple stimulation. Personal hygiene is reviewed, and the patient is made aware of signs of infection to report. A nonstress test may be performed weekly at home or in a medical setting, depending on the acuity of the situation and on maternal health factors (diabetes, pregnancy-induced hypertension [PIH]). The patient usually is provided with a 24-hr phone link to perinatal nurses in the health care system, who may contact her twice daily to discuss her situation. She is taught what to do in an emergency (bright red bleeding, membrane rupture, persisting contractions, decreased or absent fetal activity). If an incompetent cervix has been diagnosed based on the patient's history, insertion of a purse-string suture (cerclage) as reinforcement at 14 to 18 weeks gestation may prevent premature labor. If labor is inevitable, it is carried out as for a low-birth-weight, readily compromised fetus. During the postpartum period, care focuses on helping the family to understand their infant's special needs, and to participate as fully as possible in care, or, in a worst-case scenario, to come to terms with the baby's death. In such a case, the family is assisted in their grieving, with encouragement to hold the swaddled infant, and look at pictures of the child if they are able. Psychological counseling may be required.

prodromal l. The initial changes that precede actual labor, usually occurring 24 to 48 hr before the onset of labor. Some women report a surge of energy. Findings include lightening, excessive mucoid vaginal discharge, softening and beginning effacement of the ripe cervix, scant bloody show associated with expulsion of the mucus plug, and diarrhea.

prolonged l. Abnormally slow progress of labor, lasting more than 20 hr. SEE: *dystocia*.

prolonged latent phase l. Abnormally slow progress of the latent phase, lasting more than 20 hr in a nullipara or 14 hr in a multipara. SEE: *dystocia*.

protracted l. Abnormally slow dilation of the cervix in the active phase of labor; defined as less than 1.2 cm/hr in a nullipara and 1.5 cm/hr in a multipara. SYN: *protraction disorder; primary dysfunctional labor*. SEE: *arrested l.; precipitate l.*

spontaneous l. Labor that begins and progresses without pharmacological, mechanical, or operative intervention.

stage I l. SEE: *labor; Nursing Diagnoses Appendix*.

stage II l. SEE: *labor; Nursing Diagnoses Appendix*.

trial of l. Permitting labor to continue long enough to determine if normal vaginal birth appears to be possible, e.g., in vaginal birth after cesarean delivery.

laboratorian (lab″(ŏ-)ră-tor′ē-ăn) A person who works in a clinical or research laboratory, e.g., performing assays, pre-

paring or analyzing specimens, designing protocols, or managing workflow.

laboratory (lab′(ŏ-)ră-tor″ē) [L. *laboratorium*, workshop] A room or building equipped for scientific experimentation, research, testing, or clinical studies of materials, fluids, or tissues obtained from patients.

labret (lā′brĕt) [L. *labrum*, lip] A decorative piercing through the center of the lower lip.

labrocyte (lāb′rŏ-sīt″) [Gr. *labros*, greedy, + *-cyte*] A mast cell.

labyrinth (lab′ĭ-rinth) [L. *labyrinthus*, fr Gr. *labyrinthos*, maze, labyrinth] **1.** A series of intricate communicating passages. **2.** The inner ear, the bony and vestibular labyrinths, which contain the receptors for hearing and equilibrium.

bony l. Osseous **l.**

ethmoidal l. The lateral mass of the ethmoid bone, which includes the superior and middle conchae and encloses the ethmoid sinuses.

membranous l. Vestibular **l.**

osseous l. The complex, hollow space in the temporal bone that consists of the vestibule, three semicircular canals, and cochlea, all filled with perilymph. SYN: *bony l.*

vestibular l. The vestibular (balance and equilibrium) portion of the membranous labyrinth of the internal ear. It has two divisions, the utricle and saccule, and the semicircular ducts. The vestibular labyrinth is filled with endolymph and is suspended in the osseous labyrinth. SYN: *membranous l.*

labyrinthectomy (lab″ĭ-rin-thek′tŏ-mē) [*labyrinth* + *-ectomy*] Excision of the labyrinth.

labyrinthine (lab″ĭ-rin′thĭn, -thīn″, -thēn″) **1.** Pert. to a labyrinth. **2.** Intricate or involved, as a labyrinth. **3.** Pert. to speech that wanders aimlessly and unconnectedly from subject to subject, as seen in schizophrenia.

labyrinthitis (lab″ĭ-rin-thīt′ĭs) [*labyrinth* + *-itis*] An inflammation of the labyrinth. Symptoms include vertigo, vomiting, and nystagmus. It may result from viral infections, bacterial infections, or head trauma. SYN: *otitis interna*. SEE: *Ménière disease*.

labyrinthotomy (lab″ĭ-rin-thot′ŏ-mē) [*labyrinth* + *-tomy*] Surgical incision into the labyrinth.

labyrinthus (lab″ĭ-rin′thŭs) [L. *labyrinthus*, fr Gr. *labyrinthos*, maze, labyrinth] A labyrinth.

Lacazia loboi (lă-koz′ē-ă lō′bō-ī″, -lō-bō′ī″, lō′bō-ē″, -lō-bō′ē″) The spherical yeast that causes lobomycosis. It is structurally similar to *Paracoccidioides brasiliensis*. SYN: *Loboa loboi*; ***Paracoccidioides loboii***.

lacerate (las′ĕ-rāt″) [L. *lacerare*, to tear]

To tear, as into irregular segments. **lacerable** (las'ĕ-ră-bĕl), *adj.*; **lacerated** (las'ĕ-rāt"ĕd), *adj.*

laceration (las"ĕ-rā'shŏn) A wound or irregular tear of the flesh. SEE: illus.

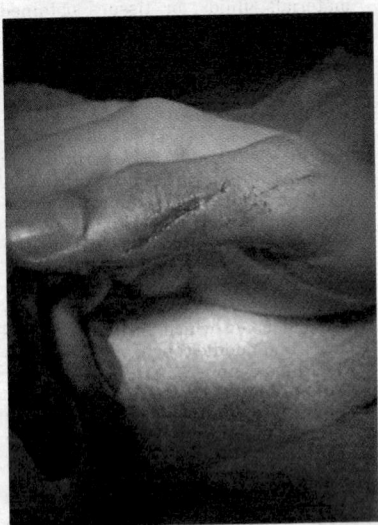

LACERATION OF THE THUMB

l. of cervix A bilateral, stellate, or unilateral tear of the cervix uteri caused by childbirth.

l. of perineum An injury of the perineum caused by childbirth. The lacerations may be classified as first-, second-, third-, or fourth-degree, depending on the extent of injury. A first-degree laceration may not require repair, but a fourth-degree laceration, which involves the vaginal mucosa, perineal muscles, and the sphincter ani, requires extensive repair. SEE: *episiotomy.*

stellate l. A tear in the skin or in an internal organ caused by blunt trauma. Several lines emanate outward from the tear's center.

lacertus (lă-sĕrt'ŭs) [L. *lacertus*, lizard] **1.** The muscular part of the arm. **2.** A muscular or fibrous band.

Lachesis muta (lak'ĕ-sĭs mūt'ă) SEE: *bushmaster.*

Lachman test (lok"măn) [John Lachman, contemporary U.S. orthopedic surgeon] A test evaluate the integrity of the anterior cruciate ligament of the knee. The examiner stands on the side being examined and grasps the tibia at the level of the tibial tubercle while stabilizing the femur with the other hand. The patient relaxes the leg while the examiner holds the knee flexed at 25° to 30° and pulls forward on the tibia while stabilizing the femur. Excessive motion relative to the opposite knee or no dis-

cernible end point determine a positive result. SEE: illus.

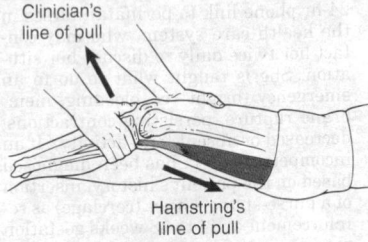

LACHMAN TEST

Biomechanics of the Lachman test for anterior cruciate laxity

lacquer (lak'ĕr) [Portuguese *lacre*, ult. fr Persian *lâk*, (tree) resin, lac] A resin or varnish that leaves a tough coating on a surface. It may be impregnated with medication, e.g., in the treatment of diseases of the toenails or fingernails.

lacrimal, lachrymal (lak'rĭ-măl) Pert. to tears. SEE: *lacrimal apparatus.*

lacrimal apparatus Structures concerned with the secretion and conduction of tears. It includes the lacrimal gland and its secretory ducts, lacrimal canaliculi, lacrimal sac, and nasolacrimal duct, which empties into the nasal cavity. SEE: illus.

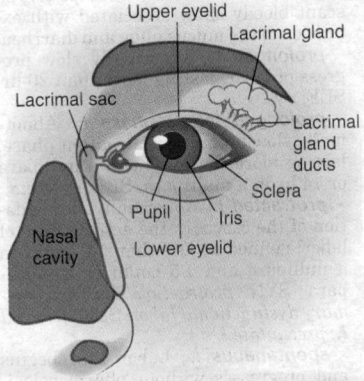

LACRIMAL APPARATUS

Anterior view

Patency of the lacrimal duct may be tested by placing a dilute solution of sugar in the conjunctival sac; if the duct is patent, the individual will report the sensation of sweetness in the mouth; if not, the sugar will not be perceived.

lacrimation, lachrymation (lak"rĭ-mā'shŏn) The secretion and discharge of tears; weeping.

lacrimator, lachrymator (lak'rĭ-māt"ŏr)

A substance that increases the flow of tears. **lacrimatory, lachrymatory** (-mă-tōr″ē), adj.

lactacid (lakt″as′ĭd) Lactic **acid**.

lactacidemia (lakt-as″ĭ-dē′mē-ă) [lactacid + -emia] Excessive accumulation of lactic acid in the blood. It occurs normally after strenuous and prolonged exercise. SYN: lactic *acidemia; lacticemia.*

lactaciduria (lakt″as″ĭ-door′ē-ă, -dūr′) [lactacid +-uria] Lactic acid excreted in the urine.

lactagogue (lak′tă-gog″) [lacto- + -agogue] Galactagogue.

lactalbumin (lak″tal″bū-mĭn) [lacto-albumin] The albumin found in the whey portion of milk.

lactam (lak′tam″) An organic chemical that contains the —NH—CO group in a ring form. It is formed by the removal of a molecule of water from certain amino acids.

lactase (lak′tās″) [lacto- + -ase] An intestinal sugar-splitting enzyme converting lactose into dextrose and galactose; found in intestinal juice. SEE: *enzyme; maltase; sucrase; sugar.*

¹lactate (lak′tāt″) [lacto- + -ate] A salt derived from lactic acid.

²lactate (lak′tāt″) To secrete milk.

lactate dehydrogenase An enzyme that catalyzes the oxidation of lactate. It is found in a variety of tissues (lung, kidney, heart, liver, blood) in slightly different forms called isoenzymes. Detection of these isoenzymes in the bloodstream is used in the diagnosis and management of a variety of illnesses. SYN: *lactic dehydrogenase.*

lactation (lak-tā′shŏn) [²lactate] **1.** The production and release of milk by mammary glands. **2.** The period of breastfeeding after childbirth, beginning with the release of colostrum (the nutrient-rich substance that precedes milk production) and continuing until the infant is weaned. Many hormonal factors are involved in lactation. The process depends on secretion of the hormone prolactin by the pituitary gland, but it begins only after the marked decreases in estrogen and progesterone that follow childbirth. Nursing by the infant stimulates pulsatile increases in prolactin secretion. Oxytocin, secreted by the hypothalamus, also contributes to the release of milk by stimulating the contraction of muscular cells in the milk ducts and mammary glands.

DIET: The dietary needs of the mother are increased during lactation, usually by about 500 kcal daily. In addition, maternal needs for calcium, folate, and other vitamins increase while breastfeeding. SEE: *breastfeeding; colostrum.*

lacteal (lak′tē-ăl) [L. *lacteus,* milky + -al (1)] The small terminal lymphatic vessel inside each villus of the small intestines. Lacteals, which are surrounded by muscle cells, absorb and actively propel chyle into the lymphatic system. SEE: *chyle.*

lactic (lak′tik) [lac] Pert. to milk or lactic acid.

lactic dehydrogenase Lactate dehydrogenase.

lactiferous (lak-tif′ĕ-rŭs) [lacti- + -ferous] Pert. to the secretion and conveying of milk.

lactigenous (lak-tij′ĕ-nŭs) [lacti- + -genous] Producing milk.

lacto-, lacti-, lact- [L. *lac,* stem *lact-,* milk] Prefixes meaning *milk* (including dairy products), *lactate,* or *lactic acid.*

Lactobacillus (lak-tō-bă-sil′ŭs) [lacto- + *Bacillus*] A genus of gram-positive, anaerobic, non–spore-forming bacilli of the family Lactobacillaceae. They produce lactic acid from carbohydrates and are responsible for the souring of milk. Some are part of the normal flora of the gastrointestinal tract and are considered probiotic.

L. acidophilus A species that produces lactic acid by fermenting the sugars in milk. It is found in milk and in the feces of bottle-fed infants and adults whose diets include a high milk content. It is also part of oral and vaginal flora.

L. bulgaricus A species found in fermented milk. Milk fermented with this organism is known as Bulgarian milk.

L. casei A species found in milk and cheese.

L. helveticus A species found in Swiss cheese.

Lactococcus (lak″tō-kok′ŭs) [lacto- + coccus] A genus of nonmotile, gram-positive cocci that grow in pairs or short chains. Most organisms in the genus were previously grouped with the enterococci, lactobacilli, and streptococci. They produce large quantities of the L-isomer of lactic acid. Members of the species are used in dairy industry, e.g., in the fermentation of cheeses. A few cause human disease.

lactoferrin (lak″tō-fer′ĭn) An enzyme released in phagocytosis by neutrophils and macrophages that combines with iron in the blood. As a result, the iron is unavailable to invading pathogens that require iron for their reproduction.

lactogen (lak′tŏ-jĕn, -jen″) [lacto- + -gen] Any substance that stimulates milk production. SEE: *prolactin.*

human placental l. ABBR: HPL. A hormone produced by the placenta and released into maternal blood. It acts in the last stage of gestation to prepare the breasts for milk production. **lactogenic** (lak″tō-jen), adj.

lactoglobulin (lak″tō-glob′yŭ-lĭn) [lacto- + globulin] A protein found in milk. Casein and lactoglobulin are the most common proteins in cow's milk.

immune l. Antibodies present in the colostrum.

lacto-ovo-vegetarian (lak″tō-ō″vō-vej′ĕ-ter′ē-ăn) A person consuming a vegetarian diet that includes eggs and dairy products.

lactophosphate (lak″tō-fos′fāt) [*lacto- + phosphate*] A salt derived jointly from lactic and phosphoric acids.

lactoprotein (lak″tō-prō′tēn, -prŏt′ē-ĭn) [*lacto- + protein*] Any protein present in milk.

lactorrhea (lak-tŏ-rē′ă) [*lacto- + -rrhea*] The discharge of milk between nursings and after weaning of offspring. SYN: *galactorrhea.*

lactose (lak-tōs″, -tōz″) [*lacto- + ²-ose*] **1.** A disaccharide that on hydrolysis yields glucose and galactose. Bacteria can convert it into lactic and butyric acids, as in the souring of milk. The milk of mammals contains 4% to 7% lactose. Its presence in the urine may be indicative of obstruction to flow of milk after cessation of nursing. Commercial lactose is a fine white powder that will not dissolve in cold water. **2.** A sugar, $C_{11}H_{22}O_{11}$, obtained from evaporation of cow's milk. It is used in manufacturing tablets and as a diluent.

lactose intolerance An inability to digest milk and some dairy products, leading to abdominal bloating, cramping, and diarrhea. The intolerance may be congenital or may begin in childhood, adolescence, or young adulthood.

ETIOLOGY: A deficiency of the enzyme lactase, which digests lactose in the small intestine, causes this intolerance.

TREATMENT: Those affected should limit consumption of milk and other lactose-containing foods. Yogurt or milk from which lactose has been reduced or eliminated may be substituted.

lactose tolerance test A test for deficiency of lactase in the small intestine that consists of the administration of a weighed amount of lactose, followed by successive measurements of blood glucose at timed intervals. Low levels of glucose indicate a lactase deficiency.

lactosuria (lak-tō-s(h)oor′ē-ă, -tōs-ūr′) [*lactose + -uria*] The presence of milk sugar (lactose) in the urine, a frequent occurrence during pregnancy and lactation.

lactotherapy (lak-tō-ther′ă-pē) [*lacto- + therapy*] Galactotherapy (2).

lactotroph (lak′tō-trōf″, -trof″) [*lacto- + -troph*] A prolactin producer. The term typically applies to prolactin-secreting cells or adenomas in the pituitary gland.

lactovegetarian, **lacto-vegetarian** (lak″tō-vej″ĕ-ter′ē-ăn) [*lacto- + vegetarian*] **1.** Pert. to milk and vegetables. **2.** One who lives on a diet of milk, other dairy products, and vegetables.

lactulose (lak′tū-lōs″, ′tū-, -lōz″) A syn-

thetic disaccharide, 4-*O*-β-D-galactopyranosyl-D-fructofuranose, that is not hydrolyzed or absorbed in humans. It is metabolized by bacteria in the colon with the production of organic acids and is used to treat constipation and the encephalopathy that develops in patients with advanced cirrhosis of the liver. The unabsorbed sugar produces diarrhea, and the acid pH helps to contain ammonia in the feces.

lacuna (lă-koo′nă, lă-koo′nē″) *pl.* **lacunae** [L., *lacuna*, pit, gap, deficiency] **1.** An empty space, gap, or hollow area. **2.** The space occupied by cells of calcified tissues (e.g., cementocytes, chondrocytes, and osteocytes). **3.** A focal loss of brain tissue due to a stroke involving a small penetrating artery in the brain.

Howship l. A tiny pit in a living bone where osteoclasts are resorbing structural minerals and collagen.resorption bay; resorption lacuna.

l. vasorum A space for passage of femoral vessels to the thigh.

venous l. A lateral pouch or diverticulum of the superior sagittal sinus of the brain into which protrude arachnoid villi that return cerebrospinal fluid to the venous circulation.

LAD *left anterior descending* (branch of the left coronary artery); *leukocyte adhesion* **deficiency**.

LADA *left acromion-dorsal-anterior* fetal position.

LADP *left acromion-dorsal-posterior* fetal position.

Laënnec, René (lā′nek) René-Théophile-Hyacinthe Laënnec, Fr. physician, 1781–1826

L. cirrhosis Cirrhosis associated with chronic excessive alcohol ingestion. SYN: *hobnail liver.*

L. pearls Round gelatinous masses seen in asthmatic sputum.

L. thrombus Globular thrombus in the heart.

Laetrile (lā′ĕ-tril) A glycoside drug derived from pits or other seed parts of plants, including apricots and almonds. Laetrile contains enough cyanide to be fatal when taken in large doses. There is no evidence that Laetrile is effective in treating cancer, and it has no known therapeutic or nutritional value.

⚠ Complications of Laetrile treatment include acute or chronic cyanide poisoning.

SYN: *vitamin B_{17}.* SEE: *amygdalin.*

Lafora, Gonzalo R (lă-fō′ră) Spanish physician, 1887–1971.

L. bodies Cytoplasmic inclusion bodies made of acid mucopolysaccharides. They may be found in neuronal tissues taken from patients with Lafora disease.

L. disease A fatal autosomal recessive disease marked by Lafora bodies within neurons and the cells of the heart, liver, muscle, and skin. Symptoms include seizures, drop attacks, myoclonus, ataxia, and a quickly developing and severe dementia. SYN: *familial myoclonic* **epilepsy**.

lag 1. The period of time between the application of a stimulus and the resulting reaction. **2.** The early period following bacterial inoculation into a culture medium, characterized by slow growth. SYN: *lag phase; latent period.*

Lagochilascaris (lă″gō-kī-lăs′kă-rĭs) [Gr. *lagōs,* hare, + *cheilos,* lip, + *askaris,* intestinal worm] A genus of parasitic worms that may infect the skin, esp. in residents of or travelers to the Caribbean.

lagophthalmos, lagophthalmus (lăg″ŏf-thăl′mōs, -mŭs) [Gr. *lagos,* hare, + *ophthalmos,* eye] An incomplete closure of the palpebral fissure when an attempt is made to shut the eyelids. This results in exposure and injury to the bulbar conjunctiva and cornea. This condition is caused by contraction of a scar of the eyelid, facial nerve injury, atony of the orbicularis palpebrarum, or exophthalmos.

TREATMENT: Artificial tears or other ocular lubricants are needed to prevent corneal ulceration.

   nocturnal l. Failure of the eyelids to remain closed during sleep, which may be due to chronic keratitis.

laity (lā′ĭ-tē) [Gr. *laos,* the people] Individuals who are not members of a particular profession such as law, dentistry, medicine, or the ministry.

LAIV *live attenuated influenza* **vaccine**.

LAK cell SEE: under *cell.*

lake [L. *lacus*] **1.** A small cavity of fluid. SEE: *lacus.* **2.** The appearance of plasma after blood cells in it have broken down, releasing their hemoglobin pigment.

   lacrimal l. The small pouch formed by the junction of the conjunctiva at the medial canthus of the eye. Tears collect in this area before they drain through the lacrimal canaliculi into the nasolacrimal duct. The lacrimal lake can hold a normal amount of tears, but when excess tears are secreted (e.g., during crying), the tears overflow the lipid-coated edge of the lower lids and spill onto the cheeks. SYN: *lacus lacrimalis.*

   venous l. 1. A small subcutaneous bleb filled with blood. It may be present on the lips, mouth, or ears. **2.** A lateral pouch or diverticulum of the superior sagittal sinus of the brain into which protrude arachnoid villi that return cerebrospinal fluid to the venous circulation.

laked (lākd) A term used to describe the blood in hemolysis or disintegration of the red blood cells, freeing the hemoglobin into the blood plasma.

laking (lāk-ĭng) The freeing of hemoglobin from red blood cells.

LAL *limulus amebocyte lysate.*

La Leche League International (la lā″chā) [Sp. *la leche,* the milk] An organization whose purpose is to promote breastfeeding. Mailing address: PO Box 4079, Schaumburg, IL 60168–3243 (USA). Phone: 1–800–525–3243. Website: www.llli.org

-lalia [Gr. *lalia,* talking, chat, conversation] Suffix meaning *speech* (for a speech disorder of a specific kind, e.g., *coprolalia, echolalia*).

lallation (lă-lā′shŭn) [L. *lallatio*] An infantile form of speech in which the letter "l" is incorrectly used or pronounced.

lalophobia (lăl″ō-fō′bē-ă) [″ + *phobos,* fear] Fear of speaking.

laloplegia (lăl-ō-plē′jē-ă) [″ + *plege,* a stroke] A paralysis of the speech muscles without affecting the action of the tongue.

lalorrhea (lăl″ō-rē′ă) [″ + *rhoia,* flow] An abnormal flow of speech.

Lamaze method (lă-moz′) [Fernand Lamaze, Fr. obstetrician, 1890–1957] A method of preparing couples for childbirth through education of the birth process and instruction in breathing and relaxation techniques during contractions that will promote comfort for the mother and facilitate delivery. Those who are able to use the method require little if any anesthesia during delivery. SEE: *labor.*

lambda, Λ, λ (lam′dă) **1.** Λ or λ, the uppercase and lowercase symbols, respectively, for the 11th letter of the Greek alphabet. **2.** The point or angle of junction of the lambdoid and sagittal sutures.

lambdacism (lăm′dă-sĭzm) [Gr. *lambdakismos*] **1.** Stammering of the "l" sound. **2.** An inability to pronounce the "l" sound properly. **3.** Substitution of "l" for "r" in speaking.

lambdoid, lambdoidal (lăm′doyd, lăm-doyd′ăl) [Gr. *lambda,* + *eidos,* form, shape] Shaped like the Greek letter Λ.

lambert (lăm′bĕrt) [Johann H. Lambert, Ger. physicist, 1728–1777] A unit of brightness equal to that seen when a perfectly diffusing surface radiates or reflects one lumen of light per square centimeter. SEE: *lumen* (2).

Lambert-Eaton myasthenic syndrome (lam′bĕrt-ēt′ŏn) [Edward Howard Lambert, U.S. physiologist, 1915–2003; Lee McKendree Eaton, U.S. physician, 1905–1958] An autoimmune syndrome in which weakness of the proximal muscles (e.g., around the shoulder and the hip girdle), diminished reflexes, and autonomic dysfunction are found. The syndrome is often associated with small cell carcinoma of the lung or other malignancies. Its cause is a unique antibody against presynaptic calcium channels. SYN: *Eaton-Lambert syndrome.*

lame Disabled in one or more limbs, esp. in a leg or foot, impairing normal locomotion.

lamella (lă-měl′ă) *pl.* **lamellae** [L., a little plate] **1.** A thin layer, sheet, or plate. **2.** A medicated disk of gelatin inserted under the lower eyelid and against the eyeball; used as a local application to the eye.

　bone l. Plates of collagen fibers, 3 to 7 μm thick, found in secondary (mature, adult) bone and surrounded by cementing substance, the mineralized bone matrix. Some lamellae are parallel to each other. Other lamellae are aligned concentrically around a vascular canal — a structure known as a haversian system or osteon.

　circumferential l. A layer of bone that underlies the periosteum, encircling the medullary cavity.

　concentric l. One of the cylindrical plates of bone surrounding a haversian canal. SYN: *haversian l.*

　enamel l. Microscopic cracks or calcification imperfections in the enamel surface of a tooth. They may be shallow or extend into the underlying dentin and occur as a developmental defect or a microfracture caused by temperature change or shearing forces.

　ground l. Interstitial **l.**

　haversian l. Concentric **l.**

　interstitial l. The bone lamella filling the irregular spaces within the haversian system. SYN: *ground l.*

　periosteal l. The bone lamella next to and parallel with the periosteum, forming the external portion of bone.

lamellar (lă-měl′ăr) **1.** Arranged in thin layers, plates or scales. **2.** Pert. to the lamella.

lameness Limping, abnormal gait, or hobbling resulting from partial loss of function in a leg. The symptom may be due to maldevelopment, injury, or disease.

lamin (lam′ĭn) A filament, intermediate in size between microtubules and microfilaments, that makes up a part of the cytoskeleton of the nucleus of a cell.

lamina (lam′ĭ-nă) *pl.* **laminae** [L. *lamina,* thin plate] **1.** A thin flat layer or membrane. **2.** The flattened part of either side of the arch of a vertebra.

　alar l. The alar plate of the neural tube, which later develops into sensory nuclei and tracts of the central nervous system.

　alar l. of neural tube Alar **plate.**

　basal l. An 80 nm thick extracellular layer of fibrils and proteoglycans along the basal surface of a variety of cells, including many epithelia, capillary endothelia, Schwann cells, and muscle cells.

Basal laminae anchor cells, organize cell-cell interactions, and act as semipermeable membranes.

　dental l. A U-shaped internal growth of the oral epithelium in the embryonic maxillary and mandibular regions that forms into enamel organs which produce the teeth. SEE: *enamel* **organ.**

　l. dura In radiography, the compact bone (alveolar bone proper) that surrounds the roots of teeth. In a state of health, it appears on a radiograph as a dense radiopaque line.

　epithelial l. The epithelial layer covering the choroid layer of the eye.

　l. papyracea A thin, smooth plate of bone on the lateral surface of the ethmoid bone; it forms part of the orbital plate.

　perpendicular l. A thin sheet of bone forming the perpendicular plate of the ethmoid bone. It supports the upper portion of the nasal septum.

　l. propria mucosae The thin layer of areolar connective tissue, blood vessels, and nerves that lies immediately beneath the surface epithelium of mucous membranes.

　pterygoid l. Either of two plates, the internal and external, that make up the pterygoid process of the sphenoid bone. They are areas of attachment for the muscles of mastication.

　l. quadrigemina The two pairs of bulges on the top of the midbrain section of the brainstem. The rostral pair are the superior colliculi, which are concerned with visual stimuli. The caudal pair are the inferior colliculi, which are concerned with auditory stimuli. Synonymous with tectum.

　rostral l. A continuation of the rostrum of the corpus callosum and the terminal lamina of the third ventricle of the brain.

　spiral l. A thin, bony plate projecting from the modiolus into the cochlear canal, dividing it into two portions, the upper scala vestibuli and lower scala tympani. SYN: *l. spiralis.*

　l. spiralis Spiral **l.**

　l. terminalis The frontmost (rostral) wall of the neural tube. In the developed brain, the lamina terminalis remains as the thin rostral wall of the third ventricle, stretching from the bases of the major cerebral commissures (the anterior commissure, the commissure of the fornix, and the rostrum of the corpus callosum) to the dorsal surface of the optic chiasm.

　l. of vertebral arch One of the laminae extending from the pedicles of the vertebral arches and fusing together to form the dorsal portion of the arch. The spinous process extends from the center of these laminae.

laminae (lăm′ĭ-nē) Pl. of lamina.

laminar (lă-m′ĭ-năr) Pert. to or composed of laminae.

   l. air flow Filtered air moving along separate parallel flow planes to surgical theaters, patient rooms, nurseries, bacteriology work areas, or food preparation areas. This method of air flow helps to prevent bacterial contamination and collection of hazardous chemical fumes in areas where they would pollute the work environment.

Laminaria digitata (lăm-ĭ-năr′ē-ă dĭj-ĭ-tā′tă) A genus of kelp or seaweed that, when dried, has the ability to absorb water and expand with considerable force. It has been used to dilate the uterine cervical canal in induced abortion and to induce cervical ripening. Hazards associated with the use of seaweed include cervical lacerations, accidental rupture of membranes, and infection.

laminarin (lăm″ĭ-nā′rĭn) A polysaccharide obtained from *Laminaria* species of seaweed. It consists principally of glucose residues.

lamination (lam″ĭ-nā′shŏn) A layer-like arrangement. **laminated** (lam′ĭ-nāt″ĕd), *adj.*

laminectomy (lăm″ĭ-něk′tō-mē) [″ + Gr. *ektome,* excision] The excision of a vertebral posterior arch, usually to remove a lesion or herniated disk.

   It is recommended only after conservative treatment (physical therapy, antiinflammatory medication) has been exhausted. Minimally invasive spine surgery can be used to treat conditions such as herniated or ruptured lumbar discs, bone spurs, synovial cysts, and lumbar spinal stenosis. Patients with a history of open spine surgery may be poor candidates for minimal procedures because of scar tissue. SEE: *Nursing Diagnoses Appendix; illus.*

   PATIENT CARE: *Preoperative:* The patient's knowledge of the procedure is determined, misconceptions are corrected, additional information is provided as necessary, and a signed informed consent form is obtained. A baseline assessment of the patient's neurological function and of lower extremity circulation is documented. Health care providers discuss postoperative care concerns, demonstrate maneuvers such as log-rolling, assure the patient of the availability of pain medications on request, and prepare the patient for surgery according to the surgeon's or institutional protocol.

   Postoperative: Vital signs and neurovascular status (motor, sensory, and circulatory) are monitored; antiembolism stockings or pneumatic dressings are applied, and anticoagulants are given if prescribed. The dressing is inspected for bleeding or cerebrospinal fluid leakage; either problem is documented and reported immediately, and the incision is

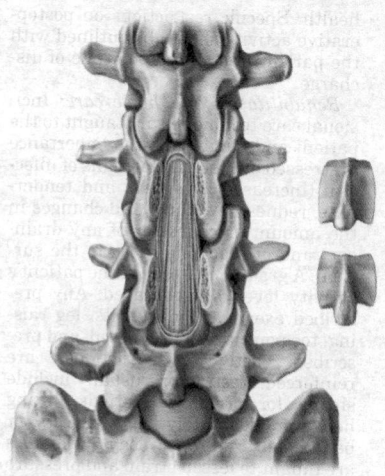

LAMINECTOMY

redressed as necessary. The patient is maintained in a supine position, with the head flat or no higher than 45° according to the surgeon's preference, for the prescribed time (usually 1 to 2 hr), then repositioned side to side every 2 hr by log-rolling the patient with a pillow between the legs to prevent twisting and hip adduction and to maintain spinal alignment. Deep breathing (with use of an inspirometer in most cases) is encouraged, and assistance is provided with range-of-motion, gluteal muscle setting, and quadriceps setting exercises. Adequate assistance should be available when the patient is permitted to dangle his or her feet, stand, and walk in the early postoperative period. Prescribed anti-inflammatory, muscle-relaxant, and antibiotic agents are administered. Noninvasive measures to prevent and relieve incisional discomfort are provided in addition to prescribed analgesics. Fluid balance is monitored by administering prescribed intravenous fluids and by assessing urine output. The patient is encouraged to void within 8 to 12 hr postsurgery and is assessed for bladder distention, which may indicate urinary retention. Catheterization is used only after other measures to promote voiding have been attempted. The abdomen is auscultated for return of bowel sounds, and adequate oral nutrition is provided as prescribed. Patients who have undergone minimally invasive procedures are out of bed and resuming some normal activities (e.g., showering, engaging in activities around the house) within a day or two of surgery. Responses vary and may depend on the patient's personality, presurgical activity level, and overall health. Specific restrictions on postoperative activity should be outlined with the patient in detail at the time of discharge.

Rehabilitative and home care: Incisional care techniques are taught to the patient and family, and the importance is stressed of checking for signs of infection (increased local pain and tenderness, redness, swelling, and changes in the amount or character of any drainage) and of reporting these to the surgeon. A gradual increase in the patient's activity level is encouraged. Any prescribed exercises (pelvic tilts, leg raising, toe pointing) are reviewed, and prescribed activity restrictions are reinforced. Restrictions usually include sitting for prolonged periods, lifting heavy or moderately heavy objects, or bending over. Proper body mechanics are taught to lessen strain and pressure on the spine: these include maintaining proper body alignment and good posture and sleeping on a firm mattress. Involvement in an exercise program, beginning with gradual strengthening of abdominal muscles, is encouraged after 6 weeks. Walking is encouraged. The patient should schedule and keep a follow-up appointment with the surgeon and communicate any concerns to the surgeon (if necessary) before that visit.

laminin (lăm'ĭ-nĭn) A glycoprotein found in all basement membranes that is involved in the binding of cells to the extracellular matrix, particularly to type intravenous collagen. It contributes to the growth and cellular organization of tissues and is involved in angiogenesis, invasion, and metastasis of tumor cells, and cellular attachment. SEE: *glycoprotein; extracellular* **matrix**.

laminitis (lăm-ĭn-ī'tĭs) [" + Gr. *itis,* inflammation] The inflammation of a lamina.

laminopathy (lă-mĭn-ŏp'ă-thē) Any disease caused by defective construction of lamins within cells.

laminotomy (lăm''ĭ-nŏt'ō-mē) [" + Gr. *tome,* incision] A division of one of the vertebral laminae.

lamp [Gr. *lampein,* to shine] A device for producing and applying light, heat, radiation, and various forms of radiant energy for the treatment of disease, resolution of impairments, or palliation of pain.

   infrared l. A lamp that develops a high temperature, emitting infrared rays; a heat lamp. The rays penetrate only a short distance (5 to 10 mm) into the skin. Its principal effect is to cause heating of the skin.

   slit l. A lamp so constructed that an intense light is emitted through a slit; used for examination of the eye. SEE: illus.

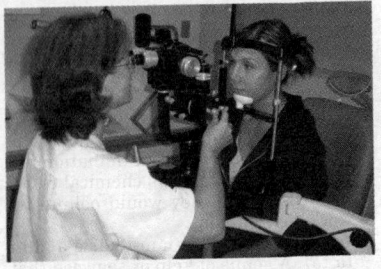

SLIT LAMP EXAMINATION

   sun l. Ultraviolet **l.**

   ultraviolet l. A lamp that produces light with a wavelength in the range of 180 to 400 nm. It is used to treat certain skin conditions such as psoriasis or T-cell lymphoma, to promote wound healing by destroying bacteria, and to tan the skin. Ultraviolet lamps produce light within specific ranges: ultraviolet-A (UV-A) lamps generate light having a wavelength of 320 to 400 nm; ultraviolet-B (UV-B) produces light in the range of 290 to 320 nm; ultraviolet-C (UV-C) has a wavelength of 180 to 290 nm. SYN: *sun l.*

⚠ Patients and operators must wear ultraviolet-resistant goggles during treatment. Overexposure to ultraviolet light produces burning and blistering of the skin and may predispose patients to skin cancers.

   Wood l. Wood filter.

lance (lăns) [L. *lancea*] **1.** A two-edged surgical knife. **2.** To incise with a lancet or other cutting instrument.

Lance-Adams syndrome (lăns-ăd'ămz) Myoclonus occurring after any disease or condition that limits the flow of blood and oxygen to the brain.

Lancefield classification (lans'fēld") [Rebecca Craighill Lancefield, U.S. bacteriologist, 1895–1981] A classification of hemolytic streptococci into various groups according to antigenic structure.

lancet (lăn'sĕt) [L. *lancea,* lance] **1.** A pointed surgical knife with two edges. **2.** A spring-loaded or manual blade used to make a limited skin incision as for collection of blood specimen.

lancinating (lăn'sĭ-nāt''ĭng) [L. *lancinare,* to tear] Sharp or cutting, as pain.

L and A Abbreviation for the reaction of the pupils of the eye to *light* and *accommodation.*

Landau-Kleffner syndrome (klĕf'nĕr) [William M. Landau, Frank R. Kleffner, American neurologists] A rare disease in which children (usually between the ages of 3 and 7) lose the ability to understand spoken language and to express themselves. Children with this disorder have seizures and sometimes hyperactivity or other behavioral or psychiatric disorders. Lost language skills are sometimes recovered by affected children in adolescence. SYN: *acquired epileptiform **aphasia;** infantile acquired **aphasia**.*

Landau reflex (lan'dō, 'dow) [A. Landau, Ger pediatrician] An infantile reflex in which the body flexes when the head is passively flexed forward in a prone position. It appears normally at 3 months and is absent in children with cerebral palsy and gross motor retardation.

landmark A recognizable skeletal or soft tissue structure used as a reference point in measurements or in describing the location of other structures. SEE: *cephalometry; craniometry.*

   bony l. A structure or spot on a bone used as a reference for measurement.

   cephalometric l. A bony point that is used in living persons or radiographs for measurements of the head or face or orientation of the head in certain positions.

   craniometric l. A bony point or area on the skull used for measurements or orientation of the skull.

   radiographic l. A cephalometric, craniometric, or soft tissue landmark used for orientation or measurements.

   soft tissue l. An area or point on a soft tissue used as a point of reference for measurements of the body or its parts.

land mines Explosive devices placed in or on the ground to injure, kill, or destroy humans, animals, or equipment passing over or near them. These are activated on contact. They remain active after armed conflict has ceased and, if they are not removed, can detonate years later, causing unexpected traumatic injury and death.

Landry-Guillain-Barré syndrome (lăn' drē-gē-yă') Guillain-Barré syndrome.

Landsteiner classification (land'stīn"ĕr) [Karl L. Landsteiner, Austrian-born U.S. biologist, 1868–1943; Nobel prize winner in medicine in 1930] A classification of blood types designating O, A, B, and AB based on the presence of antigens on red blood cells.

Lane kinks (lān) [Sir William Arbuthnot Lane, Brit. surgeon, 1856–1943] Bending or twisting of the last few centimeters of the ileum with external adhesions between the folded loops of intestines. This may cause intestinal obstruction.

Langerhans islands (lang'ĕr-han") Islets of Langerhans.

Langer lines (lang'ĕr) [Carl Ritter von Edenberg Langer, Austrian anatomist, 1819–1887] The structural orientation of the fibrous tissue of the skin, forming the natural cleavage lines that, though present in all body areas, are visible only in certain sites such as the creases of the palm. These lines are of particular importance in surgery. Incisions made parallel to them make a much smaller scar upon healing than those made at right angles to the lines. SYN: *skin tension lines.* SEE: illus.

Langhans layer (lang'hans") [Theodor Langhans, Ger. pathologist, 1839–1915] A cellular layer present in the chorionic villi of the placenta. SYN: *cytotrophoblast.*

language The spoken or written words or symbols used by a population for communication.

language bias The tendency for editors and readers to pay greater attention to scientific studies reported in English than to those studies written in other languages.

languor (lăng'gĕr) [L. *languere,* to languish] A feeling of weariness or exhaustion as from illness; lack of vigor or animation; lassitude.

lanolin (lan'ŏ-lĭn) [L. *lana,* wool] The purified, fatlike substance obtained from the wool of sheep; used as an ointment base.

   anhydrous l. Wool fat.

Lanoxin SEE: *digoxin.*

lansoprazole (lan-soh'pra-zohl) A proton pump inhibitor that decreases gastric acid production and is used to treat peptic ulcers, gastroesophageal reflux, *Helicobacter pylori* infections, and related diseases.

lanthanum (lan'thă-nŭm) [Gr. *lanthanein,* to escape notice + -(i)um (1)] SYMB: La. A metallic element, one of the lanthanides, atomic mass (weight) 138.906; atomic number 57. Lanthanum-139 is stable.

lantibiotic (lan'tī-bī-ŏt"ĭk) Any peptide antibiotic whose chemical structure includes a bridge maintained by the rare amino acid lanthionine. Subtilin and nisin are examples of lantibiotics.

lanugo (lă-nū'gō) [L. *lanugo,* down] **1.** Downy hair covering the body. **2.** Fine downy hairs that cover the body of the fetus, esp. when premature. The presence and amount of lanugo aids in estimating the gestational age of preterm infants. The fetus first exhibits lanugo between weeks 13 and 16. By gestational week 20, it covers the face and body. The amount of lanugo is greatest between weeks 28 and 30. As the third trimester progresses, lanugo disappears from the face, trunk, and extremities.

lanuginous, *adj.*

Lanz point (lants) [Otto Lanz, Swiss surgeon in the Netherlands, 1865–1935] The point situated on the line between the two anterosuperior iliac spines one third of the distance from the right spine that indicates the origin of the vermiform appendix.

LAO *left anterior oblique* position.

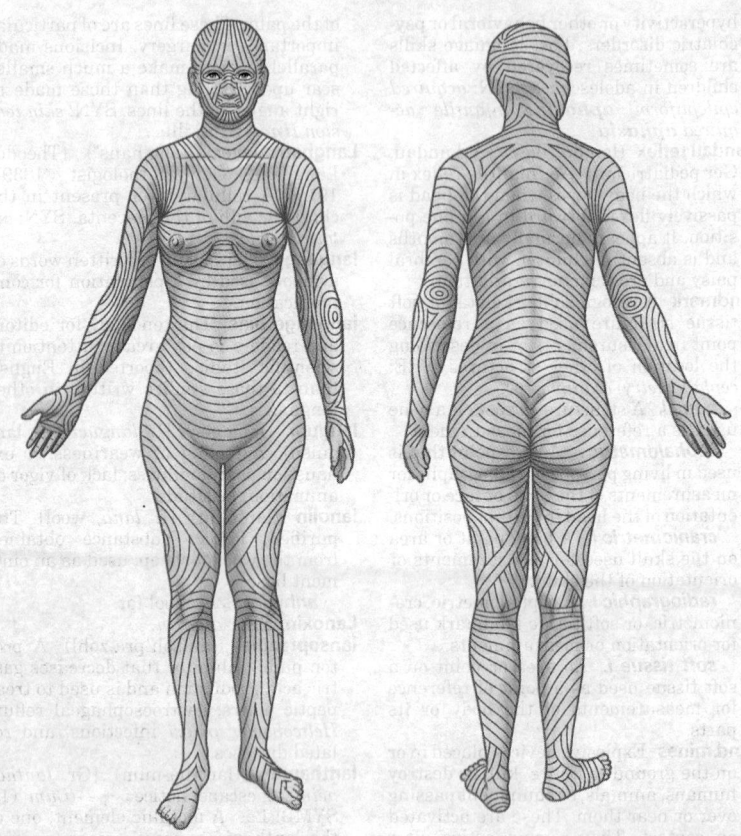

LANGER LINES

laparo-, lapar- [Gr. *lapara*, flank] Prefixes meaning *flank* or *abdominal wall*.

laparocele (lăp″ă-rō-sēl) [″ + *kele*, tumor, swelling] An abdominal hernia.

laparocolectomy (lăp″ă-rō-kō-lĕk′tō-mē) [″ + *kolon*, colon, + *ektome*, excision] Colectomy.

laparogastrostomy (lăp″ăr-ō-găs-trŏs′tō-mē) [″ + ″ + *stoma*, mouth] The surgical formation of a permanent gastric fistula through the abdominal wall. SYN: *celiogastrostomy*.

laparogastrotomy (lăp″ă-rō-găs-trŏt′ō-mē) [″ + ″ + *tome*, incision] An incision into the stomach through the abdominal wall. SYN: *celiogastrotomy*.

laparohepatotomy (lăp″ăr-ō-hĕp″ă-tŏt′ō-mē) [″ + *hepar*, liver, + *tome*, incision] An incision of the liver through the abdominal wall.

laparonephrectomy (lăp″ăr-ō-nĕ-frĕk′tō-mē) [″ + *nephros*, kidney, + *ektome*, excision] Renal excision through the loin.

laparorrhaphy (lăp-ă-ror′ă-fē) [″ + *rhaphe*, seam, ridge] Suture of a wound in the abdominal wall. SYN: *celiorrhaphy*.

laparosalpingectomy (lăp″ăr-ō-săl-pĭn-jek′tō-mē) [″ + *salpinx*, tube, + *ektome*, excision] Excision of a fallopian tube through an abdominal incision.

laparosalpingo-oophorectomy (lăp″ăr-ō-săl-pĭn″gō-ō″ŏf-ō-rĕk′tō-mē) [″ + ″ + *oon*, ovum, + *phoros*, bearer, + *ektome*, excision] The removal of the fallopian tubes and ovaries through an abdominal incision.

laparosalpingotomy (lăp″ăr-ō-săl-pĭn-gŏt′ō-mē) [″ + ″ + *tome*, incision] Incision of a fallopian tube through an abdominal incision. SYN: *celiosalpingectomy*.

laparoscope (lap′ă-rŏ-skōp″) [*laparo-* + *-scope*] An endoscope permitting visual examination of the abdominal cavity. SYN: *peritoneoscope*. SEE: illus.

laparoscopic gastric banding (lap″ă-rō-skōp′ik) A bariatric surgical treatment in which an adjustable band is placed around the upper stomach, restricting the volume of food that can be ingested

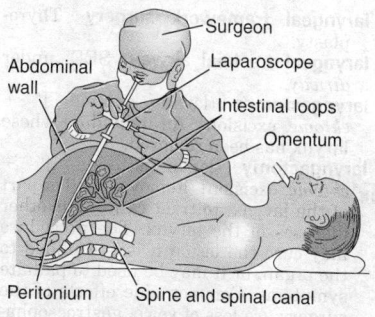

Surgeon
Abdominal wall
Laparoscope
Intestinal loops
Omentum
Peritonium
Spine and spinal canal

LAPAROSCOPE

and increasing the sense of satiety after a meal. Relative to other forms of bariatric surgery, gastric banding is less effective; patients who undergo gastric banding achieve less weight loss. However the procedure is commonly employed and achieves the intended weight loss for appropriately chosen patients.

laparoscopic ovarian drilling (lap″ă-rŏ-skop′ik) ABBR: LOD. Cautery applied directly to the ovaries of patients with polycystic ovary syndrome. It is a surgical technique for treating anovulation. SYN: *laparoscopic ovarian **diathermy***.

laparoscopy (lap″ă-ros′kŏ-pē) [*laparo- + -scopy*] Abdominal exploration with an endoscope. **laparoscopic** (lap″ă-rŏ-skop′ik), *adj*.

   diagnostic l. Laparoscopy for identifying and managing intraperitoneal diseases or injuries, e.g., after penetrating trauma to the chest and/or abdomen.

   gasless l. Laparoscopy in which the abdominal wall is lifted or elevated without insufflating gas into the peritoneum. It is designed to avoid the respiratory and circulatory complications sometimes associated with pneumoperitoneum and in cancer surgeries, to reduce the spread of malignant cells to the puncture site. SYN: *isobaric **l.***

   isobaric l. Gasless **l.**

laparosplenectomy (lăp″ăr-ō-splĕn-ĕk′tō-mē) [″ + *splen,* spleen, + *ek-tome,* excision] Abdominal excision of the spleen.

laparotomy (lap-ă-rot′ŏ-mē) [*laparo- + -tomy*] The surgical opening of the abdomen. SYN: *celiotomy.*

   PATIENT CARE: *Preoperative:* The patient's knowledge of the surgery is determined, misconceptions clarified, and a signed informed consent form is obtained. A baseline assessment of all body systems is conducted. The patient is encouraged to express feelings and concerns, and reassurance is offered. Preoperative teaching should focus on explaining the procedure, postoperative care, and expected sensations. Preoperative blood tests (including complete blood counts and serum chemistries), urinalysis, ECG, and chest X-ray usually are carried out, and consultations with appropriate specialists are conducted. Physical preparation of the patient is carried out according to protocol regarding diet; removal of abdomen and pubic area hair; enemas, douches, administration of intravenous fluids, measurements of vital signs and intake and output. Antiembolic measures are applied as prescribed.

   Postoperative: Vital signs and dressing status are monitored; the latter includes checking any drains in place and for the presence of vaginal bleeding if applicable. Ventilatory status is assessed by auscultating for adventitious or decreased breath sounds, and respiratory toilet (deep breathing, coughing, incentive spirometry, oral hygiene, and repositioning) is provided as determined by the patient's response. The nurse assists the patient to use noninvasive pain relief measures and prescribed analgesia for pain relief or monitors patient-controlled analgesia for effectiveness. Fluid balance is monitored, and prescribed fluid and electrolyte replacement therapy is administered. The patient is encouraged to void after surgery; the bladder assessed for distention, which may indicate urinary retention; and catheterization is instituted only when nursing measures are unsuccessful. The abdomen is auscultated for the return of bowel sounds, and a high-protein, high vitamin C diet is initiated following clear to full liquids as prescribed. Leg mobilization, turning, and early ambulation are encouraged, to promote gastrointestinal activity and prevent venous thrombosis. The hospital staff initiates early discharge planning, which includes carrying out patient teaching focused on incisional care, obtaining adequate nutrition, complications to report (e.g., nausea, vomiting, fevers, chills, constipation or wound dehiscence), and activity resumption and restrictions; arranging referral for home care as appropriate; and ensuring that the patient has scheduled (and plans to keep) a follow-up appointment with the surgeon.

   damage-control l. Abdominal surgery to reverse life-threatening conditions, e.g., massive bleeding or overwhelming bacterial infection. This procedure is followed by definitive surgery performed at a later time.

lap board SEE: under *board.*

lard [L. *lardum,* fat] Purified fat from the hog. The sole nutrient is fat; a 100-g portion contains 902 kcal.

   benzoinated l. Lard containing 1% benzoin, used as a vehicle for certain types of topically applied medicines.

lardaceous (lăr-dā'shŭs) [L. *lardum*, fat] Resembling lard; waxy, fatty.

large for gestational age ABBR: LGA. Term used of a newborn whose birth weight is above the 90th percentile on the intrauterine growth curve. Such babies should be monitored for signs of hypoglycemia during the first 24 hr after birth.

large loop excision of the transformation zone ABBR: LLETZ. loop electrosurgical excision procedure

L-arginine An amino acid promoted as a dietary supplement and sometimes employed by athletes to increase energy levels, human growth hormone levels, or performance in sports.

Larmor frequency In magnetic resonance imaging (MRI), the frequency of the radio wave that will resonate with all the protons in the nucleus of a given element. The Larmor radio frequency induces the magnetic resonance used to create MRI images.

Laron syndrome [Z. Laron, contemporary Israeli physician] Primary insensitivity or resistance to the effects of growth hormone. It is a common cause of dwarfism. Affected individuals have high levels of circulating growth hormone, but do not make insulin-like growth factor-1 (IGF-1). They can be treated with IGF-1. SYN: *growth hormone insensitivity syndrome.*

Larsen syndrome [Loren Joseph Larsen, Am. orthopedic surgeon, b. 1914] A rare autosomal disorder characterized by multiple joint dislocations and flattening of the face with widely spaced eyes, among other findings.

larva (lar'vă, 'vē", 'vī") *pl.* **larvae** [L. *larva*, a ghost, mask] **1.** A general term for the developing form of an insect after it has emerged from the egg and before it transforms into a pupa, from which it emerges as an adult. **2.** The immature forms of other invertebrates such as worms. **larval** (lăr'văl), *adj.*

   l. currens A type of larva migrans. The organism, *Strongyloides stercoralis,* travels subcutaneously at the rate of about 10 cm an hour rather than at the slow rate of larva migrans.

   cutaneous l. migrans A skin lesion characterized by a tortuous elevated red line that progresses at one end while fading out at the other. It is caused by the subcutaneous migration of the larvae of certain nematodes, esp. *Ancylostoma braziliense* and *A. caninum,* that occur as parasitic infections in humans.

   visceral l. migrans Toxocariasis.

larvicide (lăr'vĭ-sīd) [" + *caedere*, to kill] An agent that destroys insect larvae.

laryngeal (lăr-ĭn'jē-ăl) [Gr. *larynx*, larynx] Pert. to the larynx.

laryngeal framework surgery Thyroplasty.

laryngeal tracheal airway SEE: under *airway.*

laryngectomee (lăr"ĭn-jĕk'tō-mē) [" + *ektome*, excision] An individual whose larynx has been removed.

laryngectomy (lăr"ĭn-jĕk'tō-mē) [" + *ektome*, excision] Removal of all or part of the larynx, to treat cancers or other diseases of the larynx. The procedure may cure the lesion if it is confined to the organ, or it may be used to palliate symptoms. Common side effects of the surgery are loss of voice, gastroesophageal reflux, and adjustment disorders or depression as a result of the changes in body image produced by the operation. SEE: *Nursing Diagnoses Appendix.*

   PATIENT CARE: *Preoperative:* The patient is prepared for vocal and airway changes and for other functional losses after surgery. Explanations are supplemented with diagrams and samples of required equipment. Postsurgical communication methods most appropriate for and agreeable to the particular patient (e.g., simple sign language, flash cards, magic slate, alphabet board) are explained. The postoperative setting and care are described to the patient, including assessment procedures and sensations; and equipment used (suctioning, nasogastric [NG] tube feeding, laryngectomy tube care, wound drainage). Other functional losses that may be expected are explored (loss of smell, nose-blowing, whistling, gargling, sipping, sucking on a straw). The patient is encouraged to discuss emotions, sensations, and thoughts; and the use of familial, psychological, or spiritual forms of support is presented. Informed consent is obtained.

   Postoperative: If a partial laryngectomy is performed, a tracheostomy tube will be in place until edema subsides, and the patient should not use his voice until permitted to do so and then should whisper until healing is complete. If a total laryngectomy is performed, a laryngectomy tube (shorter and thicker than a tracheostomy tube) will be in place until the stoma heals (7 to 10 days). Vital signs are monitored, especially ventilatory rate and effort, as well as level of consciousness, arterial blood gas values, peripheral oxygen saturation levels, and the status of dressings and drains, including the posterior area. The airway is assessed for patency; the tracheostomy or laryngectomy tube is gently (but not deeply) suctioned to protect the suture line, as are the oral cavity and nose, as needed. Crust formation is prevented by increasing humidity and fluid intake, and frequent oral hygiene and assistance in managing saliva are provided. The patient usually is positioned on one side, with the head elevated to 30 to 45°. Support is provided to the patient's neck posteriorly during movement. The patient is taught to provide support by interlocking fingers of both hands behind his neck when moving. Fluid balance is monitored, prescribed replacement therapy is provided, and urination is encouraged. The patient is assessed for early complications such as respiratory distress due to edema, infection, dehydration, and hemorrhage (remembering to check the posterior aspect of the neck, as well as dressings, drains, and vital signs); and for later ones such as fistula formation, tracheal stenosis, and carotid artery rupture. If the carotid artery ruptures, pressure is applied to the site immediately, assistance called for, and the patient quickly returned to the operating theater for carotid ligation. If a fistula occurs, continued tube feeding is necessary to prevent food leakage that would interfere with healing (over a period of weeks to months). Tracheal stenosis requires fitting the patient with tracheal/laryngectomy tubes that are gradually increased in size until a tracheal opening of adequate size can be achieved. Protein-rich, high vitamin C nutrition is provided, via the prescribed route (usually NG tube feeding initially), to aid healing. Frequent oral hygiene is provided and encouraged as part of self-care. Noninvasive measures and prescribed analgesics to relieve pain are provided. When the wound drainage system is removed, dressings are checked for any further drainage, and the wound redressed according to protocol. The patient is allowed time for communication and is reassured that verbal communication ability will be reestablished through tracheoesophageal puncture, esophageal speech, or external mechanical or electronical voice boxes. Professional staff supports the patient and family through their grief over losses (including loss of voice, whistling, sucking ability, sense of smell and taste, nose blowing, activities such as swimming) and damage to self-image and self-esteem. The patient is prepared for possible follow-up therapies, such as radiation and chemotherapy and adverse effect as well as their management are discussed. Patient education also should include stoma care activities (including the need to limit exposures to dusts, fumes, and vapors). Information is also provided about the management of colds and respiratory illnesses, the removal of crust or mucus from the stoma, the need for warming and humidification of inhaled air, and the risk of postoperative tracheal stenosis. A list of the resources in the community should be provided for support, counseling, and further education. Patients are encouraged to join local branches of groups such as the American Speech-Learning-Hearing Association, American Cancer Society, National Association of Laryngectomee Clubs, or Lost Chord Club. A rapid return to employment is encouraged. Tobacco smokers and alcohol users are encouraged to seek help in quitting.

laryngismus (lăr″ĭn-jĭs′mŭs) [″ + -ismos, condition] Spasm of the larynx.

laryngitic (lăr-ĭn-jĭt′ĭk) [Gr. larynx, larynx] Pert. to or resulting from laryngitis.

laryngitis (lar″ĭn-jĭt′ĭs) [laryngo- + -itis] Inflammation of the larynx. SEE: croup; Nursing Diagnoses Appendix.

  acute l. Inflammation of the laryngeal mucosa and the vocal cords; acute congestive laryngitis. It is characterized by hoarseness and aphonia and occasionally pain on phonation and deglutition. It may be caused by improper use or overuse of the voice, exposure to cold and wet, infections in nose and throat, inhalation of irritating vapors and dust, or systemic diseases such as whooping cough or measles.
  TREATMENT: Treatment includes vocal rest, liquid or soft diet, steam inhalations, and codeine or nonnarcotic cough suppressants for pain and cough. If the laryngitis is viral, no specific therapy exists; if bacterial, appropriate antibiotics should be given.

  allergic l. Laryngitis due to inhaling dander, dust, molds, or pollen.

  atrophic l. Laryngitis leading to diminished secretion and atrophy of the mucous membrane. Symptoms are a tickling sensation in the throat, hoarseness, cough, and dyspnea when the crusts are thick and accumulate on the vocal cords, narrowing the breathing aperture. Inhalants and medicated sprays should be used to loosen the crusts, along with strict attention to associated nose and throat pathology.

  chronic l. Laryngitis caused by a recurrent irritation, or following the acute form. It is often secondary to sinus or nasal pathology, improper use of the voice, excessive smoking or drinking, or neoplasms. The patient experiences a tickling in the throat, huskiness of the voice, and dysphonia. The treatment is correction of the condition of the nose and throat, discontinuing alcohol and tobacco, and avoiding excessive use of the voice.

  contact l. Laryngitis due to inhalation of irritating aerosols, such as those that are present in tobacco smoke, paints, caustic cleansers, or inhaled medications.

  croupous l. Laryngitis occurring mainly in infants and young children and characterized by a barking cough, hoarseness, and stridor.

   diphtheritic l.   Invasion of the larynx by diphtheria, usually with formation of a membrane.

   mechanical l.   Laryngitis due to direct trauma to the vocal folds or, more commonly, from straining the voice during coughing, singing, or public speaking.

   membranous l.   Laryngitis characterized by inflammation of the larynx, with the formation of a false, nondiphtheritic membrane.

   posterior l.   Reflux **l.**

   reflux l.   Hoarseness, clearing of the throat, and alterations in voice quality thought to be due to injury to the posterior vocal folds by acid reflux. SYN: *posterior l.*

   l. sicca   Loss of normal lubrication of the vocal folds as a result of dehydration, breathing through the mouth, or medications that dry the mucus membranes, e.g., antihistamines or anticholinergic drugs.

   syphilitic l.   A rare, chronic form of laryngitis produced by secondary or tertiary involvement of the larynx by syphilis.

   tuberculous l.   Laryngitis secondary to infection with *Mycobacterium tuberculosis*. Infectious granuloma may be present in the interarytenoid area, vocal cords, epiglottis, or false cords.

laryngo-, laryng-   [Gr. *larynx,* stem *laryng-,* larynx] Prefixes meaning *larynx.*

laryngocele (lăr-ĭn'gō-sēl) [" + *kele,* tumor, swelling] A congenital air sac connected to the larynx. Its presence is normal in some animals but abnormal in humans.

laryngocentesis (lăr-ĭn"gō-sĕn-tē'sĭs) [" + *kentesis,* puncture] Incision or puncture of the larynx.

laryngogram (lă-rĭng'gō-grăm) [" + *gramma,* something written] A radiograph of the larynx.

laryngograph (lăr-ĭng'ō-grăf) [" + *graphein,* to write] A device for making a record of laryngeal movements.

laryngography (lăr"ĭn-gŏg'ră-fē) **1.** A description of the larynx. **2.** Radiography of the larynx using a radiopaque contrast medium.

laryngologist (lăr"ĭn-gŏl'ō-jĭst) [" + *logos,* word, reason] A specialist in laryngology.

laryngology (lăr"ĭng-gŏl'ŏ-jē) The specialty of medicine concerned with the pharynx, throat, larynx, nasopharynx, and tracheobronchial tree.

laryngomalacia (lăr-ĭng"gō-mă-lā'shē-ă) [" + *malakia,* softness] A softening of the tissues of the larynx.

laryngopathy (lăr"ĭn-gŏp'ă-thē) [" + *pathos,* disease] Any disease of the larynx.

laryngopharyngeal (lăr-ĭn"gō-făr-ĭn'jē-ăl) [" + *pharynx,* throat] Rel. jointly to the larynx and pharynx.

laryngopharyngeal reflux   The backward flow of gastric contents into the voice box and throat. It may cause vocal cord damage, hoarseness, and habitual throat clearing.

laryngopharyngectomy (lăr-ĭn"gō-făr-ĭn-jĕk'tō-mē) [" + " + *ektome,* excision] Surgical removal of the larynx and pharynx. It is usually only performed for cancers of the head and neck.

laryngopharyngeus (lă-rĭng"gō-fă-rĭn'jē-ŭs) The muscle that constricts the inferior pharynx.

laryngopharynx (lăr-ĭn"gō-făr'ĭnks) [Gr. *larynx,* larynx, + *pharynx,* throat] Hypopharynx.

laryngoplasty (lăr-ĭn'gō-plăs"tē) [" + *plassein,* to form] Plastic surgery of the larynx.

laryngoplegia (lă-rĭng"gō-plē'jē-ă) [" + *plege,* stroke] Paralysis of the laryngeal muscles.

laryngorhinology (lăr-ĭn"gō-rīn-ŏl'ō-jē) [" + *rhis,* nose, + *logos,* word, reason] The branch of medical science concerned with diseases of the larynx and nose.

laryngoscleroma (lăr-ĭn"gō-sklē-rō'mă) [" + *skleros,* hard, + *oma,* tumor] Scleroma affecting the larynx.

laryngoscope (lă-ring'gŏ-skōp") [-*scope* + *laryngo-*] An instrument consisting of a blade and a fiber-optic light source, used to examine the larynx (e.g., during endotracheal intubation).

laryngoscopic (lăr"ĭn-gō-skŏp'ik) [" + *skopein,* to examine] Pert. to observation of the interior of the larynx with the aid of a small long-handled mirror. SEE: *laryngoscopy.*

laryngoscopist (lăr"ĭng-gŏs'kō-pĭst) [" + *skopein,* to examine] An individual trained in laryngoscopy.

laryngoscopy (lăr"ĭn-gŏs'kō-pē) Visual examination of the interior of the voice box (the larynx) to determine the cause of hoarseness, obtain cultures, remove a foreign body, manage the upper airway, or take biopsies of potentially malignant lesions.

   PATIENT CARE: Short-acting intravenous sedation or anesthesia is administered along with oxygen. Vital signs and cardiac status are monitored throughout the procedure. After the procedure, the patient is placed in the semi-Fowler position, and vital signs are monitored until stable. Oral intake is withheld until the patient's swallowing reflex has returned, usually within 2 to 8 hr. An emesis basin is provided for saliva. Sputum is inspected for blood. Excessive bleeding is reported. Application of an ice collar helps to minimize edema; subcutaneous crepitus around the face or neck should be reported immediately because it may indicate tracheal perforation. The patient should not cough or clear the throat for at least 24 hr to minimize irritation. Smokers who undergo laryngoscopy should be encouraged to quit; preparation for the procedure and after-procedure care provide teachable moments.

⚠️ 1. Visualization of the larynx is associated with aerosolization of upper airway secretions. Standard precautions and droplet precautions are required during the procedure to limit the spread of infectious diseases such as severe acute respiratory distress syndrome (SARS) or tuberculosis.
2. Laser safety precautions must be employed when lasers are used.

direct l. Laryngoscopy with a laryngeal speculum or laryngoscope.

indirect l. Laryngoscopy with a mirror.

laryngospasm (lăr-ĭn′gō-spăzm) [″ + spasmos, a convulsion] Spasm of the laryngeal muscles.

laryngostenosis (lăr-ĭng″gō-stĕ-nō′sĭs) [″ + stenosis, a narrowing] Stricture of the larynx.

compression l. Stricture of the larynx owing to outside causes such as abscess, tumor, or goiter.

occlusion l. Stricture of the larynx owing to congenital bands or membranes, foreign bodies, tumors, scarring following ulceration as in diphtheria and tertiary syphilis, penetrating wounds, or corrosive fluid. Patients experience dyspnea, esp. on inspiration and exertion, often accompanied by stridor. Treatment depends on the cause. Tracheotomy is often necessary.

laryngostomy (lăr-ĭn-gŏs′tō-mē) [″ + stoma, mouth] Establishing a permanent opening through the neck into the larynx.

laryngostroboscope (lăr″ĭn-gō-strō′bō-skōp) [″ + strobos, whirl, + skopein, to view] An instrument for inspecting vibration of the vocal cords.

laryngotomy (lăr-ĭn-gŏt′ō-mē) [″ + tome, incision] Incision of the larynx.

inferior l. Surgical incision of the larynx through the cricoid cartilage.

median l. Surgical incision of the larynx through the thyroid cartilage.

subhyoid l. Surgical incision of the larynx through the thyroid membrane. SYN: superior l.

superior l. Subhyoid l.

laryngotracheal (lă-rĭng″gō-trā′kē-ăl) [″ + tracheia, trachea] Pert. to the larynx and trachea.

laryngotracheitis (lăr-ĭn″gō-trā-kē-ī′tĭs) [″ + ″ + itis, inflammation] Inflammation of the larynx and trachea.

laryngotracheobronchitis (lă-rĭng″gō-trā″kē-ō-brŏng-kī′tĭs) [″ + ″ + bronchos, windpipe, + itis, inflammation] Inflammation of the larynx, trachea, and bronchi. SEE: croup.

laryngotracheotomy (lăr-ĭn″gō-trā-kē-ŏt′ō-mē) [″ + ″ + tome, incision] Incision of the larynx with section of upper tracheal rings.

larynx (lăr′ĭnks) pl. **larynges** [Gr.] A tube built of cartilage that begins at the pharynx and that forms the initial segment of the respiratory tree, extending from the base of the tongue to the trachea. Its closing mechanisms prevent the aspiration of liquids and solids during swallowing and allow coughing and the production of vocalizations. SEE: illus.

ANATOMY: The framework of the larynx is built of three single cartilages and three paired cartilages. The unpaired cartilages are: the cricoid cartilage, a thick cartilage ring on top of the trachea; the thyroid cartilage, a V-shaped cartilage that sits on the cricoid with the point of its 'V' facing forward; and above this, the epiglottic cartilage, shaped like an upright paddle, with its handle held inside the front angle of the thyroid cartilage. The three smaller paired cartilages are: the arytenoids, the corniculates, and the cuneiforms. These nine cartilages are held together by membranes and ligaments, usually named by the structures that are interconnected; for example, the cricothyroid membrane connects the front of the cricoid cartilage with the base of the thyroid cartilage in the midline.

The intrinsic muscles of the larynx (cricothyroid, posterior cricoarytenoid, lateral cricoarytenoid, thyroarytenoid, transverse and oblique arytenoids, and vocalis) alter the length and tension of the vocal cords and the size and shape of the opening between them (the rima glottis). The vagus nerve supplies motor and sensory innervation to the larynx; the cricothyroid muscle is innervated by the external laryngeal branch of the vagus, while the other intrinsic muscles are innervated by the recurrent laryngeal branch of the vagus.

The cavity within the larynx comprises three consecutive chambers. The first chamber, the vestibule of the larynx, is a tube between the pharynx and a pair of folds, the vestibular folds (the "false vocal cords"), that protrude into the larynx. The second chamber, the ventricle of the larynx, is a short segment between the vestibular folds and the vocal folds; the ventricle has lateral recesses extending laterally under the vestibular folds. The third chamber, the infraglottic cavity (infraglottic larynx, subglottic space), is a tube between the vocal folds and the trachea.

foreign bodies in l. An inhaled or as-

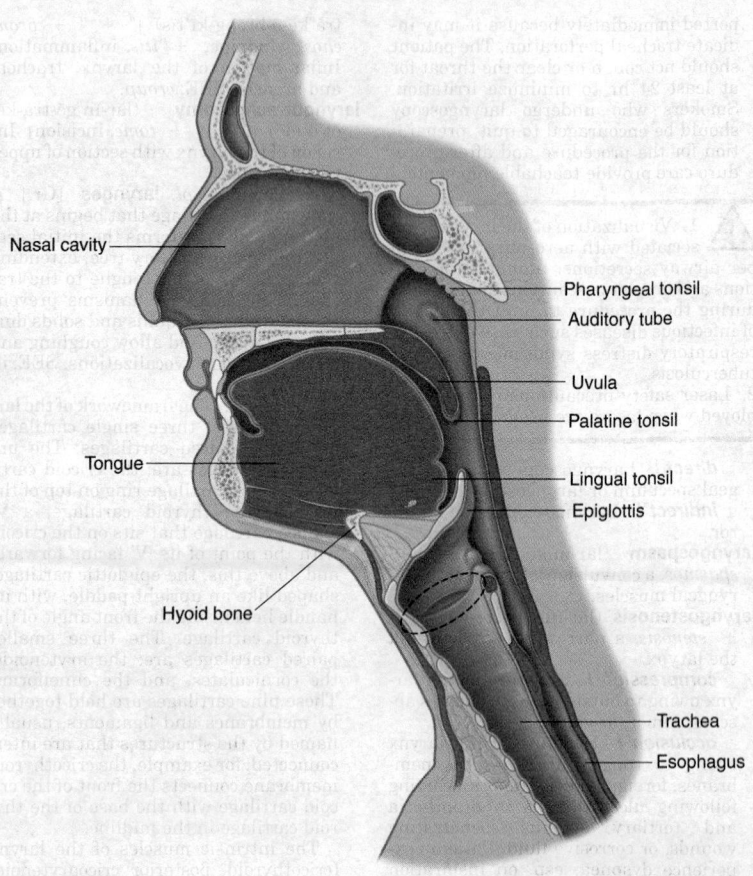

Nasal cavity

Pharyngeal tonsil

Auditory tube

Uvula

Palatine tonsil

Tongue

Lingual tonsil

Epiglottis

Hyoid bone

Trachea

Esophagus

LARYNX

pirated solid object, such as a piece of meat, hard candy, safety pin, or coin, in the larynx. Any aspirated object poses an imminent risk of airway obstruction.

SYMPTOMS: Symptoms may include coughing, choking, dyspnea, fixed pain, or loss of voice.

PATIENT CARE: If the patient is able to speak or cough, the rescuer should not interfere with the patient's attempts to expel the object. If the patient is unable to speak, cough, or breathe, the rescuer should apply the Heimlich maneuver 6 to 10 times rapidly in succession. Using air already in the lungs, the thrusts create an artificial cough to propel the obstructing object out of the airway. If the patient loses consciousness, carefully assist him or her to the ground in a supine position. Next the rescuer should begin CPR since compressions have been shown to be effective in clearing an obstruction. With each time attempt to ventilate, the rescuer should first look in the mouth to see if

there is an object that can be pulled out of the airway with gloved fingers. Previously chest thrusts were taught for an obese or pregnant patient or a child with a foreign body airway obstruction. To simplify this procedure the Emergency Cardiac Care Guidelines 2005 recommend all patients receive chest compressions following CPR. For an infant, the rescuer uses back slaps before chest thrusts. Direct laryngoscopy and the use of Magill forceps may be required to remove a foreign object. If the object cannot be readily removed with these measures, an emergency cricothyrotomy, or emergency tracheotomy may be required. SEE: *Heimlich maneuver.*

Lasègue sign (lă-seg′) [Ernest C. Lasègue, Fr. physician, 1816–1883] In lumbar disk disease, pain that radiates into the leg after the hips and knees are flexed and the knee is extended. SYN: *Bragard test.*

laser (lā′zĕr) [Acronym for light amplification by stimulated emission of radiation] A device that emits intense heat and power at close range upon a very small target by converting various frequencies of light into a small, extremely intense unified beam of a single frequency or wavelength. Lasers can influence cellular chemistry (the *photochemical* effects) and damage tissues by generating heat (e.g., producing coagulation, the *photothermal* effects). They can drill into, cavitate, or explode tissues (*photomechanical* effects) and can ablate tissues after transforming them into plasma. Lasers can also be used diagnostically (e.g., by illuminating cells or tissues, as in fluorescence). They have many applications in laboratories and in surgical procedures. In ophthalmology, they are used to treat cataracts, diabetic retinopathy, macular degeneration, and retinal detachment; in cardiology, to vaporize arterial obstructions; in dermatology, to obliterate blood vessels and to remove warts, skin cancers, nevi, excess tissue, and tattoos; in gynecology, to remove vulval lesions, including genital warts; in gastroenterology, to control bleeding in the gastrointestinal tract; and in oral surgery and dentistry, to remove tumors. Many kinds of lasers are used depending upon the wavelength and power required, including argon, carbon dioxide, copper vapor, dye, excimer, helium-neon, ion, krypton, neodymium:yttrium-aluminum garnet, and ruby lasers.

⚠️ Laser safety precautions must be observed: Warning signs should be posted indicating that a laser is being used; equipment must be checked before the procedure; conventional endotracheal tubes must be wrapped with aluminum foil tape (flexible metallic endotracheal tubes insulated with silicone may be used); skin preparation solution may not contain combustible agents; and towels draped around the site must be kept wet. The laser equipment must be moved carefully to avoid jarring the mirrors out of alignment. Alcohol-based skin preparations should not be used.

argon l. A gas-produced laser (in the blue and green visible light spectrum) with a wavelength 488 nm to 633 nm, used in the coagulation of tissue and in photodynamic therapy. Argon lasers are used to treat skin lesions, bleeding ulcers, hemangiomas, periodontal disease, glaucoma, and retinal diseases.

carbon dioxide l. ABBR: CO_2 laser. A gas-produced colorless laser with a wavelength of 10,600 nm (infrared), used in dermatological surgeries to remove scars, wrinkles, and solar skin damage. Carbon dioxide lasers can also be used as a scalpel in stereotactic neurosurgeries and gynecological surgeries.

PATIENT CARE: Laser precautions must be observed. The staff support the patient by answering questions and explaining the need for eye covering during the procedure. The procedure is documented in a laser log.

cutaneous l. Any of several lasers, e.g., argon, CO_2, used for cosmetic and plastic surgery. The procedures include treatment of pigmented lesions, wrinkles, vascular malformations, and other skin surface irregularities.

diode l. A compact laser designed with semiconductors, with wavelengths from 800 to 1000 nm, used in skin, eye, and urological surgeries.

PATIENT CARE: Care involves general support, giving explanations, and answering questions. Equipment must be checked and regulations followed, esp. those that involve fire safety. The surgeon is given assistance, as needed.

dye l. A laser with wavelengths of 510 nm for green and 577 nm–600 nm for yellow, whose energy reacts with various dyes and, modified by a tunable crystal, is applied in pulses, used primarily to manage skin lesions.

PATIENT CARE: Care involves giving general emotional support, explanations, and answering questions regarding the procedure. The equipment is checked, and all rules are observed. The needs of the surgeon are anticipated, and the procedure is recorded in the laser log.

excimer l. An ultraviolet laser used to remove tissue from the cornea, e.g., in LASIK surgery, or to remove plaque from arteries. This rare gas (halide) energy source laser breaks chemical bonds instead of destroying tissue with heat; it penetrates less than 1 mm into tissue. Halide combines with an active medium (an excited dimer), from which it derives its name. The dimeric media are excited, emitting laser energy. The chemical composition of the medium determines the ultraviolet wavelength. The four most popularly used are: the argon fluoride (ArF) laser at 193 nm, the krypton fluoride (KrF) at 248 nm, the xenon chloride (XeCl) at 308 nm, and the xenon fluoride (XeFl) at 351 nm.

grid l. A laser that scatters light energy across the macula; used to treat eye diseases, e.g., diabetic retinopathy.

yttrium-aluminum-garnet l. ABBR: YAG laser. A laser with a crystal made of yttrium, aluminum, and garnet, used for skin resurfacing, or tissue penetration in oral, urological, ophthalmic, cardiac, orthopedic applications. The depth of the penetration of the laser energy, its tissue absorption, and tissue-sparing characteristics vary with the materials used as additives to the crystal, e.g., erbium, holmium, or neodymium.

PATIENT CARE: Care involves general support, giving explanations, and answering questions. All equipment must be checked and all rules observed. The nurse assists the surgeon as necessary.

laser lipolysis The destruction of fat cells in the hypodermis with an Nd:YAG laser. In cosmetic surgery, it is used as an alternative to *liposuction* in reducing localized collections of fat under the skin.

laser microdissection SEE: under *microdissection.*

laser tissue welding (wĕld'ĭng) To bring the edges of a wound together with heat generated by a laser.

laser treatment for kidney stone removal The use of a laser to disintegrate renal calculi. A fiber-optic device is inserted through the urethra, bladder, and ureter to the calculus. The laser is activated, and the stone is destroyed without injuring adjacent tissues. SEE: *extracorporeal shock-wave lithotriptor.*

LASIK *laser-assisted in-situ keratomileusis.*

LASIK-associated neurotrophic epitheliopathy (noor″ŏ-trof'ik, -trōf′ ep″ĭ-thē″lē-rop′ă-thē) Drying of the cornea resulting from laser-assisted in-situ keratomileusis (LASIK). Tear production by affected eyes is reduced, and the patient experiences dry eye sensations, reduced blinking, and sometimes eye pain. The condition is believed to result from an injury to the nerves that supply the cornea. It may be treated with artificial tear solutions, medications like cyclosporine, serum eye drops, or plugging of the puncta of the eye.

Lasix (lā′sĭks) SEE: *furosemide.*

Lassa fever (las′ă) [*Lassa,* a town in Borno State, Nigeria] SEE: under *fever.*

lassitude (lăs′ĭ-tūd) [L. *lassitudo,* weariness] Weariness; exhaustion.

last menstrual period SEE: under *period.*

LAT *licensed athletic trainer.*

latah (lă′tă) A behavior identified in Southeast Asian women marked by imitation, swearing, repetitive speech, and obedient gestures. It may be provoked by startling, tickling, or frightening affected persons. Some researchers believe it is a social convention rather than a psychiatric or neurological illness.

latanoprost (lă-tăn′ō-prŏst) A prostaglandin agonist used as an ocular hypotensive and an antiglaucoma agent. It is administered as eye drops to manage glaucoma or to lower intraocular pressure.

latch, latch-on (lach, lach′on″) The attachment of the baby's mouth to the mother's nipple. Effective and comfortable latch-on is a crucial element in successful breast-feeding.

latchkey children Children who have a key to their home, needed for when they return home when no adult is present to supervise them. These children are at a higher risk of accidents, abusing drugs, and smoking cigarettes.

LATCH score An assessment tool to evaluate the effectiveness of early breast-feeding. A numerical score of 0, 1, or 2 is assigned to the five letters of the acronym: *L*atching of infant onto the breast, *A*mount of audible swallowing, *T*ype of nipple, *C*omfort of mother, *H*elp needed by mother to hold baby to breast. Lower scores (<5) can indicate the need for assistance for better success at breast-feeding.

late luteal phase dysphoric disorder SEE: *premenstrual dysphoric disorder.*

latency (lā′tĕn-sē) [L. *latens,* lying hidden] State of being concealed, delayed, dormant, inactive, or inapparent.

    sleep l. The amount of time between reclining in bed and the onset of sleep.

latency period The time from the stimulus to the response of a cell, organism, or tissue that has been stimulated.

latent (lāt′ĕnt) [L. *latens,* lying hidden] 1. Lying hidden. 2. Quiet; not active.

latent content In psychoanalysis, that part of a dream or unconscious mental content that cannot be brought into the objective conscious memory through any effort of will.

latent heat SEE: under *heat.*

latent period SEE: under *period.*

late-phase reaction Inflammation of any part of the body caused by the release of cytokines; leukotrienes B4, C4, and D4; and prostaglandin D2, occurring approx. 6 hr after the body's initial response to an antigen, during a type I hypersensitivity response. Late-phase reactions play a significant role in prolonging illnesses such as asthma after the initial, immediate histamine-based response has subsided. These are treated with and prevented by the use of corticosteroids, such as prednisone, and other drugs.

latera (lat′ĕ-ră) Plural of latus.

laterad (lăt′ĕr-ăd) [L. *latus,* side, + *ad,* toward] Toward a side or lateral aspect.

lateral (lăt′ĕr-ăl) [L. *lateralis*] 1. Pert. to the side. 2. Farther from the midline plane; away from the midline plane.

lateral geniculate body SEE: under *body.*

lateralis (lăt″ĕr-ā′lĭs) [L.] Located away from the mid-plane of the body.

laterality (lăt″ĕr-ăl′ĭ-tē) Rel. to one side of the body, i.e., the left or right; used, e.g., to specify which side of the body or brain is dominant.

    crossed l. Mixed dominance of body parts, e.g., preferring to use the left arm for throwing a ball but the right leg for kicking it.

    dominant l. Preferential dominance

and use of the parts of one side of the body such as the eye, arm, leg, or hand.

lateral medullary syndrome Wallenberg syndrome.

latero-, later-, lateri- [L. *latus,* stem *later-,* side] Prefixes meaning *side* or *lateral.*

lateroflexion (lăt″ĕr-ō-flĕk′shŭn) [″ + *flexis,* bending] Bending or curvature toward one side.

lateropulsion (lăt″ĕr-ō-pŭl′shŭn) [L. *lateralis,* pert. to side, + *pulsus,* driving] In cerebellar and labyrinthine disease, the involuntary tendency to fall to one side.

late tester A patient with HIV/AIDS whose immunity has already become severely impaired by the time the disease has been first diagnosed. This designation includes those who have a CD4 T-lymphocyte count of less than 200 cells/μL at the time of diagnosis and those who are first recognized as having HIV/AIDS because they have an AIDS-defining illness even though they did not seek medical care earlier.

latex (lā′tĕks) A viscous, aqueous solution of hydrocarbons, adsorbed proteins, ash, and resin produced mostly by tropical trees and used in the manufacture of rubber products, e.g., surgical gloves.

lathyrism (lăth′ĭ-rĭzm) [Gr. *lathyros,* vetch] A neurotoxic disorder caused by eating the grass pea, *Lathyrus sativus.* Its hallmarks are irreversible muscular paralysis and spasticity.

lathyrogen (lăth′ĭ-rō-jĕn) [″ + *gennan,* to produce] Something that produces lathyrism.

Latino (lah-tēn′ō) **1.** Pert. to Latin-American language, culture, or ethnicity. **2.** A person of Latin-American or Spanish-speaking ancestry.

latitude (lăt′ĭ-tood″, -tūd″) In radiology, a range of exposure that would produce a technically correct radiograph.

latrine (lă-trēn′) [L. *latrina, lavatrina,* washroom] A toilet, typically a large open receptacle excavated in the ground, often used in military settings.

   pit l. A type of outdoor latrine, used where it is impractical to provide a standard, flushing-type toilet. The structure, which is excavated in the soil, may be manufactured and installed so that odors and flies are minimized.

Latrodectus (la″trŏ-dek′tŭs) A genus of poisonous spiders that includes the black widow spider.

   L. mactans Black widow spider.

LATS *long-acting thyroid stimulator.*

lattice (lăt′ĭs) **1.** A network or framework formed by structures intertwined usually at right angles with each other. **2.** In physics, the arrangement of atoms in a crystal.

lattice degeneration SEE: under *degeneration.*

¹latus (lăt′ŭs) [L. *latus,* wide, broad]

Broad, e.g., as the uterine broad ligament.

²latus (lat′ŭs, lat′ĕ-ră) *pl.* **latera** [L. *latus,* side] The side; flank.

laudable (lawd′ă-bĭl) [L. *laudabilis,* praiseworthy] Commendable; healthy; normal; formerly said erroneously of pus.

laugh (lăf) **1.** The sound produced by laughing. SYN: *risus.* **2.** To express emotion, usually happiness or mirth, by a series of inarticulate sounds. Typically the mouth is open and a wide smile is present.

   sardonic l. Risus sardonicus.

laughter (laf′tĕr) A series of inarticulate sounds produced as an expression of emotion, usually happiness or mirth. The role of humor and laughter in promoting a positive attitude and health and in preventing the progress of some diseases has been documented esp. when it is combined with proven medical therapies.

   compulsive l. Laughter without cause, occurring in certain psychoses, esp. schizophrenia.

   pathological l. Uncontrolled laughter (occasionally accompanied by, or alternating with, uncontrolled crying), caused by pseudobulbar lesions of the brain. These lesions may result from lacunar strokes, multiple sclerosis, anoxic brain injury, and other forms of brain injury.

launch The release of a new drug or medical device into broad clinical use, that is, into the marketplace.

Laurence-Moon-Biedl syndrome (law′rĕns-moon′bē′dĕl) [John Zachariah Laurence, Brit. ophthalmologist, 1829–1870; Robert C. Moon, U.S. ophthalmologist, 1844–1914; Arthur Biedl, Prague endocrinologist, 1869–1933] The combination of girdle-type obesity, sexual underdevelopment, mental retardation, retinal degeneration, polydactyly, and deformity of the skull. The condition is inherited as an autosomal recessive trait.

lavage (lă-vazh′) [Fr. *lavage,* a washing] Washing out of a cavity. SYN: *irrigation.*

   bronchoalveolar l. The removal of secretions, cells, and protein from the lower respiratory tract by insertion of sterile saline solution into the airways through a fiber-optic bronchoscope or a blindly inserted catheter. The fluid may be used to treat cystic fibrosis, pulmonary alveolar proteinosis, or bronchial obstruction due to mucus plugging, or to obtain specimens for diagnostic purposes. SYN: *bronchopulmonary l.*

   bronchopulmonary l. Bronchoalveolar l.

   colonic l. Colonic **irrigation**.

   ductal l. The injection of a small

amount of saline into the ducts of the breast through a miniature catheter, followed by collection of the fluid and the cells that wash out with it. The cells are analyzed for evidence of early changes that may suggest an increased risk of future cancers. Occasionally they may reveal an already established cancer.

gastric l. Rinsing or irrigating the stomach to remove or dilute irritants or poisons or to cleanse the stomach before or after surgery. Gastric lavage, colloquially called *stomach pumping,* is used most often to manage patients who have ingested potentially toxic medications, street drugs, hydrocarbons, or other noncorrosive poisons. Its use in overdose is controversial. Effectiveness depends on absorption speed and the time between ingestion and removal. It has not been shown to improve clinical outcomes except perhaps in those instances in which the patient presents for care within an hour of ingesting a life-threatening amount of poison. The procedure has some risks: the trachea, instead of the stomach, may be intubated; gastric contents may be aspirated; and the mouth, teeth, pharynx, or esophagus may be injured.

PATIENT CARE: The following equipment is needed: plastic large-lumen nasogastric tube; water-soluble lubricant; disposable irrigation set with bulb syringe; adhesive tape or other device; clamp, safety pins, and rubber band; gloves and stethoscope; tissues; glass of water with straw; emesis basin; container for aspirant; at least 500 to 1000 mL of prescribed irrigating solution; and any specified antidote.

Physical restraints are applied only if prescribed and required. The patient's clothing is removed and a hospital gown put on. If conscious and cooperative, the patient is placed in the high Fowler position (head elevated 80 to 90°), and the chest is covered with a water-impermeable bib or drape. If unconscious, the patient is positioned to prevent aspiration of stomach contents; suction equipment is provided, and the airway is protected.

The distance for tube insertion is measured by placing the tip of the tube at the tip of the patient's nose and extending the tube to the earlobe and then to the xiphoid process. The length of tubing that will remain outside the patient after insertion is marked on the tube. Nostril patency is checked and the nostril with the least obstruction is selected. While the patient or an assistant holds the emesis basin, the nurse lubricates the tip of the tube and inserts it. A downward and backward motion aids passage through the back of the nose and down into the nasopharynx, thus avoiding producing a gag reflex. The patient is instructed to dry-swallow during this phase of passage. The tube should not be forced. If obstruction is met, the tube is removed, the patient permitted to rest briefly, the tube relubricated, and the procedure attempted again. If the tube cannot be passed without traumatizing the mucosa, the physician is notified.

When the tube is in the nasopharynx, the patient is instructed to flex the neck slightly to bring the head forward. A sip of water (if permitted) is given to the patient, and the patient is encouraged to swallow the tube. Rotating the tube toward the opposite nostril often helps direct toward the esophagus and away from the trachea. Placing the nondominant hand on the nose to secure the tube, the practitioner advances it with the dominant hand as the patient swallows.

The back of the throat is periodically inspected for any evidence of coiled tubing, esp. if the patient is gagging or uncomfortable, or unconscious. When the tube has been passed, placement is verified by aspirating gastric contents with the bulb syringe. The tube is then secured to the nostrils with adhesive tape or another securing device according to protocol.

⚠ Gastric lavage should never be performed on a patient who has ingested corrosive acids or alkalis. It also should never be performed on patients who cannot protect their own airways unless they are already intubated.

The irrigation fluid is instilled, and care is taken to prevent the entrance of air. A Y-connector can be attached to the nasogastric tube, with one tubing exiting to the bulb syringe or irrigant container and the other to a drainage set. The return line is clamped, and the solution, usually 500 mL or more, instilled to distend the stomach and expose all areas to the solution. The large volume also dilutes harmful liquids and thins or dissolves other materials.

The patient is monitored throughout for retching. If retching occurs, the flow is stopped, suction is applied to the bulb syringe, or the drainage line is opened to remove some of the instilled fluid. The stomach is then drained, and the procedure is repeated as necessary to cleanse and empty the stomach of harmful materials and irrigant. Alternatively, 150 to 200 mL may be removed and the same amount added on an alternating basis. The process is repeated until a total of 1000 mL has been employed and drained. An activated charcoal slurry is then instilled as appropriate and prescribed.

A specimen of the aspirant is sent to the laboratory for analysis as directed. The tube may remain in place, attached to intermittent low suction, or be removed immediately after the procedure.

For removal, the tube is clamped securely. Any securing devices are removed, and the tube is rotated gently to ensure that it moves freely and then is gently but steadily pulled out of the nose and coiled. The patient is handed tissues to wipe the eyes and blow the nose and is assisted with oral hygiene. A fresh gown or linens are provided as necessary.

After the procedure, the tube and prescribed suction are maintained as necessary, drainage is documented, comfort measures (oral misting, anesthetic throat sprays) are provided, and the patient is assessed and treated for any complications of lavage or of the toxic exposure.

nasal l. Flushing of the nose and/or sinuses with fluid, e.g., with a device such as a bulb syringe or neti pot. It is used to treat nasal congestion and allergies. SYN: *nasal **irrigation***.

peritoneal l. Irrigation of the peritoneal cavity, e.g., to diagnose blunt abdominal trauma; to diagnose, by obtaining cytologic specimens, or treat tumors of the peritoneum with chemotherapeutic agents; and to treat peritonitis, assist in evacuation of blood, fecal soilage, and/or purulent secretions as in hemorrhage or peritonitis.

pulsatile l., pulse l., pulsed l. Irrigation of a tissue surface or body cavity with intermittent sprays or splashes of fluid. It is used in several procedures to reduce the bacterial burden of contaminated surfaces, but it may occasionally cause tissue damage or infection if nonsterile solutions are accidentally employed.

lavender (lav′ĕn-dĕr) [Fr. *lavendre,* fr L. *lavendula, livendula*] An aromatic, flowering plant (*Lavandula angustifolia Miller*) whose essential oils are used for bathing, perfuming, and making ointments. Some people develop allergic reactions on contact.

law (lo) **1.** A scientific statement that is found to apply to a class of natural occurrences. **2.** A body of rules, regulations, and legal opinions of conduct and action that are made by controlling authority and are legally binding.

administrative l. Body of law in the form of decisions, rules, regulations, and orders created by administrative agencies under the direction of the executive branch of the government used to carry out the duties of such agencies. Regulations of nursing practice, for example, are considered administrative laws.

all-or-none l. The weakest stimulus capable of producing a response produces the maximum contraction of cardiac and skeletal muscle cells, and the maximal impulse transmission rate in neurons.

apology l. A colloquial term for any legal statute that encourages health care providers to acknowledge and disclose medical errors openly. Although apology laws vary from one jurisdiction to another, most include some measure of legal protection for the individual or agency making the apology.

Avogadro l. SEE: under *Avogadro, Amedeo*.

Beer l. SEE: *Beer law*.

Bell l. SEE: under *Bell, Sir Charles*.

biogenetic l. Ontogeny recapitulates phylogeny, i.e., an individual in its development recapitulates stages in its evolutionary development. SYN: *Haeckel l.*

Boyle l. SEE: *Boyle law*.

case l. Opinions or decisions made by the courts.

Charles l. SEE: *Charles law*.

common l. A system of law that originated in medieval England and is based on former legal decisions (precedent) and custom, not on legislation. Common law constantly evolves from previous decisions and changing custom. It forms the basis of the legal system in the U.S. (except Louisiana), the U.K. and most other English-speaking countries and is therefore the most frequent source of legal precedent for malpractice cases.

cosine l. **1.** A physical law that describes the relationship between the sides and angles of any triangle. **2.** When applied to physical treatment of the body, it describes the effectiveness of radiant energy and the angle at which it strikes tissue. The maximum amount of energy transfer occurs when the energy strikes tissue at a 90° angle. As the angle changes, the effectiveness of the energy is reduced by the multiple of the cosine of the angle: Effective energy = applied energy × cosine of the angle.

l. of contiguity 1. A law stating that if two ideas occur together, then the recollection of one will likely stimulate recall of the other. **2.** A law stating that if combined stimuli precede contraction of a muscle, then, when those stimuli are repeated, the muscle will contract again.

criminal l. The area of the law relating to violations of statutes that pertain to public offenses or acts committed against the public. For example, a health care provider can be prosecuted for criminal acts such as assault and battery, fraud, and abuse.

Dalton l. SEE: *Dalton law*.

l. of definite proportions Two or more elements when united to form a new substance do so in a constant and fixed proportion by weight. SEE: *Dalton law*.

l. of effect The psychological principle that positively reinforced behaviors will be repeated and negatively reinforced behaviors will diminish or be extinguished.

Fick l. SEE: under *Fick, Adolf Eugen*.

Frank-Starling l. SEE: under *Starling law*.

fraud and abuse l. A statute that regulates the appropriateness of health care provider behavior in billing practices, receipt of payments, and provision of medically necessary services.

Good Samaritan l. The legal protection given to those who stop and render care in an emergency situation without expectation for remuneration. The necessity for this legislation arose when physicians who assisted in giving emergency care were later accused of malpractice by the patient.

Hellin l. SEE: *Hellin law*.

Henry l. SEE: *Henry law*.

Hooke l. SEE: *Hooke law*.

inverse-square l. The intensity of radiation or light at any distance is inversely proportional to the square of the distance between the irradiated surface and a point source. Thus, a light with a certain intensity at a 4-ft distance will have only one-fourth that intensity at 8 ft and would be four times as intense at a 2-ft distance.

l. of Laplace SEE: *law of Laplace*.

l. of mass action In any chemical reaction, the ratio of the mathematical products of the concentrations of the products (raised to the power of the chemical coefficients in the balanced equation) to the mathematical products of the concentrations of the reactants (similarly raised) is constant at a given temperature.

Mendel l. SEE: *Mendel laws*.

l. of multiple proportions When two substances unite to form a series of chemical compounds, the proportions in which they unite are simple multiples of one another or of one common proportion. SEE: *Dalton law*.

Ohm l. SEE: *Ohm law*.

periodic l. The physical and chemical properties of chemical elements are periodic functions of their atomic number. A natural classification of elements is made according to their atomic number. When arranged in order (through calcium, atomic number 20), elements show regular variations in most of their physical and chemical properties.

Poiseuille l. SEE: *Poiseuille law*.

Q l. As temperature (in degrees Kelvin) decreases, chemical activity decreases.

l. of reciprocal proportions In chemistry, the proportions in which two elementary bodies unite with a third one are simple multiples or simple fractions of the proportions in which these two bodies unite with each other.

reciprocity l. Any milliamperage multiplied by an exposure time setting that gives the same milliamperage-second outcome should give the same relative density to an image. However, this law is dramatically affected by the image receptor response curve, esp. when it is not a 45° linear curve. In radiographic intensifying film and screen technologies, the reciprocity law does not hold at long exposure times because of the reversal of the D log E response curve.

right-to-know l. A law that dictates that employers must inform their employees of the health effects and chemical hazards of the toxic substances used in each workplace. The employer must provide information concerning the generic and chemical names of the substances used; the level at which the exposure is hazardous; the effects of exposure at hazardous levels; the symptoms of such effects; the potential for flammability, explosion, and reactivity of the substances; the appropriate emergency treatment; proper conditions for safe use and exposure to the substances; and procedures for cleanup of leaks and spills. The law provides that an employee may refuse to work with a toxic substance until he or she has received information concerning its potential for hazard. SEE: *hazardous material; health hazard; material safety data sheet; permissible exposure limits*.

Starling l. SEE: *Starling law*.

Stoke l. SEE: *Stoke law*.

Weber l. SEE: *Weber law*.

law of Laplace (lah-plhas´) [Pierre-Simon Laplace, Fr. scientist, 1749–1827] A law stating that pressure within a tube is inversely proportional to the radius. The larger the diameter of a tubular structure, the less chance that it will rupture when subjected to an increase in pressure.

lawn A layer of microorganisms growing on a culture medium.

lawrencium (lo-ren´sē-ŭm) [Ernest O. Lawrence, U.S. physicist, 1901–1958 + *-ium*] SYMB: Lr. A synthetic transuranic chemical element, atomic weight (mass) (most stable isotope) 260, atomic number 103.

lax (lăks) [L. *laxus,* slack] **1.** Without tension. **2.** Loose and not easily controlled; said of bowel movements.

laxative (lăk´să-tĭv) [L. *laxare,* to loosen]

A food or chemical substance that acts to loosen the bowels and prevent or treat constipation. Laxatives may act by increasing peristalsis by irritating the intestinal mucosa, lubricating the intestinal walls, softening the bowel contents by increasing the amount of water in the intestines, and increasing the bulk of the bowel contents. Many people feel that it is essential to have one or more bowel movements a day, and, if they do not, they may develop the habit of taking some form of laxative daily. They should be instructed that missing a bowel movement is not harmful and that bowel movements do not necessarily occur at regular intervals. SYN: *aperient; cathartic; purgative*. SEE: *constipation; enema*.

l. regimen A diet modified to avoid chronic constipation by eating high-bulk foods that contain a high fiber content, eating foods that tend to stimulate bowel activity (e.g., stewed fruits and vegetables), maintaining adequate fluid intake, and participating in regular exercise.

laxity (lăk′sĭ-tē) [L. *laxitas,* openness] The amount a joint or ligament deviates from its initial position when a force is applied to it.

layer (lā′ĕr) A thin sheetlike structure of more or less uniform thickness; a stratum.

ameloblastic l. The enamel layer of the tooth. SYN: *enamel l.*

bacillary l. The rod and cone layer of the retina of the eye.

basal l. The outermost layer of the uterine endometrium lying next to the myometrium. SYN: *basilar l.*

basilar l. Basal layer.

Bernard glandular L. SEE: *Bernard glandular layer.*

choriocapillary l. Lamina choriocapillaris.

clear l. The stratum lucidum of the epidermis.

columnar l. A layer of tall, narrow epithelial cells forming a covering or lining.

compact l. The compact surface layer of the uterine endometrium.

cuticular l. of epithelium A layer of dense cytoplasm at the luminal end of some epithelial cells, esp. that at the surface of columnar epithelium of the intestine.

enamel l. Ameloblastic layer.

ependymal l. The inner layer of cells of the embryonic neural tube.

epitrichial l. Epitrichium.

feeder l. A population of connective tissue cells that are used to nourish cultured tissue cells in the laboratory. The feeder cell layer is often derived from mouse fibroblasts. Feeder cells supply metabolites to the cells they support, do not grow or divide, and can be inactivated by gamma irradiation.

functional l. The portion of the endometrium adjacent to the uterine cavity. After it is shed in menstruation, it is regenerated by the basilar layer.

ganglionic l. **1.** The fifth layer of the cerebral cortex. **2.** The inner layer of ganglion cells in the retina whose axons form the fibers of the optic nerve.

germ l. Any of the three primary layers of the developing embryo from which the various organ systems develop. SEE: *ectoderm; endoderm; mesoderm.*

germinative l. The innermost layer of the epidermis, consisting of a basal layer of cells and a layer of prickle cells (stratum spinosum). SYN: *malpighian l.; stratum germinativum.*

granular exterior l. The second layer of the cerebral cortex, consisting of pyramidal cells.

granular interior l. The fourth layer of the cerebral cortex, consisting principally of closely packed stellate cells.

half-value l. ABBR: HVL. The amount of lead, copper, cement, or other material that would dissipate a beam of radiation by 50%. The number of half-value layers required for safety in blocking the area on a patient is five, because that represents 50% of 50% and 50% of that, and so forth. For example, 50% + 25% + 12.5% + 6.23% + 3.12% = 96.9%. Thus the patient would be shielded from all but about 3% of the radiation. (Examples of the thickness of material required to protect from radiation are 2 in [5 cm] of lead or 2 ft [61 cm] of cement.)

Henle l. SEE: under *Henle, Friedrich G. J.*

horny l. Outermost layer of the skin, consisting of clear, dead, scalelike cells, those of the surface layer being constantly desquamated. SYN: *stratum corneum.*

Huxley l. SEE: under *Huxley, Thomas H.*

Langhans l. SEE: *Langhans layer.*

mantle l. The middle layer of the neural tube of the developing embryo.

malpighian l. Germinative layer.

molecular l. **1.** The outermost layer of the cerebral or cerebellar cortex. **2.** The inner or outer plexiform layer of the retina.

molecular l. (of the cerebral cortex) The most superficial layer of the cortex of the brain, consisting of outer stellate cells and granule cells.

mucus l. Mucus **barrier**.

odontoblastic l. The layer of connective tissue cells at the outer edge of the pulp where they produce the dentin of the tooth.

Ollier l. SEE: under *Ollier, Louis Xavier Edouard.*

osteogenic l. Ollier layer.

papillary l. The superficial layer of the dermis lying immediately under the epidermis into which it extends, forming dermal papillae. SYN: *stratum papillare*.

pigment l. The outermost layer of the retina. Cells contain a pigment called fuscin.

prickle cell l. Stratum spinosum epidermidis; the layer between the granular and basal layers of the skin. Prickle cells are present in this layer. SYN: *spinous l.*

Purkinje l. SEE: *Purkinje layer*.

reticular l. The inner layer of the dermis lying beneath the papillary layer.

l. of rods and cones The layer of the retina of the eye next to the pigment layer. It contains the rods and cones.

spinous l. Prickle cell layer.

spongy l. The middle layer of the uterine endometrium; contains dilated portions of uterine glands. SYN: *stratum spongiosum*.

subendocardial l. The layer of loose connective tissue between the endocardium and the myocardium.

subendothelial l. The layer of fine fibers and fibroblasts lying immediately under the endothelium of the tunica intima of larger arteries and veins.

Tomes granular l. The layer of interglobular dentin beneath the dentinocemental junction in the root of a tooth.

Weil basal l. A relatively cell-free zone just below the odontoblastic layer in the dental pulp. It is also called subodontoblastic layer; cell-free zone of Weil; cell-poor zone.

layette (lā-et') [Fr. *laiete*, a small box] A wardrobe or complete set of clothing for a newborn infant.

Lazarus sign (laz′ă-rŭs) [Person in St. John's Gospel] Dramatic movements of the arms across the torso, which are occasionally observed in brain-dead patients after they have been disconnected from mechanical life support. These movements may be misinterpreted as signs of life, when in fact they are merely involuntary reflexes.

lb *pound*.

LBBB *left bundle branch block*.

LBW *low birth weight*.

LC50 [Fm. *lethal concentration*] An abbreviation for the concentration of a toxin that will kill 50% of organisms exposed to it.

LD *lethal dose*.

LD$_{50}$ *median lethal dose*.

LDB-CPR *load-distributing band cardiopulmonary resuscitation*.

LDH *lactic dehydrogenase*.

LDL *low-density lipoprotein*.

LDlo *lethal dose low*.

L-dopa L-3,4-dihydroxyphenylalanine; a drug used in the treatment of Parkinson's disease. SYN: *levodopa*.

LDRP An acronym for Labor, Delivery, Recovery, Postpartum that describes a maternity unit designed for family-centered care. Women in labor and their families complete normal childbearing experiences in one homelike room. The newborn may remain at the bedside throughout the stay.

LE *lupus erythematosus; lower extremity*.

leachate (lēch′āt) **1.** A contaminated liquid that leaves soil after water percolates through earth (e.g., in waste disposal sites), farmlots, or landfills. **2.** Any product of percolation.

leaching (lēch′ĭng) Extraction of a substance from a mixture by washing the mixture with a solvent in which only the desired substance is soluble. SYN: *lixiviation*.

¹lead (lēd) [Old English *laedan*, to guide] **1.** Insulated wires connecting a monitoring device to a patient. **2.** A conductor attached to an electrocardiograph. The three limb leads are lead I, right arm to left arm; lead II, right arm to left leg; lead III, left arm to left leg. These are also known as standard leads, bipolar limb leads, or indirect leads. SEE: *electrocardiogram* for illus.

bipolar l. In electrocardiography, any lead that consists of one electrode at one body site and another at a different site. A standard limb lead, I, II, or III, is a bipolar lead.

esophageal l. An ECG lead that is placed in the esophagus.

limb l. Any lead, unipolar or bipolar, in which a limb is the location of one of the electrodes.

precordial l. A lead having one electrode placed over the precordium, the other over an indifferent region.

unipolar l. An electrocardiographic lead in which one electrode is placed over the precordium, and the other over a different region of the body, e.g., a leg or the lower abdomen.

²lead (led) [Old English *lēad*] SYMB: Pb. A metallic element whose compounds are poisonous; atomic weight (mass) 207.2, atomic number 82, specific gravity 11.35. Accumulation and toxicity occur if more than 0.5 mg/day is absorbed. Any level of lead in the blood is abnormal. Most cases of lead poisoning occur in children who live in homes in which the paint contains lead. Children who eat the paint develop signs of lead toxicity. SYN: *plumbum*. SEE: *acute lead encephalopathy; acute lead poisoning; chronic lead poisoning; pica*.

l. monoxide PbO, a reddish-brown lead compound used to prepare lead subacetate.

leading zero SEE: under *zero*.

lead molecule (lēd) A chemical compound thought to be useful, safe, and distinctive enough that it might prove to be a good candidate for drug development.

lead optimization (lĕd) The synthetic refinement of a candidate drug from its crude or original state into an agent that is safer, more useful, or more marketable.

lead poisoning SEE: under *poisoning*.

lead poisoning, acute SEE: under *poisoning*.

lead poisoning, chronic SEE: under *poisoning*.

leaflet The part of a valve designed to open in the direction of flow and close to prevent backflow. Its base is typically attached to a larger structure by a fixed stalk and its unattached end moves.

leakage current In electrosurgery current that flows toward a ground along a path that the surgeon did not intend.

lean (lēn) Without excess fat. By USDA standards it means that a meat or poultry product contains less than 10 g of fat, 4.5 g of saturated fat and 95 mg of cholesterol per serving.

Leapfrog Group An initiative driven by Fortune 500 companies and other large private and public health care purchasers working to initiate breakthrough improvements in the safety, quality, and affordability of health care through technology.

learned nonuse Behavior sometimes observed in patients with hemiparesis in whom functional use of the paralyzed arm is avoided after unsuccessful attempts to use it. This phenomenon may represent a special application of learned helplessness.

learning (lĕrn′ing) A change in behavior or skill acquired by experience and practice.

action l. Learning through both direct participation in a task, followed by careful analysis of one's performance.

PATIENT CARE: It is used to improve a work processes within organizational units or address patient care issues that cross organizational lines. Team members are chosen for their technical, organizational, or managerial skills and knowledge.

asynchronous l. A method of instruction in which students access course material and engage with instructors and other students from geographically disparate locations or at different times. Techniques in asynchronous learning include on-line chats, threaded discussions, or self-directed learning modules. Before the world wide web, asynchronous learning was called correspondence education.

blended l. Academic instruction that combines computer- or web-aided instruction with direct student-teacher contact.

distance l. Distance **education**.

explicit l. Learning that results from clearly stated directions or instructions.

implicit l. Learning that takes place without directions or deliberate instruction.

interactive l. Learning in which students receive feedback for their educational efforts, usually from other students, teachers, mentors, or electronic educational resources.

latent l. Learning that is inapparent to the individual at the time it occurs, only to become evident later.

lifelong l. Learning that continues after formal education ends and fosters professional, intellectual, aesthetic, social, and leadership skills.

motor l. Any of the processes related to the acquisition and retention of skills associated with movement. They are influenced by practice, experience, and memory.

programmed l. An interactive system of education in which information is presented in small increments. As each new fact or concept is introduced, students are required to use what they have learned by responding to a prescribed series of questions. Mastery of each topic must be demonstrated before a student can proceed to more advanced subject matter. SEE: *Skinner box*.

synchronous l. Multi-site learning in which learners are linked to their instructor(s) by audio and video conferencing (includes chat, Skype, webcam) software so that they can ask questions and receive feedback in real time.

learning disorder Learning **disability**.

LEAS *lower extremity arterial studies.* SEE: *ankle-brachial index*.

least squares analysis A technique for statistical assessment of data that minimizes the sum of the squares of the distances from each data point to a line or plane. As part of the process, the slope, intercept, and correlation coefficient are also usually calculated. Once this is done, various statistical and analytical inferences can be made, so that the quality of the analytical process can be assessed.

leave, leave day, therapeutic leave day A planned and supervised furlough from care, esp. from a residential care facility. Leaves are often granted so that residents of a care facility can spend time with their family. Leave days may also be required from time to time when residents need specialized services or inpatient medical care.

Leber disease, Leber hereditary optic neuropathy (lāb′ĕr) [Theodor Leber, Ger. ophthalmologist, 1840–1917] Bilateral blindness inherited from maternal mitochondria. It primarily affects males.

Leber plexus A plexus of venules in the

eye between Schlemm's canal and Fontana's spaces.

Leboyer method (lĕ-boy-ā') [Frederick Leboyer, Fr. obstetrician, b. 1918] An approach to childbirth that employs a dark, quiet, and peaceful environment. Central to this method is the physical contact between the mother and the child immediately after delivery. The newborn is supported in a warm bath at this time. Caressing and massaging the infant begins immediately and is continued daily for several months. The method is believed to facilitate the child's mental and physical development.

lecithin (lĕs'ĭth-ĭn) [Gr. *lekithos*, egg yolk] A phospholipid (phosphoglyceride) that is part of cell membranes; also found in blood, egg yolk, and soybeans. On hydrolysis, it yields stearic acid, glycerol, phosphoric acid, and choline on hydrolysis. SYN: *phosphatidycholine*. **lecithal,** *adj.*

lecithinase (lĕs'ĭ-thĭn-ās) An enzyme that catalyzes the decomposition of lecithin.

> **cobra l.** An enzyme present in certain snake venoms.

lecithin:sphingomyelin ratio (lĕs'ĭ-thĭn sfĭng"gō-mī'ă-lĭn rā'shē-ō) ABBR: L:S ratio. The ratio of lecithin to sphingomyelin in the amniotic fluid. It is used to assess maturity of the fetal lung. Until about the 34th week of gestation, the lungs produce less lecithin than sphingomyelin. As the fetal lungs begin to mature, they produce more lecithin than sphingomyelin. Delivery before the reversal of the ratio is associated with an increased risk of hyaline membrane disease in the infant. The use of this test enables the obstetrician to determine the best time for elective termination of pregnancy. Other tests commonly used for this purpose include the amniotic lamellar body count, phosphatidylglycerol presence, and the shake test. SEE: *amniocentesis*.

lecithoblast (lĕs'ĭ-thō-blăst") [" + *blastos*, germ] One of the cells that proliferates to form the yolk sac.

lecithoprotein (lĕs"ĭ-thō-prō'tē-ĭn) [" + *protos*, first] A protein in which lecithin is part of the conjugate.

lectin (lĕk'tĭn) [L. *legere*, to pick and choose] One of several plant proteins that stimulate lymphocytes to proliferate. Phytohemagglutinin and concanavalin A are lectins. SEE: *mitogen*.

lectual (lĕkt'ū-ăl) [L. *lectus*, bed] Confining to a bed or couch, said of certain diseases.

LED *light-emitting diode.*

leech (lētch) A bloodsucking water worm, belonging to the phylum Annelida, class Hirudinea. It is parasitic on humans and other animals. Leeches were used as a means of bloodletting, a practice common up to the middle of the 19th century but now almost completely abandoned. The worms are a source of hirudin, an anticoagulant secreted by their buccal glands. In modern medicine leeches are used to evacuate periorbital hemorrhage (black eye) and to remove congested venous blood from the suture lines of reimplanted fingers. In addition to hirudin, leech saliva contains several active substances including inhibitors of platelet aggregation, that have been synthesized for use as anticoagulants in clotting disorders. SEE: *Hirudinea*.

> **artificial l.** Cup and suction pump or syringe for drawing blood.

Lee ganglion (lē) [Robert Lee, Brit. gynecologist and obstetrician, 1793–1877] A cervical uterine ganglion formed from the third and fourth sacral nerves and the hypogastric and ovarian plexuses.

LEEP *loop electrosurgical excision procedure.*

Leeuwenhoek disease (lā'vĕn-huk) [Antoni van Leeuwenhoek, Dutch microscopist, 1632–1723] Repetitive involuntary contractions ("fluttering") of the diaphragm and accessory muscles of respiration. The patient may experience shortness of breath and epigastric pulsations. The disease is caused by an abnormality of the respiratory control system of the brainstem. SYN: *diaphragmatic flutter; respiratory myoclonus*.

left The opposite of right. SYN: *sinistral*.

left-handedness Using the left hand as the dominant hand, e.g., for writing, work, or sports. SYN: *sinistrality*.

leg (leg) In common usage, the entire lower limb, or from hip to ankle; anatomically, only the lower leg, from knee to ankle, the tibia and fibula. SEE: illus.

> **bayonet l.** An uncorrected posterior displacement of the knee bones, followed by ankylosis at the joint.

> **restless l.** SEE: *restless legs syndrome*.

> **scissor l.** Scissor gait.

> **white l.** Phlegmasia alba dolens.

legal Pert. to or according to the law.

legally mandated treatment Compulsory treatment demanded by the courts even against the personal preferences of the patient. Usually, those commanded to receive particular forms of treatment are prisoners, probationers, the mentally ill (e.g., when a patient is judged to be a menace to his or her own health or the health of others), those with certain communicable diseases (e.g., tuberculosis, when a patient's refusal of treatment may threaten public health), or those with a history of substance abuse. SYN: *mandated treatment*.

legend drug SEE: under *drug*.

Legg-Calvé-Perthes disease, Legg dis-

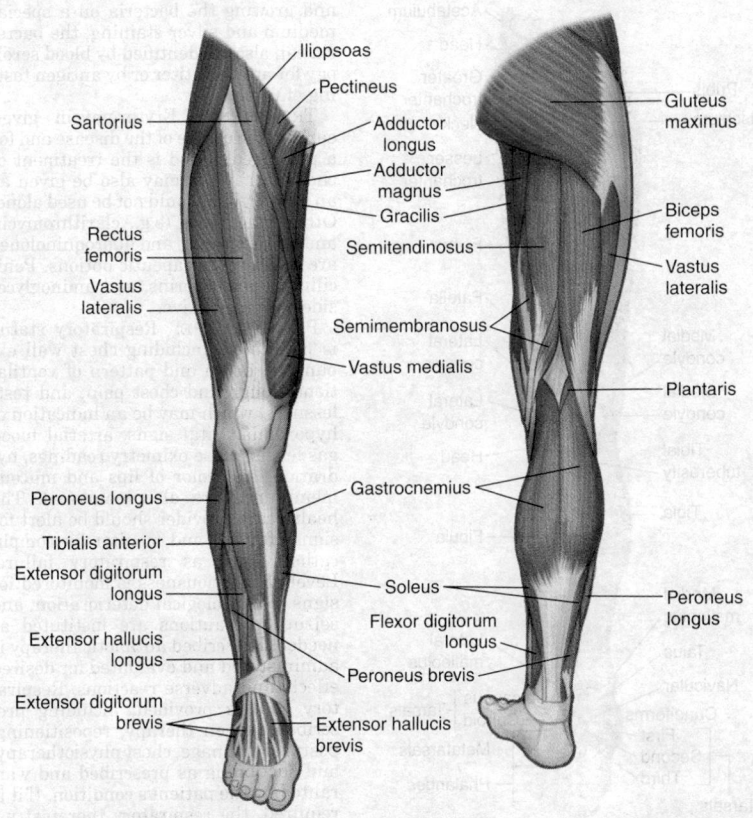

Iliopsoas
Pectineus
Sartorius
Adductor longus
Adductor magnus
Gracilis
Gluteus maximus
Rectus femoris
Semitendinosus
Biceps femoris
Vastus lateralis
Semimembranosus
Vastus medialis
Vastus lateralis
Plantaris
Peroneus longus
Gastrocnemius
Tibialis anterior
Extensor digitorum longus
Soleus
Extensor hallucis longus
Flexor digitorum longus
Peroneus longus
Extensor digitorum brevis
Peroneus brevis
Extensor hallucis brevis

MUSCLES OF THE LEG

ease (leg'kal'vā'pĕr'tē"z) [Arthur T. Legg, U.S. surgeon, 1874–1939; Jacques Calvé, Fr. orthopedist, 1875–1954; Georg C. Perthes, Ger. surgeon, 1869–1927] Osteochondritis (disintegration) of the proximal femoral epiphysis, a condition usually found in boys between 5 and 10. Symptoms include pain in the groin, hip or knee, esp. when the hip joints are moved. SYN: *coxa plana.*

leggings (leg'ingz) Stockings dressings, or drapes applied to the lower extremities, e.g., to provide compression, a sterile cover, or vascular support.

Legionella (lē"jĭ-nĕl'ă) [L., from "Legionnaire's disease"] A genus of gram-negative, motile, aerobic bacilli of the family Legionellaceae. They are found in natural water and may contaminate water used for human consumption, air-conditioning, or waste disposal.

L. longbeachae A species that causes sporadic cases of pneumonia and infections in immunocompromised hosts.

L. pneumophila (lē-jŭn-"ĕl-lă) The species that is the usual cause of Le-gionnaires' disease and Pontiac fever. SEE: *Legionnaires' disease.*

legionellosis (lē"jŭ-nĕ-lō'sĭs) Legionnaires' disease.

Legionnaires' disease (lē"jŏn-erz') [after Legionnaires stricken while attending an American Legion convention in Philadelphia, PA, in 1976] A severe, sometimes fatal disease characterized by pneumonia, dry cough, myalgia, and sometimes gastrointestinal symptoms. It may occur in epidemics or sporadically and is an important cause of nosocomial pneumonia because health care associated legionellosis, while rare, is more likely to be fatal than legionellosis acquired in the community at large. Approx. 8,000–18,000 people are infected each year in the U.S. Persons at risk include middle-aged or older adults who smoke cigarettes or have chronic lung disease and those whose immune systems are compromised by diabetes, renal failure, organ transplantation, cancer, or AIDS. The disease is responsible for about 5% of all pneumonias. SYN: *legionellosis.*

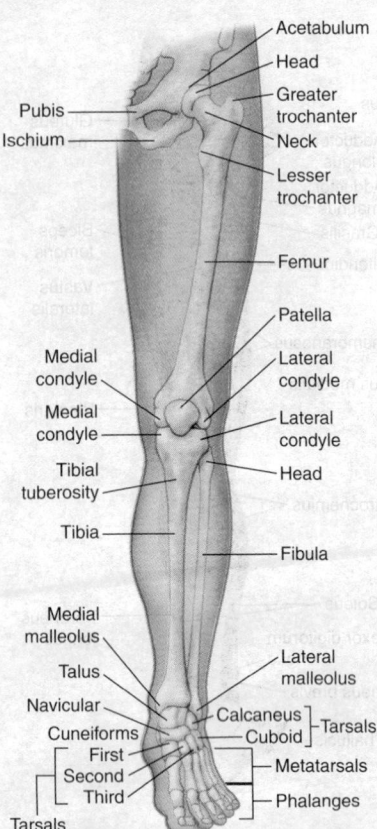

Acetabulum
Head
Greater trochanter
Pubis
Ischium
Neck
Lesser trochanter
Femur
Patella
Medial condyle
Lateral condyle
Medial condyle
Lateral condyle
Tibial tuberosity
Head
Tibia
Fibula
Medial malleolus
Talus
Lateral malleolus
Navicular
Calcaneus
Cuneiforms
Cuboid
Tarsals
First
Second
Third
Metatarsals
Phalanges
Tarsals

BONES OF THE LEG AND FOOT

Anterior view

ETIOLOGY: The infection is caused by bacteria of the genus *Legionella*. The bacteria may be inhaled or aspirated from contaminated water supplies (e.g., water cooling towers, humidifiers, air conditioning vents, hot water tanks, whirlpools, spas, showers, hydrotherapy tanks, public water fountains, and indoor waterfalls) or contaminated respiratory therapy equipment or nasogastric tubes. It thrives at temperatures about 90°–105°F (32°–41°C). Two distinct diseases occur from the various Legionella species: Legionnaires' disease or a milder influenza-like illness known as Pontiac fever.

SYMPTOMS: The signs and symptoms of Legionnaire's disease are similar to those of other pneumonias. Fatigue, anorexia, headache, malaise, myalgia, and diarrhea also may be present. The incubation period is 2 to 10 days.

DIAGNOSIS: It is diagnosed by culturing sputum or bronchial washings and growing the bacteria on a special medium and silver staining; the bacteria can also be identified by blood serology for antibody titer or by antigen testing of urine.

TREATMENT: Erythromycin given early in the course of the disease and for a prolonged period is the treatment of choice. Rifampin may also be given as an adjunct but should not be used alone. Other macrolides (e.g., clarithromycin and azithromycin) and fluoroquinolones are effective therapeutic options. Penicillin, cephalosporins, and aminoglycosides are ineffective.

PATIENT CARE: Respiratory status is monitored, including chest wall expansion, depth and pattern of ventilations, cough and chest pain, and restlessness, which may be an indication of hypoxemia. Vital signs, arterial blood gas levels, pulse oximetry readings, hydration, and color of lips and mucous membranes are also monitored. The health care provider should be alert for signs of shock and monitor for complications such as respiratory failure. Level of consciousness is monitored for signs of neurological deterioration, and seizure precautions are instituted as needed. Prescribed antibiotic therapy is administered and evaluated for desired effects and adverse reactions. Respiratory care is provided, including prescribed oxygen therapy, repositioning, postural drainage, chest physiotherapy, and suctioning as prescribed and warranted by the patient's condition. If it is required, the respiratory therapist assists with endotracheal intubation and the provision and management of mechanical ventilation or other prescribed respiratory therapies. Antipyretics are administered and tepid sponge baths given. A cooling blanket may be used as prescribed to control fever. Frequent oral hygiene is provided, and a soothing cream is applied to irritated nostrils if necessary. Fluid and electrolyte balance is monitored, and replacement therapy initiated as needed and prescribed. Prescribed antiemetics are administered if needed. The respiratory therapist or nurse teaches the patient about pulmonary hygiene, including the use of incentive spirometry. The patient is also taught how to prevent transmission of disease.

The use of sterile water only (not distilled or tap water) in respiratory therapy equipment and other aerosolizing and misting devices helps prevent nosocomial Legionella infections. Legionella can survive for long periods in plumbing systems by developing a biofilm, which forms on the inner surfaces of pipes and water tanks, provides a safe environment for the bacteria that is difficult to eradicate, and resists water disinfectants. Disruption of the biofilm then disperses the bacteria throughout the system. If Legionella is found in a facility's water supply, the system can be cleansed by hyperchlorination or superheating though recolonization may eventually occur. The Centers for Disease Control and Prevention encourage but do not require water testing, but high-risk care centers should have a testing strategy in place and should consider testing all patients with hospital-acquired pneumonia for Legionella infections. Legionnaires' infections may need to be reported to the health department, depending on state regulations. SEE: *pneumonia.*

legitimate medical practice SEE: under *practice.*

leg lifter An assistive device used to move the lower extremities from one place or surface to another; it typically consists of a large loop attached to a manually operated handle that encircles and lifts the foot or thigh. It is used by people who have difficulty moving their legs as a result of edema, joint disease, obesity, stroke, or other disabilities.

legume (leg′ūm″ lĕ-gūm′) [L. *legumen,* pulse, bean] **1.** A plant in the family Leguminosae (or Fabaceae), including alfalfa, beans, carob, clover, lentils, peas, peanuts and soybeans. **2.** The fruit or pod of a legume.

COMPOSITION: Legumes are a rich source of protein and essential amino acids. They contain legumin, a globulin, and significant quantities of dietary fiber, iron, and calcium.

VITAMINS: Sprouted beans are a good source of vitamin B complex. Vitamin A and ascorbic acid are present in small amounts.

CARBOHYDRATES: Carbohydrate is present in the form of starch in about the same proportion as in the cereals but with more cellulose.

legumin (lĕ-gū′mĭn) [L. *legumen,* pulse, bean] An albumin present in many leguminous seeds. SEE: *legume.*

Leiner disease (līn′ĕr) [Karl Leiner, Austrian pediatrician, 1871–1930] Exfoliative dermatitis.

Leininger, Madeleine (līn′ĭng-ĕr) The founder and leader of transcultural nursing who developed the Theory of Cultural Care Diversity and Universality. SEE: *Nursing Theory Appendix.*

leio-, lio- [Gr. *leios,* smooth] Prefixes meaning *smooth.*

leiodermia (lī″ō-dĕr′mē-ă) [Gr. *leios,* smooth, + *derma,* skin] Dermatitis characterized by abnormal glossiness and smoothness of the skin.

leiomyofibroma (lī″ō-mī″ō-fĭ-brō′mă) [″ + *mys,* muscle, + L. *fibra,* fiber, + Gr. *oma,* tumor] A benign tumor composed principally of smooth muscle and fibrous connective tissue.

leiomyoma (lī″ō-mī-ō′mă, ′mă-tă) *pl.* **leiomyomas, leiomyomata** [*leio- + myoma*] A benign tumor consisting principally of smooth muscle. Many leiomyomas are asymptomatic.

   epithelioid l. A leiomyoma, usually of the stomach.

   uterine l. A leiomyoma of the uterus. It is the most common tumor of the female reproductive tract.

SYMPTOMS: Leiomyomas may sometimes cause abdominal or pelvic heaviness, abnormal uterine bleeding, frequent urination, dysparunia, or pain.

Leiomyomas are classified according to their location. *Subserous leiomyomas* are found in the peritoneal covering of the uterus. They may be large or small, firm protuberances from the outer surface of the uterus or be attached by pedicles. *Intraligamentous leiomyomas* are found in the broad ligament. They may have uterine attachment. *Intramural leiomyomas* are found in the muscle wall of the uterus. If large, they can give the uterus a nodular, irregular shape. *Submucosal leiomyomas* are found next to the endometrium. Their most common symptoms are excessive, often abnormal bleeding, abdominal cramping, or pain. *Cervical leiomyomas* may cause stress incontinence, polyuria, dysparunia, or increased vaginal discharge.

TREATMENT: These tumors grow only during the reproductive years, often regressing after menopause. Surgical treatment (myomectomy or hysterectomy) may be necessary if tumors are more than 20 weeks' gestational size. Some tumors may be removed laproscopically although submucous tumors are removed by dilatation and curettage (D&C) or by hysteroscopy. Gonadotrophin-releasing hormones (GnRH) cause suppression of ovarian hormones and may cause tumors to shrink. SYN: *fibroid tumor; fibroid of uterus; fibromyoma* (2);*myoma uteri; uterine fibroma.*

leiomyosarcoma (lī″ō-mī″ō-săr-kō′mă) [″ + ″ + *sarx,* flesh, + *oma,* tumor] A combined leiomyoma and sarcoma.

leiotrichous (lī-ŏt′rĭ-kŭs) [″ + *thrix,* hair] Possessing smooth or straight hair.

Leishman, William Boog (lēsh′măn) Scottish bacteriologist and pathologist, 1865–1926. He studied tropical diseases (e.g., kala-azar) and perfected a vaccine against typhoid fever.

   L. stain A stain containing alkaline methylene blue and eosin in methanol used in genetics to identify chromosomal bands and in blood smear analysis to identify white blood cells and parasitic infections.

Leishman-Donovan bodies (lēsh′măn-don-ă-văn) [Sir William Boog Leishman, Brit. medical officer, 1865–1926; Charles Donovan, Brit. bacteriologist,

1863–1951] Nonflagellated trypanosomes found within the cytoplasm of cells infected by *Leishmania donovani,* the pathogen that causes visceral Leishmaniasis. SYN: *amastigote.*

Leishmania (lēsh-mā′nē-ă) A genus of parasitic, flagellated protozoa that cause a variety of infectious diseases in humans. These tropical organisms are usually transmitted to people by the bite of the female sandflies, although they may occasionally be transferred from person-to-person by transfusion.

   L. braziliensis The causative agent of American leishmaniasis.

   L. donovani The causative agent of kala azar (visceral leishmaniasis).

   L. major A species of *Leishmania* transmissible by sandflies and causing skin infections in humans. Infection with *L. major* is found principally in the Middle East, East Africa, and the Mediterranean.

   L. tropica The causative agent of Oriental sore (cutaneous leishmaniasis).

leishmaniasis (lēsh″mă-nī′ă-sis) [*Leishmania* + *-iasis*] Any of a group of related chronic parasitic diseases of the skin, viscera, or mucous membranes, caused by species of the genus *Leishmania.* Leishmaniasis has occurred in epidemics but occurs mostly as an endemic disease in Asia, Africa, Latin America, and the Middle East; U.S. military personnel overseas may be infected. One type of leishmaniasis, kala azar, causes visceral infection and involves the mononuclear phagocytic system, causing inflammation and fibrosis of the spleen and liver. It can be fatal if untreated. Mucosal leishmaniasis infection produces mutilating lesions that destroy the mucosa, esp. in the larynx, anus, and vulva. In the two cutaneous forms of leishmaniasis, multiple skin ulcers form on exposed areas of the face, hands, arms, and legs. These are not painful or contagious but, if left untreated, can leave permanent, disfiguring scars. Leishmaniasis organisms infect and reproduce inside macrophages and are controlled by T-cell−mediated response. The strength of the patient's immune system determines the severity of the disease. SEE: *kala azar.*

   PATIENT CARE: There is no vaccine against Leishmania. To prevent infection during exposure to sandfly vectors, topical repellants containing 30% to 35% N,N-diethyl-3-methylbenzamide (DEET) should be applied to the skin; and permethrin should be used to impregnate clothing, uniforms, bed netting, and screened enclosures. These measures also protect against infections caused by other biting insects, e.g., malaria.

   TREATMENT: Drugs used to treat leishmaniasis include amphotericin B, miltefosine, paromomycin, and sodium stibogluconate.

   American l. Mucocutaneous l.

   cutaneous l. An ulcerating, chronic, nodular skin lesion prevalent in Asia and the tropics and due to infection with *Leishmania tropica.* SYN: *Aleppo boil; Baghdad boil; Delhi boil; Oriental sore; tropical sore.*

   mucocutaneous l. A form of cutaneous leishmaniasis, involving principally the nasopharynx and mucocutaneous membranes, found in parts of Central and South America. The causative organism is *Leishmania braziliensis* usually transmitted by sandflies of the genus *Lutzomyia.* SYN: *American l.*

   tegumentary l. Leishmaniasis that involves the skin or mucous membranes.

   visceral l. Kala azar.

lemmocyte (lĕm′ō-sīt) [Gr. *lemma,* husk, + *kytos,* cell] A cell that becomes a neurilemma cell. SEE: *nerve fiber.*

lemniscus (lem-nis′kŭs, lem-nis′kī″, kē″) *pl.* **lemnisci** [Gr. *lēmniskos,* a ribbon] An axon tract originating in secondary sensory nuclei and conducting signals toward the cortex via the thalamus.

   lateral l. An axon tract originating in the cochlear nuclei and ascending to synapse in the inferior colliculi; axons from the inferior colliculi ascend to synapse in the medial geniculate nucleus of the thalamus. This lemniscus is a middle link in the circuit carrying auditory information to the auditory cortex (Heschl's gyrus).

   medial l. An axon tract originating in the cuneate and gracile nuclei, at the junction between the spinal cord and brainstem, and ascending to the ventral posterior nucleus of the thalamus. This lemniscus is a middle link in the circuit carrying somatic sensory information from the body to the primary sensory cortex.

   trigeminal l. An axon tract originating in the principal and spinal trigeminal nuclei and ascending alongside the medial lemniscus to the ventral posterior nucleus of the thalamus. This lemniscus is a middle link in the circuit carrying somatic sensory information from the face to the primary sensory cortex. SYN: *trigeminothalamic tract.*

lemon [Persian *limun,* lemon] The fruit of the tree *Citrus limon,* containing citric acid. Lemons contain enough vitamin C to prevent or treat scurvy. Lemon may be used in place of vinegar, spices, and aromatic substances by those who cannot use such items.

⚠ Food faddists who drink large quantities of lemon juice by sucking directly from the raw fruit may develop erosion of the enamel of their teeth.

lemon balm A mild herbal sedative (*Melissa officinalis*), usually taken as tea.

Lenègre disease (lĕ-neg'rĕ) [Jean Lenègre, Fr. cardiologist, 1904–1972] Atrioventricular or intraventricular conduction abnormalities resulting from fibrosis of the His-Purkinje fibers of the heart.

length (length) The measurement of the distance between two points.

basinasal l. The distance from the basion of the foramen magnum of the skull to the center of the suture between the frontal and nasal bones.

cervical l. The length between the external os and the functional internal os of the uterine cervix. At term, the average cervical length is 3.5 to 4.0 cm. A length of 2.0 cm or less is associated with an increased risk of preterm labor.

crown-heel l. In the embryo, fetus, or newborn, the length from the crown of the head to the heel.

crown-rump l. ABBR: CRL. In the embryo, fetus, or newborn, the distance from the crown of the head to the apex of the buttocks. The measurement can be used to estimate gestational age.

focal l. In optics, the length from the lens to the point of focus of light rays passing through the lens.

l. of stay The number of days between admission and discharge from an inpatient care facility.

stride l. The distance covered by the combined step length of each limb during gate.

wave l. In the line of progression of a wave, the distance from one point on the wave to the same point on the next wave. The length of a wave determines whether or not the wave is a visible light, x-ray, gamma, or radio wave.

Lennox-Gastaut syndrome, Lennox-Gastaut syndrome epilepsy (len'ŏks-gas-tō') [Henri Gastaut, Fr. neuroscientist, 1915–1995; William Gordon Lennox, U.S. neurologist, 1884–1960] A form of early childhood epilepsy marked by atypical absence and tonic-clonic seizures, slow-spike electroencephalographic waves, and a high incidence of mental retardation.

lens (lenz) [L. *lens,* lentil] **1.** A transparent refracting medium, usually made of plastic. **2.** The crystalline lens of the eye.

accommodating intraocular l. A flexible intraocular lens inserted into the eye during cataract surgery. When tugged upon by the ciliary muscle, this lens can alter its shape to focus on objects that are near, far, or middle distances from the eye.

achromatic l. A lens that transmits light without separating it into the colors of the visual spectrum.

anterior chamber intraocular l. ABBR: ACIOL. An artificial lens placed in the anterior chamber on top of the iris after natural lens has been removed. The lens may be fixated to the iris or positioned in the anterior chamber angle. SEE: *intraocular l.*

aplanatic l. A lens that corrects spherical aberrations.

apochromatic l. A lens that corrects both spherical and chromatic aberrations.

bandage l. A lens placed on the cornea to protect it while it heals, e.g., after a corneal abrasion or keratoplasty.

biconcave l. A lens that has a concave surface on each side. SEE: *biconcave* for illus.

biconvex l. A lens that has a convex surface on each side. SEE: *biconcave* for illus.

bifocal l. SEE: *bifocal eyeglasses.*

bifocal contact l. A contact lens that contains two corrections in the same lens.

concave spherical l. A lens formed of prisms with their apices together (thin at the center and thick at the edge), used for correcting myopia.

contact l. A lens made of various materials, either rigid or flexible, that fits over the cornea or part of the cornea to supplement or alter the refractive ability of the cornea or the lens of the eye. Contact lenses of any type require special care with respect to storage when they are not being worn, directions for insertion and removal, and the length of time they can be worn. The manufacturer's or dispensing health care worker's instructions should be read and followed. Failure to do this may result in serious eye diseases. Wearing contact lenses while swimming is inadvisable.

convergent l. Plus l.

convexo-concave l. A lens that has a convex surface on one side and a concave surface on the opposite side.

convex spherical l. A lens formed of prisms with their bases together (thick at the center and thin at the edge), used for correcting hyperopia.

corneal contact l. A type of contact lens that adheres to and covers only the cornea.

crystalline l. A transparent colorless biconvex structure in the eye, enclosed in a capsule, and held in place just behind the pupil by the suspensory ligament. It consists principally of lens fibers that at the periphery are soft, forming the cortex lentis, and in the center of harder consistency, forming the nucleus lentis. Beneath the capsule on the anterior surface is a thin layer of cells, the lens epithelium. The shape is changed by the ciliary muscle to focus light rays on the retina.

cylindrical l. A segment of a cylinder

parallel to its axis, used in correcting astigmatism.

disposable contact l. A soft contact lens worn for a week or two and then discarded.

divergent l. Minus l.

extended wear contact l. A contact lens made of materials that permit permeation of gas (such as oxygen) so that there is less chance for corneal irritation.

gas-permeable l. ABBR: GP lens. A contact lens that allows oxygen to pass through it, enhancing eye health, lens durability, and comfort. Gas permeability derives from the incorporation of silicone in lens plastic. GP lenses are used to manage visual conditions such as astigmatism, keratoconus, and presbyopia. SYN: *rigid gas-permeable l.*

gonio l. Gonioscopy l.

gonioscopy l. A lens with one or more tilted mirrors that is applied to the cornea for use in visualizing the anterior chamber of the eye during gonioscopy. SYN: *gonio l.*

hard contact l. A contact lens made of rigid translucent materials.

hydrophilic l. Soft contact l.

implantable collamer l. ABBR: ICL. An artificial lens that can be inserted between the cornea and a patient's own lens, used to correct severe nearsightedness.

implanted l. Intraocular l.

intraocular l. ABBR: IOL. An artificial lens made of acrylic, polymethylmethacrylate, or silicone. The lens may be placed posterior to the iris (PCIOL) or anterior to the iris (ACIOL). Posterior chamber lens may be monofocal or multifocal and can also correct an astigmatic error. A lens is removed because of abnormalities such as cataracts. If the original lens capsule is present and an IOL is placed inside it, the surgical procedure is called *posterior chamber IOL implantation.* If the capsule has been removed in a previous surgical procedure, the IOL may be placed in front of the iris, directly adjacent to the cornea. This is called *anterior chamber IOL implantation.* In another procedure, the IOL is implanted behind the iris. Which method of IOL implantation produces the best results is being investigated. SYN: *implanted l.* SEE: *cataract.*

minus l. A concave lens used to improve visual acuity in myopic patients. SYN: *divergent l.*

monofocal intraocular l. An intraocular lens inserted by the ophthalmologist during cataract surgery that allows the wearer to see clearly at a single distance (close to the eye, far from it, or in intermediate focal points). Monofocal lenses were the only lenses used in the first few decades of cataract surgery. SEE: *multifocal intraocular l.*

multifocal intraocular l. An intraocular lens inserted into the eye during cataract surgery that gives the wearer clear vision at near, intermediate, and far focal points. SEE: *monofocal intraocular l.*

multifocal l. Progressive l.

oil immersion l. A special lens with oil placed between the lens and the object being visualized. This eliminates a layer of air between the microscope slide and the lens, producing a clearer image than if the oil were not used.

orthoscopic l. A lens that produces no distortion of the periphery of the image.

plus l. A convex lens used to improve visual acuity in hyperopic patients. SYN: *convergent l.*

rigid gas-permeable l. Gas-permeable l.

posterior chamber intraocular l. ABBR: PCIOL. SEE: *intraocular l.*

progressive l. An eyeglass lens, used to treat presbyopia, that gradually changes prescription strength from the top of the lens, for distance viewing, to the bottom of the lens, for seeing objects close-up. Progressive lenses enable the eyes to adjust from one distance to another (as when one looks up from a book) without the *image jump* associated with bifocals. SYN: *multifocal l.*

silicone hydrogel contact l. ABBR: SH lens. A soft, extended-wear contact lens designed to improve the delivery of oxygen to the corneal epithelium. Depending on their design specifications, such lenses may be worn 6 to 30 days and nights consecutively.

soft contact l. A contact lens made of flexible, translucent materials. Such lenses are more comfortable, can be worn longer, and are harder to displace than hard lenses, but there are disadvantages. They may not provide the same degree of visual acuity as hard lenses, and they require more cleaning and disinfection. Production of tears may be decreased, esp. in older patients. The soft lenses may need to be replaced every 6 to 18 months. Corneal infections can prevent further use of soft lenses and also cause permanent loss of vision. SYN: *hydrophilic l.*

spherical l. A lens in which all surfaces are spherical.

toric contact l. A contact lens with two separate curvatures, used to correct astigmatism and distance vision simultaneously.

trial l. A lens used in testing the vision.

trifocal l. A corrective eyeglass lens containing three segments for near, intermediate, and distant vision.

zoom l. A type of lens that can be adjusted to focus on near or distant objects.

lensectomy, lentectomy (lĕn-zĕk′tō-mē) [L. lens, lentil, + Gr. ektome, excision] The surgical removal of the lens of the eye. SYN: lentectomy.

lensometer (len-zom′ĕt-ĕr) [lens + -meter] A device that measures the refractive power of a lens.

LENT late effect of normal tissue.

lenticonus (lĕn′tĭ-kō′nŭs) [″ + conus, cone] Conical protrusion of the anterior or posterior surface of the lens.

lenticular (lĕn-tĭk′ū-lăr) [L. lenticularis, lentil] 1. Lens shaped. SYN: lentiform. 2. Pert. to a lens.

lenticulostriate (lĕn-tĭk″ū-lō-strī′āt) [″ + striatus, streaked] Rel. to the lenticular nucleus and corpus striatum of the basal ganglia.

lenticulothalamic (lĕn-tĭk″ū-lō-thă-lăm′ĭk) Pert. to the lenticular nucleus and the thalamus.

lentiform (lĕnt′ĭ-form) [L. lens, lentil, + forma, shape] Lenticular (1).

lentiginosis (lĕn-tĭj″ĭ-nō′sĭs) [L. lentigo, freckle, + Gr. osis, condition] The presence of multiple lentigines. SEE: lentigo.

lentiginous (lĕn-tĭj′ĭn-ŭs) [L. lentigo, freckle] 1. Affected by lentigo. 2. Covered with very small dots.

lentiglobus (lĕn″tĭ-glō′bŭs) [L. lens, lentil, + globus, sphere] A lens of the eye that has extreme anterior spherical bulging.

lentigo (lĕn-tī′gō) pl. **lentigines** [L., freckle] Freckle.

   l. maligna A pigmented lesion of the skin in which a large number of superficial, atypical melanocytes are found. SYN: Hutchinson freckle. SEE: illus.

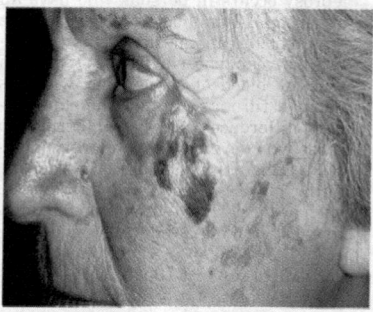

LENTIGO MALIGNA

SOURCE: Centers for Disease Control and Prevention; Carl Washington, MD

   l. senilis Solar *l.*

   solar l. A flat brown spot usually appearing on sun-exposed skin, such as the face or the back of the hands. They are commonly found on the skin of elderly individuals. Although they are popularly referred to as "liver spots," they are not caused by diseases of the liver. SYN: *l. senilis*.

lentivirus (lĕn″tĭ-vī′rŭs) [L. lentus, slow] A group of retroviruses that cause slowly developing diseases as a result of the gradual killing of lymphoid cells. Human immunodeficiency virus (HIV), the virus that causes acquired immunodeficiency syndrome (AIDS), is included in this group of viruses.

leontiasis (lē″ŏn-tī′ă-sĭs) [Gr. leon, lion, + -iasis, condition] Lionlike appearance of the face seen in certain diseases, esp. lepromatous leprosy. SYN: facies leontina.

   l. ossea Enlargement and distortion of facial bones, giving one the appearance of a lion. It can occur as a complication of hyperparathyroidism, Paget's disease, uremia, and other conditions.

Leopold maneuver (lē′ō-pōld″) [Christian Gerhard Leopold, Ger. physician, 1846–1911] In obstetrics, the use of four steps in palpating the uterus in order to determine the position and presentation of the fetus. SEE: illus.

leper (lĕp′ĕr) [Gr. lepros, scaly] A person afflicted with leprosy.

lepidic (lĕ-pĭd′ĭk) [Gr. lepis, scale] Concerning scales, or a scaly covering.

lepido-, lepid- [Gr. lepis, stem lepid-, scale (of a fish), husk] Prefixes meaning flakes or scales.

Lepidoptera (lĕp″ĭ-dŏp′tĕr-ă) [″ + pteron, feather, wing] An order of the class Insecta that includes the butterflies, moths, and skippers; characterized by scaly wings, sucking mouth parts, and complete metamorphosis.

lepidosis (lĕp″ĭ-dō′sĭs) [″ + osis, condition] Any scaly or desquamating eruption such as pityriasis.

lepothrix (lĕp′ō-thrĭks) [″ + thrix, hair] A condition in which the shaft of the hair is encased in hardened, scaly, sebaceous matter.

lepra (lĕp′ră) [Gr. lepra, leprosy] A term formerly used for leprosy. It is now used to indicate a reaction that occurs in leprosy patients consisting of aggravation of lesions accompanied by fever and malaise. It can occur in any form of leprosy and may be prolonged.

   l. alba A form of lepra in which the skin is anesthetic and white, associated with different forms of paralysis.

   l. Arabum True or nodular leprosy.

   l. maculosa A form of lepra with pigmented cutaneous areas.

leprechaunism (lĕp′rĕ-kŏn″ĭzm) An autosomal recessive disease in which elfin features of the face are accompanied by retardation of physical and mental development, a variety of endocrine disorders, emaciation, and susceptibility to infections. SYN: Donohue syndrome.

leprid (lĕp′rĭd) [Gr. lepra, leprosy, + eidos, form, shape] A leprous cutaneous lesion.

leprology (lĕp-rŏl′ō-jē) [″ + logos,

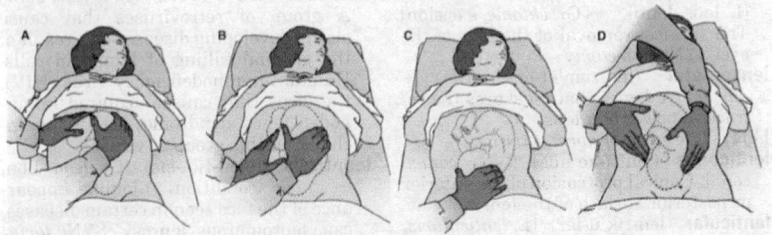

LEOPOLD'S MANEUVERS

word, reason] The study of leprosy and methods of treating it.

leproma (lĕp-rō′mă) [″ + *oma,* tumor] A cutaneous nodule or tubercle characteristic of leprosy.

lepromatous (lĕp-rō′mă-tŭs) Concerning lepromas. SEE: *leprosy.*

lepromin An extract derived from *Mycobacterium leprae,* the organism that causes leprosy. It is injected under the skin, in a fashion similar to the injection of purified protein derivative (PPD), to determine the degree of a patient's immune response to leprosy. PPD testing is used to gauge the immune response of patients to tuberculosis.

leprostatic (lĕp″rō-stăt′ĭk) [″ + *statikos,* standing] **1.** Inhibiting the growth of *Mycobacterium leprae.* **2.** An agent that inhibits the growth of *M. leprae.*

leprosy (lĕp′rō-sē) [Gr. *lepros,* scaly] A chronic infectious disease of the skin and peripheral nerves, caused by *Mycobacterium leprae.* In chronically infected persons, it may produce characteristic ring-shaped, nodular, or erosive skin changes, esp. on or near the face, and sensory and motor dysfunction, esp. of the hands and feet. Approx. 700,000 people are infected each year worldwide; leprosy is endemic in India (the site of 70% of cases) and other tropical countries. It occasionally is reported in the U.S., e.g., in Hawaii, where it was once endemic, and in the Gulf Coast states, where it is carried by an animal host, the nine-banded armadillo. SYN: *Hansen's disease.* SEE: *granuloma.*

The *lepromatous* (LL) form is characterized by skin lesions and symmetrical involvement of peripheral nerves with anesthesia, muscle weakness, and paralysis. In this form, the lesions are limited to the cooler portions of the body such as skin, upper respiratory tract, and testes. In *tuberculoid* (TT) leprosy, which is usually benign, the nerve lesions are asymmetrical and skin anesthesia is an early occurrence. Visceral involvement is not seen.

Lepromatous leprosy is much more contagious than the tuberculoid form. In the latter, *M. leprae* are found in lesions only rarely except during reactions.

Between the two major forms are *borderline* (BB) and *indeterminate* leprosy. In the borderline group, the clinical and bacteriological features represent a combination of the two principal types. In the indeterminate group, there are fewer skin lesions and bacteria are much less abundant in the lesions. In many respects, this infection resembles tuberculosis and for many years was regarded as incurable; this is no longer considered to be valid.

ETIOLOGY: The disease-producing bacterium, *M. leprae,* grows only at 32° to 34°C, the temperature of skin. A normal T cell response by the host produces tuberculoid leprosy, which can be transmitted by respiratory droplets. Once inhaled, the organisms produce granulomas in the lungs and move through the bloodstream to the skin.

In contrast, lepromatous (anergic) leprosy occurs in persons who have an abnormal T-lymphocyte response to the organism. Transmission requires contact between material from a skin lesion and the blood of a recipient, which is reached through cuts on the skin. Genetic differences have been identified in those who develop the two forms of leprosy. Other intermediate or borderline forms of the disease are well-known, such as borderline lepromatous, borderline tuberculoid, and tuberculoid leprosy.

SYMPTOMS: In tuberculoid leprosy, skin lesions initially are flat and red, but later become large, hard, irregular, and swollen, with pale depressed centers. Granulomas infiltrate the peripheral nerves, which gradually degenerate, producing loss of feeling in the skin, muscle atrophy, and contractures. Lepromatous leprosy produces large macular (flat), papular (raised), or nodular lesions without sensation on the skin, particularly on the face, hands, knees, and feet. The eyes, mucosa of the upper airway, and testes also are commonly involved. The lesions contain large numbers of infected macrophages. Infection of peripheral nerves causes loss of sensation and muscle atrophy. Nonprotective antibodies are formed, which bind with bacterial antigens; the resulting immune complexes may cause vasculitis and glomerulonephritis. In all patients with leprosy, loss of sensation leads to inadvertent trauma and skin ulcers; autoamputation may occur. The disease has a slow course and rarely causes death.

DIAGNOSIS: Biopsy of a suspected skin lesion is used for diagnosis. The bacilli may not be present in tuberculoid lesions. In vitro tests of the immunological response can be accomplished by the lymphocyte transformation test and the leukocyte migration inhibition test.

COMPLICATIONS: Bacterial skin infections, ulcers, and traumatic amputation of fingers owing to anesthesia may occur. Tuberculosis is a much more common complication in untreated cases of lepromatous leprosy than in the tuberculoid form. Amyloidosis may be the cause of death in advanced cases.

TREATMENT: Tuberculoid leprosy is treated with multiple drug therapies, such as daily oral dapsone plus one dose of rifampin each month for 6 months. Daily dapsone and clofazimine plus monthly doses of rifampin for 24 months are required to treat lepromatous leprosy. Directly observed therapy is recommended, esp. for the rifampin doses. There is concern that *M. leprae* is becoming resistant to these drugs. Treatment is complicated in pregnant women and in persons with glucose-6-phosphate dehydrogenase enzyme deficiency, because of drug intolerance. Despite effective treatments for many patients, the incidence of leprosy worldwide has not diminished in recent years.

PROGNOSIS: With proper therapy, esp. if given at the earliest time possible, the outlook is favorable.

leprous, leprotic (lĕp′rŭs) **1.** Pert. to leprosy. **2.** Affected by leprosy.

-lepsy, -lepsia [Gr. *lēpsia, -lēpsia,* seizure] Suffixes meaning *seizure.*

leptin (lĕp′tĭn) A helical peptide hormone produced by adipose tissue. Leptin acts on cells in the hypothalamus in response to increases in body fat storage to suppress appetite and increase energy expenditure. It also contributes to the onset of puberty and to the secretion of insulin by the pancreas.

lepto-, lept- [Gr. *leptos,* thin, fine, slim] Prefixes meaning *thin, fine, slight, delicate.*

leptocephalia (lĕp″tō-sĕ-fā′lē-ă) [Gr. *leptos,* slender, + *kephale,* head] Having an abnormally vertically elongated, narrow skull.

leptocephalus (lĕp″tō-sĕf′ă-lŭs) An individual possessing an abnormally vertically elongated, narrow skull.

leptochromatic (lĕp″tō-krō-măt′ĭk) [″ + *chromatin*] Having a fine chromatin network.

leptomeninges (lĕp″tō-mĕn-ĭn′jēs) *sing.,* **leptomeninx** [″ + *meninx,* membrane] The pia mater and arachnoid as distinct from the dura mater. SYN: *pia-arachnoid.* **leptomeningeal,** *adj.*

leptomeningitis (lĕp″tă-mĕn-ĭn-jīt′ĭs) [″ + ″ + *itis,* inflammation] Meningitis in which infection, carcinoma, or inflammation involves only the pia mater and arachnoid membranes of the brain, not the dura mater. SEE: *meningitis.*

SYMPTOMS: Patients have an acute headache, pain in the back, spinal rigidity, irritability, and drowsiness ending in coma. SYN: *piarachnitis.*

leptomeningopathy (lĕp″tō-mĕn″ĭn-gŏp′ă-thē) [″ + ″ + *pathos,* disease] A disease of the leptomeninges of the brain.

leptomeninx (lĕp″tō-mĕn′ĭnks) Sing. of leptomeninges.

leptonema (lĕp″tō-nē′mă) [″ + *nema,* thread] The early stage of prophase in meiosis. At this stage the chromatin coils into visible filaments. SEE: *cell division.*

leptophonia (lĕp″tō-fō′nē-ă) [″ + *phone,* voice] Weakness of the voice.

leptoprosopia (lĕp″tō-prō-sō′pē-ă) [″ + *prosopon,* face] Narrowness of the face.

leptorhine, leptorrhine (lĕp′tor-rīn) [″ + *rhis,* nose] Having a very thin or slender nose.

leptoscope (lĕp′tō-skōp) [″ + *skopein,* to examine] An optical device for measuring the thickness of cell membranes.

Leptospira (lĕp-tō-spī′ră) [″ + *speira,* coil] A genus of slender spirochetes with hooked ends.

L. interrogans icterohaemorrhagiae The species that causes hemorrhagic, spirochetal jaundice (Weil's disease). The bacteria are found worldwide; the natural hosts are wild animals and dogs, which develop chronic kidney infection. Humans acquire the bacteria from exposure to animal urine, often in water such as ponds and puddles. Symptomatic infection ranges from mild gastrointestinal upset to fatal liver failure often in association with meningitis. A vaccine is available for dogs.

leptospire (lĕp′tō-spīr) Any organism belonging to the genus *Leptospira.*

leptospirosis (lĕp″tō-spī-rō′sĭs) [*Leptospira* + *-osis*] Any of several infectious diseases affecting humans and domestic animals (dogs, horses, pigs), caused by spirochetes of the genus *Leptospira.* SYN: *Canefield fever; spirochetal jaundice.*

leptospiruria (lĕp″tă-spīr-ūr′ē-ă, -oor′) [″ + ″ + *ouron,* urine] The presence of *Leptospira* in the urine.

leptotene (lĕp′tō-tēn) [″ + *tainia,* ribbon] The initial stage of the prophase of cell division. The chromosomes become visible as separate entities but are not yet paired.

leptothricosis (lĕp″tō-thrĭ-kō′sĭs) [″ + *thrix*, hair] Disease caused by the gram-negative bacillus *Leptothrix*.

Leptus autumnalis (lĕp′tŭs) Parasitic mite larvae causing itch and sometimes wheals. SEE: *chiggers*.

Leriche syndrome (lĕ-rēsh′) [René Leriche, Fr. surgeon, 1879–1955] Occlusion of the abdominal aorta by a thrombus at its bifurcation. This causes intermittent ischemic pain (i.e., claudication) in the lower extremities and buttocks, impotence, and absent or diminished femoral pulses.

Leri pleonosteosis (lā′rē) [André Leri, Fr. physician, 1875–1930] A form of hereditary physical malformation characterized by upward slanting palpebral fissures, broad thumbs, short stature, and flexion contractures of the fingers.

lesbian (lĕs′bē-ăn) [Gr. *lesbios*, pert. to island of Lesbos] **1.** Pert. to lesbianism or sexual intercourse between women. SEE: *bisexual; homosexual*. **2.** A woman who has sex exclusively with women.

lesbianism (lĕz′bē-ăn-ĭzm) Sexual congress preferentially or exclusively between women. It was named for the Island of Lesbos, where the practice of lesbianism was reputed to have been widespread in ancient Greek history. SYN: *sapphism*.

Lesch-Nyhan disease (lĕsh′nī′ăn) [Michael Lesch, b. 1939, William Leo Nyhan, b. 1926, U.S. pediatricians] An X-linked recessive metabolic disease, in which mental retardation, aggressive behavior, self-mutilation, and renal failure are exhibited by affected boys. The disease is caused by faulty purine metabolism, resulting in excessive uric acid levels in the body.

lesion (lē′zhŏn) [L. *laesio*, a wound] **1.** A circumscribed area of pathologically altered tissue. **2.** An injury or wound. **3.** A single infected patch in a skin disease.

Primary or initial lesions include macules, vesicles, blebs or bullae, chancres, pustules, papules, tubercles, wheals, and tumors. Secondary lesions are the result of primary lesions. They may be crusts, excoriations, fissures, pigmentations, scales, scars, and ulcers. **4.** To form or make a lesion.

    anal squamous intraepithelial l. ABBR: ASIL. Anal intraepithelial **neoplasia**.

    Bankart l. SEE: *Bankart lesion*.

    coin l. Solitary pulmonary **nodule**.

    degenerative l. A lesion caused by or showing degeneration.

    destructive l. A pathological change such as an infection, tumor, or injury that causes the death of tissue or an organ.

    Dieulafoy l. SEE: under *Dieulafoy, Georges*.

    diffuse l. A lesion spreading over a large area.

    focal l. A lesion of a small definite area.

    gross l. A lesion visible to the eye without the aid of a microscope.

    high-grade squamous intraepithelial l. ABBR: HGSIL. A premalignant squamous lesion, found on the Papanicolaou test, which may be moderate dysplasia, severe dysplasia, or carcinoma in situ.

PATIENT CARE: Treatment requires removal or destruction of the affected cells, usually with loop electrosurgical excision procedure (LEEP) or ablation. Left untreated, HGSIL may progress to invasive cervical cancer.

    Hill-Sachs l. SEE: *Hill-Sachs lesion*.

    indiscriminate l. A lesion affecting separate systems of the body.

    initial l. of syphilis A hard chancre. SEE: *chancre; syphilis*.

    Janeway l. SEE: *Janeway lesion*.

    lower motor neuron l. An injury occurring in the anterior horn cells, nerve roots, or peripheral nervous system that results in diminished reflexes, flaccid paralysis, and atrophy of muscles.

    low-grade squamous intraepithelial l. ABBR: LGSIL. A cytological abnormality found in Papanicolaou tests (Pap tests) where there are early mild changes in the epithelial cells covering the outside of the cervix. Causes include infection with human papillomavirus, cervical trauma, or postmenopausal changes. Risk factors include intercourse with multiple sex partners or a partner with multiple sex partners, unprotected sex at a young age, history of sexually transmitted disease, and tobacco use. About 60% of LGSIL will spontaneously resolve. If left untreated, a small number of women eventually develop cervical cancer.

    peripheral l. A lesion of the nerve endings.

    primary l. The first lesion of a disease, esp. used in referring to chancre of syphilis.

    reverse Hill Sachs l. An indentation fracture of the anteromedial humeral head that occurs following a posterior dislocation of the glenohumeral joint. The cartilage of the humeral head is damaged, causing instability that may predispose the individual to subsequent posterior glenohumeral dislocations.

TREATMENT: Usually no surgical intervention is required when less than approx. 25% of the articular surface is involved in the fracture. When the glenoid fossa is also fractured, shoulder arthroplasty may be required.

    storage l. In blood banking and transfusion therapy, the biochemical and structural degradation of blood cells that occurs over time.

   structural l. A lesion that causes a change in tissue.

   systemic l. A lesion confined to organs of common function.

   toxic l. A lesion resulting from poisons or toxins from microorganisms.

   upper motor neuron l. Neurological damage to the corticospinal or pyramidal tract in the brain or spinal cord. This lesion results in hemiplegia, paraplegia, or quadriplegia, depending on its location and extent. Clinical signs include loss of voluntary movement, spasticity, sensory loss, and pathological reflexes.

   vascular l. A lesion of a blood vessel.

lesionectomy (lē″zhŏn-ek′tŏ-mē) [*lesion* + *-ectomy*] Surgical removal of a lesion. In neurosurgery, it is the removal of a structural abnormality in which epileptic seizures are not controlled by medications.

lesioning (lē′zhŏ-nĭng) The injuring of tissue, esp. neurologic tissue, for therapeutic purposes, e.g., with radiofrequency or radioactive energy.

LET *linear energy transfer.* A measure of the rate of energy transfer from ionizing radiation to soft tissue.

lethal [Gr. *lethe*, oblivion] Pert. to or that which causes death.

lethal factor SEE: under *factor*.

lethal injection SEE: under *injection*.

lethality (lē-thăl′ĭ-tē) The propensity for a disease or injury to cause death, rather than disability, illness, or pain.

lethal triad SEE: under *triad*.

lethargy (lĕth′ăr-jē) [Gr. *lethargos*, drowsiness] Sleepiness, drowsiness, somnolence, or mental sluggishness.

   induced l. A hypnotic trance. **lethargic** (lă-thahr′jĭk), *adj.*

lethe (lē′thē) [Gr., oblivion] Amnesia.

Letterer-Siwe disease (lĕt′ĕr-ĕr-sī′wē) [Erich Letterer, Ger. physician, b. 1895; S. August Siwe, Ger. physician, 1897–1966] The most common of three distinct histiocytosis syndromes collectively known as Langerhans cell histiocytosis, marked by proliferation of histiocytes in the viscera, bones, and skin. It is believed that this disease and the other two forms—eosinophilic granuloma of bone and Hand-Schüller-Christian syndrome—share a common pattern of granulomatous lesions with histiocyte proliferation.

   The cutaneous lesions often develop during infancy or early childhood and in some cases are present at birth. These lesions include papulovesicular eruptions; inflamed, pruritic diaper area rashes; and scaly scalp lesions, all of which can be misdiagnosed as "cradle cap" (seborrheic dermatitis of the scalp) or severe diaper rash. When the disease is confined to the skin, spontaneous resolution in infancy may occur. In sys-

temic presentations, the spleen and liver are enlarged, pulmonary infiltration is widespread, and bone marrow failure is accompanied by fever and infections. The cause of the disease is unknown.

   DIAGNOSIS: Diagnosis is based on results of a skin biopsy performed with special staining techniques.

   TREATMENT: No specific treatment exists. Corticosteroids and antineoplastic drugs are used in the more severe forms of the disease, but many children die of pulmonary failure or overwhelming infections despite treatment. SEE: *histiocytosis, Langerhans cell.*

letter of intent Formal written notice given by one party to another of a commitment to pursue an action, e.g., of a plan to bring suit against another party or to take on an assignment on behalf of that party.

Leu Conventional symbol for the amino acid leucine.

leuc-, leuco- SEE: *leuko-*.

leucine (loo′sĭn) [Gr. *leukos*, white] An essential amino acid, $C_6H_{13}NO_2$; it cannot be synthesized by the liver and must be present in the diet; required for protein synthesis. It is present in body tissues and is essential for normal growth and metabolism.

leucine aminopeptidase ABBR: LAP. A proteolytic enzyme present in the pancreas, liver, and small intestine. Its serum level is elevated in disease of the pancreas, esp. acute pancreatitis, and in obstruction of the common bile duct.

leucine-rich repeat kinase 2 ABBR: LRRK2. Dardarin.

leucinosis (loo″sĭn-ō′sĭs) [″ + *osis*, condition] Maple syrup urine disease.

leucinuria (loo″sĭn-ū′rē-ă) [″ + *ouron*, urine] The presence of leucine in urine.

leucovorin, leukovorin (loo-kov′ŏ-rĭn) Folinic acid, the active form of folic acid in the body. It is used to treat anemia and as an antidote to protect normal cells from high doses of the anticancer drug methotrexate and to increase the antitumor effects of fluorouracil (5-FU) and tegafur-uracil. SYN: *citrovorum factor*.

leukapheresis, leukopheresis (loo″kă-fĕ-rē′sĭs) [*leuko-* + *aphairesis*] The separation of leukocytes from blood.

leukemia, leucemia (loo-kē′mē-ă) [*leuko-* + *-emia*] Any of a class of hematological malignancies of bone marrow cells in which immortal clones of immature blood cells multiply at the expense of normal blood cells. As normal blood cells are depleted from the body, anemia, infection, hemorrhage, or death result. The leukemias are categorized as chronic or acute; by the cell type from which they originate; and by the genetic, chromosomal, or growth factor aberration present in the malignant cells.

Chronic leukemias, which have a relatively slow course, include chronic lymphocytic (CLL), chronic myelogenous or granulocytic (CML), and hairy cell leukemia (a subtype of CLL). Median survival in these illnesses is about 4 yr.

Acute leukemias include acute lymphocytic (ALL) and acute myeloid (myelogenous) (AML) leukemia. If untreated, these diseases are fatal within weeks or months. Each of these types of leukemia is discussed in subentries, below. SEE: *Nursing Diagnoses Appendix.*

ETIOLOGY: All the different molecular events leading to the development of unchecked cellular reproduction in the leukemias result from genetic or chromosomal lesions in blood-forming cells. Duplications of genetic material (hyperdiploidy), loss of genetic information (hypodiploidy), inactivation of genes that normally suppress tumor development, chromosomal translocations, and the release of abnormal fusion proteins can all cause leukemia. These genetic lesions in turn can be produced by viruses, ionizing radiation, chemotherapeutic drugs, and toxic chemicals. Rarely, leukemias are caused by familial genetic syndromes (e.g., as ataxia telangiectasia, Bloom syndrome, or Fanconi syndrome).

SYMPTOMS: Clinical findings such as anemia, fatigue, lethargy, fever, and bone and joint pain may be present. Physical findings include combinations of pallor, petechiae, or purpura; mucous membrane bleeding; enlarged liver, spleen, and kidneys; and tenderness over the sternum and other bones.

DIAGNOSIS: Microscopic examination of peripheral blood and specimens of bone marrow are used to establish the diagnosis. These studies are followed by cytochemical and cytogenetic studies of abnormal cells found in the marrow or the peripheral blood to confirm the diagnosis with special stains and chromosomal analysis. Leukemic cells can also be identified by flow cytometry and immunocytochemistry, which rely on antibodies binding to and helping to identify malignant cells. The spread of leukemias to internal organs (e.g., the brain, the kidneys, or the lungs) may be evaluated with imaging tests (e.g., MRI studies, CT scans, or ultrasound).

TREATMENT: Chemotherapy, bone marrow transplantation, or both are used to treat leukemias. Regimens are devised regularly and are tailored to specific illnesses. Treatment is often given in several phases, with a period of induction chemotherapy to induce remission by completely eliminating leukemic cells from the bone marrow, followed by consolidation and maintenance phases. This multiphase treatment is designed to further deplete malignant cells from the bone marrow and to achieve complete cure.

PATIENT CARE: Patient care measures focus on eradicating the illness; managing complications; minimizing the effects of chemotherapy; preserving veins (often an indwelling port is inserted to administer chemotherapy); and providing comfort, education, and psychological support. The specific needs of patients (many of whom are children) and their families must be considered. Instruction is provided about drugs the patient will receive, including any adverse reactions and measures that will be taken to prevent or alleviate these effects. Prescribed chemotherapy is administered with special precautions when indicated for infusion and drug disposal. If the chemotherapy causes weight loss or anorexia, nutritional guidance is provided. Oral, skin, and rectal care must be meticulous, e.g., the nurse must thoroughly clean the skin before all invasive procedures, inspect the patient for perirectal erosions, use strict aseptic technique when starting an intravenous line, and change sets (i.e., intravenous tubing and associated equipment) according to chemotherapeutic protocols. Ports are irrigated according to agency protocol. If the patient is receiving intrathecal chemotherapy, the lumbar puncture site is checked frequently for bleeding or oozing. The patient and family are taught to recognize signs of infection (fevers, chills, sore throat, cough, urinary difficulties) and are urged to report these to the oncologist or hematologist promptly. To prevent infection in neutropenic patients, strict hand hygiene protocols, special diets, and (in hospitalized patients) laminar airflow or other reverse isolation measures are instituted. The patient is monitored for bleeding. If bleeding occurs, compresses are applied and the bleeding site is elevated. Transfusions of platelets and other blood cells are often needed. Complications associated with specific chemotherapeutic regimens (e.g., hair loss, nausea and vomiting, anemia, neutropenia, and low platelets) are explained to the patient, along with management strategies that will be employed. Prescribed analgesics are administered as needed, and noninvasive pain relief techniques and comfort measures (e.g., position changes, cutaneous stimulation, distraction, relaxation breathing, and imagery) may be used. Gentle oral hygiene measures and protective skin care are explained. Fluid intake should be increased to eliminate chemotherapy metabolites, and the patient advised to void more frequently to prevent cystitis. Dietary fiber is important, and stool softeners may be used to ensure normal bowel movements. Antidiarrheals usually control diarrhea, but the patient should be monitored for signs of dehydration. Fatigue is an anticipated adverse effect of treatment; therefore the patient is encouraged to alternate activity with rest periods and to obtain assistance with daily activities as necessary. Reproductive issues should be discussed with the patient. Patient care routines and visiting times should be flexible when hospitalization is required. The patient and family are encouraged to participate in care as much as possible. Referrals are made to social service agencies, home health care agencies, and support groups. If the patient does not respond to treatment and has reached the terminal phase of the disease, supportive nursing, palliative care, or hospice care should be discussed sensitively with patients and their caregivers.

acute lymphoblastic l. *Acute lymphocytic l.*

acute lymphocytic l. ABBR: ALL. A hematological malignancy marked by the unchecked multiplication of immature lymphoid cells in the bone marrow, blood, and body tissues. In 2008 the American Cancer Society estimated about 5400 Americans would be diagnosed with ALL. It is rapidly fatal if left untreated. SYN: *acute lymphoblastic l.* SEE: illus; *leukemia.*

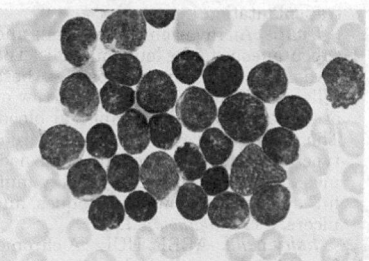

ACUTE LYMPHOCYTIC LEUKEMIA

Peripheral blood smear

ETIOLOGY: Any of a wide range of acquired or congenital chromosomal abnormalities can cause ALL, including lesions that result in the release of excess growth factors from cells and those that cause the loss of cancer-suppressing genes.

SYMPTOMS: Fatigue, lethargy, bleeding, bone and joint pain, and a predisposition to fever and infection are characteristic of ALL and other leukemias.

DIAGNOSIS: The disease is suggested by the presence of abnormalities on the complete blood count or peripheral blood smear and is confirmed by immunophenotyping.

TREATMENT: In childhood, ALL induction chemotherapy often begins with steroids, vinca alkaloids, and asparaginase. This is followed, after bone marrow recovery, by consolidation chemotherapy with multidrug regimens, including high-dose methotrexate. Maintenance therapies, which may last 2 years or longer, include methotrexate, mercaptopurines, and other cytotoxic agents. Prophylaxis against central nervous system disease is accomplished by intrathecal drug administration. In referral hospitals, allogeneic stem cell transplantation is sometimes used for refractory disease. About 90% of treated children achieve remission. The 5-year survival of children with ALL is about 85%. Adult ALL is much less responsive to therapy; only about a third of adult patients are cured. In both childhood and adult ALL, allopurinol and hydration precede induction chemotherapy to prevent hyperuricemia caused by tumor lysis.

PROGNOSIS: Late complications of therapy are not uncommon.

acute myelogenous l. ABBR: AML. *Acute myeloid l.*

acute myeloid l. ABBR: AML. Any of a group of hematological malignancies in which neoplastic cells develop from myeloid, monocytic, erythrocytic, or megakaryocytic precursors. AML is four times more common in adults than acute lymphocytic leukemia (ALL). In 2008, the American Cancer Society estimated about 13,300 Americans would be diagnosed with AML, and that the disease would cause 8,800 deaths. It occasionally follows a myelodysplastic disorder or aplastic anemia and sometimes occurs as a consequence of a familial disorder of fragile chromosomes (e.g., Fanconi's syndrome).

All forms of AML are marked by neoplastic replacement of normal bone marrow and circulation of blasts (immature cells) in the peripheral blood. Anemia and thrombocytopenia commonly occur. The central nervous system and other organs are occasionally invaded. Complete remissions occur in approximately 65% of treated patients; responses to treatment lasting 5 years are achieved in 15% to 25% of treated patients. SYN: *acute myelogenous l.; acute nonlymphocytic l.*

ETIOLOGY: Genetic and chromosomal aberrations, such as are found in other leukemias, are characteristic.

SYMPTOMS: Exertional fatigue as a result of anemia, bleeding due to thrombocytopenia, and infections due to a lack of normal white blood cells are common.

TREATMENT: Cytotoxic chemotherapies, with an induction phase followed by consolidation, are used. Typically, cytosine arabinoside and an anthracycline are used during induction for AML. Allogeneic bone marrow transplantation is used when a matching donor is available; stem cell transplantation is an option for some patients with specific cytogenetic abnormalities.

acute nonlymphocytic l. ABBR: ANLL. *Acute myeloid l.*

aleukemic l. **L.** cutis.

chronic lymphocytic l. ABBR: CLL. A malignancy in which abnormal lymphocytes (usually B cells) proliferate and infiltrate body tissues, often causing lymph node enlargement and immune dysfunction. Infectious complications are common. Median life expectancy is about 4 years. Chronic lymphocytic leukemia is the most common leukemia in industrialized nations. It usually occurs in people (older men) above age 60. Its incidence rises to 20 cases per 100,000 in people over 80. In 2008 the American Cancer Society estimated that 15,100 people would be diagnosed with CLL and that 4,400 would die of the disease. The timing of treatment and the prognosis in CLL depend on the stage of the disease. Staging includes such factors as the number of abnormal lymphocytes in the bloodstream, how quickly they double, and the presence of lymphadenopathy, organomegaly, or cytopenias. SEE: illus.

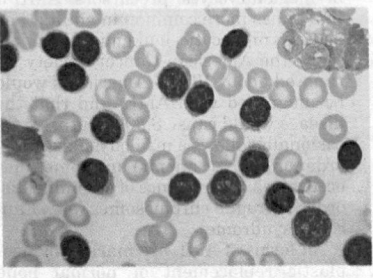

CHRONIC LYMPHOCYTIC LEUKEMIA

Peripheral blood smear

TREATMENT: Patients with advanced stages of the illness are often treated with chlorambucil, fludarabine, or other cytotoxic agents, often with rituximab (a monoclonal antibody) added to enhance response. Patients with early-stage disease are not usually given therapy.

chronic myelogenous l. ABBR: CML. *Chronic myeloid l.*

chronic myeloid l. ABBR: CML. A hematological malignancy marked by a sustained increase in the number of granulocytes, splenic enlargement, and a specific cytogenetic anomaly (the Philadelphia chromosome) in the bone marrow of more than 90% of patients. The

disease affects one or two people per 100,000. In 2008 the American Cancer Society estimated that 4830 people would be diagnosed with CML and that 450 would die of the disease. The course of the disease has three phases: a chronic one in which blood counts are relatively easy to control with medications; an accelerated phase in which granulocyte counts become more resistant to chemotherapy; and a "blast" crisis, which resembles acute leukemia. Median survival is about 4 years. It generally occurs between ages 40 and 50, affecting slightly more men than women (4600 adults in the U.S. in 2005). SYN: *chronic myelogenous l.* SEE: *leukemia.*

ETIOLOGY: CML results from a translocation of genetic material between chromosomes 9 and 22. The translocation results in the production of an abnormal tyrosine kinase that makes affected cells immortal.

SYMPTOMS: CML often is diagnosed in asymptomatic patients who are found to have an unexplained leukocytosis when their complete blood counts are checked. Subsequent evaluation, including bone marrow aspiration and biopsy with cytogenetic analysis, reveal the Philadelphia chromosome.

TREATMENT: Imatinib mesylate (a drug that blocks an abnormal kinase made by Philadelphia chromosome positive CML cells) effectively reduces the number of tumor cells in the chronic phase of CML to normal in nearly 90% of patients. An alternative is stem cell transplantation.

l. cutis An invasion of the dermis and subcutaneous fat by leukemic cells. The invasion often happens before these cells proliferate in the bone marrow or are detectable in the peripheral blood. The cells may cause several different types of skin rashes, including blue nodules (giving the skin a "blueberry muffin" appearance), papules, plaques, and ulcers. SYN: *aleukemic l.*

hairy cell l. ABBR: HCL. A chronic, low-grade hematological malignancy of abnormally shaped B lymphocytes (hairy cells). The disease is marked by pancytopenia and splenomegaly. Median survival in untreated patients is about 5 years. The disease is rare, being only 1% to 2% of all leukemias. The median age of patients is 50 years; men are affected more commonly than women by a 4-to-1 ratio. SEE: illus.

SYMPTOMS: Weight loss, hypermetabolism, infectious complications, and abdominal discomfort due to splenic enlargement are common.

TREATMENT: Cladribine, pentostatin, interferon alfa, and rituximab (a monoclonal antibody) are representative chemotherapeutic options.

leukemic (loo-kēm′ĭk) [″ + *haima,*

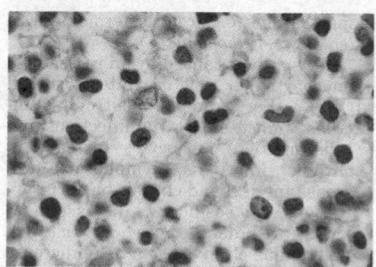

HAIRY CELL LEUKEMIA

Bone marrow aspirate

blood] **1.** Pert. to leukemia. **2.** Affected with leukemia.

leukemid (loo-ke′mĭd) Any nonspecific skin lesion associated with leukemia. The lesions may or may not contain leukemic cells.

leukemogenesis (loo-ke″mō-jĕn′ĕ-sĭs) [″ + ″ + *genesis,* generation, birth] The induction of leukemia.

leukin (loo′kĭn) A thermostable bactericidal substance present in leukocytes.

leuko-, leuk-, leuc-, leuco- [Gr. *leukos,* white] Prefixes meaning *white, white corpuscle,* or *white matter of the brain.*

leukoagglutinin (loo″kō-ă-gloo′tĭ-nĭn) [″ + L. *agglutinans,* gluing] An antibody that agglutinates white blood cells.

leukoareosis (loo-koh-ar-ee-oh′sis) An abnormal appearance of the periventricular white matter of the brain, seen in people with poorly controlled hypertension, Alzheimer disease, and other conditions.

leukocidin (loo-kō-sī′dĭn) [″ + L. *caedere,* to kill] A bacterial toxin that destroys leukocytes.

leukocoria, leukokoria (loo″kō-kŏr′ē-ă) [″ + Gr. *kore,* girl, pupil of the eye] White or abnormal pupillary reflex. This reflex may be present in infants and children who have retinoblastoma, cataract, retinal detachment, and intraocular infections. Patients with this reflex should be referred to an ophthalmologist without delay.

leukocyte (loo′kŏ-sīt″) [*leuko-* + *-cyte*] Any of several kinds of colorless or nearly colorless cells of the immune system that circulate in the blood and lymph. Leukocytes comprise granulocytes and agranulocytes. SYN: *white blood cell; white cell; white blood corpuscle; white corpuscle.* SEE: *blood* for illus.

Neutrophils, 55% to 70% of all leukocytes, are the most numerous phagocytic cells and are a primary effector cell in inflammation. Eosinophils, 1% to 3% of total leukocytes, destroy parasites and are involved in allergic reactions. Basophils, less than 1% of all leukocytes, contain granules of histamine and

heparin and are part of the inflammatory response to injury. Monocytes, 3% to 8% of all leukocytes, become macrophages and phagocytize pathogens and damaged cells, esp. in the tissue fluid. Lymphocytes, 20% to 35% of all leukocytes, have several functions: recognizing foreign antigens, producing antibodies, suppressing the immune response to prevent excess tissue damage, and becoming memory cells.

Leukocytes are formed from the undifferentiated stem cells that give rise to all blood cells. Those in the red bone marrow may become any of the five kinds of leukocytes. Those in the spleen and lymph nodes may become lymphocytes or monocytes. Those in the thymus become lymphocytes called T lymphocytes.

FUNCTION: Leukocytes are the primary effector cells against infection and tissue damage. They not only neutralize or destroy organisms, but also act as scavengers, engulfing damaged cells by phagocytosis. Leukocytes travel by ameboid movement and are able to penetrate tissue and then return to the bloodstream. Their movement is directed by chemicals released by injured cells, a process called chemotaxis. After coming in contact with and recognizing an antigen, neutrophils or macrophages phagocytize (engulf) it in a small vacuole that merges with a lysosome, to permit the lysosomal enzymes to digest the phagocytized material. When leukocytes are killed along with the pathogenic organisms they have destroyed, the resulting material is called pus, commonly found at the site of localized infections. Pus that collects because of inadequate blood or lymph drainage is called an abscess.

Microscopic examination: Leukocytes can be measured in any bodily secretion. They are normally present in blood and, in small amounts, in spinal fluid and mucus. The presence of leukocytes in urine, sputum, or fluid drawn from the abdomen is an indication of infection or trauma. The type of white blood cell (WBC) present is identified by the shape of the cell or by the use of stains (Wright) to color the granules: granules in eosinophils stain red, those in basophils stain blue, and those in neutrophils stain purple.

Clinically, WBC counts are important in detecting infection or immune system dysfunction. The normal WBC level is 5000 to 10,000/mm^3. An elevated (greater than 10,000) leukocyte count (leukocytosis) indicates an acute infection or inflammatory disease process (such as certain types of leukemia), whereas a decrease in the number of leukocytes (less than 5000) indicates either immunodeficiency or an overwhelming infection that has depleted

WBC stores. In addition to the total WBC count, the differential count is also frequently important. A differential count measures the percent of each type of WBC (e.g., neutrophils, monocytes, lymphocytes). The differential also measures the number of immature cells of each cell type as an indication of production by the bone marrow. Immature cells are called blasts (e.g., lymphoblasts, myeloblasts). During infections or in certain types of leukemia, blasts may be present in peripheral blood. SEE: *inflammation.*

acidophilic l. Eosinophil.

agranular l. Agranulocyte.

basophilic l. Basophil.

eosinophilic l. Eosinophil.

granular l. A leukocyte containing granules in cytoplasm.

heterophilic l. A neutrophilic leukocyte of certain animals whose granules stain with an acid stain.

lymphoid l. Agranulocyte.

neutrophilic l. Neutrophil.

nongranular l. Agranulocyte.

polymorphonuclear l. ABBR: PMN. A white blood cell with a nucleus made of two or more lobes, i.e., the granular leukocytes: neutrophils, eosinophils, or basophils. SYN: *polysegmented neutrophil.* SEE: *basophil; eosinophil; neutrophil.*

leukocyte reduction SEE: under *reduction.*

leukocytic (loo″kō-sĭt′ĭk) [″ + *kytos,* cell] Pert. to leukocytes.

leukocytoblast (loo″kō-sī′tō-blast) [″ + ″ + *blastos,* germ] A cell from which a leukocyte arises.

leukocytogenesis (loo″kō-sī″tō-jĕn′ĕ-sĭs) [″ + *kytos,* cell, + *genesis,* generation, birth] Leukopoiesis.

leukocytoid (loo′kō-sī″toyd) [″ + ″ + *eidos,* form, shape] Resembling a leukocyte.

leukocytolysin (loo″kō-sī-tŏl′ĭ-sĭn) A lysin that destroys leukocytes. SEE: *leukocidin.*

leukocytolysis (loo″kō-sī-tŏl′ĭ-sĭs) [″ + *kytos,* cell, + *lysis,* dissolution] Destruction of leukocytes.

leukocytoma (loo″kō-sī-tō′mă) [″ + ″ + *oma,* tumor] **1.** A tumor composed of cells resembling leukocytes. **2.** A tumorlike mass of leukocytes.

leukocytopenia (loo″kō-sī″tō-pē′nē-ă) [″ + ″ + *penia,* want] Leukopenia.

leukocytopoiesis (loo″kō-sī″tō-poy-ē′sĭs) [″ + ″ + *poiein,* to make] The formation of white blood cells.

leukocytosis (loo″kō-sī-tō′sĭs) [″ + *kytos,* cell, + *osis,* condition] An increase in the number of leukocytes (usually above 10,000/mm³) in the blood. It occurs most commonly in disease processes involving infection, inflammation, trauma, or stress, but it also can result occasionally from the use of some

medications (e.g., corticosteroids). SEE: *leukocyte; leukopenia.*

It usually is caused by an increase in one particular type of white blood cell (WBC). For example, neutrophils increase in acute bacterial infections and inflammation, monocytes increase in chronic infections, lymphocytes increase in viral and chronic bacterial infections, and eosinophils increase in allergic disorders, such as asthma. Leukemias often cause a huge increase in circulating cells, owing to the unchecked reproduction of a single clone of malignant cells.

basophilic l. An increase in the basophils in the blood.

mononuclear l. An increase in the monocytes in the blood.

pathological l. Leukocytosis due to a disease such as an infection.

leukocytotaxis (loo″kō-sī″tō-tăk′sĭs) [Gr. *leukos,* white, + *kytos,* cell, + *taxis,* arrangement] The movement of leukocytes either toward or away from an area such as a traumatized or infected site.

leukocytotoxin (loo″kō-sī″tō-tŏk′sĭn) [″ + ″ + *toxikon,* poison] A toxin that destroys leukocytes. SYN: *leukotoxin.*

leukocyturia (loo″kō-sī-tū′rē-ă) [″ + ″ + *ouron,* urine] Leukocytes in the urine.

leukoderma (loo″kŏ-děr′mă) [*leuko-* + *derma*] Deficiency of skin pigmentation, esp. in patches. SEE: *vitiligo.*

leukodystrophy (loo″kō-dĭs′trō-fē) Any disease (such as globoid cell leukodystrophy, adrenoleukodystrophy, or metachromatic leukodystrophy) whose hallmarks are metabolic defects in the formation of myelin. Bone marrow transplantation can cure some affected children.

metachromatic l. A type of hereditary leukodystrophy caused by a deficiency of the enzyme cerebroside sulfatase, an enzyme that is essential for the degradation of sulfatide. Deficiency of the enzyme allows excess deposition of sulfatide in nerve tissues. Clinical signs of this disease usually appear at about 1 year of age. They include gait disturbance, inability to learn to walk, spasticity of the limbs, hyperreflexia, dementia, and eventually death. The disease, for which there is no specific therapy, is usually fatal by age 10.

leukoedema (loo″kō-ĕ-dē′mă) [″ + *oidema,* swelling] A benign leukophakia-like abnormality of the mucosa of the mouth or tongue. The affected areas are opalescent or white, and wrinkled.

leukoencephalitis (loo″kō-ĕn-sĕf-ă-lī′tĭs) [″ + *enkephalos,* brain + *itis,* inflammation] Inflammation of the white matter of the brain.

acute hemorrhagic l. A neurological syndrome marked by rapidly progressive neurological findings, associated with asymmetric inflammatory pathological changes in the brain, and bleeding. SYN: *Weston Hurst syndrome.*

leukoencephalopathy (loo″kō-ĕn-sĕf-ă-lŏ'pă-thē) [Gr. *leukos,* white, + *enkephalos,* brain, + *pathos,* disease, suffering] Damage to the white matter of the brain, especially to myelin.

leukoencephalopathy, progressive multifocal ABBR: PML. A disease characterized by the presence of widespread demyelinating lesions of the brain, brainstem, and/or cerebellum. It is caused by infection with polyoma JC virus. PML is usually associated with chronic, immune suppressing illnesses, such as AIDS, and some lymphomas or leukemias. Clinical findings include aphasia, ataxia, blindness, dementia, dysarthria, and eventual coma. The disease is sometimes diagnostically confused with multiple sclerosis.

leukoencephalopathy, toxic Damage to the white matter of the brain caused by exposure to chemicals, radiation, and certain viruses, including HIV. The chemical agents include, but are not limited to, alcohol, carbon monoxide, cocaine, toluene, and some cytotoxic drugs.

SYMPTOMS: Confusion, disinterest, lethargy, memory losses, and psychiatric symptoms are common in early stages. Profoundly ill patients may display stupor or coma. Language disturbances are unusual.

leukoerythroblastosis (loo″kō-ĕ-rĭth″rō-blăs-tō'sĭs) [″ + *erythros,* red, + *blastos,* germ, + *osis,* condition] Anemia due to any condition that causes the bone marrow to be infiltrated and thus inactivated.

leukokeratosis (loo″kō-kĕr-ă-tō'sĭs) [″ + *keras,* horn, + *osis,* condition] Leukoplakia.

leukokraurosis (loo″kō-kraw-rō'sĭs) [″ + *krauros,* dry, + *osis,* condition] Lichen sclerosis et atrophicus.

leukolymphosarcoma (loo″kō-lĭm″fō-săr-kō'mă) [″ + L. *lympha,* lymph, + Gr. *sarx,* flesh, + *oma,* tumor] Lymphosarcoma cell leukemia.

leukoma (loo-kō'mă) [″ + *oma,* tumor] A white, dense corneal opacity.

   l. adherens A corneal opacity to which the iris is attached.

leukomatous (loo-kō'mă-tŭs) [Gr. *leukos,* white, + *oma,* tumor] **1.** Pert. to leukoma. **2.** Suffering from leukoma.

leukomyelitis (loo″kō-mī-ĕ-lī'tĭs) [″ + *myelos,* marrow, + *itis,* inflammation] Inflammation of the white matter of the spinal cord.

leukomyelopathy (loo″kō-mī-ĕl-ŏp'ă-thē) [″ + ″ + *pathos,* disease] Disease involving the white matter of the spinal cord.

leukonecrosis (loo″kō-nĕ-krō'sĭs) [″ +

nekrosis, state of death] Dry, light-colored, or white gangrene.

leukonychia (loo″kō-nĭk'ē-ă) [″ + *onyx,* nail] White spots or streaks on the nails. SYN: *canities unguium; leukopathia unguium.*

leukopathia (loo″kō-păth'ē-ă) [″ + *pathos,* disease] **1.** The absence of pigment in the skin. SEE: *leukoderma.* **2.** A disease involving leukocytes.

   l. unguium Leukonychia.

leukopedesis (loo″kō-pĕ-dē'sĭs) [″ + *pedan,* to leap] The passage of leukocytes through the walls of the blood vessels.

leukopenia (loo″kō-pē'nē-ă) [″ + *penia,* lack] Abnormal decrease of white blood cells usually below 5000/mm³. A great number of drugs may cause leukopenia, as can failure of the bone marrow. SYN: *granulocytopenia; leukocytopenia.*

leukoplakia (loo″kō-plā'kē-ă) [*leuko-* + Gr. *plax,* plate + *-ia*] Formation of white spots or patches on the mucous membrane of the tongue or cheek. The spots are smooth, irregular in size and shape, hard, and occasionally fissured. The lesions may become malignant. SYN: *leukokoria; leukoplasia; smoker's* **tongue.** SEE: illus.

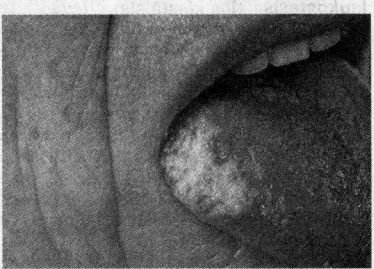

LEUKOPLAKIA

   l. buccalis Leukoplakia of the mucosa of the cheek.

   oral hairy l. Leukoplakia of the tongue. It is typically found in immunocompromised patients is a result of Epstein-Barr virus infection.

   l. vulvae Lichen sclerosis et atrophicus.

leukoplasia (loo-kō-plā'zē-ă) Leukoplakia.

leukopoiesis (loo″kō-poy-ē'sĭs) [″ + *poiesis,* formation] Leukocyte production. SYN: *leukocytogenesis.* **leukopoietic** (-ĕt'ĭk), *adj.*

leukoreduction (loo″kō-rē-dŭk'shŭn) [Gr. *leukos,* white, + L. *reductio,* leading back] The loss of white blood cells from a unit of packed red cells by filtration of the blood before transfusion. White blood cells in red cell transfusions have been associated with immunosuppression in recipients. Leukoreduction typically lowers the white cell content of packed red cells from about 3 × 10⁹ per unit of blood to about 2.5×10^5 per unit. It has been associated with a decrease in post-transfusion fevers, and, in some studies, with decreased post-transfusion mortality.

leukorrhagia (loo″kō-rā′jē-ă) [″ + *rhegnynai*, to burst forth] Leukorrhea.

leukorrhea (loo″kō-rē′ă) [*leuko*- + *-rrhea*] A white, estrogen-related, scant-to-moderate, odorless, physiological vaginal discharge, normally preceding menarche and occurring during ovulation, during pregnancy, and in response to sexual excitement. Some women note an increased discharge related to oral contraceptive or hormone replacement therapy. Chronic cervicitis and vaginal infections are the most common causes of abnormal genital discharge. Signs of infection include increased discharge, change in color and consistency, odor, vulvar irritation, dysuria, and itching. SYN: *leukorrhagia; physiological l.* SEE: *vaginitis.*

    physiological l. Leukorrhea.

leukosarcoma (loo″kō-săr-kō′mă) [Gr. *leukos*, white, + *sarx*, flesh, + *oma*, tumor] A variant of lymphoma in which malignant cells enter the blood stream and circulate.

leukostasis (loo″kō-stā′sĭs) [*leuko*- + *stasis*] Obstruction of blood vessels by excessive numbers of immature white blood cells, esp. in patients who have leukemia. The excessive concentration of white blood cells increases the viscosity of the blood, causing it to turn into sludge in small vessels, such as those in the brain and the lung.

leukotactic (loo″kō-tăk′tĭk) [″ + *taxis*, arrangement] Possessing the power of attracting leukocytes.

leukotaxis (loo″kō-tăks′ĭs) Possessing the power of attracting (positive leukotaxis) or repelling (negative leukotaxis) leukocytes.

leukotomy (loo-kŏt′ō-mē) [″ + *tome*, incision] Lobotomy.

leukotoxic (loo″kō-tŏks′ĭk) [″ + *toxikon*, poison] Destructive to leukocytes.

leukotoxin (loo″kō-tŏk′sĭn) [″ + *toxikon*, poison] Leukocytotoxin.

leukotrichia (loo″kō-trĭk′ē-ă) [″ + *thrix*, hair] Whiteness of the hair. SYN: *canities.*

leukotriene (loo″kō-trī′ēn) Any of a group of arachidonic acid metabolites that functions as a chemical mediator of allergic reactions and inflammation. Leukotrienes C_4, D_4, and E_4 are derived from the precursor molecule leukotriene A_4. The subscripted number specifies the number of double bonds in the molecule. All are synthesized by cells in response to inflammation or tissue injury. Leukotrienes have been implicated in the development of the inflammatory responses in asthma, psoriasis, rheumatoid arthritis, and inflammatory bowel disease. They are powerful bronchoconstrictors and vasodilators and mediate the adverse vascular and bronchial effects of systemic anaphylaxis.

leumorphin (loo-mŏr′fĭn) [″ + Morpheus, ancient Gr. god of dreams or sleep] An endogenous endorphin derived from proenkephalin. It decreases the secretion of vasopressin and fluid intake but increases feeding and opposes apoptosis.

Levaquin SEE: *levofloxacin.*

levator (lē-vā′tor) *pl.* **levatores** [L., lifter] **1.** A muscle that raises or elevates a part; opposite of depressor. **2.** An instrument that lifts depressed portions.

    l. ani A broad muscle that helps to form the floor of the pelvis.

    l. palpebrae superioris A muscle that elevates the upper eyelid.

levator ani syndrome Chronic pain and/or pressure felt in the anus or high in the rectum. The cause is unknown, but muscular tension or spasm, nerve irritation, or tendinitis may contribute. Some patients improve with injections of corticosteroid medications.

LeVeen shunt (lă-vēn′) [Harry LeVeen, U.S. surgeon, 1917–1997] A shunt from the peritoneal cavity to the venous circulation used to help control ascites by allowing ascitic fluid to enter the venous circulation.

level of health care SEE: *health care system.*

lever (lĕv′ĕr, lē′vĕr) [L. *levare*, to raise] A rigid bar used to modify direction, force, and motion. A type of simple machine that provides the user with a mechanical advantage. Levers are used to facilitate the moving and lifting of objects too heavy or awkward for one to move unassisted.

Levey-Jennings chart (lev′ē-jen′ingz) [S. Levey, 20th-cent. U.S. statistician; E.N. Jennings, 20th-cent. U.S. statistician] A graphical representation of control data, arranged in chronological order, that shows a mean or target value and one or more sets of acceptable limits.

Levine, Myra (lĕ-vēn′) A nursing educator, died 1996, who developed the Conservation Model of Nursing. SEE: *Nursing Theory Appendix.*

Levine-Critchley syndrome (lĕ-vēn′-krĭch′lē) Neuroacanthosis.

Levine sign (lĕ-vēn″) [Samuel A. Levine, 20th-cent. U.S. cardiologist] Holding a clenched fist over the sternum, a characteristic gesture of those who frequently experience anginal chest pain.

Levin tube (lĕ-vin′) [Abraham L. Levin, U.S. physician, 1880–1940] A catheter usually introduced through the nose and extending into the stomach. It is used to help prevent accumulation of intestinal liquids and gas during and after intestinal surgery. This tube is often referred to as a nasogastric tube. A variant includes the addition of a sump channel, which helps to reduce gas build-up in the upper gastrointestinal tract. SEE: *Salem sump tube.*

levitation (lěv″ĭ-tā′shŭn) [L. *levitas,* lightness] The subjective sensation of rising in the air or moving through the air unsupported. It occurs in dreams, altered states of consciousness, and certain mental disorders.

levo-, lev- [L. *laevus,* (on the) left] Prefixes meaning *left, on the left,* or *levorotatory.*

levocardia (lē″vō-kăr′dē-ă) [L. *laevus,* left, + Gr. *kardia,* heart] A term describing the normal position of the heart when other viscera are inverted. SEE: *dextrocardia.*

levocarnitine (lĕ″vō-kăr′nĭ-tēn) An amino acid-derived drug used in treating primary carnitine deficiency. SEE: *carnitine.*

levoclination (lē″vō-klĭ-nā′shŭn) [″ + *clinatus,* leaning] Torsion or twisting of the upper meridians of the eyes to the left. SYN: *levotorsion* (2).

levocycloduction (lē″vō-sī″klō-dŭk′shŭn) [″ + Gr. *kyklos,* circle, + L. *ducere,* to lead] Levoduction.

levodopa (lĕv″ō-dō′pă) L-3,4-dihydroxyphenylalanine; a drug used in the treatment of Parkinson's disease. Also called L-dopa.

levoduction (lē″vō-dŭk′shŭn) [L. *laevus,* left, + *ducere,* to lead] Movement or drawing toward the left, esp. of an eye. SYN: *levocycloduction.*

levofloxacin (lěv″ō-flŏk′să-sĭn) A fluoroquinolone and anti-infective, administered orally to treat urinary tract and gynecological infections and gonorrhea. It is also used to treat prostatitis; infectious diarrhea; and infections of the respiratory tract, abdomen, skin, bones, and joints.

levophobia (lĕv″ō-fō′bē-ă) [″ + Gr. *phobos,* fear] A morbid dread of objects on the left side of the body.

levorotation (lē″vō-rō-tā′shŭn) [″ + *rotare,* to turn] Levotorsion (1).

levorotatory (lē″vō-rō′tă-tor-ē) Causing to turn toward the left, applied esp. to substances that turn polarized light rays to the left.

levothyroxine sodium (lē″vō-thī-rok′sēn″, sēn) [*levo-* + *thyroxine*] ABBR: T₄. The sodium salt of the natural isomer of thyroxine used to treat thyroid deficiency. A typical dosage used to treat hypothyroidism is1.6 mcg/kg/day given orally.

levotorsion, levoversion (lē″vō-tor′shŭn, lē″vō-věr′shŭn) [″ + *torsio,* a twisting] **1.** A twisting to the left. SYN: *levorotation.* **2.** Levoclination.

levulinic acid (lěv″yŭ-lin′ik) SEE: under *acid.*

levulose (lev′yŭ-lōs″) SEE: *fructose.*

levulosemia (lěv″ū-lō-sē′mē-ă) [″ + Gr. *haima,* blood] The presence of fructose in the blood.

levulosuria (lěv″ū-lō-sū′rē-ă) [″ + Gr. *ouron,* urine] The presence of fructose in the urine.

Lewis, Gilbert Newton U.S. physical chemist, 1875–1946. He discovered the covalent bond and was the first to produce pure heavy water (deuterium oxide).

   L. acid A substance that accepts an electron pair from a base, forming a covalent bond with the base.

   L. base A substance that donates an electron pair to an acid, forming a covalent bond with the acid.

lewisite (lū′ĭ-sīt) [Warren Lee Lewis, U.S. chemist, 1878–1943] A toxic gas similar in action to mustard gas, used in warfare to disable and kill. It acts as a vesicant in the lungs. Dimercaprol is the treatment drug of choice.

Lewy body (loo-wē) [Frederic H. Lewy, Ger. neurologist, 1885–1950] A neuronal cell with pigmented inclusion bodies. They are found in the brain in the substantia nigra and locus ceruleus, esp. in patients with a unique form of dementia with some Parkinsonian features, known as "dementia with Lewy bodies."

Leydig cell (lī′dĭg) [Franz von Leydig, Ger. anatomist, 1821–1908] One of the interstitial cells in the testes that produce testosterone.

LFA *left frontoanterior* fetal position.

L-forms [named for *Lister* Institute] Spontaneous variants of bacteria that replicate as filterable spheres with defective or absent cell walls. They are filterable because of their flexibility rather than their size. Stable forms may grow for an indefinite time in a wall-less state. Organisms of the unstable form are capable of regenerating their cell walls and reverting to their antecedent bacterial form. The ability of L-forms to cause disease is unknown. SYN: *L-phase variants.*

LFP *left frontoposterior* fetal position.

LFT *left frontotransverse* fetal position.

LFT *liver function test.*

LGA *large for gestational age.*

LGSIL *low-grade squamous intraepithelial lesion.*

LH *luteinizing hormone.*

Lhermitte sign (lăr-mĕt′) [Jacques Jean Lhermitte, Fr. neurologist, 1877–1959] The symptom (rather than a sign) of a pain resembling a sudden electric shock throughout the body produced by flexing the neck. It is caused by trauma to the cervical portion of the spinal cord, multiple sclerosis, cervical cord tumor, or cervical spondylosis.

LHRH *luteinizing hormone–releasing hormone.*

Li Symbol for the element lithium.

liability (lī″ă-bil′ĭt-ē) Legal responsibility. A health care provider is legally responsible for actions that fail to meet the standards of care or are grossly negligent, thereby causing harm to the patient.

   abuse l. The propensity of a drug to produce compulsive use, to cause addiction.

   school-specific l. The legal standard that holds licensed practitioners liable only for those actions that violate the standards of their own education and training. As a result, chiropractic liability is judged based on standards of care in the school of chiropractic, while surgical liability is based on the standards set forth among surgeons.

   enterprise l. The legal and financial liability of a health care institution for injuries that result from the actions, behaviors, or negligence of its staff.

   genetic l. The heritability of a disease, e.g., the likelihood that two identical twins, even if separated at birth and raised apart, will develop the same disease.

   strict l. Liability attributed to a manufacturer or seller of a dangerous or defective product regardless of proven negligence or fault.

   vicarious l. Legal responsibility of a health care professional or health care institution for the negligent actions of its trainees and employees.

libel (lī′bĕl) [L. *libellus,* little book, pamphlet] Defaming the character of another by means of the written word. To qualify legally as libel, written communication must intentionally impugn the reputation of another person and be both malicious and demonstrably false.

libidinous (lĭ-bĭd′ĭ-nŭs) [L. *libidinosus,* pert. to desire] Pert. to or marked by sexual desires.

libido (lĭ-bī′dō, -bē′dō) [L., desire] **1.** The sexual drive, conscious or unconscious. **2.** In psychoanalysis, the energy that is the driving force of human behavior. It has been variously identified as the sex urge, desire to live, desire for pleasure, or satisfaction.

   low l. A sexual dysfunction marked by inhibited sexual desire and inability to sustain arousal during sexual activities. Diminished sexual drive may be related to advanced age, psychogenic causes, general illness, side effects of some medications, or substance abuse. In men it manifests as partial or complete failure to attain or maintain erection until completion of the sex act. In women there is partial or complete failure to attain or maintain the vaginal lubrication-swelling response of sexual excitement until completion of the sex act. SEE: table.

Some Classes of Drugs That Inhibit Libido

Class	Examples
alcohol	beer, liquor, wine
antidepressants	amitriptyline, fluoxetine
alpha blockers	clonidine
beta blockers	atenolol, propranolol
drugs of abuse	amphetamines, cocaine, heroin
histamine₂ blockers	cimetidine
major tranquilizers	clozapine, fluphenazine, thioridazine
oral contraceptives	many types
sedative/hypnotics	benzodiazepines

Libman-Sacks endocarditis An eponym for nonbacterial thrombotic endocarditis.

library A stored, retrievable collection of data.

lice Pl. of louse.

licensed occupational therapist ABBR: LOTR; OTR/L. An occupational therapist who has met the requirements to practice in states with licensure laws governing occupational therapy. Usually, licensed therapists have been certified by the National Board for Certification in Occupational Therapy as a registered occupational therapist (OTR). Some state governments, as part of their licensure statutes, permit use of the OTR/L or LOTR designations.

licensing, compulsory A law granting a government access to patented drugs and other intellectual property before the patent formally expires. Drug companies have opposed compulsory licensing on the grounds that it limits the financial value of patent holding. Some nations have sought obligatory access to drugs, or their generic copies, to limit pharmaceutical costs or address national health emergencies.

licensure (lī′sĕn-shŭr) In the health care professions, the granting of permission (official, legal, or both) to perform professional actions that may not be legally performed by those who do not have such permission. Qualification for a license in health care is usually determined by an official body representing the state or federal government.

   individual l. In the health care profession, licensure of an individual to perform certain medical actions.

   institutional l. In the health care industry, the authorization of hospitals, clinics, or corporations to provide specific forms of care.

mandatory l. Licensure that regulates the practice of a profession such as nursing or medicine by requiring compliance with the licensing statute if an individual engages in activities defined within the scope of that profession.

multistate nurse l. In the U.S., authority or permission to practice nursing in several states, granted after making a single application.

licentiate (lī-sen′shē-ăt) [L. *licentiare,* to authorize, license] **1.** One who practices a profession by the authority granted by a license. **2.** In some countries, a medical practitioner who has no medical degree.

lichen (lī′kĕn) [Gr. *leichēn,* lichen] **1.** Any form of papular skin disease, esp. lichen planus. **2.** In botany, any of numerous plants consisting of a fungus growing symbiotically with algae. They form characteristic scaly or branching growths on rocks or barks of trees.

l. nitidus A rare skin condition characterized by small, chronic, asymptomatic papules that are usually pink and are usually located only on the penis, abdomen, and flexor surfaces of the elbows and palms.

l. pilaris Keratosis pilaris.

l. planopilaris A follicular papulosquamous eruption, typically found on the scalp, and often associated with lichen planus.

l. planus An inflammatory rash marked by the presence of itchy, red to violet, polygon-shaped papules, which typically appear on the scalp, in the oral cavity, or on the limbs. The papules may merge into plaques crisscrossed by Wickham striae. Typically, the rash persists for 1 to 2 years and then spontaneously improves although about one in five patients will suffer a recurrence. SYN: *l. ruber planus.* SEE: illus.

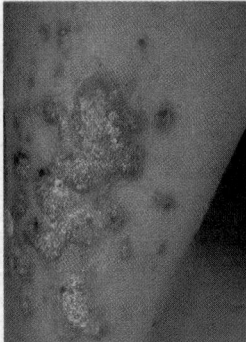

LICHEN PLANUS

ETIOLOGY: The cause of the rash is unknown, but it is occasionally associated with the use of chemicals (such as photoprocessing compounds, gold) or medications (such as beta blockers, diuretics, nonsteroidal anti-inflammatory drugs).

TREATMENT: Corticosteroids, applied topically, taken orally, or injected into the lesions, are often effective.

l. ruber planus L. planus.

l. sclerosus et atrophicus A chronic atrophic skin disorder marked by the appearance of discrete, flat-topped, white papules, which may coalesce and degenerate. The skin affected by the rash, which occurs most often on the vulva, is often thin, shiny, and scarred. Although this condition is not considered precancerous, squamous cell carcinomas arise in 1% to 5% of cases. SEE: illus.

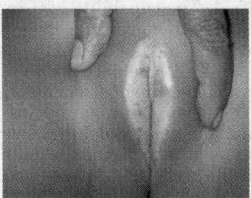

LICHEN SCLEROSUS ET ATROPHICUS

SYMPTOMS: Itching of the vulva, which may be intractable, is the most common complaint.

TREATMENT: Potent topical corticosteroids produce remission, but not cure, in the great majority of patients. SYN: *vulvar dystrophy; vulvar pruritus.*

l. spinulosus Keratosis pilaris.

l. striatus A papular eruption usually seen on one extremity of a child. It is arranged in linear groups and consists of pink papules. The disease, though self-limiting, may last for a year or longer.

lichenification (lī-kĕn″ĭ-fĭ-kā′shŭn) [Gr. *leichen,* lichen, + L. *facere,* to make] **1.** Cutaneous thickening and hardening from continued irritation. **2.** The changing of an eruption into one resembling a lichen.

lichenoid (lī′kĕn-oyd) [″ + *eidos,* form, shape] Resembling lichen.

licorice (lik′(ĕ-)rish, ris) [Ult. fr *glycyrrhiza*] An extract of the dried root of *Glycyrrhiza glabra* used as a flavoring agent, demulcent, and mild expectorant. Ingestion of large amounts of licorice can cause retention of salt, excessive loss of potassium in the urine, and elevated blood pressure. SYN: *Glycyrrhiza glabra.*

lid [ME.] An eyelid.

lidocaine (līd′ŏ-kān″) $C_{14}H_{22}N_2O$, a local anesthetic drug.

l. hydrochloride A local anesthetic also used intravenously to treat certain cardiac arrhythmias, esp. ventricular dysrhythmias.

PATIENT CARE: When lidocaine is injected into the skin, it causes a stinging or burning sensation that many patients find as unpleasant as a bee sting. This sensation can be reduced by injecting directly (perpendicularly) into the skin with a small needle (such as a 30-gauge) and by diluting the anesthetic with a 10% solution of sodium bicarbonate.

lien (lī′ĕn) [L. *lien*, spleen] The spleen. **lienal** (lī-ĕn-ăl), adj.

lienomyelomalacia (lī-ē″nō-mī″ĕl-ō-mă-lā′shē-ă) [″ + ″ + *malakia*, softening] Softening of the spleen and bone marrow.

lienorenal (lī″ĕ-nō-rēn′ăl) [*lien* + *renal*] Pert. to the spleen and kidney.

life (līf) **1.** The capability of using metabolic or biochemical processes to grow, reproduce, and adapt to the environment. **2.** The time between the birth or inception and the death of an organism. The life of an organism begins at conception and ends at death; however, for legal and other reasons the definition of when life begins and death occurs has been subject to a variety of interpretations. **3.** The sum total of those properties that distinguish living things (animals or plants) from nonliving inorganic chemical matter or dead organic matter.

life care retirement community ABBR: LCRC. A residential facility, typically for older adults, that provides several levels of supervision and access to registered health care professionals. LCRCs are typically at a location that combines independent apartments with assisted living residences and skilled nursing facilities. Residents relocate from one level of care to another, depending on their immediate needs for assistance. For example, an older woman who undergoes a knee replacement procedure may spend several weeks recuperating and undergoing rehabilitation in the nursing facility before returning to semi-independent apartment living (in which meals are provided in a common cafeteria) or to independent housing (e.g., with a healthy spouse).

life expectancy The number of years that an average person of a given age may be expected to live. Numerous factors influence life expectancy, including habits (e.g., smoking); chronic illnesses (e.g., congestive heart failure, end-stage renal disease, or cancers); gender (women live longer than men); and socioeconomic status. In the U.S., the average life expectancy at birth is about 78 years. SEE: tables; *years of life lost*.

life extension The prolongation of life with healthful practices, e.g., regular exercise, balanced diet, abstaining from tobacco, and limiting consumption of alcohol. SYN: *age retardation; biomedical gerontology; experimental gerontology*.

life review therapy A type of insight-oriented therapy that focuses on conflict resolution. It is usually conducted with people near the end of their lives and is

Life Expectancy by Sex, Age, and Race: 2008

Age (years)	White Male	White Female	Black Male	Black Female	Total Male	Total Female
Birth	75.9	80.8	70.9	77.4	75.5	80.5
1	75.4	80.2	71.0	77.4	75.1	80.0
5	71.5	76.3	67.1	73.5	71.2	76.1
10	66.5	71.3	62.2	68.5	66.2	71.1
15	61.6	66.3	57.2	63.6	61.3	66.1
20	56.8	61.4	52.6	58.7	56.5	61.2
25	52.2	56.6	48.0	53.9	51.9	56.4
30	47.5	51.7	43.5	49.1	47.2	51.5
35	42.8	46.9	39.0	44.3	42.6	46.7
40	38.1	42.1	34.5	39.6	37.9	41.9
45	33.6	37.4	30.1	35.1	33.4	37.2
50	29.2	32.8	26.0	30.8	29.0	32.7
55	25.0	28.3	22.2	26.7	24.9	28.3
60	21.0	24.0	18.7	22.7	20.9	24.0
65	17.3	19.9	15.5	18.9	17.2	19.9
70	13.7	16.0	12.6	15.4	13.7	16.0
75	10.6	12.4	10.0	12.2	10.6	12.5
80	7.9	9.3	7.8	9.5	7.9	9.4
85	5.7	6.8	6.0	7.1	5.8	6.8
90	4.1	4.8	4.6	5.3	4.1	4.8
95	2.9	3.3	3.5	3.8	2.9	3.3
100	2.0	2.2	2.6	2.8	2.1	2.3

SOURCE: Adapted from U.S. National Center for Health Statistics, National Vital Statistics Reports (NVSR), *Deaths: Preliminary Data for 2008, Vol. 59, No. 2, December 2010.*

Expectation of Life at Birth, 1970 to 2008, and Projections, 2010 to 2020**

Year	Total		White		Black	
	Male	Female	Male	Female	Male	Female
1970	67.1	74.7	68.0	75.6	60.0	68.3
1980	70.0	77.4	70.7	78.1	63.8	72.5
1981	70.4	77.8	71.1	78.4	64.5	73.2
1982	70.8	78.1	71.5	78.7	65.1	73.6
1983	71.0	78.1	71.6	78.7	65.2	73.5
1984	71.1	78.2	71.8	78.7	65.3	73.6
1985	71.1	78.2	71.8	78.7	65.0	73.4
1986	71.2	78.2	71.9	78.8	64.8	73.4
1987	71.4	78.3	72.1	78.9	64.7	73.4
1988	71.4	78.3	72.2	78.9	64.4	73.2
1989	71.7	78.5	72.5	79.2	64.3	73.3
1990	71.8	78.8	72.7	79.4	64.5	73.6
1991	72.0	78.9	72.9	79.6	64.6	73.8
1992	72.3	79.1	73.2	79.8	65.0	73.9
1993	72.2	78.8	73.1	79.5	64.6	73.7
1994	72.4	79.0	73.3	79.6	64.9	73.9
1995	72.5	78.9	73.4	79.6	65.2	73.9
1996	73.1	79.1	73.9	79.7	66.1	74.2
1997	73.6	79.4	74.3	79.9	67.2	74.7
1998	73.8	79.5	74.5	80.0	67.6	74.8
1999	73.9	79.4	74.6	79.9	67.8	74.7
2000	74.1	79.3	74.7	79.9	68.2	75.1
2001	74.2	79.4	74.8	79.9	68.4	75.2
2002	74.3	79.5	74.9	79.9	68.6	75.4
2003	74.5	79.6	75.0	80.0	68.8	75.6
2004	74.9	79.9	75.4	80.4	69.3	76.0
2005	74.9	79.9	75.4	80.4	69.3	76.1
2006	75.1	80.2	75.7	80.6	69.7	76.5
2007	75.4	80.4	75.9	80.8	70.0	76.8
2008 (preliminary)	75.5	80.5	75.9	80.8	70.9	77.4
Projections:†						
2010	75.7	80.8	76.5	81.3	70.2	77.2
2015	76.4	81.4	77.1	81.8	71.4	78.2
2020	77.1	81.9	77.7	82.4	72.6	79.2

* In years. Excludes deaths of nonresidents of the United States.
† Based on middle mortality assumptions.

SOURCE: Adapted from U.S. National Center for Health Statistics, National Vital Statistics Reports (NVSR), *Deaths: Preliminary Data for 2008, Vol. 59, No. 2, December 2010.*

designed to allow them to come to terms with conflict with others, gain meaning from their lives, and die peacefully.

life satisfaction Successful aging.

life skills Any personal ability that helps an individual to cope with people, problems, situational changes, or stress. Life skills include adaptability, creativity, critical thinking, decision making; emotional intelligence, listening, negotiation, relationship building, and self-awareness.

lifespan (līf'span") The time beginning with the birth of an organism to the time of its death.

lifestyle A person's pattern of living and behavior, esp. as distinguished from the behavior patterns or life choices of others. SEE: *lifestyle, sedentary.*

lifestyle, sedentary Reports a habit of life that is characterized by a low physical activity level. SEE: *Nursing Diagnoses Appendix.*

life support Any technique, therapy, or device that assists in sustaining life.

advanced cardiac l.s. ABBR: ACLS. **1.** The resuscitation of dying patients. ACLS involves management of the airway, reestablishment of breathing, and the restoration of spontaneous heart rhythm, blood pressure, and organ perfusion. It begins with the recognition of cardiac or respiratory emergencies, and includes cardiopulmonary resuscitation, defibrillation, endotracheal intubation, oxygenation and ventilation, medications for restoring normal cardiac rhythms and cardiac output, cardiac pacing (when needed), and post-resuscitation care. It may begin in the out-of-hospital setting or take place in the hospital. SEE: illus. **2.** SEE: *Ad-*

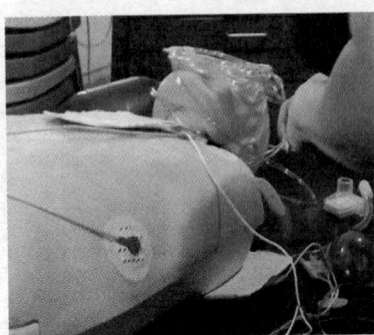

ADVANCED CARDIAC LIFE SUPPORT

Mannequin used for training

vanced Cardiac Life Support. SEE: *basic cardiac l.s.; cardiopulmonary resuscitation; emergency cardiac care.*

   Advanced Medical L.S. SEE: *Advanced Medical Life Support.*

   advanced trauma l.s. ABBR: ATLS. **1.** Treatment for managing a critically injured patient. **2.** SEE: *Advanced Trauma Life Support.*

   basic cardiac l.s. ABBR: BCLS. The phase of cardiopulmonary resuscitation (CPR) and emergency cardiac care that either (1) prevents circulatory or respiratory arrest or insufficiency by prompt recognition and early intervention or by early entry into the emergency care system or both; or (2) externally supports the circulation and respiration of a patient in cardiac arrest through CPR. When cardiac or respiratory arrest occurs, basic life support (BLS) should be initiated by anyone present who is familiar with CPR. SEE: *advanced cardiac l.s.; bag mask device; cardiopulmonary resuscitation; emergency cardiac care; Heimlich maneuver.*

   basic l.s. ABBR: BLS. **1.** A level of out-of-hospital emergency service. **2.** Cardiopulmonary resuscitation. SEE: *defibrillation; defibrillator.*

   Basic Trauma L.S. SEE: *Basic Trauma Life Support.*

   pediatric advanced l. s. ABBR: PALS. The treatment, including basic and advanced life support, for stabilizing a critically ill or injured child.

   prehospital trauma l.s. SEE: *Prehospital Trauma Life Support.*

   withholding l.s. SEE: *withholding life support.*

life-sustaining intervention Any method, medicine, or device used to prolong life. Whether, when, and how to use life-sustaining treatments are difficult topics that require careful consideration by patients, their surrogates, and health care professionals. SEE: *advance directive; living will.*

life-sustaining therapy Therapy of a crit-

ically ill patient that, if discontinued, would cause the patient to die. SEE: *life support.*

life table SEE: under *table.*

Li-Fraumeni syndrome [Fredrick Pei Li, Chinese-born U.S. epidemiologist, b. 1940; Joseph F. Fraumeni, Jr., U.S. epidemiologist, b. 1933] An inherited condition in which individuals develop multiple primary tumors, including breast cancer, osteosarcoma, chondrosarcoma, soft tissue sarcoma, brain tumors, adrenal cortex tumors, etc. Mutations of the p53 gene on chromosome 17 are responsible for this disease.

lift (lift) **1.** To raise or elevate. **2.** A material used to equalize the length of a shortened side of the body with the unshortened, normal, side, as on a shoe. SYN: *wedge* (3).

lift team Patient lift team.

ligament (lig′ă-mĕnt) [L. *ligamentum,* a band] **1.** A band or sheet of strong fibrous connective tissue connecting the articular ends of bones, binding them together to limit motion. **2.** A thickened portion or fold of peritoneum or mesentery that supports a visceral organ or connects it to another viscus. **3.** A band of fibrous connective tissue connecting bones, cartilages, and other structures and serving to support or attach fascia or muscles. **4.** A cordlike structure representing the vestigial remains of a fetal blood vessel.

   accessory l. A ligament that supplements another, esp. one on the lateral surface of a joint. This type of ligament lies outside of and independent of the capsule of a joint.

   acromioclavicular l. The ligament supporting the acromioclavicular joint; it joins the acromial process of the scapula and the distal end of the clavicle and, in combination with the coracoclavicular ligaments, holds the clavicle down.

   alar l. One of a pair of short round ligaments extending up from the sides of the dens, through the foramen of the atlas, and attaching to the sides of the foramen magnum of the skull. They limit side flexion and rotation of the head in relation to the vertebral column

   annular l. A circular ligament, esp. one enclosing a head or radius or one holding the footplate of the stapes in the oval window.

   anococcygeal l. A band of fibrous tissue joining the tip of the coccyx with the external anal sphincter.

   anterior cruciate l. ABBR: ACL. The ligament of the knee that originates on the anteromedial portion of the tibia's intercondylar eminence, passes laterally to the posterior cruciate ligament, and attaches on the medial portion of the posterior aspect of the lateral femoral condyle. The ACL prevents anterior displacement of the tibia relative to the femur, internal and external rotation of the tibia on the femur, and hyperextension of the tibiofemoral joint.

SYMPTOMS: A torn ACL causes pain and functional instability in the knee.

TREATMENT: Arthroscopic surgery is usually necessary to repair torn ACLs. Sometimes open surgery, or arthrotomy, is necessary for particularly complex repairs.

anterior longitudinal l. The thick wide connective tissue band running along the front of the entire vertebral column. The anterior longitudinal ligament attaches to the front and sides of the bodies of the vertebrae and the intervertebral disks.

anterior talofibular l. The ligament of the ankle that connects the lateral talus and fibular malleolus, preventing anterior displacement of the talus in the mortise. This ligament is injured with an excessive inversion and plantar flexion motion (supination) and is the most commonly injured ligament of the ankle.

anterior tibiofibular l. A broad ligament located on the anterior half of the distal fibula, superior to the lateral malleolus, that binds the fibula to the tibia. The anterior tibiofibular ligament is part of the distal ankle syndesmosis. SEE: *crural interosseous l.; posterior tibiofibular l.*

apical l. A single median ligament extending from the odontoid process to the occipital bone.

arcuate l. The lateral, medial, and exterior ligaments that extend from the 12th rib to the transverse process of the first lumbar vertebra, to which the diaphragm is attached.

calcaneofibular l. ABBR: CFL. An extracapsular ligament of the lateral ankle joint. The calcaneofibular ligament originates from the inferior apex of the lateral malleolus and courses at approximately a 133° angle to attach to the calcaneus. It is the primary restraint against talar inversion when the ankle is in its neutral position.

capsular l. Heavy fibrous structures, lined with synovial membrane and surrounding articulations.

check l. A ligament that restrains the motion of a joint, esp. the lateral odontoid ligaments.

collateral l. One of the ligaments that provide medial and lateral stability to joints. They include the medial (ulnar) and lateral (radial) collateral ligaments at the elbow, the medial (tibial) and lateral (fibular) collateral ligaments at the knee, the medial (deltoid) and lateral collateral ligaments at the ankle, and the collateral ligaments of the fingers.

conoid l. The posterior and inner portion of the coracoclavicular ligament.

coracoacromial l. The broad triangular ligament attached to the outer edge of the coracoid process of the scapula and the tip of the acromion.

coracoclavicular l. The ligament uniting the clavicle and coracoid process of the scapula. It has two parts, the conoid and the trapezoid ligaments. SEE: illus.

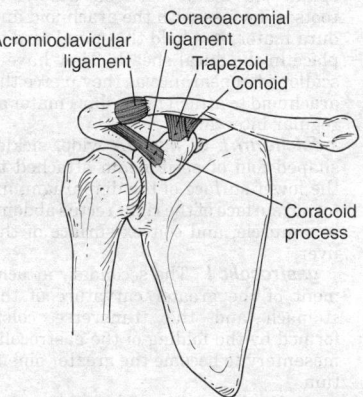

CORACOCLAVICULAR LIGAMENT

coracohumeral l. The broad ligament connecting the coracoid process of the scapula to the greater tubercle of the humerus.

costotransverse l. The ligaments uniting the ribs with the transverse processes of the vertebrae.

cricothyroid l. The ligament uniting cricoid and thyroid cartilages and the location for the horizontal incision (called coniotomy) to prevent choking.

cruciate l. **1.** The ligament of the ankle passing transversely across the dorsum of the foot that holds tendons of the anterior muscle group in place. **2.** A cross-shaped ligament of the atlas consisting of the transverse ligament and superior and inferior bands, the former passing upward and attaching to the margin of the foramen magnum, the latter passing downward and attaching to the body of the atlas. **3.** Either of two ligaments of the knee, the anterior (from the posterior femur to the anterior tibia), and the posterior (from the anterior femur to posterior tibia). They provide rotary stability for the knee and prevent displacement of the tibia. SYN: *cruciform l.* SEE: *anterior cruciate l.*

SYMPTOMS: A torn cruciate ligament causes instability and pain in the knee. The type of instability depends on which cruciate ligament is damaged.

TREATMENT: Arthroscopic surgery is usually necessary to repair torn cruciate ligaments. Sometimes open surgery, or arthrotomy, is necessary for particularly complex repairs.

cruciform l. Cruciate l.

deltoid l. The collective term for the medial ankle ligaments, formed by the anterior tibiotalar, tibionavicular, tibiocalcaneal, and posterior tibiotalar ligaments. As a group, the deltoid ligament limits eversion and rotation of the talus within the ankle mortise.

dentate l. Lateral extensions of the spinal pia mater between the nerve roots; they fuse with the arachnoid and dura mater, and hold the spinal cord in place in the dural sheath. They have a scalloped appearance as they pierce the arachnoid to attach to the dura mater at regular intervals.

falciform l. of liver A wide, sickle-shaped fold of peritoneum attached to the lower surface of the diaphragm, internal surface of the right rectus abdominis muscle, and convex surface of the liver.

gastrocolic l. The secondary attachment of the greater curvature of the stomach and the transverse colon formed by the folding of the gastrocolic mesentery to become the greater omentum.

gastrophrenic l. A fold of peritoneum between the esophageal end of the stomach and the diaphragm.

gastrosplenic l. The fold of visceral peritoneum that connects the edge of the stomach and the hilum of the spleen.

Gimbernat l. SEE: *Gimbernat ligament*.

glenohumeral l. One of the fibers of the coracohumeral ligament passing into the joint and inserted into the inner and upper part of the bicipital groove.

iliofemoral l. The Y-shaped bundle of fibers forming the upper and anterior portion of the capsular ligament of the hip joint. This ligament extends from the ilium to the intertrochanteric line. SYN: *Y ligament*.

iliolumbar l. The ligament extending from the fourth and fifth lumbar vertebrae to the iliac crest.

inguinal l. The ligament extending from the anterior superior iliac spine to the pubic tubercle. SYN: *crural l.; Poupart's l.*

interclavicular l. The bundle of fibers between the sternal ends of the clavicles, attached to the interclavicular notch of the sternum.

lacunar l. SEE: *Gimbernat ligament*.

medial l. A broad ligament that connects the medial malleolus of the tibia to the tarsal bones.

median umbilical l. The fibrous cord extending from the apex of the bladder to the umbilicus. It represents the remains of the urachus of the fetus.

meniscofemoral l. Two small ligaments of the knee, one anterior and one posterior. The anterior one attaches to the posterior area of the lateral meniscus and the anterior cruciate ligament. The posterior one attaches to the posterior area of the lateral meniscus and the medial condyle of the femur.

nuchal l. The upward continuation of the supraspinous ligament, extending from the seventh cervical vertebra to the occipital bone.

palpebral l. Two ligaments, medial and lateral, extending from tarsal plates of the eyelids to the frontal process of the maxilla and the zygomatic bone, respectively. The orbicularis oculi muscles attach to the medial palpebral ligaments.

patellar l. The continuation of the tendon of the quadriceps femoris muscle; it encloses the patella and secures it in front of the knee joint.

pectineal l. A triangular ligament that extends from the medial end of the inguinal ligament along the pectineal line of the pubis.

periodontal l. ABBR: PDL. The connective tissue attached to the cementum on the outer surface of a dental root and the osseous tissue of the alveolar process. The periodontal ligament holds the teeth in the sockets of the bone. SYN: *dentoalveolar l.; alveolar periosteum*.

phrenicocolic l. A fold of peritoneum joining the left colic flexure of the colon to the adjacent costal portion of the diaphragm.

posterior longitudinal l. The continuous narrow band of connective tissue lining the front inner surface of the entire vertebral canal. It attaches the vertebral bodies and intervertebral disks and forms the smooth front wall of the vertebral foramen.

posterior tibiofibular l. A broad ligament that binds the fibula to the tibia; located on the posterior half of the distal fibula, superior to the lateral malleolus. The posterior tibiofibular ligament is part of the distal ankle syndesmosis. SEE: *anterior tibiofibular l.; crural interosseous l.*

Poupart l. Inguinal l.

pulmonary l. A fold of pleura that extends from the hilus of the lung to the base of the medial surface of the lung.

round l. of liver A fibrous cord extending upward from the umbilicus and enclosed in lower margin of the falciform ligament; represents obliterated left umbilical vein of the fetus.

sacroiliac l. Two ligaments (anterior and posterior) that connect sacrum and ilium.

sacrospinous l. The ligament extending from the spine of the ischium to the sacrum and coccyx in front of the sacrotuberous ligament.

sacrotuberous l. The ligament extending from the tuberosity of the ischium to the posterior superior and inferior iliac spines and to the lower part of the sacrum and coccyx.

sphenomandibular l. The ligament attached superiorly to the spine of the sphenoid and inferiorly to the lingula of the mandible. The sphenomandibular ligament is a key part of the temporomandibular joint, helps support the weight of the mandible when the mandibular muscles are relaxed, and also controls and guides the swing of the mandible as it moves.

spring l. The interior calcaneonavicular ligament of the sole of the foot. It joins the calacaneus to the navicular.

stylohyoid l. A thin fibroelastic cord between the lesser cornu of the hyoid bone and the apex of the styloid process of the temporal bone.

stylomandibular l. A thin fibrous band of tissue extending between the styloid process of the temporal bone and the lower part of the posterior border of the ramus of the mandible. It is one of the structures that separates the parotid gland from the submandibular gland. SYN: *stylomaxillary l.*

supraspinal l. A ligament uniting the apices of the spinous processes of the vertebrae.

temporomandibular l. The thickened portion of the joint capsule that passes from the articular tubercle at the root of the zygomatic arch to attach to the subcondylar neck of the mandible.

transverse humeral l. A fibrous band that bridges the bicipital groove of the humerus in connecting the lesser and greater tuberosities.

trapezoid l. The lateral portion of the coracoclavicular ligament.

triangular l. One of two ligaments (right and left) connecting posterior portions of the right and left lobes of the liver with corresponding portions of the diaphragm.

uterosacral l. SEE: *Petit ligament.*

Y l. Iliofemoral ligament.

yellow l. One of the ligaments connecting the laminae of adjacent vertebrae.

ligamenta (lĭg-ă-mĕn′tă) Pl. of ligamentum.

ligamentous (lĭg″ă-mĕn′tŭs) [L. *ligamentum,* band] **1.** Relating to a ligament. **2.** Like a ligament.

ligamentum (lĭg″ă-mĕn′tŭm) *pl.* **ligamenta** [L., a band] Ligament.

l. arteriosum In the adult, the cordlike remnant of the fetal ductus arteriosus between the left pulmonary artery and the arch of the aorta. Just after birth, the ductus arteriosus constricts and begins to fill with endothelial cells,

and within a few months the ductus arteriosus is completely closed. For the remainder of one's life, the closed duct remains as a connecting cord attaching the two large outflow arteries of the heart.

l. flavum A ligament that binds adjacent vertebral laminae to each other.

l. teres In the adult, the closed remnant of the fetal umbilical vein. It runs inside the free edge of the falciform ligament from the underside of the umbilicus to the liver.

ligand (lig′ănd, lĭg′) [L. *ligandus,* for binding] **1.** In chemistry, an organic molecule attached to a central metal ion by multiple bonds. **2.** Any chemical that binds to a specific receptor site, e.g., on a cell membrane. **3.** In immunology, a small molecule bound to another chemical group or molecule.

fas l. ABBR: FasL. A protein on the surface of activated T cells that binds to Fas receptors on the surface of the same or other T cells and triggers a series of events causing apoptosis. This process is involved in the activation-induced cell death necessary to ensure that autoreactive T cells do not attack "self" antigens.

neuroimmunophilin l. Any of the small molecules that can stimulate neurons to grow new axons and dendrites. They can cross the blood-brain barrier, and therefore may be used to treat neurodegenerative diseases or central nervous system injuries.

ligase (lī′gās, lĭg′ās) The general term for a class of enzymes that catalyze the joining of the ends of two chains of DNA.

ligase chain reaction A technique for amplifying the quantity of specific sequences of nucleic acid in a specimen. The patient's DNA, or specimens thought to contain pathogenic DNA, are mixed with DNA ligase and oligonucleotide probes. Double-stranded DNA is denatured. Probes bind to the complementary strands on any denatured target DNA. Ligase joins the bound probes, and multiple copies of the DNA of interest are made. In clinical practice, ligase chain reactions are used primarily in urinary (noninvasive) assays to detect genital infections with chlamydia or gonorrhea.

ligate (lī′gāt) To apply a ligature.

ligation (lī-gā′shŏn) [L. *ligatio,* tying, binding] The application of a ligature.

band l. Rubber-band l.

rubber-band l. The application of a rubber band around a superficial bit of tissue, such as an internal hemorrhoid or an esophageal varix. Because its blood supply is thereby cut off, the tissue dies and sloughs. SYN: *band l.*

tubal l. A surgical method of contraception in which the fallopian tubes are severed and their cut ends are tied. It is used to prevent eggs, released from the ovaries, from entering the uterus where they might be penetrated by sperm.

ligature (lĭg′ă-chūr) [L. *ligatura*, a binding] **1.** Process of binding or tying. **2.** A thread or wire for tying a blood vessel or other structure in order to constrict or fasten it. The cord or material used may be catgut, synthetic suture materials such as nylon or Dacron, polyglycolic acid, or natural fibers such as silk or cotton. Sometimes strips of fascia obtained from the patient are used as a ligature. SEE: *suture*.

    wire l. A soft, thin wire, elastic cord, or elastic loop used in orthodontics to anchor an arch wire or other dental devices or to tie two structures together.

light (līt) Radiant electromagnetic energy limited to a wavelength of about 400 nm (extreme violet) to 770 nm (extreme red).

    axial l. Light whose rays are parallel to each other and to the optic axis.

    call l. A device used by a patient to signal his or her need for assistance from professional staff. It typically consists of a wireless remote control at the bedside, linked to a beeper, buzzer, cellular phone, chime, or light panel.

    cold l. Any form of light that is not perceptibly warm. The heat of ordinary light rays is dissipated when they are passed through some medium such as quartz.

    diffused l. Light rays broken by refraction.

    intrinsic l. The sensation of light when there are no retinal stimuli to produce that sensation. SYN: *idioretinal l.*

    oblique l. Light rays that strike a surface obliquely.

    polarized l. Light in which waves vibrate in one direction only.

    reflected l. Light rays thrown back by an illuminated object such as a mirror.

    refracted l. Light rays bent from their original course.

    transmitted l. Light that passes through an object.

    white l. Light that contains all of the visible wavelengths of light.

    Wood l. SEE: *Wood rays*.

light difference The difference between the two eyes with respect to sensitivity to light intensity.

lightening The descent of the presenting part of the fetus into the pelvis. This often occurs 2 to 3 weeks before the first stage of labor begins. It may not occur in multiparas until active labor begins. SYN: *engagement*. SEE: *labor*.

light-headedness The feeling of dizziness or of being about to faint; a nonspecific symptom of many conditions, including for example, anemia, anxiety, cardiac rhythm disturbances, fever, low blood pressure, many infections, and some drugs.

lightning The discharge of atmospheric electricity from cloud to cloud or from cloud to earth. About 100 lightning strokes hit the earth every second. In the U.S. each year, about 500 to 1000 people are struck by lightning; between 150 and 300 of these die as a result of being struck.

lightning safety rules SEE: under *rule*.

light pointer A head-mounted input device to enable those who are paralyzed or have limited movement to use computers. These devices typically operate through visible or invisible light sources at the tip of the pointer, which transmits a signal to a computer-mounted light sensor or receiver.

light reaction That stage of photosynthesis in which photons are captured by cells and used to supply the energy needed to synthesize carbohydrates. Chlorophyll is the light-trapping molecule of most plants. Bacteriochlorophyll is a related compound used by bacteria to capture the energy supplied by light.

light sleep SEE: under *sleep*.

light therapy SEE: *phototherapy*.

light unit A foot-candle, or the amount of light 1 ft from a standard candle. The ideal amount of light required for work varies with the specific type of work being done. The term *foot-candle* took the place of *candle power*, but light intensity in the International System of Units is indicated by lumen. SEE: *candela; lumen*.

lightwand (līt′wănd) A stylet that transilluminates the soft tissues of the neck. It is used in endotracheal intubation.

lignan (lĭg′năn) A steroid-like chemical found in flaxseed and related plants that may be beneficial in the management of hormone-sensitive illnesses. SEE: *phytoestrogen*.

lignin (lĭg′nĭn) A polymer present in plants that combines with cellulose to form cell walls. It is one of the components of dietary fiber in fruits and vegetables. Lignin is not digestible at all by the bacterial enzymes in the colon.

lignoceric acid (lĭg″nō-ser′ĭk) SEE: under *acid*.

likelihood ratio (līk′lē-hood″) ABBR: LR. A statistical tool used to help determine the usefulness of a diagnostic test for including or excluding a particular disease. An LR = 1 suggests that the test ordered neither helps to diagnose the disease in question nor helps to rule it out. Higher LRs increase the probability that the disease will be present; LRs <1.0 decrease the probability that the disease is present.

    A positive LR can be thought of as the probability that someone with a suspected condition will, accurately, have a positive test result, divided by the probability that a healthy person will, inaccurately, test positive for the disease. Mathematically this can be represented by the following equation: LR+ = sensitivity of the test/ (1− specificity of the test). A negative LR is the probability that a sick person will fail to be detected by the test, divided by the probability that a healthy person will be accurately shown by the test to have no sign of disease. Mathematically: LR− = (1 − sensitivity of the test) / specificity of the test.

Likert scale A graduated scale that reflects the degree of agreement or disagreement to a given question or questions. For example, there may be five possible responses: strongly agree, agree, don't know, disagree, or strongly disagree.

LILACS database (lī′laks″) [Abbrev. of Portuguese *Literatura Latino-Americana e do Caribe em Ciências da Saúde,* Latin American and Caribbean Literature on Health Sciences] A registry of health science and technical literature maintained by the Latin American and Caribbean Health Science Information Center.

limb (lĭm) **1.** An arm or leg. **2.** An extremity. **3.** A limblike extension of a structure.

   anterior l. of internal capsule The lenticulocaudate portion that lies between the lenticular and caudate nuclei.

   pectoral l. The upper extremity.

   pelvic l. The lower extremity.

   phantom l. SEE: *phantom sensation*.

   residual l. Stump.

   thoracic l. The upper extremity.

limbal relaxing incision ABBR: LRI. SEE: under *incision*.

limbic (lĭm′bĭk) [L. *limbus,* border] Pert. to a limbus or border. SYN: *marginal*.

limbic system A group of brain structures, including the hippocampus, amygdala, dentate gyrus, cingulate gyrus, gyrus fornicatus, the archicortex, and their interconnections and connections with the hypothalamus, septal area, and a medial area of the mesencephalic tegmentum. The system is activated by motivated behavior and arousal, and it influences the endocrine glands and autonomic nervous system. SEE: illus.

limb perfusion SEE: under *perfusion*.

limb reduction defect SEE: under *defect*.

limb replantation, limb reimplantation The surgical reattachment of a traumatically amputated limb or part.

limb salvage surgery SEE: under *surgery*.

limbus (lĭm′bŭs) *pl.* **limbi** [L. *limbus,* border] The edge or border of a part.

   l. corneae The edge of the cornea where it unites with the sclera.

   corneoscleral l. In the eye, a transitional dome 1 or 2 mm wide where the cornea joins the sclera and conjunctiva.

lime [Ult. fr. Persian *limūn,* lemon] **1.** The fruit of *Citrus aurantifolia,* which contains vitamin C. **2.** The yellowish green fruit of a lime with an acid pulp used as a preservative, flavoring agent, and high in vitamin C.

limen (lī′měn, lim′ĭ-nă) *pl.* **limina** [L. *limen,* threshold] Entrance; threshold.

   difference l. Just noticeable difference.

limestone A rock formed of organic fossil remains of shells, composed mostly of calcium carbonate.

liminal (lĭm′ĭ-năl) [L. *limen,* threshold] Hardly perceptible; relating to a threshold as of consciousness or vision.

limit (lĭ′mĭt) [Fr. *limite,* fr. L. *limes,* stem *limit-,* boundary] **1.** A boundary. **2.** A point or line beyond which something cannot or may not progress.

   assimilation l. The amount of carbohydrate that can be absorbed or ingested without causing glycosuria.

   l. of detection ABBR: LOD. The smallest amount of an analyte that can be detected by an analytical system.

   elastic l. The extent to which something may be stretched or bent and still be able to return to its original shape.

   exposure l. The maximum concentration of a substance with which an organism can have contact without suffering adverse effects.

   l. of flocculation The amount of a toxin or toxoid that causes the most rapid flocculation when combined with its antitoxin.

   l. of perception The smallest stimulus that can be perceived by any of the senses: e.g., the faintest light or the smallest amount of pressure.

   l. of quantitation ABBR: LOQ. The smallest amount of analyte that can be measured with stated and acceptable imprecision and inaccuracy e.g., the smallest number of viral particles detectable in a milliliter of blood. SEE: *l. of detection; sensitivity*.

   quantum l. The minimum wavelength present in the spectrum produced by x-rays.

   l. of stability ABBR: LOS. The largest angle from vertical that can be reached and maintained before balance is lost. In normal adults, the sagittal plane limit is 12°, the coronal plane limit, 16°.

   PATIENT CARE: Patients with decreased limits of stability have an increased likelihood of falling when they shift their body from side to side and therefore an increased risk of injuring themselves. Physical therapy, occupa-

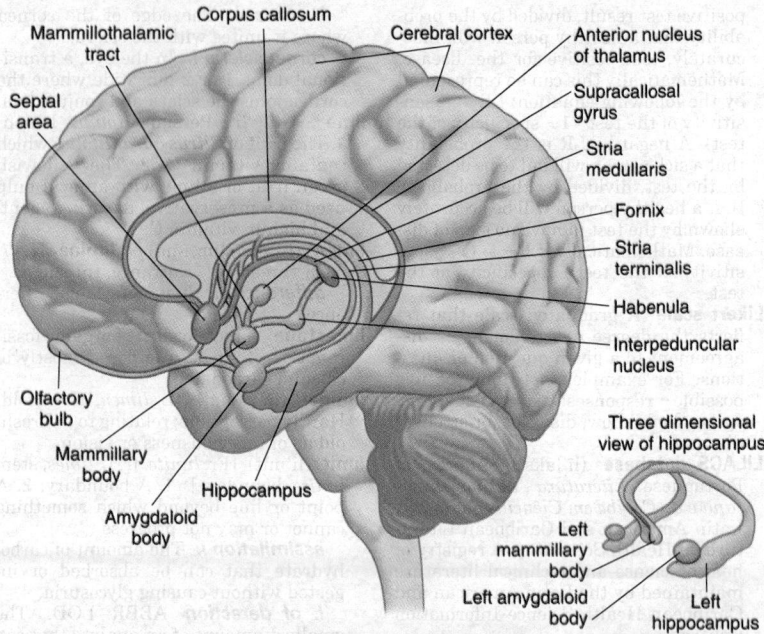

Mammillothalamic tract

Corpus callosum

Cerebral cortex

Anterior nucleus of thalamus

Septal area

Supracallosal gyrus

Stria medullaris

Fornix

Stria terminalis

Habenula

Interpeduncular nucleus

Olfactory bulb

Mammillary body

Hippocampus

Amygdaloid body

Three dimensional view of hippocampus

Left mammillary body

Left amygdaloid body

Left hippocampus

THE LIMBIC SYSTEM OF THE BRAIN

tional therapy, personal assistance, or assistive devices may reduce this risk.

tolerable upper l. ABBR: TUL. The maximum amount of a mineral or vitamin supplement that a person may consume in a day without incurring health risk.

limitans (lĭm'ĭ-tăns) [L. *limitare,* to limit] **1.** A term used in conjunction with other words to denote limiting. **2.** Membrane limitans.

limitation (lĭm″ĭ-tā'shŭn) The condition of being limited.

activity l. Functional limitation.

functional l. In rehabilitation science, any restriction in the performance of activities resulting from disease, injury, or environmental restrictions. SYN: *activity l.; disability.*

l. of motion The restriction of movement or range of motion of a part or joint, esp. that imposed by disease or trauma to joints and soft tissues.

limited data set The minimum necessary and sufficient information about a patient's medical care (e.g., dates of admission and discharge from hospital; the patient's dates of birth, death, and age; and the zip code in which the patient resides). Under regulations of the Health Insurance Portability and Accountability Act (HIPAA), data that reveal more about a patient (e.g., name, address, social security number) cannot be divulged in communication between

health care agencies or professionals without the patient's explicit approval.

limited-service provider SEE: under *provider.*

limited-stage (lĭ′mĭ-tĕd-stāj′) **1.** Not widely spread; localized. **2.** In oncology, pert. to tumors that have not metastasized outside the organ or tissue from which they arose.

limnology (lĭm-nŏl′ō-jē) [Gr. *limne,* pool, + *logos,* study] The scientific study of fresh water in the environment (i.e., potability, pH, degree of pollution, mineral content, and variation with seasonal and climatic changes).

limonene (lĭm′ō-nēn) An essential oil derived from orange or lemon peel. It is used as a flavoring agent in cough syrups.

limp To walk with abnormal, jerky movements.

limulus amebocyte lysate test (lĭm′ū-lŭs) ABBR: LAL test. A test used to detect minute quantities of bacterial endotoxins and to test for pyrogens in various materials; it is also used to detect septicemia due to gram-negative bacteria. Limulus amebocyte lysate is formed from the lysed circulating amebocytes of the horseshoe crab *(Limulus polyphemus).*

linac (li′nak″) [*lin(ear)* + *ac(celerator)*] Linear accelerator.

lindane (lĭn′dān) Gamma benzene hexachloride.

Lindau disease (lin'dow") [Arvid Lindau, Swedish pathologist, 1892–1958] Lindau–von Hippel disease.

Lindau–von Hippel disease (lin'dow" von-hip'ĕl) [Eugen von Hippel, Ger. ophthalmologist, 1867–1939] Angiomata of the retina and cysts and angiomata of the brain and certain visceral organs. SYN: *Lindau disease*.

line (līn) [L. *linea*, string, thread] **1.** A narrow straight mark. **2.** A boundary, edge, or outline. **3.** A wrinkle. **4.** An imaginary anatomical line used as a reference standard. **5.** A catheter attached to a patient, e.g., an intravenous line or an arterial line.

abdominal l. Any of the standard imaginary surface lines delineating abdominal regions. SEE: *abdominal regions*.

absorption l. A black line in the continuous spectrum of light passing through an absorbing medium.

arcuate l. 1. The lower edge of the iliac fossa of the ilium. The arcuate line is a continuation of the pectineal line of the pubis, and it continues up and back along the ilium to merge with the edge of the sacral ala and then the sacral promontory. The continuous bony ridge, of which the arcuate line is one segment, encircles the pelvic inlet and is called the pelvic brim. **2.** In the anterior abdominal wall, below the level of the umbilicus, the lower horizontal edge of the posterior layer of the rectus sheath; (the anterior (superficial) layer of the sheath continues caudally beyond this level.) At this level, the inferior epigastric vessels enter the sheath and run along the underside of the rectus abdominus muscles.

arterial l. A hemodynamic monitoring system consisting of a catheter in an artery connected to pressure tubing, a transducer, and an electronic monitor. It is used to measure systemic blood pressure and to provide ease of access for the drawing of blood (e.g., in intensive care, when regular monitoring of blood gases is necessary).

axial l. A line running in the main axis of the body or a body part, such as a limb. E.g., the axial line of the hand runs longitudinally through the middle digit; the axial line of the foot runs longitudinally through the second digit.

axillary l. The anterior axillary line, the midaxillary line, or the posterior axillary line (imaginary lines that extend in parallel down the side of the body from the axilla).

base l. An imaginary cephalometric line from the infraorbital ridge through the middle of the external auditory meatus to midline of occiput.

blue l. Lead l.

canthomeatal l. An imaginary cephalometric line extending from the lateral canthus of the eye to the center of the external auditory meatus.

cement l. The edge of a new (secondary) osteon; it contains glycoproteins and proteoglycans and has little or no collagen.

central l. A venous access device inserted into and kept in the vena cava, innominate, or subclavian veins. It is used to infuse fluids and medicines, or for gaining access to the heart to measure pressures in the venous circulation. Keeping the line open permits later venous access when the veins might be collapsed and difficult to enter. SEE: *central venous catheter*.

central intravenous l. SEE: *central venous catheter; central l.*

cervical l. 1. A line of junction of cementum and enamel of a tooth. **2.** A line on the neck of the tooth where the gum is attached.

cleavage l. Langer lines.

l. of demarcation A line of division between healthy and diseased tissue.

l. of Douglas SEE: under *Douglas, James*.

epiphyseal l. A line marking the junction of the epiphysis and diaphysis of a long bone. It is the remnant of the epiphyseal disk.

l. of fixation In descriptions of vision, the visual line.

gingival l. SEE: *gumline*.

gluteal l. The posterior, the anterior, or the inferior gluteal line, which are bony ridges on the posterior (exterior) surface of the ilium parallel to the iliac crest. The posterior gluteal line runs along the outer edge of the iliac crest and marks the upper edge of the origin of the gluteus medius muscle. The anterior gluteal line has the same contour as the iliac crest but runs a few centimeters lower and marks the upper edge of origin of the gluteus minimus muscle. The inferior gluteal line has a contour similar to, but fainter than, the other gluteal lines, it runs a few centimeters above the acetabulum, and it marks the lower edge of the origin of the gluteus minimus muscle on the ilium.

gum l. SEE: *gumline*.

iliopectineal l. The segment of the pelvic brim from the pubic symphysis to the sacrum; this includes the pubic crest, the pectineal line, and the arcuate line.

incremental l. Any of the lines seen in a microscopic section of tooth enamel. They mark the sequential layers of added enamel, similar to the growth lines in a tree.

inferior nuchal l. On the posterior outer surface of the occipital bone, a ridge extending laterally from either side of the greater occipital crest 1to 2 cm below the greater external occipital protuberance and curving slightly upward at its end.

interauricular l. An imaginary cephalometric line passing through the left and right through the external auditory meatus.

interpupillary l. An imaginary horizontal line drawn between the centers of the pupils of the eyes. The length of the line is the interpupillary distance.

intertrochanteric l. A roughened circumferential ridge at the base of the neck of the femur interconnecting the greater and lesser trochanters.

intraperiod l. SEE: *major dense l.*

Langer l. SEE: *Langer lines.*

lead l. An irregular dark line in the gingival margin. The line is present in chronic lead poisoning and is caused by the deposition of lead in that portion of the gum. SYN: *blue l.*

lip l. The highest or lowest point the lips reach on the teeth or gums during a broad smile.

M l. In high power micrographs of striated muscle, the thin, dark line in the center of the H band of a sarcomere. It contains myomesin (a protein that connects thick (myosin) filaments), C protein, and creatinine kinase. SYN: *M band; M disk.*

magnetic l. of force The lines indicating the direction of the magnetic force in the space surrounding a magnet or constituting a magnetic field.

major dense l. In electron microscopic images of myelin sheaths, the compacted cytoplasmic side of the Schwann cell membranes, which alternates in multiple layered sheaths with tightly opposed external membrane surfaces called the minor dense line or the intraperiod line. SYN: *period l.* SEE: *intraperiod l.*

mammillary l. An imaginary line through the center of the nipple along the long axis of the breast.

mammary l. Milk l.

median l. An imaginary vertical line dividing the body (or one of its parts) into a right and a left side.

midclavicular l. An imaginary median line used to describe locations on the trunk. At its top, it passes through the midpoint of the clavicle, and on a male, it runs just medial to the nipple. It crosses the costal margin near the end of the 9th costal cartilage and it extends to the thigh, passing through the fold of the groin halfway between the anterior superior iliac spine and the symphysis pubis. At one point, the milk line (mammary line) intersects the midclavicular line.

milk l. An imaginary longitudinal line along each side of the chest and abdomen of mammals marking the current location of the mammary ridge of the embryo. Mammary glands and nipples (both normal and supernumerary) develop along the milk line. The milk line and the midclavicular line intersect at one point. SYN: *mammary l.* SEE: *mammary ridge.*

mucogingival l. SEE: *mucogingival junction.*

mylohyoid l. A ridge on the inner surface of the mandible. It extends from a point beneath the mental spine upward and back to the ramus past the last molar. The mylohyoid muscle and the superior constrictor muscle of the pharynx attach to this ridge.

nasal l. A line from the lower edge of the ala nasi curving to the outer side of the orbicularis oris muscle.

nasobasilar l. A line through the basion and nasion.

neonatal l. A prominent incremental line in the tooth enamel and dentine made partly after birth. Its existence indicates that the infant survived for at least a few days after birth.

nuchal l. The inferior or the superior nuchal line.

oblique l. of mandible On the outside of the body of the mandible, a ridge continuing from the line of the anterior border of the mandibular ramus. As it passes the region below the first molar, the oblique line curves forward and runs (below the mental foramen) parallel to the lower edge of the mandible; it finally disappears into the mental tubercle. The oblique line marks the attachments of the depressor labii inferioris, depressor anguli oris, and parts of the platysma muscles.

oblique l. of thyroid cartilage A curving vertical ridge running from the top to the bottom of the posterior external surface of each of the two laminae composing the thyroid cartilage. Three muscles attach to this ridge: the sternothyroid, the thyrohyoid, and the thyropharyngeus portion of the inferior pharyngeal constrictor.

orbitomeatal l. The imaginary line running through the outer (lateral) canthus of the eye and the ipsilateral external auditory meatus. It is commonly used for radiographic positioning.

parasternal l. The line midway between the midclavicular line and the ipsilateral border of the sternum.

pectinate l. On the lumenal wall, the transition zone between the anal canal and the rectum. Inside the anal canal, the anal valves are located along the pectinate line; outside the anal canal, the superficial portion of the external anal sphincter is located at the pectinate line. The pectinate line marks where, in the embryo, two separate epithelia (the endoderm of the developing hindgut and the ectoderm of the invaginating proctodeum) meet and fuse.

pectineal l. **1.** A ridge along the upper edge of the superior ramus of the pubis (pubic bone) extending from the pubic tubercle to the ilium, where it continues as the arcuate line. Together, the pectineal line and the arcuate line form the iliopectineal line, which is a large portion of the pelvic brim. SYN: *pecten* pubis. **2.** A short, rough ridge on the posterior surface of the femur extending downward from the lesser trochanter to the linea aspera. The pectineus muscle attaches to this ridge.

period l. Major dense **l.**

pure l. 1. The progeny of a single homozygous individual obtained by self-fertilization. **2.** The progeny of an individual reproducing asexually by simple fission, or by buds, runners, or stolons. **3.** The progeny of two homozygous individuals reproducing sexually.

resting l. A smooth cement line seen in microscopic sections of bone; it marks a place where bone growth stopped temporarily and then resumed.

reversal l. A cement line seen in microscopic sections of bone that shows scallops and irregularities representing earlier bone resorption. Resorption to that point occurred before the process reversed and new bone was formed by apposition. SEE: *Howship lacuna*.

scapular l. In anatomical descriptions, an imaginary vertical line parallel to the midline and passing through the tip of the inferior angle of the scapula when the ipsilateral arm is hanging at the side of the body.

Schwalbe l. SEE: under *Schwalbe, Gustav Albert*.

semilunar l. **Linea** semilunaris.

Shenton l. SEE: *Shenton line*.

sight l. An imaginary line from the center of the pupil to a viewed object.

skin tension l. Langer lines.

soleal l. A roughened diagonal line on the posterior surface of the upper quarter of the tibia. It descends from the back of the tibial tuberosity to the medial edge of the shaft of the tibia. Part of the soleus muscle originates from the soleal line.

sternal l. An imaginary vertical midline passing through the sternum.

superior nuchal l. On the posterior outer surface of the occipital bone, a ridge extending laterally from either side of the greater occipital protuberance and curving slightly downward at its end.

temporal l. The superior or the inferior temporal line. The superior temporal line is an arching ridge along the lateral surface of the skull; it begins as a continuation of the upper posterior border of the zygomatic bone and continues as a broad arch along the frontal and parietal bones, above and roughly parallel to the upper edge of the temporal

bone. The inferior temporal line begins with the superior temporal line and separates from its lower edge to form a parallel but tighter and lower arch. The inferior temporal line marks the origin of the temporalis muscle; the superior temporal line marks the attachment of the muscle's fascia.

visual l. An imaginary line connecting the fovea of the eye to the object being viewed. SYN: *visual* ***axis***.

white l. Along the inner wall of the anal canal, a bluish-pink circumferential line below which the canal is lined by skin containing sweat and sebaceous glands; it marks the lower edge of the pectinate line. A digital exam can palpate the lower end of the internal anal sphincter at the level of the white line.

Z l. Regular dark striations visible in high power micrographs of skeletal muscle fibers. Z lines mark the ends of sarcomeres and are the anchors for the sarcomere's actin filaments. SYN: *Z* **band**. SEE: *Z disk*.

linea (lĭn′ē-ă) *pl.* **lineae** [L. *linea,* line] An anatomical line.

l. alba 1. A midline stripe of connective tissue in the abdominal wall from sternum to pubis. It is the raphe of the transverse tendons of the abdominal oblique and abdominal transverse muscles where they meet and interweave along the midline of the rectus abdominis muscle. The linea alba can be seen as a shallow midline groove along the abdominal skin of a lean muscular person, especially above the level of the umbilicus. **2.** A raised white line on the buccal mucosa along the occlusal plane, often caused by clenching the teeth. No treatment is necessary.

l. aspera A thick longitudinal ridge on the posterior surface of the middle third of the femur. Tendons of the aductor longus and biceps femoris muscles attach along this ridge.

l. nigra A dark line or discoloration of the abdomen that may be seen in pregnant women during the latter part of term. It runs from above the umbilicus to the pubes.

l. semilunaris A gently curving groove in the abdominal skin of a lean muscular person along the right and the left edges of the rectus abdominis muscle.

l. terminalis 1. Pelvic **brim**. **2.** The portion of the pelvic brim that does not include the sacral promintory.

lineage (lĭn′ē-ĭj) A group of individuals, animals, cells, or genes that share a common ancestor.

lineage-restricted In cell biology, functionally and structurally limited to behave in a differentiated manner, e.g. like a fibroblast rather than a neuron, a myocyte, or a blood cell.

linear (lĭn'ē-ăr) [L. *linea,* line] Pert. to or resembling a line.

linear accelerator A device that uses high-frequency electromagnetic waves to speed up charged particles such as electrons to high energies within a linear tube for use in radiation therapy, the creation of radioisotopes, and research. SYN: *linac.*

linear IgA bullous dermatosis SEE: under *dermatosis.*

linearity (lĭn-ē-ăr'ĭ-tē) In radiography, the production of a constant amount of radiation for different combinations of milliamperage and exposure time, commonly used as a quality management benchmark.

line pairs per millimeter ABBR: lp/mm. A measurement of fine radiographic image detail demonstrated by the number of pairs of lead lines per millimeter that can be imaged.

liner (lĭn'ĕr) Anything applied to the inside of a hollow body or structure.

cavity l. A layer of material applied to a cavity preparation to protect the pulp of the tooth. It is usually a suspension of zinc phosphate or calcium hydroxide and is used to neutralize the acidity of the base or cement material.

soft l. The material applied to the underside of a denture to provide a soft surface contact with the oral tissues. Some acrylic or silicone resins have been made resilient and are used as liners.

lingua (ling'gwă) *pl.* **linguae** [L. *lingua,* tongue, language] The tongue or a tonguelike structure.

l. plicata Fissured **tongue.**

lingual (lĭng'gwăl) [L. *lingua,* tongue, language] **1.** Pert. to the tongue. **2.** Tongue-shaped. SYN: *linguiform.* **3.** In dentistry, pert. to the tooth surface that is adjacent to the tongue. **4.** Pert. to languages. **5.** In languages and linguistics, made or articulated with the (tip of) the tongue, e.g., *t.*

lingual goiter SEE: under *goiter.*

Linguatula serrata (ling-gwa'chŭ-lă se-răt'ă) An arthropod parasite in snakes, commonly known as the tongue worm. Its larvae, nymphs, and adults occasionally infect humans. Ingested infective larvae migrate to the nasal passages and may cause a parasitic nasopharyngeal obstruction known as linguatulosis.

linguiform (lĭng'gwĭ-form) [" + *forma,* shape] Tongue-shaped. SYN: *lingual* (2).

lingula (lĭng'gyŭ-lă) [L. *lingula,* little tongue] A tongue-shaped process of some structure.

lingulectomy (ling"gyŭ-lek'tŏ-mē) [*lingula* + *-ektomy*] Surgical removal of the lingula of the upper lobe of the left lung.

linguo-, lingu-, lingua-, lingui- [L. *lingua,* tongue] Prefixes meaning *tongue.*

liniment (lĭn'ĭ-mĕnt) [L. *linimentum,* smearing substance] A liquid vehicle (usually water, oil, or alcohol) containing a medication to be rubbed on or applied to the skin. It may be applied by the friction method or on a bandage.

linitis (lĭn-ī'tĭs) [Gr. *linon,* flax, + *itis,* inflammation] Inflammation of the lining of the stomach.

l. plastica An infiltrating cancer of the stomach wall. SEE: *leather-bottle* **stomach.**

linkage In genetics, the association between distinct genes that occupy closely situated loci on the same chromosome. This results in an association in the inheritance of these genes.

sex l. A genetic characteristic that is located on the X or Y chromosome.

linkage mapping SEE: under *mapping.*

linker (lingk'ĕr) A chemical structure that binds two distinctly different chemicals to each other.

linseed (lĭn'sēd) Seed of the common flax, *Linum usitatissimum;* the source of linseed oil. Linseed is used as a demulcent and emollient. SYN: *flaxseed.*

lip (lip) **1.** A soft external structure that forms the boundary of the mouth or opening to the oral cavity. SYN: *labium oris.* **2.** One of the lips of the pudendum (labia majora or minora). SEE: *labia; labium.* **3.** A liplike structure forming the border of an opening or groove.

PATHOLOGY: *Chancre:* It is not unusual to have the initial lesion of syphilis appear on the lip of the mouth as an indurated base with a thin secretion and accompanied by enlargement of the submaxillary glands. *Condyloma latum:* This appears as a mucous patch, flattened, coated with gray exudate, with strictly delimited area, usually at the angle of the mouth. *Eczema:* This is characterized by dry fissures, often covered with a crust, bleeding easily, and occurring on both lips. *Epithelioma:* This may be confused with chancre. It seldom appears before the age of 40, but there are exceptions. It may appear as a common cold sore, a painless fissure, or other break of the lower lip. A crust or scab covers the lesion, leaving a raw surface if removed. Pain does not appear until the lesion is well advanced. It is much more common on the lower lip than on the upper. *Herpes:* These lesions may appear on the lips in pneumonia, typhoid, common cold, and other febrile diseases. *Tuberculous ulcer:* This type of ulcer is located at the inner portion of the lip, close to the angle of the mouth. Pathological examination is necessary for verification.

DIAGNOSIS: Examination is considered to be incomplete unless the lips are everted to expose buccal surfaces. *Bluish or purplish:* This sign may appear in the aged, in those exposed to great cold, and in hypoxemia. *Dry:* Mouth dryness may be seen in fevers or be caused by drugs such as atropine, by thirst, or by mouth breathing. *Fissured:* This may occur after exposure to cold, in avitaminosis, and in children with congenital syphilis. *Pale:* Pallor may be seen in anemia and wasting diseases, in prolonged fever, and after a hemorrhage. *Rashes:* These may be manifestations of typhoid fever, meningitis, or pneumonia. Mucous patches may appear in secondary syphilis, chancre, cancer, and epithelioma.

cleft l. A vertical cleft or clefts in the upper lip. This congenital condition, resulting from the faulty fusion of the median nasal process and the lateral maxillary processes, is usually unilateral and on the left side, but may be bilateral. It may involve either the lip or the upper jaw, or both, and often accompanies cleft palate. Nongenetic factors may also be responsible for causing this condition. The incidence of cleft lip is from one in 600 to one in 1250 births. SYN: *harelip.*

double l. A redundant fold of mucous membrane in the mouth on either side of the midline of the lip.

oral l. Upper and lower lips that surround the mouth opening and form the anterior wall of the buccal cavity.

lipase (lĭ′pās, lī′pās) [″ + *-ase,* enzyme] A fat-splitting enzyme found in blood, pancreatic secretion, and tissues. Emulsified fats are changed in the stomach to fatty acids and glycerol by gastric lipase. SEE: *digestion; enzyme.*

pancreatic l. The pancreatic enzyme that digests fats emulsified by bile salts to fatty acids and glycerol.

lip bumper In orthodontics, a removable appliance to push the lower molars posteriorly to create additional space for the lower anterior teeth. It consists of an archwire that attaches posteriorly to the lower mandible and anteriorly to a plastic mold. The plastic sits just behind the lips and in front of the lower incisors. It forces the molars back when the jaw moves.

lipectomy (li-pek′tŏ-mē) [*lipo-* + *-ectomy*] Excision of fatty tissues.

belt l. Surgical removal of rolls of fat that encircle the entire trunk. It is used to treat morbid accumulations of fat surrounding the abdomen. SYN: *circumferential belt l.*

circumferential belt l. Belt lipectomy.

submental l. Surgical removal of the fat that constitutes a "double chin."

suction l. SEE: *liposuction.*

ultrasound-assisted l. The use of sound waves to disrupt fatty tissues so

that they can be removed surgically. It is used in reducing the size of the breast during mammaplasty.

lipedema (lip″ĕ-dē′mă) [*lipo-* + *edema*] Swelling of the skin, esp. of the lower extremity, owing to the subcutaneous accumulation of fat and fluid.

lipemia (li-pē′mē-ă) [*lipo-* + *-emia*] An abnormal amount of fat in the blood.

alimentary l. An accumulation of fat in the blood after eating.

l. retinalis A condition in which retinal vessels appear reddish white or white; found in cases of hyperlipidemia. SEE: *hyperlipoproteinemia.* **lipemic** (-mik), *adj.*

lipid, lipide (lip′id, lip′īd″) [*lipo-* + *-ide*] Any of a group of fats or fatlike substances, characterized by their insolubility in water and solubility in fat solvents such as alcohol, ether, and chloroform. "Lipid" is descriptive rather than a chemical name such as "protein" or "carbohydrate." Lipids include true fats (esters of fatty acids and glycerol); lipoids (phospholipids, cerebrosides, waxes); and sterols (cholesterol, ergosterol). SEE: *fat; cholesterol* for table.

lipidemia (lip″ĭ-dē′mē-ă) Lipemia. SEE: *atherosclerosis; cholesterol.*

lipid histiocytosis SEE: *histiocytosis.*

lipidomics (lip″id-om′iks) [*lipid* + *-omics*] The study of the variety of fatty molecules in the body, their cellular and extracellular functions and interactions, and the diseases to which they contribute.

lipidosis (lip″ĭ-dō′sĭs) Any disorder of fat metabolism.

arterial l. Arteriosclerosis.

cerebroside l. Gaucher disease.

lipid-soluble (lip′ĭd-sol′yŭ-bĕl) Capable of dissolving in fats, oils, or fatty tissues (e.g., the fatty tissue within the peritoneum or the lipid-rich membranes of neurons).

lipid storage disease A group of rare inherited disorders of fat metabolism in which lipids are metabolized abnormally and accumulate in tissues such as the brain and peripheral nerves.

lipiduria (lip″ĭ-dū′rē-ă) [″ + Gr. *ouron,* urine] Lipids in the urine.

Lipitor (lip′ĭ-tŏr) SEE: *atorvastatin.*

lipo-, lip- [Gr. *lipos,* fat] Prefixes meaning *fat.* SEE: *adipo-; steato-.*

lipoaspiration (lip″ō-as″pĭ-rā′shŏn) Liposuction.

lipoatrophy (lip″ō-ă-trŏ′fē) [*lipo-* + *atrophy*] Atrophy of subcutaneous fatty tissue. This may occur at the site of insulin injection. SEE: *lipodystrophy.*

lipoblast (lip′ō-blăst) [″ + *blastos,* germ] An immature fat cell.

lipoblastoma (lip″ō-blăs-tō′mă) [″ + ″ + *oma,* tumor] A benign tumor of the fatty tissue. SEE: *lipoma.*

lipochondrodystrophy (lip″ō-kon″drō-dis'trŏ-fē) [*lipo-* + *chondro-* + *dystrophy*] Mucopolysaccharidosis IH.

lipochrome (lĭp'ō-krōm) [″ + *chroma*, color] Any one of a group of fat-soluble pigments (e.g., carotene, the fat-soluble yellow pigment found in carrots, sweet potatoes, egg yolk, butter, body fat, and corpus luteum).

lipocyte (lĭp'ō-sīt) SEE: *cell, fat*.

lipodermatosclerosis Thickening and red discoloration of the skin as a result of diminished blood flow, usually caused by local or regional venous obstruction.

lipodystrophy (lĭp″ō-dĭs'trŏ-fē) [*lipo-* + *dystrophy*] Disturbance of fat metabolism. Common findings include the localized accumulation of fat under the skin and on the trunk, or fatty atrophy. SYN: *fat maldistribution*. SEE: *lipoatrophy*.

   insulin l. A complication of insulin administration characterized by changes in the subcutaneous fat at the site of injection. The changes may take the form of atrophy or hypertrophy; rarely are both types present in the same patient. Atrophy develops in as many as one third of children and women who use insulin regularly, but rarely in men. The defect in subcutaneous fat leaves a saucer-like depression. Hypertrophy at the injection site occurs in the form of a spongy localized area. This complication of insulin administration is slightly more common in males than in females. It is usually associated with a history of repetitive use of one injection site.

   intestinal l. A disease characterized principally by fat deposits in intestinal and mesenteric lymphatic tissue, fatty diarrhea, loss of weight and strength, and arthritis. SYN: *granulomatous lipophagia*.

   progressive l. A pathological condition in which there is progressive, symmetrical loss of subcutaneous fat from the upper part of the trunk, face, neck, and arms.

lipodystrophy syndrome A side effect encountered in the treatment of HIV patients with protease inhibitors in which they develop abnormal accumulations of body fat (e.g., over the upper back), hypercholesterolemia, hyperglycemia, hypertriglyceridemia, and insulin resistance.

   antiretroviral treatment-related l. s. HIV-related fat redistribution syndrome.

   facial l. s. Facial lipoatrophy syndrome.

lipofibroma (lĭp″ō-fī-brō'mă) [″ + L. *fibra*, fiber, + Gr. *oma*, tumor] A lipoma having much fibrous tissue. SYN: *fibrolipoma*.

lipofilling (lĭp'ŏ-fĭl″ĭng) Lipostructure.

lipofuscin (lĭp″ō-fŭs'sĭn) [″ + L. *fuscus*, brown] An insoluble fatty pigment found in aging cells. It is the residue of cellular or extracellular material that the cells have ingested but not completely digested. SEE: *brown atrophy; free radical*.

lipofuscinosis (lĭp″ō-fū″sĭn-ō'sĭs) [″ + ″ + Gr. *osis*, condition] Abnormal deposition of lipofuscin in tissues.

   neuronal ceroid l. Batten disease.

lipogenesis (lĭp″ō-jen'ĕ-sĭs) [*lipo-* + *-genesis*] Formation of fat. **lipogenetic** (-jĕ-net'ĭk), *adj*.

lipogenous, lipogenic (li-poj'ĕ-nŭs, lĭp″ōjen'ik) Producing or produced by fat.

lipogranuloma (lĭp″ō-grăn-ū-lō'mă) [″ + L. *granulum*, granule, + Gr. *oma*, tumor] Inflammation of fatty tissue with granulation and development of oily cysts.

lipogranulomatosis (lĭp″ō-grăn″ū-lō-mă-tō'sĭs) [″ + ″ + ″ + *osis*, condition] A disorder of fat metabolism in which a nodule of fat undergoes central necrosis and the surrounding tissue becomes granulomatous.

lipohyalinosis (lī-pō-hī′ă-lĭn-ō″sĭs) Degenerative changes in small blood vessels, marked by the accumulation of a glassy- or waxy-appearing lipid within the vessel wall. This type of vascular degeneration occurs in hypertension and atherosclerosis, and predisposes patients to small infarcts, esp. in penetrating arteries of the brain.

lipoid (lĭp'oyd) [″ + *eidos*, form, shape] **1.** Similar to fat. **2.** Lipid(e).

lipoidosis (lĭp″oyd-ō'sĭs) [*lipoid* + *-osis*] Excessive lipid accumulation. SEE: *xanthomatosis; lipidosis*.

lipolysis (li-pol'ĭ-sĭs, lī-) [*lipo-* + *-lysis*] The decomposition of fat. **lipolytic** (lĭp″ōlit'ik), *adj*.

lipoma (li-pō'mă) [*lipo-* + *-oma,*] A benign fatty tumor. They often appear in crops on the arms or trunk but are not metastatic. **lipomatous** ('măt-ŭs), *adj*. SEE: illus.; *chondrolipoma*.

   l. arborescens An abnormal treelike accumulation of fatty tissue in a joint.

   diffuse l. A lipoma not definitely circumscribed.

lipomatosis (lĭp″ō-mă-tō'sĭs) [″ + *oma*, tumor + *osis*, condition] A condition marked by the excessive deposit of fat in a localized area.

   l. renis **Lipoma** diffusum renis.

lipomeningocele (lĭp″ō-mĕ-nĭng'gō-sēl) [″ + *meninx*, membrane, + *kele*, tumor, swelling] A meningocele associated with lobules of fat tissue.

lipometabolism (lip-ō-mĕ-tab'ŏ-lizm) [*lipo-*″ + ″ + *metabolism*] Metabolism of fat.

lipomyelomeningocele (lĭp″ō-mī″ĕ-lō-me-ning'ŏ-sēl″) [*lipo-* + *myelomeningocele*] A rare defect in which a fatty tumor grows from beneath the surface of the skin of the lower back toward the spinal cord, compressing and tethering

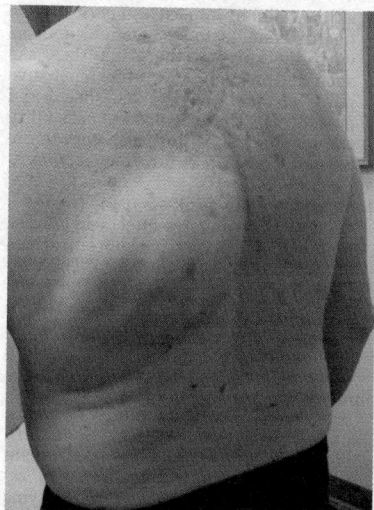

MASSIVE LIPOMA ON THE BACK

the cord in place instead of allowing it to move freely in the cerebrospinal fluid. The condition is usually identified in childhood. The fat mass can damage motor and sensory function in the lower part of the body and cause bowel and bladder problems.

lipopenia (lip″ŏ-pē′nē-ă) [*lipo-* + *-penia*] A deficiency of lipids. **lipopenic** (-nĭk), *adj.*

lipopeptide (lip″ŏ-pep′tīd″) [*lipo-* + *peptide*] A complex of lipids and amino acids.

lipophil (lĭp′ŏ-fĭl) [″ + *philein*, to love] **1.** Having an affinity for fat. **2.** Absorbing fat.

lipophilia (lip″ŏ-fĭl′ē-ă) [*lipo-* + *-philia*] Affinity for fat.

lipoplasty [″ + Gr. *plastikos*, fit for molding] Laser lipolysis.

lipopolysaccharide (lĭp″ŏ-pŏl″ē-săk′ă-rīd) The linkage of molecules of lipids with polysaccharides.

lipoprotein (lip″ŏ-prō′tēn″, prŏt′ē-ĭn) [*lipo-* + *protein*] Any of the conjugated chemicals in the bloodstream consisting of simple proteins bound to fat. Cholesterol, phospholipids, and triglycerides are all fatty components of lipoproteins. Analyzing the concentrations and proportions of lipoproteins in the blood can provide important information about patients' risks of atherosclerosis, coronary artery disease, and death.

Lipoproteins are classified as very low-density (VLDL), low-density (LDL), intermediate-density (IDL), and high-density (HDL). Increased levels of LDL and total cholesterol directly raise one's chances of having coronary heart disease (CHD). For this reason LDL has

been referred to colloquially as "bad" cholesterol. By contrast, increased levels of HDL ("good" cholesterol) are linked with a lowered risk of CHD. The National Cholesterol Education Program has designated 70–100 mg/dl or less as a desirable level of LDL in those already affected by CHD; for people without CHD, a desirable level of LDL is 100 mg/dl or less. SEE: *atherosclerosis; coronary artery disease; hyperlipoproteinemia; statin; cholesterol* for table.

ETIOLOGY: Elevated levels of lipoproteins usually are the result of a diet too rich in fats, saturated fats, and cholesterols. Genetic disease also plays a part in some patients with extremely high lipoprotein levels.

SYMPTOMS: High lipoprotein levels may cause no symptoms until patients develop arterial blockages. If arteries become blocked by lipoproteins, ischemic symptoms may develop.

TREATMENT: Abnormal lipoprotein levels become normal in many patients who consume less dietary fat and increase their exercise. When lipoproteins do not reach expected levels despite diet and exercise, medications to improve lipoprotein profiles are prescribed. These include drugs such as niacin, bile-acid binding resins, and the statins.

l. (a) ABBR: Lp(a). A lipid-protein complex found normally in the plasma in small amounts in all people, but in very high concentrations in some people with familial atherosclerosis. It consists of a low-density lipoprotein molecule bound to apolipoprotein A.

alpha l. High-density **l.**

high-density l. ABBR: HDL. Plasma lipids bound to albumin, consisting of lipoproteins. They contain more protein than either very low-density lipoproteins or low-density lipoproteins. High-density lipoprotein cholesterol is the so-called good cholesterol; a high level is desirable. SYN: *alpha l.*

intermediate-density l. ABBR: IDL. Plasma lipids bound to albumin, consisting of lipoproteins with less protein than high-density, but more than low-density lipoproteins.

l. lipase ABBR: Lp(a). An enzyme produced by many cells. On the surface of cells lining the vasculature, Lp(a) hydrolyzes fat (chylomicrons) from VLDL to monoglycerides to free fatty acids and IDL. Lp(a) is similar to plasminogen and is an important regulator of lipid and lipoprotein metabolism. Even though the physiological functions of Lp(a) and apoprotein(a) are not fully understood, there is a positive association of plasma Lp(a) with premature myocardial infarction. Deficiency of this enzyme leads to an increase in chylomicrons and VLDLs, and to low levels of HDL. Diseases associated with acquired causes of decreased lipoprotein lipase include acute ethanol ingestion, diabetes mellitus, hypothyroidism, chronic renal failure, and nephrotic syndrome.

  low-density l. ABBR: LDL. Any of the plasma lipids that carry most of the cholesterol in plasma. Bound to albumin, LDLs are a proven cause of atherosclerosis. Lowering LDLs with a low-fat diet or with drugs helps prevent and treat coronary artery disease.

  Lp(a) l. A low-density lipoprotein in which apolipoprotein B-100 is linked to apoprotein(a). It contributes to the obstruction of blood vessels in atherosclerosis.

  small, dense low-density l. Any of the low-density lipoproteins that measure less than 197 angstrom units. They are considered to be the most likely fraction of the low-density lipoprotein molecule to cause atherosclerotic vascular disease.

  very low-density l. ABBR: VLDL. Either of the plasma lipids, chylomicrons and prelipoproteins, that are bound to albumin. This class of plasma lipoproteins contains a greater ratio of lipid than the low-density lipoproteins and is the least dense.

liposarcoma (lĭp″ō-săr-kō′mă) [Gr. *lipos*, fat, + *sarx*, flesh, + *oma*, tumor] A malignant tumor derived from embryonal fat cells.

liposculpture (lip″ō-skŭlp′chĕr) The surgical removal of fat from one part of the body to another in order to smooth wrinkles, fill hollows, or create new body contours. SYN: *lipofilling*.

liposoluble (lĭp″ō-sŏl′ū-b'l) [″ + L. *solubilis*, soluble] Soluble in fats.

liposome (lĭp′ō-sōm) [″ + *soma*, body] The sealed concentric shells formed when certain lipid substances are in an aqueous solution. As it forms, the liposome entraps a portion of the solution in the shell. Liposomes may be manufactured and filled with a variety of medications. These have been used to deliver substances to particular organs. These drug forms may be more effective and less toxic than drugs given by other means.

lipostructure (lip′ō-strŭk″chŭr) The injection of fat cells or fatty tissue to fill body contours, reduce skin wrinkles, or eliminate other perceived defects in appearance. SYN: *lipofilling*.

liposuction (lip′ō-sŭk″shŏn, lī′pō-) [*lipo-* + *suction*] A form of plastic surgery for removing adipose tissue by suction from the abdomen, hips, knees, buttocks, thighs, face, arms, or neck with a blunt-tipped cannula introduced into the fatty area through a small incision. To be cosmetically successful, the skin should be elastic enough to contract after the underlying fat has been removed. Liposuction will not benefit dimpled or sagging

skin or flabby muscles. There are no health benefits to liposuction, and, as with any surgery, there may be risks such as infection, severe postoperative pain, cardiac arrhythmias, shock, and even death. There is also the possibility the results will be unsatisfactory to the patient. SYN: *lipoaspiration; suction lipectomy*.

lipotoxicity (lip″ŏ-tok-sis′ĭt-ē) [*lipo-* + *toxicity*] The adverse effects on glucose metabolism of excessive concentrations of free fatty acids in the blood. These effects include an increase in the resistance of the liver and muscle to the effects of insulin, an increase in glucose production, and reductions in insulin secretion by the pancreas.

lipotropic (lip″ō-trō′pik, trop′ik) [*lipo-* + *-tropic*] Having an affinity for lipids, as with certain dyes (e.g., Sudan III, which stains fat readily). **lipotropism** (-trö′pizm), *n.* **lipotropy** (-trö′pē), *n.*

lipoxidase (li-pŏk′sĭ-dās) An enzyme that catalyzes the oxidation of the double bonds of an unsaturated fatty acid. SYN: *lipoxygenase*.

lipoxin (li-pŏk′sĭn) Any of a group of eicosanoids formed by the action of phospholipases on cell membrane phospholipids. Some lipoxins have anti-inflammatory effects, but some promote inflammation and hypersensitivity reactions. SEE: *leukotriene; prostaglandin*.

lipoxygenase (li-pŏks′ĭ-jĕ-nās) Lipoxidase.

Lippes loop (li′pēz) [Jack (Jacob) Lippes, U.S. obstetrician, b. 1924] A serpentine-shaped intrauterine contraceptive device no longer used in the U.S.

lipping (lĭp′ĭng) A growth of bony tissue beyond the joint margin in degenerative joint disease.

lip reading Interpreting what is being said by watching the speaker's lip and facial movements and expression. This method is used as a means of speech discrimination by people with hearing impairments.

liquefaction (lĭk″wĕ-făk′shŭn) **1.** The conversion of a solid into a liquid. **2.** The conversion of solid tissues to a fluid or semifluid state.

liquescent (li-kwe′sĕnt) [L. *liquescere*, to become liquid] Being or becoming liquid.

liquid (lik′wĭd) [L. *liquidus*, fr *liquere*, to flow] One of the four states of matter, characterized by free flow, but a constant volume when bounded by a container.

liquid-based cytology SEE: under *cytology*.

liquid crystal display ABBR: LCD. A type of electronic display unit used on devices from watches to clinical laboratory instruments. It is very efficient and consumes little energy or power.

liquid measure A measure of liquid capacity.

liquor (lĭk′ĕr) [L. *liquor*, a fluid] **1.** Any liquid or fluid. **2.** An alcoholic beverage. **3.** A solution of medicinal substance in water.

    l. amnii Amniotic fluid.

    l. folliculi The fluid contained in the graafian follicle.

    l. sanguinis Blood serum or plasma.

lisinopril (lī-sĭn′ō-prĭl) An angiotensin-converting enzyme inhibitor used, e.g., to treat high blood pressure and congestive heart failure.

lisp (lĭsp) A substitution of sounds owing to a defect in speech, as of the "th" sounds of "thin" and "then" for "s" and "z."

Lissauer tract (lĭs′ow-ĕr) [Heinrich Lissauer, Ger. neurologist, 1861–1891] A long narrow axon tract in the spinal cord between the dorsolateral tip of the dorsal horn and the outer edge of the cord. The tract is filled with unmyelinated and thinly myelinated axons running rostrally or caudally for a few cord segments before entering the dorsal horn and synapsing. Some of these axons are secondary sensory axons that arise from cells in the dorsal horn; others are primary sensory axons of dorsal root ganglia cells. As it enters the hindbrain, Lissauer tract becomes the spinal trigeminal tract. SYN: *dorsolateral fasciculus; dorsolateral tract.*

Lister, Lord Baron Joseph (lĭs′tĕr) British surgeon, 1827–1912, who developed the technique of antiseptic surgery, subsequently evolving into aseptic surgery, without which modern surgery would not be possible.

Listeria (lis-tēr′ē-ă) [*Lister* + *-ia*] A genus of gram-positive, non–spore-forming coccobacilli that may be found singly or in filaments. They are normal soil inhabitants.

    L. monocytogenes The causative agent of listeriosis. This species lives in soil or the intestines of animals and may contaminate food, esp. milk or meat. Its growth is not inhibited by refrigeration.

listeriosis, listerosis (lĭs-tēr″ē-ō′sĭs, lĭs″tĕr-ō′sĭs) Infection with *Listeria monocytogenes,* which causes mild food poisoning in the healthy and severe systemic disease in immunosuppressed patients, older adults, pregnant women, fetuses, and neonates (during the first 3 weeks of life). The organism may be found in unpasteurized milk, unprocessed soft cheeses, processed foods (e.g., lunch meats) contaminated after production, or vegetables contaminated by soil or water containing the organism. Unlike other food-borne pathogens, Listeria grows in refrigerated food; it also grows on the walls of refrigerators and can infect other foods. The organism is destroyed by heat; therefore the risk of contracting listeriosis derives from consuming foods served cold or not heated to 158°F for at least 2 min. The Department of Agriculture recommends that people at risk for infection should not eat hot dogs, lunch meats, dried sausage, raw milk, and soft cheese (e.g., brie, blue cheese) or cheese made from raw milk. In pregnant women, Listeria infects the amniotic fluid and causes spontaneous abortion, stillbirth, or premature birth with lethal listeriosis; in immunosuppressed adults and neonates, it most commonly causes meningitis.

Person-to-person transmission is primarily in utero or during passage through an infected birth canal. Other modes of transmission include inhalation of contaminated dust; contact with infected animals, contaminated sewage, mud, or soil, or with feces containing the bacteria. Most often contact with *L. monocytogenes* results in a transient asymptomatic carrier state, but sometimes bacteremia and a generalized febrile illness is produced. Transplacental infections may cause abortion, premature delivery, stillbirth, or early neonatal death, though the pregnant woman herself may experience only mild illness.

TREATMENT: Ampicillin or penicillin G IV for 3 to 6 weeks is the treatment of choice, esp. since these drugs easily cross the blood-brain barrier to treat meningitis. Ampicillin plus ceftriaxone or cefotaxime or ampicillin plus an aminoglycoside also have proven effective against Listeria meningitis. Pregnant patients must be treated promptly and vigorously to manage fetal infection. If the patient is allergic to penicillin, then trimethoprim or sulfamethoxazole should be used. Dexamethasone may be given before antibiotic therapy to decrease cerebral edema.

PATIENT CARE: Public education is needed to inform pregnant women, older adults, people on immunosuppressive drug therapy, or those with HIV infection of the danger of ready-to-eat foods such as cold cuts and soft cheeses. Safe food handling techniques to minimize the risk of infection include washing hands well (at least 20 sec) when handling ready-to-eat cold foods, washing cutting boards and other utensils with hot soapy water before using them for another food, keeping uncooked foods separated from cooked foods, and washing all fruits and vegetables before eating, even those that come from a private garden.

Listing plane (lĭst′ing) [Johann Benedict Listing, Ger. physiologist, 1808–1882] A transverse vertical plane lying perpendicular to the anteroposterior axis of the eye and containing the center of motion of the eyes. It also contains the transverse and vertical axes of voluntary ocular rotation.

liter (lēt′ĕr) [Fr. *litre,* liter] ABBR: L, I. SI. SI (metric) fluid measure; equivalent to 1000 mL, 270 fl drams, 61 cu in, 33.8 fl oz, or 1.0567 qt. It is the volume occupied by 1 kg of water at 4°C and 760 mm Hg pressure. SEE: *metric system.*

NOTE: It is common to define a liter as 1000 cubic centimeters (cc). This is not quite correct because 1 milliliter (mL) equals 1.000028 cc. Thus, liquid volume should be expressed in milliliters (mL) rather than in cubic centimeters (cc).

literate (lit′ĕ-rāt) [L. *litteratus,* marked with letters] Being able to read and write, and to use written language as in understanding graphs, charts, tables, maps, symbols, and formulas. **literacy** (-ră-sē), *n.*

lithemia (lith-ē′mē-ă) [*litho-* + *-emia*] An outdated term for hyperuricemia.

lithiasis (lĭth-ī′ă-sĭs) Stone formation.

lithium (lĭth′ē-ŭm) [*litho-* + *-ium* (1)] SYMB: Li. A chemical element, atomic weight (mass) 6.941, atomic number 3.

l. carbonate Li_2CO_3, a crystalline salt used to treat bipolar disorder. Given orally, it is readily absorbed and eliminated at a fast rate for 5 to 6 hr and much more slowly over the next 24 hr. SEE: *bipolar disorder.*

The dose is adjusted as needed to produce a plasma level of 0.8 mEq/L. When the dose has been found to produce the optimal plasma concentration, blood analysis is done every 3 months unless symptoms suggestive of toxicity are present. Plasma levels of 2 mEq/L or more cause serious toxic effects, e.g., stupor or coma, muscular rigidity, marked tremor, and, in some cases, epileptic seizure.

Side effects include fatigue, weakness, fine tremor of the hands, nausea and vomiting, thirst, dry mouth, and polyuria and may be noticed in the first week of therapy. Most Side effects will disappear, but the thirst, polyuria, and tremor tend to persist. Dry mouth may be severe enough to promote dental decay.

⚠️ Decreased dietary sodium intake lowers the excretion rate of lithium. It should not be administered to patients following a salt-free diet. The risk of toxicity is very high in patients with significant renal or cardiovascular disease, severe debilitation, dehydration, sodium depletion, or in patients receiving diuretics or nonsteroidal anti-inflammatory drugs. It is essential to monitor the blood level of the drug in patients taking this therapy; samples should be taken 8 to 10

hr after the last dose and at intervals after medication.

litho-, lith- [Gr. *lithos,* stone] Prefixes meaning *stone* or *calculus.*

lithoclast (lĭth′ō-klăst) [″ + *klastos,* broken] Forceps for breaking up large stones.

lithogenesis (lĭth″ō-jĕn′ĕ-sĭs) [″ + *gennan,* to produce] Formation of calculi.

lithology (lĭth-ŏl′ō-jē) [″ + *logos,* word, reason] The science dealing with calculi.

litholysis (lĭth-ol′ĭ-sĭs) [*litho-* + *-lysis*] Dissolving of stones.

lithopedion (lĭth″ō-pē′dē-on″) [*litho-* + Gr. *paidion,* child] A rare condition in which a uterine or extrauterine fetus has died and become calcified. SYN: *ostembryon; osteopedion.*

lithotomy (lĭth-ot′ō-mē) [*litho-* + *-tomy*] The incision of a duct or organ, esp. of the bladder, for removal of a stone. SEE: *lithotomy **position**.*

PATIENT CARE: Noninvasive measures and prescribed analgesic agents are provided to relieve pain. Fluid balance is monitored, and, unless otherwise contraindicated by cardiac or renal status, fluid intake of 4 L/day is recommended to maintain a urine output of 3 to 4 L/day, which aids in the passage of small calculi (up to 5 mm in diameter) and prevents ascending infections. Supplemental IV fluids are provided if the patient is unable to tolerate the required volume by mouth. Vital signs and laboratory studies are monitored for signs of infection, and prescribed antibiotics are administered. The health care professional prepares the patient for lithotripsy or surgery, as indicated, by explaining postoperative equipment, care procedures, and expected sensations. Any incisions are assessed for drainage and healing; the character and amount of drainage are documented, usually via a ureteral catheter or nephrotomy tube (which should never be irrigated unless specifically prescribed). Using aseptic techniques, the health care professional protects surrounding skin from excoriation by redressing frequently. All urine is strained for evidence of stones, and any solid material is sent for analysis. Splinting the incision with a small pillow assists the patient to mobilize and to carry-out pulmonary hygiene. Based on laboratory analysis of the stone, treatments are prescribed to prevent recurrence.

high l. A lithotomy performed through a suprapubic incision.

lateral l. A lithotomy performed with the incision from the front of the rectum to one side of the raphe.

lithotripsy (lĭth′ō-trĭp″sē) [*litho-* + Gr. *tripsis,* rubbing] **1.** The use of sound waves to fragment or crush stones obstructing the bladder, gallbladder, ureter, or urinary bladder. **2.** The production of shock waves by use of an external energy source in order to crush renal stones. SYN: *lithotrity.*

extracorporeal shock-wave l. ABBR: ESWL. The fragmentation of kidney stones with an extracorporeal shock-wave lithotriptor. SEE: illus.

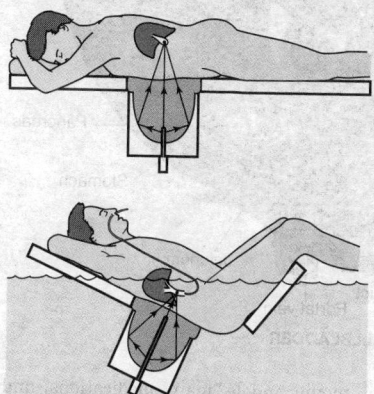

EXTRACORPOREAL SHOCK WAVE LITHOTRIPSY

Shock waves are transmitted through water to break up gallstones. A. Position for stones in gallbladder. Patient is lying on a fluid-filled bag; B. Position for stones in common bile duct. Patient is in a water bath.

lithotripter, lithotriptor (lith′ŏ-trip″tĕr) [*litho-* + Gr. *trip(sis)*, rubbing] A device for breaking up kidney stones. SYN: *lithotrite.*

electrohydraulic l. An intracorporeal lithotripter. It is a fluid-filled device that uses electrically generated shock waves next to stones to fragment them.

percutaneous ultrasonic l. A lithotripter that uses ultrasound to break up kidney stones and gallstones. The sound waves are applied to the outside of the body and penetrate to the calculi. SEE: *extracorporeal shock wave lithotripsy.*

lithotriptic (lith-ŏ-trip′tik) **1.** Pert. to lithotripsy. **2.** An agent that dissolves stones.

lithotrite (lith′ŏ-trīt″) [From *lithotrity*] Lithotripter.

lithotrity (lith-o′trĭ-tē) [*litho-* + L. *tritus*, rubbed] Lithotripsy.

litigation (lĭt″ĭ-gā′shŭn) [L. *litigatio*, dispute, lawsuit] A lawsuit or legal action that determines the legal rights and remedies of the person or party.

litmus (lit′mŭs) A blue dye made by treating coarsely powdered lichens, such as those of the genus *Roccella*, with ammonia.

litter (lĭt′tĕr) [O.Fr. *litiere*, offspring at birth, bed] **1.** A stretcher for carrying the wounded or the sick. **2.** The young produced at one birth by a multiparous mammal.

littritis (li-trīt′ĭs) [*Littré* + *-itis*] An inflammation of the urethral glands.

lived experience (līvd) The subjective perception of one's experience of health or illness. Associated with Rosemarie Parse's Nursing Theory of Human becoming, universal lived experiences are people's perceptions of their personal health-related experiences. SEE: *Nursing Theory Appendix.*

livedo (lĭv-ē′dō) [L. *livedo*, lividness] A mottled staining of the skin, often blue or purple, as may be seen in a bruise. SEE: *lividity.*

l. reticularis Semipermanent bluish mottling of the skin of the legs and hands. It is aggravated by exposure to cold.

liver (liv′ĕr) The largest solid organ in the body, situated on the right side below the diaphragm. The liver occupies the right hypochondrium, the epigastrium, and part of the left hypochondrium, and is level with the bottom of the sternum. Its undersurface is concave and covers the stomach, duodenum, hepatic flexure of colon, right kidney, and adrenal capsule. The liver secretes bile and is the site of numerous metabolic functions. SEE: illus.

ANATOMY: The liver has four lobes, five ligaments, and five fissures and is covered by a tough fibrous membrane, Glisson's capsule, which is thickest at the transverse fissure. At this point the capsule carries the blood vessels and hepatic duct, which enter the organ at the hilus. Strands of connective tissue originating from the capsule enter the liver parenchyma and form the supporting network of the organ and separate the functional units of the liver, the hepatic lobules.

The many intrahepatic bile ducts converge and anastomose, finally forming the secretory duct of the liver, the hepatic duct, which joins the cystic duct from the gallbladder to form the common bile duct or the ductus choledochus, which enters the duodenum at the papilla of Vater. A ring of smooth muscle at the terminal portion of the choledochus, the sphincter of Oddi, permits the passage of bile into the duodenum by relaxing. The bile leaving the liver enters the gallbladder, where it undergoes concentration principally through loss of water absorbed by the gallbladder mucosa. When bile is needed in the small intestine for digestive purposes, the gallbladder contracts and the sphincter relaxes, thus permitting escape of the viscid gallbladder bile. Ordinarily, the sphincter of Oddi is con-

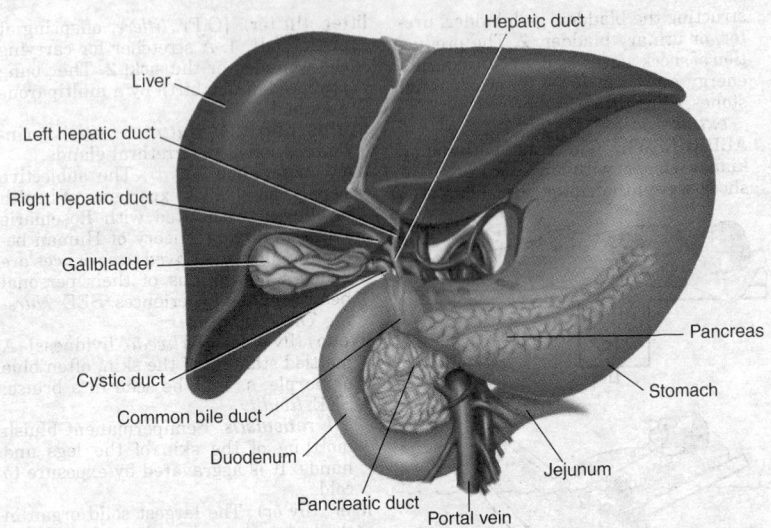

LIVER AND GALLBLADDER

Labels: Hepatic duct, Liver, Left hepatic duct, Right hepatic duct, Gallbladder, Cystic duct, Common bile duct, Duodenum, Pancreatic duct, Portal vein, Pancreas, Stomach, Jejunum

tracted, shutting off the duodenal entrance and forcing the bile to enter the gallbladder after leaving the liver.

The functional units of the liver are the liver lobules, six-sided aggregations of hepatocytes permeated by capillaries called sinusoids. Lining these sinusoids are Kupffer cells, the macrophages of the liver.

BLOOD SUPPLY: The blood supply consists of oxygenated blood from the hepatic artery, a branch of the celiac artery, and blood from all the digestive organs and spleen by way of the portal vein. The end products of digestion and other materials thus pass through the liver before entering general circulation.

NERVE SUPPLY: The nerve supply consists of parasympathetic fibers from the vagi and sympathetic fibers from the celiac plexus via the hepatic nerve.

FUNCTION: The liver is one of the most metabolically active organs of the body. *Amino acid metabolism:* It synthesizes nonessential amino acids, deaminates excess amino acids for use in energy production, and forms urea, which the kidneys excrete. *Bile production:* It is responsible for the production of bile salts, which emulsify fats in the small intestine; 800 to 1000 mL of bile is secreted in 24 hr, and the secretion rate is increased greatly during digestion of meals rich in fats. *Carbohydrate metabolism:* It converts monosaccharides other than glucose to glucose, and stores excess glucose as the starch glycogen, until such energy is needed. *Detoxification:* It produces enzymes to metabolize potentially harmful substances found in the portal circulation (e.g., alcohol, am-

monia, indole, many medications, and skatole) into less toxic ones. *Endocrine functions:* It facilitates the conversion of levothyroxine to the more metabolically active thyroid hormone, triiodothyronine. *Excretion:* It discharges the breakdown products of hemoglobin (bilirubin and biliverdin) into the bile; these are eliminated in feces. *Fat metabolism:* It synthesizes cholesterol as well as lipoproteins for the transport of fat to other body tissues; it converts fatty acids to acetyl groups or ketones, so they may be used as energy sources. *Phagocytosis:* Its macrophages (Kupffer cells) scavenge bacteria, other pathogens, and senescent red blood cells from the portal circulation. *Protein synthesis:* It manufactures albumin, alpha-globulins and beta-globulins, complement components, and clotting factors, some of which are dependent on vitamin K. *Storage:* It stores copper, iron, vitamin B_{12}, and the fat-soluble vitamins A, D, E, and K.

EXAMINATION: The liver is examined by inspection, auscultation, percussion, and palpation. Inspection of the organ includes indirect assessments (e.g., for jaundice [skin color], palmar erythema, and spider telangiectasias and other signs of chronic liver disease. Auscultation of the liver may reveal bruits associated with liver cancer; auscultation also is used to make a crude estimate of organ size. Percussion of the liver, which is performed in the right midclavicular line, provides another method for roughly estimating size. Palpation of the organ may reveal tenderness, irregular edges, masses, or tumors.

amyloid l. An enlargement of the liver caused by the deposition of amyloid proteins. SYN: *lardaceous l.*

SYMPTOMS: The liver is enlarged, smooth, firm, and painless. Infiltration of other organs may cause kidney failure, intercerebral bleeding, heart failure, anemia, and other diseases and conditions.

PROGNOSIS: The prognosis is unfavorable.

artificial l. A biomechanical device typically combining a system of filters to remove toxins from the blood with hepatic cells or tissue. It is designed to support patients with hepatic failure temporarily until a donor liver becomes available for transplantation.

fatty l. Degenerative changes in liver cells owing to fat deposits in hepatocytes. SYN: *steatohepatitis.*

nutmeg l. Chronic passive congestion of the liver, which produces a reddened central portal area and a yellowish periportal zone.

shock l. A colloquial term for injury to the liver resulting from insufficient blood flow, e.g., in patients who have suffered an episode of severe hypotension. A hallmark of this condition is a sudden and marked elevation in liver enzyme levels, such as alanine aminotransferase (ALT).

liver function, risk for impaired At risk for liver dysfunction. SEE: *Nursing Diagnoses Appendix.*

liver function test ABBR: LFT. A blood test for a specific aspect of liver metabolism. Because of the diversity of liver functions and the disorders that may affect those functions, no single test provides a reliable measure of overall liver function. The ability to excrete bile pigments is measured by determining the serum bilirubin level; the levels of serum enzymes such as the aminotransferases aspartate and alanine may be used to assess damage to the liver cells and biliary tract obstruction or dysfunction. Levels of the serum proteins albumin and globulin and their ratio are used to judge the synthetic functions of the liver. Certain blood clotting factors are also synthesized in the liver, and abnormalities may indicate impairments in hepatic synthesis. Blood ammonia levels are elevated in some patients with either acute or chronic liver disease; marked elevations may suggest acute or chronic liver failure. SEE: *liver.*

liver transplantation SEE: under *transplantation.*

livid (lĭv′ĭd) [L. *lividus,* lead-colored] **1.** Ashen, cyanotic. **2.** Discolored, black and blue.

lividity (liv-id′ĭt-ē) **1.** Skin discoloration, as from a bruise or venous congestion. SYN: *livor.* **2.** The state of being livid.

postmortem l. A dark blue staining

of the dependent surface of a cadaver, due to the pooling and congestion of blood. SEE: *livor mortis.*

living needs benefit Accelerated living benefit.

living will An advance directive, prepared when a person is still alive, competent, and able to make decisions, regarding his or her specific instructions about end-of-life care. Living wills allow people to specify whether they would want to be intubated, ventilated, treated with pressor drugs, shocked with electricity (to stop life-threatening heart rhythms), and fed or hydrated intravenously (if unable to take food or drink). SEE: *advance directive.*

livor (lī′vor″) [L. *livor,* a black-and-blue mark] Lividity (1).

l. mortis SYN: *Postmortem lividity.*

lixiviation (lik″siv″ē-ā′shŏn) [L. *lixivium,* lye] Leaching.

LLE *left lower extremity.*

LLETZ *large loop excision of the transformation zone.*

LLL *left lower lobe* of the lung.

LLQ *left lower quadrant* of abdomen.

LM *licensed midwife.*

LMA *left mentoanterior* fetal position. SEE: *presentation* for illus.

LMA *laryngeal mask airway.*

LMP *left mentoposterior* fetal position; *last menstrual period.* SEE: *presentation* for illus.

LMT *left mentotransverse* fetal position. SEE: *presentation* for illus.

LMWH *low molecular weight heparin.*

LOA *left occipitoanterior* fetal position. SEE: *presentation* for illus.

LOAD An acronym for *l(ate-)o(nset) A(lzheimer's) d(isease),* the most common form of the disease, usually diagnosed after age 65.

loading (lōd′ing) The rapid or repeated administration of a drug to quickly achieve a therapeutic level.

bicarbonate l. The ingestion of sodium bicarbonate to neutralize excessive lactic acid produced in the muscles during exercise or to treat acidosis in chronic renal failure.

carbohydrate l. Dietary increase of glycogen stored in muscle tissue. It is used by athletes before high-intensity endurance events such as a marathon. Phase I, to deplete glycogen from specific muscles, is begun 7 days before competition. The glycogen exhaustion is maintained by a high-fat, high-protein diet for 3 days. It is important to include 100 g of carbohydrate to prevent ketosis. Phase II consists of a high-carbohydrate diet of at least 1000 to 2000 kcal for 3 days. This, the supersaturation phase, enhances glycogen storage. Glycogen synthesis is facilitated by the extended period of depletion (phase I). The carbohydrates should be complex (as in grain-derived foods such as bread and pasta) rather than simple carbohydrates (as in candy and soft drinks). Phase III begins on the day of the event. Any type of food may be eaten up to 4 to 6 hr before competition. Food eaten from that time up to the time of competition is a matter of individual preference. SYN: *glycogen* **supercompensation**.

glycogen l. A dietary regimen used to fill the body's glycogen storage areas, i.e., the liver and muscles.

loading test The administration of a substance to determine the individual's ability to metabolize or excrete it. Thus, a glucose tolerance test is one form of this test.

Loa loa (lō′ă) The African eyeworm, a species of filarial worm that infests the subcutaneous tissues and conjunctiva of humans. Its migration causes itching and a creeping sensation. Sometimes it causes itchy edematous areas known as Calabar swellings. It is transmitted by flies of the genus *Chrysops*.

lobar (lō′băr) [Gr. *lobos*, lobe] Pert. to a lobe.

lobate (lō′bāt) [L. *lobatus*, lobed] **1.** Pert. to a lobe. **2.** Having a deeply undulated border. **3.** Producing lobes.

lobbying Attempting to shape legislation, influence legislators, or mold public opinion.

lobe (lōb) [Gr. *lobos*, lobe] **1.** A fairly well-defined part of an organ separated by boundaries, esp. glandular organs and the brain. **2.** A major part of a tooth formed by a separate calcification center.

anterior l. Adenohypophysis.

anterior l. of pituitary gland Adenohypophysis.

azygos l. An anomalous lobe at the apex of the right lobe of the lung.

central l. The island of Reil, which forms the floor of the lateral cerebral fossa.

cerebellar l. One of the three major divisions of the cerebellum. The anterior lobe or paleocerebellum is largely concerned with coordinating posture and with the muscle tone of the trunk and limbs. The posterior lobe or neocerebellum is in a loop with the cerebral cortex and is concerned with muscle coordination and cybernetic adjustment of movements. The flocculonodular lobe or archicerebellum is part of the vestibular system and is concerned with balance.

flocculonodular l. The lobe of the cerebellum consisting of the flocculi, nodulus, and their connecting peduncles.

frontal l. The anterior part of a cerebral hemisphere in front of the central fissure and above the lateral (Sylvian) fissure.

hepatic l. A lobe of the liver.

limbic l. The marginal section of a cerebral hemisphere on the medial aspect. SYN: *gyrus fornicatus*.

l. of lung One of the large divisions of the lungs: superior and inferior lobes of the left lung; superior, middle, and inferior lobes of the right lung.

occipital l. The posterior region of a cerebral hemisphere that is shaped like a three-sided pyramid.

olfactory l. The olfactory bulb and tract. SYN: *rhinencephalon*. SEE: *olfactory nerve* for illus.

orbital l. The convolutions above the orbit.

paracentral l. Paracentral **lobule**.

parietal l. The division of each cerebral hemisphere lying beneath each parietal bone.

posterior l. Neurohypophysis.

posterior l. of hypophysis Neurohypophysis.

posterior l. of pituitary gland Neurohypophysis.

prefrontal l. The frontal portion of the frontal lobe of the brain.

Riedel l. SEE: under *Riedel, Bernhard M. K. L.*

temporal l. The portion of the cerebral hemisphere lying below the lateral fissure of Sylvius. It is continuous posteriorly with the occipital lobe.

lobectomy (lō-bĕk′tō-mē) [Gr. *lobos*, lobe, + *ektome*, excision] The surgical removal of a lobe of any organ or gland.

lobelia Indian tobacco, also known colloquially as "puke weed." It is a perennial, flowering plant that is an expectorant and emetic. It has been used in complementary medicine as a treatment for asthma.

lobeline (lō′bĕ-lēn″) [*lobelia* + *-ine*] A nicotine receptor agonist.

lobi (lō′bī) Pl. of lobus.

lobo-, lobi-, lob- [L. *lobus*, husk, pod fr. Gr. *lobos*, lobe (of ear or liver)] Prefixes meaning *lobe*.

Lobo disease (lō′bō) [Jorge Lobo, 20th-cent. Brazilian physician] Lobomycosis.

lobomycosis (lō″bō-mī-kō′sĭs) [(*Lacazia*) *loboi* + *mycosis*] A fungal infection of the cutaneous and subcutaneous tissues in which nodules resembling keloids, plaques, or warts form on the skin, caused by *Lacazia loboi*. Treatment is surgical. SYN: *keloidal* **blastomycosis**; *Lobo disease*.

lobotomy (lō-bŏt′ō-mē) [Gr. *lobos*, lobe, + *tome*, incision] The incision of a lobe of the brain or the lung.

lobular (lŏb′ū-lăr) [L. *lobulus*, small lobe] Lobulate.

lobular capillary hemangioma SEE: under *hemangioma*.

lobulate, lobulated (lŏb′ū-lāt, -lāt-ĕd) **1.** Consisting of lobes or lobules. **2.** Pert.

to lobes or lobules. **3.** Resembling lobes. SYN: *lobular.*

lobule (lob′ūl″) [L. *lobulus,* small lobe] **1.** A physically defined subsection of an organ. **2.** A functionally defined subsection of an organ -- usually, an organ that is composed of many such functional units.

  breast l. The basic functional unit of the mammary gland, consisting of a tree of several intralobular ducts (also called alveolar ducts), each of which can develop a terminal alveolus composed of milk-secreting epithelial cells. Together, the breast lobules that empty into the same lactiferous duct form a breast lobe.

  ear l. Earlobe

  hepatic l. Liver **l.**

  liver l. A small subunit of the liver composed of cells (hepatocytes) that process blood from an incoming portal venule and send the resulting blood to an outgoing hepatic venule. There are two types of liver lobule, which look at the same cluster of liver cells from opposite ends. Focusing on the outflow of blood, the classical lobule is composed of those cords of hepatocytes that drain blood into an individual hepatic venule. Focusing on the inflow of blood, the portal lobule is defined to be those cords of hepatocytes that drain blood from an individual portal venule. SYN: *hepatic l.* SEE: illus.

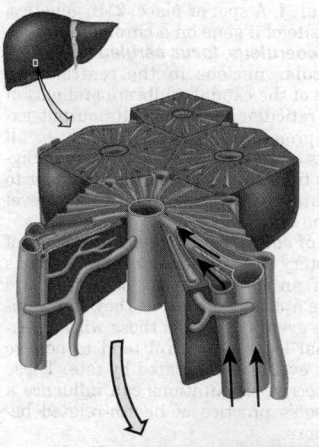

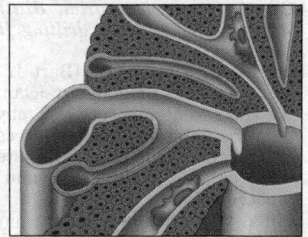

LIVER LOBULE

  paracentral l. A gyrus on the upper medial surface of each cerebral hemisphere, behind the medial frontal gyrus and above the cingulate gyrus. This lobule is the continuation, from the lateral brain surface, of the precentral (motor) and postcentral (sensory) gyri and contains cortical areas representing the lower leg, foot, toes, bladder, rectum, and genitalia. SYN: *paracentral **gyrus;** paracentral **lobe.***

  parietal l. Either the inferior or the superior parietal lobule.

  secondary pulmonary l. The smallest functionally complete unit in the lung. It is about 1 cm wide and 2 cm long, contains a few acini, and is connected to the bronchial tree by a small bronchiole. Each secondary pulmonary lobule is supplied by a pulmonary arteriole, pulmonary venule, and lymphatics and is separated from neighboring secondary pulmonary lobules by connective tissue septa.

  superior parietal l. The upper half of the posterior segment of the parietal lobe of the brain. SYN: *superior parietal **gyrus.***

lobus (lō′bŭs) *pl.* **lobi** [L.] Lobe.

LOC 1. *levels of consciousness.* **2.** *loss of consciousness.*

local (lō′kăl) [L. *locus,* place] Limited to one place or part.

local effect of a drug The impact of a therapeutic agent on specific tissues rather than on the whole body, esp. on those tissues where the agent is absorbed, metabolized, or most chemically active.

localization (lō″kă-lĭ-zā′shŏn) [*local*] **1.** Limitation to a definite area. **2.** Determination of the site of an infection. **3.** Relation of a sensation to its point of origin. **4.** Identification of a lesion in three-dimensional space, e.g., radiographically, or by reference to anatomical landmarks, skin tattoos, or hemoclips.

  cerebral l. Determination of centers of various faculties and functions in particular parts of the brain.

  tactile l. An individual's ability to accurately identify the site of tactile stimulation (touch, pressure, or pain). Tactile localization is often tested in sensory evaluations following disease or trauma of the nervous system.

  wire l. The insertion of a thin, radiographically guided metal wire into a small suspicious lesion to direct the surgeon to the lesion, making it easier for biopsy or removal.

localized (lō′kăl-īzd) Restricted to a limited region.

localized alveolar ridge augmentation Dental surgery done to repair defects in the jaw due to the extraction or loss of a tooth. A bone graft is placed into the socket formed at the base of the extracted tooth. Alternatives to a bone graft include a soft-tissue graft or bone substitutes. The surrounding gum is sutured in place to cover the graft. The grafted bone can repair aesthetic defects or be used as a foundation for dental implants. Results generally include an increase in the width and/or height of the alveolar ridge. SYN: *ridge augmentation.*

localizer (lō′kăl-ī″zĕr) An apparatus used for finding foreign bodies or exact anatomical locations during radiography.

locally advanced Large or bulky; said of a malignant tumor that has grown substantially at its site of origin.

locally advanced breast cancer SEE: under *breast cancer.*

local radiation injury SEE: under *injury.*

local reaction A reaction occurring at the point of stimulation or injection of foreign substances.

local recurrence The reappearance of a cancer after treatment at the site at which it was originally detected.

locator (lō′kā-tĕr) A device for locating or discovering an object such as a foreign body.

locavore (lō′kă-vor″) [*loca(l)* + L. *vorare,* to devour] One who eats foods grown and/or produced within approximately a 100-mile radius of his or her home.

lochia (lō′kē-ă) [Gr. *lochia,* childbirth] The puerperal discharge of blood, mucus, and tissue from the uterus. The character of the discharge progresses through three stages in the normal autolytic healing process. or **lochial** (-ăl), *adj.*

loci [L.] Pl. of locus.

locked-in state A paralytic condition, superficially resembling coma, in which a person has no voluntary control over somatic muscles but nonetheless remains awake and alert. The locked-in state is usually the result of a lesion of the brainstem, esp. the pons. Because in some patients eye blinking is preserved, communication with locked-in patients is occasionally possible. SEE: *akinetic mutism.*

Locke solution, Locke-Ringer solution (lok, lok′ring′ĕr) [Frank S. Locke, Brit. physician, 1871–1949; Sydney Ringer, Brit. physiologist, 1835–1910] A solution used in experiments in physiology. It is a buffered isotonic solution containing 9.0 g sodium chloride, 0.42 g potassium chloride, 0.24 g calcium chloride, 0.5 g sodium bicarbonate, 0.2 g magnesium chloride, 0.5 g dextrose, and distilled water to make 1000 mL.

lock-in (lok′in″) **1.** In a health care insurance plan, a provision that requires that the insured party receive all health care services from providers who partic-

ipate in the plan. **2.** In biomedical engineering, a forcing function that requires that certain actions be undertaken in a specified sequence to avoid mishaps or errors.

lockjaw (lŏk′jăw) Tonic spasm of muscles of jaw. SEE: *tetanus; trismus.*

lock-out (lok′owt″) In biomedical engineering and computer science, a forcing function that limits access to computer software, medications, or supplies unless the user performs a required sequence of actions, such as entering a unique access code.

locomotion (lō″kŏ-mō′shŭn) [L. *locus,* place, + *movere,* to move] Movement or the capacity to move from one place to another.

locomotor (lō″kō-mō′tor) Pert. to locomotion.

locoweed (lō′kō-wēd) A poisonous plant from the bean family that causes behavioral, visual, and gait disturbances, usually in cattle.

locular (lŏk′ū-lăr) [L. *loculus,* a small space] Loculated.

loculated (lŏk′ū-lāt-ĕd) Containing or divided into loculi.

loculus (lŏk′ū-lŭs) *pl.* **loculi** [L.] A small space or cavity.

locum tenens (lō′kŭm tē′nenz″, -nĕnz) [L. *locum tenens,* holding the place (of), lieutenant] A physician who temporarily substitutes for another.

locus (lō′kŭs, lō′sī″) *pl.* **loci** [L. *locus,* a place] **1.** A spot or place. **2.** In genetics, the site of a gene on a chromosome.

l. coeruleus, locus ceruleus A bluish reticular nucleus in the central gray area of the caudal midbrain and part of the reticular formation. Its output axons project widely and diffusely to all parts of the central nervous system. Signals from the locus coeruleus appear to enhance the overall attentiveness level of the brain.

l. of control An individual's sense of mastery or control over events. Persons with an internal locus of control are more apt to believe that they can influence events, whereas those with an external locus of control tend to believe that events are dictated by fate. These respective orientations can influence a person's practice of health-related behaviors.

LOD *laparoscopic ovarian **diathermy;** laparoscopic ovarian drilling **limit** of detection.*

Loeys-Dietz syndrome [Bart L. Loeys, contemporary Belgian physician; Harry C. Dietz, contemporary U.S. physician] A rare autosomal dominant cause of aortic aneurysm, often associated with cleft palate, a split uvula, and widely spaced eyes.

Löffler endocarditis (lef′lĕr) [Wilhelm Löffler, Swiss physician, 1887–1972] Endocarditis associated with hypereosinophilia and fibroplastic thickening of the endocardium. SYN: *eosinophilic cardiomyopathy.*

log A continuously kept record of important events, such as medical records or progress notes.

-log, -logue [Gr. *logos*, word, reason] Prefixes meaning *words* or *speech.*

log book A diary; a register of important names, places, dates, or other practical and useful information.

logorrhea (lŏg″ō-rē′ă) [″ + *rhoia*, flow] Repetitious, continuous and excessive speech. It may be a symptom of mania or some forms of intoxication.

log phase (log) [Fr. *log(arithm)*] SEE: under *phase.*

log roll An assessment maneuver in which the hip joint is internally and externally rotated while the patient is lying on his or her back with the lower extremity extended. Pain during the maneuver is indicative of joint disease in the hip.

-logy [Gr. *logos*, word, reason] Suffix meaning *science* or *study of.*

loiasis, loaiasis (lō-ī′ă-sĭs, lō″ă-ī′sĭs) [*Loa loa* + *-iasis*] Infection with the African eyeworm, *Loa loa.*

loin (loyn) [Fr. *loigne*, ult fr L. *lumbus*, the loins, genitals] The lower part of the back and sides between the ribs and pelvis; the lumbus.

loneliness The anxious, depressed, or dysphoric mood that occurs as a result of physical or psychic isolation.

   risk for l. The risk for experiencing discomfort associated with a desire or need for more contact with others. SEE: *Nursing Diagnoses Appendix.*

long-acting thyroid stimulator ABBR: LATS. An IgG autoantibody that binds to the thyroid-stimulating hormonereceptor, stimulating the excessive production of thyroid hormones and causing hyperthyroidism. This immunoglobulin is found in the blood of about 75% of patients with Graves' disease but is used rarely for diagnostic purposes, because the diagnosis usually can be established on clinical grounds, i.e., on finding a patient with hyperthyroidism with a diffuse, nontender goiter, exophthalmos, and/or pretibial myxedema.

longevity (lŏn-jĕv′ĭ-tē) [L. *longaevus*, aged] Long duration of life.

longevity extension Life extension.

longing A persistent desire or craving for something, usually that which is remote or unattainable.

longissimus (lŏn-jĭs′ĭ-mŭs) [L.] An anatomical term indicating a long structure.

longitudinal (lŏn″jĭ-tood′ĭ-năl, ĭ-tū′) [L. *longitudo*, length] **1.** Parallel to the long axis of the body or part. **2.** Continuing or lasting for some time. A longitudinal study follows its subjects from month to month or year to year

longitudinal arch SEE: under *arch.*

long-lever adjustment SEE: under *adjustment.*

long slow distance workout An exercise program in which a low level of exertion is maintained for a long period of time, e.g., more than an hour, without resting.

long-term care facility ABBR: LTCF. An institution such as a nursing home that is capable of providing continuous care for older or chronically ill persons.

longus (lŏng′gŭs) [L.] An anatomical term indicating a long structure.

lookback A colloquial term for retrospective research, that is, for any investigation that attempts to review the underlying causes of an event.

loop (loop) A curve or bend in a cord or cordlike structure, forming roughly an oval.

   capillary l. Minute blood vessels in the papillae of the dermis.

   cervical l. The part of an enamel organ in which the inner enamel epithelium is continuous with the outer enamel epithelium. This establishes the limit of enamel formation and therefore represents the site of the cementoenamel junction. The cells of the cervical loop become Hertwig's epithelial root sheath, induce dentinogenesis, and determine the number, size, and shape of the tooth roots.

   closed l. **1.** A biological system in which a substance produced affects the output of the substance by a feedback mechanism. **2.** In the learning of motor skills, the process of using sensory feedback to modify fine motor control or skilled movements.

   flow-volume l. A graphic record of lung function in which the amount of gas inhaled and exhaled is recorded on the horizontal axis and the rate at which the gas moves on the vertical axis. It is used to detect abnormalities in pulmonary function such as those accompanying restrictive or obstructive lung disease.

   Henle l. SEE: under *Henle, Friedrich G.J.*

   Lippes l. SEE: *Lippes loop.*

loop diuretic SEE: under *diuretic.*

loop electrosurgical excision procedure ABBR: LEEP. A technique for resecting abnormal tissue of the cervix. Colposcopic examination or Pap smear may indicate tissue abnormality. An electrical current is passed through a thin wire loop, heating it so that acts as a scalpel, removing a thin layer of tissue suitable for a biopsy. Formerly known as loop electrode excision procedure. SYN: *large loop excision of the transformation zone.*

loop recorder A portable heart rhythm monitor worn by a patient to determine the cause of palpitations or loss of consciousness. The monitor attaches to the skin of the chest with monitoring electrodes. When a patient experiences symptoms, he or she presses a button on the monitor to record a rhythm strip for analysis. SYN: *event monitor*.

loose body SEE: under *body*.

loosening (loos′ĭn-ĭng) **1.** Loss of linkage with or fixation to another structure. **2.** In speech, loss of connection to the usual rules of grammar, diction, or reason.

loosening of association A sign of disordered thought processes in which the person speaks with frequent changes of subject and the content is only obliquely related, if at all, to the subject matter. This may be seen in mania or schizophrenia.

LOP *left occipitoposterior* fetal position. SEE: *presentation* for illus.

lophotrichous (lŏ-fo′trĭ-kŭs) [Gr. *lophos,* crest + *tricho-*] Having collections of flagella at one end.

LOQ *limit of quantitation*.

loratadine (lor-ăh′tă-dēn) A piperidine administered orally to relieve nasal and non-nasal symptoms of seasonal allergies and to manage chronic idiopathic urticaria. Its therapeutic class is antihistamines.

lorazepam (lō-rā′zĕ-pam) A relatively short-acting benzodiazepine used to treat anxiety, insomnia, seizures, and alcohol withdrawal.

lordoscoliosis (lor″dŏ-skō″lē-ō′sĭs) [Gr. *lordos,* bent back + *scoliosis*] Forward curvature of the spine complicated by lateral curvature.

lordosis (lor-dō′sĭs) [Gr *lordōsis,* a bending backward.] Anterior convexity of the lumbar spine.

lordotic (-dot′ik), *adj*.

Lorenzo oil (lō-ren′zō) [Lorenzo Odone, U.S. citizen diagnosed with adrenoleukodystrophy in 1984, 1979–2008] A mixture of two fats (glyceryl-trioleate and glyceryl-trierucate) used to treat neurological disorders, including adrenoleukodystrophy. The Myelin Project is an international scientific research organization dedicated to research on myelin repair and the regeneration of the myelin sheath. Its website is: http://www.myelin.org/LorenzosOil/

losartan (lō-săr′tăn) An antihypertensive and angiotensin II receptor antagonist, administered orally to manage hypertension. SYN: *Cozaar*.

loss (los) **1.** The basis of claim on the part of a party to a lawsuit or an insurance carrier. In litigation, loss may be expressed in monetary terms. **2.** Destruction, degeneration, or the wasting of cells, tissues, organs, or capabilities.

    bone l. Osteoporosis.

    central vision l. Loss of the ability to see things directly in front of the eye, often occurring in patients with macular degeneration. The macula of the retina contains the greatest concentration of cone photoreceptors in the eye and is the location on the retina where vision is sharpest and colors are perceived with greatest clarity. When diseases like macular degeneration disturb the integrity of the macula, central vision loss occurs. A sudden loss of central vision is an ophthalmological emergency, requiring referral to a retinal specialist as soon as possible.

    conductive hearing l. Hearing loss due to any condition that prevents sound waves from being transmitted to the auditory receptors. It may result from wax obstructing the external auditory meatus, inflammation of the middle ear, ankylosis of the ear bones, or fixation of the footplate of the stirrup. SYN: *conduction* **deafness**. SEE: *otosclerosis; Rinne test; Weber test*.

    l. of consciousness Syncope.

    functional visual l. A reduction in vision with no identifiable lesion of the visual pathways. It may be caused by an occult disease of the eye or of the optical centers in the brain. It may also occur in certain psychiatric disorders.

    hearing l. A decreased ability to perceive sounds as compared with what the individual or examiner would regard as normal. In the U.S., about 1 million school-age children and 25 million adults have some degree of hearing loss. SEE: *audiogram; audiometry*.

    insensible fluid l. Insensible **l.**

    insensible l. A loss of body fluid that is not easily measured, e.g., the moisture released in exhalation and perspiration. The amount of fluid typically lost is about 200 mL a day. Insensible fluid losses increase in any disease or condition that increases diffusion of liquid from the skin or the lungs, e.g., in burns, climatic changes, fever, or heavy exercise. SYN: *insensible fluid l.*

    noise-induced hearing l. Hearing loss from exposure to very loud sounds (over 85 dB). The loss is usually most profound at a frequency of 4000 Hz. Common causes include working with noisy machinery, listening to loud music, or discharging rifles, guns, or explosives. Wearing ear plugs or earmuffs may be preventive.

    peripheral vision l. Tunnel **vision** (1).

    pregnancy l. Miscarriage or stillbirth.

    recurrent pregnancy l. ABBR: RPL. Three or more consecutive miscarriages that occur before the 20th week of gestation.

    sensible l. A measurable loss of body fluid, e.g., blood, diarrhea, urine, vomit. If sensible losses consistently exceed fluid intake, dehydration may result.

sensorineural hearing l. Hearing loss from permanent or temporary damage to the sensory cells or nerve fibers of the inner ear.

sudden hearing l. Hearing loss that occurs in 72 hr or less. It may be temporary or permanent. Some of the most common causes include cerumen impaction, medication toxicities, acute infections, ear trauma, Ménière's disease, and ischemia.

vitamin l. Loss of vitamin content in food products from oxidation or heating. Methods of preserving foods such as pickling, salting, curing, fermenting, and canning enhance vitamin loss. Vitamin C is esp. labile; up to 85% is lost in commercial canning and pasteurization. Vitamin B_1 in wheat is lost through milling because the vitamin B_1 wheat embryo is removed.

weight w. A measurable decline in body weight (BW) either intentionally or from malnutrition or illness. It is considered mild when 5% of BW is lost, moderate when 5-10% of BW is lost, and high when more than 10% of BW is lost. PATIENT CARE: Intentional weight loss achieved through dieting and/or exercise has significant health benefits for the overweight or obese. It reduces the risk of many common illnesses, including coronary artery disease, type 2 diabetes mellitus, hyperlipidemia, and hypertension. Unintentional weight loss, esp. of more than 10% of BW may be a marker of serious disease, such as AIDS, cancer, depression, hyperthyroidism, parasitosis, peptic ulceration, or food insecurity (starvation due to an inadequate food supply).

loss aversion In psychology and economics, the principle that individuals are more likely to make decisions that minimize their losses than maximize their gains, i.e., that a loss is more uncomfortable than an equal-sized gain is pleasurable.

loss of consciousness SEE: under *loss*.

lost time SEE: under *time*.

lost to follow-up In clinical medicine and research, a person who has not returned for continued care or evaluation (e.g., because of death, disability, relocation, or drop-out).

LOT *left occipitotransverse* fetal position. SEE: *presentation* for illus.

Lotensin SEE: *benazepril*.

lotion (lō'shŭn) [L. *lotio*] A liquid medicinal preparation for local application to, or bathing of, a part.

lot number SEE: under *number*.

LOTR *Licensed Occupational Therapist.*

loudness The perceived intensity of sound. It often reflects the amplitude and frequency of a sonic stimulus, but because it varies from person to person, it is a subjective, rather than a purely measurable entity. SEE: *decibel*.

Lou Gehrig disease Motor neuron disease.

Louis-Bar syndrome (loo-ē-bar') [Denise Louis-Bar, 20th-cent. Belgian neuropathologist] Ataxia-telangiectasia.

loupe (loop) [Fr.] A magnifying lens used in the form of a monocular or binocular lens. Surgeons, dentists, jewelers, and watchmakers frequently use this device.

louse (lows) Pediculus.

body l. *Pediculus humanus corporis.*

crab l. *Phthirus inguinalis* and *Phthirus pubis;* the louse that infests the pubic region and other hairy areas of the body. SEE: *pediculosis*.

head l. *Pediculus humanus capitis.* SEE: illus.

LOUSE

SOURCE: Centers for Disease Control and Prevention; James Gathany

love 1. Profound concern and affection for another person. **2.** In psychoanalysis, love may be equated with pleasure, particularly as it applies to the gratifying sexual experiences between individuals.

low birth weight SEE: under *weight*.

lower gastrointestinal tract SEE: under *tract*.

low intensity laser therapy Any of several lasers that cause photochemical changes in body tissues without producing thermal changes.

low level laser therapy The use of low-intensity laser light, typically in the near-infrared region of the electromagnetic spectrum, to stimulate body tissues, relieve inflammation and pain, improve wound healing, or regenerate damaged cells. SYN: *cold laser therapy; photo-biomodulation*.

low-level radiation SEE: *low-level radiation*.

lox (lŏks) *liquid oxygen*.

Loxosceles (lŏks-ŏs′sĕ-lēz) A genus of spiders, family Loxoscelidae, which includes the brown recluse spider.

loxoscelism (lŏk-sŏs′sĕ-lĭzm) The disease produced by the bite of the brown recluse spider, *Loxosceles laeta* or *L. reclusa*. Symptoms include a painful red vesicle that eventually becomes necrotic, leaving a skin ulcer. Rarely, the spider bite may produce hemolytic anemia or renal failure.

lozenge (lŏz′ĕnj) A small, dry, medicinal solid to be held in the mouth until it dissolves. SYN: *troche*.

LP *lumbar* **puncture**.

Lp(a) *lipoprotein (a)*.

L-phase variants L-forms.

LPO *left posterior oblique* position.

Lr Symbol for the element lawrencium.

LRF *luteinizing hormone releasing factor*.

LSA *left sacroanterior* fetal position. SEE: *presentation* for illus.

LScA *left scapuloanterior* fetal position. SEE: *presentation* for illus.

LScP *left scapuloposterior* fetal position. SEE: *presentation* for illus.

LSD *lysergic acid diethylamide*.

LSI *life satisfaction index*.

LSP *left sacroposterior* fetal position.

L/S ratio *lecithin / sphingomyelin ratio*.

LST *left sacrotransverse* fetal position.

LTBI *latent tuberculosis infection*. Active tuberculosis may emerge in patients who have latent (inactive) infections when their immune systems fail, either because of malnutrition, or because they contract other diseases. The eradication of latent tuberculosis infection is a worldwide public health goal.

LTC *long-term* **care**.

LTCF *long-term care facility*.

LTH *luteotropic* **hormone**

Lu Symbol for the element lutetium.

lubb-dupp, lub-dup, lub-dub (lŭb′dŭp″, dŭb″) The two sounds heard in auscultation of the heart technically referred to as S₁ ("lubb") and S₂ ("dupp"). The pause following the sounds is slightly longer than that between the two sounds. SEE: *auscultation*.

lubricant (loo′brĭ-kănt) [L. *lubricans*] An agent, usually a liquid oil, that reduces friction between parts that brush against each other as they move. Joints are lubricated by synovial fluid.

lucent (loo′sĕnt) [L. *lucere*, to shine] Shining, translucent, clear.

lucid (loo′sĭd) [L. *lucidus*, clear] Clear, esp. applied to clarity of the mind.

lucid dream SEE: under *dream*.

lucidity (lū-sĭd′ĭ-tē) The quality of clearness or brightness, esp. with regard to mental conditions.

luciferase (loo-sĭf′ĕr-ās) An enzyme that acts on luciferins to oxidize them and cause bioluminescence. It is present in certain organisms (e.g., fireflies, other insects) that emit light either continuously or intermittently.

luciferin (loo-sĭf′ĕr-ĭn) The general term for substances present in some organisms, which become luminescent when acted on by luciferase.

Lucilia sericata (loo-sil′ē-ă ser-ĭ-kāt′ă) SEE: *sheep* **blowfly**.

Ludwig angina (lood′vig) [Wilhelm F. von Ludwig, Ger. surgeon, 1790–1865] A suppurative inflammation of subcutaneous connective tissue adjacent to a submaxillary gland.

LUE *left upper extremity*.

lues (lū′ēz) [L.] Syphilis.

luetic (lū-ĕt′ĭk) Syphilitic.

Lugol solution (lu-gol′) [Jean G. A. Lugol, Fr. physician, 1786–1851] An antiseptic disinfectant iodine solution occasionally used to treat iodine deficiency.

LUL *left upper lobe* of the lung.

lumbago (lŭm-bā′gō) [L. *lumbus*, loin] A general, nonspecific term for dull, aching pain in the lumbar region of the back. SYN: *lumbodynia*.

lumbar (lŭm′băr, bar″) [L. *lumbus*, loin] Pert. to the loins (the part of the back between the thorax and pelvis).

lumbarization (lŭm″băr-ĭ-zā′shŏn) Nonfusion of the first sacral vertebra with the sacrum, therefore functioning as an additional (sixth) lumbar vertebra.

lumbo-, lumb- [L. *lumbus*, loin] Prefixes meaning *loins*.

lumbosacral (lŭm″bō-sā′krăl) Pert. to the lumbar vertebrae and the sacrum.

lumbrical (lŭm′brĭ-kăl) [L. *lumbricus*, earthworm] Vermiform.

lumbricalis (lŭm″brĭ-kăl′ĭs) One of the worm-shaped muscles of the hand or foot.

lumbricide (lŭm′brĭ-sīd) [″ + *caedere*, to kill] An agent that kills lumbricoid worms, i.e., ascarides or intestinal worms.

Lumbricus (lŭm′brĭ-kŭs) [L. *lumbricus*, (intestinal) worm] A genus of worms that includes earthworms.

lumbus (lŭm′bŭs) [L. *lumbus*, the loins, genitals] SEE: *loin*.

lumen (lū′mĕn) *pl.* **lumina** [L., light] **1.** The space within an artery, vein, intestine, or tube. **2.** A unit of light, the amount of light emitted in a unit solid angle by a uniform point source of one international candle. SEE: *light unit; candela*.

luminal (lū′mĭ-năl) Relating to the lumen of a tubular structure, such as a blood vessel.

luminescence (loo″mĭ-nes′ĕns) [L. *lumen*, a light] **1.** Production of light without production of heat. It includes both fluorescence and phosphorescence.

SEE: *bioluminescence*. **2.** In radiology, the light produced by a fluorescent phosphor when exposed to radiation. Phosphorescence produces light for a much longer period of time than fluorescence does and is undesirable in radiologic applications.

luminiferous (loo″mĭ-nĭf′ĕr-ŭs) [L. *lumen*, light, + *ferre*, to bear] Producing or conveying light.

luminometer (loo-mĭn-ŏm′ĕ-tĕr) A luminescence photometer used to assay chemiluminescent and bioluminescent reactions. It is used clinically to assay for bacteria and living cells.

luminophore (loo′mĭ-nō-for″) [″ + Gr. *phoros*, bearing] A chemical present in organic compounds that permits luminescence of those compounds.

luminous (loo′mĭ-nŭs) Emitting light.

lumirhodopsin (loo″mi-rō-dop′sĭn) [*lumen* + *rhodopsin*] A chemical in the retina of the eye, intermediate between rhodopsin and all-*trans*-retinal plus opsin, formed during the bleaching of rhodopsin by exposure to light.

lumpectomy (lŭm-pek′tŏ-mē) [*lump* + *-ectomy*] Surgical removal of a tumor and the immediately adjacent tissue from the breast. If cancer is identified in the lump or in neighboring lymph nodes, adjunctive therapies may be recommended, e.g., chemotherapy or radiation therapy.

lunar (loon′ĕr) Pert. to the moon, a month, or silver.

lunate (loo-nāt) **1.** Moon-shaped or crescent. **2.** A bone in the proximal row of the carpus. SYN: *semilunar bone*.

lung (lŭng) Either of two cone-shaped spongy organs of respiration contained within the pleural cavity of the thorax. SEE: illus.; *alveolus* for illus.

ANATOMY: The lungs are connected with the pharynx through the trachea and larynx. The base of each lung rests on the diaphragm, and each lung apex rises from 2.5 to 5 cm above the sternal end of the first rib, the collarbone, supported by its attachment to the hilum or root structures. The lungs include the lobes, lobules, bronchi, bronchioles, alveoli or air sacs, and pleural covering.

The right lung has three lobes and the left two. In men, the right lung weighs approx. 625 g, the left 570 g. The lungs contain 300,000,000 alveoli and their respiratory surface is about 70 sq m. Respirations per minute are 12 to 20 in an adult. The total capacity of the lung varies from 3.6 to 9.4 L in men and 2.5 to 6.9 L in women.

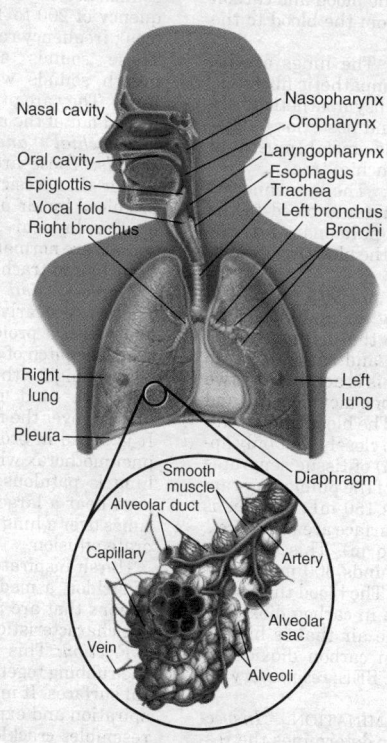

Nasal cavity
Oral cavity
Epiglottis
Vocal fold
Right bronchus
Nasopharynx
Oropharynx
Laryngopharynx
Esophagus
Trachea
Left bronchus
Bronchi
Right lung
Left lung
Pleura
Diaphragm
Smooth muscle
Alveolar duct
Capillary
Artery
Vein
Alveolar sac
Alveoli

LUNGS

The left lung has an indentation, called the cardiac depression, for the normal placement of the heart. Behind this is the hilum, through which the blood vessels, lymphatics, and bronchi enter and leave the lung.

Air travels from the nasal passages to the pharynx, larynx, and trachea. Two primary bronchi, one on each side, extend from the trachea. The primary bronchi divide into secondary bronchi, one for each of five lobes. These further divide into a great number of smaller bronchioles. The pattern of distribution of these into the segments of each lobe is important in pulmonary and thoracic surgery. There are about 10 bronchopulmonary segments in the right lung and eight in the left, the actual number varying. There are 50 to 80 terminal bronchioles in each lobe. Each of these divides into two respiratory bronchioles, which in turn divide to form two to 11 alveolar ducts. The alveolar sacs and alveoli arise from these ducts. The spaces between the alveolar sacs and alveoli are called atria.

In the alveolus, blood and inspired air are separated only by the cell of the alveolus and that of the pulmonary capillary. This respiratory membrane is thin (0.07 to 2.0 μm) and permits oxygen to diffuse into the blood and carbon dioxide to diffuse from the blood to the air.

NERVE SUPPLY: The lungs are innervated by parasympathetic fibers via the vagus nerve and sympathetic fibers from the anterior and posterior pulmonary plexuses to the smooth muscle in the walls of the bronchial tree.

BLOOD VESSELS: The bronchial arteries and veins circulate blood to the bronchial tree. The pulmonary arteries and veins circulate the blood involved in gas exchange.

FUNCTION: The primary purpose of the lung is to bring air and blood into intimate contact so that oxygen can be added to the blood and carbon dioxide removed from it. This is achieved by two pumping systems, one moving a gas and the other a liquid. The blood and air are brought together so closely that only approx. 1 μm (10^{-6} m) of tissue separates them. The volume of the pulmonary capillary circulation is 150 mL, but this is spread out over a surface area of approx. 750 sq ft (69.68 sq m). This capillary surface area surrounds 300 million air sacs called alveoli. The blood that is low in oxygen but high in carbon dioxide is in contact with the air that is high in oxygen and low in carbon dioxide for less than 1 second. SEE: *respiratory defense mechanism.*

PHYSICAL EXAMINATION: *Inspection:* The examiner determines the respiratory rate by unobtrusively watching the patient's chest rise and fall and counting the number of breaths per minute. In adults a normal respiratory rate at rest is about 12 breaths per minute. While counting the respiratory rate, the examiner can observe other breathing characteristics. Dyspneic patients breathe rapidly, often laboring to draw breath even when at rest. Retractions of the intercostal and supraclavicular spaces are visible during inspiration. Sleep apnea is characterized by episodes of stalled breathing followed by periods of respiratory compensation. Regular slow breathing is normal.

Palpation: In health, the chest and lung transmit a vibration, called fremitus, during speech. Fremitus abnormalities may be felt in chronic obstructive lung diseases or obesity, in which the vibration is diminished, and in pneumonia, in which it is increased over the infected lobe.

Percussion: Tapping on the chest wall over healthy lung results in a hollow resonant sound. The hollow character of the resonance sometimes is exaggerated in emphysematous lungs or in pneumothorax, and muffled by pleural effusions or pulmonary consolidation.

AUSCULTATION: *Normal breath sounds:* In the healthy person, breath sounds are low-pitched and have a frequency of 200 to 400 cycles per second (cps); frequency rarely exceeds 500 cps. These sounds are called vesicular breath sounds when heard over the lungs. They are produced by air passing in and out of the airways.

Bronchial and tracheal breath sounds: These are higher-pitched and louder than vesicular sounds, and are produced by air passing over the walls of the bronchi and trachea. These sounds are normally heard only over the bronchi and trachea.

Amphoric and cavernous breathing: These two nearly identical sounds are loud, with a prolonged, hollow expiration. The pitch of amphoric breathing is slightly higher than that of the cavernous type, and may be imitated by blowing over the mouth of an empty jar. It is heard in bronchiectatic cavities or pneumothorax when the opening to the lung is patulous; in the consolidation area near a large bronchus; and sometimes over a lung compressed by a moderate effusion.

Harsh inspiratory sounds are typical of stridor, a medical emergency. Expirations that are prolonged and musical are characteristic of wheezing.

Friction: This sound is produced by the rubbing together of roughened pleural surfaces. It may be heard in both inspiration and expiration. Friction often resembles crackle, but is more superficial and localized than the latter and is not modified by cough or deep inspiration.

Metallic tinkling: A silvery bell-like sound heard at intervals over a hydropneumothorax or large cavity. Speaking, coughing, and deep breathing usually induce this sound. It must not be confused with a similar sound produced by liquids in the stomach.

Crackles: Abnormal bubbling sounds heard in air cells or bronchi.

Succussion-splash or hippocratic succussion: A splashing sound produced by the presence of air and liquid in the chest. It may be elicited by gently shaking the patient during auscultation. This sound nearly always indicates either a hydropneumothorax or a pyopneumothorax, although it has also been detected over very large cavities. The presence of air and liquid in the stomach produces similar sounds.

black l. Lay term for a form of pneumoconiosis in which carbon and silica deposits accumulate in the lungs due to coal dust inhalation SYN: *anthracosilicosis; coal worker's pneumoconiosis.*

blast l. The shredding-type effect that takes place in the alveolar surfaces of the lung caused by the shock of an explosion or blast, which can cause alveolar contusion.

farmer's l. A form of hypersensitivity alveolitis caused by exposure to moldy hay that has fermented. *Actinomyces micropolyspora faeni* and *Thermoactinomyces vulgaris* are the causative microorganisms. SEE: *alveolitis; bagassosis; hypersensitivity.*

honeycomb l. An abnormal appearance of the lungs seen on chest x-ray exam, in which small cystic spaces alternate with coarsely increased interstitial markings. This pattern is typical of pulmonary injury caused by inhalation of dusts, minerals, toxic gases, or fibers; rheumatological diseases; and interstitial pneumonitis.

humidifier l. Humidifier **fever**.

iron l. Drinker respirator.

shock l. A diffuse lung injury, causing reduced perfusion, pulmonary edema, and alveolar collapse, associated with acute respiratory distress syndrome. SYN: *wet l.*

trapped l. Lung that cannot expand and contract during respiration because it is restricted by the visceral pleura.

wet l. Shock **l.**

lung collapse SEE: under *collapse.*

lung-protective strategy, lung-protective ventilatory strategy In patients treated with mechanical ventilation, the use of tidal volumes of 6 mL/kg of predicted body weight or less for each machine-generated breath. Higher tidal volumes have been consistently associated with increased mortality in patients with acute lung injuries and acute respiratory distress syndrome.

lungworm (lŭng′wĕrm) Any of the nematodes that infest the lungs of humans and animals.

lunula (loo′nyŭ-lă, -lē) *pl.* **lunulae** [L. *lunula,* little moon] **1.** A crescent-shaped area. **2.** An active area of nailbed growth at the base of the fingernails and toenails. The cells develop and keratinize to form nails. SYN: *albedo unguium.*

lupoid (loo′poyd) [″ + Gr. *eidos,* form, shape] **1.** Resembling lupus. **2.** Boeck sarcoid.

lupous (loo′pŭs) **1.** Pert. to lupus. **2.** Affected with lupus.

lupus (loo′pŭs) [L. *lupus,* wolf] Originally any chronic, progressive, usually ulcerating, skin disease. In current usage, when the word is used alone, it has no precise meaning.

discoid l. erythematosus ABBR: DLE. A chronic skin disease characterized by periodic acute appearances of a scaling, red, macular rash. DLE is caused by an autoimmune process involving both B-cell− and T-cell−mediated mechanisms that destroy the skin's basal cells. DLE is treated with topical corticosteroids. It is found in about 5% to 30% of patients who have systemic lupus erythematosus (SLE) (esp. those who smoke) but also may occur alone (without other findings of SLE). SEE: *autoimmune disease; systemic l. erythematosus.*

TREATMENT: The patient should avoid exposure to the sun. Skin lesions should be treated with topical corticosteroids, but overuse of these preparations should be avoided.

drug-induced systemic l. erythematosus A group of signs and symptoms similar to those of systemic lupus erythematosus, caused by an adverse reaction to drugs, esp. procainamide, hydralazine, and isoniazid. Joint inflammation and pain, skin rash, pleurisy, and fever are the most common manifestations; kidney and central nervous system involvement are rare. Antinuclear antibodies, specifically against the histones that fold DNA, are common. Some patients develop antinuclear antibodies but do not develop lupus-like symptoms. The lupus-like syndrome usually disappears when the drug causing it is discontinued. SEE: *antinuclear **antibodies**; systemic l. erythematosus.*

l. erythematosus Any of several chronic, progressive, ulcerating, skin diseases, esp. systemic lupus erythematosus.

neonatal l. Rash, abnormally low platelet counts, liver and brain disease, and congenital heart block occurring in an infant whose mother has systemic lupus erythematosus. The disease results from the passage of maternal autoantibodies to the developing fetus. Although most of the findings resolve spontaneously, congenital heart block does not, and it may require the insertion of a pacemaker.

l. panniculitis L. profundus.

l. pernio Purple, noncaseating granulomas occurring on the face, esp. around the nose, eyes, cheeks, lips, and ears. *Lupus* in lupus pernio is misleading because it suggests a connection with systemic lupus erythematosus; lupus pernio is actually a finding of the skin in sarcoidosis.

l. profundus A deeply scarring, atrophic rash found in patients with systemic lupus erythematosus, caused by inflammation of subcutaneous fatty tissue. SYN: **l. panniculitis**.

systemic l. erythematosus ABBR: SLE. A chronic autoimmune inflammatory disease of connective tissue involving multiple organ systems and marked by periodic acute episodes. Its name is derived from the characteristic erythematous butterfly rash over the nose and cheeks, which resembles a wolf's snout, although this is present in less than 50% of patients. The disease is most prevalent in women (ratio of 8:1 women:men) of childbearing age (ratio of 15:1). Although it occurs worldwide, it is most prevalent among black and Asian peoples. SEE: *Nursing Diagnoses Appendix.*

ETIOLOGY AND PATHOLOGY: SLE is classified as an autoimmune disease in which the body seems to be unable to maintain normal mechanisms of tolerance to autoantigens. Activation of T helper cells and B cells results in the production of autoantibodies that attack antigens in the cytoplasm and nucleus of cells and on the surface of blood cells. The exact cause of SLE is unknown: genetic defects, hormonal changes, infection, physical or mental stress, some drugs, immunizations, and environmental triggers (sunlight, UV light exposure) are possible predisposing factors. SEE: *autoimmune disease; glomerulonephritis.*

Autoantibodies can react with autoantigens to form immune complexes in such large numbers that they cannot be completely excreted; the immune complexes may precipitate within blood vessels, producing inflammation at the site and disrupting the flow of blood and oxygen to tissues. These deposits are particularly damaging in the glomeruli. Autoantibodies also promote the destruction of cells by stimulating neutrophil and macrophage phagocytic activity, which increases cell destruction from trauma, infection, or drugs.

DIAGNOSIS: In 1997, revised criteria for diagnosis of SLE were established. The diagnosis can be made if four or more of the following criteria are present, either at one time or sequentially: (1) butterfly rash; (2) raised, scaly discoid skin lesions; (3) abnormal titer of antinuclear antibodies seen by immunofluorescence; (4) other autoantibodies (anti-Sm; serological tests for syphilis); (5) pleuritis or pericarditis (together called "serositis"); (6) hemolytic anemia, leukopenia (white blood cell count less than 4,000 mm^3), lymphopenia (lymphocyte count less than 1,500/mm^3), or thrombocytopenia of less than 100,000/mm^3; (7) oral or nasopharyngeal ulcers; (8) nonerosive arthritis; (9) psychosis or seizures without other clear cause; (10) photosensitivity skin rash; and (11) proteinuria greater than 0.5 g/day or cellular casts in the urine.

Some drugs can cause a lupus-like syndrome; the most common of these are procainamide, isoniazid, and hydralazine. SEE: *drug-induced systemic l. erythematosus.*

SYMPTOMS: The onset of the disease may be acute or insidious. Patients have a wide variety of clinical symptoms, signs, and laboratory findings, but anemia, thrombocytopenia, polyarthritis, (polyarthralgia) skin rashes, glomerulonephritis, fever, malaise, weight loss, fatigue, and low blood levels of complement are the most common. Other signs include pleuritis, pericarditis, myocarditis, neurological changes including behavioral changes and seizure activity (neural lupus), gastrointestinal ulcerations, Raynaud's phenomenon (present in about 20% of patients), and other problems caused by inflammatory changes of the blood vessels or connective tissue. Most patients are prone to infection.

TREATMENT: No cure for SLE exists, and complete remission is rare. About 25% of patients have mild disease, demonstrating only minor skin and hematological signs, and can be treated with nonsteroidal anti-inflammatory drugs for their arthritis symptoms and topical treatment (sometimes with corticosteroid creams) for skin lesions. Rashes may respond to antimalarials, e.g., hydroxychloroquine, but patients must be observed closely for the possibility of drug-induced retinal damage. Other treatments for skin rash include quinacrine, retinoids, and dapsone. Life-threatening and severely disabling conditions should be treated with high doses of corticosteroids and supplemental calcium to minimize osteoporosis, which may be an undesired side effect of long-term glucocorticoid use. Immunosuppressive drugs are used for severe exacerbations and to reduce steroid dosage.

PROGNOSIS: The prognosis depends on which organ systems are involved, how severely they are damaged, and how rapidly the disease progresses. Ten-year survival rates are high (80%). Renal failure and infections are the most common causes of death.

PATIENT CARE: Patient education related to the disease, diagnostic procedures, and treatment is essential in lupus, as in any chronic disease. Ongoing assessment is carried out to assess flares of the illness. The purpose, proper dosage, use, and side effects of drugs is taught. Patients need emotional support to help cope with changes in appearance. Patients should be taught to wear clothing and hats that block direct sunlight, use a sunscreen with a 15 or higher protection factor, and to maintain a diet appropriate for their renal functional status. The health care professional should help establish a regimen for adequate relief of both the musculoskeletal pain and chronic fatigue experienced by most patients, encouraging adequate rest. Heat packs relieve joint stiffness and pain, and regular gentle exercise helps to maintain full range of motion. Physical and occupational therapy consultations are provided as appropriate. Additional support and teaching depend on the organ system most affected by the disease. If the female patient of childbearing age has no renal or neurologic impairment, she can have a safe, successful pregnancy if desired. Over time, patients with severe progressive disease need assistance in coping with chronic illness and the possibility of mortality. Referrals to the Lupus Foundation of America (202-349-1155; www.lupus.org) and the Arthritis Foundation (800-283-7800; www.arthritis.org) are helpful. SEE: illus.

l. vulgaris Tuberculosis of the skin; characterized by patches that break down and ulcerate, leaving scars on healing.

lupus-like syndrome A cluster of symptoms resembling an autoimmune disease (including arthritis, pleural or pericardial effusions, and rashes) sometimes seen in patients with widespread malignancy.

LUQ *left upper quadrant* of abdomen.

Luque wires (loo´kä) [Eduardo Roberto Luque, 20th-cent. Mexican orthopedic surgeon] Wires used in the surgical stabilization of scoliosis. Transverse traction on each vertebra is accomplished by wrapping flexible wires around the affected vertebrae and attaching the wires to flexible rods.

Luschka, Hubert von (lush´kä) Ger. anatomist, 1820–1875.

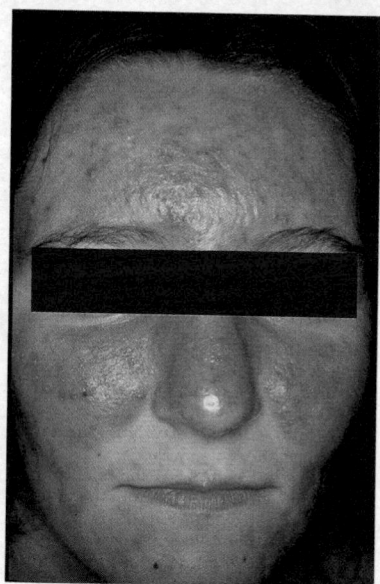

SYSTEMIC LUPUS ERYTHEMATOSUS
Facial manifestations of systemic lupus erythematosus.

foramen of L. Any of the passages for cerebrospinal fluid from the fourth ventricle to the subarachnoid space. SYN: *Key-Retzius foramina.*

lusitropy (loo-si´trŏ-pē) [Gr. *lusis,* variant of *lysis* + Gr. *tropē,* a turning] The relaxation of cardiac muscle.

lute (loot) [L. *lutum,,* clay, mud] A compound used in dentistry to bond surfaces together and make them impermeable. Compounds identified as luting agents may be cements, resins, or glass ionomers. SYN: *luting agent.*

luteal (loo´tē-ăl) [L. *luteus,* yellow] Pert. to the corpus luteum, its cells, or its hormones.

luteal phase defect SEE: under *defect.*

lutein (lū´tē-ĭn) A yellow, antioxidant pigment (a "carotenoid") derived from leafy green vegetables, the corpus luteum, egg yolk, and fat cells or lipochromes. Its consumption in the diet has been linked to a decreased risk of age-related macular degeneration.

luteinic (loot˝ē-ĭn´ik) [*lutein* + *-ic*] Pert. to the corpus luteum of the ovary.

luteinization (lū˝tē-ĭn-ĭ-zā´shŭn) The process of development of the corpus luteum within a ruptured graafian follicle.

luteinized unruptured follicle syndrome A cause of female infertility in which the maturing ovarian follicle develops into a corpus luteum without ever releasing an egg.

luteinizing hormone surge ABBR: LH surge. The abrupt increase in levels of

LH that precedes the release of an egg from an ovarian follicle.

luteinizing hormone urine test A colorimetric analysis in which a few drops of urine are placed on a strip of paper coated with an immunoassay to identify luteinizing hormone in the urine, and therefore, the presence of ovulation. SYN: *ovulation prediction test*.

Lutembacher syndrome (loot″ĕm-bok″ĕr) [René Lutembacher, Fr. physician, 1884–1968] Atrial septal defect of the heart with mitral stenosis.

luteolysin (loo″tē-ō-lī′sĭn) [L. *luteus*, yellow, + Gr. *lysis*, dissolution] Something that promotes disintegration of the corpus luteum.

luteoma (loot″ē-ō′mă) [L. *luteus*, yellow + *-oma*] A mass of lutein cells.

luteotropin (loo″tē-ō-trō′pĭn) Luteinizing hormone.

lutetium, lutecium (loo-tē′sh(ē-)ŭm) [*Lutetia (Parisiorum)*, Roman name of Paris + *-ium* (1)] SYMB: Lu. A rare element, atomic weight (mass) 174.97, atomic number 71. It is used in clinical medicine as a photosensitizing agent.

luteum (lū′tē-ŭm) [L.] Yellow.

luting Cementation.

LUTS A commonly used abbreviation for "lower urinary tract symptoms," such as difficulty in initiating or maintaining a strong and comfortable urinary stream.

Lutzomyia A genus of bloodsucking sandflies. They are vectors of leishmaniasis and Oroyo fever.

lux (lŭks) [L., light] A unit of light intensity equivalent to 1 lumen/m².

luxatio erecta (lŭk-sā′shē-ō ĕ-rek′tă) Subglenoid displacement of the head of the humerus associated with disruption of the rotator cuff.

luxation (lŭk″sā′shŭn) [L. *luxatio*, dislocation] **1.** Complete dislocation of a joint, in which organs or articular surfaces are displaced. SEE: *subluxation*. **2.** In dentistry, injury to supporting tissues that results in the loosening of the teeth with rotation or partial displacement.

Luxol fast blue (lŭks′ŏl″) An alcohol-soluble sulfonated copper phthalcyanine stain, used primarily in neuropathology. It is taken up by phospholipids and choline and stains myelin blue.

LV *left ventricle.*

LVAD *left ventricular assist **device**.*

LVEDP *left ventricular end-diastolic pressure.*

LVH *left ventricular **hypertrophy**.*

LY *lymphocyte* clinical laboratory.

lyase (lī′ās) The class name for enzymes (such as decarboxylase, aldolase, and synthases) that remove organic bonds between carbon atoms, carbon and oxygen atoms, or carbon and nitrogen atoms without hydrolysis or oxygenation.

One of the molecules that is created has a double bond.

lycanthropy (lī-kăn′thrō-pē) [Gr. *lykos*, wolf, + *anthropos*, man] A mania in which one believes oneself to be a wild beast, esp. a wolf.

lycopene (lī′kō-pēn) A red-pigmented carotenoid with antioxidant properties found in tomatoes, watermelon and red grapefruit.

lycopodium (lī″kŏ-pōd′ē-ŭm) [Gr. *lykos*, wolf + *podo-* + *-ium*] A yellow powder formed from spores of *Lycopodium clavatum*, a club moss.

lye (lī) **1.** Liquid from leaching of wood ashes. **2.** Any strong alkaline solution, esp. sodium or potassium hydroxide. SEE: *alkali; potassium hydroxide; sodium hydroxide*.

lying-in **1.** Historical term for the puerperal state. **2.** Being hospitalized for the purpose of childbearing.

Lyme disease (līm) [*Lyme*, CT, where a cluster of cases was reported in 1975] ABBR: LD. A multisystem disorder caused by the spirochete *Borrelia burgdorferi* and the most common tick-borne disease in the U.S. The disease is endemic in New England, but cases have been reported in all 50 states and in 20 other countries, including Germany, Switzerland, France, and Australia. It occurs most often in the spring and summer, when its deer tick vectors (genus *Ixodes*) are most active. Prompt removal of visible ticks from the skin before they become attached or gain access to the bloodstream (in the first 24 to 48 hr) decreases the risk of transmission. SEE: *Nursing Diagnoses Appendix*.

ETIOLOGY: The infected tick injects its spirochete-laden saliva into the bloodstream, where they incubate for 3 to 32 days and then migrate to the skin, causing the characteristic erythema migrans (EM) rash.

DIAGNOSIS: The disease is best diagnosed by the presence of EM, which begins as a red macule or papule at the site of the tick bite and expands in a red ring, leaving a clear center like a target or bull's eye. The lesion usually feels hot and itchy and may grow to over 20 in (50.8 cm) as more lesions erupt. The lesion is later replaced by red blotches or diffuse urticaria. Conjunctivitis, malaise, fatigue, and flulike symptoms and lymphadenopathy may occur. Antibody tests for *Borrelia burgdorferi* with an enzyme-linked immunosorbent assay (ELISA) test are also used for diagnosis in patients with a history of exposure and signs and symptoms of Lyme disease but with no evidence of rash. The antibodies are developed against flagellar and outer surface proteins on the spirochete.

SYMPTOMS: The course of Lyme disease is divided into three stages.

1 localized infection: begins with the tick bite and proceeds as above.

2 disseminated infection: begins weeks to months later. The spirochetes spread to the rest of the body through the blood, in some cases causing arthritis (esp. of the knee joints), muscle pain, cardiac dysrhythmias, pericarditis, lymphadenopathy, or meningoencephalitis. Nonprotective antibodies develop during this stage.

3 chronic infection: begins weeks to years after the initial bite. Patients develop mild to severe arthritis, encephalitis, or both, which rarely are fatal.

TREATMENT: Oral doxycycline or ampicillin (14–21 or –28 day course) effectively eradicates early uncomplicated Lyme disease. Erythromycin or cefuroxime axetil may be administered to patients allergic to penicillin. Patients with cardiac and neurological involvement may need to be treated with intravenous cephalosporins.

PROGNOSIS: When the disease is treated early, results are good. If treated late, convalescence is prolonged, but complete recovery is the usual outcome in most patients.

PREVENTION: The Centers for Disease Control recommends that people should discuss with their health care providers the possibility of getting a Lyme disease vaccination if they are between 15 and 70 years old; live, work, or vacation in endemic areas; or frequently go into wooded or grassy areas. The vaccine is not recommended for children, pregnant women, and those who do not live in or visit endemic areas.

When planning to spend time in places where ticks may be located, people should wear clothing impregnated with insect repellents, hats, long sleeves, pants tucked into socks, heavy shoes, and a tick repellent containing DEET (N,N-diethyltoluamide). Tick repellent should not be directly applied to an infant or toddler's skin because of the danger of neurotoxicity. If possible, people should stay on paths and away from high grass or brush. They should check clothing carefully for ticks when leaving those areas although tick nymphs, which are smaller than 1 mm in length, may not be easily seen. Once home, people should remove and wash clothing and check their entire body, esp. the hairline and ankles, for ticks or nymphs. If a tick or nymph is found, it should be carefully removed with tweezers, esp. the head and mouth parts, but the body of the tick or nymph must not be squeezed. The site may then be cleansed with an antiseptic, but should be observed for signs of infection (redness, swelling, pain, rash), and the primary health care provider contacted if infection is suspected. Some people make the mistake of trying to remove ticks or nymphs with alcohol, a lighted match, or petroleum jelly. These measures are ineffective and may increase the risk of transmission of tick-borne diseases. Prophylactic antibiotics generally should not be requested (or given). Although pet dogs may receive Lyme vaccine, they should still be checked to prevent them from bringing ticks into the house.

PATIENT CARE: The patient is checked for any drug allergies. Prescribed pharmacologic therapy is explained to the patient, including dosing schedule, the importance of completing the course of therapy even if he feels better, and adverse effects. Patients being treated for Lyme disease often require antibiotics for a prolonged period, esp. in advanced stages, which increases their risk for developing adverse effects (e.g., diarrhea). Methods for dealing with these problems are explained. Patients with chronic Lyme disease often require assistance to deal with changes in lifestyle, family interactions, and ability to perform daily activities. Available local and national support groups can assist with such problems. Patients should be made aware that one occurrence of Lyme disease does not prevent recurrences. The U.S. Department of Health and Human Services has made Lyme disease prevention a priority under its program "Healthy People 2010." Patients can be referred to the Lyme Disease Foundation (860-870-0070; http://www.lyme .org) or the American Lyme Disease Foundation (http://www.aldf.com) for information and support.

lymph (lĭmf) [L. *lympha*, water] Interstitial fluid being returned to the venous circulation via the branching set of tubular conduits called lymphatics. In most parts of the body, lymph is fluid that has been filtered out of arterial capillaries but not absorbed by the local tissues. The salt concentrations of lymph are similar to those of blood serum, but the protein concentration of lymph varies according to the secretions of local tissues, from 0.0 g/dl in the choroid plexus of the brain to 6.2 g/dl in the liver (vs. 5.5-8.0 g/dl in blood serum). Lymph from the small intestines is called chyle and is filled with lipids after a meal of fats. Lymph from most regions of the body is thin and colorless, however lymph containing chyle from the small intestines is thick and milky. chyle. Lymph also contains cells (mainly lymphocytes), particulate matter, debris, and micro-organisms. SEE: *lymphatic system.*

lymph-, lympho- [L. *lympha, limpa*, water] Prefixes meaning *lymph.*

lymphadenectomy (lĭm″fad″ĕn-ek′tŏ-mē) [*lymph-* + *adenectomy*] Surgical removal of a lymph node, as in a biopsy. It may be a simple or a radical regional procedure.

lymphadenitis (lĭm-făd″ĕn-ī′tĭs) [″ + ″ + *itis*, inflammation] Inflammation of lymph nodes, caused by the activation of phagocytes and lymphocytes, which encounter large numbers of microorganisms, cancer cells, or other antigenic material. Local swelling and pain are common symptoms and often help clinicians diagnose regional diseases (e.g., the anterior cervical lymph nodes become tender and enlarged in people with strep throat; the inguinal lymph nodes enlarge and hurt in some sexually transmitted diseases).

Lymph node inflammation sometimes is associated with inflammation of the lymphatic vessels (lymphangitis) leading into the node. Lymphatic inflammation subsides when the underlying infection is treated. Lymphadenitis of unknown cause may require lymph node biopsy (e.g., excisional or needle biopsies) or aspiration. SEE: *inflammation; lymphangitis.*

SYMPTOMS: The disease is characterized by a marked increase of tissue, with possible suppuration. Swelling, pain, and tenderness are present. The disease usually accompanies lymphangitis.

ETIOLOGY: The condition is caused by drainage of bacteria or toxic substances into the lymph nodes. The etiology may be specific, as when caused by the organisms of typhoid, syphilis, or tuberculosis, or nonspecific, in which the causative organism is not identified.

TREATMENT: Hot, moist dressings should be applied. Incision and drainage are necessary if abscesses occur. Antibiotics should be given as indicated.

Kikuchi l. SEE: *Kikuchi lymphadenitis.*

    tuberculous l. Lymph node inflammation caused by *Mycobacterium tuberculosis* (MTB), with granuloma formation and caseating necrosis within the node. The most common presentation is the finding of a neck mass in a febrile patient (a condition called "scrofula"), although MTB and other mycobacteria also can invade lymph nodes in other parts of the body. SEE: *tuberculosis.*

lymphadenoid (lĭm-făd′ĕ-noyd) [″ + *eidos*, form, shape] Resembling a lymph node or lymph tissue.

lymphadenopathy (lĭm″fad″ĕ-nop′ă-thē) [*lymph-* + *adenopathy*] Enlargement of lymph nodes (LN), typically to greater than 1.5 cm. The increased size is caused by activation and proliferation of lymphocytes and phagocytic white blood cells within the node or by invasion of the node by tumor. Most often, lym-

phadenopathy is found in nodes involved in local, regional, or systemic infections; it results occasionally from cancers. Lymphadenopathy may also be found in an array of other, less common illnesses, including thyroiditis, thyrotoxicosis, autoimmune diseases (e.g., rheumatoid arthritis), sarcoidosis, and drug reactions (e.g., phenytoin). SEE: illus.

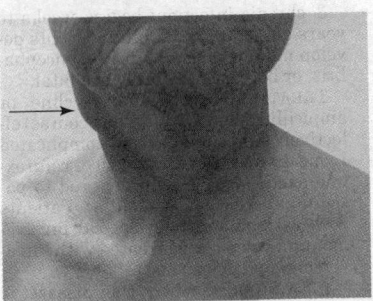

CERVICAL LYMPHADENOPATHY

Squamous cell carcinoma of the neck

Enlarged LNs may be tender or not; tenderness often is present when lymph nodes swell rapidly (e.g., in response to infections, hypersensitivity reactions, or some fulminant lymphomas). Rock-hard, enlarged, and immobile LNs are typical of metastatic cancer, whereas rubbery LNs are found in lymphomas. LNs that do not resolve spontaneously within 4 to 6 weeks, or for which no obvious explanation exists, usually are sampled by biopsy or aspiration.

    dermatopathic l. Widespread lymphadenopathy secondary to various skin disorders. SEE: table.

lymphadenosis benigna cutis (lĭm″fad″ĕ-nō′sĭs bē-nĭ′nă cū′tĭs) [L., benign lymphadenosis of the skin] A benign collection of lymphocytes in the skin.

lymphangiectasis (lĭm-făn″jē-ĕk′tă-sĭs) [″ + ″ + *ektasis*, dilatation] Benign swelling in all or part of an extremity, as the result of dilation of the subcutaneous and deep lymphatic vessels. It occurs mostly in children and may be severe enough to cause deformity. Acquired lymphangiectasis can occur as a complication of surgery or radiation therapy for cancer. SYN: *lymphectasia.*

lymphangiography (lĭm-făn″jē-ŏg′ră-fē) [″ + ″ + *graphein*, to write] Immediate radiological investigation of the lymphatic vessels after injection of a contrast medium via cutdown, usually on the dorsum of the hand or foot. Delayed films are taken to visualize the nodes. This technique has been replaced by computed tomography and magnetic resonance imaging. SYN: *lymphography.*

Causes of Swollen Glands

Category	Examples	Location	Age of Patient	Texture	Size	Associated Signs or Symptoms	Diagnostic Tests	Necessity for Biopsy or Aspirate
Bacterial infection	Strep throat; cat scratch disease	Angle of the jaw; axilla, neck	Child or preteen; any	Relatively soft and tender; relatively soft and tender	1 sq. cm; > 1 cm	Fever, sore throat, tonsillar exudate, malaise, headache, difficulty swallowing; may have fever, night sweats, weight loss	Can be diagnosed clinically; antibody blood tests	No; not usually
Granuloma	Tuberculosis; sarcoidosis	Neck, chest; hilum of the lung and other locations	Any; usually adults	Relatively soft and tender; rubbery	> 1 cm; > 1 cm, sometimes massive	May have fever, night sweats, weight loss, productive sputum; cough, shortness of breath, may have systemic illness, or be asymptomatic	Tuberculin (purified protein derivative), interferon blood test, sputum for acid-fast bacilli; blood for ACE levels	Occasionally; often
Metastatic cancer	Breast cancer	Axilla next to the breast	Adults	Stone	Especially likely if > 2 cm	Lump in the breast	Mammography, ultrasound, other imaging techniques	Yes
Lymphoma	Hodgkin lymphoma	Chest, neck, axilla, groin, or all of these	Young adult	Rubbery	> 1 cm	May have fever, night sweats, weight loss, enlarged spleen	Radiologic imaging	Yes
Viral infection	Mononucleosis; HIV/AIDS	Head and neck; spleen; generalized	Young adult; any, but most often young adult or adult	Rubbery; firm	About 1 cm; variable	May have fever, night sweats, weight loss; fever, night sweats, weight loss, or symptoms of opportunistic infection	Tests for Epstein-Barr virus, heterophile antibody; antibody blood tests	No; not usually

lymphangioma (lim″fan″jē-ō′mă) [*lymph-* + *angioma*] A tumor composed of lymphatic vessels.

    cavernous l. Dilated lymph vessels filled with lymph.

    cystic l. Multilocular cysts filled with lymph. The condition is usually congenital.

lymphangiosarcoma (lĭm-făn″jē-ō-săr-kō′mă) [″ + ″ + *sarx*, flesh, + *oma*, tumor] A malignant neoplasm that develops from the endothelial lining of lymphatics.

lymphangitis, lymphangiitis (lim″fan″ jĭt′ĭs, jē-ĭt′ĭs) [*lymph-* + *angi-* + *-itis*] Inflammation of the lymphatic vessels draining an inflamed or infected body part. There are red streaks accompanied by heat, pain, and swelling along the inflamed vessels; lymph nodes in the area are enlarged and tender. Treatment consists of antibiotics specific to the organism causing the infection, most commonly group A beta-hemolytic streptococci (occasionally staphylococci). If the infection is not contained, it can produce septicemia.

    SYMPTOMS: The condition is characterized by the onset of chills and high fever, with moderate swelling and pain.

    PATIENT CARE: Elevating the affected part of the body so that local lymphatics can drain reduces pain and helps the underlying infection to resolve. Antibiotics and, often, antipyretic and analgesic drugs are administered. SYN: *angiolymphitis*.

lymphatic (lim-fat′ik) [L. *lymphaticus*] **1.** 1. Pert. to lymph and to the system of endothelial vessels that carry it. **2.** An endothelial tube that carries lymph through lymph nodes and toward lymphatic collecting ducts. Lymphatics also provide pathways for the inter-tissue transport of lymph cells, bacteria, and tumor cells; lymphatics are the most common routes for metastases of carcinomas. Throughout the body, interstitial fluid volume is kept low by movement of excess fluid into lymph capillaries, and a significant increase of fluid movement into the interstitial space (e.g., from heart failure) or a decrease of fluid movement into the lymphatics (e.g., from surgical removal of lymph nodes and lymphatics) will lead to edema. Inside lymphatics, lymph is moved by contractions of muscle cells surrounding the lymph vessels and by secondary compressions from other muscles in the environment. In the embryo, lymphatics develop just after and alongside veins. Like veins, the larger lymphatics have walls consisting of three layers (the intima, media, and adventitia). The one-way, centripetal flow of lymph is maintained by valves. Lymphatics regenerate quickly after injury.

SYN: *lymphatic vessel*. SEE: *lymphatic capillary*. SEE: *lymphatic capillary*. SEE: *lymphatic system*.

    afferent l. Any of the small vessels carrying lymph toward a lymph node.

    efferent l. Any of the small vessels carrying lymph away from a lymph node.

lymphatic system A component of the circulatory system comprising: the lymphatics, and the lymphoid tissues, SEE: illus.; *immune response; immune system; lymph*.

    LYMPHATICS: The lymphatics begin with lymphatic capillaries, permeable endothelial vessels one-cell thick, which absorb interstitial tissue fluid, particles, microbes, debris, and, from the small intestines, fat. Lymphatic capillaries empty into larger lymph vessels that eventually empty their contents (lymph) into the venous circulation through lymphatic ducts.

    LYMPHOID TISSUES: Lymph nodes are interposed between lymph vessels at some of the junctions between vessels. As it percolates through a lymph node, lymph is modified: debris is filtered out, lymphocytes are activated, and antibodies and lymphocytes are added to the fluid. Other lymphoid tissues have similar functions: The spleen filters the circulating blood, to which it adds antibodies and lymphocytes. Tonsils, Peyer's patches, and other unencapsulated lymphoid tissues line epithelia that are in contact with the outside environment; unencapsulated lymphoid tissues activate lymphocytes and manufacture antibodies against foreign antigens. Lymphoid tissues in the bone marrow are proliferation and activation centers for lymphocytes, and the thymus is a proliferation and maturation center for T lymphocytes, esp. during the neonatal and early postnatal years.

lymphedema (lim″-fi-dē′mă) [*lymph* + *edema*] An abnormal accumulation of tissue fluid in the interstitial spaces due to the removal of lymph nodes or to the blockage or destruction of lymphatics. Stagnant flow of tissue fluid through body structures may make them prone to infections that are difficult to treat; as a result lymphedematous limbs should be protected from cuts, scratches, burns, and blood drawing. SEE: illus.

    Common causes of lymphedema include neoplastic obstruction of lymphatic flow (as in the axilla, in metastatic breast cancer); postoperative interference with lymphatic flow (as, after axillary dissection); infectious blockade of lymphatics (as in filariasis); radiation damage to lymphatics (as after treatment of pelvic, breast, or lung cancers). All of these are secondary (ac-

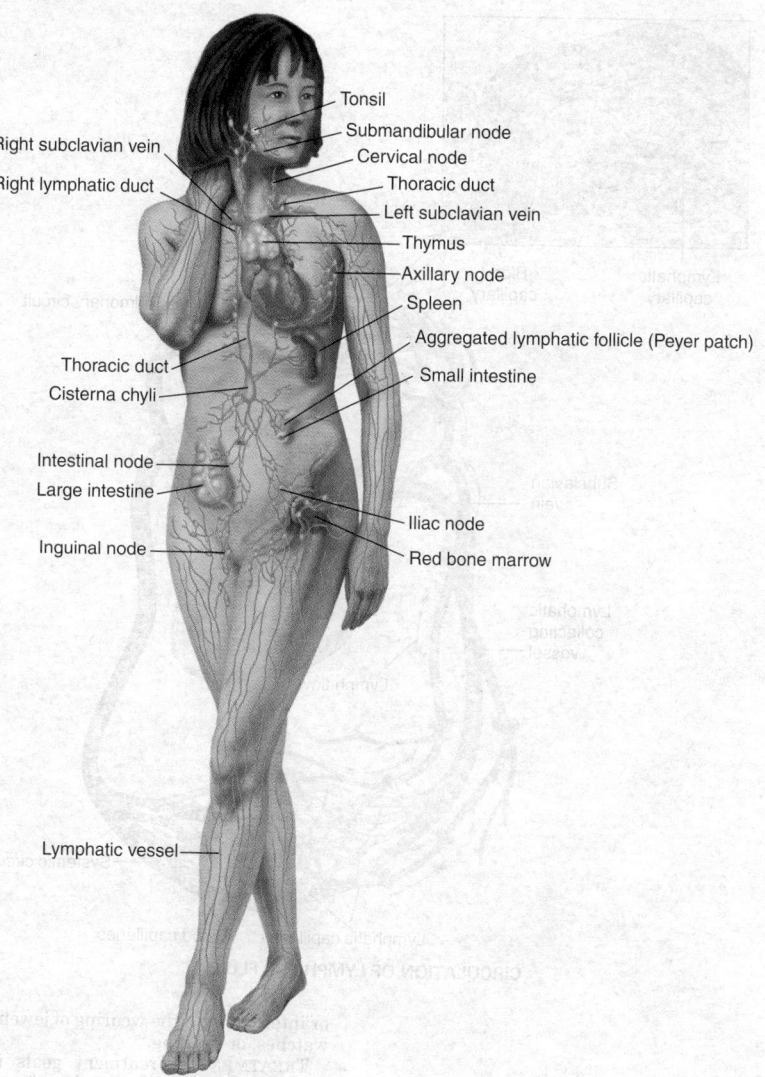

Tonsil
Submandibular node
Right subclavian vein
Cervical node
Right lymphatic duct
Thoracic duct
Left subclavian vein
Thymus
Axillary node
Spleen
Aggregated lymphatic follicle (Peyer patch)
Thoracic duct
Small intestine
Cisterna chyli
Intestinal node
Large intestine
Iliac node
Inguinal node
Red bone marrow

Lymphatic vessel

THE LYMPHATIC SYSTEM

quired) lymphedemas. Rarely, lymph-edema also may occur congenitally (Milroy disease), or develop at the onset of puberty or during adulthood from an unknown cause that may be related to vascular anomalies (primary lymph-edema). In the U.S. and other developed countries, the leading cause of second-ary lymphedema is surgical or radiation therapy for cancer, esp. if accompanied by lymph node dissection. SEE: *lymphatic blockade; elephantiasis; lymphedema pump*.

Lymphedema occurs in four stages (0 to 3): 0. Subclinical stage in which

lymph transport is known to be impaired, but no signs or symptoms are obvious (may last for years); 1. Tissue is soft with pitting edema; swelling decreases with elevation; 2. Tissue is swollen but firmer and thus may not show pitting; edema does not resolve completely with elevation; and 3. The affected limb is grossly enlarged and misshapen; skin breakdown and infection often occur.

SYMPTOMS: Symptoms of lymphedema may include a feeling of heaviness, tiredness, aching, weakness, and fullness in a limb that impairs flexibility

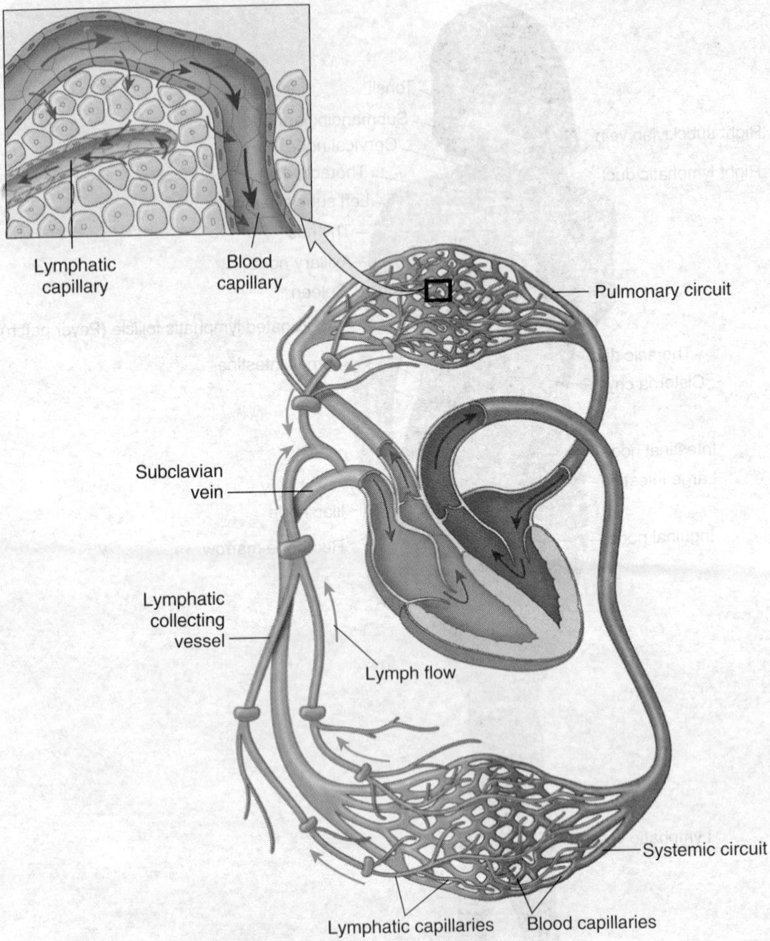

Lymphatic capillary   Blood capillary

Pulmonary circuit

Subclavian vein

Lymphatic collecting vessel

Lymph flow

Systemic circuit

Lymphatic capillaries   Blood capillaries

CIRCULATION OF LYMPHATIC FLUID

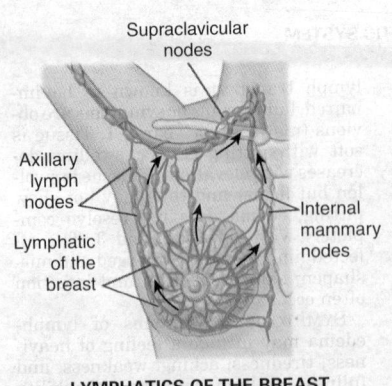

Supraclavicular nodes

Axillary lymph nodes

Internal mammary nodes

Lymphatic of the breast

LYMPHATICS OF THE BREAST

or interfers with the wearing of jewelry, watches, or clothing.

TREATMENT: Treatment goals include maintaining use of the affected limb and preventing complications.

PATIENT CARE: A combination of manual lymphatic drainage, compression devices, and protection of the affected limb can make a positive difference in a patient's quality of life. Patient management by physiatrists, other physicians experienced in lymphedema care, certified nurses, and therapists is crucial. Careful measurement of the affected limb with comparison to its opposite and diagnostic testing help to rule out other causes. If necessary, lymphangioscintigraphy can be used to examine the anatomy and functioning of the lymph system. Patients and their partners can be taught effective tech-

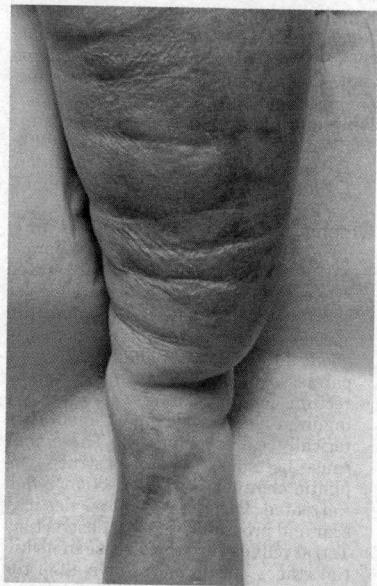

LYMPHEDEMA OF THE LEG

niques to use at home. Compression devices are fitted over the affected limb to help maintain or reduce swelling. Compression pumps use air or fluid pressure to mimic massage's beneficial effects. They are designed to move lymphatic fluid back toward functional nodes by providing sequential, even pressure from the distal to the proximal portions of the affected limb. Compression sleeves or stockings should be fitted by a professional, as an improperly fitted device may irritate skin and other tissues, resulting in additional swelling.

Sensible weight reduction programs based on mild caloric restriction and gentle exercise help to alleviate symptoms. Overexertion of affected limbs should be avoided. Using the affected limb for activities of daily living (bathing, hair-brushing) helps to drain lymph fluid. Supporting the arm on the back of a chair or couch provides helpful elevation for lymph drainage. In acute care settings, the affected limb should be identified by the patient and by health care providers using a loose-fitting, colored (bright pink) armband to ensure that blood drawings, injections, and blood pressure readings are not done on that limb. Skin should be kept clean and moisturized to limit chapping or chafing leading to breakdown. The patient is taught to avoid cuts and abrasions, as when using kitchen knives or other implements, to wear gloves when gardening and to wash and inspect skin after such activities, and to clean any skin

breaks that occur, treating them with an antibacterial cream or ointment and a sterile dry dressing. In cases of lower extremity edema, sitting with the legs in a dependent position, crossing the legs, or standing for prolonged periods should be avoided. Extremes of heat and cold exposure should be avoided. The health care provider should be notified if the limb develops a rash or itching or pain or if the patient develops fever or flulike symptoms. Local support groups can assist patients in dealing with body image issues, and fitting clothing to asymmetrical limbs. Resources for further information on lymphedema management include The National Lymphedema Network and other support organizations such as the American Cancer Society.

congenital l. Chronic pitting edema of the lower extremities. SYN: *Milroy disease.*

l. praecox Obstruction of the lymphatic channels, producing edema and occurring mostly in women between the ages of 10 and 25. Its cause is unknown. The interstitial fluid that accumulates first appears in the feet but can travel proximally to the trunk and continues to accumulate throughout life. When the edema becomes severe, it predisposes the patient to chronic ulcers and superimposed infections of the legs.

lymph node basin SEE: under *basin.*

lymphoblast (lĭm′fō-blăst) [″ + Gr. *blastos,* germ] An immature cell that gives rise to a lymphocyte. SYN: *lymphocytoblast.* **lymphoblastic,** *adj.*

lymphoblastoma (lĭm″fō-blăst-ō′mă) [″ + ″ + *oma,* tumor] Lymphosarcoma.

lymphocele (lĭm′fō-sēl) [L. *lympha,* lymph, + Gr. *kele,* tumor, swelling] A cyst that contains lymph.

lymphocytapheresis (lim″fō-sīt″ă-fă-rē′sĭs) [*lymphocyte* + Gr. *aphairesis,* removal] Removal of lymphocytes from the blood after it has been withdrawn. The blood is then returned to the donor.

lymphocyte (lim′fō-sīt″) [*lymph-* + *-cyte*] ABBR: LY. A white blood cell responsible for much of the body's immune protection. Less than 1% are present in the circulating blood; the rest lie in the lymph nodes, spleen, and other lymphoid organs, where they can maximize contact with foreign antigens. SEE: *B cell; T cell; blood* for illus.; *natural killer cell; plasma cell; cell-mediated immunity; humoral immunity.*

Lymphocytes vary from 5 to 12 μm in diameter; subpopulations can be identified by unique protein groups on the cell surface called clusters of differentiation. T cells, derived from the thymus, make up approx. 75% of all lymphocytes; B cells, derived from the bone marrow, 10%. A third classification is natural killer cells. In the blood, 20% to 40% of the white cells are lymphocytes.

activated l. A lymphocyte stimulated by exposure to a specific antigen or by macrophage processing so that it is capable of responding to a foreign antigen by neutralizing or eliminating it.

autoreactive l. A lymphocyte that reacts with autoantigens. Most of these cells are eliminated during lymphocyte maturation or by activation-induced cell death. SYN: *self-reactive l.*

B l. A lymphocyte formed from pluripotent stem cells in the bone marrow that migrates to the spleen, lymph nodes, and other peripheral lymphoid tissue where it comes in contact with foreign antigens and becomes a mature functioning cell. Mature B cells are able to independently identify foreign antigens and differentiate into antibody-producing plasma cells or memory cells; their activity also may be stimulated by IL-2 (formerly called B-cell growth factor). Plasma cells are the only source of immunoglobulins (antibodies). Memory cells enable the body to produce antibodies quickly when it is invaded by the same organism at a later date. SYN: *B cell.* SEE: *humoral **immunity**; immune response.*

reactive l. A lymphocyte that has become enlarged as a result of stimulation by antigens. Such a lymphocyte can be over 30 μm in diameter and of varying sizes and shapes.

T l. T cell.

tumor-infiltrating l. A lymphocyte found in solid tumors, e.g., lung cancers, melanomas, and renal cell carcinomas. Tumor-infiltrating lymphocytes include helper T cells and cytotoxic T cells; they participate in tumor recognition and, in some cases, tumor destruction.

lymphocyte activation The use of an antigen (or mitogen in vitro) to stimulate lymphocyte metabolic activity.

lymphocytic colitis (lim″fŏ-sit′ik) SEE: under *colitis.*

lymphocytopenia (lĭm″fŏ-sīt″ō-pē′nē-ă) [″ + ″ + *penia,* lack] Lymphopenia.

lymphocytopoiesis (lim″fŏ-sīt″ŏ-poy-ē′sĭs) [*lymphocyte* + *-poiesis*] Lymphocyte production.

lymphocytosis (lĭm″fŏ-sī-tō′sĭs) [″ + ″ + *osis,* condition] An excess of lymph cells in the blood.

lymphoepithelioma (lĭm″fŏ-ĕp″ĭ-thē-lē-ō′mă) [″ + Gr. *epi,* at, + *thele,* nipple, + *oma,* tumor] A poorly differentiated squamous cell carcinoma, usually found in the nasopharynx. The tumor is infiltrated by massive numbers of lymphocytes.

lymphogenesis (lim″fŏ-jen′ĕ-sĭs) [*lympho- genesis*] Production of lymph.

lymphogenous (lĭm-fŏj′ĕn-ŭs) [″ + Gr. *gennan,* to produce] **1.** Forming lymph. **2.** Derived from lymph.

lymphogranuloma inguinale (lim″fŏ-gran″yŭ-lō′mă ing″gwĭ-nal′ē, -nāl′) [*lympho-* + *granuloma* + L. *inguinalis,* pert. to the groin] Lymphogranuloma venereum.

lymphogranulomatosis (lĭm″fŏ-grăn-ū-lō″mă-tō′sĭs) [″ + *granulum,* granule, + Gr. *oma,* tumor, + *osis,* condition] **1.** Infectious granuloma of the lymphatics. **2.** Hodgkin's disease.

lymphogranuloma venereum (vĭ-nir′ē-ŭm) [L. *venereus,* pert. to Venus] ABBR: LGV. A sexually transmitted disease, affecting about 300 patients per year in the U.S., caused by *Chlamydia* species. It has an incubation period of about 3 to 30 days. Its hallmarks are a painless, red erosion on the genitals or rectum, followed 1 to 2 weeks later by inguinal lymph node enlargement (historically called "buboes"). These may cause fistulous tracts or obstruct lymphatic channels if the infection is left untreated. Perirectal lymph nodes may scar and produce late rectal obstruction. Tetracyclines cure the disease in its initial stages but do not resolve all of the complications brought on by scarring or lymphatic obstruction. SYN: *lymphogranuloma inguinale; lymphopathia venereum.* SEE: *pelvic inflammatory disease; sexually transmitted disease.*

SYMPTOMS: Because up to 75% of women and 50% of men have no symptoms, patients do not know they have the disease, continue to spread it, and develop more severe infection. Symptomatic patients may develop ulcerating vesicles on the genitals, urethral inflammation, abdominal pain, and swollen lymph nodes in the groin and rectum; men often have swollen testicles. Approx 40% of women develop pelvic inflammatory disease (PID), leading to chronic pain, infertility, and an increased risk of having a tubal pregnancy.

The CDC recommends that all sexually active women under 20 years old be screened yearly for *Chlamydia;* sexually active women over 20 with multiple sex partners who do not use condoms also should be screened yearly. The infection is diagnosed using fluorescent anti-*Chlamydia* antibodies. Women, rather than men, are targeted for screening because of their increased use of health care and the risk of developing PID associated with this disease.

TREATMENT: The disease can be treated effectively with a 3-week course of doxycycline; erythromycin is used for pregnant women. Recurrent infection is common if barrier contraception is not used during intercourse.

lymphography (lĭm-fŏg′ră-fē) [L. *lympha,* lymph, + Gr. *graphein,* to write] Lymphangiography.

lymphoid (lim′foyd″) [*lymph-* + *-oid*] **1.** Consisting of lymphocytes. **2.** Resembling lymphatic tissue.

   l. nodule Small, unencapsulated aggregations of immune cells in the submucosa of the respiratory, intestinal, and genitourinary epithelia; examples are tonsils and Peyer's patches. lymph nodule.

   l. tissue The fixed collections of cells of the immune system. Immune cells (lymphocytes and related cells) frequently move throughout the body, carried in the blood and lymph or crawling through tissues. Lymphoid tissues are specific places where immune cells proliferate, aggregate, and congregate, including lymph nodes, lymphoid nodules, the spleen, the thymus, and the bone marrow.

lymphokine (lĭm′fō-kīn) A cytokine released by lymphocytes, including many of the interleukins, gamma interferon, tumor necrosis factor beta, and chemokines. SEE: *cytokine*.

lymphology (lĭm-fŏl′ō-jē) [″ + Gr. *logos,* word, reason] The science of the lymphatics.

lymphoma (lim-fō′mă, ′măt-ă) *pl.* **lymphomaslymphomata** [*lymph-* + *-oma*] A malignant neoplasm originating from lymphocytes. Common forms of lymphoma are listed in the subentries below. These include Hodgkin disease, mycosis fungoides, and non-Hodgkin lymphoma. **lymphomatous** (′măt-ŭs), *adj.* SEE: *Hodgkin disease*.

   STAGING: Staging of both Hodgkin and non-Hodgkin lymphoma is as follows: Stage I: involvement of a single lymph node or localized involvement. Stage II: Involvement of two or more lymph node regions on the same side of the diaphragm. Stage III: Involvement of several lymph node regions on both sides of the diaphragm. Stage IV: Involvement of extralymphatic tissue, such as the bone marrow.

   anaplastic large cell l. ABBR: ALCL. A rare form of non-Hodgkin, T-cell lymphoma that may behave indolently when limited to the skin or may be more aggressive and spread to lymph nodes throughout the body.

   body cavity l. Primary effusion l.

   Burkitt l. SEE: *Burkitt lymphoma*.

   cutaneous T-cell l. ABBR: CTCL. A malignant non-Hodgkin lymphoma with a predilection for infiltrating the skin. In its earliest stages, it often is mistaken for a mild, chronic dermatitis because it appears as itchy macules and patches, often on the chest or trunk. Later, the lesions may thicken, become nodular, or spread throughout the entire surface of the skin, the internal organs, or the bloodstream. SEE: illus.

   follicular l. A B-cell, non-Hodgkin lymphoma found in adult and older pa-

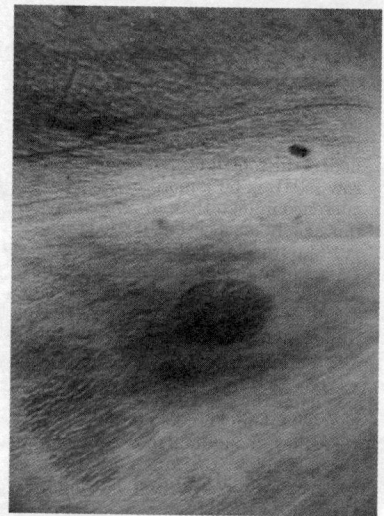

CUTANEOUS T-CELL LYMPHOMA
Raised reddish-purple plaque on the skin of the hip

tients. It results from a translocation of an oncogene from chromosome 14 to chromosome 18 [t(14;18)]. Most instances of this lymphoma are indolent or slow growing.

   hepatosplenic T-cell l. A rare, rapidly progressive lymphoma that develops in the liver, spleen, and bone marrow. It has been identified in patients taking immunosuppressive drugs for diseases such as inflammatory bowel disease.

   Hodgkin l. SEE: under *Hodgkin, Thomas*.

   non-Hodgkin l. ABBR: NHL. Any of a group of malignant tumors of B or T lymphocytes. In 2008, the American Cancer Society estimated that about 66,100 Americans would be newly diagnosed with the disease. SEE: illus; *Hodgkin disease*.

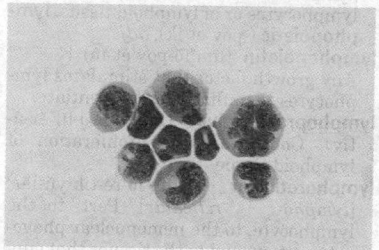

NON-HODGKIN LYMPHOMA
Bizarre-appearing lymphocytes revealing active mitosis (orig. mag. ×1000)

   SYMPTOMS: Painless lymphadenopathy in two thirds of patients is the most frequent presenting symptom. Others have fever, night sweats, and loss of 10% or more of body weight in the 6 months before presenting with symptoms of infiltration into nonlymphoid tissue. Additional involvement is in peripheral areas such as epitrochlear nodes, the tonsillar area, and bone marrow. NHL is 50% more frequent in occurrence in men than in women of similar age. In most cases the cause of NHL is unknown, but patients who have received immunosuppressive agents have an over 100 times greater chance of developing NHL, probably because the immunosuppressive agents activate tumor viruses.

TREATMENT: Specific therapy depends on the type, grade, and stage of the lymphoma. Combination chemotherapies, bone marrow transplantation, radiation therapy, and photochemotherapy may be given, depending on the specific diagnosis.

primary effusion l. A non-Hodgkin B-cell lymphoma that typically arises in body cavities such as the pleural, peritoneal, or pericardial spaces. It is caused by Kaposi sarcoma herpesvirus (human herpes virus 8) and is usually found in patients with advanced immune suppression. SYN: *body cavity l.*

lymphomatoid (lĭm-fō′mă-toyd) [L. *lympha,* lymph, + Gr. *oma,* tumor, + *eidos,* form, shape] Resembling lymphoma.

lymphomatosis (lĭm″fō-mă-tō′sĭs) [″ + ″ + *osis,* condition] Dissemination of lymphoma throughout the body.

lymphopathia venereum, lymphopathia venerea (lĭm″fō-path′ē-ă) Lymphogranuloma venereum.

lymphopenia (lĭm″fō-pē′nē-ă) [*lymph-* + *-penia*] A deficiency of lymphocytes in the blood. It is often associated with susceptibility to infection. SYN: *lymphocytopenia.*

lymphopoiesis (lĭm″fō-poy-ē′sĭs) [*lymph-* + *-poiesis*] The formation of lymphocytes or of lymphoid tissue. **lymphopoietic** (-poy-et′ik), *adj.*

lymphopoietin (lĭm″fō-poy′ĕt-ĭn) [″ + ″] Any growth factor that stimulates lymphocytes to multiply or differentiate.

lymphoproliferative (lĭm″fō-prō-lĭf′ĕr-ă-tĭv) Concerning the proliferation of lymphoid tissue.

lymphoreticular (lĭm″fō-rĕ-tik′yŭ-lăr) [*lympho-* + *reticular*] Pert. to the lymphocyte, to the mononuclear phagocyte system, and to the tissues that support their growth.

lymphoreticular disorder Any benign or malignant disease in which lymphocytes or lymphatic tissues proliferate. The disorders include self-limited proliferation of lymph glands, lymphocytes,

and monocytes; infectious mononucleosis; benign abnormalities of immunoglobulin synthesis; leukemias; lymphomas such as Hodgkin's disease, lymphosarcoma, reticulum cell sarcoma, and mycosis fungoides; malignant proliferative response or abnormal immunoglobulin synthesis such as plasma cell myeloma, macroglobulinemia, and amyloidosis; histiocytosis; and lipid storage disease.

lymphorrhea (lĭm″fō-rē′ă) [*lymph-* + *-rhea*] The flow of lymph from ruptured lymph vessels. SYN: *lymphorrhagia.*

lymphosarcoma (lĭm″fō-săr-kō′mă) [″ + Gr. *sarx,* flesh, + *oma,* tumor] An infrequently used term for lymphoma, used most often in veterinary medicine. SYN: *lymphoblastoma.*

lymphoscintigraphy (lĭm″fō-sin-tig′ră-fē) [*lymph-* + *scintigraphy*] The use of radioactive tracers to identify the lymphatic drainage basin of a tumor. The technique is used to guide the surgeon in performing biopsies and in the removal of tumors.

lymphostasis (lĭm″fos′tă-sĭs) [*lymph-* + *stasis*] Stoppage of the flow of lymph.

lymphotropic (lĭm″fō-trōp′ĭk) Attracted to lymph cells. For example, HIV and human T-cell leukemia-lymphoma virus are lymphotropic for CD4+ lymphocytes and Epstein-Barr virus is lymphotropic for B lymphocytes.

Lynch syndrome (lĭnch) An autosomal dominant predisposition to colon cancer and other solid tumors. People with Lynch I syndrome are susceptible to colon cancer alone, whereas those with Lynch II syndrome have an additional tendency to get cancers of the colon, ovaries, breasts, and/or uterus. It is also known as *hereditary nonpolyposis colorectal cancer.*

lyo- [Gr. *lyein,* to loose, dissolve] Prefix meaning to *loosen* or *dissolve.*

Lyon hypothesis (lī′ŏn) [Mary Lyon, Brit. geneticist, b. 1925] The idea that one of the X chromosomes of the female is inactivated during embryogenesis and becomes hyperpyknotic. This chromosome forms, in the cell nucleus, the sex chromatin mass, or Barr body. This X chromosome remains in this state throughout the cell's progeny so that in the adult only one X chromosome is active in each cell.

lyophilization (lī-ŏf″ĭ-lī-zā′shŭn) The process of rapidly freezing a substance at an extremely low temperature and then dehydrating the substance in a high vacuum. SYN: *freeze-drying.*

lys *lysine.*

lysate (lī′sāt) **1.** The products of hydrolysis. **2.** The material that remains when cells are lysed by enzymes, inorganic chemicals, or physical means.

lyse (līz) [Gr. *lysis,* dissolution] **1.** To

kill. **2.** To dissolve; to destroy or fragment.

lysergic acid diethylamide (lī-sĕr′jĭk, lĭ-) [*lyso-* + *erg(ot)* *-ic*] ABBR: LSD. $C_{20}H_{25}N_3O$, a hallucinogenic derivative of an alkaloid in ergot. LSD is used legally only for experimental purposes.

lysin (līs′+ĭn) [*lyso-* + *-in*] A substance that causes cell destruction and death. SEE: *antibody.*

lysine (lī′sēn″) [*lyso-* + *-ine*] ABBR: lys. An amino acid that is a hydrolytic cleavage product of digested protein. It is essential for growth and repair of tissues.

> **l. acetate** An amino acid.

> **l. hydrochloride** An amino acid.

lysis (lī′sĭs) [Gr., dissolution] **1.** The gradual decline of a fever or disease; the opposite of crisis. **2.** The death of cells or microorganisms, caused by antibodies, complement, enzymes, or other substances.

-lysis [Gr. *lysis*, a loosening, fr. *lyein*, to loosen] **1.** Suffix meaning to *decomposition, dissolving* or *loosening.* **2.** In medicine, a suffix meaning *reduction* or *relief of.*

lysis-centrifugation A technique for detecting microorganisms in a specimen of body fluid, in which the cells in the fluid are mixed in a tube, and then allowed to stand (usually for an hour) to allow its cellular components to break down. After cellular breakdown ("lysis") the tube is centrifuged to concentrate its sediment. The sediment is subsequently spread on culture media.

> Lysis-centrifugation is used to detect bacteria, fungi, mycobacteria, and other microorganisms in blood or body fluids.

lyso-, lysi-, lys- [Gr. *lysis,* a loosening, releasing] Prefixes meaning *decomposition, lysis, dissolution.*

lysogen (lī′sŏ-jĕn) [*lyso-* + *-gen*] Something capable of producing a lysin.

lysogenesis (lī″sŏ-jen′ĕ-sĭs) [*lyso(gen)* + *-genesis*] The production of lysin.

lysogenic (lī-sŏ-jen′ik) [*lyso-* + *lysogenic*] Producing lysins.

lysogeny (lī-sŏj′ĕ-nē) [*lyso-* + *-geny*] A special type of virus-bacterial cell interaction maintained by a complex cellular regulatory mechanism. Bacterial strains freshly isolated from their natural environment may contain a low concentration of bacteriophage. This phage will lyse other related bacteria.

lysolecithin (lī″sŏ-les′ĭ-thĭn) [*lyso-* + *lecithin*] A substance obtained from lecithin through the action of an enzyme present in cobra venom. It demyelinates nerves and destroys red blood cells.

lysosomal storage disease (lī″sŏ-sō′măl) A disease caused by deficiency of specific lysosomal enzymes that normally degrade glycoproteins, glycolipids, or mucopolysaccharides. The substances that cannot be catabolized accumulate in lysosomes. Specific enzymes account for specific storage diseases. Included in this group are Gaucher's, Hurler's, Tay-Sachs, Niemann-Pick, Fabry's, Morquio's, Scheie's, and Maroteaux-Lamy diseases.

lysosome (lī′sŏ-sōm″) [*lyso-* + *-some*] An organelle that is part of the intracellular digestive system. The lysosome contains within its limiting membrane hydrolytic enzymes that break down proteins and carbohydrates. Lysosomal enzymes contribute to the digestion of pathogens phagocytized by a cell and also to the tissue damage that accompanies inflammation. **lysosomal** (lī″sŏ-sōm′ăl), *adj.*

lysozyme (lī′sŏ-zīm″) [*lyso-,* + *-zyme*] An enzyme found in neutrophils, macrophages, tears, saliva, and other body secretions. It inhibits the growth of bacteria by damaging their cell walls.

lyssa (lĭs′ă) [Gr., frenzy] Obsolete term for rabies.

Lyssavirus (lĭs″ă-vī′rŭs) The genus of the family Rhabdoviridae, which includes the rabies virus.

-lyte [Gr. *lytos,* loosened, untied, fr. *lyein,* to loosen] Suffix for a substance capable of undergoing lysis, formed from a noun ending in *-lysis,* e.g., *electrolyte* from *electrolysis.*

lytic (lĭt′ĭk) Pert. to lysis (cellular destruction) or a lysin.

-lytic [Gr. *lytikos,* able to loosen, fr. *lyein,* to loose] Suffix meaning *lysis.*

LZ Landing zone for a helicopter, usually a minimum of 100×100 feet and free of overhead obstructions such as trees and power lines.

M

μ (mū, moo) [*mu*, the twelfth letter of the Greek alphabet] Symbol for *micro-*. SEE: *micro-*.

μμ Symbol for micromicro-; micromicron.

μCi *microcurie*.

μg *microgram*.

μm Symbol for micrometer.

μsec Symbol for microsecond.

μV Symbol for microvolt.

M *master* or *medicine* in professional titles; *mille*, a thousand; *misce*, mix; *molar*.

m *meter; minim; meta-* (in chemistry); *metastasis* (in oncology).

mμ Symbol for millimicron.

M0 Minimally differentiated acute myeloblastic leukemia, a relatively rare form of acute myeloid leukemia with large myeloblasts found in the bone marrow and the peripheral blood.

M1 *acute myeloblastic leukemia without maturation.*

M2 *acute myeloblastic leukemia with maturation.*

M3 *acute promyelocytic leukemia.*

M4 ABBR: AMMoL. Acute myelomonocytic leukemia.

M5 ABBR: AMoL. *acute monoblastic leukemia.*

M6 ABBR: AEL. *acute erythroleukemia.*

M7 ABBR: AMegaL. *acute megakaryoblastic leukemia.*

MA *mental age.*

ma *milliampere.*

-mab (mab) [Abbr. of *m(onoclonal) a(nti)b(ody)*] A suffix for *monoclonal antibody*.

MAC *maximum allowable concentration; monitored anesthesia care; Mycobacterium avium complex.*

MACE An abbreviation for "major adverse cardiac events." In trials of experimental therapies for heart diseases, researchers monitor patients for MACE to see if the treatments are hazardous. MACE includes but is not limited to unstable chest pain, heart attack, cardiac dysrhythmias, congestive heart failure, and death.

macerate (măs'ĕr-āt) To soften by steeping or soaking in water; usually pertains to the skin.

maceration (măs-ĕr-ā'shŭn) [L. *macerare*, to make soft] **1.** The process of softening a solid by steeping in a fluid. **2.** The dissolution of the skin of a dead fetus retained in utero.

Machado-Joseph disease (mă-chä'dō-jō'zĕf) ABBR: MJD. An autosomal-dominant form of spinocerebellar ataxia, first identified in inhabitants of the Azores Islands. It is caused by an abnormal repetition of nucleotides (cytosine-adenine-guanine) on chromosome 14. Affected people may have difficulty speaking, swallowing, or moving their eyes and may exhibit other neurological symptoms.

machine Any mechanical device or apparatus.

macies (mā'shē-ēz) [L., wasting] Atrophy.

macrencephalia, macrencephaly (măk-rĕn"sĕ-fā'lē-ă, -sĕf'ă-lē) [Gr. *makros*, large, + *enkephalos*, brain] Abnormally large size of the brain.

macro-, macr- [Gr. *makros*, large] Prefixes meaning *large* or *long*.

macroadenoma (măk"rō-ăd"ĭn-ō'mă) A tumor of the pituitary gland that is a centimeter or greater in diameter. Some macroadenomas secrete excessive quantities of hormones (e.g., adrenocorticotropic hormone, prolactin, or growth hormone). Growth of the tumor may also cause damage to the sella turcica or impinge on the optic chiasm or cranial nerves. Symptoms of macroadenomas vary but may include headaches, visual field deficits, galactorrhea, acromegaly, or Cushing's disease. The tumors may be treated medically or surgically.

macroamylase (mak"rō-am'ĭ-lās") [*macro-* + *amylase*] A form of amylase with a molecular weight much greater than ordinary amylase. The macroamylase molecule is too large to be excreted by the glomerulus of the kidney. It is clinically important because its presence in the bloodstream may falsely suggest the diagnosis of pancreatitis. In patients with macroamylasemia, the urinary amylase would be within normal limits, which would not be true if the elevation of blood amylase were due to an increase in pancreatic amylase.

macroamylasemia (măk"rō-ăm"ĭl-ă-sē'mē-ă) Macroamylase in the serum. The presence of increased amounts of macroamylase in the blood has not been correlated with disease.

macrocephalia, macrocephaly (mak"rō-sĕ-fā'lē-ă, mak"rō-sef'ă-lē) [*macro-* + *cephal- + -ia*] Abnormally large size of the head. It is found in acromegaly, hydrocephalus, rickets, Paget's disease, leontiasis ossea, myxedema, leprosy, and pituitary disturbances. **macrocephalic, macrocephalous** (mak"rō-sĕ-fal'ik, mak"rō-sef'ă-lŭs), *adj.*

macrocheilia (măk"rō-kī'lē-ă) [" + *cheilos*, lip] Abnormal size of a lip characterized by swelling of the glands of the lip. It is a congenital condition. SEE: *macrolabia*.

macroconidium (măk″rō-kō-nĭd′ē-ŭm) A large conidium or exospore.

macrocyclic (mak″rō-sik′lik) [*macro- + cyclic*] Composed of two or more linked, ring-shaped chemical structures.

macrocyst (măk′rō-sĭst) [″ + *kystis*, bladder] A large cyst.

macrocyte (măk′rō-sīt) [″ + *kytos*, cell] Abnormally large red blood cell, with a mean corpuscular volume more than 100 fL.

macrocythemia, macrocytosis (măk″rō-sī-thē′mē-ă, măk″rō-sī-tō′sĭs) [″ + ″ + *haima*, blood] Condition in which erythrocytes are larger than normal, (e.g., in folate or vitamin B_{12} deficiencies).

macrodontia (măk″rō-dŏn′shē-ă) [″ + *odous*, tooth] Abnormal increase in size of the teeth. SYN: *megadontia*.

macroesthesia (măk″rō-ĕs-thē′zē-ă) [Gr. *makros*, large, + *aisthesis*, sensation] State in which objects seen or felt appear to be greatly magnified. SYN: *macropsia*.

macrogamete (măk″rō-găm′ĕt) [″ + *gamete*, wife] A large immobile reproductive cell formed in certain protozoa and simple plants. It corresponds to the ovum in higher forms.

macrogametocyte (măk″rō-gă-mē′tō-sīt) A large nonmotile reproductive cell developing from the merozoite of certain protozoans and fungi. Macrogametocytes are found in red blood cells infected with malaria. SEE: *Plasmodium*.

macroglia (măk-rŏg′lē-ă) [″ + *glia*, glue] Astrocyte.

macroglobulin (măk″rō-glŏb′ū-lĭn) A globulin of high molecular weight over about 400,000. Macroglobulin is normally present in the blood but is increased in disease states such as multiple myeloma, connective tissue disease, cirrhosis of the liver, and amyloidosis.

alpha-2 m. Plasma glycoprotein made principally by the liver that inhibits serine proteases, leukocyte elastase, and proteinase 3, but not matrix metalloproteinases.

macroglobulinemia (măk-rō-glŏb″ū-lĭn-ē′mē-ă) Presence of globulins of high molecular weight in serum.

Waldenström's m. A disease of plasma cells in which there is macroglobulinemia marked by excess production of immunoglobulin M (IgM). Peak incidence is in the sixth and seventh decades. The disease is more common in men. Findings include anemia due to infiltration of the bone marrow with lymphocytes and plasma cells, weight loss, neurological disturbances, blurred vision, bleeding disorders, cold sensitivity, generalized lymphadenopathy, and hyperviscosity of the blood.

TREATMENT: Plasma exchange therapy decreases the viscosity of the blood by removing excess IgM. The procedure may need to be performed every 4 to 6 weeks in some patients. Other specific treatments include the use of chemotherapeutic drugs to decrease the production of IgM by abnormal clones of B lymphocytes.

macroglossia (măk″rō-glŏs′ē-ă) [Gr. *makros*, large, + *glossa*, tongue] Hypertrophy of the tongue.

macrography (măk-rŏg′ră-fē) [″ + *graphein*, to write] Writing with large letters.

macrogyria (măk″rō-jē′rē-ă) [″ + *gyros*, circle] Excessively large size of convolutions (gyri) of the cerebral hemispheres.

macrolide (măk′rō-līd) A class of antibiotics that inhibits protein synthesis by bacteria at the 50S ribosome. They are usually used for respiratory tract, skin, and genitourinary infections. Examples of macrolides are erythromycin, clarithromycin, and azithromycin.

macromastia (măk-rō-măs′tē-ă) [″ + *mastos*, breast] Abnormally large breasts.

macromelus (măk-rŏm′ĕ-lŭs) [″ + *melos*, limb] An individual with abnormally large extremities.

macromere (măk′rō-mēr) [″ + *meros*, a part] A blastomere of large size.

macromethod (mak′rō-meth″ŏd) [*macro- + method*] An imprecise term for the use of visible, rather than minute, quantities of a substance in a chemical examination or assay

macromolecule (măk″rō-mŏl′ĕ-kūl) A large molecule such as a protein, polymer, or polysaccharide.

macronucleus (măk″rō-nū′klē-ŭs) The larger of the two nuclei of ciliated protozoa.

macronutrient (măk′rō-nū′trē-ĕnt) Any essential nutrient required in large amounts in a balanced diet. There are six categories of macronutrients: carbohydrates, fats, minerals, proteins, vitamins, and water. SEE: *micronutrient; trace element*.

macropathology (măk″rō-pă-thŏl′ō-jē) Pathological changes in gross anatomical structures.

macrophage (mak′rō-făj″) [*macro- + -phage*] A monocyte that has left the circulation and settled and matured in a tissue. Macrophages are found in large quantities in the spleen, lymph nodes, alveoli, and tonsils. About 50% of all macrophages are found in the liver as Kupffer cells. They are also present in the brain as microglia, in the skin as Langerhans cells, in bone as osteoclasts, as well as in serous cavities and breast and placental tissue. Along with neutrophils, macrophages are the major phagocytic cells of the immune system.

They have the ability to recognize and ingest foreign antigens through receptors on the surface of their cell membranes; these antigens are then destroyed by lysosomes. Their placement in the peripheral lymphoid tissues enables macrophages to serve as the major scavengers of the blood, clearing it of abnormal or old cells and cellular debris as well as pathogenic organisms.

Macrophages also serve a vital role by processing antigens and presenting them to T cells, activating the specific immune response. They also release many substances that participate in inflammation, including chemokines and cytokines, lytic enzymes, oxygen radicals, coagulation factors, and growth factors. SEE: illus.; *chemokine; cytokine; inflammation; oxygen radical.*

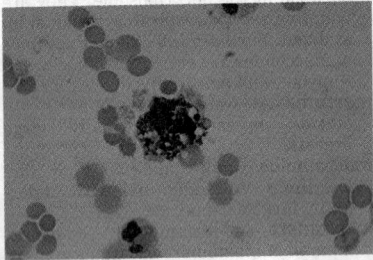

MACROPHAGE
with aggregated hemosiderin granules
(×500)

macrophthalmia (măk″rŏf-thăl′mē-ă) [″ + *ophthalmos*, eye] Abnormally large eyeball.

macropodia (măk-rō-pō′dē-ă) [″ + *pous*, foot] Abnormally large feet.

macropsia (măk-rŏp′sē-ă) [″ + *opsis*, vision] Macroesthesia.

macroscopic (măk-rō-skŏp′ĭk) [″ + *skopein*, to examine] Large enough to be seen by the naked eye. Opposite of microscopic.

macroscopy (măk-rŏs′kō-pē) Examination of an object with the naked eye.

macrosmatic (măk″rŏs-măt′ĭk) [″ + *osmasthai*, to smell] Having an abnormally keen sense of smell.

macrosomia, macrosomatia (mak″rŏ-sō-mē-ă, mak-rŏ-sŏ-mā′sh(ē-)ă) [Gr. *makros*, large, + *soma*, body] An abnormally large body.

fetal m. In a newborn, birth weight above the 90th percentile on the intrauterine growth curve or 4000 grams. SEE: *large for gestational age.*

macrospore (măk′rō-spor) The larger spore type in certain fungi and protozoa with two spores.

macrostomia (măk-rō-stō′mē-ă) [″ + *stoma*, mouth] Excessively large mouth.

macrostructure (măk′rō-strŭk″tūr) The overall or gross structure of an entity.

macrothrombocyte (măk″rō-thrŏm′bō-sīt) [″ + *thrombos*, clot, + *kytos*, cell] A large platelet seen in some leukemias and rare disorders of platelets.

macrothrombocytopenia (măk″rō-thrŏm″bō-sīt-ō-pē′nē-ă) [″ + ″ + ″ + *penia*, lack] Deficiency of macrothrombocytes. SEE: *Alport's syndrome.*

macrotia (măk-rō′shē-ă) [″ + *ous*, ear] Abnormally large ears.

macrovascular (mak″rō-vas′kyŭ-lăr) [*macro-* + *vascular*] Pert. to the large blood vessels, esp. the aorta and its branches or the coronary arteries or both.

macula (măk′ū-lă) *pl.* **maculae** [L., spot] **1.** A small spot or colored area. SEE: *roseola.* **2.** Macule. **3.** The specialized central region of the retina that surrounds the fovea and contains a high concentration of cone photoreceptors. It is responsible for central vision, fine visual detail, and color vision. It is located anatomically between the superior and inferior temporal vessels of the retina. SYN: *m. lutea retinae; yellow spot.* **macular** (-lăr), *adj.*

m. acusticae The site of the hair cells (receptors) in the wall of the saccule and utricle of the inner ear. These receptors respond to changes in the pull of gravity (position of the head) and generate impulses carried by the vestibular branch of the acoustic nerve. They include the macula sacculi and macula utriculi.

m. albida A white mark found on the visceral layer of the peritoneum or epicardium in some contagious diseases.

m. atrophica A glistening white spot on the skin due to atrophy.

m. caerulea A steel-gray or blue stain of epidermis without elevation. It does not disappear on pressure and occurs esp. with pediculosis pubis or flea bites.

cerebral m. A reddened line that becomes deeper and persists for some time when the fingernail is drawn across the skin, esp. in tuberculous meningitis. SYN: *tache cérébrale.*

m. corneae An opaque spot in the cornea.

m. cribrosa One of several tiny foramina in the wall of the vestibule of the bony labyrinth of the ear through which pass filaments of the acoustic nerve.

m. densa A group of cells in the wall of the distal renal tubule, next to the juxtaglomerular cells, that are sensitive to changes in the salt concentration of the filtrate in the tubule.

m. flava laryngis A small yellow spot at the ventral end of each vocal cord formed by a small mass of elastic tissue or, sometimes, cartilage.

m. folliculi The point on the ovarian follicle where it ruptures.

m. gonorrhoeica A red spot at the orifice of Bartholin's gland; seen in gonococcal vulvitis.

m. lutea retinae Macula(3).

m. of retina An oval, light pink area in the center of the retina (and to the temporal side of the optic disk) containing the fovea, the place of highest visual acuity. SYN: *macular area*.

m. sacculi The site of the hair cells in the saccule; receptors stimulated by the pull of gravity. These cells generate impulses carried by the vestibular branch of the acoustic nerve.

m. utriculi The site of the hair cells in the utricule; receptors stimulated by the pull of gravity. These cells generate impulses carried by the vestibular branch of the acoustic nerve.

macular area (măk'ū-lĕr ăr'ē-ă) Macula of retina.

macular hole A tear or discontinuity in the central portion of the retina, resulting in central visual loss.

macular pucker A wrinkling and eventual scarring of the retina in the macular area, resulting in visual distortion. SYN: *premacular fibrosis; cellophane maculopathy*.

macular translocation Surgery involving movement of a flap of retina containing the fovea to an area of healthy retinal pigment. It is performed experimentally to treat age-related macular degeneration. SYN: *macular rotation surgery*.

maculate(d) (măk'ū-lāt, -lāt-ĕd) Spotted, as with macules.

maculation (măk-ū-lā'shŭn) [L. *macula,* spot] Process of becoming maculate; development of macules.

macule (mak'ūl″) [L. *macula,* spot] A flat spot on the skin whose color may be lighter or darker than the surrounding skin. Some common examples are freckles, petechiae, and vitiligo. SYN: *macula (2)*.

café au lait m. Pale brown areas of increased melanin in the skin. The sites are usually 0.8 to 8 in. (2 to 20 cm) in diameter with irregular borders. They appear in infancy and tend to disappear with age. These macules are occasionally markers for systemic disease (e.g., neurofibromatosis).

melanotic m. A small, brown to black lesion of the oral mucosa that is usually less than 1 cm in diameter, solitary, and asymptomatic. In most instances, this type of macule is benign and requires no therapy. It can, however, be due to melanoma, which requires immediate, vigorous therapy. When it is benign, it may be due to Peutz-Jeghers syndrome, physiologic pigmentation, Addison's disease, or healing of traumatic lesions; or it may be secondary to a variety of medications.

syphilitic m. A small red eruption manifested in secondary syphilis. These eruptions often cover the entire body and are associated with chancre or scar, alopecia, pain in bones, swollen glands, and sore throat.

maculopapular (măk″ū-lō-păp'ū-lăr) A rash that has both flat stained regions (macules) and small elevated bumps or pimples (papules).

maculopathy (mak″yŭ-lop'ă-thē) [*macula + -pathy*] Retinal pathology affecting the macula of the eye.

crystalline m. Benign refractile crystals in the retinal macula without visual impairment.

drug-induced m. Damage to the macula of the eye due to exposure to certain drugs, e.g., hydroxychloroquine (to treat autoimmune disorders) or tamoxifen. Patients experience a painless decrease in visual acuity that may resolve when the responsible drug is discontinued.

hypotony m. Folding or wrinkling of the retina or choroid that results from excessively low intraocular pressure, usually less than 5 mm Hg.

myopic m. Macular injury due to extreme nearsightedness SYN: *myopic traction m.*

myopic traction m. Myopic **m.**

neovascular m. Any macular disease, including age-related macular degeneration, in which new, abnormal blood vessels grow in the retina, leak blood, and interfere with vision.

radiation m. Damage to the macula of the eye due to irradiation. It may occur after radiotherapy for ocular melanoma.

torpedo m. A congenital nevus of the retinal pigment epithelium, usually an asymptomatic finding on retinal examination.

Valsalva m. SEE: under *Valsalva, Antonio M.*

mad 1. Not rational. **2.** Angry. **3.** Rash, foolish, frantic. **4.** Suffering from infection with rabies.

madarosis (măd-ă-rō'sĭs) [Gr. *madaros,* bald] Loss of eyelashes or eyebrows.

mad cow disease Bovine spongiform encephalopathy.

madder (măd'ĕr) Root of the plant *Rubia tinctorum,* a source of the red dye alizarin.

Madelung deformity (mod'ĕ-lung″) [Otto W. Madelung, Ger. surgeon, 1846–1926] Displacement of the hand to the radial side due to relative overgrowth of the ulna.

Madelung disease Generalized symmetrical deposits of fatty tissue (lipomas) on the upper back, shoulders, and neck. SYN: *Madelung neck.*

made with organic ingredients A designation for food that specifies that 70% of its components are organic.

Madura foot (mă-door'ă) [from the *Madur* district in India where the disease was first described in 1842] A local, painless maduromycosis (mycetoma) of an exposed area, esp. bare feet. It consists of swollen infected tissues with sinus tracts and a purulent, grainy discharge. Madura foot is usually found in adult males who work outside and have poor footwear or inadequate wound care. SYN: *white-grain mycetoma*. SEE: *maduromycosis*.

ETIOLOGY: This mycetoma is caused by various fungi, e.g., actinomycetes. In the U.S., the most frequent cause is *Pseudallescheria boydii*.

TREATMENT: The antibiotic given depends on the specific organism involved. Clindamycin is used for actinomycetoma; ketoconazole or itraconazole has been used for eumycetomas. Surgery should not be necessary, but drug treatment often takes several months.

maduromycosis (mad″yŭ-rō-mī-kō′sĭs) [*Madura* (foot) + *mycosis*] A type of chronic mycetoma of the foot or hand characterized by marked swelling and development of nodules, vesicles, abscesses, and sinuses. **maduromycotic** (-kot′ik), *adj*.

magenta (mă-jĕn′tă) The dye basic fuchsin.

maggot (măg′gŭt) Larva of an insect, esp. the soft-bodied footless larva of flies (order Diptera). Many are parasitic, giving rise to myiasis.

maggot treatment A method of treating septic wounds. In the 1930s, scientific studies indicated that neglected and infected compound fractures were aided in healing when blackbottle fly, bluebottle fly, and blowfly maggots accidentally infested the wounds. The maggots removed necrotic tissue and left healthy granulating tissue. Modern therapy, including antibiotics, has made this method of treating wounds and osteomyelitis obsolete. Nevertheless, it is possible to culture sterile blowfly maggots for this use. In severe skin infections when all other forms of therapy have failed, this method has been used.

magical thinking The belief that one's thoughts or actions have the ability to cause actions or effects that defy the normal laws of cause and effect.

Magill forceps (mă-gĭl′) Angulated forceps used during direct laryngoscopy to remove a foreign body from an obstructed airway.

magma (măg′mă) [Gr.] **1.** Mass left after extraction of principal. **2.** Salve or paste. **3.** A suspension of finely divided material in a small amount of water.

magnesemia (mag″nĕ-sē′mē-ă) [*magnesium* + *-emia*] Hypermagnesemia.

magnesium (mag-nē′zē-ŭm, -zhĕm) [*magnesia* + *-ium*] SYMB: Mg. A white mineral element, atomic weight (mass) 24.312, atomic number 12, specific gravity 1.738. It is a naturally occurring element, abundant in sea water. Magnesium is found in soft tissue, muscles, bones, to some extent in body fluids, and is the second most common cation in intracellular fluid. The human body contains approx. 25 mg of magnesium, mostly in the bones. Muscles contain less magnesium than calcium. Concentration of magnesium in the serum is between 1.5 and 2.5 mmol/L.

Magnesium deficiency is rare because it is common in foods, e.g., fish, whole grains, fruits, and green vegetables. A typical diet contains 200 to 400 mg of magnesium, about one third of which is absorbed through the small intestine, the rest being excreted in the stool. The major function of magnesium is to enhance neuromuscular integration, but magnesium also stimulates secretion of parathyroid hormone, thus regulating intracellular fluid calcium levels.

FUNCTION: Magnesium is needed for DNA repair. It moderates cellular differentiation and proliferation and improves tissue sensitivity to circulating insulin. It is a component of enzymes required for the synthesis of adenosine triphosphate (ATP) and the release of energy from ATP. It is also a component of enzymes involved in muscle contraction and protein synthesis.

PATIENT CARE:

Magnesium is often administered orally or parenterally to patients with asthma, constipation, preeclampsia, eclampsia, or torsades de pointes. Excessive oral intake (resulting in hypermagnesemia) may promote diarrhea (compounds containing magnesium are given as laxatives).

Hypermagnesemia (excess of magnesium in blood serum) is rare in patients with normal kidney function but may develop in patients taking magnesium supplementation for impaired renal function. It may cause slowing of the heart rate, low blood pressure, decreased level of consciousness, and muscle weakness or flaccid paralysis. Severe hypermagnesemia may cause cardiac arrest. Treatment for hypermagnesemia includes withholding magnesium, increasing fluid intake, and administering loop diuretics. Calcium gluconate 10% may be administered for temporary relief of symptoms in an emergency or for magnesium intoxication. Peritoneal dialysis or hemodialysis may be needed if renal function fails or excess magnesium cannot be eliminated.

Hypomagnesemia (deficiency of magnesium in blood serum) may cause hypokalemia, hypoparathyroidism, hypocalcemia, tetany, irritability, confusion, delusions, cardiac arrhythmias, and chronic diarrhea.

⚠️ During treatment of magnesium disorders, careful monitoring is needed of serum electrolyte and fluid balance, vital signs, level of consciousness, flaccidity, clonus, and cardiac rhythm.

magnet (măg′nĕt) [Gr. *magnes,* magnet] Any body that has the property of attracting iron. This may be a natural iron oxide or a mass of iron or steel that has this property given to it artificially. A piece of iron may be magnetized by passage of an electric current through an insulated wire wound around it. **magnetic** (măg-nĕt′ĭk), *adj.*

magnetic activated cell sorting ABBR: MACS. Technology used to separate unique populations of cells from an undifferentiated specimen of blood, bone marrow, or other tissue. It relies on the use of antibodies to specific cell types. A multicomponent specimen that contains some desirable cells is bathed in a solution of magnetically tagged antibodies. The cells of interest are attracted into a magnetic field and then collected for identification, experimentation, or therapeutic manipulation.

magnetic cortical stimulation SEE: under *stimulation.*

magnetic field SEE: under *field.*

magnetic field homogeneity The uniformity of the main magnetic field in a magnetic resonance imaging device.

magnetic field therapy Magnetotherapy.

magnetic lines of force SEE: under *line.*

magnetic resonance angiography SEE: under *angiography.*

magnetic resonance cholangiopancreatography (kŏ-lan″jē-ō-pang″krē-ă-tog′ră-fē) SEE: under *cholangiopancreatography.*

magnetic resonance imaging SEE: under *imaging.*

magnetic resonance imaging-guided ultrasound therapy ABBR: MRgFUS. A treatment for uterine fibroids in which a focused ultrasonic beam is directed at the abnormal tissue, destroying it by raising its temperature. Magnetic resonance imaging is used during the procedure to monitor the course of treatment and limit damage to neighboring organs, e.g., the healthy uterus, the colon, and the bladder.

magnetism (măg′nĕ-tĭzm) [Gr. *magnes,* magnet, + *-ismos,* condition] The property of repulsion and attraction of certain substances that have magnetic properties. SEE: *magnet.*

magnetization (mag″nĕt-ĭ-zā′shŏn) SYMB: M. A measure of the degree to which a body displays magnetic properties. It is a vector field whose magnitude is equal to the local value of the magnetic moment per unit volume.

magnetoelectricity (măg-nē″tō-ē″lĕk-trĭs′ĭ-tē) [″ + *elektron,* amber] Electricity generated by use of magnets.

magnetoencephalography (măg-nē″tō-ĕn-sĕf″ă-lŏg′ră-fē) ABBR: MEG. The detection of the small amount of magnetic activity that results from electrical discharges within the brain. MEG may be used, e.g., prior to neurological surgery to provide a map of the part of the brain that needs to be removed.

magnetometer (măg″nĕ-tŏm′ĕ-tĕr) [″ + *metron,* measure] Device for measuring magnetic fields.

magneton (mag′nĕ-ton″) The unit of nuclear magnetic force. The nuclear magneton is the unit for magnetic dipole moments of heavy particles. The Bohr magneton is used to measure the dipole moment of the electron, which is much higher.

magnetotherapy (măg-nē″tō-thĕr′ă-pē) [″ + *therapeia,* treatment] Application of magnets or magnetism in treating diseases. SYN: *magnetic field therapy.*

magnet program, magnet recognition program A health care institution that has demonstrated leadership in nursing care, recruitment, retention, education, and excellence, and has circulated its findings to other facilities, as certified by the American Nurses Credentialing Center (ANCC).

magnet therapy The application of permanent magnets to painful regions of the human body in an attempt to alleviate chronic diseases or chronic pain.

magnification (măg-nĭ-fĭ-kā′shŭn) [L. *magnus,* great, + *facere,* to make] Process of increasing apparent size of an object, esp. under a microscope.

magnification endoscopy SEE: under *endoscopy.*

magnification factor SEE: under *factor.*

magnitude Size, extent, or dimensions.

magnocellular (măg′nō-sĕl″ū-lĭr) [L. *magnus,* great, large + ″] Having a large body; said of cells, esp. those in the hypothalamus and lateral geniculate nucleus of the thalamus.

ma huang (mă wŏng) Ephedra.

Maillard reaction A chemical reaction between sugars and proteins that results in cellular damage or aging; the making of advanced glycosylation end products; the chemical deterioration of proteins during food processing or storage. Also known in nutritional science as the "browning reaction."

maim (mām) [ME. *maymen,* to cripple] **1.** To injure seriously; to disable. **2.** To deprive of the use of a part, such as an arm or leg.

main (măn) [Fr.] Hand.
    m. en griffe Clawhand.

mainlining (mān′līn″ĭng) A colloquial term for injecting an illicit drug directly into a vein.

mainstreaming The practice of educating

disabled children in the general classroom instead of in specialized institutions, so as not to deprive them of normal social experiences.

mainstream smoke (mān′strēm″) SEE: under *smoke.*

maintain (mān-tān′) [L. *manu tenēre,* to hold in the hand] **1.** To hold, support, or preserve. **2.** To continue, e.g., a healthy behavior.

maintainer Something that supports or keeps another thing in existence or continuity.

    space m. SEE: *space maintainer.*

maintenance (mān′tĕ-nănts) [L. *manu tenēre,* to hold in the hand] **1.** The preservation of a desired condition. **2.** The prevention of recurrence or progression of an illness.

maintenance of wakefulness test An assessment of excessive daytime sleepiness in which the subject is asked to remain awake while resting comfortably in a quiet, dark room.

maitake (mī′tă-kā) [Japanese, "dancing mushroom"] An edible mushroom, *Grifola frondosa,* also known as *hen of the woods,* used in traditional Asian medicine as an immune booster. Its effectiveness as a therapy has not been proved in human studies.

major histocompatibility complex SEE: under *complex.*

majority, age of The age (usually 18 or 21) at which a person achieves full legal rights to make one's own decisions, enter into contracts, and be held personally accountable for the consequences of one's actions.

majority language (mă-jor′ĭt-ē) The language spoken by most of the people living in a multilingual nation.

mal (măl) [Fr., from L. *malum,* an evil] A sickness or disorder.

    m. de mer Seasickness.

mal- [L. *malus,* bad, evil] Prefix meaning *bad, poor,* or *abnormal.*

mala (mā′lă) [L. *mala,* cheek] **1.** The cheek. **2.** The cheekbone. **malar** (mā′lăr), *adj.*

malabsorption syndrome (măl″ăb-sŏrb′shŭn) Disordered or inadequate absorption of nutrients from the intestinal tract, esp. the small intestine. The syndrome may be associated with or due to a number of diseases, including those affecting the intestinal mucosa, such as infections, tropical sprue, celiac disease, pancreatic insufficiency, or lactase deficiency. It may also be due to surgery such as gastric resection and ileal bypass or to antibiotic therapy such as neomycin.

malacia (mă-lā′shē-ă) [Gr. *malakia,* softening] Abnormal softening of tissues of an organ or of tissues themselves.

-malacia [Gr. *malakia,* softness, weakness] Suffix meaning *softening.*

malacoplakia (măl″ă-kō-plā′kē-ă) [Gr. *malakos,* soft, + *plax,* plaque] Existence of soft patches in mucous membrane of a hollow organ.

maladjusted Poorly adjusted; unhappy or unsuccessful because of inability or failure to adjust to life's stresses. Marked by depression, anxiety, and irritability.

malady (măl′ă-dē) [Fr. *maladie,* illness, from L. *malum,* an evil] A disease or disorder. SYN: *disease.*

malaise (mă-lāz′) [Fr.] A subjective sense of discomfort, weakness, fatigue, or feeling rundown that may occur alone or accompany other symptoms and illnesses.

malalignment (măl″ă-līn′mĕnt) Improper alignment of structures such as teeth or the portions of a fractured bone. SEE: *malocclusion.*

malaria (mă-ler′ē-ă) [It. *mala aria,* bad air] A febrile hemolytic disease caused by infection with protozoa of the genus *Plasmodium.* Worldwide malaria is responsible for about 3 million deaths a year. There are four species of malaria: the *benign* malarias: *P. vivax, P. ovale,* and *P. malariae;* and the potentially *malignant* malaria, *P. falciparum.* Each has its own geographic distribution, incubation period, symptoms, and treatment. **malarial, malarious** (mă-ler′ē-ăl, mă-ler′ē-ŭs), *adj.*

Although malaria has been virtually eliminated from temperate climates, it is widespread throughout the tropics and subtropics. It is most prevalent in Asia, Africa and Latin America. As many as half a billion people may be infected with the disease worldwide; 300 to 500 million new infections occur annually In the U.S., less than 1500 cases are diagnosed each year, usually in those who have just come from tropical or subtropical regions. The malaria parasite is transmitted by the bite of an infected female *Anopheles* mosquito or, rarely, by transfusions or the sharing of needles during illicit drug use.

The life cycle of the parasite is complex. Once the parasitic sporozoite enters the bloodstream, it quickly invades organs such as the liver (the tissue phase of the infection). There, the organism matures as a schizont. After an incubation period ranging from about 10 to 30 days, malarial merozoites are released into the blood, where they invade red blood cells (the erythrocytic phase). Some dormant forms (hypnozoites) remain in the liver in *P. vivax* and *P. ovale* malaria, where they may serve as a reservoir for relapse. In the red blood cells, the organisms mature into ring forms and feeding forms (trophozoites). When the parasites break out of red cells to infect other cells in the circulation, they cause hemolysis and periodic symptoms (see below).

After several reproductive cycles, microgametocytes and macrogametocytes develop. Mosquitoes consume these when the parasites take their blood meal from infected humans. Further developmental stages occur within the mosquitoes, resulting in the production of the infectious sporozoites that are injected into human hosts when the mosquitoes feed again.

SYMPTOMS: Initially, the symptoms are nonspecific and resemble those of a minor febrile illness with malaise, headache, fatigue, abdominal discomfort, and muscle aches, followed by fever and chills. The three stages of the malarial paroxysm are the defining characteristics of the illness. In the first (or chill) stage, patients complain of feeling cold and experience shaking chills that last from a few minutes to several hours. During the second (or hot) stage, minimal sweating occurs, although temperature rises to as high as 106°F (41°C). This stage lasts for several hours, and patients are at risk for febrile convulsions and hyperthermic brain damage. The patient also may exhibit tachycardia, hypotension, cough, headache, backache, nausea, abdominal pain, vomiting, diarrhea, and altered consciousness. The third (sweating) stage begins within 2 to 6 hr. In this period, the sweating is marked as the fever subsides and is followed by profound fatigue and by sleep. If untreated, malarial paroxysms caused by *P. ovale* or *P. vivax* will occur cyclically every 48 hr. If due to *P. malariae*, paroxysms will occur every 72 hr. Infections with *P. falciparum* may have a 48-hr cycle of paroxysms, but continuous fever is more characteristic. A severe form of falciparum malaria (cerebral malaria) is characterized by coma and, in spite of treatment, is associated with a 20% mortality rate in adults and 15% in children. About 10% of children who survive cerebral malaria have persistent neurological deficits. Residual deficits in adults who survive this form of malaria are unusual. Progressive, possibly severe anemia and enlargement of the spleen and liver are characteristic of all forms of malaria.

A rare but serious hematological complication of malaria is acute intravascular hemolytic anemia, associated with infection with *P. falciparum*. This condition is called blackwater fever because of the accompanying hemoglobinuria.

DIAGNOSIS: Malaria should be suspected in any febrile person who has returned in the last several months from an area where malaria is endemic. Giemsa-stained thick and thin blood films are examined to confirm the diagnosis (parasites may be seen in red blood cells).

PREVENTION: In areas where malaria is endemic, pools of standing or stagnant water, in which mosquitoes breed, should be eliminated. People traveling to the tropics should wear protective clothing to which insect repellent has been applied. Protective screen netting impregnated with long-lasting insecticide should cover beds. People should apply DEET or other effective insect repellents to exposed skin (but not hands or face) or to children's clothing, esp. between dusk and dawn, when mosquitoes feed most actively. Antimalarial vaccines may reduce the incidence of disease.

PROPHYLAXIS: Chemoprophylaxis is begun 1 week before arriving in an area where malaria is endemic and is continued throughout the stay and for 4 weeks after leaving the area. Chemoprophylaxis is never perfectly effective; thus, malaria should always be considered when treating patients who have a febrile illness and who have traveled to an area where malaria is endemic even if they have taken prophylactic antimalarial drugs. The drug(s) advised for prophylaxis depend on the sensitivity of local parasites and whether infection is likely. Because of the changing sensitivity of the malaria parasites to drugs, it is not possible to be certain that a particular drug will be effective in all areas where malaria is endemic. The prophylactic drugs used for *P. falciparum* are usually effective in preventing infections with *P. ovale* and *P. vivax*. For nonimmune people traveling in areas where malaria is due to chloroquine-resistant *P. falciparum* and *P. vivax*, mefloquine, doxycycline, or atovaquone plus proguanil hydrochloride may be recommended. In areas where *P. falciparum* is chloroquine-sensitive, chloroquine is the drug of choice. Chloroquine may be used prophylactically during pregnancy.

TREATMENT: The parasites that cause malaria constantly evolve, making drug treatment difficult. Patients and health care professionals are advised to contact the Centers for Disease Control in Atlanta to obtain current recommendations (Phone: 800-311-3435; Web address: http://www.cdc.gov). Effective nonantibiotic therapy for malaria sometimes includes exchange transfusion and iron chelation.

PATIENT CARE: Health care providers in areas where malaria is endemic must work toward prompt detection and effective treatment of malaria. People traveling in areas where malaria is endemic and military personnel assigned to such areas must be made aware that missing even one dose of the prophylactic regimen increases the risk of contracting malaria. When an outbreak occurs among military personnel, it usually is found that only a small percentage of personnel have been taking the drug as prescribed in dosages sufficient to provide protection. Standard precautions are used in patient care; gloves are worn when handling blood or body fluids. Fluid balance should be closely monitored (hourly urine output) and urine checked for hematuria. The patient is also observed for signs of internal bleeding or electrolyte imbalance.

cerebral m. Falciparum malaria in which the brain is affected. This fulminant disease often produces coma, shock, or sudden death.

falciparum m. Malaria caused by *Plasmodium falciparum.* It is more prevalent in the tropics. Symptoms are more severe than in other types but it runs a shorter course without relapses. It is treated with artesunate and other drugs.

quartan m. Malaria with short and less severe paroxysms. Sporulation occurs each 72 hr, causing seizures every 4 days. It is caused by *Plasmodium malariae.*

quotidian m. Malaria in which paroxysms occur with daily periodicity due to 24-hr sporulation of two groups of *P. vivax.* Temperature rises and falls abruptly.

tertian m. Malaria in which sporulation occurs each 48 hr. Symptoms are more common during the day. Paroxysms are divided into chill, fever, and sweating stages. Cold stage is usually 10 to 15 min but may last an hour or more. Febrile stage varies from 4 to 6 hr. Benign tertian malaria is caused by *Plasmodium vivax,* malignant tertian malaria by *Plasmodium falciparum.*

vivax m. Malaria caused by *Plasmodium vivax.* It is the most common form of malaria, marked by frequent recurrence.

malariology (mă-lār-ē-ŏl′ō-jē) The scientific study of malaria.

Malassezia (măl″ă-sē′zē-ă) [Louis Charles Malassez, Fr. physiologist, 1842–1909] A genus of fungi that is a common cause of superficial skin infections. The organisms are lipophilic. In hospitals, malassezian infections tend to occur in patients receiving lipid infusions. Malassezian infections of the bloodstream result in sepsis.

M. pachydermatis A species that has been transferred from the pet dogs of health care workers to the infants in a neonatal unit.

malassimilation (măl″ă-sĭm-ĭ-lā′shŭn) [L. *malus,* ill, + *assimilatio,* making like] Defective, incomplete, or faulty assimilation, esp. of nutritive material. SEE: *malabsorption syndrome.*

malate (mā′lāt) A salt or ester of malic acid.

malathion (măl″ă-thī′ŏn) An effective pesticide; an organophosphate that inhibits the enzyme cholinesterase.

mal de ojo (mŏl′ dā ō′hō) [Sp., evil eye] In many Hispanic cultures early childhood diarrhea, vomiting, colic, and dehydration. Many cultures, other than Hispanic cultures, include a concept of the "evil eye." These include, but are not limited to, certain sects of Arabic, gypsy, and Jewish cultures, and many widely dispersed native tribes. SYN: *evil eye.*

maldigestion (măl″dī-jĕs′chŭn) Disordered digestion.

male [O.Fr.] **1.** Masculine. **2.** The sex that has organs for producing sperm for fertilization of ova.

male erectile disorder The persistent or recurrent inability to attain, or to maintain until completion of the sexual activity, an adequate erection. The disturbance causes marked distress or interpersonal difficulty. The difficulty cannot be attributed to a medical condition, substance abuse, or medications. SEE: *erectile dysfunction; female sexual arousal disorder.*

male factor SEE: under *factor.*

maleficence (mă-lĕf′ĭ-sĕns) [L. *maleficentia,* evildoing] Acting in a deliberately harmful manner toward others.

malformation (măl″for-mā′shŏn) [*mal-* + *formation*] Abnormal shape or structure, esp. congenital; deformity.

arteriovenous m. ABBR: AVM. Angiodysplasia.

spinal cavernous m. A cavernous malformation in the spinal cord. If the abnormal veins in the malformation rupture, a patient may suffer stroke-like symptoms that correspond to the nerves at the level of the spinal cord where the hemorrhage occurs.

malfunction (măl-fŭnk′shŭn) Defective function.

malic (mā′lĭk, măl′ĭk) [L. *malum,* apple] Pert. to apples.

malice (măl′ĭs) [L. *malus,* bad] Desire or intent to harm someone or to see others suffer.

malign (mă-līn′) [ME. *maligne*] Tending to injure or harm; malignant.

malignancy (mă-lĭg′năn-sē) [L. *malignus,* of bad kind] **1.** State of being malignant. **2.** A neoplasm or tumor that is cancerous as opposed to benign. SYN: *virulence.*

malignant (mă-lĭg′nănt) Growing worse; resisting treatment, said of cancerous growths. Tending or threatening to produce death; harmful. SYN: *virulent.*

malignant angioendotheliomatosis Intravascular large cell lymphoma that is typically found in the blood vessels of the skin and central nervous system and is often rapidly fatal.

TREATMENT: Current treatment is based on polychemotherapy.

malignant disease 1. Cancer. 2. A disease, including but not limited to cancer, in which the progress is extremely rapid and generally threatening or resulting in death within a short time.

malinger (mă-lĭng′ĕr) [Fr. *malingre,* weak, sickly] To feign illness, usually to arouse sympathy, to escape work, or to continue to receive compensation. SEE: *factitious disorder; Munchausen syndrome.*

malingerer (mă-lĭng′gĕr-ĕr) 1. One who pretends to be ill or suffering from a nonexistent disorder to arouse sympathy. 2. One who pretends slow recuperation from a disease once suffered in order to continue to receive benefits of medical insurance and work absence.

Mallampati classification (ma-lam-pot′ē) A four-point scale used to assess the relative ease of oral (endotracheal) intubation of a patient based on the size and position of the tongue relative to the size of the pharyngeal opening. The patient should be assessed in the sitting position, with the neck in neutral position, the mouth maximally opened, and the tongue protruded as far as possible. The four classifications of the scale are: 1.full visibility of the soft palate, uvula, tonsillar pillars, and fauces; 2.visibility of the soft palate and part of the pendant uvula; 3.visibility of the soft palate and only the base of the uvula; and 4.visibility of only the hard palate.

malleable (măl′ē-ă-bl) [L. *mallere,* to hammer] Having the property of being shaped by pressure.

malleolus (măl-ē′ŏ-lŭs) pl. **malleoli** [L. *malleolus,* little hammer] The protuberance on both sides of the ankle joint; the lower extremity of the fibula is the lateral malleolus and lower end of the tibia is the medial malleolus. **malleolar** (-ō-lăr), *adj.*

 external m. Lateral malleolus.

 lateral m. Process on outer edge of fibula at lower end. SYN: *external m.*

 medial m. Round process on inner edge of tibia at lower end.

mallet (mal′ĕt) 1. In dentistry, a hammer-like tool to condense direct filling gold. 2. In orthopedics, a small hammer. 3. Malleus.

malleus (mal′ē-ŭs, mal′ē-ī″, mal′ē-ē″) pl. **mallei** [L., *malleus,* hammer] The largest of the three auditory ossicles. It is attached to the eardrum and articulates with the incus. SYN: *hammer* (2); *mallet* (3). SEE: *ear.*

Mallophaga (măl-ŏf′ă-gă) [Gr. *mallos,* wool, + *phagein,* to eat] An order of insects that includes biting lice.

Mallory body (mal′ŏ-rē) [G. Kenneth Mallory, U.S. pathologist, 1900–1986]

An inclusion body found in liver cells, especially in diseases caused by the excessive consumption of alcohol. Mallory bodies are composed of collections of intermediate filaments.

Mallory-Weiss syndrome (măl′lŏr-ē-wīs′) [G. Kenneth Mallory, U.S. pathologist, 1900–1986; Soma Weiss, U.S. internist, 1898–1942] Hemorrhage from the upper gastrointestinal tract due to a tear in the mucosa of the esophagus or gastroesophageal junction. Violent retching usually precedes the bleeding. SEE: *Nursing Diagnoses Appendix.*

malnutrition (mal″noo-tri′shŏn) [*mal- + nutrition*] Any disease-promoting condition due to either an inadequate or an excessive exposure to nutrients, i.e., undernutrition or overnutrition. Common causes of malnutrition are inadequate calorie consumption; inadequate intake of essential vitamins, minerals, or other micronutrients; improper absorption and distribution of foods within the body; overeating; and intoxication by nutrient excesses. SEE: table; and names of specific nutritional disorders, e.g., obesity, pellegra, scurvy.

Worldwide, malnutrition is a disease that results typically from inadequate consumption of foods, esp. proteins, iron, and vitamins. In industrialized nations, overnutrition is more common than undernutrition. In the U.S., 50% of the population is considered to be overweight, and 22% have a body mass index greater than 30 kg/m^2 and are obese. Undernutrition in Western nations typically results from poverty, alcoholism, chronic illnesses, or extreme dieting.

 protein-calorie m. Protein-energy **m.**

 protein-energy m. ABBR: PEM. Malnutrition due to inadequate intake of calories or protein, or both. It usually is seen in children under 5 or in patients undergoing the stress of a major illness. In the critically ill patient, hypoalbuminemia results from the depletion of stored protein and/or hepatic dysfunction. It may increase a patient's vulnerability to the toxicities of drugs, skin breakdown, infections, gastrointestinal ulcerations, and other illnesses. SYN: *protein-calorie m.* SEE: *kwashiorkor.*

SYMPTOMS: Symptoms of PEM include generalized muscle wasting and weakness. In the elderly, these symptoms are sometimes incorrectly attributed to advanced age, and as a result, PEM is underdiagnosed.

malocclusion (mal″ō-kloo′zhŏn) [*mal- + occlusion*] Malposition of teeth and/or an imperfect relationship between the mandibular and maxillary teeth and/or dental arches. Malocclusion is classified as dental, skeletal, or dento-

Physical Signs of Malnutrition

Infants and Children	Adolescents and Adults
Lack of subcutaneous fat	Red, swollen lingual papillae
Wrinkling of skin on light stroking	Glossitis
Poor muscle tone	Papillary atrophy of tongue
Pallor	Stomatitis
Rough skin (toad skin)	Spongy, bleeding gums
Hemorrhage of newborn, vitamin K deficiency	Muscle tenderness in extremities
Bad posture	Poor muscle tone
Nasal area is red and greasy	Loss of vibratory sensation
Sores at angles of mouth, cheilosis	Increase or decrease of tendon reflexes
Rapid heartbeat	Hyperesthesia of skin
Red tongue	Purpura
Square head, wrists enlarged, rib beading	Dermatitis: facial butterfly, perineal, scrotal, vulval
Vincent's angina, thrush	Thickening and pigmentation of skin over bony prominences
Serious dental abnormalities	Nonspecific vaginitis
Corneal and conjunctival changes	Follicular hyperkeratosis of extensor surfaces of extremities
Adolescents and Adults	Rachitic chest deformity
Nasolabial sebaceous plugs	Anemia not responding to iron
Sores at angles of mouth, cheilosis	Fatigue of visual accommodation
Vincent's angina	Vascularization of cornea
Minimal changes in tongue color or texture	Conjunctival changes

SOURCE: Committee on Medical Nutrition, National Research Council, with permission.

skeletal in origin. SYN: *abnormal occlusion*.

malpighian layer SEE: under *layer*.

malposition (mal″pŏ-zish′ŏn) [*mal-* + *position*] **1.** Faulty or abnormal position or placement, esp. of the body (or one of its parts) or of an inserted catheter or device. **2.** Abnormal position of the fetal presenting part in relation to the maternal pelvis. SEE: *persistent occiput posterior*.

malpractice [″ + Gr. *praxis*, an action] An action taken by a health care professional that injures a patient, and fails to meet reasonable standards of professional care.

malpresentation (măl″prĕz-ĕn-tā′shŭn) [″ + *praesentatio*, a presenting] Abnormal position of the fetal presenting part, making natural delivery difficult or impossible. Labor is longer, and fetal descent may be impaired. SEE: *presentation* for illus.

malreduction (măl-rē-dŭk′shŭn) Imperfect replacement of a dislocated or fractured bone.

malrotation (măl″rō-tā′shŭn) Failure during embryogenesis of normal rotation of all or a portion of an organ or system, esp. the viscera.

MALT *mucosa-associated lymphoid tissue.*

malt [AS. *mealt*] Germinated grain, usually barley, used in manufacture of ale and beer. It contains carbohydrates (dextrin, maltose), a diastase, and proteins.

maltase (mawl′tās) [AS. *mealt*, grain] An enzyme of the small intestine that digests maltose, converting it by hydrolysis to glucose. SEE: *digestion; enzyme.*

maltose (mawl′tōs) A disaccharide, $C_{12}H_{22}O_{11}$, that is present in malt products, and sprouting seeds. It is formed by the hydrolysis of starch and is converted into glucose by the enzyme maltase. SYN: *malt sugar*. SEE: *carbohydrate.*

maltreatment (măl-trēt′mĕnt) [″ + ″] Neglect or abuse of people.

malunion (măl-ūn′yŭn) [L. *malus*, evil, + *unio*, oneness] The joining of the fragments of a fractured bone in a faulty position, forming an imperfect alignment, shortening, deformity, or rotation. SYN: *vicious union.*

mamelon (măm′ĕ-lŏn) [Fr., nipple] One of three rounded protuberances present on the cutting edge of an incisor tooth when it erupts. These are worn away by use.

mamill- SEE: words beginning with *mammill-*

mammal (măm′ăl) An animal of the class Mammalia, marked by having hair and by having mammary glands that produce milk to nourish the newborn.

mammaplasty, mammoplasty (mam′ă-plas″tē) [*mamma* + *-plasty*] Plastic reconstructive surgery of the breast.

    augmentation m. Surgical breast enlargement, either to increase breast size or to make an artificial breast to replace one surgically removed. It is performed by inserting autogenous tissue with mobilization of myocutaneous flap or a prosthesis filled with gel or saline.

⚠️ The long-term health risks of some implant materials are unknown.

SYN: *breast **augmentation**.*

  reduction m. Plastic surgery to re-shape and decrease the size of the breast(s). SYN: *breast **reduction**.*

mammary (măm′ă-rē) [L. *mamma*, breast] Pert. to the breast.

mammary glands Compound glands of the female breast that can secrete milk. They are made up of lobes and lobules bound together by areolar tissue. The main ducts number 15 to 20 and are known as lactiferous ducts, each one discharging through a separate orifice upon the surface of the nipple. The dilatations of the ducts form reservoirs for the milk during lactation. The pink, or dark-colored, skin around the nipple is called the areola.

mammectomy (mă-mĕk′tŏ-mē) SEE: *mastectomy.*

mammillary body (măm′ĭ-lĕr″ē) A spherical complex of hypothalamic nuclei that bulges out of the base of the brain behind the pituitary gland on either side of the midline. The mammillary body is an integral component of the limbic circuitry, receiving signals from the hippocampus via the fornix and sending signals to the anterior thalamus via the mammillothalamic tract. SEE: *medial mammillary **nucleus**; limbic system* for illus.

mammillated (măm′mĭl-lā-tĕd) Having protuberances like a nipple.

mammillitis (mam″ĭ-līt′ĭs) [L. *mam(m)illa*, breast, nipple + *-itis*] Inflammation of a nipple. SYN: *thelitis.*

mammitis (mă-mī′tĭs) SEE: *mastitis.*

mammogram (măm′ō-grăm) [″ + Gr. *gramma*, something written] Radiography of the breast. SEE: *mammography.*

mammographic breast density SEE: under *density.*

mammography (ma-mog′ră-fē) [*mamma* + *-graphy*] Radiographic imaging of the breast to screen for and detect breast cancer. Mammography detects about 85% to 90% of existing breast cancers and, along with breast self-examination and regular professional check-ups, increases the rate of early breast cancer detection. Mammography detects more cancers when more than one radiologist interprets each image, a technique called *double reading.* The American Cancer Society and expert panels convened by the federal government publish guidelines for the frequency of mammographic evaluation

in the U.S. Although these guidelines change occasionally, evidence shows that mammographic screening can reduce the risk of dying from breast cancer in women between 40 and 69. SEE: *breast cancer* for table.

Palpable abnormalities of the breast that appear mammographically benign should nonetheless be further evaluated, e.g., with ultrasonography, fine-needle or core biopsy, or close follow-up examinations.

  digital m. Mammography in which the image is collected electronically instead of on film. Compared to standard mammography, it improves the ability to visualize abnormalities in the breasts of women under 50.

    full-field digital m. ABBR: FFDM. Digital **m.**

mammose (măm′ōs) [L. *mammosus*] **1.** Having unusually large breasts. **2.** Shaped like a breast.

Mammotome (măm′ō-tōm) A minimally invasive vacuum core biopsy instrument used to collect breast tissue for pathological analysis. It consists of a probe with an opening in the tip that connects to a vacuum source, a thumbwheel that controls the direction of the opening, a hollow, high-speed rotating cutter, and a tissue collection chamber. SEE: *percutaneous breast biopsy.*

mammotrophic (măm″ō-trŏf′ĭk) [″ + Gr. *trophe*, nourishment] To have the effect of stimulating size or function of the breast.

man [AS. *mann*] **1.** Member of the human species, *Homo sapiens.* **2.** Male member of the species as distinguished from female. **3.** The human race, collectively; mankind.

managed care SEE: under *care.*

managed competition In health care practice, the requirement that health care organizations compete with each other in terms of price and quality of delivered services. SEE: *managed care; resource-based relative value scale.*

management (man′ăj-mĕnt) **1.** Administration, as of a health care enterprise or one of its functions. **2.** Guidance, as of a patient's treatment. **3.** Coping skills or autonomous control, e.g. self-management. Particular kinds of management are listed under the first word. SEE: e.g., *case management; risk management; stress management.*

manchette (măn-chĕt′) [Fr., a cuff] A circular band consisting of microtubules around the caudal pole of developing sperm.

manchineel (măn″kĭ-nēl′) [Sp. *manzanilla*, small apple] A tree, *Hippomane mancinella,* native to tropical America that contains a milky, poisonous sap. Contact with the sap causes blistering of the skin. The fruit is also poisonous.

mandala (măn′dă-lă) [Sanskrit *man-*

dala, circle] An ancient Hindu and Buddhist representation of the universe, used as a focal point for meditation.

mandate (măn′dāt) **1.** A legal, ethical, or political requirement to execute actions or orders. **2.** An order from a higher authority to an officer of a lower court. **mandatory,** *adj.*

mandated treatment Legally mandated treatment.

mandatory reporting (măn′dă-tŏr″ē) [LL. *mandatorius,* commissioned, obligatory] Legally required notification to a state, federal, or police agency of a criminal act, e.g., domestic violence, or of a disease that poses a menace to public health.

mandible (man′dĭ-běl) [L. *mandibula,* lower jawbone] The horseshoe-shaped bone forming the lower jaw. SEE: illus. **mandibular** (-dib′yŭ-lăr), *adj.*

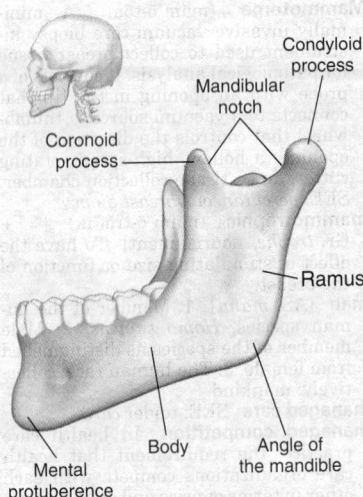

LEFT LATERAL VIEW OF MANDIBLE

Condyloid process
Mandibular notch
Coronoid process
Ramus
Mental protuberence
Body
Angle of the mandible

mandibular advancement splint SEE: under *splint.*

mandrel, mandril (măn′drěl) Handle that holds a dental tool so that it may be easily positioned by the operator. A spindle or shaft designed to fit a dental handpiece for the purpose of using a variety of tools for grinding, polishing, or buffing.

mandrin (măn′drĭn) [Fr.] A guide or stylet for a flexible catheter in order to give it shape and firmness, especially for use in the urinary meatus.

maneuver [Fr. *manoeuvre,* from L. *manu operari,* to work by hand] **1.** Any dexterous or skillful procedure. **2.** In obstetrics, manipulation of the fetus to aid in delivery. SEE: *labor.* Particular maneuvers are listed under the first word. SEE: e.g, *canalith repositioning maneu-*

ver; Heimlich maneuver; vagal maneuver.

manganese (mang′gă-nēz″, -nēs″) [L. *manganesium, magnesia,* a mineral of the philosophers' stone] SYMB: Mn. A metallic element, specific gravity 7.21, atomic weight (mass) 54.94, atomic number 25. It is found in many foods (bananas, bran, beans, beets, blueberries, chard, chocolate, peas, leafy vegetables, and whole grains) and in the tissues of the higher animals. It is an essential element needed for normal bone metabolism and many enzyme reactions. Deficiency in humans has not been demonstrated.

mange (mānj) [Fr. *mangeue,* a biting, itch] A cutaneous communicable disease of domestic animals, including dogs and cats. A number of mites, such as *Chorioptes, Demodex, Psoroptes,* and *Sarcoptes* are causative agents. A similar condition in humans is known as scabies.

mangled (măng′gŭld) Torn, shredded, or blasted apart; said for example of the limbs of severely traumatized patients.

Mangled Extremity Severity Score ABBR: MESS. An assessment tool used in trauma patients to predict the likelihood that an injured arm or leg will require amputation. MESS takes into account the age and blood pressure of the patient, the type of injury, and the perfusion of the injured limb.

mangosteen A tropical fruit that grows on an evergreen tree *Garcinia mangostana Linn.,* found in Indonesia and Indochina. Its hull has been used as a traditional medicine in Thailand. Extracts from the hull have antioxidant, antihistaminic, and anti-inflammatory effects in laboratory experiments.

mania (mā′nē-ă) [Gr. *mania,* madness] **1.** A mental disorder characterized by excessive excitement, elation, delusions of grandeur, distractibility, impulsivity, irritability, restlessness, speech and/or poor judgment. SEE: *bipolar disorder; bipolar I mood disorder; bipolar II mood disorder.*

drug-induced m. Mania that follows the prescription of psychically active medications, such as anabolic steroids, corticosteroids, or antidepressants.

juvenile m. Bipolar disorder that begins in childhood or adolescence.

late-life m. Late-onset mania.

late-onset m. Manic behavior that begins in middle-aged, or older, individuals. Some experts have proposed that it is caused by cardiovascular disease or small strokes. SYN: *late-life m.*

mixed m. Mania in which euphoric or irritable symptoms coincide with symptoms of depression for at least one week.

religious m. Mania resulting from excessive religious fervor.

vascular m. Manic symptoms that occur after a stroke.

-mania Suffix meaning *frenzy* or *madness*.

manic (măn′ĭk) Mood state characterized by excessive energy, poor impulse control, psychosis, agitation, flight of ideas, frenzied movement, and decreased sleep.

manifest **1.** To reveal in an obvious manner. **2.** Clearly apparent to the senses, esp. to the sight.

manifestation The demonstration of the presence of a sign, symptom, or alteration, esp. one that is associated with a disease process.

manikin (man′ĭ-kĭn) [Dutch *manneken*, little man] A model of the human body or its parts, used esp. in teaching anatomy and emergency medical and nursing procedures.

manipulation (mă-nip″yŭ-lā′shŏn) **1.** A conscious or unconscious process by which one person attempts to influence another in order to obtain his or her own needs or desires. **2.** A joint mobilization technique, sometimes involving a rapid thrust or the stretching of a joint, with or without anesthesia. SEE: *joint* **m.** **3.** A method of realigning a fractured long bone with manual pressure, traction, or angulation. **4.** The skillful and precise use of the fingers and hands.

cervical m. Manipulation of the bones and soft tissues of the neck.

endocrine m. Hormonal **m.** (1).

genetic m. Modification of the genotype or the gene expression of an organism or a cell.

hormonal m. **1.** The treatment of diseases, e.g., endometriosis, or endocrine-responsive tumors (such as breast and prostate cancer) with drugs that block the action of hormones or releasing factors. SYN: *endocrine* **m.** **2.** The use of hormones to affect menstrual cycles or fertility. **3.** The use of hormones like testosterone to enhance athletic performance or increase muscle mass.

joint m. Any of the passive therapeutic techniques used to stretch restricted joints or reposition a subluxation. The techniques are sometimes applied with rapid thrust movements and may be applied with the patient under anesthesia to ensure maximum relaxation. SEE: *joint* **mobilization**.

long-lever m. Long-lever **adjustment**.

nutritional m. An alteration or restriction of the natural diet for therapeutic or experimental purposes.

short-lever m. Short-lever **adjustment**.

spinal m. Manipulation of any of the spinal vertebrae, from the neck (the cervical spine) to the lower back (the lumbar spine). The procedure is commonly performed by chiropractors, osteopaths, and massage therapists.

static m. The exertion of a force on an unmoving object, e.g. when grasping it with the hands.

stem cell m. Experimentation on human or animal stem cells that alters either their genetic makeup or the biochemicals that those cells produce.

manipulation task **1.** Movement of the hands to accomplish a goal. **2.** In physical or occupational therapy, the use of the hands to move objects or to propel the body.

manna (măn′ă) [L.] **1.** The sweet juice obtained from the flowering ash, *Fraxinus ornus*. **2.** General term applied to sweetish juices obtained from a variety of plants.

mannans (măn′ănz) Any of several polysaccharides of mannose.

mannequin (măn′ĭ-kĭn) [Fr. fr. D. *manneken*, little man] SEE: *manikin*.

mannerism A peculiar modification or exaggeration of style or habit of dress, speech, or action.

mannitol (man′ĭ-tol″) An osmotic diuretic used primarily to treat oliguric renal failure and reduce intracranial pressure (e.g., in patients with threatened herniation of the brain through the foramen magnum).

mannitol sugar agar ABBR: MSA. A selective laboratory medium used to grow and isolate specimens of *Staphylococcus aureus*. Those colonies that ferment mannitol are selected for further study with other growth media.

mannose (măn′ōs) A simple sugar, molecular weight 180.16 kD, present in certain plants, such as legumes. It is an aldohexose.

mannoside (măn′ō-sīd) A glycoside of mannose.

mannosidosis (măn″ōs-ĭ-dō′sĭs) One of several congenital lysosomal storage diseases in which the deficiency of α-mannosidase is associated with mental retardation, kyphosis, and accumulation of mannose in tissues. The disease, which is lethal, can be treated with bone marrow transplantation.

manometer (mă-nom′ĕt-ĕr) [Gr. *manos*, thin + *-meter*] A device for determining liquid or gaseous pressure. The measurement is expressed in SI units of the differential height of the columns of fluid, typically millimeters or centimeters.

saline m. A manometer that uses a special tube shaped like the letter U and open at both ends. The tube is partially filled with saline. Pressure is determined by connecting one end of the U tube to the system in which pressure is to be measured. The pressure is the measured distance between the fluid level in one side of the U tube and that in the other side. The pressure is reported in millimeters of saline.

manometry (măn-ŏm′ĕ-trē) The measurement of the pressures exerted by muscles in the gastrointestinal tract, e.g., in the anus, rectum, or esophagus.

    esophageal m. A test that measures the strength of the contractions of the muscles of the esophagus and the resistance of the lower esophageal sphincter to reflux. The test is performed invasively, by inserting a tube directly into the esophagus.

manslaughter (măn″slăw-tĕr) A form of homicide in which the killing of another person is not the result of malice. On occasion, health care professionals who have withheld certain forms of treatment have been charged and convicted of manslaughter. Patients also may be charged with manslaughter (e.g., if failure to follow medical advice not to drive an automobile results in a fatal crash).

Mansonella (măn″sō-nĕl′ă) A genus of filarial nematodes.

    M. ozzardi A species found in humans in Central and South America and the Caribbean. It is transmitted by blackflies and midges. The parasites are unsheathed and most patients are asymptomatic.

    M. perstans A species of filaria that is transmitted to humans by Culicoides insects (midges). It was formerly known at *Acanthocheilonema perstans.*

    SYMPTOMS: Angioedema, urticaria, high blood eosinophil levels, and other findings.

Mansonia (măn-sō′nē-ă) A genus of mosquitoes found in tropical countries that transmit microfilariae to humans.

mantle (măn′tĭl) [AS. *mentel,* a garment] A covering structure or layer.

Mantoux test (man-tū′) [Charles Mantoux, Fr. physician, 1877–1947] An intradermal test that determines sensitivity to tuberculin by indicating present or past infection by the tubercle bacillus. Following an injection of 0.1 mL of intermediate strength purified protein derivative (PPD), the needle is removed after a brief period to minimize leakage of the PPD at the puncture site. Within 48 to 72 hr, an induration of the injected area with a diameter greater than 10 mm Hg provides unequivocal evidence of current or previous infection with tuberculosis. In people infected with HIV, an induration with a diameter 5 mm or more should be considered evidence of a positive test result. HIV-infected patients who are anergic (that is, they do not react to PPD or to control antigens) should be considered positive as well esp. if they come from demographic groups known to have high rates of infection with tuberculosis, e.g., the homeless and people born in Asia. SEE: *tuberculosis; tuberculin skin test.*

mantra (măn-tră) A word, phrase, or sound repeated to oneself to focus the mind or reduce stray thoughts during meditation.

manual (măn′ū-ăl) [L. *manus,* hand] **1.** Pert. to the hands. **2.** Performed by or with the hands.

manual muscle test A technique for estimating the relative strength of specific muscles. SEE: table.

manual therapy A collection of techniques in which hand movements are skillfully applied to mobilize joints and soft tissues. These techniques may be used to alleviate pain, improve motion, induce relaxation, reduce edema, and improve pulmonary and musculoskeletal function. SEE: *manipulation; joint mobilization; soft-tissue mobilization.*

manus (mā′nŭs) *pl.* **manus** [L.] The hand.

manuscript (man′yŭ-skript″) [L. *manuscriptus,* written by hand] A handwritten or typed document, used, for example, to inform students or health care workers or to report research findings.

MAO *monoamine oxidase.*

MAP *mean airway pressure; mean arterial pressure.*

map (map) [L. *mappa (mundi),* map (of the world)] A graphic presentation in two dimensions of the location of all or part of an area.

Grading Systems for Manual Muscle Tests

Verbal	Numerical	Clinical Finding
Normal	5/5	The patient can resist against maximal pressure; the examiner is unable to break the patient's resistance
Good	4/5	The patient can resist against moderate pressure
Fair	3/5	The patient can move the body part against gravity through the full range of motion
Poor	2/5	The patient can move the body part in a gravity-eliminated position through the full range of motion
Trace	1/5	The patient cannot produce movement, but a muscle contraction is palpable
Zero	0/5	No contraction is felt

SOURCE: Starkey, C, Brown, S, and Ryan, J: Examination of Orthopedic and Athletic Injuries, ed 3, FA Davis, Philadelphia, 2010.

map **1455** marasmus

body m. A map showing a patient's injuries, lesions, or wounds. It is used to record maltreatment by another person in a case of physical abuse or violence.

care m. Clinical **pathway**.

choropleth m. A map on which areas are colored or shaded according to variables, e.g., where a disease is active and where quiescent.

chromosomal m. SEE: *gene mapping*.

fate m. A map showing the regions of embryonic cells that will develop into specific differentiated organs and tissues in the body of the adult.

genetic m. SEE: *gene mapping*.

linkage m. Gene mapping.

mind m. A method of learning or organizing data in which a person starts with a central concept and then arranges related concepts, facts, and ideas around it in a way that helps the cartographer make sense of the material.

maple syrup urine disease An autosomal recessive metabolic disease involving defective metabolism of branched chain amino acids. The disease is so named because of the characteristic odor of the urine and sweat. The amino acids involved are leucine, isoleucine, valine, and alloisoleucine. Clinically there is rapid deterioration of the nervous system in the first few months of life and then death at an early age.

TREATMENT: Treatment includes controlling the dietary intake of the involved amino acids, exchange transfusion, peritoneal dialysis, and occasionally, liver transplantation. SYN: *leucinosis*.

mapping (map′ing) **1.** The location of genes on a chromosome. **2.** The locating of organs or tissues in health or in disease.

brain m. Cortical **m.**

cardiac m. The measurement of the electrical potentials generated by regions of the heart, often to identify a treatable source of an arrhythmia.

cortical m. Establishing the relationship between various structures of the brain and their functions. It is a technique used in neurosurgery to determine which parts of a diseased brain may be safely excised. Maps made of eloquent brain structures help surgeons minimize the damage they do when they remove tumors or seizure foci. SYN: *brain m.*

functional m. 1. Determining those brain structures that are responsible for cognitive, intellectual, speech, sensory or motor functions. SEE: *cortical m.* **2.** Locating the specific parts of a gene, or of its enhancers or silencers, that influence how the gene is expressed.

gene m. Determining the location of hereditary information carried on chromosomes. In humans, this requires determining the base pairs (chemical code) of each of the estimated 20,000 to 25,000 genes. Once a gene is mapped, that information may be used to compare abnormal genes with normal ones. Molecular biological techniques may then be used to search for methods of treating and preventing conditions resulting from genetic abnormality. SYN: *genome m.; linkage map.* SEE: *gene splicing*.

genome m. Gene **m.**

linkage m. Determination of how close two genes on the same chromosome are to each other. The further apart the two genes are, the more likely there is to be crossing over during meiosis.

lymphatic m. In the staging of cancers, injection of a tracer material near a tumor to determine the regional lymph nodes into which metastatic disease may first spread. SEE: *sentinel node* (1).

peptide m. A means of identifying proteins electrophoretically after partially hydrolyzing them. Each protein leaves a characteristic pattern of light and dark peptide bands on the electrophoretic paper or gel.

retinal m. Studying the vascular structures and thickness of the retina in order to diagnose its diseases, or study its response to medical or surgical therapies.

MAR *medication administration record.*

marantic (mă-ran′tik) [Gr. *marantikos*] Pert. to marasmus; marasmic.

marasmus (mă-raz′mŭs) [Gr. *marasmos*, a wasting away] A generalized wasting and absence of subcutaneous fat caused by malnutrition; emaciation. It results from caloric deficiency secondary to acute diseases, esp. diarrheal diseases of infancy, deficiency in nutritional composition, inadequate food intake, malabsorption, child abuse, failure-to-thrive disorders, deficiency of vitamin D, or scurvy. SYN: *athrepsia; pedatrophy; wasting.* SEE: *kwashiorkor; protein-energy malnutrition.* **marasmic** (mă-raz′mik), *adj.*

SYMPTOMS: Signs include loss of muscle mass and other soft tissues and a wizened, sunken face, resembling that of an elderly person, from loss of temporal and buccal fat pads. Failure to gain weight is followed by a loss of weight. Brain and skeletal growth continues, resulting in a long body and a head too large in proportion to the body. Subcutaneous fat is minimal, the eyes are sunken, and tissue turgor is lost. The skin appears loose and sags. The infant is not active, muscles are flabby and relaxed, and the cry is weak and shrill. The absence of pitting edema of the hands and feet and of a protuberant abdomen differentiate this condition from kwashiorkor, but in marasmic kwashiorkor, features of both conditions are combined.

TREATMENT: Initial feedings should be small and low in calories because digestive capacity is poor and a "refeeding" syndrome can occur, marked by hypophosphatemia, congestive heart failure, respiratory distress, convulsions, coma, and death. Diluted formula or breast milk is best. The amount of calories and protein, carbohydrates, and fat should be increased gradually. The goal for protein intake is 5 g/kg of body weight per day. If diarrhea due to disaccharidase deficiency is present, a low-lactose diet is beneficial. Parenteral fluid therapy is indicated if shock or fluid and electrolyte imbalance exists.

PROGNOSIS: Death occurs in 40% of affected children.

marble bone disease Osteopetrosis.

Marburg virus disease (măr′bĕrg) [Marburg, Germany] A frequently fatal disease caused by a virus classed as a member of the family Filoviridae. Clinically this disease is identical to that caused by the Ebola virus. SEE: *Ebola virus hemorrhagic fever*.

marc (mărk) [Fr.] The residue remaining after a drug has been percolated. SEE: *percolation*.

Marcus Gunn dots, pupil, syndrome SEE: under *Gunn, Robert Marcus*.

Marfan syndrome (mar′fan) [Bernard-Jean Antonin Marfan, Fr. physician, 1858–1942] An autosomal dominant degenerative disorder of connective tissue, bones, muscles, and ligaments. It affects about one person in 5000 to 7500.

SYMPTOMS: Distinguishing features include tall, lean body type with long extremities including fingers and toes, pectus carinatum or excavatum, dilation of the ascending aorta or aortic dissection, abnormal joint flexibility, flat feet, scoliosis, lumbosacral dural ectasia, a high arched palate, and dislocation of the optic lens and other ocular problems.

DIAGNOSIS: Because some of these features may be present in many individuals, the diagnosis is established after careful review of major and minor criteria and consultation with specialists in orthopedics, ophthalmology, cardiology, and medical genetics.

ETIOLOGY: It is caused by a mutation on chromosome 15, which alters the manufacture of fibrillin molecules in the extracellular matrix, resulting in elastin and collagen abnormalities.

PATIENT CARE: Treatment for Marfan syndrome is mainly symptomatic rather than curative. Ocular deformities, aortic aneurysms, or prolapsed heart valves can be repaired, but the connective tissue defect responsible for them cannot. Beta-blocking drugs such as atenolol or metoprolol may decrease blood pressure and heart rate and protect the aorta in patients with early dilatation. Angiotensin receptor blockers and angiotensin converting enzyme inhibitors also help prevent aortic dissection. Patients with dural ectasia, who often suffer with low back pain, may benefit from analgesic medications. Individuals diagnosed with Marfan syndrome should avoid sports like football, in which collisions are common, or excessive weight lifting. Patients and their families benefit from referral to the National Marfan Foundation for support and information (www.marfan.org).

margarine Butter substitute made from refined vegetable oils or a combination of vegetable oils and fats. Coloring material and vitamins A and D are added. It contains 9 kcal/g.

margin (mar′jĭn) [L. *margo*, border] **1.** A border or boundary such as the edge of a structure, or of a pathological specimen removed from the body surgically. SEE: *margo*. **2.** In dentistry, the apical extent or boundary of enamel adjacent to the cementum of the tooth root; the junction of a restoration with the cavo-surface angle of a prepared cavity in enamel.

   costal m. The lower (abdominal) border of the front of the rib cage formed by the costal cartilages of ribs 7 to 10.

   free gingival m. Gumline.

   gingival m. Gumline.

   m. of resection Surgical **m.**

   surgical m. The border of a tissue specimen that has been removed surgically from the body. It is often marked with an indelible dye to make it easily visible to the pathologist.

   PATIENT CARE: When obtaining biopsy specimens from a patient, the practitioner's goal is to obtain a tissue specimen that completely surrounds the lesion, so that the margins are free, i.e. not visibly penetrated by tumor cells. SYN: **m.** *of resection*.

marginal (mar′jĭn-ăl) Concerning a margin or border. SYN: *limbic*.

margination (mar′jĭ-nā′shŭn) Adhesion of leukocytes to the walls of blood vessels in the first stages of inflammation.

margin of resection SEE: under *margin*.

margo (măr′gō) *pl.* **margines** [L.] A border or edge.

Marie, Pierre (ma-rē′) Fr. neurologist, 1853–1940.

   M. ataxia Hereditary cerebellar ataxia caused by bilateral cortical atrophy of the cerebellum.

   M. disease Acromegaly.

   M. sign Hand tremor seen in exophthalmic goiter.

marijuana, marihuana (mar″ĭ-wan′ă) [Mexican Sp. *marihuana, mariguana*] The dried flowering tops of *Cannabis sativa*, the hemp plant. Marijuana has many colloquial and street names, e.g., dope, ganja, Mary Jane, pot, and weed. SEE: *Cannabis sativa; tetrahydrocannabinol.*

Its active ingredient, delta-9-tetrahydrocannabinol (THC), may produce euphoria, alterations in mood and judgment, and changes in sensory perception, cognition, and coordination. Driving and machine-operating skills may be impaired. Users of marijuana have impaired short-term memory; memory deficits are transient, however, and return to normal within about a week of abstinence. Depending on the dose of the drug and the underlying psychological conditions of the user, marijuana may cause transient episodes of confusion, anxiety, or delirium. Its use may exacerbate mental illness, esp. schizophrenia. Long-term, relatively heavy use may be associated with behavioral disorders and a kind of ennui called the amotivational syndrome, but it is not known whether use of the drug is a cause or a result of this condition. Transient symptoms occur on withdrawal, indicating that the drug can lead to physical dependence. There has been considerable interest in the effects of marijuana on pregnancy and fetal growth, but substance abusers often abuse more than a single substance, making it difficult to evaluate the effects of individual substances on the outcome of pregnancy or fetal development.

There is no definitive evidence that prolonged heavy smoking of marijuana leads to impaired pulmonary function. The possibility that chronic marijuana use is associated with an increased risk of developing head and neck cancer exists, but it has not been proven.

Delta-9-tetrahydrocannabinol, also known as dronabinol, is approved for use in treating nausea and vomiting associated with cancer chemotherapy in patients who have failed to respond adequately to conventional antiemetic treatment, and treatment of anorexia associated with weight loss in patients with acquired immunodeficiency syndrome. Marijuana has also been approved for other medical uses in some states, although such use violates federal Drug Enforcement Administration standards.

⚠️ Dronabinol is a controlled substance. Prescriptions are limited to the amount necessary for a single cycle of chemotherapy.

medical m. Legally sanctioned use of marijuana for people with a variety of conditions, including chronic pain, glaucoma, or nausea and vomiting caused by chemotherapy. SEE: illlus.

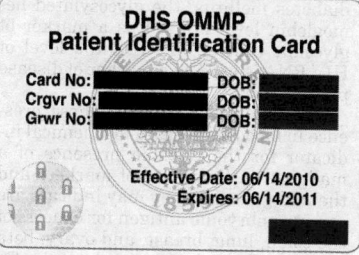

MEDICAL MARIJUANA CARD

marionette line SEE: under *line.*

marital counseling Services provided to married couples (and their families) about how to manage addictions, differences of opinion, finances, genetic illnesses, schedules, sexuality, and other topics.

Marjolin ulcer (mar′jŏ-lĭn, mar-zhō-len′) [John Nicholas Marjolin, Fr. physician, 1780–1850] A carcinoma that grows at the site of a chronic wound (e.g., a nonhealing scar or burn). The tumor is most often a squamous cell carcinoma and often metastasizes.

mark (mark) A nevus, bruise, cut, or spot on the surface of a body.

   mother's m. A birthmark.

   strawberry m. Infantile **hemangioma**. SEE: *nevus flammeus.*

   stretch m. **Stria** atrophica.

marker (mark′ĕr) **1.** A device or substance used to indicate or mark something. **2.** An identifying characteristic or trait that allows apparently similar materials or disease conditions to be differentiated.

   biochemical m. Any biochemical compound such as an antigen, antibody, abnormal enzyme, or hormone that is sufficiently altered in a disease to serve as an aid in diagnosing or in predicting susceptibility to the disease.

   fecal m. A substance, such as carmine, ingested to mark the beginning and end of fecal collection periods.

   genetic m. An identifiable physical location on a chromosome (e.g., a gene or segment of DNA with no known coding function) whose inheritance can be monitored.

   process m. A measurable component of the health care given to patients with a specific disease or condition, used as an indicator of the overall quality of care given to patients with other conditions.

   prognostic m. Any finding or characteristic that indicates that a disease is likely to improve, remit, or relapse.

risk m. Risk **factor.**

surrogate m. An indirect indicator of a disease state or of its response to therapy. Such markers often include laboratory tests thought to represent clinical progress accurately. For example, in diabetes mellitus, the glycosylated hemoglobin level is used as a marker of glycemic control; in AIDS the level of HIV RNA is used as a marker of disease progression.

tumor m. A substance whose presence in blood serves as a biochemical indicator for the possible presence of a malignancy. Examples of markers and the malignancies they may indicate are carcinoembryonic antigen for cancers of the colon, lung, breast, and ovary; beta subunit of chorionic gonadotropin for trophoblastic and testicular tumors; alpha-fetoprotein for testicular teratocarcinoma and primary hepatocellular carcinoma; and prostate-specific antigen for prostate cancer.

Markle sign (mark′ĕl) Jar **tenderness.**

Marlex mesh (măr′lĕks) A monofilament, biologically inert mesh used in surgical procedures to help cover or strengthen areas, as in hernia repair.

Maroteaux-Lamy syndrome Mucopolysaccharidosis VI.

marrow (mar′ō) **1.** The soft tissue in the marrow cavities of long bones (yellow marrow) and in the spaces between trabeculae of spongy bone in the sternum and other flat and irregular bones (red marrow). Yellow marrow consists principally of fat cells and connective tissue and does not participate in hematopoiesis. Red marrow produces red blood cells. SYN: *bone m.; medulla* (1). SEE: illus. **2.** The substance of the spinal cord. SYN: *spinal m.*

    bone m. Marrow (1).

    spinal m. Marrow (2).

marrow aspiration Bone marrow aspiration and biopsy.

MARS (marz) *Molecular adsorbent recirculating system.*

Marshall-Marchetti-Krantz procedure (mar′sähl-mar-ket′ē-krants′) A surgical procedure to treat urinary stress incontinence in women. The incontinence is caused by a weakness in the support of the bladder neck and proximal urethra. Sutures are placed periurethrally in the vaginal wall and anchored to the perichondrium of the pubic symphysis, offering a better cystourethral angle and firm support.

    PATIENT CARE: Vital signs are checked and the drain managed. Intake and output are monitored, and fluids encouraged.

marshmallow (marsh′mel′ō) A flowering herb (*Althaea officinalis*), that grows in wetlands. Its root has many uses in herbal medicine, e.g., as a treatment for sore throat and oral and gastric ulcers.

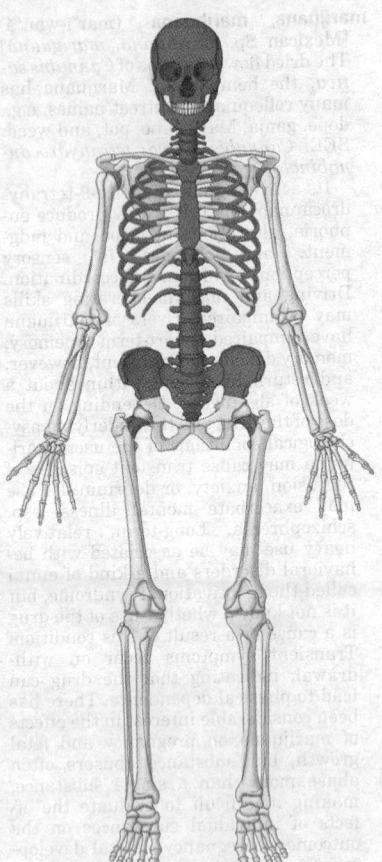

RED BONE MARROW

Red bone marrow can only be found in the ribs, sternum, vertebrae, skull, pelvis, and upper parts of both the humerus and femur. All other bones contain yellow marrow.

marsupialization (măr-sū″pē-ăl-ĭ-zā′shŭn) [L. *marsupium*, pouch] The process of raising the borders of an evacuated tumor, cyst, or abscess to the edges of the surgical wound and stitching them there to form a pouch. The interior of the sac suppurates and gradually closes by granulation.

marsupium (măr-sū″pē-ŭm) [L., pouch] **1.** Scrotum. **2.** A sac or pouch that serves to hold the young of a marsupial.

MAS, mAs *milliampere second.*

masculine (măs′kū-lĭn) **1.** Pert. to the male sex. **2.** Having male characteristics. SYN: *virile.*

masculinization (măs″cū-lĭn″ĭ-zā-shŭn) **1.** The normal development of secondary male sex characteristics that occur at puberty. **2.** The abnormal development of masculine characteristics in the female. This may be caused by certain testosterone-producing tumors, medication that contains testosterone, or anabolic steroids. SEE: *virilization*.

maser (mā'zĕr) Acronym for *m*icrowave *a*mplification by *s*timulation *e*mission of *r*adiation. It is a device that produces a small, nondiverging radiation beam. SEE: *laser*.

mask (mask) [Fr. *masque*, disguise] **1.** A covering for the face that serves as a protective barrier. SEE: *Standard Precautions Appendix*. SEE: *bag mask device; respirator*. **2.** The immobile appearance of the face occurring in certain pathological conditions. **3.** To conceal or prevent detection. **4.** A change in facial pigmentation resulting from pregnancy or from disease.

  aerosol m. A mask used for the therapeutic administration of a nebulized solution, humidity, or high airflow with oxygen enrichment. It has a large-bore inlet and an exhalation port.

  ecchymotic m. Cyanotic facies accompanying traumatic asphyxia.

  face m. **1.** A barrier device used in infection control to prevent health care providers from breathing or coughing on patients. It is also employed to prevent patients' sneezes and sputum from making contact with the health care provider's face or eyes or from being inhaled. **2.** A device that covers the mouth, nose, or both of a patient who requires positive-pressure, noninvasive ventilation or continuous positive pressure-ventilation (CPAP).

  high air flow with oxygen enrichment m. ABBR: HAFOE mask. A term applied to Venturi-type devices. SEE: *Venturi mask*.

  Hutchinson m. SEE: under *Hutchinson, Sir Jonathan*.

  luetic m. Blotchy brown pigmentation of cheeks, forehead, and temples, seen in tertiary syphilis.

  Mikulicz m. SEE: under *Mikulicz-Radecki, Johann von*.

  N95 m. N95 **respirator**.

  nonrebreathing m. An oxygen administration device with one-way valves for inspiration and expiration and a reservoir bag, used to attain high concentrations of oxygen.

  oxygen m. A device that fits over the mouth and nose and provides oxygen or other therapeutic gas. It includes a simple, partial rebreathing type and a nonrebreathing type.

  Parkinson m. A colloquialism for Parkinson facies.

  pocket face m. A folding mask that can be carried in a pocket and used for artificial ventilation. Most pocket face masks have an inlet for oxygen and a one-way valve for infection control.

  m. of pregnancy **Chloasma** gravidarum.

  surgical m. A single-use filtration device made of fabric and wornover the nose and mouth of surgical staff to prevent contamination of the operative field and to protect the wearer from splashes and splatter.

  ventilation m. A face mask device that applies mechanical ventilation.

  Venturi m. SEE: *Venturi mask*.

masked (maskt) **1.** Concealed, esp. an infection. Women exposed to rubella during the first trimester of pregnancy may be given immune globulin, which may prevent clinical symptoms of rubella in the mother; yet the fetus may be adversely affected and born with congenital defects. **2.** Blind (2).

masked hypertension SEE: under *hypertension*.

masking (mask'ing) In the perception of sounds, the alteration of the audibility of one sound by another.

Maslach Burnout Inventory (măz'lăk) ABBR: MBI. A series of three surveys of workers' interest in their fields. It consists of :

1. a general survey,
2. an educator's survey,
3. a human services survey.

Each assesses psychological factors such as emotional exhaustion, dehumanization, and sense of personal accomplishment.

Maslow, Abraham H. (măz'lō) [U.S. psychologist, 1908–1970] Articulator of a theory of human motivation based on a synthesis of holistic and dynamic principles. A contemporary of Carl Rogers, Maslow is considered one of the major theorists of humanistic psychology.

masochism (măs'ō-kĭzm) [Leopold von Sacher-Masoch, Austrian novelist, 1835–1895] A general orientation to life based on the belief that suffering relieves guilt and leads to a reward. Opposite of sadism. SEE: *algolagnia; flagellation*.

  sexual m. Sexual excitement produced in an individual by being humiliated or hurt by another.

masochist (măs'ō-kĭst) A person who derives pleasure from masochism.

mass (mas) [L. *massa*, mass fr Gr. *maza*, (barley) cake] **1.** A quantity of material, such as cells, that unite or adhere to each other. **2.** Soft solid preparation for internal use and of such consistency that it may be molded into pills. **3.** A fundamental scalar property of an object that describes the amount of acceleration an object will have when a given force is applied to it. The metric unit of mass is the kilogram. One kilogram equals 2.205 pounds. SEE: *weight*. **4.** Large, extensive, or encompassing an entire organ or population group (e.g., a mass vaccination).

cell m. In embryology, the mass of cells that develops into an organ or structure.

fat m. Total body fat. It can be measured with dual energy absorptiometry or bioelectrical impedance techniques.

fat-free m. The lean body mass plus the skeletal mass.

formula m. Gram molecular **m.**

gram molecular m. The mass or weight in grams of a substance equal to its molecular mass/weight. SYN: *formula m.; gram molecular weight.*

inner cell m. In embryology, the group of cells within the blastocyst from which the embryo, yolk sac, and amnion develop. SEE: *blastocyst.*

lateral m. of the atlas The parts of the first cervical vertebra that articulate with the occipital bone superiorly and the axis inferiorly.

lean body m. The weight of the body minus the fat content. It includes bones, muscles, and internal organs.

molecular m. Molecular weight.

massage therapist A person trained in the art and science of massage.

massage therapy Therapeutic manipulation of skin and underlying soft tissue, including ligaments, muscles, and tendons.

mass effect Evidence on a radiological study of the brain that midline structures of the central nervous system have shifted. This finding suggests that pressures within the cranium are abnormally high, that vital anatomical structures may be compressed, and that herniation of the brain and subsequent death may be imminent.

masseter (măs-sē′tĕr) [Gr. *maseter*, chewer] The muscle that closes the mouth and is the principal muscle in mastication.

masseur (mă-sĕr′) [Fr. *masseur*] A male massage therapist.

masseuse (mă-sĕz′) [Fr. *masseuse*] A female massage therapist.

mass fraction SEE: under *fraction.*

massive (măs′sĭv) [Fr. *massif*] Bulky; consisting of a large mass; huge.

massive collapse of the lung Deflation or compression of lung tissues caused either by obstruction of a main bronchus by a mucus plug, tumor, or foreign body; major trauma; or a tension pneumothorax. SEE: *lung; pneumothorax.*

SYMPTOMS: This condition is marked by dyspnea, cyanosis, shock, and chest pain.

TREATMENT: If caused by mucus or foreign body, therapy consists of bronchoscopy, pulmonary toilet, antibiotics, and oxygen.

mass sociogenic illness SEE: under *illness.*

MAST *medical antishock trousers; military antishock trousers.* SEE: *anti-G suit.*

mastalgia (mas-tal′jă) [*masto-* + *-algia*] Pain in the breast. SYN: *mammalgia; mastodynia.*

cyclical m. Breast pain that occurs during each menstrual cycle.

mastatrophia, mastatrophy (măst-ă-trō′fē-ă, măst-ăt′rō-fē) [″ + *atrophia*, want of nourishment] Atrophy of the mammary gland.

mast cell SEE: under *cell.*

mastectomy (măs-tĕk′tŏ-mē) [Gr. *mastos*, breast, + *ektome*, excision] Surgical removal of the breast. The procedure usually is performed as treatment for or prophylaxis against breast cancer; it can be curative in more than 90% of cases in which the disease is histologically noninvasive and grossly confined to the breast. In patients with more extensive disease, it is one part of a treatment strategy for breast cancer that also may include chemotherapy, radiation therapy, and/or hormone therapy. Radical mastectomy (no longer performed) involved the removal of the breast tissue as well as the pectoralis major muscle, pectoral fascia, axillary contents, nipple, and areola. In modified radical mastectomy, the pectoral fascia is removed but the pectoralis major muscle is left intact. The rest of the operation mimics radical mastectomy. In simple mastectomy, only breast tissue, pectoral fascia, nipple, areola, and axillary fat pad are removed. In tissue-saving mastectomy (modified-radical or simple) tissue is removed through a nipple and alveolar area circular incision, to limit muscle and nerve incisions and prepare the patient for immediate or delayed saline or silicone implant(s) or flap reconstruction. In the management of breast cancer, because none of these techniques has been proven superior to lumpectomy followed by radiation treatment, patient and practitioner preferences often determine which therapy is used. Mastectomy still is preferred in some breast cancer patients (e.g., pregnant women) who should not receive radiation therapy. SEE: *breast cancer; lumpectomy; Nursing Diagnoses Appendix.*

PATIENT CARE: *Preoperative:* The patient is encouraged to discuss treatment options with her surgeon and her partner, as well as with other women who have had the various treatment options. Preoperatively, the patient may be scheduled for bone, lung, and liver studies (scans, etc.) to determine the presence of metastatic disease and assist in determining staging and the needed treatment regimen. A chest x-ray, ECG, blood work, urinalysis, and anesthesia consult are carried out. Postoperative care measures are discussed, and sensation messages provided (drains, dressings, analgesia, pulmonary and thromboembolytic concerns, etc). Surgery may be in a same-day center with discharge to home or in an overnight hospital facility. In either case, a home health nurse will be needed postdischarge to assist in patientcare.

Intravenous access for fluids, sedation, and/or anesthesia is established, and cardiac monitor leads applied. Graduated compression hose or intermittent pneumatic dressings usually are applied for the surgical period. Before any sedation is given, the surgeon and patient together identify and mark the breast requiring surgery in the presence of a nurse, and this information is documented. An informed consent is obtained. Vital signs, cardiac rhythm, and the quantity and character of wound drainage are monitored throughout the surgery. Sentinel lymph node biopsy is done and sent to the pathologist to assess for cancer cells. If this node is negative, axillary nodes can be spared; if positive, axillary node dissection is carried out.

Postoperative: Postoperatively, vital signs are monitored until stable, and the patient is positioned with the arm on the affected side elevated on a pillow above heart level. Suction drain(s) will be in place, and drainage should be monitored for character and volume. Drains are removed when volume decreases to a minimal amount daily. Dressings also are inspected (anteriorly and posteriorly) for drainage. Intake and output should be monitored for 48 hr, if general anesthesia was employed. Active and passive exercise of the arm is encouraged to prevent joint contracture and muscle shortening. Prescribed analgesics are provided as ordered.

Turning, ambulating, deep breathing (incentive spirometry), and coughing are encouraged, and the patient is reminded that all will be more easily accomplished if analgesic drugs are used to prevent pain from escalating, rather than waiting until it is severe. The patient is taught not to allow any blood draws, intravenous devices, injections, or BP measurements to be done on the affected arm, and advised to carry/wear identifying information concerning this need. In the acute care setting, a bright pink bracelet provides this warning to health care providers. The incision is inspected for healing by the nurse/home-health nurse, and the patient and her partner are encouraged to view the incision as soon as they feel able to do so.

The patient and partner should both be made aware that breast surgery does not interfere with sexual function, although sensation may be absent in the surgical area; thus sexual activity and esp. foreplay touching, stroking, and other loving gestures may be resumed as soon as the patient desires. Sometimes tingling or pins-and-needles sensations (phantom breast syndrome) occur, so the patient should be prepared for this possibility. Emotional and psychological support is provided to help the patient and family to cope with the diagnosis and subsequent grief response and/or depression, and to adjust to changes in body image and self-concept. The patient is taught protective measures for lymphedema and is offered information about breast prostheses and reconstructive surgery.

The patient is prepared for adjuvant therapies that may be required, depending upon staging, estrogen receptor and Her2 status. Referrals are provided to local support groups as available, and to the American Cancer Society's Reach for Recovery group, which provides counseling, instruction, caring and sharing, and sometimes prosthetics or wigs or other head coverings for chemotherapy patients. (ACS: 800-ACS-2345; www.cancer.org).

preventive m. Prophylactic **m.**

prophylactic m. The removal of one or both breasts in an attempt to prevent the development of breast cancer. Surgical removal of the breasts to prevent breast cancer is sometimes used by women with a BRCA gene or a strong history of breast cancer in first-degree relatives. SYN: *preventive m*.

radical m. Treatment of breast cancer in which the breast, involved skin, pectoral muscles, axillary lymph nodes, and subcutaneous fat are removed. SEE: *lumpectomy*.

simple m. Treatment of breast cancer in which the breast, nipple, areola, and the involved overlying skin is removed. SEE: *lumpectomy*.

master (mas'tĕr) In robotic surgery, a device driven by the hand movements of the surgeon or interventionist. The movements of the master are mimicked, reduced, or refined by the surgical instrument (the "slave") in the operative field.

Master two-step test [Arthur Matthew Master, U.S. physician, 1895–1973] A standardized exercise test formerly used to assess cardiopulmonary function. It has been replaced by exercise treadmill testing, pharmacological stress testing, and other tests of fitness and cardiovascular reserve. SEE: *exercise tolerance test*.

mastic (mas'tik) [L. *mastiche* fr Gr. *mastichē*, chewing gum] A resin obtained from the mastic tree (*Pistacia lentiscus*), native to the Mediterranean. It is used in industry and in coating tablets.

mastication (măs-tĭ-kā'shŭn) [L. *masticare*, to chew] Chewing. Coordination of the large temporal, masseter, pterygoid muscles, and other smaller muscles of the mandible and tongue is required, under the influence of the mandibular division of cranial nerve V. **masticatory** (măs′tĭk-ă-tō″rē), *adj.*

masticatory apparatus (măs″tĭ-kă-tŏr″ē ăp″ă-răt′ĭs, -rā′tĭs) The teeth, jaws, muscles of mastication, and the temporomandibular joints; used for chewing.

mastic gum The chewed resin of the mastic tree (*Pistacia lentiscus*), used as a spice, flavoring, and as a gum in medicinal preparations such as toothpaste and lotions for the hair and skin.

Mastigophora (măs″tĭ-gŏf′ō-ră) Formerly a division of protozoa characterized by one or more flagella. Now called Zoomastigophora, a phylum of the kingdom Protista.

mastigote (măs′tĭ-gōt) A member of the protozoon group formerly called Mastigophora.

mastitis (mas-tīt′ĭs) [*masto-* + *-itis*] Inflammation or infection of the breast.

    cystic m. Mastitis resulting in formation of cysts that give the breast a nodular feeling upon palpation.

    granulomatous m. A rare inflammatory disease of the breast, often presenting as a tender mass. Symptoms usually appear within two years after a pregnancy. Even with mammography or ultrasonography, granulomatous mastitis may be difficult to distinguish from breast cancer without biopsy. Once the diagnosis is definitively established, the disease is treated with corticosteroids or by surgical removal of the mass.

    lactation m. Mastitis that occurs during breastfeeding, typically in the second or third postpartum week. Lactation mastitis may occur at any age. It occurs in about 1% of postpartum women, primarily in breast-feeding primiparas, but it can occur in nonlactating females and, rarely, in males. SYN: *lactational m.* SEE: *Nursing Diagnoses Appendix.*

    ETIOLOGY: Infection may be due to entry of disease-producing germs through cracks in the nipple. Most commonly, the offending microorganism is *Staphylococcus aureus*. Other predisposing factors include blocked milk ducts (from a tight bra or prolonged intervals between breastfeedings) and an incomplete let-down reflex (possibly related to emotional trauma). Infection begins in one lobule but may extend to other areas.

    SYMPTOMS: The woman complains of breast swelling and tenderness and shooting pains during and between feedings, in addition to fever, headache, and malaise. A triangular flush underneath the affected breast is an early sign. Abnormal vital signs include fever and tachycardia.

    TREATMENT: Heat should be applied locally; appropriate antibiotics, such as beta-lactamase–stable penicillins, are prescribed; and analgesics are given for discomfort. Although symptoms usually are relieved after 2 to 3 days of antibiotic therapy, treatment should be continued for 10 days. Frank abscesses require incision and drainage; pumping the breasts may be recommended to avoid engorgement and maintain lactation.

    PATIENT CARE: Health care professionals should encourage mothers to get adequate rest and hydration. Patient teaching emphasizes personal hygiene, breast care, wearing a supportive bra, and feeding the infant frequently to empty the breast. The mother is taught to recognize early signs of potential infection such as nipple redness and cracking. The patient and infant should be isolated from other nursing mothers and other infants to prevent spreading the infection, and the mother taught always to wash her hands before touching her breast and after feeding. The mother should be reassured that breastfeeding during mastitis will not harm her infant. The affected breast should be offered first to promote complete emptying and prevent clogged ducts. If an open abscess necessitates not feeding from this breast, it should be pumped until the abscess heals, while the mother continues feeding from the unaffected breast. The application of warm, wet towels to the affected breast or taking a warm shower should be suggested. Adequate fluid intake and rest should be encouraged. SEE: *breastfeeding.*

    lactational m. Lactation mastitis.

    puerperal m. Mastitis, often accompanied by suppuration, occurring in the later portion of the puerperium. The breast may become indurated due to retention of milk.

masto-, mast- [Gr. *mastos,* breast] Prefixes meaning *breast.*

mastocyte (măs′tō-sīt) [Gr. *masten,* to feed, + *kytos,* cell] Mast cell.

mastocytoma (măs″tō-sī-tō′mă) [″ + ″ + *oma,* tumor] An accumulation of mast cells that resembles a neoplasm.

mastocytosis (măs″tō-sī-tō′sĭs) [″ + ″ + *osis,* condition] A general term for a variety of rare disorders in which there is proliferation of excessive numbers of normal mast cells systemically or in the skin. Lesions present on the skin are termed urticaria pigmentosa. Firm stroking of the skin lesion will cause the area to become raised and pruritic with surrounding erythema; this is Darier's sign.

    Systemic mastocytosis is marked by infiltration of mast cells into the bone marrow, abdominal organs, and lymph nodes. Many of the signs and symptoms of this illness are due to the mast cells releasing granules containing histamine, prostaglandins, and arachidonic metabolites. SEE: *Darier's sign* for illus.

mastodynia (măst-ō-dĭn'ē-ă) [Gr. *mastos,* breast, + *odyne,* pain] Pain in the breast. SYN: *mammalgia; mastalgia.*

mastoid (măs'toyd) [″ + *eidos,* form, shape] **1.** Shaped like a breast. **2.** The mastoid process of temporal bone. **3.** Pert. to mastoid process. **mastoidal** (măs-toy'dăl), *adj.*

mastoid antrum SEE: under *antrum.*

mastoidectomy (măs″toy-d-ĕk'tō-mē) [″ + ″ + *ektome,* excision] Surgical excision of the mastoid sinuses used to treat mastoiditis when it has not responded to antibiotic therapy. Recurrent or persistent infections (e.g., cholesteatoma) or signs of intracranial complications (meningitis) are reasons for surgical treatment. The operation may be simple, involving complete removal of the mastoid sinuses, or radical, involving the middle ear, often with surgical reconstruction of the eardrum. SEE: *Nursing Diagnoses Appendix.*

PATIENT CARE: The patient is prepared physically and psychologically for the surgery, and postoperative care procedures are explained. An informed consent is obtained. Wound dressing is inspected daily and changed as necessary. Aseptic technique is used during dressing changes. Drains usually are removed in 72 hr. The patient is observed postoperatively for bleeding, fever, neck stiffness, vomiting, dizziness, disorientation, headache, or facial paralysis. The patient should be assessed for hearing loss after simple mastoidectomy; hearing loss usually precedes the need for radical surgery. After radical surgery, the wound is either drained with a tube, or packed with petroleum gauze or antibiotic-treated gauze, and the patient should have analgesia administered prior to its removal on postoperative day 4 or 5. Antibiotic therapy is continued for several weeks postsurgery. Analgesics are administered as needed and prescribed. Nausea and vertigo are common for several days postoperatively, so side rails should be in place, the patient assisted to ambulate, and antiemetics administered as needed. Other potential complications include damage to the facial nerve with facial muscle paralysis or difficulty swallowing. The patient and family are taught how to change and care for dressings prior to discharge, and advised of the importance of completing the prescribed antibiotic regimen.

mastoiditis (mas″toyd″ī'tĭs) [*mastoid* + *-itis*] Inflammation of the mastoid sinuses, usually due to the spread of infection from acute otitis media (OM). The disease is relatively rare now that effective antibiotics for OM are generally available. The causative organisms usually are the same as those that cause OM: streptococcal species, *Haemophilus influenzae,* and *Staphylococcus aureus* although sometimes mycobacteria or fungi cause the disease.

SYMPTOMS: The patient complains of pain behind the ear and sometimes of fever and systemic symptoms such as malaise and chills. Physical examination may reveal redness and tenderness behind the affected ear, with swelling of the external auditory canal.

TREATMENT: Early in the course of the infection, patients may be treated with several days of intravenous antibiotics followed by outpatient medications and close follow-up. Mastoidectomy or other neurosurgical procedures may be needed if the infection has spread to beneath the periosteum, or if intracranial infection or thrombosis of neighboring veins develops. All these complications may be detected with imaging (e.g., computerized tomographic scanning of the head).

mastoid process SEE: under *process.*

mastology (măs-tŏl'ō-jē) [″ + *logos,* word, reason] The branch of medicine concerned with study of the breast.

mastopathy (măs-tŏp'ă-thē) [Gr. *mastos,* breast, + *pathos,* disease] Any disease of the mammary glands.

mastopexy (măs'tō-pĕks-ē) [″ + *pexis,* fixation] Correction of a pendulous breast by surgical fixation and plastic surgery.

mastoplasty (măs'tō-plăs″tē) [″ + *plassein,* to form] Plastic surgery of the breast. SEE: *mammoplasty.*

masturbate (măs'tĕr-bāt) [L. *masturbari,* fr. *manus,* hand, + *stuprare,* to defile] To practice masturbation.

masturbation (măs″tĕr-bā'shŭn) Stimulation of genitals or other erogenous areas, usually to orgasm, by some means other than sexual intercourse.

At one time practicing masturbation was believed to cause a great variety of mental and physical disorders. There is no scientific basis for such beliefs.

matched unrelated donor SEE: under *donor.*

matching 1. Comparison in order to select objects or persons with similar characteristics. **2.** Being identical, equal, or exactly alike.

m. of controls In medical research, ensuring that the group of actively treated subjects has as many relevant similarities as possible to a group of untreated or placebo-treated persons. Matching subjects with controls increases the likelihood that the findings demonstrated by the study are the result of the treatment itself and not another variable.

cross-m. of blood Technique and procedure for determining the immunologic and genetic characteristics of the patient's blood so that appropriate blood may be used for transfusion.

human leukocyte antigen m. ABBR: HLA matching. In organ transplantation, determining the compatibility of the antigens present on donor organs with those of the patient who will receive the organ. In general, the more closely the donor and recipient match, the greater the likelihood of a successful graft. Mismatching of organ and recipient increases the chances of organ rejection. SYN: *histocompatibility locus* **antigen**.

residency m. The assignment of medical students to postgraduate medical residency training programs.

treatment m. Using patient profiles and preferences to individualize and optimize therapeutic regimens for patients (e.g., in the management of psychiatric or substance abuse disorders).

maté (mă-tā′) [Sp., vessel for preparing leaves] Tea made from the leaves of *Ilex paraguayensis*. It contains caffeine and tannin.

USES: Diaphoretic and diuretic when taken in large quantities.

mater (māt′ĕr) [L. *mater,* mother] Nonneural tissue coverings of the brain and spinal cord; meninges.

arachnoid m. Arachnoid membrane.

dura m. The outermost meninx, a tough sheet of fibrous connective tissue that completely envelops the brain and spinal cord inside the skull and vertebral canal. Inside the skull, there is no epidural space, and the dural envelope is fused with the inner periosteum of the skull bones. Inside the vertebral canal, however, the dural envelope is separated from the vertebral bone by an epidural space filled with fat and a network of veins. SYN: *dural membrane.*

pia m. The innermost meninx, a delicate membrane coating the surfaces of the brain and spinal cord and closely following all their surface contours. In most places, the pia mater is one cell thick. It encloses the surface blood vessels of the brain, and it follows the arteries as they dive into the brain tissue. It appears that the pial membrane is part of the blood-brain barrier, a set of physiological constraints that restrict diffusion of many blood-borne molecules into the tissues of the brain. SYN: *pial membrane.*

materia alba (mă-tē′rē-ă ăl′bă) [L., white matter] Yellow or grayish white, soft, sticky deposit that collects along the junction between the teeth and gingiva. Materia alba consists of microorganisms, desquamated epithelial cells, leukocytes, and a mix of salivary proteins and lipids, with few or no food particles. Materia alba lacks the regular

structure of plaque and is clearly visible without the use of disclosing agents.

material (mă-tir′ē-ăl) [L. *materialis,* pert. to matter, material] **1.** Pert. to or consisting of matter. **2.** A substance from which something may be made, constructed, or created. Particular materials are listed under the first word. SEE: e.g., *denture base material; impression material; spent material.*

material safety data sheet ABBR: MSDS. Descriptive sheet required by U.S. federal law, and by laws of other countries and states, that accompanies a chemical or a chemical mixture. The sheet provides identity of the material, physical hazards (e.g., flammability), and acute and chronic health hazards associated with contact with or exposure to the compound. It is estimated that there are almost 600,000 hazardous chemical products in American workplaces. SEE: *right-to-know law.*

materia medica (mă-tē′rē-ă mĕd′ĭ-kă) [L., medical matter] **1.** Pharmacology. **2.** A substance used to treat disease.

maternal [L. *maternus*] **1.** Relating to the mother. **2.** From a mother.

maternal mortality rate SEE: under *rate.*

maternal serum alpha-fetoprotein Alpha-fetoprotein present in the blood of a pregnant woman. SEE: *alpha-fetoprotein.*

maternal serum screen SEE: under *screen.*

maternity (mă-tĕr′nĭ-tē) **1.** Motherhood. **2.** The obstetrical department of a hospital.

mating [ME. *mate,* companion] Pairing of male and female that occurs by chance, that is, with no external influence or control.

assortative m. Pairing of male and female that is controlled in some manner.

random m. Pairing of male to female when each individual has the same chance of mating with those of other genetic makeup.

mating strategy (strat′ĕ-jē) [Gr. *stratēgia,* generalship] Any of various techniques used by organisms to increase the likelihood that they produce offspring. Common mating strategies used by animals include having brightly colored hair or feathers; making elaborate, ritualized movements to attract members of the opposite sex; defeating rivals in battle; guarding and protecting lifelong territories and mates; and entering the territories of others during mating season.

Matricaria recutita (ma″trĭ-kar′ē-ă rē″kū-tīt′ă) SEE: German **chamomile.**

matricide (măt′rĭ-sīd) [L. *mater,* mother, + *caedere,* to kill] Killing one's mother.

matrilineal (mā″trĭ-lĭn′ē-ăl) [L. *mater,* mother, + *linea,* line] Pert. to or affecting inheritance from the mothers in a family, but not the fathers.

matrilysin A member of the matrix metalloproteinase enzyme family that is expressed by many tumor cells and plays a part in tissue invasion and metastasis.

matrix (mā′triks, ′trī-sēz″) *pl.* **matrices** [L. *matrix,* female animal kept for breeding (not a woman)] **1.** The basic substance from which a thing is made or develops. **2.** The intercellular material of a tissue. **3.** Mold for casting amalgams in dental restoration.

> **bone m.** The acellular part of bone.

> **extracellular m.** ABBR: ECM. The solid or liquid material that is produced by and surrounds the cells of connective tissues.

> **nail m.** Nailbed.

> **territorial m.** That component of cartilage immediately surrounding clusters of chondrocytes. It has a rich concentration of glycosaminoglycans, and stains darkly (it is basophilic).

> **umbilical cord m.** Wharton's jelly.

> **m. unguis** Nailbed.

matrix-assisted laser desorption-ionization ABBR: MALDI. A form of mass spectrometry used to analyze proteins, peptides, carbohydrates, and other biologically important molecules.

matrix stem cell SEE: under *cell.*

matted (măt′ĭd) [LL. *matta,* mat of rushes] Tangled or connected; said of diseased lymph nodes that have grown into one another, creating a clump or mass of tissue.

matter (măt′ĕr) [L. *materia,* stuff, material, wood, matte] **1.** Tissue, esp. nerve tissue. **2.** Pus. **3.** In physics, anything that has mass and occupies space.

> **gray m.** Regions of the central nervous system with few myelinated axons. Gray matter is usually rich in neuronal cell bodies, dendrites, and the ramifying terminals of axons.

> **white m.** Regions of the central nervous system filled with myelinated axons.

mattress overlay SEE: under *overlay.*

maturate (măt′ū-rāt) [L. *maturus,* ripe] **1.** To ripen; to mature. **2.** To suppurate.

maturation (mach″ū-rā′shŏn) [L. *maturatio,* ripening] **1.** Maturing; ripening, as a graafian follicle. **2.** Suppuration. **3.** The process in the development of germ cells (spermatozoa and ova) occurring in spermatogenesis or oogenesis in which the number of chromosomes is reduced from the diploid number to the haploid number (one half of diploid). This process includes two cell divisions. SEE: *oogenesis; spermatogenesis.* **4.** The completion of the mineralization pattern or crystalline structure of calcified tissues.

> **affinity m.** The mechanism during an immune response that produces antibodies with a strong ability to bind to a foreign antigen over time. Affinity maturation is produced by changes in the genes that encode immunoglobulin G (IgG) and by increased survival of those B lymphocytes that produce antibodies with the greatest ability to destroy a particular antigen. Increased affinity occurs only when B-cell activation is stimulated by helper T cells.

> **enamel m.** The process of changing from about 30% inorganic mineral in enamel matrix of the teeth to the 96% inorganic content in mature enamel. The maturation is accomplished by the ameloblast cells over a long period, with a decrease in water and organic content, and an increase in mineral content and size or density of hydroxyapatite crystals. The final stages of enamel maturation occur after the tooth has erupted into the oral cavity.

> **fetal m.** Fetal development.

> **in vitro m.** ABBR: IVM. An assisted reproduction technique in which an immature oocyte is nurtured in the laboratory until fertilized.

maturation effect A change in the condition of a disease or organism that occurs naturally over time and not as a result of treatment.

mature (mă-tūr′) **1.** Fully developed or ripened. **2.** To become fully developed.

mature minor Any teenager who can demonstrate competence to consent to or refuse treatment. In the common law, a teenager who demonstrates adequate maturity may choose or reject some forms of care, including contraceptive and pregnancy care, mental health and chemical dependency consultations, and treatments for sexually transmitted diseases. In these instances the consent of the parent or guardian is not necessarily needed.

⚠️ Although the concept of the mature minor recognizes the autonomy of the teen, before care is provided without parental consent health care professionals must be able to obtain evidence of and clearly document both the teen's maturity and his or her understanding of any proposed treatment.

maturity **1.** The state of completed growth or development. **2.** The stage of growth at which an individual becomes capable of reproducing.

> **fetal lung m.** The ability of the developing lung to oxygenate and ventilate effectively outside the womb. The lungs are the last fetal organ to mature. Surfactant, which allows the alveoli in the lungs to expand and not stick together, is secreted by the fetal lungs after 28 weeks. The readiness of the fetal lung can be assessed with several inva-

sive, e.g., amniocentesis, and noninvasive, e.g., ultrasound, tests, all of which have some shortcomings. Some tests on amniotic fluid include: measurements of surfactant; phosphatidylglycerol; the lecithin/sphingomyelin ratio; and the number of lamellar bodies.

PATIENT CARE: Premature infants born with immature lungs have a high likelihood of developing infantile respiratory distress syndrome. Antenatal treatment with glucocorticoids improves most amniotic fluid indices of fetal lung maturity. Infants born with immature lungs are also often treated with continuous positive airway pressure, other forms of mechanical ventilation, and surfactant.

matutinal (mă-tū′tĭ-năl) [L. *matutinalis,* morning] Pert. to morning or occurring early in the day, such as morning sickness.

maxilla (măk-sĭl′ă) [L., jawbone] A paired bone with several processes that forms most of the upper face, roof of the mouth, sides of the nasal cavity, and floor of the orbit. The alveolar process of the maxilla supports the teeth, which is the basis for calling the maxilla the upper jaw. SEE: *skull* for illus; *skeleton.*

maxillary (măk′sĭ-lĕr″ē) **1.** Pert. to the upper jaw. **2.** Pert. to the maxilla.

maxillotomy (măk″sĭ-lŏt′ō-mē) [″ + Gr. *tome,* incision] Surgical incision of the maxilla.

maximal oxygen uptake SEE: *maximum aerobic capacity.*

maximum (măks′ĭ-mŭm) *pl.* **maxima** [L. *maximus,* greatest] **1.** The greatest quantity or effect. **2.** Height of a disease.
    maximal (-măl), *adj.*

maximum allowable concentration SEE: under *concentration.*

maximum breathing capacity ABBR: MBC. The greatest amount of air that can be breathed in a specified period, usually 15 sec. It is expressed in liters of air per minute.

maximum lifespan 1. The age of the oldest known member of a species. **2.** The theoretical age that any organism, drug, or structure can survive intact. The term is sometimes used in geriatrics for the maximum lifespan potential of an individual or, in pharmacology, for the effective shelf life of a drug.

maximum tolerated dose SEE: under *dose.*

Mayer reflex (mī′ĕr) [Karl Mayer, Austrian neurologist, 1862–1932] Opposition and adduction of the thumb, flexion at the metacarpophalangeal joint, and extension at the interphalangeal joint in response to downward pressure on the index finger.

Mayer wave (mī′ĕr) A low-frequency oscillation in arterial blood pressure observed in humans and other animals. This type of wave reflects the physiological variations corresponding to baroreflex feedback. It appears to diminish in elderly people. SEE: *autonomic nervous system; baroreflexes.*

May-Hegglin anomaly (mā′hĕg′lin, mī′) [Richard May, Ger. physician, 1863–1936; Robert Hegglin, Swiss physician, 1907–1969.] An autosomal-dominant blood disorder marked by the presence of Dohle bodies in granulocyte leukocytes. Platelets vary in size and may be decreased in number. Purpura and excessive bleeding may occur, although some affected persons are asymptomatic.

mayhem (mā′hĕm) **1.** Interpersonal violence or disfigurement. **2.** Chaos (e.g., in the organization of the workplace, in the administration of clinical, managerial, or research activities). **3.** Physiological disruption (e.g., by a virulent infection or a severe metabolic illness).

Mayo scissors (mā′ō″) [Mayo Clinic, Rochester, MN] A sturdy curved or straight scissors with sharp edges and a blunt tip used in a wide variety of operations.

maze A labyrinth of communicating paths.

m.b. Prescription sign meaning L. *misce bene,* mix well.

MBC *maximum breathing capacity.*

MBD *minimal brain dysfunction; minimal brain damage.*

MC *Medical Corps; microscopic colitis; monochorionic.*

mc Former abbreviation for *millicurie.*

MCADD *Medium-chain acyl-CoA dehydrogenase deficiency.*

McArdle disease (măk-ard′ĭl) [Brian McArdle, Brit. pediatrician, 1911–2002] A glycogen storage disease caused by deficient myophosphorylase B (a muscle phosphorylase.) SYN: *glycogen storage disease type V; muscle phosphorylase deficiency.*

McBurney, Charles (măk-bŭr′nē) U.S. surgeon, 1845–1913.
    M.'s incision An incision made halfway between the umbilicus and the interior superior spine, a point of extreme tenderness in appendicitis.
    M.'s point A point 1 to 2 in (2.5 to 5.1 cm) above the anterosuperior spine of the ilium, on a line between the ilium and umbilicus, where pressure produces tenderness in acute appendicitis.
    M.'s sign Tenderness and rigidity at the McBurney point, probably indicative of appendicitis.

McCune-Albright syndrome (mĭ-kūn′al′brīt″) [Fuller Albright, U.S. physician, 1900–1969] Polyostotic fibrous dysplasia accompanied by café au lait macules and endocrine disorders. It is associated esp. with precocious puberty in girls. Those affected are prone to bone fractures. Deformed and shortened bones may also develop. SYN: *Alb-*

right disease. SEE: *polyostotic fibrous dysplasia.*

mcg *microgram.*

McGill Pain Questionnaire (mă-gĭl′) [McGill University, Montreal, Canada, where the questionnaire was developed] ABBR: MPQ. An instrument used to quantify the perceived location, type, and magnitude of pain. A typical McGill Pain Questionnaire consists of three parts: location of the source of pain as depicted by marking one or more X's on a diagram; the intensity of pain as indicated by a visual analog scale; and the magnitude of pain by selecting words from a pain rating index.

MCH 1. *mean corpuscular hemoglobin.* 2. *maternal-child health.*

mch *millicurie hour.*

MCHC *mean corpuscular hemoglobin concentration.*

MCi *megacurie.*

mCi *millicurie.*

McKenzie derangement syndrome (mă-ken′zē) [Robin McKenzie, contemporary New Zealand physical therapist] Back pain resulting from structural malformations and biomechanical malfunctioning of the intervertebral disk or disks.

McLeod neuroacanthocytosis syndrome (mă-klowd′) [Hugh McLeod, U.S. student in whom the disorder was first discovered in 1961] A rare, X-linked disorder in which spiculation of blood cells is accompanied by delayed neurological, psychiatric, and cardiac muscle disease.

McMurray, Thomas Porter (măk-mŭ′rē) Brit. orthopedic surgeon, 1887–1949.

    M. sign McMurray test.

    M. test A test for a torn meniscus of the knee. The examiner flexes the patient's knee completely, rotates the tibia outward, and applies a valgus force against the knee while slowly extending it. A painful click indicates a torn medial meniscus. If a click is felt when the tibia is rotated inward and a varus force is applied against the knee during extension, the lateral meniscus is torn. SYN: *McMurray sign.*

MCP *metacarpophalangeal joint.*

MCS *multiple chemical sensitivity.*

MCT *microwave coagulation therapy.*

MCV *mean corpuscular volume.*

MCV4 *meningococcal (groups A, C, Y, and W-135) conjugate vaccine.*

Md Symbol for the element mendelevium.

MDC An abbreviation for the *congenital muscular dystrophies,* a group of autosomal recessive diseases characterized by significant muscular weakness and often cognitive disorders. All of the congenital muscular dystrophies first become evident in infancy. Examples include MDCs 1A-1D and Fukuyama disease.

MDI *metered-dose inhaler.*

MDR *multiple drug resistance.*

meadowsweet (mĕd′ō-swēt″) Any of three perennial herbs, *Filipendula ulmaria, Spiraea alba,* or *S. latifolia,* that grow in moist biomes. Meadowsweet is a source of aspirin-like chemicals used to treat chronic pain and is promoted as a digestive aid.

meal (mēl) [AS. *mael,* measure, meal] 1. Portion of food eaten at a particular time to satisfy the appetite. 2. The edible portion of any cereal grain that has been coarsely ground, as in corn meal.

meal replacement A low-calorie snack or drink taken in place of breakfast, lunch, or dinner, often as part of a weight-loss regimen.

Meals on Wheels Programs that provide to the elderly and infirm home-delivered meals that meet federally mandated criteria.

mean (mēn) [Fr. *meen,* fr. L. *medianus,* in the middle] In statistics, the average of a set of values. SEE: *arithmetic mean; median.*

    arithmetic m. The result obtained by adding all of the values in a set of data and dividing by the number of items that were added. SYN: *average.* SEE: *median.*

means testing The determination of a person's financial eligibility for subsidized health care services.

measles (mē′zĕlz) A highly communicable disease caused by the rubeola virus and marked by fever, general malaise, sneezing, nasal congestion, brassy cough, conjunctivitis, spots on the buccal mucosa (Koplik spots), and a maculopapular eruption over the entire body. The occurrence of measles before age 6 months is relatively uncommon because of passively acquired maternal antibodies from the immune mother. SYN: *first disease; rubeola.*

    An attack of measles almost invariably confers permanent immunity. Active immunization can be produced by administration of measles vaccine, preferably that containing the live attenuated virus although temporary immunity can be attained by administration of measles vaccine containing the inactivated virus for those in whom the live attenuated type is contraindicated. Vaccination has reduced the occurrence of measles during childhood, making it more prevalent during adolescence and adulthood. Measles remains a major cause of death in children in underdeveloped countries, where vaccination is less frequently employed. Passive immunization is afforded by administration of gamma globulin. SEE: *Nursing Diagnoses Appendix.*

    SYMPTOMS: Measles is spread by inhalation of contaminated air. The incubation period is from 8 to 14 days. Greatest communicability occurs during the prodromal period, which occurs approximately 11 days after exposure to the virus. The onset of symptoms is gradual and includes coryza, rhinitis, drowsiness, loss of appetite, and gradually increasing temperature for the first 2 days up to 101° to 103°F (38.3° to 39.4°C). Koplik spots appear on the buccal mucosa opposite the molars on the second or third day. The fever peaks about the fourth day, at times as high as 104° to 106°F (40° to 41.1°C). Photophobia and cough soon develop; when this happens, the temperature may fall somewhat.

At this time, the rash appears, first on the face as small red maculopapular lesions that grow rapidly and coalesce in places, often causing a swollen, mottled appearance. The somewhat pruritic rash extends outward to the rest of the body and extremities and in some areas may resemble the rash of scarlet fever. Ordinarily, the rash lasts 4 to 5 days; as it subsides, the temperature declines. Consequently, 5 days after the appearance of the rash, the temperature should be normal or about normal in uncomplicated cases. Early in the disease, leukopenia may be present. More severe symptoms and complications occur in the very young, in adolescents and adults, and in anyone who is immunocompromised or vitamin A deficient.

COMPLICATIONS: Encephalitis is a grave complication; among patients who develop this, about one in eight will die, about half will have permanent central nervous system injury, and the remainder will recover completely. Bronchopneumonia is a serious complication. Otitis media, followed by mastoiditis, brain abscess, or even meningitis, is not rare, and unilateral or bilateral nerve deafness may be a permanent consequence. Cervical adenitis, with marked cellulitis, sometimes proves fatal. Tracheitis and laryngeal stenosis, due to edema of the glottis, are sometimes seen in the course of measles. A marked conjunctivitis usually occurs.

DIFFERENTIAL DIAGNOSIS: Signs and symptoms of scarlet fever and German measles may mimic those of measles. Koplik spots are pathognomonic for measles, however, and if seen, virtually rule out other diagnoses.

PROGNOSIS: The prognosis is favorable in the healthy child, but the seriousness of the possible complications of measles should not be minimized. As said above, an attack of measles nearly always confers permanent immunity.

PREVENTION: All children who have not had measles or who have been vaccinated before age 12 months should be immunized with live attenuated measles vaccine at 12 to 15 months of age. A second dose is recommended at the start of school (5 to 6 yr) or at junior high school age (11 to 12 yr). Measles vaccine is often given in conjunction with mumps and/or rubella virus vaccines. SEE: *vaccine*.

Live attenuated vaccine is contraindicated in pregnant women or in those who have leukemia, lymphomas, and other generalized neoplasms; in those taking agents such as steroids and antimetabolites; in persons with active, untreated tuberculosis, HIV, or other severe illness; in those who are sensitive to neomycin or duck or chicken eggs; and after blood transfusion or injection of immune serum globulin. In the latter situation, a 12-week waiting period is necessary before administering the vaccine. Although people with AIDS or HIV infection with signs of serious immunosuppression should not be given MMR, those with HIV infection without symptoms can and should be vaccinated against measles.

Measles is endemic in many developing countries. In 2000, in nations where measles vaccination was unavailable, more than three quarters of a million children died of the disease.

Measles immune serum globulin is used for passive protection in unimmunized, high-risk patients (such as those who have cancer or are taking antimetabolic drugs); if given later than the third day of the incubation period, however, it may only extend the incubation period instead of preventing the disease.

PATIENT CARE: The importance of immunization of children to prevent measles should be emphasized to parents and family caregivers. Patients who contract the disease should remain isolated (droplet isolation) from diagnosis until 4 days after the rash appears. Bedrest and a quiet, calm environment are provided. A dimly lit room can help to counteract the effects of photophobia should it occur. Eye secretions are removed with warm saline or water. The child should avoid rubbing his eyes. Supportive care includes adequate fluid intake, antipyretics as necessary, a cool mist vaporizer to relieve cough and coryza, and antipruritic medication to prevent itching. Parents also should be made aware that cough preparations and antibiotics are usually ineffective. The parents are taught about the importance of hand hygiene and care of contaminated articles. Assessments are made for complications of otitis media, pneumonia, mastoiditis, brochiolitis, laryngotracheitis with obstructive edema, and encephalitis, all of which require early management. The severity of the illness in adults may be reduced by IV ribavirin administration, but this medication is not approved for use by the Food and Drug Administration. Because of vaccination programs, measles is rare in the U.S. In 2004, about 35 cases of measles were reported. Before vaccination, approx. 450,000 cases were reported in the U.S. annually.

    black m. A colloquial term used to denote hemorrhagic measles, i.e., measles in which there is bleeding into the rash.

    German m. Rubella.

    three-day m. Rubella.

measly (mē′zlē) Description of pork that is infected with the cysticerci of *Taenia solium* or *saginata*.

measurable disease (mezh′ŭr-ă-bĕl) The amount of tumor or infection that can be detected in the body by conventional means. It may be equal to or less than the total body disease burden. Treatment of detectable disease may result in durable disease remission or apparent cure even when some cancerous or infected cells remain undetected in the body.

measurand (mĕzh′ĕr-ănd″) Any quantity subject to measurement.

measure (mĕ′zhŭr) [L. *mensura,* a measuring] **1.** The dimensions, capacity, or quantity of anything that can be so evaluated. Length, area, volume, and mass are basic properties of matter and materials that can be measured. **2.** To determine the extent of length, area, mass, or volume of a substance or object. SEE: *mensuration.* **3.** A device used in measuring, for example, a marked tape or a graduated beaker. SEE: *Weights and Measures Appendix.*

meat (mēt) The flesh of animals (such as cows, pigs, and poultry) eaten as food. Meat is a concentrated source of proteins, fats, cholesterol, calories, and many vitamins and micronutrients. It contains significant amounts of B complex vitamins (thiamine, riboflavin, niacin), iron, and other minerals. It has limited amounts of calcium and fiber. Its metabolic by-products include organic acids.

    Western diets contain far more meat than is needed for growth and development. Excessive consumption of meats and of other calorically dense, high-fat foods contributes to obesity and atherosclerotic heart disease. SEE: *Food Guide Pyramid.*

meat glue A colloquial term for "transglutaminase." SEE: *transglutaminase.*

meatoplasty (mē-ăt′ō-plăs-tē) Surgical construction of an external auditory canal.

meatotomy (mē″ă-tŏt′ō-mē) Incision of urinary meatus to enlarge the opening.

meatus (mē-ā′tŭs) *pl.* **meatus** [L.] A passageway or an opening. **meatal** (mē-ā′tăl), *adj.*

    acoustic m. The opening to either the external or internal auditory canal.

It can also be a synonym for either the external or internal auditory canal.

    m. acusticus externus External auditory **canal.**

    m. acusticus internus Internal auditory **canal.**

    external acoustic m. External auditory **meatus.**

    external auditory m. The outer opening of the external auditory canal, or the canal itself. SEE: *external acoustic meatus.*

    internal acoustic m. Internal auditory **m.**

    internal auditory m. The opening of the internal auditory canal into the cranial cavity located on the posterior surface of the petrous portion of the temporal bone, or the canal itself. SYN: *internal acoustic* **m.**

    urethral m. External opening of the urethra. SYN: *urinary* **m.**; **m.** *urinarius.*

    m. urinarius Urethral **m.**

    urinary m. Urethral **meatus.**

mechanical laryngitis SEE: under *laryngitis.*

mechanical thrombolysis SEE: under *thrombolysis.*

mechanic's hand Cracking of the skin of the radial surface of the fingers and of the thenar eminence (the bulge between the thumb and the index finger). It is a characteristic skin finding in patient's with polymyositis.

mechanics [Gr. *mechane,* machine] The science of force and matter.

    body m. Application of biomechanics to use of the body in daily life activities and to the prevention and correction of problems related to posture and physical activity.

    dynamic m. The continuous automated analysis of simultaneous measurements of lung variables affecting mechanical ventilation.

mechanism (mek′ă-nizm) [L. *mechanismus* fr. Gr. *mēchanē,* instrument, machine] **1.** Involuntary, consistent response to a stimulus. **2.** A habit or response pattern formed to achieve a result. **3.** A machine or machine-like structure.

    m. of action The means by which a drug exerts its effects on cells or tissues. It may have specific binding sites, receptor activation, enzymatic activity, or solubility.

    countercurrent m. A mechanism used by the kidneys, making it possible to excrete excess solutes in the urine with little loss of water from the body.

    cycling m. In mechanical ventilation the technology or mechanism that switches a breath from inspiration to expiration.

    defense m. Defense.

    extensor m. The structures that work together to move a joint into an extended position. For most joints, this mechanism is its group of extensor tendons; for other joints, additional structures are involved, such as the patella (a sesamoid bone), which is part of the extensor mechanism of the knee.

host defense m. A complex interacting system that protects the host from endogenous and exogenous microorganisms. It includes physical and chemical barriers, inflammatory response, reticuloendothelial system, and immune responses. SEE: *cytokine; interleukin-1; interferon.*

m. of injury ABBR: MOI. The manner in which a physical injury occurred (e.g., fall from a height, ground-level fall, high- or low-speed motor vehicle accident, ejection from a vehicle, vehicle rollover). The MOI is used to estimate the forces involved in trauma and, thus, the potential severity for wounding, fractures, and internal organ damage that a patient may suffer as a result of the injury.

mechanoreceptor (měk″ă-nō-rē-sěp′tor) A receptor that receives mechanical stimuli such as pressure from sound or touch.

mechanotherapy (měk″ăn-ō-thĕr′ă-pē) [Gr. *mechane*, machine, + *therapeia*, treatment] Use of various types of mechanical apparatus to perform passive movements and to exercise various parts of the body.

Meckel, Johann Friedrich (the younger) (mek′ĕl) Ger. anatomist, 1781–1833, grandson of J.F. Meckel, the elder.

M.'s cartilage A cartilaginous bar about which the mandible develops.

M.'s diverticulum A congenital sac or blind pouch found in the lower portion of the ileum. It represents the persistent proximal end of the yolk stalk. Sometimes it is continued to the umbilicus as a cord or as a tube forming a fistulous opening at the umbilicus. The diverticulum may become a focal point for intestinal obstruction progressing to strangulation; become inflamed with symptoms mimicking acute appendicitis; and as a result of the variable presence of gastric mucosa, may develop peptic ulcer symptoms, including hemorrhage. Surgery is necessary for any of these clinical presentations. SEE: *diverticulitis.*

M. plane A plane through the auricular and alveolar points.

M. scan A radionuclide scan to demonstrate the presence of a Meckel's diverticulum. The diverticulum may be difficult to visualize with plain films, barium studies, colonoscopy, or CT imaging.

mecobalamin A form of vitamin B_{12} in which a methyl group replaces a cyanide moiety found in cyanocobalamin.

meconium (mē-kō′nē-ŭm) [L. *meconium*, fr Gr. *mēkōnion*, poppy juice]

1. Opium; poppy juice. 2. First feces of a newborn infant, made up of salts, amniotic fluid, mucus, bile, and epithelial cells. This substance is greenish black, almost odorless, and tarry. The first meconium stool should appear during the first 24 hr. Meconium should persist for about 3 days.

meconium aspiration syndrome ABBR: MAS. Fetal inhalation of meconium in utero during episodes of severe fetal hypoxia or with the first few breaths after birth. Symptoms and signs occur in varying degrees and include respiratory distress, tachypnea, rales, and wheezes throughout the lung fields. Chest x-ray may show areas of increased density from the aspirated meconium, evidence of chemical pneumonitis, and areas of atelectasis caused by bronchiolar obstruction and collapse of alveoli distally. A pneumothorax also may occur from the ball-valve effect of obstruction by meconium in the small bronchioles. These complications can produce hypoxia, acidosis, respiratory failure, persistent fetal circulation, and persistent pulmonary hypertension of the infant (PPHN). SYN: *fetal meconium aspiration.* SEE: *meconium.*

ETIOLOGY: Preeclampsia, pregnancy-induced hypertension, postmaturity (with oligohydramnios), intrauterine hypoxia and asphyxia, or other forms of stress on the fetus may be contributory factors. Fetal stress may produce increased intestinal peristalsis, anal sphincter relaxation, and expulsion of meconium into the amniotic fluid. When the fetus gasps in utero, or with the first few breaths of air after delivery, the fluid enters the respiratory tree.

PREVENTION: Preventive measures include gentle suctioning of the baby's nose and mouth by the obstetrician while the baby's head is still on the mother's perineum, followed by immediate tracheal suctioning via endotracheal intubation to remove as much airway meconium as possible before the baby's first breath.

TREATMENT: Oxygen, endotracheal intubation, surfactant replacement therapy, and assisted ventilation may be required. For severe cases, extracorporeal membrane oxygenation (ECMO) may be used to rest and heal the lung tissue.

meconium ileus SEE: under *ileus.*

meconium staining Fetal defecation of meconium while in utero during labor. It may cause staining of the amniotic fluid or of the infant.

PATIENT CARE: Meconium must be suctioned from the newborn's mouth and trachea before the first breath in order to prevent aspiration.

MED *minimal effective dose; minimal erythema dose.*

Medevac The evacuation of injured persons from the scene of an emergency by air ambulance, usually a helicopter. Air transport of trauma patients is esp. useful in rural locations, to provide definitive care as quickly as possible. SEE: *golden hour.*

media (mē′dē-ă) [L.] **1.** Pl. of medium. **2.** The middle or muscular layer of an artery or vein. SYN: *tunica media.*

mediad (mē′dē-ăd) [L. *medium,* middle, + *ad,* toward] Toward the median line or plane of the body.

medial (mē′dē-ăl) [L. *medialis*] **1.** Pert. to the middle. **2.** Nearer to the midline plane; toward the midline plane.

medial geniculate body SEE: under *body.*

medialis (mē″dē-ā′lĭs) [L.] Term indicating something that is closer to the midline of the body.

medial tibial stress syndrome, medial tibial syndrome ABBR: MTSS. Shin splints.

median (mē′dē-ăn) [L. *medianus,* in the middle] **1.** In statistics, a number obtained by arranging a given series in order of magnitude and selecting that number that has an equal number of values above and below it. Thus, in the series 5, 7, 100, 101, 102, the median is 100. SEE: *mean; mesial.* **2.** In anatomy, a point in the midline plane.

mediastinal (mē″dē-ăs-tī′năl) [L. *mediastinalis*] Relating to the mediastinum.

mediastinitis (mē″dē-ăs″tĭ-nī′tĭs) [″ + Gr. *itis,* inflammation] Inflammation or infection of the mediastinum, such as may occur after injury to the neck, perforation of the esophagus, or after surgical procedures on the heart or lungs.

mediastinoscopy (mē″dē-ăs″tĭ-nŏs′kō-pē) [″ + *skopein,* to examine] Endoscopic examination of the mediastinum.

mediastinotomy (mē″dē-ăs″tĭ-nŏt′ō-mē) [″ + *tome,* incision] Surgical incision of the mediastinum.

mediastinum (mē″dē-ăs-tī′nŭm) *pl.* **mediastina** [L., in the middle] **1.** A septum or cavity between two principal portions of an organ. **2.** The mass of organs and tissues separating the lungs. It contains the heart and its large vessels, trachea, esophagus, thymus, lymph nodes, and connective tissue.

mediate (mē′dē-āt) **1.** Accomplished by indirect means. **2.** Between two parts or sides.

mediation (mē″dē-ā′shŭn) The action of a mediating agent.

mediator (mē′dē-ā″tŏr) **1.** Any substance or anatomical structure that transmits information between two reagents, cells, tissues, or organs. **2.** Neutral third party who facilitates agreements by helping disputing parties to identify their needs and work toward mutually agreeable solutions.

medic (mĕd′ĭk) **1.** Medical corpsman. SEE: *corpsman.* **2.** Slang for paramedic.

Medicaid (mĕd′ĭ-kād) A federally aided, but state operated and administered, program for providing medical care for certain low-income individuals.

medical (mĕd′ĭ-kăl) **1.** Pert. to medicine or the study of the art and science of caring for those who are ill. **2.** Requiring therapy with medicines as distinct from surgical treatment.

medical access The right or ability of an individual to obtain medical and health care services.

medical anthropology SEE: under *anthropology.*

medical assistance In the U.S., a state-administered program designed to pay for health care provided to medically indigent patients. SEE: *Medicaid.*

medical assistant One who assists a qualified physician in an office or other clinical setting, performing administrative and technical tasks as delegated and in accordance with state laws governing medical practice. The administrative tasks include those of a secretary, receptionist, or bookkeeper; the clinical include checking vital signs, height, and weight, and performing laboratory tests. SYN: *medical office assistant.*

medical audit A systematic approach to reviewing, analyzing, and evaluating medical care in order to identify discrepancies in the quality of care and to provide a mechanism for improving that quality. SEE: *medical outcomes study.*

medical control The person or agency responsible for making final decisions about emergency medical care provided by first responders and emergency medical technicians.

medical corpsman Corpsman.

Medical Dictionary for Regulatory Activities ABBR: MedDRA. A standardized vocabulary used internationally to describe and report adverse effects caused by pharmaceutical agents.

medical direction Physician input to and overseeing of policies, protocols, medical procedures, training, and quality assurance for an emergency medical service system.

Medic Alert A nonprofit foundation that provides a bracelet or pendant with an emblem on which is contained crucial information about a patient's medical history and a warning in case of emergency. The company also keeps a file of the medical information and provides an emergency phone number that medical personnel can call collect. The goal is to prevent a serious or fatal mistake in rendering aid or medical care to an injured or unconscious person who may have an additional condition or allergy (e.g., diabetes, penicillin allergy). Applications may be obtained from Medic Alert, 2323 Colorado Ave, Turlock, CA 95382. Telephone: 1-800-IDALERT. Website: www.medicalert.org. Persons wishing to donate organs may also acquire an emblem from the Medic Alert company stating that fact. SEE: illus.

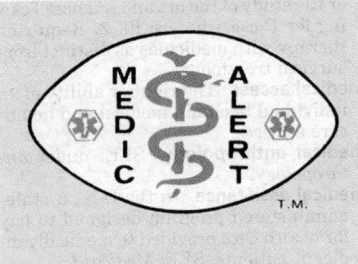

MEDIC ALERT SYMBOL

medical examiner A physician who is trained and qualified for the task of investigating the cause of death and the circumstances surrounding it. Training usually includes study of pathology and forensic medicine. The examiner is empowered by governmental agencies to represent them, and is expected to make a comprehensive report of findings to judicial or police authorities. The skill of a medical examiner is esp. important in investigating deaths wherein malpractice, homicide, suicide, or other criminal actions are suspected of being a contributing factor. SEE: *coroner; death investigation; medicine, forensic.*

medical expulsion therapy ABBR: MET. The treatment of ureteral stones with alpha-adrenergic blocking agents, which help relax the distal ureter, permitting small, lodged stones to pass into the urinary bladder.

medical geography The study of disease patterns as influenced by regional or global climate, microbiology, pollution, or other environmental factors; the relationship between the health of populations and the places in which they live.

medical geology The study of the effects of local or regional concentrations of chemicals or minerals (in air, soil, or water) on animal and human health.

medical home A form of health care delivery in which patients receive services from a team composed of a supervising personal primary care provider and a cooperative group of midlevel providers, registered nurses, nursing assistants, allied health professionals, and patient educators. The model relies on evidence-based interventions to coordinate inpatient and outpatient care, facilitate patient access to staff, and disseminate medical information either by face-to-face contact or by asynchronous communications, e.g., electronically. SYN: *patient-centered medical home.*

medical informatics SEE: under *informatics.*

medical intuitive An individual who claims to be able to make diagnoses or treat illnesses on the basis of his or her feelings and intuition rather than grounded in specialized education, training, or scientifically evaluated experience.

medical jurisprudence SEE: *jurisprudence, medical.*

medical laboratory technician ABBR: MLT. A technician who performs biological and chemical tests requiring limited independent judgment or correlation competency under the supervision of a medical technologist, pathologist, or physician.

medically attended Cared for by a health care professional.

medical monitoring The legal or ethical mandate that a manufacturer of a potentially hazardous product pay for diagnostic tests to determine whether individuals exposed to the product may be developing early signs of injury or disease before they demonstrate any clinical evidence of disease.

medical nutrition therapy ABBR: MNT. Nutritional counseling and drug prescriptions provided to patients with type 2 diabetes by dietitians or other nutritional specialists.

PATIENT CARE: The goal of MNT is to maintain blood glucose and lipid levels and blood pressure readings within normal limits. Unlike more restrictive diet plans, MNT allows the patient to eat a regular diet (including sugar), which enhances compliance, as long as carbohydrate intake is consistent each day. Consistent carbohydrate intake helps the provider and patient regulate insulin doses.

medical outcomes study ABBR: MOS. A Study to provide valid comparisons between medical care processes and outcomes as they are affected by system of care and clinician's specialty, as well as by patients' diagnoses and the levels of severity of illness. MOS provides a model for monitoring the results of medical care. SEE: *medical audit.*

Medical Outcomes Study 36-Item Short-Form Health Survey ABBR: SF-36. A study used to provide perceived health status in eight domains. These domains include:

    1. limitation of physical activity resulting from health problems;

    2. limitation of social activity caused by physical or emotional problems;

    3. physical health problems limiting usual activities;

    4. bodily pain;

5. general mental health (psychological distress or well-being);

6. limitation of usual activities due to emotional problems;

7. vitality (energy and fatigue); and

8. general health perceptions.

The SF-36 is designed for use in those over the age of 14 and is useful in comparing the impact of disease and the efficacy of treatments, and identifying those at risk.

Medical Practice Acts Any laws that govern the practice of medicine.

medical preparations Preparation (3).

medical problems of musicians SEE: *musicians, medical problems of.*

medical record SEE: under *record.*

medical record, problem-oriented SEE: *problem-oriented medical record.*

medical technologist A technologist who works in conjunction with pathologists, physicians, and scientists in all general areas of the clinical laboratory. Independent and correlational judgments are made in a wide range of complex procedures. A medical technologist may teach and supervise laboratory personnel.

medical tourism Travelling abroad to undergo expensive invasive procedures in countries where high-quality, low-cost care is available, e.g., India. The funds saved on the care received are used to sponsor recuperation and vacation in the host country. Medical tourism is a form of outsourcing of health care and is typically used for highly technical, costly surgical procedures such as coronary artery bypass graft surgery.

medical transcriptionist One who transcribes and prepares written records from dictations concerning the patient's medical care and records. A transcriptionist who has met the requirements of the American Association of Medical Transcription is certified by that body as a Certified Medical Transcriptionist.

medical waste SEE: under *waste.*

medicament (mĕ-dĭk′ă-mĕnt) [L. *medicamentum*] A medicine or remedy.

Medicare (mĕd′ĭ-kar″) In the U.S., a federally sponsored health insurance program for people over age 65, some younger disabled people, and those with end-stage renal disease. American Medicare consists of four parts. Medicare Part A provides hospital insurance. Part B (an option some participants choose to purchase) provides general medical insurance. Part C provides health plan choices to beneficiaries who choose to pay for this option. Part D provides a drug benefit. In the U.S., Medicare also administers its own managed care plan. In Canada, Medicare is administered by the provinces.

original M. Medicare Part A (inpatient or hospital health insurance) and Medicare Part B (outpatient health insurance).

Medicare Advantage plan Enrollment in Medicare mediated by a private health insurer, which manages a person's Medicare Part A and Part B benefits on behalf of the federal government.

Medicare Part C A component of Medicare that gives beneficiaries the option of receiving health care from privately managed health plans.

Medicare Part D The prescription drug benefit plan offered by Medicare beginning in January 2006. Detailed information about the plan can be obtained at Medicare's website: www.medicare.gov

medicate (mĕd′ĭ-kāt) [L. *medicatus*] **1.** To treat a disease with drugs. **2.** To permeate with medicinal substances.

medication (med-ĭ-kā′shŏn) **1.** A medicinal substance; a drug. **2.** Treatment with remedies. **3.** Impregnation with medicine.

forced m. Psychotropic medication to treat the mental illness or incompetence of a person too violent, oppositional, paranoid, or disorganized to agree to be treated. It is sometimes used to help prepare mentally ill defendants for trial.

hypodermic m. Treatment by injection of medicine by a needle and syringe through the skin.

intravenous m. The injection of a sterile solution of a drug or an infusion into a vein.

ionic m. Iontophoresis.

patient-delivered partner m. Patient-delivered partner treatment.

medication error SEE: under *error.*

medication event monitoring system A method of evaluating a patient's compliance with a medication regimen that is tied to microprocessors that are built into the medicine bottle or pill dispenser.

medication pass The administering of prescribed drugs by nurses or aides to a group of patients or residents, in accordance with state and federal standards.

medication possession ratio ABBR: MPR. The number of dispensed medication doses divided by the number of days in a unit of time (e.g., 1 year). The MPR can be used to estimate the degree to which patients with chronic medical conditions comply with prescribed drug therapies.

medication reconciliation Any process that ensures that the medications given to and taken by the patient are the same as those prescribed by the health care provider.

PATIENT CARE: Medication errors occur frequently when patients suffer new illnesses or when they are admitted to or discharged from health care facilities. Some of these errors may be limited by making certain that patients are educated about new drugs they may need to take and that they understand which of their old drugs must be eliminated from their regimen. The crucial times to reconcile prescribed medications occur at hospital admission, during transfer to and from special care units such as intensive care units, and at hospital discharge.

medication route The way that a drug is introduced into the body. The route of administration is chosen according to the speed of absorption desired and the site of action of the medication. Some medications are formulated for a specific route only and must be given in that manner. It is important that medicines be administered as directed by the manufacturer. Various routes of administration used are as follows:

Oral and *enteral* administration require that the medication not be destroyed by the environment of the stomach and digestive enzymes. It is too slow if rapid absorption is required, and cannot be used if the patient is vomiting. Rectal administration in the form of liquids or suppositories circumvents this problem in enteral administration.

Mucosal routes of administration other than the above include absorption through the nasal mucosa, the buccal mucosa, sublingually, or the bronchioles, the latter usually achieved through inhalation of an aerosol. Vaginal and rectal administration are also mucosal routes of medication.

Percutaneous administration is used for iontophoresis or by direct absorption through the skin.

Parenteral administration is used when a drug cannot be given by mouth. The speed of absorption varies greatly with the specific route used, which may be subcutaneous, intravenous, intramuscular, intra-arterial, intraperitoneal, intrathecal, intracardiac, or intrasternal.

medicinal (mĕ-dĭ′sĭn-ăl) [L. *medicina*, medicine] Pert. to medicine.

medicine (med′ĭ-sin) [L. *(ars) medicina*, healing (art)] **1.** A drug or remedy. **2.** The act of maintenance of health, and prevention and treatment of disease and illness. **3.** Treatment of disease by medical, as distinguished from surgical, treatment.

    aerospace m. The branch of medicine concerned with the selection of individuals for duty as pilots or crew members for flight and space missions. Includes study of the pathology and physiology of persons and animals who travel in airplanes and spacecraft in the earth's atmosphere and in outer space. SYN: *aviation* **m.**

    alternative m. Complementary and alternative **m.**

    anthroposophic m. A holistic approach to health care widely employed in Europe, e.g., for the care of patients with advanced cancer. Although its effectiveness remains unproven, it has gained significant acceptance by patients and some insurers.

    arts m. The study and practice of medical problems of performing artists, including musicians, vocalists, and dancers.

    aviation m. Aerospace **m.**

    Ayurvedic m. Ayurveda.

    bloodless m. Medical care of patients with anemia that avoids the use of transfusion therapy except for autologous transfusions.

    clinical m. Observation and treatment at the bedside; the practice of medicine in the clinical setting as distinguished from laboratory science.

    community m. Medical care to provide preventive and clinical services to anyone in need, rather than only to those who are insured or are able to pay for such services.

    complementary and alternative m. ABBR: CAM. Any of the therapies designed and promoted to improve health and well-being that are usually considered to be outside the scope of Western, allopathic, medical practice. The National Institute Health's National Center for Complementary and Alternative Medicine for research and scholarly purposes has defined five broad categories of CAM: 1) Biological therapies, e.g., herbs, dietary supplements, special nutritional programs; 2) Mind-Body therapies, e.g., relaxation therapies, meditation, biofeedback, hypnosis; 3) Manual therapies, e.g., massage therapy, chiropractic, and other body-based manipulative therapies like Rolfing; 4) Bioenergetic therapies, e.g., magnets, healing touch, therapeutic touch, qi gong; 5) Alternative systems of care., e.g., ayurveda, traditional Chinese medicine, naturopathy, homeopathy. SEE: Integrative Therapies: Complementary and Alternative Medicine appendix. SYN: *alternative* **m.** SEE: *integrative* **m.**

    cookbook m. The use of algorithms (in place of individualized care) in medicine; the reliance by practitioners on protocol and rules rather than on a comprehensive, individual approach to the medical needs of a patient.

    correctional m. Health care provided to inmates of prisons and jails.

    critical care m. ABBR: CCM. The care of the sickest patients (those with acutely life-threatening illnesses such as major trauma, myocardial infarction, respiratory failure, sepsis, severe hemorrhage, or shock).

    defensive m. Any health care practice used primarily to fend off malpractice litigation or to reduce a perceived risk of liability, rather than to advance patient care. It may include: ordering excessive blood tests or radiological studies; requesting unneeded consultations; or declining to participate in certain forms of care. In some cases, defensive medicine results in the early retirement of the practitioner. It is most commonly used by health care providers in specialties known to be at high-risk for litigation: emergency physicians; general surgeons; neurosurgeons; obstetricians; and orthopedic surgeons.

dental m. The branch of medicine concerned with the preservation and treatment of the teeth and other orofacial tissues. It includes preventive measures such as oral hygiene, as well as restorative procedures or prostheses and surgery. The results are widespread, including better nutrition and digestion from restored and balanced occlusion, and improved mental health from the control of oral and dental infections that often are overlooked but jeopardize the success of other medical treatments.

disaster m. Large-scale application of emergency medical services in a community, following a natural or man-made catastrophe. The aim is to save lives and restore every survivor to maximum health as promptly as possible. Its success depends on prompt sorting of patients according to their immediate needs and prognosis. SEE: *triage.*

diving m. The study, diagnosis, and treatment of diseases and injuries that occur underwater, esp. in SCUBA diving, submarines, or diving chambers, where the body is exposed to unusually high pressures. SYN: *undersea m.*

electronic m. Telemedicine.

emergency m. The branch of medicine specializing in emergency care of the acutely ill and injured. Board-certified physicians who successfully complete a residency and qualifying examination and who meet other requirements of the American College of Emergency Physicians may use the abbreviation FACEP (Fellow of the American College of Emergency Physicians). SEE: *nurse, certified emergency; Emergency Nurses Association; FACEP.*

environmental m. The branch of medicine concerned with the effects of the environment (temperature, rainfall, population size, pollution, radiation) on humans.

essential m. A medicine used to meet the fundamental health care needs of a population.

evidence-based m. Evidence-based **health care**.

experimental m. The scientific study of disease or pathological conditions through experimentation on laboratory animals or through clinical research.

family m. The branch of medicine concerned with providing or supervising the medical care of all members of the family.

folk m. The use of home remedies and informal healing practices to treat disease.

forensic m. Medicine in relation to the law, e.g., in autopsy proceedings, the determination of time or cause of death, or in the determination of sanity. It also includes the legal aspects of medical ethics and standards. SYN: *legal m.*

frontier m. Any field within complementary and alternative medicine that lacks basic scientific credibility. According to the National Center for Complementary and Alternative Medicine, reiki and therapeutic touch are examples of frontier medicine.

front-line m. Tactical **m.**

gender-specific m. Health care that pertains only to men or to women but not to individuals of both genders, e.g., those affected with diseases and conditions produced by sex hormones.

genomic m. Personalized **m.**

geriatric m. Geriatrics.

group m. 1. Practice of medicine by a group of physicians, usually consisting of specialists in various fields who pool their services and share laboratory and x-ray facilities. Such a group is commonly called a clinic. **2.** Securing of medical services by a group of individuals who, on paying definite sums of money, are entitled to certain medical services or hospitalization in accordance with prearranged rules and regulations.

high-tech m. Engineered advances in medical knowledge and technique that have resulted in improved diagnostic, therapeutic, and rehabilitative procedures.

holistic m. A patient-centered approach to healing that strives to meet the cognitive, emotional, physical, social, and spiritual needs of patients. SYN: *wholistic health.* SEE: *holism.*

industrial m. Occupational and environmental **m.**

integrative m. The branch of medicine that uses evidenced-based approaches to combine conventional medical practices with therapies from complementary and alternative medicine. SEE: *complementary and alternative m.*

internal m. ABBR: IM. The branch of medicine concerned with the overall health and well-being of adults. The internist uses the tools of history taking, physical examination, and diagnostic testing to diagnose and prevent disease. Patient education, lifestyle modification, psychological counseling, use of medications, inpatient medical care, and referral to other specialists are responsibilities of the internist.

legal m. Forensic **m.**

lifestyle m. The study of lifestyle choices in preventing and/or managing chronic disease and optimizing wellness.

mind-body m. An approach to medicine that recognizes the effect of thought, feeling, and belief on health, as well as the impact of health and illness on attitude and thought. Common therapies used in this field are biofeedback, hypnosis, imagery, meditation, psychoeducation, and relaxation therapies. SYN: *psychosomatic* **m.**

Native American m. Traditional, culturally specific beliefs and practices of Native Americans regarding health that emphasize awareness of self and spirit, rest, connection with nature, herbal medicine, social support, and ceremonial or ritualistic healing.

naturopathic m. The philosophy and practice of healing that relies primarily on the use of nutrition, herbal remedies, homeopathy, massage, and counseling to promote wellness and healthy lifestyles. Other modalities include disciplines as aromatherapy, color therapy, traditional Chinese medicine, and iridology.

The underlying principle of naturopathy is that the power of nature is the ultimate healer. Seminal figures in the founding of naturopathic medicine include Benedict Lust and Sebastian Kneipp. There are several naturopathic medical schools in the U.S. leading to an ND (Doctor of Naturopathic Medicine) degree. Fourteen states in the U.S. currently license naturopathic practice.

nuclear m. The branch of medicine involved with the use of radioactive substances for diagnosis, therapy, and research.

occupational and environmental m. ABBR: OEM. The branch of medicine concerned with work-related diseases, hazards, and injuries; working conditions; employee rehabilitation; and the regulations that pertain to these issues. SYN: *industrial* **m.**

osteopathic m. Osteopathy.

patent m. A drug or medical preparation protected by patent and sold without a physician's prescription. The law requires that it be labeled with names of active ingredients, the quantity or proportion of the contents, and directions for its use, and that it not have misleading statements as to curative effects on the label. SEE: *nonproprietary name; prescription*.

personalized m. The study of an individual's unique biochemical and genetic makeup, in order to determine his susceptibility to disease or potential responses to treatment. SYN: *genomic* **m.**, *theranostics*.

physical m. A branch of medicine that uses natural methods, including physical agents, therapeutic exercise, mechanical apparatus, and pharmaceutical agents. SYN: *physiatrics; physiatry*.

preclinical m. 1. Preventive **m.** 2. Medical education that takes place in classes, laboratories, and symposia, preceding the training that occurs through the direct care of patients.

preventive m. The anticipation and thwarting of disease or injury in individuals and populations. SYN: *preclinical m.* (1). SEE: *prevention*.

psychosomatic m. Mind-body **m.**

regenerative m. The use of stem cells to treat diseases caused by the loss or degeneration of cells in vital organs such as the brain, heart, or kidneys. SYN: *reparative* **m.** (1).

reparative m. 1. Regenerative **m.** 2. Medicine concerned primarily with repair, such as microsurgery for limb reattachment.

socialized m. A health care delivery system in which the provision of services is controlled by the government.

space m. The branch of medicine concerned with the physiological and pathological problems encountered by humans who enter the area beyond the earth's atmosphere. It includes investigation of effects of zero gravity (weightlessness), sensory deprivation, motion sickness, enforced inactivity during lengthy travels in space, and the heat and decelerative forces encountered at the time of reentry into the earth's atmosphere. With prolonged flights into space, a number of medical problems have arisen, including anemia, loss of blood volume, loss of bone, and loss of muscle mass. These changes also make adjustment to gravity after returning to earth difficult.

sports m. The branch of medicine concerned with the physiology, psychology, and pathology of athletes. Important aspects of sports medicine are the prevention of injuries, and their diagnosis, treatment, and rehabilitation.

tactical m. Emergency medical care that is provided during battlefield, terrorist, or police operations. SYN: *frontline m.* SEE: *tactical emergency medical support*.

Tibetan m. The traditional health care practices of Tibet, based primarily on the use of meditation, herbals, chanting, and other healing rituals.

traditional Chinese m. ABBR: TCM. Medical practice as it developed in early Chinese civilization and philosophy and widely used today by both Asians and non-Asians. It is an alternative system of medicine which uses acupuncture, diet, exercise therapies, e.g., tai chi and qi gong, herbal remedies, and massage. SEE: *acupuncture; tai chi.*

tropical m. The branch of medicine that deals principally with diseases common in tropical or subtropical regions, esp. diseases of parasitic origin.

undersea m. Diving **m.**

vedic m. Ayurveda.

veterinary m. The branch of medical science that deals with diagnosis and treatment of diseases of animals.

wireless m. Telemedicine.

medicine lodge Sweat lodge.

medicine wheel SEE: under *wheel.*

medicochirurgical (měd″ĭ-kō-kī-rŭr′jĭ-kăl) [L. *medicus,* medical, + Gr. *cheir,* hand, + *ergon,* work] Concerning both medicine and surgery.

medicolegal (měd″ĭ-kō-lē′găl) [″ + *legalis,* legal] Relating to medical jurisprudence or forensic medicine. SEE: table.

Medigap (měd′ĭ-găp″) One of several optional, supplemental insurance programs that augment a Medicare beneficiary's health care coverage. The costs and benefit structures of these programs vary. Some provide comprehensive health care services for relatively high prices; others provide more limited benefits for lower costs.

medio-, medi-, med- [L. *medius,* middle] Prefixes meaning *middle.*

mediolateral (mē″dē-ō-lăt′ĕr-ăl) Concerning the middle and side of a structure.

medionecrosis (mē″dē-ō-nē-krō′sĭs) [″ + *nekrosis,* state of death] Necrosis of the tunica media of a blood vessel.

meditation The art of contemplative thinking. It is used to control stress and improve relaxation, focus attention, and lower heart rate and blood pressure.

mindfulness m. A form of meditation or induced relaxation that focuses awareness on breathing and encourages positive attitudes to achieve a healthy, balanced mental state. Mindful meditation is advocated for reducing reactions to stress by inducing the relaxation response, lowering the heart rate, reducing anxiety, and encouraging positive thought patterns and attitudes. Practitioners of mindfulness meditation aim to cultivate self-awareness, and a nonjudgmental, loving, kind, and compassionate feeling toward themselves and others. SEE: *relaxation response.*

transcendental m. ABBR: TM. A type of meditation based on ancient Hindu practices in which a person tries to relax by sitting quietly for regular periods while repeating a mantra. The value of TM in treating various conditions is under investigation. It was first popularized in the West by Maharishi Mahesh Yogi. SEE: *relaxation response.*

Mediterranean spotted fever SEE: under *fever.*

medium (mē′dē-ŭm, ′dē-ă) *pl.* **media** **1.** An agent through which an effect is obtained. **2.** A substance used for the cultivation of microorganisms or cellular tissue. SEE: *culture m.* **3.** A substance through which impulses are transmitted.

Amies transport m. SEE: *Amies transport medium.*

BG m. *Bordet-Gengou medium.*

clearing m. A substance that renders histological specimens transparent.

contrast m. In radiology, a substance used to fill hollow organs or blood vessels to highlight their internal structure or distinguish them from neighboring anatomical features. The substance can be radiopaque and positive (such as barium sulfate, tri-iodinated media) or radiolucent and negative (such as air). Barium sulfate is a commonly used contrast agent for the gastrointestinal tract; it may be swallowed (for upper GI studies) or given as an enema (to visualize the colon). SYN: *radiocontrast.*

culture m. A substance on which microorganisms may grow. Those most commonly used are broths, gelatin, and agar, which contain the same basic ingredients.

defined m. In bacteriology, a medium in which the composition is accurately defined and carefully controlled. One use of this culture medium is to investigate the influence of altering ingredients on bacterial cell growth characteristics.

dispersion m. A liquid in which a colloid is dispersed.

high-osmolarity contrast m. ABBR: HOCM. A water-soluble contrast medium with high osmolarity. These agents increase the probability of an adverse reaction and are generally ionic.

low-osmolarity contrast m. ABBR: LOCM. A water-soluble contrast medium with low osmolarity. These agents produce fewer undesired effects after intravascular administration than do high-osmolarity contrast media. They are generally nonionic, with the exception of Hexabrix (an ionic dimer).

nonionic contrast m. A water-soluble contrast medium whose molecules do not dissociate into cations and anions in solution. These agents tend to have low osmolarity. They decrease the risk of adverse reactions but are costly.

nutrient m. A fortified culture medium with added nutrient materials.

radiolucent m. A substance injected into an anatomical structure to decrease the density, producing a dark area on the radiograph.

radiopaque m. A substance injected into a cavity or region or passed through the gastrointestinal tract to increase x-

Seminal Medicolegal Court Decisions in the U.S.

Case	Legal Issue Involved	Summary
Cruzan v. Director, Missouri Department of Health [1990]	End-of-life care; role of surrogate decision makers	After a motor vehicle accident left Nancy Cruzan in a persistent vegetative state, her parents asked that life support be withdrawn on the basis of statements she had made to a friend approx. a year prior to her accident. The Supreme Court ruled that a higher standard of evidence for the withdrawal of life support was required ("clear and convincing evidence") because it could not guarantee that family members would always act in the patient's best interests.
Diamond v. Chakrabarty [1980]	Limits of genetic engineering	Patents issued on man-made or genetically engineered microorganisms are legally valid.
Gonzalez v. Oregon [2006]	Do terminally ill patients have a right to "physician-assisted" suicide?	The Supreme Court ruled that Oregon's "Death With Dignity" Law was constitutional and did not constitute a violation of Federal Laws limiting the use of Controlled Substances to those instances where the drugs would cure or ameliorate disease.
Jacobson v. the Commonwealth of Massachusetts [1905]	Can the State mandate the use of vaccines?	Mr. Jacobson challenged the scientific basis of vaccination and refused inoculation against smallpox. The Supreme Court ruled that 'restraints and burdens [... can be imposed on individuals ...] in order to secure the general comfort, health, and prosperity of the state.'
Katskee v. Blue Cross/ Blue Shield (BC/BS) [1994]	Contractual obligations of insurers	Ms. Katskee, who had a strong family history of breast and ovarian cancer, but no active cancer, requested reimbursement from BC/BS for prophylactic surgery. BC/BS denied coverage; but the Nebraska Supreme Court ruled that in this particular instance it was warranted.
O'Connor v. Donaldson [1975]	Rights of the mentally ill	Mr. Donaldson, a paranoid schizophrenic, was held in a Florida state institution for the insane for 15 years because of an inability to care for himself. The Supreme Court ruled he could not be confined unless he posed a threat either to his own life or to the life of other individuals.
In re Quinlan [1976]	End-of-life care; withdrawal of life support	The parents of Karen Ann Quinlan petitioned the courts for the right to withdraw life support (mechanical ventilation and artificial respiration) from Ms. Quinlan, who was in a vegetative state after an overdose and motor vehicle accident. The request was granted. [The patient survived for several years without ventilation.]
Roe v. Wade [1973]	Legality of abortion	The Supreme Court ruled that a Texas state law restricting abortions to only those instances in which pregnancy threatened the life of the mother was unconstitutional and a violation of the Due Process Clause of the 14th Amendment to the U.S. Constitution.

Table continued on following page

ray absorption, producing an image with enhanced contrast between solid and hollow structures.

refracting m. The fluids and transparent tissues of the eye that refract light rays passing through them toward the retina: the cornea, aqueous humor, lens, and vitreous humor.

Seminal Medicolegal Court Decisions in the U.S. (Continued)

Case	Legal Issue Involved	Summary
Tarasoff v. Regents of University of California [1969]	Limits of confidentiality	After a psychologist learned that one of his patients had thoughts of killing another person, he and the University for whom he worked had a "duty to warn" (i.e., breach confidentiality) and "duty to protect" the patient and her family from the threat. Ms. Tarasoff was killed by the patient.
Vacco v. Quill [1997]	Limits on the legality of physician-assisted suicide	The U.S. Supreme Court did not support a claim that patients suffering terminal illnesses have a constitutional right to die in New York State, where a law prohibiting physician-assisted suicide was in force.

separating m. In dentistry, a substance applied to the surface of an impression or mold to prevent interaction of the materials and to facilitate their separation after casting.

Thayer-Martin m. SEE: *Thayer-Martin medium.*

transport m. A nutrient solution used to maintain the freshness or viability of patient specimens as they are being carried to the laboratory for culture.

tri-iodinated contrast m. A derivative of tri-iodobenzoic acid that is the base for water-soluble contrast media. It contains three atoms of iodine per molecule.

viral transport m. ABBR: VTM. A nutrient substance (usually a buffered liquid) used to carry and maintain the viability of specimens to a microbiology laboratory for identification and analysis of disease-producing viruses.

medium-chain triglycerides SEE: *triglycerides, medium-chain.*

medius (mē′dē-ŭs) [L.] Middle. Indicating the middle one of three similar structures.

MEDLARS (měd′lahrz″) [*Med*ical *L*iterature *A*nalysis and *R*etrieval *S*ystem] A computerized system of databases and data banks available from the National Library of Medicine. A person may search the computer files to produce a list of publications (bibliographic citations) or retrieve factual information on a specific question. MEDLARS databases cover medicine, nursing, dentistry, veterinary medicine, and the preclinical sciences. They are used by universities, medical schools, hospitals, government agencies, commercial and nonprofit organizations, and private individuals. In 2008, MEDLARS databases included about 18 million references.

MEDLINE [*MEDLARS* on *line*] The computer-accessible bibliographic database of the National Library of Medicine. It is the system that links telephone lines to the MEDLARS databases. It includes references that appear in more than 3800 research, medical, dental, veterinary, and nursing journals. SEE: *MEDLARS.*

medroxyprogesterone acetate (měd-rŏk″sē-prō-jĕs′tĕr-ōn) A progestational agent used to treat secondary amenorrhea, abnormal uterine bleeding related to hormone imbalance, and advanced endometrial and renal malignancies. It also is used with estrogens in hormone replacement therapy and administered intramuscularly as a long-term contraceptive (it is effective for up to 90 days).

medulla (mĕ-dŭl′ă, dul′) *pl.* **medullae** [L. *medulla,* marrow, pith] **1.** Marrow (1). **2.** In anatomy, the innermost or central portion of an organ in contrast to the cortex. **3.** The caudal segment of the hindbrain. SYN: *m. oblongata; bulb (2).* **4.** The medulla ossium. **medullary** (med′ŭl-er″ē, mej″), *adj.*

adrenal m. The central tissue of the adrenal gland. It is filled with pheochromocytes, which are derived from the neural crest and resemble postsynaptic sympathetic ganglion cells. In response to stimulation by presynaptic sympathetic axons, the pheochromocytes secrete epinephrine and norepinephrine into the bloodstream. SEE: illus. SEE: *adrenal gland.*

m. of hair The central axis of a hair.

m. of kidneys SEE: *pyramid, renal.*

m. oblongata Medulla (3).

m. of ovary The central portion of the ovary, composed of loose connective tissue, blood vessels, lymphatics, and nerves.

medullectomy (měd″ū-lěk′tō-mē) [L. *medulla,* marrow, + Gr. *ektome,* excision] Surgical excision of a part of the medulla of the brain.

medulloblast (mĕ-dŭl′ō-blăst) [″ + Gr. *blastos,* germ] An immature cell of the neural tube that may develop into either a nerve or neuroglial cell.

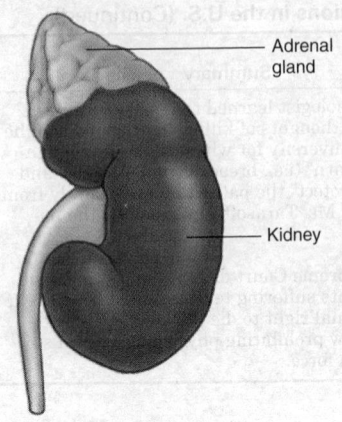

— Adrenal gland

— Kidney

ADRENAL MEDULLA

medulloblastoma (mĕ-dŭl″ō-blas-tō′mă) [*medulla* + *blast-* + *-oma*] A malignant tumor of the roof of the fourth ventricle and cerebellum. The tumor is the most common malignant brain tumor in childhood. SYN: *primitive neuroectodermal tumor*.

medulloepithelioma (mĕ-dŭl″ō-ĕp″ĭ-thēl-ē-ō′mă) [″ + Gr. *epi,* upon, + *thele,* nipple, + *oma,* tumor] Tumor composed of retina epithelium and of neuroepithelium. SYN: *glioma; neuroepithelioma*.

MedWatch (mĕd′wătch) A voluntary and confidential program of the Food and Drug Administration (FDA) for monitoring the safety of drugs, biologicals, medical devices, and nutritional products such as dietary supplements, medical foods, and infant formulas. The FDA provides forms for reporting adverse events associated with any of these products. Health professionals may obtain the form by calling 1-800-332-1088. Information may be faxed to the FDA by calling 1-800-332-0178.

Mees lines (mēz, mēs, mās) [R.A. Mees, 20th-cent. Dutch scientist] Transverse white lines that appear above the lunula of the fingernails about 5 weeks after exposure to arsenic.

mega- [Gr. *megas,* large] **1.** SEE: *megalo-*. **2.** In the International System of Units (SI), a prefix meaning 1 million (10^6).

megacode (meg′ă-kōd″) [*mega-* + *code*] A simulated cardiac arrest used as an educational tool for health care professionals during advanced cardiac life support training. It is intended to sharpen the technical and interpersonal skills needed during the resuscitation of patients with arrhythmias.

megacolon (mĕg′ă-kō″lŏn) [″ + *kolon,* colon] Massive dilation of the colon,

which, if left untreated, may result in perforation and peritonitis.

    aganglionic m. Hirschsprung's disease.

    toxic m. Marked enlargement of the colon, esp. the transverse colon. Clinically, tachycardia, fever, and leukocytosis occur. There may be abdominal tenderness, a palpable abdominal mass, confusion, cramping, and change in number of bowel movements per day. SYN: *toxic dilatation of colon*.

    ETIOLOGY: The most common causes of toxic megacolon in adults are ulcerative colitis, pseudomembranous colitis, Crohn's disease, drugs that slow intestinal motility (such as narcotics), and severe electrolyte disturbances. Megacolon in children may result from Hirschsprung's disease.

    TREATMENT: Patients with toxic megacolon are treated by withholding oral intake, providing nasogastric suction, giving broad-spectrum antibiotics (and corticosteroids, in inflammatory bowel disease), and carefully resuscitating fluids and electrolytes. Surgery is required if the patient fails to improve or deteriorates.

megacurie (mĕg″ă-kū′rē) [″ + *curie*] ABBR: MCi. A unit of radioactivity equal to 10^6 curies.

megadontia (mĕg″ă-dŏn′shē-ă) [″ + *odous, odont-,* tooth] Macrodontia.

megadose (mĕ′gă-dōs″) A dose of a nutrient, such as a vitamin supplement, that is 10 times greater than the recommended daily allowance for that nutrient.

megadyne (mĕg′ă-dīn) A unit equal to 1 million dynes. SEE: *dyne*.

megaesophagus (mĕg″ă-ĕ-sŏf′ă-gŭs) [″ + *oisophagos,* esophagus] A grossly dilated esophagus usually associated with achalasia. SYN: *megaloesophagus*.

megahertz (mĕg′ă-hĕrtz) ABBR: MHz. One million cycles per second, or 10^6 hertz.

megakaryoblast (mĕg″ă-kăr′ē-ō-blăst) An immature megakaryocyte.

megakaryocyte (mĕg″ă-kăr′ē-ō-sīt″) [″ + *karyon,* nucleus, + *kytos,* cell] Large bone marrow cell with large or multiple nuclei from which platelets are derived. SEE: *platelet;* illus.

megakaryocytosis (mĕg″ă-kăr″ē-ō-sī-tō′sĭs) [″ + ″ + ″ + *osis,* condition] An increased number of megakaryocytes in the bone marrow; presence of megakaryocytes in the blood.

megalencephaly (mĕg″ăl-ĕn-sĕf′ă-lē) [″ + *enkephalos,* brain] Abnormally large size of the brain, usually accompanied by mental deficiency.

megalo-, mega- [Gr. *megas,* stem *megal-,* large] Prefixes meaning *abnormally large*.

megaloblast (mĕg′ă-lō-blăst) [″ + *blastos,* germ] An abnormally large red

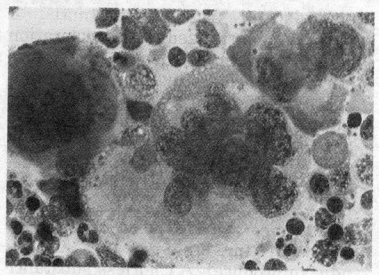

MEGAKARYOCYTE

(Orig. mag. ×640)

blood cell, with a mean corpuscular volume larger than 105 fL. It may be found in the blood in patients with folate or vitamin B_{12} deficiency, among other less common illnesses.

megaloblastoid (meg″ă-lō-blas′toyd″) [*megaloblast* + *-oid*] Tending to produce or resembling large, nucleated, abnormal red blood cells; tending to produce or resembling megaloblasts.

megalocephaly (mĕg″ă-lō-sĕf′ă-lē) [″ + *kephale*, head] **1.** Abnormal size of the head. SEE: *macrocephalia*. **2.** A rare disease characterized by hyperostosis of bones of the skull. SYN: *leontiasis ossea*.

megalocornea (mĕg″ă-lō-kor′nē-ă) [″ + L. *cornu*, horn] Abnormally enlarged cornea due to a developmental anomaly. SEE: *macrocornea*.

megalomania (mĕg″ă-lō-mā′nē-ă) [″ + *mania*, madness] A psychosis characterized by ideas of personal exaltation and delusions of grandeur.

megaloureter (mĕg″ă-lō-ū-rē′tĕr, -ūr′ĕ-tĕr) [″ + *oureter*, ureter] Increase in diameter of the ureter.

-megaly, -megalia [Gr. *megas*, stem *megal-*, large] Suffix meaning *abnormal enlargement* of a specified body part.

megarectum (mĕg-ă-rĕk′tŭm) [″ + L. *rectum*, straight] Excessive dilatation of the rectum.

megavitamin (mĕg″ă-vī′tă-mĭn) A dose of one or more vitamins that is much in excess of the normal daily requirements (up to 10 times the recommended daily intake).

megavolt (mĕg′ă-vŏlt) One million, 10^6, volts.

meglitinide (meg-lit′ĭn-īd″) Any of a class of oral agents used to treat type 2 diabetes mellitus, including nateglinide and repaglinide. Side effects include hypoglycemia and weight gain. SYN: *glinide*.

meglumine (mĕg′lū-mēn) A radiopaque compound used in x-ray studies.

megohm (mĕg′ōm) One million, 10^6, ohms.

meibomian cyst (mī-bō′mē-ăn) [Heinrich Meibom, Ger. anatomist, 1638–1700] Chalazion.

meibomitis, meibomianitis (mī″bō-mīt′is, mī-bō″mē-ă-nīt′is) Inflammation of the meibomian glands. SYN: *adenophthalmia*.

Meige syndrome (mĕg, mĕzh) [Henri Meige, French physician, 1866–1940] A dystonic movement disorder that can involve dry eyes and excessive eye blinking, with involuntary movements of the jaw muscles, neck, lips, and tongue.

Meigs syndrome (mēgz) [Joe V. Meigs, U.S. gynecologist, 1892–1963] Benign tumor of the ovary associated with ascites and pleural effusion.

meio- SEE: *mio-*.

meiosis (mī-ō′sĭs) [Gr. diminution] A process of two successive cell divisions, producing cells, egg or sperm, that contain half the number of chromosomes (haploid) in somatic cells. When fertilization occurs, the nuclei of the sperm and ovum fuse and produce a zygote with the full chromosome complement (diploid). SEE: illus.; *chromosome; mitosis; oogenesis*.

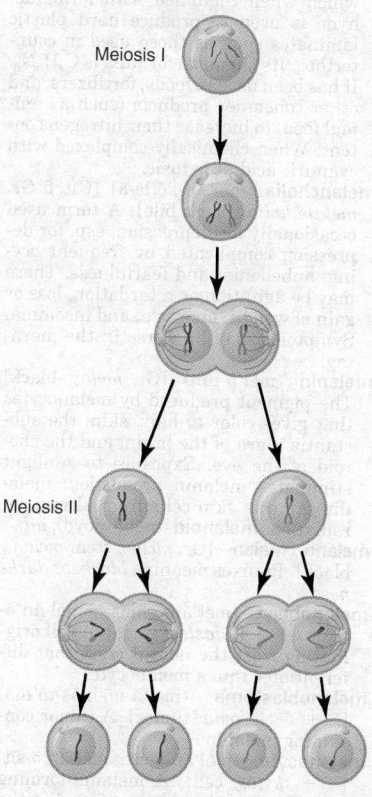

MEIOSIS

Meissner corpuscle (mīs′nĕr) [Georg Meissner, Ger. histologist, 1829–1905] A sensory end-organ in which the bare tips of 1–4 sensory axons spiral inside a sphere of ordered epithelial cells. The corpuscle is covered with a capsule that is continuous with the sheaths of the innervating axons. Meissner's corpuscles are found inside the papillary ridges (which underlie the epidermal ridges of fingerprints) of the skin of the volar surfaces. They are also found on other hairless skin (e.g., lips, eyelids, and the tip of the tongue). The corpuscles are receptors for tactile discrimination.

Meissner plexus An autonomic plexus in the submucosa of the alimentary tube that regulates secretions of the mucosa.

Melaleuca alternifolia (mĕl″ă-look′ă ăl-tĕr″nĭ-fō′lē-ă) [NL, lit. "alternate-leaved white-black" (referring to the trunk and branches, respectively)] The Australian tea tree. An evergreen from which an essential oil is made for cosmetics, fragrances, and some alternative and conventional medicines.

melalgia (mĕl-ăl′jē-ă) [″ + *algos,* pain] Pain of neural origin in the limbs.

melamine A chemical derivative of urea, which when combined with formaldehyde is used to produce hard plastic laminates such as those used in countertops. Its chemical formula is $C_3H_6N_6$. It has been used in foods, fertilizers, and other consumer products (such as animal feed) to increase their nitrogen content. When chemically complexed with cyanuric acid, it is toxic.

melancholia (mel″ăn-kō′lē-ă) [Ult. fr Gr. *melankholia,* black bile] A term used occasionally for depression, esp. for depression complicated by frequent crying, anhedonia, and fearfulness. There may be agitation or retardation, loss or gain of weight, anorexia, and insomnia. Symptoms may be worse in the morning.

melanin (mĕl′ă-nĭn) [Gr. *melas,* black] The pigment produced by melanocytes that gives color to hair, skin, the substantia nigra of the brain, and the choroid of the eye. Exposure to sunlight stimulates melanin production; melanin protects skin cells from ultraviolet radiation. **melanoid** (mĕl′ă-noyd), *adj.*

melano-, melan- [Gr. *melas,* stem *melan-,* black] Prefixes meaning *black,* or *darkness.*

melanoblast (mĕl′ăn-ō-blăst″, mĕl-ăn′ō-blăst) [″ + *blastos,* germ] A cell originating from the neural crest that differentiates into a melanocyte.

melanoblastoma (mĕl″ă-nō-blăs-tō′mă) [″ + ″ + *oma,* tumor] A tumor containing melanin.

melanocyte (mĕl′ăn-ō-sīt, mĕl-ăn′ō-sīt) [″ + *kytos,* cell] A melanin-forming cell. Those of the skin are found in the lower epidermis.

melanocytoma (mĕl″ă-nō-sī-tō′mă) [″ + *kytos,* cell, + *oma,* tumor] A rare pigmented benign tumor of the optic disk.

melanoderma (mĕl″ăn-ō-dĕr′mă) A patchy or generalized skin discoloration caused by either an increase in the production of melanin by the normal number of melanocytes or an increase in the number of melanocytes. SYN: *melanopathy.*

melanoepithelioma (mĕl″ăn-ō-ĕp″ĭ-thē-lē-ō′mă) [″ + *epi,* upon, + *thele,* nipple, + *oma,* tumor] A malignant epithelioma containing melanin.

melanogen (mĕ-lăn′ō-jĕn) [″ + *gennan,* to produce] A colorless substance that can be converted into melanin.

melanogenesis (mĕl″ăn-ō-jĕn′ĕ-sĭs) [″ + *genesis,* generation, birth] Formation of melanin.

melanoma (mel″ă-nō′mă) [*melano-* + *-oma*] A malignant tumor of darkly pigmented cells (melanocytes) that often arises in a brown or black mole. The tumor can spread aggressively throughout the body (e.g., to the brain and other internal organs). The incidence of the disease is rising rapidly in the US, esp. among people over 60. In 2008, the American Cancer Society estimated that 62,480 Americans would be diagnosed with melanoma and that more than 8,400 would die from the disease. More than 90% of melanomas develop on the skin; about 5% occur in the eye, and 2.5% occur on mucous membranes. SEE: illus.

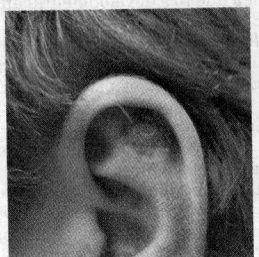

MELANOMA

The likelihood of long-term survival depends on the depth of the lesion (thicker lesions are more hazardous), whether it is ulcerated, the histological type (nodular and acral lentiginous melanomas are more dangerous than superficial spreading or lentigo malignant melanomas), the patient's age (older patients do more poorly), and gender (men tend to have a worse prognosis than women). SEE: *ABCD; skin cancer.*

ETIOLOGY: Excessive exposure to ultraviolet light, esp. sunlight, contributes to the development of melanoma, as does a family history of the disease. It is more common in fair-skinned than dark-skinned people and more common in people who have many moles on the skin than in those who have few. Total body skin examinations should be performed periodically on high-risk patients. On average, consistent screening identifies melanomas at an earlier stage (when they are thinner, or localized, rather than after they have spread) than those found on routine examination.

PREVENTION: People spending considerable time outside should wear protective clothing to shield against ultraviolet radiation and use sunscreens (at least SPF15) on exposed skin.

Common melanoma sites are the back, shoulders, head and neck (men), the legs (women), and the backs. A skin biopsy and histologic examination can distinguish malignant melanoma from a benign nevus, seborrheic keratosis, or pigmented basal cell epithelioma; it also determines tumor thickness and tumor stage. Staging is based on the TNM system and Clark's levels system, which classifies tumor progression according to skin layer penetration. Once diagnosed, patients need physical, psychological, and social assessment and care. Treatment options should be explained.

TREATMENT: Melanomas are treated with surgery to remove the primary cancer and adjuvant therapies (chemotherapy and biotherapy) to reduce the risk of metastasis. Closure of a wide resection around an excised tumor may require skin grafting. Vaccines have been developed against melanoma; they appear to improve prognosis in affected patients.

PATIENT CARE: After surgery, dressings are inspected for drainage and signs of infection, and the patient is taught about prevention and signs to report. The patient should be taught that close follow-up care will be needed to detect recurrences at an early stage, and that this must continue for years (13% of recurrences develop more than 5 yrs after the primary lesion). When therapy fails, the patient and family will need referrals for palliative (hospice) care and may also require social services and spiritual care.

desmoplastic m. A rare type of malignant melanoma in which the typical melanotic pigmentation may be absent. It often occurs on the head or neck. Microscopically, the tumor cells are spindle-shaped. Local recurrences after surgical excision are common, as are metastases, esp. to the lungs.

in situ m. A superficial melanoma that has not yet invaded deep layers of the skin or spread to local or distant tissues.

TREATMENT: The lesion should be removed by an experienced surgeon.

PATIENT CARE: Patients diagnosed with melanoma in situ need careful follow-up examinations in case the tumor recurs, spreads, or is associated with other skin cancers.

melanomatosis (měl″ă-nō″mă-tō′sĭs) [″ + ″ + osis, condition] Formation of numerous melanomas on or beneath the skin.

melanonychia (měl″ă-nō-nĭk′ē-ă) [″ + onyx, nail] Black pigmentation of the nails.

melanopathy (měl″ă-nŏp′ă-thē) Melanoderma.

melanophage (měl″ă-nō-fāj″) [″ + phagein, to eat] A phagocytic cell that contains ingested melanin.

melanophore (měl″ăn-ō-for) [″ + phoros, bearing] Cell containing dark pigment.

melanosarcoma (měl″ă-nō-sär-kō′mă) [″ + sarx, flesh, + oma, tumor] Sarcoma containing melanin.

melanosis (měl-ăn-ō′sĭs) [″ + osis, condition] A disorder of pigment metabolism characterized by excessive deposits of melanin (a brown, black, or blue pigment) in the skin or other tissues.

m. coli A benign brown or black discoloration of the colon that results from the use of laxatives, such as senna derivatives.

neurocutaneous m. A rare disorder marked by the presence of multiple or large pigmented nevi on the skin and in the leptomeninges of the central nervous system.

melanosome (měl′ă-nō-sōm″) [″ + soma, body] The pigment granule produced by melanocytes.

melanotic (měl′ă-nŏt′ĭk) **1.** Black. **2.** Pert. to melanosis.

melanotic macule SEE: under macule.

melanotroph (měl′ă-nō-trōf″) [″ + trophe, nutrition] A cell of the pituitary that produces melanocyte-stimulating hormone.

melanuria (měl-ăn-ū′rē-ă) [″ + ouron, urine] Dark pigment in urine.

melasma (měl-ăz′mă) [Gr., a black spot] Chloasma.

melatonin (měl″ă-tō′nĭn) A peptide hormone produced by the pineal gland that influences sleep-wake cycles and other circadian rhythms. It is available in supplement form. It has a sedative effect and has been used to treat sleep disorders and jet lag, even though its impact on these conditions remains unclear.

melena (mě-lē′nă) [Gr. melaina, black] Black tarry feces caused by the digestion of blood in the gastrointestinal tract. It is common in the newborn and in adult patients with gastrointestinal bleeding from the esophagus, stomach, or proximal small intestine. **melenic** (mě-lēn′ĭk), adj.

m. neonatorum Melena in the newborn.

melenotic (mel-ĕ-not′ĭk) Pert. to melena; melenic.

melioidosis (mē″lē-oy-dō′sĭs) [Gr. *melis,* a distemper of asses, + *eidos,* form, shape, + *osis,* condition] An acute or chronic disease caused by *Burkholderia pseudomallei,* formerly in the genus *Pseudomonas.* The acute form causes pneumonia, multiple abscesses, and sepsis and may be fatal.

Melissa officinalis (mĕ-lis′ă ŏ-fis″ĭ-nā′lis) SEE: *lemon balm.*

melitis (mĕl-ī′tĭs) [Gr. *melon,* cheek, + *itis,* inflammation] Inflammation of the cheek.

¹ **melo-, mel-** [Gr. *melos,* limb] Prefixes meaning *limb* or *extremity.*

² **melo-, mel-** [Gr. *meli,* stem *melit-,* honey] Prefixes meaning *honey.*

³ **melo-, mel-** [Gr. *mēlon,* cheek, apple] Prefixes meaning *cheek.*

meloplasty, melonoplasty (mel′ŏ-plast″ē) [³*melono-* + *-plasty*] Plastic surgery of the cheek.

melorheostosis (mĕl″ō-rē″ŏs-tō′sĭs) [Gr. *melos,* limb, + *rhein,* to flow, + *osteon,* bone, + *osis,* condition] A rare sclerotic tumor of long bones in which new bone formation resembles a candle with wax dripping down the sides.

melting point SEE: under *point.*

member [L. *membrum*] **1.** An organ or part of the body, esp. a limb. **2.** In managed care, a person who contracts with a prepaid health care program to receive medical services.

membrane (mem′brān″) [L. *membrana,* parchment] **1.** A thin, pliable layer of tissue that lines a tube or cavity, covers an organ or structure, or separates one part from another. **2.** A very thin sheet of polymer, ceramics, glass, or metal.

    alveolocapillary m. The structures and substances through which gases must pass as they diffuse from air to blood (oxygen) or blood to air (carbon dioxide), including the alveolar fluid and surfactant, cell of the alveolar wall, interstitial space (tissue fluid), and cell of the capillary wall. SYN: *respiratory m.* SEE: illus.

    alveolodental m. Periodontium.

    arachnoid m. The delicate middle membrane of the three meninges, which enclose the brain and spinal cord. The arachnoid membrane is 5–6 cells thick. It adheres to the inner surface of the dura and is connected to the pia by a spiderweb of thin connections. Thee space between the arachnoid and pia (the subdural space) is filled with cerebrospinal fluid. SYN: *arachnoid; arachnoid mater.*

    atlanto-occipital m. A single midline ligamentous structure that extends from the arch of the atlas to the borders of the foramen magnum.

    basement m. A two-part extracellular layer found at the interface between some tissues, e.g., skin and dermis.. The basement membrane is made of a basal lamina along the cell surfaces, coated by a stronger collagen-rich layer, the reticular lamina

    basilar m. The membrane extending from the tympanic lip of the osseous spiral lamina to the crest of the spiral ligament in the cochlea of the ear. It separates the tympanic canal from the cochlear duct and supports the organ of Corti. SEE: illus. under *organ of Corti.*

    black m. An artificially constructed membrane made of lipids arranged in a bilayer.

    Bowman m. SEE: under *Bowman, Sir William.*

    Bruch m. SEE: under *Bruch, Karl.*

    buccopharyngeal m. In the embryo, the membrane that separates the oral cavity from the foregut until the fourth week of development. SYN: *pharyngeal m.*

    cell m. The membrane that forms the outer boundary of a cell; it is made of phospholipids, protein, and cholesterol, with carbohydrates on the outer surface. SYN: *plasma m.* SEE: illus.

    choroid m. SEE: *choroid.*

    costocoracoid m. The dense fascia between the pectoralis minor and subclavius muscles.

    cricothyroid m. The membrane connecting the thyroid and cricoid cartilages of the larynx.

    croupous m. False membrane.

    decidual m. One of the membranes formed in the endometrium of a pregnant uterus. SEE: *decidua.*

    Demours m. SEE: *Demours membrane.*

    Descemet m. SEE: *Descemet membrane.*

    diphtheritic m. The fibrinous false membrane on the mucous surfaces in diphtheria.

    dural m. Dura mater.

    egg m. Any of the protective membranes or envelopes enclosing an ovum. It may be primary (formed by egg itself, as in vitelline membrane), secondary (formed by follicle cells, as in zona pellucida), or tertiary (formed by oviduct or uterus, as in albumin and shell of hen's egg).

    elastic m. Any of several membranes formed of elastic connective tissue fibers.

    enamel m. **1.** Nasmyth membrane. **2.** The thin internal layer of cells of the enamel organ.

    epiretinal m. An excessive proliferation of retinal pigment epithelial cells and extracellular proteins on the retinal surface. This condition, which can distort vision, is typically found in people older than 50. Marked visual blurring caused by epiretinal membranes occurs in macular pucker. SEE: *macular pucker.*

    external limiting m. **1.** The outer

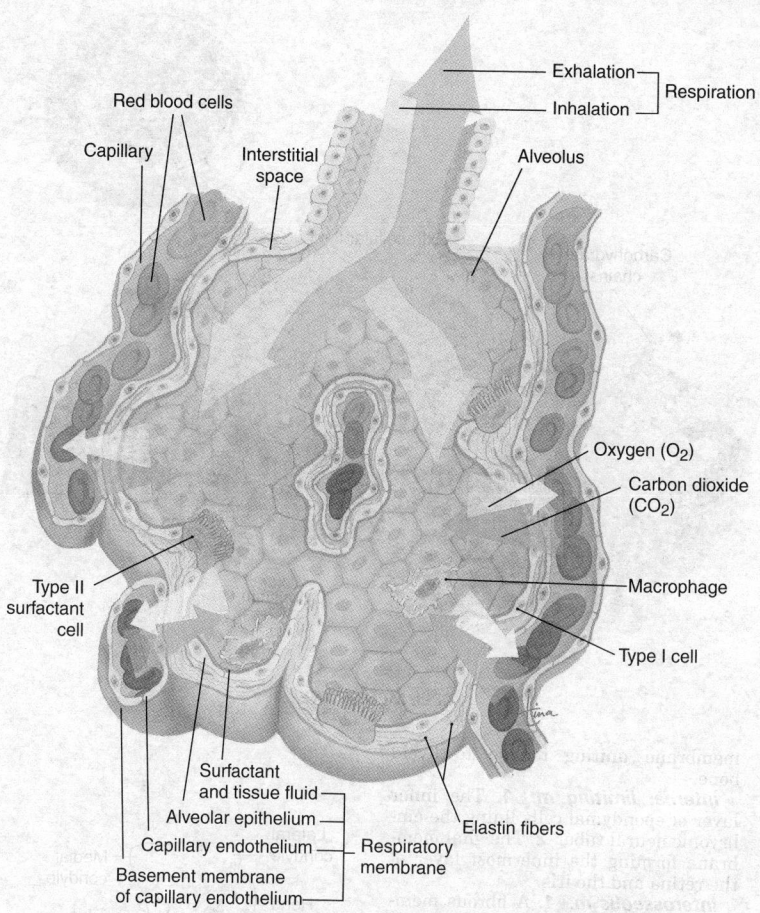

ALVEOLOCAPILLARY MEMBRANE

layer of cells of the embryonic neural tube. **2.** The membrane in the retina of the eye through which the receptor portions of the rods and cones protrude.

false m. Fibrinous exudate on a mucous surface of a membrane, as in croup or diphtheria. SYN: *croupous **m.***

fenestrated m. A layer of elastic connective tissue possessing minute round or oval openings. It is found in the tunica intima and tunica media of medium-sized and large arteries.

fetal m. Any of the membranous structures that protect and support the embryo and provide its nutrition, respiration, and excretion. The structures are yolk sac, allantois, amnion, chorion, decidua, and placenta.

fibrous m. A membrane composed entirely of fibrous connective tissue. Examples include the fasciae, aponeuroses, perichondrium, periosteum, dura mater, and the capsules of some organs.

glassy m. **1.** The transparent capsule that separates membrana granulosa from the theca of the graafian follicle. **2.** The internal layer of a hair follicle separating the epithelial and connective tissues.

glial cell m. An extremely delicate membrane, formed of foot plates of astrocytes, that surrounds all the blood vessels in the brain, spinal cord, and the lining of the pia mater, separating these vessels from the nervous tissue proper. This membrane is thought to be one of the components of the blood-brain barrier.

Huxley m. SEE: under *Huxley, Thomas H.*

hyaline m. The membrane between the outer root sheath of a hair follicle and the inner fibrous layer.

hyaloid m. The membrane that envelops the vitreous humor.

hyoglossal m. A transverse fibrous

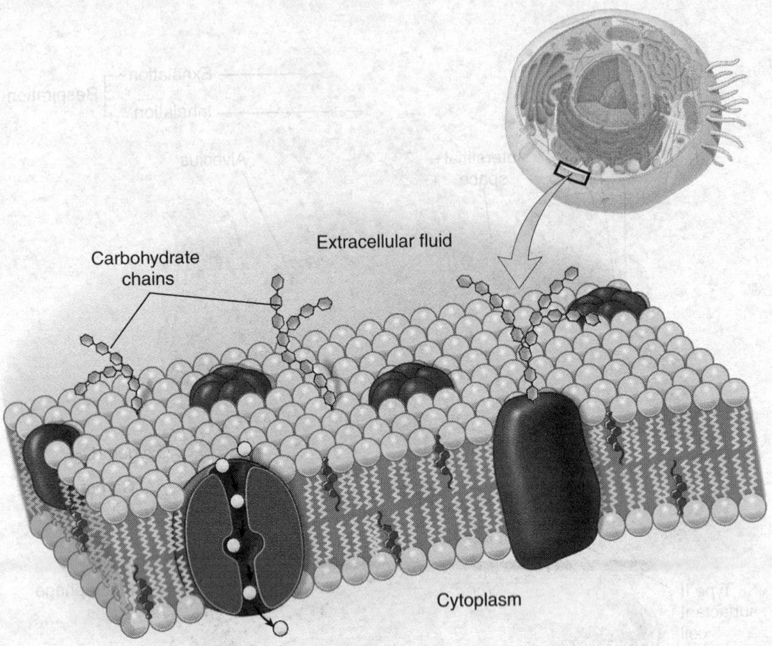

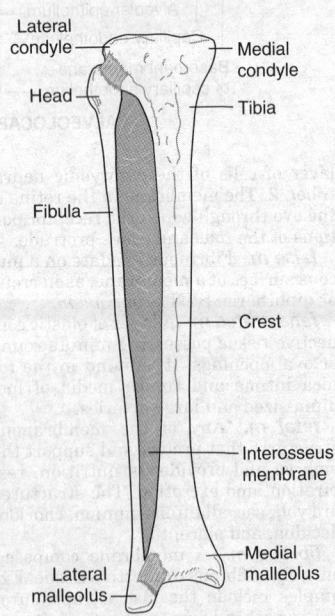

CELL MEMBRANE

membrane uniting tongue to hyoid bone.

internal limiting m. **1.** The inner layer of ependymal cells lining the embryonic neural tube. **2.** The glial membrane forming the innermost layer of the retina and the iris.

interosseous m. **1.** A fibrous membrane in the arm connecting ulna to radius. **2.** A fibrous membrane in the leg connecting tibia to fibula. SEE: illus.

masticatory mucous m. The mucosa of the mouth involved in the masticatory process. It is characterized by a keratinized surface epithelium, and includes the hard palate, gingiva, and dorsum of the tongue.

mucous m. Any of the membranes that line passages and cavities communicating with the air, consisting of epithelium, a basement membrane, and an underlying layer of connective tissue (lamina propria). Mucus-secreting cells or glands are usually present in the epithelium but may be absent. In humans, mucous membranes and the skin prevent the entry of pathogens. Mucous membranes are normally colonized with nonpathogenic organisms that discourage colonization by pathogens because the resident organisms compete for the nutrients essential to their survival. Some mucosal surfaces in the digestive tract have special characteristics that

INTEROSSEOUS MEMBRANE

tend to repel or kill organisms, such as the extremely high acid level on the mucosa of the stomach.

Noninvasive examination of membranes should reveal the degree of moisture, cyanosis, pallor, hyperemia, pigmentation, lesions or their absence, and hemorrhage. Pallor is seen in all anemias. If the pallor is temporary, it may indicate shock or vasomotor spasm, or it may occur in severe hemorrhages. Blanching and flushing alternately accompany aortic regurgitation.

Hyperemia of the mucous membranes is indicative of certain pathological changes in particular tissues, e,g., of the buccal mucous membrane, due to decayed teeth, traumatism, or stomatitis; of the nasal mucosa, due to ulceration of the nose, rhinitis, or inflammation; of the eyes (local irritation), due to a foreign body, ulcer, inflammation. Dryness is seen in fevers, chronic gastritis, some liver disturbances, excitement, shock, prostration, fatigue, thirst, and certain drugs.

nasal mucous m. The mucosa lining the nasal cavity and characterized by pseudostratified ciliated columnar epithelium with goblet cells.

Nasmyth m. SEE: *Nasmyth membrane.*

nuclear m. The two-layered membrane surrounding the chromosomes of a cell. The membrane has pores and its outer layer is continuous with the endoplasmic reticulum of the cell. SEE: *nuclear envelope.*

obturator m. A fibrous membrane closing the obturator foramen.

olfactory m. The membrane in the upper part of the nasal cavity that contains olfactory receptors.

otolithic m. A layer of gelatinous substance containing otoconia or otoliths, found on the surface of maculae in the inner ear.

palatal mucous m. The lining of the mouth on the hard and soft palates. The hard palate has heavily keratinized epithelium and copious mucous glands or fat in the submucosa. The mobile soft palate contains muscle in addition to mucous glands, and is much less keratinized on the surface.

peridental m. An obsolete term for the periodontal ligament.

periodontal m. Periodontium.

permeable m. A membrane that permits passage of water and certain substances in solution. SEE: *osmosis; selectively permeable* **m.**; *semipermeable* **m.**

persistent pupillary m. SEE: *pupillary membrane.*

pharyngeal m. Buccopharyngeal **m.**

pharyngeal mucous m. The lining of the pharynx. The mucosa of the nasopharynx is pseudostratified ciliated epithelium; the mucosa of the oropharynx

and laryngopharynx is stratified squamous epithelium.

pial m. Pia mater.

placental m. The membrane of the placenta that separates the maternal blood from fetal blood.

plasma m. Cell membrane.

pseudoserous m. A membrane resembling a serous membrane but differing in structure as the endothelium.

pupillary m. The transparent membrane closing the fetal pupil. If it persists after birth, it is called persistent pupillary membrane.

pyogenic m. The granular lining of an abscess or fistula.

quadrangular m. The upper portion of the elastic membrane of the larynx extending from the aryepiglottic folds to the level of the ventricular folds below.

Reissner m. SEE: *Reissner membrane.*

respiratory m. Alveolocapillary **m.**

reticular m. The membrane formed by the cuticular plates of the distal ends of supporting cells in the organ of Corti.

Ruysch m. SEE: *Ruysch membrane.*

selectively permeable m. A membrane that allows one substance, such as water, to pass through more readily than another, such as salt or sugar.

semipermeable m. A membrane that allows passage of water but not substances in solution. SEE: *osmosis.*

serous m. A membrane consisting of mesothelium lying on a thin layer of connective tissue that lines the closed cavities (peritoneal, pleural, and pericardial) of the body and is reflected over the organs in the cavity. Serous fluid, similar to lymph, decreases friction between the two layers.

Shrapnell m. SEE: *Shrapnell membrane.*

submucous m. SEE: *submucosa.*

synovial m. The membrane lining the capsule of a joint and secreting synovial fluid. The synovial membrane is pink, smooth, and shiny and is made of an intima lining a stronger, vascular fibrous membrane. The intima contains synoviocytes (fibroblast- and macrophage-like cells), which remove debris from the synovial fluid and synthesize some of the mucin (specifically, hyaluronic acid) of the synovial fluid. Most of the synovial fluid is filtered from the blood vessels of the outer fibrous layer of the synovial membrane. SYN: *synovium.*

tectorial m. The thin, jelly-like membrane projecting from the vestibular lip of the osseous spiral lamina and overlying the spiral organ of Corti of the ear.

thyrohyoid m. The membrane joining the hyoid bone and the thyroid cartilage.

tympanic m. The three-layered membrane at the inner (medial) end of the external auditory canal, forming the lateral boundary of the middle ear cavity. The outer layer of the tympanic membrane is keratinized skin, continuous with the skin lining the external ear canal. SYN: *drum; eardrum*. SEE: *ear thermometry; tympanum*.

unit m. The phospholipid bilayer first described as the typical cell membrane, then as the membrane of intracellular structures.

vapor-permeable m. A membrane, usually transparent, that is permeable to oxygen and water vapor. It may be prepared with an adhesive backing that will stick only to dry skin. This type of membrane has been used in covering wounds. The membrane must be applied properly without wrinkles and changed as often as necessary to prevent excess accumulation of fluid and bacteria under it.

vestibular m. The membrane in the cochlea of the inner ear that separates the cochlear duct from the vestibular canal.

virginal m. An obsolete term for the hymen.

vitelline m. The membrane that forms the surface layer of an ovum. SYN: *yolk m.; zona pellucida*.

vitreous m. 1. The inner membrane of the choroid. 2. The innermost layer of the connective tissue sheath surrounding a hair follicle.

yolk m. Vitelline **m.**

membranectomy (mĕm″brăn-nĕk′tō-mē) [L. *membrana*, membrane, + Gr. *ektome*, excision] Surgical removal of a membrane.

membranelle (mĕm″bră-nĕl′) A thin membrane composed of fused cilia and present in the buccal area of some ciliated protozoa.

membrane potential SEE: *potential*, *membrane*.

membranous (mĕm′bră-nŭs) Resembling a membrane. SYN: *membranoid*.

memory (mem′ō-rē) [L. *memoria*] 1. The mental registration, retention, and recollection of past experiences, sensations, or thoughts. This group of functions relies on the coordinated activities of the association regions of the cerebral cortex, specific sensory areas of the brain, subcortical centers, the hypothalamus, the midbrain, and a wide array of neurochemicals and neurotransmitters. Injury or damage to any of these regions of the brain (e.g., as a result of intoxication, stroke, atrophy, or infection) impairs the ability to incorporate new memories or recall and use earlier ones. 2. The capacity of the immune system to respond to antigens to which it has previously been exposed. Immunological memory depends on the activities of T and B lymphocytes, macrophages, major histocompatibility molecules, adhesion molecules, chemokines, and many other biochemicals.

anterograde m. Anterograde amnesia.

declarative m. The conscious recollection of learned information. It is a memory function that is improved by the association of learning with highly charged emotional experiences. SYN: *explicit m.*

episodic m. The ability to recall discrete events (e.g., in one's personal history).

explicit m. Declarative memory.

false m. An inaccurate or incomplete remembrance of a past event. Memory accuracy, validity, and reliability are affected by the following factors: age; serious illness, injury, or psychological trauma; prolonged medication therapy or use of a substance of abuse; mental retardation; mental illness; anxiety; preoccupation; fatigue; guilt and fear of penalty; coercion; or incentive to testify falsely. These factors must be considered in the evaluation of the reliability of patient-reported memories.

immediate m. Memory for events or information in the last few hours or days. Brain damage that limits one's ability to store new information may impair immediate memory but have no effect on memories of the distant past. SYN: *short-term m.* SEE: *digit span test*.

impaired m. A state in which a person is unable to remember or recall bits of information or behavioral skills. Impaired memory may be attributed to pathophysiological or situational causes that are either temporary or permanent. SEE: *Nursing Diagnoses Appendix*.

implicit m. Recall that is preserved when the patient is given a cue to help retrieve information but deficient without such cues. SYN: *nondeclarative m.*

incidental m. The mental storage of information that occurs passively (i.e., without conscious effort).

long-term m. Recall of experiences or of information acquired in the distant past.

It includes both explicit memory and procedural memory.

nondeclarative m. Implicit memory.

procedural m. The ability to recall how to perform activities or functions, e.g., how to brush one's teeth or ride a skateboard. This type of memory is often preserved when other memory functions are lost. SEE: *declarative m.*

recovered m. A memory recalled after having been forgotten. Recall may be the result of psychotherapy or suggestion. Not all instances of recovered memory are accurate (some are the result of suggestion). SEE: *false m.*

remote m. Recollection of information that was stored in the distant past.

retrograde m. Retrograde amnesia.

selective m. The recollection only of particular aspects of an event or experience; limited recall.

short-term m. Immediate memory.

sensory m. The momentary storage in the brain of images or sensations just felt, heard, seen, smelled, or tasted. Sensory memories typically last only a few seconds.

spatial m. The ability to recall three-dimensional objects or places, e.g., the location of an object in space, the position of one object in relation to another, or the correct path through a maze.

topographic m. 1. The ability to recall the contours, design, shape, or structure of a previously experienced environment. **2.** The ability to hold in the mind a map of a person, place, or thing.

working m. The ability to store and use those facts and ideas necessary for performing immediate tasks.

MEN *multiple endocrine neoplasia.*

Menactra (měn-ăk′trǎ) Meningococcal vaccine.

menarche (měn-ăr′kē) [Gr. *men,* month, + *arche,* beginning] The initial menstrual period, normally occurring between the 9th and 17th year. SEE: *adrenarche; puberty.* **menarchal, menarcheal, menarchial,** *adj.*

Mendel, Kurt (mend′ĕl) Ger. neurologist, 1874–1946.

M.-Bechterew reflex SEE: *Mendel-Bechterew reflex.*

Mendel-Bechterew reflex [*Mendel,* Kurt + *Bechterew,* Vladimir Mikhailovich] Plantar flexion of the toes in response to percussion of the dorsum of the foot.

mendelevium (men″dĕ-lē′vē-ŭm) [Dmitri *Mendeleyev,* Russian chemist, 1834–1907 + *-ium* (1)] SYMB: Md. A transuranium element; atomic weight (mass) 256, atomic number 101.

mendelism (měn′dĕl-ĭzm) The principles of heredity expressed in Mendel's laws.

Mendel laws (men′dĕl) [Gregor Johann Mendel, Austrian monk, 1822–1884] The laws governing the genetic transmission of dominant and recessive traits. By carefully studying the heredity characteristics of garden peas, Mendel was able to explain the transmission of certain traits from one generation to the next.

Many inherited characteristics are controlled by the interaction of two genes, one from each parent. During meiosis, parent cells divide and contribute half their chromosome complement to the egg or sperm. After fertilization, the zygote contains a pair of each chromosome; each pair has genes for the same traits at corresponding locations. Alternate forms of the gene for a specific trait are called *alleles,* which may be dominant or recessive. SEE: *allele; chromosome; gamete; gene; meiosis.*

Mendel's law of segregation states that as the gametes are formed, the gene pairs separate and do not influence each other.

Mendel's law of dominance resulted from his observation that crossing a tall strain of peas with a short strain resulted in the expression of the dominant trait, in this case tallness. Thus, a dominant trait will appear in the individual even if only one allele for it is present in the genome.

Mendel's law of independent assortment states that traits controlled by different gene pairs (such as height and color) pass to the offspring independently of each other.

Ménétrier disease (mā-nā-tre-ā′) [Pierre Ménétrier, Fr. physician, 1859–1935] Giant hypertrophic gastritis.

Ménière disease (mān″ē-ār′) [Prosper Ménière, Fr. physician, 1799–1862] A syndrome characterized by recurring episodes of hearing loss, tinnitus, vertigo, and aural fullness, often resulting in gradually progressive deafness. Exacerbations (e.g., of vertigo) may occur suddenly and last for as long as 24 hr. When one ear is affected, the other ear will become involved in approx. 50% of the cases.

ETIOLOGY: The etiology is unknown, but edema of the membranous labyrinth has been found in autopsy studies.

TREATMENT: In acute attacks, bedrest is the most effective treatment. Also effective are antihistamines, sedatives, discontinuation of smoking, and, rarely, surgical treatment. A low-salt diet (less than 2 g/day) and diuretics may be of benefit.

meninges (měn-ĭn′jēz) *sing.,* **meninx** [Gr.] **1.** Membranes. **2.** The three membranes covering the spinal cord and brain: dura mater (external), arachnoid (middle), and pia mater (internal). SEE: illus. **meningeal** (měn-ĭn′jē-ăl), *adj.*

meningioma (měn-ĭn″jē-ō′mǎ) [Gr. *meninx,* membrane, + *oma,* tumor] A slow-growing tumor that originates in the meninges.

meningiomatosis (mě-nĭn″jē-ō-mǎ-tō′sĭs) [″ + ″ + *osis,* condition] Multiple meningiomas.

meningism (měn-ĭn′jĭzm) [″ + *-ismos,* condition] Irritation of the brain and spinal cord with symptoms simulating meningitis, but without actual inflammation. SYN: *meningismus.*

meningismus (měn″ĭn-jĭz′mŭs) Meningism.

meningitis (men-ĕn-jīt′ĭs, -jĭt′ĭ-dēz″) *pl.* **meningitides** [*meningo- + -itis*] Inflammation of the membranes of the spinal cord or brain, usually but not always caused by an infectious illness. Bacterial meningitis is a medical emergency

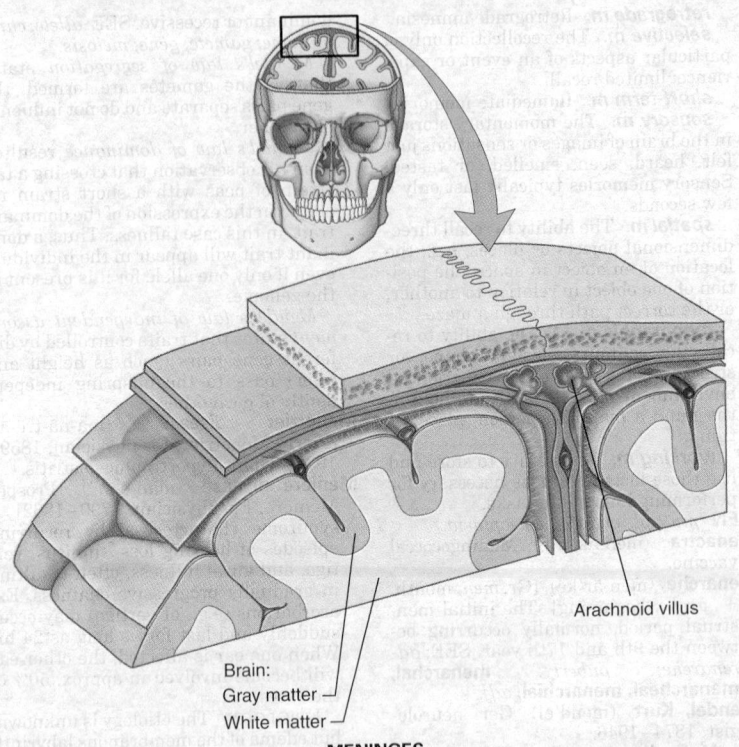

Arachnoid villus

Brain:
Gray matter
White matter

MENINGES

Frontal section of top of skull

that must be diagnosed and treated quickly to obtain the best outcome. It is fatal in 10% to 40% of cases, even with optimal therapy, and may result in persistent neurological injury in about 10% of patients who survive the initial infection. In the U.S., bacterial meningitis formerly affected infants and children more than adults; the demographics of the disease changed in the 1990s after vaccines against *Haemophilus influenzae* were introduced into pediatric care. Infectious meningitis now is largely a disease of adults and usually is caused by *Streptococcus pneumoniae* or *Neisseria meningitidis,* although other microbes may be responsible. Intravenous steroids (such as dexamethasone) given at the beginning of therapy decreases the risk of death and disability. SEE: *Standard Precautions Appendix.* **meningitic** (men-ĕn-jit′ik), *adj.*

ETIOLOGY: Meningitis may result from infection with bacteria, viruses, mycobacteria, fungi, amebas, or noninfectious sources, such as chemical irritation. Occasionally, infectious meningitis follows head trauma or sinus or ear infection. It also may result from the spread of blood-borne infection.

SYMPTOMS: The symptoms of meningitis include fever, chills, headache, stiff neck, altered mental status, vomiting, and photophobia. Many patients with meningitis present with only two or three of these clinical indicators. Acute bacterial meningitis and meningitis caused by some fungi and amebas may also cause rapid deterioration in mental status, seizures, shock, and death.

DIAGNOSIS: Cerebrospinal fluid (CSF) must be examined. A cell count to assess the level of inflammation, a Gram stain to look for infectious organisms, measurement of spinal fluid pressure, and levels of bacterial antigens, glucose, lactate, and protein are typically obtained. CSF may appear milky-white due to the large numbers of white blood cells present.

PREVENTION: All children in the U.S. are now vaccinated against *H. influenzae* type b (Hib) and pneumococcus (Prevnar) as primary prevention against the disease. Meningococcal polysaccharide vaccines are highly effective in preventing the disease during epidemic outbreaks with this organism. Close family contacts of patients with meningococcal meningitis, day care center contacts of infected children, or any persons (including health care workers) with direct contact with the saliva of infected patients are to be treated with antibiotics to prevent disease transmission.

TREATMENT: Definitive treatment depends on identification of the underlying causes, but empirical therapies for infectious meningitis must be given immediately, hours before the causative agent is identified. Dexamethasone is administered intravenously before starting antibiotic therapy for best response to reduce the incidence of deafness in children (a common complication) and to help prevent death in adults with pneumococcal meningitis. The evolution of penicillin-resistant strains of pneumococci has altered traditional empirical treatments. Third-generation cephalosporins, ampicillin and gentamicin, chloramphenicol, or vancomycin plus rifampin have been given, depending on the patient's age, level of immune function, or clinical presentation. Antibiotic therapy is usually administered intravenously for 2 weeks, then orally for a prescribed period for bacterial infections. Viral meningitis treatment is supportive; recovery usually is complete (within 7 to 10 days). Antipyretic analgesics relieve headache and fever.

PATIENT CARE: Specific measures for coexisting conditions and for shock and other complications (disseminated intravascular coagulation, metabolic acidosis, or seizures) should be initiated when indicated. Supportive therapies include bed rest, a dimly lit room, and reduced sensory stimulation. Standard precautions apply, and airborne/droplet precautions are initiated if nasal cultures are positive. Neurologic function is closely monitored for changes in level of consciousness, signs of increasing intracranial pressure (ICP), and indications of cranial nerve involvement. Fluid and electrolyte balance is monitored, and fluids are provided in quantities to prevent or treat dehydration while avoiding fluid overload and resultant cerebral edema. The patient is assessed for adverse effects of antibiotic therapy with peak and trough blood levels assessed to ensure therapeutic levels and avoid toxic overdose. The patient is repositioned carefully and assisted with range-of-motion exercises to prevent skin, muscle, and joint complications. Frequent mouth care is provided and adequate nutrition and elimination are maintained. Small frequent meals, nasogastric or parenteral feedings are provided as required. Constipation is prevented by stool softeners or mild laxatives to prevent straining, which could increase ICP. Basic explanations,

realistic reassurance, and support are provided, with reorientation if delirium or confusion is present. Questions from the patient and family should be answered honestly, with reassurance that behavioral changes usually resolve.

The patient with infectious meningitis may need monitoring in an ICU. Patients with neurologic deficits that appear to be continuing should be referred to a rehabilitation program once the acute phase of illness has ended. To help prevent meningitis, patients with chronic sinusitis or other chronic infectious or inflammatory illnesses should be taught the importance of proper hand hygiene and of following through with prescribed treatments. Sterile techniques should be strictly enforced when treating patients with head wounds, skull fractures, or lumbar puncture, ventricular shunting, or other invasive therapies.

acute aseptic m. A nonpurulent form of meningitis often due to viral infection. It usually runs a short, benign course, marked by fever and headache and ending with recovery.

aseptic m. Meningitis without obvious evidence of bacterial infection. It typically results from a viral infection (such as coxsackievirus or other enteroviruses) although frequently no causative organism is identified.

SYMPTOMS: Patients report fever, headache, stiff neck, malaise, and sometimes altered mental status or photophobia.

PATIENT CARE: Treatment is supportive, with antipyretics and pain-relieving medications administered as prescribed. The virus can be spread by direct contact with saliva, sputum, mucus, or stools of an infected person. Standard precautions apply, with droplet precautions if nasal cultures are positive; contaminated articles are disposed of by double bagging. Neurological status is monitored for changes in level of consciousness and for increases in intracranial pressure. Personal hygiene is provided, and measures to prevent complications due to immobility are implemented. Gentle position changes are performed to reduce excessive stimulation. Artificial airway, suction, and oxygen are readily available. A quiet, dark atmosphere is provided, and siderails are padded to reduce the risk of injury. Prescribed analgesics are administered, and cool compresses are applied to the forehead to relieve headache. Intravenous fluids or tube feedings are administered as ordered, and intake and output are monitored. Assessments are made for complications such as shock, respiratory distress, and disseminated intravascular coagulation.

Since mosquitoes can spread some viruses that cause meningitis, avoiding mosquito bites during the warm months of the year by wearing insecticides (DEET) and barrier protection, and eliminating standing pools of water, where mosquitoes breed, may help prevent the disease. The public should be made aware of meningitis symptoms (fever, headache, stiff neck, altered levels of consciousness) and the importance of prompt attention for any patient suspected of meningitis.

bacterial m. Meningitis caused by disease-causing and potentially life-threatening organisms, esp. *Streptococcus pneumoniae, Haemophilus influenzae, Neisseria meningitidis,* and *Listeria monocytogenes.*

basal m. Meningitis at the base of the brain, usually due to tuberculosis.

carcinomatous m. Meningitis by metastatic tumor cells. It may produce symptoms such as headache, backache, confusion, nerve palsies, or seizures and should be suspected when these symptoms arise in patients with known cancers. The diagnosis is confirmed by lumbar puncture with analysis of the cerebrospinal fluid for tumor cells.

cerebral m. Acute or chronic meningitis of the brain.

cerebrospinal m. Meningitis of the brain and spinal cord.

chronic m. Meningitis marked by persistent fever, headache, and stiff neck (associated, on lumbar puncture, with cerebrospinal fluid pleocytosis and elevated spinal fluid pressure). The underlying cause of this cluster of findings may be initially difficult to determine. Syphilis, cryptococcosis, HIV infection, or invasion of the meninges by cancer cells may be responsible. Occasionally, repeated lumbar punctures reveal a vasculitis of the central nervous system or a partially treated bacterial meningitis.

cryptococcal m. Fungal meningitis due to *Cryptococcus neoformans.* A rare cause of disease in healthy hosts, cryptococcal meningitis is an opportunistic infection usually seen in patients with advanced AIDS or patients taking high-dose steroids. It usually presents with gradually progressive headache and fever. The serum cryptococcal antigen test is a useful screening test. The diagnosis is established by the results of analysis and culture of cerebral spinal fluid.

TREATMENT: Treatment options include amphotericin B, often with flucytosine. Fluconazole and/or related antifungals are sometimes used for maintenance therapy.

meningococcal m. Meningitis caused by various serogroups of *Neis-seria meningitidis.* SEE: *Nursing Diagnoses Appendix.*

Mollaret m. SEE: *Mollaret meningitis.*

pneumococcal m. Meningitis due to *Streptococcus pneumoniae,* a disease predominantly found in adults. In the U.S., about 20% of affected patients die. Because of the worldwide emergence of streptococcal resistance to penicillins, chloramphenicol, and cephalosporins, vancomycin, rifampin, and other antibacterial agents are used to treat this infection. Intravenous steroids (such as dexamethasone) given at the beginning of therapy decrease the risk of death and disability caused by this infection.

serous m. Meningitis with serous exudation into the cerebral ventricles.

spinal m. Inflammation of the spinal cord membranes.

traumatic m. Meningitis resulting from trauma to the meninges.

tuberculous m. Meningitis resulting from the spread of *Mycobacterium tuberculosis* to the central nervous system, usually from a primary focus of infection in the lungs.

viral m. A form of aseptic meningitis due to infection with adenovirus, coxsackievirus, echovirus, HIV, mumps virus, lymphocytic choriomeningitis virus, polio viruses, and others. Patients report fever, headache, and stiff neck. Lumbar puncture reveals an excessive number of lymphocytes, typically without a decrease in cerebrospinal fluid glucose levels.

meningo-, meningi-, mening- [Gr. *mēninx,* stem *mēning-,* membrane] Prefixes meaning *meninges.*

meningocele (měn-ĭn′gō-sēl) [″ + *kele,* tumor, swelling] Congenital hernia in which the meninges protrude through a defect in the skull or spinal column.

meningococcal, meningococcic (mě-ning″gō-kok′ăl, mě-ning″gō-kok′sik) Pert. to meningococcus.

meningococcal vaccine (mě-ning″gō-kok′ăl) SEE: under *vaccine.*

meningococcemia (měn-ĭn″gō-kŏk-sē′mē-ă) [″ + *kokkos,* berry, + *haima,* blood] Meningococci in the blood, a serious illness that may cause a disseminated rash, altered mental status, shock, and death. SEE: illus.

meningococcus (měn-ĭn″gō-kŏk′ŭs) pl. **meningococci** A microorganism of the species *Neisseria meningitidis,* one of the causative agents of meningitis.

meningoencephalitis (mě-ning″gō-ĕn-sef″ă-līt′ĭs) [*meningo- + encephalitis*] Inflammation of the brain and its meninges. SYN: *encephalomeningitis.* SEE: *encephalitis; meningitis.*

primary amebic m. Meningoencephalitis caused by free-living amebae ordinarily found in water, soil, and decaying vegetation. Organisms that can

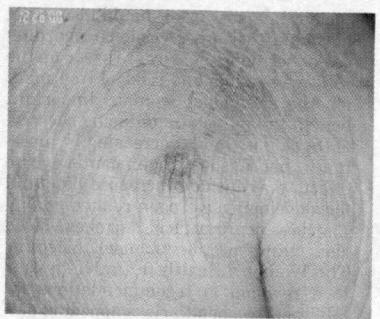

MENINGOCOCCEMIA
Typical rash

cause primary amebic meningoencephalitis include *Naegleria fowleri, Acanthamoeba culbertsoni,* and other species of *Acanthamoeba.* The amebae are acquired by swimming in freshwater lakes and sniffing water into the nasal cavities.

SYMPTOMS: The symptoms are similar to those of acute meningococcal meningitis.

TREATMENT: For *Naegleria* infections, amphotericin B, miconazole, and rifampin are effective if given early in the disease, but diagnosis of this rare disease is often delayed, and few patients survive. *Acanthamoeba* species are sensitive to pentamidine, propamidine, ketoconazole, miconazole, neomycin, and flucytosine.

meningoencephalocele (měn-ĭn″gō-ĕn-sĕf′ăl-ō-sēl) [″ + ″ + *kele,* tumor, swelling] Hernial protrusion of brain and meninges through a defect in the skull.

meningoencephalomyelitis (měn-ĭn″gō-ĕn-sĕf″ăl-ō-mī-ĕl-ī′tĭs) [″ + ″ + *myelos,* marrow, + *itis,* inflammation] Inflammation of the brain and spinal cord, and their meninges.

meningomyelitis (měn-ĭn″gō-mī″ĕl-ī′tĭs) [″ + *myelos,* marrow, + *itis,* inflammation] Inflammation of the spinal cord and its enveloping membranes.

meningomyelocele (mě-nĭng″gō-mī′ě-lō-sēl″) [″ + ″ + *kele,* tumor, swelling] Myelomeningocele.

meningoradiculitis (mě-nĭng″gō-ră-dĭk″ū-lī′tĭs) [″ + ″ + Gr. *itis,* inflammation] Inflammation of the meninges and roots of the spinal nerves.

meninx (mē′nĭnks) *pl.* **meninges** [Gr., membrane] **1.** Membrane. **2.** Any of the three membranes investing the spinal cord and brain: dura mater (external), arachnoid (middle), and pia mater (internal).

meniscectomy (měn″ĭ-sěk′tō-mē) [″ + *ektome,* excision] Removal of a torn meniscus from the knee, typically done because of pain, loss of function, or ar-

thritic changes. It may be performed via open surgery, but is often done arthroscopically in a same-day surgical setting. SEE: *Nursing Diagnoses Appendix.*

PATIENT CARE: The patient's dressing, peripheral pulses, and sensory and motor status of the affected area are evaluated every 2 hr after surgery. Knee immobility is maintained for a specified period. Use of crutches or walker with partial weight bearing may often begin in 1 to 2 days. The affected leg is kept elevated to prevent or reduce swelling, and ice is applied to control swelling. Analgesics are prescribed. On discharge, the patient is advised to continue to perform appropriate exercises at home and after a week or so of reduced activities, to begin a gradual return to normal weight-bearing on the limb. Rehabilitation to help restore muscle strength and range of motion is also indicated.

meniscus (měn-ĭs′kŭs) *pl.* **menisci** [Gr. *meniskos,* crescent] **1.** Convexoconcave lens. **2.** Interarticular fibrocartilage of crescent shape, found in certain joints, esp. the lateral and medial menisci (semilunar cartilages) of the knee joint. **3.** The curved upper surface of a liquid in a container.

lateral m. A circular, somewhat moveable plate of fibrocartilage lying horizontally in the articular surface of the lateral condyle of the tibia inside the knee joint. The meniscus cushions and deepens the articular face of the tibia. SEE: *knee* for illus.

Menkes disease (měn′kāz) Metabolic defect resulting from a mutation on the X chromosome that alters the transport of copper within the human body, resulting in neurological degeneration, connective tissue disorders, and premature death. SEE: *kinky hair disease.*

meno-, men- [Gr. *mēn,* month] Prefixes meaning *menstruation.*

menometrorrhagia (měn″ō-mět-rō-rā′jē-ă) [Gr. *men,* month, + *metra,* womb, + *rhegnynai,* to burst forth] Excessive bleeding during and between menstrual periods. SEE: *menorrhagia.*

Menomune (men′ŏ-mūn″) A freeze-dried preparation of the group-specific polysaccharide antigens from *Neisseria meningitidis.*

menopause (men′ŏ-poz″) [*meno-* + *pause*] The period that marks the permanent cessation of menstrual activity, normally occurring in the U.S. between the ages of 40 and 58. Menopause is said to have occurred once the woman has experienced 12 full months without any menstrual bleeding. The mean age of menopause in the U.S. is 51. The menses may stop suddenly, but this phenomenon is relatively rare. For most women there is first a *menopausal tran-*

sition often lasting a few years, during which ovulation becomes infrequent, menstrual cycles become irregular, brief periods of amenorrhea, polymenorrhea, or hypermenorrhea occur, and follicle-stimulating hormone levels rise. Natural menopause will occur in 25% of women by age 47, 50% by age 50, 75% by age 52, and 95% by age 55. Pathologic or premature menopause due to surgical removal of the ovaries, chemotherapy, radiation therapy, or to disorders such as malnutrition, debilitation, or extreme emotional stress can occur at any age. Women with short menstrual cycles, lower body weight, a history of smoking, nulliparity, and lower socioeconomic status may reach menopause earlier than the rest of the population. Obesity and overweight may contribute to a delayed onset of menopause. SYN: *change of life.* SEE: *climacteric; osteoporosis; perimenopause.*

SYMPTOMS: The symptoms associated with menopause begin soon after the functional decline of the ovaries results in decreased estrogen levels, or after medical, radiation, or surgical treatments destroy the reproductive glands. Symptoms, which may last from a few months to years, vary from hardly noticeable to severe. Included are vasomotor instability (hot flashes and night sweats), insomnia, atrophy of vulvovaginal tissues, vaginal dryness, and dyspareunia. Vaginal pH becomes more alkaline, increasing the chance for infections. Atrophic cystitis due to the effects of decreased estrogen levels on bladder mucosa and associated structures can occur. Breast size may decrease, skin turgor and elasticity decrease, and pubic and axillary hair may be reduced. A panel of the National Institutes of Health in 2005 found limited, if any, evidence that anxiety, fatigue, apathy, depression, poor concentration, lapses in memory, palpitations, headache, numbness, tingling, myalgia, or urinary disturbances (e.g., frequency and incontinence) had any provable relation to menopause. The long-term effects of lower estrogen levels include incremental bone loss (osteopenia or osteoporosis).

TREATMENT: Menopausal hormone replacement therapy (HRT) may be used cautiously for relief of symptoms. This therapy consists of estrogen alone (in women who have had a hysterectomy) and estrogen combined with progesterone (in patients with an intact uterus). HRT is contraindicated in women who smoke or in women with a history of an estrogen-dependent breast cancer, endometrial cancer, thromboembolic disease, acute liver disease, and vaginal bleeding of unknown cause. Many women with a strong family his-

tory of breast cancer should also avoid hormone therapy. Decisions regarding use of hormone therapy are based on the relative benefits and risks of treatment for the individual woman. Important benefits may include reducing the risk of bone loss and decreasing symptomatic hot flashes. Significant adverse effects may include increased potential for developing estrogen-related malignancies, heart attacks, strokes, blood clots, and postmenopausal bleeding. The Women's Health Initiative has led to a revision in recommendations for HRT because health risks appear to outweigh benefits. The advantages and disadvantages of hormonal therapies should be openly discussed with patients so that they may make informed choices about treatment. Because of the known risks, HRT should be used at the lowest effective dose for the shortest amount of time until treatment goals are met. Some antidepressants (e.g., fluoxetine, paroxetine, or venlafaxine) and some anticonvulsant medications, such as gabapentin, may be prescribed for hot flashes and other menopausal symptoms. Although researchers have not proved the effectiveness of herbal compounds and soy products, some women take them for relief of menopausal symptoms. Relaxation techniques, yoga, tai chi, or meditation also help. SEE: *estrogen replacement therapy; hormone replacement therapy.*

PATIENT CARE: Because women may experience a variety of symptoms during this period of their lives, their nature, severity, and personal impact need to be sensitively addressed by health care professionals. Menopause is a normal phase in the reproductive cycle. The postmenopausal woman should be encouraged to maintain a diet high in calcium, vitamins, and minerals to maintain strong bones. Any vaginal bleeding or spotting that occurs after menopause should be promptly reported and investigated. If a woman is in a sexual relationship, remaining sexually active will help to preserve vaginal elasticity, and lubricants can be used before intercourse to reduce dryness. Performing Kegel exercises strengthens vaginal and pelvic musculature.

artificial m. Menopause following oophorectomy (surgical removal of the ovaries), radiation therapy, or chemotherapy.

male m. SEE: *climacteric.*

premature m. Natural or artificial menopause occurring before age 35.

surgical m. Menopause that results from oophorectomy (surgical removal of the ovaries).

menopause transition, menopausal transition The time in most women's lives just before their monthly periods cease and when they begin to experience irregular menstrual cycles, abnormal vaginal bleeding, hot flashes, disturbed sleep, atrophy of vaginal tissues, and decreased vaginal lubrication.

PATIENT CARE: Fluctuating hormone levels are responsible for these changes. Educating women about the transition and treating individual symptoms are typically advocated. Menopausal hormone replacement therapy is controversial: its risks and benefits should be thoroughly examined and discussed. Alternatives include dietary modification, exercise, and nonhormone drug therapy. Patients should be advised to report any abnormal vaginal bleeding. SEE: *perimenopause.*

menorrhagia (měn″ō-rā′jē-ă) [″ + *rhegnynai,* to burst forth] Excessive menstrual bleeding or menstrual bleeding that lasts longer than seven days. SYN: *hypermenorrhea.* SEE: *uterine hemorrhage.*

ETIOLOGY: Common causes of excessive menstrual blood loss include: spontaneous abortion or ectopic pregnancy; pituitary, hypothalamic, thyroid, ovarian, or other endocrine disorders; bleeding disorders, such as von Willebrand disease; anticoagulant use; use of contraceptive hormones and devices; endometrial cancers and fibroids; among many other diseases and conditions.

menotropins (měn″ō-trō′pĭns) A combination of follicle-stimulating hormone (FSH) and luteinizing hormone (LH) used to treat infertility by promoting growth and maturation of the follicle of the ovary. Menotropins is obtained from the urine of postmenopausal women. A standard extract is used with human chorionic gonadotropin to induce ovulation.

menses (měn′sēz) [L., month] The monthly flow of bloody fluid and cellular debris from the uterus.

mens rea (măns rā′ă, měnz rē′ă) [L. "guilty mind"] Criminal intent. In legal matters an unlawful act is considered to be a criminal act only when the person who commits it acts with criminal intent. From a psychological perspective, this means that minors, the mentally ill, and those affected by organic brain disease may commit unlawful acts but not be culpable of them in a court of law because they may not understand the nature and consequences of such acts.

menstrual cramps (men′stroo-ăl) SEE: under *cramp.*

menstrual cycle SEE: under *cycle.*

menstrual dating An estimate of the age of a fetus or of a term, preterm, or postterm newborn infant determined by the number of days or weeks since the mother's last menstrual period.

menstrual epilepsy SEE: under *epilepsy.*

menstrual extraction SEE: under *extraction.*

menstrual period SEE: under *period.*

menstrual regulation Vacuum or suction curettage of the uterus done within the first two weeks following the expected date of the onset of menstruation. If the amenorrhea was due to pregnancy, the procedure is classed as a form of fertility control.

menstrual suppression SEE: under *suppression.*

menstrual synchrony The simultaneous occurrence of ovulatory cycles and menstrual bleeding among women who live or work together or socialize closely with one another.

menstruant (měn′stroo-ănt) [L. *menstruare,* to discharge the menses] **1.** In the condition of menstruating. **2.** One who menstruates.

menstruate (měn′stroo-āt) To discharge menses.

menstruation (měn-stroo-ā′shŭn) [L. *menstruare,* to discharge the menses] The cyclic, hormonally generated sloughing of the uterine endometrium, which occurs between puberty and menopause and is accompanied by bloody vaginal discharge. The onset of menstruation (menarche) usually occurs during puberty (9 to 17 years of age). When a woman's ovum is not fertilized, the corpus luteum undergoes involution, which causes progesterone levels to drop, which in turn triggers menses. SYN: *catamenia.* SEE: *ovary* for illus; *lactation amenorrhea method; menstrual cycle.* **menstrual** (měn′stroo-ăl), *adj.*

The average menstrual period displays the following characteristics: an intermenstrual interval that varies between 18 and 40 days, with an average of 27 to 30 days; and a menstrual flow that lasts between 3 and 7 days, 4 to 5 days average. Menstrual blood contains normal, hemolyzed, and sometimes agglutinated red blood cells; disintegrated endometrial and stromal cells; and glandular secretions. In general, menstrual blood does not coagulate, but passage of occasional clots is not unusual.

Blood loss varies widely among women; however, it usually is consistent from month to month in the same individual. Average monthly blood loss ranges from 44 to 80 mL but may be lessened by the use of oral contraceptives and increased by the presence of an intrauterine device. Menstrual blood loss is the most common single cause of female iron-deficiency anemia. Estimating a patient's blood loss from interviewing is difficult because many women are poor judges of the volume of their flow. A rough estimate of blood loss may be made by querying the number, type, and amount of saturation of tampons or sanitary pads used each day of the period. When noting the number of pads or tampons used daily, the historian should determine the reason for changes; some women may change for reasons other than pad saturation.

Indications of excessive or abnormal menstrual flow include a need to change saturated tampons or pads hourly; passage of clots, esp. when larger than 2 cm in diameter or occurring on other than the first full day of menses; and duration of flow exceeding 7 days in one or more cycles. Menstruation normally ceases during pregnancy, may or may not occur during lactation, and permanently ceases with menopause. SEE: *sanitary napkin; tampon, menstrual.*

Menstrual irregularities: Failure to menstruate may be caused by congenital abnormalities; physical disorders (e.g., obesity, malnutrition, or disease); excessive exercise; emotional and hormonal disturbances affecting the ovaries, pituitary, thyroid, or adrenal glands. An absence of flow when normally expected is called *amenorrhea;* scanty flow is known as *oligomenorrhea;* painful menstruation is *dysmenorrhea.* Excessive loss of blood is termed *menorrhagia;* loss of blood during intermenstrual periods is known as spotting or *metrorrhagia.*

    retrograde m. Backflow of menstrual fluid through the fallopian tubes into the peritoneal cavity.

    suppressed m. Failure of menstruation to occur when normally expected.

    vicarious m. Menstruation from a site other than the uterus when the menstrual flow is expected.

menstruum (měn′stroo-ŭm) [L. *menstruus,* menstrual fluid] A solvent; a medium. It was once believed that menstrual fluid had solvent qualities. SEE: *vehicle.*

mensual (měn′sū-ăl) [L. *mensis,* month] Monthly.

mensuration (měn-sū-rā′shŭn) [L. *mensuratio*] The process of measuring.

¹mental (men′tăl) [L. *mens,* stem *ment-,* mind] Pert. to the mind.

²mental [L. *mentum,* stem *ment-,* chin] Pert. to the chin.

mental fog Clouding of consciousness, usually with some loss of memory.

mentality Mental power or activity.

mentally ill Affected by any condition that affects mood or behavior, such as depression, dysphoria, personality disorders, phobias, schizophrenia, or substance abuse, among others.

Mental Measurements Yearbook A widely used index of commercially published, standardized tests.

mental retardation Below average intelligence evident before the age of 18 associated with impaired learning or communication; poor social, community, or interpersonal adjustment; and inability to function independently, e.g., to support oneself, to live safely and healthfully.

    ETIOLOGY: In many persons, the cause is not identified. Injuries that occur during fetal or embryonic development (such as exposure to infections or toxins in utero); genetic syndromes (such as Tay-Sachs disease or Down syndrome); childhood exposure to toxins (such as lead); or social and emotional deprivation during infancy or childhood all may contribute to impairments in intellectual development.

    DIAGNOSIS: Tests of intelligence (*intelligence quotient* or *IQ* tests) are used to diagnose mental retardation, esp. when poor scores on these tests correlate with observed difficulties in adaptation to the environment.

mentation (měn-tā′shŭn) Mental activity.

mentha piperita (měn′tă pǐ-pě-rē′tă, rī′) [NL, lit. "peppermint"] Peppermint.

menthol (měn′thŏl) $C_{10}H_{20}O$; an alcohol obtained from oil of peppermint or other mint oils. Menthol may be prepared synthetically. It occurs in crystalline form. When applied to the skin in a 0.25% to 2% solution, it is an antipruritic.

menton (měn′tŏn) [L. *mentum,* chin] A craniometric landmark, being the lowest point of the mandibular symphysis seen in a lateral radiograph. It is similar to, but not necessarily the same as, gnathion, which is the lowest point of the mandible in the midline as palpated in the living.

mentoplasty (měn′tō-plăs-tē) Cosmetic surgery designed to enhance the appearance of the chin.

mentor (men′tor″, ′tŏr) [Fr. *Mentor,* Odysseus′ adviser and Telemachus′ guardian in Homer′s *Odyssey*] A trusted advisor, educator, guide, guardian, and tutor.

M4Eo *acute myelomonocytic leukemia with abnormal eosinophils.*

MEOS *microsomal ethanol oxidizing system.*

mephitic (mě-fīt′ĭk) [L. *mephiticus, mephitis,* foul exhalation] Noxious, foul, as a poisonous odor.

mEq Symbol for milliequivalent.

meralgia (měr-ăl′jē-ă) [Gr. *meros,* thigh, + *algos,* pain] Pain in the thigh.

    m. paresthetica Pain and hyperesthesia on the outer femoral surface from lesion or disease of the lateral cutaneous nerve of the thigh. SYN: Bernhardt-Roth syndrome.

mercaptan (měr-kăp′tăn) Any organic chemical that contains the —SH radical. It is formed when the oxygen of an alcohol is replaced by sulfur.

Merchant view An x-ray study of the knee while it is in 30° of flexion, with the patellofemoral joint viewed tangentially. This radiographical view of the knee shows the position of the dorsal surface of the patella as it sits in the trochlear groove between the femoral condyles.

mercurial (mĕr-kū′rē-ăl) [L. *mercurialis*] **1.** Pert. to mercury. **2.** A substance containing mercury.

mercurialism (mĕr-kū′rē-ăl-ĭzm) [L. *mercurius*, mercury, + Gr. *-ismos*, condition] Chronic poisoning by mercury. It is seen as a result of continuous administration of mercury or occurs in persons who work with the metal or inhale its vapors.

SYMPTOMS: Chronic mercury poisoning causes soreness of gums and loosening of teeth; increased salivation; tremor; and behavioral mood disorders.

mercurialized (mĕr-kū′rē-ăl-īzd) **1.** Impregnated with mercury. **2.** Influenced by or treated with mercury.

mercuric (mĕr-kūr′ĭk) [*mercury* + *-ic*] Pert. to divalent mercury.

mercuric chloride HgCl₂, a highly toxic inorganic salt of mercury. SYN: **mercury** bichloride; **mercury (II)** chloride. SEE: *mercuric chloride poisoning; mercuric chloride in Poisons and Poisoning Appendix.*

mercuric chloride poisoning SEE: under *poisoning.*

mercurous (mĕr-kū′rŭs, mĕr′kū-rŭs) Relating to monovalent mercury.

mercurous chloride Mercury (I) chloride.

mercury (mĕr′kyŭ-rē) [L. *Mercurius*, a Roman god] SYMB: Hg. A metallic element, atomic weight (mass) 201, atomic number 80. Mercury is a silvery liquid at room temperature. It forms two series of salts: *mercurous*, in which it has a valence of one (univalent), and *mercuric*, in which it has a valence of two (divalent). SEE: *dental amalgam.*

⚠ Mercury is insoluble in ordinary solvents but soluble in hydrochloric acid on boiling. Boiling releases irritating, highly toxic fumes into the air.

m. bichloride A former name for mercury (II) chloride.

m. dichloride A former name for mercury (II) chloride.

m. (I) chloride HgCl, a heavy white powder formerly used in small doses in medicine as a laxative. It is also used as a component of certain reference electrodes, e.g., the calomel electrode. SYN: *mercurous chloride.*

m. (II) chloride HgCl₂, a highly toxic inorganic salt of mercury. SYN: *mercuric chloride.*

mercury poisoning SEE: under *poisoning.*

mercy (mĕr′sē) [L. *merces*, reward] In medicine, the compassionate provision of relief or mitigation of physical pain, mental suffering, or psychological distress.

-mere, -mer [Gr. *meros*, a part] Suffixes meaning *part, segment.*

meridian (mĕ-rĭd′ē-ăn) [L. *meridianus*, pert. to noon] **1.** An imaginary line encircling a globe at right angles to its equator and passing through the poles, or half of such a line. **2.** In complementary medicine, traditional Chinese medicine, and acupuncture, any of several pathways believed to conduct energy between the surface of the body and the internal organs. Blockage along these pathways is believed to disrupt energy flow (chi or qi) and to cause imbalances that are reflected in symptoms or disease. Meridians and the energy flows they are thought to direct have eluded identification by western scientific methods. SEE: illus. **3.** In visual field testing, a line that denotes an equal level of visual registration. **meridional,** *adj.*

meroblastic (mĕr-ō-blăst′ĭk) [″ + *blastos*, germ] Pert. to a type of ovum containing considerable yolk or a type of cleavage in which cleavage divisions are restricted to the protoplasmic region of the animal pole.

merocele (mer′ŏ-sēl″) [Gr. *meros*, a part +*-cele*] Femoral hernia.

merocrine (mĕr′ō-krĭn) [″ + *krinein*, to separate] Denoting a type of secretion in which the glandular cell remains intact during the process of elaborating and discharging its product. SEE: *apocrine; eccrine; holocrine.*

merodiastolic (mer″ō-dī-ă-stol′ik) [Gr. *meros*, a part + *diastolic*] Pert. to a part of the diastole of the cardiac cycle.

merogony (mĕ-rŏg′ō-nē) [″ + *gonos*, procreation] Incomplete development of fragments of an ovum.

meromelia (mĕr″ō-mē′lē-ă) [″ + *melos*, limb] Partial absence of a limb.

meromyosin (mer″ō-mī′ō-sĭn) Either of the subunits produced by tryptic digestion of myosin.

merosin A glycoprotein normally found in the basement membrane of muscles; it helps muscle cells adhere to and interact with each other and the extracellular matrix. Deficiencies of merosin produce several rare autosomal recessive forms of muscular dystrophy.

merozoite (mĕr″ō-zō′ĭt) [″ + *zoon*, animal] A body formed by segmentation or breaking up of a schizont in asexual reproduction of certain sporozoans, such as *Plasmodium*. When formed, merozoites are liberated and invade other corpuscles, where they repeat the process of schizogony or develop into gametocytes.

merozygote (mer″ō-zī′gŏt) [″ + *zygotos*, yoked together] A bacterial mechanism of gene transfer in which part of

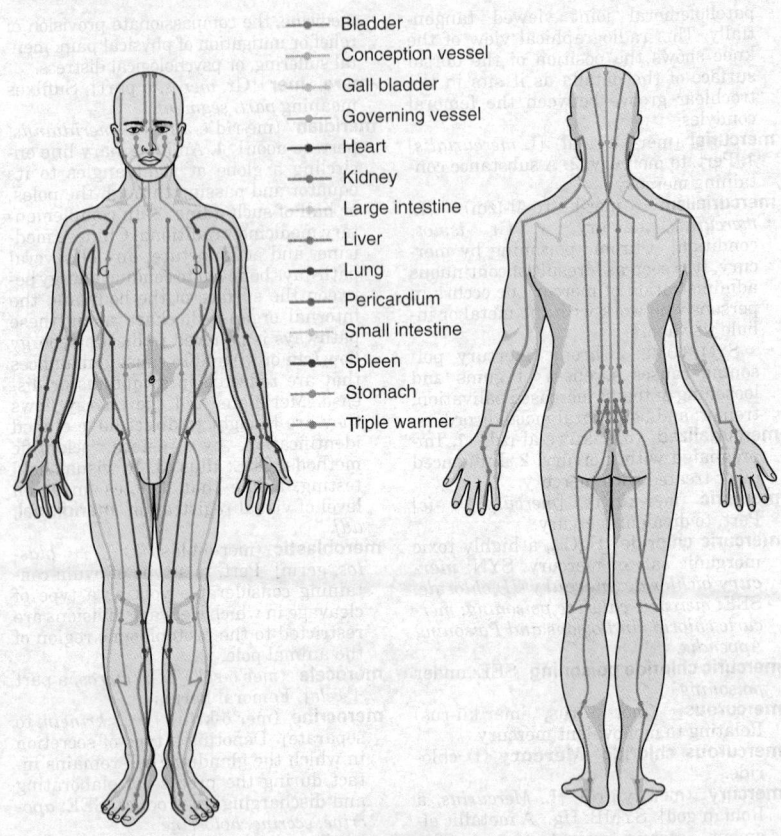

- Bladder
- Conception vessel
- Gall bladder
- Governing vessel
- Heart
- Kidney
- Large intestine
- Liver
- Lung
- Pericardium
- Small intestine
- Spleen
- Stomach
- Triple warmer

QI MERIDIANS

Qi meridians are used in the Chinese medicine techniques of acupressure and acupuncture.

the genome, or chromosome complement, is transferred into an intact recipient cell.

mesangium (mĕs-ăn′jē-ŭm) The suspensory structure of the renal glomerulus.

mesangial, *adj.*

mesaortitis (mĕs″ā-or-tī′tĭs) [″ + *aorte,* aorta, + *itis,* inflammation] Inflammation of the middle aortic layer.

mesatipellic, mesatipelvic (mĕs-ăt″ĭ-pĕl′lĭk, -pĕl′vĭk) [″ + *pella,* bowl] Having a pelvis of medium size with an index between 90 and 95.

mesaxon (mĕz-ăks′ŏn, mĕs-ăks′ŏn) The area of contact of the Schwann cell membrane and the membrane of the axon it encircles.

mescaline (mĕs′kă-lēn) A poisonous alkaloid, the active ingredient of the mescal buttons of the cactus plant *Lophophora williamsii.* It produces its euphoric effects through its impact on serotonergic neurons in the brain and causes hallucinations, esp. of color and sound.

mescalism (mĕs′kă-lĭzm) Intoxication produced by ingesting mescal.

mesectoderm (mĕs-ĕk′tō-derm) Migratory cells derived from ectoderm, esp. from the neural crest of the cephalic area in young embryos, that become pigment cells.

mesencephalon (mĕs-ĕn-sĕf′ă-lŏn) [″ + *enkephalos,* brain] The midbrain; one of three primitive cerebral vesicles from which develop the corpora quadrigemina, the crura cerebri, and the aqueduct of Sylvius. **mesencephalic,** *adj.*

mesencephalotomy (mĕs″ĕn-sĕf′ă-lŏt′ō-mē) [″ + ″ + *tome,* incision] Surgical incision of the midbrain, usually done to relieve intractable pain.

mesenchymoma (mĕs″ĕn-kī-mō′mă) A neoplasm containing a mixture of mesenchymal and fibrous tissue.

mesenteritis (mĕs″ĕn-tĕr-ī′tĭs) [″ + ″ + *itis,* inflammation] Inflammation of the mesentery.

mesentery (mĕs′ĕn-tĕr″ē) [″ + *enteron,* intestine] Commonly, the peritoneal fold that encircles the small intestine and connects it to the posterior abdominal wall. Other abdominal organs, however, also have a mesentery. **mesenteric** (měs″ĕn-tĕr′ĭk), *adj.*

MESH *Medical Subject Headings.* A list of the medical words used in storing and retrieving medical references by the U.S. National Library of Medicine. SEE: *MEDLARS.*

mesh A prosthetic patch or fabric used to repair or reinforce hernias, burns, and other defects. A split-thickness skin graft may be formed into a mesh which may be applied to a burn or other cutaneous defects requiring extensive covering. SEE: *mesh graft.*

mesh graft SEE: under *graft.*

mesiad, mesad (mē′zē-ăd, mē′săd) [Gr. *mesos,* middle, + L. *ad,* toward] Toward the median plane of a body or part.

mesial, mesal (mē′zē-ăl, mē′săl) **1.** Toward the middle point or midline plane. **2.** In dentistry, ventral or nearer to the center of the dental arch.

mesial drift SEE: under *drift.*

mesio- [*mesi(al)*] **1.** Prefix meaning *toward the middle.* **2.** In dentistry, a prefix meaning *mesial.*

mesiobuccal (mē″zē-ō-bŭk′ăl) [*mesio- + buccal*] Pert. to the mesial and buccal surfaces of a tooth or the surfaces involved in a cavity in the tooth. **mesiobuccally** (ă-lē), *adv.*

mesiodens (mē′zē-ō-dĕnz) A supernumerary tooth, often paired, which typically appears between the maxillary central incisors.

TREATMENT: Surgical removal of the mesiodens is usually indicated.

mesiodistal (mē″zē-ō-dis′tăl) [*mesio- + distal*] In dentistry, pert. to the plane defined by the mesial and distal surfaces of a tooth. **mesiodistally** (tăl-ē), *adv.*

mesiolabial (mē″zē-ō-lā′bē-ăl) [*mesio- + labial*] In dentistry, pert. to the mesial and labial surfaces of a tooth or cavity.

mesiolingual (mē″zē-ō-ling′gwăl) [*mesio- + lingual*] In dentistry, pert. to the mesial and lingual surfaces of a tooth or cavity. **mesiolingually** (gwăl-ē), *adv.*

mesmerism (měs′měr-ĭzm) [Franz Anton Mesmer, Austrian physician, 1734–1815] Originally Mesmer's theory of animal magnetism, mesmerism now means therapeutics employing hypnotism or hypnotic suggestion. **mesmeric** (měs-měr′ĭk), *adj.*

mesna (měz′nă) A detoxifying agent used to inhibit the hemorrhagic cystitis induced by ifosfamide.

meso- [Gr. *mesos,* middle] **1.** Prefix *middle.* **2.** In anatomy, a prefix meaning *mesentery.* **3.** In medicine, a prefix meaning *secondary* or *partial.*

mesoappendix (měs″ō-ă-pĕn′dĭks) [Gr. *mesos,* middle, + L. *appendix,* an appendage] Mesentery of the vermiform appendix.

mesoblast (měs′ō-blăst) [″ + *blastos,* germ] Mesoderm.

mesocardia (měs′ō-kăr′dē-ă) [″ + *kardia,* heart] Location of the heart in the midline of the thorax. This position is normal in the fetal stage, but a malposition after birth.

mesocardium (měs-ō-kăr′dē-ŭm) An embryonic mesentery supporting the heart. The dorsal mesocardium connects the heart to the foregut, and the ventral mesocardium connects the heart to the central body wall.

mesocecum (měs″ō-sē′kŭm) [″ + L. *caecum,* blindness] Part of the mesentery that connects the cecum to the right iliac fossa.

mesocephalic (měs″ō-sě-făl′ĭk) [″ + *kephale,* head] **1.** Pert. to the midbrain. **2.** Having a medium-sized head, with a cranial index of 76.0 to 80.9.

mesocolon (měs″ō-kō′lŏn) [″ + *kolon,* colon] Mesentery of the colon. **mesocolic** (měs″ō-kŏl′ĭk), *adj.*

mesoderm (měs′ō-děrm) [″ + *derma,* skin] A primary germ layer of the embryo lying between ectoderm and endoderm. From it arise all connective tissues; muscular, skeletal, circulatory, lymphatic, and urogenital systems; and the linings of the body cavities. SEE: *ectoderm; endoderm.* **mesodermic, mesodermal,** *adj.*

   axial m. Portion of the mesoderm that gives rise to the notochord and prechordal plate.

   extraembryonic m. Mesoderm lying outside the embryo proper and involved in the formation of amnion, chorion, yolk sac, and body stalk.

   intermediate m. Mesoderm lying between somite and lateral mesoderm, and giving rise to embryonic and definitive kidneys and their ducts.

   lateral m. Unsegmented mesoderm lying lateral to the intermediate mesoderm. In it develops a cavity (coelom), separating it into layers (somatic and splanchnic mesoderm). SYN: *hypomere.*

   paraxial m. Mesoderm lying immediately lateral to the neural tube and notochord.

   somatic m. The outer layer of the lateral mesoderm. It becomes intimately associated with the ectoderm, forming the somatopleure, from which the ventral and lateral walls of the embryo develop.

   splanchnic m. The inner layer of the lateral mesoderm. It becomes intimately associated with the endoderm, forming the splanchnopleure, from which the gut and the lungs and their coverings arise.

mesoduodenum (měs″ō-dū″ō-dē′nŭm)

Mesentery connecting the duodenum to the abdominal wall.

mesogastrium (měs″ō-găs′trē-ŭm) [″ + *gaster*, belly] **1.** The umbilical region. **2.** The part of the mesentery of the embryo attached to the primitive stomach. **mesogastric** (-trĭk), *adj.*

mesoileum (měs″ō-ĭl′ē-ŭm) The mesentery of the ileum.

mesomelic dwarfism An autosomal dominant form of dwarfism in which short stature is accompanied by shortening of the lower legs and the forearms.

mesometrium (měs″ō-mē′trē-ŭm) **1.** The uterine musculature. **2.** The broad ligament below the mesovarium. **mesometric, mesometrial,** *adj.*

mesomorph (měs′ō-morf) A body build characterized by predominance of tissues derived from the mesoderm (i.e., muscle, bone, and connective tissues); a well-proportioned individual. SEE: *ectomorph; endomorph; somatotype.*

mesonephroma (měs″ō-nē-frō′mă) [″ + *nephros*, kidney, + *oma*, tumor] A relatively rare tumor derived from mesonephric cells developing in reproductive organs, esp. the ovary, or the genital tract.

mesonephros (mez″ō-nef′rŏs) *pl.* **mesonephroi** [*meso-* + *nephros*] A type of kidney that develops in all vertebrate embryos of classes above the Cyclostomes. It is the permanent kidney of fishes and amphibians but is replaced by the metanephros in reptiles and mammals. SYN: *archinephron; wolffian body.* SEE: *embryo; paroophoron; parovarium.* **mesonephric** (-nef′rĭk), *adj.*

mesophile (měs′ō-fīl) [″ + *philein*, to love] Organisms preferring moderate temperatures, as some bacteria, which develop best at temperatures between 15° and 43°C. **mesophilic** (měs-ō-fīl′ĭk), *adj.*

mesoporphyrin (mě″zō-pŏr′fĭr-ĭn) $C_{34}H_{38}O_4N_4$; an iron-free derivative of hemin.

mesorchium (měs-or′kē-ŭm) [″ + *orchis*, testicle] Peritoneal fold that holds the fetal testes in place.

mesorectum (měs″ō-rěk′tŭm) Mesentery of the rectum.

mesosalpinx (měs″ō-săl′pĭnks) [″ + *salpinx*, tube] The free margin of the upper division of the broad ligament within which lies the oviduct.

mesosigmoid (měs-ō-sĭg′moyd) Mesentery of the sigmoid colon.

mesosome (měs′ō-sōm) [″ + *soma*, body] In bacteria, one or more invaginations of the cell membrane, believed to contain the enzymes for cellular respiration.

mesosternum (měs″ō-stěr′nŭm) [″ + *sternon*, chest] The middle (second) section of the sternum.

mesothelioma (měs″ō-thē-lē-ō′mă) A malignant tumor derived from the mesothelial cells of the pleura, peritoneum, or pericardium. It is found most often in smokers or persons with a history of exposure to asbestos.

mesothelium (měs″ō-thē′lē-ŭm) [″ + ″ + ″] Epithelium derived from embryonic mesenchymal cells. Mesolthelium forms the serous epithelia throughout the inside of the body. **mesothelial** (měs″ō-thē′lē-ăl), *adj.*

mesovarium (měs″ō-vā′rē-ŭm) The portion of the peritoneal fold that connects the anterior border of the ovary to the posterior layer of the broad ligament.

MESS (mes) *Mangled Extremity Severity Score.*

MET *metabolic equivalent.*

meta- [Gr. *meta*, after, among, beyond, over, with] **1.** Prefix meaning *after, along with, among, behind, beyond.* **2.** In chemistry, denoting the 1,3 position of benzene derivatives. **3.** In chemistry, isomeric with or closely related to.

meta-analysis (mět′ă-ă-năl′ĭ-sĭs) The combination of data from several different research studies to gain a better overview of a topic than what was available in any single investigation. Data obtained from combined studies must be comparable and compatible for a meta-analysis to reach logical conclusions. SYN: *pooled analysis.*

metabolic (mět″ă-bŏl′ĭk) Pert. to metabolism.

metabolic activation The chemical conversion of a relatively benign substance into a more hazardous one by normal biochemical processes in cells and tissues.

metabolic body size Body weight in kilograms to the three-fourths power ($kg^{0.75}$), representative of the active tissue mass or metabolic mass of an individual.

metabolic disease A disease due to abnormal biochemistry, usually as a result of an absent or deficient enzyme. Metabolic diseases also are known as inborn errors of metabolism.

metabolic gradient SEE: under *gradient.*

metabolic rate SEE: under *rate.*

metabolic syndrome The presence of three or more of the following interrelated atherosclerotic risk factors: insulin resistance, elevated fasting blood sugar; hypertension, elevated triglyceride level, reduced high-density lipoprotein cholesterol, and abdominal obesity (increased waist circumference). This syndrome affects an estimated 40 percent of all Americans and places patients at high risk for type 2 diabetes, cardiovascular disease, and stroke. SYN: *dysmetabolic syndrome; syndrome X.*

metabolism (mě-tab′ō-lizm) [Gr. *metabolē*, a change + *-ism*] All of the energy and material transformations that occur within living cells. It includes material changes undergone by substances during all periods of life (growth, maturity, and senescence) and energy changes (transformations of chemical energy of foodstuffs to mechanical energy or heat). Metabolism involves the two fundamental processes of anabolism and catabolism. SEE: *anabolism; catabolism*. **metabolic** (met″ă-bol′ik), *adj.*

> **basal m.** The lowest level of energy expenditure, determined when the body is at complete rest. For an average person, basal metabolism is measured in various ways. In terms of large calories (Cal), measurement is about 1500 to 1800 per day; in terms of body weight, measurement is 1 Cal/kg per hour; in terms of body surface, measurement is 40 Cal/m²/hr.

> **carbohydrate m.** The sum of the physical and chemical changes involved in the breakdown and synthesis of carbohydrates in the body. Carbohydrates are digested to hexose monosaccharides that are absorbed by the small intestine; the liver converts fructose and galactose to glucose. In the liver and muscles, glucose may be converted to glycogen. In all cells, glucose is oxidized to carbon dioxide and water, with energy released in the forms of adenosine triphosphate and heat. Lactic acid, a product of the anaerobic breakdown of glucose, causes muscle fatigue.

> **constructive m.** Anabolism.

> **destructive m.** Catabolism.

> **fat m.** The sum of the physical and chemical changes involved in the breakdown and synthesis of fats in the body. Dietary fats are digested to fatty acids and glycerol in the small intestine, absorbed, and reformed into triglycerides that are transported in the form of chylomicrons. Fats may be stored in adipose tissue as potential energy or may be broken down to provide immediate energy. The liver has enzymes for the beta-oxidation of fatty acids and their use in the Krebs cycle. Fats may be formed from excess dietary carbohydrate or amino acids. Synthetic reactions produce phospholipids and steroids.

> **first-pass m.** The metabolism of a substance that occurs immediately as it enters the body, and before it can exert any effect, or before it can be measured at its target organ.

> **intermediary m.** The series of intermediate compounds formed during digestion before the final excretion or oxidation products are formed or eliminated from the body.

> **muscle m.** The consumption of energy by all cells, including those of muscle tissue, to perform work. The source of chemical energy, adenosine triphosphate (ATP), is metabolized to adeno-

sine diphosphate (ADP). If the energy requirement is short-term, the ADP is converted back to ATP. This process is too slow to keep up with energy demands during long-term exercise; thus, consumption of other fuels is required. The main sources of fuel for muscles are carbohydrates and lipids. Before being available for intracellular metabolism, glycogen is obtained when glucose is converted to glycogen. The main lipid fuel is free fatty acids present in plasma. Carbohydrates can be metabolized either in the presence of oxygen (aerobically) or in its absence (anaerobically), but lipids can be metabolized only aerobically. During light exercise or when the body is at rest, muscle metabolism is usually entirely aerobic, and the source of fuel is the free fatty acids in plasma. During intense exercise, metabolism of the fatty acids cannot keep up with the demand, and glycogen is used for energy. However, as intense exercise continues, glycogen stores are exhausted, and free fatty acids become the principal source of energy. Trained athletes have an increased ability to metabolize fatty acids as compared with sedentary people; this permits athletes to exercise longer and at higher work rates than untrained people. Athletic trainers have found that muscle glycogen stores can be increased by carbohydrate loading.

> **protein m.** The sum of the physical and chemical changes involved in the breakdown and synthesis of proteins in the body. Dietary proteins are digested to amino acids, which are absorbed by the small intestine and used to synthesize enzymes and the structural proteins essential for growth and repair of tissue. Amino acids in excess of protein synthesis requirements are deaminated; the amino group (NH_2) is removed and converted to urea, which is excreted by the kidneys. The remaining carbon chain may be converted to a simple carbohydrate and oxidized to produce energy.

> **purine m.** Metabolism involving nucleic acids, present in nuclei of cells, in which they are combined with proteins to form nucleoproteins. In the breakdown of nucleic acid, uric acid, a nitrogenous waste product, is formed.

metabolite (mě-tăb′ō-līt) Any product of metabolism.

metabolize (mě-tab′ŏ-līz″) [Gr. *metaballein*, to change] **1.** To alter the character of a food biochemically. **2.** To break down a compound to its constituents by biological mechanisms. **metabolization** (mě-tab″ŏ-lǐ-zā′shŏn), *n.*

metabolomics (mě-tăb″ă-lŏm′ĭks) [*metabolome*, the collective metabolites in an organism + ″] **1.** The study of all the metabolic processes of cells and

their impact on health and disease.
2. The study of the metabolic profile of an organism, including the identification, categorization, and quantification of its metabolites.

metabotropic (mĕ-tab″ō-trō′pik, -trop′) [*metabo(lism)* + *-tropic*] Linked to G proteins and influenced by metabolism; said of specific cell surface receptors.

metacarp-, metacarpo- [*meta-*+Gr. *karpos,* wrist] Prefixes meaning *metacarpal* or *metacarpus*.

metacarpal (mĕt″ă-kăr′păl) [Gr. *meta,* after, beyond, over, + *karpos,* wrist] **1.** Pert. to the bones of the metacarpus. **2.** Any of the bones of the metacarpus. SEE: *hand.*

metacarpophalangeal (mĕt″ă-kăr″pō-fă-lăn′jē-ăl) Concerning the metacarpus and the phalanges.

metacarpus (mĕt″ă-kăr′pŭs) [″ + *karpos,* wrist] The five metacarpal bones of the palm of the hand. SEE: *carpometacarpal.*

metacentric (mĕt″ă-sĕn′trĭk) Term indicating a chromosome with the centromere in the median position, making the arms of the chromosome equal in length.

metacercaria (mĕt″ă-sĕr-kā′rē-ă) The encysted stage in the life of a trematode. This stage occurs in an intermediate host prior to transfer to the definitive host.

metachromasia, metachromatism (mĕt″ă-krō-mā′zē-ă, -krōm′ă-tĭzm) [Gr. *meta,* change, + *chroma,* color] Histological staining in which one stain may produce a variety of colors in the tissues. The colors are different from that of the dye used. **metachromatic** (mĕt″ă-krō-măt′ĭk), *adj.*

metachromatic granule (mĕt″ă-krōmat′ĭk) SEE: under *granule.*

metachromatic leukodystrophy SEE: *leukodystrophy, metachromatic.*

metachronous (mĕ-tăk′ră-nŭs) [″ + Gr. *chronos,* time] Occurring at a different time than another similar event. The term is the antonym of *synchronous.* It is often used to describe two or more tumors of similar pathological type detected at different times within the body.

metacognition (mĕt-ă-kŏg-nĭsh′ŭn) *pl.* **metacognitions** Awareness of the knowledge one possesses and one's ability to apply that knowledge. SEE: *insight.*

metacone (mĕt′ă-kōn) [Gr. *meta,* after, beyond, over, + *konos,* cone] The distobuccal cusp of an upper molar tooth.

metaconid (mĕt-ă-kŏn′ĭd) The mesiolingual cusp of a lower molar tooth.

metaconule (mĕt-ă-kŏn′ūl) The distal intermediate cusp of an upper molar tooth.

metagenesis (mĕt″ă-jĕn′ĕ-sĭs) [″ + *genesis,* generation, birth] Alternation of generations, esp. involving regular alternation of sexual with asexual reproduction, as seen in some fungi.

Metagonimus (mĕt″ă-gŏn′ĭ-mŭs) [″ + *gonimos,* productive] A genus of flukes belonging to the family Heterophyidae.

M. yokogawai A species of intestinal flukes common in the Middle and Far East that normally infests the intestines of dogs, cats, and other animals, but is also commonly found in humans. Intermediate hosts are snails and fish, esp. a species of trout, *Plecoglossus altivelis.*

metaiodobenzylguanidine (mĕt″ă-ī-ō″dōbĕn″zĭl-gwah′nĭ-dēn″) ABBR: MIBG. A precursor of a neurotransmitter that is used for a variety of nuclear medicine studies, including the detection of neuroectodermal tumors (e.g., neuroblastoma or pheochromocytoma) and myocardial perfusion imaging.

metakinesis (mĕt″ă-kĭ-nē′sĭs) Moving apart, esp. the moving of the two chromatids of each chromosome away from each other as they move to opposite poles in the anaphase of mitosis.

metal (met′ăl) [L. *metallum,* fr. Gr. *metallon,* mine, quarry, metal] Any of a class of elements (such as gold, silver, nickel) and their alloys (such as brass, bronze), all of which are crystalline when solid and many of which are opaque, shiny, capable of conducting electrons, and can be shaped by heat and pressure. Most elements are metals.

base m. A metal that spontaneously corrodes in an electrolyte containing a less reactive metal such as gold. Examples include aluminum, brass, nickel, and steel.

noble m. A metal that resists corrosion or oxidation. Examples are gold, platinum, and silver.

transition m. One of a series of chemical elements that have properties that exhibit a change from more metallic properties (metals) to less metallic properties (nonmetals) as one moves from left to right in the periodic table of elements. For example, many of the elements between calcium and arsenic display this phenomenon, e.g., titanium, chromium, and manganese.

metalbumin (mĕt-ăl-bū′mĭn) The mucin present in ovarian cysts. SYN: *pseudomucin.*

metal fume fever SEE: under *fever.*

metallic **1.** Pert. to metal. **2.** Composed of or resembling a metal.

metallic tinkling A peculiar ringing or bell-like auscultatory sound in pneumothorax over large pulmonary cavities.

metalloenzyme (mĕ-tăl″ō-ĕn′zīm) An enzyme that contains a metal ion in its structure.

metalloid (mettă-loyd″) [*metal* + *-oid*]

An element with physical and chemical characteristics intermediate between those of metals and nonmetals, located in the periodic table at the border between metals and nonmetals. The metalloids include antimony, arsenic, boron, germanium, polonium, silicon, and tellurium. Unlike metals, which conduct electricity, metalloids are semiconductors.

metalloporphyrin (mě-tăl″ō-por′fĭ-rĭn) Porphyrin combined with a metal, such as iron to form hemoglobin, or with magnesium to form chlorophyll.

metalloprotein (mě-tăl″ō-prō′tē-ĭn) A protein bound to metal ions.

metallurgy (mět″ăl-ŭr′jē) [″ + *ergon*, work] Science of obtaining metals from their ores, refining them, and making them into various shapes and forms.

metamer (mět′ă-měr) Something similar to but different from something else (e.g., isomers of chemical compounds).

metamere (mět′ă-mēr) [Gr. *meta*, after, beyond, over, + *meros*, part] One of a series of similar segments arranged in a linear series and making up the body of an animal such as an earthworm.

metamerism (mě-tăm′ěr-ĭzm) **1.** Isomerism. **2.** Isomerism consisting of segments or metameres. **metameric** (mět-ă-měr′ĭk), *adj.*

metamorphopsia (mět″ă-mor-fŏp′sē-ă) [Gr. *meta*, after, beyond, over, + *morphe*, form, + *opsis*, vision] Distortion of vision, esp. of the central visual field.

metamyelocyte (mět″ă-mī-ĕl′ō-sīt) A transitional cell intermediate in development between a myelocyte and a mature granular leukocyte. SYN: *juvenile cell.*

metanephrine (mět″ă-něf′rĭn) An inactive metabolite of epinephrine.

metanephros (mět″ă-něf′rŏs) *pl.* **metanephroi** [″ + *nephros*, kidney] The permanent kidney of amniotes (reptiles, birds, and mammals). Part of the metanephros develops from the caudal portion of the intermediate cell mass or nephrotome; the remaining portion is derived from a bud of the mesonephric duct.

metaparadigm (mět-ă-păr-ă-dĭm′) The concepts that identify the phenomena of central interest to a discipline; the propositions that describe those concepts and their relationships to each other.

metaphase (mět′ă-fāz) [″ + *phasis*, an appearance] The second stage of mitosis in which the pairs of chromatids line up on the equator of the cell. Each pair is connected at the centromere, which is attached to a spindle fiber. Metaphase follows prophase and precedes anaphase, in which the chromatids become chromosomes and are pulled to opposite poles of the cell. SEE: *cell division* for illus; *mitosis.*

metaphysis (mě-tăf′ĭ-sĭs) *pl.* **metaphy-ses** [Gr. *meta*, after, beyond, over, + *phyein*, to grow] The portion of a developing long bone between the diaphysis, or shaft, and the epiphysis; the growing portion of a bone. **metaphyseal**, *adj.*

metaplasia (mět″ă-plā′zh(ē-)ă) [*meta-* + *-plasia*] Conversion of one kind of tissue into a form that is not normal for that tissue. **metaplastic** (-plas′tik), *adj.*
    myeloid m. Extramedullary hema-topoiesis.

metarteriole (mět″ăr-tē′rē-ōl) A small vessel connecting an arteriole to a venule from which true capillaries are given off. SYN: *precapillary.*

metastasectomy (mě-tăs″tă-sěk′tă-mē) [″ + ″] Surgical removal of cancerous growths that have spread from the original tumor to other locations around the body.

metastasis (mě-tăs′tă-sĭs) *pl.* **metastases** [″ + *stasis*, stand] **1.** Movement of bacteria or body cells (esp. cancer cells) from one part of the body to another. **2.** Change in location of a disease or of its manifestations or transfer from one organ or part to another not directly connected. SEE: illus.

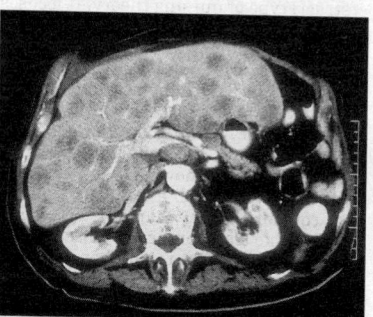

METASTASES

CT scan of liver (upper left) with round metastatic tumors (Courtesy of Harvey Hatch, MD, Curry General Hospital)

The usual application is to the manifestation of a malignancy as a secondary growth arising from the primary growth in a new location. The malignant cells may spread through the lymphatic circulation, the bloodstream, or avenues such as the cerebrospinal fluid. **metastatic** (mět″ă-stăt′ĭk), *adj.*

metastasize (mě-tăs′tă-sīz) To invade distant structures of the body. To disseminate widely.

metastatic survey (mět″ă-stăt′ĭk) Procedure in which various structures of the body are investigated, esp. by x-ray or imaging, to demonstrate any spread of cancer.

metasynthesis A technique used to gain insights from two or more thematic or categorical analyses of the same phenomenon by listing common elements in

metatarsal (mĕt″ă-tăr′săl) ABBR: MT. **1.** Concerning the metatarsal arch of the foot. **2.** Any of the bones of the metatarsus.

metatarsalgia (met″ă-tar-sal′j(ē-)ă) [*metatarsalgia* + *-algia*] Pain that emanates from the heads of the metatarsal bones and worsens with weight bearing or palpation. SEE: *Morton* **neuralgia**.

metatarsophalangeal (mĕt″ă-tăr″sŏ-fă-lăn′jē-ăl) [″ + ″ + *phalanx,* closely knit row] ABBR: MTP. Concerning the metatarsus and phalanges of the toes.

metatarsus (met″ă-tar′sŭs) [*meta-* + *tarsus*] The region of the foot between the tarsus and phalanges that includes the five metatarsal bones. SEE: *foot.*

    m. primus varus Inturning of the first metatarsal bone of the foot.

    m. varus A congenital deformity of the foot involving adduction of the forefoot. When the child walks, the foot toes in.

metatheory (mĕt″ă-thē′ă-rē, -thĕr′ē) **1.** Knowledge about a discipline. For nursing theory, it is the most global (abstract) type of nursing theory. It focuses on broad issues that address the profession's most important concepts: the relationships among human beings, health, the environment, and nursing itself. SEE: *metaparadigm.*

    2. A theory about the knowledge of a discipline, such as the nature and structure of nursing knowledge.

metathesis (mĕ-tăth′ĕ-sĭs) [″ + *thesis,* placement] **1.** A changing of places. **2.** Forcible transference of a disease process from one part to another, where it will be more accessible for treatment or where it causes less inconvenience. **3.** Double decomposition of two chemical compounds.

metatropic dwarfism A form of short-limbed dwarfism in which affected persons are born with a normal or long thorax but eventually develop kyphoscoliosis with a short trunk.

metatypical (mĕt″ă-tĭp′ĭ-kăl) Tissue elements similar to those of other tissues at the same site, but having components that are disorganized.

metazoa (mĕt″ă-zō′ă) [″ + *zoon,* animal] A term used for the multicellular animals, in contrast to unicellular forms called protozoa.

Metchnikoff theory (mech′nĭ-kof″) [Elie Metchnikoff, Russian biologist and zoologist in France, 1845–1916] The theory, developed in 1883, that the body is protected against infection by cells, such as leukocytes and phagocytes, that attack and destroy invading microorganisms. SEE: *phagocytosis.*

metencephalon (mĕt″ĕn-sĕf′ă-lŏn) [Gr. *meta,* after, beyond, over, + *enkephalos,* brain] The anterior portion of the embryonic rhombencephalon, from which the cerebellum and pons arise. SEE: *hindbrain.*

meteorism (mē′tē-or-ĭzm) [Gr. *meteorizein,* to raise up] Distention of the abdomen or intestines due to the presence of gas. SYN: *tympanites.*

meter (mēt′ĕr) [Gr. *metron,* measure] ABBR: M. A linear standard of measurement in the Système International d' Unités (SI system) that is equal to about 39.37 inches. It is the distance travelled by light in a vacuum in $\frac{1}{299,792,458}$ of a second.

-meter [Gr. *metron,* a measure] Suffix meaning *instrument for measuring.*

metestrus (met-es′trŭs) [*meta-* (3) + *estrus*] The period after estrus and before diestrus in female mammals that do not have menstrual cycles. SEE: *estrus.*

metformin (met-for′min) An oral antidiabetic agent used to treat elevated blood sugar levels in patients with type 2 diabetes mellitus. It normalizes blood sugar levels by reducing the production of glucose by the liver and by increasing sensitivity of peripheral tissues to the effects of insulin. It is a good choice for obese diabetic patients because it helps reduce body weight. On average, it lowers hemoglobin A1c levels by about 0.4%.

⚠️ This agent should not be used in patients with renal failure, because of the risk of metabolic acidosis. The most common side effect of the drug is diarrhea.

methacholine challenge test (mĕth″ă-kō′lĭn) A test for airway hyperresponsiveness, e.g., asthma or occupational asthma, in which a person is given various dilutions of the drug methacholine hydrochloride to inhale, after which spirometric measurements are taken. Decreases in the forced expiratory volume in the first second of expiration of 20% or more or decreases in specific conductance of 35% or more are indicative of airway hyper-responsiveness.

methacholine chloride (mĕth″ă-kō′lēn) A parasympathomimetic bronchoconstrictor similar to acetylcholine, used as an aerosol in different strengths in airway challenge tests.

⚠️ This substance should be used only for diagnostic purposes under the supervision of a physician trained in and thoroughly familiar with all aspects of the technique. Emergency resuscitation devices and medication should be available to treat respiratory distress.

methadone hydrochloride (mĕth′ă-dōn) A synthetic opioid analgesic with a long duration of action, used primarily to treat pain and to detoxify or maintain patients who are addicted to narcotic pain relievers. Methadone is habit-forming and subject to abuse; its use should be carefully supervised. In well-run treatment programs, its use has been associated with reductions in illegal drug use, transmission of human immunodeficiency virus, and criminal behaviors.

methamphetamine **hydrochloride** (mĕth″ăm-fĕt′ă-mēn) A sympathomimetic drug used as a stimulant or weight-loss promoter. It is a controlled substance that causes euphoria and has a high potential for abuse.

methane (meth′ān″) [*meth(yl)* + *-ane*] CH_4; a colorless, odorless, inflammable gas. It is produced as a result of putrefaction and fermentation of organic matter. It is a major component of natural gas. SYN: *marsh gas.*

methanol (mĕth′ă-nŏl) Alcohol, methyl.

methemalbumin (mĕt″hĕm-ăl-bū′mĭn) The abnormal combination of heme with albumin instead of globulin. It is present in blackwater fever (malaria complicated by massive hemolysis) and paroxysmal nocturnal hemoglobinuria.

methemoglobin (mĕt-hē′mō-glō′bĭn) [Gr. *meta,* across, + *haima,* blood, + L. *globus,* globe] SYMB: metHb. A form of hemoglobin in which the ferrous iron has been oxidized to ferric iron. Methemoglobin cannot transport oxygen. The presence of metHb in the blood may be due to toxic substances such as aniline dyes, potassium chlorate, or nitrate-contaminated water and to atypical responses to benzocaine-like analgesics, among other causes. Methemoglobin also is present in patients with a hereditary deficiency of methemoglobin reductase.

> **m. reductase** An enzyme found in significant amounts in erythrocytes that catalyzes the reduction of methemoglobin in conjunction with the coenzyme nicotine adenine dinucleotide phosphate and other enzymes.

methemoglobinemia (mĕt″hē-mō-glōb″ĭ-nē′mē-ă) [″ + ″ + ″ + *haima,* blood] The clinical condition in which more than 1% of hemoglobin in blood has been oxidized to the ferric (Fe^{3+}) form. The most common sign is cyanosis, because the oxidized hemoglobin does not transport oxygen. Very high concentrations of methemoglobin in the blood (i.e., greater than 30%) may produce dizziness, drowsiness, headache, or more severe neurological symptoms. Coma, seizures, and cardiac arrhythmias may occur with levels greater than 55%. Methylene blue is used as an antidote.

> **congenital m.** Elevated levels of methemoglobin in the blood, resulting

from one of several hereditary deficiencies of methemoglobin reductase. Affected persons may appear mildly cyanotic but are rarely symptomatic.

methene (mĕth′ēn) Methylene.

methicillin-resistant Staphylococcus aureus (mĕth″ĭ-sĭl′ĭn) ABBR: MRSA. SEE: under *Staphylococcus.*

methicillin sodium (mĕth″ĭ-sĭl′ĭn) A semisynthetic penicillinase-resistant penicillin.

methiodal sodium (mĕth-ī′ō-dăl) A radiopaque compound used in x-ray examination of the urinary tract.

methionine (mĕth-ī′ō-nīn) A sulfur-containing essential amino acid.

method (meth′ŏd) [L. *methodus,* fr Gr. *methodos,* systematic procedure] The systematic manner, procedure, or technique in performing details of an operation, tests, treatment, or any act. SEE: *algorithm; maneuver; stain; test; treatment.*

> **Abbott m.** SEE: *Abbott method.*

> **Billings m.** SEE: *Billings method.*

> **blotting m.** A technique for analyzing a tiny portion of the primary structure of genomic material (DNA or RNA).

> **caloric m.** An estimation of the total fluid and electrolyte requirements of a hospitalized patient, based on the patient's body weight, body temperature, mobility, ventilation, and other factors.

> **clean-catch m.** A procedure for obtaining a urine specimen that exposes the culture sample to minimal contamination. For females, the labia are held apart and the periurethral area is cleaned with a mild soap or antibacterial solution, rinsed with copious amounts of plain water, and dried from front to back with a dry gauze pad. The urine is then passed and the specimen collected in a sterile container. It is important that the labia be held apart and that the urine flow directly into the container without touching the skin. If possible, the sample should be obtained after the urine flow is well established, i.e., a midstream specimen. For males, the urethral meatus is cleaned and the midstream specimen is collected in a sterile container. If the male is uncircumcised, the foreskin is retracted before the penis is cleaned.

> **Credé m.** SEE: under *Credé, Carl.*

> **Delphi m.** The polling of experts in a field to reach consensus, make decisions, or disseminate knowledge. Individual specialists are organized in a virtual group, i.e., one that does not meet face-to-face in one place. They are each given a standard set of questions to answer or review. Their responses are tallied by the group's organizers, and then the preliminary data analysis is shared with all members of the group for further comments and revisions. A final report summarizing the opinions of the

group is drafted. The Delphi method is one means of publishing criteria for standards of care or the state of the art of a particular discipline in health care.

Duke m. SEE: *Duke method*.

Feldenkrais m. SEE: *Feldenkrais method*.

Fick m. SEE: under *Fick, Adolf Eugen*.

flash m. **1.** A means of pasteurizing milk by rapidly raising its temperature to 178°F (80.1°C), maintaining it there for a few minutes, and rapidly chilling it until the temperature is 40°F (4.4°C). SEE: *pasteurization*. **2.** A fast low-angle shot method of obtaining magnetic resonance images.

Ilizarow m. SEE: *Ilizarow method*.

Ivy m. SEE: *Ivy method*.

lactation amenorrhea m. ABBR: LAM. The method of causing decreased fertility in a woman by nursing a child for a lengthy period (several years or more). In general, the longer a woman breastfeeds, the longer ovulation is delayed. For this method to work, a baby must be exclusively breastfed on demand, around the clock. Once other food and drinks are added to the infant's diet, this method is not considered reliable. In addition, most breastfeeding women ovulate before their first postpartum menses and within 4 to 18 months after delivery.

Lamaze m. SEE: *Lamaze method*.

Leboyer m. SEE: *Leboyer method*.

Northern blotting m. A blot analysis technique for analyzing a small portion of RNA. Operationally, this test is identical to Southern blotting except for the target (RNA) and the specific reagents used.

rhythm m. of birth control SEE: *rhythm method of birth control*.

Southern blotting m. A technique used in molecular genetics to analyze a small portion of DNA first by purifying it, then by controlled fragmentation, electrophoretic separation, and fixing the fragment identity using specific DNA probes. It is used most commonly for G cell and T cell rearrangement analysis, bcr gene rearrangement analysis, and fragile X syndrome analysis.

Western blotting m. An electrophoretic technique for analyzing protein antigens in which proteins in a mixed specimen are moved from an electrophoretic gel to nitrocellulose, where they are analyzed. The technique is commonly used in the diagnosis of HIV/AIDS.

Ziehl-Neelsen m. SEE: *Ziehl-Neelsen method*.

methodology (měth″ō-dŏl′ō-jē) [″ + *logos*, word, reason] The system of principles and procedures used in scientific endeavors.

methotrexate (měth″ō-trĕk′sāt) An in-

hibitor of dihydrofolate reductase used to treat rheumatoid arthritis, Crohn's disease, psoriasis, and several cancers. It also has been used with misoprostol to induce abortion. Side effects from this drug include suppression of bone marrow production of blood cells and hepatitis.

methyl (měth′ĭl) [Gr. *methy,* wine + -*yl*] In organic chemistry, the radical CH_3^-, seen, for instance, in the formula for methyl alcohol, CH_3OH.

m. alcohol SEE: *methyl alcohol*.

m. mercury Methylmercury.

m. orange A dye used as a pH indicator.

m. purine An oxidation product of purine. It includes caffeine, theophylline, and theobromine. SEE: *aminopurine; oxypurine*.

m. violet A stain used in histology and bacteriology.

methylate (měth′ĭ-lāt) **1.** A compound of methyl alcohol and a base. **2.** To introduce the methyl group, CH_3, into a chemical compound. **3.** To mix with methyl alcohol.

methylation (měth″ĭ-lā′shŭn) The addition of methyl groups to a compound.

methylbenzene (měth″ĭl-běn′zēn″) [*methyl* + *benzene*] Toluene.

methylcellulose (měth″ĭl-sĕl′ū-lōs) A tasteless powder that becomes swollen and gummy when wet. Methylcellulose is used as a bulk substance in foods and laxatives and as an adhesive or emulsifier.

methylcytosine (měth″ĭl-sī′tō-sĭn) A derivative of pyrimidine present in some nucleic acids.

methylene (měth′ĭ-lēn) The chemical radical $=CH_2^-$.

methylene blue (měth′ĭ-lēn) A dark green dye available as a crystalline powder. It produces a distinct blue stain. It is used for treatment of severe methemoglobinemia.

methylglyoxal (měth″ĭl-glī-ŏk′sĭl, -awl) An aldehyde formed from the metabolic degradation of glucose. Methylglyoxal can bind to proteins and DNA, causing metabolic damage to tissues (e.g., in diabetes mellitus), mutations, or cell death.

methylhydroxychalcone polymer (měth″ĭl-hī-drok″sē-kal′kōn″) [*methyl* + *hydroxy* + *chalcone,* an aromatic ketone] ABBR: MHCP. An ingredient in cinnamon that in vitro improves insulin sensitivity.

methylmalonic acidemia (měth″ĭl-mă-lon′ik) SEE: under *acidemia*.

methylmercury, methyl mercury (mě-thĭl-mĕr′kū-rē) An organic mercury compound produced from inorganic mercury by the addition of a methyl group (CH_3) by marine and soil bacteria. This compound is readily taken up by plankton, which are then consumed by marine invertebrates, and subsequently by marine predators, in which it concentrates. Finally, it can enter the human body when people eat fish having high concentrations of the compound, such as salmon or halibut (among others). It can also be absorbed into the body through the skin and respiratory tract. Methylmercury is neurotoxic to humans, esp. children. SEE: *mercury poisoning; Minamata disease.*

methyl methacrylate (mĕth″ĭl-mĕth-ăk′crē-layt) A polymer, made from methacrylic acid, used as a bone cement, bonding agent, drug-delivery vehicle, and tissue adhesive. Its operative use is sometimes associated with hypotension, fat or air embolism, or other complications.

2-methylnaphthalene (meth″ĭl-naf′thă-lēn″) [*methyl* + *naphthalene*] $C_{11}H_{10}$, a polycyclic aromatic hydrocarbon made from coal tar. It is used in the manufacture of detergents, insecticides, solvents, and vitamins. It has been found as a contaminant in rivers and other water sources and in some food packaging.

methylparaben (mĕth″ĭl-pár′ă-bĕn) An antifungal agent used as a preservative in pharmaceuticals.

methyltransferase (meth″ĭl-trans′fĕr-ās″) An enzyme that catalyzes the transfer of a methyl group from one compound to another. SYN: *transmethylase.*

methylxanthine (mĕth″ĭl-zăn′thēn) A group of naturally occurring agents present in caffeine, theophylline, and theobromine. They act on the central nervous system, stimulate the myocardium, relax smooth muscle, and promote diuresis. A commonly prescribed methylxanthine is theophylline, which is used primarily to treat asthma and chronic obstructive pulmonary disease.

metmyoglobin (mĕt-mī″ō-glō′bĭn) Myoglobin with the ferrous ion in the heme oxidized to the ferric ion.

metol (mē′tŏl) Monomethy-*p*-aminophelol sulfate, one of two developing agents used in radiographic developing solutions. Its primary function is to act quickly to bring out the shades of gray in a radiographic image.

metonymy (mĕ-tŏn′ĭ-mē) [Gr. *meta*, after, beyond, over, + *onyma*, name] **1.** In rhetoric, a figure of speech in which one word is used for another, related one (e.g., "crown" for "king," "queen," "monarch," or "sovereign"). **2.** In psychiatry, mental confusion exhibited in some schizophrenic disorders in which an imprecise but loosely related term is used for the correct one (e.g., "rifle" for "war," or "apple" for "ball").

metopic (mē-tŏp′ĭk) [Gr. *metopon*, forehead] Relating to the forehead.

metopism (mĕt′ō-pĭzm) Persistence of the metopic suture in an adult.

metoprolol tartrate (mĕ-tŏp′ră-lŏl″, -lŏl″) A beta-1 selective beta blocker that lowers blood pressure, slows the heart rate, and reduces the heart's contractility but is less likely than nonselective beta blockers to cause wheezing. Trade names include Toprol and Toprol XL.

metria (mē′trē-ă) Inflammation of the uterus during the puerperium.

metric (me′trik) [L. *metricus*, fr Gr. *metrikos*, pert. to meter, metrical] **1.** Pert. to the meter or the metric system. **2.** A standard of measurement; a benchmark.

metrically (′tri-k(ă-)lē), *adv.*

metric system A system of weights and measures based on the meter as the unit of distance, the kilogram as the unit of mass, and the cubic meter as the unit of volume.

SEE: *Weights and Measures Appendix.*

metritis (mĕ-trī′tĭs) [Gr. *metra*, uterus, + *itis*, inflammation] Inflammation of the uterus. Metritis is designated endometritis if the endometrium is involved and myometritis if the musculature (myometrium) is involved.

chronic m. Metritis with an increase in fibrous tissue and infiltration of lymphocytes.

metrizamide (mĕ-trī′ză-mīd) A water-soluble radiographic contrast medium used to outline structures in the spinal canal during myelography. It occasionally may cause the patient to have seizures after the procedure.

¹ **metro-, metr-, metra-** [Gr. *mētra*, womb] Prefixes meaning *uterus.* SEE: *hystero-; utero-.*

² **metro-, metr-** [Gr. *metron*, a measure] Prefixes meaning *measure.*

metrology The science and technology of measurement (e.g., of body parts or chemical reagents).

metronidazole (mĕt″rō-nī′dă-zŏl) An antibiotic used to treat infections caused by *Trichomonas vaginalis, Giardia lamblia,* amebic dysentery, anaerobic bacterial infections, and colitis caused by *Clostridium difficile.*

⚠ This drug may depress the white blood cell count. Drinking alcohol while taking it may cause abdominal pain, nausea, or vomiting, as well as central nervous system symptoms such as vertigo, dizziness, and ataxia.

metrorrhagia (mē″trō-rā′jă, jē-ă) Intermenstrual bleeding. Bleeding between regular menses may be associated with either benign or malignant conditions and warrants investigation.

-metry [Gr. *metrein*, to measure, fr. *met-*

ron, a measure] Suffix meaning *to measure*.

metyrapone (mĕ-tēr′ă-pōn) A drug that inhibits adrenocortical secretion from the adrenal gland. It is used to treat excessive adrenocortical hormone secretion and to test the function of the adrenal gland.

metyrapone test One of several diagnostic tests to assess the integrity of the pituitary-adrenal axis, esp. used in the diagnosis of adrenocorticotropic hormone (ACTH) deficiencies and Cushing's disease. The drug metyrapone, which inhibits the secretion of cortisol by the adrenal glands, may be given at timed intervals during the day, or as a single nighttime dose. Depending on the method of administration, plasma levels of cortisol, 11-deoxycortisol, or ACTH, or urinary levels of 17-hydroxysteroid, are evaluated to assess the patient's response.

Metzenbaum scissors (mets′ĕn-bawm″) [M. Metzenbaum, U.S. otorhinolaryngologist, 1876–1944] A surgical scissors with a long shank, used for delicate tissue dissection.

Mev, mev *million electron volts*.

mevalonic acid (mĕv″ă-lŏn′ĭk) An intermediate compound in the metabolic processes that make cholesterol. Its synthesis is blocked by statins, medications used to lower serum lipid levels.

Meyer, Adolf (mī′ĕr) Swiss-born U.S. psychiatrist, 1866–1950. He proposed a theory of psychobiology that emphasizes the connections between occupational and social experiences and mental illness.

Meynert, Theodor H. (mī′nĕrt) Austrian neurologist, 1833–1892
  nucleus basalis of M. A nucleus with large cells in the substantia innominata. The nucleus basalis is interconnected with the amygdala, and it innervates most of the cortex of the cerebral hemisphere. Axons from this nucleus are cholinergic. The neurons in this nucleus degenerate if the brain develops Alzheimer disease. SYN: *basal nucleus; nucleus basalis*.

MFD *minimum fatal dose*.

Mg Symbol for the element magnesium.

mg *milligram*.

mgh *milligram hour*. Dosage of radiation obtained by application of 1.0 mg radium for 1 hr.

MGUS Monoclonal gammopathy of unclear significance.

MHC *major histocompatibility complex*.

mHealth The use of mobile communication devices (such as personal digital assistants, smart phones) to enhance the delivery of health care services and the technology for health care in the developing world.

mho (mō) [ohm spelled backward] Siemens.

MHz *megahertz*.

MI *myocardial infarction*.

miasm (mī′ăz-ĭm) [Gr. *miasma*, pollution, stain] In homeopathy, a toxic or noxious influence on the body, producing illness.

MIC *minimal inhibitory concentration*.

mica (mī′kă) [L. *mica*, morsel, crumb] A mineral composed of various silicates of metals. It occurs in thin, laminated scales. **micaceous** (mī-kā′shŭs), *adj*.

micella, micelle (mī-sĕl′ă, mī-sĕl′) A sphere of bile salt molecules, essential for the absorption of fatty acids in the small intestine, composed of a water-soluble exterior and a lipid-rich core.

Michigan alcoholism screening test ABBR: MAST. A questionnaire composed of 25 questions designed to determine the likelihood of a person's dependency on alcohol.

micra Pl. of micron.

micrencephalon (mī″krĕn-sĕf′ă-lon) [Gr. *mikros*, small, + *enkephalos*, brain] **1.** Cerebellum. **2.** Smallness of the brain. SEE: *cretinism*.

micrencephaly (mī″krĕn-sĕf′ă-lē) Abnormal smallness of the brain. **micrencephalous** (mī″krĕn-sĕf′ă-lŭs), *adj*.

micro-, micr- [Gr. *mikros*, small] SYMB: μ. **1.** Prefixes meaning *small, abnormally small, minute*. **2.** In the International System of Units (SI), prefixes meaning one millionth (10^{-6}), e.g., μg or 0.000001 g.

microabrasion (mī″krō-ă-brā′zhŭn) [″ + ″] The slow grinding down, polishing, or wearing away of a surface, esp. of dental enamel or rough skin.

microabscess (mī″krō-ăb′sĕs) [″ + L. *abscessus*, a going away] A very small abscess.

microadenoma (mī″krō-ad″ĕn-ō′mă) [*micro-* + *adenoma*] A tumor of the pituitary gland that is less than 1 cm in diameter.

microaerophilic (mī″krō-ā′ĕr-ō-fīl″ĭk) [″ + *aer*, air, + *philein*, to love] Growing at low amounts of oxygen; said of certain bacteria.

microaerosol (mī″krō-ĕr′ō-sŏl) A fine aerosol whose particles are of uniform size, usually less than 1 μm in diameter. Particles of this size are usually so small they pass in and out of the respiratory tract without depositing on its epithelium.

microaggregate (mī″krō-ăg′rĭ-gĭt, -gāt″) A very small amount of detectable solid material that precipitates from a saturated solution. Microaggregates found in intravenous infusions are usually caused by the incompatibility of the infused components, or by the presence of cellular fragments (e.g., in transfusion).

microalbuminuria (mī″krō-ăl″bĭn-ūr′ē-ă) The excretion of very small amounts of albumin in the urine, (too small to be detected by simple dipstick testing). The loss of 30 to 300 mg of albumin in a 24-hr urinary specimen defines microalbuminuria. In a spot urine test, microalbuminuria is defined by an albumin-to-creatinine ratio of 30 to 300.

TREATMENT: Angiotensin-converting enzyme inhibitors and angiotensin receptor blockers (and other blood pressure reducing drugs) limit urinary albumin losses.

PATIENT CARE: Patients with diabetes mellitus, in whom microalbuminuria is an indicator of progressive renal disease, should strive for optimal blood pressure and glucose control. Microalbuminuria is also a recognized risk factor for strokes, heart attacks, and death from cardiovascular diseases.

microanalysis (mī″krō-ă-nal′ĭ-sĭs) [*micro-* + *analysis*] An imprecise term for an analytical examination of minute amounts of material.

microanatomy (mī″krō-ănăt′ŏ-mē) Histology.

microaneurysm (mī″krō-ăn′ū-rĭzm) [″ + *aneurysma,* a widening] A microscopic aneurysm.

microangiopathy (mī″krō-ăn″jē-ŏp′ă-thē) [″ + *angeion,* vessel, + *pathos,* disease, suffering] Pathology of small blood vessels.

    thrombotic m. The formation of blood clots in small blood vessels, such as occurs in thrombotic thrombocytopenic purpura and hemolytic uremic syndrome.

microarray (mī″krō-ă-rā″) A biological semiconductor that uses DNA to make biochemical calculations, esp. those involving genes and the expression of mRNA by cells. SYN: *DNA m.; gene chip.*

    DNA m. Microarray.

    protein m. A laboratory tool for studying the genome or proteome of an organism, in which binding proteins are affixed to a scaffold in order to capture specific proteins from a tissue or blood sample. The captured proteins can then be analyzed individually or in aggregate.

microatelectasis (mī″krō-ăt″ĕ-lĕk′tă-sĭs) Microscopic collapse of alveoli that does not involve the airways and may not appear on radiographic examination.

microbalance (mī′krō-bal′ăns) [*micro-* + *balance*] A scale or balance for measuring very small weight (mass) changes.

microbe (mī′krōb″) [*micro-* + Gr. *bios,* life] A unicellular or small multicellular organism including bacteria, protozoa, some algae and fungi, viruses, and some worms, esp. those that are injurious to other organisms. **microbial, microbic** (mī-krō′bē-ăl, mī-krōb′ĭk), *adj.*

microbial keratitis SEE: *keratitis.*

microbial mat Biofilm.

microbicide (mī-krō′bĭ-sīd) [″ + *bios,* life, + L. *cidus,* kill] An agent that kills microscopic organisms (bacteria, fungi, and viruses). **microbicidal** (mī-krō″bĭ-sī′dăl), *adj.*

microbiology (mī″krō-bī-ŏl′ō-jē) [″ + *bios,* life, + *logos,* word, reason] The scientific study of microorganisms, that is, of bacteria, fungi, intracellular parasites, protozoans, viruses, and some worms. **microbiologic** (mī″krō-bī-ŏ-loj′ĭk), *adj.* **microbiological** (mī″krō-bī-ŏ-loj′ĭ-kăl), *adj.*

microbiostatic Bacteriostatic.

microbiota (mī″krō-bī-ō′tă) Microscopic organisms within a defined area, organism, or physiological environment. SEE: *macrobiota.* **microbiotic** (mī″krō-bī-ŏt′ĭk), *adj.*

microbleed (mī′krō-blēd″) [*micro-* + *bleed*] Leakage of a tiny amount of blood from a small blood vessel into the tissue that immediately surrounds it. It is seen as a hemosiderin deposit on magnetic resonance imaging.

microcalcification (mī″krō-kăl-sĭ-fĭ-kā′shŭn) A minute deposit of calcium in breast tissue that can be detected with a mammogram but not felt on physical examination. A grouping of microcalcifications suggests that cancer may be present in the organ.

microcentrum (mī″krō-sĕn′trŭm) [″ + *kentron,* center] The cytoplasm that contains the centrioles.

microcephalia (mī″krō-sĕf-ā′lē-ă) [″ + *kephale,* head] Microcephaly.

microcephalus (mī″krō-sĕf′ă-lŭs) Individual with an exceptionally small head.

microcephaly (mī″krō-sef′ă-lē) Abnormal smallness of head (below 1350 cc capacity) often seen in mental retardation. **microcephalic, microcephalous** (mī″krō-sĕ-fal′ĭk, mī″krō-sef′ă-lŭs), *adj.*

microchemistry (mī″krō-kĕm′ĭs-trē) [″ + *chemeia,* chemistry] Branch of chemistry analyzing specimens of minute quantity.

microchimerism (mī″krō-kī-mĭr′ĭ-zĭm, kī′mĭ-rĭz″ĭm) [″ + ″] The presence in a tissue of some cells of alien origin, e.g., of fetal cells in a pregnant woman's bloodstream.

microcinematography (mī″krō-sĭn″ĕ-mă-tŏg′ră-fē) [″ + *kinema,* motion, + *graphein,* to write] Motion pictures of microscopic objects.

microcirculation (mī″krō-sĭr″kū-lā′shŭn) Blood flow in the very small vessels (arterioles, capillaries, and venules). **microcirculatory,** *adj.*

Micrococcaceae (mī″krō-kŏk-ă′sē-ē) A family of gram-positive cocci that includes the genera *Acaricomes, Arthrobacter, Citricoccus, Kocuria, Micrococcus, Nesterenkonia, Renibacterium, Rothia, Sinomonas, Stomatococcus,* and *Zhihengliuella.*

Micrococcus (mī″krō-kŏk′ŭs) [Gr. *mik-*

ros, small, + *kokkos,* berry] A genus of gram-positive cocci; species are saprophytes found throughout the environment.

micrococcus (mī″krō-kŏk′ŭs) *pl.* **micrococci** An organism of the genus *Micrococcus.*

microcolon (mī′krō-kō″lŏn) Abnormally small colon.

microcoria (mī″krō-kō′rē-ă) [″ + *kore,* pupil] Smallness of the pupil of the eye.

microcornea (mī″krō-kŏr′nē-ă) Abnormally small cornea.

microcoulomb (mī″krō-koo′lŏm) A microunit of current electricity; one-millionth part (10^{-6}) of a coulomb.

microcrystalline (mī″krō-krĭs′tăl-īn, -ēn) Composed of microscopic crystals.

microcurie ABBR: μCi. One millionth of a curie.

microcyst (mī′krō-sĭst) A very small cyst.

microcyte (mī′krō-sīt″) A small red blood cell, having a mean corpuscular volume less than 80 fL. Common causes of microcytic anemia are iron deficiency, lead poisoning, and thalassemia. **microcytic,** *adj.*

microdebrider (mī″krō-dĕ-brēd′ĕr) An electromechanical cutting instrument used in endoscopic surgeries to remove tissues with a series of rotating blades and a suction device. This tool is often used in sinus and endobronchial procedures and other applications in which healthy tissues need to be spared while navigating inflamed or cancerous lesions.

microdeletion The loss or removal of a small amount of genetic information (a small number of nucleotides) from a chromosome.

microdialysis (mī″krō-dī-al′ĭ-sĭs) [*micro-* + *dialysis*] The sampling of extracellular fluid, e.g., in the brain, to assess the concentration of local chemical components or to perfuse drugs directly into small clusters of cells.

microdissection (mī″krō-di-sek′shŏn) [*micro-* + *dissection*] Dissection with the aid of a microscope, esp. by use of a micromanipulator.

   laser capture m. The collection of selected cell groups from tissue sections for analysis, e.g., of morphological or genetic characteristics.

   laser m. The combined use of lasers (for cutting or heating tissue) and microscopy (for identification of cells of interest) to obtain small, pure samples of tumor cells and other cell-rich specimens for analysis.

microdontia (mī″krō-dŏn′shē-ă) [″ + *odous,* tooth] Having abnormally small teeth or a single small tooth.

microdrop (mī′krō-drŏp″) **1.** A tiny drop of fluid. **2.** One sixtieth of a milliliter (mL).

microelectrophoresis (mī″krō-ĕ-lĕk″trō-fō-rē′sĭs) Electrophoresis of minute quantities of a solution.

microembolus (mī″krō-ĕm′bō-lŭs) *pl.* **microemboli** [″ + *embolos,* plug] A tiny embolus, made up of small clumps of platelets, fat, tumor cells, or intravascular debris.

microencapsulation (mī″krō-ĕn-kăp″sū-lā′shŭn) Insertion of a drug or other active substance within a coating to improve the delivery of the active agent to a particular organ or tissue.

microencephaly (mī″krō-ĕn-sĕf′ă-lē) [″ + *enkephalos,* brain] Micrencephaly.

microenvironment (mī″krō-ĕn-vī′rŏn-mĕnt) The environment at the microscopic or cellular level.

microfarad (mī-krō-făr′ăd) A microunit of electrical capacity; one millionth of a farad.

microfauna (mī″krō-faw′nă) In a specific location, the animal life that is microscopic in size.

microfibril (mī″krō-fī′brĭl) A very small fibril.

microfiche (mī′krō-fēsh″) [Gr. *mikros,* small, + Fr. *fiche,* index card] A sheet of microfilm that enables a large number of library data and medical records to be stored in a small space.

microfilament (mī″krō-fĭl′ă-mĕnt) Fibrils of the protein actin that form the cytoskeleton, which provides support and contributes to cellular movement.

microfilaremia (mī″krō-fĭl″ă-rē′mē-ă) Presence of microfilariae in the blood.

microfilaria (mī″krō-fĭ-lar′ē-ă, -lar′ē-ē″) *pl.* **microfilariae** [*micro-* + *filaria*] The embryo of a filarial worm. Microfilariae are present in the blood and tissues of those infected with filariasis and are of importance in the diagnosis of filarial infections. **microfilarial** (-lar′ē-ăl), *adj.*

microfilm (mī′krō-fĭlm″) A film containing a greatly reduced photoimage of printed or graphic matter.

microflora (mī″krō-flō′ră) In a specific area, the plant life that is microscopic in size.

microform (mī′krō-fŏrm″) [″ + ″] An incomplete or minor expression of a trait or illness.

microgamete (mī-krō-găm′ēt) [″ + *gametes,* spouse] Male reproductive cell in conjugation of protozoa.

microgastria (mī″krō-găs′trē-ă) [″ + *gaster,* stomach] Unusual smallness of the stomach.

microgenia (mī″krō-jĕn′ē-ă) [″ + *geneion,* chin] Abnormal smallness of the chin.

microglia (mī-krŏg′lē-ă) [″ + *glia,* glue] Cells of the central nervous system (CNS) present between neurons or next to capillaries. These cells may function as macrophages when they migrate to damaged CNS tissue. SEE: *gitter cell;* illus.

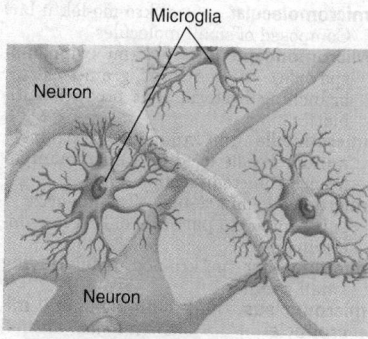

Microglia

Neuron

Neuron

MICROGLIA

microglioma (mī″krō-glī-ō′mă) [″ + ″ + *oma,* tumor] A tumor composed of microglial cells.

microglossia (mī-krō-glŏs′ē-ă) [″ + *glossa,* tongue] Abnormally small tongue.

micrognathia (mī-krō-nā′thē-ă) [″ + *gnathos,* jaw] Abnormal smallness of jaws, esp. the lower jaw.

microgram (mī′krō-grăm) ABBR: μg or mcg. One-millionth part of a gram; one-thousandth part of a milligram.

micrograph (mī′krō-grăf) [Gr. *mikros,* small, + *graphein,* to write] **1.** Apparatus for magnifying and recording minute movements. **2.** Photograph of an object seen through a microscope. SYN: *photomicrograph.*

micrography (mī-krŏg′ră-fē) **1.** Study of the physical appearance and characteristics of microscopic objects. **2.** Study of an object by use of a microscope.

microgyria (mī-krō-jīr′ē-ă) [″ + *gyros,* circle] Abnormal smallness of cerebral convolutions.

microgyrus (mī″krō-jī′rŭs) [″ + *gyros,* circle] A small, malformed gyrus of the brain.

microhematuria (mī″krō-hē-mă-tŭr′ē-ă) Microscopic hematuria.

microhm (mī′krōm) A microunit of electrical resistance; one-millionth of an ohm.

microincineration (mī″krō-ĭn-sĭn-ĕr-ā′shŭn) Determination of the presence and distribution of inorganic matter in tissues by subjecting a microscopic section of tissue to high temperatures, which destroys organic matter and leaves mineral matter as ash.

microinjection (mī′krō-ĭn-jĕk″shŭn) Injection of substances into cells or minute vessels by means of a micropipette.

microinvasion (mī″krō-ĭn-vā′zhŭn) Invasion of the tissue adjacent to a carcinoma in situ. **microinvasive,** *adj.*

microkeratome (mī″krō-kĕr′ă-tōm) A tool used in ophthalmology to remove a precisely measured depth of cornea.

microleakage (mī′krō-lē″kăj) The microscopic seepage of oral fluids between the interface of the tooth and a dental restoration. Microleakage may lead to sensitivity or discoloration of the tooth. Caused by discrepancies between the coefficient of thermal expansion of the tooth structure and the restorative material, microleakage is an inherent weakness of many restorative materials, although it is minimal with glass ionomer and polycarboxylate cements.

microlesion (mī″krō-lē′zhŭn) A very small lesion.

microliter (mī′krō-lē″tĕr) ABBR: μl. One-millionth part of a liter; i.e., 10^{-6} L.

microlith (mī′krō-lith″) [*micro-* + Gr. *lithos,* stone] A microscopic calculus or concretion (< 2 mm in diameter).

microlithiasis (mī″krō-lith-ī′ă-sĭs) [*microlith* + *-iasis*] The development of microliths within tissues. Microlithiasis is found in the gallbladder in some patients with otherwise unexplained pancreatitis.

    pulmonary alveolar m. Microlithiasis throughout the lungs.

    testicular m. Microlithiasis within the testicles. Although rarely identified during ultrasound examinations of the testes, this condition is clinically important, because it is often associated with testicular cancer.

micromanipulation (mī″krō-mă-nĭp″yū-lā′shŏn) [micro- + manipulation] The use of minute instruments and magnification aids to perform surgical or other procedures on cells or tissues. SEE: *gene splicing; micromanipulator; microsurgery.* **micromanipulative** (-nĭp′yū-lā″tiv), *adj.*

micromanipulator (mī″krō-mă-nĭp′ū-lā-tŏr) An apparatus by which extremely minute pipettes or needles can be manipulated under a microscope for microdissection, microinjection, or microsurgery.

micromechanical system (mī″krō-mĕ-kăn′ĭ-kĭl) ABBR: MEMS. Any miniature electromechanical device implanted into a prosthesis used to determine if the implanted body part is functioning optimally, e.g., tolerating body temperature, load, or pressure or other forms of biological stress. Micromechanical systems are biological sensors that transmit data obtained from within body parts via radio waves to a receiver located outside the body. They have been used as adjuncts to surgery, to identify subtle bleeding from aneurysms or endografts, or to indicate when orthopedic implants are failing or likely to fail.

micromelia (mī″krō-mē′lē-ă) [″ + *melos,* limb] Abnormally small or short limbs.

micromere (mī′krō-mĕr) [″ + *meros,* part] A small blastomere.

micrometastasis (mī″krō-mĕ-tas′tă-sĭs, ′tă-sēz″) *pl.* **micrometastases** [*micro-*

+ *metastasis*] Any of the foci of tumor cells that are invisible to the naked eye or by routine imaging techniques but may be seen using microscopy with special stains or antibodies or by other laboratory techniques.

¹ **micrometer** (mī-krŏm-mēt-ĕr) [*micro-* + *-meter*] ABBR: μm. One millionth of a meter (10^{-6}); one thousandth of a millimeter (0.001 mm). It was formerly called a *micron*.

² **micrometer** (mī-krŏm'ĕt-ĕr) [*micro-* + *-meter*] A device used for measuring small lengths, i.e., those not visible to the naked eye.

micromethod (mī″krō-mĕth'ŏd) Any chemical or physical procedure involving small amounts of material or tissue.

micrometry (mī-krŏm'ĕ-trē) [″ + *metron*, measure] Use of device, esp. a micrometer, to measure small objects or thickness.

micromicro- (μμ) Prefix formerly used to indicate one trillionth (10^{-12}). The term currently used is *pico*.

micromole (mī′krō-mōl) One millionth, 10^{-6}, of a mole. SEE: *mole* (1).

micromolecular (mī″krō-mō-lĕk′ū-lăr) Composed of small molecules.

Micromonospora (mī″krō-mŏn-ă-spawr′ă) A genus of gram-positive, branching bacteria that produce antibiotics.

microneedle (mī′krō-nē″dl) Extremely minute needle used in a micromanipulator for microdissection.

micronize (mī′krō-nīz) To pulverize a substance into particles only a few micra in size.

micronodular (mī″krō-nŏd′ū-lăr) Having small nodules.

micronucleus (mī-krō-nū′klē-ŭs) *pl.* **micronuclei** (″ + L. *nucleus*, kernel] **1.** A small nucleus. **2.** The smaller of the two nuclei of ciliated protozoa; it contains the chromosomes.

micronutrient (mī″krō-nū′trē-ĕnt) A vitamin or mineral required by the body in very small amounts (micrograms or milligrams daily), such as beta carotene, biotin, chromium, copper, folate, manganese, and selenium. SEE: table.

microorganism (mī″krō-or′gă-nĭzm) [*micro-* + *organism*] A living organ-

Micronutrients, Sources, and Deficiency Diseases

Nutrient	Results of Deficiency	Artificial Sources	Natural Sources
Biotin	Dermatitis, hair loss; neuropsychiatric symptoms	Dietary supplements	Swiss chard; raw egg yolks; cow's milk; liver; peanuts
Folate	Neural tube defects; macrocytic anemia	Fortified cereals; dietary supplements	Fruits & vegetables
Iodine	Brain damage/ intellectual disability in developing children (cretinism)	Additive to salt	Fish, seafood, seaweed (kelp)
Iron	Iron-deficiency anemia; mental impairment in children	Additive to salt ("double-fortified salt"); dietary supplements	Green, leafy vegetables; red meats; almonds; bran; beans; egg yolk; and others
Manganese	Possible impact on bone and joint disease; seizure disorders; skin diseases and impaired wound healing	Dietary supplements	Green, leafy vegetables; fruits, nuts; teas; whole grains
Selenium	Rare cause of: hypothyroidism, impaired immunity	Dietary supplements	Corn, soybean, wheat, brazil nuts
Vitamin A & other carotenoids	Blindness/low vision; increased child mortality	Milk and fortified foods	Liver, whole milk, palm oil, sweet potatoes
Zinc	Diarrheal illnesses, impaired immunity, and impaired wound healing	Added to oral rehydration solutions and crop fertilizers	Oysters (and other seafood), meats, nuts, whole grains, & beans

ism too small to be perceived with the naked eye, esp. a virus, bacterium, fungus, protozoan, or intracellular parasite, and some helminths. SYN: *germ; microbe.*

pathogenic m. Any microorganism capable of injuring its host, e.g., by competing with it for metabolic resources, destroying its cells or tissues, or secreting toxins. The injurious microorganisms include viruses, bacteria, mycobacteria, fungi, protozoa, and some helminths. Pathogenic microorganisms may be carried from one host to another as follows: *Animal sources:* Some organisms are pathogenic for animals as well as humans and may be communicated to humans through direct or indirect contact. *Airborne:* Pathogenic microorganisms such as rhinoviruses, mycobacteria, or varicella may be discharged into the air, from which infectious droplets may be inhaled by exposed persons. *Bloodborne:* Infections such as cytomegalovirus, hepatitis B or C, HIV/AIDS, malaria, or West Nile virus may be spread from person-to-person by injection drug use, organ transplantation, or transfusion. *Contact infections:* Direct transmission of microorganisms can occur by skin-to-skin or intimate body contact, as in many sexually transmitted diseases. *Foodborne:* Food and water may contain pathogenic organisms acquired from the handling of the food by infected persons or through fecal or insect contamination. *Fomites:* Inanimate objects such as linens, books, cooking utensils, or clothing that can harbor microorganisms and could serve to transport them from one location to another. *Human carriers:* Asymptomatic individuals (e.g., "typhoid Mary") may harbor microorganisms without injury but transmit disease to others. *Arthropod vectors:* Insects, ticks, fleas, mosquitoes, and mites may transmit diseases by biting their hosts and depositing microorganisms into the blood. *Soilborne:* Spore-forming organisms (e.g., tetanus) in the soil may enter the body through a cut or wound. Vegetables and fruits, esp. root crops, may transmit microorganisms to the gastrointestinal tract.

PATIENT CARE: In health care settings such as clinics, hospitals, nursing homes and care facilities, hand hygiene before and after patient contact can do more than any other intervention to limit the spread of pathogenic microorganisms to patients. Hand hygiene is also the most effective preventive measure in the home and should be taught when handling food, after using the toilet, after handling nasal secretions or sputum, and before or after providing care to children, sick relatives, or other close contacts who have transmissible illnesses or risk factors (such as immune-suppressing illnesses) that predispose them to infection. Vaccination is another potent tool against the spread of pathogenic microorganisms, as is quarantine or "social distancing."

micropannus (mī″krō-păn″ŭs) Pathological condition in which abnormal vessels and fibrous tissue infiltrate the cornea. SEE: *pannus.*

microparasite (mī″krō-păr′ă-sīt) A parasitic microorganism.

microparticle (mī″krō-part′ĭ-kĕl) [*micro- + particle*] ABBR: MP. **1.** A microscopic particle. **2.** A fragment of cytoplasm and cell membrane, released into the circulation when the cell is injured.

micropathology (mī″krō-păth-ŏl′ō-jē) [Gr. *mikros,* small, + *pathos,* disease, + *logos,* word, reason] The study of disease caused by microorganisms.

micropenis (mī″krō-pē′nĭs) An abnormally small penis. SYN: *microphallus.*

microphage, microphagus (mī′krō-fāj, mī-krŏf′ă-gŭs) [″ + *phagein,* to eat] A small phagocyte.

microphakia (mī″krō-fā′kē-ă) [″ + *phakos,* lens] Abnormally small crystalline lens. SYN: *microlentia.*

microphallus (mī-krō-făl′ŭs) [″ + *phallos,* penis] Micropenis.

microphone (mī′krō-fōn) [″ + *phone,* voice] Device for detecting and converting sound energy into an electronic signal, which is then transmitted.

microphotograph (mī″krō-fō′tō-grăf) [″ + *phos,* light, + *graphein,* to write] **1.** A photograph of extremely small size. **2.** A photograph on microfilm. **3.** Photomicrograph.

microphthalmia, microphthalmus (mī-krŏf-thăl′mē-ă, -mŭs) [″ + *ophthalmos,* eye] Abnormally small size of one or both eyes.

micropipette, micropipet (mī′krō-pī-pĕt) An extremely small pipette used for measuring small amounts of fluid substances.

microplate (mī′krō-plāt″) [*micro- + plate*] **1.** An anchoring device to hold tissues together or to hold implants placed during neurosurgery. **2.** A stimulatory electrode device implanted in the brain.

micropolitan area A small city, i.e., one with a population of 10,000 to 49,999 people.

microprobe (mī′krō-prōb) A very small probe, suitable for use in microsurgery.

microprojection (mī″krō-prō-jĕk′shŭn) Projection of images of microscopic objects upon a screen.

micropsia (mī-krŏp′sē-ă) [″ + *opsis,* vision] Visual disorder in which objects seem smaller than they actually are. It is seen in paralysis of accommodation, retinitis, and choroiditis.

micropuncture (mī″krō-pŭnk′chŭr) A

very small incision or puncture of a structure such as a single cell.

micropus (mī-krō′pŭs) [″ + *pous*, feet] One with unusually small feet.

micropyle (mī′krō-pīl) [″ + *pyle*, gate] The opening in the ovum for entrance of the spermatozoon. It is seen in the ova of some animals.

microradiography (mī″krō-rā″dē-ŏg′ră-fē) Technique of x-raying microscopic objects. The pictures are usually enlarged.

microrespirometer (mī″krō-rĕs″pĭ-rŏm′ĕ-tĕr) Device for measuring oxygen consumption of minute amounts of tissue.

microRNA (mī′krō-ăr′ĕn″ā′) [″ + ″] ABBR: miRNA. Oligonucleotides that prevent a variety of messenger RNAs from being transcribed from DNA or translated into proteins. They typically consist of 21 to 25 linked nucleotides.

microsampling (mī′krō-sam″pling) [*micro-* + *sampling*] Performing a laboratory analysis on a very small amount of blood or tissue. **microsample** (mī′krō-sam″pĕl), *n*.

microscope (mī′krŏ-skōp″) [*micro-* + *-scope*] An optical instrument that greatly magnifies minute objects. **microscopic, microscopical** (mī″krŏ-skŏp′ĭk, mī″krŏ-skŏp′ĭ-kăl), *adj*.

 binocular m. A microscope possessing two eyepieces or oculars.

 compound m. A microscope with two or more objective lenses with different magnifications.

 dark-field m. A microscope by which objects invisible through an ordinary microscope may be seen by means of powerful side illumination. SEE: *illumination, dark-field*.

 electron m. A microscope that uses streams of electrons deflected from their course by an electrostatic or electromagnetic field for the magnification of objects. The final image is viewed on a fluorescent screen or recorded on a photographic plate. Because of greater resolution, images may be magnified up to 400,000 diameters. SEE: *scanning electron m*.

 light m. A microscope that uses visible light to allow viewing of the object.

 operating m. A microscope designed for use during surgery involving small tissue such as nerves, vessels, the inner ear, eye, or fallopian tubes. SEE: *microsurgery*.

 phase m. A compound microscope to which a diffraction or phase plate and a specialized condenser diaphragm have been added. These make it possible to view details of objects characterized by differences in refractive index and thus delineate a change of phase, such as brightness or color. This microscope is particularly useful for viewing living cells and observing cytoplasmic organelles.

 polarization m. A microscope for examining specimens that polarize light or have double refraction.

 scanning electron m. ABBR: SEM. An electron microscope that scans an object point by point and displays the image on film or digitally. It scans the specimen with a beam of electrons that reveal its three-dimensional topography and other characteristics. Its magnification ranges from 20 to 100,000 times.

 simple m. A microscope with a single magnifying lens.

 slit-lamp m. A microscope with slit illumination for examining the eye, esp. the cornea.

 specular m. A camera that takes high-magnification images of the cellular layer of the inner surface of the cornea. It is used, e.g., to evaluate the healing of the corneal epithelium after corneal injury or corneal surgery ("keratectomy").

 stereoscopic m. A binocular microscope with an objective lens for each eyepiece, permitting objects to be viewed stereoscopically.

 ultraviolet m. A microscope using ultraviolet radiations as a light source and having an optical system for transmitting them. Used in observing specimens that fluoresce, such as tissues stained with a fluorescent dye.

 x-ray m. A microscope using x-rays to reveal the structure of objects through which light cannot pass. The image is usually reproduced on film.

microscopic colitis SEE: under *colitis*.

microscopy (mī″kros′kŏ-pē) [*micro-* + *-scopy*] Inspection with a microscope.

 confocal m. Microscopy that permits high-resolution analysis of serial optical sections (microscopic tomograms) into the depths of tissues or cells.

 epiluminescence m. Dermatoscopy.

 multiphoton m. ABBR: MPM. A means of imaging tissues deep within the body by infrared fluorescence. The technique relies on the absorption of two photons directed into tissues by a pulsed infrared laser. It can be applied to the visualization of tissues beneath the body surface and to optical biopsy.

 video m. The use of movie-making techniques, such as time-lapse photography, to obtain highly magnified microscopic images of tissues, thereby allowing observation of cellular processes as they occur.

microsecond (mī′krō-sĕk″ŭnd) One-millionth (10^{-6}) of a second.

microsmatic (mī″krŏs-măt′ĭk) [″ + *osmasthai*, to smell] Having a poorly developed sense of smell.

microsomal ethanol oxidizing system (mī′krō-sōm′ăl) ABBR: MEOS. A hepatic enzyme system that catabolizes drugs and other potentially toxic substances. Ethanol ingested in relatively small amounts is catabolized by the hepatic enzyme alcohol dehydrogenase. Whenever ingested amounts of ethanol are large enough to overcome or deplete the alcohol dehydrogenase system, the MEOS becomes the major route for ethanol catabolism. Ethanol breakdown by the MEOS is not thought to produce as much energy as alcohol dehydrogenase breakdown, resulting in less weight gain than would be expected from the ethanol calories consumed.

microsome (mī'krō-sōm) Ribosome.

microspectrophotometry (mī"krō-spĕk"trō-fō-tŏm'ĕ-trē) Method for the histochemical study of substances present in cells, such as nucleic acid, based on absorption in the ultraviolet spectrum. This method permits quantitative and qualitative studies of certain cellular components.

microspectroscope (mī"krō-spĕk'trō-skōp) [" + L. *spectrum,* image, + Gr. *skopein,* to examine] A combined spectroscope and microscope.

microsphere (mī'krō-sfēr) Minute container suitable for implantation or injection into the body or circulatory system. Microspheres may be used for delivering medicines to certain sites or, if radioactive, to study the blood flow to an area. If microspheres are used as a drug-delivery system, the container is designed to be dissolved in body fluids.

magnetic m. Microscopic magnetic particles that are used experimentally in autologous bone marrow transplant. The particles are coated with or coupled to antibodies and exposed to certain types of malignant cells in order to bind to them. The microspheres so bound can be removed by passing the cells through a magnetic field.

microspherocytosis (mī"krō-sfē"rō-sī-tō'sĭs) [" + " + *osis,* condition] Spherocytosis; marked by an excessive number of microspherocytes.

microsporid (mī-krŏs'pō-rĭd) A skin eruption distant from the site of infection with *Microsporum* and due to hypersensitivity to the organism.

microsporidiosis (mī"krō-spō-rĭd"ē-ō'sĭs) Intracellular spore-forming protozoa that infect many animals and are known to cause human disease, esp. in those with AIDS. The genera of microsporidia implicated are *Encephalitozoon, Pleistophora, Septata, Nosema,* and *Enterocytozoon.* They cause a variety of pathological conditions, including diarrhea, wasting, keratoconjunctivitis, peritonitis, myositis, and hepatitis.

microsporosis (mī"krō-spō-rō'sĭs) Ringworm infection due to fungi of the genus *Microsporum.*

Microsporum (mī"krŏs'por-ŭm) A genus of fungi that causes disease of the skin, hair, and nails.

M. audouinii The causative agent of tinea capitis (ringworm of scalp).

M. canis The causative agent of ringworm in cats and dogs. It may be easily transmitted to children.

M. gypseum A dermatophyte species that like other Microsporum species, causes ringworm.

microstomia (mī-krō-stō'mē-ă) [" + *stoma,* mouth] Abnormal smallness of the mouth.

microstrabismus (mī"krō-stră-bĭs'mŭs) [" + *strabismos,* a squinting] Movement of the eyes in divergent directions or at different speeds. These movements are too small and too quick to be seen, but they have been detected through analysis of high-speed motion pictures.

microstreaming (mī"krō-strēm'ĭng) The flow of interstitial fluids, or the pulsation of tissue particles associated with the application of therapeutic ultrasound. In physical medicine, microstreaming can promote soft-tissue healing. In dentistry, it is used in the removal of plaque and scale. SEE: *cavitation.*

microsurgery (mī"krō-sŭr"jĕ-rē) Surgery in which various types of magnification, specialized instrumentation, fine sutures, and meticulous techniques are used to repair, anastomose, or restore delicate tissues.

microthrombus (mī"krō-thrŏm'bŭs) [" + "] A microscopic clump of fibrin, platelets, and red blood cells.

microtia (mī-krō'shē-ă) [" + *ous,* ear] Unusually small size of the auricle or external ear.

microtome (mī'krō-tōm) [" + *tome,* incision] Instrument for preparing thin sections of tissue for microscopic study.

freezing m. Microtome equipped to cut frozen tissues.

sliding m. Microtome in which the tissue being sectioned slides along a track.

microtomy (mī-krŏt'ō-mē) The process of incising thin sections of tissues.

microtrauma (mī"krō-traw'mă) A very small injury.

microtropia (mī"krō-trō'pē-ă) [" + *trope,* a turning] Strabismus with very small deviation, usually less than 4°.

microtubule (mī"krō-tū'būl) An elongated (200 to 300 Å), hollow or tubular structure present in the cell. Microtubules are important in helping certain cells maintain their rigidity, in converting chemical energy into work, and in providing a means of transporting substances in different directions within a cell. They increase in number during mitosis.

microtus (mī-krō'tŭs) [" + *ous,* ear] A person with abnormally small ears.

microvasculature (mī"krō-văs'kū-lă-chur) The smallest arterioles and venules, and the capillary networks of the body. **microvascular** (mī″krō-văs′kū-lăr), *adj.*

microvillus (mī″krō-vĭl′ŭs) *pl.* **microvilli** [L., tuft of hair] A microscopic fold of the free surface of a cell membrane. Microvilli greatly increase the exposed surface area of the cell. SEE: *border, brush.*

microvillus inclusion disease A rare congenital disorder in which newborns or infants develop severe watery diarrhea (caused by intestinal malabsorption) resulting in dehydration, metabolic disarray, and malnutrition. It can be treated with small bowel transplantation when donor organs are available. SYN: *microvillous **atrophy.***

microvolt (mī′krō-vōlt) One millionth of a volt.

microwave (mī′krō-wāv) That portion of the radio wave spectrum between a wavelength of 1 mm and 30 cm.

microwave ablation, microwave tissue ablation Microwave coagulation therapy.

microwave coagulation therapy ABBR: MCT. The use of locally applied microwave energy to coagulate and destroy diseased tissues, e.g., in the cardiac conduction system, the endometrium, the liver, or prostate. SYN: *microwave ablation.*

microwave oven An oven that uses microwave energy for cooking or heating food.

⚠ Food prepared or reheated in a microwave should be tested with a thermometer to make certain it has reached the lethal temperature for potentially hazardous microorganisms.

Micruris fulvius (mĭ-kroo′rĭs fool′vĭ-ŭs) The scientific name for the eastern coral snake, a venomous snake of the Elapidae family.

Micrurus (mī-kroor′ŭs) [*micro-* + L. *-urus,* fr Gr. *oura,* tail] A genus of small venomous snakes of the family *Elapidae* including the coral snakes and found in the southern U.S. and tropical America.

miction (mĭk′shŭn) Urination.

micturate (mĭk′tū-rāt) [L. *micturire*] To pass urine from the bladder. SYN: *urinate.*

micturition (mĭk-tū-rĭ′shŭn) Urination.

micturition syncope SEE: *syncope, micturition.*

MICU *medical intensive care unit.*

MID *minimum infective dose.*

midbody (mĭd′bŏd-ē) Microtubules that appear as a granule between daughter cells during telophase of mitosis.

midbrain (mĭd′brān) [AS. *mid,* middle, + *braegen,* brain] The corpora quadrigemina, the crura cerebri, and aqueduct of Sylvius, which connect the pons and cerebellum with the hemispheres of the cerebrum. It contains reflex centers for eye and head movements in response to visual and auditory stimuli. SYN: *mesencephalon.*

MIDCAB (mid′kab″) [Acronym for *m(inimally) i(nvasive) d(irect) c(oronary) a(rtery) b(ypass)*] An alternative to coronary artery bypass graft surgery (CABG) performed via a sternotomy. In conventional CABG, the aorta is cannulated, the heart is chilled, and the patient's blood is routed through a perfusion pump that oxygenates the blood outside the body and then recirculates it to the patient. In MIDCAB by contrast, a small incision is made between the ribs (instead of dividing the sternum), and only those arteries easily accessible on the anterior of the heart, e.g., the left anterior descending artery, are bypassed. Because of the smaller incision made in this procedure, it is sometimes referred to as cardiac*keyhole surgery.*

midcarpal (mĭd-kăr′păl) Between the two rows of carpal bones.

midclavicular (mĭd″klă-vĭk′ū-lĕr) [mid + ″] In the middle of the clavicle.

middle lobe syndrome Atelectasis, bronchiectasis, or chronic pneumonitis of the middle lobe of the right lung, possibly due to calcified lymph nodes compressing the right middle lobe bronchus.

middle-molecular-weight solute Middle molecule.

middle molecule A molecule having a size of at least 500 daltons (Da) and no more than 30,000 Da, presumed to be an endogenous poison that accumulates in the body of patients with chronic kidney disease or uremia. Clearance of these molecules is a goal of hemodialysis. SYN: *middle-molecular-weight solute.*

middle-old (mid′ĕl-ōld″) Between 75 and 85 years old.

midfoot The area of the foot surrounding the cuboid, cuneiform, and navicular bones that lies between the forefoot and hindfoot.

midge (mĭj) [ME. *migge*] Small, gnat-like flies including those from the families Chironomidae and Ceratopogonidae. Some cause painful bites.

midget (mĭj′ĭt) A nontechnical term for a very small person; an adult who is perfectly formed but has not attained and will not attain normal size.

midgut (mĭd-gŭt′) [AS. *mid,* middle, + *gut,* intestine] The middle section of the embryonic gut tube; the caudal section of the duodenum, the jejunum, the ileum, the caecum (and appendix), the ascending colon (and approx. two thirds of the transverse intestine develop from the midgut.

midlife (mĭd′līf) Denoting (approximately) the ages from 35 to 55 years.

midline (mĭd′līn) Any line that bisects a

structure that is bilaterally symmetrical.

midplane (mĭd′plān) **1.** The plane bisecting a symmetrical structure; the median plane. **2.** In obstetrics, the plane of least dimensions in the pelvic outlet.

midriff (mĭd′rĭf) [″ + *hrif,* belly] The diaphragm; the middle region of the torso.

midsection (mĭd-sĕk′shŭn) [″ + L. *secare,* to cut] A section through the middle of a structure.

midstream specimen of urine A urine specimen collected after the first few milliliters of urine are voided and discarded. SEE: *clean-catch* **method**.

midtarsal (mĭd-tär′săl) Between the two rows of bones that make up the tarsus of the foot.

midwife (mĭd′wīf) [″ + *wif,* wife] Nurse midwife.

midwifery (mĭd-wīf′ĕr-ē) The practice of assisting at childbirth. SEE: *obstetrics*.

Midwives Alliance of North America ABBR: MANA. A professional certification and advocacy group for midwives and midwifery care, students of midwifery, and their supporters.

MIF *maximum inspiratory force.*

mifepristone (mĭf′ĕ-prĭs′tōn) An abortifacient drug that blocks the action of progesterone. It is not used more than 47 days after the last menstrual period. A prostaglandin is administered by injection or as a suppository as an adjunct.

migraine (mī′grān″) [Fr. fr L. *hemicrania,* fr Gr. *hemikrania,* (headache in) half (of the) skull] A familial disorder marked by periodic, usually unilateral, pulsatile headaches that begin in childhood or early adult life and tend to recur with diminishing frequency in later life. Migraine consists of two closely related syndromes: classic migraine (migraine with aura) and common migraine (migraine without aura). The classic type may begin with aura, which consists of episodes of well-defined, transient focal neurologic dysfunction that develops over the course of minutes and may last an hour. Visual symptoms include seeing stripes, spots, or lines and scotomata. In most people, the aura precedes the headache; however, occasionally the aura will appear or recur at the height of the headache. Before the onset of symptoms, some people experience mood changes, fatigue, difficulty thinking, depression, sleepiness, hunger, thirst, urinary frequency, or altered libido. Others report a feeling of well-being, increased energy, clarity of thought, and increased appetite, esp. for sweets. The headache follows. Pain is usually confined on one side but is occasionally bilateral. Nausea and vomiting may be present and may last a few hours or a day or two. Common migraine has a similar onset with or without nausea. Sensitivity to light and noise is present in both types. Migraine is a common problem that affects about 30 million Americans, three times as many females as males. During their reproductive years, women experience a much higher rate of migraine, and their headaches tend to occur during periods of premenstrual tension and fluid retention. Many patients link their attacks to ingesting certain foods, exposure to glare, or to sudden changes in barometric pressure. SYN: *migraine headache*.

ETIOLOGY: A family history of migraine will be found in over 70% of patients. Migraine may be precipitated by allergic hypersensitivity or emotional disturbances.

TREATMENT: Many medications help migraine sufferers. For most mild-to-moderate headaches, nonsteroidal anti-inflammatory drugs (such as ibuprofen or naproxen) alleviate pain and restore the ability to function normally within a few hours. These agents work best when combined with antiemetic drugs such as metoclopromide or promethazine, as well as rest or relaxation. Triptan drugs (such as sumatriptan or naratriptan), ergotamine derivatives (such as dihydroergotamine or ergotamine with caffeine), prednisone, and other agents are also helpful although each has its own side effect profile and precautions for use. Patients who experience many migraine headaches each month may benefit from preventive medications such as beta-blocking drugs (such as propranolol), calcium channel blocking drugs (such as verapamil), or tricyclic antidepressants taken on a regular basis. Narcotics (morphine, fentanyl, and others) are given to abort some severe migraine attacks, but habitual use of narcotics may result in tolerance to their effects and drug dependence.

PATIENT CARE: The nurse monitors the nature and character of the patient's pain, helps the patient relax by creating a dark and quiet environment, helps the patient recognize and avoid exacerbating factors (based on history), and teaches the patient methods for coping with discomfort (such as imagery, relaxation techniques). The patient is taught to take prescribed medications at the first signs of headache and to increase fluid intake to prevent dehydration once nausea is controlled. Prescribed medications are administered and evaluated for desired effects and adverse reactions. To enhance the effects of medications and pain relief, noninvasive pain relief measures should be instituted before pain becomes severe. Many headache experts recommend that patients with migraines learn to keep detailed diaries of their illness. Analysis of the diary may help headache sufferers to recognize factors such as lack of sleep; irregular meals; and particular foods, odors, or stresses that are likely to trigger a migraine (and therefore should be avoided). Headache diaries are also used to help distinguish migraine headaches from other types of head pain.

abdominal m. Intermittent attacks of prolonged and intense upper abdominal pain, often associated with nausea or vomiting. The condition is considered a variant of migraine headache. SYN: *cyclic vomiting syndrome*.

migraine variant Any of several intermittent disorders, usually in patients with a family history of migraine headaches, characterized by attacks of head, neck, or abdominal pain; transient confusion or paralysis; or visual disturbances. Typical migraine headaches often develop in children and young adults who suffer from migraine variants.

migration (mī-grā'shŏn) [L. *migratio*, removal, migration] **1.** Movement from one location to another. **2.** Unwanted movement of an implanted device from its original therapeutic location to another part of the body, where it may cause injury. **migratory** (mī'gră-tor″ē), *adj*.

m. of leukocytes Passage of white blood cells through walls of capillaries. SYN: *diapedesis*.

tooth m., m. of teeth The movement of teeth during eruption or out of their normal position in the dental arch due to periodontal disease or missing adjacent teeth.

Mikulicz-Radecki, Johann von (mē-koo′lich-ra-det′skē) Polish-born Ger. surgeon, 1850–1905.

M.'s drain A large-scale capillary drain that also serves as a tampon to arrest bleeding. It consists of a tubular piece of iodoform gauze of proper size, placed in a cavity and filled with narrow strips of plain gauze until the necessary degree of compression is secured. This is used if there is parenchymatous oozing. SYN: *Mikulicz tampon*.

M.'s mask A gauze-covered frame worn over the nose and mouth during an operation.

M.'s pad A folded gauze pad for packing of the viscera in abdominal operations and as a sponge in general.

M.'s syndrome Chronic infiltration with lymphocytes and painless enlargement of lacrimal and salivary glands.

M.'s tampon Mikulicz drain.

mild cognitive impairment SEE: under *impairment*.

mildew [AS. *mildeaw*] Lay term for a discoloration or superficial coating on various materials caused by the growth of fungi. It occurs in damp conditions.

milia (mĭl′ē-ă) Pl. of milium.

miliaria (mil-ē-ar′ē-ă) [L. *miliaria*, pert. to millet (seeds)] An inflamed papular or vesicular rash that results from obstruction of the flow of sweat from sweat glands, esp. by occlusive clothing in warm and humid conditions. **miliary** (mil′ē-er″ē), *adj*.

TREATMENT: The rash often improves after the patient returns to a cooler climate or the affected area is cooled and dried.

m. crystallina A noninflammatory eruption from sweat glands marked by whitish vesicles caused by the retention of sweat in the cornified layer of the skin, appearing after profuse sweating or in certain febrile diseases. SYN: *sudamina*.

m. rubra Prickly **heat**.

miliary tubercle SEE: *tubercle, miliary*.

miliary tuberculosis SEE: under *tuberculosis*.

milieu (mē-lyŭ′) [Fr.] Environment.

milieu therapy A method of psychotherapy that controls the environment of the patient to provide interpersonal contacts that will develop trust, assurance, and personal autonomy.

military antishock trousers ABBR: MAST. Antishock garment.

milium (mĭl′ē-ŭm) *pl.* **milia** [L., millet seed] White pinhead-size, keratin-filled cyst. Treatment consists of the use of mechanical keratolytics (pumice stone, soap), salicylic acid and sulfur ointment, or incision and expression of contents. In the newborn, milia occur on the face and, less frequently, on the trunk, and usually disappear without treatment within several weeks.

colloid m. Tiny papule formed beneath the epidermis due to colloid degeneration.

milk (milk) A secretion of the mammary glands for the nourishment of the young.

COMPOSITION: Milk from cows consists of water, organic substances, and mineral salts. *Organic substances:* Proteins: The principal proteins are caseinogen, lactoalbumin, and lactoglobulin; in the presence of calcium ions, soluble caseinogen is converted into insoluble casein by the action of acids, rennet, or pepsin. This brings about the curdling of milk. Lactoglobulin is identical with serum globulin of the blood and hence contains maternal antibodies. Carbohydrates: Lactose (milk sugar) is the principal sugar, although small quantities of other sugars are present. Fats: The principal fats are glycerides of oleic, palmitic, and myristic acids. Smaller quantities of stearic acid and short-chain fatty acids with carbon chains of C_4 to C_{24} are present. Sterols and phosphatides (lecithin and cephalin) are also present. Churning causes the fat globules to unite into a solid mass and separate from the whey to form butter.

Mineral salts: The principal cations are calcium, potassium, and sodium; the principal anions are phosphate and chloride. Citrates and lactates are present in small quantities. Milk is low in iron and magnesium.

Vitamins: Vitamin A and those of the B complex (thiamine, riboflavin, and pantothenic acid) are present in adequate quantities to meet the needs of a growing child. Milk is low in vitamins C and D.

Milk contains antibodies that are present in the mother's blood and a number of enzymes (catalase, oxidase, reductase, phosphatase).

acidophilus m. Milk inoculated with *Lactobacillus acidophilus,* a bacterium that grows best in an acid medium. It is a probiotic food, used to modify the bacterial flora of the digestive tract.

breast m. Milk obtained from the mammary glands of the human breast. It is the ideal source of nutrition for most infants, since it contains maternal antibodies that protect the child from infection, and other substances that promote development of the brain and the gastrointestinal tract, among other organs. Human breast milk that is collected and refrigerated immediately may be used for up to 5 days. If it is collected, frozen, and stored at −17.7°C (0°F), it is safe for 6 months.

⚠️ breast-feeding by mothers with human immunodeficiency virus (HIV) is not recommended, because of the risk of transmission of HIV to the child.

butter m. SEE: *buttermilk.*

casein m. Milk prepared with a large quantity of casein and fat but little sugar and salt, e.g., a product like whole fat milk.

condensed m. Milk from which water has been removed and sugar has been added to make it thick and sweet. It is an ingredient in dessert recipes.

cow's m. Milk obtained from cows.

donor m. Pasteurized donor breast milk.

evaporated m. Cow's milk that has been concentrated by evaporating some of the water. It can be canned after pasteurization and stored for long periods of time. SEE: *lactic acid evaporated m.*

fermented m. Any cultured dairy product, such as buttermilk, cheese, kefir, koumiss, and yogurt. SEE: *koumiss.*

fore m. Milk released at the beginning of each breast-feeding that contains a high percentage of water, protein, and vitamins but a lower percentage of fat than the hind milk that is released later.

goat's m. Milk obtained from goats, which, like cow's milk, should be pasteurized before use. Goat's milk differs from cow's milk in that is has a higher fat content, and is deficient in folacin and vitamin B_{12}.

hind m. Milk released at the end of a breast-feeding, distinguished by its high fat content.

homogenized m. Milk that has been processed in such a manner that fats are combined with the body of the milk and the cream does not separate.

low-fat m. 1% Cow's milk with 1% fat, which represents 22% of the calories.

low-fat m. 2% Cow's milk with 2% fat, which represents 35% of the calories.

mature m. Milk released once lactation has become fully established. SEE: *fore m.; hind m.*

modified m. Cow's milk altered so that its composition more closely approximates that of human milk.

mother's m. Breast **m.**

nonfat m. Skim **m.**

pasteurized m. Milk heated to a specified temperature for a precise length of time and then cooled rapidly. This process kills pathogenic bacteria without appreciably altering the taste of the milk. SEE: *pasteurization.*

protein m. Milk modified to be high in protein and low in carbohydrate and fat content.

red m. Milk contaminated by blood, chromogenic bacteria, or plant pigments.

ropy m. Milk that has become viscid as a result of the presence of exopolysaccharides produced by bacterial contamination.

skim m. Cow's milk from which the fat has been removed.

sour m. Milk with lactic acid caused either by lactic acid–producing bacteria or by the addition of vinegar. It is most commonly used in baked goods.

soy m. A beverage derived from soybeans. It can take the place of cow's milk in people who have lactose intolerance and those who are allergic to milk proteins.

sterilized m. Milk that has been boiled to kill bacteria.

transitional m. The first breast milk produced as colostrum production fades. It has more triglyceride and medium-chain fatty acid content than colostrum. Its other components include lactose, water-soluble vitamins, and immunoglobulins.

vegetable m. **1.** The latex of plants. **2.** A beverage prepared from juices of various plants, such as soybean.

vitamin D m. Milk in which vitamin D content has been increased by addition of concentrates, ultraviolet irradiation, or feeding of irradiated yeast to milk-producing animals.

whole m. Milk whose fat content is unaltered. It is homogenized, pasteurized, and often fortified with vitamins A and D. It may in some instances be treated with lactase-destroying enzymes. SEE: *pasteurization.*

witch's m. 1. Milk secreted by the newly born infant's breast, stimulated by the lactating hormone circulating in the mother. **2.** A rarely used synonym for galactorrhea.

milk-alkali syndrome Elevated blood calcium without an increase in calcium or phosphate in the urine, renal insufficiency, and alkalosis due to prolonged intake of excessive amounts of milk and soluble alkali. This condition is usually found as an undesired side effect of treating a peptic ulcer with calcium-containing antacids. SYN: *Burnett's syndrome.*

milk fever SEE: under *fever.*

milking 1. Removal of the contents of a tubular structure, such as the urethra, by compressing the tube with the fingers and moving them along the course of the tube and away from the origin of the urethra. This maneuver forces material out of the tube that might not otherwise be seen or available for study. **2.** Stroking or tugging on the soft tissue near a joint space to determine if it holds an abnormal collection of fluid (an effusion). SEE: *effusion; strip.*

milk leg Phlegmasia alba dolens.

milk letdown, letdown The ejection of a mother's milk from the alveoli of the breast into the mammary ducts and to the nipple.

Milkman syndrome (milk′măn) [Louis A. Milkman, U.S. roentgenologist, 1895–1951] Failure of reabsorption of phosphate by the renal tubules. This failure causes osteomalacia that produces a transverse striped area of multiple pseudofractures in bone x-rays.

milk thistle (milk this′il) An annual or biennial herb (*Silybum marianum*) promoted as a treatment for liver disorders. SYN: *Silybum marianum; silymarin.*

Miller-Abbott tube (mil′ĕr-ăb′ŏt) [Thomas Grier Miller, U.S. physician, 1886–1981; William Osler Abbott, U.S. physician, 1902–1943] A double-channel intestinal tube used to relieve intestinal obstruction. Inserted through a nostril, the tube is passed through the stomach into the small intestine.

Miller Analogies Test (mil′ĕr) ABBR: MAT. A test to assess a person's ability to see the connections between words or concepts. The test consists of 100 core items designed in the following format: X is to Y as ? is to B, where ? denotes a blank that must be filled in with one of several choices. The test may be administered to children to measure their language ability, knowledge, and ability to

reason, and to others as part of a battery of neuropsychiatric tests.

Miller Assessment for Preschoolers [Lucy Jane Miller, Ph.D., contemporary occupational therapist] ABBR: MAP. A widely used standardized developmental screening test for youngsters from 2 to 5 years of age. It contains sensory, motor, and cognitive performance items.

Miller-Fisher syndrome (mil′ĕr-fish′ĕr) An acute polyneuropathy thought to represent a variant of Guillain-Barré syndrome. Its characteristic features include: difficulty walking, loss of reflexes, and extraocular paralysis. The disease often follows infections with and may be caused by an abnormal immune response to certain pathogens, esp. *Campylobacter jejuni* and certain viruses. It is treated with plasmapheresis. Recovery is usually complete within a few months.

milli- [L. *mille,* thousand] In the International System of Units (SI), a prefix meaning *one-thousandth* (10^{-3}).

milliammeter (mil″ē-am′ĕt″ĕr) [*milli-* + *ammeter*] An ammeter registering in milliamperes. SEE: *ammeter.*

milliampere (mil″ē-am′pēr″) [*milli-* + *ampere*] ABBR: mA. One thousandth of an ampere.

milliampere second ABBR: mAs. A unit used in radiographic imaging that is equal to the product of the current used in milliamperes and the time in seconds. It is the primary unit for determining the density or brightness of an ionizing radiation image.

millibar (mil′ĭ-băr) One thousandth of a bar, which is 100 newtons/sq m. The normal atmospheric pressure of 14.7 lb/sq in is equal to 1013 millibars.

millicurie (mil″ĭ-kū′rē) ABBR: mCi. One thousandth of a curie. A practical unit of dosage for a radioactive source: 1 mCi of a radioactive substance applied for 1 hr.

milliequivalent (mi″l-ē-ē-kwiv′ă-lĕnt) ABBR: mEq. One thousandth of a chemical equivalent. The concentration of electrolytes in a certain volume of solution is usually expressed as milliequivalent per liter (mEq/L). It is calculated by multiplying the milligrams per liter by the valence of the chemical and dividing by the molecular weight of the substance.

milligram (mil′ĭ-grăm) ABBR: mg. One thousandth of a gram.

millilambert (mil″ĭ-lăm′bĕrt) One thousandth of a lambert, a unit of light intensity. About one foot-candle, but more accurately, it is 0.929 lumens per square foot.

milliliter (mil′ĭ-lēt″ĕr) [*milli-* + *liter*] ABBR: mL, ml. One thousandth of a liter. The U.S. National Institute of Standards and Technology recommends the use of mL instead of ml because of the possible confusion of lower case l and the Arabic numeral 1.

millimeter (mĭl′ĭ-mē″tĕr) ABBR: mm. One thousandth of a meter.

millimicro- (mμ) Prefix formerly used to indicate one billionth (10^{-9}). The term currently used is *nano*.

millimicrogram (mĭl″ĭ-mī′krō-grăm) A nanogram, or 10^{-9} g.

millimicron (mĭl-ĭ-mī′krŏn) ABBR: mμ. An obsolete term for distance in the metric system, usually applied to light wavelength. SEE: *nanometer*.

millimole (mĭl′ĭ-mōl) ABBR: mM or mmol. One thousandth of a mole.

milliosmole (mĭl″ē-ŏs′mōl) One thousandth of an osmole; the osmotic pressure equal to one thousandth of the molecular weight of a substance divided by the number of ions that the substance forms in a liter of solution.

millipede (mĭl′ĭ-pēd) A wormlike arthropod with two pairs of legs on each body segment. Some produce an irritating venom.

millirem (mĭl′ē-rĕm) ABBR: mrem. One thousandth of a rem.

milliroentgen (mĭl′ē-rĕnt″gĕn) ABBR: mR. One thousandth of a roentgen.

millisecond (mĭl″ĭ-sĕk′ŏnd) One thousandth of a second.

millivolt (mĭl′ĭ-vōlt) One thousandth of a volt.

Milroy disease (mĭl′roy″) [William Forsyth Milroy, U.S. physician, 1855–1942] Chronic hereditary lymphedema of the legs.

Milwaukee brace (mil-wo′kē) SEE: under *brace*.

mimesis (mĭ-mē′sĭs) [Gr. *mimēsis*, imitation, mimicry] In medicine, a phenomenon in which a disease exhibits symptoms of another disease or in which conditions in functional illnesses simulate organic disease. **mimetic** (mĭ-met′ik), *adj*.

mimic (mim′ik) [L. *mimicus*, fr. Gr. *mimikos*, pertaining to a mime or buffoon, imitative] **1.** To copy, resemble, or simulate; imitate. **2.** A person or thing that imitates or mimics.

mimicry (mim′i-krē) The practice or instance of one organism copying or mimicking another organism or object, sometimes for concealment from predators.

mimivirus (mĭ′mĭ-vī″rŭs) [Fr. *mimi(c)* + ″] A massive double-stranded DNA virus, first identified in an ameba in 2003, so large that it appears to be a bacterium when seen under light microscopy. It has been identified in some patients with pneumonia.

mimotope, mimetope (mĭm′ŏ-tōp″) [From *mim(ic)* + *(epi)tope*] A small peptide that elicits a stronger antibody response than the polysaccharide or nucleic acid antigen that it is designed to

mimic. Polysaccharide and nucleic acid antigens are often weakly immunogenic.

min *minim; minimum; minute*.

Minamata disease (mĭn″ă-maw′tă) [Minamata Bay, Japan] A degenerative neurological disease due to ingestion of alkyl mercury, an organic mercury used industrially. Peripheral nerve injury, ataxia, and dysarthria are common consequences. SYN: *yushi*.

mind [AS. *gemynd*] Psyche; integration and organization of functions of the brain resulting in the ability to perceive surroundings, to have emotions, imagination, memory, and will, and to process information in an intelligent manner. The quality and quantity of the functions of the mind vary with experience and development.

mind-body duality Dualism (2).

mindfulness (mīnd′fool-nĕs″) [ME.] Attentiveness; self-awareness.

mindfulness-based stress reduction SEE: under *reduction*.

mind map SEE: under *map*.

mineral [L. *minerale*] **1.** An inorganic element or compound occurring in nature, esp. one that is solid.

FUNCTION: Minerals are essential constituents of all cells; they form the greater portion of the hard parts of the body (bone, teeth, nails); they are essential components of respiratory pigments, enzymes, and enzyme systems; they regulate the permeability of cell membranes and capillaries; they regulate the excitability of muscular and nervous tissue; they are essential for regulation of osmotic pressure equilibria; they are necessary for maintenance of proper acid-base balance; they are essential constituents of secretions of glands; they play an important role in water metabolism and regulation of blood volume.

DAILY REQUIREMENTS: Because mineral salts and water are excreted daily from the body, they must be replaced through food intake. Daily values for principal minerals for a healthy adult are as follows: calcium, 800 to 1200 mg; copper, 2 mg; iodine, 150 μg (micrograms); magnesium, 400 mg; phosphorus, 1000 g; selenium, 55 to 70 mcg; zinc, 15 mg. Daily intake of sodium chloride should be limited to 6 g (2.4 g of sodium) or less each day. SEE: *Recommended Daily Dietary Allowances Appendix*.

2. Inorganic; not of animal or plant origin. **3.** Impregnated with minerals, as mineral water. **4.** Pert. to minerals.

mineralization (mĭn″ĕr-ăl-ī-zā′shŭn) **1.** Normal or abnormal deposition of minerals in tissues. **2.** In the food chain, the degradation by bacteria and fungi of complex organic molecules to simpler organics and inorganics.

mineralocorticoid (mĭn″ĕr-ăl-ō-kor′tĭ-koyd) A steroid hormone (e.g., aldosterone) that regulates the retention and excretion of fluids and electrolytes by the kidneys. SEE: *aldosterone*.

mineral spring A natural water source which contains dissolved mineral salts, including calcium, fluoride, magnesium, potassium, and sodium (among others). SEE: *spa*.

mineral water SEE: under *water*.

mini-cog (mĭn′ē-kŏg″) A screening test used to detect cognitive deficits present in patients with dementia. Patients are asked to draw a clock face and to remember three objects. The test is easier to administer than the 30-component Mini-Mental State Examination, another screening test for cognitive impairment.

minification (mĭn″ĭ-fĭ-kā′shŭn) In radiography, the reduction in the size of a fluoroscopic image to intensify the brightness of that image.

minilaparotomy (mĭn″i-lap″ă-rot′ŏ-mē) A limited incision of the abdominal wall into the peritoneum.

minimal (mĭn′ĭ-măl) Least; the smallest possible.

minimal cerebral dysfunction Learning disability. SEE: *attention-deficit hyperactivity disorder*.

minimal change disease The form of nephrotic syndrome most often found in children, in which renal biopsies reveal little if any pathological change under the light microscope. With electron microscopy, effacement of the foot processes of the glomerulus becomes evident. SEE: *nephrotic syndrome*.

minimally conscious state ABBR: MCS. A severe alteration in consciousness that does not meet the diagnostic criteria for either coma or a persistent vegetative state, in which patients respond to some sounds and unpleasant stimuli and have a sleep-wake cycle but do not attend to their environment consistently.

minimally invasive total knee arthroplasty SEE: under *arthroplasty*.

Mini-Mental State Examination SEE: under *examination*.

Mini–Mental Status Examination SEE: *Mini-Mental State Examination*.

minimum (mĭn′ĭ-mŭm) pl. **minima** Least quantity or lowest limit. SEE: *threshold*.

minimum daily requirements ABBR: MDR. The quantity of vitamins and minerals needed in the diet to prevent symptoms of deficiency. SEE: *Recommended Daily Dietary Allowances Appendix*.

Minimum Data Set ABBR: MDS. A comprehensive computer-compatible form for assessment of Medicare- or Medicaid-certified nursing home residents. It was developed as a result of the Omnibus Reconciliation Act of 1987 and mandated for use in nursing homes in the U.S. Resident assessment protocols are used to identify multiple triggers for the assessment of various conditions. Under the current prospective payment system, the form must be completed and sent electronically to the federal government within 5 days of admission to a nursing home and at frequent intervals thereafter. SEE: *Nursing Minimum Data Set*.

mining (mī′nĭng) [ME] **1.** The extraction of useful information from a database. SYN: *data m.* **2.** The extraction from the earth of materials with industrial value, such as coal, silver, or gold. Miners are exposed to various occupational disorders, including respiratory diseases (e.g., pneumoconiosis), allergies, and traumatic injuries.

   data m. Mining (1).

minipill (mĭn′ē-pĭl″) A colloquial term for an oral contraceptive consisting of only progestins. It may be used during breastfeeding (estrogen-containing pills are contraindicated during lactation). The minipill works by thickening cervical mucus. Some formulations are somewhat less effective contraceptives than birth control pills that contain both estrogens and progestins. However, the absence of estrogens reduces the risk of blood clots.

minipool (mĭn′ē-pool″) A small sample of blood or blood products derived from a large group of blood donors. Minipools taken from 14 to 48 blood donors are screened in clinical medicine for the presence of dangerous infections, such as hepatitis B, hepatitis C, or HIV. Minipool testing is more efficient and more cost effective than the more expensive method of testing each individually donated specimen. If a minipool is negative for infection, all of its components are cleared for use. If a minipool tests positive, the individual components in the pool are tested to determine which of the donors has given a specimen that needs to be discarded.

miniscope, mini-scope, mini scope (mĭn′ē-skŏp″) A miniature endoscope (i.e., one whose external diameter is about 2 mm). It is used inside small ducts or narrow organs (e.g., the common bile duct or the pancreatic ducts).

Minnesota Multiphasic Personality Inventory ABBR: MMPI. SEE: *personality test*.

Minnesota Rate of Manipulation Test ABBR: MRMT. A measure of fine motor (hand) coordination and dexterity. It uses turning and placing of objects to assess unilateral and bilateral manual dexterity and eye-hand coordination. Both accuracy and speed are assessed. It is useful as a measure of how visual deficits affect manual performance. SEE: *fine motor skill.*

minor (mī′nŏr) [L. *minor,* smaller, lesser] **1.** Of lesser or inferior importance, size, scope, or effect. **2.** A person not of legal age and thus requiring consent for medical, surgical, or dental care. The legal age of consent in the U.S. varies from state to state.

 emancipated m. A person not of legal age who is in the armed services, married, the mother of a child whether married or not, or has left home and is self-sufficient. Some state legislatures do not require such a person to have parental consent to receive medical or surgical care, or advice on contraception or abortion.

mio-, mi-, meio- [Gr. *meiōn,* less] Prefixes meaning *less* or *fewer.*

miopus (mī′ō-pŭs) [″ + *ops,* face] Conjoined twins with one having a rudimentary face.

miosis (mī-ō′sĭs) [Gr. *meiosis,* a lessening] Abnormal contraction of the pupils, possibly due to irritation of the oculomotor system or paralysis of dilators. Pupillary contraction may occur after a stroke that affects the brainstem or after administration of drugs such as opiates or eyedrops that inactivate acetylcholinesterase.

miotic (mī-ŏ′tĭk) **1.** An agent that causes the pupil to contract, such as eserine or pilocarpine. **2.** Pert. to or causing contraction of the pupil. **3.** Diminishing.

MIP *maximum inspiratory pressure.*

miracidium (mī″ră-sĭd′ē-ŭm) *pl.* **miracidia** [Gr. *meirakidion,* lad] The ciliated free-swimming larva of a digenetic fluke. On emerging from an ovum, it penetrates a snail of a particular species and metamorphoses into a sporocyst. SEE: *fluke.*

miracle, medical The unexplained spontaneous remission or cure of a medical condition thought to be invariably fatal or incurable or both.

mire (mēr) [L. *mirari,* to look at] A test object on the ophthalmometer, the images of which denote the amount of astigmatism.

Mirizzi syndrome (mĭ-riz′ē) [Pablo Luis Mirizzi, Argentinian surgeon, 1893–1964] Impaction of a gallstone in the infundibulum of the gallbladder or the cystic duct resulting in obstruction of the common hepatic duct, occasionally associated with fistula formation. The syndrome is a rare but surgically important cause of jaundice.

miRNA MicroRNA: short nucleotide sequences that regulate DNA expression but are not themselves transcribed.

mirror (mir′ŏr) [Fr. *miroir*] A polished surface that reflects light and thus reproduces visible images of objects in front of it.

 dental m. An instrument commonly used for viewing occlusal and distal surfaces of teeth.

 dichroic m. An optical device used in some spectrophotometers to split a beam of light into reference and sample beams.

mirror writing Writing in which letters and/or words are reversed by the writer—a characteristic of some persons with dyslexia and some who have suffered a left hemispheric stroke.

misanthropy (mĭs″ăn′thrō-pē) [″ + Gr. *anthropos,* man] Hatred of mankind.

misarticulation (mĭs″ăr-tĭk″ū-lā′shŭn) Inaccurately produced speech.

misattribution (mis″a-trĭ-bū′shŏn) A false, incorrect, or mistaken attribution, assignment, or ascription.

misbranding (mĭs-brănd′ĭng) Ambiguous, deceptive, false, incomplete, incorrect, or misleading labeling of a drug or medical device.

miscarriage (mis′kar-ăj) Termination of pregnancy at any time before the fetus has attained the potential for extrauterine viability.

 late m. A miscarriage that occurs after 10 weeks of pregnancy.

 recurrent m. Three consecutive pregnancy losses. SYN: *spontaneous **abortion.***

miscegenation (mĭs″ĕ-jē-nā′shŭn) [L. *miscere,* to mix, + *genus,* race] Sexual relations or marriage between those of different races.

miscible (mĭs′ĭ-bl) Capable of being mixed.

misclassification (mis-kla″sĭ-fĭ-kā′shŏn) Inaccurate diagnosis; incorrect assignment of an individual to a group that appears to have some similar characteristics. **misclassify** (-kla′sĭ-fī″), *v.*

misconduct (mis″kon′dŭkt) **1.** Behavior that is professionally unethical and/or illegal, e.g., negligence, incompetence, impairment from drugs or alcohol. **2.** Behavior that is unethical or immoral, but not necessarily illegal, e.g., adultery.

misconnection error SEE: under *error.*

misdemeanor A lesser crime than a felony, usually punishable by fines, imprisonment, penalty, or forfeiture.

misery Extreme mental or emotional unhappiness.

misfeasance The performance of a legal act in an improper or unlawful manner.

misidentification syndrome (mĭs″ī-dĕn″tĭ-fĭ-kā′shŭn) The delusion that a person, an object, or an environment has been duplicated and placed in a new location distant from the location of the original.

misinformation Data or information concerning a patient that may be erroneously assumed to be accurate (e.g., inaccurate laboratory data, unreliable historical data from the patient or the family, and transcription errors in recording data).

mismatch V-Q mismatch.

mismatched related donor SEE: under *donor.*

misogynist (mĭs-ŏj'ĭ-nĭst) [" + *gyne,* woman] One who hates women.

misogyny (mĭs-ŏj'ĭn-ē) [Gr. *miseio,* to hate + *gyne,* woman] Aversion to or hatred of females. SEE: *misandry.*

misrepresentation An incorrect, dishonest, or false represenation of facts.

missed period SEE: under *period.*

mist Aerosolized liquid or particles.

Mister In England and other parts of the British Commonwealth, the title of address of a surgeon.

misting 1. The therapeutic use of mists, e.g., as a means of administering a drug for inhalation. **2.** The use of aerosols to coat objects, e.g., to protect the skin with insect repellent.

mistletoe (mis'ĕl-tō") A small flowering shrub (*Viscum album*) native to Eurasia, that grows high on the limbs of leafy trees. It is used in homeopathy to treat conditions associated with high blood pressure.

⚠ Viscumin, a toxic lectin, has been isolated from *Viscum album.*

mistura (mĭs-tū'ră) Mixture.

mite (mīt) A minute arachnid of the order Acarina. Some mites are parasitic and cause asthma, mange, and scabies; others are vectors of disease organisms and are intermediate hosts for certain cestodes.

 dust m. A species, *Dermatophagoides pteronyssinum* or *D. farinae,* that ingests shed human skin cells. The mite is a common cause of allergic reactions.

 harvest m. Chigger.

 itch m. SEE: *Sarcoptes; scabies.*

 mange m. Any mite of the families Sarcoptidae and Psoroptidae, which causes mange in many species of animals. SEE: *mange; scabies.*

 red m. Chigger.

miticide (mī'tĭ-sīd) [AS. *mite,* mite, + L. *caedere,* to kill] A substance that kills mites.

mitigate (mit'ĭ-gāt") [L. *mitigare,* to soften] To reduce the intensity of an effect; alleviate. **mitigated** (-gāt"ĕd), *adj.* **mitigation** (mit"ĭ-gā'shŏn), *n.*

mitis (mī'tĭs) [L.] Mild.

mitochondrial disease (mī"tō-kŏn'drē-ăl) Any of hundreds of congenital illnesses that result from mutations in the DNA of mitochondria. Mitochondrial diseases are transmitted from mother to child.

mitochondrion (mīt"ō-kŏn'drē-ŏn) *pl.* **mitochondria** [Gr. *mitos,* thread, + *chondros,* cartilage] A cell organelle of rod or oval shape 0.5 μm in diameter. Mitochondria can be seen by using phase-contrast or electron microscopy. They contain the enzymes for the aerobic stages of cell respiration and thus are the sites of most ATP synthesis. SEE: *cell; organelle* for illus.

mitochondriopathy (mīt"ō-kon"drē-op'ă-thē) [*mitochondrion* + *-pathy*] Any disease caused by a mutation in mitochondrial DNA.

mitogen (mī'tō-jĕn) A plant-derived protein used in the laboratory to stimulate cell division (mitosis). It is frequently used in vitro to study the proliferation of lymphocytes from blood drawn during a research study. The most commonly used mitogens are phytohemagglutinin and concanavalin A. SEE: *concanavalin A; lectin; phytohemagglutinin.*

 pokeweed m. ABBR: PWM. A mitogen isolated from the pokeweed plant, *Phytolacca americana.* In the presence of T lymphocytes, it has the capacity to induce primed B lymphocytes to proliferate and differentiate into plasma cells.

mitogenesis (mī"tō-jĕn'ĕ-sĭs) [" + *osis,* condition, + *genesis,* generation, birth] The production of cell mitosis.

mitoma, mitome (mī-tō'mă, mī'tōm) [Gr. *mitos,* thread] The network of microtubules in the cytoplasm of a cell.

mitosis (mī-tō'sĭs, mī-tō'sēz") *pl.* **mitoses** [Gr. *mitos,* thread + *-osis*] A type of cell division of somatic cells in which each daughter cell contains the same number of chromosomes as the parent cell. Mitosis is the process by which the body grows and dead somatic cells are replaced. Mitosis is a continuous process divided into four phases: prophase, metaphase, anaphase, and telophase. **mitotic** (mī-tot'ĭk), *adj.* SEE: illus.; *meiosis.*

 Prophase: The chromatin granules of the nucleus stain more densely; the DNA strands coil extensively and become visible as chromosomes. These first appear as long filaments, each consisting of two identical chromatids, the result of DNA replication. Each pair of chromatids is joined at a region called the centromere, which may be central or toward one end. As prophase progresses, the chromosomes become shorter and more compact and stain densely. The nuclear membrane and the nucleoli disappear. At the same time, the centriole divides and the two daughter centrioles, each surrounded by a centrosphere, move to opposite poles of the cell. They are connected by fine protoplasmic fibrils, which form an achromatic spindle.

 Metaphase: The chromosomes (paired chromatids) arrange themselves in an equatorial plane midway between the two centrioles.

 Anaphase: The chromatids (now called daughter chromosomes) diverge

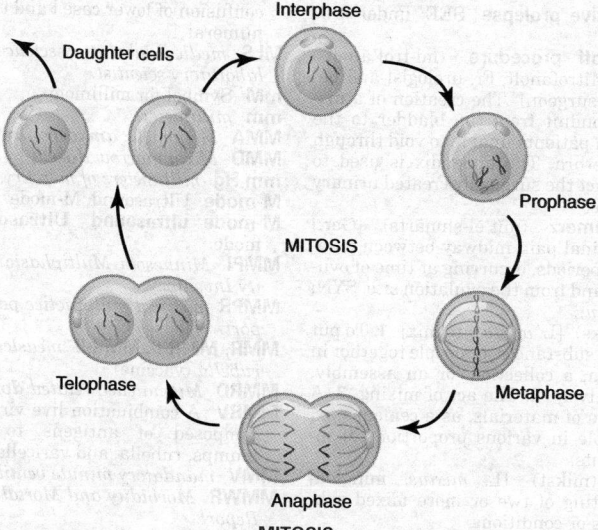

Interphase

Daughter cells

Prophase

MITOSIS

Telophase

Metaphase

Anaphase

MITOSIS

and move toward their respective centrioles. The end of their migration marks the beginning of the next phase.

Telophase: The chromosomes at each pole of the spindle uncoil, the reverse of prophase, each becoming a long, loosely spiraled thread. The nuclear membrane re-forms and nucleoli reappear. Outlines of chromosomes disappear, and chromatin appears as granules scattered throughout the nucleus and connected by a lightly staining net. The cytoplasm divides (cytokinesis), resulting in two complete cells. This is accomplished in animal cells by constriction in the equatorial region; in plant cells, a cell plate develops in the same region and becomes the new cell wall. The period between two successive divisions is called interphase.

Mitosis is of particular significance in that genes are distributed equally to each daughter cell, and the diploid number of chromosomes is maintained in all somatic cells of an organism.

mitosome (mī′tō-sōm) [Gr. *mitos,* thread, + *soma,* body] A stainable portion of the spindle fibers following mitosis.

mitotic index (mī-totik) SEE: under *index.*

mitral (mī′trăl) [mit(e)r + -al] **1.** Shaped like a miter (the official headdress of a bishop). **2.** Pert. to the bicuspid or mitral valve.

mitral area Area of the chest wall over the apex of the heart where mitral valve sounds are heard best (usually between intercostal spaces 5–6 to the left of the midclavicular line).

mitral commissurotomy A surgical procedure for treating stenosis of the mitral valve of the heart, in which the stenosed valve leaflets are separated from each other. Patients may undergo an open or a closed procedure.

PATIENT CARE: Prior to mitral valve surgery, cardiac catheterization is performed to evaluate coronary artery anatomy, the severity of the mitral stenosis, and the presence of other cardiac pathologies. Specially trained cardiac surgery nurses provide general care for the patient undergoing open heart surgery including support of oxygenation, ventilation, fluid status, blood pressure, and pain relief. The types of access lines and endotrachial and drainage tubes in place after surgery, as well as the reasons for their use, are explained. The type of postoperative pain to be expected is also explained, and the patient is encouraged to report pain before it becomes severe to maintain a comfortable state necessary for healing. General patient care concerns apply throughout the patient's hospitalization. The caregivers support the patient and family throughout recovery. Anticoagulant therapy may be prescribed for patients with artificial valves postoperatively. Antibiotic prophylaxis is required prior to dental procedures to prevent endocarditis. After discharge, the patient begins a gradual return to activity. Regular medical follow-up to assess valve function, and to detect heart failure, heart blocks, or dysrhythmias such as atrial fibrillation are a necessary part of care. Participation in a cardiac rehabilitation program, if recommended by the physician, should be encouraged.

mitral stenosis SEE: under *stenosis.*

mitral valve SEE: under *valve.*

mitral valve prolapse SEE: under *prolapse*.

Mitrofanoff procedure (mi-trof'ă-nof") [Paul Mitrofanoff, Fr. urologist and pediatric surgeon] The creation of a urinary conduit from the bladder to the skin, in patients unable to void through the urethra. The appendix is used to construct the surgically created urinary passage.

mittelschmerz (mĭt'ĕl-shmārts) [Ger.] Abdominal pain midway between menstrual periods, occurring at time of ovulation and from the ovulation site. SYN: *midpain*.

mix (mĭks) [L. *mixtus,* to mix] **1.** To put things, substances, or people together in solution, a collection, or an assembly, respectively. **2.** The act of mixing. **3.** A mixture of materials, as a cement mix, available in various proportions of ingredients.

mixed (mĭkst) [L. *mixtus,* mingled] Consisting of two or more mixed substances or conditions.

mixed connective tissue disease ABBR: MCTD. A rare disease that combines the signs and symptoms of several connective tissue diseases, including systemic lupus erythematosus, scleroderma, rheumatoid arthritis, and/or polymyositis. The cause is unknown.

mixed dementia SEE: under *dementia*.

mixed lymphocyte culture reaction A laboratory test in which lymphocytes from different individuals are mixed to identify the presence of particular HLA class II antigens. The T cells from the "responder" will synthesize DNA and proliferate only if they do not have the same histocompatibility antigens as the "donor cells," homozygous cells with known HLA types. The donor cells are irradiated to prevent their proliferation during the test.

mixing study SEE: under *study*.

mixing vessel SEE: under *vessel*.

mixture (mĭks'chĕr) A combination of two or more substances with or without chemical union. SYN: *mistura*.

Miyoshi myopathy (mĭ-yō'shē) An autosomal recessive form of muscular dystrophy in which mutations in the skeletal muscle gene that codes for dysferlin results in weakness of distal muscles, esp. the muscles that control plantar flexion of the feet. The disease first becomes clinically obvious in early adulthood.

MKS, mks *meter-kilogram-second*. It indicates a measurement system using meter for length, kilogram for weight, and second for time.

MLA *Medical Library Association*.

MLD *minimum lethal dose*.

MLF *medial longitudinal fasciculus*.

mL, ml *Milliliter*. National patient safety organizations suggest the use of mL instead of ml because of the possible confusion of lower case l and the Arabic numeral 1.

MLS *medical laboratory science; medical laboratory scientist*.

mM Symbol for millimole.

mm *millimeter*.

MMA *Monomelic **amyotrophy***.

MMD *Mean marrow **dose***.

mm Hg *millimeters of mercury*.

M-mode Ultrasound, M-mode.

M-mode ultrasound Ultrasound, M-mode.

MMPI *Minnesota Multiphasic Personality Inventory*.

MMPR *medical malpractice payment report*.

MMR, MMR II, MMR-II *measles, mumps, rubella* (vaccine).

MMRD *Mismatched related **donor***.

MMRV A combination live viral vaccine composed of antigens to measles, mumps, rubella, and varicella.

MMV *mandatory minute ventilation*.

MMWR *Morbidity and Mortality Weekly Report*.

Mn Symbol for the element manganese.

mnemic (nē'mĭk) Relating to memory.

mnemonic (nē-mŏn'ĭk) *pl.* **mnemonics** [Gr. *mnemonikos,* pert. to memory] Anything intended to aid memory.

MNL *mononuclear leukocyte* (e.g., monocytes and macrophages).

MO *Medical Officer; Monocyte*

Mo Symbol for the element molybdenum.

mo *month*.

MoAb *Monoclonal **antibody***.

mobile [L. *mobilis*] Movable.

mobility [L. *mobilitas*] State or quality of being mobile; facility of movement. In rehabilitation, mobility refers to an individual's ability to move within a living environment, including the community.

   functional m. The ability to move from one place to another to complete an activity or task.

   impaired wheelchair m. Limitation of independent operation of wheelchair within one's environment. SEE: *Nursing Diagnoses Appendix*.

   powered m. SEE: *powered mobility device*.

mobility device SEE: under *device*.

mobility training SEE: under *training*.

mobilization (mō"bĭ-lĭ-zā'shŏn) The process of making a fixed part movable or releasing stored substances, as in restoring motion to a joint, freeing an organ, or making available substances held in reserve in the body as glycogen or fat.

   early controlled m. A method of rehabilitating flexor and extensor injuries through splinting and active exercises, beginning the first week after injury or surgical repair.

   joint m. The movement of previously injured, frozen, or limited joints to reduce pain and improve range of motion, thereby improving function. Joint mobilization is not synonymous with joint manipulation: joint manipulation involves high-velocity thrusting; joint mobilization does not. These passive techniques are joint-specific and should be performed close to joint surfaces. SEE: *joint manipulation*.

soft-tissue m. The therapeutic manipulation of connective tissue, including muscle, fascia, tendons, and ligaments, for mechanical and physiological effects on blood flow, temperature, metabolism, and autonomic reflex activity. It includes techniques such as myofascial release, muscle energy, Rolfing, scar massage, and traditional massage.

stapes m. A surgical procedure to restore mobility to the stapes, used to treat deafness.

stem cell m. The stimulation of bone marrow (with intensive cancer chemotherapies or blood-forming growth factors) to release stem cells into the peripheral blood. The cells that appear in the blood can be harvested for use in autologous bone marrow transplantation. Mobilized cells (identified by the cell surface marker CD34) are returned to the patient after chemotherapy or radiation therapy so that the treated patient can ultimately resume making healthy blood cells on his own.

mobilize (mō'bĭl-īz) **1.** To incite to physiological action. **2.** To render movable; to put in movement.

Mobiluncus (mō"bĭ-lŭngk'ŭs) [L. *mobilis*, motile + *uncus*] A genus of anaerobic motile bacteria shaped like a curved rod. It can be isolated from vaginal fluid samples in patients with bacterial vaginosis.

Möbius, Paul Julius, Moebius (mū'bē-ŭs, mē', mö') Ger. neurologist, 1853–1907.

M. disease Migraine accompanied by paralysis of the oculomotor nerves.

M. sign A symptom of Graves disease in which one eye converges and the other diverges when one looks at the tip of one's nose.

M. syndrome Congenital paralysis of the facial nerve occurring in the absence of other neurological deficits. It may be unilateral or bilateral.

modal (mōd'l) [L. *modus*, mode] **1.** Pert. to, or characteristic of, a mode. **2.** In statistics, pert. to the most frequent, common, or typical measure of the variables being investigated.

modality (mō-dăl'ĭt-ē) **1.** method of application or the employment of any therapeutic agent, device, or treatment. **2.** Any specific sensory stimulus such as taste, touch, vision, pressure, or hearing.

modal personality SEE: under *personality*.

mode (mōd) [L. *modus*, measure, mode] **1.** In a set of data, the value of the most frequently occurring variable. **2.** In res-

piratory therapy, any of several approaches to continuous mechanical ventilation including volume- and pressure-targeted application with full or partial ventilatory support.

control m. Continuous mandatory ventilation in which the ventilator generates breaths at a preset rate regardless of the respiratory efforts of the patient.

model (mod'ĕl) **1.** A pattern or form used to make a replica, as a cast or impression of teeth in dentistry. **2.** A person or thing worthy of emulation or imitation. **3.** A diagram representing an idea, phenomenon, or statistical relationship among variables. **4.** A framework or system for organizing ideas and representing hypotheses or theories. SEE: *Nursing Theory Appendix.*

animal m. The study of anatomy, physiology, or pathology in laboratory animals in order to apply the results to human function and disease.

conceptual m. A set of abstract and general concepts and statements about those concepts. SYN: *conceptual framework; conceptual system; paradigm* (2).

conceptual m. of nursing SEE: *conceptual models of nursing.*

fluid mosaic m. A representation of the structure of the cell membrane, in which protein molecules are dispersed in a phospholipid bilayer.

m. of human occupation ABBR: MOHO. A conceptual framework for viewing occupational therapy practice, aimed at improving the patient's organization of time, overall function, and adaptation as reflected in the performance of occupations. Within this framework, intervention includes strategies for fostering skill development and habit changes through role acquisition, improved self-image, and environmental changes.

mortality prediction m. ABBR: MPM. A rating system of the severity of illness of patients admitted to an ICU. It includes the patient's age, need for vasoconstricting drugs (blood pressure), kidney function, urinary output, coagulation status, oxygenation, need for mechanical ventilation, mental status, liver health, cancer diagnosis (if any), and the presence of mass lesions in the brain.

Nagi disablement m. SEE: *Nagi disablement model.*

nursing m. A conceptual model that refers to abstract and general ideas about human beings, their environments and health, and nursing. SEE: *conceptual models of nursing.*

stochastic m. A statistical model that attempts to account for randomness. The model aims to reproduce the sequence of events likely to occur in real life.

study m. A diagnostic cast of an impression of the dental arches or a part thereof, trimmed with the arches articulated and the edges perpendicular to the occlusal plane. The study model serves as the basis for construction of dental appliances, dentures, or orthodontic treatment.

Model of Human Occupational Screening Tool ABBR: MOHOST. A screening assessment tool used by occupational therapists and based on the Model of Human Occupation. The measure includes items related to a client's motivation for and patterns of activity, communication and interactive skills, cognitive skills, and living environment, viewed from the perspective of everyday activities.

modeling (mod'ling) A form of behavior therapy involving the patient's acquisition of social behavior and mental response by following the example of associates, esp. parents and siblings.

moderated (mod'ĕ-rāt″ĕd) [L. *moderari,* to restrain] Diminished in severity; mitigated, allayed.

moderation (mŏd-ĕr-ā'shŭn) [L. *moderatio*] The limited use of a substance; the avoidance of excessive or hazardous exposure to a potentially harmful agent.

modification (mŏd″ĭ-fĭ-kā'shŭn) The act or result of changing something, such as the shape or character of an object or structure.

posttranslational m. The alteration of a protein, e.g., by phosphorylation or by the addition of carbohydrates to its structure. This process changes both the structure of proteins and their functions in biochemical reactions.

modified Ottawa ankle rules ABBR: MOAR. A 1998 modification of the 1992 Ottawa ankle rules that extended the palpation zone from the lateral malleolus to the midportion of the malleolus. This change significantly increased the specificity of the examination for ankle fracture.

modified vaccinia virus Ankara ABBR: MVA. An attenuated form of vaccinia virus that does not replicate itself efficiently. It has been used as an antigen carrier and as an adjuvant in the development of vaccines against both infectious illnesses and cancers.

modifier In medicine, esp. in therapeutics and clinical medicine, use of or addition of something that alters that to which it is added.

biological response m. ABBR: BRM. **1.** An agent that intensifies normal immune responses. Examples include interferon, interleukin-2, and monoclonal antibodies. **2.** A nutrient with hormonal or anti-inflammatory effects. Examples include botanical enzymes and hormones. Usually, these agents are used as adjuncts to other pharmacolog-

ical agents and therapies in the management of selected malignancies, immunodeficiency and autoimmune disorders, and certain viral infections such as hepatitis C. SEE: *biotherapy.*

modiolus (mō-dī'ō-lŭs) [L., hub] Central pillar or axial part of cochlea extending from the base to the apex.

modulation (mŏd″ū-lā'shŭn) **1.** The alteration in function or status of something in response to a stimulus or altered chemical or physical environment. **2.** In electronics, the manner in which a signal is used to vary either the amplitude, frequency, or phase of a normally constant carrier signal; a method of coding information onto a carrier.

module (mŏj'ool) [L. *modulus,* a small unit of measure] **1.** In education, a unit of study. **2.** In engineering, a structural element used in the design or architecture of a device.

modulus (mŏj'ŭ-lŭs) [L., a small measure] In physics, a constant or coefficient that indicates to what extent a substance possesses some property.

modus operandi (mō'dŭs ŏp″ĕ-răn'dē) Method of performing an act.

MOHOST *Model of Human Occupational Screening.*

MOI *mechanism of injury.*

moiety (moy'ĕ-tē) [Fr. *moitié,* fr. L. *medietas,* middle] **1.** One of two equal parts. **2.** A portion of something that has been divided.

moist (moyst) Damp, wet.

moisture vapor transmission rate ABBR: MVTR. The rate at which a barrier permits moisture to penetrate or escape. In pharmaceutical packaging the moisture vapor transmission rate is one element that determines the shelf life and expiration of a medication.

mol SEE: ² *mole.*

² mol *molecular; molecule.*

molal (mō'lăl) One mole of solute per kilogram of solvent. SEE: *mole.*

molality (mō-lal'ĭt-ē) [*molal*] The number of moles of a solute per kilogram of solvent. It is the unit of choice when dealing with colligative properties such as osmotic pressure.

¹ molar (mō'lăr) [L. *moles,* a mass] **1.** Pert. to a mole. **2.** Gram-molecule. SYN: *mole* (1). **3.** Pert. to solutions having a concentration of solute of 1 mol/L at 25°C.

² molar (mō'lăr) [L. *molaris,* grinding] A grinding or back tooth, one of three on each side of each jaw. The first permanent molar erupts between 6 and 7 years; the second between the 13th and 16th years. The third molars (wisdom teeth) are extremely variable, usually erupting between the 18th and 25th years; however, they may erupt later or not at all. SEE: *dentition* for table; *teeth.*

impacted m. A tooth that is unable to erupt into its place in normal occlusion, typically because there is not enough space in the dental arch to accept it. This condition is commonly related to the third molar (wisdom tooth).

molar concentration The number of moles of a substance in a specified volume of solution.

molariform (mōl-ăr'ĭ-form) Resembling a molar tooth.

molarity (mō-lar'ĭt-ē) [*molar*] The number of gram molecular mass (moles) of a substance per liter of solution.

molar solution SEE: under *solution*.

mold, mould 1. A fuzzy coating due to growth of a fungus on the surface of decaying vegetable matter or on nonorganic objects. **2.** One of the parasitic or saprophytic fungi that grow in a mycelium pattern; genera include *Aspergillus* and *Penicillium*. SYN: *filamentous fungus*. **3.** To shape a mass or the container in which the mass is shaped.

molding 1. Shaping of the fetal head to adapt itself to the dimensions of the birth canal during its descent through the pelvis. **2.** A protective border used in plastic surgery. **3.** The casting of a reproduction.

   border m. In dentistry, the shaping of impression material at the edges by the oral tissues.

¹ **mole** [Old English *māl*, blemish] A birthmark or nevus. SEE: illus.

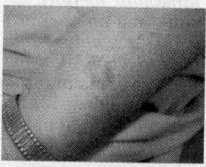

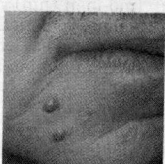

MOLES

⚠ Moles should be examined and, if necessary, be removed by experienced professionals.

PATIENT CARE: The patient is encouraged to regularly inspect areas of the skin that have moles and consult a health care professional about any mole that changes color or shows signs of growth or changes in appearance, as such changes may indicate neoplasm.

   pigmented m. Nevus pigmentosus.

   vascular m. Hemangioma.

² **mole, mol** (mōl) [Ger. *Mol*, abbr. for *Molekulargewicht*, molecular weight] In the Système International d' Unités (SI system), 1 mole of a substance contains as many atoms as exist in 0.012 kg of carbon 12.

³ **mole** (mōl) [L. *moles*, a shapeless mass] A uterine mass arising from a poorly developed or degenerating ovum.

   hydatid m. A rare form of gestational trophoblastic disease in which there is overproduction of chorionic villi normally destined to develop into the placenta. A partial mole is characterized by an abnormal placenta and some fetal development; a complete mole, by an abnormal placenta and no fetal development. Complete and partial moles differ in karyotype. Complete moles show an absence of maternal chromosomes and a duplication of spermatozoal chromosomes. Partial moles exhibit either karyotype 69 XXY or karyotype 69 XYY due to the presence of the maternal X chromosome. Symptoms of molar pregnancy may include abnormal uterine growth (usually increased), nausea and vomiting, vaginal bleeding, and high blood pressure. Diagnosis is made by measuring serum human chorionic gonadotropin levels and ultrasonography, and definitive treatment is complete surgical removal of the mole, usually with curettage. Moles that are not removed may become malignant. Eighty percent of all moles are benign. SEE: *gestational trophoblastic disease*.

   true m. A mole representing the degenerated embryo or fetus.

molecular (mŏ-lek'yŭ-lăr) ABBR: mol. Pert. to molecules.

molecular adsorbent recirculating system ABBR: MARS. An artificial liver that removes toxins from the blood. It is used temporarily to support and treat patients with fulminant hepatic failure while awaiting liver transplantation.

molecular diagnostics SEE: under *diagnostics*.

molecular disease Disease due to a defect in a single molecule. An example is sickle cell anemia, in which a single amino acid substitution in the hemoglobin molecule causes the abnormally shaped red cells characteristic of this disease.

molecular farming The study of plants and animals for their potential uses in pharmacology.

molecular histology The study of the functional molecules within tissues, using techniques such as immunocytochemistry or in situ hybridization.

molecular layer (of the cerebral cortex) SEE: under *layer*.

molecular mimicry (mĭm'ĭk-rē) Antigenic similarity between molecules found on some disease-causing microorganisms and on specific previously healthy body cells or tissues. Molecular mimicry is one explanation for autoimmune diseases. After infection with a microorganism whose surface contains antigens similar to those found in the body, the immune system may respond inappropriately by trying to damage these cells with similar surface antigens in otherwise healthy joints, blood vessels, or other organs.

molecule (mol′ĕ-kūl″) [L. *molecula,* little mass] ABBR: mol. Any electrically neutral aggregate of atoms held together strongly enough to be considered as a unit. The individual atoms in the molecule may be of the same type or different. Combinations of dissimilar atoms form chemical compounds. The positive and negative electrical charges balance exactly. Excess or deficiency of either positive or negative charge by the loss or acquisition of electrons results in the formation of an ion.

A molecule is designated by the number of atoms it contains, as monatomic (one atom); diatomic (two); triatomic (three); tetratomic (four); pentatomic (five); or hexatomic (six).

molimen (mō-lī′mĕn) *pl.* **molimina** [L., effort] Effort to establish any normal function, esp. that necessary to establish the menstrual flow.

Mollaret meningitis (mō-lă-rā′) [Pierre Mollaret, Fr. physician, 1898–1987] A form of meningitis characterized by recurring bouts of headache with fever, cerebrospinal fluid leukocytosis, and signs of meningeal irritation. It is often associated with recurrences of herpes simplex virus infection (HSV-1 and HSV-2).

Mollicutes (mol′ĭ′kūt-ēz) [L. *mollis,* soft + *cutis,* skin] A class of very small bacteria, some of which have cell walls and others of which have no cell walls but are surrounded instead by a cell membrane. It includes several genera that cause human diseases, including *Erysipelothrix* (a gram-positive rod shaped bacterium that has a cell wall), *Mycoplasma,* and *Ureaplasma.*

Mollusca (mŏl-lŭs′kă) A phylum of animals that includes the bivalves (mussels, oysters, clams), slugs, and snails. Snails are intermediate hosts for many parasitic flukes. Oysters, clams, and mussels, esp. if inadequately cooked, may transmit the hepatitis A virus or bacterial pathogens.

molluscum (mŏ-lŭs′kŭm) [L., soft] A mildly infective skin disease marked by tumor formations on the skin. **molluscous** (mŏ-lŭs′kŭs), *adj.*

   m. contagiosum A rash composed of small dome-shaped papules with a central crater that is said to be "umbilicated" (dimpled or belly button–shaped). Cheesy (caseous) material fills the dimple's core. A pox virus causes the

rash, which is commonly spread by person-to-person contact among children and young adults. Widespread lesions are sometimes identified on the skin of immunosuppressed patients (e.g., patients with AIDS). Lesions in the groin, on the genitals, or on the upper thighs usually are sexually transmitted. SEE: illus.

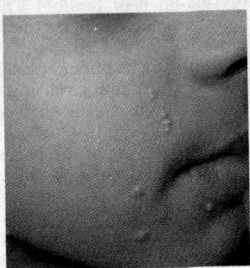

MOLLUSCUM CONTAGIOSUM

TREATMENT: Some lesions may heal spontaneously and require no therapy. Persistent papules can be removed with curettage or frozen with liquid nitrogen.

mollusk, mollusc (mŏl′ŭsk) Any member of the phylum Mollusca.

molt (mōlt) To shed a covering such as feathers or skin that is replaced by new growth.

mol. wt. *Molecular weight.*

molybdenum (mŏ-lib′dĕ-nŭm) [L. *molybdaena* fr Gr. *molybdaina,* (fisherman's) sinker] SYMB: Mo. A hard, heavy, metallic element, atomic weight 95.94, atomic number 42. It is a trace element crucial to plant nutrition and is found in certain enzymes, including xanthine oxidase.

momentum (mō-mĕn′tŭm) [L.] **1.** In physics, the quantity obtained by multiplying the mass of a body by its linear velocity. **2.** Force of motion acquired by a moving object as a result of continuance of its motion; impetus.

mometasone (mō-mĕt′ă-sōn) A corticosteroid, administered as a nasal spray to treat seasonal allergic rhinitis and other chronic nasal inflammatory conditions, including nasal polyps. Its therapeutic classes are corticosteroids and allergy, cold, and cough remedies.

momism (mŏm′ĭzm) [Coined by Phillip Wylie in his book *A Generation of Vipers*] In American culture, undue dependence on one's mother, esp. in very early life. This was alleged to cause the individual to be immature.

monacolin (mŏn″ŭ-kŏl′ĭn) One of a class of chemicals that reduce high cholesterol levels. Monacolin K is marketed as an alternative medicine called "red yeast rice extract" and as the proprietary medication lovastatin.

monad (mō′-năd) [Gr. *monas,* a unit] **1.** A univalent element. **2.** A unicellular organism. **3.** One of the four components of a tetrad.

monamine (mŏn-ăm′ĭn) Monoamine.

monarticular (mŏn-ăr-tĭk′ŭ-lăr) Concerning or affecting one joint. SYN: *monarthric.*

-monas [L. fr. Gr. *monas,* stem *monad-,* unit, unity] Suffix meaning *unit, single-celled* (organism), esp. in taxonomic names, e.g., *Pseudomonas.*

Monascus purpureus (mŏn-ăs′kŭs pŭr-pūr′ē-ŭs) [NL fm. Gr. "purple single-bag"'] Red yeast, a traditional Chinese medicine used as a food preservative in the past and as a contemporary alternative medication to lower serum cholesterol levels.

monaster (mŏn-ăs′tĕr) [″ + *aster,* star] Single starlike figure formed in mitosis.

monatomic (mŏn″ă-tŏm′ĭk) [″ + *atomos,* indivisible] **1.** Concerning a single atom. **2.** Univalent.

monaural (mŏn-aw′răl) Concerning or affecting one ear.

Mönckeberg calcification (mungk′ĕ-bĕrg, mengk′) [Johann Georg Möngkeberg, Ger. pathologist, 1877–1925] Calcium deposition in the media of arteries.

Mondini syndrome [Carlo Mondini, Italian anatomist, 1729–1803] Congenital deafness in which the cochlea develops with one and a half instead of its usual two and a half turns.

Mondor disease (mon′dor″) [Henri Mondor, Fr. physician, 1885–1962] Thrombosis, sclerosis, or phlebitis of a subcutaneous vein or veins in the breast or chest wall sometimes extending from the axilla to the epigastrium. It may occur after trauma or appear without apparent cause. Although a benign, self-limiting disease, its appearance may be confused with breast cancer.

moneme The smallest unit of intelligible or meaningful speech, e.g., a word composed of a single syllable.

Monera (mō-nē′ră) In taxonomy, the kingdom of organisms with prokaryotic cell structure, that is, they lack membrane-bound cell organelles and a nuclear membrane around the chromosome Included are the bacteria and cyanobacteria (formerly the blue-green algae). SYN: *Prokaryotae.*

monestrous (mŏn-ĕs′trŭs) Having a single estrous cycle in a single sexual season.

mongolism (mŏn′gŏl-ĭzm) An inaccurate and inappropriate term for Down syndrome.

mongoloid (mŏn′gō-loyd) **1.** Concerning Mongols. **2.** Characterized by mongolism (i.e., Down syndrome).

monilethrix (mŏn-ĭl′ĕ-thrĭks) [L. *monile,* necklace, + Gr. *thrix,* hair] A genetic defect of the hair shaft in which the hair becomes beaded and brittle. The defect

usually appears by the second month of life. There is no effective treatment.

Monilia (mă-nĭl′ē-ă) [L. *monile,* necklace] Former name for the genus of fungi now called *Candida.* **monilial** (mō-nĭl′ē-ăl), *adj.*

moniliasis (mō″nĭ-lī′ă-sĭs) Candidiasis.

moniliform (mŏn-ĭl′ĭ-form) [″ + *forma,* shape] Resembling a necklace or string of beads.

monitor (mon′ĭt-ŏr) [L. *monitor,* adviser] **1.** One who observes a condition, procedure, or apparatus, esp. one responsible for detecting and preventing malfunction. **2.** A device that provides a warning signal when another device fails or malfunctions or when a measurement threshold is reached. **3.** To check by using an electronic device.

   apnea m. SEE: *apnea monitoring.*

   blood glucose m. Glucometer.

   blood pressure m. A device that automatically obtains and usually records the blood pressure at certain intervals, using the direct or indirect method of determining pressure. In some models, an alarm or light signal is activated if the pressure rises or falls to an abnormal level.

   cardiac m. A visual and/or audible recording of each electrical impulse or physical contraction of the heart.

   event m. Loop recorder.

   fetal m. 1. A monitor that detects and displays fetal heartbeat. **2.** Assessment of fetus in utero with respect to its heart rate by use of electrocardiogram or by chemical analysis of the amniotic fluid or fetal blood. SEE: *fetal heart rate monitoring; fetal monitoring in utero.*

   glucose m. Glucometer.

   Holter m. SEE: *Holter monitor.*

   impedance m. A device used to detect variations in respiratory rate and volume. It measures changes in the electrical impedance of the chest as the patient breathes. It may be used in intensive care units to monitor critically ill patients or in private residences to detect apnea, esp. in sleeping infants.

   peak flow m. A handheld device used to assess the maximum expiratory flow (in liters/minute) in patients with asthma and chronic obstructive lung disease. SEE: illus.

   respiratory m. Respiratory function monitoring

   temperature m. A monitor for measuring and recording temperature of the body or some particular portion of the body.

   unit m. In radiation therapy, a calibrated unit of dose that determines the length of the treatment.

   vaccine vial m. A heat-sensitive indicator on the outside of a vaccine bottle that changes color when the vaccine has been exposed to excessively high tem-

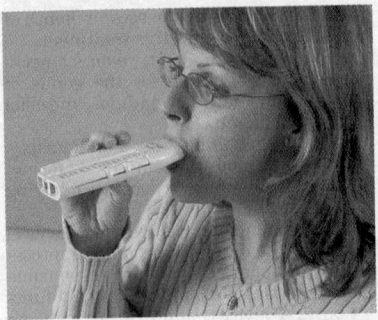

PEAK FLOW MONITORING

peratures, making it unsafe for patient use.

monitrice (mŏn'ĭ-trĭs) [Fr. *female,* instructor] In the Lamaze technique of childbearing, a labor coach or doula.

monkeypox (mŭn'kē-pŏks) ABBR: MoxV. A poxviral illness clinically similar to smallpox. The CDC recommends that persons exposed to MoxV be vaccinated against smallpox to prevent the disease.

mono Infectious **mononucleosis**.

mono-, mon- [Gr. *monos,* single] Prefixes meaning *one, single.*

monoacidic (mŏn″ō-ă-sĭd'ĭk) Having one replaceable hydroxyl (OH) group.

monoamide (mŏn″ō-ăm'ĭd) An amide with only one amide group.

monoamine (mŏn″ō-ăm'ēn) An amine with only one amine group.

monoamine oxidase inhibitor SEE: under *inhibitor.*

monoarthritis (mŏn″ō-ăr-thrī'tĭs) [″ + ″ + *itis,* inflammation] Arthritis affecting a single joint.

monobactam (mŏn'ō-băk-tăm) A beta-lactam antibiotic, similar in structure to penicillins and cephalosporins, except with respect to its nucleus: monobactams have a single cyclical nucleus, while penicillins and cephalosporins have two linked cyclical nuclei.

monobacterial (mŏn″ō-băk-tē'rē-ăl) Concerning a single species of bacteria.

monobasic (mŏn-ō-bā'sĭk) [″ + *basis,* a base] Having only one hydrogen atom replaceable by a metal or positive radical.

monoblast (mŏn'ō-blăst) [″ + *blastos,* germ] A cell that gives rise to a monocyte.

monobromated (mŏn″ō-brō'māt-ĕd) Pert. to chemical compound with only one atom of bromine in each molecule.

monocelled (mŏn'ō-sĕld) Composed of a single cell.

monochord (mŏn'ō-kord) [″ + *chorde,* cord] A single-string instrument used for testing upper tone audition.

monochorionic (mŏn-ō-kor″ē-ŏn'ĭk) Pos-

sessing a single chorion, as in the case of identical twins.

monochromatic (mŏn″ō-krō-măt'ĭk) [″ + *chroma,* color] 1. Having one color. 2. A color-blind person to whom all colors appear to be of one hue. 3. In radiology and physics, having a single wavelength and energy.

monochromatism (mŏn″ō-krō'mă-tĭzm) [Gr. *monos,* single, + *chroma,* color, + *-ismos,* condition] Complete color blindness in which all colors are perceived as shades of gray. SYN: *monochromasy.*

monochromator (mŏn-ō-krō'mă-tor) A spectroscope modified for selective transmission of a narrow band of the spectrum.

monoclinic (mŏn″ō-klin'ĭk) [″ + *klinein,* to incline] Pert. to crystals in which the vertical axis is inclined to one lateral axis but at right angles to the other.

monoclonal (mŏn″ō-klōn'ăl) Arising from a single cell.

monoclonal antibody ABBR: MoAb. SEE: *antibody.*

monoclonal antibody therapy The use of monoclonal antibodies to suppress immune function, kill target cells, or treat specific inflammatory diseases. Because of their high level of specificity, they bind to precise cellular or molecular targets. A potential problem associated with the use of monoclonal antibodies is an allergic reaction to the foreign antigens in the antibody, since they are created from mouse cells. Monoclonal antibodies have numerous uses in health care. SEE: table; *hybridoma; monoclonal antibody.*

monoclonal B-cell lymphocytosis The presence of excessive numbers of B lymphocytes in the bloodstream, all derived from a single parent cell. This condition sometimes precedes chronic lymphocytic leukemia, although it is often found in patients who never develop the disease.

monocontaminated (mŏn″ō-kŏn-tăm'ĭ-nāt″ĕd) Infected with a single species of organism.

monocular (mŏn-ŏk'ū-lar) [″ + L. *oculus,* eye] 1. Concerning or affecting one eye. 2. Possessing a single eyepiece, as in a monocular microscope.

monoculus (mŏn-ŏk'ū-lŭs) 1. A bandage for shielding one eye. 2. A fetus with only one eye. SYN: *cyclops.*

monocyclic (mŏn″ō-sī'klĭk) Concerning one cycle.

monocyte (mŏn'ō-sīt″) [*mono-* + *-cyte*] ABBR: MO. A mononuclear phagocytic white blood cell derived from myeloid stem cells. Monocytes circulate in the bloodstream for about 24 hr and then move into tissues, at which point they mature into macrophages, which are long lived. Monocytes and macrophages

Some Monoclonal Antibodies and Their Uses

Name of Antibody	Condition Treated or Prevented
Adalimumab	Rheumatoid arthritis; psoriasis
Bevacizumab	Solid tumors
Edrecolomab	Solid tumors
Efalizumab	Psoriasis
Enlimomab	Organ transplant rejection
Ibritumomab	Follicular lymphoma
Infliximab	Crohn's disease; rheumatoid arthritis
Natalizumab	Relapsing forms of multiple sclerosis
Omalizumab	Allergic rhinitis
OKT3	Organ transplant rejection
Palivizumab	Respiratory syncytial virus
Rituximab	Leukemias and lymphomas
RhuMAb/ VEGF	Solid tumors
Tositumomab	B cell lymphoma
Transtuzumab	Metastatic breast cancer

are one of the first lines of defense in the inflammatory process. This network of fixed and mobile phagocytes that engulf foreign antigens and cell debris previously was called the reticuloendothelial system and is now referred to as the mononuclear phagocyte system (MPS). SEE: illus.; *blood* for illus.; *macrophage*.

monocytic (mŏn-ō-sĭt′ĭk), *adj.*

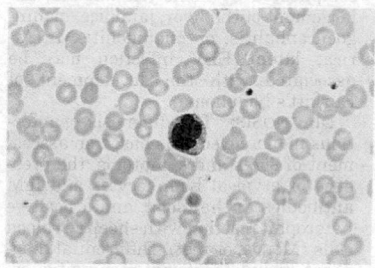

MONOCYTES

(Orig. mag. ×640)

monocyte chemotactic protein ABBR: MCP. Any of a family of cytokines that attract mononuclear cells (monocytes and lymphocytes), eosinophils, and neutrophils to inflamed or injured parts of the body.

monocytopenia (mŏn″ō-sī″tō-pē′nē-ă) [″ + *kytos,* cell, + *penia,* lack] Diminished number of monocytes in the blood.

monocytosis (mŏn″ō-sī-tō′sĭs) [″ + ″ + *osis,* condition] Excessive number of monocytes in the blood.

monodose (mon′ŏ-dōs″) [*mono- + dose*] Unit **dose**.

monoecious (mŏn-ē′shŭs) [″ + *oikos,* house] Pert. to the presence of functioning male and female sex organs in the same individual.

monofilament (mŏn′ō-fĭl″ă-mĕnt) [″ + *filum,* thread] A strand of nylon used to assess sensation in peripheral nerves, especially in the feet of patients with diabetes mellitus and other neuropathic conditions. The inability to feel the prodding of a strand of monofilament on the foot in one or more locations is diagnostic of diabetic peripheral neuropathy.

monofixation syndrome (mŏn″ō-fĭk-sā′shĭn) [″ + ″] An inability of the eyes to bifixate.

monogamy (mō-nŏg′ă-mē) [″ + *gamos,* marriage] A long-term exclusive sexual affiliation.

monogenesis (mŏn″ō-jĕn′ĕ-sĭs) [Gr. *monos,* single, + *genesis,* generation, birth] **1.** Production of offspring of only one sex. **2.** The theory that all organisms arise from a single cell. **3.** Asexual reproduction.

monogenic (mŏn″ă-jĕn′ĭk) Caused by, relating to, or affecting a single gene.

monogenic disease SEE: under *Disease*.

monograph (mŏn′ō-grăf) [″ + *graphein,* to write] A treatise dealing with a single subject.

   drug m. A publication that specifies for a drug (or class of related drugs) the kinds and amounts of ingredients it may contain, the conditions and limitations for which it may be offered, directions for use, warnings, and other information that its labeling must contain. The monograph may contain important information concerning interactions with other drugs.

monogyny (mō-nŏj′ă-nē) [″ + *gyne,* woman] Practice whereby a male has only one female mate.

monohybrid (mŏn″ō-hī′brĭd) [″ + L. *hybrida,* mongrel] Offspring of a cross between parents differing in a single genetic characteristic.

monohydrated (mŏn-ō-hī′drāt-ĕd) [″ + *hydor,* water] United with only one molecule of water.

monohydric (mŏn″ō-hī′drĭk) Having a single replaceable hydrogen atom.

monoinfection (mŏn″ō-ĭn-fĕk′shŭn) Infection with a single species of organism.

monoiodotyrosine (mŏn″ō-ī-ō″dō-tī′rō-sēn) An amino acid intermediate in the synthesis of thyroxine and triiodothyronine.

monokine (mŏn′ō-kīn) A chemical mediator released by monocytes and macrophages during the immune response.

Monokines affect the growth and activity of other white blood cells. Interleukin-1 is an important monokine. SEE: *cytokine; inflammation; interleukin-1; lymphokine; paracrine.*

monolayer (mŏn″ō-lā′ĕr) A single layer, esp. of cells growing in culture.

monolingual (mŏn″ō-lĭng′gwĭl) Being able to speak only one language in a semantically correct and fluent manner.

monolocular (mŏn″ō-lŏk′ū-lar) [″ + L. *loculus,* a small chamber] Having only one cell or cavity. SYN: *unilocular.*

monomania (mŏn-ō-mā′nē-ă) [″ + *mania,* madness] Mental illness characterized by distortion of thought processes concerning a single subject or idea.

monomaniac (mŏn″ō-mā′nē-ăk) One afflicted with monomania.

monomelic (mon″ō-mēl′ik) [″ + *melos,* limb] Affecting a single limb.

monomelic amyotrophy (mon″ō-mēl′ik) SEE: under *amyotrophy.*

monomer (mŏn′ō-mĕr) Any molecule that can be bound to similar molecules to form a polymer.

monomeric (mŏn-ō-mĕr′ĭk) [″ + *meros,* part] Consisting of, or affecting, a single piece or segment of a body.

monometallic (mŏn″ō-mĕ-tăl′ĭk) Containing a single atom of a metal per molecule.

monomolecular (mŏn″ō-mō-lĕk′ū-lăr) Concerning one molecule.

monomorphic (mŏn-ō-mor′fĭk) [″ + *morphe,* form] Unchangeable in form; keeping the same form throughout every stage of development.

mononeural (mŏn-ō-nū′răl) [″ + *neuron,* nerve] Supplied by or concerning a single nerve.

mononeuritis (mŏn″ō-nū-rī′tĭs) [″ + ″ + *itis,* inflammation] Peripheral nerve damage affecting several distinct nerves in different regions of the body. Mononeuritis multiplex is found in vasculitis and in some patients with diabetes mellitus, among other diseases and conditions.

   m. multiplex Inflammation of nerves in separate body areas. SYN: *multiple mononeuropathy.*

mononeuropathy (mon″ō-noo-rop′ă-thē) [*mono-* + *neuropathy*] Disease of a single nerve.

   focal appendicular m. Nerve disease or impairment that affects motor function on the face or limbs. Examples include Bell's palsy, diabetic amyotrophy, median neuropathy (carpal tunnel syndrome), and ulnar neuropathy.

   multiple m. Mononeuritis multiplex.

mononuclear (mŏn-ō-nū′klē-ăr) [″ + L. *nucleus,* kernel] Having one nucleus, particularly a blood cell such as a monocyte or lymphocyte. SYN: *uninuclear.*

mononuclear phagocyte system ABBR: MPS. The system of fixed macrophages and circulating monocytes that serve as phagocytes, engulfing foreign substances in a wide variety of immune responses. This system formerly was called the reticuloendothelial system.

mononucleosis (mŏn-ō-nū″klē-ō′sĭs) [″ + *nucleus,* kernel, + *osis,* condition] Presence of an abnormally high number of mononuclear leukocytes in the blood.

   infectious m. An acute infectious disease caused by the Epstein-Barr virus (EBV), a member of the herpesvirus group. It is most common in the U.S. in people between 15 and 25 years of age (i.e., in high school- and college-age adolescents and young adults); beyond that age, most people are immune to EBV. The disease is sometimes referred to colloquially as the "kissing disease" because of its mode of transmission from person to person. SEE: *Epstein-Barr virus; Nursing Diagnoses Appendix.*

ETIOLOGY: The virus is transmitted in saliva and infects the epithelial cells of the oropharynx, nasopharynx, and salivary glands before spreading to lymphoid tissue (e.g., lymph nodes, spleen, liver) via infected B lymphocytes. The incubation period is 30 to 45 days.

SYMPTOMS: Typically, infectious mononucleosis causes a sudden or gradual onset (7 to 14 days) of flulike symptoms. Findings include enlarged tender cervical lymph nodes (lymphadenopathy), exudative tonsillitis, possible splenic enlargement and tenderness, and an enlarged spleen. Leukocytosis with atypical lymphocytes is present on blood smears. A maculopapular rash may be present early on. The infection usually lasts 2 to 4 weeks.

Rarely, infectious mononucleosis is complicated by hemolytic anemia, enlargement of the liver, jaundice, meningoencephalitis, or pneumonitis. In Africa, latent EBV infection may be associated with the development of Burkitt's lymphoma.

DIAGNOSIS: The diagnosis of infectious mononucleosis is based on assessment of signs and symptoms, the presence of atypical lymphocytes and IgM antibodies in the blood, and a positive heterophil reaction with sheep red blood cells (Monospot test). Differential diagnoses include bacterial meningitis, cytomegalovirus infection, cat scratch disease, allergic reactions to drugs (e.g., sulfa or phenytoin), German measles, strep throat, *Toxoplasma gondii* infection, and the acute onset of infection with HIV/AIDS.

TREATMENT: There is no specific therapy for infectious mononucleosis; NSAIDs are used to treat fever, headache, sore throat, and myalgias. Corticosteroids may be used for complications. Full recovery is usual, after a period of convalescence lasting weeks or months.

PATIENT CARE: During the acute phase, the patient is encouraged to refrain from activity and to maintain adequate rest to reduce fatigue. Gargling with saline mouthwash, drinking noncitrus fruit juices, milk shakes, and broth, and eating cool, bland foods help to relieve sore throat. Generally, patients may resume activity that does not involve heavy exertion after 1 to 2 weeks and their normal activity level in 4 to 6 weeks. Students generally are advised to carry out routine school assignments but delay arduous projects until recovery is complete. If the spleen is enlarged, patients should avoid contact sports and not lift more than 10 lb until cleared by their health care provider to prevent traumatizing or rupturing the spleen.

⚠️ To decrease the risk of inducing splenic rupture, health care providers should avoid deep palpation of the abdomen of patients with infectious mononucleosis.

mononucleotide (mŏn″ō-nū′klē-ō-tīd″) A product resulting from hydrolysis of nucleic acid, containing phosphoric acid combined with a glucoside or pentoside. SYN: *nucleotide*.

monoparesis (mŏn-ō-păr-ē′sĭs) [Gr. *monos,* single, + *paresis,* weakness] Paralysis of a single part of the body.

monophyletic (mŏn″ō-fīl-ĕt′ĭk) [″ + *phyle,* tribe] Originating from a single source; opposite of polyphyletic.

monoplegia (mŏn-ō-plē′jē-ă) [″ + *plege,* stroke] Paralysis of a single limb or a single group of muscles. **monoplegic,** *adj.*

monopodia (mŏn″ō-pō′dē-ă) [″ + *pous,* foot] Condition of having only one foot; usually the two feet are fused.

monopolar (mŏn-ō-pōl′ăr) [″ + L. *polus,* pole] **1.** Having one pole. SYN: *unipolar.* **2.** In therapeutic electrical stimulation, the application of a current using large dispersive electrodes and smaller active electrodes under which the treatment effects occur.

monorchid (mŏn-or′kĭd) [″ + *orchis,* testicle] Person having only one testicle.

monosaccharide (mŏn-ō-săk′ă-rīd) [″ + Sanskrit *sarkara,* sugar] A simple sugar that cannot be decomposed by hydrolysis, such as fructose, galactose, or glucose.

monosodium glutamate (mŏn″ō-sō′dē-ŭm) ABBR: MSG. $C_5H_8NNaO_4 \cdot H_2O$; sodium salt of glutamic acid; a white crystalline substance used to flavor foods, esp. meats. When ingested in large amounts, it may cause chest pain, a sensation of facial pressure, headaches, burning sensation, and excessive sweating. Allergy to MSG is common, and those persons who are allergic should avoid eating foods containing this ingredient. The use of MSG to enhance the flavor of foods prepared for infants is controversial. MSG is sold under various trade names, such as Ajinomoto, Accent, Vetsin.

monosodium urate deposition disease Gout.

monosome (mŏn′ō-sōm) [″ + *soma,* body] An unpaired sex chromosome, X or Y, sometimes called an accessory chromosome.

monosomy (mŏn′ō-sō″mē) Condition of having only one of a pair of chromosomes, as in Turner's syndrome, in which there is one X chromosome rather than the normal pair.

monospermy (mŏn′ō-spĕr″mē) [″ + *sperma,* seed] Fertilization by a single spermatozoon entering an ovum.

monostotic (mŏn″ŏs-tŏt′ĭk) [″ + *osteon,* bone] Concerning a single bone.

monosubstituted (mŏn″ō-sŭb′stĭ-tūt″ĕd) Having only a single molecule replaced.

monosymptomatic (mŏn″ō-sĭmp-tō-măt′ĭk) [″ + *symptomatikos,* pert. to symptom] Having only one dominant symptom.

monosynaptic (mŏn″ō-sĭ-năp′tĭk) Transmitted through only a single synapse.

monotherapy (mŏn′ō-thĕr-ă-pē) Treatment with a single drug, for example, a single antihypertensive agent.

monotocous (mō-nŏt′ō-kŭs) [Gr. *monos,* single, + *tokos,* birth] Producing a single offspring per birth.

monotrichous (mŏn-ŏt′rĭ-kŭs) Pert. to or having a single flagellum.

monovalent (mŏn-ō-vā′lĕnt) [″ + L. *valere,* to have power] Having a single electron available in the outermost orbital for chemical bonding. SYN: *univalent* (1).

monovision (mŏn′ō-vĭzh″un) [Gr. *monos,* single, + L. *visio,* fr. *vidēre,* to see] A treatment for presbyopia in which the dominant eye is corrected to improve distance vision and the other eye is corrected for near and intermediate tasks. Standard lenses, contact lenses, or refractive surgery may be used for the corrections.

monoxenous (mō-nŏks′ĕn-ŭs) [″ + *xenos,* stranger] Said of a parasite that requires only one species as a host.

monoxide (mŏn-ŏk′sīd) An oxide having only one atom of oxygen.

monozygotic (mŏn″ŏ-zī-gŏt′ĭk) [*mono-* + *zygotic*] ABBR: MZ. Originating from a single fertilized ovum, said of identical twins.

Monsel solution Ferric subsulfate.

Monteggia, Giovanni Battista (mon-tej′ă) Italian surgeon, 1762–1815.

M. fracture Fracture of the proximal portion of the ulna with dislocation of the radial head.

montelukast (mŏn-tē-lūk′ăst) An oral leukotriene inhibitor used to treat asthma.

Montevideo unit (mon″tā-vi-dā′ō) [*Montevideo*, Uruguay, where the procedure was developed] ABBR: MVU. The sum of the intrauterine pressures (measured in mm Hg) recorded during all the contractions of the uterus during a consecutive 10-min period of labor.

PATIENT CARE: After an intrauterine pressure catheter is inserted, the baseline intrauterine pressure is recorded. The difference between the baseline pressure and the pressure during each contraction of the uterus in a 10-min period is calculated. For example, in a patient with a baseline uterine pressure of 15 mm Hg, and four intrauterine contractions, each of which has a peak pressure of 70 mm Hg, the difference is $(70 - 15 = 55)$. The sum of these four pressure differences (in this idealized case: $MVU = 4 \times 55 = 220$) is compared to a normal standard. An MVU of >200 predicts normally progressive labor 90% of the time. An MVU < 200 suggest protraction of labor or frank arrest of labor.

Montgomery, William F. (mŏnt-gŭm′ĕ-rē) Irish obstetrician, 1797–1859.

Montgomery straps Paired adhesive straps applied to either side of a wound (usually abdominal), the central sections of which are folded back on themselves with several perforations at the leading edges. This provides a method of securing a bandage and subsequently changing it without having to replace the tape each time. SEE: illus.

month, lunar Four calendar weeks (28 days), a measurement of time used in obstetrics. Pregnancy is calculated in terms of 10 lunar months.

monthly period SEE: under *period*.

mood [AS. *mod,* mind, feeling] A pervasive and sustained emotion that may have a major influence on a person's perception of the world. Examples of mood include depression, joy, elation, anger, and anxiety. SEE: *affect*.

mood disorder Any mental disorder that has a disturbance of mood as the predominant feature. In DSM-IV, these have been divided into mood episodes, mood disorders, and specifications describing either the most recent mood episode or the course of recurrent episodes. Mood disorders, including dysthymic disorder, are divided into the depressive disorders (unipolar depression), the bipolar disorders, and two disorders based on cause (i.e., due to a general medical condition or substance-induced mood disorder). Depressive disorders are distinguished from the bipolar disorders by the absence of a history of a manic, mixed, or hypomanic episode. Bipolar I disorder and bipolar II disorder involve the presence of or history of manic episodes, mixed episodes, or hypomanic episodes, usually with a history or presence of major depressive episodes. SEE: *Nursing Diagnoses Appendix.*

dysthymic m.d. Dysthymic disorder.

hypomanic episode m.d. A mood disorder characterized by a period of persistently elevated, expansive, or irritable mood lasting for at least 4 days. Three or more of the following must be present:

1. inflated self-esteem,
2. decreased need for sleep,
3. talking more than usual,
4. flight of ideas or feeling that thoughts are racing,
5. distractibility,
6. increase in goal-directed activities, and
7. excessive involvement in pleasur-

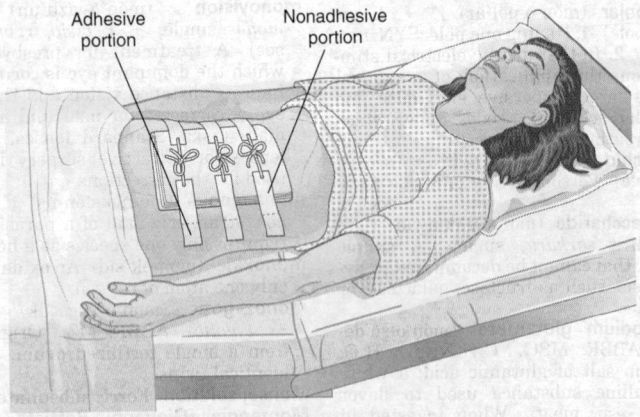

Adhesive portion   Nonadhesive portion

MONTGOMERY STRAPS

able activities with a high potential for painful consequences.

The episode is not severe enough to cause marked impairment in social or occupational functioning or to necessitate hospitalization, and there are no psychotic features. These changes are not due to drugs or to a general medical condition.

    major depressive episode m.d. Major depression.

    postpartum m.d. SEE: *postpartum blues; postpartum depression.*

    substance-induced m.d. A prominent and persistent disturbance in mood characterized by either or both of the following: depressed mood or markedly diminished interest or pleasure in all, or almost all, activities; and elevated, expansive, or irritable mood. The clinical and laboratory findings must support that either the symptoms developed during, or within a month of, substance intoxication or withdrawal, or that the medication (i.e., substance) is causally related to the disturbance. The condition cannot be better accounted for by a mood disorder that is not substance induced. The disturbance does not occur exclusively during the course of a delirium. The symptoms cause clinically significant distress or impairment in social, occupational, or other important areas of functioning.

mood stabilizer Any agent or therapy that prevents or relieves wide fluctuations in affective range, e.g., as occur in bipolar disorder.Examples of mood stabilizing drugs are carbamazepine and lithium carbonate.

mood swings Periods of variation in how one feels, changing from a sense of well-being to one of depression. This occurs normally, but may become abnormally intense in persons with manic-depressive states.

moon face SEE: *face, moon.*

Mooren ulcer (mōr′ĕn, moor′) [Albert Mooren, Ger. ophthalmologist, 1828–1899] A rare, inflammatory lesion of the peripheral cornea that causes significant eye pain and blindness if untreated. This condition is found in some patients with hepatitis C, other infectious diseases, or prior eye trauma or eye surgery. It may be an example of autoimmune molecular mimicry. Treatments include the use of immunosuppressant drugs, keratoplasty, or both. SEE: *molecular mimicry.*

moral reasoning Ethical reasoning.

moral treatment An approach to treating mental illness in the 19th century influenced by humanistic philosophy and a belief that a rational, caring approach would enable patients to normalize their thoughts and actions.

Moraxella (mor-ăx-ĕl′ă) A genus of gram-negative coccobacilli in the family Neisseriaceae; most are nonpathogenic inhabitants of mammalian mucous membranes.

    M.catarrhalis A species that is a frequent cause of upper and lower respiratory tract infections, including otitis media in children and bronchitis and pneumonia in the elderly. It is resistant to beta-lactam antibiotics such as most penicillins, but can be treated with many cephalosporins, macrolides, and sulfa drugs.

    M.lacunata A species that is a cause of conjunctivitis in humans.

morbid (mor′bĭd) [L. *morbidus,* sick] **1.** Diseased. **2.** Pert. to disease. **3.** Preoccupied with unwholesome ideas and circumstances.

morbidity (mor-bid′ĭt-ē) [L. *morbidus,* sickly] **1.** The state of being diseased. **2.** The number of sick persons or cases of disease in relationship to a specific population.

Morbidity and Mortality Weekly Report ABBR: MMWR. The weekly report of illness and death rates for a variety of diseases and conditions, published by the Centers for Disease Control and Prevention, Atlanta, Georgia. Prominent in the material are statistics on communicable diseases in the states, territories, and major cities in the U.S. Articles on outbreaks of disease or accidents appear in the MMWR, sometimes including reports of importance to public health as a result of an international event.

morbidity rate SEE: under *rate.*

morbific (mor-bĭf′ĭk) [″ + *facere,* to make] Causing or producing disease.

morbilli (mor-bĭl′ī) [L. *morbillus,* little disease] Measles.

morbillous (mor-bĭl′ŭs), *adj.*

morbilliform (mŏr-bĭl′ĭ-form) [″ + *forma,* shape] Resembling measles or its rash.

morcellate (mor′sĕ-lāt″) [Fr. *morceler,* to divide into small pieces] To divide tissue into fragments or pieces for surgical removal. **morcellation** (mor″sĕ-lā′shŏn), *n.*

morcellement (mor″sel-mon′) [Fr. *morceler,* to divide into small pieces] Division of tissue into fragments for surgical removal; morcellation.

mordant (mor′dănt) [L. *mordere,* to bite] A substance that fixes a stain or dye, as alum and phenol.

mores (mō′rāz) [L.] Habits and customs of society; usually those that come to be regarded as being essential to the survival and well-being of the society.

Morgagni, Giovanni B (mŏr-găg′nē, -găn′yē) Italian pathological anatomist, 1682–1771. **morgagnian** (mor-găn′ē-ăn), *adj.*

    M.'s cataract Cataract that is hypermature with a softened cortex and a hard nucleus.

M.'s cyst A cystlike remnant of the müllerian duct that is attached to the fallopian tube.

M.'s hydatid Cystlike remains of müllerian duct attached to testicle or oviduct.

M.'s hyperostosis Hyperostosis of the frontal bones of the head, possibly associated with obesity, headache, amenorrhea, diabetes, multiple endocrine abnormalities, and various neuropsychiatric disturbances. SYN: *frontal internal hyperostosis.*

Morganella morganii (mŏr″găn-ĕl′lă mōr-găn′ē-ī) [Harry de R. Morgan, Brit. physician, 1863–1931] A gram-negative bacillus that is part of colon flora; it may cause urinary tract infections, wound infections, bacteremia, meningitis, keratitis, and acute enteritis.

morgue (morg) [Fr.] A place for holding dead bodies until they are identified or claimed for burial.

moria (mō′rē-ă) [Gr. *moria,* folly] **1.** Simple dementia. **2.** Foolishness. SEE: *witzelsucht.*

moribund (mor′ĭ-bŭnd) [L. *moribundus*] In a dying condition; dying.

morning care Care provided for a patient, which includes measuring temperature, pulse, and respiration, assistance with oral hygiene and bathing, changing bed linen, and providing breakfast.

morning sickness SEE: under *sickness.*

morning stiffness Limitations of joint and muscle movement that are present on awakening or after resting, but which subside with activity. This is one of the principal symptoms of inflammatory, rather than degenerative, arthritis.

Moro reflex (mo′rō) [Ernst Moro, Ger. pediatrist, 1874–1951] A reflex seen in infants in response to stimuli, such as that produced by suddenly striking the surface on which the infant rests. The infant responds by rapid abduction and extension of the arms followed by an embracing motion (adduction) of the arms. SYN: *embrace reflex; startle reflex.*

morph-, morpho- [Gr. *morphē,* shape, form] Prefixes meaning *form, shape,* or *structure.*

morphea (mor-fē′ă) [Gr. *morphe,* form] Localized or widespread sclerotic plaques of the skin, often arrayed in lines or bands. The lesions typically have an ivory-colored to yellow slightly firm center, with a violet border. SEE: *progressive systemic sclerosis.*

generalized m. A severe form of localized morphea. There are multiple indurated plaques, hyperpigmentation, and possible muscle atrophy. It is not associated with systemic disease. The disease may become inactive in 3 to 5 years.

localized m. A localized form of scleroderma that does not progress to the systemic form of the disease.

morpheme (mor′fĕm) The smallest meaningful grammatical unit in a language (e.g., the *s* in "beds"). SEE: *phoneme.*

morphia (mor′fē-ă) Morphine.

morphine (mor′fēn″) [Ger. *Morphin,* fr. *morph-* +*-ine*] The principal alkaloid found in opium, occurring as bitter colorless crystals.

m. sulfate An opiate commonly used in oral or injectable form to control severe acute or chronic pain. Its side effects include sedation, respiratory depression, constipation, itching, hallucinations, tolerance, and dependence.

⚠️ Like other narcotic analgesics, morphine sulfate is a controlled substance with a potential for abuse. The commonly used abbreviation for morphine sulfate, MSO_4, is considered a dangerous abbreviation because it may be confused with an abbreviation for magnesium sulfate.

morphinism (mor′fĭn-ĭzm) [L. *morphina,* morphine, + *-ismos,* condition] Morbid condition due to habitual or excessive use of morphine. SEE: *morphine poisoning.*

morphodifferentiation (mor″fō-dĭf″fĕr-en-chē-ā′shŭn) The stage of tooth formation that determines the shape and size of the tooth crown. SEE: *enamel organ.*

morphogen (mŏr′fō-gĕn) [Gr. *morphe,* form, + *genesis,* generation, birth] A protein that influences the development, differentiation, growth, and patterning of embryonic tissues.

morphogenesis (mor″fō-jen′ĕ-sĭs) [Gr. *morphe,* form, + *genesis,* generation, birth] **1.** Various processes, including cell migration, cell aggregation, localized growth, splitting (delamination and cavitation), and folding (invagination and evagination), occurring during development by which the form of the body and its organs is established. SYN: *morphosis.* **2.** The assembly of virion from its components. **morphogenetic** (mor″fō-jĕ-net′ĭk), *adj.*

morphography (mor-fŏg′ră-fē) [″ + *graphein,* to write] The classification of organisms by form and structure.

morphology (mor-fŏl′ō-jē) [Gr. *morphe,* form, + *logos,* word, reason] The science of structure and form of organisms without regard to function.

morphometry (mor-fŏm′ĕ-trē) [″ + *metron,* measure] The measurement of forms.

morphosis (mor-fō′sĭs) Morphogenesis.

morsicatio (mor″sĭ-kā′sh(ē-)ō) [L. *mor-*

sicatio, a biting] Habitual or repetitive chewing or biting of a body part.

mortal (mŏr'tl) [L. *mortalis*] **1.** Causing death. **2.** Subject to death.

mortality (mor-tal'ĭt-ē) [*mortal*] **1.** The condition of being mortal. **2.** The number of deaths in a population. In the U.S. about 2,300,000 people die each year. The most common causes of death, according to the National Center for Health Statistics, are (in descending order) heart disease, cancer, stroke, chronic obstructive lung disease, accidents, pneumonia and influenza, diabetes mellitus, suicide, kidney failure, cirrhosis, and other chronic liver diseases. The causes of death vary by age group: accidents are the most common cause of death among infants, children, adolescents, and young adults; cancers are the most common cause of death among people ages 45 to 64. Heart disease predominates after age 65. SEE: table.

    all-cause m. All of the deaths that occur in a population, regardless of the cause. It is measured in clinical trials and used as an indicator of the safety or hazard of an intervention. SEE: *disease-specific m.*

    disease-specific m. All of the deaths that occur in a population from a specific illness. In clinical trials that study the effect of a treatment on that illness, it is used as a measure of the treatment's effectiveness. SEE: *all-cause m.*

    infant m. The number of deaths of children younger than 1 year of age per 1000 live births per year.

    neonatal m. The death of a newborn.

    perinatal m. The number of fetal deaths plus the number of deaths of infants younger than 7 days of age per 1000 live births per year.

mortality prediction model SEE: under *model.*

mortality table SEE: under *table.*

mortar (mŏr'tĕr) [L. *mortarium*] A vessel with a smooth interior in which crude drugs are crushed or ground with a pestle.

mortician (mŏr-tĭsh'ăn) [L. *mors,* death] Undertaker; person trained to prepare the dead for burial.

mortification (mŏr″tĭ-fĭ-kā'shŭn) SEE: *gangrene; necrosis.*

mortise A depression, groove, or hole into which another anatomical structure fits.

mortise joint (mor'tĭs) SEE: under *joint.*

Morton, Dudley Joy (mort'ŏn) U.S. orthopedic surgeon, 1884–1960.

    M. disease Morton toe.

    M. toe A seldom-used term for shortening of a metatarsal bone, usually the first metatarsal, or the pain around that bone caused by such a shortening (metatarsalgia) or the pain along the course of the nearby nerve (neuralgia). The condition is sometimes but not always congenital. SYN: *Morton syndrome; Morton toe.* SEE: illus.

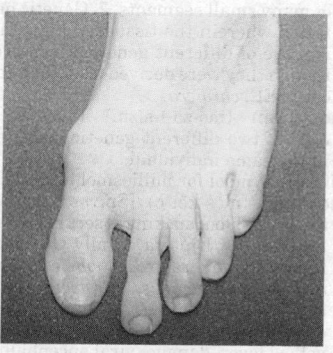

MORTON TOE

    M. syndrome Morton toe.

Morton, Thomas George (mort'ŏn) U.S. surgeon, 1835–1903.

    M. neuralgia Pain in the metatarsal area due to a fallen transverse arch with pressure on the lateral plantar nerve. SEE: *metatarsalgia.*

Leading Causes of Death in Children Under Five Years of Age, Estimates for 2000-2003

Rank	Cause	Numbers (thousands per year)	% of all deaths
1	Neonatal causes	3,910	37
2	Acute respiratory infections	2,027	19
3	Diarrheal diseases	1,762	17
4	Malaria	853	8
5	Measles	395	4
6	HIV/AIDS	321	3
7	Injuries	305	3
	Other causes	1,022	10
	Total	10,596	100.0

Worldwide, 50% of all deaths under the age of five are caused by infectious diseases.
SOURCE: World Health Organization, The World Health Report 2005.

M. neuroma A neuroma-like mass of the neurovascular bundle of the inter-metatarsal spaces. SYN: *interdigital neuropathy.*

mortuary (mor'chū-ā-rē) [L. *mortuarium*, a tomb] **1.** Temporary place for keeping dead bodies before burial. SEE: *morgue.* **2.** Relating to the dead or to death.

morula (mor'ū-lǎ) [L. *morus,* mulberry] **1.** Solid mass of cells, resembling a mulberry, resulting from cleavage of an ovum. **2.** A mulberry-shaped body found in white blood cells in patients afflicted with human granulocyte ehrlichiosis. SEE: *fertilization* for illus.

Morvan disease (mor-van') [Augustin M. Morvan, Fr. physician, 1819–1897] A form of syringomyelia in which there are trophic changes in the extremities with slowly healing ulcers.

MOS *medical outcomes study.*

mosaic (mō-zā'ĭk) **1.** A pattern made up of many small segments. **2.** Genetic mutation wherein the tissues of an organism are of different genetic kinds even though they were derived from the same cell. SEE: *chimera.*

mosaicism (mō-zā'ĭ-sĭzm) Presence of cells of two different genetic materials in the same individual.

mOsm Symbol for milliosmol(e).

mosquito (mǒs-kēt'ō) [Sp. *mosquito,* little fly] A bloodsucking insect belonging to the order Diptera, family Culicidae. Important genera are *Anopheles, Culex, Aedes, Haemagogus, Mansonia,* and *Psorophora.* They are vectors of many diseases, including malaria, filariasis, yellow fever, dengue, viral encephalitis, and dermatobiasis. Illnesses carried by mosquitoes cause millions of deaths annually, esp. in underdeveloped countries.

moss Any low-growing green plant of the class Musci.

   Iceland m. An edible lichen, *Cetraria islandica.* It is a demulcent that has been promoted as a treatment for bladder, kidney, and lung diseases.

   Irish m. **1.** Carrageen. **2.** Carrageenan.

   peat m. **1.** Any moss of the large genus *Sphagnum* whose decomposed and compacted remains form peat. The moss is absorptive and acidic and inhibits growth of bacteria and fungi. SYN: *sphagnum m.* **2.** The decomposed and compacted remains of the mosses, used as a soil conditioner and as a dressing for wounds. It has also been used by some primitive people as a form of external menstrual protection. SYN: *sphagnum m.*

   sphagnum m. Peat **m.**

mother (mŏth'ĕr) **1.** A female parent. **2.** A structure that gives rise to others.

   biological m. A woman whose ovum

was fertilized and became a fetus. This term does not apply to a woman who provided the uterus for the gestation of a fertilized ovum obtained from a donor. SEE: *birth m.; surrogate parenting.*

   birth m. The woman who gives birth to a child, whether or not she is the biological mother. SEE: *surrogate parenting.*

   social m. The woman who raises a newborn child, regardless of whether she is genetically related to it.

   surrogate m. A woman who, through in vitro fertilization, gives birth to a child to which she may not have a genetic relationship.

mother tongue Native language.

motile (mō'tĭl, mō'tīl″) [L. *motilis,* moving] Able to move.

motilin (mō-tĭl'ĭn) A polypeptide that stimulates and controls contractions of the gastrointestinal tract. It is secreted by the mucosa of the small intestine.

motility (mō-tĭl'ĭ-tē) Ability to move.

motion (mō'shŏn) [L. *motio,* movement] **1.** A change of place or position; movement. **2.** Evacuation of the bowels. **3.** Matter evacuated from bowels. SEE: words beginning with *cine-* and *kine-.*

   accessory m. Joint play.

   accessory joint m. Joint play.

   active m. Movement caused by the patient's own intention. SEE: *active range of motion.*

   continuous passive m. ABBR: CPM. Use of a mechanical device following surgery to passively and gradually move a repaired joint through a prescribed range of motion continuously over an extended period. The goal is to reduce recovery time by decreasing soft tissue stiffness, increasing range of motion, promoting healing of joint surfaces and soft tissue, and preventing the development of motion-limiting adhesions.

⚠️ Patients should be monitored closely during use of these devices.

   paradoxical vocal cord m. Vocal cord dysfunction.

   passive m. A therapeutic exercise technique used to move a patient's joint through a range of motion without the patient's use of the involved extremity. The motion is accomplished by a therapist, an assistant, the use of a machine, or by the patient's use of the non-involved extremity. SYN: *passive exercise; passive movement.*

   physiological m. Physiological movement.

   total active m. ABBR: TAM. A measure of hand range of motion in which the sum of the extension at the metacarpophalangeal (MCP), proximal interphalangeal (PIP), and distal interphalangeal (DIP) joints is subtracted from the total achievable flexion of the same joints.

motion artifact Blurring of a radiographic image, produced by respiratory, muscular, or other movement of the patient.

motion-mode display M-mode **ultrasound**.

motion scaling In robotic surgery, the conversion of the surgeon's large hand movements into smaller movements of the surgical instrument in the operative field.

motion sickness SEE: under *sicknes*.

motivation (mō"ĭ-vā'shŏn) The internal drive or externally arising stimulus to action or thought. **motivational** (shŏn-ăl), *adj*.

motivational enhancement therapy A form of psychotherapy to overcome ambivalence and help people to reach desired goals. It is used to treat alcoholism, drug dependency, and anorexia/bulimia.

motivational interviewing A form of directive, client-centered psychotherapy in which patients are encouraged to explore the discrepancies between what they hope to attain in their lives and how they currently live and behave. The therapist uses empathy while helping patients explore how change may positively affect their lives. Patients' natural resistance to change is accepted as normal and natural. Autonomy is fostered so that changes in speech and behavior are developed by the patient, not by the therapist. The technique is used in a variety of settings, including alcohol and drug rehabilitation.

motive (mō'tĭv) A need, reason, or want that impels action.

motofacient (mō"tō-fā'shĕnt) Producing motion.

motoneuron (mō"tō-nū'rŏn) Motor neuron.

motor [L. *motor*, mover] **1.** Causing motion. **2.** In anatomy, pert. to neurons or axons involved in the output of the nervous system; efferent. **3.** In psychology, pert. to neural events relating to motions made by the body. **4.** A part or center that induces movements, as nerves or muscles. **5.** A structural mechanism producing motion. **motorial,** *adj*.

motor area Posterior part of the frontal lobe anterior to the central sulcus, from which impulses for volitional movement arise.

Motor Assessment Scale SEE: under ¹*scale*.

motor control The neural and biomechanical basis of planned, coordinated movement. SEE: *motor learning*.

Motor-Free Visual Perception Test A standardized test of visual perception

that does not require motor performance.

motor lag An unusually long delay before a movement is initiated in response to a stimulus.

motor neuron disease Any of several impairments in motorneurons, including progressive muscular atrophy, primary lateral sclerosis, progressive bulbar paralysis, and amyotrophic lateral sclerosis. These diseases occur principally in males and are characterized by degeneration of anterior horn cells of the spinal cord, the motor cranial nerve nuclei, and the corticospinal tracts. These illnesses limit the ability to use the upper and lower extremities and/or to speak and swallow. SYN: *Lou Gehrig's disease*.

motor recovery SEE: under *recovery*.

motor sense SEE: under *sense*.

motor speech area Broca's area.

motor unit A somatic motor neuron and all the muscle cells it innervates.

mottle (mot'ĕl) [Possibly fr *motley*] **1.** To mark with irregular spots of different color or colors. **2.** An irregular spot of different color. **3.** A pattern or condition of irregular spots of different color or colors. SYN: *mottling* (1). **4.** In radiography, the variation or fluctuation of x-ray photons. Images with increased mottle have a lower ratio of accurate signal to interference.

    quantum m. In radiography, a speckled, snowy-looking, nonuniform mottle caused by an insufficient number of x-ray photons striking the radiographic image receptor during an exposure. The mottle is corrected by increasing milliampere seconds.

mottled (mot'ĕld) Blotchy or marbled in appearance. It is often used to describe the skin of patients who are cold or inadequately perfused, e.g., in shock.

mottling (mot'lĭng) **1.** Mottle (3). **2.** In dentistry, discoloration of enamel. SEE: *mottled **enamel***.

moulage (moo-lăzh') [Fr.] **1.** A wax model or reproduction of the configuration of some part of the anatomy such as the face or nose, or of a pathological skin lesion. **2.** Molding of a wax model.

mounding (mŏwn'dĭng) [origin uncertain] The rising of a lump, as the mounding of a wasting muscle when struck a quick, firm blow. SYN: *myoedema* (1).

mount (mownt) [ME. *mounten*, to mount] **1.** To place on a support or backing. **2.** To place specimens or sections in special containers or on slides for study.

mounting (mownt'ĭng) **1.** The arrangement of specimens on slides, frames, chart boards, display boards, or any background for study. **2.** In dentistry, the attachment of a cast of the mandible or maxilla to an articulator.

mourning [AS. *murnan*] The observable

expression of grief after a death, esp. of a loved one. Mourning is not synonymous with depression or melancholia. SEE: *grief.*

mouse (mows) **1.** A small rodent of the genus *Mus.* Mice are used extensively in research. **2.** A small piece of tissue that has become free or unattached, esp. in a body cavity or joint.

New Zealand black m. ABBR: NZB m. A mouse bred for the genetic trait of spontaneously developing autoimmune hemolytic anemia.

nude m. A mutant mouse, completely devoid of hair and lacking T lymphocytes, bred for use in immunological investigations.

mouth [AS. *muth*] **1.** The opening of any cavity. **2.** The cavity within the cheeks, containing the tongue and teeth, and communicating with the pharynx. SYN: *buccal cavity; oral cavity.*

ABNORMALITIES: *Tongue:* dry, coated, smooth, strawberry, large, pigmented, geographic, deviated, tremulous, sore. *Gums and teeth:* gingivitis, sordes, lead line, pyorrhea, atrophy, hypertrophy, dental caries, alveolar abscesses. *Mucous membranes and other parts of mouth:* eruptions accompanying exanthematous diseases, stomatitis, canker sores, herpes simplex, thrush, trench mouth, cysts, tumors, carcinoma, lesions of syphilis such as chancre, mucous patches, gumma, lesions of tuberculosis, abscesses.

Disorders of the mouth cavity may be indications of purely local diseases or they may be symptoms of systemic disturbances such as dehydration, pernicious anemia, and nutritional deficiencies, esp. avitaminosis.

Rashes of the mouth may indicate stomatitis, measles, or scarlet fever. Rashes on lips may indicate typhoid fever, meningitis, or pneumonia. In secondary syphilis, chancre, cancer, and epithelioma, mucous patches appear.

EXAMINATION: In addition to visual examination, careful digital examination should be made because it reveals areas of tenderness and alterations of texture characteristic of leukoplakia, cancer, cystic swellings, and lymphadenopathy.

Excessive moisture of the mouth is seen in stomatitis, irritation of the vagus nerve, ingestion of irritating drugs or foods, nervous disorders, teething, seeing appetizing foods, and smelling pleasant odors. SEE: *burning mouth syndrome.*

trench m. Necrotizing ulcerative gingivitis.

mouth guard A removable dental appliance used to protect the teeth and investing tissues during contact sports.

PATIENT CARE: Mouth guards, like other dental appliances, should be cleaned daily. SEE: *occlusal guard.*

mouthrinse Mouthwash.

mouthstick Assistive technology device consisting of a stick attached to a molded dental mouthpiece that permits page turning and other tasks by means of head movement.

mouthwash A medicated solution used to cleanse or treat diseases of the oral mucosa, reduce halitosis, or add fluoride to the teeth for control or prevention of dental caries. It may contain various chemical compounds, such as fluoride or zinc chlorides, alcohol, glycerin, detergents, essential oils for flavoring, and coloring agents. According to the composition and proposed function, mouthwashes may be described as antibacterial, astringent, buffered, concentrated, cosmetic, deodorizing, or therapeutic. SYN: *mouthrinse.*

MOV *minimal occluding volume.*

movement (moov'měnt) [Fr. fr L. *movere,* to move] **1.** The act of passing from place to place or changing position of the body or its parts. **2.** Bowel movement.

accessory m. Joint play.

active m. Voluntary movement of joints and muscles through their usual range of motion, accomplished without external assistance.

ameboid m. Cellular movement like that of an ameba. A protoplasmic pseudopod extends, and then the remaining cell contents flow into the pseudopod, which swells gradually. This type of movement allows cells such as leukocytes to move through very small openings. SEE: *diapedesis.*

angular m. The change in the joint position between long bones. Flexion, extension, abduction, and adduction are examples of angular movement.

associated m. **1.** Synchronous correlation of two or more muscles or muscle groups that, although not essential for the performance of some function, normally accompany it, as the swinging of arms in normal walking. Associated movements are characteristically lost in cerebellar disease. **2.** An involuntary movement in one limb accompanying a voluntary movement on the other side of the body.

bodily m. Movement of a tooth by natural or orthodontic forces so that the crown and root maintain their same vertical axis. SEE: *rotational m.; tipping m.*

bowel m. Evacuation of feces from the gastrointestinal tract. The number of bowel movements varies in healthy individuals, some having a movement after each meal, others one in the morning and one at night, and still others only in several days. SYN: *defecation.*

⚠️ A persistent change in bowel habits should be investigated thoroughly because it may be a sign of cancer or inflammation in the gastrointestinal tract.

Bloody bowel movements may be caused by a variety of lesions in the upper or lower gastrointestinal tracts, including hemorrhoids, anal fissures, dysentery, bleeding diverticuli, arteriovenous malformations, inflammatory bowel diseases (such as ulcerative colitis), or cancers. Black (melenic) bowel movements may result from bleeding in the upper gastrointestinal tract but may be mimicked by other conditions, e.g., the use of iron supplements or bismuth-containing medications. Clay-colored stools are often seen in biliary obstruction. Constipation with a decrease in the caliber of stools may indicate a malignant obstruction of the large intestine.

PATIENT CARE: A history is obtained of the patient's usual bowel habits, and any change is documented. The patient is questioned and the stool is inspected for color, shape, odor, consistency, and other characteristics, as well as the presence of any unusual coatings or contents (mucus, blood, fat, parasites). Privacy is provided for the patient when using a bed pan, toilet, or bedside commode. The area should be ventilated or a deodorant spray used after the bowel movement to limit the patient's embarrassment and to reduce the discomfort of others sharing the area. The patient is taught the importance of fluid intake, diet, and activity to help prevent constipation, supportive therapies for diarrhea, and the importance of hand hygiene after toileting. The rationale for testing the stool for occult blood or other laboratory studies, if this is required, is explained.

brownian m. The oscillatory movement of particles resulting from chance bombardment by other particles.

ciliary m. Rhythmic movement of the cilia of a ciliated cell or epithelium. SYN: *vibratile* **m.**

circus m. **1.** A phenomenon appearing after injury to a corpus striatum, optic thalamus, or crus cerebri, and causing an odd circular gait. **2.** In cardiac rhythm disturbances caused by re-entry, the conduction of electrical activity cyclically through tissue, a process that continues indefinitely as long as the tissue ahead of the electrical wave has adequate time to recover before the electrical stimulus reappears. The movement occurs because of a conduction block in one limb of a circuit, in which the electrical impulse is permitted to travel in only one direction.

decreased fetal m. A mother's perception that her fetus is less active than usual. It may be monitored by assessing the number of fetal kicks in a specified time.

fetal m. Muscular movements performed by the fetus in utero.

gliding m. Movement of one surface over another without angular or rotatory movement, as well. This type of movement occurs in the temporomandibular joint after opening when the condyles and disks move forward, as in protrusion of the jaw.

hinge m. Movement in a joint around a transverse axis, as occurs in the lower compartment of the temporomandibular joints at the beginning of jaw opening when the occluding teeth are separated or in the final stage of wide opening of the mouth.

independent living m. Any of the societal programs that support a philosophy of full participation, self-reliance, and social inclusion of people with functional impairment. Emphasis on self-help, interdependence, environmental accessibility, freedom of choice, and programs to enable community living characterize this movement.

jaw m. Movement of the mandible. SEE: *gliding* **m.**; *hinge* **m.**

masticatory m. One of the movements of the jaw that results in the cutting and grinding of food. It may involve unilateral chewing, alternating bilateral chewing according to the learned automatic pattern of activity, or consciously initiated movements.

molecular m. The rotational, translational, and vibrational movement of molecules, primarily as a function of absolute temperature. The higher the temperature, the greater the movement, i.e., the greater the kinetic energy. SEE: *brownian* **m.**

orthodontic m. Movement of teeth and bone produced by orthodontic appliances.

passive m. Passive **motion**.

pendular m. Swaying movements of the intestines caused by rhythmic contractions of the longitudinal muscles of the walls of the intestines.

peristaltic m. Peristalsis.

physiological m. A movement normally executed by muscles under voluntary control (e.g., flexion, extension, abduction, adduction, and rotation). SYN: *physiological* **motion**.

physiological tooth m. Mesial **drift**.

purposeful m. Motor activity requiring the planned and consciously directed involvement of the patient. It is hypothesized that evoking cortical involvement in movement patterns during sensorimotor rehabilitation will enhance the development of coordination and voluntary control.

rapid eye m. ABBR: REM. Cyclic

movement of the closed eyes observed or recorded during sleep.

relaxed m. Passive **exercise.**

respiratory m. Any movement resulting from the contraction of respiratory muscles or occurring passively as a result of elasticity of the thoracic wall or lungs. SEE: *compliance* (1); *expiration; inspiration; respiration.*

rotational m. Movement around an axis, as in hinge movement of the temporomandibular joint or rotation of a tooth around its longitudinal axis in tooth movement or extraction.

saccadic m. Jerky movements of the eyes as they move from one point of fixation to another.

tipping m. Movement of a tooth crown while the root apex remains essentially stationary, resulting in an inclination of the axis of the tooth in one direction. SEE: *bodily m.; rotational m.*

tooth m. The change in position of a tooth or teeth in the dental arch. This may be due to abnormal pressure from the tongue, pathological changes in tooth-supporting structures, malocclusion, missing teeth, or a therapeutic orthodontic procedure. Thumb sucking, if prolonged, may cause malocclusion and, eventually, displacement of teeth. SEE: *pathological tooth* **migration***; physiological tooth* **migration.**

transitive m. Any movement in which physical objects, such as tools or utensils, are employed. Using a bottle-opener, carving a turkey, brushing the teeth, and drinking from a glass are all examples of transitive movement.

movement disorder Any brain-based motor system disorder marked by disturbed muscle movement. These disorders include hemiplegia, ataxia, monoplegia, tremors, rigors, chorea, athetosis, convulsions, spasm (clonic or tonic), reflex (hysterical, habit spasm, tics), and spastic paralysis. Movement disorders are common in the elderly (e.g., those with degenerative neurological diseases). When they occur acutely, they are often caused by a new medication or toxin, stroke, or trauma. SEE: *hyperkinetic disorder; hypokinetic movement disorder.*

movement system The physiological components that function together to produce motion at a joint or multiple body segments. The components include the support and base; modulating nerves and muscles; cardiovascular and pulmonary reserves; and cognitive-affective elements. Specialists in physical medicine are trained to manage the components of the movement system.

moxa (mŏk′sa) [Japanese] The use of a soft combustible substance, such as the herb *Artemisia vulgaris,* burned on the skin. It is popular in eastern Asia, Ja-

pan, and complementary medicine as a cautery and counterirritant. SEE: *moxibustion.*

moxibustion (mok″sĭ-bŭs′chŏn) [*moxa* + *(com)bustion*] In traditional Asian and alternative medicine, cauterization and counterirritation to treat disease with a cylinder or cone of cotton wool (moxa) placed on the skin and fired at the top.

M-Oxy Oxycodone.

MPD *Maximum permissible* **dose.**

MPM *Mortality prediction* **model.**

MPN *most probable number* (of bacteria present in a quantity of solution, esp. water).

MPS *mucopolysaccharidosis; mononuclear phagocytic system*

MPSV *meningococcal polysaccharide vaccine.*

MPSV4 *tetravalent meningococcal polysaccharide vaccine.*

MR *magnetic resonance; mitral regurgitation.*

mR *milliroentgen.*

MRA *magnetic resonance* **angiography.**

MRCP *Magnetic resonance* **cholangiopancreatography***; Member of the Royal College of Physicians.*

MRCP(C) *Member of the Royal College of Physicians of Canada.*

MRCS *Member of the Royal College of Surgeons.*

MRCS(C) *Member of the Royal College of Surgeons of Canada.*

mrem *millirem.*

MRI *magnetic resonance* **imaging.**

mRNA *messenger RNA.*

MRSA methicillin-resistant *Staphylococcus aureus.*

MRSE Methicillin-resistant *Staphylococcus epidermidis.*

MS *multiple sclerosis.*

ms *millisecond.*

MSAFP *maternal serum alpha-fetoprotein.*

MSDS *material safety data sheets.*

msec *millisecond.*

MSH *melanocyte-stimulating hormone.* SEE: under *hormone.*

mSv *milliSievert* (one thousandth of a sievert).

MTD *Maximum tolerated* **dose.**

MTP *metatarsophalangeal.*

MTSS *Medial tibial stress syndrome.*

Mu *Mache unit.*

mu (mū, moo) SYMB: μ; u. **1.** M or μ, the uppercase and lowercase symbols, respectively, for the 12th letter of the Greek alphabet. **2.** Symbol used for the prefix *micro-* which stands for multiplication by 10^{-6}. Thus, μm would stand for 10^{-6} m.

mucigen (mū′sĭ-jĕn″) [″ + Gr. *gennan,* to produce] A substance present in mucous cells that, upon being extruded from the cell, is converted into mucin.

mucilage (mū′sĭ-lĭj) [L. *mucilago,* moldy

juice] Thick, viscid, adhesive liquid, containing gum or mucilaginous principles dissolved in water, usually employed to suspend insoluble substances in aqueous liquids or as a demulcent.
mucilaginous (mū-sĭl-ăj'ĭn-ŭs), *adj.*
mucilloid (mū'sĭl-loyd) A mucilaginous preparation.
 psyllium hydrophilic m. Mucilloid prepared from psyllium seeds. It is used as a bulk-type laxative.
mucin (mū'sĭn) [L. *mucus,* mucus] A glycoprotein found in mucus. It is present in saliva, bile, skin, glandular tissues, connective tissues, tendon, and cartilage. Mucin is formed from mucigen and forms a slimy solution in water.
mucinoid (mū'sĭn-oyd), *adj.*
mucinase (mū'sĭ-nās) Any enzyme that acts on mucin.
muco-, muc-, muci- [L. *mucus,* snot, mucus] Prefixes meaning *mucus.*
mucoactive (mū'kō-ak'tiv) [*muco- + active*] Tending to enhance the clearance of mucus from an organ, esp. from the lung. SEE: *mucolytic.*
mucocele (mū'kŏ-sēl") [*muco- + -cele*] **1.** Enlargement of the lacrimal sac. **2.** A mucous cyst. **3.** A mucous polypus. **4.** Cystic disease of the air cavities of the cranial bones causing erosion of the bone.
mucociliary (mū'kō-sĭl'ē-ăr-ē) Pert. to ciliated mucosa.
mucocutaneous (mū'kō-kū-tā'nē-ŭs) [" + *cutis,* skin] Pert. to mucous membrane and the skin.
mucocutaneous lymph node syndrome Kawasaki disease.
mucoid (mū'koyd) [" + Gr. *eidos,* form, shape] **1.** Glycoprotein similar to mucin. **2.** Muciform, similar to mucus. SYN: *blennoid.*
mucokinetic (mū'kŏ-kĭ-net'ik) [*muco- + kinetic*] Mucolytic.
mucolipidosis (mū'kō-lĭp-ĭ-dō'sĭs) ABBR: ML. One of several rare, inherited lysosomal storage diseases in which abnormalities in the transport of lysosomal enzymes into lysosomes result in their accumulation in extracellular fluids or plasma. Findings include muscle and skeletal anomalies, coarsened facial features, eye abnormalities (including a visible "cherry-red spot" on the retina), and mental retardation.
 m. type II ABBR: ML II. A rare autosomal recessive disease that results in death in infancy or early childhood. Characteristic findings include severe mental retardation, poor muscle tone, kyphosis, and coarsened facial features. SYN: *I cell disease.*
mucolytic (mū'kŏ-lit'ik) [*muco- + -lytic*] Tending to liquefy sputum or reduce its viscosity. SYN: *mucokinetic; mucoregulatory.* SEE: *cystic **fibrosis**; mucoactive.*
mucomembranous (mū'kō-měm'bră-

nŭs) [" + *membrana,* membrane] Concerning mucous membrane.
mucoperiosteum (mū'kō-pěr"ē-ŏs'tē-ŭm) Periosteum that has a mucous surface, as in the middle ear and hard palate.
mucopolysaccharide (mū'kō-pŏl"ĭ-săk'ă-rīd) A group of polysaccharides, containing hexosamine and sometimes proteins, that forms chemical bonds with water. The thick gelatinous material is found in many places in the body, forming intercellular ground substance and basement membranes of cells and found in mucous secretions and synovial fluid.
mucopolysacchariduria (mū'kō-pŏl"ē-săk'ă-rī-dū'rē-ă) Mucopolysaccharides in the urine.
mucoprotein (mū'kō-prō'tē-ĭn) A complex of protein and mucopolysaccharide. Usually, the polysaccharide contains hexosamine.
 Tamm-Horsfall m. SEE: *Tamm-Horsfall mucoprotein.*
mucopurulent (mū-kō-pūr'ū-lěnt) [L. *mucus,* mucus, + *purulentus,* made up of pus] Consisting of mucus and pus.
Mucor (mū'kor) [L.] A genus of mold found in dead and decaying matter. Some species can cause infections of external ear, skin, and respiratory passageways. SEE: *mucormycosis.*
mucoregulatory (mū'kō-reg'yŭ-tor"ē) [*muco- + regulatory*] Mucolytic.
mucoriferous (mū'kor-ĭf'ěr-ŭs) [L. *mucor,* mold, + *ferre,* to carry] Covered with mold or a moldlike substance.
mucormycosis (mū'kor-mĭ-kō'sĭs) [" + Gr. *mykes,* fungus, + *osis,* condition] An invasive and frequently fatal infection with fungi of the family Mucoraceae and the class Zygomycetes. SYN: *zygomycosis.*
 PATHOLOGY: The fungi responsible have an affinity for blood vessels, in which they cause thrombosis and infarction. The form of this disease that affects the head and face usually causes paranasal sinus infections, esp. during periods of ketoacidosis in persons with diabetes mellitus. This form may also disseminate to the brain. The pulmonary form of the disease causes infarcts of the lung; the gastrointestinal form causes mucosal ulcers and gangrene of the stomach. The disease is contracted by inhalation or ingestion of the fungus by susceptible individuals. Most persons have a natural resistance to the fungus, accounting for the rarity of the disease.
 TREATMENT: Radical surgery may sometimes be used to remove the invasive fungal mass. Potent antifungal agents, such as amphotericin B, may be given intravenously. Control of underlying immunosuppressive conditions may be helpful.
 RISK FACTORS: The infection occurs

most commonly in persons with immunosuppressive conditions, such as AIDS, or poorly controlled diabetes mellitus, or in recipients of transplanted organs who are taking immunosuppressive drugs.

mucorrhea (mū″kō-rē′ă) [″ + *rhoia*, to flow] Increased cervical discharge at ovulation, usually covering a span of 3 to 4 days. The discharge has the character and appearance of raw egg white. SEE: *spinnbarkeit*.

mucosa (mū-kō′să) *pl.* **mucosae** [L., mucous] A mucous membrane or moist tissue layer that lines the hollow organs and cavities of the body that open to the environment. It consists of an epithelial layer on a basement membrane and a connective tissue layer called the lamina propria. The tissue lining the alimentary canal also contains a smooth muscle layer called the muscularis mucosae. The type of epithelium, thickness, and presence or absence of glands vary with the function or location of the mucosa. **mucosal** (mū-kō′săl), *adj.*

   alveolar m. A thin, nonkeratinized mucosal layer covering the alveolar process of maxillae and mandible and loosely attached to underlying bone. It is continuous with the mucosa of the cheek, lips, tongue, and palate.

   buccal m. The lining of the cheeks of the oral cavity. It is characterized by stratified squamous nonkeratinized epithelium that may become keratinized in local areas due to cheek-biting. It may also contain ectopic sebaceous glands. SEE: *Fordyce's disease*.

   lingual m. The keratinized, papillated covering of the dorsum of the tongue that contains nerve endings for the sense of taste.

   masticatory m. Those areas of the mucosa of the mouth that have become keratinized due to the friction and abrasion of the masticatory process, esp. the gingivae and hard palate.

   nasal m. The lining of the nasal cavities and paranasal sinuses, made of pseudostratified ciliated epithelium with goblet cells. The nasal mucosa warms and humidifies the inhaled air, and the cilia sweep mucus-entrapped dust and microbes to the pharynx.

   oral m. The stratified squamous epithelial lining of the oral cavity in its many locations: the gingiva, hard palate, soft palate, cheek, vestibule, lip, tongue, and oropharynx.

mucosal immune system Clusters of lymphoid cells beneath the mucosal endothelium of the gastrointestinal, respiratory, and genitourinary tracts that help protect the body from inhaled, consumed, or sexually transmitted infections. The system has two parts: organized and diffuse. The organized part (the mucosal-associated lymphoid tissue of the gastrointestinal and respiratory tracts) is composed of nodules containing lymphocytes and macrophages that are activated by ingested or inhaled microorganisms. The diffuse part is composed of loose clusters of macrophages and mature B and T lymphocytes found within the folds of the intestinal walls. The B cells secrete antibodies, primarily immunoglobulin A; the T cells directly lyse microorganisms.

   The mucosal immune system is augmented by the presence of normal microflora; by peristalsis and cilia, which move mucus outward; and by various chemicals, such as gastric acid and pancreatic enzymes, which destroy pathogens. Normally all of these components must be functioning to prevent infection.

mucosectomy (mū″kō-sek′tŏ-mē) [*mucosa* + *-ectomy*] Surgical resection of the mucous membrane of an organ, e.g., of the large intestine.

   endoscopic m. Mucosectomy performed when cancer is present only in the lining of an organ. It is sometimes used to treat superficial cancers of the esophagus.

mucoserous (mū″kō-sēr′ŭs) Composed of mucus and serum.

mucositis (mū″kō-sīt′ĭs) [*muco-* + *-itis*] Inflammation of a mucous membrane.

   chemotherapy-induced m. Oral inflammation caused by medications, esp. those used to treat cancers or autoimmune diseases.

   PATIENT CARE: Mucositis may alter a person's ability to brush his teeth, drink fluids, eat foods, sleep, or talk comfortably. If the patient has severe, painful sores, he may need a feeding tube for hydration and nutrition.

   radiation-induced m. Inflammation of the lining of the mouth due to radiation injury to the head and/or neck. SEE: *gingivitis, acute necrotizing ulcerative*.

mucous (mū′kŭs) **1.** Having the nature of or resembling mucus. **2.** Secreting mucus. **3.** Depending on presence of mucus.

mucous membrane SEE: under *membrane*.

mucoviscidosis (mū″kō-vĭs″ĭ-dō′sĭs) Cystic fibrosis.

mucus (mū′kŭs) [L.] A viscid fluid secreted by mucous membranes and glands, consisting of mucin, leukocytes, inorganic salts, water, and epithelial cells. A good example is the almost ropy secretion from the sublingual and submandibular glands.

   cervical m. The discharge secreted by the endocervical glands of the uterine cervix. Characteristic assessment findings correlate with normal hormonal changes of the menstrual cycle that influence the type and amount of mucus secreted. Immediately before ovulation, high estrogen levels stimulate secretion of a large amount of thin, watery mucus that is hospitable to sperm transit. After ovulation, high progesterone levels stimulate secretion of a thick, viscous mucus that is less hospitable to sperm. SEE: *ferning; spinnbarkeit.*

MUD *Matched unrelated **donor**.*

Mueller maneuver (mū'lĕr) Inspiration against a blocked upper airway, a maneuver that generates negative pressure within the thorax. The Mueller maneuver can be performed voluntarily, by trying to suck air into the lungs with the mouth closed and the nostrils pinched. It also occurs spontaneously during obstructive sleep apnea when a person with an occluded airway struggles to breathe.

MUFA *monounsaturated fatty acid.*

muffle (mŭf'ĕl) To wrap or cover something in order to suppress sound or to clothe or protect the body.

mugwort (mŭg'wŏrt", 'wort") A perennial herb (*Artemisia vulgaris*) that is burned on or near the skin by acupuncturists during moxibustion to warm acupuncture points and nearby structures.

 The herb is toxic if eaten.

Muir-Torre syndrome (mūr'-taw'rā, tŏ're) An autosomal dominant condition marked by internal organ malignancies and sebaceous skin lesions. SYN: *Torre-Muir syndrome.*

mull (mŭl) To grind or pulverize.

Müller, Johannes P. (mül'ĕr) German physician, 1801–1858.

    M. **duct** Müllerian duct.

    M. **maneuver** Inspiratory effort with a closed glottis at the end of expiration. This technique is used during radiographic studies to produce negative intrathoracic pressure and cause engorgement of blood vessels, thus allowing visualization of esophageal varices.

    M. **ring** The muscular ring at the junction of the cervical canal and the gravid uterus.

    M. **tubercle** The projection on the dorsal wall of the cloaca at which Müller's ducts terminate.

mult-, multi- [L. *multus,* stem *mult-,* much, many] Prefixes meaning *many, much.*

multangular (mŭl-tăng'ū-lăr) Having many angles (e.g., the trapezium and trapezoid bones in the wrist).

multiallelic (mŭl"tē-ă-lĕl'ĭk) Concerning a large number of genes affecting hereditary characteristics.

multiarticular (mŭl"tē-ăr-tĭk'ū-lăr) [L.

multus, many, + *articulus,* joint] Polyarticular.

multicellular (mŭl"tĭ-sĕl'ū-lăr) [" + *cellula,* small chamber] Consisting of many cells.

Multiceps (mŭl'tĭ-sĕps) A genus of tapeworms.

multicolored Asian lady beetle (mŭlt'ē-kŏl'ŏrd) Harmonia axyridis.

multicuspid, multicuspidate (mŭl"tĭ-kŭs'pĭd, -pĭ-dāt) [" + *cuspis,* point] Having several cusps.

multicystic (mŭl"tē-sĭs'tĭk) Composed of or having many cysts.

multidirectional instability SEE: under *instability.*

multidisciplinary (mŭl"tĭ-dĭs'ĭ-plĭ-năr-ē) Relating to multiple fields of study involved in the care of patients. The term suggests that the various disciplines are working in collaboration, but in a parallel mode of interaction. Each distinctive discipline is accountable and responsible for its tasks and functions regarding patient care.

multifactorial (mŭl"tē-fak-tor'ē-ăl, mŭl"tĭ") Resulting from many factors, e.g., a disease caused by the combined effects of several components. **multifactorially** ('ē-ă-lē), *adv.*

multifamilial (mŭl"tĭ-fă-mĭl'ē-ăl) Concerning a familial disease that affects children in several generations.

multifid (mŭl'tĭ-fĭd) [" + *fidus,* from *findere,* to split] Divided into many sections.

multifocal (mŭl"tĭ-fō'kăl) Concerning or arising from many locations.

multifocal intraocular lens SEE: under *lens.*

multiform (mŭl'tĭ-form) [" + *forma,* shape] Having many forms or shapes. SYN: *polymorphic; polymorphous.*

multigenic (mŭl"tē-jĕn'ĭk, -jēn') Caused by, affecting, or relating to more than one gene.

multiglandular (mŭl"tĭ-glănd'ū-lar) [" + *glandula,* a little acorn] Concerning several glands.

multigravida (mŭl"tĭ-grăv'ĭ-dă) [" + *gravida,* pregnant] A woman who has been pregnant more than once. The number of pregnancies may be recorded as gravida II, gravida III, and so on. SEE: *multipara.*

Multilevel Assessment Instrument A questionnaire (used primarily for community-based geriatric patients) that evaluates instrumental activities of daily living. It assesses cognitive and physical limitations in activities such as telephone use, shopping, housework, and money management.

multilineage (mŭl"tē-lĭn'ē-ĭj) [" + "] Derivation from multiple ancestors. In hematology, it is applied to cellular proliferation affecting several blood cell types.

multilingual (mŭl"tē-ling'gwăl, tĭ-)

[*multi-* + *lingual*] **1.** Capable of speaking, reading, and/or understanding more than one language. **2.** Communicated in more than one language.

multilingual aphasia examination (mŭl″tē-ling′gwăl) [*multi-* + *lingual*] SEE: under *examination.*

multilobular (mŭl″tĭ-lŏb′ū-lar) [″ + *lobulus,* a small lobe] Formed of or possessing many lobules.

multilocular (mŭl″tĭ-lŏk′ū-lar) [″ + *loculus,* a cell] Having many cells or compartments.

multimodal (mŭl″tē-mō′dăl) [L. *multi-,* many, + *modus,* measure] **1.** Multidisciplinary. **2.** Using or relying on multiple methods, e.g., to treat an illness.

multinodular (mŭl-tĭ-nŏd′ū-lar) [″ + *nodulus,* little knot] Possessing many nodules or small knots.

multinuclear, multinucleate (mŭl-tĭ-nū′klē-ăr, -āt) Possessing several nuclei. SYN: *polynuclear.*

multipara (mŭl-tĭp′ă-ră) [″ + *parere,* to bring forth, to bear] A woman who has carried more than one fetus to viability, regardless of whether the offspring were born alive. The number of deliveries may be recorded as para II, para III, and so on. SEE: *multigravida.*

  grand m. A woman who has given birth seven or more times.

multiparity (mŭl-tĭ-păr′ĭ-tē) The condition of having carried one or more fetuses to viability, regardless of whether the infants were alive at birth. SEE: *multipara.*

multiparous (mŭl-tĭp′ăr-ŭs) Having borne more than one child.

multiphasic screening (mŭl″tĭ-fā′zĭk) SEE: *screening test, multiphasic.*

multiple (mŭl′tĭ-pl) [L. *multiplex,* many folded] **1.** Consisting of or containing more than one; manifold. **2.** Occurring simultaneously in various parts of the body.

multiple chemical sensitivity syndrome ABBR: MCSS. The association of multiple physical symptoms with prolonged or recurrent exposures to low levels of environmental pollutants. Clinical research has failed to establish the precise nature of the syndrome, its causes, the functional limitations it may cause, or the best course of treatment. Many hypotheses have been suggested: some proponents of the syndrome believe that it results from allergic or immune-mediated mechanisms; skeptics have suggested that the symptoms are a form of masked depression, adverse conditioning to unusual odors, or, in some instances, a form of malingering. None of these hypotheses has been definitively proven.

multiple drug resistance SEE: under *resistance.*

multiple-ejaculate resuspension and centrifugation ABBR: MERC. A method of isolating viable sperm from men previously thought to be sterile for in vitro fertilization. The patient ejaculates three or four times in a 24-hr period, and the semen is collected and concentrated. The small number of sperm isolated from the specimens can be used to impregnate the man's partner.

multiple endocrine neoplasia SEE: under *neoplasia.*

multiple malformation syndrome Any of the developmental anomalies affecting two or more systems in the fetus. The anomalies may be caused by chromosomal and genetic abnormalities or by teratogens, including certain drugs and chemicals. In determining causes, it is important to obtain a complete family history and the history of exposure to known teratogens and infectious diseases. SEE: *amniotic band disruption sequence syndrome.*

multiple myeloma SEE: *myeloma, multiple.*

multiple organ dysfunction syndrome ABBR: MODS. Progressive failure of two or more organ systems, resulting from acute, severe illnesses or injuries (sepsis, systemic inflammatory response, trauma, burns) and mediated by the body's inability to sufficiently activate its defense mechanisms. SYN: *multiple systems organ failure; multisystem organ failure.*

  PATIENT CARE: Patients at risk should be closely monitored to help prevent MODS by prompt recognition and correction of perfusion problems, infection, and organ dysfunction. Patients with MODS often have pulmonary, cardiovascular, renal, and hepatic failure, often followed or accompanied by gram-negative sepsis and disseminated intravascular coagulation. Appropriate medical interventions are initiated for each failing system's problems. Nursing responsibilities include assessing for hemodynamic, acid-base and fluid and electrolyte balance, monitoring and assessing diagnostic study results, coordinating and carrying out prescribed therapies and evaluating patient responses while simultaneously assessing for adverse effects, protecting the patient from nosocomial infections and environmental stressors, and providing emotional support for the patient and family through this type of devastating illness, which has a 90% mortality rate.

  The respiratory therapist assists the physician in determining when to intubate the patient and initiate mechanical ventilation. Mechanical ventilation ensures adequate oxygenation and carbon dioxide retention, protects the patient against aspiration, and serves to rest the muscles of breathing and reduce oxygen consumption. The health care provider frequently measures arterial blood gases and pulse oximetry, continually monitors cardiac rhythms, assesses electrolyte and renal function, ensures patient and family comfort and understanding, and protects the patient against complications, including deep venous thrombosis, pressure ulcers, malnutrition, and hospital-acquired infections.

multiple personality SEE: under *personality*.

multiple sclerosis SEE: under *sclerosis*.

multiple sleep latency test A test to diagnose any of several causes of excessive daytime sleepiness. Causes include insomnia, narcolepsy, and obstructive sleep apnea.

multiple subpial transection ABBR: MST. A surgical treatment for partial seizures in which the seizure focus cannot be resected in its entirety. Small cuts are made in the involved cortex of the brain to disrupt the occurrence of seizures. About 20% of patients suffer some new neurological symptoms as a result of the surgery. MST has been used in particular to treat seizures in Landau-Kleffner syndrome.

multipolar (mŭl-tĭ-pōl′ăr) [L. *multus,* many, + *polus,* a pole] **1.** Possessing more than two poles. **2.** Possessing more than two processes, said of neurons.

multipotent (mŭl-tĭp′ă-tĕnt) Of stem cells, having the ability to differentiate into several types of specialized cells.

multirooted (mŭl′tĭ-root″ĕd) In dentistry, referring to a tooth having several roots.

multitalker babble SEE: under *babble*.

multitask (mŭl′ti-task″) To work on several projects at the same time.

multiterminal (mŭl″tĭ-tĕr′mĭ-năl) [″ + Gr. *terma,* a limit] Providing several sets of terminals, making possible the use of several electrodes.

multivalent (mŭl-tĭ-vā′lĕnt) [″ + *valere,* to have power] **1.** Having ability to combine with more than two atoms of a univalent element or radical. **2.** Active against several strains of an organism.

multivariate, multivariable (mŭl-tē-var′ē-āt″, mŭl-tē-var′ē-ă-bĕl) **1.** In statistics, having more than one variable. **2.** Pert. to a research study in which two or more parameters are allowed to assume several values.

mummification (mŭm″mĭ-fĭ-kā′shŭn) [Arabian *mumiyaa,* mummy, + L. *facere,* to make] **1.** Mortification producing a hard, dry mass. SYN: *dry gangrene*. **2.** Drying and shriveling of a body, as a dead and retained fetus.

mumps (mŭmps) An acute, contagious disease caused by the mumps paramyxovirus, which results in inflammation of the salivary glands and other organs. The incidence in the U.S. is extremely low because of childhood immunization with the measles, mumps, and rubella (MMR) vaccine. SEE: *Nursing Diagnoses Appendix.*

SYMPTOMS: Following an incubation period of 12 to 25 days, patients develop prodromal symptoms of fever, malaise, headache, followed by earache that increases with chewing, pain when chewing or drinking sour or acidic fluids, and swollen salivary glands, esp. the parotid glands. The virus is present in saliva 6 days before to 9 days after the onset of parotid swelling. Lifelong immunity is conferred in almost all cases by one attack (even if unilateral). Occasionally, involvement of other organs results in deafness, pancreatitis, or meningitis (about 10% of cases, usually with complete recovery). In boys or men, mumps orchitis or epididymo-orchitis may occur. Testicular swelling and tenderness, lower abdominal pain, nausea, vomiting, fever, and chills are present; the testicles may atrophy, but infertility (sterility) as a result of inflammatory testicular destruction is rare.

TREATMENT: Treatment is generally supportive, with bedrest, antipyretics, analgesics, and adequate fluid intake to prevent dehydration from fever. Intravenous fluids are given if they are needed.

PATIENT CARE: Immunization with MMR is encouraged for all children between ages 12 and 15 months and again between ages 4 and 6 years to prevent the disease. If mumps occurs, the patient is kept in droplet-isolation precautions to prevent transmission of the disease to others. Bedrest is encouraged during the febrile period. The patient's temperature is monitored closely and fluids are encouraged, with tepid sponge baths as needed. Analgesics, salt water gargles, local application of heat or cold, and a liquid or soft diet help reduce pain from swollen glands. Foods that require a great deal of chewing are poorly tolerated and should be avoided. Discomfort from mumps orchitis may be eased with heat or cold applications as the patient prefers, scrotal support, and bedrest. The patient is observed for signs and symptoms of neurological and other complications and is encouraged to gradually resume activity as symptoms subside. All cases of mumps should be reported to local health authorities.

Munchausen syndrome (mĕn′chow″zĕn) [Baron Karl F. H. von Munchausen, fictional character created by Rudolph Erich Raspe, Ger. librarian and scientist, 1736–1794] A type of malingering or factitious disorder in which the patient may practice self-multilation or deception to feign illness. When detected, patients with Munchausen syndrome may leave one hospital and appear in the emergency room of another. They are often misdiagnosed, frequently operated upon, and seldom receive timely psychiatric diagnoses and therapy, which might be beneficial. SEE: *factitious disorder*.

Munchausen syndrome by proxy The fabrication of symptoms or physical evidence of another's illness, or the deliberate causing of another's illness, to gain medical attention. SYN: *Medical child abuse*.

Munro point (mŭn-rō') [John Cummings Munro, U.S. surgeon, 1858–1910] The point halfway between the left anterior iliac spine and the umbilicus.

mural (mū'răl) [L. *murus,* a wall] Pert. to a wall of an organ or part.

muramidase (mŭr-ăm'ĭ-dās) An enzyme found in blood cells of the granulocytic and monocytic series. Its serum and urine level is increased in patients with acute or chronic leukemia. It is also normally present in saliva, sweat, and tears. Also called lysozyme.

murein (mūr'ē-ĭn, -ēn") [Fr *mur(amic acid),* an amino sugar] Peptidoglycan.

murine (mū'rĭn) [L. *mus,* mouse] Concerning rodents, esp. rats and mice.

murmur (mŭr'mŭr) [L. *murmur*] An abnormal sound or extra beat heard when listening to the heart or neighboring large blood vessels. Murmurs may be soft, blowing, rumbling, booming, loud, or variable in intensity. They may be heard during systole, diastole, or both. A murmur does not necessarily indicate heart disease, and many heart diseases do not produce murmurs. SEE: *heart*.

   aortic m. An abnormal, soft sound heard on auscultation that may be due to stenosis or regurgitation. It is a sign of aortic valvular disease. SEE: *aortic regurgitant m.*

   aortic regurgitant m. A blowing or hissing following the second heart sound.

   apex m. An inorganic murmur over the apex of the heart.

   Austin Flint m. SEE: *Austin Flint murmur*.

   cardiac m. A sound arising due to blood flow through the heart.

   continuous m. A murmur that extends throughout systole and diastole.

   crescendo m. A murmur that progressively builds up in intensity and then suddenly subsides.

   diastolic m. A murmur occurring during relaxation of the heart.

   ejection m. A systolic murmur that is most intense at the time of maximum flow of blood from the heart. This murmur is associated with pulmonary and aortic stenosis.

   functional m. A murmur occurring in the absence of any pathological change in the structure of the heart valves or orifices. It does not indicate organic disease of the heart, and may disappear upon a return to health. It may be mis-

taken for a pathological murmur by an inexperienced listener.

   heart m. Cardiac **m.**

   holosystolic m. Pansystolic **m.**

   machinery m. Gibson's murmur.

   mitral m. A murmur produced at the orifice of the mitral (bicuspid) valve.

   musical m. A cardiac murmur with sounds that have an intermittent harmonic pattern.

   organic m. A murmur due to structural changes.

   pansystolic m. A heart murmur heard throughout systole.

   presystolic m. A murmur occurring just before systole, due to mitral or tricuspid obstruction.

   regurgitant m. A murmur due to leakage or backward flow of blood through a dilated valvular orifice.

   systolic m. A cardiac murmur during systole.

   to-and-fro m. A pericardial murmur heard during both systole and diastole.

   tricuspid m. A murmur produced at the orifice of the tricuspid valve and caused by stenosis or incompetency of the valve.

   vascular m. A murmur occurring over a blood vessel.

   vesicular m. Normal breath sounds.

Murphy, John Benjamin (mŭr'fē) U.S. surgeon, 1857–1916.

   M. button A device consisting of two button-like hollow cylinders, used for intestinal anastomosis. Each cylinder is sutured to an open end of the intestine, and the ends are fitted together. After firm union of the ends of the intestine, the sutures separate, and the cylinders are passed in stools.

   M. sign Pain on deep inspiration when an inflamed gallbladder is palpated under the rib cage.

MUS *Medically unexplained symptom*.

Mus (mŭs) [L., mouse] A genus of rodents including mice and rats.

   M. musculus The common house mouse.

Musaceae (mū-zās'ē-ē") [L. *Musa,* banana (the name of the type genus) + *-aceae*] The family of flowering tropical plants that includes the fruit-bearing banana and plantain tree.

Musca (mŭs'kă) [L., fly] A genus of flies belonging to the order Diptera, family Muscidae.

   M. domestica The common house fly. It may mechanically transmit the causative agents of typhoid fever, bacillary and amebic dysentery, cholera, trachoma, and many other diseases to humans.

muscae volitantes (mŭs'sē vōl-ĭ-tăn'tēz) [L., flitting flies] The Latin term for a "floater."

muscarine, muscarin (mŭs'kă-rin, -rēn) [L. *muscarius,* pert. to flies + *-ine*] A toxic organic compound present in *Am-*

anita muscaria (fly agaric mushroom). SEE: *mushroom and toadstool poisoning; amanita in Poisons and Poisoning Appendix.*

muscarinic (mŭs″kă-rĭn′ĭk) Pert. to the effect of acetylcholine at parasympathetic postganglionic effector sites.

muscle (mŭs′ĕl) [L. *musculus,* diminutive of *mus,* mouse] A type of tissue composed of contractile cells. Each muscle cell is filled with parallel actin and myosin filaments. When activated by an internal release of calcium, the filaments use the energy in ATP to crawl along each other in opposite directions. This movement shortens the length of the cell, which then contracts.

The three general classes of muscle cells (myocytes) are skeletal (striated), cardiac (striated), and smooth; most of the muscle in humans is skeletal. A typical muscle has a central portion called the belly and two or more attachment ends with tendons; the more stationary of the attachments is called the muscle's origin, while the more movable attachment is called the muscle's insertion. SEE: illus.

abdominal m. The abdominal muscles are made up of the cremaster, external abdominal oblique, iliacus, psoas major, pyramidalis, quadratus lumborum, rectus abdominis, and transversus abdominis muscles.

abductor digiti minimi m. Hand muscle. Origin: pisiform bone of wrist. Insertion: base of proximal phalanx of digit 5. Nerve: ulnar (C8-T1). Action: abducts digit 5.

abductor pollicis brevis m. Hand muscle. Origin: flexor retinaculum of wrist, scaphoid and trapezium bones. Insertion: lateral base of proximal phalanx of thumb. Nerve: median (C8-T1). Action: abducts thumb, aides in opposition with digit 5. SEE: *arm* for illus. (Muscles of the Arm).

adductor longus m. Hip and thigh muscle. Origin: front of pubis (below crest). Insertion: linea aspera. Nerve: obturator (L2-L4). Action: adducts, flexes, and rotates thigh medially. SEE: *leg* for illus. (Muscles of the leg).

adductor magnus m. Hip and thigh muscle. Origin: inferior ramus of pubis, ramus of ischium, ischial tuberosity. Insertion: linea aspera and adductor tubercle of femur. Nerve: obturator and sciatic (L2-L4). Action: adducts, flexes, and rotates thigh medially. SEE: *leg* for illus. (Muscles of the leg).

adductor pollicis m. Hand muscle. Origin: capitate bone of wrist and metacarpals 2-3. Insertion: proximal phalanx of thumb and medial sesamoid bone. Nerve: ulnar (C8-T1). Action: adducts thumb, aids in opposition with digit 5.

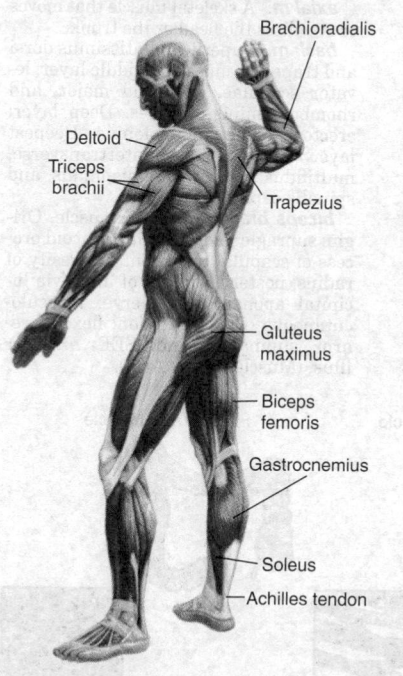

Brachioradialis
Deltoid
Triceps brachii
Trapezius
Gluteus maximus
Biceps femoris
Gastrocnemius
Soleus
Achilles tendon

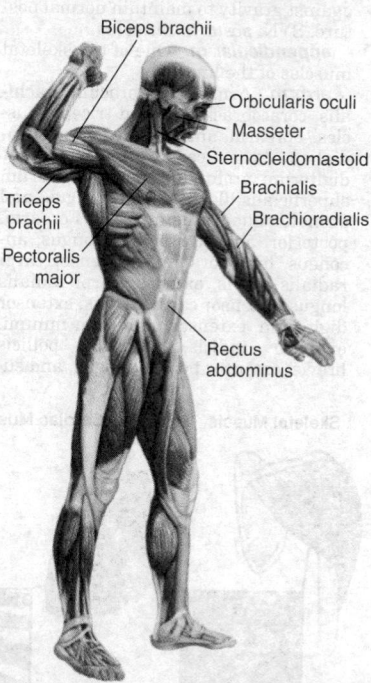

Biceps brachii
Orbicularis oculi
Masseter
Sternocleidomastoid
Brachialis
Brachioradialis
Triceps brachii
Pectoralis major
Rectus abdominus

SELECTED MUSCLES OF THE BODY

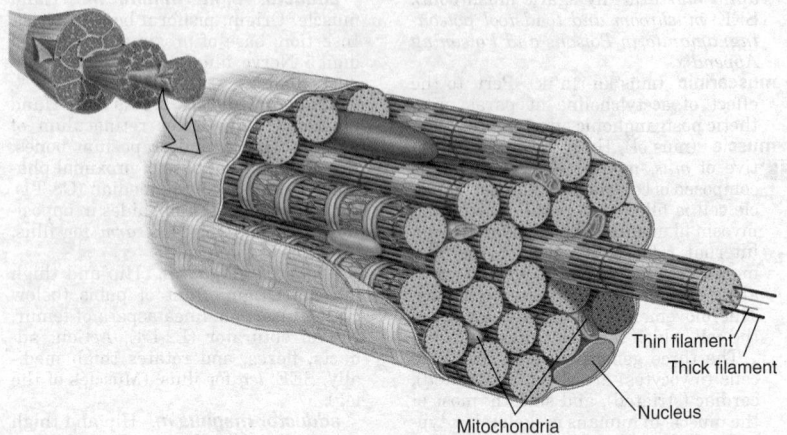

Thin filament

Thick filament

Nucleus

Mitochondria

MUSCLE FIBER

agonist m. Controlled movements involve two opposing muscles: the agonist muscle produces the main action, while the antagonist muscle produces the opposite action to a lesser degree. The balance between agonist and antagonist muscles allows precise control of the final action. SYN: *antagonist m.*

antagonist m. Agonist **muscle.**

antigravity m. Muscles that pull against gravity to maintain normal posture. SYN: *postural muscles.*

appendicular m. One of the skeletal muscles of the limbs.

arm m. Arm: biceps brachii, brachialis, coracobrachialis, and triceps muscles. Forearm, anterior: flexor carpi radialis, flexor carpi ulnaris, flexor digitorum profundus, flexor digitorum superficialis, flexor pollicis longus, and pronator quadratus muscles. Forearm, posterior: abductor pollicis longus, anconeus, brachioradialis, extensor carpi radialis brevis, extensor carpi radialis longus, extensor carpi ulnaris, extensor digitorum, extensor digitorum minimi, extensor indicis, extensor pollicis brevis, extensor pollicis longus, and su-

pinator muscles. SEE: *arm* for illus. (Muscles of the Arm).

arytenoid m. The oblique or the transverse arytenoid -- laryngeal muscles. Origins: arytenoid cartilage. Insertions: contralateral arytenoid cartilage. Nerve: recurrent laryngeal and superior laryngeal of the vagus (CN X). Action: closes laryngeal inlet by bringing arytenoid cartilages toward each other.

axial m. A skeletal muscle that moves or stabilizes the head or the trunk.

back m. Superficial: latissimus dorsi and trapezius muscles. Middle layer: levator scapulae, rhomboid major, and rhomboid minor muscles. Deep layer: erector spinae and splenius. Deepest layer: interspinalis, intertransverse, multifidus, rotatores, semispinalis, and spinalis capitis.

biceps brachii m. Arm muscle. Origin: supraglenoid tubercle, coracoid process of scapula. Insertion: tuberosity of radius, posterior border of ulna (via bicipital aponeurosis). Nerve: musculocutaneous (C5-C6). Action: flexes forearm, supinates hand. SEE: *arm* for illus. (Muscles of the Arm).

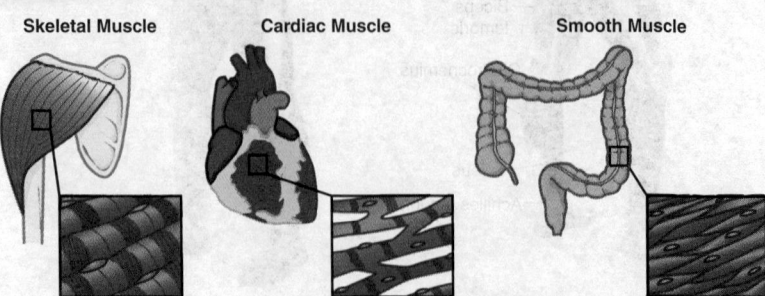

Skeletal Muscle   Cardiac Muscle   Smooth Muscle

MORPHOLOGICAL FORMS OF MUSCLE

biceps femoris m. Leg muscle. Origin: ischial tuberosity, linea aspera and second supracondylar ridge of femur. Insertion: lateral condyle of tibia, head of fibula. Nerve: sciatic (L5-S2). Action: flexes leg, rotates leg laterally, extends thigh. SEE: *leg* for illus. (Muscles of the leg).

brachialis m. Arm muscle. Origin: anterior surface of lower (distal) humerus. Insertion: coronoid process of ulna. Nerve: musculocutaneous and radial (C5-C7). Action: flexes forearm. SEE: *arm* for illus. (Muscles of the Arm).

brachioradialis m. Arm muscle. Origin: lateral supracondylar ridge of distal humerus. Insertion: distal end of radius. Nerve: radial (C5-C7). Action: flexes forearm. SEE: *arm* for illus. (Muscles of the Arm).

buccinator m. Facial muscle. Origin: pterygomandibular raphe and alveolar processes of jaws. Insertion: orbicularis oris muscle at angle of mouth. Nerve: facial (CN VII). Action: compresses check against teeth, retracts angle of mouth.

cardiac m. A tissue composed of mitochondrion-filled muscle cells that also contain neatly packed actin and myosin filaments; the filaments are arranged in cylindrical bundles called myofibrils. In each cell, the myofibrils are all aligned in the same direction and are parceled into longitudinal blocks (called sarcomeres) of similar lengths. Under the microscope, the ends of the blocks appear as lines, making cardiac muscle cells appear to have regularly arranged striations. In the muscle tissue, the cardiac muscle cells are connected in branching networks.

Cardiac muscle is innervated by both sympathetic and parasympathetic autonomic motor axons. In addition, cardiac muscle is stimulated by blood-borne molecules, can conduct electrical impulses from cell to cell, and can independently generate rhythmical contractions. Cardiac muscle, which is found only in the heart, cannot be controlled consciously. SEE: table.

chest wall m. Pectoralis major, pectoralis minor, serratus anterior, subclavius, subscapularis, or teres major muscle.

chewing m. Mastication **m.**

ciliary m. Internal eye muscle. Origin: edges of sclera. Insertion: ciliary process of lens. Nerve: oculomotor (CN III). Action: allows lens to become more curved to focus on near objects.

core m. One of the major muscles that stabilizes and controls the pressure inside the trunk; these are the pelvic floor, abdominal wall, back, and diaphragm muscles.

corrugator m. Facial muscle. Origin: medial part of supraorbital margin. Insertion: skin above middle of eyebrow. Nerve: facial (CN VII). Action: pulls eyebrows toward midline and downward. SYN: *Corrugator supercilii.*

cremaster m. Spermatic cord muscle. Origin: inguinal ligament and pubic tubercle. Insertion: cremasteric fascia covering spermatic cord. Nerve: genitofemoral (L1-L2). Action: elevates testis in males. SEE: *penis* for illus.

cricoarytenoid m. Either of two laryngeal muscles—the lateral or the posterior. Origin: cricoid cartilage. Insertion: muscular process of arytenoid cartilage. Nerve: recurrent laryngeal of the vagus (CN X). Action: rotates arytenoid cartilages for vocalizations.

cricothyroid m. Laryngeal muscle. Origin: cricoid cartilage. Insertion: lower edges of thyroid cartilage. Nerve: superior laryngeal of the vagus (CN X). Action: tenses (stretches) vocal cords SEE: *thyroid* for illus.

deltoid m. Shoulder muscle. Origin: a bony ellipse from the lateral third of the clavicle over the acromial process and along the spine of the scapula. Insertion: deltoid tuberosity on the lateral shaft of the humerus. Nerve: axillary (C5-C6). Action: abducts arm. SEE: *arm* for illus. (Muscles of the Arm).

detrusor m. The three-layered muscular wall of the urinary bladder. Nerve: primarily parasympathetic (S2-S4), sec-

Comparison of Properties of Three Types of Muscle

	Smooth	Cardiac	Striated
Synonyms	Involuntary Nonstriated Visceral	Myocardial	Voluntary Skeletal
Fibers			
Length (in/m)	50–200		25,000
Thickness (in/m)	4–8		75
Shape	Spindles		Cylinders
Markings	No striation	Striation	Marked striation
Nuclei	Single	Single	Multiple
Effects of cutting related nerve	Slight	Regulation of heart rate is lost	Complete paralysis

ondarily sympathetic (T11-L2). Action: empties bladder.

diaphragm m. Origin: internal surfaces of lower six ribs, xiphoid process, vertebral bodies L1-L3. Insertion: central tendon (of diaphragm). Nerve: phrenic, lower six intercostals. Action: inflates lungs

digastric m. Neck muscle with two bellies. Origin: anterior belly attaches to the digastric fossa in mandible at base of anterior midline, posterior belly attaches to mastoid process. Insertion: tendon connecting both bellies in a loop of fascia that is attached to hyoid bone. Nerve: anterior belly -- trigeminal (CN V), posterior belly -- facial (CN VII). Action: lowers mandible and raises hyoid bone. SEE: *neck* for illus.

erector spinae m.'s Three adjacent vertical bands of deep back muscles -- the iliocostalis, longissimus, and spinalis muscles. Origins: a wide tendon running along the iliac crest to the sacrum, the lower lumbar and sacral spinous processes. Insertions: along the back in the angles of the lower ribs, transverse processes of the thoracic and cervical vertebrae. Nerves: dorsal rami of the spinal nerves. Actions: extends (bends backward) the vertebral column and neck, twists the back.

extensor carpi ulnaris m. Forearm muscle. Origin: lateral epicondyle of humerus, proximal edge of ulna. Insertion: proximal end of fifth metacarpal. Nerve: radial (C7-C8). Action: adducts hand, extends wrist. SEE: *arm* for illus. (Muscles of the Arm).

extensor digitorum m. Forearm muscle. Origin: lateral epicondyle of humerus. Insertion: common extensor tendon of fingers. Nerve: radial (C7-C8). Action: extends fingers and wrist. SEE: *arm* for illus. (Muscles of the Arm).

extensor digitorum brevis m. Foot muscle. Origin: dorsolateral surface of calcaneus. Insertion: extensor tendons of toes. Nerve: deep peroneal (S1-S2). Action: extends toes. SEE: *leg* for illus. (Muscles of the leg).

extensor digitorum longus m. Foot muscle. Origin: lateral condyle of tibia, upper three-fourths of fibula. Insertion: extensor tendons of toes 2-5. Nerve: deep peroneal (L5-S1). Action: extends toes, dorsiflexes foot. SEE: *leg* for illus. (Muscles of the leg).

extensor hallucis longus m. Foot muscle. Origin: middle of fibula. Insertion: base of proximal phalanx of big toe. Nerve: deep peroneal (S1-S2). Action: dorsiflexes big toe. SEE: *leg* for illus. (Muscles of the leg).

external oblique m. Abdominal wall muscle. Origin: lower costal margin. Insertion: anterior half of iliac crest, rectus sheath, inguinal ligament. Nerve: intercostals 8-12, iliohypogastric, ilioin-

guinal (L1). Action: tenses and compresses abdomen, flexes and laterally rotates spine, lowers rib cage.

external pterygoid m. Lateral pterygoid **m.**

extraocular m. ABBR: EOM. Six muscles that attach outside the eyeball and that move the eye in its socket. The EOM are: the inferior and superior oblique muscles, and the lateral, medial, inferior, and superior rectus muscles. SEE: *extraocular* for illus.

m.s of facial expression Thin muscles that insert into the skin of the face; all are innervated by the facial nerve (CN VII). Scalp: frontalis and occipitalis muscles. Ear: anterior, posterior, and superior auricular muscles. Eye: orbicularis oculi. Nose: depressor septi, nasalis, and procerus muscles. Mouth: buccinator, depressor anguli oris, depressor labii inferioris, levator anguli oris, levator labii superioris, mentalis, orbicularis oris, risorius, and zygomaticus muscle. Neck: platysma. SEE: *face* and *head* for illus.

m. of facial expression Facial muscles.

fibularis m. The newer name for the peroneus muscles.

flexor carpi radialis m. Forearm muscle. Origin: medial epicondyle of humerus. Insertion: bases of second and third metacarpals. Nerve: median (C6-C7). Action: abducts hand, flexes wrist. Arm, muscles of the arm (illus.).

flexor carpi ulnaris m. Forearm muscle. Origin: medial epicondyle of humerus, medial side of olecranon, proximal posterior edge of ulna. Insertion: pisiform, hamate, and base of fifth metacarpal. Nerve: ulnar (C7-C8). Action: adducts hand, flexes wrist.

flexor digitorum longus m. Foot muscle. Origin: posterior surface of middle tibia. Insertion: distal phalanges of toes 2-5. Nerve: tibial (S2-S3). Action: flexes toes 2-5, plantarflexes foot. SEE: *leg* for illus. (Muscles of the leg).

flexor digitorum profundus m. Forearm muscle. Origin: proximal three-fourths of ulna. Insertion: distal phalanges of fingers (digits 2-5). Nerve: ulnar, median (C8-T1). Action: flexes distal finger joints, aids in wrist flexion.

flexor digitorum superficialis m. Forearm muscle. Origin: medial epicondyle of humerus, coronoid process of ulna. Insertion: middle phalanges of fingers (digits 2-5). Nerve: median (C7-T1). Action: flexes fingers and wrist. SEE: *arm* for illus. (Muscles of the Arm).

flexor hallucis longus m. Foot muscle. Origin: distal two-thirds of posterior tibia. Insertion: plantar side of distal phalanx of big toe. Nerve: tibial (S2-S3). Action: flexes big toe, plantarflexes foot.

flexor pollicis longus m. Forearm muscle. Origin: coronoid process of ulna, anterior surface of radius. Insertion: distal phalanx of thumb. Nerve: median (C8-T1). Action: flexes thumb. SEE: *arm* for illus. (Muscles of the Arm).

foot m. Dorsal: dorsal interosseous, extensor digitorum brevis, extensor digitorum longus, extensor hallucis longus, and tibialis anterior muscles. Plantar: abductor digiti minimi, abductor hallucis, adductor hallucis, flexor digitorum brevis, flexor digiti minimi brevis, flexor hallucis brevis, lumbrical, plantar interosseous, and quadratus plantae muscles. SEE: *leg* for illus. (Muscles of the leg).

frontalis m. Front half of occipitofrontalis muscle, one of the facial muscles. Origin: epicranial (scalp) aponeurosis. Insertion: skin of eyebrows, root of nose. Nerve: facial (CN VII). Action: elevates eyebrows, wrinkles forehead. SEE: *face* and *head* for illus.

gastrocnemius m. Leg muscle. Origin: medial condyle of femur, lateral condyle of femur. Insertion: calcaneus (via Achilles tendon). Nerve: tibial (S1-S2). Action: plantarflexes foot, flexes knee. SEE: *leg* for illus. (Muscles of the leg).

genioglossus m. Tongue muscle. Origin: genial tubercle on inside of mandibular symphysis. Insertion: ventral tongue, hyoid bone. Nerve: hypoglossal (CN XII). Action: protrudes and depresses tongue.

gluteus maximus m. Thigh muscle. Origin: upper outer edge of ilium and sacrum. Insertion: iliotibial tract of fascia lata, gluteal tuberosity of femur. Nerve: inferior gluteal (L5-S2). Action: extends, abducts, and laterally rotates thigh.

gluteus medius m. Thigh muscle. Origin: lower half of ilium. Insertion: proximal medial tibia. Nerve: obturator (L2-L3). Action: adducts, flexes, and medially rotates thigh.

gracilis m. Thigh muscle. Origin: lower half of pubis. Insertion: proximal medial tibia. Nerve: obturator (L2-L3). Action: adducts, flexes, and medially rotates thigh. SEE: *leg* for illus. (Muscles of the leg).

hamstring m. Posterior thigh muscles that originate on the ischial tuberosity and act across both the hip and knee joints; they are the biceps femoris, gracilis, sartorius, semitendinosus, and semimembranosus muscles.

hand m. Abductor digiti minimi, abductor pollicis brevis, adductor pollicis, dorsal interosseous, flexor digiti minimi, flexor pollicis brevis, lumbrical, opponens digiti minimi, opponens pollicis, palmaris brevis, and palmar interosseous muscles.

iliacus m. Thigh muscle. Origin: iliac fossa. Insertion: lesser trochanter of fe-

mur, psoas major tendon. Nerve: femoral (L2-L3). Action: flexes thigh.

iliopsoas m. The iliacus and psoas major muscles considered together. SEE: *leg* for illus. (Muscles of the leg).

inferior oblique m. Extraocular muscle. Origin: inside front lower margin of maxillary part of orbit. Insertion: lateral surface of eyeball behind its equator. Nerve: oculomotor (CN III). Action: turns eye up and outward with lateral rotation. SEE: *extraocular* for illus.

inferior rectus m. Extraocular muscle. Origin: tendinous ring around optic nerve at rear of orbit. Insertion: lower edge of eyeball in front of its equator. Nerve: oculomotor (CN III). Action: turns eye down and medially. SEE: *extraocular* for illus.

infraspinatus m. Shoulder muscle. Origin: medial two-thirds of infraspinatus fossa of scapula. Insertion: posterior side of greater tubercle of humerus. Nerve: suprascapular (C4-C6). Action: rotates arm laterally.

internal pterygoid m. Medial pterygoid **muscle.**

involuntary m. A muscle not under conscious control: smooth, cardiac, and some skeletal muscles.

laryngeal m. Any of six short muscles inside the larynx that move the vocal apparatus and (except for the cricothyroid muscle) are innervated by the recurrent laryngeal branch of the vagus nerve (CN X).

lateral pterygoid m. One of the mastication muscles. Origin: greater wing of sphenoid bone, lateral pterygoid plate. Insertion: pterygoid fovea of condyle of mandible. Nerve: trigeminal (CN V). Action: opens mouth, protrudes mandible. SYN: *external pterygoid* **m.** SEE: *arm* for illus.

lateral rectus m. Extraocular muscle. Origin: tendinous ring around optic nerve at rear of orbit. Insertion: temporal edge of eyeball in front of its equator. Nerve: abducens (CN VI). Action: turns eye laterally. SEE: *extraocular* for illus.

latissimus dorsi m. Back muscle. Origin: spinous processes of vertebrae T7-S3, thoracolumbar fascia, iliac crest. Insertion: bicipital groove of humerus. Nerve: thoracodorsal (C6-C8). Action: adducts, extends, and medially rotates arm.

leg m. Anterior and lateral: extensor digitorum longus, extensor hallucis longus, peroneus, peroneus longus, peroneus tertius, and tibialis anterior muscles. Posterior: flexor digitorum longus, flexor hallucis longus, gastrocnemius, plantaris, popliteus, soleus, and tibialis posterior muscles. SEE: *leg* for illus. (Muscles of the leg).

levator ani m. The set of pelvic floor muscles, which include the iliococcygeus, levator prostatae or vaginal sphincter, pubococcygeus, and puborectalis muscles. Origins: insides of pelvic bones (pubis, arcus tendinaeus, ischial spine, and sacrospinous ligament). Insertions: perineal body, coccyx, anococcygeal ligament, lower sacrum. Nerve: perineal of spinal S4, pudendal. Action: supports pelvic viscera, contributes to urethral, vaginal, and anal sphincter actions.

levator palpebrae m. Eyelid muscle. Origin: inner roof of orbit. Insertion: skin and tarsal plate of upper eyelid. Nerve: oculomotor (CN III). Action: raises upper eyelid. SEE: *extraocular* for illus.

lumbrical m. Hand and foot muscles. Origins: tendons of flexor digitorum profundus or flexor digitorum longus. Insertions: extensor tendons of digits 2-5. Nerve, hand: median (C8-T1), ulnar (C8-T1). Nerve, foot: medial plantar (S2-S3), lateral plantar (S2-S3). Action: flex the straightened digits (specifically, flex the metacarpophalangeal or metatarsophalangeal joints while extending the interphalangeal joints).

masseter m. Muscle of mastication. Origin: zygomatic process of maxilla, zygomatic arch. Insertion: coronoid process, lower half of ramus, and angle of mandible. Nerve: trigeminal (CN V). Action: elevates mandible to close jaw. SEE: *head* for illus.

mastication m. The chewing muscle, which is innervated by the mandibular division of the trigeminal nerve (CN V). These muscles include the masseter, temporalis, and medial and lateral pterygoid muscles. SYN: *chewing* **m.**

medial pterygoid m. Muscle of mastication. Origin: lateral pterygoid plate. Insertion: medial surface of ramus and angle of mandible. Nerve: trigeminal (CN V). Action: closes mouth, protrudes mouth, moves jaw sideways. SYN: *internal pterygoid* **m.**

medial rectus m. Extraocular muscle. Origin: tendinous ring around optic nerve at rear of orbit. Insertion: nasal edge of eyeball in front of its equator. Nerve: oculomotor (CN III). Action: turns eye medially.

mentalis m. Facial muscle. Origin: incisive fossa at front of mandible. Insertion: skin of chin. Nerve: facial (CN VII). Action: raises and protrudes lower lip. SEE: *face* and *head* for illus.

mimetic m. Facial muscles. SYN: *muscles of facial expression.*

mylohyoid m. Neck muscle. Origin: mylohyoid line of mandible. Insertion: hyoid bone, mylohyoid raphe. Nerve: trigeminal (CN V). Action: elevates hyoid and larynx, lowers jaw.

neck m. Anterior and lateral: digastric, geniohyoid, mylohyoid, omohyoid, platysma, sternocleidomastoid, sterno-

hyoid, sternothyroid, stylohyoid, and thyrohyoid muscles. Posterior: levator scapulae, scalene muscles, and trapezius. Suboccipital: obliquus capitis and rectus capitis muscles. SEE: *head* for illus.

nonstriated m. Smooth **m.**

orbicularis oculi m. Facial muscle. Origin: completely surrounds eye, attaches to medial palpebral ligament (and adjacent bones) and lacrimal crest (and adjacent bones). Insertion: medial palpebral raphe (after encircling orbit), lateral palpebral raphe, tarsi of eyelids. Nerve: facial (CN VII) Action: closes eyelids, lifts cheeks, compresses lacrimal sac. SEE: *face* and *head* for illus.

orbicularis oris m. Facial muscle. Origin: adjacent facial muscles that surround mouth. Insertion: into itself and skin of lips while encircling mouth. Nerve: facial (CN VII). Action: closes and purses lips. SEE: *face* and *head* for illus.

m. of the palate Levator veli palatini, musculus uvulae, palatoglossus, palatopharyngeus, pharyngeal constrictor, salpingopharyngeus, and tensor veli palatine muscles.

palmaris longus m. Forearm muscle. Origin: medial epicondyle of humerus. Insertion: palmar surface of flexor retinaculum, palmar aponeurosis. Nerve: median (C7-C8). Action: flexes hand. SEE: *arm* for illus. (Muscles of the Arm).

papillary m. Internal conical heart muscles. Origin: ventricular wall. Insertion: tricuspid and mitral valve leaflets via chordae tendinae. Action: anchor leaflets of valves during heart contractions.

pectoralis major m. Chest wall muscle. Origin: medial half of clavicle, sternum, costal cartilages 4-6. Insertion: lateral edge of bicipital groove of humerus. Nerve: lateral and medial pectoral (C5-T1). Action: adducts and medially rotates arm.

pectoralis minor m. Chest wall muscle. Origin: Anterior medial surface of ribs 3-5. Insertion: coracoid process of scapula. Nerve: lateral and medial pectoral (C6-C8). Action: pulls shoulder forward and down, elevates rib cage.

peroneus longus m. Leg muscle. Origin: lateral two-thirds of fibula. Insertion: medial cuneiform bone, base of first metatarsal. Nerve: superficial peroneal (L5-S1). Action: everts and plantar flexes foot. SYN: *fibularis longus* **m.** SEE: *leg* for illus. (Muscles of the leg).

pharynx and tongue m. Cricothyroid, genioglossus, geniohyoid, hyoglossus, palatoglossus, pharyngeal constrictor, styloglossus, stylopharyngeus, salpingopharyngeus, and thyrohyoid muscles.

piriformis m. Thigh muscle. Origin: anterior surface of sacrum. Insertion: upper part of greater trochanter of femur. Nerve: spinal L5-S2. Action: laterally rotates thigh.

platysma m. Neck and facial muscle. Origin: superficial fascia of upper chest. Insertion: skin of lower face. Nerve: facial (CN VII). Action: lowers jaw, widens neck. SEE: *face* and *head* for illus.

postural m. Antigravity **muscles.**

pronator teres m. Arm muscle. Origin: medial epicondyle of humerus, coronoid process of ulna. Insertion: lateral side of middle of radius. Nerve: median (C6-C7). Action: pronates forearm.

psoas major m. Thigh muscle. Origin: bodies of vertebrae T12-L1. Insertion: lesser trochanter of femur. Nerve: lumbar L1-L3. Action: flexes thigh.

pterygoid m. The lateral or the medial pterygoid muscle.

puborectalis m. Pelvic muscle, part of levator ani. Origin: back surface of pubis. Insertion: joins other levator ani muscles forming a bowl shaped diaphragm, encircles anal canal, and attaches to sacrum and coccyx. Nerve: inferior rectal and sacral (S4). Action: supports pelvis, holds anal canal at right angle to rectum.

quadriceps m. The rectus femoris, vastus intermedius, vastus lateralis, and vastus medius muscles together.

rectus abdominis m. Abdominal wall muscle. Origin: crest and symphysis of pubis. Insertion: xiphoid process, costal cartilages 5-7. Nerve: spinal T7-T12. Action: tenses abdomen, flexes vertebral column.

rectus femoris m. Thigh muscle. Origin: anterior inferior iliac spine, upper edge of acetabulum. Insertion: tibial tuberosity (via the patellar ligament). Nerve: femoral (L2-L4). Action: extends leg, flexes thigh. SEE: *leg* for illus. (Muscles of the leg).

red m. Twitch skeletal muscle cells containing myoglobin and many mitochondria. These cells largely generate energy via aerobic oxidation and are suited for maintaining contractions for an extended time.

m. of respiration Any of the muscles used in breathing, including the diaphragm, the muscles of the rib cage, and the abdominal muscles. SEE: *diaphragm; expiration; inspiration*.

rhomboid m. The major or the minor rhomboid muscle, two of the many shoulder muscles. Origins: nuchal ligament, spinous processes of vertebrae C7-T5. Insertion: vertebral edge of scapula. Nerve: dorsal scapular (C4-C5). Action: pulls scapulae toward each other. illus. (Muscles of the Trunk).

rotator cuff m. Shoulder muscles -- the infraspinatus, subscapularis, supraspinatus, and teres minor muscles -- which hold the head of the humerus in the glenoid fossa of the scapula.

sartorius m. Thigh muscle. Origin:

anterior superior iliac spine. Insertion: medial side of proximal tibia. Nerve: femoral (L2-L3). Action: flexes thigh and leg, laterally rotates thigh. SEE: *leg* for illus. (Muscles of the leg).

scalene m. The anterior, the middle, or the posterior scalene muscle -- neck muscles. Origins: transverse processes of vertebrae C1-C7. Insertions: upper surfaces of ribs 1-2. Nerves: cervical spinal C4-C8. Actions: raises ribs 1-2, bends neck ipsilaterally.

semimembranosus m. Thigh muscle. Origin: ischial tuberosity. Insertion: medial condyle of tibia. Nerve: sciatic (L5-S2). Action: extends thigh, flexes and medially rotates leg. SEE: *leg* for illus. (Muscles of the leg).

semitendinosus m. Thigh muscle. Origin: ischial tuberosity. Insertion: upper medial tibia near tuberosity. Nerve: sciatic L5-S2). Action: extends thigh, flexes and medially rotates leg. SEE: *leg* for illus. (Muscles of the leg).

serratus anterior m. Chest muscle. Origin: outer surface of ribs 1-8. Insertion: anterior side of vertebral edge of scapula. Nerve: long thoracic (C5-C7). Action: pulls scapula forward (anterior) and laterally (abduction), rotates scapula upward.

shoulder m. Deltoid, infraspinatus, subscapularis, supraspinatus, teres major and teres minor muscles.

skeletal m. A tissue composed of muscle cells (often multinucleated) that contain neatly packed actin and myosin filaments; these filaments are arranged in cylindrical bundles called myofibrils. In each cell, the myofibrils are all aligned in the same direction and are parceled into longitudinal blocks (called sarcomeres) of similar lengths. Under the microscope, the ends of the blocks look like lines, making skeletal muscle cells appear to have regularly arranged striations.

Skeletal muscle is innervated by somatic (as opposed to autonomic) motor axons at a synaptic structure called a motor endplate, where acetylcholine is the neurotransmitter. Most skeletal muscles can be controlled consciously, and skeletal muscle is sometimes referred to as voluntary muscle. Skeletal muscle cells contract more forcefully than smooth or cardiac muscle cells.

Skeletal muscle got its name because it usually attaches at one end to bone. Skeletal muscle is by far the most common type of muscle in the body and it plays a major role in normal metabolism, e.g., after a meal, excess glucose is removed from the blood stream primarily by skeletal muscle.

smooth m. A tissue composed of muscle cells that contain loosely organized actin and myosin filaments. The lack of tight organization means that smooth muscle cells do not appear striated when examined under a microscope. Smooth muscle tissue tends to occur as sheets and is typically found in the walls of tubes, e.g., arteries, and sacs, e.g., the gastrointestinal system.

Smooth muscles are innervated by both sympathetic and parasympathetic autonomic motor axons; they are also stimulated by blood-borne molecules. Smooth muscles cannot be consciously controlled, and this form of muscle tissue is called involuntary muscle. Smooth muscle cells contract more slowly than skeletal or cardiac muscle cells. SYN: *nonstriated* **muscle.**; *unstriated* **muscle.** SEE: table.

soleus m. Leg muscle. Origin: proximal ends of tibia and fibula. Insertion: calcaneus via Achilles tendon. Nerve: tibial (S1-S2). Action: plantarflexes foot. SEE: *leg* for illus. (Muscles of the leg).

somatic m. Muscle derived from mesodermal somites, including most skeletal muscle.

sphincter m. A muscle that encircles a duct, tube, or orifice, thus controlling its opening.

stapedius m. Middle ear muscle. Origin: posterior wall of middle ear. Insertion: neck of stapes. Nerve: facial (CN VII). Action: tilts stapes, dampens excessive vibrations.

sternocleidomastoid m. Neck muscle. Origin: upper edge of manubrium, middle of upper clavicle. Insertion: mastoid process. Nerve: accessory (CN XI), spinal C2. Action: contralaterally rotates head. SEE: *face* and *head* for illus.

striated m. SEE: table.

subscapularis m. Shoulder muscle. Origin: medial subscapular fossa. Insertion: lesser tubercle of humerus. Nerve: upper and lower subscapular (C5-C7). Action: medially rotates arm.

superior oblique m. Extraocular muscle. Origin: sphenoid bone deep in medial side of orbit. Insertion: lateral surface of eyeball behind its equator. Nerve: trochlear (CN IV). Action: turns eye down and outward with medial rotation.

superior rectus m. Extraocular muscle. Origin: tendinous ring around optic nerve at rear of orbit. Insertion: upper edge of eyeball in front of its equator. Nerve: oculomotor (CN III). Action: turns eye up and medially. SEE: *extraocular* for illus.

supraspinatus m. Shoulder muscle. Origin: medial supraspinous fossa of scapula. Insertion: greater tubercle of humerus. Nerve: suprascapular (C4-C6). Action: abducts arm.

temporalis m. Muscle of mastication. Origin: temporal fossa of skull. Insertion: coronoid process of mandible. Nerve: trigeminal (CN V). Action: closes

mouth, clenches teeth, retracts jaw. SEE: *head* for illus.

tensor fascia lata m. Thigh muscle. Origin: iliac crest, anterior superior iliac spine. Insertion: iliotibial tract of fascia lata. Nerve: superior gluteal (L4-L5). Action: stabilizes (abducts) thigh, extends and laterally rotates leg.

tensor tympani m. Middle ear muscle. Origin: wall of auditory tube. Insertion: handle of malleus. Nerve: trigeminal (CN V). Action: tenses tympanic membrane, dampens excessive vibrations.

teres major m. Shoulder muscle. Origin: lower lateral edge of scapula. Insertion: bicipital groove of humerus. Nerve: lower scapular (C6-C7). Action: adducts and medially rotates arm.

teres minor m. Shoulder muscle. Origin: upper lateral side of scapula. Insertion: greater tubercle of humerus. Nerve: axillary (C4-C6). Action: laterally rotates arm.

thigh m. Anterior: iliopsoas, quadriceps (rectus femoris, vastus intermedius, vastus lateralis, and vastus medius), and sartorius muscles. Medial: adductor brevis, adductor longus, adductor magnus, gracilis, and pectineus muscles. Gluteal region: gemelli, gluteus maximus, gluteus medius, gluteus minimus, obturator externus, obturator, internus, piriformis, quadratus femoris, and tensor fasciae lata muscles. Posterior: biceps femoris, semimembranosus, and semitendinosus muscles. SEE: *leg* for illus. (Muscles of the leg).

tibialis anterior m. Leg muscle. Origin: lateral side of proximal tibia. Insertion: medial side of cuneiform bone, base of metatarsal 1. Nerve: deep peroneal (L4-L5). Action: inverts and dorsiflexes foot.

tibialis posterior m. Leg muscle. Origin: anterior tibia and fibula. Insertion: navicular, cuneiform, and cuboid bones; metatarsals 2-4. Nerve: tibial (L4-L5). Action: inverts and plantarflexes foot.

tonic m. Skeletal muscle fibers that contract slowly and that cannot propagate an action potential along their cell membranes. Tonic muscles are uncommon in humans and are found only in the extraocular muscles, stapedius muscle, and intrafusal fibers of the muscle spindles. The remainder of human skeletal muscle contains only twitch fibers.

trapezius m. Neck and back muscle. Origin: occipital bone (superior nuchal line), nuchal ligament, spinous processes of vertebrae C7-T12. Insertion: posterior edge of lateral clavicle, acromion, posterior edge of spine of scapula. Nerve: accessory (CN XI), spinal C3-C4. Action: elevates, retracts, and rotates scapula. SEE: *face* and *head* for illus.

triceps m. Arm muscle. Origin: infraglenoid tubercle of scapula, posterior of proximal humerus, posterior of distal humerus. Insertion: olecranon process. Nerve: radial (C6-C8). Action: extends forearm. SYN: *triceps brachii m.* SEE: *arm* for illus. (Muscles of the Arm).

triceps brachii m. Triceps **muscle**.

twitch m. Muscle fibers that can conduct axon potentials along their cell membranes. Almost all skeletal muscle in humans is twitch muscle. A very small number of muscles in humans are tonic muscles. Twitch muscles cells can be categorized into a number of types on the basis of the biochemical cycle that they use to produce their energy: red (oxidative), white (glycolytic), or intermediate (oxidative/glycolytic). Most human muscles are composed of a mix of twitch muscle cell types.

unstriated m. Smooth **m.**

uterine m. SEE: *myometrium*.

vastus intermedius m. Thigh muscle. Origin: anterior and lateral sides of proximal femur. Insertion: common tendon of quadratus muscles, tibial tuberosity via patellar ligament. Nerve: femoral (L2-L4). Action: extends leg.

vastus lateralis m. Thigh muscle. Origin: lateral side of proximal femur. Insertion: common tendon of quadratus muscles, tibial tuberosity via patellar ligament. Nerve: femoral (L2-L4). Action: extends leg. SEE: *leg* for illus. (Muscles of the leg).

vastus medialis m. Thigh muscle. Origin: medial side of femur Insertion: common tendon of quadratus muscles, tibial tuberosity via patellar ligament. Nerve: femoral (L2-L4). Action: extends leg.

vocalis m. Laryngeal muscle. Origin: midline of inner surface of thyroid cartilage. Insertion: arytenoid cartilage. Nerve: recurrent laryngeal of vagus (CN X). Action: changes tension of vocal cords.

voluntary m. A muscle that can be controlled voluntarily; most skeletal muscles are voluntary.

muscle cramps SEE: under *cramp*.

muscle dysmorphia, muscle dysmorphic disorder A body image disorder principally experienced by males, characterized by excessive fear about one's body size, esp. a concern that one's muscles are not large enough. Boys affected by muscle dysmorphia often take drugs, e.g., androgenic or anabolic steroids, to increase their body size. The syndrome is also known colloquially as *bigorexia* or *vigorexia*. SYN: *reverse* **anorexia**. SEE: *body dysmorphic disorder*.

muscle fiber SEE: under *fiber*.

muscle metabolism SEE: under *metabolism*.

muscle phosphorylase deficiency SEE: under *deficiency*.

muscle recovery SEE: under *recovery*.

muscle relaxer Muscle **relaxant**.

muscle soreness A nonspecific term used to describe general discomfort in a muscle or muscle group that is the result of disease, trauma, or exertion. SEE: *delayed onset m.s.*

delayed-onset m.s. ABBR: DOMS. Muscle tenderness, decreased strength, and decreased range of motion that develops 12 to 24 hr following strenuous exercise and peaks in intensity between 24 to 48 hr, although symptoms may persist 72 hr or more. DOMS may result from microtearing of muscular fibers, lactic acid accumulation, local inflammatory response, and/or physiochemical changes within the muscle fibers. Muscle soreness is most pronounced following eccentric exercise. SEE: *eccentric exercise; inflammation*.

muscle synergy, muscular synergy The association of several muscle groups contracting simultaneously as a single functional unit, e.g., the back, trunk, abdominal, and leg muscles working together to maintain balance while walking.

muscular (mŭs′kū-lăr) [L. *muscularis*] **1.** Pert. to muscles. **2.** Possessing well-developed muscles.

muscular dystrophy SEE: under *dystrophy*.

muscularis (mŭs-kū-lā′rĭs) [L.] The smooth muscle layer of an organ or tubule.

m. mucosae Smooth muscle tissue of a mucous membrane.

muscular system The system that includes the skeletal muscles and their tendons. SEE: *muscle*.

muscular tissue SEE: under *muscle*.

musculature (mŭs′kū-lă-chūr) [L. *musculus*, muscle] The arrangement of muscles in the body or its parts.

musculo-, muscul- [L. *musculus*, muscle] Prefix meaning muscle. SEE: *myo-*.

musculoaponeurotic (mŭs-kū-lō-ăp″ō-nū-rŏt′ĭk) Composed of muscle and an aponeurosis of fibrous connective tissue.

musculocutaneous (mŭs″kū-lō-kū-tān′ē-ŭs) [″ + *cutis*, skin] **1.** Pert. to the muscles and skin. **2.** Supplying or affecting the muscles and skin. **3.** The specific nerve from the brachial plexus that innervates the coracobrachialis, biceps brachii, and brachialis muscles and provides cutaneous sensory distribution to the forearm.

musculofascial (mŭs″kū-lō-făsh′ē-ăl) Composed of muscle and fascia.

musculomembranous (mŭs″kū-lō-mĕm′brăn-ŭs) Pert. to or consisting of muscle and membrane.

musculophrenic (mŭs″kū-lō-frĕn′ĭk) Pert. to muscles of the diaphragm.

musculoskeletal (mŭs″kū-lō-skĕl′ĕ-tăl) Pert. to the muscles and skeleton.

musculospiral (mŭs″kū-lō-spī′răl) [″ +

spira, coil] Concerning the musculospiral (radial) nerve.

musculotendinous (mŭs″kū-lō-těn-dĭ-nī′tĭs) Composed of both muscle and tendon.

musculus (mŭs′kū-lŭs) [L.] Muscle.

mushroom [Fr. *mousseron*] Umbrella-shaped fungus belonging to the class Basidiomycetes. Mushrooms grow on decaying vegetable matter and are generally found in woods and dark, damp places. Some of the poisonous varieties include *Amanita* species and toadstools. SEE: *amanita; toadstool.*

COMPOSITION: Mushrooms are low in carbohydrates and fats, and high in protein. Their relationship and similarity to poisonous fungi are so close that only those who are thoroughly capable of distinguishing the poisonous varieties from the edible ones should attempt to gather and eat them.

musicians, medical problems of Profession-related injuries, most commonly overuse injuries involving muscle-tendon units. The pain associated with this type of injury may be mild or severe enough to prevent use of the affected part. Those who play string instruments have more difficulty than those who use percussion instruments; women are more commonly affected than men. Focal dystonias may involve the hands or the muscles of the face and lips, and may be severe. Stress and anxiety may interfere with or prevent performing.

TREATMENT: Treatment consists of rest for physical difficulties and beta-adrenergic blocking agents for stress and anxiety.

musicogenic (mū″zĭ-kō-jĕn′ĭk) [L. *musica,* music, + *gennan,* to produce] Caused by music, esp. epileptic convulsions.

musicogenic epilepsy SEE: under *epilepsy.*

music therapy [″ + *therapeia,* treatment] Treatment of disease, esp. mental illness, with music.

musk (mŭsk) [Sanskrit *muska,* testicle] An oily secretion obtained from a gland beneath the abdominal skin of male mammals. It has a strong odor and plays a part in animal communication. It is commercially used in manufacturing perfume.

mussel A bivalve mollusk belonging to the class Pelecypoda.

must A mandatory educational requirement that has to be completed in order to finish a course of study or attain health care certification.

mustard (mŭs′tărd) [Fr. *moustarde*] Yellow powder of mustard seed used as a counterirritant, rubefacient, emetic, stimulant, and condiment. SEE: *plaster.*

    nitrogen m. **1.** Any of the alkylating drugs used to treat several solid and hematological malignancies such as Hodgkin's disease, multiple myeloma, and some leukemias. Nitrogen mustards include mechlorethamine, cyclophosphamide, uracil mustard, melphalan, and chlorambucil. **2.** Any of the gases used in chemical warfare (e.g., mustard gas, vesicant gas).

mustard gas SEE: under *gas.*

Mustard procedure (mŭs′tărd) [William Thornton Mustard, Canadian cardiac surgeon, 1914–1987] A surgical procedure to repair transposition of the great vessels, in which a baffle is placed to shunt blood between the right and left atria, allowing more oxygenated blood to be circulated systemically.

mutagen (mū′tă-jĕn) [L. *mutare,* to change, + Gr. *gennan,* to produce] Any agent that causes genetic mutations. Many medicines, chemicals, and physical agents such as ionizing radiation and ultraviolet light have this ability. SEE: *teratogen.* **mutagenic,** *adj.*

mutagenesis (mū″tă-jĕn′ĕ-sĭs) The induction of genetic mutation. SEE: *mutation; teratogenesis.*

mutant (mū′tănt) [L. *mutare,* to change] SEE: under *gene.*

mutase (mū′tās) [″ + *ase,* enzyme] **1.** Enzyme that accelerates oxidation-reduction reactions through activation of oxygen and hydrogen. **2.** A food preparation made from leguminous plants high in protein content.

mutation (mū-tā′shŏn) [L. *mutatio,* a change] **1.** Change; transformation; instance of such change. **2.** A permanent variation in genetic structure with offspring differing from parents in a characteristic. It is differentiated by gradual variation through many generations. **3.** A change in a gene potentially capable of being transmitted to offspring.

    conservative m. A change in DNA or RNA that results in the replacement of an amino acid with one that has a similar structure, e.g., glycine replaced by alanine.

    escape m. The ability of a microorganism to defend itself from host immune responses by making mutations in its genotype and phenotype. Organisms with a high rate of mutations, e.g., human immunodeficiency virus, rely on mutational escape as one mechanism to avoid destruction by host cells. SYN: *mutational escape.*

    factor V Leiden m. An autosomal dominant mutation in coagulation factor V that is found in about 5% of all whites. It produces a hypercoagulable state as a result of inherited resistance to activated protein C. Clinically, it is found in many patients with deep venous thrombosis.

    founder m. An altered gene that proliferates in a kinship or community from a single identifiable ancestor.

frameshift m. The deletion or insertion of one or two DNA nucleotides that alters the transcription of each subsequent triplet.

gain-of-function m. A change in DNA that results in the synthesis of a protein with a new or different function. Gain-of-function mutations are typically dominant.

germline m. A mutation in the genetic content of a sperm or egg.

inactivating m. Loss-of-function **m.**

induced m. Mutation resulting from exposure to x-rays, radioactive substances, and certain drugs and chemicals.

JAK2 m. A mutation found on chromosome 9 in myeloproliferative disorders such as polycythemia vera.

loss-of-function m. A change in DNA that results in the decreased production of a protein or a protein with impaired function. Loss-of-function mutations are usually recessive. SYN: *inactivating* **m.**

missense m. A substitution of a single DNA nucleotide for another. This results in the transcription of a different amino acid than is normally found in the protein coded by the gene. Missense mutations are found in diseases such as sickle cell anemia. Red blood cell sickling is caused by the replacement of the amino acid glutamic acid by valine in the sixth position of the beta hemoglobin chain.

natural m. Mutation occurring without artificial external intervention. Natural mutation is thought to be a primary factor in evolutionary change.

nonconservative m. A change in DNA that results in the replacement of an amino acid with one that is not biochemically similar, e.g., serine replaced by proline.

nonsense m. A change in a single DNA nucleotide that creates a stop codon (TGA, TAA, TAG) that results in the premature termination of protein synthesis.

null m. **1.** A change in DNA or RNA that does not result in any change in the protein product or content of a cell. **2.** A change in a nucleotide that results in the complete failure of protein synthesis by a cell.

point m. A change in only one nucleotide in the DNA sequence of a gene. Frame-shift, conservative, nonconservative, missense, nonsense, and silent mutations are examples of point mutations.

regulatory m. A change in DNA or RNA that alters the expression of other genes by a cell.

silent m. A change in a single nucleotide that does not change the amino acid sequence of a protein (e.g., in DNA, the codons AAA and AAG both designate the amino acid phenylalanine).

somatic m. Mutation occurring in somatic cells.

mutational escape Escape mutation.

mute (mūt) [L. *mutus,* dumb] **1.** Lacking the ability to speak. **2.** One who is unable to speak. **3.** Refraining from speech; silent.

deaf m. SEE: *deaf-mute.*

mutein (mū″tē-ĭn, tēn″) [Fm. *mut(ation)* + *(pro)tein*] A protein produced by a genetically engineered mutation.

mutilate [L. *mutilatus,* to maim] To deprive of a limb or a part; to maim or disfigure.

mutilation (mū″tĭ-lā′shŭn) The removal, destruction, or injury of a conspicuous or essential body part or organ; maiming.

mutism (mū′tĭzm) [L. *mutus,* dumb] **1.** Inability or unwillingness to speak. **2.** Persistent inhibition of speech, seen in some severe forms of mental illness.

akinetic m. The condition of being immobile and silent while partially or fully awake. This may be caused by lesions of the frontal lobes of the brain or by hydrocephalus.

elective m. Selective **m.**

selective m. A form of social phobia, typically first identified in young children, in which the child fails to speak in certain public settings but has normal speech at other times. SYN: *elective* **m.**

mutual help group SEE: under *group.*

mutualism (mū′tū-ăl-ĭzm) [L. *mutuus,* exchanged] A form of symbiosis in which organisms of two different species live in close association to the mutual benefit of each.

mutualist (mū′tū-ăl-ĭst) Organism associated with another organism to the mutual benefit of each.

mv *millivolt.*

M-VAC Methotrexate, vinblastine, doxorubicin, and cisplatin, chemotherapeutic drugs used to treat cancers of the urinary tract.

MVU *Montevideo unit.*

MW *Molecular weight.*

MWIA *Medical Women's International Association.*

myalgia (mī-ăl′jē-ă) [″ + *algos,* pain] Tenderness or pain in the muscles; muscular rheumatism.

myasthenia (mī″ăs-thē′nē-ă) [*my-* + *-asthenia*] Muscular weakness and abnormal fatigue. **myasthenic** (-then′ik), *adj.*

m. gravis ABBR: MG. An autoimmune motor disorder marked by muscular fatigue that develops with repetitive muscle use and improves with rest or with the application of a cold pack. It is caused by antibodies to the acetylcholine receptor in the neuromuscular junction and a decrease in receptor sites for acetylcholine. Because the smallest concentration of acetylcholine receptors in the body is in the cranial nerves, weakness and fatigue of the eye muscles, muscles of mastication, and pharyngeal muscles are the most prominently affected in most patients, but any (skeletal) muscle group may be involved. The disease is rare, affecting about 14 people out of 100,000. SEE: *Nursing Diagnoses Appendix.*

DIAGNOSIS: Diagnosis is made on the basis of patient history, a thorough neurological examination, electromyography, repetitive nerve stimulation, a Tensilon test, or a combination of these tests. Intravenous injection of Tensilon significantly improves muscle weakness within 60 sec, lasting up to 30 min Acetylcholinesterase receptor antibody titers in the blood are elevated in about 50% to 70% of patients with myasthenia gravis.

SYMPTOMS: Clinical signs include ptosis of the eyelid and double vision due to fatigue and weakness in the extraocular muscles, and difficulty chewing and swallowing from impaired facial and pharyngeal muscles. Speech that becomes progressively more dysarthric during prolonged dialogue is another common symptom. Symptoms are exacerbated by repetitive muscle use, and, in some patients, by menses, emotional stress, prolonged exposure to sunlight or cold, and infections. Myasthenia gravis crisis is a sudden exacerbation of symptoms with respiratory failure.

TREATMENT: The primary treatment is with anticholinesterases and immunosuppressive agents. Anticholinesterase therapy often becomes less effective as the disease worsens. In selected patients, removal of the thymus, plasmapheresis, or immunoglobulin therapy is used.

PATIENT CARE: The patient with MG should seek medical attention immediately if he or she experiences difficulty breathing, talking, chewing, or swallowing. These symptoms may herald a myasthenic crisis. In crisis the patient's cardiovascular, neurologic, and respiratory status should be monitored in an intensive care unit. Suctioning the airway and postural changes may sometimes maintain adequate oxygenation and ventilation. If not, the patient will need intubation and positive-pressure ventilation. Exercise, meals, and care activities should be planned around medication-induced energy peaks. The patient should be taught that soft but solid foods are more easily managed than liquids when swallowing is difficult. Additional help for patients is available through support groups and Internet-based resources such as the Myasthenia Gravis Foundation of America (www.myasthenia.org).

⚠️ Because edrophonium (Tensilon) occasionally causes significant bradycardia or asystole, atropine should be kept at the bedside of any patient given this medication.

myatonia (mī-ă-tō′nē-ă) Deficiency or loss of muscular tone.

mycelioid (mī-sē′lē-oyd) [″ + *helos,* nail, + *eidos,* form, shape] Moldlike; resembling mold colonies in which filaments radiate from a center, said of bacterial colonies.

mycelium (mī-sē′lē-ŭm) [Gr. *mykes,* fungus, + *helos,* nail] The mass of filaments (hyphae) that constitutes the vegetative body of fungi such as molds.

mycetes (mī-sē′tēz) The fungi.

myceto-, mycet- [Gr. *mykēs,* stem *mykēt-,* fungus, mushroom] Prefixes meaning *fungus.* SEE: *myco-.*

mycetoma (mī-sĕ-tō′mă, ′mă-tă) pl. **mycetomas, mycetomata** [*mycet-* + -*oma*] A syndrome caused by a variety of aerobic actinomycetes and fungi. It is characterized by swelling and suppuration of subcutaneous tissues and formation of sinus tracts, with granules present in the pus draining from the tracts. These tracts usually appear on the foot or leg. SEE: *actinomycetoma; eumycetoma.*

TREATMENT: Sulfones, trimethoprim and sulfamethoxazole, or sulfonamides may benefit lesions caused by actinomycetes. If lesions are due to fungi, there is no specific therapy.

white-grain m. Madura foot. **mycetomatous** (′mă-tŭs), *adj.*

-mycin [*myco-* + -*in*] A suffix used in pharmacology to designate any antibiotic derived from species of *Streptomyces.*

myco-, myc- [Gr. *mykēs,* stem *mykēt-,* fungus, mushroom] Prefixes meaning *fungus.* SEE: *myceto-.*

mycobacteriosis (mī″kō-băk-tē″rē-ō′sĭs) An infection caused by any mycobacterium.

Mycobacterium (mī″kō-bak-tir′ē-ŭm) [*myco-* + *bacterium*] A genus of acid-fast, nonmotile, non–spore-forming bacilli of the family Mycobacteriaceae, which includes the causative agents of tuberculosis and leprosy. The organisms are slender, nonmotile, gram-positive rods and do not produce spores or capsules.

Species include *M. africanum, M. avium intracellulare, M. bovis, M. chelonei, M. fortuitum, M. gastri, M. gordonae, M. kansasii, M. marinum, M. scrofulaceum, M. terrae, M. triviale, M. smegmatis,* and *M. xenopi.*

M. bovis The causative species of tuberculosis in cows and, less commonly, in humans.

M. kansasii A causative species of tuberculosis-like pulmonary disease in humans.

M. leprae The causative species of leprosy.

M. marinum An atypical mycobacterium that thrives in water and produces skin infection resembling sporotrichosis. It is the cause of swimming pool granuloma.

nontuberculous M. ABBR: NTM. Any mycobacterium that does not cause tuberculosis. There are four main classes. Three of these groups grow more slowly than *M. tuberculosis* and one group grows more rapidly. These organisms may cause various skin, lung, or other conditions or they may be harmless.

M. tuberculosis The causative agent of tuberculosis in humans. SEE: *tuberculosis*.

M. ulcerans A causative agent of infections of the skin and the underlying soft tissues. It is a common cause of illness in tropical and subtropical Africa and South America, where it is responsible for Buruli ulcer. It is thought to be the third most common disease-causing mycobacterium (after *M. tuberculosis* and *M. leprae*) in humans.

mycoderma (mī″kō-děr′mă) [Gr. *mykos*, mucus, + *derma*, skin] Mucous membrane.

mycology (mī-kŏl′ō-jē) [″ + *logos*, word, reason] The science and study of fungi.

mycophenolate (mī-kō-fě′nō-lāt) An immunosuppressive drug used to prevent organ rejection after transplantation.

Mycoplasma (mī″kō-plăz′mă) A group of bacteria that lack cell walls and are highly pleomorphic. There are more than 70 organisms in this group, including 12 species that infect humans. Tetracyclines or erythromycins are effective for treatment of *M. pneumoniae* and *M. hominis* infections. Other treatment choices include some cephalosporins or fluoroquinolones.

M. genitalium A species of *Mycoplasma* that is the smallest free-living organism known. It, like *M. hominis,* can cause nongonococcal urethritis.

M. hominis A species of *Mycoplasma* that can cause genital tract infections (nongonococcal urethritis).

M. pneumoniae A species of *Mycoplasma* that can cause infections of the upper respiratory tract and the lungs (mycoplasma pneumonia).

mycoprotein (mī″kō-prō′tēn, -tē-ĭn) [″ + ″] A meat substitute made from fungi. It can be shaped, textured, and flavored, provides protein and fiber, and is low in saturated fats.

mycose (mī′kōs) Trehalose.

mycosis (mī-kō′sĭs) [″ + *osis*, condition] Any disease induced by a fungus, or resembling a fungal disease.

m. fungoides ABBR: MF. Cutaneous T-cell lymphoma, esp. when the disease is first clinically apparent on the skin. The skin is marked by irregularly shaped macules, plaques, or nodules, which usually first appear on the trunk and may sometimes cause considerable itching. The rash may be difficult to diagnose or may be misdiagnosed as another form of dermatitis. Biopsy specimens may reveal atypical-appearing lymphocytes in the epidermis or collections of malignant lymphocytes in clusters called Pautrier's microabscesses. Eventually (e.g., 10 or more years after diagnosis), the malignant cells disseminate throughout the skin and into lymph nodes and internal organs.

TREATMENT: Topical nitrogen mustard, phototherapy with psoralens and ultraviolet light, systemic chemotherapy, interferons, extracorporeal phototherapy, and electron beam radiation of the skin have all been used. The disease may be curable when treated in its very earliest stage.

NOTE: The name "mycosis fungoides" is deceptive, as the disease is not fungal in origin.

superficial m. Any of a group of fungus infections of the skin. Included in this group are erythrasma, tinea barbae, tinea capitis, tinea corporis, tinea cruris, tinea favosa, tinea pedis, tinea unguium, and trichomycosis axillaris.

systemic m. Any of a group of deep fungus infections involving various bodily systems or regions. Included in this group are aspergillosis, blastomycosis, chromoblastomycosis, coccidioidomycosis, cryptococcosis, geotrichosis, histoplasmosis, maduromycosis, moniliasis, mucormycosis, nocardiosis, penicilliosis, rhinosporidiosis, and sporotrichosis.

mycostasis (mī-kŏs′tă-sĭs) [Gr. *mykes*, fungus, + *stasis,* standing] Stopping the growth of fungi.

mycotic (mī-kŏt′ĭk) Caused by or infected with fungus; concerning mycosis. The term is also used improperly to signify a bacterial infection, esp. one that has metastasized from one part of the body (e.g., a heart valve) to another (e.g., the wall of a blood vessel).

mycotoxicosis (mī″kō-tŏk″sĭ-kō′sĭs) [″ + *toxikon*, poisoning, + *osis,* condition] Disease either caused by toxins on molds or produced by molds.

mycotoxins (mī′kō-tŏk″sĭnz) Substances produced by mold growing in food or animal feed and causing illness or death when ingested by humans or animals. SEE: *ergotism*.

mydriasis (mĭ-drī′ă-sĭs) [L., Gr. *mydriasis,* of uncertain origin] Dilation of the pupil.

ETIOLOGY: Causes include fright and other causes of sympathetic nervous system activation, first and third stages of anesthesia, drugs, coma, botulism, and irritation of the cervical sympathetic nerve.

mydriatic (mĭd-rē-ăt′ĭk) **1.** Causing pupillary dilatation. **2.** A drug that dilates the pupil, such as atropine, cocaine, ephedrine, euphthalmine, and homatropine. In certain eye diseases, it is essential that the pupil be dilated during the course of treatment to prevent adhesions of the pupils.

myectomy (mī-ĕk′tō-mē) [Gr. *mys*, muscle, + *ektome*, excision] Excision of a portion of a muscle.

myelencephalon (mī″ĕl-ĕn-sĕf′ă-lŏn) [Gr. *myelos*, marrow, + *enkephalos*, brain] The most posterior portion of the embryonic hindbrain (rhombencephalon), which gives rise to the medulla oblongata.

myelic (mī-ĕl′ĭk) Pert. to the spinal cord.

myelin (mī′ĕ-lĭn) The phospholipid-protein of the cell membranes of Schwann cells (peripheral nervous system) and oligodendrocytes (central nervous system) that forms the myelin sheath of neurons. It acts as an electrical insulator and increases the velocity of impulse transmission. Another difference between central and peripheral myelin sheaths is that a single oligodendroglial cell can put out many tongues of cell membrane and form separate myelin sheaths for many different axons, whereas each Schwann cell ensheaths only one axon. SEE: *neuron* for illus.
myelinic (mī-ĕl-ĭn′ĭk), *adj.*

myelination (mī′ĕl-ĭn-ā′shŭn) [Gr. *myelos*, marrow] Process of growth of a myelin sheath around nerve fibers. SYN: *myelinization.*

myelinization (mī′ĕl-ĭn-ĭ-zā′shŭn) Myelination.

myelinolysis (mī′ĕ-lĭ--nol′ĭ-sĭs) [*myelin* + *-lysisn*] Destruction of the myelin sheaths of nerves.
   central pontine m. Osmotic demyelination syndrome.

myelinopathy (mī″e-lĭ-nŏp′ă-thē) Degeneration of the myelin sheaths of neurons, esp. in the central nervous system. SEE: *multiple sclerosis.*

myelinosis (mī′ĕl-ĭn-ō′sĭs) [″ + *osis*, condition] Fatty degeneration during which myelin is produced.

myelitis (mī-ĕ-lī′tĭs) [″ + *itis*, inflammation] **1.** Inflammation of the spinal cord, resulting from either an infection (e.g., a viral or bacterial infection) or a noninfectious necrosing or demyelinating lesion of the cord. Patients often exhibit flaccid limb paralysis, incontinence, weakness or numbness of the limbs, and other symptoms. SEE: *poliomyelitis.* **2.** Inflammation of bone marrow. SEE: *osteomyelitis.* **myelitic** (mī-ĕl-ĭt′ĭk), *adj.*
   acute m. Myelitis that develops rap-

idly, that is, in hours or days. Myelitis of rapid onset is more likely to be reversible than chronic or slowly developing inflammation of the spinal cord.
   acute ascending m. Myelitis that moves progressively upward in the spinal cord.
   acute transverse m. An acute form of myelitis involving the entire thickness of the spinal cord, developing, for example, subsequent to injury to the spinal cord.
   compression m. Myelitis caused by pressure on the spinal cord, as by a hemorrhage or tumor.
   disseminated m. Inflammation of several separate areas of the spinal cord.
   transverse m. Myelitis involving the whole thickness of the spinal cord, but limited longitudinally.

myelo-, myel- [Gr. *myelos*, marrow] Prefixes meaning *spinal cord, bone marrow.*

myeloablation (mī″ĕ-lō-a-blā′shŏn) [*myelo-* + *ablation*] Suppression of the ability of bone marrow to produce blood cells, e.g., by chemotherapy or radiation therapy.

myeloblast (mī′ĕl-ō-blăst) [″ + *blastos*, germ] Immature bone marrow cell that develops into a myelocyte. It matures to develop into a promyelocyte, and eventually into a granular leukocyte.

myeloblastosis (mī″ĕ-lō-blăs-tō′sĭs) [″ + ″ + *osis*, condition] Excess production of myeloblasts and their presence in circulating blood.

myelocele (mī′ĕ-lō-sēl) [″ + *kele*, tumor, swelling] A form of spina bifida with spinal cord protrusion.

myelocystocele (mī″ĕl-ō-sĭst′ō-sēl) [″ + ″ + *kele*, tumor, swelling] Protrusion of the spinal cord through a defect in the vertebral canal.

myelocyte (mī′ĕl-ō-sīt) [″ + *kytos*, cell] A large immature, granular blood cell from which leukocytes are derived.

myelocytic (mī″ĕl-ō-sĭt′ĭk) Characterized by presence of, or pert. to, myelocytes.

myelodysplasia (mī″ĕl-ō-dĭs-plā′zē-ă) [″ + *dys*, bad, + *plassein*, to form] ABBR: MDS. **1.** Any of a group of hematological diseases which primarily affect people over 60, in which there is inadequate bone marrow production of normal blood cells. These conditions begin when an abnormal clone of cells dominates the marrow; they may evolve into acute leukemia. Under the French-American-British classification there are five types of myelodysplasia:
   1. refractory anemia;
   2. refractory anemia with ringed sideroblasts;
   3. refractory anemia with excess blasts;

4. refractory anemia with excess blasts in transformation; and

5. chronic myelomonocytic leukemia.

The World Health Organization has proposed a different classification system:

1. refractory anemia (with or without ringed sideroblasts);

2. refractory anemia with multilineage dysplasia (with or without ringed sideroblasts);

3. refractory anemia with excess blasts;

4. the 5q-syndrome; and

5. unclassified myelodysplasia.

PATIENT CARE: Patients gradually become more and more anemic and often require frequent blood transfusions. Bone marrow transplantation, when a matching donor is available for young, otherwise healthy patients, can cure the disease. Several forms of chemotherapy based on thalidomide-like drugs may improve symptoms and outcomes. Drugs that stimulate the bone marrow to produce more cells (hematopoietic growth factors) alleviate symptoms caused by anemia and other cytopenias. **2.** Defective formation of the spinal cord.

myelodysplastic syndrome (mī″ĕ-lō-dĭs-plăs′tĭk) ABBR: MDS. Myelodysplasia.

myeloencephalitis (mī″ĕl-ō-ĕn-sĕf″ă-lī′tĭs) [″ + ″ + itis, inflammation] Inflammation of the spinal cord and the brain.

myelofibrosis (mī″ĕ-lō-fī-brō′sĭs, ′sēz″)pl. **myelofibroses** [myelo- + fibrosis] A myeloproliferative disorder marked by the overproduction of a single stem cell clone, reactive bone marrow fibrosis, and enlargement of the spleen.

myelogenesis (mī″ĕl-ō-jĕn′ĕ-sĭs) [″ + genesis, generation, birth] **1.** Development of the brain and the spinal cord. **2.** Development of the myelin sheath of nerve fiber.

myelogenic, myelogenous (mī-ĕ-lō-jĕn′ĭk, -lŏj′ĕn-ŭs) [″ + gennan, to produce] Producing or originating in marrow.

myelogram (mī′ĕ-lō-grăm) [″ + gramma, something written] **1.** A radiograph of the spinal cord and associated nerves. **2.** A differential count of bone marrow cells.

myelography (mī-ĕ-lŏg′ră-fē) [″ + graphein, to write] Radiography of the spinal cord and associated nerves after intrathecal injection of a radiopaque, water-soluble contrast medium. This technique has limited use, owing to computed tomography and magnetic resonance imaging.

air m. Myelography using a radiolucent contrast medium, usually air or oxygen.

myeloid (mī′ĕ-loyd) [″ + eidos, form, shape] **1.** Pert. to or produced in the bone marrow. **2.** Resembling cells produced in the bone marrow. **3.** Pert. to the spinal cord.

myelokathexis (mī″ĕ-lō-kă-thek′sĭs) [myelo- + cathexis] A congenital form of neutropenia in which mature granulocytic white blood cells are not released from the bone marrow to circulate in the bloodstream. It is often inherited as an autosomal dominant condition associated with warts, low levels of gamma globulins, and recurrent infections (WHIM syndrome).

myeloma (mī-ĕ-lō′mă) [″ + oma, tumor] A tumor originating in cells of the hematopoietic portion of bone marrow.

multiple m. A malignant disease characterized by infiltration of the bone marrow by cancerous plasma cells. These cells produce excessive levels of monoclonal immunoglobulins, antibodies that are normally made by plasma cells to recognize foreign antigens and fight infection. In myeloma, inadequate production of normal antibodies makes patients susceptible to infection. Tumors composed of malignant plasma cells also grow within the skeleton, making bones fragile and prone to fracture.

DIAGNOSIS: Characteristics include: 10% or more plasma cells in the bone marrow; monoclonal or "M" protein (produced by the myeloma cells) in serum and/or urine; at least one of four organ dysfunctions indicated by elevated serum calcium or creatinine levels, lytic bone lesions, or osteoporosis.

SYMPTOMS: The disease accounts for about 1% of all cancers. The cause is unknown. The median age at diagnosis is 62, and only 30% of patients survive 5 years or more. Patients typically report fatigue, weakness, shortness of breath and dyspnea on exertion (resulting from anemia (present in about 75% of patients at diagnosis), due to plasma cells inhibiting hemoglobin production in the bone marrow. They also may have bone pain, fevers, hypercalcemia, and infections with bacteria such as Streptococcus pneumoniae.

TREATMENT: Chemotherapies include melphalan and prednisone. Drugs that modulate the immune system and improve outcome include thalidomide and arsenic derivatives. Patient care focuses on helping the patient manage signs and symptoms, forestalling infection, preserving adequate levels of hemoglobin, relieving pain, preserving or restoring neurologic function, maintaining spinal stability, and controlling tumor growth. Acetaminophen, opioids or opiates, antiseizure medications, or tricyclic antidepressants may be prescribed for pain. Radiation therapy may be applied to affected bones. Chemotherapy alleviates or prevents hypercalcemia and tumor metastasis. Early recognition and immediate, vigorous treatment are needed for infection. Prophylactic antibacterial, antiviral, and antifungal drugs may be prescribed. Pneumococcal vaccine and annual influenza immunization are standard therapies. Plasmapheresis can decrease serum viscosity in an emergency. Exercise and occupational therapy can be helpful in retaining or restoring function.

nonsecretory m. Multiple myeloma is which there is infiltration of the bone marrow by abnormal plasma cells, hypercalcemia, anemia, renal failure, or pathological bone fractures, but in which a monoclonal protein cannot be detected in either the urine or the blood.

myelomalacia (mī″ĕ-lō-mă-lā′shē-ă) [Gr. *myelos,* marrow, + *malakia,* softening] Abnormal softening of the spinal cord.

myelomeningocele (mī″ĕ-lō-me-ning′ō-sēl″, -mĕ-nin′jō-) [*myelo-* + *meningo-* + *-cele*] A hernia of the spinal cord and meninges through the posterior vertebral column that results from failure of the neural tube to close during embryonic development (about 28 days after conception). The defect usually is found in the lumbosacral spine and often results in significant impairment in urination, defecation, and walking (spastic or flaccid paralysis).

PREVENTION: Folic acid supplementation is recommended for all women of childbearing age because maternal dietary folate deficiency is a known risk factor. It reduces but does not eliminate the risk of severe neural tube defects (NTDs) like myelomeningocele.

PATIENT CARE: When an NTD has been diagnosed by amniocentesis, the parents should be referred for genetic counseling, information, and support regarding decisions to terminate or continue the pregnancy. Myelomeningoceles are common, occurring in about 1 in 2000 live births. After birth, the defect is cleansed gently, and foam or sheepskin support provided to prevent pressure, skin breakdown, and infection. Parental bonding is encouraged: the infant needs cuddling and loving, and should be held facedown held on the parent's lap. Fluid balance is monitored and adequate nutrition provided. Passive range of motion exercises help minimize contractures. Surgical repair of the defect is followed by careful monitoring for hydrocephalus, infection, shock, and increased intracranial pressure (bulging fontanels are the most common indicator in infants). The wound is inspected and redressed according to protocol. Leg casts may be needed to treat hip and knee deformities. Close assessment of the child's growth and development, and ongoing physical and occupational

therapy will be needed throughout the child's life, along with psychological support for the child and parents who may feel guilt, anger, or helplessness. Mental stimulation helps to ensure maximum development. Bladder and bowel training are taught, with management dependent on the severity of the deficit. Social services may be able to assist parents with financial needs. Counseling and careful follow-up are needed to optimize outcomes and the adaptation of the child and parents to the illness. Parents may acquire additional support and information from the Spina Bifida Association of America (800-621-3141; www.sbaa.org). SYN: *meningomyelocele.*

myelopathy (mī″ĕ-lop′ă-thē) [*myelo-* + *-pathy*] Any disease or condition affecting the spinal cord.

focal m. Myelopathy of small areas.

HTLV-1–associated m. Tropical spastic paraparesis.

transverse m. Myelopathy extending across the spinal cord.

traumatic m. Myelopathy due to trauma to the spinal cord.

myeloperoxidase (mī-ĕl″ō-pĕr-ŏks′ĭ-dās″) [″ + peroxidase] ABBR: MPO. An enzyme found principally in neutrophils and monocytes that generates hypochlorous acid from hydrogen peroxide and chloride ions. The enzyme is released into plasma in infectious and inflammatory diseases. Measurement of plasma levels of MPO has been used in some risk assessments for patients with acute coronary syndrome.

myelophthisis (mī-ĕ-lŏf′thĭ-sĭs) [″ + *phthisis,* a wasting] 1. Atrophy of the spinal cord. 2. Replacement of the bone marrow by a disease process such as a neoplasm.

myelopoiesis (mī″ĕl-ō-poy-ē′sĭs) [″ + *poiein,* to form] Development of bone marrow or formation of cells derived from bone marrow.

extramedullary m. Development of myeloid elements (erythrocytes and granular leukocytes) in regions other than bone marrow. SYN: *ectopic myelopoiesis.*

myeloproliferative (mī″ĕ-lō-prō-lĭf″ĕr-ā′tĭv) Concerning abnormal proliferation of hematological stem cells.

myeloproliferative disorder Any of several hematologic malignancies marked by the excessive multiplication of one or more types of blood cells. These disorders include polycythemia rubra vera, essential thrombocytosis, chronic myeloid leukemia, and idiopathic myelofibrosis.

myeloradiculitis (mī″ĕ-lō-ră-dĭk″ū-lī′tĭs) [″ + L. *radiculus,* rootlet, + Gr. *itis,* inflammation] Inflammation of the spinal cord and the dorsal roots of spinal nerves.

myeloradiculopathy (mī″ĕ-lō-ră-dĭk″ū-lŏp′ă-thē) [″ + ″ + Gr. *pathos*, disease, suffering] Disease of the spinal cord and spinal nerves.

myelorrhaphy (mī-ĕl-or′ă-fē) [″ + *rhaphe*, seam, ridge] Suture of a cut or wound of the spinal cord.

myelosarcoma (mī″ĕl-ō-săr-kō′mă) [″ + *sarx*, flesh, + *oma*, tumor] Sarcoma composed of bone marrow cells and tissue. SYN: *osteosarcoma*.

myeloschisis (mī″ĕ-lŏs′kĭ-sĭs) [″ + *schisis*, a splitting] Cleft spinal cord resulting from failure of the neural tube to close. SEE: *rachischisis; spina bifida cystica*.

myelosclerosis (mī″ĕ-lō-sklĕr-ō′sĭs) [″ + *sklerosis*, hardening] Sclerosis of the spinal cord.

myelosis (mī-ĕ-lō′sĭs) [″ + *osis*, condition] Formation of a myeloma or medullary tumor.

    erythremic m. A malignancy involving the erythropoietic tissue. Symptoms and signs include anemia, fever, hepatosplenomegaly, bleeding tendency, and abnormal cells in the circulating blood. Also known as Di Guglielmo syndrome.

myelosuppression (mī″ĕ-lō-sŭ-prĕsh′ŏn) [*myelos- + suppression*] Inhibition of bone marrow function (i.e., of the production of cells or chemicals normally produced by the marrow).

myelotomy (mī-ĕl-ŏt′ō-mē) Surgical severance of nerve fibers of the spinal cord.

myenteric reflex (mī″ĕn-ter′ik) SEE: under *reflex*.

myiasis, myasis (mī-ī′ă-sĭs, -sēz″) *pl.* **myiases** [Gr. *myia*, fly + *-sis*] Infestation by the larvae (maggots) of flies. It may be caused by cutaneous, intestinal, or atrial (within a cavity such as mouth, nose, eye, sinus, vagina, urethra).

Mylabris (mī-lăb′rĭs) The scientific name for a genus of blister beetle, several species of which (*Mylabris phalerata* and *M. cichorii*) have been used in traditional Chinese medicine as a vesicant and antitumor agent. Skin exposure to the crushed body of the beetle results in contact dermatitis. The blistering agent in the beetle, cantharides, is also known as Spanish fly.

mylohyoid (mī″lō-hī′oyd) [Gr. *myle*, mill, + *hyoid*, U-shaped] **1.** Pert. to the hyoid bone and the molar teeth. **2.** The paired muscles attached to the mandible that fuse in the midline and form the floor of the mouth.

myo-, my- [Gr. *mys*, muscle] Prefixes meaning *muscle*. SEE: *musculo-*.

myoblast (mī′ō-blăst) [″ + *blastos*, germ] An embryonic cell that develops into muscle cell.

myoblastoma (mī″ō-blăs-tō′mă) [″ + ″ + *oma*, tumor] A tumor consisting of cells resembling myoblasts.

myocardial, myocardiac (mī-ŏ-kar′dē-ăl, -ak″) [*myo-* + *cardiac* (2)] Pert. to the myocardium.

myocardial infarction SEE: under *infarction*.

myocardial insufficiency SEE: under *insufficiency*.

myocardial ischemia SEE: under *ischemia*.

myocardiograph (mī″ō-kăr′dē-ō-grăf) [″ + ″ + *graphein*, to write] Instrument for recording heart movements.

myocardiopathy (mī″ō-kăr″dē-ŏp′ă-thē) [″ + ″ + *pathos*, disease, suffering] Any disease of the myocardium.

myocarditis (mī″ō-kar-dīt′ĭs) [*myo-* + *carditis*] Inflammation of the heart muscle, usually in the U.S. as a consequence of *infections* (viruses, esp. coxsackie virus, and occasionally as a consequence of bacterial, protozoan or fungal infections); *immunological-rheumatological conditions* (e.g., systemic lupus erythematosus, ulcerative colitis, hypersensitivity reactions, or transplant rejection); exposure to chemicals or *toxins* (e.g., cocaine, doxorubicin, methamphetamine); *nutritional or metabolic abnormalities* (e.g., thiamine deficiency or hypophosphatemia); or *radiation*. Myocarditis also is occasionally found in pregnancy and with advanced age. The myocardium is infiltrated by leukocytyes, lymphocytes, and macrophages, leading to inflammation, necrosis of muscle cells, and fibrosis. Inflammatory damage to heart muscle fibers may resolve spontaneously or may cause progressive deterioration of the heart with pericarditis, arrhythmias, chronic dilated cardiomyopathy, and heart failure. SEE: *cardiomyopathy*.

    SYMPTOMS: Patients may be entirely asymptomatic or may seek medical attention because of vague symptoms consistent with a viral infection, or because of sudden onset of palpitations, pleuritic chest pain, shortness of breath, cough, edema, heart failure, or arrhythmias. When chest pain is reported, it may be described as sharp, stabbing precordial pain or as substernal squeezing pain (like that of myocardial infarction). In children, symptoms tend to be very nonspecific, but can include poor feeding, respiratory distress, and cyanosis. Often the initial infection has resolved or subsided by the time the patient seeks medical advice and care.

    DIAGNOSIS: Diagnosis is based on history, physical examination, and occasionally on endomyocardial biopsy.

    TREATMENT: Any identifiable causes are corrected or treated. Symptomatic management also may include drugs such as angiotensin-converting enzyme (ACE) inhibitors or diuretics (for heart failure), beta-blocking agents, sodium restriction, supplemental oxygen, steroids and immunoglobulins, and anticoagulant therapy when needed.

PATIENT CARE: Hospitalization may be required so that patients can be monitored for arrhythmias and signs of heart failure (e.g., increasing dyspnea, edema, weight gain, fatigue). Diuretics and ACE inhibitors or angiotensin receptor blockers are used to reduce fluid retention and afterload on the heart. Beta blockers like carvedilol may improve survival. Bed rest is maintained to decrease the work of the heart and to minimize myocardial damage. Elastic or pneumatic stockings and passive and resistive exercises are used to decrease the risk of venous stasis and thrombosis. Activity is increased gradually after the acute phase, and a progressive exercise program is developed for use after recovery. Patients are cautioned to stop exercising if shortness of breath occurs. The patient is taught prescribed drug and dietary regimens and to recognize and report signs of heart failure. In patients with refractory heart failure, options for management include a left-ventricular assist device or a heart transplant.

myocardium (mī-ō-kăr′dē-ŭm) [″ + *kardia*, heart] The middle layer of the walls of the heart, composed of cardiac muscle. The layers of cardiac muscle form a complex spiral. When they contract they twist or wring blood from the ventricles. The muscle layers are attached to an internal "skeleton" of the heart composed of dense connective tissue.

myocilin (mī″ō-sĭl′ĭn) A glycoprotein that influences or regulates intraocular pressure. Mutations in the myocilin gene are found in some people with glaucoma.

myoclonia (mī-ō-klō′nē-ă) Myoclonus.

myoclonus (mī″ok′lŏ-nŭs) [*myo-* + *clonus*] Twitching or clonic spasm of a muscle or group of muscles.

　　nocturnal m. Restless legs syndrome.

　　palatal m. Rapid, rhythmic clonus of one or both sides of the soft palate. It may cause a clicking sound in the throat or, occasionally, tinnitus.

myocyte (mī′ō-sīt) [″ + *kytos*, cell] A muscle tissue cell.

myodynamia (mī″ō-dī-năm′ē-ă) [″ + *dynamis*, force] Muscular force or strength.

myodystrophy (mī″ō-dĭs′trō-fē) [″ + ″ + *trophe*, nutrition] Muscular dystrophy. SEE: *spinal muscular atrophy.*

myoedema (mī″ō-ĕ-dē′mă) [″ + *oidema*, swelling] **1.** Mounding. **2.** Edema of a muscle.

myoelastic (mī″ō-ē-lăs′tĭk) Pert. to smooth muscle and elastic tissue.

myoelectric prosthesis SEE: under *prosthesis.*

myoepithelial cell (mī″ō-ep-ĭ-thē′lē-ăl) SEE: under *cell.*

myoepithelioma (mī″ō-ĕp″ĭ-thē″lē-ō′mă) [″ + *epi*, upon, + *thele*, nipple, + *oma*, tumor] A slow-growing tumor of the sweat gland.

myoepithelium (mī″ō-ĕp″ĭ-thē′lē-ŭm) [″ + ″ + *thele*, nipple] Modified smooth muscle cells found in some glands. **myoepithelial** (mī″ō-ĕp″ĭ-thē′lē-ăl), *adj.*

myofascial pain syndrome (mī″ă-făsh′ăl, shē-ăl) ABBR: MFP. A chronic musculoskeletal pain disorder characterized by the presence of trigger points; decreased range of motion in affected muscle groups; weakness; and, on occasion, local autonomic disturbances such as localized perspiration.

myofasciitis (mī″ō-făs″ē-i′tĭs) [″ + L. *fascia*, band, + Gr. *itis*, inflammation] Inflammation of a muscle and its fascia.

myofiber (mī″ō-fī′bĕr) A skeletal muscle cell.

myofibril, myofibrilla (mī-ō-fī′brĭl, -fī-brĭl′lă) [″ + L. *fibrilla*, a small fiber] A microscopic fibril found in muscle cells, grouped into bundles that run parallel to the long axis of the cell. It is made of sarcomeres placed end-to-end, which in turn are made of myofilaments of myosin and actin, the contractile proteins.

myofibroma (mī″ō-fī-brō′mă) [″ + L. *fibra*, fiber, + Gr. *oma*, tumor] Tumor containing muscular and fibrous tissue.

myofibrosis (mī″ō-fī-brō′sĭs) [″ + ″ + Gr. *osis*, condition] Increase of connective or fibrous tissue with degeneration of muscular tissue.

myofibrositis (mī″ō-fī″brō-sī′tĭs) [Gr. *mys*, muscle, + L. *fibra*, fiber, + Gr. *itis*, inflammation] Inflammation of the perimysium, the fibrous tissue that encloses muscle tissue.

myofilament (mī″ō-fīl′ă-mĕnt) A filament within the myofibrils of muscle cells. Thick ones are made primarily of myosin; thin ones are made primarily of actin, troponin, and tropomyosin.

myofunctional (mī″ō-fŭnk′shŭn-ăl) Concerning muscle function.

myogenesis (mī-ō-jĕn′ĕ-sĭs) [″ + *genesis*, generation, birth] Formation of muscular tissue, esp. in embryos.

myoglobin (mī″ō-glō′bĭn) The iron-containing protein found in muscle cells that stores oxygen for use in cell respiration.

myoglobinuria (mī″ō-glō″bĭn-ū′rē-ă) Myoglobin in the urine. It may occur following muscular activity, trauma, or as a result of a deficiency of muscle phosphorylase.

myoglobulin (mī″ō-glŏb′ū-lĭn) [″ + L. *globulus*, globule] A coagulable globulin present in muscular tissue.

myogram (mī′ō-grăm) [″ + *gramma*, something written] Tracing made by the myograph of muscular contractions.

myograph (mī'ō-grăf) [" + *graphein,* to write] Instrument for tracing movements caused by muscular contractions. **myographic** (mī-ō-grăf'ĭk), *adj.*

myography (mī-ŏg'ră-fē) **1.** Recording of muscular contractions by a myograph. **2.** Description of the muscles and their action.

myohemoglobin (mī"ō-hē"mō-glō'bĭn) Myoglobin.

myoid (mī'oyd) [Gr. *mys,* muscle, + *eidos,* form, shape] Resembling muscle.

myokinase (mī"ō-kĭn'ās) An enzyme present in muscle that catalyzes the synthesis of adenosine triphosphate.

myokymia (mī-ō-kim'ē-ă) [*myo-* + Gr. *kyma,* wave + *-ia*] Twitching of isolated segments of muscle. The condition may be functional, but it is also seen in organic diseases and general paresis. SYN: *kymatism.*

myolemma (mī"ō-lĕm'ă) [" + *lemma,* sheath] Sarcolemma.

myolipoma (mī"ō-lĭ-pō'mă) [" + *lipos,* fat, + *oma,* tumor] Muscle tissue tumor containing fatty elements.

myology (mī-ŏl'ō-jē) [" + *logos,* word, reason] The scientific study of the structure and function of muscles.

myolysis (mī-ŏl'ĭ-sĭs) [" + *lysis,* dissolution] Fatty degeneration and infiltration with destruction of muscular tissue accompanied by separation and disappearance of muscle cells.

myoma (mī-ō'mă, 'mă-tă) *pl.* **myomas-myomata** [*myo-* + *-oma*] A tumor containing muscle tissue. SEE: *chondromyoma; leiomyoma.* **myomatous** (-tŭs), *adj.*

  m. uteri Uterine **leiomyoma.**

myomalacia (mī"ō-mă-lā'sē-ă) [Gr. *mys,* muscle, + *malakia,* softening] Softening of muscular tissue.

myomatosis (mī"ō-mă-tō'sĭs) [" + *oma,* tumor, + *osis,* condition] The development of multiple myomas.

myomectomy (mī"ō-mĕk'tō-mē) [" + *oma,* tumor, + *ektome,* excision] **1.** Removal of a portion of muscle or muscular tissue. **2.** Removal of a myomatous tumor, generally uterine, usually by abdominal section, leaving the uterus in place.

myomere (mī'ō-mēr) [" + *meros,* part] Myotome (2).

myometer (mī-ŏm'ĕt-ĕr) [" + *metron,* measure] Device for measurement of muscular contractions.

myometrial (mī"ō-mē'trē-al) Concerning the myometrium.

myometritis (mī"ō-mē-trī'tĭs) [" + *metra,* uterus, + *itis,* inflammation] Inflammation of the muscular wall of the uterus. SYN: *mesometritis.*

myometrium (mī"ō-mē'trē-ŭm) [*myo-* + ¹*metro-* + *-ium*] The smooth muscle layer of the uterine wall, forming the main mass of the uterus. The myometrium contracts for labor and delivery.

myon (mī'ōn) [Gr. *mys,* muscle] A single muscle unit.

myonecrosis (mī"ō-nĕ-krō'sĭs) [" + *nekrosis,* state of death] Necrosis of muscle tissue.

myoneural (mī"ō-nŭr'ăl) Pert. to muscle and nerve, esp. nerve terminations in muscles.

myoneural junction SEE: under *junction.*

myopathic facies (mī"ō-păth'ĭk) SEE: under *facies.*

myopathy (mī-op'ă-thē) [*myo-* + *-pathy*] Any congenital or acquired muscle disease, marked clinically by focal or diffuse muscular weakness. **myopathic** (mī"ō-path'ik), *adj.*

  centronuclear m. Myopathy in which the muscle fibers resemble those seen in fetal development. The nuclei of the cells are surrounded by a clear zone. SYN: *myotubular m.*

  critical illness m. Intensive care **m.**

  distal m. Distal muscular dystrophy.

  myotubular m. Centronuclear myocerosis. SEE: *myocerosis.*

  nemaline m. Congenital nonprogressive weakness, esp. of the proximal muscles. The muscles are thin and resemble rods.

  ocular m. Hereditary dystrophy of the extraocular muscles. This may progress to complete paralysis of these muscles.

  thyrotoxic m. A progressive muscular weakness and atrophy as a result of hyperthyroidism.

myope (mī'ōp) [Gr. *myein,* to shut, + *ops,* eye] One afflicted with myopia (nearsightedness).

myopericarditis (mī"ō-pĕr-ĭ-kar-dī'tĭs) [Gr. *mys,* muscle, + *peri,* around, + *kardia,* heart, + *itis,* inflammation] Inflammation of the pericardium and cardiac muscular wall.

myopia (mī-ō'pē-ă) [Gr. *myein,* to shut, + *ops,* eye] An error in refraction in which light rays are focused in front of the retina, enabling the person to see distinctly for only a short distance. A negative (concave) lens of proper strength will correct this condition. SYN: *nearsightedness.* SEE: *emmetropia* for illus. **myopic** (mī-ŏp'ĭk), *adj.*

  axial m. Myopia due to elongation of the axis of the eye.

  index m. Myopia resulting from abnormal refractivity of the media of the eye.

  progressive m. Myopia that increases steadily during adult life.

  transient m. Myopia seen in spasm of accommodation, as in acute iritis or iridocyclitis.

myoplasm (mī'ō-plăzm) [Gr. *mys,* muscle, + LL. *plasma,* form, mold] The contractile part of the muscle cell, as differentiated from the sarcoplasm.

myoplastic (mī'ō-plăs'tĭk) [" + *plas-*

sein, to form] Pert. to the plastic use of muscle tissue or plastic surgery on muscles.

myoplasty (mī-ō-plăs″tē) Plastic surgery of muscle tissue.

myorhythmia (mī″ō-rĭth′mē-ŭ) [″ + ″] A coarse muscular tremor of the hands or feet.

myosarcoma (mī″ō-sar-kō′mă) [″ + *sarx,* flesh, + *oma,* tumor] A malignant tumor derived from myogenic cells.

myosin (mī′ō-sĭn) [*my-* + ²*-ose* + *-in*] A protein present in muscle fibrils and constituting about 45% of total muscle protein. It consists of long chains of polypeptides joined by side chains. Myosin and actin are the contractile proteins in muscle fibers. Myosin catalyzes the removal of the third phosphate from adenosine triphosphate (ATP), thereby releasing the energy needed for contraction. SEE: *sarcomere; actin.*

myositis (mī-ō-sī′tĭs) [″ + *itis,* inflammation] Inflammation of muscle tissue, esp. voluntary muscles caused, for example, by infection, trauma, autoimmunity, or infestation by parasites. SEE: *fibromyalgia.*

   interstitial m. Myositis with hyperplasia of connective tissue.

   m. ossificans Bone formation occurring at an abnormal anatomical site, usually in soft tissue, e.g. ossification of the intramuscular fascia after an injury.

   traumatic m. Myositis due to physical injury. The condition may be simple, with accompanying pain and swelling, or may be suppurative.

myospasm (mī′ō-spăzm) [″ + *spasmos,* a convulsion] Spasmodic contraction of a muscle.

myostatin (mī′ō-stăt′ĭn) A growth-regulating protein that limits the size of muscles by inhibiting excessive growth.

myotactic (mī″ō-tăk′tĭk) [″ + L. *tactus,* touch] Pert. to muscle or kinesthetic sense.

myotenositis (mī″ō-tĕn-ō-sī′tĭs) [″ + ″ + *itis,* inflammation] Inflammation of a muscle and its tendon.

myothermic (mī″ō-thĕrm′ĭk) [Gr. *mys,* muscle, + *therme,* heat] Pert. to rise in muscle temperature due to its activity.

myotome (mī′ō-tōm) [″ + *tome,* incision] **1.** Instrument used for cutting muscles. **2.** That portion of an embryonic somite that gives rise to somatic (striated) muscles. SYN: *myomere.*

myotomy (mī-ŏt′ō-mē) Surgical division or anatomical dissection of muscles.

myotonia (mī″ō-tō′nē-ă) [*myo-* + *tono-* + *-ia*] Tonic spasm of a muscle or temporary rigidity after muscular contraction. **myotonic** (-tŏn′ĭk), *adj.*

   m. atrophica Myotonia dystrophica.

   m. congenita A benign disease characterized by tonic spasms of the muscles

induced by voluntary movements. The condition is usually congenital and is transmitted by either dominant or recessive genes. SYN: *amyotonia congenita; myotonic atrophy; Oppenheim's disease; Thomsen's disease.*

   SYMPTOMS: The disease appears in early childhood and is manifested by a tonic spasm of the muscles every time the muscles are used. In a few minutes, rigidity wears away, and the movements become free from repeated contractions, the muscles becoming firm and extremely well developed.

   TREATMENT: Quinine or procainamide are indicated for relief of myotonia. Neostigmine is contraindicated. Avoidance of obesity is important.

   PROGNOSIS: The disease is incurable but may improve with age.

   m. dystrophica A dominantly inherited disease characterized by muscular wasting, myotonia, and cataract. SYN: *m. atrophica; Steinert's disease.*

myotonic (mī-ă-tŏn′ĭk) Pert. to tonic muscular spasm, as differentiated from myokinetic spasm.

myotropic (mī″ō-trŏp′ĭk) [″ + *trope,* a turn] Attracted to muscle tissue.

myotube (mī′ō-tūb) The developing stage of skeletal muscle. The central nucleus occupies most of the cell.

My Plate A compendium of resources designed to help individuals make good choices in selecting their diet. Website: www.ChooseMyPlate.gov

My Pyramid A compendium of dietary recommendations for Americans of all ages, body weights, and exercise levels. Website: www.mypyramid.gov

Myriapoda (mĭr-ē-ăp′ō-dă) [Gr. *myrios,* numberless, + *pous,* foot] Group of arthropods including millipedes and centipedes.

myringitis (mĭr-ĭn-jī′tĭs) [L. *myringa,* drum membrane, + Gr. *itis,* inflammation] Inflammation of the tympanic membrane (eardrum).

myringo-, myring- [L. *myringa, mininga, meninga,* membrane fr. Gr. *mēning-,* membrane] Prefixes meaning *tympanic membrane* or *eardrum.* SEE: *tympano-.*

myringoplasty (mĭr-ĭn′gō-plăst″ē) [″ + Gr. *plassein,* to form] Plastic surgery of the tympanic membrane.

myringotomy (mĭr-ĭn-gŏt′ō-mē) Incision of the tympanic membrane with placement of a tympanostomy tube. This procedure is most often performed on children with recurrent otitis media or medically refractory middle ear effusion. SEE: *Nursing Diagnoses Appendix.*

   PATIENT CARE: Because this procedure is most often performed on young children in response to a recurring condition, parents are taught to recognize the signs of otitis media and to seek medical assistance when their child complains of recurring ear pain, esp. if it is associated with evident loss of hearing. The parents are advised that tubes inserted after myringotomy gradually come out of the eardrum (usually falling out within 9 to 12 months), and that the child should not swim in the early period after surgery.

Postoperatively, the outer ear may be lightly packed with material selected by the surgeon. Parents are taught to change this packing when it is damp, using hand hygiene prior to and following handling of these materials. A common complication of the procedure is otorrhea. It is often prevented by instillation of topical medications including antibiotics and steroids. Parents are also taught to report headache, fever, severe pain, or disorientation, which may signal infection. Parents should not feed infants in a supine position or put them to bed with a bottle because reflux of nasopharyngeal flora into the middle ear can result. For patients old enough to understand, performing Valsalva's or Politzer's maneuver gently, several times each day, helps to promote Eustachian tube patency. Vigorous Valsalva maneuver may dislodge the tympanostomy tube.

Myristica fragrans (mi-ris'tĭ-kă) An evergreen tree whose fruit produces the spice nutmeg. The tissue surrounding this seed is used for a variety of culinary purposes and in folk medicine.

myrmecia (mŭr-mē'shē-ă) [Gr. *myrmex*, ant] A dome-shaped wart.

myrrh (mŭr) [L. *myrrha*, fr Gr. *myrra*, ult fr a Semitic language] A gum resin obtained from a number of species of plants of the genus *Commiphora*, used in antiquity to make incense and perfume. Its most important use today is as an aromatic, astringent mouthwash. Tincture of myrrh provides symptomatic relief when applied to canker sores. SEE: *Commiphora*.

myth (mĭth) [Gr. *mythos*, story] **1.** A narrative whose plot, characters, and themes are well known culturally or globally. It may have a variety of cultural meanings and may become an emblem of psychological, religious, or social truth. Alternatively, it may be used to summon inspiration or courage or provide a source of fear or wonder. **2.** A falsehood; an unscientific proposition, often one that is demonstrably untrue. SYN: *urban legend*.

myxadenoma (mĭks"ăd-ĕ-nō'mă) [" + " + *oma*, tumor] **1.** A tumor with the structure of a mucous gland. SYN: *myxoadenoma*. **2.** A tumor of glandular structure containing mucous elements.

myxedema (mik-sĕ-dē'mă) [*myx-* + *edema*] **1.** Infiltration of the skin by mucopolysaccharides, which give it a waxy or coarsened appearance and create nonpitting edema. Myxedematous skin is seen particularly in patients with hypothyroidism. **2.** The clinical and metabolic manifestations of hypothyroidism in adults, adolescents, and children. **myxedematous** (-dem'ăt-ūs, -dēm'), adj.

SYMPTOMS: The hypothyroid patient often complains of sluggishness, intolerance of cold, apathy, fatigue, and constipation. Findings may include infiltration of the subcutaneous layers of the skin by mucopolysaccharides. The hair may become dry and brittle. If the syndrome is left untreated, hypothermia, coma, and death may result.

TREATMENT: Thyroid hormone replacement reverses the symptoms and reestablishes normal metabolic function.

pretibial m. Edema of the anterior surface of the legs following hyperthyroidism and exophthalmos.

myxedema madness A colloquial term for a wide range of psychiatric manifestations accompanying profound hypothyroidism, including personality disorders, neurotic traits, and psychotic features.

myxo-, myx- [L. fr. Gr. *myxa*, snot, slime] Prefixes meaning *mucus*.

Myxobacterales (mĭks"ō-băk-tĕ-rā'lēz) The gliding bacteria, gram-negative and of various shapes; they are soil inhabitants and do not cause disease in humans. They form a slimy spreading colony.

myxoedema (mĭks"ĕ-dē'mă) [" + *oidema*, swelling] Myxedema.

myxofibroma (mĭks"ō-fī-brō'mă) [" + L. *fibra*, fiber, + Gr. *oma*, tumor] Tumor composed of mucous and fibrous elements.

myxofibrosarcoma (mĭk"sō-fī"brō-săr-kō'mă) [" + " + Gr. *sarx*, flesh, + *oma*, tumor] Fibrosarcoma that contains primitive mesenchymal tissue.

myxoid (mĭk'soyd) [" + *eidos*, form, shape] Similar to or resembling mucus.

myxolipoma (mĭk"sō-lĭ-pō'mă) [" + *lipos*, fat, + *oma*, tumor] Mucous tumor with fatty tissue elements. SYN: *lipomyxoma*.

myxoma (mĭk-sō'mă) *pl.* **myxomas or myxomata** [" + *oma*, tumor] Tumor composed of mucous connective tissue similar to that present in the embryo or umbilical cord. Cells are stellate or spindle-shaped and separated by mucoid tissue. The tumors are usually soft, gray, lobulated, and translucent and are not completely encapsulated. Myxomas may be pure or of mixed types involving other types of tissue.

cystic m. A tumor with parts fluid enough to resemble cysts.

myxomatosis (mĭk"sō-mă-tō'sĭs) [" + " + *osis,* condition] **1.** Formation of multiple myxomas. **2.** Myxomatous degeneration.

Myxomycetes (mĭk″sō-mī-sē′tēz) [Gr. *myxa*, mucus, + *mykes*, fungus] In one system of taxonomy, a class of fungi, the slime molds, which do not cause diseases in humans. This class is equivalent to the subkingdom Myxomycota in another system of taxonomy.

myxosarcoma (mĭk″sō-săr-kō′mă) [″ + *sarx*, flesh, + *oma*, tumor] Tumor containing myxomatous and sarcomatous components, having undergone partial degeneration. **myxosarcomatous** (mĭk″sō-săr-kō′mă-tŭs), *adj.*

myxospore (mĭks′ō-spor) [″ + *sporos*, seed] A spore that is embedded in a gelatinous mass. It is seen in some fungi and protozoa.

Myxosporidia (mĭks-ō-spor-ĭd′ē-ă) Parasitic sporozoans most commonly found in the epithelial cells of lower vertebrates.

myxovirus (mĭk″sō-vī′rŭs) Any of a family of viruses including those that cause influenza. Subgroups include paramyxovirus and orthomyxovirus. SEE: *paramyxovirus.*

Myzomyia (mī″zō-mī′ă) [Gr. *myzan*, to suck, + *myia*, fly] Subgenus of anopheline mosquitoes. Some species transmit malarial parasites.

N **1.** Symbol for the element nitrogen. **2.** *normal* (no longer in technical use). **3.** *neuraminidase*.

n **1.** Symbol for *index of refraction*. **2.** *nasal; number*. **3.** In statistics, *sample size*. **4.** In the TNM system of cancer staging, the number of lymph nodes that have been invaded by a cancer.

¹⁵N The symbol for the isotope of nitrogen with mass number 15; radioactive; atomic mass (weight) 15.

N, N-diethyl-3-methylbenzamide (ĕn′ĕn′ dī-ĕth′ĭl thrē′ mĕth″ĭl-bĕn′ză-mīd) DEET.

N, N-dimethyltryptamine (dī-mĕth″ĭl-trĭp′tă-mĭn) [*dimethyl + tryptamine*] ABBR: DMT. A hallucinogenic compound found in ayahuasca, a woody vine, *Banisteriopsis caapi*, and in other tropical plants. It has also been manufactured synthetically.

NA *nicotinic acid; Nomina Anatomica; not applicable; numerical aperture; nurse's aide.*

Na [L. *natrium*] Symbol for the element sodium.

NAACCR *North America Association of Central Cancer Registries.*

nabothian cyst (nă-bō′thē-ăn) [Martin Naboth, Ger. anatomist and physician, 1675–1721] SEE: under *cyst*.

N-acetyl-p-aminophenol (ă-mē″nō-fē′nōl″, am″ĭ-nō-) ABBR: APAP. SEE: *acetaminophen*.

NaCl Sodium chloride.

nacreous (nā′krē-ŭs) [L. *nacer*, mother of pearl] Having an iridescent pearl-like luster, as bacterial colonies.

NAD *nicotinamide adenine dinucleotide; no appreciable disease.*

N.A.D. *no appreciable disease.*

NADH *nicotinamide adenine dinucleotide*, reduced form.

nadir (nā′dĕr) [Arabic] **1.** A low point in any measurement. **2.** The lowest concentration of blood cells (esp. white blood cells) found after taking a drug that suppresses the bone marrow. The term is usually used for the low blood cell counts that occur after cancer chemotherapy. When the absolute neutrophil count reaches a nadir below 1000 cells/mm³, the risk of life-threatening infections increases dramatically.

NADP *nicotinamide adenine dinucleotide phosphate.*

NADPH *nicotinamide adenine dinucleotide phosphate*, reduced form.

NAD⁺ *nicotinamide adenine dinucleotide*, oxidized form.

NADP⁺ *nicotinamide adenine dinucleotide phosphate*, oxidized form.

Naegele, Franz Carl (nā′gĕ-lē) [German obstetrician, 1777–1851]

  N. obliquity. Anterior parietal presentation of the fetal head in labor. SYN: *anterior asynclitism*.

  N. rule A numerical formula for estimating the date labor will begin; by subtracting 3 months from the first day of the last menstrual period and adding 7 days to that date, a provisional date of delivery is identified.

Naegleria (nā-glēr′ē-ă) A genus of ameba present in soil, ground water, and sewage. One species, *N. fowleri*, is the cause of a rapidly lethal form of hemorrhagic meningoencephalitis (brain and meningeal infection). Other species include *N. gruberi* and *N. lovaniensis*. SEE: *acanthamebiasis; meningoencephalitis*.

NAEMSE *National Association of Emergency Medical Services Educators.*

NAEMSP *National Association of EMS Physicians.*

NAEMT *National Association of Emergency Medical Technicians.*

NaF Sodium fluoride.

Nagi disablement model A descriptive scheme that describes the progression from pathology or disease to disability. The components are pathology, impairment, functional limitation, and disability. Physical therapists use a modification of this model to make diagnoses and to help direct intervention.

NaHCO₃ Formula for sodium bicarbonate.

NaHSO₃ Formula for sodium hydrogen sulfite.

nail (nāl) **1.** A rod made of metal, bone, or other solid material used to attach the ends or pieces of broken bones. **2.** A horny cell structure of the epidermis forming flat plates upon the dorsal surface of the fingers and toes. SYN: *onyx; unguis*. SEE: illus.

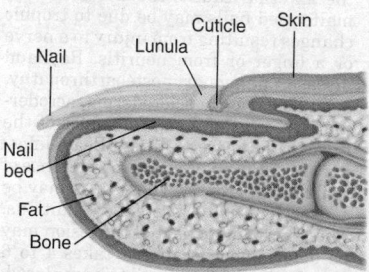

FINGERNAIL

A fingernail or toenail consists of a body composed of keratin (the exposed portion) and a root (the proximal portion hidden by the nail fold), both of which rest on the nailbed (matrix). The latter consists of epithelium and corium continuous with the epidermis and dermis of the skin of the nail fold. The crescent white area near the root is called the lunula. The epidermis extending from the margin of the nail fold over the root is called eponychium; that underlying the free border of the distal portion is called hyponychium.

A nail grows in length and thickness through cell division in the stratum germinativum of the root. The average rate of growth in fingernails is about 1 mm per week. Growth is slower in toenails and slower in summer than in winter. Nail growth varies with age and is affected by disease and certain hormone deficiencies. The onset of a disease that briefly interferes with nail growth and development may be estimated by measuring the distance of the line (Beau line) across the nail from the root of the nail.

DIFFERENTIAL DIAGNOSIS: Changes in the nails, such as ridges, may occur after a serious illness or indicate defective nutrition. In achlorhydria and hypochromic anemia, excessively spoon-shaped nails that are depressed in the center may occur. In chronic pulmonary conditions and congenital heart disease, a spongy excess of soft tissue at the base of the nails may be associated with clubbed fingers. SEE: *clubbing.*

Atrophy may occur as a result of hereditary or congenital tendencies. Permanent atrophy may follow injuries, scars from disease, frostbite, nerve injuries, and hyperthyroidism. Nail shedding is due to the same causes. Fragile or split nails often occur as a congenital condition or may be due to prolonged contact with chemicals or too frequent buffing or filing of the flat surface of the nail during manicuring. In a healthy person brittle nails are usually caused by exposure to solvents, detergents, and soaps. The brittleness disappears when the external causes are avoided. Dry, malformed nails may be due to trophic changes resulting from injury to a nerve or a finger or from neuritis, Raynaud disease, pulmonary osteoarthropathy, syphilis, onychia, scleroderma, acrodermatitis, or granuloma fungoides of the fingers. Transverse lines (Beau lines) may result from previous interference of nail matrix growth. These lines may be caused by local or systemic conditions. The approximate date of the lesion may be determined because it takes 4 to 6 months for the fingernail to be replaced. Chancre may be suspected if a small in-

dolent ulcer appears near the nail, esp. if indurated and associated with enlarged lymph glands above the inner condyle. Quincke capillary pulsation, indicated by a rhythmic flushing and blanching under the nails, is seen most frequently in aortic regurgitation and often in anemia.

Discoloration of nails is seen in various medical conditions. *Black* discoloration may be seen in diabetic and other forms of gangrene. *Blue-black* discoloration is a common condition due to hemorrhage caused by bleeding diseases, such as hemophilia, or trauma. This condition may be painful and can be relieved by drilling a small hole in the nail at the site of the hemorrhage. A dental drill, the heated tip of a paper clip, or a similar rigid wire of small diameter may be used. *Brown* discoloration may be due to arsenic poisoning. *Brownish-black* discoloration often indicates chronic mercury poisoning due to the formation of sulfide of mercury in the tissues. *Cyanosis* of the nails usually indicates anemia, poor circulation, or venous stasis. *Green* staining of the nail fold or under the nail is associated with the growth of *Pseudomonas* in a wet area. *Slate* discoloration is an early manifestation of argyria, and intake of silver should be stopped at once. *White* spots or striate lesions may be due to trauma and are more frequently seen in women. Transverse white bands in all nails may be a sign of acute or chronic arsenic poisoning or, rarely, of thallium acetate poisoning. SEE: *Mees lines.*

eggshell n. A condition in which the nail plate is soft and semitransparent, bends easily, and splits at the end. The condition is associated with arthritis, peripheral neuritis, leprosy, and hemiplegia. It may be the only visible sign of late syphilis.

fungal infection of n. SEE: under *infection.*

habit deformity n. Disruption of the nail surface by the habit of abrading or stroking that area. This produces a wavy or washboard-like nail surface.

hang n. Broken epidermis at the edge of a nail.

ingrown n. Growth of the nail edge into the soft tissue, causing inflammation and sometimes an abscess. Ingrown nails may be due to improper paring of the nails or pressure on a nail edge from improperly fitted shoes. In many cases, this condition may be prevented by cutting the nails straight across.

intramedullary n. A surgical rod inserted into the intramedullary canal to act as an immobilization device to hold the two ends of a fractured long bone in position.

reedy n. A nail marked by longitudinal fissures.

Smith-Petersen n. SEE: *Smith-Petersen nail.*

spoon n. A nail with a depressed center and elevated lateral edges. This condition may follow trauma to the nail fold or iron deficiency anemia or may develop naturally. SEE: *koilonychia* for illus.

nailbed The portion of a finger or toe covered by the nail. SYN: *nail matrix.*

nail biting An anxious behavior in which the free edges of the nails are chewed down as a means of expressing or relieving stress. SYN: *onychophagy.*

nail bur A small rotating tool used in podiatry to remove layers of keratin (or other materials) from dystrophic toenails.

nail fold SEE: under *fold.*

nailing Fixing fragments of bone by use of a nail.

nail-patella syndrome Onycho-osteodysplasia.

nail root SEE: under *root.*

nail wall Epidermis covering edges of the nail. SYN: *vallum unguis.*

nairovirus (nā′rō-vī″rŭs, nī′) A genus of RNA viruses that includes the causative agent of Crimean-Congo hemorrhagic fever.

naive, naïve (nī-ēv′) [Fr. *naif, naïve,* natural, inborn, fr. L. *nativus,* native, innate] **1.** In psychology, lacking experience, sophistication, or skepticism. **2.** In research, previously untreated. **3.** Having no history of exposure to a disease or drug.

Naja (nā′jă) [L fr Sanskrit *naga,* snake] A genus of venomous snakes of the family Elapidae, native to Africa, India, Asia, and Australia, commonly known as cobras. Their venom contains tissue-destroying enzymes that cause local necrosis at the site of a bite and produce cardiotoxic and neurotoxic polypeptides. SEE: *cobra; Ophiophagus.*

naked (nā′kĕd) Uncovered, exposed to view, nude, bare, devoid of clothing.

nalorphine hydrochloride (năl-or′fēn) A narcotic antagonist used in the treatment of narcotic overdose.

naloxone hydrochloride (na-lok′sōn″) A drug that is antagonistic to the actions of narcotics and opiates such as morphone, methadone, and opium. It is helpful in reversing the respiratory depression caused by an overdose of the narcotics.

⚠ The half-life of many opiates is longer than the half-life of naloxone. Patients treated for overdose often need close monitoring and/or repeated dosing to ensure their safety.

naltrexone (năl-trĕk′sōn) An opioid antagonist used to treat addiction to narcotics and alcohol.

⚠ Naltrexone may cause liver damage when given in high doses.

NANDA *North American Nursing Diagnosis Association.*

nanism (nā′nĭzm) [L. *nanus,* dwarf, + Gr. *-ismos,* condition] Dwarfism.

symptomatic n. Nanism with deficient dentition, sexual development, and ossification.

nano-, nan-, nanno-, nann- [Gr. *nanos, nannos,* dwarf] **1.** In the International System of Units (SI), prefixes meaning *one billionth* (10⁻⁹). **2.** Prefixes meaning *dwarfism.*

nanobacteria (nă′nō-băk-tēr-ē-ă) A controversial entity, formerly thought to be the smallest known bacteria with intact gram-negative cell walls. They are now suspected of being inorganic precipitates of calcium carbonate.

nanocurie (nā″nō-kū′rē) A unit of radioactivity equal to 10⁻⁹ curie.

nanodiagnostics (nan″ŏ-dī″ăg-nos′tiks) [*nano-* + *diagnostics*] Molecular **pathology** (2).

nanogram (năn′o-grăm) One billionth (10⁻⁹) of a gram.

nanometer (nā″nō-mē′tĕr) A unit of length equal to 10⁻⁹ meter.

nanomole (năn′ō-mōl) One billionth (10⁻⁹) mole.

nanoparticle (nan′ŏ-part″ĭ-kĕl) [*nano-* + *particle*] A microscopic particle (<100 nm in diameter) containing a drug or a radiologic contrast agent used in cancer treatment to identify and eradicate tiny metastatic tumors.

nanophyetus Any species of parasitic flatworms (flukes) that live in freshwater fish. They may infest humans who consume raw, smoked, or partially cooked salmon and steelhead. Characteristic symptoms include nausea, vomiting, and abdominal pain.

nanoscale (nă′nō-skāl″) [*nano-* + ¹*scale*] Pert. to objects approx. 1 nanometer (nm) in size, i.e., about the size of an atom.

nanosecond (nā″nō-sĕk′ŏnd) A unit of time measurement equal to 10⁻⁹ second.

nanotechnology (nā″nō-tĕk-nŏl′ŏ-jē) [*nano-* + *technology*] The scientific study and engineering of chemical or biological objects measuring between 1 and 1000 nanometers. Objects this small are about the size of atoms or small molecules. "Wet" nanotechnology is the manipulation of organic or biological compounds in solution. "Dry" nanotechnology is the engineering of objects on silicon or carbon surfaces, such as those used in computing.

NaOH Sodium hydroxide.

nap (nap) **1.** To slumber. **2.** A short sleep; a doze. SEE: *sleep.*

napalm (nā′pălm) [*na*phthene +

*palm*itate] Gasoline made thick or jelly-like for use in incendiary bombs and flame throwers.

nape (nāp, năp) The back of the neck.

naphtha (năf'thă) **1.** A volatile inflammable liquid distilled from carbonaceous substances. **2.** Petroleum, esp. more volatile varieties.

naphthalene (năf'thă-lēn) A toxic hydrocarbon, $C_{10}H_8$. It is used as a disinfectant, in moth balls, and in the manufacture of dyes and explosives.

naphthol (năf'thōl) $C_{10}H_8O$; a toxic petroleum derivative used as an antiseptic and in some dyes. It is prepared from naphthalene.

NAPNAP *National Association of Pediatric Nurse Associates and Practitioners.*

NAPNES *National Association for Practical Nurse Education and Services.*

naprapathy [Czech *naprapravit*, to correct + *-pathy*] The use of electrical stimulation of the body, topical application of heat and cold, manipulation, massage, nutritional counseling, stretching, and ultrasonography to improve neuromuscular and connective tissue diseases. Practitioners of naprapathy are called naprapaths. The first school of naprapathy was founded in the U.S. in 1907 by Dr. Oakley Smith.

Naprosyn, Naprelan, Napron X Naproxen.

naproxen (nă-prŏk'sĕn) A propionic acid, administered orally to relieve mild to moderate pain, dysmenorrhea, fever, and inflammatory disorders, including rheumatoid arthritis and osteoarthritis. Its therapeutic classes are nonopioid analgesic, nonsteroidal anti-inflammatory agent, and antipyretic. SYN: *Naprosyn*.

Nar-Anon (nar'ă-non") A nonprofit organization that provides group support for the family and close friends of drug addicts. SEE: *Alateen; Alcoholics Anonymous; Al-Anon; 12-step program*.

narcissism (năr'sĭs-ĭzm) [*Narcissus*, a Gr. mythical character who fell in love with his own reflection] **1.** Self-love or self-admiration. **2.** Sexual pleasure derived from observing one's own naked body. **narcissistic** (năr-sĭs-sĭst'ĭk), *adj*.

narcissistic object choice (năr"sĭ-sĭs'tĭk) Selection of another like one's own self as the object of love, friendship, or liking.

narco-, narc- [Gr. *narkē*, numbness, stiffness] Prefixes meaning *numbness, stupor.*

narcolepsy (năr'kō-lĕp"sē) [Gr. *narke*, numbness, + *lepsis*, seizure] A disorder marked by recurrent, uncontrollable attacks of daytime sleepiness, often associated with temporary muscular paralysis (cataplexy), which may occur after powerful emotional experiences. People affected by this condition may have several sleep attacks each

day. Typically, narcoleptic patients arouse from sleep relatively easily. **narcoleptic** (năr-kō-lĕp'tĭk), *adj*.

ETIOLOGY: Narcolepsy occurs in families, and about 90% of affected people have specific human leukocyte antigens (HLA-DQw6 or HLA-DR2). People with narcolepsy have diminished levels of peptides in the brain, called orexins, that influence sleep and consciousness.

TREATMENT: Scheduled naps during the day may prevent sleep attacks, especially if the naps are timed to occur when the patient usually experiences sleep attacks. Drugs used to treat narcolepsy include stimulants such as dextroamphetamine sulfate, pemoline, or methylphenidate hydrochloride.

⚠ Narcoleptics should avoid activities that require constant alertness (e.g., driving or flying). At the first sign of drowsiness, affected patients should seek a safe place to sleep. In many states in the U.S., loss of consciousness is grounds for revocation of driving privileges. Patients with narcolepsy should review their motor vehicle usage with their health care professionals.

narcosis (nar-kō'sĭs) [*narco-* + *-sis*] Unconsciousness or stupor produced by drugs.

    basal n. Initial narcosis produced by sedatives used before administration of a general anesthetic.

    carbon dioxide n. Personality changes, confusion, and coma due to an increase in carbon dioxide content of the blood. This may occur during oxygen therapy of patients with chronic obstructive pulmonary disease or in patients receiving inadequate levels of artificial respiration.

    medullary n. General anesthesia induced by a local anesthetic injected into the sheath of the spinal cord in lumbar region. SYN: *spinal anesthesia*.

    nitrogen n. A condition of euphoria, impaired judgment, and decreased coordination and motor ability seen in people exposed to high atmosphere pressure (e.g., divers and submariners). The effects, caused by the increased concentration of nitrogen gas in body tissues (including the brain), are similar to those produced by alcohol intoxication.

narcotic (năr-kŏt'ĭk) [Gr. *narkotikos*, benumbing] **1.** Producing stupor or sleep. **2.** A drug that depresses the central nervous system, thus relieving pain and producing sleep. Most narcotics are habit-forming. Excessive doses produce unconsciousness, stupor, coma, respiratory depression, pulmonary edema, and sometimes death. Opium, morphine, codeine, papaverine, and heroin are examples of narcotics. A more precise term is *opioid analgesic.* SEE: *pain.*

narcotism (năr′kō-tĭzm) [Gr. *narke,* stupor, + *-ismos,* condition] An addiction to the use of narcotics. Addiction may be said to exist when discontinuance causes abstinence symptoms that are speedily relieved by a dose of the drug. SEE: *withdrawal.*

TREATMENT: Treatment is ordinarily successful only during hospitalization. Relapses are frequent. Participation in group therapy (e.g., in a program such as Narcotics Anonymous) may be helpful.

narcotize (năr′kŏt-īz) [Gr. *narkotikos,* benumbing] To place under the influence of a narcotic.

narcotrafficking (nar′kō-traf″ik-ing) The illegal production, distribution, and sale of controlled narcotic substances.

naris (nā′rĭs) *pl.* **nares** [L.] The nostril. SEE: *nose.*

narrative competence (năr′ĭ-tĭv) [L. *narrativus*] A communication skill with two components: the ability to listen actively and empathetically to the underlying meanings of patient's histories, and the ability to craft a narrative for use in relaying meanings to patients.

narrowing Decreasing the width or diameter of some space or channel (e.g., narrowing of the size of the coronary arteries), usually due to some pathological process.

NASA *National Aeronautics and Space Administration.*

nasal (nā′zl) [L. *nasus,* nose] **1.** Pert. to the nose. **2.** Uttered through the nose. **3.** A nasal bone.

nasal cavity SEE: under *cavity.*

nasal challenge SEE: under *challenge.*

nasal flaring Intermittent outward movement of the nostrils with each inspiratory effort; indicates an increase in the work of breathing.

nasal gavage SEE: *enteral tube feeding.*

nasal height Distance between the lower border of the nasal aperture and the nasion.

nasal index SEE: under *index.*

nasal meatus SEE: under *meatus.*

nasal obstruction SEE: under *obstruction.*

nasal reflex SEE: under *reflex.*

nasal septum SEE: *septum, nasal.*

nasal tip The inferior third of the nose.

nasal trumpet Nasopharyngeal **airway**.

nasal width The maximum width of the nasal aperture.

nascent (năs′ĕnt; nā′sĕnt) [L. *nascens,* born] **1.** Just born; incipient or beginning. **2.** Pert. to a substance being set free from a compound.

nasendoscope (năz″ĕn′dŏ-skōp″) [″ + ″] A small, angled endoscope that is inserted into a nostril and used to visualize the nose, sinuses, pharynx, and larynx.

nasion (nā′zē-ŏn) [L. *nasus,* nose] The point at which the nasofrontal suture is cut across by the median anteroposterior plane.

Nasmyth membrane (nā′smith) [Alexander Nasmyth, Scottish dental surgeon, d. 1848] A thin cuticle consisting of the cellular remnants of the enamel organ and the mucopolysaccharide basement membrane that attaches them to the enamel surface. This covering is very friable and usually lost after eruption of the tooth into the oral cavity; however, it may persist in protected areas, such as the labial surface of maxillary incisors. SYN: *cuticula dentis; enamel* **membrane***.*

naso- [L. *nasus,* nose] Prefix meaning *nose.* SEE: *rhino-.*

nasociliary (nā″zō-sĭl′ē-ār-ē) Pert. to the nose, eyebrow, and eyes. Applied esp. to the nerve supplying these structures.

nasoduodenal tube (nā″zō-dū-ă-dē′năl,-doo, nā″zō-dū-ŏd′ĕ-năl,-doo) A flexible tube of silicone or a similar synthetic material, inserted through the nose into the duodenum for short-term enteral feeding. The small weight on the distal end of the tube moves the tube into place through the stomach into the duodenum. Aspiration is less likely than with a nasogastric tube.

nasofrontal (nā″zō-frŏn′tăl) [″ + *frontalis,* forehead] Pert. to nasal and frontal bones.

nasogastric (nā″zō-găs′trĭk) [″ + Gr. *gaster,* belly] Pert. to the nasal passages and the stomach, esp. relating to intubation.

nasogastric tube A tube inserted through the nose and extending into the stomach. It may be used for emptying the stomach of gas and liquids or for administering liquids to the patient. SEE: illus.

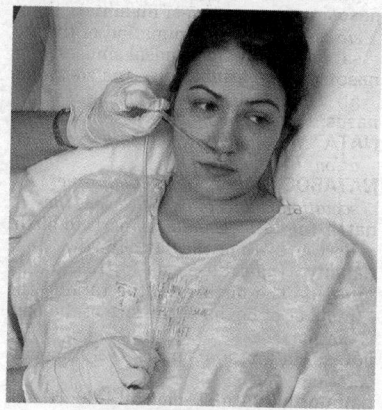

NASOGASTRIC TUBE

nasointestinal tube A long tube inserted through the nose into the stomach for decompression. A weight at the end promotes its advancement into the small intestine. The most common use is to relieve the abdominal distention associated with intestinal obstruction.

nasojejunal tube (nā″zō-jĕ-joon′ăl) A tube passed through the nose into the jejunum for formula feeding.

nasolabial (nā″zō-lā′bē-ăl) [″ + *labium*, lip] Pert. to the nose and lip.

nasolacrimal (nā″zō-lăk′rĭm-ăl) [″ + *lacrima*, tear] Pert. to the nose and lacrimal apparatus.

nasomental reflex SEE: under *reflex*.

Nasonex SEE: *mometasone*.

naso-oral (nā″zō-ō′răl) [″ + *oralis*, pert. to the mouth] Pert. to the nose and oral cavity.

nasopalatine (nā″zō-păl′ă-tĭn) [L. *nasus*, nose, + *palatum*, palate] Pert. to the nose and palate.

nasopharyngeal airway, maintenance of (nā″zō-fă-rĭn′jē-ăl) By means of a flexible tube that is inserted into the nose of an unresponsive patient and rests above the hypopharynx, the airway is maintained. Used in patients with intact gag reflexes to prevent retching during attempts to maintain an open airway.

nasopharyngitis (nā″zō-făr-ĭn-jī′tĭs) [″ + Gr. *pharynx*, throat + *itis*, inflammation] Inflammation of the nasopharynx.

nasopharyngoscope (nā″zō-fă-rĭn′jō-skōp) Device used to visualize the nasal passage and pharynx.

nasopharyngoscopy Inspection of the nasopharynx and posterior nares. SYN: *pharyngorhinoscopy*.

nasopharynx (nā″zō-făr′ĭnks) [L. *nasus*, nose, + Gr. *pharynx*, throat] The part of the pharynx situated above the soft palate (postnasal space). **nasopharyngeal** (nā″zō-făr-ĭn′jē-ăl), *adj*.

nasosinusitis (nā″zō-sī″nū-sī′tĭs) [″ + *sinus*, cavity] Inflammation of the nasal cavities and paranasal sinuses.

nasotracheal intubation (nā″zō-trā′kē-ăl) SEE: under *intubation*.

nasus (nā′sŭs) [L.] The nose.

NATA *National Athletic Trainers Association, Inc.*

NATABOC *National Athletic Trainers Association Board of Certification, Inc.*

natal (nāt′ăl) [L. *natalis*, pert. to birth] Pert. to birth or the day of birth.

natality (nā-tăl′ĭt-ē, nă-) [L. *natalis*, birth] The birth rate; the ratio of the number of births to the size of the population.

nates (nā′tēz) *sing.*, **natis** [L.] The buttocks.

natimortality (nā″tĭ-mor-tăl′ĭ-tē) [L. *natus*, birth, + *mortalitas*, death] Rate of stillbirths in proportion to birth rate.

National Academy of Sciences, National Academies ABBR: NAS. An organization comprising a selected group of honored or distinguished engineers and scientists who are called upon to review and explore the uses of science and technology as they may further or enlighten national interests in the U.S.

National Academy of Sports Medicine ABBR: NASM. An international health, fitness and sports medicine organization offering evidence-based education, training, certification, and advanced specialization programs to qualified athletic and health care professionals.

National Adult Reading Test ABBR: NART. An intelligence test in which subjects are asked to read and pronounce words with unusual spellings.

National Association of Area Agencies on Aging ABBR: N4A. A U.S. nonprofit organization that oversees and supports the work of local Area Agencies on Aging by providing them with home and community-based services to help older adults and the disabled live in the environments that meet their needs.

National Association of EMS Educators A trade association of professionals who provide course work and training for health care professionals who want to study how to assess and manage health care crises.

National Association of School Psychologists ABBR: NASP. An advocacy and educational group of psychologists who work with children in grades K–12. The association ensures that children adapt as best as possible to school and that the psychologists who serve them use evidence-based approaches and high ethical standards in their work.

National Association of Social Workers ABBR: NASW. An international organization of professional social workers.

National Athletic Trainers' Association, Inc. ABBR: NATA. A not-for-profit organization dedicated to advancing the quality of health care provided by athletic trainers and advancing the athletic training profession.

National Athletic Trainers' Association Board of Certification, Inc. ABBR: NATABOC, BOC. The national certification agency for athletic trainers. It establishes standards for certification and develops the continuing education requirements that a certified athletic trainer must satisfy. The BOC credential is recognized by many states as the standard for licensure.

National Board for Certification in Occupational Therapy ABBR: NBCOT. An independent agency to certify the eligibility of occupational therapists and occupational therapy assistants to practice in the U.S.

National Board for Respiratory Care ABBR: NBRC. The national accrediting agency for pulmonary function technologists and respiratory care practitioners.

National Center for Advancing Translational Sciences A division of the National Institutes of Health whose mission is to foster the development of new drugs. It plays a key role in shaping future research directions.

National Center for Complementary and Alternative Medicine ABBR: NCCAM. National Institutes of Health center for research into alternative medical treatments. It was established in 1992 as the Office of Alternative Medicine.

National Center for Environmental Health A U.S. federal agency that maintains a database of hazardous chemicals, the risks of exposure to them, and methods of preparedness for dealing with toxic spills and the casualties they may cause.

National Center for Health Statistics ABBR: NCHS. A branch of the Centers for Disease Control and Prevention that gathers and analyzes a broad array of data about the health of Americans.

National Clinicians' Post-Exposure Prophylaxis Hotline ABBR: PEPline. A public health resource that offers up-to-the minute advice on managing occupational exposures; i.e., needle sticks or splashes to HIV, hepatitis, and other blood-borne pathogens. Telephone: 1-888-448-4911; Website: www.nccc.ucsf.edu/about_nccc/pepline/

National Conference of Gerontological Nurse Practitioners ABBR: NCGNP. An advanced-practice nursing organization that provides continuing education and peer support for gerontological nurse practitioners. Website: www.ncgnp.org

National Council Licensure Examination–Practical Nurse ABBR: NCLEX–PN. A computer-administered standardized test taken by new applicants for state licensure as practical nurses that attempts to determine the candidate's minimum competence for safe practice. Examinations are available in all states and are administered by the National Council of State Boards of Nursing.

National Council Licensure Examination–Registered Nurse ABBR: NCLEX–RN. A computer-administered standardized test taken by new applicants for state licensure as registered nurses that measures the competencies needed to perform safely and effectively as a newly licensed, entry-level nurse. Examinations are available in all states and are administered by the National Council of State Boards of Nursing.

National Disaster Medical System ABBR: NDMS. A partnership between U.S. federal and state health care institutions that provides emergency responses to catastrophes, including emergency on-site health care, evacuation, and interstate hospital coordination.

National Drug Code ABBR: NDC. A numerical designation assigned by the Food and Drug Administration to each drug marketed and used in the U.S.

National Formulary ABBR: NF. A collection of officially recognized drug names originally issued by the American Pharmaceutical Association but now published by the United States Pharmacopeial Convention, Inc. The NF includes drugs of established usefulness that are not listed in the United States Pharmacopeia. SEE: *United States Pharmacopeia; United States Pharmacopeial Convention, Inc.*

National Gerontological Nursing Association ABBR: NGNA. A national nursing organization for improving clinical care for older adults. Members include researchers, clinicians, educators, clinical nurse specialists, and other advanced practice nurses. Website: http://www.ngna.org

National Health and Nutrition Examination Survey ABBR: NHANES. A survey of the population of the U.S., conducted periodically by the National Center for Health Statistics, that reviews the height, weight, and nutritional habits of Americans (and other demographic, environmental, and socioeconomic variables) and links those data to health outcomes, such as the incidence of heart disease, hypertension, hyperlipidemia, kidney disease, diabetes mellitus, obesity, osteoporosis, psychiatric illnesses, sexually transmitted illnesses, and stroke.

Other accomplishments of NHANES have included the development of normal growth charts for children and infants and the reduction of blood lead levels among this population and the diseases caused by excessive exposure to lead.

national health insurance A form of health insurance coverage whereby all citizens receive care financed by their government. Countries with national health insurance include Canada and the United Kingdom.

National Health Safety Network ABBR: NHSN. A voluntary association of health care institutions that share information about patient safety concerns and best practices via software maintained and supervised by the CDC.

National Highway Traffic Safety Administration ABBR: NHTSA. The division of the U.S. Department of Transportation that conducts research on driver behavior and traffic safety, and investigates and enforces safety standards for motor vehicles and their operation. It is also responsible for developing the national standard emergency medical services training curriculum. Website: http://www.nhtsa.gov

National Incident Management System ABBR: NIMS. A U.S. federal agency that coordinates responses to major disasters, such as, earthquakes, fires, hurricanes, spills, terrorist attacks, and major transportation accidents.

National Institute of Arthritis and Musculoskeletal and Skin Diseases A U.S. federal agency of the National Institutes of Health that supports research in diseases associated with aging. The diseases include osteoporosis, Paget disease, degenerative joint diseases, and skin diseases such as psoriasis.

National Institute of Environmental Health Sciences ABBR: NIEHS. A U.S. federal agency that conducts research on aging, the effects of environmental agents, and the combined effects of aging and exposure to environmental agents.

National Institute of Mental Health ABBR: NIMH. The division of the National Institutes of Health that sponsors and promotes research, education, and training in the study of the brain and behavioral science. The stated goals of the organization are to understand, treat, and prevent mental illness. The website address is www.nimh.nih.gov/.

National Institute of Neurological Disorders and Stroke ABBR: NINDS. A U.S. federal agency that conducts research on nervous system disorders, including Alzheimer disease, Parkinson disease, and stroke, which occur with greater frequency in the elderly.

National Institute of Occupational Safety and Health ABBR: NIOSH. A research branch of the Centers for Disease Control and Prevention that investigates workplace hazards and makes recommendations for the prevention of worker injuries, illnesses, and disabilities.

National Institute on Aging ABBR: NIA. A U.S. federal agency of the National Institutes of Health that conducts and supports biomedical, social, and behavioral research and training related to aging.

National Institute of Standards and Technology ABBR: NIST. A U.S. federal agency that proposes and develops standards of measurement and the means to support advances in technology. It was formerly known as the National Bureau of Standards.

National League for Nursing ABBR:

NLN. An organization originally formed by the merging of three other nursing organizations. The principal concern of the League is improvement of nursing education and service.

Nationally Registered Emergency Medical Technician ABBR: NREMT. The designation awarded after successful completion of written and practical examinations administered by the National Registry of Emergency Medical Technicians. There are three NREMT designations: NREMT-Basic, NREMT-Intermediate, and NREMT-Paramedic. Website: http://www.nremt.org

National Marrow Donor Program ABBR: NMDP. The coordinating center for bone marrow donors. Telephone: 1-800-654-1247; Website: http://www.marrow.org

National Nursing Staff Development Organization A national organization that represents the interests of those who foster the professional advancement of nursing. Website: http://www.nnsdo.org

National Organization for Rare Disorders ABBR: NORD. An organization created by a group of voluntary agencies, medical researchers, and private citizens concerned about orphan diseases and orphan drugs.

Address: P.O. Box 8923, New Fairfield, CT 06812; telephone: (203) 746-6518; Website: www.rarediseases.org

National Practitioner Data Bank ABBR: NPDB. A national databank, created by the Health Care Quality Improvement Act of 1986, that receives, stores, and disseminates records on the conduct and competence of medical professionals. Health care facilities use the information contributed to the databank during hiring and credentialing. The databank stores information relating to medical malpractice payments made on behalf of health care practitioners; information relating to adverse actions taken against clinical privileges of physicians, osteopaths, or dentists; and information concerning actions by professional societies that adversely affect membership.

national provider identifier ABBR: NPI. A unique 10-digit identification number used to identify health care personnel (e.g., physicians and other clinicians) and facilities (e.g., hospitals and laboratories). The NPI is used by all health plans for administrative and financial transactions.

National Quality Forum ABBR: NQF. A private nonprofit organization, founded in 1999 and devoted to the systematic study of the implementation of optimal practices in the delivery of U.S. health care.

National Safety Council A nonprofit organization whose mission is to promote and influence safety and health at work, on the road, at home, and in the environment.

National Stroke Association ABBR: NSA. A nonprofit organization devoted to stroke prevention, treatment, rehabilitation, and research and to the support of people who have had strokes as well as their partners and families. Telephone: 1-800-STROKES; Website: www.stroke.org

National Student Nurses Association ABBR: NSNA. The primary organization for student nurses in the U.S., a counterpart of the American Nurses Association.

native (nā'tĭv) [L. *nativus*] **1.** Born with; inherent. **2.** Natural, normal. **3.** Belonging to, as place of one's birth.

native language The first language a person learns. It is usually the language he or she is most proficient in and uses with the greatest comfort, confidence, and precision. SYN: *first language; mother tongue.*

natremia (nă-trē'mē-ă) [L. *natrium,* sodium, + Gr. *haima,* blood] Sodium in the blood.

natrium (nā'trē-ŭm) [Ult. fr Gr. *natron* + *-ium* (1)] SYMB: Na. SEE: *sodium.*

natriuresis (nā"trē-ū-rē'sĭs) [" + Gr. *ouresis,* make water] The excretion of abnormal amounts of sodium in the urine.

natriuretic (nā"trē-yŭ-ret'ik) [*natrium* + Gr. *ourētikos,* pert. to urine] **1.** Pert. to the excretion of sodium in the urine. **2.** A drug that increases the rate of sodium excretion in the urine. SYN: *saluretic.* SEE: *diuretic.*

natural [L. *natura,* nature] Not abnormal or artificial.

natural childbirth SEE: under *childbirth.*

natural history (of disease) SEE: under *history.*

natural killer cells SEE: under *cells.*

natural selection SEE: under *selection.*

nature and nurture The combination of a person's genetic constitution and the environmental conditions to which he is exposed. The interplay of these forces produces physical and mental characteristics that make each human being different from another.

nature of illness ABBR: NOI. The expression of a disease and its meaning to the patient and significant others.

naturopath (nā'tūr-ō-păth) [" + Gr. *pathos,* disease, suffering] One who practices naturopathic medicine.

naturopathy (nā"tūr-ŏp'ă-thē) Naturopathic medicine.

nausea (naw'sē-ă, naw-zē-ă) [Gr. *nausia,* seasickness] An unpleasant, queasy, or wavelike sensation in the back of the throat, epigastrium, or abdomen that may or may not lead to the urge or need to vomit. SEE: *Nursing Diagnoses Appendix.*

PATIENT CARE: Any materials or environmental factors that precipitate the nausea should be removed. Frequency, time, amount, and characteristics of nausea-associated emesis are noted. Vomitus is tested for blood when indicated. Oral hygiene and comfort measures are provided. If nausea persists, professional evaluation may be advisable.

   n. gravidarum Morning sickness. SEE: *hyperemesis gravidarum.*

nauseant (naw'shē-ănt, naw'sē-ănt) **1.** Provoking nausea. **2.** An agent that causes nausea.

nauseate (naw'shē-āt, naw'sē-āt) To cause nausea.

nauseous (naw'shŭs, naw'shē-ŭs) **1.** Producing nausea, disgust, or loathing. **2.** Affected with nausea.

navel (nā'věl) Umbilicus.

navicular (nă-vĭk'ū-lăr) **1.** Shaped like a boat. **2.** Scaphoid bones in the carpus (wrist) and in the tarsus (ankle). SEE: *skeleton.*

navicular drop test A test used to quantify pronation of the foot. While the patient's foot is in a non–weight-bearing position, the examiner places a mark over the navicular tuberosity. Next, the foot is placed on the floor, again in a non–weight-bearing position, and a mark is made on a 3 × 5 index card to measure the distance between the floor and the navicular tubercle. The measure is repeated when the patient bears weight on the foot and the distance between the two marks is recorded. Inferior displacement of greater than 10 mm while bearing weight is considered hyperpronation of the foot. SEE: illus.

navicular fossa SEE: *navicular fossa.*

navigation (năv"ĭ-gā'shŭn) [L. *navigatio,* voyage] **1.** Determining, calculating, and guiding an action in which an object, e.g., a catheter or a surgical instrument, is directed to a particular anatomic position, typically with radiological guidance. **2.** The ability to direct one's movements through space, i.e., through both familiar and new environments.

navigational deficits Any difficulties in orienting oneself in one's environment or in finding a sure path through a maze. It is more common in elderly persons than in the young and esp. in those who have suffered traumatic brain injury or neurodegenerative diseases that cause dementia.

-navir A suffix used in pharmacology to designate an antiviral protease inhibitor.

Nb Symbol for the element niobium.

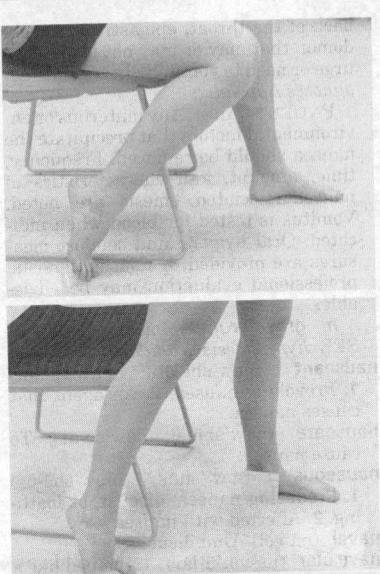
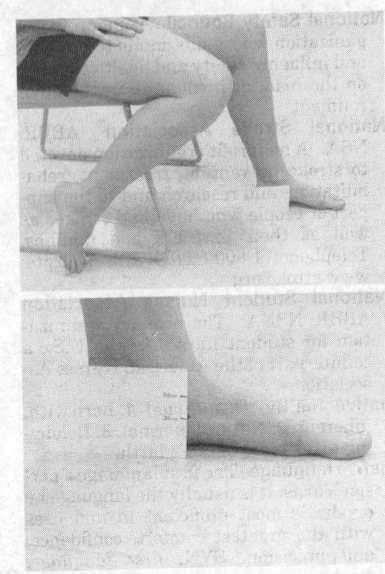

NAVICULAR DROP TEST

NBCOT *National Board for Certification in Occupational Therapy.*

N-benzylpiperazine (běn″zĭl-pĭ-pĕr′ŭ-zēn, zĭn, pĭp′er) ABBR: BZP. An amphetamine-like drug used illicitly for its euphoric effects. Originally marketed as an antiparasitic agent.

NBT-PABA test The N-benzoyl-L-tyrosyl-p-aminobenzoic acid test, a noninvasive test primarily used to measure the function of the exocrine pancreas. The test is performed by administering NBT-PABA to patients with suspected chronic pancreatitis and measuring the amount of PABA excreted in the urine. In patients with chronic pancreatitis, chymotrypsin is not released by the exocrine pancreas into the gastrointestinal tract; NBT is not cleaved from PABA, and thus the excretion of PABA in the urine is diminished.

NCC *National Certification Corporation.*

NCHS *National Center for Health Statistics.*

NCI *National Cancer Institute.*

nCi *nanocurie.*

NCLEX–PN *National Council Licensure Examination–Practical Nurse.*

NCLEX–RN *National Council Licensure Examination–Registered Nurse.*

NCMHD *National Center on Minority Health and Health Disparities.*

nCPAP Nasal continuous positive airway pressure, a treatment for sleep apnea, and in neonates, for respiratory distress.

NCRR *National Center for Research Resources*

NCSBN *National Council of State Boards of Nursing.*

Nd Symbol for the element neodymium.

NDA *National Dental Association.*

NE *Neutrophil;* (clinical laboratory).

Ne Symbol for the element neon.

NEA-BC *Nurse Executive, Advanced, Board-Certified.*

near-death experience ABBR: NDE. The perception held by certain individuals that they have glimpsed an afterlife when coming close to death. SEE: *out-of-body experience.*

near-drowning Survival after immersion in water. This term has been replaced with "submersion," which is more accurate and was agreed upon at the Utstein Guidelines Conference for uniform reporting of drowning and submersion incidents.

About 330,000 persons, mostly children, adolescents, or young adults, survive an immersion injury in the U.S. each year; of these, about 10% receive professional attention. Many who suffer near-drowning do so because of preventable or avoidable conditions, such as the use of alcohol or drugs in aquatic settings or the inadequate supervision of children by adults. Water sports (e.g., diving, swimming, surfing, or skiing) and boating or fishing accidents also are common causes of near-drowning. A small percentage of near-drowning episodes occur when patients with known seizure disorders convulse while swimming or boating. SEE: *drowning.*

ETIOLOGY: The injuries suffered result from holding one's breath ("dry drowning"), the aspiration of water into the lungs ("wet drowning"), and/or hypothermia.

SYMPTOMS: Common symptoms of near-drowning result from oxygen deprivation, retention of carbon dioxide, or direct damage to the lungs by water. These include cough, dyspnea, coma, and seizures. Additional complications of prolonged immersion include aspiration pneumonitis, noncardiogenic pulmonary edema, electrolyte disorders, hemolysis, disseminated intravascular coagulation, and arrhythmias.

TREATMENT: In unconscious patients rescued from water, the airway is secured, ventilation is provided, and cardiopulmonary resuscitation is begun. Oxygen, cardiac, and blood pressure monitoring, rewarming techniques, and other forms of support are provided, e.g., anticonvulsants for seizures; electrolyte and acid-base disorders are corrected.

PROGNOSIS: Most patients who are rapidly resuscitated from a dry drowning episode recover fully. The recovery of near-drowning victims who have inhaled water into the lungs depends on the underlying health of the victim, the duration of immersion, and the speed and efficiency with which oxygenation, ventilation, and perfusion are restored.

near fall An event in which a person feels a fall is imminent but avoids it by compensatory action, such as grabbing a nearby object or controlling the fall. People who experience near falls may be at risk of falling and require preventive intervention to avoid potential injury.

near-infrared fluorescence imaging SEE: under *imaging.*

near point SEE: under *point.*

nearsighted Able to see clearly only those objects held close to the eye. SEE: *myopia.*

nearsightedness Myopia.

nebula (nĕb′ū-lă) *pl.* **nebulae** [L., mist, cloud] **1.** Slight haziness on the cornea. **2.** A translucent corneal scar. **3.** Cloudiness in urine. **4.** Aqueous or oily substance for use in an atomizer.

nebulization (nĕb″ū-lĭ-zā′shŭn) Production of particles such as a spray or mist from liquid. The size of particles produced depends upon the method used. SEE: *nebulizer.*

nebulizer (nĕb′ū-lī″zĕr) [L. *nebula,* mist] An apparatus for producing a fine spray or mist. This may be done by rapidly passing air through a liquid or by vibrating a liquid at a high frequency so that the particles produced are extremely small. SEE: *aerosol; atomizer; vaporizer;* illus.

ultrasonic n. An aerosol produced by

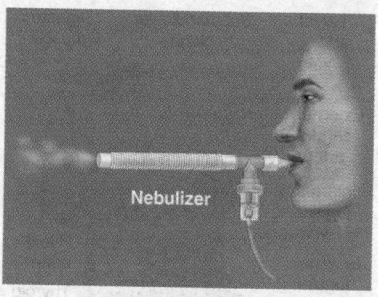

NEBULIZER

the action of a vibrating ultrasonic transducer under water.

NEC *necrotizing enterocolitis.*

Necator (nē-kā′tor) [L., murderer] A genus of parasitic hookworms belonging to the family Ancylostomidae.

N. americanus A parasitic hookworm found worldwide that is responsible for iron-deficiency anemia and impaired growth in children. SEE: *hookworm;* illus.

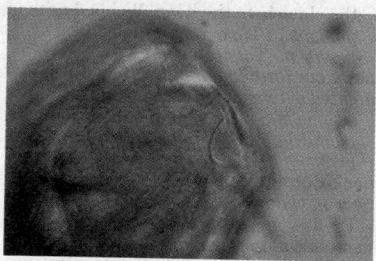

NECATOR AMERICANUS

necatoriasis (nē-kā″tō-rī′ă-sĭs) Hookworm.

neck (nek) **1.** The part of the body between the head and shoulders. SEE: illus.; *muscle* for illus. **2.** The constricted portion of an organ, or that resembling a neck. **3.** The region between the crown and the root of a tooth.

n. of the femur The heavy column of bone that connects the head of the femur to the shaft.

Madelung n. Madelung disease.

n. of the mandible The constricted area below the articular condyle; the area of attachment for the articular capsule and the lateral pterygoid muscle.

surgical n. of the humerus The segment of the shaft of the humerus just distal to the greater and lesser tubercles. It is a region prone to fractures.

n. of the tooth The constricted area that connects the crown of a tooth to the root of a tooth.

webbed n. A broad neck as seen anteriorly or posteriorly. The breadth is due to a fold of skin that extends from

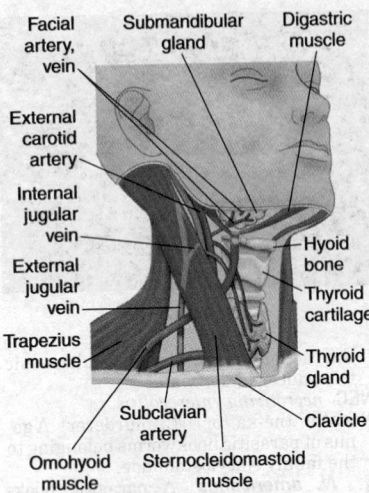

Facial artery, vein — Submandibular gland — Digastric muscle — External carotid artery — Internal jugular vein — External jugular vein — Trapezius muscle — Hyoid bone — Thyroid cartilage — Thyroid gland — Clavicle — Subclavian artery — Sternocleidomastoid muscle — Omohyoid muscle

LATERAL ASPECT OF THE NECK

the clavicle to the head. Webbed neck is present in Turner syndrome.

wry n. Torticollis.

neck conformer A splint, usually fabricated of thermoplastic material, that positions the neck to prevent flexion contractures due to burns of the anterior neck.

neck-righting reflex SEE: under *reflex*.

necro-, necr- [Gr. *nekros*, corpse] Prefixes meaning *death, necrosis*.

necrobacillosis (nĕk″rō-bas″ĭ-lō′sĭs) [*necro-* + *bacillosis*] Any of several infections with *Fusobacterium necrophorum* that affect farm animals.

necrobiosis (nĕk-rō-bī-ō′sĭs) [″ + *biosis*, life] Gradual degeneration and swelling of collagen bundles in the dermis. SEE: *necrosis*. **necrobiotic** (nĕ″krō-bī-ŏt′ĭk), *adj.*

n. lipoidica diabeticorum A skin disease marked by necrotic atrophy of connective and elastic tissue. The lesions have a central yellowish area surrounded by a brownish border and telangiectases and usually present on the anterior surface of the legs. The disease is commonly found in people who have had diabetes mellitus for many years. Beginning as 1 to 3 mm papules or nodules, the lesions enlarge to become waxy or shiny round plaques that are reddish brown at first and later become yellow atrophic lesions. SYN: diabetic *dermopathy*.

PATIENT CARE: Infection and, occasionally, ulceration result when an affected area is traumatized. A variety of treatments have been tried for patients who find the rash unsightly; none are definitively effective. The patient also

should be taught methods for protecting legs and other affected areas from injury. Graduated compression stockings should be worn, and the legs should be rested frequently.

necrogenic, necrogenous (nĕ-krō-jĕn′ĭk, -krŏj′ĕn-ŭs) [″ + *gennan*, to produce] Pert. to, caused by, or originating in dead matter.

necrology (nĕk-rŏl′ō-jē) The study of mortality statistics.

necrolysis (nĕ-krŏl′ĭ-sĭs) [″ + *lysis*, dissolution] Necrosis and dissolution of tissue.

toxic epidermal n. ABBR: TEN. A rare, often life-threatening illness marked by scaling and shedding of the skin and mucous membranes. It usually is caused by an adverse reaction to a drug. Treatment is similar to that for patients with extensive burns. SYN: *Lyell disease*.

necrolytic migratory erythema SEE: under *erythema*.

necromania (nĕk-rō-mā′nē-ă) [″ + *mania*, madness] Abnormal interest in dead bodies or in death.

necroparasite (nĕk″rō-păr′ă-sīt) [″ + *para*, beside, + *sitos*, food] Saprophyte.

necrophagous (nĕ-krof′ă-gŭs) [*necro-* + Gr. *-phagos*, fr. *phagein*, to eat] Feeding on dead flesh.

necrophile (nĕk′rō-fīl) [″ + *philein*, to love] One who is affected with necrophilia.

necrophilia (nĕk″rō-fīl′ē-ă) [″ + *philein*, to love] **1.** Abnormal interest in corpses. **2.** Sexual intercourse with a dead body.

necrophilic (nĕk″rō-fīl′ĭk) [″ + *philein*, to love] **1.** Pert. to necrophilia. **2.** Pert. to bacteria that thrive best in dead tissue.

necropsy (nek′rop″sē) [*necro-* + *-opsy*] Autopsy.

necroscopy (nĕ-kros′kŏ-pē) [*necro-* + *-scopy*] Autopsy.

necrose (nĕk-rōs′) [Gr. *nekroun*, to make dead] To cause or to undergo necrosis.

necrosis (nĕ-krō′sĭs, ′sēz″) pl. **necroses** [Gr. *nekrōsis*, (state of) death] The death of cells, tissues, or organs. Necrosis may be caused by insufficient blood supply, pathogenic microorganisms, physical agents such as trauma or radiant energy (electricity, infrared, ultraviolet, roentgen, and radium rays), and chemical agents acting locally, acting internally after absorption, or placed into the wrong tissue. Some medicines cause necrosis if injected into the tissues rather than the vein, and some, such as iron dextran, cause necrosis if injected into areas other than deep muscle or vein. SEE: illus.; *gangrene*; *mortification*.

necrotizing (nek′rŏ-tīz″ing), *adj.*

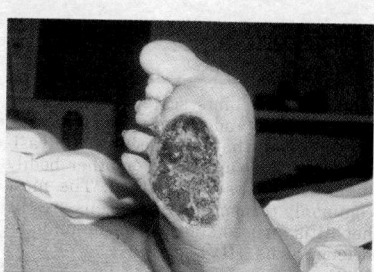

NECROSIS

Necrotic wound of the foot

acute esophageal n. Necrotizing **esophagitis**.

acute tubular n. ABBR: ATN. Acute damage to the renal tubules; usually due to ischemia associated with shock. SEE: *acute renal failure*.

anemic n. Necrosis due to inadequate blood flow to a body part.

aseptic n. Necrosis without infection, e.g., as a result of trauma or drug use.

avascular n. Osteonecrosis.

caseous n. Necrosis with soft, dry, cheeselike formation, seen in diseases such as tuberculosis or syphilis. SYN: *cheesy n.*

central n. Necrosis that affects only the center of a body part.

cheesy n. Caseous **n.**

coagulation n. Necrosis occurring esp. in infarcts. Coagulation occurs in the necrotic area, converting it into a homogeneous mass and depriving the organ or tissue of blood. SYN: *fibrinous n.; ischemic n.*

colliquative n. Necrosis caused by liquefaction of tissue due to autolysis or bacterial putrefaction. SYN: *liquefactive n.*

dry n. Dry **gangrene**.

embolic n. Necrosis due to an embolic occlusion of an artery.

fat n. Necrosis of fatty tissues, seen, for example, in patients with severe cases of pancreatitis.

fibrinous n. Coagulation **n.**

focal n. Necrosis in small scattered areas, often seen in infection.

gummatous n. Necrosis forming a dry rubbery mass resulting from syphilis.

ischemic n. Coagulation **n.**

liquefactive n. Colliquative **n.**

medial n. Necrosis of cells in the tunica media of an artery.

moist n. Necrosis with softening and wetness of the dead tissue.

postpartum pituitary n. Sheehan syndrome.

putrefactive n. Necrosis due to bacterial decomposition.

radiation n. Necrosis caused by radiation exposure.

subcutaneous fat n. of newborn An inflammatory disorder of unknown cause affecting fat tissue that may occur in the newborn at the site of application of forceps during delivery and occasionally in premature infants.

superficial n. Necrosis affecting only the outer layers of bone or any tissue.

thrombotic n. Necrosis due to thrombus formation.

total n. Necrosis affecting an entire organ or body part.

necrotizing (nek″rŏ-tī′zing) Causing or undergoing necrosis.

necrotizing sialometaplasia (sī″ă-lō-met″ă-plā′zh(ē-)ă) [*sialo-* + *metaplasia*] An ulcerative oral lesion usually found on the palate, caused by inflammation of the salivary glands. It may simulate an oral malignancy.

necrotomy (nĕ-krŏt′ō-mē) [″ + *tome*, incision] **1.** Dissection of a cadaver. **2.** Incision into necrotic tissue.

need (nēd) **1.** Something required, wanted, or essential. **2.** A duty or obligation. **3.** Any disease or condition for which a patient seeks a remedy. **4.** A motivation. **5.** Extreme want or poverty.

needle (nēd′l) A pointed instrument for stitching, ligaturing, puncturing, or cannulating. It may be straight, half-curved, full-curved, semicircular, double-curved (sometimes called "S-" or sigmoid-shaped), double-ended, sharp or blunt-tipped, solid, or hollow. Cutting edge and round point are the two classifications of needles. Cutting edge needles are used in skin and dense tissue; round point needles are used for more delicate operations, esp. on soft tissues. When a needle is used for stitching, the suture material may be attached via an eye, french eye, or more commonly, an easily detachable swaged needle.

aneurysm n. A blunt, curved needle with an eye in the tip used for passing a suture around a vessel.

aspirating n. A needle, usually fitted to a syringe, for withdrawing fluids from a cavity.

atraumatic n. Pencil-point needle.

cataract n. A needle used in removing a cataract.

discission n. A special cataract needle for making multiple cuts into the lens capsule.

Hagedorn n. SEE: *Hagedorn needle*.

hypodermic n. A hollow needle of varying length and diameter used for intradermal, subcutaneous, intramuscular, and intravenous injection.

knife n. A narrow, needle-pointed knife.

ligature n. Aneurysm needle.

obturator n. A device that fits into the lumen of a needle to prevent blockage during the puncture procedure.

pencil-point n. A needle with a tapered tip that does not damage tissue as much as a beveled needle. Pencil-point needles are commonly used in lumbar puncture to reduce leakage of cerebrospinal fluid from the subarachnoid space. SYN: *atraumatic n.*

Reverdin n. SEE: *Reverdin needle.*

scalp vein n. A specially designed needle for the administration of intravenous fluids, with a flat flange on each side to facilitate anchoring it after its placement in a small vein.

stop n. A needle with an eye at its tip, with a flange or shelf extending out from its shank end that prevents the needle from being inserted farther than the shelf.

Tuohy n. SEE: *Tuohy needle.*

needle exchange program A public health program for collecting used hypodermic syringes and exchanging them for sterile ones. Such programs are designed to decrease the spread of diseases (like AIDS and hepatitis C) that are transmitted by the sharing of contaminated needles.

PATIENT CARE: Syringe-exchange programs not only reduce the spread of blood-borne illnesses but also serve as gateways to other vital medical services for patients at risk, e.g., drug abusers who want to stop, or pregnant women, the mentally ill, malnourished, or those who need vaccination. In its position statement on needle exchange and HIV/AIDS, the American Nursing Association states, "nurses support the availability of needle exchange programs (that) include adherence to public health and infection control guidelines, access for referral to treatment and rehabilitative services, and education about the transmission of HIV disease." Health care professionals must be familiar with federal and state laws about needle exchange. Most programs operate by providing a single sterile needle for each contaminated needle brought in by a client. Contaminated needles brought to exchange programs are treated as biomedical waste products and are managed by these programs according to public health guidelines. SYN: *syringe exchange program.*

needleholder (nēd'ĭl-hōld'ĕr) A forceps used to drive a needle with an attached suture into tissue.

needleless intravenous infusion system A device for administering intravenous solutions that permits intravascular access without the necessity of handling a needle. These systems were developed to reduce the number of needle-stick injuries related to traditional intravenous administration of fluids. SEE: *needlestick injury.*

needlestick, needle-stick, needle-stick injury (nēd'ĕl-stik") Accidental penetration of the skin by any sharp object used in health care. It is estimated that more than 600,000 needlesticks occur each year among healthcare providers in the U.S.

⚠️ Needle points, scalpels, sutures, syringes, and other penetrating objects (sharps) that have been used invasively may transmit blood or other bodily fluids from person to person. The most commonly transmitted pathogens are the hepatitis viruses and human immunodeficiency virus (HIV).

PATIENT CARE: Under the provisions of the Needlestick Safety and Prevention Act of 2001, all health care facilities are required to develop exposure and engineering control plans that limit penetrating injuries and are required to maintain logs of such injuries at their facilities.

needling (nēd'lĭng) Inserting an acupuncture needle into the body.

dry n. Intramuscular stimulation.

trigger point dry n. ABBR: TrP-DN. Intramuscular stimulation.

needs assessment SEE: under *assessment.*

Neer test (nēr) A clinical assessment to identify impingement of the rotator cuff tendons beneath the acromion. With the elbow extended, the patient's humerus is placed in internal rotation, and the forearm is pronated. The glenohumeral joint is then passively forced through forward flexion as the scapula is stabilized. The test is positive if the patient experiences pain in the anterior or lateral shoulder, typically above 90 degrees.

NEFA *nonesterified fatty acids.*

negation (nē-gā'shŭn) [L. *negare,* to deny] Denial.

negative (nĕg'ă-tĭv) [L. *negare,* to deny] **1.** Possessing a numerical value that is less than zero. **2.** Lacking results or indicating an absence, as in a test result. **3.** Marked by resistance or retreat.

negative crossmatch In organ transplantation, a lack of reaction between recipient and donor cells.

negative predictive value The proportion of people whose test results are true negatives and who are truly disease free.

negative pressure pulmonary edema SEE: under *edema.*

negative pressure wound therapy, negative-pressure wound therapy Vacuum-assisted wound closure.

negative sign SEE: under *sign.*

negative study SEE: under *study.*

negativism (nĕg'ă-tĭv-ĭzm) **1.** A behavioral peculiarity marked by not performing suggested actions (passive negativism) or in doing the opposite of what one has been asked to do (active negativism). **2.** Pervasive doubt or skepticism. **3.** Pessimism.

neglect (nĕ-glĕkt) **1.** In neurology, absence of perception of—or disregard for—the nondominant part of the body in patients who have had a stroke that has damaged the nondominant hemisphere of the brain. **2.** Inattention to one's responsibilities, esp. to those dependent on one's care.

altitudinal n. Unilateral **inattention.**

hemispatial n. Unilateral **inattention.**

negligence The failure of a health care professional to meet his or her responsibilities to a patient, with resultant injury. There are four elements of negligence: duty owed, breach of duty or standard of care, proximate cause or causal connection (between the breach and damages), and damages or injuries or harm. Medical professionals are legally liable for their own negligence or can be held liable for negligence of others of which they have knowledge but fail to report or intercede.

comparative n. SEE: *comparative negligence.*

contributory n. In forensic medicine, the concept that the plantiff's negligence in combination with the defendant's negligence is the cause of the plaintiff's injuries or damages.

corporate n. Failure of a corporation to meet its legal obligations to its clients. With regard to health care facilities, responsibilities included under the doctrine of corporate negligence are monitoring and supervision of the competence of medical and nursing personnel within the facility; investigating physicians' credentials before granting staff privileges; and negligent hiring of health care professionals (including failure to conduct appropriate background investigations).

gross n. Any voluntary, intentional, and conscious act or omission committed by an individual, with reckless disregard for the consequences, esp. how they may affect another person's life or property.

ordinary n. Failure to exercise the care that an ordinary prudent person would exercise under similar circumstances.

negotiation (nĕ-gō″shē-ā′shŭn) [L. *negotium,* business] A form of conflict resolution in which two or more parties discuss their differences in the hope of reaching a mutually acceptable conclusion. SEE: *alternative dispute resolution; conflict resolution.*

Negri bodies (nā′grē) [Adelchi Negri, It. physician, 1876–1912] Inclusion bodies found in the cells of the central nervous system of animals infected with rabies. They are acidophilic masses appearing in large ganglion cells or in cells of the brain, esp. those of the hippocampus and cerebellum. Their presence is considered conclusive proof of rabies.

NEI *National Eye Institute.*

Neisseria (nī-sē′rē-ă) [Albert Neisser, Ger. physician, 1855–1916] A genus of gram-negative diplococci of the family Neisseriaceae. The most significant human pathogens are *Neisseria meningitidis* (the meningococcus) and *Neisseria gonorrhoeae* (the gonococcus)

N. catarrhalis SEE: under *Moraxella catarrhalis.*

N. gonorrhoeae The species causing gonorrhea. SYN: *gonococcus.* SEE: *gonorrhea.*

N. meningitidis The species causing epidemic cerebrospinal meningitis. SEE: *meningitis.*

N. sicca Species found in mucous membrane of the respiratory tract. Occasionally, this species may cause bacterial endocarditis.

Neisseriaceae (nīs-sē″rē-ā′sē-ē) A family of bacteria that are spherical, gram-negative, and nonmotile.

Nélaton line (nā-lă-ton′) [Auguste Nélaton, Fr. surgeon, 1807–1873] A line from the anterior superior spine of the ilium to the tuberosity of the ischium.

Nemathelminthes (nĕm″ă-thĕl-mĭn′thēz) The phylum of the roundworms.

nematocide (nĕm′ă-tō-sīd″) [Gr. *nema,* thread, + L. *caedere,* to kill] An agent that kills nematodes.

nematocyst (nĕm′ă-tō-sĭst) [″ + *kystis,* bladder] The small stinging barb present in jellyfish and some other coelenterates. It can penetrate the skin of saltwater swimmers or divers and cause painful stings. In some rare cases, multiple contact can be fatal.

Nematoda (nĕm″ă-tō′dă) [″ + *eidos,* form, shape] A class of the phylum Nemathelminthes that includes the true roundworms or threadworms, many species of which are parasitic. They are cylindrical or spindle-shaped worms that possess a resistant cuticle, have a complete alimentary canal, and lack a true coelom. The sexes usually are separate, and development usually is direct and simple.

nematode (nĕm′ă-tōd) [Gr. *nema,* thread, + *eidos,* form, shape] A member of the class Nematoda. **nematoid,** *adj.*

nematodiasis (nĕm″ă-tō-dī′ă-sĭs) [″ + ″ + *-iasis,* condition] Infestation by a parasite belonging to the class Nematoda.

nematology (nĕm″ă-tŏl′ō-jē) The division of parasitology that deals with worms belonging to the class Nematoda.

neo- [Gr. *neos,* new] Prefix meaning *new, recent.*

neoadjuvant therapy (nē″ō-ad′joo-vănt) In treating cancer, the use of chemotherapy before radiation or surgery.

neoantigen (nē″ō-ăn′tĭ-jĕn) [″ + *anti,*

against, + *gennan,* to produce] A nonspecific term for various tumor antigens.

neobladder (nē-ō-blăd′dĕr) A surgically constructed urinary reservoir, usually made from a segment of small bowel, that is used to replace a bladder removed during radical cystectomy. It is surgically connected to the patient's natural urethra and, typically, maintains urinary continence, and limits or eliminates the need for self-catheterization. Neobladders are often used after bladder cancer surgery as an alternative to a urostomy. They cannot be used in patients whose malignancy involves the distal urethra.

neoblastic (nē′ō-blăs′tĭk) [″ + *blastos,* germ] Pert. to or constituting a new growth of tissue.

neocerebellum (nē″ō-sĕr-ĕ-bĕl′ŭm) [Gr. *neos,* new, + L. *cerebellum,* little brain] The portion of the corpus cerebelli of the cerebellum that lies between the primary and prepyramidal fissures and consists principally of the ansiform lobules. Phylogenetically, it develops last, in conjunction with the cerebral cortex, and is concerned with the integration of voluntary movements. It is the posterior lobe of the cerebellum.

neocortex (nē″ō-kor′teks) [*neo-* + *cortex*] The nonolfactory portion of the cerebral cortex. It is composed of six layers of neurons and nerve fibers having a similar distribution pattern. Phylogenetically, it is the new part of the cerebral cortex. SYN: *isocortex.*

neodymium (nē″ō-dim′ē-ŭm) SYMB: Nd. A shiny, silvery, rare-earth element, atomic weight 144.24, atomic number 60.

neoformation (nē″ō-for-mā′shŭn) [″ + L. *formatio,* a shaping] **1.** Regeneration. **2.** A neoplasm or new growth.

neogenesis (nē-ō-jĕn′ĕ-sĭs) [″ + *genesis,* generation, birth] Regeneration; reformation, as of tissue. **neogenetic** (nē″ō-jĕn-ĕt′ĭk), *adj.*

neointima (nē″ō-ĭn′tĭ-mă) New growth of intimal tissue.

neointimal hyperplasia (nē″ō-ĭn′tĭ-măl) [*neo-* + *intima*] SEE: under *hyperplasia.*

neologism (nē-ŏl′ă-jĭzm) [″ + *logos,* word, reason, + *-ismos,* state] **1.** A newly invented word. **2.** A nonsensical word, or verbal tic, the use of which is sometimes associated with neuropsychiatric disorders, such as psychoses or Tourette syndrome.

neomembrane (nē-ō-mĕm′brān) [″ + L. *membrana,* membrane] Pseudomembrane.

neon (nē′on″) [Gr. *neos,* new] SYMB: Ne. A chemical element, one of the noble gases, atomic weight (mass) 20.183, atomic number 10. Neon makes up only 18 parts per million parts of air. SEE: *noble gas.*

neonatal (nē″ō-nāt′ăl) [*neo-* + *natal*] Pert. to the first 28 days after birth.

neonatal abstinence syndrome Any of the adverse consequences in the newborn of exposure to addictive or dangerous intoxicants during fetal development. The consequences include preterm delivery, intrauterine growth retardation, asphyxia, low birth weight, drug withdrawal symptoms after delivery, and behavioral, psychiatric, and learning disabilities later in life.

neonatal hemochromatosis ABBR: NH. A rare congenital disorder causing iron overload in the fetus and newborn, resulting in intrauterine growth retardation, premature birth, end-stage liver disease at birth, or intrauterine death.

neonatal mortality rate SEE: under *rate.*

neonate (nē′ō-nāt) A newborn infant up to 1 month of age. SEE: *Nursing Diagnoses Appendix.*

neonaticide (nē″ō-nāt′ĭ-sīd″) [″ + (hom)icide] Killing of a newborn child, usually during the first day of life.

neonatologist (nē″ō-nă-tŏl′ō-jĭst) [″ + ″ + Gr. *logos,* word, reason] A physician who specializes in the study, care, and treatment of neonates.

neonatology (nē″ō-nă-tŏl′ō-jē) The study, care, and treatment of neonates.

neophallus (nē″ō-făl′ŭs) [Gr. *neos,* new, + *phallos,* penis] A surgically constructed penis, made, e.g., from tissue grafts taken from other parts of the body.

neopharynx (nē-ō-făr′ĭnks) A surgically reconstructed pharynx. The surgery reestablishes the integrity of the throat after laryngectomy.

neoplasia (nē″ō-plā′zh(ē-)ă) [*neo-* + *-plasia*] The development of neoplasms (new tissues or tumors).

  anal intraepithelial n. ABBR: AIN. A precancerous change in the squamous cells of the anus that may eventually develop into anorectal cancer. It is similar to cervical intraepithelial neoplasia in that it is a premalignant lesion that arises in squamous cells, is found primarily in sexually active people, and is associated with human papillomavirus and HIV. SYN: *anal **dysplasia;** anal squamous intraepithelial lesion.*

  cervical intraepithelial n. ABBR: CIN. Dysplasia of the basal layers of the squamous epithelium of the uterine cervix. This may progress to involve deeper layers of the epithelium. Grades 1, 2, and 3 represent increasing progression of the pathological process. Grade 3 (CIN 3) represents carcinoma in situ. CIN 3 is also classed stage 0 of cancer of the cervix. SEE: *Bethesda System, The; cervical cancer.*

  intraepithelial n. Abnormal cell

growth that is found within epithelial cells but has not yet spread to neighboring, underlying, or distant tissues. Intraepithelial neoplasia is thought to be an early marker of some cancers, e.g., breast, prostate, or uterine cervix. SEE: *cervical intraepithelial* **n.**

multiple endocrine n. ABBR: MEN. Any of several inherited syndromes caused by a defect in tumor suppressor genes that produces benign and malignant tumors of many endocrine glands. Angiofibromas and collagenomas of the skin also are common findings. This group of diseases has been classed according to the glands affected. SYN: *multiple endocrine* **neoplasm**.

multiple endocrine n., type I ABBR: MEN I. Multiple endocrine neoplasia in which there are tumors of the parathyroid, pituitary, and islet cells of the pancreas. SYN: *Wermer syndrome*.

multiple endocrine n., type II Multiple endocrine neoplasia characterized by medullary thyroid carcinoma, pheochromocytoma, and parathyroid hyperplasia. SYN: *Sipple syndrome*.

multiple endocrine n., type III Multiple endocrine neoplasia that is similar to MEN II but in which there are marked facial aberrations with neuromas of the conjunctiva, labial mucosa, tongue, larynx, and gastric intestinal tract.

vaginal intraepithelial n. ABBR: VAIN. Vulvar intraepiethelial **n.**

vulvar intraepithelial n. ABBR: VIN. Precancerous, noninvasive lesions of the squamous epithelium of the vulva.

SYMPTOMS: Symptoms are vulvar pain, itching, or burning. Risk factors include exposure to human papilloma virus 16 and 18, herpes simplex virus 2, and smoking.

DIAGNOSIS: Diagnosis is made by biopsy of the lesion.

TREATMENT: Treatments include brief observation to see if the condition spontaneously remits, topically applied chemotherapy, laser ablation, or wide surgical excision. SYN: *vaginal intraepithelial* **n.**

neoplasm (nē′ŏ-plazm)   [*neo-* + *-plasm*]   A tumor or abnormal clump of tissue that may be benign or malignant. It serves no useful function but grows at the expense of the healthy organism. **neoplastic** (nē″ŏ-plas′tik), *adj*.

benign n. Growth not spreading by metastases or infiltration of tissue.

histoid n. Neoplasm in which structure resembles the tissues and elements that surround it.

malignant n. Growth that infiltrates tissue, metastasizes, and often recurs after attempts at surgical removal. SYN: *cancer*.

mixed n. Neoplasm composed of tissues from two of the germinal layers.

multiple endocrine n. Multiple endocrine **neoplasia**.

noninvasive n. A tumor that has not spread or does not spread.

organoid n. Neoplasm in which the structure is similar to that of some organ of the body.

neoplastic (nē″ŏ-plas′tik) [*neo-* + *plastic* (2)] Pert. to neoplasia or to a neoplasm. **neoplastically** (ti-k(ă-)lē), *adv*.

Neorickettsia (nē″ŏ-rĭ-kĕt′sēă) [″ + ″] A genus of bacteria of the family Anaplasmataceae. They are intracellular parasites transmitted to mammals by insect or animal vectors, including trematodes that infest salmon and trout.

neostomy (nē-ŏs′tō-mē) [″ + *stoma*, mouth] Surgical formation of artificial opening into an organ or between two organs.

neostriatum (nē″ŏ-strī-ā′tŭm) [″ + L. *striatum*, grooved] The caudate nucleus and the putamen considered together.

neoteny (nē-ŏt′ĕ-nē) [″ + *teinein*, to extend] Sexual maturation in larvae.

neotropics (nē″ŏ-trop′iks) [*neo-* + *tropics*] That portion of the Western hemisphere that extends between the Tropic of Cancer and the Tropic of Capricorn. It includes southern Mexico, Central America, the West Indies, and parts of South America. Its unique climate and geography favor the growth of a variety of animals, plants, and microbial species not found in more temperate regions. Living in or traveling to the neotropics predisposes people from other geographic areas to a wide variety of illnesses, e.g., parasitic diseases, not normally found farther north or south.

neovascular (nē″ŏ-văs′kū-lăr) Pert. to new blood vessels.

neovascularization (nē″ŏ-văs″kū-lă-rĭ-zā′shŭn) The formation of new blood vessels, e.g., in the retina, in inflamed tissue or in a malignant tumor.

neper (nē′pĕr, nā′) [John Napier, Scot. mathematician, 1550–1617] ABBR: Np. A unit of measure denoting the ratio of two amplitudes. It is similar to the decibel but is expressed as a natural logarithm instead of a logarithm of the base 10. 1 Np = 8.687 dB.

nephelometer (nef″ĕ-lom′ĕt-ĕr) [Gr. *nephelē*, cloud + *-meter*] A device used to measure the turbidity of a fluid and estimate the number of particles in solution. For example, it is used to measure the turbidity of a fluid and also may be used to estimate the degree of contamination of air by particulate matter. SEE: *turbidimeter*.

nephelometry (nef″ĕ-lom′ĕ-trē) [Gr. *nephelē*, cloud + *-metry*] A technique for detecting proteins in body fluids, based on the tendency of proteins to scatter light in identifiable ways. SEE: *turbidimetry*.

nephralgia (nĕ-frăl'jē-ă) [" + *algos*, pain] Renal pain. **nephralgic** (nĕ-frăl'jĭk), *adj.*

nephrectomy (nĕ-frĕk'tō-mē) [" + *ektome*, excision] Surgical removal of a kidney, e.g., to remove a renal cell carcinoma or injured organ, or to harvest an organ for transplantation. The surgery may be performed with a large, open incision or laparoscopically. Complications sometimes include spontaneous pneumothorax, infection, azotemia, or secondary hemorrhage. SEE: *Nursing Diagnoses Appendix*.

PATIENT CARE: The patient is prepared for surgery according to protocol. Aspirin or other medications that may cause postoperative hemorrhage are withheld. The patient and family are assured that, in most instances, the body will adapt to functioning with only one kidney. Postoperatively, vital signs are checked frequently; analgesics are administered (often by intravenous or epidural patient-controlled analgesia); and excessive bleeding is reported. Dressings are changed according to the surgeon's directions or agency protocol. Fluid intake and output, body weight, and electrolytes are carefully monitored. Hemodynamics are monitored closely; the patient is assessed for evidence of post-operative complications such as stroke, myocardial infarction, pneumonia, or atelectasis. The patient is encouraged to breathe deeply (using incentive spirometry) and to cough to prevent atelectasis and other pulmonary complications. Oral hygiene is provided, and early fluid and food intake encouraged. Antithrombotic or sequential compression hose are applied, and the patient is assisted to turn and move in bed. Positioning on the surgical side helps other organs fill operative dead space. Early ambulation is encouraged, usually within 24 hr. Discharge teaching focuses on the components of a renal diet (if necessary), incisional care, recommended activities and restrictions, medications, and the need for follow-up.

abdominal n. Nephrectomy through an incision in the abdominal wall.

paraperitoneal n. Removal of a kidney through an extraperitoneal incision.

nephric (nĕf'rĭk) [Gr. *nephros*, kidney] Pert. to the kidney or kidneys. SYN: *renal*.

nephritic (nĕ-frĭt'ĭk) **1.** Pert. to the kidney. **2.** Pert. to nephritis. **3.** An agent used to treat nephritis.

nephritis (nĕ-frīt'ĭs, nē-frīt'ĭ-dēz") *pl.* **nephritides** [*nephr-* + *-itis*] Inflammation of the kidneys. The condition, whether either acute or chronic, is caused by bacteria or their toxins (e.g., pyelonephritis), autoimmune disorders (e.g., poststreptococcal glomerulonephritis, systemic lupus erythematosus), or toxic chemicals (e.g., pesticides, mercury, arsenic, lead, alcohol). The glomeruli, tubules, interstitial tissues, and renal pelvis may be affected.

PATIENT CARE: Renal function is assessed by measuring serum creatinine, blood urea nitrogen, and urine creatinine clearance levels. Signs of renal failure (oliguria, azotemia, acidosis) are reported. Hemoglobin, hematocrit, electrolyte levels, intake and output of fluids, and body weights are monitored. The health care provider observes, records, and reports hematuria and monitors blood pressure using the same cuff, arm, and position each time. Antihypertensive drugs are administered as prescribed. The patient is encouraged to maintain adequate hydration and follow the prescribed dietary restrictions, which may include limits on the amounts of sodium, potassium, fluid volume, and protein ingested. Intravenous fluid intake is monitored. Complications of hypertension are anticipated and prevented.

acute n. An inflammatory nephritis involving the glomeruli, the tubules, or the entire kidney. It may be degenerative, diffuse, suppurative, hemorrhagic, interstitial, or parenchymal, depending upon the portion of the kidney involved.

analgesic n. Analgesic nephropathy.

chronic n. A progressive nephritis in which the entire structure of the kidney or only the glomerular or tubular processes may be affected.

glomerular n. Glomerulonephritis.

hereditary n. Alport syndrome.

interstitial n. Nephritis associated with pathological changes in the renal interstitial tissue. The diseased tissue may be primary or due to a toxic agent such as a drug or chemical. Common findings include fever, rash, itch, and eosinophiles in the urine. The result is the destruction of the nephrons and serious impairment of renal function.

scarlatinal n. Acute glomerulonephritis complicating scarlet fever.

suppurative n. Nephritis associated with abscesses in the kidney.

transfusion n. Renal failure and tubular disease caused by transfusion of incompatible blood.

tubulointerstitial n. Pyelonephritis.

nephritogenic (nĕ-frĭt"ō-jĕn'ĭk) [" + *gennan*, to produce] Causing nephritis.

nephro-, nephr- [Gr. *nephros*, kidney] Prefixes meaning *kidney*. SEE: *reno-*.

nephroblastoma (nĕf'rō-blăs-tō'mă) [" + *blastos*, germ, + *oma*, tumor] Wilms tumor.

nephrocalcinosis (nĕf-rō"kăl"sĭn-ō'sĭs) The

deposition of calcium phosphate in the renal tubules.

nephrogenetic (nĕf″rō-jĕn-ĕt′ĭk) [″ + *gennan,* to produce] Arising in or from the renal organs; capable of giving rise to kidney tissue.

nephrolithiasis (nĕf″rō-lĭth-ī′ă-sĭs) The presence of calculi (stones) in the kidney. SEE: *calculus, renal.*

nephrolithotomy (nĕf″rō-lĭth-ŏt′ō-mē) [″ + *lithos,* stone, + *tome,* incision] Renal incision for removal of kidney stones.

nephrology (nĕ-frŏl′ă-jē) [″ + ″] The branch of medical science concerned with the structure and function of the kidneys and the prevention and treatment of kidney disease.

nephroma (nĕ-frō′mă) [″ + *oma,* tumor] Renal tumor.

nephron (nĕf′rŏn) [Gr. *nephros,* kidney] The structural and functional unit of the kidney, consisting of a renal (malpighian) corpuscle (a glomerulus enclosed within Bowman's capsule), the proximal convoluted tubule, the loop of Henle, and the distal convoluted tubule. These connect by arched collecting tubules with straight collecting tubules. Urine is formed by filtration in renal corpuscles and selective reabsorption and secretion by the cells of the renal tubule. There are approx. one million nephrons in each kidney. SEE: *kidney* for illus.; *malpighian capsule; urine.*

nephronophthisis [*nephron* + *phthisis*] ABBR: NPH, NPHP. Any of a group of autosomal recessive cystic diseases of the kidneys that may result in juvenile-onset renal failure.

nephropathia epidemica (nĕf″rō-păth′ē-ă ĕp″ĭ-dĕm′ĭ-kă, -dĕm′) [NL, "epidemic nephropathy"] ABBR: NE. A mosquito-borne viral infection found almost exclusively in northern Europe, e.g., Finland and Sweden. Its principal symptoms are fever, abdominal pain, and renal failure.

nephropathy (nĕ-frŏp′ă-thē) [*nephro-* + *-pathy*] Disease of the kidney. It includes inflammatory (nephritis), degenerative (nephrosis), and sclerotic lesions of the kidney.

   analgesic n. Damage to the tubules and interstitium of the kidneys due to overuse of pain relievers such as acetaminophen, aspirin, ibuprofen, or phenacetin.

   cast n. Deterioration in kidney function resulting from the deposition of immunoglobulin light chains (and other proteins) in the distal kidney tubules. SYN: *myeloma kidney.*

   diabetic n. Proteinuria (or microalbuminuria) in a patient with long-standing diabetes mellitus. The disease is often accompanied by high blood pressure, and, eventually, chronic kidney disease. In the U.S. it is the most common cause of end-stage kidney disease.

   TREATMENT: It may be delayed or prevented with scrupulous control of blood glucose and hemoglobin A1c levels, and by controlling blood pressure with angiotensin-converting enzyme inhibitors or angiotensin receptor blockers.

   HIV-associated n. ABBR: HIVAN. Renal failure with nephrotic-range (massive) protein loss in the urine caused by infection of the kidneys with HIV. Biopsy of kidneys of affected patients reveals focal segmental glomerulosclerosis.

   hypercalcemic n. Renal damage due to hypercalcemia. It is usually caused by hyperparathyroidism; sarcoidosis; excess intake of vitamin D; excess use of calcium-containing antacids; multiple myeloma; malignant disease; and, occasionally, by immobilization or Paget disease.

   hypokalemic n. Renal damage due to abnormal depletion of potassium, regardless of the basic cause of the electrolyte abnormality. Characteristically, there are multiple vacuoles in microscopic sections of the renal tubular epithelium. Clinically, the patient is unable to concentrate urine. Therapy for the primary cause of the hypokalemia may allow the kidney lesions to become completely reversed.

   immunoglobulin A n. ABBR: IgA n. A form of glomerulonephritis in which immunoglobulin A molecules are deposited in the glomeruli. The disease, more common in males than females, may eventually cause renal failure in as many as 40% of patients. It is treated with glucocorticoids. SYN: *Berger disease.* SEE: *glomerulonephritis.*

   membranous n. A glomerular disease of unknown cause that produces nephrotic syndrome. It may be distinguished from lipoid nephrosis by immunofluorescence and electron microscopy. SEE: *glomerular disease; nephrotic syndrome.*

   TREATMENT: Treatment consists of corticosteroids with or without other immunosuppressive drugs.

   obstructive n. Kidney damage resulting from the blockage of urinary blood flow out of the kidneys, ureters, or bladder, e.g. as a result of prostatic hyperplasia, or a tumor compressing urinary outflow. It can be identified by bladder scanning, which will reveal a large amount of retained urine or by ultrasonography of the kidneys, which will show hydronephrosis.

   phosphate n. Precipitation of phosphate crystals in the renal tubules, e.g., after phosphate-containing laxatives are administered.

   pigment n. Injury to the kidney that

results from the deposition of myoglobin and other myocyte debris in rhabdomyolysis. It is suggested by the identification of blood on urine dipstick testing in the absence of red blood cells on urine microscopy..

radiocontrast-induced n. Nephropathy caused by the use of radiological contrast media, e.g., the dye used during angiography. It is usually defined as one of the following: an increase in the serum creatinine of 0.5 mg/dL within 48 hr of exposure to contrast agents when no other cause is apparent; a decrease in renal function of 25%; or any deterioration in renal function that results in clinically significant adverse effects on a patient's health.

PATIENT CARE: Kidney damage due to injected contrast occurs most often in people who are dehydrated or have diabetes mellitus, heart failure, impaired renal blood flow or kidney disease, liver failure, or multiple myeloma. It sometimes results in serious illness and death, increased hospital length of stay, and end-stage renal disease. Health care professionals should acquire complete medical histories and baseline blood tests to identify at-risk patients. Aggressive preprocedure hydration with sodium bicarbonate in saline decreases the incidence of radiocontrast nephropathy (RCN) in at-risk patients. Maintaining a urine volume more than 150 mL/hr before, during, and after contrast-requiring procedures reduces the rate of RCN significantly.

reflux n. Chronic kidney disease due to kidney damage from vesicoureteral reflux (and repeated episodes of pyelonephritis).

nephropexy (nĕf′rō-pĕks-ē) [″ + *pexis*, fixation] Surgical fixation of a floating kidney.

nephroprotective (nef″rō-prŏ-tek′tiv) [*nephro-* + *protective*] Pert. to the preservation of kidney function, esp. when the kidneys are exposed to unusual or unique stresses. **nephroprotection** (′shŏn), *n.*

nephros (nĕf′rŏs) [Gr.] The kidney.

nephrosclerosis (nef″rō-sklĕ-rō′sĭs) [*nephro-* + *sclerosis*] Hardening of the connective tissues of the kidneys. SYN: *renal sclerosis*.

arterial n. Arteriosclerosis of the renal arteries resulting in ischemia, atrophy of parenchyma, and fibrosis of the kidney.

arteriolar n. Sclerosis of the smaller renal arterioles, esp. the afferent glomerular arterioles with resulting fibrosis, ischemic necrosis, and glomerular degeneration and failure. This type of nephrosclerosis occurs in most cases of essential hypertension.

malignant n. Nephrosclerosis that

develops rapidly in patients with severe hypertension. SEE: *hypertension.*

nephroscope (nĕf′-ră-skōp″) A rigid or flexible endoscope used to inspect and/or treat conditions present inside the urinary tract.

nephrosis (nĕf-rō′sĭs) *pl.* **nephroses** **1.** Clinical classification of kidney disease in which protein loss is so extensive that edema and hypoproteinemia are produced. **2.** Degenerative changes in the kidneys, esp. the renal tubules, without the occurrence of inflammation. SEE: *nephrotic syndrome.*

amyloid n. A nephrotic syndrome from amyloid deposits in the kidney.

lipoid n. Idiopathic nephrotic syndrome.

nephrosonephritis (nĕ-frō″sō-nĕ-frīt′ĭs) [*nephros(is)* + *nephritis*] Renal disease with characteristics of nephritis and nephrosis.

hemorrhagic n. An acute infectious disease caused by the Hanta virus, with abrupt onset of fever that lasts 3 to 8 days, conjunctival injection, prostration, anorexia, and vomiting. Renal involvement may be mild or progress to acute renal failure, which may last several weeks. The mode of transmission is unknown but is apparently not from person to person. The incubation period varies from 9 to 35 days. Shock and renal failure should be treated symptomatically. There is no specific therapy. SYN: *epidemic hemorrhagic **fever**; Korean hemorrhagic **fever**.*

nephrostomy (nĕ-frŏs′tō-mē) The formation of an artificial fistula into the renal pelvis. It may be used to drain an obstructed kidney or relieve hydronephrosis.

percutaneous n. The placement of a catheter into the renal pelvis from the posterolateral aspect of the body below the 11th rib using radiologic guidance.

nephrotic (nĕ-frŏt′ĭk) [Gr. *nephros*, kidney] Pert. to or caused by nephrosis.

nephrotic syndrome ABBR: NS. A condition marked by increased renal glomerular permeability to proteins, resulting in massive loss of proteins in the urine, edema, hypoalbuminemia, hyperlipidemia, and hypercoagulability. Several types of glomerular injury can cause the syndrome, including membranous glomerulopathy, minimal-change disease (lipoid nephrosis), focal segmental glomerulosclerosis, glomerulonephritis, and membranoproliferative glomerulonephritis. These pathological findings in the kidney result from a broad array of diseases such as diabetic injury to the glomerulus, amyloidosis, immune-complex deposition disease, vasculitis, systemic lupus erythematosus, allergic reactions, infections, and toxic injury to the kidneys by drugs or heavy metals. The prognosis depends on the cause. For example, if the cause is exposure to a drug or toxin, the removal of that substance may be curative. When the disease results from glomerulosclerosis caused by AIDS, death may occur within months. Renal biopsy is usually needed to determine the precise histological cause, treatment, and prognosis. Idiopathic NS is diagnosed when the known causes of NS have been excluded. It is usually diagnosed in adults by use of renal biopsy. Causes are classified according to the changes found in the capillaries of the glomerulus when examined by use of electron microscopy. SEE: *proteinuria; Nursing Diagnoses Appendix.*

SYMPTOMS: Patients with nephrotic syndrome may initially present with fluid retention in the legs (occasionally with presacral or periorbital edema) or symptoms caused by blood clotting, e.g., in the renal vein. The hyperlipidemia that often accompanies the syndrome may lead to symptoms caused by atherosclerosis.

TREATMENT: Angiotensin-converting enzyme inhibitors significantly reduce the degree of protein loss. Diuretics are used to treat symptomatic edema, antibiotics to treat infection. Anticoagulants may be used to treat and prevent clotting. Antihypertensive agents and lipid-lowering medications are used to prevent atherosclerotic complications. Renally tailored diets, with defined quantities of sodium, potassium, and protein, often are recommended.

Corticosteroids and immunosuppressive drugs (such as cyclophosphamide, cyclosporin A, or tacrolimus) are used to manage nephrosis caused by some histological subtypes. Infusions of salt-poor albumin help to replace protein. When renal failure accompanies nephrotic syndrome, dialysis may be required.

PATIENT CARE: Patients are weighed every day at the same time (usually on awakening) and fluid intake and output checked at that time so that changes in fluid retention can be documented, and, if necessary, remediated. The skin over edematous areas must be handled carefully to prevent trauma. Urine protein levels are checked frequently. Because of the loss of protein through the urine and lack of appetite, patients with nephrosis often have protein-calorie malnutrition. Many patients find it difficult to adjust to the low-sodium, moderate-to-low–protein, low-potassium diet recommended for disease management. Small, frequent meals using as many of the patients' food preferences as possible may help improve nutritional status. Antithrombotic stockings are provided and incentive spirometry and leg exercises, and other preventive activities are encouraged. Symptoms such as leg pain, pleuritic chest pain, or shortness of breath should be evaluated carefully for evidence of thromboses. Psychosocial support is often needed by patients to help them cope with the changes in their appearance and functioning that accompany the edema.

nephrotomogram (nĕf″rō-tō′mō-grăm) A tomogram of the kidney.

nephrotomography (nĕf″rō-tō-mŏg′ră-fē) [″ + ″ + *graphein*, to write] Tomograph of the kidney after the intravenous injection of a radiopaque contrast medium that is excreted by the kidney.

nephrotomy (nĕ-frŏt′ō-mē) [″ + *tome*, incision] Surgical incision of the kidney.

nephrotoxin (nef″rŏ-tok′sĭn) [*nephro-* + *toxin*] A substance that is toxic to and damages kidney tissues. Common nephrotoxins include aminoglycoside antibiotics (such as amikacin, gentamicin, or tobramycin), glycopeptide antibiotics (vancomycin), nonsteroidal anti-inflammatory drugs (such as indomethacin), lead (as in moonshine [whiskey] and some paints), and some ionic radiocontrast agents.

nephrotropic (nĕf″rō-trŏp′ĭk) [″ + *tropos*, turning] **1.** Affecting the kidneys. **2.** An agent or drug that exerts its effect on the kidneys or renal function.

neptunium (nep-too′nē-ŭm, -tū′) [*Neptune* (the planet) + *-ium*] SYMB: Np. A radioactive chemical element obtained by bombarding uranium with neutrons, atomic weight (mass) 237, atomic number 93.

nerve (nĕrv) [L. *nervus,* sinew] Parallel axons running together inside a thick connective tissue sheath (an epineurium). In the nerve, axons are wrapped into small bundles by thin connective tissue sheaths (endoneuria); each small bundle of axons is called a fascicle. The neuronal cell bodies of a nerve's axons are in the brain, the spinal cord, or ganglia, but the nerves run only in the peripheral nervous system. Nerves with axons that conduct electrochemical impulses toward the CNS are afferent, nerves with axons that conduct impulses away from the CNS are efferent, and nerves with both afferent and efferent axons are mixed. Nerves in the peripheral nervous system are roughly analogous to tracts in the CNS and, like tracts, act as highways that axons can join or leave on the way from their origin to their target. SEE: *ansa; cell; nervus.* illus.

SYMPTOMS: A broad array of insults may damage nerves, including direct trauma, repetitive motion injuries, compression by neighboring structures, gly-

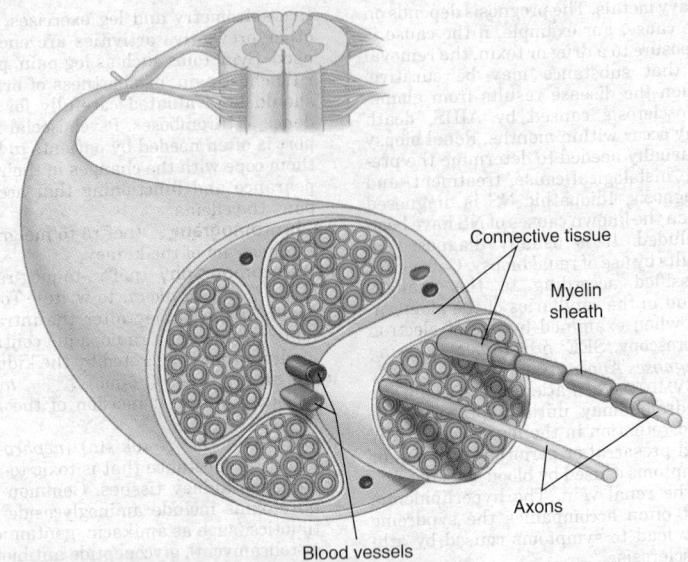

Connective tissue

Myelin
sheath

Axons

Blood vessels

NERVE STRUCTURE

cosylation, infections, drugs, toxins, and paraneoplastic syndromes. Symptoms of nerve injury include paresthesias, loss of sensation and position sense, impaired motor function, cranial nerve malfunction, changes in reflexes, and impairments in glandular secretion.

TESTS FOR LOSS OF FUNCTION: The assessment of nerve injury includes a careful neurological examination, sometimes accompanied by tests, e.g., electromyography or nerve conduction studies.

abducens n. A somatic motor nerve originating in the abducens nucleus in the pons. It runs in the subarachnoid space and the cavernous sinus inside the skull, enters the back of the orbit through the superior orbital fissure, and innervates the lateral rectus muscle. SYN: *abducent n.; sixth cranial n.* SEE: *cranial n.*

abducent n. Abducens **n.**

accessory n. Spinal accessory nerve. SEE: *cranial nerve* for illus.

acoustic n. Auditory **n.** SEE: illus.

adrenergic n. A nerve that uses a catecholamine as its main neurotransmitter.

afferent n. A nerve that conducts impulses toward the brain or spinal cord. SEE: *sensory n.*

alveolar n. Any of the sensory nerves to the teeth; they are branches of the trigeminal nerve (CN V). The superior alveolar nerves innervate the upper teeth and gingivae; the inferior alveolar nerves innervate the lower teeth and gingivae. The anterior superior alveolar nerves, branches of the infraorbital

nerve (from CN V2), run in canals in the anterior wall of the maxillary sinus and innervate the upper incisors, canines, premolars, and often part of the first molar. Sometimes there is a middle superior alveolar nerve that innervates the premolars and first molar. The posterior superior alveolar nerves (also from CN V2) innervate the rest of the upper molars. The inferior alveolar nerve (from CN V3) runs in the mandibular canal, giving off branches to the lower teeth and gingivae as it passes. SYN: *dental n.*

antebrachial cutaneous n. SEE: *lateral antebrachial cutaneous n.; medial antebrachial cutaneous n.; posterior antebrachial cutaneous n.*

auditory n. The component of the vestibulocochlear nerve (CN VIII) that carries axons conveying sound information between the spiral ganglion in the inner ear and the cochlear nuclei in the brainstem. SYN: *acoustic n.; cochlear n.*

auricular n. Any of three nerves, the great auricular nerve, the posterior auricular nerve, or the auricular branch of the vagus nerve (CN X). The great auricular nerve is a sensory branch of the cervical plexus composed of axons from spinal cord segments C2–C3; it innervates the skin and fascia behind the ear, on the lower part of the pinna of the ear, and over the angle of the jaw. The posterior auricular nerve is a motor branch of the facial nerve (CN VII) that innervates the posterior and intrinsic auricular muscles. The auricular branch of the vagus nerve is a sensory nerve

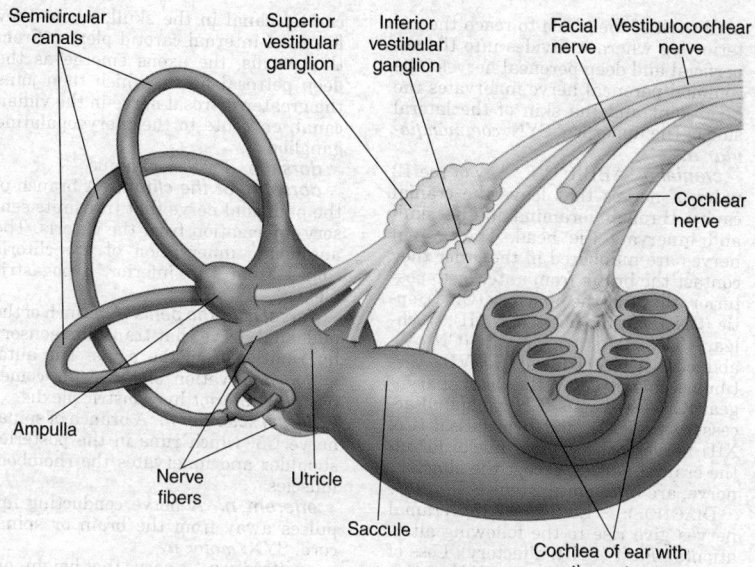

Semicircular canals · Superior vestibular ganglion · Inferior vestibular ganglion · Facial nerve · Vestibulocochlear nerve · Cochlear nerve · Ampulla · Nerve fibers · Utricle · Saccule · Cochlea of ear with portion cut away

ACOUSTIC NERVE (8th CRANIAL)

emerging from the superior ganglion of the vagus nerve, joined by branches from the glossopharyngeal (CN IX) and facial nerves, and innervating the lower part of the tympanic membrane and the floor of the external auditory canal.

autonomic n. A visceral motor (visceral efferent) nerve, innervating smooth muscle, cardiac muscle, or glands. Visceral motor nerves can contain pre- or postganglionic sympathetic or parasympathetic axons. Visceral sensory (visceral afferent) axons can run in autonomic or somatic nerves.

axillary n. A mixed nerve of the posterior upper arm originating in the posterior cord of the brachial plexus and composed of axons from spinal cord segments C5-C6.

SENSORY: It innervates skin over the shoulder joint and the lower portion of the deltoid muscle.

MOTOR: It innervates the teres minor and deltoid muscles.

buccal n. 1. A branch of the mandibular nerve (CN V3).

SENSORY: It innervates skin over the lower cheek, mucous membranes inside the cheek, and the buccal gingivae along the second and third lower molar.

MOTOR: It innervates the lateral pterygoid muscle. 2. A motor branch of the facial nerve (CN VII) that innervates the buccinator and neighboring facial muscles.

carotid n. 1. Any of the nerves from the superior cervical ganglion of the sympathetic trunk that form plexuses around the carotid arteries. The inter-nal carotid nerves form a plexus around the internal carotid artery inside the carotid canal; the external carotid nerves form a plexus around the external carotid artery. 2. Carotid sinus nerve.

carotid sinus n. A sensory branch of the glossopharyngeal nerve (CN IX) carrying signals from the baroceptors (blood pressure receptors) in the bifurcation of the carotid artery to the nucleus of the solitary tract (nucleus solitarius). SYN: *carotid n.*

cervical n. 1. Any of the eight pairs of spinal nerves that originate in the cervical segments of the spinal cord. They are abbreviated C1 to C8. The first cervical spinal nerve (C1) emerges from the spinal canal above the first cervical vertebra; the eighth cervical spinal nerve (C8) emerges from between the seventh cervical vertebra and the first thoracic vertebra. Cervical spinal nerves innervate the neck, shoulders, and arms. 2. A motor branch of the facial nerve (CN VII) that emerges from the lower end of the parotid gland and runs down behind the angle of the jaw to innervate the platysmus muscle.

cholinergic n. A nerve that uses acetylcholine as its main neurotransmitter.

collateral n. An offshoot nerve composed of branches of some of the axons in the main nerve.

common peroneal n. One of the two divisions of the sciatic nerve in the leg. The sciatic nerve branches into the tibial and common peroneal nerves in the apex of the popliteal fossa. The common peroneal nerve winds around the proximal neck of the fibula to reach the anterior leg where it divides into the superficial and deep peroneal nerves. The common peroneal nerve innervates the knee joint and the skin of the lateral side of the upper leg. SYN: *common fibular n.*

cranial n. ABBR: CN. Any of the 12 pairs of nerves that leave the cranial cavity through foramina in the skull and innervate the head. The cranial nerves are numbered in the order they contact the brain; from anterior to posterior, they are the olfactory (CN I), optic (CN II), oculomotor (CN III), trochlear (CN IV), trigeminal (CN V), abducens (CN VI), facial (CN VII), vestibulocochlear (CN VIII), glossopharyngeal (CN IX), vagus (CN X), spinal accessory (CN XI), and hypoglossal (CN XII) nerves. The central nuclei for all the cranial nerves, except the olfactory nerve, are in the brainstem. SEE: illus.

DIAGNOSIS: Lesions of the cranial nerves give rise to the following alteration(s): *First* (CN I; olfactory): Loss of the sense of smell. *Second* (CN II; optic): Blindness in all or part of a visual field. *Third* (CN III; oculomotor): Ptosis (drooping) of the eyelid, deviation of the eyeball outward, immobility of the pupil, double vision. *Fourth* (CN IV; trochlear): Rotation of the eyeball upward and outward, double vision. *Fifth* (CN V; trigeminal):

SENSORY: Pain or loss of sensation in the face.

MOTOR: Weakness of the jaw, difficulty chewing. *Sixth* (CN VI; abducens): Deviation of the eye outward, double vision. *Seventh* (CN VII; facial): Paralysis of muscles of facial expression. *Eighth* (CN VIII; vestibulocochlear): Deafness; ringing in the ears; dizziness; nausea and vomiting; reeling. *Ninth* (CN IX; glossopharyngeal): Disturbance of taste; difficulty in swallowing; loss of gag reflex. *Tenth* (CN X; vagus): hoarseness; difficulty swallowing; autonomic disturbances of the viscera. *Eleventh* (CN XI; spinal accessory): Drooping of the shoulder; inability to rotate the head. *Twelfth* (CN XII; hypoglossal): Paralysis of the tongue; deviation of the tongue toward one side; thick speech.

deep peroneal n. One of the two major branches of the common peroneal nerve formed as the latter winds around the proximal neck of the fibula. The deep peroneal nerve runs along the interosseous membrane (between the fibula and tibia) into the dorsal foot. It innervates anterior leg muscles and the skin of the dorsal surface of the foot. SYN: *deep fibular n.*

deep petrosal n. A bundle of postganglionic sympathetic axons from the superior cervical ganglion. These axons take the internal carotid nerve into the carotid canal in the skull, where they form the internal carotid plexus. From this plexus, the axons emerge as the deep petrosal nerve, which then joins the greater petrosal nerve in the vidian canal, en route to the pterygopalatine ganglion.

dorsal n. Posterior ramus.

dorsal n. of the clitoris A branch of the pudendal nerve that transmits sensory information from the clitoris. The autonomic innervation of the clitoris comes from the inferior hypogastric plexus.

dorsal n. of the penis A branch of the pudendal nerve that transmits sensory information from the penis. The autonomic innervation of the penis comes from the inferior hypogastric plexus.

dorsal scapular n. A branch of spinal nerve C5, which runs in the posterior shoulder and innervates the rhomboid muscles.

efferent n. A nerve conducting impulses away from the brain or spinal cord. SYN: *motor n.*

excitatory n. A nerve that heightens, increases, or starts the activity of its target.

facial n. A mixed nerve consisting of efferent fibers supplying the facial muscles, the platysma muscle, the submandibular and sublingual glands; and of afferent fibers from taste buds of the anterior two thirds of the tongue and from the muscles.

SENSORY: Taste fibers from the anterior two thirds of the tongue and the soft palate follow the chorda tympani to their neuronal cell bodies in the geniculate ganglion; the axons of these neurons follow the nervus intermedius (the sensory root of the facial nerve) into the pons where they synapse in the nucleus of the tractus solitarius (the gustatory nucleus).

MOTOR: Somatic motor axons from the motor nucleus of the facial nerve in the pons emerge as the motor root of the facial nerve and enter the bone of the skull through the internal auditory meatus. The motor axons follow the facial canal inside the temporal bone and exit the skull through the stylomastoid foramen. From there, the axons innervate all the muscles of facial expression. Preganglionic parasympathetic axons from the superior salivatory nucleus take the nervus intermedius to the region of the geniculate ganglion inside the facial canal. From there, some of the axons join the chorda tympani and later reach the submandibular ganglion by following the lingual nerve. Other preganglionic parasympathetic axons follow the major superficial petrosal nerve and the vidian nerve to reach the pterygopalatine ganglion. SYN: *seventh cranial n.* SEE: illus.; *cranial nerve.*

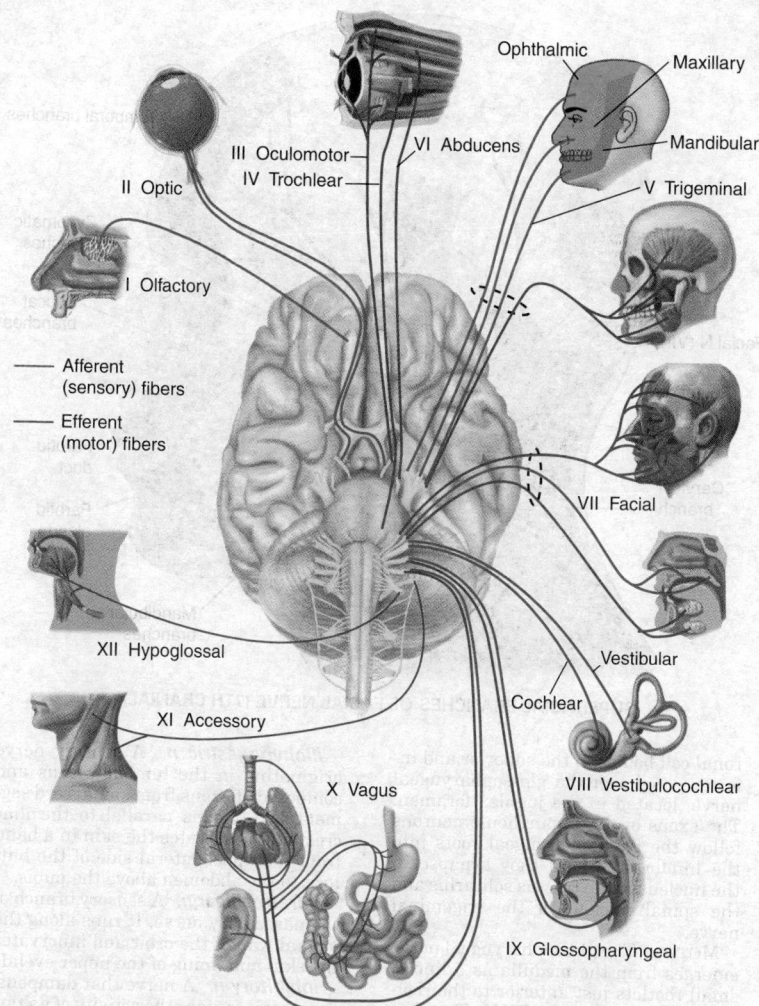

CRANIAL NERVES AND THEIR DISTRIBUTIONS

femoral n. 1. A mixed nerve originating in the lumbar plexus and composed of axons from spinal cord segments L2–L4. It runs into the thigh, passing under the inguinal ligament, on the lateral side of the femoral vessels. It then divides into a number of branches, including the anterior cutaneous nerves of the thigh and the saphenous nerve.

SENSORY: The femoral nerve and its branches innervate the skin along the distal anterior thigh, the front and medial side of the knee, and the medial leg and foot. They also innervate the hip and knee joints.

MOTOR: The femoral nerve and its branches innervate the pectineus, sartorius, and quadriceps muscles. **2.** A sensory branch of the genitofemoral nerve that runs in the femoral sheath and innervates skin over the femoral triangle.

first cranial n. ABBR: CN I. Olfactory **n.**

fourth cranial n. ABBR: CN IV. Trochlear **n.**

glossopharyngeal n. A mixed nerve that is sensory for taste and for the carotid sinus and body, and motor for secretion of saliva and contraction of the pharynx.

SENSORY: Taste fibers from the posterior third of the tongue join visceral sensory fibers from the pharynx, auditory tube, middle ear, carotid sinus, and carotid body and run back to their neu-

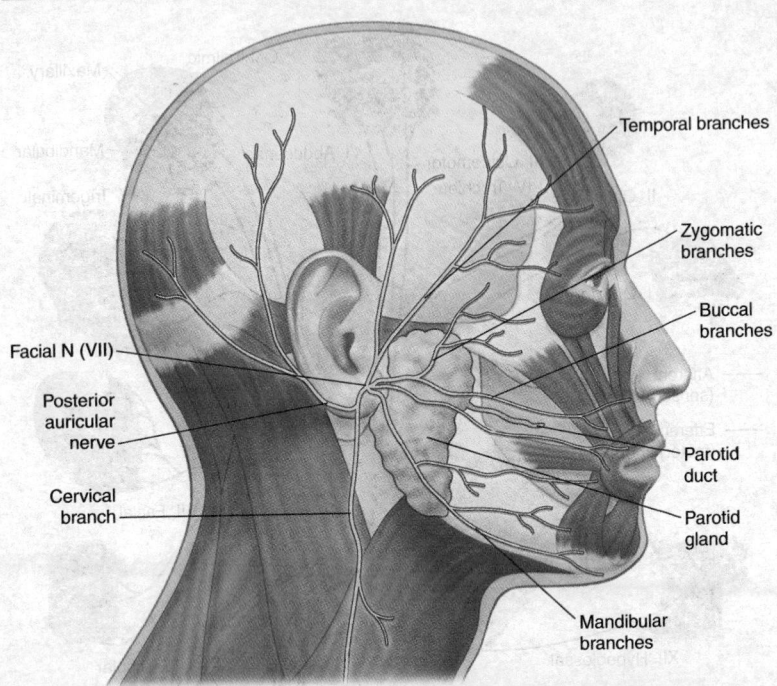

SUPERFICIAL BRANCHES OF FACIAL NERVE (7TH CRANIAL)

ronal cell bodies in the superior and inferior ganglia of the glossopharyngeal nerve, located in the jugular foramen. The axons of these ganglionic neurons follow the glossopharyngeal roots into the hindbrain where they synapse in the nucleus of the tractus solitarius and the spinal nucleus of the trigeminal nerve.

MOTOR: The glossopharyngeal nerve emerges from the medulla as a line of small rootlets just anterior to the rootlets of the vagus nerve (CN X). The glossopharyngeal rootlets collect into a single nerve that emerges from the skull through the jugular foramen, along with the vagus and spinal accessory (CN XI) nerves. The glossopharyngeal nerve then divides into branches as it runs along the stylopharyngeus muscle.

COURSE: CN IX. SYN: *ninth cranial n.* SEE: illus.

hypoglossal n. A somatic motor nerve originating in the hypoglossal nucleus of the hindbrain. The nerve collects from a short line of rootlets and exits the skull through the hypoglossal canal. It then innervates the intrinsic muscles of the tongue (the superior and inferior longitudinal, transverse, and vertical muscles) and three of the extrinsic muscles of the tongue (the styloglossus, hyoglossus, and genioglossus muscles). SYN: *twelfth cranial n.*

iliohypogastric n. A sensory nerve originating in the lumbar plexus and composed of axons from spinal cord segment L1. It runs parallel to the iliac crest and innervates the skin in a band from the upper lateral side of the buttock to the abdomen above the pubis.

infratrochlear n. A sensory branch of the nasociliary nerve. It runs along the medial wall of the orbit and innervates the skin and lining of the upper eyelid.

inhibitory n. A nerve that dampens, decreases, or stops the activity of its target.

intermediate n. Nervus intermedius.

lateral plantar n. A mixed nerve that is a terminal branch of the tibial nerve; it angles laterally from the medial plantar nerve along the sole of the foot.

SENSORY: It innervates the skin on the lateral one-third of the sole and on the plantar side of the last 1 1/2 toes.

MOTOR: It innervates the quadratus plantae, abductor digiti minimi, flexor digiti minimi brevis, plantar and dorsal interossei, lateral three lumbricals, and adductor hallucis muscles.

lumbar n. Any of the five pairs of spinal nerves originating in the lumbar segments of the spinal cord. Each lumbar spinal nerve emerges from the spinal canal through the intervertebral foramen below its corresponding vertebra. Lumbar spinal nerves innervate the lower limbs.

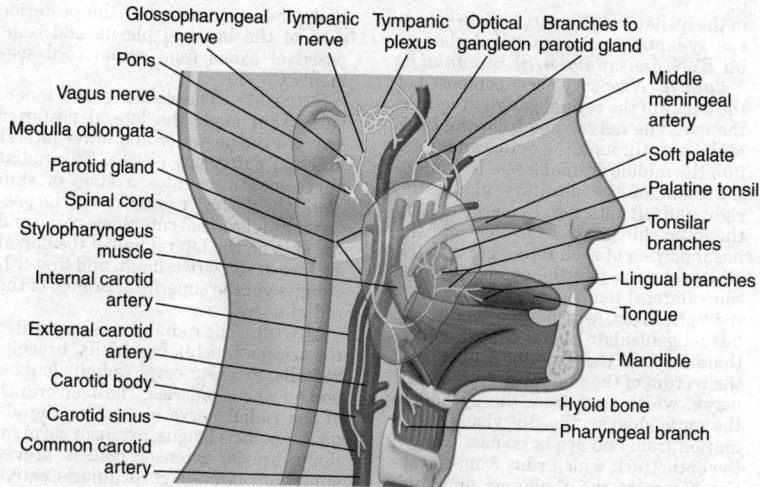

GLOSSOPHARYNGEAL NERVE

mandibular n. ABBR: CN V3. **1.** The inferior trunk of the trigeminal cranial nerve. The mandibular nerve is both sensory and motor.

SENSORY: The major sensory branches are the auriculotemporal, lingual, and inferior alveolar nerves, which innervate the lower teeth and gingivae and the skin of the lower lip, chin, and jaw up into the "sideburn area" in front of the ear.

MOTOR: The major motor branches are the lateral pterygoid, masseteric, deep temporal, and buccal nerves, which innervate the muscles of mastication (lateral and medial pterygoids, masseter, and temporalis).

COURSE: The mandibular nerve leaves the skull via the foramen ovale. **2.** A motor branch of the facial nerve (CN VII) that innervates the facial muscles of the lower lip and chin.

medial cutaneous n. of the forearm Medial antebrachial cutaneous nerve.

median n. A mixed nerve of the upper limb originating in the lateral and medial cords of the brachial plexus and composed of axons from spinal cord segments C6–T1.

SENSORY: It innervates the skin of the first 3 1/2 digits and the palm proximal to them.

MOTOR: In the forearm, it innervates the flexor carpi radialis, palmaris longus, pronator teres, flexor digitorum profundus, flexor digitorum superficialis, flexor pollicis longus, and pronator quadratus. In the hand, it innervates the thenar muscles (other than the adductor pollicis and the deep head of the flexor pollicis brevis) and the lumbricals of digits 2 and 3.

COURSE: It runs in the anterior fore-arm, roughly midway between the radial and ulnar arteries; it becomes superficial near the wrist and then runs inside the carpal tunnel.

mixed n. A nerve containing both afferent (sensory) and efferent (motor) axons.

motor n. A nerve conveying efferent information to an effector target, such as a muscle or a gland. SYN: *efferent n.*

ninth cranial n. ABBR: CN IX. Glossopharyngeal nerve

oculomotor n. A somatic and visceral motor nerve originating in the midbrain oculomotor nucleus and the adjacent Edinger-Westphal nucleus. The oculomotor nerve runs in the subarachnoid space and cavernous sinus inside the skull and enters the orbit through the superior orbital fissure. Its somatic motor axons innervate the superior, medial, and inferior rectus muscles, the inferior oblique muscle, and the superior levator palpebrae muscle. Its preganglionic parasympathetic axons synapse in the ciliary ganglion; the ganglion cell axons (postganglionic parasympathetic axons) follow the short ciliary nerves into the eyeball to innervate the ciliary muscle of the lens of the eye and the pupillary constrictor muscles. SYN: *third cranial n.*

olfactory n. A sensory nerve with neuronal cell bodies located in the olfactory epithelium (a yellowish-brown thickened patch of epithelium found along the upper back walls of the nasal cavity). Axons from the receptor cells join into approximately 20 small nonmyelinated bundles (the olfactory nerves). These nerves pass into the skull through holes in the cribriform plate of the ethmoid bone and terminate in the ipsilateral olfactory bulb in spherical synaptic structures called glomeruli. SYN: *first cranial n.* SEE: *cranial n.*

optic n. A sensory nerve composed of the axons of the retinal ganglion cells in the eye. The nerve runs from the back of the eye, through the optic canal, and into the middle cranial fossa. In front of the stalk of the pituitary gland, the right and left optic nerves merge to form the optic chiasm. Here axons from the nasal portion of each retina cross to the other side and join the axons from the contralateral temporal retina to run as the optic tract, which synapses in the lateral geniculate bodies (nuclei) of the thalamus and the superior colliculus of the tectum of the midbrain. In the optic nerve, which runs from the eyeball to the optic chiasm, the full visual information from one eye is transmitted; in the optic tract, which runs from the optic chiasm to the thalamus and midbrain, the full visual information from one visual field is transmitted. SYN: *second cranial nerve.*

parasympathetic n. A nerve composed of axons of the parasympathetic division of the autonomic nervous system. Parasympathetic innervation is always a chain of two consecutive axons. The first axon, the preganglionic parasympathetic axon, has its cell body in the brainstem or in the intermediate gray column of spinal cord segments S2–S4; the first axon leaves the brainstem through the oculomotor (CN III), facial (CN VII), glossopharyngeal (CN IX), or vagus (CN X) nerve, or it leaves the sacral spinal cord through a pelvic splanchnic nerve. The second axon in the chain, the postganglionic parasympathetic axon, has its cell body in a peripheral ganglion near its target tissue. The main transmitter used by both pre- and postganglionic parasympathetic axons is acetylcholine. Stimulation of parasympathetic nerves usually relaxes the body tone.

peripheral n. A nerve outside the central nervous system (CNS).

pharyngeal n. 1. An autonomic nerve from the pterygopalatine ganglion that innervates the mucosa of the nasopharynx. 2. A sympathetic nerve from the superior cervical ganglia that innervates the pharynx and its surrounding pharyngeal plexus.

phrenic n. A mixed nerve composed of axons from spinal nerves C3 –C5. It descends through the neck behind the carotid sheath; in the chest, it lies between the mediastinal pleura and the pericardium. It is sensory and motor to the diaphragm and sensory to the pericardium.

posterior cutaneous n. of the arm Posterior brachial cutaneous **n.**

radial n. A mixed nerve of the upper limb, the continuation of the posterior cord of the brachial plexus and composed of axons from spinal cord segments C5–T1.

SENSORY: The radial nerve innervates skin along the lateral posterior arm via the posterior and lower lateral brachial cutaneous nerves. The radial nerve also innervates a strip of skin along the posterior forearm via the posterior antebrachial cutaneous nerve and the skin on the lateral half of the dorsal surface of the wrist, hand, and first 2 1/2 digits via the superficial branch of the radial nerve.

MOTOR: The radial nerve innervates the triceps brachii, brachialis, brachioradialis, extensor carpi radialis longus, and anconeus muscles. The deep branch of the radial nerve innervates the abductor pollicis longus, extensor carpi radialis brevis, extensor pollicis brevis, supinator, extensor carpi ulnaris, extensor digitorum, extensor indicis, extensor pollicis longus, extensor digiti minimii, and abductor digiti minimi muscles.

COURSE: From the posterior cord of the brachial plexus, the radial nerve runs with the deep brachial artery along the back of the humerus; it comes laterally around the humerus and continues distally, passing over the lateral condyle of the humerus. There it divides into the superficial and deep branches of the radial nerve, which continue into the forearm.

sciatic n. The largest nerve in the body. It originates in the sacral plexus and is composed of axons from spinal cord segments L4–S3. It runs along the back wall of the pelvis, exits through the greater sciatic foramen under the piriformis muscle, passes under the gluteus maximus muscle, and runs deeply along the posterior thigh. As it enters the popliteal fossa, its two internal components separate as the tibial and common peroneal nerves. The sciatic and its branches innervate the posterior thigh muscles (the flexors of the knee) and all the muscles, joints, and skin of the leg and foot.

secretory n. A nerve that behaves like an endocrine gland by secreting neurohormones into the blood stream. Secretory neurons are a characteristic of the hypothalamus, where they release vasopressin, oxytocin, somatostatin, corticotropin-releasing hormone, and thyrotropin-releasing hormone.

sensory n. A nerve that conveys afferent information, e.g., visual information from the eye or proprioceptive information from a joint.

somatic n. A peripheral nerve that contains axons of the dorsal root ganglia or the cranial ganglia (i.e., somatic sensory nerves) or axons of the ventral horn or cranial nuclei motor neurons (i.e., somatic motor nerves). Somatic nerves innervate skin, skeletal muscles, and joints.

spinal accessory n. A motor nerve originating in the nucleus ambiguus in the medulla and in a column of motor neurons in the ventral horn of the upper cervical spinal cord. After exiting the skull through the jugular foramen, the nerve splits; its cranial trunk joins the vagus (CN X) and innervates striated muscles in the soft palate, pharynx, larynx, and esophagus; its spinal trunk continues down the neck to innervate the sternocleidomastoid and trapezius muscles. SYN: *accessory n.; eleventh cranial n.*spinal accessory nucleus.

spinal n. Any of the 31 sets of nerves originating in the spinal cord and emerging from the spinal canal through intervertebral foramina. Each spinal nerve is the concatenation of two sets of axons that emerge separately from the spinal cord: sensory axons (the dorsal root) and motor axons (the ventral root). SEE: illus.

splanchnic n. Any one of the paired, purely autonomic nerves from the thoracic sympathetic ganglia. The major splanchnic nerves are the greater, lesser, and least (smallest, renal) splanchnic nerves, which carry preganglionic sympathetic axons from ganglia 6–10 of the thoracic sympathetic trunk to the prevertebral ganglia (celiac, superior mesenteric, and aorticorenal ganglia) in the abdomen.

sympathetic n. A nerve composed of axons of the sympathetic division of the autonomic nervous system. Sympathetic innervation is always a chain of two consecutive axons. The first axon, the preganglionic sympathetic axon, has its cell body in the intermediolateral column of spinal cord segments T1–L1; the first axon leaves the spinal cord through a ventral root and synapses in a peripheral sympathetic ganglion, either in the sympathetic trunk (the paraspinal ganglia) or in the prevertebral ganglia. The second axon in the chain, the postganglionic sympathetic axon, has its cell body in a peripheral ganglion, and it follows a splanchnic or other sympathetic nerve to its target tissue. The main transmitter used by preganglionic sympathetic axons is acetylcholine; for postganglionic sympathetic axons, it is norepinephrine. In general, stimulation of sympathetic nerves activates the body, putting it in "fight or flight" mode.

temporal n. **1.** Any of the two or three branches of the anterior division of the mandibular nerve (CN V3) that innervates the temporalis muscle. SYN: *deep temporal n.* **2.** Any of the branches of the facial nerve (CN VII) that run over the zygomatic arch to innervate facial muscles of the upper eyelid and forehead.

thoracic n. Any of the twelve pairs of spinal nerves originating in the thoracic segments of the spinal cord. Each thoracic nerve emerges from the spinal canal through the intervertebral foramen below its corresponding vertebra. Thoracic spinal nerves innervate the trunk.

trigeminal n. A mixed nerve arising from the pons in a large sensory root and a smaller motor root.

SENSORY: Somatic sensory fibers from the face collect into three major trunks: the ophthalmic, from the region of the eyes and above; the maxillary, from the region of the lower eyelids and cheeks down to the upper lip, teeth, and gingivae; and the mandibular, from a region that follows the sideburns down along the jaw and that includes the lower lips, teeth, and gingivae. Neuronal cell bodies for these fibers are located in the trigeminal (Gasserian, semilunar) ganglion along the floor of the middle cranial fossa; the axons of the ganglion cells synapse in the pons and medulla.

MOTOR: Somatic motor axons originate in motor nuclei in the pons and, running only in the mandibular trunk of the trigeminal nerve, innervate the muscles used in chewing.

COURSE: The trigeminal nerve emerges from the pons via a large sensory root and a small adjacent motor root; both run together to the trigeminal ganglion. From the ganglion, three trunks leave the cranial cavity separately: the ophthalmic trunk (ophthalmic nerve, CN V1) enters the back of the orbit through the superior orbital fissure, the maxillary trunk (maxillary nerve, CN V2) leaves through the foramen rotundum, and the mandibular trunk (mandibular nerve, CN V3) leaves through the foramen ovale. SYN: *fifth cranial n.*

ulnar n. A mixed nerve of the upper limb originating in the medial cord of the brachial plexus and composed of axons from spinal cord segments C7–T1.

SENSORY: It innervates the skin of the last 1 1/2 digits and the palm proximal to them.

MOTOR: In the forearm, it innervates the flexor digitorum profundus, abductor digiti minimi, flexor carpi ulnaris, and flexor digiti minimi. In the hand, it innervates most of the intrinsic muscles (the hypothenar, interosseous, adductor pollicis, deep head of the flexor pollicis brevis, opponens digiti minimi, and palmaris brevis muscles and the medial lumbricals of digits 4 and 5).

COURSE: It runs along the medial side of the anterior forearm. It becomes superficial near the wrist and passes

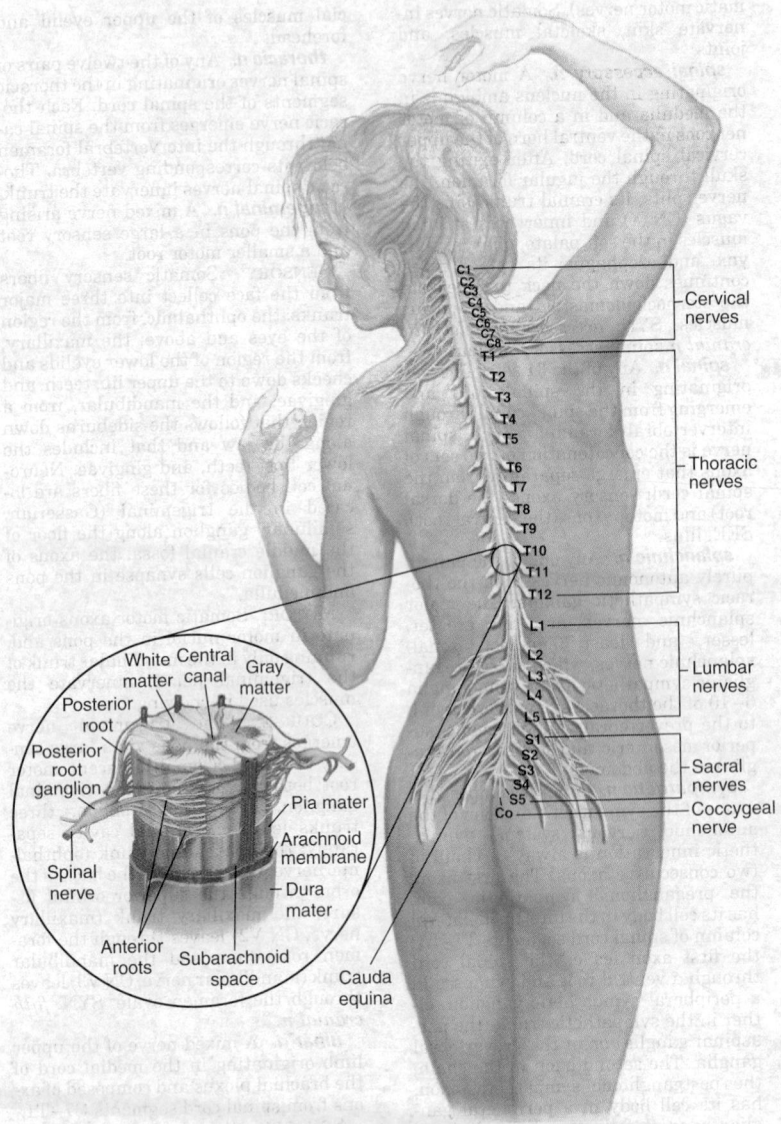

SPINAL NERVES

into the hand above (superficial to) the flexor retinaculum.

vagus n. A nerve that arises from the medulla and has branches to many organs

SENSORY: Visceral sensory fibers from the lower pharynx, larynx, thoracic organs, and abdominal viscera join proprioceptive sensory fibers from the muscles of the soft palate, pharynx, and larynx and sensory taste fibers from the root of the tongue and the epiglottis. These axons enter the vagus nerve along its length and run to the superior and inferior (nodosal) ganglia of the vagus nerve; these ganglia lie within and just below the jugular foramen of the skull. The axons of cell bodies in the ganglia then take the vagus nerve to their various synaptic sites in the medulla.

MOTOR: Somatic motor axons from

Labels on figure: Cervical nerves, Thoracic nerves, Lumbar nerves, Sacral nerves, Coccygeal nerve; C1–C8, T1–T12, L1–L5, S1–S5, Co; White matter, Central canal, Gray matter, Posterior root, Posterior root ganglion, Pia mater, Arachnoid membrane, Dura mater, Spinal nerve, Anterior roots, Subarachnoid space, Cauda equina hindbrain motor nuclei run in the vagus nerve and innervate the soft palate, pharynx, and larynx. Preganglionic parasympathetic axons from the dorsal motor nucleus of the vagus take the vagus nerve to provide most of the parasympathetic innervation of the body below the neck and above the pelvis, including the lungs, heart, and abdominal viscera.

COURSE: The vagus forms from a line of small rootlets along the lower medulla; the rootlets collect into a single nerve, which emerges from the skull through the jugular foramen, along with the glossopharyngeal (CN IX) and spinal accessory (CN XI) nerves. The vagus nerve continues caudally in the carotid sheath between the internal jugular vein and the carotid artery, giving off branches along the way. It then joins the esophageal plexus and continues along the esophagus as it passes through the diaphragm; in the abdomen, the vagus nerve splits into branches that innervate all the abdominal viscera. SYN: *tenth cranial n.*

vasoconstrictor n. A sympathetic nerve that stimulates the constriction of smooth muscle cells in arterial walls.

vestibulocochlear n. The eighth cranial nerve, a sensory nerve for hearing and equilibrium. Cell bodies of the vestibular neurons are located in the vestibular ganglion in the inner ear; their receptor terminals end in the saccule, utricle, and semicircular ducts. Cell bodies of the cochlear neurons are located in the spiral ganglion in the inner ear; their receptor terminals end in the spiral organ of Corti. Axons of the neuron cell bodies in the vestibular and spiral ganglia run to the CNS side-by-side in the petrous process of the temporal bone; they exit through the internal acoustic meatus and enter the brainstem at the junction of the pons and the medulla.

vidian n. A short efferent nerve formed from the merger of the deep petrosal and greater petrosal nerves. The vidian nerve carries postganglionic sympathetic axons from the superior cervical ganglion and preganglionic parasympathetic axons from the superior salivatory nucleus (in the pons); it also carries taste axons from the palate. The vidian nerve exits the skull through the pterygoid (vidian) canal and connects to the pterygopalatine ganglion inside pterygopalatine fossa. SYN: *n. of the pterygoid canal.*

nerve block SEE: under *block.*

nerve cell SEE: under *cell.*

nerve ending The termination of a nerve fiber (axon or dendrite) in a peripheral structure. It may be sensory (receptor) or motor (effector). Sensory endings can be nonencapsulated (e.g., free nerve endings, peritrichal endings, or tactile corpuscles of Merkel) or they can be encapsulated (e.g., end-bulbs of Krause, Meissner's corpuscles, Vater-Pacini corpuscles, or neuromuscular and neurotendinous spindles).

nerve entrapment syndrome Compression of a nerve or nerves resulting in nerve damage. This may cause anesthesia or pain if a sensory nerve is affected and paralysis if a motor nerve is involved. The compression may be due to physical pressure on the nerve (i.e., sleeping in a position in which a nerve is pressed upon by surrounding tissue) or to swelling of tissue in a compartment through which the nerve passes. SEE: *carpal tunnel syndrome;* .

nerve fiber **1.** An axon. Nerve fibers are identified by intrinsic characteristics (e.g., diameter, presence of myelin, or neurotransmitter type) or by extrinsic characteristics, e.g., whether they conduct sensory or motor information (e.g., a myelinated, large-diameter, cholinergic motor fiber).

"Nerve fiber," or simply "fiber," is more often used in anatomical descriptions, and "fiber tract" is more commonly used than "axon tract." "Axon" is more commonly used in histological descriptions.

2. An axon or a small group of axons bundled together by glia or Schwann cells. **3.** In informal usage, a small peripheral nerve.

A delta n.f. A myelinated sensory fiber that rapidly relays painful sensations to the central nervous system.

B n.f. A myelinated nerve fiber that transmits autonomic impulses.

C n.f. An unmyelinated nerve fiber that slowly relays sensations of pain from the periphery or viscera to the central nervous system.

nerve gas SEE: under *gas.*

nerve growth factor SEE: under *factor.*

nerve plexus SEE: *plexus, nerve.*

nerve-sparing (nĕrv″spar″ing) Pert. to surgery that does not remove or injure nerves adjacent to or within the organ being removed from the body. In prostatectomy, a nerve-sparing procedure preserves the parasympathetic and sympathetic nerves that control penile erection and ejaculation.

nerve tissue SEE: under *tissue.*

nerve trunk The main stem of a peripheral nerve.

nervous (nĕr′vŭs) [L. *nervosus,* sinewy, vigorous, nervous] **1.** Anxious. **2.** Characterized by excitability. **3.** Pert. to the nerves.

nervous breakdown A colloquial term for any incapacitating mental illness, esp. one having acute onset and interfering with normal function, thought, or behavior.

nervousness Anxiety; tension.

nervous system One of the regulatory systems, made of millions of neurons in precise pathways to transmit electrochemical impulses, and of neuroglial cells that have several functions, including formation of myelin sheaths of neurons. It consists of the brain and spinal cord (central nervous system [CNS]) and the cranial nerves and spinal nerves (peripheral nervous system), which include the nerves of the autonomic nervous system and its ganglia. SEE: *autonomic nervous system; central nervous system*.

FUNCTION: Receptors detect external and internal changes and transmit impulses along sensory nerves to the CNS. Receptors are found in the skin, muscles and joints, viscera, and the organs of special sense: the eyes, the ears, and the organs of taste and smell. The CNS uses this sensory information to initiate appropriate responses to changes; reflexes involving muscle contraction or glandular secretion, or voluntary movement, all mediated by motor nerves. A function specific to the brain is the integration, analysis, and storage of information for possible later use; this function is learning and memory.

nervus (nĕr′vŭs) [L. *nervus*, sinew] Nerve.

    n. erigens Pelvic splanchnic nerve.

    n. intermedius The smaller of the two roots of the facial nerve (CN VII). It emerges between the large motor root of the facial nerve and the vestibulocochlear nerve (CN VIII) on the lateral side of the hindbrain along the lower (caudal) edge of the pons SYN: *intermediate nerve*.

    nervi nervorum Nerve fibers that innervate sheaths of nerves.

    n. terminales A terminal nerve accompanying the olfactory nerve to the brain and consisting principally of sensory fibers from the mucosa of the nasal septum.

    nervi vasorum Vasomotor nerve.

nesidioblastoma (nē-sĭd″ē-ō-blăs-tō′mă) [″ + *blastos*, germ, + *oma*, tumor] Islet-cell tumor of the pancreas.

nesidioblastosis (nē-sĭd″ē-ō-blăs-tō′sĭs) Diffuse hyperplasia of the beta cells in the islets of Langerhans of the pancreas. It is a rare cause of hypoglycemia.

nest A small cluster of unusual cells found within normal tissue. SYN: *rest* (4).

    cancer n. A mass of cells extending from a common center seen in cancerous growths.

    cell n. A mass of epithelial cells set apart from surrounding cells by connective tissue.

net reproductive rate ABBR: NRR. A measure of whether a population is reproducing at a greater or lesser rate than needed for its replacement. It is determined by calculating the average number of surviving daughters born to the women in that population during their reproductive years. An NRR of 1 indicates that each woman in the population has one surviving daughter during her lifetime.

nettle (nĕt′ĕl) Any plant of the genus *Urtica*. Its sawtoothed leaves contain hairs that secrete a fluid that irritates the skin. Extracts from nettles are used as herbal remedies to treat allergic rhinitis and kidney stones. SYN: *stinging n.*

    stinging n. Nettle.

network (net′wŏrk″) Fiber arrangement in a structure resembling a net. SYN: *rete; reticulum*. Particular networks are listed under the first word. SEE: e.g., *Advanced Research Projects Agency Network; neural network*.

Neuman, Betty (nū′măn) Nursing educator, born 1924, who developed Neuman's systems model, a conceptual model of nursing. SEE: *Nursing Theory Appendix*.

    N. systems model A conceptual model of nursing developed by Betty Neuman in which individuals and groups are considered client systems made up of physiological, psychological, sociocultural, developmental, and spiritual variables that respond to stress The goal of nursing is to facilitate optimal wellness through retention, attainment, or maintenance of client system stability. These three goals are referred to respectively, as primary prevention, secondary prevention, and tertiary prevention interventions.

neural (nū′răl) [L. *neuralis*] Pert. to nerves or connected with the nervous system.

    n. crest A band of cells extending longitudinally along the neural tube of an embryo from which cells forming cranial, spinal, and autonomic ganglia arise as well as the cells (ectomesenchyme) that migrate into the forming facial region and become odontoblasts, which form the dentin of the teeth.

    n. fold One of two longitudinal elevations of the neural plate of an embryo that unite to form the neural tube.

    n. grafting An experimental procedure for transplanting tissue into the brain and spinal cord. Possible sources of material to be used include human fetal tissue, cultured and genetically engineered cells, and tissues from the patient's own body.

    n. plate SEE: under *plate*.

neuralgia (noo-ral′jă, nū-) [*neuro-* + *-algia*] Pain occurring along the course of a nerve. It may be caused by pressure on nerve trunks, nutritional deficiencies, toxins, or inflammation. SYN: *neurodynia*. SEE: *sciatica*. **neuralgic** (-ral′jik), *adj.*

facial n. Trigeminal **n.**

geniculate n. Ramsay hunt syndrome.

glossopharyngeal n. Neuralgia along the course of the glossopharyngeal nerve, characterized by severe pain in back of the throat, tonsils, and middle ear.

Hunt n. Ramsay Hunt syndrome.

idiopathic n. Neuralgia without structural lesion or pressure from a lesion.

intercostal n. Pain between the ribs. It is frequently associated with eruption of herpes zoster on the chest, and with costochondritis, an inflammatory condition of the ribs and their cartilage. SYN: *pleuralgia.*

mammary n. Neuralgia of the breast. SYN: *mastodynia.*

Morton n. SEE: *Morton neuralgia.*

nasociliary n. Neuralgia of the eyes, brows, and root of the nose.

occipital n. Neuralgia involving the upper cervical nerves, usually caused by nerve entrapment.

otic n. Geniculate **n.**

postherpetic n. Neuralgia that persists for more than three months after the rash of herpes zoster (shingles) resolves.

sphenopalatine n. Neuralgia of the sphenopalatine ganglion, causing pain in the area of the upper jawbone and radiating into the neck and shoulders. There is pain on one side of the face radiating to the eyeball, ear, and occipital and mastoid areas of the skull, and sometimes to the nose, upper teeth, and shoulder on the same side.

stump n. Neuralgia due to irritation of nerves at the site of an amputation.

symptomatic n. Neuralgia not primarily involving the nerve structure but occurring as a symptom of local or systemic disease.

trigeminal n. Neuralgia of the trigeminal (fifth cranial) nerve marked by brief attacks of lightning-like stabs along the distribution of one or more of its branches, but usually along the maxillary nerve. The attacks typically last from a few seconds to 2 min and may be triggered by light touch to a hypersensitive area, drinking hot or cold beverages, chewing, brushing teeth, smiling, or talking. It occurs most frequently in people over 40 and in women more often than men and on the right side of the face more often than the left. SYN: *facial n.; tic douloureux.* SEE: *Nursing Diagnoses Appendix.*

SYMPTOMS: Symptoms include episodes of facial pain, often accompanied by painful spasms of facial muscles. Between attacks the patient may be pain-free. When observed during an attack, the patient will often try to splint or in other ways protect the affected area. In long-standing cases, the hair on the affected side sometimes becomes coarse and bleached. Physical examination shows no motor or sensory function impairment.

ETIOLOGY: The cause is thought to be the pressure of blood vessels on the trigeminal nerve root at its point of entrance into the brainstem. Magnetic resonance imaging is used to identify other potentially hazardous causes of facial pain.

TREATMENT: Carbamazepine, phenytoin, or other anticonvulsant drugs in gradually increasing doses are often effective. Other therapies include narcotic analgesics or muscle relaxers such as lioresal. Nerve block provides temporary relief. Surgical therapies include rhizotomy, microsurgical nerve root decompression, or nerve root injections. Radiation therapy is sometimes employed.

PATIENT CARE: The characteristics of each attack are observed and recorded. Analgesic drugs are administered as prescribed and observed for desired and adverse effects. Before surgery is contemplated, an effort should be made to reduce factors that make symptoms worse, e.g., by having the patient use a cotton pad to cleanse the face and a blunt-toothed comb to comb the hair.

After surgery, sensory deficits are assessed to prevent trauma to the face and affected areas. The patient who has had an ophthalmic branch resection should avoid rubbing his or her eye, avoid using aerosol sprays, wear glasses or goggles outdoors, blink often, and examine the eye for foreign substances with a hand mirror frequently. The patient who has had a mandibular or maxillary branch resection should eat carefully to avoid oral injuries from hot food or drinks or chewing, e.g., by eating food on the unaffected side to prevent inner cheek injury. Frequent dental examinations detect abnormalities that the patient cannot feel. The patient and significant others require emotional support throughout treatment. Expression of feelings should be encouraged, and independence promoted, helping the patient to avoid trigger stimulation while carrying out self-care and physical activities.

neuralgiform (nū-răl′jĭ-form) [″ + ″ + L. *forma,* form] Resembling neuralgia.

neurally adjusted ventilatory assistance ABBR: NAVA. A form of mechanical ventilation in which each machine-generated breath initiates after the detection of diaphragmatic muscle depolarization. A lead inserted into the esophagus detects signals from the diaphragm.

neural network A form of artificial intelligence that relies on a group of interconnected mathematical equations that accept input data and calculate an output. The more often the equations are used, the more reliable and valuable they become in drawing conclusions from data. Neural networks have been used in health care to interpret electrocardiograms and to make and suggest diagnoses.

neural provocation test Neurodynamic test.

neural tension test Neurodynamic test.

neural tension tests Various assessment techniques that stretch neural tissues (meninges, nerve roots, axons, and peripheral nerves) and assess the mobility and/or length of the structures and their ability to withstand tensile forces. Positive signs may include the reproduction of symptoms, limitation of motion, or asymmetric responses. The tests include the slump test, the straight leg raise, and the upper limb tension test.

neural tube Tube formed from fusion of the neural folds from which the brain and spinal cord arise.

neural tube defect SEE: under *defect*.

neuraminidase (noor″ă-min-ĭ-dās″) ABBR: N. An enzyme present on the surface of influenza virus particles. The activity of neuraminidase enables the virus to separate itself from cells in the respiratory tract of its host, allowing it to spread to other hosts. People with increased levels of antibodies against neuraminidase in their serum have increased resistance to influenza infection. Mutations in neuraminidase occur commonly, giving the influenza virus differing abilities to cause disease from year to year. Annual vaccines are made to prevent influenza target neuraminidase (N) and also hemagglutinin (H), another important disease-causing antigen on the viral surface.

neurapraxia (nūr″ă-prăk′sē-ă) A temporary impairment in nerve conduction, typically caused by an injury that does not produce permanent structural damage to the nerve.

neurasthenia (nū″răs-thē′nē-ă) [″ + *astheneia*, weakness] An old term for functional (psychosomatic) illness, marked by symptoms such as chronic fatigue, weakness, lassitude, noncardiogenic chest pain, panic attacks, irritability, anxiety, depression, headache, insomnia, joint and muscle discomfort, and sexual disorders. Contemporary terms for neurasthenia include chronic fatigue, anxiety, fibromyalgia, depression, and dysphoria. SYN: *nervous debility*.

neuraxial blockade (noor-aks′ē-ăl, nūr-) SEE: under *blockade*.

neuraxial infusion SEE: under *infusion*.

neuraxis (nūr-ak′sĭs, nūr-, nūr-ak′sēz″, nūr-) *pl.* **neuraxes** [*neuro-* + *axis*] The cerebrospinal axis. **neuraxial** (nūr-ak′sē-ăl, nūr-), *adj.*

neurectomy (nū-rĕk′tō-mē) [″ + *ektome*, excision] Partial or total excision or resection of a nerve.

    presacral n. Surgical procedure for removing the hypogastric (presacral) nerve plexus. This is done to treat conditions such as dysmenorrhea and chronic idiopathic pelvic pain.

neurepithelium (nūr″ĕp-ĭ-thē′lē-ŭm) [″ + *epi*, upon, + *thele*, nipple] Neuroepithelium.

neurilemma, neurolemma (nū′ră-lĕm″mă) [″ + *lemma*, husk] In the peripheral nervous system, the cytoplasm and nuclei of Schwann cells wrapped around the myelin sheath or the unmyelinated processes of nerve fibers. This contributes to regeneration of damaged nerve fibers by producing growth factors and serving as a tunnel or guide for regrowth. SEE: *nerve fiber; neuron* for illus.

neurilemmoma, neurolemmoma (nū″ră-lĕm-ō′mă) [″ + *eilema*, tight sheath, + *oma*, tumor] A firm, encapsulated fibrillar tumor of a peripheral nerve. SYN: *neurinoma; schwannoma*.

neurinoma (nū-rĭ-nō′mă) [″ + *oma*, tumor] Neurilemmoma.

neurite (nū′rīt) [Gr. *neuron*, nerve, sinew] An axon or a dendrite.

neuritis (noo-rī′tĭs, nū-) [*neuro-* + *-itis*] Inflammation of a nerve, usually associated with a degenerative process. SEE: *Guillain-Barré syndrome; polyneuritis; Nursing Diagnoses Appendix*.

    SYMPTOMS: There are many forms of neuritis, which produce a variety of symptoms, including neuralgia in the part affected, hyperesthesia, paresthesia, dysesthesia, hypesthesia, anesthesia, muscular atrophy of the body part supplied by the affected nerve, paralysis, and lack of reflexes.

    ETIOLOGY: Neuritis may be caused by mechanical factors (e.g., compression or contusion of the nerve) or localized infection involving direct infection of a nerve. It may accompany diseases such as leprosy, tetanus, tuberculosis, malaria, or measles. Toxins, esp. poisoning by heavy metals (arsenic, lead, mercury), alcohol, or carbon tetrachloride, may also be a cause. Neuritis may accompany thiamine deficiency, gastrointestinal dysfunction, diabetes, toxemias of pregnancy, or peripheral vascular disease.

    PATIENT CARE: Changes in motor and sensory function are monitored. Correct positioning and prescribed analgesic drugs are used to relieve pain. Rest is provided, and affected extremities are rested by limiting their use and by using supportive appliances. Passive range-of-motion exercises are performed to help prevent contracture formation. Skin care is provided, and proper nutrition and dietary therapy are prescribed for metabolic disorders. Health care providers remove causative factors or counsel the patient about their avoidance. After pain subsides, prescribed activities are performed (e.g., massage, electrostimulation, and exercise).

adventitial n. Neuritis of a nerve sheath.

ascending n. Neuritis moving upward along a nerve trunk away from the periphery.

axial n. Neuritis of the inner portion of a nerve.

degenerative n. Neuritis with rapid degeneration of a nerve.

descending n. Neuritis that leads away from the central nervous system toward the periphery.

disseminated n. Neuritis involving a large group of nerves.

interstitial n. Neuritis involving the connective tissue of a nerve.

intraocular n. Neuritis of the retinal fibers of the optic nerve causing disturbed vision, contracted field, enlarged blind spot, and fundus findings such as exudates, hemorrhages, and abnormal condition of the blood vessels. Treatment depends on the cause (e.g., brain tumor, meningitis, syphilis, nephritis, diabetes). SEE: *optic n.*

n. migrans Neuritis that ascends or descends along a nerve trunk, affecting one area and then another.

multiple n. Neuritis that affects a number of peripheral nerves simultaneously. SYN: *polyneuritis.*

SYMPTOMS: Symptoms are related to the suddenness of onset and severity. Usually, lower limbs are affected first, with weakness that may progress until the entire body is affected. Muscle strength, deep tendon reflexes, sensory nerves, and autonomic nerves become involved.

ETIOLOGY: Causes include infectious diseases (e.g., diphtheria), metabolic disorders (e.g., alcoholism, diabetes, pellagra, beriberi, sprue), and various poisons, including lead. In some instances, the disease arises without apparent cause.

TREATMENT: Causative factors should be removed if possible. Treatment includes skilled nursing, with particular care taken to prevent bedsores, and dietary therapy (depending upon the cause).

optic n. Neuritis of the optic nerve, causing varying degrees of visual loss. It is often the first recognized symptom in patients with multiple sclerosis.

peripheral n. Neuritis of terminal nerves or end organs.

retrobulbar n. Neuritis of the portion of the optic nerve behind the eyeball.

SYMPTOMS: The main symptom is acute loss of vision in one or both eyes. Pain may be absent or may be unbearable, lasting for only a brief period or for days.

ETIOLOGY: This type of neuritis may be caused by a variety of illnesses, but in adults it is most frequently associated with multiple sclerosis.

segmental n. Neuritis affecting segments of a nerve interspersed with healthy segments.

sympathetic n. Neuritis of the opposite nerve without attack of the nerve center.

syphilitic n. Neuritis in locomotor ataxia caused by syphilis. SYN: *tabetic n.*

toxic n. Neuritis resulting from metallic poisons (e.g., arsenic, mercury, and thallium) or nonmetallic poisons (e.g., various hydrocarbons and organic solvents).

traumatic n. Neuritis following an injury.

vestibular n. Neuritis accompanied by vertigo, nausea and vomiting, and gait disturbance of relatively acute onset, usually caused by inflammatory processes within the bony labyrinth of the ear.

neuro-, neuri-, neuro- [Gr. *neuron,* nerve, sinew] Prefixes meaning *nerve, nervous tissue, nervous system.*

neuroablation (nūr″ō-ăb-lā′shŭn) The destruction or inactivation of nerve tissue, with surgery, cautery, injections of sclerosing agents, lasers, or cryotherapy.

neuroacanthosis (noor″ō-ăk″ăn-thō′sĭs, nūr″) [″ + ″] An autosomal recessive neurological disorder associated with acanthosis of red blood cells beginning between the ages of 25 and 45. It is marked by the development of choreiform movements, oral dystonias, motor and vocal tics, and other neurological abnormalities. SYN: *Levine-Critchley syndrome.*

neuroactive [Gr. *neuron,* nerve, sinew + *active*] Capable of modifying the activities of nerves or the behavior of organisms. The term is applied to the actions of many chemicals, drugs, foods, or toxins.

neuroanastomosis (nū″rō-ă-năs″tō-mō′sĭs) [″ + *anastomosis,* opening] Surgical attachment of one end of a severed nerve to the other end.

neuroanatomy (nū″rō-ăn-ăt′ō-mē) The anatomy of the nervous system.

neuroarthropathy (noo″rō-ar-throp′ă-thē, nū″) [*neuro-* + *arthropathy*] Disease of a joint associated with disease of the central nervous system.

diabetic n. Charcot foot.

neuroastrocytoma (nū″rō-ăs″trō-sī-tō′mă) [″ + *kytos,* cell, + *oma,* tumor] A tumor of the central nervous system composed of neurons and glial cells.

neuroaugmentation (nūr″ō-ăwg-měn-tā′shŭn) Any method used to increase the function of a nerve, esp. in managing pain. One example is transcutaneous electrical nerve stimulation.

neurobiology (nū″rō-bī-ŏl′ō-jē) [″ + *bios,* life, + *logos,* word, reason] Biology of the nervous system.

neuroblast (nū′rō-blăst) [″ + *blastos,* germ] An embryonic cell derived from the neural tube or neural crest, giving rise to a neuron.

neuroblastoma (nū″rō-blăs-tō′mă) [″ + ″ + *oma,* tumor] A malignant hemorrhagic tumor composed principally of cells resembling neuroblasts that give rise to cells of the sympathetic system, esp. adrenal medulla. This tumor occurs chiefly in infants and children. The primary sites are in the mediastinal and retroperitoneal regions.

neurocanal (nū″rō-kă-năl′) [″ + L. *canalis,* passage] The central canal of the spinal cord.

neurocardiac (nū″rō-kăr′dē-ăk) [″ + *kardia,* heart] **1.** Pert. to the nerves supplying the heart or nervous system and the heart. **2.** Pert. to a cardiac neurosis.

neurocentral (nū″rō-sĕn′trăl) [″ + *kentron,* center] Pert. to the centrum of a vertebra and the neural arch.

neurocentrum (nū″rō-sĕn′trŭm) The body of a vertebra.

neurochemistry (nū″rō-kĕm′ĭs-trē) The chemistry of the nervous system.

neurochorioretinitis (nū″rō-kō″rē-ō-rĕ″tĭn-ī′tĭs) [Gr. *neuron,* nerve, sinew, + *chorion,* skin, + L. *retina,* retina, + Gr. *itis,* inflammation] Inflammation of choroid and retina combined with optic neuritis.

neurochoroiditis (nū″rō-kō-roy-dī′tĭs) [″ + ″ + *eidos,* form, shape, + *itis,* inflammation] Inflammation of the choroid coat and optic nerve.

neurocirculatory (nū″rō-sŭr′kū-lă-tō″rē) [″ + L. *circulatio,* circulation] Pert. to circulation and the nervous system.

neurocladism (nū-rŏk′lă-dĭzm) [″ + *klados,* a young branch, + *-ismos,* condition] A phenomenon occurring after a nerve is severed, in which an outgrowth of axons meet to reestablish the nerve's integrity. SYN: *odogenesis.*

neuroclonic (nū″rō-klŏn′ĭk) [″ + *klonos,* spasm] Marked by spasms of neural origin.

neurocranium (noor″ō-krā′nē-ŭm) [*neuro-* + *cranium*] The portion of the skull that surrounds the brain, eyes, nose, and ears. The skull has two separate embryonic portions: the neurocranium and the viscerocranium. The neurocranium develops from the mesenchyme surrounding the cerebral vesicles. SEE: *viscerocranium.*

neurocrine (nū″rō-krĭn) [″ + *krinein,* to secrete] **1.** Pert. to an endocrine influence on nerves or the influence of nerves on endocrine tissue. **2.** A chemical transmitter.

neurocutaneous (nū″rō-kū-tā′nē-ŭs) [″ + L. *cutis,* skin] Pert. to the nervous system and skin.

neurocytolysis (nū″rō-sī-tŏl′ĭ-sĭs) [″ + *kytos,* cell, + *lysis,* dissolution] Dissolution or destruction of nerve cells.

neurocytoma (nū″rō-sī-tō′mă) [″ + ″ + *oma,* tumor] A tumor formed of cells of nervous origin (usually ganglionic). SEE: *neuroma.*

neurodegeneration with brain iron accumulation (nū″rō-dē-gĕn″ĕr-ā′shŭn) ABBR: NBIA. Hallervorden-Spatz disease.

neurodegenerative (noor″ō-dĕ-jen′ĕ-rāt″ĭv, nūr″, ĕ-răt-ĭv) Pert. to wasting, necrosis, or deterioration of nerves, neurons, or components of the central or peripheral nervous system.

neurodendrite, neurodendron (nū″rō-dĕn′drīt, -drŏn) [Gr. *neuron,* nerve, sinew, + *dendron,* tree] Cytoplasmic branched process of a nerve cell. SEE: *dendrite* for illus.

neurodermatitis (noor″ō-dĕr-mă-tīt′ĭs, nūr″ō-) [*neuro- + dermatitis*] Inflammation and itching of the skin, associated with, but not entirely due to, emotional stress. After an initial irritant, scratching becomes habitual and prolongs the condition. Treatment is corticosteroid ointment or cream. SEE: illus.

circumscribed n. **Lichen** simplex chronicus.

disseminated n. Chronic superficial inflammation of the skin characterized by thickening, excoriation, and lichenification, usually beginning in infancy. It is common in families with a high incidence of allergic diseases. SYN: *atopic* ***dermatitis.***

neurodermatosis (nū″rō-dĕr-mă-tō′sĭs) [″ + ″ + *osis,* condition] Any skin disease of neural origin, including neurofibromatosis, von Hippel-Lindau disease, Sturge-Weber syndrome, and tuberous sclerosis. SYN: *phacomatosis.*

neurodevelopmental treatment (nūr″ō-dē-vĕl″ŏp-mĕn′tăl) ABBR: NDT. A rehabilitation treatment approach for cerebral palsy, hemiplegia, and other central nervous system deficits that emphasizes the use of carefully considered handling to inhibit abnormal reflexes and movement patterns and facilitate higher level reactions and patterns in order to attain normal movement. This method was first promoted by Karel and Bertha Bobath (German physiotherapists).

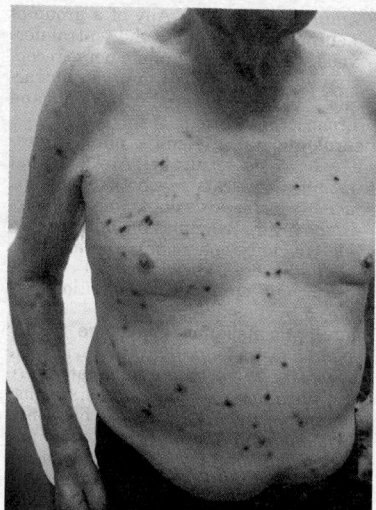

NEURODERMATITIS

excoriations on chest and arms

neurodynamic (nū″rō-dī-năm′ĭk) Pert. to nervous energy.

neurodynamic test, neurodynamic testing Any of several physical diagnostic maneuvers in which the examiner mechanically stresses the spine to determine if spinal nerve roots are the cause of a patient's back pain. Examples include the straight leg raising test and the slump test. SYN: *neural provocation test; neural tension test.*

neuroectoderm (nū″rō-ĕk′tō-dĕrm) [″ + *ektos,* outside, + *derma,* skin] The embryonic tissue that gives rise to nerve tissue.

neuroendocrine (nū″rō-ĕn′dō-krĭn) Pert. to the nervous and endocrine systems as an integrated functioning mechanism.

neuroendocrinology (nū″rō-ĕn″dō-krĭ-nŏl′ō-jē) [″ + *endon,* within, + *krinein,* to secrete, + *logos,* word, reason] The study of the relationship between the nervous and endocrine systems.

neuroenteric (nū″rō-ĕn-tĕr′ĭk) Pert. to the nervous system and the gastrointestinal tract.

neuroepidermal (nū″rō-ĕp-ĭ-dĕr′măl) [″ + *epi,* upon, + *derma,* skin] Pert. to or giving rise to the nervous system and epidermis.

neuroepithelioma (nū″rō-ĕp″ĭ-thē-lē-ō′mă) [″ + ″ + *thele,* nipple, + *oma,* tumor] A relatively rare tumor of the neuroepithelium in a nerve of special sense.

neuroepithelium (nū″rō-ĕp″ĭ-thē′lē-ŭm)
1. A specialized epithelial structure forming the termination of a nerve of special sense, including gustatory cells, olfactory cells, hair cells of the inner ear,

and the rods and cones of the retina.
2. The embryonic layer of the epiblast from which the cerebrospinal axis is developed. SYN: *neurepithelium.*

neurofibril, neurofibrilla (nū-rō-fī′brĭl, -fī-brĭl′ă) [″ + L. *fibrilla,* a small fiber] Any of the many fibrils that extend in every direction in the cytoplasm of the neuron cell body. They maintain the shape of the neuron and extend into the axon and dendrites. SEE: *neuron.*

neurofibroma (nū″rō-fī-brō′mă) *pl.* **neurofibromata, -mas** [Gr. *neuron,* nerve, + L. *fibra,* fiber, + Gr. *oma,* tumor] A tumor of the connective tissue (esp. Schwann cells) of a nerve. SYN: *fibroneuroma.* SEE: *neurofibromatosis.*

neurofibromatosis (noor″rō-fī-brō″mă-tō′sĭs, nūr″) [*neuro-* + *fibromatosis*] Any of a group of genetic disorders affecting the cell growth of neural tissues. A characteristic of the disease is the growth of neurofibromas in many locations within or on the surface of the body. For those with affected family members, genetic assessment and counseling of parents may be indicated. Genetic assessment and counseling can identify the parents' risk of being a gene carrier and passing the disease on to subsequent offspring.

  type 1 n. ABBR: NF-1. An autosomal dominant disease that affects about 1 in 3000 people. Its clinical hallmarks include hyperpigmented macules on the skin (café au lait spots) and multiple cutaneous and subcutaneous tumors that appear in late childhood (there may be only a few or thousands). When the tumors are pressed, they pass through a small opening in the skin, leaving the space previously occupied vacant. This characteristic, called buttonholing, helps to distinguish these tumors from lipomas. In about 2% to 5% of cases, the tumors become malignant. No cure has yet been found. Tumors that give rise to symptoms or those that become malignant should be excised; however, if the tumor is on a vital nerve, excision may be impossible. Radiation therapy and surgery are of benefit. SYN: *Recklinghausen disease.*

  type 2 n. ABBR: NF-2. An autosomal dominant disease affecting 1 in 50,000 people. It causes intracranial and spinal tumors, esp. of the eighth cranial nerve. Although the disease is incurable, its symptoms can be palliated with multidisciplinary care.

neurofibromin (nū″rō-fī-brō′mĭn, noo″) [″ + ″] A tumor suppressor protein whose expression is reduced in the neurons of patients with neurofibromatosis and increased in the skin of patients who suffer tissue trauma.

neurofibrosarcoma (nū″rō-fī″brō-săr-kō′mă) [″ + ″ + Gr. *sarx,* flesh, +

oma, tumor] A malignant neurofibroma.

neuroganglion (nū″rō-găn′glē-ōn) A group of neuron cell bodies outside the central nervous system.

neurogenesis (nū″rō-jĕn′ĕ-sĭs) [″ + *genesis,* generation, birth] **1.** Growth or development of nerves. **2.** Development from nervous tissue. **neurogenetic** (nū″rō-jĕn-ĕt′ĭk), *adj.*

neurogenic (nū-rō-jĕn′ĭk) **1.** Originating from nervous tissue. **2.** Due to or resulting from nerve impulses.

neurogenic communication disorder Inability to exchange information with others because of hearing, speech, or language problems caused by impaired functioning of the nervous system.

neuroglia (nū-rŏg′lē-ă) [″ + *glia,* glue] The interstitial and supporting tissue of the nervous system, also called glia. The cells, of ectodermal origin, are astrocytes, oligodendrocytes, satellite cells, ependymal cells, and Schwann cells. Microglia are phagocytic cells that are esp. active during injury or infection. **neuroglial** (nū-rŏg′lē-ăl), *adj.*

neuroglioma (nū″rō-glī-ō′mă) [Gr. *neuron,* nerve, + *glia,* glue, + *oma,* tumor] Glioma.

    n. **ganglionare** A glioma containing ganglion cells. SYN: *ganglioneuroma.*

neuroglycopenia (nūr″ō-glī-kō-pē′nē-ă) Hypoglycemia of sufficient duration and degree to interfere with normal brain metabolism. Patients with an insulinoma or hypoglycemia due to an insulin overdose may have this condition, which produces confusion, agitation, coma, or brain damage. SYN: *glucopenic brain injury.*

neurography (noor-ŏg′rŭ-fē, nūr-) [″ + ″] Radiological imaging of the brain, spinal cord, or peripheral nerves.

neurohistology (nū″rō-hĭs-tŏl′ō-jē) [″ + *histos,* tissue, + *logos,* study] The microscopic anatomy of peripheral nerves and the central nervous system.

neurohypophysis (noor″ō-hī-pof′ĭ-sĭs, nūr″) [*neuro* + *hypophysis*] The posterior lobe of the pituitary gland (hypophysis), consisting of the pars intermedia and the infundibulum. SYN: *posterior pituitary; posterior lobe; posterior lobe of hypophysis; posterior lobe of pituitary gland.*

neuroimaging (noor″ō-im′ă-jing) [*neuro* + *imaging*] The visual or graphic representation of the anatomy, blood flow, electrical activity, metabolism, oxygen usage, receptor sites, or other physiological functions of the central nervous system.

    volumetric n. Volumetric brain imaging.

neurokeratin (nū″rō-kĕr′ă-tĭn) [″ + *keras,* horn] The type of keratin found in myelinated nerve fibers.

neurokinin (noor″ō-kī′nĭn) [*neuro-* +

kinin] ABBR: NK. Any of a group of neuropeptides found in the central nervous system that stimulate nerve receptors and cause smooth muscle contraction, blood pressure reduction, and bronchoconstriction.

neuroleptic (noor″ō-lep′tik, nūr″) [*neuro-* + Gr. *lēpsis,* seizure] **1.** Any drug that modifies or treats psychotic behaviors, usually by blocking dopamine receptors in the brain. Examples include haloperidol (a butyrophenone), thorazine (a phenothiazine), and clozapine (a tricylic dibenzodiazepine). **2.** A condition produced by a neuroleptic agent.

neuroleptic malignant syndrome ABBR: NMS. A potentially fatal syndrome marked by hyperthermia; catatonic rigidity; altered mental status; profuse sweating; and, occasionally, rhabdomyolysis, renal failure, seizures, and death. It typically occurs after exposure to drugs that alter levels of dopamine in the brain (such as antipsychotic agents) or after the withdrawal of agents that increase central nervous system dopamine levels (such as levodopa or carbidopa). The death rate may be as high as 30%. Antipyretics, curare-based paralytic drugs, bromocriptine, and dantrolene are used to treat the syndrome. SEE: *malignant hyperthermia.*

neurologist (nū-rŏl′ō-jĭst) A specialist in diseases of the nervous system.

neurology (noo-rol′ō-jē, nū-) [″ + *logos,* word, reason] The branch of medicine that deals with the nervous system and its diseases. **neurologic, neurological** (noo-rō-loj′ĭk, nū-, noo-rō-loj′ĭ-kăl), *adj.*

    clinical n. The branch of medicine concerned with the study and treatment of people with diseases of the nervous system.

neurolymphomatosis (nū″rō-lĭm″fō-mă-tō′sĭs) [″ + L. *lympha,* lymph, + Gr. *oma,* tumor, + *osis,* condition] Malignant lymphoma involving the nervous system.

neurolysin (nū-rŏl′ĭs-ĭn) [″ + *lysis,* dissolution] A peptide-cleaving enzyme that destroys nerve cells.

neurolysis (nū-rŏl′ĭs-ĭs) **1.** The loosening of scar tissue surrounding a nerve. **2.** The disintegration or destruction of nerve tissue. It is often used to treat peripheral nerve diseases, esp. those that cause intolerable pain. The painful nerve may be destroyed with drugs or chemicals, extremely cold probes, radio frequency ablation, or surgery. Painful conditions that can be treated with neurolysis include trigeminal neuralgia and glossopharyngeal neuralgia. **neurolytic** (nū-rō-lĭt′ĭk), *adj.*

neuroma (noo-rō′mă) [*neuro-* + *-oma*] Former term for any type of tumor composed of nerve cells. Classification is now made with respect to the specific portion of the nerve involved. SEE: *gan-*

glioneuroma; neurilemmoma. **neuromatous** ('mă-tŭs), *adj.*

acoustic n. A benign neuroma of the eighth cranial nerve. The symptoms may include hearing loss, balance disturbances, pain, headache, and tinnitus.

amputation n. A neuroma occurring on the nerves of a stump after amputation.

appendiceal n. A neuroma found in the mucosa and submucosa of the appendix.

n. cutis A neuroma in the skin.

cystic n. A neuroma with cystic formations.

false n. A tumor arising from the connective tissue of nerves, including the myelin sheath. SYN: *neurofibroma; pseudoneuroma.*

ganglionated n. A neuroma composed of true nerve cells.

Joplin n. SEE: *Joplin neuroma.*

plexiform n. A neuroma of nerve trunks that appear to be twisted.

n. telangiectodes A neuroma containing an abundance of blood vessels.

traumatic n. An unorganized neuroma occurring in wounds or on an amputation stump, resulting after accidental or intentional incision of the nerve.

neuroma-in-continuity Localized nerve injury caused by compression or friction on a nerve by nearby tendons or bones.

neuromatosis (nū-rō″mă-tō′sĭs) [″ + *oma,* tumor, + *osis,* condition] A condition characterized by the occurrence of multiple neuromas in the body.

neuromechanical dyssynchrony SEE: under *dyssynchrony.*

neuromere (nū′rō-mēr) [″ + *meros,* part] One of a series of segmental elevations on the ventrolateral surface of the rhombencephalon. SYN: *rhombomere.*

neuromodulation (nū″rō-mŏd″ū-lā′shŭn) Controlled stimulation of the peripheral or central nervous system with electricity.

neuromodulator (nūr″ō-mŏd′ū-lā-tŏr) Any of the biologically active substances produced by neurons that enhance or diminish the effects of neurotransmitters. Some neuromodulators are substance P, cholecystokinin, and somatostatin. SEE: *neuron; neurotransmitter.*

neuromonitoring (noor″ō-mon′ĭt-ŏ-ring, nūr″) [*neuro-* + *monitor*] The measurement of the physiological activity of the brain and spinal cord.

PATIENT CARE: Neuromonitoring includes cerebral microdialysis, used to identify metabolic disturbances in the brain, e.g., abnormalities of glucose metabolism, and measurements of cerebral blood flow, jugular venous oximetry (SjvO2), and brain tissue oxygen tension (PbtO2). These techniques are used

after neurosurgery and in some patients with embolic strokes, epilepsy, subarachnoid hemorrhage, or traumatic brain injury to help identify neurological damage before it becomes irreversible.

neuromotor (noor″ō-mōt′ŏr, nūr″) [*neuro-* + *motor*] **1.** Pert. to nerves and muscles. **2.** Pert. to nerve impulses to muscles.

neuromuscular (nū″rō-mŭs′kū-lăr) [″ + L. *musculus,* a muscle] Pert. to both nerves and muscles.

neuromyelitis (noor″ō-mī-ĕ-līt′ĭs, nūr″) [*neuro-* + *myelitis*] Inflammation of nerves and the spinal cord.

n. optica ABBR: NMO. A rare syndrome in which there is a severe transverse myelitis and optic nerve damage, probably as a result of immunological injury to the optic nerve and spinal cord. It shares some features with multiple sclerosis (i.e., predilection for young women, demyelination of nerve cells) but is believed to be a distinct disease. An IgG antibody test (for NMO-IgG autoantibodies) can be used to distinguish it from multiple sclerosis.

neuromyopathy (nū″rō-mī-ŏp′ă-thē) [″ + *mys,* muscle, + *pathos,* disease, suffering] A pathological condition involving both muscles and nerves.

neuromyositis (nū″rō-mī″ō-sī′tĭs) [″ + ″ + *itis,* inflammation] Neuritis complicated by inflammation of muscles that come in contact with the affected nerves.

neuromyotonia (nū″rō-mī″ō-tō′nē-ă) [+ Gr. *mys,* muscle + *tonikos,* tone] SYN: *Isaac syndrome.*

neuron (noo′ron″) [Gr. *neuron,* nerve, sinew] A nerve cell, the structural and functional unit of the nervous system. A neuron consists of a cell body (perikaryon) and its processes, an axon and one or more dendrites. Neurons function in the initiation and conduction of impulses. They transmit impulses to other neurons or cells by releasing neurotransmitters at synapses. Alternatively, a neuron may release neurohormones into the bloodstream. SYN: *nerve cell.* SEE: illus. **neuronal** (noor′′ŏn-ăl), *adj.*

afferent n. A neuron that conducts sensory impulses toward the brain or spinal cord. SYN: *sensory n.*

association n. Interneuron.

associative n. A neuron that mediates impulses between a sensory and a motor neuron.

bipolar n. **1.** A neuron that bears two processes. **2.** A neuron of the retina that receives impulses from the rods and cones and transmits them to a ganglion neuron. SEE: *retina* for illus.

central n. A neuron confined entirely to the central nervous system.

commissural n. A neuron whose

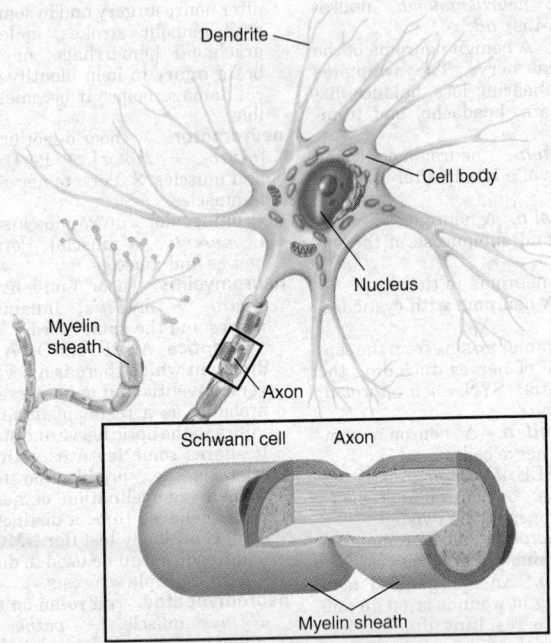

Dendrite

Cell body

Nucleus

Myelin sheath

Axon

Schwann cell   Axon

Myelin sheath

NEURON STRUCTURE

axon crosses to the opposite side of the brain or spinal cord.

efferent n. A neuron whose axon carries motor impulses away from the brain or spinal cord.

gamma motor n. A small nerve originating in the anterior horns of the spinal cord that transmits impulses through type A gamma fibers to intrafusal fibers of the muscle spindle for muscle control.

ganglion n. A neuron of the retina that receives impulses from bipolar neurons. Axons of ganglion neurons converge at the optic disk to form the optic nerve. SEE: *retina* for illus.

internuncial n. Interneuron.

lower motor n. A peripheral motor neuron that originates in the ventral horns of the gray matter of the spinal cord and terminates in skeletal muscles. Lesions of these neurons produce flaccid paralysis of the muscles they innervate. SYN: *lower* **motoneuron**.

mirror n. Any of a group of neurons that become active both when an animal moves in a certain way and when the animal observes others performing the same action. Learning by simulation or imitation is thought to be a function of the system of mirror neurons in the brain.

motor n. A neuron that carries impulses from the central nervous system either to muscle tissue to stimulate con-

traction or to glandular tissue to stimulate secretion.

multipolar n. A neuron with one axon and many dendrites.

peripheral n. A neuron whose process constitutes a part of the peripheral nervous system (cranial, spinal, or autonomic nerves).

peripheral motor n. A motor neuron that transmits impulses to skeletal muscle. SYN: *peripheral* **motoneuron**.

postganglionic n. A neuron of the autonomic nervous system whose cell body lies in an autonomic ganglion and whose axon terminates in a visceral effector (smooth or cardiac muscle or glands).

preganglionic n. A neuron of the autonomic nervous system whose cell body lies in the central nervous system and whose axon terminates in a peripheral ganglion, synapsing with postganglionic neurons.

sensory n. Afferent **n.**

serotonergic n. A nerve cell that uses serotonin as its neurotransmitter.

unipolar n. A neuron whose cell body bears one process.

neuronal intestinal dysplasia SEE: under *dysplasia*.

neuronal migration disorder ABBR: NMD. Any of a group of rare neurological disorders in which embryological development of the central nervous system is flawed, resulting in structural abnormalities of the brain. Developmental delays, mental retardation, movement and muscle disorders, and seizures are common consequences. Specific diseases include agyria, lissencephaly, microgyria, and porencephaly.

neuronavigation (nū″rō-năv′ĭ-gā′shŭn) Radiological guidance for neurosurgery. The surgeon may rely on information obtained from ultrasonic images (sononavigation), magnetic resonance images, PET scans, or CT data, to select tissues for excision while avoiding eloquent (speech-controlling) regions of the brain.

neuronitis (nū-rō-nī′tĭs) [Gr. *neuron,* nerve, + *itis,* inflammation] Inflammation of nerve cells; e.g., inflammation of middle ear nerve cells is called vestibular neuronitis.

Neurontin (noor′ŏn-tĭn) SEE: *gabapentin.*

neuro-ophthalmology (nū″rō-ŏf″thăl-mŏl′ŏ-jē) [″ + *ophthalmos,* eye, + *logos,* word, reason] The branch of ophthalmology concerned with the neurology of the visual system.

neuro-optic (nū″rō-ŏp′tĭk) [″ + *optikos,* pert. to vision] Pert. to the central nervous system and the eye.

neuro-otology (nū″rō-ō-tŏl′ă-jē) [″ + *ous,* ear, + *logos,* word, reason] Otoneurology.

neuropacemaker (nūr″ō-pās′mā-kĕr) An implantable device used to stimulate the brain or spinal cord (e.g., in the management of motor movement disorders or chronic and intractable pain). The electrical energy is provided in pulses at an appropriate rate to inhibit the perception of pain.

neuropathic arthritis SEE: under *arthritis.*

neuropathogenesis (nū″rō-păth″ō-jĕn′ē-sĭs) [″ + *pathos,* disease, suffering, + *genesis,* generation, birth] The origin and development of a neural disease.

neuropathogenicity (nū″rō-păth″ō-jĕnĭs′ĭ-tē) [″ + *pathos,* disease, suffering, + *gennan,* to produce] The ability to cause pathological changes in nerves.

neuropathology (nū″rō-pă-thŏl′ō-jē) [″ + ″ + *logos,* word, reason] The study of diseases of the nervous system and the structural and functional changes occurring in them. Neurological diseases may affect the peripheral nerves or the central nervous system and may be congenital or acquired. Congenital defects tend to occur during embryonic or fetal development and become obvious in the early years of life. Acquired diseases that affect neurological function include vascular injuries (e.g., strokes), inflammatory diseases (e.g., encephalitis or meningitis), autoimmune diseases (multiple sclerosis), toxic illnesses (lead or mercury exposure), trauma (closed head injury), or neoplastic diseases (metastatic or primary brain tumors).

neuropathy (noo-rop′ă-thē) [*neuro-* + *-pathy*] Any disease of the nerves. **neuropathic** (noor″ŏ-path′ĭk), *adj.* SEE: table; *polyneuropathy.*

AIDS peripheral n. Direct infection of peripheral nerves by HIV, resulting in sensory and motor changes due to destruction of axons or their myelin covering. Acute or chronic inflammatory myelin damage may be the first sign of peripheral nerve involvement. Patients display gradual or abrupt onset of motor weakness and diminished or absent reflexes. Diagnostic biopsies of peripheral nerves show inflammatory changes and loss of myelin. Distal sensory neuropathy occurs in up to 30% of patients with AIDS, usually late in the disease. There is increased risk in older patients and those with diabetes mellitus, nutritional deficiencies, low CD4 cell counts, and vitamin B_{12} deficiencies. Patients report sharp pain, numbness, or burning in the feet. Destruction of dorsal root ganglions and degeneration of central peripheral axons are seen on autopsy. Some older antiretroviral drugs (ddI, ddC, and d4T) also cause a reversible peripheral neuropathy in about 20% of patients. SEE: *AIDS; Guillain-Barré syndrome; chronic inflammatory demyelinating* **polyneuropathy***.*

TREATMENT: Nonsteroidal anti-inflammatory drugs, opioids, gabapentin, anticonvulsants, and topical agents have all been used with variable success to treat the pain of AIDS-related sensory neuropathy. Acupuncture is not effective. Human nerve growth factor, which stimulates regeneration of damaged nerve fibers, is being studied, esp. to minimize the neuropathy that antiretroviral drugs cause.

ascending n. Neuropathy that ascends from the lower part of the body to the upper.

auditory n. ABBR: AN. Impaired hearing in children due to an absence of auditory evoked potentials, despite the presence of normal cochlear hair cell structure and function. SYN: *auditory dyssynchrony.*

descending n. Neuropathy that descends from the upper part of the body to the lower.

diabetic n. Damage to autonomic, motor, and/or sensory nerves due to metabolic or vascular derangements in patients with long-standing diabetes mellitus. In Western nations, diabetes is the most common cause of neuropathy. Symptoms usually include loss of sensation or unpleasant sensations in the feet, erectile dysfunction, focal motor deficits, gastroparesis, loss of the ability to maintain postural blood pressure, and diseases of cardiac innerva-

Common Neuropathies

Name	Affected nerve(s)	Affected part(s)	Affects sensation?	Affects movement?	Clinical features	Type of neuropathy
Bell's palsy	Facial	Eye, nasolabial fold, lip (corner of the mouth)	Occasionally	Yes	Paralysis of the facial muscles, usually on just one side of the face	Inflammatory
Carpal tunnel syndrome	Median	Wrist and hand	Yes	Yes	Pain and numbness of the hand and wrist, often caused by repetitive movements or overuse such as typing, sawing, hammering, or polishing	Entrapment
Diabetic sensory neuropathy	Multiple	Feet, lower extremities; sometimes hands late in the course	Yes	No	Burning, stinging pain beginning in both feet, typically occurring after several years of poorly controlled diabetes. Can predispose to foot injury and infections.	Metabolic
Idiopathic brachial plexopathy (neuralgic amyotrophy; Parsonage-Turner syndrome; shoulder girdle syndrome)	Brachial	Shoulder	Yes	Yes	Pain in the shoulder, esp. after vigorous physical activity. Occasionally followed by shoulder girdle muscle atrophy	Entrapment
Meralgia paresthetica	Lateral femoral cutaneous	Thigh	Yes	No	Stinging pain in the anterolateral thigh. Usually found in obesity or in diabetes mellitus	Entrapment
Morton's neuroma (interdigital neuropathy)	Interdigital nerves of the feet	Ball of foot	Yes	No	Pain often occurring between the web spaces of the 3rd and 4th toes during walking or standing	Entrapment
Piriformis syndrome	Sciatic	Buttock, with radiation into the leg	Yes	No	Buttock pain *without* back pain that is worsened by sitting and is relieved by walking	Entrapment/compression

Radial nerve palsy (musculospiral paralysis; Saturday night palsy)	Radial nerve (spiral groove entrapment)	Wrist, hand, and forearm	Yes	Yes	Temporary paralysis and numbness of the hand and arm, which may mimic a stroke. Caused by nerve compression, e.g., falling asleep on one's side on a hard surface	Entrapment compression
Suprascapular neuropathy	Suprascapular	Back of the shoulder	Yes	Yes	Shoulder pain and muscular atrophy. Decreased ability to rotate or abduct the shoulder	Entrapment
Tarsal tunnel syndrome	Posterior tibial	Sole of the foot	Yes	No	Pain under the foot that is worsened by walking	Entrapment
Trigeminal neuralgia	Trigeminal	Cheek, nose, upper lip	Yes	No	Intense, repetitive facial pains that are often worsened by chewing, shaving, or toothbrushing, usually accompanied by spasm on the affected side of the face	Entrapment

NEUROPATHIC FOOT DUE TO DIABETES

tion. Sensory loss in the feet may result in undetected injuries that become infected or gangrenous. SYN: *diabetic polyneuropathy*. SEE: illus.

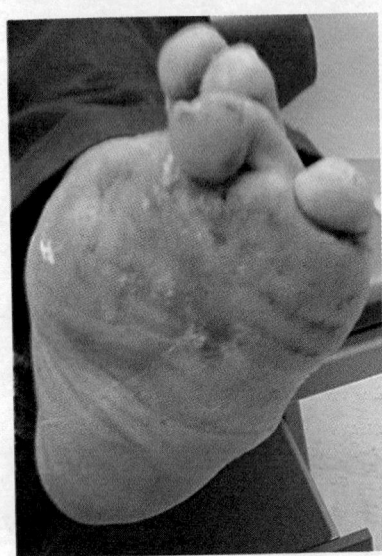

NEUROPATHIC FOOT DUE TO DIABETES

TREATMENT: Tight control of blood sugar levels may prevent some neuropathic symptoms in patients with diabetes mellitus.

dysthyroid optic n. Crowding of and damage to the optic nerve in patients with Grave disease. It is characterized by loss of visual acuity and color vision, swelling of the optic disk, and compression of the optic nerve at the apex of the orbit. SYN: *apical crowding*.

entrapment n. Nerve entrapment syndrome.

facial sensory n. Trigeminal **neuralgia**.

focal n. Any nerve disease or injury, e.g., carpal tunnel syndrome or peroneal nerve palsy, that affects a single nerve.

glue-sniffer's n. Malfunction of sensory and motor nerves due to inhaling toxic hydrocarbons. The lower extremities and trigeminal nerve are most often damaged.

interdigital n. SEE: under *Morton, Thomas George*.

multifocal motor n. An asymmetrical motor weakness occasionally found in middle-aged men.

optic n. Pathological injury to the optic nerves or the blood supply to them. Usually, only one eye is affected. Several forms have been described, including ischemic optic neuropathy, which, if prolonged, leads to blindness in the affected eye; optic neuritis due to acute demyelination of optic nerve fibers; in-filtrative optic neuropathy, in which the optic nerve is compressed by a tumor or aneurysm; and optic neuropathy due to toxic nutritional factors, e.g., methanol or a combined nutritional and vitamin deficiency.

peripheral n. Any syndrome in which muscle weakness, paresthesias, impaired reflexes, and autonomic symptoms in the hands and feet are common. This syndrome occurs in patients with diabetes mellitus, renal or hepatic failure, alcoholism, or in those who take certain medications such as phenytoin and isoniazid.

plantar n. Any of several conditions in which nerves that supply sensation to the sole of the foot are injured or chronically compressed, resulting in burning and tingling sensations and difficulty standing, walking, or running.

subacute myelo-optic n., subacute myelo-optico neuropathy ABBR: SMON. Neuropathy that usually begins with abdominal pain or diarrhea, followed by sensory and motor disturbances in the lower limbs, ataxia, impaired vision, and convulsions or coma. It is reported mostly in Japan and Australia. Most patients survive, but neurological disability remains. Many of those who have the disease have a history of taking drugs of the halogenated oxyquinoline group such as clioquinol (formerly called iodochlorhydroxyquin).

sural n. A relatively rare form of sensory neuropathy affecting the lateral ankle, typically associated with the wearing of poorly fitting work boots or shoes that compress the sural nerve.

tomaculous n. The presence of sausage-shaped areas of thickened myelin with secondary axon constriction in some cases of familial recurrent brachial neuropathy.

toxic-nutritional optic n. Bilateral visual impairment with central scotomas. This is usually associated with a toxic or nutritional disorder (e.g., the ingestion of methyl alcohol).

vibration-induced n. Hand-arm vibration syndrome.

neuropeptidase (noor″ō-pĕp′tĭ-dās, nūr″) [″ + ″] An enzyme that cleaves peptides in neurons.

neuropharmacology (nū″rō-fär″mă-kŏl′ō-jē) [″ + *pharmakon*, drug, + *logos*, word, reason] The branch of pharmacology concerned with the effects of drugs on the nervous system.

neurophilic (nū″rō-fĭl′ĭk) [″ + *philos*, fond] Having an affinity for nervous tissue.

neurophthalmology (nū″rŏf-thăl-mŏl′ō-jē) [″ + *ophthalmos*, eye, + *logos*, word, reason] Neuro-ophthalmology.

neurophysin (nū″rō-fī′zĭn) Proteins secreted by the hypothalamus that are involved in the transport of oxytocin and antidiuretic hormone (vasopressin).

neurophysiological treatment approach (nūr″ō-fĭz″ē-ō-lŏj′ĭ-kăl) In occupational and physical therapy, various techniques used in sensorimotor rehabilitation that rely on voluntary and involuntary activation, facilitation, and inhibition of muscle action through the reflex arc.

neurophysiology (noor″ō-fĭz″ē-ol′ŏ-jē, nūr″) [*neuro-* + *neurophysiology*] The physiology of the nervous system.

neuropil (nū′rō-pīl) [″ + *pilos,* felt] The gray matter of the central nervous system, a network of neurons, neuroglia, and their cell processes resembling intermingled fibers of felt.

neuroplasm (nū′rō-plăzm) [″ + LL. *plasma,* form, mold] The cytoplasm of a neuron. **neuroplasmic** (nū″rō-plăz′mĭk), *adj.*

neuroplasticity (nūr″ō-plăs-tĭs′ĭ-tē) The ability of the nervous system to adapt to trauma or disease; the ability of nerve cells to grow and form new connections to other neurons.

neuroplasty (nū′rō-plăs″tē) [″ + *plassein,* to form] Plastic surgery of the nerves.

neuropodium (nū″rō-pō′dē-ŭm) *pl.* **neuropodia** [″ + *podion,* little feet] The expanded tips of the axon terminals at a synapse.

neuropore (nū′rō-por″) [″ + *poros,* an opening] Embryonic opening from the neural canal to the exterior.

neuroprosthetics (noor″ō-pros-thet′iks, nūr″) [*neuro-* + *prosthetics*] Any biomedically engineered device designed to be linked to the peripheral or central nervous system and enhance the cognitive, motor, or sensory abilities of an organism. SYN: *neural* **prosthetics**.

neuroprotection (nūr″ō-prō-těk′shŭn) The science of minimizing secondary neurologic damage following stroke or trauma. Certain drugs, enzymes, hormones, and physical actions, such as inducing hypothermia, may act as neuroprotectors.

neuropsychiatrist (nū″rō-sī-kī′ă-trĭst) [″ + *psyche,* mind, + *iatreia,* healing] A specialist in neuropsychiatry.

neuropsychiatry (nū″rō-sī-kī′ă-trē) The branch of medicine concerned with the study and treatment of both neurological and psychiatric diseases.

neuropsychopharmacology (nū″rō-sī″kō-făr″mă-kŏl′ō-jē) [″ + ″ + *pharmakon,* drug, + *logos,* word, reason] The study of the effects of drugs on mental illness.

neuroradiography (nū″rō-rā″dē-ŏg′ră-fē) [″ + L. *radius,* ray, + Gr. *graphein,* to write] Radiography of the structures of the nervous system.

neuroradiology (nū″rō-rā″dē-ŏl′ō-jē) [″ + ″ + Gr. *logos,* word, reason] The branch of medicine that utilizes radiography for diagnosis of pathology of the nervous system.

neuroretinitis (nū″rō-rět″ĭn-ī′tĭs) [″ + L. *retina,* retina, + Gr. *itis,* inflammation] Inflammation of the optic nerve and retina.

neuroretinopathy (nū″rō-rět″ĭ-nŏp′ă-thē) [″ + ″ + Gr. *pathos,* disease, suffering] Pathology of the retina and optic nerve.

neurorrhaphy (nū-ror′ă-fē) [″ + *rhaphe,* seam, ridge] The suturing of the ends of a severed nerve.

neurosarcoma (nū″rō-săr-kō′mă) [″ + ″ + *oma,* tumor] A sarcoma containing neuromatous components.

neuroscience (nū″rō-sī′ěns) Any one of the various branches of science (e.g., embryology, anatomy, physiology, histopathology, biochemistry, pharmacology) concerned with the growth, development, and function of the nervous system.

neurosecretion (nū″rō-sē-krē′shŭn) [″ + L. *secretio,* separation] The manufacture and discharge of chemicals by neurons, such as the secretion of hormones by cells of the hypothalamus or anterior pituitary.

neurosensory (nū″rō-sěn′sō-rē) [″ + L. *sensorius,* pert. to a sensation] Pert. to a sensory nerve.

neurosis (nū-rō′sĭs) *pl.* **neuroses** [″ + *osis,* condition] **1.** In traditional (e.g., Freudian) psychiatry, an unconscious conflict that produces anxiety and other symptoms and leads to maladaptive use of defense mechanisms. **2.** An unpleasant or maladaptive psychological disorder that may affect personality, mood, or certain limited aspects of behavior but that does not distract the affected individual from carrying out most activities of daily living. **3.** A term formerly used to describe anxiety disorders, phobias, obsessions and compulsions, or somatoform disorders. SYN: *psychoneurosis.*

TREATMENT: Psychotherapy, cognitive therapy, behavioral therapy, family therapy, minor tranquilizers, and/or sedatives may be used.

Many neuroses are chronic and debilitating; others are minor, manageable, or adaptive. Treatment may be difficult in some cases.

   anxiety n. Anxiety disorder. SEE: *effort syndrome.*

   cardiac n. Neurasthenia.

   compensation n. A form of malingering that develops subsequent to an injury in the belief that financial or other forms of compensation can be obtained or will be continued by being ill. SEE: *factitious* **disorder**.

   compulsion n. Compulsion.

   expectation n. Anxiety disorder.

obsessional n. Obsessive-compulsive disorder.

war n. Post-traumatic stress disorder.

neurosonography (nū″rō-sō-nŏg′ră-fē) The use of ultrasound to obtain diagnostic images of the brain, cranial bones, intracranial and extracranial vascular structures, ventricles, and spinal cord. SYN: *neurosonology.*

neurosonology (nū″rō-sō-nŏl′ŏ-gē) [″ + L. *sonus,* sound + ″] Neurosonography.

neurospasm (nū′rō-spăzm) [″ + *spasmos,* a convulsion] Spasmodic muscular twitching due to a neurological disorder.

Neurospora (nū-rŏs′pō-ră) Genus of fungi belonging to the Ascomycetes class. It includes certain bread molds.

neurostimulation (noor″ō-stim″yă-lā′shŏn, nūr″) [*neuro-* + *stimulation*] The delivery of low voltage electricity to a specific nerve or target in the spinal cord or brain in an attempt to affect neuronal transmission. It can be used to treat neuropathic pain or to modulate motor function (e.g., in the treatment of gastroparesis). **neurostimulator** (noor″ō-stim′yă-lāt″ŏr, nūr″), *n.*

neurosurgeon (nū″rō-sŭr′jŭn) A physician specializing in surgery of the nervous system.

neurosurgery (nūr′ō-sŭr″jĕ-rē) [Gr. *neuron,* nerve, sinew, + L. *chirurgia,* hand, + *ergon,* work] Surgery of the brain, spinal cord, cranial nerves, or peripheral nerves.

functional n. The treatment of diseases of the nervous system in which structurally normal-appearing nerves behave abnormally. Examples of diseases treated with functional neurosurgery include Parkinson disease and other movement disorders, seizure disorders, and some types of chronic nerve pain.

neurosyphilis (nū″rō-sĭf′ĭ-lĭs) Infection of the central nervous system with *Treponema pallidum,* the spirochete that causes syphilis. It may produce acute or chronic meningitis, dementia, damage to the posterior columns, gummatous lesions, or myelopathy. The disease is diagnosed most often when cerebrospinal fluid tests positive for syphilis on standard serological testing with Venereal Disease Research Laboratories. In patients with AIDS, neurosyphilis is more common and more difficult to eradicate than in those with intact immunity.

asymptomatic n. Neurosyphilis that is clinically occult. It is diagnosed by changes in spinal fluid.

meningovascular n. Meningovascular syphilis.

paretic n. Dementia paralytica.

tabetic n. Tabes dorsalis.

neurotensin (nū″rō-tĕn′sĭn) A peptide containing 13 amino acids that is produced by cells of the brain and the small intestine. It is released after the consumption of fats and acts both as a neurotransmitter with psychostimulant properties and as a peripheral hormone that stimulates colonic motility, pancreatic and biliary secretion, and the growth of developing gastrointestinal tissues.

neurotension (nū″rō-tĕn′shŭn) [″ + L. *tensio,* a stretching] Neurectasia.

neurotic (nū-rŏt′ĭk) [Gr. *neuron,* nerve, sinew] **1.** One suffering from a neurosis. **2.** Pert. to neurosis. **3.** Nervous.

neurotic disorder Neurosis.

neuroticism (nū-rŏt′ĭ-sĭzm) [″ + *-ismos,* condition] A condition or trait of neurosis.

neurotization (nū″rŏt-ĭ-zā′shŭn) [Gr. *neuron,* nerve, sinew] **1.** Regeneration of a nerve after division. **2.** Surgical introduction of a nerve into a paralyzed muscle.

neurotmesis (nū″rŏt-mē′sĭs) [″ + *tmesis,* cutting] Nerve injury with complete loss of function of the nerve even though there is little apparent anatomic damage.

neurotome (nū′rō-tōm) A fine knife used in the division of a nerve.

neurotomy (nū-rŏt′ō-mē) [″ + *tome,* an incision] Division or dissection of a nerve.

neurotonic (nū″rō-tŏn′ĭk) [″ + *tonos,* tension] **1.** Pert. to neural stretching. **2.** Having a stimulating effect upon nerves or the nervous system.

neurotony (nū-rŏt′ō-nē) Nerve stretching, usually to ease pain.

neurotoxicity (nū″rō-tŏk-sĭs′ĭ-tē) [″ + *toxikon,* poison] The capability of harming nerve cells or tissues.

neurotoxin (nū″rō-tŏks′ĭn) A substance that attacks or damages nerve cells. **neurotoxic** (-ĭk), *adj.*

neurotransmitter (nūr″ō-trans-mit′-ĕr, noor″, -tranz-,) [*neuro-* + *transmitter*] A molecule released by axon terminals to influence target cells.. Typically, the molecule (e.g., acetylcholine, glutamate, or norepinephrine) is released into a synaptic cleft; it diffuses to a receptor on the membrane of the postsynaptic target cell, and the activated receptor then triggers a reaction that excites or inhibits the activity of the target cell. Often, the activation is quickly stopped when the released neurotransmitter molecules are inactivated or taken up by the presynaptic axon terminal or by nearby glial cells. However, longer term effects of neurotransmitters may be involved in more permanent cellular changes, such as occur in learning.

neurotrauma (nū-rō-traw′mă) [″ + *trauma,* wound] Injury to peripheral nerves or the central nervous system.

neurotripsy (nū″rō-trĭp′sē) [″ + *tripsis,* a rubbing] Surgical crushing of a nerve.

neurotubule (nū″rō-too′būl) [″ + L. *tubulus,* a tubule] A microtuble within the cytoplasm of a neuron.

neurovaccine (nū″rō-văk′sĭn) A standardized vaccine virus of specific strength, usually prepared by cultivation in a rabbit's brain.

neurovascular (nū″rō-văs′kū-lăr) [″ + L. *vasculus,* a small vessel] **1.** Pert. to both the nervous and vascular systems. **2.** Pert. to the nerves that innervate the blood vessels.

Neurovax (noor′ŏ-văks, nūr′) T-cell vaccination for multiple sclerosis.

neurovegetative (nū″rō-vĕj′ĕ-tā″tĭv) Pert. to the autonomic nervous system.

neurovirus (nū″rō-vī′rŭs) Virus that has been modified by its growth in nervous tissue and used in preparing vaccines.

neurula (nū′roo-lă) The stage in the development of an embryo (esp. amphibian embryos) during which the neural plate develops and axial embryonic nervous structures are elaborated.

neurulation (nū″roo-lā′shŭn) Formation of the neural plate in the embryo and the development and closure of the neural tube.

neutral (noo′trăl, nū′) [L. *neutralis,* neuter (gender), fr. *neuter,* neither (of two)] **1.** Neither alkaline nor acid. **2.** Indifferent; having no positive qualities or opinions. **3.** Pert. to electrical charges that are neither positive nor negative.

neutralization (nū″trăl-ĭ-zā′shŭn) **1.** The opposing of one force or condition with an opposite force or condition to such degree as to cause counteraction that permits neither to dominate. **2.** In chemistry, the process of destroying the peculiar properties or effect of a substance (e.g., the neutralization of an acid with a base or vice versa). **3.** In medicine, the process of checking or counteracting the effects of any agent that produces a morbid effect.

neutralization test A test of the ability of an antibody to neutralize the effects of an antigen.

neutralize (noo′tră-līz″, nū′) **1.** To counteract and make ineffective. **2.** In chemistry, to destroy peculiar properties or effect; to make inert. **3.** To make into a substance that is neither acidic or basic.

neutral reaction In chemistry, a reaction indicating the absence of acid or alkaline properties; expressed as pH 7.0.

neutral thermal environment SEE: under *environment.*

neutrino (nū-trē′nō) In physics, a subatomic particle at rest, with no mass and no electric charge. These particles are constantly flowing through the universe and are not known to affect the matter through which they pass.

neutro-, neutr- [L. *neuter,* stem *neutr-,* neither] Prefixes meaning *neutral.*

neutroclusion (nū″trō-kloo′zhŭn) [L. *neuter,* neither, + *occludo,* to close] A condition in which the anteroposterior occlusal positions of the teeth or the mesiodistal positions are normal but malocclusion of other teeth exists.

neutron (noo′tron″, nū′) [L. *neuter,* neither] A subatomic particle very slightly greater in mass to a proton but without an electric charge. It is believed to be a particle of all nuclei of mass number greater than one.

neutron capture analysis The use of the ability of a neutron to be absorbed (captured) by an atomic nucleus to detect the presence of various substances.

neutropenia (noo″trō-pē′nē-ă, nū″) [*neutro-* + *-penia*] The presence of an abnormally small number of neutrophils in the blood, usually less than 1500 per microliter. Severely low levels of neutrophils predispose patients to infection. **neutropenic** (-pē′nik), *adj.*

  cyclic n. A rare blood disorder in which patients suffer recurring fevers and infections, oral ulcers, and malaise and are found to have periodically depressed numbers of neutrophils in the blood. Cyclic neutropenia can be treated with drugs that stimulate neutrophil production.

  malignant n. Agranulocytosis.

  severe congenital n. One of several autosomal recessively inherited blood diseases in which inadequate neutrophils are made by the bone marrow, predisposing affected children to the risk of repeated, severe bacterial infections.

neutrophil, neutrophile (noo′trŏ-fil″, nū′, -fīl″) [*neutro-* + *-phile*] ABBR: NE. A granular white blood cell (WBC), the most common type (55% to 70%) of WBC. Neutrophils are responsible for much of the body's protection against infection. They play a primary role in inflammation, are readily attracted to foreign antigens (chemotaxis), and destroy them by phagocytosis. Neutrophils killed during inflammation release destructive enzymes and toxic oxygen radicals that eradicate infectious microorganisms. An inadequate number of neutrophils (neutropenia) leaves the body at high risk for infection from many sources and requires protective precautions on the part of health care workers. Cancer patients receiving chemotherapy, which destroys leukocytes, must be carefully protected from infections during the course of therapy and until the bone marrow produces additional leukocytes.

  As part of a severe inflammatory response or autoimmune disorder, neutrophils may begin attacking normal cells and cause tissue damage. This occurs in adult respiratory distress syndrome, inflammatory bowel disease, myocarditis, and rheumatoid arthritis. Corticosteroids are the most commonly used drugs to minimize the damage caused by severe inflammation. SYN: *neutrophilic leukocyte*. SEE: illus; *blood* for illus.

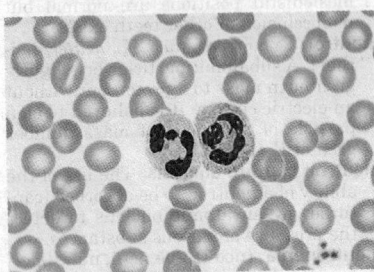

NEUTROPHILS

two segmented neutrophils

polysegmented n. Polymorphonuclear **leukocyte**.

neutrophilia (nū″trō-fĭl′ē-ă) Increase in the number of neutrophils in the blood (e.g., as a result of inflammation, infection, corticosteroid drugs, or malignancies).

neutrophilic, neutrophilous (nū-trō-fĭl′ĭk, -trŏf″ĭ-lŭs) [″ + Gr. *philein,* to love] Staining readily with neutral dyes.

neutrophilic dermatoses SEE: under *dermatosis.*

neutrophil recovery In neutropenic patients, esp. those who have been treated with chemotherapy or bone marrow transplantation, the return of neutrophil counts to higher than 500 cells/mm³.

neutrotaxis (nū″trō-tăk′sĭs) [*neutrophil* + Gr. *taxis,* arrangement] The phenomenon in which neutrophils are repelled by or attracted to a substance.

nevocarcinoma (nē″vō-kăr″sĭ-nō′mă) [L. *naevus,* birthmark, + Gr. *karkinos,* crab, + *oma,* tumor] Malignant melanoma.

nevoid (nē′voyd) [″ + Gr. *eidos,* form, shape] Resembling a nevus.

nevose (nē′vōs) [L. *naevus,* birthmark] Spotted or marked with nevi. SEE: *nevus.*

nevus (nē′vŭs, nē′vī″) *pl.* **nevi** [L. *naevus,* birthmark] **1.** A congenital discoloration of a circumscribed area of the skin due to pigmentation. SYN: *birthmark; mole.* **2.** A circumscribed vascular tumor of the skin, usually congenital, due to hyperplasia of the blood vessels. SEE: *angioma.*

n. anemicus A patch of pale skin in which blood vessels are narrowed or contracted and blood flow is locally limited.

n. araneus Spider **angioma**.

blue n. A dark blue nevus covered by smooth skin. It is composed of melanin-pigmented spindle cells in the mid-dermis.

blue rubber bleb n. An erectile, easily compressible, bluish, cavernous hemangioma present in the skin and gastrointestinal tract.

capillary n. A nevus of dilated capillary vessels elevated above the skin. It is usually treated by ligature and excision.

n. comedonicus A horny nevus that contains a hard plug of keratin. It is caused by failure of the pilosebaceous follicles to develop normally.

compound n. A cluster of melanocytes found in both the epidermis and the dermis.

connective tissue n. A nevus composed of collagenous tissue.

cutaneous n. A nevus formation on the skin.

dysplastic n. A nevus composed of cells having some malignant characteristics.

eclipse n. A benign nevus often found on the scalp, having a pale or tan center enclosed within a darker encircling rim.

epidermal n. A raised nevus present at birth. It may be hyperkeratotic and widely distributed.

faun tail n. In newborns, a tuft of hair over the lower spinal column. It may be associated with spina bifida occulta.

n. flammeus A large reddish-purple nevus of the face or neck, usually not elevated above the skin. It is considered a serious deformity due to its large size and color. In children, these have been treated with the flashlamp-pulsed tunable dye laser. SYN: *port-wine* **mark**; *port-wine* **stain**. SEE: illus.

hairy n. A nevus covered by a heavy growth of hair. It is usually darkly pigmented.

halo n. A papular brown nevus with an oval halo occurring in the first three decades of life. This type of nevus is usually benign but should be evaluated for malignancy.

intradermal n. A nevus in which the melanocytes are found in nests in the dermis and have no connection with the deeper layers from which they were formed.

Ito n. SEE: *Ito nevus.*

junctional n. A nevus in the basal cell zone at the junction of the epidermis and dermis. It is slightly raised, pigmented, and does not contain hair. This type of nevus may become malignant. SEE: illus.

n. lipomatous A tumor composed of fatty connective tissue. It is probably a degenerated nevus containing numerous blood vessels. SYN: *nevolipoma.*

melanocytic n. Any nevus that contains melanocytes. SEE: illus.

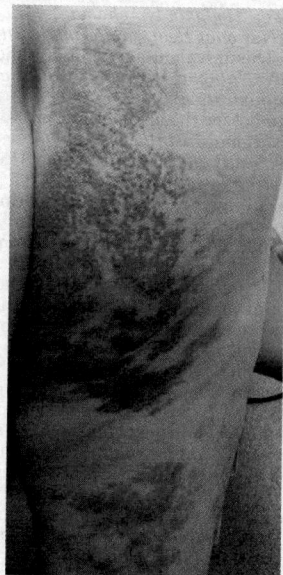

NEVUS FLAMMEUS

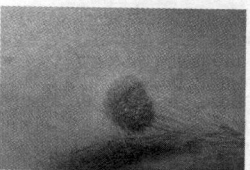

MELANOCYTIC NEVUS

nevocytic n. A common mole. Moles may appear at any age. They are classified according to their stage of growth and whether or not they are still growing.

Ota n. SEE: *Ota nevus.*

pigmented n. A congenital nevus varying in color from light yellow to black. Intradermal or nevocytic nevi are benign. Other types of nevi may become malignant. SYN: *n. pigmentosus.*

TREATMENT: Malignant or suspicious lesions should be treated by wide surgical excision. Benign lesions do not require treatment except when located at sites of friction causing bleeding or ulceration. Some nevi are removed for cosmetic reasons.

n. pigmentosus pigmented **n.**

sebaceous n. n. sebaceus.

n. sebaceus An epidermal nevus containing sebaceous gland tissue. SYN: *sebaceous n.*

spider n. Spider **angioma**.

n. spilus A pigmented nevus with a smooth, unraised surface.

n. spongiosus albus mucosae White sponge **n.**

strawberry n. 1. Vascular **n. 2.** Infantile **hemangioma**.

telangiectatic n. A nevus containing dilated capillaries.

n. unius lateris A congenital nevus that occurs in streaks or linear bands on one side of the body. It usually occurs between the neurotomes of the lumbar or sacral area.

vascular n. A nevus in which superficial blood vessels are enlarged. Nevi of this type are usually congenital. They are of variable size and shape, slightly elevated, and red or purple in color. They generally appear on the face, head, neck, and arms, though no region is exempt. The nevi usually disappear spontaneously, but wrinkling, pigmentation, and scarring are sometimes seen. SYN: *strawberry n. (1); n. vascularis.*

n. vascularis Vascular **n.**

n. venosus Venous **n.**

venous n. A nevus formed of dilated venules. SYN: *n. venosus.*

verrucous n. A nevus with a raised, wartlike surface. SYN: *n. verrucosus.*

n. verrucosus Verrucous **n.**

white sponge n. A white, spongy nevus that may occur in the mouth, labia, vagina, or rectum. SYN: *n. spongiosus albus mucosae.*

newborn 1. Born recently. **2.** A term applied to human infants less than 28 days old. SEE: *neonate.*

Newcastle disease (nū′kăs-ĕl) [Newcastle, England] An acute viral disease of birds, particularly chickens. It occasionally produces incidental infections in humans, usually in the form of a mild conjunctivitis.

new drug application ABBR: NDA. An application requiring approval by the Food and Drug Administration before any new drug is marketed to the general public. Before approval, the manufacturer must provide the FDA with scientifically acceptable evidence of the new drug's safety and efficacy.

New Freedom Initiative A comprehensive U.S. federal program to promote the participation of persons with disabilities in society by increasing access to built environments and transportation, making devices usable despite physical

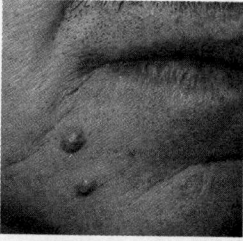

JUNCTIONAL NEVI

and sensory limitations, expanding educational and employment opportunities, and promoting increased access to community life.

newly born Born within the past few minutes. Contrast the terms *newborn* and *neonate*.

Newman, Margaret (nū'măn) Nursing educator, born 1933, who developed the Theory of Health as Expanding Consciousness. SEE: *Nursing Theory Appendix*.

new molecular entity ABBR: NME . A unique, pharmacologically active product that has never previously been synthesized or used to treat disease.

newsgroup (nooz'groop", nūz') An Internet-based support group that shares information about a particular topic, e.g., advances in the management of a disease (including diagnosis, treatment, or prognosis) or developments in prosthesis.

newton (nū'tŭn) SYMB: N. The name of a measure of force derived from the base units used in SI units of measurement. It is equal to the force that will accelerate one kilogram a meter per second squared, 10^5 dynes. SEE: SI Units.

newton meter SYMB: Nm. In SI units, one newton per square meter. This is called one pascal (Pa). Thus 1 Pa = 1 N/m^2.

New World The Western hemisphere. Used in the biological sciences to designate plants, animals, and infections that live or thrive primarily in North, South, and Central America.

New York Heart Association ABBR: NYHA. The professional society that promulgated four classes of heart failure. *Class 1* is asymptomatic, but there is risk because of hypertension with evidence of organ stress; *Class 2* is mildly symptomatic during significant exertion; *Class 3* is moderately symptomatic during light exertion; and in *Class 4* the patient is unable to leave the room or bed without severe shortness of breath.

nexus (něk'sŭs) *pl.* **nexus** [L., bond] A connection or link; a binding together. It is used to designate a bond between components of a group.

NF *National Formulary.*

NFLPN *National Federation of Licensed Practical Nurses.*

NFPA *National Fire Protection Association.* Website: NFPA.org

ng *nanogram.*

NG tube *nasogastric tube.*

NH₃ Ammonia.

NHANES *National Health and Nutrition Examination Survey.*

NHBLI *National Health Lung and Blood Institute.*

NH₄Cl *Ammonium chloride.*

NHGRI *National Human Genome Research Institute.*

NHI *National Heart Institute.*

NHL *non-Hodgkin lymphoma.*

NHLI *National Heart and Lung Institute.*

NH₄⁺ The univalent ammonium radical.

NHTSA *National Highway Traffic Safety Administration.*

Ni Symbol for the element nickel.

NIA *National Institute on Aging.*

NIAAA *National Institute on Alcohol Abuse and Alcoholism.*

niacin (nī'ă-sĭn) A B vitamin existing in two forms, nicotinic acid (niacin) and nicotinamide, both of which are modified within cells to form NAD and NADP, coenzymes that are essential for cellular metabolic processes. It naturally occurs in mushrooms, wheat bran, fish, poultry, meat, asparagus, and peanuts. The many products made with flour fortified with niacin are good sources of this nutrient. As tryptophan is readily converted to niacin, foods such as eggs and milk that lack niacin are good sources of this vitamin. Niacin is the form used orally or parenterally for the treatment of pellagra; oral administration of niacin is used to treat hyperlipidemia. SYN: *nicotinic acid.*

⚠ The use of niacin is sometimes associated with nausea, vomiting, flushing, abnormal liver function tests, hyperglycemia, dry skin, itching, muscle injury, and rarely liver failure. In doses much higher than the Recommended Daily Allowance, niacin lowers the production of very low-density lipoproteins (VLDLs) precursors to low-density lipoproteins (LDLs), increases blood high-density lipoproteins (HDLs), and reduces blood triglycerides. Common side effects of high doses of niacin include red, scaly, itchy skin; stomach irritation and ulcers; liver disease; and elevations of blood sugar, uric acid, and homocysteine.

niacinamide (nī"ă-sĭn-ăm'īd) Nicotinamide.

NIAID *National Institute of Allergy and Infectious Diseases.*

NIAMD *National Institute of Arthritis and Metabolic Diseases.*

NIAMSD *National Institute of Arthritis and Musculoskeletal and Skin Diseases.*

nib (nĭb) In dentistry, the smooth or serrated blade of a condensing instrument that contacts the restorative material placed in a cavity preparation.

NIBIB *National Institute of Biomedical Imaging and Bioengineering.*

NICE *National Institute for Health and Clinical Excellence* (in the U.K.).

niche (nĭch) [Fr.] **1.** A depression or recess on a smooth surface, esp. an erosion in the wall of a hollow organ, detected by radiography. **2.** A habitat and way of life to which a particular organism is adapted.

    enamel n. One of two depressions

that develop between the dental lamina and the enamel organ.

NICHHD *National Institute of Child Health and Human Development.*

nick 1. To cleave or cut a molecular bond. **2.** A gap made in the backbone of a DNA molecule.

nickel (nik'ĕl) SYMB: Ni. A metallic element, atomic mass 58.70; atomic number 28.

n. carbonyl Ni(CO)$_4$, an industrial chemical used in plating metals. It is toxic when inhaled, causing pulmonary edema. SYN: *tetracarbonyl n.*

tetracarbonyl n. **Nickel** carbonyl.

nicking, A-V nicking (nik'ing) **1.** Compression of the retinal vessels of the eye at the point where a vein and an artery cross, seen in hypertensive cardiovascular disease. **2.** To notch a tissue.

Nicolas-Favre disease (nē″kō-lă-făv'r) [Josef Nicolas, b. 1868, and M. Favre, 1876–1954, Fr. physicians] Lymphogranuloma venereum.

Nicolau syndrome (nik-ŏ-low') [Stefan George Nicolau, contemporary Romanian physician] Localized necrosis of the skin and subcutaneous tissues after an intramuscular or intra-articular drug injection. SYN: *embolia cutis medicamentosa; livedo-like dermatitis.*

nicotinamide (nik″ŏ-tiē′nă-mīd″, tin'ă) [*nicotine* + *amide*] A basic amide that is a member of the vitamin B complex, used in the prophylaxis and treatment of pellagra. SYN: *niacinamide.*

n. adenine dinucleotide ABBR: NAD. An enzyme important in accepting electrons in the course of metabolic reactions. In its oxidized form, NAD$^+$ gives up its electron and is converted to the reduced form, NADH. SYN: *V factor.*

n. adenine dinucleotide-dehydrogenase SEE: *nicotinamide adenine dinucleotide phosphate.*

n. adenine dinucleotide phosphate ABBR: NADP. A coenzyme that contains adenosine, nicotinamide, and phosphoric acid. When in its oxidized form (NADP$^+$), it serves as an electron carrier in catabolic and anabolic reactions. In its reduced form (NADPH or NADPH-diaphorase), it is important in reducing the ferric iron (Fe^{+++}) to its ferrous (Fe^{++}) form, thus converting methemoglobin (which is unable to transport oxygen) to hemoglobin (which can transport oxygen). Deficiency of NADPH-diaphorase causes congenital methemoglobinemia. SYN: *methemoglobin reductase.*

nicotine (nik'ŏ-tēn, -tĭn) [L. *nicotiana,* tobacco] A poisonous, highly addictive alkaloid found in all parts of the tobacco plant, but esp. in the leaves. When pure, it is a colorless oily fluid with little odor but a sharp burning taste. On exposure to air or in crude materials, it becomes deep brown with a characteristic

tobacco-like smell. Cigarettes, cigars, and chewing tobacco contain varying amounts of nicotine. During cigarette smoking the blood nicotine level rises 10 to 15 sec after each puff. A person's average daily nicotine intake varies with the number and type of tobacco products used, the depth of inhalation during smoking, and any exposure to secondhand smoke. Many smokers experience withdrawal symptoms when their daily nicotine exposures fall below 5 mg/day. SEE: *cancer, lung; cotinine; nicotine chewing gum; nicotine poisoning, acute; patch, nicotine; tobacco, smokeless.*

Smoking during pregnancy is associated with high risk for low-birth-weight infants, prematurity, and perinatal respiratory infections.

SYMPTOMS: In healthy subjects who are not accustomed to using nicotine, nausea, vomiting, dizziness, headache, sleep disturbances, and sweating are commonly reported.

TREATMENT: Nicotine replacement therapy, administered by chewing gum, nasal spray, transdermal patch, or inhaler, can help motivated smokers to abstain from tobacco use. This type of therapy should be offered to patients who have specific plans to quit and who have received some form of structured counseling about smoking cessation.

Nicotine replacement is sometimes helpful in managing active ulcerative colitis, esp. in former smokers with the disease. Other treatments for nicotine addiction include some antidepressant medications (e.g., bupropion) and nicotine-receptor blocking drugs.

nicotine chewing gum The oral form of nicotine, used primarily as an aid to stop smoking.

nicotine patch SEE: under *patch.*

nicotinic (nĭk″ŏ-tĭn'ĭk) Pert. to the stimulating effect of acetylcholine on the parasympathetic and sympathetic ganglionic or somatic skeletal muscle receptors.

nicotinism (nĭk'ŏ-tĭn-ĭzm) Poisoning from excessive use of tobacco or nicotine.

nictitate (nik'tĭ-tāt″) [L. *nictitare,* to wink] To wink.

NICU *neonatal intensive care unit.*

NIDA *National Institute on Drug Abuse.*

nidation (nī-dā'shŭn) Implantation (2).

NIDCD *National Institute on Deafness and Other Communication Disorders.*

NIDDK *National Institute of Diabetes and Digestive and Kidney Diseases.*

NIDDM *Noninsulin–dependent diabetes mellitus,* the former abbreviation for the disease now known as type 2 diabetes mellitus.

NIDR *National Institute of Dental Research.*

NIDRR *National Institute of Disability*

and Rehabilitation Research (U.S. Department of Education.)

nidus (nī′dŭs) *pl.* **nidi** [L., nest] **1.** A nestlike structure. **2.** Focus of infection. **3.** A nucleus or origin of a nerve. **nidal** (nī′dăl), *adj.*

Niemann-Pick cell A foamy, lipid-filled cell present in the spleen and bone marrow in Niemann-Pick disease.

Niemann-Pick disease (nē′măn-pĭk) [Albert Niemann, Ger. pediatrician, 1880–1921; Ludwig Pick, Ger. physician, 1868–1944] A disturbance of sphingolipid metabolism characterized by enlargement of liver and spleen, anemia, lymphadenopathy, and progressive mental and physical deterioration. It is an autosomal recessive lysosomal storage disease, with its onset in early infancy. Death usually occurrs before the third year. A typical cell, having a foamy appearance and filled with a lipoid believed to be sphingomyelin, can be found in the bone marrow, spleen, or lymph nodes, and aids in establishing the diagnosis. SYN: *lipid histiocytosis.*

night blindness SEE: under *blindness.*

nightguard A dental prosthesis worn at night to prevent traumatic grinding of the teeth during sleep. SEE: *occlusal guard.*

Nightingale, Florence (nīt′ĭn-gāl) A British philanthropist, 1820–1910, the founder of nursing as a profession, a statistician, and a pioneering hospital reformer. She was one of many trained nurses to serve in Crimea and greatly lowered the death rate in the British army by advocating cleanliness and reform of sanitary conditions in hospitals at the battlefront. The decrease in morbidity and mortality at the front attracted the public in Britain, Europe, and the U.S., and the Nightingale Fund gained large contributions from donors around the world. The fund was used to establish a school of nursing at St. Thomas' Hospital in London, England, in 1860. The school became a model for nursing schools around the world; the first nursing school based on the Nightingale model to be established in the U.S. was at Bellevue Hospital in New York City.

nightmare (nīt′mār) [AS. *nyht*, night, + *mara*, a demon] A frightening dream. SYN: *incubus; oneirodynia.* SEE: *sleep disorder.*

nightshade (nīt′shād) Any of several of the poisonous plants of the genus *Solanum,* which contain atropine-like toxins.

   deadly n. Belladonna.

night sweat Profuse sweating during sleep. It may be a symptom of lymphoma or other cancers, numerous infectious diseases, or menopause.

night terrors [″ + L. *terrere,* to frighten] A form of nightmare typically experienced by children in which a frightening hallucination is accompanied by an inability to awaken from sleep. The fear continues for a period after the return to consciousness. SYN: *pavor nocturnus.* SEE: *sleep disorder.*

nightwalking Sleepwalking. SEE: *sleep disorder.*

night work, maladaptation to Difficulty in adapting to sleeping during the day and working at night. In the U.S. about 7.3 million people work at night and are forced to attempt to readjust their day-night schedule for working and sleeping. Adaptation may be facilitated by making the work space as light as possible and scheduling the sleep period (8 hours) in a totally dark environment. SEE: *clock, biological; shift work.*

NIGMS *National Institute of General Medical Sciences.* A division of the National Institutes of Health of the U.S. Department of Health and Human Services.

nigra (nī′gră) [L., black] Substantia nigra.

nigricans (nī′grĭ-kăns) Blackened.

nigrities (nī-grĭsh′ĭ-ēz) Blackness; black pigmentation.

   n. linguae A black pigmentation of the tongue.

nigrostriatal (nī′grō-strī-ā′tăl) Concerning a bundle of nerve fibers that connect the substantia nigra of the brain to the corpus striatum.

NIH *National Institutes of Health* (of the U.S. Department of Health and Human Services).

nihilism (nī′ĭ-lĭzm) [L. *nihil,* nothing, + Gr. *-ismos,* condition] **1.** Disbelief in efficacy of medical therapy. SYN: *therapeutic pessimism.* **2.** In psychiatry, a delusion in which everything is unreal or does not exist.

Nikolsky sign (nĭ-kol′skē) [Pyotr Nikolsky, Russian dermatologist, 1855–1940] A condition seen in pemphigus, where the external layer of the skin can be detached from the basal layer and rubbed off by slight friction or injury.

NIMH *National Institute of Mental Health,* a division of the National Institutes of Health of the U.S. Department of Health and Human Services.

NINCDS *National Institute of Neurological and Communicative Disorders and Stroke.*

NINDB *National Institute of Neurological Diseases and Blindness,* a division of the National Institutes of Health of the U.S. Department of Health and Human Services.

Nine-Hole Peg Test ABBR: 9-HPT. A timed performance test in which a subject places nine dowels in nine holes and then removes them, first with the dominant hand and then with the nondominant one. The more rapidly the test is performed, the greater the dexterity of the subject.

ninhydrin test (nĭn-hī′drĭn) A neurological test of sensation following peripheral nerve injury; used to detect a sympathetic response as indicated by sweat.

NINR *National Institute of Nursing Research.*

ninth cranial nerve Glossopharyngeal nerve.

niobium (nī-ō′bē-um) [*Niobe,* a character in Gr. mythology + *-ium*] SYMB: Nb. A chemical element, atomic number 41, atomic weight (mass) 92.906.

nip-it (nip′it) [Acronym from *Nursing Initiative Promoting Immunization Training*] A Web-based curriculum designed to educate nurses and nursing students about vaccine-preventable illnesses and contemporary immunization practices. Website: www.nip-it.org

nipple (nip′ĕl) **1.** The erectile protuberance at the tip of each breast from which the lactiferous ducts discharge. The nipple projects from the center of the more heavily pigmented areola. Both the nipple and the areola contain small sebaceous glands (Montgomery glands) that secrete a protective oily substance. SYN: *mammae papilla; teat.* SEE: *breast* for illus.

PATIENT CARE: *Assessment:* Instructions and demonstrations to help patients examine their own breasts should include inspecting the nipples and areolae for symmetry of shape, size, color, and texture and reporting any sign of retraction or evidence of discharge.

Pregnancy-related: Prenatal instructions about breast-feeding and postpartum breast care emphasize the signs to report promptly to the health care provider, e.g., nipple cracking, inversion, redness, or bleeding. SEE: *breast cancer; breast-feeding.*

2. An artificial substitute for a female nipple, used for bottle-feeding infants. Nipple-shaped pacifiers may be used to satisfy infant needs for sucking as a self-consoling activity.

crater n. Retracted **n.**

retracted n. A nipple whose tip is pulled inward or folded on itself. It differs from an inverted nipple in that it will not come out when stimulated. Causes include aging, ductal ectasia, or breast cancer. Any change in nipple position, esp. if accompanied by discharge or change in surrounding skin, should be reported to a health care provider. SYN: *crater **n.***

nipple stimulation SEE: under *stimulation.*

nisin (nī′sĭn) An antibiotic that is active against gram-positive bacteria; it is used primarily as a food preservative.

Nissl, Franz (nis′ĕl) Ger. neurologist, 1860–1919.

N. body Large granular bodies found in nerve cells. They can be demonstrated by selective staining. They are rough endoplasmic reticulum (with ribosomes) and are the site of protein synthesis. Nissl bodies show changes under various physiological conditions, and in pathological conditions they may dissolve and disappear (chromatolysis). SYN: *N. granule.* SEE: *tigroid bodies.*

N. degeneration Nerve cell degeneration after division of the axon.

N. granule **N.** body.

NIST *National Institute of Standards and Technology.*

nit (nĭt) [AS. *hnitu*] The egg of a louse or any other parasitic insect. SEE: *Pediculus.*

Ni-Ti *nickel-titanium* (an alloy used in some bone grafts and other dental and orthodontic applications).

nitrate (nī′trāt″) [*nitro-* + *-ate*] A salt of nitric acid. Agents in this class include isosorbide dinitrate or mononitrate and nitroglycerin. They are arteriovenous dilators used to treat angina pectoris, hypertension, and heart failure.

nitration (nī-trā′shŭn) Combination with nitric acid or a nitrate.

nitrazine A chemical indicator used to determine pH, especially of vaginal secretions. It is often used in gynecological and obstetrical evaluations, e.g., to determine whether a pregnant woman has premature rupture of membranes with leaking amniotic fluid in the vaginal vault.

nitric acid (nī′trik) SEE: under *acid.*

nitric oxide NO, a soluble gas normally produced in the human body and present in expired air at a concentration of about 10 parts per billion. Nitric oxide is a potent vasodilator produced by endothelial cells, neurons in the brain, and macrophages during inflammation. Nitric oxide has many other roles: it inhibits the adhesion, activation, and aggregation of platelets and the inflammatory process induced by mast cells; controls chemotaxis of lymphocytes; regulates smooth muscle cell proliferation, penile erection, and other sexual functions; participates in programmed cell death; and interacts with oxygen radicals to form metabolites that destroy pathogens. When nitric oxide is given as part of a mixture of inhaled gas, it decreases recruitment of lymphocytes. In the acute respiratory distress syndrome, nitric oxide improves oxygenation but does not affect patient survival. Nitric oxide was formerly called *endothelium-derived relaxing factor.* SYN: **nitrogen** *monoxide.* SEE: *nitric oxide **gas;** oxygen radical; phagocytosis.*

nitride (nī'trīd) A binary compound formed by direct combination of nitrogen with another element (e.g., lithium nitride [Li$_3$N], formed from nitrogen and lithium).

nitrification (nī"trĭ-fĭ-kā'shŭn) The process by which the nitrogen of ammonia or other compounds is oxidized to nitric or nitrous acid or their salts (nitrates, nitrites). This process takes place continually in the soil through the action of nitrifying bacteria.

nitrifying bacteria (nī'trĭ-fī-ĭng) Bacteria that induce nitrification, including the nitrite bacteria of the genus *Nitrosomonas,* which convert ammonia to nitrites, and nitrate bacteria of the genus *Nitrobacter,* which convert nitrites to nitrates.

nitrile (nī'trĭl) An organic compound in which trivalent nitrogen is attached to a carbon atom. It is used to make latex-free gloves for use in health care.

nitrite (nī'trīt) [Gr. *nitron,* salt] A salt of nitrous acid. Nitrites dilate blood vessels, reduce blood pressure, depress motor centers of the spinal cord, and act as antispasmodics.

nitro-, [Gr. *nitron,* salt] Prefix meaning *combination with nitrogen* or presence of the group NO$_2$.

nitrobenzene (nī"trō-bĕn'zēn) A toxic derivative of benzene used esp. in making aniline.

nitroblue tetrazolium test (nī'trō-blū) A test of the ability of leukocytes to reduce nitroblue tetrazolium from a colorless state to a deep blue. It is used as a marker of nitric oxide synthase. The reduction of NBT may be used in the rapid diagnosis of urinary tract infections and in the study and diagnosis of chronic granulomatous disease and other illnesses in which there are defects in the oxidative metabolism of phagocytic white blood cells.

nitrocellulose (nī"trō-sel'yŭ-lōs") [*nitro-* + *cellulose*] Pyroxylin.

nitrogen (nī'trō-jĕn) [*nitro-* + *-gen*] SYMB: N. A colorless, odorless, tasteless, gaseous chemical element, atomic weight (mass) 14.0067, atomic number 7. It occurs free in the atmosphere and forms approx. 80% of the volume of the atmosphere.

    A component of all proteins, nitrogen is essential to plant and animal life for tissue building. Generally it is found organically only in the form of compounds such as ammonia, nitrites, and nitrates. These are transformed by plants into proteins and, being consumed by animals, are converted into animal proteins of the blood and tissues.

    liquid n. Nitrogen cooled to 77K (77°C above absolute zero). Liquid nitrogen is used to cool or freeze body parts, esp. the skin, in anesthesia and some surgeries. SEE: illus.

LIQUID NITROGEN

    n. monoxide Nitric oxide.

    nonprotein n. Compounds in animal nutrition that can be converted to nitrogen sources in ruminant animals. Urea, biuret, and ammonia are three examples.

nitrogenase (nī'trō-jĕn-ās) [*nitrogen* + *-ase,* enzyme] An enzyme that catalyzes the reduction of nitrogen to ammonia.

nitrogen lag The length of time required after a given protein is ingested before an amount of nitrogen equal to that in the protein has been excreted.

nitrogenous (nī-trŏj'ĕn-ŭs) Pert. to or containing nitrogen. Foods that contain nitrogen are the proteins; those that do not contain nitrogen are the fats and carbohydrates. The retention of nitrogenous waste products such as urea in the blood indicates kidney disease.

nitrogen plasma skin regeneration Plasma skin regeneration.

nitroglycerin (nī"trō-glĭs'ĕr-ĭn) [Gr. *nitron,* salt, + *glycerin*] ABBR: NTG. Any nitrate of glycerol, but specifically the trinitrate. The trinitrate is a heavy, oily, colorless liquid obtained by treating glycerol with nitric and sulfuric acids, well known as the explosive constituent of dynamite. In medicine it is used as an arterial and venous dilator, esp. to treat angina pectoris, congestive heart failure, and acute pulmonary edema.

    It is available as an intravenous infusion (in critical care), as an ointment that can be applied to the chest, as transdermal patches, and as an oral drug (either a tablet that dissolves under the tongue or a spray that can be applied to the mucous membranes of the mouth). Its most common side effects include lowering of blood pressure and headache.

PATIENT CARE: Nitroglycerin tablets used at home should be stored in a tightly sealed dark glass container and replaced every 6 months to ensure that the drug maintains optimal activity. Patients using nitroglycerin during episodes of angina pectoris should take a single dose and sit quietly or lie down for 5 min while waiting for relief of chest discomfort. If, after 5 min the discomfort has not abated, the patient may take a second dose. He may take a third dose of medication if symptoms have not resolved in another 5 min, but if this dose is also ineffective, the patient or a family member should call for emergency assistance (dial 911). For patients who are prescribed long-acting nitrates (e.g., nitroglycerin patches or pills containing isosorbide), an interval overnight during which no nitrates are used may improve the effectiveness of prescribed nitrates and prevent drug tolerance.

⚠️ Nitroglycerin should not be taken by men using sildenafil (Viagra) or related compounds for erectile dysfunction because of the risk of fatal hypotension.

nitromersol (nī"trō-mĕr'sŏl) An organic mercurial antiseptic.

nitrous (nī'trŭs) [Gr. *nitron,* salt] Containing nitrogen in its lowest valency.

nitrous acid HNO_2; a chemical reagent used in biological laboratories.

nitrous oxide N_2O, a flammable, anesthetic and analgesic gas, used in both general and outpatient dental anesthesia. Its use has been associated with miscarriage, organ injuries, and dependence and abuse, although the data linking nitrous oxide to these problems are controversial. The informal name of nitrous oxide is *laughing gas.* SYN: *dinitrogen monoxide.*

Nitrous oxide has little or no effect on body temperature, metabolism, blood pressure, volume, or composition, or on the genitourinary system. Diaphoresis, increased muscle tone, or both may occur with induction of anesthesia with nitrous oxide.

Asphyxiation may occur if it is not administered properly. Prolonged administration of nitrous oxide will cause depression of bone marrow.

SYMPTOMS: Signs of deep nitrous oxide anesthesia include a slight increase in respirations and some dyspnea. The pupils become fixed and dilated, and there is muscular rigidity and cyanosis that increases to a grayish pallor.

TREATMENT: Patients suffering from an overdose should be oxygenated and ventilated.

exhaled n.o. The concentration of nitrous oxide (N_2O) in expired air.

NK cells *natural killer cells.*

NLM *National Library of Medicine.*

NLN *National League for Nursing.*

NLP *Natural language* **processing**.

nm *nanometer.*

NMDP *National Marrow Donor Program.*

NMDS *Nursing Minimum Data Set.*

NME *Necrolytic migratory* **erythema**; *new molecular entity.*

NMO *neuromyelitis optica.*

NMRI *Naval Medical Research Institute* (U.S. Navy); *nuclear magnetic resonance imaging.*

NMR spectroscopy *nuclear magnetic resonance spectroscopy.*

NMSS *National Multiple Sclerosis Society.*

NND *New and Nonofficial Drugs,* a former publication of the American Medical Association, which described new drugs that had not been admitted to the U.S. Pharmacopeia.

NNRTI *nonnucleoside analog reverse transcriptase inhibitor.*

NO *nitrogen monoxide.*

No Symbol for the element nobelium.

no [L. *numero*] *to the number of.*

NOADN *National Organization for Associate Degree Nursing.*

nobelium (nō-bel'lē-ŭm) [*Nobel* Institute, Sweden, where it was first isolated in 1957] SYMB: No. An element obtained from the bombardment of curium. Its atomic number is 102. The atomic mass of the most stable isotope of nobelium is 254; other isotopes vary in weight from 252 through 256.

Nobel Prize (nō-bĕl') [Alfred B. Nobel, Swedish chemist and philanthropist who developed nitroglycerin, 1833–1896, and whose will provided funds for awarding the annual prizes] Awards given almost every year since 1901 to honor distinguished contributions to world peace, chemistry, physics, literature, economics, physiology, and medicine.

Noble position (nō'bĕl) [Charles Percy Noble, U.S. physician, 1863–1935] A position in which the patient is standing, leaning forward, and supporting the upper body by bracing the arms against a wall or a chair. This position is useful in renal examinations.

Nocardia (nō-kăr'dē-ă) [Edmund I. E. Nocard, Fr. veterinary pathologist, 1850–1903] A genus of gram-positive aerobic bacilli that often appear in filaments. Some species are acid-fast and thus may be confused with the causative organism for tuberculosis when stained. A species pathogenic for humans causes the disease nocardiosis. **nocardial** (nō-kăr'dē-ăl), *adj.*

N. asteroides A species pathogenic for humans in which abscesses called mycetomas arise in the skin. The invasion site may be the lungs or skin. SEE: *nocardiosis*.

N. brasiliensis A species pathogenic for humans in which chronic subcutaneous abscesses are formed.

nocardiosis (nō-kăr″dē-ō′sĭs) A pulmonary or brain infection caused by the bacteria *Nocardia asteroides* or, less commonly, by other *Nocardia* species that are found in soil. *Nocardia* are considered opportunistic pathogens, primarily infecting patients with a compromised immune system (e.g., patients with AIDS or end-stage renal disease), but approx. 15% of cases occur in healthy persons. Inhalation of contaminated dust causes the infection.

SYMPTOMS: Infection occurs in the lungs in 75% of patients, causing pneumonia characterized by a productive cough, hemoptysis, and, at times, abscesses; pleural invasion may occur, producing pain. The remaining 25% of patients develop brain abscesses marked by headache, nausea, vomiting, and changes in mental status.

DIAGNOSIS: Infection is diagnosed through cultures of sputum or transtracheal aspirates, which may require 4 weeks of growth.

TREATMENT: Nocardiosis usually is treated with 6 months of oral sulfasoxazole or trimethoprim/sulfamethoxazole; persons with AIDS need lifelong suppressive therapy. Pneumonia producing severe respiratory distress is treated with intravenous cefotaxime plus imipenem, followed by oral therapy. In patients with brain abscesses, mortality is approx. 40%; in patients with pneumonia, it ranges from 10% to 30%.

nocebo (nō-sē′bō) [L., I will harm] A substance (such as a sugar pill) or an exposure (such as to an odor or fragrance) that makes a person feel ill, even though it has no measurable negative effects. The nocebo effect can be contagious, as in cases of mass sociogenic illness. SEE: *placebo*.

noci-, noc- [L. *nocere*, to injure] Prefixes meaning *pain, injury*.

nociception (nō″si-sep′shŏn) [*noci-* + (re)ception] The stimulus-response process involving the stimulation of peripheral pain-carrying nerve fibers and the transmission of impulses along peripheral nerves to the central nervous system, where the stimulus is perceived as pain. SEE: *nociceptor; nociceptive impulse*.

abnormal cardiac n. Chest pain in patients undergoing coronary angiography or simultaneous electrocardiography without abnormal findings found inside the coronary arteries. The symptoms can occur during catheterization of the right atrium, right ventricle, coronary arteries, or other intracardiac locations.

nociceptive impulse (nō″si-sĕp′tĭv) Impulse giving rise to sensations of pain.

nociceptor (nō″sē-sĕp′tor) [″ + *receptor*, receiver] A free nerve ending that is a receptor for painful stimuli. **nociceptive** (nō″sĭ-sĕp′tĭv), *adj.*

nociperception (nō″sĭ-pĕr-sĕp′shŭn) [″ + *perceptio*, apprehension] The perception by the nerve centers of injurious influences or painful stimuli.

no code orders (nō-kōd) An indication on the chart of a patient that he or she does not want heroic or lifesaving measures to be instituted when death is imminent.

no-CPR order A formal, often written request by a patient with a terminal illness for emergency assistance with comfort care at the end of life, without cardiopulmonary resuscitation. Such orders include emergency and hospital care for dyspnea, pain, excessive secretions, or psychological discomfort.

noct-, nocti-, nocto- [L. *nox*, stem *noct-*, night] Prefixes meaning *night*. SEE: *nycto-*.

nocturia (nŏk-tū′rē-ă) [″ + Gr. *ouron*, urine] Excessive or frequent urination after going to bed, typically caused by excessive fluid intake, congestive heart failure, uncontrolled diabetes mellitus, urinary tract infections, diseases of the prostate, impaired renal function, or the use of diuretics. Less often, diabetes insipidus is the cause. SYN: *nycturia*. SEE: *enuresis*.

PATIENT CARE: Patients may find that they can reduce the need to void at night by limiting fluid intake during the evening. Safety is emphasized for patients who need to get up to go to the bathroom at night because they may not be fully awake or alert. Specific recommendations include use of night lights and removal of objects blocking the route from the bedroom to the bathroom. The patient should be assessed for cause and treatment instituted to resolve the problem if possible.

nocturnal (nok-tŭr′năl) [L. *nocturnus*, belonging to the night, at night] Pert. to or occurring in the night. SEE: *diurnal*. See words beginning with *nyct-*.

nocturnal eating (drinking) syndrome A rare disorder involving frequent awakenings from sleep to eat or drink. Those affected are unable to return to sleep without eating a meal. The condition is most commonly observed in infants, young children, and people being treated with some sedatives. In adults it is considered to be both a sleep disorder and a binge eating disorder.

nocturnal hypoglycemia SEE: under *hypoglycemia*.

nocturnal penile tumescence ABBR: NPT. Erection occurring during sleep.

In the normal male, erections during sleep begin in early childhood and continue to at least the eighth decade. The total time of NPT averages 100 minutes per night. In evaluating erectile dysfunction (ED), the presence of NPT suggests the patient has psychogenic ED rather than neurogenic or vascular ED.

NOD   *nucleotide-binding oligomerization domain proteins.*

nodal (nō′dăl) [L. *nodus,* knot] Pert. to a protuberance.

   n. **rhythm**   Cardiac rhythm with origin at the atrioventricular node.

nodding (nŏd′ĭng) Involuntary motion of the head downward, as when momentarily dozing.

nodding spasm   SEE: under *spasm.*

node (nōd) [L. *nodus,* knot] **1.** A knot, knob, protuberance, or swelling. **2.** A constricted region. **3.** A small rounded organ or structure.

   atrioventricular *n.*   ABBR: AV node. A node of specialized cardiac muscle fibers in the lower interatrial septum that receives impulses from the sinoatrial node and transmits them to the bundle of His. SYN: *Aschoff **n.*** SEE: *atrioventricular **bundle**; conduction system of the **heart*** for illus.

   Bouchard *n.*   In osteoarthritis, bony enlargement of the proximal interphalangeal joints.

   ectopic lymph *n.*   A cluster of immunologically active cells inside a malignant tumor. The node may represent an attempt by the body to destroy foreign antigens on the tumor cell surface.

   Haygarth *n.*   Joint swelling seen in rheumatoid arthritis.

   Heberden *n.*   SEE: *Heberden nodes.*

   Hensen *n.*   SEE: under *Hensen, Christian Andreas Victor.*

   lymph *n.*   A small encapsulated lymphoid organ that filters lymph. Lymph nodes are found at junctions or branches along the lymphatics. They provide sites where immune responses can be generated through the interaction of antigens, macrophages, dendritic cells and lymphocytes. SEE: illus.; *immune response; inflammation; lymph; lymphocyte.*Lymph nodes are 0.1-2.5 cm long kidney-shaped aggregates of lymphocytes and macrophages embedded in a meshwork reticulum composed of thin collagen fibers. At each lymph node, an artery enters through a surface indentation (the hilum) alongside an exiting vein and an exiting (efferent) lymphatic vessel; a number of afferent lymphatic vessels enter the lymph node at other sites. Inside lymph nodes, lymph slowly flows through endothelial sinuses lined by lymphocytes and macrophages. Macrophages remove macromolecules, particles, debris, and microorganisms from the lymph stream. Lymphocytes and antibodies move through the walls of

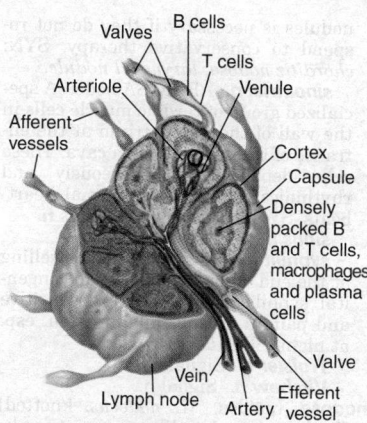

LYMPH NODE

the sinuses and into the passing lymph, while dendritic cells pass from the lymph into the lymphatic follicles, carrying antigens from the body's epithelia and from infected tissues. In the cortical region of the lymph node, the sinuses wind around lymphatic follicles, which are ovoid germinal centers packed with differentiating and proliferating B lymphocytes and surrounded by loose T lymphocytes. Lymphocytes and antibodies also enter and exit blood capillaries throughout the lymph node. Lymph nodes are most numerous in the neck, mediastinum, abdominal mesenteries, pelvis, the proximal limbs (the axillae and the groin), and along the posterior abdominal wall. Inside the chest and trunk, lymph nodes tend to be found along the veins near viscera.

   neurofibril *n.*   Ranvier node.

   Osler *n.*   SEE: *Osler nodes.*

   Parrot *n.*   SEE: *Parrot nodes.*

   piedric *n.*   A node on the hair shaft seen in piedra.

   Ranvier *n.*   SEE: *Ranvier node.*

   Schmorl *n.*   A node seen in radiographs of the spine. It is caused by prolapse of the nucleus pulposus into the end plate of the vertebra.

   sentinel *n.*   **1.** A lymph node that receives drainage from a tumor and is likely to harbor metastatic disease before cancer cells have the opportunity to spread elsewhere. **2.** Signal node.

   signal *n.*   Enlargement of one of the supraclavicular lymph nodes; usually indicative of primary carcinoma of thoracic or abdominal organs. SYN: *sentinel **n.** (2); Troisier's **n.**; Virchow node.*

   singer's *n.*   Noncancerous, callus-like growths on the inner parts of the vocal cords, usually caused by voice abuse or overuse. It is marked by a singer's hoarseness and an inability to produce the desired notes. It is treated by resting the voice. Surgical removal of the nodules is necessary if they do not respond to conservative therapy. SYN: *chorditis nodosa; laryngeal nodule.*

sinoatrial n. ABBR: SA node. A specialized group of cardiac muscle cells in the wall of the right atrium at the entrance of the superior vena cava. These cells depolarize spontaneously and rhythmically to initiate normal heartbeats. SYN: *pacemaker* (2); *sinus n.*

  sinus n. Sinoatrial node.

  syphilitic n. Circumscribed swelling at the end of long bones due to congenital syphilis. The nodes are sensitive and painful during inflammation, esp. at night. SEE: *Parrot nodes.*

  Troisier n. Signal n.

  Virchow n. Signal n.

nodose (nō'dōs) [L. *nodosus,* knotted] Swollen or knotlike at intervals; marked by nodes or projections.

nodosity (nō-dŏs'ĭ-tē) [L. *nodositas,* a knot] **1.** A protuberance or knot. **2.** The condition of having nodes.

nodular (noj'ŭ-lăr) Pert. to, containing, or resembling nodules.

nodular worm SEE: under *worm.*

nodule (noj'ool") [L. *nodulus,* little knot] **1.** A small node. **2.** A small cluster of cells.

  aggregate n. A group of unencapsulated lymph nodules, such as Peyer patches of the small intestine.

  apple jelly n. The jelly-like lesion of lupus vulgaris.

  Aschoff n. SEE: *Aschoff nodules.*

  laryngeal n. Singer's n.

  lymph n. A mass of compact, densely staining lymphocytes forming the structural unit of lymphatic tissue. These nodules may occur singly, in groups (as in Peyer's patches), or in encapsulated organs such as lymph nodes. Each contains a lighter-staining germinal center where new lymphocytes are formed.

  miliary n. A small round density, 1 to 5 mm in diameter, as seen on the chest radiograph (e.g., in disseminated tuberculosis).

  milker's n. A painless smooth or warty lesion due to a poxvirus that is transmitted from the udders of infected cows to the hands of milkers. SEE: *paravaccinia.*

  rheumatic n. A subcutaneous node of fibrous tissue that may be present in patients with rheumatic fever. SEE: *subcutaneous n.* for illus.

  Schmorl n. Schmorl node.

  n. of the semilunar valve Arantius body.

  siderotic n. A small brown nodule seen in the spleen and other organs and consisting of necrotic tissue encrusted by iron salts.

  solitary n. An isolated nodule of lymphatic tissue such as occurs in mucous membranes.

  solitary pulmonary n. Any isolated mass lesion found in the lung, usually during an x-ray study performed for another reason. Most small masses that are identified in this way are benign, although smokers, patients already known to have cancer in another organ system, and older patients have an increased risk that a solitary nodule will be a new malignancy or a metastasis from another source.

  PATIENT CARE: The first step in evaluating a solitary lung nodule is to search for prior chest x-ray films. If the nodule can be found on films done many months or years earlier and has not changed in size, shape, or calcification, it is likely to be benign and can be followed conservatively. Newly identified lesions within the lung that were not previously present usually are evaluated with further studies, such as computed tomography of the lungs, sputum studies, or biopsies.

  subcutaneous n. A small, nontender swelling resembling Aschoff bodies and found over bony prominences in persons with rheumatic fever or rheumatoid arthritis (in rheumatoid arthritis, it is called a rheumatoid nodule). SEE: illus.

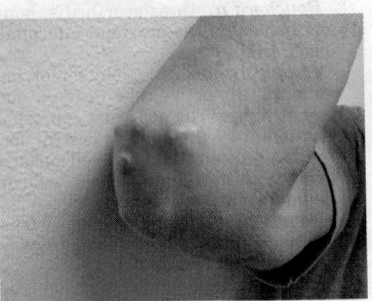

SUBCUTANEOUS NODULES

  surfer's n. Nodular swelling and possible bone changes of the area of the lower leg and foot exposed to pressure and trauma while on a surfboard. The nodules may be painful. SYN: *surfer's knots.* SEE: illus.

  thyroid n. A visible or palpable mass in the thyroid gland, benign about 90% to 95% of the time. A history of radiation to the head or neck increases the likelihood that the lesion will be malignant, as does the appearance of the nodule in the first decades of life. Fine-needle aspiration biopsy is the first and often the definitive diagnostic test.

  typhoid n. A nodule characteristic of typhoid fever and found in the liver.

  typhus n. A small nodule of the skin seen in typhus. They are composed of mononuclear cell infiltration around vessels.

nodulus (nŏd'ū-lŭs) *pl.* **noduli** [L.]

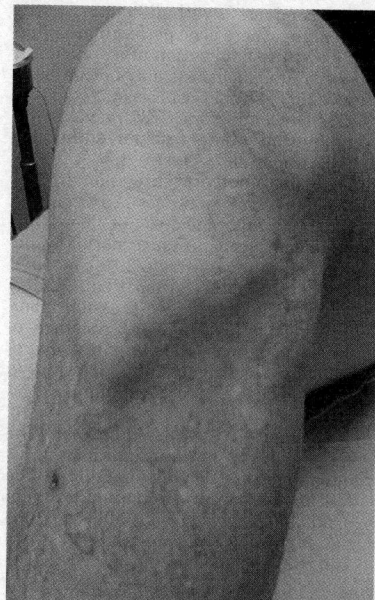

SURFER'S NODULES

1. Nodule. 2. The anterior portion of the vermis of the cerebellum.

nodus (nō′dŭs) *pl.* **nodi** [L.] 1. Node. 2. Anatomically, a small circumscribed mass of undifferentiated tissue.

noesis (nō-ē′sĭs) [Gr. *noesis,* thought] The act of thinking; cognition.

noetic therapy (nō-ĕt′ĭk) [Gr. *noetikos,* intelligent] Any therapy based on deeply held belief systems, prayer, or spirituality rather than on tangible or visible interventions, e.g., the use of drugs, radiation, or surgery.

no-fault error SEE: under *error.*

noise [O.Fr. *noise,* strife, brawl] 1. Sound of any sort, including that which is loud, harsh, confused, or senseless. SEE: table; *acoustic trauma; pollution, noise.* 2. In electronics or physics, any electronic disturbance that interferes with the signal being recorded or monitored. In electrocardiography, the 60-cycle alternating current used to power the machine may be inadvertently recorded. This obscures the signal from the electrical activity of the heart. 3. Unwanted information on a radiograph caused by fogging or scattered radiation.

   ambient n. The total noise from all sources in a given environment.

   n. pollution A level of environmental noise of such nature or intensity as to cause mental or physical discomfort or damage to the hearing system.

NOM *Nonoperative management.*

noma (nō′mă) [Gr. *nome,* a spreading] Cancrum oris.

   n. pudendi An infected ulcer affecting the labia majora, esp. in young children.

nomadism (nō′măd-ĭzm) [Gr. *nomas,* roaming about] Having a constantly migratory lifestyle, as is practiced by some animals and humans.

nomenclature (nō′měn-klā″chŭr) [L. *nomen,* name, + *calare,* to call] A classified system of technical or scientific names. SEE: *terminology.*

   binomial n. The system of classifying living organisms by the use of two Latin-derived words to indicate the genus and species.

nomen nudum (nō′měn noo′dŭm, nū′) [L. mere name] A named but as yet undescribed organism.

Nomina Anatomica (nō′mĭ-nă ăn-ă-tŏm′ĭ-kă) [″ + Gr. *anatome,* dissection] ABBR: NA. Formerly, the official anatomical nomenclature prepared by revising the Basle Nomina Anatomica and adopted by the Sixth International Congress of Anatomists at meetings held periodically since 1955. It was replaced by the Terminologia Anatomica in 1998. SEE: *Basle Nomina Anatomica; Terminologia Anatomica.*

nomogram (nŏm′ō-grăm) [Gr. *nomos,* law, + *gramma,* something written] Representation by graphs, diagrams, or

Typical Noise Levels in Decibels and Their Effect

Situation	Level (decibels)	Effect
Jet engine (close by)*	140	Harmful to hearing
Jet takeoff*	130	
Propeller aircraft*	120	
Live rock band	110	Risk of hearing loss
Jackhammer	100	
Heavy-duty truck	90	
Private car; business office	70	Probably no risk of permanent damage to hearing
Wooded residential area	50	No harm
Whisper	30	
Rustle of leaf	10	

* Outside aircraft

charts of the relationship between numerical variables.

Rumack n. A nomogram that predicts both the severity of acetaminophen overdose and the need for specific treatment.

weight-based n. A nomogram used to prescribe medications based on patient size.

nomography (nō-mŏg′ră-fē) [″ + *graphein*, to write] The construction of a nomogram.

non- [L. *non*, not] Prefix meaning *not*.

nonabandonment (nŏn″ă-băn′dŭn-mĕnt) The ethical obligation of a health care provider to remain in a continuous caring partnership with his or her patient. This partnership remains in place during periods of health and illness and is particularly important when the patient has a chronic or life-threatening disease. Several aspects of modern medical care, in which the patient's choice of physician may be limited and disrupt the continuity of the physician-patient relationship, make carrying out this obligation difficult. SEE: *abandonment*.

nonagenarian (nŏn″ă-jĕ-nār-ē-ăn) A person whose age is between 90 and 99 years.

noncombatant (nŏn″kom′bă-tănt, nŏn″kŏm-bat′ănt) **1.** A member of the military who does not engage in combat, such as a chaplain or physician. **2.** A civilian, esp. in a combat zone.

noncommunicable disease (nŏn″kŭm-ū′nĭ-kă-bĭl) An infectious disease such as tetanus or botulism that cannot be transmitted from one person to another.

noncompliance (nŏn″cŏm-plī′ăns) The failure or refusal of a patient to cooperate by carrying out that portion of the medical care plan under his or her control (e.g., not taking prescribed medicines or not adhering to the diet or rehabilitation procedures ordered). SEE: *Nursing Diagnoses Appendix*.

noncompliance [adherence, ineffective] (specify) Behavior of person and/or caregiver that fails to coincide with a health-promoting or therapeutic plan agreed upon by the person (and/or family, and/or community) and health care professional. In the presence of an agreed-on health-promoting or therapeutic plan, person's or caregiver's behavior is fully or partially adherent or nonadherent and may lead to clinically ineffective, partially ineffective outcomes. SEE: *Nursing Diagnoses Appendix*.

non compos mentis (nŏn kŏm′pŏs mĕn′tĭs) [L.] Not of sound mind; mentally incompetent to handle one's affairs.

nonconductor (nŏn″cŏn-dŭk′tŏr) [L. *non*, not, + *con*, with, + *ductor*, a leader] Any substance that does not transmit heat, sound, or electricity or

that conducts it with difficulty. Strictly speaking, there is no perfect nonconductor. On the application of a sufficiently high voltage, current may be caused to flow through materials usually spoken of as nonconductors. SEE: *insulator*.

nondihydropyridine calcium antagonist SEE: under *antagonist*.

nondipping blood pressure (nŏn″dĭp′ĭng) Blood pressure that does not drop by at least 10% after the onset of sleep. During sleep blood pressure normally decreases by about 10% to 20% compared to daytime values. In patients undergoing ambulatory blood pressure monitoring, a failure of blood pressure to drop has been associated with several health concerns, including an increased risk of obstructive sleep apnea and stroke.

nondisclosure (nŏn″dis-klō′zhŭr) The withholding of relevant information.

nondisjunction (nŏn″dĭs-jŭnk′shŭn) The failure of a pair of chromosomes to separate during meiosis, allowing one daughter cell to have two chromosomes and the other to have none. SEE: illus.

Nondisjunction

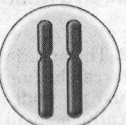

In **nondisjunction**, a pair of chromosomes fails to separate: both chromosomes go to the same daughter cell while the other daughter cell doesn't receive a chromosome.

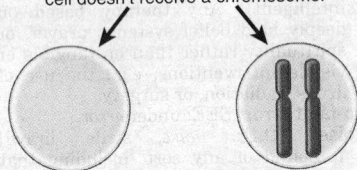

When fertilization adds the matching chromosome, one daughter cell has three of that particular chromosome (called **trisomy**) while the other daughter cell has one chromosome with no mate (called **monosomy**)

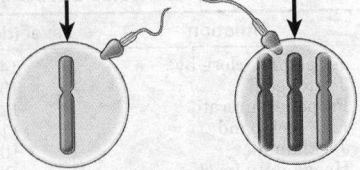

NONDISJUNCTION

nondominant (nŏn″dŏm′ĭ-nĭnt) In neurology, that hemisphere of the brain that does not control speech or the preferentially used hand. SEE: *cerebral dominance*.

nonelectrolyte (nŏn″ē-lĕk′trō-līt) [″ + Gr. *elektron*, amber, + *lytos*, dissolved] A solution that will not conduct electricity because its chemical constituents are not sufficiently dissociated into ions.

nonepileptic attack disorder Pseudoseizure.

nonfeasance (nŏn-fē′zĕns) [L. *non*, not + O.Fr. *faisance*, doing, action] In law, failure to meet an obligation, esp. an official duty or a legal one.

nonformulary (non″for′myŭ-ler″ē) [*non-* + *formulary*] Not approved for use. The term is applied to a drug whose prescription is not usually reimbursed by a health insurer because it is absent from its formulary.

nongonococcal urethritis (non″gon″ŏ-kok′ăl) [*non-* + *gonococcal*] SEE: under *urethritis*.

nonheartbeating organ donation ABBR: NHBOD. An organ (e.g., a kidney or liver) derived from a patient who is asystolic, apneic, and unresponsive to stimulation. Organs used in transplantation may be donated by living donors such as friends or relatives or deceased donors who have chosen to donate their body parts.

non-Hodgkin lymphoma (non″hoj′kĭn) SEE: *non-Hodgkin **lymphoma***.

noni (nō′nē) [Hawaiian] A tropical fruit tree, *Morinda citrifolia,* studied for its possible use as an immune booster and a treatment for cancer.

nonigravida (nō″nĭ-grā′vĭ-dă) [L. *nonus*, ninth, + *gravida*, pregnant] A woman pregnant for the ninth time. Written gravida IX. SEE: *nonipara*.

nonimmediate allergic reaction Delayed hypersensitivity reaction.

noninferior (non″in-fēr′ē-ŏr) [*non-* + *inferior*] In a clinical trial, jargon for *at least as good as*.

non-inferiority trial (non″in-fēr″ē-or′ĭt-ē) SEE: under *trial*.

noninvasive (nŏn″ĭn-vā′sĭv) **1.** Not tending to spread, as certain tumors. **2.** A device or procedure that does not penetrate the skin or enter any orifice in the body.

nonipara (nō-nĭp′ăr-ă) [″ + *parere*, to bring forth, to bear] ABBR: para IX. A woman who has given birth nine times.

nonlinear (non″lin′ē-ăr) Not linear; not obeying a linear relationship. In mathematics, a linear equation may be given in the form $y = mx + b$, where x is the independent variable, and y is the dependent variable. A nonlinear relationship cannot be represented by such an equation.

nonmaleficence (non″mă-lĕf′ĭ-sĭns) The principle of not doing something that causes harm. Hippocrates felt this was the underpinning of all medical practice. He advised his students, *primum non nocere* ("first, do no harm").

nonmyelinated (nŏn-mī′ĕ-lĭ-nāt″ĕd) [″ + Gr. *myelos*, marrow] Containing no myelin.

nonmyeloablative, nonablative (nŏn-mī″ĕl-ō-ă-blā′tĭv, nŏn-ă-blā′tĭv) [L. *non*, not, + Gr. *myelos*, narrow, + L. *ablatus*, taken away] Not completely destructive of bone marrow. The term describes chemotherapeutic treatments for cancer that do not deplete the marrow of all its blood cells.

nonnucleated (nŏn-nū′klē-āt″ĕd) [″ + *nucleatus*, having a kernel] Containing no nucleus.

nonocclusion (nŏn″ŏ-kloo′zhŭn) [″ + *occlusio*, occlusion] A type of malocclusion in which the teeth fail to make contact.

nonopaque (nŏn″ō-pāk′) Not opaque, esp. to x-rays.

nonoperative management (non″op′ĕ-ră-tiv) ABBR: NOM. The treatment of patients who have suffered serious illnesses, injuries, or trauma without urgent surgery, as with a period of fluid resuscitation, stabilization of vital signs, antibiotics, and analgesics. It is used for some relatively stable patients who have experienced blunt trauma and gunshot wounds and is sometimes used for orthopedic injuries and vascular diseases. SYN: *selective nonoperative management*.

nonose (nŏn′ōs) [L. *nonus*, ninth] A nine-carbon carbohydrate.

nonoxynol (nō-nŏks′ĭ-nŏl) A general class of surface-active agents with the basic formula of $C_{15}H_{24}O(C_2H_4O)_n$, named with respect to the value of *n*. Nonoxynol 9 is a spermicide.

nonpalpable (nŏn-păl′pă-b′l) [L. *non*, not + ″] Not detectable during manual examination but identified instead with radiological or other diagnostic means.

nonpolar (nŏn-pō′lăr) [″ + *polus*, a pole] Not having separate poles; sharing electrons.

   n. compound A compound formed by the sharing of electrons.

nonproblematic drinking (non″prŏb-lĕ-măt′ĭk) In alcohol-related research, alcohol consumption that does not adversely affect a person's physical or mental health, or his or her occupation, family life, or functioning in society. The consumption of less than one standard drink daily normally constitutes nonproblematic drinking.

nonprogressor (nŏn″prŏ-grĕs′ŏr) An individual infected with the human immunodeficiency virus who does not develop worsening immune function or symptoms of active disease.

nonproprietary (non″prŏ-prī′ĕ-ter″ē) [*non-* + *proprietary*] Not protected by trademark or patent. SEE: *generic* (3, 4); *proprietary* (3).

nonproprietary name (non″prŏ-prī′ĕ-ter″ē) The name of a drug other than its trademarked (proprietary) name.

The nonproprietary name for a new drug is usually the same as that selected by the United States Adopted Name (USAN) Council. The official names for older drugs may differ from the nonproprietary names. In some cases the generic name is the same as the nonproprietary name. Drugs also have chemical names; in most cases those names are too long and complex to permit their use. The use of a USAN-selected name simplifies and standardizes drug nomenclature. SEE: *generic* (3, 4); *proprietary* (3); *United States Adopted Names.*

nonprotein (nŏn-prō'tēn) [*non-* + *protein*] Any substance not derived from protein.

nonprotein nitrogen SEE: under *nitrogen.*

nonresectable (nŏn"rē-sĕk'tă-bĭl) Not removable by surgery.

nonresponder (nŏn"rĕ-spŏn'dĕr) **1.** An individual who does not achieve an immunological response to a vaccine. **2.** A person who does not respond in the expected way to therapy, particularly medication.

nonresponse bias (nŏn"rĭ-spŏns') Distortion introduced into a research investigation by incomplete collection of data from all possible respondents. This bias is most likely to influence the results of a study when those who do not participate or who refuse to be sampled have other crucial characteristics that the study is designed to identify.

nonrestraint (nŏn"rē-strānt') [L. *non*, not, + *re*, back, + *stringere*, to bind back] Treatment of the uncooperative without using mechanical restraints.

nonsecretor (nŏn"sē-krē'tor) [" + *secretio*, separation] An individual whose saliva and other body fluids do not contain the ABO blood antigens.

nonself, non-self (non'sĕlf") In immunology, pert. to matter recognized by the body as foreign, e.g., pathogens or pollen, and thereby provoking an attack by the body's immune system. **nonself,** *n.*

nonsexual (nŏn-sĕk'shū-ăl) Asexual.

nonspecific 1. Inexact, imprecise, not well delimited or defined. **2.** Vague. **3.** Poorly identified; described without certainty.

nonspecific therapy The use of injections of foreign proteins or bacterial vaccines in the treatment of infection to stimulate general immunological responses. SEE: *specific therapy.*

nonstochastic effect (nŏn-stă-kăs'tĭk) A radiation effect whose severity increases in direct proportion to the dose and for which there usually is a threshold. An example is radiation-induced cataracts.

nonstress test ABBR: NST. An external electronic monitoring procedure to assess fetal well-being. An acceleration in fetal heart rate should be evident in response to fetal movement. *Reactive test:* Two criteria indicate satisfactory fetal status. The monitor records a minimum of two episodes of heart rate acceleration accompanying fetal movement within one 20-min period, and accelerations of 15 beats per minute (BPM) persist for a minimum of 15 sec per episode. *Nonreactive test:* The monitor record does not meet either criterion for reactivity. This indicates the need for a second test within the next several hours—contraction stress testing, a fetal biophysical profile, or all three. *Inconclusive test:* The monitor records less than one acceleration in 20 min or an acceleration less than 15 BPM lasting less than 15 sec.

nontarget (non"tar'gĕt) **1.** Pert. to a person, area, structure, or organ that is not the target of an action or operation **2.** Such a person, area, structure, or organ. In radiology, a nontarget is only accidentally or incidentally exposed to or affected by an exposure, and not intentionally.

nontoxic (nŏn-tŏk'sĭk) [L. *non*, not, + Gr. *toxikon*, poison] Not poisonous or productive of poison. SEE: *Poisons and Poisoning Appendix.*

nonunion (nŏn-ūn'yŭn) [" + *unio*, oneness] Failure to unite, as a fractured bone that fails to heal completely. Diagnosis of nonunion is established when a minimum of 9 months has elapsed since the injury and the fracture site shows no progressive signs of healing for a minimum of 3 months and is not complicated by a synovial pseudoarthrosis.

nonverbal IQ test (nŏn"vŭr'bŭl) Any of several standard psychometric tests that measure intelligence without the confounding effect posed by differences in speech, reading, and language ability. Such tests include visuospatial tests, pattern recognition tests, and picture-completion tests.

nonviable (nŏn-vī'ă-b'l) [L. *non*, not, + *via*, life] Incapable of life or of living. This term is frequently used to indicate a fetus that has either died in utero or been born prior to 20th week of gestation.

non–weight bearing Pert. to the support or suspension of a lower extremity so that it does not touch the ground.

nonyl (nŏ'nĭl) A univalent radical, $CH_3(CH_2)_8^-$, that contains nine carbon atoms.

nootropic (nō"ă-trŏp'ĭk) [Gr. *nous*, mind + *tropikos*, turning, affecting] Capable of improving or preserving memory, of potentiating learning, or of preventing cognitive decline or dementia.

nopal (nō-păl') *pl.* **nopales** [Sp. fm. Nahuatl] Prickly pear cactus.

noradrenergic (nor″ad″rĕ-nĕr′jik) [*nor (mal)* + *adrenergic*] **1.** Pert. to norepinephrine, esp. its pharmacologic actions on blood vessels and nerves. **2.** Pert. to nerves that release norepinephrine from their axons.

NORD *National Organization for Rare Disorders.*

norepinephrine (nor-ĕp″ĭ-nĕf′rĭn) **1.** A hormone produced by the adrenal medulla, similar in chemical and pharmacological properties to epinephrine but chiefly a vasoconstrictor with little effect on cardiac output. **2.** A neurotransmitter released by most sympathetic postganglionic neurons and by some neurons of the brain. A disturbance in its metabolism at important brain sites has been implicated in affective disorders. It is used to manage severe hypotension, esp. in patients with neurogenic or septic shock.

   n. bitartrate A standardized preparation of norepinephrine. The former name was levarterenol bitartrate.

norgestimate (nŏr-jĕs′tĭ-māt) An estrogen/progestin used as a tricyclic contraceptive hormone. It is administered orally to healthy women and girls over 14 years of age to prevent pregnancy, regulate the menstrual cycle, and manage acne if topical treatment has failed.

norm [L. *norma*, rule] **1.** A standard or ideal for a specific group. **2.** Normal.

norma (nŏr′mă) [L., rule] A view or aspect, esp. with reference to the skull.

   anterior n. N. frontalis.

   n. basilaris N. ventralis.

   n. facialis N. frontalis.

   n. frontalis The outline of the skull viewed from the front. SYN: *anterior n.; n. facialis.*

   inferior n. N. ventralis.

   n. lateralis A view of the skull as seen from the side; a profile view.

   n. occipitalis A view of the skull as seen from behind.

   n. sagittalis A view of the skull as seen in sagittal section.

   superior n. N. verticalis.

   n. ventralis A view of the inferior surface of skull. SYN: *n. basilaris; inferior n.*

   n. verticalis A view of the skull as seen from above. SYN: *superior n.*

normal (nor′măl) [L. *normalis*, according to pattern] **1.** Performing proper functions; standard; regular. **2.** In biology, not affected by experimental treatment; occurring naturally and not because of disease or experimentation. **3.** In psychology, free from mental disorder; of average development or intelligence.

normalize (nor′mă-līz″) To modify in order to attain a normal standard. Example: *The drug was given to normalize the platelet level.* To enforce or impose a criterion or a standard on a person,

place, or thing. **normalization** (nor″mă-li-zā′shŏn), *n.*

normetanephrine (nor-mĕt″ă-nĕf′rĭn) A metabolite of epinephrine.

normo- [*norm(al)*] Prefix meaning *normal.*

normoblast (nor′mō-blăst) [″ + Gr. *blastos*, germ] An immature nucleated red blood cell similar in size to a mature erythrocyte and usually found in the bone marrow. SYN: *erythroblast.* **normoblastic** (-blăs-tĭk), *adj.*

normoblastosis (nor″mō-blăs-tō′sĭs) [″ + ″ + *osis*, condition] Increased production and circulation of normoblasts. This indicates a need for greater oxygen-carrying capacity of the blood, as when mature erythrocytes are being rapidly destroyed.

normocalcemia (nor″mō-kăl-sē′mē-ă) Normal level of blood calcium.

normocapnia (nor″mō-kăp′nē-ă) The presence of a normal concentration of carbon dioxide in the blood and serum. **normocapnic** (-kăp′nĭk), *adj.*

normocholesterolemia (nor″mō-kō-lĕs″tĕr-ō-lē′mē-ă) The presence of a normal concentration of cholesterol in the blood.

normochromasia (nor″mō-krō-mā′zē-ă) [″ + Gr. *chroma*, color] Average staining capacity in a cell or tissue.

normocyte (nor′mō-sīt) [″ + Gr. *kytos*, cell] An average-sized red blood cell. SYN: *erythrocyte.*

normoglycemia (nor″mō-glī-sē′mē-ă) [″ + Gr. *glykys*, sweet, + *haima*, blood] Normal sugar content of the blood. **normoglycemic** (-sē′mĭk), *adj.*

normokalemia (nor″mō-kă-lē′mē-ă) Normal level of blood potassium.

normospermic (nor″mō-spĕr′mĭk) [″ + Gr. *sperma*, seed] Producing normal spermatozoa.

normotensive (nor″mō-tĕn′sĭv) **1.** Normal blood pressure. **2.** A person with normal blood pressure.

normothermia (nor″mō-thĕr′mē-ă) [″ + Gr. *therme*, heat] Normal body temperature.

normovolemia (nor″mō-vō-lē′mē-ă) [″ + *volumen*, volume, + Gr. *haima*, blood] Normal blood volume. **normovolemic**, *adj.*

norovirus (nŏr′ō-vī″-rŭs) Any Norwalk-like virus. Diarrheal outbreaks caused by norovirus infections of the gastrointestinal tract have been reported in nursing homes, schools, and cruise ships, settings in which large groups of people congregate in relatively confined spaces. SEE: *Norwalk virus.*

Norrie disease (nor′ē) [Gordon Norrie, Danish ophthalmologist, 1855–1941] A rare form of x-linked blindness due to retinal malformation. Also present are peripheral vascular pathology, vitreous opacities, microphthalmia, and sometimes mental retardation and loss of hearing.

Norton scale (nort'ŏn) A scale used to predict the likelihood a patient will develop pressure ulcers. The patient is rated from 1 (low risk) to 4 (high risk) using the following five criteria: physical condition, mental condition, activity, mobility, and incontinence. SEE: table.

Norvasc SEE: *amlodipine.*

Norwalk agent (nor'wok") [A virus first identified in Norwalk, Ohio] SEE: under *agent.*

Norwegian itch (nŏr-wē'jĭn) SEE: *Norwegian scabies.*

Norwegian scabies A rare form of scabies in which the mites are present in great number. It often is found in patients with human immunodeficiency virus infection. Ivermectin is used to treat the infestation.

Norwood procedure (nor'wood) [W.I. Norwood, Jr., contemporary U.S. surgeon] Surgical correction of congenital underdevelopment of the left ventricle and the ascending aorta. The procedure is performed in three stages. An alternative to this procedure for children with severe hypoplasia of the left side of the heart is heart transplantation.

NOS *not otherwise specified.* In medical billing and coding, it refers to a diagnosis without specific or distinguishing features.

nose (nōz) The projection in the center of the face that is the organ of smell and the entrance to the nasal cavities. The nose is a triangle composed of and bounded by bone and cartilage covered with skin and lined with mucous membrane. Hairs just inside the nostrils block the entrance of dusts and small insects. SYN: *nasus; organum olfactus.*

EXAMINATION: Note the shape, size, color, and state of the alae nasi, and any discharge, interference with respiration, evidence of injury, deflected or perforated septum, enlarged turbinates, or tenderness over frontal and maxillary sinuses.

DIAGNOSIS: *Chronic red nose:* Dilated capillaries as a result of alcoholism, lupus erythematosus, acne rosacea, pustules, and boils. *Superficial ulceration:* Basal cell carcinoma, tuberculosis, syphilis, tuberculous ulcer, epithelioma. *Broad and coarse:* Cretinism, myxedema, acromegaly. *Sunken:* Syphilis or injury. *Pinched with small nares:* Hypertrophied adenoid tissue or chronic obstructions; tumors. *Inoffensive watery discharge:* Allergic rhinitis, the common cold, early stages of measles. *Offensive discharge:* Nasopharyngeal diphtheria, lupus, local infection, impacted foreign bodies, caries, rhinitis, glanders, syphilitic infection.

   foreign body in the n. Presence of material in the nasal cavity that was either inhaled or accidentally placed there. A child may place a foreign object in his or her own or another child's nose.

SYMPTOMS: Coughing or watery or purulent discharge; occasionally pain and obstruction of nose. The foreign body may cause a nasal obstruction and infection, often with a foul-smelling discharge. If the foreign body is very small, symptoms may be absent.

TREATMENT: Vigorous nose blowing should be discouraged because it may spread infection to the various cavities and sinuses about the nose or to the middle ear. The foreign body should be removed by a health care professional.

   hammer n. Rhinophyma.

   saddle n. A nose with a depressed bridge due to congenital absence of bony or cartilaginous support, to a disease such as leprosy or congenital syphilis, or to postoperative complications of suppuration and destruction of the supporting framework.

nosebleed Hemorrhage from the nose. SEE: *epistaxis; Kiesselbach area.*

Nosema (nō-sē'mă) A genus of parasites of the order Microsporidia. SEE: *microsporidiosis.*

nosepiece (nōz'pēs) The portion of a microscope to which the objective lenses attach.

nose springs A springlike device applied

The Norton Scale*

Physical Condition		Mental State		Activity		Mobility		Incontinence	
Good	4	Alert	4	Ambulatory	4	Full	4	Not	4
Fair	3	Apathetic	3	Walks with help	3	Slightly limited	3	Occasionally	
Poor	2	Confused	2	Chairbound	2	Very limited	2	Usually urinary	2
Very bad	1	Stuporous	1	Bedfast	1	Immobile	1	Double	1

* The patient is rated from 1 to 4 on the five risk factors listed. A score of ≤14 indicates risk for decubitus ulcers, or pressure sores.

SOURCE: Doreen Norton, Rhoda McLaren, and A.N. Exton-Smith. An investigation of geriatric nursing problems in the hospital. London: National Corporation for the Care of Old People (now the Centre for Policy on Ageing), 1962.

to the bridge of the nose that pulls the nostrils open slightly. The device may reduce nasal airway resistance, thereby improving sleep quality and decreasing snoring.

noso-, nos- [Gr. *nosos,* disease] Prefixes meaning *disease.*

nosocomial (nŏs″ō-kō′mē-ăl) [Gr. *nosokomos,* one who tends the sick] Pert. to or occurring in a health care setting, such as a hospital or nursing home.

nosocomial infection SEE: under *infection.*

nosode (nŏs′ōd) [″] A homeopathic vaccination. A very dilute pathological tissue sample, taken from the blood, feces, mucus, pus, or tissue of an infected or diseased organism, administered to a human to promote immunity against disease.

nosology (nō-sŏl′ō-jē) [″ + *logos,* word, reason] The science of description or classification of diseases.

nosophyte (nŏs′ō-fīt) [″ + *phyton,* plant] A disease-causing plant microorganism.

Nosopsyllus (nŏs″ō-sĭl′ŭs) [″ + *psylla,* flea] A genus of fleas belonging to the order Siphonaptera.

    N. fasciatus A species of rat fleas responsible for transmission of murine typhus and possibly plague.

nostalgia (nŏs-tăl′jē-ă) [Gr. *nostos,* a return home, + *algos,* pain] **1.** Homesickness; longing to return home. **2.** A longing to return to a previously experienced time or place.

nostril (nos′trĭl) [Old English. *nosu,* nose + *thyrel,* a hole] One of the external apertures of the nose. SYN: *naris.* SEE: *nose.*

nostrum (nŏs′trŭm) [L., our] A patent, secret, or quack remedy.

notalgia (nō-tal′j(ē-)ă) [*noto-* + *-algia*] Pain in the back. SYN: *dorsalgia.*

    n. paresthetica A localized area of skin, usually of the upper back below the scapula, that itches and then becomes darkly pigmented as a result of habitual scratching. The itch (and the rash that accompany it) are thought to be the result of a focal sensory neuropathy.

notch (nŏch) A deep indentation or narrow gap in the edge of a structure. SYN: *incisure.*

    antegonial n. A depression in the inferior border of the mandible at the anterior edge of the insertion of the masseter muscle.

    aortic n. The notch in a sphygmogram caused by rebound at the aortic valve closure.

    cardiac n. The concavity on the anterior border of the left lung into which the heart projects.

    cardial n. The angle or indentation on the top of the stomach between its orifice (the cardia) and its fundus.

    cerebellar n. Either of two deep notches (anterior and posterior) separating the hemispheres of the cerebellum.

    clavicular n. A notch at the upper angle of the sternum with which the clavicle articulates.

    costal n. Any of seven pairs of indentations on the lateral surfaces of the sternum, for articulation with costal cartilages.

    greater sciatic n. A large notch on the posterior border of the hip bone between the posterior inferior iliac spine and the spine of the ischium.

    interclavicular n. A rounded notch at the top of the manubrium of the sternum between the surfaces articulating with the clavicles.

    jugular n. (of sternum) A notch on the upper surface of the manubrium of the anterior superior chest between the two clavicular notches. SYN: *sternal n.; suprasternal n.*

    labial n. A notch in the labial flange of a denture at the point where it crosses the frenum.

    lesser sciatic n. A notch immediately below the spine of the ischium on the posterior border of the hip bone, which is converted into a foramen by the sacrotuberous ligament.

    mandibular n. A notch on the superior border of the ramus of the mandible separating the coronoid and condyloid processes.

    manubrial n. A depression on the superior edge of the sternum.

    nasal n. **1.** A deep notch on the anterior surface of the maxilla, forming the lateral border of the piriform aperture. **2.** A notch between the internal angular processes of the frontal bone.

    pancreatic n. A notch on the lateral surface of the head of the pancreas for the superior mesenteric artery and vein. It separates the uncinate process of the head from the remaining portion.

    radial n. A notch on the lateral surface of the coronoid process of the ulna for receiving the circumference of the head of the radius.

    scapular n. A deep notch on the superior border of the scapula that transmits the suprascapular nerve.

    semilunar n. A notch on the anterior aspect of the proximal end of the ulna for articulation with the trochlea of the humerus. SYN: *trochlear n.*

    sphenopalatine n. A notch between the orbital and sphenoidal processes of the palatine bone.

    sternal n. Jugular **n.** (of sternum).

    superior thyroid n. Thyroid notch.

    suprasternal n. Jugular **n.** (of sternum).

    tentorial n. An arched cavity in the free border of the tentorium cerebelli through which the brainstem passes.

thyroid n. A notch on the superior border of the thyroid cartilage of the larynx that separates the two laminae. SYN: *superior thyroid n.* SEE: *thyroid cartliage.*

   trochlear n. Semilunar notch.

   ulnar n. The notch on the distal end of the radius that receives the head of the ulna.

   vertebral n. A concavity on the inferior surface of the vertebral arch for transmission of a spinal nerve.

notchplasty (nŏch'plăs-tē) A surgical procedure to enlarge the intercondylar notch and space available for an anterior cruciate ligament graft during knee reconstruction. The lateral wall of the notch, which is the medial portion of the lateral femoral condyle, may be removed by various means.

notch width index SEE: under *index.*

note [L. *nota,* a mark] **1.** A sound of definite pitch. **2.** A brief comment or condensed report.

NOTES *Natural orifice transluminal endoscopic surgery.*

nothing by mouth ABBR: NPO. An instruction used in patient care to indicate that the patient is not to take or receive food, solids, liquid, or medicine orally.

notifiable disease SEE: under *disease.*

noto-, not- [Gr. *nōton,* the back] Prefixes meaning the *back.*

notochord (nō'tō-kord) [" + *chorde,* cord] An embryonic rod of cells lying dorsal to the intestine and extending from the anterior to the posterior end. The notochord forms the axial skeleton in embryos of all chordates. In vertebrates it is replaced partially or completely by the bodies of vertebrae. A remnant persists in humans as a portion of the nucleus pulposus of the intervertebral disk.

Nottingham Extended Activities of Daily Living Scale (not'ing-ăm) [*Nottingham,* England] SEE: under *scale.*

nourishment [L. *nutrire,* to nurse] **1.** Sustenance; nutriment; food. **2.** The act of nourishing or of being nourished. SEE: *trophic.*

Novocaine (nō'vō-kān″) A trade name for procaine, a local anesthetic. "Novocaine" is often loosely used to signify any local or topical anesthetic in discussions with laypersons.

Novolin 70/30 Human insulin consisting of 70% NPH and 30% regular insulins. SEE: *human insulin.*

noxious (nŏk'shŭs) [L. *noxius,* injurious] Harmful; not wholesome.

NP *nucleoprotein; nurse practitioner; nursing practice; nursing procedure; neuropsychiatrist; neuropsychiatry.*

Np Symbol for the element neptunium.

NPA *Nasopharyngeal airway.*

NPC *nodal premature complex.*

NPDB *National Practitioner Data Bank.*

NPH insulin A pancreatic hormone and antidiabetic, administered intravenously or subcutaneously to manage type 1 and some cases of type 2 diabetes mellitus.

NPN *nonprotein nitrogen.*

NPO, npo [L.] *nihil per os,* nothing by mouth.

NPPV *noninvasive positive pressure ventilation.*

NPT *normal pressure and temperature; nocturnal penile tumescence.*

NREM *nonrapid eye movement.* SEE: *sleep, nonrapid eye movement.*

NREMT *National Registery of Emergency Medical Technicians.*

NRMS *National Registry of Medical Secretaries.*

NRTI *nucleoside reverse transcriptase inhibitor.*

NS *normal saline.*

ns **1.** *nanosecond.* **2.** *nonsignificant.*

NSA *National Stroke Association; Neurosurgical Society of America.*

NSAID *nonsteroidal anti-inflammatory drug.*

NSCC *National Society for Crippled Children.*

NSCLC *non–small-cell lung cancer.*

NSD in ret *nominal standard dose* in radiation equivalent therapy.

nsec *nanosecond.*

NSNA *National Student Nurses' Association.*

NSR *normal sinus rhythm.*

NSTEMI *non–ST-segment elevation myocardial infarction.*

N-telopeptide ABBR: NTx. A biomarker of osteoclast-induced bone resorption. Detection of NTx is used, for example, to detect bone breakdown in patients with osteopenia or osteolysis.

   Also known as *cross-linked N-telopeptide of type 1 collagen.*

NTG *nitroglycerin.*

nth (enth) A symbol used in statistics to indicate the continuation of data or subjects to large numbers in a progression or series. Patients in a series are designated as P1, P2,....patients, with Pnth the last patient.

nuad bo rarn (noo'ăd bō rărn) [Thai, literally, "traditional massage"] A traditional Thai method of massage, practiced for centuries in Thailand as a means of improving health and well-being.

nucha (nū'kă) [L.] The nape (back) of the neck. **nuchal** (nū'kăl), *adj.*

nuchal translucency measurement (trăns-loos'ĕn-sē) Intrauterine ultrasonography of the nape of the fetal neck, measured in the first trimester of pregnancy. Abnormal thickening of this part of the body has been associated with a variety of congenital, chromosomal diseases.

Nuck canal (nŭk) [Anton Nuck, Dutch

anatomist, 1650–1692] A rare condition in which a pouch of peritoneal membrane, formed during embryonic development, extends through the inguinal canal.

nuclear (nū′klē-ăr) [L. *nucleus,* a kernel] Pert. to a cellular, atomic, or anatomical nucleus.

nuclear matrix protein 22 SEE: under *protein.*

nuclear medicine scanning examination Any exam that uses radioactive tracers to diagnose disease. Radioactive isotopes are either injected into the body or inhaled. The dose of radiation is minimal, and the substances used either lose their radioactivity in a short time or are excreted. Nuclear medicine scans may be used to diagnose tumors, biliary disease, gastrointestinal emptying or bleeding, coronary artery disease, valvular heart disease, red blood cell survival time, renal dysfunction, deep vein thrombosis, pulmonary embolus, thyroid function, osteomyelitis (or other infections), fractures, and cardiac ejection fraction. Isotopes of thallium, iodine, or other metals are used. In 2007, about 18 million nuclear medicine exams were performed in the U.S. alone, most for obtaining images of the heart and coronary arteries.

nuclear medicine technologist A health care professional who prepares radioactive compounds for use in diagnostic imaging procedures; gives those compounds to patients (usually by injection); scans patients to determine how radiation is emitted from the body after injection and circulation of the compounds; and then processes and analyzes the images derived so that they can be used as diagnostic aids.

nuclear pharmacy SEE: under *pharmacy.*

nuclease (nū′klē-ās) [L. *nucleus,* kernel, + *-ase,* enzyme] Any enzyme in animals or plants that facilitates hydrolysis of nuclein and nucleic acids.

nucleate (nū′klē-āt) [L. *nucleatus,* having a kernel] **1.** Having a nucleus. **2.** To form a nucleus.

nucleic acid (noo-klē′ik, nū-) SEE: under *acid.*

nucleic acid probe (noo-klē′ik, nū-) A labelled single-strand of DNA used to detect complementary DNA in a laboratory specimen.

nucleic acid test (noo-klē′ik, nū-) ABBR: NAT. A test for the presence of specific genetic material in a laboratory specimen, e.g., a specific segment of viral DNA or RNA in a blood sample. NATs are used, e.g., to detect contamination of blood by hepatitis viruses and HIV during the initial period of infection, before viral antigens appear in the blood of infected patients.

nuclein (nū′klē-ĭn) [L. *nucleus,* a kernel] The breakdown product of the nucleoproteins of chromosomes.

nuclein base Any of the bases formed from decomposition of nuclein, such as adenine, guanine, xanthine, and hypoxanthine.

nucleo-, nucle-, nuclei- [L. *nucleus,* kernel] Prefix meaning *nucleus.*

nucleocapsid (nū″klē-ō-kăp′sĭd) In a virus, the protein coat and the viral nucleic acid.

nucleofugal (nū-klē-ŏf′ū-găl) [″ + *fugere,* to flee] Directed or moving away from a nucleus.

nucleohistone (nū″klē-ō-hĭs′tŏn, -tōn) [″ + Gr. *histos,* tissue] A substance composed of nuclein and histone, found in sperm of various animals.

nucleoid (nū′klē-oyd) [″ + Gr. *eidos,* form, shape] Resembling a nucleus.

nucleoloid (nū′klē-ō-loyd) Similar to a nucleus.

nucleolonema (nū″klē-ō″lō-nē′mă) [″ + Gr. *nema,* thread] A fine network in the nucleolus of a cell.

nucleoli (nū-klē′ō-lŭs) *pl.* **nucleoli** [L., little kernel] A spherical structure in the nucleus of a cell made of DNA, RNA, and protein. It is the site of synthesis of ribosomal RNA (rRNA); a cell may have more than one. Embryonic cells and those in malignancies actively synthesize rRNA; therefore, their nucleoli are larger than those of cells that do not require increased amounts of rRNA. **nucleolar** (nū-klē′ō-lăr), *adj.*

nucleon (nū′klē-ŏn) Any of the particles that collectively make up the nucleus of an atom.

nucleopetal (nū-klē-ŏp′ĕ-tăl) [L. *nucleus,* kernel, + *petere,* to seek] Seeking or moving toward the nucleus.

nucleophilic (nū″klē-ō-fĭl′ĭk) [″ + Gr. *philein,* to love] Having an attraction to nuclei.

nucleoplasm (nū′klē-ō-plăzm″) [″ + L. *plasma,* form, mold] The protoplasm of a cell nucleus. **nucleoplasmic,** *adj.*

nucleoprotein (nū′klē-ō-prō′tē-ĭn) [″ + Gr. *protos,* first] The combination of protein and nucleic acid (DNA or RNA).

nucleosidase (nū″klē-ō-sī′dās) An enzyme that catalyzes the hydrolysis of nucleosides.

nucleoside (nū′klē-ō-sīd) A glycoside formed by the union of a purine or pyrimidine base with a sugar (pentose).

nucleosome (nū′klē-ō-sōm) The combination of positively charged histone proteins and negatively charged DNA; the first step in the folding of DNA into chromatin.

nucleospindle (nū″klē-ō-spĭn′d′l) A spindle-shaped body occurring in karyokinesis.

nucleotidase (nū″klē-ŏt′ĭ-dās) An enzyme (nucleophosphatase) that splits phosphoric acid from nucleotides, leaving a nucleoside.

5′-nucleotidase An enzyme present in the serum in abnormal amounts in diseases that affect the liver or obstruct the biliary tree.

nucleotide (nū′klē-ō-tīd) [L. *nucleus,* kernel] A compound formed of phosphoric acid, a pentose sugar, and a base (purine or pyrimidine), all of which constitute the structural unit of nucleic acid. SYN: *mononucleotide.*

nucleotide-binding oligomerization domain proteins SEE: under *protein.*

nucleotidyl (nū″klē-ō-tīd′ĭl) The residue of a nucleotide.

nucleotidyltransferase (nū″klē-ō-tīd″ĭl-trăns′fĕr-ās) An enzyme that transfers nucleotidyls from nucleosides into dimer or polymer forms.

nucleotoxin (nū″klē-ō-tŏk′sĭn) [″ + Gr. *toxikon,* poison] A toxin acting upon or produced by cell nuclei.

nucleus (noo′klē-ŭs, nū′, noo′klē-ī″, nū′) *pl.* **nuclei** [L., *nucleus,* kernel] **1.** A central point about which things are clustered. **2.** The organelle in a eukaryotic cell that contains the chromosomes. SYN: *cell* **n. 3.** In the central nervous system, a group of neuronal cell bodies that are clustered together and form a coherent demarcated mass in stained brain sections. **4.** Atomic nucleus.

    n. abducens A nucleus of the somatic motor column in the hindbrain. It lies in the floor of the fourth ventricle near the midline, and it is the origin of the abducens nerve (CN VI).

    n. accumbens A limbic nucleus that sits at the ventral head of the striatum, contiguous with the caudate and putamen and adjacent to the olfactory tubercle. The nucleus accumbens is part of the ventral striatum nuclei. Synapses in the nucleus accumbens use dopamine as their neurotransmitter. Increasing the activity of these synapses (i.e., increasing the level of dopamine in the nucleus) leads to a rewarding or pleasurable sensation. This is thought to partly explain the addictive effect of those drugs, such as cocaine and amphetamine, that increase the level of dopamine in the nucleus accumbens.

    n. ambiguus A long, thin nucleus of the branchial motor column in the medulla. It is the origin of motor axons in both the glossopharyngeal and vagus nerves, and its axons innervate the muscles of swallowing and vocalization.

    amygdaloid n. Amygdala (2).

    anterior thalamic n. The most rostral of the thalamic nuclei. The anterior thalamic nucleus is the only thalamic nucleus that is directly part of the limbic circuitry. This nucleus receives axons from the mammillary body via the mammillothalamic tract, from the hip-

pocampus via the fornix, and from cholinergic nuclei in the basal forebrain. The anterior thalamic nucleus sends axons to medial cerebral cortices: the cingulate gyrus, the anterior limbic area, and the parahippocampal gyrus. SEE: *limbic system* for illus.

    anterior olfactory n. The neurons clustered along the olfactory tract. Some axons from the mitral cells in the olfactory bulb synapse on anterior olfactory neurons, and anterior olfactory neurons contribute axons to the olfactory tract. The anterior olfactory nucleus, which is distinct in most mammals, is sparse in primates.

    arcuate n. A hypothalamic nucleus in the ventral wall of the third ventricle near the pituitary stalk. The arcuate nucleus produces inhibiting and releasing factors (adrenocorticotrophic hormone, beta-lipotrophic hormone, and beta-endorphin) for pituitary hormones. SYN: *infundibular* **n.**

    atomic n. In chemistry, the heavy, positively charged, central part of an atom, which contains protons, neutrons, and most of the atomic mass. SYN: *nucleus* (4).

    n. basalis of Meynert SEE: under *Meynert, Theodor H.*

    caudate n. A large basal ganglion nucleus shaped like a tadpole. With its interconnected neighbor, the putamen, the caudate forms a single functional nucleus called the striatum. The caudate lies deep in the cerebral hemisphere; its head forms the base of the anterior horn of the lateral ventricle, and its tail follows the ventricle as it arches over the thalamus and curves down and outward to become the inferior horn of the lateral ventricle, inside the temporal lobe of the cerebral hemisphere. The tip of the tail of the caudate ends alongside the caudal end of the amygdala, and many axons that originate in the amygdala synapse in the caudate and other parts of the striatum. SYN: **n.** *caudatus; intraventricular* **n.**

    cell n. Nucleus (2).

    cerebellar n. One of the four deep (i.e., below the cerebellar cortex) nuclei of each half of the cerebellum (from lateral to medial): the dentate, the emboliform, the globose, and the fastigial nuclei.

    cochlear n. SEE: *dorsal cochlear* **n.;** *ventral cochlear* **n.**

    cuneiform n. A nucleus in the midbrain reticular formation lying directly under the superior and inferior colliculi. Axons from the cuneiform nucleus project widely, caudally as far as the hindbrain and rostrally as far as the the diencephalon. SEE: *reticular formation.*

    n. of Darkschewitsch SEE: *nucleus of Darkschewitz.*

Deiter n. The lateral vestibular nucleus. SEE: *vestibular n.*

dentate n. The largest and most lateral of the four pairs of deep cerebellar nuclei; in cross-sections it has a serpentine shape. The nucleus receives axons from the cerebellar cortex and from the brainstem, and it sends axons to the red nucleus and the thalamus via the superior cerebellar peduncle.

n. of the diagonal band A collection of large cholinergic neurons intermingled with the diagonal band, an axon tract interconnecting the septal area of the cerebral hemispheres with the substantia innominata. The nucleus of the diagonal band has reciprocal connections with the hippocampus. Like the large cholinergic neurons in the nucleus basalis, the neurons in the nucleus of the diagonal band degenerate if the brain develops Alzheimer's disease.

diploid n. A cell nucleus that contains double the normal number of chromosomes.

dorsal cochlear n. A nucleus of the special sensory column in the hindbrain. It forms a bump (the acoustic tubercle) on the lateral edge of the floor of the fourth ventricle. Axons of the primary sensory cells in the spiral ganglion (in the cochlea of the inner ear) run in the vestibulocochlear nerve (CN VIII) and synapse in the dorsal and ventral cochlear nuclei. About half of the axons from neurons in the cochlear nuclei cross the midline in a tract called the trapezoid body and then join the uncrossed axons from the contralateral cochlear nuclei. Together, these axons ascend in a tract called the lateral lemniscus to synapse in the inferior colliculus in the midbrain.

dorsal n. of the lateral lemniscus One of the two distinguishable nuclei clustered in the upper (rostral) end of the lateral lemniscus near the inferior colliculi. These nuclei are part of the auditory circuitry.

dorsal motor n. of the vagus A nucleus of the visceral motor column in the hindbrain; it lies in the floor of the fourth ventricle lateral to the hypoglossal nucleus. The dorsal motor nucleus of the vagus is the origin of preganglionic parasympathetic axons via which the vagus nerve (CN X) modulates secretory activity in the gastrointestinal system. SYN: *n. of the vagus; dorsal n. of the vagus.*

dorsal raphe n. A midbrain nucleus that lies in the midline in the tegmentum, below the periaqueductal gray. It sends serotonergic axons to the striatum via the medial forebrain bundle, and it receives axons from the interpeduncular nucleus. SYN: *raphe n.*

dorsal n. of the vagus Dorsal motor n. of the vagus.

dorsolateral septal n. One of the four major septal nuclei.

Edinger-Westphal n. SEE: *Edinger-Westphal nucleus.*

emboliform n. A deep nucleus of the cerebellum, lying between the dentate and globose nuclei.

external cuneate n. A secondary sensory nucleus in the caudal hindbrain lying along the lateral edge of the cuneate nucleus. It receives proprioceptive information from the upper half of the body, it is the source of the cuneocerebellar tract, and it is the homologue of the nucleus called "Clarke column", which receives proprioceptive information from the lower half of the body. SYN: *lateral cuneate n.*

facial motor n. A nucleus of the branchial motor column in the pontine region of the hindbrain. This nucleus is a column of cholinergic neurons in the ventrolateral tegmentum. It is the origin of motor axons in the facial nerve (CN VII), which innervate the muscles of facial expression.

fastigial n. The most medial of the four pairs of deep cerebellar nuclei. The fastigial nucleus receives inputs from the vestibular nuclei and from the medial cerebellar cortex. Outputs from the fastigial nucleus synapse in the vestibular nuclei and the medial part of the hindbrain reticular formation.

free n. A cell nucleus that is no longer surrounded by the other intracellular components.

germinal n. A cell nucleus resulting from the union of male and female pronuclei.

globose n. A deep nucleus of the cerebellum, lying between the emboliform and fastigial nuclei. SYN: *posterior interposed n.*

gracile n. A secondary sensory nucleus medial to the cuneate nucleus in the caudal hindbrain near the junction with the spinal cord. Axons of the fasciculus gracilis in dorsal columns synapse in this nucleus, and neurons in the nucleus send their axons in the contralateral medial lemniscus to synapse in the ventral posterior lateral (VPL) nucleus of the thalamus. The gracile nucleus is a way station for discriminative somatic sensory information from the leg and trunk. SYN: *n. gracilis.*

n. gracilis Gracile **n.**

habenular n. A small set of nuclei in the limbic system found just rostral to the pineal gland in the roof of the third ventricle. The habenula receives axons from the limbic forebrain via a compact tract, the stria medullaris. In turn, the habenula sends a compact bundle of axons, the fasciculus retroflexus (habenulo-interpeduncular tract), to innervate the interpeduncular nuclei of the midbrain. SEE: *limbic system* for illus.

haploid n. A cell nucleus with half the normal number of chromosomes, as in germ cells (ova and sperm) following the normal reduction divisions in gametogenesis.

hypoglossal n. A nucleus of the somatic motor column, found near the midline in the caudal hindbrain. It innervates all the muscles in the tongue and is the origin of the hypoglossal nerve (CN XII)

hypothalamic n. w2A set of nuclei in the ventral diencephalon on either side of the lower recess of the third ventricle. These nuclei (a) regulate the preganglionic motor neurons of the sympathetic and parasympathetic nervous systems, (b) control the secretions of the anterior lobe of the pituitary gland, (c) secrete hormones (e.g., oxytocin and vasopressin) through the posterior lobe of the pituitary gland, and (d) modulate the limbic system (e.g., via the mammillary bodies). SEE: *limbic system* for illus.

inferior olivary n. Inferior **olive**.

interpeduncular n. A ventral nucleus of the midbrain tegmentum lying between the left and right substantia nigrae, which cap the two cerebral peduncles. The interpeduncular nucleus receives axons from the habenula (via the habenulo-interpeduncular tract), and it sends axons dorsally, to the midbrain raphe nuclei. SEE: *limbic system* for illus.

interstitial n. of Cajal A midbrain nucleus found both interspersed among and lateral to the medial longitudinal fasciculus (MLF), just rostral to the oculomotor nucleus. The interstitial nucleus of Cajal is one of the accessory oculomotor (preoculomotor) nuclei, which are composed of interneurons concerned with eye movements and reflex gaze coordination and which receive axons from the MLF.

lateral geniculate n. The visual relay nucleus of the thalamus. It is a set of nuclei located on the bottom rear edges of the thalamus, lateral to the medial geniculate nucleus. Axons from the retinal ganglion cells of the retina reach the lateral geniculate via the optic nerve and optic tract and then synapse in topographic order. The outflow axons from the lateral geniculate neurons run in the optic radiation and synapse in the primary visual cortex in the occipital hemisphere, again maintaining their topographic organization.

lateral posterior n. of the thalamus A nucleus that lies dorsal to the ventral posterior nucleus. SEE: *thalamic n.*

lentiform n. The putamen and the globus pallidus considered together. This is an artificial grouping of basal ganglia nuclei determined purely by physical appearance.

medial geniculate n. The auditory relay nucleus of the thalamus. It is on the back undersurface of the thalamus, above the cerebral peduncle. It receives auditory axons from the inferior colliculus, and it sends axons to the auditory cortex (superior temporal gyrus of Heschl [area 41]) in which the neurons are organized according to auditory pitch.

mother n. A cell nucleus that divides into two or more parts to form daughter nuclei.

motor n. A nucleus participating in the formation or the execution of the output programs of the central nervous system.

oculomotor n. A nucleus in the grey matter below the cerebral aqueduct in the midbrain at the rostral end of the somatic motor column. It is the origin of the axons that innervate four extraocular eye muscles -- the medial, the inferior, and the superior rectus muscles and the inferior oblique muscle -- via the oculomotor nerve (CN III).

n. of origin When referring to an axon in the central nervous system, the nucleus that contains the neuronal cell body of that axon.

paraventricular n. A large-celled nucleus beneath the ependymal layer lining the third ventricle in the supraoptic region of the hypothalamus. Axons of the paraventricular nucleus, along with axons from the neighboring supraoptic n., form the supraopticohypophyseal tract. The axons of this tract regulate water balance in the body, secreting vasopressin, the antidiuretic hormone, from their terminals in the posterior lobe of the pituitary gland. Its cells also seem to stimulate the sensation of thirst. Finally, the supraoptic and paraventricular nuclei produce oxytocin, which causes uterine muscle contraction and milk secretion. SEE: *hypothalamic n.*

pontine n. Any of the neurons interspersed with the corticospinal axons in the ventral pontine hindbrain. The inputs to the pontine nuclei are mainly axons from sensory and motor areas of the cerebral cortex; the outputs are axons that cross the midline and ascend into the cerebellum via the middle cerebellar peduncle (brachium pontis).

n. pulposus The center cushioning gelatinous mass lying within an intervertebral disk. It is the remnant of the notochord.

reticular n. A column of neurons in the spinal cord, brainstem, and thalamus.

segmentation n. The cell nucleus of a zygote formed by fusion of the male and female pronuclei.

sensory n. A nucleus participating in the reception or the interpretation of input to the central nervous system.

sperm n. The head of the spermatozoon.

subthalamic n. A basal ganglia nucleus that is found under the thalamus in the base of the diencephalon; it lies between the thalamus and the cerebral peduncle, just rostral to the substantia nigra. The subthalamic nucleus is a satellite of the globus pallidus with which it has reciprocal connections. Lesions of the subthalamic nucleus on one side of the brain produce hemiballismus.

superior olivary n. Superior **olive**.

supraoptic n. A large-celled nucleus of the hypothalamus lying above the rostral ends of the optic tracts and lateral to the optic chiasm. SEE: *paraventricular* **n.**

thalamic n. Any of the more than 27 nuclei of the thalamus. The thalamic nuclei are named according to their position in the thalamus, and the medial and dorsal nuclei are separated from the lateral and ventral nuclei by a partitioning layer of axons, called the internal medullary lamina. The thalamic nuclei filter and modify the signals that the nervous system sends to the cerebral cortices. Thalamic nuclei can be divided into five groups by their patterns of connectivity: (a) The nuclei in the base of the thalamus -- the ventroposterior (also called, ventrobasal), the lateral geniculate, and the medial geniculate nuclei -- receive all the sensory information from the body, except olfaction, and send information to the primary sensory areas of the cerebral cortices. (b) The ventral anterior and ventral lateral nuclei (the VA-VL complex) receive motor programs from the globus pallidus (of the basal ganglia) and the cerebellum and send information to the motor areas of the cerebral cortices. (c) The dorsomedial nucleus, the lateral posterior and lateral dorsal nuclei, and the pulvinar nucleus receive information from the association areas of the cerebral cortices and from noncortical regions of the brain and send information back to the association cortices. (d) The anterior nucleus -- part of the limbic circuitry -- receives information from the mammillary body and from the fornix and sends information to the cingulate gyrus of the cerebral cortex. (e) The small nuclei in the internal medullary lamina (intralaminar nuclei) and the nuclei along the midline of the thalamus receive information from the cerbral cortices,

the cererebellum, the reticular formation, and elsewhere and send information widely throughout the cerebral cortices.

ventral cochlear n. A nucleus of the special sensory column in the hindbrain; it forms a bulge around the entering cochlear nerve. Axons of the primary sensory cells in the spiral ganglion (in the cochlea of the inner ear) run in the vestibulocochlear nerve (CN VIII) and synapse in the dorsal and ventral cochlear nuclei. About half of the axons from neurons in the cochlear nuclei cross the midline in a tract called the trapezoid body and join the uncrossed axons from the contralateral cochlear nuclei. Together, these axons ascend in a tract called the lateral lemniscus to synapse in the inferior colliculus in the midbrain.

vesicular n. A cell nucleus having a deeply staining membrane and a pale center.

vestibular n. The inferior, lateral, medial, or superior vestibular nucleus.

yolk n. Vitelline nucleus.

nucleus of Darkschewitsch (dark-she′vich) [Liverij Osipovich Darkschewitsch, Russian neurologist, 1858–1925] A midbrain nucleus in the ventrolateral periaqueductal gray matter, dorsal to the interstitial nucleus of Cajal and rostral to the oculomotor nucleus. The nucleus of Darkschewitsch is one of the accessory oculomotor (preoculomotor) nuclei, which are composed of interneurons concerned with eye movements and reflex gaze coordination and which receive axons from the medial longitudinal fasciculus.

nucleus-to-cytoplasm ratio, nuclear-to-cytoplasmic ratio The proportion of a nucleated blood cell occupied by the nucleus. In white blood cells, the larger the nucleus (relative to the cytoplasm), the more immature the cell.

nuclide (nū′klīd) An atomic nucleus identified by its atomic number, mass, and energy state.

nude [L. *nudus,* naked] **1.** Bare; naked; unclothed. **2.** An unclothed body.

nude mouse SEE: under *mouse*.

nudism 1. In psychiatry, a morbid desire to remove clothing. **2.** The practice of living without clothing.

NUG *necrotizing ulcerative gingivitis.*

nuisance Anything that causes inconvenience, annoyance, or disturbance of normal physiology.

null cell (nul) SEE: under *cell.*

null hypothesis The assumption that the observed difference between two groups of subjects in a research study results from chance and not from the intervention that is being studied.

nulligravida (nŭl″ĭ-grăv′ĭ-dă) A woman who has never conceived a child.

nullipara (nŭl-ĭp′ă-ră) [L. *nullus,* none, + *parere,* to bear] A woman who has never produced a viable offspring.

nulliparity (nŭl″ĭ-păr′ĭ-tē) The condition of not having given birth to a child.

numb (nŭm) **1.** Insensible; lacking in feeling. **2.** Deadened or lacking in the power to move.

numb chin syndrome Loss of sensation in the area from the lower lip to the chin, caused by a lesion of the third division of the trigeminal nerve (fifth cranial nerve).

number (nŭm′bĕr) [L. *numerus,* number] **1.** A total of units. **2.** A symbol graphically representing an arithmetical sum.

> ***atomic mass n.*** A number equal to the sum of all the neutrons and the protons in an atom's nucleus. SEE: *mass **n.***

> ***atomic n.*** SYMB: Z. The number of negatively charged electrons in an uncharged atom, or the number of protons in the nucleus. This number determines the position of elements in the periodic table of elements. It is used to describe isotopes of an element, each of which has a different mass number but the same atomic number.

> ***Avogadro n.*** SEE: under *Avogadro, Amedeo.*

> ***Drug Enforcement Administration n.*** SEE: *Drug Enforcement Administration number.*

> ***hardness n.*** A number on a calibrated scale indicating the relative hardness as determined by a particular system of testing, e.g., Knoop, Mohs, Rockwell, Vickers hardness tests. A steel ball or diamond point is applied with a known variable load for a determined period of time to produce an indent whose depth or diameter can be measured.

> ***lot n.*** An identifier assigned to a batch of medications. It facilitates drug manufacturing inventory control and tracing adverse incidents in a batch of contaminated medications.

> ***low density lipoprotein particle n.*** Low density lipoprotein particle concentration.

> ***mass n.*** The mass of the atom of a specific isotope relative to the mass of hydrogen. In general, this number is equal to the total of the protons and neutrons in the atomic nucleus of that specific isotope.

> ***OMIM n.*** MIM #.

> ***saponification n.*** In analysis of fats, the number of milligrams of potassium hydroxide needed to saponify 1 g of oil or fat.

> ***Unique Physician Identification N.*** SEE: *Unique Physician Identification Number.*

number needed to harm The number of patients needed to be exposed to a noxious agent or medical intervention in order that one might suffer an adverse event. This concept is important in the assessment of the relative hazard of medical interventions, the relative toxicities of poisons, or the relative value of certain experimental interventions. Generally, the smaller the value, the more dangerous the therapy or noxious agent.

number needed to treat The number of patients who must receive a specific therapy (or undergo a specific medical test) so that one of them will benefit. This concept is important in assessing the relative values and costs of interventions for specific illnesses. For example, to prevent one death from breast cancer, the number of patients who need annual mammography can be calculated. Similarly, the number of patients with cancer who will survive because of the use of a particular chemotherapy can be assessed. Generally, the smaller the number needed to treat, the greater the value of the intervention. This comparative information can be used to decide how to allocate resources, plan studies, or make recommendations to patients about their care.

numbness Lack of sensation in a part.

numeral (nū′mĕr-ăl) [L. *numerus,* number] **1.** Pert. to or denoting a number. **2.** A conventional symbol expressing a number.

nummular (nŭm′yŭ-lăr) [L. *nummus,* coin] **1.** Circular or oval. **2.** Stacked like coins, as in a rouleau of red blood cells.

nunnation (nŭn-ā′shŭn) [Heb. *nun,* letter N] The frequent and abnormal use of the "n" sound.

Nuremberg Code (nŭr′ĕm-bĕrg) A set of principles established after World War II to protect the rights of research participants (subjects).

nurse (nŭrs) [Fr. fr. L. *nutrix,* nurse] **1.** One who provides health care. The extent of participation varies from simple patient care to the most expert professional techniques necessary in acute life-threatening situations. The ability of a nurse to make self-directed judgments and to act independently will depend on professional background, motivation, and opportunity for professional development. The health care team includes the technical nurse, who is technique-oriented, deals with commonly recurring nursing problems and knows standardized procedures and medically delegated techniques. Also included is the professional nurse, who is prepared to assume responsibility for the care of individuals and groups in collaboration with a physician. The roles of nurses constantly change in response to the growth of biomedical knowledge, changes in patterns of demand for health services, and the evolution of professional relationships among nurses, physicians, and other health care professionals. **2.** To feed an infant at the breast. **3.** To perform the duties of caring for the sick. **4.** To care for a young child.

advanced practice n. A registered nurse with additional education, skill, and specialization in various fields of medicine. SEE: **n.** *anesthetist; clinical* **n.** *specialist;* **n.** *midwife;* **n.** *practitioner.*

n. anesthetist ABBR: CRNA. A registered nurse who administers anesthesia to patients in the operating room and delivery room. The knowledge and skill required to provide this service are attained through an organized program of study recognized by the American Association of Nurse Anesthetists. Nurse anesthetists hold at least a master's degree.

certified emergency n. ABBR: CEN. A nurse who has passed the examination administered by the Board of Certification of Emergency Nursing. To maintain certification as a CEN, a nurse must recertify every 4 years; a formal examination is required every 8 years, and continuing education credits can be submitted as proof of professional competence during alternate 4-year cycles.

charge n. A nurse responsible for supervising the nursing staff on a hospital or nursing home unit. This nurse reports to the nurse manager.

circulating n. A nurse who participates in surgeries by taking a preoperative history, educating the patient about the upcoming operation, monitoring the patient's vital functions, ensuring the sterility of instruments to be used, and making certain that operating room equipment is available for the procedure and functions well.

clinical n. specialist ABBR: CNS. A nurse with particular competence in certain areas such as intensive care, cardiology, oncology, obstetrics, or psychiatry. A CNS holds a master's degree in nursing, preferably with emphasis in clinical nursing. Clinical Nurse Specialists are licensed registered nurses who have graduate preparation (Master's or Doctorate) in nursing as a Clinical Nurse Specialist. Clinical practice areas may be organized according to population (pediatrics, geriatrics, women's health, etc.), setting (critical care, emergency room, etc.), disease or medical subspecialty (diabetes, oncology, etc.), type of care (psychiatric, rehabilitation, etc.), and/or type of problem (pain, wounds, stress, etc.).

n. clinician A registered nurse with preparation in a specialized educational program. At present this preparation may be in the context of a formal continuing education program, a baccalaureate nursing program, or an advanced-degree nursing program. The nurse clinician is capable of working independently in solving patient-care problems..

community health n. A nurse who combines the principles and practices of nursing and public health to provide care to the people in a community rather than in an institution. A 1985 consensus conference report of the U.S. Department of Health and Human Services defined community health nurses as any nurses working in the community, whether or not they had preparation in public health nursing. Public health nurses are nurses with specialty education and clinical practice in public health nursing. Public health nursing specialists have advanced nursing preparation, either a master's degree or a doctorate, with an emphasis on public health sciences.

dental n. A dental auxiliary trained to provide oral hygiene instruction and dental health care to school children. Formerly, the term applied to dental hygienists, but now it refers to persons trained according to a program developed in New Zealand.

enterostomal therapy n. Wound ostomy continence **n.**

epidemiologist n. A registered nurse with special training and certification in the prevention of hospital-acquired infections in patients. SEE: *infection control* **n.**

flight n. A nurse who cares for patients being transported in an aircraft.

general duty n. A nurse not specializing in a particular field but available for any nursing duty.

graduate n. A nurse who is a graduate of a state-approved school of nursing but has not yet passed the National Council Licensure Examination–Registered Nurse (NCLEX-RN).

head n. An obsolete term for nurse manager.

health n. A community or visiting nurse whose responsibility is to give information on hygiene and prevention of disease. SEE: *community health* **n.**

home health n. A nurse who visits patients in their homes to provide skilled nursing services, such as assessment and patient and family teaching.

infection control n. A registered nurse employed by an agency to monitor the rate and causes of nosocomial infections and to promote measures to prevent such infections.

licensed practical n. ABBR: LPN. A graduate of a school of practical nursing who has passed the practical nursing state board examination and is licensed to administer care, usually working under the direction of a licensed physician or a registered nurse. SYN: *licensed vocational* **n.**

licensed vocational n. ABBR: LVN. Licensed practical **n.**

n. manager A nurse responsible for a unit in a hospital, nursing home, or ambulatory care setting. The nurse manager supervises staff performance and patient care.

n. midwife A registered nurse who has completed specialized theory and clinical courses in obstetrics and gynecology and is certified by the American College of Nurse Midwives. The nurse midwife's practice includes providing primary obstetrical, neonatal, and preventive gynecological care to essentially healthy women and their normal newborns, usually in collaboration with an obstetrician-gynecologist.

oncology certified n. ABBR: OCN. A nurse with special training and experience, who has passed a certifying examination in core areas of knowledge pertinent to the care of adult cancer patients.

n. practitioner ABBR: NP. A licensed registered nurse who has had advanced preparation for practice that includes 9 to 24 months of supervised clinical experience in the diagnosis and treatment of illness. Most contemporary NP programs are at the master's degree level; graduates are prepared for primary care practice in family medicine, women's health, neonatology, pediatrics, school health, geriatrics, or mental health. Nurse practitioners may work in collaborative practice with physicians or independently in private practice or in nursing clinics. Depending upon state laws, NPs may be allowed to write prescriptions for medications. SEE: **n. clinician; n. midwife; advanced practice nursing.**

prescribing n. A nurse who is allowed to prescribe drugs. Certain U.S. states permit nurses to prescribe only certain types and classes of drugs; most states require that prescribing nurses work with a supervising or collaborating physician; approval for prescribing is granted only to nurse practitioners.

private duty n. A nurse who cares for a patient on a fee-for-service basis, usually in an institution. The nurse is not a staff member of the institution.

psychiatric n. practitioner A registered nurse with advanced preparation who combines medical and nursing skills in the care and treatment of psychiatric or mental health patients.

public health n. A community health nurse with primary responsibility for the health concerns of large groups of individuals within a community.

registered n. ABBR: RN. A nurse who has graduated from a state-approved school of nursing, has passed the professional nurse licensure examination (NCLEX-RN), and has been granted a license to practice within a given state.

school n. A nurse practicing in a school or college who is responsible for the health of enrolled children, adolescents, or adults.

scrub n. An operating room nurse who directly assists the surgeon, primarily by passing instruments and supplies.

special n. Private duty **n.**

specialist n. Clinical **n.** specialist.

visiting n. A community health nurse with primary responsibility for individual patients in their homes.

wet n. A woman who breast-feeds someone else's child.

wound ostomy continence n. A nurse specially trained in the use of ostomies, the care of the patients who use them, and the problems associated with them. SYN: *enterostomal therapy* **n.**

nurse's aide, nurse aide ABBR: NA. An individual who assists nurses by performing the patient-care procedures that do not require special technical training, such as feeding and bathing patients.

nurse-led chronic disease management Nurse-led disease management.

nurse-led disease management Case management of complex or costly diseases by registered nurses who have primary responsibility for patient contact and feedback, usually based on well-accepted, proven, disease-specific guidelines. SYN: *nurse-led chronic disease management.*

Nurse Reinvestment Act Public law 107-205, a federal law enacted in 2002 that creates incentives to enter or remain in the nursing profession. It provides funding to recruit students, retain nurses in current assignments, train nurse educators, and ensure the competency of nurses who care for the elderly.

nursery A hospital department in which newborns are cared for.

day n. Day care center.

nurse supply estimate The number of licensed, registered nurses in active full-time practice, plus half the number of licensed nurses who work part-time. The estimate includes all associate-, baccalaureate-, and graduate-level nurses.

NurseTIP (nŭrs′tip″) [Acronym from *Nurse Training on Immunization Project*] A national education project whose goal is to increase nursing knowledge and competency in contemporary immunization practices. Website: www.nursetip.org

nurse-to-patient ratio The number of nurses assigned to care for a patient, esp. in a hospital. Low nurse-to-patient ratios have been associated with a decrease in the quality of hospital care and an increase in complications in care.

nursing (nŭrs′ing) **1.** The care and nurturing of healthy and ill people, individually or in groups and communities. The American Nurses Association identifies four essential features of contemporary nursing practice: attention to the full range of human experiences and responses to health and illness without restriction to a problem-focused orientation; integration of objective data with knowledge gained from an understanding of the patient or group's subjective experience; application of scientific knowledge to the processes of diagnosis and treatment; and provision of a caring relationship that facilitates health and healing. SEE: *nurse.* **2.** Breast-feeding.

advanced practice *n.* Primary medical care provided by nurses prepared at the master's or doctoral level, including nurse practitioners, nurse-midwives, clinical nurse specialists, and nurse anesthetists. These nurses may practice independently or with a supervising or collaborating physician.

barrier *n.* The use of special gloves, masks, and gowns to prevent contact between sources of infection and medical personnel caring for critically ill patients. Situations in which one would use these precautions include care of the patient with gas gangrene, fulminant sepsis, burns, tuberculosis, and other highly contagious conditions.

forensic *n.* A subspecialty of nursing requiring formal preparation (a master's or other postgraduate degree) in which nurses conduct sexual assault examinations and participate in a wide variety of other legal matters affecting health care.

geriatric *n.* The branch of nursing concerned with the care of the older population, including promotion of healthy aging as well as prevention, assessment, and management of physiological, pathological, psychological, economic, and sociological problems. SYN: *gerontological n.*

gerontological *n.* Geriatric **n.**

holistic *n.* The art and science of caring for the whole person. SEE: *holism.*

preventive *n.* The branch of nursing concerned with preventing the occurrence of both mental and physical illness and disease. The nurse is an essential part of the health care team and has the opportunity to emphasize and implement health care services to promote health and prevent disease. Nursing expertise and general professional competence can also be used in supporting community action at all levels in order to promote public health measures. There are three levels of preventive nursing:

Primary. Nursing care aimed at general health promotion. This includes intervention necessary to provide a health-promoting environment at home, in the schools, in public places, and in the workplace by ensuring good nutrition, adequate clothing and shelter, rest and recreation, and health education (including sex education and, for the aging group, plans for retirement). Areas of emphasis are specific protective measures such as immunizations, environmental sanitation, accident prevention, and protection from occupational hazards. Changes in lifestyle through behavior therapy, although difficult, must be attempted in those areas known to represent major health risk factors (i.e., smoking, obesity, sedentary lifestyle, improper diet, alcohol and drug abuse, sexual promiscuity and unsafe sex, and falls). Major efforts must be made to prevent automobile accidents.

Secondary. Nursing care aimed at early recognition and treatment of disease. It includes general nursing interventions and teaching of early signs of disease. Infectious diseases, glaucoma, obesity, and cancer fall into this category.

Tertiary. Nursing care for patients with incurable diseases, e.g., Parkinson's disease, multiple sclerosis, or cancer, and patient instruction on how to manage them. The goal is to prevent further deterioration of physical and mental function and to have the patient use residual function for maximum enjoyment of and participation in life. Rehabilitation is an essential part of tertiary prevention. SEE: *preventive medicine; public health.*

primary *n.* A nursing system in which all nursing care for a patient is managed by one nurse for a 24-hr period. Primary nursing includes scheduling of activities, tests, and procedures.

nursing assessment The systematic collection of all data and information relevant to the care of patients, their problems, and needs. The initial step of the assessment consists of obtaining a careful and complete history from the patient. If this cannot be done because the mental or physical condition of the patient makes communication impossible, the nursing history is obtained from those who have information about the patient and the reason(s) for his or her need of medical and nursing care. Obtaining an accurate and comprehensive history requires skill in communicating with individuals who are ill, including those who are reluctant or unable to share important life experiences and medical data. The skilled nurse will be able to obtain the essential information despite resistance. Next in the assessment is the physical examination of the patient in order to determine how the disease has altered physical and mental status. To do this requires that the nurse be capable of performing visual and tactile inspection, palpation, percussion, and auscultation and have knowledge of what represents deviation from the norm and how disease and trauma alter the physical and mental condition of a patient. After these two steps have been completed, the nurse will be able to establish a nursing diagnosis. SEE: *evaluation; nursing process.*

nursing assistant ABBR: NA. An unlicensed nursing staff member who assists with basic patient care such as giving baths, checking vital signs, bedmaking, and positioning. Nursing assistants usually must complete a training course, including classroom instruction and clinical practice under supervision. Each state regulates nursing assistant practice. Nursing assistants who meet specified federal standards are referred to as certified nursing assistants (CNAs).

   geriatric n.a. ABBR: GNA. An unlicensed caregiver who provides basic care needs, such as bathing and feeding, to residents in nursing homes or other health care facilities. According to federal regulations, GNAs must successfully complete at least a prescribed training course and register in the state in which they are practicing. Geriatric nursing assistants are a specially trained class of certified nursing assistants. SEE: *nursing assistant.*

nursing association, nursing organization Any professional nursing group that clarifies, researches, educates, and promotes the continued development of nurses and nursing.

nursing audit A procedure to evaluate the quality of nursing care provided for a patient. Established criteria for care are the yardstick for the evaluation. SEE: *nursing process; problem-oriented medical record.*

nursing-bottle syndrome Baby bottle syndrome.

nursing care plan SEE: under *plan.*

nursing diagnosis The patient problem identified by the nurse for nursing intervention by analysis of assessment findings in comparison with what is considered to be normal. Nurses, esp. those involved in patient care, are in virtually constant need to make decisions and diagnoses based on their clinical experience and judgment. In many instances, that process dictates a course of action for the nurse that is of vital importance to the patient. As the nursing profession evolves and develops, nursing diagnosis will be defined and specified in accordance with the specialized training and experience of nurses, particularly for nurse practitioners and clinical nurse specialists. SEE: *nursing process; planning.*

nursing dose SEE: under *dose.*

nursing goal A specific expected outcome of nursing intervention as related to the established nursing diagnosis. A goal is stated in terms of a desired, measurable change in patient status or behavior. Nursing goals provide direction for selection of appropriate nursing interventions and evaluation of patient progress.

nursing history SEE: under *history.*

nursing home An extended-care facility for patients who need continued health care, usually after a hospital stay. Nursing homes provide 24-hr nursing supervision, rehabilitation services, activity and social services, a safe environment, careful attention to nutritional needs, and measures to prevent complications of decreased mobility. In addition, some nursing homes have specialty units for patients with dementia, chronic ventilator support, or head injuries. Some nursing homes provide subacute units for patients who are not as medically stable as patients in the typical nursing home setting.

   Most nursing homes are licensed and certified to provide an intermediate or skilled level of care or both. Medicare reimbursement is available for patients receiving skilled care in a skilled nursing facility (approximately 40% of nursing home payments come from state Medicaid funding for intermediate nursing home care).

   Patients who are admitted to nursing homes are called residents. In the U.S. about 1.5 million people reside in nursing homes. The nursing home should provide a homelike environment for each resident. Residents vary in age from 18 to over 100. Many facilities support residents who stay for several days or weeks to receive rehabilitation services (e.g., for orthopedic surgeries and strokes). Other residents may remain in the nursing home for the remainder of their lives.

   PATIENT CARE: Vaccination of health care workers in nursing homes against communicable diseases (e.g., hepatitis, influenza) decreases infections among the residents.

nursing informatics SEE: under *informatics.*

nursing intervention In the nursing process, the step after planning. This step involves all aspects of actual caring for the patient and requires full knowledge of the assessment and planning stages of the nursing process. The goals of nursing intervention are stated in the planning step of the nursing process. Included in this step are patient care in the areas of hygiene and mental and physical comfort, including assistance in feeding and elimination; controlling the physical aspects of the patient's environment; and instructing the patient about the factors important to his or her care and what actions to take to facilitate recovery. After the patient's acute and immediate needs are met, he or she should be instructed concerning actions that could be taken to help prevent a recurrence of the condition. SEE: *nursing process; planning; problem-oriented medical record*.

Nursing Minimum Data Set ABBR: NMDS. A standardized set of data identifying essential, common, and core data elements collected in all settings for any patients/clients receiving nursing care. They include the three broad elements of nursing care, patient or client demographics, and service.

nursing model SEE: under *model*.

nursing process An orderly approach to administering nursing care so that the patient's needs are met comprehensively and effectively. The object of health care is to provide comprehensive care of patients. Nursing is dedicated to this concept and, from the holistic viewpoint, has formalized the processes that contribute to the prevention of illness and the restoration and maintenance of health. In so doing, the traditional approaches used in problem solving have been used. Therefore the nurse needs skills in the following five areas to provide comprehensive care of patients:

1. *assessment:* the systemic collection of all data relevant to the patients, their problems, and needs;

2. *problem identification:* the analysis and interpretation of the information obtained during assessment that establishes the nursing diagnosis;

3. *planning:* the determination of individualized patient-centered goals and the optimum course of action to solve the problem;

4. *intervention:* determination of expected patient-centered outcomes, objective methods of evaluating patient progress toward the contributory goals, and optimum courses of action to resolve the problems identified and achieve the desired results;

5. *evaluation:* assessment of the effectiveness of the plan in terms of measurable progress toward established nursing goals and altering the approach and goals as needed. SEE: *evaluation; nursing assessment; nursing intervention; planning; problem-oriented medical record*.

nursing protocol A specific written procedure that prescribes nursing actions in a given situation. Health agencies and physicians establish protocols to ensure consistency and quality of care. A protocol may describe mandatory nursing assessments, behaviors, and documentation for establishing and maintaining invasive appliances; methods of administering specific drugs; special-

care modalities for patients with certain disorders; other components of patient care; lines of authority; or channels of communication under particular circumstances.

nursing research SEE: under *research*.

nursing rounds A procedure in nursing education and in later practice in which one or more visits to a hospital patient are scheduled by two or more nurses to coordinate care, troubleshoot, respond to patient needs, and share insights.

nursing standards The criteria established by professional nursing organizations that describe peer expectations for safe, competent, ethical performance of professional responsibilities. Documents such as the American Nurses' Association Standards of Clinical Practice and Standards of Professional Performance describe general behaviors expected of all professional nurses. Criteria established by specialty nursing organizations, such as the Standards for the Nursing Care of Women and Newborns developed by the Association of Women's Health, Obstetric, and Neonatal Nurses, contain both universal and specialty-specific expectations. Standards are used to develop nursing curricula and occupational descriptions and to evaluate nursing effectiveness and accountability. SEE: *Code for Nurses; standard of care*.

nursing student An individual enrolled in a nursing program.

nursing supervisor A nurse responsible for an individual practice area, reporting to the nursing director or vice president. This position is also commonly seen in nursing home settings, where it may be called *house supervisor*.

nursing theorist, nurse theorist An individual who develops theories regarding the purpose, meaning, structure, and functions of the profession and discipline of nursing. SEE: *nursing theorist*.

nursing theory SEE: under *theory*.

NURSYS A centralized nationwide nursing databank that contains information about nursing licensure.

Nuss procedure (nus) [Donald Nuss, contemporary U.S. surgeon] A minimally invasive surgical treatment to correct pectus excavatum.

nutation (nū-tā'shŭn) [L. *nutare*, to nod] **1.** Nodding, as of the head. SEE: *nodding*. **2.** A complex movement of the sacrum.

nutgall (nŭt'gawl) A growth on certain oak trees produced by insect eggs and larvae. Gallic and tannic acids are obtained from these growths.

nutraceutical, nutriceutical (nū-trăsēū'tĭ-kŭl) Any food component used for medicinal purposes. Examples include minerals, vitamins, amino acids, and hormones. Rules for the sale and promotion of these agents have been set forth in the Dietary Supplement Health and Education Act of 1994.

nutrient (nū′trē-ĕnt) [L. *nutriens*] Any food that supplies the body with the chemicals necessary for metabolism. Essential nutrients are those that the body either cannot synthesize or cannot synthesize quantities sufficient to meet needs. Nutrients can be subdivided into the macronutrients, consisting of protein, carbohydrate, and fat; the micronutrients, which include vitamins and minerals; and water.

nutrigenomics The use of knowledge of an individual's genetic makeup to devise a personally appropriate eating strategy. Also known as "personalized nutrition."

nutriment (nū′trĭ-mĕnt) [L. *nutrimentum,* nourishment] That which nourishes; food.

nutrition (noo-trish′ŏn, nū-) [L. *nutritio,* feeding] **1.** The ingestion and utilization of food by which growth, repair, and maintenance of activities in the body are accomplished. The body is able to store some nutrients (glycogen, calcium, iron) for times when food intake is insufficient. Vitamin C is an example of a nutrient that is not stored. SEE: *total parenteral n.* **2.** The professional discipline that includes both the scientific study and the practical use of nutrients in health. **nutritional** (-trish′ŏn-ăl), *adj.*

   enteral ***n.*** Nutrition provided through a tube placed into the stomach or small intestine. This may be accomplished through a nasogastric tube, a percutaneous gastrostomy tube, or a jejunostomy.

   hemotrophic n. Transplacental passage of nutrients from the maternal bloodstream to the fetal circulation.

   n.: less than body requirements, imbalanced Intake of nutrients insufficient to meet metabolic needs. SEE: *Nursing Diagnoses Appendix.*

   n.: more than body requirements, imbalanced Intake of nutrients that exceed metabolic needs. SEE: *Nursing Diagnoses Appendix.*

   partial enteral n. Supplemental tube feeding or oral feeding of foods that are rich in protein, calories, and other nutrients to patients receiving partial parenteral nutrition. SEE: *enteral n.*

   partial parenteral n. ABBR: PPN. Intravenous administration of nutrients to patients whose nutritional requirements cannot be fully met via the enteral route. An amino acid–dextrose solution (usually 10%) and a lipid emulsion (10% to 20%) are delivered into a peripheral vein through a cannula or catheter.

   n.: risk for more than body requirements, imbalanced At risk for an intake of nutrients that exceeds metabolic needs. SEE: *Nursing Diagnoses Appendix.*

   total enteral n. Enteral tube **feeding**.

   total parenteral n. ABBR: TPN. The intravenous provision of dextrose, amino acids, emulsified fats, trace elements, vitamins, and minerals to patients who are unable to assimilate adequate nutrition by mouth. Patients with many illnesses become malnourished if they are unable to eat a balanced diet for more than a few weeks. Patients who have been hospitalized for a prolonged period, have had no oral intake for several days, or have a cachectic disorder should be assessed for the need for nutritional support. However, only a small percentage of these patients clearly benefit from parenteral nutritional support in clinical trials. Patients who benefit most from TPN are those at the extremes of nutritional risk, e.g., preterm or newborn infants who require surgery or the 5% of adult surgical candidates who are the most nutritionally deficient. Patients who may occasionally benefit from TPN include those with inflammatory bowel disease, radiation enteritis, bowel obstruction, and related intestinal diseases. In many other patients, the anticipated risks of malnutrition and starvation are exceeded by the potential risks of TPN, which include injury during central line placement, sepsis as a result of infectious contamination of intravenous lines, and metabolic complications, e.g., refeeding syndrome.

Patients requiring 7 to 10 days of nutritional support may benefit from the administration of parenteral nutrition through a peripheral venous catheter. This method limits the caloric intensity of TPN to about 2300 kcal/day (ca. 900 mOsm/kg) because more concentrated formulas cause peripheral vein inflammation. With central TPN, patients have been occasionally supported for several months with limited overt complications. The superior vena cava tolerates feedings of up to 1900 mOsm/kg. Typically, central TPN includes individually tailored amounts of dextrose, amino acids, lipids, vitamins, trace elements, heparin, insulin, and other substances. In patients with specific diseases, some nutrients may be limited, for example, sodium (in congestive heart failure), protein content (in liver failure), and potassium (in renal failure).

PATIENT CARE: The procedure is explained to the patient, and a nutritional assessment is obtained. Intake and output are monitored and recorded. The nurse assists with catheter insertion and observes for adverse effects, documents procedure and initial fluid administration, and continues to monitor fluid intake. The catheter insertion site is inspected and redressed every 24 to 48 hr according to agency protocol; a strict aseptic technique is used for this procedure. The condition of the site and position of the catheter are documented, and the catheter is evaluated for leakage; if present, this should be reported to the physician. Electrolytes are monitored. Vitamin supplements are administered as prescribed. The patient is observed for edema and dehydration. If diarrhea or nausea occurs, the infusion rate is slowed. Urine sugar and acetone tests are performed every 6 hr, and blood sugar levels are monitored as prescribed. Daily weights are obtained. The solution should never be discontinued abruptly but tapered off with isotonic glucose administered for several hours. In the event of catheter blockage or accidental removal, the physician should be notified immediately. Patients should be encouraged to ambulate. Some patients recuperating from long illnesses are released from the hospital with self-administered TPN until they are able to resume eating. These patients need to be taught how to use TPN in the home.

Although TPN is often necessary, in most instances the best way to nourish a patient is by mouth or enterally (by intestinal tube). Oral and enteral feedings preserve the integrity of the intestinal mucosa, maintain a normal pH in the stomach, prevent the entry of bacteria into the body through the walls of the gastrointestinal tract, and are less expensive than parenteral nutrition. Chronic liver failure is the most common, potentially life-threatening complication in patients who need to be maintained on TPN for more than a year.

nutrition, readiness for enhanced A pattern of nutrient intake that is sufficient for meeting metabolic needs and can be strengthened. SEE: *Nursing Diagnoses Appendix.*

nutritional adequacy The relationship between intake of nutrients and individual requirements.

nutritional preemption The reduction of risk factors for disease by consuming a healthy or personally tailored diet.

nutritional recovery SEE: under *recovery.*

nutritional support The giving of nutrients either by intravenous infusion (parenterally) or by drip feeding through a tube placed in the upper gastrointestinal tract (enterally).

nutritious (nū-trĭsh′ŭs) [L. *nutritius*] Affording nourishment.

nutritive (nū′trĭ-tĭv) **1.** Pert. to the process of assimilating food. **2.** Having the property of nourishing.

nux vomica (nŭks vŏm′ĭ-kă) The poisonous seed from an East Indian tree that contains several alkaloids, the principal ones being brucine and strychnine.

NWB *non-weight bearing.*

nyctalopia (nik-tă-lō′pē-ă) [*nyct-* + Gr. *alaos,* blind + *opia,* eye] **1.** Inability to see well in a faint light or at night. This condition occurs in retinitis pigmentosa and choroidoretinitis; it may also be due to vitamin A deficiency. Smoking tobacco may impair the ability to see at night. Hypoxia associated with being above sea level in an aircraft will also decrease night vision. SYN: *night blindness.* **2.** An incorrect term for hemeralopia (day blindness). SEE: *hemeralopia.*

nyctamblyopia (nĭk″tăm-blē-ō′pē-ă) [Gr. *nyx,* night, + *amblyopia,* poor sight] Reduction or dimness of vision at night without visible eye changes.

nycto-, nyct-, nycti- [Gr. *nyx,* stem *nykt-,* night] Prefixes meaning *night.* SEE: *noct-.*

nyctohemeral, nycthemerus (nĭk″tō-hĕm′ĕr-ăl, nĭk-thĕm′ĕ-rŭs) Pert. to both day and night.

nycturia (nĭk-tū′rē-ă) [″ + *ouron,* urine] Nocturia.

NYHA *New York Heart Association.*

nylon (nī′lŏn) A synthetic polymer that can be formed into fibers, lines, sutures, sheets, and fabrics. It is used in a variety of medical applications, including nonabsorbable sutures.

nymph (nĭmf) [Gr. *nymphe,* a maiden] The immature stage of insect development in which wings and genitalia have not fully developed.

nymphomania (nĭm″fō-mā′nē-ă) [″ + *mania,* madness] A colloquial term for excessive sexual desire or promiscuous sexual behavior by a female.

nymphomaniac (nĭm″fō-mā′nē-ăk) [″ + *mania,* madness] A colloquial term for a female perceived to behave in an excessively sexual manner.

nystagmograph (nĭs-tăg′mō-grăf) [″ + *graphein,* to write] An apparatus for recording the oscillations of the eyeball in nystagmus.

nystagmus (nis-tag′mŭs) [Gr. *nystagmos,* nodding] Involuntary back-and-forth or cyclical movements of the eyes. The movements may be rotatory, horizontal, or vertical and often are most noticeable when the patient gazes at objects moving by rapidly or at fixed objects in the peripheral field of view.

ETIOLOGY: Lesions of the labyrinth, vestibular nerve, cerebellum, and brainstem commonly produce rhythmic eye movements. Drug intoxications, e.g., with alcohol or phenytoin, also may be responsible.

aural n. Nystagmus due to a disorder in the labyrinth of the ear. Eye movement is spasmodic.

convergence n. Slow abduction of eyes followed by rapid adduction.

dissociated n. Nystagmus in one eye that is not synchronized with that in the other eye.

end-position n. Nystagmus that occurs when eyes are turned to extreme positions. It may occur normally in debilitation or fatigue, or it may be due to pathology of the subcortical centers for conjugate gaze.

fixation n. Nystagmus that occurs only when the eyes gaze at an object.

gaze-evoked n. Nystagmus upon holding the eyes in an eccentric position. It is due to dysfunction of the brainstem, or it may be caused by drugs such as sedatives or anticonvulsants. The direction of the nystagmus may change when the individual is fatigued or returns fixation to the primary position. This is called *rebound nystagmus*.

labyrinthine n. Nystagmus due to disease of the labyrinthine vestibular apparatus.

latent n. Nystagmus that occurs only when one eye is covered.

lateral n. Horizontal movement of the eyes from side to side.

manifest n. Nystagmus present at all times whether or not one's gaze is directed toward a visual stimulus.

miner's n. Nystagmus occurring in those who work in comparative darkness for long periods.

opticokinetic n. A rhythmic jerk nystagmus occurring when one is looking at constantly moving objects, e.g., viewing telephone poles from a moving car or train.

pendular n. Nystagmus characterized by movement that is approx. equal in both directions. It is usually seen in those who have bilateral congenital absence of central vision or who lost it before the age of 2.

postrotatory n. A form of vestibular nystagmus that occurs when the body is rotated and then the rotation is stopped. If, while sitting upright in a chair that can be swiveled, the body is rapidly rotated to the right, the nystagmus during rotation has its slow component to the left. When the rotation stops, the slow component is to the right. Stimulation of the semicircular canals causes this type of nystagmus, and it is a normal reaction.

rebound n. Gaze-evoked **n.**

retraction n. Nystagmus associated with the drawing of the eye backward into the orbit.

rhythmic n. Nystagmus in which the eyes move slowly in one direction and then jerk back rapidly. SYN: *jerk* **n.**

rotatory n. Nystagmus in which eyes rotate about the visual axis.

seesaw n. Nystagmus in which the inturning eye moves up and the opposite eye moves down, and then both eyes move in the opposite direction.

vertical n. Involuntary up-and-down ocular movements.

vestibular n. Nystagmus caused by disease of the vestibular apparatus of the ear, or due to normal stimuli produced when the semicircular canals are tested by rotating the body. SEE: *postrotatory* **n.**

voluntary n. A rare type of pendular nystagmus in those who have learned to oscillate their eyes rapidly, usually by extreme convergence.

NZB mouse SEE: *New Zealand black mouse*.

ω Lower-case Greek letter omega.

Ω Capital of the Greek letter omega. Symbol for ohm.

O **1.** Symbol for the element oxygen. **2.** *oculus,* eye. **3.** Symbol for a particular blood type. **4.** The diameter of a suture.

    PATIENT CARE: The greater the number of O's, the smaller the diameter of the suture. Thus, a 6-O or 7-O suture is used for delicate surgeries, e.g., in plastic surgery on the face. A 3-O or 4-O suture is wider and stronger, may be used to close a deep laceration on a limb or the trunk but is more likely to leave a scar.

O_2 Symbol for the molecular formula for oxygen.

O_3 Symbol for ozone.

o- In chemistry, an abbreviation of *ortho-.*

OA *occiput anterior; ongoing assessment.*

OAE *otoacoustic emissions test.*

OAF *osteoclast activating factor.*

oak bark (ōk bark) The external layer of woody plants of the genus *Quercus,* sometimes used by alternative medicine practitioners as an anti-inflammatory and antidiarrheal.

OASIS *Outcome and assessment information set.*

oasis (ō-ā′sĭs) *pl.* **oases** [Gr., a fertile area in an arid region] An area of healthy tissue surrounded by a diseased portion.

oat [AS. *ate,* oat] Grain or seed of a cereal grass used as food.

oath [AS. *ooth*] A solemn attestation or affirmation. SEE: *Hippocratic oath; Nightingale Pledge.*

oatmeal [AS. *ate,* oat, + *mele,* meal] Ground, rolled, or steel-cut oats from which a cereal can be made. Oatmeal has several therapeutic uses. In the diet, it provides fiber, lowers cholesterol levels, and can safely be consumed by patients with wheat allergies or celiac sprue because it has no gliaden. Oatmeal is also sometimes used in tepid baths or soaps to sooth inflamed or irritated skin.

OB *obstetrics.*

obelion (ō-bē′lē-ŏn) [Gr. *obelos,* a spit] A craniometric point on the sagittal suture between the two parietal foramina.

Ober test (ō′bĕr) **1.** A clinical test for tightness of the iliotibial band. The patient lies on the uninvolved side and abducts the hip maximally in neutral flexion. The examiner stands behind the patient, with the patient's foot resting on the examiner's arms with the thigh

supported. The thigh is then released. The result is negative if the abducted knee falls into adduction. It is positive if the knee does not fall into adduction. The specificity of the Ober Test is improved by the use of an inclinometer. SEE: illus. **2.** A modification of the traditional Ober test in which the knee is flexed to an angle of 90 deg.

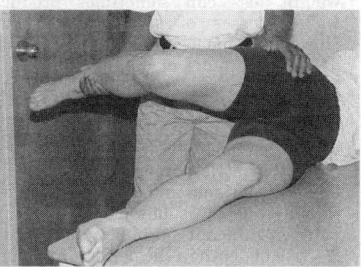

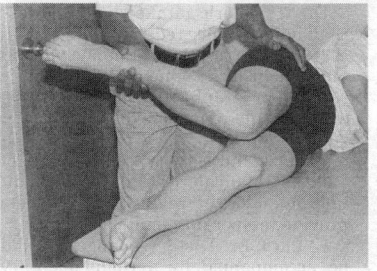

OBER TEST

obese (ō-bēs′) [L. *obesus*] Having a body mass index in excess of 30 kg/m².

obesity (ō-bē′sĭt-ē, -bes′) [*obese*] A body mass index of >30 kg/m², an unhealthy accumulation of body fat. In adults, damaging effects of excess weight are seen when the body mass index exceeds 25 kg/m². A person 5′7″ tall and weighing more than 191 lb would be obese by this standard. SYN: *adiposis; adiposity; corpulence; liposis.* SEE: *body mass index* for table; *Nursing Diagnoses Appendix; Recommended Daily Dietary Allowances Appendix; weight.*

    Obesity is the most common metabolic/nutritional disease in the U.S., with more than 65% of the adult population being overweight. Obesity is more common in women, minorities, and the poor. The obese have an increased risk of developing diabetes mellitus, hypertension, heart disease, stroke, fatal cancers, and other illnesses. Obese people may also suffer psychologically and socially.

ETIOLOGY: Obesity is the end result of an imbalance between food eaten and energy expended, but the underlying causes are more complex. Genetic, hormonal, and neurological influences all contribute to weight gain and loss. In addition, some medications (such as tricyclic antidepressants, insulin, and sulfonylurea agents) may cause patients to gain weight.

TREATMENT: Attempts to lose weight are often unsuccessful, but mild caloric restriction, an increase in physical activity, and supportive therapies all have a role. Medications to enhance weight loss can sometimes produce weight losses of several kilograms. However, some weight loss agents (such as amphetamines or amphetamine-like agents) have unacceptable side effects (such as cardiac valvular injuries with fenfluramine/phentermine, addiction with other anorexiants). Surgical remedies (bariatric surgery) are available for some patients and can result in sustained weight loss, but such surgery involves significant morbidity and a 1% to 2% risk of death in the perioperative period.

DIET: Caloric intake should be less than maintenance requirements, but all essential nutrients must be included in any weight-loss regimen. Severe caloric restriction is unhealthy and should be avoided unless undertaken under strict supervision. For many patients of average size and activity, consumption of 1200 to 1600 calories a day will result in gradual loss of weight. Most fad diets provide temporary results at best.

EXERCISE: Dietary changes should be accompanied by a complementary program of regular exercise. Exercise improves adherence to weight loss diets and consumes stored fat. For many people 35 minutes of low-level exercise performed daily (either in one long workout session or in several shorter intermittent sessions) will aid weight loss and improve other cardiovascular risk factors. Exercise programs may be hazardous for some patients; professional supervision may be recommended for some people who start an exercise program, e.g., people with a history of heart or lung disease, arthritis, or diabetes mellitus.

PATIENT CARE: The U.S. Preventive Services Task Force and other promoters of public health recommend that clinicians screen all adults for obesity and offer incentive behavioral counseling to obese adults. Patients who are overweight should be screened for conditions worsened by obesity, e.g., hypertension, diabetes mellitus, and hyperlipidemia. Health care professionals can aid patients in making permanent life-style changes by discussing diet and exercise, being familiar with various eating plans, and by providing patients with a list of local weight loss centers. The patient's feelings about weight and body image should be explored to understand the individual's motivations. People who diet and exercise for health reasons tend to be the most successful. Family support is also important.

abdominal o. Android o.

acquired o. Obesity that results primarily from environmental rather than genetic causes. It can be most clearly identified in identical twins one of whom is of normal weight and the other markedly overweight

adult-onset o. Obesity first appearing in the adult years. SYN: *Recent o.*

android o. Obesity in which fat is located largely in the waist and abdomen. It is associated with an increased risk of heart disease, hypertension, and diabetes. People with android obesity are often described as having an *apple-shaped* body. SYN: *abdominal o.*

developmental o. Juvenile o.

endogenous o. Obesity associated with some metabolic or endocrine abnormality.

exogenous o. Obesity due to an excessive intake of food.

gluteal-femoral o. Obesity in which fat deposits are located primarily below the waist in the hips and thighs. The health risks of gluteal-femoral fat appear to be less than those associated with abdominal obesity. SYN: *gynecoid o.*

gynecoid o. Gluteal-femoral o.

hypothalamic o. Obesity resulting from dysfunction of the hypothalamus, esp. the appetite-regulating center.

juvenile o. Obesity that occurs before adulthood. It is associated with an increased risk of obesity in adulthood. SYN: *developmental o.*

PATIENT CARE: About one third of American children and 15% of teenagers are overweight or obese. A variety of factors contributes to childhood obesity, including learned patterns of behavior, genetics, a decreased emphasis on physical activity and exercise, and access to inexpensive, calorically dense fast foods (typically rich in fats and sugars but limited in fiber, vitamins, minerals, and other essential nutrients). School nurses, pediatricians, and other health care professionals who provide care to children should help educate children about healthy food choices and portion sizes and the need to increase activity and decrease caloric intake. Parents should be taught to avoid overfeeding infants and to familiarize themselves with nutritional needs and optimum growth rates. The overweight child should be assisted in keeping a record of what, where, and when he/she eats to help identify situations that lead to overeating. Unhealthy weight loss behaviors, such as fad diets or purging, are discouraged. Children and teens benefit from weight loss support programs. Snacks should consist of foods such as raw vegetables rather than cookies, candies, or sugary drinks. Families that exercise together (as by walking, hiking, biking, swimming) provide children with interest in, knowledge of, and practice in activities that help to maintain desired weight levels.

    morbid o. 1. Having a body mass index >40. Approx. 5% of Americans 20 years and older are morbidly obese. **2.** 2. Having a BMI > 95 or 99% of the population (expert opinion varies). SYN: *severe o.*

    recent o. Adult-onset **o.**

    severe o. Morbid **o.**

obesogenic (ŏ-bēs″ŏ-jen′ik) [*obes(ity)* + *-genic*] Tending to promote or contribute to obesity. It is said of unhealthy, calorie-rich diets and sedentary behavior. **obesogenicity** (-jĕ-nis′ĭt-ē), *n.*

obex (ō′bĕks) [L., a band] A thin, crescent-shaped band of tissue covering the calamus scriptorius at the point of convergence of nervous tissue at the caudal end of the fourth ventricle of the brain.

obfuscation (ŏb-fŭs-kā′shŭn) [L. *obfuscare,* to darken] **1.** The act of making obscure or confusing. **2.** Mental confusion.

OB/GYN, OB-GYN *obstetrics and gynecology.*

object (ŏb′jĕkt) [L. *objectus*] That which is visible or tangible to the senses.

object, sex 1. An individual regarded as being of little interest except for providing sexual pleasure. **2.** A person to whom one is sexually attracted.

objective (ŏb-jĕk′tĭv) **1.** Able to be analyzed, measured, or counted. **2.** Objective findings are those findings that are obtained during the physical examination (ROM, girth, and strength). Opposite of subjective. **3.** The lens of a microscope that is closest to the object.

    achromatic o. A microscope objective in which chromatic aberration is corrected for red and blue light.

    apochromatic o. A microscope objective in which chromatic aberration is corrected for red, blue, and green light.

    immersion o. A microscope objective designed so that the space between the objective lens and the specimen is filled with oil or water.

object permanence The thought process, first described by Piaget, whereby infants perceive that objects have constancy. This process normally develops by 6 to 12 months of age.

object relations Emotional attachment to other persons or objects.

obligate (ŏb′lĭ-gāt) [L. *obligatus*] Necessary or required; without alternative. SEE: *obligate anaerobe* .

obligatory thermogenesis The energy cost to a cell or organism of consuming, digesting, and metabolizing ingested nutrients.

oblique (ō-blĕk′, ō-blīk′) [L. *obliquus*] Slanting, diagonal.

obliquity (ō-blik′wĭt-ē) [L. *obliquitas,* a slant, slanting direction] The state of being oblique or slanting.

    Litzmann o. SEE: *Litzmann obliquity.*

    Naegele o. SEE: *Naegele obliquity.*

    o. of the pelvis Inclination of pelvis.

obliteration (ŏb-lĭt″ĕr-ā′shŭn) [L. *obliterare,* to remove] Destruction or complete occlusion of a part or a reflex by degeneration, disease, or surgery.

oblongata (ŏb″lŏng-gă′tă) [L. *oblongus,* long] Medulla oblongata.

obnubilation (ŏb-nū″bĭ-lā′shŭn) A rarely used term for clouding of consciousness or confusion.

obscure (ŏb-skūr′) [L. *obscurus,* hide] **1.** Hidden, indistinct, as the cause of a condition. **2.** To make less distinct or to hide.

observational study SEE: under *study.*

observer bias (ŏb-zĕr′vĕr) [″] Distortions introduced into a research investigation by the expectations and/or knowledge of the individuals collecting the data.

obsession [L. *obsessus,* besiege] A persistent or recurring idea or feeling, esp. one that causes emotional distress or that interferes with effective living. SYN: *compulsive idea.*

obsessive-compulsive disorder (ob-ses′iv-kŏm-pŭl′siv) [*obsess(ion)* + *compuls(ion)*] ABBR: OCD. A disorder whose hallmarks are recurring thoughts, ideas, feelings, or actions that either cause significant psychological distress or interfere with effective living. Common obsessions include concerns about cleanliness, injury, or aggressive or sexual impulses. Common compulsions include repetitive handwashing, cleaning, praying, counting, or making things orderly. A diagnosis of OCD is established if distress is present, the acts are time-consuming (i.e., take more than an hour a day), or the illness significantly interferes with the individual's normal routine, occupation, or social activities. In the general population, the lifetime prevalence of this disorder is approximately 2.5%. It is estimated to be present in 35% to 50% of patients with Tourette's syndrome.

    TREATMENT: Cognitive behavioral therapy, and drugs such as selective serotonin reuptake inhibitors are used to treat OCD. If successful, repeated sessions gradually decrease the anxiety, and the patient may be able to refrain from the compulsive actions. SYN: *obsessional neurosis; obsessive-compulsive personality; obsessive-compulsive personality disorder.*

obstetrician (ŏb-stĕ-trĭsh′ăn) A physician who treats women during pregnancy and parturition and delivers infants.

obstetrics (ŏb-stĕt′rĭks) [L. *obstetrix,* midwife] The branch of medicine that concerns the management of pregnancy, childbirth, and the puerperium. **obstetric** (ŏb-stĕt′rĭk), *adj.*

obstipation (ŏb-stĭ-pā′shŭn) Severe obstruction to the normal flow of feces through the bowels.

obstruction (ŏb-strŭk′shŏn) [L. *obstructio,* blockade] **1.** Blockage of a structure that prevents it from functioning normally. **2.** A thing that impedes; an obstacle.

 aortic o. Blockage of the aorta, which prevents the flow of blood.

 biliary o. Blockage of the flow of bile from the gallbladder. It is typically caused by gallstones but occasionally from other causes, e.g., cancer, cholangitis, cirrhosis, or parasites.

 SYMPTOMS: Biliary obstruction may cause right upper quadrant abdominal pain that radiates to the right flank, nausea, vomiting, jaundice, clay-colored stools, and green or dark urine.

 bladder outlet o. ABBR: BOO. The inability to pass urine. BOO is caused by prostatic hyperplasia, drug therapy, or urethral injury and may produce bladder pain, urinary tract infection (esp. in elderly men), or kidney failure. SEE: *benign prostatic* **hyperplasia.**

 central airway o. Compression of the upper airways by a tumor, esp. lung cancer, or a goiter; inhalation of a foreign body into the airway; or narrowing of the trachea by a stricture or tracheomalacia or bronchiomalacia. It is a potentially life-threatening condition that in many cases requires bronchoscopy to clear the airway, often followed by placement of a stent.

 chronic airflow o. ABBR: CAO. Chronic obstructive pulmonary disease.

 foreign body airway o. Blockage of the free passage of air from the mouth and nose to the lungs by any object accidentally inhaled into the trachea, bronchus, or pharynx. Common causes of this type of obstruction are red meat, hard candy, hot dogs, coins, and marbles. SEE: *Heimlich maneuver.*

 gastric outlet o. Blockage of the flow of food or liquids from the stomach to the duodenum. In children, the cause may be pyloric stenosis or atresia. In adults, ulcers and cancer are frequent causes.

 intestinal o. A partial or complete blockage of the lumen of the large or small intestine. SEE: *Nursing Diagnoses Appendix.*

 SYMPTOMS: Patients typically complain of colicky abdominal pain, nausea, vomiting (if the obstruction is in the proximal small intestine), or inability to pass gas or stool. Thirst, dizziness, malaise, and other symptoms of dehydration may be present. The physical examination may show a distended, gas-filled abdomen, which is often tympanitic and diffusely tender. Auscultation reveals bowel sounds, borborygmi, and rushes, which may be loud enough to hear without the stethoscope. The examiner may sometimes find a palpable mass or an incarcerated hernia.

 TREATMENT: The patient is given nothing orally, and when nausea and vomiting are present, a nasogastric (Levin, Salem Sump) or intestinal (Cantor, Miller-Abbott) tube is placed to remove upper intestinal contents and decompress the bowel. Fluids and electrolytes are given intravenously. A large intestinal obstruction due to fecal impaction may be relieved by disimpaction or enemas. When obstructions do not resolve with conservative measures and supportive care, surgery may be needed.

 PATIENT CARE: In partial obstruction, the patient's condition is monitored closely, including assessment of bowel sounds, vital signs, abdominal girth, fluid and electrolyte balance, and acid-base balance. The patient is assessed for signs of dehydration. Frequent oral hygiene is provided. Prescribed pain medications, antiemetics, and antibiotics are administered. Opioids are sometimes withheld or used sparingly because they may slow peristalsis. Noninvasive pain relief strategies (e.g., relaxation techniques, imagery, repositioning, massage, and music therapy) may be effective for individual patients. The patient is asked to alert health care providers if pain changes from colicky to constant, because this may signal perforation. Throughout, the patient receives support and encouragement. Ischemia is the most serious consequence of intestinal obstruction, because it leads to peritonitis, perforation, hemorrhage, and gangrene. Ischemia makes the bowel more permeable, allowing normal intestinal flora such as *Escherichia coli* and *Klebsiella* to penetrate the bowel wall and enter the peritoneal cavity, potentially leading to peritonitis and/or septic shock. Intravenous fluids are required; blood products and antibiotics may be needed, depending on complications experienced by the patient.

 If conservative treatment fails for

partial or incomplete mechanical obstruction, or if the obstruction is initially diagnosed as vascular or mechanical and complete, the patient is prepared for nasogastric suctioning, endoscopy, or surgery. If the patient requires a colostomy or ileostomy (which may be a temporary measure or may be permanent, depending on the cause of the obstruction), an enterostomal therapist makes recommendations regarding stoma location and provides further positive reinforcement and emotional support. Postoperative care is explained; if the patient is well enough to understand, he is taught exercises to aid ventilation and prevent complications due to immobility. Following surgery, all necessary postoperative care is given, including care of the surgical wound, maintenance of ventilatory status and fluid and electrolyte balance, and relief of pain and discomfort. Vital signs are closely monitored. Oral care is provided, along with misting of mucous membranes while the decompression tube remains in place, and the amount and color of drainage are recorded. Clear fluids may be initiated with the tube clamped to determine toleration. The tube is removed and diet advanced as bowel sounds return. Incentive spirometry, antiembolic or pneumatic hose, and early ambulation help to prevent complications related to immobility. Any necessary postoperative activity limitations are discussed with the patient. Before discharge, any prescribed medications, their proper use, desired responses, and adverse effects are reviewed. Incision and/or colostomy care is taught and signs of infection, activity restrictions, and signs or symptoms for which the surgeon should be called are reviewed with the patient before discharge. The importance of following a structured bowel regimen is emphasized (particularly if the cause of obstruction was a fecal impaction). The patient is encouraged to eat a high-fiber diet, drink plenty of fluids, and exercise daily.

nasal o. Blockage of the nasal passages. Common causes of nasal obstruction in adults are irregular septum, enlarged turbinates, and nasal polyps. In children, a common cause is a foreign body, such as food, buttons, or pins. Complications such as infections, sinusitis, and otitis may develop. TREATMENT: Depending upon the cause of the obstruction, nasal douches, inhalations, or operative care, including resection of septum, turbinectomy, removal of polyp, opening and draining sinuses, or removal of foreign body.

upper airway o. ABBR: UAO. Any potentially life-threatening abnormality in which the flow of air into and out of the lungs is partially or completely blocked by such conditions as laryngeal swelling, foreign bodies, or angioedema. SEE: *cardiopulmonary resuscitation; tracheostomy.*

obstruent (ŏb′stroo-ĕnt) [L. *obstruens*] **1.** Blocking up. **2.** That which closes a normal passage in the body. **3.** Any agent or agency causing obstruction.

obtrusive (ŏb-troo′siv) [L. *obtrudere,* to thrust against] **1.** Aggressively and unpleasantly noticeable. **2.** Forced into one's awareness. **3.** Starkly contrasted with the environment. **obtrusiveness** (′siv-nĕs), *n.*

obtund (ŏb-tŭnd′) [L. *obtundere,* to beat against] To dull or blunt, as sensitivity or pain. SEE: *consciousness, levels of.*

obturation (ŏb-tūr-ā′shŭn) [L. *obturare,* to stop up] Closure of a passage or opening, as in intestinal obstruction.

obturator (ob′t(y)ŭ-rāt″ŏr) [L. *obturare,* to stop up, block] **1.** Anything that obstructs or closes a cavity or opening. **2.** A prosthetic bridge for spanning the gap in a cleft palate. **3.** A device for closing the end of an instrument in order to introduce a taper-tipped device into a cavity (e.g., sigmoidoscope). **4.** Pert. to the obturator foramen, the obturator membrane, and other related structures such as obturator muscles, nerve, and plexus.

obturator sign SEE: under *sign.*

obtuse (ŏb-tūs′) [L. *obtusus*] **1.** Not pointed or acute; dull or blunt. **2.** Of dull mentality.

obtusion (ŏb-tū′zhŭn) Blunting or weakening of normal sensation.

OC *oral contraceptive.*

Occam's razor (ok′ămz) [William of Occam, or Ockham, Brit. Franciscan and philosopher, c. 1285–1349] The concept that the simplest explanation for a phenomenon is the best one, i.e., "what can be done with fewer (assumptions) is done in vain with more."

occipital (ŏk-sĭp′ĭ-tăl) [L. *occipitalis*] Concerning the back part of the head.

occipital area The back of the head, the portion of the skull made of the occipital bone, and the part of the cerebrum below the occipital bone.

occipitalis (ŏk-sĭp″ĭ-tā′lĭs) [L.] The posterior portion of the occipitofrontalis muscle at the back of the head.

occipitalization (ŏk-sĭp″ĭ-tăl-ĭ-zā′shŭn) Fusion of the atlas and occipital bones.

occipital neuralgia A type of headache that originates from the upper neck, often radiating toward the back of the head and the scalp on one or both sides. The pain may be chronic or intermittent and may extend all the way up the scalp to the forehead. It is associated with head and neck injury, osteoarthritis of the cervical spine, and, less often, with spinal infections or tumors. Treatments vary but sometimes include analgesic injections, corticosteroids, or other pain relievers.

occipito-, occipit- [L. *occiput*, stem *occipit-*, back of the head] Prefixes meaning *occiput*.

occipitocervical (ŏk-sĭp″ĭ-tō-sĕr′vĭ-kăl) Concerning the occiput and the neck.

occipitofrontal (ŏk-sĭp″ĭ-tō-frŏn′tăl) Concerning the occiput and the forehead.

occiput (ŏk′sĭ-pŭt) [L.] The back part of the skull. On the fetal head, it is used to determine the position of cephalic presentations in relation to the maternal pelvis.

    persistent o. posterior A fetal malposition; a cephalic presentation with the occiput directed toward the mother's sacrum. Labor often is longer and the woman complains of back pain.

occlude (ŏ-klūd′) [L. *occludere*, to shut up] To close up, obstruct, or join together, as bringing the biting surfaces of opposing teeth together.

occluder (ŏ-klood′ĕr) A device used in ophthalmology to cover one eye while the other is being examined.

occlusal (ŏ-kloo′zăl) **1.** Pert. to the closure of an opening. **2.** Pert. to the opposing surfaces of the molars and premolars that make contact with each other, e.g., during chewing.

occlusal pattern The appearance and anatomical location of the occluding surfaces of teeth.

occlusal wear The attritional loss of substance on opposing occlusal surfaces in natural or artificial teeth; the modification of tooth cusps, ridges, and grooves by functional use.

    TREATMENT: Excessive wear is treated by wearing an occlusal guard.

occlusion (ŏ-kloo′zhŭn) [L. *occlusio*, a closing up] **1.** The acquired or congenital closure, or state of being closed, of a passage. SYN: *imperforation*. **2.** Alignment of the mandibular and maxillary teeth when the jaw is closed or in functional contact. SYN: *dental o.* SEE: *malocclusion*. **3.** The covering of an eye in order to improve vision in the other, e.g., in treating strabismus.

    acquired centric o. Centric **o.**

    abnormal o. Malocclusion.

    adjusted o. SEE: *equilibration*.

    anatomical o. In dentistry, an occlusion in which the posterior teeth of a denture have masticatory surfaces that resemble natural, healthy dentition and articulate with the surfaces of similar or opposing teeth. The opposing teeth may be artificial or natural.

    arterial o. A blockage of blood flow through an artery. It may be acute or chronic and occurs, for example, in coronary or in peripheral arteries. Patients with acute arterial occlusion have severe pain (as in angina pectoris), decreased or absent pulses, and mottling

of the skin of an affected extremity. The occlusion is removed and blood flow restored if possible.

    balanced o. The ideal and equal contact of the teeth of the working side of the jaw by the complementary contact of the teeth on the opposite side of the jaw. SYN: *balanced bite*.

    central retinal artery o. ABBR: CRAO. Blockage of blood flow to the retina (that is, to the central retinal artery or one of its branches), resulting in sudden visual loss. The condition usually affects one eye. When the retinal artery is blocked by a blood clot, early thrombolysis sometimes provides sight-preserving therapy.

    ETIOLOGY: CRAO is typically caused by a tiny embolus that lodges in the retinal circulation. It usually occurs in people with high blood pressure, diabetes mellitus, cardiac valve disease, or atrial fibrillation, which predispose to atherosclerosis or arterial embolization. Other causes include inflammatory or autoimmune diseases affecting the circulation (arteritis), clotting disorders, hyperlipidemia, injected drugs or contaminants, and tumor metastases.

    centric o. In dentistry, the vertical and horizontal position of the mandible that produces maximal interdigitation of the cusps of the maxillary and mandibular teeth. This is the ideal position or type of occlusion. SYN: *acquired centric o.; habitual centric o.; intercuspal position*.

    coronary o. Complete or partial obstruction of a coronary vessel by thrombosis or as a result of spasm. SYN: *cardiac **thrombosis;** coronary **thrombosis**.* SEE: *myocardial **infarction;*** illus.

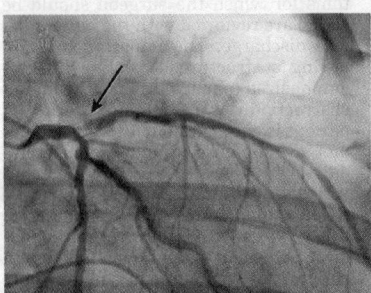

CORONARY OCCLUSION

    dental o. Occlusion (2).

    eccentric o. Any dental occlusion other than centric.

    habitual o. The usual relationship between the teeth of the maxilla and mandible that represents the maximum contact. This occlusion varies from person to person and is seldom ideal or true centric occlusion.

habitual centric o. Centric **o.**

o. of the pupil In the eye, a pupil with an opaque membrane shutting off the pupillary area.

traumatic o. Injury to the tissues that support the teeth because of malocclusion, missing teeth, improper chewing habits, or a pathological condition that causes a person to chew abnormally.

working o. The usual method of contact of teeth as the mandible is moved to one side during chewing.

occlusive cerebrovascular disease Any disease that limits blood flow to the brain, e.g., through the basilar, carotid, or vertebral arteries.

occlusive dressing SEE: under *dressing.*

occlusorehabilitation (ŏ-kloo″zō-rē″hă-bil″ĭ-tā′shŏn) [*occlus(ion)* + *rehabilitation*] Rehabilitation (2).

occult (ŏ-kŭlt′) [L. *occultus,* hidden] Not easily understood; obscure; concealed, as a hemorrhage.

occult blood Blood that is present in such small quantities that it is not apparent to the eye. Blood may be present in feces but of such color and consistency as to be unnoticed by the patient. Occult blood is usually detected only by chemical tests or by microscopic or spectroscopic examination. SEE: table.

occult blood test A screening test for disorders of the gastrointestinal tract, including anemias that may be caused by gastrointestinal blood loss. SEE: *fecal occult blood test.*

occupation (ok″yŭ-pā′shŏn) **1.** Any goal-

Diagnostic Tests for Occult Bleeding

Diagnostic Test	Purpose/Considerations
Hemoglobin and hematocrit levels	Essential for ongoing assessment. Results are unreliable during or immediately after acute hemorrhage—levels may not accurately reflect early blood loss. Low baseline levels may indicate pre-existing anemia.
A coagulation profile	Detects actual or potential abnormalities, especially in a patient taking an anticoagulant or drugs that affect platelet function. Factor assay may reveal clotting disorders such as hemophilia, low platelet count or elevated prothrombin time, activated partial thromboplastin time, or international normalized ratio indicating coagulopathy.
Serum lactate level and arterial blood gases	Evaluate tissue perfusion. A rising lactate level signals insufficient perfusion. An arterial pH less than 7.35 and a falling bicarbonate level indicate impaired perfusion and metabolic acidosis.
CT scan	May suggest fluid collections or injury to solid organs; free fluid may indicate bleeding into organs or spaces.
X-rays	May reveal fluid in the thorax or hemothorax, aortic injury, pelvic fracture, or fracture of other large bones, such as the femur, which can cause significant blood loss.
Arteriography	Helps detect arterial disruption caused by trauma or vascular abnormality. It may be used to guide injection of a clot-forming substance into the bleeding vessel. Aortic imaging helps rule out traumatic disruption or dissecting thoracic aneurysm.
Ultrasound	Helps detect bleeding in the peritoneal cavity, thorax, pericardium, retroperitoneum, pelvis, or uterus. It permits simultaneous procedures, such as placing IV lines or an endotracheal tube.
Endoscopy	Allows visualization of a gastrointestinal bleeding source and may allow the physician to sclerose bleeders.
Diagnostic peritoneal lavage	May be performed at the bedside to rapidly identify intraperitoneal hemorrhage in an unstable or critical patient. It does not identify retroperitoneal bleeding or pinpoint hemorrhage site. If results are positive, the patient may require laparotomy.
Laparoscopy	May help rule out intra-abdominal hemorrhage. It is not appropriate for acute hemorrhage because setup is time-consuming and surgical access is limited.
Transesophageal echocardiography	May be performed at the bedside to detect cardiac injury, such as aortic dissection. It is contraindicated in esophageal trauma.

SOURCE: Used with permission from *Nursing 97,* 27(9):38, © Springhouse Corporation/Springnet.com.

directed pursuit in which one works for a wage, salary, or other income. **2.** Any goal-directed use of time. **3.** Any activity or pursuit in which one is engaged outside one's work, e.g., a hobby or sport.

secondary o. Employment in addition to that for which one is primarily hired.

occupational (ŏk″yŭ-pā′shŏn-ăl) Pert. to or engaged in goal-directed use of time.

occupational disease A disease resulting from factors associated with the occupation in which the patient is engaged.

occupational injustice Any undue limitation on a person's freedom to have or to pursue meaningful occupational engagement in society.

occupational justice A concept describing the social inequity that results when people are deprived of the opportunity to engage in productive, meaningful daily activity.

occupational performance In occupational therapy, a person's ability to perform the required activities, tasks, and roles of living.

occupational therapist ABBR: OT. One who provides assessment and intervention to address environmental, physical, and psychological factors that interfere with the performance of activities and tasks of everyday living.

occupational therapy ABBR: OT. Any of the activity-based interventions to help people to develop, regain, or maintain the skills and capacities necessary for health, productivity, and participation in everyday life. It may include the use of training, environmental modification, assistive technologies, or orthotics to enhance function or prevent disability. SEE: *rehabilitation.*

occupational therapy aide An individual with on-the-job training or experience in occupational therapy who performs routine tasks under the direction of an occupational therapist.

occupational therapy assistant ABBR: OTA. One who works under the supervision of an occupational therapist to assist with patient or client assessment and intervention. The degree and scope of supervision required depend on practice statutes and the levels of competency of the assistant. SEE: *certified occupational therapy assistant.*

occurrence report An incident report.

Ochlerotatus (ō-klĕr″ō-tā′tŭs) A subgenus of the *Aedes* mosquito that sometimes carries infectious diseases.

ochronosis (ō-krō-nō′sĭs) [″ + *nosos,* disease] A rare illness whose hallmark is abnormally dark pigmentation of the skin, urine, and connective tissues. There are two variants: Endogenous ochronosis, also known as alkaptonuria, is familial (transmitted genetically in autosomal recessive inheritance). Exogenous ochronosis results from exposure to specific drugs or chemicals, such as hydroquinone or phenol.

Ocimum sanctum (os′ĭ-mŭm sangk′tŭm) SEE: *holy basil.*

Ockelbo disease (ŏk′ĕl-bō″) [Ockelbo, a town in Sweden] A viral infection, predominantly found in northern Europe, characterized by fever, headache, rash, and arthritis. It is caused by infection with a Sindbis virus.

OCN *Oncology certified* **nurse.**

O'Connor Finger Dexterity Test [Johnson O'Connor, U.S. psychometrician, 1891–1973] A standardized test that measures a person's ability to manipulate small objects rapidly. The test, designed for those 13 and older, requires sticking pins in a board containing multiple holes.

O'Connor Tweezer Dexterity Test A standardized, timed test of finger and eye-hand coordination requiring placement of pins in holes using tweezers. The test is designed for adults and children ages 13 and above.

OCP *oral contraceptive pill.*

OCT *oxytocin challenge test; optical coherence tomography.*

octa-, octo-, oct- [Gr. *oktō,* L. *octo*] Prefixes meaning *eight.*

octahedron (ŏk-tă-hē′drŏn) An eight-sided solid figure.

octane (ŏk′tān) C_8H_{18}; a hydrocarbon of the paraffin series.

octapeptide (ŏk″tă-pĕp′tĭd) A peptide that contains eight amino acids.

octaploid (ŏk′tă-ployd″) **1.** Pert. to octaploidy. **2.** Having eight sets of chromosomes.

octaploidy (ŏk′tă-ploy″dē) The condition of having eight sets of chromosomes.

octavalent (ŏk′tă-vā′lĕnt) [L. *octo,* eight, + *valeo,* to have power] Having a valence of eight.

octigravida (ŏk″tĭ-grăv′ĭ-dă) [″ + *gravida,* pregnant] A woman who has been pregnant eight times.

octipara (ŏk-tĭp′ă-ră) [″ + L. *parere,* to bring forth, to bear] A woman who has given birth to eight children.

octocrylene (ok″tō-kril′ēn) An ultraviolet filtering chemical found in some topical sunscreens. It is an occasional cause of photoallergic contact dermatitis.

octogenarian (ŏk″tō-jĕn-ĕr′ē-ĕ-) [L. *octogenarius,* containing eighty] A person who is 80 to 89 years old.

ocular (ŏk′ū-lăr) [L. *oculus,* eye] **1.** Concerning the eye or vision. **2.** The eyepiece of a microscope.

ocular histoplasmosis syndrome ABBR: OHS. A disease of the macula found in young and middle-aged adults from the Ohio and Mississippi river valleys, in which loss of vision occurs with central scotoma. It is also known as presumed ocular histoplasmosis syndrome (POHS), since the macular lesion is thought to be caused by *Histoplasma* *capsulatum,* a fungus that does not grow in cultures of pathological specimens from affected lesions.

ocular ischemic syndrome A rare syndrome in which gradual or sudden loss of vision results from blockage of blood flow through the carotid arteries to the eyes. The disease is found most often in patients with other risk factors for cardiovascular disease, such as diabetes mellitus, hyperlipidemia, and hypertension. Ophthalmic examination may reveal neovascularization of the retina, retinal microinfarcts, or elevated intraocular pressures.

ocularist (ŏk′ū-lăr-ĭst) An allied health specialist who is prepared by training and experience to make and fit artificial eyes.

ocular masquerade syndrome Presentation of a cancer of the eyelid as inflammation of the eyelid, conjunctiva, or tarsal glands, mimicking a benign condition.

oculi (ŏk′ū-lī) Pl. of oculus.

oculo-, ocul- [L. *oculus,* eye] Prefixes meaning *eye.*

oculocutaneous (ŏk″ū-lō-kū-tā′nē-ŭs) Concerning the eyes and the skin.

oculofacial (ŏk″ū-lō-fā′shē-ăl) Concerning the eyes and the face.

oculogyration (ŏk″ū-lō-jī-rā′shŭn) [″ + Gr. *gyros,* circle] The circular motion of the eyeball around its antero-posterior axis. SEE: *nystagmus.*

oculogyria (ŏk″ū-lō-jī′rē-ă) The limits of rotation of the eyeballs.

oculogyric (ŏk″ū-lō-jī′rĭk) Producing or concerning movements of the eye. SYN: *oculomotor.*

oculomotor (ŏk″ū-lō-mō′tor) [″ + *motor,* mover] Relating to eye movements. SYN: *oculogyric.*

oculomycosis (ŏk″ū-lō-mī-kō′sĭs) [″ + Gr. *mykes,* fungus, + *osis,* condition] Any disease of the eye or its parts caused by fungus.

oculonasal (ŏk″ū-lō-nā′săl) [″ + *nasus,* nose] Concerning the eyes and the nose.

oculopharyngeal muscular dystrophy (ŏk″yū-lō-far″in-jē′ăl) SEE: under *dystrophy.*

oculoplastics (ŏk″ū-lō-plăs′tĭks) Plastic surgery of the eyelids and other periorbital tissues, performed to treat ectropion, exophthalmos, ptosis, trauma, or other conditions.

oculopupillary (ŏk″ū-lō-pū′pĭ-lăr-ē) Concerning the pupil of the eye.

oculovestibular test (ŏk″ū-lō-věs-tĭb′ū-lăr) Caloric test.

oculus (ŏk′ū-lŭs) *pl.* **oculi** [L.] Eye; the organ of vision made up of the eyeball and optic nerve.

    o. dexter ABBR: OD. The right eye.

    o. sinister ABBR: OS. The left eye.

    o. uterque ABBR: OU. Each eye.

OD *overdose;* [L.] *oculus dexter,* right eye.

odaxesmus (ō″dăk-sěz′mŭs) [Gr. *odaxesmos,* an irritation] The biting of the tongue, lip, or cheek during an epileptic attack.

odaxetic (ō″dăk-sět′ĭk) Producing a stinging or itching sensation.

OD′d (ō′dēd′) Slang term for a death or illness due to a drug overdose, esp. a drug of abuse.

odds In statistics, the probability that an event may appear or occur. This probability is estimated from known rates of occurrence of the event in a specific setting, e.g., from the known number of patients with a particular disease on a particular island. In practice most patients do not live on islands, and many have diseases whose presentation varies from the norm. The use of odds in health care always implies some degree of probability rather than of proof.

odds ratio In epidemiological case-control studies, a relative measure of the occurrence of disease. The odds in favor of a particular disease occurring in an exposed group are divided by the odds in favor of its occurring in an unexposed group. If the condition being studied is rare, the odds ratio is a close approximation to the relative risk. SYN: *events odds ratio.* SEE: *relative* **risk.**

odogenesis (ō″dō-jěn′ĕ-sĭs) [Gr. *hodos,* pathway, + *genesis,* generation, birth] Neural regeneration.

odont-, odonto- [Gr. *odous,* stem *odont-,* tooth] Prefixes meaning *tooth, teeth.*

odontalgia (ō″don″tal′j(ē-)ă) [*odont-* + *-algia*] Toothache. **odontalgic** (jik), *adj.*

    phantom o. Pain felt in the area from which a tooth has been extracted.

odontectomy (ō-dŏn-těk′tō-mē) [″ + *ektome,* excision] Surgical removal of a tooth.

odonterism (ō-dŏn′těr-ĭzm) [″ + *erismos,* quarrel] Chattering of the teeth.

odontic (ō-dŏn′tĭk) [Gr. *odous,* tooth] Concerning the teeth.

odontitis (ō″dŏn-tī′tĭs) [″ + *itis,* inflammation] Inflammation of a tooth.

odontoblast (ō-dŏn′tō-blăst) [″ + *blastos,* germ] One of the cells forming the surface layer of the dental papilla that is responsible for the formation of the dentin of a tooth. After a tooth is formed, the odontoblasts line the pulp cavity and continue to produce dentin for years after the tooth has erupted.

odontoblastoma (ō-dŏn″tō-blăs-tō′mă) [″ + ″ + *oma,* tumor] A tumor composed principally of odontoblasts.

odontocele (ō-dŏn′tō-sēl) [″ + *kele,* tumor, swelling] An alveolodental cyst.

odontoclasis (ō″dŏn-tŏk′lă-sĭs) [″ + *klasis,* fracture] The breaking or fracture of a tooth.

odontogenesis, odontogeny (ō-dŏn″tō-jen′ĕ-sĭs, -toj′ĕn-ē) [*odonto-* + *-gene-*

sis] The origin and formation of the teeth. **odontogenic** (-jen'ik), *adj.*

o. imperfecta A congenital anomaly of the developing teeth in which there is deficient production of enamel and dentin in affected teeth, producing decreased density and enlarged pulp chambers.

odontoid (ō-dŏn'toyd) [" + *eidos,* form, shape] Toothlike.

odontoma (ŏ"don"tō'mă, "tō'mă-tă) *pl.*
odontomas, odontomata [*odont-* + *-oma*] A tumor originating in the dental tissue.

ameloblastic o. Ameloblastic fibro-odontoma.

complex o. A benign, radioopaque dental mass that consists of a mixture of enamel, dentin, cementum, and pulp. It is most often found in the posterior mandible and can prevent the eruption of teeth.

compound o. Ameloblastic fibro-odontoma.

coronary o. A bony tumor at the crown of a tooth.

follicular o. A bony shell in the gums below the tooth margin, usually appearing after the second dentition. It is due to an excessive number of dental follicles. The tumor often involves one or more teeth and is crepitating to pressure. SYN: *dentigerous cyst.*

radicular o. Odontoma close to or on the root of a tooth.

odontonomy (ŏ"dŏn-tŏn'ō-mē) [" + *onoma,* name] Dental nomenclature.

odontoprisis (ō-dŏn"tō-prī'sĭs) [" + *prisis,* sawing] Bruxism.

odontoschism (ō-dŏn'tō-skĭzm) [" + *schisma,* cleft] Fissure of a tooth.

odontoscopy (ŏ"dŏn-tŏs'kō-pē) [" + *skopein,* to examine] **1.** Examination of the teeth and oral cavity by use of an odontoscope. **2.** An impression made of the biting marks made by teeth. It is used as a means of identification.

odor (ō'dĕr) [L.] That quality of a substance that renders it perceptible to the sense of smell.

Odors have been classed as (1) pure, (2) those mixed with sensations from the mucous membrane, and (3) those mixed with the sensation of taste. Although classification attempts are useful, it is important to realize that most complex substances do not produce a single odor.

In the past, body and breath odors were sometimes relied on to suggest diagnoses; this is rarely done in contemporary health care. Examples are a "mousy" odor present in the breath of patients with liver failure (liver breath); an odor of stale urine (uremic breath) in uremia; and the sweet smell of acetone in diabetic ketoacidosis. The characteristic smell of some alcoholic beverages can be detected in the breath. In some hospitals, the employees and staff who work in the presence of patients are asked to refrain from wearing scented substances such as perfumes, hair sprays, underarm deodorants, or aftershave lotions. This is done to prevent olfactory discomfort to patients. Individuals who have just returned from surgery or who have asthma or other respiratory problems are particularly sensitive to odors. Electronic devices for detecting and characterizing odors have been developed. SEE: *breath; odorimetry; pheromone.*

body o. The aroma or fragrance emanating from the human body. It may be derived from sweat gland secretions, urine, feces, expiration, saliva, breasts, skin, and sex organs. The major sources are the eccrine and apocrine sweat glands. Sebaceous gland secretions from the skin contribute to these odors. Eating garlic or onions or taking certain drugs may add to the odors produced by sweat glands, but the major sources of body sweat odor are the volatile fatty acids, steroids, and amines emitted by apocrine glands. Bacteria and fungi in and around these glands can intensify the odors. The secretions increase at puberty and decrease after menopause, are enhanced by stress, and are partially genetically controlled. SEE: *halitosis.*

odorant (ō'dor-ănt) Something that stimulates the sense of smell.

odoriferous (ō"dor-ĭf'ĕ-rŭs) [L. *odor,* smell, + *ferre,* to bear] Bearing an odor; fragrant; perfumed.

odorimetry (ō"do-rĭm'ĕ-trē) The measurement of odors.

odorography (ō"dor-ŏg'ră-fē) [" + Gr. *graphein,* to write] A description of odors.

odorous (ō'dŏr-ŭs) [L. *odor,* smell] Having an odor, scent, or fragrance.

odynacusis (ō"dĭn-ă-kū'sĭs) [Gr. *odyne,* pain, + *akousis,* hearing] A condition in which noise causes pain in the ear.

-odynia [Gr. *odynē,* pain + *-ia*] Suffix meaning *pain.*

odynometer (ō"dĭn-om'ĕt-ĕr) [" + *metron,* measure] A device for measuring pain.

odynophagia (ŏd"ĭn-ō-fā'jē-ă) [" + *phagein,* to eat] Pain upon swallowing.

Oedipus complex (ĕd'ĭ-pŭs) [Oedipus, a character in Gr. tragedy who unwittingly killed his father and married his mother] Abnormally intense love of the child for the parent of the opposite sex. This love continues in adulthood, and usually involves jealous dislike of the other parent. Most often, it is the love of a son for his mother. SEE: *Electra complex; Jocasta complex.*

oesophago- SEE: *esophago-.*

oesophagostomiasis (ē-sŏf"ă-gō-stō-mī'ă-sĭs) [Gr. *oisophagos,* esophagus,

+ *stoma*, mouth, + *-iasis*, state] Infection with the nematode of the genus *Oesophagostomum*.

Oesophagostomum (ē-sŏf″ă-gŏs′tō-mŭm) [Gr. *oisophagos*, esophagus, + *stoma*, mouth] A genus of nematodes belonging to the suborder Strongylata that is parasitic in the intestinal tract of animals and humans.

oestrus (es′trŭs, ēs′) Estrus.

Oestrus ovis (es′trŭs ō′vis) A botfly whose maggots (larvae) may cause ocular myiasis in humans. SEE: *myiasis; ophthalmomyiasis.*

offal (of′fel) Animal parts discarded during the process of butchering or slaughtering, typically including the brain, viscera, skin, hooves, and blood. These by-products have been implicated in the transmission of some infectious illnesses, like mad cow disease.

office (ŏf′is) **1.** A room, suite, or building used for professional, commercial, or bureaucratic work. **2.** An outpatient facility where patients are seen, examined, and treated; a clinic.

office-based (ŏf′is-bāst″) Occurring in an outpatient setting rather than in a hospital or another inpatient setting.

official Said of medicines authorized as standard in the U.S. Pharmacopeia and in the National Formulary.

officinalis (ō-fis″ĭ-nā′lis) [L. *officinalis*, pert. to a workshop, storeroom, pharmacy] Part of the scientific name of a species pert. to a plant or herb traditionally sold in pharmacies, readily available without special preparation, and considered to have medicinal properties, e.g., *Calendula officinalis*, the pot marigold. **officinale** (ō-fis″ĭ-nā′lē), *adj.*

off-label drug use The use of a drug to treat a condition for which it has not been approved by the U.S. Food and Drug Administration (FDA), esp. when such use may relieve unpleasant symptoms, or prove compassionate. During the drug approval process in the U.S., drug manufacturers present carefully accumulated data to the FDA about the safety and effectiveness of their products. Drugs are labeled for specific uses when manufacturers make an application to the FDA with data that describe their drug's performance during clinical trials. If the data withstand rigorous scrutiny the drug is labeled for a specific use. Drug effects that have been observed but not specifically proven (and for which no application has been made) may be exploited for unproven or "off-label" uses by licensed medical practitioners.

Ofuji disease (ō-foo′jē) Eosinophilic pustular folliculitis.

ogbanje (ŏg-băn′jä) [Igbo (Nigeria), lit. "children who come and go"] Among the Igbo people of Nigeria, a person who is reborn after birth. In the Igbo culture all humans undergo reincarnation, but some particularly evil children are born over and over again. They suffer terrible illnesses (typically their signs and symptoms match those of sickle cell disease) that inflict revenge upon families that have been cursed.

Ogilvie syndrome (ō′gĭl-vē) [Sir William Heneage Ogilvie, Brit. physician, 1887–1971] Acute intestinal pseudo-obstruction due to intestinal dilatation, mostly of the colon. A patient displaying this syndrome has usually undergone recent severe surgical or medical stress (such as myocardial infarction, sepsis, or respiratory failure), may be hospitalized or in intensive care, may have metabolic and electrolyte disturbances, and may have received narcotics.

PATIENT CARE: Treatment consists of therapy for the underlying disease, correction of electrolyte disturbances, avoidance of drugs that inhibit intestinal motility, and intubation of the small intestine for decompression. Colonoscopy may be required to avoid ischemic necrosis and perforation of the bowel.

OGTT *Oral glucose tolerance test.*

⁻OH Symbol for the hydroxyl ion.

OHA *Oral hypoglycemic agent.*

OHCA *out-of-hospital cardiac arrest.*

ohm (ōm) [Georg S. Ohm, Ger. physicist, 1787–1854] The unit of electrical resistance equal to that of a conductor in which a current of one ampere is produced by a potential of one volt across the terminals. SEE: *electromotive force.*

Ohm's law (ōmz) [Georg S. Ohm, Ger. physicist, 1787–1854] The strength of an electric current, expressed in amperes, is equal to the electromotive force, expressed in volts, divided by the resistance, expressed in ohms (V=IR). SEE: *electricity.*

ohmmeter (ōm′mē-tĕr) A device for determining the electrical resistance of a conductor.

Ohtahara syndrome (ō-tă-ha′ră) [S. Ohtahara, Japanese pediatric neurologist] A form of progressive epileptic encephalopathy in newborns. The disease is difficult to treat and has a poor prognosis. SYN: *early infantile epileptic **encephalopathy** with suppression bursts.*

-oid [Gr. *-oeidēs*, fr. *eidos*, form, shape] Suffix indicating partial or imperfect resemblance to the item designated in the first part of the word.

oil (oyl) [Fr. *oile* fr L. *oleum*, olive oil, oil] A greasy liquid not miscible with water, usually obtained from and classified as mineral, vegetable, or animal. According to character, oils are subdivided principally as fixed (fatty) and volatile (essential).

Examples of fixed oils are castor oil, olive oil, and cod liver oil. Examples of volatile oils are oils of mustard, peppermint, and rose.

canola o. A light, clear oil derived from the pods of an oilseed plant in the rapeseed family. The oil is composed of 7% saturated fat (the lowest saturated fat content of any vegetable oil), 61% monounsaturated fat, and 22% polyunsaturated fat.

castor o. A fixed oil expressed from the seed of the castor-oil plant (*Ricinus communis*), used externally as an emollient and internally as a cathartic. It is hydrolyzed to ricinoleic acid, which acts as an irritant type of laxative.

chaulmoogra o., chaulmugra oil, chaulmaugra oil A vegetable oil used to treat leprosy and some dermatoses. Although generally replaced by sulfones in treatment of leprosy, chaulmoogra oil is still used in areas where leprosy is endemic because of its availability and low cost.

coconut o. A colorless cooking oil, derived from the nut of the palm tree (*Cocos nucifera*). It has the highest level of saturated fat (about 91%) of all cooking oils.

cod liver o. An oil obtained from cod-fish liver, rich in vitamins A and D.

ACTION/USES: Cod liver oil was widely used in cases of nutritional deficiency to supply vitamins A and D, esp. for prophylaxis of rickets in infants. It is rarely used now because more efficient and more palatable agents are available.

croton o. A fixed oil expressed from the seed of the croton plant (*Croton tiglium*). It is toxic to skin, heart, muscle, and the gastrointestinal tract.

essential o. A volatile oil, esp. one that has an odor and taste, extracted from plants by various means. Some of these oils have been used since antiquity as preservatives and antiseptics, e.g., thymol and eugenol. Some are used in flavorings, perfumes, and medicines. They are usually complex chemicals difficult to purify. SYN: *volatile o.*

eucalyptus o. Eucalyptol.

evening primrose o. An oil derived from *Oenothera biennis*, a biennial herb with yellow flowers, that contains omega-6 fatty acids. It is promoted for the treatment of inflammatory conditions, e.g., of the skin or joints.

fish o. A popular term for omega-3 fatty acids, which when consumed in the diet in the form of salmon, halibut, and other cold-water fish, reduce the risk of coronary artery disease (CAD). Dietary supplements of fish oil capsules containing omega-3 and/or omega-6 fatty acids, by contrast, have shown inconsistent results in the prevention of CAD.

fixed o. Any of the oils in plants and animals that are glyceryl esters of fatty acids. These oils serve as food reserves in animals. They are nonvolatile and contain no acid.

flaxseed o. Oil extracted from the seeds of the flax plant (*Linum usitatissimum*), used as a nutritional supplement. Flaxseed oil contains alpha-linolenic acid, an essential omega-3 fatty acid promoted for its effect in preventing heart disease, inflammatory bowel disease, and arthritis. SEE: *essential fatty acid; flaxseed; linolenic acid; omega-3 (ω3) fatty acids.*

halibut liver o. An oil obtained from the liver of the halibut fish (genus *Hippoglossus*), rich in vitamins A and D.

lavender o. An essential oil derived from *Lavandula angustifolia*, a plant with lavender flowers. The oil is used in aromatherapy to alleviate pain, e.g., during acupressure, massage, and childbirth.

Lorenzo's o. SEE: *Lorenzo's oil.*

medium-chain triglyceride o. A cooking oil of medium-chain triglycerides, used therapeutically as a source of calories and fatty acids, esp. in patients with long-chain and very long-chain fatty acid metabolism disorders. These triglycerides are more readily absorbed from the gut than are most long-chain triglycerides.

mineral o. Liquid **petrolatum**.

olive o. An oil obtained by pressing ripe olives (*Olea europaea*). It is the major fat used in Mediterranean cooking. It has a relatively high content of monounsaturated fatty acids (which reduce levels of low-density lipoprotein cholesterol) and polyphenols (which act as antioxidants). It can be consumed in the diet or used on the skin as an emollient.

peanut o. A refined oil obtained from the seed kernels of one or more of the cultivated varieties of *Arachis hypogaea,* used as a solvent for some medicines that are injected intramuscularly.

safflower o. The oil expressed from the seeds of the safflower plant, *Carthamus tinctorius.* It is high in linoleic acid and low in saturated fatty acids. Diets rich in safflower oil produce less serum cholesterol and apolipoproteins A-I and B than similar diets in which butter or coconut oil is used as the primary fat source.

sesame o. Oil obtained from the seeds of *Sesamum indicum,* used as a pharmaceutical aid and as a cooking oil. Sesame oils occasionally cause contact dermatitis.

silicone o. Injectable **silicone**.

soybean o. A commonly used oil obtained from the seeds of the soya plant (soybeans) that is low in unsaturated fat and rich in linolenic acid, an essential fatty acid.

tea tree o. The aromatic essential oil of *Melaleuca alternifolia,* used as a topical antibacterial, anti-inflammatory, and antifungal in a range of herbal medicines. Skin irritation may occur in some sensitized people exposed to the oil or if the oil is used in high concentrations.

    volatile o. Essential **o.**

    wheat germ o. The oil expressed from the germ of the wheat seed. It is a rich source of vitamin E.

    wintergreen o., oil of wintergreen A colorless, yellowish, or reddish liquid derived from methyl salicylate. It has a characteristic taste and odor and is used as a flavoring substance and as a counterirritant applied topically in the form of salves, lotions, and ointments. SEE: ***methyl*** *salicylate.*

oil red-O A fat-soluble dye primarily used in microscopic tissue examination to highlight triglycerides.

ointment (oynt′mĕnt) [Fr. *oignement*] A viscous, semisolid vehicle used to apply medicines to the skin. Ointments differ from creams or lotions in their superior ability to occlude the skin and improve the uptake of drugs. The base or vehicle of an ointment typically includes petrolatum, fats, oils, resins, or water-based or water-soluble compounds. SYN: *salve; unguent.*

    hydrophilic o. An oil-in-water emulsion in the form of a standardized ointment preparation used topically as an emollient.

OIRD *object-film distance.* Distance from the radiographic film to the object being radiographed.

OKT3 An immunosuppressive monoclonal antibody used in organ transplantation.

ol L. *oleum,* oil.

-ol [(*alcoh*)*ol* or (*phen*)*ol*] Suffix used in chemical names for an *alcohol* or, occasionally, a *phenol*.

OLA L. *occipitolaeva anterior* (fetal presentation). SYN: *LOA.* SEE: *position.*

olanzapine An atypical antipsychotic agent used to treat psychosis and schizophrenia. It controls both the "positive" symptoms of schizophrenia (delusions, hallucinations) and the "negative" symptoms (passivity, blunted affect, social isolation). Extrapyramidal side effects are less commonly associated with the use of olanzapine than with conventional neuroleptic drugs, such as haloperidol. Common side effects include drowsiness, dizziness, and weight gain.

Older Americans Resources and Services Scale—Instrumental Activities of Daily Living ABBR: OARS-IADL. A modified activity of daily living assessment scale to quantify a person's ability to perform tasks considered essential for community living. The seven tasks assessed are telephone use, traveling, shopping, preparing meals, performing housework, taking medications, and handling finances.

old-old (ōld′ōld″) Over 85 years old.

Old World The Eastern hemisphere. It is used in the biological sciences to distinguish plants, animals, and infections that live and thrive primarily in Africa, Asia, and Europe.

olea (ō′lē-ă) [L.] **1.** Olive. **2.** Pl. of oleum.

Olea europaea (ō′lē-ă ūr″ŏ-pē′ă) [L., European olive] The scientific name for the olive tree. Allergens in the fruit may cause anaphylaxis in susceptible individuals. Abbreviated Ole by the World Health Organization.

oleaginous (ō-lē-ăj′ĭ-nŭs) [L. *oleaginus*] Greasy; oily; unctuous.

oleander (ō″lē-ăn′dĕr) A poisonous ornamental evergreen shrub, *Nerium oleander.*

oleate (ō′lē-āt) [L. *oleatum*] **1.** Any salt of oleic acid. **2.** A salt of oleic acid dissolved in an excess of the acid and used as an ointment.

olecranon (ō-lĕk′răn-ŏn) [Gr., elbow] A large process of the ulna projecting behind the elbow joint and forming the bony prominence of the elbow. In treating a fracture of the olecranon, it is important to prevent spasm of the triceps muscle (to avoid separation of the fracture fragments by placing the arm in a sling or bandaging the arm to the side). The fragments may have to be wired. SYN: *olecranon process.* SEE: *elbow; skeleton; ulna.* **olecranal** (ō-lĕk′răn-ăl), *adj.*

oleic (ō-lē′ĭk) [L. *oleum,* oil] Derived from or pert. to oil.

olein (ō′lē-ĭn) [L. *oleum,* oil] An oleate of glyceryl found in nearly all fixed oils and fats; an important part of oils. SYN: *triolein.*

oleo-, ole-, olei- [L. *oleum,* oil] Prefixes meaning *oil.*

oleoresin (ō″lē-ō-rĕz′ĭn) [″ + *resina,* resin] An extract of a plant containing a resinous substance and oil, which is prepared by dissolving the crude extract in ether, acetone, or alcohol.

Olestra (ō-lĕs′tră) Trade name for a synthetic mixture of sucrose and fatty acids that pass through the digestive tract without absorption. While this fat replacement has been approved for use in savory snacks, it can interfere with uptake of fat-soluble vitamins, such as A, D, E, and K and may result in loose stools.

oleum (ō′lē-ŭm) *pl.* **olea** [L.] Oil.

olfaction (ŏl-făk′shŭn) [L. *olfacere,* to smell] **1.** The sense of smell. **2.** The act of smelling.

olfactometer (ŏl″făk-tŏm′ĕt-ĕr) [″ + Gr. *metron,* measure] Apparatus for testing the power of the sense of smell.

olfactory (ŏl-făk′tō-rē) Pert. to smell.

oligo-, olig- [Gr. *oligos,* little, few] Prefixes meaning *small, few.*

oligoanalgesia (ol″ĭ-gō-an″ăl-jē′zhă) [*oligo-* + *analgesia*] Inadequate treatment of pain.

oligoanovulatory (ol″i-gō-an″ov′yū-lă-tor″ē) [*oligo-* + *anovulatory*] Pert. to or characterized by intermenstrual periods that are no shorter than 35 days but no longer than 180 days.

oligoarthritis Inflammation that involves four or fewer joints. Inflammation involving a single joint is known as monoarticular arthritis, and that involving more than four joints as polyarthritis.

oligodendroblast (ŏl″ĭ-gō-dĕn′drō-blăst) [″ + Gr. *dendron*, tree, + *blastos*, germ] A glial cell precursor that develops from a neuroectoderm cell in the neural tube or from a subependymal cell in the nervous system and that gives rise to a mature oligodendrocyte, which can myelinate axons.

oligodendrocyte (ŏl″ĭ-gō-dĕn′trŏ-sīt) [″ + ″ + *kytos*, cell] A glial cell found most commonly in axon tracts; it myelinates axons in the central nervous system just as Schwann cells myelinate axons in the peripheral nervous system. Oligodendrocytes are neuroectodermal cells that originate from different precursors in the neural tube than astrocytes; later, stem cells in the subependymal layer can continue to generate new oligodendrocytes. Mature oligodendrocytes wrap neighboring axons in myelin, and some oligodendrocytes can simultaneously wrap many axons. However, not all oligodendrocytes myelinate axons. SYN: *oligodendroglia*. SEE: illus.

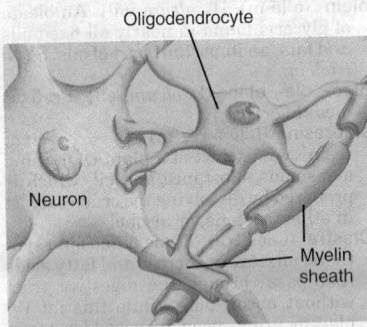

Oligodendrocyte

Neuron

Myelin sheath

OLIGODENDROCYTE

oligodendroglia (ŏl″ĭ-gō-dĕn-drŏg′lē-ă) [″ + ″ + *glia*, glue] Oligodendrocyte.

oligodendroglioma (ŏl″ĭ-gō-dĕn″drō-glī-ō′mă) [″ + ″ + ″ + *oma*, tumor] A malignant tumor of unknown etiology that consists mostly of oligodendrocytes and occurs principally in the cerebrum.

oligodontia (ŏl″ĭ-gō-dŏn′shē-ă) [″ + *odont*, tooth] A hereditary developmental anomaly characterized by fewer teeth than normal.

oligogenic (ŏl″ĭ-gō-jĕn′ĭk, -jēn′) Caused by, affecting, or relating to a small number of genes.

oligohydramnios (ŏl″ĭg-ō-hī-drăm′nē-ōs) [″ + *hydor*, water, + *amnion*, amnion] An abnormally small amount of amniotic fluid. It is a rare condition in which the volume of amniotic fluid during the third trimester is less than 300 ml. Insufficient fluid surrounding the fetus increases the potential for cord compression, fetal hypoxia, fetal malformation, perinatal demise, and dysfunctional and prolonged labor. Although the etiology is unknown, the disorder is associated with amniotic fluid leakage, placental insufficiency, postmaturity, intrauterine growth retardation, and major congenital abnormalities of the fetal kidney or lungs.

oligomeganephronia (ŏl″ĭ-gō″meg″ă-ne-frŏn′ē-ă) [*oligo-* + *mega-* + *nephron* + *-ia*] A hypoplastic renal disease in which the kidneys are small and have a reduced number of functional nephrons and calyces. The glomeruli and tubules that are present are hypertrophied.

oligomenorrhea (ŏl″ĭ-gō-mĕn″ō-rē′ă) [″ + *men*, month, + *rhoia*, flow] Scanty or infrequent menstrual flow.

oligonucleotide (ŏl″ĭ-gō-nū″klē-ō-tīd) [″ + *nucleotide*] A compound made up of a small number of nucleotide units.

oligoovulation (ŏl″i-gō-ov″yŭ-lā′shŏn) [*oligo-* + *ovulation*] Infrequent ovulation. It is a potential cause of infertility.

oligosaccharide (ŏl″ĭ-gō-săk′ă-rīd) A compound made up of a small number of monosaccharide units. Some are found on the outer surface of cell membranes as part of antigens.

oligospermia, oligozoospermatism (ŏl″ĭ-gō-spĕr′mē-ă, -zō″ō-spĕr′mă-tĭzm) [″ + *sperma*, seed] A temporary or permanent deficiency of spermatozoa in seminal fluid.

oligotrichia (ŏl″ĭ-gō-trĭk′ē-ă) [″ + *thrix*, hair] Congenital scantiness of hair.

oligotyping (ŏl″ĭ-gō-tīp′ĭng) [″ + ″] The detection of particular oligonucleotides in a nucleic acid specimen.

oliguria (ŏl-ĭg-ū′rē-ă) [″ + *ouron*, urine] Urinary output of less than 400 mL/day. Oliguria results in renal failure if it is not reversed.
ETIOLOGY: Diminished urinary output may result from inadequate perfusion of the kidneys (e.g., in shock or dehydration), from intrarenal diseases (e.g., acute tubular necrosis), or from obstruction to renal outflow (as in bilateral hydronephrosis). **oliguric,** *adj.*

olive (ol′ĭv) [L. *oliva*, olive] **1.** Inferior olive. **2.** An ovoid device small enough to fit on the tip of a vein stripper. This prevents damaging the vein as the stripper is pushed into it. **3.** Olivary **complex**. **4.** An enlarged, stenotic pylorus in infantile hypertrophic pyloric stenosis.

accessory o. The inferior, the medial, or the dorsal accessory olivary nuclei, which together form the inferior olive. SYN: *accessory olivary* **nucleus**.

inferior o. A large ovoid nucleus in the hindbrain just caudal to the pons; in cross-section, the inferior olive appears wavy or serpentine. Inputs to the inferior olive include axons from the midbrain reticular formation via the central tegmental tract. Outputs of the inferior olive project to the contralateral cerebellar hemisphere via the olivocerebellar tract in the inferior cerebellar peduncle. SYN: *inferior olivary* **complex**; *inferior olivary* **nucleus**.

superior o. A small nucleus located in the mid-lateral tegmental region of the pons. It is embedded in the lateral lemniscus just beyond the trapezoid body, and it receives axons from and sends axons to the lateral lemniscus. SYN: *superior olivary* **nucleus**; *superior olivary* **complex**. SYN: *olivary* **complex**.

olive oil SEE: under *oil*.

Ollier, Louis Xavier Edouard (ol″ē-ā′, ol-yā′) French surgeon, 1830–1900.

O.'s disease SEE: *chondrodysplasia*.

O.'s graft A split-thickness skin graft that is quite thin.

-olol A suffix used in pharmacology to designate any beta blocker similar in chemical structure to propranolol.

OLP L. *occipitolaeva posterior* (fetal presentation). SYN: *LOP*. SEE: *position*.

OM [o(*btuse*) + m(*arginal*)] Any of the coronary arteries that branch from the circumflex coronary artery. They are designated *OM1, OM2,* etc., in numerical order, from the most proximal artery to the most distal.

om L. *omni mane,* every morning.

-oma, -omas, -omata [Gr. *-ōma,* stem *-ōmat-,* tumor] Suffixes meaning *tumor*.

OMAP *Office of Medical Assistance Programs*.

ombudsman (ŏm′bŭdz-măn) In medicine, an advocate, esp. for patients or clients of health care institutions. The ombudsman verifies complaints and advocates for their resolution. SEE: *Patient's Bill of Rights*.

-ome [Fr. (*gen*)*ome*] Suffix meaning *complete set,* e.g., *genome, proteome*.

omega-3 (ω3) **fatty acids** (ō-meg′ă, -mā′gă, ō′mĕg-ă) SEE: under *acid*.

omentectomy (ō-mĕn-tĕk′tō-mē) [″ + Gr. *ektome,* excision] Surgical removal of all or part of the omentum.

omentopexy (ō-mĕn′tō-pĕks″ē) [″ + Gr. *pexis,* fixation] Fixation of the omentum to the abdominal wall or adjacent organ.

omentoplasty (ō-mĕn′tō-plăs″tē) [L. *omentum,* covering, + Gr. *plassein,* to form] The use of tissue from the greater omentum as a graft in reinforcing tissues.

omentotomy (ō-mĕn-tŏt′ō-mē) [″ + Gr. *tome,* incision] Surgical incision of the omentum.

omentum (ō-ment′ŭm) *pl.* **omenta** [L. *omentum,* adipose membrane] A double fold of peritoneum attached to the stomach and connecting it with certain of the abdominal viscera. It contains a cavity, the omental bursa (lesser peritoneal cavity). SEE: illus.

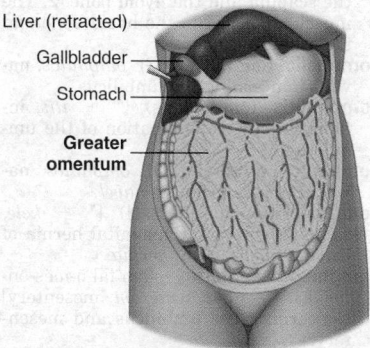

Liver (retracted)
Gallbladder
Stomach
Greater omentum

OMENTUM

gastrocolic o. Greater **o.**

gastrohepatic o. Lesser **o.**

greater o. The portion of the omentum that is suspended from the greater curvature of the stomach and covers the intestines like an apron. It is the largest of the folds of the peritoneum. It dips in among the folds of the intestines and is attached to the transverse colon and mesocolon. It contains fat, prevents friction, and aids in localizing infections. SYN: *gastrocolic* **o.**

lesser o. The portion of the omentum that passes from the lesser curvature of the stomach to the transverse fissure of the liver. **omental** (ō-ment′ăl), *adj.*

omeprazole (ō-mĕp′ră-zōl″) A potent inhibitor of the formation of gastric acid. It is used to treat erosive esophagitis, gastritis, gastroesophageal reflux, and peptic ulcer.

-omic [*-ome* + *-ic*] Suffix meaning *pertaining to a comprehensive field of study*.

OMIM *Online Mendelian Inheritance in Man*.

OML *orbitomeatal line*.

Ommaya reservoir (ō-mī′yă) [A. K. Ommaya, contemporary U.S. neurosurgeon] A mushroom-shaped infusion port, implanted in the ventricles of the brain, to allow access to cerebrospinal fluid (CSF), measurement of CSF pressure, or intrathecal drug administration (e.g., antibiotics, cancer-fighting drugs, or opiates). The reservoir may be used to help treat malignancies or infections of the central nervous system, or control chronic cancer pain. It may occasionally become infected or clogged during use.

omnipotence of thought In psychiatry, the infantile concept of reality in which one expects all of one's wishes to be instantly gratified.

omnivorous (ŏm-nĭv'ō-rŭs) [L. *omnis*, all, + *vorare*, to eat] Consuming foods of both vegetable and animal origin.

omo-, om- [Gr. *ōmos*, shoulder] Prefixes meaning *shoulder*.

omohyoid (ō-mō-hī'oyd) **1.** Concerning the scapula and the hyoid bone. **2.** The muscle attached to the hyoid bone and the scapula.

omphalic (ŏm-făl'ĭk) [Gr. *omphalos*, navel] Concerning the umbilicus.

omphalitis (ŏm-făl-ī'tĭs) [" + *itis*, inflammation] Inflammation of the umbilicus.

omphalo-, omphal- [Gr. *omphalos*, navel] Prefixes meaning *navel*.

omphalocele (ŏm-făl'ō-sēl) [" + *kele*, tumor, swelling] Congenital hernia of the umbilicus. SEE: *hernia*.

omphalomesenteric (ŏm″făl-ō-měs-ěn-těr'ĭk) [" + *mesenterion*, mesentery] Concerning the umbilicus and mesentery.

omphalopagus (ŏm″fă-lŏp'ă-gŭs) [" + *pagos*, thing fixed] Conjoined twins united at the abdomen.

omphalophlebitis (ŏm″făl-ō-flĕ-bī'tis) [" + *phleps*, vein, + *itis*, inflammation] Inflammation of the umbilical veins.

omphalotomy (ŏm-făl-ŏt'ō-mē) [" + *tome*, incision] Cutting of the umbilical cord at birth.

Omsk hemorrhagic fever virus (omsk) [*Omsk*, a city in eastern Russia] SEE: under *virus*.

ON orthopedic nurse.

on L. *omni nocte*, every night.

onanism (ō'năn-ĭzm) [So named because it was practiced by the biblical character Onan, son of Judah] Coitus interruptus; withdrawal before ejaculation. The term is erroneously used to designate masturbation.

Onanoff reflex (on-ă-nof') [Jacques Onanoff, Fr. physician, b. 1859] Contraction of the bulbocavernous muscle resulting from compression of the glans penis.

Onchocerca, Oncocerca (ong″kŏ-sěr'kă) [Gr. *onkos*, barb (of an arrow) + Gr. *kerkos*, tail] A genus of filarial worms that live in the subcutaneous and connective tissues of their hosts, usually enclosed in fibrous cysts or nodules.

O. volvulus A species of *Onchocerca*, a parasitic worm that is transmitted to people by the bite of black flies of the genus *Simulium*. Tiny, threadlike offspring of the worm migrate to the skin and eyes and produce inflammatory reactions that result in skin swellings and river blindness. The inflammation produced by the parasites may be mediated by a bacterium, *Wolbachia*, which in turn infests the parasitic worm.

onchocerciasis (ong″kŏ-sěr″kī'ă-sĭs, -sēz″) *pl.* **onchocerciases** [*Onchocerca* + -*iasis*] Infection with *Onchocerca volvulus*. SYN: *onchocercosis; river blindness*.

onco- [Gr. *onkos*, bulk, mass] Prefix meaning *tumor, swelling, mass*.

oncocyte (ŏn'kō-sīt) [" + *kytos*, cell] A large columnar cell with granular, acidophilic cytoplasm and a large number of mitochondria. They may become neoplastic.

oncocytoma (ŏng″kō-sī-tō'mă) [" + " + *oma*, tumor] A benign adenoma composed of eosinophilic epithelial cells, esp. one of the salivary or parathyroid glands.

oncofetal (ŏng″kō-fē'tăl) Concerning tumors in the fetus.

oncogene (ŏng'kō-jēn″) [*onco-* + *gene*] A gene in a virus that has the ability to induce a cell to become malignant. Oncogenes have been identified in human tumors. In addition to genes that can induce tumor formation, there are antioncogenes that suppress tumors.

oncogenesis (ŏng″kō-jěn'ě-sĭs) [" + *genesis*, generation, birth] Tumor formation and development. **oncogenic** (-jěn'ĭk), *adj.*

oncologist (ŏng-kŏl'ō-jĭst) [Gr. *onkos*, bulk, + *logos*, word] A specialist in oncology.

oncology (ŏng-kŏl'ō-jē) [" + *logos*, word, reason] The branch of medicine dealing with cancer.

   radiation o. The branch of medical therapeutics in which radioactive energy is used to cure or palliate cancer. The objective is to deliver a therapeutic dose of radiation to malignant tissue, leaving healthy, surrounding tissues unharmed. Radiation therapy is used to treat many cancers, including cancers of the bone, brain, breast, cervix, lymphoid tissues, and uterus.

oncology certified nurse SEE: under *nurse*.

Oncology Nursing Society ABBR: ONS. A professional nursing organization for nurses who specialize in one or more elements of cancer care: administration, education, patient care, or research. The society's website is www.ons.org.

oncolysis (ŏng-kŏl'ĭ-sĭs) [" + *lysis*, dissolution] The absorption or dissolution of tumor cells.

onconeural antigen (ong″kō-noor'ăl, on″, -nūr') SEE: under *antigen*.

oncoplastic surgery SEE: under *surgery*.

oncornaviruses (ŏn-kŏr'nă-vī'rŭ-sěz) A group of RNA viruses that can cause cancer in humans or animals.

oncosphere (ŏng'kō-sfēr) [" + *sphaira*, sphere] Hexacanth.

oncotherapy (ŏng″kō-thĕr'ă-pē) [" +

therapeia, treatment] The treatment of tumors.

oncotic (ŏng-kŏt′ĭk) [Gr. *onkos,* bulk, mass] Concerning, caused by, or marked by swelling.

oncovirus (ŏn′kō-vī″rŭs) [″ + *virus*] Any virus that causes malignant neoplasms.

Ondine's curse (on′dēnz″) [Fr. *ondine,* fr. L. *undina,* mythical water nymph whose human lover was cursed to continuous sleep] **1.** Primary alveolar hypoventilation caused by reduced responsiveness of the respiratory center to carbon dioxide. **2.** Loss of automatic respiratory function owing to a lesion in the cervical portion of the spinal cord.

-one [Gr. *-ōnē,* a feminine suffix] Suffix in biochemistry used in naming *ketones,* e.g., *quinone.*

oneirism (ō-nī′rĭzm) [″ + *-ismos,* state of] A dreamlike hallucination in a waking state.

oneirology (ō″nī-rŏl′ō-jē) [Gr. *oneiros,* dream, + *logos,* word, reason] The scientific study of dreams.

onion (ŭn′yŭn) [AS. *oignon*] The edible bulb of the onion plant (genus: *Allium*), cultivated as a vegetable.

onlay (ŏn′lā) **1.** A graft applied to the surface of a tissue, esp. a bone graft applied to bone. **2.** In dentistry, a cast metal restoration that overlays the cusps of the tooth, thereby providing additional strength to the restored tooth.

online database Any library of information accessible via linked computers, e.g., via the World Wide Web.

Online Mendelian Inheritance in Man ABBR: OMIM. A database of known genetic diseases and conditions.

on-off phenomenon In Parkinson patients, the alternating periods of good control (*on*) and poor control (*off*) of their symptoms. The on-off phenomenon is often experienced in patients undergoing L-dopa therapy.

onomatopoiesis, onomatopoeia (on″ō-mat″ŏ-poy-ē′sĭs, on″ō-mat″ō-pē′ă) [Gr. *onoma,* name + *-poiesis,*] **1.** The formation of words that imitate the sounds with which they are associated, e.g., hiss, buzz. **2.** In psychiatry, imitative words and sounds created by patients with schizophrenia. **onomatopoeic, onomatopoietic** (on″ō-mat″ŏ-pē′ik, on″ō-mat″ŏ-pō-et′ik), *adj.*

ONS *Oncology Nursing Society; oral nutritional supplement.*

onset of action The time between the administration of a medication or other form of treatment and the first evidence of its effect.

on site Available at an institution. Many medical or surgical services are available in specialized or tertiary care facilities but not in smaller, rural, or less technologically developed hospitals or clinics.

ontogeny (ŏn-tŏj′ĕn-ē) [Gr. *on,* being, + *gennan,* to produce] The developmental history of an organism, beginning with the germ cell(s).

onychauxis (ŏn″ĭ-kawk′sĭs) [″ + *auxein,* to increase] Overgrowth of the nails.

onychectomy (ŏn″ĭ-kĕk′tō-mē) [″ + *ektome,* to cut] Surgical removal of the nail of a finger or toe.

onychia (ō-nĭk′ē-ă) [Gr. *onyx,* nail] Inflammation of the nailbed with possible suppuration and loss of the nail. SYN: *matrixitis; onychitis.* SEE: *paronychia.*

onychitis (ŏn″ĭ-kī′tĭs) [″ + *itis,* inflammation] Onychia.

onycho-, onych- [Gr. *onyx,* stem *onych-,* nail] Prefixes meaning *fingernail, toenail.*

onychodystrophy (ŏn″ĭ-kō-dĭs′trō-fē) [″ + *dys,* bad, + *trophe,* nutrition] Any maldevelopment of a nail.

onychogryposis (ŏn″ĭ-kō-grī-pō′sĭs) [″ + *gryposis,* a curving] Abnormal overgrowth of the nails with inward curvature.

onychoid (ŏn′ĭ-koyd) [″ + *eidos,* form, shape] Similar to a nail, esp. a fingernail.

onycholysis (ŏn″ĭ-kŏl′ĭ-sĭs) [″ + *lysis,* dissolution] Loosening or detachment of the nail from the nailbed. SEE: *photoonycholysis.*

onychomadesis (on′ĭ-kō-mă-dē′sĭs, -dē′sēz″) *pl.* **onychomadeses** [*onycho-* + Gr. *madēsis,* loss of hair] The complete loss or shedding of the proximal fingernails or toenails.

onychomycosis (on′ĭ-kō-mī-kō′sĭs) [*onycho-* + *mycosis*] A fungal infection of the nails usually caused by *Trichophyton* and *Tinea* species and occasionally by *Candida* or other fungi. The hallmarks of the disease are thickening, scaling, and discoloration of the nailbed. PATIENT CARE: Foot and nail care include keeping the feet and toes clean and dry, wearing fresh socks, changing shoes daily, and applying topical creams to the foot if the skin has cracked from athlete's foot. Paring away excessive nail growth ("debridement") reduces the thickness and length of affected nails and may enhance the effectiveness of medications. Some patients may have debridement performed professionally by a podiatrist.

Topical medications or oral (systemic) medications improve the appearance of fungal nail changes, but both are expensive and efficacy is only moderate. Oral antifungal drugs also carry the risk of liver damage and should be avoided by those with underlying liver compromise. Relapse rates after treatment are high. SYN: *tinea unguium.* SEE: illus.

onycho-osteodysplasia (ŏn″ĭ-kō-ŏs″tē-ō-dĭs-plā′zē-ă) A genetic disease involving ectodermal and mesodermal tissues.

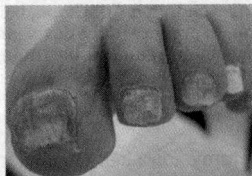

ONYCHOMYCOSIS

The nails and patellae may be absent; other bones and joints are affected. SYN: *nail-patella syndrome*.

onychopathy (ŏn-ĭ-kŏp′ăth-ē) [″ + *pathos*, disease, suffering] Any disease of the nails. SYN: *onychosis*.

onychophosis (ŏn″ĭk-ō-fō′sĭs) An accumulation of horny layers of epidermis under the toenail.

onychorrhexis (ŏn″ĭ-kō-rĕk′sĭs) [″ + *rhexis*, a rupture] Abnormal brittleness and splitting of the nails.

onychoschizia (ŏn″ĭ-kō-skĭz′ē-ă) [″ + *schizein*, to split] Loosening and eventual separation of the nail from its bed; nail splitting.

onychotomy (ŏn″ĭ-kŏt′ō-mē) [″ + *tome*, incision] Surgical incision of a fingernail or toenail.

onyx (ŏn′ĭks) [Gr., nail] **1.** A fingernail or toenail. **2.** Pus collection between the corneal layers of the eye. SYN: *hypopyon*.

oo- [Gr. *ōion*, egg] Prefix meaning *egg* or *ovary*.

oocyst (ō′ō-sĭst) [Gr. *oon*, egg, + *kystis*, bladder] The encysted form of a zygote occurring in certain sporozoa. SEE: *ookinete*.

oocyte (ō′ŏ-sīt″) [*oo-* + *-cyte*] The stage in the development of an egg cell between the oogonium and the ovum. SEE: *ovocyte*. SEE: *oogenesis* for illus.

   primary o. The oocyte produced by mitosis of an oogonium.

   secondary o. The larger of the two cells produced by the first meiotic division of the primary oocyte. SEE: *polar body*.

oogenesis (ō″ō-jĕn′ĕ-sĭs) [″ + *genesis*, generation, birth] The developmental process by which the mature human ovum (the female reproductive cell) is formed. Formation begins during the first 3 months of female embryonic life with the development of ovarian follicles. Each follicle contains one oogonium which, through the process of mitosis, becomes a primary oocyte containing 46 chromosomes. The oocyte then undergoes the first meiotic reduction division, resulting in formation of a secondary oocyte and a polar body, each containing 22 autosomes (half the number of chromosomes that are found in nongerm cells) and one X heterosome. Further division is arrested in prophase

until the female reaches puberty. The second meiotic division begins at ovulation and reaches metaphase where, once again, division is arrested until the ovum is fertilized. The second meiotic division is completed at fertilization, ending with formation of the mature haploid ovum and one polar body. SYN: *ovigenesis*. SEE: illus.; *meiosis*. **oogenetic** (-jĕ-nĕt′ĭk), *adj*.

oogonium (ō″ō-gō′nē-ŭm) *pl.* **oogonia** [″ + *gone*, seed] **1.** The primordial cell from which an oocyte originates. **2.** A descendant of the primordial cell from which the oocyte arises.

ookinete (ō″ō-kĭ-nēt′) [″ + *kinetos*, motile] An elongated motile zygote occurring in the life cycle of certain sporozoan parasites, esp. those of the genus *Plasmodium*. It penetrates the stomach wall of a mosquito and gives rise to an oocyst.

oolemma (ō″ō-lĕm′ă) [″ + *lemma*, sheath] The plasma membrane of the oocyte.

oophagy (ō-ŏf′ă-jē) [″ + *phagein*, to eat] Eating of eggs.

oophorectomy (ō″ŏf-ō-rĕk′tō-mē) [Gr. *oophoros*, bearing eggs, + *ektome*, excision] Excision of an ovary. SEE: *ovariectomy*.

   PATIENT CARE: Teaching is individualized according to the reason for removal of the ovary and the surgical method employed. Often the procedure is carried out to remove a benign ovarian cyst, but it may also be performed to remove a tumor of the ovary or an ovary that has twisted. Care before and after surgery is similar to that for other types of laparoscopic or open abdominal surgery. The procedure and expected sensations are explained, deep-breathing and coughing exercises are taught, and the importance of incentive spirometry, early ambulation, and other activity after surgery is emphasized. Vital signs are monitored, and intravenous fluids provided until the patient is able to tolerate oral intake. Urinary output is checked to be certain the patient is able to void and is emptying her bladder completely. After removal of a large cyst or mass, the decrease in intra-abdominal pressure may result in abdominal distention. Use of an abdominal binder may help to prevent this. The effectiveness of care is evaluated. If further treatment is required, the patient is given the opportunity to ask questions and to verbalize her feelings and concerns. Support and reassurance are provided. Appropriate reassurance is offered regarding the patient's concerns about infertility or cancer. Discharge instructions include gradually increasing activities and abstaining from use of tampons and sexual intercourse until her postoperative visit to the surgeon or gynecologist has been completed.

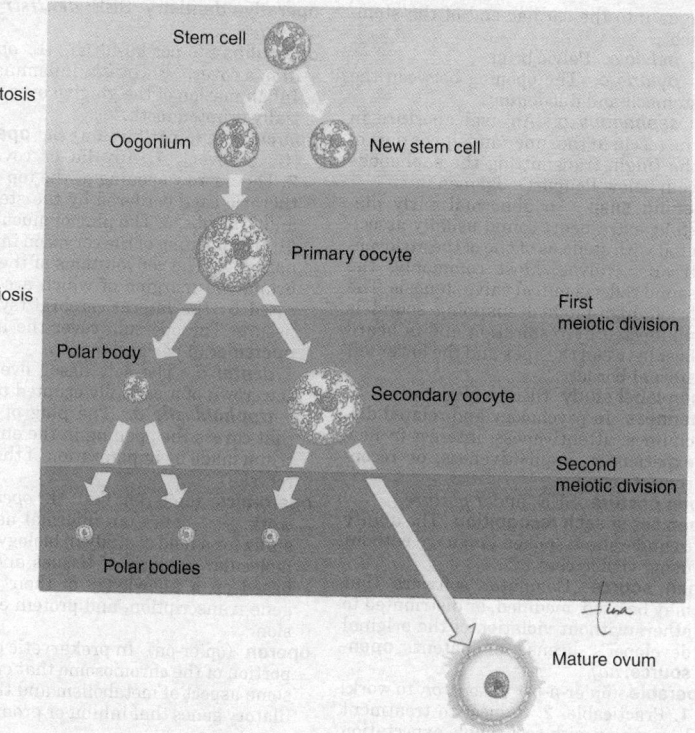

OOGENESIS

oophoritis (ō″ŏf-ō-rī′tĭs) [″ + *itis*, inflammation] Inflammation of an ovary. SEE: *ovaritis*.

   follicular o. Inflammation of the graafian follicles.

oophoro-, oophor- [Gr. *ōiophoros*, bearing eggs] Prefixes meaning *ovary*.

oophoropexy (ō-ŏf″ō-rō-pĕk′sē) [″ + *pexis*, fixation] Fixation of a displaced ovary.

ooplasm (ō′ō-plăzm) [Gr. *oon*, egg, + LL. *plasma*, form, mold] The cytoplasm of an ovum.

oospore (ō′ō-spor) [″ + *sporos*, seed] A spore formed by the union of opposite sexual elements.

ootid (ō′ō-tĭd) The ovum after first maturation has been completed and the second meiotic division has begun.

OP *operative procedure; outpatient; occiput posterior.*

OPA *Oropharyngeal airway.*

opacification (ō-păs″ĭ-fĭ-kā′shŭn) [L. *opacitas*, shadiness, + *facere*, to make] **1.** The process of making something opaque. **2.** The formation of opacities.

opacity (ō-păs′ĭ-tē) [L. *opacitas*, shadiness] **1.** The state of being opaque. **2.** An opaque area or spot. **3.** The ratio of incident light to transmitted light in a specific area or on a radiograph.

opalescent (ō″păl-ĕs′ĕnt) Iridescent; similar to an opal with respect to the colors produced.

opaque (ō-pāk′) [L. *opacus*, dark] **1.** Impenetrable by visible light rays or by other forms of radiant energy such as x-rays. **2.** Not transparent or translucent.

open [AS.] **1.** Not closed. **2.** Uncovered or exposed, as a wound to air. **3.** To puncture, as to open a boil. **4.** Interrupted, as in an electric circuit when current cannot pass because a switch is open.

open bite SEE: under *bite*.

open enrollment A defined time of the month or year when eligible individuals may obtain insurance from a health benefits provider.

open enrollment period SEE: under *period*.

open head injury SEE: under *injury*.

opening (ōp′ĕ-ning) **1.** The act of making or becoming open. **2.** A hole, aperture, entrance, or open space.

   aortic o. The opening in the diaphragm through which the aorta passes.

   cardiac o. The opening of the esophagus into the cardiac end of the stomach.

pelvic o. Pelvic brim.

pyloric o. The opening between the stomach and duodenum.

saphenous o. An oval aperture in the fascia in the inner and upper part of the thigh, transmitting the saphenous vein below Poupart's ligament.

opening snap An abnormal early diastolic extra heart sound usually associated with stenosis of one of the atrioventricular valves. Most commonly, the sound reflects mitral valve stenosis. The brief, high-pitched snapping sound is unaffected by respiration and is heard best between the apex and the lower left sternal border.

open-label study SEE: under *study*.

openness In psychology and related disciplines: attentiveness, interest in new experiences, inquisitiveness, or receptivity to change.

open posture SEE: under *posture*.

open set speech recognition The ability to understand spoken language without using visible cues.

open source Computer software that may be used, modified, or distributed to others without violation of the original developer's license or patent. **open-source**, *adj.*

operable (ŏp′ĕr-ă-bl) [L. *operor*, to work] **1.** Practicable. **2.** Subject to treatment by surgery with reasonable expectation of cure, palliation, or improvement.

operant (ŏp′ĕr-ănt) Producing effects.

operant conditioning SEE: *conditioning*, *operant*.

operate (ŏp′ĕr-āt) [L. *operatus*, worked] To perform a surgical procedure.

operation (op″ĕ-rā′shŏn) [L. *operatio*, a working] **1.** The act of operating. **2.** A surgical procedure. **3.** The effect or method of action of any type of therapy. SEE: *surgery*.

Abbe-Wharton-McIndoe o. SEE: *Abbe-Wharton-McIndoe operation*.

Alexander-Adams o. SEE: *Alexander-Adams operation*.

Amussat o. SEE: *Amussat operation*.

Babcock o. SEE: *Babcock operation*.

Bassini o. SEE: *Bassini operation*.

Beer o. SEE: *Beer operation*.

Billroth I o. Gastroduodenostomy.

Billroth II o. Gastrojejunostomy.

Emmet o. SEE: *Emmet operation*.

Halsted o. SEE: under *Halsted, William Stewart*.

Kader o. SEE: *Kader operation*.

Kondoleon o. SEE: *Kondoleon operation*.

McIndoe o. SEE: *Abbe-Wharton-McIndoe operation*.

Morrow o. SEE: *Morrow operation*.

Syme o. SEE: *Syme operation*.

operative (ŏp′ĕr-ă-tĭv) [L. *operativus*, working] **1.** Effective, active. **2.** Pert. to or brought about by an operation.

operative dentistry SEE: *dentistry*, *operative*.

operculitis (ō-pĕr″kū-lī′tĭs) [L. *operculum*, a cover, + Gr. *itis*, inflammation] Inflammation of the gingiva over a partially erupted tooth.

operculum (ō-pĕr′kū-lŭm) *pl.* **opercula** [L., a cover] **1.** Any lid or covering. **2.** The narrow opening at the top of the thoracic cage bordered by the sternum and first ribs. **3.** The plug of mucus that fills the opening of the cervix on impregnation. **4.** The convolutions of the cerebrum, the margins of which are separated by the lateral cerebral (sylvian) fissure. The opercula cover the insula. **opercular** (ō-pĕr′kū-lăr), *adj.*

dental o. The soft tissue overlying the crown of a partially erupted tooth.

trophoblastic o. The plug of fibrin that covers the opening in the endometrium made by implantation of the blastocyst.

operomics (ŏp″ē-rŏm′ĭks) [L. *operor*, to work, + *-omics*, an informal neologic suffix for a field of study in biology] The molecular analysis of tissues and cells based on a knowledge of their genes, gene transcription, and protein expression.

operon (ŏp′ĕr-ŏn) In prokaryotic cells, a portion of the chromosome that encodes some aspect of metabolism and the regulatory genes that inhibit or promote its expression.

ophiasis (ō-fī′ă-sĭs) [Gr. *ophis*, snake] Baldness occurring in winding streaks across the head.

ophidism (ō′fĭd-ĭzm) [″ + *-ismos*, condition] Poisoning from snake bite.

Ophiophagus (ō″fē-of′ă-gŭs) [Gr. *ophis*, snake + Gr. *phagein*, to eat] A genus of venomous snakes of the family Elapidae that includes the king cobra (*Ophiophagus hannah*). SEE: *cobra*; *Naja*.

ophryon (ŏf′rē-ŏn″) The meeting point of the facial median line with a transverse line across the forehead's narrowest portion.

ophryplasty (ŏf′rē-plăs″tē) Cosmetic surgery to reduce forehead wrinkling or furrowing and sagging of the eyebrows. SEE: *browlift*.

ophthalmia (of-thal′mē-ă) [*ophthalmo-* + *-ia*] Severe inflammation of the eye, usually including the conjunctiva.

Egyptian o. Trachoma.

electric o. Ophthalmia marked by eye pain, intolerance to light, and tearing (lacrimation). The condition occurs following prolonged exposure to intense light such as that encountered in arc welding.

gonococcal o. Purulent conjunctivitis due to infection with gonococcus.

granular o. Trachoma.

metastatic o. Sympathetic inflammation of the choroid due to pyemia or metastasis.

o. neonatorum Severe purulent conjunctivitis in the newborn.

ETIOLOGY: Infection of the birth canal at the time of delivery. *Neisseria gonorrhoeae* and *Chlamydia trachomatis* are responsible for the great majority of cases. Symptoms are present 12 to 48 hr after birth when due to gonorrhea and 1 week or more after birth for *Chlamydia* infections.

PROPHYLAXIS: Erythromycin ophthalmic ointment or other approved agents are introduced into the conjunctival sac of each eye of the newborn to prevent gonorrheal or chlamydial conjunctivitis. SEE: *Credé method* (2).

neuroparalytic o. Ophthalmia resulting from injury or disease involving the semilunar ganglion or the branches of the trigeminal nerve supplying the affected eye.

phlyctenular o. Vesicular formations on the epithelium of the conjunctiva or cornea.

purulent o. Purulent inflammation of the eye, usually due to gonococcus.

spring o. Conjunctivitis occurring in the spring, usually due to an allergic reaction to pollen. SYN: *vernal conjunctivitis*.

sympathetic o. Granulomatous inflammation of the uvea of both eyes after a penetration injury to one eye.

ophthalmic (ŏf-thăl'mĭk) Pert. to the eye.

o. nerve A branch of the trigeminal (fifth cranial) nerve. It is sensory and has lacrimal, frontal, and nasociliary branches.

ophthalmic laboratory technician A technician who makes eyewear by following ophthalmic prescriptions. The work involves coating, cutting, grinding, polishing, tinting, and ensuring the quality of corrective lenses as well as the preparation and adjustment of eyewear.

ophthalmitis (ŏf"thăl-mī'tĭs) [" + *itis*, inflammation] Inflammation of the eye.

ophthalmo-, ophthalm- [Gr. *ophthalmos*, eye] Prefixes meaning *eye*.

ophthalmodynamometer (ŏf-thăl"mō-dī"nă-mŏm'ĕ-tĕr) [" + *dynamis*, power, + *metron*, measure] An instrument for determining the pressure in the ophthalmic arteries. The device is placed against the conjunctiva of the eye. If the pressure is higher on one side than on the other, appropriate studies to attempt to define the cause are indicated.

ophthalmodynamometry (ŏf-thăl"mō-dī"nă-mŏm'ĕ-trē) Determination of pressure in the ophthalmic artery by use of an instrument that produces pressure on the eyeball until pulsations in the ophthalmic artery are seen

through the ophthalmoscope, indicating the diastolic pressure. As the pressure is increased, the vessel collapses and the systolic pressure is obtained.

ophthalmologist (ŏf-thăl-mŏl'ō-jĭst) [" + *logos*, word, reason] A physician who specializes in the treatment of disorders of the eye. SEE: *optician; optometrist*.

ophthalmology (ŏf-thăl-mŏl'ō-jē) [" + *logos*, word, reason] The health science dealing with the eye and its diseases.

ophthalmometer (ŏf-thăl-mŏm'ĕt-ĕr) [" + *metron*, measure] **1.** An instrument for measuring errors of eye refraction. **2.** An instrument for measuring the volume of various chambers of the eye. **3.** An instrument for measuring the anterior curvatures of the eye. **4.** An instrument for measuring the size of the eye.

ophthalmomyiasis (of-thal"mō-mī-ī'ă-sĭs) [*ophthalmo-* + *-myiasis*] Infestation of the eye by maggots (larvae) of the fly *Oestrus ovis*. SEE: *myiasis; Oestrus ovis*.

ophthalmopathy (ŏf"thăl-mŏp'ă-thē) Any disease of the eye.

ophthalmoplegia (of-thal"mō-plē'j(ē-)ă) [*ophthalmo-* + *-plegia*] Paralysis of ocular muscles. SEE: illus.

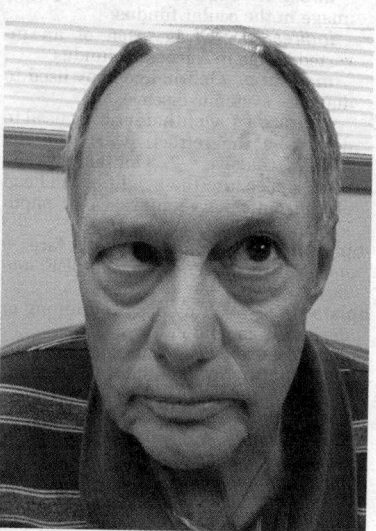

OPHTHALMOPLEGIA

o. externa Paralysis of extraocular muscles.

o. interna Paralysis of the iris and ciliary muscle.

internuclear o. ABBR: INO. Loss of the normal paired movements of the eyes when tracking an object to the left or right. An INO is marked by the failure of one eye, e.g., the left, to cross the midline during an attempt to see an object on the opposite side of the body, e.g., the right.

ETIOLOGY: This failure of adduction of the affected eye is caused by a lesion of the medial longitudinal fasciculus of the brain. SYN: *Roth-Bielschowsky syndrome*.

nuclear o. Paralysis due to a lesion of the nuclei of the ocular motor nerves.

Parinaud o. SEE: *Parinaud ophthalmoplegia syndrome.*

o. partialis Incomplete paralysis involving only one or two of the ocular muscles.

o. progressiva Ocular muscle paralysis in which all the muscles become involved slowly due to deterioration of the motor nerve nuclei.

o. totalis Paralysis that affects both internal and external ocular muscles.

ophthalmorrhea (ŏf-thăl″mō-rē′ă) [″ + *rhoia*, flow] Discharge from the eye.

ophthalmoscope (of″thal′mŏ-skōp″) [*ophthalmo-* + *-scope*] An instrument used for examining the interior of the eye, esp. the retina. **ophthalmoscopic** (″thal″mŏ-skop′ik), *adj.*

ophthalmoscopy (of″thal-mos′kŏ-pē) [*ophthalmo-* + *-scopy*] Examination of the interior of the eye with an ophthalmoscope. SYN: *funduscopy.*

direct o. Observation of an upright image in the ocular fundus.

indirect o. Observation of an inverted image in the ocular fundus.

medical o. Ophthalmoscopy used to diagnose systemic disease.

metric o. **1.** Ophthalmoscopy used to determine the refractive error of the lens of the eye. **2.** Ophthalmoscopy used to measure the height of the head of the optic nerve in cases of papilledema.

-opia, -opy [Gr. *-ōpia*, fr. *ōps*, eye, face + *-ia*] Suffixes meaning *vision*. SEE: *-opsia.*

opiate (ō′pē-ăt) Any drug containing or derived from opium.

opiate receptor SEE: under *receptor.*

opiate treatment agreement SEE: *drug contract.*

opiate withdrawal syndrome Physiological responses to abrupt cessation of the use of addictive substances. The symptoms include chills, runny nose, yawn-

ing, irritability, insomnia, and cramping. Physical signs of withdrawal include elevated blood pressure, diaphoresis, diarrhea, and muscle spasms. Discomfort peaks at 48 to 72 hr; however, symptoms persist for 7 to 10 days. Treatment includes methadone and psychological support and counseling.

OPIM Acronym for *o*ther *p*otentially *i*nfectious *m*aterials.

opioid (ō′pē-oyd) [L. *opium*, opium, + Gr. *eidos*, form, shape] **1.** Any synthetic narcotic not derived from opium. **2.** Indicating substances such as enkephalins or endorphins occurring naturally in the body that act on the brain to decrease the sensation of pain.

opisthion (ō-pĭs′thē-ŏn″) [NL. fr. Gr. *opisthen*, back, in the rear] The craniometric point at the middle of the lower border of the foramen magnum.

opistho-, opisth- [Gr. *opisthen*, behind, in the rear] Prefixes meaning *backward, behind.*

opisthorchiasis (ō″pĭs-thor-kī′ă-sĭs) Infestation of the liver by flukes of the genus *Opisthorchis.*

Opisthorchis (ō″pĭs-thor′kĭs) [″ + *orchis*, testicle] A genus of liver flukes endemic to Asia.

O. felineus SEE: *O. tenuicollis.*

O. sinensis A species common throughout Asia, acquired by humans who eat poorly cooked fish that contains the larval forms. *O. sinensis* is a relatively uncommon cause of biliary obstruction in Western nations.

O. tenuicollis A species found in cats and other mammals. Humans become infected by eating raw or poorly cooked fish containing the larval forms. It was formerly called *O. felineus.*

opisthotonos (ō″pĭs-thŏt′ŏ-nŏs) [″ + *tonos*, tension] A tetanic spasm in which head and heels are bent backward and the body is bowed forward. This type of spasm is seen in strychnine poisoning, tetanus, epilepsy, the convulsions of rabies, and in severe cases of meningitis. In the latter case, the patient's neck is rigid and the head retracted, seeming to press into the pillow. SEE: illus.; *emprosthotonos; pleurothotonos.* **opisthotonic,** *adj.*

opium (ō′pē-ŭm) [L.] **1.** The substance

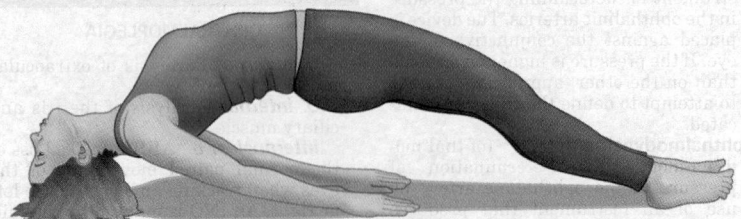

OPISTHOTONOS

obtained by air-drying the juice from the unripe capsule of the poppy, *Papaver somniferum*. It contains a number of important alkaloids, such as morphine, codeine, heroin, and papaverine. The growing and transportation of the poppy as well as the manufacture of drugs from the juice are controlled by national and international laws. **2.** A standardized preparation of the air-dried milky exudate from unripe capsules of the poppy, *Papaver somniferum* or *P. album*. It contains not less than 9.5% anhydrous morphine.

¹ opo- [Gr. *opos*, juice] Prefix meaning *juice*. It is used in trade names of some organic extracts.

² opo- [Gr. *ops*, stem *op-*, eye, face] Prefix meaning *face*.

Oppenheim, Hermann (ŏp′ĕn-hīm″) Ger. neurologist, 1858–1919.

    O.'s disease Myotonia congenita.

    O.'s gait A manner of walking in which there is a wide swinging motion of the head, body, and extremities. It is a variation of the gait seen in multiple sclerosis.

opponens (ō-pō′nĕns) [L.] Opposing, a term applied to muscles of hand or foot by which one of the lateral digits may be opposed to one of the other digits.

opportunistic infection SEE: under *infection*.

opposition The ability to move the thumb into contact with the other fingers across the palm of the hand.

-opsia, -opsy [-*opsis* + -*ia*] Suffixes meaning *vision*. SEE: -*opia*; -*opsy*.

opsin (ŏp′sĭn) The protein portion of the rhodopsin molecule in the retina of the eye.

opsinogen (ŏp-sĭn′ō-jĕn) An antigen that causes the production of opsonins.

-opsis [Gr. *opsis*, look, eyesight, vision, appearance, face] Suffix meaning *having a (specified) likeness* in the name of an organism or organic structure, e.g., *xanthopsis*.

opsoclonus (ŏp″sō-klō′nŭs) Conjugate irregular and nonrhythmical jerking movements of the eyes. The eyes move in any linear or rotating direction at a rate of up to 10 times per second. Any one of several areas of the brain, including the cerebellum and brainstem, may be diseased and cause this condition.

opsoclonus myoclonus syndrome A rare brain and eye disease characterized by abnormal muscle jerking, unsteady gait, poor speech, and abnormal eye movements. The disease is most often identified in children with recent viral infections or brain tumors. SYN: *dancing eyes-dancing feet syndrome; Kinsbourne syndrome*.

opsonin (ŏp-sō′nĭn) [Gr. *opsonein*, to purchase food] A substance that coats foreign antigens, making them more susceptible to macrophages and other leukocytes, thus increasing phagocytosis of the organism. Complement and antibodies are the two main opsonins in human blood. **opsonic** (-sŏn′ĭk), *adj.*

    immune o. Opsonin formed after stimulation by a specific antigen.

opsonization (ŏp″să-nĭ-zā′shŭn) The action of opsonins to facilitate phagocytosis.

opsonocytophagic (ŏp″sŏn-ō-sī″tō-fā′jĭk) [″ + *kytos*, cell, + *phagein*, to eat] Pert. to the phagocytic action of the blood when serum opsonins are present.

-opsy [-*opsia*] **1.** Suffix meaning (medical) *examination* or *inspection*, e.g., *autopsy, biopsy* **2.** Variant of -*opsia*. SEE: -*opsia*.;

opt To select one thing rather than another.

optic (ŏp′tĭk) [Gr. *optikos*] Pert. to the eye or to sight.

optical (ŏp′tĭ-kăl) [Gr. *optikos;* L. *opticus*] Pert. to vision, the eye, or optics.

    o. transmission The amount of light that passes through a laboratory specimen. It can be used to measure the concentration of components in the specimen (e.g., the amount of solute contained in a solution).

    o. tweezers A laser device used to alter or manipulate microorganisms, molecules, or living cells.

optician (ŏp-tĭsh′ăn) One who is a specialist in filling prescriptions for corrective lenses for eyeglasses and contact lenses.

optico- [Gr. *optikos*] Combining form denoting *eye, vision*.

opticokinetic (ŏp″tĭ-kō-kĭ-nĕt′ĭk) [Gr. *optikos*, of or for sight, + *kinesis*, movement] Concerning the movement of the eye.

optics (op′tĭks) [*opt(ic)* + -*ics*] The science dealing with light and its relationship to vision.

    fiber o., fiberoptics The transmission of light through flexible glass or plastic fibers by reflections from the side walls of the fibers. This permits transmission of visual images around sharp curves and corners. Devices that use fiberoptic materials are useful in endoscopic examinations.

optimal cutting temperature compound SEE: under *compound*.

optimism **1.** The philosophical doctrine that this world is the best possible one. **2.** The personal characteristic of regarding only the bright side of a condition or event and of expecting a favorable result. SEE: *pessimism*.

optimistic bias (ŏp″tĭ-mis′tĭk) The tendency of people beginning a course of treatment to assume that it will succeed even when the outcome is uncertain. Thus investigators tend to assume that their research will yield positive findings.

optimum (ŏp′tĭ-mŭm) *pl.* **optima** [L. *op-*

timus, best] Most conducive to a function.

optional surgery SEE: under *surgery.*

opto- [Gr. *optos,* seen, visible] Prefix meaning *optic, vision, eye.*

optogram (ŏp′tō-grăm) [Gr. *optos,* seen, + *gramma,* something written] The image of an external object that is fixed on the retina by the photochemical bleaching action of light on the visual purple.

optokinetic (ŏp″tō-kĭ-nĕt′ĭk) [″ + *kinesis,* movement] Concerning the appearance of a twitching movement of the eyes, as in nystagmus when the eyes gaze at moving objects.

optometer (ŏp-tŏm′ĕ-tĕr) [″ + *metron,* measure] An instrument used to measure the eye's refractive power.

optometrist (ŏp-tŏm′ĕ-trĭst) A doctor of optometry (OD); a primary health care provider who practices optometry (trained to prescribe eyeglasses and contact lenses, examine eyes, and detect diseases), as regulated and permitted by state laws. SEE: *optometry.*

optometry (op-tom′ĕ-trē) [*opto-* + *-metry*] The science of dealing with visual measurement and correction with eyeglasses, other visual aids, and prisms. **optometric** (op″tŏ-me′trik), *adj.* **optometrical** (-me′tri-kăl), *adj.*

optotype (ŏp′tō-tīp) The variable-sized type used in testing visual acuity.

PATIENT CARE: Figures, letters, numbers, or pictures may be used in optotype tests of visual acuity. Traditionally the symbols have been printed on a wall-mounted card and presented to the patient to identify, e.g., the Snellen test. The patient stands at a predetermined distance (usually 20 ft) from the symbols, covers one eye, and then reads or interprets the symbols for the examiner, and then repeats the process covering the other eye. In illiterate patients or young children directional symbols may be used, e.g., "tumbling E's" instead of numbers or randomly chosen letters of the alphabet. Optotype testing is subject to a number of flaws, e.g., patients may try to memorize listed letters or objects to improve their scores; alternately, some patients with learning disabilities may not understand how to respond to the test.

opt-out (ŏpt′owt′) [L. *optare,* to wish for] To choose not to participate in a program or not to receive information about a particular product or service. In health care, to decline to participate in a recommended program, e.g., in health screening, vaccination, or research.

OPUS *One-port umbilical* **surgery.**

OPV *oral poliovirus vaccine.*

OR *operating room.*

ora (ō′ră) [L.] Plural of os.

oral (ōr′ăl, or′) [L. *oralis*] Pert. to the mouth. **orally** (′ă-lē), *adv.*

oral allergy syndrome A form of contact dermatitis of the lips, tongue, or other tissues of the mouth, usually triggered by exposure to fresh fruits or vegetables. SYN: *pollen-food allergy syndrome.*

oral contraceptive SEE: *contraceptive.*

orale (ō-rā′lē) The point on the hard palate where lines drawn tangent to the lingual margins of the alveoli of the medial incisor teeth intersect the midsagittal plane.

oral fat load test ABBR: OFLT. Measurement of serum triglyceride levels (and other circulating fat molecules) after consumption of a specified amount of liquid fat or cream (e.g., 50 g).

oral glucose tolerance test ABBR: OGTT. A screening test for diabetes mellitus (DM), in which plasma glucose levels are measured after the patient consumes an oral glucose load. In screening patients for type 2 DM, measuring fasting plasma glucose levels or checking a hemoglobin A1c level is generally preferable to an OGTT because the former tests are simpler, cheaper, and better tolerated by patients. An OGTT reveals type 2 DM when plasma glucose levels exceed 200 mg/dL 2 hr after drinking a 75-g glucose load. Plasma glucose levels between 140 mg/dL and 199 mg/dL suggest impaired glucose tolerance.

GESTATIONAL DIABETES MELLITUS: In pregnancy, a modified OGTT is used to screen women with risk factors for gestational diabetes (GDM), including obesity, family history of type 2 DM, age greater than 25 years, and a history of unexplained stillbirths. At 24 to 28 weeks' gestation, a 50-g glucose load is given; 1-hr plasma glucose levels greater than 140 mg/dL constitute a positive screening result. Any patient having a positive test result should then undergo a 2-hr, 100-g OGTT to determine whether GDM is present. SEE: table.

International Criteria for Diabetes Mellitus in Pregnancy[*1,2]

Time:	Glucose level exceeds:
Fasting	92 mg/dL
60 min	180 mg/dL
120 min	155 mg/dL
180 min	140 mg/dL

Screen high-risk women at first visit, and screen all women at 24–28 weeks' gestation with 75g oral glucose tolerance test.
American Diabetes Association revised Standards of Medical Care, published in *Diabetes Care* special supplement, January 2011.
International Association of Diabetes and Pregnancy Study Groups published in Leary, J. et al. (2010). *Best Practice Research Clinical Endocrinology and Metabolism* 24 (4), 673.

oral hypoglycemic agent SEE: under *agent.*

oralism (or″ăl-ĭzm) The instruction of hearing-impaired students with speech or speech reading rather than with signed or finger-spelled words.

orality (ō-răl′ĭ-tē) The oral stage of psychosexual development, which involves sucking or chewing on objects other than food.

orally disintegrating In pharmacology, rapidly absorbed after contact with tiny amounts of saliva in the mouth.

oral mucous membrane, impaired Disruptions of the lips and soft tissue of the oral cavity. SEE: *Nursing Diagnoses Appendix.*

oral nutritional supplement ABBR: ONS. Supplement (1).

oral rehydration solution SEE: under *solution.*

oral rehydration therapy ABBR: ORT. The administration by mouth of a solution of electrolytes in sufficient quantity to correct the deficits produced by dehydration due to diarrhea. The earlier this therapy is begun, the more effective it is (i.e., the fluid should be given before the patient is dehydrated). Because this therapy is simple and economical and can be supervised by nonprofessionals, it has been extremely effective in treating diarrhea in countries lacking health care resources.

In many parts of the world, commercially prepared ORT solutions are not available or are too expensive. In these areas, very inexpensive and effective solutions can be prepared from sources such as cooled water from a pot in which rice is boiled or two pinches of salt and one ounce of molasses added to a quart of boiled water. SEE: *oral rehydration solution; viral gastroenteritis.*

orange book The "Approved Drug Products with Therapeutic Equivalence Evaluations" published by the U.S. Food and Drug Administration in both bound and electronic formats.

orb [L. *orbis,* circle, disk] A spherical body, esp. the eyeball.

orbicular (or-bĭk′ū-lăr) [L. *orbiculus,* a small circle] Circular.

orbicularis (or-bik″yŭ-lar′ĭs, or-bik″yŭ-lar′ēz″) *pl.* **orbiculares** A muscle surrounding an orifice; a sphincter muscle.

orbiculus (or-bĭk′ū-lŭs) *pl.* **orbiculi** [L., little circle] Muscle surrounding an orifice; a sphincter muscle.

   o. ciliaris The portion of the ciliary body consisting of a bandlike zone lying directly anterior to the ora serrata. SYN: *ciliary ring.*

   o. oris The circular muscle surrounding the mouth. It is a muscle of facial expression, innervated by the facial nerve.

orbit (or′bĭt) [L. *orbita,* track] The bony pyramid-shaped cavity of the skull that contains and protects the eyeball. It is pierced posteriorly by the optic foramen (which transmits the optic nerve and ophthalmic artery), the superior and inferior orbital fissures, and several foramina. It is formed by the frontal, zygomatic, ethmoid, maxillary, lacrimal, sphenoid, and palatine bones. **orbital** (-bĭ-tăl), *adj.*

orbitale (ŏr″bĭ-tă′lē) An anthropometric landmark, being the lowest point along the inferior margin of the orbit. It is one of two landmarks (the other is the porion) used to establish the Frankfort horizontal plane, most frequently in positioning the head for radiographs or measurements.

orbitonasal (or″bĭ-tō-nā′zăl) Concerning the orbit and nasal cavity of the skull.

orbitopathy (ŏr-bĭ-tŏp′ăthē) Disease of the orbit.

   dysthyroid o. Ocular dysfunction present in Graves' disease, including protrusion of the eyeball, exposure of the cornea, lid retraction, and occasionally, optic neuropathy. SEE: *Graves' disease.*

orbitotomy (or-bĭ-tŏt′ō-mē) [″ + Gr. *tome,* incision] Surgical incision into the orbit.

orcein (awr′sē-ĭn) An orcinol stain specific for elastic connective tissue.

orchialgia (or-kē-ăl′jē-ă) [″ + *algos,* pain] Pain in the testes. SYN: *orchiodynia; testalgia.*

orchichorea (or″kĭ-kō-rē′ă) [″ + *chorea,* a dance] Involuntary jerking movements of the testicles.

orchidectomy (or″kĭ-dek′tŏ-mē) [*orchido-* + *-ectomy*] Orchiectomy.

orchiditis (or″kĭ-dī′tĭs) [″ + *itis,* inflammation] Orchitis.

orchido-, orchid-, orchio-, orchi- [Gr. *orchidion,* fr. *orchis,* testicle] Prefixes meaning *testicle.*

orchidopexy (or′kĭd-ō-pĕk″sē) [″ + *pexis,* fixation] Orchiopexy.

orchidoptosis (or″kĭd-ŏp-tō′sĭs) [″ + *ptosis,* a dropping] Downward displacement of the testes.

orchidorrhaphy (or″kĭ-dor′ă-fē) [″ + *rhaphe,* seam, ridge] Orchiopexy.

orchiectomy, orchectomy (or″kē-ek′tŏ-mē) [*orchio-* + *-ectomy*] Surgical excision of a testicle or the testicles. SYN: *androgen deprivation; male castration; orchidectomy.* SEE: illus.

PATIENT CARE: The plan of care and expected outcome of the surgery are explained, and information is provided about scrotal prostheses. Patient teaching is modified according to the extent of surgery. Deep-breathing and coughing exercises are taught, and the importance of early ambulation and activity after surgery is emphasized. Pain control measures are discussed, and the patient is advised to seek pain relief in the postoperative period before pain be-

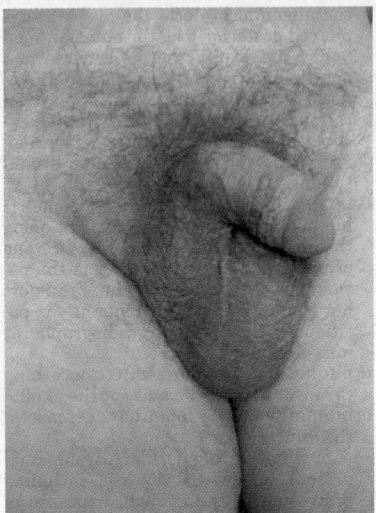

ORCHIECTOMY
the right testicle has been surgically removed

comes severe. If only one testicle is removed and the other one is healthy, impotence does not occur. If both testicles are removed, the patient may require hormone replacement therapy. Support and reassurance are offered to the patient and family. Patients having this surgery for testicular cancer are offered the opportunity to bank sperm prior to the surgery.

orchiepididymitis (or″kē-ĕp″ĭ-dĭd″ĭ-mī′tĭs) [″ + *epi*, upon, + *didymos*, testis, + *itis*, inflammation] Inflammation of a testicle and epididymis.

orchio-, orchi- SEE: *orchido-*.

orchiopathy (or″kē-ŏp′ăth-ē) [″ + *pathos*, disease, suffering] Any disease of the testes.

orchiopexy (or″kē-ō-pĕk′sē) [″ + *pexis*, fixation] The suturing of an undescended testicle to fix it in the scrotum. SYN: *orchidopexy; orchiorrhaphy*.

orchioplasty (or′kē-ō-plăs″tē) [″ + *plassein*, to form] Plastic repair of the testicle.

orchiotomy (or″kē-ŏt′ō-mē) [″ + *tome*, incision] Surgical incision of a testicle.

orchis (or′kĭs) [Gr.] Testis.

orchitis (or-kī′tĭs) [Gr. *orchis*, testicle, + *itis*, inflammation] Inflammation of a testis due to trauma, ischemia, metastasis, mumps, or infection elsewhere in the body. SYN: *testitis*.

SYMPTOMS: The symptoms of orchitis include swelling, pain, chills, fever, vomiting, hiccough, and in some patients, delirium. Atrophy of the organ may be an end result.

INCIDENCE AND PREVALENCE: With the widespread use of the mumps vac-

cine in childhood, infectious orchitis is uncommon, as are the atrophy and infertility resulting from it.

TREATMENT: The patient is confined to bed with the organ elevated and supported. An ice bag is applied. Nonsteroidal anti-inflammatory drugs are given.

gonorrheal o. Orchitis due to gonococcus.

metastatic o. Orchitis due to a bloodborne infection that spreads to the testicle.

syphilitic o. Orchitis due to syphilis. This type of orchitis usually begins painlessly in the body of the gland and is apt to be bilateral. It causes dense, irregular, knotty induration but little enlargement in size.

tuberculous o. A rare form of orchitis generally arising in the epididymis. It may be accompanied by formation of chronic sinuses and destruction of tissues. With the widespread use of antituberculosis drugs for primary pulmonary tuberculosis, this condition is rarely seen. **orchitic** (-kĭt′ĭk), *adj.*

orcin, orcinol (or′sĭn, -ol″) A chemical derived from lichens and used as a histological stain.

order (or′dĕr) [L. *ordo*, a row, series] **1.** Instructions from a health care provider specifying patient treatment and care.A directive mandating the delivery of specific patient care services. **2.** An arrangement or sequence of events; rules; regulations; procedures. **3.** In biological classification, the main division under class, superior to family.

no-CPR o. A formal, often written request by a patient with a terminal illness requesting emergency assistance with palliative care at the end of life but without cardiopulmonary resuscitation. Such orders include emergency and hospital care for dyspnea, pain, secretions, or psychological discomfort.

stop o. A standing medical order in a patient's chart requiring discontinuation of a specific drug or treatment after a specified time. The order may be reinstated by an authorized health care provider at a later date.

orderly (or′dĕr-lē) An attendant in a hospital who does general work to assist nurses. Orderlies are responsible for lifting and transporting patients and preparing them for surgery (e.g., shaving, catheterizing, or administering enemas).

ordinate (or′dĭ-năt) The vertical line parallel to the y-axis in a graph in which horizontal and perpendicular lines are crossed in order to provide a frame of reference. The abscissa is the horizontal line parallel to the x-axis. SEE: *abscissa* for illus.

ordure (or′dūr) Feces or other excrement.

Orem, Dorothea (or'ĕm) [Nursing educator, 1914–2007] Nursing educator, who developed the Self-Care Framework, also known as the Self-Care Deficit Theory of Nursing and the Self-Care Deficit Nursing Theory. SEE: *Nursing Theory Appendix.*

orexins (ŏ-rĕk-sĭnz) Neuropeptides produced by the hypothalamus that influence sleep and wakefulness. SYN: *hypocretins; hypocretin.*

orf (orf) A contagious pustular dermatitis caused by the orf virus, a DNA virus of the Parapoxvirus genus, which is related to the vaccinia-variola subgroup of poxviruses. Orf mainly affects lambs and occurs in the spring. The disease rarely occurs in humans. When it does, it is usually confined to a single pustular lesion on a finger, which encrusts and finally heals. Antibiotics are not indicated except for secondary bacterial infections.

organ (or'găn) [L. *organum* fr Gr. *organon*, tool, (musical) instrument, (bodily) organ] A body structure made of several tissues that all contribute to specific functions. Many organs occur in pairs. In such pairs, one organ may be extirpated and the remaining one can perform all necessary functions peculiar to it. One third to two fifths of some organs may be removed without loss of function necessary to support life. SEE: table.

accessory o. An organ that has a subordinate function.

acoustic o. SEE: under *Corti, Alfonso Giacomo Gaspare.*

o. of Corti SEE: under *Corti, Alfonso Giacomo Gaspare.*

enamel o. A cup-shaped structure that forms on the tooth buds of an embryo. It produces the enamel and serves as a mold for the remainder of the tooth.

end o. The expanded end of a nerve fiber in a peripheral structure.

excretory o. An organ that is concerned with the excretion of waste products from the body. SEE: *excretion.*

Golgi tendon o. SEE: under *Golgi, Camillo.*

gustatory o. The organ of taste; a taste bud.

o. of Jacobson SEE: under *Jacobson, Ludwig.*

lymphatic o. A structure composed principally of lymphatic tissue. It includes the lymph nodes, spleen, tonsils, and thymus.

lymphoid o.'s The spleen, lymph nodes, thymus, Peyer patches, and tonsils, where more than 98% of T lymphocytes are found. SEE: *T cell.*

neuromuscular end o. A spindle-shaped bundle of specialized fibers in which sensory nerve fibers terminate in muscles.

neurotendinous end o. A specialized tendon fasciculus in which sensory nerve fibers terminate in the tendon. SYN: *tendon spindle.*

reproductive o. Any organ concerned with the production of offspring. These include the primary organs (testes and ovaries) and accessory structures (penis and spermatic cord in the male and fallopian tubes, uterus, and vagina in the female). SYN: *sex o.*

sense o. A sensory receptor; a structure consisting of specialized sensory nerve endings that are capable of reacting to a stimulus (an external or internal change) by generating nerve impulses that pass through afferent nerves to the central nervous system. These impulses may give rise to sensations or reflexly bring about responses in the body.

sensory end o. Any of the special clusters of cells that form a capsule around the receptor ends of certain sensory axons and affect the response of the axons. They include Meissner corpuscles, Pacinian corpuscles, Ruffini corpuscles, and Golgi tendon organs. SEE: *sensory receptor.*

sex o. Reproductive **o.**

solid o. An internal organ that has a firm tissue consistency and is neither hollow (such as the organs of the gastrointestinal tract) nor liquid (such as blood). Such organs include the heart, kidney, liver, lungs, and pancreas.

special sense o. Any of the organs of smell, taste, sight, balance, and hearing.

spiral o. SEE: under *Corti, Alfonso Giacomo Gaspare.*

target o. **1.** An organ upon which a chemical or hormone acts. **2.** An organ adversely affected by a disease or condition.

vestigial o. An organ that is underdeveloped in humans but is fully functional in some animals.

o.'s of Zuckerkandl SEE: under *Zuckerkandl, Emil.*

organ-confined disease An illness, such as a tumor or an abscess, that has not spread beyond the organ in which it originated. One example is prostate cancer that is confined within the prostate gland and has not entered the seminal vesicles or pelvic lymph nodes.

organ donation The removal of a body part from one person for transplantation into another, typically to restore functional capacity.

PATIENT CARE: Organ donation may occur during life, as when a matched individual chooses to give bone marrow or a kidney to another; or it may occur at death, by those who have agreed to donate their organs if they suffer fatal accidents. Health care professionals working with trauma patients have a significant effect on increasing the num-

Size, Weight, and Capacity of Various Organs and Parts of the Adult Body
♂ Male ♀ Female

Description	Size	Weight	Capacity
Adrenal gland	5 cm high 3 cm across 1 cm thick	5 g	
Bladder	12 cm in diameter		500 mL (when moderately full)
Blood volume			♂ 4–6 L ♀ 3–5 L
Brain		♂ 1240–1680 g ♀ 1130–1570 g	
Ear, external canal	2.5 cm long (from concha)		
Esophagus	23–25 cm		
Eye	23.5 mm vertical diameter 24 mm anteroposterior diameter		
Fallopian tube	10 cm		
Gallbladder	7–10 cm long 3 cm wide		30–50 mL
Heart	12 × 8–9 × 6 cm	♂ 280–340 g ♀ 230–280 g	
Intestines—small	Variable 6–7 m long		
Intestines—large	1.5 m long		
Intestines—vermiform appendix	2–20 cm long, average 9 cm		
Intestines—rectum	12 cm long		
Kidney	11 cm long 6 cm broad 3 cm thick	♂ 150 g ♀ 135 g	
Larynx	♂ 44 × 43 × 36 mm ♀ 36 × 41 × 26 mm		
Liver		♂ 1.4–1.8 kg ♀ 1.0–2.5 kg	6500 mL
Lung		Right 625 g Left 565 g	
Ovaries	3 × 1.5 × 1 cm	2–3.5 g	
Pancreas	15 cm long	♂ 74–106 g ♀ 70–100 g	
Parathyroid	6 × 3–4 × 1–2 mm	50 mg	
Pharynx	12.5 cm long		
Prostate	2 × 4 × 3 cm	8 g	
Skeleton		Average adult male, 4957 g	
Skull		Average (without teeth), 642 g	Variable ♂ 406 mL ♀ 207 mL
Spinal cord	42–45 cm long	30 g	
Spleen	12 × 7 × 3–4 cm	150 g 80–300 g Decreases with age	
Stomach	Variable 25 cm long 10 cm wide		Variable 1500 mL
Testes	4–5 × 2.5 × 3 cm	10.5–14 g	
Thoracic duct	38–45 cm long		
Thymus		Newborn, 10.9 g 10–15 yr, 29.5 g 20–25 yr, 18.6 g	

Size, Weight, and Capacity of Various Organs and Parts of the Adult Body
♂ Male ♀ Female (Continued)

Description	Size	Weight	Capacity
Thyroid	Each lobe 5 × 3 × 2 cm	30 g total	
Trachea	11 cm long 2–2.5 cm in diameter		
Ureter	28–34 cm long		
Urethra	♂ 17.5–20 cm long ♀ 4 cm long		
Uterus	7.5 × 5.0 × 2.5 cm	30–40 g (nonpregnant)	
Vagina	Anterior wall length 7.5 cm Posterior wall length 9.0 cm		

SOURCE: Adapted from Gray's Anatomy, ed 27. Lea & Febiger, Philadelphia, 1959; Gray's Anatomy, ed 37. Churchill Livingstone, London, 1987; Growth. Federation of American Societies for Experimental Biology, Washington, DC, 1962; Jandl, JH, Blood. Little, Brown and Co., Boston, 1987.

ber of organ donations through prompt identification of possible donors and the provision of hemodynamic management to preserve organ function and health. SEE: *donor card; transplantation.*

organelle (or′gă-nĕl″) A specialized structure within a cell that performs a distinct function. Examples of organelles are the endoplasmic reticulum, the Golgi apparatus, lysosomes, mitochondria, proteasomes, and ribosomes.

organic (or-găn′ĭk) [Gr. *organikos*] **1.** Pert. to an organ or organs. **2.** Structural. **3.** Pert. to or derived from animal or vegetable forms of life. **4.** Denoting chemicals containing carbon.

organic brain syndrome ABBR: OBS. Any of a large group of acute and chronic mental disorders associated with brain damage or impaired cerebral function.

SYMPTOMS: The clinical characteristics vary not only with the nature and severity of the underlying organic disorder but also occasionally among individuals. Consciousness, orientation, memory, intellect, judgment and insight, and thought content may be impaired (e.g., hallucinations, illusions).

ETIOLOGY: Any acute or chronic disease or injury that interferes with cerebral function may trigger symptoms. Possible causes include infection, intoxication, trauma, circulatory disturbance, epilepsy, metabolic and endocrine diseases, or intracranial trauma or neoplasms.

DIAGNOSIS: Difficulty in diagnosis may be encountered because of the possibility of attributing all of the signs and symptoms to a psychiatric disorder, thereby ignoring the possibility of organic disease. However, it must be noted that purely functional psychiatric diseases are much more common than OBS.

TREATMENT: Treatment of the basic organic disease and provision of psychiatric care are indicated.

organic disease A disease resulting from recognizable anatomical changes in an organ or tissue of the body.

organic dust toxic syndrome, organic dust toxicity syndrome ABBR: ODTS. An acute nonallergenic, noninfectious, influenza-like respiratory disorder caused by inhalation of organic dusts, such as molds that contaminate grasses, hay, and other agricultural products. The most important sources are cotton dust, which causes byssinosis; grain dust; and exposure to moldy hay. It is also known scientifically as pulmonary mycotoxicosis and colloquially as farmer's lung or grain lung. Prominent symptoms are cough, chest tightness, muscle ache, and low-grade fever. SEE: *byssinosis; pneumonitis, hypersensitivity.*

organism (or′găn-ĭzm) [Gr. *organon,* organ, + *-ismos,* condition] Any living thing, plant or animal. An organism may be unicellular (bacteria, yeasts, protozoa) or multicellular (all complex organisms including humans).

organization (or″găn-ĭ-zā′shŭn) **1.** The process of becoming organized. **2.** Systematic arrangement. **3.** That which is organized.

organize (or′găn-īz) To develop from an amorphous state to that having structure and form.

organized thrombus SEE: under *thrombus.*

organo- [Gr. *organon,* tool, bodily organ] Prefix meaning *organ.*

organogel (or-găn′ō-jĕl) A water-in-oil emulsion used, e.g., as a drug delivery vehicle.

organogenesis (or″găn-ō-jĕn′ĕ-sĭs) [″ + *genesis,* generation, birth] The formation and development of body organs from embryonic tissues.

It is important that an embryo-fetus not be exposed to harmful chemicals, particularly during organogenesis. The embryo-fetus is most vulnerable to the damaging effects of infections or teratogenic drugs between the second and eighth weeks of gestation (and during the first trimester in general).

organoleptic (or″gă-nō-lep′tik) **1.** Pert. to or affecting a sense organ or its functions, e.g., the ear (hearing), the eye (vision), the nose (smell), the skin (touch), or the tongue (taste). **2.** Susceptible to sensory impressions.

organomegaly (or″gă-nō-mĕg′ă-lē) [″ + *megas,* large] The enlargement of visceral organs.

organometallic (or-gă-nō-mĕ-tăl′ĭk) A compound containing a metal combined with an organic molecule.

organophosphate (or-gan″ō-fos′fāt″) [*organo-* + *phosphate*] ABBR: OP. Any of the neurotoxic pesticides that are esters of phosphoric acid.

⚠ These agents have been employed in chemical warfare. Examples of organophosphates include the insecticides malathion and diazinon and the nerve gases sarin, tabun, and VX.

organotherapy (or″găn-ō-thĕr′ă-pē) [″ + *therapeia,* treatment] Hormonotherapy.

organotropism (ŏr″gă-nō-trōp′ĭzm) [″ + *trope,* a turn, + *-ismos,* condition] The attraction or affinity of chemicals or biological agents for body organs or tissues.

organ perfusion system A mechanical device equipped to supply metabolic, oxygen, and electrolyte needs to an organ obtained from a cadaver or donor in order to keep it viable for transplantation. The organ and the perfusion solution pumped through it can be kept at the ideal temperature for organ survival. They can be transported as necessary.

organ procurement organization ABBR: OPO. An institution that facilitates organ transplantation by obtaining cadaveric tissues and organs for use in living patients with end-stage diseases of the heart, kidneys, liver, and lungs.

organ recovery The surgical removal of a body part from one person to be used in organ transplantation in another patient.

organ-specific (or′găn-spĕ-sĭf′ĭk) Originating in a single organ or affecting only one specific organ.

organ system A group of tissues or organs, often with a common embryological origin, that participate in the same major systemic activity, e.g., circulation or digestion. SEE: table.

Particular organ systems are listed under the first word. SEE: *e.g., digestive system; nervous system; reproductive system.*

orgasm (or′găzm) [Gr. *orgasmos,* swelling] A state of physical and emotional excitement that occurs at the climax of sexual intercourse. In the male it is accompanied by the ejaculation of semen. SYN: *climax.*

orientation (ōr″ē-ĕn-tā′shŏn) [L. *oriens,* to arise] **1.** The ability to comprehend and to adjust oneself with regard to time, location, and identity of persons. This ability is partially or completely lost in some neurological and psychiatric disorders. **2.** The formal introduction of a new employee to the facilities, practices, regulations, resources, and staff with which he will work.

Orientia tsutsugamushi (ŏr″ē-ĕn′tē-ă, shē-, shē-ă soo-tsoo-gă-moo′shē, tsoo-) An intracellular parasite, formerly known as *Rickettsia tsutsugamushi,* that is the causative agent of scrub typhus. It is transmitted to humans by the bites of infected trombiculid mites, which prey in the wild on rodents.

orifice (or′ĭ-fĭs) [L. *orificium,* outlet] The mouth, entrance, or outlet of any anatomical structure. **orificial** (-fĭ′shăl), *adj.*

    anal o. The anus.

    atrioventricular o. The opening between the atrium and the ventricle on each side of the heart.

    cardiac o. The opening of the esophagus into the stomach.

    external urethral o. The exterior opening of the urethra. In the male, it is located at the tip of the glans penis; in the female, it is located anterior and cephalad to the vaginal opening.

    ileal o. Ileocecal valve.

    internal urethral o. The opening from which the urethra makes its exit from the bladder.

    mitral o. The opening between the left atrium and the left ventricle.

    pyloric o. Pylorus.

    ureteric o. The opening of the ureter into the bladder.

origin (or′ĭ-jĭn) [L. *origo,* beginning] **1.** The source of anything; a starting point. **2.** The beginning of a nerve. **3.** The more fixed attachment of a muscle.

original Medicare SEE: under *Medicare.*

Orlando, Ida Jean (or-lăn′dō) [1926 –

Organ Systems

System	Chief Components	Major Activities
Circulatory or Cardiovascular	Heart, arteries, veins, blood capillaries, lymphatic vessels	Moves blood, oxygen, and nutrients to tissues. Transports hormones, leukocytes, and lymphocytes. Removes wastes and carbon dioxide from tissues.
Digestive or Alimentary	Oral cavity (incl., mouth, teeth, tongue, oropharynx), esophagus, stomach, duodenum, jejunum, colon, liver, pancreas	Transforms consumed materials into absorbable molecules; absorbs water and small molecules.
Endocrine	Pituitary (adenohypophysis and neurohypophysis), pineal gland, thyroid gland, parathyroid glands, suprarenal (adrenal) glands, pancreatic islets, neuroendocrine system, ovaries, testes	Regulates metabolic processes, blood pressure, body temperature, reproductive cell cycles, and levels of blood molecules (e.g., glucose, sodium, water).
Hemolymphoid	Erythrocytes, leukocytes, lymphocytes, platelets, hemal generating tissues, lymphoid generating tissues (e.g., thymus, lymph nodes, spleen, lymphoid nodules)	Carries oxygen, facilitates clotting, attaches to threatening antigenic substances, and generates immune reactions.
Integumental	Skin, hair, nails, subcutaneous tissues	Isolates internal tissues from the environment to help maintain body temperature, hydration, and composition; provides a barrier against infection and injury.
Muscular	Skeletal, smooth, and cardiac muscles	Changes the relative position of tissues in the body. Provides stability and support. Generates heat. Helps to maintain internal metabolic homeostasis (e.g., normal blood glucose levels).
Nervous	Brain, spinal cord, peripheral nerves, peripheral ganglia, sensory receptors (e.g., retina, cochlea), glia, Schwann cells	Receives sensory input and generates motor output. Coordinates the metabolic state and the activity types and levels throughout the body.
Reproductive	Female: ovaries, fallopian tubes, uterus, vagina, clitoris, breasts. Male: testes, ductus deferens, spermatic cord, prostate, penis	Stimulates maturation and gender specificity of tissues. Allows formation and maturation of an embryo.
Respiratory	Nose, paranasal sinuses, larynx, trachea, bronchi, lungs	Oxygenates blood and removes carbon dioxide. Generates sounds for communication.
Skeletal	Bones, cartilage, joints	Supports, stabilizes and protects the body. Gives the body its 3D shape.
Urinary	Kidney, ureters, bladder, urethra	Maintains the body's normal concentrations of salts, waters, and small molecules. Adjusts blood volume of body.

2007] Nursing educator who developed the Theory of the Deliberative Nursing Process, also known as the Theory of the Nursing Process Discipline. SEE: *Nursing Theory Appendix.*

Ormond disease (or'mond") [John K.

Ormond, U.S. physician, b. 1886] Retroperitoneal fibrosis.

ornithine (or″nĭ-thēn″) An amino acid formed when arginase hydrolyzes arginine. It is not present in proteins.

Ornithodoros (or″nĭ-thŏd′ō-rōs) A genus of ticks (family Argasidae) that infests mammals, including humans. Several species are vectors of the causative agents of disease, including spotted fever, tick fever, Q fever, tularemia, Russian encephalitis, and relapsing fever.

Ornithonyssus (or″nĭ-thon-ĭ′sŭs) [Gr. *ornis, ornithos,* bird + Gr. *nyssein,* to prick] A genus of parasitic mites of the family Macronyssidae.

    O. sylviarum The northern fowl mite. Its bite may cause an itchy rash, esp. prevalent in owners of infected farm animals or pets.

    O. bacoti The tropical rat mite. Its bite may cause itchy papules on the skin.

ornithosis (or″nĭ-thō′sĭs) [Gr. *ornithos,* bird, + *osis,* condition] Any acute, generalized, infectious disease of birds and domesticated fowls sometimes communicated to humans. SEE: *Chlamydophila psittaci.*

oro- [L. *os,* stem *ori-,* mouth] Prefix meaning *mouth.*

orofacial (or″ō-fā′shē-ăl) [L. *oris,* mouth, + *facies,* face] Concerning the mouth and face.

oromandibular sleep movement disorder (ŏr″ō-măn-dĭb′ū-lĭr) [″ + ″] Bruxism.

oropharyngeal airway (or″ō-fă-rin′j(ē-)ăl) SEE: under *airway.*

oropharynx (or″ō-făr′ĭnks) [″ + Gr. *pharynx,* throat] The central portion of the pharynx lying between the soft palate and the upper portion of the epiglottis.

orosomucoid (or″ō-sō-mū′koyd) An alpha 1-globulin in blood plasma.

orotic aciduria (or-ot′ik) SEE: under *aciduria.*

orotracheal (or″ō-trā′kē-ăl) Pert. to the passageway between the mouth and the trachea.

Oroya fever (ō-rŏy′ă) [*Oroya,* a region of Peru] SEE: under *fever.*

orphan (or′făn) [L. *orphanus,* fr Gr. *orphanos,* destitute, without parents] A minor whose parents have died or are unknown.

orris root (or′ĭs) [Variant of *iris*] SEE: under *root.*

ORS *oral rehydration solution.*

ORT *oral rehydration therapy.*

ortho-, orth- [Gr. *orthos,* straight] Prefixes meaning *straight, correct, normal, in proper order;* in chemical formulas, the first position clockwise to the primary on aromatic ring structures. SEE: *o-.*

orthoacid (or″thō-ăs′ĭd) An acid with as many hydroxyl groups as the number of

valences of the acid-forming portion of the molecule.

orthochromatic (or″thō-krō-măt′ĭk) [″ + *chroma,* color] Having normal color or staining normally.

orthochromophil (or″thō-krō′mō-fĭl) [″ + ″ + *philein,* to love] Staining normally with neutral dyes.

orthodeoxia (or″thō-dē-ŏk′sēă) Decreased arterial oxygen concentration while in an upright position. The condition improves when the patient assumes the supine position. SEE: *syndrome, hepatopulmonary.*

orthodiagraph (or″thō-dī′ă-grăf) [″ + *dia,* through, + *graphein,* to write] An instrument invented in 1912; formerly used to record the outlines and positions of internal organs or foreign bodies seen radiographically. The device is obsolete.

orthodontia, orthodontics (or″thō-dŏn′shē-ă, -dŏn′tĭks) [″ + *odous,* tooth] The area of dentistry concerned with the correction of abnormal dentofacial structures. It includes treatment of malocclusion of the teeth and the surrounding muscles and nerves. The design, application, and control of functional and corrective oral appliances are aspects of orthodontic practice.

orthodontist (or″thō-dŏn′tĭst) A dental specialist with postgraduate training in the diagnosis and treatment of dentoskeletal abnormalities.

orthodox Conventional; conforming with generally accepted standards of practice.

orthodromic (or″thō-drŏm′ĭk) [Gr. *orthodromein,* to run straight forward] Moving in the normal direction; said of nerve and cardiac impulses. SEE: *antidromic.*

orthogenic (or″thō-jĕn′ĭk) Pert. to, or related to, the correction, treatment, or rehabilitation of children with mental or emotional difficulties.

orthogenics (or″thō-jĕn′ĭks) Eugenics.

orthograde (or′thō-grād) [″ + L. *gradi,* to walk] Walking with the body vertical or upright; pert. to bipeds, esp. humans. Opposite of pronograde.

orthokeratology (or″thō-ker″ă-tol′ŏ-jē) [*ortho-* + *kerato-* + *-logy*] ABBR: Ortho-K. The use of special hard contact lenses to treat myopia by altering the curvature of the cornea. The lens presses on the center of the cornea, decreasing the protrusion.

orthokinetics (or″thō-kĭ-nĕt′ĭks) A variety of tactile stimulation techniques and orthoses used to stimulate proprioceptors and enhance motor performance in rehabilitation.

orthomolecular (or″thō-mō-lĕk′ū-lăr) Indicating the normal chemical constituents of the body or the restoration of those constituents to normal.

orthomyxovirus (or″thō-mĭk″sō-vī′rŭs)

A virus in the family of influenza viruses.

orthopantogram (or'thō-pan"tŏ-gram") [*ortho-* + *panto-* + *-gram*] ABBR: OPG. A panoramic x-ray of all the teeth and the surrounding bones of the face and jaw. It is obtained by rotating the imaging source around the front of the mouth and is used for orthodontic assessments, evaluations of the wisdom teeth, and periodontal imaging.

orthopedic, orthopaedic (or"thō-pē'dĭk) Concerning the prevention or correction of bone, joint, ligament, and muscular disorders.

orthopedics, orthopaedics (or"thō-pē'dĭks) [" + *pais,* child] The branch of medical science that deals with prevention or correction of disorders involving locomotor structures of the body, esp. the skeleton, joints, muscles, fascia, and other supporting structures such as ligaments and cartilage.

orthopedic technician A health care professional who is skilled in maintaining traction devices, applying traction, making casts, and applying splints.

orthopedist, orthopaedist (or"thō-pē'dĭst) A specialist in orthopedics.

orthophoria (or"thō-fō'rē-ă) [" + *pherein,* to bear] Coordination (alignment) of the visual axes.

orthophthalaldehyde (or-thof"thăl-al'dĭ-hīd") [*ortho-* + *(na)phthal(ene)* + *aldehyde*] ABBR: OPA. A microbicidal chemical used to disinfect surfaces, endoscopes, and other heat-sensitive instruments.

⚠️ Personnel who use OPA must wear gloves, goggles, and gowns to prevent contact with mucous membranes or skin.

orthopnea (or"thŏp'nē-ă) [" + *pnoia,* breath] Labored breathing that occurs when lying flat and improves when standing or sitting up. This is one of the classic symptoms of left ventricular heart failure, although it occasionally occurs in other cardiac or respiratory illnesses.

Orthopoxvirus (or"thō-pŏks'vī-rŭs) A genus of virus that includes the virus causing smallpox (variola) and monkeypox.

orthopsychiatry (or"thō-sī-kī'ă-trē) [" + *psyche,* soul, + *iatreia,* treatment] The branch of psychiatry concerned with mental and emotional development. It encompasses child psychiatry and mental hygiene.

orthoptic (or-thŏp'tĭk) [" + *optikos,* pert. to vision] Pert. to or producing normal binocular vision.

orthoptics 1. The science of correcting defects in binocular vision resulting from defects in optic musculature. 2. The technique of eye exercises for correcting faulty eye coordination affecting binocular vision. The technique is also referred to as orthoptic training.

orthoptist A health care professional who specializes in the evaluation and treatment of eye movement and eye muscle disorders, that is, disorders that typically impact binocular vision, e.g., strabismus.

orthoroentgenography (or"thō-rĕnt-gĕn-ŏg'ră-fē) A technique for obtaining accurate measurement of the size and position of the internal organs using radiographic apparatus. A radiographic procedure used for the accurate measurement of long bones. SEE: *orthodiagraph.*

orthosis (or-thō'sĭs) [Gr. *orthōsis,* guidance, straightening] Any device added to the body to stabilize or immobilize a body part, prevent deformity, protect against injury, or assist with function. Orthotic devices range from arm slings to corsets and finger splints. They may be made from a variety of materials, including rubber, leather, canvas, rubber synthetics, and plastic. **orthotic** (-thot'ik), *adj.*

ankle-foot o. ABBR: AFO. Any of a class of external orthopedic appliances, braces, or splints devised to control, limit, or assist foot and ankle motion and provide leg support. Typically, orthotics are made of lightweight materials such as thermoplastics. SEE: illus.

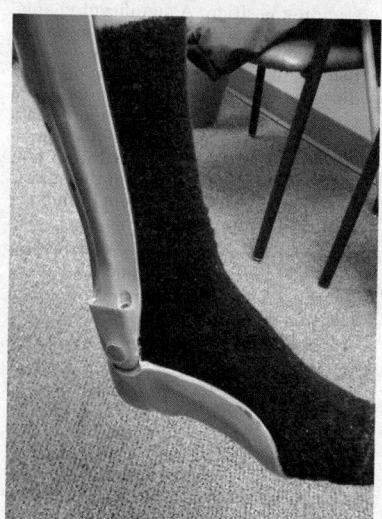

ANKLE-FOOT ORTHOSIS

PATIENT CARE: A variety of ankle-foot orthoses are used. In the treatment of Achilles' tendon rupture, e.g., the orthosis holds the foot at a right angle to the horizontal plane of the body, in plantar flexion.

balanced forearm o. Mobile arm support.

halo vest o. Halo vest.

spinal o. A supportive device applied to the back (and often encircling the trunk) that limits the movement of the vertebrae, alleviates pain, or unloads mechanical stress; back brace.

wrist-driven hand o. ABBR: WDHO. An orthotic that uses the muscles of the wrist, esp. the extensor muscles, to drive the fingers together into a grasping motion. It can be used by people with paralysis of the hand to improve the ability to hold on to and release objects.

wrist-driven wrist-hand o. ABBR: WDWHO. A dynamic splint used for functional grasp by people with C6 tetraplegia. SEE: *tenodesis (2); universal cuff.*

orthostatic (or″thō-stat′ĭk) [*ortho-* + *static*] Pert. to or caused by an erect position.

orthostatic intolerance Loss of consciousness, near fainting, or light-headedness occurring when a person stands up from a seated or resting position. It is caused by insufficient blood flow to the brain, typically brought on by inability to raise blood pressure during changes in posture.

orthostatic vital signs determination The measurement of patient blood pressure and pulse rate, first in the supine, then in the sitting, and finally in the standing position. A significant change in both of these vital signs signifies hypovolemia or dehydration. A positive test result occurs if the patient becomes dizzy or loses consciousness, or if the pulse rate increases by 20 or more beats per minute and the systolic blood pressure drops by 20 mm Hg within 3 min of the patient's arising from the supine to the sitting position or from the sitting to the standing position.

⚠ For patient safety, measurements may sometimes be made with the patient on a tilt table.

orthotic (or″thŏt′ĭk) [Gr. *orthosis,* straightening] Relating to orthosis.

orthotics (or-thŏt′ĭks) **1.** The science pert. to mechanical appliances for orthopedic use. **2.** The use of orthopedic appliances. **3.** Custom-built or over the counter shoe insoles used to correct the biomechanics of the feet and legs.

orthotist (or′thō-tĭst) [Gr. *orthosis,* straightening] A health care professional who helps design, construct, and adjust orthotics, orthopedic braces, and other structures that support the body or its parts.

orthotonos, orthotonus (or-thŏt′ō-nŏs, -nŭs) [″ + *tonos,* tension] Tetanic

spasm marked by rigidity of the body in a straight line.

orthotopic (or″thō-tŏp′ĭk) **1.** In the correct place. **2.** Pert. to a tissue graft to a site where that tissue would normally be present.

orthotopic bladder replacement Neobladder.

orthotripsy (or″thō-trĭp′sē) [″ + ″] The use of extracorporeal shock wave technology to treat musculoskeletal disorders.

orthovoltage (or″thō-vōl′tĭj) The median voltage used in x-ray therapy, approx. 250 kV.

Ortner syndrome (ort′nĕr) [Norbert Ortner, Austrian physician, 1865–1935] Vocal paralysis caused by pressure from an enlarged heart on the recurrent laryngeal nerve.

Ortolani maneuver (or-tŏ-lon′ē) [Marius Ortolani, 20th-cent. Italian orthopedic surgeon] A test to detect congenital subluxation or dislocation of the hip. The examiner places the infant on the back with hips and knees flexed while abducting and lifting the femurs. When the result is positive, a palpable click is felt as the femur enters the dysplastic joint.

-ory [Fr. *-oire,* fr. L. *-orius,* adj. suffix] Suffix meaning *pertaining to,* or *relating to.*

oryza sativa (ō-rīz′ă să-tīv′ă) [L. *oryza sativa,* sown rice] The scientific name for rice, a cereal grain in the grass family consumed as a staple source of carbohydrates.

OS, os L. *oculus sinister,* left eye. SEE: *OD.*

Os Symbol for the element *osmium.*

¹os (ōs, ōr′ă) *pl.* **ora** [L. *os,* mouth] Mouth, opening.

incompetent cervical o. A uterine cervix that cannot maintain a diameter small enough to support the increasing weight of the fetus. This condition usually results in early second trimester abortion. The cause is a congenital structural defect or previous trauma to the cervix. It is treated with a pursestring ligature that encircles, encloses, and reinforces the cervix.

o. uteri The mouth of the uterus. It opens into the vagina.

o. uteri externum The opening of the cervical canal of the uterus into the vagina.

o. uteri internum The internal opening of the cervical canal into the uterus.

o. ventriculi The cardia of the stomach.

²os (os, os′ă) *pl.* **ossa** [L. *os,* bone] Bone.

o. innominatum The innominate (hip) bone.

o. peroneum A bone occasionally found in the tendon of the peroneus longus muscle.

o. planum **1.** Flat bone; any bone

that has only a slight thickness. **2.** The orbital plate of the ethmoid bone.

   o. pubis The pubic bone; the antero-inferior part of the hip bone. In the adult, it and the ilium and ischium form the pelvic bone. The superior and inferior rami unite medially to form the pubic symphysis; at its lateral end the pubic bone forms approx. one fifth of the acetabulum.

   o. vesalianum A bone that develops from the ossification of the posterior tubercle of the fifth metatarsal.

OSA *obstructive sleep apnea.*

osazone (ō′sā-zōn) Any of a series of compounds resulting from heating sugars with acetic acid and phenylhydrazine.

oscheo- [Gr. *oscheon*] Combining form meaning *scrotum.*

oscillate To rapidly move back and forth between two locations or physical states.

oscillation (ŏs″sĭl-ā′shŭn) [L. *oscillare,* to swing] A swinging, pendulum-like movement; a vibration or fluctuation.

oscillator (ŏs′ĭ-lā″tor) **1.** Device for producing oscillations. **2.** An electronic circuit that will produce an oscillating current of a certain frequency.

oscillogram (ŏs′ĭl-ō-grăm) [″ + Gr. *gramma,* something written] A graphic record made by the oscillograph.

oscillograph (ŏs′ĭl-ō-grăf) [″ + Gr. *graphein,* to write] An electronic device used for detecting, displaying, and recording variations in electrical phenomena. In medicine, electrocardiographs and electroencephalographs are examples of the application of this technique.

oscillometer (ŏs-ĭl-ŏm′ĕ-tĕr) [″ + Gr. *metron,* measure] A machine used to measure oscillations, esp. those of the bloodstream.

oscillometry (ŏs-ĭl-ŏm′ĕ-trē) The measurement of oscillations.

oscillopsia (os″ĭ-lop′sē-ă) The visual perception that stationary objects are swinging. This perception is an illusion, usually associated with vestibular dysfunction, but also with multiple sclerosis. SYN: *oscillating vision.*

oscilloscope (ŏ-sĭl′ō-skōp) [L. *oscillare,* to swing, + Gr. *skopein,* to examine] An instrument that makes visible the presence, nature, and form of oscillations or irregularities of an electric current. SEE: *oscillograph.*

osculation (ŏs″kū-lā′shŭn) [L. *osculum,* little mouth, kiss] **1.** The union of two vessels or structures by their mouths. **2.** Kissing.

osculum (ŏs′kū-lŭm) *pl.* **oscula** [L.] A tiny aperture or pore.

¹**-ose** [Fr. *-us, -ous,* fr. L. *-osus,* adj. suffix] Suffix meaning *pertaining to* or *relating to.* SEE: *-ous.*

²**-ose** [Fr. (*gluc*)*ose*] **1.** Suffix in chemistry meaning *carbohydrate,* such as glucose. **2.** Suffix in chemistry meaning *primary alteration product of a protein,* such as proteose.

Osgood-Schlatter disease (oz′good-shlat′ĕr) [Robert B. Osgood, U.S. orthopedist, 1873–1956; Carl Schlatter, Swiss surgeon, 1864–1934] Inflammation of the insertion of the patellar tendon on the tibia. This condition is a common cause of anterior knee pain in active adolescents.

OSHA (ō′shă) *Occupational Safety and Health Administration.* A U.S. governmental regulatory agency concerned with the health and safety of workers. Website: www.osha.gov/.

-osis [Gr. *-ōsis,* fr. *-sis*] Suffix indicating *condition, status, process,* whether normal or diseased, or sometimes an *increase.* SEE: *-sis.*

Osler, Sir William (ŏs′lĕr) Canadian physician, 1849–1919, he is considered a leading figure in contemporary medicine, diagnosis, and the humanitarian care of patients. During his career he was associated with McGill, Johns Hopkins, and Oxford Universities, where he prepared a number of editions of his monumental *The Principles and Practice of Medicine.*

   O.'s nodes Small, tender cutaneous nodes, usually present in the fingers and toes, that may be seen in subacute bacterial endocarditis. The nodes are caused by emboli dislodged from infected heart valves. SEE: *infective endocarditis* for illus.

osmatic (ŏz-măt′ĭk) [Gr. *osmasthai,* to smell] Pert. to or having a keen sense of smell.

osmesthesia (ŏz″mĕs-thē′zē-ă) [Gr. *osme,* odor, + *aisthesis,* sensation] Olfactory sensibility; the power of perceiving and distinguishing odors.

-osmia [Gr. *osmē,* odor + *-ia*] Suffix meaning *odor, smell.* SEE: *osmo-.*

osmidrosis (ŏz-mĭ-drō′sĭs) [″ + *hidros,* sweat] Bromidrosis.

osmiophilic (ŏz″mē-ō-fĭl′ĭk) Having an affinity for the staining material osmium tetroxide.

osmiophobic (ŏz″mē-ō-fō′bĭk) Having resistance to the staining material osmium tetroxide.

osmium (oz′mē-ŭm) [¹*osmo-* + *-ium* (1)] SYMB: Os. A metallic element, atomic weight (mass) 190.2, atomic number 76.

   o. tetroxide OsO_4, a volatile, colorless acid formed by heating osmium in air. It is used as a caustic, a stain for fats, and a tissue fixative for electron microscopy. SYN: *osmic* **acid**.

⚠ Its vapors are extremely toxic to the eyes, skin, and respiratory tract.

¹ osmo-, ² osm- [Gr. *osmē*, odor] Prefixes meaning *odor, smell*.

² osmo- [Gr. *ōsmos*, impulse, thrust] A prefix meaning *osmosis*.

osmol, osmole (oz′mōl″, os′) The standard unit of osmotic pressure based on a one molal concentration of an ion in a solution. **osmolal** (oz-mō′lăl), *adj.*

osmolality (oz″mō-lal′ĭt-ē, os″) The characteristic of a solution determined by the particulate concentration of the dissolved substances per unit of solvent. SYN: *osmotic concentration*.

    fecal o. The concentration of solutes in stool. In health, this is equivalent to the concentration of solutes in plasma.

    plasma o. The osmotic concentration of plasma. Normally the ionic concentration in the plasma is maintained within a narrow range: 275 to 295 mOsm/kg. When plasma osmolality increases above normal, antidiuretic hormone (ADH [vasopressin]) is released. ADH prevents loss of water by the kidney and thus decreases plasma osmolality. An increase in plasma osmolality also produces the sensation of thirst, which stimulates the person to drink fluids; this, too, serves to decrease plasma osmolality.

    serum o. The osmotic concentration of the serum.

    urine o. The osmotic concentration of the urine.

osmolar (oz-mō′lăr) Pert. to the osmolality of a solution.

osmolarity (os″mō-lăr′ĭ-tē) The concentration of osmotically active particles in solution.

osmolyte (oz′mō-līt″, os′) [²*osmo* + *-lyte*] An organic solute, esp. one that helps cells adapt to dehydration or fluid excess. Osmolytes are generated within cells in response to osmotic stresses. Examples include glutamine, glycine, inositol, sorbitol, and taurine. SYN: *idiogenic* **osmole**.

osmometer (ŏz-mŏm′ĕt-ĕr) [Gr. *osmos*, impulse, + *metron*, measure] A device for measuring osmotic pressure either directly or indirectly. It was formerly used to assess the extent of dehydration or blood loss.

osmometry (ŏz-mŏm′ĕ-trē) **1.** The study of osmosis. **2.** The measurement of osmotic forces using an osmometer.

osmoreceptor (ŏz″mō-rē-sĕp′tor) **1.** A receptor in the hypothalamus that is sensitive to the osmotic pressure of the serum. **2.** A receptor in the brain that is sensitive to olfactory stimuli.

osmoregulation (ŏz″mō-rĕg″ū-lā′shŭn) The regulation of osmotic pressure.

osmosis (oz-mō′sĭs) [Gr. *osmos*, impulse, + *osis*, condition] The passage of solvent through a semipermeable membrane that separates solutions of different concentrations. The solvent, usually water, passes through the membrane from the region of lower concentration of solute to that of a higher concentration of solute, thus tending to equalize the concentrations of the two solutions. The rate of osmosis is dependent primarily upon the difference in osmotic pressures of the solutions on the two sides of a membrane, the permeability of the membrane, and the electric potential across the membrane and the charge upon the walls of the pores in it. SEE: illus.

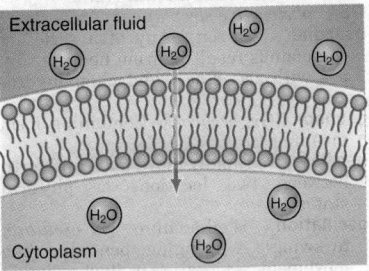

OSMOSIS

    reverse o. A form of water treatment that removes infectious particles and dissolved ions more effectively than other water purification techniques. Water so purified can be used in hemodialysis. **osmotic** (oz-mot′ik), *adj.*

osmotherapy (ŏz″mō-thĕr′ă-pē) [″ + *therapeia*, treatment] Intravenous administration of highly concentrated or hypertonic solutions to increase the serum osmolarity. This therapy is used to treat cerebral edema, among other conditions.

osmotic demyelination syndrome (oz-mot′ik dē-mī″ĕ-lĭ-nā′shŏn) Damage to the myelin sheaths that surround nerves, usually as a result of excessively rapid correction of very low serum sodium levels.

    PATIENT CARE: It can be prevented by carefully monitoring serum sodium (Na+) concentrations when hyponatremic patients are rehydrated, limiting the increase in Na+ concentration to less than 10 meq/L in the first 24 hours, and 18meq/L in the first 2 days. SYN: *myelinolysis*.

osmotic pressure (oz-mot′ik) SEE: under *pressure*.

osmotoxicity (ŏz″mō-tŏk′sĭs′ĭ-tē) [″ + ″] The adverse effects of highly concentrated fluids on body structures. These effects are often observed when radiological contrast media with a dense concentration of solute are injected into the body during imaging procedures. Patients may experience a sense of warmth, have low or high blood pressures, or suffer adverse effects caused by cell membrane dysfunction, e.g., alterations in the flexibility of red blood cell membranes or in the permeability of the lungs to gas exchange.

OspA The outer surface protein A of the spirochete *Borrelia burgdorferi*. It was formerly used as an antigen in Lyme disease immunization.

ossa (ŏs′ă) [L., bones] Pl. of os.

ossein (ŏs′ē-ĭn) [L. *ossa*, bones] The collagen of bone. It forms the framework of bone.

osseocartilaginous (ŏs″ē-ō-kăr″tĭ-lăj′ĭ-nŭs) Concerning bone and cartilage.

osseofibrous (ŏs″ē-ō-fī′brŭs) [″ + *fibra*, fiber] Composed of bone and fibrous tissue.

osseointegration (ŏs″sē-ō-ĭn-tĕ-grā′shŭn) The anchoring of prosthetic material into bone.

osseous (ŏs′ē-ŭs) [L. *osseus*, bony] Bonelike; concerning bones. SYN: *bony*.

osseous system The bony structures of the body; the skeleton. SEE: *skeleton*.

osseous tissue SEE: under *tissue*.

ossicle (os′ĭ-kĕl) [L. *ossiculum*, little bone] Any small bone, esp. one of the three bones of the ear. **ossicular** (o-sĭk′yŭ-lăr), *adj*.

     auditory o. Any of the three bones of the middle ear: malleus, incus, and stapes. SEE: *incus; malleus; stapes; ear* for illus.

ossiculectomy (ŏs″ĭk-ū-lĕk′tō-mē) [L. *ossiculum*, little bone, + Gr. *ektome*, excision] Excision of an ossicle, esp. one of the ear.

ossiculum (ŏ-sĭk′ū-lŭm) *pl.* **ossicula** [L.] Tiny bone, esp. one of the three in the middle ear.

ossific (ŏs-ĭf′ĭk) [″ + *facere*, to make] Producing or becoming bone.

ossificans (ŏ-sĭf′ĭ-kănz″, kăns″) [L. "bone-making"] Becoming or forming bony growth.

ossification (ŏs″ĭ-fĭ-kā′shŭn) [″ + *facere*, to make] **1.** The formation of bone matrix. **2.** The replacement of other tissue by bone, esp. during fetal development. SEE: *osteogenesis*.

     endochondral o. The formation of bone in cartilage, as in the formation of long bones, involving the destruction and removal of cartilage and the formation of osseous tissue in the space formerly occupied by the cartilage.

     intramembranous o. The formation of bone in or underneath a fibrous membrane, such as occurs in the formation of the cranial bones.

     pathologic o. The formation of bone in abnormal sites or abnormal development of bone.

     periosteal o. The formation of successive thin layers of bone by osteoblasts between the underlying bone or cartilage and the cellular and fibrous layer that covers the forming bone. Also called subperiosteal ossification.

ossify (ŏs′ĭ-fī) [″ + *facere*, to make] To become bone tissue.

osteal (ŏs′tē-ăl) Pert. to bone.

ostectomy, osteectomy (ŏs-tĕk′tō-mē, -tē-ĕk′tō-mē) [″ + *ektome*, excision] Surgical excision of a bone or a portion of one.

osteitis (ŏs-tē-ī′tĭs) [″ + *itis*, inflammation] Inflammation of a bone. SYN: *ostitis*.

     condensing o. **1.** Osteitis in which the marrow cavity becomes filled with osseous tissue, causing the bone to become denser and heavier. SYN: *sclerosing o.* **2.** A form of osteomyelitis, esp. noted in dentistry.

     o. deformans Paget's disease.

     o. fibrosa cystica An osteitis resulting from overactivity of the parathyroid glands with resulting disturbances in calcium and phosphorus metabolism. It is characterized by decalcification and softening of bone, nephrolithiasis, elevation of blood calcium, and lowering of blood phosphorus. Cysts form and tumors may develop. SEE: *hyperparathyroidism*.

     gummatous o. Chronic osteitis associated with syphilis and characterized by the formation of gummas.

     localized alveolar o. A localized inflammation of a tooth socket following extraction. Destruction of the primary clot results in denuded bone surfaces. Treatment includes irrigation and placement of medications into the bony void. SYN: *dry socket*.

     o. pubis A chronic osteitis due to repetitive stress to the symphysis pubis by the muscles that attach in the groin area, causing pain with simple daily movements and activities over the pubis symphysis. It occurs in such athletic activities as distance running, soccer, football, skating, and hockey. It is best treated with rest and anti-inflammatory medication.

     rarefying o. Chronicosteitis marked by development of granulation tissue in marrow spaces with absorption of surrounding hard bone.

     sclerosing o. Condensing **o.**

ostensible agency In malpractice law, the responsibility an employer bears for the negligent actions of professional employees or contractors; among other duties, the employer is assumed to have diligently researched its agents, credentials, licensure, and suitability to provide care. SYN: *ostensible authority*.

ostensible authority (ŏs-tĕn′sĭ-bĭl) Ostensible agency.

osteo-, oste- [Gr. *osteon*, bone] Prefixes meaning *bone*.

osteoanesthesia (ŏs″tē-ō-ăn″ĕs-thē′zē-ă) [″ + *an-*, not, + *aisthesis*, sensation] The condition of the bone being insensitive, esp. to stimuli that would normally produce pain.

osteoarthritis (ŏs″tē-ō-ăr-thrī′tĭs) [″ + *arthron*, joint, + *itis*, inflammation]

ABBR: OA. A type of arthritis marked by progressive cartilage deterioration in synovial joints and vertebrae. Risk factors include aging, obesity, overuse or abuse of joints (repetitive motions, bending, lifting), as in sports or strenuous occupations, instability of joints, excessive mobility, immobilization, and trauma. Signs and symptoms include pain and inflammation in one or more joints, typically in the hands, knees, hips, and spine. The dominant side of the body is involved somewhat more often than the nondominant side. Affected joints become enlarged, lose range of motion, make sounds, or feel noisy or creaky. Diagnostic testing includes joint and symptom evaluation, including assessment of the location and pattern of pain and tests to rule out other diseases, including x-rays, joint fluid analysis, and blood tests. SYN: *degenerative joint disease.* SEE: *Nursing Diagnoses Appendix;* illus.

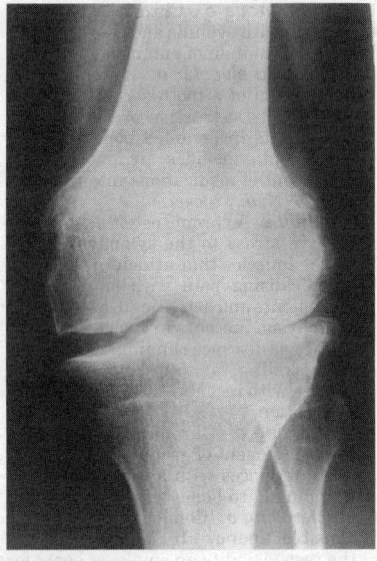

OSTEOARTHRITIS OF THE KNEE

It is especially prominent in the area above the fibula

PATIENT CARE: Treatment is supportive, using exercise balanced with rest and locally applied heat. Weight reduction, if needed, can ease joint pain and improve mobility; a body mass index below 24.9 is desirable. Aerobic exercise and flexibility routines can prevent joint stiffness related to lack of movement, and strong muscles provide better joint support. Swimming and aquatic exercises, which improve aerobic fitness without stressing joints, are encouraged. Meditation and other forms of relaxation may be beneficial as part of the patient's daily routine. Analgesics provide pain relief. Acetaminophen is the drug of choice, unless contraindicated. Nonsteroidal anti-inflammatory drugs (NSAIDs) are good alternatives for pain that is unresponsive to acetaminophen, although these agents increase the risk of gastrointestinal injury, bleeding, and renal failure. Other useful drugs include low doses of narcotic pain relievers, steroids, and intraarticular injections. Some patients, esp. those with osteoarthritis of the knee, benefit from joint bracing. If degeneration reaches the point where a joint is "bone on bone," joint replacement surgery usually is recommended, providing greatly improved mobility and function as well as pain relief.

osteoarthropathy (os″tē-ō-ar-throp′ă-thē) [*osteo-* + *arthropathy*] Any disease involving the joints and bones.

    diabetic o. Charcot foot.

    hypertrophic pulmonary o. A disorder characterized by enlargement of the distal phalanges of the fingers and toes and a thickening of their distal ends, accompanied by a peculiar longitudinal curving of nails. The wrists and interphalangeal joints may become enlarged, as may the distal ends of the tibia, the fibula, and the jaw. This condition may be associated with emphysema, pulmonary tuberculosis, chronic bronchitis, bronchiectasis, and congenital heart disease.

osteoarthrotomy (ŏs″tē-ō-ăr-thrŏt′ō-mē) [″ + ″ + *tome,* incision] Surgical excision of the articular end of a bone.

osteoblast (ŏs′tē-ō-blăst) [Gr. *osteon,* bone, + *blastos,* germ] A cell derived from mesenchymal cells. It manufactures bone matrix.

osteoblastoma (ŏs″tē-ō-blăs-tō′mă) [″ + ″ + *oma,* tumor] A large, benign tumor of osteoblasts in a patchy osteoid matrix. It occurs mostly in the vertebral columns of young people.

osteocalcin (os″tē-ō-kal′sĭn) A protein produced by osteoblasts, believed to increase insulin secretion by the pancreas and decrease fat storage by adipose tissue. Osteocalcin serves as a marker of bone turnover.

osteocarcinoma (ŏs″tē-ō-kăr-sĭn-ō′mă) [″ + *karkinos,* cancer, + *oma,* tumor] **1.** Combined osteoma and carcinoma. **2.** Carcinoma of a bone.

osteocartilaginous (ŏs″tē-ō-kăr″tĭ-lăj′ĭ-nŭs) Concerning bone and cartilage.

osteochondral (ŏs″tē-ō-kŏn′drăl) Concerning bone and cartilage.

osteochondritis (ŏs″tē-ō-kŏn-drī′tĭs) [″ + *chondros,* cartilage, + *itis,* inflammation] Inflammation of bone and cartilage.

    o. deformans juvenilis Chronic inflammation of the head of the femur in children, resulting in atrophy and shortening of the neck of the femur with a wide flat head. SYN: *Perthes' disease; Waldenström's disease.*

   o. dissecans A condition affecting a joint in which a fragment of cartilage and its underlying bone become detached from the articular surface. It commonly occurs in the knee joint. SYN: *osteochondrolysis.*

osteochondrodysplasia (ŏs″tē-ō-kŏn-drō-dĭs-plā′zē-ă, -zhă) [″ + ″ + ″] Any of several diseases or conditions in which bone and cartilage develop abnormally.

osteochondrodystrophy (ŏs″tē-ō-kŏn″drō-dĭs′trō-fē) [″ + ″ + *dys,* bad, + *trephein,* to nourish] A disorder of skeletal growth resulting from bone and cartilage malformation. The condition produces a form of dwarfism. SYN: *Morquio's syndrome.*

   familial o. Morquio's syndrome. SEE: *mucopolysaccharidosis IV.*

osteochondroma (os″tē-ō-kon″drō′mă, os″tē-ō-kon″drō′mă-tă) *pl.* **osteochondromas, osteochondromata** [*osteo-* + *chondroma*] A tumor composed of both cartilaginous and bony substance.

osteochondromatosis (ŏs″tē-ō-kŏn″drō-mă-tō′sĭs) [″ + ″ + ″ + *osis,* condition] A disease in which there are multiple osteochondromata.

osteochondrosarcoma (ŏs″tē-ō-kŏn″drō-săr-kō′mă) [″ + ″ + *sarx,* flesh, + *oma,* tumor] Chondrosarcoma occurring in bone.

osteochondrosis (ŏs″tē-ō-kŏn-drō′sĭs) [″ + ″ + *osis,* condition] A disease causing painful degenerative changes in the ossification centers of the epiphyses of bones, particularly during periods of rapid growth in children (Osgood-Schlatter disease). It is most likely to result from trauma before fusion of the epiphysis to the main bone that occurs between ages 10 and 15; thus it is most common in active adolescent boys (rather than girls) and may affect one or both knees. Other causes are a deficiency in local blood supply or genetic factors. The process may result in aseptic necrosis of bone, or there may be gradual healing and repair.

   SYMPTOMS: The patient experiences constant aching pain and tenderness over the tibial tubercle, which worsens when running, jumping, going up or down stairs, or forcefully flexing the leg. Soft-tissue swelling and localized heat and tenderness may be present.

   DIAGNOSIS: Diagnosis is based on clinical examination, x-ray studies, and bone scans.

   PATIENT CARE: The disease usually is self-limiting; treatment is conservative, supportive, and palliative. Bedrest is encouraged, and support is offered through disruption of normal activity. The knee may be immobilized in exten-

sion for 6 to 8 weeks if necessary. Quadriceps strengthening, hip extension, abductor strengthening, and hamstring and quadriceps stretching exercises are taught and practiced, with ice applications after exercise and for pain. The patient learns the correct use of crutches. Neurocirculatory function distal to supportive devices (splint, elastic support, or cast) is evaluated. Joint mobility and limitation of motion are assessed daily. If conservative treatment is ineffective (which is rare), the orthopedic surgeon removes or fixates the epiphysis or drills holes through the tubercle to the main bone, forming channels for rapid revascularization.

   o. deformans tibiae Degeneration or aseptic necrosis of the medial condyle of the tibia.

osteoclasia, osteoclasis (ŏs″tē-ō-klā′zē-ă, -ŏk′lă-sĭs) [″ + *klasis,* a breaking] **1.** Surgical fracture of a bone in order to remedy a deformity. SYN: *diaclasis.* **2.** Bony tissue absorption and destruction.

osteoclast (ŏs′tē-ō-klăst) [″ + *klan,* to break] **1.** A device for fracturing bones for therapeutic purposes. **2.** A giant, multinucleated cell derived from blood cell (monocyte) precursors formed in the bone marrow of growing bones. Osteoclasts are found in depressions (called Howship's lacunae) on the surface of the bone. By absorbing calcium salts, they remove excess bone tissue, as in the remodeling of growing bones or damaged bone in the repair of fractures. **osteoclastic** (-klăs′tĭk), *adj.*

osteoclast-activating factor SEE: under *factor.*

osteoclastoma (ŏs″tē-ō-klăs-tō′mă) [″ + ″ + *oma,* tumor] Giant cell tumor of bone.

osteocranium (ŏs″tē-ō-krā′nē-ŭm) [″ + *kranion,* skull] The portion of the cranium formed of membrane bones in contrast to that formed of cartilage (chondrocranium).

osteocyte (ŏs′tē-ō-sīt″) [″ + *kytos,* cell] A mesodermal bone-forming cell that has become entrapped within the bone matrix. It lies within a lacuna with processes extending outward through canaliculi and, by its metabolic activity, helps to maintain bone as a living tissue.

osteodentin (ŏs″tē-ō-dĕn′tĭn) Dentin that forms very rapidly or in response to severe trauma so that cells and blood vessels are incorporated, resembling bone.

osteodystrophy (ŏs″tē-ō-dĭs′trō-fē) [″ + *dys,* ill, + *trophe,* nourishment] Defective bone development.

   renal o. Bony degeneration that results from the secondary hyperparathyroidism of chronic renal failure. Its hallmarks are increased bone resorption by osteoclasts, decreased new bone formation, and decreased bone mass.

osteofibroma (ŏs″tē-ō-fī-brō′mă) [″ + L. *fibra,* fiber, + Gr. *oma,* tumor] A tumor composed of bony and fibrous tissues. SYN: *fibro-osteoma.*

osteogen (ŏs′tē-ō-jĕn) [″ + ″] A tissue layer of the inner periosteal layer from which bone is formed.

osteogenesis, osteogeny (ŏs″tē-ō-jĕn′ĕ-sĭs, -ŏj′ĕ-nē) The formation and development of bone. SEE: *ossification.* **osteogenic,** *adj.*

   distraction o. ABBR: DO. A method of lengthening bones by making a series of controlled fractures which are then spread to desired locations and held in place with hinges, rods, and/or wires. The technique is used primarily in orthopedic or maxillofacial surgery to repair deficits in long bones or facial bones.

   o. imperfecta An inherited disorder of the connective tissue marked by defective bone matrix, short stature, and abnormal bony fragility. Additional clinical findings are multiple fractures with minimal trauma, blue sclerae, early deafness, opalescent teeth, a tendency to capillary bleeding, translucent skin, and joint instability. Although the disease is heterogeneous, two different classifications of osteogenesis imperfecta are used for clinical distinction. *Osteogenesis imperfecta congenita* manifests in utero or at birth. *Osteogenesis imperfecta tarda* occurs later in childhood with delayed onset of fracturing and much milder manifestations. The healing of bone fractures progresses normally. Later in life, the tendency to fracture decreases and often disappears. The vast majority of cases are inherited as an autosomal dominant trait, although a small percentage of congenital cases are transmitted as an autosomal recessive. There is no known cure for osteogenesis imperfecta; therefore, treatment is supportive and palliative. SYN: *Bruck's disease.*

osteogenic (ŏs″tē-ō-jĕn′ĭk) Pert. to osteogenesis.

osteoid (ŏs′tē-oyd) [″ + *eidos,* form, shape] **1.** Resembling bone. **2.** The noncalcified matrix of young bone. Also called prebone.

osteokinematics (ŏs″tē-ō-kĭn″ĕ-măt′ĭks) The branch of biomechanics concerned with the description of bone movement when a bone swings through a range of motion around the axis in a joint, such as with flexion, extension, abduction, adduction, or rotation.

osteologist (ŏs″tē-ŏl′ō-jĭst) [″ + *logos,* word, reason] A specialist in the study of the bones.

osteology (ŏs-tē-ŏl′ō-jē) [″ + *logos,* word, reason] The science concerned with the structure and function of bones.

osteolysis (ŏs″tē-ŏl′ĭ-sĭs) [″ + *lysis,* dissolution] A softening and destruction of bone without compensatory osteoclastic activity. Osteolysis occurs within compact bone and results from a breakdown of the organic matrix and subsequent leaching out of the inorganic fraction. The condition is probably caused by localized metabolic disturbances, vascular changes, or the release of hydrolytic enzymes by osteocytes.

osteoma (os-tē-ō′mă, măt-ă) *pl.* **osteomata, osteomas** [*osteo-* + *-oma*] A bonelike structure that develops on a bone or at other sites; a benign bony tumor. SYN: *exostosis.*

   cancellous o. A soft, spongy tumor. It has thin, delicate trabeculae that enclose large medullary spaces like those in cancellous bone.

   choroidal o. A rare, benign tumor of the eye, composed of calcified bone. On examination of the retina, it appears as an orange-yellow lesion usually located near the optic disc, often bilaterally. It is most often identified in young women. The tumor frequently compromises visual acuity. It can be treated with laser photocoagulation.

   o. cutis A benign formation of bone nodules in the skin.

   dental o. A bony outgrowth of the root of a tooth.

   o. durum A very hard osteoma in which the bone is ivory-like.

   osteoid o. A rare benign bone tumor composed of sheets of osteoid tissue that is partially calcified and ossified. The condition occurs esp. in the bones of the extremities of the young.

osteomalacia (ŏs″tē-ō-măl-ā′shē-ă) [Gr. *osteon,* bone, + *malakia,* softening] A vitamin D deficiency in adults that results in a shortage or loss of calcium salts, causing bones to become increasingly soft, flexible, brittle, and deformed. An adult form of rickets, osteomalacia can also be traced to liver disease, cancer, or other ailments that inhibit the normal metabolism of vitamin D. **osteomalacic** (-măl-ā′sĭk), *adj.*

   SYMPTOMS: Clinical findings are pains in the limbs, spine, thorax, and pelvis; fractures; anemia; and progressive weakness.

   ETIOLOGY: The disease is caused by any of the many vitamin D disorders or by deranged phosphorus metabolism.

   TREATMENT: In patients with vitamin D–deficient diets, ergocalciferol and calcium are given as nutritional supplements.

   oncogenic o. A rare disorder in which low serum phosphorus levels and excessive wasting of phosphorus by the kidneys accompany weakening and softening of bone. The disease is found in patients with cancer and is caused by excessive circulating levels of fibroblast growth factor. SYN: *tumor-induced o.*.

tumor-induced osteomalacia Oncogenic osteomalacia.

osteomatosis (ŏs″tē-ō″mă-tō′sĭs) [″ + ″ + *osis,* condition] The formation of multiple osteomas.

osteomeatal complex (ŏs″tē-ō-mē-ā′tăl) SEE: under *complex.*

osteometry (ŏs-tē-ŏm′ĕt-rē) [″ + *metron,* measure] Measurement of bones and their relationships within the skeleton.

osteomyelitis (os″tē-ō-mī″ĕ-līt′ĭs) [*osteo- + myelitis*] Inflammation of bone and marrow, usually caused by infection (and less often by radiation or other causes). It most commonly occurs in the long bones or spine. SEE: *bone scan; Nursing Diagnoses Appendix.*

ETIOLOGY: Infections may reach the bone by several routes. Usually, disease-causing germs are carried to the bone as a result of a bloodborne infection (hematogenous spread). Organisms also may invade bone from an adjacent site such as a decubitus ulcer or an infected tooth socket (contiguous infection) or be introduced during traumatic injury or bone surgery. Pyogenic bacteria, esp. *Staphylococcus aureus,* are the most common cause, but gram-negative bacteria, mycobacteria, fungi, and viruses also cause bone infection; no organism can be identified in approx. 50% of patients. Osteomyelitis occurs more commonly in children than adults, and in boys more frequently than in girls. The risk of osteomyelitis is increased by peripheral vascular disease, sickle cell disease, urinary tract infections, prosthetic joints, inadequate nutrition, injection drug use, indwelling vascular catheters, diabetes mellitus, aging, animal bites, and soft tissue infections.

SYMPTOMS: Clinical presentation of osteomyelitis may be overt or very subtle. Severe throbbing pain over the affected part, fever, and malaise are commonly seen in hematogenous infection. However, only mild pain, swelling, and redness, with or without fever, are seen in more localized infection. Purulent drainage may be present. In chronic osteomyelitis, symptoms are similar, persisting over years and flaring up after minor trauma. Sometimes persistent purulent drainage from a pocket in an old sinus tract is the only indication of chronic infection.

DIAGNOSIS: Laboratory studies may reveal an elevated white blood cell count or erythrocyte sedimentation rate; x-ray studies or nuclear medical scans may show bone destruction. Biopsies and bone cultures are necessary to determine the causative organism.

TREATMENT: All forms of osteomye-litis require long courses of treatment with high-dose antibiotics, although many of them, including most cases of osteomyelitis that are found in the limbs of diabetics and many infections associated with prosthetic hardware, will not be cured without surgery. SEE: *diabetic foot infection.*

PATIENT CARE: The patient may be hospitalized initially for intravenous antibiotics and débridement, incision and drainage of any abscesses, and/or intracavitary instillation of antibiotics, or he or she may be cared for at home. Activity and weight-bearing may be restricted to minimize the risk of pathological fractures. The affected part is immobilized and elevated, and adequate analgesics are given to relieve the severe pain and muscle spasms. Gentle passive range of motion is performed on the joints above and below the site of infection. Warm soaks may be applied to enhance blood flow and, thus, delivery of antibiotics to the area. If surgery has been performed and/or drainage is present, the site is monitored for healing; strict sterile technique is used for all dressing changes, and all dressings are disposed of carefully. Adequate hydration and a diet high in protein and vitamin C are provided to promote healing. If the patient is at home, family members are taught the principles of infection control and the need for follow-up to prevent recurrence. Emotional support and diversionary activities should be provided.

osteon (ŏs′tē-ŏn) [Gr., bone] The microscopic unit of compact bone, consisting of a haversian canal and the surrounding lamellae. SEE: *haversian system.*

osteonecrosis (os″tē-ō-nĕ-krō′sĭs) [*osteo- + necrosis*] The death of a segment of bone, usually caused by insufficient blood flow to a region of the skeleton. This is a relatively common disorder, and an estimated 10% of total joint replacements are for osteonecrosis. From 5% to 25% of patients receiving prolonged therapy with corticosteroids will develop this condition. Treatment is symptomatic, but in some cases of osteonecrosis of the knee or hip joint prosthetic replacement is required. SYN: *avascular **necrosis**.*

osteonectin (ŏs″tē-ō-nĕk′tĭn) A glycoprotein present in the noncollagenous portion of the matrix of bone.

osteopath (ŏs′tē-ō-păth) [″ + *pathos,* disease] A practitioner of osteopathy.

osteopathic medicine Osteopathy.

osteopathology (ŏs″tē-ō-păth-ŏl′ō-jē) [″ + *pathos,* disease, + *logos,* word, reason] **1.** Any bone disease. SYN: *osteopathy* (1). **2.** The study of bone diseases.

osteopathy (os-tē-op′ă-thē) [*osteo- + -pathy*] **1.** Any bone disease. **2.** A system of medicine founded by Dr. Andrew

Taylor Still, MD (1828–1917). Although manipulation was historically the primary method used in osteopathy to restore balance to the body, contemporary osteopaths rely much more heavily on the use of medications and surgery than upon body adjustments. Osteopathy is recognized as a standard method or system of medical and surgical care. Physicians with a degree in osteopathy use the designation DO. SYN: *osteopathic medicine*. **osteopathic** (-path'ik), *adj.*

diabetic o. Charcot foot.

osteopenia (ŏs″tē-ō-pē′nē-ă) [″ + *penia,* lack] A significant decrease in the amount of bone mineral density (BMD) normally found in a population or group. The World Health Organization specifies that when BMD is between 1 and 2.5 standard deviations below normal, osteopenia exists. Decreases in BMD that exceed 2.5 standard deviations below normal are called osteoporosis. SEE: *osteoporosis*.

osteoperiostitis (ŏs″tē-ō-pĕr″ē-ŏs-tī′tĭs) [″ + ″ + ″ + *itis,* inflammation] Periostitis.

osteopetrosis (ŏs″tē-ō-pĕ-trō′sĭs) [″ + *petra,* stone, + *osis,* condition] A rare hereditary dysplastic disease of bone with at least four subtypes, two of which are *Type I:* the infantile (malignant) form, an autosomal recessive trait; and *Type II:* the adult (benign) form (also known as Albers-Schönberg disease), an autosomal dominant trait. In both types of osteopetrosis, normal bone metabolism is disrupted. Although bone continues to be formed, normal resorption diminishes, and the bones become increasingly dense. Radiographs reveal the spotted, marble-like appearance of abnormally calcified bone. In severe cases, this leads to cranial nerve entrapment, bone marrow failure, and recurrent fractures.

PROGNOSIS: If untreated, the infantile form is usually fatal during the first decade of life.

TREATMENT: Some infants have responded to bone marrow transplants. Children who are not candidates for bone marrow transplants have improved considerably with long-term administration of interferon gamma-1b. Therapy for the adult type is symptomatic.

osteophlebitis (ŏs″tē-ō-flē-bī′tĭs) [″ + *phleps, phleb-,* vein, + *itis,* inflammation] Inflammation of the veins of a bone.

osteophyte (ŏs′tē-ō-fīt) [″ + *phyton,* plant] A bony excrescence or outgrowth, usually branched in shape.

osteoplastic (ŏs″tē-ō-plăs′tĭk) [″ + *plastikos,* formed] **1.** Pert. to bone repair by plastic surgery or grafting. **2.** Concerning bone formation.

osteopoikilosis (ŏs″tē-ō-poy″kĭ-lō′sĭs) [″

+ *poikilos,* spotted] A benign, hereditary disease of the bones marked by excessive calcification in spots less than 1 cm in diameter.

osteopontin (ŏs″tē-ō-pŏn′tĭn) An extracellular matrix glycoprotein (approximate molecular weight 44 to 64 kD). It has been implicated in the pathophysiology of inflammatory, autoimmune, and malignant disorders as well as in wound repair.

osteoporosis (os″tē-ō-pŏ-rō′sĭs) [*osteo-* + *-porosis*] Loss of bone mass throughout the skeleton, predisposing patients to fractures. Healthy bone constantly remodels itself by taking up structural elements from one area and patching others. In osteoporosis, more bone is resorbed than laid down, and the skeleton loses some of the strength that it derives from its intact trabeculation. Aging causes bone loss in both men and women, predisposing them to vertebral and hip fractures. This is called type II osteoporosis (formerly "senile" osteoporosis). Type I osteoporosis (also known as "involutional" bone loss) occurs as a result of the loss of the protective effects of estrogen on bone that takes place at menopause. SYN: *bone loss; rarefaction* of bone. **osteoporotic** (-rot′ik), *adj.* SEE: illus; Nursing Diagnoses Appendix.

ETIOLOGY: Several modifiable factors contribute to bone mass and strength: increased body weight, higher levels of sex hormones, and frequent weight-bearing exercise all build up bone and prevent fractures. Bone loss and the risk of fractures increase with age, immobilization, excess of thyroid hormone, use of corticosteroids and some anticonvulsant drugs, the consumption of alcohol, tobacco, and caffeine, and after menopause. Genetics (a nonmodifiable risk factor) also contributes to osteoporosis. SEE: table.

SYMPTOMS: Bone loss progresses for many years without causing symptoms. When it results in fractures, bone pain and loss of mobility may be disabling. Signs of osteoporosis include deformities of the skeleton, e.g., kyphosis ("dowager's hump"), and loss of height, esp. if vertebral compression fractures occur.

TREATMENT: Supplemental calcium and regular exercise help slow or prevent the rate of bone loss and are recommended for most men and women. Bisphosphonate drugs, e.g., alendronate, calcitonin, sodium fluoride, and other agents are useful for patients of both sexes. In menopausal women, estrogen supplementation or the selective estrogen receptor modulators help prevent bone loss and fractures, but calcium supplementation has not been shown to be helpful.

PATIENT CARE: Protection against

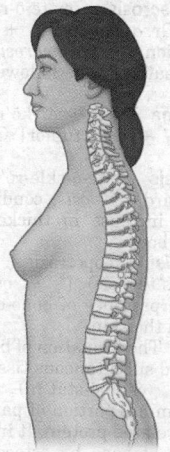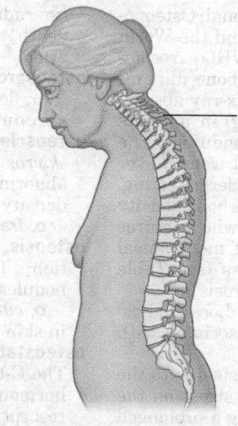

— Deterioration of
vertebral support
due to osteoporosis

OSTEOPOROSIS

osteoporosis should begin in childhood and adolescence and focus on building bone mass. Children should be encouraged to eat foods rich in calcium; parents should be taught to encourage regular exercise, including school gym

Risk Factors for Osteoporosis

Female
Advanced age
White or Asian
Thin, small-framed body
Positive family history
Low calcium intake
Early menopause (before age 45)
Sedentary lifestyle
Nulliparity
Smoking
Excessive alcohol or caffeine intake
High protein intake
High phosphate intake
Certain medications, when taken for a long time (e.g., aromatase inhibitors, glucocorticoid, phenytoin, proton pump inhibitors, selective serotonin reuptake inhibitors, thiazolidinediones, thyroid medication)
Endocrine diseases (hyperthyroidism, Cushing's disease, acromegaly, hypogonadism, hyperparathyroidism)
Diseases such as anorexia nervosa, autoimmune disorders, celiac disease, HIV/AIDS, multiple myeloma, multiple sclerosis, Parkinson disease, sickle cell disease

SOURCE: Stanley, M and Beare, PG: Gerontological Nursing, FA Davis, Philadelphia, 1995. National Osteoporosis Foundation website, 2011.

classes and sports programs, to build strong bones and establish healthy habits. Parents should also be informed about the effects that eating disorders, excessive dieting, excessive exercise, alcohol consumption, and smoking have on bone density. From the mid-20s through age 35, focus continues to be placed on building and maintaining bone mass through a calcium-rich diet. After age 35, bone resorption exceeds bone formation. Emphasis is placed on preventing bone loss through a healthy diet, use of calcium (plus vitamin D) supplements (an intake of at least 1000 mg of calcium per day), and weight-bearing exercises, e.g., weight-lifting, walking, jogging, dancing, and climbing stairs. High-impact aerobics may create too much stress on the bones of older adults and should be avoided.

After patients have been diagnosed with osteoporosis, time should be spent assessing their diets and activity levels. Although patients should engage in walking or other weight-bearing activity for 30 to 60 min three to four times a week, this goal may need to be approached slowly. Foods rich in calcium include dairy products, spinach, sardines, and nuts. Calcium supplements totaling 1000 to 1500 mg per day should be consumed and can prevent further bone loss. Based on bone density testing, alendronate or another drug that inhibits bone resorption may be prescribed in a daily or weekly formulation. Bisphosphonates like alendronate should be taken on an empty stomach with a full glass (8 oz) of water. The patient should remain in an upright position for 30 min after taking these medications to avoid pill-induced esophagitis.

DIAGNOSIS: The National Osteoporosis Foundation (NOF) and the World Health Organization (WHO) recommend tests to determine bone mineral density, e.g., dual energy x-ray absroptiometry (DEXA scanning) in patients with specific diseases or conditions. The NOF recommends that all women over 65 and all men over 70 undergo testing. The NOF also recommends bone density testing for anyone over 50 who fractures a bone and for women of menopausal age who have risk factors (see Table "Risk Factors for Osteoporosis").

o. circumscripta cranii Localized osteoporosis of the skull associated with Paget's disease.

o. of disuse Osteoporosis due to the lack of normal functional stress on the bones. It may occur during a prolonged period of bedrest or as the result of being exposed to periods of weightlessness, e.g., astronauts in outer space.

glucocorticoid o. Bone loss that results from prolonged treatment with oral or inhaled steroids, e.g., prednisone, beclomethasone, or triamcinolone.

idiopathic juvenile o. Juvenile **o.**

juvenile o. A rare childhood disease of inadequate bone mineral density, characterized by poor bone formation that usually improves spontaneously during puberty or young adulthood. Affected children often complain of bone or back pain, muscle weakness, or impaired gait. Fractures of long bones and vertebral compression fractures are common. Other diseases of bone formation, such as osteogenesis imperfecta, must be excluded before a diagnosis of juvenile osteoporosis is made. Affected children are usually asked to refrain from participation in sports to lessen the risk of fractures. SYN: *idiopathic juvenile o.*

post-traumatic o. Loss of bone tissue following trauma, esp. when there is damage to a nerve supplying the injured area. The condition may also be caused by disuse secondary to pain.

osteoporosis risk assessment instrument ABBR: ORAI. A questionnaire to gauge a woman's probability of developing bone loss (osteoporosis). It optimizes the selection of women who need or do not need bone mineral density testing.

osteoporosis self-assessment tool ABBR: OST. A decision-making rule to determine patients at high, medium, or lowrisk for osteoporosis and to identify those who would benefit most from bone mineral density testing. The tool was originally used in Asian women but has been found to be reliable in other populations of postmenopausal women and in men.

osteoradionecrosis (ŏs″tē-ō-rā″dē-ō-nĕ-krō′sĭs) [Gr. *osteon,* bone, + L. *radiatio,* radiation, + Gr. *nekrosis,* state of death] Death of bone following irradiation.

osteosarcoma (ŏs″tē-ō-săr-kō′mă) [″ + *sarx,* flesh, + *oma,* tumor] Osteogenic **sarcoma**.

osteosclerosis (ŏs″tē-ō-sklē-rō′sĭs) [″ + *skleros,* hard, + *osis,* condition] An abnormal increase in thickening and density of bone.

o. fragilis Osteopetrosis.

osteosis (ŏs″tē-ō′sĭs) [″ + *osis,* condition] The presence of bone-containing nodules in the skin.

o. cutis The formation of bone tissue in skin and subcutaneous tissue.

osteostatin (ŏs″tē-ō-stăt′ĭn) [″ + ″] The C-terminal portion of parathyroid-hormone-related protein. It inhibits the resorption of bone by osteoclasts and participates in metastasis of cancer cells into bone.

osteosynthesis (ŏs″tē-ō-sĭn′thĕ-sĭs) [″ + *synthesis,* a joining] Surgical fastening of the ends of a fractured bone by mechanical means, such as a screw or plate.

osteotome (ŏs′tē-ō-tōm) [″ + *tome,* incision] A chisel beveled on both sides for cutting through bones.

osteotomy (ŏs-tē-ŏt′ō-mē) [″ + *tome,* incision] The operation of cutting through a bone.

C-form o. A C-shaped cut through the ramus of the mandible to allow forward placement of the mandible in correcting a retrognathic condition.

condylar neck o. Surgery on the condylar neck of the mandible to correct prognathism.

cuneiform o. The excision of a wedge of bone from the cuneiform.

linear o. The lengthwise division of a bone.

Macewen's o. Supracondylar section of the femur for correction of genu valgum.

subtrochanteric o. Division of the shaft of the femur below the lesser trochanter to correct ankylosis of the hip joint.

transtrochanteric o. Section of the femur through the lesser trochanter for correction of a deformity about the hip joint.

osteotribe (ŏs′tē-ō-trīb″) [″ + *tribein,* to rub] A bone rasp.

osteotrite (ŏs′tē-ō-trīt) [″ + *tribein,* to grind or rub] An instrument used to scrape away diseased bone.

ostitis (ŏs-tī′tĭs) [Gr. *osteon,* bone, + *itis,* inflammation] Osteitis.

ostium (ŏs′tē-ŭm) *pl.* **ostia** [L. *ostium,* a little opening] A small opening, esp. one into a tubular organ. **ostial** (-ăl), *adj.*

o. primum The opening in the first

septum of the embryonic heart; it closes as the ventricles form.

o. primum defect An atrial septal defect located low in the septum, resulting from the incomplete closure of the ostium primum.

o. secundum An opening in the higher part of the septum of the atria of the embryonic heart. This becomes the foramen ovale and closes shortly after birth.

o. secundum defect An atrial septal defect located high in the septal wall, usually resulting from incomplete formation of the edge of the ostium secundum.

ostomate (ŏs′tō-māt) [L. *ostium*, little opening] One who has a surgically formed fistula connecting the intestinal or urinary tract to a site on the skin surface (stoma), usually through the abdominal wall. SEE: *colostomy; ileostomy*.

ostomy (ŏs′tō-mē) A surgically formed fistula connecting a portion of the intestine or urinary tract to the exterior (usually through the abdominal wall). SEE: *colostomy; ileostomy*. SEE: illus.

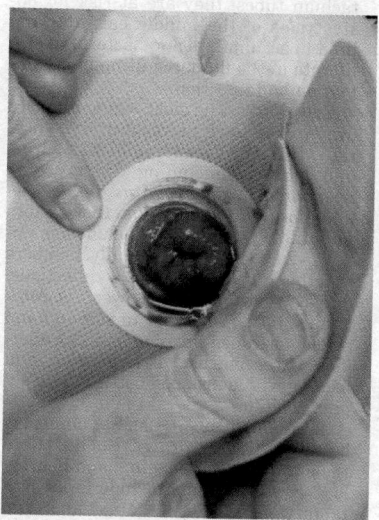

OSTOMY APPLIANCE

OSTOMY CARE: Whether the ostomy is temporary or permanent, the patient should be assured that it will be possible to carry on normal activities with a minimum of inconvenience. Prior to being discharged from the hospital, the patient and/or family should be provided full explanation and demonstration of ostomy care. Consultation with another patient who has become competent in ostomy care will be esp. helpful. Those individuals may be contacted through ostomy clubs that have been organized in various cities. The patient should be provided with precise directions concerning places that sell ostomy care equipment. Detailed instructions for care and use of ostomy devices are included in the package.

Specific care involves the stoma (enterostomal care) and irrigation of the bowel, when appropriate, leading to the stoma. In caring for a double-barrel colostomy, it is important to irrigate only the proximal stoma.

STOMA CARE: The character of the material excreted through the stoma will depend on the portion of the bowel to which it is attached. Excretions from the ileum will be fluid and quite irritating to skin; those from the upper right colon will be semifluid; those from the upper left colon are partly solid; and those from the sigmoid colon will tend to be solid. Care of the stoma, whether for ileostomy or colostomy, is directed toward maintaining the peristomal skin and mucosa of the stoma in a healthy condition. This is more difficult to achieve with an ileostomy than with a lower colon colostomy. The skin surrounding the stoma can be protected by use of commercially available disks (washers) made of karaya gum or hypoallergenic skin shields. The collecting bag or pouch can be attached to the karaya gum washer or skin shield so that a watertight seal is made. The karaya gum washers can be used on weeping skin, but the skin shields cannot. New skin will grow beneath the karaya gum. The stoma may require only a gauze pad covering in the case of a sigmoid colostomy that is being irrigated daily or every other day. If a plastic bag is used for collecting drainage, it will need to be emptied periodically and changed as directed. At each change of the bag, meticulous but gentle skin care will be given. The stoma should not be digitally dilated except by those experienced in enterostomal care.

IRRIGATION OF COLOSTOMY: Many individuals will be able to regulate the character of their diet so that the feces may be removed from the colonic stoma at planned intervals. The stoma is attached to a plastic bag held in place with a self-adhering collar or a belt. Tap water at 40°C (104°F), is introduced slowly through a soft rubber catheter or cone. The catheter is inserted no further than 10 to 15 cm, and the irrigating fluid container is hung at a height that will allow fluid to flow slowly. The return from the irrigation may be collected in a closed or open-ended bag. The latter will allow the return to empty into a basin or toilet. The return of fluid and feces should be completed in less than one-half hour after irrigating fluid has entered the bowel.

At the completion of the irrigating

process, the skin and stoma should be carefully cleaned and the dressing or pouch replaced. The equipment should be cleaned thoroughly and stored in a dry, well-ventilated space. When irrigation of an ostomy is provided for a hospitalized patient, charting is done on the amount and kind of fluid instilled, the amount and character of return, the care provided for the stoma, the condition of the stoma, and if a pouch or bag is replaced.

MISCELLANEOUS CONSIDERATIONS: Odor may be controlled by avoiding foods that the individual finds to cause undesirable odors. Chlorophyll or bismuth subgallate tablets may control odor as well. Gas may be controlled by avoiding foods known to produce gas, which will vary from patient to patient, and with the use of simethicone products. The diet should be planned to provide a stool consistency that will be neither hard and constipating nor loose and watery. The patient may learn this by trial and error and by consulting with nutritionists and ostomy club members. Daily physical activity, sexual relations, and swimming are all possible.

Oswestry Disability Index (oz-wes′trē) [Fr. the Robert Jones and Agnes Hunt Orthopaedic Hospital, *Oswestry,* Shropshire, U.K.] SEE: under *index.*

OT *occupational therapy.*

otalgia (ō-tăl′jē-ă) [Gr.] Pain in the ear. SYN: *earache; otodynia.*

TREATMENT: Local treatment consists of application of heat in the form of compresses or a hot water bottle or instillation of warm glycerin in the affected ear. Generally, nasal astringents help maintain the patency of the eustachian tube, and appropriate systemic antibiotics may be used if there is an infection.

> ⚠ Medicines should not be placed in the external auditory canal unless the eardrum is intact.

Ota nevus (ō′tă) [Mokutaro Kinoshita Ota, Japanese dramatist, poet, art historian, and dermatologist, 1885–1945] Blue, gray, or black macular discoloration of the skin, typically above or just below the eyes. It may be congenital or appear in childhood or adolescence. Close follow-up of this lesion is needed because malignant melanoma may develop in it. SEE: *mongolian spot.*

OTC *over the counter;* refers to drugs and devices available without a prescription.

OT(C) *occupational therapist (Canada);* one who is certified by the Canadian Association of Occupational Therapists.

OTD *organ tolerance dose;* the maximum amount of radiation tolerated by specific tissues.

Othello syndrome (ŏ-thel′ō) [Fr. Shakespeare's *Othello* (1604)] The paranoid delusion that one's spouse is unfaithful. It is a form of delusional jealousy.

otic (ō′tĭk) [Gr. *otikos*] Concerning the ear.

OTIS (ōt′is) [Acronym from *Organization of Teratology Information Specialists*] A nonprofit organization that provides information about potential health risks during pregnancy and lactation. Website: www.otispregnancy.org

otitis (ō-tīt′ĭs) [*oto-* + *-itis*] Inflammation of the ear. It is differentiated as externa, media, and interna, depending upon which portion of the ear is inflamed. **otitic** (ō-tit′ik), *adj.*

   acute o. media ABBR: AOM. The presence of fluid in the middle ear accompanied by signs and symptoms of local or systemic infection. In the U.S. 12,000,000 cases of otitis media are estimated to occur each year. More than 90% of children experience at least one episode by age 2 years. Because infants and children have short, horizontal eustachian tubes, they are at risk for obstructions of the middle ear, allowing fluid to accumulate and bacteria to proliferate in the fluid, resulting in inflammation and infection.

   ETIOLOGY: The most common causes are viruses, such as respiratory syncytial virus (RSV) and influenza virus, and bacteria, including *Streptococcus pneumoniae, Haemophilus influenzae,* and *Moraxella catarrhalis.* Risk factors for middle ear infection include age under 2 years, exposure to family members or others with respiratory infections, day care attendance, lower socioeconomic status, exposure to second-hand smoke or wood-burning stoves, allergies, excessive use of a pacifier, and feeding with a propped bottle or in a supine position.

   SIGNS AND SYMPTOMS: There may be pain in the ear, drainage of fluid from the ear canal, ear-tugging, and hearing loss. Systemic signs include fever, irritability, headache, lethargy, anorexia, and vomiting. Diarrhea is also a common sign of AOM in infants. History of a recent upper respiratory infection is common.

   TREATMENT: Since AOM is usually self-limiting and resolves in 1 to 2 weeks without antibiotics, the best approach is to watch and wait. Parents should be told that if the child does not show improvement in 2 to 3 days, an antibiotic may be needed, but that inappropriate use of antibiotics leads to bacteria that are resistant to these drugs. Antibiotics, however, should be prescribed for the child under age 2 or when the eardrum is bulging and fever is present. Amoxicillin is the drug of choice when antibiotics are required. Parents should be warned that if improvement is not seen in 2 to 3 days on this therapy, the primary care provider should be notified, because this may indicate that the causative bacteria are amoxicillin-resistant, requiring a different drug, such as amoxicillin-clavulanate (Augmentin), cefuroxime (Ceftin) or ceftriaxone (Rocephin). Anesthetic eardrops may be prescribed if the tympanic membrane is intact and there is no discharge from the ear. Antihistamines, decongestants, homeopathic, and naturopathic remedies are not beneficial in AOM and should not be given. Pain is usually treated with acetaminophen or ibuprofen. Cold or hot pack applications help to ease the pain, as does positioning the child with the head propped up. Some evidence suggests that vaccinations against common viral illnesses (such as influenza and RSV) will diminish the incidence of AOM.

Vaccination against *Streptococcus pneumoniae* prevents ear infections and limits the need for giving antibiotics in children.

DIAGNOSIS: Clinical diagnosis relies on the visualization of a red tympanic membrane with limited mobility (established by pneumatic otoscopy or tympanogram). Definitive diagnosis of the causative organism relies on tympanocentesis, that is, puncturing the eardrum with a needle to aspirate and culture the fluid in the middle ear. This test is rarely performed in routine outpatient care.

PATIENT CARE: Because some children are prone to recurrences, parents should be taught to recognize signs of otitis media and seek medical assistance when their child complains of pain or when they observe the child tugging his ears or demonstrating pain in other ways. Parents should be taught to help prevent recurrent AOM by not smoking or allowing smoking around children. Parents who smoke should be encouraged to quit or at least to limit their smoking to out-of-doors. Use of pacifiers should be limited because the pressure of vigorous sucking opens the eustachian tubes and allows nasopharyngeal secretions to enter the middle ear. Breast-feeding should be encouraged for at least the first 3 months to enhance transfer of antibodies and reduction of infections. Bottle-fed infants should never be propped with the bottle and should have the head elevated during feedings. Parents should be reminded that good hand hygiene is the best way to prevent the spread of infections and that, if the child is in day-care, they should make sure the facility has soap and sinks readily available and enforces

hand hygiene policies. Failure to treat acute and chronic ear infections may lead to spontaneous rupture of the eardrum, temporary or permanent hearing loss in children, and subsequent communication disorders; therefore, parents must understand the importance of proper medical follow-up. The child should be referred to an ear, nose, and throat (ENT) specialist for evaluation in the presence of recurrent AOM (6 episodes in 12 months), associated complications (mastoiditis), AOM that does not respond to treatment, and problems with hearing, speech, or language.

allergic o. media Otitis media with effusion.

o. externa Infection or inflammation of the external auditory canal. It may be caused by a contact allergy, an acute bacterial infection, or by fungi. In diabetics and the immunosuppressed patient, the infection may invade the base of the skull, resulting in deep bone infection.

o. interna Labyrinthitis.

o. labyrinthica Inflammation of the labyrinth of the ear.

o. mastoidea Inflammation of the middle ear, involving the mastoid spaces.

o. media Acute o. media.

o. media with effusion The presence of fluid in the middle ear without signs or symptoms of acute infection. This causes retraction of the eardrum. Upon examination, a level of air fluid may be seen through the tympanic membrane. The cause of the obstruction may be enlarged adenoid tissue in the pharynx, inflammation in the pharynx, tumors in the pharyngeal area, or allergy. SYN: *allergic o. media; nonsuppurative o. media; secretory o. media; serous o. media.*

TREATMENT: Nasal decongestants may afford symptomatic relief. The use of antibiotics is controversial. Adenoidectomy and bilateral myringotomy may be necessary if conservative measures, including insertion of a ventilation or tympanostomy tube, are not effective. Adenoidectomy is not advisable in children under 4 years of age. SEE: *tympanocentesis; tympanostomy tube.*

⚠ The routine use of grommets, also called ventilation tubes, as part of the initial therapy for otitis media is not advised. Their use should be reserved for persistent or recurrent infections that have failed to respond to appropriate therapy.

o. mycotica Inflammation of the ear caused by a fungal infection.

necrotizing o. externa Infection of the base of the skull that originates in the external auditory canal. It is usually caused by infection with the bacterium *Pseudomonas aeruginosa*. The disease occurs most often in diabetic and other immunocompromised patients. It may be life-threatening and requires prolonged antibiotic therapy. Hyperbaric oxygen treatments are used in patients with the most advanced and refractory disease.

    nonsuppurative o. media **Otitis** media with effusion.

    secretory o. media **Otitis** media with effusion.

    serous o. media **Otitis** media with effusion.

oto-, ot- [Gr. *ous*, stem,*ōt-* ear] Prefixes meaning *ear*.

otoacoustic (ō″tō-ă-koo′stĭk) [″ + ″] **1.** Pert. to or aiding hearing. **2.** A device to aid hearing; an ear trumpet.

otoacoustic emissions test ABBR: OAE test. A screening test for deafness that assesses the functioning of the cochlea. It is used esp. in newborns as a quick way of identifying possible congenital hearing loss. The test is performed by placing a probe in the external ear canal. The probe emits a series of clicks and then measures the echoes returning from the cochlea.

otocephaly (ō″tō-sĕf′ă-lē) [″ + *kephale*, head] A congenital absence of the lower jaw and fusion or near fusion of the ears on the front of the neck.

otocyst (ō′tō-sĭst) [″ + *kystis*, sac, bladder] An embryonic chamber from which the membranous labyrinth arises.

otodynia (ō″tō-dĭn′ē-ă) [″ + *odyne*, pain] Otalgia.

otogenic, otogenous (ō″tō-jĕn′ĭk, ō-tŏj′ĕn-ŭs) [″ + *gennan*, to produce] Originating in the ear.

otolaryngologist (ō″tō-lar″ĭn-gŏl′ō-jĭst) [″ + *larynx*, larynx, + *logos*, word, reason] A specialist in otolaryngology.

otolaryngology (ō″tō-lar″ĭn-gŏl′ō-jē) The division of medical science that includes otology, rhinology, and laryngology.

otolith Microscopic crystals of calcium carbonate on the hair cells of the maculae of the utricle and saccule of the middle ear. These are important in sensing the orientation to gravity. SYN: *statoconia; statolith*.

otologist (ō-tŏl′ō-jĭst) One knowledgeable in the anatomy, physiology, and pathology of the ear; a specialist in diseases of the ear.

otology (ō-tŏl′ō-jē) [Gr. *otos*, ear, + *logos*, word, reason] The science dealing with the ear, its function, and its diseases.

otomycosis (ō″tō-mī-kō′sĭs) [″ + *osis*, condition] An infection of the external auditory meatus of the ear caused by a fungus. SYN: *myringomycosis*.

otoneurology (ō″tō-nū-rŏl′ō-jē) [″ + ″

+ *logos*, word, reason] The division of otology that deals with the inner ear, esp. its nerve supply, nerve connections with the brain, and auditory and labyrinthine pathways and centers within the brain. SYN: *neuro-otology*.

otoplasty (ō′tō-plăs″tē) [″ + *plassein*, to form] Plastic surgery of the ear to correct defects and deformities.

otorhinolaryngology (ō″tō-rī″nō-lăr″ĭn-gŏl′ō-jē) [″ + *rhis*, nose, + *larynx*, larynx, + *logos*, word, reason] The science of the ear, nose, and larynx, and their functions and diseases.

otorhinology (ō″tō-rī-nŏl′ō-jē) [″ + ″ + *logos*, word, reason] The branch of medicine dealing with the ear and nose and their diseases.

otorrhea (ō″tō-rē′ă) [″ + *rhein*, flow] Inflammation of ear with purulent discharge. SEE: *otitis*.

    cerebrospinal fluid o. Leakage of cerebrospinal fluid from the external auditory canal. It is usually the result of prior surgery to the ear or mastoid bone or of trauma to the skull, and may predispose patients to meningitis.

otosclerosis (ō″tō-sklē-rō′sĭs) [″ + *sklerosis*, hardening] Chronic progressive deafness, esp. for low tones. It is caused by the formation of spongy bone, esp. around the oval window, with resulting ankylosis of the stapes. In the late stages of this condition, atrophy of the organ of Corti may occur. The cause of this condition is unknown, but it may be familial. It is more common in women and may be made worse by pregnancy.

TREATMENT: Because the three bones of the middle ear become fused, patients cannot normally transmit sound to the inner ear from the vibrations of the tympanic membrane. Various surgical procedures, including stapedectomy, have been used with considerable improvement in hearing.

otoscope (ō′tō-skōp) [″ + *skopein*, to examine] A device for examination of the ear.

otoscopy (ō-tŏs′kō-pē) The use of an otoscope in examining the ear.

otospongiosis (ō″tō-spŭn″jē-ō′sĭs) The growth of bony tissue within the labyrinth of the inner ear, which may cause significant hearing loss.

ototoxic (ō″tō-tŏk′sĭk) [″ + *toxikon*, poison] Having a detrimental effect on the eighth nerve or the organs of hearing.

OTR/L *Licensed Occupational Therapist*.

Ottawa ankle rules ABBR: OAR. Practice guidelines developed in Canada in 1992 to reduce the number of unnecessary ankle x-rays in emergency departments. The inability to walk four steps or the presence of point tenderness over the posterior half of the lateral malleolus or the base of the fifth metatarsal warrant radiographic examination. SEE: *modified Ottawa ankle rules*.

Ottawa knee rules Clinical prediction rules used to determine the appropriate use of knee x-rays after an injury. Variables that suggest a knee fracture or dislocation include a patient over 55 years old, tenderness at the head of the fibula, isolated tenderness of the patella, inability to flex the knee to 90°, and inability to bear weight on the affected leg both immediately after the injury and in the ER.

Otto pelvis (ŏt′ō) [Adolph W. Otto, Ger. surgeon, 1786–1845] The protrusion of the acetabulum into the pelvic cavity. This condition may occur in association with severe osteoarthritis of the hip.

O.U., o.u. L. *oculus uterque,* each eye.

-ous [Fr. *-us, -ous,* fr. L. *-osus,* adj. suffix] **1.** Suffix meaning *possessing, full of.* **2.** Suffix meaning *pertaining to.* **3.** Suffix used in chemistry in meaning *the lower of two valencies.* SEE: *-ic.* SEE: ¹ *-ose.*

outborn (owt′born″) A premature infant who is delivered at a health care facility and then transferred to a tertiary care medical center. SEE: *inborn.*

outbreak The sudden increase in the incidence of a disease or condition.

outbreeding (owt′brēd″ing) The mating of unrelated (or very distantly related) members of a species. It increases the heterozygosity and genetic diversity of offspring. SYN: *outcrossing.* SEE: *inbreeding.*

outcome A result or consequence, e.g., of a disease, an interpersonal interaction, a chemical reaction, drug, or operation.

   o. criteria Predetermined goals for quality assurance and improvement.

   expected o. **1.** The anticipated results of a therapeutic intervention. **2.** The anticipated findings of a scientific investigation. Expected outcomes are most useful when they are described in precisely defined terms.

   functional o. In rehabilitation therapy, a measurable goal that helps a patient perform specific activities of daily living.

   positive o. In health care, the remediation of functional limitations or disability; the prevention of illness or injury; or an improvement in patient satisfaction.

outcome and assessment information set ABBR: OASIS. A group of items that represent the core of a comprehensive assessment for adult home health patients. It forms the basis for measuring patient outcomes for purposes of Outcomes Based Quality Improvement (OBQI) and Medicare reimbursement. The data set is composed of 79 health and functional status patient assessment items that are discipline-neutral. When measured at two or more points in time, they serve as outcome measures.

outcrossing (owt′kros″ing) Outbreeding.

outflow In neurology, the passage of impulses outwardly from the central nervous system.

   craniosacral o. Impulses passing through parasympathetic nerves.

outlay (owt′lā″) **1.** Payment for a health care service. **2.** Expenditure.

outlet 1. A vent or opening through which something can escape. **2.** The lower pelvic opening between the tip of the coccyx, the ischial tuberosities, and the lower margin of the symphysis pubis. **3.** A pharmacy or other agency that dispenses medications.

   pelvic o. Outlet (2).

   quick-connect o. A device that allows a compressed gas container to be quickly connected to and disconnected from the delivery unit.

outlier In a research study, a data point that falls so far from the rest of the data points that it may be suspected of reflecting a bias, a measurement error, or a unique circumstance.

out-of-body experience The perception of being away from and overlooking oneself; the feeling that the mind has separated from the body.

out-of-hospital A term used in emergency medicine to mean "in the field," "in the community," "at the patient's home or workplace," or "prehospital." Assessments performed and treatments given out-of-hospital often stabilize a patient or initiate critically needed care.

out-of-network Pert. to a health care provider or service that is not a part of an individual's health insurance plan. Most health insurers do not pay for services that are provided out of network. The recipient must pay for these services out of his or her own funds.

out-of-pocket expenses Out-of-pocket medical expense.

out-of-pocket medical expenses Those health-related costs that are not reimbursed by a health insurance plan, including copayments, deductibles, and the cost of services that are not covered by the insurer. SYN: *out-of-pocket expenses.*

outpatient (owt′pā″shĕnt) One who receives treatment that does not involve hospitalization.

outpocketing Evagination.

output (owt′put″) **1.** Information sent from a computer to an external device such as a display screen, disk drive, printer, or modem. **2.** That which is produced, ejected, or expelled.

   acoustic o. A measure of the intensity, pressure, or power generated by an ultrasonic transducer.

   cardiac o. The amount of blood discharged from the left or right ventricle per minute. For an average adult at rest, cardiac output is approx. 3.0 L per sq m of body surface area each minute. Cardiac output is determined by multiplying the stroke volume by the heart rate. SYN: *minute volume.*

   decreased cardiac o. A state in which the blood pumped by the heart is inadequate to meet the metabolic demands of the body. Cardiac output and tissue perfusion are interrelated. When cardiac output is decreased, tissue perfusion problems will develop. Tissue perfusion also can be impaired when there is normal or high cardiac output, for example, in septic shock.)

⚠️ In a hypermetabolic state, although cardiac output may be within normal range, it may still be inadequate to meet the needs of the body's tissues.

SEE: *Nursing Diagnoses Appendix.*
   energy o. The work expended by the body per unit of time.
   urinary o. ABBR: UOP. The amount of urine produced by the kidneys.

outrigger An attachment for hand splints that permits the fingers to be placed in elastic traction.

outsource (owt′sors″) To contract with employees or managers to perform specific duties as independent contractors or to purchase goods and services from consultants or third parties instead of maintaining or developing goods and services on site. In health care, for example, radiology services are often obtained from off-shore locations, and intensive care unit expertise is provided by telemedicine and robots to small hospitals by staff in tertiary care hospitals.
   outsourcing (sor″sing), *n.*

outsourcing A method in which services usually provided by the health care agency are now allocated to another firm or agency.

ova (ō′vă) [L. *ovum,* egg] Pl. of ovum.

oval (ō′văl) [L. *ovalis,* egg-shaped] **1.** Pert. to an ovum. **2.** Shaped like an egg or an ellipse, esp. with one end larger than the other; elliptical. **3.** Something shaped like an oval.

ovalbumin (ō″văl-bū′mĭn) [″ + *albumen,* white of egg] Albumin occurring in egg white. Ovalbumin is one of the major allergens found in egg white. Allergens present in ovalbumin are designated *Gad d* by the World Health Organization.

ovalocyte (ō′văl-ō-sīt″) [″ + Gr. *kytos,* cell] An elliptical red blood corpuscle.

ovalocytosis (ō-văl″ō-sī-tō′sĭs) [″ + ″ + *osis,* condition] An abnormally large amount of elliptical red blood cells in the blood.

ovaralgia, ovarialgia (ō″văr-ăl′jē-ă, -ē-ăl′jē-ă) [LL. *ovarium,* ovary, + Gr. *algos,* pain] Ovarian pain.

ovarian (ō-vā′rē-ăn) [LL. *ovarium,* ovary] Concerning or resembling the ovary.

ovarian cyst SEE: under *cyst.*

ovarian factor SEE: under *factor.*

ovarian hyperstimulation syndrome ABBR: OHSS. A potentially life-threatening complication that may occur in women receiving drugs to stimulate ovulation. The acute onset occurs within the first week ovulation is induced and is characterized by marked cystic ovarian enlargement, ascites, hydrothorax, arterial hypotension, tachycardia, hemoconcentration, oliguria, sodium retention, hypernatremia, and in severe cases renal failure. The condition is usually mild if the diameter of the ovary is less than 8 cm; moderate if 8 to 12 cm; and severe if greater than 12 cm.

Treatment includes symptomatic therapy to maintain circulatory function, bedrest, a low-sodium diet, and diuretic therapy. The life-threatening possibility can be avoided with close monitoring and withholding of drugs if ovarian response becomes excessive.

ovarian remnant syndrome The finding of a pelvic mass (often in a woman with chronic pelvic pain), in a patient who has previously undergone surgical removal of the ovaries. It results from incomplete oophorectomy and the growth or cystic degeneration of the retained ovarian tissue and can lead to unilateral ureteral obstruction. It can be treated by removal of the tissue using laparoscopy or laparotomy.

ovarian reserve SEE: under *reserve.*

ovarian stimulation SEE: under *stimulation.*

ovariectomy (ō″vă-rē-ĕk′tō-mē) [″ + Gr. *ektome,* excision] The partial or complete excision of an ovary. SEE: *oophorectomy.*

ovario-, ovari- [L. *ovarium,* ovary, fr. *ovum,* egg] Prefixes meaning *ovary.*

ovariotomy (ō-vā″rē-ŏt′ō-mē) [LL. *ovarium,* ovary, + Gr. *tome,* incision] **1.** The incision or removal of an ovary. **2.** The removal of a tumor of the ovary.

ovariotubal (ō-vā″rē-ō-tū′băl) [″ + *tuba,* a narrow duct] Concerning the ovary and oviducts.

ovaritis (ō″vă-rī′tĭs) [″ + Gr. *itis,* inflammation] The acute or chronic inflammation of an ovary, usually secondary to inflammation of the oviducts or pelvic peritoneum. It may involve the substance of the organ (oophoritis) or its surface (perioophoritis).

ovarium (ō-vā′rē-ŭm) *pl.* **ovaria** [LL.] The ovary.

ovary (ō′vă-rē) [LL. *ovarium,* ovary] One of two almond-shaped glands in the female that produces the reproductive cell, the ovum, and three hormones: estrogen, progesterone, and inhibin. The ovaries lie in the fossa ovarica on either side of the pelvic cavity, attached to the uterus by the utero-ovarian ligament, and close to the fimbria of the fallopian tube. Each ovary is about 4 cm long, 2 cm wide, and 8 mm thick and is attached to the broad ligament by the mesovarium and to the side of the pelvis by the suspensory ligament. At menarche, the surface of the ovary is smooth; at menopause, the rupture and atrophy of follicles make it markedly pitted.

Each ovary consists of two parts. The outer portion (cortex) encloses a central medulla, which consists of a stroma of connective tissue containing nerves, blood and lymphatic vessels, and some smooth muscle tissue at region of hilus. The cortex consists principally of follicles in various stages of development (primary, growing, and mature or graafian). Its surface is covered by a single layer of cells, the germinal epithelium, beneath which is a layer of dense connective tissue, the tunica albuginea. Each of the 400,000 follicles present in the ovaries at birth has the potential for maturity, but fewer than 600 mature during a woman's reproductive years (usually one per cycle). Other structures (corpus luteum, corpus albicans) may be present. The blood supply is mainly derived from the ovarian artery, which reaches the ovary through the infundibulopelvic ligament. SEE: *fertilization* for illus.; *oogenesis* for illus.

PHYSIOLOGY: The functional activity of the ovary is controlled primarily by gonadotropins of the hypophysis, follicle-stimulating hormone (FSH), and luteinizing hormone (LH). The hormones produced are estrogen, progesterone, and inhibin. Estrogen is secreted by the developing follicle and by the corpus luteum if the ovum is fertilized. Estrogen stimulates development of the secondary sexual characteristics, growth of the mammary glands, and growth of the endometrium for possible implantation of a fertilized egg. Progesterone is secreted by the corpus luteum; it contributes to growth of the endometrium and mammary glands. Inhibin is secreted by cells of the follicle and the corpus luteum; it decreases the secretion of FSH.

resistant o. An ovary that does not produce follicles when stimulated by the release or injection of follicle stimulating hormone (FSH). It is one cause of amenorrhea. Laboratory studies reveal increased levels of FSH and luteinizing hormone (LH).

overbite The vertical extension of the incisal ridges of the upper teeth over the incisal ridges of the lower anterior teeth when the jaws are in occlusion. SYN: *closed bite;; overclosure.*

overclosure Overbite.

overcompensation The process by which a person substitutes an opposite trait or

exerts effort in excess of that needed to compensate for, or conceal, a psychological feeling of guilt, inadequacy, or inferiority. It may lead to maladjustment.

overcorrection The use of too powerful a lens to correct a defect in the refractive power of the eye.

overcrowding (ō″vĕr-krowd′ing) The act of filling past capacity or the state of being filled past capacity or comfort.In geography, having more inhabitants in a region than can be supported locally with life's necessities.In health care facilities, being burdened by excessive demands for services, esp. in emergency departments or urgent care settings. **overcrowded** (-krowd′ĕd), *adj.*

overdenture A denture supported by the soft tissue and whatever natural teeth remain. These have been altered so the denture will fit over them.

PATIENT CARE: Patients with overdentures must remove and thoroughly clean the denture daily.

overdetection (ō″vĕr-dĕ-tek′shŏn) The identification of clinically insignificant disease during screening programs designed to detect severe or malignant illnesses.

overdetermination The idea in psychoanalysis that every symptom and dream may have several meanings, being determined by more than a single association.

overdistention (ō′vĕr-dĭs-tĕn′shĭn) Excessive stretching, insufflation, or inflation of an organ, e.g., of the lungs during mechanical ventilation or of the urinary bladder in bladder outlet obstruction.

overdose ABBR: OD. An excessive and potentially toxic amount of a medication, given in error or taken intentionally (e.g., by patients making suicide gestures or suicide attempts).

overeruption A condition in which the occluding surface of a tooth projects beyond the line of occlusion. SYN: *supereruption; supraocclusion.*

overexertion Physical exertion to a state of abnormal exhaustion.

overexposure (ō′vĕr-ĕk-spō′zhŭr) Excessive contact with chemicals, drugs, physical agents, or psychological stimuli.

overexpress (ō″vĕr-ek-spres′) **1.** To transcribe and translate more genetic product than normal. The process is a characteristic of cancer cells. **2.** To display more antigenic markers on a cell surface than are normally seen.

overextension In dentistry, the assessment of the vertical extent of a root canal filling, denoting an extrusion beyond the apical foramen.

overflow The continuous escape of fluid from a vessel or viscus, as of urine or tears.

overgrowth **1.** Excessive growth. SYN: *hyperplasia; hypertrophy.* **2.** In bacteriology, the growth of one type of micro-organism on a culture plate so that it covers and obscures the growth of other types.

overgrowth syndrome A general term for a group of disorders of childhood physical development in which head circumference and height are larger than normal, and there is a tendency to develop malignant tumors.

overhang The undesirable extension of filling material beyond the margins of a cavity preparation.

TREATMENT: Treatment includes reshaping or replacing the restoration.

overhydration (ō″vĕr-hī-drā′shŭn) An excess of fluids in the body.

overjet (ō′vĕr-jĕt) Horizontal overlap of the teeth, esp. between the lingual surface of the maxillary incisors and the labial surfaces of the mandibular incisors.

overlap Something that covers the tissue or object but also extends past the border.

overlap syndrome A rheumatological disorder with features suggestive of several kinds of connective tissue disease, but not definitively diagnostic of any single syndrome. Overlap syndromes typically have elements of systemic lupus erythematosus, rheumatoid arthritis, and progressive systemic sclerosis, among other illnesses.

overlay (ō′vĕr-lā″) 1. An addition superimposed upon an already existing state. 2. In dentistry, a cast restoration for the occlusal surface of one or more cusps of a tooth but not a three-quarter or full-cast crown.

functional o. The emotional response to physical illness. It may take the form of a conversion reaction, affective overreaction, prolonged symptoms of physical illness after signs of the illness have subsided, or combinations of these. Functional overlay may appear to be the primary disease; skill may be required to determine the actual cause of illness.

mattress o. A cushioned surface placed on top of a bed to decrease pressure on bony prominences and reduce the chance of the patient's developing pressure ulcers.

psychogenic o. The emotional component of a symptom or illness that has an organic basis.

overlaying (ō′vĕr-lā′ĭng) The asphyxiation of an infant when a larger person lies on top of the baby and presses his or her face into the bed, preventing the infant from breathing.

overload (ō′vĕr-lōd″) To exceed the capacity of a cell, physiological process, organism, or system, causing it to fail. **overload**, *n.*

circulatory o. Volume **o.**

fluid o. Volume **o.**

iron o. Organ failure caused by excessive accumulation of iron in the body, usually from frequent transfusions or hemochromatosis.

pressure o. Demand placed on muscle, esp. heart muscle, in response to high blood pressure or stenotic valves. Over time pressure overload results in cardiac hypertrophy and, eventually, heart failure.

sensory o. A condition in which sensory stimuli are received at an excessive rate or intensity. Sensory overload can produce increases in heart rate, breathing, blood pressure, confusion, anxiety, mental distress, and/or erratic behavior.

stress o. Excessive amounts and types of demands that require action. SEE: *Nursing Diagnoses Appendix.*

volume o. An excess of blood or body fluids in the circulation or extracellular tissues. It is usually caused by transfusions or excessive fluid infusions that increase the venous pressure, esp. in patients with heart disease, and it can result in heart failure, pulmonary edema, and cyanosis. SYN: *circulatory o.; fluid o.; hypervolemia.*

overmedication Side effects, drug interactions, or other potential problems that result from the excessive use or excessive prescription of medications. Overmedication is a common problem in the elderly, who may have multiple diseases and conditions and multiple health care providers.

overpressure (ō′vĕr-presh″ŭr) A manual force applied passively to a joint and surrounding soft tissue at the end of the range of motion in order to determine the end feel of the tissues.

overproduction Excessive output of an organic element during the reparative process, as in excessive callus development after a bone fracture. SEE: *keloid.*

overprotection Limitation of the behavior or autonomy of another person due to excessive concern for that person's safety or ability to function independently.

over-response An abnormally intense reaction to a stimulus; an inappropriate degree of response.

overriding The slipping of one end of a fractured bone past the other part. SYN: *overriding fracture.*

overshoot A response to a stimulus that is greater than would normally be expected.

overt (ō-vĕrt) [O.Fr. "open"] Easily observable; clinically obvious; symptomatic. When said of diseases, it is the opposite of occult.

overtoe (ō′vĕr-tō) Hallux varus of the great toe to the extent that it rests over the other toes.

overtreatment (ō″vĕr-trēt′mĕnt) The treatment of clinically insignificant disease, that is, minor or indolent illnesses that do not require aggressive or invasive therapy.

overtriage (ō″vĕr-trē-azh″) The misidentification of patients who have minor illnesses or injuries but who on initial assessment appear to be critically ill.

overuse syndrome An injury that results from repetitive use or overuse of a part of the body or from external pressure or environmental conditions, that can affect bones, joints bursae, muscles, tendons, nerves or other anatomical structures. Resulting disorders include carpal tunnel syndrome, tenosynovitis, tendinitis, pronator syndrome, peritendinitis, thoracic outlet syndrome, and cervical syndrome. Treatment for these conditions involves flexibility and strengthening exercises; severe or recurrent cases may require immobilization or surgery. There is a growing awareness of the importance of prevention through education, task modification, and workplace design based on ergonomic principles. SYN: *cumulative trauma disorder; cumulative trauma syndrome; repetitive motion **injury**; repetitive strain **injury**.* SEE: *ergonomics.*

overvalued idea SEE: under *idea.*

overweight (ō-vur-wāt′) **1.** Having weight in excess of what is normal for a person's age, height, and build. **2.** Having a body mass index (BMI) that exceeds the 95th percentile of other people of the same age. **3.** Having a body mass index greater than 25 and less than 30.

ovi-, ovo-, ov- [L. *ovum*, egg] Prefixes meaning *egg.*

ovicide (ō′vĭ-sīd) [L. *ovum*, egg, + *caedere*, to kill] An agent destructive to ova.

oviduct (ō′vĭ-dŭkt) [″ + *ductus*, a path] Fallopian tube.

oviform (ō′vĭ-form) [″ + *forma*, shape] **1.** Having the shape of an egg. **2.** Resembling an ovum.

ovigenesis (ō″vĭ-jĕn′ĕ-sĭs) [″ + Gr. *gennan*, to produce] Oogenesis.

ovine (ō′vīn) [L. *ovinus*, of a sheep] Concerning sheep.

oviparity (ō″vĭ-păr′ĭ-tē) The quality of being oviparous.

oviparous (ō-vĭp′ăr-ŭs) [L. *ovum*, egg, + *parere*, to produce] Producing eggs that are hatched outside the body; egg laying; the opposite of ovoviviparous.

oviposition (ō″vĭ-pō-zĭsh′ŭn) [″ + *ponere*, to place] The laying of eggs as in oviparous reproduction.

ovipositor (ō″vĭ-poz′ĭt-ŏr) A specialized tubular structure found in many female insects, through which they lay their eggs in plants or soil.

ovocyte (ō′vŏ-sīt″) [*ovo-* + *-cyte*] Oocyte.

ovogenesis (ō″vō-jĕn′ĕ-sĭs) [″ + Gr. *genesis*, generation, birth] Production of ova. SYN: *oogenesis.*

ovoglobulin (ō″vō-glŏb′ū-lĭn) [″ + *glob-*

ulus, globule] The globulin found in egg white. SEE: *albumin; protein, simple.*

ovoid (ō′voyd) [L. *ovum*, egg, + Gr. *eidos*, form, shape] **1.** Shaped like an egg. **2.** A cylindrical apparatus attached to a handle, used as a pair to hold a radioactive source during brachytherapy of the cervix.

ovomucin (ō″vō-mū′sĭn) A glycoprotein in the white of an egg.

ovomucoid (ō″vō-mū′koyd) [″ + *mucus,* mucus, + Gr. *eidos,* form, shape] A glycoprotein derived from egg whites. It is a major allergen for people who are allergic to egg whites. Abbreviated *Gal d* by the World Health Organization.

ovotestis (ō″vō-tĕs′tĭs) A gonad that contains both testicular and ovarian tissue.

ovoviviparous (ō″vō-vī-vĭp′ă-rŭs) [″ + *vivus,* alive, + *parere,* to bring forth, to bear] Reproducing by eggs that have a well-developed membrane and that hatch inside the maternal organism; opposite of oviparous.

ovular (ō′vū-lăr) [L. *ovulum,* little egg] Concerning an ovule or ovum.

ovulation (ŏv″ū-lā′shŭn) [L. *ovulum,* little egg] The periodic ripening and rupture of the mature graafian follicle and the discharge of the ovum from the cortex of the ovary. Under the influence of follicle-stimulating hormone secreted by the anterior pituitary, the follicle matures. The enlarging and maturing follicle causes a slight protrusion of the ovarian surface. Final follicular maturation and rupture occur in response to a sudden surge of luteinizing hormone. The ovum is expelled, captured by the fimbriae, and guided into the fallopian tube. Rapid changes occur in the ruptured follicle as it becomes the corpus luteum and secretes large amounts of progesterone. In the absence of fertilization, the corpus luteum degenerates within about a week, forming a fibrous scar known as corpus albicans. SEE: *conception; fertilization* for illus; *menstrual cycle* for illus.

ovulation induction SEE: under *induction.*

ovulation prediction test Luteinizing hormone urine test.

ovule (ō′vūl) [L. *ovulum*] **1.** The ovum in the graafian follicle. **2.** A small egg.

ovulogenous (ō-vū-lŏj′ĕn-ŭs) **1.** Giving rise to ovules or ova. **2.** Originating from an ovule or ovum.

ovum (ō′vŭm) *pl.* **ova** [L., egg] **1.** The female reproductive or germ cell. **2.** A cell that is capable of developing into a new organism of the same species. Usually fertilization by a spermatozoon is necessary, although in some lower animals ova develop without fertilization (parthenogenesis). SEE: *conception; fertilization; menstrual cycle; menstruation.*

   human o. The female gamete, required for reproduction. The ovum develops from an oogonium within the graafian follicle of the ovary and matures through the meiotic process of oogenesis. A mature ovum is about 0.13 to 0.14 mm (0.0051 to 0.0055 in) in diameter. At ovulation, the ovum is bounded by a translucent cellular membrane (the zona pellucida), which is connected to a layer of follicular cells (the corona radiata); these cells enclose the cytoplasm, nuclei, and chromatin material. The exact time during which a human ovum is capable of fertilization and further development before degenerating is not known; however, it is probably 24 hr. SEE: illus.; *oogenesis; ovulation.*

    mature o. A secondary oocyte that has completed its second meiotic division as a result of contact with a sperm. The nucleus of the mature ovum becomes the female pronucleus.

    meroblastic o. An ovum in which only the protoplasmic region undergoes cleavage, characteristic in ova containing a large amount of yolk.

    permanent o. An ovum ready for fertilization.

    primordial o. A germ cell that arises very early in the development of the embryo, usually in the yolk sac endoderm, migrates into the urogenital ridge, and

is the precursor for the functional gamete.

Owren disease (ō′rĕn) [Paul A. Owren, Norwegian hematologist, 1905–1990] Parahemophilia.

oxa-, ox- Prefixes indicating the *presence of oxygen in place of carbon.*

oxal-, oxalo- [Fr. *(acide) oxalique*] Prefixes indicating *derivation from oxalic acid.*

oxalate (ŏk′să-lāt) [Gr. *oxalis,* sorrel] A salt of oxalic acid.

oxaloacetic acid (ŏk″să-lō-ă-sēt′ik) SEE: under *acid.*

Oxalobacter formigenes (ŏk″să-lō-bak′tĕr for-mij′ĕ-nēz) A gram-negative, anaerobic bacterium that inhabits the gastrointestinal (GI) tract and metabolizes oxalates. The absence of this species from the GI tract or its elimination by antibiotic therapy may increase the likelihood of the patient's developing calcium oxalate stones in the urine.

oxaluria (ŏk″săl-ūr′ē-ă) [*oxalo-* + *-uria*] Excess excretion of oxalates in the urine, esp. calcium oxalate. It is often caused by excessive oxalate absorption from the gut. It can be reduced by increasing dietary calcium (which binds intestinal oxalate).

oxazolidinone (ŏk-să″zō-lī′dī-nōn) Any of a class of antibiotics effective against

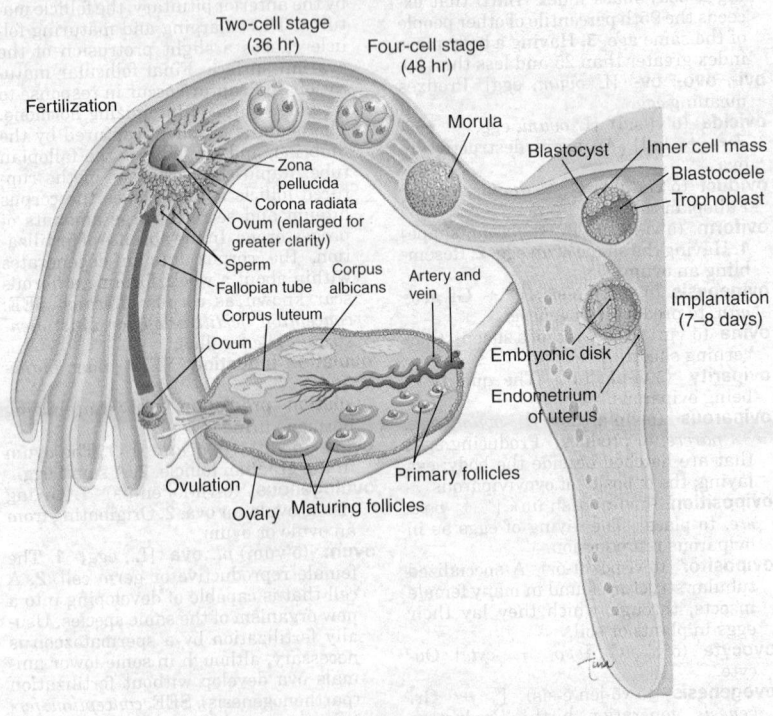

HUMAN OVUM

Ovulation, fertilization, and implantation

gram-positive organisms that inhibit the manufacture of bacterial proteins. An example is linezolid.

oxidant (ok′sĭd-ănt) **1.** In oxidation-reduction reactions, the acceptor of an electron. **2.** A chemically reactive form of oxygen, e.g., an oxygen ion or peroxide. SYN: *reactive oxygen species.*

oxidase (ok′sĭ-dās″, -dāz″) [*oxide* + *-ase*] A class of enzymes present in plant and animal cells that catalyzes an oxidation reaction; a respiratory enzyme.

> **cytochrome o.** An enzyme present in most cells that oxidizes reduced cytochrome to cytochrome.

> **urate o.** Uricase.

oxidation (ŏk′sĭ-dā′shŭn) [Gr. *oxys,* sharp] **1.** The process of a substance combining with oxygen. **2.** The loss of electrons in an atom with an accompanying increase in positive valence. SEE: *reduction* (2).

oxidation-reduction reaction A chemical interaction in which one substance is oxidized and loses electrons, and thus is increased in positive valence, while another substance gains an equal number of electrons by being reduced and thus is decreased in positive valence. This is called a redox system or reaction.

oxide (ŏk′sīd) Any chemical compound in which oxygen is the negative radical.

oxidize (ŏk′sĭ-dīz) **1.** To combine with oxygen. **2.** To increase the positive valence or to decrease the negative valence by bringing about a loss of electrons. SYN: *oxygenize.* SEE: *oxidation-reduction reaction.*

oxidoreductase (ŏk′sĭ-dō-rē-dŭk′tās) An enzyme that catalyzes oxidation-reduction reactions.

oxim, oxime (ŏk′sĭm) Any compound produced by the action of hydroxylamine on an aldehyde or ketone. When an aldehyde is involved, the general formula RCH = NOH is produced. When a ketone is acted upon, R_2CH = NOH is produced.

oximeter (ok-sim′ĕt-ĕr) [²*oxy-* + *-meter*] An electronic device for determining the percentage of hemoglobin in arterial blood saturated with oxygen. The oximeter is usually attached to the tip of a finger (preferably the index, middle, or ring finger) but may sometimes be placed on a toe (if there is adequate circulation to the foot) or the bridge of the nose, the forehead, or an earlobe.

⚠️ The oximeter should not be so tight that it prevents circulation to the finger, toe, or ear lobe.

> **ear o.** An oximeter clipped to the pinna of the ear.

> **finger o.** A pulse oximeter that attaches to the finger.

> **pulse o.** An oximeter that selectively measures oxygen saturation of pulsed (arterial) blood.

oximetry (ok-sim′ĕ-trē) [²*oxy-* + *-metry*] The use of an oximeter to determine the oxygen saturation of blood.

> **jugular venous o.** SYMB: $SjvO_2$. A form of indirect neuromonitoring in which a catheter placed at the jugular bulb measures the oxygen saturation of blood as it leaves the brain. Normal jugular venous oximetry levels are 60%–75%.

> **pulse o.** A noninvasive method of measuring oxygen saturation of pulsed (arterial) blood with a pulse oximeter.

oxindole (ŏk′sĭn-dōl) Natural derivatives of tryptophan that are present in high concentrations in the brains of patients with hepatic encephalopathy. Chemicals from this class have sedative and antioxidant effects. Some evidence suggests oxindoles may be useful in the treatment of Alzheimer's dementia.

¹ **oxy-** [Gr. *oxys,* sharp] Prefix meanings-harp, keen, acute, acid, pungent.

² **oxy-** [Fr. *oxy(gène)*] **1.** Prefix indicating the presence of oxygen in a compound. **2.** Prefix indicating the presence of a hydroxyl group.

oxybenzene (ŏk″sē-bĕn′zēn) Phenol.

oxycellulose (ŏks″ē-sĕl′lū-lōs) Cellulose that has undergone oxidation.

oxychloride (ŏk″sē-klō′rīd) [Gr. *oxys,* sharp, + *chloros,* green] A compound consisting of an element or radical combined with oxygen and chlorine or the hydroxyl radical and chlorine.

oxycodone (ŏk″sē-kō′dōn) An opioid agonist administered orally or rectally to manage moderate to severe pain. Its therapeutic class is opioid analgesic.

Oxycontin Oxycodone in a long-acting form.

OxyFAST Oxycodone in a long-acting form.

oxygen (ok′sĭ-jĕn) [¹*oxy-* + *-gen*] SYMB: O. A colorless, odorless, tasteless, gaseous chemical element, atomic weight (mass) 15.9994, atomic number 8. It occurs free in the atmosphere and makes up approx. 21% of the volume of the atmosphere. Oxygen is a constituent of animal, vegetable, and mineral substances and is essential to respiration for most living organisms. At sea level, oxygen represents 10% to 16% of venous blood and 17% to 21% of arterial blood.

Oxygen is absorbed by most living organisms. During photosynthesis it is produced by green plants from carbon dioxide and water. When oxygen is used in cell respiration, the end products are water and carbon dioxide; the carbon dioxide is returned to the atmosphere.

Oxygen combines readily with other elements to form oxides. When oxygen combines with another substance, the process is called oxidation. When combination takes place rapidly enough to produce light and heat, the combination is called combustion.

Oxygen is used medicinally to manage anemia, bleeding, ischemia, shock, pulmonary edema, pneumonia, respiratory distress, ventilatory failure, obstructive lung diseases, pulmonary embolism, myocardial infarction, mountain sickness, smoke inhalation, carbon monoxide or cyanide poisoning, and gangrene, where oxygen is temporarily or chronically insufficient. Oxygen is administered by mask, nasal tube, tent, or in an airtight chamber in which pressure may be increased. No matter how much oxygen is given, it is important to have it adequately humidified. It is desirable to administer oxygen at whatever rate is necessary to increase the oxygen content of inspired air to 50%. SEE: *hypoxia; oxygen therapy.*

hyperbaric o. The administration of oxygen under greater than normal atmospheric pressure (usually two to three times absolute atmospheric pressure). It has been used to treat air embolism, decompression sickness, severe carbon monoxide poisoning, some anaerobic infections, and to facilitate healing of indolent wounds. SEE: *hyperbaric* **oxygenation.**

singlet o. A highly active form of oxygen produced during reactions of hydrogen peroxide with superoxide and hypochlorite ions. It is believed that this free radical is bactericidal.

transtracheal o. Oxygen that is delivered to the lungs via a cannula placed directly into the trachea. SEE: *transtracheal* **oxygenation.**

oxygenase (ŏk′sĭ-jĕn-ās″) [Gr. *oxys,* sharp, + *gennan,* to produce, + *-ase,* enzyme] An enzyme that enables an organism to use atmospheric oxygen in respiration.

oxygenate (ŏk′sĭ-jĕn-āt) To combine or supply with oxygen.

oxygenation (ŏk″sĭ-jĕn-ā′shŭn) Saturation or combination with oxygen, as the aeration of the blood in the lungs.

apneic o. Providing oxygen to the upper airway of an anesthetized patient or a patient who has had cardiac arrest. Oxygenation is maintained, but carbon dioxide is not eliminated.

hyperbaric o. ABBR: HBO. Administration of oxygen under increased pressure while the patient or the patient's extremity is in an airtight chamber. Pressure chambers in which the oxygen is hyperbaric have been used to treat carbon monoxide poisoning, anaerobic infections such as gas gangrene, necrotizing fasciitis, crush injuries with acute ischemia of tissues, compromised skin grafts and flaps, mixed soft tissue reactions, burns, smoke inhalation, car-

bon monoxide poisoning, soft tissue radiation necrosis, chronic refractory osteomyelitis, decompression sickness (bends), and gas embolism. Appliances that use hyperbaric oxygen topically (colloquially called boots) have been used to treat localized infections of the extremities.

> ⚠ Hyperbaric oxygenation should not be used in untreated pneumothorax, inner ear infection, or premature infants.

tissue o. The oxygen level in tissues. Measurement of the oxygen concentration in body fluids is not as important as knowing the oxygen level in the tissues themselves. Determining the gastrointestinal interstitial pH provides an indication of the adequacy of tissue oxygenation. Decreased oxygen supply leads to anaerobic metabolism in cells, which produces a fall in pH. Thus the tissue pH serves as a marker for the adequacy of oxygen supply in the tissues.

transtracheal o. The application of oxygen via a catheter system inserted into the trachea.

oxygenation index SEE: under *index.*

oxygenator (ok″sĭ-jĕ-nāt′ŏr) A device for mechanically oxygenating something, but esp. blood, e.g., during thoracic or open-heart surgery.

bubble o. A device for bubbling oxygen through the blood during extracorporeal circulation.

extracorporeal membrane o. ABBR: ECMO. A device that circulates blood, removes carbon dioxide from it, and adds oxygen to it. The blood is warmed to an appropriate temperature and recirculated to the patient. ECMO is used in patients with acute respiratory distress that has not responded to conventional mechanical ventilation, as well as in patients with meconium aspiration syndrome, pneumonia, and persistent pulmonary hypertension.

intravenous membrane o. An artificial lung that has been used experimentally to assist in the exchange of oxygen and carbon dioxide, esp. in patients with chronic obstructive pulmonary disease (COPD), respiratory failure, or chest trauma.

rotating disk o. A device for oxygenating blood during extracorporeal circulation. A thin film of blood attaches to a disk as it dips into the blood flow. The portion of the disk not in the blood is rotating in an atmosphere of oxygen.

screen o. A device for oxygenating blood during extracorporeal circulation. The blood passes over a series of screens that are in an oxygen atmosphere. Oxygen is exchanged in the thin film of blood on the screens.

oxygen capacity The maximum amount of oxygen expressed in volume percent (cc per 100 mL) that a given amount of blood will absorb. Normal blood contains about 20 cc.

oxygen concentrator A device used for home oxygen therapy that removes most of the nitrogen from room air and delivers the oxygen at a low flow rate. SYN: *oxygen enricher*.

oxygen-conserving device SEE: under *device*.

oxygen content The amount of oxygen in volume percent that is present in the blood at any one moment. Arterial oxygen content = (Hemoglobin x 1.36 x SaO2) + (0.0031 x PaO2).

oxygen content of blood, total The sum of the oxygen bound to hemoglobin plus the oxygen dissolved in the blood.

oxygen debt SEE: under *debt*.

oxygen delivery The amount of oxygen carried to the tissues, i.e., the cardiac output multiplied by the oxygen content of arterial blood.

oxygen delivery system An apparatus that provides a concentration of inhaled oxygen greater than that of room air. A *fixed-performance* oxygen delivery system provides a consistent oxygen concentration. A *variable-performance* oxygen delivery system provides an oxygen concentration that may vary with changes in the patient's breathing pattern.

oxygen enricher Oxygen concentrator.

oxygen extraction SEE: under *extraction*.

oxygen hood Head hood.

oxygenic (ŏk″sĭ-jĕn′ĭk) [″ + *gennan*, to produce] Concerning, resembling, containing, or consisting of oxygen.

oxygenize (ŏk′sĭ-jĕ-nīz) Oxidize.

oxygen-powered ventilation device SEE: under *device*.

oxygen radical SEE: under *radical*.

oxygen saturation ABBR: SaO₂. Percent of arterial hemoglobin saturated with oxygen. SaO₂ can be monitored noninvasively with a pulse oximeter. It is normally higher than 96%.

oxygen therapy The administration of oxygen at higher levels than are normally found in the atmosphere to patients needing enhanced tissue oxygen uptake. Oxygen can be administered via nasal cannulae, Venturi masks, nonbreathing masks, continuous positive-pressure ventilation devices, endotracheal tubes, or in airtight or hyperbaric chambers, depending on the needs of the patient. Each of these modes of therapy has its own benefits and limitations. Nasal cannulae facilitate speaking and eating but can deliver oxygen in concentrations only up to 40%. Venturi masks can deliver more oxygen (approx. 50%) more precisely than nasal devices, but they interfere with some communication and oral intake. The highest levels of noninvasive oxygen therapy are delivered by nonrebreather masks (approx. 90%). One hundred percent oxygen can be given through endotracheal tubes, but patients are often uncomfortable or hemodynamically unstable with these devices and may need sedation or paralytic or pressor drugs to support them. Continuous positive-pressure ventilation devices can be used to administer oxygen, but they are not tolerated by some patients because of claustrophobia and poor adaptation to the fit of the mask. Supplemental oxygen is also available for home use through an oxygen concentrator that uses a molecular sieve to remove nitrogen from room air. SEE: *hyperbaric oxygen; oximeter*.

⚠ Inhalation of high concentrations of oxygen, esp. at pressures of more than one atmosphere, may produce deleterious effects such as irritation of the respiratory tract, reduced vital capacity, and, sometimes, neurological symptoms. Serious eye defects may result if premature infants are exposed to a high concentration of oxygen as part of their therapy. Because oxygen provides a perfect environment for combustion, it should not be used in the presence of oil, lighted cigarettes or open flames, or where there is the possibility of electrical or spark hazards.

transtracheal o.t. The delivery of oxygen via a small plastic cannula inserted directly into the trachea through a small surgical opening in the cricothyroid membrane of the neck. SEE: illus.

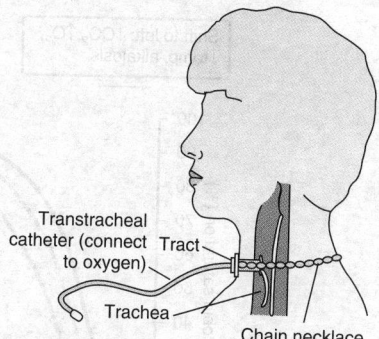

Transtracheal catheter (connect to oxygen)

Tract

Trachea

Chain necklace

TRANSTRACHEAL OXYGEN THERAPY

oxygen toxicity SEE: under *toxicity*.

oxyhemoglobin (ŏk″sē-hē″mō-glō′bĭn) [″ + *haima*, blood, + L. *globus*, a sphere] That hemoglobin that is reversibly bound to oxygen. Hemoglobin is oxygenated as blood passes through capillaries in the lungs. It is circulated to body tissues by the muscular contraction of the heart. In the tissues oxygen unbinds from hemoglobin and is used for cellular respiration.

fractional o. SYMB: FO_2Hb. The ratio of the substance fraction of oxyhemoglobin to the substance fraction of all forms of hemoglobin. This quantity takes into account the effects of abnormal hemoglobins such as carboxyhemoglobin, methemoglobin, or sulfhemoglobin. Thus, in the presence of abnormal hemoglobins, the fractional oxyhemoglobin may be decreased while the oxygen saturation is normal.

oxyhemoglobin dissociation curve The mathematical relationship between the partial pressure of oxygen and the percentage of saturation of hemoglobin with oxygen (i.e., the proportion of oxyhemoglobin to reduced hemoglobin). Factors that favor a shift of the curve to the right, accelerating the decomposition of hemoglobin, are a rise in temperature and an increase of H ions that results from liberation of CO_2 and formation of lactic acid. SEE: illus.

oxyiodide (ŏk″sē-ī′ō-dīd) [″ + *ioeides*, violet colored] A compound of iodine and oxygen with an element or radical.

oxymyoglobin (ŏk″sē-mī″ō-glō′bĭn) The compound formed when myoglobin is exposed to oxygen.

oxyntic (ŏk-sĭn′tĭk) [Gr. *oxynein*, to make acid] Producing or secreting acid.

oxyntomodulin (ŏk-sĭn″tō-mŏj′ū-lĭn) A 37-amino acid peptide secreted by the small intestine. It inhibits gastric acid secretion and reduces food intake.

oxyphil, oxyphile (ok′sĭ-fil″, -fīl″) [′*oxy-* + *-phile*] **1.** Staining readily with acid

dyes. **2.** A cell that stains readily with acid dyes.

oxypurine (ŏk″sē-pū′rēn) [″ + L. *purus*, pure, + *urina*, urine] An oxidation product of purine; includes hypoxanthine, xanthine, and uric acid. SEE: *aminopurine; methyl purine.*

oxytalan (ŏks-ĭt′ă-lăn) A type of connective tissue fiber present in periodontal tissues.

oxytocic (ŏk″sē-tō′sĭk) **1.** Agent that stimulates uterine contractions. **2.** Accelerating childbirth.

oxytocin (ok″sē-tōs′ĭn) **1.** A 9-amino acid peptide hormone secreted by the magnocellular cells of the hypothalamus and stored in the pituitary gland. It stimulates the uterus to contract. During labor it helps expel the fetus. After delivery of the placenta, it helps the uterus to contract.

    Its other function in breast-feeding is to stimulate milk letdown.

    2. A synthetic version of the same peptide. It is used to induce labor, contract the uterus, and control postpartum hemorrhage.

oxytocin challenge test ABBR: OCT. The intravenous infusion of ten very small doses of oxytocin in order to determine whether contraction of the uterus in response to the oxytocin will cause signs of fetal distress. The results of the test provide a basis of making a decision concerning continuation of high-risk pregnancies. Uterine contractions can also be induced by manual stimulation of the nipple. This process stimulates the hypothalamus, which causes the posterior lobe of the pituitary

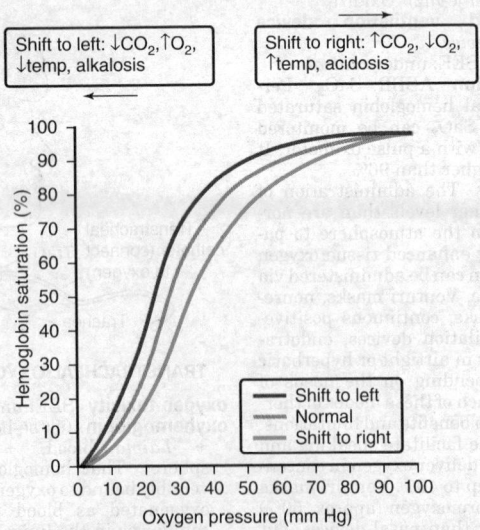

Shift to left: $\downarrow CO_2$, $\uparrow O_2$, $\downarrow$temp, alkalosis

Shift to right: $\uparrow CO_2$, $\downarrow O_2$, $\uparrow$temp, acidosis

Hemoglobin saturation (%)

Shift to left
Normal
Shift to right

Oxygen pressure (mm Hg)

OXYHEMOGLOBIN DISSOCIATION CURVE

to release oxytocin. SYN: *contraction stress test.*

Criteria for Interpretation: Negative result: The monitor records a minimum of three uterine contractions and an absence of late decelerations within 10 min. The fetal heart rate exhibits average baseline variablity and acceleration associated with movement. *Positive result:* The monitor records late decelerations with more than 50% of uterine contractions. *Suspicious result:* The monitor records late decelerations associated with fewer than 50% contractions. *Hyperstimulation:* The monitor records uterine hypertonus and uterine contractions occurring more often than every 2 min or lasting longer than 90 sec.

PATIENT CARE: The test is explained, and the patient is supported through the procedure. Oxytocin solution is piggybacked into the tubing of the main intravenous line and delivered via infusion pump or controller to ensure accurate dosing. Uterine contractions and fetal heart rate are monitored until three uterine contractions occur in a 30-min period. The fetal heart rate pattern is then interpreted for the absence or presence of late decelerations.

If the result is negative, the infusion of oxytocin is then discontinued, the intravenous line is removed, and the patient is assisted with discharge preparations.

oxyuriasis (ŏk″sē-ū-rī′ăs-ĭs) [Gr. *oxys*, sharp, + *oura*, tall, + *iasis*, infection] Infestation with *Enterobius vermicularis* (pinworm). SYN: *enterobiasis.*

Oxyuris vermicularis (ŏk″sē-ūr′ĭs vĕr-mĭk″ū-lăr′ĭs) [″ + *oura,* tail] *Enterobius vermicularis.*

oyster [AS. *oistre*] A shellfish that, when eaten raw or only partially cooked, may be a source of hepatitis A virus and bacterial pathogens. SEE: *travelers' diarrhea.*

oyster mushroom An edible fungus, *Pleurotus ostreatus,* used in the diet as an antioxidant and cholesterol-lowering agent.

oz *ounce.*

ozena (ō-zē′nă) [Gr. *oze,* stench] A disease of the nose characterized by atrophy of the turbinates and mucous membrane accompanied by considerable crusting, discharge, and an offensive odor. It is present in various forms of rhinitis.

ozone (ō′zōn) [Gr. *ozein,* to smell] A form of oxygen present in the stratosphere in which three atoms of the element combine to form the molecule O_3. Depletion of the ozone in the stratosphere permits increased exposure to ultraviolet light. This favors the development of skin cancers and cataracts and may impair cellular immunity.

Persons exposed to arc welding, flour bleaching, fumes from copying equipment, or photochemical air pollutants may be in contact with toxic levels of ozone. The signs and symptoms include asthma, mucous membrane irritation, pulmonary hemorrhage and edema, and transient reduced pulmonary function when exposed to summer haze. SEE: *greenhouse effect.*

ozone therapy Treatment with ozone for lumbar disk disease, cancer, and infectious diseases. It is used primarily in European alternative medicine. Proof of the safety and effectiveness of ozone therapy has never been established. Unlike many other alternative and complementary therapies that are promoted for their antioxidant properties, ozone is an oxidant and toxic in high concentrations.

ozonization (ō″zō-nĭ-zā′shŭn) The act of converting to, or impregnating with, ozone.

ozonize (ō′zō-nīz) [Gr. *ozein,* to smell] **1.** To convert oxygen to ozone. **2.** To impregnate the air of a substance with ozone.

P

P 1. *position; posterior; postpartum; pressure; pulse; pupil.* **2.** Symbol for the element phosphorus. **3.** Symbol for partial pressure, preferably italicized. **4.** Probability.

p *page; probability* (in statistics); *pupil.*

^{32}P Symbol for the isotope of phosphorus with mass number 15; radioactive; atomic mass (weight) 15.

P_2 *pulmonic second sound.*

p- In chemistry, an abbreviation of *para-*.

$\overline{p}$ *after-* or *post-*.

p53 SEE: under *gene*.

P 0.1 The inspiratory mouth occlusion pressure measured 0.1 seconds after a breath initiates. Higher pressures are found in those mechanically ventilated patients who are more difficult to wean from ventilatory support. A more negative pressure implies a patient with an increased ventilatory demand (shortness of breath) and a less negative pressure means a patient is obtunded or has weak respiratory muscles.

PA *physician assistant; posteroanterior; pulmonary artery.*

P & A *percussion and auscultation.*

Pa 1. Symbol for the element *protactinium.* **2.** Abbreviation of *pascal.*

P-A, PA *posteroanterior.*

P.A. *physician assistant.*

paan (pon) [Hindi *pān*] The chewing of betel leaf, common in the Indian subcontinent and Southeast Asia, which is a stimulant and is associated with the development of oral cancers.

P(A–a)O$_2$ The oxygen pressure gradient between the alveoli and the arterial blood.

pabulum (păb'ū-lŭm) [L.] Food or nourishment; esp. in an absorbable solution.

PAC *premature atrial contraction.*

pacchionian depressions Small pits produced on the inner surface of the skull by protuberance of the pacchionian bodies (arachnoid villi).

PACE (pās) *Patient Advise and Consent Encounter.*

pacemaker (pās'māk"ĕr) **1.** Anything that influences the rate and rhythm of occurrence of some activity or process. **2.** In cardiology, a specialized cell or group of cells that automatically generates impulses that spread to other regions of the heart. The normal cardiac pacemaker is the sinoatrial node, a group of cells in the right atrium near the entrance of the superior vena cava. **3.** A generally accepted term for artificial cardiac pacemaker.

    artificial cardiac p. A device that can trigger mechanical contractions of the heart by emitting periodic electrical discharges. If the device delivers electricity through the chest wall, it is called a transcutaneous pacemaker; if it works via electrodes inserted inside the body, it is called an internal or implantable pacemaker. Pacemakers are used most often to treat patients with symptomatic slow heart rates or long pauses between heart beats (such as patients with third-degree heart block, symptomatic second-degree heart block, bifascicular block with first-degree heart block, carotid sinus hypersensitivity, and tachybrady syndrome) and slow ventricular response rates. Occasionally, though, they also are used for other purposes, such as to capture and override some tachyarrhythmias. SEE: illus.

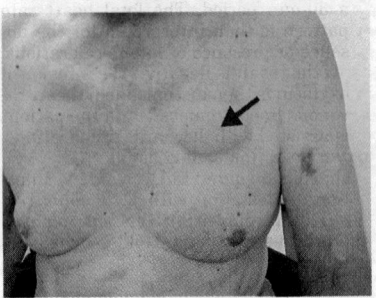

PACEMAKER

Pacemaker defibrillator beneath the skin

    All artificial cardiac pacemakers have a pulse generator (a device that gives off an electrical impulse at prescribed intervals), electrical leads (which transmit the impulse to the myocardium), and a battery (usually made of lithium iodide) encased in titanium and implanted surgically in a subcutaneous pocket (usually in the chest). The pacing leads are threaded through a subclavian vein into the right heart, with the primary lead placed in the ventricle, and the second lead (if required) in the atrium. For biventricular pacing, a third lead is placed in the left ventricle. A biventricular pacemaker also may have a built-in cardiovertor-defibrillator. Pacemakers typically have the ability to pace the ventricle, the atrium, or both; to sense electrical discharges coming from cardiac chambers; and to respond to sensed beats. Most pacemakers in the U.S. also are programmable, and many are rate responsive. The features of each pacemaker are identified in its three- to five-letter NASPE/BPG code (developed and revised by the North American Society of Pacing & Electrophysiology and the British Pacing & Electrophysiology Group). The five positions describe the pacer's functions as follows:

1. Chambers paced (O=none, A=atrium, V=ventricle, D=dual [atria and ventricles], S=manufacturer's designation for single [atrium or ventricle];

2. Chambers sensed (O=none, A=atrium, V=ventricle, D=Dual, S=Single;

3. Response to sensed event (O=none, T=triggered, I=inhibited, D=dual [inhibited and triggered];

4. Rate modulation (O=none, R=rate modulation in response to sensor technology;

5. Multisite pacing (O=none, A=atrium, V=ventricle, D=dual [atrium and ventricle]).

Thus a pacemaker with the letter I in position 3 of its code will inhibit firing when it senses an intrinsic beat but will pace the cardiac chamber if no beat is sensed. The letter D in position 5 indicates that both atria and both ventricles are paced, with the left and right chambers stimulated simultaneously to maintain coordination and thus improve cardiac output. When the pacemaker has a rate modulation feature (R in position 4), also known as an adaptive rate mechanism, it works to copy the abilities of a normally functioning heart, such as detecting exercise and triggering pacer rate acceleration to meet the increased metabolic need. Other pacemaker features include hysteresis, which delays unnecessary pacing (which can harm the right ventricle), and allows the patient's intrinsic impulse to provide an atrial kick, which stokes the ventricle and increases cardiac output by 15% to 30% over a beat without atrial kick. Pacers with a "rate-smoothing algorithm" limit heart rate changes to a programmed percentage from one beat to the next, allowing the heart rate to increase or decrease more slowly and providing time for the body to adjust the stroke volume as it would normally in such situations.

PATIENT CARE: After pacemaker implantation, follow-up care is provided to ensure that the device is working optimally. A chest x-ray confirms correct placement of the leads and also can identify some complications, such as pneumothorax. Since pacemakers usually are implanted under moderate sedation and analgesia, the patient may still be drowsy on return to the unit from recovery; however, he or she should arouse easily and be able to answer questions and follow commands. Supplemental oxygen is provided (nasal cannula or mask) until the patient is fully awake and his/her oxygen saturation has returned to baseline. Immobilizing the patient's shoulder and arm on the operative side with a sling or ace-wrap for 24 to 48 hr limits movement that could dislodge the tip of the pacing electrode(s) from the endocardial wall, preventing sensing of intrinsic beats or needed pacing. The incision is assessed for bleeding, infection, and incisional discomfort, which is controlled with prescribed analgesia. The patient also is assessed for chest pain, palpitations, dizziness, shortness of breath, hiccuping, and a sensation of pacing in the abdomen, and the cardiologist or surgeon notified if any of these occur. The chest x-ray usually is repeated the following day to document positioning and rule out pneumothorax. Pacer function is checked, and the patient discharged with instructions for activity restrictions and further care. Follow-up care typically includes monitoring the pacemaker's performance, either in the cardiologist's office or by telephonic link-up to ensure, for example, that the pulse generator is triggering a heart rate that is appropriate for the patient's needs, that the leads are working, and that the battery's strength is adequate.

Health care professionals should ascertain the type of pacemaker employed and expectations for its function based on its NASPE/BPG code; monitor the cardiac rate and rhythm for evidence of pacemaker function; assess the patient for evidence of pacemaker failure or noncapture (vertigo, loss of consciousness, hypotension, chest discomfort, dyspnea) and evaluate the patient for effects on cardiac output; teach the patient technique and rationale for monitoring own pulse rate and for care and protection of insertion site; and counsel concerning telephone monitoring checkup, battery replacement, medication regimen, physical activity, and follow-up care. They should encourage the patient to wear or carry medical identification and information indicating the presence and type of pacemaker implanted, along with an electrocardiogram rhythm strip showing pacemaker activity and capture.

⚠️ Patients with artificial cardiac pacemakers should avoid MR imaging.

demand p. An implanted pacemaker that is designed to permit its electrical output to be inhibited by the heart's electrical impulses. This decreases the chances for the pacemaker to induce discomfort or dysrhythmias.

dual-chamber p. A pacemaker that is also known as an atrioventricular sequential pacemaker because it stimulates both atria and ventricles sequentially.

ectopic p. Any endogenous cardiac pacemaker other than the sinoatrial node.

fixed-rate p. A pacemaker that stimulates the heart at a predetermined rate.

internal p. A cardiac pacemaker placed within the body.

programmable p. An electronic permanent pacemaker in which one or more settings can be changed electronically.

rate-responsive p. An electronic pacemaker that senses changes in the body's need for adjustment of the cardiac rate as can occur in sleeping, waking, sitting, walking, or running. The device alters cardiac rate by sensing body motion, changes in breathing, or slight changes in blood temperature, which improves the quality of life for active patients. It is also called a *rate-adaptive pacemaker*.

temporary p. An electronic device for temporary cardiac pacing (e.g., during cardiac surgery and emergencies). The device consists of an electrode catheter inserted transvenously in the right ventricular apex that receives impulses from an external generator.

wandering p. A cardiac arrhythmia in which the site of origin of the pacemaker stimulus shifts from one site to another, usually from the atrioventricular node to some other part of the atrium.

pacemaker lead malposition, pacemaker malposition Misplacement of an artificial pacemaker in an undesired location, e.g., into the wrong chamber of the heart through an atrial or ventricular septal defect.

pacemaker syndrome A group of unpleasant symptoms associated with unsynchronized atrioventricular timing in patients who have single-chamber (ventricular) pacemakers. The symptoms may include syncope or presyncope, orthostatic dizziness, cough, dyspnea, palpitations, and others. The symptoms are produced by the contraction of the atria against closed atrioventricular valves and by the loss of cardiac output that the atria would normally contribute to ventricular filling during diastole. DDD pacing reduces the incidence of this condition by allowing restoration of atrioventricular synchrony.

pacer Pacemaker.

pachometer (pa-kom′ĕt-ĕr) [*pachy-* + *-meter*] A device for determining the thickness of the cornea.

pachy-, pach- [Gr. *pachys,* thick] Prefixes meaning *thick.*

pachyderma (păk-ē-dĕr′mă) [″ + *derma,* skin] Unusual thickness of the skin. SEE: *elephantiasis.*

pachydermoperiostosis (păk″ē-dĕr″mō-pĕr″ē-ŏs-tō′sĭs) A hereditary form of osteoarthropathy of unknown origin marked by thickening of the skin over the face and extremities. If associated with an underlying disease, treatment of the disease may cause the symptoms and signs of this condition to disappear.

pachygyria (păk-ē-jī′rē-ă) [″ + *gyros,* a circle] Flat, broad formation of the cerebral convolutions.

pachymeningitis (păk-ē-mĕn″ĭn-jī′tĭs) [″ + *meninx,* membrane, + *itis,* inflammation] Inflammation of the dura mater. SYN: *perimeningitis.*

pachymeter (pă-kim′ĕt-ĕr) [*pachy-* + *-meter*] A device to determine the thickness of a material or object, such as the cornea.

pachymetry (pă-kĭm′ĕ-trē) Measurement of the thickness of a body part, esp. the thickness of the cornea.

pachyonychia (păk″ē-ō-nĭk′ē-ă) [Gr. *pachys,* thick, + *onyx,* nail] Abnormal thickening of the fingernails or toenails.

p. congenita A congenital condition characterized by thickening of the nails, thickening of the skin on the palms of the hands and the soles of the feet, follicular keratosis at the knees and elbows, and corneal dyskeratosis.

pachytene (păk′ē-tēn) [″ + *tainia,* band] The stage in meiosis following zygotene, in which the paired homologous chromosomes become shorter, thicker, and form tetrads; crossing over may take place.

pacifier (pas′ĭ-fī″ĕr) A nipple, usually made of a synthetic material,, provided for infants to satisfy their need to suck.

pacing (pās′ing) [L. *passus,* a step] **1.** Setting the rate or tempo of an event, esp. the heartbeat. SEE: *pacemaker.* **2.** Walking forward and back or side to side without a defined destination. It is a symptom of anxiety, stress, or of some people affected by dementia.

asynchronous p. Cardiac pacing set at a rate independent of the heart's own pacemakers. This allows pacemaking at heart rates that are faster or slower than the patient's diseased pacemaker.

DDD p. SEE: *DDD pacemaker.*

epicardial p. Electrical pacing of the heart by conductive leads inserted surgically, usually during bypass graft or valvular operations. The leads are used in the postoperative period for the management of heart blocks or dysrhythmias and are removed as the patient stabilizes.

gastric p. Artificial stimulation of gastrointestinal contractions with an implanted pulse generator. It is used to treat gastric motility disorders and morbid obesity. SYN: *gastric electrical p.*

gastric electrical p. Gastric **p.**

overdrive p. Using a pacemaker to generate a heart rate that is faster than the spontaneous heart rate of the patient. This is used in attempts to capture and terminate tachycardias or, in some cases, to try to trigger and study tachycardias in patients who have suffered them in the past.

synchronous p. Cardiac pacing set at a rate matching the underlying rate of one of the heart chambers.

transcutaneous p. The application of an electrical current between electrodes placed on the skin to stimulate the heart to beat. Typically, the electrodes are placed on the anterior and posterior chest, or to the right of the sternum and below the clavicle and on the midaxillary line at the level of the sixth to seventh ribs. Also called *external pacing, noninvasive pacing, external thoracic pacing,* and *transchest pacing.*

pacing wire SEE: under *wire.*

pacinian corpuscles (pă-sĭn'ē-ăn) [Filippo Pacini, It. anatomist, 1812–1883] Encapsulated sensory nerve endings found in subcutaneous tissue and many other parts of the body (pancreas, penis, clitoris, nipple). These corpuscles are sensitive to deep or heavy pressure. SYN: *Vater corpuscles.*

pack (pak) **1.** A dry or moist, hot or cold blanket or sheet wrapped around a patient and used for treatment. **2.** To fill up a cavity with cotton, gauze, or a similar substance.

cold p. **1.** A bulky dressing containing icewater, cubed or crushed ice, or refrigerated gel which is used topically to control pain and inflammation. SYN: *ice p.* **2.** A rarely used form of physical restraint, once popular in psychiatric practice. The restless, insomniac, or uncooperative patient was wrapped in two or more sheets that had been placed in cold water and wrung out before application, and then in heavy blankets to prevent loss of cooling and evaporation of moisture.

dry p. A procedure that is used in combination with a hot bath to induce perspiration. When leaving the hot bath, the patient is placed in a dry warm sheet and wrapped in several warm blankets.

half p. A wet-sheet pack extending from the axillae to below the knees.

hot p. A type of superficial moist heat applied to reduce pain and promote muscle relaxation. The pack is heated to 65° to 90°C in hot water. The pack is then wrapped with terrycloth prior to application. SYN: *moist heat p.*

ice p. Cold **p.**

moist heat p. Hot **p.**

starter p. A small number of pills given to a patient to initiate treatment, esp. when the treatment begins in the middle of the night or on a weekend, when a pharmacy may not be available to fill a prescription.

wet p. A form of bath given by wrapping a patient in hot or cold wet sheets, covered with a blanket, formerly used to reduce fever.

package insert An informational leaflet placed inside the container or package of prescription drugs. The U.S. Food and Drug Administration requires that the drug's generic name, indications, contraindications, adverse effects, dosage, and route of administration be described in the leaflet. SYN: *patient package insert.*

packed (pakt) In hematology, reduced in volume; concentrated. It describes the red blood cells that remain after the plasma and platelets are removed from a unit of whole blood.

packed cells, packed red blood cells ABBR: PRBCs. Red blood cells that have been separated from plasma. They are used to treat conditions such as hemorrhage or symptomatic anemias that require transfusions of red blood cells but not the liquid components of whole blood. The transfusion of PRBCs in place of whole blood elevates hemoglobin levels and reduces the likelihood of fluid overload in the recipient.

packer (păk'ĕr) A device for packing a cavity or a wound.

packing (păk'ĭng) **1.** The process of filling a cavity or wound with gauze sponges or gauze strips. **2.** Material used to fill a cavity or wound.

pack-year The consumption of a pack of cigarettes daily for a year (approx. 365 packs of cigarettes annually). The number of pack-years that people smoke correlates closely with the amount of damage that tobacco does to their hearts, lungs, and other organs.

PaCO$_2$ Partial pressure of carbon dioxide in the arterial blood; arterial carbon dioxide concentration or tension. It is usually expressed in millimeters of mercury (mm Hg).

PACS *picture archiving and communication.*

PAC-TD [An acronym for *p(ulmonary) a(rtery) c(atheter) t(hermo)d(ilution)*] An invasive technique used to measure cardiac output in the intensive care unit.

pad (pad) **1.** A cushion of soft material, usually cotton or rayon, used to apply pressure, relieve pressure, or support an organ or part. **2.** A fleshlike or fatty mass.

abdominal p. A dressing for absorbing discharges from surgical wounds of the abdomen.

buccal fat p. Sucking **p.**

dorsocervical fat p. Buffalo hump.

fat p. **1.** Sucking **p.** **2.** A layer of adipose tissue (usually capsulated) that protects structures from direct impact. Fat pads are found in various locations in the body: beneath the patellar tendon; under the calcaneus; or behind the elbow. SEE: illus.

FAT PAD

Prolapse of orbital fat pad at the lateral canthus of the eye

knuckle p. A congenital condition in which small nodules appear on the dorsal side of fingers.

laparotomy p. A gauze pad with radioopaque marker employed to absorb fluids and/ or to pack off mobile viscera intraoperatively; commonly referred to as lap pad.

Mikulicz p. SEE: under *Mikulicz-Radecki, Johann von*.

perineal p. A pad covering the perineum; used to cover a wound or to absorb the menstrual flow.

Paederus (pēd′ĕr-ŭs) [NL] A genus of beetles that contain the toxin pederin.

paedo- SEE: ² *pedo-*.

PAF *paroxysmal atrial fibrillation; platelet aggregating factor*.

Page kidney (pāj) Compression of a kidney, usually by a hematoma or tumor, with resulting hypertension.

Paget, Sir James (paj′ĕt) Brit. surgeon, 1814–1899.

extramammary P. disease A plaque with a definite margin found in the anogenital area and in the axilla. It is a rare malignant disease and is treated by surgical excision.

P. disease A chronic form of osteitis of unknown cause affecting older people, causing thickening and hypertrophy of the long bones and deformity of the flat bones. SYN: *osteitis deformans*.

SYMPTOMS: Symptoms are insidious in onset and include pain in the lower limbs (esp. the tibia), frequent fractures, waddling gait, and shortened stature. The skull often becomes enlarged, and hearing may be affected.

TREATMENT: Common treatments include bisphosphonate drugs (e.g., alendronate and etidronate). Acetaminophen, aspirin, and other nonsteroidal anti-inflammatory drugs are often used to control pain.

P. disease of the breast Carcinoma of the mammary ducts. The tumor extends to the nipple and aureola, often presenting as a red, crusty rash, scaly skin, or an oozing, eczematous discharge. The patient may complain of itching or burning. Biopsy confirms the diagnosis.

pagetoid (paj′ĕ-toyd) [*Paget* + Gr. *eidos*, form, shape] Similar to Paget's disease.

page turner An assistive technology device for persons with limited or absent upper extremity movement; used to turn the pages of a book.

pagophagia (pā″gō-fā′jē-ă) [Gr. *pagos*, frost, + *phagein*, to eat] A form of pica characterized by excessive consumption of ice or ice drinks. Causally associated with iron-deficiency anemia.

-pagus [Gr. *pagos*, fixation, thing fixed] Suffix meaning twins joined together at the site indicated in the initial part of the word.

PAH, PAHA *para-aminohippuric acid*.

pain (pān) [Fr. *peine*, fr L. *poena*, a fine, a penalty, punishment] As defined by the International Association for the Study of Pain, an unpleasant sensory and emotional experience arising from actual or potential tissue damage or described in terms of such damage. Pain includes not only the perception of an uncomfortable stimulus but also the response to that perception. About half of those who seek medical help do so because of the primary complaint of pain. Acute pain occurs with an injury or illness; is often accompanied by anxiety, diaphoresis, nausea, and vital sign changes such as tachycardia or hypertension; and should end after the noxious stimulus is removed or any organ damage heals. Chronic or persistent pain is discomfort that lasts beyond the normal healing period. Pain may arise in nearly any organ system and may have different characteristics in each. Musculoskeletal pain often is exacerbated by movement and may be accompanied by joint swelling or muscle spasm. Myofascial pain is marked by trigger-point tenderness. Visceral pain often is diffuse or vaguely localized, whereas pain from the lining of body cavities often is localized precisely, very intense, and exquisitely sensitive to palpation ormovement. Neuropathic (nerve) pain usually stings or burns, or may be described as numbness, tingling, or shooting sensations. Colicky pain fluctuates in intensity from severe to mild, and usually occurs in waves.

Usual Adult Doses and Intervals of Drugs for Relief of Pain

Nonopioid Analgesics			
Generic Name	Dose, mg *	Interval	Comments
Acetylsalicylic acid	325–650	4–24 hr	Enteric-coated preparations available
Acetaminophen	650	4 hr	Avoid in liver failure
Ibuprofen	400–800	4–8 hr	Available without prescription
Indomethacin	25–75	8 hr	Gastrointestinal and kidney side effects common
Naproxen	250–500	12 hr	Delayed effects may be due to long half-life
Ketorolac	15–60 IM	4–6 hr	Similar to ibuprofen but more potent

Opioid Analgesics			
Generic Name	Parenteral Dose (mg)	PO Dose (mg)	Comments
Codeine	30–60 every 4 hr	30–60 every 4 hr	Nausea common
Hydromorphone	1–2 every 4 hr	2–4 every 4 hr	Shorter acting than morphine sulfate
Levorphanol	2 every 6–8 hr	4 every 6 hr	Longer acting than morphine sulfate; absorbed well PO
Methadone	10–100	6–24 hr	Delayed sedation due to long half-life
Meperidine	25–100	300 every 4 hr	Poorly absorbed PO; normeperidine is a toxic metabolite
Morphine	10 every 4 hr	60 every 4 hr	
Morphine, sustained release	30–90	60–180 2 or 3 times daily	
Oxycodone	—	5–10 every 4–6 hr	Usually available with acetaminophen or aspirin

* By mouth unless indicated otherwise.
PO—by mouth only.
SOURCE: Adapted from Isselbacher, K.J., et al.: *Harrison's Principles of Internal Medicine,* ed 13. McGraw-Hill, New York, 1994.

Referred pain results when an injury or disease occurs in one body part but is felt in another.

Several factors influence the experience of pain. Among these are the nature of the injury or illness causing the symptom, the physical and emotional health of the patient, the acuity or chronicity of the symptom, the social milieu and/or cultural upbringing of the patient, neurochemistry, memory, personality, and other features. SEE: table.

SYMPTOMS: Many clinicians use the mnemonic "COLDER" to aid the diagnosis of painful diseases. They will ask the patient to describe the *C*haracter, *O*nset, *L*ocation, and *D*uration of their painful symptoms, as well as the features that *E*xacerbate or *R*elieve it. For example: The pain of pleurisy typically is sharp in character, acute in onset, located along the chest wall, and long-lasting; it is worsened by deep breathing or coughing and relieved by analgesics or holding still. By contrast, the pain of myocardial ischemia usually is dull or heavy, gradual in onset, and located substernally. It may be worsened by activity (but not by taking a breath or coughing) and relieved by nitroglycerin.

In 2000, the Joint Commission on Accreditation of Healthcare Organizations (JCAHO), since 2007 called The Joint Commission, issued pain-management standards, in 2001 began surveying for compliance, and in 2004 added patient-safety goals, thus most U.S. health care facilities have devised policies and procedures that require pain-intensity rating as a routine part of care (the fifth vital sign). Pain intensity usually is assessed on a numerical scale, in which 0 = no pain, 1 to 3 = mild pain, 4 to 6 = moderate pain, and 7 to 10 = severe pain. However, obtaining a numerical rating of pain intensity is possible only if the patient is able to provide this report of the pain being experienced, which infants, children, the critically ill, and cognitively impaired usually are unable to do. The Wong-Baker FACES scale, developed for pediatric use, has been used successfully in other patient populations. It uses visual representations of smiles or grimaces to depict the level of pain apatient feels.

PATIENT CARE: Health care professionals must be aware that pain in nonverbal patient can easily be overlooked and must make a conscious effort to ensure that pain in these patients is assessed and treated. Observing subtle behaviors and being sensitive to contextual clues are two pain methods used by health care professionals to try to determine when nonverbal patients are in pain. When this judgment is made, a trial of pain-relieving medication may be used. The responses of the patient and any complications of treatment should be carefully observed and appropriate changes made in dosing or the type of analgesic drug as indicated.

Because pain is a subjective phenomenon, sympathetic care is an important part of its relief. In addition to administering analgesic drugs, health care professionals should use a wide range of techniques to help alleviate pain, including local application of cold and heat, tactile stimulation, relaxation techniques, diversion, and active listening, among others.

acute p. Pain that typically is produced by sudden injury (e.g., fracture) or illness (e.g., acute infection) and is accompanied by physical signs such as increased heart rate, elevated blood pressure, pupillary dilation, sweating, or hyperventilation. Acute pain is typically sharp in character. It is relayed to the central nervous system rapidly by A delta nerve fibers. Depending on the severity of the underlying stimulus, acute pain may be managed with acetaminophen or anti-inflammatory drugs, immobilization and elevation of the injured body part, or the topical application of heat or ice. Severe acute pain, such as that of broken ribs or of an ischemic part, may require narcotics, often with adjunctive agents like hydroxyzine for relief, or antiemetics. Acute pain should be managed aggressively. SYN: *fast p.* SEE: *Nursing Diagnoses Appendix.*

back p. Pain felt in or along the spine or musculature of the posterior thorax. It is usually characterized by dull, continuous pain and tenderness in the muscles or their attachments in the lower lumbar, lumbosacral, or sacroiliac regions. Back pain is often referred to the leg or legs, following the distribution of the sciatic nerve.

ETIOLOGY: Common causes of back pain include pain caused by muscular or tendon strain, herniated intervertebral disk, lumbar spinal stenosis, or spondylolisthesis. Patients with a history of cancer may have back pain caused by metastatic tumors to the vertebrae and should be evaluated to be certain that damage to the spinal cord is not imminent. Patients with back pain and fever (esp. those with a history of injection drug use, tuberculosis, or recent back surgery) should be evaluated for epidural abscess or osteomyelitis.

TREATMENT: Depending on the underlying cause of the back pain, treatment may include drugs, rest, massage, physical therapy, chiropractic, stretching exercises, injection therapy, and surgery. Most nonmalignant causes of back pain improve with a few days of rest, analgesics, and antiinflammatory drugs, followed by 2 to 4 weeks of antiinflammatory treatment, appropriate muscle strengthening, and patience. Pain caused by an osteoporotic fracture may prove more debilitating and longer-lasting. Back pain produced by a spinal metastasis can improve with corticosteroids, radiation therapy, intravenous bisphosphonates, and/or surgical decompression. Patients with a spinal epidural abscess will need surgical drainage of the infection and antibiotics.

PATIENT CARE: Prolonged bedrest is inadvisable in most patients with back pain. The treatment regimen is explained, implemented, and reinforced. Factors that precipitate symptoms are identified and preventive actions are discussed.

bearing-down p. Rectal pressure and discomfort occurring during the second stage of labor, related to fetal descent and the woman's straining efforts to expel the fetus.

boring p. Piercing pain felt deep within the body.

breakthrough p. Transient episodes of pain that occur in patients with chronic pain that has been previously reduced to tolerable levels. Breakthrough pain disrupts the well-being of cancer or hospice patients who have been prescribed regular doses of narcotic analgesics. The painful episodes may occur as a previous dose of pain-relieving medication wears off ("end-of-dose pain"), or after unusual or unanticipated body movements ("incident pain").

burning p. Pain experienced in heat burns, superficial skin lesions, herpes zoster, and circumscribed neuralgias.

central p. Pain due to a lesion in the central nervous system.

chest p. Pain in the upper abdomen, thorax, neck, or shoulders. Chest pain is one of the most common potentially serious complaints offered by patients in emergency departments, hospitals, outpatient settings, and physicians' offices. A broad array of diseases and conditions may cause it, including (but not limited to) angina pectoris or myocardial infarction; anxiety and hyperventilation; aortic dissection; costochondritis or injured ribs; cough, pneumonia, pleurisy, pneumothorax, or pulmonary emboli; esophageal diseases, such as reflux or esophagitis; gastritis, duodenitis, or peptic ulcer; and stones in the biliary tree.

chronic p. **1.** Long-lasting discomfort, with episodic exacerbations, that may be felt in the back, one or more joints, the pelvis, or other parts of the body. **2.** Pain that lasts more than 3–6 months. **3.** Pain that lasts more than a month longer than the usual or expected course of an illness. **4.** Pain that returns periodically every few weeks or months for many years. Chronic pain is often described by sufferers as being debilitating, intolerable, disabling, or alienating and may occur without an easily identifiable cause. Studies have shown a high correlation between chronic pain and depression or dysphoria, but it is unclear whether the psychological aspects of chronic pain precede or develop as a result of a person's subjective suffering. Chronic pain is the leading cause of disability in the U.S. SEE: *acute p.; Nursing Diagnoses Appendix.*

PATIENT CARE: The management of chronic, nonmalignant pain is often difficult and may be frustrating for both sufferer and caregiver. The best results are usually obtained through multimodal therapy that combines sympathetic guidance that encourages patients to recover functional abilities, by combinations of drugs (e.g., nonsteroidal anti-inflammatories, narcotic analgesics, and/ or antidepressants), physical therapy and regular exercise, occupational therapy, physiatry, psychological or social counseling, and alternative medical therapies (e.g., acupuncture, massage, or relaxation techniques). Placebos, although rarely employed clinically, effectively treat chronic pain in about a third of all patients. Surgery and other invasive strategies are occasionally employed, with variable effectiveness.

dental p. Pain in the oral area, which, in general, may be of two origins. Soft tissue pain may be acute or chronic, and a burning pain is due to surface lesions and usually can be discretely localized; pulpal pain or tooth pain varies according to whether it is acute or chronic, but it is often difficult to localize.

diskogenic p. Low back pain resulting from degeneration of an intervertebral disk. Discogenic pain differs from neuropathic pain in that it does not radiate into the extremities or torso.

dull p. A mild discomfort, often difficult to describe, that may be associated with some musculoskeletal injuries or some diseases of the visceral organs.

epigastric p. Pain located between the xiphoid process and the umbilicus. It may suggest a problem in one of many different organs, including the stomach, pancreas, gallbladder, small or large bowel, pleura, or heart. SYN: *gastralgic* **p.** SEE: *cardialgia.*

fast p. Acute **p.**

gas p. Pain in the intestines caused by an accumulation of gas therein.

girdle p. Zonesthesia.

growing p. An imprecise term indicating ill-defined pain, usually in the shin or other areas of the legs, typically occurring after bedtime in children age 5 to 12. There is no evidence that the pain is related to rapid growth or to emotional problems. If these symptoms occur during the daytime, are accompanied by other symptoms, or become progressively more severe, evaluation for infection, cancer, and other diseases of muscle and bone should be undertaken. In the majority of cases, this evaluation is not necessary.

TREATMENT: The child should be reassured and given acetaminophen or ibuprofen; heat and massage can be applied locally. Children with growing pains benefit from concern and reassurance from their parents and health care providers.

incident p. Pain due to a sudden, forceful, unanticipated, or unusual body movement or posture.

inflammatory p. Pain in the presence of inflammation that is increased by pressure.

intractable p. Chronic pain that is difficult or impossible to manage by usual means. Common causes include metastatic cancer, chronic pancreatitis, radiculopathy, spinal cord transection, or peripheral neuropathy. Intractable pain may also accompany somatoform disorders, depression, fibromyalgia, irritable bowel syndrome, and opiate dependence. Various combinations of the following management strategies are often used to treat intractable pain: antidepressant medications, counseling, deep brain stimulation, injected anesthetics, narcotic analgesics, neurological surgery, and pain clinic consultations.

labor p. Uncomfortable, intermittent, rhythmic, girdling sensations associated with uterine contractions during childbearing. The frequency, duration, and intensity of the events increase, climaxing with the delivery of the fetus.

lancinating p. Acute **p.**

menstrual p. Dysmenorrhea.

movement p. Kinesalgia.

neuropathic p. Pain that originates in peripheral nerves or the central nervous system rather than in other damaged organs or tissues. A hallmark of neuropathic pain is its localization to specific dermatomes or nerve distributions. Some examples of neuropathic pain are the pain of shingles (herpes zoster), diabetic neuropathy, radiculopathy, and phantom limb pain.

TREATMENT: Drugs like gabapentin or pregabalin provide effective relief of neuropathic pain for some patients. Other treatments include regional nerve blocks, selective serotonin and norepinephrine reuptake inhibitors, psychological counseling, acupuncture, transcutaneous electrical nerve stimulation, and physical therapy.

night p. Pain that awakens the patient at night or interferes with sleep; may be due to infection, inflammation, neurovascular compromise, or severe structural damage.

objective p. Pain induced by some external or internal irritant, by inflammation, or by injury to nerves, organs, or other tissues that interferes with the function, nutrition, or circulation of the affected part. It is usually traceable to a definite pathologic process.

phantom limb p. The sensation of pain felt in the nerve distribution of a body part that has been amputated. Phantom pain can lead to difficulties in prosthetic training. SYN: *phantom sensation*.

PATIENT CARE: Phantom limb pain or nonpainful sensations are reported by most amputees. A multimodal or combination approach to management is appropriate. Drugs used to treat neuropathic pain may be helpful, including some anticonvulsant drugs, tricyclic antidepressants, selective serotonin inhibitors, and muscle relaxants. Nerve blockade and/or transcutaneous electrical stimulation may also be helpful. Health care professionals should encourage amputees to move the affected extremity, seek counseling or group therapy, engage in physical and occupational therapy, and use distraction techniques.

postprandial p. Abdominal pain after eating.

precordial p. Pain felt in the center of the chest (e.g., below the sternum) or in the left side of the chest.

psychogenic p. Pain having mental, as opposed to organic, origin.

radicular p. Pain that radiates away from the spinal column through an extremity or the torso resulting from the compression or irritation of a spinal nerve root or large paraspinal nerve. It may be accompanied by numbness or tingling.

referred p. Pain that arises in one body part or location but is perceived in another. For example, pain caused by inflammation of the diaphragm often is felt in the shoulder; pain caused by myocardial ischemia may be referred to the neck or jaw; and pain caused by appendicitis may first be felt near the umbilicus rather than in the right lower quadrant, where the appendix lies. SEE: table. SYN: *heterotopic p.; sympathetic p.* SEE: illus.

rest p. Pain due to ischemia that comes on when sitting or lying.

root p. Cutaneous pain caused by disease of the sensory nerve roots.

shooting p. Pain that seems to travel like lightning from one place to another.

slow p. Pain that is perceived a second or more after a stimulus. It is transmitted to the central nervous system by

Sites of Referred Pain

Organ of Origin	Location Felt
Head	External or middle ear
Nose & sinuses	
Teeth, gums, tongue	
Throat, tonsils	
Parotid gland, TMJ joint	
Thorax	
Diaphragm	Shoulder, upper abdomen
Heart	Upper chest, L shoulder, inside L arm, L jaw
Abdomen	
Stomach & spleen	L upper abdomen
Duodenum	Upper abdomen, R shoulder
Stomach & spleen	L upper abdomen
Stomach & spleen	L upper abdomen
Stomach & spleen	L upper abdomen
Colon	Lower abdomen
Appendix	Periumbilical and R lower abdomen
Pelvis	
Appendix	Periumbilical and R lower abdomen

NOTE: L = left; R = right.

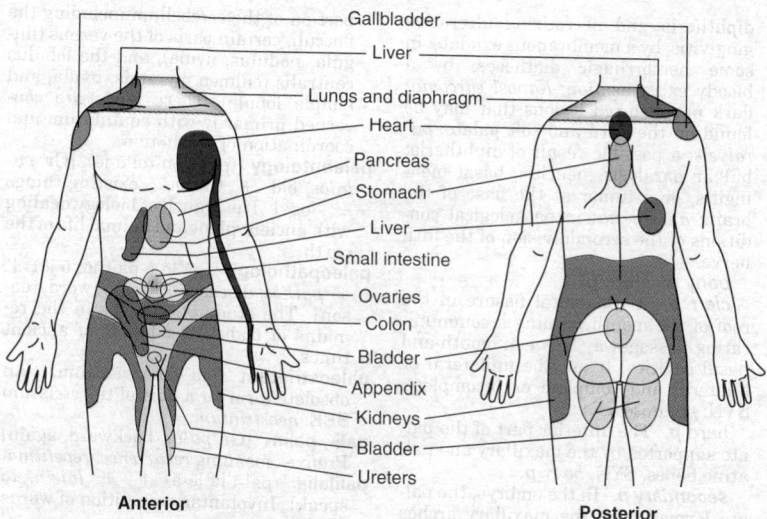

- Gallbladder
- Liver
- Lungs and diaphragm
- Heart
- Pancreas
- Stomach
- Liver
- Small intestine
- Ovaries
- Colon
- Bladder
- Appendix
- Kidneys
- Bladder
- Ureters

Anterior   **Posterior**

SITES OF REFERRED PAIN

C (nerve) fibers, which are not myelinated, and therefore conduct sensations more slowly than A delta fibers. Slow pain lasts longer than sudden pain. It is usually perceived by patients as burning, cramping, dull, itchy, or warm.

   sympathetic p. Referred **p.**

   thalamic p. SEE: *thalamic syndrome.*

   thoracic p. Chest pain.

   throbbing p. Pain found in dental caries, headache, and localized inflammation. The pain is often thought to be caused by arterial pulsations.

   vascular p. Pain that throbs or pulses, such as the pain of a migraine headache.

   wandering p. Pain that changes its location repeatedly.

pain agreement Drug contract.

pain and suffering Psychological distress or discomfort experienced as a result of an injury. Estimates of pain and suffering are used to determine the extent of a patient's award in malpractice cases and the residual disability a patient may have.

pain disorder A disorder in which pain is the predominant symptom, is of such severity to warrant clinical attention, and interferes with function. Psychological factors are important in the onset, severity, exacerbation, or maintenance of the pain. The condition is not intentionally produced or feigned.

painful arc SEE: under *arc.*

painful bladder syndrome A colloquial, commonly used term for interstitial nephritis.

painkiller, pain killer (pān'kil"ĕr) A colloquial term for a medication or a procedure that decreases a patient's dis-

comfort caused by pain or alleviates hurtful or unpleasant sensations.

paint (pānt) **1.** A solution of medication for application to the skin. **2.** To apply a medicated liquid to the skin.

pain threshold SEE: under *threshold.*

pair (par) Two of anything similar in shape, size, and conformation.

   base p. In the double-stranded helical arrangement of DNA, the complementary purine-pyrimidine nucleotide bases (adenine-thymidine or guanine-cytosine) that are linked by weak chemical bonds. The order of these base pairs encode the genetic information in each segment of DNA.

   ion p. Two particles of opposite charge, usually an electron and a proton.

PAL *posterior axillary line.*

palatable (pǎl'ăt-ă-b'l) [L. *palatum,* palate] Pleasing to the palate or taste, as food.

palatal (pǎl'ă-tăl) Pert. to the roof of the mouth, the palate.

palatal myoclonus SEE: under *myoclonus.*

palate (pal'ăt) [L. *palatum,* palate] The horizontal structure separating the mouth and the nasal cavity; the roof of the mouth, supported anteriorly by the maxillae and palatine bones. SEE: *mouth* for illus.

   DISEASES AFFECTING THE PALATE: *Koplik spots*: a rash frequently seen on the palate in measles; *secondary syphilis*: mucous patches on the palate; *herpes of the throat*: vesicles on the pharyngeal walls and soft palate; *swelling of uvula*: noted in inflammations of pharynx and tonsil and in nephritis, severe anemia, and angioneurotic edema; in diphtheria and necrotizing ulcerative gingivitis, by a membranous exudate; in some hemorrhagic diatheses, by a bloody extravasation; *Kaposi sarcoma*: dark purplish-red lesions that may be found on the hard and soft palate; *paralysis*: a possible result of diphtheria, bulbar paralysis, neuritis, basal meningitis, or a tumor at the base of the brain; *anesthesia*: in pathological conditions of the seconddivision of the fifth nerve.

    bony p. Hard **p.**

    cleft p. A congenital fissure in the roof of the mouth forming a communicating passageway between mouth and nasal cavities. It may be unilateral or bilateral and complete or incomplete. SYN: *palatoschisis.*

    hard p. The anterior part of the palate supported by the maxillary and palatine bones. SYN: *bony p.*

    secondary p. In the embryo, the palate formed from the maxillary arches and frontonasal processes.

    soft p. A musculomembranous fold that partly separates the mouth and the pharynx; the posterior roof of the mouth. It is elevated during swallowing to block the nasopharynx.

palatine (păl′ă-tīn) [L. *palatinus*] **1.** Pert. to the palate. **2.** Pert. to the rear palatal bone.

palatoglossal (păl″ă-tō-glŏs′ăl) Pert. to the palate and tongue.

palatoglossus (păl″ă-tō-glŏs′ŭs) [″ + Gr. *glossa*, tongue] The muscle arising from the sides and undersurface of the tongue. Fibers pass upward through glossopalatine arch and are inserted in palatine aponeurosis. It constricts the faucial isthmus by raising the root of the tongue and drawing the sides of the soft palate downward.

palatopharyngeal (păl″ă-tō-fă-rĭn′jē-ăl) Pert. to the palate and pharynx.

palatopharyngeus (păl″ăt-ō-fă″rĭn′jē-ŭs) [″ + Gr. *pharynx*, throat] The muscle arising from thyroid cartilage and pharyngeal wall, extending upward in posterior pillar, and inserting into aponeurosis of soft palate. It constricts the pharyngeal isthmus, raises the larynx, and depresses the soft palate.

palatopharyngoplasty (păl″ă-tō-fă-rĭng′gō-plăs″tē) Plastic surgical procedure for decreasing the size of the opening of the nasopharyngeal passageway. It has been used to treat chronic snoring.

palatoplasty (păl′ăt-ō-plăs″tē) [″ + Gr. *plassein*, to form] Plastic surgery of the palate, usually to correct a cleft. SEE: *staphylorrhaphy.*

palatoschisis (păl-ă-tŏs′kĭ-sĭs) [″ + *schisis*, a splitting] Cleft palate.

paleocerebellum (păl″ē-ō-sĕr″ĕ-bĕl′ŭm) [Gr. *palaios*, old, + L. *cerebellum*, little brain] Phylogenetically, the older portion of the cerebellum including the flocculi, certain parts of the vermis (lingula, nodulus, uvula), and the lobulus centralis (culmen, pyramis, uvula, and simple lobule). These parts are concerned primarily with equilibrium and coordination of locomotion.

paleontology (pā″lē-on″tol′ŏ-jē) [Gr. *palaios*, old + Gr. *onta*, existing things + *-logy*] The branch of biology dealing with ancient plant and animal life of the earth.

paleopathology (pā″lē-ō-pă-thŏl′ō-jē) [″ + *pathos*, disease, + *logos*, word, reason] The study of diseases in the remains of bodies and fossils of ancient times.

paleostriatum (pā″lē-ō-strī-ā′tŭm) An obsolete term for a part of the striatum SEE: *neostriatum.*

pali-, palin- [Gr. *palin*, backward, again] Prefixes meaning *recurrence, repetition.*

palilalia (păl-ĭ-lā′lē-ă) [″ + *lalein*, to speak] Involuntary repetition of words or phrases.

palindromic (păl-ĭn-drŏm′ĭk) Relapsing.

palinopsia (păl″ĭn-ŏp′sē-ă) [″ + *opsis*, vision] Persistence of a visual image after the object has been removed. It may be associated with a lesion in the occipital lobe of the brain. SEE: *afterimage.*

palladium (pă-lād′ē-ŭm) [L. *palladium,* named after the contemporaneous (1803) discovery of the asteroid *Pallas* (Athena)] SYMB: Pd. A transition metal; atomic weight 106.4; atomic number 46. It is used in dentistry and surgical instruments.

palliate (păl′ē-āt) [L. *palliatus,* cloaked] To ease or reduce effect or intensity, esp. of a disease; to allay temporarily, as pain, without curing.

palliation (păl″ē-ā′shŭn) [L. *palliare,* to cloak, conceal] The alleviation of some aspects of a disease, e.g., the reduction of the pain and suffering accompanying an illness.

palliative (păl′ē-ā″tĭv) **1.** Relieving or alleviating without curing. **2.** An agent that alleviates or eases a painful or uncomfortable condition.

palliative sedation SEE: under *sedation.*

palliative treatment Treatment designed to relieve symptoms of disease rather than to cure it. SEE: table.

pallid (păl′ĭd) [L. *pallidus,* pale] Lacking color, pale, wan.

pallidal (păl′ĭ-dăl) Concerning the pallidum of the brain.

pallidotomy (păl″ĭ-dŏt′ō-mē) [″ + Gr. *tome,* incision] Surgical destruction of the globus pallidus done to treat involuntary movements or muscular rigidity. The procedure is used experimentally in treating patients with Parkinson's disease.

pallidum (păl′ĭ-dŭm) [L.] The globus pallidus of the lenticular nucleus in the corpus striatum.

Important Considerations in Palliative Care

Communication

How should patients be informed of their illness and prognosis?
Who meets the ongoing information needs of patients and their loved ones?

Symptom Management

Does the patient have pain? How is it to be alleviated?
Does the patient have difficulty breathing?
Does the patient have nausea and/or vomiting?
Does the patient have difficulties with nutrition?
With oral ulcerations or dry mouth?
With constipation or bowel obstruction?
With dehydration?
With incontinence?
With immobility?
With insomnia and other sleep disturbances?
With delirium?
With depression?
With adverse drug reactions?
With excessive sedation?
What techniques will be used to help manage patients with specific illnesses (e.g., AIDS, cancer, dementias, heart failure, renal failure, stroke, among others)?

Treatment Issues

Which procedures or treatments would the patient like to have?
Which should patient like to avoid?
How will complementary or alternative therapies be incorporated into management of the illness?
When are transfusions indicated?
What role does chemotherapy, radiotherapy, or surgery play in palliation?

Social Needs

How will family or friends support the patient during the illness?
How will their needs be met?
Will someone be designated to serve as family spokesperson?
How will children learn about the illness, or the impending death of a family member?
Do patients have culturally specific issues the care team needs to address?

Institutional Issues

Where will palliative care take place? (Home? Day care? Hospice? Nursing home? Hospital? Prison? Psychiatric institution?)
What staff members will help provide care for the affected person?
How are professional staff educated in the art and science of palliation?
How is continuing education to be provided to staff?
How will errors in palliation be addressed?
What mechanisms are in place for feedback from patients or their loved ones?
For self-criticism by the palliative team?

Legal Issues

What laws or regulations govern the use of palliative methods in the community?
Does the patient have an advanced directive regarding life-sustaining therapies?
Has the patient designated a decision maker to guide palliative efforts, should the need arise?

Financial Issues

Who pays for care?
How do budget constraints limit or define care?

Important Considerations in Palliative Care (Continued)

Spiritual Needs

Are the philosophical and/or spiritual needs of the patient being met?
Is the patient having difficulties with existential issues (meaning of life? meaning of death? imminence of death?)?

Issues at the End of Life

Has the patient expressed an interest in life support? What limits, if any, has the patient specified?
Has the patient expressed an interest in hospice care?
Has the patient expressed an interest in physician assistance to hasten death?

Issues after Death

How will the grief and bereavement issues of the patient's closest partners be addressed?
What follow-up will be provided to grieving friends and family?

pallium (păl′ē-ŭm) [L., cloak] The cerebral cortex and its adjacent white matter.

pallor (păl′or) [L. *pallor,* paleness] Lack of color; paleness.

palm [L. *palma,* hand] The anterior or flexor surface of the hand from the wrist to the fingers. SYN: *palma; vola manus.* SEE: *thenar.*

palma (păl′mă) [L.] Palm.

palm and sole system of identification A system based on prints of the palmar surface of the hand and the plantar surface of the foot. SEE: *dermatoglyphics.*

palmar (păl′măr) Pert. to the palm of the hand.

    p. cuff Universal cuff.

palmaris (păl-mā′rĭs) One of two muscles, palmaris brevis and palmaris longus.

palmar-plantar erythrodysesthesia A toxic effect of chemotherapy, characterized by burning or tingling discomfort in the hands and the soles of the feet occurring after the administration of cancer chemotherapy. Red, violet, and swollen skin may develop on the hands and feet and may shed, crust, or ulcerate. Additional cycles of chemotherapy worsen the effect.

palmitin (păl′mĭ-tĭn) An ester of glycerol and palmitic acid, derived from fat of both animal and vegetable origin.

palmoplantar (păl″mō-plăn′tăr) Pert. to the palms of the hands and soles of the feet.

palpable (păl′pă-b'l) [L. *palpabilis,* stroke, touch] Perceptible, esp. by touch.

palpate (păl′pāt) [L. *palpare,* to touch] To examine by touch; to feel.

palpation (păl-pā′shŭn) [L. *palpatio*] **1.** Examination by application of the hands or fingers to the external surface of the body to detect evidence of disease or abnormalities in the internal organs. **2.** In obstetrics, a technique used to evaluate fetal presentation and position; frequency, duration, and strength of uterine contractions; status of membranes; cervical effacement and dilation; and fetal station.

palpebra (păl′pĕ-bră) *pl.* **palpebrae** [L.] An eyelid.

    p. superior The upper eyelid.

palpebral (păl′pĕ-brăl) Concerning an eyelid.

palpitate (păl′pĭ-tāt) [L. *palpitatus,* throbbing] **1.** To cause to throb. **2.** To throb or beat intensely or rapidly, usually said of the heart.

palpitation (păl-pĭ-tā′shŭn) A sensation of rapid or irregular beating of the heart. The beating may be described as a thudding sensation, a fluttering, or a throbbing that is felt beneath the sternum or in the neck. In clinical practice, most palpitations are felt by patients with benign premature ventricular or atrial contractions. In these patients, the sensation, although disturbing, is not associated with serious heart disease. Occasionally palpitations are caused by sustained arrhythmias, such as atrial fibrillation, atrial flutter, paroxysmal supraventricular tachycardia, or ventricular tachycardia. Electrocardiography, outpatient cardiac monitoring, or cardiology consultation may be needed to determine whether a patient's symptoms are benign or hazardous. **palpitant,** *adj.*

palpography (păl-pŏg′ră-fē) [Fm. *palp(ate)* + ″] A method of imaging atherosclerotic plaques with intravascular ultrasonography, in which the movement of arterial walls in response to arterial pulse pressure is measured. The greater the deformation of the arterial wall, the more the strain on the wall and therefore the greater its soft lipid content.

PALS (pălz) *pediatric advanced life support.*

palsy (pal′zē) [Fr. *palesie, paralisie,* fr L. *paralysis,* fr Gr. *paralysis,* loosening, disabling] Paralysis.

    birth p. SEE: *birth paralysis.*

brachial p. SEE: *birth paralysis.*

bulbar p. Palsy caused by degeneration of the nuclear cells of the lower cranial nerves. This causes progressive muscular paralysis.

cerebral p. ABBR: CP. SEE: *cerebral palsy.*

Erb p. SEE: *Duchenne-Erb paralysis.*

facial p. SEE: *Bell palsy.*

facial nerve p. SEE: *Bell palsy.*

lead p. Paralysis of the extremities in lead poisoning.

night p. A form of paresthesia characterized by numbness, esp. at night.

peroneal nerve p. Paralysis of the peroneal nerve, often caused by automobile accidents in which a pedestrian's leg is injured, by fractures of the tibia, or by other occurrences of nerve disruption or compression. It produces footdrop.

pressure p. SEE: *compression paralysis.*

progressive supranuclear p. A chronic progressive degenerative disease of the central nervous system that has its onset in middle age. Common symptoms include difficulty walking (with frequent falls), impairments in speech and in swallowing, and an inability to gaze upward.

Saturday night p. Paralysis due to prolonged ischemia of the musculospiral nerve incident to compressing an arm against a hard edge. It occurs if the patient has been comatose or in a stupor or has fallen asleep with the arm hanging over the edge of a bed or chair. In some cultures individuals traditionally become intoxicated on Saturday night; while stuporous, they may remain in a position that allows nerve compression. SYN: *musculospiral paralysis; radial paralysis; Saturday night paralysis; Sunday morning paralysis.*

Palv *pressure in the alveolus.*

PAMP *pathogen-associated molecular patterns.*

pampiniform (păm-pĭn'ĭ-form) [L. *pampinus,* tendril, + *forma,* shape] Convoluted like a tendril.

pan-, pano- [Gr. *pas, pan,* all] Prefixes meaning *all.*

panacea (păn-ă-sē'ă) [Gr. *panakeia,* universal remedy] A remedy for all ills; a cure-all.

panagglutinin (păn″ă-glu'tĭn-ĭn) [Gr. *pan,* all, + L. *agglutinare,* to glue to] A substance capable of agglutinizing corpuscles of every blood group.

panarteritis (păn″ăr-tĕ-rī'tĭs) [Gr. *pan,* all, + *arteria,* artery, + *itis,* inflammation] Inflammation of all three layers of an artery (intima, media, and adventitia).

Panax (pā'naks″) [L. *panax,* fr Gr. *panax,* fr *panakēs,* all-healing] A genus of slow-growing perennial plants with fleshy roots, native to the cooler climates of Korea, northern China, and eastern Siberia, certain species of which are used in alternative medicine. SEE: *ginseng.*

P. ginseng The variety of ginseng used most often in herbal remedies. SYN: *Asian ginseng; Chinese ginseng; Korean ginseng.*

P. japonicus SEE: *Japanese ginseng.*

P. notoginseng A species native to China and Japan, used in Chinese medicine to treat blood deficiencies and as a hemostatic. SYN: *P. pseudoginseng.*

P. pseudoginseng *P.* notoginseng.

P. quinquefolius SEE: *American ginseng.*

panbronchiolitis, diffuse (păn″brŏng-kē-ō-lī'tĭs) [Gr. *pan,* entire, + L. *bronchiolus,* air passage, + Gr. *-itis,* inflammation of] A rare chronic obstructive lung disease in which small lung nodules form, sometimes in association with sinus disease. It is typically found in people of Japanese ancestry.

pancarditis (păn-kăr-dī'tĭs) [″ + *kardia,* heart, + *itis,* inflammation] Inflammation of all the structures of the heart.

PANCE *Physician Assistant National Certifying Exam.*

Pancoast syndrome (pan'kōst″) [Henry Khunrath Pancoast, U.S. physician, 1875–1939] A cluster of signs and symptoms that include upper extremity or shoulder pain, Horner syndrome, and atrophy of muscle or bone of the affected arm. It almost always is caused by a malignant neoplasm invading the brachial plexus and cervical sympathetic nerves. Rarely, it results from a tubercular or fungal infection of the same nerves.

Pancoast tumor A tumor (usually from lung cancer) that spreads from the superior pulmonary sulcus into the brachial plexus and cervical sympathetic chain, producing Pancoast syndrome.

pancreas (pang'krē-ăs, pan', pan-krē'ăt-ă) *pl.* **pancreata** [*pan-* + Gr. *kreas,* flesh, meat] A compound acinotubular gland located behind the stomach and in front of the first and second lumbar vertebrae. The head lies within the curve of the duodenum, the tail lies near the spleen, and the middle portion constitutes the body. The pancreas is both an exocrine and an endocrine organ. The exocrine glands are acini, each with its own duct; these ducts anastomose to form the main pancreatic duct or duct of Wirsung, which joins the common bile duct and empties into the duodenum at the hepatopancreatic ampulla. An accessory pancreatic duct or duct of Santorini is often present and opens into the duodenum directly. Scattered throughout the exocrine glandular tissue are

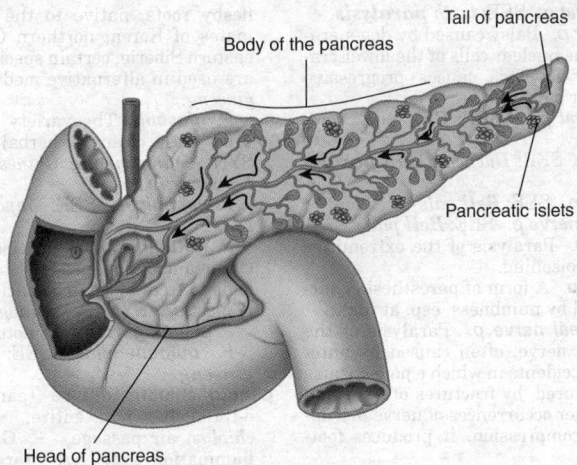

Tail of pancreas

Body of the pancreas

Pancreatic islets

Head of pancreas

PANCREAS

masses of cells called islets of Langerhans, endocrine glands that secrete hormones. SEE: illus.

FUNCTION: The exocrine secretion of the pancreas consists of enzymes that digest food in the small intestine, and sodium bicarbonate to neutralize hydrochloric acid from the stomach in the duodenum. SEE: *pancreatic juice.*

The islets of Langerhans contain alpha, beta, and delta cells. Alpha cells secrete glucagon, which raises blood glucose; beta cells secrete insulin, which lowers blood glucose; delta cells secrete somatostatin, which inhibits the secretion of insulin, glucagon, growth hormone from the anterior pituitary, and gastrin from the stomach.

DISEASES OF THE PANCREAS: Autoimmune damage to the islets of Langerhans results in type 1 diabetes mellitus, a disease in which insulin secretion is insufficient or completely absent. Insulin-secreting tumors of the pancreas, called insulinomas, produce hypoglycemia; they are exceptionally rare. Inflammation of the pancreas, known as pancreatitis, is a common condition that often results from excessive use of alcohol or from obstruction of the exocrine secretions of the pancreas by gallstones. Pancreas divisum is a common congenital anomaly in which the main duct of the exocrine pancreas drains into an accessory pancreatic papilla instead of the duodenal papilla; it has been associated with recurring episodes of pancreatitis. SEE: *diabetes mellitus; insulin; pancreatic function test.*

    accessory p. A small mass of pancreatic tissue close to the pancreas but detached from it.

    annular p. An anomalous condition in which a portion of the pancreas encircles the duodenum.

    p. divisum A congenital anomaly in which the dorsal and ventral pancreatic ducts fail to unite during embryonic development. It has been associated with pancreatitis.

    dorsal p. A dorsal outpocketing of the embryonic gut that gives rise to the body and tail of the adult pancreas.

    ventral p. An outgrowth at the angle of the hepatic diverticulum and the embryonic gut that migrates and fuses with the dorsal pancreas. It forms the head of the definitive organ.

pancreat-, pancreato- [L. fr. Gr. *pankreas,* stem *pankreat-,* pancreas] Prefixes meaning *pancreas.*

pancreatectomy (păn″krē-ă-těk′tō-mē) [″ + ″ + *ektome,* excision] An operation for removal of part or all of the pancreas. Total pancreatectomy produces diabetes mellitus due to the removal of insulin-producing cells. Exogenous insulin must be administered. After a subtotal (or partial) pancreatectomy, diabetes may develop some time later because the remaining islets may be unable to take care of the increased demands placed on them. SEE: *diabetes.*

pancreatic (păn″krē-ăt′ĭk) [Gr. *pan,* all, + *kreas,* flesh] Pert. to the pancreas.

pancreatic function tests Any of several noninvasive tests used to assess the health of the exocrine pancreas, typically by assessing the levels of certain enzymes or digestive products in blood, feces, or urine. Some examples are the amino acid consumption test, the NBT-PABA test, and the pancreatolauryl test. None of these tests perfectly reflects pancreatic function. SEE: *oral glucose tolerance test.*

pancreatic juice SEE: under *juice.*

pancreaticoduodenal (păn″krē-ăt″ĭ-kō-dū-ō-dē′năl) [″ + ″ + L. *duodeni,* twelve] Pert. to the duodenum and pancreas.

pancreaticoduodenectomy (pang″krē-at″ĭ-kō″doo″ŏ-dē-nek′tŏ-mē) A surgical treatment for cancer of the head of the pancreas in which the pancreatic head is surgically removed, along with adjacent organs (the last portion of the bile duct and the stomach and the duodenum). SYN: *Whipple procedure.*

pancreaticogastrostomy (păn″krē-ăt″ĭ-kō-găs-trŏs′tō-mē) [″ + ″ + *gaster,* belly, + *stoma,* mouth] Surgical creation of a passage between the transected end of the pancreas and the stomach. Pancreaticocystogastrostomy is the anastomosis of pancreatic pseudocyst and the stomach.

pancreaticojejunostomy (păn″krē-ăt″ĭ-kō-jĕ″jū-nŏs′tō-mē) [″ + ″ + L. *jejunum,* empty, + Gr. *stoma,* mouth] Surgical creation of a passage between the pancreatic duct or the transected end of the pancreas and jejunum.

pancreatin (păn′krē-ă-tĭn) [Gr. *pan,* all, + *kreas,* flesh] **1.** One of the enzymes of the pancreas. **2.** A mixture of enzymes, chiefly amylase, lipase, and protease.

ACTION/USES: It is used chiefly in patients with chronic pancreatitis, who do not secrete adequate amounts of their own pancreatic enzymes.

pancreatitis (pang″krē-ă-tīt′ĭs, pan″) [*pancreat-* + *-itis*] Inflammation of the pancreas, sometimes accompanied by damage to neighboring organs (e.g., the bowel, lungs, spleen, or stomach) or by a systemic inflammatory response. SEE: *acute* ***p.****; chronic* ***p.****; Nursing Diagnoses Appendix.*

acute p. Pancreatitis of sudden onset, marked by epigastric pain, nausea, vomiting, and elevated serum pancreatic enzymes. Varying degrees of pancreatic inflammation, autodigestion, necrosis, hemorrhage, gangrene, or pseudocyst formation may develop. The disease may be relatively mild, resolving in 3 or 4 days, or severe enough to cause multiple organ system failure, shock, and death (in about 5% of patients). The patient may assume a sitting or fetal position in attempting to ease the pain because lying supine or walking tends to increase discomfort.

ETIOLOGY: Alcohol abuse and obstruction of the pancreatic duct by gallstones are the most common causes of the disease. Pancreatitis may also result from exposure to drugs (e.g., thiazide diuretics or pentamidine), hypertriglyceridemia, hypercalcemia,

abdominal trauma, or viral infections (e.g., mumps or coxsackievirus).

TREATMENT: The patient receives nothing by mouth until pain, nausea, and vomiting have resolved and diagnostic markers (e.g., serum lipase level) show evidence of normalizing. Standard supportive measures include the administration of fluids and electrolytes, sometimes in massive quantities if dehydration or third-spacing of fluids in the abdomen occurs.

⚠ Refeeding patients before pancreatic inflammation has resolved may cause a relapse.

PROGNOSIS: Several techniques are used to determine how well (or how poorly) patients with pancreatitis will progress during their illness and whether they may benefit from intensive care. The best of these is the Acute Physiology and Chronic Health Evaluation (APACHE II) system; it grades patients with pancreatitis on the basis of 14 measurable physiological parameters, including the patient's body temperature, heart rate, mean arterial pressure, respiratory rate, serum creatinine and sodium levels, arterial pH, white blood cell count, Glasgow coma scale, and age.

Other methods for determining the severity of illness in pancreatitis rely on abnormalities seen on computed tomography (CT) imaging or the measurement of other physiological criteria, including the serum calcium and glucose levels, fluid deficit, and liver function.

PATIENT CARE: Intravenous fluids, antiemetics, and pain relievers are administered parenterally. A nasogastric tube may be inserted and placed on low, intermittent suctioning for patients with intractable nausea and vomiting or to reduce hydrochloric acid levels or relieve distention. Required nutritional support is best provided by jejunal enteral feedings that maintain gut integrity. These are as effective as parenteral feeding is and have the benefit of reducing the potential for infection and hypoglycemia. Total parenteral nutrition may be needed for patients with evidence of severe pancreatitis. Such patients may be critically ill and will require close monitoring of vital signs, oxygenation and ventilation, body temperature, cardiac and hemodynamic status, fluid and electrolytes, balance, body weight, serum calcium levels, renal function, level of consciousness, peripheral circulation, possible delirium, and possible multiorgan system failure. Severepancreatitis often results in a prolonged and complicated hospitalization. Throughout the illness, range-of-motion exercises, correct positioning, prophylaxis against deep venous thrombosis, oral hygiene, and other physical support measures prevent debilitation and complications of prolonged illness. Both patient and family may need support, esp. in the presence of complications (pulmonary, cardiovascular, renal, immune, and coagulation abnormalities). After pancreatitis has resolved, alcoholic patients should be encouraged to seek help from Alcoholics Anonymous or other supportive programs. Follow-up with a gastroenterologist, primary care provider, or nutritionist may be helpful during convalescence and recovery. Patients should return for prompt reevaluation if they have nausea, vomiting, epigastric pain, fevers, or jaundice after discharge.

   alcoholic p. Pancreatitis due to excessive (typically chronic) alcohol consumption. It is the second most common cause of pancreatitis, after ductal obstruction by gallstones.

   autoimmune p. Chronic pancreatitis, usually found in association with other autoimmune disorders (e.g., inflammatory bowel disease, rheumatoid arthritis, or Sjogren's syndrome). It is a relatively rare disease, suggested by the finding of antibodies against lactoferrin and carbonic anhydrase in the blood of affected patients. Biopsy specimens reveal infiltration of the organ by lymphocytes. It is treated with corticosteroids. SYN: *autoimmune-related p.*

   autoimmune-related p. Autoimmune pancreatitis.

   chronic p. Pancreatitis due to repeated or massive pancreatic injury, marked by the formation of scar tissue, which leads to malfunction of the pancreas. The disease may be diagnosed with endoscopic procedures, with radiographic studies (e.g., x-rays of the abdomen showing pancreatic calcification), or with so-called tubeless tests that assess malabsorption caused by failure of the pancreas to release digestive enzymes into the gastrointestinal tract.

   SYMPTOMS: The pain may be mild or severe, tending to radiate to the back. Jaundice, weakness, emaciation, malabsorption of proteins and fats, and diarrhea are present.

   drug-induced p. Pancreatitis due to medications, such as antiretroviral agents used to treat HIV/AIDS.

   gallstone p. Pancreatitis caused by the obstruction of the ampulla of Vater by a biliary stone.

   interstitial p. Pancreatitis with overgrowth of interacinar and intra-acinar connective tissue.

   suppurative p. Purulent pancreatitis.

   tropical p. ABBR: TP. Pancreatitis

of unclear cause, found primarily in children in Northern Africa and Southeast Asia.

pancreatoduodenectomy (păn″krē-ă-tō-dū″ō-dē-něk′tō-mē) [Gr. *pan,* all, + *kreas,* flesh, + L. *duodeni,* twelve, + Gr. *ektome,* excision] Excision of the head of the pancreas and the adjacent portion of the duodenum.

pancreatogenic, pancreatogenous (păn″krē-ă-tō-jěn′ĭk, -tŏj′ě-nŭs) [″ + ″ + *gennan,* to produce] Produced in or by the pancreas; originating in the pancreas.

pancreatography (păn″krē-ă-tŏg′ră-fē) [″ + ″ + *graphein,* to write] Endoscopic and radiological examination of the pancreas after injection of a radiopaque contrast medium through the duct of Wirsung.

pancreatolithiasis (păn″krē-ă-tō-lĭ-thī′ă-sĭs) [″ + ″ + ″ + *-iasis,* condition] Stones in the duct system of the pancreas.

pancreatopathy (păn″krē-ă-tŏp′ă-thē) [″ + ″ + *pathos,* disease, suffering] Any pathologic state of the pancreas. SYN: *pancreopathy.*

pancreatoscopy (pang″krē-ă-tos′kŏ-pē, pan″) [*pancreat-* + *-scopy*] Endoscopic examination of the pancreatic ducts.

pancrelipase (păn″krē-lī′pās) A standardized preparation of enzymes, principally lipase, with amylase and protease, obtained from the pancreas of the hog. It is used in treating conditions associated with deficient secretion from the pancreas.

pancytopenia (păn″sī-tō-pē′nē-ă) [″ + *kytos,* cell, + *penia,* poverty] A reduction in all cellular elements of the blood. It is sometimes present in patients with bone marrow failure, cirrhosis and portal hypertension, or leukemia.

pandemic (paăn-dem′ĭk) [*pan-* + Gr. *dēmos,* people] **1.** Pert. to an exceptionally widespread, even worldwide, disease affecting a very high percentage of people, e.g., HIV/AIDS, the bubonic plague in the Middle Ages, or malaria. **2.** Such a disease.

panel 1. A number of patients or normal subjects who participate in medical investigations, esp. studies in which new drugs, devices, or procedures are tested. **2.** A group of patients who obtain their primary medical care from a single health care provider.

panel reactive antibody SEE: under *antibody.*

panencephalitis (păn″ĕn-sĕf″ă-lī′tĭs) [Gr. *pan,* all, + *enkephalos,* brain, + *itis,* inflammation] A diffuse inflammation of the brain.

   subacute sclerosing p. ABBR: SSPE. A disease of childhood and adolescence marked by gradual and progressive intellectual and behavioral deterioration followed by seizures, muscle jerking, gait disturbances, and eventually coma. The illness is a late complication of measles infection (usually developing about 5 years after the child had measles). It has been almost completely eradicated in the U.S. as a result of universal measles vaccination. SYN: *Dawson disease.*

panendoscope (păn-ĕn'dō-skōp) ["" + *endon,* within, + *skopein,* to view] A cystoscope that gives a wide view of the bladder. SEE: *endoscope.*

Paneth cells (pah'nĕt) [Josef Paneth, Ger. physician, 1857–1890] Large secretory cells containing coarse granules, found at the blind end of the crypts of Lieberkühn (the intestinal glands). They secrete lysozyme.

pang 1. A paroxysm of extreme agony. 2. A sudden attack of any emotion.

panhypopituitarism (pan"hī"pō-pī-too'ĭt-ă-rizm, -tū') [*pan-* + *hypopituitarism*] Defective or absent function of the entire pituitary gland. SYN: *pituitary cachexia; Simmonds disease.*

panhysterectomy (păn"hĭs-tĕr-ĕk'tō-mē) ["" + *hystera,* womb, + *ektome,* excision] Excision of the entire uterus including the ovaries, oviducts, and uterine cervix. SEE: *hysterectomy.*

panic (pan'ik) [Gr. *panikos,* pert. to (the god) Pan] Acute anxiety, terror, or fright that is usually of sudden onset and may be uncontrollable.

   homosexual p. 1. In Freudian psychiatry, fear, anxiety, aggression, or psychosis that originates in conflicts that arise from an attraction to members of one's own gender. 2. An irrational fear of contracting illnesses from casual contact with people who have sex with members of their own gender.

panic disorder An anxiety disorder characterized by panic attacks (e.g., agoraphobia with panic attacks).

panic value A laboratory test result so far outside the normal range that it requires immediate notification of a health care provider.

panlobular (păn"lŏb'ū-lăr) ["" + ""] Pert. to or involving all the lobes of an organ.

panmyeloid (păn-mī'ĕ-loyd) [Gr. *pan,* all, + *myelos,* marrow, + *eidos,* form, shape] Pert. to all of the elements of the bone marrow.

panneuritis (păn"ū-rī'tĭs) ["" + *neuron,* sinew, + *itis,* inflammation] Generalized neuritis.

panniculectomy (pă-nĭk"ū-lĕk'tă-mē) The excision of an apron of abdominal subcutaneous fat that lacks adequate supportive tissue from people who are morbidly obese. Cosmesis can be achieved by panniculectomy and concomitant abdominoplasty.

panniculitis (păn-ĭk"ū-lī'tĭs) [L. *panniculus,* a small piece of cloth, + *itis,* inflammation] Inflammation of subcuta-

neous fatty tissue. The most common form of the disease is erythema nodosum.

   nodular nonsuppurative p. Weber-Christian disease.

panniculus (păn-ĭk'ū-lŭs) [L., a small piece of cloth] Any clothlike sheet or layer of tissue.

   p. adiposus The subcutaneous layer of fat; the fat cells in the superficial fascia.

   p. carnosus The thin layer of muscle tissue in the superficial fascia of mammals. SEE: *platysma myoides.*

pannus (păn'nŭs) [L., cloth] 1. Superficial vascular inflammation of the cornea. The area is cloudy, and its surface is uneven because it is infiltrated with a film of new capillary blood vessels. This condition may be seen in trachoma, acne rosacea, eczema, and as a result of irritation in granular conjunctivitis. SEE: *micropannus.* 2. Inflamed synovial granulation tissue seen in chronic rheumatoid arthritis.

   corneal p. An overgrowth of vascular tissue in the periphery of the cornea, occurring in response to inflammation of the cornea, esp. in trachoma.

   p. crassus Pannus that is highly vascularized, thick, and opaque.

   phlyctenular p. Pannus that occurs in conjunction with phlyctenular conjunctivitis.

   p. siccus Pannus accompanying xerophthalmia. It is composed principally of connective tissue that is dry and poorly vascularized.

   p. tenuis Pannus that is thin, poorly vascularized, and slightly opaque.

panoptic (păn-ŏp'tĭk) ["" + *optikos,* vision] Making every part visible.

panproctocolectomy (pan"prŏk"tō-kŏlek'tŏ-mē) [*pan-* + *procto-* + *colectomy*] Surgical removal of the entire large intestine, from the anus, to the rectum, and the length of the large bowel. It is a treatment for severe cases of inflammatory bowel disease and is followed by the creation of an ileostomy.

PANRE *Physician Assistant National Recertifying Exam.*

pansinusitis (păn"sī-nŭs-ī'tĭs) ["" + L. *sinus,* curve, hollow, + *itis,* inflammation] Inflammation of all of the paranasal sinuses.

Panstrongylus (pan"stron'jĭ-lŭs) A genus of insects belonging to the order Hemiptera, family Reduviidae. Members of this genus are vectors for *Trypanosoma cruzi,* the causative agent of Chagas disease.

pansystolic (păn-sĭs-tŏl'ĭk) Throughout systole; used to describe the murmur of mitral regurgitation. SYN: *holosystolic.*

pant (pănt) 1. To gasp for breath. 2. A short and shallow breath. Panting is produced by physical overexertion, as in running, or from fear.

pant-, panto-, panta- [Gr. *pas*, stem *pant-*, all] Prefixes meaning *all, whole.*

pantanencephaly (păn″tăn-ĕn-sĕf′ă-lē) [″ + *an-*, not, + *enkephalos*, brain] Complete absence of the brain in the fetus.

pantetheine (păn-tĕ-thē′ĭn) The naturally occurring amide of pantothenic acid. It is a growth factor for *Lactobacillus bulgaricus.*

panting (pănt′ĭng) Short, shallow, rapid respirations. SYN: *polypnea.*

pantograph (păn′tō-grăf) [Gr. *pantos*, all, + *graphein*, to write] A device that will reproduce, through a system of levers connected to a stylus, a duplicate of whatever figure or drawing is being copied by the device.

pantomography (păn″tō-mŏg′ră-fē) Panoramic radiograph.

Pantopaque (păn-tō′păk) An oil-based, iodine-containing contrast medium used to outline body structures during radiographic or fluoroscopic examinations, such as myelograms.

pantothenate (păn-tō′thĕn-āt) A salt of pantothenic acid, a B vitamin.

pantothenic acid (pant-ŏ-then′ik) SEE: under *acid.*

Pan troglodytes troglodytes A subspecies of chimpanzee believed to be the primary host of human immunodeficiency virus (HIV) before the illness became epidemic in humans.

panuveitis (păn-ū″vīt′ĭs) Inflammation that affects all the structures of the eye. SYN: *diffuse uveitis.*

panzootic (păn″zō-ŏt′ĭk) [″ + *zoon*, animal] Any animal disease that is widespread.

PaO The pressure of gases at the opening of the patient's airway

PaO₂ The partial pressure of oxygen in arterial blood; arterial oxygen concentration, or tension; usually expressed in millimeters of mercury (mm Hg).

pap (păp) [L. *pappa*, infant's sound for food] Any soft, semiliquid food.

papain (pă-pā′ĭn) Proteolytic enzyme obtained from the fruit of the papaya, *Carica papaya;* used to tenderize meat.

Papanicolaou test, Pap test (păp″-ă-nē′kă-low″) [George Nicholas Papanicolaou, Gr.-born U.S. scientist, 1883–1962] ABBR: Pap test. A cytological study used to detect cancer in cells that an organ has shed. The Pap test has been used most often in the diagnosis and prevention of cervical cancers, but it also is valuable in the detection of pleural or peritoneal malignancies and in the evaluation of cellular changes caused by radiation, infection, or atrophy. SYN: *Pap smear.*

Cellular material is collected and smeared on a glass slide. DNA hybrid testing for HPV can be done on the liquid-based specimen. When suspicious cells are identified, further testing may be performed on the same sample. Testing for human papilloma virus (HPV) is often performed if results show abnormal changes of uncertain significance. HPV is the primary risk factor for cervical cancer. Currently the two available technologies are Thin Prep Pap Test and Sure Path. SEE: illus.

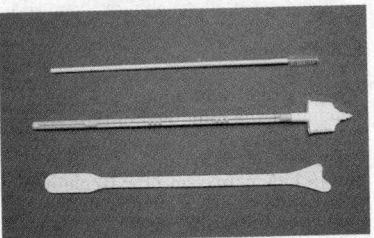

TOOLS FOR PAP TEST

(top to bottom) Cytobrush, cervical cytobroom, and wooden paddle

Since the introduction of the Pap test, death from cervical cancer in the U.S. has declined by 70%. Although interpretation of the test is subject to human error, a variety of developments have improved test accuracy, including use of computer-generated procedures for detection and examination of abnormal cells and mandated reexamination of sample batches to test quality control. A woman may augment the accuracy and value of the Pap test by following these guidelines: Asking her health care provider about the quality of the laboratory evaluating the results; having an annual Pap test beginning by age 21 or when the woman becomes sexually active; scheduling the test during a time when she does not expect to be bleeding; abstaining from sexual intercourse and and putting nothing in her vagina; providing a detailed medical history, including use of birth control pills or other exogenous hormones and results of past Pap tests; and requesting a secondopinion on the Pap test if she is at risk for cancer of the reproductive tract.

⚠️ As with any test, it is possible that human errors may influence results. It is important that the quality of performance of the technicians and physicians be periodically reviewed by persons not employed by the laboratory or hospital.

SCREENING RECOMMENDATIONS: The American Cancer Society (ACS) and the American College of Obstetricians and Gynecologists (ACOG) both recommend that screening for cervical cancer begin about 3 years after a woman begins having vaginal intercourse, but no later than age 21. Annual Pap testing should continue until age 30. After age 30, the ACS says women can reduce test frequency to every 2 to 3 years if their health care provider uses the newer liquid-based Pap tests, which include human papillomavirus (HPV) typing. In young, sexually active women, certain types of HPV cause precancerous changes that can lead to cervical cancer. Women who have had a hysterectomy for benign conditions and who do not have a cervix no longer need to undergo screening.

Screening can stop at age 65 or 70 for those women who have never had positive findings on previous examinations, as long as they have no new risk factors for cervical cancer.

Certain women are at high risk for cervical cancer and may need more frequent testing than the general population. These include women with HPV, chlamydial, or HIV infection and those who are immunosuppressed as a result of other illnesses. Additional risk factors for cervical cancer include early age at first intercourse, a history of sexually transmitted illnesses, cigarette smoking or substance abuse, a previous history of cervical dysplasia, a history of multiple sexual partners, or having a sexual partner who has other partners with cervical cancer.

PATIENT CARE: Because Pap testing has been effective in detecting the early stages of cervical cancer, health care professionals should advocate this procedure for their female patients and participate in health promotion efforts to increase the number of women who have the test done regularly.

papaya (pă-pä′yă) [Sp. Amerind.] **1.** *Carica papaya,* a large herb of the family Caricaceae, native to the American tropics and cultivated for its edible fruit and latex-bearing leaves and stem, which contain digestive enzymes. **2.** Large, oblong, edible fruit of the *Carica papaya* plant; the source of the digestive enzyme papain.

paper (pā′pĕr) [L. *papyrus,* papyrus, paper] **1.** Cellulose pulp prepared in thin sheets from fibers of wood, rags, and other substances. **2.** Charta. **3.** A thin sheet of cellulosic material impregnated with specific chemicals that react in a definite manner when exposed to certain solutions. This permits use of these papers for testing purposes.

   articulating p. Paper coated on one or both sides with a pigment that marks the teeth during dental occlusion. This allows the contact points of the teeth to be demonstrated.

   PATIENT CARE: It is often used to assess the patient's bite after restorative procedures.

   bibulous p. Paper that absorbs water readily.

   filter p. A porous, unglazed paper used for filtration of solids from liquids or gases. It is manufactured in different pore sizes so as to retain different sized particles.

   indicator p. Paper saturated with a solution of known strength and then dried; used for testing the pH (or other properties) of a solution.

   litmus p. Chemically prepared blue paper that contains a hydrogen-ion sensitive dye, is turned red by acids, and remains blue in alkali solutions; pH range is 4.5 to 8.5. SEE: *indicator.*

   test p. Paper impregnated with a substance that will change color when exposed to solutions of a certain pH or to specific chemicals.

papilla (pă-pil′ă, pă-pil′ē″, ī″) *pl.* **papillae** [L. *papilla,* nipple, teat] A small nipple-like protuberance or elevation.

   Bergmeister p. SEE: *Bergmeister papilla.*

   circumvallate p. Any of the large papillae near the base on the dorsal aspect of the tongue, arranged in a V-shape. The taste buds are located in the epithelium of the trench surrounding the papilla. SYN: *vallate p.*

   conical p. **1.** Any of the papillae on the dorsum of the tongue. **2.** Any of the papillae in the ridgelike projections of the dermis. SYN: ***p.** of corium.*

   p. of corium Conical papilla (2).

   dental p. A mass of connective tissue that becomes enclosed by the developing enamel organ. It gives rise to dentin and dental pulp.

   dermal p. Any of the small elevations of the corium that indent the inner surface of the epidermis.

   duodenal p. Papilla of Vater.

   filiform p. Any of the very slender papillae at the tip of the tongue.

   foliate p. Any of the folds in the sides of the tongue. They are rudimentary papillae.

   fungiform p. Any of the broad flat papillae resembling a mushroom, chiefly found on the dorsal central area of the tongue. SYN: *clavate p.*

   gingival p. The gingivae that fill the spaces between adjacent teeth. They are rudimentary papillae.

   gustatory p. Taste papilla of tongue; one of those possessing a taste bud. SYN: *taste p.*

   p. of hair A conical process of the corium that projects into the undersurface of a hair bulb. It contains capillaries that nourish the hair root. SYN: ***p.** pili.*

   incisive p. A small bump in the mucosa above and just forward of the incisive foramen at the very front of the hard palate. The papilla is used as an injection site when anesthetizing the nasopalatine nerve. SYN: *palatine p.*

interdental p. The triangular part of the gingivae that fills the area between adjacent teeth. The papilla includes free gingiva and attached gingiva and projections seen from the lingual, buccal, or labial sides of the tooth. SYN: *interproximal p.*

interproximal p. Interdental papilla.

lingual p. Any of the papillae covering the anterior two thirds of the tongue. These include circumvallate, filiform, fungiform, and conical papillae.

optic p. Blind spot (1).

parotid p. The projections around the opening of the parotid duct into the oral cavity.

p. pili Papilla of hair.

renal p. The apex of a renal pyramid in the kidney, enclosed by a calyx of the renal pelvis.

tactile p. A dermal papilla that contains a sensory receptor for touch.

taste p. Gustatory **p.**

urethral p. The small projection in the vestibule of the female perineum at the entrance of the urethra.

vallate p. Circumvallate **p.**

p. of Vater SEE: under *Vater, Abraham.*

papillary (păp′ĭ-ler″ē) [L. *papilla,* nipple] **1.** Pert. to a nipple or papilla. **2.** Resembling or composed of papillae.

papillary carcinoma of the thyroid A well-differentiated thyroid cancer, and the most common form of thyroid cancer in the US. Most thyroid cancers of this type grow slowly and respond well to treatment. They are usually identified as a thyroid nodule and are best diagnosed with fine needle aspiration biopsy. Treatment includes surgical removal of the thyroid gland, followed by radioactive iodine treatment to destroy any residual tissue or metastasis. Survival ten years after diagnosis and treatment exceeds 90%.

papillate (păp′ĭ-lāt) [L. *papilla,* nipple] Having nipple-like growths on the surface, as a culture in bacteriology.

papillectomy (păp″ĭ-lĕk′tō-mē) [″ + Gr. *ektome,* excision] Excision of any papilla or papillae.

papilledema (păp″ĭl-ĕ-dē′mă) [*papilla* + *edema*] Swelling of the optic disk with dilated veins, blurred optic disc margins, flame-shaped hemorrhages in the nerve fiber layer adjacent to the disk, and an enlarged blind spot on the visual field. It is caused by increased intracranial pressure, often due to a tumor of the brain pressing on the optic nerve. Blindness may result very rapidly unless relieved. SYN: *choked disk.*

papilliform (pă-pĭl′ĭ-form) [″ + *forma,* shape] Having the characteristics or appearance of papillae.

papillitis (păp-ĭ-lī′tĭs) [″ + Gr. *itis,* inflammation] Optic disc swelling caused by local inflammation; usually acute.

papilloma (pap-ĭ-lō′mă, ′măt-ă) *pl.* **papillomas, papillomata** [*papilla* + *-oma*] **1.** A benign epithelial tumor. **2.** An epithelial tumor of skin or mucous membrane consisting of hypertrophied papillae covered by a layer of epithelium. Included in this group are warts, condylomas, and polyps. **papillomatous** (′măt-ŭs), *adj.* SEE: *acanthoma; papillomavirus.*

p. durum A hardened papilloma, e.g., a wart or corn.

fibroepithelial p. A skin tag containing fibrous tissue.

hard p. A papilloma that develops from squamous epithelium.

Hopmann p. SEE: under *Hopmann, Carl Melchior.*

intracystic p. A papilloma within a cystic adenoma.

intraductal p. A papilloma in the milk ducts of the breast, composed of fibrous tissue and blood vessels. It is the most common cause of spontaneous nipple discharge. Breast biopsies, ductograms, or examination of the discharge for malignant cells are used to evaluate the lesion. Surgery is the preferred treatment.

p. molle Condyloma.

soft p. A papilloma formed from columnar epithelium; applies to any small, soft growth.

villous p. A papilloma with long, thin excrescences, present in the urinary bladder, breast, intestinal tract, or choroid plexus of the cerebral ventricles.

papillomatosis (păp″ĭ-lō-mă-tō′sĭs) [″ + Gr. *oma,* tumor, + *osis,* condition] **1.** Widespread formation of papillomas. **2.** The condition of being afflicted with many papillomas.

papillomavirus (păp″ĭ-lō′mă-vī″rŭs) Any of a group of viruses that cause papillomas or warts in humans and animals. They belong to the papovavirus family or group. SEE: *wart, genital.*

human p. ABBR: HPV. A papillomavirus that is specific to humans and is a common viral sexually transmitted disease in the U.S. A number of HPV types, esp. HPV 16, 18, 31, and 45, have been shown to contribute to squamous cell cancers of the anogenital region, including cancers of the anus, cervix, penis, and vulva. Others (types 6 and 11) are responsible for genital warts. Cervical cancer kills nearly 4,000 women in the U.S. annually.

A vaccine (trade name Gardasil) has proven 100% effective in preventing the two strains of HPV responsible for 70% of cervical cancer and two responsible for most genital warts. In June 2006, the FDA approved the vaccine, and the CDC includes the HPV vaccine in its recommended vaccination schedule for girls age 11 or 12.

The vaccine costs approx. $360.00, for girls and women age 9 to 26. The organization "Vaccines of Children" may cover the expense for some girls if a health care company refuses coverage.

TREATMENT: Imiquimod is used to treat warts of the genitals or anus. An alternative drug treatment is podophyllum. Cervical HPV lesions may be removed by loop electrosurgical excision procedure. Cryotherapy and laser surgery also may be used in treatment.

Papillon-Lefèvre syndrome (pa-pē-yon'lĕ-fev'ĕr) [M. M. Papillon, P. Lefèvre, 20th-cent. Fr. dermatologists] A rare autosomal recessive disorder occurring between the first and fifth years of life marked by hyperkeratosis of the palms and soles, ectopic calcifications of the skull, severe periodontal disease, and early loss of teeth.

papillophlebitis (păp"ĭ-lō-flĕ-bī'tĭs, pă-pĭl"ō) [" + "] Nonischemic central retinal vein occlusion, typically but not exclusively occurring in an otherwise young or healthy patient.

papillotome (pă-pĭl'ŏ-tōm") [papilla + -tome] An instrument used to incise a papilla, e.g., the papilla of Vater.

papovavirus (păp"ō-vă-vī'rŭs) [papilloma, + polyoma, + vacuolating agent + virus] Any of a group of viruses important in investigating viral carcinogenesis; including polyoma virus, simian virus 40 (SV 40), and papillomaviruses.

pappose (păp'pōs) [L. pappus, down] Covered with fine, downy hair.

pappus (păp'pŭs) [L.] The first growth of beard hair appearing on the cheeks and chin as fine, downy hair.

Pap smear, Pap test (păp) Papanicolaou test.

papular mucinosis (păp'yă-lĕr mū-sĭ-nō'sĭs) A rare rash of unknown cause, in which mucin deposits are found in the dermis, creating a bumpy (papular) eruption often found on the face or arms. The condition is often associated with lesions of the internal organs and the presence of paraproteins in the bloodstream.

papular-purpuric "gloves and socks" syndrome (păp'yŭ-lăr-pŭr"pūr'ik) ABBR: PPGSS. The sudden development of well-defined, itchy, or painful red and swollen papules on the hands, feet, wrists, and ankles, usually appearing in the spring or summer and typically associated with a viral infection, e.g., coxsackievirus, cytomegalovirus, or human parvovirus B19.

papule (păp'ūl) [L. papula, pimple] A small bump or pimple, typically larger than a grain of salt but smaller than a peppercorn, that rises above the surface of the neighboring skin. Papules may appear in numerous skin diseases, including prickly heat, psoriasis, xanthomatosis, eczema, and skin cancers. Their color may range from pale, to yellow, red, brown, or black. SEE: illus.
papular (ū-lăr), adj.

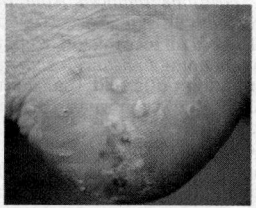

PAPULES ON HEEL

dry p. Chancre.

moist p. Condyloma latum.

pearly penile p. An asymptomatic white papule with a pink, white, or pearly surface on the dorsum of the penis of blacks and uncircumcised men. No treatment is indicated, just reassurance.

piezogenic pedal p. A soft, painful, skin-colored papule present on the non–weight-bearing portion of the heel. It disappears when weight is taken off the foot and heel. This papule is caused by herniation of fat through connective tissue defects.

split p. Fissures at the corners of the mouth; seen in some cases of secondary syphilis.

papulo- [L. papula, pimple] Combining form indicating pimple, papule.

papulopustular (păp"ū-lō-pŭs'tū-lăr) [" + pustula, blister] Denoting the presence of both pustules and papules.

papulosis (păp"yŭ-lō'sĭs) [papulo- +-sis] The presence of numerous and generalized papules.

malignant atrophic p. Degos disease.

papulosquamous (păp"ū-lō-skwā'mŭs) [" + squamosus, scalelike] Denoting the presence of both papules and scales.

papulovesicular (păp"ū-lō-vē-sĭk'ū-lăr) [" + vesicula, tiny bladder] Denoting the presence of both papules and vesicles.

papyraceous (păp-ĭ-rā'shŭs) [L. papyraceus, made of papyrus] In obstetrics, pert. to a fetus that is retained in the uterus beyond natural term and appears mummified.

par [L., equal] A pair, esp. a pair of cranial nerves.

para (păr'ă) [L. parere, to bring forth, to bear] A woman who has produced a viable infant (weighing at least 500 g or of more than 20 weeks' gestation) regardless of whether the infant is alive at birth. A multiple birth is considered to be a single parous experience. SEE: gravida; multipara.

para- [Gr. *para*, by, beyond, alongside, beyond] **1.** Prefix meaning *near, beside, past, beyond, opposite, abnormal, irregular.* **2.** A prefix frequently used in the names of ancillary or subordinate roles, e.g., *paramilitary, paramedical* **3.** In chemical formulas, a prefix meaning *three positions removed from the primary locus.* SEE: *p-*.

-para [L. *parere*, to bring forth (offspring)] Suffix meaning *to bear, give birth.*

para-aminohippuric acid (par″ă-ă-mēn″ō-hĭp-ūr′ĭk, par″ă-ăm″ĭ-nō-) SEE: under *acid.*

parabiosis (păr″ă-bī-ō′sĭs) [″ + *biosis*, living] **1.** The joining together of two individuals. It may occur congenitally as with conjoined twins or may be produced surgically for experimentation in animals. **parabiotic** (-ŏt′ĭk), *adj.*

paracasein (păr-ă-kā′sē-ĭn) An insoluble protein formed when rennin or pepsin acts on the casein in milk; this reaction, which results in the curdling of milk, occurs only in the presence of calcium ions.

paracellular (păr″ă-sĕl′ū-lĭr) [″ + ″] Pertaining to pathways or junctions between or around cells. It is used for ions that pass through an epithelial membrane without entering its cells.

paracentesis (par″ă-sen-tē′sĭs) [*para-* + *centesis*] The puncture of a cavity with removal of fluid, as in pleural effusion or ascites. Paracentesis commonly refers to aspiration of fluid from within the peritoneum. **paracentetic** (-tet′ĭk), *adj.*

PATIENT CARE: The procedure is explained to the patient and an informed consent is obtained. The patient is assessed for allergies, including local anesthetics and antiseptic agents, and for bleeding and coagulation abnormalities. The patient should have an intravenous access and should empty his/her bladder before the procedure. Emotional support is offered during the procedure, and the patient is encouraged to express feelings. The patient is positioned as directed by the physician. Vital signs are monitored, esp. for changes in respiratory rate, pulse, and blood pressure. The amount of fluid removed is measured and recorded, and its appearance, color, consistency, odor, and specific gravity are noted. The puncture site is observed, a pressure dressing applied, and redressed as necessary. Specimens are sent to laboratories as directed. The procedure and the patient's response are documented, and the patient is monitored for several hours after theprocedure, e.g., for bleeding or drainage from the puncture site, or worsening internal pain.

paracentral lobule SEE: under *lobule.*

Paracoccidioides (par″ă-kok-sid″ē-oyd′ēz) A genus of yeastlike fungi.

P. brasiliensis The species of dimorphic yeast that causes South American blastomycosis. It was formerly called *Blastomyces brasiliensis.* SEE: *Blastomyces brasiliensis.*

P. loboii Lacazia loboi.

paracoccidioidomycosis (păr″ă-kŏk-sĭd″ē-ŏy″dō-mī-kō′sĭs) A chronic granulomatous disease of the skin caused by *Paracoccidioides brasiliensis.* SYN: *South American blastomycosis.*

paracone (păr′ă-kōn) [″ + *konos*, cone] The mesiobuccal cusp of an upper molar tooth.

paraconid (păr″ă-kō′nĭd) The mesiobuccal cusp of a lower molar tooth.

paracrine (păr″ă-krēn) Secreting macromolecules that diffuse and influence other nearby cells. One of three general mechanisms (the others being autocrine and endocrine) by which ductless glands regulate or control the activities of cells.

p. regulation, paracrine signaling The secretion of macromolecules, such as clotting factors, to regulate the activities of neighboring cells.

paracytic (păr″ă-sĭt′ĭk) [″ + *kytos*, cell] Pert. to cells other than those normally present in a specific location.

paradental (păr″ă-dĕn′tăl) [″ + L. *dens*, tooth] **1.** Pert. to the practice of dentistry. **2.** Periodontal.

paradidymis (păr-ă-dĭd′ĭ-mĭs) [″ + *didymos*, testicle] The atrophic remnants of the tubules of the wolffian body, situated on the spermatic cord above the epididymis.

paradigm (par′ă-dīm″, -dim″) [L. *paradigma* fr Gr. *paradeigma*, example] **1.** An example that serves as a model. **2.** Conceptual **model.**

paradox (par′ă-doks″) [Gr. *paradoxos*, contrary to expectation] A condition or statement that on superficial examination seems contradictory or illogical.

prevention p. A preventive measure that brings benefits to the community at large but affords little benefit to each participating individual.

paradoxical disinhibition An unexpected increase in aggressiveness, hostility, impulsivity, or talkativeness in a patient after treatment with a tranquilizing drug, esp. a sedative/hypnotic. SEE: *paradoxical excitement.*

paradoxical excitement Paradoxical disinhibition.

paraffin (păr′ă-fĭn) [L. *parum*, too little, + *affinis*, neighboring] **1.** A waxy, white, tasteless, odorless mixture of solid hydrocarbons obtained from petroleum; used as an ointment base or wound dressing. SEE: *petrolatum.* **2.** One of a series of saturated aliphatic hydrocarbons having the formula C_nH_{2n+2}. Paraffins constitute the methane or paraffin series. **3.** A series of solid waxes prepared according to their melting point, to be used to infiltrate and embed tissues for sectioning in the preparation of microscope slides.

paraformaldehyde (păr″ă-for-măl′dĕ-hīd) A white, powdered antiseptic and disinfectant, a polymer of formaldehyde.

paraganglia (păr″ă-găng′lē-ă) *sing.*, **paraganglion** [″ + *ganglion*, knot] Groups of chromaffin cells, similar in staining reaction to cells of the adrenal medulla, associated anatomically and embryologically with the sympathetic system. They are located in various organs and parts of the body.

paraganglioma (par″ă-gang″glē-ō′mă) [*paraganglion* + *-oma*] An extra-adrenal tumor composed of neural crest cells. The cells may release catecholamines into the systemic circulation and cause symptoms of sustained or episodic hypertension, with sweating, palpitations, and headache. Paragangliomas usually are found in the paravertebral ganglia or the carotid bodies. SYN: *chromaffinoma.* SEE: *pheochromocytoma.*

   extra-adrenal catecholamine-secreting p. A pheochromocytoma that arises in the sympathetic ganglia instead of the adrenal glands.

paraganglion (păr″ă-găng′lē-ŏn) [″ + *ganglion*, knot] Sing. of paraganglia.

paragonimiasis (păr″ă-gŏn″ĭ-mī′ă-sĭs) [*Paragonimus* + *-iasis*, condition] Infection with worms of the genus *Paragonimus.* The clinical signs depend on the path the worm takes in migrating through the body, after the larvae contained in partially cooked freshwater crabs or crayfish are eaten. The larvae migrate from the duodenum to various organs, including the lungs, intestinal wall, lymph nodes, brain, subcutaneous tissues, and genitourinary tract. When the lungs are involved, the symptoms are cough and hemoptysis. In peritoneal infections, there may be an abdominal mass, pain, and dysentery. When the larvae invade the brain, paralysis, epilepsy, homonymous hemianopsia, optic atrophy, and papilledema are common. In some cases, the infected person may appear to be well. This infection is treated by administration of praziquantel.

Paragonimus (păr″ă-gŏn′ĭ-mŭs) A genus of trematode worms.

   P. westermani The lung fluke, a common parasite of certain mammals including humans, dogs, cats, pigs, and minks. Human infestation occurs through eating partially cooked crabs or crayfish, the second intermediate host. This infestation is endemic in certain parts of Asia.

paragranuloma (păr″ă-grăn″ū-lō′mă) [Gr. *para,* beside, + L. *granulum,* little grain, + Gr. *oma,* tumor] A benign form of Hodgkin's disease usually limited to lymph nodes.

parahemophilia (pă″ră-hēm″ō-fēl′ē-ă) A rare, autosomal recessive bleeding disorder in which there is a deficiency in blood clotting factor V. SYN: *Owren disease.*

parahypnosis (pă-ră-hĭp-nō′sĭs) [″ + *hypnos,* sleep] Abnormal or disordered sleep.

parainfectious (par″ă-in-fek′shŭs) [*para-* + *infectious*] Occurring as an indirect result of an infection.

parainfluenza viruses (pă-ră-ĭn-floo-ĕn′ză) A group of viruses that cause acute respiratory infections in humans, esp. in children. Virtually all children in the U.S. have been infected by age 6.

parakeratosis (par″ă-ker″ă-tō′sĭs, ′sēz″) *pl.* **parakeratoses** [*para-* + *keratosis*] The persistence of nuclei within the keratinocytes of the stratum corneum of epidermis or mucosal layers. It indicates a partial keratinization process and is a general term applied to disorders of the keratinized layer of the skin.

   p. ostracea Parakeratosis scutularis.

   p. psoriasiformis Scab formation resembling that of psoriasis.

   p. scutularis A scalp disease with hairs encircled by epidermic crust formation. SYN: *p. ostracea.*

paralanguage (par″ă-lang′gwăj) [*para-* + *language*] Nonverbal elements in communication, including loudness, tone of voice, and, at times, facial expressions and body language.

paralexia (păr″ă-lĕk′sē-ă) [″ + *lexis,* speech] An inability to comprehend printed words or sentences, together with substitution of meaningless combinations of words.

parallax (păr′ă-lăks) [Gr. *parallaxis,* change of position] The apparent movement or displacement of objects caused by change in the observer's position or by movement of the head or eyes.

   binocular p. The basis of stereoscopic vision; the difference in the angles formed by the lines of sight to two objects at different distances from the eyes. This is important in depth perception.

   heteronymous p. Parallax in which, when one eye is closed, the object viewed appears to move closer to the closed eye.

   homonymous p. Parallax in which, when one eye is covered, the object viewed appears to move closer to the uncovered eye.

parallel trial SEE: under *trial.*

paralysis (pă-ral′ĭ-sĭs, -sēz″) *pl.* **paralyses** [Gr. *paralyein,* to disable] **1.** Loss of sensation; anesthesia. **2.** Loss of purposeful movement, usually as a result of neurological disease (such as strokes, spinal cord injuries, poliomyelitis), drugs, or toxins. Loss of motor function may be complete (paralysis) or partial (paresis), unilateral (hemiplegic) or bilateral (diplegic), confined to the lower extremities (paraplegic) or present in all four extremities (quadraplegic), accompanied by increased muscular tension and hyperactive reflexes (spastic) or by loss of reflexes and tone (flaccid). SYN: *palsy*.

PATIENT CARE: Rehabilitation therapists evaluate the patient's motor and sensory capabilities (muscle size, tone and strength, reflex or involuntary movement, response to touch or to painful stimuli). The patient must be positioned to prevent deformities. Passive range of motion is performed on the involved extremities to prevent contractures. The patient is repositioned frequently to prevent pressure sores. Local and systemic responses, including fatigue, are evaluated. The rehabilitation team assesses and attends to any self-care deficits the patient may have. Support is offered to the patient and family to help them deal with psychological concerns and the response to grief and loss. Assistance is provided to help the patient in achieving an optimal level of function and in adapting to the disability.

Important concerns include functional positioning, the prevention of deformities secondary to spasticity, and the prevention of injury when sensation is absent. A plan may be prescribed for muscle reeducation and compensatory training. Functional orthoses and assistive technology devices may be necessary to assist the patient in performing self-care and other tasks of daily living.

p. of accommodation Inability of the ciliary muscles to alter the lens to focus on near or far objects.

acoustic p. Deafness.

p. agitans Parkinson disease.

alcoholic p. Paralysis caused by the toxic effect of alcohol on spinal nerves. SYN: *alcoholic **paraplegia***.

birth p. Loss of function due to nerve injury during delivery. Trauma to the baby during delivery may result in damage to the brachial nerves, facial nerves, or diaphragm. Asymmetrical movements or reflexes of the affected part are present. Prognosis depends on the amount of nerve damage sustained; permanent damage is rare. Most newborn paralyses resolve without sequelae within a few weeks or a few months after birth. SYN: *birth **palsy**; brachial **palsy**; obstetrical **p***.

brachial p. Paralysis arising from an injury received at birth to the brachial nerve.

brachiofacial p. Paralysis of the face and an arm.

bulbar p. Paralysis caused by changes in the motor centers of the medulla oblongata. SYN: *progressive bulbar p*.

complete p. Paralysis in which there is total loss of function and sensation.

conjugate p. Paralysis of the conjugate movement of the eyes in all directions even though the fixation axis remains parallel.

crossed p. Paralysis affecting muscles of one side of the face and those in the limbs on the opposite side of the body.

crutch p. Paralysis due to pressure on nerves in the axilla caused by improper use of a crutch.

decubitus p. Paralysis caused by compression of a nerve after lying on it, e.g., in sleep or a coma.

diphtheritic p. Paralysis of the muscles of the palate, eyes, limbs, diaphragm, and intercostal muscles as a complication of diphtheria. It is caused by a bacterial toxin. SYN: *postdiphtheritic p*.

diver's p. Decompression illness.

Duchenne-Erb p. SEE: *Duchenne-Erb paralysis*.

facial p. Bell palsy.

facial nerve p. Bell palsy.

familial periodic p. A rare familial disease marked by attacks of flaccid paralysis, often at awakening. This condition is usually associated with hypokalemia but is sometimes present when the blood potassium level is normal or elevated. In affected individuals the condition may be precipitated by administration of glucose in patients with hypokalemia, and by administration of potassium chloride in those with hyperkalemia.

TREATMENT: Acetazolamide is used to prevent either hypokalemia or hyperkalemia. Oral potassium chloride is given in attacks accompanied by hypokalemia.

flaccid p. Paralysis in which there is loss of muscle tone, loss or reduction of tendon reflexes, and atrophy and degeneration of muscles. It is caused by lesions of the lower motor neurons of the spinal cord.

general p. Paresis.

ginger p. Jamaica ginger **p**.

glossolabial p. Paralysis of the tongue and lips occurring in bulbar paralysis.

hyperkalemic p. A rare form of periodic paralysis characterized by brief (1- to 2-hr) attacks of limb weakness. Respiratory muscles are involved in some cases. "Hyperkalemic" is misleading because the potassium levels may be normal. But, because an attack is precipitated by the administration of potassium, this form of paralysis is better termed "potassium-sensitive periodic paralysis."

TREATMENT: Emergency treatment is seldom necessary. Oral glucose hastens recovery. Attacks may be prevented by acetazolamide or thiazide diuretics.

hypokalemic periodic p. A form of periodic paralysis with onset usually before adulthood. An attack typically comes on during sleep, after strenuous exercise during the day. The weakness may be so pronounced as to prevent the patient from being able to call for help. The attack may last from several hours to a day or more. The diagnosis is established by determining that the serum potassium level is decreased during an attack.

TREATMENT: Administration of oral potassium salts improves the paralysis. If the patient is too weak to swallow, intravenous potassium salts are required. Attacks may be prevented by oral administration of 5 to 10 g of potassium chloride daily.

immunological p. The inability to form antibodies after exposure to large doses of an antigen.

incomplete p. Partial paralysis of the body or a part.

infantile p. Poliomyelitis.

infantile cerebral ataxic p. Cerebral palsy.

ischemic p. Volkmann contracture.

Jamaica ginger p. Paralysis due to polyneuropathy that affects the muscles of the distal portions of the limbs. It is caused by drinking Jamaica ginger, an alcoholic beverage containing the toxin triorthocresylphosphate.

Klumpke p. SEE: *Klumpke paralysis.*

Landry p. Flaccid paralysis that begins in the lower extremities and rapidly ascends to the trunk.

laryngeal p. Loss of vocal fold mobility. Common causes include surgical trauma to the recurrent laryngeal nerve or invasion of the nerve by a tumor. SYN: *vocal* **p.**

lead p. Paralysis due to lead poisoning.

leaden p. Extreme fatigue, a symptom of atypical depression.

local p. Paralysis of a single muscle or one group of muscles.

mimetic p. Paralysis of the facial muscles.

mixed p. Paralysis of the motor and sensory nerves.

muscular p. Loss of the capacity of muscles to contract. It may be due to a structural or functional disorder in the muscle at the myoneural junction, in efferent nerve fibers, in cell bodies of nuclei of origin of the brain or of the gray matter of the spinal cord, in conducting pathways of the brain or spinal cord, or in motor centers of the brain.

musculospiral p. Saturday night **palsy**.

nuclear p. Paralysis caused by lesion of nuclei in the central nervous system.

obstetrical p. Birth **p.**

ocular p. Paralysis of the extraocular and intraocular muscles.

postdiphtheritic p. Diphtheritic **p.**

posticus p. Paralysis of the posterior cricothyroid muscles.

potassium-sensitive periodic p. SEE: *hyperkalemic* **p.**

Pott p. SEE: under *Pott, John Percivall.*

primary periodic p. The occurrence of intermittent weakness, usually following rest or sleep and almost never during vigorous activity. The condition usually begins in early life and rarely has its onset after age 25. The attacks may last from a few hours to a day or more. The patient is alert during an attack.

The causes include hypokalemia, hyperkalemia, thyrotoxicosis, and a form of paramyotonia. Both forms of the disease in which potassium regulation is a factor respond to acetazolamide. The thyrotoxicosis-related disorder is treated by correcting the underlying thyrotoxicosis. Spironolactone is the treatment for cases of paramyotonia congenita with periodic paralysis.

progressive bulbar p. Bulbar **p.**

pseudobulbar p. Paralysis caused by cerebral center lesions, simulating the bulbar types of paralysis.

pseudohypertrophic muscular p. SEE: *pseudohypertrophic muscular dystrophy.*

radial p. Saturday night **palsy**.

Saturday night p. Saturday night **palsy**.

sensory p. Loss of sensation due to a structural or functional disorder of the sensory end organs, sensory nerves, conducting pathways of the spinal cord or brain, or the sensory centers in the brain.

sleep p. Brief, temporary inability to move or speak when falling asleep or awakening.

spastic p. Paralysis usually involving groups of muscles. It is caused by an upper motor neuron lesion and is characterized by excessive tone and spasticity of muscles, exaggeration of tendon reflexes but loss of superficial reflexes, and positive Babinski reflex.

Sunday morning p. Saturday night **palsy**.

supranuclear p. Paralysis resulting from disorders in pathways or centers above the nuclei of origin.

tick-bite p. Paralysis resulting from bites of some species of ticks whose saliva contains a toxin, esp. of the genera *Ixodes* and *Dermacentor*. It affects domestic animals and humans, esp. children, and causes a progressive ascending, flaccid motor paralysis. Recovery usually occurs after removal of the ticks.

Todd p. SEE: *Todd paralysis.*

tourniquet p. Paralysis, esp. of the arm, resulting from a tourniquet being applied for too long a time.

vasomotor p. Paralysis of the vasomotor centers, resulting in lack of tone and dilation of the blood vessels.

vocal p. Laryngeal **p.**

Volkmann p. Volkmann contracture.

wasting p. Spinal muscular **atrophy.**

paralytic (par″ă-lit′ik) [Gr. *paralytikos,* a paralytic] **1.** Pert. to paralysis. **2.** One afflicted with paralysis. **3.** A drug or other agent that causes muscular paralysis.

paralytic ileus Paralysis of the intestinal smooth muscles with distention of the abdomen, nausea or vomiting, abdominal pain, and inability to pass stool or gas. It may occur after abdominal surgery, during an episode of peritonitis, or after the administration of some drugs (e.g., narcotics).

paralyzant (păr′ă-līz″ănt) [Fr. *paralyser,* paralyze] **1.** Causing paralysis. **2.** A drug or other agent that induces paralysis.

paralyze (păr′ă-līz) [Fr. *paralyse*] **1.** To cause temporary or permanent loss of muscular power or sensation. **2.** To render ineffective.

paramagnetic (par″ă-mag-net′ik) [*para-* + *magnetic*] Pert. to a substance that is attracted by the poles of a magnet and becomes parallel to the lines of magnetic force. Paramagnetic contrast agents (usually incorporating gadolinium) are used in magnetic resonance imaging to help identify blood vessels and different tissue types. **paramagnetism** (-mag′nĕ-tizm), *n.*

paramedian (păr″ă-mē′dē-ăn) [″ + L. *medianus,* median] Near to the midline. SYN: *paramesial.*

paramedian incision SEE: under *incision.*

paramedic (păr″ă-mĕd′ik) [Gr. *para,* beside, + L. *medicus,* doctor] A health care professional trained in the emergency care of patients who suffer from acute illnesses or injuries. Paramedics typically function in the out-of-hospital setting, under the medical direction of a physician. They are trained to provide assessment and management including cardioversion, defibrillation, electrocardiographic interpretation, external pacing, IV therapy, thoracic decompression, endotracheal intubation, and drug and fluid therapy. SEE: *emergency medical technician.*

paramedical (pă-ră-mĕd-ĭ-lăl) Supplementing the work of medical personnel.

paramedical personnel Health care workers who are not physicians or nurses. These include medical technicians, emergency medical technicians, and physician assistants. SEE: *allied health professional.*

paramesial (păr″ă-mē′sē-ăl) [″ + *mesos,* middle] Paramedian.

parameter (pă-răm′ĕ-tĕr) [″ + *metron,* measure] **1.** In mathematics, an arbitrary constant, each value of which determines the specific form of the equation in which it appears. The term is often misused for variable. **2.** In biostatistics, a measurable or adjustable characteristic; a named value. **parametric** (păr″ă-mĕ′trĭk), *adj.*

parametric statistics SEE: under *statistics.*

parametritis (par″ă-mĕ-trīt′ĭs) [*parametrium* + *-itis*] An inflammation of the parametrium,. It may occur in puerperal fever or septic conditions of the uterus and appendages. SYN: *pelvic cellulitis.* **parametritic** (par″ă-mĕ-trĭt′ik), *adj.*

parametrium (păr-ă-mē′trē-ŭm) [″ + *metra,* uterus] Loose connective tissue around the uterus.

paramnesia (păr″ăm-nē′zē-ă) [″ + *amnesia,* loss of memory] **1.** Use of words without meaning. **2.** Distortion of memory in which there is inability to distinguish imaginary or suggested experiences from those that have actually occurred. **3.** Seeming recall of events that never have occurred.

paramyloidosis (păr-ăm″ĭ-loy-dō′sĭs) [″ + L. *amylum,* starch, + Gr. *eidos,* form, shape, + *osis,* condition] The presence and buildup of atypical amyloid in tissues.

paramyoclonus multiplex (păr-ă-mī-ŏk′lō-nŭs mŭl′tĭ-plĕks) [″ + *mys,* muscle, + *klonos,* tumult] Sudden and frequent shocklike contractions usually affecting the muscles of both legs, and particularly the trunk muscles. The contractions, which disappear during sleep and motion, may occur 10 to 50 times each minute. Usually the condition develops spontaneously, but it has been known to follow fright, trauma, infectious diseases, and poliomyelitis. SYN: *polymyoclonus.*

paramyotonia (par″ă-mī″ŏ-tō′nē-ă) [*para-* + *myotonia*] A disorder marked by muscular spasms and abnormal muscular tonicity.

ataxic p. Tonic muscular spasm with slight ataxia or paresis during any attempt at movement.

p. congenita A congenital condition of tonic muscular spasms when the body is exposed to cold. SYN: *Eulenburg disease.*

symptomatic p. Temporary muscular rigidity when one first tries to walk, as in Parkinson's disease.

paramyxovirus (pă-ră-mĭk′sō-vī-rŭs) Any virus of a subgroup of the myxoviruses that are similar in physical, chemical, and biological characteristics, even though they are quite different pathogenetically. The group includes parainfluenza, measles, mumps, Newcastle disease, and respiratory syncytial viruses.

paraneoplastic syndromes (pă-ră-nēō-plăs'-tĭk) Indirect effects of cancers, such as metabolic disturbances or hormonal excesses produced by chemicals released by tumor cells. Tumors such as small-cell carcinoma of the lung, hypernephroma, and neuroendocrine cancers are often responsible.

paraneuron (păr"ă-noor'ŏn, -nūr') A cell of epithelial origin with a membrane that can generate an action potential and with the ability to secrete neurotransmitter at a synaptic junction but without dendrites or axon, e.g., the primary sensory cells in taste buds.

paranoia (păr"ă-noy'ă) [Gr. *para*, beside, + *nous*, mind] A condition in which patients show persistent persecutory delusions or delusional jealousy. The disorder must last at least 1 week. It may be accompanied by delusional jealousy or by symptoms of schizophrenia (e.g., bizarre delusions or incoherence). There are no prominent hallucinations; a full depressive or manic syndrome is either absent or brief. The illness is not due to organic disease of the brain. SYN: *paranoid disorder; paranoid ideation.* SEE: *paranoid reaction type.*

This disorder, which usually occurs in middle or late adult life and may be chronic, often includes resentment and anger that may lead to violence. Paranoid people rarely seek medical attention but are brought for care by associates or relatives.

litigious p. Paranoia in which the patient institutes or threatens to institute legal action because of the imagined persecution.

somatic p. The delusion that one's body is malodorous, infested with an internal or external parasite, or misshapen or ugly.

paranoiac (păr-ă-noy'ăk) **1.** Pert. to or afflicted with paranoia. **2.** One suffering from paranoia.

paranoid (păr'ă-noyd) [" + *nous*, mind, + *eidos*, form, shape] **1.** Resembling paranoia. **2.** A person afflicted with paranoia.

paranoid disorder Paranoid personality disorder (under *personality disorder*). SEE: *Nursing Diagnoses Appendix.*

paranoid ideation Paranoia.

paranormal (pă-ră-nŏr-măl) **1.** Pert. to experiences that are not explainable scientifically. SEE: *extrasensory perception.* **2.** Moderately abnormal.

paranuclear (păr"ă-nū'klē-ăr) Adjacent to the nucleus of a cell.

paranucleus (păr"ă-nū'klē-ŭs) [Gr. *para*,

beside, + L. *nucleus*, a kernel] A structure next to the nucleus of a cell.

para-occupational (par"ă-ok"yŭ-pā'shŏn-ăl) [*para-* + *occupational*] Occurring as an indirect effect of work or of exposure to a work environment.

paraparesis (păr"ă-păr-ē'sĭs, -păr'ĕ-sĭs) [" + *parienai*, to let fall] Partial paralysis affecting the lower limbs.

tropical spastic p. A gradually progressive disease of the spinal cord caused by infection with human T-cell lymphotropic virus—I. SYN: *HTLV-1-associated myelopathy.*

SYMPTOMS: Symptoms include back pain with gradual loss of motor function in one or both legs, ataxia, and urinary incontinence.

paraphasia (păr-ă-fā'zē-ă) [" + *aphasis*, speech loss] A form of aphasia in which a meaningless or inappropriate word or syllable is substituted for the correct spoken word or word combinations. SYN: *paraphemia; paraphrasia.* **paraphasic** (-fā'zĭk), *adj.*

paraphilia (pă-ră-fēl'ē-ă) [" + *philein*, to love] A psychosexual disorder in which unusual or bizarre imagery or acts are necessary for realization of sexual excitement. This disorder includes bestiality, fetishism, transvestism, zoophilia, pedophilia, exhibitionism, voyeurism, sexual masochism, and sexual sadism.

paraphimosis (păr"ă-fī-mō'sĭs) [" + *phimoun*, to muzzle, + *osis*, condition] Strangulation of the glans penis due to retraction of a narrowed or inflamed foreskin.

paraplegia (par-ă-plē'j(ē-)ă) [*para-* + *-plegia*] Paralysis of the lower portion of the body and of both legs. It is caused by a lesion involving the spinal cord that may be due to maldevelopment, epidural abscess, hematomyelia, acute transverse myelitis, spinal neoplasms, multiple sclerosis, syringomyelia, or trauma. SEE: *Nursing Diagnoses Appendix.*

PATIENT CARE: Patient care during the acute period, immediately following traumatic injury, aims at stabilizing the patient and preventing further injury or deterioration. Initial and ongoing neurological assessment by nurses, the neurologist, and the neurosurgeon helps to determine the level and degree of paralysis and the patient's potential for recovery. Supportive medical therapy, based on assessment results, is provided. Specific medical, neurological, and neurosurgical interventions depend on the etiology of the paraplegia. Prescribed therapies are administered, and desired and adverse effects assessed for.

The patient should have early consultations with physical and occupational therapy staff, because correct body alignment, positioning, and exercise can prevent complications, encouraging the patient to think about rehabilitation from the beginning. The respiratory therapist also is involved early on to monitor ventilatory activity and help prevent respiratory complications. If intensive care is required, the health care provider recognizes the need to limit sensory overload by controlling and moderating environmental stimuli and to avoid sleep deprivation by planning an uninterrupted sleep time. Because immobility affects all body systems, they must each be monitored for expected and complicating changes. Medical consultations (as with a pulmonologist or a urologist) are made as necessary, and treatment regimens are developed based on each patient's needs.

The patient experiences paraplegia as a profound loss, affecting not only independent mobility but also self-image and self-esteem. Although the loss may be sudden or gradual, predictable or unexpected, and temporary or permanent, depending on the cause of the patient's paraplegia, it is present, nevertheless. Because family members also are affected, the health care provider includes them when helping the patient with grief work and mourning, recognizing that anger and despondency are expected responses. Referral to a mental health care provider can help patients cope with their loss.

Patients with paraplegia are usually transferred to a rehabilitation facility once the acute period has passed. This move often engenders transfer anxiety, as the patient and family fear a lesser level of care as a threat to security and well-being. Behavioral and psychosomatic manifestations may occur. A liaison nurse from the new facility can help the patient bridge the transition by providing information about the facility and the vigorous program the patient will encounter. The family should be encouraged to visit the facility and to bring any questions or concerns to their liaison, while giving the patient positive input.

Rehabilitation requires the patient's active participation to achieve his or her highest potential, and this participation begins with planning. The patient's individualized plan of care should be developed by the entire rehabilitation team, which includes the patient and significant others who make up the support system, as well as the primary physician, nurse, physiatrist, physical therapist, occupational therapist, vocational counselor, dietitian, social worker, psychologist, and neuropsychologist. The goals of the plan include learning to manage neuromuscular deficits and being able to perform activities of daily living (ADLs) with enough independence to function successfully in the home, workplace, and social situations. Activities include proper positioning, range-of-motion exercises, balancing and sitting, transfer activities, ambulation, and use of equipment to aid ambulation (if the patient will be able to walk with the aid of braces, canes, or crutches) or adjustment to being in a wheelchair. Skin care is of great importance, as persons with paraplegia are at risk for pressure sore development because of their motor, sensory, and vasomotor deficits. Poor nutrition, infection, debilitation, edema, and prolonged immobility are contributing factors. Assessment and prevention of breakdown, as well as treatment of most areas of broken skin, fall within the purview of nursing, although severe pressure sores may require surgical débridement and plastic surgery.

Cystometric studies help to assess bladder function and determine the patient's ability to participate in a bladder-retraining program, as opposed to requiring catheter or condom-catheter drainage methods. Bowel incontinence also demands assessment of cause and contributing factors (autonomic dysfunction, sacral injury, immobility, decreased food intake, esp. roughage). Incontinence is managed matter-of-factly, getting the patient involved, observing behavioral cues related to the need for defecation, noting defecation habits and using them for appropriate toileting, and supporting the patient's self-esteem. Bowel retraining involves establishing and maintaining a defecation routine. All members of the rehabilitation team, but esp. mental health care providers, are involved in helping the patient and family cope with the lifestyle changes necessitated by the illness or injury. Psychosocial care begins with listening to the patient's and family's perceptions of the impact of the disability, their expectations for the future, and learning about their personalities, previous coping abilities, and previous adjustment patterns.

The adjustment to discharge to home or group living adds its own set of transfer anxieties. The team teaches the patient and family any special procedures they will need and determines home and vehicle modifications needed to provide access for wheelchair or other necessary equipment. Group sessions with others who have faced similar situations often help both the patient and family. Initiating the move with a "weekend pass," followed by a return to process feelings and activities, can also help. It is important to note that rehabilitation, instead of ending with discharge, is an ongoing process central to living a worthwhile life. Involvement in paraplegic group activities including a variety of sports (wheelchair basketball, swimming) helps patients to focus on what they can learn, enjoy, and accomplish.

alcoholic p. Alcoholic **paralysis**.

ataxic p. Lateral and posterior sclerosis of the spinal cord characterized by slowly progressing ataxia and paresis.

cerebral p. Paraplegia from a bilateral cerebral lesion.

congenital spastic p. Infantile spastic **p.**

p. dolorosa Paraplegia due to pressure of a neoplasm on the posterior spinal cord and nerve roots; extremely painful despite paralysis.

hereditary spastic p. Any of a group of inherited diseases of the central nervous system characterized by muscle spasticity, esp. of the lower extremities. SYN: *Troyer syndrome*.

infantile spastic p. Spastic paraplegia that occurs in infants, usually due to birth injury. SYN: *congenital spastic p.*

peripheral p. Paraplegia due to pressure on, injury to, or disease of peripheral nerves.

Pott p. SEE: under *Pott, John Percivall.*

primary spastic p. Paraplegia from degeneration in corticospinal tracts.

superior p. Paralysis of both arms.

paraplegic (păr-ă-plē′jĭk) [Gr. *paraplegia*, stroke on one side] Pert. to or afflicted with paraplegia.

Parapoxvirus (par″ă-poks′vī″rŭs) [*para- + poxvirus*] A genus of very large DNA viruses that primarily infect ungulates such as deer and cattle. Transmission to humans occasionally occurs, e.g., when farmers, hunters, and ranchers butcher or dress animals.

paraprofessional (păr″ă-prō-fĕsh′ŭn-ăl) A person with education and training in a specific area of one of the professions (e.g., medicine or law) who provides services in that profession as an extension of an individual licensed to practice independently.

paraprotein (păr″ă-prō′tē-ĭn) An abnormal plasma protein, such as a macroglobulin, cryoglobulin, or immunoglobulin. SEE: *paraproteinemia*.

paraproteinemia (pă-ră-prō-tēn-ē′mē-ă) The presence of abnormal or excessive amounts of proteins, such as immunoglobulins or cryoglobulins, in the blood. Paraproteinemias include amyloidosis, cryoglobulinemia, cryofibrinogenemia, cold IgM antibody disease, light chain disease, monoclonal gammopathy, multiple myeloma, and Waldenström's macroglobulinemia. Plasma exchange therapy, immunomodulating drugs, or specific chemotherapeutic agents are used to treat these disorders.

parapsoriasis (păr″ă-sō-rī′ă-sĭs) [″ +

psoriasis, an itching] A chronic disorder of the skin marked by scaly red lesions.

p. en plaque A form of parapsoriasis that is often the precursor of mycosis fungoides.

p. lichenoides chronica A form of parapsoriasis that forms a widespread network over the extremities and trunk that is red to blue, sometimes resembling psoriasis or lichen planus.

parapsychology (păr″ă-sī-kŏl′ō-jē) A brand of psychology that deals with alleged instances of extrasensory perception, telepathy, psychokinesis, clairvoyance, and associated phenomena.

paraquat (păr′ă-kwăt) A toxic chemical used in agriculture to kill certain weeds. It damages the skin on contact and if ingested may cause vomiting, diarrhea, and liver, renal, and pulmonary disease. This chemical is sometimes present as a contaminant in marijuana.

pararectal (păr″ă-rĕk′tăl) [″ + L. *rectum,* straight] Near the rectum.

pararenal (păr″ă-rē′năl) [″ + L. *ren,* kidney] Near the kidneys.

parasexuality (păr″ă-sĕks″ū-ăl′ĭ-tē) [″ + L. *sexus,* sex] Recombination without sexual reproduction, as in fungi.

parasite (păr′ă-sīt) [″ + *sitos,* food] **1.** An organism that lives within, upon, and at the expense of another organism (its host), causing harm. **2.** The smaller or incomplete element of conjoined twins that is attached to and dependent on the more nearly normal twin (autosite).

accidental p. A parasite infesting a host that is not its normal host. SYN: *incidental p.*

external p. A parasite that lives on the outer surface of its host, such as a flea, louse, mite, or tick. SYN: *ectoparasite.*

facultative p. A parasite capable of living independently of its host at times; the opposite of an obligate parasite.

incidental p. Accidental **p.**

intermittent p. A parasite that visits its host at intervals for nourishment. SYN: *occasional p.*

internal p. A parasite such as a protozoon or worm that lives within the body of the host, occupying the digestive tract or body cavities, or living within body organs, blood, tissues, or cells. SYN: *endoparasite.*

obligate p. A parasite completely dependent on its host; the opposite of a facultative parasite.

obligate intracellular p. A parasite such as a virus or rickettsia that can reproduce only when within a living cell, although it may survive outside cells.

occasional p. Intermittent **p.**

periodic p. A parasite that lives on the host for short periods of time.

permanent p. A parasite, such as a

fluke or an itch mite, that lives on its host until maturity or spends its entire life on its host.

specific p. A parasite that requires a specific host in order to complete its life cycle. **parasitic** (păr″ă-sĭt′ĭk), *adj.*

parasitemia (păr″ă-sī-tē′mē-ă) [″ + ″ + *haima,* blood] The presence of parasites in the blood.

parasitic disease A disease resulting from the growth and development of parasitic organisms (plants or animals) in or on the body.

parasiticide (păr″ă-sĭt′ĭ-sīd) [″ + ″ + L. *caedere,* to kill] **1.** Destructive to parasites. **2.** An agent that kills parasites.

parasitism (păr′ă-sīt″ĭzm) [″ + ″ + *-ismos,* condition] **1.** The state or condition of being infected or infested with parasites. **2.** The behavior of a parasite.

parasitize (păr′ă-sĭt-īz″, -sĭt-īz″) To infest or infect with a parasite.

parasitologist (păr″ă-sī-tŏl′ō-jĭst) [″ + *logos,* word, reason] One who specializes in the science of parasitology.

parasitology (păr″ă-sī-tŏl′ō-jē) [″ + *logos,* word, reason] The study of parasites and parasitism.

parasitosis (păr″ă-sī-tō′sĭs) [″ + ″ + *osis,* condition] A disease or condition resulting from parasitism.

delusional p. The psychotic obsession or belief that one is infested with insects or parasites.

parasomnia (păr″ă-sŏm′nē-ă) [″ + L. *somnus,* sleep] Any of several abnormal experiences or behaviors occurring during sleep (e.g., bruxism, night terrors, or sleepwalking). SEE: *sleep disorder.*

paraspinal (par″ă-spīn′ăl) [*para- + spinal*] Adjacent to the spine.

parasternal (par″ă-stĕr′năl) [*para- + sternal*] Alongside the sternum.

Parastrongylus (păr″ă-strŏn′jĕ-lus) The former name for the roundworm genus *Angiostrongylus.* SEE: *Angiostrongylus.*

parasuicide (pă″ră-sū′ĭ-sīd″) The intentional act of injuring or harming oneself without intending to commit suicide.

parasympathetic (păr″ă-sĭm″pă-thĕt′ĭk) [″ + *sympathetikos,* sympathetic nerve] Of or pert. to the craniosacral division of the autonomic nervous system.

parasympathetic nervous system In the autonomic nervous system, those efferent (motor) circuits in which the preganglionic neurons are located in the brainstem or the most caudal segments of the spinal cord and the main postganglionic neurotransmitter is acetylcholine.

ANATOMY: The primary motor cells of the parasympathetic nervous system are found in the brainstem visceral motor nuclei (including, the Edinger-Westphal nucleus, superior and inferior salivatory nuclei, dorsal motor nucleus of the vagus, and nearby reticular nuclei) and in the lateral horns of the sacral segments of the spinal cord. The axons, the "preganglionic axons," of these neurons exit through cranial nerves (specifically, CN III, CN VII, CN IX, and CN X) or through sacral ventral roots (specifically, S2, S3, and S4) and synapse on neurons in small peripheral parasympathetic ganglia, all of which are located near the effector cells. The vagus nerve (CN X) is the major conduit for those preganglionic parasympathetic axons that innervate the autonomic ganglia of the viscera, including the gastrointestinal tract, lungs, heart, pancreas, liver, gallbladder, kidney, and ureters. In general, preganglionic parasympathetic axons tend to be long, while postganglionic parasympathetic axons are usually short.

PHYSIOLOGY AND PHARMACOLOGY: Activation of the parasympathetic nervous system relaxes an organism and allows it to focus inward, to digest food, and to rebuild. Parasympathetic activity constricts pupils, decreases heart rate, narrows airways, increases motility of the gastrointestinal tract, and increases storage of glucose.

Most of these effects are produced by acetylcholine interacting with cholinergic receptors on effector cells (smooth muscle, cardiac muscle, and secretory cells, although parasympathetic postganglionic axons also affect target cells by secreting other active chemicals, such as nitric oxide and a number of peptides.) There are two main classes of cholinergic receptors— muscarinic and nicotinic; autonomic effector cells typically have muscarinic receptors. Drugs other than acetylcholine can act on cholinergic receptors, and receptor subtypes differ in their sensitivity to specific drugs. For example, bethanechol, carbachol, muscarine, and pilocarpine selectively activate muscarinic cholinergic receptors and atropine, ipratropium, and scopolamine selectively block muscarinic cholinergic receptors. The availability of selective drugs allows some autonomic medical symptoms to be targeted selectively. SEE: *autonomic nervous system* for illus. and table; *sympathetic nervous system.*

parasympatholytic (par″ă-sim″pă-thō-lit′ik) [*para- + sympatholytic*] Anticholinergic.

parasympathomimetic (păr″ă-sĭm″pă-thō-mĭm-ĕt′ĭk) [″ + ″ + *mimetikos,* imitative] Producing effects similar to those resulting from stimulation of the parasympathetic nervous system.

parasystole (păr-ă-sĭs′tō-lē) [″ + *systole,* contraction] An ectopically originating cardiac rhythm independent of the normal sinus rhythm.

paratenic host SEE: under *host.*

paratenon (păr″ă-tĕn′ŏn) [″ + *tenon,* tendon] Fatty and areolar tissue that fills the spaces within the facscia around a tendon.

paratestis (păr″ă-tĕs′tĭs) [″ + ″] The anatomical structures immediately adjacent to the testis.

parathion (par″ă-thī′ŏn, ′on″) [*para-* + *thio-* + *-one*] An agricultural insecticide that is highly toxic to humans and animals.

parathormone (păr″ă-thor′mōn) [Gr. *para,* beside, + *thyreos,* shield, + *eidos,* form, shape, + *hormaein,* to excite] Parathyroid hormone.

parathyroidectomy (păr″ă-thī-royd-ĕk′tō-mē) [″ + ″ + ″ + *ektome,* excision] Surgical removal of one or more of the parathyroid glands; used as a treatment for hyperparathyroidism or neoplasm. Because the parathyroid glands maintain serum calcium levels, removal of the parathyroid glands may produce profound hypocalcemia. SEE: *Nursing Diagnoses Appendix.*

PATIENT CARE: The patient's understanding of the procedure and postoperative care is assessed. The health care provider gives additional information and answers questions. Baseline levels of serum potassium, calcium, phosphate, and magnesium are obtained prior to treatment and are carefully monitored in both blood and urine throughout preoperative treatment and the postoperative period. Preoperatively serum calcium levels are reduced by forcing fluids, limiting calcium in the diet, using intravenous normal saline solution plus furosemide or ethacrinic acid to promote diuresis and increase sodium and calcium excretion, and administering sodium or potassium phosphate, subcutaneous calcitonin, intravenous biphosphonates, or intravenous plicamycin. During this period of hydration, fluid intake and output are recorded, with total intake of at least 3 L/day. All urine is strained for calculi. Breath sounds are auscultated frequently to assess the patient for volumeoverload. Because the patient is at risk for pathologic fractures, safety precautions are taken to minimize potential injuries. The bed is kept in low position with side rails in place. The patient is moved and turned gently and carefully, and assisted with walking. Postoperatively, all general patient care concerns apply. The head of the patient's bed should be slightly elevated (semi-Fowler's position) and the patient watched closely for respiratory distress. A tracheostomy tray should be available at the bedside for emergency use. The patient is also assessed for laryngeal nerve damage (hoarseness or loss of voice) and hemorrhage. The operative site is checked for swelling, dressings (and esp. the posterior neck) checked for bleeding, and the head and

neck supported with sandbags to reduce edema, which can result in pressure on the trachea and other vital structures. The patient is assessed for signs of tetany (tingling around the mouth or in thehands), which should subside. Calcium gluconate or calcium chloride is kept available for intravenous administration should neuromuscular irritability or other signs of severe tetany occur. During the first 4 to 5 days postoperatively, supplemental calcium may be needed as serum calcium falls to low normal levels, and vitamin D or calcitriol also may be given to help raise calcium levels. If serum levels of magnesium or phosphate are low, magnesium phosphate or sodium phosphate is administered intravenously, or given orally or by retention enema. Listlessness, irritability, and muscle weakness may indicate persistent hypercalcemia. Pain is monitored, and pain control is provided by patient-controlled analgesia or by round-the-clock preventive dosing. Well-supported ambulation is begun early in the postoperative period, as pressure on long bones encourages bone recalcification. Before discharge, the patient is taught about prescribed drug therapies, includingadverse effects that should be reported, and about the importance of recognizing and seeking medical attention for signs of calcium deficiency. Instruction is provided in incisional care. The importance of ambulation and activity is emphasized. Arrangements are made for initial postoperative visits to the surgeon and/or endocrinologist.

paratope (păr′ă-tōp) [″ + *topos,* a place] The site on an antibody to which an antigen attaches. SEE: *epitope.*

paratracheal (par″ă-trā′kē-ăl) [*para-* + *tracheal*] Adjacent to the trachea.

paratyphoid fever (par″ă-tī′foyd″) [*para-* + *typhoid*] SEE: under *fever.*

paraumbilical (păr″ă-ŭm-bĭl′ĭk-ăl) [″ + L. *umbilicus,* navel] Periumbilical.

paravalvular (par″ă-val′vyŭ-lăr) [*para-* + *valvular*] Surrounding or adjacent to a heart valve.

paravenous (păr″ă-vē′nŭs) [″ + L. *vena,* vein] Located close to a vein.

paravertebral (păr″ă-vĕr′tĕ-brăl) [″ + L. *vertebralis,* pert. to vertebrae] Alongside or near the vertebral column.

paraxial (păr-ăk′sē-ăl) [″ + L. *axis,* axis] On either side of the axis of the body or one of its parts.

parched (părch) Extremely dry or shriveled.

Paré, Ambroise (păr-ā′) French surgeon, 1510–1590, who instituted certain refined techniques into surgery, obstetrics, and wound care.

paregoric (păr-ĕ-gor′ĭk) [L. *paregoricus,* soothing] **1.** Camphorated tincture of opium, a narcotic-containing drug that in large doses is poisonous; used in the symptomatic treatment of diarrhea. **2.** Soothing.

parenchyma (păr-ĕn′kĭ-mă) [Gr. *parenkheim*, to pour in beside] The essential parts of an organ that are concerned with its function in contradistinction to its framework.

parenchymatous (păr″ĕn-kĭm′ă-tŭs) Concerning the essential tissues of an organ.

parent (par′ĕnt) [L. *parere*, to bring forth, bear] **1.** One who begets or bears offspring; a father or a mother. **2.** In radiation physics, a radioactive substance that decays into another nuclide.

   adoptive p. One who assumes legally authorized parental responsibilities for another person's child.

   birth p. One of the biological parents of a child. SEE: *surrogate parenting.*

parentage, determination of (păr-ĕntj) SEE: *paternity test.*

parental consent SEE: under *consent.*

parental leave (păr-ĕn-tăl) The policy of allowing one or both parents to have leave from work following the birth of their child.

parenteral (păr-ĕn′tĕr-ăl) [Gr. *para,* beside, + *enteron,* intestine] Denoting any medication route other than the alimentary canal, such as intravenous, subcutaneous, intramuscular, or mucosal. SEE: *medication route.*

   p. nutrition SEE: *total parenteral nutrition.*

parenteral therapy A medicine or solution administered via a route other than ingestion.

parenting (păr-ĕn-tēng) **1.** Caring for and raising a child or children. **2.** Producing offspring.

   impaired p. Inability of the primary caretaker to create an environment that promotes the optimum growth and development of the child. SEE: *Nursing Diagnoses Appendix.*

   impaired p., risk for Risk for inability of the primary caretaker to create, maintain, or regain an environment that promotes the optimum growth and development of the child. SEE: *Nursing Diagnoses Appendix.*

   surrogate p. An alternative method of childbearing for an infertile couple in which the wife is unable to bear a child. The surrogate mother agrees to be artificially inseminated by the husband's sperm and to relinquish the baby to the couple. Another approach is to retrieve eggs from the infertile wife and have them impregnated in vitro by her husband. The fertilized ovum is then implanted in the surrogate mother. SEE: *fertilization, in vitro; GIFT.*

parenting, readiness for enhanced A pattern of providing an environment for children or other dependent persons that is sufficient to nurture growth and development and can be strengthened. SEE: *Nursing Diagnoses Appendix.*

parent-of-origin The parent from whom a particular gene or trait is inherited.

paresis (pă-rē′sĭs, par′ĕ-sĭs, pă-rē′sēz″, par′ĕ-sēz″) *pl.* **pareses** [Gr. *paresis,* paralysis] **1.** Partial or incomplete paralysis. SEE: *paralysis.* **2.** A dated but occasionally used term for neurological complications of syphilis. **paretic** (pă-ret′ik), *adj.*

paresthesia (par″es-thē′zh(ē-)ă) [*para-* + *esthesi-* + *-ia*] An abnormal or unpleasant sensation that results from injury to one or more nerves. It is often described by patients as numbness and tingling, or as a prickly, stinging, or burning feeling.

pareunia (păr-ē-ū′nē-ă) [Gr. *pareunos,* lying beside] Sexual intercourse. SEE: *dyspareunia.*

paries (pă′rē-ēs) *pl.* **parietes** [L., a wall] The enveloping wall of any structure; applied esp. to hollow organs.

parietal (pă-rī′ĕ-tăl) [L. *parietalis*] **1.** Pert. to, or forming, the wall of a cavity. **2.** Pert. to the parietal bone.

   p. cell A large cell on the margin of the gastric glands of the stomach that secretes hydrochloric acid and intrinsic factor. SYN: *oxyntic cell.* SEE: *achlorhydria; anemia, pernicious; intrinsic factor.*

Parietaria judaica (păr-ī″ĕ-tār′ē-ă joo-dā′ĭ-kă) [L., Jew's pellitory] ABBR: Par j. The scientific name for a weed found primarily in southern Europe and the Mediterranean. Allergens derived from the pollen of this weed are a common cause of seasonal allergies. SYN: *pellitory-of-the-wall.*

parietofrontal (pă-rī″ĕ-tō-frŏn′tăl) Pert. to both the parietal and frontal bones of the skull or the parietal and frontal lobes of the brain.

parieto-occipital (pă-rī″ĕ-tō-ŏk-sĭp′ĭ-tăl) Pert. to both the parietal and occipital bones of the skull or the parietal and occipital lobes of the brain.

parietotemporal (pă-rī″ĕ-tō-tĕm″pō-răl) Pert. to the parietal and temporal bones or lobes.

parietovisceral (pă-rī″ĕ-tō-vĭs′ĕr-ăl) Pert. to the wall of a body cavity and the viscera within.

Parinaud, Henri (pă-rĭ-nō′) French ophthalmologist, 1844–1905.

   P. oculoglandular syndrome Conjunctivitis with palpable preauricular lymph nodes.

   P. ophthalmoplegia syndrome Dorsal midbrain syndrome with palsy of vertical gaze. It is caused by a brainstem lesion near the vertical gaze center. Sometimes associated with inability to converge the eyes and poor pupillary response to light.

pari passu (păr′ē-păs′ū) [L., with equal

speed] Occurring at the same time or at the same rate; side by side.

¹parity (par′ĭt-ē) [Fr. *parité*, fr L. *paritas*, equality, parity] Equality, similarity.

²parity (par′ĭt-ē) [L. *parere*, to bring forth, to bear] The number of live children a woman has delivered. SEE: *multiparity; nulliparity*.

Parkinson, James (par′kĭn-sŏn) Brit. physician, 1755–1824.

     P. disease ABBR: PD. A common, chronic degenerative disease of the central nervous system that produces progressive movement disorders and changes in cognition and mood. Its hallmarks include a pill-rolling tremor of the hands, muscular rigidity, loss of facial expression, difficulty initiating movements (akinesia, bradykinesia), and gait disturbances (esp. shuffling gait, festination, and sometimes difficulty initiating forward movements). Parkinson's disease is usually found in people over the age of 65. Its underlying cause is unknown; it is clear, however, that dopamine production by brain cells in the substantia nigra is diminished in the disease. Although PD often clusters in families, it is uncertain whether this is the result of genetics or of exposure to common precipitating agents (viruses, toxins, or drugs). In the U.S. about 1.5 million people have PD, with about 50,000 new cases diagnosed each year. SEE: *Nursing Diagnoses Appendix.*

     SYMPTOMS: Most patients report gradual onset of fatigue, or malaise, followed by evidence of a tremor in one or more extremities, typically a hand when it is at rest. Such tremors increase during periods of anxiety or stress but decrease during purposeful motion or sleep. Other common symptoms include difficulty getting up from a chair or turning over in bed, a change in vocal quality (a softer, less audible, more monotonous voice), shuffling gait that becomes faster after a few steps (festination), and a stooped posture. As the years pass, frequent falls may occur. Occasionally a tendency to fall backward (retropulsion) replaces festination. Facial expressiveness may diminish (patients are said to have masklike facies), swallowing often becomes impaired, and handwriting may become smaller or more cramped (micrographia).

     TREATMENT: The goal of treatment is to maintain function for as long as possible and relieve symptoms. Medical therapies include selegiline, levodopa/carbidopa; dopamine agonists (e.g., bromocriptine); inhibitors of catechol-o-methyltransferase (e.g., entacapone), and monoamine oxidase-B inhibitors (e.g., deprenyl). Surgical therapy, which is performed at a small number of hospitals, may involve transplantation of dopamine-secreting cells (fetal brain tissue, nerve cells from other parts of the patient's body) into affected areas of the brain or insertion of electrical brain stimulators into the subthalamic nucleus, globus pallidus internus, or ventral intermediate nucleus. Physical therapy is a very important part of the treatment, helping to maintain muscle tone and function.

     PATIENT CARE: Teamwork benefits the PD patient, who may require a social worker, nurses, primary care providers, a neurologist, registered dietitian, physical therapist, occupational therapist, and speech therapist. Patients should be monitored for the efficacy and safety of drug therapy, particularly when a new drug is prescribed. Drug-drug interactions are common but may be avoided with careful dose titration and prescribing. Elderly patients are at increased risk for adverse effects because of reduced drug tolerance and should be assessed for postural hypotension, pulse irregularities, blepharospasm, and anxiety and confusion. Drug dosages should be reduced if adverse side effects occur. If patients have periods of immobility alternating with periods of severely impaired mobility, they may need changes in their medication schedule or new, additional medications. The patient and family are taught safety measures to prevent injury caused by falling, aswell as swallowing techniques to deal with dysphagia. Prescribed drugs are administered and evaluated for desired effects and adverse reactions; the patient is instructed in their use and potential side effects so that the dosage can be adjusted to minimize the side effects. The nurse, physician, or occupational or physical therapist teaches the patient and family about safety measures to prevent injury, about drug-related dietary restrictions, and about the need for frequent small feedings to provide needed fluids, calories, and dietary bulk. Drinking at least 2 L/day of liquids and eating a high-fiber diet help to establish a regular bowel routine; an elevated toilet seat and frame can help the patient in moving from sitting to standing position. Independence is encouraged. The patient should plan daily activities for when he or she feels rested to prevent fatigue, but even so, the patient needs to exercise regularly (active and passive range of motion,walking, massage, baths, carrying out activities of daily living) to help relax muscles and prevent contractures and muscle atrophy. Education about progression of the disease and emotional support are provided; the family is assisted to recognize and fulfill the patient's need for intellectual stimulation and recreation. The patient is also referred to national organizations (e.g., the National Parkinson Foundation, Inc.; www.parkinson.org) for additional information.

P. facies The immobile, masklike, facial expression that is a hallmark of Parkinson disease and postencephalitic states. Its is informally called "Parkinson's mask."

parkinsonian (păr″kĭn-sōn′ē-ăn) Concerning Parkinson disease and/or its characteristic signs and symptoms.

parkinsonism (păr′kĭn-sŏn-ĭzm″) A neurological disorder in which a few but not all of the symptoms of Parkinson disease are present.

Parkland formula (park′lănd) [*Parkland Memorial Hospital , Dallas, TX*] A formula used to compute the approximate need for intravenous hydration in patients who have suffered burns, based on the percent of body surface area that has been injured.

PAR nurse *postanesthesia recovery room nurse.*

parodontitis (păr″ō-dŏn-tī′tĭs) [″ + *odous,* tooth, + *itis,* inflammation] Inflammation of the tissues around a tooth.

parodontium (păr″ō-dŏn′shē-ŭm) Periodontium.

parole (pă-rōl′) [Fr. *parole,* short for *parole d'honneur,* word of honor] **1.** In psychiatry, the release of a patient from the hospital on a trial basis. **2.** In the criminal justice system, the release of an prisoner from to monitored life in society at large. SYN: *community supervision.*

paronychia (păr-ō-nĭk′ē-ă) [″ + *onyx,* nail] An acute or chronic infection of the marginal structures about the nail. SYN: *felon; runaround; whitlow.* SEE: illus.

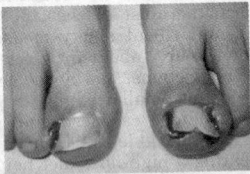

PARONYCHIA

SYMPTOMS: The nail edge shows redness, swelling, and suppuration.
TREATMENT: Therapy may involve moist heat application, oral antibiotics, or surgical drainage.

paroophoron (pă″-ō-ŏf′ă-rŏn″) [″ + *oophoros,* bearing eggs] A group of minute tubules located in the mesosalpinx between the uterus and ovary. It is a vestigial structure consisting of the remains of the caudal group of mesonephric tubules and is a homologue of the paradidymis of the male.

parosmia (păr-ŏz′mē-ă) [″ + *osme,* odor] Any disorder or perversion of the

sense of smell; a false sense of odors or perception of those that do not exist. Agreeable odors are considered offensive, and disagreeable ones pleasant. Intravenous fluid therapy, esp. postoperatively, may create temporary parageusia and parosmia. SYN: *parosphresia.* SEE: *cacosmia.*

parosteal (păr-ŏs′tē-ăl) Concerning the outermost layer of the periosteum.

parosteosis, parostosis (par″os-tē-ō′sĭs, par″os-tō′sĭs) [″ + *osteon,* bone, + *osis,* condition] **1.** Bone formation outside of the periosteum. **2.** Bone development in an unusual location.

parotidectomy (pă-rŏt″ĭ-děk′tō-mē) [″ + *ous,* ear, + *ektome,* excision] Excision of the parotid gland. This procedure is most often performed to excise a malignancy and less often to remove a stone (calculus) that cannot be extracted from Stenson's duct in the mouth.

PATIENT CARE: The patient's understanding of the procedure and postoperative care is assessed, including suctioning and the nasogastric tube for drainage. The patient is encouraged to express feelings and anxiety about the surgery and alterations in body image. After surgery, the patient is asked to perform facial movements such as smiling, frowning, and exposing teeth to observe for possible damage to the facial nerve. Pain is managed. Drainage should be observed for excessive bleeding. A patent airway is maintained, and good oral hygiene and nutrition are encouraged.

parotitis, parotiditis (pă-rŏt″ĭ-dī′tĭs, pă″rō-tī′tĭs) [″ + *ous,* ear, + *itis,* inflammation] Inflammation of the parotid gland.

granulomatous p. Granulomatous inflammation of the parotid gland, usually due to tuberculosis or sarcoidosis.

suppurative p. Bacterial infection of the parotid gland, usually in patients with decreased salivary flow. It is often caused by *Staphylococcus aureus.*

parous (păr′ŭs) [L. *pario,* to bear] Parturient; fruitful; having borne at least one child.

parovarian (păr-ō-vā′rē-ăn) [Gr. *para,* beside, + LL. *ovarium,* ovary] **1.** Situated near or beside the ovary. **2.** Pert. to the parovarium, a residual structure in the broad ligament.

parovarium (păr″ō-vā′rē-ŭm) Epoophoron.

paroxetine (păr-ŏx′ĕ-tēn) A selective serotonin reuptake inhibitor used as an antianxiety agent and antidepressant. It is administered orally to manage depression, panic, obsessive-compulsive disorder, social anxiety, and general anxiety. It may be used as an adjunct to psychotherapy.

paroxysm (păr′ŏk-sĭzm) [Gr. *paroxys-*

mos, irritation] **1.** A sudden, periodic attack or recurrence of symptoms of a disease; an exacerbation of the symptoms of a disease. **2.** A sudden spasm or convulsion of any kind. **3.** A sudden emotional state, as of fear, grief, or joy.

paroxysmal (păr″ŏk-sĭz′măl) Occurring repeatedly and without warning.

> **p. nocturnal hemoglobinuria** SEE: under *hemoglobinuria.*

paroxysmal nocturnal dyspnea SEE: under *dyspnea.*

PARQ conference [park] [Acronym fm *p(rocedure), a(lternative), r(isk),* and *q(uestion)*] A conference to establish informed consent for medical treatment or surgery in which the proposed procedure, alternatives to the procedure, and its risks are discussed, and the patient has the opportunity to ask questions and have them answered.

Parrot, Joseph Marie Jules (păr-ō′) French physician, 1829–1883.

> **P. disease 1.** Osteochondritis that occurs in infants with congenital syphilis. **2.** A form of dwarfism that is transmitted as an autosomal dominant.

> **P. nodes** Bony nodules on the skull of infants with congenital syphilis. Also called *Parrot's sign.*

> **P. pseudoparalysis** Pseudoparalysis caused by syphilitic osteochondritis.

> **P. sign Parrot** nodes.

> **P. ulcer** Lesions seen in thrush or stomatitis.

Parry-Romberg syndrome (păr′ē rŏm′bĕrg) Progressive hemifacial atrophy.

pars (pärz) *pl.* **partes** [L.] A part; portion of a larger structure.

> **p. flaccida membranae tympani** The portion of the membrane of the eardrum that fills the notch of Rivinus. This portion of the drum is not taut. SYN: *Shrapnell membrane.*

> **p. interarticularis** The region between the superior and inferior articulating facets of a vertebra; the region where fracture frequently occurs with spondylolysis.

> **p. squamosa ossis temporalis** The flat portion of the temporal bone that forms part of the lateral wall of the skull.

> **p. tensa membranae tympani** The larger portion of the tympanic membrane, a tightly stretched membrane lying inferior to the malleolar folds. SEE: *p. flaccida membranae tympani.*

Parse, Rosemarie (pärsē) A nursing educator who developed the Theory of Human Becoming and the Human Becoming School of Thought. SEE: *Nursing Theory Appendix.*

parsley (pars′lē) A root herb, *Petroselinum crispum,* of the carrot family used primarily in cooking as a spice. In herbal medicine it is used to promote menstruation, to treat high blood pressure, and to cleanse the bowels (when given as an enema). Parsley has a high content of oxalates (the chemical component of many kidney stones). It also contains chemicals that may cause rashes in patients exposed to ultraviolet light.

Parsonage-Turner syndrome Idiopathic brachial plexopathy.

pars planitis (pärs plā-nī′tĭs) Inflammation of the anterior chamber, the anterior vitreous, and/or the peripheral retina of the eye. It commonly causes floaters and blurring of vision. The disease may occur in childhood or adulthood. It is associated with autoimmune diseases such as multiple sclerosis or sarcoidosis and infectious diseases such as Lyme disease, syphilis, or tuberculosis. Treatments include treatment of the underlying illness and/or laser or cryotherapy. SYN: *intermediate uveitis.*

partes (pär′tēs) Pl. of pars.

Parthenium argentatum (par-then′ē-ŭm ar″jĕn-tāt′ŭm) SEE: *guayule.*

parthenogenesis (par″thĕ-nō-jen′ĕ-sis) [Gr. *parthenos,* virgin, + *-genesis*] Reproduction arising from a female egg that has not been fertilized by the male; unisexual reproduction. **parthenogenetic** (-jĕ-net′ik), *adj.* **parthenogenetically** (-i-k(ă-)lē), *adv.* **parthenogenic** (-jen′ik), *adj.*

partial-thickness (par′shăl-thik′nĕs) Pert. to a graft, wound, or pressure sore affecting the epidermis and part of the dermis.

participant observation (păr-tĭ-sĭ-pănt) A method of field research in which the investigator observes and records information about the characteristics of a setting through experience as a participant in that setting.

participation (par″ti″sĭ-pā′shŏn) In rehabilitation, a person's involvement in life situations despite physical impairments, limitations on activity, or contextual factors, such as social or physical barriers in the environment. Participation in life activities, tasks, and roles is an aspect of living that is considered important within the framework of the World Health Organization's International Classification of Functioning, Disability, and Health (ICF). SEE: *International Classification of Functioning, Disability, and Health.*

participation restriction Any of the difficulties that a person with physical limitations may experience in the course of daily life. The term*participation restriction* has replaced *handicap.*

particle (part′-ĭ-kĕl) [L. *particula*] **1.** A very small piece or part of matter; a tiny fragment or trace. **2.** Any of several subatomic components of the nuclei of radioactive elements, such as alpha and beta particles. **3.** An attraction particle or centriole of the nucleus of a cell. **4.** Virion.

   alpha p. A charged particle emitted from a radioactive substance made up of a helium nucleus consisting of two protons and two electrons. The particle has very low penetrability but an extremely high linear energy transfer.

   beta p. Beta **ray**.

   charged p. Any ion or subatomic particle that carries an electrical charge, e.g., in medicine, a proton used in radiation therapy. By convention, protons are positively charged particles; electrons, negatively charged.

   Dane p. SEE: *Dane particle.*

   elementary p. The subatomic parts of the atomic nucleus.

   large low density lipoprotein p. ABBR: large LDL particle. A low density lipoprotein larger than 213 angstroms. The particles are thought to represent the least atherogenic fraction of the LDL molecule.

particle therapy, particle beam therapy The use of heavy nuclear particles, e.g., protons, neutrons, or helium ions, to bombard and destroy diseased tissues, esp. cancers. SYN: *hadron therapy.*

particulate (par-tik′yŭ-lăt, -lāt″) [L. *particula,* a little part] **1.** Made up of particles. **2.** A substance made up of particles.

particulate matter ABBR: PM. Small but discrete airborne or waterborne solids, such as fragments of ash, dust, pollen, or soot. They may be generated by the burning of fossil fuels, agricultural or construction projects, incineration, mining, and other natural and artificial processes. Higher levels of PM in air have been associated with increases in lung disease and mortality in exposed populations.

partner (part′nĕr) **1.** A colleague or co-worker. **2.** A member of a partnership. **3.** A spouse or confidant. **4.** A person with whom one has sex.

partner notification A public health practice in which the sexual contacts of persons diagnosed with sexually transmitted diseases are made aware of their exposure and are advised to seek medical attention. Two methods are used to contact persons at risk. They may be notified directly by their sexual partner or partners, or they may be contacted by public health authorities who have obtained their names from their sexual partner or partners.

partogram (part′ŏ-gram″) In obstetrics, a graphical representation of labor that in a healthy delivery results in the birth of a child.

   PATIENT CARE: The parameters recorded on the graph include changes in fetal heart rate, rate of dilation of the maternal cervix, and rate of fetal de-

scent. These data can be compared with known norms to help identify delays in the expected progress of labor and improve intrapartum care.

parts per million ABBR: PPM; ppm. The concentration of a solute in a liquid or gas. For example, a pollutant such as soot may be said to be present in air at a level of 50 parts per million (parts of air). The units also may be expressed as weight of one substance to the weight of another or the volume of a fluid in the volume of another.

parturient (păr-tū′rē-ĕnt) [L. *parturiens,* in labor] Concerning childbirth or parturition; giving birth.

parturition (păr-tū-rĭsh′ŭn) [L. *parturitio*] The act of giving birth to young. SYN: *childbirth.* SEE: *delivery; labor.*

party (păr′tē) A person or entity who acts as petitioner, plaintiff, or defendant in a legal action.

parulis (pă-roo′lĭs) [Gr. *para,* beside, + *oulon,* gum] Gumboil.

parv-, parvi-, parvo- [L. *parvus,* small] Prefixes meaning *small.*

parvocellular, parvicellular (par″vō-sel′yŭ-lăr) [*parvo-* + *cellular*] Having a small cell body. It is said esp. of cells found in the lateral geniculate nucleus of the thalamus.

parvovirus (par″vō-vī′rŭs) [*parvo-* + *virus*] Any of a group of viruses similar to adeno-associated viruses. They are pathogenic in animals and humans.

   p. B19 SEE: *erythrovirus B19.*

PAS, PASA *para-aminosalicylic acid.*

pascal (pas-kal′) [Blaise Pascal, Fr. mathematician, physicist, philosopher of religion, 1623–1662] ABBR: Pa. A unit of pressure equal to the force of one newton acting uniformly over 1 m². SEE: *newton;* SI Units Appendix.

PASG *pneumatic antishock garment.* SEE: *MAST.*

pass (pas) [Fr. *passer,* fr L. *passare,* to step, pace] To release or discharge matter from the body, e.g., feces, urine, or a kidney stone.

passage (pas′ij) **1.** A channel between cavities and body structures or with the external surface of an organ. **2.** An evacuation of the bowels. **3.** Introduction of a probe or catheter. **4.** Incubation of a pathogenic organism, esp. a virus, in one or a series of tissue cultures or living organisms. **5.** In cell biology, a cycle of cellular proliferation of cells maintained in culture. **6.** In obstetrics, a colloquial term for the pelvis or birth canal.

passion (pash′ŏn) [L. *passio,* suffering] **1.** Suffering. **2.** Great emotion or zeal.

passion flower An herbal remedy from the American shrub or vine *Passiflora incarnata,* used primarily as a sedative or calming agent. Its effectiveness has not been systematically tested in human beings.

passivation (păs″ĭ-vā′shĭn) [″] The stabilization and protection of a surface from outside influences, e.g., the treatment of an atherosclerotic plaque to keep it from rupturing or of a metal to keep it from corroding.

passive (păs'ĭv) [L. *passivus,* capable of suffering] **1.** Not reacting or participating. **2.** Secondhand; unintentional (e.g., passive smoking). **3.** Submissive.

passive smoking The exposure of nonsmokers to the toxic gases released by the burning of tobacco products in their homes, workplaces, or recreational environments. Exposure to second-hand smoke has been linked to allergies, asthma, cardiovascular diseases, lung diseases, and stroke. Passive smoking causes about 30,000 deaths from heart disease and another 3,000 lung disease deaths annually in the U.S. SYN: *second-hand smoking.* SEE: *tobacco.*

passive transfer of antibodies SEE: under *transfer.*

passivity (păs-sĭv'ĭ-tē) [L. *passivus,* capable of suffering] **1.** Dependence on others. **2.** A reluctance to be self-determined or assertive.

paste (pāst) In pharmacy, a mixture of an ointment and a powder, having a semisolid consistency.

Pasteur, Louis (pas-tŭr'-tör') [Fr. chemist and bacteriologist, 1822–1895] Fr. chemist and bacteriologist, 1822–1895. He was the founder of microbiology. He also developed the technique of eliminating bacteria from food products and produced the first vaccines.

Pasteurella (păs-tă-rĕl'ă) [Louis Pasteur] A genus of gram-negative coccobacilli that causes disease in animals and humans. Pathogens once classed in this genus include *Yersinia pestis* (the microbe that causes plague) and *Francisella tularensis* (tularemia).

    P. multocida A species found in the oral cavities of cats, dogs, and other animals. It may be transmitted to humans by animal bites, and may cause cellulitis, abscesses, osteomyelitis, pneumonia, peritonitis, or meningitis. Penicillins, doxycycline, or cephalosporins are used to treat the infection.

pasteurellosis (păs″tĕr-ĕ-lō'sĭs) A disease caused by infection with bacteria of the genus *Pasteurella.*

pasteurization (păs″tūr-ī-zā'shŭn) [Louis Pasteur] The process of heating a fluid at a moderate temperature for a definite period of time to destroy undesirable bacteria without changing to any extent the chemical composition of the fluid. In pasteurization of milk, pathogenic bacteria are destroyed by heating at 62°C for 30 min, or by "flash" heating to higher temperatures for less than 1 min. The pasteurization process, reducing total bacterial count of the milk by 97% to 99%, is effective because the common milk-borne pathogens (tu-

bercle bacillus, and *Salmonella, Streptococcus,* and *Brucella* organisms) do not form spores and are quite sensitive to heat. SEE: *flash method; milk.*

pastille (păs-tēl', -tĭl') [L. *pastillus,* a little roll] **1.** A medicated disk used for local action on the mucosa of the throat and mouth. SYN: *lozenge; troche.* **2.** A small cone used to fumigate or scent the air of a room.

past-pointing (păst-pŏyn-tēng) The inability to place a finger or some other part of the body accurately on a selected point; seen esp. in cerebellar disorders.

PAT (păt) *Paroxysmal atrial tachycardia.* The contemporary, and more accurate, term is paroxysmal supraventricular tachycardia (PSVT).

patau syndrome Trisomy 13.

patch (pach) **1.** A small circumscribed area distinct from the surrounding surface in character and appearance. **2.** A drug delivery system that enhances the uptake of a medicine through the skin. **3.** Any substance or object used to repair a defect in the body. **patchy** (pach'ē), *adj.*

    blood p. An injection of a patient's own blood over the dura to repair a cerebrospinal fluid leak that may be caused by a lumbar puncture, esp. one performed with a large-bore needle. It is used to treat post–lumbar puncture headache. SYN: *epidural blood p.* SEE: *post–lumbar puncture headache.*

    cotton-wool p., cotton-wool spot A fluffy looking lesion in the nerve fiber layer caused by infarction; usually seen in hypertension, diabetes, collagen vascular disease, or AIDS.

    epidural blood p. Blood patch.

    herald p. A solitary oval patch of scaly skin that appears several days before the generalized rash of pityriasis rosea.

    Hutchinson p. SEE: under *Hutchinson, Sir Jonathan.*

    mucous p. A syphilitic eruption having an eroded, moist surface; usually on the mucous membrane of the mouth or external genitals, or on a surface subject to moisture and heat.

    nicotine p. A transdermal method of administering nicotine, used as an aid in quitting smoking.

    Peyer p. SEE: *Peyer patch.*

    salmon p. An oval pale retinal hemorrhage seen in sickle cell disease. SEE: *Hutchinson patch.*

    smoker's p. Leukoplakia of the oral mucosa.

    white p. A white, thickened area of oral mucosa that will not rub off and represents a benign hyperkeratosis. SEE: *leukoplakia.*

patch test A skin test in which a low concentration of a presumed allergen is applied to the skin beneath an occlusive dressing. The test is the primary method used to determine the presence of allergic contact dermatitis. If the concentration of the agent is too high or an allergy exists to the material used in the dressing, false-positive reactions can occur as a result of local irritation. False-negative reactions may result if the concentration of the suspected allergen is too low, or if the duration of the test is too short. Commercially available, standardized kits to facilitate patch testing include the T.R.U.E. test and Finn Chambers. SEE: illus.; *skin test*.

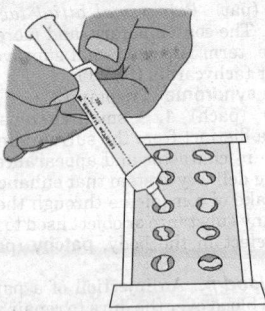

Patch tests are prepared

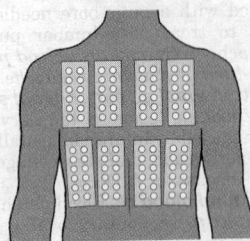

Patches are affixed to upper back

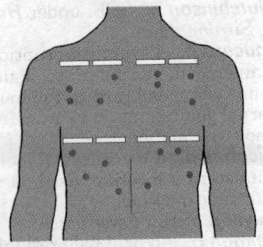

Hypersensitivity is determined

APPLYING PATCH TEST

patchy anesthetic block SEE: under *block*.

patella (pă-tel′ă, -tel′ē, -tel′ī″) *pl.* **patellae, patellas** [L. *patella*, a small pan] A lens-shaped sesamoid bone situated in front of the knee in the tendon of the quadriceps femoris muscle. SYN: *kneecap*. SEE: *osteochondritis* dissecans.

p. alta A high-riding patella (high po-

sitioning of patella). When a person is standing, the patella rests in a more superior position than normal.

p. baja A low-riding patella (low positioning of patella). When a person is standing, the patella rests in a more inferior position than normal.

ballotable p. Floating **p.**

bipartite p. The developing patella that matures from two centers rather than one. This usually congenital condition causes no symptoms but may be mistaken for a fracture.

dislocated p. Displacement of the patella from its normal position in the femoral trochlea. Most patellar dislocations are marked by obvious deformity and occur laterally. They result in the tearing or stretching of the medial patellar retinaculum and the oblique fibers of the vastus medialis muscle. The patella may spontaneously reduce as the patient attempts to straighten the knee.

floating p. A patella that rides up from the condyles owing to a large effusion in the knee. SYN: *ballotable p.*

fracture of p. A break in the continuity of the kneecap. Treatment may consist of suturing the bone fragments. A long-leg immobilizer is applied for 6 to 8 weeks. Following removal of the brace, gradual exercise may be started and weight placed on the leg for a few weeks, after which the patient may walk.

hypermobile p. Excessive medial and/or lateral motion of the patella. A medially hypermobile patella can be moved greater than 75% of its width medially. A laterally hypermobile patella can be moved greater than 75% of its width laterally. SEE: *hypomobile p.; apprehension test*.

ETIOLOGY: Increased medial patellar hypermobility can result from laxity of the lateral patellar retinaculum. Lateral patellar hypermobility indicates laxity of the medial patellar retinaculum and/or weakness of the oblique fibers of the vastus medialis.

SYMPTOMS: Increased motion of the patella within the femur's trochlea can lead to chondromalacia patellae, producing pain in weight-bearing activities, esp. squatting or climbing or descending stairs. Lateral patellar hypermobility is a predisposition to patellar dislocation or subluxation.

TREATMENT: Treatment and rehabilitation consists of strengthening the muscles on the side opposite the hypermobility. Neuromuscular reeducation may be needed to restore the normal recruitment sequence of the oblique fibers of the vastus medialis and the vastus lateralis.

hypomobile p. Lack of normal medial and/or lateral motion of the patella.

A medially hypomobile patella cannot be moved more than 25% of its width medially. A laterally hypomobile patella cannot be moved more than 15% of its width laterally. SEE: *hypermobile p.*

ETIOLOGY: Medial hypomobility often results from adhesions of the lateral patellar retinaculum or tightness of the iliotibial band. Lateral hypomobility can result from tightness of the medial patellar retinaculum or hypertrophy or spasm of the oblique fibers of the vastus medialis.

SYMPTOMS: The patient will complain of pain and demonstrate decreased strength during weight-bearing activities. Improper tracking of the patella as the result of hypomobility can lead to chondromalacia patellae.

TREATMENT: Physical agents such as moist heat and/or ultrasound and manual therapy techniques can be used to encourage the elasticity of the offending tissues. A surgical release of the patellar retinaculum may be required.

squinting p. A condition in which the patella appears to be pointing inward when the patient is standing; caused by excessive femoral anteversion.

patellar (pă-tĕl′ăr) Pert. to the patella.

patellectomy (păt″ĕ-lĕk′tō-mē) [″ + Gr. *ektome*, excision] Surgical removal of the patella.

patellofemoral (pă-tĕl″ō-fĕm′ō-răl) Concerning the patella and femur.

patellofemoral pain syndrome Pain in the knee that occurs with exertion (e.g., walking upstairs) and is associated with stiffness after prolonged sitting and tenderness when the patella is compressed on the femoral condyle or when it is moved laterally. SEE: *patellofemoral instability.*

patency (pā′tĕn-sē) [L. *patens,* open] The state of being freely open.

patent (pat′ĕnt (senses 1, 2), pāt′ (senses 2, 3)) [L. *litterae patentes,* open letters] ABBR: . **1.** Protected by trademark or trade name; patented. SEE: *proprietary* (3).

2. Evident; accessible. **3.** Having or offering free, unobstructed passage.

patent ductus arteriosus Persistence, after birth, of a communication between the main pulmonary artery and the aorta. This condition in preterm infants has been treated successfully with drugs, such as indomethacin, that inhibit prostaglandin synthesis. SEE: *prostaglandin.*

patent period SEE: under *period.*

paternal (pă-tĕr′năl) [L. *paternis,* fatherly] Pert. to or inherited from the father.

paternalism (pă-tĕr-năl-ĭzm) A type of medical decision making in which health care professionals exercise unilateral authority over patients. When patients are competent to make their own choices and health care professionals seek to act in the patients' best interests, shared decision making is preferable, because it encourages dialogue, preserves autonomy, fosters responsibility, and allows for adaptation.

paternity test (pă-tĕr-nĭ-tē) A test to determine the father of a child. Because paternity is a clinical estimate, there is the need to have tests to determine whether it would be possible for an individual to have fathered a specific child. At one time, the tests used to prove or exclude the possibility of paternity used blood type data from the child and the suspected father. Tests involving the technique of molecular genetic fingerprinting and of determining genetic markers are available and have the ability to exclude almost all except the father. Use of these techniques makes it possible to distinguish differences between the genotype of all individuals except identical twins.

path (păth) A particular course that is followed or traversed. SEE: *pathway.*

circulation p. SEE: *circulation path.*

p. of closure The path traversed by the mandible as it closes when its neuromuscular mechanisms are in a balanced functional state.

condyle p. The path traversed by the condyle during various mandibular movements.

incisor p. An arc described by the incisal edge of the lower incisors when the mandible closes to normal occlusion.

p. of instantaneous center of rotation ABBR: PICR. The plotted trajectory of the axis of rotation of a joint through its entire range of movement. The center of rotation moves due to translation, the accessory gliding or sliding motion that accompanies the rotation. The fact that this is instantaneous infers that the PICR is not constant, but changes with the moment.

PATIENT CARE: Deviation from the ideal PICR for any joint may result from muscle strength or length imbalance, internal joint derangement, or joint capsule restriction. These conditions may occur because of previous joint surgery, scar tissue, traumatic injury, or simply from aging, and may affect the quality, quantity, efficiency, or pain of joint movement and gait mechanics. Physical therapists try to improve their patients' awareness of their center of gravity and of shifts that can throw this off balance by employing balance exercises and posture training. Correct patient positioning for bed or chair rest should be practiced by all health care providers, as asymmetry can affect the patient's comfort and lead to further joint concerns over time. An orthotist or prosthetist measuring and fitting a patient for any joint brace must consider the desired PICR, as the brace must allow the joint to move through full PICR. If proper joint movementis restricted, the device could lead to further pathology.

-path [Gr. *-pathēs*, fr. *paschein*, to feel] Suffix meaning *one affected by a disease*, e.g., sociopath; or *one practicing a method of treatment*, e.g., osteopath

pathergy (path'ĕr-jē) [*path-* + Gr. *ergon*, work] A skin reaction at the site of a sterile needle prick (or other injuries) that results in a pustule and reddened skin. This reaction is a sign of skin hyperreactivity consistent with Behçet syndrome and neutrophilic dermatoses, such as Sweet syndrome.

pathetic (pă-thĕt'ĭk) [L. *patheticus*] **1.** Pert. to, or arousing, the emotions of pity, sympathy, or tenderness. **2.** Pert. to the trochlear nerve.

pathfinder (păth-fīn-dĕr) **1.** An instrument for locating stricture of the urethra. **2.** A dental instrument for tracing the course of root canals.

-pathic [*-pathy* + *-ic*] Suffix meaning *affected by a disease*, e.g., psychopathic; or pertaining to a *method of treating disease*, e.g. allopathic.

patho-, path- [Gr. *pathos*, disease, suffering] Prefixes meaning *disease*. SEE: *-pathy*.

pathoanatomy (păth"ŏ-ă-năt'ŏ-mē) Anatomic pathology.

pathobiology (păth"ŏ-bī-ŏl'ŏ-jē) Pathology.

pathogen (path'ŏ-jĕn) [*patho-* + *-gen*] A microorganism capable of producing a disease.

bloodborne p. A pathogen present in blood that can be transmitted to an individual who is exposed to the blood or body fluids of an infected individual. Three common bloodborne pathogens are hepatitis C, hepatitis B, and human immunodeficiency virus 1 (HIV-1). SEE: *hepatitis B; human immunodeficiency virus; Standard Precautions Appendix.*

opportunistic p. A microorganism that is usually harmless but may become pathogenic in certain circumstances, e.g., when it is introduced into a part of the body where it normally does not reside or when it infects an immunocompromised host.

pathogen-associated molecular patterns ABBR: PAMP. Any of several molecular sequences associated with or found in many different disease-causing microorganisms to which the innate immune system reacts without initiating an antigen-antibody response. Examples of pathogen-associated molecular patterns are

1. bacterial DNA,
2. lipoteichoic acids found in the cell walls of gram-positive bacteria,
3. lipopolysaccharides found in the cell walls of gram-negative bacteria, and
4. sugars like glucans or mannose, found in fungi or bacteria, respectively, but not in mammalian cells.

pathogenesis (păth"ŏ-jĕn'ĕ-sĭs) The origin and development of a disease. SYN: *pathogeny.*

bacterial p. The development of a bacterial disease. There are three stages: entry and colonization in the host, bacterial invasion and reproduction with the production of toxic substances, and the response of the host. The mere presence of an organism in the body does not necessarily mean that disease will follow. This progression of the infection will depend upon a number of interacting factors, including the virulence and number of invading organisms and the ability of the host's immune system to destroy the bacteria.

pathogenetic, pathogenic (path"ŏ-jĕnet'ĭk, path"ŏ-jen'ĭk) Productive of disease. SYN: *morbific.*

pathogenicity (path"ŏ-jĕ-nis'ĭt-ē) The act of producing or ability to produce pathological changes and disease. It can be estimated as the number of organisms that develop a disease, divided by the number exposed to its causes.

pathogeny (păth-ŏj'ĕn-ē) Pathogenesis.

pathognomonic (păth"ŏg-nō-mŏn'ĭk) [Gr. *pathognomonikos*, skilled in diagnosing] Indicative of a disease, esp. its characteristic symptoms.

pathognomy (păth-ŏg'nō-mē) [Gr. *pathos*, disease, suffering, + *gnome*, a means of knowing] Diagnosis of the cause of an illness after careful study of the signs and symptoms of a disease.

pathologic, pathological (path"ŏ-loj'ĭk, path"ŏ-loj'ĭ-kăl) [Gr. *pathos*, disease, suffering, + *logos*, word, reason] **1.** Pert. to pathology. **2.** Diseased; due to a disease. SYN: *morbid.*

pathologist (pă-thŏl'ŏ-jĭst) [" + *logos*, word, reason] A medical professional trained to examine tissues, cells, and specimens of body fluids for evidence of disease.

pathology (pă-thol'ŏ-jē) [*patho-* + *-logy*] **1.** The study of the nature and cause of disease, which involves changes in structure and function. **2.** A condition produced by disease.

anatomic p. The field of pathology that deals with structural changes in disease.

cellular p. Pathology based on microscopic changes in body cells produced by disease.

chemical p. The study of chemical changes that occur in disease.

clinical p. The analysis of blood and body fluids (e.g., plasma, serum, cerebrospinal fluid, or urine) in the laboratory to aid in the diagnosis and treatment of disease.

comparative p. The study of the distinctions between human diseases and the diseases that affect other animals, or plants.

dental p. The science of diseases of the mouth. SYN: *oral p.*

digital p. ABBR: DP. The analysis of pathological specimens after the slides made from a tissue are scanned and converted to binary images that can be viewed, stored, analyzed, and archived by a computer.

experimental p. The study of diseases induced artificially and intentionally, esp. in animals.

functional p. The study of alterations of functions that occur in disease processes without associated structural changes.

geographical p. Pathology in its relationship to climate and geography.

humoral p. Pathology of the fluids of the body.

medical p. Pathology of disorders that are not accessible for surgical procedures.

molecular p. **1.** The study of the pathological effects of specific molecules. **2.** The identification of specific proteins in body fluids or tissue samples as a means of diagnosing specific diseases, e.g., the cancers that release those proteins. SYN: *molecular diagnostics; nanodiagnostics.*

oral p. Dental **p.**

special p. Pathology of particular diseases or organs.

surgical p. The application of pathological procedures and techniques for investigating tissues removed surgically.

pathomechanics (păth″ō-mĭ-kăn′ĭ-ks) Changes in the normal biomechanical function of a joint, an extremity, or the torso as the result of trauma or disease. SEE: *biomechanics.*

pathomimesis (păth″ō-mĭm-ē′sĭs) [Gr. *pathos,* disease, suffering, + *mimesis,* imitation] Intentional (conscious or unconscious) imitation of a disease. SYN: *pathomimicry.*

pathomimicry (păth″ō-mĭm′ĭ-krē) Pathomimesis.

pathophysiology (păth″ō-fĭz″ē-ŏl′ō-jē) [″ + *physis,* nature, + *logos,* word, reason] The study of how normal physiological processes are altered by disease.

pathotype (păth′ō-tīp) [Gr. pathos, disease, + typos, type] A disease-causing variant of a microorganism. It is distinguishable from other members of its species by its virulence and by unique molecular markers.

pathway (path′wā″) **1.** A path or a course, e.g., one formed by neurons (cell bodies and their processes) over which impulses pass from their point of origin to their destination. **2.** A metabolic sequence; a predictable series of chemical reactions, such as those of cellular respiration. **3.** A course of study or a means to attain professional certification.

afferent p. A sensory pathway from a receptor to the central nervous system.

biosynthetic p. The chemical and metabolic events that lead to the formation of substances in the body.

central p. An axon tract within the brain or spinal cord.

clinical p. An administrative method to organize, evaluate, and limit variations in patient care. Development of a clinical pathway usually begins with establishment of a multidisciplinary committee that examines data to determine which patients will benefit most. Usually, diagnoses that involve costly or complex care (such as multidisciplinary care) or common illnesses are selected for study. The following aspects of care are evaluated: consultations and assessments, tests and treatments, nutrition and medications, activity and safety, and teaching and discharge planning. Clinical pathways address timelines, actions, and outcomes, and ensure that essential components of care are provided.

Agencies using clinical pathways report the following advantages: reduced length of stay for patients in given diagnosis-related groups (DRGs), greater accountability for patient care, greater patient and family satisfaction, enhanced staff and physician satisfaction and communication, an improved and integrated process for care delivery, lower patient charges and costs, and less time spent on documentation. SYN: *critical p.; care map.*

complement alternative p. A complement cascade initiated by a foreign protein, usually a bacterium. SEE: *complement.*

complement classic p. A complement cascade initiated by an antibody-antigen reaction that activates complement factor 1 (C1). SEE: *complement.*

conduction p. A group of fibers in the heart, nerves, spinal cord, or brain that conduct impulses that trigger responses in the same or other tissues.

critical p. Clinical **p.**

efferent p. A pathway from the central nervous system to an effector.

Embden-Meyerhof p. SEE: *Embden-Meyerhof pathway.*

exposure p. The route that an infectious, toxic, or radioactive substance takes as it enters the body. Foodborne toxins typically enter the body by ingestion. Airborne toxins usually enter the body by inhalation although they may be deposited on the skin and be absorbed transcutaneously.

fifth p. A form of postgraduate medical education, in which graduates of international medical training programs undergo supervised clinical clerkships in the U.S. to complete their residency training.

p. of incidence The path of a penetrating foreign object from the point of entry into the body to the point where it stops, e.g., the path of a bullet from where it enters the body to where it lodges.

metabolic p. The sequence of chemical reactions that occur as a substance is metabolized.

motor p. A pathway over which motor impulses are carried from the central nervous system to muscles or glands.

pentose phosphate p. The pathway of glucose metabolism in tissues during which five-carbon sugars are formed.

sensory p. A pathway over which sensory impulses are conveyed from sense organs or receptors to sensory or reflex centers of the spinal cord or brain.

-pathy [Gr. *patheia*, feeling, suffering] Suffix meaning *feeling*, e.g., sympathy; *disease*, e.g., neuropathy; and a *method of treating disease*, e.g. homeopathy.

patient (pā′shĕnt) [L. *patiens*, suffering] **1.** One who is sick with, or being treated for, an illness or injury. **2.** One who is receiving medical care. SEE: table.

standard p., standardized patient An actor who is trained to represent a patient during a clinical encounter with a health care provider. His or her performance is used in health care education to help trainees recognize the signs and symptoms of diseases and how to gather and relay information during a patient interview.

surrogate p. A normal, healthy individual who is employed to be examined and perhaps interviewed by health care students. The purpose is to provide students with the opportunity to examine an individual in a less stressful setting than would be the case if the person being examined were indeed sick. This also prevents persons who are ill from being subjected to multiple examinations by students. In some cases, the surrogate patient is an actor who has been instructed to pretend to be sick, injured, disabled, or hostile.

Patient Advise and Consent Encounter ABBR: PACE. An interactive computer program to assist a patient to understand certain medical and surgical procedures and their risks. The program uses touch-screen technology, animation, and an actor-doctor narrator to communicate with the patient. At the end of each program, the patient may take an interactive quiz that evaluates understanding of the presentation. A printout of the entire session is available for the patient and the physician.

patient advocate An individual, such as an attorney, friend, nurse, ombudsman, physician, or social worker, who pleads for and preserves a patient's rights to health care. Patient advocates address many common and important health care issues, including the right to access a health care provider, the right to obtain confidential care, and the right for the patient to work after diagnosis or treatment.

patient autonomy The right of an informed patient to choose to accept or refuse therapy. SEE: *advance directive; informed consent; living will; quality of life.*

Patient's Bill of Rights A declaration of the entitlements of hospital patients, compiled by the American Hospital Association. First published in 1973, it emphasizes the responsibilities of hospitals and patients and the need for communication and collaboration between them. The patient is entitled to consideration and respect while receiving care; accurate, understandable information about the condition and treatment; privacy and confidentiality; an appropriate response to the request for treatment; and continued care as necessary after leaving the hospital. The patient may also have an advance directive regarding treatment; designate a surrogate to make decisions; review his or her medical records; be informed of hospital policies or business relationships that may affect care; and agree or refuse to participate in treatments or research studies. Patient responsibilities include providing any information (e.g., an advance directive) that may influence treatment; providing the needed information for insurance claims; and understanding how lifestyle affects health. The fulltext of the Patient's Bill of Rights is available from the American Hospital Association, One North Franklin, Chicago, IL 60606, phone number: 312-422-3000.

patient care advisory committee A multidisciplinary group that advises health care agencies facing ethical dilemmas. The committee usually consists of health care professionals, clergy, legal counsel, and administrative personnel. SYN: *institutional ethics committee*. SEE: *institutional review board.*

patient care data set ABBR: PCDS. A terminology data set recognized by the American Nurses Association and developed by Dr. Judith Ozbolt primarily for use in the acute care arena. The data set includes terms and codes for patient problems, therapeutic goals, and patient care orders.

patient-centered (pā′shĕnt-sent′ĕrd) Pert. to health care that is focused on the patient or consumer of health care rather than on health care providers, financiers, insurers, or institutions.

A Patient's Perception of Quality Health Care

Quality Indicator	The Patient's Viewpoint
Access	Scheduling a visit with my health care provider was easy and convenient.
Attentiveness	My concerns were heard, and my needs were anticipated and addressed.
Availability of primary care	I saw someone who knows me personally.
Availability of specialty care	I saw someone who is skilled in managing my specific problems.
Communication	I was able to contact my health care providers easily. We were able to talk to each other simply and directly. I was told what to expect during my care.
Continuity	Follow-up care was easy to arrange with professionals I already know.
Cost	My care was affordable and was worth its cost.
Craftsmanship	I was carefully examined, and my treatment was technically competent.
Dignity	I was treated with respect.
Hygiene	The facilities where I received care were spotless.
Outcome	Things turned out well. (If things did not turn out well, problems were anticipated and explained to me in advance.)
Time management	I was not left waiting for long. My health care providers respected my schedule.

patient-centered medical home ABBR: PCMH. Medical home.

patient circuit The artificial conduit that relays gases between a mechanical ventilator and a patient.

patient compensation fund A governmentally administered account used as a treasury from which disbursements are made to those injured as a result of incompetence or malpractice by health care providers.

patient concern A complaint or grievance raised by a patient (or a personal representative of a patient) about care rendered to him or her.

patient day The basic time unit for calculating the cost of keeping a patient in a hospital for one day.

patient delay Delay by a patient in seeking medical attention or in taking prescribed medicines or advice given by a physician.

patient-delivered partner therapy Patient-delivered partner treatment.

patient-delivered partner treatment (pā′shĕnt-dĕ-liv′ĕrd) ABBR: PDPT. A method to prevent the spread of sexually transmitted diseases, e.g., gonorrhea or chlamydial infections, in which an infected person is given a prescription for an antibiotic agent to be shared with his or her sexual partner(s). SYN: *expedited partner therapy; patient-delivered partner medication; patient-delivered partner therapy.*

patient education SEE: under *education.*

patient information system Hospital information system.

patient lift team A team of physically fit people who assist the nursing staff in moving patients with mobility problems.

PATIENT CARE: Moving patients from beds to gurneys or from chairs to beds is a frequent cause of nursing injuries, esp. in critical care units and medical-surgical wards, where many patients are incapacitated and unable to manage their own transfers. Back injuries afflict approx. 50 percent of nurses during their professional lives. Lift teams are specially trained in the ergonomics of assisting patients with transfers and turning or repositioning them, thereby reducing the number of injuries that nurses receive while moving patients. SYN: *lift team.*

patient management A description of the interaction, from intake to discharge, between the patient and the health care team. It includes communication, empathy, examination, evaluation, diagnosis, prognosis, and intervention. The last element, intervention (or treatment), depends on the others.

patient mix The numbers and types of patients served by a hospital or other health care program.

patient outcomes research team ABBR: PORT. Those involved in investigating the results of disease interventions and comparing the benefit or lack of benefit of various therapeutic measures.

patient package insert Package insert.

patient portal SEE: under *portal.*

patient-prosthesis mismatch, prosthesis-patient mismatch, prosthesis mismatch Insertion of an inappropriately sized prosthesis in a patient in need of organ repair.

patient-reported outcome (pā′shĕnt-rĕ-port′ĕd) ABBR: PRO. Any report by a patient or group of patients about their experiences during an illness, e.g., the symptoms felt or the treatment received from health care providers and health care systems.

patient return electrode In electrosurgery, an electrode that collects the current used to operate on the patient and returns it to a current generator.

Patient Self-Determination Act ABBR: PSDA. A 1991 act of the U.S. Congress that preserves individual rights to decisions related to personal survival. There are several methods for preserving autonomy: filing appropriate forms for durable power of attorney for health care, making a living will, or giving a directive to the physician.

patient self-testing Monitoring laboratory results at home to guide day-to-day decisions about health care. Examples include ambulatory blood pressure monitoring, capillary glucose monitoring, and point-of-care testing of warfarin (by measuring the prothrombin time/international normalized ratio [PT/INR] levels).

patient-specific (pā′shĕnt-spĕ-sif′ik) Customized to the precise anatomy, physiology, or health care needs of one person.

patients′ rights Those culturally and legally specified rights, claims, powers, privileges, and remedies due to a person receiving health care services. They include, but are not limited to, the following:

1. access to care;
2. aftercare assistance or aid;
3. an appeals process when one has a grievance;
4. choice in the selection of one's health care providers;
5. confidentiality and privacy;
6. freedom from discrimination;
7. information;
8. respectful treatment;
9. safety;
10. shared decision making; and
11. respect for patient preferences and wishes.

patient transporter Someone who conveys patients from one health care location to another.

patient-ventilator interaction SEE: under *interaction*.

patient-year A patient experience of 1 year's duration, e.g., on a waiting list, in a treatment program, under observation, or suffering an illness. One patient-year is equal to, for example, the experience of two patients for 6 months, or 12 patients for 1 month each.

Patrick test (pa′trik) [Hugh Talbot Patrick, U.S. neurologist, 1860–1939] A test for arthritis of the hip or for sacroiliac dysfunction. The thigh and knee of the supine patient are flexed, and the external malleolus of the ankle is placed over the patella of the opposite leg. The test result is positive if depression of the knee produces pain. This test is also called the FABERE maneuver (FABERE is a mnemonic for the position the hip assumes during this test). SYN: *FABERE maneuver*.

patrilineal (păt-rĕ-lĭn′ē-ăl) [L. *pater,* father, + *linea,* line] Tracing descent through the father.

pattern (păt-tĕrn) **1.** A design, figure, model, or example. **2.** In psychology, a set or arrangement of ideas or behavior reactions. Particular patterns are listed under the first word. SEE: e.g., *functional health pattern; synergy patterns; wear pattern*.

patterning (păt-tĕrn-ēng) A therapeutic method used in treating children and adults with brain damage. The patient is guided through movements such as creeping or crawling, based on the theory that undamaged sections of the brain are capable of developing the ability to perform these functions.

pattern recognition receptor SEE: under *receptor*.

patulous (păt′ū-lŭs) [L. *patulus*] Patent.

pauciarticular (păw-sē-ăr-tĭk′ū-lăr) A classification of juvenile rheumatoid arthritis that indicates that four or fewer joints are affected at the time of onset of the disease.

Pau d′Arco (pow dăr′koo) [Portuguese] The inner bark of the *Tabebuia avellanedae,* an evergreen tree of the rain forests of Central and South America. It is marketed as a tea that is promoted as a treatment for cancer, fungal diseases, inflammation, and pain.

pause (poz) [L. *pausa* fr Gr. *pausis,* a stop, halt.] An interruption; a temporary cessation of activity.

    compensatory p. The long interval following a premature ventricular contraction, so called because it does not disturb the normal sinus pacing of the heart.

    end-inspiratory p. ABBR: EIP. The brief, normal period of breath-holding between inhalation and exhalation.

    noncompensatory p. The interval on the electrocardiogram that follows a premature atrial contraction (PAC). Because PACs reset the sinus pacemaker, the next sinus beat does not appear when it would have if there had been no extra beat.

    sinus p. An interruption in the normal pacemaking function of the sinus (sinoatrial) node of the heart, resulting in a decrease in the number of heartbeats per minute. When sinus pauses are rare, the condition may be asymptomatic. When they occur frequently, patients may note palpitations or experience loss of consciousness.

Pavlik harness (pŏv'lĭk) A device used to stabilize the hip in neonates with congenital hip dislocation.

Pavlov, Ivan Petrovich (păv'lŏv) Russian physiologist, 1849–1936; winner of Nobel Prize in medicine in 1904. He is remembered particularly for his work on conditioning. SEE: *conditioned reflex*.

pavor (pā'vor) [L.] Anxiety, dread.

  p. diurnus Attacks of terror or fright during the day, esp. in children.

  p. nocturnus A night terror; a nightmare.

PAWP *pulmonary artery wedge pressure*.

PAX8 A protein product of one of the *PAX* family of genes. It is used clinically as a biomarker of follicular thyroid cancer.

PAX-2 An embryonic cellular transcription factor that can be used in the laboratory diagnosis of renal cell carcinoma.

Paxil, Paxil CR SEE: *paroxetine*.

pay for performance ABBR: PFP, or, P4P. The use of specific indicators of health care efficiency or quality to increase or decrease the funds paid to health care providers for the services they render.

Pb [L. *plumbum*] Symbol for the element lead.

P.B. *Pharmacopoeia Britannica,* British pharmacopeia.

PBA *pseudobulbar affect*.

PBI *protein-bound iodine*.

Pbto2 *brain tissue oxygen tension*.

P.B.W. *posterior bitewing* in dentistry.

PBZ *pyribenzamine*.

p.c. L. *post cibum,* after a meal.

PCA *patient-controlled analgesia; percutaneous coronary angiography; posterior cerebral artery*.

PCG *phonocardiogram*.

pCi *picocurie*.

PCMH *patient-centered medical home*.

Pco₂ Symbol for *partial pressure of carbon dioxide*.

PCOS *polycystic ovary syndrome*.

PCP *phencyclidine hydrochloride; Pneumocystis carinii pneumonia; primary care physician; primary care provider*.

PCR *polymerase chain reaction; prehospital care report*.

PC-SPES (pē-sē-spēs') A mixture of the herbs chrysanthemum *Ganoderma lucidum,* isatis, licorice, *Panax pseudoginseng, Rabdosia rubescens,* saw palmetto, and scutellaria, which have estrogen-like effects. The mixture was formerly promoted as an alternative therapy for prostate cancer. It has been taken off the market in the U.S. because of contamination and adulteration with pharmaceuticals.

PCV *packed cell volume*.

PCV7 An abbreviation for a pneumococcal polyvalent vaccine with antigens from seven common serotypes of *Strep-*

tococcus pneumoniae. It is used, like PCV13, to immunize children against pneumococcal diseases, e.g., otitis media, pneumonia, meningitis.

PCV13 An abbreviation for a pneumococcal polyvalent vaccine composed of 13 capsular antigens of *Streptococcus pneumoniae*. It is used, like PCV7, to immunize children against pneumococcal diseases, e.g., otitis media, pneumonia, meningitis.

PCWP *pulmonary capillary wedge pressure*.

Pd Symbol for the element palladium.

p.d. *prism diopter; pupilla diameter; pupillary distance*.

PDA *patent ductus arteriosus; personal digital assistant; posterior descending artery*.

PDE *phosphodiesterase*.

PDE-5i *phosphodiesterase-5 inhibitor*.

PDO *polydioxanone*.

PDPT *patient-delivered partner treatment*.

PDR *Physicians' Desk Reference*.

PDS *polydioxanone*.

PEA *phenylethylamine; pulseless electrical activity*.

Peabody Developmental Motor Scales (pē'bŏd"ē, pē'bĭ-dē") ABBR: PDMS; PDMS-2. A standardized performance test of gross and fine motor development for infants and children. The PDMS is suitable for newborns, infants, and children up to 6 years of age. Subtests include reflexes, stationary, locomotion, object manipulation, grasping, and visual-motor manipulation. The PDMS-2 includes both subtests and training and remediation programs.

Peabody Individual Achievement Test (Revised) (pē'bŏd"ē, pē'bĭ-dē") ABBR: PIAT-R. A test typically administered to school-aged children designed to measure scholastic achievement. It includes six sections that gauge general knowledge; reading comprehension and recognition; spelling; writing; and math skills.

peak (pēk) A high point or the highest point of a course of events, esp. as represented on a chart or graph. To reach a high point or the highest point.

peak and trough The highest and lowest concentrations of a drug in plasma. Measurement of peak and trough drug levels are used to determine whether an intravenously administered medication is consistently within therapeutic range. The trough is drawn just before a drug is scheduled to be given; the peak is drawn after the drug is administered (30 to 60 min after infusion). These measurements may guide therapy in the use of potentially toxic medications, e.g., aminoglycosides, which can have serious adverse effects if therapeutic levels are exceeded or can fail to work effectively if adequate drug levels are not attained.

peak power of a muscle The maximum amount of force that a muscle can exert over a distance in a specified period of time.

peanut (pē'nŭt") An oily herb of the legume family, *Arachis hypogaea,* whose seeds are consumed for their nutritional value and whose oil, derived from the seeds, is used in cooking.

pearl (pĕrl) 1. A small, tough mass in the sputum in asthma. 2. A small capsule containing a medicinal fluid for inhalation. The capsule is crushed in a handkerchief and inhaled. 3. A small mass of cells.
> ***enamel p.*** A small, benign projection of enamel attached to cementum at or near the root furcation. Pearls are usually found on maxillary molars.
> ***epithelial p.*** Concentric squamous epithelial cells in carcinoma.
> **Epstein p** SEE: *Epstein pearls.*
> ***gouty p.*** Tophus (1).

Pearl index (pĕrl) [Raymond Pearl, U.S. biologist, 1879–1940] A measure of the reliability of any birth control method. A Pearl index of 1.0 signifies that if 100 women use a particular contraceptive method for 1 year, only one of them will become pregnant. The most effective contraceptive methods have Pearl indexes of about 0.7.

peau d'orange (pō"dō-rănj') [Fr., orange skin] Dimpling, pitting, and swelling, seen in inflamed skin (e.g., in acne rosacea) or in the skin that overlies inflammatory carcinoma of the breast. SEE: illus.

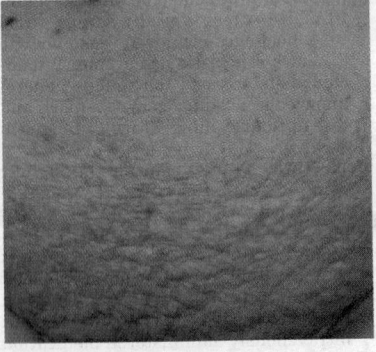

PEAU D' ORANGE

peccant (pĕk'ănt) [L. *peccans,* sinning] 1. Corrupt; producing disease. 2. Sinning, or violating a law.

pecten (pĕk'tĕn) *pl.* **pectines** [L., comb] 1. A comblike organ. 2. Pubic bone. 3. The middle portion of the anal canal.
> ***p. pubis*** Pectineal **line** (1).

pectic acid (pek'tik) SEE: under *acid.*

pectin (pĕk'tĭn) [Gr. *pektos,* congealed] Water-soluble carbohydrate polymers, found in ripe fruits, such as the apple, grape, peach, or plum. Pectins are colloids; they form gels in solution. They are used to make jams, jellies, and some medications.

pectinase (pĕk'tĭ-nās) An enzyme that catalyzes the formation of sugars and galacturonic acid from pectin.

pectinate (pĕk'tĭ-nāt) [L. *pecten,* comb] Having teeth like a comb.

pectineal (pĕk-tĭn'ē-ăl) Pert. to the pubic bone or the pectineal muscle.

pectineus (pĕk-tĭn-ē'ŭs) [L. *pecten,* comb] A flat quadrangular muscle at the upper and inner part of the thigh, arising from the superior ramus of pubis and inserted between the lesser trochanter and linea aspera of the femur, which flexes and adducts the thigh.

pectora (pĕk'tor-ă) [L.] Pl. of pectus.

pectoral (pĕk'tō-răl) [L. *pectoralis*] 1. Concerning the chest. 2. Efficacious in relieving chest conditions, as a cough.

pectoralis (pĕk"tō-rā'lĭs) [L.] 1. Pert. to the chest. 2. Any of the two overlapping muscles on each side of the anterior upper portion of the chest.
> ***p. major*** A large triangular muscle that extends from the sternum to the humerus and functions to flex, horizontally adduct, and internally rotate the arm, and aids in chest expansion when the upper extremities are stabilized.
> ***p. minor*** A muscle beneath the pectoralis major, attached to the coracoid process of the scapula that depresses as well as causes anterior tipping of the scapula.

pectoriloquy (pĕk"tō-rĭl'ō-kwē) [L. *pectoralis,* chest, + *loqui,* to speak] The distinct transmission of vocal sounds during auscultation of the chest with a stethoscope. The words seem to emanate from the spot that is auscultated. Pectoriloquy is heard over cavities that communicate with a bronchus and areas of consolidation near a large bronchus, over pneumothorax when the opening in the lung is patulous, and over some pleural effusions. SYN: *pectorophony.* SEE: *chest.*

pectose (pĕk'tōs) [Gr. *pektos,* congealed] A carbohydrate found in the pulp of unripe fruits. It does not dissolve in water. When fruit ripens it converts to pectin..

pectus (pĕk'tŭs) *pl.* **pectora** [L.] The chest.
> ***p. carinatum*** Pigeon chest.
> ***p. excavatum*** A congenital condition in which the sternum is abnormally depressed. SYN: *funnel breast;* **p.** *recurvatum.* SEE: illus.
> ***p. recurvatum*** **P.** excavatum.

[1]ped- SEE: [1]*pedo-.*

[2]ped- SEE: [2]*pedo-.*

pedagogy (pĕd'ŭ-gŏj"ē, -gō"jē) [Gr. *pai-*

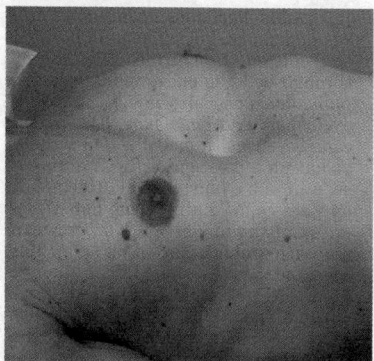

PECTUS EXCAVATUM

dagogos, an assistant who takes children to school] The art, sciences, techniques, and professional methods used in teaching, esp. the teaching of school-age children.

pedal (pĕd'l) [L. *pedalis*] Pert. to the foot.

pedal spasm SEE: under *spasm.*

pederast (ped'ĕ-rast″) [Gr. *paiderastēs,* a lover of boys] A man who indulges in anal intercourse with young boys.

pederasty (ped'ĕ-ras″tē) [Gr. *paiderastia,* love of boys] Anal intercourse between a man and a young boy.

pedi- SEE: ¹*pedo-.*

pedia- [Gr. *pais,* child] Combining form denoting *child.*

pediatric (pē-dē-ăt'rĭk) [Gr. *pais,* child, + *iatreia,* treatment] Pert. to the medical treatment of children.

pediatric advanced life support SEE: under *life support.*

pediatric autoimmune neuropsychiatric disorder associated with streptococci ABBR: PANDAS. Any of the childhood behavioral disorders (esp. tic disorders, Tourette syndrome, and obsessive-compulsive disorder) that begin before puberty and are associated with and worsened by group A beta-hemolytic streptococcal infections (e.g., strep throat or scarlet fever). Researchers suspect that an autoimmune response to the infection is responsible for the syndrome.

pediatrician (pē-dē-ă-trĭsh'ăn) [″ + *iatrikos,* healing] A specialist who examines children, provides preventive care, and diagnoses and treats childhood illnesses.

pediatrics (pē-dē-ăt'rĭks) [Gr. *pais,* child, + *iatreia,* treatment] The care of children and the treatment of their diseases. SEE: *mortality* for table.

Pediatric Sexual Assault Nurse Examiner ABBR: Pediatric SANE. A Sexual Assault Nurse Examiner (SANE) specially trained to examine children.

pediatric trauma score ABBR: PTS. A method for scoring and quantifying the severity of trauma in pediatric patients. SYN: *revised trauma score.*

pedicel (pĕd'ĭ-sĕl) **1.** Foot process or footplate. **2.** A secondary process of a podocyte that in conjunction with other podocytes forms the inner layer of Bowman's capsule of a renal corpuscle.

pedicle (pĕd'ĭ-k'l) **1.** The stem that attaches a new growth. SYN: *peduncle* (1). **2.** The bony process that projects backward from the body of a vertebra, connecting with the lamina on each side. It forms the root of the vertebral arch.

pedicle screw A rigid surgical implant used to stabilize adjacent spinal segments in spinal fusion surgery. Pedicle screws have been used to treat spinal disorders, including those caused by spinal cancer, congenital anomalies, trauma, and chronic pain syndromes. Potential complications may include increased pain, infection, or mechanical failure (breakage of the screws or the rods that connect them).

pedicular (pĕ-dik'yŭ-lăr) [L. *pediculus,* a louse] Pert. to or infested with lice.

pediculate (pē-dĭk'ū-lāt) [L. *pediculus,* a little foot] Pedunculate.

pediculicide (pi-dik'yŭ-lĭ-sīd″) [*Pediculus* + *-cide*] **1.** Pert. to the killing of lice. **2.** An agent that kills lice.

Pediculidae (pĕd″ŭ-kŭl'ĭ-dē) A family of lice belonging to the order Anoplura. It includes the species parasitic on primates, including humans. SEE: *Pediculus.*

pediculosis (pē-dĭk″ū-lō'sĭs) [″ + Gr. *osis,* condition] Infestation with lice. SEE: *Pediculus.*

    p. capitis A scalp infection caused by head lice, *Pediculus humanus capitis,* a common parasite in children. Outbreaks are common in schools, esp. among children between the ages of 5 and 11. The infection is transmitted through use of personal items such as hair ornaments, combs, hairbrushes, hats, scarves, or coats or through direct contact between the heads of two children. Lice, which feed on blood obtained by biting the skin, cause itching, esp. around the ears, in the occipital area, and at the nape of the neck. Long-standing infestations may produce chronic inflammation. The adult louse is seen rarely; diagnosis usually is made through the presence of eggs (nits), which appear as whitish sacs attached to the hair.

    SYMPTOMS: Itching and eczematous dermatitis. In long-standing, neglected cases, scratching may result in marked inflammation. Secondary infection by bacteria may occur, with formation of pustules, crusts, and suppuration. Hair may become matted and malodorous.

    TREATMENT: Therapies for lice infestations are modified frequently, to match the resistance of lice to current therapies and to minimize the toxicities of medications. Manual removal of lice always is appropriate and is strongly recommended by lice specialists. Others recommend the use of insecticides (pediculocides).

PATIENT CARE: The patient and family are taught how to apply medication (lindane, permethrin, pyrethrins, piperonyl butoxide, malathion) to dry hair for lice and are warned that the eyes should be immediately flushed with copious amounts of water if the medication accidentally contacts them. They are informed about minimizing the spread of infection by washing or dry cleaning all clothing and linen used in the home, delousing of rugs and upholstered furniture with sprays or vacuuming, keeping combs and brushes separate, and using medicinal shampoos if there has been contact with the patient.

p. corporis Pediculosis caused by the body louse, *Pediculus humanus*. It is transmitted by direct contact or by wearing infested clothing and is often transmitted in crowded or unhygienic conditions. The body louse is an occasional vector for several important transmissible illnesses, including epidemic typhus, trench fever, and relapsing fever.

SYMPTOMS: Infestation with body lice is marked by intense itching, esp. on the neck, trunk, and thighs. Tiny hemorrhagic points identify the bites. Generalized excoriation, mild fever, and fatigue characterize heavy infestations. In severe cases, pustules may develop.

TREATMENT: The patient first bathes with hot soap and water and then applies prescribed creams containing approved pesticides to affected areas.

PATIENT CARE: The patient should be assessed for diseases that body lice may transmit. If the patient is homeless or impoverished, social services agencies should be contacted to assist him or her to find shelter and clean clothing. If the patient lives with others, close personal contacts or family members should be screened for lice. All clothing, furniture, rugs, and bedding must be washed with hot water or dry cleaned. To prevent transmission of pediculosis among hospitalized patients, all high-risk patients should be examined for evidence of hair or body lice infestation on admission. Health care professionals should be careful to include older adults who are dependent on others for care, those coming from nursing homes or other assisted living facilities, and people living in crowded conditions.

p. palpebrarum Infestation by lice of the eyebrows and eyelashes.

p. pubis Pediculosis caused by *Phthirus pubis*, also known as crab lice. It is transmitted by direct contact and through bedding or shared towels. The pubic louse can also infest the axillae, eyelashes, and head hair. The patient can present with pruritus. On occasion visual identification of the lice may be seen in pubic hair as oval attachments on pubic hair shafts, black dots (feces) on skin and underwear, or crusts or scabs in pubic area from scratching. Treatment is the same as for other ectoparasitic (skin parasite) infestations.

Pediculus (pē-dĭk′ū-lŭs) A genus of parasitic insects, commonly called lice, that infest humans and other primates. Lice are sucking insects belonging to the family Pediculidae, order Anoplura. They transmit the causative organisms of epidemic typhus, trench fever, and relapsing fever to animal hosts.

P. humanus capitis The head louse that lives in the fine hair of the head, including the beard and eyebrows. Its eggs, commonly called nits, may be found glued to hairs. They form nests in the vicinity of the ears. This organism is the cause of pediculosis capitis.

P. humanus corporis The body louse that inhabits the seams of clothing worn next to the body and feeds on regions of the body covered by that clothing. Eggs are attached to fibers of the clothing. This organism causes human illnesses including pediculosis corporis and trench fever.

pediculus (pē-dĭk′ū-lŭs) *pl.* **pediculi** [L.] **1.** A little foot. **2.** Louse. SEE: *Pediculus.*

pedicure (pĕd′ĭ-kūr) [L. *pes,* foot, + *cura,* care] **1.** Care of the feet. **2.** Cosmetic care of the feet and toenails. **3.** Podiatrist.

pediform (pĕd′ĭ-form) [″ + *forma,* shape] Having the shape of a foot.

pedigree (pĕ-dĭ-grē) A chart, diagram, or table of an individual's ancestors used in genetics to analyze or reveal inherited traits and illnesses.

¹pedo-, ped-, pedi- [L. *pes,* stem *ped-,* foot] Prefixes meaning *foot.* SEE: *podo-.*

²pedo-, ped- [Gr. *pais,* stem *paid-,* child] Prefixes meaning *child.* The variant *paed-* is used outside the U.S.

pedodontics (pĕd′ō-dont′ĭks) [²*pedo-* + *odont-* + *-ics*] Dentistry for children. **pedodontic** (-dont′ĭk), *adj.* **pedodontist** (-dont′ĭst), *n.*

pedodontist (pē″dō-dŏn′tĭst) A dentist who specializes in care of children's teeth.

pedometer (pĕd-ŏm′ĕ-tĕr) [L. *pes,* foot, + Gr. *metron,* measurement] An instrument that indicates the number of steps taken while walking.

pedophilia (pē″dō-fĭl′ē-ă) [″ + *philein,* to love] An unnatural desire for sexual relations with children.

pedorthics (pēd'ŏr-thĭks) [L. *pes*, foot + Gr. *orthos*, straight] The making and fitting of shoes and other foot support products to alleviate and prevent foot injury and disease.

pedorthist (pēd'ŏr-thĭst) A footwear specialist. Pedorthists design and produce individually fitted shoes and foot support products to alleviate and prevent foot injury and disease.

peduncle (pĕ-dŭn'kl) [L. *pedunculus*, a little foot] **1.** Pedicle (1). **2.** A band of tissue connecting parts of the brain. SEE: *crus; sessile; stalk*.

　　cerebellar n The inferior, the middle, or the superior cerebellar peduncle. SYN: *crura cerebelli*.

　　cerebral p. One of two large rope-like longitudinal axon tracts, which cover the ventral surface of the midbrain. The cerebral peduncles contain axons originating in the cerebral cortices and traveling the brainstem and spinal cord, including the corticospinal tract axons. SYN: *crus cerebri*.

　　inferior cerebellar p. A thick band of axons running dorsally along the caudal hindbrain and over the fourth ventricle terminating in medial regions of the cerebellar cortex. The inferior cerebellar peduncle contains the olivocerebellar tract, the dorsal spinocerebellar tract, and the cuneocerebellar tract. A segment of this peduncle – the juxtarestiform body – contains both incoming and outgoing vestibular axons. SYN: *restiform body*.

　　inferior thalamic p. An axon tract running dorsally into the dorsomedial nucleus of the thalamus from the amygdala, the temporal cortex, and the substantia innominata. SEE: *thalamic radiation*.

　　mammillary p. An axon tract carrying secondary sensory information from the tegmentum of the midbrain to the mammillary body.

　　middle cerebellar p. A thick band of axons running dorsally along the pontine (rostral) hindbrain and over the fourth ventricle to terminate in lateral regions of the cerebellar cortex. The middle cerebellar peduncle contains axons from the pontine nuclei; i.e., the pontocerebellar tract axons SYN: *brachium pontis*.

　　olfactory p. The long stalk of the olfactory bulb, which contains the olfactory tract.

　　olivary p. A reciprocal axon tract between the superior olive and the abducens nucleus.

　　superior cerebellar p. A thick band of axons running ventrally and rostrally along the front edges of the fourth ventricle and into the midbrain. The superior cerebellar peduncle contains the outflow axons originating in the dentate, embolliform, and globose nuclei and travels to the red nucleus and thalamus. SYN: *brachium conjunctivum*.

peduncular (pĕ-dŭn'kū-lăr) [L. *pedunculus*, a little foot] Concerning a peduncle.

pedunculate, pedunculated (pĕ-dŭng' kyū-lāt", pĕ-dŭng'kyū-lāt"-ĕd) Possessing a stalk or peduncle. SYN: *pediculate*.

pedunculotomy (pĕ-dŭng"kū-lŏt'ō-mē) [" + Gr. *tome*, incision] Surgical section of a cerebral peduncle. It has been used to treat involuntary movement disorders.

peeling (pē-lēng) Shedding of the surface of the skin. SEE: *desquamation*.

　　chemical p. Agents applied to skin to produce a mild, superficial burn; done to remove wrinkles.

PEEP (pēp) *positive end-expiratory pressure.*

PEEP decrement (trial) SEE: under *trial.*

peer (pēr) One who has an equal standing with another in age, class, or rank.

　　p. review The evaluation of the quality of the work effort of an individual by his or her colleagues. It could involve evaluation of articles submitted for publication or the quality of medical care administered by an individual, group, or hospital.

peer victimization (vik"tĭ-mĭ-zā'shŏn) Teasing, harassing, bullying, or belittling of a person by another person from the same, general group, e.g., of one child by another.

PEG (pĕg) *percutaneous endoscopic gastrostomy.*

peg, rete Rete ridge.

Peganum harmala (pĕ-gahn' ŭm hahr' mŭ-lŭ) A weed, commonly known as Syrian rue and considered a livestock toxin, used for medicinal and spiritual purposes in many regions of the world. Extracts (tea) made from its seeds are consumed ceremonially in certain cultures. They contain beta-carboline alkaloids, a class of chemicals that increase levels of serotonin in the brain. Use of the extracts may induce hallucinations. Overdose may result in the serotonin syndrome.

pegylation (pĕg'ĭ-lā'-shŭn) The chemical linking of a drug (e.g., interferon) to polyethylene glycol. Pegylation increases the half-life of interferon.

PEJ *percutaneous endoscopic jejunostomy.*

pejorative (pĭ-jawr'ă-tĭv, pē"jă-rā'tĭv) [L. *pejor*, worse] **1.** Tending to become or make worse. **2.** Disparaging or belittling.

PEL *permissible exposure limits.*

pelade (pĕl-ăd') [Fr., to remove hair] Alopecia areata.

pelage (pĕl'ĭj) [Fr.] The collective hair of the body.

Pelamis (pel′ă-mis) A genus of poisonous sea snakes with only one species (*Pelamis platurus*).

PELD score [Acronym for *pediatric end-stage liver disease*] A tool for characterizing the severity of liver disease in pediatric patients (under 12), used to determine their priority for receipt of donor organs. Patients with higher scores (more severe disease) are given a higher priority for transplantation. The score is based on repeated measurements of five variables: the patient's age, serum albumin level, serum bilirubin level, INR (international normalized ratio), and growth failure, entered into the following equation: PELD score = 0.436 (if patient is listed before age 1 year) — 0.687Ln (serum albumin) + 0.480Ln (serum bilirubin) +1.857Ln (INR) +0.667 (for growth failure that is more than 2 standard deviations below normal).

Pelger-Huët anomaly (pel″gĕr hū′ĕt) [Karel Pelger, Dutch physician, 1885–1931; Gauthier Jean Huët, Dutch physician, 1879–1970] ABBR: PHA. A benign autosomal dominant disorder of neutrophil maturation, in which granulocytes form with rodlike, dumbbell, peanut-shaped, and spectacle-like nuclei. The chromatin of the nuclei is unusually coarse. Despite their unusual shape, the oddly formed cells function normally. An anomaly in white blood cell formation called *Pseudo-PHA* or *acquired PHA* appears structurally similar to PHA and occurs in myelodysplasia and some leukemias.

peliosis (pē-lē-ō′sĭs) Purpura.

   bacillary p. A complication of an infection due to *Bartonella henselae* and *B. quintana*, esp. in immunocompromised patients. The infection causes vascular lesions in the visceral organs, esp. the liver and spleen.

   p. hepatis Multiple cystic, blood-filled spaces in the liver associated with dilatation of the sinusoids. These cause enlargement of and pain in the liver. These lesions are associated with use of oral contraceptives, certain types of anabolic steroids, and infections with *Bartonella* organisms. If the condition is due to infection, treatment consists of parenteral doxycycline for several weeks followed by several months of oral therapy. SEE: *bacillary angiomatosis; cat scratch disease.*

Pelizaeus-Merzbacher disease (pĕl-ĭ-zā′ŭs-mŭrts′ bŏk-ĕr, -mă rts′) [F. Pelizaeus, Ger. neurologist, 1850–1917; L. Merzbacher, Ger. neurologist, 1875–1942] An X-linked disorder of myelin formation marked by cognitive deficits, nystagmus, spasticity, and gait disturbance.

pellagra (pĕl-ă′gră, pĕ-lăg′ră) [L. *pellis*, skin, + Gr. *agra*, rough] The clinical consequences of profound niacin deficiency characterized by cutaneous, gastrointestinal, mucosal, and neurological symptoms. It is found in regions of the world where malnutrition is endemic.

SYMPTOMS: In advanced cases, stomatitis and glossitis, diarrhea, dermatitis, and central nervous system involvement occur. Cutaneous lesions include erythema followed by vesiculation, crusting, and desquamation. The skin may become dry, scaly, and atrophic. The mucous membranes of the mouth, esophagus, and vagina may atrophy; ulcers and cysts may develop. Anemia is common. Nausea, vomiting, and diarrhea occur, the last being characteristic. Involvement of the central nervous system is first manifested by neurasthenia, followed by organic psychosis characterized by disorientation, memory impairment, and confusion. Later, delirium and clouding of consciousness may occur.

ETIOLOGY: This condition is due to inadequate intake or absorption of niacin (nicotinic acid) or its amide (niacinamide, nicotinamide). It is commonly associated with restricted or limited diets in which a single cereal grain, esp. corn, is consumed without adequate consumption of wheat, eggs, beef, poultry, or other foods rich in niacin or tryptophan. The condition is often found in chronic alcoholism.

TREATMENT: The disease is treated by following a diet adequate in all vitamins, minerals, and amino acids supplemented by 500 to 1000 mg of niacinamide given orally three times daily. If there is any doubt about the ability of the intestinal tract to absorb vitamins, the vitamins should be given parenterally.

pellagrin (pĕ-lă′grĭn, -lăg′rĭn) A person afflicted with pellagra.

pellet (pĕl′ĕt) [Fr. *pelote*, a ball] **1.** A tiny pill or small ball of medicine or food. **2.** A solid that condenses at the bottom of a centrifuged solution. **3.** Any small round object, such as a bit of buckshot or a BB, that may enter the body in gunshot injuries.

   cotton p. A small rolled cottonball, less than ⅜ in (about 1 cm) in diameter, used for desiccation or topical application of medicaments, particularly in dentistry; also called pledgets.

   foil p. Loosely rolled gold foil used for direct filling in dental restoration. SEE: *foil.*

pellicle (pĕl′ĭ-k'l) [L. *pellicula*, a little skin] **1.** A thin piece of cuticle or skin. **2.** Film or surface on a liquid. **3.** Scum.

   salivary p. The thin layer of salivary proteins and glycoproteins that quickly adhere to the tooth surface after the tooth has been cleaned; this amorphous, bacteria-free layer may serve as an attachment medium for bacteria, which in turn form plaque.

pellucid (pĕl-lū′sĭd) [L. *pellucidus*] Clear.

pelv-, pelvi-, pelvo- [L. *pelvis,* basin, bowl] Prefixes meaning *pelvis.*

pelvic (pĕl′vĭk) [L. *pelvis,* basin] Pert. to a pelvis, usually the bony pelvis.

pelvic congestion syndrome   A cause of chronic, nonmenstrual pelvic pain, typically occurring in multiparous women and associated with dilated veins near the ovaries and uterus.

pelvic floor   SEE: under *floor.*

pelvic floor muscle training   SEE: under *training.*

pelvic inflammatory disease   ABBR: PID. Infection of the uterus, fallopian tubes, and adjacent pelvic structures that is not associated with surgery or pregnancy. PID usually is caused by an ascending infection in which disease-producing germs spread from the vagina and cervix to the upper portions of the female reproductive tract. SEE: *chlamydia; gonorrhea; Nursing Diagnoses Appendix.*

ETIOLOGY: *Chlamydia trachomatis* and *Neisseria gonorrhoeae* are the most frequent causes of PID, although anaerobic microorganisms, *Escherichia coli,* and other microorganisms also are often involved.

SYMPTOMS: The most common symptom is lower abdominal or pelvic pain, typically beginning after the start of a menstrual period. Exquisite tenderness during physical examination of the cervix, fallopian tubes, or ovaries is a common sign. Clear, white, or purulent vaginal discharge is sometimes present. Fevers, chills, nausea, vomiting, vaginal bleeding, dysuria, dyspareunia, or anorectal pain are seen in smaller numbers of patients.

DIAGNOSIS: Distinguishing PID from other causes of lower abdominal or pelvic pain can be difficult. The disease may be confused with appendicitis, diverticulitis, tubo-ovarian abscess, endometritis, ectopic pregnancy, and other serious illnesses. PID is most likely to be found in young, sexually active patients with multiple sexual partners, esp. if there is a history of previous sexually transmitted illnesses or of substance abuse. Leukocytosis and an elevated sedimentation rate are commonly found, and a mucopurulent discharge is often present on pelvic examination. Cultures from the vagina or cervix may be helpful in identifying the causative organism. In patients for whom the diagnosis is unclear, laparoscopy, ultrasonography, or computed tomography may be needed.

COMPLICATIONS: PID may result in adhesions or scarring of the fallopian tubes and pelvis, and is a common cause

of pelvic pain and ectopic pregnancy. About a third of all women who are infertile have lost the ability to conceive because of PID. Occasionally, PID causes intraperitoneal abscesses.

TREATMENT: Antibiotics effective against gonococci, chlamydiae, anaerobes, and gram-negative rods usually are used to treat PID. Typical therapy includes a tetracycline derivative, like doxycycline, and a cephalosporin. Early therapy prevents infertility caused by fallopian tube adhesions or scarring. In patients with tubal or pelvic abscesses, drainage is required. Sexual partners should be examined for evidence of sexually transmitted diseases and treated if culture results are positive. SEE: *safe sex.*

pelvic support   Pelvic **floor.**

pelvic tilt   An exercise to strengthen the abdominal muscles and reduce the risk of backache or back stiffness (e.g., during pregnancy). The patient assumes a supine position and flattens the hollow of her back against the floor. The abdominal, gluteal, and levator muscles are contracted with each exhalation and relaxed with each inhalation. The effects are maximized by concurrent abdominal breathing.

pelvimeter (pĕl-vĭm′ĕ-tĕr) [″ + Gr. *metron,* measure] A device for measuring the pelvis.

pelvimetry (pĕl-vĭm′ĕ-trē)   Measurement of the pelvic dimensions or proportions, a technique which was formerly thought to be useful in obstetrics.

pelvis (pel′vĭs, pel′vēz″, pel′vĭ-sĕz) *pl.* **pelves, pelvises** [L. *pelvis,* basin] **1.** A basin-shaped structure or cavity. **2.** The bony compartment comprising the innominate bones, the sacrum, and the coccyx, joined at the symphysis pubis, sacroiliac, and sacrococcygeal articulations by a network of cartilage and ligaments. The structure supports the vertebral column and articulates with the lower limbs. SEE: illus. **3.** The cavity encompassed by the innominate bones, the sacrum, and the coccyx.

ANATOMY: The pelvis is separated into a false or superior pelvis and a true or inferior pelvis by the iliopectineal line and the upper margin of the symphysis pubis. The circumference of this area constitutes the inlet of the true pelvis. The lower border of the true pelvis, termed the outlet, is formed by the coccyx, the protuberances of the ischia, the ascending rami of the ischia, and the descending rami of the ossa pubis and the sacrosciatic ligaments. The floor of the pelvis is formed by the perineal fascia, the levator ani, and the coccygeus muscles. All diameters normally are larger in the female than in the male.

EXTERNAL DIAMETERS: *Interspinous:* The distance between the outer

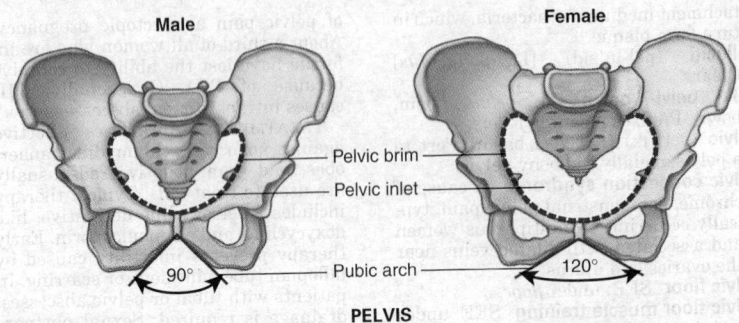

PELVIS

edges of the anterosuperior iliac spines, the diameter normally measuring 26 cm (10¼ in). *Intercristal:* The distance between the outer edges of the most prominent portion of the iliac crests, the diameter normally being 28 cm (11 in). *Intertrochanteric:* The distance between the most prominent points of the femoral trochanters, 32 cm (12½ in). *Oblique* (right and left): The distance from one posterosuperior iliac spine to the opposite anterosuperior iliac spine, 22 cm (8½ in), the right being slightly greater than the left. *External conjugate:* The distance from the undersurface of the spinous process of the last lumbar vertebra to the upper margin of the anterior surface of the symphysis pubis, 20 cm (7⅞ in).

INTERNAL DIAMETERS: *True conjugate:* The anteroposterior diameter of the pelvic inlet, 11 cm (4¼ in), the most important single diameter of the pelvis. *Diagonal conjugate:* The distance between the promontory of the sacrum to the undersurface of the symphysis pubis, 13 cm (5⅛ in). Two cm (¾ in) are deducted for the height and inclination of the symphysis pubis to obtain the diameter of the conjugate. *Transverse:* The distance between the ischial tuberosities, 11 cm (4¼ in). *Anteroposterior* (of outlet): The distance between the lower border of the symphysis pubis and the tip of the sacrum, 11cm (4¼ in). *Anterior sagittal:* The distance from the undersurface of the symphysis pubis to the center of the line between the ischial tuberosities, 7 cm (2¾ in). *Posterior sagittal:* The distance from the center of line between the ischial tuberosities to the tip of the sacrum, 10 cm (4 in).

android p. The normal shape of the male pelvis. About 30% of women share this bony configuration; however, the heart-shaped inlet, convergent sidewalls, slanted sacrum, and narrow sacrosciatic notch pose problems for childbearing. The narrowed dimensions increase the risk of fetopelvic disproportion, obstructed labor, and cesarean delivery. SYN: *masculine* **p.**

anthropoid p. A deviation from the normal gynecoid configuration of the pelvic bones in which the anterior-posterior diameter is greater than the transverse diameter. It is found in approx. 20% of women. Deviations from the normal gynecoid configuration include a long, oval, narrow inlet and narrow sacrum, straight sidewalls, and a wide sacrosciatic notch. The shape increases the potential for fetal posterior positions during childbearing.

assimilation p. A structural abnormality that results from a developmental lumbosacral fusion or from a sacrococcygeal fusion.

bony pelvis The skeleton of the pelvis, consisting of the right and left hip bones (each made of an ilium, an ischium, and a pubis), the sacrum, and the coccyx.

brachypellic p. An oval pelvis in which the transverse diameter is at least 1 cm longer, but no more than 3 cm longer, than the anteroposterior diameter of the pelvis.

brim of the p. Brim (2).

contracted p. A pelvis in which one or more of the principal diameters is reduced to a degree that parturition is impeded.

cordate p. A pelvis possessing a heart-shaped inlet.

coxalgic p. A pelvis deformed subsequent to hip joint disease.

dolichopellic p. An abnormal pelvis in which the anteroposterior diameter is greater than the transverse diameter.

dwarf p. An unusually small pelvis in which all diameters are symmetrically reduced.

elastic p. Osteomalacic **p.**

extrarenal p. A renal pelvis located outside the kidney.

false p. The portion of the pelvic cavity that lies above the pelvic brim, bounded by the linea terminalis and the iliac fossae. It supports the weight of the growing uterus during the middle and last trimesters of pregnancy. SYN: *p. major.*

fissured p. A structural malformation in which the ilia are pushed forward to an almost parallel position; caused by rickets.

flat p. A pelvis in which the antero-posterior diameters are shortened.

frozen p. Adhesion of the female reproductive organs to the peritoneum or bowel by cancer, endometriosis, or pelvic infection.

funnel-shaped p. A pelvis in which the outlet is considerably contracted but the inlet dimensions are normal.

gynecoid p. A normal female pelvis. Relative to the male pelvis, it has a wider bone structure and a more oval shape.

infantile p. An adult pelvis that retains its infantile characteristics. SYN: *juvenile p.*

p. justo major An unusually large pelvis.

juvenile p. Infantile **p.**

kyphoscoliotic p. A deformed pelvis caused by rickets.

kyphotic p. A deformed pelvis characterized by an increase of the conjugate diameter at the brim with reduction of the transverse diameter at the outlet.

lordotic p. A deformed pelvis in which the spinal column has an anterior curvature in the lumbar region.

p. major False **p.**

masculine p. A female pelvis that resembles a male pelvis, esp. in that it is narrower, more conical, and heavier-boned and has a heart-shaped inlet. SYN: *android p.*

p. minor True **p.**

p. obtecta A deformed pelvis in which the vertebral column extends across the pelvic inlet.

osteomalacic p. A pelvis distorted because of osteomalacia. SYN: *elastic p.*

Otto p. SEE: *Otto pelvis.*

platypellic p. A rare structural malformation that resembles a flattened gynecoid pelvis with shortened anteroposterior and wide transverse diameters.

pseudo-osteomalacic p. A rachitic pelvis similar to that of a person with osteomalacia.

rachitic p. A pelvis deformed from rickets.

renal p. The expanded proximal end of the ureter. It is within the renal sinus of the kidney and receives the urine through the major calyces.

reniform p. A pelvis shaped like a kidney.

round p. A pelvis with a circular inlet.

scoliotic p. A deformed pelvis resulting from spinal curvature.

simple flat p. A pelvis with a shortened anteroposterior diameter.

split p. A pelvis with a congenital division at the symphysis pubis.

spondylolisthetic p. A pelvis in which the last lumbar vertebra is dis-

located in front of the sacrum, causing occlusion of the brim.

true p. The portion of the pelvis lying below the iliopectineal line. The dimensions of the true pelvis are of obstetrical significance in determining the success of fetal descent. SYN: *p. minor.*

pelviscopy (pĕl-vĭs′kŭ-pē) Visual examination of the female reproductive organs with a laparoscope.

Pemberton sign (pem′bĕr-tŏn) [Hugh Spear Pemberton, Brit. physician, 1890–1956] Facial plethora that develops when a patient with a large substernal goiter raises his or her arms over the head. When the arms are elevated the enlarged thyroid gland compresses other structures in the neck, collapsing the jugular veins and congesting the head and neck with blood.

pemphigoid (pem′fĭ-goyd″) [*pemphigus* + *-oid*] A skin condition similar to pemphigus.

bullous p. A blistering disease found almost exclusively in older adults. Large, tense bullae filled with clear serum form on normal and urticarial skin. Lesions predominate in the flexural aspects of the limbs and abdomen. This condition is treated with corticosteroids and immunosuppressive agents, such as azathioprine or cyclophosphamide.

cicatricial p. Pemphigus in which blisters form in the mucous membranes, e.g., in the mouth, the throat, the anus, or the conjunctiva.

pemphigus (pem′fĭ-gŭs) [L. *pemphigus,* fr Gr. *pemphix,* a blister, bubble] An acute or chronic autoimmune disease principally of adults but sometimes found in children, characterized by occurrence of successive crops of bullae that appear suddenly on apparently normal skin and disappear, leaving pigmented spots. Antibodies form against cellular adhesion molecules in the epidermis, causing layers of the skin to separate and blister. A characteristic sign is a positive Nikolsky sign: when pressure is applied to an area as if trying to push the skin parallel to the surface, the skin will detach from the lower layers.

erythematous p. Scaling, erythematous macules and blebs of the scalp, face, and trunk. The lesions have a "butterfly" distribution over the face. The disease resembles pemphigus foliaceus.

familial benign chronic p. Hailey-Hailey disease.

p. foliaceus Pemphigus in which keratinocyte adhesion is disrupted beneath the stratum corneum. Once lesions develop, they may spread to the entire body and mimic generalized exfoliative dermatitis. The positive Nikolsky sign helps to make the correct diagnosis. The condition is treated with systemic corticosteroids.

paraneoplastic p. Pemphigus that arises together with or sometimes before malignancy, particularly B-cell lymphomas and chronic lymphocytic leukemia.

p. vegetans A form of pemphigus vulgaris characterized by pustules instead of bullae. Pustules are followed by warty vegetations. Prognosis is good, even before therapy with corticosteroids.

p. vulgaris The most common form of pemphigus. Blisters develop suddenly and are round or oval, thin-walled, tense, and translucent and bilateral in distribution. The lesions have little tendency to heal, and bleed easily when they burst. Since the introduction of corticosteroids, the prognosis for this autoimmune disease is favorable, but the mortality rate is still 5% to 15%. Immunosuppressive agents (such as azathioprine or cyclophosphamide) are used with corticosteroid therapy. SEE: *photochemotherapy*.

penalization (pĕn″ĭl-ĭ-zā′shĭn, pĕn″) An ophthalmological treatment for an eye with weak vision in which the vision from the healthier eye is blunted, blurred, or blocked so that the weaker eye must be relied upon. It is one form of treatment for amblyopia.

pencil (pĕn-sĭl) A material rolled into cylindrical form; may contain a caustic substance or a therapeutic paste or ointment.

Pender, Nola J. (pĕn′ dĕr) A U.S. nursing educator and researcher, born 1941, who developed and refined the Health Promotion Model nursing theory. SEE: *Health Promotion Model*.

Pendred syndrome (pen′dred″) [Vaughan Pendred, Brit. surgeon, 1869–1946] An autosomal recessive disease that causes progressive childhood sensorineural hearing loss and often causes goiter either with or without hypothyroidism.

pendular (pĕn′dū-lĕr) [L. *pendulus*] Hanging so as to swing by an attached part; oscillating like a pendulum.

pendulous (pĕn′dū-lŭs) Swinging freely like a pendulum; hanging.

penectomy (pĕn-ĕk′tŏ-mē) Surgical or traumatic removal of the penis.

penetrance (pĕn′ĕ-trăns) **1.** The frequency of manifestation of a hereditary condition in individuals. In theory, if the genotype is present, penetrance should be 100%. That is not usually the case, as a result of the modifying effects of other genes. **2.** The extent to which something enters an object.

penetrate (pĕn′ĕ-trāt) [L. *penetrare*] To enter or force into the interior; pierce.

penetrating (pĕn′ĕ-trāt-ĭng) Entering beyond the exterior.

p. power The capacity of a lens to see into an object.

penetration (pĕn″ĕ-trā′shŭn) [L. *penetrare*, to go within] **1.** The process of entering within a part. **2.** The capacity to enter within a part. **3.** The power of a lens to give a clear focus at varying depths. **4.** The ability of radiation to pass through a substance.

penetrometer (pĕn″ĕ-trŏm′ĕ-tĕr) [″ + Gr. *metron*, measure] An instrument that compares roughly the comparative absorption of x-rays in various metals, esp. silver, lead, and aluminum; hence, it gives a rough estimation of the ability of x-rays to penetrate tissues. SYN: *qualimeter*.

-penia [Gr. *penia*, lack, poverty] Suffix meaning *decrease, deficiency*.

penicillin (pĕn-ĭ-sĭl′ĭn) Any of a group of antibiotics biosynthesized by several species of molds, esp. *Penicillium notatum* and *P. chrysogenum*. Penicillin is bactericidal, inhibiting the growth of some gram-positive bacteria and some spirochetes by interfering with cell wall synthesis. There are many different penicillins, including synthetic ones, and their effectiveness varies for different organisms. SEE: *penicillin allergy*.

beta-lactamase resistant p. Synthetic penicillins that resist the action of the enzyme beta-lactamase, produced by some microorganisms. Bacteria that produce the enzyme are not susceptible to the action of non–beta-lactamase resistant penicillins.

p. G benzathine An antibiotic of the penicillin class available in a variety of dosage forms, used orally and parenterally.

penicillinase-resistant p. Any of a group of penicillins that are not inactivated by the enzyme penicillinase. These penicillins retain their effectiveness as antibiotics used for infections caused by bacteria that produce penicillinase. SEE: *bacterial resistance; beta-lactamase resistance; Staphylococcus aureus, methicillin-resistant*.

p. V potassium An antibiotic of the penicillin class. It is relatively stable in an acid medium and is therefore not inactivated by gastric acid when taken orally.

penicillin allergy SEE: under *allergy*.

penicillinase (pĕn-ĭ-sĭl′ĭ-nās) A bacterial enzyme that inactivates most but not all penicillins.

penicillinase-producing Neisseria gonorrhoeae ABBR: PPNG. Penicillin-resistant strains of *Neisseria gonorrhoeae*.

penicilliosis (pen″ĭ-sil′ē-ō′sĭs) [*Penicillium* + *-osis*] Infection with the fungi of the genus *Penicillium*, e.g., *P. marneffei*.

Penicillium (pĕn″ĭ-sĭl′ē-ŭm) [L. *penicillum*, brush] A genus of molds belonging to the Ascomycetes (sac fungi). They form the blue molds that grow on fruits, bread, and cheese. A number of species (*P. chrysogenum, P. notatum*) are the

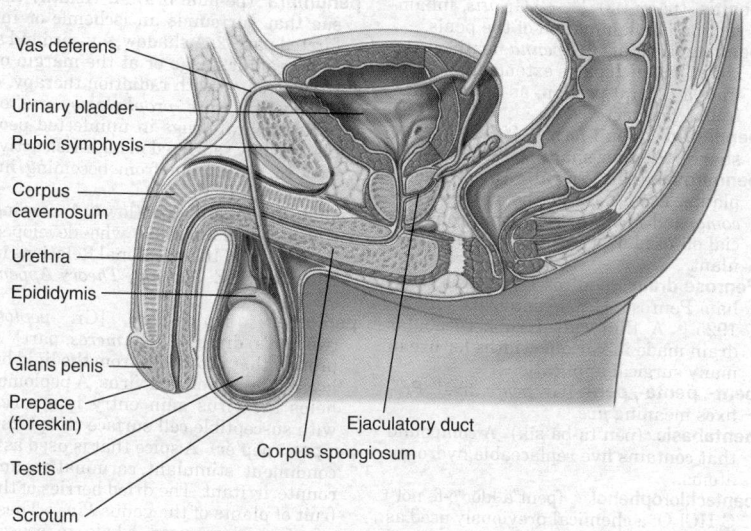

Vas deferens
Urinary bladder
Pubic symphysis
Corpus cavernosum
Urethra
Epididymis
Glans penis
Prepace (foreskin)
Testis
Scrotum
Ejaculatory duct
Corpus spongiosum

PENIS AND OTHER MALE ORGANS

sources of penicillin. Occasionally in humans they produce infections of the external ear, skin, or respiratory passageways. They are common allergens.

P. marneffei A species that may cause systemic infections, esp. in immunocompromised patients. It is found most often in Southeast Asia, where it frequently infects patients who have AIDS.

penicilloyl-polylysine (pen″ĭ-sil′ō-il″pol″ĭ-lī′sēn″) The major antigenic determinant of penicillin. It is used in skin testing for penicillin sensitivity.

PATIENT CARE: When it is injected intradermally into a sensitive person, an allergic reaction occurs within 20 min. Tested patients should be monitored for wheals, hives, angioedema, or anaphylaxis. SYN: *benzylpenicilloyl polylysine*.

penicillus (pĕn″ĭ-sĭl′ŭs) *pl.* **penicilli** [L., paint brush] A group of the branches of arteries in the spleen that are arranged like the bristles of a brush. Each consists of successive portions: the pulp arteries, sheathed arteries, and terminal arteries.

penile (pē′nĭl, -nīl) [L. *penis,* penis] Pert. to the penis. SEE: *penile prosthesis.*

penile fracture SEE: under *fracture.*

penis (pē′nĭs) *pl.* **penes, penises** [L.] The male organ of copulation and, in mammals, of urination. It is a cylindrical pendulous organ suspended from the front and sides of the pubic arch. It is homologous to the clitoris in the female. SEE: illus.; *circumcision; penile prosthesis; Peyronie's disease; priapism.*

ANATOMY: The penis is composed mainly of erectile tissue arranged in three columns, the whole being covered with skin. The two lateral columns are the corpora cavernosa penis. The third or median column, known as the corpus spongiosum, contains the urethra. The body is attached to the descending portion of the pubic bone by the crura of the penis. The cone-shaped head of the penis, the glans penis, contains the urethral orifice. It is covered with a movable hood known as the foreskin or prepuce, under which is secreted the substance called smegma.

Hyperemia of the genitals fills the corpora cavernosa with blood as the result of sexual excitement or stimulation, thus causing an erection. The hyperemia subsides following orgasm and ejaculation of the seminal fluid. The organ then returns to its flaccid condition. The size of the flaccid penis does not necessarily correlate with that of the erect penis.

buried p. A penis that is covered by overlying pubic skin and fat.

The occult location of the organ can interfere with normal urination and with sexual penetration.

clubbed p. The condition in which the penis is curved during erection.

double p. A congenital deformity in which the penis in the embryo is completely divided by the urethral groove.

p. envy In psychoanalysis, the female's desire to have a penis.

p. lunatus Chordee.

p. palmatus A penis enclosed by the scrotum. SYN: *webbed p.*

webbed p. **P.** palmatus.

penitis (pĕ-nī'tĭs) [" + Gr. *itis,* inflammation] Inflammation of the penis.

pennate (pĕn'āt) [L. *penna,* feather] An object in which parts extend at an angle from a central portion, as do the barbs from a feather.

penniform (pĕn'ĭ-form) [" + *forma,* shape] Feather-shaped.

pennyroyal (pĕn'ĭ-roy'ăl) Any of several plants, esp. those of the genera *Hedeoma* and *Mentha,* that yield commercial oil used as a carminative and stimulant.

Penrose drain (pen'rōz") [Charles Bingham Penrose, U.S. gynecologist, 1862–1925.] A thin-walled rubber tubular drain made in various widths for use in many surgical applications.

pent-, penta-, pen- [Gr. *pente,* five] Prefixes meaning *five,*

pentabasic (pĕn"tă-bā'sĭk) A compound that contains five replaceable hydrogen atoms.

pentachlorophenol (pent"ă-klōr"ŏ-fē'nōl") C_6HCl_5O; a chemical previously used as a wood preservative for termite control and as a defoliant. It is extremely toxic on its own, but some grades are additionally contaminated with dioxin.

pentad (pĕn'tăd) [Gr. *pente,* five] **1.** A radical or element with a valence of five. **2.** A group of five.

pentadactyl (pĕn"tă-dăk'tĭl) [" + *daktylos,* finger] Having five digits on each hand and foot.

pentane (pĕn'tān) C_5H_{12}; one of the hydrocarbons of the methane series. It is a product of petroleum distillation.

pentapeptide (pĕn"tă-pĕp'tĭd) A polypeptide with five amino acid groups.

pentaploid (pĕn'tă-ployd) [" + *ploos,* a fold, + *eidos,* form, shape] Having five sets of chromosomes.

pentastarch (pĕn' tŭ-stahrch) A plasma volume expander derived from amylopectin. It is a colloidal solution similar to hetastarch, but with a lower average molecular weight. It is used to support blood pressure in critical situations, such as the treatment of sepsis, shock, or trauma.

pentavalent (pĕn"tă-vā'lĕnt, -tăv'ă-lĕnt) [Gr. *pente,* five, + L. *valens,* having power] Having a chemical valence of five.

pentose (pĕn'tōs) [Gr. *pente,* five] $C_5H_{10}O_5$; a monosaccharide containing five carbon atoms, such as ribose in RNA and deoxyribose in DNA.

pentoside (pĕn'tō-sīd) Pentose combined with some other substance. Pentoses combined with purine or pyrimidine bases are present in nucleic acids, DNA, and RNA.

pentosuria (pĕn"tō-sū'rē-ă) A condition in which pentose is found in the urine.

pentoxide (pĕn-tŏk'sīd) A chemical molecule containing five atoms of oxygen.

penumbra (pĕ-nŭm'bră) **1.** Healthy tissue that surrounds an ischemic or infarcted part. **2.** A shadow, e.g., around a radiographic image or at the margin of tissue treated with radiation therapy.

PEP *post-exposure prophylaxis* (use of antiretroviral drugs in uninfected people who have engaged in high-risk activities to keep them from becoming infected with HIV).

Peplau, Hildegard (pĕp'low) A nursing educator (1909–1999) who developed the Theory of Interpersonal Relations in Nursing. SEE: *Nursing Theory Appendix.*

peplomer (pĕp'lă-mĕr) [Gr. *peplos,* (woman's) dress + Gr. *meros,* part] A protein that protrudes from the lipid bilayer of an enveloped virus. A peplomer helps the virus gain entry into a cell with susceptible cell surface receptors.

pepper (pĕp'ĕr) A spice that is used as a condiment, stimulant, carminative, and counterirritant. The dried berries of the fruit of plants of the genus *Piper.* These are ground or used whole to season foods. Although pepper irritates the oral mucosa, it does not produce peptic ulcers.

The Scoville scale is used for judging the level of "heat" or spiciness of peppers. Using this scale, the hottest peppers have a rating of 250,000 to 400,000 units. The active ingredient in chile peppers, capsaicin, may cause nasal or ocular irritation; it is wise to wear gloves, or to wash one's hands frequently when handling esp. spicy peppers.

peppermint (pĕp'ĕr-mĭnt) A perennial herb, *Mentha piperita,* cultivated for its aromatic leaves and used as a flavoring agent, carminative, antiemetic, and gastrointestinal antispasmodic.

-pepsia [L. fr Gr. *pepsis,* warming, cooking, digestion + *-ia*] Suffix meaning *digestion.*

pepsin (pĕp'sĭn) [Gr. *pepsis,* digestion] The chief enzyme of gastric juice, which converts proteins into proteoses and peptones. It is formed by the chief cells of gastric glands and produces its maximum activity at a pH of 1.5 to 2. It is obtainable in granular form. In the presence of hydrochloric acid, it digests proteins in vitro.

pepsinogen (pĕp-sĭn'ō-jĕn) [" + *gennan,* to produce] The antecedent of pepsin existing in the form of granules in the chief cells of gastric glands.

pepsinuria (pĕp"sĭ-nū'rē-ă) [" + *ouron,* urine] Excretion of pepsin in the urine.

peptic (pĕp'tĭk) [Gr. *peptikos*] **1.** Pert. to digestion. **2.** Pert. to pepsin. SYN: *pepsic.*

peptic ulcer SEE: under *ulcer.*

peptidase (pĕp'tĭ-dāz) An enzyme that converts peptides to amino acids.

peptide (pep'tīd") [*pept(ic)* + *-ide*] A

compound containing two or more linked amino acids.

atrial natriuretic p. ABBR: ANP. Atrial natriuretic **factor**.

brain natriuretic p. B-type natriuretic peptide.

B-type natriuretic p. ABBR: BNP. A hormone secreted by the left or right ventricle of the heart Concentration of this peptide in the bloodstream rises during episodes of decompensated heart failure. SEE: *brain natriuretic p.*

cell-penetrating p. A peptide that readily crosses cell membranes and therefore can influence cellular functions or carry other molecules that can directly or indirectly perform the same tasks.

endogenous opioid p. Any of a group of more than 15 substances present in the brain, certain endocrine glands, and the gastrointestinal tract. They have morphine-like analgesic properties, behavioral effects, and neurotransmitter and neuromodulator functions. Included in this group of chemicals are endorphins, enkephalins, and dynorphin.

glucose-dependent insulinotropic p. A hormone released by cells in the upper gastrointestinal tract in response to sugary or fatty meals. It stimulates beta cells in the pancreas to secrete insulin.

immunodominant p. Any of the peptides having a strong affinity for binding with class I or II histocompatibility antigens and for stimulating a response by T lymphocytes. Immunodominant peptides are produced by antigen processing, are expressed on the surface of macrophages and other antigen-presenting cells, and may be useful both in desensitizing people to allergens and in vaccine production. SYN: *immunodominant epitope*.

natriuretic p. Any peptide that stimulates the kidneys to excrete salt and water.

p. YY An appetite-regulating protein released by L cells of the mucosa of the gastrointestinal tract in response to a meal. It binds to cells in the arcuate nucleus of the brain, decreases the desire to eat, and creates a feeling of fullness.

peptide mapping SEE: under *mapping*.

peptidoglycan (pĕp-tĭ-dōglīsăn) A large, complex carbohydrate that forms layers in the cell walls of bacteria. Gram-positive cell walls have many peptide-linked layers; gram-negative cell walls have few layers.

peptidolytic (pĕp″tĭ-dō-lĭt′ĭk) [″ + *lytikos*, dissolving] Causing the splitting up or digestion of peptides.

peptidomimetics (pĕp″tĭ-dō-mĭ-mĕt′ĭks, pĕp-tĭd′ō-mĭ-) [″ + ″] The synthetic alteration of a natural peptide to make a new molecule that works in a specific biological or therapeutic application.

peptization (pĕp″tĭ-zā′shŭn) [Gr. *pep-tein,* to digest] In the chemistry of colloids, the process of making a colloidal solution more stable; conversion of a gel to a sol.

Peptococcaceae (pĕp-tō-kō-kā-sēī) A family of gram-positive, anaerobic cocci that includes the genus *Peptococcus* and may be normal or pathogenic inhabitants of the upper respiratory and intestinal tracts.

Peptococcus (pĕp″tō-kŏk′ŭs) A genus of gram-positive, anaerobic cocci that are normally present in the oral cavity, on the skin, and in the intestinal tract. When associated with infection, they usually act synergistically with other organisms.

peptone (pĕp′tōn) [Gr. *pepton,* digesting] A secondary protein formed by the action of proteolytic enzymes, acids, or alkalies on certain proteins.

peptonization (pĕp″tō-nĭ-zā′shŭn) [Gr. *pepton,* digesting] The action by which proteolytic enzymes break proteins into peptones.

peptonize (pĕp′tō-nīz) To convert into peptones; to predigest with pepsin.

peptonuria (pĕp″tō-nū′rē-ă) [″ + *ouron,* urine] Excretion of peptones in the urine.

Peptostreptococcus (pep″tŏ-strep″tŏ-kok′ŭs) A genus of gram-positive anaerobic cocci of the Peptostreptococcaceae family. They may be normal or pathogenic inhabitants of the upper respiratory and intestinal tracts and are an important cause of infections. Two species of *Peptostreptococcus* (*P. magnus* and *P. micros*) have been renamed as *Finegoldia magnus* and *Micromonas magnus,* respectively.

per (per) [L. *per,* through] **1.** Through, by, by means or agency of. **2.** For each unit or entity, e.g., milligrams per kilogram, usually written as *mg/kg*.

per- [L. *per,* through] Prefix meaning *throughout, through, utterly, intense;* in chemistry, the highest valence of an element.

peracid (pĕr-ăs′ĭd) **1.** An acid that contains the highest valence possible. **2.** An acid containing the peroxide group, O—OH.

peracute (pĕr″ă-kūt′) [″ + *acutus,* keen] Very acute or violent.

per anum (pĕr ā′nŭm) [L.] Through or by way of the anus.

perceived control (pĕr-sēvd′) The degree to which people feel they are in charge of their own lives, instead of feeling helpless, hopeless, or buffeted by events or other people. People who report that they have significant control tend to feel mentally and physically healthier than those who do not.

percent (pĕr-sĕnt) Per hundred; one of each hundred. The symbol % is used to indicate that the preceding number is a percentage rather than an absolute number. Thus, 8% of 50 is 4; whereas 8% of 500 is 40.

percentage depth dose SEE: under *dose*.

percentile (pĕr-sen'tĭl") One of 100 equal divisions of a series of items or data. Thus if a value such as a test score is higher than 92% of all the other test scores, that result is above the 92nd percentile of the range of scores. SYN: *centile*.

percept (pĕr'sĕpt) The mental image of an object seen.

perception (pĕr-sep'shŏn) [L. *perceptio*, taking, receiving] **1.** Awareness of objects; consciousness. **2.** The observation or receipt of sensory information. **3.** The elaboration of a sensory impression; the ideational association modifying, defining, and usually completing the primary impression or stimulus. Vague or inadequate association occurs in confused and depressed states.

    anomalous p. **1.** An infrequently used term for extrasensory perception. **2.** The subjective experience of one of the five senses when another sense is stimulated, e.g., the sensing of poetry as color, or sound as taste.

    auditory p. **1.** Hearing. **2.** Ability to identify, interpret, and attach meaning to sound.

    depth p. The perception of spatial relationships; three-dimensional perception.

    extrasensory p. ABBR: ESP. The reported perception of external events by other than the five senses.

    gustatory p. Taste.

    olfactory p. Smell.

    risk p. Concern about the probability of succumbing to a potential illness.

    stereognostic p. The recognition of objects by touch.

    tactile p. Touch.

    visual p. Sight.

perceptual completion An optical illusion in which a boundary, color, texture, light, or object is seen where one does not actually exist. This defect in visual perception, also known as "filling-in," commonly is experienced by people with visual field cuts or defects (scotoma).

percolate (pĕr'kō-lāt) [L. *percolare*, to strain through] **1.** To allow a liquid to seep through a powdered substance. **2.** Any fluid that has been filtered or percolated. **3.** To strain a fluid through powdered substances in order to impregnate it with dissolved chemicals.

percolation (pĕr"kŏ-lā'shŏn) [L. *percolare*, to filter] **1.** The process of extracting soluble portions of a drug of powdered composition by filtering a liquid solvent through it. **2.** Filtration.

percolator (pĕr'kō-lā"tor) An apparatus used for extraction of a drug with a liquid solvent.

percuss (pĕr-kŭs') [L. *percutere*] To tap parts of the body to aid diagnosis by listening carefully to the sounds they emit.

percussion (pĕr-kŭsh'ŭn) [L. *percussio*, a striking] **1.** Striking the body surface (usually with the fingers or a small hammer) to determine the position, size, or density of underlying structures. **2.** A technique for mobilizing secretions from the lungs by striking the chest wall with cupped hands. **3.** Any of the techniques of body massage in which the hands are used to strike the body and are drawn back after contact in order to control the impact. These techniques include beating with a loosely closed fist, clapping with the palm of the hand, cupping with a cupped hand, hacking with the ulnar border of the hand, and tapping with the knuckles or tips or flats of the fingers. SYN: *¹tapping; tapotement*.

    auscultatory p. Percussion combined with auscultation.

    bimanual p. Mediate **p.**

    deep p. Forceful percussion used to elicit a note from a deeply seated tissue or organ.

    direct p. Immediate **p.**

    finger p. Striking of the examiner's finger as it rests upon the patient's body with a finger of the examiner's other hand.

    immediate p. Percussion performed by striking the surface directly with the fingers. SYN: *direct p.*

    indirect p. Mediate **p.**

    mediate p. Percussion performed by using the fingers of one hand as a plexor and those of the opposite hand as a pleximeter. SYN: *bimanual p.; indirect p.*

    palpation p. Percussion in which the examiner uses his or her fingers to feel vibrations that are produced within the body, instead of listening for the sounds produced by striking the body.

    threshold p. Percussing lightly with the fingers on a glass-rod pleximeter, the far end of which is covered with a rubber cap. The cap is usually placed on an intercostal space. This technique is used to confine the percussion to a very small area.

percussor (pĕr-kŭs'or) [L., striker] A device used for diagnosis by percussion, consisting of a hammer with a rubber or metal head.

percutaneous (pĕr"kū-tā'nē-ŭs) [L. *per*, through, + *cutis*, skin] Effected through the skin; pert. to the application of a medicated ointment by friction, or the removal or injection of a fluid by needle.

percutaneous cord blood sampling Cordocentesis.

percutaneous coronary intervention ABBR: PCI. Any procedure in which catheters are placed within the coronary arteries to study them or open them when they are obstructed. Examples of this are balloon angioplasty, atherectomy, and stent placement.

PATIENT CARE: When the patient returns to the nursing unit after a PCI procedure, the nurse should be alerted to the type of procedure performed, the site of the sheath, the type of the sheath, the flush system in use, and any adverse events that have occurred. A cardiovascular assessment is performed immediately, including vital signs and an ECG. The invaded artery, peripheral perfusion in the limb on the side of the intervention (typically the right foot), urine output, and pain level are assessed and documented. The physician's orders are reviewed concerning vital signs, intravenous fluids (IV), activated clotting time, and the plan for sheath removal. If any bleeding is suspected, hemoglobin and hematocrit levels are checked and compared to preprocedural values. During sheath removal, two nurses work together, one monitoring the patient, the other removing the sheath. The patient's IV line must be patent, with fluid infusing and 500 mL normal saline available. A bedside monitor with noninvasive blood pressure capability, an ECG, and pulse oximeter should also be available. The patient is placed in a supine position, the dressing removed, and the arterial puncture site inspected for bleeding or hematoma. The patient should be advised that he or she will probably feel mild to moderate discomfort and pressure during and after removal of the sheath. Pain relievers are provided as prescribed. A syringe is attached to the stopcock, and blood is drawn to ensure there is no clot in the sheath. If a suture has been used to close the access site, it is removed. The femoral artery is palpated, and pressure is applied with fingers placed along the artery, beginning about 1 cm above the puncture site (because the sheath is inserted on an angle and therefore enters the artery proximal to the skin puncture site). Using the free hand, the nurse then gently withdraws the sheath (pulling it toward the patient's foot). Manual pressure is maintained on the site to stop bleeding but should not be strong enough to obscure the pedal pulse (checked by the other nurse). The site is re-examined for bleeding, swelling, and hematoma formation. Vital signs are assessed every 3 to 5 min after the sheath is removed. Continuous manual pressure or mechanical compression should be applied to an arterial site for 10 to 20 min or longer and to a venous site for 10 min. When bleeding has ceased, compression is discontinued, and a dressing is applied to the insertion site. The head of the bed may now be elevated slightly.

Frequent patient assessment continues according to protocol, typically q15m X4, then q30m X4, then q1h X4. Bedrest is maintained for 2 to 6 hr (longer if the patient is not stable), with the affected leg kept straight to minimize bleeding at the insertion site. This position may be uncomfortable, and the patient may require reminders to maintain it. Oral intake can be resumed once the sheath has been removed and the potential for vasovagal-induced vomiting has passed. The dressing is removed after 24 hr and the wound assessed for complications. Vascular closure devices (suture-placement and collagen-delivery) may be employed. Adverse reactions to sheath removal include bleeding, hypotension (during or following removal), or vasovagal-induced bradycardia. The patient is assessed for symptoms such as dizziness, altered mental status, nausea, bradycardia, or hypotension. Patients must be monitored for complications related to PCI (e.g., coronary ischemia, contrast-induced nephropathy, and problems at the site of insertion). Trauma to the femoral vessels may be minor or serious. When patients have both femoral arterial and venous sheaths, the arterial sheath is removed first to reduce the risk of vascular complications. Bleeding frequently complicates the procedure. For mild bleeding, pressure is applied to the puncture site; for more serious bleeding (e.g., bleeding that compromises vital signs or the punctured limb), pressure is applied, and the cardiologist or a vascular surgeon notified. Ecchymosis is common at the site immediately or after dressing removal, often extending into surrounding tissues and accompanied by pain and minor swelling. Retroperitoneal hematoma should be suspected if the patient experiences flank, abdominal, or back pain, unexplained hypotension, or a marked drop in hematocrit. Other complications include arterial occlusion by clot formation, pseudoaneurysm, arteriovenous fistula, and infection. The patient and family should receive clear written and verbal instructions for home care before discharge. The patient should be advised to avoid strenuous activities for 3 days after a PCI and not to attempt to lift anything heavier than 10 lb until after a follow-up visit with the cardiologist. Reclining is recommended rather than sitting. The patient may shower but should not take tub baths or swim until the groin is fully healed. If a dressing is in place, it may be removed in 24 hr, and the site kept clean and dry. Some bruising and development of a small lump at the site are normal. If light bleeding occurs, the patient or a family member should apply pressure to the site for 10 min and then apply an adhesive bandage. For heavy bleeding, pressure should be applied 1 in above the puncture site and 911 should be called. The site should also be observed for infection (redness, warmth, pain, drainage) and the physician notified if any of these signs occur.

percutaneous electrical nerve stimulation SEE: under *stimulation*.

percutaneous heart valve replacement ABBR: PHVR. Surgical placement of a prosthetic heart valve delivered by a catheter into the heart instead of by the approach of sternotomy.

percutaneous nephrolithotomy ABBR: PNL. The removal of stones from the urinary tract with a needle inserted through the skin and into the urinary collecting system. The collecting system near the stone is dilated, and the stone is grasped and/or crushed.

percutaneous pinning SEE: *external fixation*.

percutaneous vertebral augmentation SEE: under *augmentation*.

per diem cost (pĕr-dē-ĕm) Daily expenses.

perennial Throughout the entire year. Said of diseases, such as some cases of allergic rhinitis, which do not have a peak incidence in one season.

perfectionism (pĕr-fĕk′shŭn-ĭzm) A personality trait in which the individual strives for achievement in a manner that borders on the obsessive or the depressive.

perfluorocarbon (pĕr-floor″-ă-kahr′ bŭn, -floo″ă-rō-) A class of solvent molecules that can carry nonpolar gases, such as oxygen, nitrogen, and carbon dioxide. They have been used experimentally in transfusion medicine and in some ophthalmic surgeries. Perfluorocarbons are also used as blood gas controls when prepared in buffered solutions equilibrated with CO_2 and O_2.

perforans (pĕr′fō-răns) [L.] Perforating or penetrating, as a nerve or blood vessel through a nerve or a muscle.

perforate (pĕr′fō-rāt) [L. *perforatus*, pierced with holes] **1.** To puncture or to make holes. **2.** Pierced with holes.

perforation (pĕr″fō-rā′shŏn) [L. *perforatio*, a boring through] **1.** The act or process of making a hole, such as that caused by ulceration. **2.** A hole made through a structure or part.

   Bezold p. SEE: under *Bezold, Friedrich*.

   glove p. A tear or puncture through the protective membrane of a glove. It exposes both the surgeon and the patient to potentially transmissible infectious diseases. Loss of glove integrity occurs most often on the thumb of the dominant surgical hand and on either index finger. It is often unrecognized. Its frequency increases with the duration of the operation.

   intestinal p. P. of stomach or intestine.

   nasal septal p. A hole through the nasal septum, usually the result of chronic inflammation caused by infection or repeated cocaine inhalation.

   p. of stomach or intestine An abdominal crisis in which a hole forms in a wall of the gastrointestinal tract, resulting in the release of intestinal fluids into the peritoneum. The leakage may produce a localized abscess, phlegmon, or diffuse peritonitis. SYN: *intestinal p.* SEE: *peritonitis*.

   SYMPTOMS: The onset is accompanied by acute pain, beginning over the perforated area and spreading all over the abdomen. Nausea and vomiting, tachycardia, hypotension, fevers, chills, sweats, confusion, and decreased urinary output are common.

   TREATMENT: Surgical treatment is necessary. Pending operation, the patient is given no oral fluids; parenteral fluids, antibiotics, and other medications are administered.

   tooth p. Pulp **exposure**.

perforator (pĕr′fō-tor) [L., a piercing device] **1.** An instrument for piercing the skull and other bones. **2.** A blood vessel that penetrates an organ (e.g. the septal perforator arteries of the heart); any of the perforating veins of the lower extremities

   tympanum p. An instrument used to perforate the tympanum.

perforatorium (pĕr″fō-ră-tō′rē-ŭm) The pointed tip of the acrosome of the spermatozoa.

perforin (pĕr′ fŭ-rĭn) One of a group of membrane-altering proteins released from natural killer cells and cytotoxic T cells that drill holes in cell membranes, causing affected cells to die. Perforins contribute to innate immune defenses against viruses and tumors.

performance (pĕr-fŏr-măns) **1.** The undertaking and completion of mental or physical work. In rehabilitation, a person's performance is observed and measured to determine functional capability. **2.** Fulfillment of a task; accomplishment.

performance area Functional classification of tasks and roles used by occupational therapists for assessment and goal-setting, including activities of daily living, work and other productive activities, and leisure and play.

Performance Assessment of Self-Care Skills ABBR: PASS. A formal means of gauging an adult's capacity to thrive independently that measures home management and personal care skills, mobility, safety, and outcome.

performance-based physical function test ABBR: PPF. A four-component assessment of physical functioning. The PPF includes:

1. the time it takes a subject to walk 10 feet;

2. the time it takes to stand up from a seated position in a chair five consecutive times;

3. the grip strength in the dominant hand; and

4. a test of balance and stability.

Each component of the test is given a score from 0 to 4. The highest possible score on the test, indicating optimal physical functioning, is 16.

performance improvement ABBR: PI. Any enhancement in health care operations (e.g., communications, laboratory operations, patient safety, profitability, resource utilization).

Performance IQ A synonym for "nonverbal intelligence" as measured by standard psychometric tests.

performance measure Any criterion used to assess the efficiency or the quality of health care.

perfusate (pĕr-fū′zāt) The fluid used to perfuse a tissue or organ.

perfuse (pĕr-fūz′) [L. *perfundere*, to moisten (all over)] To force or instill (fluids) into an organ or a vessel.

perfusion (pĕr-fū′zhŏn) [L. *perfusio*, a pouring through, drenching] **1.** The circulation of blood through tissues. **2.** Passing of a fluid through spaces. **3.** Pouring of a fluid. **4.** Supplying of an organ or tissue with nutrients and oxygen by injecting blood or a suitable fluid into an artery.

   coronary p. The passage of blood through the arteries of the heart.

   isolated limb p. Limb **p.**

   limb p. A method for concentrating a dose of chemotherapy in an arm or leg affected by cancer. Large blood vessels near the tumor are cannulated; the limb is wrapped in a tourniquet, and chemotherapy is circulated into the limb. Isolated limb perfusion has been used to treat melanomas or sarcomas. SYN: *isolated limb p.*

   machine p. In organ transplantation, the infusion of donated organs with fluids that supply necessary nutrients and wash away metabolic by-products. It is used to improve the viability of the organs before and after they are transplanted into recipients.

perfusionist (pĕr-fū′zhŭn-ĭst) A health care professional, formally known as a clinical perfusion scientist, who manages extracorporeal circulation of blood and operates the heart-lung machine.

peri- [Gr. *peri*, around, about] Prefix meaning *around, about.*

periadenitis (pĕr″ē-ā″dĕ-nī′tĭs) [″ + *aden*, gland, + *itis*, inflammation] Inflammation of the tissues surrounding a gland.

   p. mucosa necrotica recurrens An obsolete term for recurrent aphthous ulcers of the mouth, also known as Sutton ulcers.

perianal (pĕr″ē-ā′năl) [″ + L. *anus*, anus] Around or close to the anus.

periaortic (pĕr″ē-ā-or′tĭk) [″ + *aorte*, aorta] Around the aorta.

periaortitis (pĕr″ē-ā-or-tī′tĭs) [″ + *aorte*, aorta, + *itis*, inflammation] Inflammation of adventitia and tissues around the aorta.

periapex (pĕr″ē-ā′pĕks) [″ + L. *apex*, tip] The area around the apex of a tooth.

periapical (pĕr″ē-ăp′ĭ-kăl) [″ + L. *apex*, tip] Around the apex of the root of a tooth.

periappendicitis (pĕr″ē-ă-pĕn″dĭ-sī′tĭs) [″ + L. *appendix*, appendage, + Gr. *itis*, inflammation] Inflammation of the tissues surrounding the appendix secondary to either appendicitis or other intraperitoneal inflammatory process.

   p. decidualis A condition in which decidual cells exist in the peritoneum of the appendix vermiformis in cases of tubal pregnancy owing to adhesions between fallopian tubes and the appendix.

periappendicular (pĕr″ē-ăp″ĕn-dĭk′ū-lăr) [″ + L. *appendix*, appendage] Surrounding an appendix.

periarterial (pĕr″ē-ăr-tē′rē-ăl) [″ + *arteria*, artery] Placed around an artery.

periarteriolar lymphoid sheath (pĕr″ē-ahr-tīr′ē-ō′lĕr) ABBR: PALS. A region of the spleen that encircles the splenic arteries and is composed mostly of T cells. It comprises the tissues sometimes referred to as the white pulp of the organ.

periarteritis (pĕr″ē-ăr-tĕr-ī′tĭs) [″ + ″ + *itis*, inflammation] Inflammation of the external coat of an artery.

   p. gummosa Gummas in the blood vessels in syphilis.

   p. nodosa Polyarteritis nodosa. SEE: *Nursing Diagnoses Appendix.*

periarthritis (pĕr″ē-ăr-thrī′tĭs) [″ + ″ + *itis*, inflammation] Inflammation of the area around a joint.

periarticular (pĕr″ē-ăr-tĭk′ū-lăr) Circumarticular.

periauricular (pĕr″ē-ăw-rĭk-ū-lăr) Around the ear.

periaxial (pĕr-ē-ăk′sē-ăl) [″ + *axon*, axis] Located around an axis.

peribronchiolar (pĕr″ĭ-brŏng″kē-ō′lăr) [″ + L. *bronchiolus*, bronchiole] Surrounding a bronchiole.

peribronchiolitis (pĕr″ĭ-brŏng″kē-ō-lī′tĭs) [″ + ″ + Gr. *itis*, inflammation] Inflammation of the area around the bronchioles.

pericardiectomy (pĕr″ĭ-kăr-dē-ĕk′tō-mē) [″ + ″ + *ektome*, excision] Puncturing or perforation of the pericardium or creation of a pericardial window, for example, to relieve a pericardial effusion responsible for cardiac tamponade.

pericardiocentesis (per″ĭ-kard″ē-ō-sen-tē′sĭs) [*peri-* + *cardiocentesis*] Insertion of a needle into the pericardium to remove accumulated fluid. The procedure can save the lives of patients with pericardial tamponade.

pericardiophrenic (pĕr-ĭ-kăr″dē-ō-frĕn′ĭk) [″ + *kardia,* heart, + *phren,* diaphragm] Pert. to the pericardium and diaphragm.

pericardiostomy (pĕr″ĭ-kăr″dē-ŏs′tō-mē) [″ + *kardia,* heart, + *stoma,* mouth] Formation of an opening into the pericardium for drainage.

pericardiotomy (pĕr″ĭ-kăr-dē-ŏt′ō-mē) [″ + ″ + *tome,* incision] Incision of the pericardium.

pericarditis (per″ĭ-kar-dīt′ĭs) [*pericard(ium)* + *-itis*] Inflammation of the pericardium, marked by chest pain, fever, and an audible friction rub. SEE: *Dressler syndrome; Nursing Diagnoses Appendix.*

ETIOLOGY: Many diseases and conditions can inflame the membranous covering of the heart, including infections (bacterial, tubercular, viral, fungal); collagen-vascular diseases (e.g., rheumatic fever, rheumatoid arthritis, or systemic lupus erythematosus); drugs (hydralazine, procainamide, isoniazid, minoxidil); myocardial infarction; cancer; renal failure; cardiac surgery; or trauma. In many instances the precise cause is unknown (in these cases the inflammation is called idiopathic).

SYMPTOMS: Chest pain that varies with respiration is a hallmark of pericarditis. The pain often worsens when the patient lies down and improves when he sits up and leans forward. The pain is usually described as sharp, constant, and located in the mid-chest (retrosternally), but it may radiate to the neck, shoulder, and back. Fever, cough, dyspnea, and palpitations are also characteristic. The classic sign of pericarditis is the pericardial rub (found in about 50% of cases), a multicomponent abnormal heart sound that some observers describe as high-pitched, scratchy, raspy, grating, or leathery. It is best heard with the diaphragm of the stethoscope at the left lower sternal border as the patient sits up, leans forward, and holds his breath after expiration.

DIAGNOSIS: Diagnosis is usually based on the clinical presentation, electrocardiogram changes, and echocardiography.

TREATMENT: Therapy depends on the cause of the syndrome. Uremic pericarditis is treated with dialysis; pyogenic pericarditis requires antibiotic therapy and drainage. Nonsteroidal anti-inflammatory drugs and colchicine improve outcomes in patients with idiopathic disease. Many cases of pericarditis are self-limiting, but without treatment others may progress to chronic constrictive pericarditis or cardiac tamponade.

PATIENT CARE: The patient is observed closely for symptoms of cardiac tamponade, such as pallor and clammy skin, pulsus paradoxus (systolic blood pressure at least 10 mm Hg lower during slow inspiration than during expiration), weak or absent peripheral pulses, distended neck veins, decreased blood pressure, and narrowing pulse pressure. Patients with chronic constrictive pericarditis usually require a total pericardectomy to permit adequate filling and contraction of the heart. If surgery is required, the patient is taught deep-breathing and coughing (incentive spirometry) exercises beforehand as time permits. Postoperative care will be similar to that for other cardiothoracic surgical patients. Medications are administered as prescribed. Activities are restricted and vigorous exercise should be avoided until pain and fever subside, which may take weeks to months. In the convalescent phase, the patient is taught about the importance of taking prescribedmedications, their purposes, and any potentially recurring symptoms to report. The patient is encouraged to keep all scheduled follow-up appointments and to notify the primary health care provider immediately if changes in symptoms occur, such as return or worsening of pain, difficulty with breathing, irregular heart beats, or loss of consciousness.

adhesive p. An old term for constrictive pericarditis.

constrictive p. Scarring of the pericardium after one or more episodes of pericarditis. This limits normal cardiac filling during diastole. Impaired filling of the heart chambers reduces the volume of blood ejected by the heart with each contraction. The patient often complains of shortness of breath. On physical examination, elevated neck veins, ascites, hepatic enlargement, and lower extremity edema often are found. Surgical stripping of the pericardium (pericardiectomy) relieves the constriction. The disease can be distinguished from restrictive cardiomyopathy by echocardiography or cardiac magnetic resonance imaging.

external p. Inflammation of the exterior surface of the pericardium.

fibrinous p. Pericarditis in which the membrane is covered with a butter-like exudate that organizes and unites the pericardial surfaces.

SYMPTOMS: The condition is characterized by symptoms of heart failure (e.g., dyspnea, generalized edema, cyanosis).

hemorrhagic p. Pericarditis in which the exudate contains blood.

ischemic p. Pericarditis resulting from myocardial infarction.

neoplastic p. Pericarditis due to invasion of the pericardium by cancer.

p. obliterans Pericarditis causing adhesions and obliteration of the pericardial cavity.

serofibrinous p. Pericarditis in which there is a considerable quantity of serous exudate but little fibrin.

uremic p. Pericarditis associated with end-stage renal failure or hemodialysis. It indicates the need for more frequent or more intensive dialysis.

pericardium (pĕr″ĭ-kăr′dē-ŭm) [Gr. *peri,* around, + *kardia,* heart] The membranous fibroserous sac enclosing the heart and the bases of the great vessels. Its three layers are the fibrous pericardium (the outer layer); the parietal pericardium, a serous membrane that lines the fibrous pericardium; and the visceral pericardium (epicardium), a serous membrane on the surface of the myocardium. The space between the two serous layers is the pericardial cavity, a potential space filled with serous fluid that reduces friction as the heart beats. Its base is attached to the diaphragm, its apex extending upward as far as the first subdivision of the great blood vessels. It is attached in front to the sternum, laterally to the mediastinal pleura, and posteriorly to the esophagus, trachea, and principal bronchi.

adherent p. A condition in which fibrous bands form between the two serous layers of the pericardium, obliterating the pericardial cavity. SEE: *pericarditis, constrictive.*

bread-and-butter p. A pathological appearance seen in fibrinous pericarditis, in which the pericardium has a peculiar appearance as a result of fibrinous deposits on the two opposing surfaces.

fibrous p. The outer fibrous layer of the pericardium; it extends over the bases of the great vessels and the upper surface of the diaphragm.

parietal p. The middle layer of the pericardial sac, a serous membrane lining the fibrous pericardium.

serous p. A flattened sac formed of a single layer of cells and connective tissue.

shaggy p. A condition occurring in fibrinous pericarditis in which loose shaggy deposits of fibrin are seen on the surfaces of the pericardium.

visceral p. The side of the sac attached to the external surface of the heart. SYN: *epicardium.*

pericellular (pĕr″ĭ-sĕl′ū-lăr) [″ + L. *cellula, cell*] Around a cell.

pericholangitis (pĕr″ĭ-kō-lăn-jī′tĭs) [Gr. *peri,* around, + *chole,* bile, + *an-*

geion, vessel, + *itis,* inflammation] Inflammation of tissues surrounding a bile duct. SYN: *periangiocholitis.*

pericholecystitis (pĕr″ĭ-kō-lē-sĭs-tī′tĭs) [″ + ″ + *kystis,* a sac, + *itis,* inflammation] Inflammation of tissues situated around the gallbladder.

perichondritis (pĕr-ĭ-kŏn-drī′tĭs) [″ + ″ + *itis,* inflammation] Inflammation of the perichondrium.

perichondrium (pĕr-ĭ-kŏn′drē-ŭm) [″ + *chondros,* cartilage] Fibrous connective tissue that surrounds cartilage.

pericolic (pĕr-ĭ-kō′lĭk) [″ + *kolon,* colon] Around or encircling the colon.

pericolitis (pĕr″ĭ-kō-lī′tĭs) [″ + ″ + ″] Inflammation surrounding the colon.

pericorneal (pĕr-ĭ-kor′nē-ăl) [″ + L. *cornu,* horn] Placed around the cornea.

pericoronal (pĕr″ĭ-kor′ō-năl) [″ + *korone,* crown] Around the crown of a tooth.

pericoronitis (pĕr″ĭ-kor″ō-nī′tĭs) [″ + ″ + *itis,* inflammation] Abscess around the crown of an unerupted molar. SYN: *pericoronal abscess.*

pericranial (pĕr″ĭ-krā′nē-ăl) [″ + *kranion,* skull] Pert. to the periosteum of the skull.

pericranium (pĕr″ĭ-krā′nē-ŭm) The fibrous membrane surrounding the cranium; periosteum of the skull.

pericystic (pĕr″ĭ-sĭs′tĭk) [″ + *kystis,* bladder] Surrounding a cyst.

pericyte (pĕr′ĭ-sīt) [″ + *kytos,* cell] A stem cell that may give rise to smooth muscle cells; often found around capillaries.

peridental (pĕr″ĭ-dĕn′tăl) [″ + L. *dens,* tooth] Surrounding a tooth or part of one. SYN: *periodontal.*

periderm (pĕr′ē-dĕrm) [″ + *derma,* skin] A thin layer of flattened cells forming a transient layer of embryonic epidermis. SYN: *epitrichial layer; epitrichium.*

peridiverticulitis (pĕr″ĭ-dī″vĕr-tĭk″ū-lī′tĭs) [″ + L. *diverticulare,* to turn aside, + Gr. *itis,* inflammation] Inflammation of tissues situated around an intestinal diverticulum.

periductal (pĕr-ĭ-dŭk′tăl) [″ + L. *ductus,* a passage] Situated around a duct.

peridural (pĕr″ĭ-dū′răl) [″ + L. *durus,* hard] Outside the dura mater.

perienteric (pĕr″ē-ĕn-tĕr′ĭk) [Gr. *peri,* around, + *enteron,* intestine] Around the intestines.

perifocal (pĕr″ĭ-fō′kăl) [″ + L. *focus,* hearth] Around a focus, esp. around an infected focus.

perifollicular (pĕr″ĭ-fŏl-lĭk′ū-lăr) [″ + L. *folliculus,* a little sac] Around a follicle.

perifolliculitis (per″ĭ-fŏ-lĭk″yŭ-līt′ĭs) [*peri-* + *folliculitis*] Inflammation around hair follicles.

p. capitis abscedens et suffodiens Dissecting **cellulitis** of the scalp.

periganglionic (pĕr″ĭ-găng″glē-ŏn′ĭk) [″ + *ganglion*, knot] Around a ganglion.

perihepatic (pĕr″ĭ-hē-păt′ĭk) [Gr. *peri*, around, + *hepar*, liver] Around the liver.

perihepatitis (pĕr″ĭ-hĕp-ă-tī′tĭs) [″ + ″ + *itis*, inflammation] Inflammation of the peritoneal covering of the liver, e.g., in Fitz-Hugh-Curtis syndrome.

perikaryon (pĕr″ĭ-kăr′ē-ŏn) [″ + *karyon*, nucleus] The cell body of a neuron.

perikeratic (pĕr″ĭ-kĕr-ă′tĭk) [″ + *keras*, horn] About the cornea. SYN: *pericorneal*.

perikymata (pĕr″ĭ-kī′mă-tă) [″ + *kyma*, wave] The transverse wavelike grooves most apparent in the surface enamel of newly erupted anterior teeth; they are more pronounced at eruption and are reduced in depth with wear in advancing age.

perilaryngeal (pĕr″ĭ-lă-rĭn′jē-ăl) [″ + *larynx*, larynx] Around the larynx.

perilymph, perilympha (per′ĭ-limf″, per″ĭ-lim′fă) [″ + L. *lympha*, serum] The pale, transparent fluid within the bony (not the vestibular) labyrinth of the inner ear.

perimenopause (pĕr-ē-mĕn′ō-păwz) The phase before the menopause transition and the first year after menopause. It includes three distinct elements: the time during which menstrual cycles become increasingly less regular and follicle-stimulating hormones rise; the last menstrual period; and the first 12 consecutive months during which no menses occur. SEE: *menopause transition*.

perimeter (pĕr-ĭm′ĕ-tĕr) [″ + *metron*, measure] **1.** The outer edge or periphery of a body or measure of the same. **2.** A device for determining the extent of the field of vision. SEE: *perimetry*.

¹perimetric (per″ĭ-me′trĭk) [*peri-* + *¹metro-* + *-ic*] Situated around the uterus.

²perimetric (per″ĭ-me′trĭk) [*peri-* + *-metry*] Pert. to perimetry.

perimetritis (per″ĭ-mē-trīt′ĭs) [*perimetrium* + *-itis*] Inflammation of the peritoneal covering of the uterus; may be associated with parametritis. **perimetritic** (per″ĭ-mē-trit′ĭk), *adj*.

perimetrium (per″ĭ-mē′trē-ŭm) [*peri-* + *¹metro-* + *-ium*] The serous layer of the uterus. It is the visceral peritoneum that covers the uterus, except for the portion that rests on the bladder and the vaginal part of the cervix.

perimetry (pĕ-rim′ĕ-trē) [*peri-* + *-metry*] **1.** Circumference; edge; border of a body. **2.** Measurement of the scope of the field of vision with a perimeter. SYN: *campimetry*.

kinetic p. A test of visual field impairment in which a person's ability to see peripherally placed objects is assessed by moving the objects but keeping their size and brightness unchanged.

static p. A test of visual field impairment in which a person's ability to see objects at the edges of the visual field is assessed by changing the brightness or size of the objects but not their position.

perimysium (pĕr″ĭ-mĭs′ē-ŭm) *pl.* **perimysia** A connective tissue sheath that envelops each primary bundle of muscle fibers; sometimes called perimysium internum.

perinatal (per″ĭ-nāt′ăl) [*peri-* + *¹natal*] Pert. to the period beginning between the 20th to 28th week of pregnancy and ending 28 days after birth.

perinatal asphyxial encephalopathy SEE: under *encephalopathy*.

perinatal programming The triggering of illnesses in adults by events that occurred during development within the womb.

perinatology (pĕr-ē-nā-tŏl′ō-jē) The study of the fetus and infant during the perinatal period. SEE: *perinatal*.

perineal (pĕr″ĭ-nē′ăl) [Gr. *perinaion*, perineum] Pert. to or situated on the perineum.

perineal body SEE: under *body*.

perineo- [Gr. *perinaion*] Prefix meaning *perineum*.

perineometer (pĕr″ĭ-nē-ŏm′ĕ-ter) [Gr. *perinaion*, perineum, + *metron*, measure] An apparatus for measuring the pressure or force that is produced in the vagina when the pubococcygeus and levator ani muscles are contracted voluntarily. SEE: *Kegel exercise*.

perineoplasty (pĕr″ĭ-nē′ō-plăs″tē) [″ + *plassein*, to form] Reparative surgery on the perineum.

perineorrhaphy (pĕr″ĭ-nē-or′ă-fē) [″ + *rhaphe*, a sewing] Suture of the perineum to repair a laceration that occurs or is made surgically during the delivery of the fetus.

PATIENT CARE: Caregivers should implement standard precautions, wearing disposable gloves throughout perineal assessment, patient care, and disposal of biohazardous wastes, and performing thorough hand hygiene before and after procedures. Assessments focus on diet and fluid intake, bowel elimination, and the status of the suture line. To minimize potential for autoinfection, patient care and teaching should emphasize cleansing the perineum from front to rear after urination or defecation with a cascade of warm fluid or an antiseptic towelette. Perineal pads also should be applied and removed from front to rear. Application of an ice pack immediately after delivery and intermittently during the first 24 hr postpartum aids in reducing edema and relieving discomfort. To maximize effects, the ice pack should be removed 20 min after its placement and reapplied 10 min later and the mother taught this 20 min on, 10 min off regimen. The use of warm Sitz baths for 20 min several times daily is encouraged. Personal portable Sitz baths avoid the possibility of cross-contamination and may be sent home with the mother. Pain is assessed and analgesics are administered as prescribed. Ambulation also is encouraged. Gluteal splinting (i.e., tensing the buttocks while sitting or rising from a seated position) reduces discomfort. Health care professionals should provide support and reassurance because the patient may experience anxiety about the ability to resume normal physical functions and sexual activity and should provide opportunities for the patient to express feelings and to ask questions.

anterior p. Surgical repair of anterior perineum and vaginal wall to correct a cystocele.

posterior p. The removal and repair of a rectocele.

perineoscrotal (pĕr″ĭ-nē-ō-skrō′tăl) [″ + L. *scrotum*, a bag] Concerning the perineum and scrotum.

perineotomy (pĕr″ĭ-nē-ŏt′ō-mē) [″ + *tome*, incision] Surgical incision into the perineum. SYN: *perineal section*.

perinephric (pĕr″ĭ-nĕf′rĭk) [Gr. *peri*, around, + *nephros*, kidney] Located or occurring around the kidney.

perinephritis (pĕr″ĭ-nĕ-frī′tĭs) [″ + ″ + *itis*, inflammation] Inflammation of peritoneal tissues around the kidney.

perineum (pĕr″ĭ-nē′ŭm) [Gr. *perinaion*] **1.** The structures occupying the pelvic outlet and constituting the pelvic floor. **2.** The external region between the vulva and anus in a female or between the scrotum and anus in a male. It is made up of skin, muscle, and fasciae. The muscles of the perineum are the anterior portion of the intact levator ani muscle and the transverse perineal muscle. SEE: illus.; *perineal body*.

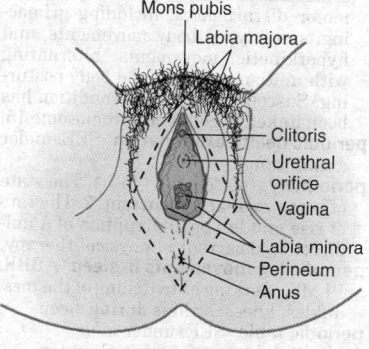

Mons pubis
Labia majora
Clitoris
Urethral orifice
Vagina
Labia minora
Perineum
Anus

PERINEUM

perineural (pĕr″ĭ-nū′răl) [Gr. *peri*, around, + *neuron*, nerve] Around a nerve.

perineurial (pĕr″ĭ-nū′rē-ăl) [″ + *neuron*, sinew] Concerning the perineu-

rium, the sheath around a bundle of nerve fibers.

perineuritis (pĕr″ĭ-nū-rī′tĭs) [″ + ″ + *itis*, inflammation] Inflammation of the sheath enveloping nerve fibers.

perineurium (pĕr″ĭ-nū′rē-ŭm) [″ + *neuron*, sinew] A connective tissue sheath investing a fasciculus or bundle of nerve fibers.

perinuclear (pĕr″ĭ-nū′klē-ăr) [″ + L. *nucleus*, a kernel] Around a nucleus.

periocular (pĕr″ē-ŏk′ū-lăr) [″ + L. *oculus*, eye] Located around the eye. SYN: *circumocular*.

period (pēr′ē-ŏd) [Gr. *periodos*, circuit, period of time] **1.** The interval between two successive occurrences of any regularly recurring phenomenon or event; a cycle. **2.** Colloquial expression for the menstrual flow. **3.** Time occupied by a disease in running its course, or by a stage of a disease, such as an incubation period.

absolute refractory p. The period of time in which a stimulus, no matter how strong, will not elicit a response after contraction of a muscle fiber or transmission of a nerve impulse by a neuron.

childbearing p. The period in the life of the female puberty to menopause during which she is capable of procreation.

comment p. The time during which public discussion of health care regulations is invited, e.g., by federal health care agencies. When new governmental rules affecting health care are enacted, their potential effects are usually discussed in advance during open meetings. During this period members of the public, health care insurers, hospitals, clinics, and other agencies make known their interpretation of the effects of these new rules.

communicable p. In epidemiology and infectious diseases, the time during which an infectious agent is transmissible, directly or indirectly, from an infected person or animal to a susceptible person.

effective refractory p. In electrocardiography, the interval during which a second action potential cannot occur in an excitable fiber unless the stimulus is much stronger than usual. The membrane is still in the repolarization phase of the previous action potential.

exclusivity p. In drug marketing, the time during which a manufacturer of a proprietary drug is allowed exercise monopoly rights to its sales.

gestation p. The period of pregnancy from conception to parturition. Average length is 10 lunar months or 280 days measured from the onset of the last menstrual period, but length varies from 250 to 310 days. SEE: *gestation*; *pregnancy* for table.

incubation p. Incubation (1).

isoelectric p. 1. The time when no electrical energy is produced in an action that normally produces an electric force, such as a muscle contraction,. **2.** In an electrocardiogram, the period when the electrical tracing is neither positive nor negative.

isometric p. Postsphygmic **p.**

last menstrual p. ABBR: LMP. The date of the first day of menstruation before a presenting illness or the advent of pregnancy-related amenorrhea. The date is used in estimating the expected date of delivery. SEE: *Naegeli rule.*

latent p. 1. The time between stimulation and the resulting response. SYN: *lag.* **2.** Incubation (1). **3.** The time from exposure to ionizing radiation to the first visible sign of the effects.

menstrual p. Menstruation.

missed p. Menstruation not occurring at the time it was expected or regularly occurs monthly.

monthly p. The time of menstrual flow.

open enrollment p. A time of the year when a health plan allows subscribers to choose new forms of health care coverage. During this period subscribers to one benefit plan may choose to disenroll from one component of a health plan and enroll in another.

patent p. The time during a parasitic disease that organisms are demonstrable in the body.

postsphygmic p. The short period in diastole when the ventricles are relaxed and no blood is entering. This lasts until the atrioventricular valves open. SYN: *isometric p.*

prepatent p. The period between the time of introduction of parasitic organisms into the body and their appearance in the blood or tissues.

presphygmic p. The short period in systole beginning with closing of the atrioventricular valves and ending with opening of the valves connecting the right and left ventricles to the pulmonary artery and aorta, respectively.

p. of reactivity In obstetrics, an initial episode of activity, alertness, and responsiveness to interaction, characteristic of the physiological and social responses of newborns to stimuli. The first period of reactivity begins with birth, lasts approx. 30 min, and ends when the infant falls into a deep sleep. Common assessment findings include transient tachypnea, nasal flaring, sternal retraction, crackles, tachycardia, and irregular heart rhythms. The second period of reactivity begins when the infant awakens and usually lasts 4 to 6 hr. Common assessment findings include signs of excessive respiratory and gastric mucus, hunger, apneic episodes, and the passing of a meconium stool.

relative refractory p. The brief period during repolarization of a neuron or muscle fiber when excitability is depressed. If stimulated, the cell may respond, but a stronger than usual stimulus is required.

safe p. The time during the menstrual cycle when conception is supposedly not possible. It typically extends from five days before ovulation to the day ovulation occurs. Because of the great variability of the menstrual cycle, it is either extremely difficult or impossible to predict the portion of the cycle in which intercourse may take place with no chance of conception. SYN: *fertile interval.*

silent p. 1. The time in the course of a disease in which the signs and symptoms are so mild as to be difficult to detect. **2.** A pause in normally continuous electrical events such as an electrocardiogram (ECG) or electroencephalogram (EEG). **3.** The period in a tendon reflex that immediately follows the contraction of the responding muscles during which the motor neurons do not respond to afferent impulses entering the reflex center.

wear p. 1. The maximum length of time that a radiation badge is worn before it is exchanged and the dose of radiation is measured. **2.** The length of time that a transdermal medication delivery system is applied to the skin before it should be removed or replaced.

Wenckebach p. SEE: under *Wenckebach, Karel F.*

periodic (pēr-ē-ŏd′ĭk) [Gr. *periodikos*] Recurring after definite intervals.

periodic abstinence A method of birth control in which a couple tries to avoid pregnancy by refraining from sexual intercourse during certain times within the menstrual cycle.

periodic catatonia An inherited form of schizophrenia characterized by psychomotor disturbances, including grimacing, stereotyped body movements, and hyperkinetic movements alternating with mutism, staring, and body posturing. Susceptibility to this condition has been linked to genes on chromosome 15.

periodic health examination SEE: under *examination.*

periodicity (pēr″ē-ō-dĭs′ĭ-tē) **1.** The state of being regularly recurrent. **2.** The rate of rise and fall or interruption of a unidirectional current in physical therapy.

periodic leg movements in sleep ABBR: PLMS. Jerking or twitching of the toes, ankles, knees, or hips during sleep.

periodic table SEE: under *table.*

periodontal (per″ē-ō-don′t′ăl) [*peri-* + *odont-* + *-al*] **1.** Located around a tooth. **2.** Pert. to the periodontium. SYN: *peridental.*

periodontal disease A disease of the periodontium. The most common initial symptom is bleeding gums, but loosening of the teeth, receding gums, abscesses in pockets between the gums and the teeth, and necrotizing ulcerative gingivitis may be present as the disease worsens. Proper dental hygiene (proper brushing of the teeth, use of dental floss, gum massage, and periodic removal of plaque) will help prevent periodontal disease.

TREATMENT: In the early stages of the disease, curettage of plaque and calculus from the crown and root surfaces of the teeth may be the only treatment required. In more advanced stages, procedures such as gingivectomy, gingivoplasty, and correction of the bony architecture of the teeth may be necessary. Adjustment of the occlusion of the teeth and orthodontic treatment may help prevent recurrences. SEE: *plaque; teeth; tooth; toothbrushing.*

PATIENT CARE: Dental professionals teach the patient about the importance of proper dental care (brushing for two minutes twice a day, flossing, and regular dental examinations and prophylaxis). Patients should consult a dentist if recession of teeth from gums, drainage from the gums, or bleeding gums occur because these symptoms may indicate periodontal disease. The patient may also need medical follow-up to ascertain whether or not hypovitaminosis, blood dyscrasias, diabetes mellitus, or use of hormonal contraceptive drugs are contributing to or causing the dental problems.

periodontal pocket SEE: under *pocket.*

periodontia (pĕr″ē-ō-dŏn′shē-ă) [Gr. *peri,* around, + *odous,* tooth] **1.** Plural of periodontium. **2.** Periodontics.

periodontics (pĕr″ē-ō-dŏn′tĭks) [″ + *odous,* tooth] The branch of dentistry dealing with treatment of diseases of the supporting tissues of the teeth, the periodontium. SYN: *periodontia (2); periodontology.*

periodontist (per″ē-ō-dont′ist) A dentist who specializes in the diagnosis, treatment, and prevention of gum diseases, e.g., gingivitis and periodontitis.

periodontitis (per″ē-ō-don′tīt′is) [*periodonti(um)* + *-itis*] Inflammation or degeneration, or both, of the dental periosteum, alveolar bone, cementum, and adjacent gingiva. Suppuration usually occurs, supporting bone is resorbed, teeth become loose, and recession of gingivae occurs. This condition usually follows chronic gingivitis, necrotizing ulcerative gingivitis, or poor dental hygiene. Systemic factors may also predispose one to this condition. SYN: *Riggs disease.* SEE: table.

aggressive p. ABBR: AgP. Periodontitis in which alveolar bone loss and ligament failure occur rapidly, resulting in dental mobility and sometimes exfoliation (loss of teeth). The disease often

Symptoms and Signs of Periodontitis

- Gums bleed during brushing or flossing
- Gums are puffy or swollen
- Gums have a bright red appearance
- Gum line has receded, giving the teeth a longer appearance
- Bad breath persists even after brushing and flossing

begins in adolescence and may cluster in families. SYN: *generalized progressive p.*

apical p. Dental **granuloma.**

chronic p. Periodontitis in which there is gradual and persistent evidence of periodontal pocket formation, injury to the ligamentous attachments of the teeth, alveolar bone destruction, and eventually, dental loosening.

early p. Periodontitis in which, despite mild-to-moderate pocket formation and some bone loss, there is no evidence of abnormal tooth movement.

moderate p. Periodontitis in which moderate bone loss and pocket formation are accompanied by abnormal tooth mobility.

generalized progressive p. Aggressive **p.**

periodontium (pĕr-ē-ō-dŏn′shē-ŭm) The structures that support the teeth, cushion the shock of chewing, and keep the teeth firmly anchored in the bone. These structures are the gingivae, periodontal membrane or ligament, cementum, and alveolar bone. SYN: *alveolodental* **membrane.**

periodontoclasia (pĕr″ē-ō-dŏn″tō-klā′zē-ă) [″ + *odous,* tooth, + *klasis,* breaking] A condition marked by inflammation with degenerative and retrogressive changes in the periodontium. SYN: *peridentitis.*

periodontology (pĕr″ē-ō-dŏn-tŏl′ō-jē) [″ + ″ + *logos,* word, reason] Periodontics.

periodontosis (pĕr″ē-ō-dŏn-tō′sĭs) [″ + ″ + *osis,* condition] Any degenerative disease of the periodontal tissues.

perionychium (pĕr″ē-ō-nĭk′ē-ŭm) The epidermis surrounding a nail.

perionyx (pĕr″ē-ō′nĭks) [″ + *onyx,* nail] The remnant of the eponychium that persists as a band across the root of the nail.

perioophorosalpingitis (per″ē-ō-ŏ-for″ŏ-sal″pĭn-jīt′ĭs) [*peri-* + *oophorosalpingitis*] Perithecal salpingitis. SYN: *perioothecosalpingitis.*

perioperative (pĕr-ē-ŏp′ĕr-ă-tĭv) Occurring in the period immediately before, during, and/or after surgery.

perioral (pĕr″ē-or′ăl) [″ + L. *oralis,* mouth] Surrounding the mouth. SYN: *circumoral.*

periorbita (pĕr″ē-or″bĭ-tă) [″ + L. *orbita*, orbit] Connective tissue lining the socket of the eye.

periorbital (pĕr″ē-or′bĭ-tăl) Surrounding the socket of the eye. SYN: *circumorbital*.

periorbititis (pĕr″ē-or″bĭ-tī′tĭs) [″ + L. *orbita*, orbit, + Gr. *itis*, inflammation] Inflammation of the periorbita.

periorchitis (pĕr″ē-or-kī′tĭs) [″ + *orchis*, testicle, + *itis*, inflammation] Inflammation of the tissues investing a testicle.

   p. hemorrhagica A chronic hematocele of the tunica vaginalis of the testis.

periosteum (pĕr-ē-ŏs′tē-ŭm) [Gr. *periosteon*] The fibrous membrane that forms the covering of bones except at their articular surfaces; consists of a dense external layer containing numerous blood vessels and an inner layer of connective tissue cells that function as osteoblasts when the bone is injured and then participate in new bone formation. Periosteum serves as a supporting structure for blood vessels nourishing bone and for attachment of tendons and ligaments.

   alveolar p. Periodontal ligament.

   p. externum Periosteum covering external surfaces of bones.

   p. internum Interior periosteum lining the marrow canal of a bone.

periostitis, periosteitis (per″ē-os-tīt′ĭs, per″ē-ost″ē-īt′ĭs) [*periosteum* + *-itis*] Inflammation of the periosteum. Findings include pain over the affected part, esp. under pressure; fever; sweats; leukocytosis; skin inflammation, and rigidity of overlying muscles. Infectious diseases, esp. syphilis, and trauma cause this condition. SYN: *osteoperiostitis; periosteitis.*

   albuminous p. Periostitis with albuminous serous fluid exudate beneath the membrane affected.

   alveolar p. Periodontitis.

   diffuse p. Periostitis of the long bones.

   hemorrhagic p. Periostitis with extravasation of blood under the periosteum.

periostosis (pĕr″ē-ŏs-tō′sĭs) [″ + ″ + *osis*, condition] A bony neoplasm around a bone or arising from it.

periotic (pĕr-ē-ō′tĭk) [″ + *ous*, ear] Situated around the ear, esp. the internal ear.

periovular (pĕr″ē-ō′vū-lăr) [″ + L. *ovulum*, little egg] Around an ovum.

peripatetic (pĕr″ĭ-pă-tĕt′ĭk) [L. *peripateticus*, to walk about while teaching] Moving from place to place.

peripersonal (pĕr″ĭ-pŭr′sŭn-ĭl) Near the body; within arm's reach.

peripheral (pĕ-rif′(ĕ-)răl) [*peripher(y)* + *-al*] Pert. to or located at the periphery or away from the center. In anatomy and physiology, it refers to the outer part or surface of an organ or body or to the part of the nervous system outside the central nervous system or to the blood flow of the systemic circulation; in ophthalmology, to vision perceived near the outer edges of the retina. **peripherally** (-rif′răl-ē), *adv.*

peripheral arterial disease ABBR: PAD. Atherosclerotic disease of the aortoiliac, axillary, carotid, or femoral arteries. It affects more than 8 million Americans, many of whom also have ischemic disease of the coronary arteries or a history of heart attack or stroke. PAD contributes to claudication, amputation, stroke, and other diseases and conditions. SEE: *peripheral vascular disease.*

peripheral nervous system ABBR: PNS. The neurons and axons that populate the body outside the central nervous system.

   NERVES: The peripheral nervous system includes somatic and autonomic motor nerves with cell bodies inside the central nervous system, autonomic nerves and axons with cell bodies in peripheral ganglia and in the enteric nervous system, and sensory nerves and axons from cell bodies in dorsal root ganglia, in cranial sensory ganglia, and in the enteric nervous system.

   CELL BODIES: Neurons in the peripheral nervous system are derived from the neural crest and from ectodermal placodes.

peripheral neurovascular dysfunction, risk for A state for which an individual is at risk of experiencing a disruption in circulation, sensation, or motion of an extremity. SEE: *Nursing Diagnoses Appendix.*

peripheral vascular disease ABBR: PVD. Any condition that causes partial or complete obstruction of the flow of blood to or from the arteries or veins outside the chest. Peripheral vascular disease includes atherosclerosis of the carotid, aortoiliac, femoral, and axillary arteries, as well as deep venous thromboses of the limbs, pelvis, and vena cava. SEE: *atherosclerosis; claudication; deep venous thrombosis; Nursing Diagnoses Appendix.*

peripheral zone SEE: under *zone.*

periphery (pĕr-ĭf′ĕ-rē) [Gr. *periphereia*] The outer part or surface of a body; the part away from the center.

periphlebitis (pĕr″ĭ-flĕ-bī′tĭs) [Gr. *peri*, around, + *phleps*, vein, + *itis*, inflammation] Inflammation of the external coat of a vein or tissues around it.

Periplaneta (per″ĭ-plă-nēt′ă) [L. *periplaneta*, fr *peri-* + Gr. *planētēs*, wanderer] A genus of large cockroaches (order Orthoptera). SEE: *cockroach.*

   P. americana SEE: *American cockroach.*

   P. australasiae SEE: *Australian cockroach.*

periradicular (pĕr-ē-ră-dĭk'ū-lăr) Around a root or a rootlike process, esp. relating to a tooth.

perirectal (pĕr″ĭ-rĕk'tăl) [″ + L. *rectus,* straight] Extending around the rectum.

perirenal (pĕr″ĭ-rē'năl) [″ + L. *ren,* kidney] Extending around the kidney. SYN: *perinephric.*

periscopic (pĕr″ĭ-skŏp'ĭk) [″ + *skopein,* to examine] Viewing on all sides; providing a wide range of vision.

perisinusitis (pĕr″ĭ-sī″nŭ-sī'tĭs) [″ + L. *sinus,* cavity, + Gr. *itis,* inflammation] Inflammation of membranes about a sinus, esp. a venous sinus of the dura mater.

perisplenic (pĕr″ĭ-splĕn'ĭk) [″ + *splen,* spleen] Near or around the spleen.

perisplenitis (pĕr″ĭ-splĕ-nī'tĭs) [″ + ″ + *itis,* inflammation] Inflammation of the peritoneal coat of the spleen, the splenic capsule.

peristalsis (pĕr-ĭ-stăl'sĭs) [Gr. *peri,* around, + *stalsis,* contraction] A progressive wavelike movement that occurs involuntarily in hollow tubes of the body, esp. the alimentary canal. It is characteristic of tubes possessing longitudinal and circular layers of smooth muscle fibers.

Peristalsis is induced reflexly by distention of the walls of the tube. The wave consists of contraction of the circular muscle above the distention with relaxation of the region immediately distal to the distended portion. The simultaneous contraction and relaxation progresses slowly for a short distance as a wave that causes the contents of the tube to be forced onward.

> ***mass p.*** Forceful peristaltic movements of short duration in which contents are moved from one section of the colon to another, occurring three or four times daily.

> ***reverse p.*** Peristalsis in a direction opposite to the normal direction. SYN: *antiperistalsis.*

peristome (pĕr'ĭ-stōm) [″ + *stoma,* mouth] The channel leading to the cytosome or mouth in certain types of protozoa.

peritendinitis, peritenonitis (per″ĭ-ten″dĭ-nīt'ĭs, per″ĭ-ten″ŏ-nīt'ĭs) [″ + ″ + Gr. *itis,* inflammation] Tenosynovitis.

> ***p. calcarea*** Calcific tendinitis.

> ***p. serosa*** Peritendinitis with effusion into the sheath.

peritenon (pĕr″ĭ-tē'nŏn) [″ + *tenon,* tendon] The sheath of a tendon.

perithelioma (pĕr″ĭ-thē-lē-ō'mă) [″ + *thele,* nipple, + *oma,* tumor] A tumor derived from the perithelial layer of the blood vessels.

peritomy (pĕr-ĭt'ō-mē) [″ + *tome,* incision] **1.** A 360° incision of the conjuctiva and subconjunctival tissue around the

limbus as part of retinal surgery or enucleation. SYN: *syndectomy.* **2.** Circumcision.

peritoneal (per″ĭt-ō-nē'ăl) [*peritoneal + -al*] Pert. to the peritoneum.

peritoneo- [*peritoneum*] Prefix meaning *peritoneum.*

peritoneoscope (per″ĭt-ŏnē'ō-skōp″) [*peritoneum + -scope*] Laparoscope.

peritoneoscopy (pĕr″ĭ-tŏ″nē-ŏs'kō-pē) Examination of the peritoneal cavity with a laparoscope.

peritoneotomy (pĕr″ĭ-tŏ″nē-ŏt'ō-mē) The process of incising the peritoneum.

peritoneum (pĕr″ĭ-tō-nē'ŭm) [LL., Gr. *peritonaion*] The largest serous membrane of the body, made up of the following five different folds: the greater omentum, lesser omentum, falciform ligament, mesentery, and mesocolon. These folds line the abdominal cavity and are reflected over the viscera. They connect organs within the abdomen together and protect and support the organs.

> EXAMINATION: Diseases that affect the peritoneum can be assessed with gentle and careful percussion and palpation of the abdomen. Localized or diffuse peritonitis, for example, may be evident when the abdomen is tapped with a percussing finger (the patient will wince, guard the abdomen, and complain that the percussion is very painful); it may also be evident when the abdominal wall is gently depressed and then released (release of the examining hand causes guarding and discomfort). Fluid within the peritoneum (ascites) may be suggested by shifting dullness on percussion of the abdominal wall, or by the detection of a fluid wave when one hand depresses and releases on one side of the abdomen, while the other hand gently holds the opposite side. SEE: illus.

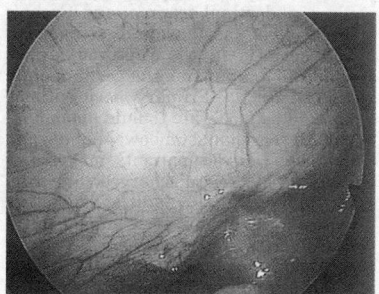

PERITONEUM

Seen laparoscopically (mag. ×½)

> ***parietal p.*** Peritoneum lining the abdominal walls and the undersurface of the diaphragm.

> ***visceral p.*** Peritoneum that invests the abdominal organs. The peritoneum

holds the viscera in place by its folds, which are called the *mesentery*.

peritonism (pĕr′ĭ-tō-nĭzm) [Gr. *peritonaion*, peritoneum, + *-ismos*, condition] **1.** A condition having the clinical signs of shock and peritonitis. **2.** Symptoms similar to peritonitis, but without actual inflammatory process, due instead to functional disease.

peritonitic (pĕr″ĭ-tō-nĭt′ĭk) [″ + *itis*, inflammation] Pert. to or affected with peritonitis.

peritonitis (per″ĭt-ŏn-īt′ĭs) [*peritoneum* + *-itis*] Inflammation of the serous membrane that lines the abdominal cavity and its viscera. SEE: *chemical p.; primary p.; secondary p.*

ETIOLOGY: Peritonitis is caused by infection of the abdominal cavity without obvious organ rupture (primary peritonitis), by perforation (rupture) of one of the internal organs (secondary peritonitis), or by instillation of a chemical irritant into the abdominal cavity (chemical peritonitis).

Primary peritonitis occurs in patients with cirrhosis and ascites, in some patients with tuberculosis (esp. those with AIDS), and in patients who use the peritoneum for dialysis. Cirrhotic patients develop peritonitis from infection of the peritoneal contents by microorganisms such as *Streptococcus pneumoniae*, enterococci, or *Escherichia coli*. Patients who use the peritoneum for dialysis (chronic ambulatory peritoneal dialysis patients) sometimes contaminate their dialysate with hand-borne microbes such as staphylococci or streptococci. Dialysis patients may also develop peritonitis after the infusion of irritating substances (e.g., antibiotics like vancomycin) into the peritoneal cavity during treatment for these infections.

Common causes of secondary peritonitis are ruptured appendix, perforated ulcer, abdominal trauma, and Crohn's disease. The gases, acids, fecal material, and bacteria in the ruptured organs spill into and inflame the peritoneum.

SYMPTOMS: Primary peritonitis is marked by moderate to mild abdominal pain, fever, change in bowel habits, and malaise. Dialysis patients may notice clouding of their discharged dialysate. Fever, weight loss, inanition, and other systemic symptoms are common in tuberculous peritonitis.

Secondary peritonitis is marked by intense, constant abdominal pain that worsens on body movement. It is often associated with nausea, loss of appetite, and fever or hypothermia. On examination the abdomen is typically distended and quiet, and the patient holds very still in order to limit discomfort.

DIAGNOSIS: In patients with organ rupture, a plain x-ray examination of the abdomen may reveal air trapped beneath the diaphragm. Ultrasonography or abdominal computed tomography is used to visualize intraperitoneal fluid, abscesses, and diseased organs. Paracentesis or peritoneal lavage are also helpful in the diagnosis of some cases.

TREATMENT: Primary peritonitis may respond to the administration of antibiotics or antitubercular drugs, but the prognosis is guarded. Secondary peritonitis is treated with surgical drainage, repair or removal of the ruptured viscus, fluid resuscitation, and antibiotics. The prognosis depends on the patient's underlying condition, the rapidity of the diagnosis and of subsequent medical intervention, and the skill of the surgeon.

acute diffuse p. Diffuse **p.**

adhesive p. Peritonitis characterized by the adherence of adjacent visceral and parietal surfaces.

aseptic p. Peritonitis due to causes other than bacterial, fungal, or viral infection (e.g., trauma, presence of chemicals produced naturally or introduced into the cavity, or irradiation).

bile p. Peritonitis caused by the escape of bile into the peritoneal cavity. It usually results from an injury to the gallbladder or bile ducts during cholecystectomy.

chemical p. Peritonitis due to presence of chemicals (e.g., intestinal juices, pancreatic secretions, or bile) in the peritoneal cavity.

chronic p. Peritonitis usually caused by tuberculosis or cancer. Findings include slight or absent fever, pain, diffuse tenderness, anemia, and emaciation.

circumscribed p. Localized **p.**

p. deformans Chronic peritonitis with a thickened membrane and adhesions that contract and cause retraction of the intestines.

diaphragmatic p. Peritonitis in which the peritoneal surface of the diaphragm is mainly affected.

diffuse p. Peritonitis that is widespread, involving most of the peritoneum. SYN: *generalized p.*

fibrocaseous p. Peritonitis with fibrosis and caseation, usually caused by tuberculosis.

gas p. 1. Peritonitis in which gas is present in the peritoneal cavity. **2.** Peritonitis caused by group A streptococci (GAS).

generalized p. Diffuse **p.**

localized p. Peritonitis confined to the area immediately surrounding an abscess, inflamed organ, or leak. SYN: *circumscribed p.*

meconium p. Peritonitis in the newborn caused by perforation of the gastrointestinal tract in utero. It most often occurs in newborns with cystic fibrosis.

Neonatal intestinal obstruction is also usually present.

pelvic p. Peritonitis involving the peritoneum of the pelvis, usually as a result of endometrial, tubal, or ovarian infections.

periodic p. Familial Mediterranean fever.

primary p. Peritonitis resulting from infectious organisms transmitted through blood or lymph.

puerperal p. Peritonitis that develops after childbirth.

secondary p. Peritonitis resulting from extension of infection from adjoining structures, rupture of a viscus, abscess, or trauma.

septic p. Peritonitis caused by a pyogenic bacterium.

serous p. Peritonitis in which there is copious liquid exudation.

silent p. Peritonitis in which there are no signs or symptoms.

talc p. Peritonitis due to particles of talcum powder in the peritoneal cavity (e.g., postoperatively).

traumatic p. Acute peritonitis due to injury or wound infection.

tuberculous p. Peritonitis caused by tuberculosis.

peritonsillar (pĕr″ĭ-tŏn′sĭ-lăr) [Gr. *peri*, around, + L. *tonsilla*, tonsil] Extending around a tonsil.

peritonsillitis (pĕr″ĭ-tŏn″sĭ-lī′tĭs) [″ + ″ + Gr. *itis*, inflammation] Inflammation of tissues around the tonsils.

peritrichous, peritrichal, peritrichic (pĕ-ri′trĭ-kŭs, pĕ-ri′trĭ-kăl, per″ĭ-trik′ĭk) [″ + *thrix*, hair] Pert. to microorganisms that have cilia or flagella covering the entire surface of the cell.

perityphlitis (pĕr″ĭ-tĭf-lī′tĭs) [″ + ″ + *itis*, inflammation] Inflammation about the cecum; it may be secondary to appendicitis.

periumbilical (pĕr″ē-ŭm-bĭl′ĭ-kăl) [″ + L. *umbilicus*, a pit] Located around or near the navel (i.e., umbilicus). SYN: *paraumbilical*.

periungual (pĕr″ē-ŭng′gwăl) [″ + L. *unguis*, nail] Around a nail.

periureteritis (pĕr″ē-ū-rē″tĕr-ī′tĭs) [″ + ″ + *itis*, inflammation] Inflammation of parts around the ureter.

periurethral (pĕr″ē-ū-rē′thrăl) [″ + *ourethra*, urethra] Located around the urethra.

periurethral bulking The injection of collagen, plastic polymers, or other substances around the bladder sphincter. It is used as a surgical treatment for stress urinary incontinence. Also known as urethral bulking.

periuterine (pĕr″ē-ū′tĕr-ĭn) [″ + L. *uterus*, womb] Around the uterus. SYN: *perimetric*.

perivaginal (pĕr″ĭ-văj′ĭ-năl) [″ + L. *vagina*, sheath] Around the vagina.

perivascular (pĕr″ĭ-văs′kŭ-lăr) [″ + L. *vasculus*, a little vessel] Around a vessel, esp. a blood vessel.

perivasculitis (pĕr″ĭ-văs″kū-lī′tĭs) [″ + ″ + Gr. *itis*, inflammation] Inflammation of the tissues surrounding a blood vessel. SYN: *periangiitis*.

periventricular (pĕr″ĭ-vĕn-trĭk′ū-lăr) Pert. to the area surrounding or near the ventricles, esp. the ventricles of the brain.

perivertebral (pĕr″ĭ-vĕr′tĕ-brăl) [″ + L. *vertebra*, vertebra] Around a vertebra.

perivesical (pĕr″ĭ-vĕs′ĭ-kăl) [″ + L. *vesicula*, little bladder] Around the urinary bladder.

perle (pĕrl) [Fr., pearl] A soft capsule containing medicine.

perlèche (pĕr-lĕsh′) [Fr.] Angular cheilosis.

Perls stain (pŭrlz stān) [Max Perls, Ger. pathologist, 1843–1881] A histochemical stain that demonstrates iron when it is present in body tissues.

permanent (pĕr′mă-nĕnt) [″ + *manere*, to remain] Enduring; without change.

permanganate (pĕr-măn′gă-nāt) Any one of the salts of permanganic acid.

permeability (pĕr″mē-ă-bĭl′ĭ-tē) [L. *permeabilis*] The quality of being permeable; that which may be traversed.

capillary p. The condition of the capillary wall that enables substances in the blood to pass into tissue spaces or into cells, or vice versa.

permeable (pĕr′mē-ă-b′l) Capable of allowing the passage of fluids or substances in solution. SYN: *pervious* (1).

permeation (pĕr″mē-ā′shŭn) [L. *permeare*, permeate] Penetration of and spreading throughout an organ, tissue, or space.

permethrin (pĕr-mĕth-rĭn) An insecticide and insect repellent that has been used to treat scabies and lice infestations, and to protect people from tick exposure while working or playing outdoors.

permissible (pĕr-mis′ĭ-bĕl) [L. *permissibilis*] Acceptable or allowable.

permissible exposure limits (pĕr-mĭs-să-bl) The limits, usually expressed as a combination of time and concentration, to which humans may be safely exposed to physical agents, ionizing radiation, or chemical substances in the environment in general and in work areas specifically. SEE: *hazardous material; health hazard; maximum allowable concentration; right-to-know law.*

permselectivity (pĕrm″sĕ-lek-tiv′ĭt-ē) [*perm(eability)* + *selectivity*] Any limitation of the permeability of a filter, e.g., the renal glomerulus, to the passage of macromolecules.

permucosal (pĕr-mū-kō′săl) Across mucous membranes.

permutation (pĕr″mū-tā′shŭn) [L. *per*, completely, + *mutare*, to change]

Transformation; complete change; act of altering objects in a group.

pernicious (pĕr-nish′ŭs) [L. *perniciosus*, destructive] Very destructive or harmful.

pernio (pĕr′nē-ō) [L.] Chilblain.

peroneal (pĕr″ō-nē′ăl) [Gr. *perone*, pin] Pert. to the fibula.

    p. sign Eversion and dorsiflexion of the foot resulting from tapping the peroneal nerve with a reflex hammer.

peroneo- [Gr. *perone*, pin] Combining form meaning *fibula*.

peroneus (pĕr″ō-nē′ŭs) [Gr. *perone*, pin] One of three muscles of the leg that act to move the foot.

    p. brevis The muscle arising from the distal two thirds of the lateral fibula and attaching to the styloid process of the base of the fifth metatarsal. The peroneus brevis assists in plantar flexion of the foot and eversion of the ankle.

    p. longus The muscle arising from the lateral tibial condyle and the upper two thirds of the fibula and inserting on the lateral aspect of the first metatarsal and the associated portion of the first cuneiform. The peroneus longus is the primary contributor to the plantar flexion of the foot and the eversion of the ankle.

    p. tertius The muscle arising from the anterior portion of the distal one third of the tibia and the adjacent portion of the interosseous membrane and attaching on the dorsal surface of the fifth metatarsal. The peroneus tertius is a secondary contributor to ankle dorsiflexion and eversion. This muscle is absent in a significant proportion of the population.

peroral (pĕr-or′ăl) [L. *per*, through, + *oris*, mouth] Administered through the mouth.

per os (pĕr ōs) [L.] ABBR: po. By mouth.

peroxidase (pĕr-ŏk′sĭ-dās) [″ + Gr. *oxys*, acid, + *-ase*, enzyme] An enzyme that catalyzes the decomposition of hydrogen peroxide to water and oxygen; common in plant cells. This process is essential to intracellular respiration.

peroxide (pĕr-ŏk′sīd) In chemistry, a compound containing more oxygen than the other oxides of the element in question.

peroxisome (pĕ-rok′sĭ-sōm″) A class of single-membrane-bound vesicles that contain a variety of oxidase enzymes. They are present in most human cells but are concentrated in the liver. The absence of functional peroxisomes is involved in a number of diseases. The most severe is Zellweger syndrome, which affects newborns, and is usually fatal before 1 year of age, and consists of cirrhosis of the liver and congenital malformations of the central nervous system and skeleton in newborns, and is usually

per rectum (pĕr rĕk′tŭm) [L.] By way of or through the rectum.

PERRLA (pŭr′lă) *pupils equal, round, reactive to light and accommodation.*

perseveration (pĕr-sĕv″ĕr-ā′shŭn) [L. *perseverare*, to persist] **1.** Abnormal, compulsive, and inappropriate repetition of words or behaviors, a symptom observed, for example, in patients with schizophrenia or diseases of the frontal lobes of the brain. **2.** The repetition of rhythmic but meaningless actions, behaviors, or movements.

Persian Gulf syndrome ABBR: PGS. A term used to describe a variety of symptoms experienced by veterans of the Persian Gulf war, including fatigue, loss of memory, muscle and joint pains, shortness of breath, and gastrointestinal complaints. The cause of these complaints is obscure.

persistent light reaction Photosensitivity.

persistent vegetative state A continuing and unremitting clinical condition of complete unawareness of the environment accompanied by sleep-wake cycles with either complete or partial preservation of hypothalamic and brainstem autonomic functions. The diagnosis is established if the condition is present for 1 month after acute or nontraumatic brain injury or has lasted for 1 month in patients with degenerative or metabolic disorders or developmental malformations. SYN: *vegetative state*.

person (pĕr′sŭn) A human being.

persona (pĕr-sō′nă) [L., mask] **1.** The attitude or appearance a person presents to others. **2.** Personality.

personal care attendant An employee hired to assist a functionally limited person with activities of daily living.

personal digital assistant ABBR: PDA. A handheld or pocket-sized computer used to store information or communicate with others.

personal emergency alert system (pĕr-sŭn-ăl) A device consisting of a portable battery-powered help button and a machine that automatically dials a monitoring station. The device is connected to the individual's telephone or to a phone jack. When the system is activated, it either allows a two-way communication between the monitoring station and the individual or alerts the station personnel to phone the individual. In the latter case, if there is no response the station may call a neighbor or family member or dispatch emergency medical technicians to the person's home.

personal equation SEE: under *equation*.

personal item In health care, any object designed for use by a single consumer, e.g., bars of soap, cosmetics, shaving razors, toothbrushes, or towels.

PATIENT CARE: These items may be colonized by microorganisms such as antibiotic-resistant bacteria. Safeguarding them so that they are used by only one individual, or carefully cleaned or discarded after use can prevent the spread of health care associated infections.

personality (pĕr″sŏn-al′ĭt-ē) [L. *personalitas*] The unique organization of traits, characteristics, and modes of behavior of an individual, setting that individual apart from others and at the same time determining how others react to the individual. SYN: *persona* (2). SEE: *personality test*.

   alternating p. Dissociative identity disorder.

   anal p. In Freudian psychology, a personality disorder marked by excessive orderliness, stinginess, and obstinacy. If carried to an extreme, these qualities lead to the development of obsessive-compulsive behavior. SYN: *anal characteristic*.

   borderline p. SEE: *borderline personality disorder*.

   callous-unemotional p. ABBR: CU. A group of personality traits including lack of empathy, manipulativeness, and remorselessness. These traits are considered to be indicators of conduct disorder in childhood and adolescence and are uniquely characteristic of antisocial personality disorder in adults.

   compulsive p. Obsessive-compulsive **personality disorder**.

   distressed p. Type D **p.**

   double p. Dissociative identity disorder.

   extroverted p. SEE: *extrovert*.

   inadequate p. A personality type in which the individual is ineffective and is physically and emotionally unable to cope with the normal stress of living.

   introverted p. SEE: *introvert* (1).

   modal p. The individual traits or characteristics typical of the society in which a person lives.

   multiple p. A term formerly used for dissociative identity disorder. SEE: *dissociative identity disorder*. SEE: *Nursing Diagnoses Appendix*.

   obsessive-compulsive p. Obsessive-compulsive disorder.

   paranoid p. Paranoid **personality disorder**.

   psychopathic p. Antisocial **personality disorder**.

   type A p. SEE: under *behavior*.

   type B p. SEE: under *behavior*.

   type D p. A personality type in which the individual is inhibited and uncomfortable in social situations, has difficulty making friends, and who tends to experience, but repress, feelings of anger, anxiety, depression, and discontent with others. Some studies have found correlations between this personality type and an increased risk of atherosclerotic vascular disease. SYN: *distressed p.*

personality disorder A pathological disturbance of the patterns of perception, communication, and thinking that impairs a person's ability to function effectively. Personality disorders are manifested in at least two of the following areas: cognition, affect, interpersonal functioning, or impulse control. Generally, the disorder is of long duration, and its onset can be traced to early adolescence.

TREATMENT: Psychotherapy, psychopharmacological drugs, or a combination of the two is used in treating these disorders although many personality disorders resist treatment.

   antisocial p.d. A type of personality disorder characterized by disregard for the rights and feelings of others. It usually begins before age 15. In early childhood, lying, stealing, fighting, truancy, and disregard of authority are common. In adolescence, aggressive sexual behavior, excessive use of alcohol, and drug use may be characteristic. In adulthood, these behaviorial patterns continue with the addition of poor work performance, inability to function responsibly as a parent, and inability to accept normal restrictions imposed by the law. Affected people may repeatedly perform illegal acts (e.g., destroying property, harassing others, or stealing) or pursue illegal occupations. They disregard the safety, wishes, rights, and feelings of others. This type of personality disorder is not due to mental retardation, schizophrenia, or manic episodes. It is much more common in males than females. This condition has been referred to as psychopathy, sociopathy, or dyssocial personality disorder.

   avoidant p.d. A personality disorder marked by a pervasive pattern of social inhibition, feelings of inadequacy, and hypersensitivity to criticism. This begins by early adulthood and is present in various situations (e.g., school, work, or activities involving contact with others). People with this disorder desire affection, security, certainty, and acceptance and may fantasize about idealized relationships with others.

   borderline p.d. A personality disorder in which there is difficulty in maintaining stable interpersonal relationships and self-image. This manifests as unpredictable and impulsive behavior, outbursts of anger, irritability, sadness, and fear. Self-mutilation or suicidal behavior may also be present. Sometimes there is a chronic feeling of emptiness or boredom. SEE: *Nursing Diagnoses Appendix*.

Cluster A p.d. A grouping of personality disorders sharing traits of odd behavior and social isolation. This group of diagnoses includes paranoid, schizoid, and schizotypal personality disorders.

Cluster B p.d. A grouping of personality disorders sharing traits of attention-seeking, highly excitable emotional states, and unpredictable behavior. This group includes antisocial, borderline, narcissistic, and histrionic personality disorders.

Cluster C p.d. A group of personality disorders in which anxious and fearful behavior is a prominent feature. This group includes dependent, avoidant, and obsessive-compulsive personality disorders.

histrionic p.d. A personality disorder marked by excessive emotionalism and attention-seeking. Those affected are active, dramatic, prone to exaggerate, and subject to irrational, angry outbursts or tantrums. They express boredom with normal routines and crave novelty and excitement. Behavior in interpersonal relationships is shallow, vain, demanding, and dependent.

obsessive-compulsive p.d. Obsessive-compulsive disorder. SYN: *obsessive-compulsive personality.*

narcissistic p.d. A personality disorder marked by a grandiose sense of self-importance and preoccupation with fantasies of unlimited success, power, brilliance, or beauty. The individual believes that his problems are unique and can only be understood by other "special" people. There is an exhibitionistic need for admiration and attention, a lack of empathy, and an inability to understand how others feel.

paranoid p.d. A personality disorder characterized by unwarranted suspiciousness and mistrust of others, hypervigilance directed at hidden motives or intent to harm, hypersensitivity to criticism, tendency to hold grudges and to be easily offended, and reluctance to confide in others. SYN: *paranoid disorder.*; SEE: *paranoid disorder in Nursing Diagnoses Appendix.*

passive-aggressive p.d. A personality disorder marked by indirect resistance to demands for adequate occupational or social performance through procrastination, dawdling, stubbornness, inefficiency, or forgetfulness. The disorder begins in early childhood and may manifest itself in refusal to complete routine tasks, complaints of being misunderstood or unappreciated, sullen or argumentative attitude, pronounced envy of others, and behavior that alternates between hostile defiance and contrition.

schizoid p.d. A personality disorder characterized by shyness, oversensitiv-ity, seclusiveness, dissociation from close interpersonal or competitive relationships, eccentricity, daydreaming, preference for solitary activities, and inability to express anger or joy in situations that normally call for such a reaction. In most social interactions, those affected seem cold or aloof.

personality test A neuropsychiatric assessment tool, such as the Minnesota Multiphasic Personality Inventory–2, used to identify an individual's predominant emotional makeup. Personality tests measure adjustment, adventurousness, agitation, anxiety, coping styles, depression, introversion, hypochondriasis, paranoia, and other variables.

personal projects analysis A structured method of gathering information about the key activities in which people participate on a regular basis.

personal protective equipment Clothing, masks, gloves, or other gear that protects a person from exposure to noxious chemicals or transmissible diseases.

personal representative (pĕr′sĭn-ĭl rĕp″rĭ-zĕn′-tă-tĭv) Someone designated to make health care decisions for another if that other person becomes incapable of making such decisions.

perspiration (pĕr″spĭr-ā′shŭn) [L. *perspirare,* breathe through] **1.** The secretion of the sweat (sudoriferous) glands of the skin; sweating. **2.** The salty fluid secreted through the sweat glands of the skin; sweat. Essentially, the fluid is a weak solution of sodium chloride, but it also contains potassium, lactate, and urea.

Perspiration is a means of removing heat from the body. Evaporation of 1 L of sweat removes 580 kcal of heat from the body. Sweat loss varies from 100 to 1000 mL/hr but may exceed those amounts in a hot climate.

Perspiration is increased by temperature and humidity of the atmosphere, exercise, pain, nausea, nervousness, mental excitement, dyspnea, diaphoretics, and shock. It is decreased by cold, diarrhea, other causes of profound dehydration, and using certain drugs.

insensible p. Evaporation of water vapor from the body without appearing as moisture on the skin. SYN: *insensible sweating.*

sensible p. Perspiration that forms moisture on the skin.

perspire (pĕr-spīr′) [L. *perspirare,* breathe through] To secrete fluid through the pores of the skin. SYN: *sweat* (3).

persuasion (pĕr-swā′zhŭn) The act of influencing the thinking or behavior of others.

persulfate (pĕr-sŭl′fāt) One of a series of

sulfates containing more sulfuric acid than the others in the same series.

Perthes disease (pĕr′tēz) [Georg C. Perthes, Ger. surgeon, 1869–1927] Osteochondritis deformans juvenilis.

pertinent Relevant; clinically meaningful.

    p. negative An element of the patient's history that aids diagnosis because the patient denies that it is present.

    p. positive An element of a patient's history that aids diagnosis because the patient affirms that it is present.

perturbation (pĕr″tĕr-bā′shŭn) [L. *perturbare,* thoroughly disordered] **1.** The state of being greatly disturbed or agitated; uneasiness of mind. **2.** A disturbance or a change in a structure or function, usually as a result of an external influence.

pertussis (pĕr-tŭs′ĭs) [L. *per,* through, thorough + *tussis,* cough] An acute, contagious disease characterized by paroxysmal coughing, vomiting that follows the cough, and whooping inspiration. The disease is caused by the bacillus *Bordetella pertussis.* The incubation period is 7 to 10 days. Treatment is symptomatic and supportive. Antibiotics, e.g., erythromycin, are given to treat bacterial pneumonia and otitis media, esp. in infants and young children, early in the course of the infection. SYN: *whooping* **cough** (1).

    PREVENTION: Pertussis may be prevented by immunization of infants beginning at 3 months of age. Booster vaccination (Tdap) should be given to adolescents (at ages 11 to 18) and to susceptible adults. All adults should receive one dose of TdaP to bolster immunity and prevent epidemic spread of the disease.

    SYMPTOMS: Pertussis is often divided into the following three stages:

    Catarrhal: At this stage the symptoms are chiefly suggestive of the common cold (slight elevation of fever, sneezing, rhinitis, dry cough, irritability, and loss of appetite).

    Paroxysmal: This stage sets in after approx. 2 weeks. The cough is more violent and consists of a series of several short coughs, followed by a long drawn inspiration during which the typical whoop is heard, brought on by spasmodic contraction of the glottis. With the conclusion of the paroxysm, vomiting is common. The number of paroxysms in 24 hr may vary from 3 or 4 to 40 or 50. The cough may be precipitated by eating, drinking, or pressing on the trachea.

    Decline: This stage begins after an indefinite period of several weeks. Paroxysms become less frequent and less violent, and, after a period that may be prolonged for several months, the cough finally ceases.

    PATIENT CARE: Parents are to be advised that immunization prevents pertussis. Vaccination should be given to children and adults, except for those with a history of known allergy. Polymerase chain reaction (PCR) is a valuable diagnostic tool when specimens are carefully collected. For those who contract the disease, precautions are to be taken to prevent spread after the onset of symptoms. Bedrest, isolation, and a quiet environment are to be provided. Because the cough may be severe and debilitating, remedies such as guaifenesin or benzonatate may be given. Comfort measures are provided as indicated.

pertussis vaccine SEE: under *vaccine.*

per vaginam (pĕr vă-jī′năm) [L.] Through the vagina.

pervasive (pĕr-vā′sĭv) [L. *pervadere,* to go through] Spreading widely and deeply; affecting all aspects of something.

pervasive developmental disorder A synonym for the autism spectrum of disorders, e.g., "classical" autism, Asperger disorder, childhood disintegrative disorder (regressive autism), and Rett syndrome.

perversion (pĕr-vĕr′zhŭn) [L. *perversus,* perverted] Deviation from the normal path, whether it be in the area of one's intellect, emotions, actions, or reactions.

    sexual p. A maladjustment of sexual behavior in which satisfaction is sought in ways that veer far from accepted cultural norms.

pervert (pĕr-vĕrt′) [L. *pervetere,* to turn the wrong way] **1.** To turn from the normal; to misuse. **2.** One who has turned from the normal or socially acceptable path, esp. sexually.

pervious (pĕr′vē-ŭs) [L. *pervius*] **1.** Permeable. **2.** Penetrating.

pes (pĕs, pēz, pē′dēz) *pl.* **pedes** [L.] The foot or a footlike structure.

    p. abductus Talipes valgus.

    p. adductus Talipes varus.

    p. anserinus **1.** The network of branches of the facial nerve as it passes through the parotid gland **2.** The combined tendinous expansions of the sartorius, gracilis, and semitendinosus muscles at the medial border of the tibial tuberosity. SEE: illus.

    p. cavus Talipes arcuatus.

    p. contortus Talipes equinovarus.

    p. equinovalgus A condition in which the heel is elevated and turned laterally.

    p. equinovarus A condition in which the heel is turned inward and the foot is plantar flexed.

    p. equinus A deformity marked by

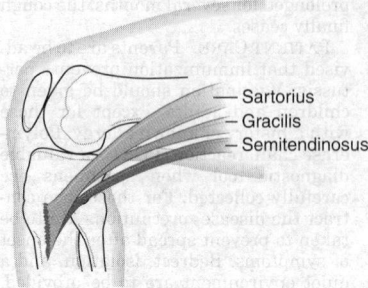

— Sartorius
— Gracilis
— Semitendinosus

PES ANSERINUS

walking without touching the heel to the ground. SYN: *talipes equinus*.

p. gigas Macropodia.

p. hippocampi The lower portion of the hippocampus major.

p. planus Flatfoot.

p. valgus Talipes valgus.

p. varus Talipes varus.

pessary (pes′ă-rē) [L. *pessarium,* suppository] A device inserted into the vagina to function as a supportive structure for the uterus. A pessary may be inserted to treat symptomatic uterine displacements. After manually repositioning the uterus, the physician inserts the appropriate-size device; a woman should not feel a well-fitted pessary. Pessaries should be removed and cleaned frequently; however, this requires manual dexterity and is difficult for elderly patients. Use of an antibacterial cream or gel will help decrease odor. Unless discomfort arises, the device is removed about 6 weeks later. If relief and anteversion occur, no further treatment is necessary. If not, the pessary is reinserted for another 6 weeks.

cup p. A pessary that has a cup-shaped hollow that fits over the os uteri. It is used to treat a mild uterine prolapse.

diaphragm p. A cup-shaped rubber pessary used as a contraceptive device.

ring p. A round pessary.

pessimism (pes-ĭ-mĭ-zĭm) A frame of mind marked by loss of hope, confidence, or trust in a good outcome, even when such an outcome is likely. SEE: *optimism*.

therapeutic p. Nihilism (1).

pest (pest) [L. *pestis,* plague] **1.** A noxious, destructive insect. **2.** A fatal epidemic disease, esp. plague.

pesticide (pes′tĭ-sīd″) [*pest* + *-cide*] Any chemical used to kill pests, esp. rodents and insects.

restricted-use p. In the U.S., a pesticide known to have adverse effects on the environment or on people; only individuals who have been specially trained and certified as pesticide applicators may use it.

pesticide residue The amount of any pesticide remaining on or in food or beverages intended for human consumption.

pestilence (pes′tĭl-ĕns) [L. *pestilentia*] An epidemic contagious disease. **pestilential** (pĕs-tĭ-lĕn′shăl), *adj.*

pestis (pes′tĭs) [L.] Plague.

p. ambulans Ambulatory plague.

p. fulminans The most severe form of plague.

pestle (pes′l) [L. *pistillum*] A device for macerating drugs in a mortar.

PET *positron emission **tomography**.*

peta- [Fm. *penta,* representing the fifth power of a thousand] In the International System of Units (SI), a prefix signifying 10^{15}.

Petasites hybridus (pet″ă-sīt′ēz hī′brid-ŭs) butterbur.

PETCO₂ *end-tidal carbon dioxide tension; partial **pressure** of exhaled carbon dioxide.*

PET-CT *positron emission tomography, and computed tomography* (used together to identify metastases in patients with cancer).

petechiae (pē-tē′kē-ē) *sing.,* **petechia** [It. *petecchia,* skin spot] **1.** Small, purplish, hemorrhagic spots on the skin that appear in patients with platelet deficiencies (thrombocytopenias) and in many febrile illnesses. SEE: illus. **2.** Red spots from the bite of a flea.

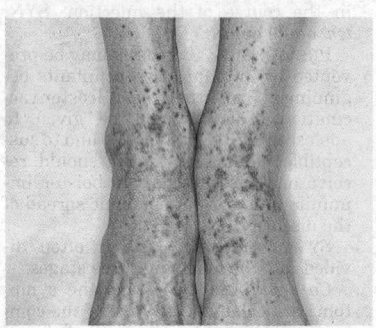

PETECHIAE

petechial (pē-tē′kē-ăl) Pert. to or marked by the presence of petechiae.

petiole (pĕt′ē-ōl) [L. *petiolus*] A slender stalk or stem, as petiole of the epiglottic cartilage.

petition Complaint (2).

petit mal SEE: *epilepsy.*

Petri dish (pē′trē) [Julius Petri, Ger. bacteriologist, 1852–1921] A shallow covered dish made of plastic or glass, used to hold solid media for culturing bacteria.

petrifaction (pĕt-rĭ-făk′shŭn) [L. *petra,* stone, + *facere,* to make] The process of changing into stone or hard substance.

petrify (pĕt′rĭ-fī) To convert into stone; make rigid.

pétrissage (pā″trĕ-sazh′) [Fr. *pétrissage,* kneading] A massage technique that uses kneading or squeezing of muscle groups across muscle fibers and is performed generally by the tips of the thumbs, with the index finger and thumb, or with the palm of the hand. It is used principally on the extremities. The operator picks up a special muscle or tendon and, placing one finger on each side of the part, proceeds in centripetal motion with a firm pressure. SYN: *kneading.*

petro- [L. *petra,* stone] Combining form meaning *stone;* pert. to the petrous portion of the temporal bone.

petrolatum (pe″trŏ-lāt′ŭm) [*petroleum* + *-ate*] A purified semisolid mixture of hydrocarbons obtained from petroleum. This occlusive substance is used as a base for ointments. It is not suitable for use as a vaginal lubricant because it is not miscible in body secretions. SYN: *soft paraffin.*

    liquid p. A mixture of liquid hydrocarbons obtained from petroleum. This mixture is used as a vehicle for medicinal substances for local applications. Light petrolatum is employed as a topical spray, whereas heavy petrolatum was once used internally to treat constipation. SYN: *mineral oil.*

petroleum (pĕ-trō′lē-ŭm) [L. *petra,* stone, + *oleum,* oil] An oily inflammable liquid found in the upper strata of the earth; a hydrocarbon mixture.

petro-occipital (pĕt″rō-ŏk-sĭp′ĭ-tăl) [″ + *occipitalis,* occipital] Concerning the petrous portion of the temporal bone and the occipital bone.

petrosa (pĕ-trō′să) [L. *petrosus,* stony] The petrous part of the temporal bone.

petrosal (pĕt-rō′săl) [L. *petrosus,* stony] Pert. to or situated near the petrous portion of the temporal bone.

Petroselinum crispum (pe″trō-sĕ-lī′nŭm kris′pŭm) SEE: *parsley.*

petrositis (pĕt″rō-sī′tĭs) [″ + Gr. *itis,* inflammation] Inflammation of the petrous region of the temporal bone.

petrosquamous (pĕt″rō-skwā′mŭs) [″ + *squamosus,* scaly] Pert. to the petrous and squamous portions of the temporal bone.

petrous (pĕt′rŭs) [L. *petrosus*] **1.** Resembling stone. **2.** Pert. to the petrous portion of the temporal bone. SYN: *petrosal.*

pet therapy The therapeutic use of animals, e.g., as pets or companions for the socially isolated or infirm.

Peutz-Jeghers syndrome (pūtz-jā′kĕrs) [Johannes Laurentius Augustinus Peutz, Dutch physician, 1886–1957; Harold J. Jeghers, U.S. physician, 1904–1990] An inherited disorder characterized by the presence of polyps of the small intestine and melanin pigmentation of the lips, mucosa, fingers,

and toes. Anemia due to bleeding from the intestinal polyps is a common finding.

PEx *physical examination.*

pexin (pĕk′sĭn) Rennet.

-pexy [Gr. *pēxis,* a fixing] Suffix meaning *fixation,* usually surgical.

Peyer patch (pī′ĕr) [Johann Conrad Peyer, Swiss anatomist, 1653–1712] A group of diffuse lymphoid nodules in the mucosa of the small bowel. Part of the mucosa-associated lymphoid tissue (MALT), Peyer patches detect and respond to foreign antigens in the gastrointestinal tract. Antibodies secreted by B cells in Peyer's patches provide a significant defense against ingested pathogens.

peyote (pā-ō′tē) [Nahuatl *peyotl*] **1.** The cactus plant, *Lophophora williamsii,* from which the hallucinogen mescaline is obtained. **2.** The drug from the flowering heads, buttons, of *L. williamsii,* used by some Native Americans to produce altered states of consciousness. In certain tribes the buttons are used in religious ceremonies.

Peyronie disease (pā-rō-nē′) [François de la Peyronie, Fr. surgeon, 1678–1747] A dorsal deformity or curvature of the penis caused by fibrous tissue within the tunica albuginea. When the distortion of the penis is severe, the affected individual may experience erectile dysfunction or pain during sexual intercourse.

    TREATMENT: In many cases the contracture is mild, and those patients do not require treatment. When pain is present for more than 12 months, however, or when the deformity is severe or interferes with erectile function, surgical repair of the defect may prove helpful.

Peyrot thorax (pā-rō′) [Jean J. Peyrot, Fr. surgeon, 1843–1918] A chest that has an obliquely oval deformed shape, seen with large pleural effusions.

Pfannenstiel incision (făn′ĕn-stēl) A transverse curvilinear incision immediately above the pubic symphysis extending from the skin into the peritoneum. The skin incision is continued transversely to include the anterior rectus sheath, which is then reflected superiorly; the bellies of the rectus muscle are separated longitudinally and the peritoneum is incised vertically. This surgical approach is used most often in gynecological procedures.

PFAPA syndrome *periodic fever, aphthous stomatitis, pharyngitis, cervicaladenitis* (a syndrome that is a relatively rare cause of relapsing and remitting fevers in otherwise healthy children aged 5 to 10 and occasionally in adults). Febrile episodes typically resolve with corticosteroids such as prednisone.

PFD *Personal flotation **device**.*

Pfeiffer, Richard F. (fī'fĕr) German bacteriologist, 1858–1945.

    P. bacillus *Haemophilus influenzae.*

    P. phenomenon The serum of guinea pigs immunized with cholera vibrios destroys cholera organisms in the peritoneal cavity of immune and nonimmune guinea pigs and that the same reaction occurs in vitro. That same lytic reaction occurred with typhoid and *Escherichia coli.*

Pfiesteria piscicida (fēs-tĕr'ē-ă pĭs-ĭ-sīd'ä) A unicellular marine organism, which may or may not produce a toxin, depending on environmental conditions. When toxic, it has been implicated in the death of millions of fish in the estuaries of North Carolina, Delaware, and Maryland. The toxin can become aerosolized, and if humans are exposed to it, severe neurological, mental, and physical illness may occur. Specific therapy to combat the toxin is not available, but concomitant infections can be treated with tetracyclines.

PFKM *Phosphofructokinase **deficiency**.*

P:F ratio The ratio of arterial partial pressure of oxygen to inspired fractional concentration of oxygen; used to measure oxygen transfer.

PFS *Progression-free survival.*

PFT *platelet function test; pulmonary function test.*

PG *prostaglandin.*

pg *picogram.*

PGA *pteroylglutamic acid.*

Ph **1.** *Pharmacopoeia.* **2.** Symbol for phenyl.

pH [Ger. *Potenz*, power + *H*, symbol for hydrogen] In chemistry, a measure of the hydrogen ion concentration of a solution. The degree of acidity or alkalinity of a substance is expressed in a pH value. A solution that is neither acid nor alkaline has a pH of 7. Increasing acidity is expressed as a number less than 7, and increasing alkalinity as a number greater than 7. Maximum acidity is pH 0 and maximum alkalinity is pH 14. Because the pH scale is logarithmic, there is a 10-fold difference between each unit. For example, pH 5 is 10 times as acid as pH 6 and pH 4 is 100 times as acid as pH 6. The general mathematical formula defining pH is: pH = −log[H+], in which pH is the negative logarithm of the hydrogen ion concentration. The pH of a solution may be determined electrically by a pH meter or colorimetrically by the use of indicators. A list of indicators and the pH range registered by each is given under the indicator. SEE: illus.; table; *indicator.*

PHA *phytohemagglutinin.*

phaco-, phac-, phak-, phako- [Gr. *phakos*, lentil, wart, mole] Prefix meaning *lens.*

phacoanaphylaxis (făk"ō-ăn"ă-fĭ-lăk'sĭs)

[Gr. *phakos*, lens, + *ana*, excessive, + *phylaxis*, protection] Hypersensitivity to protein of the crystalline lens.

phacoemulsification (fak"ō-ĕ-mŭl"sĭ-fĭ-kā"shŏn) [*phaco-* + *emulsification*] A method for removing the lens of the eye in order to treat cataracts. An ultrasonic device is used to fragment the lens, which is then removed via aspiration through a small incision. SYN: *phacofragmentation.* SEE: *cataract; extracapsular **extraction**.*

phacofragmentation (făk"ō-frăg"mĕn-tā'shŭn) Phacoemulsification.

phacomatosis (fā"kō-mă-tō-sĭs) Phakomatosis.

phaeohyphomycosis (fē"ō-hī"fō-mī-kō'sĭs) [Gr. *phaeos*, gray + Gr. *hyphos, hyphe*, web, net + "] Tissue infection with fungi that have darkly pigmented hyphae. SEE: *hyalohyphomycosis.*

phage (fāj) [Gr. *phagein*, to eat] Bacteriophage.

-phage [Gr. *-phagos*, fr. *phagein*, to eat] Suffix meaning *one that eats,* esp.*a cell,* e.g., a bacteriophage, *that destroys cells*

phagedena (făj-ĕ-dē'nă) [Gr. *phagedaina*] A sloughing ulcer that spreads rapidly.

    sloughing p. Hospital gangrene; bedsores.

phagedenic (făj-ĕ-dĕn'ĭk) Concerning, or of the nature of, phagedena.

-phagia, -phagy [Gr. *phagein*, to eat] Suffixes meaning *eating, ingestion, devouring.*

phago-, phag- [Gr. *phagein*, to eat] Prefixes meaning *eating, ingestion, devouring.*

phagocyte (făg'ō-sīt) [Gr. *phagein*, to eat, + *kytos*, cell] White blood cells (neutrophils and macrophages) that can ingest and destroy microorganisms, cell debris, and other particles in the blood or tissues. SEE: *endocytosis; macrophage; mononuclear phagocyte system; neutrophil; phagocytosis; pinocytosis.*

phagocytic (făg'ō-sĭt'ĭk) **1.** Pert. to phagocytes. **2.** Pert. to phagocytosis.

phagocytize (făg'ō-sīt"ĭz) To ingest bacteria and foreign particles by phagocytosis.

phagocytose (făg"ō-sī'tōs) [" + *kytos*, cell] Phagocytize.

phagocytosis (făg"ō-sī-tō'sĭs) [" + " + *osis*, condition] A three-stage process by which phagocytes (neutrophils, monocytes, and macrophages) engulf and destroy microorganisms, other foreign antigens, and cell debris. Generally, these substances must be covered with opsonins, such as antibodies or complement, to initiate binding with cell receptors on the phagocytes, the first stage in phagocytosis. In the second stage, the particle is engulfed and enclosed in a vacuole (phagosome). During the third stage, the phagosome merges with lysosomes whose

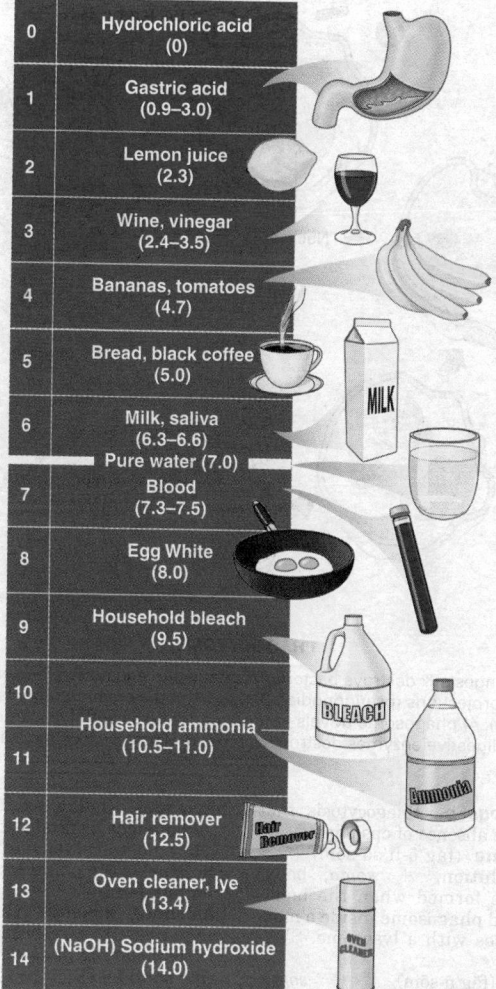

pH SCALE

Values of body fluids and some familiar solutions

pH of Some Fluids

Material	pH
10% HCl	1.0
Gastric juice	1.0–5.0
0.1% HCl	3.0
Pure water (neutral) at 25°C	7.0
Blood plasma	7.35–7.45
Pancreatic juice	8.4–8.9
0.1% NaOH	11.0
10% NaOH	13.0

HCl—hydrochloric acid; NaOH—sodium hydroxide

enzymes destroy the engulfed particle. SEE: illus.; *defensin; lysozyme; macrophage; neutrophil; oxygen radical.*

Most bacteria are killed during phagocytosis by oxygen radicals, which are formed during the respiratory burst when phagosomes and lysosomes merge. When oxygen radical production is excessive, tissue damage occurs. Lysozymes, defensins, and bacteriocidal permeability-increasing (BPI) protein also destroy bacteria and other organisms; their actions do not depend on the generation of oxygen radicals.

induced p. Phagocytosis that is stimulated by the presence of opsonins such as antibodies.

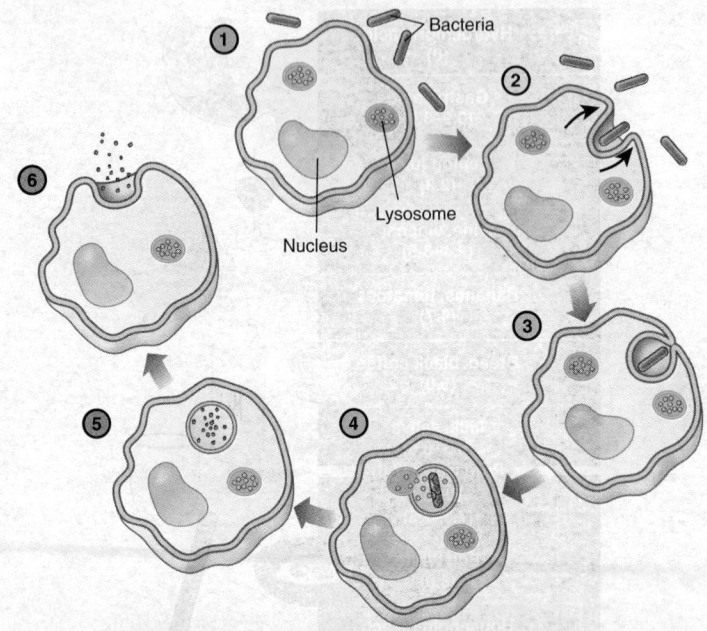

PHAGOCYTOSIS

1) Phagocyte ingests & destroys bacteria; 2) phagocyte encounters bacteria & sends out membrane projections (pseudopodia); 3) pseudopodia envelop organism, forming sac (phagosome); 4) phagosome travels to inner cell & fuses with lysosome; 5) lysosome's digestive enzymes destroy bacteria; 6) waste products released.

spontaneous p. Phagocytosis that occurs in the absence of opsonins.

phagolysosome (făg″ō-lī′sō-sōm) [″ + *lysis*, dissolution, + *soma*, body] The vacuole formed when the membrane-bound phagosome inside a macrophage fuses with a lysosome. SEE: *phagosome.*

phagosome (făg′ō-sōm) [″ + *soma*, body] A membrane-bound vacuole inside a phagocyte that contains material waiting to be digested. Digestion is facilitated by the fusion of the vacuole with the lysosome. The phagosome is then called a phagolysosome or a secondary lysosome. SEE: *phagolysosome.*

phakoma, phacoma (fă-kō′mă) [*phaco- + -oma*] **1.** A tumor of glial tissue. **2.** An area of myelinated nerve fibers rarely seen in the retina in association with neurofibromatosis.

phakomatosis (fă″kō-mă-tō′sĭs) [Gr. *phakos*, lens, + *oma*, tumor, + *osis*, condition] Any genetic neurocutaneous disorders, in which anomalies are spread unevenly through the body. SYN: *phacomatosis.* SEE: *Hippel disease; neurofibromatosis; sclerosis, tuberous; Sturge-Weber syndrome.*

phalangeal (fă-lăn′jē-ăl) [Gr. *phalanx*, closely knit row] Pert. to a phalanx.

phalanges (fă-lăn′jēz) Pl. of phalanx. "Phalanges" is used as the plural of only the anatomical sense of "phalanx;" "phalanxes" is the plural for all other senses of "phalanx."

phalango-, phalang- [Gr. *phalanx*, stem *phalang-*, line of battle, center] Prefixes meaning *phalanges* (bones of fingers and toes).

phalanx (făl′ănks) *pl.* **phalanges** [Gr., closely knit row] **1.** Any of the bones of the fingers or toes. SEE: *skeleton.* **2.** One of a set of plates formed of phalangeal cells (inner and outer) forming the reticular membrane of the organ of Corti.

distal p. The phalanx most remote from the metacarpus or metatarsus. SYN: *terminal p.; ungual p.*

metacarpal p. Any phalanx that articulates with a metacarpal bone. SEE: *proximal p.*

metatarsal p. Any phalanx that articulates with a metatarsal bone. SEE: *proximal p.*

middle p. When there are three phalanges, the phalanx intermediate between distal and proximal phalanges.

proximal p. Any phalanx that articulates with a metacarpal or metatarsal bone.

terminal p. Distal **p.**

ungual p. Distal **p.**

Phalen test (fā'lĕn) A maneuver used in the physical diagnosis of carpal tunnel symptoms. The patient is asked to flex the wrists while keeping the fingers extended, typically by placing the dorsa of the wrists together. The test is positive (suggestive of carpal tunnel syndrome) when wrist flexion produces numbness in the distribution of the median nerve. The accuracy of the test is limited. Also known as Phalen's sign.

phall-, phallo- [Gr. *phallos*, penis] Prefix meaning *penis*.

phallic (făl'ĭk) Pert. to the penis.

phalloid (făl'oyd) [" + *eidos*, form, shape] Resembling a penis.

phalloidin (fă-loyd'ĭn) A poisonous peptide from the mushroom *Amanita phalloides*. Ingestion of this can cause death from fulminant hepatic failure.

phalloplasty (făl'ō-plăs"tē) [" + *plassein*, to form] Reparative or plastic surgery on the penis.

phallus (făl'ŭs) [Gr. *phallos*, penis] **1.** The penis. **2.** An artificial penis, used as a symbol. **3.** Embryonic structure developing at the tip of the genital tubercle that in the male develops into the penis and in the female, the clitoris.

phanero-, phaner- [Gr. *phaneros*, visible] Prefixes meaning *evident, visible*.

phantasm (făn'tăzm) [Gr. *phantasma*] An optical illusion; an apparition, or illusion of something that does not exist.

phantasy (făn'tă-sē) [Gr. *phantasia*, imagination] Fantasy.

phantom (făn'tŭm) [Gr. *phantasma*, an appearance] **1.** An apparition. **2.** A model of the body or of one of its parts.

Pharma The colloquial name for the pharmaceutical industry. The largest companies in the industry, in terms of market capitalization, are sometimes referred to as "Big Pharma."

pharmacal (făr'mă-kăl) [Gr. *pharmakon*, drug] Pert. to pharmacy.

pharmaceutical (făr-mă-sū'tĭ-kăl) [Gr. *pharmakeutikos*] Pert. to drugs or pharmacy.

pharmaceutical clean room A controlled, typically aseptic environment within a pharmacy in which the concentration of airborne particles is reduced by particle filtration and by air locks or positive pressure ventilation and in which surfaces are easily cleaned or decontaminated. It is used to compound sterile drugs and infusions for dispensing. Operators within the clean room wear gowns, hoods, and masks to avoid shedding cellular debris.

pharmaceutics (făr-mă-sū'tĭks) Pharmacy (1).

pharmacist (făr'mă-sĭst) [Gr. *pharmakon*, drug] A druggist; one licensed to prepare and dispense drugs. SYN: *apothecary*.

pharmaco- [Gr. *pharmakon*, drug] Prefix meaning *drug, medicine*.

pharmacochemistry (făr"mă-kō-kĕm'ĭs-trē) [" + *chemeia*, chemistry] Pharmaceutical chemistry.

pharmacodynamics (făr"mă-kō-dī-năm'ĭks) [" + *dynamis*, power] The study of drugs and their actions on living organisms.

pharmacoepidemiology (făr'mă-kō-ĕ-pĭ-dĕm-ē-ŏl"ō-jē) The application of the science of epidemiology to the study of the effects of drugs, desired and undesired, and uses of drugs in human populations.

pharmacogenetics (făr"mă-kō-jĕn-ĕt'ĭks) [" + *genesis*, generation, birth] The study of the influence of hereditary factors on the response of individual organisms to drugs.

pharmacogenomics (făr"mă-kō-jĕ-nŏm'ĭks, -nōm') The study of the effects of genetic differences among people and the impact that these differences have on the uptake, effectiveness, toxicity, and metabolism of drugs.

pharmacogeriatrics (făr-mă-kō-jĕr-ē-ă'trĭks) The study of the dynamics of medication use in the elderly.

pharmacognosy (făr-mă-kŏg'nō-zē) [Gr. *pharmakon*, drug, + *gnōsis*, knowledge] The scientific study of drugs originating in nature, i.e., derived from animals, minerals, and plants. The field includes the characterization and cultivation, production, and standardization of such drugs.

pharmacokinetics (făr"mă-kō-kī-nĕt'ĭks) The study of the metabolism and action of drugs with particular emphasis on the time required for absorption, duration of action, distribution in the body, and method of excretion.

pharmacological stress test SEE: under *stress test*.

pharmacologist (făr"mă-kŏl'ō-jĭst) An individual who by training and experience is a specialist in pharmacology.

pharmacology (făr"mă-kol'ŏ-jē) [*pharmaco- + -logy*] The study of drugs and their origin, nature, properties, and effects upon living organisms. **pharmacologic** (-kŏ-loj'ĭk), *adj.* **pharmacological** (-kŏ-loj'ĭ-kăl), *adj.*

pharmacopeia (far"mă-kŏ-pē'ă) [L. *pharmacopoeia*, fr Gr. *pharmakopoiia*, preparation of drugs] An authorized treatise on drugs and their preparation, esp. a book containing formulas and information that provide a standard for preparation and dispensation of drugs. **pharmacopeial** (-pē'ăl), *adj.*

pharmacophore (făr'mă-kō-for) [" + *phoros*, bearing] The three-dimensional shape of a molecule that makes it fit and activate cellular receptors.

pharmacoresistant (for"mă-kō-ri-zis'tănt) [*pharmaco- + resistant*] Not easily treated with drugs; drug resistant. The term is used to describe refractory infections or tumors. **pharmacoresistance** (-zis′tăns), *n.*

pharmacotherapy (far″mă-kō-ther′ă-pē) [*pharmaco-* + *therapy*] Use of drugs to treat disease; drug therapy.

pharmacovigilance (făr″mă-kō-vīj′ĭ-lĭns) [″ + ″] The analysis, detection, and prevention of adverse effects caused by medications.

pharmacy (făr′mă-sē) [Gr. *pharmakon*, drug] **1.** The practice of compounding and dispensing medicinal preparations. **2.** A drugstore.

    nuclear pharmacy The compounding and dispensing of radioactive isotopes, such as technetium-99m, for use in nuclear medicine procedures such as cardiac or gallbladder imaging. Special techniques in nuclear pharmacy include working behind radioactive shielding, testing compounded products with chromatography, and distributing radionuclides in leaded syringes.

pharmacy technician A technician who assists the pharmacist in certain activities such as medication profile reviews for drug incompatibilities, typing of prescription labels, prescription packaging, handling of purchase records, and inventory control, and may, where state law and hospital policy permit, dispense drugs to patients under the supervision of a registered pharmacist.

Pharm D *Doctor of Pharmacy.*

pharyngeal (făr-ĭn′jē-ăl) [L. *pharyngeus*] Pert. to the pharynx.

pharyngectomy (făr-ĭn-jĕk′tō-mē) [Gr. *pharynx*, throat, + *ektome*, excision] Partial excision of the pharynx to remove growths or abscesses.

pharyngitis (făr″ĭn-jīt′ĭs) [*pharyng-* + *-itis*] Inflammation of the mucous membranes and lymphoid tissues of the pharynx, usually as a result of infection.
    ETIOLOGY: The disease typically is caused by viral or bacterial infections, including influenza virus, *Streptococcus pyogenes*, or *Mycoplasma pneumoniae*. Occasionally, diphtheria or *Candida albicans* is responsible.
    SYMPTOMS: The predominant symptom is throat pain. Fever, malaise, muscle aches, and painful swallowing are often present.
    TREATMENT: Gargling with warm salty water provides topical relief. Analgesic drugs, fluids, throat lozenges, or topical anesthetics also are helpful. If clinical suspicion, rapid tests, or culture results identify streptococci, penicillin or an erythromycin is usually curative.

    acute p. Inflammation of the pharynx with pain in the throat.
    SYMPTOMS: Symptoms include malaise, fever, dysphagia, throat pain, and difficulty swallowing.
    PATIENT CARE: Comfort measures for sore throat include gargling (e.g., with salty water), throat lozenges, or

OTC topical anesthetics. Many patients benefit from rest, hydration, and analgesics. An appropriate antibiotic (if prescribed) is given when there is evidence of bacterial infection.

    atrophic p. A chronic form of pharyngitis with some atrophy of mucous glands and abnormal secretion.

    bacterial p. Severe, epidemic, pseudomembranous inflammation of the fauces and tonsils caused by group A beta-hemolytic streptococcus. It was formerly known as *septic sore throat.*

    chronic p. Pharyngitis associated with pathology in the nose and sinuses, mouth breathing, excessive smoking, and chronic tonsillitis. Dryness and irritation of the throat and a cough characterize this condition. Intranasal medication and removal of pathological factors in sinuses and tonsillectomy are the treatment choices.

    diphtheritic p. Sore throat with general symptoms of diphtheria and formation of a true membrane.

    granular p. Chronic pharyngitis with granulations seen on the pharynx.

    p. herpetica Pharyngitis characterized by formation of vesicles and ulcers.

    hypertrophic p. Chronic pharyngitis with thickened red mucous membrane on each side with a glazed central portion.

    membranous p. Pharyngitis characteristic of diphtheria, in which an exudate in the pharynx or on the tonsils forms a false membrane.

    streptococcal p. A common bacterial infection of the throat and tonsils, esp. in children between the ages of 5 and 15, typically characterized by fever, sore throat, painful swallowing, exudates on the tonsils, and swollen anterior cervical lymph nodes. The disease is caused by infection with group A beta-hemolytic streptococci and may be treated with a variety of antibiotics, including penicillins and macrolides. It may occasionally produce late complications, including rheumatic fever or poststreptococcal glomerulonephritis. SYN: *strep throat.*

    p. ulcerosa Pharyngitis with fever, pain, and the formation of ulcerations.

pharyngo-, pharyng- [Gr. *pharynx*, stem *pharyng-*, throat] Prefixes meaning *throat.*

pharyngoepiglottic, pharyngoepiglottidean (fă-rĭng″gō-ep″ĭ-glot′ĭk, fă-rĭng″gō-ep″ĭ-glŏ-tid′ē-ăn) [″ + *epi*, upon, + *glottis*, glottis] Pert. to the pharynx and glottis.

pharyngoesophageal (fă-rĭng″gō-ē-sŏf′ă-jē″ăl) [″ + *oisophagos*, esophagus] Pert. to the pharynx and esophagus.

pharyngolaryngeal (fă-rĭng″gō-lă-rĭn′jē-ăl) [″ + *larynx*, larynx] Pert. to the pharynx and larynx.

pharyngomaxillary (fă-rĭng″gō-măk′sĭ-lĕr″ē) [″ + L. *maxilla,* jawbone] Pert. to the pharynx and maxillae.

pharyngoplasty (făr-ĭn′gō-plăs″tē) [″ + *plassein,* to form] Reparative surgery of the pharynx (e.g., to treat obstructive sleep apnea).

pharyngoscope (făr-ĭn′gō-skōp) [″ + *skopein,* to examine] An instrument for visual examination of the pharynx.

pharyngoscopy (făr″ĭn-gŏs′kō-pē) Visual examination of the pharynx.

pharyngotomy (făr-ĭn-gŏt′ō-mē) Incision of the pharynx.

pharyngotonsillitis (fă-rĭng″gō-tŏn″sĭ-lī′tĭs) [″ + L. *tonsilla,* almond, + Gr. *itis,* inflammation] Inflammation of the pharynx and tonsils.

pharynx (făr′ĭnks) *pl.* **pharynges** [Gr.] The passageway for air from the nasal cavity to the larynx and for food from the mouth to the esophagus. The pharynx participates in speech as a resonating cavity. SEE: *pharyngitis; mouth* for illus.

ANATOMY: The pharynx is a musculomembranous tube extending from the base of skull to the level of the sixth cervical vertebra, where it becomes continuous with the esophagus. The upper portion, the nasopharynx, is above the soft palate, lined with pseudostratified ciliated epithelium, and has openings to the posterior nares and eustachian tubes. The middle part, the oropharynx, is lined with stratified squamous epithelium and has an opening to the oral cavity. The lowest part, the laryngopharynx, is also lined with stratified squamous epithelium and opens inferiorly to the larynx anteriorly and the esophagus posteriorly.

The nerve supply is from the autonomic nervous system and from the vagus and glossopharyngeal nerves. Blood vessels branch from the external carotid artery. Veins form an extensive pharyngeal plexus and drain into the internal jugular vein.

phase (fāz) [Gr. *phasis,* an appearance] **1.** A stage of development. **2.** A transitory appearance. **3.** In chemistry, a distinct component of a larger, heterogeneous system, as oil or water when the two are mixed.

   aqueous p. The water portion of a mixture of liquids and solids or of immiscible liquids and of gases.

   continuous p. The state of a substance in a heterogeneous system in which particles are continuous, e.g., the water particles in which oil has been dispersed.

   death p. In cellular biology, the period that begins when cells in culture exhaust their nutrient supply and begin to die.

   disperse p. The state of a substance in a heterogeneous system in which particles are separated from each other, e.g., oil particles in water.

   eclipse p. The phase of the viral life cycle during which a virus enters a cell to parasitize it. The phase includes the attachment of the virus to the cell membrane, penetration of the cell by the virus, and the uncoating of the virus once it has entered the cytoplasm. During this phase in its life cycle, no progeny virus is found within the cell.

   isometric contraction p. The first phase in contraction of the ventricle of the heart in which ventricular pressure increases but there is no decrease in volume of contents because semilunar valves are closed.

   lag p. Lag (2).

   latent p. Incubation (1).

   log p. That portion of the bacterial growth curve at which bacteria are reproducing at an exponential rate.

-phasia, -phasy [Gr. *phasis,* statement, utterance + *-ia*] Suffixes meaning *speech* (for a speech disorder of a specific kind, e.g., *aphasia, paraphasia*).

phasic (fā′sĭk) Pert. to a phase.

PhD *Doctor of Philosophy.*

phe *phenylalanine.*

phenanthrene (fĕ-nan′thrĕn″) $C_{14}H_{10}$, a carcinogenic derivative of coal tar.

phenate (fē′nāt) A salt of phenic acid (phenol).

phencyclidine hydrochloride (fĕn-sĭk′lĭ-dĭn″, -sī′klĭ, -dĭn) ABBR: PCP. An anesthetic used in veterinary medicine. It is also used illegally as a hallucinogen, and referred to in slang as "PCP" or "angel dust." The drug is potent; intoxication can occur from passive smoking, and even small doses can produce excitement, hallucinations, and psychotic or extremely violent behavior. Moderate doses also cause elevated blood pressure, rapid pulse, increased skeletal muscle tone, and sometimes, myoclonic jerking. Large doses can cause seizures, ataxia, nystagmus, respiratory depression, and death. The pupils of patients intoxicated with PCP are usually of normal size or small but not the pinpoint size seen in opiate use. This, together with the other physical findings, may help clinicians diagnose overdosed patients.

TREATMENT: For agitation caused by acute intoxication, diazepam is indicated. Because PCP abusers are often hostile, aggressive, and dangerous, efforts to pacify these patients are contraindicated. Instead, the patient should be isolated in a quiet room and protective measures taken to avoid injury to self or others.

PROGNOSIS: Despite medication and psychotherapy, the psychotic symptoms produced by PCP may persist for weeks or months.

phenethylamine (fen-eth′ĭl-ă-mēn″) Any

of a class of toxic, controlled, and sometimes addictive central nervous system stimulants that suppress appetite and induce euphoria or hallucinations. Members of this class include amphetamines and methamphetamines.

phenobarbital (fē″nō-băr′bĭ-tăl) Phenylbarbituric acid, a sedative, hypnotic, and anticonvulsant drug.

phenocopy (fē′nō-kŏp″ē) [Gr. *phainein*, to show, + *copy*] An individual with a biochemical or physical characteristic that resembles that produced by a genetic mutation but is instead due to an environmental condition.

phenol (fē′nōl) **1.** C_6H_5OH; a crystalline, colorless or light pink solid, melting at 43°C, obtained from the distillation of coal tar. It has a characteristic odor and is dangerous because of its rapid corrosive action on tissues. SYN: *carbolic acid*. **2.** Any of the aromatic derivatives of benzene with one or more hydroxyl groups attached.

phenology (fē-nŏl′ō-jē) [Gr. *phainesthai*, to appear, + *logos*, word, reason] The study of the effects of climate on living things.

phenolsulfonphthalein (fēn″ŏl-sŭl″fon-thal′ē-ĭn, -thal′ēn″) ABBR: P.S.P. A bright red organic chemical $C_{19}H_{14}O_5S$ used diagnostically in studies of kidney function, bladder emptying, and, after intra-amniotic injection, in invasive tests for premature rupture of membranes. SYN: *phenol red*.

phenomenology (fē-nŏm″ĕ-nŏl′ō-jē) [Gr. *phainomenon*, appearing, + *logos*, word, reason] **1.** The study and classification of phenomena. **2.** The science of the subjective processes by which phenomena are presented, with emphasis on mental processes and essential elements of experiences. A phenomenological study emphasizes a person's descriptions of and feelings about experienced events.

phenomenon (fē-nom′ĕ-non″, -nŏn, ′ĕ-nă) *pl.* **phenomena** [Gr. *phainomenon*, appearance] Any observable or objective symptom, sign, event, or fact. Particular phenomena are listed under the first word. SEE: e.g., *alien limb phenomenon; breakaway phenomenon; dawn phenomenon.*

phenothiazines (fē″nō-thī′ă-zēnz) A class of major tranquilizers used to treat psychotic illnesses such as schizophrenia. They have neuroleptic and antiemetic effects. Among the most commonly used agents in this class are chlorpromazine, haloperidol, prochlorperazine, and thioridazine. Side effects of these drugs include dystonic reactions, tardive dyskinesia, seizures, and sedation. SEE: *neuroleptic*.

phenotype (fē′nŏ-tīp″) [Gr. *phainein*, to show + *type*] The expression of the genes present in an individual. This may be directly observable (e.g., eye color) or apparent only with specific tests (e.g., blood type). Some phenotypes (e.g., the blood groups) are completely determined by heredity; others are readily altered by environmental agents. SEE: *genotype.*

phenozygous (fē-nŏz′ĭ-gŭs) [″ + *zygon*, yoke] Possessing a cranium much narrower than the face.

phentermine (fĕn′tĕr-mēn) An amphetamine-like substance that enhances weight loss. When used with fenfluramine hydrochloride, a similar drug, it has been implicated in the destruction of the pulmonary valve of a small percentage of patients.

phenyl (fĕn′ĭl, fē′nĭl) The univalent radical of phenol, C_6H_5.

phenylalanine (fĕn″ĭl-ăl′ă-nĭn) ABBR: phe. An essential amino acid, one of the two linked amino acids in the sugar substitute aspartame. The genetically determined inability to dispose of excess phenylalanine is known as phenylketonuria (PKU). SEE: *phenylketonuria.*

phenylamine (fĕn″ĭl′ă-mēn′) Aniline.

phenylethylamine (fĕn″ĭl-ĕth″ĭl-ăl′ă-mēn″) ABBR: PEA. An alkaloid synthesized from the amino acid phenylalanine. It is found in the brain, where it contributes to the release of dopamine and endorphins. It is concentrated in chocolate and thought to be an antidepressant.

phenylhydrazine (fĕn″ĭl-hī′dră-zēn″) [*phenyl* + *hydrazine*] An oily nitrogenous base used as a test for the presence of sugar in the urine.

phenylketonuria (fĕn″ĭl-kēt″ŏn-ū′rē-ă, fĕn″) [*phenyl* + *ketone* + *-uria*] ABBR: PKU. A congenital autosomal recessive disease marked by failure to metabolize phenylalanine to tyrosine. It results in severe neurological deficits in infancy if it is unrecognized and left untreated. PKU is present in about 3.5 in 10,000 newborns in the U.S. In this disease, phenylalanine and its by-products accumulate in the body, esp. in the nervous system, where they cause severe mental retardation (IQ test results often below 40), seizure disorders, tremors, gait disturbances, coordination deficits, and psychotic or autistic behavior. Eczema and an abnormal skin odor also are characteristic. The consequences of PKU can be prevented if it is recognized in the first weeks of life and a phenylalanine-restricted (very low protein) diet is maintained throughout infancy, childhood, and young adulthood. SYN: *Folling's disease.*

PREVENTION: The U.S. Preventive Services Task Force recommends that all newborns be screened for PKU before discharge from the nursery or in the first 2 weeks of life. The test's accuracy is highest if it is performed no sooner than 24 hr after birth. Mass screening for the disease began in the 1960s. Some women with PKU are now of childbearing age. During their pregnancies, strict adherence to a low-phenylalanine diet will help to prevent fetal malformations. Chorionic villus sampling can detect PKU prenatally.

PATIENT CARE: Testing newborns for PKU is typically performed with a heel-stick specimen of blood, which is allowed to dry on blotting paper before being sent to the lab for the Guthrie test. The presence of phenylpyruvic acid in the urine also confirms the diagnosis (a few drops of 10% ferric acid are added to a wet diaper, resulting in a deep, bluish coloration if the test is positive. Since urinary levels of the acid vary according to the amount of protein ingested, testing should be repeated 4 to 6 weeks after birth. If elevated levels of phenylalanine are found, additional tests are performed to confirm the diagnosis.

Effective treatment requires that phenylalanine blood levels be maintained between 3 and 9 mg/dL. This means severely limiting natural proteins in the diet, as most contain 5% phenylalanine. An enzymatic hydrolysate of casein (Lofenalac or Pregestimil) is substituted for milk for affected infants, providing normal amounts of protein other than phenylalanine, plus additional carbohydrates and fat. As the child grows, breads, cheese, eggs, flour, meat, poultry, fish, nuts, milk, legumes, and phenylalanine-type sugar substitutes must be avoided. Frequent blood and urinary testing evaluates dietary effects. Overzealous restriction can cause phenylalanine deficiency. Parents also need to understand normal growth and development to help them to recognize development delays related to PKU. As the child becomes older and dietary supervision by parents less possible, restriction deviations are more likely to occur, putting the child at risk for neurological damage. Involving the child from early on in choosing permitted low-protein foods that he/she prefers helps to develop responsible behaviors.

phenylpyruvic acid (fĕn″ĭl-pī-roo′vĭk) A metabolic derivative of phenylalanine.

phenylthiocarbamide (fĕn″ĭl-thī″ō-kär′bă-mīd) ABBR: PTC. A chemical used in studying medical genetics to detect the presence of a marker gene. About 70% of the population inherit the ability to note the taste of phenylthiocarbamide to be extremely bitter. To the remainder of the population, it is tasteless. The gene for tasting is dominant and is expressed in both homozygous and heterozygous individuals. SYN: *phenylthiourea.*

phenylthiourea (fĕn″ĭl-thī″ō-ū-rē′ă) Phenylthiocarbamide.

phenytoin (fĕn′ĭ-tō-ĭn) An anticonvulsant drug used primarily to treat patients with seizure disorders, including tonic-clonic and partial complex seizures and status epilepticus. It also can be used as an antiarrhythmic drug. Side effects of phenytoin include hyperplasia of the gums, ataxia, nystagmus, and neurological depression. Its use alters the metabolism of many other drugs that the liver degrades. SYN: *diphenylhydantoin sodium.*

⚠️ Because of the drug's effects on heart rhythm, cardiac monitoring is required during intravenous infusions.

pheochromocytoma (fē″ō-krō″mŏ-sĭ-tō′mă, -sī-) [*pheochromocyte* + *-oma*] A tumor derived from neural crest cells of the sympathetic nervous system, responsible for about 0.1% to 2% of all cases of hypertension. The tumor releases catecholamines, which cause episodic or sustained signs and symptoms (e.g., palpitations, sweating, headaches, fainting spells, tremor, nausea, dyspepsia, pallor, chest or abdominal pain, hyperglycemia, weakness, anxiety, feelings of impending doom, and hypertensive emergencies). It may result from an inherited autosomal dominant trait. All races and both sexes are affected, with symptoms most commonly beginning between ages 30 and 40. SEE: *catecholamine; multiple endocrine neoplasia; paraganglioma; Nursing Diagnoses Appendix.*

This neuroendocrine tumor is one of the surgically correctable forms of hypertension. It may be difficult to diagnose because the symptoms it causes are found in other, more common, conditions (e.g., anxiety disorders, alcohol withdrawal, and hyperthyroidism).

The tumor is located in the adrenal gland itself in about 85% of cases, but sympathetic tissues are distributed widely throughout the body. As a result, catecholamine-releasing tumors may be found in the urinary bladder, carotid bodies, paravertebral tissues, and other sites in the neck, thorax, abdomen, or pelvis. Neuroendocrine tumors found outside the adrenal glands are called paragangliomas. Some patients have multiple tumors. About 10% of patients with pheochromocytoma also have multiple endocrine neoplasias, one of several genetic syndromes in which pheochromocytomas are associated with adenomas or tumors of other glands.

DIAGNOSIS: The patient's urine or blood is tested to determine whether it contains excessive levels of catecholamines or their metabolites. If so, imaging studies (e.g., computed tomography, magnetic resonance imaging, or radioisotope or nuclear scanning) are used to locate the tumor before surgery.

PATIENT CARE: Anesthesia for this surgery is challenging because of the hemodynamic instability that can occur during and after the procedure. Hypotension is treated with dopamine, and hypertensive episodes, occurring most commonly during induction, intubation, or tumor manipulation, are treated with nitroprusside or alpha blockers. For the first 24 hr postoperatively when vasopressors, plasma volume expanders, and IV fluids may be required, ICU monitoring is recommended. Other postoperative care includes continuous cardiac monitoring for arrhythmias, hemodynamic monitoring, and assessment for heart failure and angina. Postoperative hypertension is common due to the stress of surgery and adrenal gland manipulation that stimulates catecholamine secretion. Blood pressure must be closely monitored, a quiet, cool environment provided, and clothing and bedding changed as needed in response to the sweating that may occur. Careful blood pressure assessment continuesthrough the first 2 postoperative days, when blood pressure may fall. Postoperative orthostatic hypotension may be a threat to patient safety. Until it resolves, patients need to be taught to get up from the bed or chair slowly and hold on to a solid object. To collect diagnostic specimens from stress-free subjects, the patient is often placed on bedrest. Drugs are withheld that may block or augment test results for catecholamines or metanephrines. If a tumor is identified and surgery is planned, preoperative hydration of the patient prevents hypotension during anesthetic induction. Medications to blunt the effect of catecholamines (e.g., alpha-adrenergic blocking agents and then beta-adrenergic blocking agents) are administered for 1 to 2 weeks before surgery. Postoperatively, vital signs (esp. blood pressure, via an arterial line), cardiac rhythms, fluid balance, and electrolytes are monitored closely. Analgesics are provided to manage pain, and the bloodpressure response is assessed closely so that dosing can be titrated to prevent hypotensive episodes. The abdomen is auscultated for returning bowel sounds and observed for distention. The health care team reassures the patient and family throughout diagnosis and management because the symptoms of this condition often fluctuate dramatically. After discharge, long-term follow-up should be provided by an endocrinologist experienced in the care of patients with pheochromocytoma.

pheomelanins (fē-ō-mĕl′ă-nĭnz) [″ + Gr. *melas*, black] Yellow-brown, sulfur-containing pigments present as the pigment in human red hair.

pheresis (fĕ-rē′sĭs) [Gr. *aphairesis*, separation] Apheresis.

pheromone (fĕr′ō-mōn) A chemical released by one animal that acts as a form of communication with other animals of the same species. It is often detected by smell and may affect the development, reproduction, or behavior of other individuals.

Ph.G. *German Pharmacopeia; Graduate in Pharmacy.*

PHI *protected health information.*

phial (fī′ăl) [Gr. *phiale*, a bowl] A small vessel for medicine; a vial.

Philadelphia collar (fĭl″ă-del′fē-ă) SEE: under *collar.*

-phile, -phil [Gr. *philos*, one's own, dear] Suffixes meaning *lover of, having an affinity or enthusiasm for.*

-philia [Gr. *philia*, love] Suffix meaning *love for, tendency toward* or *excessive appetite or craving for.* **-phil,** *adj.* **-philic,** *adj.*

-philic [-*phile* + -*ic*] Adjectival suffix for nouns ending in -*phile*, e.g., *acidophilic* from *acidophile.*

philosophy (fĭ-lŏs′ō-fē) **1.** The love or pursuit of knowledge. **2.** A culturally determined system of beliefs, concepts, theories, or convictions.

philtrum (fĭl-trŭm) The median groove on the external surface of the upper lip.

phimosis (fĭ-mō′sĭs) [Gr., a muzzling] Stenosis or narrowness of the preputial orifice so that the foreskin cannot be pushed back over the glans penis. The condition is treated by circumcision.
    p. vaginalis Narrowness or closure of the vaginal orifice.

phlebectasia,   phlebectasis   (flĕb″ek″ tă″zh(ē-)ă, flĕb″ek′tă-sĭs) [*phlebo-* + *ektasis,* dilatation] Varicosity.

phlebectomy (fleb-ek′tŏ-mē) [*phlebo-* + -*ectomy*] Surgical removal of a vein or part of a vein.
    stab p. The surgical excision of varicose veins through tiny incisions made through the skin along the course of the vein.

phlebitis (flĕ-bī′tĭs) [″ + *itis,* inflammation] Inflammation of a vein. SYN: *thrombophlebitis.* SEE: *Nursing Diagnoses Appendix.* **phlebitic,** *adj.*
    ETIOLOGY: Common causes include chemical or mechanical irritation of veins by sclerosing intravenous fluids or indwelling catheters, thrombosis, or venous infections.
    SYMPTOMS: When a superficial vein is affected, the affected vein often is painful, tender, red, warm to touch, indurated along its length, or swollen. Inflammation or occlusion of large or deep veins may be asymptomatic or may produce edema distal to the lesion, as well as chills and fever and pain.

PREVENTION: Immobilized patients are at risk for phlebitic disorders. To prevent phlebitis, concentrated or irritating infusions should be given through central venous catheters or ports. Irritated or reddened intravenous sites should be changed, and peripheral catheters should never be left in place longer than 96 hr in adults, according to CDC guidelines. Patients with a history of deep venous thrombosis should adhere closely to anticoagulant drug regimens and avoid prolonged sitting or bedrest. They should avoid medications that increase the risk of thrombosis, such as compounds that contain estrogen.

PATIENT CARE: The Infusion Nurses Society has established the following clinical criteria to grade phlebitis:

0. no symptoms;

1. erythema at access site with or without pain;

2. pain at access site with erythema or edema;

3. pain at access site with erythema, streak formation, or palpable venous cord;

4. pain at access site with erythema, streak formation, palpable venous cord longer than 1 inch (2.5 cm), or purulent drainage.

Superficial and deep vein phlebitis are treated by elevating the extremity along its length and applying warm continuous moist heat for 72 hr to reduce inflammation and relieve pain. Analgesics and anti-inflammatory drugs also are provided to manage discomfort. Any offending solution or catheter is removed from the vein. Phlebitis caused by clots may be treated with antiplatelet or anticoagulant drugs, thrombolytic agents (streptokinase), or, in rare cases, surgery. Antibiotics and/or surgery may be required for venous infections. The circumference of the affected extremity should be measured daily at the same location and compared to the unaffected one. When anticoagulant therapy is used, precautions are taken to monitor its effects and limit the risk of bleeding.

adhesive p. Phlebitis in which the vein tends to become obliterated.

chemical p. Inflammatory damage to the lining of blood vessels, caused by infusions of highly acidic, highly basic, hypertonic, or sclerosing fluids.

migrating p. A transitory phlebitis that appears in a portion of a vein and then clears up, only to reappear later in another location.

p. nodularis necrotisans Circumscribed inflammation of cutaneous veins resulting in nodules that ulcerate.

obliterative p. Phlebitis in which the lumen of a vein becomes permanently closed.

puerperal p. Venous inflammation following childbirth.

sclerosing p. Phlebitis in which the veins become obstructed and hardened.

sinus p. Inflammation of a sinus of the cerebrum.

suppurative p. Phlebitis characterized by the formation of pus.

phlebo-, phleb- [Gr. *phleps*, stem *phleb-*, vein] Prefixes meaning *vein*.

phlebogram (flĕb'ō-grăm) [Gr. *phlebos*, vein, + *gramma*, something written] An infrequently used term for venogram.

phlebography (flĕ-bŏg'ră-fē) [" + *graphein*, to write] An infrequently used term for venography.

phlebolith, phlebolite (flĕb'ō-lith", flĕb'ō-līt") [" + *lithos*, a stone] A stone within a vein.

phlebology (flĕ-bol'ŏ-jē) [*phlebo-* + *-logy*] The study of veins and their diseases.

phlebosclerosis (flĕb"ō-sklē-rō'sĭs) [" + *sklerosis*, hardening] Fibrous hardening of a vein's walls.

phlebostatic axis (fleb-ō-stat'ĭk) SEE: under *axis*.

phlebothrombosis (flĕb"ō-thrŏm-bō'sĭs) [" + *thrombos*, a clot] Clotting in a vein; phlebitis with secondary thrombosis.

phlebotomist (flĕ-bŏt'ō-mĭst) [" + *tome*, incision] One who draws blood.

phlebotomize (flĕ-bŏt'ō-mīz) To take blood from a person.

Phlebotomus (flĕ-bŏt'ō-mŭs) [" + *tome*, incision] A genus of insects, the sandflies, belonging to the family Psychodidae, order Diptera. These bloodsucking insects transmit various forms of leishmaniasis, sandfly (pappataci) fever, and Oroya fever.

P. argentipes In India, the transmitter of *Leishmania donovani*, causative agent of kala-azar.

P. chinensis Transmitter of kala-azar in China.

P. papatasii Transmitter of the causative agent of sandfly fever. The virus is capable of being transmitted through the offspring of flies.

P. sergenti Transmitter of kala-azar in the Middle East and India.

P. verrucarum The transmitter of *Bartonella bacilliformis*, causative agent of Oroya fever (Carrion's disease), in South America.

phlebotomy (flĕ-bot'ŏ-mē) [*phlebo-* + *-tomy*] The puncturing of a vein or the surgical opening of a vein to withdraw blood. SYN: *blood draw*. SEE: illus.

phlebovirus (flĕ'bō-vī-rŭs) A genus of RNA viruses, transmitted to people by the bite of infected insects. Common examples include Rift Valley fever virus and Toscana virus. Phleboviruses can cause hemorrhagic fevers, meningitis,

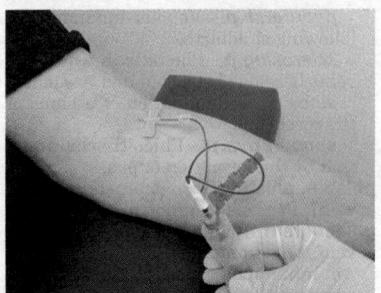

**BLOOD DRAWING FROM THE
ANTECUBITAL VEIN**

and meningoencephalitis, among other illnesses. SEE: *Toscana virus*.

phlegm (flĕm) [Gr. *phlegma*] **1.** Thick mucus, esp. that from the respiratory passages. **2.** One of the four humors of early physiology.

phlegmasia (flĕg-mā′zē-ă) [Gr. *phlegmasia*] Inflammation.

    p. alba dolens A complication of deep venous thrombosis of the iliofemoral veins in which the affected leg becomes extremely pale, swollen, and tender. SYN: *milk leg; white leg*. SEE: *deep venous thrombosis*.

    cellulitic p. Septic inflammation of the connective tissue of the leg following childbirth.

    p. cerulea dolens A complication of deep venous thrombosis of the iliofemoral veins, in which the entire limb distal to the clot becomes swollen, purple, and painful.

phlegmatic (flĕg-măt′ĭk) [Gr. *phlegmatikos*] Of sluggish or dull temperament; apathetic.

phlegmon (flĕg′mŏn) [Gr. *phlegmone*, inflammation] Acute suppurative inflammation of subcutaneous connective tissue, esp. a pyogenic inflammation that spreads along fascial planes or other natural barriers.

    diffuse p. Diffuse inflammation of subcutaneous tissues with sepsis.

    gas p. Gas gangrene.

phlegmonous (flĕg′mŏn-ŭs) Pert. to inflammation of subcutaneous tissues.

Phleum pratense (flē′ŭm prā-ten′sē) SEE: *timothy grass*.

phlorhizin, phlorizin, phloridzin (flōr′ĭ-zĭn, flŏ-rīz′ĭn, flōr′ĭd-zĭn, flŏ-rid′zĭn) [Gr. *phloios, phloos*, bark + *rhizo-* + *-in*] A glycoside present in the bark of some fruit trees. It is a powerful inhibitor of sugar transport in some animals.

phlyctenular (flĭk-tĕn′ū-lăr) Pert. to or resembling vesicles or pustules.

phobia (fō′bē-ă) [Gr. *phobos*, fear] Any persistent and irrational fear of a specific object, activity, or situation that results in a compelling desire to avoid the feared stimulus. SEE: *Nursing Diagnoses Appendix; Phobias Appendix*.

    social p. Persistent irrational fear of, and the need to avoid, any situation in which one might be exposed to potentially embarrassing or humiliating scrutiny by others. Even the anticipation of a phobia-producing situation, such as speaking or eating in public, socializing, or using a public toilet, may cause anxiety or terror. Cognitive therapies, desensitization, relaxation therapy, selective serotonin-reuptake inhibitors, and beta-blocking drugs such as atenolol are used to treat this condition.

-phobia [Gr. *phobia*, fear] Suffix meaning *fear, aversion*.

phobic (fō′bĭk) [Gr. *phobos*, fear] Concerning a phobia.

phocomelia (fō″kō-mē′lē-ă) [Gr. *phoke*, seal, + *melos*, limb] A congenital malformation in which the proximal portions of the extremities are poorly developed or absent. Thus the hands and feet are attached to the trunk directly or by means of a poorly formed bone. In some cases this condition was due to the pregnant woman taking thalidomide, a sleeping pill, during early pregnancy. That drug is no longer approved for such use. SYN: *amelia*.

phon (fon) [Gr. *phōnē*, voice, sound] A unit of measure of perceived loudness.

phonal (fō′năl) [Gr. *phone*, voice] Concerning the voice.

phonation (fō-nā′shŭn) The production of sounds used in speech.

phone (fōn) [Gr. *phone*, voice] A single speech sound.

    cell p., cellular phone A portable telephone, used, for example, in ambulance-to-hospital communications and in 12-lead electrocardiogram transmission in some emergency medical systems. Although many people speculate that cellular phone use may increase the risk of brain cancers (e.g., gliomas or meningiomas), no correlation between moderate usage and cancer has been definitively identified.

phoneme (fō′nēm) [Gr. *phonema*, an utterance] In linguistics, the smallest unit of speech that distinguishes one sound from another.

phonetics (fō-net′iks) [Gr. *phōnētikos*, vocal, spoken] The study of the production (pronunciation) and reception (hearing) of speech sounds. SEE: *phonology*.

-phonia, -phony [Gr. *-phōnia*, fr. *phōnē*, sound of the voice, voice, speech] Suffixes meaning *speech* (for a speech disorder of a specific kind, esp. of phonation, e.g., *egophony, tragophony*).

phoniatrics (fō″nē-ăt′rĭks) [Gr. *phone*, voice, + *iatrikos*, treatment] The study of the voice and treatment of its disorders.

phonic (fŏ'nĭk) Pert. to the voice or sound.

phono-, phon- [Gr. *phonē*, voice] Prefixes meaning *sound, voice.*

phonocardiogram (fō"nō-kăr'dē-ō-grăm) [" + *kardia*, heart, + *gramma*, something written] A graphic recording of the heart sounds.

phonocardiography (fō"nō-kăr"dē-ŏg'ră-fē) [" + " + *graphein*, to write] The mechanical or electronic registration of heart sounds.

phonogram (fō'nō-grăm) [" + *gramma*, something written] A graphic curve indicating the intensity and duration of a sound.

phonograph (fō'nō-grăf) [" + *graphein*, to write] An instrument used for the reproduction of sounds recorded on vinyl.

phonology (fŏ-nol'ŏ-jē) [*phono-* + *-logy*] The study of the speech sounds of a particular language at a particular time or place, e.g., 17th-century Mexican Spanish. SEE: *phonetics.*

phonophobia (fō"nō-fō'bē-ă) [" + *phobos*, fear] **1.** A morbid fear of sound or noise. **2.** A fear of speaking or hearing one's own voice.

phonophoresis (fō-nō-fŏr-ē'sĭs) The use of ultrasound to introduce medication into a tissue. This has been used in treating injuries to soft tissues. Not all medicines are suitable for application using this technique.

⚠️ The use of phonophoresis should be supervised by persons skilled in using the technique.

-phore, -phor [L. *-phorus*, fr Gr. *-phoros*, bearing] Suffixes meaning *bearer of*, e.g., *chromatophore, conidiophore.*

-phoresis [Gr. *phorēsis*, being borne] Suffix meaning *transmission.*

-phoria [Gr. *-phoros*, a carrying + *-ia*] In ophthalmology, a suffix meaning *a turning*, with reference to the visual axis, e.g., *cyclophoria.*

Phormia (for'mē-ă) A genus of blowflies belonging to the family Calliphoridae. Their larvae normally live in decaying flesh of dead animals, but they may infest neglected wounds or sores, causing myiasis. SEE: *blowfly; myiasis.*

phoropter (fŏ-rop'tĕr) In optometry, an instrument with multiple lenses to measure the refractive ability of the eye and aid in the prescription of appropriate corrective lenses.

phose (fōz) [Gr. *phos*, light] A subjective sensation of light or color. SEE: *chromophose; .*

phosgene (fŏs'jēn) [" + *genes*, born] Carbonyl chloride, $COCl_2$, a poisonous gas that causes nausea and suffocation when inhaled; used in chemical warfare.

phosphagen (fŏs'fă-jĕn) Several chemicals, including phosphocreatine, that re-

lease energy when split. They are high-energy phosphate compounds.

phosphatase (fos'fă-tās") [*phosphate* + *-ase*] One of a group of enzymes that catalyze the hydrolysis of phosphoric acid esters. They are of importance in absorption and metabolism of carbohydrates, nucleotides, and phospholipids and are essential in the calcification of bone.

    acid p. A phosphatase whose optimum pH is between 4.0 and 5.4. It is present in kidney, semen, serum, and prostate gland, and particularly in osteoclasts or odontoclasts in which it is associated with demineralization or resorption of bone and teeth.

    alkaline p. ABBR: ALP. An enzyme whose optimal pH is about 9.8. It is present in the liver, kidneys, intestines, teeth, plasma, and developing bone. Alkaline phosphatase levels greater than 300% of normal usually signify cholestatic disorders like obstructive jaundice or intrahepatic biliary disease.

    CDc25 p. A group of intracellular enzymes that regulate cell division, some of which may contribute to the conversion of normal cells to cancer cells.

    placental alkaline p. ABBR: PLAP. A form of heat-stable alkaline phosphatase released by trophoblast cells in the human placenta, i.e. during pregnancy. Cancers of colon, lung, ovary, and testes, esp. seminoma, produce the enzyme ectopically.

phosphate (fos'fāt") [*phosph(orus)* + *-ate*] Any salt of phosphoric acid containing the radical PO_4. Phosphates are important in the maintenance of the acid-base balance of the blood, the principal ones being monosodium and disodium phosphate. The former is acid, the latter alkaline. In the blood, because of their low concentration, they exert a minor buffering action.

    acid p. A phosphate in which only one or two hydrogen atoms of phosphoric acid have been replaced by a metal. SYN: *superphosphate.*

    calcium p. Any one of three salts of calcium and phosphate; used as an antacid and dietary supplement.

    creatine p. Phosphocreatine.

    triple p. Calcium, ammonium, and magnesium phosphate.

phosphate-bond energy SEE: under *energy.*

phosphatemia (fŏs"fă-tē'mē-ă) [Gr. *phosphas*, phosphate, + *haima*, blood] Phosphates in the blood.

phosphatide (fŏs'fă-tīd) Phospholipid.

phosphatidylcholine (fŏs-fă-tī'dăl-kō'lĭn, lēn) [" + "] Lecithin.

phosphatidyl glycerol (fŏs-fă-tī'dĭl) ABBR: PG. A phospholipid found in amniotic fluid, pulmonary effluent, and semen. It first appears in amniotic fluid during week 36 of pregnancy, confirms fetal gestational age, and is an accurate predictor of fetal lung maturity.

phosphaturia (fŏs″fă-tū′rē-ă) [″ + *ouron*, urine] An excessive amount of phosphates in the urine; often causing renal stones. SYN: *phosphoruria; phosphuria*.

SYMPTOMS: This condition is characterized by cloudy, opaque, alkaline, and pale urine and pearly or pink-white deposits of phosphates in standing urine.

phosphene (fŏs′fēn) [Gr. *phos*, light, + *phainein*, to show] A sensation of light caused by electrical or mechanical stimulation of the retina.

   accommodation p. Phosphene resulting from contraction of the ciliary muscles in accommodation. This is seen esp. in the dark.

phosphide (fŏs′fīd) [″ + *phorein*, to carry] A binary compound of phosphorus with an element or radical.

   aluminum p. A pesticide used to protect stored grains from insects and rodents. After exposure to water it is converted to hydrogen phosphide, a poison that inhibits cellular oxidative metabolism, esp. in metabolically active organs. It may be toxic or deadly to humans if ingested or inhaled. Its chemical formula is AlP.

   TREATMENT: There is no specific antidote. Cardiopulmonary support is given to intoxicated patients.

   hydrogen p. A poison that is released when phosphide pesticides react with water. It inhibits oxidative metabolism in cells and may be deadly if eaten or inhaled. Chemical formula is PH_3. SYN: *phosphine*.

   zinc p. A toxic pesticide that releases hydrogen phosphide after exposure to water. Its chemical formula is Zn_3P_2.

phosphine Hydrogen **phosphide**.

phosphite (fŏs′fīt) A salt of phosphoric acid.

phospho-, phosph- [Fr. *phosphorique*, phosphoric] Prefixes meaning *phosphorus*. SEE: *phosphoro-*.

phosphoamidase (fŏs″fō-ăm′ĭ-dās) An enzyme that catalyzes the conversion of phosphocreatine to creatine and orthophosphate.

phosphocholine (fŏs-fō-kō′lĭn, lēn) [Fm. *phospho(rus)* + ″] ABBR: Pcho. A choline metabolite.

phosphocreatine (fŏs″fō-krē′ă-tĭn) A compound found in muscle. It is important as an energy source, yielding phosphate and creatine in this process, and releasing energy that is used to synthesize adenosine triphosphate. SYN: *creatine phosphate.*

phosphodiesterase (fos″fō-dī-es′tĕ-rās″, -rāz″) ABBR: PDE. An enzyme critical for the breakdown of cyclic adenosine monophosphate.

phosphodiesterase inhibitor SEE: under *inhibitor.*

phosphofructokinase (fŏs″fō-frŭk″tō-kī′nās) A glycolytic enzyme that catalyzes phosphorylation of fructose-6-phosphate by adenosine triphosphate.

phosphofructokinase deficiency SEE: under *deficiency.*

phospholipase (fŏs″fō-lĭp′ās) An enzyme that catalyzes hydrolysis of a phospholipid.

phospholipid (fŏs″fō-lĭp′ĭd) [Gr. *phos*, light, + *phorein*, to carry, + *lipos*, fat] A diglyceride containing phosphorus, such as lecithin. The lipid portion of cell membranes is primarily phospholipids. SYN: *phosphatide; phospholipin.*

phospholipin (fŏs″fō-lĭp′ĭn) Phospholipid.

phosphoprotein (fŏs″fō-prō′tē-ĭn) [″ + ″ + *protos*, first] One of a group of proteins in which the protein is combined with a phosphorus-containing compound. Caseinogen and vitellin are examples. Phosphoprotein was formerly called nucleoalbumin.

phosphor (fos′fŏr, ′for″) [Fr. *phosphore*, fr L. *phosphorus*, morning star, fr Gr. *phŏsphoros*, light-bringer] A substance that in radiographic intensifying screens, fluoroscopic image intensifiers, or other image receptors converts photons of ionizing radiation into light, thereby amplifying the image.

   rare-earth p. An element such as yttrium, gadolinium, or lanthanum, used for ultra-high-speed radiographic intensification screens.

phosphorated (fŏs″fō-rā″tĕd) [″ + *phorein*, to carry] Impregnated with phosphorus.

phosphorescence (fŏs-fō-rĕs′ĕns) The induced luminescence that persists after cessation of the irradiation that caused it; the emission of light without appreciable heat.

phosphoribosyltransferase (fŏs″fō-rī″bō-sĭl-trăns′fĕr-ās) An enzyme that catalyzes reconversion to the ribonucleotide stage of the purine bases, hypoxanthine and guanine. The deficiency of this enzyme is inherited as an X-linked trait.

phosphoro-, phosphor- [L. *phosphorus*, morning star, fr. Gr. *phŏsphoros*, light-bearing] Prefixes meaning *phosphorus*. SEE: *phospho-.*

phosphorolysis (fŏs″fō-rŏl′ĭ-sĭs) The chemical reaction of incorporating phosphoric acid into a molecule.

phosphorous acid (fos′flŏ-)rŭs, fosfŏr′ŭs) SEE: under *acid.*

phosphorus (fos′fō-rŭs) [L. *phosphorus*, morning star, fr Gr. *phŏsphoros*, light-bringer] SYMB: P. A nonmetallic chemical element, atomic weight (mass) 30.9738; atomic number 15, not found in a free state but in combination with oxygen and cations such as calcium, sodium, and potassium. The normal serum value of phosphorus is 2.5 to 4.5 mg/dL. Normally, plasma concentrations of phosphorus and calcium have a reciprocal relationship: as one increases, the other decreases.

The adult body contains from 600 to 900 g of phosphorus in various forms: 70% to 80% in bones and teeth, principally combined with calcium; 10% in muscle; and 1% in nerve tissue. Minimum daily requirement is approx. 800 mg. This amount should be increased during pregnancy and lactation. Vitamin D is important in the absorption and metabolism of phosphorus. Excess phosphorus is excreted by the kidneys and intestines, about 60% being excreted in urine principally as phosphates. Phosphorus deficiency is characterized by impaired appetite, weight loss, retarded growth, weakness, and malformation of bones and teeth. Bony malformation resulting from disorders of phosphorus metabolism is known either as rickets or osteomalacia.

Phosphorus compounds are found in the nucleic acids DNA and RNA; in adenosine triphosphate, the principal energy source in cells; and in phosphocreatine, a secondary energy source for muscle contraction.

ETIOLOGY: Deficiencies or excesses of serum phosphorus are caused most often by abnormalities in the excretion of phosphorus by the kidneys.

SOURCES: Phosphorus is found in many foods. Excellent sources are almonds, beans, barley, bran, cheese, cocoa, chocolate, eggs, lentils, liver, milk, oatmeal, peanuts, peas, rye, walnuts, and whole wheat. Good sources are asparagus, beef, cabbage, carrots, celery, cauliflower, chard, chicken, clams, corn, cream, cucumbers, eggplant, fish, figs, meat, prunes, pineapples, pumpkin, raisins, and string beans.

phosphoryl (fŏs′for-ĭl) The radical [PO]⁻.

phosphorylase (fŏs-for′ĭ-lās) An enzyme that catalyzes the formation of glucose-1-phosphate from glycogen.

phosphorylation (fŏs″for-ĭ-lā′shŭn) The combining of a phosphate with an organic compound.

phot (fōt) [Gr. *photos*, light] ABBR: ph. The unit of photochemical energy equal to 1 lumen/cm² or about 929 foot-candles.

photic (fōt′ik) [*phot-* + *-ic*] **1.** Pert. to light. **2.** In biology, pert. to the production of light by certain organisms.

photic driving Exposing a subject to flashing lights during an electroencephalographic (EEG) recording.

photo-, phot- [Gr. *phōs*, stem *phōt-*, light] Prefixes meaning *light.*

photoaging Skin damage as a result of exposure to ultraviolet rays. SYN: *dermatoheliosis.*

photoallergy (fō″tō-ăl′ĕr-jē) [Gr. *photos*, light, + *allos*, other, + *ergon*, work] A contact dermatitis produced by the interaction between ultraviolet light rays and topically applied chemicals such as sunscreens, perfumes, phenothiazines, sulfonamides, and some components in soaps. Sunlight changes the structure of these chemicals, causing them to become allergens. An eczematous rash results. Avoiding the inciting agent is preventive; topical corticosteroid drugs provide relief from the rash. SEE: *persistent light reaction; photosensitivity; phototoxic.*

photoautotrophic (fō″tō-aw″tō-trŏf′ĭk) [″ + ″] Capable of synthesizing nutrients from light and inorganic chemicals. Said of certain microorganisms, such as bacteria that contain chlorophyll.

Photobacterium damsela (fō″tō-băk-tēr′ē-ŭm dăm′sĕl-ă) [″ + ″] A gram-negative bacillus formerly classified in the genus *Vibrio*. It is a cause of fulminant wound infections.

photobiology (fō″tō-bī-ŏl′ō-jē) [″ + *bios*, life, + *logos*, word, reason] The study of the effect of light on living things.

photobiomodulation (fōt″ō-bī″ō-moj″ŭ-lā′shŏn) [*photo-* + *bio-* + *modulation*] Low level laser therapy.

photocarcinogenesis (fō-tō-căr-sĭn-ō-jĕn′ĕ-sīs) Malignant skin damage caused by exposure to ultraviolet rays.

photochemistry (fō″tō-kĕm′ĭs-trē) [″ + *chemeia*, chemistry] The branch of chemistry concerned with the effects of light rays.

photochemotherapy (fō-tō-kē-mō-thĕr′ă-pē) The use of light and chemicals together to treat certain conditions, such as psoriasis or cutaneous T cell lymphoma.

   extracorporeal p. The exposure of blood that is temporarily removed from the body to ultraviolet A radiation. This is used to treat several diseases, including pemphigus vulgaris and cutaneous T cell lymphoma.

⚠️ Patients exposed to photosensitizing agents, such as psoralens in conjunction with ultraviolet light, have an increased risk of melanoma and squamous cell carcinoma. They should be examined regularly so that any developing skin cancers will be detected early.

photochromogen (fō-tō-krō′mō-jĕn) [″ + *chroma*, color, + *gennan*, to produce] Certain microorganisms in which a pigment develops when it is grown in the presence of light, such as *Mycobacterium kansasii.*

photocoagulation (fōt″ō-kō-ag″yŭ-lā′shŏn) [*photo-* + *coagulation*] The use of intense light or laser to burn or destroy tissue under direct observation; used for treatment of diabetic retinopathy and glaucoma. SYN: *scatter p.*

grid laser p., laser grid photocoagulation A treatment for macular edema in which tiny burns are made in the pigment epithelium of the macula of the eye, while taking care to avoid the fovea. The burns are made with a laser along precise vertical and horizontal lines.

panretinal p. ABBR: PRP. The use of high-intensity light or laser to create hundreds of tiny retinal burns outside of the vascular arcades. This treatment has been shown to produce regression of abnormal blood vessels in patients with proliferative retinopathy from diabetes or retinal vein occlusion. SYN: *scatter p.*

scatter p. 1. Photocoagulation. **2.** Panretinal **p.**

photodermatitis (fō″tō-dĕr-mă-tī′tĭs) [″ + *dermatitis*] Sensitivity of the skin to light due to photoallergy or to phototoxic reaction.

photodynamic (fōt″ō-dī-nam′ĭk) [*phot-* + *dynamic*] Pert. to the effects of light on biological, chemical, or physical systems.

photodynamic therapy 1. In ophthalmology, the use of laser-activated photosensitizing drugs to treat a variety of tumors and nonmalignant conditions such as exudative age-related macular degeneration. **2.** A method of treating cancer by using light-absorbing chemicals that are selectively retained by malignant cells. When these cells are exposed to light in the visible range, the cancer cells are killed. SYN: *photoradiotherapy.*

photoelectric effect (fō″tō-ē-lĕk′trĭk) An interaction between x-rays and matter in which the x-ray photon ejects an inner-shell electron, causing a cascade of outer-shell electrons to fill the hole. The changing of energy shells releases secondary radiation equal to the difference in the binding energies. This absorption reaction increases the patient dose and creates contrast on the radiographic film. It usually occurs at low photon energies.

photoelectricity (fō″tō-ē-lĕk-trī′sĭ-tē) [″ + *elektron,* amber] Electricity formed by the action of light.

photoelectron (fō″tō-ē-lĕk′trŏn) [″ + *elektron,* amber] An electron that is ejected from its orbit around the nucleus of an atom by interaction with a photon of energy (light, x-radiation, and so on).

photofluorography (fō″tō-flū″ĕr-ŏg′ră-fē) Photographing the images seen during fluoroscopic examination.

photogenic, photogenous (fōt″ō-jen′ik, fō-tŏj′ĕ-nŭs) Induced by, or inducing, light.

photokinetic (fō″tō-kĭn-ĕt′ĭk) [″ + *kinetikos,* motion] Reacting with motion to stimulation by light.

photolabile (fō-tō-lā′bĭl) The characteristic of being destroyed or inactivated by light.

photoluminescence (fō″tō-lū-mĭ-nĕs′ĕns) [″ + L. *lumen,* light] The power of an object to become luminescent when acted on by light.

photolysis (fō-tŏl′ĭ-sĭs) [″ + *lysis,* dissolution] Dissolution or disintegration under stimulus of light rays.

photomedicine (fō″tō-mĕd′ĭ-sĭn) [″ + ″] The use of light to treat certain conditions. SEE: *hemolytic disease of the newborn; phototherapy; psoriasis.*

photometer (fō-tom′ĕt-ĕr) [*photo-* + *-meter*] A device for measuring the intensity of light.

reflectance p. An instrument used to measure reflectance. It is used clinically in some chemical analyzers, glucometers, and dipstick readers.

photometry (fō-tŏm′ĕ-trē) Measurement of light rays.

photomicrograph (fō″tō-mī′krō-grăf) [″ + *mikros,* small, + *graphein,* to write] A photograph of an object under a microscope.

photomultiplier tube (fō″tō-mŭl′tĭ-plī″ĕr) ABBR: PMT. In radiography, an electronic vacuum tube designed to convert light photons into electrical pulses. It is used to digitize incoming light photons prior to the creation of computerized images in nuclear medicine and other imaging modalities.

photon (fō′tŏn) [Gr. *photos,* light] A light quantum or unit of energy of a light ray or other form of radiant energy. It is generally considered to be a discrete particle having zero mass, no electric charge, and indefinitely long life.

photo-onycholysis (fō-tō-ŏ-nĭ-kō-lī′sĭs) Separation of the nail from the distal nailbed in conjunction with sun exposure and simultaneous use of drugs such as antibiotics.

photopatch testing (fō′tō-păch″) A test used to identify allergic reactions triggered by ultraviolet (UV) light (specifically, to UVA).

PATIENT CARE: Two equivalent samples of the putative allergen are prepared. Each is applied to one side of the upper back of the patient. One side is shielded from exposure to ultraviolet light, and the other is treated with UVA at standardized doses and intervals. The reactions of the skin on either side are compared.

photoperceptive (fō″tō-pĕr-sĕp′tĭv) [″ + L. *percipere,* to receive] Capable of perceiving light.

photoperiod (fō″tō-pĕr′ē-ŏd) [″ + L. *periodus,* period] The daily duration of exposure to light of a living thing.

photoperiodism (fō″tō-pĕr′ē-ō-dĭzm) [″ + ″ + Gr. *-ismos,* condition] The periodic occurrence of biological phenomena in relationship to the presence or absence of light. In most animals, the sleep-wake cycle is a form of photoperiodism.

photophilic (fō-tō-fīl′ĭk) [″ + *philein,* to love] Seeking, or fond of, light.

photophobia (fō″tō-fō′bē-ă) [″ + *phobos,* fear] Unusual intolerance of light, occurring in measles, rubella, meningitis, and inflammation of the eyes. SYN: *photodysphoria.*

photophoresis (fō-tō-fŏr-ē′sĭs) A technique used in treating cutaneous T-cell lymphoma. It incorporates exposure of a lymphocyte-enriched blood fraction, obtained by use of apheresis to ultraviolet A light after the patient has ingested the cytotoxic agent 8-methoxypsoralen. SYN: *extracorporeal photochemotherapy.*

photopsia, photopsy (fō-top′sē-ă, fō-top′sē) [Gr. *photos,* light, + *opsis,* vision] The subjective sensation of sparks or flashes of light in retinal, optic, or brain diseases.

photoreaction (fō″tō-rē-ăk′shŭn) [″ + LL. *reactus,* reacted] A chemical reaction produced or influenced by light.

photoreactivation (fō″tō-rē-ăk″tĭ-vā′shŭn) Enzymatic repair of lesions such as can be produced in DNA by ultraviolet light.

photoreception (fō″tō-rē-sĕp′shŭn) [″ + L. *recipere,* to receive] The perception of light rays in the visible light spectrum.

photoreceptor (fō″tō-rē-sĕp′tor) Sensory nerve endings or cells that are capable of being stimulated by light. In humans, these include the rods and cones of the retina.

photorejuvenation (fō″tō-rē-jū-vĕ-nā′shun) [Gr. *photos,* light, + L. *re,* again, + *juvenis,* young] The cosmetic repair of skin damaged by sunlight or other ultraviolet radiation. It may involve dermabrasion, chemical peels, or pulsed-light therapy.

photoscan (fō′tō-skăn″) A representation of the concentration of a radioisotope outlining an organ in the body. The map is printed on photographic paper. SEE: *scintiscan.*

photosensitivity (fō″tō-sĕn″sī-tĭv′ĭ-tē) [″ + ″] Sensitivity to light either because of an autoimmune illness (e.g., systemic lupus erythematosus), or because of the use or application of sensitizing drugs or chemicals.

DRUG-INDUCED PHOTOSENSITIVITY: Individuals using certain drugs or other chemicals may develop dermatitis or sunburn after exposure to light of an intensity or duration than normally would not have affected them. These phototoxic reactions result from interaction between ultraviolet light and chemicals contained in the drug, but are not mediated by the immune system. Agents associated with photosensitizing reactions include coal tar derivatives found in perfumes and dyes, antiemetics, estrogens and progestins, psoralens, sulfonamides, sulfonylureas (oral hypoglycemic agents), thiazide diuretics, and tetracyclines. Persons known to have increased sensitivity to light caused by the medications they are taking should avoid exposure to sunlight or, when in the sun, should use sunscreens or clothing to cover exposed areas of the skin. SEE: *photoallergy.*

photosensitization (fŏt″ō-sen″sĭt-ĭ-zā′shŏn) [*photo-* + *sensitization*] A condition in which the skin reacts abnormally to light, esp. ultraviolet radiations or sunlight. The skin may burn easily, become itchy, or change color dramatically. It is frequently caused by drugs, foods, hormones, heavy metals, or exposure to natural oils or dusts. SEE: *photoallergy.*

photosensitizer (fō″tō-sĕn′sĭ-tī″zĕr) A substance that, in combination with light, will cause a sensitivity reaction in the substance or organism.

photosensor (fō″tō-sĕn″sĕr) A device that detects light.

photostable (fō″tō-stā″b′l) [″ + L. *stabilis,* stable] Uninfluenced by exposure to light.

photosynthesis (fō″tō-sĭn′thĕ-sĭs) [″ + *synthesis,* placing together] The process by which plants manufacture carbohydrates and oxygen by combining carbon dioxide and water, using light energy in the presence of chlorophyll.

phototaxis (fō″tō-tăk′sĭs) [Gr. *photos,* light, + *taxis,* arrangement] The reaction and movement of cells and microorganisms under the stimulus of light.

phototest (fō′tō-tĕst″) The use of controlled exposures to ultraviolet light (and ambient or polychromatic light) to determine the cause, or presence of, a rash, thought to be triggered by sunlight exposure.

phototherapy (fō″tō-thĕr′ă-pē) [″ + *therapeia,* treatment] Exposure to sunlight or to ultraviolet (UV) light for therapeutic purposes. One example of phototherapy is the treatment of neonatal jaundice, in which the jaundiced infant is exposed to UV light to decrease bilirubin levels in the bloodstream, thereby reducing the risk of bilirubin deposition in the brain. Phototherapy also is used to treat some skin diseases, including cutaneous T-cell lymphoma and psoriasis, and to relieve the symptoms of seasonal affective disorder. SYN: *light therapy.* SEE: *photodynamic therapy; seasonal affective disorder.*

⚠️ The eyes and often the gonads of treated patients are shielded from the light source to prevent them from being damaged.

photothermal (fō″tō-thĕr′măl) [″ + *therme*, heat] Pert. to heat produced by light.

photothermolysis (fō″tō″thĕr-mol′ĭ-sĭs) [*photo-* + *thermolysis*] The use of light produced by lasers to produce heat damage. **photothermolytic** (-mŏ′lit-ik), *adj.*

   fractional p. A method of laser skin resurfacing in which laser energy is directed at pinpoint, broadly separated islands of skin instead of larger swaths to remove cosmetically unappealing blemishes in skin color and texture. The technique is used to minimize the time it takes to restore normal epithelium to the treated surface. SYN: *fractional ablation.*

   selective p. The use of short pulses of light to treat skin conditions. This method causes less damage to normal tissue than do continuous beam lasers.

phototimer (fō′tō-tīm″ĕr) Automatic exposure control.

phototoxic (fōt″ō-tok′sik) [*photo-* + *toxic*] Pert. to the harmful reaction produced by light energy, esp. that produced in the skin. Simple sunburn of the skin is a kind of phototoxicity. **phototoxicity** (-tok-sis′ĭt-ē), *n.*

phototrophic (fō″tō-trŏf′ĭk) [″ + *trophe*, nutrition] Pert. to the ability to use light in metabolism.

phototropism (fō-tŏt′rō-pĭzm) [″ + *tropos*, turning, + *-ismos*, condition] A tendency exhibited by green plants and some microorganisms to turn toward or grow toward light.

-phrasia [Gr. *phrasis*, speech, enunciation + *-ia*] Suffix meaning *speech* (for a speech disorder of a specific kind, e.g., *aphrasia, polyphrasia*).

phrenectomy (frĕ-nĕk′tō-mē) [Gr. *phren*, diaphragm, + *ektome*, excision] **1.** Surgical excision of all or part of the diaphragm. **2.** Surgical resection of part of the phrenic nerve.

-phrenia [Gr. *phrēn*, diaphragm, region around the heart, seat of emotion, mind] Suffix meaning *mental disorder.*

phrenic (fren′ik) [Gr. *phrēn*, diaphragm, region around the heart, seat of emotion, mind] **1.** Pert. to the diaphragm. **2.** Pert. to the mind.

phrenicotomy (frĕn″ĭ-kŏt′ō-mē) [″ + *tome*, incision] Cutting of the phrenic nerve to immobilize a lung by inducing paralysis of one side. This causes the diaphragm to rise, compressing the lung and diminishing respiratory movement, thus resting the lung on that side.

phreno-, phren-, phreni- [Gr. *phrēn*, diaphragm, region around the heart, seat of emotion, mind] **1.** Prefixes meaning *mind.* **2.** Prefixes meaning *diaphragm.*

phrynoderma (frī″nō-dĕr′mă) [Gr. *phrynē*, toad + *derma*] Toad skin.

phthalates (thăl′ātes) Chemical compounds used to improve the flexibility of plastics. In health care, phthalates are used in devices such as intravenous tubing. They are also used in numerous consumer goods, including nail polish, soaps, shampoos, and vinyl, among many others. Some evidence suggests these compounds may have carcinogenic, endocrine disruptive, or other toxic effects on adults or the developing fetus.

Phthirus (thĭr′ŭs) [Gr. *phtheir*, louse] A genus of sucking lice belonging to the order Anoplura.

   P. pubis The crab louse. It infests primarily the pubic region but it may also be found in armpits, beard, eyebrows, and eyelashes. SEE: *pediculosis pubis.*

phthisis A wasting illness.

   p. bulbi The wasting of ocular tissue.

phyco-, phyc- [Gr. *phykos*, seaweed] Prefixes meaning *seaweed.* or *algae.*

phycology (fī-kŏl′ō-jē) [Gr. *phykos*, seaweed, + *logos*, word, reason] The study of algae.

phycotoxin (fī″kō-tŏk′sĭn) [″ + ″] Any natural poison produced by algae, e.g., marine phytoplankton. Examples of phycotoxins include okadaic acid, domoic acid, and yessotoxin.

phylactic (fī-lăk′tĭk) [Gr. *phylaktikos*, preservative] Pert. to or producing phylaxis.

phylaxis (fī-lăk′sĭs) [Gr., protection] The active defense of the body against infection.

phyletic (fī-lĕt′ĭk) [Gr. *phyletikos*] Phylogenetic.

phylloquinone (fĭl″ō-kwĭn′ōn) Vitamin K1

phylogenesis (fī″lō-jĕn′ĕ-sĭs) [Gr. *phyle*, tribe, + *genesis*, generation, birth] The evolutionary development of a group, race, or species. SEE: *phylogeny.*

phylogenetic (fī″lō-jĕ-nĕt′ĭk) Pert. to the development of a race or phylum. SYN: *phyletic.*

phylogeny (fī-lŏj′ĕ-nē) The family tree of an organism, going back enough generations to include predecessors that differed significantly.

phylum (fī′lŭm) *pl.* **phyla** [Gr. *phylon*, tribe] In taxonomy, one of the primary divisions of a kingdom, one division higher than a class.

physaliphorous (fĭs″ă-lĭf′ō-rŭs) Pert. to a highly vacuolated cell present in a chordoma.

physalis (fĭs′ă-lĭs) [Gr. *physallis*, bubble] A large vacuole present in the cell of certain malignancies such as a chondroma.

Physaloptera (fĭs″ă-lŏp′tĕr-ă) [″ + *pteron*, wing] A genus of nematode worms belonging to the suborder Spirurata.

   P. caucasica A species that occurs in and damages the upper gastrointestinal tract.

physiatrist (fĭz″ē-ăt′rĭst) A physician who specializes in physical medicine.

physiatry (fiz-ī′ă-trē) Physical **medicine**.

physic (fĭz′ĭk) [Gr. *physikos*, natural] **1.** An obsolete term for medicine and healing. **2.** An obsolete term for a medicine, esp. a cathartic.

physical (fĭz′ĭ-kăl) [L. *physicalis*, pert. to medicine] **1.** Pert. to nature or material things. **2.** Pert. to the body; bodily. **3.** Pert. to the science of physics.

physical activity and exercise A general term for any sort of muscular effort but esp. that intended to train, condition, or increase flexibility of the muscular and skeletal systems of the body.

physical mobility, impaired A limitation in independent, purposeful physical movement of the body or of one or more extremities. SEE: *Nursing Diagnoses Appendix.*

physical therapist ABBR: PT. A licensed practitioner of physical therapy who has graduated from an accredited physical therapy education program.

physical therapist assistant ABBR: PTA. A graduate of an accredited physical therapist assistant education program. The physical therapist assistant is a paraprofessional who assists the physical therapist, providing selected interventions under the direction and supervision of the physical therapist.

physical therapy A profession that is responsible for management of the patient's movement system. This includes conducting an examination; alleviating impairments and functional limitation; preventing injury, impairment, functional limitation, and disability; and engaging in consultation, education, and research. Direct interventions include the appropriate use of patient education, therapeutic exercise, and physical agents such massage, thermal modalities, hydrotherapy, and electricity. SYN: *physiotherapy.*

physical therapy diagnosis SEE: under *diagnosis.*

physician (fĭ-zish′ŏn) [*physic* (2)] One who has successfully completed the prescribed course of studies in medicine in a medical school officially recognized by the country in which it is located and has acquired the requisite qualifications for licensure in the practice of medicine.

    attending p. A physician who is on the staff of a hospital and regularly cares for patients therein. SEE: *following p.*

    family p. SEE: *primary care p.*

    primary care p. ABBR: PCP. A physician to whom a family or individual goes initially when ill or for a periodic health check. This physician assumes medical coordination of care with other physicians for the patient with multiple health concerns. A related term, primary care provider, includes both physicians and mid-level practitioners. SYN: *family p.*

    resident p. A physician who works full or part time in a hospital to continue training after internship; commonly called a resident.

physician assistant ABBR: PA. A specially trained and licensed individual who performs tasks usually done by physicians and works under the direction of a supervising physician. The PA training programs are accredited by the American Medical Association. All states require PAs to pass the certification examination of the National Commission on Certification of Physician Assistants.

physician orders for life-sustaining therapy ABBR: POLST. A part of a patient's health record that specifies his or her preferences regarding end-of-life care, specifically directives regarding life support, the use of antibiotics, artificial feeding, and medically administered hydration.

Physicians′ Desk Reference ABBR: PDR. An annual compendium of information concerning drugs, primarily prescription and diagnostic products. The information is largely that included by the manufacturer in the labeling or package insert as required by the Food and Drug Administration: indications for use, effects, dosages, administration, warnings, hazards, contraindications, drug interactions, side effects, and precautions.

physician shortage area A geographic region with an inadequate supply of physicians, usually one where more than 400 people live for each physician in residence.

physicist (fĭz′ĭ-sĭst) [L. *physics*, natural sciences] A specialist in the science of physics.

physico- [Gr. *physikos*, fr. *physis*, nature] Prefix meaning *physical, natural.*

physicochemical (fĭz″ĭ-kō-kĕm′ĭ-kăl) [″ + *chemeia*, chemistry] Pert. to the application of the laws of physics to chemical reactions.

physics (fĭz′ĭks) [Gr. *physis*, nature] The study of the laws of matter and their interactions with energy. Included are the fields of acoustics, optics, mechanics, electricity, thermodynamics, and ionizing radiation.

physio-, physi- [Gr. *physis*, nature] Prefixes meaning *nature, physical,* or *physiological.*

physiochemical (fĭz″ē-ō-kĕm′ĭ-kăl) [Gr. *physis*, nature, + *chemeia*, chemistry] Pert. to clinical chemistry.

physiognomy (fĭz″ē-ŏg′nō-mē) [Gr. *physis*, nature, + *gnomon*, a judge] **1.** The countenance. **2.** Assumed ability to diagnose a disease or illness based on the appearance and expression(s) on the face.

physiological, physiologic (fĭz″ē-ŏ-lŏj′ĭ-kăl, fĭz″ē-ŏ-lŏj′ĭk) [*physiology* + *-ic*] **1.** Pert. to physiology. **2.** Pert. to normal, healthy body function. **physiologically** (fĭz″ē-ŏ-lŏj′ĭ-k(ă)lē), *adv.*

physiologically based pharmacokinetic modeling ABBR: PBPK. A means of assessing the behavior of various chemical compounds in living organisms based upon their apparent absorption, distribution, and elimination from the body, and such in vitro characteristics as their plasma protein binding and cell membrane permeability. PBPK mathematical modeling is used in pharmacology to select promising new agents for therapeutic use, and in toxicology to estimate the potential harm that chemicals may cause when ingested by animals or released into the environment.

physiologist (fĭz″ē-ŏl′ō-jĭst) One who studies the functioning of the body.

physiology (fĭz″ē-ŏl′ō-jē) [Gr. *physis,* nature, + *logos,* study] The science of the functions of the living organism and its components and of the chemical and physical processes involved.

aviation p. The branch of physiology that deals with conditions encountered by humans in flying, mountain climbing, or space flight. The conditions studied are hypoxia, extreme temperature and radiation, effects of acceleration and deceleration, weightlessness, motion sickness, enforced inactivity, mental stress, acclimatization, and disturbance of biological rhythm.

cell p. The functioning of cells.

comparative p. The study and comparison of the physiology of different species.

general p. The broad scientific basis of physiology.

pathologic p. The physiological explanation of pathologic events.

physiopathologic (fĭz″ē-ō-păth″ō-lŏj′ĭk) [″ + *pathos,* disease, suffering, + *logos,* word, reason] **1.** Pert. to physiology and pathology. **2.** Pert. to a pathologic alteration in a normal function.

physiotherapy (fĭz″ē-ō-thĕr′ă-pē) [″ + *therapeia,* treatment] Physical therapy.

decongestive p. Physical therapy designed to mobilize localized collections of fluid, e.g., in lymphedema.

physique (fĭ-zēk′) [Fr.] Body build; the structure and organization of the body.

physo-, phys- [Gr. *physa,* bellows, bladder] Prefixes meaning *gas or air bladder.*

physostigmine salicylate (fĭ″sŏ-stig′mēn″) Eserine

phytanic acid storage disease (fĭ-tăn′ĭk) Refsum disease.

phytase (fĭ′tās) [″ + *ase,* enzyme] An enzyme found in grains and present in the kidneys; important in splitting phy-tin or phytic acid into inositol and phosphoric acid.

phytin (fĭ′tĭn) A calcium or magnesium salt of inositol and hexaphosphoric acid, present in cereals. SEE: *inositol.*

phyto-, phyt- [Gr. *phyton,* a plant] Prefixes meaning *plant.*

phytoagglutinin (fĭ″tō-ă-gloo′tĭ-nĭn) [Gr. *phyton,* plant, + L. *agglutinans,* gluing] A lectin that agglutinates red blood cells and leukocytes.

phytobezoar (fĭ″tō-bē′zor) [″ + Arabic *bazahr,* protecting against poison] A mass composed of vegetable matter found in the stomach. SYN: *food ball.* SEE: *bezoar.*

phytochemical (fĭ-tō-kĕm′ĭ-kăl) Any of the hundreds of natural chemicals present in plants. Many have nutritional value; others are protective (e.g., antioxidants) or cause cell damage (e.g., free radicals). Important phytochemicals include allyl sulfur, phytosterol, polyphenol, saponin, phenolic acids, protease inhibitors, carotenoids, capsaicin, and lignans.

phytochemistry (fĭ″tō-kĕm′ĭs-trē) [″ + *chemeia,* chemistry] The study of plant chemistry.

phytoestrogen (fĭ′tō-ĕs′trō-jĕn) Estrogen-like steroid compound found in beans, sprouts, fruits, vegetables, cereals, and some nuts. Phytoestrogens are being examined for their potential role in the management of hormone-sensitive cancers, cardiovascular disease, lipid disorders, and menopause.

phytohemagglutinin (fĭt″ō-hēm-ă-gloot′ĭ-nĭn) [″ + *haima,* blood, + *agglutinin*] ABBR: PHA. A chemical derived from red kidney beans, used in the laboratory as a mitogen, stimulating T-lymphocyte growth in cultures.

phytonutrient (fĭ″tō-nūt′rē-ĕnt) A metabolically active or nourishing substance derived from plants. Examples of phytonutrients are carotene, lutein, and lycopene.

phytopharmacology (fĭ″tō-făr″mă-kŏl′ō-jē) [″ + *pharmakon,* drug, + *logos,* word, reason] The study of drugs obtained from plants.

phytophotodermatitis (fĭ″tō-fō″tō-dĕr″mă-tī′tĭs) [″ + *photos,* light, + *derma,* skin, + *itis,* inflammation] A dermatitis produced by exposure to certain plants and then sunlight.

phytoremediation (fĭ″tō-rĕ-mēd′ē-ā′shŭn) The use of trees and plants to remove pollutants from the environment.

phytosis (fĭ-tō′sĭs) [″ + *osis,* condition] **1.** The presence of a plant parasite. **2.** A disease caused by a plant parasite.

phytosterol (fĭ-tos-tĕ-rol″, -rōl″) [*phyto-* + *sterol*] Any sterol present in vegetable oil or fat. A common phytosterol is sitosterol.

phytotherapy (fī″tō-thĕr″ă-pē) The use of plant extracts in the maintenance of health or the treatment of disease.

phytotoxin (fīt″ŏ-tok′sĭn) [*phyto-* + *toxin*] A toxin produced by or derived from a plant. SYN: *plant toxin.* SEE: *ricin.*

P&I *pneumonia and influenza; protection and indemnification.*

pI The pH at which a molecule or ion carries no net charge.

pia (pī′ă, pē′ă) [L. *pia,* loyal, pious] SEE: under *mater.*

pia-arachnoid, piarachnoid (pī″ă-ă-rak′noyd″, pē″, pī″ă-răk′noyd″, pē″) [″ + ″ + *eidos,* form, shape] **1.** Pert. to the leptomeninges. **2.** Leptomeninges.

Piaget, Jean (pē-ă-zhā′) Swiss philosopher and psychologist, 1896–1980, whose work provided understanding of how children's thinking differs from adults' and of how children learn. Concerning education, he explained, "The goal of education is not to increase the amount of knowledge but to create the possibilities for a child to invent and discover, to create men who are capable of doing new things."

pial (pī′ăl) Pert. to the pia mater.

pian (pē-an′, pyan) [Fr. *pians*] Yaws.

pica (pī′kă) [L. *pica,* magpie] An eating disorder manifested by a craving to ingest material not normally considered food, e.g., starch, clay, ashes, crayons, cotton, grass, cigarette butts, soap, wood, paper, or plaster. This condition is seen in pregnancy, chlorosis, hysteria, helminthiasis, and certain psychoses. It may also be associated with iron-deficiency anemia. The importance of this condition, whose cause is unknown, stems from the toxicity of ingested material, e.g., paint that contains lead, or from ingesting materials in place of essential nutrients. The inclusion of compulsive ingestion of nonfood and food items such as licorice, croutons, chewing gum, coffee grounds, or oyster shells as examples of pica is controversial. SYN: *perverted appetite.* SEE: *allotriophagy; geophagia; taste.*

picaridin (pĭ-kar′ĭd-ĭn) 1-methyl-propyl 2-(2-hydroxyethyl)-1-piperidinecarboxylate, an insect repellent.

PICC *peripherally inserted central venous catheter.*

pick 1. A sharp, pointed, curved dental instrument used to explore tooth surfaces and restorations for defects. **2.** To remove bits of food from teeth.

Pick, Arnold (pĭk) Czechoslovakian physician, 1851–1924.
     P. disease Dementia associated with atrophy of the frontal and/or temporal lobes of the brain. The disease has three variants: one in which affected patients develop a progressively worsening fluent aphasia; one in which aphasia is not

fluent; and one in which loss of social skills and intellectual functions, apathy, and disorientation are most prominent. SYN: *frontotemporal dementia.* SEE: *Alzheimer disease.*

Pick, Friedel (pĭk) Czechoslovakian physician, 1867–1926.
     P. disease Chronic constrictive pericarditis.

Pick, Ludwig (pĭk) German physician, 1868–1944.
     P. cell A foamy, lipid-filled cell present in the spleen and bone marrow in Niemann-Pick disease. SYN: *Niemann-Pick cell.*
     P. disease Niemann-Pick disease.

pickling 1. A method of preserving and flavoring food in which the food is soaked in a solution of salt and vinegar. **2.** The use of a chemical solution to remove scales and oxides from metals after casting or before plating them.

pickup (pĭk′ŭp″) A colloquial term for forceps.

pickwickian syndrome (pĭk-wĭk′ē-ăn) [Inspired by Joe, an obese character in Pickwick Papers by Charles Dickens.] Obesity, decreased pulmonary function, and polycythemia.

pico- [Sp. *pico,* bit, beak] In the International System of Units (SI), a prefix meaning *one trillionth* (10^{-12}).

picocurie (pī′kō-kū-rē) ABBR: pCi. An amount of radiation equal to 10^{-12} curies. SEE: *becquerel.*

picogram (pē′kō-gram″, kŏ-) [*pico-* + *gram*] ABBR: pg. 1×10^{-12} g; colloquially, 1 trillionth of a gram.

picornavirus (pī-kor″nă-vī′rŭs) [″ + RNA, ribonucleic acid, + L. *virus,* virus] Any of a group of very small ether-resistant viruses that includes enteroviruses and rhinoviruses.

picrate (pĭk′rāt) A salt of picric acid.

picro-, picr- [Gr. *pikros,* bitter] Prefixes meaning *bitter.*

pictograph (pĭk′tō-grăf) A set of test pictures used for testing vision in children and illiterate adults.

picture archiving and communication system ABBR: PACS. Computers or networks dedicated to the storage, retrieval, distribution, and presentation of images.

PID *pelvic inflammatory disease; position-indicating device.*

piedra (pē-ā′dră) [Sp., stone] Sheath-like nodular masses in the hair of the beard and mustache from growth of either *Piedraia hortai,* which causes black piedra, or *Trichosporon beigelii,* which causes white piedra. The masses surround the hairs, which become brittle; hairs may be penetrated by fungus and thus split. SYN: *tinea nodosa.*

pierce To penetrate body tissue, usually in order to place an ornamental ring or stud on the surface of the skin.

Pierre Robin syndrome (pē-ăr′rō-băn′)

[Pierre Robin, French physician, 1867–1950] A congenital facial anomaly characterized by an unusually small jaw, cleft palate, downward displacement of the tongue, and absent gag reflex. Affected children may suffer episodes of upper airway obstruction.

Pierson syndrome (pēr'sŏn) An autosomal recessive form of nephrotic syndrome with diffuse mesangial sclerosis found in association with developmental abnormalities of the eyes, esp. microcoria.

PIE syndrome Eosinophilic **pneumonia**.

piezoelectric effect (pē-ā'zō-ē-lĕk'trĭk) In ultrasound, a change of the mechanical action of ceramic crystals into an electrical impulse and vice versa. SEE: *triboluminescence.*

piezoelectricity (pē-ā'zō-ē-lĕk-trĭs''ĭ-tē) [" + *elektron,* amber] Production of an electric current by application of pressure to certain crystals such as mica, quartz, or Rochelle salt. SEE: *triboluminescence.*

PIF *proliferation inhibiting factor.*

pigeon breeder's disease (pĭ'jŭn) Bird breeder's lung.

pigeon-toed With feet turned inward.

pigment (pĭg'mĕnt) [L. *pigmentum,* paint] Any organic coloring matter in the body. SEE: *albino; carotene; carotenoid;* words beginning with *chrom-.*

   bile p. Any of the complex, highly colored waste products of the hemoglobin of old red blood cells, found in the bile. Included are bilirubin (orange), biliverdin (green), their derivatives (urobilinogen, urobilin, bilicyanin, and bilifuscin), and stercobilin, which gives brown color to intestinal contents and feces. Van den Bergh test is used to detect the type of bilirubin in the blood serum. SYN: *hepatogenous p.*

   blood p. A pigment in blood (hemoglobin) or a derivative of it (hematin, hemin, methemoglobin, hemosiderin).

   endogenous p. A pigment produced within the human body, as melanin.

   exogenous p. A pigment produced outside the human body.

   hematogenous p. A pigment from hemoglobin of the erythrocytes.

   hepatogenous p. Bile pigment.

   respiratory p. Any pigment such as hemoglobin, myoglobin, or cytochrome that has a part in the metabolism of oxygen within the body.

   skin p. Melanin, melanoid, and carotene.

   urinary p. Urochrome and sometimes urobilin.

   uveal p. Melanin in the choroid layer of the eye, the ciliary processes, and the posterior surface of the iris. Uveal pigment absorbs light within the eyeball to prevent glare.

   visual p. A light-absorbing compound in the photoreceptor cells of the retina that converts light energy into a nerve impulse that is passed from the receptor cells to the optic nerve.

pigmentary (pĭg'mĕn-tĕr''ē) [L. *pigmentum,* paint] Pert. to or resembling a pigment.

pigmentation (pĭg''mĕn-tā'shŭn) Coloration caused by deposition of pigments. SEE: *albinism; carotenemia;* words beginning with *chrom-.*

   hematogenous p. Pigmentation produced by the collection of hemoglobin, or pigment carried to a site through the blood.

pigmented (pĭg'mĕnt-ĕd) Colored by a pigment.

pigtail (pĭg'tal'') In surgery, a coil on the end of a device such as a wire, a stent, or a catheter used to hold the device in place within a hollow organ or chamber.

pil L. *pilula,* pill, or *pilulae,* pills.

pil-, pili-, pilo- [L. *pilus,* hair] Prefixes meaning *hair.*

pila (pī'lă) *pl.* **pilae** [L., pillar] A pillarlike spicule in spongy bone.

pilar, pilary (pī'lăr, pī'lă-rē) [L. *pilaris*] Pert. to or covered with hair.

pile (pīl) [L. *pila,* a ball, a pillar] **1.** A single hemorrhoid. SEE: *hemorrhoid.* **2.** The hair. **3.** A battery for production of electricity. **4.** An apparatus for producing and regulating a nuclear chain-reaction fission process.

   sentinel p. A localized thickening of the skin at the distal end of an anal fissure. SYN: *sentinel fold; sentinel tag.*

piles (pīls) [L. *pila,* a mass] Hemorrhoids. SEE: *hemorrhoid.*

pili (pī'lē) [L. *pili,* hairs] In bacteria, filamentous appendages of which there may be hundreds on a single cell. One function of pili is to attach the bacterium to cells of the host; another is to conjugate bacteria with each other.

   p. incarnati The condition of ingrowing hair, esp. in the beard area.

   p. tactiles Sensitive or tactile hairs.

   p. torti A condition in which hairs are broken and twisted.

   p. trianguli et canaliculi A condition in which the hair shaft is triangular in cross section and often has a groove; seen in children with uncombable hair syndrome. SEE: *uncombable hair syndrome.*

piliation (pī-lē-ā'shŭn) [L. *pilus,* hair] The formation and development of hair.

piliform (pī'lĭ-form) [" + *forma,* shape] Hairlike.

pill (pil) [L. *pilula,* little ball] **1.** Medicine in the form of a tiny solid mass or pellet to be swallowed or chewed; may be coated. **2.** Birth control pill.

   birth control p. A class of medicines taken orally to control conception. They contain synthetic forms of estrogen and progesterone or synthetic progesterone alone. SEE: *contraceptive.*

   morning-after p. A pill containing

estrogen, progesterone, or both that must be taken within 72 hr after intercourse to prevent pregnancy.

pep p. A colloquial term for a stimulant drug, e.g., an amphetamine.

pillar (pĭl'ĕr) [L. *pila*, a column] An upright support, column, or structure resembling a column.

p. cell One of two groups of cells (inner and outer) resting on the basement membrane of the organ of Corti in which elongated bodies (pillars) develop. These enclose the inner tunnel (Corti tunnel).

p. of the fauces Folds of mucous membrane, one on each side of the fauces and between which is situated the palatine tonsil. The anterior pillar (in front of the tonsil) is also called the glossopalatine arch; the posterior pillar (behind the tonsil) is also called the pharyngopalatine arch.

pill burden A complex medication regimen, i.e., one that taxes a patient's adherence.

pill-induced esophagitis (pĭl'ĭn-doost') SEE: under *esophagitis*.

pillion (pĭl'yŭn) [L. *pellis*, skin] A temporary form of artificial leg, esp. a peg-leg type of stump.

pillow A postsurgical cushion or support for a body part (e.g., the head, chest, hip, or knee). Therapeutic pillows are used as buttresses or wedges to relieve stress on parts of the body that have been operated on. Chest pillows are used after sternotomy to support the chest wall and limit pain from deep breathing or coughing. Pillows placed under or between the lower extremities are often used to maintain neutral or desired alignment of joints after joint replacement surgeries.

abductor p. A pillow or cushioned wedge placed between the legs of a patient to maintain proper positioning and prevent dislocation of the hip joint. It is used in patients with some congenital disorders of the hip, other conditions in which the patient is unduly prone to hip dislocation, and following surgeries (such as total hip replacement).

piloerection (pī-lō-ē-rĕk'shŭn) Elevation of the hair above the skin as a result of contraction of the arrector pili muscles. This may occur after exposure to the cold or during adrenergic stimulation. SYN: *cutis anserina; goose flesh; horripilation*.

pilomotor (pī″lō-mō'tor) [″ + *motor*, mover] Causing movements of hairs, as the arrectores pilorum.

pilonidal (pī″lō-nī'dăl) [″ + *nidus*, nest] Containing hairs; most often seen in a dermoid cyst, esp. in the saccrococcygeal region.

pilosebaceous (pī″lō-sē-bā'shŭs) [″ + *sebaceus*, fatty] Concerning the hair and sebaceous glands.

pilot study pī'lŏt SEE: under *study*.

pilus (pī'lŭs) *pl.* **pili** [L.] A hair.

p. cuniculatus A hair that burrows into the skin.

p. incarnatus An ingrown hair.

p. tortus A twisted hair.

PI_max *maximum inspiratory pressure.* SEE: *force, maximum inspiratory*.

pimel-, pimelo [Gr. *pimelē*, soft fat, lard] Prefixes meaning *fat* or *fatty*.

pimp (pimp) A person, usually a male, who brokers sexual relationships between one or more sex workers and their customers.

pimple (pĭm'pl) A papule or pustule of the skin often seen in clusters on skin of the adolescent with acne.

pin A short, slim piece of wire, plastic, or metal. It may have one end blunt and the other sharp.

endodontic p. A straight or threaded filling that is passed through the root canal to the alveolar bone beyond the apex of the tooth root.

self-threading p. A pin screwed through a small hole into dentin.

sprue p. In dentistry, a wax, plastic, or metal pattern used to make the channel or channels through which molten metal flows into a mold to make a casting. Also called *sprue former*.

pinch A type of hand prehension. The pinch of the human hand is achieved principally through holding objects between the thumb and index finger or the index and long fingers.

Hand pinch is classified according to the anatomical parts involved, as follows:

Pinch, fingertip—pinch using the tips of strongly arched digits, primarily the thumb and index finger; used to pick up very small objects such as pins and needles.

Pinch, palmar tripod or three-jaw chuck—pinch using the palmar pads of the thumb and index and long fingers.

Pinch, lateral—pinch accomplished by clamping the palmar surface of the distal portion of the thumb against the side of the index finger.

pinched nerve A colloquial term for *nerve entrapment syndrome*.

pinch meter A device for objectively measuring the strength of hand pinch in grams or pounds.

Pindborg tumor (pind'borg″, pin'bor″) [Jens Jørgen Pindborg, Danish oral pathologist, 1921–1995] A rare tumor, typically of the jaw, consisting of malignant epithelial cells with a polyhedral shape and deposits of cementum. It is often associated with an impacted tooth. SYN: *calcifying epithelial odontogenic tumor*.

pineal (pĭn'ē-ăl) [Fr., pine cone] **1.** Shaped like a pine cone. **2.** Pert. to the pineal gland.

pineal body Pineal **gland**.

pinealectomy (pĭn″ē-ăl-ĕk′tō-mē) [L. *pineus*, of the pine, + Gr. *ektome*, excision] Removal of the pineal gland.

pinealoblastoma (pĭn″ē-ă-lō-blăs-tō′mă) [″ + Gr. *blastos*, germ, + *oma*, tumor] Pineoblastoma.

pinealocyte (pĭn′ē-ă-lō-sīt″) [″ + Gr. *kytos*, cell] The principal cell of the pineal gland. It contains pale-staining cytoplasm and has long processes that terminate in bulbous expansions.

pinealoma (pĭn″ē-ă-lō′mă) [″ + Gr. *oma*, tumor] A tumor of the pineal gland, usually encapsulated; often associated with precocious puberty.

Pinel, Philippe (pē-nĕl′) French psychologist, 1745–1826, who developed a method or system of treating the mentally ill without the use of restraint, at a time when use of restraint was the accepted form of therapy.

pineoblastoma (pĭn″ē-ō-blăs-tō′mă) [L. *pineus*, of the pine, + Gr. *blastos*, germ, + *oma*, tumor] A malignant tumor of the pineal gland that may occur in childhood and early adulthood. SYN: *pinealoblastoma*.

pineocytoma (pĭn-ē-ō-sī-tō′mă) A malignant tumor of the pineal gland of the brain.

ping-pong fracture (ping′pong″) SEE: under *fracture*.

pinguecula (pĭn-gwĕk′ū-lă) [L. *pinguiculus*, fatty] A yellow triangular thickening of the bulbar conjunctiva on the inner and outer margins of the cornea. The base of the triangle is toward the limbus. The yellow color is due to an increase in elastic fibers.

pinhole (pĭn′hōl) A small perforation made by, or the size of that made by, a pin.
　p. os A very small opening to the uterus from the vagina. It may be present in very young women.

pink disease Acrodynia.

pinkeye Inflammation of the conjunctiva, usually characterized by redness, watery discharge, lid edema, itching, and a gritty sensation. Most commonly caused by a contagious viral infection. Depending on the cause, pinkeye may be treated conservatively (e.g., with warm, moist compresses) or with antibiotics when bacteria are the cause.

pinna (pĭn′ă) *pl.* **pinnae** [L. *pinna, penna*, feather] **1.** The mostly cartilaginous, projected part of the external ear. It directs sound waves into the external acoustic meatus toward the tympanic membrane. SYN: *auricle* (1). **2.** A feather, fin, wing, or similar appendage.

pinnaplasty (pĭn′ă-plas″tē) [*pinna* + *-plasty*] Cosmetic surgery on the external ear.

pinocyte (pī′nō-sīt) [Gr. *pinein*, to drink, + *kytos*, cell] A cell that exhibits pinocytosis.

pinocytosis (pĭn″ō-sī-tō′sĭs, pīn″, -sī″) [*pinocyte* + *-osis*] The process by which cells absorb or ingest nutrients and fluid. An invaginating portion of the cell membrane encircles the nutrient, enclosing it in a membrane-bound sac. The contents of the sac are then digested.

pinosome (pī′nō-, pĭn′ō-sōm) [″ + *soma*, body] The fluid-filled vacuole formed during pinocytosis.

pinprick test A test for cutaneous pain receptors. A small, clean, sharp object such as a pin or needle is gently applied to the skin and the patient is asked to describe the sensation. One must be certain the patient is reporting the sensation of pain rather than that of pressure. Usually, application of the sharp object is interspersed with application of a dull object, and the patient is asked to state each time whether a sharp or dull sensation was felt. The patient is not, of course, allowed to observe the test procedure.

⚠ The sharp object should not penetrate the dermis, and to prevent passage of infectious material from one patient to another, the test objects should be either discarded after use or sterilized before their use on another patient.

PINS (pĭnz) *persons in need of supervision.*

pint (pīnt) ABBR: pt. In the U.S. a measure of capacity equal to ½ qt.; 16 fl. oz; 473.2 mL. SEE: *Weights and Measures Appendix.*

pinta (pēn′tă) [Sp., paint] A nonvenereal disease spread by body contact, caused by the spirochete *Treponema carateum*. It is manifested by depigmented spots or patches. The treatment is administration of penicillin.

pinwheel (pĭn′(h)wēl″) A spiked rotating instrument that is rolled along the patient's skin to gauge the ability of the patient to perceive pain or light touch. SYN: *neuro p.; Wartenberg neurological pinwheel.*
　neuro p. Pinwheel.

pinworm (pĭn′wŭrm″) Any of numerous long, slender nematode worms, esp. of the genus *Enterobius*. They parasitize humans. SEE: *Enterobius vermicularis.*

pioglitazone (pī″ ō-glīt′ ŭ-zōn″) A thiazolidinedione administered orally as an adjunct to diet and exercise for the management of type 2 diabetes mellitus. Its therapeutic class is antidiabetic (oral).

PIP *peak inspiratory pressure; proximal interphalangeal (joint)*

Piper (pī′pĕr) [L.] Genus of plants that produce pepper. The species *Piper nigrum* is a flowering vine that produces black pepper.

pipet, pipette (pī-pet′) [Fr. *pipette*, small

pipe] A narrow glass tube with both ends open for transferring and measuring liquids by suctioning them into the tube. Some are graduated through their length and can measure increments of fluid; others are graduated at one point and are intended to dispense a fixed amount; others are not graduated and are intended to simply transfer fluid or droplets of fluid.

PIQ *Performance Intelligence Quotient.*

piriform, pyriform (pĭr′ĭ-form) [L. *pirum,* pear, + *forma,* shape] Pear-shaped.

piriformis syndrome (pĭr-ē-fŏr′mĭs) A condition marked by pain in the hip and buttock that radiates up into the lower back and down the leg. In women, the pain may occur during sexual intercourse. This is caused by entrapment of the sciatic nerve as it passes through the piriformis muscle in the buttock. Because the symptoms mimic those caused by a herniated lumbar disk, the syndrome may be confused with that disease. Treatment includes physical therapy to relieve pressure, ultrasound to reduce muscle spasm, and anti-inflammatory medicines. Surgical therapy to free the entrapped nerve may be necessary. SEE: *sciatica.*

piroplasm (pī′rō-plăzm) A sporozoan protozoan of the subclass Piroplasia, such as the genus *Babesia.*

pisiform (pī′sĭ-form) [L. *pisum,* pea, + *forma,* shape] 1. Pea-shaped. 2. The smallest carpal bone, located in the flexor carpi ulnaris tendon as a sesamoid bone, on the ulnar side in the proximal row of carpals.

pit (pit) 1. A tiny hollow or pocket. SYN: *depression; fossa.* 2. To be or become marked with a shallow depression; to cause a depression on pressure in edema. 3. A small depression in the enamel surface of a tooth often connected with one or more developmental grooves. It contributes to pit and fissure caries. SYN: *occlusal p.*

   anal p. Proctodeum.

   gastric p. Any of many foveolae in the gastric mucosa into which the gastric glands open. SEE: illus.

   nasal p. In the embryo, one of two horseshoe-shaped depressions on the ventrolateral surface of the head bounded by lateral and median nasal processes. It gives rise to nostrils and a portion of the nasal fossa. SYN: *olfactory p.*

   occlusal p. Pit (3).

   olfactory p. Nasal **p.**

   optic pit A small indentation of the optic nerve head. It may sometimes release fluid below the retina, which can cause central retinal detachment.

   primitive p. A minute depression at the anterior end of the primitive groove

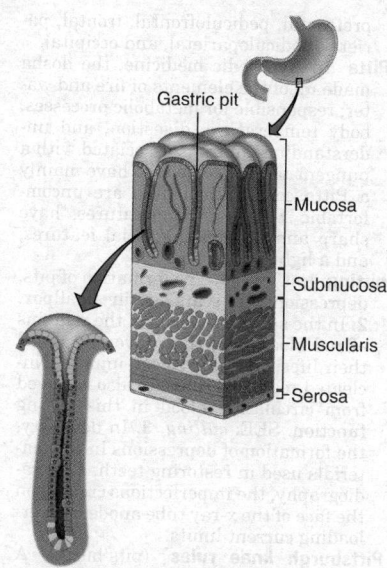

Gastric pit

Mucosa

Submucosa

Muscularis

Serosa

GASTRIC PIT

or streak and immediately posterior to the primitive knot.

   p. of the stomach 1. A colloquial term for the depression at the end of the xiphoid process. 2. A colloquial term for the center of the abdominal region above the navel.

pitch (pĭch) 1. That quality of the sensation of sound that enables one to classify it in a scale from high to low. It is dependent principally on frequency of vibrations. 2. Residue obtained from distillation of coal or wood tar. 3. In radiography, the table speed divided by the width of the x-ray beam.

pitchblende (pĭch′blĕnd) Uraninite, the principal source of uranium. It is a mineral that resembles pitch.

pith (pĭth) 1. The center of a hair or the soft material in the stalk of a plant. 2. Destruction of a part of the central nervous system of an animal being prepared for certain experiments. A blunt probe is inserted in the brain or spinal cord through a foramen.

pithing (pĭth′ĭng) Destruction of the central nervous system by the piercing of brain or spinal cord, as in vivisection. This is done on experimental animals to render them insensible to pain and to inhibit controlling effects of the central nervous system during research and experimentation. SEE: *decerebration.*

Pitres section (pē-trĕs′) [Jean A. Pitres, Fr. physician, 1848–1927] Any of the series of six coronal vertical sections of the brain for study. The sections are prefrontal, pediculofrontal, frontal, parietal, pediculoparietal, and occipital.

Pitta In Ayurvedic medicine, the dosha made up of the elements of fire and water; responsible for metabolic processes, body temperature, digestion, and understanding, and it is associated with a pungent taste. People who have mainly a Pitta constitution often are uncomfortable with hot temperatures, have sharp and penetrating facial features, and a light body frame.

pitting (pĭt′ĭng) **1.** The formation of pits, depressions, or scars, as in smallpox. **2.** In the spleen, removal of the remains of red blood cells that have completed their lifespan or have been injured. Nucleated red blood cells are also removed from circulating blood in this pitting function. SEE: *culling.* **3.** In dentistry, the formation of depressions in the materials used in restoring teeth. **4.** In radiography, the imperfections created on the face of the x-ray tube anode by overloading current limits.

Pittsburgh knee rules (pits′bŭrg″) A clinical prediction rule used to determine whether an individual requires plain x-rays to rule out a knee fracture after an acute or blunt injury. Predictive variables include a fall or blunt trauma as the mechanism of injury, inability to ambulate initially or in the ER (i.e., the inability to take four steps), or patients younger than 12 or older than 50.

pituicyte (pĭ-tū′ĭ-sīt) [L. *pituita,* phlegm, + Gr. *kytos,* cell] A modified branched neuroglia cell characteristic of pars nervosa of the posterior lobe of the pituitary gland; also present in the infundibular stalk.

pituitary (pĭ-tū′ĭ-ter″ē) [L. *pituitarius,* phlegm] The pituitary body or gland. SYN: *hypophysis.* SEE: *releasing hormone; inhibitory* **hormone;** *pituitary* **gland.**

    anterior p. 1. Adenohypophysis. **2.** A preparation of dried, defatted, powdered anterior lobe of the pituitary gland of domestic animals.

    posterior p. Neurohypophysis. **2.** The dried, powdered posterior lobe of the pituitary gland of animals used as food by humans.

pituitary body SEE: under *body.*

pituitary gland SEE: under *gland.*

pityriasis (pĭt″ĭ-rī′ă-sĭs) [Gr. *pityron,* bran, scale + *-iasis*] A skin disease characterized by scales that resemble bran.

    p. alba A form of decreased melanin in the skin marked by patches of round or oval macular skin lesions with fine adherent scales. The lesions are commonly seen in the facial areas of children. They are virtually painless and usually require no therapy. They may disappear spontaneously. The cause is

unknown, but the disease is regarded as a mild form of eczema.

    p. capitis Dandruff.

    p. lichenoides et varioliformis, acuta ABBR: PLEVA. A skin disorder characterized by development of an edematous pink papule that undergoes central vesiculation and hemorrhagic necrosis. The lesions clear spontaneously after weeks or months but leave scars.

    p. linguae Transitory benign plaques of the tongue. SYN: *geographic tongue.*

    p. nigra Tinea nigra.

    p. rosea An acute inflammatory skin disease sometimes associated with human herpes virus 6 or 7 infection, marked by a macular eruption on the trunk, obliquely to the ribs, and on the upper extremities. The initial (herald) patch appears in more than half of the cases. In a few days it enlarges to several centimeters. Then, within 2 to 21 days, secondary eruptions occur. They are rose-red and somewhat scaly with a clearing in the center, or reddish ring-shaped patches symmetrically distributed over the limbs. The symptoms disappear spontaneously within 2 to 10 weeks. Treatment consists of the local application of antipruritics.

    p. rubra pilaris Persistent general exfoliative dermatitis of unknown cause SEE: *exfoliative* **dermatitis.**

    p. versicolor Tinea versicolor.

Pityrosporum (pī″tĭ-rō-spawr′ŭm, -rŏs′pŭ-rŭm) SEE: *Malasesezia.*

pivot (pĭv′ŭt) In dentistry, a part used for attaching an artificial crown to the base of a natural tooth.

pivotal (pĭv′ŏt-ăl) **1.** Pert. to a pivot **2.** Of central importance; said, e.g., of a drug or treatment.

pixel (pĭk′sĭl, -sel) [Fr. *pix,* slang for *picture* + *el(ement)*] An individually adjustable picture element in a digital image. Variations in its size and brightness contribute to the resolution and contrast of the image.

PJC *premature junctional contraction.*

PK *psychokinesis.*

pK Abbreviation for the negative logarithm of the ionization constant (K) of an acid. The closer the pK to the pH, the greater the buffering power of the system. It is a key component value in the Henderson-Hasselbalch equation.

PKU *phenylketonuria.*

placebo (plă-sē′bō) [L. *placebo,* I shall please] **1.** An inactive substance or treatment given instead of one that has a proven effect. **2.** A drug or treatment used as a nonspecific or inactive control in a test of a therapy that is suspected of being useful for a particular disease or condition. The placebo is given to one group of patients, and the drug being tested is given to a similar group; then the results obtained in the two groups are compared. Placebos often elicit a re-

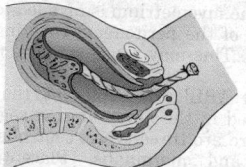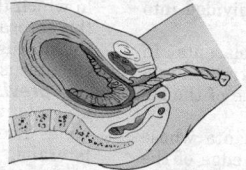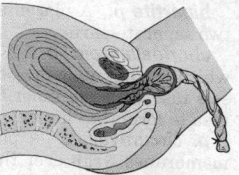

DELIVERY OF THE PLACENTA

sponse, possibly because of patient expectations that they will produce a cure or prove harmful.

⚠ Placebos are not legitimate treatments and should be prescribed and administered only under tightly controlled conditions as part of a clinical trial approved by an institutional review board (IRB). Placebos should not be used without the informed consent of the patient, i.e., an explicit understanding that a patient in a trial may receive an inactive agent. When clinical use of a placebo involves deceiving the patient, such use is unethical. Deception of a patient constitutes a failure to respect his rights to make informed decisions and undermines the element of trust that is crucial to every interaction between patient and caregiver.

placement (plăs′mĭnt) **1.** The positioning or implantation of a object, such as a catheter or stent, within or near a body part. **2.** The assignment of a patient to a particular care facility, treatment program, or level of care. **3.** The assignment of a student in a health profession to a specialized learning environment, such as a clinic, hospital, or ward, where he or she performs professional activities under supervision.

placenta (plă-sent′ă, -sent′ē″) *pl.* **placentae, placentas** [L. *placenta,* flat cake] The oval or discoid spongy structure in the uterus of eutherian mammals from which the fetus derives its nourishment and oxygen. SEE: illus. **placental** (′ăl), *adj.*

ANATOMY: The placenta consists of a fetal portion, the chorion frondosum, bearing many chorionic villi that interlock with the decidua basalis of the uterus, which constitutes the maternal portion. The chorionic villi lie in spaces in the uterine endometrium, where they are bathed in maternal blood and lymph. Groups of villi are separated by placental septa forming about 20 distinct lobules called cotyledons.

Attached to the margin of the placenta is a membrane that encloses the embryo. It is a composite of several structures (decidua parietalis, decidua capsularis, chorion laeve, and amnion).

At the center of the concave side is attached the umbilical cord through which the umbilical vessels (two arteries and one vein) pass to the fetus. The cord is approx. 50 cm (20 in) long at full term.

The mature placenta is 15 to 18 cm (6 to 7 in) in diameter and weighs about 450 gm (approx. 1 lb). When expelled following parturition, it is known as the afterbirth.

Maternal blood enters the intervillous spaces of the placenta through spiral arteries, branches of the uterine arteries. It bathes the chorionic villi and flows peripherally to the marginal sinus, which leads to uterine veins. Food molecules, oxygen, and antibodies pass into fetal blood of the villi; metabolic waste products pass from fetal blood into the mother's blood. Normally, there is no admixture of fetal and maternal blood. The placenta is also an endocrine organ. It produces chorionic gonadotropins, the presence of which in urine is the basis of one type of pregnancy test. Estrogen and progesterone are also secreted by the placenta.

abruption of p. Abruptio placentae.

accessory p. A placenta separate from the main placenta.

p. accreta A placenta in which the cotyledons have invaded the uterine musculature, resulting in difficult or impossible separation of the placenta. Complications of manually separating the placenta include hemorrhage, damage to the uterus, and, in rare cases, hysterectomy. SYN: *p. creta.*

adherent p. A placenta that remains adherent to the uterine wall after the normal period following childbirth. SEE: *p. accreta.*

annular p. A placenta that extends like a belt around the interior of the uterus. SYN: *zonary p.*

battledore p. A form of insertion of the umbilical cord into the margin of the placenta in which it spreads out to resemble a paddle or badminton racket.

bidiscoidal p. A placenta with two separate portions attached to separate sites on the wall of the uterus, occasionally found in humans.

bilobate p. A placenta consisting of two lobes. SYN: *dimidiate p.*

bipartite p. A placenta divided into two separate parts.

chorioallantoic p. A placenta in which the allantoic mesoderm and vessels fuse with the inner face of the serosa to form the chorion.

p. circumvallata A placenta whose membranes wrap over the edge of the fetal surface of the organ.

circumvallate p. P. circumvallata.

cordiform p. A placenta having a marginal indentation, giving it a heart shape.

p. creta P. accreta.

deciduate p. A placenta whose maternal part is shed with delivery.

dimidiate p. Bilobate **p.**

discoid p. A placenta with a flat, circular shape.

double p. A placental mass of the two placentae of a twin gestation.

endotheliochorial p. A placenta in which the syncytial trophoblasts of the chorion penetrate to the blood vessels of the uterus.

epitheliochorial p. A placenta in which the chorion is next to the lining of the uterus but does not invade or erode the lining.

p. fenestrata A placenta in which a portion of the placental tissue is thinning or absent.

fetal p. That part of the placenta formed by aggregation of chorionic villi in which the umbilical vein and arteries ramify.

fundal p. A placenta attached to the uterine wall within the fundal zone.

hemochorial p. A placenta in which the maternal blood is in direct contact with the chorion. The human placenta is of this type.

hemoendothelial p. A placenta in which the maternal blood is in contact with the endothelium of the chorionic vessels.

horseshoe p. A formation in which the two placentae of a twin gestation are united.

incarcerated p. A placenta retained in the uterus due to incomplete separation from the uterine wall or by irregular uterine contractions after delivery.

p. increta A form of placenta accreta in which the chorionic villi invade the myometrium.

lateral p. A placenta attached to the lateral wall of the uterus.

maternal p. A portion of the placenta that develops from the decidua basalis of the uterus.

membranous p. Thinning of the placenta from atrophy.

multilobate p. A placenta with more than three lobes.

nondeciduate p. A placenta that does not shed the maternal portion.

p. percreta A type of placenta accreta in which the myometrium is invaded to the serosa of the peritoneum covering the uterus. This may cause rupture of the uterus.

p. previa ABBR: PP. A placenta that is implanted in the lower uterine segment. There are three types: centralis, lateralis, and marginalis. Placenta previa centralis (total or complete PP) is the condition in which the placenta has been implanted in the lower uterine segment and has grown to completely cover the internal cervical os. Placenta previa lateralis (low marginal implantation) is the condition in which the placenta lies just within the lower uterine segment. Placenta previa marginalis is the condition in which the placenta partially covers the internal cervical os (partial or incomplete PP). SEE: *Nursing Diagnoses Appendix.*

SYMPTOMS: The condition is more common in multigravidas than primigravidas, and occurs in about 1 in every 200 pregnancies. Slight hemorrhage, recurrent with greater severity, appears in the seventh or eighth month of pregnancy. Gradual anemia, pallor, rapid weak pulse, air hunger, and low blood pressure occur.

DIAGNOSIS: Painless bleeding during the last 3 months and a placenta found in the lower portion of the uterus are diagnostic.

TREATMENT: The blood supply before and during delivery should be conserved. Postpartum hemorrhage should be prevented or controlled. Anemia should be treated before and after labor. Prevention of sepsis is necessary.

PROGNOSIS: The prognosis for the mother is good with control of hemorrhage and prevention of sepsis. Prognosis for the fetus depends on gestational age and the amount of blood lost, but continuous monitoring and rapid intervention help to prevent neonatal death.

PATIENT CARE: In a calm environment, the patient is told what is happening; then the procedure of vaginal ultrasound is explained. The patient is told that if the ultrasound examination reveals a placenta previa, sterile vaginal examination will be delayed if possible until after 34 weeks' (preferably 36 weeks') gestation (to enhance the chances for fetal survival) and then will be carried out only as a "double-setup" procedure, with all preparations needed for immediate vaginal or cesarean delivery. (If, however, the ultrasound examination reveals a normally implanted placenta, a sterile vaginal speculum examination is performed to rule out local bleeding causes, and a laboratory study is ordered to rule out coagulation problems.)

The patient is maintained on absolute

bedrest and under close supervision (usually in the hospital) to extend the period of gestation until 36 weeks, when fetal lung maturity is likely (or can be stimulated to mature 48 hr before delivery). Intravenous access is established using a large-bore catheter, and continuous external electrode fetal monitoring is initiated. Maternal vital signs are closely monitored, and the amount of vaginal bleeding is assessed. The laboratory types and cross-matches blood for emergency use; the number of units is based on the assessment of the particular patient's possible requirements. The patient's hematocrit level is kept at 30% or greater. The patient is prepared physically and emotionally for cesarean delivery; vaginal delivery may be attempted, but only if the previa is marginal, bleeding is minimal, and labor is rapidly progressing.

After delivery, the patient is monitored closely for continued bleeding, which may occur from the large vascular channels in the lower uterine segment, even if the fundus is firmly contracted. Prophylactic antibiotic therapy may be prescribed because of the patient's propensity for infection. Oxytocic drugs are given to control bleeding; packed cells or whole blood also are given. The obstetrical surgery team remains available, in case further intervention is required. The patient's hemodynamic status is monitored continuously, to provide blood and fluid replacement needed to prevent and treat hypovolemia while avoiding hypervolemia.

Although maternal mortality remains a concern, the patient and her family should be assured that this is unlikely but not impossible in most large treatment centers because of the conservative regimen that is followed. A pediatric team is present at delivery to assess and treat neonatal hypoxia, anemia, blood loss, and shock. In the event of fetal distress or death, the family is informed that these are related to detachment of a significant portion of the placenta or to maternal hypovolemic shock, or both. All parents are provided opportunities to be with and touch their (usually premature) neonate in the critical care nursery. In cases of fetal demise, the infant is carefully wrapped and the parents encouraged to hold their baby, and to examine it as they desire. Infant photographs may be taken to provide memories for the family. The patient and family require the health care providers' empathetic concern and support. A social serviceconsultation is set up if financial or home and family care concerns require agency referrals; spiritual counseling is supplied according to the patient's wishes. Reducing maternal anxiety helps reduce uterine irritability, and therefore a mental health practitioner should be consulted if the patient does not respond to nursing interventions (e.g., relaxation techniques, guided imagery) or if the patient's previous coping skills are known to be ineffective.

p. previa partialis A placenta that only partially covers the internal os of the uterus.

p. reflexa An abnormal placenta in which the margin is thickened and appears to turn back on itself.

reniform p. A kidney-shaped placenta.

retained p. A placenta not expelled within 30 min after completion of the second stage of labor.

p. spuria An outlying portion of the placenta that has not maintained its vascular connection with the decidua vera.

succenturiate p. An accessory placenta that has a vascular connection to the main part of the placenta.

trilobate p. A placenta with three lobes.

tripartite p. A three-lobed placenta attached to a single fetus.

triple p. A placental mass of three lobes in a triple gestation.

p. uterina The maternal part of the placenta.

velamentous p. A placenta with the umbilical cord attached to the membrane a short distance from the placenta, the vessels entering the placenta at its margin.

villous p. A placenta in which the chorion forms villi.

zonary p. Annular **p.**

placental (plă-sĕn′tăl) [L. *placenta*, a flat cake] Rel. to the placenta.

p. blood banking The use of human placental tissue as a source of fetal blood and hematopoietic stem cells.

placental site trophoblastic tumor SEE: under *tumor*.

placentation (plă″sĕn-tā′shŭn) The process of formation and attachment of the placenta.

placentitis (plă″sĕn-tī′tĭs) [″ + Gr. *itis*, inflammation] Inflammation of the placenta.

placentography (plas″ĕn-tog′ră-fē) [*placenta* + *-graphy*] Examination of the placenta by radiography.

placode (plăk′ōd) [Gr. *plax*, plate, + *eidos*, form, shape] In embryology, a platelike thickening of epithelium, usually the ectoderm, that serves as the precursor of an organ or structure.

auditory p. A dorsolateral placode located alongside the hindbrain that gives rise to the otocyst, which in turn develops into the internal ear.

lens p. A placode developing in the ectoderm directly overlying the optic vesicle. It forms the lens vesicle, which becomes enclosed in the optic cup and eventually becomes the lens of the eye.

olfactory p. A placode that first gives rise to the olfactory pit and later to the major portion of the nasal cavity.

placoid (plak'oyd") [Gr. *plax,* plate + *-oid*] Shaped like a plate.

plagio- [Gr. *plagios,* slanting, sideways] Prefix meaning *slanting, oblique.*

plagiocephaly (plă"jē-ō-sef'ă-lē) [*plagio- + -cephaly*] A malformation of the skull producing the appearance of a twisted and lopsided head, caused by irregular closure of the cranial sutures.

deformational p. Plagiocephaly on one side the skull of an infant, usually after repeatedly sleeping in a single position, e.g. on the infant's back, to prevent SIDS.

It can usually be treated nonoperatively by repositioning the developing infant frequently, or by having the child wear a protective, adjustable helmet while resting. SYN: *positional p.*

positional p. Deformational **p.**

plague (plāg) [L., *plaga,* blow, injury] **1.** Any widespread contagious disease associated with a high death rate. **2.** An often fatal disease caused by *Yersinia pestis.* The natural hosts are ground squirrels, wild rodents, and rats; the vector is the rat flea. In the U.S., hunters, trappers, and campers may encounter infected mammals. Outbreaks are also associated with crowded living conditions and poor sanitation. Although plague was responsible for millions of deaths during the Middle Ages, improvements in sanitation, medical care, and the availability of antibiotics now prevent widespread epidemics. Plague is characterized by high fever, restlessness, confusion, prostration, delirium, shock, and coma. Streptomycin (the antibiotic of choice), gentamicin, tetracyclines, doxycycline, fluoroquinolones, and chloramphenicol are effective in treating plague. In the U.S., about 15 cases of plague are reported annually , primarily in western and southwestern regions. If treated promptly, plague is rarely fatal; however, in the U.S. about 1 in 7 people infected dies, usually because of delayed diagnosis ortreatment.

ambulatory p. A mild form of bubonic plague.

black p. Plague.

bubonic p. Plague.

hemorrhagic p. A severe form of bubonic plague in which there is hemorrhage into the skin.

murine p. A plague infecting rats.

pneumonic p. A highly virulent form of plague spread from person to person by respiratory secretions. It occurs as a sequela of bubonic plague or as a primary infection.

septicemic p. Severe bubonic plague; septicemia may precede the formation of buboes.

sylvatic p. Bubonic plague that is endemic among wild rodents and their fleas.

plaintiff The person, entity, or party who sues or brings a legal action against another and seeks damages or other legal relief. SEE: *defendant.*

plait (plāt) To braid; to make separate strands of tissue into a ropelike structure (e.g., during tendon repair).

plan (plan) [Fr. *plan,* ground, groundwork, plan] The conscious design of desired future states and of the goals, objectives, and activities required.

birth p. Written specifications for the management of labor, delivery, and recovery as desired by the expectant mother or couple and approved by the physician or midwife. Components usually include pain management techniques and comfort during labor; medications that may be used; family participation and other maternal supporters; methods that may be employed for anesthesia, delivery and monitoring; and early care of the newborn. SEE: *Lamaze method; Leboyer method.*

care p. A description of the goals, prognosis, and proposed interventions for a particular patient, including criteria for discharge and the optimal duration and frequency of therapeutic interventions.

dental care p. **1.** The statement of the goals and procedures related to the dentist's care for the patient, based on medical history, oral examination, and oral radiographs. **2.** Third-party insurance that covers part or all of the cost for regular dental care.

disaster recovery p. A document defining the resources, actions, tasks, and data for managing the recovery of lost databases, programs, or other computing functions in the event of catastrophic damage to the computing infrastructure of an organization.

eating p. Diet (2).

emergency action p. **1.** A protocol used during catastrophic events or mass casualties. **2.** A protocol for use during hectic, or rapidly changing conditions in patient care.

health p. A corporation that provides medical insurance.

individual education p. ABBR: IEP. A federally required, individual program of goals and methods for addressing needs of students receiving special education and related services in public schools. The goals and methods are required under the provisions of federal legislation providing for a free and appropriate public education for individuals with disabilities, as amended (Individuals with Disabilities Education Act [IDEA]-PL 101–476, amended in 2004).

The law mandates that for each child receiving special education services under the act, a written plan, involving input from teachers, service providers, and parents, will document the needs of the child, how those special needs will be addressed, and when and how the effectiveness of the services will be evaluated.

individualized family service p. ABBR: IFSP. A written document, developed by service personnel and parents of young children with disabilities, that describes plans for intervention and educational placement. Twenty-five percent of occupational therapists now practice in school settings in order to meet the legislated mandate for public schools to provide related services for children with disabilities.

medical care p. The goals of the physician's care and the treatment instituted to accomplish them.

nursing care p. The statement of the goals and objectives of the nursing care provided for the patient and the activities or tasks required to accomplish the plan, including the criteria to be used to evaluate the effectiveness and appropriateness of the plan.

treatment p. A therapeutic strategy that may incorporate patient education, dietary adjustment, an exercise program, drug therapy, and the participation of nursing and allied health professionals. Treatment plans are esp. important in the optimal management of complex or chronic illnesses.

written action p. ABBR: WAP. A flexible script that patients may use to guide their own outpatient therapy when they experience deterioration in a chronic condition.

PATIENT CARE: WAPs were initially introduced into asthma therapy to guide the use of inhaled and oral steroids, but they can be used for other conditions.

WAPs typically include: 1. How to recognize signs of worsening illness; 2. treatment protocols; 3. the duration of and how to modify or increase the intensity of treatments; 4. When to seek additional help from health care professionals.

planaria (plă-năr′ē-ă) Free-living flatworms of the Turbellaria class.

planchet (plăn′chĕt) A small, flat container or dish on which a radioactive sample is placed.

plane (plān) [L. *planum,* flat surface] **1.** A flat or relatively smooth surface. **2.** A flat surface formed by making a cut, imaginary or real, through the body or a part of it. Planes are used as points of reference by which positions of parts of the body are indicated. In the human subject, all planes are based on the body being in an upright anatomical position. SEE: illus.; *anatomical* **position**. **3.** A

certain stage, as in levels of anesthesia. **4.** To smooth a surface or rub away.

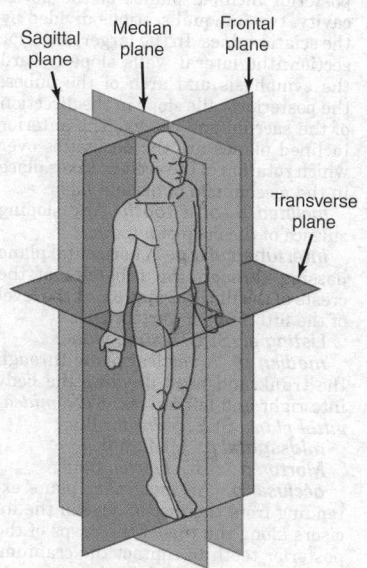

Sagittal plane · Median plane · Frontal plane · Transverse plane

BODY PLANES

Addison p. SEE: *Addison plane.*

alveolocondylar p. A plane tangent to the alveolar point with most prominent points on lower aspects of condyles of the occipital bone.

axiolabiolingual p. A plane that passes through an incisor or canine tooth parallel to the long axis of the tooth and in a labiolingual direction.

axiomesiodistal p. A plane that passes through a tooth parallel to the axis and in a mesiodistal direction.

Baer p. SEE: *Baer plane.*

bite p. A plane formed by the biting surfaces of the teeth.

coccygeal p. The fourth parallel plane of the pelvis.

coronal p. A vertical plane at right angles to a sagittal plane. It divides the body into anterior and posterior portions. SYN: *frontal* **p.**

datum p. An assumed horizontal plane from which craniometric measurements are taken.

Daubenton p. SEE: *Daubenton plane.*

focal p. One of two planes through the anterior and posterior principal foci of a dioptric system and perpendicular to the line connecting the two.

Frankfort horizontal p. SEE: *Frankfort horizontal plane.*

frontal p. Coronal **p.**

Hodge p. SEE: under *Hodge, Hugh Lennox.*

horizontal p. A transverse plane at

right angles to the vertical axis of the body.

inclined p. of the pelvis Anterior and posterior inclined planes of the pelvic cavity, two unequal sections divided by the sciatic spines. In the larger, anterior section, the lateral walls slope toward the symphysis and arch of the pubes; the posterior walls slope in the direction of the sacrum and coccyx. The anterior inclined planes are the declivities over which rotation of the occiput takes place in the mechanism of normal labor.

inclined p. of a tooth Any sloping surface of the cusp of a tooth.

intertubercular p. A horizontal plane passing through the tubercles of the crests of the ilia; lies approx. at the level of the fifth lumbar vertebra.

Listing p. SEE: *Listing plane.*

median p. A vertical plane through the trunk and head dividing the body into right and left halves. SYN: *midsagittal plane.* SEE: *plane* for illus.

midsagittal p. Median **p.**

Morton p. SEE: *Morton plane.*

occlusal p. An imaginary plane extending from the incisal edge of the incisors along the tips of the cusps of the posterior teeth to contact the cranium. Although not a true plane, it represents the mean of the curvature of the occlusal surface.

parallel p. of the pelvis The planes intersecting the axis of the pelvic canal at right angles. The first plane is that of the superior strait; the second that extending from the middle of the sacral vertebra to the level of the subpubic ligament. The third plane is at the level of the spines of the ischia, and the fourth plane is at the outlet.

p. of the pelvis Imaginary planes touching the same parts of the pelvic canal on both sides.

p. of refraction A plane passing through a refracted ray of light and drawn perpendicular to the surface at which refraction takes place.

p. of regard A plane through the fovea of the eye; fixation point.

sagittal p. A vertical plane through the longitudinal axis of the body or part of the body, dividing it into right and left parts. If it is through the anteroposterior midaxis and divides the body into right and left halves, it is called a *median* or *midsagittal plane.*

subcostal p. A horizontal plane passing through the lowest points of the 10th costal cartilages. It lies approx. at the level of the third lumbar vertebra.

transverse p. A plane that divides the body into a top and bottom portion.

treatment p. A plane in the concave joint surface that defines the direction of joint mobilization techniques. The plane is perpendicular to a line drawn from the axis of rotation in the convex joint surface to the center of the concave surface. Joint distraction techniques are applied perpendicular to, and gliding techniques parallel to, the treatment plane.

vertical p. Any body plane perpendicular to a horizontal plane.

visual p. A plane passing the visual axis of the eye.

planigraphy (plă-nĭg′ră-fē) [″ + Gr. *graphein,* to write] Tomography.

planimeter (plă-nĭm′ĕ-tĕr) [″ + Gr. *metron,* measure] An apparatus used to measure the area of a plane figure by passing a tracer around the boundaries.

planing (plā′nĭng) **1.** Dermabrasion. **2.** In dentistry, a meticulous deep scaling procedure designed to remove calculus, diseased cementum or dentin, microbial flora, and bacterial toxins on the root surface of a tooth or in a gingival pocket. The smooth, healthy root facilitates reattachment of the soft tissues of the periodontium. SYN: *root planing.*

plankton (plănk′tŏn) [Gr. *planktos,* wandering] A freely floating organism, not anchored to a surface, e.g., some algae, bacteria, crustaceans, and diatoms.

planned parenthood The concept that a couple or a woman may choose when to conceive and give birth. This is, of course, accomplished only by the careful and proper use of some form of birth control.

planning (plan′ing) In the nursing process, the step following nursing diagnosis. After the nursing diagnoses have been established, the next action is noting the priority of the diagnoses and indicating the actions that will accomplish the immediate and long-range goals of the nursing process. Specific nursing interventions are indicated, and the expected outcomes of these actions are recorded on the chart. This portion of the nursing process is dynamic and will need to be altered as the patient's course evolves. The evaluation of the effectiveness of the nursing process will be essential to restating the plan for administering nursing care. SEE: *nursing process; nursing assessment; evaluation; nursing intervention; problem-oriented medical record.*

planocellular (plā″nō-sĕl′ū-lăr) [L. *planus,* plane, + *cellula,* cell] Composed of flat cells.

planoconcave (plā″nō-kŏn′kāv) [″ + *concavus,* hollow] An optical lens that is flat on one side and concave on the other.

planoconvex (plā″nō-kŏn′vĕks) [″ + L. *convexus,* arched] An optical lens that is flat on one side and convex on the other.

Planorbis (plăn-or′bĭs) A genus of freshwater snails that is the intermediate host for some species of schistosomal blood flukes.

plant (plănt) [L. *planta*, a sprout] An organism that contains chlorophyll and synthesizes carbohydrates and oxygen from carbon dioxide and water. Plants make up one of the five kingdoms of living things. SEE: *chlorophyll.*

planta pedis (plăn′tă pē′dŭs) *pl.* **plantae** [L.] The sole of the foot.

plantar (plăn′tăr) Pert. to the sole of the foot.

plantar flexion Extension of the foot so that the forepart is depressed with respect to the position of the ankle. SEE: *dorsiflexion.*

plantaris (plăn-tăr′ĭs) [L.] A long slim muscle of the calf between the gastrocnemius and soleus. It is sometimes double and at other times missing.

plantar neuropathy SEE: under *neuropathy.*

plantation (plăn-tā′shŭn) [L. *plantare*, to plant] Insertion of a tooth into the bony socket from which it may have been removed by accident, or transplantation of a tooth into the socket from which a tooth has just been removed. The transplanted tooth may come from the patient or a donor.

plantigrade (plăn′tĭ-grād) [L. *planta*, sole of the foot, + *gradi*, to walk] A type of foot posture in which the entire sole of the foot is placed on the ground in walking, as in the bear, rabbit, or human.

planula (plăn′ū-lă) The larval stage of a coelenterate.

planum (plā′nŭm) *pl.* **plana** [L.] A flat or relatively smooth surface; a plane.

   nuchal p. The outer surface of the occipital bone between the foramen magnum and superior nuchal line.

   occipital p. The outer surface of the occipital bone lying above the superior nuchal line.

   popliteal p. A smooth triangular area on the posterior surface of distal end of femur. It is bordered by the medial and lateral supracondylar lines and forms the floor of the popliteal fossa.

   sternal p. The anterior or ventral surface of the sternum.

PLAP *placental alkaline phosphatase.*

plaque (plak) [Fr. *plaque*, metal plate] A patch on the skin or on a mucous membrane.

   atheromatous p. An obstruction in the lining of an artery, formed by the abnormal accumulation of lipids (fats) and sometimes calcium.

   bacterial p. Dental **p.**

   dental p. A biofilm that accumulates and grows on the crowns of teeth. Plaque is colorless, transparent, and the forerunner of dental caries and periodontal disease. Measures to prevent plaque buildup include daily self-care of the teeth, careful use of dental floss, and

periodic prophylaxis by a dentist or dental hygienist.

   TREATMENT: Treatment should include removal on a daily basis. Brushing and flossing are typical methods of plaque removal. Additional techniques may include water irrigation, chemical plaque control, and auxiliary oral hygiene aids. SYN: *bacterial p.* SEE: *calculus; caries; periodontal disease; periodontitis.*

   fibrous p. SEE: *arteriosclerosis.*

   mucous p. Condyloma latum.

   senile p. Accumulations of bundled amyloid fibrils surrounding normal and damaged neurons in the brain, a finding on pathological inspection of brain tissue from patients with Alzheimer dementia.

plaque cracker A device used in endovascular surgery to cut out an obstructing atheromatous plaque from the intima of an artery.

-plasia, -plasy [Gr. *plasis*, molding, fr. *plassein*, to mold, form] Suffixes meaning *formation, growth, proliferation.*

plasm (plazm) [L. fr. Gr. *plasma*, form, mold, image] Plasma.

plasm- [Gr. *plasma*, anything formed] Prefix meaning *living substance, tissue.*

-plasm [Gr. *plasma*, anything formed] Suffix meaning *living substance, tissue.*

plasma (plaz′mă) [L. *plasma*, fr Gr. *plasma*, something formed or mold] **1.** An ointment base of glycerol and starch. **2.** The liquid part of blood and of lymph. SYN: *blood p.*

   Plasma forms 52% to 62% of the total blood volume and is a transport medium and a medium for chemical reactions. It is about 91.5% water, and about 7% protein, including albumin, globulins, and the clotting factors. Also found in plasma are electrolytes that determine osmotic pressure and pH balance, nutrients and waste products, and hormones. Most carbon dioxide is transported in plasma in the form of bicarbonate ions. Plasma from which clotting factors have been removed is called serum.

   antihemophilic factor p. Human plasma in which factor VIII, the antihemophilic globulin, has been preserved; used to correct temporarily the bleeding tendency in some forms of hemophilia. SEE: *hemophilia.*

   blood p. Plasma (2).

   fresh frozen p. ABBR: FFP. The fluid portion of one unit of human blood that has been centrifuged, separated, and frozen solid within 6 hr of collection. SEE: *blood component therapy.*

   hyperimmune p. Plasma with a high titer of a specific antibody, administered to create passive immunity to the antigen.

   normal human p. Pooled plasma from a number of human donors. The plasma is selected from screened donors and sterilized.

p. skimming The natural separation of red blood cells from plasma at bifurcations in the vascular tree, dividing the blood into relatively concentrated and relatively dilute streams.

platelet-rich p. A concentrate of platelets and plasma proteins derived from a patient's whole blood, centrifuged to remove red blood cells and other unwanted components. It has a greater concentration of growth factors than whole blood and has been used as a tissue injection in a variety of disciplines, including dentistry, orthopedic surgery, and sports medicine.

plasmablast (plăz′mă-blăst) [L. *plasma,* form, mold, + Gr. *blastos,* germ] The undifferentiated cell that will mature into a B lymphocyte and ultimately into a plasma cell.

plasma cell balanitis SEE: under *balanitis.*

plasmacytoma (plăz″mă-sī′tō′mă) [″ + ″ + *oma,* tumor] A tumor composed of plasma cells. SEE: *multiple myeloma.*

plasmacytosis (plăz″mă-sī-tō′sĭs) [″ + ″ + *osis,* condition] An excess of plasma cells in the blood.

plasma exchange therapy The removal of plasma from a patient (usually to treat an immmunologically mediated illness such as thrombotic thrombocytopenic purpura or myasthenia gravis) and its replacement with normal plasma. Plasma exchange therapy can also be used to replace excessively viscous plasma in patients with Waldenström macroglobulinemia. Pathological antibodies, immune complexes, and protein-bound toxins are removed from the plasma by plasma exchange.

    Immunoglobulin infusions are an alternative to plasma exchange when treating some immunological illnesses, including Guillain-Barré syndrome and chronic inflammatory demyelinating polyneuropathy. SYN: *hemapheresis; plasmapheresis.*

plasmagene (plăz′mă-jēn″) [″ + Gr. *gennan,* to produce] A cytoplasmic hereditary determiner.

plasmalemma (plăz″mă-lĕm′ă) [″ + Gr. *lemma,* husk] Plasma, or cell, membrane.

plasmapheresis (plăz″mă-fĕr-ē′sĭs) [″ + Gr. *aphairesis,* separation] Plasma exchange therapy.

plasma protein fraction SEE: under *fraction.*

plasma skin regeneration ABBR: PSR. A treatment for removing abnormal skin pigmentation, fine lines, acne scarring, and abnormal skin texture, in which ionized gas (plasma) is used to remove superficial or deeper skin layers. Nitrogen gas is typically stripped of its electrons, and then applied to the skin as a spray. This heats the dermis (the layer of skin beneath the epidermis). The epidermal layer peels off a few days after treatment, while new collagen grows within the dermis, giving the skin a smoother appearance. PSR is an alternative to laser skin resurfacing.

plasmatherapy (plăz″mă-thĕr′ă-pē) [″ + Gr. *therapeia,* service] Plasma exchange therapy.

plasmatic (plăz-măt′ĭk) **1.** Pert. to plasma. **2.** Formative or plastic.

plasma transglutaminase Fibrin-stabilizing **factor**.

plasma very-long-chain fatty acid assay SEE: under *assay.*

plasma volume expander SEE: *volume expander.*

plasmid (plăz′mĭd) A piece of extrachromosomal, double-stranded DNA found in most bacteria. Plasmids replicate when a bacterium divides and are passed to subsequent cells. The products of plasmid genes are enzymes that provide resistance to antibiotics or that synthesize bacteriocins or other toxins. SYN: *episome.* SEE: *bacteriocin; transposon.*

plasmin (plăz′mĭn) A fibrinolytic enzyme derived from its precursor plasminogen. SYN: *fibrinolysin.*

plasminogen (plăz-mĭn′ō-jĕn) A protein found in many tissues and body fluids; important in preventing fibrin clot formation.

plasminogen activator inhibitor-1 A protein that degrades extracellular tissues. It has been linked to the invasive and metastatic spread of cancers.

plasmo-, plasm- Prefixes meaning *plasma* or *cytoplasm.*

plasmocyte, plasmacyte (plăz′mă-sīt) [″ + Gr. *kytos,* cell] The malignant cells found in the bone marrow and occasionally in the blood of persons with multiple myeloma.

plasmodesmata (plăz″mō-dĕz′mă-tă) *sing.,* **plasmodesma** [″ + Gr. *desmos,* bond] Tunnels in plant cell walls. These facilitate communication between cells.

plasmodial (plăz-mō′dē-ăl) Pert. to plasmodia.

Plasmodium (plaz-mōd′ē-ŭm) A genus of protozoa belonging to subphylum Sporozoa, class Telosporidia; includes causative agents of malaria in humans and lower animals. SEE: *malaria; mosquito.*

P. falciparum The causative agent of malignant (falciparum) malaria.

P. knowlesi A species found in Southeast Asia. It is structurally similar to *P. malariae.* Although it primarily infects other primates, it can infect humans and produce a debilitating febrile illness.

P. malariae The causative agent of quartan malaria.

P. ovale The causative agent of benign tertian or ovale malaria.

P. vivax The causative agent of benign tertian or vivax malaria.

plasmodium (plăz-mō'dē-ŭm) *pl.* **plasmodia** [L. *plasma,* form, mold, + Gr. *eidos,* form, shape] **1.** A multinucleate mass of naked protoplasm, occurring commonly among slime molds. **2.** An organism in the genus *Plasmodium.*

plasmogamy (plăs-mŏg'ă-mē) [″ + Gr. *gamos,* marriage] The fusion of cells.

plasmolysis (plăz-mŏl'ĭ-sĭs) [″ + Gr. *lysis,* dissolution] Shrinking of cytoplasm in a living cell caused by loss of water by osmosis.

plasmotomy (plăz-mŏt'ō-mē) [″ + Gr. *tome,* incision] Cell division with unequal separation of cytoplasm.

-plast [Gr. *plastos,* molded] Suffix meaning *cell, organelle, granule.*

plastein (plăs'tē-ĭn) A massive polypeptide formed by the hydrolysis of proteins and the subsequent recombination of amino acid esters. Plasteins can be derived from nonconventional sources of protein (e.g., cassava leaves or other plants) and used to make protein-rich foods.

plaster [Gr. *emplastron*] **1.** A material, usually plaster of Paris, that is applied to a part and allowed to harden in order to immobilize the part or to make an impression. In many settings, plaster of Paris has been replaced with synthetic cast materials, such as fiberglass. **2.** A topical preparation in which the constituents are formed into a tenacious mass of substance harder than an ointment and spread upon muslin, linen, skin, or paper.

dental p. A powder, when mixed with water, that hardens to form a stonelike investment or model material. It is composed of a hemihydrate of gypsum ($CaSO_4 \cdot 2H_2O$), which differs in compression strength and expansion coefficient according to how it is treated and rehydrated. There are four classes of dental plaster, with differing uses as materials for casts, impressions, or stone models, based on the differences of characteristics.

mustard p. Sinapsim.

p. of Paris Gypsum cement, hemihydrated calcium sulfate ($CaSO_4 \cdot 2H_2O$), mixed with water to form a paste that sets rapidly; used to make casts and stiff bandages.

salicylic acid p. A uniform mixture of salicylic acid spread on an appropriate base such as paper, cotton, or fabric. It is applied topically for use as a keratolytic agent.

plastic (plăs'tĭk) [Gr. *plastikos,* fit for molding] **1.** Capable of being molded. **2.** Contributing to building tissues.

plastic deformation of bone A bow-shaped deformity of bone from trauma strong enough to cause the bone to bend but not break. It is typically seen in children, esp. in the ulna or fibula. SYN: *bend* **fracture**.

plasticity (plăs-tĭs'ĭ-tē) **1.** The ability to be molded. **2.** The ability of tissues to grow, to adapt, or to integrate with others during development, after trauma, or after an illness.

plastid (plăs'tĭd) [Gr. *plastos,* formed] An organelle in plant cells. It includes chloroplasts (which contain chlorophyll), leukoplasts (colorless), chromoplasts (which contain pigment), and amyloplasts (which store starch). Chloroplasts are the site of photosynthesis.

-plasty [Gr. *plastos,* molded, fr. *plassein,* to mold, form] Suffix meaning *surgical repair.*

plate (plāt) [Fr. *plate,* something flat] **1.** A thin, flattened part or portion, such as a flattened process of a bone. SYN: *lamella; lamina.* **2.** An incorrect reference to a full denture. **3.** A shallow covered dish for culturing microorganisms. **4.** To inoculate and culture microorganisms in a culture plate.

alar p. In the embryo, the upper (dorsal) half of the neural tube (above the sulcus limitans). SYN: *alar* **lamina** *of neural tube.*

belay p. A metal, steel, or aluminum plate that has one or more slots in it, designed to weave a rope through, to create friction with a carabiner.

bite p. In dentistry, a plate made of some suitable plastic material into which the patient bites in order to have a record of the relationship between the upper and lower jaws. The device may be reinforced with wire and used as a splint in the mouth or to treat temporomandibular joint difficulties. SYN: *interocclusal record; occlusal template.*

bone p. A flat, round or oval decalcified bone or metal disk, employed in pairs, used in approximation.

chorionic p. The fetal surface of the placenta.

cortical p. The compact layers of bone forming the surfaces of the alveolar processes of the mandible and maxilla.

cribriform p. **1.** The thin, perforated, medial portion of the horizontal plate of the ethmoid bone; the olfactory foramina are passages for the olfactory nerve. **2.** Alveolar bone, the spongy bone that makes up the wall of the socket for a tooth; found in the maxillae and mandible.

dental p. An old term for the denture base of metal or acrylic material that rests on the oral mucosa and to which artificial teeth are attached; by extension, *incorrectly* used to mean the complete denture.

epiphyseal p. The thin layer of cartilage between the epiphysis and the shaft of a bone. Growth in length of the bone occurs at this layer. SYN: *growth p.* SEE: illus.

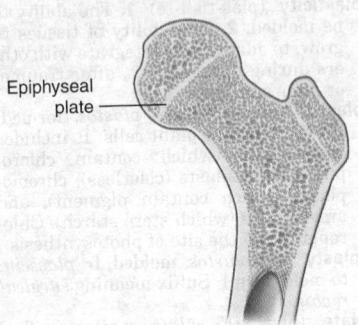

Epiphyseal plate

EPIPHYSEAL PLATE

equatorial p. The platelike mass of chromosomes at the equator of the spindle in cell division.

floor p. In the embryonic neural tube, the wedge of cells in the ventral midline. These cells are primitive radial glia and do not give rise to neurons. The ventral commissures and decussations eventually develop through this structure. SYN: *ventral p.*

force p. A flat, floor-mounted instrument, similar to a scale, for determining weight-bearing loads and biomechanical forces placed on the foot during walking or running. It is used to detect subtle body movements in order to identify postural deficits, or to develop (in athletes or people with balance disorders) more fluid and safer coordination and locomotion.

growth p. Epiphyseal **p.**

image p. A photostimulable image detector used in computed tomography in place of x-ray cassettes. It gathers the energy from x-ray photons on a layer of phosphor that can repeatedly store and release information in digitized form for enhancement, recording, and image display.

medullary p. The central portion of the ectoderm in the embryo developing into the neural canal.

neural p. A thickened band of ectoderm along the dorsal surface of an embryo. The nervous system develops from this tissue.

palate p. The part of the palatine bone forming the dorsal half of the roof of the mouth.

polar p. In some cells, the flattened platelike bodies seen at the end of the spindle during mitosis.

pterygoid p. Either of a pair of thin, bony processes that arise from the sphenoid bone. They are termed medial and lateral pterygoid plates on each side, serve to bound the infratemporal fossa, and give origin to muscles of mastication.

pusher p. A device that moves fluids in a specific direction.

tarsal p. The dense connective tissue structure that supports the eyelid. It was formerly called *tarsal cartilage;* however, it is not true cartilage.

ventral p. Floor **p.**

plateau (plă-tō′) **1.** An elevated and usually flat area; a steady and consistent fever appears as a plateau on the patient's chart of vital signs. **2.** The stage in training or skill acquisition when progress occurs at a very slow or flat rate in comparison with earlier phases.

ventricular p. The flat portion of the record of intraventricular pressure during the end of the ejection phase of ventricular systole.

platelet (plāt′lĕt) [Gr. *plate,* flat] A round or oval disk, 2 to 4 μm in diameter, found in the blood of vertebrates. Platelets number 130,000 to 400,000/mm³. They are fragments of megakaryocytes, large cells found in the bone marrow. SYN: *thrombocyte.* SEE: *blood* for illus.; *megakaryocyte* for illus.; *thrombopoietin.*

FUNCTION: Platelets contribute to chemical blood clotting and to other aspects of hemostasis. Platelet factors are the chemicals released by platelets to initiate the first stage of (intrinsic pathway) chemical clotting. When a capillary ruptures, platelets adhere to each other and to the cut edges of the vessel, forming a platelet plug. Blood clotting may be beneficial (e.g., in preventing blood loss from wounds) or may be harmful when it occurs within arteries or veins inside the body (e.g., during coronary thrombosis). Blood clotting is a positive feedback cascade that may continue and occlude an unbroken vessel.

DISORDERS: Thrombocytopenia (reduced platelet count) occurs in acute infections, anaphylactic shock, and certain hemorrhagic diseases and anemias. Thrombocytosis (increased platelet count) occurs after operations, esp. splenectomy, and after violent exercise and tissue injury.

platelet-activating factor antagonist SEE: under *antagonist.*

platelet antiaggregant (ant″ē-ag′rĕ-gănt) A medicine, such as aspirin, that prevents platelets from forming blood clots.

platelet concentrate Platelets prepared from a single unit of whole blood or plasma and suspended in a specific volume of the original plasma. This blood fraction must be used before the expiration date shown on its label. Platelets are stored at room temperature (22°C) either in plasma or in a concentrated form as platelet-rich plasma.

platelet distribution width ABBR: PDW. A measure of the variation in the size of platelets found in the circulating blood. Platelets recently released from bone marrow tend to be larger and to contain more RNA than older, smaller platelets, which discard their endoplasmic reticulum as they mature.

plateletpheresis (plăt-lĕt-fĕr-ē′sĭs) The separation of platelets from other components of whole blood (e.g. for use in transfusion or to treat hematologic disease).

platelet reactivity test Any laboratory test that assesses the degree to which platelets aggregate to form clots, esp. in response to treatment with drugs, e.g., clopidogrel or ticlopidine, that inhibit the aggregation of platelets.

platelet transfusion refractoriness A failure of circulating platelet levels to rise after platelet transfusion. Alloimmunization against platelet antigens, disseminated intravascular coagulation, fever, hypersplenism, and sepsis are among the potential causes. A typical platelet transfusion should normally raise platelet counts by more than 20,000 platelets μm.

-platin [Fm. *platin(um)*] A suffix used in pharmacology to designate any chemotherapeutic agent that contains platinum.

plating In bacteriology, inoculation of liquefiable, solid media (gelatin or agar) with microorganisms and pouring of medium into a shallow flat dish.

platinic (plă-tĭn′ĭk) Pert. to a compound containing quadrivalent platinum.

platinum (plat′ĭn-ŭm, plat′nŭm) [L. *platinum* fr Sp. *platina*] SYMB: Pt. A heavy silver-white metallic chemical element, atomic weight (mass) 195.09, atomic number 78, specific gravity 21.45.

platy-, plat- [Gr. *platys*, broad] Prefixes meaning *broad* or *flat*.

platybasia (plăt″ē-bā′sē-ă) A developmental defect of the skull in which the floor of the posterior fossa of the skull around the foramen magnum protrudes upward.

platyhelminth (plăt″ē-hĕl′mĭnth) The common name for any flatworm.

Platyhelminthes (plăt″ē-hĕl-mĭn′thēz) [″ + *helmins*, worm] A phylum of flatworms including the classes Turbellaria, Trematoda (flukes), and Cestoidea (tapeworms). The last two are parasitic and include many species of medical importance. SEE: *Cestoda; Cestoidea; fluke; tapeworm; trematode.*

platypnea (plă-tĭp′nē-ă) [″ + *pnoia*, breath] Shortness of breath, dyspnea, only when the patient is upright or seated. SEE: *orthopnea.*

platyrrhine (plăt′ĭr-īn) [″ + *rhis*, nose]

1. Pert. to a very wide nose in proportion to length. **2.** Pert. to a skull with a nasal index between 51.1 and 58.

platysma myoides (plă-tĭz′mă mī-oy′dēz) [Gr. *platysma*, plate, + *mys*, muscle, + *eidos*, form, shape] A broad, thin, platelike layer of muscle that extends from the fascia of both sides of the neck to the jaw and muscles around the mouth. It acts to wrinkle the skin of the neck and depress the jaw.

platysmaplasty (plă-tĭz′mă-plas″tē) [*platysma* + *-plasty*] Surgery to minimize sagging skin under the jaw or to remove a double chin; a neck lift.

Plavix SEE: *clopidogrel.*

play 1. Involvement in a sport, amusement, or any form of recreation, esp. an activity other than that in which one is usually engaged as an occupation. From the medical standpoint, it is important that the recreational activity be enjoyable and that participation in it be safe and satisfactory. **2.** Unimpeded motion, as of a joint.

play assessment The evaluation of the personal styles and interactions of children engaged in pleasurable activities, often to determine levels of development and functioning and to assess needs.

play therapy The use of play, esp. with dolls and toys, to allow children to express their feelings. This may permit insight into their thought processes that could not be obtained through verbal communication.

pleadings (plēd′ĭngz) The written accusations or claims of the defendant and the plaintiff in a lawsuit.

pleasure [L. *placere*, to please] The feeling of being delighted or pleased.

pleasure principle SEE: under *principle.*

pledger (plej′ĕr) A colloquial term for an adolescent or preteen-ager who promises to abstain from sexual intercourse. Conversely, a *nonpledger* is a young person who does not promise to maintain sexual abstinence.

pledget (plĕj′ĕt) [origin uncertain] **1.** A small, flat compress, usually of gauze or absorbent cotton, used to apply or absorb fluid, to protect, or to exclude air. **2.** A small spherical mass of cotton about ⅛ in. (3 mm) in diameter that is used with forceps for topical application of medicinal substances, particularly in dentistry.

-plegia [Gr. *plēgē*, blow, stroke] Suffix meaning *paralysis, stroke.*

pleio-, pleo-, plio- [Gr. *pleiōn*, more] Prefixes meaning *more.*

pleiotropism (plī-ŏt′rŏ-pĭzm) [″ + ″ + *-ismos*, condition] The ability of a gene to have many effects SYN: *pleiotropia.*

Pleistophora (plī-stō-fō′ră) A genus of microsporidia that usually parasitizes fish. SEE: *microsporidiosis.*

pleocytosis (plē″ō-sī-tō′sĭs) [″ + *kytos*,

cell, + *osis,* condition] An excessive number of cells in a body fluid; used esp. to denote excessive lymphocytes in the cerebrospinal fluid.

pleomorphic (plē″ŏ-mor′fĭk) [*pleio-* + *-morph* + *-ic*] Having many shapes.

pleomorphism (plē″ŏ-mor′fĭzm) [*pleio-* + *-morph* + *-ism*] Polymorphism.

pleomorphous (plē″ŏ-mor′fŭs) Having many shapes or crystallizing into several forms.

plerocercoid (plĕr-ō-sĕr-kŏyd) The wormlike larvae of certain tapeworms, which develop in secondary hosts.

Plesiomonas shigelloides (plē-sē-ō-mon′ăs, shĭ-gĕl-oi′dēz″) [Gr. *plesios,* close, nearby + ″ + ″] A gram-negative facultative anaerobic rod-shaped bacterium. It is thought to be a cause of gastroenteritis/infectious diarrhea acquired from contaminated water.

plethora (plĕth′ō-ră) [Gr. *plethore,* fullness] **1.** Overfullness of blood vessels or of the total quantity of any fluid in the body. SEE: *sanguine.* **2.** Congestion causing distention of the blood vessels.

plethoric (plĕ-thor′ĭk, plĕth′ō-rĭk) Pert. to, or characterized by, plethora; overfull.

plethysmograph (plĕ-thiz′mŏ-graf″) [Gr. *plĕthysmos,* an increase, multiplication + *-graph*] A device for finding variations in the size of a part owing to variations in the amount of blood passing through or contained in the part.

   body p. A body box used to measure lung volume and pressure in pulmonary function tests.

   impedance p. A device that uses gas-to-tissue ratio to set an alarm or measure a volume.

plethysmography (pleth″iz-mog′ră-fē) [Gr. *plĕthysmos,* an increase, multiplication + *-graphy*] The use of or an examination with a plethysmograph to record the changes in volume of an organ or extremity.

   air displacement p. A technique for measuring body composition (body volume and percentage of body fat) that relies on the relative volume and pressure of gas displaced by the body when it is placed inside a plethysmograph.

   electrical impedance p. ABBR: EIP. Impedance **cardiography.**

pleur-, pleuro- [Gr. *pleura,* rib, side] Prefixes meaning *pleura, side, rib.*

pleura (ploo′ră) *pl.* **pleurae** [Gr., side] A serous membrane that enfolds both lungs and is reflected upon the walls of the thorax and diaphragm. The pleurae are moistened with a serous secretion that reduces friction during respiratory movements of the lungs. SEE: *pleural effusion; mediastinum; thorax;* illus.

   costal p. Parietal **p.**

   mediastinal p. The portion of the pa-

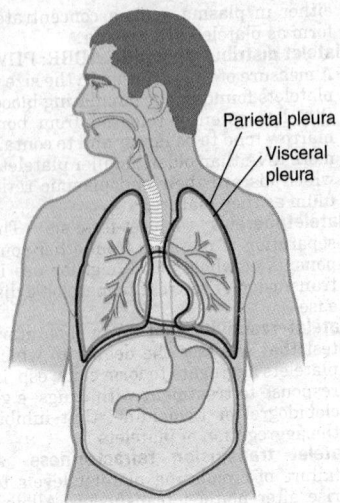

Parietal pleura
Visceral pleura

PLEURAE

rietal pleura that extends to cover the mediastinum.

   parietal p. The serous membrane that lines the chest cavity; it extends from the mediastinal roots of the lungs and covers the sides of the pericardium to the chest wall and backward to the spine. The visceral and parietal pleural layers are separated only by a lubricating secretion. These layers may become adherent or separated by air or by blood, pus, or other fluids, when the lungs and chest wall are injured or inflamed. SYN: *costal p.*

   visceral p. The pleura that covers the lungs and enters into and lines the interlobar fissures. It is loose at the base and at the sternal and vertebral borders to allow for lung expansion.

pleural (ploor′ăl) [*pleur-* + *-al*] Pert. to the pleura.

pleural drainage unit ABBR: PDU. A device to evacuate fluids from the pleural cavity. Most PDUs consist of three chambers: one to collect fluids such as blood, pus, or pleural effusions; a second to maintain a water seal; and a third to control suction.

pleural reaction Thickening of the pleura or of the pleural shadow on an x-ray. It may be an indication of pleural disease, pleural effusion, or infiltration by cancer.

pleurectomy (ploo-rĕk′tō-mē) [″ + *ektome,* excision] Excision of part of the pleura.

pleurisy (ploo′rĭs-ē) [Gr. *pleuritis*] Inflammation of the visceral and parietal pleurae that surround the lungs and line the thoracic cavity. It may be primary or secondary; unilateral, bilateral, or local; acute or chronic; fibrinous, serofibrinous, or purulent. Common causes of pleurisy include viral infections, pneumonia, pulmonary embolism, rib fracture, and serositis from autoimmune diseases. SYN: *pleuritis*. SEE: *Nursing Diagnoses Appendix*.

SYMPTOMS: Sharp stabbing pain exacerbated by breathing is characteristic.

PATIENT CARE: Respiratory function is monitored by auscultation, observation of breathing pattern, and oximetry. The patient is positioned in the high Fowler position to facilitate chest expansion. Rest is encouraged. Deep breathing using incentive spirometry is encouraged every 1 to 2 hr to prevent atelectasis. To reduce discomfort when coughing, the patient should splint the chest with a pillow and administer analgesic drugs and use noninvasive measures, such as local application of warm or cool compresses. Respiratory toilet is provided if secretions are present. Rest is recommended. Prescribed medical regimens are carried out, with treatment directed at the underlying cause, and the patient's responses evaluated. Severe pain may be managed with intercostal nerve block. Thoracentesis may be required if pleural effusion is present.

adhesive p. Pleurisy in which the exudate causes the parietal pleura to adhere to the visceral. If this is extensive, the pleural space is obliterated.

diaphragmatic p. Inflammation of the diaphragmatic pleura. Symptoms include intense pain under the margin of the ribs, sometimes referred into the abdomen, with tenderness upon pressure; thoracic breathing; tenderness over the phrenic nerve referred to the supraclavicular region in the neck on the same side; hiccough; and extreme dyspnea.

dry p. A condition in which the pleural membrane is covered with a fibrinous exudate.

p. with effusion Pleural effusion.

tuberculous p. Inflammation of the pleura as a result of tuberculosis. The effusion may be bloody.

typhoid p. Pleurisy with symptoms of typhoid.

pleuritic (ploo-rĭt′ĭk) [Gr. *pleuritis*, pleurisy] Relating to, or resembling, pleurisy.

pleuritis (ploo-rī′tĭs) [Gr.] Pleurisy.

pleurocentesis (ploo″rō-sĕn-tē′sĭs) [″ + *kentesis*, a piercing] Thoracentesis.

pleurodesis (ploor″ō-dē′sĭs) [*pleuro-* + *-desis*] Production of adhesions between the parietal and visceral pleura. It is usually done surgically or by instillation of drugs or chemicals and is used to treat recurrent pneumothorax and malignant pleural effusions.

mechanical p. Rubbing or scrubbing the pleura with a sponge to inflame the parietal and visceral pleura, and heal-

ing by forming a scar that unifies them. SYN: *pleural abrasion*.

pleurodynia (ploo″rō-dĭn′ē-ă) [″ + *odyne*, pain] Pain of sharp intensity in the intercostal muscles due to chronic inflammatory changes in the chest fasciae; pain of the pleural nerves.

epidemic p. Bornholm disease.

pleuropericarditis (ploo″rō-pĕr″ĭ-kăr-dī′tĭs) [″ + ″ + ″ + *itis*, inflammation] Pleuritis accompanied by pericarditis.

pleuropneumonia (ploo″rō-nū-mō′nē-ă) [″ + *pneumon*, lung] Pleurisy accompanied by pneumonia.

pleuroscopy (ploo-rŏs′kō-pē) [″ + *skopein*, to examine] Inspection of the pleural cavity with an endoscope inserted through an incision into the thorax.

pleurothotonos (ploo″rō-thŏt′ō-nŏs) [Gr. *pleurothen*, from the side, + *tonos*, tension] A tetanic spasm in which the body is arched to one side.

pleurotomy (ploo-rŏt′ō-mē) [Gr. *pleura*, side, + *tome*, incision] Incision of the pleura.

plexal (plĕk′săl) [L. *plexus*, a braid] Pert. to, or of the nature of, a plexus.

plexectomy (plĕk-sĕk′tō-mē) [″ + Gr. *ektome*, excision] Surgical removal of a plexus.

plexiform (plĕk′sĭ-form) [″ + *forma*, shape] Resembling a network or plexus.

pleximeter (plĕks-ĭm′ĕ-tĕr) [Gr. *plexis*, stroke, + *metron*, measure] A device for receiving the blow of the percussion hammer, consisting of a disk that is struck in mediate percussion while being held over the surface of the body. SYN: *plessimeter; plexometer*.

plexitis (plĕk-sī′tĭs) [L. *plexus*, a braid, + Gr. *itis*, inflammation] Inflammation of a nerve plexus.

plexopathy (plek-sŏp′ă-thē) [Gr. *plēxis*, stroke + *-pathy*] **1.** A peripheral neuropathy. **2.** Any disease of a (peripheral) nerve plexus.

idiopathic brachial p. A peripheral neuropathy that affects movement and sensation in the shoulder. Idiopathic brachial plexopathy usually results from brachial nerve entrapment by vigorous exercise. It may cause atrophy of the muscles surrounding the shoulder (the shoulder girdle). Nonidiopathic (i.e., readily identifiable) causes of the neuropathy sometimes are found in those with brachial nerve injury caused by tumors or radiation. SYN: *neuralgic amyotrophy; Parsonage-Turner syndrome; shoulder girdle syndrome*.

plexor (plĕks′or) A hammer or other device for striking on the pleximeter in percussion. SYN: *plessor*.

plexus (pleks′ŭs) *pl.* **plexus, plexuses** [L., *plexus*, a braid] An interwoven network of nerves, blood vessels, or lymphatics. SEE: *rete*.

aortic p., thoracic A nerve plexus that coats the thoracic aorta; it is composed of axons from the upper thoracic ganglia of the sympathetic trunk along with axons from the greater splanchnic nerve. This plexus connects with the celiac plexus, further caudally.

arterial p. A network of anastomosing arteries.

Auerbach p. SEE: *Auerbach plexus*.

autonomic p. A nerve plexus of sympathetic or parasympathetic axons, often containing autonomic neurons or ganglia. Such a plexus typically extends along major arteries and is named for its underlying artery. The large autonomic nerve plexuses are the cardiac, pulmonary, celiac, superior hypogastric, and inferior hypogastric.

basilar p. A venous sinus filled with anastomosing vascular channels; it is located in the dura that covers the clivus of the skull, under the brainstem. Rostrally, the basilar plexus interconnects with the cavernous sinuses, laterally with the superior and inferior petrosal sinuses, and caudally with the occipital and marginal sinuses and the vertebral venous plexuses, which continue outside the foramen magnum.

brachial p. A nerve plexus extending from the lower neck to the axilla; in it, axons from spinal nerves C4-T1 (or C5-T2) rearrange to form the nerves of the shoulder, upper trunk, and arm. These nerves include the dorsal scapular, suprascapular, long thoracic, lateral pectoral, medial pectoral, upper scapular, thoracodorsal, subscapular (upper, middle, and lower), musculocutaneous, axillary, lower subscapular, medial (brachial and antebrachial) cutaneous, radial, median, and ulnar. In the rearranging segments, the spinal nerves merge to form three trunk nerves (upper, middle, and lower), and the trunks divide and merge to form two divisions (anterior and posterior) and then three nerve cords (lateral, posterior, and medial); individual nerves emerge from all segments of the plexus.

capillary p. An anastomosing network of blood capillaries or of lymphatic capillaries, i.e., lymphatics.

cardiac p. The autonomic nerve plexus at the base of the heart. It is composed of parasympathetic axons from the vagus nerves and sympathetic axons from the sympathetic trunks; it also contains cells of the cardiac ganglion. The cardiac plexus provides both afferent and efferent axons to the heart and the great vessels. SYN: *p. cardiacus*.

carotid p. 1. Any of the autonomic nerve plexuses that coat the carotid arteries; all carotid plexuses receive postganglionic sympathetic axons from the superior cervical ganglia. The external carotid plexus sends axons to the smooth muscles of the face and upper neck, along branches of the external carotid artery. The internal carotid plexus sends axons to the trigeminal and ciliary ganglia, and the oculomotor, trochlear, ophthalmic, abducens, and glossopharyngeal nerves. Some axons leave the internal carotid artery at the foramen lacerum, inside the skull, to form the deep petrosal nerve, which runs to the pterygoid ganglion. Other carotid plexus axons continue along the anterior and middle cerebral arteries to provide sympathetic innervation of arteries of the brain. 2. A venous plexus that exits the skull through the carotid canal and interconnects the cavernous sinus inside the skull with the internal jugular vein outside the skull.

cavernous p. A plexus of a cavernous part of the body, including a venous plexus in the mucosa covering the superior and middle conchae of the nasal cavity, an autonomic nerve plexus at the base of the penis giving rise to large and small cavernous nerves, an autonomic nerve plexus at the base of the clitoris, and an autonomic plexus of the cavernous sinus in the skull.

celiac p. A dense nerve plexus along the celiac artery and the trunk of the superior mesenteric artery; this plexus interconnects the two large celiac ganglia. The plexus's parasympathetic axons come from the vagus, while the sympathetic axons come from the greater and lesser splanchnic nerves. The celiac plexus gives rise to a number of secondary autonomic plexuses including the phrenic, hepatic, left gastric, splenic, suprarenal, renal, testicular, ovarian, superior mesenteric, and inferior mesenteric plexuses. SYN: *solar p.*

cervical p. A nerve plexus, beneath the internal jugular vein in the neck, in which axons from cervical spinal nerves C1-C4 rearrange to form nerves to the neck muscles, to the diaphragm, and to the skin of parts of the head, neck, and chest. These nerves include the lesser occipital, great auricular, transverse cutaneous, supraclavicular, and phrenic nerves. (In general, axons from C1-C3 innervate parts of the head and neck, while axons from C3-C4 innervate parts of the shoulder and chest.)

choroid p. Small, tufted projections into the third, fourth, and lateral ventricles of the brain that are made of blood vessels of the pia mater covered by a thin coat of ependymal cells. These projections secrete cerebrospinal fluid.

dermal p. Any of the nerve plexuses found throughout the dermis of the skin; these plexuses contain autonomic axons and cutaneous sensory axons.

enteric p. A complex autonomic

nerve plexus inside the walls of the gastrointestinal tract, from esophagus to anus. The plexus contains intrinsic sensory and motor axons connected through local ganglionic interneurons. It is also joined by postganglionic sympathetic axons from external autonomic ganglia and preganglionic parasympathetic axons from the vagus nerve. Peristalsis, vasodilation, vasoconstriction, and secretion and absorption of substances from the intestinal lumen are controlled by this intrinsic neural network. The ganglion cells and axons of the enteric plexus that are found between the circular and longitudinal layers of muscles in the lamina externa are collectively called the myenteric division of the enteric plexus; the ganglion cells and axons found in the submucosa are called the submucosal division of the enteric plexus. SEE: *enteric nervous system.*

esophageal p. An autonomic nerve plexus surrounding the lower half of the thoracic esophagus. The plexus is formed by the vagus nerves: the left vagus nerve spreads around the front surface of the esophagus, while the right vagus nerve spreads around the back surface. The plexus is joined by sympathetic axons from the thoracic sympathetic trunk.

gastric p. Any of the secondary autonomic nerve plexuses, derived from the celiac plexus, that follow the gastric arteries to the stomach.

hemorrhoidal p Rectal **p.**

hypogastric p. The superior or the inferior hypogastric plexus.

inferior hypogastric p. ABBR: IHP. A long, thin descending extension from the superior hypogastric plexus on the right and the left sides. The inferior hypogastric plexus, which feeds into the pelvic, middle rectal, vesical, prostatic, and uterovaginal plexuses, contains sympathetic axons from the superior hypogastric plexus and the lowest lumbar splanchnic nerves and parasympathetic axons from the pelvic splanchnic nerves. The inferior hypogastric plexus (or a portion of it) is sometimes called the hypogastric nerve or the pelvic plexus.

inferior mesenteric p. A secondary nerve plexus found along the inferior mesenteric artery and its branches. It is connected to the celiac plexus and it also receives axons from the lumbar splanchnic (sympathetic) nerves. The inferior mesenteric plexus contains one or more inferior mesenteric ganglia found near the trunk of the inferior mesenteric artery.

lumbar p. A nerve plexus lying within the psoas major muscle, along the posterior abdominal wall. In this plexus, axons from spinal nerves L1-L4 rearrange to form nerves to muscles of the thigh and to skin of the thigh and leg. These nerves include the iliohypogastric, ilioinguinal, genitofemoral, lateral femoral cutaneous, femoral, obturator, and accessory obturator nerves.

lumbosacral p. The lumbar plexus and the sacral plexus.

lymphatic p. An anastomosing network of lymphatics.

Meissner p. SEE: *Meissner plexus.*

mesenteric p. The superior or the inferior mesenteric plexus.

mucosal p. An autonomic nerve plexus without ganglia found in the lamina propria in the wall of the gastrointestinal tract and is part of the enteric nervous system.

myenteric p. The division of the enteric plexus found in the external muscular layer (muscularis externa) of the walls of the gastrointestinal tract. SYN: *Auerbach plexus.*

nerve p. A meshwork of axons, fascicles of axons, or nerves outside the central nervous system. Axons, which join the meshwork from incoming nerves, resort and exit the meshwork singly or with new companions.

ovarian p. A secondary autonomic nerve plexus that follows the ovarian artery to the ovary and the Fallopian tube. This plexus is connected to the celiac plexus and gets additional sympathetic axons from the lowest thoracic spinal segments and parasympathetic axons from the inferior hypogastric plexus.

pampiniform p. In males, a venous plexus that surrounds the testicular artery inside the distal segment of the spermatic cord. The pampiniform plexus drains the testicular veins (from the testis and epididymis). Before the spermatic cord enters the inguinal canal from the scrotum, the pampiniform plexus empties into 3-4 parallel veins. After exiting the inguinal canal, these veins merge to form two testicular veins. In females, there is a homologous venous plexus located in the broad ligament; it intervenes between the veins draining the ovary and the final ovarian veins, which empty blood back into the systemic circulation.

papillary p. A nerve plexus that ramifies throughout the junction between the reticular and papillary layers of the dermis of the skin. The plexus contains autonomic axons and cutaneous sensory axons.

pelvic p. SEE: *inferior hypogastric p.*

perivascular p. An autonomic nerve plexus coating an artery.

pharyngeal p. 1. A nerve plexus along the posterior surface of the middle pharyngeal constrictor muscle. The plexus contains sympathetic, parasympathetic, and somatic (branchial) axons from the pharyngeal branch of the vagus nerve, the glossopharyngeal and external laryngeal nerves, and the sympathetic trunk. Axons from the pharyngeal plexus innervate the muscles and mucosa of the pharynx and soft palate. **2.** A venous plexus that drains the pharynx and that empties into the internal jugular and facial veins; it interconnects with the pterygoid plexus.

prostatic p. 1. In males, an autonomic nerve plexus that is an extension of the inferior hypogastric plexus. It sends axons to the prostate gland, the erectile tissue of the penis, and the seminal vesicles. **2.** In males, a venous plexus anterior to the bladder and prostate gland. Its tributaries include the deep dorsal vein of the penis. It connects with the vesical plexus and the internal pudendal vein, and it empties into the vesical veins and internal iliac vein.

pterygoid p. A venous plexus lying between the temporalis, lateral pterygoid, and medial pterygoid muscles. Many of the deeper veins of the front of the head, e.g., deep temporal, sphenopalatine, inferior ophthalmic, dental, connect with this plexus, which empties into the deep facial vein and which is thus in communication with the cavernous sinus inside the skull.

pulmonary p. An autonomic nerve plexus extending from the cardiac plexus into the lungs along the right and left pulmonary arteries. Parasympathetic axons come from the vagus nerves, and sympathetic axons from the sympathetic trunk. Axons from the pulmonary plexus follow the bronchi and the bronchial vessels and provide the autonomic innervation inside the lungs.

rectal p. 1. Any of three autonomic nerve plexuses — superior, middle, and inferior — innervating the rectum. The rectal plexuses are extensions of the inferior hypogastric plexus and they follow the three corresponding rectal arteries. **2.** Any of three venous plexuses — external, internal, and superior — in and around the rectum. The external rectal plexus empties via the internal rectal vein, into the internal pudendal vein; the internal and the superior rectal plexuses empty into the superior rectal vein. When veins in the internal rectal plexus develop varices, the varicose segments are called hemorrhoids. SYN: *hemorrhoidal p.*

renal p. A dense autonomic nerve plexus along the renal artery; it contains small ganglia and its axons follow the branches of the renal artery into the kidney.

sacral p. 1. A nerve plexus lying along the posterior wall of the pelvis, deep to the internal iliac blood vessels and anterior to the piriformis muscle. In this plexus, axons from spinal nerves L4-S4 rearrange to form sensory and motor nerves to the thigh, leg, and foot. These nerves include the superior gluteal, inferior gluteal, posterior femoral cutaneous, sciatic, and pudendal nerves. The lower portion of the sacral plexus also gives rise to the preganglionic parasympathetic axons of the pelvic splanchnic nerves. **2.** A venous plexus, on the pelvic surface of the sacrum, that interconnects the lateral sacral veins.

solar p. Celiac **p.**

subdermal p. A nerve plexus found in the deep dermis and between the dermis and the subcutaneous tissue; it contains autonomic axons and cutaneous sensory axons.

submucous p. Submucosal **p.**

submucosal p. The division of the enteric plexus found in the submucosal layer of the walls of the gastrointestinal tract. The most superficial (closest to the lumen) layer of the submucosal plexus is also called the Meissner plexus. SYN: *submucous p.* SEE: *Meissner plexus.*

superior mesenteric p. A continuation of the celiac nerve plexus. It runs along the superior mesenteric artery and it provides autonomic innervation to the same intestinal segments supplied by the artery.

sympathetic p. An autonomic plexus composed of sympathetic axons. Large sympathetic plexuses surround the midline (prevertebral) sympathetic ganglia, which are found near major midline arteries such as the celiac trunk.

tympanic p. A nerve plexus along the medial wall of the tympanic cavity. The axons of this plexus come from the glossopharyngeal nerve and the caroticotympanic nerves, i.e., sympathetic axons from the internal carotid plexus.

vaginal p. 1. The autonomic nerve plexus that supplies axons to the walls of the vagina. **2.** A venous plexus surrounding the vagina; it empties, via the internal pudendal vein, into the internal iliac vein.

venous p. A network of interconnecting veins.

vertebral p. 1. An autonomic nerve plexus that runs along each vertebral artery and carries sympathetic axons to arteries inside the skull. **2.** Any of the anastomosing networks of valveless veins draining the vertebral column and spinal cord. Outside the spinal canal, anterior vertebral plexuses lie in front of the vertebral bodies, while posterior plexuses surround the vertebral spines and other vertebral processes. Inside the spinal canal, dense vertebral plexuses run between the bone and the dura; at the top of the cord, the internal vertebral plexuses communicate with intracranial sinuses.

vesical p. 1. An autonomic nerve plexus that is an extension of the inferior hypogastric plexus; it supplies nerves to the bladder muscles and, in males, to the seminal vesicles and the ductus deferens. **2.** A venous plexus surrounding and draining blood from the upper part of the urethra and the neck of the bladder. It empties, via vesical veins, into the internal iliac vein. In males, it connects to the prostatic plexus∞ females, it connects to the vaginal plexus.

pliability (plī″ă-bĭl′ĭ-tē) [O.Fr. *pliant*, bend, + L. *abilis*, able] Capacity of being bent or twisted easily.

plica (plī′kă, plī′kē″, sē″) *pl.* **plicae** [L. *plica*, a fold] A fold. SEE: *fold*.

circular p. One of the transverse folds of the mucosa and submucosa of the small intestine. Collectively they resemble accordion pleats, do not disappear with distention of the intestine, and increase the surface area for absorption. SEE: *circular folds*.

semilunar p. of the colon The transverse fold of mucosa of the large intestine lying between sacculations.

semilunar p. of the conjunctiva The mucosal fold at the inner canthus of the eye.

transverse p. of the rectum One of the mucosal folds in the rectum.

plica syndrome Patellar pain and a sensation of instability, clicking, or locking of the knee as a result of inflammation of the synovial plicae (folds) of the knee joint

plicate (plī′kāt) [L. *plicatus*] Braided or folded.

plication (plī-kā′shŏn) [L. *plicare*, to fold] The stitching of folds or tucks in tissue at an organ's walls to reduce its size.

esophageal p. Esophagoplication.

p. of the stomach A surgical procedure for obesity supplanted by partial gastric bypass. SEE: *fundoplication*.

pliers (plī′ĕrz) **1.** Commonly, a scissor-action, pointed-jawed tool for bending or cutting metal wires or grasping small objects. **2.** In dentistry, a variety of instruments that have been shaped or adapted for special uses such as cutting arch wires or metal clasps, shaping metal crown details, applying cotton pledgets or rolls, carrying metal foils, tying ligatures, and placing or removing matrix bands.

plinth (plinth) [Gr. *plinthos*, squared stone, tile] A table, seat, or apparatus on which a patient lies or sits while doing remedial exercise or undergoing examination.

plio- SEE: *pleio-*.

-ploid [(*ha*)*ploid*] Suffix meaning the *number of chromosome pairs* of the root word to which it is added.

ploidy (ploy′dē) [Gr. *ploos*, a fold, + ei-*dos*, form, shape] The number of chromosome sets in a cell (e.g., haploidy, diploidy, and triploidy for one, two, and three sets, respectively, of chromosomes).

plug (plŭg) **1.** A mass obstructing a hole or intended to close a hole. **2.** A plastic or metallic device for closing the end of an instrument or tube.

ear p. A device for preventing sound from entering the ear by occluding the external auditory canal.

⚠ Ear plugs should not be used during swimming, diving, or flying because they may interfere with pressure equalization.

epithelial p. A mass of epithelial cells temporarily closing up an orifice in the embryo, esp. the nasal openings.

lacrimal p. Punctal **p.**

mucous p. 1. A mass of cells and mucus that closes the cervical canal of the uterus during pregnancy and between menstrual periods. **2.** A mass of cells and mucus that obstructs an airway, limiting respiratory gas exchange.

punctal p., punctum plug A small plastic device inserted into a tear duct to block the drainage of tears and treat dry eye syndromes. SYN: *lacrimal* **p.**

vaginal p. A closed tube for maintaining patency of the vagina following surgery for fistula.

plugger (plŭg′ĕr) A hand- or machine-operated tool for condensing amalgam or gold foil in the cavity preparation of a tooth. SEE: *condenser (2).*

automatic p. A plugger that is run by a machine rather than by hand.

back-action p. A plugger with a bent shank so that the pressure applied is back toward the operator.

foot p. A plugger with a broad, foot-shaped tip.

plumbism (plŭm′bĭzm) [L. *plumbum*, lead, + Gr. *-ismos*, condition] Poisoning from lead.

plume (ploom) A wisp or puff of smoke, esp. one that may rise from a surgical field in which electrocautery or lasers are used to cut, coagulate, or destroy tissue. Surgical plumes may contain carbon monoxide, among other potentially toxic gases.

Plummer-Vinson syndrome (plŭm′ĕr-vĭn′sŏn) [Henry S. Plummer, U.S. physician, 1874–1937; Porter P. Vinson, U.S. surgeon, 1890–1959] Iron-deficiency anemia, associated with dysphagia, gastric achlorhydria, splenomegaly, and spooning of the nails due to an esophageal web. It occurs most commonly in premenopausal women. Treatment consists of disrupting the web. SEE: *esophageal web.*

plumper (plŭm′pĕr) A pad for filling out

sunken cheeks, sometimes in the form of a flange or extension from artificial dentures.

pluri- [L. *plus*, stem *plur-*, more] Prefixes meaning *several, more.*

pluriglandular (ploo″rĭ-glănd′ū-lăr) [″ + *glandula*, gland] Polyglandular.

plurilocular (ploo″rĭ-lŏk′ū-lăr) [″ + *loculus*, a cell] Multilocular.

pluripotent, pluripotential (ploo-rip′ŏt-ĕnt, ploor″ĭ-pŏ-ten′shăl) [″ + *potentia*, power] **1.** Pert. to an embryonic cell that can form different kinds of cells. **2.** Having a number of different actions.

plutonium (ploo-tō′nē-ŭm) [*Pluto*, (the planet) + *-ium*] SYMB: Pu. A radioactive chemical element obtained from neptunium, which in turn is obtained from uranium; atomic weight (mass) (most stable isotope) 244, atomic number 94.

PLWA *people living with HIV/AIDS.*

plyometrics (plī-ō-mĕt′rĭks) An exercise technique that combines strength with speed to achieve maximum power in functional movements. This regimen combines eccentric training of muscles with concentric contraction.

Pm Symbol for the element promethium.

PMD *powered mobility device.*

PMDD *premenstrual dysphoric disorder.*

PML *progressive multifocal leukoencephalopathy.*

PMMA *polymethylmethacrylate.*

PMP *prescription monitoring program.*

PMS *premenstrual syndrome.*

PMSG *pregnant mare serum gonadotropin.* SEE: *gonadotropin, human chorionic.*

PMT *photomultiplier tube; premenstrual tension.*

P$_{mus}$ The pressure generated by the respiratory muscles during inspiration or expiration.

PNA *peptide nucleic acid; pneumonia.*

PNC *premature nodal contraction* or *complex.*

PND *paroxysmal-nocturnal dyspnea.*

-pnea [Gr. *pnoia*, *pnoē*, breath, fr. *pnein*, to breathe] Suffix meaning *breath, breathe,* or *breathing.* The variant *-pnoea* is used outside the U.S.

PNES *psychogenic nonepileptic seizure.*

pneum-, pneumo- [Gr. *pneuma*, air, breath] Prefixes meaning *air, gas, respiration, pneumonia.* SEE: *pneumato-; pneumono-.*

pneumatic (nū-măt′ĭk) [Gr. *pneumatikos*, pert. to air] **1.** Pert. to gas or air. **2.** Pert. to respiration. **3.** Pert. to rarefied or compressed air.

pneumatic antishock garment ABBR: PASG. Antishock garment.

pneumatics (nū-măt′ĭks) The branch of physics that is concerned with the physical and mechanical properties of gases and air.

pneumatization (nū″mă-tĭ-zā′shŭn) The

formation of air-filled cavities, usually in bone (e.g., the paranasal sinuses and mastoid sinuses).

pneumatized (noo′mŭ-tīzd, nū′) Filled with air or gas.

pneumato-, pneumat- [Gr. *pneuma*, stem *pneumat-*, air, breath] Prefixes meaning *air, gas, pneumatic, respiration.* SEE: *pneum-; pneumono-.*

pneumatocele (nū-măt′ō-sēl) [″ + *kele*, tumor, swelling] **1.** A hernia of the lung tissue. **2.** A swelling containing gas or air, esp. a swelling of the scrotum. SYN: *pneumonocele.*

    extracranial p. A collection of gas under the scalp, caused by a fracture of the skull that communicates with a paranasal sinus.

    intracranial p. A collection of gas within the skull. SYN: *pneumocephalus; pneumocranium.*

pneumatosis (nū″mă-tō′sĭs) [Gr. *pneumatosis*] The presence of air or gas in an abnormal location in the body.

    p. cystoides intestinalis The presence of thin-walled gas-filled cysts in the intestines. The cause is unknown. The cysts usually disappear but occasionally rupture and cause pneumoperitoneum.

pneumaturia (noo″mă-toor′ē-ă) [Gr. *pneuma*, air, + *ouron*, urine] Excretion of urine containing free gas.

pneumectomy (noo″mek′tŏ-mē, nū″) [*pneum-* + *-ectomy*] Pneumonectomy.

pneumobilia (noo″mō-bil′ē-ă, nū″) [*pneum-* + *bile* + *-ia*] Air or gas within the bile ducts. It is a finding associated primarily with cholecystitis caused by gas-forming organisms.

pneumocephalus (nū″mō-sĕf′ă-lŭs) [Gr. *pneuma*, air, + *kephale*, head] Intracranial pneumatocele.

pneumococcal (nū″mō-kŏk′ăl) [″ + *kokkos*, berry] Concerning or caused by pneumococci.

pneumococcemia (nū″mō-kŏk-sē′mē-ă) The presence of pneumococci in the blood.

pneumococcus (nū″mō-kŏk′ŭs) *pl.* **pneumococci** [″ + *kokkos*, berry] *Streptococcus pneumoniae.*

pneumocolon (nū″mō-kō′lŏn) [″ + *kolon*, colon] Air in the colon. This may be introduced as an aid in radiological diagnosis.

pneumoconiosis (nū″mō-kō″nē-ō′sĭs) [″ + *konis*, dust, + *osis*, condition] Any disease of the respiratory tract owing to inhalation of dust particles; an occupational disorder such as that caused by mining or stonecutting. SYN: *pneumonoconiosis.* SEE: table.

pneumocranium (nū″mō-krā′nē-ŭm) [″ + *kranion*, skull] Intracranial pneumatocele.

Pneumocystis carinii (noo″mō-sis′tĭs kă-rī′nē-ē″) [A. Carini, Italian microbiolo-

The Pneumoconioses

Asbestosis*
Black lung disease (coal worker's
  pneumoconiosis)
Mixed dust pneumoconiosis
Silicosis
Talcosis

*Asbestosis is currently the most common
lung disease caused by the inhalation of mineral dusts

gist, 1872–1950] SEE: *Pneumocystis jiroveci.*
Pneumocystis jiroveci (jĭr-ō′vĕ-sī″) [Otto
Jirovec, Czech parasitologist, 1910–
1972] An opportunistic fungus that
causes lung infections in those with immunosuppressive diseases and conditions. It was formerly called *pneumocystis carinii.* SEE: illus.

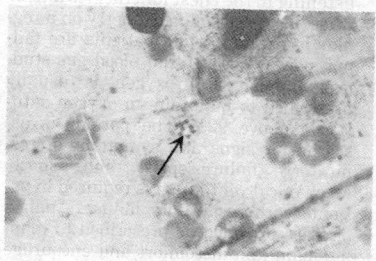

PNEUMOCYSTIS JIROVECI (×1000)

pneumocystography (nū″mō-sĭs-tŏg′ră-
fē) [Gr. *pneuma,* air, + *kystis,* bladder, + *graphein,* to write] A cystogram done after air has been introduced
into the urinary bladder.
pneumocystosis (nū″mō-sĭs-tō′sĭs)
Pneumocystis carinii pneumonia.
pneumocyte (nū′mō-sīt) Either of the
two types of cells that form the alveoli
of the lung. Type I cells are simple squamous epithelium that permit gas exchange. Type II cells are rounded and
produce surfactant.
pneumodynamics (noo″mō-dī-nam′iks,
nū″) [*pneumo-* + *dynamics*] The
branch of science dealing with force employed in respiration.
pneumoencephalitis (nū″mō-ĕn-sĕf″ă-
lī′tĭs) [″ + *enkephalos,* brain, + *itis,*
inflammation] Newcastle disease.
pneumoencephalography (nū″mō-ĕn-sĕf
″ă-lŏg′ră-fē) [″ + ″ + *graphein,* to
write] An obsolete technique of radiography of the ventricles and subarachnoid spaces of the brain following withdrawal of cerebrospinal fluid and
injection of air or gas via lumbar puncture. This technique has been replaced
by computed tomography and magnetic
resonance imaging.
pneumogram (nū′mō-grăm) [″ +

gramma, something written] **1.** A
record of respiratory movements. **2.** A
radiograph following injection of air.
pneumograph (nū′mō-grăf) [″ +
graphein, to write] A device for recording the frequency and intensity of respiration.
pneumography (nū-mŏg′ră-fē) **1.** An anatomical description or illustration of
the lung. **2.** The recording of respiratory
movements on a graph. **3.** Radiography
of a part or organ after injection of air.
pneumohemopericardium (nū″mō-
hēm″ō-pĕr-ĭ-kăr′dē-ŭm) [Gr. *pneumon,*
lung, + *haima,* blood, + *peri,*
around, + *kardia,* heart] The accumulation of air and blood in the pericardium.
pneumohemothorax (nū″mō-hēm″ō-
thō′răks) [″ + ″ + *thorax,* chest]
Gas or air and blood collected in the
pleural cavity.
pneumolysin (nū-mŏl′ĭ-sĭn) A hemolytic
toxin produced by pneumococci.
pneumomassage (nū″mō-mă-săzh′)
[Gr. *pneuma,* air, + *massein,* to knead]
Massage of the tympanum with air to
cause movement of the ossicles of the inner ear.
pneumomediastinum (nū″mō-mē″dē-ăs-
tī′nŭm) [″ + L. *mediastinum,* in the
middle] The presence of air or gas in
the mediastinal tissues, either owing to
disease or following injection of air into
the area. It is a cause of intense chest
pain that worsens with movement.
pneumonectomy (noo″mŏ-nek′tŏ-mē, nū″)
[*pneumono-* + *-ectomy*] Excision of an
entire lung. SYN: *pneumectomy.*
  extrapleural p. Surgery that removes
  a lung, the adjacent pleural and the pericardium. It is used as a treatment for
  malignant mesothelioma.
pneumonia (noo-mōn′yă, nū-) [*pneu-
mono-* + *-ia*] ABBR: PNA. Inflammation of the lungs, usually due to infection with bacteria, viruses, or other
pathogenic organisms. Clinically, *pneumonia* indicates an infectious disease.
Pulmonary inflammation due to other
causes is called *pneumonitis.* In the
U.S., about 4,500,000 people contract
pneumonia each year, and pneumonia is
the sixth most common cause of death
in the U.S. and the most common cause
of death due to infectious disease. Pneumonia occurs most commonly in weakened people (those with cancer, heart or
lung disease, immunosuppressive illnesses, diabetes mellitus, cirrhosis,
malnutrition, and renal failure), but virulent pathogens can cause pneumonia
in the healthy, as well. Smoking, general anesthesia, and endotracheal intubation increase the risk for developing
pneumonia by inhibiting airway defenses and helping disease-causing
germs reach the alveoli of the lungs.
SEE: *aspiration; pleural* **effusion***; em-*

pyema; pleurisy; pneumonitis; tuberculosis (and names of lung pathogens); *Nursing Diagnoses Appendix.*

ETIOLOGY: Pneumonias are categorized by site and cause. *Lobar pneumonia* affects most of a single lobe; *bronchopneumonia* involves smaller lung areas in several lobes; *interstitial pneumonia* affects tissues surrounding the alveoli and bronchi of the lung. *Atypical pneumonias* diffusely affect lung tissues rather than anatomical lobes or lobules. *Community-acquired pneumonia* is a lung infection that occurs in noninstitutionalized people, typically involving organisms such as viruses, *Streptococcus pneumoniae, Klebsiella pneumoniae, Mycoplasma pneumoniae, Legionella pneumophila, Chlamydia pneumoniae, Moraxella* spp, or *Pneumocystis carinii*. *Nosocomial pneumonia* develops in patients in the hospital or nursing home; this type is most likely to be caused by gram-negative rods or staphylococcal species. *Aspiration pneumonias* result from the inhalation of oropharyngeal microorganisms and often involve anaerobic organisms. Pneumonias in immunocompromised patients sometimes are caused by *Pneumocystis jiroveci* or by fungal species such as *Aspergillus.* or *Candida.* Some fungal pneumonias occur in specific geographical regions of the U.S. For example, histoplasmosis is common in the Ohio River Valley, and coccidioidomycosis is found in the San Joaquin River Valley of southern California. Viral pneumonias may be caused by influenza,varicella-zoster, herpes, or adenoviruses.

SYMPTOMS: Most patients with pneumonia have cough, shortness of breath, and fever although these symptoms are not universal. Bacterial pneumonias are marked by abrupt onset, with high fevers, shaking chills, pleuritic chest pain, and prostration. Patients with atypical pneumonias usually have lower temperatures and nonproductive coughs and appear less ill.

PREVENTION: Pneumococcal vaccine effectively prevents many forms of streptococcal pneumonia. This vaccine is recommended for people over 65; those with chronic respiratory, cardiac, or neuromuscular diseases; and patients with diabetes mellitus or renal failure.

TREATMENT: Treatment is based on the clinical presentation (such as community-acquired versus nosocomial), results of the Gram stain of sputum specimens, the radiographical appearance of the pneumonia, the degree of respiratory impairment, and the results of cultures. Many patients hospitalized with pneumonia require supplemental oxygen and analgesics. Initial antibiotic treatments for pneumonia should be given without delay and typically involve powerful, broad-spectrum drugs. The antibiotic used for subsequent therapy is guided by the results of cultured specimens taken on presentation.

PATIENT CARE: A large percentage of patients with pneumonia are not admitted to hospitals but are treated with antibiotics given on an outpatient basis. However, older adults, people with serious chronic diseases, and those with evidence of organ dysfunction, poor oxygenation, or acute decompensation may need hospitalization to reduce the risk of injury or death. Supportive care is provided to the patient to remove secretions and improve gas exchange. Such care includes position changes, deep breathing and coughing exercises, incentive spirometry, active and passive limb exercises, and assistance with self-care. Respiratory status is monitored by listening to the chest for crackles and/or wheezing, performing oximetry on a regular basis, and, when patients are failing, performing arterial blood gas studies. Supplemental oxygen is usually prescribed to maintain an oxygen saturation above 92%. The patient is assessed for signs and symptoms of respiratory failure,sepsis, and shock. Mechanical ventilation is required in patients with respiratory failure. Analgesics are provided as prescribed to manage pain and discomfort and encourage good pulmonary toilet. A large percentage of patients receive care to remove secretions and to improve gas exchange. Such care includes position changes, deep-breathing, and coughing exercises. The patient is encouraged to verbalize concerns; diagnostic studies and therapeutic measures are explained, and the patient is taught about the importance of follow-up care. Outpatient therapy of community-acquired pneumonia can be recommended for selected patients who are young, otherwise healthy, and not hypoxic, hypotensive, hypothermic, or in renal failure. Activities are scheduled to allow for plenty of rest. The patient is taught hand hygiene and encouraged to wash hands with soap and water or use an alcohol-based hand wipe entirely over both hands after blowing the nose, coughing, using thebathroom, or eating or drinking. Only disposable tissues are used for sneezing and coughing. Used tissues are deposited in a lined bag taped to the bedside and are disposed of frequently according to agency policy. Unless otherwise restricted, the patient should drink eight 12-ounce glasses of water daily to help thin and loosen mucous secretions. Each patient's meal preferences and restrictions are discussed to plan a diet that ensures adequate high-caloric intake. Emotional support is provided, and all procedures and treatments are explained. The patient who smokes is taught the relationship between smoking and lung diseases (including the increased risk of respiratory infections) and referred for support group assistance with quitting as needed. Pneumonia prevention is aided by encouraging individuals to avoid indiscriminate antibiotic use, receive pneumonia and influenza vaccinations, perform deep-breathing and coughing exercises when confined to bedand after surgery, and ambulate early after surgery. Aspiration pneumonia is prevented in tube-fed patients by correct positioning and slow, low-volume feedings. The chronically ill and debilitated in nursing homes should have swallowing function assessed as necessary; caregivers should be taught correct feeding techniques to prevent aspiration.

acute lobar p. Lobar **p.**

aspiration p. Pneumonia caused by inhalation of gastric contents, food, or other substances. A frequent cause is loss of the gag reflex in patients with central nervous system depression or damage or alcoholic intoxication with stupor and vomiting. This condition also occurs in newborns who inhale infected amniotic fluid, meconium, or vaginal secretions during delivery.

atypical p. Pneumonia caused by a virus or *Mycoplasma pneumoniae.* The symptoms are low-grade fever, nonproductive cough, pharyngitis, myalgia, and minimal adventitious lung sounds.

bacterial p. Pneumonia caused by bacteria such as streptococcus, *Staphylococcus aureus, Klebsiella,* or coliforms.

chlamydial p. An atypical pneumonia caused by *Chlamydia* spp, characterized clinically by cough, low-grade fever, sore throat, and malaise. A chest x-ray taken during the illness is more likely to show diffuse lung involvement than a lobar pneumonia.

community-acquired p. Pneumonia occurring in outpatients, often caused by infection with streptococcus, *Haemophilus influenzae, Staphylococcus aureus,* and atypical organisms such as *Legionella* spp. Mortality is approx. 15% but depends on many host and pathogen features.

desquamative interstitial p. Pneumonia of unknown cause, accompanied by cellular infiltration or fibrosis in the pulmonary interstitium. Progressive dyspnea and a nonproductive cough are symptoms characterizing this disease. Clubbing of the fingers is a common finding. Diffusion of oxygen and carbon dioxide is abnormal. Diagnosis is made by lung biopsy. The condition is treated by corticosteroids.

double p. Pneumonia that involves both lungs or two lobes.

embolic p. Pneumonia following embolization of a pulmonary blood vessel.

eosinophilic p. Infiltration of the lung by eosinophils, typically found in patients with peripheral eosinophilia. The cause is usually unknown; occasionally, the condition responds to the administration of corticosteroids. In some cases, a specific underlying cause is found, such as the recent initiation of cigarette smoking or an allergic drug reaction. Infection with some parasites or fungi also can trigger the disease. SYN: *pulmonary **infiltration** with eosinophilia.*

fibrous p. Pneumonia followed by formation of scar tissue.

Friedländer p. SEE: *Friedländer pneumonia.*

gangrenous p. Pulmonary gangrene.

giant cell p. An interstitial pneumonitis of infancy and childhood. The lung tissue contains multinucleated giant cells. The disease often occurs in connection with measles.

healthcare-associated p. Nosocomial **p.**

hypostatic p. Pneumonia occurring in elderly or bed-ridden patients who remain constantly in the same position. Ventilation is greatest in dependent areas. Remaining in one position causes hypoventilation in many areas, causing alveolar collapse (atelectasis) and creating a pulmonary environment that supports the growth of bacteria or other organisms. Development of this condition is prevented by having the patient change positions and take deep breaths to inflate peripheral alveoli.

PATIENT CARE: Prevention is the most important factor, esp. in older and immobile persons. Patients should be moved and turned frequently at least every 1 to 2 hr. The nurse and respiratory therapist should monitor respiratory status by frequently auscultating for crackles, gurgles, and wheezes and encourage the patient to engage in active movement and to perform deep-breathing and coughing exercises frequently and regularly. Incentive spirometry may prove useful in patients who need added encouragement to deep breathe periodically.

intrauterine p. Pneumonia contracted in utero.

Legionella p. Legionnaires' disease.

lipoid p. Damage to lung tissue that results from aspiration of oils. It may occur repeatedly in patients with impaired swallowing mechanisms or in persons affected by esophageal disorders, such as esophageal carcinoma, achalasia, or scleroderma. Mineral oils and cooking oils often are responsible. Most cases resolve spontaneously, but corticosteroids sometimes are used as treatment to reduce inflammatory changes. Distinguishing lipoid pneumonia from bacterial pneumonia may require endoscopy.

lobar p. Pneumonia infecting one or more lobes of the lung, usually caused by *Streptococcus pneumoniae*. The pathologic changes are, in order, congestion; redness and firmness due to exudate and red blood cells in the alveoli; and, finally, gray hepatization as the exudate degenerates and is absorbed. SYN: *acute lobar p.*

neonatal p. Lung infection occurring in the first few days of life due to uterine exposure to infectious microorganisms or to infection during or immediately after birth. Common causes include viruses (such as herpes simplex) and bacteria (such as group B streptococcus, *Chlamydia, Escherichia coli, Listeria*).

nosocomial p. Pneumonia occurring after 48 hr of confinement in a hospital, intensive care unit, or nursing home. It is often the result of infection with gram-negative pathogens or multiply drug-resistant bacteria and includes both ventilator-associated pneumonias and other lower respiratory tract infections. SYN: *healthcare-associated p.*

pneumococcal p. The most common form of pneumonia in the U.S., affecting about half a million people each year. It often begins with hard-shaking chills and may be fatal, esp. in the elderly or those with underlying diseases. It usually strikes smokers, people with underlying lung diseases, those recently infected with influenza or those with sickle-cell anemia, chronic or heavy alcohol use, or cirrhosis.

SYMPTOMS: Fevers, body-shaking chills, productive cough, pleurisy, prostration, and sweating.

TREATMENT: Penicillin may be used when the pneumococcus is sensitive to this agent, but the incidence of penicillin resistance in pneumococci is rapidly growing. Third-generation cephalosporins, erythromycin, vancomycin, and linezolid, are alternative agents.

PATIENT CARE: Vaccination provides passive immunity against many serotypes of pneumococcal pneumonia. People over the age of 65 or those with heart, lung, liver, kidney, or immunosuppressive diseases should be immunized as should infants under the age of two.

Pneumocystis carinii p. ABBR: PCP. A subacute opportunistic infection marked by fever, nonproductive cough, tachypnea, dyspnea, and hypoxemia. It is caused by *Pneumocystis carinii*, the former name of *Pneumocystis jiroveci*, an organism formerly thought to be a protozoan but now generally accepted as a fungus. The disease is seen principally in immunosuppressed patients, such as those with AIDS or who have received an organ transplant and immunosuppressant drugs. Without treatment, the progressive respiratory failure that the infection causes is ultimately fatal.

DIAGNOSIS: The disease should be suspected in patients with human immunodeficiency virus infection or other risk factors for the disease who present with cough and shortness of breath. Chest x-ray examination may reveal diffuse interstitial infiltrates, upper lobe disease, spontaneous pneumothorax, or cystic lung disease. The diagnosis is confirmed with special stains of sputum, bronchial washings, or lung biopsy specimens.

TREATMENT: Oral trimethoprim-sulfamethoxazole effectively protects against PCP, and is also the drug of choice for active infection. Other drugs that are active against PCP include pentamidine, trimethoprim in combination with dapsone, and atovaquone. Corticosteroids are used as adjunctive therapy when treating markedly hypoxic patients, e.g., those who present with an alveolar-arterial oxygen gradient of more than 35 mm Hg. The introduction of highly active antiretroviral drug cocktails for AIDS patients has markedly reduced the incidence of PCP.

secondary p. Pneumonia that occurs in connection with a specific systemic disease such as typhoid, diphtheria, or plague.

tuberculous p. Pneumonia caused by *Mycobacterium tuberculosis*. SEE: *tuberculosis*.

tularemic p. Pneumonia caused by *Francisella tularensis*. It may be primary or associated with tularemia.

ventilator-associated p. In patients receiving invasive mechanical ventilation, a new and persistent infiltrate seen on chest x-ray associated with fever, elevated or depressed white blood cell counts, and sputum that is either purulent or full of disease-causing bacteria. SYN: *artificial airway-associated p.*

viral p. Any infections of the lower respiratory tract (the lungs, bronchioles, and trachea) caused by viral species such as adenovirus, coronavirus, herpesviruses, influenza viruses, and respiratory syncytial viruses. Viral pneumonias may range from mild respiratory infections (with nonproductive cough and low-grade fevers) to life-threatening and highly contagious illnesses (such as SARS). SEE: *bronchitis; bronchiolitis*.

Pneumonia PORT score [Patient Outcomes Research Team] Pneumonia Severity **Index**.

Pneumonia severity index SEE: under *index.*

pneumonic (nū-mŏn'ĭk) [Gr. *pneumon,* lung] Pert. to the lungs or pneumonia.

pneumonitis (nū″mō-nī'tĭs) [″ + *itis,* inflammation] Inflammation of the lung, usually due to hypersensitivity (allergy), radiation exposure, aspiration, viral infection, or autoimmune illnesses, such as systemic lupus erythematosus.

 hypersensitivity p. Immunologically induced inflammation of the lungs of a susceptible host caused by repeated inhalation of a variety of substances including organic dusts. Included are molds and other fungi from sources such as cheese, vegetables, mushrooms, flour, mushroom compost, bark of trees, detergents, and contaminated humidification systems. In the acute stage, patients may present with cough, fever, chills, malaise, and shortness of breath. In the subacute and chronic forms, the onset of symptoms is gradual and prolonged. Treatment includes identifying and avoiding causative agents.

 mycoplasma p. A form of atypical pneumonia caused by *Mycoplasma pneumoniae.*

 pneumococcal p. Pneumonia caused by pneumococci. SEE: *Streptococcus pneumoniae.*

pneumono-, pneumon- [Gr. *pneumōn,* lung] Prefixes meaning *lung.* SEE: *pneum-; pneumato-.*

pneumonoconiosis (noo″mă-nō-kō″nē-ō'sĭs) [″ + *konis,* dust, + *osis,* condition] Pneumoconiosis.

pneumonocyte (nū-mō'nō-sīt) Either a type I or a type II alveolar cell of the lungs.

pneumonolysis (nū″mŏ-nŏl'ĭ-sĭs) [″ + *lysis,* dissolution] The loosening and separation of an adherent lung from the costal pleura.

 extrapleural p. Separation of the parietal pleura from the chest wall. SEE: *apicolysis.*

 intrapleural p. Separation of adhering visceral and parietal layers of pleura.

pneumonorrhapy (nū″mō-nor'ă-fē) [″ + *rhaphe,* seam, ridge] Suture of a lung.

pneumopericardium (nū″mō-pĕr-ĭ-kăr'dē-ŭm) [Gr. *pneuma,* air, + *peri,* around, + *kardia,* heart] Air or gas in the pericardial sac; caused by trauma or pathological communication between the esophagus, stomach, or lungs and the pericardium. On examination one finds unusual metallic heart sounds and tympany over the precordial area.

pneumoperitoneum (nū″mō-pĕr-ĭ-tō-nē'ŭm) [″ + *peritonaion,* peritoneum] **1.** A condition in which air or gas collects in the peritoneal cavity. This may occur catastrophically when internal organs rupture. **2.** Air or gas that has been injected into the peritoneal cavity to facilitate laparoscopy.

pneumoretroperitoneum (nū″mō-rĕt″rō-pĕr″ĭ-tō-nē'ŭm) [″ + L. *retro,* backwards, + Gr. *peritonaion,* peritoneum] Air or gas in the retroperitoneal space.

pneumoscopy (noo-mos'kō-pē, nū-) [*pneum-* + *-scopy*] Insufflation of air into the external auditory canal during otoscopy. The procedure is performed to see if the tympanic membrane moves normally or if its movements are dampened by fluids or a mass in the middle ear.

pneumotaxic (nū″mō-tăk'sĭk) [″ + *taxis,* arrangement] Pert. to the regulation of breathing.

pneumothorax (noo″mŏ-thōr'aks″, nū″, -thŏr'ă-sēz″) *pl.* **pneumothoraces, pneumothoraxes** [*pneum-* + *thorax*] A collection of air or gas in the pleural cavity. The gas enters following a perforation through the chest wall, e.g., due to traumatic or iatrogenic injury, or the pleura, e.g., from the rupture of an emphysematous bleb or superficial lung abscess. Some tall, slender young men and women suffer repeated episodes of spontaneous pneumothorax. SEE: illus.; *Nursing Diagnoses Appendix.*

SYMPTOMS: The onset is sudden, usually with a severe sharp pain in the side of the chest, and dyspnea. The physical signs are those of a distended unilateral chest, increased resonance, decrease in or absence of breath sounds, and, if fluid is present, a splashing sound on succussion (shaking) of the patient. Patients often report chest pain is worsened by coughing, deep breathing, or movement.

DIAGNOSIS: Chest x-rays confirm the diagnosis, revealing air in the pleural space, often identified as a line seen outlining a partially collapsed lung. A shift of the mediastinum toward one side of the chest or the other may be seen in tension pneumothorax. SEE: *tension p.*

TREATMENT: Treatment varies according to type and amount of lung collapse. Traumatic or iatrogenic pneumothorax requires chest tube insertion to closed (water-sealed) chest drainage for lung re-expansion. Surgical repair also may be required. Spontaneous pneumothorax may be treated conservatively with bedrest if there is no sign of increased pleural pressure, less than 15% lung collapse, no dyspnea or other indication of physiological compromise. If the patient's condition worsens or if more than 15% of the lung is collapsed, a thoracostomy tube may be placed anteriorly in the second intercostal space and attached to a Heimlich flutter valve or chest-drainage unit. If fluid is present in the pleural space, a thoracostomy tube is placed in the fourth, fifth, or

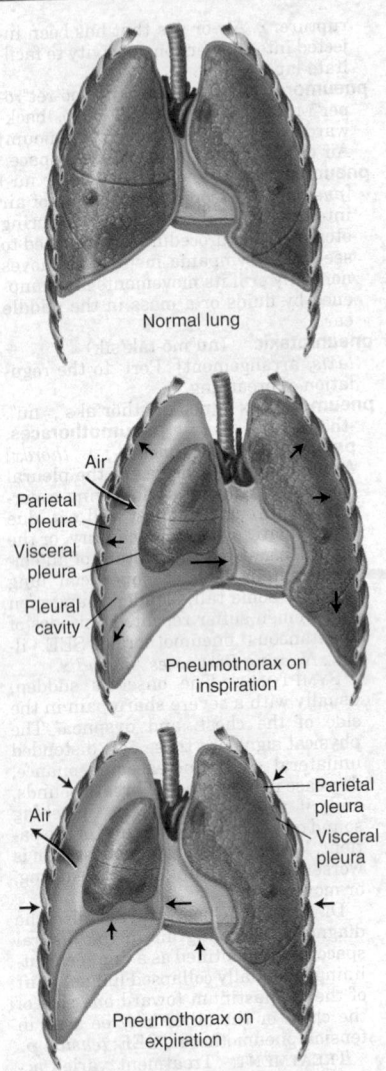

Normal lung

Air
Parietal pleura
Visceral pleura
Pleural cavity

Pneumothorax on inspiration

Parietal pleura
Visceral pleura
Air

Pneumothorax on expiration

PNEUMOTHORAX

sixth intercostal space more posteriorly to drain it.

PATIENT CARE: The patient's vital signs, chest expansion, oximetry and/or blood gases are monitored and oxygen administered to prevent hypoxia. The purpose and process for placing a chest tube are explained to the patient to allay anxiety and foster cooperation with the procedure. After the surgeon prepares and drapes the patient in sterile fashion, and administers local anesthesia, a small incision is made. A thoracostomy tube is attached to a water-sealed drainage device. The patient is placed in the semi-Fowler position to promote drainage, comfort, and ease of breathing. Vital signs and ventilatory status are monitored. Once the tube is placed, deep breathing (incentive spirometry) and coughing are encouraged (at least hourly) to promote lung expansion, with prescribed analgesics provided to control pain and discomfort (due in part to the tube itself). Ambulation is encouraged to facilitate full inspiration and enhance lung expansion. The thoracostomy tube site is kept sealed, generally by using a purse-string suture and occlusive dressing. Care is taken to avoid tension on the tubing, and all connections also are sealed to avoid air leaks. If the tube is accidentally dislodged, an occlusive (petroleum gauze) dressing is placed over the opening immediately to prevent lung collapse. When chest x-ray demonstrates adequate lung re-expansion that remains stable without suction, the thoracostomy tube is carefully removed, and the incision is covered with an occlusive dressing. The importance of follow-up examination, x-ray, and any needed care is explained prior to discharge. Patients who smoke are urged to stop smoking and exercise is increased gradually as determined by follow-up evaluation.

artificial p. An intentionally and artificially induced pneumothorax, used to facilitate transcutaneous mediastinal biopsy and, infrequently, to treat pulmonary tuberculosis and pneumonia. Pneumothorax allows the diseased lung to rest temporarily. The lung collapses when the air enters the pleural space.

Scattered adhesions may afford only a partial collapse. Effusion may occur in about one third of the cases. Hazards include pain, infection, and respiratory distress.

extrapleural p. The formation of a pneumothorax by introducing air into the space between the pleura and the inside of the rib cage.

occult p. A pneumothorax that is not detected by physical examination of the patient or by plain x-rays but is identified instead by other means, usually a computed tomography scan of the chest and abdomen. The condition may be life-threatening.

open p. A pneumothorax in which the pleural cavity is exposed to the atmosphere through an open wound in the chest wall.

spontaneous p. The spontaneous entrance of air into the pleural cavity. The pressure may collapse the lung and displace the mediastinum away from the side of the lesion.

SYMPTOMS: Although some patients with pneumothorax have few symptoms, most people who come to clinical attention report the sudden onset of left- or right-sided chest pain, often accompanied by shortness of breath. Breath sounds may be absent on the affected side, or the lung percussion note on that side may reveal increased resonance.

tension p. A type of pneumothorax in which air can enter the pleural space but cannot escape via the route of entry. This leads to increased pressure in the pleural space, resulting in lung collapse. The increase in pressure also compresses the heart and vena cavae, which impairs circulation.

PATIENT CARE: The patient is assessed for evidence of respiratory failure or the need for immediate intervention. The development of tension pneumothorax is a medical emergency; if it is not promptly relieved, the patient will experience inadequate cardiac output and hypoxemia (and may die). To prevent rapid decompensation, a large-bore needle is inserted emergently into the pleural space at the second intercostal space, mid-clavicular line (needle decompression, needle thoracotomy). This temporizing procedure must be followed by thoracostomy tube placement and water-sealed chest drainage unit.

pneumotonometry (noo″mō-tō-nom′ĕ-trē) [*pneumo-* + *tonometry*] A noninvasive method of estimating the intraocular pressure of the eye by exposing the cornea to a sudden puff or blast of air. It is less reliable than applanation tonometry.

Pneumovax 23 (noo″mō-văks″) Pneumococcal vaccine, polyvalent.

PNH *paroxysmal nocturnal* **hemoglobinuria**.

-pnoea SEE: *-pnea*.

Po Symbol for the element polonium.

PO₂ *partial pressure of oxygen.*

p.o. L. *per os,* by mouth.

pock (pŏk) A pustule of an eruptive fever, esp. of smallpox.

pocket (pŏk′ĕt) A saclike cavity.

gingival p. Periodontal **p.**

periodontal p. A pathologically deepened gingival sulcus enlarged beyond normal limits as a result of the destructive effects of bacterial plaque; the space bordered on one side by the tooth and the other side by ulcerated sulcular epithelium. The pocket contains inflammatory cells and destructive enzymes released by bacteria, and is surrounded by diseased gum tissue. SYN: *gingival* **p.**

pockmarked (pŏk-mărkd) Pitted or marked with scars from healed pustules, esp. those due to smallpox.

POCT *point-of-care testing.*

podagra (pō-dăg′ră) [Gr. *podos,* foot, + *agra,* seizure] Gout, esp. of the joints of the great toe.

podalic (pō-dăl′ĭk) [Gr. *podos,* foot] Pert. to the feet.

podcast A World Wide Web feed of audio or video files for playing on mobile devices such as MP3 players at a later time and at a listener's or viewer's convenience.

podiatrist (pō-dī′ă-trĭst″) [″ + *iatreia,* treatment] A health professional responsible for the examination, diagnosis, prevention, treatment, and care of conditions and functions of the human foot. A podiatrist performs surgical procedures and prescribes corrective devices, drugs, and physical therapy as legally authorized in the state in which he or she is practicing. SYN: *chiropodist.*

podiatry (pō-dī′ă-trē) The diagnosis, treatment, and prevention of conditions of human feet. SYN: *chiropody.*

podium (pō′dē-ŭm) [Gr. *podos,* foot] A footlike projection.

podo-, pod- [Gr. *pous,* stem *pod-,* foot] Prefixes meaning *foot.* SEE: *¹pedo-.*

podocyte (pŏd′ō-sīt) [″ + *kytos,* cell] A special epithelial cell with numerous footplates (pedicels). These form the inner layer of Bowman's capsule of the renal corpuscle and have spaces for the passage of renal filtrate from the glomerulus.

podosome (pod′ŏ-sōm″) [*podo-* + *-some*] A cellular structure composed of actin and integrins, used by mesenchymal cells to hold them to each other or to neighboring cells. Podosomes are found, e.g., on osteoclasts attached to bone matrix.

poecilo-, poecil- SEE: *poikilo-.*

POEMS syndrome (pō′ ĭmz) [Acronym fr. p*o*lyneuropathy, *o*rganomegaly, *e*ndocrinopathy, *m*onoclonal gamm*o*pathy, and *s*kin changes] A rare multisystem disease characterized by polyneuropathy, organomegaly, endocrinopathy, monoclonal gammopathy, and skin changes. It often presents with osteosclerotic bone lesions associated with plasma cell dyscrasia. The cause is unknown. SYN: *Crow-Fukase syndrome.*

-poiesis [Gr. *poiēsis,* making, formation, fr. *poiein,* to make] Suffix meaning *formation, production.* **-poietic,** *adj.*

poikilo-, poikil-, poecilo-, poecil- [Gr. *poikilos,* many-colored, spotted, variegated] Prefixes meaning *irregular, varied.*

poikilocyte (pŏy-kĭl-ō-sīt) A teardrop or pear-shaped red blood cell, seen in myelofibrosis and certain anemias. SEE: illus.

poikilocytosis (poy″kĭl-ō-sī-tō′sĭs) [″ + ″ + *osis,* condition] A term used to describe variations in shape of red blood cells (e.g., elliptocytes, spherocytes, dacryocytes, sickle cells, schizocytes, echinocytes, and acanthocytes).

poikiloderma (poy″kĭl-ō-dĕr′mă) [*poikilo-* + Gr. *derma,* skin] A skin disorder characterized by pigmentation,

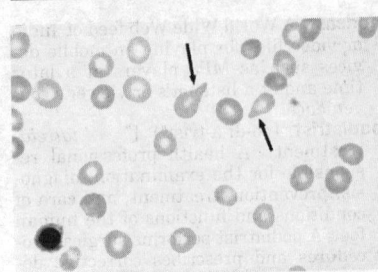

POIKILOCYTES

teardrop-shaped cells (arrows): peripheral
blood smear in patient with
myelofibrosis

telangiectasia, purpura, pruritus, and atrophy.

p. atrophicans vasculare A generalized dermatitis of unknown cause. It is symmetrical and occurs almost exclusively in adults. There is widespread telangiectasia, pigmentation, and atrophy of the skin.

p. of Civatte Reticulated pigmentation and telangiectasia of the sides of the face and neck; seen quite commonly in middle-aged women. SYN: *Berkshire neck.*

poikilotherm (poy′ki′lŏ-thĕrm″) [*poikilo-* + *thermo-*] Cold-blooded animal. **poikilothermal, poikilothermic** (-thĕr′măl, -thĕr′mik), *adj.*

poikilothermy, poikilothermism (poy″ki-lŏ-thĕr′mē, -thĕr′mizm) [*poikilo-* + *thermo-*] The quality of being cold-blooded, in which the temperature of an organism or animal, e.g., a reptile or an amphibian, matches the temperature of the environment. SEE: *ectotherm; endotherm.*

point (poynt) [Fr. *point,* a prick, a dot fr L. *punctum*] **1.** The sharp end of any object. **2.** The stage at which the surface of an abscess is about to rupture. **3.** A minute spot. **4.** A position in space, time, or degree. **5.** An area of skin that overlies a bony prominence and is subject to pressure injury or ulceration.

absorbent p. A cone of paper used in drying or in keeping liquid medicines in a root canal of a tooth.

active trigger p. A trigger point that is painful without stimulation. Palpation will reproduce the patient's symptoms.

acupuncture p. Any anatomical location used in acupuncture to relieve symptoms or treat disease.

ah-shi p. A tender point on the body; a trigger point.

auricular p. The center of the external orifice of the auditory canal.

boiling p. The temperature at which a liquid boils. The boiling point of a liquid varies according to the chemicals present in it. Under ordinary conditions water boils at 212°F (100°C) at sea level. To kill most vegetative forms of microorganisms, water should be boiled for 30 min.

Capuron p. SEE: *Capuron point.*

cardinal p. 1. Any of six points determining the direction of light rays emerging from and entering the eye. SEE: *nodal p.; principal p.* **2.** Capuron point.

p. of care Any location where patient care is provided, e.g., the bedside, radiology suite, emergency room, clinic, or ambulance.

cold rigor p. The temperature at which cell activity ceases.

contact p. The point on a tooth that touches an opposed tooth.

convergence p. 1. The point to which rays of light converge. **2.** The closest point to the patient on which the eyes can converge as the object is moved closer and closer.

corresponding p. The point in the retina of each eye that, when stimulated simultaneously, results in a single visual sensation.

craniometric p. Any of the fixed points of the skull used in craniometry. SEE: *craniometry* for illus.

critical p. of gases The temperature at or above which a gas is no longer liquefied by pressure.

critical p. of liquids The temperature above which no pressure may retain a substance in a liquid form.

cut p. In an analysis of data, a specified value used to sort continuous variables into discrete categories. It may be set according to its usefulness in predicting abnormal clinical events or arbitrarily.

Blood pressure measurements, for example, are continuous variables: in general, the higher one's pressure, the greater one's risk of congestive heart failure, kidney disease, myocardial infarction, or stroke. The analysis of blood pressure measurements has shown that the risk for these events climbs sharply as systolic blood pressures rise above 139 mm Hg. Therefore hypertension is defined by the cut point of 140 mm Hg, even though lower pressures may be harmful for some patients and higher pressures may be relatively well tolerated by a small number of other patients.

deaf p. of the ear Any of several points or areas close to the external auditory meatus where a vibrating tuning fork is not heard.

disparate p. Points on the retinas that are unequally paired.

end p., endpoint 1. The final objective, result, or resolution of an illness, treatment, or research protocol. **2.** The measurement or time designated as the completion of an activity.

p. of entry In dental or medical radiography, the location on the face toward which the central ray is directed. Points of entry are typically in the region of the apices of the teeth.

equal pressure p. During forced exhalation, the point at an airway where the pressure inside the airway equals the intrapleural pressure. When the pleural pressure is greater than the pressure inside the airway, it tends to cause bronchiolar collapse.

Erb p. SEE: *Erb, Wilhelm.*

external orbital p. The prominent point at the outer edge of the orbit above the frontomalar suture.

far p. The point (normally 20 ft [6.1 m]) at which distinct vision is possible without aid of the muscles of accommodation. It may be nearer than 20 ft (6.1 m) according to the degree of myopia. There is no far point in the hypermetropic eye.

fixation p. The fovea or point on the retina where the visual axes (lines) meet the point of clearest vision.

flash p. The temperature at which a substance bursts into flame spontaneously.

focal p. The point at which a group of light rays converge.

freezing p. The temperature at which the liquid phase and solid phase of a substance coexist in equilibrium.

fusion p. Melting **p.**

Guéneau de Mussy p. SEE: *Guéneau de Mussy point.*

gutta-percha p. A cone made of gutta-percha combined with other material that is used in filling root canals of teeth.

Halle p. SEE: *Halle point.*

hazard analysis and critical control p. SEE: *hazard analysis and critical control point.*

hot p. A spot on the skin that perceives hot but not cold stimuli.

ice p. The temperature at which there is equilibrium between ice and air-saturated water at one atmosphere of pressure.

identical retinal p. The points in the two retinas upon which the images are seen as one.

isoelectric p. The particular pH of a solution of an amphoteric electrolyte such as an amino acid or protein in which the charged molecules do not migrate to either electrode. Proteins are least soluble at this point. Thus at the appropriate pH, proteins may be precipitated.

isoionic p. The pH at which a solution of ionized material has as many negative as positive ions.

J p. On the electrocardiogram, the juncture between the end of the QRS complex and the beginning of the T wave (between the representations of ventricular depolarization and repolarization).

lacrimal p. The outlet of the lacrimal canaliculus. SYN: *punctum lacrimale.*

Lanz p. SEE: *Lanz point.*

latent trigger p. Any of the trigger points that are not symptomatic when the involved muscle is at rest, but produce pain during palpation. Range of motion and strength may also be limited.

p. of maximal impulse ABBR: PMI. The point on the chest wall over the heart at which the contraction of the heart is best seen or felt; normally at the fifth intercostal space in the midclavicular line.

maximum occipital p. The point on the occipital bone farthest from the glabella.

Mayo-Robson p. SEE: *Mayo-Robson point.*

McBurney p. SEE: under *McBurney, Charles.*

melting p. The temperature at which the solid and liquid phases of a material exist in equilibrium. SYN: *fusion p.*

mental p. The most anterior point of the midline of the chin.

metopic p. Glabella.

motor p. The point usually about the middle of a muscle where a motor nerve enters the muscle at which a minimal electrical stimulus to the overlying skin will elicit a visible contraction.

Munro p. SEE: *Munro point.*

nasal p. Nasion.

near p. ABBR: np. The closest point of distinct vision with maximum accommodation. This point becomes more distant with age, varying from about 3 in (7.62 cm) at age 2 to 40 in. (101.60 cm) at age 60. SYN: *punctum proximum.*

neutral p. A point on the pH scale (pH 7.0) that represents neutrality, i.e., the solution is neither acid or alkaline in reaction.

p. of no return A colloquial term for a critical biochemical event that indicates lethal, irreversible changes in cells following ischemic cell injury.

nodal p. Either of a pair of points situated on the axis of an optical system so that any incident ray sent through one will produce a parallel emergent ray sent through the other.

occipital p. The most posterior point on the occipital bone.

pressure p. 1. A cutaneous area that can be used for exerting pressure to control bleeding. For control of hemorrhage, pressure above the bleeding point when an artery passes over a bone may be sufficient. SEE: *bleeding* for table. 2. An anatomical location used in shiatsu (acupressure) to relieve pain or improve the health of organs or tissues.

principal p. One of two points so situated that the optical axis is cut by the two principal planes.

p. of regard The point at which the eye is looking.

saturation p. The point at which a solution contains all the solute it can dissolve; the maximum concentration of a solution. SEE: *saturated solution; supersaturated solution*.

p. of service A form of extended health care coverage granted to members of managed care plans who opt to pay additional premiums for medical services provided by special panels of providers.

set p. A homeostatic mechanism that maintains a variable (such as body temperature, body weight, blood glucose level, or hormone levels) within specific limits. SYN: *settling p.* SEE: *homeostasis*.

silver p. An elongated, tapered silver plug used to fill the root canal in the endodontic treatment of teeth.

spinous p. A spot over a spinous process very sensitive to pressure.

subnasal p. The center of the base of the anterior nasal spine. SYN: *spinal p.*

supra-auricular p. The point on the skull on the posterior root of the zygomatic process of the temporal bone, directly above the auricular point.

supraorbital p. A neuralgic point just above the supraorbital notch.

tender p. One of the anatomic locations used to identify fibromyalgia. The deep diffuse muscular pain is localized to a number of reproducible (from patient to patient) areas that are tender when palpated. Tender points differ from trigger points in that pain does not radiate to referred areas. SEE: *fibromyalgia* for table.

thermal death p. In bacteriology, the degree of heat that will kill organisms in a fluid culture in 10 min.

trigger p. **1.** An area of tissue that is tender when compressed and may give rise to referred pain and tenderness. **2.** An area of the cerebral cortex that, when stimulated, produces abnormal reactions similar to those in acquired epilepsy. SYN: *trigger zone*.

triple p. The temperature and pressure that allow the solid, liquid, and vapor forms of a substance to exist in equilibrium.

viral set p. The balance in a viral infection between the viral load and the response by the immune system to initial infection. It may be one of the predictors of disease progression in illnesses such as HIV infection.

visual p. The center of vision.

vital p. The point in the medulla oblongata close to the floor of the fourth ventricle, the puncture of which causes instant death owing to destruction of the respiratory center.

point of care SEE: under *point*.

point of dispensing Any of the locations to which the public is directed to obtain necessary drugs, vaccines, or supplies during a catastrophe or public health emergency.

point of entry SEE: under *point*.

pointing **1.** Reaching a point. **2.** Forming a localized collection of pus near the body surface.

point-of-care testing ABBR: POCT. A clinical laboratory measurement made at the bedside, in the clinic, or in a satellite lab, rather than at a centralized laboratory. POCT is designed to improve the turnaround time and usefulness of lab testing. Examples of POCT are nitrazine strips for measuring vaginal pH, refractometers for measuring urine specific gravity, glucometers for measuring blood sugar, and immunoassays for measuring the creatine phosphokinase isoenzymes, myoglobin, and troponin I.

point of service SEE: under *point*.

point source A geographically limited, fixed location from which a disease or an environmental pollutant spreads.

poise (poyz) [J. M. Poiseuille] The unit of viscosity; the tangential shearing force required to be applied to an area of 1 cm^2 between two parallel planes of 1 cm^2 in area and 1 cm apart in order to produce a velocity of flow of the liquid of 1 cm/sec.

Poiseuille law (pwa-zŭy′) [Jean Marie Poiseuille, Fr. physiologist, 1799–1869] A law that states that the rapidity of the capillary current is directly proportional to the fourth power of the radius of the capillary tube, the pressure on the fluid, and inversely proportional to the viscosity of the liquid and the length of the tube.

POISINDEX℠ (pŏy-zĭn-dĕks) A computerized database, revised quarterly, on over 300,000 commercial compounds. For information, contact Micromedex, Inc., 600 Grant St., Denver, CO 80203; (800) 525-9083.

poison (poyz′ŏn) [Fr. *poison*, fr L. *potio*, a poisonous draft] Any substance taken into the body by ingestion, inhalation, injection, or absorption that interferes with normal physiology. Virtually any substance can be poisonous if consumed in sufficient quantity; therefore *poison* more often implies an excessive degree of dosage rather than a specific group of substances. Aspirin is not usually thought of as a poison, but overdoses of this drug kill more children accidentally each year than any of the traditional poisons. SEE: *poisoning; Poisons and Poisoning Appendix*.

cellular p. Anything that damages or kills cells.

pesticidal p. Chemicals whose toxic properties are commercially exploited in agriculture, industry, or commerce to increase quantity, improve quality, or generally promote consumer acceptability of a variety of products. Common types include insecticides, rodenticides, herbicides, defoliants, fungicides, insect repellents, molluscicides, and some kinds of food additives. The wide variety of poisons commonly found in and around the home constitutes an important source of accidental poisonings. SEE: *Poisons and Poisoning Appendix.*

poison control center SEE: under *center.*

poisoning (poy'zŏn-ĭng) **1.** Illness caused by a toxic substance introduced into the body. **2.** Administration of a noxious substance. SEE: *intoxication; Poisons and Poisoning Appendix.*

PATIENT CARE: Poisoning should be suspected in many clinical circumstances but esp. when a patient has otherwise unexplained alterations in consciousness. The standard care of the poisoned patient begins with immediate stabilization of the patient's airway, breathing, circulation, and neurological status if these are compromised. This may require oximetry, blood gas analysis, electrocardiographic monitoring, airway placement, endotracheal intubation, fluid resuscitation, administration of naloxone and dextrose, or the use of pressors for some severely intoxicated patients. If the poison can be identified, reference texts or local poison control centers should be contacted to determine specific antidotes or treatments. When the poison is unidentified or when rescuers are uncertain about its cause, it is safest to test blood and urine for acetaminophen, aspirin, and commonly abused drugs. Blood testing should also include assessments of electrolytes, kidney function, liver function, and a complete blood count. Women of childbearing age should also be routinely screened for pregnancy.

Decontamination of the gastrointestinal tract includes activated charcoal if the patient has ingested a drug or chemical to which the charcoal can bind; or whole bowel irrigation, which sweeps toxins from the bowel before they are absorbed. Inducing vomiting, formerly relied on in poisonings, is now rarely used because it has not been shown to improve outcome and may cause complications such as aspiration pneumonia. After decontamination procedures, specific antidotes, if available, should be administered.

The elimination of many drugs from the body can be enhanced by other means, including the administration of alkaline fluids, hemodialysis, or hemoperfusion.

Once the patient is stabilized, the cause for the intoxication should be addressed. Patients with substance abuse problems should be referred for detoxification, support, and counseling; suicidal and depressed patients may benefit from counseling or drug therapy. Demented patients who have poisoned themselves because of confusion about their medications should have the administration of their medications supervised. In some cases, poisonings are iatrogenic

⚠️ Many illnesses (such as massive strokes, postictal states, insulin reactions, sepsis, meningitis, uremia) mimic the symptoms of poisoning, esp. when the patient has altered mental status.

acetaminophen p. Poisoning resulting from an overdose of acetaminophen, causing injury to or necrosis of the liver, or liver failure. Because acetaminophen is one of the most commonly used over-the-counter pain relievers and prescription drugs, this is one of the most common poisonings encountered in emergency departments and hospitals. If a reliable history of the amount of drug can be obtained, ingestions that exceed 7.5 g in the adult or about 150 mg/kg in children should always be considered potentially toxic. In most cases, data about overdoses are not reliable, and plasma levels of acetaminophen concentration are routinely measured and compared with standard nomograms to decide whether a patient will need antidotal therapy with N-acetylcysteine.

CLINICAL COURSE: Shortly after ingestion, patients may suffer nausea, vomiting, and malaise. If appropriate treatment is not instituted, hepatitis develops, with elevated liver enzymes in the first day, and jaundice and coagulation disorders by about 36 hr. Encephalopathy may follow. A prolonged course of recovery or complete liver failure may result, depending on the amount of drug ingested and the severity of the liver injury.

PATIENT CARE: Gastrointestinal (GI) decontamination with activated charcoal absorbs toxin from the GI tract, but it should be given within 4 hr of ingestion of the drug. A specific antidote, *N*-acetylcysteine, is given orally within 8 to 10 hr after ingestion in an initial dose of 140 mg/kg and then in 70 mg/kg doses every 4 hr for 17 doses if acetaminophen levels are toxic. Alternatively, acetylcysteine may be administered intravenously. Blood should be drawn for stat acetaminophen level, complete blood count, electrolyte levels, blood urea nitrogen, serum creatinine, serum glucose, liver function, prothrombin time, and further toxicology screens. Urine should also be analyzed for drug content. If the patient with a suspected overdose is a female of child-bearing age, a pregnancy test should be done as a part of routine laboratory studies. The overdosed patient should be cared for in an intensive care unit until medical-lyand psychiatrically cleared for discharge. SEE: *Poisons and Poisoning Appendix; Rumack nomogram.*

⚠️ Taking more than 4 g of acetaminophen in one day (adults) or more than 90 mg/kg (children) can damage the liver and may lead to coma, kidney failure, and death.

acetanilid p. Poisoning caused by acetanilid ingestion. Symptoms are cyanosis caused by formation of methemoglobin, cold sweat, irregular pulse, dyspnea, and unconsciousness. Sudden cardiac failure may occur.

FIRST AID: Irrigate exposed skin with soap and water, e.g., in the safety shower. Support breathing and oxygenation. Notify the local poison control center. SEE: *Poisons and Poisoning Appendix.*

acetylsalicylic acid p. Aspirin **p.**
acid p. Poisoning caused by ingestion of a toxic acid. SEE: *acids in Poisons and Poisoning in Appendix.*

FIRST AID: Dilute with large volumes of water. Give demulcents and morphine for pain. Treat as a chemical burn.

⚠️ The use of emetics and stomach tubes is contraindicated.

acute cocaine hydrochloride p. The acute, toxic, systemic reaction to an overdose of cocaine that has been eaten, smoked, inhaled, or injected. SEE: *Nursing Diagnoses Appendix.*

SYMPTOMS: An overdose of cocaine is an accelerated version of the classic physiological and psychological responses to cocaine use. Initial euphoria is followed by excitability, delirium, tremors, convulsions, tachycardia, and angina pectoris, all of which are signs of overwhelming sympathetic stimulation of the brain, heart, and lungs. Death is usually caused by a cardiovascular event or to respiratory failure. Plasma and liver pseudocholinesterase detoxify cocaine into water-soluble metabolites that are excreted in urine. Anyone with low plasma cholinesterase activity (such as a fetus, infant, pregnant woman, or someone with liver disease) is very prone to cocaine toxicity. People who congenitally lack pseudocholinesterase are highly sensitive to the effects of any dose of cocaine.

Many chronic cocaine users overdose while taking no more than their usual amount of the drug, when, e.g., the purity (pharmacological strength) of an ingested dose is greater than usual or the drug has been mixed with another psychoactive substance. Lethal overdoses are usually caused by acute coronary syndromes. Some cocaine users may die instead of intracerebral hemorrhage. The presenting findings may include seizures, hemiplegia, aphasia, or coma. Patients admitted for trauma may also be cocaine intoxicated (two thirds of cocaine-related deaths result from traumatic injuries, not drug overdose). Because many signs and symptoms that cocaine produces resemble those from injuries, and because cocaine poisoning is life-threatening, emergency department care providers must quickly distinguish drug-related problems from traumatic injury problems.

TREATMENT: Oxygen and aspirin should be given with benzodiazepines to reduce agitation and calcium channel blockers to reduce high blood pressure. Beta blockers should be avoided.

PATIENT CARE: Vital signs are checked frequently, the patient is attached to a cardiac monitor, and an intravenous line is initiated. Large volumes of fluids are infused to help remove protein breakdown products from the body (a result of rhabdomyolysis). Bilateral lung sounds are auscultated frequently during fluid resuscitation because aggressive fluid therapy can worsen heart failure. Care providers try to physically control patients to prevent them from injuring themselves. If patients demonstrate violent or aggressive behavior, chemical or physical restraints may be necessary. Calcium channel blockers or a benzodiazepine is administered as prescribed to reduce the patient's blood pressure and heart rate. Seizures, which occur because the seizure threshold is lowered by cocaine, are treated with diazepam. Because cocaine causes hypothalamic thermal regulatory dysfunction, core body temperature must be monitored closely. Elevated temperature is treatedwith acetaminophen and cooling blankets, cool-air ventilation, and cool saline gastric lavage. Central Nervous System (CNS) stimulation may be followed by CNS depression (flaccid paralysis, coma, fixed and dilated pupils, respiratory failure, and cardiovascular collapse).

Cocaine smuggling often involves body packing (swallowing balloons, condoms, or other objects filled with cocaine). If these items leak, the patient becomes intoxicated and is at high risk for death.

If the patient survives the acute poisoning episode, treatment is directed toward helping the patient abstain from drugs and preventing relapses. The patient benefits from consultation with an addictions specialist or mental health nurse practitioner. Studies support the effectiveness of a 12-step program, such as Cocaine Anonymous, to help build a solid recovery program. Other community resources also can be accessed to provide various types of support and to help the patient identify and manage relapse triggers.

acute lead p. Poisoning caused by ingestion or inhalation of a large amount of lead, causing abdominal pain, metallic taste in mouth, anorexia, vomiting, diarrhea, headache, stupor, renal failure, convulsions, and coma. SEE: *Nursing Diagnoses Appendix.*

TREATMENT: Adequate urine flow should be established; convulsions may be controlled with diazepam. Calcium disodium edetate and dimercaprol are administered to remove lead from the body. After acute therapy is completed, penicillamine is given orally for 3 to 6 months for children and up to 2 months for adults. The exposure to lead should be reduced or eliminated.

⚠️ Patients receiving penicillamine therapy must be monitored weekly for adverse reactions, including diffuse erythematous rashes, angioneurotic edema, proteinuria, and neutropenia. Penicillamine is contraindicated in patients with a history of penicillin sensitivity, renal disease, or both.

acute nicotine p. Poisoning resulting from nicotine exposure, causing excessive stimulation of the autonomic nervous system. Usually nicotine poisoning occurs when young children accidentally consume nicotine chewing gum or patches found in the home. SEE: *Poisons and Poisoning Appendix.*

SYMPTOMS: Nausea, salivation, abdominal pain, vomiting, diarrhea, sweating, dizziness, and mental confusion. If the dose is sufficient, the patient will collapse, develop shock, convulse, and die of respiratory failure caused by paralysis of respiratory muscles.

TREATMENT: Activated charcoal may be given to conscious patients who are not vomiting. Unconscious patients should be intubated and supported in an intensive care unit. Anticonvulsants are used to treat seizures.

alkali p. Poisoning caused by ingestion of an alkali.

TREATMENT: Large amounts of water are given by mouth. Consultation with an ear, nose, and throat specialist is often advisable. Tracheostomy or intubation is performed if necessary to protect the airway. Morphine is useful to allay pain. Rest, heat, quiet, and adequate fluid intake are necessary.

⚠️ Emetics, strong acids, and lavage should be avoided. Fluid balance and electrolytes should be carefully monitored.

aluminum p. Poisoning caused by excessive exposure to aluminum, causing nausea, vomiting, renal dysfunction, and cognitive disorders. Aluminum poisoning (impaired cognition or dialysis dementia in patients with end-stage renal disease) has been nearly eliminated now that dialysates no longer contain aluminum.

aminophylline p. SEE: *Poisons and Poisoning Appendix.*

amnesic shellfish p. Poisoning caused by consumption of crabs and shellfish contaminated with domoic acid, causing permanent short-term memory loss, brain damage, and, in severe cases, death.

amphetamine p. SEE: *Poisons and Poisoning Appendix.*

aniline p. SEE: *Poisons and Poisoning Appendix.*

antihistamine p. SEE: *Poisons and Poisoning Appendix.*

antimony p. Poisoning caused by ingestion of antimony. Symptoms include an acrid metallic taste, cardiac failure, sweating, and vomiting about 30 min after ingestion. In large doses it causes irritation of the lining of the alimentary tract, resembling arsenic poisoning.

FIRST AID: British antilewisite can be used as an antidote. SEE: *arsenic in Poisons and Poisoning Appendix.*

arsenic p. Poisoning produced by ingestion of arsenic.

SYMPTOMS: Symptoms include a burning pain throughout the gastrointestinal tract, vomiting, dehydration, shock, dysrhythmias, coma, convulsions, paralysis, and death.

FIRST AID: The stomach should be lavaged with copious amounts of water. Dimercaprol (British antilewisite) or other chelators (such as penicillamine) should be given immediately.

TREATMENT: After first aid, fluid and electrolyte balance must be maintained. Morphine should be given for pain. The patient is treated for shock and pulmonary edema. Blood transfusion may be required. SEE: *arsenic in Poisons and Poisoning Appendix.*

arum family p. Poisoning caused by ingestion of plants of the genus *Arum*, e.g., dieffenbachia, caladium, and philodendron, which contain poisonous calcium oxalate crystals. Symptoms include irritation, pain, burning, and swelling of the affected areas. The affected area should be washed with water, and ice should be applied. If pain is severe, corticosteroids are of benefit.

aspirin p. Poisoning caused by ingestion of an overdose of aspirin. In acute poisoning, signs vary with increasing doses from mild lethargy and hyperpnea to coma and convulsions. Sweating, dehydration, hyperpnea, hyperthermia, and restlessness may be present with moderate doses. In chronic poisoning, tinnitus, skin rash, bleeding, weight loss, and mental symptoms may be present. Aspirin poisoning in very young infants may produce very few signs and symptoms other than dehydration or hyperpnea.

TREATMENT: Activated charcoal is given by mouth. Intravenous (IV) fluids are given for dehydration but must not be overloaded. Enough IV fluids should be given to establish 3 to 4 mL/kg/hr of urine flow. Alkalinization of urine is achieved by administering bicarbonate. The goal is a urine pH of 8 or higher. After urine flow is established, potassium 30 mEq/L of administered fluid should be added. After serum potassium levels reach 5 mEq/L, potassium should be discontinued. If alkalinization of the urine is not attained, hemodialysis may be needed. SYN: *acetylsalicylic acid p.* SEE: *salicylates in Poisons and Poisoning Appendix.*

atropine sulfate p. Poisoning caused by ingestion of atropine, resulting in anticholinergic side effects of restlessness, dry mouth, fever, hot and dry skin, pupillary dilation, tachycardia, hallucinations, delirium, and coma. SYN: *atropinism.*

PATIENT CARE: Oxygen is given; a cardiac monitor, oximeter, and automated blood pressure cuff are applied; and intravenous fluids are administered. Patients experiencing restlessness may respond to the administration of a benzodiazepine (such as lorazepam or diazepam). If the atropine has been ingested orally, gastric lavage with activated charcoal may absorb some of the toxin from the gastrointestinal tract. Severe neurological side effects (such as seizures) may be treated with physostigmine. SEE: *Poisons and Poisoning Appendix.*

barbiturate p. Poisoning caused by an overdose of barbiturates, reslting in excessive sedation, sometimes accompanied by an inability to protect the airway; coma; shock; and hypothermia. Agents commonly taken in overdose include secobarbital, phenobarbital, or butalbital.

TREATMENT: When oxygenation and ventilation are compromised, intubation and mechanical ventilation may be needed. Other supportive treatments include activated charcoal, bicarbonate-containing fluids (to make the urine al-

kaline and increase barbiturate excretion), rewarming techniques, and fluids or drugs to support blood pressure.

blood p. An obsolete term for septicemia.

boric acid p. Poisoning caused by the consumption of or exposure to boric acid.

SYMPTOMS: Symptoms include nausea, vomiting, diarrhea, convulsions, weakness, central nervous system depression, livid skin rash characterized as "boiled lobster rash," and shock. Acute renal failure and cardiac failure may result from large ingestions.

TREATMENT: Activated charcoal may prevent absorption of boric acid from the gastrointestinal tract. Hemodialysis is sometimes required for severe intoxications. SEE: *Poisons and Poisoning Appendix.*

brass p. Poisoning caused by the inhalation of fumes of zinc and zinc oxide, causing destruction of tissue in the respiratory passage. It is rarely fatal. Symptoms include dryness and burning in respiratory tract, coughing, headache, and chills.

 Call the nearest poison control center to determine proper therapy.

---

brodifacoum p. Poisoning caused by the ingestion of brodifacoum. Brodifacoun, a long-acting derivative of warfarin, is often found in rodenticides.

SYMPTOMS: Hemorrhage is the most common side effect and may occasionally be life-threatening. Bleeding within the kidneys and urinary tract produces acute renal failure.

TREATMENT: Because warfarin interferes with the liver's use of vitamin K to produce clotting factors, brodifacoum poisoning is treated with vitamin K, fresh frozen plasma, and supportive therapy.

bromide p. Poisoning caused by an overdose of bromide.

SYMPTOMS: Symptoms include vomiting, abdominal pain, respiratory and eye irritation if inhaled, corrosion of the mouth and intestinal tract if swallowed, cyanosis, tachycardia, and shock.

FIRST AID: If bromide is inhaled, oxygen is administered, respiratory support provided, and pulmonary edema treated. If bromide is swallowed, gastric lavage may reduce intestinal absorption. SEE: *Poisons and Poisoning Appendix.*

buckthorn p. Poisoning caused by eating the fruit of the buckthorn (a species of *Bumelia*), which grows in the southeastern U.S., resulting in motor paralysis.

camphor p. SEE: *Poisons and Poisoning Appendix.*

carbon dioxide p. Poisoning caused by inhalation of carbon dioxide (CO_2). In small quantities (up to approx. 5%) in inspired air, CO_2 stimulates respiration in humans; in greater quantities it produces an uncomfortable degree of mental activity with confusion. Although not toxic in low concentrations, CO_2 can cause death by suffocation. Poisoning is rarely fatal unless exposure occurs in a closed space.

SYMPTOMS: Symptoms include a sensation of pressure in the head, ringing in the ears, an acid taste in the mouth, and a slight burning in the nose. With massive exposures to very concentrated CO_2, respiratory depression and coma may occur.

TREATMENT: The patient should be removed to fresh air and given oxygen and, if needed, ventilatory assistance.

carbon monoxide p. Poisoning caused by inhalation of small amounts of carbon monoxide (CO) over a long period or from large amounts inhaled for a short time. In the U.S., where exposure to smoke, car exhaust, and other sources of incomplete combustion of carbon fuels is common (particularly during winter), CO poisoning is one of the most frequent, and potentially deadliest, intoxications. CO poisoning results from the avid chemical combination of the gas with hemoglobin, forming carboxyhemoglobin (COHb). SEE: *Poisons and Poisoning Appendix*.

⚠ Pulse oximetry is not a useful measure in CO intoxication: it cannot differentiate between carboxyhemoglobin and oxyhemoglobin and therefore gives a falsely elevated indication of oxygenation.

SYMPTOMS: The symptoms of CO poisoning vary with the level of exposure and the concentration of COHb in the bloodstream. At levels of less than 10%, patients may be symptom-free or may complain only of headache. (Heavy cigarette smoking may produce levels as high as 7% to 9%.) COHb levels of 30% produce mild neurological impairment (dizziness, fatigue, difficulty concentrating), and levels of 50% may cause seizures or coma. Death is likely when COHb levels exceed 70%.

PATIENT CARE: Arterial or venous COHb levels should be obtained immediately, and serial levels checked hourly to monitor treatment effectiveness. Blood glucose, ethyl alcohol, acetaminophen, and other drug levels should be measured on all patients who come to the ER with altered mental status. Computed tomography or MR imaging of the brain may also be necessary. The patient should be removed immediately from exposure to CO. If the patient has

severe CO poisoning (indicated by carboxyhemoglobin levels above 25%) or cardiovascular and neurologic impairment regardless of levels, hyperbaric oxygen therapy should be employed if available, and the patient admitted to the hospital. 100% oxygen is given with a tight-fitting non-rebreather mask, under pressure (hyperbaric) if possible. Intubation and mechanical ventilation should be used if indicated. A venous access is used to provide saline infusion, and cardiac and hemodynamic monitoring is established. The patient should be kept at bedrest to reduce the body's oxygen requirements.

Potential complications of hyperbaric therapy include sinus and middle ear barotrauma, hyperoxic seizure, anxiety, and oxidative stress. Intubation and mechanical ventilation should be used for patients with diminished level of consciousness or respiratory distress, esp. if hyperbaric treatment is not available. An antiemetic may be prescribed to manage nausea and prevent vomiting. Bedrest limits exertion and tissue oxygen demand, reducing organ ischemia. Patients with cardiac or renal disease are necessarily at increased risk for CO complications. In general, people with more severe initial symptoms are at higher risk for sequelae.

Clinical improvement after treatment is indicated by the presence of hemodynamic stability without IV support, mechanical ventilation, or supplemental oxygen; sufficient urine output; the return of an appetite; and a stable neurological status. A follow-up visit with a health care professional is advisable shortly after discharge. Patients should be taught about the major causes of CO exposure and should not return home until the source of carbon monoxide has been eliminated, e.g., by a certified heating and ventilation specialist. The importance of having the home heating furnace inspected and cleaned annually should be stressed. Patients should also be cautioned about working on an automobile in a garage with the engine running or burning items indoors. The Consumer Product Safety Commission recommends that CO detectors be installed on each level of the home and just outside the sleeping areas. Most are battery operated and easilyinstalled. Patients should be advised to evacuate the home if an alarm sounds, leaving windows or doors open for ventilation, and to call 911. Alarms should never be turned off or ignored, and batteries should be replaced when the clocks are changed in spring and fall, as for smoke alarms. SEE: table.

carbon tetrachloride p. Poisoning caused by prolonged inhalation of carbon tetrachloride. Consequences in-

Toxicity of Carbon Monoxide

Carbon Monoxide Concentration in Air		Comment
Percent in Air	**Parts per Million**	
0.005	50	Occupational Safety and Health Administration (OSHA) maximum permissible exposure limit averaged over an 8-hr day
0.01	100	OSHA standard: Maritime worker peak concentration limit
0.02	200	OSHA standard: Brief exposures during loading and unloading cargo are permissible
0.04	400	The level of CO in cigarette smoke is eight times higher than the OSHA permissible exposure limit
0.08	800	Headache, dizziness, and nausea in 45 min; collapse and possible unconsciousness in 2 hr
0.16	1600	Headache, dizziness, and nausea in 20 min; collapse and possible death in 2 hr
0.32	3200	Headache and dizziness in 5–10 min; unconsciousness and possible death in 10–15 min
0.64	6400	Headache and dizziness in 1–2 min; possible death in 10–15 min
1.28	12,800	Immediate unconsciousness; possible death in 1–3 min

SOURCES: Adapted from Hamilton, A, and Hardy, H: Industrial Toxicology, ed 3. Publishing Sciences Group, Littleton, MA, 1974. Occupational Safety and Health Administration (OSHA).

clude irritation of the eyes, nose, and throat, headache, confusion, central nervous system depression, visual disturbances, nausea, anorexia, hepatitis, nephropathy, and cardiac arrhythmias.

TREATMENT: Clothes contaminated with carbon tetrachloride are removed. Oxygen, artificial respiration, gastric decontamination, and management of cardiac rhythms are often needed. SEE: *Poisons and Poisoning Appendix.*

chloride p. SEE: *barium salts, absorbable, in Poisons and Poisoning Appendix.*

chlorpromazine p. SEE: *Poisons and Poisoning Appendix.*

chromium p. Poisoning caused by excess chromium (e.g., in mining, welding, or pigment manufacturing). It may cause contact dermatitis, skin burns, or lung, liver, or kidney damage. Treatment after ingestion consists of gastrointestinal irrigation followed by forced diuresis and alkalinization of urine.

chronic lead p. Poisoning caused by chronic ingestion or inhalation of lead, which damages the central and peripheral nervous systems, kidneys, the blood-forming organs, and the gastrointestinal tract. Early symptoms include loss of appetite, weight loss, anemia, vomiting, fatigue, weakness, headache, lead line on gums, apathy or irritability, and a metallic taste in the mouth. Later, symptoms of paralysis, sensory loss, lack of coordination, and vague pains develop. Laboratory diagnosis is made through evidence of anemia, blood lead level above 5 μg/dL, elevated free erythrocyte protoporphyrin (FEP), increased excretion of lead in urine, and characteristic x-ray changes in the ends of growing bones. SEE: *Nursing Diagnoses Appendix.*

TREATMENT: Exposure to lead should be eliminated and an adequate diet with added vitamins provided. Chelating agents such as dimercaprol, dimercaptosuccinic acid (succimer), or EDTA are given to reduce lead levels to normal.

PATIENT CARE: A history is obtained to determine whether the sources of lead ingestion or inhalation are caused by the environment, work, or folk remedies, and preparations are made for their removal. (In many states, removal of household lead must be done by state-licensed specialists, not homeowners. The CDC and local poison-control centers provide relevant information. A 1-cm square chip of lead-based paint may contain a thousand times the usual safe daily ingestion of lead.) A history is obtained of pica; recent behavioral changes, particularly, in children, a lack of interest in playing; and behavioral problems such as aggression and hyperirritability. The patient is assessed for developmental delays or loss of acquired skills, esp. speech. central nervous system signs indicative of lead toxicity may be irreversible. The younger child is assessed for at-risk characteristics such as the high level of oral activity in late infancy and toddlerhood; smallstature, which enhances inhalation of contaminated dust and dirt in areas heavily contaminated with lead; and nutritional deficiencies of calcium, zinc, and iron, the single most important predisposing factor for increased lead absorption. Older children are assessed for gasoline sniffing, which is esp. prevalent among children in some cultures. The parent-child interaction is assessed for indications of inadequate child care, including poor hygienic practices, insufficient feeding to promote adequate nutrition, infrequent use of medical facilities, insufficient rest, less use of resources for child stimulation, less affection, and immature attitudes toward maintaining discipline. Prescribed chelating agents are administered to mobilize lead from the blood and soft tissues by enhancing its deposition in bones and its excretion in urine. A combination of drugs may result in fewer side effects and better removal of lead from the brain. If encephalopathy ispresent, fluid volume is restricted to prevent additional cerebral edema. Injections are administered intramuscularly, and injection sites are rotated for painful injections (which may include simultaneous procaine injection for local anesthesia). The child is allowed to express pain and anger, and physical and emotional comfort measures are provided to relieve related distress. If there is no encephalopathy, injections are administered intravenously, and hydration is maintained. The patient is evaluated for desired drug effects measured by blood levels and urinary excretion of lead and for signs of toxicity from the chelating agents. (Special blood collection and urine collection containers are necessary for some of the monitoring tests. The laboratory should be consulted before collection.) . Prescribed anticonvulsants are administered as necessary to control seizures (often severe and protracted), an antiemetic for nausea and vomiting, an antispasmodicfor muscle cramps, and analgesics and muscle relaxants for muscle and joint pain. Serum electrolytes are monitored daily, and renal function is evaluated frequently. Whole bowel irrigation is used when lead is visible in the GI tract (or for episodes of acute lead ingestion). Adequate nutrition is provided, and nutritional deficiencies are corrected, by administering prescribed supplements (e.g., of iron). An active, active-assisted, or passive range-of-motion exercise program is established to maintain joint

mobility and prevent muscle atrophy. Parents are taught and supported to prevent recurrence, and the public is educated about the dangers of lead ingestion, the importance of screening young (esp. preschool) children at risk, the signs and symptoms indicative of toxicity, and the need for treatment.

ciguatera p. A form of fish poisoning caused by eating certain types of bottom-dwelling shore fish, e.g., grouper, red snapper, sea bass, and barracuda. The toxin, ciguatoxin, is present in fish that feed on dinoflagellates. It acts within 5 hr of ingestion, and symptoms may persist for 8 days or longer. Symptoms include tingling of the lips, tongue, and throat, abdominal cramps, nausea, vomiting, diarrhea, paresthesia, hypotension, and respiratory paralysis. Treatment is supportive, but treatment of respiratory paralysis may be required.

codeine p. SEE: *opiate p; Poisons and Poisoning Appendix.*

cone shell p. A toxic reaction to the neurotoxin delivered by the pointed, hollow teeth of the marine animal contained in the cone shell. Intense local pain, swelling, and numbness may last several days. In severe poisoning, muscular incoordination and weakness can progress to respiratory paralysis. Although death can occur, recovery within 24 hr is the usual outcome. There is no specific therapy, but supportive measures including artificial respiration and supplemental oxygen may be needed.

corrosive p. Poisoning by strong acids, alkalies, strong antiseptics including bichloride of mercury, carbolic acid (phenol), Lysol, cresol compounds, tincture of iodine, and arsenic compounds. These agents cause tissue damage similar to that caused by burns. If the substances have been swallowed, any part of the alimentary canal may be affected. Tissues involved are easily perforated. Death may result from shock or from asphyxiation caused by swelling of the throat and pharynx. Esophageal injury and stricture may be a late complication. SEE: *individual poisons in Poisons and Poisoning Appendix.*

SYMPTOMS: This type of poisoning is marked by intense burning of the mouth, throat, pharynx, and abdomen; abdominal cramping, retching, nausea, and vomiting, and often collapse. There may be hematemesis and diarrhea; the stools are watery, mucoid, bloody, and possibly stained with the poison or its products, resulting from its action on the contents of the alimentary tract. Stains of the lips, cheeks, tongue, mouth, or pharynx are often a characteristic brown; stains on the mucous membranes may be violet or black. Carbolic acid (phenol) stains are white or gray, resembling boiled meat; hydrochloric acid stains are grayish, nitric acid, yellow; sulfuric acid leaves tan or dark burns.

TREATMENT: Immediate treatment in a hospital is mandatory. It is important to try to discover the chemical substance ingested, and all materials such as food, bottles, jars, or containers should be saved. This is essential if the patient is comatose or an infant.

⚠️ In treating corrosive poisoning, vomiting must not be induced; gastric lavage must not be attempted; and no attempt should be made to neutralize the corrosive substance.

Vomiting will increase the severity of damage to the esophagus by renewing contact with the corrosive substance. Gastric lavage may cause the esophagus or stomach to perforate. If the trachea has been damaged, tracheostomy may be needed. Emergency surgery must be considered if there are signs of possible perforation of the esophagus or of the abdominal viscera. Opiates will be needed to control pain. For esophageal burns, broad-spectrum antibiotic and corticosteroid therapy should be started. Intravenous fluids will be required if esophageal or gastric damage prevents ingestion of liquids. Long-range therapy will be directed toward preventing or treating esophageal scars and strictures.

cyanide p. Poisoning caused by any of several cyanide-containing compounds, very potent blockers of cellular oxygenation. They inhibit respiration by blocking oxidative phosphorylation at the cellular level. SEE: *Poisons and Poisoning Appendix.*

The most common patients are jewelers, metal platers, those who handle rodenticides, victims of smoke inhalation, and patients treated with very high doses of sodium nitroprusside. Rarely, cyanide poisoning results from the ingestion of certain fruits (e.g., the bitter cassava and some stone fruits).

SYMPTOMS: Palpitations, disorientation, and confusion may be rapidly followed by respiratory failure, seizures, coma, and death in patients who suffer large exposures. Smaller exposures may produce anxiety, dizziness, headache, and shortness of breath. Patients may report that they have detected an odor of bitter almonds at the time of exposure to cyanide.

TREATMENT: The patient is immediately treated with gastric lavage, and activated charcoal is given to adsorb to whatever toxin may remain in the gastrointestinal tract. Emesis is contraindicated. Oxygen is immediately provided; intubation and mechanical ventilation may be needed when the patient has suffered respiratory failure. Antidotes to cyanide poisoning include hydroxocobalmin and sodium thiosulfate.

digitalis p. Acute or chronic poisoning caused by the cumulative effect of digitalis. Its most common adverse effects include anorexia, nausea, vomiting, atrial tachycardia and other dysrhythmias, atrioventricular heart blocks, confusion, dizziness, or neurological depression. Digitalis toxicity is a potentially life-threatening, and frequently a drug-related, complication. SEE: *Nursing Diagnoses Appendix.*

SYMPTOMS: Extracardiac signs develop initially in most patients, the first of which is almost always anorexia. Nausea and vomiting, sometimes with abdominal pain and increased salivation, usually appear 1 to 2 days later. Other symptoms include fatigue, drowsiness, general muscle weakness, and visual disturbances such as blurring of vision, yellow-green or white halos around visual images, light flashes, photophobia, and diplopia. Mental disturbances (such as agitation, hallucinations, and disorientation) are very common in elderly atherosclerotic patients. If the early signs are unheeded, 80% of patients eventually will show more serious cardiac signs. Toxic concentrations of digitalis can cause nearly every known arrhythmia. They can decrease heart rate by slowing conduction and increasing the refractory period at the AV node, or they can increase the rate by creating abnormal pacemaker activity in the conductive tissue.

PATIENT CARE: The distinction between therapeutic and toxic levels digoxin is narrow; therefore, health care providers must be alert to signs of digitalis poisoning in patients. Elderly patients and those with liver or kidney disease are at esp. high risk because their absorption, metabolism, and excretion rates are unpredictable. Health care providers should consider health status changes that can alter a patient's response to digitalis, including vomiting, diarrhea, or other gastrointestinal upset; acid-base or electrolyte disturbances (such as hypokalemia, hypomagnesemia, or hypercalcemia), which alter the heart's sensitivity to digitalis; hypothyroidism, which disrupts the patient's ability to metabolize digitalis; and liver or kidney disease, which modifies metabolism and excretion. Changes in a treatment regimen also can predispose the patient to toxicity, esp. the addition of or increase in dosages of drugs such as antiarrhythmics, calcium channelblockers, or potassium-wasting diuretics. Assessment for digitalis toxicity is necessary if electrical cardioversion is used to restore a patient to sinus rhythm because this procedure increases the heart's sensitivity to digitalis.

Because digitalis toxicity develops quickly and insidiously, the patient is taught early symptoms to report. Extracardiac signs can be missed or mistaken for complications of another condition being treated, e.g., pneumonia. Health care providers need to compare the patient's current appetite and activity to the patient's previous health status, and carefully monitor the patient for electrolyte imbalances. Significant decreases or increases in heart rate and rhythmic irregularities must be reported because toxic concentrations may lead to ventricular fibrillation and death. If toxicity is suspected, an electrocardiogram is performed. Electrocardiographic signs of digitalis toxicity include first-degree atrioventricular (A-V) block with depressed S-T segments, shortened Q-T intervals, and flattened T waves. In the presence of such changes a serum digoxin level and basic chemistries may be used to confirm toxicity. Because hypokalemia is amajor cause of digitalis toxicity, adequate potassium intake in the diet and prescribed supplementations are essential. The patient is advised about conditions such as diarrhea, which may deplete the body of potassium or contribute to dehydration and renal insufficiency. The patient is advised not to take over-the-counter medications without notifying his health care provider because these may alter his sensitivity to digitalis.

Digitalis poisoning may sometimes occur because of accidental or deliberate overdose. Emergency department personnel may sometimes remove the drug from the stomach by lavage or activated charcoal, administer intravenous fluids, provide potassium, monitor cardiac status, and/or treat cardiac arrhythmias as they arise. They may also administer digoxin immune FAB (ovine) to bind serum digoxin, preventing it from binding to cardiac receptors.

disulfiram p. SEE: *Antabuse in Poisons and Poisoning Appendix.*

ergot p. Poisoning caused by eating bread made with grain contaminated with the *Claviceps purpurea* fungus, or from an overdose of ergot. SYN: *ergotism.*

SYMPTOMS: Within several hours of ingestion, the patient may develop anticholinergic symptoms (such as abdominal cramping, bradycardia, pupillary dilation, urinary retention) and vasoconstriction (with ischemia and gangrene of the extremities).

TREATMENT: Sodium nitroprusside may counteract the vascular spasm produced by ergots. SEE: *Poisons and Poisoning Appendix.*

fish p. Food poisoning caused by eating fish that are inherently poisonous or poisonous because they had decomposed, become infected, or had fed on other poisonous life forms.

fluoride p. SEE: *Poisons and Poisoning Appendix.*

food p. Illness from ingestion of foods containing poisonous substances. These include mushrooms; shellfish; foods contaminated with pesticides, lead, or mercury; milk from cows that have fed on poisonous plants; foods that have putrefied or decomposed, or foods in which bacterial toxins have accumulated. SEE: *staphylococcal food poisoning.*

formaldehyde p. Poisoning caused by ingestion of formaldehyde.

SYMPTOMS: Symptoms include local irritation of the eyes, nose, mouth, throat; respiratory and gastrointestinal tracts; central nervous system disorders (including vertigo, stupor, convulsions, unconsciousness); and renal damage. SEE: *Poisons and Poisoning Appendix.*

gasoline p. The reaction of the body to ingested or inhaled gasoline.

SYMPTOMS: The most hazardous symptom of gasoline exposure is a potentially fatal inflammation of the lungs, caused by aspiration of even small quantities of distilled petroleum. Symptoms of oral ingestion may also include dizziness, disorientation, seizures, and other neurological difficulties; gastric irritation and vomiting; rashes; and cardiac rhythm disturbances.

PATIENT CARE: The patient should be observed for at least 6 hr. If no evidence of respiratory distress or dysfunction is found, and if a chest x-ray exam shows no signs of chemical pneumonitis, the patient may be safely discharged home.

Patients with evidence of chemical pneumonitis should be treated with oxygen and monitored in a hospital. Patients in full respiratory failure will require mechanical ventilation. Those who have deliberately ingested gasoline may benefit from supportive psychotherapy or psychiatric referral.

heavy metal p. Poisoning due to ingestion, inhalation, or absorption of a heavy metal, esp. lead or mercury. Symptoms are determined by the type and duration of exposure and may include pulmonary, neurological, integumentary, or gastrointestinal disorders.

hemlock p. Poisoning caused by ingesting hemlock *Conium maculatum*, which causes weakness, drowsiness, nausea, vomiting, difficult breathing, paralysis, and death.

TREATMENT: Oral activated charcoal may be given to decrease the absorption of the toxin from the gastrointestinal tract. Respiratory failure should be treated with intubation and mechanical ventilation. The local Poison Control Center should be contacted for additional instructions.

herbicide p. Poisoning caused by the use of a toxic herbicide such as 2,4-D.

hyoscyamus p. SEE: *atropine in Poisons and Poisoning Appendix.*

hypochlorite salt p. SEE: *Poisons and Poisoning Appendix.*

iron p. Acute poisoning usually caused by the accidental ingestion (usually by infants or small children) of iron-containing medications intended for use by adults. In the US, about 20,000 accidental iron exposures are reported each year.

SYMPTOMS: The victim vomits, usually within an hour of taking the iron. Vomiting of blood and melena may occur. If untreated, restlessness, hypotension, rapid respirations, and cyanosis may develop, followed within a few hours by coma and death.

TREATMENT: Whole bowel irrigation should be used to force ingested iron out of the gastrointestinal tract. Chelation of iron can be performed with deferoxamine, which binds circulating iron from the bloodstream.

ivy p. SEE: *poison ivy* **dermatitis**.

lead p. Poisoning caused by ingestion or inhalation of substances containing lead. Symptoms of acute poisoning include a metallic taste in the mouth, burns in the throat and pharynx, and later abdominal cramps and prostration. Chronic lead poisoning is characterized by anorexia, nausea, vomiting, excess salivation, anemia, a lead line on the gums, abdominal pains, muscle cramps, kidney failure, encephalopathy, seizures, learning disabilities, and pains in the joints.

PATIENT CARE: *Acute poisoning*: Seizures are treated with benzodiazepines. Fluid and electrolyte balance is maintained. Cerebral edema is treated with mannitol and dexamethasone. The blood lead level is determined. If it is above 50 to 60 μg/dL, the lead is removed from the body with a chelator, e.g., edetate calcium disodium, dimercaprol, D-penicillamine, or succimer [DMSA]. Succimer has the advantage of being orally active and is esp. helpful in treating children. The effect of treatment is monitored; it may have to be continued for a week or longer or repeated if the lead level rebounds. *Chronic lead poisoning*: A blood lead level equal to or > 10 mcg/dL in a child may impair normal development of the central nervous system. Parents of exposed children should be educated about potential environmental or nutritional sources of lead exposure, and the child should be rechecked in a month. Rising levels, e.g., above 25 mcg/dL or higher, may warrant treatment with chelators. Public health officials should be notified when a child's lead level is elevated so that environmental remediation or relocation of the patient and family, as indicated, may be undertaken.

lye p. SEE: *Poisons and Poisoning Appendix.*

manganese p. An uncommon cause of toxicity in workers exposed to manganese on a regular basis.

SYMPTOMS: Symptoms include muscular weakness, difficulty walking, tremors, central nervous system disturbances, and salivation.

mercuric chloride p. Acute toxic reaction to ingested or inhaled salt of mercury. This form of mercury may also be absorbed through the skin.

SYMPTOMS: Symptoms include severe gastrointestinal irritation with pain, cramping, constriction of the throat, vomiting, and a metallic taste in the mouth. Abdominal pain may be severe. Bloody diarrhea, bloody vomitus, scanty or absent urine output, prostration, convulsions, and unconsciousness may follow. Death from uremia is the usual outcome unless treatment is begun immediately.

TREATMENT: Oxygen and intravenous fluids are given. Gastric lavage (not emesis) is used to empty the gastrointestinal tract. Dimercaprol or D-penicillamine is used for chelation. Similar treatment is given for mercurous chloride poisoning. SEE: *Poisons and Poisoning Appendix.*

mercurous chloride p. Acute toxic reaction to ingestion or absorption through the skin of mercurous chloride, a mercury salt. Acute poisoning is rare because it is poorly absorbed. Symptoms include increased salivation, abdominal discomfort, and diarrhea. SEE: *mercuric chloride in Poisons and Poisoning Appendix.*

mercury p. The acute or chronic consequences of the ingestion or inhalation of mercury. These include nausea, vomiting, abdominal pain, renal failure, gingivitis, behavioral and cognitive deficits, seizures, paralysis, pneumonitis, and/or death.

TREATMENT: Gastric lavage or whole bowel irrigation may be used to empty the gastrointestinal tract. Hemodialysis or chelation therapy, e.g., with succimer or penicillamine, may also be helpful. SEE: *mercuric chloride in Poisons and Poisoning Appendix.*

methyl alcohol p. Intoxication with methanol (methyl alcohol). The initial primary consequences are depression of central nervous system function (including coma or convulsions), visual disturbances (including permanent blindness) caused by the concentration of the toxin in the vitreous humor and optic nerve, headache, abdominal cramping, nausea, weakness, and an anion-gap metabolic acidosis.

TREATMENT: Fluids and electrolyte and acid-base balance should be carefully monitored and adjusted. Methanol may be removed from the bloodstream by hemodialysis. SEE: *Poisons and Poisoning Appendix.*

morphine p. Acute intoxication by injected, inhaled, or orally consumed morphine sulfate. SEE: *opiate poisoning; Poisons and Poisoning Appendix.*

mushroom p., mushroom and toadstool poisoning Poisoning caused by ingestion of mushrooms such as *Amanita muscaria*, which contains muscarine, or species that contain phalloidin, a component of the amanita toxin. The nearest poison control center should be called for emergency treatment. SYN: *toadstool p.* SEE: *amanita in Poisons and Poisoning Appendix.*

mussel p. Poisoning common on the U.S. Pacific coast caused by eating mussels or clams that have ingested a poisonous dinoflagellate that is not destroyed by cooking. Mussel poisoning typically occurs from June to October.

narcotic p. Poisoning caused by narcotic or sleep-producing drugs such as opium and its derivatives.

SYMPTOMS: The patient may experience brief exhilaration followed by drowsiness, respiratory depression, or coma, or, in massive overdoses, death.

TREATMENT: An airway should be established and ventilation provided. A narcotic antagonist such as naloxone should be given.

nitric acid p. Injury sustained from contact with nitric acid. Symptoms include pain, burning, vomiting, thirst, and shock.

TREATMENT: Emergency measures include oral administration of activated charcoal and large volumes of water. Emetics and stomach tubes should be avoided because they may cause rupture of the esophagus or stomach.

opiate p. Poisoning caused by injected, inhaled, dermal, or orally consumed opiate or opioid analgesics.

SYMPTOMS: The patient may experience brief mental exhilaration followed by drowsiness, respiratory depression, pulmonary edema, coma, or, in massive overdoses, death.

TREATMENT: An airway should be established and ventilation provided. A narcotic antagonist such as naloxone is given, which may be repeated periodically if symptoms return. Pulmonary edema may be treated with diuretics,

nitrates, and/or positive pressure ventilation. SEE: *Poisons and Poisoning Appendix.* SYN: *codeine p.; opium p.*

opium p. Opiate p.

oxalic acid p. Acute poisoning occurring when oxalic acid is accidentally ingested or when large quantities of foods rich in oxalic acid are eaten. Ingestion of 5 g of oxalic acid may be fatal. Chronic poisoning may result from inhalation of vapors. SEE: *Poisons and Poisoning Appendix.*

SYMPTOMS: Signs and symptoms include a corrosive action on the mucosa of the mouth, esophagus, and stomach; a sour taste; burning in the mouth, throat, and stomach; great thirst; bloody vomitus; collapse; and, sometimes, convulsions and coma.

TREATMENT: Gastric lavage should be used to empty the gastrointestinal tract. Activated charcoal can be given to bind the acid. Vomiting should not be induced.

paraldehyde p. Poisoning in which symptoms resemble those of chloral hydrate poisoning. Symptoms include cardiac and respiratory depression, dizziness, and collapse with partial or complete anesthesia; it may also produce severe lactic acidosis.

TREATMENT: There is no specific antidote. Supportive care includes airway management, ventilation, and hemodialysis.

paralytic shellfish p. ABBR: PSP. Poisoning after ingestion of shellfish contaminated by toxic marine algae that produce saxitoxin. Saxitoxin alters cell membrane permeability to sodium ions. It causes numbness and tingling, nausea and vomiting, and, in severe intoxications, paralysis and respiratory failure. Care includes the administration of intravenous fluids, respiratory support, and the oral administration of activated charcoal.

paraquat p. Poisoning caused by ingestion of paraquat. Patients may be treated with oral activated charcoal and, if kidney failure is present, hemodialysis.

parathion p. Poisoning contracted by accidental inhalation or ingestion while working with the pesticide or because of the inadvertent contamination of food products eaten. Shortly after exposure, headache, sweating, salivation, lacrimation, vomiting, diarrhea, muscular twitching, convulsions, dyspnea, and blurred vision occur. SEE: *Poisons and Poisoning Appendix.*

paregoric p. SEE: *opiate p.*

phenol p. Intoxication or chemical burns of the skin caused by exposure to carbolic acid—containing compounds, as found in some dyes, deodorizers, and disinfectants. These substances are corrosive to the skin and mucous membranes. SEE: *Poisons and Poisoning Appendix.*

SYMPTOMS: The patient may present with coagulative necrosis of affected skin or mucous membranes or with evidence of internal organ damage.

TREATMENT: Contaminated clothing should be removed immediately. The skin should then be irrigated with copious amounts of water and either isopropyl alcohol or a solution containing polyethylene glycol. Patients who have ingested phenols should be treated with activated charcoal to absorb as much toxin as possible and be given general supportive care. Consultation with specialists in toxicology, otorhinolaryngology, and critical care medicine, may be necessary in cases of massive or severe exposure.

phosphorus p. Poisoning caused by the ingestion of substances containing yellow phosphorus, such as rat poison or roach poison. Yellow phosphorus is used in manufacturing fireworks and fertilizers. SEE: *Poisons and Poisoning Appendix.*

SYMPTOMS: Liver failure may follow acute irritation of the gastrointestinal tract. There may also be kidney damage. Other symptoms include profound weakness, hemorrhage, and heart failure. Occasionally nervous system symptoms predominate.

PATIENT CARE: Gastric lavage is performed if phosphorus was swallowed. The airway is protected by cuffed endotracheal intubation. Charcoal and a cathartic drug are administered. Depending on the length of time since ingestion, intravenous fluids may be used to flush the poison out of the system by diuresis. In some cases, peritoneal or hemodialysis may be needed. The patient requires close monitoring for delayed effects for at least 24 hr. If the poison was intentionally ingested, the patient is placed on suicide precautions and referred for further psychological counseling.

pokeroot p. Poisoning caused by ingestion of pokeroot. Nausea, vomiting, drowsiness, vertigo, and possible convulsions and respiratory paralysis characterize this type of poisoning. Treatment includes administration of whole bowel irrigation or gastric lavage.

potassium chlorate p. Poisoning caused by potassium chlorate, large doses of which cause abdominal discomfort, vomiting, diarrhea, hematuria with nephritis, and disturbances of the blood. Gastric lavage should be used to empty the stomach. Other treatment is symptomatic.

⚠ Vomiting should not be induced.

potassium chromate p. Poisoning caused by potassium chromate, possibly contracted by inhalation or from touching the nose with contaminated fingers, causing deep indolent ulcers.

SYMPTOMS: When taken by mouth, potassium chromate has a disagreeable taste; it causes cramping, pain, vomiting, diarrhea, slow respiration; and it may affect the liver and kidneys.

 Vomiting should not be induced.

PATIENT CARE: For ingestion, the patient is treated as if poisoned with a strong acid. Gastric lavage is administered through a nasogastric tube. Bronchoalveolar lavage or penicillamine may be used.

potassium hydroxide p. Poisoning caused by potassium hydroxide, characterized by nausea, soapy taste, and burning pain in the mouth; bloody, slimy vomitus; abdominal cramping; bloody purging and prostration.

⚠ Vomiting should not be induced.

PATIENT CARE: The patient requires hospitalization, morphine for pain, and, often, treatment for shock. If the patient's airway has been burned, topical care is provided; tracheostomy may be required. Corticosteriods and antibiotics may be given.

potato p. Poisoning caused by ingestion of potatoes containing excess amounts of solanine. Solanine is a poisonous alkaloid present in the potato peel and in the green sprouts. Potatoes usually contain about 7 mg of solanine per 100 g; the toxic dose of solanine is about 20 to 25 g. Boiling, but not baking, removes most of the solanine from the potato. Symptoms of poisoning include headache, vomiting, abdominal pain, diarrhea, and fever. Neurological disturbances include apathy, restlessness, drowsiness, confusion, stupor, hallucinations, and visual disturbances. There is no specific therapy. With appropriate supportive and symptomatic therapy, prognosis is good.

quail p. Acute myoglobinuria caused by eating game birds of the species *Coturnix coturnix.* The cause is unknown but is suspected to be toxic rather than genetic (as was once believed).

salicylate p. Poisoning caused by aspirin or one of its derivatives. It causes a metabolic acidosis and respiratory alkalosis in adults. Ringing in the ears (tinnitus), nausea, vomiting, and diaphoresis are other common symptoms. Severe intoxications produce hyperthermia, mental status changes, and pulmonary edema.

PATIENT CARE: Patients who have overdosed on aspirin are treated with bicarbonate to increase the systemic pH and enhance excretion of salicylates in the urine. Hemodialysis is used to remove salicylates from the blood in life-threatening intoxications. SEE: *aspirin poisoning*.

salt p. Poisoning caused by excessive intake of table salt (sodium chloride), which usually occurs in hospitalized patients treated with concentrated sodium solutions. It typically results in acute hypernatremia.

scombroid fish p. Poisoning caused by eating raw or inadequately cooked fish of the suborder Scombroidea, such as tuna and mackerel, as well as certain non-scombroid fish, including amberjack, mahimahi, and bluefish. Certain bacteria act on the fish after they are caught to produce a histamine-like toxin. Therefore, these fish should be either properly cooked and eaten shortly after being caught or refrigerated immediately.

SYMPTOMS: Nausea, vomiting, abdominal cramps, diarrhea, flushing, headache, urticaria, a burning sensation and metallic taste in the mouth, dizziness, periorbital edema, and thirst may develop 30 min after eating the fish and last a few hours.

TREATMENT: Antihistamines reverse many of the symptoms of the syndrome.

shellfish p. Poisoning caused by eating shellfish that have fed on plankton during a red tide. There are several recognized syndromes that may result, including amnesic shellfish poisoning, diarrheal shellfish poisoning, and paralytic shellfish poisoning.

silver nitrate p. Poisoning caused by repeated exposure to silver compounds, marked by a bluish pigmentation of the skin or occasionally of the eyes. In the past, many medications contained biologically available silver; the incidence of this intoxication nowadays is very low. SEE: *argyria*.

sodium fluoride p. A reaction to exposure to a toxic dose of sodium fluoride, which is normally used in dentistry or in fluoridating water supplies. Symptoms include conjunctivitis, nausea, vomiting, kidney disturbances, and interference with blood coagulation.

FIRST AID: The affected areas of the skin should be washed and the compound precipitated by addition to the wash solution of soluble calcium salts such as lime water, calcium gluconate, or calcium lactate. SEE: *Poisons and Poisoning Appendix*.

staphylococcal food p. Poisoning caused by food containing any one of several heat-stable enterotoxins produced by certain strains of staphylococci. When ingested, the toxin causes nausea, vomiting, diarrhea, intestinal cramps, and, in severe cases, prostration and shock. The attack usually lasts less than a day, and fatalities are rare. Hygienic preparation techniques can prevent this form of food poisoning. Food handlers must cook all foods thoroughly, refrigerate them during storage, wash their hands, and clean equipment and surfaces used in food preparation before and after handling foods. Certain foods (meat, poultry, fish, and those containing mayonnaise, eggs, or cream) must be refrigerated and used as soon as possible and cooked until their internal temperatures equal or exceed safe limits.

PATIENT CARE: Patients who contract food poisoning should ingest clear fluids until abdominal pain subsides and then gradually return to a normal diet. Fluid and electrolyte balance is monitored, and supportive therapy is maintained as indicated. Enteric precautions are used until evidence of infection subsides.

stramonium p. Poisoning caused by the dried leaves of *Datura stramonium*, a powerful anticholinergic agent (containing belladonna alkaloids) that produces atropine-like effects. Common signs and symptoms include delirium and hallucinations, tachycardia and hypertension, fever, pupillary dilation, and, sometimes, seizures, coma, cardiac rhythm disturbances, or death. SEE: *atropine sulfate p.*

PATIENT CARE: After the gastrointestinal tract is decontaminated with activated charcoal, stimulation of the intoxicated person should be minimized. Severely poisoned people (those with seizures, extremely high body temperatures, or cardiac dysrhythmias) may be treated with intravenous physostigmine, given slowly.

strychnine p. Poisoning caused by ingestion of strychnine.

PATIENT CARE: Overdoses should be treated with gastric decontamination, e.g., activated charcoal, and drugs, e.g., diazepam that limit muscular contraction. Supportive care includes intravenous hydration with alkalinization of the urine to prevent or treat the consequences of rhabdomyolysis. SEE: *Poisons and Poisoning Appendix*.

sulfuric acid p. Poisoning from contact with, or ingestion of, sulfuric acid, e.g., in laboratories, agriculture, or weapons manufacturing.

SYMPTOMS: Early local effects of acid injury, e.g., necrosis of the skin or the upper gastrointestinal tract, result from direct contact of sulfuric acid with the epithelium. The patient may complain of intense pain, e.g., in the mouth or throat. If acid contacts the eye, it may cause pain and corneal injury, sometimes resulting in blindness. Several days to 2 weeks after massive acid ingestion, perforation of internal organs may occur. When the stomach is involved, the perforation may leak acid into the mediastinum or peritoneum, causing pain, dyspnea, hypotension, tachycardia, or shock.

TREATMENT: Exposed surfaces should be promptly washed in water to dilute the concentration of acid and minimize the depth of acid penetration. If the airway is compromised, the patient should be immediately intubated and ventilated, before undergoing dilutional therapy. Activated charcoal, which is helpful in many other exposures, is not useful. Neutralizing substances such as diluted alkalies are probably not helpful.

Most patients who ingest significant quantities of acid will undergo upper gastrointestinal endoscopy to evaluate the extent of the acid burn. Strictures, e.g., esophageal strictures, that develop as a result of scarring from acid burns are treated with dilation. People with ocular exposures need immediate ophthalmological consultation. Immediate surgery is warranted for patients with internal organ perforation. SEE: *acids in Poisons and Poisoning Appendix.*

⚠️ Blind nasogastric intubation is generally contraindicated because it may damage the upper gastrointestinal tract. Gastric intubation and lavage should be performed by experienced endoscopists.

tellurium p. A rare poisoning caused by ingestion of tellurium, usually in the workplace. Characteristic findings include a strong garlicky odor of the mouth and excreta; dry skin and mouth; anorexia; weakness; and, in severe cases, respiratory or circulatory collapse. Treatment is supportive.

thallium p. Poisoning caused by ingesting thallium, characterized by severe abdominal pain, vomiting, diarrhea, tremors, delirium, convulsions, paralysis, coma, and death. SYN: *thallotoxicosis.* SEE: *Poisons and Poisoning Appendix.*

theophylline p. Poisoning caused by excessive levels of compounds containing theophylline in the blood, characterized by nausea, vomiting, agitation, cardiac arrhythmias, and, in some instances, seizures or death. For young patients with asthma, theophylline levels exceeding 20 mg/dL are typically toxic; even lower levels, e.g., 15 mg/dL, may produce toxic effects in people over 60. Theophylline levels above 30 mg/dL have a high likelihood of adverse effects at any age.

PATIENT CARE: Theophylline toxicity may occur if the patient's symptoms and drug levels while using compounds containing theophylline are not monitored regularly. Many commonly used drugs such as cimetidine, ciprofloxacin, erythromycin, and rifampin alter the metabolism of theophylline and may produce toxic reactions if they are taken during theophylline therapy; these drugs should be avoided. Because of the risk of theophylline poisoning, most patients with reactive airway diseases such as asthma or asthmatic bronchitis are treated with inhaled bronchodilators instead of theophylline.

The patient may require monitoring in a critical care unit, where blood pressure and cardiac rhythm can be observed closely and early interventions taken in the case of seizures or potentially fatal arrhythmias. Anticonvulsants are given for seizures (or to prevent seizures when theophylline levels exceed 100 mg/dL); the gastrointestinal tract should be decontaminated with activated charcoal, and antiarrhythmic drugs are administered, as indicated, for disturbances in cardiac rhythm. Severe overdoses or ones with refractory symptoms should be treated with charcoal hemoperfusion.

thiram p. Poisoning caused by exposure to thiram. This may occur in those engaged either in manufacturing or applying this compound in agriculture.

tin p. Poisoning caused by exposure to organic compounds containing tin or tin arsenites. Most of the symptoms are neurological: changes in behavior, cognition, or awareness. Some toxic effects of tin are found on electroencephalographic examination.

tincture of iodine p. Iodine **p.**

toadstool p. Mushroom **p.**

toluene p. SEE: *benzene in Poisons and Poisoning Appendix.*

turpentine p. Poisoning usually caused by inhalation of turpentine. SEE: *Poisons and Poisoning Appendix.*

SYMPTOMS: Symptoms include a warm or burning sensation in the esophagus and stomach, followed by cramping, vomiting, and diarrhea. Pulse and respiration become weak, slow, and irregular. Irritation of the urinary tract and central nervous system resembles alcoholic intoxication.

FIRST AID: The airway should be secured and breathing assessed. Other therapies are supportive (intravenous fluids, oxygen, etc.).

p. by unknown substances Poisoning in which there is no information concerning the nature of the poison taken, and in which the signs and symptoms are not recognized as being caused by any particular substance, and for which specific antidotes cannot be given in this situation. There are some agents that act in a general manner and may be efficacious. One of these is activated charcoal, which binds most organic toxins. Whole bowel irrigation can be used to flush ingested substances from the gastrointestinal tract. When dermal exposures are suspected, the patient should be showered to remove chemicals from the skin.

verdigris p. Poisoning caused by ingestion of verdigris, which contains copper salts. Symptoms are identical to those caused by ingesting copper sulfate. SEE: *copper salts in Poisons and Poisoning Appendix*.

warfarin p. Poisoning caused by administration of an overdose of warfarin, causing excessive anticoagulation and resulting in bleeding or an increased risk of bleeding. SEE: *Poisons and Poisoning Appendix*.

⚠️ Many drugs interact with warfarin. To prevent problems with clotting or bleeding, patients taking anticoagulants should consult with health care professionals before adding or deleting medicines from their drug regimens.

PATIENT CARE: The patient is instructed to observe for signs of bleeding such as epistaxis, bleeding gums, hematuria, hematochezia, hemetemesis, melena, and bleeding into the skin (ecchymosis, purpura, or petechia). The importance of regular blood tests (to assess the prothrombin time and international normalized ratio) and medical follow-up is stressed. Maintaining constant intake levels of foods containing vitamin K also is stressed, as intermittent intake can result in widely varied coagulation levels. The patient should wear or carry a medical identification tag listing the prescribed drug, dosage, and frequency of administration. Patients who have mild to moderately elevated INRs should be treated with vitamin K; patients who have serious bleeding and warfarin poisoning should be treated emergently with infusions of prothrombin complex concentrate, factor IX complex concentrate, and recombinant activated factor VII. If these are not readily available, fresh frozen plasma may be used.

xylene p. Injury to body tissues caused by a benzene-like compound. SEE: *benzene in Poisons and Poisoning Appendix*.

zinc phosphate p. Poisoning with zinc phosphide, a rodenticide that causes fatal lung and cardiac injury. There is no specific antidote.

poison ivy (ī'vē) A climbing vine, *Toxicodendron radicans,* that on contact may produce severe pruritic dermatitis. *Toxicodendron* species contain urushiol, an extremely irritating oily resin, which stimulates a hypersensitivity reaction. First contact produces sensitization; later contacts cause severe blistering, eczema, and itching. SEE: *poison ivy dermatitis*.

poison oak A climbing vine, *Toxicodendron diversiloba,* closely related to poison ivy and having the same active substances. SEE: illus.

POISON OAK

poisonous (poy'zŏn-ŭs) [L. *potio,* a poisonous draft] Having the properties or qualities of a poison. SYN: *toxic; venomous*.

poisonous plants Plants containing a poisonous substance that may be fatal if ingested, including azalea, castor bean, chinaberry, European bittersweet, wild or black cherry, oleander, berries of holly and mistletoe, dieffenbachia, horse chestnuts, poison hemlock, laurel, death cup, black nightshade or deadly nightshade, rhododendron, choke cherry, Japanese yew, unripe fruit of akee, cassava roots, betel nut, seeds and pods of bird-of-paradise, belladonna, angels trumpet, fava bean (if eaten by a person with glucose-6-phosphate deficiency), foxglove, bulb of hyacinth, Indian tobacco, iris root, poinsettia, pokeroot, apricot kernels, apple seeds, green tubers and new sprouts of potatoes, privet, rhubarb leaves, wild tomatoes, skunk cabbage, and jimsonweed; and plants containing irritating substances, such as poison ivy, poison oak, and poison sumac.

poison sumac SEE: under *sumac*.

Poland syndrome (pō′lĭnd) A rare developmental anomaly in which one pectoralis muscle and the fingers on the same side of the body are hypoplastic or aplastic. The disease is not genetically transmitted but occurs spontaneously.

polar [L. *polaris*] Pert. to a pole.

polar body SEE: under *body.*

polarimeter (pō″lă-rĭm′ĕ-tĕr) [″ + Gr. *metron,* measure] An instrument for measuring amount of polarization of light or rotation of polarized light.

polarimetry (pō″lăr-ĭm′ĕ-trē) The measurement of the amount and rotation of polarized light.

polariscope (pō-lăr′ĭ-skōp) [L. *polaris,* pole, + Gr. *skopein,* to examine] An apparatus used in the measurement of polarized light.

polarity (pō-lăr′ĭ-tē) 1. The quality of having poles. 2. The exhibition of opposite effects at the two extremities in physical therapy. 3. The positive or negative state of an electrical battery. 4. In cell division, the relation of cell constituents to the poles of the cell.

polarization (pō″lăr-ĭ-zā′shŭn) [L. *polaris,* pole] 1. A condition in a ray of light in which vibrations occur in only one plane. 2. In a galvanic battery, collection of hydrogen bubbles on the negative plate and oxygen on the positive plate, whereby generation of current is impeded. 3. The electrical state that exists at the cell membrane of an excitable cell at rest; the inside is negatively charged in relation to the outside. The difference is created by the distribution of ions within the cell and in the extracellular fluid. SYN: *resting potential.* SEE: *depolarization* for illus.

polarizer (pō′lă-rīz″ĕr) The part of a polariscope that polarizes light.

pole (pōl) [L. *polus*] 1. The extremity of any axis about which forces acting on it are symmetrically disposed. SYN: *polus.* 2. One of two points in a magnet, cell, or battery having opposite physical qualities. 3. In biology, the regions around each endpoint of a diameter (esp. an axis) of a sphere.

    animal p. The pole opposite the yolk in an ovum. At this point, polar bodies are formed and pinched off and protoplasm is concentrated and has its greatest activity.

    p. of the eye The anterior and posterior extremities of the optic axis.

    frontal p. The most forward tip of the frontal lobe of the cerebral hemisphere.

    germinal p. The pole of an ovum at which the development begins.

    p. of the kidney The upper and lower extremities of the kidney.

    occipital p. The posterior extremity of the occipital lobe.

    pelvic p. The breech of a fetus.

    placental p. of the chorion The spot

at which the domelike placenta is situated.

    temporal p. The anterior extremity of the temporal lobe.

policosanol (pŏl″ē-kŏs′ăn-ŏl) A mixture of long-chain alcohols derived from sugar cane and other natural sources. It has been promoted as a natural lipid-lowering agent. Studies sponsored by the manufacturer of policosanol have shown striking results, but no effect on lipid levels was found during an independent trial performed in Germany.

polio *acute anterior poliomyelitis.*

polio-, poli- [Gr. *polios,* gray] Prefixes meaning *gray.*

polioencephalitis (pŏl″ē-ō-ĕn-sĕf″ă-lī′tĭs) [″ + *enkephalos,* brain, + *itis,* inflammation] A condition characterized by inflammatory lesions of the gray matter of the brain.

    anterior superior p. Inflammatory changes in the gray matter around the third ventricle, the anterior portion of the fourth ventricle, and the aqueduct of Sylvius. It is characterized by ocular abnormalities, mental disturbances, and ataxia. The origin of the disease is thiamine (vitamin B_1) deficiency. SYN: *Korsakoff syndrome.*

    p. hemorrhagica Polioencephalitis accompanied by hemorrhagic lesions.

    posterior p. Polioencephalitis involving the gray matter around the fourth ventricle.

polioencephalomyelitis (pŏl″ē-ō-ĕn-sĕf″ăl-ō-mī″ĕl-ī′tĭs) Inflammation of the gray matter of the brain and spinal cord.

polioencephalopathy (pŏl″ē-ō-ĕn-sĕf″ăl-ŏp′ă-thē) [Gr. *polios,* gray, + *enkephalos,* brain, + *pathos,* disease, suffering] Disease of the gray matter of the brain.

poliomyelitis (pŏl″ē-ō-mī″ĕl-ī′tĭs) [″ + ″ + *itis,* inflammation] An acute infectious inflammation of the anterior horns of the gray matter of the spinal cord.

    abortive p. Poliomyelitis in which the illness is mild with no involvement of the central nervous system.

    acute anterior p. An acute infectious inflammation of the anterior horns of the gray matter of the spinal cord, a rare illness in the U.S. since the introduction of effective polio vaccines. In this disease, paralysis may or may not occur. In the majority of patients, the disease is mild, being limited to respiratory and gastrointestinal symptoms, such constituting the minor illness or the abortive type, which lasts only a few days. In the major illness, muscle paralysis or weakness occurs with loss of superficial and deep reflexes. In such cases characteristic lesions are found in the gray matter of the spinal cord, medulla, motor area of cerebral cortex, and cerebellum.

    ETIOLOGY: The causative agent is the poliovirus. The virus is excreted in the feces and remains viable for months outside the body. Three immunological types exist. The incubation period for infected people ranges from 5 to 35 days but is usually 7 to 12 days.

SYMPTOMS: The onset is often abrupt although the ordinary manifestations of a severe cold or constipation may come on gradually, accompanied by slight elevation of temperature, frequently enduring for not more than 3 days. At the end of this period, paralysis may or may not develop. The extent of paralysis necessarily depends on the degree of nerve involvement: paralysis may be confined to one small group of muscles or affect one or all extremities. When the pharyngeal or respiratory muscles are involved, death is likely to occur unless mechanical ventilation is provided. Extensor muscle paralysis is typical of the disease.

DIFFERENTIAL DIAGNOSIS: The various types of meningitis, postinfection encephalomyelitis, and, rarely, conversion disorders can be confused with polio.

PROPHYLAXIS: Active immunization with inactivated poliovirus vaccine has greatly reduced the incidence of paralytic poliomyelitis. SEE: *inactivated poliovirus* **vaccine**.

COMPLICATIONS: Paralysis and muscle atrophy are common long-term complicatons of paralytic polio.

PROGNOSIS: Ordinarily the outcome is good (mortality less than 10%). When paralysis develops, 50% of the patients make a full recovery, and about 25% have mild permanent paralysis.

Progressive paralysis (postpolio syndrome) may occur years after the acute attack, often first appearing decades after the initial infection. SEE: *postpoliomyelitis muscular* **atrophy***; postpolio syndrome*.

INCIDENCE: Poliomyelitis is endemic throughout the world but occurs in epidemics in poorer countries. Thanks to a worldwide effort to eradicate polio through mass vaccination, reported cases have declined from 350,000 annually about 25 years ago, to slightly more than 1000 cases in 2007. Polio no longer occurs in epidemics in the U.S. (virtually all cases for the last several years have been vaccine-associated). In countries where polio vaccine has not been used extensively, epidemics are seasonal, occurring in summer and fall. Children are more susceptible than adults. Infection is spread by direct contact with infected oropharyngeal secretions or feces, the virus probably entering the body via the mouth. It reaches the central nervous system through the blood.

TREATMENT: Treatment is supportive. Mechanical ventilation is used for patients whose respiratory muscles are paralyzed. Physical therapy is used to attain maximum function and prevent deformities that are late manifestations of the disease.

PATIENT CARE: Strict isolation with concurrent disinfection of throat discharge and feces is enforced to prevent transmission of poliovirus. A patent airway is maintained; the patient is observed closely for signs of respiratory distress; oxygen is administered as necessary, and intubation equipment or a tracheostomy tray should be available on a nearby crash-cart.

The patient should be kept on strict bedrest during the acute phase. Gentle passive range-of-motion exercises and application of hot moist packs at 20-min intervals (or tub baths for children) help alleviate muscle pain. Proper body alignment is maintained, and the patient turned frequently to prevent deformity and decubiti. A mild sedative or analgesic is administered to decrease pain and anxiety and to promote rest. The patient is observed for distended bladder due to transitory paralysis. Personal hygiene is provided, and oral hygiene is promoted. Standard precautions are employed to dispose of fecal excretions, which contain live virus. Fluids are provided orally (intravenously if necessary) to ensure adequate hydration and urinary output. Appetizing food is offered because anorexia is common. Antipyretics are administered to reduce fever. Fluid and electrolyte balance and elimination are monitored closely. A foot board or T-foot supportsare used to prevent footdrop. Emotional support is provided. A personalized rehabilitation program is developed to assist the patient in regaining the fullest possible function. Cases must be reported to the local health department and CDC.

anterior p. Inflammation of the anterior horns of the spinal cord.

ascending p. Poliomyelitis in which paralysis begins in the lower extremities and progresses up the legs, thighs, and trunk, and finally involves the respiratory muscles.

bulbar p. Poliomyelitis in which the gray matter of the medulla oblongata is involved, affecting respiratory nerves and muscles supplied by the cranial nerves, resulting in paralysis and usually respiratory failure.

chronic anterior p. Progressive wasting of the muscles; myelopathic progressive muscular atrophy.

nonparalytic p. Pain and stiffness in the muscles of the axial skeleton, esp. of the neck and back; mild fever; increased proteins and leukocytes in the cerebrospinal fluid. Diagnosis depends on the isolation of the virus and serological reactions.

paralytic p. Poliomyelitis with a variable combination of signs of damage of the central nervous system. These include weakness, incoordination, muscle tenderness and spasms, flaccid paralysis, and disturbance of consciousness. SEE: *postpolio syndrome*.

provocative p. During an epidemic of poliomyelitis, the onset of paralysis in the area close to the site of an invasive procedure. Thus an injection in muscle increases the risk of paralysis of the side of the body injected; and tonsillectomy and adenoidectomy increases the risk that poliomyelitis will affect the brain stem.

poliosis (pŏl″ē-ō′sĭs) [Gr. *polios*, gray, + *osis*, condition] Whiteness of the hair, esp. when due to a hereditary condition or as a result of infection. SYN: *canities*.

poliovirus (pō″lē-ō-vī′rŭs) The etiological agent of poliomyelitis, separable into three serotypes based on the specificity of the neutralizing antibody. The three serotypes are types I, II, and III. A virus once found worldwide, it spreads directly or indirectly from infected persons or convalescent carriers. Epidemics of poliomyelitis that were characteristic of this virus have been greatly reduced by the poliovirus vaccine. SEE: *inactivated poliovirus vaccine*.

polished rice (pol′isht) Rice that has been milled to produce the commercially available white rice commonly consumed in Western countries. Milling removes most of the protein and thiamine from the grain. Beriberi, a thiamine deficiency, is caused when polished rice is the major source of calories in the diet.

polishing (pŏl′ĭsh-ĭng) Producing a smooth, glossy finish on a denture or a dental restoration.

Polistes (pō-lis′tēz″) [Gr. *polistēs*, founder of a city] A genus of stinging paper wasps of the order Hymenoptera, so-called because of the structural material used to build their nests.

Politzer bag (pŏl′ĭt-sĕr) [Adam Politzer, Hungarian otologist, 1835–1920] A soft rubber bag with a rubber tip for inflating the middle ear by increasing the pressure in the nasopharynx. SEE: *aerotitis*.

politzerization (pŏl″ĭt-sĕr-ĭ-zā′shŭn) The inflation of the middle ear by means of a Politzer bag.

pollen (pol′ĕn) [L. *pollen*, fine flour] The microspores of a seed plant that develop in the anther at the tip of the stamen. Each pollen grain develops a pollen tube and constitutes the male gametophyte. Within it develops a tube nucleus and two sperm nuclei, which are the male reproductive cells. Many airborne pollens are allergens. SEE: *hay fever*.

bee p. A mixture of pollens and honey, gathered by bees from flowering plants and used by them to feed their larvae. It has been as an ergogenic aid by some athletes but has no proven effect. Exposure to bee pollen sometimes produces allergic reactions in users. SYN: *bee bread*.

grass p. Pollens released by grasses such as Kentucky blue grass (*Poa pratensis*) or Timothy grass (*Phleum pratense*). They are a common source of seasonal allergies and asthma, esp. in summer.

tree p. Pollen released by coniferous trees (e.g., cedar), deciduous trees (e.g., birch), or fruit trees (e.g., olive). It is a major source of seasonal rhinitis and asthma.

pollen-food allergy syndrome Oral allergy syndrome.

Polle syndrome (pol′ē) [*Polle,* a town in Germany] A form of Munchausen syndrome by proxy and also of child abuse in which a dependent child is a victim of parentally induced or fabricated illnesses without any external incentives for this behavior, which is usually caused by a mentally unstable person.

pollex (pŏl′ĕks) *pl.* **pollices** [L.] The thumb.

p. extensus Posterior deviation of the thumb.

p. flexus Permanent flexion of the thumb.

p. valgus Abnormal deviation of the thumb toward the ulnar side.

p. varus Abnormal deviation of the thumb toward the radial side.

pollicization (pŏl″ĭs-ĭ-zā′shŭn) [L. *pollex,* thumb] The plastic surgical procedure of constructing a thumb from adjacent tissues.

pollinosis (pŏl-ĭn-ō′sĭs) [L. *pollen,* dust, + Gr. *osis,* disease] Hay fever.

pollute (pŭ-loot′) To ruin, contaminate, or spoil; to make something, such as water, food, or the environment, unfit for use or unsafe for living things.

pollution (pŭ-loo′shŭn) The state of making impure or defiling.

polonium (pŏ-lō′nē-ŭm) [L. *Polonia,* Poland, native country of its discoverers, the Curies + *-ium* (1)] SYMB: Po. A radioactive metallic chemical element isolated from pitchblende, atomic weight 210, atomic number 84.

poly (pŏl′ē) *polymorphonuclear leukocyte.*

poly- [Gr. *polys,* much, many] Prefix meaning *many, much.*

polyacid (pŏl″ē-ăs′ĭd) An alcohol or a base with two or more hydroxyl groups that will combine with an acid.

polyacrylonitrile (pŏl′ ĭ-ăk″ rĭ-lō-nī′ trĭl, trĕl″) A synthetic polymer used in the fabrication of dialysis membranes with high biocompatibility.

polyadenopathy (pŏl″ē-ăd″ĕ-nŏp′ă-thē)

[" + " + *pathos,* disease, suffering] Any disease in which many glands are involved.

polyagglutination (pŏ-lē-a-glŭ-tĭ-nā′shŭn) Red cells that are agglutinated by a large proportion of adult human sera regardless of blood group.

polyalkene (pŏl″ē-al′kēn″) [*poly-* + *alkene*] Polyolefin.

polyamide (pŏl″ē-ăm′ĭd, ĭd) [" + "] A polymer used in catheters, sutures, other biomedical devices, and clothing.

polyandry (pŏl″ē-ăn′drē) [Gr. *polyandria*] The practice of having more than one husband at the same time. SEE: *polygamy.*

polyangiitis (pŏl″ē-ăn″jē-ī′tĭs) [Gr. *polys,* many, + *angeion,* vessel, + *itis,* inflammation] Inflammation of a number of blood vessels.

polyarteritis nodosa (pŏl″ē-ăr″tĕr-ī′tĭs) [" + *arteria,* artery, + *itis,* inflammation] ABBR: PAN. A form of vasculitis affecting medium and small arteries, particularly at the point of bifurcation and branching. Segmental inflammation and fibrinoid necrosis of blood vessels lead to diminished blood flow (ischemia) to the areas normally supplied by these arteries. Although signs and symptoms depend on the location of the affected vessels and organs, patients usually present with symptoms of multisystem disease, including fever, malaise, weight loss, hypertension, renal failure, myalgia, peripheral neuritis, and gastrointestinal bleeding; these may occur episodically. Unlike most types of vasculitis, polyarteritis nodosa does not affect glomerular capillaries, although other renal vessels are involved. The disease is associated with hepatitis B and C, among other illnesses. SYN: *periarteritis nodosa.* SEE: *Nursing Diagnoses Appendix.*

ETIOLOGY: The cause is unknown, but the disease is associated with immunological disorders. Hepatitis B antigens are present in the blood of approx. 30% of patients.

polyarthritis (pŏl″ē-ăr-thrī′tĭs) [" + *arthron,* joint + *itis,* inflammation] Inflammation of more than one joint, seen in rheumatoid arthritis, juvenile rheumatoid arthritis, and psoriatic arthritis. It usually refers to involvement of more than four joints. **polyarthritic** (pŏl″ē-ăr-thrĭt′ĭk), *adj.*

    acute p. rheumatica An obsolete term for acute rheumatic fever.

    chronic villous p. Chronic inflammation of the synovial membrane of multiple joints.

polyarticular (pŏl″ē-ăr-tĭk′ū-lăr) [" + L. *articulus,* a joint] Concerning, having, or affecting many joints. SYN: *multiarticular.*

polyatomic (pŏl″ē-ă-tŏm′ĭk) [" + *atomon,* atom] Having several atoms.

polybasic (pŏl″ē-bā′sĭk) [Gr. *polys,* many, + *basis,* base] Pert. to an acid with two or more hydrogen ions that will combine with a base.

polybrominated diphenyl ethers (pŏl″ē-brōm′ĭ-nāt″ĕd) ABBR: PBDE. A class of chemicals used as flame retardants. They are chemically related to polychlorinated biphenyls and are thought to have similar biological toxicity. They have been found in streams, marine animals, human fetuses, and human breast milk.

polycarbonate (pŏl″ē-kăr′bĭ-nāt, -nĭt) [" + "] A transparent polymer used to manufacture eye protectors, shields, and other medical devices.

polycarbophil (pŏl″ē-kăr′bō-fĭl) A hydrophilic substance that is used as a bulk-forming laxative.

polycentric (pŏl″ē-sĕn′trĭk) [" + *kentron,* center] The condition of having many centers.

polychemotherapy (pŏl″ē-kē″mō-thĕr′ă-pē) [" + *chemeia,* chemistry, + *therapeia,* treatment] Treatment with several chemotherapeutic agents at once.

polychlorinated biphenyl (pŏ-lē-klŏr′ĭ-nā-tĕd) ABBR: PCB. Any of a group of complex chemicals classed as chlorinated aromatic hydrocarbons. They were widely used in industry as a component of transformers and capacitors; in paints and hydraulic systems; and in carbonless NCR paper. Because of their extremely low rate of biodegradation, accumulation in animal tissues (particularly in adipose tissue), and their potential for chronic or delayed toxic effects, the manufacture of PCBs was discontinued in the U.S. in 1977.

polychondritis (pŏl″ē-kŏn-drī′tĭs) [" + *chondros,* cartilage, + *itis,* inflammation] Inflammation of several cartilaginous areas.

    relapsing p. A rare inflammatory disease of cartilage associated with polyarthritis and involvement of the cartilage of the nose, ears, joints, bronchi, and trachea. It is most common between the ages of 40 and 60 years but may occur at any time. The cause is unknown. Because of the collapse of the bronchial walls, repeated infections of the lungs may occur, and death may result from respiratory compromise.

    TREATMENT: Prednisone is the treatment of choice. Immunosuppressive drugs such as cyclophosphamide or azathioprine are used if patients fail to respond to prednisone. Heart valve replacement or repair of aortic aneurysm may be necessary.

polychromasia (pŏl″ē-krō-mā′zē-ă) [" + *chroma,* color] The quality of having many colors.

polychromatic (pŏl″ē-krō-măt′ĭk) **1.** Multicolored. **2.** Having a wide spectrum of energies or wavelengths; said of radiation.

polychromatophil,   **polychromatophile** (pŏl″ē-krō-măt′ō-fĭl) [Gr. *polys,* many, + *chroma,* color, + *philein,* to love] A cell, esp. a red blood cell that is stainable with more than one kind of stain.

polychromatophilia (pŏl″ē-krō-măt″ō-fĭl′ē-ă) **1.** The quality of being stainable with more than one stain. **2.** An excess of polychromatophils in the blood.

polyclinic (pŏl″ē-klĭn′ĭk) [″ + *kline,* bed] A hospital or clinic treating patients with various medical and surgical conditions; a general hospital.

polyclonal (pŏl″ē-klōn′ăl) Arising from different cell lines.

polycoria (pŏl″ē-kō′rē-ă) [″ + *kore,* pupil] The state of having more than one pupil in one eye.

polycystic (pŏl″ē-sĭs′tĭk) [″ + *kystis,* cyst] Composed of many cysts.

polycystic kidney disease ABBR: PKD. Any of several hereditary disorders in which cysts form in the kidneys and other organs, eventually destroying kidney tissue and function. The autosomal recessive form usually appears in early childhood; the autosomal dominant form usually develops later in life. Definitive treatments are dialysis and kidney transplant. Because cerebral aneurysms are commonly found in adults with PKD, patients with this disorder are often screened with computed tomography or magnetic resonance imaging studies of the brain.

polycystic ovary syndrome ABBR: PCOS. Chronic anovulation in the setting of obesity, hyperinsulinemia, type 2 diabetes mellitus, lipid abnormalities, hirsutism, infertility, and ovarian cysts. SYN: *Stein-Leventhal syndrome.*

polycythemia (pŏl″ē-sī-thē′mē-ă) [*poly-* + *cyto-* + *-emia*] An excess of red blood cells. In a newborn, it may reflect hemoconcentration due to hypovolemia or prolonged intrauterine hypoxia, or hypervolemia due to intrauterine twin-to-twin transfusion or placental transfusion resulting in delayed clamping of the umbilical cord. SYN: *erythrocytosis.*

  Chuvash p. An autosomal recessive erythrocytosis in which patients respond to normal oxygen levels as if they were in a hypoxic environment and make more red blood cells than are needed. Sludging of blood, pulmonary hypertension, and vascular infarcts are common sequelae.

  relative p. A relative (rather than an absolute) increase in the number of erythrocytes due to a reduction of plasma volume, e.g., in patients with burns or dehydration.

  secondary p. Polycythemia due to a physiological condition that stimulates erythropoiesis, e.g., lowered oxygen tension in blood.

  spurious p. Gaisböck syndrome.

  p. vera A chronic, life-shortening myeloproliferative disorder due to the reproduction of a single stem-cell clone. It is characterized by proliferation or hyperplasia of all bone marrow cells, with an increase in red blood cell mass and hemoglobin concentration that occurs independently of erythropoietin stimulation. SYN: *erythremia.* SEE: illus.; Nursing Diagnoses Appendix.

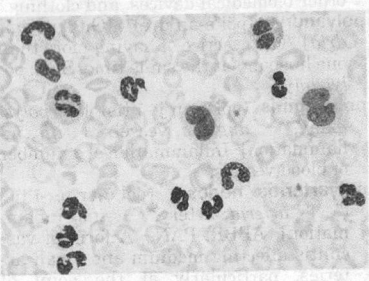

POLYCYTHEMIA VERA

peripheral blood smear in polycythemia vera (X 400)

SYMPTOMS: Usually occurring between ages 40 and 60 and most common in males with Jewish ancestry, polycythemia seldom affects children or those of African ancestry. Weakness, fatigue, headache, blood clotting, vertigo, tinnitus, irritability, dyspnea, visual disturbances, flushing of face, redness, or ruddy cyanosis, pruritus, ecchymosis, hypertension, epigastric distress, weight loss, and pain in joints or extremities occur commonly. The bone marrow shows uncontrolled, rapid cellular reproduction and maturation (increased cellularity). Peptic ulcers are often reported.

TREATMENT: The mainstay of patient care is the reduction in red blood cell mass with recurrent phlebotomy to lower the hematocrit to 45% or less. Vitals signs are monitored during and after phlebotomy, and the patient is provided with oral fluids and protected from orthostatic hypotension. The symptoms and the need to seek medical attention when signs and symptoms of bleeding and thrombus formation occur are explained to the patient. Rest should be balanced with exercise, but the patient should be advised that activity and ambulation help prevent thrombotic complications. Reassurance and support are provided to the patient and family, and opportunities are provided for questions and discussion of concerns. Patients who have a history of blood clotting or very high platelet counts are treated with myelosuppressive drugs, such as hydroxyurea. During myelosuppressive therapy the patient is informed about adverse effects that may occur and is assessed for leukopenia and thrombocytopenia. Protective measures are instituted.

polydactylism (pŏl″ē-dăk′tĭ-lĭzm) [Gr. *polys,* many, + *daktylos,* digit, + *-ismos,* condition] The state of having supernumerary fingers or toes.

polydactyly (pŏl″ē-dăk′tĭ-lē) [″ + *daktylos,* finger] The condition of having more than the normal number of fingers and toes.

polydioxanone (pol″ē-dī″ok′să-nōn″) ABBR: PDO, PDS. A bioabsorable synthetic material used to make self-absorbing sutures.

polydipsia (pol″ē-dip′sē-ă) [*poly-* + Gr. *dipsa,* thirst] Excessive thirst, a symptom suggestive of dehydration, hyperglycemia, or hypovolemia.

polydrug use (pŏ-lē-drŭg′) In drug abusers, the practice of concurrent use of several dissimilar drugs, such as alcohol, cocaine, opiates, and other drugs. The toxic potential of multiple drug use is increased as compared with use of a single drug.

polydystrophy (pŏl″ē-dĭs′trō-fē) [″ + ″ + *trophe,* nourishment] The condition of having multiple congenital anomalies of the connective tissues.

   pseudo-Hurler p. Mucolipidosis type III.

polyendocrine deficiency syndrome (pol″ē-en′dŏ-krĕn, -krīn″, -krēn″) Polyglandular autoimmune syndrome.

polyene (pŏl-ē′ēn) An organic compound containing alternating, or conjugate, double bonds. An example is butadiene, $CH_2=CHCH=CH_2$.

polyepitope (pŏl″ē-ĕp′ĭ-tōp″) [″ + ″] A synthetic merger of immunogenic protein sequences, used (e.g., in the manufacture of vaccines).

polyestrous (pŏl″ē-ĕs′trŭs) [″ + *oistros,* mad desire] Having two or more estrous cycles in each mating season.

polyether impression material (pol″ē-ē′thĕr) [*poly-* + *ether*] The stiffest of the dental final impression materials, used to construct restorations, prosthetics, and other appliances. It is made from a base containing a polyether polymer, silica, filler, and plasticizer, and an accelerator, made of an alkylaromatic sulfonate, filler, and plasticizer.

polyethylene (pŏl″ē-ĕth′ĭ-lēn) A polymerized resin of ethylene; used to make a wide variety of products, including tubing used in intravenous sets.

polygamy (pō-lĭg′ă-mē) [″ + *gamos,* marriage] The practice of having several wives, husbands, or mates at the same time. SEE: *polyandry; polygyny.*

polygen (pŏl′ĕ-jĕn) **1.** An element that has more than one valency and that can form more than one series of compounds. **2.** An antigen that will cause

the formation of two or more specific antibodies.

polygenic (pŏl″ē-jĕn′ĭk) [″ + *gennan,* to produce] Pert. to or caused by several genes.

polyglactin (pol″ē-glak′tĭn) An absorbable polymer used to manufacture sutures and surgical mesh.

polyglandular (pŏl″ē-glăn′dū-lăr) [″ + L. *glandula,* a little kernel] Pert. to or affecting many glands. SYN: *pluriglandular.*

polyglandular autoimmune syndrome Any of several syndromes that combine endocrine and autoimmune disorders. SYN: *autoimmune endocrine failure syndrome; autoimmune polyglandular syndrome; polyendocrine deficiency syndrome.*

   type 1 p.a.s. A polyglandular autoimmune syndrome that begins at about age 12 and is characterized by hypoparathyroidism, primary adrenal insufficiency, and mucocutaneous candidiasis. Alopecia, pernicious anemia, malabsorption, and chronic hepatitis may also be present.

   type 2 p.a.s. Schmidt syndrome.

polyglucosan (pŏl″ē-gloo′kŏ-săn″) Glucose polymers. Abnormal collections of glucose polymers in tissue specimens are sometimes called "polyglucosan bodies," "Lafora bodies," or "corpora amylacea."

polyglucose, poly-D-glucose (pŏl″ē-gloo′kōs) A water-soluble polymer made of linked dextrose subunits. It is used as a peritoneal dialysis solution and as a sweetener in foods.

polyglycolic acid (pol″ē-glī-kol′ik) SEE: under *acid.*

polygram (pŏl′ē-grăm) [″ + *gramma,* something written] A tracing or record made by a polygraph.

polygraph (pol′ē-graf″) [*poly-* + *-graph*] An instrument for determining minor physiological changes assumed to occur under the stress of lying (or other emotion). Variations in respiratory rhythm, pulse rate, blood pressure, and sweating of the hands are among the functions monitored. Increased perspiration lessens resistance to passage of electrical current. The test has popular appeal among law enforcement departments, but results obtained are presumptive and not absolute; nevertheless, interpretations of polygraph data have been admitted as evidence in some legal proceedings. The advisability of accepting the results of polygraph tests is controversial. SYN: *lie detector.*

polygyny (pŏ-lĭg′ŏ-nē) The practice of having more than one female mate at a time. SEE: *polygamy.*

polyhedral (pŏl″ē-hē′drăl) [Gr. *polys,* many, + *hedra,* base] Having many surfaces.

polyhydramnios (pŏl″ē-hī-drăm′nē-ŏs) [″

+ *hydor,* water, + *amnion,* amnion]
A condition in which the volume of amniotic fluid exceeds 2000 mL during the last half of pregnancy. Acute polyhydramnios occurs suddenly between 20 and 24 weeks' gestation and is marked by a rapid (within a few days) increase in volume. Chronic polyhydramnios, a continuous, gradual increase in volume throughout the last trimester, is more common. Uterine overdistention may result in preterm labor.

ETIOLOGY: The cause is unknown; however, the condition occurs more frequently in association with congenital fetal anomalies that interfere with swallowing, in anencephaly, in monozygotic multiple gestation, and in 10% of pregnancies in diabetic women.

SYMPTOMS: Suspicious clinical signs include a taut abdomen, a fundal height increased out of proportion to gestation, and difficulty in auscultating the fetal heart rate. When the amniotic fluid volume exceeds 3000 mL, interference with diaphragmatic excursion and vena caval compression are reflected in maternal shortness of breath and increased dependent edema.

DIAGNOSIS: Ultrasonography confirms the presence of polyhydramnios and will identify fetal anomalies such as anencephaly or exposed fetal meninges.

TREATMENT: Amniocentesis is performed to reduce the amniotic volume in women who are experiencing severe discomfort and/or respiratory embarrassment. In most cases, however, conservative management includes bedrest in the left lateral position to encourage placental perfusion and diuresis.

polykaryocyte (pŏl″ē-kăr′ē-ō-sīt) [″ + *karyon,* nucleus, + *kytos,* cell] A cell possessing several nuclei.

polylactide (pol″ē-lak′tīd″) A bioabsorbable, heat-sensitive polymer made from lactic acid and used in the manufacture of sutures, meshes, patches, and stents. SYN: *polylactic acid.*

polylysine (pŏl″ē-lī′sīn) A polypeptide in which two lysine molecules are joined.

polymastia (pŏl″ē-măs′tē-ă) [Gr. *polys,* many, + *mastos,* breast] The condition of having more than two breasts. SYN: *multimammae.*

polymenorrhea (pŏl″ē-mĕn-ō-rē′ă) [″ + ″ + *rhoia,* to flow] Menstrual bleeding that occurs regularly, but at intervals of less than 21 days.

polymer (pŏl′ĭ-mĕr) [″ + *meros,* a part] A natural or synthetic substance formed by a combination of two or more molecules (and up to millions) of the same substance. SYN: *polymerid.*

polymerase (pŏl-ĭm′ĕr-ās) An enzyme that catalyzes polymerization of nucleotides to form DNA molecules before cell division, or RNA molecules before protein synthesis.

RNA p. Transcriptase.

polymerase chain reaction ABBR: PCR. A process that permits making, in the laboratory, unlimited numbers of copies of genes. This is done beginning with a single molecule of the genetic material DNA. The technique can be used in investigating and diagnosing numerous bacterial diseases, viruses associated with cancer, genetic diseases such as diabetes mellitus, human immunodeficiency virus, pemphigus vulgaris, and various diseases of the blood (e.g., sickle cell anemia) and of muscles.

polymeric (pŏl″ĭ-mĕr′ĭk) **1.** Having the characteristics of a polymer. **2.** Muscles derived from more than one myotome. **3.** Consisting of repeating, linked elements.

polymerization (pŏl″ĭ-mĕr″ĭ-zā′shŭn) The process of changing a simple chemical substance or substances into another compound having the same elements usually in the same proportions but with a higher molecular weight.

polymerize (pŏl′ĭ-mĕr-īz) To cause polymerization.

polymersome (pŏl′ĭ-mĕr-sōm″) A vesicle made artificially of linked, helix-shaped proteins.

polymethylmethacrylate, polymethyl methacrylate (pol′ē-meth′ĭl-meth″ak′rĭ-lāt″) [*poly-* + *methyl* + *methacryl(ic acid)* + *-ate*] ABBR: PMMA. $C_5H_8O_2$, a transparent, colorless acrylic polymer. It is used in optics and ophthalmology to make intraocular lenses for cataract surgery, in dentistry as a denture base material, in cosmetic surgery as a soft-tissue filler, and in the fabrication of dialysis membranes with high biocompatibility.

polymicrobial (pŏl″ē-mī-krō′bē-ăl) [Gr. *polys,* many, + *mikros,* small, + *bios,* life] Concerning a number of species of microorganisms.

polymicrogyria (pŏl″ē-mī″krō-jī′rē-ă) [″ + ″ + *gyros,* convolution] A developmental malformation of the brain in which the gyri form with abnormally small convolutions. It often results from chromosomal deletions, e.g., from chromosome 22.

polymorph (pŏl′ē-morf) [″ + *morphe,* form] A polymorphonuclear leukocyte.

polymorphic (pŏ-lē-mŏr-fĭk) Occurring in more than one form. SYN: *multiform; polymorphous.*

polymorphism (po″lē-mor′fĭzm) [*poly-* + *morph-* + *-ism*] **1.** The property of crystallizing into two or more different forms. **2.** The occurrence of more than one form in a life cycle. **3.** An allelic variation within a species. SYN: *pleomorphism.*

single nucleotide p. ABBR: SNP. A change in one nucleotide in a strand of DNA. An SNP may alter a single codon, resulting in the transcription of one substituted amino acid in a protein. This small *point mutation* may be all that is needed to modify the function of the protein, which in turn may be responsible for the development of a particular disease. SNPs have been identified that increase the propensity for macular degeneration, sickle cell anemia, and other illnesses. Studies that aim to determine if SNPs underlie common illnesses are known as *genome-wide association studies.*

restriction fragment length p. DNA fingerprinting with a specific nucleotide insertion sequence.

polymorphocellular (pŏl″ē-mor′fō-sĕl′ū-lăr) [″ + ″ + L. *cellula,* a small chamber] Composed of cells of many forms.

polymorphonuclear (pŏl″ē-mor′fō-nū′klē-ăr) [″ + ″ + L. *nucleus,* a kernel] Possessing a nucleus consisting of several parts or lobes connected by fine strands.

polymorphous (pŏl″ē-mor′fŭs) Polymorphic.

polymorphous light eruption, polymorphic light eruption SEE: under *eruption.*

polymyalgia arteritica (pŏl″ē-mī-ăl′jē-ă) [″ + *mys,* muscle, + *algos,* pain] Polymyalgia rheumatica.

polymyalgia rheumatica ABBR: PMR. A rheumatologic illness marked by fevers, malaise, weight loss, muscle pain and stiffness (esp. of the shoulders and pelvis), and morning stiffness. It occurs primarily, but not exclusively, in white individuals over age 60. The cause of the syndrome is unknown. Although there is no single diagnostic test for this condition, patients typically have a markedly elevated erythrocyte sedimentation rate (>50 mm/hr) and no evidence of another disease (e.g., infection, cancer, rheumatoid arthritis, or lupus) as the underlying cause. Patients with the syndrome obtain rapid and durable relief from corticosteroids but usually require a course of treatment lasting 6 to 18 months. Pathologically, and sometimes clinically, the syndrome is related to giant cell arteritis. Mild cases may sometimes respond to nonsteroidal antiinflammatory drugs. SYN: *polymyalgia arteritica.*

polymyositis (pŏl″ē-mī″ō-sī′tĭs) [″ + ″ + *itis,* inflammation] A relatively uncommon inflammatory disease of skeletal muscles, marked by symmetrical weakness of the proximal muscles of the limbs, elevated serum muscle enzymes, evidence of muscle necrosis on biopsy, and electromyographic abnormalities.

PATIENT CARE: Treatment regimens may include corticosteroids, methotrexate, or other immunosuppressive agents. Physical therapy is employed after disease activity lessens.

polymyxin (pŏl″ē-mĭk′sĭn) [*polymyxa* + *-in*] Any of the group of cationic polypeptide antibiotics produced by the bacterium *Bacillus polymyxa.* Although these antibiotics are toxic to the brain and kidney and are poorly absorbed from the gastrointestinal tract, they are occasionally used to treat resistant infections caused by gram-negative microorganisms.

polyneural (pŏl″ē-nū′răl) [″ + *neuron,* nerve, sinew] Pert. to, innervated, or supplied by many nerves.

polyneuritic (pŏl″ē-nū-rĭt′ĭk) [″ + ″ + *itis,* inflammation] Inflammation of several nerves at once.

polyneuritis (pŏl″ē-noo-rīt′ĭs) [*poly-* + *neuritis*] Multiple neuritis.

acute idiopathic p. Guillain-Barré syndrome.

diabetic p. Diabetic **neuropathy.**

Jamaica ginger p. Jamaica ginger **paralysis.**

metabolic p. Polyneuritis due to metabolic disorders such as nutritional deficiency, esp. the lack of thiamine; gastrointestinal disorders; or pathologic conditions such as diabetes, pernicious anemia, and toxemias of pregnancy.

toxic p. Polyneuritis due to poisons such as heavy metals, alcohol, carbon monoxide, or organic compounds.

polyneuropathy (pŏl″ē-noo-rŏp′ă-thē) [*poly-* + *neuropathy*] Any disease that affects multiple peripheral nerves.

acute inflammatory demyelinating p. Guillain-Barré syndrome.

amyloid p. Polyneuropathy characterized by deposition of amyloid in nerves.

chronic inflammatory demyelinating p. ABBR: CIDP. A gradually progressing autoimmune muscle weakness in arms and legs caused by inflammation of the myelin sheath covering peripheral nerve axons. Demyelination slows or blocks conduction of impulses to muscles. Numbness and paresthesia may accompany or precede loss of motor function, which varies from mild to severe. Laboratory findings include elevated protein levels in the cerebrospinal fluid. The inflammatory damage involves not only phagocytes (neutrophils and macrophages), but also immune complexes and complement activation by myelin autoantigens. Immunosuppressive drugs are used to treat this illness. Plasma exchange therapy or infusions of immunoglobulins often are used first, to produce a remission. CIDP is considered to be a chronic counterpart to Guillain-Barré syndrome.

critical illness p. ABBR: CIP. A complication occurring in patients in intensive care in which failure to wean from mechanical ventilation is associated with distal limb weakness, loss of distal sensation from light touch or pinprick, and diminished reflexes; facial muscles and nerves are spared. Recovery typically occurs several weeks or months after resolution of the underlying disease. It is associated with the use of drugs, such as corticosteroids or paralytic agents, and neurological illnesses, such as Guillain-Barre syndrome.

diabetic p. Diabetic **neuropathy**.

familial amyloiditic p. An inherited form of amyloid polyneuropathy in which abnormal forms of transthyretin are deposited in nerves and brain tissue, making multiple nerves malfunction.

paraproteinemic p. Polyneuropathy due to excessive levels of immunoglobulin in the blood. The most commonly implicated immunoglobulins are immunoglobulin M and immunoglobulin G.

porphyric p. Polyneuropathy due to acute porphyria, characterized by pains and paresthesias in the extremities and by flaccid paralysis.

progressive hypertrophic p. Déjérine-Sottas disease.

polynuclear, polynucleate (pol″ē-noo′klē-ăr, -nū′, pol″ē-noo′klē-āt″) [″ + L. *nucleus,* a kernel] Possessing more than one nucleus. SYN: *multinuclear; multinucleate.*

polynucleotide (pŏl″ē-nū′klē-ō-tīd) Nucleic acid composed of two or more nucleotides.

polynucleotide kinase ABBR: PNK. An enzyme that facilitates the transfer of a phosphate group from adenosine triphosphate to the 5′ terminus of a nucleic acid (RNA or DNA).

polyolefin (pol″ē-ō′lĕ-fin) A flexible, synthethic hydrocarbon polymer. It is produced from a simple olefin (alkene) with the general formula C_nH_{2n}. Its health-related uses include storage bags and containers for blood components, infusion devices and tubes for intravenous fluids, and prosthetic body parts. SYN: *polyalkene.*

polyomavirus (pŏl″ē-ō-mă-vī′rŭs) A double-stranded DNA virus that causes kidney, nerve, and lymphoid disease in humans.

polyopia, polyopsia (pol″ē-ō′pē-ă, pol″ē-op′sē-ă) [*poly-* + *-opia*] Perception of more than one image of the same object. SYN: *multiple vision.*

polyorchidism (pŏl″ē-or′kĭ-dīzm) [″ + *orchis,* testicle, + *-ismos,* condition] The condition of having more than two testicles.

polyorchis (pŏl″ē-or′kĭs) An individual with more than two testicles.

polyostotic (pŏl″ē-ŏs-tŏt′ĭk) [″ + *osteon,* bone] Involving several bones.

polyovulatory (pŏl″ē-ŏv′ū-lă-tō″rē) [″ + L. *ovulum,* little egg] Releasing several ova in a single ovulatory cycle.

polyp (pol′ĭp) [Gr. *polypous,* many-footed, octopus, nasal tumor] A swelling or excrescence (tumor) emanating from a mucous membrane; commonly found in vascular organs such as the nose, uterus, colon, and rectum. Polyps bleed easily; if there is a possibility that they will become malignant, they should be removed surgically. SYN: *polypus.*

adenomatous p. Benign neoplastic tissue originating in the glandular epithelium.

antrochoanal p. A nasal polyp found near the posterior wall of the maxillary sinus.

aural p. Polypoid granulation tissue in the external canal of the ear attached to the tympanic membrane or middle ear structures.

bleeding p. An angioma of the nasal mucous membrane.

cardiac p. A pedunculated tumor attached to the inside of the heart. If situated close to a valve, it may cause blockage of the valve intermittently.

cervical p. A usually benign growth of the cervical mucosa.

choanal p. A nasal polyp that extends into the pharynx.

colonic p. An abnormal tissue growth within the lumen of the colon. It may be benign or malignant. SEE: illus.

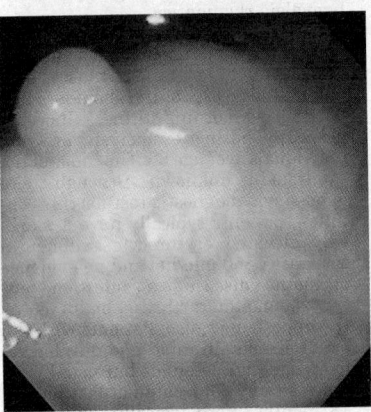

POLYPS

Polyps in the colon, seen endoscopically

fibrinous p. A polyp containing fibrin and blood, located in the uterine cavity.

fibroepithelial p. A smooth-surfaced polyp of the oral mucosa, usually developing after trauma to the area. SEE: *acrochordon.*

fleshy p. A submucous myoma in the uterus, consisting of benign neoplastic tissue from smooth muscle.

gelatinous p. **1.** A polyp made up of loose swollen edematous tissue. **2.** A myxoma.

Hopmann p. SEE: under *Hopmann, Carl Melchior.*

hydatid p. A cystic polyp.

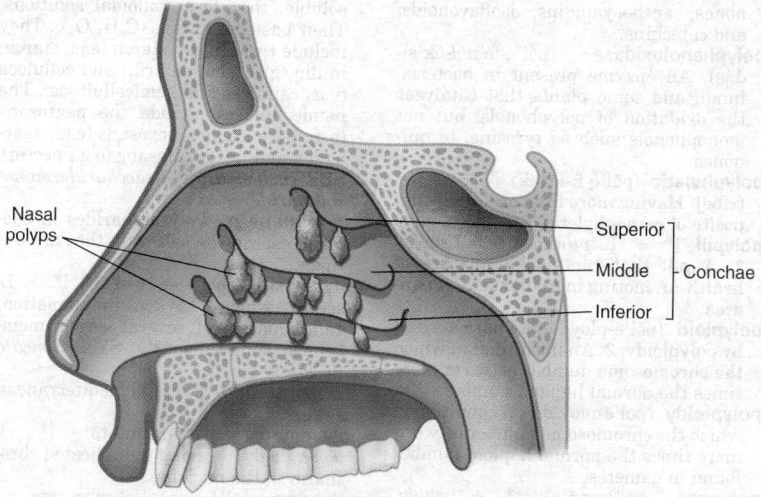

NASAL POLYPS

juvenile p. A benign rounded mucosal hamartoma of the large bowel. This type of polyp may be present in large numbers in infants and is commonly associated with rectal bleeding. SYN: *retention p.*

laryngeal p. A polyp attached to the vocal cords and extending to the air passageway.

lymphoid p. A benign lymphoma of the rectum.

mucous p. A polyp of soft or jelly-like consistency and exhibiting mucoid degeneration.

nasal p. A pedunculated polyp of the nasal mucosa. SEE: illus.

Nasal polyps are the most commonly identified nonmalignant tumor of the nasal passages. They are more commonly identified in men than in women.

SYMPTOMS: The most common symptom of nasal polyposis is obstruction to the flow of air into and out of the nasal passages.

TREATMENT: Steroid nasal sprays may improve airflow through the nasal passages. Surgical removal of polyps may occasionally be necessary when medical treatment is unsuccessful.

placental p. A polyp composed of retained placental tissue.

retention p. Juvenile **p.**

vascular p. A pedunculated angioma.

polypectomy (pŏl″ĭ-pĕk′tō-mē) [″ + *pous*, foot, + *ektome*, excision] The surgical removal of a polyp. In the U.S., about 1 million colonic polypectomies are performed each year.

polypeptidase (pŏl″ē-pĕp′tĭ-dās) An enzyme that catalyzes the hydrolysis of peptides.

polypeptide (pŏl″ē-pĕp′tīd″) [poly- + Gr. *peptein*, to digest] A union of two or more amino acids.

islet amyloid p. Amylin. SEE: *peptide.*

polyphagia (pŏl″ē-fā′jē-ă) [Gr. *polys*, many, + *phagein*, to eat] Eating abnormally large amounts of food; gluttony.

polypharmacy (pŏl″ē-făr′mă-sē) [″ + *pharmakon*, drug] **1.** Concurrent use of a large number of drugs. It increases the likelihood of unwanted side effects and adverse drug-to-drug interactions.

PATIENT CARE: The more complicated an illness, and the more illnesses one suffers, the greater the likelihood that a patient will have a complex, difficult to manage, and costly drug regimen. Any person taking more than one medication should keep a careful record of all of his drug therapies, including how often they are taken, for what purpose, and by whom they have been prescribed. The medical regimen should be reviewed at each visit with health care professionals to avoid misunderstandings and prescribing errors. Frequent physical examinations and laboratory studies may be needed to ensure that complex drug regimens are not causing preventable side effects. Medical regimens should be simplified whenever possible to those with the greatest beneficial effect and the least likelihood of causing harm.

2. Excessive use of drugs.

polyphenol (pŏl″ē-fē′nŏl) [″ + ″] Any of a large group of colorful phytochemicals found in plants, many of which are antioxidants. Polyphenols include several thousand flavonoids, including flavanones, anthocyanidins, isoflavonoids, and catechins.

polyphenoloxidase (pŏl″ē-fē″nŏl-ŏk′sĭ-dās) An enzyme present in bacteria, fungi, and some plants that catalyzes the oxidation of polyphenols, but not monophenols such as tyrosine, to quinones.

polyphyletic (pŏl″ē-fī-lĕt′ĭk) [″ + *phyle*, tribe] Having more than one origin; opposite of monophyletic.

polypill [″ + L. *pilula*, a small mass] **1.** A pill that contains a mixture of health-promoting ingredients. **2.** A panacea.

polyploid (pŏl′ē-ployd) **1.** Characterized by polyploidy. **2.** An individual in which the chromosome number is two or more times the normal haploid number.

polyploidy (pŏl″ē-ploy″dē) A condition in which the chromosome number is two or more times the normal haploid number found in gametes.

polypnea (pŏl″ĭp-nē′ă) [″ + *pnoia*, breath] Panting.

polypoid (pŏl′ē-poyd) [″ + ″ + *eidos*, form, shape] Like a polyp.

polyposis (pŏl″ē-pō′sĭs) [″ + GR. *pous*, foot, + ″] Any disease resulting in the growth of multiple polyps.

    p. **coli** Polyposis of the large intestine.

    familial adenomatous p. SEE: *familial adenomatous polyposis.*

    multiple intestinal p. Familial adenomatous polyposis.

    p. **ventriculi** The presence of numerous polyps in the stomach, sometimes involving the entire mucosa, accompanied by chronic atrophic gastritis.

polyprotein (pŏl′ĭ -prō′tēn″) [″ + ″] A polypeptide that contains the linked transcripts of several proteins. Cleavage of the polypeptide releases the contained protein sequences.

polypus (pŏl′ĭ-pŭs) *pl.* **polypi** [L.] Polyp.

polyradiculitis (pŏl″ē-ră-dĭk″ū-lī′tĭs) [″ + L. *radix*, root, + Gr. *itis*, inflammation] Inflammation of nerve roots, esp. the roots of spinal nerves. SEE: *Nursing Diagnoses Appendix.*

polyradiculoneuritis (pŏl″ē-ră-dĭk″ū-lō-nū-rī′tĭs) [″ + ″ + Gr. *neuron*, nerve, + *itis*, inflammation] Inflammation of the peripheral nerves and spinal ganglia.

polyribosome (pŏl″ē-rī′bō-sōm) A cluster or group of ribosomes. They are the site of attachment for mRNA in the cytoplasm and the translation of genetic information into the synthesis of specific proteins. SYN: *polysome.*

polysaccharide (pŏl″ē-săk′ă-rīd) [″ + Sanskrit *sarkara,* sugar] One of a group of carbohydrates that, upon hydrolysis, yield more than 20 monosaccharide molecules. They are complex carbohydrates of high molecular weight, usually insoluble in water, but when soluble, they form colloidal solutions. Their basic formula is $(C_6H_{12}O_6)_n$. They include two groups: starch (e.g., starch, inulin, glycogen, dextrin) and cellulose (e.g., cellulose and hemicelluloses). The hemicelluloses include the pentosans (e.g., gum arabic), hexosans (e.g., agar-agar), and hexopentosans (e.g., pectin). SEE: *carbohydrate; disaccharide; monosaccharide.*

    immune p. Polysaccharides in bacteria, esp. in the cell wall, that are antigenic.

polyserositis (pŏl″ē-sē-rō-sī′tĭs) [″ + L. *serum,* whey, + *itis,* inflammation] Inflammation of several serous membranes simultaneously. SYN: *Concato disease.*

    recurrent p. Familial Mediterranean fever.

polysomaty (pŏl″ē-sō′mă-tē) [″ + *soma,* body] Having reduplicated chromatin in the nucleus.

polysome (pŏl′ē-sōm) Polyribosome.

polysomnography (pŏ-lē-sŏm-nŏ′gră-fē) The simultaneous monitoring of respiratory, cardiac, muscle, brain, and ocular function during sleep. It is used most often to diagnose sleep apnea. SYN: *sleep study.*

polysorbates (pŏl″ē-sor′bāts) Nonionic surface-active agents composed of polyoxyethylene esters of sorbitol. They usually contain associated fatty acids. The series includes polysorbates 20, 40, 60, and 80, which are used in preparing pharmaceuticals. These polysorbates have the trade names of Tween 20, Tween 40, etc.

polyspermia (pŏl″ē-spĕr′mē-ă) [Gr. *polys,* many, + *sperma,* seed] **1.** The excessive secretion of seminal fluid. **2.** The entrance of several spermatozoa into one ovum. SYN: *polyspermism.*

polyspermy (pŏl″ē-spĕr′mē) [*poly-* + *sperm*] The fertilization of an ovum by multiple spermatozoa. This is normal in some species but abnormal and rare in humans.

polystyrene (pŏl″ē-stī′rēn) A synthetic resin produced by the polymerization of styrene from ethylene and benzene. The formula is $(CH_2CHC_6H_5)_n$. It is used in the plastics industry.

polysulfide impression material (pol″ē-sŭl′fīd″) [*poly-* + *sulfide*] An elastic final dental impression used to construct restorations, prosthetics, and appliances, which is made from a paste composed of polysulfide polymer, filler, sulfur, plasticizer, and an accelerator paste containing lead dioxide (which causes it to turn dark-brown).

polysulfone A synthetic polymer used in the fabrication of dialysis membranes with high biocompatibility.

polysynaptic (pŏl″ē-sĭ-năp′tĭk) [″ + *synapsis,* point of contact] Pert. to nerve pathways involving multiple synapses.

polysyndactyly (pŏl″ē-sĭn-dăk′tĭl-ē) [″ + *syn*, together, + *daktylos*, finger] Multiple syndactyly.

polysystole (pol″ē-sis′tŏ-lē) [*poly-* + *systole*] In labor and delivery, the presence of 6 or more uterine contractions during a 10-minute period. SYN: *hypertonic uterine* **dysfunction**.
   uterine p. Polysystole.

polytene (pŏl′ĕ-tēn) [″ + *tainia*, band] Composed of many filaments of chromatin.

polyteny (pŏl″ĕ-tē′nē) [″ + *tainia*, band] Multiple lateral duplication of the chromosome. This produces a giant chromosome.

polytetrafluoroethylene (pŏ-lē-tĕ-tră-flŏ-rō-ĕth′ĭ-lēn) ABBR: PTFE. A synthetic polymer that has slippery, nonsticking properties. It is used in a variety of products, including vascular grafts used to bypass obstructed blood vessels and grafts used for dialysis access.

polythelia (pŏl″ē-thē′lē-ă) [″ + *thele*, nipple, + *-ismos*, condition] The presence of more than one nipple on a mamma.

polytherapy (pŏl′ē-thĕr′ă-pē) Therapy with two or more drugs used at the same time to treat a condition. The term is used most often to describe treatment of seizure disorders with more than one drug; however, it is also used to describe multidrug therapy in Parkinson disease, schizophrenia, and other brain diseases.

polytrauma (pŏl″ē-traw′mă) [″ + ″] Simultaneous injury to several organs or body systems.

polytrichia (pŏl″ē-trĭk′ē-ă) [″ + *thrix*, hair] Hypertrichosis.

polytropic (pŏl″ē-trŏp′ĭk) [″ + *trope*, a turning] Affecting more than one type of cell, said of viruses, or affecting more than one type of tissue, said of certain poisons.

polyunsaturated (pŏ-lē-ŭn-săch′ŭr-ā-tĕd) In chemistry, relating to long-chain carbon compounds, esp. fats that have many carbon atoms joined by double or triple bonds.

polyuria (pŏl″ē-ūr′ē-ă) [*poly-* + *-uria*] Excessive secretion and discharge of urine; specifically, urination in excess of 50mL/kg of body weight per day. The urine generally does not contain abnormal constituents. Several liters in excess of normal may be voided each day. The urine is virtually colorless. Specific gravity is 1.000 to 1.002 (higher in diabetes mellitus). Polyuria occurs in diabetes insipidus, diabetes mellitus, chronic nephritis, nephrosclerosis, hyperthyroidism, following edematous states (esp. those induced by heart failure treated with diuretics), and following excessive intake of liquids.

polyvalent (pŏl″ē-vā′lĕnt, pō-lĭv′ă-lĕnt) [″ + L. *valere*, to be strong] Multivalent; having a combining power of more than two atoms of hydrogen.

polyvinyl chloride (pŏl″ ē-vī″ nĭl) ABBR: PVC. A thermoplastic polymer formed from vinyl chloride, used in the manufacture of many products such as rainwear, garden hoses, and floor tiles.

⚠ Exposure to toxic fumes of PVC can cause respiratory irritation, asthma, or decompensation. Some evidence suggests PVCs can cause cancer.

polyvinylsiloxane, polyvinyl siloxane (pŏl″ē-vīn′il-sĭ-lok′sān″) Vinyl polysiloxane.

Pompe disease (pomp) [Johann Cassianus Pompe, 20th-cent. Dutch physician] Glycogen storage disease type II.

pompholyx (pŏm′fĕ-lĭks) A blistering itchy rash of the hands and feet, marked by episodic and recurring deep-seated vesicles or bullae. The rash is most often found in adolescents and young adults, esp. during spring and summer. SYN: *dyshidrosis; dyshidrotic eczema*.
   ETIOLOGY: Although the cause is unknown, emotional stress, an allergic predisposition, and fungal infections have each been associated with episodes of the rash.
   TREATMENT: Burow or permanganate solution and potent topical steroids sometimes are effective. The rash tends to appear less often as patients reach middle age.

POMR *problem-oriented medical record.*

Poncet disease (pon-sā′) [Antonin Poncet, Fr. surgeon, 1849–1913] Noninfectious polyarthritis in patients with active infection with tuberculosis.

ponderal (pŏn′dĕr-ăl) [L. *pondus*, weight] Relating to weight.

pons (pŏnz, pŏn′tēz) *pl.* **pontes** [L., bridge] **1.** The rostral segment of the hindbrain, under the cerebellum. This segment – the pontine hindbrain – has two major parts. First, there is the pontine tegmentum, which extends ventrally from the gray matter along the floor of the fourth ventricle to the longitudinal axons of the corticospinal tracts. Second, there is the pons "proper," the ventral half of the pontine hindbrain, containing axons of the corticospinal tract, pontine nuclei, and the axons from the pontine nuclei -- these axons sweep dorsally along the edges of the brainstem into the cerebellum forming the middle cerebellar peduncle, also called the brachium pontis. **2.** The ventral half of the pontine hindbrain, comprising axons of the corticospinal tract and the pontine nuclei. SYN: *pons varolii.*

Pontiac fever (pon′ tē-ăk″) [*Pontiac,*

Michigan, where an outbreak occurred in a building in 1986] SEE: under *fever.*

pontic (pŏn′tĭk) [L. *pons, pontis,* bridge] An artificial tooth set in a bridge.

pontile (pŏn′tēl) Pert. to the pons varolii.

pontine (pŏn′tēn) Pert. to the pons varolii.

pontobulbar (pŏn″tō-bŭl′bar) Pert. to the pons and medulla oblongata.

pool (pool) **1.** To mix blood from several donors. **2.** The accumulation of blood in a body site. **3.** A source of similar substances or cells.

    amino acid p. The amino acids available for protein synthesis at any given time; the liver regulates the blood level of amino acids based on tissue needs and converts excess amino acids to carbohydrates for energy production.

    gene p. The sum of the genetic material in the members of a specified population.

    metabolic p. All of the chemical compounds included in metabolic processes in the body.

    risk p. A government-administered health insurance program for people who cannot obtain insurance privately, e.g., because of costly preexisting medical conditions.

    vaginal p. The mucus and cells that are present in the posterior fornix of the vagina when the patient is in a supine position. Material obtained from this site is used in cancer detection and in evaluating the character of the vaginal fluid in investigating infertility problems.

pooled analysis Meta-analysis.

POP (pop) *pelvic organ **prolapse.***

Popeye sign (pop′ī″) A bulging of the body of the biceps brachii muscle that results from rupture of the muscle's tendon. It superficially resembles an exaggerated attempt to flex the biceps muscle. SEE: illus.

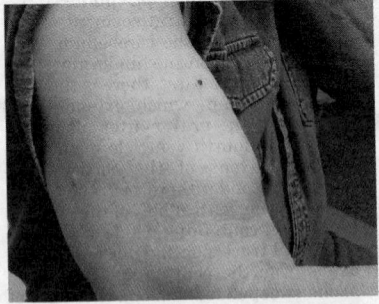

POPEYE SIGN

popliteal entrapment syndrome Cramping of the calf muscles after exercise or during dorsiflexion of the ankle. It is a relatively rare type of claudication typically identified in young athletes rather than in patients with established atherosclerotic vascular disease. The cause is compression of the popliteal artery by muscles in the popliteal fossae.

popliteus (pŏp-lĭt′ē-ŭs, -lĭt-ē′ŭs) [L. *poples,* ham of the knee] Muscle located in the hind part of the knee joint that flexes the leg and aids it in rotating.

popliteal (pŏp″lĭt-ē′ăl, pŏp-lĭt′ē-ăl), *adj.*

pop-off valve (pop′of″) SEE: under *valve.*

poppy (pŏp′ē) Any of the several plants of the genus *Papaver.* Opium is obtained from the juice of the unripe pods of *P. somniferum.*

populate (pop′yŭ-lāt″) [L. *populare,* to inhabit] In an electronic health record, to add identifying information, clinical history, medication and allergy lists, and other pertinent identifiers about a patient to the patient's database.

population 1. All persons, plants, or animals inhabiting a specified area. **2.** The group of persons from which a research sample is drawn.

population density SEE: under *density.*

Populus candicans (pop′yŭ-lŭs kan′dĭ-kanz″, -kons″) SEE: **balm** *of Gilead* (2).

POR *problem-oriented record.*

porcelain (por′sĕ-lĭn) A hard, translucent ceramic made by fusing clay, quartz, and feldspar. The combination is colored by glazing with fusible pigments. It is used in dentistry to construct restorations and prosthetics.

porcelaneous, porcelanous (por′sĕ-lā″nē-ŭs, por-sel′ă-nŭs) [Fr. *porcelaine*] Translucent or white like porcelain.

porcine (por′sīn) [L. *porcus,* pig] Relating to or concerning swine.

pore (por) [Gr. *poros,* passage.] **1.** A minute opening, esp. one on an epithelial surface. SEE: *porus.* **2.** The opening of the secretory duct of a sweat gland. SEE: *skin; stoma; sweat glands.*

    alveolar p. A minute opening that is thought to exist between adjacent alveoli of the lung.

    gustatory p. Taste **p.**

    taste p. The external opening of a taste bud. SYN: *gustatory p.* SEE: *taste.*

pori (pŏr-ē) Pl. of porus.

Porifera (pŏ-rĭf′ĕ-ră) [NL. *porus,* opening + *ferre,* to bear] The phylum of sea sponges, some of which are toxic to humans.

porin (pŏr′ĭn) [Gr. *poros,* passageway] A channel-forming protein in cell membranes that facilitates the diffusion of water and small molecules in and out of the cell.

Porocephalus (pō″rō-sĕf′ă-lŭs) a genus of helminthoid arthropods. The species parasitic in humans have been assigned to other genera. SEE: *Armillifer.*

porokeratosis (pō″rō-kĕr″ă-tō′sĭs) [″ + *keras,* horn, + *osis,* condition] A rare skin disease marked by thickening of the stratum corneum in a linear arrangement, followed by its atrophy. Porokeratosis appears on smooth areas. It is irregular in form and size with a circumscribed outline and affects the hands and feet, forearms and legs, the face, neck, and scalp.

poroma (pō-rō'mă) [Gr.] **1.** Callosity. **2.** A tumor of cells lining the opening of the sweat glands.

cerebral p. At postmortem examination, the presence of cavities in the brain substance caused by gas-forming bacteria.

eccrine p. A tumor arising from the duct of an eccrine gland; usually occurring on the palm or sole.

porosis (pō-rō'sĭs) [Gr. *poros*, passage, + *osis*, condition] Callus formation in repair of fractured bone. SEE: *callus*.

porosity (pō-rŏs'ĭ-tē) [Gr. *poros*, passage] The state of being porous.

porous (pō'rŭs) Full of pores; able to let liquid pass.

porphin (por'fĭn) The basic ring structure forming the framework of all porphyrins. It consists of four pyrrole rings united by methene couplings.

porphobilinogen (por"fō-bī-lĭn'ō-jĕn) An intermediate product in heme synthesis sometimes found in the urine of patients with acute porphyria. The urine may appear normal when fresh but will change to a burgundy wine color or even to black when heated with dilute hydrochloric acid to 100°C.

porphyria (por-fir'ē-ă) [*porphyro-* + *-ia*] A group of disorders that result from a disturbance in any of the sequential steps involved in the synthesis of heme, causing increased formation and excretion of porphyrin or its precursors.

acute intermittent p. A rare autosomal dominant disorder characterized by excessive excretion of porphyrins, episodes of acute abdominal pain, sensitivity to light, and neurological disturbances. The disorder is sometimes precipitated by the excessive use of sulfonamides, barbiturates, or other drugs.

congenital erythropoietic p. A rare autosomal recessive disorder characterized by severe skin lesions, hemolytic anemia, and splenomegaly.

p. cutanea tarda Porphyria in which patients develop liver disease and rashes on parts of their bodies exposed to the sun, e.g., on the knuckles or face. The use of alcohol or estrogens may aggravate the condition. The cause is a deficiency of uroporphylinogen decarboxylase.

p. erythropoietica A mild form of porphyria characterized by cutaneous lesions and excess protoporphyrin in the erythrocytes and feces. SYN: *protoporphyria*.

p. hepatica Porphyria caused by a disturbance in liver metabolism such as occurs following hepatitis, poisoning by heavy metals, and certain anemias.

South African genetic p. Variegate p.

variegate p. Hepatic porphyria in which there are recurrent episodes of abdominal pain and neuropathy. The skin is esp. fragile. SYN: *South African genetic p.*

porphyrin (por'fĭ-rĭn) [*porphyro-* + *-in*] Any of a group of nitrogen-containing organic compounds obtained from hemoglobin and chlorophyll and forming the basis of animal and plant respiratory pigments.

porphyrinuria (por"fĭ-rĭ-noor'ē-ă, -nŭr') [*porphyrin* + *-uria*] Excretion of an increased amount of porphyrin in the urine. SYN: *porphyruria*.

porphyro-, porphyr- [L. fr Gr. *porphyra*, purple fish, murex, purple] Prefixes meaning *purple, dark red*.

Porphyromonas (pōr"fĭ-rō-mōn'ăs) [Gr. *porphyra*, purple + *monas*, single] A genus of gram-negative, rod-shaped, anaerobic bacteria that inhabits the oral cavity. One species, *Porphyromonas gingivalis*, is a common cause of gingivitis and periodontal infection.

PORT (pŏrt) *patient outcomes research team.*

porta (pŏr'tă) [L., gate] The point of entry of nerves and vessels into an organ or part.

p. hepatis The fissure of the liver where the portal vein and hepatic artery enter and the hepatic duct leaves.

portable (pŏr'tă-bul) [L. *portare*, to carry] Movable or transferable from one place to another, e.g., a portable oxygen supply.

portacaval (por"tă-kā'văl) Pert. to the portal system and the vena cava.

portal (pŏr'tăl) [L. *porta*, gate] **1.** An entryway. **2.** Concerning a porta or entrance to an organ, esp. that through which the blood is carried to the liver. **3.** A website that serves as a point of entry into other websites or computer programs.

p. of entry The pathway by which infectious organisms gain access to the body (e.g., respiratory tract, breaks in skin).

p. of exit The pathway by which pathogens leave the body of a host (e.g., respiratory droplets, feces, urine, blood).

intestinal p. The opening of the midgut or yolk sac into the foregut or hindgut of an embryo.

patient p. A domain in an electronic health record that allows patients to access their records or communicate with their health care providers.

positioning p. Surgical **p.**

surgical p. An opening in the skin through which a surgical instrument (e.g., a fiberoptic scope) may be placed. SYN: *positioning p.*

p. vein Vein formed by the union of

veins from the abdominal viscera, which then takes blood into the liver. It is made of the combined superior and inferior mesenteric, splenic, gastric, and cystic veins.

portal system A system of vessels in which blood passes through a capillary network, a large vessel, and then another capillary network before returning to the systemic circulation (e.g., the circulation of blood through the liver).

port film (pŏrt) [L. *porta*, door, gate] In radiation oncology an x-ray image used to verify the positioning of the patient within the planned treatment field.

portoenterostomy, hepatic (pŏr-tō-ĕn-tĕr-ŏs′tō-mē) A surgical procedure performed to establish bile flow in an infant who has external biliary atresia associated with absence of the extrahepatic biliary system. A section of the jejunum is attached to the liver at the normal exit site of the hepatic duct to allow bile drainage into the small intestine. The jejunal segment may be looped to form a cutaneous double-barreled ostomy. Postoperatively, liver function continues to deteriorate in most children, and liver transplantation is often needed. SYN: *Kasai procedure*.

portogram (por′tō-grăm) [L. *porta*, gate, + Gr. *gramma*, something written] A radiograph of the portal vein after injection of a contrast medium.

portography (por-tŏg′ră-fē) [″ + Gr. *graphein*, to write] Radiography of the portal vein after injection of a radiopaque contrast medium.

    portal p. Portography after injection of opaque material into the superior mesenteric vein. This is usually done during laparotomy.

    splenic p. Radiography of the splenic and portal veins after injection of a contrast medium into the splenic artery.

portosystemic (por″tō-sĭs-tĕm′ĭk) Joining the portal and systemic venous circulation.

PORT score (port) [*Patient Outcomes Research Team*] Pneumonia Severity **Index**.

Portuguese man-of-war A type of jellyfish, *Physalia physalis*, whose tentacles contain a neurotoxin that produces a burning sensation on contact. SEE: *bite*.

porus (pō′rŭs) *pl*. **pori** [L.] A meatus or foramen; a tiny aperture in a structure; a pore.

    p. acusticus, internal The opening of the internal acoustic meatus into the cranial cavity.

    p. gustatorius The small taste pore openings in the taste buds of the tongue.

position (pŏ-zish′ŏn) [L. *positio*, a placing] **1.** The place or arrangement in which something is put. **2.** The manner in which a body is arranged, as by the nurse or physician for examination. **3.** In obstetrics, the relationship of a se-

lected fetal landmark to the maternal front or back, and on the right or left side. SEE: table; *presentation* for illus.

    abdominal p. Horizontal abdominal p.

    anatomical p. The position assumed when a person is standing erect with arms at the sides, palms forward. SYN: *orthograde p.*

    anteroposterior p. A radiographical examination position in which the central ray enters the front of the body and exits from the back.

    antideformity p. Any of several postures that reduce edema and the shortening of ligaments and tendons caused by abnormal muscle tone, e.g., in patients with injuries or burns.

    axial p. A radiographical examination position in which an image is obtained with the central ray entering the body at an angle.

    Bonnet p. In inflammation of the hip joint, the flexion, abduction, and out-

Positions of Fetus in Utero

Vertex Presentation (point of designation—occiput)	
Left occiput anterior	LOA
Right occiput posterior	ROP
Right occiput anterior	ROA
Left occiput posterior	LOP
Right occiput transverse	ROT
Occiput anterior	OA
Occiput posterior	OP

Breech Presentation (point of designation—sacrum)	
Left sacroanterior	LSA
Right sacroposterior	RSP
Right sacroanterior	RSA
Left sacroposterior	LSP
Sacroanterior	SA
Sacroposterior	SP
Left sacrotransverse	LST
Right sacrotransverse	RST

Face Presentation (point of designation—mentum)	
Left mentoanterior	LMA
Right mentoposterior	RMP
Right mentoanterior	RMA
Left mentoposterior	LMP
Mentoposterior	MP
Mentoanterior	MA
Left mentotransverse	LMT
Right mentotransverse	RMT

Transverse Presentation (point of designation—scapula of presenting shoulder)	
Left acromiodorso-anterior	LADA
Right acromiodorso-posterior	RADP
Right acromiodorso-anterior	RADA
Left acromiodorso-posterior	LADP

ward rotation of the thigh, which produces relief.

Brickner **p**. A method of obtaining traction, abduction, and external rotation of the shoulder by securing the patient's wrist to the head of the bed.

butterfly **p**. Frog-leg **p**.

centric **p**. The most posterior position of the mandible in relation to the maxilla.

closed-packed **p**., *close-packed* **position** Of a joint, the position in which there is maximum congruency of the articular surfaces and joint stability is derived from the alignment of bones. This is the opposite of the maximum loose-packed position.

decubitus **p**. The position of the patient on a flat surface. The exact position is indicated by which surface of the body is closest to the flat surface: in left or right lateral decubitus, the patient is flat on the left or right side, respectively; in dorsal or ventral decubitus, the patient is on the back or abdomen, respectively.

dorsal elevated **p**. A position in which the patient lies on the back with the head and shoulders elevated at an angle of 30° or more. It is employed in digital examination of genitalia and in bimanual examination of the vagina.

dorsal recumbent **p**. A position in which the patient lies on the back with the lower extremities moderately flexed and rotated outward. It is employed in the application of obstetrical forceps, repair of lesions following parturition, vaginal examination, and bimanual palpation.

dorsosacral **p**. Lithotomy **p**.

Edebohls **p**. Simon position.

Elliot **p**. SEE: *Elliot position*.

English **p**. Left lateral recumbent **p**.

fetal **p**. The relationship of a specified bony landmark on the fetal presenting part to the quadrants of the maternal pelvis.

Fowler **p**. SEE: illus.; *Fowler position*.

frog-leg **p**. A body position used in physical examination to evaluate the genitals and perineum in which the patient lies on the back or sits on the buttocks, bends the knees, abducts the thighs, and draws the heels toward the pelvis. SYN: *butterfly* **p**.

genucubital **p**. A position with the patient on the knees, thighs upright, body resting on elbows, head down on hands. It is used when it is not possible to use the classic knee-chest position. SYN: *knee-elbow* **p**.

genupectoral **p**. A position with the patient on the knees, thighs upright, the head and upper part of the chest resting on the table, arms crossed above the head. It is employed in displacement of a prolapsed fundus, dislodgment of the impacted head of a fetus, management

of transverse presentation, replacement of a retroverted uterus or displaced ovary, or flushing of the intestinal canal. SYN: *knee-chest* **p**. SEE: illus. (Positions: knee-chest).

gravity-dependent **p**. Placement of a limb so that its distal end is lower than the level of the heart. Gravity affects the fluids within the limb, drawing or retaining them to the distal aspect. When limbs, esp. injured limbs, are placed below the level of the heart, interstitial pressure is increased, encouraging the formation and retention of edema within the extremity.

head-down **p**. Trendelenburg position.

horizontal **p**. A position in which the patient lies supine with feet extended. It is used in palpation, in auscultation of fetal heart, and in operative procedures.

horizontal abdominal **p**. **1.** A position in which the patient lies flat on the abdomen with the feet extended. It is used in examination of the back and spinal column. **2.** Face down. SYN: *abdominal* **p**.

intercuspal **p**. Centric **occlusion**.

jackknife **p**. A position in which the patient lies on the back, shoulders elevated, legs flexed on thighs, thighs at right angles to the abdomen. It is used when introducing a urethral sound. SYN: *reclining* **p**.

knee-chest **p**. Genupectoral **p**.

knee-elbow **p**. Genucubital **p**.

lateral **p**. In radiology, a side-lying position, which allows the central ray to enter the upright side.

laterosemiprone **p**. SEE: *Sims position*.

lawn-chair **p**. A colloquial term for a dorsal recumbent position with the hips and knees flexed slightly (approx. 5°–10°).

left lateral recumbent **p**. A position with the patient on the left side, right knee and thigh drawn up; employed in vaginal examination. SYN: *English* **p**.; *obstetrical* **p**.

lithotomy **p**. A surgical position used in gynecologic, rectal, and urologic procedures in which the patient lies on her back, thighs flexed on the abdomen, legs on thighs, thighs abducted. It is used in genital tract operations, vaginal hysterectomy, and the diagnosis and treatment of diseases of the urethra and bladder. SYN: *dorsosacral* **p**. SEE: illus. (Positions).

loose-packed **p**. The position of a joint where it is unlocked and free to move. SYN: *open-packed* **p**. SEE: *closed-packed* **p**.

maximum loose-packed **p**. Of a joint, the position where maximum joint play occurs, where ligaments and capsule have the least amount of tension. SYN: *resting* **p**.

Noble **p**. SEE: *Noble position*.

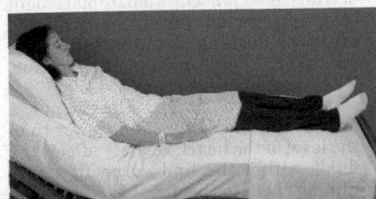

Fowler

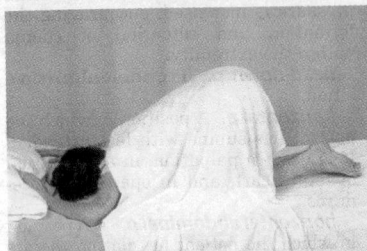

Knee-chest

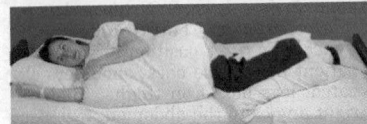

Lateral

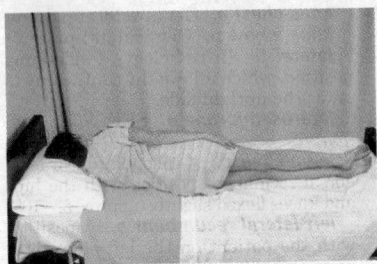

Lateral recumbent

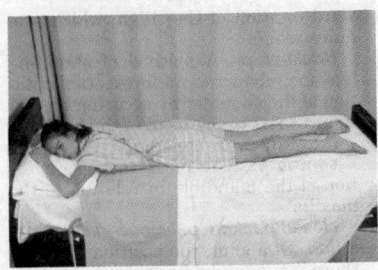

Prone

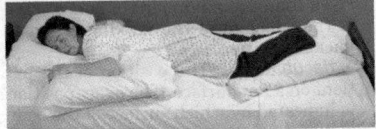

Sims

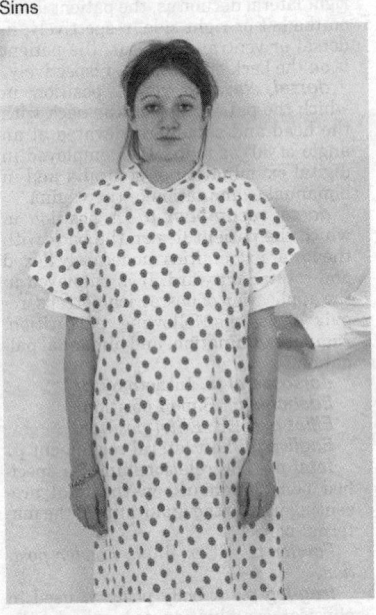

Standing

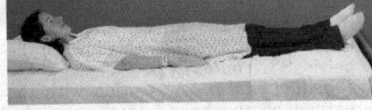

Supine

POSITIONS

oblique p. In radiology, an alignment of the body between a lateral and an anteroposterior or posteroanterior position. The angle formed by the body surface and the image receptor may vary. The central ray enters the aspect of the body that is upright and facing away from the image receptor.

obstetrical p. Left lateral recumbent **p.**

orthograde p. Anatomical **p.**

orthopneic p. The upright or nearly upright position of the upper trunk of a patient in a bed or chair. It facilitates breathing in those with congestive heart failure and some forms of pulmonary disease.

physiological rest p. In dentistry, the position of the mandible at rest when the patient is sitting upright and the condyles are in an unstrained position. The jaw muscles are relaxed. SYN: *rest p.*

posterior-anterior p. ABBR: PA position. In radiology, a position in which the central ray enters the posterior surface of the body and exits the anterior surface.

prone p. A position in which the patient is lying face downward. SEE: illus. (Positions: prone).

prone-on-elbows p. ABBR: POE. A position in which the body is lying face down with the upper trunk and head elevated, propped up by the arms, while the lower body is in contact with the supporting surface. The weight of the upper body rests on the elbows and forearms.

PATIENT CARE: This position, a component of the developmental sequence, is used in physical therapy to improve weight bearing and stability through the shoulder girdle. Elbow joint stability is not required, because the joint is not involved.

reclining p. Jackknife **p.**

recovery p. A position in which the patient is placed on the left side with the left arm moved aside and supported to allow for lung expansion and the right leg crossed over the left. This position affords the unconscious, breathing patient the best protection from airway occlusion or aspiration of fluids into the lungs.

rest p. Physiological rest **p.**

resting p. Maximum loose-packed **p.**

semi-Fowler p. A position in which the patient lies on the back with the trunk elevated at approx. 30°. SEE: *Fowler position.*

semiprone p. Sims' position.

Sims p. SEE: *Sims position.*

subtalar neutral p. of the foot The middle range of the subtalar joint with no pronation or supination measured. It is usually one third of the way from the fully everted position.

tangential p. In radiology, a position in which the central ray separates the images of anatomical parts by skimming between them.

Trendelenburg p. SEE: under *Trendelenburg, Friedrich.*

tripod p. A position that may be assumed during respiratory distress to facilitate the use of respiratory accessory muscles. The patient sits leaning forward, with hands placed on the bed or a table with arms braced.

unilateral recumbent p. The position in which the patient lies on the right side is used in acute pleurisy, lobar pneumonia of the right side, and in a greatly enlarged liver; the position in which the patient lies on left side is used in lobar pneumonia, pleurisy on the left side, and in large pericardial effusions. SEE: illus. (Positions).

Walcher p. SEE: *Walcher position.*

positioner (pŏ-zish'ŏn-ĕr) **1.** An apparatus for holding or placing the body or body part in a certain position. **2.** In orthodontics, a flexible, removable apparatus worn over the teeth esp. during sleep to obtain minor adjustments in the position or stabilization of teeth after removal of orthodontic appliances.

positioning (pŏ-zish'ŏn-ing) **1.** In rehabilitation, the placing of the body and extremities so as to aid treatment by inhibiting undesirable reflexes and preventing deformities. In treatment of children with developmental disabilities involving neuromotor function, the position of the body affects the degree to which some primitive reflexes affect muscle tone. Alignment of the head, neck, and trunk is important to reduce unnecessary influences on muscle tone, and the careful placement of the limbs is important to reduce or prevent contractions and deformities. **2.** The use of supportive devices, e.g., bolsters, wedges, and rolls, to optimize client position, comfort, and support during massage therapy.

position statement (stāt'mĕnt) The official, published editorial taken by a professional organization regarding best practices, standard care, or inconclusive evidence-based research. Position statements are typically updated regularly. SEE: *consensus statement.*

positive (pŏz'ĭ-tĭv) [L. *positivus,* ruling] **1.** Definite; affirmative; opposite of negative. **2.** Indicating an abnormal condition in examination and diagnosis. **3.** Having a value greater than zero. In laboratory findings and mathematical expressions, positive is indicated by a plus $(+)$ sign.

positive predictive value The proportion of people whose test results are true positives and who are actually ill.

positron (pŏz'ĭ-trŏn) A particle having the same mass as a negative electron but possessing a positive charge.

posology (pō-sol'ŏ-jē) [Gr. *posos,* how much + *-logy*] In pharmacology, the determination of proper dosages, esp. of the beneficial or adverse effects of drugs administered at specific doses. It includes the study of errors made in calculating the doses of medications given to patients.

post In dentistry, a cast restoration that extends into the root of a tooth to anchor a dental crown or prosthesis.

post- (L. *post,* after, behind] A prefix meaning *behind, after, posterior.*

postabortal (pōst″ă-bor′tăl) [L. *post,* behind, after, + *abortus,* abortion] Happening subsequent to abortion.

postadolescent (pōst″ăd-ō-lĕs′ĕnt) [″ + *adolescens,* to grow up] An individual who has passed adolescence.

post-anesthesia care unit ABBR: PACU. A unit to which patients are admitted after surgery for the monitoring of signs and symptoms that suggest that they may have poorly tolerated their anesthesia or operation. The typical PACU is staffed by nurses who evaluate patients for symptoms of instability (e.g., bleeding, chest pain, or labored breathing), or unstable vital signs (e.g., excessive pain, low blood pressure, poor oxygenation, or tachycardia). Anesthesiologists, hospitalists, and/or surgeons may be available for consultation or the management of emergencies.

postanesthetic (pōst″ăn-ĕs-thĕt′ĭk) [″ + Gr. *an-,* not, + *aisthesis,* sensation] Pert. to the period following anesthesia.

postbrachial (pōst″brā′kē-ĭl) [″ + *brachiolis,* arm] Pert. to the posterior portion of the upper arm.

post–cardiac arrest syndrome Neurological impairment, myocardial stunning, internal organ injury, and systemic inflammation resulting from inadequate blood flow to vital organs during cardiac arrest. The syndrome may be attenuated by targeted lowering of body temperature, mechanical ventilation, circulatory support, and keeping blood glucose levels less than 180mg/dL.

postcardiotomy (pōst-kăr″dē-ŏt′ō-mē) [″ + ″ + *tome,* incision] The period after open-heart surgery.

postcardiotomy syndrome Postpericardiotomy syndrome.

postcholecystectomy   **syndrome** (pōst″kō″lĕ-sis″tek′tŏ-mē) [*post-* + *cholecystectomy*] Persistent right upper quadrant pain or indigestion or both after surgical removal of the gallbladder for similar symptoms.

postcibal (pōst-sī′băl) [″ + *cibum,* food] ABBR: pc. Occurring after meals.

postclimacteric (pōst″klī-măk-tēr′ĭk, -măk′tēr-ĭk) [″ + Gr. *klimakter,* rung of a ladder] Occurring after menopause.

postcoital (pōst-kō′ĭt-ăl) [″ + *coitio,* a coming together] Subsequent to sexual intercourse.

postcoital test In the evaluation of infertile couples, sampling of the woman's cervical mucus within two hr after male ejaculation, to determine the number of actively moving sperm in the specimen. In a favorable specimen, between 6 and 20 motile sperm should be seen per high-power microscopic field.

postcoital test (pōst″kō-ĭ-tăl) [″ + ″] Huhner test.

postconcussion syndrome (pōst″kŏn-kŭsh′ŏn) [*post-* + *concussion*] A consequence of traumatic brain injury, in which patients experience headaches, dizziness, confusion or mental sluggishness, and insomnia. SEE: *traumatic brain injury.*

postconvulsive (pōst″kŏn-vŭl′sĭv) [″ + *convulsus,* pull violently] Occurring after a convulsion.

postcranial (pōst-krā′nē-ăl) Behind or below the cranium; used to describe the bones of the trunk and limbs.

postdiphtheritic (pōst″dĭf-thĕr-ĭt′ĭk) Following diphtheria.

postencephalitis (pōst″ĕn-sĕf-ă-lī′tĭs) [″ + Gr. *enkephalos,* brain, + *itis,* inflammation] Occurring after encephalitis; an abnormal state remaining after the acute stage of encephalitis has passed.

postepileptic (pōst″ĕp-ĭ-lĕp′tĭk) [″ + Gr. *epi,* upon, + *lepsis,* a seizure] Following an epileptic seizure. SEE: *postictal.*

posterior (pŏs-tē′rē-or) [L. comparative of *posterus,* coming after] **1.** In quadrupeds, pert. to or located at or toward the rear of the body; caudal; opposite of anterior. **2.** In human anatomy, pert. to or located at or toward the back; dorsal. In human anatomy, "caudal," "dorsal," and "posterior" mean the same thing. **3.** Situated behind; coming after.

posterior teeth The bicuspid and molar teeth.

posterior vitreous detachment ABBR: PVD. Separation of the vitreous gel from the retinal surface, often as a result of aging or diabetes mellitus.

postero- [L. *poster(us),* following, coming after] Prefix meaning *posterior, situated behind, toward the back.*

posteroanterior (pŏs″tĕr-ō-ăn-tēr′ē-or) [L. *posterus,* behind, + *anterior,* anterior] Indicating the flow or movement from back to front.

posterolateral (pŏs-tĕr-ō-lă′tĕr-ăl) [″ + *lateralis,* side] Located behind and at the side of a part.

posteromedial (pŏs″tĕr-ō-mē′dē-ăl) [″ + *medius,* middle] Toward the back and toward the median plane.

posterosuperior (pŏs″tĕr-ō-sū-pē′rē-or) [″ + *superior,* upper] Located behind and above a part.

posterotemporal (pŏs″tĕr-ō-tĕm′pō-răl) [″ + *temporalis,* temporal] Located at the back of the temporal bone.

posteruption (pōst″ĕr-ŭp-shŭn) The stage of tooth eruption in which the tooth has reached the occlusal plane and is functional, but continues to erupt to compensate for loss of tooth substance because of wear. SEE: *eruption; preeruption.*

postesophageal (pōst″ē-sŏf″ă-jē′ăl) [L. *post,* behind, after, + Gr. *oisophagos,* gullet] Located behind the esophagus.

postexposure (pōst″ĕx-pō′zhĕr) [″ + ″] The period following actual or potential contact with a pathogen or a toxic agent. SEE: *exposure.*

postfebrile (pōst-fē′brĭl) [″ + *febris,* fever] Occurring after a fever.

postganglionic (pōst″găn-glē-ŏn′ĭk) [″ + Gr. *ganglion,* knot] Posterior or distal to a ganglion.

posthemorrhagic (pōst-hĕm″ō-răj′ĭk) [″ + Gr. *haima,* blood, + *rhegnynai,* to burst forth] Occurring after hemorrhage.

posthepatic Originating after bile leaves the liver, as in posthepatic jaundice, in which obstruction of bile ducts causes the jaundice.

posthepatitic (pōst″hĕp-ă-tĭt′ĭk) [″ + Gr. *hepar,* liver, + *itis,* inflammation] Occurring after hepatitis.

posthitis (pos-thīt′ĭs) [Gr. *posthē,* penis + *-itis*] Inflammation of the foreskin. SYN: *acroposthitis.*

post hoc (pōst hŏk) [L., after this] After the fact.

posthumous (pŏs′tū-mŭs) [L. *postumus,* last] **1.** Occurring after death. **2.** Born after the death of the father. **3.** Pert. to a child taken by cesarean section after the death of the mother.

posthypnotic (pōst″hĭp-nŏt′ĭk) [L. *post,* behind, after, + Gr. *hypnos,* sleep] Occurring or performed after hypnosis.
p. suggestion SEE: under *suggestion.*

postictal (pōst″ĭk′tăl) [*post-* + *ictal*] Occurring after a sudden attack or stroke, as an epileptic seizure or apoplexy.

post-ICU syndrome Any of a group of neuropsychiatric disorders that limit the functioning of patients after a prolonged hospitalization in an intensive care unit (ICU). Symptoms include anxiety, depression, post-traumatic stress disorder, as well as motor weakness and muscular deconditioning.

postlingual (pōst″lĭng′gwĭl) [″+ ″] Occurring after the development and use of speech and language.

postmalarial (pōst″mă-lā′rē-ăl) [″ + It. *malaria,* bad air] Occurring after malaria.

postmature (pōst″mă-tūr′) [″ + *maturus,* ripe] Pert. to an infant born after an estimated 42 weeks' gestation, who exhibits findings consistent with postmaturity syndrome.

postmaturity (pōst″mă-toor′ĭt-ē, -tūr′, -choor′) Perinatal compromise related to diminished intrauterine oxygenation and nutrition secondary to placental insufficiency occurring in infants born after 42 weeks' gestation. During labor the fetal monitor may display late decelerations, and fetal hypoxia may result in the expulsion and aspiration of meconium. Characteristic assessment findings include skin desquamation and an absence of lanugo and vernix caseosa. Laboratory findings may include polycythemia and hypoglycemia. Postmature infants may also be at increased risk of cold stress due to diminished subcutaneous fat.

postmenopausal (pōst″mĕn-ō-paw′zăl) [″ + Gr. *men,* month, + *pausis,* cessation] Occurring after permanent cessation of menstruation.

postmenopause (pōst″mĕn′ō-pawz″) [″ + ″] The phase of a woman's life that begins 1 year after her final menstrual period.

postmortem (pōst″mŏr-tĕm) [L.] **1.** Occurring or performed after death. **2.** Autopsy.

postmyocardial infarction syndrome (pōst″mī″ō-kard′ē-ăl) [*post-* + *myocardial*] Nonischemic chest pain that occurs in a patient who has had a myocardial infarction, typically worsens when the patient breathes in deeply, improves when the patient is sitting, and is aggravated when the patient is lying down. The syndrome is caused by pericardial inflammation. Patients may develop a low-grade fever, an elevated erythrocyte sedimentation rate, and elevated levels of antimyocardial antibodies. Patients are usually treated with nonsteroidal anti-inflammatory drugs or corticosteroids. A similar syndrome occurs in some patients who have undergone cardiac surgery (postpericardiotomy syndrome). SEE: *Dressler syndrome.*

postnasal (pōst-nā′zăl) [L. *post,* behind, after, + *nasus,* nose] Posterior to the nasal cavities.

postnasal drip syndrome ABBR: PNDS. A frequent cause of chronic cough, often associated with chronic or allergic rhinitis, in which nasal secretions drain via the posterior pharynx.

postnatal (pōst′nā′tăl) [″ + *natus,* birth] Occurring after birth.

postnecrotic (pōst″nĕ-krŏt′ĭk) [″ + Gr. *nekros,* corpse] Occurring after the death of a tissue or a part.

postoperative (pōst″ŏp′ĕ-răt-ĭv) [*post-* + *operative*] **1.** Occurring after surgery or other invasive procedure. **2.** Pert. to the first hours and days after surgery.
PATIENT CARE: During the postoperative period patients often experience considerable pain, difficulty in moving, nausea, vomiting, and changes in nutritional status and fluid balance. Patients may also be at risk of infection from the surgical wound and indwelling catheters. Other high-risk possibilities after surgery include heart attack, atelectasis/ pneumonia, stroke, delirium, bleeding, clotting, adverse reactions to medications, peptic ulceration, and depression.

postparalytic (pōst″păr-ă-lĭt′ĭk) [″ +

para, beside, + *lyein,* to loosen] Subsequent to an attack of paralysis.

postpartum, postpartal (pōst-part'ŭm, pōst-part'ăl) [*post-* + L. *partus,* birth] **1.** Being or following the period after childbirth. **2.** Pert. to the 6-week period after childbirth, during which the mother undergoes progressive physiological changes that restore uterine size and system functions to nonpregnant status. SEE: *Nursing Diagnoses Appendix.*

postpartum mood disorder SEE: *postpartum* **blues***; postpartum* **depression***.*

postpericardiotomy syndrome (pōst"kär-dē-ŏt'ŭ-mē) Fever, pericardial friction rub, and chest pain occurring several days or weeks after cardiac surgery. The syndrome appears to be an autoimmune response to damaged cardiac cells. Congestive heart failure may ensue. SYN: *postcardiotomy syndrome.* SEE: *postmyocardial infarction syndrome.*

postphlebitic (pōst"flē-bit'ik) [*post-* + *phlebitic*] Occurring after a blood clot forms in a vein.

postphlebitic syndrome Pain and swelling felt in a limb that has been affected by a blood clot in its deep veins (a deep vein thrombosis). It is usually relieved somewhat by elevating the limb and worsened when the limb is dependent. SYN: *postthrombotic syndrome.*

postpneumonic (pōst"nū-mŏn'ik) [" + Gr. *pneumon,* lung] Occurring after pneumonia.

post-polio syndrome (pōst"pō'lē-ō") The development of motor and respiratory muscle weakness, limb muscle atrophy, fatigue, and diminished endurance occurring approx. 15–25 years after an initial bout of paralytic poliomyelitis. The syndrome results from progressive motor denervation.

PATIENT CARE: Affected patients benefit from the use of mobility aids, regular, supervised exercise, modifications of their homes and workplaces, planned rest periods, and orthoses to maintain optimal function and prevent excessive fatigue and bone, joint, or muscle injury. Patients with dysphagia are at risk for aspiration pneumonia and benefit from speech consultation.

SYN: *postpoliomyelitis muscular atrophy.*

postprandial (pōst-prăn'dē-ăl) Following a meal.

    p. dumping syndrome Dumping syndrome.

postpuberty (pōst-pū'bĕr-tē) [" + *pubertas,* puberty] The period after puberty. **postpubertal** (-tăl), *adj.*

postpubescent (pōst"pū-bĕs'ĕnt) [" + *pubescens,* becoming hairy] Following puberty.

postpyloric feeding SEE: under *feeding.*

postradiation (pōst"rā-dē-ā'shŭn) Occurring after exposure to ionizing radiation.

poststenotic (pōst"stĕ-nŏt'ĭk) [" + Gr. *stenosis,* act of narrowing] Distal to a stenosed or constricted area, esp. of an artery.

postsynaptic (pōst"sĭ-năp'tĭk) [" + Gr. *synapsis,* point of contact] Located distal to a synapse.

post-tachycardia syndrome Secondary ST and T wave changes associated with decreased filling of the coronary arteries and subsequent ischemia during tachycardia.

postterm pregnancy (pōst'tĕrm') SEE: under *pregnancy.*

posttesticular structures (pōst"tes-tik'yŭ-lăr) [*post-* + *testicular*] The epididymis and vas deferens.

postthrombotic syndrome (pōst"thrombot'ik) [*post-* + *thrombotic*] Postphlebitic syndrome.

posttibial (pōst"tib'ē-ăl) [*post-* + *tibial*] Behind the tibia.

posttransfusion purpura (pōst"transfū'zhŏn) [*post-* + *transfusion*] SEE: under *purpura.*

post-traumatic (pōst"tră-mat'ik, "tro-) [*post-* + *traumatic*] Following an injury or traumatic event.

post-traumatic stress disorder ABBR: PTSD. Intense psychological distress, marked by horrifying memories, recurring fears, and feelings of helplessness that develop after a psychologically traumatic event, such as combat, rape, criminal assault, life-threatening accident, or natural disaster. The symptoms of PTSD include flashback; avoidance of stimuli associated with the trauma; disturbances of memory; psychological or social withdrawal, increased aggressiveness; irritability, insomnia, startle responses, and vigilance. The symptoms may last for years after the event but can often be managed with supportive psychotherapy or medications such as antidepressants.

post-traumatic syndrome A sustained maladaptive response to a traumatic, overwhelming event. SEE: *Nursing Diagnoses Appendix.*

postulate (pŏs'tū-lāt) [L. *postulare,* to request] A supposition or view, usually self-evident, that is assumed without proof. SEE: *Koch postulate.*

postural (pŏs'tū-răl) [L. *postura,* position] Pert. to or affected by posture.

postural control An involuntary neurological loop consisting of motor, sensory, and integrative processes used to maintain the body's position relative to gravity and of its segments relative to each other for stability. Postural control relies on information from the vestibular and somatosensory systems and visual cues. Balance is a hallmark of postural control. SEE: *balance; proprioception.*

postural drainage SEE: under *drainage*.

postural orthostatic tachycardia syndrome ABBR: POTS. Inability to tolerate a standing position as a result of a sudden increase in heart rate when rising from a seated or recumbent position. It is thought to be one of the dysautonomic syndromes.

postural vital signs SEE: under *sign*.

posture (pŏs′chŭr) [Italian *postura*, fr. L. *positura*, fr. *ponere*, to place] Attitude or position of the body.

   coiled p. Posture in which the body is on one side with legs drawn up to meet the trunk. It is used sometimes during lumbar punctures.

   decerebrate p. A rigid posture of stiff, extended arms, pronated forearms, and exaggerated deep tendon reflexes. It is a posture of a patient who has lost cerebral control of spinal reflexes, usually as a result of an intracranial catastrophe.

   decorticate p. A rigid posture of flexed arms, clenched fists, and extended legs. It is the characteristic posture of a patient with a lesion at or above the upper brainstem. SYN: *decorticate* **rigidity**.

   dorsal rigid p. Posture in which the patient lies on the back with both legs drawn up. This is a position that is maintained by some patients suffering the pain of peritonitis.

   hyperlordotic p. Increased lumbar lordosis without compensation in the thoracic or cervical spine. It is a component of the condition colloquially referred to as sway-back. SEE: illus.

   kyphosis-lordosis p. A stance in which the pelvis is tilted forward, causing hip flexion, increased lumbar lordosis, and thoracic kyphosis.

   modified plantigrade p. A standing position with the lower extremities on the ground and the upper extremities bearing weight on a table or other surface. The body weight is stabilized on all four extremities. This posture is used developmentally and in physical therapy to prepare for independent standing and gait.

   open p. Positioning the body with the torso leaning toward the person being addressed, the arms at one's sides, and the chest, abdomen, and lower extremities easily seen. This form of body positioning during communication implies that one is actively listening and emotionally available to the client or patient. By contrast, a *closed posture* (in which one leans back, crosses one's arms on the chest and crosses the legs) implies that a person is less receptive to the other person.

   orthopnea p. Posture in which the patient sits upright, hands or elbows resting upon some support; seen in

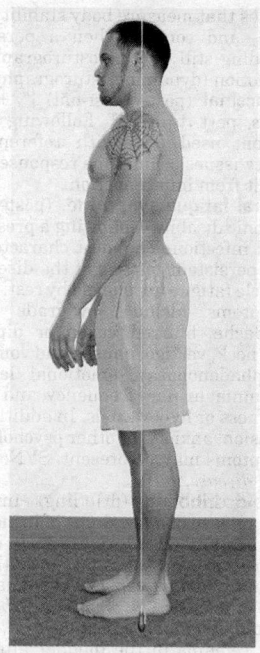

HYPERLORDOTIC POSTURE

asthma, emphysema, dyspnea, ascites, effusions into the pleural and pericardial cavities, and congestive heart failure.

   prone p. Prone.

   semireclining p. Posture used instead of lying supine, by patients who are short of breath, e.g., because of heart failure.

   slouched p. Swayback **p.**

   standard p. The skeletal alignment accepted as normal; used for evaluating posture. There is equilibrium around the line of gravity and the least amount of stress and strain on supporting muscles, joints, and ligaments. From either the front or the back, a plumb bob would bisect the body equally. From the side, a plumb bob would be anterior to the lateral malleolus and the axis of the knee, posterior to the axis of the hip and the apex of the coronal suture, and through the bodies of the lumbar vertebrae, the tip of the shoulder, the bodies of the cervical vertebrae, and the external auditory meatus.

   swayback p. A relaxed stance in which the pelvis is shifted forward, resulting in hip extension, and the thorax is shifted backward, resulting in an increased thoracic kyphosis and forward head. SYN: *slouched* **p.**

posturography (pos″chŭr-og′ră-fē) [*posture* + *-graphy*] Any of several techniques that measure body stability, balance, and control when a person is standing still (static posturography) or in motion (dynamic posturography).

postvaccinal (pŏst-văk′sĭ-năl) [″ + *vaccinus,* pert. to cows] Following vaccination; used esp. with reference to safety issues or immune responses that result from immunization.

postviral fatigue syndrome (pŏst-vī-răl) Chronic disability following a presumed viral infection. The most characteristic and persistent feature of the disease is muscle fatigue unrelieved by rest. Other symptoms include low-grade fever, headache, blurred vision or diplopia, stiff neck, vertigo, nausea and vomiting, lymphadenopathy, emotional lability, insomnia, urinary frequency, and either deafness or hyperacusis. In addition depression, anxiety, or other psychological symptoms may be present. SYN: *Royal Free disease.*

postvoid dribbling (drib′ling) Involuntary release of a few drops of urine from the urethra after urinating. It differs from other types of urinary incontinence in that it always consists of a small volume of urine. SYN: *terminal dribble.*

postvoid residual (pŏst″voyd′) Urine that remains in the bladder after urination; e.g., in prostate hypertrophy.

pot (pot) SEE: *marijuana.*

potable (pō′tă-bl) [LL. *potabilis*] Suitable for drinking, esp. pert. to water free of harmful organic or inorganic ingredients.

Potain, Pierre Charles Édouard (pō-ten′) Fr. cardiologist, 1825–1901.

    P. sign In dilatation of the aorta, dullness on percussion over the area extending from the body of the sternum toward the third costal cartilage on the right, and to the base of the sternum.

potassemia (pŏt-ă-sē′mē-ă) [L. *potassa,* potash, + Gr. *haima,* blood] Hyperkalemia.

potassium (pŏ-tas′ē-ŭm) [L. *potassa,* potash + *-ium*] SYMB: K. A metallic chemical element, atomic weight (mass) 39.0983, atomic number 19. It is a mineral that serves as both the principal cation in intracellular fluid and an important electrolyte in extracellular fluid. Along with other electrolytes (such as sodium, magnesium, calcium, and chloride), potassium participates in many functions, including cell membrane homeostasis, nerve impulse conduction, and muscle contraction.

    Potassium, which constitutes 0.35% of body weight, is found in most foods, including cereals, dried peas and beans, fresh vegetables, fresh or dried fruits, fruit juices, sunflower seeds, nuts, molasses, cocoa, and fresh fish, beef, ham, or poultry. The usual dietary intake of potassium is 50 to 150 mEq/day. In healthy people, the kidneys excrete any potassium excess consumed in the diet. In patients with renal failure, congestive heart failure, hypertension, and many other illnesses, serum potassium levels must be adjusted carefully to avoid adverse consequences of deficiency or excess.

    DEFICIENCY: Muscle weakness, dizziness, thirst, confusion, changes in the electrocardiogram, and life-threatening arrhythmias may develop during potassium deficiency (hypokalemia).

    EXCESS: Extracellular potassium is increased in renal failure; in destruction of cells with release of intracellular potassium in burns, crush injuries, or severe infection; in adrenal insufficiency; in overtreatment with potassium salts; and in metabolic acidosis. This causes weakness and paralysis, impaired electrical conduction in the heart, and eventually ventricular fibrillation and death. Hyperkalemia can be treated by withholding potassium, by using drugs such as sodium polystyrene sulfonate, a cation exchange resin, to lower the potassium concentration in cells, and by using calcium gluconate to counteract the effects on the heart.

    ⚠ Rapid infusion of potassium is painful and may cause severe hyperkalemia, complicated by cardiac arrhythmias. Institutional protocols for the use of intravenous potassium should be followed carefully.

    p. alum $KAl(SO_4)_2 \cdot 12(H_2O)$, an astringent and styptic. SYN: *aluminum potassium sulfate.*

    p. aminosalicylate Para-aminosalicylic **acid**.

    p. chloride KCl, a mineral/electrolyte administered orally to treat and prevent potassium depletion in patients unable to digest adequate dietary potassium. It is also administered to treat urinary tract infections and to prevent kidney stones. Its therapeutic classes are antiurolithics and mineral and electrolyte replacements/supplements.

    p. chromate K_2CrO_4, carcinogenic lemon-yellow crystals used as a dye and furniture stain, in manufacture of batteries, in photography, and in laboratories to preserve tissue.

    p. citrate, tri-potassium citrate $C_6H_5K_3O_7 \cdot H_2O$, transparent prismatic crystals used as an alkalizer.

    p. cyanide KCN, a highly poisonous compound used as a fumigant.

    p. gluconate $C_6H_{11}KO_7$, a drug used orally to replenish loss of potassium ion.

    p. hydrogen carbonate K_2CO_3, a white crystalline powder used in pharmaceutical and chemical preparations. SYN: *potash.*

    p. iodide KI, colorless or white crystals having a faint odor of iodine, used as an expectorant. Potassium iodide is recommended for use following exposure to radioactive iodides downwind from a nuclear reactor accident because it blocks the uptake of radioactive iodides by the thyroid gland, thus preventing or decreasing the chance of developing thyroid cancer many years later.

p. permanganate $KMnO_4$, crystals of dark purple prisms that are sweet and odorless. Concentrated solutions irritate and even corrode the skin and, when swallowed, induce gastroenteritis. The solutions have considerable power as disinfectants because their oxidizing ability destroys bacteria. They fail to penetrate deeply in an active form, which renders them of less value than many other disinfectants, except for use in very superficial infections.

total body p. The sum of all the potassium in the human body, used as one indicator of muscle mass. More than half of the potassium in the human body is within skeletal muscle.

potbelly (pŏt-bĕl-ē) Slang term for the selective deposition of adipose tissue in the abdominal subcutaneous tissue. It is seen, e.g., in patients with the metabolic syndrome (syndrome X).

potency (pō′tĕn-sē) [L. *potentia,* power] **1.** Strength; force; power. **2.** Strength of a medicine. **3.** The ability of a man to perform coitus. **4.** For a cell, the range of specialized cell types into which it can differentiate. The major cell types are: totipotent cells, which can form any cell in an organism; pluripotent cells, which can form most cell types in an organism; multipotent cells, which can form many cells types in an organism; and unipotent (or monopotent) cells, which can differentiate into only one specialized cell type.

potent (pō′tĕnt) [L. *potens,* powerful] **1.** Powerful. **2.** Highly effective medicinally. **3.** Having the power of procreation.

potential (pō-ten′chăl) [L. *potentialis,* powerful] **1.** Existing in possibility; latent. **2.** In electricity, voltage or electrical pressure. It is a condition in which a state of tension or pressure, capable of doing work, exists. When two electrically charged bodies of different potentials are brought together, an electric current passes from the body of high potential to that of low.

action p. ABBR: AP. A local reversal of the charge across an excitable cell membrane that is propagated quickly along the length of the membrane. In humans, most of the cells that conduct action potentials are neurons or muscles. As with all cells, neuron and muscle cell membranes actively maintain an excess of negative ions inside the cell,

which gives them, at rest, a cross-membrane charge of about -75 to -80 mV. If ion channels in one area of the membrane are caused to open briefly (as when the membrane is stimulated by a neurotransmitter), then charged ions move across the membrane, reducing the charge differential. When the cross-membrane charge reaches a threshold level (often about -40 to -60 mV), sodium ion channels (voltage-sensitive or voltage-gated channels) briefly open in the vicinity. Sodium ions rush into the cell, and temporarily the cross-membrane potential rises to a peak of about $+40$ to $+50$ mV, the height of the action potential in that region. This flood of ions also depolarizes adjacent membrane regions, which quickly reach their threshold levels, opening their voltage-gated channels. In this way, the depolarization spreads rapidly along the membrane.

after p. The small ionic changes across an excitable membrane that follow an action potential.

demarcation p. The difference in electrical potential between an intact longitudinal surface and the injured end of a muscle or nerve. SYN: *injury p.*

evoked p. The electroencephalographic record of electrical activity produced at one of several levels in the central nervous system by stimulation of an area of the sensory nerve system. Evoked potentials differ from the spontaneous electrical activity in the nervous system in that they are potentials that arise in response to an induced stimulus, such as exposure to sound, touch, or a source of light. Analysis of the response can provide important information concerning the function of the peripheral and central nervous systems. SYN: *evoked* **response.**

injury p. Demarcation **p.**

late p. Deflections found on signal-averaged electrocardiograms that follow the QRS complex and point to an increased likelihood of ventricular dysrhythmias. These deflections represent delays in electrical conduction through the ventricles.

liquid junction p. The potential voltage developed in an electrode measurement system at the point where two solutions are in contact. Most often the solutions are the test solution and a liquid bridging solution such as saturated KCl although any liquid-liquid interface may be involved. An example is the pH reference electrode.

membrane p. The electrical charge or potential difference between the inside and outside of a cell membrane.

resting p. Polarization (3).

spike p. A change in potential that occurs when a cell membrane is stimulated.

transcranial magnetic motor-evoked p. ABBR: tcMMEP. Intraooperative electrical stimulation of scalp nerves to monitor the responses of structures in the central nervous system and prevent neurosurgical trauma.

potential space SEE: under *space*.

potentiate (pō-tĕn'shē-āt) To increase the potency or action.

potentiation (pō-tĕn"shē-ā'shŭn) The synergistic action of two substances, such as hormones or drugs, in which the total effects are greater than the sum of the independent effects of the two substances.

potentiometer (pō-tĕn"shē-ŏm'ĕ-tĕr) A voltmeter.

   calibration p. A mechanically adjusted resistance used as a calibration control on many instruments. It adjusts a voltage or current within the device.

potion (pō'shŭn) [L. *potio,* draft] A drink or draft; a dose of poison or liquid medicine.

Pott, John Percivall (pot) Brit. surgeon, 1714–1788. He pioneered research into chemical carcinogenesis by describing scrotal cancer in chimney sweeps.

   P. disease Infection of the vertebrae caused by miliary (disseminated) tuberculosis. About 1% to 3% of patients with tuberculosis have infections in the bone; the spine is the most common site. Organisms spread from the site of primary infection through the blood. Once established in the spine, the infection moves through the intervertebral disks to multiple vertebrae. When it extends into the surrounding soft tissue, abscesses may be created. SYN: *spinal caries; tuberculous spondylitis.*

   SYMPTOMS: Patients report pain when they move their back. Signs include a low-grade fever, weight loss, and local tenderness. When several upper vertebrae are involved, compression fractures, curvature of the spine (kyphosis), or nerve injury may occur.

   TREATMENT: See Treatment section under tuberculosis.

   P. fracture Fracture of the lower end of the fibula and medial malleolus of the tibia, with dislocation of the foot outward and backward.

   P. paraplegia **P.** paralysis.

   P. paralysis Paralysis of the lower half of the body due to vertebral infection with tuberculosis and subsequent spinal cord injury SYN: **P.** *paraplegia.*

Potter-Bucky diaphragm (pot'ĕr) Bucky diagram. SEE: *Bucky, Gustav P.*

pouchitis (pŏw-chī'tĭs) Acute or chronic inflammation of the surgically produced pouch used in restorative proctocolectomy.

poudrage (pū-drăzh') Application of an irritating, but otherwise nontoxic, powder to the pleura to produce adhesions, e.g., in patients with recurring pleural effusions.

poultice (pōl'tĭs) [L. *pultes,* thick paste] A hot, moist, usually medicated mass that is placed between cloth sheets and applied to the skin to relieve pain, soothe the injured tissues, stimulate the circulation, or act as a counterirritant. SEE: *plaster.*

pound (pownd) [L. *pondus,* weight] SYMB: lb. A measure of weight of the avoirdupois and the apothecaries' systems that is equal to 16 oz. SEE: *Weights and Measures Appendix.*

   avoirdupois p. Sixteen ounces, equal to 453.59 g.

   troy p. Twelve ounces, 5760 gr, equal to 373.242 g.

Poupart ligament (poo-par') [François Poupart, Fr. anatomist, 1661–1708] SYN: *inguinal* **ligament**.

poverty (pov'ĕrt-ē) [Fr. *poverté,* fr L. *paupertas*] The condition of having an inadequate supply of money, resources, or means of subsistence. In 2010 in the U.S., for example, a family of four earning less than $22,000 was considered to live in poverty.

   p. of thought The mental state of being devoid of thought and having a feeling of emptiness.

poverty level The relative standard of living of individuals or families who have inadequate funds to afford basic needs, such as shelter, food, clothing, or health care.

povidone (pō'vĭ-dōn) A synthetic polymer used as a dispersing and suspending agent in manufacturing drugs.

povidone-iodine A complex of iodine with povidone. It contains not less than 9% and not more than 12% available iodine. This iodophor is used in dilute concentration as a surgical scrub, in aerosol spray, in vaginal douche solutions, and in ointments and gels.

Powassan virus (pō-wa'săn) [*Powassan,* Ontario] SEE: under *virus*.

powder (powd'ĕr) An aggregation of fine particles of one or more substances that may be passed through fine meshes.

power [ME. *power*] **1.** The rate at which work is done; the work/time ratio. The SI unit of power is the watt, equal to 1 joule per second. **2.** The capacity for action. **3.** In optics, the degree to which a lens or optical instrument magnifies. **4.** In microscopy, the number of times the diameter of an object is magnified, indicated by placing an $\times$ after the number (e.g., $10\times$ indicates magnification of 10 times. **5.** In mathematics and in scientific nomenclature, the number of times a value is to be multiplied by itself, the exponent (i.e., $10^2 = 10 \times 10 = 100$; $10^3 = 10 \times 10 \times 10 = 1000$). **6.** In statistics, the probability that a planned investigation will yield a statistically significant result. This is estimated by calculating how many individuals need to be randomly assigned to each group studied and how many would have to demonstrate improvement after receiving therapy in order to be able to conclude that one result meaningfully differs from another.

power, readiness for enhanced A pattern of participating knowingly in change that is sufficient for well being and can be strengthened. SEE: *Nursing Diagnoses Appendix.*

power of attorney ABBR: POA. A legal document by which a person identifies someone to make financial decisions if he or she is unable to perform this task independently. SEE: *power of attorney, durable, for health care.*

powerlessness (pŏw′ĕr-lĕs-nĕs) **1.** Lack of control or influence. **2.** The perception of lacking control or influence on one's environment. SEE: *helplessness; Nursing Diagnoses Appendix.*

    p., risk for At risk for perceived lack of control over a situation and/or one's ability to significantly affect an outcome. SEE: *Nursing Diagnoses Appendix.*

pox (pŏks) **1.** An eruptive, contagious disease. **2.** A papular eruption that becomes pustular. SEE: *chickenpox; smallpox.*

poxvirus, pox virus (pŏks′vī-rŭs) One of a group of DNA viruses that produce characteristic spreading vesicular lesions, often called pocks. It is the largest of the true viruses and includes viruses responsible for smallpox, vaccinia, molluscum contagiosum, and orf.

pp *punctum proximum,* the near point of accommodation (in vision).

ppb *parts per billion,* usually based on a mass or volume of a substance.

PPD *purified protein derivative.*

PPE *personal protective equipment.*

PPGSS *papular-purpuric "gloves and socks" syndrome.*

PPI *proton pump inhibitor.*

ppm *parts per million,* usually based on mass or volume or a combination of the two.

PPSV *pneumococcal polysaccharide vaccine.*

ppt *parts per trillion* (based on mass, volume or a combination of the two); *powerpoint; precipitate; prepared.*

Pr 1. *presbyopia.* **2.** Symbol for the element praseodymium.

pr L. *punctum remotum,* the far point of visual accommodation.

PRA *Panel reactive antibody*

practice (prak′tis) [L. *practica,* practical work, fr Gr. *praktikē*] **1.** The use by a health care professional of knowledge and skill to provide a service in the prevention, diagnosis, and treatment of illness and in the maintenance of health. **2.** The continuing, repetitive effort to become proficient and to improve one's skill in the practice of medicine.

    blocked p. A means of gaining mastery over a skill by drilling, i.e., by performing tasks or movements repeatedly according to a fixed procedure. Research shows that while blocked practice is superior at improving immediate performance, it is not as effective as other approaches, such as random practice, for retained learning. SEE: *random p.*

    evidence-based p. ABBR: EBP. Evidence-based **health care.**

    family p. Comprehensive medical care with particular emphasis on the family unit, in which the physician's continuing responsibility for health care is not limited by the patient's age or sex or by a particular organ system or disease entity.

    legitimate medical p. Any form of treatment that is accepted under the Medical Practice Acts enacted by each of the fifty U.S. states.

    patient safety p. A systematic health care practice that reduces the likelihood that patients will suffer undesirable side effects from treatment.

    private p. The practice by a health care professional, usually a physician or dentist, in a setting in which the practice and the practitioner are independent of external policy control other than ethics of the professional and state licensing laws.

    random p. A means of gaining mastery over a skill through training exercises that vary the sequence of elements in the skill. Compared with blocked practice, in which a skill is learned by fixed, repetitive drilling, random practice, with its frequently modified routine, results in better retention of the skill after training is completed. SEE: *blocked p.*

    recommended p. ABBR: RP. A protocol for care about which there is general agreement, e.g., a practice guideline or officially sanctioned technique, esp. one that enhances the safety or reliability of care.

    wear and care p. Guidelines for the use and cleansing of contact lenses, designed to optimize their healthful and safe use. SYN: *wear and care regimen.*

practice guidelines Consensus statements by professional societies or agents suggesting appropriate diagnostic and therapeutic options for patients with a specified diagnosis.

practice parameter A guideline published by a panel of experts or reviewers to help health care professionals provide patient care based on the best current evidence and/or academic or professional consensus.

practice pattern A preferred or standard method of care, esp. one about which authorities, experts, or experienced practitioners generally agree. SYN: *preferred practice pattern.*

practice variation A euphemism for a deviation from normal standards of care.

practitioner (prak-tish'ĭ-nĕr) One who has met the professional and legal requirements necessary to provide a health care service, such as a nurse, dentist, dental hygienist, or physical therapist.

   acute care nurse p. An advanced-practice nurse who is credentialed to manage the care of select patient groups that have acute and specialized health care needs. Acute care nurse practitioners practice in hospitals and in community care settings.

   adult nurse p. ABBR: ANP. A nurse practitioner credentialed to care for people over 18 years of age.

   advanced nurse p. An umbrella term for the following health care professionals: certified nurse-midwife, certified registered nurse anesthetist, clinical nurse specialist, and nurse practitioner.

   emergency room p. A nurse certified in the area of urgent care, who possesses skills in triage and the knowledge to meet the emergent needs of clients.

   family nurse p. ABBR: FNP. A nurse practitioner who has been educated and credentialed to care for people across the lifespan. Family nurse practitioners hold a graduate nursing degree. They practice autonomously and in collaboration with other health care professionals to assess, diagnose, treat, and manage a patient's health problems and needs. They teach and counsel individuals and families and serve as researchers, consultants, and patient advocates. SEE: *adult nurse p.*

   geriatric nurse p. ABBR: GNP. An advanced practice registered nurse with a graduate specialty degree in the diagnosis, treatment, and management of acute and chronic conditions commonly found among older adults and generally associated with aging. Generally GNPs are required to have specialty certification by a nationally recognized credentialing organization. The functions of the GNP are defined by individualized scope of practice and collaborative agreements with physicians and other health-care providers based on state nurse practice acts and experience, education, knowledge, and abilities. SYN: *gerontologic nurse practitioner.*

   gerontologic nurse p. Geriatric nurse **p.**

   mid-level p. Mid-level **provider**.

   nurse p. SEE: under *nurse.*

   pediatric nurse p. A certified nurse who focuses on the common acute and chronic illnesses experienced by children and adolescents. The pediatric nurse practitioner integrates concepts of growth and development in assessing health care needs.

Practitioners' Reporting Network, USP ABBR: USP-PRN. Three separate programs designed to collect practitioners' experience with unreliable drug products, defective medical devices, drug problems with radiopharmaceuticals, and medication errors. Practitioners and pharmacists report their experience to the United States Pharmacopeia, 12601 Twinbrook Parkway, Rockville, MD 20852. The USP receives the reports and publishes the results. Drug problem reports and medical device and laboratory product problem reports may be made by calling (800) 638-6725; medication errors may be reported by calling (800) 23ERROR.

Prader-Willi syndrome (prah' dĕr-vĭl' ē) A rare inherited condition marked by genetic obesity, hyperphagia, mental retardation, inadequate growth hormone secretion, short stature, sexual infantilism, and hypotonia. The cause is an abnormal chromosome 15 of maternal origin. SEE: *Angelman* **syndrome.**

prae- SEE: *pre-.*

praecox (prē'kŏks) [L.] Early.

praevia, praevius (prē'vē-ă, prē'vē-ŭs) [L.] Going before in time or place.

pragmatics (prăg-măt' ĭks) In speech and language pathology, the social or interpersonal context of language (i.e., knowing how to use spoken language appropriately with other speakers).

pragmatism (prăg'mă-tĭzm) [Gr. *pragma,* a thing done, + *-ismos,* condition] The belief that the practical application of a principle should be the determining factor in decision making.

pragmatic (prăg-măt'ĭk), *adj.*

pragmatist (prăg'mă-tĭst) A person whose goals are achieved or attempted from a practical concept, action, or approach; a practical person.

pranayama (pra-na-ya'mă) [Sanskrit *prānā,* life force, breath + *yāmā,* extension, self-control] A pattern of regulated, rhythmic breathing used in yoga and meditation to clear the mind and relieve stress or distraction. It has also been suggested as an alternative treatment for asthma. SYN: *yogic breathing.*

prandial (prăn'dē-ăl) [L. *prandium,* breakfast] Pert. to a meal.

praseodymium (prā″zē-ō-dim′ē-ŭm, sē) SYMB: Pr. A metallic element in the lanthanide series; atomic weight 140.907; atomic number 59.

Prausnitz-Küstner reaction (prows′nĭts-kĭst′nĕr) [Carl Willi Prausnitz, Ger. bacteriologist, 1876–1963; Heinz Küstner, Ger. gynecologist, 1897–1963] The intracutaneous injection of a hypersensitive patient's serum into a nonallergic person followed, 24 to 48 hr later, by the application of the suspected antigen to the injection site. If a wheal and flare occur, there is evidence that the suspected antigen is causing the hypersensitivity. Because of the danger of transmitting viral hepatitis and AIDS, this test is no longer used.

Pravachol SEE: *pravastatin*.

pravastatin (prăʹvă-stătʹĭn) An HMG-CoA reductase inhibitor and lipid-lowering agent. It is administered orally, as an adjunct to diet and exercise, to manage hypercholesterolemia and mixed dyslipidemias.

praxis (prăkʹsĭs) [Gr., action] The ability to plan and execute coordinated movement.

-praxis, -praxes, -praxises [Gr. *praxis*, act, action] Suffix meaning *act, activity, practice, therapy*.

PRBCs packed red blood cells.

pre- [L. *prae*, before] Prefix meaning *before, in front of*. *Prae*-is an uncommon variant except in words pertaining to Roman law and history.

preadmission certification (prēʺăd-mishʹŏn) SEE: under *certification*.

preagonal (prē-ăgʹō-năl) [L. *prae*, before, in front of, + Gr. *agonia*, agony] Pert. to the condition immediately before death.

preanesthesia (prēʺăn-ĕs-thēʹzē-ă) A light anesthesia produced by a medication given before anesthesia.

preanesthetic (prēʺanʺĕs-thetʹĭk) [*pre- + preanesthetic*,] A preliminary drug given to facilitate induction of general anesthesia. SYN: *premedication (2)*.

preauthorization (prēʺ awthʺ ĕr-ĭ-zāʹshŭn) The agreement of a health care funding agent (e.g., a health maintenance organization, health insurer, or governmental agency) to defray the costs of a proposed treatment or procedure before its occurrence.

preaxial (prē-ăkʹsē-ăl) [ʺ + Gr. *axon*, axis] In front of the axis of a limb or of the body.

prebiotic (prē-bī-ŏtʹĭk) [ʺ + ʺ] A nutrient that stimulates the growth or health of bacteria living in the large intestine. Prebiotics are typically neither absorbed nor digested by the mammalian gastrointestinal tract. Their effects on human health occur indirectly, through their promotion of commensal organisms in the colon.

precachexia (prē-kă-kekʹsē-ă) [*pre- + cachexia*] Weight loss resulting from any chronic disease.

precancer (prēʹkăn-sĕr) [ʺ + *cancer*, crab] A condition that tends to become malignant.

precancerous (prē-kănʹsĕr-ŭs) [ʺ + *cancer*, crab] Pertaining to a growth that is not yet, but probably will become, cancerous. SYN: *premalignant*.

precapillary (prēʺkăpʹ ĭ-lĕrʺē) [ʺ + *capillaris*, hairlike] Before or at the beginning of a capillary network, such as a precapillary sphincter.

precaution (pri-koʹshŏn) [*pre- + caution*] An action taken in advance to protect against danger, harm, or possible failure.

> **airborne p.** Airborne **isolation**.
> **contact p.** Contact **isolation**.
> **droplet p.** Droplet **isolation**.

precautionary principle SEE: under *principle*.

precautions, blood and body fluid Universal precautions. SEE: *Standard Precautions Appendix*.

precautions, standard Guidelines recommended by the Centers for Disease Control and Prevention to reduce the risk of the spread of infection in hospitals. These precautions (e.g., handwashing and wearing personal protective equipment such as gloves, mask, eye protection, gown) apply to blood, all body fluids, secretions, excretions (except sweat), nonintact skin, and mucous membranes of all patients and are the primary strategy for successful nosocomial infection control. SEE: *Standard Precautions Appendix*.

precautions, universal SEE: *Standard Precautions Appendix*.

precedent (preʹsĕ-dĕnt) [L. *praecedere*, to go before, precede] In law, an action, ruling, or verdict that may be used as an example to be followed in the future.

preceptor (prĭ-sepʹtĕr, prēʹsĕp-) [L. *praecipere*, to direct] 1. A teacher or instructor. 2. An expert who supervises and instructs students in clinical practice experiences, esp. medicine or nursing.

preceptorship (prĭ-sepʹtĕr-shĭp) A period of practical training under the supervision of an experienced or certified practitioner or specialist. SEE: *preceptor*.

precipitant (prē-sĭpʹĭ-tănt) [L. *praecipitare*, to cast down] A substance bringing about precipitation.

precipitate (prē-sĭpʹĭ-tāt) 1. A deposit separated from a suspension or solution by precipitation, the reaction of a reagent that causes the deposit to fall to the bottom or float near the top. 2. To separate as a precipitate. 3. Occurring suddenly or unexpectedly.

precipitation (prē-sĭpʺĭ-tāʹshŭn) [L. *praecipitatio*] 1. The process of a substance being separated from a solution by the action of a reagent so that a precipitate forms. 2. The sudden and unprepared-for delivery of an infant. SEE: *precipitous delivery*.

precipitation test A test in which a positive reaction is indicated by formation of a precipitate in the solution being tested.

precipitin (prē-sĭpʹĭ-tĭn) An antibody formed in the serum of an animal owing to the presence of a soluble antigen, usually a protein. When added to a solution of the antigen, it brings about precipitation. The injected protein is called the antigen, and the antibody produced is the precipitin. It was originally thought that these antibodies were members of a unique class, but most antibodies are capable of precipitating when combined with their antigens. SEE: *autoprecipitin; precipitinogen.*

precipitinogen (prē-sĭp″ĭ-tĭn′ō-jĕn) Any protein that, acting as an antigen, stimulates the production of a specific precipitin.

precipitin test A test in which two dissolved substances in a solution join to form a visible solid. The results depend on the strength of the attraction between the Fab fragment on the antibody and the corresponding epitope on the antigen (affinity) and on the stability of the complex (antibody avidity). The test demonstrates how immune complexes form in the circulation and are deposited in blood vessel walls. SEE: *precipitation test.*

preclinical (prē-klĭn′ĭ-kăl) [L. *prae,* before, in front of, + Gr. *klinike,* medical treatment in bed] **1.** Occurring before definitive diagnosis of a disease is possible. **2.** Classroom training and education that occurs before actual observation and treatment of patients.

precocious (prē-kō′shŭs) [L. *praecox,* ripening early] Achieving mental or physical development earlier than expected.

precocity (prē-kos′ĭt-ē) [Fr. *précosité* fr L. *praecox,* ripening early] Premature development of physical or mental traits.

   isosexual p. Sexual **p.**

   sexual p. Onset of secondary sex characteristics at an earlier age than expected, typically before age 6 to 8 in girls or 9 in boys. SYN: *isosexual **p.*** SEE: *precocious **puberty.***

precognition (prē″kŏg-nĭsh′ŭn) [L. *prae,* before, in front of, + *cognoscere,* to know] Prior knowledge that an event will occur acquired pre-rationally.

precoital (prē-kō′ĭ-tăl) [″ + *coitio,* a going together] Before sexual intercourse.

precoma (prē-kō′mă) [″ + Gr. *koma,* a deep sleep] An imprecise term for lethargy or stupor.

preconception (prē″kŏn-sep′shŏn) **1.** Occurring before fertilization of an ovum, as in genetic counseling. **2.** An idea or a belief held before analysis or investigation.

precondition (prē″kŭn-dĭsh′ĭn) [″ + ″] To protect tissues from future injury with anesthetics, drugs, physical exercises, or other therapies.

preconscious (prē-kŏn′shŭs) [″ + *conscius,* aware] Not present in consciousness but able to be recalled as desired.

preconvulsive (prē″kŏn-vŭl′sĭv) [″ + *convulsio,* pulling together] Before a convulsion.

precordia (prē-kor′dē-ă) [L. *praecordia*] Plural of precordium.

precordial thump SEE: under *thump.*

precordium (prē-kor′dē-ŭm, prē-kor′dē-ă) *pl.* **precordia** The area on the anterior surface of the body overlying the heart and lower part of the thorax. **precordial** (prē-kor′dē-ăl), *adj.*

precursor (prē-kĕr′sĕr) A substance that precedes another substance (e.g., in a series of chemical reactions); or a substance from which another is synthesized.

predentin (prē-dĕn′tĭn) Uncalcified dentinal matrix.

prediabetes (prē-dī″ă-bē′tēz) [″ + Gr. *diabetes,* passing through] Early evidence either of autoimmune disease or impaired carbohydrate metabolism in patients who later develop overt diabetes mellitus. The condition includes impaired fasting glucose and impaired glucose tolerance. In the U.S. in 2007 more than 50 million people were affected by prediabetes.

predict (pri-dikt′) [L. *praedicere,* to foretell] To declare what will happen; foretell. In clinical observations, it is to make an educated estimate about the natural history of a disease or its prognosis. **predictable** (-dikt′ă-bĕl), *adj.* **predictive** (-dik′tiv), *adj.*

prediction (pri-dik′shŏn) **1.** An act of predicting. **2.** Something predicted.

prediction rules Any of the rules for identifying and estimating the factors in formulating a diagnosis in order to establish the probability that a disease is present.

predictive factor SEE: under *factor.*

predictive value SEE: *negative predictive value; positive predictive value.*

predigestion (prē″dī-jĕs′chŭn) [″ + *digestio,* carrying apart] Artificial proteolysis or digestion of proteins and amylolysis of starches before ingestion.

predisposing (prē″dĭs-pōz′ĭng) [″ + *disponere,* to dispose] Pert. to a tendency to, or susceptibility to, disease.

predisposition (prē″dis″pŏ-zish′ŏn) The potential to develop a certain disease or condition in the presence of specific environmental stimuli; susceptibility.

prednisolone (prĕd-nĭs′ō-lōn) A glucocorticosteroid drug, available in a variety of dosage forms. It is similar in action to cortisone.

prednisone (prĕd′nĭ-sōn) A glucocorticosteroid with the same effects as cortisone.

preeclampsia (prē″ĕ-klămp′sē-ă) [*pre- + eclampsia*] An increase in hypertension (HTN), proteinuria, and edema, a complication occurring in about 3% to 5% of pregnancies. It may progress rapidly from mild to severe and, if untreated, to eclampsia. It is the leading cause of fetal and maternal morbidity and death, esp. in underdeveloped countries. SEE: *eclampsia; HELLP syndrome; pregnancy-induced* **hypertension;** *Nursing Diagnoses Appendix.*

ETIOLOGY: The cause is unknown. Incidence is higher among adolescents, primigravidas, smokers, and overweight or diabetic women. The disease mechanisms found in preeclampsia include generalized vasospasm, damage to the glomerular membranes, and hypovolemia and hemoconcentration due to a fluid shift from intravascular to interstitial compartments.

SYMPTOMS: The condition develops between the 20th week of gestation and the end of the first postpartum week, usually during the last trimester. Characteristic complaints include sudden weight gain, severe headaches, and disturbances in vision. Indications of increasing severity include complaints of epigastric or abdominal pain; generalized, presacral, and facial edema; oliguria; and hyperreflexia. Objective findings include HTN, edema, proteinuria, and hyperreflexia. SEE: *deep tendon reflex.*

TREATMENT: Treatment includes bedrest, diet, drugs to manage high blood pressure (BP), intravenous magnesium sulfate, or immediate delivery of the fetus, depending on the severity of the disease and the development of the fetus.

PROGNOSIS: A history of preeclampsia increases a woman's likelihood of vascular diseases (such as heart attacks and strokes) later in life. Women with preeclampsia should be monitored postpartum for elevated BP, blood sugars, and lipid levels. Cardiovascular risk factors should be treated aggressively to prevent future atherosclerotic illness.

pre-embryo (prē″ĕm′brē-ō) The morula and blastocyst stages produced by the division of the zygote until the formation of the embryo proper at the appearance of the primitive streak about 14 days after fertilization.

pre-embryonic (prē-ĕm″brē-on′ik) [*pre- + embryonic*] In human gestation, pert. to the stage of prenatal development beginning with implantation of the fertilized egg and ending at day 4.

preemie, premie (prē′mē) [*prem(ature)*] A colloquial term for a baby born prematurely; a preterm baby.

pre-excitation, ventricular (prē-ĕk″sī-tā′shŭn) [″ + *excitare*, to arouse] Premature excitation of the ventricle by an impulse that traveled a path other than through the atrioventricular node. This produces a short P-R interval. SEE: *Wolff-Parkinson-White syndrome.*

pre-existing condition Any injury, disease, or physical condition occurring prior to an arbitrary date; usually used in reference to the date of issuance of a health insurance policy. In some cases, a pre-existing condition results in an exclusion from coverage for costs resulting from the injury, disease, or condition.

preferential looking test (prē″fĕren′shăl) [*preference + -al*] A test of visual acuity in infants in which the direction of the infant's gaze indicates whether or not a visual stimulus was seen.

preferred practice pattern Practice pattern.

preferred provider organization ABBR: PPO. An incorporated group of physicians, hospital(s), nurses, and other health care workers, who jointly assume the clinical and financial responsibilities for delivering health care to enrolled groups of insured patients. The providers are semi-independent agents who agree to provide care at reduced rates.

preformation (prē-fawr-mā′shŭn) In embryology, the development of structures from pre-existing templates, e.g., of bones from cartilage templates.

prefrontal (prē-frŏn′tăl) [″ + *frons, front*] **1.** The middle portion of the ethmoid bone. **2.** In the anterior part of the frontal lobe of the brain.

preganglionic (prē″găng-lē-ŏn′ĭk) [″ + Gr. *ganglion*, knot] **1.** Situated in front of or anterior to a ganglion. **2.** Situated before a ganglion, such as a preganglionic neuron.

preganglionic fiber SEE: under *fiber.*

pregenital (prē-jĕn′ĭ-tăl) [″ + *genitalia, genitals*] In psychology, pert. to that period when erotic interest in the reproductive organs and functions is not yet organized.

pregnancy (preg′năn-sē) [L. *praegnans*, with child, pregnant] The condition of having a developing embryo or fetus in the body after successful conception. The average duration of pregnancy is about 280 days. Estimation of the date on which delivery should occur is based on the first day of the last menstrual period. SEE: *Naegeli rule;* table; *prenatal care; prenatal* **diagnosis;** *Nursing Diagnoses Appendix.*

DEMOGRAPHICS: About 7 million American women become pregnant each year, and about two thirds of these pregnancies result in live births. In 2009, there were 4,143,000 live births in the U.S.

SIGNS AND SYMPTOMS: Presumptive and probable signs are those commonly associated with pregnancy but may be due to other causes, such as oral contraceptive therapy. *Presumptive symptoms* include amenorrhea, nausea and vomiting, breast tenderness, urinary frequency, fatigue, chloasma, vaginal hyperemia (Chadwick sign), and

Pregnancy Table for Expected Date of Delivery

Month	1	2	3	4	5	6	7	8	9	10	11	12	13	14	15	16	17	18	19	20	21	22	23	24	25	26	27	28	29	30	31	
Jan.	1	2	3	4	5	6	7	8	9	10	11	12	13	14	15	16	17	18	19	20	21	22	23	24	25	26	27	28	29	30	31	
Oct.	**8**	**9**	**10**	**11**	**12**	**13**	**14**	**15**	**16**	**17**	**18**	**19**	**20**	**21**	**22**	**23**	**24**	**25**	**26**	**27**	**28**	**29**	**30**	**31**	**1**	**2**	**3**	**4**	**5**	**6**	**7**	Nov.
Feb.	1	2	3	4	5	6	7	8	9	10	11	12	13	14	15	16	17	18	19	20	21	22	23	24	25	26	27	28				
Nov.	**8**	**9**	**10**	**11**	**12**	**13**	**14**	**15**	**16**	**17**	**18**	**19**	**20**	**21**	**22**	**23**	**24**	**25**	**26**	**27**	**28**	**29**	**30**	**1**	**2**	**3**	**4**	**5**				Dec.
Mar.	1	2	3	4	5	6	7	8	9	10	11	12	13	14	15	16	17	18	19	20	21	22	23	24	25	26	27	28	29	30	31	
Dec.	**8**	**9**	**10**	**11**	**12**	**13**	**14**	**15**	**16**	**17**	**18**	**19**	**20**	**21**	**22**	**23**	**24**	**25**	**26**	**27**	**28**	**29**	**30**	**31**	**1**	**2**	**3**	**4**	**5**	**6**	**7**	Jan.
April	1	2	3	4	5	6	7	8	9	10	11	12	13	14	15	16	17	18	19	20	21	22	23	24	25	26	27	28	29	30		
Jan.	**8**	**9**	**10**	**11**	**12**	**13**	**14**	**15**	**16**	**17**	**18**	**19**	**20**	**21**	**22**	**23**	**24**	**25**	**26**	**27**	**28**	**29**	**30**	**31**	**1**	**2**	**3**	**4**	**5**	**6**		Feb.
May	1	2	3	4	5	6	7	8	9	10	11	12	13	14	15	16	17	18	19	20	21	22	23	24	25	26	27	28	29	30	31	
Feb.	**8**	**9**	**10**	**11**	**12**	**13**	**14**	**15**	**16**	**17**	**18**	**19**	**20**	**21**	**22**	**23**	**24**	**25**	**26**	**27**	**28**	**1**	**2**	**3**	**4**	**5**	**6**	**7**	**8**	**9**	**10**	Mar.
June	1	2	3	4	5	6	7	8	9	10	11	12	13	14	15	16	17	18	19	20	21	22	23	24	25	26	27	28	29	30		
Mar.	**8**	**9**	**10**	**11**	**12**	**13**	**14**	**15**	**16**	**17**	**18**	**19**	**20**	**21**	**22**	**23**	**24**	**25**	**26**	**27**	**28**	**29**	**30**	**31**	**1**	**2**	**3**	**4**	**5**	**6**		April
July	1	2	3	4	5	6	7	8	9	10	11	12	13	14	15	16	17	18	19	20	21	22	23	24	25	26	27	28	29	30	31	
April	**8**	**9**	**10**	**11**	**12**	**13**	**14**	**15**	**16**	**17**	**18**	**19**	**20**	**21**	**22**	**23**	**24**	**25**	**26**	**27**	**28**	**29**	**30**	**1**	**2**	**3**	**4**	**5**	**6**	**7**	**8**	May
Aug.	1	2	3	4	5	6	7	8	9	10	11	12	13	14	15	16	17	18	19	20	21	22	23	24	25	26	27	28	29	30	31	
May	**8**	**9**	**10**	**11**	**12**	**13**	**14**	**15**	**16**	**17**	**18**	**19**	**20**	**21**	**22**	**23**	**24**	**25**	**26**	**27**	**28**	**29**	**30**	**31**	**1**	**2**	**3**	**4**	**5**	**6**	**7**	June
Sept.	1	2	3	4	5	6	7	8	9	10	11	12	13	14	15	16	17	18	19	20	21	22	23	24	25	26	27	28	29	30		
June	**8**	**9**	**10**	**11**	**12**	**13**	**14**	**15**	**16**	**17**	**18**	**19**	**20**	**21**	**22**	**23**	**24**	**25**	**26**	**27**	**28**	**29**	**30**	**1**	**2**	**3**	**4**	**5**	**6**	**7**		July
Oct.	1	2	3	4	5	6	7	8	9	10	11	12	13	14	15	16	17	18	19	20	21	22	23	24	25	26	27	28	29	30	31	
July	**8**	**9**	**10**	**11**	**12**	**13**	**14**	**15**	**16**	**17**	**18**	**19**	**20**	**21**	**22**	**23**	**24**	**25**	**26**	**27**	**28**	**29**	**30**	**31**	**1**	**2**	**3**	**4**	**5**	**6**	**7**	Aug.
Nov.	1	2	3	4	5	6	7	8	9	10	11	12	13	14	15	16	17	18	19	20	21	22	23	24	25	26	27	28	29	30		
Aug.	**8**	**9**	**10**	**11**	**12**	**13**	**14**	**15**	**16**	**17**	**18**	**19**	**20**	**21**	**22**	**23**	**24**	**25**	**26**	**27**	**28**	**29**	**30**	**31**	**1**	**2**	**3**	**4**	**5**	**6**		Sept.
Dec.	1	2	3	4	5	6	7	8	9	10	11	12	13	14	15	16	17	18	19	20	21	22	23	24	25	26	27	28	29	30	31	
Sept.	**8**	**9**	**10**	**11**	**12**	**13**	**14**	**15**	**16**	**17**	**18**	**19**	**20**	**21**	**22**	**23**	**24**	**25**	**26**	**27**	**28**	**29**	**30**	**1**	**2**	**3**	**4**	**5**	**6**	**7**	**8**	Oct.

The date of the last menstrual period is in the top line (light-face type) of the pair of lines. The dark number (bold-face type) in the line below will be the expected day of delivery.

"quickening." *Probable signs* include increased abdominal girth, palpable fetal outline, softening of the lower uterine segment (Hegar sign), softening of the cervix (Goodell sign), and immunodiagnostic pregnancy tests. *Positive signs and symptoms* of pregnancy are auscultation of fetal heart sounds, fetal movements felt by the examiner, and an identifiable embryonic outline on ultrasound.

PHYSICAL CHANGES: The pregnant woman experiences many physiological alterations related to the increased levels of estrogen and progesterone and to the demands of the growing fetus; every system in the woman's body responds to these changes.

Reproductive tract changes: Alterations in uterine size, shape, and consistency include an increase in uterine muscle mass over the months of pregnancy. In response to elevated estrogen and progesterone levels, the cervix and lower uterine segment soften. A thick mucous plug fills the cervical canal. Vaginal secretions increase, and vaginal pH is more acidic (pH = 3.5 to 6.0). Change in vaginal pH discourages the survival and multiplication of bacteria; however, it also encourages infection by *Candida albicans*. The vagina elongates as the uterus rises in the pelvis; the mucosa thickens, with increases in secretions, vascularity, and elasticity. SEE: *Chadwick sign; Goodell sign; Hegar sign.*

Breast changes: The breasts become enlarged, tender, and more nodular. The areolae darken; the nipples become more sensitive and erectile; and Montgomery's tubercles enlarge. Colostrum may leak out during the last trimester, as the breasts prepare for lactation.

Endocrine glands: The size and activity of the thyroid gland increase markedly. Levels of thyroid-binding globulin and triiodothyronine rise; levels of thyroid-stimulating hormone drop slightly. These changes allow the pregnant woman to meet the endocrine needs imposed by the developing fetus, and other body changes that occur during pregnancy. Pituitary activity increases; prolactin levels increase ensuring lactation; placental hormones prevent ovulation and encourage development of the corpus luteum. Parathyroid activity decreases during the first trimester, then increases throughout the pregnancy to meet the increasing calcium demands of the fetus. Insulin resistance increases; this poses a risk, for some women, of glucose intolerance or gestational diabetes mellitus.

Cardiovascular alterations: Circulating blood volume increases progressively throughout pregnancy, peaking in the middle of the third trimester. Al-

though the red blood cell count rises by about 30%, a 50% increase in blood volume creates dilutional anemia. The lower relative hematocrit decreases the viscosity of the blood . However, a hemoglobin concentration of less than 11 g is usually due to iron deficiency. Rising levels of clotting factors VII, VIII, IX, X, fibrinogen, and von Willebrand factor increase coagulability. The pulse rate increases, along with cardiac stroke volume. Peripheral vascular resistance drops. Mid-trimester blood pressure may be slightly lower than normal but remains essentially unchanged.

Skeletal system: Softening and increased mobility of the pelvic articulations is reflected in the waddling gait of pregnancy. As pregnancy progresses, the woman's center of gravity shifts, and the lumbar curve increases to compensate for the growing anterior weight of the gravid uterus. Problems with dental caries may become more prominent during pregnancy but can be prevented with oral rinses (such as chlorhexidine) and regular brushing and flossing.

Respiratory system: The effects of progesterone on smooth muscle include a decreased airway resistance, which enables the woman to meet her increased needs for oxygen by permitting a 30% to 40% increase in tidal volume and a 15% to 20% rise in oxygen consumption. The effects of estrogen include edema and congestion of the nasal mucosa, reflected in nosebleeds and nasal stuffiness.

Gastrointestinal system: Nausea and vomiting is the single most common complaint during the first trimester. Progesterone-related diminished motility contributes to common complaints of heartburn and constipation. Hemorrhoids are common and caused by increased pressure in the lower pelvis and constipation.

Immune system Alterations in T helper cell dominance produce immunological tolerance for the fetus and the placenta, both of which contain antigens that are alien to the mother. During pregnancy, autoimmune diseases such as rheumatoid arthritis or systemic lupus erythematosus tend to become less active.

Skin: Pigmentation changes in pregnancy include chloasma (the mask of pregnancy), areolar darkening, and linea nigra (a pigmented line that vertically bisects the abdomen). They reflect estrogen-related stimulation of skin melanocytes. Striae gravidarum (stretch marks) may appear in the skin of the abdomen, breasts, and thighs.

Urinary system: By the middle of the first trimester, the glomerular filtration rate has risen by about 50%; in compensation, tubular reabsorption also increases. Although urinary frequency is common in the first and last trimesters, bladder capacity actually increases; however, pressure from the growing uterus reduces the volume required to stimulate voiding. During the second trimester, the uterus rises out of the pelvis, becoming an abdominal organ and relieving bladder compression until late in the third trimester.

Weight: In average-sized women, expected first trimester weight gain is 2 to 5 lb. Total weight gain and the pattern by which it increases should be monitored to enable early signs of pregnancy-related problems common to the particular point in gestation. The Institute of Medicine recommends the following weight gains during singleton pregnancies: a woman with a pre-pregnancy body mass index less than 19.8 should gain 25 to 39 lb (11.4 to 17.7 kg); a woman with a prepregnancy body mass index from 19.8 to 26 should gain 25 to 34 lb (11.4 to 15.5 kg); and a woman with a prepregnancy body mass index from 26 to 29 should gain 15 to 24 lb (6.8 to 10.9 kg). The recommended weight gains during pregnancy are different for multiple gestations, e.g., a woman carrying triplets should gain about 50 lb (22.7 kg) during her pregnancy.

PATIENT CARE: An essential component to anticipatory guidance and patient teaching is to encourage the woman's active participation in her own health maintenance and pregnancy progress. Health care providers describe to pregnant women common complaints related to normal physiological changes of pregnancy and suggest actions to minimize discomfort.

DISORDERS: *Nausea and vomiting.* SEE: *morning sickness.*

Heartburn: Hormone-related delayed gastric emptying, cardiac sphincter relaxation, and stomach displacement by the growing uterus contribute to reflux. The use of low-sodium or combination aluminum hydroxide/magnesium hydroxide preparations is recommended for symptomatic relief. For severe, unresponsive heartburn, over-the-counter H2-receptor antagonists such as ranitidine (Zantac) or famotidine (Pepcid), may be recommended.

Constipation: The woman should increase fiber and fluid intake. She also may use stool softeners.

Muscle cramps: The woman may relieve the so-called charley horse that occurs during sleep by dorsiflexing the foot of the affected leg. A calcium-phosphorus imbalance may contribute to increased frequency of this problem, although the causes are not clear. The woman can increase calcium intake by drinking the recommended daily quart of milk or by drinking a pint of milk daily and taking a calcium supplement with vitamin D.

Back pain: Growing anterior mass, shift in center of gravity, and increased lumbar curve contribute to backaches. To relieve discomfort, the pregnant woman should wear well-fitting, low-heeled shoes and perform exercises that increase abdominal muscle tone. SEE: *pelvic rock; pelvic tilt.*

Dependent edema: Pedal edema is a common third-trimester complaint related to decreased venous return from the extremities. The woman is advised to rest frequently and to elevate her feet. She should report promptly any edema of the face, hands, or sacral area to facilitate early diagnosis and management of pregnancy-induced hypertension.

Varicose veins: Decreased venous return from the extremities and compression of vascular structures by the growing uterus aggravate any weakness in the vascular walls and valves. Varicosities often occur in the legs, vulva, and pelvis. The woman should avoid tight clothing and prolonged standing. Other preventive and therapeutic measures include wearing support stockings, resting in left Sims position, and elevating the lower limbs during sleep.

Hemorrhoids: Temporary symptomatic relief may be obtained by Sitz baths and analgesic ointments. The woman also should be instructed in how to reinsert the hemorrhoid with a well-lubricated finger, holding it in place for 1 to 2 min before releasing the pressure. SEE: *constipation.*

Vaginal discharge: A normal increase in vaginal discharge occurs during pregnancy. Common perineal hygiene usually is effective as a comfort measure; douching is contraindicated during pregnancy. The woman should contact her primary caregiver promptly if profuse, malodorous, or blood-tinged discharge occurs. SEE: *vaginitis.*

Dyspnea: Shortness of breath occurs as the growing uterus presses on the woman's diaphragm. Elevation of the head and shoulders may provide some relief. The dyspnea disappears when lightening occurs.

Pruritus: The normal stretching of the skin may generate itching on the breasts, abdomen, and vulva. Pruritic urticarial papules and plaques of pregnancy is the most common benign dermatosis of pregnancy. Occurring in the third trimester, it usually resolves spontaneously after delivery. If severe, topical emollients, steriods, and, antihistamines may provide some relief. Use of an emollient lotion may be suggested; the patient is instructed to inform her primary caregiver if vulvovaginal itching occurs in conjunction with an increase or alteration in vaginal discharge. SEE: *vaginitis.*

NUTRITION: A woman's nutritional status before and during pregnancy is an important factor that affects both her health and that of her unborn child. Nutritional assessment is an essential part of antepartal care. In addition, the presence of pre-existing and coexisting disorders, such as anemia, diabetes mellitus, chronic renal disease, and phenylketonuria, may affect dietary recommendations. Substance abuse increases the risk of inadequate nutrition, low maternal weight gain, low-birth-weight infants, and perinatal mortality.

Dietary recommendations emphasize a high-quality, well-balanced diet. Increased amounts of essential nutrients (i.e., protein, calcium, magnesium, zinc, and selenium, B vitamins, vitamin C, folate, and iron) are necessary to meet nutritional needs of both mother and fetus. Most nutritional and metabolic needs can be met by eating a balanced daily diet containing approx. 35 kcal for each kilogram of optimal body weight plus an additional 300 kcal/day during the second and third trimesters. Because it is difficult to meet all the daily dietary recommendations, vitamin and iron supplements are recommended.

CONSIDERATIONS: *Travel:* Preparing for travel during pregnancy will depend upon the number of weeks gestation, the duration of the travel, and the method (i.e., auto, boat, bus, train, airplane).

Safety belts, preferably the combined lap and shoulder type, should be worn with the lap portion below the pregnant abdomen not across it. If nausea and vomiting of pregnancy is a factor, travel by sea isn't advisable. If anti-motion-sickness medication is used, it should be one approved for use during pregnancy (or antinausea wrist bands may be used). Travel during the last part of pregnancy is not advised unless obstetrical care is available at the destination(s). It is important to have a copy of current medical records along when traveling. Travel abroad should be discussed with the obstetrician so that appropriate immunizations can be given. For travel in an area known to be endemic for malaria, certain drugs will be needed for prophylaxis.

⚠️ Live virus immunization should not be administered during pregnancy.

Working: Healthy pregnant women who are employed in jobs that present no more risk than those in daily life are encouraged to continue working if they desire until shortly before delivery.

Exercise: If the pregnancy is progressing normally, exercise should be continued. The amount and type of exercise is an individual matter. A woman who has exercised regularly before her pregnancy should experience no difficulty with continuing; however, a previously sedentary woman should not attempt to institute a vigorous exercise program such as long-distance running or jogging during her pregnancy. No matter what the type of exercise, it is important to remember that, with the progress of pregnancy, the center of gravity will change and probably prevent participation at the same level and skill as before pregnancy. Sports to avoid include water skiing, horseback riding, and scuba diving. In horseback riding, in addition to the possibility of falling from the horse, the repeated bouncing may lead to bruising of the perianal area. Scuba diving may lead to decompression sickness and bends and to intravascular air embolism in the fetus. Women who breast-feed their children should continue exercising if they maintain hydration and adequate breast support.

Sexual intercourse: Women who are experiencing normally progressing pregnancies need not avoid intercourse. Pregnant women should refrain from coitus if they have a history of preterm labor or premature rupture of membranes and if they are bleeding or have ruptured membranes.

Tests: Common tests include blood tests for nutritional or sickle cell anemia, blood type and Rh factor, rubella titers, syphilis, and serum alpha-fetoprotein for the presence of neural tube defects such as spina bifida. Additional testing may include determining HIV status and hepatitis immunity. Ultrasound may be used to determine age, rate of growth, position, some birth defects, and fetal sex. Chorionic villus sampling may be done early in pregnancy if the family history indicates potential for genetic diseases. Second trimester amniocentesis may be used to detect chromosomal abnormalities, genetic disorders, and fetal sex. In late pregnancy, nonstress tests, contraction stress tests, and fetal biophysical profiles may be done; amniocentesis may be done to evaluate fetal lung maturity. SEE: table.

Vaccinations: Influenza vaccination is recommended during pregnancy

Pregnancy in adolescence: Although pregnancy among teenagers is decreasing in the U.S., approx. 7% of all American teenage girls still become pregnant in any given year, one of the highest rates

Recommended Screening for Pregnant Women

- Assessment of pregnant women for alcohol misuse and tobacco use
- HIV antibodies (blood test)
- Chlamydia and gonorrhea (antigen or culture) tests
- Hepatitis B virus (blood test)
- Rh incompatibility (blood test)
- Syphilis (blood test)
- Urinalysis for asymptomatic bacteriuria
- Nutritional assessment
- Assessment for intimate partner violence

SOURCE: Adapted from the recommendations of the U.S. Preventive Services Task Force, Agency for Healthcare Research and Quality, "The Guide to Clinical Preventive Services 2010."

of teenage pregnancy in developed countries. Sociocultural factors are believed to contribute to the high incidence of pregnancies among this population. Demographic data indicate that teenage pregnancy is more likely to be associated with being single, having low socioeconomic status, and lacking social support systems. Pregnant teenagers are believed to be at high risk for some complications of pregnancy; if, however, they seek prenatal care early and consistently cooperate with recommendations, the risk is comparable to that for other age groups. Clinical data identify a common pattern of late entry to the prenatal care system, failure to return for scheduled appointments, and non-compliance with medical and nursing-recommendations. As a result of these behaviors, adolescents are at higher risk for pregnancy-related complications, such as iron-deficiency anemia, pregnancy-induced hypertension, preterm labor and delivery, low birthweight newborns, and cephalopelvic disproportion. Other health problems seen more commonly in pregnant adolescents include sexually transmitted diseases and substance abuse. SEE: *high-risk p.*; *Nursing Diagnoses Appendix.*

Mature pregnancy: A growing number of women are experiencing their first pregnancies after age 35. The incidence of fetal demise among this population is 6:1000 births, double the rate for women under 35. Many factors may contribute to the increased risk, including pre-existing and coexisting conditions, such as diabetes mellitus, hypertension, and uterine fibroids. Mature women are identified as being at higher risk for spontaneous abortion, preeclampsia, abruptio placentae, placenta previa, gestational diabetes, cesarean birth, and chromosomal abnormalities such as

Down syndrome. Multiple-gestation secondary assisted reproduction also may be a factor in fetal loss.

Pregnancy after menopause: Very rarely, postmenopausal women have become pregnant through embryo donation and have successfully carried the pregnancy to term delivery. Prior to undergoing this procedure, the women had been undergoing hormone replacement therapy. Previously, it had been assumed that the postmenopausal uterus would not be capable of supporting the growth and development of an embryo. Pregnancies in older women are considered high risk for reasons similar to those related to mature pregnancy. Late in the third trimester, the woman may be instructed to keep a fetal activity record and undergo regularly scheduled nonstress tests.

abdominal p. Ectopic gestation in which the embryo develops in the peritoneal cavity. SYN: *abdominocyesis.* SEE: *ectopic p.*

ampullar p. Ectopic implantation of the zygote in the ampulla of a fallopian tube; 78% of all ectopic pregnancies occur in this site.

bigeminal p. Intrauterine twin gestation.

biochemical p. A pregnancy that is confirmed by laboratory tests of blood or urine but cannot be seen using contemporary imaging techniques.

cervical p. Pregnancy with implantation of the embryo in the cervical canal.

clinical p. Any conception that is detected by ultrasonography or serum hormone levels, whether or not the pregnancy is healthy or likely to progress to delivery of a newborn child. Examples of clinical pregnancies include healthy singleton, twin, and other multiple pregnancies; ectopic pregnancies; and threatened miscarriages.

cornual p. A rare type of ectopic pregnancy (found in about 2% to 4% of all ectopic pregnancies) in which implantation takes place in one of the horns of the uterus. The uterine horn may rupture between the 12th and 16th week of gestation, causing life-threatening shock. Traditionally, cornual pregnancies have been managed with laparotomy and hysterectomy, although conservative management strategies are employed occasionally.

ectopic p. Extrauterine implantation of a fertilized ovum, usually in the fallopian tubes, but occasionally in the peritoneum, ovary, or other locations. Ectopic implantation occurs in about 1 of every 150 pregnancies. Symptoms usually occur between 6 and 12 weeks after conception. SYN: *extrauterine p.* SEE: illus.; *pregnancy.*

SYMPTOMS: Early complaints are

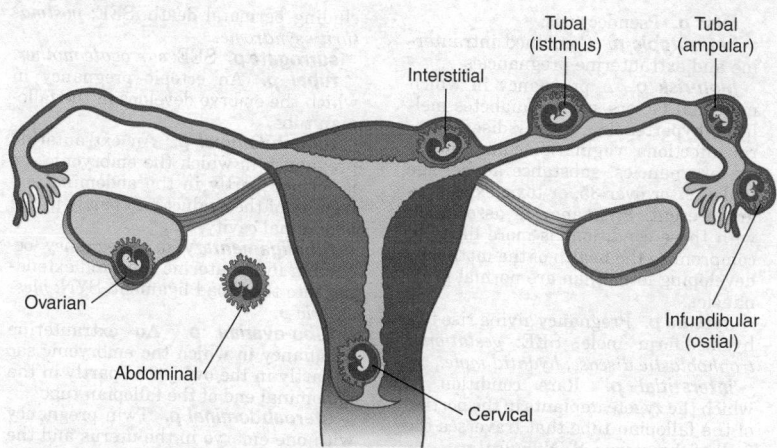

SITES FOR ECTOPIC PREGNANCY

Labels: Interstitial · Tubal (isthmus) · Tubal (ampular) · Ovarian · Infundibular (ostial) · Abdominal · Cervical

consistent with those of a normal pregnancy (i.e., amenorrhea, breast tenderness, nausea). Pregnancy test results are positive owing to the presence of human chorionic gonadotropin (hCG) in blood and urine. Signs and symptoms arise as the growing embryo distends the fallopian tube; associated complaints include intermittent, unilateral, colicky abdominal pain. Complaints associated with tubal rupture include sharp unilateral pelvic or lower abdominal pain; orthostatic dizziness and vertigo or syncope; and referred shoulder pain related to peritoneal irritation from abdominal bleeding (hemoperitoneum). Signs of hypovolemic shock may indicate extensive abdominal bleeding. Vaginal bleeding, typically occurring after the onset of pain, is the result of decidual sloughing.

LOCATIONS: *Abdominal:* The incidence of pregnancy in the abdominal cavity with the conceptus attached to an abdominal organ is between 1:3000 and 1:4000 births. *Ovarian:* Conception and implantation within the ovary itself occurs in approx. 1 in 7,000 to 1 in 50,000 pregnancies. *Tubal:* Ninety to 95% of ectopic pregnancies occur in the fallopian tube; of these, 78% become implanted in the uterine ampulla, 12% in the isthmus, and 2% to 3% in the interstices.

DIAGNOSIS: Transabdominal or transvaginal pelvic ultrasonography is used to identify the location of the pregnancy. It has also largely replaced culdocentesis for confirmation of hemoperitoneum.

TREATMENT: An operative approach is most common. Laparoscopy and linear laser salpingostomy can be used to excise early ectopic implantations; healing is by secondary intention. Segmental resection allows salvage and later reconstruction of the affected tube. Salpingectomy is reserved for cases in which tubal damage is so extensive that reanastomosis is not possible. Methotrexate has been used successfully to induce dissolution of unruptured tubal masses less than 3.5 cm. Posttreatment monitoring includes serial quantitative b-hCG levels, to be certain that the pregnancy has ended.

PATIENT CARE: *Preoperative:* The patient is assessed for pain and shock. Vital signs are monitored and oxygen administration by nonrebreather mask is started. An IV fluid infusion via a large-bore cannula is started and blood is drawn to type and cross (including Rh-compatibility) for potential transfusion. Medications (including Rho(D) immune globulin if the patient is Rh negative) may be prescribed and administered and the patient's response evaluated. The patient's and family's wishes regarding religious rites for the products of conception are determined. Both patient and family are encouraged to express their feelings of fear, loss, and grief. Information regarding the condition and the need for surgical intervention is clarified.

Postoperative: Vital signs are monitored until stable, incisional dressings are inspected, vaginal bleeding is assessed, and the patient's physical and emotional reactions to the surgery are evaluated. Prescribed analgesics and other medications are administered, and the patient evaluated for desired and adverse effects. The grieving process is anticipated, and both the patient and family are referred for further counseling as needed. SEE: *Nursing Diagnoses Appendix.*

extrauterine p. Ectopic **p.**

false p. Pseudocyesis.

heterotopic p. Combined intrauterine and extrauterine pregnancies.

high-risk p. A pregnancy in which maternal factors such as diabetes mellitus, hypertension, kidney disease, viral infections, vaginal bleeding, multiple pregnancies, substance abuse, age under 17 or over 35, or toxic exposures are present. Pregnancy in association with these conditions is more likely to compromise the health of the mother or developing fetus than are normal pregnancies.

hydatid p. Pregnancy giving rise to a hydatidiform mole. SEE: *gestational trophoblastic disease; hydatid mole.*

interstitial p. Rare condition in which the zygote implants in the portion of the fallopian tube that traverses the wall of the uterus. SYN: *mural* **p.**

intraligamentary p. Pregnancy that occurs within the broad ligament.

membranous p. Pregnancy in which the amniotic sac ruptures and the embryo comes to lie in direct contact with the uterine wall.

mesenteric p. Tuboligamentary **p.**

molar p. Pregnancy in which, instead of the ovum developing into an embryo, it develops into a mole. SEE: *gestational trophoblastic disease; hydatid mole.*

multiple p. The presence of two or more embryos in the uterus. If drugs are not used to promote fertility, the incidence of natural twin pregnancies is 1:94; however, 20% of women who have undergone treatment with fertility drugs develop multiple pregnancies. In about one-half of twin pregnancies diagnosed by ultrasound early in the first trimester, one twin will silently abort, and this may or may not be accompanied by bleeding. This has been termed the vanishing twin. The incidence of birth defects in each embryo of a twin pregnancy is twice that in singular pregnancies. SEE: *parabiosis.*

mural p. Interstitial **p.**

ovarian p. Implantation of the embryo in the substance of the ovary.

phantom p. Pseudocyesis.

postdate p. Pregnancy that extends beyond 42 wk of gestation. An average of 10% of normal pregnancies are so classified. SEE: *postterm* **p.**; *postmaturity syndrome.*

postterm p. Extension of the duration of pregnancy beyond the beginning of the 42nd week (294 days) of gestation, as counted from the first day of the last normal menstrual period. This occurs in an estimated 3% to 12% of pregnancies. Complications include oligohydramnios, passage of meconium, macrosomatia, and dysmaturity, all of which may lead to poor pregnancy outcome, including perinatal death. SEE: *postmaturity syndrome.*

surrogate p. SEE: *surrogate mother.*

tubal p. An ectopic pregnancy in which the embryo develops in the fallopian tube.

tuboabdominal p. An extrauterine pregnancy in which the embryonic sac is formed partly in the abdominal extremity of the oviduct and partly in the abdominal cavity.

tuboligamentary p. Pregnancy occurring in the uterine tube and extending into the broad ligament. SYN: *mesenteric* **p.**

tubo-ovarian p. An extrauterine pregnancy in which the embryonic sac is partly in the ovary and partly in the abdominal end of the fallopian tube.

uteroabdominal p. Twin pregnancy with one embryo in the uterus and the other in the abdominal cavity.

pregnancy-related death SEE: under *death.*

pregnancy-specific beta₁ glycoprotein SEE: under *glycoprotein.*

pregnancy test A test used to determine whether conception has occurred. In addition to the clinical signs and symptoms of pregnancy, almost none of which are reliable within the first several weeks of pregnancy, chemical tests done in the physician's office are quite accurate by as early as the time the first menstrual period is missed. There are also test kits available for purchase without a prescription. If over-the-counter tests are used, it is very important to follow the directions carefully.

A major class of pregnancy tests is those using immunodiagnostic procedures. They are the hemagglutination inhibition test, which requires a sample of urine; radioreceptor assay, which requires blood from the patient; radioimmunoassay, which requires a blood sample; and monoclonal antibody determination, which requires a sample of urine. In general, these tests are accurate beginning the 40th day following the first day of the last menstrual period; the monoclonal antibody test is somewhat more sensitive. The reliability of the test methods increases as pregnancy continues.

pregnancy wheel SEE: under *wheel.*

pregnane (prĕg′nān) $C_{21}H_{36}$; the organic compound that is a precursor of two series of steroid hormones: the progesterones and several adrenal cortical hormones.

pregnanediol (prĕg″nān-dī′ŏl) $C_{21}H_{36}O_2$; the inactive end product of metabolism of progesterone present in the urine. The amount in the urine increases during the premenstrual or luteal phase of the menstrual cycle and during pregnancy.

pregnanetriol (prĕg″nān-trī′ŏl) A metabolite of progesterone. Its presence in the urine is increased in those who have congenital adrenal hyperplasia.

pregnant (prĕg'nănt) [L. *praegnans*] Having conceived; with child. SYN: *gravid*.

pregnene (prĕg'nēn) A steroid that forms the nucleus of progesterone.

prehallux (prē-hăl'ŭks) [" + *hallux*, the great toe] A supernumerary bone, accessory naviculare pedis, or sometimes a prolongation inward of it on the foot.

prehensile (prē-hĕn'sĭl) [L. *prehendere*, to seize] Adapted for grasping or holding, esp. by encircling an object.

prehension (prē-hĕn'shŭn) [L. *prehensio*] The primary function of the hand; includes pinching, grasping, and seizing.

Prehn sign (prān, prēn) [D. T. Prehn, 20th-cent U.S. physician] A decrease in scrotal pain with elevation of the testicle. It is a physical finding in patients with epididymitis and testicular torsion.

prehormone (prē'' hawr' mōn'') A precursor of a hormone.

prehospital care SEE: under *care*.

prehospital care report ABBR: PCR. Run **sheet**.

prehospital provider SEE: under *provider*.

Prehospital Trauma Life Support ABBR: PHTLS. A continuing education course developed by the National Association of Emergency Medical Technicians designed to improve the assessment and management of trauma patients in the field.

prehypertension (prē''hī''pĕr-ten'chĭn) [*pre-* + *hypertension*] Having a systolic blood pressure between 120 and 139 mm Hg and/or a diastolic blood pressure between 80 and 89 mm Hg. People with prehypertension have an increased risk for strokes, heart attacks, and kidney failure relative to individuals whose blood pressure is below 120/80.

preictal (prē-ĭk'tăl) [" + *ictus*, stroke] The period just prior to a stroke or convulsion.

preicteric (prē-ĭk-tĕr'ĭk) [" + *ikteros*, jaundice] In liver disease, the period prior to the appearance of jaundice.

preimmunization (prē-ĭm''ū-nĭ-zā'shŭn) [" + *immunis*, safe] Immunization produced artificially in very young infants.

preimplantation (prē'' ĭm-plăn-tā' shŭn) Before one thing is secured within another, e.g., before embedding of the blastocyst in the uterine wall.

preinvasive (prē''ĭn-vā'sĭv) [" + *in*, into, + *vadere*, to go] Pert. to a stage of development of a malignancy in which the neoplastic cells have not metastasized.

prejudgment (prē-jŭj'mĕnt) A judgment made before a final ruling by a court. In malpractice litigation it refers to what occurred at the time of an injury or at the date of filing a claim.

prejudice 1. A preconceived judgment or opinion formed without factual knowledge. **2.** Irrational hostility, hatred, or suspicion of a particular group, race, or religion.

prekallikrein (prē''kal''lĭ-krē'ĭn, kă-lik'rē-ĭn) ABBR: PK. Coagulation factor XIII, a serine protease that acts with high molecular weight kininogen (HMWK) to enhance the activity of the intrinsic pathway of coagulation and is converted to kallikrein by activated coagulation factor XII. SYN: *Fletcher factor*. SEE: *blood* **coagulation;** *coagulation* **factor**.

preleukemia (prē-loo-kē'mē-ă) Myelodysplasia (1).

prelingual (prē-lĭng'gwĭl) [" + "] Occurring before the development and use of speech and language.

preload (prē'lōd) In cardiac physiology, the end-diastolic stretch of a heart muscle fiber. In the intact ventricle, this is approx. equal to the end-diastolic volume or pressure. At the bedside, preload is estimated by measuring the central venous pressure or the pulmonary capillary wedge pressure. SEE: *afterload*.

premalignant (prē-mŭ-lĭg'nĭnt) [" + "] Precancerous.

Premarin (prĕm'ĭ-rĭn) SEE: *conjugated estrogen*.

premature (prē-mă-chūr') [L. *praematurus*, ripening early] Born or manifest before full development has been achieved.

premature pubarche SEE: under *pubarche*.

premature rupture of membranes ABBR: PROM. The rupture of membranes before onset of labor. When PROM occurs at term, labor either begins spontaneously or is induced after 24 hr. Risk factors for PROM include bacterial infection, smoking, and defects of the cervix. Other factors include uterine distention due to multiple pregnancies, previous premature rupture of membranes, vaginal bleeding, sexually transmitted diseases, or low socioeconomic status of the mother. The major maternal hazard of PROM is infection, including chorioamnionitis, endometritis, and sepsis. Fetal hazards include infections, compression or prolapse of the umbilical cord, respiratory distress syndrome, or placental abruption. SEE: *prematurity*. SEE: table.

PATIENT CARE: PROM is diagnosed when amniotic fluid is found in the vaginal fornix. A sterile speculum is used to observe and collect amniotic fluid. The fluid can be tested with nitrazine paper (which will turn blue, demonstrating alkalinity), or it can be placed on a slide

Tests for Premature Rupture of Membranes

Test	How it is done	Discussion
alpha-fetoprotein (AFP) kit	Detects abnormally high concentrations of AFP in vaginal fluids	Sensitivity and specificity are high, about 90-95%
ferning	Assessment of the appearance of dried cervical mucus on a microscope slide. A branching appearance of the dried mucus represents a positive test.	Sensitivity and specificity are only fair (about 60-75%)
fetal fibronectin (fFn) test	Sample cervicovaginal secretions for fFN with a qualitative immunoassay or dipstick indicator	Sensitivity and specificity are high, about 85-95%
intra-amniotic dye injection	Phenol-sulfonphthalein (PSP) or other dye indicators are injected into the amniotic fluid, and assessments are made of the leakage of dye into the vagina.	Sensitivity and specificity are high, but the test is invasive.
nitrazine test	pH indicator test—insert a strip of paper impregnated with nitrazine into the vaginal vault and observe for change in color.	Sensitivity and specificity are only fair (about 60-75%)
ultrasonography	An ultrasound transducer is used transvaginally to determine the length of the cervix. Shorter lengths correlate with an increased risk of premature rupture of membranes.	Sensitivity and specificity are low, esp. in women at low risk for premature delivery. The test is sometimes used in conjunction with other studies.

and observed for ferning. False positives can occur with both tests. Alpha-fetoprotein (AFP) and fetal fibronectin (fFN) tests have been used with varying results. An intra-amniotic dye injection is accurate but invasive. Ultrasonography can confirm gestational age, presentation, and amniotic fluid index. Digital exams should not be performed. The Amnisure test, which identifies a specific placental protein in the amniotic fluid, can be performed at the bedside and has high sensitivity and specificity. Delivery is indicated if there are signs of maternal infection or of compromise of the fetus. Antibiotics are ordered as needed, and corticosteroids are given to increase fetal lung maturity between 24 and 34 weeks. Tocolytics are given if the mother needs to be transported to a tertiary facility.

    preterm p.r.o.m. ABBR: PPROM. Rupture of the fetal membranes before completion of week 37 of pregnancy. It is the most serious form of premature rupture of membranes. SEE: *prematurity*.

premature ventricular contraction SEE: under *contraction*.

prematurity (prē″mă-chur′ĭt-ē, -tūr′, -tūr″) The state of an infant born any time before completion of the 37th week of gestation. The normal gestation period for humans is 40 weeks. Because of the difficulty of obtaining accurate and objective data on the exact length of gestation, a birth weight of 2500 g (5.5 lb) or less has been accepted internationally as the clinical criterion of prematurity regardless of the period of gestation. Other measures suggestive of prematurity are crown-heel length (47 cm or less), crown-rump length (32 cm or less), occipitofrontal circumference (33 cm or less), occipitofrontal diameter (11.5 cm or less), and ratio of the thorax circumference to the head circumference (less than 93%).

The use of a single-criterion measure (birth weight) imposes limitations in accurately identifying those infants born before adequate development of body organs and systems has been achieved. It can easily include mature infants who are of low birth weight for reasons other than a shortened gestation period. The Expert Committee on Prematurity of the World Health Organization (1961) recommended that the concept of prematurity in the international definition be replaced by that of low birth weight. *Low birth weight* more accurately describes infants weighing less than 2500 g at birth than does *prematurity*. The latter term should be reserved for those neonates within the low birth weight group with evidence of incomplete development.

In the U.S. approx. 7.1% of white liveborn and 13.4% of nonwhite liveborn infants weigh 2500 g or less. Chances of survival depend on the degree of maturity achieved, general medical condition, and quality of care received.

Prematurity is the leading cause of death in the neonatal period. Mortality among infants weighing less than 2500 g at birth is 17 times greater than among infants with birth weight above 2500 g. Chief causes of mortality are abnormal pulmonary ventilation, infection, intracranial hemorrhage, abnormal blood conditions, and congenital anomalies. Antenatal steroids assist fetal lung development.

ETIOLOGY: The incidence of neonates of low birth weight is more frequent among females, nonwhite races, plural births, and the first- and fifth-born (and more) infants. Delivery of infants of low birth weight is reported to be more frequent among women with one or more of the following characteristics: having their children at either a very young age or between ages 45 and 49; being unmarried; having children closely spaced (less than 2 to 4 years between births); and living in a large urban area.

Another factor associated with low birth weight is the socioeconomic status of the family as measured by the mother's educational attainment. The proportion of infants of low birth weight born to mothers with 16 years or more of education was half of that of infants born to mothers with less than 9 years of education. Low birth weight is also associated with generally elevated risk of infant mortality, congenital malformations, mental retardation, and other physical and neurological impairments.

COMPLICATIONS: Frequently, premature infants are handicapped by a number of anatomical and physiological limitations. These limitations vary in direct proportion to the degree of immaturity present. Limitations include weakness of the sucking and swallowing reflexes, small capacity of stomach, impairment of renal function, incomplete development of capillaries of the lungs, immature alveoli of the lungs, weakness of the cough and gag reflexes, weakness of the thoracic cage muscles and other muscles used in respiration, inadequate regulation of body temperature, incomplete or poorly developed enzyme systems, hepatic immaturity, and deficient placental transfer and antenatal storage of minerals, vitamins, and immune compounds. Severely premature infants

have high rates of neurological deficits later in life. SEE: *intrauterine growth retardation; premature rupture of membranes.*

PATIENT CARE: Ideally, the premature birth should take place in a regional intensive care center rather than a community health facility so that specially prepared staff are available to manage the birth and the premature infant, eliminating the need for infant transfer and mother-child separation. A resuscitation team should be in attendance to take immediate charge of the neonate. A physical assessment correlated with the expected maturation for fetal age is performed. Health care providers perform a neurological evaluation, obtain an Apgar score, ensure proper environmental temperature, provide proper fluid and caloric intake, ensure parental bonding and support, assess laboratory reports, monitor intake and output, notify the pediatrician and nursery of the (impending) premature birth, weigh the infant daily at the same time without clothing and on the same scale, monitor oxygen concentration at frequent intervals, hold and cuddle the infant during feedings, cover the infant when removing from isolette, and provide adequate time for feeding.

Care of low-birth-weight infants: Care of low-birth-weight infants should be individualized and reflect the needs of the developing infant with regard to anatomical and physiological handicaps. Evaluation for degree of immaturity and identification of special problems after birth dictates care required by these infants. In general, care centers on prevention of infection, stabilization of body temperature, maintenance of respiration, and provision of adequate nutrition and hydration.

Aseptic technique is required. An incubator or heated bed provides a suitable environment for maintenance of body temperature. A high-humidity environment may be of value for infants with respiratory difficulties. Gentle nasal and pharyngeal suctioning aids in keeping airways clear. Use of oxygen should be restricted to the minimal amounts required for survival of the infant. Because of the danger of retrolental fibroplasia, the oxygen concentration should not exceed 30%.

Depending on the infant's sucking and swallowing abilities, feeding by gavage may be necessary. Some infants may not be given anything by mouth for as long as 72 hr after birth. Caloric and fluid intakes are increased gradually until 100 to 120 cal/kg and 140 to 150 mL/kg, respectively, in 24 hr are reached. The time required to achieve these intake levels depends on the newborn's condition. The infant may require small, frequent feedings to cope with the small capacity of the stomach, to prevent vomiting and distention, and to meet the body's caloric and fluid requirements. Overfeeding should be avoided. During the early days of life, clyses are sometimes administered to maintain adequate hydration. Breast milk is the optimal nutritional choice.

The infant should not be allowed to become fatigued from excessive handling, prolonged feeding procedures, or too much crying. Body position should be changed every 2 to 4 hr. Gentle handling should be practiced. The newborn and infant should receive cuddling and pleasant vocal stimulation several times a day.

Because of the possibility of retinal damage, premature infants should not be exposed to bright light. Parents are kept informed of their infant's condition, and equipment, procedures, and treatments used are explained. They are encouraged to visit, stroke and touch, and then hold and feed the neonate as this becomes possible. Home health care may be required to assist the parents in caring for special needs when the neonate is ready for discharge.

premaxilla (prē″măk-sĭl′ă) [L. *prae*, before, in front of, + *maxilla*, jawbone] A separate bone, derived from the median nasal process embryologically, that fuses with the maxilla in humans; formerly called the incisive bone.

premedication (prē″med″ĭ-kā′shŏn) [*pre-* + *medication*] **1.** Administration of drugs before treatment to enhance comfort, therapeutic effect, and/or safety of a given procedure. **2.** Preanesthetic. **premedicate** (prē″med′ĭ-kāt″), *v.*

premenarchal (prē″mĕ-nǎr′kǎl) [″ + Gr. *men*, mouth, + *arche*, beginning] Pert. to the time before the first menstrual period.

premenstrual (prē-mĕn′stroo-ăl) [″ + *menstruare*, to discharge the menses] Before menstruation.

premenstrual dysphoric disorder ABBR: PMDD. A disorder characterized by symptoms such as markedly depressed mood, anxiety, affective lability, and decreased interest in activities. It is the current term, according to *DSM-IV*, for what was previously known as premenstrual tension syndrome, now PMDD. Although the term premenstrual syndrome also is commonly used, it is not the technical term for this disorder, but may be used to identify a milder and less debilitating form of the disorder. SYN: *premenstrual tension syndrome.*

SYMPTOMS: In patients with this disease, the symptoms occur regularly during the last week of the luteal phase in most menstrual cycles during the year preceding diagnosis. These symptoms begin to remit within a few days of the onset of the menses (the follicular phase) and are always absent the week following menses.

DIAGNOSIS: Five or more of the following symptoms must be present most of the time during the last week of the luteal phase, with at least one of the symptoms being one of the first four: feeling sad, hopeless, or self-deprecating; feeling tense, anxious, or on edge; marked lability of mood interspersed with frequent tearfulness; persistent irritability, anger, and increased interpersonal conflicts; decreased interest in usual activities, which may be associated with withdrawal from social relationships; difficulty concentrating; feeling fatigued, lethargic, or lacking in energy; marked changes in appetite, which may be associated with binge eating or craving certain foods; hypersomnia or insomnia; a subjective feeling of being overwhelmed or out of control; and physical symptoms such as breast tenderness or swelling, headaches, or sensation of bloating or weight gain, with tightness of fit of clothing, shoes, or rings. There may also be joint or muscle pain. The symptoms may be accompanied by suicidal thoughts.

The pattern of symptoms must have occurred most months for the previous 12 months. The symptoms disappear completely shortly after the onset of menstruation. In atypical cases, some women also have symptoms for a few days around ovulation; and a few women with short cycles might, therefore, be symptom-free for only 1 week per cycle. Women commonly report that their symptoms worsen with age until relieved by the onset of menopause.

TREATMENT: The selective serotonin reuptake inhibitors, such as fluoxetine and sertraline, but not tricyclic antidepressants, help improve symptoms of the disorder for many patients. Other pharmacologic treatments include calcium and magnesium supplements, vitamins (esp. vitamin B6), prostaglandin inhibitors, NSAIDs, and diuretics. Some people believe that symptoms are diminished by limiting one's intake of salt, refined sugars, caffeine (e.g., in chocolate, colas, and coffee), nicotine, alcohol, red meat, and animal fat, and increasing consumption of leafy green vegetables, whole-grain cereals, vitamins B_6 and E, and complex carbohydrates. The hypothesis that dietary changes influence PMDD has not been rigorously tested.

PATIENT CARE: Support and reassurance are offered, and the woman is informed about self-help groups (as available) and encouraged to develop her own resources to help her cope with the syndrome.

premenstrual syndrome ABBR: PMS. SEE: *premenstrual dysphoric disorder.*

premenstrual tension syndrome ABBR: PTS. Premenstrual dysphoric disorder. SEE: *Nursing Diagnoses Appendix.*

premenstruum (prē-měn'stroo-ŭm) [" + *menstruus,* menstrual fluid] The period of time before menstruation.

premise (prěm'ĭs) A proposition or starting point that is accepted as true or that is agreed to be true. SEE: *assumption.*

premium (prē'mē-um) A payment made periodically to a health care insurer in exchange for benefits coverage (indemnity against future expenses).

premium support (prē'mē-ŭm sŭ-pŏrt') A form of health insurance coverage in which a third party, such as an employer or the federal government, provides a fixed contribution to an employee's health insurance costs. The employee chooses the extent of coverage (e.g., basic, catastrophic, dental, extensive) and how much he or she is willing to pay to be insured.

premixed (prē'mikst') [*pre-* + *mixed*] Prepared in standard concentrations or percentages before use. Insulins, e.g., may be pure (composed of either short or long-acting varieties but not both), or they may be combined to take advantage of the differing times of onset and peak effect of two different agents. Premixed insulins are usually labeled with two numbers, separated by a slash (/). An insulin mixture that is half long-acting and half rapid-acting is labeled 50/50; one that is 70% long-acting and 30% rapid-acting is labeled 70/30.

premolar (prē-mō'lĕr) [" + *moles,* a mass] One of the permanent teeth that erupt to replace the deciduous molars. They are often called bicuspid teeth, for the maxillary premolars have two cusps, whereas the mandibular premolars may have from one to three cusps. They are located between the canine and first molar of each quadrant of the dental arches. SEE: *dentition.*

premonition (prěm″ĕ-, prē-mě-nĭsh'ŭn) [L. *praemonere,* to warn beforehand] A feeling of an impending event.

premonitory (prē-mŏn'ĭ-tō-rē) [L. *praemonitorius*] Giving a warning, as an early symptom.

premonocyte (prē-mŏn'ō-sīt) [L. *prae,* before, in front of, + Gr. *monos,* alone, + *kytos,* cell] An embryonic cell transitional in development prior to a monocyte.

premorbid (prē-mor'bĭd) [" + *morbidus,* sick] Occurring before the development of disease.

prenatal (prē-nāt'ăl) [*pre-* + *¹natal*] Before birth. SYN: *antenatal.*

prenatal care SEE: under *care.*

prenatal counseling Instruction of pregnant women and their partners about the choices they may need to make during pregnancy, esp. about prenatal nutrition, folic acid supplementation, exercise, screening, and methods of childbirth, and how these choices may affect the outcome of the pregnancy.

prenatal screening SEE: under *screening.*

prenatal stress SEE: under *stress.*

prenatal surgery SEE: under *surgery.*

preobese (prē-ō-bēs') The term used by the World Health Organization for "overweight."

preoperative blood donation (prē-op'ě-răt-iv) SEE: *autologous blood transfusion.*

preoperative care (prē-op'ě-răt-iv) SEE: under *care.*

preoptic area (prē-ŏp-tĭk) The anterior portion of the hypothalamus. It is above the optic chiasma and on the sides of the third ventricle.

preosseous (prē″ŏs'ē-ŭs) [" + "] Pert. to the formation of partly formed bone made of developing cartilage or connective tissue.

preoxygenation (prē-ŏks″ĭ-jĭ-nā'shŭn) **1.** The administration of high-flow oxygen to a patient before endotracheal intubation or suctioning of the upper airway. **2.** Breathing of 100% oxygen via a face mask by the fully conscious patient before induction of anesthesia. Duration is 2 to 7 min. In that time the nitrogen is washed out of the lungs and is replaced by oxygen.

This same procedure is used for a longer period of time in persons before exposure to very low atmospheric pressure (e.g., aviators before flying to high altitudes) or to very high atmospheric pressure (e.g., divers descending to a great depth in water). In both cases the goal is to rid the body of nitrogen to prevent bends.

PrEP *preexposure prophylaxis* (use of antiretroviral drugs in uninfected but at-risk people to keep them from becoming infected with HIV).

prep (prep) [Abbr. of *prepare* or *preparation*] **1.** To prepare (a patient) for a medical or surgical procedure. **2.** Preparation of a patient for a medical or surgical procedure. SEE: *preoperative* ***care.***

bowel p. The administration of a clear liquid diet with laxatives, enemas, or both, in anticipation of endoscopy of the lower gastrointestinal tract to provide an optimal view of the bowel wall. It is also used in some bowel surgeries

touch p. SEE: under *preparation.*

prepaid care SEE: under *care.*

preparalytic (prē″păr-ă-lĭt'ĭk) [" + Gr. *para,* at the side, + *lyein,* to loosen] Before the appearance of paralysis.

preparation (prep″ă-rā'shŏn) [L. *praeparatio*] **1.** The making ready, esp. of a medicine for use. **2.** A specimen set up for demonstration in anatomy, pathology, or histology. **3.** A medicine made ready for use.

cavity p. The removal of dental caries and the excavation of surrounding dental structure to permit reconstruction of the tooth with dental restorative materials.

chlorine p. A disinfectant solution such as Dakin's solution or Javelle water, made from hypochlorites in water.

corrosion p. In anatomical and pathology investigations, hollow organs and structures such as vessels are filled with a liquid substance that hardens. Then the surrounding tissues are dissolved by use of suitable chemicals. This leaves a cast of the structures.

heart-lung p. In animal studies and in open-heart surgery, the use of devices that take over the function of the heart and lungs while those organs are being treated or possibly replaced.

touch p. 1. The dabbing of a clinical specimen, e.g., the cut surface of an organ or tissue, onto a microscope slide to distribute a thin layer of cells for microscopic examination. **2.** Any slide so obtained and prepared for pathological analysis. SYN: *biopsy imprint; touch print.*

preparative regimen High doses of cancer chemotherapy and/or radiation therapy, used prior to bone marrow or cord blood transplantation to eliminate the recipient's blood-forming cells. Very high doses of drugs and/or radiation are used to eliminate as many diseased cells from the recipient's marrow as possible. As a result, the recipient's normal blood cells are also destroyed. Preparative regimens temporarily make patients immunodeficient, anemic, and platelet-deficient. Immunocompetence and the ability to form red cells and platelets are restored to patients when the donated stem cells they receive engraft, i.e., begin to repopulate and reproduce in the marrow. Also known as *conditioning regimen.*

preparedness (prē-pār′ĕd-nĕs) The capability, planning, and training needed to respond to a crisis (e.g., a multiple casualty incident, chemical spill, or terrorist attack).

preparticipation (prē″par-ti″sĭ-pā′shŏn) [*pre-* + *participation*] Pert. to something occurring before or as a prerequisite for engaging in an activity, esp. a sport. A preparticipation sports physical examination, e.g., is a preventive health exam to identify those who might be harmed by playing a particular sport or engaging in a certain activity.

prepatellar (prē″pă-tĕl′ăr) [L. *prae,* before, in front of, + *patella,* pan] In front of the patella.

prepatellar bursitis SEE: under *bursitis.*

prepatent (prē-pā′tĕnt) Before becoming evident or manifest.

prepatent period SEE: under *period.*

preplacental (prē″plă-sĕn′tăl) [″ + *placenta,* a flat cake] Occurring prior to formation of the placenta.

preponderance of evidence (prē-pon′dĕ-răns) [L. *praeponderare,* to outweigh] The relative weight or strength of the claims made by opposing parties in a legal dispute. When a civil lawsuit is decided, it is determined according to this standard and not according to the standard of reasonable doubt, which is used in criminal trials.

prepotent (prē-pō′tĕnt) [″ + *potentia,* power] Pert. to the greater power of one parent to transmit inherited characteristics to the offspring.

preprandial (prē-prăn′dē-ăl) [″ + *prandium,* breakfast] Before a meal.

prepregnancy counseling Prepregnancy evaluation.

prepregnancy evaluation (prē″preg′năn-sē) [*pre-* + *pregnancy*] A health care assessment of a woman who is contemplating pregnancy to determine her risks for complications and/or to optimize her health status. It is recommended for women with diseases such as diabetes mellitus, cardiac arrhythmias or murmurs, malnutrition, chronic infectious diseases, and autoimmune disorders. SYN: *prepregnancy counseling.*

preprosthetic program (prē″pros-thet′ik) [*pre-prosthetic*] Postsurgical intervention after an amputation during which the patient is taught to take care of the stump, tolerate sitting, techniques in transferring, positioning, and other necessary skills before prosthetic training can begin.

prepuberal, prepubertal (prē-pū′bĕ-răl, prē-pū′bĕrt-ăl) [″ + *pubertas,* puberty] Before puberty.

prepubescent (prē″pū-bĕs′ĕnt) [″ + *pubescens,* becoming hairy] Pert. to the period just before puberty.

prepuce (prē′pūs) [L. *praeputium,* prepuce] Foreskin.

p. of the clitoris A fold of the labia minora that covers the clitoris. SEE: *clitoris.*

preputial (prē-pū′shăl) Pert. to the prepuce.

preputial gland SEE: under *gland.*

preretinal (prē-rĕt′ĭ-năl) [″ + *retina,* retina] In front of the retina of the eye.

presacral (prē-sā′krăl) [″ + *sacrum,* sacred] In front of the sacrum.

presby-, presbyo- [Gr. *presbys,* old man, elder] Prefixes meaning *old.*

presbycardia (prĕz-bĭ-kăr′dē-ă) [″ + *kardia,* heart] Decreased functional capacity of the heart, as a result of age-related muscular hypertrophy, loss of myocytes, and decreased cardiac elasticity and compliance.

presbycusis, presbykousis (prez-bĭ-kū′sĭs) [*presby-* + Gr. *akousis,* hearing] Progressive loss of hearing with aging, typically resulting from sensorineural hearing loss. It is the third most common disease of the elderly, after hypertension and arthritis, and can cause significant social isolation. SYN: *presbyacusia.*

presbylaryngis (prez″bē-lă-rin′jis) [*presby-* + *larynx*] Atrophy of the vocal folds occurring progressively with aging and producing a breathy, hoarse, or weakened voice.

presbyope (prĕs′bē-ōp) [″ + *ops,* eye] A person who is presbyopic.

presbyopia (prĕz-bē-ō′pē-ă) [″ + *ops,* eye] The permanent loss of accommodation of the crystalline lens of the eye that occurs when people are in their 40s, marked by the inability to maintain focus on objects held near to the eye (i.e., at reading distance). SEE: *farsightedness.*

preschool (prē′skool″) [*pre-* + *school*] An educational institution such as a nursery school or play group that encourages the cognitive, emotional, and social development of children before they enter mandatory education, i.e., kindergarten. **preschool,** *adj.*

prescribe (prē-skrīb′) [L. *praescriptio, prescription*] To indicate the medicine to be administered. This can be done orally but is usually done by writing a prescription or an order in the patient's hospital chart.

prescribing cascade SEE: under *cascade.*

prescribing error (pri-skrīb′ing) SEE: under *error.*

prescribing information A detailed description of a drug's uses, dosage range, side effects, drug-drug interactions, and contraindications that is available to clinicians and is often included in pharmaceutical packaging instructions.

prescription (prē-skrĭp′shŭn) [L. *praescriptio*] A written direction or order for dispensing and administering drugs. It is signed by a physician, dentist, or other practitioner licensed by law to prescribe such a drug. Historically, a prescription consists of four main parts:

1. *Superscription,* represented by the symbol ℞, which signifies *Recipe,* meaning "take"

2. *Inscription,* containing the ingredients

3. *Subscription,* directions to the dispenser how to prepare the drugs

4. *Signature,* directions to the patient how to take the dosage; the physician's signature, address, and telephone number; the date; and whether the prescription may be refilled. When applicable, the physician's Drug Enforcement Administration number must be included. Many states also require that the prescriber indicate on the prescription whether or not a generic drug

may be substituted for the trade name equivalent.

In the U.S. each year about 3 billion prescriptions are written in health care offices, and still more are written for inpatients.

⚠ Unused prescription pads should be kept in a secure place in order to prevent their being misused or stolen. Each prescription should be numbered consecutively. One should never sign a prescription blank in advance. The prescriber should use ink to prevent changes being made and not use prescription pads for writing notes or memos.

p. drug A drug available to the public only upon prescription written by a physician, dentist, or other practitioner licensed to do so.

exercise p. An exercise schedule usually intended to increase the physical fitness of a previously sedentary individual who has recently had a serious illness such as myocardial infarction, or who is physically fit and wants to know the amount, frequency, and kind of exercise necessary to maintain fitness. The prescription is individualized, taking into account the person's age, the availability of facilities and adequate supervision, and health, particularly if the person has had chronic diseases of the heart or lungs. SEE: *physical activity and exercise.*

shotgun p. A prescription containing many drugs, given with the hope that one of them may prove effective; it is not a recommended approach to the treatment of disease.

prescription monitoring program ABBR: PMP. A state-run agency in the U.S. that monitors the prescription of controlled substances, and provides education, trend analysis, and feedback to prescribers and to law enforcement. PMPs help promote the appropriate use of pain relieving drugs by preventing their diversion, abuse, or misuse. Health care providers and pharmacists can access reports in PMP databases about the medications their patients have recently received.

prescriptive authority (prē-skrĭp-tĭv′) The limited authority to prescribe certain medications according to established protocol. In the U.S., prescriptive authority has been granted to advanced practice nurses, optometrists, osteopaths, physicians, podiatrists, and veterinarians among other health care professionals.

presenile (prē-sē′nīl) [L. *prae,* before, in front of, + *senilis,* old] Occurring before the expected onset of age-related changes, that is, in middle age. The word is usually applied to dementia that occurs relatively early in life.

presenium (prē-sē′nē-ŭm) [″ + *senium,* old age] The time of life that precedes old age, typically the years before age 65.

present (prē-zĕnt′) [L. *praesent,* to be present before others] The presence of the patient for examination.

presentation (prē″zĕn-tā′shŭn) [L. *praesentatio*] **1.** In obstetrics, the position of the fetus presenting itself to the examining finger in the vagina or rectum (e.g., longitudinal or normal and transverse or pathologic presentation). **2.** The relationship of the long axis of fetus to that of the mother; also called *lie.* SEE: illus.; *position* for table. **3.** The fetal body part that first enters the maternal pelvis. SEE: *position* for table.

   breech p. Fetal position in which the buttocks comes first. Breech presentation is of three types: complete breech, when the thighs of the fetus are flexed on the abdomen and the legs flexed upon the thighs; frank breech, when the legs of the fetus are extended over the anterior surface of the body; and footling, when a foot or feet present. Footling can be single, double, or, if the leg remains flexed, knee presentation. SYN: *pelvic* **p.**

   brow p. Fetal position in which the brow or face of the infant comes first

during labor, making vaginal delivery almost impossible. Cesarean section may be needed if the presentation cannot be altered.

   cephalic p. Presentation of the head of the fetus in any position.

   compound p. Fetal position in which a prolapsed limb is alongside the main presenting part.

   face p. Fetal position in which the head of the fetus is sharply extended so that the face comes first.

   footling p. Fetal position in which the feet come first. SEE: *breech* **p.**

   funic p. Appearance of the umbilical cord during labor.

   longitudinal p. Presentation in which the long axis of the fetus is parallel to the long axis of the mother.

   oblique p. Presentation in which the long axis of the fetus is oblique to that of the mother.

   pelvic p. Breech **p.**

   placental p. Placenta previa.

   shoulder p. Presentation in which the shoulder of the fetus is the presenting part.

   transverse p. Presentation with the fetus lying crosswise.

   vertex p. Presentation of the upper and back part of the fetal head.

presenteeism (prē″zĕn-tē′izm) [By analogy with *absenteeism*] Presence at work without contributing to the pro-

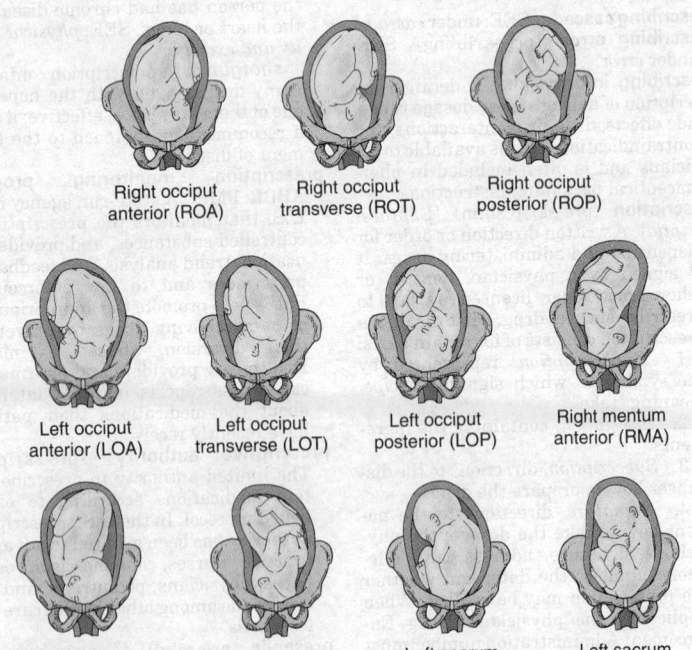

Right occiput anterior (ROA)

Right occiput transverse (ROT)

Right occiput posterior (ROP)

Left occiput anterior (LOA)

Left occiput transverse (LOT)

Left occiput posterior (LOP)

Right mentum anterior (RMA)

Right mentum posterior (RMP)

Left mentum anterior (LMA)

Left sacrum anterior (LSA)

Left sacrum posterior (LSP)

PRESENTATIONS OF FETUS

ductivity of the institution. The term is used for such behavior as working while ill or while being distracted from one's primary tasks, and thus in a less than fully functional mode; or logging excessive hours at work to impress coworkers or managers.

presenting part Before delivery, the fetal anatomical structure nearest the internal cervical os, identified by sonogram or palpation during vaginal examination. SEE: *presentation* for illus.

preservative (prē-zĕr'văt-ĭv) [L. *praeservare*, to watch beforehand] A substance added to medicines or foods to prevent them from spoiling. It may act by interfering with certain chemical reactions or with the growth of molds, fungi, bacteria, or parasites. Some common preservatives are sugar, salt, vinegar, ethyl alcohol, sulfur dioxide, and benzoic acid.

⚠️ In some cases preservatives may have undesirable effects, e.g., they may reduce the nutritional content of foods, or they may be carcinogenic or teratogenic.

prespinal (prē-spī'năl) [″ + *spina*, thorn] In front of the spine, or ventral to it.

pressor (prĕs'or) [Fr. *presser*, to press] **1.** Stimulating, increasing the activity of a function, esp. of vasomotor activity, as a nerve. **2.** Inducing an elevation in blood pressure. **3.** One of several drugs, such as dopamine, epinephrine, and norepinephrine, that are used to increase the blood pressure of patients in shock.

pressoreceptor (prĕs″ō-rē-sĕp'tor) Baroreceptor.

pressure (presh'ŭr) [L. *pressura*] **1.** A compression. **2.** Stress or force exerted on a body, as by tension, weight, or pulling. **3.** In psychology, the quality of sensation aroused by moderate compression of the skin. **4.** In physics, the quotient obtained by dividing a force by the area of the surface on which it acts.

   airway opening p. The pressure at the access point to a patient's airway, (nose, mouth, or for a mechanically ventilated patient, the trachea). When this pressure exceeds the alveolar pressure, gases tend to move into the lower airways and open the alveoli. When this pressure is less than the alveolar pressure, gases tend to move out of the lungs and into the atmosphere. SEE: *alveolar p.*

   alveolar p. Air pressure in the alveoli and bronchial tree. When this pressure is positive, it is higher than atmospheric pressure; when negative, less. Gases flow from higher to lower pressures: when alveolar pressures are higher

than atmospheric pressure, respiratory gases tend to be exhaled. When alveolar pressures are less than atmospheric pressures, gas flows into the lungs. SYN: *intrapulmonic p.*

   arterial p. The pressure of the blood in the arteries. For a normal young person at physical and mental rest and in sitting position, systolic blood pressure averages about 120 mm Hg; diastolic pressure about 80 mm Hg. A wide range of normal variation is due to constitutional, physical, and psychic factors. For women, the figures are slightly lower. For older people, they are higher. Normally there is little difference in the blood pressure recorded in the two arms. SEE: *blood pressure.*

   atmospheric p. The pressure of the weight of the atmosphere; at sea level it averages about 760 mm Hg.

   bilevel positive airway p. ABBR: BiPAP. A type of continuous positive airway pressure in which inspiratory and expiratory pressure differ from each other.

   blood p. SEE: *blood pressure.*

   capillary p. The blood pressure in the capillaries.

   central venous p. ABBR: CVP. The pressure within the superior vena cava. It reflects the pressure under which the blood is returned to the right atrium. The normal range is between 5 and 10 cm H_2O. A high CVP indicates circulatory overload (as in congestive heart failure), whereas a low CVP indicates reduced blood volume (as in hemorrhage or fluid loss). CVP can be estimated by examining the cervical veins or the dorsal veins of the hand if the neck and hand are at the level of the heart. Those veins are well filled if CVP is normal or high, and tend to collapse if it is low.

   cerebrospinal p. The pressure of the cerebrospinal fluid. This varies with body position but is normally about 100 to 180 mm H_2O when the spinal canal is initially entered during lumbar puncture with the patient lying on his or her side.

   continuous positive airway p. ABBR: CPAP. A method of ventilatory support applied to the spontaneously breathing patient in which airway pressure is maintained above atmospheric pressure throughout the respiratory cycle. CPAP can be applied by way of a nasal mask, a face mask, or an endotracheal tube. It can be used to treat congestive heart failure, acute pulmonary edema, obstructive sleep apnea syndrome, and other conditions. A potential adverse effect of CPAP is barotrauma to the lungs.

   coronary perfusion p. ABBR: CPP. The blood pressure in the aorta during diastole minus the blood pressure during right atrial diastole. For ICU patients it is an indicator of the adequacy of blood flow through the epicardial coronary arteries, e.g., during CPR. Patients whose CPP is > 15 mm Hg during CPR are more likely to regain spontaneous circulation than patients whose CPP is lower.

cricoid p. The application of manual pressure onto the cricoid cartilage during intubation and mechanical ventilation. This technique helps to occlude the esophagus and prevent the entry of air into the gastrointestinal tract during ventilation. It also diminishes the chances for regurgitation from the stomach and aspiration of gastric contents.

cuff p. The gas pressure used to inflate and hold in place the balloon surrounding a tracheal tube or laryngeal airway.

⚠️ To avoid damage to the trachea, the pressure should be carefully monitored and adjusted. Cuff pressure should be sufficient to prevent aspiration of secretions around the cuff.

driving p. **1.** In respiratory physiology, the difference between the inspiratory pressure and the expiratory pressure. **2.** In cardiovascular physiology, the difference between the arterial pressure at the source of blood flow, and the pressure at the target tissue.

effective osmotic p. That portion of the total osmotic pressure of a solution that determines the tendency of the solvent to pass through a membrane, usually one that is semipermeable. The tendency is for the solvent to pass from a solution containing a high concentration of the solute to the side of the membrane with the low concentration. SYN: *threshold p.*

end-diastolic p. Blood pressure in a ventricle of the heart at the end of diastole.

end-expiratory p. The pressure in the lungs when exhalation is complete.

expiratory p. The pressure in the lungs during the exhalation of a breath.

expiratory positive airway p. ABBR: EPAP. The amount of positive pressure in excess of the barometric pressure that is used during invasive or noninvasive ventilation while the patient is exhaling.

filling p. The average pressure in the atria or the ventricles at the end of diastole.

hydrostatic p. The pressure exerted by a fluid within a closed system.

increased intracranial p. An elevation of the pressure of the cerebrospinal fluid. In healthy people intracranial pressures range between 0 and 10 mm Hg. Pressures higher than 20 mm Hg

increase the risk of compression or herniation of the brain or brainstem.

inspiratory p. The pressure in the lungs during the inhalation of a breath.

intra-abdominal p. Pressure within the abdominal cavity, such as that caused by descent of the diaphragm.

intracranial p. The pressure of the cerebrospinal fluid in the subarachnoid space between the skull and the brain. The pressure is normally the same as that found during lumbar puncture.

intraocular p. ABBR: IOP. Fluid pressure inside the eye, normally 12 to 21 mm Hg.

intrapleural p. Pleural **p.**

intrapulmonic p. Alveolar **p.**

intrathoracic p. Pleural **p.**

intraventricular p. The pressure within the ventricles of the heart during different phases of diastole and systole.

jugular venous p. ABBR: JVP. Back pressure exerted into the jugular veins from the right side of the heart.

PATIENT CARE: To estimate jugular venous pressure, have the patient lie on his or her back with the chest, neck, and head elevated 30 degrees above the horizontal. Measure the vertical height of the fullness seen as the jugular vein fills. In the healthy (and in the dehydrated) little or no blood is seen in the jugular veins, and they appear to be flat. In right-sided heart failure, the column of blood distends the jugular veins to a height of 5 to 6 cm or more.

maximum inspiratory p. Maximum inspiratory **force**.

negative p. Any pressure less than that of the atmosphere, or less than that pressure to which the initial pressure is being compared.

oncotic p. Osmotic pressure exerted by colloids in a solution.

opening p. ABBR: OP. The pressure of the cerebrospinal fluid that is detected just after a needle is placed into the spinal canal. It is normally 100 to 180 mm H_2O.

osmotic p. The force with which a solvent, usually water, passes through a semipermeable membrane separating solutions of different concentrations. It is a colligative property, i.e., it depends on the number of particles, not on the nature of the particles, dissolved in solution. It is measured by determining the hydrostatic (mechanical) pressure that must be opposed to the osmotic force to bring the passage to a standstill.

partial p. In a gas containing several different components, the pressure exerted by each component.

partial p. of exhaled carbon dioxide ABBR: PETCO2. The carbon dioxide content of an expired breath. In a patient with normal ventilation and perfusion, it should exceed 40 mm Hg.

peak inspiratory p. The maximum

pressure in the lungs that is achieved at the peak of inhalation.

plateau p. The average pressure in the alveoli during the brief pause that follows an inhaled breath.

pleural p. The pressure in the pleural space, e.g., during mechanical ventilation or critical illness. It is normally lower than atmospheric pressure and therefore is sometimes called a negative pressure. It is rarely measured, except during mechanical ventilation, thoracentesis, or critical illness. SYN: *intrapleural p.; intrathoracic p.*

positive p. Pressure greater than atmospheric or greater than the pressure to which the initial pressure is being compared.

positive end-expiratory p. ABBR: PEEP. In respiratory medicine, a method of holding alveoli open during expiration. This is done by gradually increasing the expiratory pressure during mechanical ventilation. When PEEP is used, it is important to monitor the hemodynamic status of the patient because PEEP reduces venous return to the heart and cardiac output. The goal is to achieve adequate arterial oxygenation, without using toxic levels of oxygen and without compromising cardiac output.

⚠ The patient must be carefully monitored to allow observation for undesired side effects such as pneumomediastinum, subcutaneous emphysema, and pneumothorax.

positive end-expiratory p., auto ABBR: auto-PEEP. A complication of mechanical ventilation in which the ventilator does not permit the patient sufficient time to exhale. This causes air to be trapped in the lungs, particularly the alveoli. If continued, auto-PEEP causes respiratory muscle fatigue and can cause rupture of the lung (i.e., pneumothorax). Auto-PEEP may be corrected by increasing exhalation time, decreasing the ventilator rate, or switching the ventilation mode so that the patient's spontaneous respiratory pattern governs the inspiratory and expiratory times.

posterior cricoid p. Pressure applied by firmly placing the thumb and index finger on the lateral aspects of a patient's cricoid ring to occlude the esophagus. Once cricoid pressure is applied, it should not be discontinued until control of the airway (as by intubation to achieve a patent airway) has been established. SYN: *Sellick maneuver.*

pulmonary artery occlusive p. Pulmonary artery wedge **p.**

pulmonary artery wedge p. ABBR: PAWP. Pressure measured in the pulmonary artery after catheterization. The catheter is positioned in the pulmonary artery, and the distal portion of the catheter is isolated from pressure behind it in the artery by inflating a balloon with air. This allows the catheter to float into a wedged position and permits sensing of transmission of pressures ahead of the catheter (in the pulmonary capillary bed) by the transducer. Because no valve is present between this location and the left atrium, the measurement reflects left atrial pressure, and, in the presence of a competent mitral valve, the measurement provides an indication of left ventricular end-diastolic pressure. The balloon is then passively deflated after measurements of wedge pressure are completed. Elevated wedge pressures are found characteristically in patients with congestive heart failure or fluid overload. SYN: *pulmonary artery occlusive p.; wedge p.* SEE: *Swan-Ganz catheter.*

PATIENT CARE: The nurse prepares and sets up the transducer equipment to monitor pulmonary artery pressure and PAWP according to institutional protocol and the manufacturer's instructions. The transducer is balanced and calibrated as required (every 4 to 8 hr). Hemodynamic status is monitored, and findings are documented, including pulmonary artery pressure (normally 20 to 30 mm Hg systolic and 8 to 12 mm Hg diastolic) every hour as directed. To measure PAWP every 1 to 4 hr as directed, the nurse inflates the balloon with 0.75 to 1.5 cc of air depending on balloon size (the balloon is never inflated with fluid) while watching for change in waveform (indicating wedging) and assessing for balloon rupture (lack of resistance on inflation, with absence of wedging). If this occurs, the wedging procedure is discontinued (because of concern for air embolism), and therapy is managed based on pulmonary artery diastolic pressures. Pulmonary artery wedge pressure isread, documented (normally 4 to 12 mm Hg), and correlated to clinical findings and other hemodynamic values, and any abnormal findings are reported. The nurse then removes the syringe and permits passive deflation of the balloon while observing for reappearance of pulmonary artery pressure waveform. If the balloon remains inflated, the patient is at risk for pulmonary artery necrosis. The patient should be positioned on the right side and encouraged to take deep breaths and to cough as the nurse mobilizes the right arm. If the balloon remains wedged, the physician should be notified. Fluid and diuretic therapy are adjusted based on PAWP and other values as prescribed. Impedance cardiography may be employed as an alternative to invasive monitoring with a pulmonary artery catheter.

pulse p. The difference between systolic and diastolic pressures. The systolic pressure is normally about 40 points greater than the diastolic. A pulse pressure over 50 points or under 30 points is considered abnormal.

production p. The idea that an institution's quantity of productivity is more important than its quality. In health care institutions, the pressure to move patients quickly from one status or setting to another, or to maximize bed occupancy, may sometimes take precedence over attention to detail and the provision of optimal care. To counteract such pressures, health care professionals must communicate clearly and effectively with each other, follow established safe practices, have methods for reporting errors, and have protocols that link providers of different organizational status.

solution p. Pressure that tends to dissolve a solid present in a solution.

static p. **1.** The pressure in the circulatory system between pulses. **2.** Pressures that are present in a system when any variables that may impact the system are minimized.

systolic p. Systolic **blood pressure.**

threshold p. Effective osmotic **p.**

transpulmonary p. Alveolar pressure minus pleural pressure. When normal transpulmonary pressures are exceeded, air leaks may develop.

venous p. The pressure of the blood within the veins. It is highest near the periphery, diminishing progressively from capillaries to the heart. Near the heart the venous pressure may be below zero (negative pressure) owing to negative intrathoracic pressure.

wedge p. Pulmonary artery wedge **p.**

pressure pain threshold SEE: under *threshold.*

pressure point SEE: under *point.*

pressure sore Pressure **ulcer.**

pressure of speech Loud and emphatic speech that is increased in amount, accelerated, and usually difficult or impossible to interrupt. The speech is not in response to a stimulus and may continue even though no one is listening. It may be present in manic episodes, organic brain disease, depression with agitation, psychotic disorders, and sometimes as an acute reaction to stress.

pressure-time product ABBR: PTP. An estimate of respiratory muscle oxygen consumption during breathing. The PTP is sometimes represented mathematically as the integral of the esophageal and chest wall static recoil pressure curves. It estimates the work done

when the diaphragm moves and estimates the oxygen consumption when respiratory muscles contract isometrically but fail to move the chest wall or the diaphragm.

presymptomatic (prē″sĭmp-tō-măt′ĭk) The state of health before the clinical appearance of the signs and symptoms of a disease.

presynaptic (prē″sĭ-năp′tĭk) [″ + Gr. *synapsis,* point of contact] Anterior to the nerve synapse.

presyncope (prē″sĭng′kă-pē) Near fainting; the sensation that one is about to pass out.

presystole (prē-sĭs′tō-lē) [L. *prae,* before, in front of, + Gr. *systole,* contraction] The period in the heart's cycle just before the systole. SYN: *perisystole.*

presystolic (prē-sĭs-tŏl′ĭk) Before the systole of the heart.

pretarsal (prē-tăr′săl) [″ + Gr. *tarsos,* a broad flat surface] Anterior to the tarsus.

preterm (prē′tĕrm″) In obstetrics, occurring before the 37th week of gestation. SEE: *premature.*

late p. In pregnancy, pert. to the period between the 239th and the 259th day after the mother's last menstrual period.

preterm labor SEE: under *labor.*

prethalamus (prē-thăl′ŭ-mŭs) [″ + ″] Subthalamus.

pretibial (prē-tĭb′ē-ăl) [″ + *tibia,* shinbone] Anterior to the tibia.

pretracheal (prē′ trā′ kē-ĭl, prē-trā′kē-ĭl) [″ + ″] Anterior to the trachea.

pretreatment **1.** A priming treatment given before the main course of therapy or the main chemical modification of a substance. **2.** Before therapy.

wastewater p. In environmental practice, acting to attempt to eliminate, reduce, or alter polluted water after it enters the water treatment works.

Prevacid (prĕ′vă-sĭd) SEE: *lansoprazole.*

prevailing charge SEE: under *charge.*

prevalence (prĕv′ă-lĕns) [L. *praevalens,* prevail] The number of cases of a disease present in a specified population at a given time. SEE: *incidence.*

point p. The prevalence of a disease during a specified time.

prevention (pri-vĕn′shŏn) The anticipation of harm, disease, or injury and the measures taken to block their effects. SEE: *preventive medicine; preventive nursing.*

primary p. Limiting the spread of illness to previously unaffected patients or populations.

secondary p. Limiting the impact or the recurrence of an illness in patients already afflicted by it.

preventive (prē-vĕn′tĭv) Hindering the occurrence of something, esp. disease. SEE: *prophylactic* (1).

preventive medicine SEE: under *medicine; prevention; preventive **nursing***.

preventive nursing SEE: under *nursing*.

preventive supplementation SEE: under *supplementation*.

prevertebral (prē-věr′tē-brăl) [L. *prae,* before, in front of, + *vertebra,* vertebra] In front of a vertebra.

previa, praevia (prē′vē-ă) [L.] Appearing before or in front of.

previable (prē′ vī′ ă-bĭl) Pert. to a fetus not sufficiently mature to survive outside the uterus.

Prevnar (prěv′năr) Pneumococcal sevenvalent conjugate vaccine

prevocational evaluation (prē-vō-kā′shŭn-ăl) In rehabilitation, the assessment of those interests, aptitudes, abilities, and behavioral traits that are necessary for developing or performing specific job skills.

Prevotella (prē-vō-těl′ ă) A genus of gram-negative, rod-shaped, anaerobic bacteria that colonizes the oral cavity and genital organs. Members of the genus cause abscesses, blood-borne infections, genital infections, periodonitis, and wound infections.

prezygotic (prē-zī-gŏt′ĭk) [″ + *zygotos,* yoked] Happening before fertilization of the ovum.

priapism (prī′ă-pĭzm) [LL. *priapismus*] Abnormal, painful, and continued erection of the penis caused by disease, occurring usually without sexual desire. SEE: *erection; gonorrhea.*

ETIOLOGY: It may be due to lesions of the cord above the lumbar region; turgescence of the corpora cavernosa without erection may exist. It may be reflex from peripheral sensory irritants, from organic irritation of nerve tracts or nerve centers when libido may be lacking. It is sometimes seen in patients as a complication of sickle cell disease or acute leukemia. It can also be due to medicines injected into the penis to promote erection.

stuttering p. Painful, recurrent attacks of priapism that last 2 to 6 hr. The condition is seen in some patients with homozygous sickle cell disease.

PRICE (prīs) [An acronym for *protection, rest, ice, compression, elevation*] A regimen that supports healing in overuse injuries.

prick (prĭk) To penetrate or puncture the skin with a sharp object, e.g., with a needle during phlebotomy or a test for allergen hypersensitivity.

prickly heat (prĭk′lē) SEE: under *heat.*

prickly pear cactus (prĭk′lē păr kăk′tŭs) The fruit of any of the cacti of the genus *Opuntia,* native to and a staple food in Mexico and Central America. SYN: *nopal.*

-pril A suffix used in pharmacology to designate an angiotensin-converting enzyme (ACE) inhibitor.

Prilosec (prī′lō-sěk) SEE: *omeprazole.*

primal scene (prī′măl) In psychiatry, the term for a child's first observation of sexual intercourse, real or imagined.

primary (prī′mă-rē) [L. *primarius,* principal] First in time or order. SEE: *principal.*

primary acute respiratory distress syndrome Acute respiratory distress syndrome that results from direct injury to lung tissues. SEE: *acute respiratory distress syndrome.*

primary antiphospholipid antibody syndrome Antiphospholipid antibody syndrome that occurs in the absence of other rheumatologic disorders.

primary care provider SEE: under *provider.*

primary effusion lymphoma SEE: under *lymphoma.*

primary health care Primary **care**.

primary nursing SEE: under *nursing.*

primary progressive aphasia ABBR: PPA. SEE: under *aphasia.*

primary sore SEE: under *sore.*

primary teeth The deciduous teeth, colloquially known as baby teeth.

primate (prī′māt) [L. *primus,* first] A member of the order Primates.

Primates (prī-mā′tēz) An order of vertebrates belonging to the class Mammalia, subclass Theria, including the lemurs, tarsiers, monkeys, apes, and humans. This order is most highly developed with respect to the brain and nervous system.

prime (prīm) [L. *primus,* first] **1.** The period of greatest health and strength. **2.** To give an initial treatment in preparation for either a larger dose of the same medicine, or a different medicine.

primer (prīm′ ĕr) A sequence of nucleotides that starts the replication or transcription of a gene.

primigravida (prī″mĭ-grav′ĭd-ă, ′ĭ-dē″) *pl.* **primigravidae, primigravidas** [L. *primus,* first + *gravida*] A woman during her first pregnancy.

elderly p. A woman who is 35 years of age or older and pregnant for the first time. Congenital diseases related to chromosomal duplication may increase with maternal age, e.g., Down syndrome (trisomy 21).

primipara (prī-mĭp′ă-ră) [″ + *parere,* to bring forth, to bear] A woman who has been delivered of one infant of 500 g (or of 20 weeks' gestation), regardless of its viability.

primiparous (prī-mĭp′ă-rŭs) Pert. to a primipara.

primitive (prĭm′ĭ-tĭv) [L. *primitivus*] Original; early in point of time; embryonic.

primitive streak SEE: under *streak.*

primordial (prī-mor′dē-ăl) [L. *primordialis*] **1.** Existing first. **2.** Existing in an undeveloped, primitive, or early form.

primordium (prī-mord′ē-ŭm) *pl.* **primordia** [L. *primordium,* origin] Anlage.

primum non nocere (prī″mŭm nōn nō′sĕ-rā) [L.] "First do no harm," the goal in health care, of avoiding actions that may worsen a patient's disease or suffering. SEE: *risk-benefit analysis.*

princeps (prĭn′sĕps) [L., chief] **1.** Original; first. **2.** The name of certain arteries (e.g., princeps cervicis). **3.** Chief, principal.

principal (prĭn′sĭ-păl) **1.** Chief. **2.** Outstanding.

principle (prĭn′sĭ-pl) [L. *principium,* foundation] **1.** A constituent of a compound representing its essential properties. **2.** A fundamental truth. **3.** An established rule of action.

   active p. The ingredient of a pharmaceutical preparation that produces the therapeutic action.

   air gap p. A procedure to decrease the amount of scattered radiation reaching the radiographic film by increasing the object-image receptor distance.

   Arndt-Schultz p. SEE: *Arndt-Schultz principle.*

   Fick p. SEE: under *Fick, Adolf Eugen.*

   gastrointestinal p. An archaic term used for hormones, such as cholecystokinin, gastrin, and secretin, which are secreted by mucosal cells of the gastrointestinal tract and absorbed into the blood.

   labeled line p. A hypothesis to explain how different nerves, all of which use the same physiological principles in transmitting impulses along their axons, are able to generate different sensations. Structurally similar nerves can generate distinct sensory perceptions if they are connected to unique neurons in the central nervous system that are capable of decoding similar nerve signals in different ways.

   pleasure p. In psychoanalytic theory, the idea that people strive to avoid pain, hunger, and physical or psychological stresses in favor of pleasant experiences, e.g., food, sex, and narcissistic satisfaction

   precautionary p. A risk management principle, originally developed in the environmental movement, based on the concept of avoiding any new action (e.g., introducing a new technology or a new drug) that carries a hypothetical risk for human health or the environment, regardless of whether the hypothesis has been subjected to formal testing.

   reality p. In psychoanalysis, the idea that the striving for narcissistic pleasure can never be absolute but must be balanced against competing demands placed on the self by other persons and situations.

Pringle maneuver (pring′gĕl) [James Hogarth Pringle, Australian surgeon, 1863–1941] Securing the hepatic pedicle with a clamp during resection or hepatectomy of the liver to diminish the loss of blood.

Prinivil (prĭn′ĭ-vĭl) SEE: *lisinopril.*

Prinzmetal angina (prins′met″ăl) [Myron Prinzmetal, U.S. cardiologist, 1908–1987] Variant **angina.**

prion (prē′ŏn) A small proteinaceous infectious particle that is believed to be responsible for central nervous system diseases (*spongiform encephalopathies*) in humans and other mammals.

prion disease Any transmissible neurodegenerative disease believed to be caused by a proteinaceous infectious particle (also known as prion proteins, or PrPs). PrPs change other cellular proteins, producing intracellular vacuoles (spongiform change) that disrupt the functioning of neurons. Included in this group are Creutzfeldt-Jacob disease, Gerstmann-Strüssler-Scheinker syndrome, kuru, and fatal familial insomnia in humans, mad cow disease (bovine spongiform encephalopathy), and scrapie in sheep and goats. Prion diseases may be transmitted by hereditary changes in the gene coding PrP; by contaminated biological agents such as plasma or serum, human growth hormone, and organ transplants; and, possibly, by eating the meat of infected animals. All prion diseases are marked by a long incubation period followed by a rapidly progressive dementia.

prior authorization The approval by an insurer or other third-party payor of a health care service before the service is rendered. This approval is required in order for the insurer to pay the provider for the service.

Priorix-Tetra (prī′ŏ-riks-te′tră) Live attenuated measles, mumps, rubella, and varicella-zoster vaccine.

prism (prĭzm) [Gr. *prisma*] A transparent solid, three sides of which are parallelograms. The bases, perpendicular to the three sides, are triangles, and a transverse section of the solid is a triangle. Light rays going through a prism are deflected toward the base of the triangle and at the same time are split into the primary colors.

   enamel p. Enamel **rod.**

   Maddox p. Two base-together prisms used in testing for cyclophoria or torsion of the eyeball.

   Nicol p. A prism made by splitting a prism of Icelandic spar and rejoining the cut surfaces. This causes the light passing through to be split. Ordinary light rays are reflected by the joined surfaces, and polarized light is transmitted.

   Risley rotary p. A prism mounted in a device that allows it to be rotated.

This is used in testing eye muscle imbalance.

prismatic (prĭz-măt′ĭk) **1.** Shaped like a prism. **2.** Produced by a prism.

privacy (prī′vă-sē) In the medical context, the rights of a patient to control the distribution and release of data concerning his or her illness. This includes information the patient has provided to health care professionals and all additional information contained in the chart, medical records, and laboratory data. Failure to observe this aspect of a patient's rights is classed as an invasion of privacy.

privacy officer (prī′vĭ-sē ŏf′ĭ-sĭr) The health care administrator responsible for safeguarding patient confidentiality at a clinic or hospital. Under regulations of the Health Insurance Portability and Accountability Act (HIPAA), the privacy officer oversees institutional privacy policies, procedures, and rules.

private patient A patient whose care is the responsibility of one identifiable health care professional, usually a physician or dentist. The health care professional is paid directly, either by the patient or by the patient's insurer.

private practice SEE: under *practice.*

privilege (prĭv′ĭ-lĭj) [L. *privilegium,* law affecting a single person, prerogative] **1.** A right granted to a person in recognition of some special status, e.g., a right to practice one's profession in a health care facility. **2.** An immunity from commonly imposed standards or laws.

privileged communication SEE: under *communication.*

prn [L. *pro re nata*]; according to circumstances; as necessary. Frequently used in prescription and order writing.

pro- [L., Gr. *pro,* before] Prefix indicating *for, in front of, before, from, in behalf of, on account of,* or, in chemistry, *precursor (of).* SEE: also *ante-; pre-.*

proaccelerin (prō″ak-sel′-ĕ-rĭn) Coagulation factor V, a protein of the coagulation system, functioning as a cofactor in forming thrombin from prothrombin. SYN: *labile* **factor.** SEE: *blood* **coagulation;** *coagulation* **factor.**

proanthocyanidin (prō-ăn″thō-sī-ăn′ĭ-dĭn) A chemical in cranberry juice that is believed to inhibit the adhesion of *Escherichia coli* to the mucosa of the urinary tract.

proarrhythmia (prō-ă-rĭth′mē-ă) An arrhythmia that is stimulated, provoked, or worsened by drug therapy. **proarrhythmic,** *adj.*

probability (prob″ă-bil′ĭt-ē) [L. *probabilitas,* likelihood] **1.** Likelihood. **2.** The ratio that expresses the possibility of the occurrence of a specific event. The probability of a tossed coin landing heads or tails is one-half or 50% each. This 50% probability remains the same every time a coin is tossed. Probability ratios based on sophisticated techniques are used for estimating the chance of occurrence of diseases in a population and in projecting vital statistics such as birth and death rates.

 pretest p. An estimate of a patient's likelihood of illness. It is based on or derived from the prevalence of disease in a community.

proband (prō′bănd″) [L. *probare,* to test] The initial subject presenting a mental or physical disorder and who causes a study of his or her heredity in order to determine if other members of the family have had the same disease or carry it. SYN: *index case; propositus.*

probang (prō′băng) A slim, flexible rod with a sponge or similar material attached to the end; used for determining the location of strictures in the larynx or esophagus and for removing objects from the trachea. Medicines may also be applied to these areas by use of this device.

probation (prō-bā′shŏn) **1.** In the criminal justice system, a period of legal oversight of one's behavior after release from incarceration or instead of incarceration after conviction for a crime. **2.** A period after an employee is hired during which the employee's on-the-job performance is evaluated. During this time the employee may need to demonstrate his or her suitability for continued work and in many instances may not receive full salary or benefits.

probationer (prō-bā′shŭn-ĕr) A person being evaluated while working during a trial period, as a student nurse just after entering training.

probe (prōb) [L. *probare,* to test] **1.** A long, thin instrument for exploring the depth or direction of a wound, sinus, or sulcus. **2.** Transducer

 dental p. A dental instrument formally known as a periodontal probe.

 Florida p. A periodontal probe connected to a computer that measures the depth of periodontal pockets automatically.

 heater p. A surgical instrument that is advanced through an endoscope and used to cauterize bleeding peptic ulcers. The probe applies thermal energy directly to the bleeding vessel, and works best when it is pressed forcefully onto the lesion.

 periodontal p. A fine-caliber probe, calibrated in millimeters, designed and used to measure the depth and extent of the gingival sulcus and periodontal pockets present.

probing depth In periodontics, the measured distance from the free end of the gingival margin to the bottom of the periodontal pocket.

probiotic (prō″bī-ŏ′tĭk) [Gr. *pro,* on behalf of, + *bios,* life] Having favorable or health-promoting effect on living cells and tissues. For example, *Lactobacillus acidophilus* present in the gastrointestinal tract is probiotic because its presence inhibits the growth of harmful bacteria such as *Salmonella* and *Listeria*.

probity (prō′ bĭ-tē, prŏb′) Rectitude, integrity, or honesty; a characteristic expected of professionals.

problem drinking The consumption of any amount of alcohol that causes life problems for the drinker. Issues related to the unhealthy use of alcohol arise when drinking compromises one's job, legal standing, social relationships, or health. Problem drinking is often used as a synonym for alcohol abuse or alcoholism.

problem list (prob′lĕm) [Gr. *problēma*, obstacle] A summary of a patient's pertinent medical history or active, unresolved health concerns.

problem-oriented medical record ABBR: POMR. Method of establishing and maintaining the patient's medical record so that problems are clearly listed, usually in order of importance, and a rational plan for dealing with them is stated. These data are kept at the front of the chart and are evaluated as frequently as indicated with respect to recording changes in the patient's status as well as progress made in solving the problems. Use of this system may bring a degree of comprehensiveness to total patient care that might not be possible with conventional medical records.

problem-oriented record ABBR: POR. SEE: *problem-oriented medical record*.

problem-solving therapy ABBR: PST. A form of brief psychotherapy (typically lasting 10 sessions or less) in which patients are taught a structured approach to recognizing problems and finding workable solutions.

pro bono publico (prō bō′ nō pŭb′ lĭ-kō, poob-) Rendered for the public good (i.e., without financial reward).

procalcitonin (prō-kal″sĭ-tō′nĭn) [*pro-* + *calcitonin*] ABBR: PCT. A polypeptide produced within C cells in the thyroid gland. It is composed of 116 amino acids and has a molecular weight of 13 kD. Cleavage of the molecule liberates calcitonin. In severe bacterial infections, procalcitonin is released from the thyroid into the blood. Laboratory tests for the molecule can help distinguish bacterial infections from viral infections.

procarboxypeptidase (prō″kar-bok″sē-pep″tĭ-dās″, -dāz″) [*pro-* + *carboxypeptidase*] The inactive precursor of carboxypeptidase, which is activated by trypsin.

procarcinogen (prō″kar-sin′ŏ-jĕn) [*pro-* + *carcinogen*] An agent that may cause cancer only after it is metabolized within an organism.

procaryote (prō-kăr′ē-ōt) [Gr. *pro*, before, + *karyon*, nucleus] Prokaryote.

procedure (prō-sē′jŭr) [Fr. *procédure*, ult. fr. L. *procedere*, to go forward] A particular way of accomplishing a desired result.

Blalock-Hanlon p. SEE: *Blalock-Hanlon procedure*.

Burch p. SEE: *Burch procedure*.

Chamberlain p. SEE: *Chamberlain procedure*.

commando p. A surgical procedure for cancers of the head and neck in which the entire tumor, neighboring lymph nodes, and a portion of the mandible are removed.

ex-utero-intrapartum p. ABBR: EXIT. A modification of a cesarean delivery, in which after delivery the fetus remains attached to the umbilical cord until its airway is securely intubated. The EXIT procedure is used during those assisted births in which severe airway obstruction or respiratory insufficiency is suspected.

Fontan p. SEE: *Fontan procedure*.

Hartmann p. SEE: *Hartmann procedure*.

Heller p. SEE: *Heller procedure*.

invasive p. A procedure in which the body is penetrated or entered, e.g., by a tube, needle, or ionizing radiation.

Kasai p. SEE: *Kasai procedure*.

Marshall-Marchetti-Krantz p. SEE: *Marshall-Marchetti-Krantz procedure*.

MAZE p. A surgical treatment for atrial fibrillation, in which the right and left pulmonary veins are isolated and the left atrial appendix is surgically removed. Incisions are made to disrupt the irregular fibrillatory flow of electricity through the atrium, constructing a path shaped like a labyrinth, which directs energy solely from the sinoatrial node to the atrioventricular node. The procedure is often performed during other heart surgeries, e.g., coronary artery bypass grafting.

Mitrofanoff p. SEE: *Mitrofanoff procedure*.

Mustard p. SEE: *Mustard procedure*.

Puestow p. SEE: *Puestow procedure*.

Rashkind p. SEE: *Rashkind procedure*.

Ross p. SEE: *Ross procedure*.

staged p. Any operation undertaken in two or more separate parts, with a lull between the two stages to facilitate tissue healing or clearance of infection.

Toupet p. SEE: *Toupet procedure*.

procentriole (prō-sĕn′trē-ōl) The early form of the centrioles and ciliary basal bodies in the cell. SEE: *centriole*.

procercoid (prō-sĕr′koyd) The first larval stage in the development of certain cestodes belonging to the order Pseudophyllidea. It is an elongated structure that develops in crustaceans.

process (pros′es″) [L. *processus*, going

forwards, an advance] **1.** A method of action. **2.** The state of progress of a disease. **3.** A projection or outgrowth of bone or tissue. **4.** A series of steps or events that lead to achievement of specific results.

acromial p. Acromion.

alveolar p. The portion of the mandible and maxilla containing the tooth sockets. SYN: *alveolar* **bone**.

articular p. of vertebra One of four small, flat processes (two superior and two inferior) by which vertebrae articulate with each other.

basilar p. The narrow part of the base of the occipital bone, in front of the foramen magnum, articulating with the sphenoid bone. SYN: *pars basilaris ossis occipitalis*.

caudate p. The process of the caudate lobe of the liver extending under the right lobe.

ciliary p. One of about 70 prominent meridional ridges projecting from the corona ciliaris of the choroid coat of the eye to which the suspensory ligament of the lens is attached. These have the same structure as the rest of the choroid and secrete aqueous humor, which nourishes neighboring parts, the cornea, and lens.

clinoid p. Any of three pairs of bony processes on the top of the body of the sphenoid bone, overhanging the edges of the sella turcica.

condyloid p. A posterior process on the superior border of the ramus of the mandible consisting of a capitulum and neck. It articulates with the mandibular fossa of the temporal bone. SEE: *mandible* for illus.

coracoid p. A beak-shaped process extending upward and laterally from the neck of the scapula. The coracoid process is not part of any bone-to-bone articulation although the coracoclavicular ligament holds the clavicle against the acromium of the scapula. The muscles attaching to the coracoid process are the pectoralis major, coracobrachialis, and the short head of the biceps brachii. SEE: *scapula*.

coronoid p. **1.** The process on the proximal end of the ulna that forms the anterior portion of the semilunar notch. **2.** The process on the anterior upper end of the ramus of the mandible that serves for attachment of the temporalis muscle. SEE: *mandible* for illus.

due p. The standard or customary application of prevailing laws or rules and the protections that follow from their application.

ensiform p. Xiphoid **p.**

frontal p. An upward projection of the maxilla that articulates with the frontal bone; forms part of the orbit and nasal fossa.

lenticular p. A knob on the incus, an auditory ossicle. articulating with the stapes.

mastoid p. A horn-shaped process of the mastoid portion of the temporal bone extending downward and forward behind the external auditory meatus. It serves for attachment of the sternocleidomastoid, splenius capitis, and longissimus capitis muscles.

nursing p. SEE: *nursing process*.

odontoid p. A toothlike process extending upward from the axis and about which the atlas rotates. SYN: *dens*. SEE: illus.

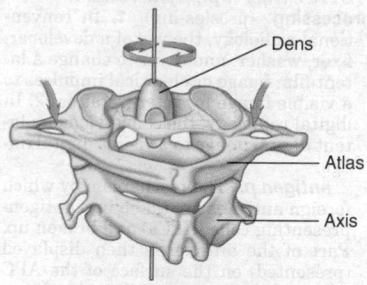

ODONTOID PROCESS

Articulation of atlas and axis

olecranon p. Olecranon.

palatine p. A process extending transversely from the medial surface of the maxilla. With the corresponding process from the other side, it forms the major portion of the hard palate.

pterygoid p. The process of the sphenoid bone extending downward from the junction of the body and great wing. It consists of the lateral and medial pterygoid plates, which are fused at the top. The top of the pterygoid process is pierced by the pterygoid canal.

spinous p. The prominence at the posterior part of each vertebra.

spinous p. of vertebrae The posteriormost part of a vertebra. This spine projects back and serves as a point of attachment for muscles of the back.

styloid p. **1.** A pointed process of the temporal bone, projecting downward, and to which some of the muscles of the tongue are attached. **2.** A pointed projection behind the head of the fibula. **3.** A protuberance on the outer portion of the distal end of the radius. **4.** An ulnar projection on the inner side of the distal end.

transverse p. The process extending laterally and dorsally from the arch of a vertebra.

unciform p. **1.** A long thin lamina of bone from the orbital plate of the ethmoid articulating with the inferior turbinate. **2.** The hook at the anterior end of the hippocampal gyrus. **3.** The hooked end of the unciform bone.

uncinate p. of the ethmoid bone A sickle-shaped bony process on the medial wall of the ethmoidal labyrinth below the concha.

vermiform p. Vermiform **appendix**.

vocal p. The process of the arytenoid cartilage that serves for attachment of the vocal cord.

xiphoid p. The lowest portion of the sternum; a sword-shaped cartilaginous process supported by bone. No ribs attach to the xiphoid process; however, some abdominal muscles are attached. The xiphoid process ossifies in the aged SYN: *ensiform p.; xiphisternum.*

processing (pros′es-ing) **1.** In conventional radiology, the use of a developer, fixer, washer, and dryer to change a latent film image or electrical impulses to a visible image for interpretation. **2.** In digital radiology, the conversion of a latent digital image to a visible digital image.

antigen p. The mechanism by which foreign antigens are taken into antigen-presenting cells (APCs) and broken up. Part of the antigen is then displayed (presented) on the surface of the APC next to a histocompatibility or self-antigen, activating T lymphocytes and cell-mediated immunity. T lymphocytes are unable to recognize or respond to most antigens without APC assistance. SEE: *antigen; macrophage p.; self.*

daylight p. An automatic system that accepts radiographic film, inserts it into the processor, and refills the cassette without the need for a darkroom.

extended p. In mammography, an increase of the development time or developer temperature to enhance image contrast and/or lower the radiation dose to the patient.

image p. Any of the computer-aided improvements in a radiological image to highlight some of its features and/or improve its contrast or definition.

macrophage p. The mechanism by which foreign antigens are taken into the macrophage by phagocytosis and broken up. Part of the antigen is then displayed on the surface of the macrophage next to a histocompatibility or self-antigen activating T lymphocytes and the specific immune response. T lymphocytes are unable to recognize or respond to most antigens without macrophage assistance.

natural language p. ABBR: NLP. **1.** The automated analysis of a text for phrases, meanings, or trends in word use. It is used in health care to extract information from electronic medical records, to classify and code the material found, to develop nomenclature, and to develop hypotheses about the data obtained. **2.** The cognitive process by which people learn how to understand words, grammar and diction.

processor (pros′es-ŏr) **1.** In radiology, a machine that helps to convert the latent image to a visible image. In digital radiology, it consists of a unit designed to convert a latent image into a visible image by computerized measurements from image detection equipment. In conventional radiology, it consists of a transporter, electrical system, temperature control, circulation system, and dryer. **2.** SEE: *tissue processor.* **3.** That portion of a computer's central processing unit that analyzes and prepares information for display.

procidentia (prō″sĭ-dĕn′shē-ă) [L.] Prolapse of the uterus.

proclination (prok″lĭ-nā′shŏn) [L. *proclinatio,* a leaning forward] Anterior inclination of one of the incisors.

procoagulant (prō″kō-ag′yŭ-lănt) [*pro- + coagulant*] **1.** Speeding or promoting blood clotting. **2.** An agent that speeds or promotes blood clotting.

procoagulant factor (prō″kō-ag′yŭ-lănt) SEE: under *factor.*

procollagen (prō-kŏl′ă-jĕn) [″ + *kolla,* glue, + *gennan,* to produce] A precursor of collagen.

proconvertin (prō″kŏn-vĕrt′ĭn) Serum prothrombin conversion accelerator.

proconvulsive (prō-kŏn-vŭl′sĭv) Able or likely to provoke seizures.

procreate (prō′krē-āt) [L. *procreare*] To beget; to be the parents of an infant.

procreation (prō″krē-ā′shŭn) The act or state of conceiving and giving birth to an infant. SYN: *reproduction.*

proctalgia (prŏk-tăl′jē-ă) [″ + *algos,* pain] Pain in or around the anus and rectum.

p. fugax Severe rectal or anal pain, usually occurring in young men, possibly as a result of muscular spasms.

proctectomy (prŏk-tĕk′tō-mē) [″ + *ektome,* excision] Excision of the rectum or anus.

proctitis (prok-tīt′ĭs) [*procto- + -itis*] Inflammation of the rectum and anus that may be caused by sexually transmitted diseases, e.g., infections with herpes simplex virus, *Neisseria gonorrhoeae, Chlamydia trachomatis*; radiation injury, e.g., after treatment of cancers of the pelvis; inflammatory bowel disease, e.g., ulcerative colitis; allergy; trauma; or ischemia.

diphtheritic p. Proctitis caused by diphtheria. It is now a rare condition when vaccination against diphtheria is routine.

dysenteric p. Proctitis due to infectious diarrhea. It may produce ulcers and scarring of the rectum and anus.

gonococcal p. Gonorrheal infection around the rectum and anus.

traumatic p. Proctitis due to anal or rectal injury.

procto-, proct- [Gr *prōktos,* anus] Prefixes meaning *anus, rectum.*

proctoclysis (prŏk-tŏk'lĭ-sĭs) [" + *klysis,* a washing] Hydration of patients using a continuous slow infusion of fluids into the rectum and colon. The treatment sometimes is used for palliation of thirst in terminally ill patients who cannot receive fluids by other means. SEE: *enteroclysis.*

THERAPEUTIC EFFECT: This procedure has the following therapeutic effects: to supply fluid in postoperative cases when fluids cannot be taken otherwise; to supply the body with fluid as in hemorrhage, vomiting, or diarrhea; to relieve thirst as in persistent vomiting; and to lower body temperature by giving ice water enemas.

PATIENT CARE: Any hydrating solution may be used, e.g., saline, free water, dextrose in water, depending on the patient's fluid or electrolyte needs. After the bowel is evacuated, a catheter is inserted approx. 40 cm into the bowel, and fluids are given at 250 to 300 mL/hr or less, depending on tolerance. If pain or distention develop, treatment should be discontinued.

proctocolitis (prŏk"tō-kō-lī'tĭs) [" + *kolon,* colon, + *itis,* inflammation] Inflammation of the colon and rectum.

proctodeum (prŏk-tō-dē'ŭm) [" + *hodaios,* a way] An ectodermal depression located caudally that, upon rupture of the cloacal membrane, forms the anal canal.

proctologic (prŏk"tō-lŏj'ĭk) [" + *logos,* word, reason] Pert. to proctology.

proctologist (prok-tol'ŏ-jĭst) [*proctology* + *-ist*] A dated term for a surgeon whose practice is restricted to the rectum and anus. SEE: *colorectal surgeon.*

proctology (prŏk-tŏl'ō-jē) The phase of medicine dealing with treatment of diseases of the colon, rectum, and anus.

proctoscope (prŏk'tă-skōp") [" + "] An instrument used to inspect the rectum visually.

proctoscopy (prŏk-tŏs'kō-pē) Inspection of the rectum with a proctoscope.

proctosigmoidectomy (prŏk"tō-sig"moyd-ek'tō-mē) [*procto-* + *sigmoidectomy*] Surgical removal of the anus, rectum, and sigmoid flexure of the colon.

proctosigmoiditis (prŏk"tō-sĭg"moyd-ī'tĭs) [" + " + *eidos,* form, shape, + *itis,* inflammation] Inflammation of the rectum and sigmoid.

proctosigmoidoscopy (prŏk"tō-sig"moy"dos'kō-pē) [*procto-* + *sigmoidoscopy*] Visual examination of the rectum and sigmoid colon. SYN: *anosigmoidoscopy.*

proctostomy (prŏk-tŏs'tō-mē) [" + *stoma,* mouth] Surgical creation of a permanent opening into the rectum.

proctotomy (prŏk-tŏt'ō-mē) Incision of the rectum or anus.

PATIENT CARE: The dressing is assessed frequently and the presence and amount of bleeding and drainage are recorded. Dressings should be changed or reinforced as prescribed by the physician. A T binder (female patients) or split T binder (male patients) is advantageous to ensure proper placement of the dressing. Pain is assessed and analgesia provided as prescribed. The wound is assessed for infection, and antibiotics prescribed as needed.

procumbent (prō-kŭm'bĕnt) [L. *procumbens,* lying down] Prone.

procure (prō-kūr') [L. *procurare,* to take care of] To obtain (e.g., an organ from a donor).

prodigiosin (prō-dĭj-ē-ō'sĭn) A bright red pigmented chemical synthesized by *Serratia marcescens* and several other bacteria. It is cytotoxic and antibacterial.

prodromal (prō-drō'măl) [Gr. *prodromos,* running before] Pert. to the initial stage of a disease; the interval between the earliest symptoms and the appearance of a rash or fever.

prodrome (prō-drōm) *pl.* **prodromes,prodromata** A symptom indicative of an approaching disease.

prodrug (prō'drŭg") An inert drug that becomes active only after it is transformed or metabolized by the body.

    carrier p. A prodrug that is transiently attached to another chemical used to ferry it to its target or in other ways improve its bioavailability and kinetics. SYN: *carrier-linked p.*

    carrier-linked p. Carrier prodrug.

product (prod'ŭkt) [L. *productum,* result (in arithmetic)] Anything that is made; also, the resulting compound after the reaction of two chemical substances. Particular reactions are listed under the first word. SEE: e.g., *decay product; pressure-time product; substitution product.*

production (prō-dŭk'shŭn) Development or formation of a substance.

production pressure SEE: under *pressure.*

productive (prō-dŭk'tĭv) Forming, esp. new tissue.

productive burping The backflow (vomiting) of food from the upper pouch of a patient who has a gastric band in place for weight loss. It can result from eating too quickly or too much, practices that overwhelm the capacity of the pouch.

productive inflammation SEE: under *inflammation.*

product liability The debt that manufacturers and sellers owe the public for any damages their products cause. In health care, the U.S. Food and Drug Administration and applicable tort law regulate the responsibility for consumer product safety of medical devices, new technologies, prostheses and implants, telecommunications machinery, office equipment, supplies, and drugs.

proenzyme (prō-ĕn'zīm) ["' + *en,* in, + *zyme,* a leaven] The inactive form of an enzyme found within a cell, which, upon leaving the cell, is converted into the active form, such as pepsinogen, which is cleaved to pepsin by hydrochloric acid in gastric juice.

proestrus (prō-ĕs'trŭs) The period preceding estrus in females, characterized by development of ovarian follicles and uterine endometrium.

professional (prō-fĕsh'ŭn-ăl) Pert. to a profession.

   p. misconduct Behavior that is professionally unsuitable, potentially dangerous to patients, incompetent, disruptive, abusive, or illegal.

   nonphysician p. Nonphysician **provider**.

professionalism (prō-fĕsh'ŏn-ăl-ĭz"m) **1.** The competence and skill expected and required of a professional. **2.** The status, practice, and methods of a professional as opposed to an amateur (e.g., in sports or music). SEE: *professional competence.*

professional liability The obligation of health care providers or their insurers to pay for damages resulting from the provider's negligent acts of omission or commission in treating patients.

professional liability insurance A type of insurance contract that provides compensation for a person or party injured by a professional's acts or omissions. Two common types of policies are as follows: (1) *Claims made.* The claim for damages by the injured party must be made during the policy coverage period in order for the professional to be covered and represented by the insurance company. (2) *Occurrence basis.* The claim for damages by the injured party is covered by the insurance company as long as the act of professional liability occurs during the policy coverage period, even though the claim is filed after the coverage period ends.

Professional Standards Review Organization ABBR: PSRO. Peer review at the local level required by Public Law 92-603 of the U.S. for the services provided under the Medicare, Medicaid, and maternal and child health programs funded by the federal government. The major goals of the PSRO program are as follows: to ensure that health care services are of acceptable professional quality; to ensure appropriate use of health care facilities at the most economical level consistent with professional standards; to identify lack of quality and overuse problems in health care and improve those conditions; to attempt to obtain voluntary correction of inappropriate or unnecessary practitioner and facility practices, and, if unable to do so, recommend sanctions against violators.

profibrinolysin (prō"fī-brĭ-nō-lī'sĭn) [Gr. *pro,* before, + L. *fibra,* fiber, + Gr. *lysis,* dissolution] The inactive precursor of the proteolytic enzyme fibrinolysin.

proficiency (prō-fĭsh'ĕn-sē) [L. *proficere,* to move forward, to accomplish] Expertise; skill.

proficiency test 1. A formal assessment of the quality of work. Proficiency tests for health care personnel are commonly performed in the clinical laboratory to ensure that standard procedures are followed and that laboratory results are reliable. **2.** The validation of a laboratory's accuracy by examination of unknown specimens submitted to the laboratory by an independent agency. In the U.S., all laboratories that examine human specimens must undergo external validation of their accuracy several times a year.

profile (prō'fīl") [Italian *proffilo,* an outline] **1.** An outline of the lateral view of an object, esp. the human head. **2.** A summary, graph, or table presenting a subject's most notable characteristics. **3.** A comprehensive history of the use of health care services. SEE: *practice p.*

   biophysical p. ABBR: BPP. A system of estimating current fetal status, determined by analyzing five variables via ultrasonography and nonstress testing. Fetal breathing movements, gross body movement, fetal tone, amniotic fluid volume, and fetal heart rate reactivity are each assigned specific values. Each expected normal finding is rated as 2; each abnormal finding is rated as 0. Scores of 8 to 10 with normal amniotic fluid volume and a reactive nonstress test (NST) indicate satisfactory fetal status. A score of 6 with normal amniotic fluid volume requires reassessment of a preterm fetus within 24 hr of delivery. Scores of less than 6 or a nonreactive NST indicate fetal compromise and require prompt delivery. SYN: *fetal biophysical p.* SEE: *Apgar score.*

   chemistry p. Chemistry panel.

   drug p. The unique characteristics of a drug or class of drugs, including their administration, absorption, metabolism, duration of action, toxicity, and interactions with foods or other medications.

   fetal biophysical p. Biophysical **p.**

   functional ambulation p. The formal evaluation of a person's ability to walk, e.g., while being filmed on a grid or walkway with pressure-sensitive sensors, during initiation of movement, while making turns, or while treading on level or uneven ground. Ambulation or gait assessments identify the risk of falling and may suggest assistive devices or therapeutic exercises that can be employed to lessen the risk. SYN: *functional gait assessment*.

iceberg p. The profile of a person with a psychological outlook characterized by more vigor and less tension, depression, anger, fatigue, and confusion than is found in others. This type of affect often is found in elite athletes and others with physically active lifestyles.

occupational p. Those components of an occupational therapy evaluation that collectively provide non–performance-related information, e.g., the individual's interests, values, experiences, occupational history, and needs.

practice p. A performance-based method of assessing the professional behaviors of individual practitioners. A typical profile may include data about a practitioner's patients, their known illnesses, their drug therapies, their immunization history, hospitalization rate, use of other services, and the cost of specific aspects of their care. The profile of an individual practitioner's performance could provide information such as the number of his or her patients who are screened for cancer or diabetes mellitus, or the number of patients treated for a particular condition who survive. The profile could be used to further a practitioner's education, to influence future care patterns, to certify or recertify health care providers, or to assist decisions about the hiring, retention, or dismissal of professionals who provide health care services. The outcome of establishing practice profiles could help to increase the quality of medical care and to provide patients the opportunity of evaluating physicians. The methods used to profile practice are constantlyevolving.

PULSES p. One of the first formal, widely used scales to assess daily living skills. PULSES is an acronym formed by the domains measured: *P*hysical condition, *U*pper extremity function, *L*ower extremity function, *S*ensory, *E*xcretory, and psychosocial *S*tatus. SEE: *activities of daily living*.

safety p. The chemistry, pharmacology, therapeutic effects, and adverse effects of an administered drug or other substance.

profunda (prō-fŭn′dă) [L.] Deep seated; applied to certain deeply located blood vessels.

profundaplasty (prō-fŭn′dă-plăs″tē) An operation to repair an obstructing lesion in a deep blood vessel, for example, of the deep femoral artery.

profundus (prō-fŭn′dŭs) [L.] Located deeper than the indicated reference point.

progastrin (prō-găs′trĭn) The inactive precursor of gastrin.

progenitor (prō-jĕn′ĭ-tor) [L.] An ancestor.

progeny (prŏj′ĕ-nē) Offspring.

progeria (prō-jē′rē-ă) [Gr. *pro*, before, + *geras*, old age] The syndrome of premature aging, which may be an inherited disorder that is transmitted as an autosomal dominant trait. The incidence appears higher in children of older fathers. Onset is from birth to 18 months of age and the average age at death is 12 to 13 years.

FINDINGS: The child has an aged and wizened appearance. In addition there is small stature, slightness of build, alopecia, thick and inelastic skin that has brownish spots on it, delayed dentition, high-pitched voice, prominent eyes, and infantile sex organs.

progestagen (prō-jĕs′tŭ-jĕn) [*progesta(tional)* + ″] A synthetic compound that mimics the physiological effects of progesterone.

progestational (prō″jĕs-tā′shŭn-ăl) **1.** Pert. to the luteal phase of the menstrual cycle, immediately after ovulation, at which time progesterone is secreted, further preparing the endometrium for implantation of a fertilized ovum. **2.** Pert. to the hormone progesterone and its actions. **3.** Pert. to a drug with actions similar to progesterone.

progestational agent SEE: under *agent*.

progesterone (prō-jes′tĕ-rōn″) [*progestin* + *-sterone*] A steroid hormone, $C_{21}H_{30}O_2$, obtained from the corpus luteum and placenta. It is responsible for changes in the endometrium in the second half of the menstrual cycle preparatory to implantation of the blastocyst. It facilitates implantation by inhibiting uterine motility and stimulates the development of the mammary glands. Progesterone is used to treat patients with menstrual disorders (secondary amenorrhea, abnormal uterine bleeding, luteal phase deficiency) and to manage renal or endometrial carcinoma. In combination with estrogen, it is used for contraception and postmenopausal hormone replacement therapy. SYN: *corpus luteum hormone; luteal hormone; progestational hormone; progestin (1)*.

progestin (prō-jĕs′tĭn) **1.** A corpus luteum hormone that prepares the endometrium for implantation of the fertilized ovum. SYN: *progesterone; progestational agent*. **2.** Progestogen.

progestin-only contraceptive ABBR: POC. A nonestrogen-containing medication, such as a "mini-pill," or an injectable progestogen, used to prevent pregnancy

progestogen (prō-jĕs′tō-jĕn) Any natural or synthetic hormonal substance that produces effects similar to those due to progesterone.

proglottid (prō-glŏt′ĭd) *pl.* **proglottides** [Gr. *pro*, before, + *glotta*, tongue] A segment of a tapeworm, containing both male and female reproductive organs. SEE: *Cestoda; tapeworm.*

prognathic (prŏg-nā'thĭk) [" + *gnathos,* jaw] Prognathous.

prognathism (prŏg'nă-thĭzm) [" + *gnathos,* jaw + *-ismos,* condition] Projection of the jaws beyond projection of the forehead.

prognathous (prŏg'nă-thŭs) Having jaws projecting forward beyond the rest of the face. SYN: *prognathic.*

prognose (prŏg-nōs') To predict the course of a disease.

prognosis (prŏg-nō'sĭs) [Gr., foreknowledge] Prediction of the course and end of a disease, and the estimate of chance for recovery.

prognosticate (prŏg-nŏs'tĭ-kāt) [Gr. *prognostikon,* knowing before] To make a statement on the probable outcome of an illness.

prognostic marker (prog-nos'tik) SEE: under *marker.*

program (prō'gram") [Fr. *programme,* fr L. *programma,* fr Gr. *programma,* public notice] A plan or system, usually printed, outlining procedures or actions to be followed. Particular programs are listed under the first word. SEE: e.g., *employee benefit program; Individualized Education Program; preprosthetic program.*

program of all-inclusive care for elderly ABBR: PACE. A form of capitation administered in the U.S. by the Centers for Medicare and Medicaid Services in which frail older adults receive adult day care, outpatient or in-home medical care, and social services. The goal of the program is to foster independent living by the elderly, thus decreasing institutionalization.

programmable (prō"gram'ă-bĕl) **1.** Able to accept new instructions; modifiable. **2.** In electronics, receptive to new instructions, manual settings, or computer code.

programming Making a set of instructions guiding the actions of a computer, a piece of equipment, an organism, or a research investigation.

progranulocyte (prō-grăn'ū-lō-sīt) [" + L. *granula,* granule, + Gr. *kytos,* cell] Promyelocyte.

progress [L. *progressus,* a going forward] The ongoing sequence of events of an illness.

progression (prŏ-gresh'ŏn) [L. *progressus,* going forward] **1.** An advance or movement forward. **2.** A worsening of a disease, e.g., of a cancer.

progression-free (prŏ-gresh'ŏn-frē") Pert. to a disease, such as cancer, that does not advance or become worse or more symptomatic.

progression-free survival ABBR: PFS. In cancer care, the time during which a patient shows no signs or symptoms of the growth or the spreading of a tumor.

progressive (prō-grĕs'ĭv) Advancing, as a disease, from bad to worse.

progressive hemifacial atrophy SEE: under *atrophy.*

progressive lens SEE: under *lens.*

progressive systemic sclerosis SEE: under *sclerosis.*

progress notes An ongoing record of a patient's illness and treatment. Physicians, nurses, consultants, and therapists record their notes concerning the progress or lack of progress made by the patient between the time of the previous note and the most recent note. In patients who are not critically ill, a note concerning progress may be made daily or less frequently; for patients in critical care, notes may be made hourly. It is important that each note be clearly written, the date and time recorded, and the note signed.

progress report The written or verbal account of a patient's present condition, esp. as compared with the previous state.

prohapten (prō-hăp'tĕn) A chemical (often a drug) that does not stimulate an immune response until it is metabolized into an immunologically reactive form by living cells.

prohormone (prō-hor'mōn) A precursor of a hormone.

proinflammatory cytokine (prō"in-flam'ă-tōr-ē) SEE: under *cytokine.*

proinsulin (prō-ĭn'sū-lĭn) A precursor of insulin produced in the beta cells of the pancreas.

projection (prŏ-jek'shŏn) [L. *projectio* a throw forward] **1.** The act of throwing forward. **2.** A part extending beyond the level of its surroundings. **3.** The mental process by which sensations are referred to the sense organs or receptors stimulated, or outside the body to the object that is the stimulus. **4.** The distortion of a perception as a result of its repression, resulting in such a phenomenon as hating without cause one who has been dearly loved, or attributing to others one's own undesirable traits. These are characteristics of the paranoid reaction. SYN: *projective identification.* **5.** In radiology, the path of the central ray of radiation from entry to exit of the body. In an anteroposterior projection, for example, the beam enters the anterior surface of the body and exits the posterior surface.

    isometric p. A projection of an x-ray photon beam that yields an image having the same dimensions as the object being examined.

    lateral skull p. A radiograph in which the central ray is directed through the acoustic meatus and perpendicular to the midsagittal plane of the cranium and the radiographical film. It is used to evaluate the skull for abnormalities caused by developmental or connective tissue diseases, cancer, and trauma. SEE: *lateral cephalometric **radiograph**.*

light p. The ability to determine the source of a visual stimulus.

prokaryote (prō″kăr′ē-ōt) [″ + *karyon*, nucleus] An organism of the kingdom Monera with a single, circular chromosome, without a nuclear membrane, or membrane-bound organelles (i.e., mitochondria and lysosomes). Included in this classification are bacteria and cyanobacteria (formerly the blue-green algae). SYN: *procaryote; prokaryon* (2). SEE: *eukaryote.*

prokinetic (prō″kĭn-ĕt′ĭk) Producing increased activity of the muscles of the stomach and the upper gastrointestinal tract.

prokineticin (prō″kĭn-ĕt′ ĭ-sĭn) A class of proteins that stimulate intestinal muscles to contract.

prolactin (prō-lăk′tĭn) [″ + *lac,* milk] A hormone produced by the anterior pituitary gland. In humans, prolactin in association with estrogen and progesterone stimulates breast development and the formation of milk during pregnancy. The act of sucking is an important stimulus for the production of prolactin in the postpartum period. Some of the metabolic effects of prolactin resemble those of growth hormone. In the female this includes amenorrhea, galactorrhea, and infertility. In the male it may cause erectile dysfunction. Hyperprolactinemia may be associated with amenorrhea in women and reduced sexual potency in men. Thyrotropin-releasing hormone and stress of all kinds can stimulate prolactin release.

prolactinoma (prō-lak″tĭn-ō′mă) [*prolactin* + *-oma*] An adenoma of the pituitary gland that produces excessive amounts of prolactin and, in some cases, endocrine effects such as galactorrhea or amenorrhea, or visual effects due to compression of the optic chiasm. It is found more often in women than in men. Treatments include surgical removal of the tumor or suppression of the gland with drugs such as cabergoline. SYN: *lactotroph **adenoma***; *prolactin-secreting **adenoma***.

prolamin, prolamine (prō′lă-mĭn, -mēn]) [*prol(ine)* + *am(monia)*] A class of vegetable proteins found in seeds and cereal grains (such as wheat, rye, barley, and corn) that contain high levels of glutamic acid and proline.

prolapse (prō′laps″) [L. *prolapsus,* a falling forward] A falling or dropping down of an organ or internal part, such as the uterus or rectum. SEE: *mitral valve prolapse; procidentia; ptosis.*

iris p. Protrusion of the iris or part of the iris through an injury in the cornea.

lumbar disk p. Herniated **disk**.

mitral valve p. ABBR: MVP. A relatively rare condition in which the cusp or cusps of the mitral valve billow into the left atrium during systole. The abnormality has many causes, but the most common and clinically significant cause is leaflet thickening and redundancy (myxomatous degeneration of the valve). Mitral valve prolapse affects about 3% of U.S. population and is the primary cause of severe nonischemic mitral regurgitation. It is found equally in men and women, but men have a higher risk of cardiovascular (CV) complications; age over 50 increases that risk. Other risk factors for CV complications include mild to moderate mitral regurgitation, atrial fibrillation, and atrial enlargement. Physical examination and two-dimensional echocardiography diagnose the problem.

In patients without evidence of mitral regurgitation, there are usually no symptoms, but in some patients, nonanginal chest pain, palpitations, dyspnea, and fatigue may be present. On auscultation, there may be a murmur at the apex that is present during all of systole (holosystolic). Sometimes only a midsystolic click and late systolic murmur are heard.

TREATMENT: Simple prolapse requires no therapy, and most MVP patients have an excellent prognosis and live a normal life. However, if mitral regurgitation is present on physical examination or echocardiogram, antibiotic prophylaxis is indicated during surgical and dental procedures. If heart failure caused by severe mitral regurgitation develops, surgical repair of the valve is helpful.

pelvic organ p. ABBR: POP. Protrusion of the pelvic organs into or through the vaginal canal. This condition is usually due to direct or indirect damage to the vagina and its pelvic support system. The damage may be related to stretching or laceration of the vaginal wall, hypoestrogenic atrophy, or injury to the nerves of the pelvic support structures. SYN: *vaginal **hernia**.*

SYMPTOMS: Symptoms include a sensation of pelvic pressure, groin pain, coital difficulty, sacral backache, bloody vaginal discharge, difficult bowel movements, and urinary frequency, urgency, or incontinence.

PROPHYLAXIS: Preventive measures include treatment of chronic respiratory disorders or constipation, estrogen replacement for menopausal women, weight control, smoking cessation, avoidance of strenuous occupational or recreational stresses to the pelvic support system, and pelvic muscle exercise to strengthen the pelvic diaphragm.

TREATMENT: Treatment may be

nonsurgical (such as use of a vaginal pessary) or surgical, including reconstructive operations, vaginal hysterectomy, and cystocele or rectocele repair.

p. of the rectum Protrusion of the rectal mucosa or full thickness of the rectum (procidentia). Internal or complete rectal prolapse can be identified radiographically or endoscopically without transanal protrusion.

p. of the umbilical cord Premature expulsion of a loop of umbilical cord into the cervical or vaginal canal during labor before engagement of the presenting part and a potentially life-threatening event that occurs in about 2 of 1000 births. The greatest danger of cord prolapse is neonatal asphyxia and death. SEE: *deceleration*.

p. of the uterus Downward displacement of the uterus from its normal position in the female reproductive tract. It can be classified by its severity: 1st degree: the cervix is within the vagina; 2nd degree: the cervix protrudes through the introitus; 3rd degree: the uterus and inverted vaginal walls lie outside of the vaginal introitus. Uterine prolapse is usually caused by relaxation of the tissues that provide support for the pelvic organs. SYN: *descensus uteri; hysteroptosia; procidentia*.

ETIOLOGY: This condition may be congenital or acquired; most often it is acquired. The etiological factors are congenital weakness of the uterine supports and injury to the pelvic floor or to the uterine supports during childbirth.

SYMPTOMS: The condition is most often seen following instrumental deliveries or when the patient has been allowed to bear down during labor before the cervix is fully dilated. Frequently associated with this is a prolapse of the anterior and posterior vaginal walls, as seen in cystocele and rectocele. In the early stages there are dragging sensations in the lower abdomen, back pain while standing and on exertion, a sensation of weight and bearing down in the perineum, and frequency of urination and incontinence of urine in cases associated with cystocele. In the later stages, a protrusion or swelling at the vulva is noticed on standing or straining, and leukorrhea is present. In procidentia, there is frequently pain on walking, an inability to urinate unless the mass is reduced, and cystitis.

TREATMENT: The treatment depends on the age of the patient, the degree of prolapse, and the associated pathology. Abdominal surgery with fixation of the uterus is required if the prolapse is complete.

prolapsus (prō-lăp′sŭs) [L.] Prolapse.

prolepsis (prō-lĕp′sĭs) [Gr. *pro*, before, + *lepsis*, a seizure] The return of paroxysmal attacks at successively shorter intervals. **proleptic,** *adj.*

proliferate (prō-lĭf′ĕr-āt) [L. *proles*, offspring, + *ferre*, to bear] To increase by reproduction of similar forms.

proliferation (prō-lĭf″ĕr-ā′shŭn) **1.** Rapid and repeated reproduction of new parts, as by cell division. **2.** The process or result of rapid reproduction.

proliferous (prō-lĭf′ĕr-ŭs) **1.** Multiplying, as by formation of new tissue cells. **2.** Bearing offspring.

prolific (prō-lĭf′ĭk) [L. *prolificus*] Fruitful; reproductive. SYN: *fertile*.

prolinase (prō′lĭn-āz) An enzyme that is found in animal tissues and yeast and that hydrolyzes proline peptides to simpler peptide and proline.

proline (prō′lēn) C_4H_8NCOOH; an amino acid formed by digestion of protein. Proline is a constituent of collagens.

proline iminopeptidase (prō′lēn″ im″ĭ-nō″pep′tĭ-dās″) ABBR: PIP. An enzyme that helps catalyze the removal of proline residues from the N-terminal portion of polypeptides. Elevated levels of PIP in vaginal fluids are an indicator of bacterial vaginosis.

prolonged QT syndrome, long QT syndrome, QT syndrome A life-threatening syndrome marked by a prolonged QT interval with episodes of electrocardiographic torsades de pointes. This condition may be inherited or may be acquired as a result of drug administration. Inherited variants of the long QT syndrome include Romano-Ward syndrome and Lange-Nielsen syndrome. It is treated with beta-blocking drugs or an implanted cardioverter defibrillator (ICD).

prolotherapy (prō″ lō-thĕr′ ŭ-pē) The injection of sclerosing solutions (or solutions that contain ingredients such as highly concentrated dextrose) into ligaments, in an attempt to strengthen the ligaments and treat musculoskeletal pain.

prolymphocyte (prō″lĭmf′ō-sīt) [″ + L. *lympha*, lymph, + Gr. *kytos*, cell] A cell intermediate between a lymphoblast and lymphocyte.

PROM *passive range of motion; premature rupture of membranes.*

promegakaryocyte (prō-mĕg″ă-kăr′ē-ō-sīt) [″ + *megas*, big, + *karyon*, nucleus, + *kytos*, cell] A cell from which a megakaryocyte develops.

prometaphase (prō-mĕt′ă-fāz) [″ + *meta*, change, + *phasis*, to appear] The stage of mitosis in which the nuclear membrane disintegrates, and the chromosomes move toward the equator of the cell.

promethium (prō-mē′thē-ŭm) [*Prometheus,* a Titan in Gr. mythology + *-ium* (1)] SYMB: Pm. A radioactive metallic element of the rare-earth series, atomic weight 144.9128, atomic number 61.

prominauris (prŏm″ĭ-nor′ĭs) Protrusion of the ears from the side of the head.

prominence (prŏm′ĭ-nĕns) [L. *prominens*, project] A projection or protrusion.

promonocyte (prō-mŏn′ō-sīt) [Gr. *pro*, before, + *monos*, single, + *kytos*, cell] In the development of white blood cells, the precursor of the monocyte. It is between the monoblast and monocyte.

promontory (prŏm′ŏn-tor″ē) [L. *promontorium*] A projecting process or part.

   p. of the sacrum The anterior projecting portion of the pelvic surface of the base of the sacrum. With the fifth lumbar vertebra, it forms the sacrovertebral angle.

   p. of the tympanic cavity The projection on the medial wall of the tympanic cavity produced by the first turn of the cochlea.

promoter (prō-mō′tĕr) A substance that assists a catalyst to act. SEE: *coenzyme*.

prompt Assistance, reinforcement, or feedback given during the acquisition or relearning of skills necessary for task completion.

prompted voiding A treatment for urinary incontinence in which patients (particularly those with limited self-awareness) are reminded to void before they urinate on themselves or are taught to seek assistance with urination periodically before an episode of incontinence occurs.

promyelocyte (prō-mī′ĕl-ō-sīt) [Gr. *pro*, before, + *myelos*, marrow, + *kytos*, cell] **1.** A large mononuclear myeloid cell seen in the blood in leukemia. **2.** Cell development between a myeloblast and a myelocyte, resembling a myeloblast. SYN: *progranulocyte*. SEE: illus.

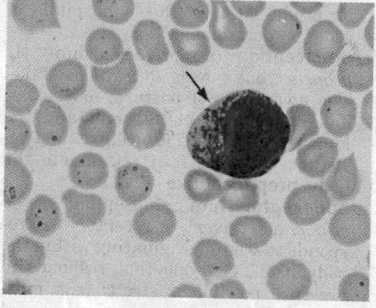

PROMYELOCYTE

pronate (prō′nāt) To place in a prone position. SEE: *supinate*.

pronation (prō-nā′shŭn) [L. *pronus*, prone] **1.** The act of lying prone or face downward. **2.** The act of turning the hand so that the palm faces downward or backward. SEE: *supination*.

pronator (prō-nā′tŏr) A muscle that pronates.

pronator syndrome, pronator teres syndrome A neurological disorder caused by entrapment of the median nerve at the elbow. Symptoms and signs include aching in the wrist with a subjective feeling of poor coordination; paresthesias extending into the hand; paresis of the thumb muscles; pain on pronation of the forearm and flexion of the wrist against resistance; and tenderness in the proximal thenar muscles. A positive Tinel sign over the pronator teres muscles may be present. The disease usually affects the dominant arm in men. The condition may be treated with corticosteroid injections or orthopedic surgery.

prone (prōn) **1.** Horizontal with the face downward. **2.** Denoting the hand with the palm turned downward. It is the opposite of supine. SYN: *prone posture*; *procumbent*.

pronephros (prō-nĕf′rŏs) The earliest and simplest type of excretory organ of vertebrates, functional in simpler forms (cyclostomes), and serving as a provisional kidney in some fishes and amphibians. In reptiles, birds, and mammals, it appears in the embryo as a temporary, functionless structure.

prong (prŏng) A cone-shaped body such as the root of a tooth.

pronograde (prō′nō-grād) [L. *pronus*, prone, + *gradus*, a step] In animals, walking on the hands and feet or resting with the body in a horizontal position. It is the opposite of orthograde.

pronormoblast (prō-nor′mō-blăst) [Gr. *pro*, before, + L. *norma*, rule, + Gr. *blastos*, germ] An early precursor of the red blood cell.

pronucleus (prō-nū′klē-ŭs) [Gr. *pro*, before, + *nucleus*, little kernel] The haploid nucleus of either the ovum or spermatozoon prior to their union in fertilization.

proof of concept An early scientific investigation of an idea; a pilot project.

proofreading (proof″rēd″ing) In genetics and cellular biology, the ability of a cell to ensure that copies of its genetic information are faithfully made with limited errors or mutations.

prootic (prō-ŏt′ĭk, -ō′tĭk) [″ + *ous*, ear] In front of the ear.

prop A device of sturdy material used to support or hold something in place.

   mouth p. A metal or rubber device inserted between the jaws to maintain the mouth in an open position. SYN: *bite block*.

propagate (prop′ă-gāt″) [L. *propagare*, to fasten down, set slips, propagate] **1.** To transmit or spread through a population, e.g., an infection or epidemic illness. **2.** To reproduce a species with a particular genotype or phenotype. **3.** To spread through a medium or part of the body , e.g., to transmit a stimulus from one nerve ending to others.

propagation (prŏp-ă-gā′shŭn) [L.] The act of reproducing or giving birth. SYN: *generation; reproduction.*

propagative (prŏp′ă-gā″tĭv) Pert. to or taking part in reproduction.

propane (prō′pān) An inflammable odorless, colorless hydrocarbon, C_3H_8, that is present in natural gas.

propellant (prŏ-pĕl′ănt) [L. *propellere,* to drive forward] Any agent that forces another to move in a desired direction. Inhaled medications rely on propellants to improve drug delivery to patients. Hydrofluoroalkane propellants are used in metered dose inhalers, i.e., in canisters that deliver drugs such as beta-agonists or anticholinergic agents to patients with asthma or chronic obstructive lung disease.

properdin (prō-pĕrd′ĭn) A plasma protein that stabilizes the enzyme C3 convertase, and helps to activate the alternative pathway of the complement cascade. SEE: *complement.*

prophase (prō′fāz) [″ + *phasis,* an appearance] The first stage of cell division. SEE: *mitosis* for illus.

prophylactic (prō-fĭ-lăk′tĭk) [Gr. *prophylaktikos,* guarding] **1.** Any agent or regimen that contributes to the prevention of infection and disease. **2.** A popular term for a condom.

prophylactic cranial irradiation SEE: under *irradiation.*

prophylaxis (prō-fĭ-lak′sĭs, -lak′sēz″) *pl.* **prophylaxes** [Gr. *prophylaktikos,* guarding against] Observance of rules necessary to prevent disease.

   oral p. The removal of bacterial plaque, calculus, and stains from surfaces of the teeth, primarily by scaling and root planing. It is a preventative measure against gingivitis, halitosis, and periodontal disease.

   postexposure p. A preventive measure taken to protect a person or community from harm after contact with disease-causing chemicals, germs, or physical agents.

   pre-exposure p. ABBR: PrEP. The use of agents to prevent a disease before an anticipated exposure to it, esp. the use of antiviral agents before sexual intercourse to prevent infection with HIV.

propiolactone (prō″pē-ō-lăk′tŏn) A disinfectant used in preparing certain viral and bacterial vaccines.

Propionibacterium acnes (prō-pē-ŏn-ĭ-băk-tĕr′ē-ŭm) A gram-positive bacillus that may be part of the normal skin flora, but can also be pathogenic in acne, wounds, and infected prosthetic devices. It was formerly called *Corynebacterium acnes.*

propionic acid (prō″pē-on′ik) SEE: under *acid.*

proplastid (prō-plăs′tĭd) An immature plastid.

propofol (prŏ′pō-fŏl) A nonbarbiturate sedative used to induce anesthesia. It has a short duration of action and a rapid recovery time. Common side effects of its use include pain during injection and bradycardia.

propolis (prō-plĭs) [Gr. *pro,* before, + *polis,* city] A sticky resin present in the buds and bark of certain trees and plants. It is collected by bees for the purpose of repairing combs, filling cracks, and making the entrance to the hive waterproof. Propolis can be used as a topical antibacterial.

proportional In medical ethics, commensurate, acceptably balanced between the risk for harm and the likelihood of benefit.

proposition (prŏp-uh-zĭsh′ĕn) A statement about a concept or about the relationship between concepts. A proposition may be an assumption, a premise, a theorem, or a hypothesis. SEE: *assumption; hypothesis; premise; theorem.*

propositus (prō-pŏz′ĭ-tŭs) [L. *proponere,* to put on view] Proband.

propoxyphene hydrochloride, propoxyphene napsylate (prō-pok′sĭ-fēn″, nap′sĭ-lāt″) A mild opioid pain reliever. It was withdrawn from the U.S. market in 2011 because of potentially hazardous effects on cardiac conduction.

proprietary (prŏ-prī′ĕ-ter″ē) [L. *proprietarius,* an owner] **1.** Pert. to property or ownership. **2.** Pert. to an owner or proprietor. **3.** Protected by trademark or patent registration from free, open competition. In pharmaceuticals, for example, it means that a drug can be made, marketed, or sold solely by the owner of the intellectual property rights or the trade mark or patent. SEE: *generic* (3, 4). **4.** Privately owned or operated run for profit, as some schools, hospitals, or other corporations.

proprioception (prō″prē-ō-sĕp′shŭn) [L. *proprius,* one's own, + *capio,* to take] The awareness of posture, movement, and changes in equilibrium and the knowledge of position, weight, and resistance of objects in relation to the body. **proprioceptive** (-tĭv), *adj.*

proprioceptor (prō″prē-ō-sĕp′tor) [″ + *ceptor,* a receiver] A receptor that responds to stimuli originating within the body itself, esp. one that responds to pressure, position, or stretch (e.g., muscle spindles, pacinian corpuscles, and labyrinthine receptors).

propriospinal (prō″prē-ō-spī′năl) [″ + *spina,* thorn] Concerned exclusively with the spinal cord.

proptosis (prŏp-tō′sĭs) An abnormal protrusion forward of the eyeball, seen in thyroid eye disease and tumors of the orbit. SEE: *exophthalmus.*

propulsion (prō-pŭl′shŭn) [L. *propulsus,* driven forward] **1.** A tendency to push or fall forward in walking. **2.** A condition seen in Parkinson disease. SEE: *festination.*

propyl (prō′pĭl) The radical of propyl alcohol or propane, $CH_3-CH_2-CH_2-$.

propylene glycol (prŏp′ĭ-lēn) A demulcent agent used as a solvent for medicines, and in cosmetics.

propylparaben (prō″pĭl-păr′ă-bĕn) Propyl *p*-hydroxybenzoate, $C_{10}H_{12}O_3$, a chemical used as an antifungal agent and as a preservative in pharmaceuticals.

pro re nata (prō rē nā′tă) [L.] ABBR: prn. According to the circumstances; as necessary.

proscription (prō-skrip′shŏn) [L. *proscriptio,* a written public notice, outlawry] Restriction of behavior based on cultural or religious beliefs. SEE: *taboo.*

prosection (prō-sĕk′shŭn) [″ + L. *sectio,* a cutting] Dissection for the purpose of demonstrating anatomical structure.

prosector (prō-sĕk′tor) [L.] One who prepares cadavers for dissection or dissects for demonstration.

prosencephalon (prŏs″ĕn-sĕf′ă-lŏn) [Gr. *proso,* before, + *enkephalos,* brain] The embryonic forebrain, which gives rise to the telencephalon and diencephalon.

proso- [Gr. *prosō,* forward] Prefix meaning *forward, anterior.*

prosody (prŏs′ă-dē) [L. *prosodia,* accent of a syllable] The normal rhythm, melody, and articulation of speech.

prosopagnosia (prŏs″ō-păg-nō′sē-ă) [Gr. *prosopon,* face, + *a-,* not, + *gnosis,* recognition] Inability to recognize faces, even one's own face. Ability to recognize other objects may be intact. SYN: *face blindness.*

prospective payment system A reimbursement method used in which a fixed, predetermined amount is allocated for treating patients with a specific diagnosis. It was originally developed for Medicare recipients. It is also called payment-by-diagnosis.

prospective study SEE: under *study.*

prostacyclin (prŏs-tă-sīk′lĭn) A compound formed from the metabolism of arachidonic acid. It is a potent vasodilator and inhibitor of platelet aggregation.

prostaglandin (prŏs″tă-glăn′dĭn) ABBR: PG. Any of a large group of biologically active, carbon-20, unsaturated fatty acids that are produced by the metabolism of arachidonic acid through the cyclooxygenase pathway. They are autacoids: local short-range hormones that are formed rapidly, act in the immediate area, and then decay or are destroyed by

enzymes. PGD_2, PGE_2, $PGF_{2\alpha}$, and PGI_1PGI_2 (prostacyclin), and TXA_2 (thromboxane) are important mediators of inflammation. Nonsteroidal anti-inflammatory drugs block the production of prostaglandins.

PGs influence a broad range of biological effects, including vasodilation, vascular permeability, bronchoconstriction, platelet aggregation, dysmenorrhea, inhibition of gastric acid secretion, stimulation of neural receptors for pain during tissue damage, sleep inhibition, and maintenance of patent ductus arteriosus. Exogenous PGE_2 gel may be used to soften the cervix before induction of labor. SEE: *arachidonic acid; nonsteroidal anti-inflammatory drug; patent ductus arteriosus.*

prostaglandin inhibitor SEE: under *inhibitor.*

prostanoids (prŏs-tă-nŏyds) The end products of the cyclooxygenase pathway of the metabolism of arachidonic acid. These are prostaglandins and thromboxanes. SEE: *eicosanoid; prostaglandin; thromboxane A_2.*

prostate (pros′tāt″) [L. *prostata,* fr. Gr. *prostatēs,* the one (gland) standing in front] A gland, consisting of a median lobe and two lateral lobes, that surrounds the neck of the bladder and the urethra in the male. It is partly muscular and partly glandular, with ducts opening into the prostatic portion of the urethra. About $2 \times 4 \times 3$ cm, and weighing about 20 g, it is enclosed in a fibrous capsule containing smooth muscle fibers in its inner layer. Muscle fibers also separate the glandular tissue and encircle the urethra. The gland secretes a thin, opalescent, slightly alkaline fluid that forms part of the seminal fluid.

PATHOLOGY: Inflammation of the prostate may occur, often the result of gonorrheal urethritis. Enlargement of the prostate is common, esp. after middle age. This results in urethral obstruction, impeding urination and sometimes leading to retention. Benign and malignant tumors, calculi, and nodular hyperplasia are common, particularly in men past 60. SEE: *benign prostatic **hypertrophy**; prostate cancer.*

    enlarged p. Benign prostatic **hyperplasia.**

prostate cancer A malignant tumor (almost always an adenocarcinoma) of the prostate gland. Other than skin cancers, it is the most common neoplasm in men. In 2008, the American Cancer Society estimated that 186,320 American men would be diagnosed with prostate cancer and that 28,660 would die as a result. Nonetheless, 93% of those diagnosed survive at least 10 years, and 77% of men with the disease survive at least 15 years. SEE: *benign prostatic hypertrophy; brachytherapy; prostatectomy.*

ETIOLOGY: Although the cancer may have many causes, it is a hormone-sensitive tumor (testosterone).

SYMPTOMS: The disease is often asymptomatic, or it may present with symptoms similar to those of benign prostatic hypertrophy (difficulty in urinating, urinary hesitancy, frequency, dribbling, steam reduction or interruption, and nocturia); symptoms of urinary tract infection; or in cases in which the cancer has spread to bone, localized or generalized bone pain. Prostatic cancer can spread locally or metastasize via the lymphatic system to lung, liver and brain in addition to bone.

DIAGNOSIS: About two thirds of those diagnosed are over age 65. Incidence is 60% higher in black men than in whites or Hispanics and lowest in Asians. The highest mortality is also in black men. Other risk factors include family history, having had a vasectomy, eating a diet high in fats and red meats and low in fruits and vegetables, and demonstrating reduced levels of vitamins D and E, lycopene, and selenium.

PATIENT CARE: Most professional medical societies recommend that men over the age of 50 or men with a strong family history of the disease discuss prostate cancer screening with their primary care providers. The available options include blood tests to assess levels of prostate specific antigen (PSA), digital rectal examination (DRE), or assessment of the gland with ultrasonography. Mass screening for prostate cancer is not recommended by any major professional group because it may result in false-positive diagnosis, unnecessary or complicated treatments, or unnecessary anxiety. However, those men at high risk (esp. black men) should begin annual testing at 45. Screening should begin at 40 for men at highest risk (several first-degree relatives having prostate cancer at early ages).

When prostate cancer is suggested by screening tests, biopsies are required to confirm the diagnosis, usually with guided imagery via transrectal ultrasound. Further studies may include MRIs, CTs and bone scans to see if the disease has spread. Once diagnosed, prostate cancer is differentiated as stages 1 to 4, with the higher stages indicating more advanced or widespread disease, and is graded on the Gleason grading system from 2 to 10, with lower numbers indicating cells more closely resembling normal cells (well differentiated) and higher number increasingly abnormal (poorly differentiated). Stage, grade, age, and overall health aid in determining treatment although all treatment options should be explored.

Patient support and education vary with the stage of the disease and the therapies to be provided. For example, for patients with early (low-grade or low-stage) disease, or for those with limited life expectancy and significant co-morbid diseases who choose expectant care (watchful waiting) to avoid the rigors of treatment and potential adverse reactions, teaching should focus on symptoms requiring prompt intervention and on the need for follow-up visits for repeat PSA and DRE, usually every 6 months. If the patient chooses external beam radiation, he is taught the most common side effects (localized skin irritation, diarrhea, urinary urgency, frequency, hesitancy and pain, erectile dysfunction, fatigue, and bone marrow suppression). If the patient chooses brachytherapy, he is taught that the radioactive seeds will be placed in the prostate while he is under sedation. Radiation precautions are needed, including following the approved method of lost seed disposal. A condom must be used when sexual activity is resumed after 2 weeks. The most common side effects are irritation and obstruction of the urinary tract. Patients who have received brachytherapy should immediately report inability to void, rectal bleeding, rectal irritation, or diarrhea to the health care providers.

Cryosurgery in which liquid-nitrogen probes are inserted into the prostate eradicates the malignant cells. Complications include erectile dysfunction, urinary incontinence, and formation of fistulas between the bladder and the rectum. Radical prostatectomy is the most effective surgery for improving long-term survival. The entire prostate, seminal vesicles, regional lymph nodes, and part of the bladder neck are removed. All patients should be taught from an early age about their risks for prostate cancer and encouraged to have regular screening at the appropriate age.

prostatectomy (prŏs″tă-tĕk′tō-mē) [Gr. *prostates*, prostate, + *ektome*, excision] Excision of part or all of the prostate gland. The operation may be performed via a laparoscopic approach through an incision in the perineum (perineal prostatectomy), into the bladder (suprapubic prostatectomy), retropubically, or through the urethra (transurethral prostatectomy, TURP). SEE: *Nursing Diagnoses Appendix.*

PATIENT CARE: *Preoperative:* To prepare the patient for surgery and postoperative recovery, the type of procedure planned and expected results are explained and informed consent is obtained.

Postoperative: Vital signs are monitored closely for indications of hemorrhage or shock. Any dressings and drainage tubes are managed, skin is protected from excoriation, and incisions or tube insertion wounds are inspected for signs of infection. If a suprapubic tube is present, patency and drainage are monitored; drainage fluid should be amber to pink tinged. Urinary catheter patency is monitored, and intermittent or continuous bladder irrigation is maintained as prescribed, usually via a three-channel indwelling catheter. Irrigation rate should be fast enough to limit drainage color change to amber to pink tinged, rather than red; rate should be increased if color deepens or clots appear. Volume of irrigant and amount of drainage are carefully tracked, and the former is subtracted from the latter to determine urinary output. Medicines are administered as prescribed to reduce bladder spasms and pain. Sitzbaths also may be used to relieve pain and discomfort.

When the catheter is removed, the patient should void every 2 hr, and serial urines are monitored for color, time, and amount of each voiding. Bladder ultrasound is used to assess for retained urine. Fluid intake of 2 to 3 L/day (unless restricted by cardiac or renal deficits), mainly as water, is encouraged; caffeine is avoided. The patient may experience urinary frequency temporarily and dribbling, but he can regain control of urinary function with Kegel exercises. Urine may be blood tinged for a few weeks, but any bright red bleeding and fever, chills, or other signs of infection should be reported. The patient should avoid straining at stool (stool softeners are often prescribed) and lifting objects of more than 10 lb, long automobile trips, and strenuous exercise for several weeks. Walking usually is considered acceptable exercise. Sexual intercourse should be delayed until the patient has been evaluated by the physician at the follow-up visit and has the physician's permission to begin such activity. The patient also should continue prescribed medications at least until the follow-up visit and should have an annual prostatic examination if prostate removal was partial.

prostatic (prŏs-tăt′ĭk) [Gr. *prostates, prostate*] Pert. to the prostate gland.

prostatic urethra That part of the male urethra surrounded by the prostate gland.

prostatism (prŏs′tă-tĭzm) [″ + *-ismos*, condition] Any condition of the prostate gland that interferes with the flow of urine from the bladder. The condition is characterized by frequent uncomfortable urination and nocturia. Retention of urine may occur with development of uremia. Causes include benign hypertrophy, carcinoma, prostatitis, and nodular hyperplasia.

prostatitis (prŏs″tă-tī′tĭs) [″ + *itis*, inflammation] Inflammation of the prostate gland, usually as a result of infection.

acute bacterial p. Inflammation of the prostate, commonly associated with urinary tract infections caused by enterococci, staphylococci, or gram-negative bacteria such as *Escherichia coli.* It often is caused by reflux of urine resulting from an anatomical abnormality. Patients present with fever, chills, urethral discharge, pain on urination, difficulty voiding, malaise, myalgias, and discomfort in the perineal area; the prostate is soft, swollen, and tender on examination.

The causative organism is identified through a culture of prostatic secretions and is treated with an extended course of antibiotics. Narcotics and antispasmodics may be needed to relieve pain.

chronic abacterial p. Inflammation of the prostate gland, marked by dull, aching pain in the perineum, usually of long duration. Although this is the most common type of chronic prostatitis, its cause is unknown. SYN: *chronic pelvic pain syndrome.*

chronic bacterial p. ABBR: CBP. Inflammation of the prostate caused by a long-standing bacterial infection that often develops insidiously; causative organisms include gram-negative bacteria and enterococci. Clinically, the patient may have mild to moderate low back pain, pain with urination, and perineal discomfort, or he may be asymptomatic. Patients may have a history of multiple urinary tract infections; bacteria can hide in the prostate, which resists penetration by antibiotics, and reinfect the urinary tract. Causal bacteria are identified by culture of prostatic secretions and urine. Treatment consists of ciprofloxacin or another fluoroquinolone antibiotic for 4 to 6 weeks. The long course is needed because of poor penetration into the prostate.

prostato-, prostat- [Gr. *prostatēs (adēn),* prostate (gland), fr. *pro-* + *-stat*] Prefixes meaning *prostate gland.*

prostatodynia (prŏs″tă-tō-dĭn′ē-ă) [″ + *odyne,* pain] The condition of having the symptoms and signs of prostatitis but no evidence of inflammation of the prostate, with negative urine culture. Use of antibiotics in patients with prostatodynia is unnecessary. SEE: *proctalgia fugax.*

prosthesis (pros′thē-sĭs, pros′thĕ-) *pl.* **prostheses** [Gr. *prosthesis,* an addition] **1.** Replacement of a missing part by an artificial substitute, such as an artificial extremity. **2.** An artificial organ or part, including arms, hands, joints, heart valves, teeth, and others. **3.** A device to augment performance of a natural function, such as a hearing aid.

dental p. A dental appliance used to restore soft and hard oral tissue. The prosthesis may be internal or external to the oral cavity. Examples include dentures, partial dentures, orthodontic retainers, obturators, fixed bridges, and removable bridges.

PATIENT CARE: Care should be taken to remove, maintain, and clean dental prostheses at least on a daily basis, with dental prophylaxis and examinations scheduled regularly, usually semiannually.

expansion p. A prosthesis that expands the lateral segment of the maxilla; used in clefts of the soft and hard palates and alveolar processes.

externally powered p. Any prosthesis in which a small electric motor has been incorporated for the purpose of providing force to control various functions.

hair p. Wig.

maxillofacial p. The repair and artificial replacement of the face and jaw missing because of disease or injury.

myoelectric p. An prosthetic device operated by battery-powered electric motors that are activated through electrodes by the myoelectric potentials provided by muscles.

neural p. Any device or electrode that improves function by substituting for an injured or diseased part of the nervous system.

ocular p. Artificial eye.

penile p. A device implanted in the penis that assists it to become erect. The device is used in patients with erectile dysfunction due to such organic causes as trauma, prostatectomy, or diabetes. It is usually in the form of inflatable plastic cylinders implanted in each corpus cavernosum of the penis. These cylinders are attached to a pump embedded in the scrotal pouch. A reservoir for the fluid used to fill the cylinders is implanted behind the rectus muscle. This system allows the cylinders to be filled when an erection is desired and the fluid to be drained back into the reservoir when the need for the erection has passed. In most patients, this device permits the attaining of a nearly physiological erection. SEE: *Peyronie disease.*

porcine valvular p. A biological prosthesis made from the heart valve of a pig, used to replace a diseased cardiac valve.

tracheobronchial p. An airway stent used to open part of the trachea or a bronchus that has become obstructed (e.g., because of airway collapse, stenosis, or compression by a tumor).

voice p. A device that synthesizes the human voice. It is used in patients who have undergone laryngeal surgery.

prosthetic (pros-thet′ik) [Gr. *prostheti-*

kos, added to] **1.** Pert. to a prosthesis. **2.** Pert. to prosthetics.

prosthetic group SEE: under *group.*

prosthetics (pros-thet′iks) The branch of surgery or physiatry (physical medicine) dealing with construction, replacement, and adaptation of missing or damaged parts.

dental p. The dental specialty dealing with the needs of patients with missing teeth or with abnormal maxillofacial or oral structures. SYN: *prosthodontology.*

neural prosthetics Neuroprosthetics.

prosthetic training program Systematic education and training provided to persons with amputations following fitting of a prosthetic device.

prosthetist, prothetist (prŏs′thĕ-tĭst) **1.** A health care professional who helps to design, construct, and adjust artificial limbs and other body parts that assist in mobility, ambulation, and use of the extremities. **2.** A specialist in artificial dentures.

prosthodontics (prŏs″thŏ-dŏn′tĭks) [″ + *odous,* tooth] The branch of dentistry pertaining to the replacement of missing teeth or soft tissues with bridges, crowns, implants, and prostheses. Replacements may be fixed or removable, and may repair defects within the mouth, or in maxillofacial structures.

prosthodontist (prŏs″thŏ-dŏn′tĭst) A dentist who specializes in the mechanics of making and fitting artificial teeth, dental appliances, and other prostheses that replace structures of the maxillofacial region.

prosthokeratoplasty (prŏs″thō-kĕr′ă-tō-plăs″tē) [″ + *keras,* horn, + *plassein,* to form] Surgical replacement of diseased or scarred corneal tissue with a transparent prosthesis.

prostitution (pros″tĭ-too′shŏn, -tū′) [L. *prostitutio,* prostitution] The exchange of sexual favors for money. It is a risk factor for the spread of sexually transmitted diseases, including chlamydia, gonorrhea, trichomoniasis, syphilis, hepatitis, and AIDS.

prostrate (prŏs′trāt) [Gr. *pro,* before, + L. *sternere,* stretch out] **1.** Lying with the body extended, usually face down. **2.** To deprive of strength or to exhaust.

prostrated (prŏs-trā-tĕd) Depleted of strength; exhausted.

prostration (pros-trā′shŏn) Total physical, mental, or psychological exhaustion.

heat p. Heat **exhaustion.**

protactinium (prōt″ak″tin′ē-ŭm) [*proto-* + *actinium*] SYMB: Pa. A radioactive element, an actinide; atomic weight 231; atomic number 91.

protal (prō′tăl) [Gr. *protos,* first] Congenital.

protamine (prōt′ă-mēn″) [*prot-* +

amine] **1.** One of a class of simple proteins that are strongly basic, noncoagulable in heat, and yield diamino acids when hydrolyzed. **2.** An amine isolated from spermatozoa and the spawn of fish, and named for the fish from which it is derived. SEE: *salmin(e)*.

protanope (prō'tă-nōp) [Gr. *protos*, first, + *an-*, not, + *opsis*, vision] A person with protanopia.

protanopia (prō-tăn-ō'pē-ă) [" + " + *opsis*, vision] Red blindness; color blindness in which there is a defect in the perception of red. SEE: *color blindness*.

protean (prō'tē-ăn) [Gr. *Proteus*, a god who could change his form] Having the ability to change form, as the ameba; variable.

protease (prōt'ē-ās", -āz") [*prote(in)* + *-ase*] Any of a class of enzymes that break down, or hydrolyze, the peptide bonds that join the amino acids in a protein. The protein is broken down into its basic building blocks, i.e., amino acids. SEE: *digestion*.

protease inhibitor (prō'tē-ās", -āz") SEE: under *inhibitor*.

proteasome, proteosome (prō'tē-ă-sōm") An enzymatic (protease) cell organelle that degrades misfolded or damaged proteins and modulates the quantity of regulatory proteins in the cell. The breakdown of proteins by proteasomes (proteolysis) is triggered when damaged proteins are tagged by ubiquitin.

protected health information ABBR: PHI. According to the Health Insurance Portability and Accountability Act (HIPAA), information in a health care record that "relates to the past, present, or future physical or mental health or condition of an individual; the provision of health care to an individual; or the past, present, or future payment for the provision of health care to an individual." PHI, esp. the recording and transmission of health information, must be held in strict confidence by health care agencies and professionals.

protection, ineffective The state in which an individual experiences a decrease in the ability to guard the self from internal or external threats such as illness or injury. SEE: *Nursing Diagnoses Appendix*.

Protection and Advocacy for Individuals with Mental Illness ABBR: PAIMI. In the U.S., programs administered by every state and territory, protecting patients with mental illness from abuse, neglect, or infringements of their rights.

protection motivation theory SEE: under *theory*.

protective (prō-tek'tiv) **1.** Covering, preventing infection, providing immunity or insulation against trauma. **2.** A dressing.

protegrin (prō'teg-rin) Any of a class of cysteine-rich compounds, derived from mammalian peptides, that protect animals from a broad range of infections, including oral and periodontal diseases.

protein (prō'tēn", tē-ĭn) [*proto-* + *-in*] Any of a class of complex nitrogen-containing compounds synthesized by all living organisms and yielding amino acids when hydrolyzed. Dietary proteins provide the amino acids necessary for the growth and repair of animal tissue.

COMPOSITION: All amino acids contain carbon, hydrogen, oxygen, and nitrogen; some also contain sulfur. About 20 different amino acids make up human proteins, which may contain other minerals such as iron or copper. A protein consists of from 50 to thousands of amino acids arranged in a very specific sequence. The essential amino acids are those the liver cannot synthesize (tryptophan, lysine, methionine, valine, leucine, isoleucine, phenylalanine, threonine, arginine, and histidine); because they cannot be made by the body, they must be consumed as food. A protein containing all of them is called a complete protein. An incomplete protein lacks one or more of the essential amino acids. The nonessential amino acids are synthesized by the liver.

SOURCES: Milk, eggs, cheese, meat, fish, and some vegetables such as soybeans are the best dietary sources of protein. Proteins are found in both vegetable and animal food sources. Many incomplete proteins are found in vegetables; they contain some but not all of the essential amino acids. A vegetarian diet can compensate for dietary protein deficiencies by combining vegetable groups that complement each other in their basic amino acid groups.

Principal animal proteins are lactalbumin and lactoglobulin in milk; ovalbumin and ovoglobulin in eggs; serum albumin in serum; myosin and actin in striated muscle tissue; fibrinogen in blood; serum globulin in serum; thyroglobulin in thyroid; globin in blood; thymus histones in thymus; collagen and gelatin in connective tissue; collagen and elastin in connective tissue; and keratin in the epidermis. Chondroprotein is found in tendons and cartilage; mucin and mucoids are found in various secreting glands and animal mucilaginous substances; caseinogen in milk; vitellin in egg yolk; hemoglobin in red blood cells; and lecithoprotein in the blood, brain, and bile.

FUNCTION: Ingested proteins are a source of amino acids needed to synthesize the body's own proteins, which are essential for the growth of new tissue or the repair of damaged tissue; proteins are part of all cell membranes. Excess amino acids in the diet may be changed to simple carbohydrates and oxidized to produce adenosine triphosphate and heat; 1 g supplies 4 kcal of heat.

Infants and children require from 2 to 2.2 g of dietary protein per kilogram of body weight each day for normal health and development. The World Health Organization recommends that healthy adults consume about 0.8 g of protein per kg of body weight daily. The calculation should be made on the basis of ideal body weight rather than the actual weight of the adult or child. High levels of exercise, menstruation, pregnancy, lactation, and convalescence from severe illness require increased protein intake. Excess protein in the diet results in increased nitrogen excretion in the urine.

accessory p. A protein that works with another protein, e.g., in helping it to fold into its normal shape or become anchored into its preferred location in a cell membrane.

activator p. A protein that stimulates the expression of a gene.

acute phase p. Any of the plasma proteins whose concentration increases or decreases by at least 25% during inflammation. Acute-phase proteins include C-reactive protein, several complement and coagulation factors, transport proteins, amyloid, and antiprotease enzymes. They help mediate both positive and negative effects of acute and chronic inflammation, including chemotaxis, phagocytosis, protection against oxygen radicals, and tissue repair. In clinical medicine the erythrocyte sedimentation rate or serum C-reactive protein level sometimes is used as a marker of increased amounts of acute-phase proteins. SYN: *acute phase reactant*. SEE: *inflammation.*

adapter p. An intracellular molecule that undergoes structural and functional changes in response to binding of cell membrane receptors by ligands. Adapter proteins participate in the immune response by acting as a bridge for enzymes in the signaling pathway needed to activate lymphocytes and initiate a response to an antigen.

amyloid precursor p. ABBR: APP. An integral membrane protein concentrated at neuron synapses that is cleaved biochemically into components, one of which is the Alzheimer disease–associated beta amyloid. Mutations in the gene for APP on chromosome 21 account for less than 5% of early-onset familial Alzheimer disease.

Bence Jones p. SEE: *Bence Jones protein.*

binding p. A protein that is linked to another chemical in the body, either transporting it through the blood or helping to convey it into cells across cell membranes. Examples of binding proteins include ceruloplasmin, sex hormone-binding globulin, and transcobalamin, which carries vitamin B12.

blood p. A broad term encompassing numerous proteins, including hemoglobin, albumin, globulins, the acute-phase reactants, transporter molecules, and many others. Normal values are hemoglobin, 13 to 18 g/dL in men and 12 to 16 g/dL in women; albumin, 3.5 to 5.0 g/dL of serum; globulin, 2.3 to 3.5 g/dL of serum. The amount of albumin in relation to the amount of globulin is referred to as the albumin-globulin (A/G) ratio, which is normally 1.5:1 to 2.5:1.

bone morphogenetic p. A bone graft substitute.

p. C A plasma protein that inhibits coagulation factors V and XIII, preventing excessive clotting. Deficiency of this protein or resistance to its effects may lead to deep venous thrombosis and pulmonary embolism. In the presence of thrombin, protein C is activated, forming activated protein C. SEE: *protein S.*

carrier p. 1. A protein that elicits an immune response when coupled with a hapten. 2. A membrane protein for facilitated diffusion of a specific substance into a cell.

CHK2 p., CHEK2 protein An abbreviation for a *checkpoint kinase* protein that stimulates cells to multiply and is found in excessive amounts in several cancers, including cancers of blood, breast, stomach, and vulva.

cholesteryl ester transfer p. ABBR: CETP. A protein that circulates in plasma and facilitates the chemical transfer of cholesteryl esters from high-density lipoproteins to other lipoproteins.

coagulated p. One of the derived (insoluble) proteins resulting from the action of alcohol, heat, or other physicochemical entities on protein solutions.

coat p. Capsid.

complement S p. Vitronectin.

complete p. A protein containing all the essential amino acids.

conjugated p. A protein that is chemically linked with a nonprotein molecule. Included are chromoproteins (e.g., hemoglobin); glycoproteins (e.g., mucin); lecithoproteins, nucleoproteins, and phosphoproteins (e.g., casein).

C-reactive p. ABBR: CRP. The first acute phase protein identified. It binds with phospholipids on foreign substances, activates the complement system, stimulates the production of cytokines, and inhibits the production of oxygen radicals by neutrophils. Increased blood levels of CRP are present in many infectious and inflammatory diseases (including in patients with coronary artery disease, in whom it is sometimes employed as a risk factor). CRP levels are sometimes monitored serially to determine if infectious or inflammatory diseases have been effectively treated. SEE: *acute phase p.*

decorin-binding p. One of two antigens released by *Borrelia burgdorferi* (the spirochete that causes Lyme disease). The antigen may be useful as a target for Lyme disease vaccination.

denatured p. A protein in which the amino acid composition and stereochemical structure (shape) have been altered by physical or chemical means. SEE: *coagulated p.*

derived p. A protein altered chemically or physically.

fusion p. A protein made from the natural or artificial hybridization and translation of two distinct genes.

G p. A cellular protein activated by the binding of an intercellular signal to its receptor on the cell membrane; the G-protein then activates the enzyme adenyl cyclase within the cell, triggering the formation of cyclic AMP and a stereotyped response.

glial fibrillary acidic p. ABBR: GFAP. An intermediate filament found only in astrocytes and astroglial cells. It forms part of the skeletal structure of neurons. Abnormalities in GFAP are found in a variety of neurological diseases, including Alzheimer's disease, Creutzfeldt-Jakob disease, and some brain tumors.

heart fatty acid-binding p. ABBR: H-FABP. A biomarker in the serum of patients with injury to myocardial cells. H-FABP is present in the serum within about an hour after heart muscle cells are deprived of blood.

heat shock p. Any of a large group of proteins that protect cells from injury caused by increased temperatures or other physical stresses. SYN: *stress response p.*

heparin-binding p. A proinflammatory, antimicrobial peptide released by neutrophils. It increases the permeability of blood vessels. It is found in high concentrations in plasma of patients with septic shock.

HFE p. A protein normally found intracellularly in duodenal crypt enterocytes and the placenta. It is closely associated with transferrin receptors for iron and regulates iron absorption. HFE is a homologue of class I major histocompatibility complex (MHC) molecules. The C2824 and H63D mutations on chromosome 6 in the HFE gene cause hemochromatosis.

high-mobility–group box chromosomal p. 1 ABBR: HMGB1. A component of chromatin, released as a cytokine in the systemic inflammatory response of sepsis.

immune p. An antibody or immunoglobulin produced by plasma cells that identifies foreign antigens and initiates their destruction.

incomplete p. A protein lacking one or more of the essential amino acids. SEE: *amino acid, essential.*

lipopolysaccharide-binding p. One of many acute-phase proteins released into the serum in patients with a gram-negative bacterial infection; it helps to defend the body against sepsis by binding and transferring bacterial endotoxin.

M p. A protein in the cell wall of group A streptococci that helps to inhibit the ingestion of bacteria by polymorphonuclear white blood cells. Some of the more than 80 identified M proteins have been linked to poststreptococcal acute rheumatic fever. Others have been linked to poststreptococcal acute glomerulonephritis.

membrane-bound p., membrane protein A protein that is part of a cell membrane and acts as a receptor for substances transported in extracellular fluid or as an agent that mediates the transport of chemicals into or out of the cell.

native p. A protein in its natural state; one that has not been denatured.

nuclear matrix p. 22 ABBR: NMP22. A tumor marker excreted in the urine of some patients with bladder cancer. NMP22 can be used to screen patients for the disease, esp. for recurrence of the disease after primary treatment.

nucleotide-binding oligomerization domain p.s ABBR: NOD. Any of a family of cytoplasmic proteins that recognize molecules associated with disease-causing bacteria and stimulate cells to secrete cytokines and costimulatory molecules. Inappropriate regulation of NODs has been linked to the pathogenesis of Crohn disease and other syndromes.

oncofetal p. Oncofetal **antigen**.

plasma p. A protein present in blood plasma, such as albumin or globulin.

pregnancy-associated plasma p. A ABBR: PAPP-A. A plasma protein that is used as a screening test between 8 and 14 weeks gestation; diminished levels of the protein suggest an increased risk for Down syndrome, intrauterine growth retardation, preeclampsia, and stillbirth.

p. S A vitamin-K dependent protein that acts with protein C to prevent blood clotting. Deficiencies may lead to venous thrombosis and pulmonary embolism. SEE: *protein C.*

sarcomeric p. Any of the proteins in a sarcomere that contribute to the contraction of a muscle fiber. These proteins include actin, myosin, troponin, and nebulin.

serum p. Any protein in the blood serum. The two main fractions are albumin and the globulins. Serum protein forms weak acids mixed with alkali salts; this increases the buffer effects of the blood but to a lesser extent than does cellular protein.

simple p. Any of the proteins that produce alpha amino acids on hydrolysis (e.g., albumins, albuminoids, globulins, glutelins, histones, prolamines, and protamines).

soy p. A type of vegetable protein found in food products derived from soybeans. Soy-based foods also contain fiber, flavones, phytoestrogens, and other potentially beneficial components. SEE: *soy milk; tofu.*

steroidogenic acute regulatory p. ABBR: StAR protein. A protein found within cells of the adrenal glands and gonads that stimulates the conversion of cholesterol to sex hormones, corticosteroids, and mineralocorticoids.

stress response p. Heat shock **p.**

transport p. One of the proteins important in transporting materials such as hormones from their site of origin to the site of cellular action and metabolism.

vascular cell adhesion p. Vascular cell adhesion molecule-1.

p. Z A vitamin-K–dependent coagulation protein that helps thrombin bind to phospholipids, a critical step in the coagulation cascade. It is made in the liver and circulates in the blood.

proteinaceous (prō″tē-ĭn-ā′shŭs) Pert. to, derived from, or resembling proteins.

proteinase (prō′tē-ĭn-ās) [Gr. *protos,* first, + *lase,* enzyme] A proteolytic enzyme; an enzyme that catalyzes the breakdown of native proteins.

protein balance SEE: under *balance.*

protein-bound Linked to polypeptides; not freely circulating in the plasma. Drugs or toxins that are heavily protein-bound have less impact on body receptors and metabolic functions than those that circulate in a free (unbound) state.

protein C SEE: under *protein.*

protein-calorie malnutrition SEE: under *malnutrition.*

protein catabolic rate ABBR: PCR. In patients receiving hemodialysis, the quantity of urea that appears in the blood between two dialysis sessions, a function of the amino acid content of the patient's diet.

protein chip A tool for evaluating very large numbers of proteins (e.g., the entire proteome of an organism) using DNA microarray technology. Uses include the evaluation of interactions between proteins and other molecules; the development of new drugs; and the diagnosis of diseases, such as immunological disorders, in which small concentrations of abnormal proteins or antigens occur in body fluids.

protein correlation profiling Protein profiling.

protein digestibility corrected amino acid score ABBR: PDCASS. A measure of a food source's amino acid content and its ability to deliver that content to growing children (its digestibility). The PDCASS is used by relief agencies to compare the protein content of foods used to prevent and treat malnutrition in impoverished, undernourished children. It is based on the total nitrogen content of a food source, the percent of essential amino acids in the food, and the ability of a child to absorb those amino acids from the food. Foods that have optimal PDCASS scores include soybeans and egg whites.

protein equivalent of nitrogen appearance ABBR: PNA. Protein catabolic rate.

protein folding The shaping of a protein into its unique three-dimensional conformation from the linked amino acids of which it is composed.

protein kinase An enzyme that activates or inactivates cell proteins or enzymes by adding a phosphate moiety, thereby changing cell functions.

protein-losing enteropathy SEE: under *enteropathy.*

protein misfolding disease Any abnormality that prevents a polypeptide chain from achieving its usual structure in the body, rendering it functionally abnormal or inactive. Examples include sickle cell disease, in which a single genetic substitution makes hemoglobin molecules distorted under low oxygen tension, or Alzheimer disease, in which structurally abnormal amyloid plaques build up in the brain, causing dementia.

proteinopathy, proteopathy (prō″tē-nop′ă-thē, prŏt″ē-op′ă-thē) [*protein, -pathy* + *-pathy*] Any disease or condition that results from the abnormal synthesis, folding, posttranslational modification, or deposition of protein in cells or tissues.

proteinosis (prō″tē-ĭn-ō′sĭs) [″ + *osis,* condition] Accumulation of excess proteins in the tissues.

alveolar p. Pulmonary alveolar **p.**

lipoid p. A rare autosomal recessive condition resulting from an undefined metabolic defect. Yellow deposits of a mixture of protein and lipoid occur, esp. on the mucous surface of the mouth and tongue. Nodules may appear on the face, extremities, and epiglottis and vocal cords, the latter producing hoarseness.

pulmonary alveolar p. A disease of unknown cause in which eosinophilic material is deposited in the alveoli. The principal symptom is dyspnea. Death from pulmonary insufficiency may occur, but complete recovery has been observed. There is no specific treatment, but general supportive measures including antibiotics and bronchopulmonary lavage have helped. In about 25% of cases, the disease clears spontaneously, but in most untreated cases the disease is progressive and leads to respiratory failure. SYN: *alveolar p.* SEE: *bronchoalveolar lavage.*

protein profiling The detection of the character and quantity of specific sets of proteins in blood or other specimens. Protein profiling has been used as a means of diagnosing specific illnesses, esp. cancers or infectious diseases known to release unique protein patterns into serum. Protein profiling may be used as a means of screening for cancer recurrence in previously treated patients or in patients with multiple risk factors for an illness. It may also aid in the crafting of therapies, e.g., by demonstrating that a particular disease is susceptible to a specific drug therapy. SYN: *protein correlation profiling; serum protein profiling; serum protein-expression profiling.*

protein synthesis The manufacturing of proteins from amino acids. Within cells this process is guided by the specific sequence of nucleotides in DNA.

protein targeting Any mechanism by which proteins that have been manufactured by cells are distributed to specific cellular membranes or organelles.

protein therapeutics The use of proteins, such as antibodies or enzymes, to treat disease.

protein transduction SEE: under *transduction.*

protein tyrosine phosphatases A family of phosphate hydrolyzing enzymes that help regulate signaling between cells. Some diseases linked to abnormalities in protein tyrosine phosphatases include allergies, asthma, diabetes mellitus, obesity, and Alzheimer's disease.

proteinuria (prōt″ĕn-ūr′ē-ă, prō″tēn″) [*protein* + *-uria*] Loss of proteins (such as albumin or globulins) in the urine. This finding may be transient and benign or may reflect severe underlying kidney or systemic illness. SYN: *hyperproteinuria.* SEE: *albuminuria; microalbuminuria; nephrotic syndrome.*

PATIENT CARE: Normally, the glomerular membrane allows only low molecular weight proteins to enter the filtrate, and then most of this protein is reabsorbed via the renal tubules. Loss of protein in the urine is a common finding in diseases that damage the glomeruli and/or tubules of the kidneys. Common illnesses that contribute to urinary protein loss include diabetes mellitus, hypertension, kidney stones, multiple myeloma, polycystic kidney disease, and renal artery stenosis. All of these

illnesses may result in progressive kidney failure. The degree of proteinuria can be measured with timed collections of all the urine a person produces (such as 24-hr collection with first specimen discarded and final specimen retained in a day) or by spot urine collections, i.e., by collecting a single specimen and estimating daily protein losses. The urine must not be contaminated with toilet tissue or feces. Controlling high blood pressure and hyperglycemia, taking ACE inhibitors or angiotensin receptor blockers, and limiting dietary protein intake can all have a beneficial effect on patients with urinary protein losses. Minimal proteinuria is more commonly associated with renal diseases that have less glomerular involvement, e.g., pyelonephritis. Moderate proteinuria occurs in various renal diseases or in diseases in which renal failure is a late complication (diabetes mellitus, heart failure). Heavy proteinuria is usually associated with nephritic syndrome. Many therapeutic agents (such as amphotericin B, aminoglucosides, gold preparations, polymixins) cause renal damage, resulting in proteinuria. Benign proteinuria can result from changes in body positioning. Functional proteinuria can be associated with physical exercise as well as emotional or physiologic stress and is usually transient. Proteinuria is associated with progressive kidney failure, the eventual need for dialysis, and an increased risk of death fromcardiovascular diseases.

   glomerular p. Loss of protein (primarily albumin and other large molecules) in the urine because of defects in the glomerular capillary membranes of the kidneys.

   massive p. A nephrotic syndrome with the largest protein losses, specifically in which the urine protein-to-creatinine ratio is greater than 10 mg/mg.

   nephrotic range p. Loss of large amounts of protein in the urine (more than 3 g/day or, when measured by a urine protein-creatinine ratio, more than 3.5 mg/mg).

   orthostatic p. Protein present in the urine only when the patient has been standing. It is not present when the patient is in bed. SYN: *postural p.*

   postural p. Orthostatic **p.**

   transient p. Loss of protein into the urine that appears only briefly or occasionally, e.g., during fevers or seizures). It should be evaluated in people over 50, but in younger people it is usually benign.

   tubular p. The loss of relatively small amino acids, immunoglobulin light chains, and other small proteins (less than 25 kD) in the urine, because of failure of the renal tubules to reabsorb proteins that have been filtered by the glomerulus.

protein Z SEE: under *protein*.

proteo-, prote- [Fr. *protéine*, protein] Prefixes meaning *protein*.

proteobacteria (prō″tē-ō-băk-tē′rē-ă) A diverse phylum of gram-negative bacteria, which includes many intestinal bacteria (e.g., *Escherichia coli, Salmonella*), the nitrogen-fixing bacteria, and the anaerobic purple bacteria.

proteoglycan (prō″tē-ō-glī′kan″) [*prote(in)* + *glycan*] Any of a family of molecules that are fundamental components of mucus and connective tissues. They are composed of sugars linked to polypeptides and are found in organs and tissues throughout the body.

proteolipid (prō″tē-ō-lĭp′ĭd) A lipid-protein complex that is insoluble in water. It is found principally in the brain.

proteolysis (prōt″ē-ol′ĭ-sis) [*protein* + *lysis*] The hydrolysis of proteins, usually by enzyme action, into simpler substances. **proteolytic** (-ŏ-lit′ik), *adj.* **proteolytically** (-i-k(ă-)lē), *adv.*

proteolytic (prō″tē-ō-lĭt′ĭk) Hastening the hydrolysis of proteins.

proteome (prō′tē-ōm″) All of the proteins that can be synthesized from the DNA of an organism.

proteomics (prō″ tē-ōm′ ĭks) The study of the proteins synthesized by living organisms and their impact on health and disease.

proteose (prō′tē-ōs) [Gr. *protos,* first] One of the class of intermediate products of proteolysis between protein and peptone.

    primary p. The first products formed during proteolysis of proteins.

    secondary p. The protein resulting from further hydrolysis of primary proteoses.

proteosome (prōt′ē-ŏ-sōm″) An intracellular enzyme that degrades misfolded or damaged proteins and modulates the quantity of regulatory proteins in the cell. The breakdown of proteins by proteosomes (proteolysis) is triggered when damaged proteins are tagged by ubiquitin.

Proteus (prō′tē-ŭs) [Gr. *Proteus,* a god who could change his form] A genus of gram-negative, facultatively anaerobic, motile bacilli that inhabits the intestinal tract and causes protein decomposition; it is a cause of human infection, esp. of the kidneys, ureters, and bladder.

    P. mirabilis A species abundant in nature and an occasional human pathogen (e.g., of the urinary tract).

    P. vulgaris An essentially saprophytic species that may produce urinary tract infections.

prothrombin (prō-throm′bĭn) [*pro-* + *thrombin*] Coagulation factor II, a plasma protein coagulation factor synthesized by the liver (vitamin K is necessary) and converted to thrombin by prothrombinase and thrombokinase (activated factor X) in the presence of calcium ions. SEE: *blood* **coagulation**; *coagulation* **factor**.

prothrombinase (prō-thrŏm′bĭn-āz) An enzyme important in blood coagulation. In a reaction with activated factors X (Xa) and V (Va) in the presence of calcium and platelets, prothrombinase catalyzes the conversion of prothrombin to thrombin.

prothrombin complex concentrate ABBR: PCC. Plasma that contains only clotting factors II, IX, X (and low levels of factor VII). It is used clinically to reverse the effects of excessive anticoagulation with warfarin.

prothrombin consumption test A test for the amount of thromboplastin present in the plasma that reacts with prothrombin. This is determined by quantitating the prothrombin that remains in the serum after coagulation is complete.

prothrombinemia (prō-thrŏm″bĭn-ē′mē-ă) [Gr. *pro,* before, + *thrombos,* clot, + *haima,* blood] The presence of prothrombin in the blood.

prothrombin time SEE: under *time*.

prothrombotic (prō″throm-bot′ik) [*pro-* + *thrombotic*] Tending to favor or promote blood clotting.

prothymocyte (prō-thī′mō-sīt) A precursor cell that matures and differentiates into a functioning T cell in the thymus gland. SEE: *T cell*.

protime (prō′tĭm′) A common colloquialism for prothrombin time.

protist (prō′tĭst) Any member of the Protista kingdom.

Protista (prō-tĭs′tă) [L., simplest organisms] In taxonomy, a kingdom of organisms that includes the protozoa, unicellular and multicellular algae, and the slime molds. The cells are eukaryotic. SEE: *Protozoa* for illus.; *eukaryote; prokaryote*.

protium (prōt-ē-ŭm, prō′shē-) [*proto-* + *-ium* (1)] SYMB: ¹H. The isotope of hydrogen with an atomic weight (mass) 1. It is most common of the three isotopes known collectively as hydrogen.

proto-, prot- [Gr. *prōtos,* first] **1.** Prefixes meaning *first,earliest, proncipal.* **2.** In chemistry, prefixes indicating the lowest of a series of compounds having the same elements.

protocol (prō′tō-kŏl) [Gr. *protokollon,* first notes glued to manuscript] **1.** Formal ideas, plans, or expectations concerning the actions of those involved in patient care, bench work, administration, or research. **2.** In computer science, the rules or conventions governing the formats and timing of information exchange between communicating devices or processes. SEE: *algorithm*. **3.** A description of the steps to be taken in an experiment or procedure.

therapist-driven p. A patient care plan initiated and carried out by a respiratory care practitioner with the approval of the hospital medical staff.

treatment p. An algorithm or recipe for managing a disease or condition.

protodiastole (prō″tō-dī-ǎs′tō-lē) [Gr. *protos*, first, + *diastole*, expansion] The first of four phases of ventricular diastole characterized by a drop in intraventricular pressure. This occurs immediately after the second heart sound.

proton (prō′tǒn) [Gr. *protos*, first] A positively charged particle forming the nucleus of hydrogen and present in the nuclei of all elements, the atomic number of the element indicating the number of protons present. Its mass is 1836 times that of an electron. SEE: *atom; atomic* **theory;** *electron; element*.

proton pump SEE: under *pump*.

proton therapy A type of particle therapy that uses a beam of protons to irradiate diseased tissue.

proto-oncogene (prōt″ō-ong″kǒ-jēn″) [*proto-* + *oncogene*] A gene that regulates the growth of cells or the signals that cells send to each other. Mutations in proto-oncogenes may cause excessive growth of cells or tissues in several diseases, including cancers.

protopathic (prō-tō-pǎth′ĭk) [″ + *pathos*, disease, suffering] Primitive, undiscriminating, esp. with respect to sensing and localizing pain stimuli. SEE: *sensibility*.

protoplasm (prō′tō-plǎzm) [″ + LL. *plasma*, form, mold] A watery colloid that forms the cytoplasm and nucleoplasm of cells; it is enclosed in a cell membrane that regulates exchanges of materials with the environment. It is a solution of organic (proteins, carbohydrates, lipids) and inorganic (minerals and gases) chemicals in water. SEE: *cell; cytoplasm; nucleus*. **protoplasmic** (prō-tō-plǎz′mǐk), *adj*.

protoplast (prō′tō-plǎst″) [″ + *plassein*, to form] In bacteriology, the sphere remaining after gram-positive bacteria are lysed and their cell walls destroyed. Gram-negative bacteria retain a partial cell wall and are called spheroplasts.

protoporphyria (prō″tō-por-fǐr′ē-ǎ) Porphyria erythropoietica.

protoporphyrin (prō″tō-por′fǐ-rǐn) A derivative of hemoglobin containing four pyrrole nuclei; $C_{34}H_{34}N_4O_4$. It occurs naturally and is formed from heme (ferriprotoporphyrin) by deletion of an atom of iron.

prototype (prō″tō-tīp) An original or initial model or type from which subsequent types arise.

Protozoa (prōt″ǎ-zō′ǎ) [*proto-* + *-zoa*] The phylum of the kingdom Protista that includes unicellular, animal-like microorganisms. Many protozoa are saprophytes that live on dead matter in water and soil. Many parasitic protozoa infect only humans without adequate immunological defenses although a few infect the immunocompetent. Infections are spread by the fecal-oral route, through ingestion of food or water contaminated with cysts or spores, or by the bite of a mosquito or other insect that has previously bitten an infected person. Common protozoan infections include malaria (*Plasmodium vivax, P. malariae*); gastroenteritis (*Entamoeba histolytica, Giardia lamblia*); leishmaniasis, an inflammatory skin or visceral disease (*Leishmania* spp.); sleeping sickness (*Trypanosoma brucei gambiense, T. b. rhodiense*); and vaginal infections (*Trichomonas vaginalis*). *Pneumocystis jiroveci*, previously classified as a protozoon, is now categorized as a fungus. Opportunistic protozoan infections caused by *Cryptosporidium parvum* and *Toxoplasma gondii* are seen in patients who are immunosuppressed by disease or drug therapy. SEE: illus.; table.

protozoa (prōt″ǎ-zō′ǎ) Pl. of protozoon.

protozoal (prō″tō-zō′ǎl) Pert. to protozoa.

protozoal disease A disease produced by parasitic protozoa. Examples include amebic dysentery, sleeping sickness, and malaria.

protozoan (prō″tō-zō′ǎn) [″ + *zoon*, animal] Concerning protozoa.

protozoology (prō″tō-zō-ŏl′ō-jē) [Gr. *protos*, first, + *zoon*, animal, + *logos*, word, reason] The branch of science dealing with the study of protozoa.

protozoon (prōt-ǎ-zō′ŏn″) *pl*. **protozoa** Unicellular organism. SEE: *Protozoa*.

protract (prō-trakt′) [L. *protrahere*, to draw out, prolong] To extend or lengthen in time or space. **2.** In anatomy, to extend or protrude forward and outward.

protraction (prō-trǎk′shŭn) [″ + L. *protractus*, dragged out] The extension forward or drawing forward of a part of the body such as the mandible.

protractor (prō-trǎk′tor) [L. *protractus*, dragged out] **1.** An instrument formerly used to remove foreign bodies from wounds. **2.** A muscle that draws a part forward; the opposite of retractor. **3.** A semicircular device for drawing angles.

protrude [L. *protrudere*] To project; to extend beyond a border or limit.

protrusion (prō-troo′zhŭn) The state or condition of being thrust forward or projecting. In dentistry, particularly related to the position of the mandible, as opposed to retrusion.

protuberance (prō-tū′bĕr-ǎns) [Gr. *pro*, before, + L. *tuber*, bulge] A part that is prominent beyond a surface, like a knob.

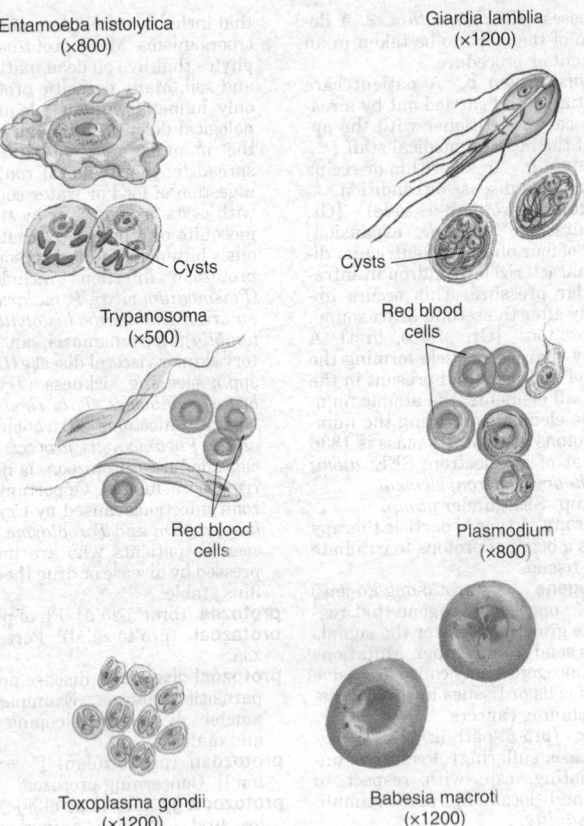

Entamoeba histolytica
(×800)

Giardia lamblia
(×1200)

Cysts

Cysts

Trypanosoma
(×500)

Red blood
cells

Red blood
cells

Plasmodium
(×800)

Toxoplasma gondii
(×1200)

Babesia macroti
(×1200)

PROTOZOA

external occipital p. A bony bump or elevation in the midline of the lower part of the back of the skull in the middle of the occipital bone. It is more prominent in males than in females.

protuberantia (prō-tū″bĕr-ăn′shē-ă) A protuberance, eminence, or projection.

proud flesh (prowd) SEE: *lobular capillary* **hemangioma**.

Proventil (prō′vĕn-tĭl, prō-vĕn′) SEE: *albuterol*.

provider (prŏ-vīd′ĕr) A professional who gives health care services, or an institution that supervises the rendering of such services.

application service p. A company that offers individuals or enterprises access over the Internet to applications and services that would otherwise have to be located on their own computers.

limited-service p. Health care providers or institutions, such as outpatient surgery centers or facilities, that provide care to a market niche, i.e., to those people with a limited number of diseases or conditions.

mid-level p. A category of health care professionals that includes physician assistants, nurse midwives, nurse anesthetists, and nurse practitioners. SYN: *mid-level practitioner*.

nonphysician health care p. Nonphysician p.

nonphysician p. A health care professional licensed to provide healing services that complement or supplement those provided by a physician. Such providers include midwives, nurse practitioners, optometrists, physican assistants, physical or occupational therapists, psychologists, social workers, and chiropractors. In many settings, physicians and nonphysician providers evaluate and treat the same patients. Most states limit the practice privileges and prescribing authority of nonphysician providers. SYN: *nonphysician* **clinician**; *nonphysician health care* **p.**; *nonphysician* **professional**.

prehospital p. A health care provider trained and certified or licensed by the state, who practices emergency assessment and care in the out-of-hospital set-

Table of Pathogenic Protozoa

Subphylum	Genus and Species	Disease Caused
Zoomastigophora (Mastigophora) Locomotion by flagella	*Giardia lamblia*	Gastroenteritis
	Leishmania donovani	Kala azar
	Leishmania braziliensis	American leishmaniasis
	Leishmania tropica	Oriental sore
	Trichomonas vaginalis	Trichomoniasis
	Trypanosoma brucei gambiense, *T. b. rhodiense*	Sleeping sickness
	Trypanosoma cruzi	Chagas disease
Rhizopoda (Sarcodinae) Locomotion by pseudopodia	*Acanthamoeba castellani* *A. culbertsonii* *A. astromyxis*	Amebic meningoencephalitis
	Dientamoeba fragilis	Diarrhea, fever
	Entamoeba histolytica	Amebic dysentery
	Naegleria fowleri	Amebic meningoencephalitis
Apicomplexa (Sporozoa) No locomotion in adult stage	*Babesia microti* *B. divergens*	Babesiosis
	Cryptosporidium parvum	Cryptosporidiosis
	Cyclospora cayetanensis	Diarrhea, gastroenteritis
	Isospora belli	Diarrhea
	Microspora (multiple spp.)	Diarrhea, chronic
	Plasmodium malariae	Quartan malaria
	Plasmodium falciparum	Malignant tertian malaria
	Plasmodium vivax	Tertian malaria
	Plasmodium ovale	Tertian malaria
	Toxoplasma gondii	Toxoplasmosis
Ciliophora Possession of cilia in some stage of life cycle	*Balantidium coli*	Balantidiasis

ting. SEE: *emergency medical technician; first responder; paramedic.*

primary care p. ABBR: PCP. The health care provider the nurse practitioner, physician's assistant, or physician) to whom a patient first goes to address a problem with his or her health.

provider report card A measurement of the compliance of a health care provider with accepted standards of care. Ratings are used as a public means of comparing health care quality and patient care experience A variety of performance factors are used as measures, such as the percentage of a provider's female patients who have undergone Pap testing or mammography, the percentage of school-age patients vaccinated against preventable diseases; or the frequency of hospital-acquired infections among patients.

proving (proo'vĭng) *pl.* **provings** In homeopathy, an assessment of the symptoms experienced by healthy volunteers after they are treated with a proposed remedy.

provirus (prō-vī'rŭs) The nucleic acid of a virus that has been incorporated into the DNA of a host cell.

provisional (prō-vĭzh'ŭn-ăl) [L. *provisio,*

provision] Serving a temporary use pending permanent arrangements.

provitamin (prō-vī'tă-mĭn) [L. *pro,* before, + *vita,* life, + *amine*] An inactive substance that can be transformed in the body to a corresponding active vitamin and thus function as a vitamin.

p. A Carotene, the precursor of vitamin A.

provocation test (prŏv"ă-kā'shŭn) A diagnostic test in which drugs, chemicals, allergens, or physical forces are systematically administered to reproduce symptoms, in order to discover the source of a symptom or the tissue origin of a lesion. Provocation tests are used by specialists in several fields of health care, such as: allergists, to determine which of several agents may produce a patient's rhinitis, wheezing, or rash; physical therapists, to identify relationships between a patient's tissue pathology or impairment and his or her functional limitations; and cardiologists and neurologists, who use tilt table provocation tests to diagnose the cause of a patient's loss of consciousness.

proxemics (prok-sē'miks) [*prox(imity)* + *(phon)emics*] The study of how people interact with each other spatially, e.g., how closely they approach each other, how directly they face each other, and how they enter or leave each other's personal space. **proxemic** (mik), *adj.*

proximad (prŏk´sĭm-ăd) [L. *proximus,* next, + *ad,* toward] Toward the proximal or central point.

proximal (prŏk´sĭm-ăl) Nearest the point of attachment, center of the body, or point of reference; the opposite of distal.

proximate (prŏk´sĭm-āt) Closely related with respect to space, time, or sequence; next to, or nearest.

proxy directive (prok´sē) A form of advanced directive that specifies the person or persons who have power of attorney to make health care decisions for the patient if he or she is no longer competent to make choices.

Prozac (prō´zăk″) SEE: *fluoxetine hydrochloride.*

prozone (prō-zōn) A portion of the low dilution range of a homologous serum that fails to agglutinate bacteria that are agglutinated by the same serum in a higher dilution.

PrP *prion protein.* SEE: *prion disease.*

prune (proon) [L. *pruna*] A dried plum, rich in carbohydrate, potassium, and iron, that contains dihydroxyphenyl isatin, a laxative. Regular consumption may lead to dependence on its laxative properties.

pruriginous (proo-rĭj´ĭ-nŭs) [L. *prurigo,* itch] Pert. to or of the nature of prurigo.

prurigo (proo-rī´gō) [L., *prurigo,* an itch] A chronic skin disease of unknown etiology, marked by constantly recurring, discrete, pale, deep-seated, intensely itchy papules on extensor surfaces of limbs. SYN: *p. nodularis.*

p. agria A severe type of prurigo that starts in childhood and persists. The skin becomes thickened and pigmented. Because of the severe itching and scratching, secondary pustules, boils, and abscesses may develop.

p. estivalis A form of polymorphic light eruption characterized by prurigo and photodermatitis. It recurs every summer and continues during hot weather.

p. mitis Mild prurigo.

p. nodularis Prurigo.

pregnancy p. A form of prurigo that usually has its onset in the middle trimester of pregnancy or later. The lesions occur on the proximal portion of the limbs and upper part of the trunk and usually improve spontaneously before term or rapidly after delivery.

simple acute p. A simple form of prurigo that often recurs. It is thought to be caused by a reaction to bites in sensitive subjects.

p. simplex Urticaria papulosa.

pruritoceptive (proo-rit″ŏ-sep´tiv) [*prurit(us)* + *(re)ceptive*] Pert. to an itch that arises from a primary skin disease as opposed to an itch that is triggered by a systemic or neurological cause.

pruritogenic (proo″rĭ-tō-jĕn´ĭk) [L. *pruritus,* itching, + *gennan,* to produce] Causing pruritus.

pruritus (proo-rīt´ŭs) [L. *pruritus,* itching] A tingling or faintly burning skin sensation that prompts a person to rub or scratch; an itch. It may be a symptom of a disease such as hyperbilirubinemia, an allergic response, or an insect bite. SEE: *Nursing Diagnoses Appendix.* **pruritic** (-rit´ik), *adj.*

TREATMENT: Any inciting or contributory cause should be identified and removed if possible.

p. ani Itching around the anus. This may be due to poor perineal hygiene; perianal skin damage caused by scratching, or abrasion due to use of harsh, dry paper; excess moisture caused by wearing tight, nonporous clothing; decreased resistance to fungi and yeasts during steroid therapy; ingestion of dietary irritants; pinworms; anal fistula or hemorrhoids; or contact with soap or detergents that remain in underclothing following improper washing.

TREATMENT: The primary cause should be removed or avoided. The anus should be kept scrupulously clean by use of a mild soap, and applications of drugs that produce sensitivity and irritation should be avoided.

aquagenic p. Pruritus produced by contact with water.

emperor of p. SEE: *emperor of pruritus.*

essential p. Pruritus without apparent skin lesion.

p. estivalis Pruritus with prickly heat occurring in hot weather.

p. hiemalis Winter **itch**.

p. senilis Pruritus in the aged with degenerative skin changes sometimes caused by loss of epidermal hydration.

vulvar p. Lichen sclerosus et atrophicus.

PSA *prostate-specific antigen.*

psammoma (săm-ō´mă) [Gr. *psammos,* sand, + *oma,* tumor] A small tumor of the brain, the choroid plexus, and other areas, containing calcareous particles.

psammoma body SEE: under *body.*

PSA response SEE: under *response.*

PSC *Posterior subcapsular* **cataract**.

PSDE *painful swollen deformed extremity.*

pseudarthrosis, pseudoarthrosis (sood″ar-thrō´sĭs, sood″ō-ar-thrō´sĭs) [″ + *arthron,* joint, + *osis*] A false joint or abnormal articulation, as one developing after a fracture that has not united. SYN: *nearthrosis*.

pseudo-, pseud- [Gr. *pseudēs,* false] Prefixes meaning *false*.

pseudoachalasia (sood″ō-ă″kă-lā′zh(ē-)ă) [*pseudo- + achalasia*] Difficulty passing food from the esophagus to the stomach not caused by a primary disorder of the swallowing muscles but attributable to another disease such as a mass in the esophagus or a nerve disease affecting lower esophageal motility. SYN: *secondary achalasia*.

pseudoagglutination (soo″dō-ă-glü″tĭ-nā′shŭn) The clumping together of red blood cells as in the formation of rouleaux, but differing from true agglutination in that the cells can be dispersed by shaking.

pseudoalleles (soo″dō-ă-lēlz′) [″ + *allelon,* of one another] A set of genes that seem to be present in the same locus in certain conditions and in closely situated loci in other conditions.

pseudoallergy (sood″ō-al′ĕr-jē) [*pseudo- + allergy*] An allergic-like reaction such as an outbreak of hives that is not caused by activation of the immune system. Some instances are attributable to exposure to food colorings or preservatives.

pseudoanemia (soo″dō-ă-nē′mē-ă) [*pseudo- + anemia*] Pallor of mucous membranes and skin without other signs of true anemia.

   p. of pregnancy A drop in hematocrit during pregnancy. The increase in circulating blood volume reflects an altered ratio of serum to red blood cells; plasma volume increases by 50%, whereas the red blood cell count increases by 30%.

pseudoaneurysm (soo″dō-ăn′ū-rĭzm) [″ + *aneurysma,* a widening] A dilation or tortuosity in a vessel that gives the impression of an aneurysm.

pseudoangina (soo″dō-ăn′jĭ-nă, -ăn-jī′nă) [*pseudo- + angina*] Chest pain in patients who have healthy coronary arteries. The syndrome may be caused by esophageal, peptic, gallbladder, musculoskeletal, pulmonary, pleural, or psychogenic illnesses.

pseudobacteremia (sood″ō-bak″tĕ-rēm′ē-ă) [*pseudo- + bacteremia*] False-positive blood culture results that occur because of contamination of blood culture bottles or other instruments used to obtain blood samples.

pseudoboutonnière deformity (sood″ō-boo″tōn-yār′) SEE: under *deformity*.

pseudocholinesterase (soo″dō-kō″lĭn-ĕs′tĕr-ās) A nonspecific cholinesterase that hydrolyzes noncholine esters as well as acetylcholine. It is found in serum and pancreatic tissue.

pseudocirrhosis (soo″dō-sĭr-ō′sĭs) [″ + ″] Any disease or condition that produces signs and symptoms that falsely suggest of cirrhosis (e.g., right-sided heart failure, constrictive pericarditis, or metastatic breast cancer).

pseudoclaudication (sood″ō-klod″ĭ-kā′shŏn) [*pseudo- + claudication*] Pain in the lower extremities that develops when patients are standing for a long time. The pain is relieved by leaning forward or by sitting. It is caused by lumbar spinal stenosis and not by impaired blood flow through the aorta, iliac, or femoral arteries. SEE: *intermittent* **claudication**.

pseudocroup (soo-dō-kroop′) False croup.

pseudo-Cushing syndrome (sood′ō-koosh′ing) The presence of signs and symptoms of high cortisol levels in people who drink alcohol excessively, have anxiety and depression, severe obesity, or severe acute illness. All these conditions may falsely raise serum cortisol levels and mimic Cushing syndrome. True Cushing syndrome and pseudo-Cushing syndrome can usually be distinguished by repeated dexamethasone suppression tests and repeated measurements of urinary or salivary cortisol.

pseudocyesis (soo″dō-sī-ē′sĭs) [″ + *kyesis,* pregnancy] A condition in which a patient has nearly all of the usual signs and symptoms of pregnancy, such as enlargement of the abdomen, weight gain, cessation of menses, and morning sickness, but is not pregnant. It is usually seen in women who either are very desirous of having children or wish to avoid pregnancy. Treatment usually is done by psychiatric means. Pseudocyesis also occurs in men. SYN: *false pregnancy; phantom pregnancy; pseudopregnancy* (2).

pseudocyst (soo′dō-sĭst) [″ + *kystis,* bladder] A collection of fluid that becomes surrounded by a capsule, esp. a fluid collection that forms in the pancreas during some cases of pancreatitis.

pseudodementia (soo″dō-dē-mĕn′shē-ă) [″ + L. *dementare,* to make insane] An impairment in thinking accompanied by a withdrawal from social interactions that resembles dementia but instead is the result of depression, esp. in the elderly.

pseudodiphtheria (soo″dō-dĭf-thē′rē-ă) [″ + *diphthera,* membrane] A condition resembling diphtheria but not due to *Corynebacterium diphtheriae*.

pseudofolliculitis barbae (soo″dō-fō-lik″yŭ-līt-ĭs bar′bē) [*pseudo- + folliculitis* + L. *barba,* beard] Inflammation of beard follicles when tightly coiled hairs become ingrown. The only sure prevention is not shaving. SYN: *razor bumps*.

pseudofracture (soo″dō-frăk′chūr) A ribbon-like zone of decalcification seen in certain types of osteomalacia.

pseudoglioma (soo″dō-glī-ō′mă) [″ + *glia*, glue, + *oma*, tumor] Inflammatory changes occurring in the vitreous body that simulate glioma of retina but are due to iridochoroiditis.

pseudoglobulin (soo″dō-glŏb′ū-lĭn) [″ + L. *globulus*, little globe] One of a class of globulins characterized by being soluble in salt-free water. SEE: *euglobulin.*

pseudogout (soo′dō-gowt″) Chronic recurrent arthritis that may be clinically similar to gout. The crystals found in synovial fluid are composed of calcium pyrophosphate dihydrate (CPPD), instead of urate (urate crystals accumulate in the synovial fluid in gout). CPPD crystals deposit in fibrocartilage (e.g., meniscus of knee, triangular fibrocartilage of wrist), and these deposits can be identified on radiographs as chondrocalcinosis. The most commonly involved joint is the knee. Multiple joints are involved in two thirds of patients. This condition is treated by joint aspiration, nonsteroidal anti-inflammatory agents, and intra-articular injection of glucocorticoids. SEE: *chondrocalcinosis.*

pseudohemophilia (soo″dō-hē″mō-fĭl′ē-ă) [″ + ″ + *philos*, to love] SEE: *Willebrand disease.*

pseudohermaphrodite (soo″dō-hĕr-măf′rō-dīt) An individual having the sex glands of only one sex but having some of the physical appearances of an individual of the opposite sex.

pseudohermaphroditism (soo″dō-hĕr″maf″rō-dīt″izm, sūd″) [*pseudo-* + *hermaphroditism*] A condition in which an individual has both male and female external genitalia but the internal reproductive organs of only one gender. SYN: *disorder of sex development; false hermaphroditism.* SEE: *intersex.*

   female p. A condition in a female marked by a large clitoris, resembling the penis, and hypertrophied labia majora, resembling the scrotum, thus producing a resemblance to male genitalia. This condition can be caused by disease of the adrenal gland.

   male p. A condition in a male marked by a small penis, perineal hypospadias, and scrotum without testes, thereby resembling the vulva. This condition can be due to disease of the adrenal gland or a feminizing tumor of the undescended testis.

pseudohypertension (soo-dō-hī-pĕr-tĕn′shŭn) The observation of elevated blood pressure when taken by conventional means (i.e., sphygmomanometer), that is in reality not elevated when compared with the actual pressure in the artery when determined by more accurate methods. Accurate blood pressure may be obtained with an intra-arterial catheter. Pseudohypertension usually is found in elderly persons, who may have arterial calcifications that interfere with blood pressure measurements obtained with a cuff. SEE: *indirect measurement of blood pressure; hypertension; infrasonic recorder.*

pseudohypertrophy (soo″dō-hī-pĕr′trō-fē) [″ + *hyper*, above, + *trophe*, nourishment] The increase in size of an organ or structure owing to hypertrophy or hyperplasia of tissue other than parenchyma. It often is accompanied by diminution of function. **pseudohypertrophic** (-trō′fĭk), *adj.*

pseudohyponatremia (sood′ō-hī″pō-nā-trē′mē-ă) [*pseudo-* + *hyponatremia*] A low measured serum sodium level that results from replacement of water and dissolved sodium by excessively high serum levels of lipids or proteins.

pseudohypoparathyroidism (soo″dō-hī″pō-păr″ă-thī′royd-ĭzm) Any of a group of hereditary diseases resembling hypoparathyroidism but caused by an inadequate response to parathyroid hormone rather than a deficiency of the hormone. Some of these patients are obese with short, stocky build and a moonface.

pseudohypopyon (sood″ō-hī-pō′pē-on″) [*pseudo-* + *hypopyon*] A collection of cells infiltrating the anterior chamber of the eye resembling an hypopyon but typically caused instead by cancer or endophthalmitis.

pseudoisochromatic (soo″dō-ī″sō-krō-măt′ĭk) [″ + *isos*, equal, + *chroma*, color] Seemingly of the same color; colors used in charts testing for color blindness.

pseudologia (soo-dō-lō′jē-ă) [″ + *logos*, word, reason] Falsification in writing or in speech, a form of pathological lying.

   p. fantastica Pathological lying, usually for psychological reasons rather than for personal gain. The condition is considered to be a type of factitious disorder.

pseudomelanosis (soo″dō-mĕl-ă-nō′sĭs) [″ + *melas*, black, + *osis*, condition] Discoloration of the tissues after death.

pseudomembrane (soo″dō-mĕm′brăn) [″ + L. *membrana*, membrane] A leaflike or shelflike exudate made of inflammatory debris and fibrin that may form on epithelial surfaces, e.g., in colitis caused by *Clostridium difficile,* or the pharyngitis caused by *Corynebacterium diphtheriae.* SYN: *neomembrane.* **pseudomembranous,** *adj.*

Pseudomonas (soo-dō-mō′năs) [″ + *monas*, single] A genus of gram-negative, aerobic, motile bacilli with polar flagella. Most are saprophytic, living in soil and decomposing organic matter. Some produce blue and yellow pigments.

   P. aeruginosa A species that produces a distinctive blue-green pigment, grows readily in water, and may cause life-threatening infections in humans, including nosocomial pneumonia, urinary tract infections, and sepsis. It may also cause folliculitis, malignant otitis externa, and skin infections in patients who have suffered burns. SEE: illus.

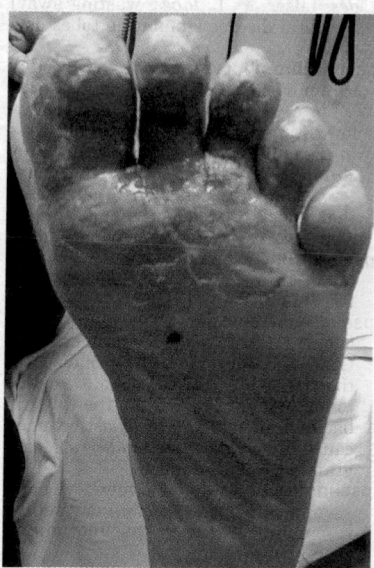

Psuedomonas Aeruginosa

infection of the distal foot

P. cepacia *Burkholderia cepacia.*

P. mallei SEE: under *Burkholderia.*

mucoid P. aeruginosa A variant of *P. aeruginosa* that resists both phagocytosis and antibiotic treatment by secreting a slimy protective coating (alginate slime). It is more virulent than nonmucoid-secreting forms of *P. aeruginosa* and often colonizes patients with bronchiectasis or cystic fibrosis.

P. oryzihabitans A gram-negative rod that can cause health care-related infections, esp. in catheterized, immunosuppressed, or critically ill patients. It was formerly known as *Flavimonas oryzihabitans.*

P. pseudomallei *Burkholderia pseudomallei.*

pseudomucin (soo-dō-mū′sĭn) [″ + L. *mucus,* mucus] A variety of mucin found in ovarian cysts.

pseudomyopia (soo″dō-mī-ō′pē-ă) [″ + *myein,* to shut, + *ops,* eye] A condition in which defective vision causes persons to hold objects close in order to see them, even though myopia is not present.

pseudomyxoma (sood″ŏ-mik-sō′mă, -sō′mă-tă) *pl.* **pseudomyxomaspseudomyxomata** [*pseudo-* + *myxoma*] A peritoneal tumor resembling a myxoma and containing a thick viscid fluid.

p. peritonei A pseudomyxoma develops in the peritoneum from metastases that spread from appendiceal, colonic, or ovarian sources. Numerous papillomas develop, attached to the abdominal wall and intestine, and the peritoneal cavity becomes filled with mucus-like fluid. SYN: *diffuse peritoneal adenomucinosis.*

pseudoneoplasm (soo-dō-nē′ō-plăsm) [″ + *neos,* new, + L. *plasma,* form, mold] A false or phantom tumor; a temporary swelling, usually of an inflammatory nature, that simulates a tumor.

Pseudo-nitzschia australis (soo″dō-nich′ē-ă, sū″, o-strāl′ĭs) A species of marine diatom that produces domoic acid, a neurotoxic amino acid. Shellfish and fish that feed on the diatom are toxic to sea mammals and humans.

pseudopapilledema (soo″dō-păp″ĭ-lĕ-dē′mă) [″ + *papilla,* nipple, + *oidema,* swelling] Elevation of the optic nerve head resembling edema, caused by elevated intracranial pressure (papilledema). It may be congenital or due to optic nerve head drusen.

pseudoparalysis (soo″dō-pă-răl′ĭ-sĭs) [″ + *para,* at the side, + *lyein,* to loosen] A loss of movement caused by the pain and inflammation of a localized injury, an infection, or a factitious disorder, rather than caused by a nerve injury or stroke.

pseudoparasite (soo″dō-păr′ă-sīt) [″ + ″ + *sitos,* food] **1.** Anything resembling a parasite. **2.** An organism that can live as a parasite, although it is normally not one. SEE: *faculative **parasite.***

pseudophakia The condition in which an artificial lens has been implanted in the eye, e.g., after cataract surgery to remove a cloudy lens.

Pseudophyllidea (soo″dō-fĭ-lĭd′ē-ă) An order belonging to the class Cestoidea, subclass Cestoda. It includes tapeworms with scolices bearing two lateral (or one terminal) sucking grooves (bothria) and includes *Diphyllobothrium latum,* the fish tapeworm of humans.

pseudophyphae Filamentous fungal structures that resemble hyphae.

pseudopod (soo′dō-pŏd) [″ + *pous,* foot] Pseudopodium (1).

pseudopodium (soo″dō-pō′dē-ŭm) *pl.* **pseudopodia 1.** A temporary protruding process of a protozoan or ameboid cell, such as a leukocyte, into which the cell flows, for locomotion and the engulfing of food particles or foreign substances, as in phagocytosis. SYN: *pseudopod.* **2.** An irregular projection at the edge of a wheal.

pseudopolyp (soo″dō-pŏl′ĭp) [″ + *polys,* many, + *pous,* foot] A hypertrophied area of mucous membrane resembling a polyp.

pseudopolyposis (soo″dō-pŏl″ĭ-pō′sĭs) [″ + ″ + ″ + *osis*, condition] A large number of pseudopolyps in the colon due to chronic inflammation.

pseudopregnancy (soo″dō-prĕg′năn-sē) [Gr. *pseudes*, false, + L. *praegnans*, with child] **1.** A condition in animals following sterile matings in which anatomical and physiological changes occur, similar to those of pregnancy. **2.** Pseudocyesis.

pseudo-pseudohypoparathyroidism (soo″dō-soo″dō-hī″pō-păr″ă-thī′royd-ĭzm) [″ + *pseudes*, false, + *hypo*, under, + *para*, beside, + *thyreos*, shield, + *eidos*, form, shape + *-ismos*, condition] Pseudohypoparathyroidism in which most of the clinical but none of the biochemical changes are present.

pseudopterygium (soo″dō-tĕr-ĭj′ē-ŭm) [″ + *pterygion*, wing] A scar on the conjunctiva of the eye that is firmly attached to the underlying tissue.

pseudoptosis (soo-dō-tō′sĭs) [″ + *ptosis*, a dropping] Apparent ptosis of the eyelid, resulting from a fold of skin or fat projecting below the edge of the eyelid.

pseudopuberty, precocious (soo-dō-pū′bĕr-tē) Feminization of a young girl due to enhanced estrogen production, but ovulation and cyclic menstruation are absent. Estrogen-secreting tumors of the ovary are the usual cause. Treatment is removal of the tumor.

pseudoreaction (soo″dō-rē-ăk′shŭn) A false reaction; a response to injection of a test substance into the tissues owing to the presence of an allergen other than one for which the test is made.

pseudorelapse of multiple sclerosis (sood″ō-rē′laps″) [*pseudo-* + *relapse*] Neurological deterioration in a patient with multiple sclerosis caused by a new medication, an infection, or another disease rather than by new demyelination in the central nervous system. The signs and symptoms of pseudorelapse improve when the patient's new medication is eliminated or the underlying disorder is treated.

pseudosclerosis (soo″dō-sklē-rō′sĭs) [″ + *sklerosis*, a hardening] A condition with the symptoms, but without the lesions, of multiple sclerosis of the nervous system.

pseudoseizure (sood″ō-sē′zhŭr) [*pseudo-* + *seizure*] A series of movements or behaviors that resemble a seizure but are not caused by abnormal electrical brain activity. Some are simulated for secondary gain, and some by psychological causes; they can be stopped by an act of will. SYN: *nonepileptic attack disorder; psychogenic nonepileptic seizure.*

pseudostenosis (soo″dō-stă-nō′sĭs) Something that mimics stenosis; a condition that gives the false impression of an ob-struction or narrowing, e.g., in a blood vessel, valve, or the spinal canal.

pseudostratified (soo-dō-străt′ĭ-fīd) [″ + L. *stratificare*, to arrange in layers] Apparently composed of layers.

pseudotabes (soo″dō-tā′bēz) [Gr. *pseudes*, false, + L. *tabes*, wasting away] A neural disease simulating tabes dorsalis.

pseudothrombocytopenia (sood″ō-throm″bŏ-sīt″pē′nē-ă, pē′nyă) [*pseudo-* + *thrombocytopenia*] An inaccurately low estimate of the number of platelets in a sample of blood that is caused by clumping of the platelets in the laboratory sample rather than by a disease that affects platelet production or destruction.

pseudotruncus arteriosus (soo″dō-trŭnk′ŭs ăr-tē″rē-ō′sŭs) The severest form of tetralogy of Fallot.

pseudotuberculosis (soo″dō-tū-ber″kū-lō′sĭs) [″ + L. *tuberculus*, tubercle, + Gr. *osis*, condition] A group of diseases that resemble tuberculosis but are due to an organism other than the tubercle bacillus. In humans the most common cause is *Yersinia pseudotuberculosis*, a gram-negative organism.

pseudotumor (sood″ō-too′mŏr) [*pseudo-* + *tumor*] An enlargement or swelling resembling a tumor. **pseudotumoral** (′mŏ-răl), *adj.*

p. cerebri A relatively uncommon neurological condition found in young, overweight women more than in other groups of the population, marked by moderately severe headaches associated with papilledema on physical examination. Imaging studies do not reveal a mass lesion in the brain. Cerebrospinal fluid pressures are markedly elevated when measured by lumbar puncture. Treatment may include diuretics or the surgical construction of a shunt to relieve intracranial hypertension.

Temporary loss of vision may be a symptom. Patients should be followed regularly with visual fields to monitor optic nerve function. If progressive loss of field is noted, optic nerve sheath decompression may be done.

SYN: *benign intracranial hypertension; indiopathic intracranial hypertension.*

pseudoword (soo′dō-wŭrd″) A string of letters that can be pronounced by literate people but has no meaning. The ability to read and pronounce pseudowords is impaired in people who have difficulty reading, e.g., children with dyslexia or some adults with brain damage or stroke.

pseudoxanthoma (soo″dō-zăn-thō′mă) [″ + *xanthos*, yellow, + *oma*, tumor] A condition resembling xanthoma.

p. elasticum An autosomal recessive disease that affects elastic tissues in cardiovascular tissues and skin. Abnormalities in the retina may result in the finding of angioid streaks on physical examination, and blindness. Arterial damage in other organs can result in ischemia. Skin lesions include yellow xanthomatoid patches and excess skin laxity.

psi *pounds per square inch.*

psilocin (sī′lō-sĭn) A hallucinogen similar to psilocybin.

psilocybin (sī″lō-sī′bĭn) A rapidly acting visual hallucinogen derived from the mushroom *Psilocybe mexicana* and related species, sometimes used by recreational substance abusers.

psittacosis (sĭt-ă-kō′sĭs) [Gr. *psittakos,* parrot, + *osis,* condition] A relatively uncommon flulike illness caused by *Chlamydia psittaci,* a microbe that is transmitted to humans from infected birds. It causes an atypical pneumonia with headache, sore throat, fevers and chills, cough, anorexia, muscle aches, and other nonspecific symptoms. It is treated with tetracyclines. SYN: *ornithosis; parrot fever.* SEE: *Chlamydia.*

psoas (sō′ăs) [Gr. *psoa*] One of two muscles of the loins, psoas major and psoas minor.

psoralen (sŏr-ă-lĕn) One of a group of plant-derived chemicals that sensitize the skin to damage by ultraviolet light. Drugs derived from psoralens, such as methoxsalen and trioxsalen, are used to treat vitiligo, psoriasis, and cutaneous T-cell lymphoma. Side effects from the use of psoralens may include drying and chapping of the skin and an increased risk of developing skin cancer. SEE: *psoriasis; PUVA therapy; vitiligo.*

psoriasiform (sō-rī′ă-sī-form) Resembling psoriasis; psoriasis-like. It applies to a rash that resembles the plaquelike erythematous lesions of psoriasis; also used in reference to joint conditions resembling those of psoriatic arthritis. SEE: *psoriasis; psoriatic arthritis.*

psoriasis (sŏ-rī′ă-sĭs) [Gr. *psōriasis,* itching] A chronic skin disorder affecting 1% to 2% of the population, in which red papules and scaly silvery plaques with sharply defined borders appear on the body surface. The rash commonly is found on the knees, shins, elbows, umbilicus, lower back, buttocks, ears, and along the hairline. Pitting of the nails also occurs frequently. Patients complain of itching and sometimes of pain from dry, cracked, or encrusted lesions. Removal of scales usually causes fine bleeding points. Widespread shedding of scales is common, and occasionally the disease becomes pustular. The severity of the disease may range from a minimal cosmetic problem to total body surface involvement. About a third of all affected patients have a family history

of the disease. **psoriatic** (sōr″ē-at′ik), *adj.* SEE: illus.

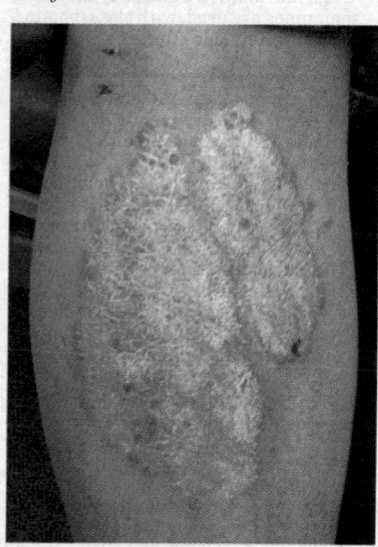

PSORIASIS

silvery plaque on the shin

Although psoriasis may begin at any time of life, the most common age of onset is between 10 and 40. Sudden onset may be related to HIV. The condition has relapses and partial remissions, but established lesions often persist for many months or years. Flare-ups may be related to specific systemic and environmental factors or may be unpredictable. About 5% of patients also develop inflammatory arthritis that commonly affect fingers and toes or sacroiliac joints, and patients with psoriasis have an increased rate of inflammatory bowel disease. SEE: *Nursing Diagnoses Appendix.*

ETIOLOGY: Although the cause of psoriasis is unknown, some evidence suggests that immune dysregulation contributes to excessive proliferation of skin. Families with psoriasis have been found to have a significantly higher-than-normal incidence of certain human leukocyte antigens. Genetic studies show that about one third of affected patients have a family history of the disease. Emotional stress, skin trauma, cold weather, infections, and some drugs may trigger attacks.

TREATMENT: The disease has no cure, and all treatments are palliative. Topical corticosteroids, coal tar derivatives, vitamin D_3 analogs (e.g., calcipotriene), retinoids (e.g., etretinate, tacarotene), ultraviolet light exposure, and saltwater immersion are among the many methods that have been used effectively to treat this condition. For severe disease, immune-modulating drugs like methotrexate or cyclosporine sometimes are used, with close monitoring to prevent side effects.

⚠ Many treatments for psoriasis carry some risk for the patient. Etretinate, for example, produces fetal abnormalities and should never be used by women of childbearing age. Phototherapy with ultraviolet light increases the risk of developing many types of skin cancer. Patients receiving PUVA therapy must wear goggles during treatments, stay out of the sun on treatment days, and protect their eyes with UVA-screening sunglasses for 24 hr after the therapy. Use of methotrexate use requires regular monitoring of liver function, renal function, complete blood counts, and lung function.

PATIENT CARE: The nurse teaches the patient the prescribed therapy to soften and remove scales, to relieve pruritus, to reduce pain and discomfort, to retard rapid cell proliferation, and to help induce remission and monitors for adverse reactions. Assistance is provided to help the patient gain confidence in managing these largely palliative treatments, many of which require special instructions for application and removal. The patient should protect against and minimize trauma. The patient's ability to manage therapies and their results are evaluated. The patient learns to identify stressors that exacerbate the condition, and to avoid and reduce these as much as possible. If the patient smokes cigarettes, participation in a smoking cessation program is recommended. The nurse helps the young patient (aged 20 to 30) to deal with body image changes and effects on self-esteem, encourages the patient to verbalize feelings, and supports the patient through loss of body image and associated grief. Psychological problems often occur. Referral for psychological counseling or cosmetic concealment therapy may be necessary. Patients and their families should be referred to the National Psoriasis Foundation and its local chapters for information and support. (800-723-9166; www.psoriasis.org)

p. annularis Circular or ringlike lesions of psoriasis.

p. buccalis Leukoplakia of the oral mucosa.

elephantine p. A rare but persistent psoriasis that occurs on the back, thighs, and hips in thick scaling plaques.

guttate p. Psoriasis characterized by small distinct lesions that generally occur over the body. The lesions appear particularly in the young after acute streptococcal infections. SEE: illus.

GUTTATE PSORIASIS

on the back

nummular p. The most common form of psoriasis with disks and plaques of varying sizes on the extremities and trunk. There may be a great number of lesions or a solitary lesion.

pustular p. Psoriasis in which small sterile pustules form, dry up, and then form a scab.

rupioid p. Psoriasis with hyperkeratotic lesions on the feet.

p. universalis Severe generalized psoriasis.

PSP *phenolsulfonphthalein.*

PSRO *Professional Standards Review Organization.*

PSV *pressure support ventilation.*

PSVT *paroxysmal supraventricular tachycardia.*

psych-, psycho- [Gr. *psychē,* breath, life, soul, mind] Prefixes meaning *mind, mental processes.*

psyche (sī'kē) [Gr. *psyche,* soul, mind] The mind and mental processes.

psychedelic (sī"kĕ-dĕl'ĭk) [" + *delos,* manifest] Mind-altering; hallucinogenic; capable of producing an altered state of awareness or consciousness. It is said of drugs such as lysergic acid diethylamide (LSD).

psychiatric (sī-kē-ă'trĭk) [" + *iatrikos,* healing] Pert. to psychiatry.

psychiatric technician A technician who works under the supervision of a professional in the care of mentally ill patients in a psychiatric care facility. This person assists in carrying out the prescribed treatment plan and assigned individual and group activities with patients.

psychiatrist (sī-kī′ă-trĭst) A physician who specializes in the study, treatment, and prevention of mental and behavioral disorders.

psychiatry (sī-kī′ă-trē) The branch of medicine that deals with the study, diagnosis, treatment, and prevention of mental illness.

consultation-liaison p. Psychiatry that addresses the needs of patients who also have active medical conditions.

descriptive p. A system of psychiatry concerned with readily observable external factors that influence the mental state of an individual. SEE: *dynamic p.*

dynamic p. The study of the origin, influence, and control of emotions. This involves investigating the factors both from within and without that alter emotions and motivation. Such analysis provides a basis for judging regression or progression.

emergency p. The treatment of patients suffering psychological crises, including those who are suicidal or homicidal, perpetrators or victims of child abuse, spousal abuse, or other intense mental anguish. Most of these people see a physician within hours or days of their violent or abusive act. Many physician training programs fail to prepare students for managing patients who need this emergency service.

forensic p. The use of psychiatry in legal matters, esp. in determining social adaptability of a person suspected of insanity; or the presence or absence of insanity, esp. at the time a person committed a crime.

orthomolecular p. The study of the impact of natural (e.g., mineral or vitamin) or artificial (e.g., neuroleptic agents) on mental health and mental illness.

transcultural p. The study, treatment, and prevention of emotional and behavioral disorders in immigrants or in members of a nondominant social group within society.

psychic, psychical (sī′kĭk, sī′ki-kăl) [Gr. *psychikos,* pert. to the soul] **1.** Pert. to the mind or psyche. **2.** Someone supposedly endowed with preternatural or supernatural powers, such as the ability to read the minds of others or to foresee the future.

psychoactive (sī″kō-ăk′tĭv) [″ + L. *actio,* action] Having an impact on thinking, mood, or behavior. The term typically is used to describe the effects of drugs or toxins.

psychoanalysis (sī″kō-ă-năl′ĭ-sĭs) [″ + *analysis,* a dissolving] A method of obtaining a detailed account of past and present mental and emotional experiences in order to make the unconscious and often irrational underpinnings of thought and behavior available to the conscious mind. The theory of psychoanalysis, first elaborated by Sigmund Freud, is that repressed thoughts and feelings have undesirable effects on behavior and personality, often eccentrically shaping, or establishing unwanted boundaries on conscious life. By making patients aware of their existence, origin, and inappropriate expression in emotions and behavior, the analyst aims to enhance human life and experience. The term "psychoanalysis" is often used synonymously with Freudianism; but the practice has grown to include many other styles of free association by patients, and the interpretation of the nuances of the patient's speech, by the analyst.

Psychoanalysis includes a study of the ego in relationship to reality and the conflicting goals so created. This conflict is solved by repressing one component. This repressed or censored emotion-laden complex of ideas exists in the subconscious, manifesting itself in the hidden content of dreams, neuroses, and tension states. Angry outbursts, rationalization of unfair attitudes, or slips of the tongue occur because the patient is unaware of the influence of the subconscious.

Repressed material is, in Freudian analysis, sexual. The peculiar conditioning of the patient is determined chiefly by emotional experiences of earlier years. Reactions of inferiority may result in a compensatory reaction of goodness or ambition. Sublimation is the escape of creative interest on levels not socially taboo. Therefore, psychoanalysis makes an effort to bring forgotten memories into the conscious mind. The patient thus is enabled to view the occurrence in its true perspective and to minimize its harm.

In addition to the Freudian tradition, other schools of psychoanalysis include analytical psychology (Jung), psychobiology (Meyer), and individual psychology (Adler).

psychoanalyst (sī″kō-ăn′ă-lĭst) [Gr. *psyche,* mind, + *analysis,* a dissolving] One who practices psychoanalysis. SYN: *analyst* (2).

psychobiology (sī″kō-bī-ŏl′ō-jē) [″ + *bios,* life, + *logos,* word, reason] **1.** The study of the biology of the psyche, including the anatomy, physiology, and pathology of the mind. **2.** A method of psychoanalysis employing distributive analysis, which includes a study of all mental and physical factors involved in an individual's growth and development.

objective p. Psychobiology in which special emphasis is placed on the relationship of the individual to his or her environment.

psychodiagnosis (sī″kō-dī″ăg-nō′sĭs) [″ + *diagignoskein*, to discern] The use of psychological tests to assist in diagnosing diseases, esp. mental illness.

psychodiagnostics (sī″kō-dī″ăg-nŏs′tĭks) The use of psychological testing as an aid in diagnosing mental disorders.

Psychodidae (sī″kŏd′ĭ-dē) A family of the order Diptera, characterized by minute size, long legs, and hairy bodies and wings. It includes moth flies, owl midges, and sandflies. SEE: *Phlebotomus*.

psychodrama (sī″kō-drăm′ă) [″ + L. *drama*, drama] A form of group psychotherapy. Patients act out assigned roles and, in so doing, are able to gain insight into their own mental disturbances.

psychodynamics (sī″kō-dī-năm′ĭks) [″ + *dynamis*, power] The scientific study of mental action or force.

psychoeducation (sī″kō-ĕj″oo-kā′shŭn) A means of providing patients with psychiatric illnesses with the skills to co-manage their illnesses. These skills include improving adherence to treatment regimens, managing stressful events and symptom relapses, enhancing social and familial integration and unity, and decreasing the need for hospitalization.

psychogenesis (sī″kō-jĕn′ĕ-sĭs) [″ + *genesis*, generation, birth] **1.** The origin and development of mind; the formation of mental traits. **2.** Origin within the mind or psyche.

psychogenetic (sī″kō-jĕn-ĕt′ĭk) **1.** Originating in the mind, as a disease. **2.** Concerning formation of mental traits.

psychogenic (sī-kō-jĕn′ĭk) [″ + *gennan*, to produce] **1.** Of mental origin. **2.** Pert. to the development of the mind. SEE: *psychogenetic*.

psychogeriatric (sī-kō-jĕr-ē-ăt′rĭk) Pert. to the psychiatric disorders that may affect elderly persons.

psycholinguistics (sī″kō-lĭng-gwĭs′tĭks) The study of linguistics as it relates to human behavior.

psychological (sī″kō-lŏj′ĭ-kăl) [″ + *logos*, word, reason] Pert. to the study of the mind in all of its relationships, normal and abnormal.

psychologist (sī-kŏl′ō-jĭst) One who is trained in methods of psychological analysis, therapy, and research.

psychology (sī-kol′ŏ-jē) [*psych-* + *-logy*] The science dealing with mental processes, both normal and abnormal, and their effects upon behavior. There are two main approaches to the study: introspective, i.e., engaging in self-examination of one's own mental processes; and objective, studying of the minds of others.

　abnormal p. The study of deviant behavior and the associated mental phenomena.

　analytic p. Psychoanalysis based on the concepts of Carl Jung, de-emphasizing sexual factors in motivation and emphasizing the "collective unconscious" and "psychological types" (introvert and extrovert).

　animal p. The study of animal behavior.

　applied p. The application of the principles of psychology to special fields (e.g., clinical, industrial, educational, nursing, or pastoral).

　clinical p. The branch of psychology concerned with diagnosing and treating mental disorders.

　cognitive p. The study of the processes of reasoning and decision making.

　criminal p. The branch of psychology concerned with the behavior and therapy of those convicted of crimes.

　depth p. The psychology of unconscious behavior, as opposed to the psychology of conscious behavior.

　dynamic p. Psychology of motivation; that which seeks the causes of mental phenomena.

　experimental p. The study of mental acts by tests and experiments.

　genetic p. The branch of psychology concerned with the inheritance of psychological characteristics.

　gestalt p. Psychology that emphasizes the importance of the wholeness of psychological processes and behavior, rather than their components.

　individual p. A system of psychological thinking developed by Alfred Adler in which an individual is regarded as having three life goals: physical security, sexual satisfaction, and social integration.

　physiological p. Psychology that deals with the structure and function of the nervous system and other bodily organs and their relationship to behavior.

　social p. The branch of psychology concerned with the study of groups and their influence on the individual's actions and mental processes.

psychometrician (sī″kō-mĕ-trĭsh′ăn) [Gr. *psyche*, mind, + *metron*, measure] A person skilled in the application of statistical analysis to psychological data.

psychometric test (sī″kō-mĕ′trĭk) Any metric used to assess cognition, behavior, or other psychological variables.

psychometry (sī-kŏm′ĕ-trē) [″ + *metron*, measure] The measurement of psychological variables, such as intelligence, aptitude, behavior, and emotional reactions.

psychomotor (sī″kō-mō′tor) [″ + L. *motor*, a mover] Concerning or causing physical activity associated with mental processes.

psychomotor and physical development of infant The physical growth of an infant and the effect of mental activity on motor skills. It is important that all concerned with the care of the newborn through infancy have guidelines for comparing the growth and development of an individual with normal standards. Certain activities of infants serve as general indicators of normal psychomotor development. The average ages for certain of these activities are shown in the accompanying table. SEE: table; *arousal level.*

Appearance and loss of certain reflexes and reactions: The Moro reflex is present at birth and disappears by 3 to 6 months; the stepping and placing reflexes are present at birth and are no longer obtainable by 6 weeks; the tonic neck reflex is usually present at 2 months and is gone by 6 months; neck righting appears at 4 to 6 months and is gone by 24 months; the parachute reaction is present at 9 months and persists; sucking and rooting are present at birth and are usually gone by 4 months if tested while awake and by 7 months if tested while the infant is asleep; palmar grasp is present from birth to 6 months; plantar grasp is present from birth to 10 months.

psychomotor retardation A generalized slowing of physical and mental reactions; seen frequently in depression, intoxications, and other conditions.

psychoneuroendocrinology (sī″kō-nū″rō-ĕn″dō-krĭn-ŏl′ō-jē) [″ + ″ + ″] The study of hormones and their effects on the brain and on animal and human behavior.

psychoneuroimmunology (sī-kō-nū″rō-

Psychomotor and Physical Development: Birth to 1 Year

		Physical Development			
		Length Range		Weight Range	
		In	Cm	Lb	Kg
Birth	boys	18¼–21½	46.4–54.4	5½–9¼	2.54–4.15
	girls	17¾–20¾	45.4–52.9	5¼–8½	2.36–3.81
1 Month	boys	19¾–23	50.4–58.6	7–11¾	3.16–5.38
	girls	19¼–22½	49.2–56.9	6½–10¾	2.97–4.92
3 Months	boys	22¼–25¾	56.7–65.4	9¾–16¼	4.43–7.37
	girls	21¾–25	55.4–63.4	9¼–14¾	4.18–6.74
6 Months	boys	25–28½	63.4–72.3	13¾–20¾	6.20–9.46
	girls	24¼–27¾	61.8–70.2	12¾–19¼	5.79–8.73
9 Months	boys	26¾–30¼	68.0–77.1	16½–24	7.52–10.93
	girls	26–29½	66.1–75.0	15½–22½	7.0–10.17
12 Months	boys	28¼–32	71.7–81.2	18½–26½	8.43–11.99
	girls	27½–31¼	69.8–79.1	17¼–24¾	7.84–11.24

Psychomotor Development	
Birth through 1st Month	Ability to suck, swallow, gag, cry, and maintain eye contact with a person. Head needs to be supported. Loud noises may cause a startle reflex.
2nd Month	May turn to either side when on their backs; will follow moving objects; able to lift head but not for a sustained period; begin to smile, frown, and turn away.
3rd Month	Greater movement and vocal response to stimuli; notice own hands and suck on them; head steady while supported.
4th and 5th Months	Able to lift head higher when lying on stomach; will reach for objects and may be able to encircle a bottle with both hands; may drool a lot; attempt to put all kinds of objects in mouth.
6th–9th Month	Develop ability to grasp and pick up food; are able to pull up to a sitting position and eventually will crawl; begin to make noises that sound like words and to recognize certain words; will play peek-a-boo.
9th–11th Month	Develop ability to handle food and to drink from a cup; may imitate sounds and say certain words; crawl by pulling body along with arms, and pull themselves to a standing position; they will point at objects and throw things; they want to feed themselves and to help with dressing and undressing; they will walk while holding a person's hand.
12th Month	Can eat food alone and drink from a cup with assistance; able to move around easily and crawl up stairs and out of crib.

ĭm-ū-nŏl'ō-jē) ABBR: PNI. The study of the relationships that exist among the central nervous system, autonomic nervous system, endocrine system, and immune system. Social scientists use the data gathered from studies as they examine the impact of psychosocial stressors and the psychophysiological stress response on the development of disease. SEE: *mind-body medicine*.

psychoneurosis (sī″kō-nū-rō'sĭs) [″ + *neuron,* sinew, + *osis,* condition] Neurosis.

psychoneurotic (sī″kō-nū-rŏt'ĭk) [Gr. *psyche,* mind, + *neuron,* sinew] **1.** Pert. to a functional disorder of mental origin. **2.** A person suffering from a neurosis.

psychopath (sī'kō-păth) [″ + *pathos,* disease, suffering] A person who consistently and repeatedly treads on, abuses, or violates the rights of others, often causing considerable harm. SEE: *antisocial personality disorder.*

psychopathic (sī″kō-păth'ĭk) **1.** Pert. to or characterized by a mental disorder. **2.** Pert. to the treatment of mental disorders. **3.** Abnormal.

psychopathology (sī″kō-păth-ŏl'ō-jē) [″ + *pathos,* disease, suffering + *logos,* word, reason] The study of the causes and nature of mental disease or abnormal behavior.

psychopathy (sī-kŏp'ă-thē) Any mental disease, esp. one associated with defective character or personality. SEE: *antisocial personality disorder.*

psychopharmacology (sī″kō-fär″mă-kŏl'ō-jē) The study and use of drugs that influence thinking, behavior, or emotion.

psychophysical (sī″kō-fĭz'ĭ-kăl) [″ + *physikos,* natural] Pert. to the relationship of the physical and the mental.

psychophysics (sī″kō-fĭz'ĭks) **1.** The study of mental processes in relationship to physical processes. **2.** The study of stimuli in relationship to the effects they produce.

psychophysiological (sī″kō-fĭz-ē-ō-lŏj'ĭ-kăl) Pert. to psychophysiology.

psychophysiological insomnia SEE: under *insomnnia.*

psychophysiology (sī″kō-fĭz″ē-ŏl'ō-jē) Physiology of the mind; science of the correlation of body and mind.

psychoprophylactic preparation for childbirth (sī″kō-prō″fĭ-lak'tik) [*psych-* + *prophylactic*] Mental and physical training of the mother for delivery. The goals of the preparation are to dispel the fear of pain and the delivery of a healthy child. SEE: *natural childbirth; prepared childbirth; Lamaze method.*

psychoprophylaxis (sī″kō-prō″fĭ-lak'sĭs) [*psych-* + *prophylaxis*] In obstetrics, a method of mental and physical preparation for natural childbirth. SEE: *natural childbirth; Lamaze method.*

psychosensory (sī″kō-sĕn'sō-rē) [″ + L. *sensorius,* organ of sensation] **1.** Understanding and interpreting sensory stimuli. **2.** Pert. to perceptions not arising in sensory organs, as hallucinations.

psychosexual (sī″kō-sĕks'ū-ăl) [Gr. *psyche,* soul, mind, + L. *sexus,* sex] Pert. to the emotional components of sexual behavior.

psychosexual development Evolution of personality through infantile and pregenital periods to sexual maturity.

psychosine (sī″kō-sīn″, sēn″) A glycosylated lipid found in the brains of patients with Krabbe disease. It produces premature death of neurons and the clinical features of Krabbe disease.

psychosis (sī-kō'sĭs) *pl.* **psychoses** [*psycho-* + *-osis*] A mental disorder in which there is severe loss of contact with reality, evidenced by delusions, hallucinations, disorganized speech patterns, and bizarre or catatonic behavior. Psychotic disorders are common features of schizophrenia, bipolar disorders, and some affective disorders. They can also result from substance abuse (e.g., the use of hallucinogens), substance withdrawal (e.g., delirium tremens), or side effects of some prescription drugs.

SYMPTOMS: In psychotic states patients may express unusual ideas (e.g., that they can read the minds of others, send radio messages directly to God or inanimate objects, travel to distant galaxies). These ideas are called delusions. Psychosis also is marked by patient reports of hearing voices (auditory hallucinations) or seeing objects or persons not visible to others (visual hallucinations). Auditory hallucinations are hallmarks of schizophrenic and manic states, while visual hallucinations are characteristic of drug intoxication or withdrawal. Disturbances in thought content and form, perception, affect, sense of self, volition, interpersonal relationships, and psychomotor behavior occur. Thorough physical and psychiatric examinations rule out organic causes of the patient symptoms and establish the diagnosis.

TREATMENT: Treatment goals focus on meeting the patient's physical and psychosocial needs, and usually combine drug therapies with behavioral therapies, long-term psychotherapy, psychosocial rehabilitation, and/or vocational counseling, requiring use of community resources. Patients with psychosis are treated effectively with neuroleptic drugs (which appear to work by blocking postsynaptic dopamine receptors), such as haloperidol, risperidone, or chlorpromazine. Side effects of some of these medications include dystonic reactions and tardive dyskinesia. The newer agents produce fewer of these extrapyramidal symptoms. Treatment drugs also have sedative, anticholinergic, and orthostatic hypotension effects, and about 1% of patients taking these agents experience neuroleptic malignant syndrome (life-threatening fever, muscle rigidity, and altered level of consciousness).

PATIENT CARE: The psychotic patient should be treated gently and with respect. A safe environment should be maintained, with suicide precautions instituted if needed. Trusting relationships are gradually developed, while avoiding promotion of dependence. Engaging the patient in reality-oriented activities that involve human contact and employing reality-orientation is helpful. Attempts to correct delusional thinking should be avoided because delusions are resistant to logical argument, and discussion about them may be misinterpreted. Because psychotic patients behave violently on occasion, careful practitioners eschew confrontation with them, and obtain immediate help to protect the safety of all involved.

⚠ 1. Unfamiliar religious experiences and rituals may have all the hallmarks of psychosis when viewed by individuals from different cultures. What constitutes an especially meaningful experience in one society may be recognized as psychosis by another.
2. When assisting a psychotic patient, most clinicians sit close to a door, so that if they feel the need to leave the room quickly, they can do so unimpeded.

Clinicians need to be honest and dependable, and should never make promises that cannot be kept. The family needs to be involved in therapies, taught to recognize adverse drug effects and signs of relapse, as well as ways to manage patient symptoms. Patients are taught to manage their drug regimens, and advised to report any adverse reactions they experience, but not to discontinue a drug without specific direction from the primary care provider. If blood testing is required, the patient is taught when and where this monitoring will take place. If slow-release formulations are used, the patient needs to know when to return for the next dose.

alcoholic p. Loss of contact with reality that results from acute or chronic alcohol use. Examples are pathological intoxication, delirium tremens, Korsakof psychosis, and acute hallucinosis. SEE: *acute alcoholism; acute alcoholic hallucinosis; delirium tremens; intoxication; Korsakoff syndrome.*

depressive p. Psychosis characterized by extreme depression, melancholia, and feelings of unworthiness.

drug p. Psychosis caused by intoxication.

functional p. A psychosis in which there is no apparent pathology of the central nervous system.

gestational p. Psychosis that occurs during pregnancy.

involutional p. Psychosis occurring during the period of bodily and intellectual decline.

manic depressive p. Bipolar disorder.

organic p. Psychosis induced by structural brain changes. Emotional instability, irritability, angry outbursts, and inattention are typical symptoms. At any time in the course of the disease, memory, comprehension, ideation, and orientation may become defective. Possible causes include alcohol, narcotics, trauma, syphilis, drugs, poisons, chronic infections, encephalitis, and brain tumors.

postinfectious p. A psychosis following an infectious disease such as meningitis, pneumonia, or typhoid fever.

postpartum p. A psychosis that develops during the 6 months after childbirth, the highest incidence being in the third to sixth day after delivery through the first month postpartum. The symptoms and signs include hallucinations, delusions, preoccupation with death, self-mutilation, infanticide, distorted reality, and interpersonal dependency. Therapies to treat this condition include estrogens, electroconvulsive therapies, lithium, and neuroleptic drugs. SYN: *puerperal p.* SEE: *postpartum depression.*

puerperal p. Postpartum **p.**

situational p. Psychosis due to excessive stress in an unbearable environmental situation.

steroid-induced p., steroid p. A psychosis that follows the administration of corticosteroids (e.g., prednisone or methylprednisolone) and cannot be clearly ascribed to another cause. The psychosis may remit after steroids are withheld or may respond to neuroleptic drugs or electroconvulsive therapy.

toxic p. Psychosis brought on by intoxication.

traumatic p. Psychosis or schizophrenia-like illnesses occurring in people who have suffered traumatic brain injury.

psychosocial (sī″kō-sō′shăl) Pert. to both psychological and social factors.

psychosomatic (sī″kō-sō-măt′ĭk) [Gr. *psyche*, mind, + *soma*, body] Pert. to the relationship of the brain and body, esp. to disorders that have a physiological component but are thought to originate in the emotional state of the patient. When the term is used, the impression is created that the brain and body are separate entities and that a disease may be purely somatic in its effect or entirely emotional. This partitioning of the human being is not possible; thus no disease is limited to only the brain or the body. A complex interaction is always present even though in specific instances a disease might on superficial examination appear to involve only the body or the mind.

psychosomatic disease Somatoform disorder.

psychostimulation (sī″kō-stim″yŭ-lā′shŏn) [*psycho-* + *stimulation*] Cognitive **stimulation**.

psychosurgery (sī″kō-sur′jĕr-ē) [″ + L. *chirurgia,* surgery] Surgical intervention for mental disorders, e.g., frontal lobotomy.

psychotherapist (sī″kō-thĕr′ă-pĭst) An individual trained or skilled in the management of psychological disorders.

psychotherapy (sī″kō-ther′ă-pē) [*psycho-* + *therapy*] A method of treating disease, esp. psychic disorders, by mental rather than pharmacological means, e.g., suggestion, reeducation, hypnotism, and psychoanalysis.

psychotic (sī-kŏt′ĭk) Pert. to or affected by psychosis.

psychotogenic (sī-kŏt″ō-jĕn′ĭk) [″ + *gennan,* to produce] Producing a psychosis, usually temporary and due to certain powerful drugs.

psychotomimetic (sī-kŏt″ō-mĭ-mĕ′tĭk) [″ + *mimetikos,* imitative] Pert. to or producing a state resembling psychosis.

psychro-, psychr- [Gr. *psykhros,* cold, chill] Prefixes meaning *cold.* SEE: also *cryo-.*

psychrometer (sī″krom′ĕt-ĕr) [*psychro-* + *-meter*] A device for measuring relative humidity of the atmosphere. Calculations are made using the readings of two thermometers, one with a dry bulb and one with a wet bulb. SYN: *wet-and-dry-bulb* **thermometer**.

psychrophile (sī′krō-fīl″) [*psychro-* + *-phile*] A microorganism that can thrive in exceptionally cold environments, e.g., from 32° to 50°F (0° to 10°C.

psychrophilic (sī″krō-fil′ik) [*psychro-* + *-philic*] Preferring cold, as bacteria that thrive at low temperatures, between 0° and 30°C (32° and 86°F).

psyllium seed (sĭl′ē-ŭm) The dried ripe seed of the psyllium plant (*Plantago afra*), grown in France, Spain, and India; used as a mild laxative. It is also used in symptomatic treatment of diarrhea. It enhances stool consistency by absorbing water from the bowel contents.

PT *prothrombin* **time**; *physical therapist.*

Pt Symbol for the element platinum.

pt *pint; patient.*

PTA *plasma thromboplastin antecedent; physical therapist assistant.*

PTAH *phosphotungstic acid-hematoxylin* **stain**.

P-tau, p-Tau (pē′tow′) Tau protein that is abnormally phosphorylated. Its concentrated presence in the cerebrospinal fluid is indicative of Alzheimer disease.

PTC *percutaneous transhepatic cholangiography; phenylthiocarbamide; plasma thromboplastin component.*

PTCA *percutaneous transluminal coronary angioplasty.*

pterion (tē′rē-ŏn) [Gr. *pteron,* wing] The point of suture of frontal, parietal, temporal, and sphenoid bones.

pterygium (tĕr-ĭj′ē-ŭm) [Gr. *pterygion,* wing] Triangular thickening of the bulbar conjunctiva extending from the inner canthus to the border of the cornea with the apex toward the pupil, probably related to chronic irritation.

    p. colli A congenital band of fascia extending from the mastoid process of the temporal bone to the clavicle.

    progressive p. A stage in which the growth extends toward the center of the cornea.

pterygoid (tĕr′ĭ-goyd) [Gr. *pterygoeides*] Wing-shaped.

    p. hamulus A small bony projection, just medial to the pterygoid process, that serves as an attachment for the tensor veli palatini muscle.

pterygomaxillary (tĕr″ĭ-gō-măk″sĭ-lĕr′ē) [″ + L. *maxillaris,* upper jaw] Pert. to the pterygoid process and upper jaw.

pterygopalatine (tĕr″ĭ-gō-păl′ă-tīn) [″ + L. *palatinus,* palate] Pert. to the pterygoid process and the palatine bone.

PTFE *polytetrafluoroethylene* (Teflon).

PTH *parathyroid* **hormone**.

ptomaine (tō′mān, tō-mān′) [Gr. *ptoma,* dead body] One of a class of nitrogenous organic bases formed by the action of putrefactive bacteria on proteins and amino acids.

ptosis (tō′sĭs) [Gr. *ptosis,* a dropping] Dropping or drooping of an organ or part, as the upper eyelid from paralysis, or the visceral organs from weakness of the abdominal muscles. SEE: illus. **ptotic** (tŏt′ĭk), *adj.*; **ptosed** (tōst), *adj.*

PTT *partial thromboplastin time.*

ptyalin (tī′ă-lĭn) [Gr. *ptyallon,* saliva + *-in*] A salivary enzyme that hydrolyzes starch and glycogen to maltose and a small amount of glucose. The optimum pH for ptyalin activity is 6.9. SYN: *amylase, salivary.* SEE: *enzyme; ptyalism; saliva.*

ptyalism (tī′ă-lĭzm) [″ + *-ismos,* condition] Excessive secretion of saliva. This may be due to pregnancy, stomatitis, rabies, exophthalmic goiter, menstruation, epilepsy, hysteria, nervous conditions, and gastrointestinal disorders

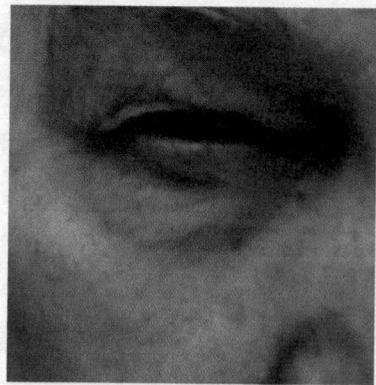

PTOSIS

involutional ptosis, associated with the loss
of elasticity of the eyelid

and may be induced by mercury, io-
dides, pilocarpine, and other drugs.
SYN: *hyperptyalism; hypersalivation;
salivation.* SEE: *xerostomia.*

ptysis (tī′sĭs) [Gr.] Spitting; the ejection
of saliva from the mouth.

Pu Symbol for the element plutonium.

pubalgia (pyū′bal-ja) Pain arising from
the groin or pubic symphysis. Diagnosis
is made after ruling out the presence of
an inguinal hernia.
    ETIOLOGY: Symptoms are often sec-
ondary to strain of the muscles that attach in the area (e.g., rectus abdominis,
iliopsoas, adductor longus, or rectus femoris), inflammation in the urogenital
system (e.g., urethritis, epididymitis),
inflammation of the hip (e.g., bursitis,
arthritis), or weaknesses in the abdominal wall.
    athletic p. Musculoskeletal pain,
typically arising from the pubic symphysis, lower abdominal muscles, or the
inguinal region of young athletes in
whom an inguinal hernia is not present.
SYN: *Gilmore groin; groin disruption;
sports hernia.*
    ETIOLOGY: Inflammation and tears
in the local muscles or abdominal wall
may result from repetitive overuse of
movements (e.g., kicking, jumping, and
sudden change of direction) that create
shear forces across the pubic symphysis
or inguinal ligament.

pubarche (pū′bar″kē) [*puber* + Gr. *archē,* beginning] **1.** The beginning of puberty. **2.** Beginning development of pubic hair. SEE: *semenarche; thelarche.*
    premature p. The development of
pubic hair on a female child before 8
years of age, or on a male before the age
of 9.

puber (pū′bĕr) [L., grown up] One at
the onset of puberty.

puberal (pū′bĕr-ăl) [L. *pubertas,* pu-
berty] Pubertal.

puberphonia (pū″bĕr-fō′nē-ă) [*puber* +
phono- + *-ia*] Persistence of a high-
pitched, childlike voice in adolescents or
young adults who have already
achieved puberty.

pubertal (pū′bĕr-tăl) Pert. to puberty.

pubertas (pū′bĕr-tăs) [L.] Puberty.
    p. praecox Precocious puberty or pu-
berty at an early age.

puberty (pū′bĕr-tē) The stage in life at
which members of both sexes become
functionally capable of reproduction. A
period of rapid change occurs between
the ages of 13 and 15 in boys and 9 to
16 in girls, ending in the attainment of
sexual maturity. There is evidence that
the onset of puberty is related to a decrease in secretion of the pineal gland.
    onset of p. *Boys:* Between the ages
of 13 and 15, a relatively rapid increase
in height and weight occurs, with broad-
ening of the shoulders and increase in
size of the penis and testicles. Pubic and
facial hair begin to grow. Endocrine and
sebaceous gland activity is increased.
Nocturnal emissions usually occur.
    Girls: Between the ages of 9 and 16, a
marked increase in growth is accompanied by breast enlargement and appearance of pubic hair. Within 1 to 2 years
after these changes, underarm hair
grows and the normal whitish vaginal
secretion (physiological leukorrhea)
characteristic of the adult female is noticed. Several months later the first
menstrual period (menarche) occurs.
Each individual will vary somewhat
from this schedule.
    PATIENT CARE: Before puberty,
young girls should be told about menstruation and the techniques of menstrual protection through use of perineal pads or tampons. In addition, they
should be told that a certain amount of
intermenstrual vaginal discharge (leukorrhea) is normal but if the secretion
is malodorous or causes irritation of the
vulva, a health care provider should be
consulted. SEE: *menstruation.*
    At puberty, boys should be assured
that the size of the penis is not related
to the degree of masculinity and is not
an important factor in experiencing or
providing sexual gratification.
    precocious p. The appearance of sec-
ondary sex characteristics before 8
years of age in girls and 9 years of age
in boys. The pituitary and hypothalamus glands may be involved, or the condition may result from premature secretion of sex hormones not caused by
pituitary or hypothalamic action. Gonadotropin-releasing hormone (GnRH)
has been used to treat this condition.

pubes (pū′bēz) *sing.,* **pubis** [L., grown
up] **1.** The region just above the geni-

talia in which pubic hair grows. **2.** An obsolete term for pubic hair.

pubescence (pū-bĕs′ĕns) [L. *pubescens*, becoming hairy] **1.** Puberty or the approach of puberty. **2.** A covering of fine, soft hairs on the body. SYN: *lanugo*. **pubescent,** *adj.*

pubic (pū′bĭk) [L. *pubes*, pubic hair] Pert. to the pubes.

pubic hair SEE: under *hair*.

pubio- Prefix meaning *pubic bone, pubic region.*

pubis (pū′bĭs) *pl.* **pubes** [NL. *(os) pubis*, bone of the groin] Pubic bone.

publication (pŭb″lĭ-kā′shŭn) [L. *publicare*, to make public] **1.** The dissemination of information in print. **2.** Any document, journal, or text distributed to a general audience or to a limited readership.

publication bias (pŭb″lĭ-kā′shŭn) [L. *publicare*, to confiscate, make public] The tendency of professional journals to publish and report the results of research trials that show a large positive clinical effect. Studies that demonstrate no association between variables or those that show neutral effects are less likely to be published or reported.

public comment period The designated time during which members of a community may testify for or against any proposed administrative action affecting health, wellness, or public safety.

public health SEE: under *health*.

Public Health Service Act One of the principal laws giving the authority for federal health activities. First enacted July 1, 1944, it provided a complete codification of all the federal public health laws. Many of the health laws since 1944 are amendments to the Public Health Service Act revising, extending, or giving new authority to the act.

PubMed An electronic database maintained by the U.S. National Library of Medicine that includes over 21 million citations in biomedicine, the life sciences, nursing, and allied health.
    Website: www.ncbi.nlm.nih.gov/entrez/

pubovesical (pū″bō-vĕs′ĭ-kl) [″ + *vesiculus*, a little sac] Pert. to the os pubis and bladder.

PUBS *percutaneous umbilical blood sampling.*

pudenda (pū-dĕn′dă) *sing.,* **pudendum** [L.] Vulva.

pudendum (pū-dĕn′dŭm) *pl.* **pudenda** [L.] **1.** The external genital organs, esp. of a female. **2.** The vulva.

puerile (pū′ĕ-rĭl) [L. *puerilis*] Pert. to a child; childlike.

puerperal (pū-ĕr′pĕ-răl) [L. *puerperalis*, pert. to childbirth] **1.** Pert. to childbirth or to a woman in childbirth. **2.** Pert. to the time from the birth of a child to approx. 6 weeks later, at which time complete involution of the uterus has occurred.

puerperal eclampsia Convulsions occurring immediately after childbirth.

puerperal fever SEE: under *fever*.

puerperium (pū″ĕr-pē′rē-ŭm) [L.] The period of 42 days following childbirth and expulsion of the placenta and membranes. The generative organs usually return to normal during this time. SEE: *postpartum*. **puerperal,** *adj.*

Puestow procedure (pūs′tow″, tō′) A lateral side-to-side pancreaticojejunostomy in Roux-en-Y configuration to relieve pain in patients with chronic pancreatitis. The pancreatic duct, which may be obstructed in chronic pancreatitis, is opened and attached to the small intestine. Alternatively, the incised or partially resected pancreas may be invaginated into the cut end of the Roux-en-Y limb.

PUFA *polyunsaturated fatty acids.* SEE: *fatty acid.*

puff A soft, short, blowing sound heard on auscultation.

Pulex (pū′lĕks″) [L. *pulex*, flea] A genus of fleas belonging to the order Siphonaptera. SEE: *flea.*
    P. irritans A species that infests humans, dogs, hogs, and other mammals. It is an intermediate host of the tapeworm *Dipylidium caninum.* SYN: *human flea.*

Pulfrich phenomenon (poolf′rik) [Carl Pulfrich, Ger. physicist, 1858–1927] An alteration in depth perception that occurs when one eye receives light from a moving object earlier than the other eye. The moving object appears to be closer to or further from the viewer than it actually is.

Pulicidae (pū-lĭs′ĭ-dē) A family of fleas belonging to the order Siphonaptera. Pulicidae includes the genera *Pulex, Echidnophaga, Ctenocephalides,* and *Xenopsylla.* SEE: *flea.*

pull A colloquial term for a muscle strain.

pullulation (pŭl″ū-lā′shŭn) The act of budding or germinating, as seen in yeast.

pulmo- [L. *pulmo*, stem *pulmon-*, lung] Prefix meaning *lung, pulmonic.*

pulmonary (pŭl′mō-nĕ-rē) [L. *pulmonarius*] Pert. to or involving the lungs.

pulmonary artery wedge pressure SEE: under *pressure.*

pulmonary autograft procedure for aortic valve disease Ross procedure.

pulmonary function test ABBR: PFT. One of several different tests used to evaluate the condition of the respiratory system. Measures of expiratory flow and lung volumes and capacities are obtained. The forced vital capacity is one of the more important pulmonary function tests; it provides a measure of the amount of air that can be maximally exhaled after a maximum inspiration and the time required for that expiration. Pulmonary function tests can also determine the diffusion ability of the alveolar-capillary membrane.

pulmonary veno-occlusive disease A condition that may complicate organ transplantation rejection. It is marked by extensive occlusion of the small and medium-sized veins of the lung by loose, sparsely cellular, fibrous tissue. Some larger veins may be involved. This disease produces severe pulmonary venous hypertension.

pulmonectomy (pŭl″mō-něk′tō-mē) [L. *pulmonis,* lung, + Gr. *ektome,* excision] Pneumectomy.

pulmonic (pŭl-mŏn′ĭk) **1.** Pert. to the lungs. **2.** Pert. to the pulmonary artery.

pulmonologist (pul″mō-nol′ŏ-jĭst, pŭl″) [*pulmo-* + *-log* + *-ist*] Respirologist.

pulmotor (pŭl′mō-tor) [″ + *motor,* mover] An apparatus for inducing artificial respiration by forcing air or oxygen into the lungs.

pulp (pŭlp) [L. *pulpa,* flesh (of a fruit), pulp] **1.** The soft part of fruit. **2.** The soft part of an organ. **3.** A mass of partly digested food passed from stomach to duodenum. SYN: *chyme.* **4.** The soft vascular portion of the center of a tooth.

    coronal p. The portion of the dental pulp in the pulp chamber or in the crown of the tooth.

    dead p. Devitalized **p.**

    dental p. The connective tissues that fill the pulp cavity enclosed by dentin of the tooth. Dental pulp includes a vascular and nerve network, a peripheral layer of odontoblasts involved with dentin formation, and other cellular and fibrous components.

    devitalized p. A dead or necrotic dental pulp as indicated by a vitalometer.
    TREATMENT: Treatment is by root canal. SYN: *dead* **p.**

    digital p. The soft, elastic prominence on the palmar or plantar surface of the last phalanx of a finger or toe.

    enamel p. Cells forming a stellate reticulum lying between outer and inner layers of the enamel organ of a tooth.

    exposed p. Pulp that, due to disease, is exposed to the air and saliva in the mouth.
    TREATMENT: Treatment includes extraction of the tooth or root canal.

    putrescent p. Dead pulp that has a foul odor because of the action of anaerobic bacteria.

    radicular p. Pulp that is in the root canal of a tooth.

    red p. The portion of splenic pulp consisting of vascular sinuses through which blood flows. The sinuses are separated by pulp cords that are made up of loosely connected macrophages that phagocytize foreign antigens and

old or damaged red blood cells. SEE: *spleen.*

    splenic p. The spongelike vascular and connective tissue of the spleen.

    tooth p. SEE: *tooth.*

    vital p. Dental pulp that is alive and healthy.

    white p. The portion of splenic pulp, consisting of T and B lymphocytes, that forms sheaths around arteries. The sheaths are thickest around the large arteries and grow progressively thinner as the arteries progress into the spleen. SEE: *spleen.*

    wood p. A soft form of cellulose, derived from wood or cotton, used as a food additive. Humans cannot digest it.

pulpa (pŭl′pă) [L. *pulpa,* flesh] Pulp.

pulpectomy (pŭl-pek′tŏ-mē) [*pulp* + *-ectomy,*] The complete removal of the pulp tissue from the pulp chamber and root canal, irrespective of the state of health of the pulp. SYN: *pulp extirpation.*

pulpitis (pŭl-pī′tĭs) *pl.* **pulpitides** [″ + *itis,* inflammation] Inflammation of the pulp of a tooth.

pulpotomy (pŭl-pot′ŏ-mē) [*pulp* + *-tomy,*] Pulp **amputation.**

pulp tester Vitalometer.

pulpy (pŭl′pē) Pert. to or resembling pulp; flabby.

pulsate (pŭl′sāt) [L. *pulsare*] To throb or beat in rhythm.

pulsatile (pŭl′să-tĭl) Pulsating; characterized by a rhythmic beat. SYN: *throbbing.*

Pulsatilla (pŭl″să-tĭl′ă) A genus of wild flowers, commonly called pasque-flowers, wind-flowers, and meadow anemones. The flowers are used in homeopathic remedies and are investigated for their cytotoxic components.

pulsation (pŭl-sā′shŭn) [L. *pulsatio,* a beating] The rhythmic beat, as of the heart and blood vessels; a throbbing. SEE: *pulse.*

pulse (pŭls) [L. *pulsus,* beating] **1.** The rate, rhythm, condition of arterial walls, compressibility and tension, and size and shape of the fluid wave of blood traveling through the arteries as a result of each heartbeat. **2.** Rhythmical throbbing. **3.** Throbbing caused by the regular contraction and alternate expansion of an artery as the wave of blood passes through the vessel; the periodic thrust felt over arteries in time with the heartbeat. SEE: illus.

A tracing of this is called a sphygmogram and consists of a series of waves in which the upstroke is called the anacrotic limb, and the downstroke (on which is normally seen the dicrotic notch), the catacrotic limb.

The normal resting pulse in adults is between 60 and 100 beats per minute. The resting pulse is faster in febrile patients, anemic or hypovolemic persons, persons in shock, and patients who have

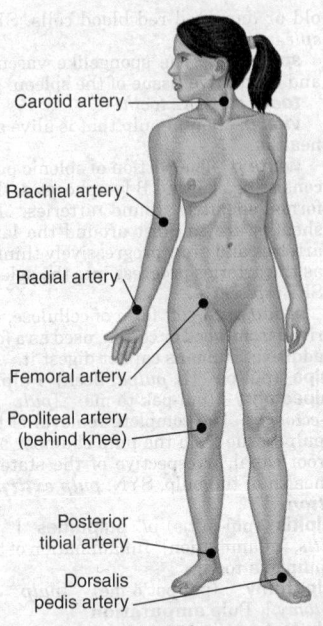

Carotid artery

Brachial artery

Radial artery

Femoral artery

Popliteal artery
(behind knee)

Posterior
tibial artery

Dorsalis
pedis artery

PULSES

taken drugs that stimulate the heart, such as theophylline, caffeine, nicotine, or cocaine. It may be slower in well-trained athletes; in patients using beta blockers, calcium channel blockers, or other agents; and during sleep or deep relaxation.

PATIENT CARE: In patients complaining of chest pain, pulses should be assessed in at least two extremities (e.g., both radial arteries). A strong pulse on the right side with a weak one on the left may suggest an aortic dissection or a stenosis of the left subclavian artery. Young patients with high blood pressure should have pulses assessed simultaneously at the radial and femoral artery because a significant delay in the femoral pulse may suggest coarctation of the aorta. Patients with recent symptoms of stroke or claudication should have pulses checked at the carotid, radial, femoral, popliteal, and posterior tibial arteries, to see whether any palpable evidence of arterial insufficiency exists at any of these locations. If a decreased pulse is detected, further evaluation might include ultrasonography or assessments of the ankle brachial index. Patients who are light-headed or dizzy or who notice palpitations may have detectable premature beats or otherpulse irregularities (e.g., the irregularly irregular pulse of atrial fibrillation).

alternating p. A pulse with alternating weak and strong pulsations. SYN: *pulsus alternans.*

anacrotic p. A pulse showing a secondary wave on the ascending limb of the main wave.

apical p. A pulse felt or heard over the part of the chest wall that lies over the apex of the heart. In healthy people this is roughly located at the left midclavicular line in the fourth intercostal space.

asymmetrical radial p. Unequal **p.**

basal p. Resting **p.**

bigeminal p. A pulse in which two regular beats are followed by a longer pause. SYN: *coupled* **p.**

bisferiens p. A pulse marked by two systolic peaks on the pulse waveform. It is characteristic of aortic regurgitation (with or without aortic stenosis) and hypertrophic cardiomyopathy.

bounding p. A pulse that reaches a higher intensity than normal, then disappears quickly. Best detected when the arm is held aloft. SYN: *collapsing* **p.**

brachial p. A pulse felt in the brachial artery.

capillary p. Visible inflow and outflow of blood from the nailbed. It is a finding in patients with aortic regurgitation when their fingernails or toenails are gently depressed by the examiner's finger. SYN: *Quincke pulse.*

carotid p. A pulse felt in the carotid artery.

catacrotic p. A pulse showing one or more secondary waves on the descending limb of the main wave.

catadicrotic p. A pulse wave with two small notches on the descending portion.

central p. A pulse recorded near the origin of the carotid or subclavian arteries.

collapsing p. Bounding **p.**

Corrigan p. SEE: *waterhammer* **p.**

coupled p. Bigeminal **p.**

dicrotic p. A pulse with a double beat, one heartbeat for two arterial pulsations, or a seemingly weak wave between the usual heartbeats. This weak wave should not be counted as a regular beat. It is indicative of low arterial tension and is noted in fevers.

dorsalis pedis p. A pulse felt over the dorsalis pedis artery of the foot.

entoptic p. Intermittent subjective sensations of light that accompany the heartbeat.

filiform p. Thready **p.**

hepatic p. A pulse due to expansion of veins of the liver at each ventricular contraction.

intermediate p. A pulse recorded in the proximal portions of the carotid, femoral, and brachial arteries.

intermittent p. A pulse in which occasional beats are skipped, caused by conditions such as premature atrial contractions, premature ventricular contractions, and atrial fibrillation. SYN: *irregular p.*

irregular p. Intermittent **p.**

irregularly irregular p. The erratic, unpredictable pulse present in atrial fibrillation.

jugular p. A venous pulse felt in the jugular vein.

Kussmaul p. SEE: under *Kussmaul, Adolph.*

monocrotic p. A pulse in which the sphygmogram shows a simple ascending and descending uninterrupted line and no dicrotism.

nail p. A visible pulsation in the capillaries under the nails.

paradoxical p. A decrease in the strength of the pulse (and of systolic blood pressure) during inspiration, a condition that may be esp. prominent in severe asthma, cardiac tamponade, obstructive sleep apnea, croup, and other conditions that alter pressure relationships within the chest. SYN: *Kussmaul p.; pulsus paradoxus.*

p. parvus **Pulsus** parvus et tardus.

peripheral p. A pulse recorded in the arteries (radial or pedal) in the distal portion of the limbs.

pistol-shot p. A pulse resulting from rapid distention and collapse of an artery as occurs in aortic regurgitation.

plateau p. A pulse associated with an increase in pressure that slowly rises but is maintained.

Quincke p. SEE: *capillary p.*

rapid p. Tachycardia.

regular p. A pulse felt when the force and frequency are the same (i.e., when the length of beat and number of beats per minute and the strength are the same).

respiratory p. Alternate dilatation and contraction of the large veins of the neck occurring simultaneously with inspiration and expiration.

resting p. A pulse rate obtained while an individual is at rest and calm. SYN: *basal p.*

retrosternal p. A venous pulse felt over the suprasternal notch.

Riegel p. SEE: *Riegel pulse.*

running p. A weak, rapid pulse with one wave continuing into the next.

short p. A pulse with a short, quick systolic wave.

slow p. A pulse rate that is less than 60 beats per minute.

small p. SEE: *pulsus parvus et tardus.*

soft p. A pulse that may be stopped by moderate digital compression.

tense p. A full but not bounding pulse.

thready p. A fine, scarcely perceptible pulse. SYN: *filiform p.*

tremulous p. A pulse in which a series of oscillations is felt with each beat.

tricrotic p. A pulse with three separate expansions during each heartbeat.

triphammer p. Waterhammer **p.**

undulating p. A pulse that seems to have several successive waves.

unequal p. A pulse in which beats vary in force. SYN: *asymmetrical radial p.*

vagus p. A slow pulse resulting from parasympathetic influence on heart rate, mediated by the vagus nerve.

venous p. A pulse in a vein, esp. one of the large veins near the heart, such as the internal or external jugular. Normally it is undulating and scarcely palpable. In conditions such as tricuspid regurgitation, it is pronounced.

vermicular p. A small, frequent pulse with a wormlike feeling.

waterhammer p. A pulse with a powerful upstroke and then sudden disappearance; a hallmark of aortic regurgitation. SYN: *triphammer p.; Corrigan pulse.*

wiry p. A tense pulse that feels like a wire or firm cord.

pulsed lavage (pŭlst) SEE: under *lavage.*

pulseless disease Takayasu arteritis.

pulseless electrical activity SEE: under *activity.*

pulse ox A colloquial term for a pulse oximeter.

pulsing electromagnetic field SEE: under *field.*

pulsion (pŭl′shŭn) Driving or propelling in any direction.

lateral p. Movement, particularly walking as if pulled to one side.

pulsus (pŭl′sŭs) [L. *pulsus,* beating] Pulse.

p. bigeminus Bigeminal pulse.

p. differens A condition in which the pulses on either side of the body are of unequal intensity. It is seen sometimes in aortic dissection, or in atherosclerotic obstruction of one of the subclavian arteries.

p. paradoxus Paradoxical **p.**

p. parvus et tardus A pulse that is small and rises and falls slowly, indicative of severe aortic stenosis. SYN: *p. parvus.*

p. tardus An abnormally slow pulse.

pulv (pŭlv) L. *pulvis,* powder.

pulverization (pŭl″vĕr-ī-zā′shŭn) [L. *pulvis,* powder] The crushing of any substance to powder or tiny particles.

pulverulent (pŭl-vĕr′ū-lĕnt) Of the nature of, or resembling, powder.

pulvinar (pŭl-vī′năr) [L. *pulvinar,* cushioned seat, couch] A large thalamic nucleus overhanging the geniculate nuclei and making up the most caudal segment of the thalamus. The pulvinar is part of the visual circuitry of the brain.

pulvinate (pŭl'vĭ-nāt) [L. *pulvinus*, cushion] Convex; shaped like a cushion.

pulvis (pŭl'vĭs) [L.] Powder.

pumice (pŭm'ĭs) An abrasive polishing agent derived from volcanic material. Pumice consists chiefly of complex silicates of aluminum, potassium, and sodium.

pump (pŭmp) **1.** An apparatus that transfers fluids or gases by pressure or suction. **2.** To force air or fluid along a certain pathway, as the heart does to blood.

 air p. A device for forcing air in or out of a chamber.

 blood p. **1.** A device for pumping blood. It is attached to an extracorporeal circulation system. **2.** A compression sleeve placed about a plastic transfusion bag.

 breast p. An apparatus for expressing milk from the human breast.

 efflux p. A cell membrane protein channel that selectively admits or excludes chemicals from the cytoplasm. In some bacteria efflux pumps prevent their cells from accumulating antibiotics, contributing to drug resistance.

 electronic implantable infusion p. ABBR: EIIP. A type of infusion pump inserted in the body. The pump, which may be programmable or nonprogrammable, is placed in a subcutaneous pocket and is connected to a dedicated catheter leading to the appropriate compartment or site.

 infusion p. A pump to administer fluids into an artery, vein, or enteral tube, beneficial in overcoming arterial resistance, controlling the rate of the fluid and drug administration, or administering thick solutions. The pump can be programmed to set the rate of administration depending on the patient's needs. SEE: ; *electronic infusion **device***. SYN: *intravenous infusion **p***.

 insulin p. A small battery-driven pump that delivers insulin subcutaneously into the abdominal wall. The pump can be programmed to deliver varying doses of insulin as a patient's need for insulin changes during the day (e.g., before exercise or meals, when physical or psychological levels of stress change). SEE: illus.

INSULIN PUMP

 intra-aortic balloon p. Intra-aortic balloon **counterpulsation**.

 intravenous infusion p. Infusion **p**.

 lymphedema p. A pneumatic compression device for application to an edematous limb. It works best when combined with elevation of the limb and manual massage. The device, which may be single-chambered or multichambered, is designed to provide calibrated, sequential pressure to the extremity. This action "milks" edema fluid from the extremity. It is essential that the device be used in the early phase of the development of lymphedema. If the affected lymph vessels develop fibrotic changes (i.e., scar tissue), then pneumatic compression devices are of questionable benefit.

 proton p. An enzyme located in the parietal cell of the stomach that excretes hydrogen ions in exchange for potassium ions. The formal name of the proton pump is hydrogen/potassium adenosine triphosphate (H^+/K^+ATPase).

 PATIENT CARE: Gastric acids produced by the proton pump aid chemical digestion of foods. Some diseases and conditions are worsened by acid in the stomach (e.g., peptic ulcers, acid reflux disease). Drugs that inhibit the proton pump (proton pump inhibitors such as omeprazole) are used to treat these illnesses.

 respiratory p. Those abdominal and thoracic structures that contribute to the expansion and contraction of the lungs. Movement of the chest and abdomen alters central pressures during inspiration and expiration. During inspiration, decreases in intrathoracic pressure draw air into the trachea, bronchi, and lungs and draw blood into the vena cava and right atrium of the heart. During expiration, intrathoracic pressures rise, and air is forced out of the lungs.

 sodium p. The active transport mechanism that moves sodium ions across a membrane to their area of greater concentration. In neurons and muscle cells, this is outside the cell. In many cells, the sodium pump is linked with the potassium pump that transports potassium ions into the cell, also against a concentration gradient, and may be called the *sodium-potassium pump*. In neurons and muscle fibers, this pump maintains the polarization of the membrane.

 smart p. A programmable infusion device used to control and administer intravenous drugs and limit medication administration errors. Its software may include some or all of the following features: infusion rate programming; dosing limit lockout features; configurations for specific hospital areas (pediatric dosing versus adult or intensive care unit dosing); surgical or anesthetic drug libraries; controls for patient-controlled analgesia; and alert features (alarms or messages that notify users of possible medication errors).

stomach p. A colloquial term for gastric lavage.

thoracic p. The negative pressure in the chest during inspiration that pulls venous blood into the vena cava and right side of the heart so that it can circulate to the lungs.

venous plexus foot p. A device that alternates between applying pressure and no pressure on the sole of the foot. The change in pressure allows venous blood vessels to alternately fill and then empty, thus imitating the effects of walking on the veins of the lower extremities. The pump is used to prevent deep vein thromboses (DVTs) in patients at high risk because of a previous history of DVTs, hypercoagulable states, or prolonged bedrest.

pumping (pŭmp'ing) Draining or emptying of fluids by hydraulic suction.

lymphatic p. In osteopathy, manipulation of the thoracic cavity to facilitate lymphatic circulation.

stomach p. SEE: *gastric lavage*.

pump-oxygenator (pŭmp-ŏk'sĭ-jĕn-ā"tŏr) A device that pumps and oxygenates blood.

pump pocket A surgically constructed pouch beneath the skin but superficial to muscle, in which implanted devices such as defibrillators, insulin pumps, or pacemakers are inserted. Hematomas, infections, and seromas sometimes develop in these locations.

pumptech (pump'tek") [Slang] A cardiovascular perfusionist.

punch An instrument for making a small circular hole in material or tissue, esp. the skin.

punchdrunk An imprecise term pert. to the behavioral consequences of traumatic brain injury in boxers who have received many blows to the head. If severe, cognitive and motor functions of the brain may be affected. Symptoms may resemble those of Parkinson disease. SYN: *dementia pugilistica*.

punched out Appearing as if holes have been made; used to describe appearance of bones (as seen on x-ray film) in diseases like multiple myeloma.

puncta (pŭnk'tă) *sing.*, **punctum** [L.] Points.

punctate (pŭnk'tāt) [L. *punctum*, point] Having pinpoint punctures or depressions on the surface; marked with dots.

p. keratoses Discrete yellow-to-brown firm papules of the palms and soles that appear after skin trauma, e.g., in walking or regular use of the hands or feet at work. The lesions are found in patients with a genetic predisposition to keratoderma.

p. pits Depressed areas of the skin, esp. of the palmar creases of the hands and soles.

p. rash A rash with minute red points.

punctiform (pŭnk'tĭ-form) [" + *forma*, shape] **1.** Formed like a point. **2.** In bacteriology, referring to pinpoint colonies of less than 1 mm in diameter.

punctum (pŭnk'tŭm) *pl.* **puncta** [L.] Point.

puncture (pŭngk'chŭr) [L. *punctura*, prick] **1.** A hole or wound made by a sharp pointed instrument. **2.** To make a hole with such an instrument.

p. of the antrum Puncture of the maxillary sinus by insertion of a trocar through the sinus wall in order to drain fluid. The instrument is inserted near the floor of the nose, approx. 1½ in (3.8 cm) from the nasal opening. SEE: *antrotomy*.

PATIENT CARE: The antrum is irrigated with the prescribed solution (often warm normal saline solution) according to protocol. The character and volume of the returned solution and the patient's response to treatment are carefully monitored and documented. Ice packs are applied as prescribed for edema and pain; these are replaced by warm compresses as healing progresses. Assessments are made for chills, fever, nausea, vomiting, facial or periorbital edema, visual disturbances, and personality changes, which may indicate the development of complications.

arterial p. Placement of a needle or catheter into an artery to sample blood gases or blood pressure, or positioning of a catheter in the aorta or the heart.

cerebrospinal p. A puncture of the meninges to collect cerebrospinal fluid or to inject contrast media or medications. Puncture sites include the spaces around the spinal cord (lumbar puncture), the cisterna magna (cisternal puncture), or open fontanelles in infants (ventricular puncture).

cisternal p. A spinal puncture with a hollow needle between the cervical vertebrae, through the dura mater, and into the cisterna at the base of the brain. This is done to inject a drug as in meningitis or cerebral syphilis, to remove spinal fluid for diagnostic purposes, or to reduce intracranial pressure. It should be used as a source of spinal fluid only if fluid cannot be obtained by lumbar puncture. SEE: *cerebrospinal fluid*.

⚠ This procedure may be lethal if not done by one skilled in this technique.

exploratory p. Piercing of a cavity or cyst in order to examine the fluid or pus removed.

heel p. A method for obtaining a blood sample from a newborn or premature infant.

⚠ The puncture should be made in the lateral or medial area of the plantar surface of the heel, while avoiding the posterior curvature of the heel. The puncture should go no deeper than 2.4 mm. Previous puncture sites should not be used.

lumbar p. ABBR: LP. Gaining entry into the subarachnoid space of the meningeal sac below the end of the spinal cord, usually at the level of the fourth intervertebral space with a hollow needle. This procedure is done to obtain cerebrospinal fluid (CSF) for analysis, as in the diagnosis of severe headache or in suspected central nervous system infection or bleeding; to administer drugs to the brain or spinal cord (such as anesthetics or chemotherapeutic agents); or to relieve the CSF of excess pressure or fluid, as in pseudotumor cerebri. SYN: *spinal p.; Quincke puncture; spinal tap.* SEE: illus.; *cisternal puncture; headache; Queckenstedt sign.*

⚠ Postprocedure headache occurs in about half of all patients who undergo lumbar puncture. Rarely reported complications of the procedure include cerebral herniation, epidural infection, epidural bleeding, paraparesis, and subdural bleeding.

PROCEDURE: Informed consent for the procedure is obtained except in dire emergencies when clinical judgment prevails. Appropriate equipment is gathered: sterile gloves and mask for the operator, skin antiseptic (povidine-iodine solution), local anesthetic (1% lidocaine), and a lumbar puncture tray containing sterile gauze sponges, fenestrated drape and towel, needles and syringe for anesthesia, spinal needles, 4 collection tubes, 3-way stopcock and manometer; and a small adhesive bandage.

The procedure and expected sensations are explained, and the patient is asked to remain still when positioned and to breathe normally. The patient is typically placed on his or her left side at the right edge of the bed or examining table with knees drawn up to the abdomen and chin down to the chest, or in a sitting position with legs over one side of the table and buttocks at the other, bending head and chest toward the knees. Either of these positions exposes the back to the operator and provides spinal flexion, allowing easy access to the lumbar subarachnoid space. The assisting nurse holds the patient appropriately to secure this position (one arm around the neck, the other around the knees, or holding both shoulders bent forward). Draping provides warmth and privacy. Next, the patient's skin is prepared with antiseptic solution, and a sterile fenestrated barrier is placed over the proposed puncture site. Local anesthetic is injected, andthen the spinal needle, with its stylet in place, is slowly advanced between the vertebra into and through the dura and arachnoid membranes. The stylet that fills the needle is removed, and initial measurements are made of the opening intracranial

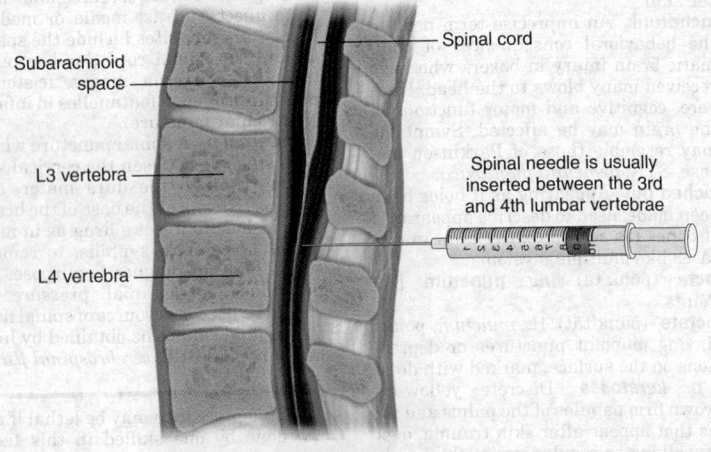

Subarachnoid space

Spinal cord

L3 vertebra

Spinal needle is usually inserted between the 3rd and 4th lumbar vertebrae

L4 vertebra

LUMBAR PUNCTURE

pressure with a manometer. When the procedure is performed for diagnosis, about 8 to 10 mL of fluid are collected and sent promptly to the clinical laboratory for analysis of cell count, glucose, protein levels, cultures stains, and special studies. The closing pressure should then be read, the needle removed, and a small impervious adhesive dressing applied, sometimes with collodion to prevent CSF leakage.

COMPLICATIONS: Pain at the puncture site, infection, bleeding, neurological injury, death, and post-spinal tap headaches are all potential complications. Of these, postural headache, caused by chronic leakage from the puncture site, is the complication most often brought to the attention of health care professionals. It may be treated with the injection of a small amount of the patient's own blood epidurally, to form a blood patch. SEE: *cerebrospinal fluid*.

PATIENT CARE: The nurse assists the operator throughout the procedure by numbering and capping specimen tubes for laboratory examination and by applying jugular vein pressure as directed. Reassurance and direction are provided to the patient throughout the procedure, and the patient is assessed for adverse reactions (elevated pulse rate, pain radiating into the limbs, pallor, clammy skin, or respiratory distress).

After the procedure, the nurse assesses vital signs and neurological status, particularly observing for signs of paralysis, weakness, or loss of sensation in the lower extremities. If CSF pressure is elevated, the patient's neurological status should be assessed every 15 min for 4 hr, if normal, every hour for 2 hr, then every 4 hr or as ordered. The puncture site should be checked hourly for 4 hr, then every 4 hr for 24 hr, assessing for redness, swelling, and drainage. To decrease the chance of headache, oral intake (for spinal fluid replacement and equalization of pressures) is encouraged, and the patient should remain in bed in a supine position or with the head elevated no more than 30° for 4 to 24 hr (per operator or institutional protocol). The patient should not lift his or her head but can move it (and himself or herself) from side to side. Noninvasive pain relief measures and prescribed analgesia are provided if headache occurs.

sternal p. Puncture of the sternum with a large-bore needle to obtain a specimen of marrow.

tracheoesophageal p. ABBR: TEP. A surgically created connection between the trachea and the esophagus for a patient who has had his or her voicebox (larynx) removed. It permits the patient to force air from the lungs through the windpipe into the esophagus, and from there out of the mouth in order to speak.

A one-way valve (shunt) is placed into the tracheoesophageal opening. The patient learns to speak using the TEP with the help of a speech therapist.

ventricular p. Puncture of a ventricle of the brain in order to withdraw fluid or introduce air for ventriculography.

pungency (pŭn'jĕn-sē) [L. *pungens*, prick] The quality of being sharp, strong, or bitter, as an odor or taste.

pungent (pŭn'jĕnt) Acrid or sharp, as applied to an odor or taste.

pupa (pū'pă) [L., girl] The stage in complete metamorphosis of an insect during which a larva transforms into an adult or imago. The pupa does not feed during this stage and appears to be inactive; the internal activity is not visible.

pupil (pū'pĭl) [L. *pupilla*, little doll (the reflection in the pupil)] The contractile opening at the center of the iris of the eye. It is constricted when exposed to strong light and when the focus is on a near object; is dilated in the dark and when the focus is on a distant object. Average diameter is 4 to 5 mm. The pupils should be equal. SEE: *pupilla;* illus.

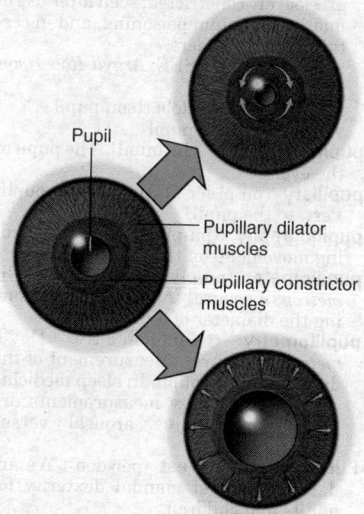

Pupil

Pupillary dilator muscles

Pupillary constrictor muscles

PUPIL DILATION AND CONSTRICTION

The upper image shows constriction; the lower, dilation.

DIFFERENTIAL DIAGNOSIS: Constriction of the pupil occurs, for example, in bright light and after exposure to drugs such as morphine, pilocarpine, physostigmine, eserine, and other miotics.

Dilation of the pupil is most often observed after treatment with mydriatic drugs (such as atropine, scopolamine, or homatropine), but may also be caused by paralysis of cranial nerve III, intracranial masses or trauma, sympathetic nervous system stimulation, and other pupillary stimuli.

Adie p. SEE: under *Adie, William John*.

Argyll Robertson p. SEE: *Argyll Robertson pupil*.

artificial p. A pupil made by iridectomy when the normal pupil is occluded.

bounding p. Rapid dilatation of a pupil, alternating with contraction.

Bumke p. Dilatation of the pupil owing to psychic stimulus.

cat's-eye p. A pupil that is narrow and slitlike.

cornpicker's p. Dilated pupils found in agricultural workers who are exposed to dust from jimsonweed. The dust contains stramonium, a mydriatic.

fixed p. A pupil that does not react to stimuli.

Gunn p. SEE: under *Gunn, Robert Marcus*.

keyhole p. A pupil with an artificial coloboma at the pupillary margin.

luetic p. Argyll Robertson pupil.

Marcus Gunn p. SEE: under *Gunn, Robert Marcus*.

pinhole p. A pupil of minute size; one excessively constricted; seen after use of miotics, in opium poisoning, and in certain brain disorders.

Robertson p. SEE: *Argyll Robertson pupil*.

stiff p. Argyll Robertson pupil.

tonic p. Adie pupil

pupilla (pū-pĭl′ă) [L., pupil] The pupil of the eye.

pupillary (pū′pĭ-lĕr-ē) [L. *pupilla*, pupil] Pert. to the pupil.

pupillography (pū-pĭl-ŏg′ră-fē) Recording movements of the pupil of the eye.

pupillometer (pū-pĭl-ŏm′ĕ-tĕr) [″ + Gr. *metron*, measure] A device for measuring the diameter of a pupil.

pupillometry (pū-pĭl-lŏm′ĕ-trē) [″ + *metron*, measure] Measurement of the diameter of the pupil. In sleep medicine research, pupillary measurements are used to determine arousal versus drowsiness.

Purdue Pegboard Test (pĕr-doo′) A standardized test of manual dexterity for adults and children.

pure (pūr) Free from pollution; uncontaminated.

pure tone SEE: under *tone*.

pure tone audiometry SEE: under *audiometry*.

purgation (pŭr-gā′shŭn) [L. *purgatio*] 1. Cleansing. 2. Evacuation of the bowels by the action of a purgative medicine. SYN: *catharsis*.

purgative (pŭr′gă-tĭv) [L. *purgativus*] 1. Cleansing. 2. An agent that will stimulate the production of bowel movements. SEE: *catharsis; cathartic*.

purge (pŭrj) [L. *purgare*, to cleanse] 1. To evacuate the bowels by means of a cathartic. 2. A drug that causes evacuation of the bowels. 3. Removal of malignant or other pathologic cells from bone marrow.

purging (pŭr′jĭng) In eating disorders, the act of eliminating ingested calories, either by vomiting or by evacuation of the bowels. Purging behaviors may include misuse of emetics, diuretics, laxatives, or enemas.

purified protein derivative ABBR: PPD. SEE: *tuberculin*.

puriform (pū′rĭ-form) [L. *pus*, pus, + *forma*, shape] Resembling pus. SEE: *puruloid*.

purine (pū′rēn″) [L. *purum*, pure, + *uricus*, uric acid] The parent compound of nitrogenous bases, including adenine, guanine, xanthine, caffeine, and uric acid. Purines (chemical formula $C_5H_4N_4$) are the end products of nucleoprotein digestion, and are catabolized to uric acid, which is excreted by the kidneys. Adenine and guanine are synthesized within cells for incorporation into DNA and RNA. SEE: *aminopurine; oxypurine; methyl purine*.

endogenous p. Purine originating from nucleoproteins within the tissues.

exogenous p. Purine present in, or derived from, foods. SEE: table.

purine base Any of a group of chemical compounds that have a purine as their base. Such bases include xanthine, hypoxanthine, uric acid, and theobromine.

purity [L. *purus*, clean, pure, unmixed] The state of being free of contamination.

Purkinje, Johannes E. von, Purkině (poor′kin-ye, -yā) Jan Evangelista Purkinje, Bohemian anatomist and physiologist, 1787–1869.

P. cell A large cerebellar cortex neuron with an ornate, antler-shaped dendritic arbor. Purkinje cells receive inputs (climbing fibers) from the inferior olive, and they send their axons (inhibitory) to the cerebellar and vestibular nuclei. SYN: **P. neuron**.

P. fiber A cardiac muscle cell beneath the endocardium of the ventricles of the heart. These extend from the bundle branches to the ventricular myocardium and form the last part of the cardiac conduction system.

P. figures Shadows of blood vessels perceived when light is projected out of focus or obliquely onto the retina.

P. layer A single row of large flask-shaped cells (Purkinje cells) lying between molecular and granular layers of the cerebellar cortex.

P. neuron P. cell.

P. phenomenon The adjustment of the pupil of the eye to light intensity. When the eye adapts from light to dark conditions, the maximum pupillary movement is caused by green instead of yellow light. SYN: *pupillomotor reflex*.

P.-Sanson images Three images of the same object, produced by reflections

Purines in Food

Group A: High Concentration (150–1000 mg/100 g)	
Liver	Sardines (in oil)
Kidney	Meat extracts
Sweetbreads	Consommé
Brains	Gravies
Heart	Fish roes
Anchovies	Herring

Group B: Moderate Amounts (50–150 mg/100 g)	
Meat, game, and fish other than those mentioned in Group A	
Fowl	Asparagus
Lentils	Cauliflower
Whole-grain cereals	Mushrooms
Beans	Spinach
Peas	

Group C: Very Small Amounts: Need Not be Restricted in Diet of Persons with Gout	
Vegetables other than those mentioned above	
Fruits of all kinds	Coffee
Milk	Tea
Cheese	Chocolate
Eggs	Carbonated
Refined cereals, spaghetti, macaroni	beverages
	Tapioca
Butter, fats, nuts, peanut butter*	
Sugars and sweets	
Vegetable soups	

* Fats interfere with the urinary excretion of urates and thus should be limited if the objective is to promote excretion of uric acid.

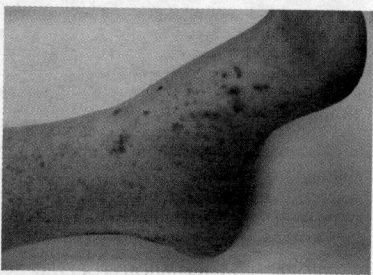

PURPURA

from the surface of the cornea and the anterior and posterior surfaces of the lens of the eye. For the most part, the viewer adapts to this phenomenon and ignores these extra images.

purple A color formed by mixing red with blue.

    visual p. Rhodopsin.

purple bacteria A colloquial term for the proteobacteria.

purpura (pŭr'pyŭ-ră) [L. *purpura*, purple] Any rash in which blood cells leak into the skin or mucous membranes, usually at multiple sites. Purpuric rashes often are associated with disorders of coagulation or thrombosis. Pinpoint purpuric lesions are called petechiae; larger hemorrhages into the skin are called ecchymoses. SYN: *peliosis*. SEE: illus.

    allergic p. Any of a group of purpuras caused by a variety of agents, including bacteria, drugs, and food. The immune complexes associated with type III hypersensitivity reaction damage the walls of small blood vessels, leading to bleeding. SYN: *nonthrombocytopenic p.*

    anaphylactoid p. Henoch-Schönlein purpura.

    p. annularis telangiectodes Majocchi disease.

    fibrinolytic p. Purpura resulting from excess fibrinolytic activity of the blood.

    p. fulminans A rapidly progressing form of purpura occurring principally in children. It is of short duration and frequently fatal.

    hemorrhagic p. Idiopathic thrombocytopenic **p.**

    Henoch-Schönlein p. SEE: *Henoch-Schönlein purpura.*

    idiopathic thrombocytopenic p. ABBR: ITP. A hemorrhagic autoimmune disease in which there is destruction of circulating platelets, caused by antiplatelet autoantibodies that bind with antigens on the platelet membrane, making platelets more susceptible to phagocytosis and destruction in the spleen. It occurs as an acute disease in children, usually between ages 2 and 6, and often follows a viral infection. Chronic ITP seldom follows an infection and is commonly linked to immunologic disorders such as lupus erythematosis or patients with acquired immunodeficiency syndrome who are exposed to the rubella virus. It also is linked to drug reactions, and occurs in cases of alcohol, heroin, or morphine abuse. It mainly affects adults under age 50, esp. women between 20 and 40. Opsonization of platelets by autoantibodies stimulates their lysis by macrophages, esp. in the spleen. SYN: *Henoch-Schönlein disease; hemorrhagic **p.**; thrombocytopenic **p.**; thrombopenic **p.** SEE: illus; *Nursing Diagnoses Appendix.*

⚠️ People with ITP should take special precautions to avoid injuries in contact sports. Aspirin and other drugs that may cause bleeding should only be taken

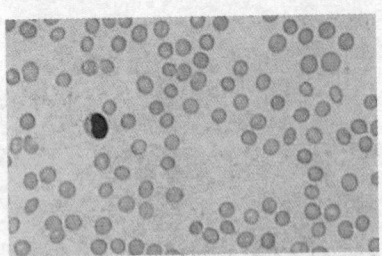

**IDIOPATHIC THROMBOCYTOPENIC
PURPURA**

Virtual absence of platelets in peripheral
blood (×400)

by people with ITP under direction of an
experienced physician.

SYMPTOMS: Symptoms include
bleeding from the nose, the gums, or the
gastrointestinal tract. Physical findings
include petechiae, esp. on the lower extremities, and ecchymoses. Laboratory
findings: The platelet count is usually
less than 20,000/mm³, bleeding time is
prolonged and may be associated with
mild anemia as a result of bleeding.

TREATMENT: If patients are asymptomatic (i.e., have no active bleeding)
and have platelet counts of about
50,000/mm³, treatment is not needed (4
out of 5 patients recover without treatment). Treatment for symptomatic patients, or patients with very low platelet
counts, usually is with glucocorticoids
or immune globulin for acute cases and
corticosteroids for chronic cases. For
those who do not respond within 1 to 4
months, treatment may include high-
dose corticosteroids, intravenous immune globulin, immunosupression, immunoabsorption apheresis using
staphylococcal protein-A columns to filter antibodies out of the bloodstream,
AntiRhD therapy for those with specific
blood types, splenectomy, or chemotherapeutic drugs such as vincristine or cyclophosphamide.

PATIENT CARE: Platelet count is
monitored closely. The patient is observed for bleeding (petechiae, ecchymoses, epistaxis, oral mucous membrane or gastrointestinal bleeding,
hematuria, menorrhagia) and stools,
urine, and vomitus are tested for occult
blood. The amount of bleeding or size of
ecchymoses is measured at least every
24 hr. Any complications of ITP are
monitored. The patient is educated
about the disorder, prescribed treatments, and importance of reporting
bleeding (such as epistaxis, gingival,
urinary tract, or uterine or rectal bleeding) and signs of internal bleeding (such
as tarry stools or coffee-ground vomi-

tus). The patient should avoid straining
during defecation or coughing because
both can lead to increased intracranial
pressure, possibly causing cerebral
hemorrhage. Stool softeners are provided as necessary to prevent tearing of
the rectal mucosa and bleeding due to
passage of constipated or hard stools.
The purpose, procedure, and expected
sensations of each diagnostic test are
explained. The role of platelets and the
way in which the results of platelet
counts can help to identify symptoms of
abnormal bleeding are also explained.
The lower the platelet count falls, the
more precautions the patient will need
to take; in severe thrombocytopenia,
even minor bumps or scrapes can result
in bleeding. The nurse guards against
bleeding by taking the following precautions to protect the patient from
trauma: keeping the side rails of the bed
raised and padded, promoting use of a
soft toothbrush or sponge-stick (toothette) and an electric razor, and avoiding
invasive procedures if possible. When
venipuncture is unavoidable, pressure
is exerted on the puncture site for at
least 20 min or until the bleeding stops.
During active bleeding, the patient
maintains strict bedrest, with the head
of the bed elevated to prevent gravity-
related intracranial pressure increases,
possibly leading to intracranialbleed-
ing. All areas of petechiae and ecchymoses are protected from further injury.
Rest periods are provided between activities if the patient tires easily. Both
patient and family are encouraged to
discuss their concerns about the disease
and its treatment. Emotional support is
provided and questions are answered
honestly. The nurse reassures the patient that areas of petechiae and ecchymoses will heal as the disease resolves.
The patient should avoid taking aspirin
in any form as well as any other drugs
that impair coagulation, including nonsteroidal anti-inflammatory drugs. If
the patient experiences frequent nosebleeds, the patient should use a humidifier at night and should moisten the
nostrils twice a day with saline. The
nurse teaches the patient to monitor the
condition by examining the skin for petechiae and ecchymoses and demonstrates the correct method to test stools
for occult blood. If the patient is receiving corticosteroid therapy, fluid ande-
lectrolyte balance is monitored and the
patient is assessed for signs of infection,
pathological fractures, and mood
changes. If the patient is receiving blood
or blood components, they are administered according to protocol; vital signs
are monitored before, during, and after
the transfusion, and the patient is observed closely for adverse reactions. If
the patient is receiving immunosup-

pressants, the patient is monitored closely for signs of bone marrow depression, opportunistic infections, mucositis, GI tract ulceration, and severe diarrhea or vomiting. If the patient is scheduled for a splenectomy, the nurse determines the patient's understanding of the procedure, corrects misinformation, administers prescribed blood transfusions, explains postoperative care and expected activities and sensations, ensures that a signed informed consent has been obtained, and prepares the patient physically (according to institutional or surgeon's protocol) and emotionally for the surgery. Postoperatively, all general patient care concerns apply. Normally, platelets increase spontaneously after splenectomy, but the patient may need initial postoperative support with blood and component replacement and platelet concentrate. The patient with chronic ITP should wear or carry a medical identification device.

    nonthrombocytopenic p. Allergic **p.**

    posttransfusion p. ABBR: PTP. An abnormal immune-mediated fall in the number of circulating platelets, caused by a recipient's reaction to foreign antigens on platelets received during a transfusion. Although the immune reaction normally starts against the donated platelets, in PTP host (recipient) platelets are also attacked, leading to a severe decrease in platelet numbers about a week, plus or minus 2 days, after the platelet transfusion. The consequences of a low platelet count may include bleeding, bruising, or discoloration of the skin.

    p. rheumatica Purpura with joint pain, colic, bloody stools, and vomiting of blood.

    p. simplex Purpura that is not associated with systemic illness.

    thrombocytopenic p. Idiopathic thrombocytopenic **p.**

    thrombopenic p. Idiopathic thrombocytopenic **p.**

    thrombotic thrombocytopenic p. ABBR: TTP. A rare, life-threatening disease marked by widespread aggregation of platelets throughout the body, neurological dysfunction, and renal insufficiency. The disease is triggered by a deficiency of an enzyme that cleaves von Willebrand factor (a blood clotting protein). This deficiency results in blood clots in small blood vessels throughout the body. Shifting neurological signs such as aphasia, blindness, and convulsions are often present. SEE: *hemolytic uremic syndrome.*

    ETIOLOGY: The disease has occurred in patients taking certain drugs (e.g., ticlopidine); in some patients with cancer or HIV-1 infection; and in some pregnant women.

    TREATMENT: Plasmapheresis or in-

fusions of fresh frozen plasma are effective in treating the disease.

    wet p. A blister filled with blood; colloquially, a blood blister.

purpuric (pŭr-pū′rĭk) [L. *purpura,* purple] Pert. to, resembling, or suffering from purpura.

purulence, purulency (pūr′ū-lĕns, -lĕn″sē) [LL. *purulentia,* collection of pus] The condition of forming or containing pus.

purulent (pūr′(y)ŭ-lĕnt) [L. *purulentus,* full of pus] Forming or containing pus; suppurative.

pus (pŭs) [L.] Protein-rich fluid (exudate) containing white blood cells, esp. neutrophils, and cell debris produced during inflammation. It commonly is caused by infection with pyogenic (pus-forming) bacteria such as streptococci, staphylococci, gonococci, and pneumococci. Normally, pus is yellow; red pus may contain blood from the rupture of small vessels, and bluish-green pus may contain *Pseudomonas aeruginosa.* Pus that has been walled off by a membrane is called an abscess. SYN: *suppuration.* SEE: *abscess; purulence.*

    blue p. Purulence with a blue tint; usually associated with infection due to *Pseudomonas aeruginosa.*

    ichorous p. Pus that is thin with shreds of sloughing tissue. It may have a fetid odor.

push (poosh) **1.** To inject rapidly. **2.** A substance that is rapidly injected. **3.** A bolus.

pustula (pŭs′tū-lă) [L., blister] Pustule.

pustular (pŭs′tū-lĕr) Pert. to, or characterized by, pustules.

pustulation (pŭs″tū-lā′shŭn) The development of pustules.

pustule (pŭs′tūl) [L. *pustula,* blister] A small, elevated skin lesion filled with white blood cells and, sometimes, bacteria or the products of broken-down cells. Pustules are found in many common skin disorders, including acne vulgaris, some drug rashes, many viral exanthems (e.g., herpes simplex or varicella-zoster viruses), and pustular psoriasis.

pustulosis (pŭs″chŭ-lō′sĭs, tyŭ) [*pustule* + *-osis*] A generalized eruption of pustules.

    acute generalized exanthematous p. ABBR: AGEP. A rare but severe allergic reaction to a drug, characterized by a widespread pustular rash, fever, and a high white blood cell count. It usually resolves within a few weeks after one stops taking the drug that caused the reaction.

putamen (pū-tā′mĕn) [L., shell] A major basal ganglia nucleus shaped like a concave-convex lens, located deep inside the cerebral hemisphere, and composing one of the two segments of the striatum. The other segment of the striatum is the caudate nucleus. The putamen and the caudate nucleus are separated by the internal capsule. A separate basal ganglia nucleus, the globus pallidus, lies like a small convex-convex lens in the concavity of the putamen. SEE: *striatum.*

putrefaction (pū″trĕ-făk′shŭn) [L. *putrefactio*] Decomposition of animal matter, esp. protein associated with malodorous and poisonous products such as the ptomaines, mercaptans, and hydrogen sulfide, caused by certain kinds of bacteria and fungi. Decomposition that occurs in previously sterile tissue after death (carried out by normal flora) is called autolysis. SEE: *sepsis.*

   intestinal p. The chemical changes by bacteria in the intestine, forming indole, skatole, paracresol, phenol, phenylpropionic acid, phenylacetic acid, paraoxyphenylacetic acid, hydroparacumaric acid, fatty acids, carbon dioxide, hydrogen, methane, methylmercaptan, and sulfurated hydrogen.

putrefactive (pū″trĕ-făk′tĭv) [L. *putrefacere,* to putrefy] **1.** Pert. to or causing putrefaction. **2.** An agent promoting putrefaction.

putrefy (pū′trĕ-fī) [L. *putrefacere,* to putrefy] To undergo putrefaction.

putrescence (pū-trĕs′ĕns) [L. *putrescens,* grow rotten] Decay; rottenness.

putrescine (pū-trĕs′ĭn) A poisonous polyamine formed by bacterial action on the amino acid arginine.

putrid (pū′trĭd) [L. *putridus*] Decayed; rotten; foul.

Puumala virus (poom′ ă-lă) [*Puumala,* a city in Finland] SEE: under *virus.*

PUVA therapy (poov′ă) [psoralen + *ul*traviolet A] The treatment of skin conditions (e.g., psoriasis or cutaneous T-cell lymphoma) with a photosensitizing drug, psoralens, and gradually increasing doses of long-wave ultraviolet light. SEE: *psoralen; psoriasis.*

PVA *percutaneous vertebral **augmentation**.*

p value The probability that a finding has occurred randomly rather than as a result of a treatment or other intervention. In a research study that compares a treated group of patients with a control group exposed only to a placebo, investigators may find that the treated population experienced benefits or suffered more side effects than the controls. Was the observed effect real, or did it occur by chance? The p value of the study helps researchers tell the difference. A p value of 0.5 suggests that there is a 50-50 chance that the findings of the study are significant. A p value of 0.05 (the value customarily used to suggest that research results are statistically significant) means that there is a

5% chance that the results of the study occurred by chance alone. The lower the value, the greater the degree of confidence in the findings: a p value of 0.01, for example, creates more confidence than a p value of 0.05.

PVC *polyvinyl chloride; premature ventricular contraction.*

P$\bar{v}$O$_2$ Symbol for partial pressure of oxygen in mixed venous blood.

PVP *polyvinylpyrrolidone.*

PVP-iodine *povidone-iodine.*

PWA *person with AIDS.*

PWB *partial weight bearing.*

P2Y$_{12}$ The adenosine diphosphate receptor on platelets. It is the target for drugs such as clopidogrel, prasugrel, or ticagrelor, which are used to inhibit platelet aggregation.

pyarthrosis (pī″ăr-thrō′sĭs) [Gr. *pyon,* pus, + *arthron,* joint, + *osis,* condition] Pus in the cavity of a joint.

pycno-, pycn-, pykno-, pykn- [Gr. *pyknos,* compact, thick] Prefixes meaning *dense, thick, compact, frequent.*

pycnogenol (pik-noj′ĕn-ol′) A mixture of antioxidant chemicals derived from the maritime pine, *Pinus pinaster,* native to the western Mediterranean, and marketed in alternative medicine as *pine bark extract.*

pyelitis (pī″ĕ-lī′tĭs) [Gr. *pyelos,* pelvis, + *itis,* inflammation] Inflammation of the pelvis of the kidney and its calices. **pyelitic,** *adj.*

   calculous p. Pyelitis resulting from a kidney stone.

   p. cystica Pyelitis associated with multiple small cysts in the mucosa of the renal pelvis.

pyelo- [Gr. *pyelos,* pelvis] Combining form meaning *pelvis.*

pyelocaliectasis (pī″ĕ-lō-kăl″ē-ĕk′tă-sĭs) [″ + *kalyx,* cup, + *ektasis,* dilation] Dilation of the pelvis and calices of the kidney.

pyelocystitis (pī″ĕ-lō-sĭs-tī′tĭs) [″ + *kystis,* bladder, + *itis,* inflammation] Inflammation of the renal pelvis and bladder.

pyelogram (pī′ĕ-lō-grăm) [Gr. *pyelos,* pelvis, + *gramma,* something written] A radiograph of the ureter and renal pelvis.

   intravenous p. ABBR: IVP. A pyelogram in which a radiopaque material is given intravenously. Multiple radiographs of the urinary tract taken while the material is excreted provide important information about the structure and function of the kidney, ureter, and bladder. This examination may be used to detect kidney stones and other lesions that may block or irritate the urinary tract.

pyelography (pī″ĕ-lŏg′ră-fē) [″ + *graphein,* to write] Radiography of the renal pelvis and ureter after injection of a radiopaque contrast medium.

pyelolithotomy (pī″ĕ-lō-lĭth-ŏt′ō-mē) [″ + ″] The surgical removal of a stone from the renal pelvis.

pyelonephritis (pī″ĕ-lō-nĕ-frīt′ĭs) [*pyelo-* + *nephritis*] Inflammation of the kidney and renal pelvis, usually due to a bacterial infection that has ascended from the urinary bladder. SYN: *tubulointerstitial **nephritis***. SEE: *Nursing Diagnoses Appendix.*

ETIOLOGY: *Escherichia coli* is usually the agent. Cultures of urine and blood are obtained to guide therapy.

SYMPTOMS: This condition is characterized by the sudden onset of chills and fever with dull pain in the flank over one or both kidneys. There is tenderness when the kidney is palpated. There may be signs of cystitis, i.e., urgency with burning, and frequency of urination. Urinalysis and culture findings include pyuria, urine sediment with leukocytes singly, in clumps, or in casts, significant bacteria (more than 100,000 organisms/μL of urine), low specific gravity and osmolarity, slightly alkaline urine pH, and sometimes proteinuria, glycosuria, and ketonuria.

TREATMENT: Antibiotics, e.g., fluoroquinolones, sulfa drugs, cephalosporins, or aminoglycosides, that effectively treat common pathogens of the urinary tract are administered, pending the results of cultures. Antiemetics are given to control nausea and vomiting. If patients are unable to take medications by mouth or if they have predisposing conditions, e.g., pregnancy or diabetes, that increase the likelihood of a bad outcome, they may be admitted to the hospital for observation, monitoring, and hydration.

PROGNOSIS: The outcome depends on the character and virulence of the infection, accessory etiological factors, drainage of the kidney, presence or absence of complications, and general physical condition of the patient.

PATIENT CARE: Antibiotics and antipyretics are administered as prescribed. The patient is encouraged to complete the full course of antibiotics and drink 2 to 3 L of fluids per day to prevent urinary stasis and to flush byproducts of the inflammatory process. Symptoms may disappear after a few days of treatment, and urine become sterile within 48 to 72 hr; however, the prescribed course of therapy should be completed (10 to 14 days). The patient is taught how to correctly collect a midstream urine specimen, and urine usually is recultured about 1 week after therapy has concluded. After the completion of therapy, the patient may require urine cultures periodically over the next year to detect recurrent or residual infections. The patient should report any signs of infection during scheduled follow-up care. Patients requiring

prolonged use of indwelling catheters are at increased risk for recurring infections. Strict aseptic technique must be carried outduring insertion and care. Females can help to prevent urinary tract infections by wiping the perineum from front to back after defecation and by washing the area before and after sexual intercourse. Chronic pyelonephritis is a persistent kidney inflammation that may scar the kidneys and lead to chronic renal failure. Its cause may be bacterial, metastatic, or urogenous and is most common in patients with histories of urinary obstructions or vesicoureteral reflux. Hypertension occurs in late stages of this condition, and effective treatment involves controlling blood pressure, surgically eliminating obstructions and/or correcting anomalies, and treating bacterial infections with long-term antimicrobial therapy.

xanthogranulomatous p. ABBR: XGP. A relatively rare form of chronic destructive kidney infection in which a kidney, usually one obstructed by stones, becomes enlarged, necrotic, and functionless. In most cases the diseased kidney is surgically removed.

pyelonephrosis (pī″ĕ-lō-nĕ-frō′sĭs) [″ + ″ + *osis,* condition] Any disease of the pelvis of the kidney. SYN: *pyelopathy.*

pyeloplasty (pī′ĕ-lō-plăs″tē) [″ + *plastos,* formed] Reparative surgery on the pelvis of the kidney.

pyelostomy (pī″ĕ-lŏs′tō-mē) [″ + *stoma,* mouth] Creation of an opening into the renal pelvis.

pyelotomy (pī″ĕ-lŏt′ō-mē) [″ + *tome,* incision] Incision of the renal pelvis.

PATIENT CARE: All catheters should be secured to the patient to prevent dislodgement. The nurse should assess and record the appearance of the urine, including color, consistency, and amount. Catheter drainage tubing must be kept free of kinks and dependent loops. Catheters should never be clamped. The nurse should monitor and record intake and output. After removal of the catheter, a stoma-bag collection device should be used to collect any drainage and maintain skin integrity while the wound heals.

pyemia (pī-ē′mē-ă) [″ + *haima,* blood] A form of septicemia due to the presence of pus-forming organisms in the blood, manifested by formation of multiple abscesses of a metastatic nature.

SYMPTOMS: The disease is characterized by intermittent high temperature with recurrent chills; metastatic processes in various parts of the body, esp. in lungs; septic pneumonia; empyema. It may be fatal.

TREATMENT: Antibiotics are effective. Prophylactic treatment consists in prevention of suppuration.

arterial p. Pyemia resulting from dissemination of emboli from a thrombus in cardiac vessels.

cryptogenic p. Pyemia of an origin that is hidden in the deeper tissues.

metastatic p. Multiple abscesses resulting from infected pyemic thrombi.

portal p. Suppurative inflammation of the portal vein. **pyemic** (-ē'mĭk), *adj.*

Pyemotes (pī-ĕ-mō'tēz) A genus of mites parasitic on the larvae of insects.

P. ventricosus A mite present in the straw of some cereals, contact with which causes a vesiculopapular dermatitis in humans. This is called grain itch.

pygal (pī'găl) [Gr. *pyge*, rump] Concerning the buttocks. SEE: *steatopygia*.

pygeum (pij'ē-ŭm) An herbal remedy extracted from the bark of *Prunus africana*. Tea and herbal capsules made from its bark are used to treat benign prostatic hyperplasia (enlarged prostate). SEE: *Prunus africana*.

Pygeum africanum (pij'ē-ŭm ăf"rĭ-kān'ŭm) Prunus africana.

pygmy (pĭg'mē) A very small person, a dwarf.

pygo-, pyg- [Gr. *pygē*, rump, buttocks] Prefixes meaning *buttocks*.

pyknic (pĭk'nĭk) [Gr. *pyknos*, thick] Pert. to a body type characterized by roundness of the extremities, stockiness, large chest and abdomen, and tendency to obesity.

pykno-, pykn- SEE: *pycno-*.

pyknodysostosis (pĭk"nō-dĭs"ŏs-tō'sĭs) [" + *dys*, bad, + *osteon*, bone, + *osis*, condition] An autosomal recessive disease that affects bones and resembles osteopetrosis, but the disease is mild and not associated with hematological or neurological abnormalities. Affected children have short stature, open fontanels, frontal bossing, hypoplastic facial bones, blue sclerae, and dental abnormalities. There may be double rows of malformed teeth. Despite the multiple abnormalities, life span is unaffected. The patient usually seeks medical care because of frequent fractures. The only treatment is surgical correction of deformities and fractures.

pyknosis (pĭk-nō'sĭs) [" + *osis*, condition] Thickness, esp. shrinking of cells through degeneration. SYN: *inspissation*.

pyle-, pylo-, pyl- [Gr. *pylē*, gate] Prefixes meaning *orifice*, esp. of the portal vein.

pylephlebitis (pī"lē-flē-bī'tĭs) [" + " + *itis*, inflammation] Inflammation of the portal vein, generally suppurative.

adhesive p. Thrombosis of the portal vein.

p. obturans Pylephlebitis with obstructed flow in the portal vein.

pylethrombophlebitis (pī"lē-thrŏm"bō-flē-bī'tĭs) [" + *thrombos*, clot, + *phleps*, vein, + *itis*, inflammation] Thrombosis and inflammation of the portal vein.

pylethrombosis (pī"lē-thrŏm-bō'sĭs) [Gr. *pyle*, gate, + *thrombos*, clot, + *osis*, condition] Occlusion of the portal vein by a thrombus.

pylon (pī'lŏn) A temporary artificial leg.

pylorectomy (pī"lō-rĕk'tō-mē) [" + *ektome*, excision] Surgical removal of the pylorus.

pyloric (pī-lor'ĭk) [Gr. *pyloros*, gatekeeper] Pert. to the distal portion of the stomach or to the opening between the stomach and duodenum.

pyloric stenosis SEE: under *stenosis*.

pyloristenosis (pī-lōr"ĭ-stĕ-nō'sĭs) [*pyloro-* + *stenosis*] Pyloric **stenosis**.

pyloro-, pylor- [Gr. *pylōros*, gatekeeper, porter] Prefixes meaning *pylorus*.

pyloromyotomy (pī-lor"ō-mī-ot'ō-mē) [*pyloro-* + *myotomy*] Incision of the pyloric sphincter to treat (infantile hypertrophic) pyloric stenosis. SEE: *pylorotomy*.

pyloroplasty (pī-lōr'ŏ-plas"tē) [*pyloro-* + *-plasty*] Operation to repair or alter the pylorus, esp. one to increase the caliber of the pyloric opening.

Finney p. SEE: *Finney pyloroplasty*.

Heineke-Mikulicz p. SEE: *Heineke-Mikulicz pyloroplasty*.

Jaboulay p. SEE: under *Jaboulay, Mathieu*.

pylorospasm (pī-lor'ō-spăzm) [" + "] Spasmodic contraction of the pyloric orifice. The usual cause is a disturbance in the motor innervation of the pyloric sphincter. It may occur secondary to lesions of the stomach or duodenum near the pyloric orifice. It may sometimes be mistaken for infantile hypertrophic pyloric stenosis.

pylorotomy (pī-lor-ŏt'ō-mē) [" + *tome*, incision] Incision of the pylorus through its muscular layers to the level of the submucosa to relieve hypertrophic stenosis.

pylorus (pī-lor'ŭs) [Gr. *pyloros*, gatekeeper] **1.** The lower portion of the stomach that opens into the duodenum, consisting of the pyloric antrum and pyloric canal. **2.** In older usage, a term for the pyloric orifice or the pyloric sphincter. **pyloric,** *adj.*

pyocele (pī'ō-sēl) [Gr. *pyon*, pus, + *kele*, tumor, swelling] A hernia or distended cavity containing pus.

pyocyanin (pī"ō-sī'ă-nĭn) A blue cytotoxic crystalline chemical (1-hydroxy-5-methylphenazine) secreted by *Pseudomonas aeruginosa*.

pyoderma (pī-ō-dĕr'mă) [" + *derma*, skin] Any acute, inflammatory, purulent bacterial dermatitis.

p. gangrenosum A rare, ulcerating skin disease in which the skin is infiltrated by neutrophils. It is often found in people with other underlying illnesses, such as inflammatory bowel disease, rheumatoid arthritis, or some hematological malignancies. SEE: illus.

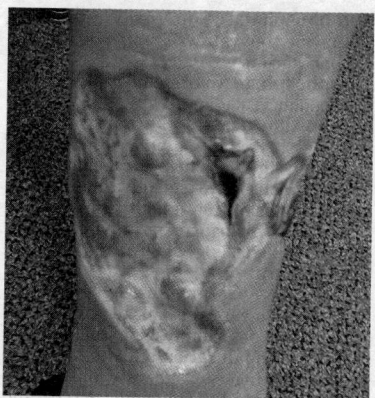

**PYODERMA GANGRENOSUM OF THE
LOWER LEG**

pyodermatitis (pī″ō-dĕr″mă-tī′tĭs) [″ +
″ + *itis*, inflammation] Pyogenic infection of the skin causing a dermatitis.

pyodermia (pī″ō-dĕr′mē-ă) Any suppurative skin disease.

pyogenic (pī-ō-jĕn′ĭk) [″ + *gennan*, to
produce] Producing pus.

pyogenic cocci Any of a group of genetically unrelated spherical bacteria that
produce pus-forming infections. They
include *Streptococcus pyogenes, Staphylococcus aureus, Neisseria gonorrhoeae,* and *Neisseria meningitidis.*

pyometra (pī″ō-mē′tră) [″ + *metra*,
uterus] Retained pus accumulation in
the uterine cavity.

pyonephrosis (pī″ō-nĕf-rō′sĭs) [″ + ″ +
osis, condition] Pus accumulation in
the pelvis of the kidney.

pyopericarditis (pī″ō-pĕr″ĭ-kăr-dī′tĭs) [″
+ *peri*, around, + *kardia*, heart, +
itis, inflammation] Pericarditis with
suppuration.

pyopericardium (pī″ō-pĕr″ĭ-kăr′dē-ŭm)
Pus formation in the pericardium.

pyopneumothorax (pī″ō-nū″mō-thō′răks)
[″ + ″ + *thorax*, chest] The presence
of pus and gas in the pleural cavity.

pyorrhea (pī″ō-rē′ă) [″ + *rhoia*, flow]
1. A discharge of purulent matter. **2.** A
dated term for periodontal disease.

pyosalpinx (pī″ō-săl′pĭnks) Pus in the
fallopian tube.

pyothorax (pī″ō-thō′răks) [″ + *thorax*,
chest] Empyema.

pyoverdin (pī-ō-vĕr′dĭn) An iron-binding
molecule, produced by *Pseudomonas*
species, that competes with transferrin
for host iron. It contributes to the virulence of *Pseudomonas* infections.

pyoxanthin(e) (pī″ō-zăn′thĭn) [″ + *xanthos*, yellow] A yellow pigment resulting from oxidation of pyocyanin, sometimes present in pus.

pyramid (pĭr′ă-mĭd) [Gr. *pyramis*, a pyr-
amid] **1.** A solid on the base with three

or more triangular sides that meet at an
apex. **2.** Any part of the body resembling
a pyramid. **3.** A compact bundle of nerve
fibers in the medulla oblongata. **4.** The
petrous portion of the temporal bone.

 p. of light The triangular light reflex
from the typanic membrane of the ear.

 p. of the medulla One of a pair of
elongated tapering prominences on the
anterior (i.e., ventral) surface of the medulla oblongata, composed of descending corticospinal fibers.

 renal p. The inner mass of the kidney
consisting of 5 to 11 conical renal pyramids separated by renal columns. The
renal pyramids contain the loops of
Henle and the collecting ducts. The renal columns contain interlobar arteries
and veins.

 p. of the thyroid A conical process
sometimes present, extending cephalad
from the isthmus of the thyroid gland.

pyramidal (pĭ-răm′ĭ-dăl) [L. *pyramidalis*] In the shape of a pyramid.

pyramidalis (pĭ-răm″ĭ-dăl′ĭs) [L.] The
muscle that arises from the crest of the
pubis and is inserted into the linea alba
upward about halfway to the navel.

pyramidal system The direct output
from the motor cortices of the cerebral
hemispheres to the brainstem and spinal cord. It deals with the regulation of
fine muscle movements.

pyramidotomy (pĭ-răm-ĭ-dŏt′ō-mē) [Gr.
pyramis, a pyramid, + *tome*, incision]
Excision of the pyramidal tracts of the
spinal cord in order to alleviate involuntary muscular movements.

pyran (pī′răn) The compound C_5H_6O,
the ring structure of which consists of
five carbon atoms and one oxygen atom.

pyranose (pī′ră-nōs) A cyclic sugar or
glycoside with a structure similar to a
pyran.

pyrethrins (pī-rē′thrĭnz) The general
name given to substances derived from
pyrethrum flowers (chrysanthemums);
used as insecticides.

pyretic (pī-rĕt′ĭk) [Gr. *pyretos*, fever]
Pert. to fever.

pyreto-, pyret- [Gr. *pyretos*, burning
heat, fever] Prefixes meaning *fever*.

pyrexia (pī-rĕk′sē-ă) [Gr. *pyressein*, to be
feverish] Fever.

pyridine (pĕr′ĭ-dēn) A colorless, volatile
liquid with a charred odor. It is obtained
by dry distillation of nitrogen-containing organic matter. It is used as an industrial solvent.

pyridoxal 5-phosphate (pĭr-ĭ-dŏk′săl) A
derivative of pyridoxine. It serves as a
coenzyme of certain amino-acid decar-
boxylases in bacteria, and in animal tissues of 3,4-dihydroxyphenylalanine
(dopa) decarboxylase.

pyridoxamine (pĭr″ĭ-dŏks′ă-mēn″) One
of the vitamin B_6 group; a 4-aminoethyl
analog of pyridoxine.

4-pyridoxic acid (pir″ĭ-dok′sik) SEE: under *acid*.

pyridoxine dependency (pir″ĭ-dok′sĕn, sĕn) [*pyrid(ine)* + *ox(ygen)* + *-ine*] A rare autosomal recessive cause of neonatal seizures. The disorder requires lifelong supplementation of pyridoxine (vitamin B₆).

pyridoxine hydrochloride (pĭ-rĭ-dŏks′ēn) One of a group of substances, including pyridoxal and pyridoxamine, that make up vitamin B₆. SEE: *Vitamins Appendix.*

pyriform, piriform (pĭr′ĭ-fŏrm″) [L. *pirum*, pear, + *forma*, shape] Shaped like a pear.

pyrimidine (pĭ-rĭm′ĭd-ĭn) The parent of a group of heterocyclic nitrogen compounds, $C_4H_4N_2$. Cytosine and thymine are found in DNA; cytosine and uracil, in RNA.

pyrithiamine (pĭr″ĭ-thī′ă-mēn) A synthetic analog of thiamine that blocks thiamine transport. It was used experimentally in studies of human lymphoblasts to mimic nutritional diseases such as beriberi and Wernicke-Korsakoff syndrome, two forms of thiamine deficiency.

pyro-, pyr- [Gr. *pyr*, fire] Prefixes meaning *fire, heat, temperature.*

pyrogallol (pī″rō-găl′ŏl″) $C_6H_6O_3$; a toxic chemical derived from gallic acid.

pyrogen (pī′rō-jĕn) [Gr. *pyr*, fire, + *gennan*, to produce] Any agent that causes fever. It may be exogenous, such as bacteria or viruses, or endogenous, produced in the body. The latter are usually in response to stimuli accompanying infection or inflammation. SYN: *pyrexin; pyrotoxin.* **pyrogenic** (pī″rō-jĕn′ĭk), *adj.*

⚠ A fluid that has been opened previously and allowed to stand should not be given intravenously, even though the top may have been closed tightly, because pyrogens may have formed within it.

leukocytic p. A protein released by phagocytes into the blood during a fever. It raises body temperature by acting on the thermoregulatory centers of the anterior hypothalamus

pyrolysis (pī-rŏl′ĭ-sĭs) [″ + *lysis*, dissolution] The decomposition of organic matter when there is a rise in temperature.

pyromania (pī″rō-mā′nē-ă) [″ + *mania*, madness] Fire madness; a mania for setting fires or seeing them.

pyrometer (pī-rŏm′ĕ-tĕr) [″ + *metron*, measure] A device for measuring a very high temperature.

pyronine (pī′rō-nĭn) A histological stain used to demonstrate the presence of ribonucleic acid and deoxyribonucleic acid.

pyrophosphatase (pī″rō-fŏs′fă-tās) An enzyme that catalyzes splitting of phosphoric groups.

pyrophosphate (pī″rō-fŏs′fāt) Any salt of phosphoric acid.

pyropoikilocytosis (pī″rō-poy″ki-lō-sī-tō′sĭs) [*pyro-* + *poikilocytosis*] An inherited form of hemolytic anemia in which cells have defective spectrin in their cytoskeleton, resulting in cellular breakdown during exposure to heat.

pyrosis (pī-rō′sĭs) [Gr. *pyrosis*, burning] Heartburn.

PATIENT CARE: The caregivers explain the meaning of this term to the patient and determine the exact location, timing, and duration of discomfort. Position changes exaggerate discomfort; precipitating factors (such as type and amount of food), method of relief, and other factors that aggravate the discomfort are determined (increased intra-abdominal pressure related to pregnancy, obesity, constipation, tight clothing, vigorous exercise, etc). Diagnostic studies such as barium swallow and endoscopy, gastric biopsies, and saliva samples for *Helicobacter pylori*, etc., may be carried out to ascertain the cause (gastroesophageal reflux, peptic ulcer, etc). Treatment may include antacids and absorbents, H_2 receptor site inhibitors, proton-pump inhibitors, and antibiotics to treat *Helicobacter pylori*. The patient is advised to sit upright after meals, take small frequent feedings, avoid highly seasoned foods, acidic juices, alcoholic drinks, bedtime snacks, and food high in fat or carbohydrates. Meals should be taken 2 to 3 hr before retiring. Elevation of the head of the bed often helps to relieve symptoms.

pyroxylin (pī-rok′sĭ-lĭn) Nitrocellulose in ether or acetone. It is colloquially known as *guncotton*. It is a toxic and extremely flammable white fiber used in lacquers, plastics, and resins, among other applications.

pyrrole (pĕr′ŏl) A heterocyclic substance that provides the building blocks for a large number of vital compounds such as hemoglobin, chlorophyll, and bile acids. It is a colorless liquid with the odor of chloroform.

pyrrolidine (pĭ-rŏl′ĭ-dĭn) Tetramethylamine, $(CH_2)_4NH$. It may be obtained from pyrrole or tobacco, which contains pyrrole.

pyruvate (pī-roo′vāt″) A salt or ester of pyruvic acid.

pyuria (pī-ūr′ē-ă) [*pyo-* + *-uria*] Pus in the urine, which is evidence of renal or bladder disease, usually a urinary tract infection.

sterile p. The presence of white blood cells in the urine in the absence of bacteria or other infectious agents. It is a sign of kidney inflammation, occurring in disorders like interstitial nephritis.

Q 1. *quality factor; quantity*. 2. Symbol for coulomb.

q Symbol for long arm of a chromosome.

QA *Quality assurance*.

Q angle SEE: under *angle*.

Qco₂ The number of microliters of CO_2 given off per milligram of dry weight of tissue per hour.

qd L. *quaque die*, every day.

> ⚠️ Most experts in the prevention of health care errors recommend that the abbreviation q.d. be written out as "daily" in order to prevent communication errors. q.d may be confused with q.i.d (four times a day), a mistake that could result in an unintentional overdose.

Q fever [Abbr. of *q(uery)*, because the cause was unknown] SEE: under *fever*.

qh, q1h L. *quaque hora*, every hour.

> ⚠️ For safety, hourly medications are almost always written as q1h.

qi, ch'i (chē) [Chinese *qì*, breath, air, spirit] In traditional Chinese medicine, the vital force or energy of life.

q.i.d. L. *quater in die*, four times a day.

> ⚠️ To avoid medication errors, this order should be written "four times daily."

qi gong, qigong, chi kung (chē goong) [Chinese *qì*, breath, air, spirit + *gōng*, work, practice] An ancient Chinese approach to healing and an exercise that combines internal energy, movement, breathing exercises, meditation, and relaxation.

Qo₂ The number of microliters of O_2 taken up per milligram of dry weight of tissue per hour.

qod *Every other day*. This abbreviation appears on the Joint Commission's "Do not use" list.

> ⚠️ The "o" may be misinterpreted as a period or an "i."

QRS complex SEE: under *complex*.

QRST complex SEE: under *complex*.

q.s. L. *quantum sufficit*, as much as suffices.

QSAR *quantitative structure-activity relationship*.

qt *quart*.

QTc In electrocardiography, the duration of the QT interval adjusted for the patient's heart rate. Prolonged QTc's are associated with an increased risk of ventricular dysrhythmia and sudden death.

Q-T dispersion SEE: under *dispersion*.

Q-T interval SEE: under *interval*.

QT/R-R ratio On an electrocardiogram, the measured QT interval of an electrocardiogram divided by the R-R interval of the same cardiac cycle.

quack (kwăk) [D. *kwaksalven*, to peddle salve] One who pretends to have knowledge or skill in medicine. SYN: *charlatan*.

quad (kwăd) Medical "shorthand" for quadriceps, quadrilateral, quadrant, quadriplegia.

quadrangular (kwŏd-răng′ū-lěr) [L. *quadri*, four, + *angulus*, angle] Having four angles.

quadrant (kwŏd′rănt) [L. *quadrans*, a fourth] 1. One quarter or fourth of a circle. 2. One of four corresponding regions, as of the abdomen, divided for descriptive and diagnostic purposes.

    dental q. One quarter of the mouth. Each arch is divided in half so that one can easily describe the location of teeth or soft tissue observations. Quadrants are labeled as maxillary right and left or mandibular right and left and are shown in diagram form for dental records.

quadrantanopia, quadrantanopsia (kwo″drănt-ă-nō′pē-ă, -op′sē-ă) [*quadrant* + *anopia*] Blindness or diminished visual acuity in one fourth of the visual field.

quadrantectomy (kwŏd″răn-tek′tŏ-mē) [*quadrant* + *-ectomy*] Surgical removal of a defined segment (approx. one quarter) of an organ, e.g., of the breast in a patient with breast cancer.

quadrate (kwŏd′rāt) [L. *quadratus*, squared] Square, or having four equal sides.

quadrate lobe A small lobe of liver located on the visceral surface and lying in contact with the pylorus and duodenum.

quadri-, quadr-, quadru- [L. *quadr-*, fr. *quattuor*, four] Prefixes meaning *four*.

quadribasic (kwŏd″rĭ-bā′sĭk) [L. *quattuor*, four + basic] Having four replaceable atoms of hydrogen.

quadriceps (kwŏd′rĭ-sĕps) [″ + *caput*, head] Four-headed, as a quadriceps muscle.

quadriceps femoris A large muscle on the anterior surface of the thigh composed of the rectus femoris, vastus lateralis, vastus medialis, and vastus intermedius muscles. These muscles are inserted by a common tendon on the tuberosity of the tibia. The quadriceps femoris is an extensor of the leg.

quadricepsplasty (kwŏd″rĭ-sĕps′plăs-tē) [″ + ″ + Gr. *plassein*, to form] Plastic surgery to repair adhesions and scars around the quadriceps femoris muscle in order to restore function.

quadricuspid (kwŏd″rĭ-kŭs′pĭd) [″ + *cuspis*, point] Having four cusps, as a tooth.

quadridigitate (kwŏd″rĭ-dĭj′ĭ-tāt) Having only four fingers on a hand or four toes on a foot.

quadrigeminal (kwŏd″rĭ-jĕm′ĭn-ăl) Fourfold; having four symmetrical parts; pert. to the corpora quadrigemina.

quadrigeminal bodies Four rounded projections from the roof of the midbrain. SEE: *colliculus inferior; colliculus superior.*

quadrilateral (kwŏd″rĭ-lăt′ĕr-ăl) [″ + *latus*, side] Having four sides.

quadrilocular (kwŏd″rĭ-lŏk′ū-lăr) [″ + *loculus*, a small space] Having four chambers, cavities, or spaces.

quadripara (kwŏd-rĭp′ă-ră) [″ + *parere*, to bring forth, to bear] A woman who has had four pregnancies that have continued beyond the 20th week of gestation. SYN: *quartipara.* SEE: *para.*

quadripartite (kwŏd″rĭ-păr′tĭt) [″ + *partire*, to divide] Divided into four parts.

quadriplegia (kwŏd″rĭ-plē′jē-ă) [″ + Gr. *plege*, stroke] Paralysis of all four extremities, usually caused by an injury to or disease of the cervical spinal cord. Quadriplegia most often results from trauma to the neck, although it may occasionally result from spinal stenosis, infections, aneurysms, vasculitis, autoimmune diseases, neurosurgery, or mass lesions. The higher the injury (the closer it is to the brainstem) the less function will be present in the arms. Injury above the third cervical vertebra paralyzes the diaphragm; in patients with high cervical lesions, life can be sustained only with mechanical ventilation. SYN: *tetraplegia.* SEE: *Nursing Diagnoses Appendix.*

PATIENT CARE: Patients with quadriplegia benefit from physical therapy, occupational therapy, and respiratory care to regain optimal functioning. Assistance is provided with self-care deficits, including bladder paralysis, skin and oral care, feeding and nutrition, elimination, respiratory toilet, positioning, and exercise. The patency of the urinary catheter is checked, and a bulk diet is provided to prevent impaction. Both patient and family are encouraged to verbalize their concerns, and support is offered to help them cope with their grief and loss. Assistance is provided to help the family set realistic plans for the future in view of the patient's functional abilities, body image, and self-concept. The patient is urged to participate in a rehabilitation program as soon as stabilized. Rehabilitative care may be provided in a skilled nursing care facility, rehabilitation center, or in the home with home health care providers and family participation. SEE: *spinal cord injury, acute.*

   transient q. The temporary state of absent or diminished sensory and motor function throughout the body caused by trauma to the cervical spine. Symptoms clear within 15 min to 48 hr.

quadripolar (kwŏd″rĭ-pō′lăr) Pert. to a cell having four poles.

quadrisect (kwŏd′rĭ-sĕkt) [″ + *sectio*, a cutting] To divide into four parts, usually of equal size.

quadrisection (kwŏd″rĭ-sĕk′shŭn) Dividing into four sections or parts.

quadrivalent (kwŏd″rĭ-vā′lĕnt) [″ + *valens*, powerful] 1. Having the ability to replace four atoms of hydrogen in a compound (i.e., a chemical valence of four). 2. Having four components, e.g., a quadrivalent vaccine.

quadruped (kwah′drŭ-ped″) [*quadri-* + L. *pes*, foot] 1. A four-footed animal. 2. Assuming a position with hands and feet on the floor. **quadrupedal** (kwo-droo′ped-ăl, kwod′ŭ-ped″ăl), *adj.*

quadrupedal reflex (kwo-droo′ped-ăl, kwod′ŭ-ped″ăl) SEE: under *reflex.*

quadruplet (kwŏd′roo-plĕt, kwŏ-droo′plĕt) [L. *quadruplus*, fourfold] One of four children born of the same mother in the same confinement.

quale (kwā′lē) [L. *qualis*, of what kind] The quality of anything, esp. of a sensation.

qualified mental retardation professional A person with more than one year's experience working with mentally retarded persons who has a bachelor's degree, a nursing degree, or another form of professional education in health care.

qualitative (kwŏl′ĭ-tā″tĭv) [L. *qualitativus*] Referring to the quality of anything. SEE: *quantitative.*

qualitative analysis Determination of the presence of a substance in a test sample or of the physicochemical characteristics of a substance in a sample.

qualitative metasummary A technique used to gain insights from two or more descriptive analyses of the same phenomenon by listing common elements in a standardized format so that patterns in analytical thought can be highlighted.

quality (kwŏl′ĭ-tē) [L. *qualitas*, quality] 1. That which constitutes or characterizes a thing; the natural character. 2. In radiology, the energy or penetrating power of the x-ray beam, which is controlled by kilovoltage peak.

quality-adjusted life-years ABBR: QALY. A measure of health that combines the duration of life and its degradation by disease or death. A year in perfect health is considered to have a QALY of 1.0; a year of life in a coma is assigned a lower QALY approaching zero.

quality assurance ABBR: QA. Activities and programs designed to achieve desired levels of care.

quality factor SEE: under *factor*.

quality indicator SEE: under *indicator*.

quality of life The objective conditions, consequences, or subjective value or satisfaction experienced in life. The concept holds varying meanings for different people and may evolve over time. For some individuals it implies access to resources, autonomy, empowerment, capability, and choice; for others, security, social integration, or freedom from stress or illness.

    health-related q.o.l. ABBR: HRQOL. The measurable impact of a person's perception of his or her health and the effect that produces on satisfaction with life and well-being. HRQOL is influenced by functional and socioeconomic status; by health risks; and by the beliefs, cultural milieu, policies, and practices of society.

quality management 1. A measurement and assessment system designed to regulate variations in equipment, procedures, processes, or evaluations. 2. The oversight and supervision within health care institutions of programs that improve patient care, patient safety, resource utilization, and ancillary services.

quanta (kwŏn′tă) [L.] Pl. of quantum.

quantal (kwant′ăl) [L. *quantum,* how much + *-al*] 1. Pert. to quantum theory. 2. Pert. to a response to a stimulus marked by the presence or absence of a specific reaction, e.g., an all or none response.

quantitative (kwont″ĭ-tāt′ĭv) [L. *quantitativus,* pert. to quantity] 1. Pert. to measurement. 2. Capable of being counted. SEE: *qualitative*.

quantitative analysis Determination of the amount of a substance in a specified material. The amount may be represented in various ways: "x" grams, "x" g/L, kPa (i.e., an absolute quantity, a concentrational quantity, an intensive quantity).

quantity (kwŏn′tĭ-tē) [L. *quantitas,* quantity] Amount; portion.

quantum (kwont′ŭm, ′ă) *pl.* **quanta** [L., *quantum,* how much; QUANTA, how many] 1. A definite amount. 2. A minimal or indivisable unit of matter or energy.

quantum mottle SEE: under *mottle*.

quarantine (kwor′ăn-tēn″) [It. *quarantina,* 40 days (of isolation)] 1. The period during which free entry to a country by humans, animals, plants, or agricultural products is prohibited, in order to limit the spread of potentially infectious diseases. 2. A period of enforced isolation from public contact to prevent the spread of a contagious disease. Quarantine is typically used to isolate only those people, animals, or plants thought to pose significant health risks to the population at large. The duration of enforced detention is typically equal to the longest known incubation period of the disease.

quart (kwort) [L. *quartus,* a fourth] ABBR: qt. A unit of fluid equal to one fourth of a gallon, or 2 pints, or 946 mL; in dry measure, one eighth of a peck.

quartan (kwor′tăn) [L. *quartana,* of the fourth] Occurring every fourth day. SEE: *malaria*.

quartile (kwor′tĭl) [L. *quartus,* a fourth] A 25% section, wedge, or slice of a consecutively arranged set of data.

quartz (kwărts) [Ger. *quarz*] Silicon dioxide, the principal ingredient of sandstone (crystallized silica; rock crystal). When crystal is clear and colorless, it permits the passage of large amounts of ultraviolet rays.

    q. applicator A quartz rod containing various shapes and angles used to conduct, by total internal reflection, ultraviolet radiation from a water-cooled mercury arc quartz lamp.

    q. glass Crystalline quartz used for prisms and lenses; fused quartz used for windows, through which ultraviolet radiations are freely transmitted.

quater in die (kwŏ′tĕr ĭn dē′ă) [L.] ABBR: q.i.d. Four times a day.

quaternary (kwŏ-tĕr′nă-rē) [L. *quaternarius,* of four] 1. The fourth in order. 2. Composed of four elements.

Queckenstedt sign (kvek′ĕn-shtet″) [Hans H. G. Queckenstedt, Ger. neurologist, 1876–1918] A test formerly used to diagnose lumbar spinal stenosis, in which a lumbar puncture is performed and the opening pressure measured, followed by manual compression of both jugular veins, causing a rise in intracranial pressure. In healthy people, the pressure rises rapidly on compression and then disappears when the compression is released. In those with vertebral canal block, the cerebrospinal fluid pressure is scarcely affected by compression of the veins of the neck, unilaterally or bilaterally.

Queen Anne sign [Queen Anne of Denmark, 1574–1619] Thinning of the eyebrows at their lateral margins, considered a diagnostic finding in hypothyroidism.

Queensland tick typhus (kwēnz′land″) [Name of a state in Australia] SEE: under *typhus*.

quellung reaction (kwĕl′ŭng, kvĕl′)

[Ger. *Quellung,* swelling] The swelling of capsules of bacteria when they are mixed with their specific immune serum.

quenching (kwĕnch'ĭng) **1.** Cooling a hot object. **2.** Decreasing the energy released from a radioactive or fluorescent object. **3.** The ability of any material to decrease the toxicity of a poison. **4.** In MRI, the emergency release of cooling cryogens that maintain the necessary super-cooling condition of the primary magnet in order to turn off the magnetic field; used as a safety measure.

   fluorescence q. A technique for investigating antigen-antibody reactions by measuring the light absorbed by an antigen mixed with a fluorescent-labeled antibody.

quercetin (kwĕr'sĕt-ĭn) [L. *quercetum,* oak forest + *-in*] An anti-inflammatory antioxidant flavonoid found in many fruits and vegetables.

Quervain disease (ker'ven) [Fritz de Quervain, Swiss surgeon, 1868–1940] De Quervain disease.

questionnaire A list of questions submitted to a patient or research subject in order to obtain data for analysis.

Quetelet index, Quételet index (ket-le', kät-) [Lambert Adolphe Quetelet, Belgian statistician, 1796–1874] Body mass index.

quick (kwĭk) [ME. *quicke,* alive] **1.** A part susceptible to keen feeling, esp. the part of a finger or toe to which the nail is attached. **2.** Pregnant and experiencing fetal movements.

quickening (kwĭk'ĕn-ĭng) A woman's initial awareness of the movement of the fetus within her womb (uterus). Most commonly, fetal activity is first reported between 18 and 20 weeks' gestation.

quicklime (kwĭk'līm) CaO; calcium oxide (unslaked lime). It forms calcium hydroxide when water is added to it.

quick-look (kwĭk'look″) A colloquial term for a rapid assessment, esp. of a cardiac rhythm during emergency cardiac resuscitation.

Quick Neurological Screening Test ABBR: QNST. A standardized test of neurological function for persons 5 years of age or older. It assesses various areas, including attention, balance, motor planning, coordination, and spatial organization.

Quick test (kwik) [Armand James Quick, U.S. physician, 1894–1978] **1.** A liver function test that measures the amount of hippuric acid excreted after a dose of sodium benzoate is given. **2.** A test for the amount of prothrombin present in plasma. **3.** Quick Neurological Screening Test.

quiescent (kwē-ĕs'ĕnt) The condition of being inactive or at rest. SYN: *dormant; latent.*

quinapril (kwĭn'ă-prĭl″) An ACE inhibitor, administered orally to manage hypertension and congestive heart failure. Its therapeutic class is antihypertensive. SYN: *Accupril.*

Quincke, Heinrich (kving'kĕ) Heinrich Irenaeus Quincke, Ger. internist, 1842–1922.
   Q. disease Angioedema.
   Q. pulse Capillary pulse.
   Q. puncture Lumbar puncture.

quinestrol (kwĭn-ĕs'trōl) An estrogen.

quinic acid (kwin'ik, kwīn') SEE: under *acid.*

quinine (kwī'nīn″, kwĭ-nēn') [Sp. *quina* + *-ine*] A bitter white crystalline alkaloid derived from cinchona bark and used as an antimalarial. It is usually administered in the form of its salts.
   q. sulfate The sulfate of a cinchona alkaloid, used to treat nocturnal leg cramps and malaria.

quininism (kwī'nĭn-ĭzm, kwĭ-nēn'ĭzm) Cinchonism.

quininium resin test (kwī-nĭ'nē-ŭm, kwĭ-nī') ABBR: QRT. A tubeless (nonendoscopic) test for insufficient gastric acid secretion. The patient consumes quininium resin. If the pH of the stomach is less than 3.5, quinine is freed from the resin and absorbed. Its presence is detectable in the blood.

quinoa (kĭ-nō'ă, kēn'wä) [Sp. *quinua* fr Quechua (an indigenous language in the Andes Mountains), *kinua, kinwa*] A protein-rich seed consumed as a staple in Peru and other Andean nations. It has a lower glycemic index than many grains (for which it serves as a food substitute), is gluten-free, contains about 15% protein by weight, and is a source of all essential amino acids.

quinolone (kwĭn'ō-lōn) Any of a class of antibiotics that inhibit bacterial DNA gyrase. Commonly prescribed agents include ciprofloxacin, levofloxacin, norfloxacin, and ofloxacin.

quinone (kwĭn'ōn) **1.** $C_6H_4O_2$; a yellow crystalline oxidation product of quinic acid. **2.** A class of organic compounds in which two atoms of hydrogen are replaced by two oxygen atoms.

quinqu- [L. *quinque,* five] Prefix meaning *five.*

Quinquaud disease (kan-kō', -kōd') [Charles E. Quinquaud, Fr. physician, 1841–1894] Purulent inflammation of the hair follicles of the scalp, resulting in bald patches. SEE: *folliculitis.*

quinquina (kwĭn-kwī'nă, kĭn-kē'nă) Cinchona.

quinsy (kwĭn'zē) [Gr. *kynanche,* sore throat] Peritonsillar **abscess**.

quintan (kwĭn'tăn) [L. *quintanus,* of a fifth] **1.** Occurring every fifth day. **2.** Trench fever.

quinti-, quint- [L. *quintus,* fifth] Prefixes meaning *fifth.*

quintipara (kwĭn-tĭp'ă-ră) [″ + *parere,* to bear] A woman who has had five pregnancies that have continued beyond the 20th week of gestation. SEE: *para*.

quintuplet (kwĭn-tŭp′lĕt, kwĭn-toop′lĕt) [LL. *quintuplex,* fivefold] One of 5 children born of a single gestation.

qui tam (kwī tam) [L., who as well, who also] A legal claim or type of litigation in which an individual alleges fraudulent billing by a government contractor. Funds recovered by the government as a result of the claim are divided between the government and the relator of the action. The government is entitled to most of the fraudulently obtained money, and the "whistleblower" is given a percentage of the recovered funds as a reward. Qui tam litigation is one way the U.S. government combats Medicare fraud and abuse.

quit line A means of aiding smoking cessation in which trained counselors staffing telephone lines assess smokers' needs and provide smoking-related advice, information, and pharmacological assistance.

Many states staff their own quit lines with money funded by the 1998 Master Settlement Agreement (between tobacco companies and state attorney generals). The federal government quit line in the U.S. is 1–800–QUITNOW.

quorum sensing (kwôr′ŭm) The ability of bacteria to sense cell density. SEE: *biofilm*.

quota (kwōt′ă) [L. *quota (pars),* how large (a part)?] A numerical threshold, target, or limit.

quota sample SEE: under *sample*.

quotidian (kwō-tĭd′ē-ăn) [L. *quotidianus,* daily] Occurring daily.

quotient (kwō′shĕnt) [L. *quotiens,* how many times] The number of times one number is contained in another.

   hazard q. ABBR: HQ. A numerical ratio used to estimate whether a toxic exposure will prove harmful to an exposed person or ecosystem. The ratio is typically expressed as the measurable toxic exposure to a screening benchmark, such as the highest concentration of the toxicant known not to cause harm. An HQ greater than 1.0 is potentially toxic. An HQ less than 1.0 is not toxic, unless the toxic exposure is to multiple substances each with its own biological or ecological risk.

   intelligence q. ABBR: IQ. An index of intelligence determined through a subject's answers to standardized test questions. It is the ratio of the individual's mental age, as determined by scoring on the test, to his or her age in years, multiplied by 100. Contemporary IQ tests, such as the Wechsler Intelligence Scale for Children or the Stanford-Binet test, measure both verbal ability, and performance (nonverbal) ability. The IQ is determined for each of these categories, and as an overall score.

The concept of the IQ, and the related concept of general intelligence, are controversial. Critics of IQ testing have argued that IQ tests are culturally biased; that they measure test-taking ability rather than intelligence; and that they favor speed rather than skill. Variations of IQ tests are used in clinical medicine as part of a battery of neuropsychiatric tests, e.g., in patients with learning disabilities, brain injury, and dementias, among other diseases and conditions. SEE: *intelligence; mental retardation; intelligence test*.

   respiratory q. **1.** The amount of energy derived from carbohydrate, rather than fat, metabolism. **2.** The result of dividing the amount of carbon dioxide exhaled per minute by the amount of oxygen consumed each minute, normally 0.9.

QUS *Quantitative **ultrasound***.

q.v. L. *quantum vis,* as much as you please; *quod vide,* which see.

R

R 1. *respiration; right; roentgen.* 2. In chemistry, a radical. It is an atom, ion or molecule with unpaired electrons. *R* is an abbreviation for that entity in a larger formula. 3. In the ideal gas equation, $PV = nRT$, R is the gas constant. Its value is 0.082 liter-atmospheres per degree per mole. 4. An abbreviation for the transmissibility of a contagious illness. An $R = 1$ implies that a single infected person (on average) transmits a given infection to one additional person. A disease with an $R = 10$ would be more contagious; one infected individual would on average transmit the infection to ten others.

R- 1. Abbr. used in organic chemistry to indicate part of a molecule. 2. Rinne negative. SEE: *Rinne test.*

R+ Rinne positive. SEE: *Rinne test.*

R0 Meaning *complete resection* (of a tumor). It is used in surgical oncology.

RA *rheumatoid arthritis; right atrium; robot-assisted; room air.*

Ra Symbol for the element radium.

RabAvert (răb′ă-vĕrt″) Rabies vaccine.

rabbetting (răb′ĕt-ĭng) [Fr. *raboter,* to plane] Interlocking the jagged edges of a fractured bone.

rabbitpox An acute viral disease of laboratory rabbits.

rabid (răb′ĭd) Pert. to or affected with rabies.

rabies (rā′bēz) [L. *rabies,* rage] A fatal infection of the central nervous system (CNS) caused by the rabies virus. Human infection occurs as the result of a bite from a wild animal in which the virus is present. It may occasionally be transmitted by inhalation of infectious aerosol particles or contamination of conjunctiva or other mucous membranes by the saliva of an infected animal. The long incubation period, before signs of rabies appear, is 3 to 12 weeks; this means that wild animals that are displaying no signs of the disease may still be infected, thereby increasing the risk of human infection. SYN: *hydrophobia* (1). SEE: *immune globulin; rabies vaccine.*

ETIOLOGY: Rabies is found almost exclusively in wild animals (raccoons, skunks, coyotes, foxes, and bats), which serve as reservoirs for infection. Domestic animal infections have been rare in the U.S. since 1960, but dogs and cats in developing countries may be infected. After infection, the virus replicates in the animal for several days to months; this period stimulates an immune response to viral antigens. The virus then spreads through the cytoplasm of peripheral nerve axons to the CNS.

SYMPTOMS: Early symptoms in humans are usually nonspecific and include fever, malaise, and headache. Progressive signs of cerebral infection are those of encephalitis (anxiety, confusion, insomnia, agitation, delirium, hallucinations, hypersalivation, hyperactive reflexes, and convulsions). Periods of stupor alternate with episodes of extreme agitation. The classic symptom of hydrophobia is probably related to the painful contracture of the pharyngeal muscles that occurs during swallowing. Once clinical signs occur, the disease is usually fatal within days.

DIAGNOSIS: The diagnosis of rabies is made in animals by a direct fluorescent antibody test on brain tissue. In humans, brain biopsies, skin biopsies from the nape of the neck, corneal impression tests, and/or spinal fluid, blood, or salivary antibody tests are conducted.

PREVENTION: Veterinarians, animal handlers, and those who come in frequent contact with wild animals should receive preexposure prophylaxis with rabies vaccine. The vaccine does not prevent infection with rabies but simplifies treatment because it eliminates the need for immune globulin and decreases the amount of rabies vaccine required after exposure.

To decrease the spread of rabies, the CDC recommends that all domestic animals be vaccinated routinely (consult local veterinarian and public health department) and that contact between pets and wild animals be minimized. Control of rabies in pets through vaccination and elimination of contact with stray animals significantly reduces the risk of human infection. Garbage containers should be designed to prevent attracting raccoons and skunks. Physical contact with raccoons, skunks, foxes, coyotes, and bats should be reported immediately. SEE: *Standard Precautions Appendix.*

PATIENT CARE: Physicians should contact the local or state health department to determine the need for postexposure prophylaxis. All wounds must be thoroughly cleaned. Intravenous immune globulin containing preformed antibodies and one dose of rabies vaccine is given immediately (day 1); an additional three doses of vaccine are administered on days 3, 7, and 14 to patients with normal immunocompetence. No cases of rabies have occurred when this postexposure prophylactic regimen has been followed promptly after exposure. Most fatalities occur when people do not seek medical assistance because they are not aware of the possibility of rabies infection.

rabies immune globulin, human rabies immune globulin ABBR: RIG, HRIG. A standardized preparation of globulins derived from blood plasma or serum from selected human donors who have been immunized with rabies vaccine and have developed high titers of rabies antibody. It is used to produce passive immunity in persons bitten by animals. SEE: *rabies*.

rabies virus group SEE: under *group*.

rabiform (rā′bǐ-form) [″ + *forma*, shape] Resembling rabies.

raccoon sign SEE: under *sign*.

race (rās) [Fr. *race*, fr Italian *razza*] **1.** The descendants of a genetically cohesive ancestral group. **2.** A group of organisms identifiable within a species. **3.** A political or social designation for a group of people thought to share a common ancestry or common ethnicity.

racemase (rā′sē-mās) An enzyme that catalyzes racemization (i.e., the production of an optically inactive compound).

racemate (rā′sē-māt) A racemic compound.

racemic (rā-sē′mǐk) Optically inactive; used of compounds.

racemization (rā″sē-mǐ-zā′shǔn) The production of a racemic form of an optically inactive compound.

racemose (răs′ě-mōs) [L. *racemosus*, full of clusters] Resembling a clustered bunch of grapes, as a gland; divided and subdivided; ending in a bunch of follicles.

rachi-, rachio- [Gr. *rhachis*, spine] Combining forms meaning *spine*.

rachial (rā′kē-ăl) [Gr. *rhachis*, spine] Spinal.

rachicele (rā′kǐ-sēl) [″ + *kele*, tumor, swelling] Protrusion of the contents of the spinal canal in spina bifida cystica.

rachidial (ră-kǐd′ē-ăl) Spinal.

rachidian (ră-kǐd′ē-ăn) Pert. to the spinal column.

rachilysis (rā-kǐl′ǐ-sǐs) [″ + *lysis*, dissolution] The mechanical treatment of lateral curvature of the spine through traction and pressure.

rachiometer (rā-kē-ŏm′ě-těr) [″ + *metron*, measure] An instrument for measuring a spinal curvature.

rachiopagus (rā″kē-ŏp′ă-gǔs) [″ + *pagos*, thing fixed] A conjoined twin deformity in which the two are joined at the vertebral column.

rachiotome (rā′kē-ō-tōm″) [″ + *tome*, incision] An instrument for dividing the vertebrae.

rachis (rā′kǐs) *pl.* **rachises** [Gr. *rhachis*] The spinal column.

rachischisis (rā-kǐs′kǐ-sǐs) [″ + *schisis*, a splitting] A congenital spinal column fissure (e.g., spina bifida).

   posterior r. Spina bifida.

rachitic (rā-kǐt′ǐk) Pert. to or affected with rickets.

rachitis (ră-kī′tǐs) [″ + *itis*, inflammatory] **1.** Inflammation of the spine. **2.** Rickets.

   r. fetalis annularis Congenital enlargement of the epiphyses of the long bones.

   r. fetalis micromelica Congenital shortness of the bones.

rachitome (răk′ǐ-tōm″) [″ + *tome*, incision] An instrument used to open the spinal canal.

rachitomy (ră-kǐt′ō-mē) [″ + *tome*, incision] Surgical cutting of the vertebral column.

rad *radiation absorbed dose.*

radectomy, radiectomy (rā-děk′tō-mē, rā″dē-ěk′tō-mē) [L. *radix*, root, + Gr. *ektome*, excision] Surgical removal of all or a portion of a dental root.

radiability (rā″dē-ă-bǐl′ǐ-tē) [L. *radius*, ray, + *habilitas*, able] The capability of being penetrated readily by ionizing radiation. **radiable** (rā′dē-ă-băl), *adj.*

radial (rā′dē-ăl) **1.** Radiating out from a given center. **2.** Pert. to the radius.

radialis (rā″dē-ā′lǐs) [L.] Pert. to the radius bone.

radian (rā′dē-ăn) **1.** A unit of angular measurement equivalent to 57.295 degrees. It is subtended at the center of a circle by an arc the length of the radius of the circle. **2.** In ophthalmometry, a lens of 1 radian would have one plane surface equal in length to the radius of curvature of the curved surface.

radiant (rā′dē-ănt) [L. *radians*, radiate] **1.** Emitting beams of light. **2.** Transmitted by radiation. **3.** Emanating from a common center. SEE: *energy; heat; radiation*.

radiant warmer A bed for stabilizing the body temperature of a newborn or premature infant. It has a heat source positioned above the baby to keep his or her temperature constant. Unlike an incubator, it is not enclosed.

radiate (rā′dē-āt) [L. *radiatre*, to emit rays] To spread from a common center.

radiation (rād-ē-ā′shŏn) [L. *radiatio*, a shining] **1.** The process by which energy is propagated through space or matter. **2.** The emission of rays in all directions from a common center. **3.** Ionizing rays used for diagnostic or therapeutic purposes. Two types of radiation therapy are commonly used for patients with cancer: teletherapy and brachytherapy. SEE: *brachytherapy*. **4.** Any form of radiant energy emission or divergence, as of energy in all directions from luminous bodies, radiographical tubes, particle accelerators, radioactive elements, and fluorescent substances.

In neurology, a group of fibers that diverge from a common origin.

acoustic r. Auditory **r.**

actinic r. Ionizing electromagnetic radiation that can produce chemical changes, e.g., the damage done to skin by ultraviolet sunlight.

auditory r. A band of fibers that connect auditory areas of the cerebral cortex with the medial geniculate body of the thalamus. SYN: *acoustic r.*

background r. Total radioactivity from cosmic rays, natural radioactive materials, and other radiation that is present in a specific area.

bremsstrahlung r. Diagnostic radiation produced at the target of the anode in an x-ray tube. An electron is accelerated at high speed from the x-ray tube cathode filament. It interacts with the nuclear field of a target atom, changing direction and losing energy that is emitted in the form of an ionizing radiation photon. The result is a heterogeneous beam. SYN: *braking radiation*.

characteristic r. In radiology, the production of radiation in an anode caused by an interaction between an electron from the electron stream and an inner-shell electron of the target material. The result is an ejected electron, a positive atom, and an x-ray photon characteristic of the difference in binding energies between the atomic shells.

corpuscular r. Radiation composed of discrete elements or particles such as elements of atomic nuclei, i.e., alpha, beta, neutron, positron, or proton particles.

cosmic r. Ionizing radiation from the sun and other extraterrestrial sources. It has a short wavelength, high velocity, and an exceptional ability to penetrate tissue. It accounts for about one tenth of the yearly total of ionizing radiation exposure for each person. Colloquially, it is known as "cosmic rays."

electromagnetic r. Photons that travel at the speed of light. They exhibit both magnetic and electrical properties. SEE: *electromagnetic spectrum* for table.

heterogeneous r. Radiation containing waves of various wavelengths.

homogeneous r. Radiation containing photons of similar wavelength.

infrared r. Infrared ray.

interstitial r. Radiation treatment accomplished by inserting sealed sources of a particle emitter directly into tissues.

ionizing r. Electromagnetic waves capable of producing ions after interaction with matter. Examples include x-rays, gamma rays, and beta particles. SEE: *ionizing radiation injury*.

irritative r. An overdose of ultraviolet irradiation resulting in erythema and, in exceptional cases, blister formation.

low-level r. Electromagnetic waves at intensity levels below that known to cause obvious damage to living things. Low-level radiation includes that emitted by power lines, nuclear power plants, and appliances such as electric blankets, television sets, and computer terminals.

nonionizing r. ABBR: NIR. Electromagnetic radiation that does not readily ionize atoms such as that in visible light, ultraviolet light, infrared light, microwaves, ultrasound, and radiofrequency emissions.

optic r. A system of fibers extending from the lateral geniculate body of the thalamus through the sublenticular portion of the internal capsule to the calcarine occipital cortex (striate area). SYN: *geniculocalcarine tract*.

photochemical r. Light rays that penetrate tissues only fractions of a millimeter, are absorbed by cells, and cause physical and biological changes. This type of radiation causes surface heating.

photothermal r. Radiation of heat by a source of light, as that from an electric bulb.

primary r. That radiation being emitted directly to the patient from an x-ray source.

remnant r. Ionizing radiation that passes through the part being examined to make the radiographical image.

scattered r. X-rays that have changed direction because of a collision with matter.

secondary r. X-rays produced by the interaction between primary radiation and the substance being radiated.

solar r. Radiation from the sun; 60% is infrared and 40% is visible and ultraviolet.

spatially fractionated r. ABBR: SFR. Radiation treatment applied in high doses to a large tumor through a grid designed to direct energy into multiple discrete regions of the mass.

striatomesencephalic r. Fibers originating in the corpus striatum and terminating principally in the substantia nigra of the midbrain.

striatothalamic r. Groups of fibers connecting the corpus striatum with the thalamus and subthalamus.

synchrotron r. Radiation released by charged particles accelerated by a synchrotron. It may be used to obtain noninvasive images of body structures (e.g., the coronary arteries) or to study the structure of proteins, tissue samples, or other objects of biological or medical interest.

thalamic r. Groups of fibers connecting the thalamus with the cerebral hemispheres. These include frontal, centroparietal, occipital, and optic radiations.

thermal r. Heat radiation.

ultraviolet r. Radiant energy extending from 3900 to 200 angstrom units (A.U.). Divided into near ultraviolet, which extends from 3900 to 2900 A.U., and far ultraviolet, which extends from 2900 to 200 A.U.

visible r. The radiation of the visible spectrum, which may be broken up into different wavelengths representing different colors:

Violet, 3900–4550 angstrom units (A.U.)

Blue, 4550–4920 A.U.

Green, 4920–5770 A.U.

Yellow, 5770–5970 A.U.

Orange, 5970–6220 A.U.

Red, 6220–7700 A.U.

x r. 1. A form of electromagnetic radiation with wavelengths in the range of 0.01 to 10 nm, frequencies from 3×10^{16} Hz to 3×10^{19} Hz, and energies in the range 120 eV to 120 keV. **2.** Treatment with or exposure to x-rays.

radiation protection Prophylaxis against injury from ionizing radiation. The only effective preventive measures are shielding the source and the operator, handlers, and patients; maintaining appropriate distance from the source; and limiting the time and amount of exposure. In general, the use of drugs to protect against radiation is not practical because of their toxicity. An exception is the use of orally administered potassium iodide to protect the thyroid from radioactive iodine.

radiation symbol An international symbol used to indicate radioactive sources, containers for radioactive materials, and areas where radioactive materials are stored and used. The presence of this symbol (a magenta or black propeller on a yellow background) on a sign denotes the need for caution to avoid contamination with or undue exposure to atomic radiation. The wording on the sign varies with the level of potential radiation in the area. SEE: illus.

UNIVERSAL RADIATION SYMBOL

radiation syndrome Illness due to overexposure to harmful electromagnetic waves, usually x-rays or gamma rays. Mild acute illness is manifested by anorexia, headache, nausea, vomiting, and diarrhea. Delayed effects resulting from repeated or prolonged exposure may result in skin ulcers, alopecia, proctitis, enteritis, amenorrhea, sterility, disturbances in blood cell formation, cataract formation, premature aging, and cancer. SYN: *radiation sickness*.

radiation therapist Radiation therapy technologist.

radiation therapy ABBR: RT, XRT. The use of energy from man-made ionizing radiation or from the radioactive decay of atomic nuclei to destroy diseased tissues, esp. cancers. SYN: *radiotherapy*.

PATIENT CARE: The radiotherapy must be directed only at the diseased tissue. The patient's body is precisely measured and marked ("tattooed"), and cradles are designed to hold the patient in a precise position for each treatment. Systemic adverse effects of radiation therapy include weakness, fatigue, anorexia, nausea, vomiting, and anemia. These may subside with antiemetics, steroids, frequent small meals, fluid maintenance, and added rest and are seldom severe enough to require discontinuation of treatment although dosage adjustment may be required. Local adverse effects of radiation depend on the organ system affected. For example, radiation of the breast may sometimes result in esophagitis or pneumonitis; cranial radiation may cause hair loss; radiation treatment of head and neck cancers may cause dry mouth (for which good oral hygiene or artificial saliva may be helpful). Because radiation may affect bone marrow, patients require frequent measurement of complete blood counts. Radiation also requires special skin care, and the patient should use a hypoallergenic moisturizer (Biafine, Radiacare Gel, and Aquaphor are popular brands). Many nurses and patients prefer using natural aloe (from the leaf of an aloe plant, split open to apply the gel from inside) or bottled aloe. Usually the radiation therapist will recommend that the skin be free of any such preparations at treatment time.

conformal r.t. Radiation therapy in which tumors are imaged in three-dimensions and then treated with small beams of radiation adjusted for their size, unique shape, and location. The objective is to deliver the radiation directly to the tumor and to make the energy conform to the unique shape of the tumor, leaving neighboring healthy tissue unaffected by the damaging effects. This therapy is used to treat tumors previously treated with external beam radiotherapy, tumors for which external beam radiation is also planned, and tumors that are difficult to reach or that have encircled healthy organs or tissues. SYN: *intensity-modulated* **r.t.**

endocavitary r.t. Intracavitary **r.t.**

intensity-modulated r.t. ABBR: IMRT. Conformal **r.t.**

intracavitary r.t. Radiation therapy for treatment of a cancer found in hollow organs (such as the rectum, the sinuses, or the vagina) by placing the source of radiation inside the affected body cavity. SYN: *endocavitary r.t.*

intraoperative r.t. ABBR: IORT. The administration of a large dose of radiation to a malignant tumor during surgery. After the tumor is debulked, the surrounding tissues are displaced, temporarily sutured, or protected by the applicator shield. The applicator then delivers a large dose of radiation directly to the affected tissues. IORT is used to manage otherwise unresectable tumors.

involved-field r.t. A treatment for lymphoma in which therapeutic radiation is directed only to those areas involved by detectable tumor masses and not to other regions of the body.

selective internal r.t. ABBR: SIRT. The treatment of solid internal organ tumors with radioactive microspheres injected directly into the target tissue, or bound to substrates that the target tissue preferentially takes up from the blood. SYN: *radioembolization; selective internal radiotherapy.*

radiation therapy technologist ABBR: RT(T). A technologist who assists specialists in nuclear medicine in the proper and safe use of radiation for patient diagnosis and treatment. The roles of the radiation therapy technologist include the operation of radiation detection equipment, the administration of radiopharmaceuticals, and the recognition and early treatment of radiation-related emergencies, among others.

radiation treatment The administration of high-energy x-ray photons, electrons, or nuclear emissions for the cure of cancer or palliation of symptoms.

radiator (rā'dē-ā″tor) [LL. *radiatus,* radiate] A device for radiating heat or light.

infrared r. A device for transmitting infrared rays.

radical (rad'ĭ-kăl) [L. *radicalis,* having roots] **1.** In chemistry, a group of atoms acting as a single unit, passing without change from one compound to another, but unable to exist in a free state. **2.** Pert. to surgery or other therapy to remove or destroy all disease or diseased tissue. SEE: *conservative; radical treatment.*

acid r. The electronegative portion of a molecule when the acid hydrogen is removed.

alcohol r. The portion of an alcohol molecule left when the hydrogen of the OH-group is removed.

free r. A molecule containing an odd number of electrons. These molecules contain an open bond or a half bond and are highly reactive. In ischemic injury to tissues (as in myocardial infarction), free radical production may play an important role at certain stages in the progression of the injury.

The body has developed methods of defending against the harmful effects of free radicals. Superoxide dismutases, enzymes in mitochondria, and antioxidants are effective in counteracting the harmful effects of free radicals. SEE: *antioxidant; oxidative* **stress**; *superoxide; superoxide dismutase.*

oxygen r. Hydrogen peroxide (H_2O_2) or the superoxide radical (O_2^-) produced by the incomplete reduction of oxygen. Oxygen free radicals are released during the respiratory burst phase of phagocytosis by neutrophils and macrophages during inflammation. They cause direct cell damage, increase vascular permeability through damage to the capillary endothelium, and promote chemotaxis. Oxygen free radicals are normally contained by antioxidant protective measures; however, with severe inflammation they cause significant damage. They are believed to be responsible for much of the cellular damage involved in adult respiratory distress syndrome (ARDS), in which massive neutrophil aggregation and phagocytosis occur.

oxygen-derived free r. SEE: *oxygen r.; superoxide.*

radical treatment An extensive or complete therapy, such as surgical removal of an entire diseased organ and its associated lymphatic drainage. Alternatives to radical treatment may include observation, palliation, modified procedures, lumpectomies, or conservative treatments.

radices (răd'ĭ-sēz) [L.] Pl. of radix.

radicle (răd'ĭ-kl) [L. *radicula,* little root] A structure resembling a rootlet, as a radicle of a nerve or vein. SYN: *radicula.*

radicotomy (răd″ĭ-kŏt'ō-mē) [L. *radix,* root, + Gr. *tome,* incision] Rhizotomy. SEE: *radiculectomy.*

radicul-, radiculo- [L. *radiculus,* little root] Prefixes meaning *nerve root.*

radicula (ră-dĭk'ū-lă) [L.] Radicle.

radiculalgia (ră-dĭk″ū-lăl'jē-ă) [L. *radix,* root, + Gr. *algos,* pain] Neuralgia of nerve roots.

radicular (ră-dĭk'ū-lăr) [L. *radix,* root] **1.** Pert. to a root or radicle. **2.** Pert. to the tissues on or around a tooth root (e.g., radicular dentin, radicular bone).

radiculectomy (ră-dĭk″ū-lĕk'tō-mē) [″ + Gr. *ektome,* excision] **1.** Excision of a spinal nerve root. **2.** Resection of a posterior spinal nerve root. SEE: *rhizot-omy.*

radiculitis (ră-dĭk″ū-lī′tĭs) [L. *radicula,* little root, + Gr. *itis,* inflammation] Inflammation of the spinal nerve roots, accompanied by pain and hyperesthesia.

radiculoganglionitis (ră-dĭk″ū-lō-găng″glē-ō-nī′tĭs) [″ + Gr. *ganglion,* knot, + *itis,* inflammation] Inflammation of the posterior spinal roots and their ganglia.

radiculomedullary (ră-dĭk″ū-lō-mĕd′ū-lĕr″ē) [″ + *medullaris,* marrow] Pert. to the nerve roots and the spinal cord.

radiculomeningomyelitis (ră-dĭk″ū-lō-mĕ-nĭn″gō-mī-ĕl-ī′tĭs) [″ + Gr. *meninx,* membrane, + *myelos,* marrow, + *itis,* inflammation] Inflammation of the nerve roots, meninges, and spinal cord.

radiculoneuritis (ră-dĭk″ū-lō″nū-rī′tĭs) [L. *radicula,* little root, + Gr. *neuron,* sinew, + *itis,* inflammation] Inflammation of the spinal nerve roots.

radiculopathy (ră-dĭk-ū-lŏp′ă-thē) [″ + ″ + *pathos,* disease, suffering] Any disease of a nerve root.

radiectomy (rā″dē-ĕk′tō-mē) [L. *radix,* root, + Gr. *ektome,* excision] SEE: *radectomy.*

radii (rā′dē-ī) [L.] Pl. of radius.

radio- [L. *radius,* ray] **1.** Prefix meaning *radiant energy, radioactive substances.* **2.** Prefix meaning *radioactive isotope.*

radioactive (rā″dē-ō-ăk′tĭv) [L. *radius,* ray, + *activus,* acting] Capable of spontaneous emission of alpha, beta, or gamma rays as a result of the disintegration of the nucleus of an atom.

radioactive patient An individual treated or accidentally contaminated with radioactive materials. The patient should be told how long to avoid close contact with children and pregnant women.

radioactivity (rā″dē-ō-ăk″tĭv′ĭ-tē) Spontaneous disintegration of an atomic nucleus resulting in the emission of alpha, beta, or gamma rays.

  artificial r. Radioactivity resulting from bombardment of a substance with high-energy particles in a cyclotron, betatron, or other apparatus.

  induced r. Temporary radioactivity of a substance that has been exposed to a radioactive element.

  natural r. Radioactivity emitted by elements in the environment, such as radon in soil. It may include alpha particles, beta particles, or gamma rays.

radioallergosorbent test (rā″dē-ō-ăl″ĕr-gō-sor′bĕnt) ABBR: RAST. A blood test for allergy that measures minute quantities of immunoglobulin E in blood. People who have type I hypersensitivity reactions to common allergens (e.g., ragweed, trees, molds, milk, eggs, and animal dander) have elevated levels of IgE. For these individuals and others, RAST

is safer than skin testing, because it carries no risk of systemic anaphylaxis. RAST is not as sensitive as skin testing, however.

radioautograph (rād″ē-ō-ot′ŏ-graf″) [*radio-* + *auto-* + *-graph*] Autoradiograph.

radiobicipital (rā″dē-ō-bī-sĭp′ĭ-tăl) Pert. to the radius and biceps muscle of the arm.

radiobiology (rā″dē-ō-bī-ŏl′ō-jē) The branch of biology that deals with the effects of ionizing radiation on living organisms.

radiocarbon (rā″dē-ō-kăr′bŏn) A radioisotope of carbon; ^{11}C and ^{14}C are used in medical studies.

radiocardiogram (rā″dē-ō-kăr′dē-ō-grăm) [L. *radius,* ray, + Gr. *kardia,* heart, + *gramma,* something written] The record or film obtained during radiocardiography.

radiocardiography (rā″dē-ō-kăr″dē-ŏg′ră-fē) [″ + ″ + *graphein,* to write] The investigation of the anatomy and function of the heart by obtaining a record or film of a radioactive substance as it travels through the heart.

radiocarpal (rā″dē-ō-kăr′păl) [″ + Gr. *karpos,* wrist] Pert. to the radius and carpus.

radiochemistry (rā″dē-ō-kĕm′ĭs-trē) [″ + Gr. *chemeia,* chemistry] The branch of chemistry dealing with radioactive phenomena.

radiocontrast (rā″dē-ō-kŏn′trăst″) Contrast medium.

radiocurable (rā″dē-ō-kūr′ă-bl) Curable by radiation therapy.

radiocystitis (rā″dē-ō-sĭs-tī′tĭs) [″ + Gr. *kystis,* bladder, + *itis,* inflammation] Inflammation of the bladder following radiation therapy as a result of cell and tissue damage.

radiodensity (rā″dē-ō-dĕn′sĭ-tē) The impenetrability of a substance or tissue by x-rays. SYN: *radiopacity.*

radiodermatitis (rā″dē-ō-dĕr″mă-tī′tĭs) [″ + Gr. *derma,* skin, + *osis,* condition] Radiation dermatitis.

radiodiagnosis (rā″dē-ō-dī″ăg-nō′sĭs) [″ + Gr. *dia,* through, + *gnosis,* knowledge] Diagnosis with radiological imaging.

radiodigital (rā″dē-ō-dĭg′ĭ-tăl) Pert. to the radius and the fingers.

radioecology (rā″dē-ō-ē-kŏl′ō-jē) [″ + Gr. *oikos,* house, + *logos,* word, reason] Investigation of the effect of radiation on the living organisms in the environment.

radioelement (rā″dē-ō-ĕl′ĕ-mĕnt) [″ + *elementum,* a rudiment] Any of the radioactive elements.

radioembolization (rād″ē-ō-em″bŏ-lĭ-zā′shŏn) [*radio-* + *embolization*] Selective internal **radiation therapy**.

radioencephalogram (rā″dē-ō-ĕn-sĕf′ă-lō-grăm″) [″ + Gr. *enkephalos,* brain,

+ *gramma,* something written] The record obtained when a radioactive tracer passes through the blood vessels of the brain.

radioencephalography (rā″dē-ō-ĕn-sĕf″ă-lŏg′ră-fē) [″ + ″ + *graphein,* to write] The recording of radio waves transmitted from the brain to a receiver but without electrodes being placed on the scalp.

radioepithelitis (rā″dē-ō-ĕp″ĭ-thē-lī′tĭs) [″ + ″ + *thele,* nipple, + *itis,* inflammation] Radiation dermatitis.

radiofrequency ablation (rād″ē-ō-frē′kwĕn-sē) [*radio +frequency*] Ablation in which an electrode delivers a low-voltage, high-frequency current to cauterize and destroy abnormal tissues. Destruction of electrical conduction pathways in the heart with an intracardiac catheter that removes the abnormal conducting tissues has been used to treat Wolff-Parkinson-White syndrome, atrioventricular re-entrant tachycardia, and other cardiac arrhythmias.

radiofrequency identification (rād″ē-ō-frē′kwĕn-sē) [*radio +frequency*] ABBR: RFID. A method of labeling a drug or device with a unique electronic code to ensure that the object has been manufactured, stored, distributed, inventoried, and marketed legitimately. RFID devices provide electronic tags to prevent adulteration, counterfeiting, or theft of health care-related products.

radiogenic (rā″dē-ō-jĕn′ĭk) [″ + *gennan,* to produce] **1.** Producing radiation. **2.** Caused by radiation. SYN: *actinogenic.*

radiogold (rā′dē-ō-gōld) A radioisotope of gold.

radiograph (rād′ē-ō-graf″) [*radio- + -graph*] **1.** An x-ray image or photograph produced on photographic film or other image receptor by x-rays or nuclear radiation that is passed through a structure to be imaged. SYN: *radiographic image; roentgenogram.* **2.** To make a radiograph. **3.** The film used to make a radiograph.

   bitewing r. A radiograph that shows the crowns and cervical third of the roots of the maxillary and mandibular teeth. Bitewing radiographs are usually taken on premolar and molar teeth. SYN: *interproximal r.*

   body section r. Tomogram.

   bregma-menton r. A radiograph taken in the submental-vertex plane, from below the chin to the top of the skull. It shows the contour of the zygomatic arches and the lateral separation of the mandibular condyles, coronoid processes, or both.

   bucket-handle r. An informal term for radiograph taken with the beam aimed from beneath the chin toward the vertex of the skull. It is used to assess facial and orbital floor injuries.

   cephalogram r. A radiograph of the jaws, teeth, and skull, used to demonstrate dental occlusion and its relation to other craniofacial structures.

   dental r. A radiograph of dental structures made on x-ray film or stored as a digital image. The radiographs may be extraoral or intraoral. Three common types of intraoral dental images are periapical, interproximal, and occlusal radiographs.

   interproximal r. Bitewing **r.**

   lateral cephalometric r. A radiograph of the entire head, taken from the side with the head in a fixed position and used to make definitive observations or measurements.

   lateral oblique r. A radiograph used to examine the body of the mandible and the ramus. Projections may be performed with conventional dental radiographical film and may cover a broader area than a typical periapical radiograph. SYN: *lateral jaw survey.*

   lateral skull r. A radiograph of the sinuses and lateral aspects of the cranial skeleton.

   maxillary sinus r. A frontal radiograph of the maxillary sinuses and the zygomas that allows direct comparison of both sides. SYN: *Water's projection.*

   panoramic r. A type of extraoral curved-surface radiograph that shows the entire upper and lower jaws in a continuous single film. SYN: *panography; pantomography.*

   periapical r. An intraoral radiograph that depicts the tooth and surrounding tissues extending to the apical region. SYN: *dental r.*

   posteroanterior r. A frontal radiograph of the skull. It is used to examine the skull for disease, trauma, and developmental abnormalities.

   rotational r. Panoramic **r.**

   transcranial r. A radiograph that includes views of the mouth in open, closed, and static positions.

radiographer (rā″dē-ŏg′ră-fĕr) A radiologic technologist specializing in the production of images for medical diagnosis. Such images include radiographs (x-ray images), computed-tomography (CT) scans, mammograms, and magnetic resonance images (MRIs).

radiography (rā-dē-og′ră-fē) [*radio- + -graphy*] The process of obtaining an image for diagnosis using a radiological modality. Radiography includes x-ray studies, computed tomography [CT] scanning, magnetic resonance imaging [MRI], bone scanning, positron emission tomography [PET] scanning, combined CT and PET scanning, ultrasonography, and mammography and digital mammography.

   body section r. Tomography.

   computed r. ABBR: CR. The capturing of a radiographic image on a solid-state imaging device (instead of on radiographic film). A photostimulable phosphor imaging plate recovers the image, which is subsequently enhanced with a digital computer and displayed on a monitor.

direct r. ABBR: DR. The conversion of x-ray energy received from an imaged body part into digital format using semiconductors, without first collecting images on an image plate or as light.

radioguided surgery (rād″gīd′ĕd) SEE: under *surgery*.

radiohumeral (rā″dē-ō-hū′mĕr-ăl) [" + *humerus*, upper arm] Pert. to the radius and humerus.

radioimmunity (rā″dē-ō-ĭ-mū′nĭ-tē) [" + *immunitas*, immunity] Apparent decreased sensitivity to radiation that may follow repeated radiation therapy.

radioimmunoassay (rā″dē-ō-ĭm″ū-nō-ăs′ā) ABBR: RIA. A method of determining the concentration of a substance, esp. hormones, based on the competitive inhibition of binding of a radioactively labeled substance to a specific antibody. Protein concentrations in the picogram (10^{-12} g) range can be measured by this technique.

radioimmunoconjugate (rād″ē-ō-ĭm″yŭ-nō-kon′jŭ-găt, -ĭm-ū″) [*radio-* + *immuno-* + *conjugate*] The chemical linkage of a monoclonal antibody to a radionuclide for therapeutic or diagnostic purposes.

radioimmunodiffusion (rā″dē-ō-ĭm″ū-nō-dĭf-fū′zhŭn) [" + " + *dis*, apart, + *fundere*, to pour] A method of studying antigen-antibody interaction by use of radioisotope-labeled antigens or antibodies diffused through a gel.

radioimmunoelectrophoresis (rā″dē-ō-ĭm″ū-nō-ē-lĕk″trō-fō-rē′sĭs) [" + " + Gr. *elektron*, amber, + *phoresis*, bearing] Electrophoresis involving the use of a radioisotope-labeled antigen or antibody. An autoradiograph is taken of the electrophoretic pattern produced.

radioimmunoguided surgery (rād″ē-ō-ĭm″yŭ-nō-gīd″ĕd, -ĭ-mū″nō-) SEE: under *surgery*.

radioimmunoimaging (rā′dē-ō-ĭm″ū-nō-ĭm′ĭ-′jĭng) Immunoscintigraphy.

radioimmunosorbent test (rā″dē-ō-ĭm″ū-nă-sör′bĕnt, -ĭ-mūn″ă) ABBR: RIST. Use of radioimmunoassay to measure the immune globulin E (IgE) antibody in serum.

radioimmunotherapy (rā″dē-ō-ĭm″ū-nō-thĕr′ă-pē) The use of radioactively labeled monoclonal antibodies to treat malignancies, e.g., breast cancers, non-Hodgkin's lymphoma, and prostate cancer. The monoclonal antibodies selectively bind with antigens on the tumor cells and deliver a dose of cell-killing radiation directly to those cells.

radioiodine (rād″ē-ō-ī′ŏ-dīn″) [*radio-* (2) + *iodine*] Any of the radioactive isotopes of iodine, used in the diagnosis and treatment of thyroid disorders. The most commonly used isotope is ^{131}I.

radioiron (rā″dē-ō-ī′ĕrn) A radioactive isotope of iron; ^{55}Fe and ^{59}Fe are used in medical studies.

radioisotope (rā″dē-ō-ī′sō-tōp) A radioactive form of an element.

radiolabel (rā″dē-ō-lā′bĕl) Tag, radioactive.

radiolead (rā″dē-ō-lĕd′) A radioactive isotope of lead.

radiolesion (rā″dē-ō-lē′zhŭn) An injury caused by radiation.

radioligand (rā″dē-ō-lī′gănd, răd″dē-ō-līg′ănd) A molecule, esp. an antigen or antibody, with a radioactive tracer attached to it.

radiological technologist A technologist trained in the safe application of ionizing radiation to portions of the body to assist the physician in the diagnosis of injuries and disease. This individual may also supervise or teach others. Technology programs approved by the Joint Review Commission on Education in the Radiologic Sciences are conducted in hospitals, medical schools, and colleges with hospital affiliations.

radiologist (rā-dē-ŏl′ō-jĭst) [L. *radius*, ray, + Gr. *logos*, word, reason] A physician who uses x-rays or other sources of ionizing radiation, sound, or radiofrequencies for diagnosis and treatment.

radiologist assistant A midlevel radiologic practitioner who works under the supervision of a radiologist. In the U.S., radiologist assistants are credentialed by the American Registry of Radiologic Technologists (AART).

radiology (rā-dē-ŏl′ō-jē) The branch of medicine concerned with radioactive substances, including x-rays, radioactive isotopes, and ionizing radiation, and the application of this information to prevention, diagnosis, and treatment of disease.

radiology information system ABBR: RIS. A computer system used in health care radiology facilities to help manage patient appointments, scheduling, and tracking of files; radiologic work flow; staff assignments; digital imaging; data storage; and the display and reporting of the interpretations of images by radiologists.

radiolucency (rā″dē-ō-lū′sĕn-sē) [" + *lucere*, to shine] The property of being partly or wholly penetrable by radiant energy.

radiolucent (rā″dē-ō-lū′sĕnt) [" + *lucere*, to shine] Penetrable by x-rays.

radiolus (rā-dē′ō-lŭs) [L., a little ray] A sound or probe.

radiometer (rā-dē-ŏm′ĕ-tĕr) [" + Gr. *metron*, measure] An instrument for measuring the intensity of radiation.

radiomicrometer (rā″dē-ō-mī-krŏm′ĕ-tĕr) [" + Gr. *mikros*, small, + *metron*, measure] An instrument for measuring small changes in radiation.

radiomimetic (rā″dē-ō-mĭm-ĕt′ĭk) [″ + Gr. *mimetikos,* imitation] Imitating the biological effects of radiation. Alkylating agents are examples of substances with this property. SEE: *alkylating agent.*

radiomuscular (rā″dē-ō-mŭs′kū-lăr) Pert. to the radius or radial artery and the muscles of the arm.

radiomutation (rā″dē-ō-mū-tā′shŭn) The permanent alteration of the genetic material of a cell caused by the effects of ionizing radiation.

radionecrosis (rā″dē-ō-nĕ-krō′sĭs) [″ + Gr. *nekrosis,* state of death] The disintegration of tissue resulting from exposure to ionizing radiation.

radioneuritis (rā″dē-ō-nū-rī′tĭs) [″ + Gr. *neuron,* sinew, + *itis,* inflammation] Inflammation of a nerve caused by exposure to radioactivity.

radionuclide (rā″dē-ō-nū′klĭd) An atom that disintegrates by emitting electromagnetic rays, known as gamma rays.

radiopacity (rā″dē-ō-păs′ĭ-tē) Radiodensity.

radiopaque (rā-dē-ō-pāk′) [″ + *opacus,* dark] Impenetrable to x-rays or other forms of radiation.

radiopathology (rā″dē-ō-pă-thŏl′ō-jē) [″ + Gr. *pathos,* disease, suffering, + *logos,* word, reason] The study of radiation injuries.

radiopelvimetry (rā″dē-ō-pĕl-vĭm′ĕt-rē) [″ + *pelvis,* basin, + Gr. *metron,* measure] Measurement of the pelvis by use of x-rays.

radiopharmaceutical (rā″dē-ō-fărm″ă-sū′tĭ-kăl) A radioactive chemical or drug (e.g., an isotope of technetium or iodine) that has a specific affinity for a particular body tissue or organ. It can be used in nuclear medicine to obtain images of structures, or to treat radiation-sensitive diseases.

⚠ Radiopharmaceuticals must be handled in accordance with prescribed methods to prevent the patient or those treating the patient from being exposed to unnecessary ionizing radiation.

radiophosphorus (rā″dē-ō-fŏs′fō-rŭs) A radioactive isotope of phosphorus. ^{32}P is used in medical studies.

radiopotassium (rā″dē-ō-pō-tăs′ē-ŭm) A radioactive isotope of potassium. ^{42}K is used in medical studies.

radiopotentiation (rā″dē-ō-pō-tĕn″shē-ā′shŭn) [″ + *potentia,* power] The augmentation of the effect of radiation. This may be produced by certain drugs and by oxygen.

radioprotective agent (rād″ē-ō-prō-tĕk′tĭv) SEE: under *agent.*

radioreaction (rā″dē-ō-rē-ăk′shŭn) The reaction of the body to radiation.

radioreceptor (rā″dē-ō-rē-sĕp′tor) Something that receives radiant energy such as light, heat, or x-rays.

radioresistant (rā″dē-ō-rē-zĭs′tănt) Resistant to the action of radiation; used esp. of a tumor that cannot be destroyed by radiation treatment.

radioresponsive (rā″dē-ō-rē-spŏn′sĭv) Radiosensitive.

radioscopy (rā-dē-ŏs′kō-pē) [L. *radius,* ray, + Gr. *skopein,* to examine] Inspection and examination of the internal structures of the body by fluoroscopic procedures. SYN: *fluoroscopy.*

radiosensibility (rā-dē-ō-sĕn-sĭ-bĭl′ĭ-tē) Radiosensitivity.

radiosensitivity (rād″ē-ō-sen″sĭ-tiv″ĭt-ē) The relative susceptibility of cells, tissues, organs, or entire organisms to the harmful effect of ionizing radiation. SYN: *radiosensibility.* SEE: table. **radiosensitive,** *adj.*

Radiosensitive Tumors

adenocarcinoma of the anus and rectum
adenoid cystic carcinoma
breast cancer
cervix
Ewing sarcoma
head and neck cancer
Hodgkin disease
Hürthle cell tumor
lymphoma
myeloma
Merkel cell tumor
neuroblastoma
plasmacytoma
prostate cancer
seminoma
thyroid

radiosodium (rā″dē-ō-sō′dē-ŭm) A radioisotope of sodium such as ^{24}Na and ^{22}Na.

radiostrontium (rā″dē-ō-strŏn′shē-ŭm) A radioisotope of strontium.

radiosulfur (rā″dē-ō-sŭl′fŭr) A radioisotope of sulfur.

radiosurgery (rā″dē-ō-sŭr′jĕr-ē) [″ + Gr. *cheirurgia,* handwork] The use of ionizing radiation in surgery. SEE: *gamma knife surgery.*

radiotelemetry (rā″dē-ō-tĕl-ĕm′ĕ-trē) [″ + Gr. *tele,* distant, + *metron,* measure] The transmission of data, including biological data, by radio from a patient to a remote monitor or recording device for storage, analysis, and interpretation.

radiotherapeutics (rā″dē-ō-thĕr″ă-pū′tĭks) 1. Radiotherapy. 2. The study of radiotherapeutic agents.

radiotherapist (rā″dē-ō-thĕr′ă-pĭst) [″ + Gr. *therapeia,* treatment] Someone trained in use of ionizing radiation for therapeutic purposes.

radiotherapy (rād″ē-ō-ther′ă-pē) [*radio-* + *therapy*] Radiation therapy.

   involved-field r. Involved-field **radiation therapy**.

   selective internal r. Selective internal **radiation therapy**.

radiothermy (rā″dē-ō-thĕr′mē) [″ + Gr. *therme*, heat] **1.** The use of radiant heat or heat from radioactive substances for therapeutic purposes. **2.** Short-wave diathermy.

radiothorium (rā″dē-ō-thō′rē-ŭm) A radioisotope of thorium.

radiotoxemia (rā″dē-ō-tŏk-sē′mē-ă) [″ + Gr. *toxikon*, poison, + *haima*, blood] A rarely used term for radiation syndrome.

radiotransparent (rā″dē-ō-trăns-păr′ĕnt) [″ + *trans*, across, + *parere*, to appear] Penetrable by radiation.

radioulnar (rā″dē-ō-ŭl′năr) [″ + *ulna*, arm] Concerning the radius and ulna.

radium (rā′dē-ŭm) [L. *radius*, ray + *-ium* (1)] SYMB: Ra. A metallic element found in very small quantities in uranium ores such as pitchblende; atomic number 88, atomic weight 226, half-life 1622 years. It is radioactive and fluorescent. Radon is produced by the breakdown of radium. The most stable isotope, ^{226}Ra, has been used as a source of radioactivity in medical research and therapy.

radius (rā′dē-ŭs) [L., ray] **1.** A line extending from a circle's center point to its circumference. **2.** The outer and shorter bone of the forearm. It revolves partially about the ulna. Its head articulates with the capitulum of the humerus and with the radial notch on the ulna and is encircled by the annular ligament. Its lower portion articulates with the ulna by the ulnar notch, and by another articulation with the navicular (scaphoid) and lunate bones of the wrist. **radial,** *adj.*

   fracture of r. A break in the radius. A common fracture of the lower end of the radius is a Colles' fracture, caused by falling on the outstretched hand. Fractures also occur along the shaft or at the upper end frequently involving the radial head. SEE: *fracture*.

radix (rā′dĭks) *pl.* **radices** [L., root] **1.** The root portion of a cranial or spinal nerve. **2.** The root of a plant.

radon (rā′dŏn) [L. *radius*, ray] SYMB: Rn. A chemical element, one of the noble gases, resulting from the disintegration of isotopes of radium, atomic weight (mass) 222, atomic number 86. Because radium is present in the earth's crust, radon and its disintegration products accumulate in caves, mines, houses (particularly those that are energy efficient), and any space where no free exchange exists between the air contained in it and the air outside it. Exposure to radon above acceptable limits is be-

lieved to be a risk factor for lung cancer. SEE: *noble* **gas**.

   PATIENT CARE: If the level of radon in a house is measured and exceeds acceptable limits, steps should be taken to reduce it. In some areas, this is a legal requirement for sale of a property. Methods for removing or decreasing radon exposure in buildings include the installation of fans for ventilation.

   r. seed A tissue implant containing radon that is used to treat internal malignancies.

RADT *Rapid antigen detection test.* SEE: *rapid antigen test*.

radura (ră-dūr′ă) The internationally recognized symbol for irradiated food. It consists of a stylized representation of a flower surrounded by a dashed semicircle.

Raeder paratrigeminal syndrome (rād′ĕr) [J. G. Raeder, Norwegian ophthalmologist, 1889–1956] An incomplete form of Horner syndrome with unilateral ptosis and miosis and preserved facial sweating. It may result from aneurysms of or injury to the internal carotid artery.

raffinose (răf′ĭ-nōs) A trisaccharide, melitose, present in certain plants, cereals, and fungi. Hydrolysis yields fructose and melibiose.

raft A liquid phase of a cholesterol-rich region on a cell membrane that carries specific chemicals across the membrane into the cell.

   lipid r. A tiny cholesterol-rich region on a cell membrane that helps selected molecules enter the cytoplasm. SYN: *lipid domain*.

rage (rāj′) [ME.] Violent anger.

   sham r. A rage reaction produced by stimuli in decorticated animals.

ragsorter's disease A febrile pulmonary disease that may occur in people who sort paper and rags. It is caused by inhalation of anthrax.

ragweed One of several species of the genus *Ambrosia,* whose pollen is an important allergen. The pollen-producing period of grasses in temperate zones is from the middle of August to the first hard frost. SEE: *allergy*.

Raillietina (rī″lē-ĕ-tī′nă) A genus of tapeworms belonging to the family Davaineidae.

   R. demerariensis A species that infests humans, reported from several South American countries, esp. Ecuador.

Raimiste phenomenon (re-mēst′) [Johann M. Raimiste, 20th-cent. Ger. neurologist] An associated reaction in hemiplegia in which resistance to hip abduction or adduction in the noninvolved extremity evokes the same motion in the involved extremity. SYN: *Raimiste sign*.

raised (rāzd) [ME. *reisen*, to rise] Elevated above a surface.

rale (rāl) Crackle.

raloxifene (ră-lŏk′sĭ-fēn″) A selective estrogen receptor modulator administered orally to treat and prevent osteoporosis in postmenopausal women. Its therapeutic class is bone resorption inhibitor.

ramal (rā′măl) [L. *ramus*, branch] Pert. to a ramus.

rami (rā′mī) [L.] Pl. of ramus.

ramicotomy (răm″ĭ-kŏt′ō-mē) [L. *ramus*, branch, + Gr. *tome*, incision] Ramisection.

ramification (răm″ĭ-fĭ-kā′shŭn) [L. *ramificare*, to make branches] **1.** The process of branching. **2.** A branch. **3.** Arrangement in branches.

ramify (răm′ĭ-fī) To branch; to spread out in different directions.

ramisection (răm′ĭ-sĕk″shŭn) [L. *ramus*, branch, + *sectio*, a cutting] The surgical division of a ramus communicans between a spinal nerve and a ganglion of the sympathetic trunk.

ramisectomy (răm-ĭs-ĕk′tō-mē) [″ + Gr. *ektome*, excision] Excision of a ramus, specifically a ramus communicans. SEE: *ramisection*.

ramitis (răm-ī′tĭs) [″ + Gr. *itis*, inflammation] Inflammation of a ramus.

ramose (rā′mōs) [L. *ramus*, branch] Branching; having many branches.

Ramsay Hunt syndrome (ram′zē hŭnt) [James Ramsay Hunt, U.S. neurologist, 1872–1937] A condition caused by herpes zoster of the geniculate ganglion of the brain or neuritis of the facial nerve and characterized by severe facial palsy and vesicular eruption in the pharynx, external ear canal, tongue, and occipital area. Deafness, tinnitus, and vertigo may be present. SYN: *herpes zoster oticus*.

ramulus (răm-ū-lŭs) [L.] A small branch or ramus.

ramus (rā′mŭs, rā′mī″) *pl.* **rami** [L. *ramus*, branch] A branch; one of the divisions of a forked structure. **ramal** (rā′măl), *adj.*

    anterior r. One of the primary branches of a spinal nerve that supplies the lateral and ventral portions of the body wall, limbs, and perineum.

    r. communicans One of the primary branches of a spinal nerve that connects with a sympathetic ganglion. Each consists of a white portion (white ramus communicans) composed of myelinated preganglionic sympathetic fibers and a gray portion (gray ramus communicans) composed of unmyelinated postganglionic fibers.

    dorsal r. Posterior ramus.

    mandibular r. The vertical portion of the mandible.

    meningeal r. One of the primary branches of a spinal nerve that reenters the vertebral foramen and supplies the meninges and vertebral column.

    posterior r. The branch of a spinal nerve carrying motor axons to sensory axons from the deep muscles of the back and the skin that overlies them. SYN: *dorsal nerve; dorsal r.*

    pubic r. Either of the two barlike processes of the pubic bone that extend laterally and posteriorly from the pubic symphysis. The inferior ramus articulates with the ischium; the superior ramus articulates with the ilium and forms the front of the acetabulum.

    ventral r. The branch of a spinal nerve that carries motor axons to and sensory axons from all parts of the body except the deep (intrinsic) muscles of the back and their overlying skin.

Rancho Los Amigos Guide to Cognitive Levels A scale widely used to classify a neurological patient's level of cognitive dysfunction according to behavior. This scale provides eight levels with descriptors, progressing from level I (no response) to level VIII (purposeful and appropriate response), as follows:

1. No response: is unresponsive to any stimuli.

2. Generalized response: exhibits limited, inconsistent, nonpurposeful responses, often to pain only.

3. Localized response: displays purposeful responses; may follow simple commands; may focus on presented object.

4. Confused, agitated: demonstrates heightened state of activity; confusion, disorientation; aggressive behavior; inability to perform self-care; unawareness of present events; agitation, which appears as internal confusion.

5. Confused, inappropriate: is nonagitated; appears alert; responds to commands; is distractible; does not concentrate on task; demonstrates agitated responses to external stimuli; is verbally inappropriate; does not learn new information.

6. Confused, appropriate: demonstrates goal-directed behavior, needs cuing; can relearn old skills, such as activities of daily living; displays serious memory problems; exhibits some awareness of self and others.

7. Automatic, appropriate: appears appropriate, oriented; frequently acts robot-like in daily routine; has minimal or no confusion; demonstrates shallow recall; exhibits increased awareness of self, interaction in environment; lacks insight into condition; shows decreased judgment and problem-solving ability; lacks realistic planning for future.

8. Purposeful, appropriate: is alert, oriented; recalls and integrates past events; learns new activities and can continue without supervision; is inde-

pendent in home and living skills; is capable of driving; demonstrates defects in stress tolerance, judgment, abstract reasoning; possibly functions at reduced levels in society.

rancid (răn′sĭd) [L. *rancidus*, stink] Having a disagreeable odor resulting from the breakdown of double bonds in fatty acids.

rancidity (răn-sĭd′ĭ-tē) The condition of being rancid.

random (răn′dŭm) Without order; unpredictable; unintentionally complex.

randomization (ran″dŏ-mĭ-zā′shŏn) In research, a method used to assign subjects to experimental groups without introducing biases into a study. SYN: *random sampling*.

randomized controlled trial SEE: under *trial*.

random sample SEE: under *sample*.

range (rānj) The difference between the highest and lowest in a set of variables or in a series of values or observations.

r. of accommodation The difference between the least and the greatest distance of distinct vision. SEE: *accommodation*.

acoustic dynamic r. The difference between the highest and lowest frequencies of sound that an individual can hear without discomfort or auditory distortion.

continuous passive r. of motion Continuous passive **motion**.

host r. All the various organisms that a parasite or pathogen is capable of infecting.

interquartile r. The middle 50% of a set of data. It represents all the data greater than or equal to the 25th percentile and less than or equal to the 75th percentile.

r. of motion ABBR: ROM. **1.** The possible excursion of motion at a joint, accomplished by an examiner, without any muscle contraction by the patient. The excursion can be measured by a goniometer and is normally slightly greater than active range of motion. The examiner assesses the maximum excursion at both its beginning and end. SEE: *range-of-motion exercise* for illus.; *goniometer*. **2.** An exercise in which an external force moves a joint through its excursion without any effort by the patient. Passive range of motion exercise is used when the patient is unable to move or when active motion is contraindicated.

passive r. of motion ABBR: PROM. **1.** The possible excursion of motion at a joint, accomplished by an examiner, without any muscle contraction by the patient. This can be measured by a goniometer. The excursion is normally slightly greater than active range of motion. The examiner assesses the end point. **2.** An exercise in which an exter-

nal force moves a joint through its excursion without any effort by the patient. PROM exercise is used when the patient is unable to move or when active motion is prohibited.

ranine (rā′nīn) [L. *rana*, a frog] **1.** Pert. to a ranula, or the region beneath the tip of the tongue. **2.** The branch of the lingual artery supplying that area. **3.** Pert. to frogs.

ranitidine (ră-nĭ′tĭ-dēn) A histamine H$_2$ antagonist and antiulcer agent, administered orally or intravenously for short-term treatment of active duodenal ulcers and benign gastric ulcers.

ranula (răn′ū-lă) [L., little frog] A cystic tumor seen on the underside of the tongue on either side of the frenum; a retention cyst of the submandibular or sublingual ducts. The swelling may be small or large.

SYMPTOMS: The tumor is semitranslucent, with soft, dilated veins coursing over it. The patient experiences fullness and discomfort, but usually no pain. The tumor contains clear fluid owing to dilatation of the salivary glands and obstruction of the sublingual mucous glands.

TREATMENT: Periodic emptying of the sac by careful needle aspiration provides temporary relief. Surgical intervention is required for complete removal.

pancreatic r. Cystic disease of the pancreas caused by obstruction of its ducts.

Ranvier node (ron-vē-ā′) [Louis A. Ranvier, Fr. pathologist, 1835–1922] A space between adjacent Schwann cells along a nerve fiber; no myelin sheath is present. SYN: *neurofibril node*. SEE: *nerve fiber; neuron* for illus.; *Schwann cell*.

RAO *right anterior oblique* position.

rape (rāp) [L. *rapere*, to seize] Sexual assault or sexual violence perpetrated on one person by another against the will of the victim. Rape involves an attempt at or actual penetration of the vagina or another body orifice by a penis, finger, other body part, or inanimate object. Complete penetration by the penis or emission of seminal fluid is not necessary to constitute rape. Most rapes include force, intimidation, or violence, but acquiescence because of verbal threats does not indicate consent. Some studies have indicated that an incident involving rape occurs about every 2.5 min, and that 1 out of 6 women will be raped sometime during her life. According to the National Sexual Assault Hotline in 2005, there were about 190,000 victims of rape, attempted rape, or sexual assault, annually. A majority of rapes are inflicted by someone known to the victim. SEE: *rape and sexual assault* *prevention; syndrome, rape-trauma; sexual abuse; Nursing Diagnoses Appendix.*

TREATMENT: The medical care of the rape victim must include timely prophylactic treatment for sexually transmitted diseases (including HIV/AIDS), prophylaxis against hepatitis B, and prophylaxis against pregnancy.

PATIENT CARE: The health care professional provides sensitive care, esp. psychological support, remains with the patient, and encourages her to express her feelings. If available, a Sexual Assault Nurse Examiner should be summoned. State regulations regarding the reporting of rape should be followed. The health care professional explains and assists with the psychological, oral, pelvic, and rectal examinations and diagnostic tests. Directions should be followed exactly in collecting rape evidence such as head and pubic hair combings, nail scrapings, and vaginal, oral, or anal specimens for police investigation. The patient should be allowed as much control as possible throughout examination, treatment, and interview procedures. An assault and sexual history is obtained, including whether the female rape victim was menstruating and, if so, the type of menstrual protection used.

Attempts are made to obtain as accurate a history of the rape as possible. Meticulous documentation is required. Medically relevant evidence of the patient's emotional reactions and state should be included, with care taken not to record one's own feelings or thoughts. The interviewer should be aware that medical records may be called in evidence in a court of law. Prior to the examination, the patient should be asked whether she has douched, bathed, or washed her perineal area before coming to the hospital. She may need to urinate, but should be cautioned not to wipe or clean the perineum in any way. As she changes into a hospital gown, her clothing is collected in paper bags, with each bag labeled accurately (with the patient's name, collector's name, chain of evidence, location, date, and time).

After determining the patient's allergy history, prescribed treatments of associated injuries are given. Topical ice packs may be used to reduce vulvar swelling and discomfort. Analgesics and sedatives or anti-anxiety agents are prescribed as needed. Photographs to document any injuries are taken. Crisis intervention services are offered to assist the patient. Assistance is offered to help the patient explain the rape to family. Arrangements are made for someone to escort the patient home. Follow-up services and written and verbal instructions for prescribed medications, including drug actions and possible side effects, are provided. The importance of returning for sexually transmitted disease testing is explained: some microbiological cultures take days or longer to reveal results. Psychological counseling is encouraged to help the patient cope with aftereffects of the rape-trauma. Legal proceedings may revive the trauma of the event for the victim. Further counseling and support is provided as needed. Female victims should be referred to Women Organized Against Rape or a local rape crisis center for ongoing empathic care and advice.

date r. Nonconsensual, unsolicited, and unwelcome sexual relations between individuals who are currently or were previously romantically involved or sexually intimate.

gang r. Forcible sexual intercourse or other sexual activity committed on an individual by several persons. SEE: *rape.*

male r. Sexual assault, usually penetrative, of a man by a man. Estimating the prevalence of male rape is difficult because it often is not reported.

marital r. Forcible sexual assault by a spouse at a time when the sexual encounter was neither solicited nor welcome.

prison r. Rape that occurs when the victim is assaulted by another prisoner or by a prison employee.

statutory r. Sexual intercourse with an individual younger than the legal age of consent.

rape and sexual assault prevention The precautions taken to decrease the chances of one's being forced to engage in unwanted sexual behaviors. In the U.S., about 700,000 to 1,000,000 sexual assaults occur each year; 75% to 85% of all sexual assaults are committed by friends, family members, or sexual partners of the victim; 95% of all sexual assaults are committed against women, the majority of whom are under 18 years old. Because of this, a crucial element in the prevention of sexual assault is the education of young men and adolescent boys about respectful sexual interactions with women. In addition, women who feel threatened, dominated, or controlled by men or boys in their home, school, or work environments should proactively seek help from sexual assault crisis services in their neighborhood.

Personal safety tips. (1) Because alcohol consumption is a related factor in many rapes, it is advisable to keep alcohol intake to a minimum, not allow another person to handle anything you are drinking, to avoid drug addition, and not allow a companion who is intoxicated into one's home. (2) As much as possible, preventive measures should be directed at remaining in a well-secured area and being close to persons who can be called for assistance day or night. (3) Emergency police and fire department telephone numbers should be kept readily available. Help should be summoned without delay if it is suspected that one's apartment or home is being illegally entered. (4) When preparing to enter a car or home, one should be constantly alert for the presence of strangers. (5) Before leaving a well-lighted and populated area, one should have the car keys in hand and ready for quick use. It is advisable to leave one arm free of packages, handbag, or other items and to carry a noise making device. (6) When driving, it is important to lock the car doors and close any open windows immediately, and stay on well-lit streets. (7) When returning home alone at night, one should enlist the assistance of a known neighbor, law enforcement officer, or friend to search the home if the door is unlocked or anything seems amiss. Once one is safely inside, the door should be locked securely. (8) If a stranger comes to the door, a security chain should be kept on and a peephole preferably used for communication until proper identification has been presented. If doubt exists about the credentials or demeanor of the stranger, admission should be refused and help summoned immediately. (9) Always walk quickly and with assurance. (10) Avoid automated teller machines at night. (11) If attacked, make as much noise and resist assault vigorously, unless you believe that to do so would increase the likelihood of physical harm or death. (12) Never leave children unattended. (13) Do not allow strangers to enter your car. (14) If you are assaulted, seek immediate help from local medical, social, and policing agencies. Do not wash or bathe. (15) Attempt to remember as many details as possible about the attacker: clothes, size, race, accent, hair color, identifying marks and scars, facial hair, vehicle, and evidence of drug or alcohol use.

rape counseling The provision of advice, comfort, and sources of therapy for victims of sexual assault. The emotional reaction and sequelae of rape may be devastating to the mental well-being of the victim. It is therefore important that the victim be reassured about what to expect from both internal feelings and the potential reactions of society. Historically, law enforcement officers have been less than sympathetic to rape victims, but now most police departments have officers trained in rape investigation who are sensitive to the emotional and physical trauma the victim has experienced. Frequently, specially trained Sexual Assault Nurse Examiners (SANE) are available to provide care

and support. Various services are available to the victim, including advocate groups and health care professionals experienced in counseling rape victims.

rapeseed (rāp-sēd) [L. *rapa,* turnip] The seed of *Brassica campestris* and other *Brassica* species, whose oil is used in the manufacture of lubricants and canola oil. The oil made from the seeds of the variety high in erucic acid is used as an industrial lubricant. Oil made from the seeds of the low-erucic-acid variety is relatively low in saturated fat and is commonly known as canola oil.

rape-trauma syndrome Sustained maladaptive response to a forced, violent sexual penetration against the victim's will and consent. SEE: *rape; Nursing Diagnoses Appendix.*

Like other posttraumatic stress disorders, this condition initially causes an acute phase of disorganization and involves a long-term reorganization of lifestyle. Sequelae may include marked changes in lifestyle and a variety of phobias.

Acute phase: Profound emotional responses mark the acute phase (i.e., fear, shame, and feelings of humiliation; self-blame and self-degradation; and anger and desire for revenge). Most commonly, rape victims exhibit crying, trembling, talkativeness, statements of disbelief, and emotional shock. Some may exhibit overt signs of hostility, which reflect their anger and feelings of powerlessness. Later, patient complaints of sleep pattern disturbances, gastrointestinal irritability, and genitourinary discomforts reflect physical responses to emotional trauma. Some victims may appear quiet, dispassionate, and smiling; however, these behaviors should not be misinterpreted as indicating a lack of concern; rather, they may represent an avoidance reaction.

Long-term phase: Many rape victims experience one or more of the following: nightmares; chronic suspicion, inability to trust, and altered interpersonal relationships; anxiety, aversion to men, and avoidance of sex; depression; and phobias. Paradoxically, patients express feelings of guilt and shame because they feel that either they invited the attack, should have prevented the episode, or that they deserved being punished.

PATIENT CARE: The nurse exhibits empathy and understanding and ensures privacy and a quiet supportive environment. The patient is encouraged to verbalize feelings, fears, and concerns. Positive self-perception and self-esteem are promoted and supported. The nurse emphasizes that rape usually is an expression of the rapist's overwhelming feelings of psychosocial impotence and anger and that the act conveys a sense of power over others; the woman was a victim of the rapist's inability to contain a violent personal rage that is not related to her or to sex. The patient is referred to community resources (support groups) and for psychological counseling. Most patients prefer to have a counselor of the same sex.

raphe (rā'fē) [Gr. *rhaphe*] A crease, ridge, or seam denoting union of the halves of a part.

abdominal r. Linea alba.

palatine r. A line or ridge in the median line of the palate. The raphe appears as a whitish line, which sometimes turns into a slight groove at its posterior end.

r. of penis A median ridge on the undersurface of the penis, a continuation of the raphe of the scrotum.

perineal r. A line or ridge in the midline of the perineum.

pterygomandibular r. A tendinous line of fusion between the buccinator and superior pharyngeal constrictor muscles that passes between the pterygoid process and the mandible, serving as an important landmark in dental anesthesia.

r. of scrotum A ridge in the midline of the scrotum.

r. of tongue A median groove on the dorsum of the tongue.

rapid alternating movement test Dysdiadochokinesia.

rapid antigen detection test ABBR: RADT. Rapid antigen test.

rapid antigen test Any laboratory test used to quickly identify the presence of a specific antigen in a body fluid sample.

PATIENT CARE: Rapid antigen tests are used to confirm diagnostic impressions or to screen large numbers of patients quickly for the possibility of infection. In rapid HIV antigen tests, a positive test is not considered definitive for infection: it requires confirmation with blood tests (serology). In screening for streptococcal pharyngitis (strep throat), clinicians often consider the test as adequate for immediate treatment even though false positive and negative results can occur. SYN: *rapid antigen detection test.*

rapid cycling Four or more episodes of depression, mania, hypomania, or other alternating mood disturbances occurring in a single year. Roughly 10% of patients with bipolar illness have this condition; more men than women are affected. Lithium carbonate is less effective in treating rapid cycling than in treating other forms of bipolar disorder.

rapid eye movement sleep behavior disorder, REM sleep behavior disorder A behavior characteristic of patients with dementia accompanied by Lewy bodies and with other neurodegenerative diseases in which the patient is physically active while dreaming. Those affected may move their arms and legs, sometimes abruptly or violently, and eat, speak, shout, or void during sleep.

rapid maxillary expansion ABBR: RME. Surgical correction of hypoplastic disorders of the midface, consisting of enlargement of the dental arch and widening of the palate.

rapid response team A group of specially trained health care professionals who respond to emergencies or developing emergencies in health care institutions. A typical team consists of a critical care nurse, respiratory therapist, intensivist, hospitalist, and an emergency physician or physician assistant.

rapid shallow breathing index ABBR: f/VT; RSBI. SEE: under *index.*

rapid strep test A commonly used rapid antigen test performed on saliva swabbed from the throat or tonsils of patients suspected of having strep throat. SEE: *rapid antigen test; streptococcal pharyngitis.*

rapid surfactant test Shake test.

rappel (ră-pĕl') To slide down a rope, as in a lifesaving rescue.

rapport (ră-por') [Fr. *rapporter,* to bring back] A relationship of mutual trust and understanding, esp. between the patient and physician, nurse, or other health care provider.

rapture A state of great joy, delight, or ecstasy.

Rapunzel syndrome (ră-pŭn'zĕl) [*Rapunzel,* a long-haired girl in a fairy tale by the Brothers Grimm] The extension of a hairball into the small intestine, causing obstruction of the small or large bowel.

rarefaction (răr"ĕ-făk'shŭn) [L. *rarefacere,* to make thin] The process of decreasing in density and weight.

r. of bone Osteoporosis.

rarefy (rār'ĕ-fī) To make less dense; to increase the porosity of something.

RAS *reticular activating system.*

rash (rash) [Fr. *rasche,* skin eruption] A general term for any eruption that appears on the skin transiently (as opposed to durable skin lesions such as scars, tattoos, or moles). SYN: *exanthem.*

PATIENT CARE: Assessments are made of the location and characteristics of the lesion: color; size (height and diameter); pattern, whether discrete or coalesced; and any secondary changes (crusting, scaling, lichenification). Associated symptoms such as pruritus or discomfort, temporal elements, history of known allergies, drugs used, and contacts with communicable diseases during prior 2-week period also are assessed. Suspected drugs are discontinued, and the potential communicable disease patient is isolated and assessed. Cool compresses are applied to relieve itching. Topical preparations and dressings are applied and systemic medications administered as prescribed. The patient is instructed to keep hands clean and nails short and even, and to avoid scratching. The patient also is taught about the treatment regimen, its actions, and its side effects and evaluates for desired effects and side effects.

butterfly r. A rash on both cheeks joined by an extension across the bridge of the nose. It is seen in systemic lupus erythematosus, esp. after the patient's face has been exposed to sunlight, and in seborrheic dermatitis, tuberous sclerosis, and dermatomyositis. SEE: *discoid lupus erythematosus*.

diaper r. Irritant contact dermatitis as a reaction to friction, maceration, and prolonged contact with urine, feces, soap retained in diapers, and topical preparations. A persistent diaper rash may be colonized by yeast or bacteria. SYN: *diaper dermatitis*.

TREATMENT: Treatment is symptomatic. Diapers should be changed frequently. If washable cloth diapers are used, they should be thoroughly washed and rinsed; occlusive plastic pants should not be used over diapers; the perianal and genital areas should be washed with warm water and mild, nonperfumed soap. If these measures and the application of a bland protective agent (such as zinc oxide paste) do not promote healing, then a small amount of 0.5% to 1% topical hydrocortisone cream should be applied to the area after each diaper change until the rash has completely resolved.

drug r. Drug **eruption**.

gum r. A red papular eruption on an infant's chin and anterior chest area seen during teething. It is a form of miliaria due to excess saliva coming in contact with the skin. SYN: *red r.; tooth r.*

heat r. Prickly **heat**.

hemorrhagic r. A rash consisting chiefly of bleeding or bruising into or under the skin. SYN: *ecchymotic r.*

macular r. A rash in which the lesions are flat and level with the surrounding skin.

maculopapular r. A rash in which there are discrete macular and papular lesions or a combination of both.

mercurial r. A rash caused by local application of mercurial preparations.

mulberry r. A dusky rash seen in typhus.

nettle r. Urticaria.

red r. Gum **r.**

serum r. A pruritic hivelike rash (urticaria or angioedema) or a vasculitis (palpable purpura) that accompanies serum sickness, usually caused by a hypersensitivity reaction to drugs or immune globulins obtained from animals.

Malaise, joint pains, fevers, and other symptoms may accompany the rash. SEE: *serum sickness*.

splash r. Hot tub **folliculitis**.

sunburn-like r. A macular rash resembling the reddened skin characteristic of a severe sunburn. SEE: *exfoliative dermatitis; toxic shock syndrome*.

tooth r. Gum **r.**

wandering r. Geographic **tongue**.

Rashkind procedure (rash'kīnd″) [William Rashkind, U.S. surgeon and pediatric cardiologist; d. 1986] Balloon atrial **septostomy**.

rasion (rā'zhŭn) [L. *rasio*] The grating of drugs by use of a file.

Rasmussen encephalitis (ras'mus-ĕn) [Theodore Brown Rasmussen, U.S. neurologist, 1910–2002.] ABBR: RE. A rare inflammatory disorder, typically involving a single hemisphere of the brain and often resulting in hemiplegia and partial seizures that are difficult to control. The condition is more common in children than in adults.

raspatory (răs'pă-tō″rē) [L. *raspatorium*] A file used in surgery, esp. for trimming bone surfaces. SYN: *xyster*.

RAST (răst) *radioallergosorbent test*.

Rastafarian (răs-tă-fă'rē-ăn) A religious cult that originated in Jamaica in the 1930s and has members in the Caribbean, Europe, Canada, and the U.S. It is of medical importance because cult members' dietary practices may lead to vitamin B_{12} deficiency with subsequent neurological disease, megaloblastic anemia, or both.

rat (rat) A rodent of the genus *Rattus*, found in and around human habitations. In addition to causing economic loss from crop destruction, rats are of primary importance in the spread of human and animal diseases. They are hosts of various protozoans, flukes, tapeworms, and threadworms, and reservoirs of amebiasis, murine and scrub typhus, and bubonic plague. Typhus and plague are transmitted to people mainly by the rat flea. Rats also transmit rat-bite fever.

rat-bite fever SEE: under *fever*.

rate (rāt) [L. *rata*, calculated] The speed or frequency of occurrence of an event, usually expressed with respect to time or some other known standard.

acquisition r. In radiology, the speed with which medical images are recorded, usually expressed in images per second.

attack r. The rate of occurrence of new cases of a disease.

basal metabolic r. ABBR: BMR. The metabolic rate as measured 12 hr after eating, after a restful sleep, with no exercise or activity preceding testing, with elimination of emotional excitement, and at a comfortable temperature. It is usually expressed in terms of kilocalories per square meter of body surface per hour. It increases, for example, in hyperthyroidism. SYN: *resting energy expenditure.*

baseline fetal heart r. ABBR: FHR. The average range of beats per minute recorded within a 10-min time frame. The normal range is between 120 and 160 beats per minute.

birth r. The number of live births per 1000 in the population in a given year.

case r. Morbidity **r.**

case fatality r. The percentage of individuals afflicted with an illness who die as a result of it.

concordance r. The frequency with which a gene will be inherited or expressed by identical or fraternal twins.

death r. The number of deaths in a specified population, usually expressed per 100,000 population over a given period, usually 1 year. SYN: *death-to-case ratio; mortality* **r.**

delivery r. In assisted reproduction technology, the number of newborn deliveries achieved in every one hundred follicular aspirations, embryo transfers, or stimulated cycles.

dose r. The quantity of medicine or radiation administered per unit of time.

erythrocyte sedimentation r. ABBR: ESR. SEE: *sedimentation* **r.**

false-negative r. The rate of occurrence of negative test results in those who have the attribute or disease for which they are being tested.

false-positive r. The rate of occurrence of positive test results in those who do not have the attribute or disease for which they are being tested.

fertility r. The number of births per year per 1000 women between ages 15 and 44 in a given population.

fetal mortality r. The number of fetal deaths per 1000 live births, usually per year.

growth r. The rate at which an individual, tissue, or organ grows over time.

heart r. ABBR: HR. The number of heartbeats per unit of time, usually expressed or written as number per minute. A normal resting heart rate for an adult is 60–100 beats per minute.

infant mortality r. The number of deaths per year of live-born infants less than 1 year of age divided by the number of live births in the same year. This value is usually expressed as deaths per 100,000 live births. SEE: *neonatal mortality* **r.***; perinatal mortality* **r.**

infusion r. The speed of administration of a solution in mL/hr.

⚠ It is calculated by the following formula: Rate = (Dose × 60 × Body weight)/Concentration, in which the dose is in mcg/kg/min; 60 is in min/hr; weight is in kg; and the concentration of the substance in solution is in mcg/mL.

---

maternal mortality r. The number of maternal deaths in 1 year from puerperal causes (such as those associated with pregnancy, childbirth, and the puerperium) within 42 days after delivery divided by the number of live births in that same year. This value is usually expressed as deaths per 100,000 live births. SEE: illus.

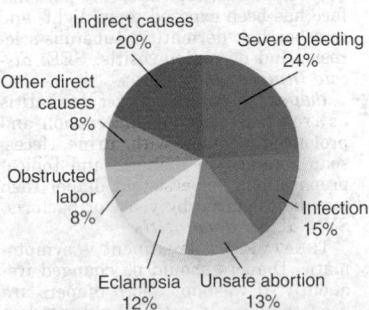

Indirect causes 20%
Severe bleeding 24%
Other direct causes 8%
Obstructed labor 8%
Infection 15%
Eclampsia 12%
Unsafe abortion 13%

CAUSES OF MATERNAL DEATH

maximum midexpiratory flow r. ABBR: MMFR. The average airflow during the middle half of a forced vital capacity effort.

metabolic r. The rate of utilization of energy. This is usually measured at a time when the subject is completely at rest and in a fasting state. Energy used is calculated from the amount of oxygen used during the test. SEE: *basal metabolic* **r.***; basal* **metabolism.**

morbidity r. The number of cases per year of certain diseases in relation to the size of the population in which they occur. SYN: *case* **r.**

mortality r. Death **r.**

neonatal mortality r. The number of deaths in 1 year of infants aged 0 to 28 days divided by the number of live births in that same year. SEE: *maternal mortality* **r.***; perinatal mortality* **r.**

peak expiratory flow r. The maximum rate of exhalation during a forced expiration, measured in liters per second or liters per minute. It is used as a test of airway obstruction.

perinatal mortality r. The number of stillbirths (in which the gestation period was 28 weeks or more) in the first 7 days of life divided by the number of live births plus stillbirths in the same year. This value is usually expressed as deaths per 100,000 live births plus stillbirths. SEE: *infant mortality* **r.***; neonatal mortality* **r.**

periodontal disease r. SEE: *periodontal (Ramfjord) index.*

pulse r. The number of heartbeats

per unit of time that can be detected by palpating any accessible artery.

respiration r. The number of breaths per unit of time.

sedimentation r. ABBR: ESR (erythrocyte sedimentation rate). A nonspecific laboratory test used as a marker of inflammation. In this test the speed at which erythrocytes settle out of unclotted blood is measured. Blood to which an anticoagulant has been added is placed in a long, narrow tube, and the distance the red cells fall in 1 hr is the ESR. Normally it is less than 10 mm/hr in men and slightly higher in women.

The speed at which the cells settle depends on how many red blood cells clump together. Clumping is increased by the presence of acute-phase proteins released during inflammation.

specific absorption r. The rate at which electromagnetic energy is absorbed by a kilogram of tissue, usually expressed as the heat absorbed by the tissue, or as the power absorbed per unit of mass.

ventilation r. ABBR: VR. The number of breaths per minute.

rate of perceived exertion ABBR: RPE. The intensity of exercise as subjectively gauged by the individual who is exercising. The corresponding written descriptions range from "very light" to "very, very hard." The scale correlates well with cardiorespiratory and metabolic variables such as minute ventilation, heart rate, and blood lactate levels. SEE: *Borg dyspnea scale*.

PATIENT CARE: Two common rating scales are used to assess RPE. One is scored from 0 (no effort) to 10 (maximal effort), with descriptions in between, such as "very light" or "very hard" exercise. The scale correlates well with cardiorespiratory and metabolic variables such as minute ventilation, heart rate, and blood lactate levels, and can be used as a substitute for monitoring these variables directly. Another RPE scale ranges from 6 to 20. In this self-scoring system "very, very light exertion" is rated as a 7, and "very, very hard exertion" is rated as 19. Optimal physical training occurs in the range that exceeds "fairly light exertion" but is less than "very hard" exertion (about 12–16). The scales help people to monitor their workouts, and may be esp. helpful in clinical settings when patients are unable to take their own pulse during exercise or if they have abnormal heart rate responses to exercise.

ratio (rā′shē-ō) [L., computation] The relationship in degree or number between two things. Particular ratios are listed under the first word. SEE: e.g., *body weight ratio; international normalized ratio; sex ratio*.

ration (ra′shŏn, rā′) [L. *ratio,* calcula-

tion] A fixed allowance of a nutrient or of a service for a specified period, e.g. of food, health care.

rational (răsh′ŭn-ăl) [L. *rationalis,* reason] **1.** Of sound mind. SYN: *sane.* **2.** Reasonable or logical; employing treatments based on reasoning or general principles; opposed to empiric.

rational drug design The study of the shape of molecules in order to determine how they will bind receptors on cells or combine with other molecules. Drug design that is based on molecular shape or architecture is an alternative to blindly testing hundreds of molecules to see if one or more of them will bind cellular or molecular targets.

rationale (răsh′ŭn-ăl′) [L.] The logical or fundamental reason for a course of action or procedure.

rationalization (răsh″ŭn-ăl-ĭ-zā′shŭn) In psychology, a justification for an unreasonable or illogical act or idea to make it appear reasonable.

rational treatment Treatment based on scientific principles.

rationing Resource allocation in health care, esp. in managed health care systems.

rattle (răt′l) [ME. *ratelen,* to rattle] A coarse crackle heard during auscultation of the chest. This finding suggests excessive airway secretions are present.

death r. A colloquial term for gurgling noises caused by movements of secretions in the upper airways with inspiration and expiration in dying patients.

rattlesnake (rat′ĕl-snāk″) A venomous snake of the genus *Crotalus.* Its bite may produce coagulation disorders, anaphylaxis, or injury to local tissues.

raucous (raw′kŭs) [L. *raucus, hoarse*] Hoarse, harsh, as the sound of a voice.

Rauscher leukemia virus (rou′shĕr) [Frank J. Rauscher, U.S. virologist, b. 1931] A virus known to cause leukemia in mice.

rauwolfia serpentina (raw-wŏlf′ē-ă) [Leonhard Rauwolf, Ger. botanist, 1535–1596] The dried roots of a tropical shrub of the family Apocynaceae, whose extracts are potent hypotensive and sedative drugs. Derivatives include reserpine, serpentine, and serpentinine.

rave (rāv) [ME. *raven,* to be delirious] **1.** To talk irrationally, as in delirium. **2.** An all-night dance party at which mind-altering drugs, e.g., ecstasy or other amphetamines, are often used.

raving 1. Irrational utterance. **2.** Talking irrationally.

RAW *airway resistance.*

raw (raw) [AS. *hreaw*] **1.** Of food: not cooked. **2.** Of the skin: damaged by abrasion. **3.** Of information or data: unstudied, unanalyzed, or unevaluated.

raw data The information obtained during an experiment, before the information has been analyzed or statistically manipulated.

ray (rā) [Fr. *rai, raie,* fr L. *radius,* ray] **1.** Any of several lines diverging from a common center. **2.** A line of propagation of any form of radiant energy, esp. light or heat; loosely, any narrow beam of light.

actinic r. A solar ray capable of producing chemical changes. SYN: *chemical r.*

alpha r. A ray composed of positively charged helium particles derived from atomic disintegration of radioactive elements. Its velocity is one tenth the speed of light. Alpha rays are completely absorbed by a thin sheet of paper and possess powerful fluorescent, photographic, and ionizing properties. They penetrate tissues less than beta rays.

beta r. A ray composed of negatively charged electrons expelled from atoms of disintegrating radioactive elements. SYN: *beta **particle**.*

border r. Grenz **r.**

cathode r. A ray composed of negatively charged electrons discharged by a cathode through a vacuum, moving in a straight line and producing x-ray photons upon hitting solid matter.

central r. The theoretical center of an x-ray beam. The term designates the direction of the x-ray photons as projected from the focal spot of the x-ray tube to the radiographical film.

characteristic r. A secondary photon produced by an electron giving up energy as it changes location from an outer to an inner shell in an atom. The wavelengths are characteristic of the difference in binding energies.

chemical r. Actinic **r.**

cosmic r. Cosmic **radiation**.

delta r. Highly penetrative waves emitted by radioactive substances.

erythema-producing r. Ultraviolet radiation (wavelengths between 2050 and 3100 A.U.) capable of reddening skin.

gamma r. Short wavelength, high-energy electromagnetic radiation emitted by disintegrating atomic nuclei.

grenz r. A low-energy x-ray photon with an average wavelength of 2 A.U. (range from 1 to 3 A.U.); obtained with peak voltage of less than 10 kV. Grenz rays lie between ultraviolet and x-rays. SYN: *border **r.**.*

hard r. An x-ray photon of short wavelength and great penetrative power.

heat r. Radiation whose wavelength is between 3,900 and 14,000 A.U. Shorter wavelength heat sources penetrate tissues better than longer (infrared) sources. SEE: *heat.*

infrared r. An invisible heat ray from beyond the red end of the spectrum. Infrared wavelengths range from 7700

angstrom units (A.U.) to 1 mm. Long-wave infrared rays (15,000 to 150,000 A.U.) are emitted by all heated bodies and exclusively by bodies of low temperature such as hot water bottles and electric heating pads; short-wave infrared rays (7,200 to 15,000 A.U.) are emitted by all incandescent heaters. The sun, electric arcs, incandescent globes, and so-called infrared burners are sources of infrared rays.

USES: Infrared ray energy is transformed into heat in a superficial layer of the tissues. It is used therapeutically to stimulate local and general circulation and to relieve pain. The infrared thermograph is useful in studying the heat of tissues. SEE: *radiation; thermography.*

luminous r. One of the visible rays of the spectrum.

medullary r. In the kidney, one of many slender processes composed of one or two collecting ducts and other straight tubules that project into the cortex from the bases of renal pyramids.

monochromatic r. Single wavelength electromagnetic radiation.

pigment-producing r. A ray between 2540 and 3100 A.U. that is most effective in stimulating pigment production in the skin. This is due to a local response to irritation of cutaneous prickle cells.

positive r. A ray composed of positively charged ions that in a discharge tube moves from the anode toward the cathode.

primary r. In radiographic imaging, the x-ray beam that originates at the source of radiation. It is usually used to differentiate those rays from the additional scatter radiation that constitutes the majority of the beam used to create images.

roentgen r. X-ray photon.

scattered r. SEE: under *radiation.*

secondary r. X-ray photons produced after the incoming, primary x-ray photons remove an inner-shell electron from the atom. Secondary rays can also be primary x-rays that have been diverted through scatter interactions with other atoms. Secondary rays are of lower energy than primary rays and are usually absorbed in matter, an interaction that produces x-ray photons via a cascade effect.

ultraviolet r. An invisible ray of the spectrum beyond the violet rays. The wavelengths of ultraviolet rays vary. They may be refracted, reflected, and polarized, but will not traverse many substances impervious to the rays of the visible spectrum. They rapidly destroy the vitality of bacteria, and are able to produce photochemical and photographic effects.

Raynaud, Maurice (rĕ-nō′) French physician, 1834–1881.

R. disease A primary vasospastic disease of small arteries and arterioles; the cause is unknown. There is an exaggerated response of vasomotor controls to cold or emotion.

SYMPTOMS: Patients have intermittent vasospastic attacks of varying severity and frequency that affect the digits of the hands bilaterally; the toes are less commonly involved. Color changes occur in sequence, first white (pallor), then blue (cyanosis), and then red (hyperemia as blood flow returns). Initially, there is numbness and sensation of cold; during the red phase patients may have throbbing and paresthesia. Normal skin color returns after the attack. Patients with long-term disease may develop atrophy of the skin and subcutaneous tissues, brittle nails, and, occasionally, skin ulcerations or gangrene.

PATIENT CARE: People with Raynaud disease should maintain warmth in their extremities by wearing warm mittens or gloves and socks. They should avoid contact with cold materials and prolonged exposure to cold environments; they should also avoid emotional stress. Use of tobacco is contraindicated because of the vasoconstrictive effects of nicotine. Other aggravating factors include alcohol, caffeine, and medications such as beta blockers, adrenergic receptor agonists, sympathomimetic agents, ergotamine drugs, antineoplastic agents, estrogens, immunosuppressants, biologic response modifiers, and stimulants such as amphetamines and cocaine. Increasing hydrostatic pressure, and therefore circulation, by vigorous exercise of the arms may be useful. Exercise increases circulation, warms the body, and can prevent or limit vasoconstriction. If attacks are prolonged and frequent, vasodilator drugs, including calcium channel blockers and sympatholytic agents (alpha-adrenergic receptor blockers) may be helpful. Direct vasodilators may be effective in primary Raynaud phenomenon, but not in secondary Raynaud phenomenon. Transdermal nitroglycerin or a long-acting oral nitrate reduces the severity and frequency of attacks and provides symptomatic relief in both conditions. Applying nitroglycerin cream to the fingers may help heal skin ulcerations, which progress to necrosis if left untreated. Investigational drugs (angiotensin II-receptor blockers such as oral losartin, intravenous prostaglandins, topical nitric acid gel, and cilostazol) are also used. A sympathectomy to prevent vasoconstriction may be tried but is not always successful.

Nonpharmacologic management include massaging the affected digits; placing hands under the armpits or placing hands and feet in warm (never hot) water; climate control (avoiding winter air and air-conditioned rooms); dressing warmly in winter (coat with snug cuffs, hat, scarf, waterproof and insulated footwear, thermal underwear); clothing made of wool, silk, down, or polypropylene synthetics that retain warmth; running the car heater for a few minutes before beginning to drive and insulating the steering wheel; wearing socks and shoes or slippers indoors and keeping indoor temperatures above 70°F; handling cold drinks and frozen foods only with barrier hand protection (insulated glasses or sleeves, mittens, pot holders). Relaxation techniques such as structured relaxation exercises with concurrent biofeedback should be encouraged because they can decrease the frequency and severity of attacks. Feet and hands must be protected from injury, examined daily for skin changes, and lotion used to prevent drying. Pavlovian conditioning takes time to master but may be beneficial: the hands are immersed in 110°F water for 45 min while the rest of the body is exposed to cold or freezing temperatures in order to condition peripheral vessels to dilate in response to cold rather than constricting. Complementary and alternative therapies include acupuncture, ginkgo biloba to increase blood flow in primary RP, omega-3 and omega-6 fatty acids (in flaxseed oil) to reduce red blood cell aggregation and improve blood flow, and niacin to dilate blood vessels and increase circulation to the skin.

R. phenomenon Intermittent attacks of pallor or cyanosis of the small arteries and arterioles of the fingers as the result of inadequate arterial blood flow. This condition is associated with scleroderma, systemic lupus erythematosus, Buerger disease, nerve entrapment, and anorexia-bulimia. The signs, symptoms, and treatment are identical to those of Raynaud disease. SEE: *Nursing Diagnoses Appendix.*

rayon, purified (rā-ŏn) A fibrous form of regenerated cellulose manufactured by the viscose process, desulfured, washed, and bleached. Once used in surgical dressings and bandages.

razor bumps (rāz′ŏr) Pseudofolliculitis barbae.

RBBB *right bundle branch block.*

RBC, rbc *red blood cell; red blood count.*

RBE *relative biological effectiveness.*

RBRVS *resource-based relative value scale.*

RCD *relative cardiac dullness.*

R-CHOP *rituximab,* plus *CHOP* (chemotherapeutic agents to treat non-Hodgkin lymphoma).

RCMD *refractory cytopenia with multilineage dysplasia.*

RCP *Royal College of Physicians; Respiratory Care Practitioner.*

RCS *Royal College of Surgeons.*

RCVS *Reversible cerebral vasoconstriction syndrome.*

R.D.A. *right dorsoanterior,* presentation position of the fetus; *recommended dietary allowance.*

RDMS *registered diagnostic medical sonographer.*

R.D.P. *right dorsoposterior,* presentation position of the fetus.

RDR *relative dose response.*

RDS *respiratory distress syndrome.*

RE *radium emanation; right eye; reticuloendothelium.*

Re Symbol for the element rhenium.

re- [L. *re-, red-* again, against, back] Prefix meaning *back, again.*

reabsorb (rē″ăb-sorb′) To absorb again.

reabsorption (rē″ăb-sorp′shŭn) The process of absorbing again. It occurs in the kidney when some of the materials filtered out of the blood by the glomerulus are reabsorbed as the filtrate passes through the nephron.

reacher (rē′chĕr) A type of extension device for assisting persons with limited reach to grasp and manipulate objects in the performance of everyday tasks.

react (rē-ăkt′) [L. *re,* again, + *agere,* to act] **1.** To respond to a stimulus. **2.** To participate in a chemical reaction.

reactant (rē-ăk′tănt) A chemical or substance taking part in a chemical reaction.

   acute phase r. Acute phase protein.

   limiting r. The substance with the lowest concentration in a chemical reaction. Its amount determines the amount of product made from that reaction.

reaction (rē-ăk′shŭn) [LL. *reactus,* reacted] **1.** The response of an organism, or part of it, to a stimulus. **2.** In chemistry, a chemical process or change; transformation of one substance into another in response to a stimulus. **3.** An opposing action or counteraction. **4.** An emotional and mental response to a stimulus. Particular reactions are listed under the first word. SEE: e.g., *adverse drug reaction; anaphylactoid reaction; late-phase reaction.*

reaction of degeneration A change in muscle reactivity to electricity, seen in lower motor neuron paralysis.

reactivate (rē-ăk′tĭ-vāt″) To make active again (e.g., to restore to a physiological response or to awaken a dormant infection).

reactivation (rē-ăk″tĭ-vā′shŭn) The process of making something active again.

reactive (rē-ak′tiv) **1.** Capable of participating in a chemical reaction. **2.** Emotionally or psychologically responsive. **3.** Of antibodies and some allergic and immune illnesses, triggered by an antigen. **4.** Inflammatory.

reactive airway disease Any disease in which there is reversible bronchospasm, such as asthma. SEE: *asthma.*

reactive airways dysfunction syndrome The development of persistent bronchospasm in a previously nonasthmatic patient after an exposure to a high concentration of an inhaled irritant, for example, a chemical fume, gas, or smoke. It may persist for months. It is treated with inhaled corticosteroids.

reactive attachment disorder A developmental disorder of infancy or early childhood marked either by social isolation and withdrawal or by indiscriminate sociability. The disorder may result from neglect of the child by his or her primary caregiver or from frequent changes in caregivers (esp. in children who have lost their parents or who have been moved frequently from one foster home to another).

reactive oxygen species ABBR: ROS. Oxidant (2).

reactive tracing A recording of the fetal heart rate in which normal accelerations of the fetal heart rate are observed during fetal movement.

reactivity (rē″ăk-tĭv′ĭ-tē) **1.** The ability to respond to a stimulus. **2.** In measurement of function or behavior, the influence that the presence of the examiner and the assessment process may have on performance and therefore on the outcome or finding.

   cross r. The ability of an antibody to bind with more than one antigen or of an antigen to bind with more than one antibody.

reactogenic (rē-ak″tŏ-jen′ik) [*react(ion)* + *-genic*] Capable of producing a physiologic response, as a vaccine that elicits an antibody response. **reactogenicity** (-jĕ-nis′ĭt-ē), *n.*

read back (rēd băk) A method of preventing errors in which information relayed to one person is repeated and verified in a slightly different form as a means of confirming its accuracy. For example, a respiratory therapist is asked to administer an aerosol to a patient named "Dabs." Before giving the medication, he repeats the name of the patient out loud as "Dabs...delta, alpha, bravo, sam. Have I spelled the name correctly?"

readiness (red′ē-nĕs) **1.** Preparation for an event or a task. **2.** In psychology, the capability or willingness to learn something new; openness.

   school r. An educational milestone in the development of a child, experienced when he or she is independent and mature enough to listen, work, and play in a structured learning environment.

reading (rēd) Interpreting or perusing written or printed characters or material. Reading may or may not include comprehension of the material.

   lip r. SEE: *lip reading.*

   pulse r. The assessment of the characteristics of the radial pulse as an aid in the diagnosis of disease, a technique used in traditional Chinese medicine, Ayurvedic medicine, among other healing traditions.

reading difficulty A deficiency in a person's fluent use and comprehension of written language. SEE: *dyslexia.*

reading disability Dyslexia.

reading disorder A condition that interferes with or prevents comprehension of written or printed material; used esp. in reference to children. In some adults, the condition may have developed from a brain injury or may have persisted from infancy. SEE: *dyslexia.*

reading machine for the blind An electronic device that converts printed matter into speech. Several machines for home use are available. Information may be obtained from the Lighthouse National Center for Vision and Aging at (800) 334-5497 or the American Foundation for the Blind at (800) 232-5463.

readmission (rē″ăd-mish′ŏn) [*re-* + * admission*] The return of a patient to inpatient hospital care shortly after discharge (typically within 30 days of discharge). **readmit** (-mit′), *v.*

ready-to-use Able to be dispensed with minimal if any effort or preparation; prepackaged.

ready-to-use therapeutic food SEE: under *food.*

reagent (rē-ā′jĕnt) [L. *reagere,* to react] **1.** A substance involved in a chemical reaction. **2.** A substance used to detect the presence or amount of another substance. **3.** A subject of a psychological experiment, esp. one reacting to a stimulus.

reagin (rē-ā-jĭn, -gĭn) [Ger. *Reagin,* fr. *reag(ieren),* to react + *-in*] A type of immunoglobulin E (IgE) present in the serum of atopic individuals that mediates hypersensitivity reactions. SYN: *sensitizing antibody.*

   rapid plasma r. ABBR: RPR. A nonspecific serological test for syphilis. The RPR titer is elevated in most patients with syphilis (and falsely elevated in some patients with other diseases). The titer decreases or returns to normal after successful eradication of the disease.

   reaginic (rē-ă-jĭn′ĭk, -gĭn′), *adj.*

reality (rē-al′ĭt-ē) **1.** The quality or state of being real or actual. **2.** All that exists, as opposed to those ideas or mental images that are imagined.

reality orientation An intervention to orient people with early dementia or delirium. It involves repetition of verbal and nonverbal information. The environment remains constant, and the person is reminded about names, dates, weather, and other pertinent information.

reality principle (rē-al′ĭt-ē) SEE: under *principle.*

reality testing The attempt by the individual to evaluate and understand the real world and his or her relation to it.

reality therapy A psychiatric treatment based on the concept that some patients deny the reality of the world around them. Therapy is directed to assist patients in recognizing and accepting the present, instead of dwelling on the past. Patients undergoing reality therapy are helped to cope with present demands, limit distortions, and anticipate future needs.

real-time **1.** Pert. to technologies that report or record events and processes as they happen; said, e.g., of imaging procedures that take moving pictures rather than static images of body structures. **2.** Pert. to computer systems that analyze data at the same rate as data is received, allowing automatic control of a process.

reamer (rē′mĕr) A small instrument used in dentistry for enlarging the root canal of a tooth.

reanastomosis, surgical (rē-ă-năs-tō-mō′sĭs) The rejoining of structures, esp. vessels or tubes, that had been previously ligated.

reanimate (rē-ăn′ĭ-māt) [L. *re,* again, + *animare,* fill with life] To reactivate, restore to life, revive, or resuscitate.

reapers' keratitis (rēp′ĕrz) SEE: under *keratitis.*

reasonable and customary fees In health care finance, the prevailing reimbursement for health services or medical care in a specific region or state. The term is vague. It reflects the reality that in differing states, regions, or health care institutions, the economics of health care may vary, owing to regional attitudes about care, or differences in professional expertise or available technologies.

reasonable care In law, the degree of care that an ordinarily prudent or reasonable person would exercise under the same or similar circumstances.

reasonable certainty Epistemological likelihood based on considerable evidence or the opinion of most experts that an event has resulted from a specific cause. The concept of reasonable certainty is a legal one; it implies a measure of proof acceptable to a jury in a court of law rather than a proof that might be acceptable to the most stringent scientist.

reasonable cost The amount a third

party (usually the medical insurer) will actually reimburse for health care. This amount is based on the cost to the provider for delivering that service.

reasoning The making of judgments or drawing of conclusions based on evidence, education, experience, training, and/or personal biases.

reasoning, narrative A means of understanding people and their behaviors in the context of their life histories and their interpretations of the important events in their lives.

reassessment (rē″ă-ses′mĕnt) [re- + assessment] The evaluation and care of patients recovered from the field, performed en route to the hospital. It includes appraisals of mental status, airway, breathing, circulation, vital signs, chief complaints, and the effectiveness of initial treatments.

reattachment (rē″ă-tăch′mĕnt) **1.** Recementing of a dental crown. **2.** Re-embedding of periodontal ligament fibers into the cementum of a tooth that has become dislodged. **3.** Rejoining of parts that have been separated, as a finger that has been traumatically detached. SEE: limb replantation.

reauthorization (rē″aw-thŏr-ĭ-zā′shŭn) The renewal of an act of legislation, e.g., one that authorizes certain forms of treatment or health care funding.

rebase (rē-bās′) To refit a denture by replacing the base material without altering the occlusal characteristics.

rebound (rē′bownd″) **1.** A reflex response in which sudden withdrawal of a stimulus is followed by increased activity, e.g., an increase in heart rate or blood pressure when beta-blocking drugs or clonidine are withheld. **2.** A return to a state or condition that existed before treatment. **rebound,** v.

rebreathing (rē′brē″thĕng) The inhalation of gases that had been previously exhaled.

Rebuck skin window test (rē′bŭk) An in vivo method of assessing inflammation. A superficial abrasion is made in the skin and a glass coverslip applied to the area. Leukocytes accumulate at the site and adhere to the coverslip.

rebuttal (ri-bŭt′ăl) In law, evidence or testimony that contradicts or sheds doubt upon the assertions of the opposing party in a dispute. **rebut** (ri-bŭt′), v.

recalcification (rē″kăl-sĭ-fĭ-kā′shŭn) [L. re, again, + calx, lime, + facere, to make] The restoration of calcium salts to tissues from which they have been withdrawn.

recalcification test A test for excessive blood clotting, used esp. in cancer-related thrombosis. Also known as the modified recalcification test.

recalcitrant Difficult to treat; resistant to commonly used treatments.

recall (rē′kăwl, rē-kăwl′) [″ + AS. ceal-

lian, to call] **1.** The act of bringing back to mind something previously learned or experienced. SEE: memory. **2.** To remove from use; to restrict marketing of a substance or product, usually as a result of problems with product safety.

 24-hr dietary r. A dietary assessment method in which a person lists the foods he or she actually consumed during the previous day. It can provide an estimate of the absolute quantity of food consumed and identify habitual food intake versus unusual consumption (or the lack of food consumption, e.g., during fasts prior to medical procedures).

recall bias Distortion introduced into a research investigation that relies on the memory of subjects, specifically, their recollections of elements that might have contributed to the eventual development of a disease or condition. A research subject's memories after the occurrence of an adverse event, e.g., the diagnosis of a serious ailment, may be unduly influenced by his or her assumptions, beliefs, expectations, or prior education about possible causes of that ailment and thus may not reflect the true breadth of exposure contributing to the occurrence of the disease.

recall rate In radiology, the percentage of individuals asked to return for follow-up imaging after an anomaly is found on an initial study, e.g., the number of women who are screened with mammography and who have to return for spot films, ultrasound, or magnetic resonance imaging.

recanalization (rē′kăn-ăl-ĭ-zā″shŭn) Reestablishment of an opening through a vessel that had been previously occluded.

receiver (rē-sēv′ĕr) [″ + capere, to take] **1.** A container for holding a gas or a distillate. **2.** An apparatus for receiving electric waves or current, such as a radio receiver.

recency bias Recency effect.

recency effect (rē′sĕn-sē) The tendency to recall recent events under the assumption that they are normal even if they are abnormal. This effect may sometimes result in misdiagnosis. SYN: recency bias.

receptaculum (rē″sĕp-tăk′ū-lŭm) pl. **receptacula** [L.] A vessel or cavity in which a fluid is received.

receptor (ri-sep′tŏr) [L. receptor, a receiver] **1.** In cell biology, a structure in the cell membrane or within a cell that combines with a drug, hormone, chemical mediator, or an infectious agent to alter an aspect of the functioning of the cell. **2.** A sensory nerve ending. SYN: ceptor.

 accessory r. Any of the proteins on the surface of T lymphocytes that enhance the response of the T-cell receptor to foreign antigens and stimulate signals from the receptor to the cytoplasm. SEE: *antigen-presenting* **cell**; *T-cell* **r.**

adrenergic r. A cell membrane protein that mediates the effects of adrenergic stimulation on target organs by catecholamines.

alpha-adrenergic r. A site in autonomic nerve pathways responsive to the adrenergic agents norepinephrine and epinephrine In general, alpha-1 receptors produce excitatory responses, and alpha-2 receptors produce inhibitory responses. SEE: *beta-adrenergic* **r.**

antigen r. Receptors, primarily on white blood cells, that bind with the epitope in foreign antigens, stimulating an immune response. SEE: *epitope.*

auditory r. One of the hair cells in the organ of Corti in the cochlea of the ear.

beta-adrenergic r. A site in autonomic nerve pathways responsive to the adrenergic agents norepinephrine and epinephrine. In general, beta-1 receptors produce excitatory responses, and beta-2 receptors produce inhibitory responses. SEE: *alpha-adrenergic* **r.**

CD r. Any of the markers on T lymphocytes and other white blood cells that, along with major histocompatibility complex (MHC) genes, is responsible for the recognition of antigens. More than 100 receptor molecules have been identified. CD4 receptors on T4 lymphocytes are the sites to which HIV binds, producing infection. SEE: *AIDS; cluster of differentiation.*

cell r. Any of the cell membrane proteins or intracellular proteins that react with chemicals, e.g., hormones, circulating in the cell's environment. The reaction triggers the cell's characteristic response to the hormone or other chemical. SEE: *drug r.*

chemokine r. ABBR: CCR. Any of several protein receptors for chemokines that spans the cell membrane and links to intracellular G proteins. The cell-to-cell signaling and regulating effects of chemokines, e.g., on inflammation or hematopoiesis, are mediated through chemokine receptors, which can be blocked with specific antagonist drugs. CCR5 and CXCR4 are chemokine receptors that are also receptors for HIV. The virus uses these receptors to gain entry into T cells, macrophages, and other CD4$^+$ cells.

cholinergic r. A site in a nerve synapse or effector cell that responds to the effect of acetylcholine.

complement r. ABBR: CR. A receptor on neutrophils, macrophages, lymphocytes, and other cells that allows complement factors to bind, thus stimulating inflammation, phagocytosis, and cell destruction.

contact r. A receptor that produces a sensation such as touch, temperature, or pain that can be localized in or on the surface of the body.

cutaneous r. A receptor located in the skin.

distance r. A sense organ that responds to stimuli arising some distance from the body, such as the eye, ear, or nose. SYN: *teleceptor.*

dopamine r. Any of at least six receptors that bind dopamine in the brain. They influence body movements and emotional states. The dopamine receptors are designated D1, D2a, D2b, D3, D4, and D5. Each has an identifiably different function. The D2a receptor, for example, has a strong affinity for antipsychotic drugs, such as haloperidol.

drug r. A complex containing protein, located on a cell membrane, capable of being stimulated by drugs in the extracellular fluid, and translating that stimulation into an intracellular response. SEE: *cell r.*

estrogen r. A cellular protein that binds female sex steroid hormones. When estrogens attach to it, they stimulate cells to transcribe DNA and manufacture proteins, typically leading to cellular growth and proliferation.

Fc r. A receptor on phagocytes (neutrophils, monocytes, and macrophages) that binds Fc fragments of immunoglobulins G and E. SEE: *immunoglobulin; macrophage* **processing**; *phagocytosis.*

gravity r. A macular hair cell of the utricle and saccule. It responds to changes in position of the head and linear acceleration.

histamine H$_3$ r. H$_3$ receptor.

homing r. An adhesion molecule on leukocytes that binds to endothelial cells in blood vessels. It is used by white blood cells to guide them to inflamed or infected tissues in the body.

H$_3$ r. A presynaptic receptor in the central nervous system that controls the release of histamine and other neurotransmitters, including acetylcholine, dopamine, and norepinephrine. It influences arousal and sleep, cognition, attention, and other body functions. SYN: *histamine H$_3$ r.*

image r. ABBR: IR. Any device used in radiology to detect the energy released by the imaging instrument after it passes through the imaged body part.

immunologic r. A receptor on the surface of white blood cells that identifies the type of cell and links with monokines, lymphokines, or other chemical mediators during the immune response.

killer cell inhibitory r. ABBR: KIR. A receptor on the surface of natural killer (NK) cells that bind with major histocompatibility complex (MHC) class I markers and inhibit the ability of NK cells to destroy target cells. Different groups of KIRs may create subsets of

NK cells that bind to and destroy different targets. SEE: *natural killer* **cell**.

olfactory r. Any of the bipolar nerve cells found in olfactory epithelium whose axons form olfactory nerve fibers.

opiate r. A specific site on a cell surface that interacts in a highly selective fashion with opiate drugs. These receptors mediate the major known pharmacological actions and side effects of opiates and the functions of the endogenous opiate-like substances (endorphins and enkephalins).

optic r. A rod or cone cell of the retina.

pattern recognition r. ABBR: PRR. A receptor on an antigen-presenting cell of the immune system that recognizes molecular sequences found on disease-causing organisms but not host cells. PRRs detect the presence of pathogen-associated chemicals such as lipopolysaccharides, mannans, and teichoic acids.

proprioceptive r. A muscle or tendon spindle. These are the receptors for muscle stretching or kinesthetic stimuli.

rotary r. Any of the hair cells in the cristae of the ampulla of the semicircular ducts of the ear. They are stimulated by angular acceleration or rotation.

ryanodine r. ABBR: RyR. The release channel for calcium ions that is found on the membranes of the sarcoplasmic reticulum of skeletal muscles.

sensory r. A sensory nerve ending, a cell or group of cells, or a sense organ that when stimulated produces an afferent or sensory impulse.

CLASSIFICATION: *Exteroreceptors* are receptors located on or near the surface that respond to stimuli from the outside world. They include eye and ear receptors (for remote stimuli) and touch, temperature, and pain receptors (for contact). *Interoceptors* are those in the mucous linings of the respiratory and digestive tracts that respond to internal stimuli; also called visceroceptors. *Proprioceptors* are those responding to stimuli arising within body tissues.

Receptors also are classified according to the nature of stimuli to which they respond. These include *chemoreceptors,* which respond to chemicals (taste buds, olfactory cells, receptors in aortic and carotid bodies); *pressoreceptors,* which respond to pressure (receptors in the aortic and carotid sinuses); *photoreceptors,* which respond to light (rods and cones); and *tactile receptors,* which respond to touch (Meissner corpuscle).

stretch r. A proprioceptor located in a muscle or tendon that is stimulated by a stretch or pull. SEE: *proprioceptor.*

taste r. A gustatory cell of a taste bud.

T-cell r. ABBR: TCR. One of two polypeptide chains (α or β) on the surface of T lymphocytes that recognize and bind foreign antigens. TCRs are antigen specific; their activity depends on antigen processing by macrophages or other antigen-presenting cells and the presence of major histocompatibility complex proteins to which peptides from the antigen are bound. SEE: *autoimmunity; immune* **response**; *T* **cell**.

temperature r. Any of the free nerve endings in the dermis that detect heat and cold.

toll-like r. ABBR: TLR. Any of several receptors on macrophages and other immune and endothelial cells that reacts with pathogen components such as bacterial peptidoglycan or lipopolysaccharide. Activation of a receptor stimulates release of cytokines and other chemical signals that are part of innate immunity.

tonic r. A sensory receptor that continues to trigger a response for minutes or hours after it is stimulated.

touch r. A Merkel disk, a Meissner corpuscle, or a nerve plexus around a hair root.

receptor-binding screening A method of identifying useful drugs by exposing large numbers of chemicals to cellular receptors and selecting those agents that attach to and activate the receptors.

receptor trafficking The movement of chemical receptors from one cellular structure to another, e.g., from the cell membrane to the cytoplasm.

receptosome (rē-sĕp′tō-sōm) Endosome.

recess (rē′ses″) [L. *recessus,* withdrawal] A small indentation, depression, or cavity.

cochlear r. A small concavity, lying between the two limbs of the vestibular crest in the vestibule of the ear, that lodges the beginning of the cochlear duct.

epitympanic r. The upper portion of the middle ear, which leads posteriorly to the mastoid antrum. SYN: *attic*.

hepatorenal r. A deep pocket inside the upper right peritoneal cavity between the liver and the peritoneal surface of the right kidney. When a person is lying on his back, fluid from the omental bursa will pool into the hepatorenal recess. SYN: *hepatorenal pouch*.

infundibular r. A small projection of the third ventricle that extends into the infundibular stalk of the hypophysis.

nasopalatine r. A small depression on the floor of the nasal cavity near the nasal septum, lying immediately over the incisive foramen.

omental r. Any of three pocket-like extensions of the omental bursa. The superior recess extends upward behind the caudate lobe of the liver; the inferior recess extends downward into the great omentum; and the lineal recess extends laterally to the hilus of the spleen.

pharyngeal r. A recess in the lateral wall of the nasopharynx lying above and behind the opening to the auditory tube. SYN: *Rosenmüller fossa.*

pineal r. The recess of the roof of the third ventricle extending into the stalk of the pineal body.

piriform r. A deep depression in the wall of the laryngeal pharynx lying lateral to the orifice of the larynx. It is bounded laterally by the thyroid cartilage and medially by the cricoid and arytenoid cartilages. It is a common site for lodgment of foreign objects.

sphenoethmoidal r. A small space in the nasal fossa above the superior concha. It lies between the ethmoid bone and the anterior surface of the body of the sphenoid bone and posteriorly receives the opening of the sphenoidal sinus.

tonsillar r. Tonsillar **fossa.**

umbilical r. A dilatation on the left main branch of the portal vein that marks the position where the umbilical vein was originally attached.

recession (rē-sĕsh′ŭn) [L. *recessus,* recess] The withdrawal of a part from its normal position.

gingival r. Apical migration of the gingiva resulting from faulty toothbrushing technique, tooth malposition, friction from soft tissues, gingival inflammation, and high frenum attachment. The incidence of recession may result in sensitivity, increased susceptibility to caries, and difficulty maintaining clean teeth. SEE: *gingivitis.*

recessive (ri-ses′iv) [L. *recessus,* withdrawal, retreat] **1.** Tending to recede or go back; lacking or not exercising control. **2.** In genetics, pert. to a trait or characteristic that is expressed only if present in the genes received from both parents

recessive disorder Any disease passed from one generation to the next by the inheritance of recessive genes.

recessus (rē-sĕs′ŭs) [L.] SEE: *recess.*

recidivation (rē-sĭd″ĭ-vā′shŭn) [L. *recidivus,* falling back] **1.** The relapse of a disease or recurrence of a symptom. **2.** The return to criminal activity.

recidivism (rē-sĭd′ĭ-vĭ-zĭm) Habitual criminality; the repetition of antisocial acts.

recidivist (rē-sĭd′ĭ-vĭst) **1.** A confirmed criminal. **2.** A patient, esp. one with mental illness, who has repeated relapses into behavior marked by antisocial acts.

recidivity (rē-sĭd-ĭv′-ĭ-tē) Tendency to relapse, or to return to a former condition.

recipe (rĕs′ĭ-pē) [L., take] **1.** Take, indicated by the sign ℞. **2.** A prescription

or formula for a medicine. SEE: *prescription.* **3.** A set of instructions for preparing food from multiple ingredients.

recipient (rĭ-sĭp′ē-ĕnt) [L. *recipiens,* receiving] One who receives something, esp. blood, tissues, or an organ, provided by a donor, as in a blood transfusion or kidney transplant. SEE: *donor.*

reciprocal (rĭ-sĭp′rō-kăl) [L. *reciprocus,* alternate] Interchangeable.

reciprocal inhibition SEE: under *inhibition.*

reciprocation (rĭ-sĭp″rō-kā′shŭn) [L. *reciprocare,* to move backward and forward] The countering of a reaction by an action. In dentistry, the action of one part of a dental device to counter the effect of another part.

reciprocity (re″sĭ-pros′ĭt-ē) The recognition and acceptance by one governmental body of the legal practices, procedures, or rulings of another.

Recklinghausen, Friedrich D. von (rek′ling-how″zĕn) Ger. pathologist, 1833–1910.

R. disease, von Recklinghausen disease Type 1 **neurofibromatosis.**

R. tumor, von Recklinghausen tumor A benign adenoleiomyofibroma on the wall of the fallopian tube or the posterior uterine wall.

reclination (rĕk″lĭ-nā′shŭn) [L. *reclinatio,* lean back] A cataract operation where the lens is turned over in the vitreous.

recline (rē-klīn′) [L. *reclinare*] To be in recumbent position; to lie down.

recognition (rĕk″ŏg-nĭsh′ĭn) The ability to identify a previously encountered item; the memory of a person, place, or thing as something familiar.

recoil (rē′koil″, rĭ-koil′) [ME. *recoilen*] The springing back of body tissues to their relaxed state after they have been squeezed or compressed.

recombinant (rē-kom′bĭ-nănt) ABBR: r. In genetics and molecular biology, pert. to genetic material combined from different sources.

recombinant DNA SEE: under *DNA.*

recombinant tPA Tissue plasminogen **activator.**

recombinase (rē-kŏm′bĭn-ās) [*recombinan(t)* + ″] Any enzyme that catalyzes nucleic acid recombination, i.e., the rearrangement of genetic material on a strand of DNA or RNA.

recombination (rē″kŏm-bĭ-nā′shŭn) **1.** Joining again. **2.** In genetics, the joining of gene combinations in the offspring that were not present in the parents.

Recombivax HB (rĭ-kŏm′bĭ-văks″) Hepatitis B (recombinant) vaccine.

recomposition (rē-kŏm-pō-zĭ′shŭn) [L. *re,* again, + *composer,* to place together] The recombination of constituents or parts.

recompression [″ + LL. *compressare,*

press together] The resubjection of a person to increased atmospheric pressure, as in the treatment of caisson disease (the bends). SEE: *aeroembolism; hyperbaric chamber.*

reconcentration (rē-kŏn″sĕn-trā′shŭn) The process of repeated concentration.

reconditioning The process of restoring normal cardiovascular and neuromuscular function following injury, disease, or inactivity. SEE: *rehabilitation.*

reconstitute (rē-kon′stĭ-toot″) [re- + L. *constituere,* to set up] **1.** In pharmacology, to restore a dried substance to a fluid form that can be used for injection. **2.** To rebuild a substance or reservoir within the body (such as bone marrow) to a natural or a functionally healthy state.

reconstitution (rē″kŏn-stĭ-tū′shŭn) The return of a substance previously altered for preservation and storage to its original state, as is done with dried blood plasma.

reconstruction (rē″kŏn-strŭk′shŏn) [re- + construction] **1.** Surgical repair or restoration of a missing part or organ. **2.** The manipulation of digitized information obtained during body imaging into interpretable pictures that represent anatomical details and diseases. SYN: *image r.*

   dose r. An estimate of the total exposure of a person or population to the environmental release of a toxic substance, such as a pollutant or a sudden burst of radiation.

   breast r. Plastic surgery to restore the appearance of the breast after mastectomy. It may rely upon techniques such as the use of breast implants or tissue flaps.

   image r. Reconstruction (2).

   r. of the knee Any procedure to reestablish stability of the knee after injury, usually to the anterior or posterior cruciate ligaments or to both.

   neovaginal r. Construction of an artificial vagina after the vagina has been removed because of cancer or trauma of the pelvic area. The tissue used may be obtained from muscle and skin tissue from the abdomen. Normal sexual function is possible after the area has healed.

   surgical ventricular r. Removal of sections of the heart that have been damaged during a heart attack and are no longer helping to push blood to the body through the aorta.

   transverse rectus abdominis musculocutaneous flap r. SEE: *transverse rectus abdominis musculocutaneous flap reconstruction.*

recontamination (rē″kŏn-tăm″ĭ-nā′shŭn) The contamination of a recently disinfected or sterilized instrument before its use in patient care. It may result from inadequate packaging or mishandling of instruments after they have been rid of microorganisms.

record (rek′ŏrd) **1.** A written account of something. SEE: *problem-oriented medical record.* **2.** In dentistry, a registration of jaw relations in a malleable material or on a device.

   anecdotal r. Notes used in nursing education to document observed incidents of a student's clinical behavior related to attainment of clinical learning objectives. Such anecdotal notes have not been treated as hearsay evidence in a court but have been upheld as documented evidence for failing a student.

   electronic health r. ABBR: EHR. Electronic medical **r.**

   electronic medical r. ABBR: EMR. A computerized database that typically includes demographic, past medical and surgical, preventive, laboratory and radiographic, and drug information about a patient. It is the repository for active notations about a patient's health. Most EMRs also contain billing and insurance information and other accounting tools. SYN: *electronic health r.*

   functional chew-in r. A record of the natural chewing action of the mandible made on an occlusion rim by the teeth or scribing studs.

   interocclusal r. Bite **plate**.

   medical r. A written transcript of information obtained from a patient, guardian, or medical professionals concerning a patient's health history, diagnostic tests, diagnoses, treatment, and prognosis.

   medication administration r. ABBR: MAR. A file maintained on hospital units that documents the schedule and dosing of medications given to patients.

   personal health r. A summary of a patient's health care status (allergies, drugs taken, past hospitalizations, lab tests, radiology results, and surgeries) that is kept by the patient privately rather than stored in a hospital or third-party database.

recover (rĭ-kŭv′ĕr) [O.Fr. *recoverer*] **1.** To regain health after illness; to regain a former state of health. **2.** To regain a normal state, as to recover from fright.

recovery (ri-kŏv′ĕ-rē) [Fr. *recoverer* fr. L. *recuperare,* to regain] **1.** The process or act of becoming well or returning to a state of health. **2.** Compensation awarded by a court to the party that prevailed in a lawsuit. **3.** Emergence from anesthesia.

   inversion r. In magnetic resonance imaging, a standard pulse sequence used to produce T1-weighted images.

   motor r. Improvement in the performance of a fatigued muscle or in the movement of a group of muscles paralyzed by stroke or injury.

   muscle r. Improvement in the performance of skeletal muscles used during intense or prolonged exercise.

nutritional r. The restoration of optimal nutrition after illness, injury, or starvation; the correction of the body's balance of macro- and micronutrients.

recovery house A residential treatment program or transitional residence for people who are overcoming the effects of drugs or alcohol or are recovering from other diseases or addictions.

recovery position SEE: under *position*.

recreation (rĕk-rē-ā'shŭn) Participation in any endeavor that is entertaining, relaxing, or refreshing. Recreational activities may be personal or private (e.g., reading, painting), social (e.g., team sports or dance), physical (e.g., hunting), or mental (e.g., meditating or praying); they may be active or passive. Many recreational activities combine more than one of these elements.

recredentialing (rē-krē-dĕn'chăl-ēng) The process whereby an individual certified in a profession completes the current requirements for certification in that profession.

recrudescence (rē"kroo-dĕs'ĕns) Relapse.

recrudescent (rē"kroo-dĕs'ĕnt) Assuming renewed activity after a dormant or inactive period.

recruitment (rĭ-kroot'mĕnt) [O.Fr. *recrute,* new growth] **1.** An increased response to a reflex when a stimulus is prolonged, even though the strength of the stimulus is unchanged, due to activation of increasingly greater numbers of motor neurons. **2.** In audiology, an increase in the perceived intensity of a sound out of proportion to the actual increase in the sound level. **3.** The addition of staff to a hospital or clinic during expansion of employment. **4.** The reopening of collapsed alveoli.

r. of end organs An increase in discharge from sensory end organs, resulting from an increase in the number of end organs discharging and an increase in frequency of discharge from each.

recruitment maneuver Any technique in which sustained high airway pressures are applied to the patent airway in order to diminish collapse of alveoli during mechanical ventilation.

rectal (rĕk'tăl) [L. *rectus,* straight] Pert. to the rectum.

rectalgia (rĕk-tăl'jē-ă) [L. *rectus,* straight, + Gr. *algos,* pain] Pain in the rectum.

rectal reflex SEE: under *reflex*.

recti-, rect- [L. *rectus,* right, straight] Prefixes meaning *right, straight*.

rectification (rĕk"tĭ-fĭ-kā'shŭn) [" + *facere,* to make] **1.** The process of refining or purifying a substance. **2.** The act of straightening or correcting. **3.** The process of changing an alternating current into a pulsating direct current.

rectified (rĕk'tĭ-fīd) Made pure or straight; set right.

rectifier (rĕk'tĭ-fī"ĕr) [L. *rectum,* straight, + *-ficare,* to make] In electricity, a device for transforming an alternating current into a pulsating direct current.

rectitis (rĕk-tī'tĭs) Proctitis.

recto-, rect- [L. *rectum (intestinum),* straight (intestine)] Prefixes meaning *rectum, rectal*.

rectoabdominal (rĕk"tō-ăb-dŏm'ĭ-năl) [L. *rectus,* straight, + *abdomen,* belly] Pert. to the rectum and abdomen.

rectocele (rek'tŏ-sēl") [*recto- + -cele*] Protrusion or herniation into the posterior vaginal wall by the anterior wall of the rectum. SEE: *cystocele*.

rectoclysis (rĕk-tŏk'lĭ-sĭs) [" + Gr. *klysis,* a washing] The slow introduction of fluid into the rectum.

rectococcygeal (rĕk-tō-kŏk-sĭj'ē-ăl) [" + Gr. *kokkyx,* coccyx] Pert. to the rectum and coccyx.

rectocolitis (rĕk"tō-kō-lī'tĭs) Proctocolitis.

rectocystotomy (rĕk"tō-sĭs-tŏt'ō-mē) [" + Gr. *kystis,* bladder, + *tome,* incision] An incision of the bladder through the rectum, usually to remove a stone.

rectolabial (rĕk"tō-lā'bē-ăl) [" + *labium,* lip] Pert. to the rectum and a labium of the vulva.

rectopexy (rĕk'tō-pĕk-sē) Suture of the rectum to some other part, for example, presacral fascia.

rectoscope (rĕk'tō-skōp) [" + Gr. *skopein,* to examine] Proctoscope.

rectoscopy (rĕk-tŏs'kō-pē) Proctoscopy.

rectosigmoid (rĕk"tō-sĭg'moyd) [" + Gr. *sigma,* letter S, + *eidos,* form, shape] The upper part of the rectum and the adjoining portion of the sigmoid colon.

rectosigmoidectomy (rĕk"tō-sĭg"moy-dĕk'tō-mē) [" + " + *ektome,* excision] Surgical removal of the rectum and sigmoid colon.

rectostenosis (rĕk"tō-stĕn-ō'sĭs) [" + Gr. *stenos,* narrow] Stricture of the rectum.

rectostomy (rĕk-tŏs'tō-mē) Proctostomy.

rectotomy (rĕk-tŏt'ō-mē) Proctotomy.

rectourethral (rĕk"tō-ū-rē'thrăl) [" + Gr. *ourethra,* urethra] Pert. to the rectum and urethra.

rectouterine (rĕk"tō-ū'tĕr-ĭn) [" + *uterus,* womb] Pert. to the rectum and uterus.

rectovaginal (rĕk"tō-văj'ĭ-năl) [" + *vagina,* sheath] Pert. to the rectum and vagina.

rectovesical (rĕk"tō-vĕs'ĭ-kăl) [" + *vesica,* bladder] Pert. to the rectum and bladder.

rectovestibular (rĕk"tō-vĕs-tĭb'ū-lăr) [" + *vestibulum,* vestibule] Pert. to the rectum and vestibule of the vagina.

rectovulvar (rĕk″tō-vŭl′văr) [″ + *vulva,* covering] Pert. to the rectum and vulva.

rectum (rĕk′tŭm) [L., straight] The lower part of the large intestine, about 5 in (12.7 cm) long, between the sigmoid colon and the anal canal. Its smooth muscle layer is the effector for the defecation reflex, the reflex centers for which are in the second, third, and fourth sacral segments of the spinal cord. SEE: illus.

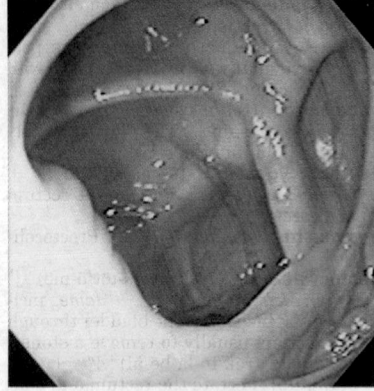

RECTUM

Rectum seen during colonoscopy

rectus (rĕk′tŭs) [L.] Straight; not crooked.

recumbency (rĭ-kŭm′bĕn-sē) [L. *recumbens,* lying down] The condition of leaning or reclining.

recumbent (rē-kŭm′bĕnt) **1.** Lying down. SEE: *position, left lateral recumbent; position, unilateral recumbent; prone.* **2.** Inactive, idle.

   dorsal r. Lying on one's back. SYN: *supine* (1).

   lateral r. Lying on one's side.

   ventral r. Lying with one's anterior side down. SYN: *prone* (1).

recuperation (rĭ-kū″pĕr-ā′shŭn) [L. *recuperare,* to recover] The process of returning to normal health following an illness.

recurrence (rĭ-kŭr′ĕns) Relapse. **recurrent** (-ĕnt), *adj.*

recurrent pregnancy loss SEE: under *loss.*

recurvation (rī″kŭr-vā′shŭn) [L. *recurvus,* bent back] The act of bending backward.

recurvatum (rē-kŭr-vā′tŭm) Backward bowing. At the knee, it is called genu recurvatum; at the elbow, it is called cubital recurvatum.

recurve (rē-kŭrv′) To bend backward.

red (red) A primary color of the spectrum that, when added to blue, forms purple, and when added to yellow, forms orange.

   Congo r. An odorless red-brown powder used in testing for amyloid. In polarized light, amyloid treated with Congo red produces a green fluorescence.

   cresol r. An indicator of pH. It is yellow below pH 7.4 and red above 9.0.

   methyl r. An indicator of pH. It is red at pH 4.4 and yellow at 6.2.

   phenol r. Phenolsulfonphthalein.

   scarlet r. A red azo dye used to stimulate healing of indolent ulcers, burns, wounds, and so on; in histology, used as a stain. SYN: *rubrum scarlatinum.*

   vital r. A stain used in preparing tissues for microscopic examination.

red bag waste SEE: under *waste.*

red blood cell Erythrocyte.

   spiculed r.b.c. Spiculed red cell.

red blood cell scan technetium Tc 99m RBC.

redbug (rĕd′bŭg) Chiggers.

red cell ghost In a blood smear, a large, pale, crescent-shaped cell devoid of internal contents and produced by hemolysis. Such cells are always indicative of disease. SYN: *achromocyte; crescent body; ghost corpuscle; phantom cell; selenoid cell.*

red cross **1.** A red cross on a white background; an internationally recognized sign of a medical installation or of medical personnel. **2.** The emblem of the American Red Cross.

redia (rē′dē-ă) *pl.* **rediae** [Francesco Redi, It. naturalist, 1626–1698] The stage in the life cycle of a trematode that follows the sporocyst stage. It is a saclike form with an oral sucker and a blind gut. Rediae are produced within the sporocyst and in turn develop into second-generation rediae or cercariae.

redifferentiation (rē″dĭf-ĕr-ĕn″shē-ā′shŭn) The respecialization of dedifferentiated cells, as occurs in the regeneration of an amphibian limb.

red. in pulv. [L., *reductus in pulverem*] Let it be reduced to powder.

redintegration (rĕd-ĭn″tĕ-grā′shŭn) [L. *redintegratio*] **1.** Restitution of a part. **2.** Restoration to health. **3.** Recall by mental association.

redistribution **1.** The matching of care personnel resources to the population's site of care. The term usually is used in discussing the maldistribution of in-hospital personnel compared with in-community personnel. **2.** The return of blood flow to an ischemic segment of myocardium. During exercise, regions of the heart supplied by partially occluded arteries are deprived of blood, a condition that may foster angina pectoris. With rest, healthy blood flow to the affected areas is restored. Radionuclide agents (e.g., thallium-201 or sestamibi) can be used to demonstrate regions of the coronary circulation where this effect occurs, and aid in the diagnosis and management of ischemic heart disease.

red lead Pb_3O_4; lead (II, IV) oxide

red man (neck) syndrome An adverse anaphylactoid reaction to vancomycin therapy, causing pruritus, flushing, and erythema of the head and upper body. The condition is caused by release of histamine. It can be prevented by slowing the infusion rate.

re-do (rē′doo″) A colloquial term for a re-operation or a revision of an operation.

redosing (rē″dōs′ing) Administration of an additional dose of a medication.

redose, *v.*

red-out (rĕd′owt) A term used in aerospace medicine to describe what happens to the vision and central nervous system (i.e., seeing red and perhaps experiencing unconsciousness) when the aircraft is doing part or all of an outside loop at high speed, or any other maneuver that causes the pilot to experience a negative force of gravity. The condition is due to engorgement of the vessels of the head including those of the retina.

redox (rē′dŏks) Combined form indicating oxidation-reduction system or reaction.

red raspberry The aromatic, sweet, and mildly tart fruit of a northern hemispheric thorny vine (Rubus idaeus), eaten raw or prepared in jams and jellies. It is a rich food source of many nutrients, including fiber, carbohydrates, minerals, and vitamin C. It is promoted in alternative medicine as a means of inducing labor, alleviating menstrual cramping, and treating colds, among other uses. SYN: *Rubis idaeus*.

red rice yeast extract SEE: under *extract*.

red rules Policies or procedures that must be adhered to without compromise to prevent avoidable error or harm.

red tide SEE: under *tide*.

reduce (rĭ-dūs′) [L. *re*, again, + *ducere*, to lead] **1.** To restore to usual relationship, as the ends of a fractured bone. **2.** To restore the normal alignment of a dislocated joint. **3.** To weaken, as a solution. **4.** To diminish, as bulk or weight.

reducible (rĭ-dūs′ĭ-bl) Capable of being replaced in a normal position, as a dislocated bone or a hernia.

reducing agent SEE: under *agent*.

reducing substance Reducing agent.

reductant (rĭ-dŭk′tănt) The atom that is oxidized in an oxidation-reduction reaction.

reductase (ri-dŭk′tās″, ′tāz″) [*reduct(ion)* + *-ase*] An enzyme that accelerates the reduction process of chemical compounds.

   5-alpha r. An enzyme that converts testosterone to dihydrotestosterone.

reduction (ri-dŭk′shŏn) [L. *reductio*, leading back] **1.** Restoration to a normal position, as a fractured bone, dislocated joint, or a hernia. **2.** In chemis-

try, a type of reaction in which a substance gains electrons and positive valence is decreased. SEE: *oxidation*.

   breast r. Reduction **mammaplasty**.

   closed r. of fractures The treatment of bone fractures by placing the bones in their proper position without surgery.

   dorsal r. Surgery to decrease the size or prominence of the bridge of the nose.

   fat r. Elimination or limitation of greasy, fatty, or oily foods from the diet (e.g., by substituting vegetables or legumes for cheeses and meats). Fat reduction is thought by some nutritionists to help reduce the risk of cancer.

   fetal r. Pregnancy **r.**

   leukocyte r. The removal of white blood cells from blood before transfusion to decrease the likelihood of transfusion reactions or infection of the recipient with viral diseases.

   mindfulness-based stress r. The use of meditation and self-awareness to enhance one's ability to cope with challenging circumstances and psychological tensions.

   multifetal pregnancy r. In multiple pregnancies (as for triplets, quadruplets), the procedure for reducing the number of fetuses, to minimize the risk of maternal and fetal complications later in the pregnancy.

   open r. of fractures The treatment of bone fractures by the use of surgery to place the bones in their proper position.

   pocket r. Surgery to eliminate deep periodontal spaces that have formed around teeth. Periodontal pockets are colonized and/or infected by numerous disease-causing bacteria. The periodontist peels away and surgically removes infected gum tissue surrounding the tooth, smooths uneven dental surfaces, and removes tartar before suturing healthy gum back onto the affected tooth.

   pregnancy r. The intentional elimination of one or more fetuses carried by a woman with a multifetal pregnancy. SYN: *fetal r.*

   risk r. **1.** A decrease in the probability of an adverse outcome. **2.** In biostatistics, the formula 1 − HR (the hazard ratio). **3.** Any lowering of factors considered hazards for a specified disease, such as wearing a condom to lower the risk for sexually transmitted diseases, ceasing smoking to prevent lung cancer or emphysema, or lowering the intake of dietary cholesterol and fats to prevent heart disease.

   salt r. Limiting the quantity of sodium chloride in the diet, usually to lower blood pressure or prevent fluid retention.

   selective r. **1.** In radiography, the reduction of exposed silver halide crystals to black metallic silver, creating a visible image. **2.** In oncology, killing or destroying tumor cells or their products with relatively little damage to healthy cells.

reduction division Meiosis.

redundant (rĭ-dŭn′dĕnt) [L. *redundare,* to overflow] More than necessary.

reduplicated (rĭ-dū′plĭ-kā″tĕd) [L. *re,* again, + *duplicare,* to double] **1.** Doubled. **2.** Bent backward on itself, as a fold.

reduplication (rĭ-dū″plĭ-kā′shŭn) **1.** A doubling, as of the heart sounds in some morbid conditions. **2.** A fold.

reduplicative paramnesia (rĭ-doop′lĭ-kāt″ĭv) A rare psychiatric disorder in which the patient is convinced that the environment in which he is living has been duplicated brick by brick and leaf by leaf in another location. It is usually diagnosed in people who have suffered a focal brain injury (e.g., to the right hemisphere of the brain).

reduviid (rĭ-doo′vē-id) [Fr. *Reduviidae*] A bug of the family Reduviidae. **reduviid,** *adj.*

Reduviidae (rej″ŭ-vī′ĭ-dē) [*Reduvia,* the name of the type genus + *-idae*] A family of the order Hemiptera, including the assassin bugs and the kissing bug.

Reduvius (ri-doo′vē-ŭs, -dū′) [L. *reduvia,* hangnail] A genus of true bugs belonging to the family Reduviidae.

   R. personatus A species that normally feeds on other insects but sometimes preys on humans. In some cases the bite may transmit *Trypanosoma cruzi,* a protozoan responsible for Chagas disease.

red wale markings Raised red streaks seen on esophageal or gastric varices during endoscopy. They suggest that the varices have a high likelihood of rupture and bleeding.

Reed-Sternberg cell (rēd′stĕrn′bĕrg″) [Dorothy Reed, U.S. pathologist, 1874–1964; Karl Sternberg, Aust. pathologist, 1872–1935] A giant, malignant, multinucleated B lymphocyte, the presence of which is the pathologic hallmark of Hodgkin's disease. SEE: illus.

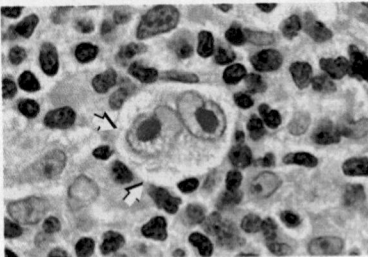

REED-STERNBERG CELL

Reed-Sternberg cell in Hodgkin Lymphoma

reeducation (rēej″ŭ-kā′shŏn) [*re-* + *education*] **1.** Training to restore compe-

tence to a person with functional limitations. **2.** A physical technique to facilitate restoration of motor control.

   sensory r. A rehabilitation regimen used after sensation is impaired by peripheral nerve injuries or surgery to the hand. Common applications include manual techniques, vibration, and electrical stimulation. The purpose is to relearn the interpretation of sensory information related to pain, temperature, and object identification.

reef (rēf) A fold or tuck, usually taken in redundant tissue.

re-entry (rē-ĕn′trē) In cardiology, the cycling of an electrical impulse through conductive tissue that has been recently stimulated. This is the cause of many tachycardic heart rhythms (e.g., those originating in the atrioventricular node).

re-experience (rē-ks″pēr′ē-ĕns) To recall an event, feeling, or thought; to have an intrusive memory or "flashback." Frequent re-experiencing of traumatic events is one of the symptoms of posttraumatic stress disorder.

refection (rē-fĕk′shŭn) [L. *reficere,* to refresh] **1.** Restoration after hunger or fatigue, esp. with food or drink. **2.** Recovery by laboratory rats from the symptoms of vitamin B deficiency caused by consuming a diet deficient in vitamin B, due to vitamin synthesis by intestinal flora.

refeeding syndrome The potentially fatal metabolic response of a starved individual to feeding, either enteral or parenteral. The correction of electrolyte imbalances is imperative before gradual refeeding to prevent hypophosphatemia, rhabdomyolysis, and other lifethreatening complications.

refer (rĭ-fĕr′, rē-) [L. *referre,* to bring back] **1.** To allude to or mention. **2.** To direct attention to. **3.** To recommend someone to another health care provider for specific testing or treatment.

reference (rĕf′ĕr-ĕns) [L. *referre,* to bring back, to report] **1.** A standard for the evaluation of objects, data, or ideas. **2.** A link or connection between data, ideas, or objects.

reference man A human being of statistically average size and physiology, used in research models of nutrition, pharmacology, population, radiologic dosimetry, or toxicology. The reference weight for men 19 and older is 76 kg. Also known as "refman" or "standard man." Similarly, *reference woman.*

reference pricing (prĭs′ĭng) A method of health care cost control in which the cost of all items in a class of roughly equivalent products or services is reimbursed at a fixed dollar amount. Patients or providers who seek care that is more expensive than the reference price pay additional fees. Those who agree to use standard services are reimbursed in full for the products or services they receive.

reference value A range of expected measurements for a laboratory test. Findings outside the range may be abnormal or worth noting. Reference ranges may be determined or set in a number of ways: statistically, e.g., all values within two standard deviations of a mean data point; by consensus (all values thought by a panel of specialists to be acceptable or healthy); or pathologically (all values within the range are to be associated with good health; those outside the range are associated with the presence of a disease).

reference woman An idealized female, used in research models, described the same as reference man, except in weight (66 kg) and caloric intake (2000 kcal/day).

referral The practice of sending a patient to another practitioner or specialty program for consultation or service. Such a practice involves a delegation of responsibility for patient care, which should be followed up to ensure satisfactory care.

referral bias The difference that arises from the study of those patient populations who receive primary care as opposed to those who receive care at tertiary care centers.

refine (rē-fīn′) [L. *re*, again, + ME. *fin*, finished] To purify or render free from foreign material.

reflectance (rē-flĕk′tăns) The fraction of total light reflected after it hits a surface, and the angle at which it is reflected. It is the inverse of absorbance.

    diffuse r. The reflectance of light from a rough or nonpolished surface in which the radiant energy tends to scatter. The angle of reflectance does not equal the angle of incidence.

    spectral r. The reflectance of light from a polished surface in which the angle of reflectance equals the angle of incidence.

reflection (rĭ-flĕk′shŭn) [L. *reflexio*, a bending back] **1.** The condition of being turned back on itself, as when the peritoneum passes from the wall of a body cavity to and around an organ and back to the body wall. **2.** The throwing back of a ray of radiant energy from a surface not penetrated. **3.** Mental consideration of something previously considered.

    diffuse r. The reflection of a light ray by a rough surface in which the angle of reflection is not equal to the angle of incidence. As opposed to *specular* reflection by a smooth surface in which the angle of reflection equals the angle of incidence. Employed in the analytical technique of reflectometry.

reflectometer (rē″flĕk″tom′ĕt-ĕr) [*reflect*

+ *-meter*] An instrument that measures the light reflected by a surface.

reflectometry (rē″flĕk″tom′ĕ-trē) [*reflect* + *-metry*] A laboratory technique for analyzing thin layers of objects, such as biological membranes or layered metallic surfaces. It is performed by measuring the scatter of energized particles from the layered surface.

reflector (rĭ-flĕk′tor) [L. *re*, again, + *flectere*, to bend] A device or surface that reflects waves, radiant energy, or sound.

reflex (rē′flĕks″) [L. *reflexus*, bending back] An involuntary response or action to a stimulus. Reflexes are specific and predictable and are usually purposeful and adaptive. They depend on an intact neural pathway between the stimulation point and a responding organ. This pathway is called the reflex arc. In a simple reflex this includes a sensory receptor, afferent or sensory neuron, reflex center in the brain or spinal cord, one or more efferent neurons, and an effector organ. Most reflexes, however, are more complicated and include internuncial or associative neurons intercalated between afferent and efferent neurons. SEE: *reflex **arc*** for illus.

    abdominal r. Contraction of the muscles of the abdominal wall when the overlying skin is stimulated. Absence of this reflex indicates damage to the pyramidal tract.

    abdominocardiac r. A change in heart rate, usually a slowing, resulting from mechanical stimulation of abdominal viscera.

    accommodation r. Any of the changes that take place as the eye adjusts to bring light rays from an object to focus on the retina. This involves a change in the size of the pupil, convergence or divergence of the eyes, and either a decrease or an increase in the convexity of the lens depending on the previous condition of the lens. SYN: *near r.*

    Achilles tendon r. SEE: *Achilles tendon reflex.*

    Achilles r. SEE: *Achilles tendon reflex.*

    acoustic blink r. Involuntary closure of the eyelids after exposure to a sharp, sudden noise. This is a normal startle response that may be exaggerated in patients with anxiety disorders or hyperacusis. It may be blunted in infants or adults with a hearing disorder or facial nerve paralysis.

    acquired r. Conditioned **r.**

    acromial r. Flexion of the forearm and internal rotation of the hand as a result of a quick blow to the acromion. It is elicited in hyperreflexic states.

    adductor r. Contraction of the adductor muscles of the thigh on applying pressure to or tapping the medial surface of the thigh or knee.

allied r. Any of the reflexes initiated by several stimuli originating in widely separated receptors whose impulses follow the final common path to the effector organ and reinforce one another.

anal r. Contraction of the anal sphincter following irritation or stimulation of the skin around the anus. This reflex is lost if the second to fourth sacral nerves are injured. SYN: *anal wink.*

ankle clonus r. A reflex elicited by quick, vigorous dorsiflexion of the foot while the knee is held in a flexed position, resulting in repeated clonic movement of the foot as long as it is maintained in dorsiflexion. In women with pregnancy-induced hypertension, this reflects hyperirritability of the central nervous system and increased risk for eclamptic convulsions.

ankle r. Achilles tendon reflex.

antagonistic r. Two or more reflexes initiated simultaneously in different receptors that involve the same motor center but produce opposite effects.

asymmetrical tonic neck r. In an infant, extension of one or both extremities on the side to which the head is forcibly turned. Flexion of the extremities occurs on the other side.

attention r. Change in the size of the pupil when attention is suddenly fixed.

audito-oculogyric r. The sudden turning of the head and eyes toward an alarming sound.

auditory r. Any reflex produced by stimulation of the auditory nerve, esp. blinking of the eyes at the sudden unexpected production of a sound.

auriculocervical nerve r. **Snellen** reflex.

auriculopalpebral r. Kisch reflex.

autonomic r. Any reflex involving the response of a visceral effector (cardiac muscle, smooth muscle, or gland). Such reflexes always involve two efferent neurons (preganglionic and postganglionic).

axon r. A reflex that does not involve a complete reflex arc and hence is not a true reflex. Its afferent and efferent limbs are branches of a single nerve fiber, the axon (axon-like dendrite) of a sensory neuron. An example is vasodilation resulting from stimulation of the skin.

Babinski r. SEE: under *Babinski, Joseph-François-Felix.*

Bainbridge r. SEE: under *Bainbridge, Francis Arthur.*

Bechterew r. SEE: under *Bechterew, Vladimir Mikhailovich.*

biceps r. Flexion of the forearm on percussion of the tendon of the biceps brachii.

blink r. Sudden closing of the eyelids in response to turning of the head, loud noises, bright lights, or visual threats. Absence of this reflex occurs in blindness and in injuries to cranial nerves III, V, and VII.

Brain r. SEE: *Brain reflex.*

bregmocardiac r. A reduced heart rate following pressure on the anterior fontanel.

Breuer-Hering r. Hering-Breur reflex.

Brissaud r. SEE: under *Brissaud, Édouard.*

bulbocavernosus r. Contraction of bulbocavernosus muscle on percussing the dorsum of the penis. SYN: *virile r.*

bulbospongiosus r. Contraction of bulbospongiosus muscle on percussing the dorsum of the penis.

cardiac r. An involuntary response consisting of a change in cardiac rate. Stimulation of sensory nerve endings in the wall of the carotid sinus by increased arterial blood pressure reflexively slows the heart (Marey law). Stimulation of vagus fibers in the right side of the heart by increased venous return reflexively increases the heart rate (Bainbridge reflex).

cardiovascular r. **1.** A sympathetic increase in heart rate when there is increased pressure in or distention of great veins. **2.** Reflex vasoconstriction resulting from reduced venous pressure.

carotid sinus r. A slowing of the heart rate and a fall in blood pressure when the carotid sinus is massaged. Carotid sinus massage may be used therapeutically to treat paroxysmal supraventricular tachycardia.

cat's eye r. In children, an abnormal pupillary flash or reflection from the eye that may be momentary; may be white, yellow, or pink; and is best seen under diminished natural illumination. This reflex, which may be noticed first by a parent, may be caused by various conditions, the most important of which is retinoblastoma. It is also observed in tuberous sclerosis, inflammatory eye diseases, and some congenital malformations of the eye. SEE: *retinoblastoma.*

Chaddock r. SEE: *Chaddock reflex.*

chain r. A reflex initiated by several separate serial reflexes, each activated by the preceding one.

chemical r. Chemoreflex.

chin r. A clonic movement resulting from percussion or stroking of the lower jaw. SYN: *jaw jerk; jaw r.*

ciliary r. The normal contraction of the pupil in accommodation of vision from distant to near.

ciliospinal r. Dilation of the pupil after stimulation of the skin of the neck by pinching or scratching.

clasp-knife r. Quick inhibition of the stretch reflex when extensor muscles are forcibly stretched by flexing the limb.

cochleo-orbicular r. Cochleopalpebral **r.**

cochleopalpebral r. Contraction of the orbicularis palpebrarum muscle resulting from a sudden noise produced near the ear. SYN: *cochleo-orbicular* **r.**

conditioned r. A reflex acquired as a result of training in which the cerebral cortex plays an essential part. Conditioned reflexes are learned, not inborn or inherited. SYN: *acquired* **r.**

conjunctival r. Closure of eyelids when the conjunctiva is touched or threatened.

consensual r. Crossed **r.**

consensual light r. The reaction of both pupils that occurs when one eye is exposed to a greater intensity of light than the other. SEE: *pupillary* **r.**

contralateral r. 1. Passive flexion of one part following flexion of another. **2.** Passive flexion of one leg, causing similar movement of the opposite leg.

convulsive r. A reflex induced by a weak stimulus and causing widespread uncoordinated and purposeless muscle contractions, seen in strychnine poisoning.

corneal r. Closure of eyelids resulting from direct corneal irritation. This reflex is mediated by the fifth cranial nerve. SYN: *lid* **r.**

corneomandibular r. Deflexion of the mandible toward the opposite side when the cornea is irritated while the mouth is open and relaxed.

cranial r. Any reflex whose origin is in the brain.

cremasteric r. Retraction of the testis when the skin is stroked on the inner front side of the thigh.

crossed r. A reflex in which stimulation of one side of the body results in response on the opposite side. SYN: *consensual* **r.**; *indirect* **r.**

crossed extension r. An extension of the lower extremity on the opposite side when a painful stimulus is applied to the skin.

cry r. 1. The normal ability of an infant to cry. It is not usually present in premature infants. **2.** The spontaneous crying by infants during sleep.

deep r. Deep tendon **r.**

deep tendon r. ABBR: DTR. An automatic motor response elicited by stimulating stretch receptors in subcutaneous tissues surrounding joints and tendons. The assessment of DTRs is typically made by striking a tendon (such as the Achilles or brachioradialis tendons) with a weighted hammer. Brisk or hyperactive responses are seen in conditions such as hyperthyroidism, stroke, preeclampsia, or spastic disorders. Diminished responses may be seen in patients with hypothyroidism, drug intox-

ication, and flaccid neuromuscular disorders. SYN: *deep* **r.**; *muscle stretch* **r.** SEE: *clonus; knee-jerk* **r.**

defense r. Retraction or tension in response to an action or threatened action.

delayed r. A reflex that does not occur until several seconds after the application of a stimulus.

depressor r. A reflex that results in slowed muscle activity, as in the heart rate.

digital r. Sudden flexion of the terminal phalanx of a finger or thumb when the nail is suddenly tapped.

direct r. A reflex in which response occurs on the same side as the stimulus.

direct light r. Prompt contraction of the sphincter of the iris when light entering through the pupil strikes the retina.

diving r. Slowing of the heart rate when a person's head is immersed in water. This reflex helps to protect a person from drowning, esp. in cold water. SEE: *drowning.*

dorsal r. Lumbar **r.**

elbow r. Triceps **r.**

elementary r. A typical reflex common to all vertebrates that includes the postural, flexion, stretch, and extensor thrust reflexes.

embrace r. Moro reflex.

epigastric r. Contraction of the upper portion of the rectus abdominis muscle when the skin of the epigastric region is scratched.

Erben r. SEE: *Erben reflex.*

erector spinae r. Lumbar **r.**

Escherich r. SEE: *Escherich reflex.*

extensor plantar r. Extension of the great toe when the sole of the foot is stimulated. SEE: *Babinski* **r.**

extensor thrust r. A quick and brief extension of a limb when pressure is applied to its plantar surface.

extrusion r. An infantile reflex in which the tongue moves outward after it has been touched. It is present from birth to 4 months.

facial r. In coma, contraction of facial muscles when pressure is applied to the eyeball. SYN: *bulbomimic* **r.***; Mondonesi* **r.**

fascial r. Muscular contraction resulting from percussing facial fascia.

femoral r. Extension of the knee and flexion of the foot resulting from irritation of the skin over the upper anterior third of the thigh.

fencing r. Tonic neck **r.**

flexor withdrawal r. Flexion of a body part in response to a painful stimulus. SYN: *withdrawal* **r.**

front-tap r. Contraction of the gastrocnemius muscle when stretched muscles of the extended leg are percussed.

gag r. Gagging and vomiting resulting from irritation of the throat or pharynx.

gastrocolic r. A peristaltic wave in the colon induced by entrance of food into the stomach.

gastroileac r. The physiological relaxation of the ileocecal valve resulting from food in the stomach.

Geigel r. SEE: *Geigel reflex.*

glabellar r. Blinking of the eyes when the forehead just above the bridge of the nose is tapped. In most people, blinking stops after a few taps on the forehead. If it does not, significant brain disease may be present, e.g., Parkinson disease or any disease that causes frontal lobe atrophy.

gluteal r. Contraction of the gluteal muscles from stimulation of the overlying skin.

Gordon r. SEE: under *Gordon reflex.*

grasp r. The grasping reaction of the fingers and toes when they are stimulated. This reflex is normal in the newborn but disappears as the nervous system matures. It may reappear later in life if a person suffers an injury to the frontal lobes of the brain.

H r. In electrodiagnostic studies of spinal reflexes, the time required for a stimulus applied to a sensory nerve to travel to the spinal cord and return down the motor nerve. SEE: *F response.*

heart r. Any reflex, such as the Bainbridge reflex, in which the stimulation of a sensory nerve causes the heart rate to increase or decrease.

Hering-Breuer r. SEE: *Hering-Breuer reflex.*

Hoffmann r. SEE: under *Hoffmann, Johann.*

hung-up r. Slowness of the relaxation phase of deep tendon reflexes. It is present in hypothyroidism.

hypochondrial r. Sudden inspiration resulting from abrupt pressure below the costal border.

inborn r. An unconditioned reflex; an innate or inherited reflex.

indirect r. Crossed **r.**

inflation r. Hering-Breuer reflex.

inguinal r. Contractions of the musculature in the female groin when the upper thigh is scratched. SEE: *Geigel r.*

interscapular r. A scapular muscular contraction after percussion or stimulus between the scapulae.

intersegmental r. A reflex involving several segments of the spinal cord. SYN: *long r.*

intestinal r. Myenteric **r.**

intrasegmental r. A reflex that involves only a single segment of the spinal cord.

jaw r. Chin **r.**

Joffroy r. SEE: *Joffroy reflex.*

Juster r. SEE: *Juster reflex.*

kinetic r. Labyrinthine righting **r.**

Kisch r. SEE: *Kisch reflex.*

knee-jerk r. Extension of the leg after percussion of the patellar tendon. This is one of the myotatic or stretch reflexes important in maintaining posture. SYN: *patellar r.; quadriceps r.*

Kocher r. SEE: *Kocher reflex.*

labyrinthine righting r. A reflex, esp. a postural reflex, resulting from stimulation of receptors in the semicircular ducts, utricle, and saccule of the inner ear. This reflex helps orient the head in space and to the rest of the body. SYN: *kinetic r.; optical righting r.; tonic labyrinthine r.*

lacrimal r. Secretion of fluid after irritation of the corneal conjunctiva.

Landau r. SEE: *Landau reflex.*

laryngeal r. Coughing from irritation of the larynx or fauces.

laughter r. Uncontrollable laughter resulting from tickling or the fear of tickling.

letdown r. The movement of breast milk from the alveoli into the lactiferous ducts in response to oxytocin-stimulated contractions. The reflex may be stimulated by suckling or by an infant's crying. Stimulation of the nipple increases the secretion of oxytocin. This technique may be used to stimulate contraction of the postpartum uterus.

lid r. Corneal **r.**

light r. Constriction of the pupil when light is flashed into the eye.

lip r. The reflex movement of the lips when the angle of the mouth is suddenly and lightly tapped during sleep.

local r. A reflex that does not involve the central nervous system, e.g., the myenteric reflex, which occurs even when extrinsic nerves to the intestine have been cut.

long r. Intersegmental **r.**

lumbar r. An irritation of the skin over the erector spinae muscles, causing contraction of the back muscles. SYN: *dorsal r.; erector spinae r.*

mandibular r. Clonic movement resulting from percussing or stroking the lower jaw.

mass r. Autonomic dysfunction that may occur as a late consequence of transection of the spinal cord. It is marked by episodes of sweating, bradycardia, hypotension, urinary incontinence, and muscular spasms of the legs.

Mayer r. SEE: *Mayer reflex.*

Mendel r. SEE: under *Mendel, Kurt.*

Mendel-Bechterew r. SEE: *Mendel-Bechterew reflex.*

monosynaptic r. A reflex involving only two neurons (afferent and efferent).

Moro r. SEE: *Moro reflex.*

muscle stretch r. Deep tendon **r.**

myenteric r. Reflex caused by distention of the intestine, resulting in contraction above the point of stimulation and relaxation below it. SYN: *intestinal r.*

myotatic r. Stretch **r.**

nasal r. Sneezing resulting from irritation of nasal mucosa.

nasomental r. Contraction of the mentalis muscle with elevation of lower lip and wrinkling of skin of chin. The reflex is elicited by percussion of the side of the nose.

near r. Accommodation **r.**

neck-righting r. In a reclining infant, rotation of the trunk in the same direction in which the head is turned. This reflex appears at age 4 to 6 months and is no longer obtainable by age 2 years.

nociceptive r. A reflex initiated by a painful stimulus.

nostril r. Reduction of the opening of the naris on the affected side in lung disease in proportion to lessened alveolar air capacity on the affected side.

obliquus r. Contraction of the entire external obliquus muscle when the skin of the thigh below the inguinal ligament is simulated.

oculocardiac r. SEE: *Aschner phenomenon.*

oculocephalic r. The deviation of a person's eyes to the opposite side when the head is rapidly rotated. This is a normal finding in neonates. In adults it is indicative of coma. SYN: *doll's eye movement.*

Onanoff r. SEE: *Onanoff reflex.*

optical blink r. Involuntary closure of the eyelids after exposure to a bright light. Shining a bright light at an infant's eyes causes the eyes to blink and the head to flex backward. If this reflex is absent, further testing of cranial nerves II, III, IV, and VI is required.

optical righting r. Labyrinthine righting **r.**

palatal r. Swallowing induced by stimulation of the soft palate.

palmar grasp r. A normal reflex in a the newborn in which the baby's fingers spontaneously curl around any object placed within them and do not spontaneously let go. This reflex usually diminishes by age 3 to 4 months and disappears before age 6 months. The reflex reappears later in life in diseases that affect the frontal lobes of the brain.

palmar r. Swallowing induced by stimulation of the soft palate.

palmomental r. A contraction of the superficial muscles of the eye and chin produced on the same side as the palmar area that is stimulated by an examiner. This is an abnormal finding and indicates frontal disease.

parachute r. Extension of an infant's arms, hands, and fingers when the infant is suspended in the prone position and dropped a short distance onto a soft surface. This reaction appears at age 9

months and persists. An asymmetrical response indicates a motor nerve abnormality. SYN: *parachute **response**.*

paradoxical r. A response to a stimulus that is unexpected and may be the opposite of what is considered normal.

patellar r. Knee-jerk **r.**

pathological r. Any abnormal reflex due to disease.

penile r. 1. Sudden downward movement of the penis when the prepuce or gland of a completely relaxed penis is pulled upward. SYN: *virile r.* 2. Contraction of the bulbocavernous muscle on percussing the dorsum of the penis. SYN: *virile r.* 3. Contraction of the bulbocavernous muscle resulting from compression of the glans penis. SYN: *virile r.*

pharyngeal r. An attempt to swallow when the pharynx is stimulated.

pilomotor r. Piloerection when the skin is cooled or as a result of emotional reaction.

placing r. Flexion and then extension of an infant's leg that occurs when the infant is held erect and the dorsum of one foot is dragged along the underedge of a table top. This reflex lasts from birth until age 6 weeks.

plantar r. SEE: *plantar **grasp**.*

plantar grasp r. A grasp reflex resulting from gentle stimulation of the sole of the foot. This reflex lasts from birth until age 10 months. SYN: *sole r.*

platysmal r. Dilation of the pupil resulting from sharp pinching of the platysma myoides.

pneocardiac r. A change in the rate and rhythm of the heart and blood pressure when an irritant vapor is inhaled.

pneopneic r. A change in respiratory depth and rate, coughing, suffocation, and pulmonary edema when an irritant vapor is inhaled.

postural r. Any reflex concerned with maintaining posture.

pressor r. A reflex in which the response to stimulation is an increase in blood pressure caused by constriction of arterioles.

proprioceptive r. A reflex initiated by body movement to maintain the position of the moved part; any reflex initiated by stimulation of a proprioceptor.

psychogalvanic r. Decreased electric resistance of the skin in response to emotional stress or stimuli.

pupillary r. 1. Constriction of the pupil upon stimulation of the retina by light. This reflex is mediated by the third cranial nerve. 2. Constriction of the pupil upon accommodation for near vision, and dilatation upon accommodation for far vision. 3. Constriction of the pupil of one eye in response to stimulation of the other by light. 4. Constriction of the pupil upon attempted closure of eyelids that are held apart.

quadriceps r. Knee-jerk **r.**

quadrupedal r. Extension of the flexed arm on assuming a quadrupedal posture.

quadrupedal extensor r. Brain reflex.

radial r. Flexion of forearm resulting when the lower end of the radius is percussed.

rectal r. The normal desire to evacuate feces present in the rectum.

red eye r. Red **r.**

red r. The red light reflection seen in ophthalmoscopic examination of the eye. SYN: *red eye* **r.**

righting r. Any of the reflexes that enable an animal to maintain its body in a definite relationship to its head and thus maintain its body right side up.

rooting r. The turning of an infant's mouth toward the stimulus when the infant's cheek is stroked. This reflex is present at birth; by age 4 months it is gone when the infant is awake; by age 7 months it is gone when the infant is asleep.

Rossolimo r. SEE: *Rossolimo reflex.*

scapular r. Muscular contraction following percussion or stimulus between the scapulae.

scapulohumeral r. A reflex in which the upper arm is adducted and rotated outward when the vertebral border of the scapula is percussed.

Schäffer r. SEE: *Schäffer reflex.*

scrotal r. Slow vermicular contraction of the scrotal muscle when the perineum is stroked or cold is applied.

segmental r. A reflex in which afferent impulses enter the cord in the same segment or segments from which the efferent impulses emerge.

sexual r. A reflex concerned with sexual activities, esp. erection and ejaculation, which results from direct genital stimulation or indirectly from emotion, whether the individual is asleep or awake.

short r. A reflex involving one or a few segments of the spinal cord.

simple r. A reflex in which only two or possibly three neurons are interposed between receptor and effector organs.

Snellen r. SEE: under *Snellen, Herman.*

solar sneeze r. A sneeze following exposure to bright sunlight. This reflex is and affects a great number of normal people; it may also be associated with rhinitis. The mechanism of the cause of this type of sneeze reflex is unknown.

sole r. Plantar grasp **r.**

somatic r. A reflex induced by stimulation of somatic sensory nerve endings.

spinal r. A reflex whose center is in the spinal cord.

startle r. Moro reflex.

static r. A reflex concerned with establishing and maintaining posture when the body is at rest.

statokinetic r. A reflex that occurs when the body is moving.

stepping r. Movements of progression elicited by holding an infant upright, inclined forward, and touching the soles of the feet to a flat surface. This reflex lasts from birth to age 6 weeks.

stretch r. The contraction of a muscle caused by quick stretching of that muscle. Stretch reflexes are of primary importance in the maintenance of posture. SYN: *myotatic* **r.**

sucking r. A sucking movement of an infant's mouth produced by stroking the lips. A primitive form of this reflex is present in the fetus by the 16th week of gestation; it is fully developed by the time of birth. In adults, the presence of a sucking reflex is an indicator of severe dementia, frontal lobe disease, or extrapyramidal diseases.

superficial r. A cutaneous reflex caused by irritation of the skin or of areas that depend on the spinal cord as a motor center (such as the scapular, epigastric, and plantar reflexes) or on centers in the medulla (such as the conjunctival, pupillary, and palatal reflexes). This reflex is induced by a very light stimulus, e.g., stroking the skin lightly with a soft cotton swab.

supraorbital r. Eyelid closure **r.**

suprapubic r. Deflection of the linea alba toward the stroked side when the abdomen is stroked above the inguinal ligament.

swallowing r. Involuntary muscular activity in the oropharynx and nasopharynx when foods, tongue depressors, or other objects stimulate the back of the throat. This reflex is mediated by the deglutition center of the medulla oblongata, i.e., by cranial nerves VII, IX, X, and XI.

symmetrical tonic neck r. In an infant, flexion or extension of the arms in response to flexion and extension, respectively, of the neck.

tendon r. A deep reflex obtained by sharply tapping the skin over the tendon of a muscle. It is exaggerated in upper neuron disease and diminished or lost in lower neuron disease.

tonic labyrinthine r. Labyrinthine righting **r.**

tonic neck r. The ipsilateral extension and contralateral flexion of the supine infant's extremities when the head is turned to one side. This normal newborn reflex may not be evident immediately after birth; however, once it appears, it persists until about the third postnatal month. SYN: *fencing* **r.**

tonic vibration r. ABBR: TVR. A polysynaptic reflex believed to depend on spinal and supraspinal pathways.

triceps r. Sharp extension of the forearm resulting from tapping of the triceps tendon while the arm is held loosely in a bent position. SYN: *elbow jerk*; *elbow r.*

   triceps surae r. Achilles tendon reflex.

   true autonomic r. A visceral response in which afferent impulses do not pass through the central nervous system but enter prevertebral ganglia where connections are made with efferent neurons.

   unconditioned r. A reflex that is not acquired but is natural or inherited.

   urinary r. A spinal cord reflex, initiated by accumulated urine stretching the bladder and the resulting contraction of the bladder to expel urine.

   vascular r. Vasomotor **r.**

   vasomotor r. The constriction or dilatation of a blood vessel in response to a stimulus, as in becoming pale from fright. SYN: *vascular* **r.**

   vesical r. An inclination to urinate caused by moderate bladder distention.

   vestibulocollic r. A reaction that stabilizes the position of the head according to sensory information from the labyrinth of the ear and the nerves in the neck.

   visceral r. Any reflex induced by stimulation of the visceral nerves.

   visceromotor r. Contraction or tenseness of the skeletal muscles resulting from painful stimuli originating in visceral organs.

   viscerosensory r. Pain or tenderness elicited in somatic structures (skin and muscle) caused by visceral disorder. SEE: *referred **pain**.*

   withdrawal r. Flexor withdrawal **r.**

   zygomatic r. The movement of the lower jaw toward the percussed side when the zygomatic bone is percussed.

reflex decay test A test used in audiometry to see how the eardrum responds to a loud tone applied either directly to the ear of interest or to the opposite (contralateral) ear. The sonic stimulus makes the stapedius muscle contract. Data from the test help to determine whether abnormal responses to the tone are the result of damage to the acoustic nerve or to the cochlea.

reflexogenic (rĭ-flĕks″ō-jĕn′ĭk) [L. *reflexus*, bend back, + Gr. *gennan*, to produce] Causing a reflex action.

reflexogenous (rĭ″flĕks-ŏj′ĕ-nŭs) Reflexogenic.

reflexology (rē″flĕk-sŏl′ō-jē) [″ + Gr. *logos*, word, reason] 1. The study of the anatomy and physiology of reflexes. 2. A system of massage in which the feet and sometimes the hands are massaged in an attempt to favorably influence other body functions.

reflexotherapy (rē-flĕks″ō-thĕr′ă-pē) [″ + Gr. *therapeia*, treatment] Treatment by manipulating, anesthetizing,

or cauterizing an area distant from the location of the disorder. SEE: *spondylotherapy.*

reflex sympathetic dystrophy SEE: under *dystrophy.*

reflex testing, reflexive testing A laboratory test that is automatically obtained when the results of a screening test indicate the need for further study. Examples of reflex tests include determination of the antibiotic sensitivity of bacteria that are identified in culture specimens; and determination of an enzyme immunoassay test for HIV when an antibody test for the virus is present in a sample of body fluids.

reflux (rē′flŭks) [L. *re*, back, + *fluxus*, flow] A return or backward flow. SEE: *regurgitation.*

   hepatojugular r. Distention of the veins of the neck when the liver is compressed during physical examination of the abdomen. Neck vein filling during liver examination commonly is seen in patients with congestive heart failure but also may be a normal finding.

   vesicoureteral r. The backward flow of urine up the ureter during urination, instead of downward into the bladder. This condition may cause recurrent urinary tract infections in infants and children and may produce kidney scarring and failure if it is untreated. Depending on the underlying cause, treatment may include endoscopic or open surgical procedures.

refluxate (rē-flŭks′āt″) The acid, gas, and liquid that rise from the upper gastrointestinal tract into the esophagus in gastroesophageal reflux disease. Its components may include gastric acids, bile, and pepsin.

reflux disease SEE: *gastroesophageal reflux disease.*

refract (rĭ-frăkt′) [L. *refractus*, broken off] 1. To turn back; to deflect. 2. To detect and correct refractive errors in the eyes.

refraction (rĭ-frak′shŏn) [L. *refractio*, a breaking back] 1. Deflection from a straight path, as of light rays as they pass through media of different densities; the change in direction of a ray when it passes from one medium to another of a different density. 2. Determination of the amount of ocular refractive errors and their correction.

   double r. Possession of more than one refractive index, resulting in a double image. SEE: *birefractive; birefringence.*

   dynamic r. The static refraction of the eye plus that accomplished by accommodation; the reciprocal of the nearpoint distance.

   r. of eye The refraction brought about by the refractive media of the eye (cornea, aqueous humor, crystalline lens, vitreous body). SYN: *ocular* **r.**

ocular r. Refraction of eye.

static r. Refraction of the eye when accommodation is at rest or paralyzed.

refractionist (rĭ-frăk′shŭn-ĭst) [LL. *refractio,* break back] A person skilled in determining and correcting ocular refractive errors.

refractive (rĭ-frăk′tĭv) [L. *refractus,* broken off] Concerning refraction. SYN: *refringent.*

refractive media The structures of the eye that deflect light: the cornea, aqueous, crystalline lens, and vitreous.

refractive power The degree to which a transparent body deflects a ray of light from a straight path. SEE: *diopter.*

refractivity (rē″frăk-tĭv′ĭ-tē) The quality of being refractive; the ability to refract.

refractometer (rē-frăk-tŏm′ĕt-ĕr) [″ + Gr. *metron,* measure] A device for measuring refractive power, as of the eye.

refractometry (rē″frăk-tŏm′ĕ-trē) Measurement of the refractive power of lenses.

refractory (rē-frăk′tō-rē) [L. *refractarius*] 1. Obstinate; stubborn. 2. Resistant to ordinary treatment. 3. Resistant to stimulation; used of muscle or nerve.

refractory cytopenia with multilineage dysplasia ABBR: RCMD. In the World Health Organization classification of myelodysplastic syndromes, a disorder in which two or more blood cell lines form aberrantly. For example, the peripheral blood shows evidence of anemia and leukopenia, or of anemia, leukopenia, and thrombocytopenia; and the bone marrow shows abnormal precursors in two or more mature blood cell precursors.

refracture (rē-frăk′chūr) [L. *refractus,* broken off] Rebreaking of a fracture united in a malaligned position.

refrangible (rē-frăn′jĭ-bl) [L. *re,* again, + ME. *frangible,* breakable] Capable of being refracted.

refresh (rĭ-frĕsh′) [O.Fr. *refreschir,* to renew] 1. To restore strength; to relieve from fatigue; to renew; to revive. 2. To scrape epithelial covering from two opposing surfaces of a wound to facilitate healing and joining together.

refrigerant (rē-frij′ĕr-ănt) [L. *refrigerans,* making cold] 1. Cooling. 2. An agent that produces coolness or reduces fever. SYN: *algefacient.*

refrigeration (rĭ-frĭj″ĕr-ā′shŭn) [L. *refrigeratio,* make cold] Cooling; reduction of heat.

refringent (rē-frĭn′jĕnt) Refractive.

Refsum disease (rĕf′sum) [Sigvald Bernhard Refsum, Norwegian physician, 1907–1991] An autosomal recessive disease caused by the inability to metabolize phytanic acid. Clinical symptoms include visual disturbances, peripheral neuropathy, ataxia, and liver, kidney, and heart disease. Diets low in animal fat and milk products may relieve some of the symptoms. SYN: *phytanic acid storage disease.*

refuge A shelter; a safe place for persons fleeing danger or distress.

refugee A person fleeing danger or distress, esp. in times of war or political persecution.

refusal of therapy 1. Denial of treatment to a patient. 2. Unwillingness of a patient to participate in treatment.

refusal to treat A deliberate, conscious decision to withhold health care services from a patient.

refuse (re′ūs″) [Fr. *refus,* denial, rejection] Anything discarded; garbage, trash, waste.

regainer (rē-gān′ĕr) 1. A device that ameliorates or restores something that was lost. 2. A device that applies pressure between teeth on either side of the space left by a missing tooth. It is used to move teeth away from the edentulous space.

regeneration (rē-jen″ĕ-rā′shŏn) [*re-* + *generation*] Reconstitution of an injured or missing part of a cell, tissue, organ, or body. SEE: *degeneration.*

guided tissue r. ABBR: GTR. Any of the techniques used in periodontics to reconstruct lost or diseased periodontal tissue in those with gingival recession. GTR often involves the use of absorbable barrier membranes or collagen.

regimen (rej′ĭ-mĕn) [L. *regimen,* rule, government] A systematic plan of activities, treatments, diet, sleep, and exercise designed to improve, maintain, and/or restore health.

regio (rē′jē-ō) [L.] Region.

region (rē′jŏn) [L. *regio,* boundary] A portion of the body with natural or arbitrary boundaries. SYN: *regio.* **regional** (-ăl), *adj.*

abdominal r.s The abdomen and its external surface, divided into nine regions by four imaginary planes: two horizontal, one at the level of the ninth costal cartilage (or the lowest point of the costal arch) and the other at the level of the highest point of the iliac crest; two vertical, through the centers of the inguinal ligaments (or through the nipples or through the centers of the clavicles) or curved and coinciding with the lateral borders of the two abdominal rectus muscles. SEE: illus.

chest r. Any of the three areas of the chest: anterior, posterior, and lateral. The anterior divisions (right and left) are the clavicular, infraclavicular, and supraclavicular, the mammary and inframammary, and the upper and lower sternal. The posterior divisions (right and left) are the scapular, infrascapular, interscapular, and suprascapular. The lateral divisions are the axillary and infra-axillary.

hypochondriac r. Hypochondrium.

hypogastric r. Hypogastrium.

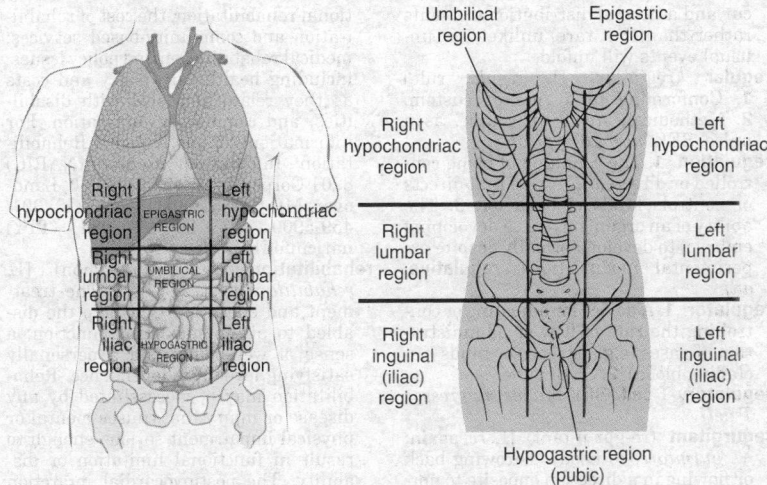

ABDOMINAL REGIONS

iliac r. The inguinal region on either side of the hypogastrium.

inguinal g. Groin.

lumbar r. That area of the abdominal surface lateral to the umbilical region, above the iliac region, and below the hypochondriac region.

r. of interest ABBR: ROI. In radiology, the object of a study or a treatment designed to affect a limited part of the body.

parasternal r. The area between the sternal border and parasternal line.

sternomastoid r. The wide area on the lateral region of the neck covered by sternocleidomastoid muscle.

register [LL. *regesta*, list] **1.** An official recording of vital statistics, including date and place of birth, marriage(s), and death. Recording these data is a legal requirement in the U.S. **2.** The compass or range of a voice. **3.** A series of tones of like quality or character, as low or high register, chest or head register.

registered pulmonary function technologist An individual who has completed the pulmonary function registry examination administered by the National Board for Respiratory Care.

registered record administrator ABBR: RRA. A person registered by the American Medical Records Association, who plans, supervises, designs, and develops medical records systems for health care facilities.

registrant (rej'ĭ-stränt) [L. *registrare*, to collect, pile up] A nurse named on the books of a registry as being on call or available to be called for duty. The term usually refers to the status of a private-duty nurse.

registrar (rĕj'ĭs-trär) [O.Fr. *registreur*] The official manager of a registry.

registration [L. *registratio*] The recording of information such as births or deaths; the recording of those who are registered or licensed to practice within a state.

registry (rej'ĭ-strē) [L. *regesta*, list, catalog] **1.** A database that holds the names of patients who share common characteristics, usually diseases. **2.** An office or book containing a list of nurses ready for duty; a placement bureau for nurses. **3.** A placement bureau for nurses.

cancer r. A list of patients diagnosed with cancer, kept to facilitate patient follow-up, as well as research about cancer causes, therapies, and outcomes.

donor deferral r. A means of tracking potential blood donors whose blood has been rejected at one location so that these people cannot attempt to donate blood products at other facilities. SYN: *donor deferral tracking.*

sexual offense r. A list of previously convicted sex offenders living or incarcerated in a community.

regression (rĭ-grĕsh'ŭn) [L. *regressio*, go back] **1.** A turning back or return to a former state. **2.** A return of symptoms. **3.** Retrogression. **4.** In psychology, an abnormal return to an earlier reaction, characterized by a mental state and behavior inappropriate to the situation. Regression may occur as a result of frustration or in states of fatigue, dreams, hypnosis, intoxication, illness, and certain psychoses (e.g., schizophrenia). **5.** In statistics, a procedure used to predict one variable on the basis of data about one or more other variables. **regressive** (-grĕs'ĭv), *adj.*

regression to the mean The likelihood that over time probable events will occur and a normal distribution of events rather than that rare, unlikely, or unusual events will unfold.

regular (rĕg′ū-lăr) [L. *regula,* rule] **1.** Conforming to a rule or custom. **2.** Methodical, steady in course, as a pulse. SEE: *normal; typical.*

regulation **1.** The condition of being controlled or directed. **2.** A rule that directs or controls kinds of behavior. **3.** The ability of an organism (e.g., a developing embryo) to develop normally despite experimental modifications. **regulative,** *adj.*

regulator **1.** A device for adjusting or controlling the rate of flow or administration of gases (e.g., oxygen) or fluids (including blood). **2.** SEE: under *gene.*

regulatory T cell SEE: under *suppressor T cell.*

regurgitant (rē-gŭr′jĭ-tănt) [L. *re,* again, + *gurgitare,* to flood] Throwing back or flowing in a direction opposite to normal.

regurgitation (rē-gŭr″jĭ-tā′shŭn) A backward flowing, as in the return of solids or fluids to the mouth from the stomach or the backflow of blood through a defective heart valve.

> **aortic r.** Aortic **insufficiency**.

> **duodenal r.** A return flow of chyme from the duodenum to the stomach.

> **functional r.** Regurgitation caused not by valvular disorder but by dilatation of ventricles, the great vessels, or valve rings.

> **mitral r.** ABBR: MR. A backflow of blood from the left ventricle into the left atrium, resulting from imperfect closure of the mitral (bicuspid) valve. It may result from congenital anomalies of the valve, connective tissue disorders (such as Marfan syndrome), infective endocarditis, ischemic damage to the valve or its supporting chordae, rheumatic valvulitis, or other degenerative conditions.
>
> Congestive heart failure or atrial fibrillation may be complications of severe MR. The degree of regurgitation can be judged by echocardiography or angiography. Valve reconstruction or valve replacement surgeries can be used to repair the defect. SYN: *mitral insufficiency.*

> **pulmonic r.** A backflow of blood from the pulmonary artery into the right ventricle.

> **tricuspid r.** A backflow of blood from the right ventricle into the right atrium.

> **valvular r.** A backflow of blood through a valve, esp. a heart valve, that is not completely closed as it would normally be.

REHABDATA (rē′hab″dāt″ă) A computerized bibliographical database of rehabilitation information supplied by the National Rehabilitation Information Center (NARIC). Topics included in the REHABDATA database include vocational rehabilitation, the cost of rehabilitation and community-based services; medical rehabilitation and policy issues, including health care policy and costs as they relate to people with disabilities; and community integration. For information, contact National Rehabilitation Information Center (NARIC) 8201 Corporate Drive, Suite 600, Landover, MD 20785 800/346-2742 (V); 301/459-5900 (V); 301/459-5984 (TTY) naricinfo@heitechservices.com

rehabilitation (rē″hă-bĭl″ĭ-tā′shŏn) [L. *rehabilitare,* to restore] **1.** The treatment and education that help the disabled to attain maximum function, a sense of well-being, and a personally satisfying level of independence. Rehabilitation may be necessitated by any disease or injury that causes mental or physical impairment serious enough to result in functional limitation or disability. The postmyocardial infarction patient, the post-trauma patient, patients with psychological illnesses, and the postsurgical patient need and can benefit from rehabilitation efforts. The combined efforts of the patient, family, friends, medical, nursing, allied health personnel, and community resources are essential to making rehabilitation possible. SYN: *restorative care.* **2.** In dentistry, the methods for restoring dentition to its optimal functional condition. It may involve restoration of teeth by fillings, crowns, or bridgework; adjustment of occlusal surfaces by selective grinding; orthodontic realignment of teeth; or surgical correction of diseased or malaligned parts. It may be done to improve chewing, to enhance the aesthetic appearance of the face and teeth, to enhance speech, or to preserve the dentition and supporting tissues. SYN: *mouth rehabilitation; occlusal rehabilitation; oral rehabilitation.*

> **aquatic r.** Aquatic therapy.

> **aural r.** Any treatment used to improve the hearing or expressiveness of a hearing-impaired person.

> **cardiac r.** A structured, interdisciplinary program of progressive exercise, psychological support, nutritional counseling, and patient education to enable attainment of maximum functional capacity by patients who have experienced a myocardial infarction.

> **cognitive r.** Cognitive retraining.

> **driver r.** Specialized assistance provided to those who need to develop or improve their skills and abilities to enable greater safety or independence in driving because of physical, cognitive, or perceptual deficits. Services typically include clinical assessment, assistance with seating and positioning, simulated driving practice, on-road evaluation and training, passenger car evaluation, and recommendations for vehicle modifica-

tions. SEE: *driver rehabilitation therapist*.

mouth r. Rehabilitation (2).

occlusal r. Rehabilitation (2).

oral r. Rehabilitation (2).

neurological r. A supervised program of formal training to restore function to patients who have neurodegenerative diseases, spinal cord injuries, strokes, or traumatic brain injury.

nutritional r. A comprehensive nutritional program for patients with especially grave nutritional deficits, such as those caused by severe eating disorders or malabsorption syndrome.

penile r. Any technique or medication that improves erectile function after radical prostatectomy.

pool r. Aquatic therapy.

psychiatric r. Any intervention that helps people with psychiatric or psychological restrictions to participate successfully in school or work, the management of their own homes, and relationships with others. SYN: *psychosocial r*.

psychosocial r. Psychiatric **r.**

pulmonary r. A structured program of activity, progressive breathing and conditioning exercises, and patient education designed to return patients with pulmonary disease to maximum function.

rehabilitation engineering The application of engineering principles and practices to the design and manufacturing of assistive technology devices, such as powered wheelchairs, environmental control systems, and augmentative or alternative communication devices.

Rehabilitation Engineering and Assistive Technology Society of North America. ABBR: RESNA. A professional organization concerned with establishing and promoting education, research, and standards of practice for rehabilitation engineers and other specialists in assistive technology.

rehabilitee (rē″hă-bĭl′ĭ-tē) A person who has been rehabilitated.

rehearse To practice or repeat an action, emotion, operation, phrase, or thought to attain mastery of it.

rehydration (rē″hī-drā′shŭn) [″ + Gr. *hydor*, water] The restoration of fluid volume to a dehydrated person, either orally or parenterally. SEE: *oral rehydration therapy*.

Reichert cartilage (rī′kĕrts) [Karl Bogislaus Reichert, Ger. anatomist, 1811–1883] The second branchial arch of the embryo, which gives rise to the stapes, styloid process, stylohyoid ligament, and lesser cornua of the hyoid bone.

Reid base line (rēdz) [Robert William Reid, Scottish anatomist, 1851–1939] The line extending from the lower edge of the orbit to the center of the aperture of the external auditory canal and backward to the center of the occipital bone.

Reid index (rēd) A measure of the relative thickness of the glandular layer of the trachea, bronchi, or bronchioli to the thickness of the entire airway wall. The index increases in patients with chronic bronchitis.

Reifenstein syndrome (rīf′ĕn-shtīn″) [Edward Conrad Reifenstein, Jr., U.S. endocrinologist, 1908–1975] A rare X-linked condition in which males have a genetic alteration in their androgen receptors, which blocks the effect of testosterone and related hormones on the development of male secondary sexual characteristics. Boys with the syndrome have both small penises and pseudovaginas at birth and therefore an intersexed appearance.

Reiki (rī′kē) A system of healing originating in Japanese metaphysics in which practitioners direct the ch'i to achieve restoration of health.

Reil island (rīl) Island of Reil.

reimbursement (rē-ĭm-bŭrs′mĕnt) Payment for health care services.

reimplantation (rē″ĭm-plăn-tā′shŭn) [L. *re*, again, + *in*, into, + *plantare*, to set] Replantation (2).

reimportation (rē″ĭm-pawr-tā′shŭn) The purchase of drugs manufactured in their source nation by another nation to which the drugs are exported. At times it yields significant price advantages to the purchaser. Drugs manufactured in the U.S. are sometimes marketed abroad to other nations at low cost. The purchase of these drugs by American consumers from foreign pharmacies may yield cost savings accompanied by the risk that they may prove to be counterfeit or contaminated versions of the originals.

reincarnation (rē-ĭn-kăr-nā′shŭn) [″ + incarnation] **1.** The belief held by members of some religious groups that a person returns in physical or spiritual form to live again after death. **2.** A renewal of interest in an old or previously discarded idea. **3.** A psychological or spiritual reawakening of someone who had previously been engaged in a wholly different set of activities or interests.

reinfarction (rē″ĭn-fărk′shĭn) [″ + ″] Repeat infarction (esp. myocardial infarction) after an initial infarct.

reinfection (rē″ĭn-fĕk′shŭn) [″ + ME. *infecten*, infect] A second infection by the same organism. SEE: *superinfection*.

reinforcement (rē″ĭn-fors′mĕnt) [″ + *inforce*, enforce] **1.** Strengthening; an augmentation of force, e.g., of a reflex. **2.** In educational theory, a reward given for an appropriate or desired response.

reinforcer (rē″ĭn-fors′ĕr) Something that produces reinforcement.

reinfusion (rē″ĭn-fū′zhŭn) [″ + *infusio*,

to pour in] The reinjection of blood serum or cerebrospinal fluid.

Reinke edema (rĭngk′ĕ) [Friedrich B. Reinke, Ger. anatomist, 1862–1919] Pathological swelling of the vocal folds as a result of smoking. It causes an alteration in the pitch of the voice and may interfere with the passage of air (or medical instruments) through the folds.

reinnervation (rē″ĭn-ĕr-vā′shŭn) [″ + in, into, + nervus, nerve] **1.** Anastomosis of a paralyzed part with a living nerve. **2.** Grafting of a fresh nerve for restoration of function in a paralyzed muscle.

reinoculation (rē″ĭn-ŏk″ū-lā′shŭn) [″ + in, into, + oculus, bud] A second inoculation with the same organism or its antigens. SEE: reinfection.

reintegration In psychology, the resumption of normal behavior and mental functioning following disintegration of personality in mental illness.

reinversion (rē″ĭn-vĕr′shŭn) [″ + in, into, + versio, turning] Correction of an inverted organ.

Reissner membrane (rīs′nĕr) [Ernst Reissner, Ger. anatomist, 1824–1878] A delicate membrane separating the cochlear canal from the scala vestibuli.

Reiter syndrome (rīt′ĕr) [Hans Conrad Julius Reiter, Ger. physician, 1881–1969] ABBR: RS. A syndrome consisting of urethritis, which usually occurs first; then arthritis and conjunctivitis. It occurs mainly in young men. When an organism is implicated, it is most frequently Chlamydia. The disease recurs frequently, and can produce debilitating arthritis and skin lesions. The prognosis is generally good; however, recurrences are common.

    TREATMENT: There is no specific therapy. Tetracyclines or erythromycins are used for urethritis. The sexual partner should be treated if RS was transmitted sexually. Arthritis and conjunctivitis are treated symptomatically.

rejection (rĕ-jek′shŭn) [L. rejectio, a throwing back] **1.** Refusal to accept or to show affection. In animals, for example, the young may be ignored or driven away by their mother. **2.** In tissue and organ transplantation, destruction of transplanted material at the cellular level by the host's immune mechanism. Transplant rejection is controlled primarily by T cells, but macrophages and B lymphocytes are also involved. Maintenance immunosuppressive therapy with cyclosporine, mycophenolate, and tacrolimus, which inhibit or block T-cell activity, lowers the risk of transplant organ rejection. Monoclonal and polyclonal antibody therapies are saved for acute rejection.

    acute r. The early destruction of grafted or transplanted material, usually beginning a week after implantation. Acute rejection is identified clinically by decreased function of the transplanted organ. High-dose corticosteroids are the first treatment of acute rejection; they are typically quite effective. Antilymphocyte globulin (ALG), the monoclonal antibody OKT 3, mycophenolate mofetil, and tacrolimus are used when corticosteroids are not effective. SEE: suppressive immunotherapy; macrophage processing; major histocompatibility complex; T cell.

    antibody-mediated r. Rejection of a transplanted organ due to the action of antibodies against antigens found on the endothelial surface of blood vessels.

    chronic r. Late and ongoing destruction of grafted or transplanted tissue. It most commonly involves vascular changes and interstitial fibrosis. Immunosuppressive therapy with tacrolimus and cyclosporine has significantly reduced this T-cell–mediated rejection process.

    hyperacute r. Immediate, intense, and irreversible destruction of grafted material due to preformed antibodies. These antibodies are most common in patients who have rejected a previously transplanted organ or who have received multiple blood transfusions. The risk of hyperacute rejection has been nearly eliminated by testing the recipient's blood for antibodies against donor lymphocytes before surgery.

    parental r. The refusal of a parent to accept or show affection for a son or daughter.

rejuvenation (ri-joo″vĕ-nā′shŏn) [re- + L. juvenis, young] A return to a youthful condition or to the normal.

    facial r. Any form of cosmetic surgery (or other skin treatment) that makes the face appear younger, e.g., by eliminating or reducing wrinkles, sun damage, or the drooping or sagging of tissues or structures.

rejuvenescence (rĭ-jū″vĕ-nĕs′ĕns) [″ + juvenescere, to become young] The renewal of youth; the return to an earlier stage of existence.

relapse (rē-lăps′) [L. relapsus] The recurrence of a disease or symptoms after apparent recovery.

relapsing (rē′lăp-sēng) Recurring after apparent recovery.

related identical donor SEE: under donor.

relation (rĭ-lā′shŭn) [L. relatio, a carrying back] The condition, connection, or state of one thing compared with another.

    jaw r. Any relation of the position of the maxilla to that of the mandible.

    occlusal jaw r. The relation of the mandibular teeth to the maxillary teeth when the teeth are in contact.

    unstrained jaw r. The position of the

jaw during normal tonus of all the jaw muscles.

relational disorder Any marked impairment in communication or other aspects of interpersonal interactions among family members, spouses, or coworkers.

relative biological effectiveness, relative biological effect ABBR: RBE. The impact of a specific radiation dose on the diseased tissue or organ into which it is directed. For a given amount of radiation, tissue destruction is greater for a larger RBE.

relative dose response SEE: under *response*.

relative refractory period SEE: under *period*.

relator (ri-lāt′ŏr) [L. *relator,* a proposer] **1.** One who reports alleged illegal behavior to a court of law. **2.** A surgical device that positions two structures so they are properly aligned.

relax [L. *relaxare,* to loosen] To decrease tension or intensity; to be rid of strain, anxiety, and nervousness.

relaxant (ri-lak′sănt) [L. *relaxare,* to loosen] **1.** Pert. to or producing relaxation. **2.** A drug that reduces tension. **3.** A laxative.

   muscle r. A drug or therapeutic treatment that specifically relieves muscular tension. SYN: *muscle relaxer*.

   neuromuscular r. A drug (e.g., succinylcholine) that prevents transmission of stimuli to muscle tissue, esp. striated muscle.

   smooth muscle r. A drug that reduces the tension of smooth muscles such as those in the intestinal tract or bronchi.

relaxation (rē-lăk-sā′shŭn) **1.** A lessening of tension or activity in a part. **2.** A phase or period in a single muscle twitch following contraction in which tension decreases, fibers lengthen, and the muscle returns to a resting position. **3.** In magnetic resonance imaging, the return of an excited atom to alignment with the applied magnetic field.

   general r. Relaxation of the entire body.

   local r. Relaxation limited to a particular muscle group or to a certain part.

   pelvic r. Diminished support of the pelvic tissues and organs, esp. in women; usually due to childbirth or aging. The organs affected and the pathological conditions associated with this condition are the bladder (cystocele), rectum (rectocele), uterus (uterine prolapse), small intestine (enterocele), and urethra (protrusion of the urethra into the vagina). Symptoms are related to the organ(s) affected. Treatment is determined by the severity of the relaxation. Medical treatments, including pelvic muscle exercises, pessaries, prompted voiding regimens, and estrogen therapy, may be helpful to patients;

however, many patients require surgery.

relaxation response SEE: under *response*.

relaxin (rĭ-lăk′sĭn) A polypeptide hormone related to insulin. It has many effects on breast, uterine, cardiac, and other tissues. In women, during pregnancy, it is secreted by the corpus luteum. In the latter part of pregnancy, for example, it facilitates labor by softening the uterine cervix and symphysis pubis. In men, it is secreted by the prostate gland.

relaxometry (rē-lăk-sŏm′ĕ-trē) [″ + ″] In magnetic resonance imaging, the measurement of the time it takes for excited nuclei to return to their basal state.

relearning Acquiring a skill or ability that had been previously present but was lost or removed as a result of physical damage to the muscles or brain.

release (ri-lēs′) **1.** A document that, if signed by the patient or the patient's legal representative, permits the treating health care provider to perform certain procedures. In addition to being signed by the patient, the release should also be signed by a witness. Most releases have a notation indicating the applicable time of the release. **2.** To discharge. **3.** To remove restraints.

   extended r. In pharmacology, the slow or gradual absorption of a drug after ingestion, e.g., one that achieves a peak concentration in the blood after about 6 hr.

   immediate r. In pharmacology, the rapid absorption of a drug after ingestion.

   myofascial r. ABBR: MFR. The manipulation of soft tissue to facilitate improved posture and range of motion and to decrease pain. SEE: *soft-tissue mobilization*.

   surgical r. Freeing tissues or organs trapped in place by adhesions or scars.

   sustained r. The delivery of a drug from a tablet or other reservoir over many hours or days (instead of minutes or hours), to provide a durable therapeutic effect.

reliability (ri-lī″ă-bil′ĭt-ē) **1.** Dependability, accuracy, or honesty. **2.** In statistics, the ability of a measuring instrument to produce reproducible results.

   interobserver r. Interrater **r.**

   interrater r. The extent to which two independent parties, each using the same tool or examining the same data, arrive at matching conclusions. Many health care investigators analyze graduated data, not binary data. In an analysis of anxiety, for example, a graduated scale may rate research subjects as "very anxious," "somewhat anxious," "mildly anxious," or "not at all anxious," whereas a binary method of rating anxiety might include just the two categories "anxious" and "not anxious." If the study is carried out and coded by more than one psychologist, the coders may not agree on the implementation of the graduated scale: some may interview a patient and find him or her "somewhat" anxious; another might assess the patient as being "very anxious." The congruence in the application of the rating scale by more than one psychologist constitutes its interrater reliability. SYN: *interobserver r.*

intrarater r. The extent to which a single individual, reusing the same rating instrument, consistently produces the same results while examining a single set of data.

test-retest r. The ability of a test to produce consistent results when it is used multiple times under nearly equivalent conditions. A test whose results fluctuate minimally when it is reused is said to have good test-retest reliability.

relief (rĭ-lēf') [ME.] **1.** The alleviation or removal of a distressing or painful symptom. **2.** Assistance given to the poor, homeless, or those whose lives have been changed by mass casualty incidents or other catastrophes. Relief may be provided in the form of food, clothing, shelter, loans, or cash, as well as other goods and services.

religiosity, impaired Impaired ability to exercise reliance on beliefs and/or participate in rituals of a particular faith tradition. SEE: *Nursing Diagnoses Appendix.*

religiosity, readiness for enhanced Ability to increase reliance on religious beliefs and/or participate in rituals of a particular faith tradition. SEE: *Nursing Diagnoses Appendix.*

religiosity, risk for impaired At risk for an impaired ability to exercise reliance on religious beliefs and/or participate in rituals of a particular faith tradition. SEE: *Nursing Diagnoses Appendix.*

reline (rē-līn') To replace or resurface the lining of a denture.

relocation stress syndrome Physiological and/or psychosocial disturbances as a result of transfer from one environment to another. SEE: *Nursing Diagnoses Appendix.*

relocation test A clinical test to identify the presence of anterior glenohumeral instability. The patient is placed supine, the glenohumeral joint abducted to 90° with the elbow flexed to 90°. While maintaining a posteriorly directed pressure on the humeral head, the examiner externally rotates the humerus. The test is used only after a positive apprehension test for glenohumeral instability. A positive relocation test is marked by decreased apprehension and pain, and increased range of motion relative

to the apprehension test. SEE: *sudden release test.*

REM (rĕm) *rapid eye movement.*

rem (rĕm) *roentgen equivalent (in) man.*

Remak sign (rā'mok") [Ernest Julius Remak, Ger. neurologist, 1849–1911] A sign or symptom pert. to perception of stimuli. It can be one of two types: a single stimulus may be perceived as if it were several stimuli applied in separate locations (polyesthesia), or there may be a delay in perception of stimuli. Both types are seen in tabes dorsalis.

REM behavior disorder, rapid eye movement sleep disorder ABBR: RBD. A relatively rare sleep disorder in which people act out their dreams during REM sleep, a phase of sleep during which most people are normally paralyzed. It is found most often in men over the age of 60. Sudden and potentially dangerous limb movements, grunting vocalizations, and disruption of the normal continuity of sleep are common findings.

remedial (rĭ-mē'dē-ăl) [L. *remedialis*] Curative; intended as a remedy.

remedy (rem'ĕd-ē) [L. *remedium,* healing, medicine] **1.** To cure or relieve a disease. **2.** Anything that relieves or cures a disease.

home r. A traditional therapy often utilizing natural products, nutritional supplements, or physical measures. Its effectiveness may be supported by familial, local, or culturally accepted stories or rituals. Also called a folk remedy.

local r. An agent used to relieve a local condition such as a sore.

systemic r. An agent used to relieve or cure a disease affecting the entire organism.

remineralization (rē-mĭn"ĕr-ăl-ĭ-zā'shŭn) Therapeutic replacement of the mineral content of the body after it has been disrupted by disease or improper diet. Remineralization of bone, e.g., is accomplished by adding mineral ions to hydroxyapatite in the bony matrix.

reminiscence therapy (rĕm-ĭn-ĭs'ĕns) A form of supportive psychotherapy for elderly patients experiencing depression or loss. Reminiscence therapy assists patients to review and highlight the meaningful components of their past. This is thought to increase self-esteem and life satisfaction. It can be conducted in groups or individually.

remission (rĭ-mĭsh'ŭn) [L. *remissio,* remit] **1.** A lessening in severity or an abatement of symptoms. **2.** The period during which symptoms abate. **3.** The period when no evidence of underlying disease exists.

remittance (rē-mĭt'ĕns) A temporary abatement of symptoms.

remittent (rē-mĭt'ĕnt) [L. *remittere,* to send back] **1.** Alternately abating and returning at certain intervals. SEE: *fever.* **2.** Episodic; periodic.

remnant Something that remains or is left over.

remnant removal disease A disorder of lipid metabolism in which the uptake of lipoproteins by the liver is impaired. The condition increases levels of both cholesterol and triglycerides in the blood, resulting in an increased risk of both coronary and peripheral vascular disease.

remodeling The reshaping or reconstruction of a part of the body, esp. to repair a part that has been injured (e.g., the walls of the heart after myocardial infarction or the airways in patients with asthma).

   airway r. Pathological changes in bronchi and bronchioles that occur in chronic asthma. These include increases in airway collagen, airway smooth muscle, and goblet cells.

   bone r. The net effect of new bone formation and absorption in which bone is resorbed and new bone formed at the same site. This process keeps the calcium content of bone stable. Bone is a dynamic tissue: it responds continuously to mechanical stress, nutritional status, hormones, and concentrations of circulating calcium.

   temporomandibular joint r. The slow changes in the articular surfaces of the temporomandibular joint as it adapts to changing occlusal forces, resulting in shape changes or irregularities of the condyle or articular eminence.

remote ischemic preconditioning ABBR: RIPC. The protection of internal organs from ischemia by transiently blocking the flow of blood, usually to an arm or a leg, and then letting the limb reperfuse before permanent injury occurs. It is used as a pretreatment before several forms of vascular surgery.

REM sleep behavior disorder A sleep disorder, most often identified in older men, in which there is frequent and sometimes violent motor activity during REM sleep, specifically during dreams. The condition often precedes the development of dementia with Lewy bodies, or other neurodegenerative disorders such as Parkinson disease.

ren (rĕn) *pl.* **renes** [L.] The kidney.

renal (rē'năl) [LL. *renalis,* kidney] **1.** Pert. to the kidney. SYN: *nephric.* SEE: *kidney* for illus. **2.** Shaped like a kidney.

renal clearance test One of several kidney function tests based on the kidney's ability to eliminate a given substance in a standard time. Urea, phenolsulfonphthalein (PSP), and other substances are employed.

renal papillary necrosis Destruction of the papillae of the kidney, usually as a result of pyelonephritis, diabetes mellitus, sickle cell disease, urinary obstruc-

tion, or the toxic effects of nonsteroidal anti-inflammatory drugs. If the necrotic tissue sloughs into the ureters, it may cause renal colic similar to the pain caused by a kidney stone.

renal scanning SEE: under *scanning.*

renal tubular acidosis SEE: under *acidosis.*

renaturation (rē"nā"chŭ-rā'shŏn) [*re-* + *(de)naturation*] The reassembly of a molecule or the shape of a molecule, e.g., the rejoining of unraveled complementary strands of DNA into a double helix. **renature** (rē-nā'chŭr), *v.* **renatured** (rē-nā'chŭrd), *adj.*

Rendu-Osler-Weber syndrome (răn-dyū'ŏs'lĕr-wĕ'bĕr) Hereditary hemorrhagic telangiectasia.

reniform (rĕn'ĭ-form) [L. *ren,* kidney, + *forma,* shape] Shaped like a kidney. SYN: *nephroid.*

renin (rĕn'ĭn) An enzyme produced by the kidney that splits angiotensinogen to form angiotensin I, which is then transformed to angiotensin II, which stimulates vasoconstriction and secretion of aldosterone. The blood renin level is elevated in some forms of hypertension.

renin substrate Angiotensinogen.

renipuncture (rĕn"ĭ-pŭnk'chūr) [" + *punctura,* a piercing] Surgical puncture of the renal capsule.

rennet (rĕn'ĕt) [ME.] **1.** The lining of the fourth stomach of a calf. **2.** A fluid containing rennin (chymosin), a coagulating enzyme, used for making junket or cheese.

rennin (rĕn'ĭn) Chymosin.

renninogen (rĕn-ĭn'ō-jĕn) [ME. *rennet,* rennet, + Gr. *gennan,* to produce] The antecedent or zymogen from which rennin is formed; the inactive form of rennin.

reno-, ren- [L. *ren(es),* kidney(s)] Prefixes meaning *kidney.* SEE: *nephro-.*

renogram (rē'nŏ-gram") [*reno-* + *-gram*] A record of the rate of removal of an intravenously injected dose of a radioactive tracer from the blood by the kidneys.

   DMSA r. A method of testing the kidneys for evidence of pyelonephritis, e.g., in children suspected of having kidney damage resulting from vesicoureteral reflux. A small dose of dimercaptosuccinic acid (DMSA) linked to radioactive technetium (technetium-99m) is injected intravenously and allowed to circulate to the kidneys. Several hours later, uptake of the tracer by the kidneys is measured with a gamma camera.

   DTPA r. A method for measuring blood flow to the kidneys and urinary excretion by the kidneys. A small dose of diethylenetriamine pentacetic acid (DTPA) linked to radioactive technetium (technetium-99m) is injected intravenously. Images of the kidneys are taken without delay. The tracer's circulation to the kidneys and its excretion by them can provide information about diseases such as renal artery stenosis, kidney transplant rejection, and ureteral or urethral obstruction.

renography (rē-nŏg'ră-fē) [" + Gr. *graphein,* to write] Radiography of the kidney.

renoprival (rē"nō-prī'văl) Pert. to loss of kidney function.

renoprotective (rē"nō-prŏ-tek'tiv) [*reno- + protective*] Protecting the kidneys, structurally or functionally.

renovascular (rē"nō-văs'kū-lăr) Pert. to the vascular supply of the kidney.

Renshaw cell (rĕn'shaw) [B. Renshaw, U.S. neurophysiologist, 1911–1948] An interneuron of the spinal cord that inhibits motor neurons.

reocclusion (rē'ŏ-kloo"zhŭn) Closure of a structure (e.g., a blood vessel) that had been previously stenosed and then unclogged by mechanical dilation or the use of medications.

Reoviridae (rē"ō-vĭr'ĭ-dē) [NL. fr. r(espiratory) + (e)nteric + o(rphan)] A family of double-stranded RNA viruses that includes many members that produce human disease, including the rotaviruses (prominent causes of nonbacterial diarrhea in children) and coltiviruses (the cause of Colorado tick fever).

reovirus (rē"ō-vī'rŭs) [*respiratory enteric orphan virus*] A double-stranded RNA virus found in the respiratory and digestive tracts of apparently healthy persons, and occasionally associated with respiratory, digestive, or neurological diseases.

repackaging The transfer of specified doses of a medication from a manufacturer's bulk container to smaller containers used by patients and/or dispensing institutions.

repair (ri-par') To remedy, replace, or heal, as in a wound or a lost part.

   mini-open r. Surgery made through a small incision, typically one that is shorter than 3 cm in length. When the surgery enters a joint space, it is often assisted by arthroscopy, e.g., in repairs of the carpal tunnel, the rotator cuff, or the spine.

   PATIENT CARE: Compared with open surgical techniques, mini-open techniques often heal more quickly and with less disability and pain.

   plastic r. Use of plastic surgery to repair tissue.

   tooth r. Professional dental care that covers defects in an injured or carious tooth or replaces missing teeth, e.g., with a crown, a bridge, or an implant. This is usually accompanied by improved health of the gingiva and the periodontal ligament.

reparative medicine (ri-par'ăt-ĭv) SEE: under *medicine.*

repeat open application test ABBR: ROAT. A skin test used to confirm or rule out the presence of allergic contact dermatitis, used after an initial patch test of a suspected allergen was negative or only weakly positive. The agent suspected of causing the reaction is applied to the skin twice a day for several days, and the skin is examined for eczema. The presence of a rash after ROAT implies the patient is truly allergic to the applied agent.

repellent [L. *repellere,* to drive back] An agent that repels noxious organisms such as insects, ticks, and mites. Repellents may be applied to the surface of the body as a liquid, spray, or dust, or they may be used to impregnate clothing.

   insect r. A commercial preparation effective in repelling insects. Many insect repellents contain diethyltoluamide, an effective agent popularly known as DEET.

⚠ When applying insect repellent, do not allow it to contact the eyes.

repercolation (rē"pĕr-kō-lā'shŭn) [L. *re,* again, + *percolare,* to filter] Repeated percolation using the same materials.

repercussion (rē-pĕr-kŭsh'ŭn) [L. *repercussio,* rebound] 1. A reciprocal action. 2. An action involved in causing the subsidence of a swelling, tumor, or eruption. 3. Ballottement.

repercussive (rē"pĕr-kŭs'ĭv) 1. Causing repercussion. 2. An agent that repels; a repellent.

reperfusion (rē-pĕr-fū'zhŏn) [*re- + perfusion*] 1. The restoration of blood flow to a part of the body deprived of adequate circulation, e.g., the heart muscle in myocardial infarction or the brain in stroke. This may be accomplished by thrombolytic agents, (e.g., streptokinase or tissue plasminogen activator), or mechanical interventions (e.g., stent placement). These interventions have improved outcomes in patients with acute coronary syndromes and in patients with stroke who come to medical attention in the first few hours of their illness. 2. The reinstitution of blood flow to tissues that have been traumatized, esp. by a long period of crushing. SEE: *crush syndrome; rhabdomyolysis.*

repetition maximum The greatest amount of weight a person can lift "n" number of times. The amount of weight that can be lifted exactly 10 times is 10 RM. The greatest amount of weight that can be lifted once is 1 RM. Repetition maximum can be used as a comparative measure of strength or as a technique in exercise prescription and strength training. During strength training 8 RM or 10 RM is used to develop strength, power, and muscle mass.

repetitive motion injury SEE: under *injury*.

replacement (ri-plās'mĕnt) **1.** The restoration of a structure to its original position. **2.** The restoration of lost fluids e.g., by fluid infusions or blood transfusion. **3.** The giving of an electrolyte or hormone to a patient to replenish a deficit and restore normal plasma concentrations. Particular replacements are listed under the first word. SEE: e.g., *fat replacement; fluid replacement; total joint replacement.*

replacement level fertility **1.** That level of reproduction in which a mother delivers a single daughter. **2.** A level of reproduction in which a population exactly replaces itself from one generation to the next.

replacement solution SEE: under *solution.*

replacement therapy The therapeutic use of a medicine to substitute for or replenish a natural substance that is either absent or diminished in disease (e.g., insulin in diabetes mellitus or thyroid hormone in hypothyroidism). SYN: *substitution therapy.*

replantation [L. *re*, again, + *planto,* to plant] **1.** Surgical reattachment or reconnection of something removed from the body, esp. the surgical procedure of rejoining a hand, arm, or leg to the body after its accidental detachment. **2.** In dentistry, the replacement of a tooth that has been removed from its socket. SYN: *reimplantation.*

repletion (rē-plē'shŭn) [L. *repletio,* a filling up] The condition of being full or satisfied.

replication (rĕp″lĭ-kā'shŭn) **1.** A doubling back of tissue. **2.** In medical investigations, the repetition of an experiment. **3.** In genetics, the duplication process of genetic material.

replicon (rĕp'lĭ-kŏn) A segment of DNA that includes the "start" and "stop" nucleotide sequences and can replicate as a unit. Self-replicating units of DNA include, for example, chromosomes, plasmids, and phages.

repolarization (rē″pō″lăr-ĭ-zā'shŭn) Restoration of the polarized state at a cell membrane (negative inside in relation to the outside) following depolarization as in muscle or nerve fibers.

report **1.** The account, usually verbal and often tape-recorded, that the nursing staff going off duty gives to the oncoming staff. The purpose is to provide continuity of care despite the change in staff. The information provided is of the utmost importance in caring for critically ill patients. **2.** A record of a drug reaction, illness, medical emergency, or other health-related statistic.

reporting (rĭ-pŏrt'ĭng) Making a record of an observation available for review.

reposition (rē″pō-zĭsh'ŭn) [L. *repositio,* a replacing] Restoration of an organ or tissue to its correct or original position.

repositioning (rē″pŏ-zish'ŏn-ing) [*re-* + *positioning*] Replacement of a structure to its original site or a new site.

  jaw r. Changing of the position of the mandible in relation to the maxilla by altering the occlusion of the teeth.

  muscle r. Surgical placement of a muscle to another attachment point to enhance function.

  patient r. Turning a patient from one side to another, or from a recumbent position to a seated one, in order to facilitate patient care, perform a procedure, prevent pressure ulcers, or improve comfort.

repositor (ri-poz'ĭt-ŏr) An instrument for restoring a tissue or an organ to its normal position.

repression (rē-prĕsh'ŭn) [L. *repressus,* press back] In psychology, the refusal to entertain distressing or painful ideas. In Freudian theory, repression involves the submersion of such thoughts in the unconscious, where they continue to influence the individual. Psychoanalysis seeks to discover and release repressions.

  coordinate r. Simultaneous reduction of the enzyme levels of a metabolic pathway.

  enzyme r. Interference with enzyme synthesis by a metabolic product.

repressor (rē-prĕs'or) [L. *repressus,* press back] Something, esp. an enzyme, that inhibits or interferes with the initiation of protein synthesis by genetic material.

reprocessing Preparation of a dialysis membrane (or other medical device) for reuse with rinses and sterilizing solutions.

reprocessing of endoscopes Preparation of endoscopes for reuse by scrupulous cleaning and sterilization. Antimicrobial agents, such as glutaraldehyde, hydrogen peroxide, orthophthalaldehyde or peracetic acid, may be used.

  PATIENT CARE: To protect patients from infections transmitted by reused endoscopes, the following procedure is followed when using glutaraldehyde:

  1. The endoscope is manually cleaned externally;

  2. Detergent is drawn through the accessory channel;

  3. The accessory channel's chamber and valves are carefully brushed;

  4. Reusable forceps are sterilized;

  5. The endoscope is treated with a 2.4% solution of glutaraldehyde, heated to 25°C for 45 min;

  6. The strength of the disinfectant solution is tested daily.

reproducibility   (rē-prō-doos-ĭ-bĭl'ĭ-tē)

1. The quality of being provable again by repeated experimentation. SEE: *research*. **2.** A quality control test of radiographical output for multiple exposures using the same exposure factors. These factors must not vary by more than ±5%.

reproduction (rē-prō-dŭk′shŭn) [L. *re*, again, + *productio*, production] **1.** The production of offspring by parents. SEE: *fertilization* for illus; *oogenesis* for illus. **2.** The creation of a similar structure or situation; duplication.

   asexual r. Reproduction without the union of gametes, as by fission, budding, or spore formation. SYN: *asexual generation*.

   cytogenic r. Reproduction by asexual single germ cells.

   sexual r. Reproduction by means of the union of germ or sex cells. Usually a male cell (spermatozoon) fuses with a female cell (egg or ovum). SYN: *sexual generation; syngamy*.

   somatic r. Asexual reproduction by cloning of somatic cells.

reproductive (rē″prō-dŭk′tĭv) Pert. to or employed in reproduction.

reproductive age In women, those years of life between menarche and menopause, roughly from ages 12 to 49. The term is imprecise, since some women can become pregnant and bear children at younger or older ages. In men, those years between the onset of puberty and loss of fertility.

reproductive system The gonads and their associated structures and ducts. In the female, this system includes the ovaries, uterine tubes (oviducts), uterus, vagina, and vulva. In the male, it includes the testes, efferent ducts, epididymis, ductus deferens, ejaculatory duct, urethra and accessory glands (bulbourethral, prostate, seminal vesicles), and penis. SYN: *genital system*. SEE: *female genitalia* and *male genitalia* for illus.

reproductive toxin SEE: under *toxin*.

reproductive tract infection SEE: under *infection*.

reptilase time (rep′tĭ-lās″) [Fr *reptil(e)* (the enzyme is a derivative of snake venom) + *-ase*] SEE: under *time*.

repulsion (rĭ-pŭl′shŭn) [L. *repulsio*, a thrusting back] **1.** The act of driving back. **2.** The force exerted by one body on another to cause separation; the opposite of attraction.

request for production of documents and things A discovery technique in which the plaintiff or defendant requests in a written form that the other party furnish information pertaining to the issues of the lawsuit.

   In medical negligence cases, the information requested may include medical records, office records, facility policies and procedures, staffing schedules, personnel records, ambulance run sheets, and autopsy protocols.

request for proposal ABBR: RFP. Notification by a foundation or government agency that funds are available for research projects and that research sponsors are seeking applicants for those funds.

required service A service that must be included in a health program for it to qualify for federal funds.

requisition (re″kwĭ-zish′ŏn) [L. *requisitio*, a searching] An order for a specific laboratory service or test, e.g., for a specimen to be analyzed.

requisition slip (re″kwĭ-zi′shŏn) [L. *requirere*, to seek] A form for ordering laboratory tests for a patient.

rescue (res′kū″) **1.** To free a person from a hazardous situation such as entrapment in an automobile, trench, cave, or burning building, or from the site of a hazardous material spill. **2.** To restore an organ to its normal function after an illness or a treatment that has damaged it.

   abdominal r. Emergency cesarean delivery of a fetus jeopardized during labor or failed vaginal birth. Indications for surgical intervention include fetal distress associated with dystocia, arrested descent, abruptio placentae, or umbilical cord prolapse.

   stem cell r. In patients being treated with high doses of chemotherapy or radiation therapy, the removal of stem cells (the precursors to red and white blood cells and platelets) from the patient's blood before treatment and their reinfusion after treatment. Granulocyte colony stimulating factor, erythropoietin, and other growth factors are administered to stimulate proliferation of the stem cells after reinfusion. Until adequate numbers of cells repopulate the patient's marrow and bloodstream, the patient is at high risk for infection and bleeding.

   Stem cell rescue is used in patients with solid tumors not involving bone marrow who require treatments that would destroy the blood-forming (hematopoietic) cells. The process is immunologically advantageous because the cells infused are the patient's own cells, and thus do not have foreign antigens.

rescue tool (rĕs′kyū) A piece of equipment used by rescuers in emergency medical service to free trapped victims. Rescue tools include a come-a-long, a hand-operated winch used to gain forceful entry during a rescue; cutting tools, used to cut open vehicles and metal to gain access to a person; a hydraulic jack, a hand-operated jack used to lift objects away from a person; pneumatic air bags, used to lift or spread heavy objects; and a power chisel, a pressure-operated device used to cut into sheet metal.

research (ri-sĕrch', rē'sĕrch″) [Fr. *re-cercher,* to go looking] Scientific study, investigation, or experimentation to establish facts and analyze their significance.

applied r. Transitional **r.**

clinical r. Research based mainly on observation of the patient rather than on laboratory work. It is often used to determine the safety and effectiveness of treatments, the natural history of disease, or the conditions that predispose to illness.

comparative effectiveness r. Any head-to-head study of alternative solutions to managing a disease, esp. when such a study examines a broadly representative population of patients and follows them for a long enough time to determine meaningful outcomes. Its goal is to identify which treatment produces the best clinical outcomes for most patients, rather than which is better than a placebo or which influences a laboratory test or other surrogate marker without having an impact on the actual health or longevity of patients.

exempt r. **1.** Research on human subjects that poses minimal risk, e.g., anonymous surveys, observation in a public place, or analysis of secondary data. **2.** Any research investigation that does not need to follow standard protocols or provide the usually expected protection to its subjects.

laboratory r. Research done principally in the laboratory.

longitudinal r. A long-term study of a cohort (a group of subjects born during a particular time period) that determines the natural history of an illness or the enduring effects of a treatment.

medical r. Research concerned with any phase of medical science.

nursing r. A formal, systematic, and rigorous process of inquiry used by nurses to generate and test the concepts and propositions that constitute middle-range nursing theories, which are derived from or linked with a conceptual model of nursing. The theories include: *Grand*: Health belief model; Transactional model of stress and coping; Life process interactive person-environment model; Roy adaptation model; Interacting systems conceptual framework. *Middle-Range*: Theory of self-care deficit; Theory of health promotion; Theory of self-regulation; Theory of uncertainty in illness; Theory of acute pain management; Theory of families, children, and chronic illness. *Practice*: Theory of interpersonal relations; Theory of representativeness heuristic; Theory of communicative action; Theory of clinical reasoning in nursing practice; Theory of end-of-life decision making.

outcomes r. An analysis of the value of provided health care services. SEE: *outcome criteria.*

participatory r. A community process in which a group of people takes an active role in defining their own health needs and devising means to meet them, including setting priorities for public health, controlling health-enhancing techniques, and evaluating results.

preembryo r. Research involving the use of the fertilized egg from its unicellular zygote stage until the embryo stage (the 14th day following fertilization). This includes studies of in vitro fertilization, conception, gene therapy, and studies of cancer.

transitional r. Scientific research that applies knowledge from fundamental research into, for example, biology, chemistry, or physics, to the solution of problems in agriculture, engineering, health care, industry, or pharmacology. SYN: *applied r.*

resect (rē-sekt') [L. *resecare,* to cut off, cut back] To cut off or cut out a portion of an entire structure or organ, as cutting off the end of a bone or removing a segment of the intestine.

resectable (rē-sĕk'tă-bl) Able to be removed surgically; usually used in reference to malignant growths.

resection (rē-sek'shŏn) [L. *resectio,* a cutting off] Partial or complete excision of a bone or other structure.

bilateral carotid body r. ABBR: BCBR. A rarely used method of treating carotid sinus syncope that relies on the bilateral surgical removal of the carotid bodies. SEE: *carotid body; carotid sinus syncope.*

gastric r. Surgical resection of all or a part of the stomach.

piecemeal r. Removal of a structure from the body, e.g., a polyp from the colon, in small bits or stages.

submucous r. Removal of tissue below the mucosa, esp. excision of cartilaginous tissue beneath the mucosal tissue of the nose.

transurethral r. of the prostate ABBR: TUR, TURP. The removal of prostatic tissue using a device inserted through the urethra. SEE: *prostatectomy;* illus.

wedge r. Surgical removal of a triangular-shaped piece of tissue, e.g., from the lung, gastrointestinal tract, uterus, ovary, or other organs. Wedge resection is often used to remove malignant tissue.

window r. Resection of a portion of the nasal septum after reflection of a flap of mucous membrane.

resectoscope (rē-sĕk'tō-skōp) [L. *resectus,* cut off, + Gr. *skopein,* to examine] An instrument for resection of the prostate gland through the urethra.

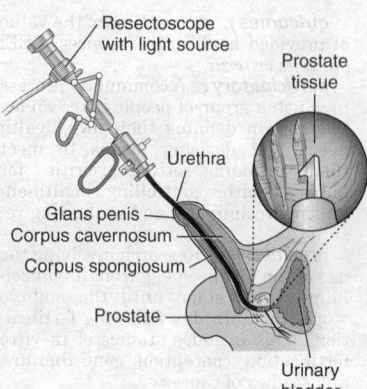

Labels: Resectoscope with light source; Prostate tissue; Urethra; Glans penis; Corpus cavernosum; Corpus spongiosum; Prostate; Urinary bladder

TRANSURETHRAL RESECTION OF THE PROSTATE

resectoscopy (rē″sĕk-tŏs′kō-pē) Resection of the prostate through the urethra.

resedation (rē″sĕ-dā′shŭn) [″ + ″] Succumbing to the effects of a sedative, hypnotic, or anesthetic drug after the drug's action has been reversed with its antagonist. The effect may occur because the half-life of the drug exceeds that of the antagonist (e.g., when the drug re-enters the bloodstream after it is released from storage in fatty tissues).

⚠️ Because many sedative/hypnotic drugs, anesthetics, or narcotic analgesics may redistribute into the blood after their effects have been temporarily reversed, patients who have received these drugs should be monitored for several hours to ensure that they are maintaining an alert mental status, an open airway, and effective respiration.

reserve (rĕ-zĕrv′) [L. *reservare,* to keep back] **1.** Something held back for future use. **2.** Self-control of one's feelings and thoughts.

    alkali r. Alkaline **r.**

    alkaline r. The amount of base in the blood, principally bicarbonates, available for neutralization of fixed acids (acetoacetate, β-hydroxybutyrate, and lactate). A fall in alkaline reserve is called acidosis; a rise, alkalosis. SYN: *alkali r.*

    cardiac r. The ability of the heart to increase cardiac output to meet the needs of increased energy output.

    coronary flow r. The ratio of the blood flow in the coronary arteries when they are at rest to their blood flow when they are maximally stimulated or dilated. SEE: *coronary blood flow.*

    fractional flow r. ABBR: FFR. The ratio of the blood pressure in the furthest reaches of a coronary artery divided by the blood pressure in the aorta.

The ratio is determined when the arteries are maximally vasodilated. The FFR determines the flow-limiting significance of a coronary artery stenosis. When the pressure in the distal portion of a healthy coronary artery is equal to the pressure in the aorta, the FFR is 1.0. Arteries with FFR less than 0.75 have large enough obstructions to cause myocardial ischemia.

    ovarian r. The number of remaining oocytes or follicles in the ovaries. The number typically falls with increasing age. It also declines as a result of some types of chemotherapy. Women with very limited ovarian reserves may have difficulty conceiving a child without assisted reproductive techniques.

reservoir (rez′ĕr-vwor) [Fr.] A place or cavity for storage.

    cardiotomy r. A device used to salvage autologous blood lost by patients as they undergo cardiac surgery.

    continent urinary r. A pouch made from the intestines used to hold urine in the abdomen, e.g., in patients who have had the urinary bladder removed. This internal pouch is an alternative to an ileostomy. It contains the urine and can be emptied by manual pressure or, more often, by catheterization. SYN: *Indiana continent urinary r.*

    Indiana continent urinary r. Continent urinary **r.**

    r. of infectious agents Any person, animal, arthropod, plant, soil, or substance in which an infectious agent normally lives and multiplies, on which it depends primarily for survival, and where it reproduces itself in a way that allows transmission to a susceptible host.

residence (rez′ĭ-dĕns) The place where one lives; a dwelling or habitation. **residential** (rez″ĭ-den′shăl), *adj.*

residency A period of at least 1 year and often 3 to 7 years of on-the-job training, usually postgraduate, that is part of the formal educational program for health care professionals.

resident (rez′ĭd-ĕnt) [L. *residere,* to sit back, remain behind, reside] A physician obtaining further clinical training after internship, usually as a member of the house staff of a hospital.

    categorical r. A trainee who enters a specialized academic health care program with the intent of completing his or her course of study in that field of study; as opposed to a resident who pursues elective instruction in the field before specializing in another.

    chief r. A house officer who participates in an additional year of residency in order to gain experience in the administration and education of other health care professionals during their training.

    surgical r. A physician who is enrolled in a hospital-based training program to complete the requirements for board certification in a surgical specialty.

residual (rĭ-zĭd′ū-ăl) [L. *residuum,* residue] **1.** Pert. to something left as a residue. **2.** In psychology, any aftereffect of experience influencing later behavior.

residual function The functional capacity remaining after an illness or injury.

residue (rez′ĭ-doo″, -dū″) [L. *residuus,* left over] **1.** The substance that remains after distillation or evaporation of a solution. **2.** Toxic materials that stay in an environment after their use or accidental discharge.

resilience (rē-zĭl′ē-ĕns) [L. *resiliens,* leaping back] **1.** Elasticity. **2.** The ability to withstand mental or physical stress.

resilient (rē-zĭl′ē-ĕnt) Elastic.

resin (rez′ĭn) [L. *resina,* fr. Gr. *rhētinē,* resin of the pine] **1.** A natural, amorphous, nonvolatile, soft or solid exudation of plants. It is practically insoluble in water but dissolves in alcohol. SEE: *rosin.* **2.** Any of a class of solid or soft organic compounds of natural or synthetic origin. They are usually of high molecular weight and most are polymers. Included are polyvinyl, polyethylene, and polystyrene. These are combined with chemicals such as epoxides, plasticizers, pigments, fillers, and stabilizers to form plastics.

    acrylic r. Quick-cure resin.

    anion-exchange r. SEE: *ion-exchange r.*

    cation-exchange r. SEE: *ion-exchange r.*

    cold-cure r. Quick-cure resin.

    ion-exchange r. An ionizable synthetic substance, which may be acid or basic, used accordingly to remove either acid or basic ions from solutions. Anion-exchange resins are used to absorb acid in the stomach, and cation-exchange resins are used to remove basic (alkaline) ions from solutions.

    quick-cure r. An autopolymer resin, used in many dental procedures, that can be polymerized by an activator and catalyst without applying external heat. SYN: *acrylic r.; cold-cure r.; self-curing r.*

    self-curing r. Quick-cure resin.

resinoid (rĕz′ĭ-noyd) [″ + Gr. *eidos,* form, shape] Resembling a resin.

resinous (rĕz′ĭ-nŭs) Having the nature of or pert. to resin.

res ipsa loquitur (rās ĭp′să lŏ′kwĭ-tur, rēz) [L. *res ipsa loquitur,* the thing speaks for itself] In malpractice a concept invoked in cases in which an injury occurs to the plaintiff in a situation solely under the control of the defendant. The injury would not have occurred had the defendant exercised due care. The defendant must then defend his or her actions. In medicine, the classic example of this situation is the leaving of an object such as a sponge or clamp in a patient's body after a surgical procedure, or the inadvertent removal of a healthy organ or extremity.

resistance (ri-zis′tăns) [L. *resistere,* to remain standing] **1.** Opposition to a disease, a toxin, or to a physical force. **2.** In psychoanalysis, a condition in which the ego avoids bringing into consciousness conflicts and unpleasant events responsible for neurosis; the reluctance of a patient to give up old patterns of thought and behavior. It may take various forms such as silence, failure to remember dreams, forgetfulness, and undue annoyance with trivial aspects of the treatment situation. **3.** Force applied to a body part by weights, machinery, or another person to load muscles as an exercise to increase muscle strength.

    airway r. The impedance to the flow of air into and out of the respiratory tract, measured in cm $H_2O/L/s$. Normal airway resistance is 4 cm $H_2O/L/s$.

    antibiotic r. The ability of microorganisms to survive in the presence of antibiotics. Mutations have provided some bacteria with genes for enzymes that destroy antibiotics such as penicillins, cephalosporins, or aminoglycosides. Other mutations have changed the structure of bacterial cell walls formerly penetrable by antibiotics or have created new enzymes for cellular functions previously blocked by drugs. SYN: *antimicrobial r.* SEE: *vancomycin-resistant enterococci; resistance transfer factor; methicillin-resistant Staphylococcus aureus.*

⚠ The indiscriminate use of antibiotics provides the selection pressure that creates ever more resistant strains.

    antimicrobial r. Antibiotic **r.**

    antiviral r. The developed resistance of a virus to specific antiviral therapy.

    bacterial r. The ability of bacteria to survive and cause continuous infection in the presence of antibiotics. SEE: *antiviral r.; antibiotic r.; multidrug r.; transfer factor.*

    bedtime r. Misbehaving, stalling tactics, or temper tantrums used by children to avoid going to bed on time. Bedtime resistance may be caused by a variety of emotional or psychological factors, e.g., fear of the dark, loneliness, or the desire for more attention.

    beta-lactamase r. The ability of microorganisms that produce the enzyme beta-lactamase (penicillinase) to resist the action of certain types of antibiotics, including some but not all forms of penicillin. Beta-lactamases make these microorganisms resistant to antibiotics by catalyzing the destruction of the beta-lactam ring that is essential for their antibacterial activity.

cross r. The ability of bacteria, viruses, or cancer cells to live and reproduce despite treatment with more than one drug. In cancer therapy, resistance to a wide range of unrelated drugs may occur after resistance to a single agent has developed. SYN: *multidrug r.; multiple drug r.* SEE: *gene amplification.*

drug r. The ability of a disease, esp. one caused by infectious pathogens, to withstand drug treatment.

expiratory r. 1. The impedence to airflow from the trachea, bronchi, mouth, or nose during exhalation. 2. The use of a restricted orifice, or flow resistor, during positive-pressure ventilation to retard the flow of exhaled gases. 3. An objective measure of bronchospasm.

extended-spectrum beta-lactamase r. ABBR: ESBL. An enzymatically mediated antibiotic resistance found in gram-negative bacilli (such as *Klebsiella pneumoniae, Enterobacter cloacae,* and *Pseudomonas aeruginosa*), that make these bacteria resistant to cephalosporins and penicillin antibiotics.

glucocorticoid r. 1. A rare genetically inherited insensitivity of peripheral tissues to the effects of steroid hormones produced by the adrenal cortex. Affected patients produce excessive compensatory quantities of ACTH and may be affected by hyperandrogenism or mineralocorticoid excess. 2. Insensitivity to treatment with glucocorticoid drugs, e.g., prednisone for asthma or Crohn disease.

insulin r. Cellular phenomena that prevent insulin from stimulating the uptake of glucose from the bloodstream and the synthesis of glycogen. Insulin resistance is one of the fundamental metabolic defects found in patients with type 2 diabetes mellitus.

manual r. SEE: *resistance exercise.*

mechanical r. SEE: *resistance exercise.*

multidrug r. ABBR: MDR. Cross **r.**

multiple drug r. Cross **r.**

peripheral r. The resistance of the arterial vascular system, esp. the arterioles and capillaries, to the flow of blood.

systemic vascular r. ABBR: SVR. The resistance to the flow of blood through the body's blood vessels. It increases as vessels constrict (as when a drug like norepinephrine is given) and decreases when vessels dilate (as in septic shock). Any change in the diameter, elasticity, or number of vessels recruited can influence the measured amount of resistance to the flow of blood through the body.

threshold r. The amount of pressure

necessary in overcoming resistance to flow.

transthoracic r. The amount of resistance to the flow of electrical energy across the chest. This is an important factor to consider when electrical therapies such as defibrillation, cardioversion, and transthoracic pacing are used to treat abnormal cardiac rhythms.

viscous r. Nonelastic opposition of tissue to ventilation due to the energy required to displace the thorax and airways.

resistance exercise SEE: under *exercise.*

resistance transfer factor SEE: under *factor.*

resistant (rē-zĭs′tĭnt, rĭ-) [L. *resistere,* to stand back, to withstand] A lack of response to, or of influence by, a pathogen, toxin, treatment, or other stressor.

resistant ovary SEE: under *ovary.*

resistin (rē-zĭs′tĭn) A cysteine-rich peptide hormone, secreted by fat, that decreases cell sensitivity to the effects of insulin.

RESNA *Rehabilitation Engineering and Assistive Technology Society of North America.*

resolution (rez-ŏ-loo′shŏn) [L. *resolutio,* a relaxing] 1. Absorption or breaking down of the products of inflammation; decomposition. 2. Cessation of illness; a return to normal. 3. The ability of the eye or a series of lenses to distinguish fine detail. 4. In radiology, the ability to record small images placed very close together as separate images.

alternative dispute r. ABBR: ADR. Any of the methods of dealing with disputes and avoiding trial or litigation that are less threatening, less costly, and less time-consuming. Examples include arbitration, facilitation, negotiation, and mediation. SYN: *conflict r.*

conflict r. Any of the methods used by disputing parties to settle their differences. Common methods include accommodating each other's needs, compromising, or working together toward shared goals; or avoiding, competing with, or attempting to defeat the opponent.

contrast r. In radiology, the ability to distinguish two images that vary very slightly in hue or color intensity.

diabetes r. Clinical improvement in a patient with diabetes mellitus, so that he no longer needs medication to maintain normal blood glucose levels. It can occur in patients who have sustained weight loss as a result of a change in body weight, e.g., after a continuing regimen of careful diet and exercise, or after bariatric surgery.

spatial r. In radiology, the ability to distinguish two adjacent points of similar density as being separate.

temporal r. In radiology, the ability

to distinguish two images that are separated by small increments of time.

resolve (rē-zŏlv′) [L. *resolvere*, to release] **1.** To return to normal as after a pathological process. **2.** To separate into components.

resolvin (ri-sol′vĭn) An anti-inflammatory lipid derived from eicosapentanoic acid (an omega-3-fatty acid).

resonance (rĕz′ō-năns) [L. *resonantia*, resound] **1.** The quality or act of resounding. **2.** The quality of the sound heard on percussion of a hollow structure such as the chest or abdomen. An absence of resonance is termed *flatness;* diminished resonance, *dullness.* **3.** In physics, the modification of sound caused by vibrations of a body that are set up by waves from another vibrating body. **4.** In electricity, a state in which two electrical circuits are in tune with each other.

   amphoric r. A sound similar to that produced by blowing across the mouth of an empty bottle.

   bandbox r. The pulmonary resonance heard during chest percussion in patients with emphysema.

   electron spin r. ABBR: ESR. A technique used in medical imaging that identifies atoms by their electron spin characteristics.

   normal r. Vesicular **r.**

   tympanic r. A low-pitched, drumlike sound heard on percussion over a large air-containing space.

   tympanitic r. The resonance obtained by percussion of a hollow structure, such as the stomach or colon, when it is moderately distended with air.

   vesicular r. The resonance obtained by percussion of normal lungs. SYN: *normal r.*

   vocal r. In auscultation, the vibrations of the voice transmitted to the examiner's ear, normally more marked over the right apex of the lung. These vibrations are abnormally increased in pneumonic consolidation, in lungs infiltrated with tuberculosis, or in cavities that communicate freely with a bronchus.

   Vocal resonance is diminished or absent in pleural effusion (air, pus, serum, lymph, or blood); emphysema; pulmonary collapse; pulmonary edema; and egophony, a modified bronchophony characterized by a trembling, bleating sound usually heard above the upper border of dullness of pleural effusions and occasionally heard in beginning pneumonia.

   whispering r. The auscultation sound heard when a patient whispers.

resonant (rĕz′ō-nănt) Producing a vibrating sound on percussion.

resonating (rĕz′ă-nāt″ĭng) [L. *resonantia*, resound] Vibrating sympatheti-

cally with a source of sound or electrical oscillations.

resonator (rĕz′ō-nā″tĕr) **1.** A structure that can be set into sympathetic vibration when sound waves of the same frequency from another vibrating body strike it. **2.** In electricity, an apparatus consisting of an electric circuit in which oscillations of a certain frequency are set up by oscillations of the same frequency in another circuit.

resorb (rē-sorb′, rē-zorb′) [L. *resorbere*, to suck in] **1.** To undergo resorption. **2.** To absorb again.

resorbent (rē-sor′bĕnt) [L. *resorbens*, sucking in] An agent that promotes the absorption of abnormal matters, as exudates or blood clots (e.g., potassium iodide, ammonium chloride).

resorcin (rē-zor′sĭn) Resorcinol.

resorcinol (rē-zor′sĭ-nŏl) An agent with keratolytic, fungicidal, and bactericidal actions, used in treating certain skin diseases. SYN: *resorcin*.

resorption (rē-sorp′shŏn) [L. *resorbere*, to suck in] **1.** Removal by absorption, as of an exudate or pus. **2.** The removal of enamel from a tooth or calcium compounds from bone. It often results from pressure or vascular changes as in root resorption of deciduous teeth prior to shedding, or bone resorption on the pressure side during tooth movement.

   bone r. The removal of bone by osteoclasts.

resource (rē′sors″, rē-sors′) [Fr. *ressourse*, relief, resource] **1.** An asset, valuable commodity, or service. **2.** Anything, e.g., medical supplies, held in reserve.

   renewable r. Any material that replenishes itself, grows naturally in the environment, or is constant, e.g., vegetable matter and wood, solar radiation, wave action, or wind.

Resource, Conservation, and Recovery Act ABBR: RCRA. An act passed in 1976 that gave the Environmental Protection Agency the authority to control hazardous waste disposal, including the disposal of infectious and radioactive medical waste products.

resource allocation 1. The management of economic and administrative reserves by choosing from among competing claims for assets and services. **2.** Health care rationing.

resource-based relative value scale SEE: under ¹ *scale*.

resource depletion The dissipation of assets or reserves, esp. (in health care and the environment) those that affect public health.

respirable (rē-spīr′ă-bl, rĕs′pĕr-ă-bl) [L. *respirare*, breathe again] Fit or adapted for respiration.

respiration (res″pĭ-rā′shŏn) [L. *respiratio*, breathing] **1.** The interchange of gases between an organism and the medium in which it lives. **2.** The act of breathing (inhaling and exhaling) during which the lungs are provided with air through inhaling and the carbon dioxide is removed through exhaling. Normal respiratory exchange of oxygen and carbon dioxide in the lungs is impossible unless the pulmonary tissue is adequately perfused with blood. SEE: *lung; ventilation;* illus.

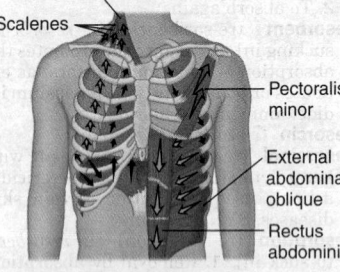

Sternocleidomastoid

Scalenes

Pectoralis minor

External abdominal oblique

Rectus abdominis

MUSCLES OF RESPIRATION

abdominal r. Respiration in which chiefly the diaphragm exerts itself while the chest wall muscles are nearly at rest; used in normal, quiet breathing, and in pathological conditions such as pleurisy, pericarditis, and rib fracture. SYN: *belly* **breathing**; *diaphragmatic* **r.**

absent r. Respiration in which respiratory sounds are suppressed or absent.

aerobic r. Cellular respiration in which oxygen is used in the production of energy.

amphoric r. Respiration having amphoric resonance. SEE: *amphoric reso-nance*.

anaerobic r. The release of energy from the reduction of metals (such as iron, manganese, or sulfur) by cells or organisms that do not use oxygen as their primary energy source.

apneustic r. Breathing marked by prolonged inspiration unrelieved by attempts to exhale. It is seen in patients who have had the upper part of the pons of the brain removed or damaged.

artificial r. Maintenance of respiratory movement by artificial means, such as rescue breathing, bag mask, pocket mask, automatic transport ventilator, manual transport ventilator, or a flow-restricted oxygen-powered ventilation device. SEE: *cardiopulmonary resuscitation*.

Biot r. Biot breathing.

cell r. The gradual breakdown of food molecules in the presence of oxygen within cells, resulting in the formation of carbon dioxide and water and the release of energy in the forms of adenosine

triphosphate and heat. In many intermediary reactions, substances other than oxygen act as oxidizing agents (hydrogen or electron acceptors). Reactions are catalyzed by respiratory enzymes, which include the flavoproteins, cytochromes, and other enzymes. Certain vitamins (nicotinamide, riboflavin, thiamine, pyridoxine, and pantothenic acid) are essential in the formation of components of various intracellular enzyme systems.

Cheyne-Stokes r. SEE: *Cheyne-Stokes respiration*.

costal r. Respiration in which the chest cavity expands by raising the ribs.

cutaneous r. The transpiration of gases through the skin.

decreased r. Respiration at less than a normal rate for the individual's age. In adults, it is a respiratory rate of less than 12 breaths per minute. Slower than normal respiratory rates occur after opiate or sedative use, during sleep, in coma, and other conditions and may result in respiratory failure or carbon dioxide retention. SYN: *slow r.*

diaphragmatic r. Abdominal **r.**

direct r. Respiration in which an organism, such as a one-celled ameba, secures its oxygen and gives up carbon dioxide directly to the surrounding medium.

electrophrenic r. Radiofrequency electrophrenic **r.**

external r. The exchange of gases in the lungs. Oxygen diffuses from the air to the blood, and carbon dioxide diffuses from the blood to the air.

fetal r. Gas exchange in the placenta between the fetal and maternal blood. SYN: *placental r.*

forced r. Voluntary hyperpnea.

internal r. The exchange of gases in body tissues. Oxygen diffuses from the blood to the cells, and carbon dioxide diffuses from the cells to the blood. Oxygen is carried in combination with hemoglobin. Oxyhemoglobin gives arterial blood its red color; reduced hemoglobin gives venous blood its dark red color. Most carbon dioxide is carried in the blood as bicarbonate ions; a small amount is bonded to hemoglobin. Normally the partial pressure of oxygen in the blood is 75 to 100 mm Hg, depending on age; for carbon dioxide it is 35 to 45 mm Hg. SYN: *tissue r.*

interrupted r. Respiration in which inspiratory or expiratory sounds are not continuous. SYN: *cogwheel r.*

intrauterine r. Respiration by the fetus before birth. SEE: *fetal r.*

Kussmaul r. SEE: under *Kussmaul, Adolph*.

labored r. Respiration that involves active participation of accessory inspiratory and expiratory muscles; dyspnea.

mitochondrial r. The stages of cell

respiration (citric acid cycle and cytochrome transport system) that take place in the mitochondria. Water is formed from oxygen and hydrogen ions, and energy is released. SEE: *cell r.*

paradoxical r. 1. Respiration occurring in patients with chest trauma and multiple rib fractures in which a portion of the chest wall sinks inward with each spontaneous inspiratory effort. **2.** A condition seen in paralysis of the diaphragm in which the diaphragm ascends during inspiration.

periodic r. Periodic **breathing**.

placental r. Fetal **r.**

radiofrequency electrophrenic r. A method of stimulating respiration in cases of respiratory paralysis from spinal cord injury at the cervical level. Intermittent electrical stimuli to the phrenic nerves are supplied by a radiofrequency transmitter implanted subcutaneously. The diaphragmatic muscles contract in response to these stimuli.

slow r. Decreased **r.**

stertorous r. Stertor.

thoracic r. Respiration performed entirely by expansion of the chest when the abdomen does not move. It is seen when the peritoneum or diaphragm is inflamed, when the abdominal cavity is restricted by tight bandages or clothes, or during abdominal surgery.

tissue r. Internal **r.**

respirator (res′pĭ-rāt″ŏr) [L. *respirare*, to breathe] **1.** A mask used to protect the user from a dusty, infectious, toxic, or hypoxic atmosphere. **2.** A machine used to assist ventilation and/or oxygenation.

air-purifying r. A face mask covering the mouth and nose that is used to filter hazardous gases, vapors, and/or particles from the environment in order to prevent them from being inhaled.

N95 r. A respirator that filters 95% of circulating particles (allergens, bacteria, dusts, or viruses) from ambient air. SYN: *N95* **mask**. SEE: table.

Rate of Respiration (breaths/min)

Premature infant	40–90
Newborn	30–60
1st yr	20–40
2nd yr	20–30
5th yr	20–25
15th yr	15–20
Adult	8–20

respirator dependent Ventilator dependent.

respirator fit testing Fit test.

respiratory (rĕs-pīr′ă-tō-rē, rĕs′pĭ-ră-tō″rē) [L. *respiratio*, breathing] Pert. to respiration.

respiratory anemometer An obsolete form of respirometer formerly used in investigating pulmonary function.

respiratory apparatus Respiratory system.

respiratory center SEE: under *center*.

respiratory defense mechanisms Ciliated epithelium, mucus, immunoglobulins, and other devices present in the trachea, bronchi, and lungs, used to defend the respiratory tract against microorganisms and other inhaled particles.

respiratory distress syndrome of the preterm infant ABBR: RDS. Severe impairment of respiratory function in a preterm newborn, caused by immaturity of the lungs. This condition is rarely present in a newborn of more than 37 weeks' gestation or in one weighing at least 2.2 kg (5 lb). RDS is the leading cause of death in prematurely born infants in the U.S. SYN: *hyaline membrane disease*. SEE: *acute respiratory distress syndrome; preterm labor; Nursing Diagnoses Appendix.*

SYMPTOMS: Shortly after birth the preterm infant with RDS has a low Apgar score and obvious difficulty breathing. Tachypnea, tachycardia, retraction of the rib cage during inspiration, cyanosis, nasal flaring, and grunting during expiration are present. Blood gas studies reflect the impaired ventilatory function (abnormally low oxygen levels and respiratory acidosis).

TREATMENT: Preterm infants with RDS require treatment in a specially staffed and equipped neonatal intensive care unit. Therapy is supportive: humidified oxygen is supplied, the airways are ventilated, and adequate hydration and electrolytes are administered. If necessary, assisted ventilation with PEEP or CPAP is used to open alveoli. Care is taken to prevent the barotrauma: traumatic formation of pulmonary air leaks that could cause pulmonary emphysema and tension pneumothorax. Instillation of surfactant into the respiratory tract via an endotracheal tube is essential in managing RDS.

PATIENT CARE: To prevent RDS, as soon after birth as possible (preferably within 15 min), the health care professional administers neonatal lung surfactant intratracheally. The neonate's response to the medication is monitored carefully, and used to guide changes in ventilation, e.g., inspiratory pressures, tidal volume, and oxygenation.

The skin and mucous membranes are frequently inspected and lubricated with a water-soluble lubricant to prevent irritation, inflammation, and perforation.

The newborn is maintained in a thermoneutral environment to stabilize body temperature at 97.6°F (36.5°C). The newborn requires gentle and minimal handling, with assessment and care procedures separated by rest periods.

Caloric intake is provided orally or by gavage feeding in quantity to prevent catabolic breakdown. When her milk comes in, the infant's mother may want to pump her breasts as her infant can receive her milk through gavage feeding until the infant is strong enough to nurse.

The neonate also is at risk for multiple complications, including bronchopulmonary dysplasia, intracerebral bleeding, learning disabilities, pneumomediastinum, pneumothorax, retinopathy of prematurity, and sepsis among others. His or her parents require ongoing support of family, friends, or clergy to help them deal with familial, financial, and emotional stresses imposed by the illness. The parents are encouraged to ask questions and raise concerns. The parents' presence at cribside is encouraged to aid normal parent-infant bonding and they are shown ways to approach and be involved in the care of the infant (maintaining sterile technique) without adding to his or her stress.

respiratory frequency to tidal volume ratio ABBR: f/VT. A measure of the speed and depth of spontaneous breathing, used to gauge a patient's dependency on mechanical ventilation. The higher the ratio, the less likely it is that the patient will be able to breathe without mechanical assistance.

respiratory function monitoring The use of various techniques to provide alarms that alert a patient's attendants to a change in the ability of the lungs to perform their functions. These techniques include noninvasive devices for measuring the oxygen content of the blood (e.g., pulse oximetry); methods of monitoring respiratory muscle function and breathing pattern; or devices for monitoring the carbon dioxide content of expired air (i.e., capnography). SEE: *apnea monitoring.*

respiratory pump SEE: under *pump.*

respiratory pump dysfunction SEE: under *dysfunction.*

respiratory system The organs involved in the interchange of gases between an organism and the atmosphere. In humans, this system consists of the air passageways and organs (nasal cavities, pharynx, larynx, trachea, and lungs, including bronchi, bronchioles, alveolar ducts, and alveoli) and the respiratory muscles. SEE: illus.; *lung* for illus.

respiratory therapist A person skilled in managing the techniques and equipment used in treating those with acute and chronic respiratory diseases.

respiratory therapy ABBR: RT. Treatment to preserve or improve pulmonary function.

respiratory therapy technician A technician who routinely treats patients requiring noncritical respiratory care and who recognizes and responds to specified respiratory emergencies.

respiratory triggering In radiology, image acquisition that is synchronized to the patient's breathing, used to minimize motion artifact.

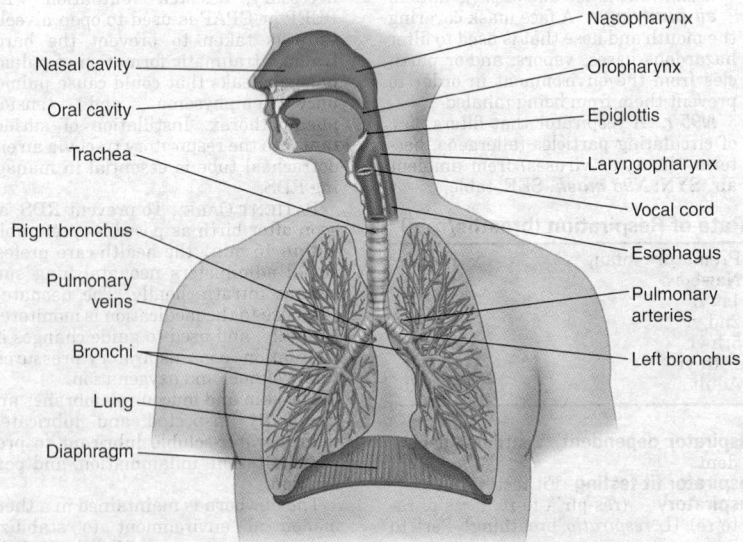

Nasal cavity — Oral cavity — Trachea — Right bronchus — Pulmonary veins — Bronchi — Lung — Diaphragm

Nasopharynx — Oropharynx — Epiglottis — Laryngopharynx — Vocal cord — Esophagus — Pulmonary arteries — Left bronchus

RESPIRATORY SYSTEM
anterior view

respire (rē-spīr′) To breathe and to consume oxygen and release carbon dioxide.

respirologist (res″pĭ-rol′ŏ-jĭst) [*respire* + *-log* + *-ist*] A physician trained and certified to treat pulmonary diseases. SYN: *pulmonologist*.

respirology (rĕs″pĭr-ŏl′ŏ-jē) [″ + ″] The study and treatment of diseases of the lungs and respiratory tract.

respirometer (rĕs″pĭr-ŏm′ĕt-ĕr) [L. *respirare*, to breathe, + Gr. *metron*, a measure] An instrument to ascertain the character of respirations. Several devices are available for measuring specific respiratory qualities such as minute ventilation and tidal volume. SEE: *respiratory anemometer*.

respite (rĕs′pĭt) [Fr. *respit*, a looking back] SEE: under *care*.

respondeat superior (rē-spŏn-dē-ăt) [L., let the master answer] A Latin term meaning "Let the master answer." The "master," or employer, is held liable for negligent or wrongful acts of the "servant," or employee, if the employee causes injury or damage while he or she is at work.

response (rĭ-spons′) [L. *responsum*, an answer] **1.** A reaction, e.g., contraction of a muscle or secretion of a gland, resulting from a stimulus. SEE: *reaction*. **2.** The total of an individual's reactions to specific conditions, e.g., the response of a patient to a certain treatment or to a challenge to the immune system.

    acute phase r. Acute phase reaction.

    auditory evoked r. Response to auditory stimuli determined by a method independent of the individual's subjective response. The electroencephalogram has been used to record response to sound. By measuring intensity of sound and presence of response, one can test the acuity of hearing of psychiatric patients, people who are asleep, and children too young to cooperate in a standard hearing test.

    brainstem auditory evoked r. Evoked response **audiometry**.

    clinical benefit r. ABBR: CBR. An improvement in at least one important symptom or element of the quality of life of a cancer patient that directly results from treatment, without any decline in any other element of the patient's quality of life.

    PATIENT CARE: Some cancers are not curable or responsive to treatment with surgery, radiation, or chemotherapy. However, one or more of their most distressing symptoms may be manageable, e.g., alleviation of pain by therapy. Palliation of pain, nausea, or breathlessness, even in the absence of cure, is a clinically beneficial goal of treatment for some incurable tumors, such as cancers of the pancreas.

    complete r. ABBR: CR. In cancer care, the eradication by treatment of all of a readily identifiable tumor. A complete response differs from a cure in that microscopic amounts of tumor may remain in the patient and later produce a relapse.

    conditioned r. SEE: *conditioned reflex*.

    Cushing r. SEE: under *Cushing, Harvey*.

    dose r. 1. The relationship between the quantity or intensity of a treatment regimen and its effect on living cells, tissues, or organisms. **2.** The relationship between the intensity of an exposure, e.g., to an infectious pathogen, physical stressor, or a toxin, and its effect on living organisms.

    durable r. In cancer care, a long-lasting positive reaction to tumor therapy, usually lasting at least a year.

    evoked r. Evoked **potential**.

    F r. In electrodiagnostic study of spinal reflexes, the time required for a stimulus applied to a motor nerve to travel in the opposite direction up the nerve to the spinal cord and return.

    galvanic skin r. The measurement of the change in the electrical resistance of the skin in response to stimuli.

    immune r. The body's reaction to foreign antigens so that they are neutralized or eliminated, thus preventing the diseases or injuries these antigens might cause. It requires that the body recognize the antigen as nonself. There are several major components to the immune response. The *nonspecific immune response*, or inflammation, is the response of the body's tissues and cells to injury from any source, e.g., trauma, organisms, chemicals, ischemia. As the initial response of the immune system to any threat, it involves vascular, chemical, and white blood cell activities. The *specific immune response*, involving T cells and B cells, is a reaction to injury or invasion by particular organisms or foreign proteins. The *cell-mediated immune response* refers to the activity of T lymphocytes (T cells) produced by the thymus in response to antigen exposure. Without T cells, the body cannot protect itself against many disease-causing microbes. The loss of T cells in patients with AIDS, for example, leads to infections with many opportunistic microbes that would otherwise be relatively well tolerated by persons with intact cellular immunity. T-cell activity also is the basis for delayed hypersensitivity, rejection of tissue transplants, and responses to cancers. The *humoral immune response* refers to the production of antigen-specific antibodies by plasma B lymphocytes (B cells); antibodies attach to foreign antigens in the bloodstream, helping to inactivate or remove them. SEE: *cell-mediated immu-*

nity; humoral immunity; inflammation.

inflammatory r. Inflammation.

minor r. In cancer care, a reduction in tumor size by less than 50% but more than 25%.

parachute r. Parachute **reflex**.

partial r. ABBR: PR. In cancer care, a reduction in the size of readily identifiable tumors by 50% or more.

physiological stress r. Stress **r.**

primary immune r. The initial reaction to an immunogen, during which T and B lymphocytes are activated and antibodies specific to the antigen are produced. This reaction is considered relatively weak but produces large numbers of antigen-specific memory cells.

PSA r. A decrease in the level of prostate-specific antigen (PSA) of at least 50% in a patient receiving treatment for prostate cancer.

relative dose r. ABBR: RDR. **1.** A progressively increasing reaction of a cell, tissue, or organism to a stimulus. **2.** A test used to estimate liver stores of vitamin A in order to identify those with marginal vitamin A deficiency.

relaxation r. The physiological responses produced when one sits quietly with the eyes closed and breathes slowly and methodically. The responses include slower heart rate, decreased blood pressure, and lowered cutaneous resistance. A brief word or phrase (such as a mantra) may be repeated to oneself to help focus the mind or reduce stray thoughts. This approach to meditation or stress reduction may be undertaken once or twice a day, usually for 10 to 30 min. The relaxation response helps reduce anxiety, high blood pressure, pain, postmenopausal symptoms, and use of medications.

reticulocyte r. An increase in reticulocyte production in response to the administration of a hematinic agent.

secondary immune r. The rapid, strong response by T and B cells to a second or subsequent appearance of an immunogen. This occurs because of the availability of T and B lymphocyte memory cells.

somatosensory evoked r. ABBR: SER. Response produced by small, painless electrical stimuli administered to large sensory fibers in mixed nerves of the hand or leg. The electroencephalographic record of the character of the subsequent waves produced helps determine the functional state of the nerves involved.

stress r. The predictable physiological response that occurs in humans as a result of injury, surgery, shock, ischemia, or sepsis. SYN: *physiological stress r.*

This response is hormonally mediated and is divided into three distinct phases:

Ebb phase (lag phase): For 12 to 36 hr after the precipitating event, the body attempts to conserve its resources. Vital signs (heart, respiration, temperature) are less than normal. *Flow phase (hypermetabolic phase):* This stage peaks in 3 to 4 days and lasts 9 to 14 days, depending on the extent of the injury or infection and the person's physical and nutritional status. Carbohydrate, protein, and fat are mobilized from tissue stores and catabolized to meet the energy needs of an increased metabolic rate (hypermetabolism). Serum levels of glucose and electrolytes such as potassium can increase dramatically. If this stage is not controlled by removal of the cause or activator, multiple system organ failure or death can result. *Anabolic phase (recovery):* The anabolic, or healing, phase occurs as the catabolism declines and electrolyte balances are restored. Aggressive nutritional support is often necessary to promote a positive nitrogen balance.

triple r. Any of the three phases of vasomotor reactions that occur when a sharp object is drawn across the skin. In order of appearance, these are red reaction, flare or spreading flush, and wheal.

unconditioned r. An inherent response rather than a learned response. SEE: *conditioned* **reflex.**

visual evoked r. ABBR: VER. A reaction produced in response to visual stimuli. While the patient is watching a pattern projected on a screen, the electroencephalogram is recorded. The characteristics of the wave form, its latency, and the amplitude of the wave can be compared with the normal, and important information concerning the function of the visual apparatus in transmitting stimuli to the brain can be obtained.

responsibility (rē-spŏn″sĭ-bĭ′lĭ-tē) **1.** Accountability. **2.** Trustworthiness.

responsible party The individual whose actions or inactions caused injury, harm, or damage to something or someone.

rest (rĕst) [AS. *raest*] **1.** Repose of the body caused by sleep. **2.** Freedom from activity, as of mind or body. **3.** To lie down; to cease voluntary motion. **4.** A remnant of embryonic tissue that persists in the adult.

restenosis (res″tĕ-nō′sĭs) [*re-* + *stenosis*] Recurrence of a blockage in a previously opened heart valve, blood vessel, or tube.

restiform (rĕs′tĭ-form) [L. *restis*, rope, + *forma*, shape] Ropelike; rope-shaped.

restiform body SEE: under *body.*

resting Inactive, motionless, at rest.

resting cell SEE: under *cell*.

resting energy expenditure Basal metabolic **rate**.

restitutio ad integrum (rĕs″tĭ-tū′shē-ō ăd ĭn-tĕ′grŭm) [L.] Complete restoration to health.

restitution (res″tĭ-too′shŏn, -tū′) [L. *restitutio*, restoration, rebuilding] **1.** The return to a former status. **2.** The act of making amends. **3.** The turning of a fetal head to the right or left after it has completely emerged through the vagina in order to align the head with the spine. SYN: *movement of restitution*. SYN: *external* **rotation**.

restless legs syndrome A condition marked by an intolerable creeping sensation or itching in the lower extremities and causing an almost irresistible urge to move the legs. The symptoms are worse at the end of the day when the patient is seated or in bed and may produce insomnia.

    TREATMENT: Treatments include levodopa/carbidopa, benzodiazepines, ropinirole, and tricyclic antidepressants. SYN: *nocturnal myoclonus*.

restoration (res″tŏ-rā′shŏn) [L. *restaurare, to fix*] **1.** The return of something to its previous state. **2.** In dentistry, any treatment, material, or device that restores a tooth surface or replaces a tooth or all of the teeth and adjacent tissues. SEE: *dental* **amalgam**.

    temporary r. A temporary dental filling, bridge, crown or retainer, made, e.g., from zinc oxide, stainless steel, aluminum, resin, or cements. Temporary restorations are designed to last from days to years after placement.

    tissue r. Any of the biologically compatible materials used to replace missing body parts or to provide a scaffolding into which cells may grow and regenerate themselves.

    vocal r. The technology used to improve speech in a patient who has had a laryngectomy.

restorative (rĭ-stor′ă-tĭv) [L. *restaurare, to fix*] **1.** Pert. to restoration. **2.** An agent that is effective in the regaining of health and strength.

restraint (rĭ-strānt′) [Fr. *restrainte,* a tying back] **1.** Refraining from any action, mental or physical. **2.** The condition of being hindered. **3.** In medicine, the use of major tranquilizers or physical means to prevent patients from harming themselves or others.

    The FDA defines restraint as "a device, usually a wristlet, anklet, or other type of strap intended for medical purposes and that limits a patient's movements to the extent necessary for treatment, examination, or protection of the patient." Protective devices include safety vests, hand mitts, lap and wheelchair belts, body holders, straitjackets, and protection nets.

Restraints should be fitted properly and comfortably. They should be applied so as to protect the patient from accidental self-injury, such as strangling or smothering by slipping down in a bed, wheelchair, or chair.

Caregivers are legally and ethically responsible for the safety and well-being of patients in their care; however, when the patient's protection or the achievement of the therapeutic goal appears to require physical or pharmacological restraint, health care providers must consider that such action limits the patient's legal rights to autonomy and self-determination. Decisions to institute restraint must be based on a clear, identifiable, documented need for their use.

With many patients, effective alternatives to physical restraint include providing companionship and close supervision of activities; explaining procedures to reduce anxiety; when possible, removing indwelling tubes, drains, and catheters to reduce discomfort and the potential for displacement; providing good lighting, ensuring that pathways are clear, and that furniture is adequately secured to minimize potential hazards; maintaining beds in low position and using bed alarm systems that signal if the patient's body is not in contact with the mattress; using an alarm system when the patient is in a chair or wheelchair; ensuring that the call button is easily accessible to facilitate patient requests for help with ambulation; reducing unwelcome distractions (e.g., background noise); enabling the patient's access to diversions such as music and videos to encourage relaxation; and encouraging ambulation and exercise to meet the patient's needs for mobility.

⚠ Informed consent must be obtained from the patient or guardian before restraints are to be used. Restraints should not be used without a specific order from the treating health care provider. Almost any type of restraint has the potential for harming the patient; thus it is extremely important to monitor use and be certain that it is applied correctly and removed periodically.

PATIENT CARE: The nurse records behavior that demonstrates a need for restraint; describes nursing actions to achieve the therapeutic objectives of without resort to restraint and the effects of the restraint; suggests the minimum amount of restraint for achieving the objectives; secures or reviews practitioner orders for specific types of restraints; validates informed consent; explains the use of the specific type of restraint to the patient and family members as a "reminder" needed for protection; and encourages verbalization of feelings and concerns and provides emotional support.

The nurse follows these guidelines for application of restraints: the device that is most appropriate for the purpose is selected (e.g., padded mitts protect against patient removal of intravenous or other invasive tubing by limiting the ability to manipulate equipment with fingers but do not elicit the restlessness and frustration that occurs when the hands are tied down with wrist restraints). The status of tissues is assessed and documented before application. Bony prominences in contact with the restraining devices are padded before application of restraints. Restraints are applied to maintain a comfortable, normal position, and mobility is limited only as much as is necessary to protect the patient (i.e., the nurse may change the position without defeating the objectives of the restraint). The nurse anchors restraint devices securely and ensures that they do not interfere with blood flow to the limbs or trunk; ensures that the restraints can be released quickly in an emergency; documents application and evaluation of current status; assesses and records at frequent intervals (e.g., every 30 min) the effects of the restraint on the patient's behavior and on the neurovascular status distal to the site of the restraint; promptly reports signs of increased agitation; releases restraints (one at a time if the patient is unreliable or combative) and allows or provides range-of-motion exercises two to four times each shift; and evaluates the need for continuing restraint at least once each shift, discontinuing the devices as soon as the patient's status permits.

automotive r. A seat belt, lap belt, shoulder harness, or child car seat designed to protect passengers in a motor vehicle from injury during an accident.

r. in bed The therapeutic use of physical restraint to prevent limb or body motion in bed. Siderails are placed on the bed full or half-length to prevent a patient from falling out of bed. Beds are maintained in low position to limit falls and injuries. A mattress alarm system may be used to alert nursing personnel if a patient's body is not contacting the mattress or a foot pad alarmed to sound if the patient attempts to stand.

PATIENT CARE: The nurse follows general guidelines for application of restraints. The nurse never ties restraints to bed siderails; rather, the restraints are anchored to a part of the bed that moves when the head is raised or lowered; the nurse uses a clove hitch to secure restraints so they will not tighten

if tension is applied and so that they can be released rapidly in an emergency. A simple body restraint can be made by folding a sheet lengthwise to a 1-ft width. This restraint is placed under the patient's back and crossed in front below the armpits. The ends are secured to the side bar of the bed. This prevents some freedom in side-to-side movement.

chemical r. A sedative or tranquilizer given to a patient to reduce agitation or potentially hazardous behavior.

⚠ Psychoactive drugs should be given to patients only when other less invasive and less hazardous means of calming or stabilizing behavior have been exhausted or when there is imminent risk of injury without their use.

clove hitch r. A device to restrain a person's arm or leg. Gauze or other soft material is placed on a flat surface in a figure eight configuration. The loops are then lifted from the underside and the tops brought together. The extremity is placed through both loops at once and the loose ends of the material are tied to an immobile surface. It is important to check circulation regularly in any extremity restrained by this device.

r. of lower extremities Physical restraint of movement of the legs and feet. A sheet is tied across the knees and the feet are tied together with a figure-eight bandage. The correct method is to start the loop under the ankles, cross it between the feet, bring the ends around the feet, and tie them on top.

⚠ The restraint should not interfere with blood circulation to an extremity and should be padded to prevent injury to soft tissue.

mechanical r. Restraint by physical devices.

medicinal r. An anxiolytic, sedative, or tranquilizer used to subdue combative or violent patients.

restrictive eating Limiting food intake to a certain number of calories or to certain foods or food groups.

restrictive lung disease Any chest disease that results in reduced lung volumes and reduced lung compliance.

resurfacing (rē-sŭr'fă-sĭng) Repair of damaged body surfaces, such as articular cartilage or skin. In cosmetic surgery, resurfacing of the skin may involve dermabrasion, chemical peels, cutaneous lasers, and other techniques.

laser r. of skin Use of laser treatments to repair wrinkled or photoaged skin for aesthetic purposes. Carbon dioxide and other lasers are used to remove the damaged dermis and repair underlying connective tissues. Whether these treatments have long-term adverse effects is unknown.

radiofrequency r. The treatment of wrinkles, scars, sun damage, and other minor cosmetic skin defects with radiofrequency energy. This method disintegrates tissues without the heat produced by laser resurfacing.

resuscitation (rē-sŭs″ĭ-tā′shŏn) [L. *resuscitare,* to raise up again, rebuild] Revival of a patient from a serious illness or injury.

    active compression decompression cardiopulmonary r. SEE: *active compression decompression cardiopulmonary resuscitation.*

    cardiopulmonary r. ABBR: CPR. In emergency cardiac care, the opening of the airway, provision of artificial breathing, and assisting the circulation until definitive treatment can restore spontaneous cardiac, pulmonary, and cerebral function. SYN: *basic life support* (2).

    PATIENT CARE: In emergency cardiac care, CPR involves either opening the airway, providing artificial breathing, and assisting circulation with chest compressions (until definitive treatments can restore spontaneous cardiac, pulmonary, and cerebral function) or providing chest compressions alone, without rescue breathing. When trained providers are available, CPR includes defibrillation with automated external defibrillators. In the U.S., the American Heart Association (AHA) develops and disseminates standard techniques for emergency cardiac care.

The first step in CPR is to ensure that an unarousable patient needs cardiopulmonary support and is not merely asleep or unconscious. If the patient does not respond to a loud voice or gentle shaking, the best thing a rescuer can do is to call for skilled assistance because successful resuscitation usually depends on the speed with which the patient can be defibrillated.

Before the defibrillator arrives, the rescuer can either position the patient for chest compressions only or begin rescue breathing. The patient should be placed supine on a firm, flat surface, with care taken to protect his cervical spine if traumatic injury is suspected. Kneeling at the level of the patient's shoulder, the rescuer performing rescue breathing may open the patient's airway, either with the jaw-thrust or the head-tilt chin-lift technique. If foreign bodies are present in the airway, they must be removed; dentures must also be removed if they interfere with resuscitation. Next, breathing is assessed by listening for breath sounds at the nose

and lips and watching for the rise and fall of the chest. If these signs are not present, the patient is apneic, and rescue breathing can be performed. Survival rates of patients undergoing CPR are roughly equivalent with or without rescue breathing.

Rescue breathing can be performed with mouth-to-mouth technique or through a mask with a one-way valve if one is available. The rescuer gives two deep, slow positive-pressure breaths to the patient, the duration of each breath depending on the patient's age. If the supplied breaths meet obvious resistance, the rescuer should make another attempt to reopen the airway, and, if this is ineffective, to clear the airway with the Heimlich maneuver in children and adults. Infants should receive chest thrusts and blows to the back instead of the Heimlich maneuver.

The AHA formerly suggested checking the victim for a pulse after the first two breaths but eliminated the pulse check in its revised guidelines of 2000. If the patient is not breathing on his own, rescue breathing continues. If there is no pulse, external chest compression is begun and continued, with periodically interposed ventilations, until a defibrillator arrives or the patient revives. The precise number of ventilations and chest compressions per minute depends on the patient's age and the number of rescuers. For a single rescuer caring for an adult patient, two breaths are given for every 15 chest compressions. According to the AHA, for resuscitation purposes, infants are those who are up to a year old, children are from 1 to 8 years old, and adults are over the age of 8.

Compressions are given to adults (the usual victims of cardiac arrest) at the center of the sternum between the nipples, with the heel of one hand below the other hand; the fingers of the two hands are interlaced for support and to minimize the possibility of fracturing the ribs. The rescuer's elbows should be locked and straight, and the direction of compression should be exactly perpendicular to the patient's chest.

The chest is depressed 1.5 to 2.0 in for a normal-sized adult. For a child, the chest is depressed 1.0 to 1.5 in; for an infant, 0.5 to 1.0 in. The chest should return to its normally inflated position after each compression.

When professional rescuers arrive, the patient should be defibrillated immediately. If a defibrillator is not available, two-person CPR continues; the two rescuers alternate in giving rescue breaths and chest compressions to minimize fatigue. Ventilation and chest compressions are held for 5 sec at the end of the first minute and every few minutes after to determine whether the patient has responded. SEE: illus.; *advanced cardiac life support; defibrillation; emergency cardiac care; Standard and Universal Precautions Appendix.*

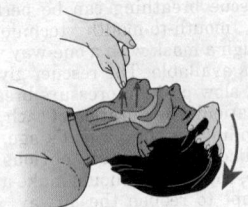

Open airway by raising chin and tilting head backward from chest

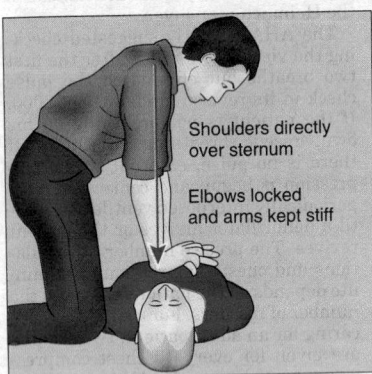

Shoulders directly over sternum

Elbows locked and arms kept stiff

External chest compression

CARDIOPULMONARY RESUSCITATION

cerebral r. The restoration of a patient's normal neurological function due to effective revival from cardiopulmonary arrest.

goal-directed r. Precise adjustments in a septic patient's hemodynamics, oxygenation, and volume status to optimize his or her chances of survival.

hypotensive r. Low-volume **r.**

low-volume r. Treatment of a seriously ill patient with small, rather than large volumes of intravenous fluids and without an explicit attempt to restore normal blood pressures. SYN: *hypotensive r.*

mouth-to-mouth r. Provision of respiratory gases, consisting of approximately 16% oxygen, to a patient in respiratory or cardiopulmonary arrest by exhaling directly into the open mouth of the unconscious victim. Because of potential exposure to infectious disease, this technique is used only when a pocket mask or other barrier device is not available. SEE: *artificial respiration; cardiopulmonary resuscitation.*

neonatal r. The prevention of death or injury to newborn infants with techniques to support the newborn's airway, breathing, circulation, and body temperature. In the U.S. about 1% of all newborns require intensive resuscitative efforts immediately after birth. Most are infants born preterm (before 37 weeks' gestation). Failure to recognize and treat neonatal emergencies may result in inadequate oxygen delivery to the brain, heart, lungs, and other organs. Seizures, cognitive impairment, encephalopathy, or cerebral palsy may result from delayed recognition of asphyxia in the neonatal period.

PATIENT CARE: The cornerstone of neonatal resuscitation is the prompt recognition of the newborn who is failing to breathe and perfuse organs effectively. Immediately after birth, the newborn should be dried, gently suctioned, and assessed for: adequate respiratory effort (versus apnea); a heart rate above 100 beats/min; good muscle tone (as opposed to flaccidity); skin color that indicates effective cardiac output (rather than cyanosis); and evidence of fullterm versus pre-term birth.

The neonate who lacks some of these findings should be professionally managed, with warming, gentle stimulation (e.g., rubbing its back gently with a towel to stimulate effective breathing) and airway suctioning. When apnea, hypothermia, respiratory distress, bradycardia, or poor skin perfusion is evident, evidenced-based interventions (e.g., those recommended by the Neonatal Resuscitation Program of the American Academy of Pediatrics and the AHA) should be begun immediately.

Positive-pressure ventilation (PPV), with breaths supplied via a bag mask device, effectively resuscitates most infants at risk for neonatal asphyxia. Those who have meconium in the upper airways (evidenced by meconium staining of the amniotic fluid), as well as inadequate breathing, slow heart rate, and poor muscle tone, require endotracheal intubation and suctioning, preferably by an experienced practitioner.

Most neonates respond favorably to airway and ventilatory management, breathe spontaneously, and maintain a heart rate above 100 beats/min. Chest compressions should be begun only if the heart rate remains below 60 beats/min despite 30 sec of PPV with 100% oxygen. Chest compressions should cease when the heart rate is above 60 beats/min, but PPV should be continued until the heart rate is above 100 beats/min and the newborn has begun to breathe on his own. PPV should always accompany chest compressions and be coordinated so that a breath is provided after every third compression. After 30 sec of PPV and chest compressions, the compressions should be stopped and the heart rate evaluated while PPV is continued. If there is no palpable pulse at the base of the umbilical cord, PPV should be stopped and the chest auscultated to determine the heart rate.

Chest compressions are most effective when the sternum is depressed to a depth equal to one third of the anteroposterior chest diameter of the newborn. The preferred technique is to use the thumbs to depress the sternum, with the hands encircling the newborn's thorax. An alternative is to perform compressions with two fingers on the same hand, so that the umbilical vein can be cannulated by another resuscitator. Ninety compressions a minute should be coordinated with 30 positive-pressure breaths, with care taken to avoid simultaneous compressions and ventilations.

Access to the circulation can be gained through the umbilical vein or intraosseously into the tibia. Normal saline or lactated Ringer's solution is the preferred fluid. Narcotic antidotes should be given to reverse any depression in respiratory or neurological status from maternal narcotic overdose. Inotropes such as epinephrine should be used when ventilation and chest compressions do not revive the dying infant.

In prolonged resuscitations, blood gases should be drawn to help guide additional therapies.

Resuscitative interventions that have not proved to be helpful include the use of high-dose epinephrine, the induction of cerebral hypothermia, and the use of carbon dioxide detectors on the endotracheal tube.

Resuscitation should not be initiated for children born with severe anomalies incompatible with life, e.g., anencephaly or birth weights of less than 400 g. Resuscitative efforts that do not resolve apnea and pulselessness after more than 10 min are rarely successful in newborns. In these circumstances, efforts may be discontinued.

oral r. SEE: *artificial respiration*.

resuscitator (ri-sŭs′ĭ-tāt-ŏr) [L. *resuscitare*, to raise up again, rebuild] A device to assist breathing, used to oxygenate and ventilate a patient who can no longer breathe spontaneously. Most resuscitators are portable and capable of delivering high concentrations of oxygen.

manual r. A handheld mask with an attached self-inflating bag, which permits air to be forced into the lungs each time it is squeezed. Manual resuscitators can be difficult to use properly. Complications can arise if the mask does not seal the patient's face properly, if excessive pressure is used during ventilation, if inadequate supplemental oxygen is provided, or if the rate or volume of ventilations is excessive or insufficient to inflate the lungs and remove carbon dioxide.

resveratrol (rĕs-vĕr′ă-trŏl) A plant-derived polyphenol that is structurally related to diethylstilbestrol. It is found in grapes and wine, and is believed to have antioxidant effects.

resynchronization therapy (rē″sing″krŏ-nĭ-zā′shŏn) [*re-* + *synchronize*] The use of left and right ventricular pacemaking in patients with congestive heart failure and bundle branch block to restore the normal timing of ventricular depolarization. Resynchronization reduces symptoms of heart failure. SYN: *cardiac resynchronization therapy*.

retail clinic SEE: under *clinic*.

retained foreign object (surgical) ABBR: RFO. Any implement used in surgery left inside the patient after the surgery is completed. The rate of retention is estimated at 1 in 7000 procedures. The most common objects left inside the patient are sponges. Surgical packing, sharp objects such as sutures or needles, and operative instruments are also occasionally unaccounted for postoperatively.

⚠️ Strict protocols for evaluation of the operating theatre and the surgical wound must be employed to prevent leaving foreign objects inside surgical wounds. These include: accounting for all surgical materials before, during, and after an operation; exploring the wound meticulously whenever a discrepancy in a surgical count is identified; performing radiological studies, as indicated, to identify lost implements; and keeping clear and complete documentation of all findings is done. In spite of these measures, an RFO may not be identified until after the patient has left the operating room (short term or long term interval) necessitating subsequent removal.

retainer (rĭ-tān′ĕr) **1.** Any device or attachment for keeping something in place. **2.** In dentistry, a fixed or removable appliance used in orthodontia for maintaining the teeth and jaws in position.

retardate (rĭ-tăr′dāt) [L. *retardare*, to delay] One who is mentally retarded.

retardation (rē″tar″dā′shŏn) [L. *retardatio*, a delay] **1.** A holding back or slowing down; a delay. **2.** Delayed mental or physical response resulting from pathological conditions. Particular retardations are listed under the first word. SEE: e.g., *intrauterine growth retardation; mental retardation; psychomotor retardation*.

retarded ejaculation SEE: under *ejaculation*.

retarder (rē-tär′dĕr) A biomaterial used in dentistry to slow the rate at which impression materials gel, set, or polymerize.

retch (rĕch) [AS. *hraecan*, to cough up phlegm] To make an involuntary attempt to vomit.

retching (rĕch′ĭng) Intense rhythmic contraction of the respiratory and abdominal muscles that may precede or accompany vomiting.

rete (rē′tē) *pl.* **retia** [L.] A network; a plexus of nerves or blood vessels.

   arterial r. A vascular arterial network just before the point where arteries become capillaries. SEE: *arterial*.

   r. cutaneum A network of blood vessels at the junction of the dermis and superficial fascia.

   malpighian r. Stratum germinativum.

   r. mirabile A plexus formed by the abrupt division of a vessel into capillaries that reunite to form one vessel, as in the glomeruli of the kidneys.

   r. ovarii A layer of cells in the broad ligament and mesovarium of the ovary. It is homologous to rete testes in men.

   r. subpapillare A network of vessels between the papillary and reticular layers of the dermis.

   r. testis A network of tubules in the mediastinum testis that receives sperm through the tubuli recti from the seminiferous tubules. From the rete testis, efferent ducts convey sperm to the epididymis.

   r. venosum Venous network.

   vertebral r. One of two plexuses within the vertebral canal that extends from the foramen magnum to the coccyx. These retia lie posteriorly and laterally to the dura and between the dura and the arches of the vertebrae.

retention (ri-ten′shŏn) [L. *retentio*, a holding back] **1.** The act or process of keeping in possession or of holding in place. **2.** The persistent keeping within the body of materials normally excreted, such as urine, feces, or perspiration. **3.** In dentistry, any of several procedures or materials used to keep a dental device or dentures in place. **4.** Memory or recall. **5.** Heavy sutures used to reinforce wound closures.

retention defect SEE: under *defect*.

retention with overflow A spasm of the urinary sphincter, causing failure to empty the bladder at one voiding, with only overflow dribbling away. It results from the same causes as urinary retention.

reteplase (rĕ′tĕ-plāz) A thrombolytic drug used to treat acute myocardial infarction.

rete ridge (rē′tē) One of the downgrowths of epithelium surrounding the connective tissue papillae in the irregular internal surface of the epidermis. Microscopic sections often appear as single downgrowths when in fact the epithelium is in a series of interconnecting ridges at the dermis-epidermis interface. SYN: *peg, rete*.

retia (rē′tē-ă) [L.] Pl. of rete.

retial (rē′tē-ăl) Pert. to a rete.

reticula (rĕ-tĭk′yŭ-lă) [L.] Pl. of reticulum.

reticular (rĭ-tĭk′ū-lăr) [L. *reticula*, net] Meshed; in the form of a network. SYN: *retiform*.

reticular activating system ABBR: RAS. The alerting system of the brain consisting of the reticular formation, subthalamus, hypothalamus, and medial thalamus. It extends from the central core of the brainstem to all parts of the cerebral cortex. This system is essential in initiating and maintaining wakefulness and introspection and in directing attention. Sedative and tranquilizing drugs may depress the RAS temporarily; some strokes may permanently injure it.

reticular dysgenesis SEE: under *dysgenesis*.

reticular fiber SEE: under *fiber*.

reticulated, reticulate (rĕ-tĭk′yŭ-lāt″ĕd, -lăt, -lāt″) [*reticulo-*] Pert. to or forming a reticulum or network. **reticulation** (rĕ-tĭk″yŭ-lā′shŏn), *n*.

reticulated platelet An incompletely developed platelet found in the peripheral blood that contains strands of mRNA or rRNA. Small numbers of circulating reticulated platelets, typically less than 5%, are found in blood as a result of normal maturation from megakaryocytes in the bone marrow. High levels of reticulated platelets appear in diseases in which platelets are rapidly destroyed, such as idiopathic thrombocytopenic purpura (ITP) or disseminated intravascular coagulation (DIC) SYN: *immature platelet; stress platelet*.

reticulin (rē-tĭk′ū-lĭn) [L. *reticula*, net] An albuminoid or scleroprotein in the connective tissue framework of reticular tissue.

reticulo-, reticul-, reticuli- [L. *reticulum*, little net, network] Prefixes meaning *network*.

reticulocyte (rĕ-tĭk′yŭ-lō-sīt″) [*reticulo-* + *-cyte*] The last immature stage of a red blood cell. Its darkly staining granules are fragments of the endoplasmic reticulum. Reticulocytes normally constitute about 1% of the circulating red blood cells. Reticulocyte counts increase as a normal response to anemia.

reticulocyte hemoglobin content The amount of hemoglobin in newly circulating red blood cells. It is an early indicator of functional iron deficiency. SEE: *functional iron **deficiency***.

reticulocytopenia (rē-tĭk″ū-lō-sī″tō-pē′nē-ă) [″ + ″ + *penia,* poverty] A decreased number of the reticulocytes of the blood. SYN: *reticulopenia.*

reticulocytosis (rē-tĭk″ū-lō-sī-tō′sĭs) [″ + ″ + *osis,* condition] An increased number of reticulocytes in the circulating blood. This condition indicates active erythropoiesis in the red bone marrow and the need for greater oxygen-carrying capacity of the blood. It occurs after hemorrhage, during acclimatization to high altitude, during any pulmonary disorder that induces hypoxia, and in all types of anemia.

reticuloendothelial (rē-tĭk″ū-lō-ĕn″dō-thē′lē-ăl) [″ + Gr. *endon,* within, + *thele,* nipple] Pert. to the reticuloendothelial system, which is the old name for the mononuclear phagocytic system.

reticuloendothelial system ABBR: RES. Old name for the system of monocytes, macrophages, and dendritic phagocytes and antigen-presenting cells found in the blood and lymphoid tissues. This system is now called the mononuclear phagocytic system. SEE: *macrophage.*

reticuloendothelioma (rē-tĭk″ū-lō-ĕn″dō-thē-lē-ō′mă) [″ + ″ + ″ + *oma,* tumor] A neoplasm composed of cells of the mononuclear phagocytic system.

reticuloendotheliosis (rē-tĭk″ū-lō-ĕn″dō-thē-lē-ō′sĭs) [″ + ″ + *thele,* nipple, + *osis,* condition] Hyperplasia of reticuloendothelium.

reticuloendothelium (rē-tĭk″ū-lō-ĕn″dō-thē′lē-ŭm) The tissue of the reticuloendothelial system, which is the old name for the mononuclear phagocytic system.

reticulohistiocytoma (rē-tĭk″ū-lō-hĭs″tē-ō-sī-tō′mă) [L. *reticula,* net, + Gr. *histion,* little web, + *kytos,* cell, + *oma,* tumor] A malignant connective tissue tumor composed of multinucleated giant cells in the skin, mucous membranes, or synovium.

reticulohistiocytosis (rē-tĭk″ū-lō-hĭs″tē-ō-sī-tō′sĭs) [″ + ″ + ″ + *osis,* condition] Reticuloendotheliosis.

reticuloid (rē-tĭk′ū-loyd) [″ + Gr. *eidos,* form, shape] Resembling reticulosis.

reticuloma (rē-tĭk″ū-lō′mă) [″ + Gr. *oma,* tumor] A neoplasm composed of cells of the mononuclear phagocytic system.

reticulopenia (rē-tĭk″ū-lō-pē′nē-ă) [″ + Gr. *penia,* lack] Reticulocytopenia.

reticulopodium (rē-tĭk″ū-lō-pō′dē-ŭm) A branching pseudopod.

reticulosarcoma (rē-tĭk″ū-lō-săr-kō′mă) [″ + Gr. *sarx,* flesh, + *oma,* tumor] A neoplasm composed of large monocytic cells that originated in the mononuclear phagocyte of the lymph and other glands.

reticulosis (rē-tĭk-ū-lō′sĭs) [″ + Gr. *osis,* condition] Reticulocytosis.

histiocytic medullary r. A form of malignant histiocytosis marked by ane-

mia; granulocytopenia; enlargement of the spleen, liver, and lymph nodes; and phagocytosis of red blood cells.

reticulum (rĕ-tĭk′yū-lŭm, -lă) *pl.* **reticula** [L. *reticulum,* a little net, network] A network.

   endoplasmic r. ABBR: ER. A cell organelle that is a complex network of membranous tubules in the cytoplasm between the nuclear and cell membranes; it is visible only with an electron microscope. One form with ribosomes attached is called *granular* or *rough ER;* another form that is free of ribosomes is called *agranular* or *smooth ER.* Rough ER transports proteins produced on the ribosomes; smooth ER synthesizes lipids. SEE: *cell* for illus.

   r. of nucleus The netlike contents of a nondividing nucleus of a cell; the chromatin, the long, uncoiled chromosomes.

   sarcoplasmic r. The endoplasmic reticulum of striated muscle cells, surrounding the sarcomeres. In response to an action potential, it releases calcium ions to induce contraction, then reabsorbs calcium ions to induce relaxation.

   stellate r. The enamel pulp of a developing tooth, consisting of stellate cells lying between the inner and outer epithelial layers of the enamel organ.

retina (rĕt′ĭ-nă) *pl.* **retinae** [L.] The innermost layer of the eye, which receives images transmitted through the lens and contains the receptors for vision, the rods and cones. SEE: illus. (Retina of Right Eye). **retinal** (-năl), *adj.*

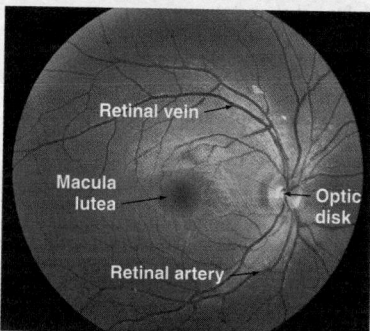

Retinal vein

Macula lutea

Optic disk

Retinal artery

RETINA OF THE RIGHT EYE

   The retina is a light-sensitive membrane on which light rays are focused. It extends from the entrance point of the optic nerve anteriorly to the margin of the pupil, completely lining the interior of the eye. It consists of three parts. The pars optica, the nervous or sensory portion, extends from the optic disk forward to the ora serrata, a wavy line immediately behind the ciliary process; the pars ciliaris lines the inner surface of the ciliary process; and the pars iridica forms the posterior surface of the iris. Slightly lateral to the posterior pole of the eye is a small, oval, yellowish spot, the macula lutea, in the center of which is a depression, the fovea centralis. This region contains only cones and is the region of the most acute vision. About 3.5 mm nasally from the fovea is the optic papilla (optic disk), where nerve fibers from the retina make their exit and form the optic nerve. This region is devoid of rods and cones and is insensitive to light; hence it is named the blind spot.

The layers of the retina, in the order light strikes them, are the optic nerve fiber layer, ganglion cell layer, inner synaptic layer, bipolar cell layer, outer synaptic layer, layer of rods and cones, and pigment epithelium. SEE: illus. (Retina).

COLOR: The retina is normally red, reflecting blood flow, and is pale in anemia or ischemia.

VESSELS: The arteries are branches of a single central artery, which is a branch of the ophthalmic artery. The central artery enters at the center of the optic papilla and supplies the inner layers of the retina. The outer layers, including rods and cones, are nourished by capillaries of the choroid layer. The veins lack muscular coats. They parallel the arteries; blood leaves by a central vein that leads to the superior ophthalmic vein.

coarctate r. A condition in which there is an effusion of fluid between the retina and choroid, giving the retina a funnel shape.

shot-silk r. A retina having an opalescent appearance, sometimes seen in young persons.

tigroid r. A retina having a spotted or striped appearance, seen in retinitis pigmentosa.

retinaculum (rĕt″ĭ-năk′ū-lŭm) *pl.* **retinacula** [L., halter] A band or membrane holding any organ or part in its place. Thickenings of the deep fascia in distal portions of limbs that hold tendons in position when muscles contract are called retinaculum tendinum.

r. cutis A fibrous band connecting the corium with underlying fascia.

extensor r. of ankle **1.** The superior extensor retinaculum, a band crossing the extensor tendons of the foot and attached to the lower portion of the tibia and fibula. **2.** The inferior extensor retinaculum, a band located on the dorsum of the foot. It consists of two limbs having a common origin on the lateral surface of the calcaneus. The upper limb is attached to the medial malleolus; the lower limb curves around the instep and is attached to the fascia of the abductor hallucis on the medial side of the foot.

extensor r. of wrist An oblique band attached medially to the styloid process of the ulna, the hamate bone, and the

medial ligament of the wrist joint. Laterally it is attached to the anterior border of the radius. It contains six separate compartments for passage of the extensor tendons to the hand.

flexor r. of ankle The retinaculum extending from the medial malleolus to the medial tubercle of the calcaneus.

flexor r. of hand The fascial band that holds down the flexor tendons of the digits.

flexor r. of wrist The retinaculum extending from the trapezium and scaphoid bones laterally to the hamate and pisiform bones medially.

r. of hip joint Any of three flat bands lying along the neck of the femur and continuous with the capsule of the hip joint.

r. mammae Strands of connective tissue in the mammary gland extending from glandular tissue through fat toward the skin, where they are attached to the dermis. Over the cephalic portion of the mammae, they are well developed and are called suspensory ligaments of Cooper.

patellar r. One of two fibrous bands (medial and lateral) lying on either side of the knee joint and forming part of the joint capsule. These bands are extensions of the insertions of the medial and lateral vastus muscles of the thigh.

peroneal r. One of two fibrous bands on the lateral side of the foot that contains the tendons of the peroneus longus and brevis muscles. The superior peroneal retinaculum extends from the lateral malleolus to the lateral surface of the calcaneus; the inferior peroneal retinaculum is attached below to the calcaneus and above to the lower border of the inferior extensor retinaculum.

r. tendinum The annular band of the wrist or ankle.

retinal (rĕt′ĭ-năl) **1.** Pertaining to the retina. **2.** The light-absorbing portion of a photopigment, a derivative of vitamin A.

retinal break A break in the continuity of the retina, usually caused by trauma to the eye. Detachment of the retina may follow the appearance of the break.

retinal correspondence A condition in which simultaneous stimulation of points in the retina of each eye results in formation of a single visual sensation. These points, called corresponding points, lie in the foveae of the two retinas, or in the nasal half of one retina and the temporal half of the other. Abnormal correspondence results in double vision (diplopia) and usually is caused by imbalance of the ocular muscles. SEE: *strabismus.*

retinal cryopexy A treatment for a retinal tear in which the retina and choroid surrounding the tear are frozen. This scars the retina around the tear, sealing

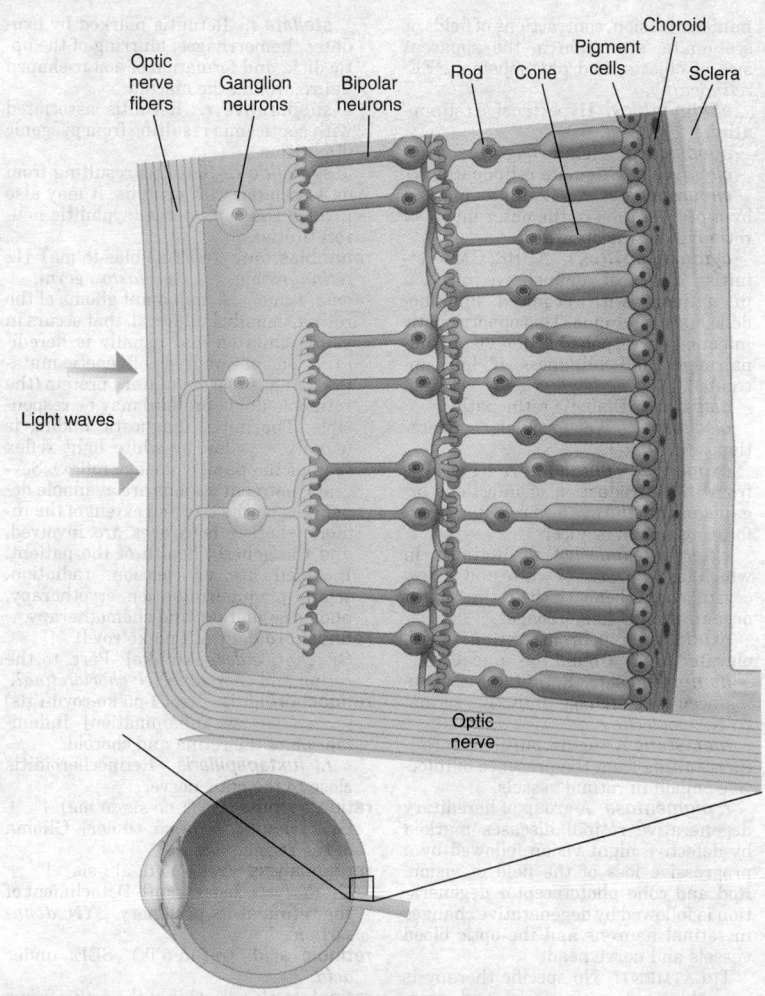

RETINA

Microscopic structure of optic disk area

the defect. Cryopexy is typically used to treat lesions at the retinal periphery, which may be difficult to treat with a laser.

retinal detachment Separation of the inner sensory layer of the retina from the outer pigment epithelium. It is usually caused by a hole or break in the inner sensory layer that permits fluid from the vitreous to leak under the retina and lift off its innermost layer. Causes include trauma and any disease that causes retinopathy, such as diabetes or sickle cell disease. Symptoms are blurred vision, flashes of light, vitreous floaters, and loss of visual acuity. The location of holes must be determined so that they can be repaired by laser ther-

apy (i.e., photocoagulation). SEE: *Nursing Diagnoses Appendix.*

TREATMENT: Scleral buckling techniques are used to treat retinal detachment in a large number of patients. Vitrectomy with laser and pneumatic retinopexy are occasionally employed as an alternative treatment.

retinal isomerase The enzyme in rods and cones that converts *trans*-retinal to *cis*-retinal, which then combines with the opsin present to form a photopigment responsive to light.

retinal vascular imaging SEE: under *imaging.*

retinitis (rĕt-ĭ-nī′tĭs) [L. *retina,* retina, + Gr. *itis,* inflammation] Inflammation of the retina. Symptoms include diminished vision, contractions of fields or scotomata, alteration in the apparent size of objects, and photophobia. SEE: *retinopathy*.

albuminuric r. Hypertensive retinopathy.

apoplectic r. Hemorrhagic **r.**

circinate r. Circinate retinopathy.

circumpapillar r. Retinitis marked by a proliferation of the outer layers of retina about the optic disk.

cytomegalovirus r. ABBR: CMV retinitis. The most common eye infection in patients with acquired immunodeficiency syndrome. This opportunistic infection is responsible for visual impairment and blindness if left untreated.

diabetic r. Diabetic retinopathy.

disciform r. Wet macular degeneration.

exogenous purulent r. Retinitis from the introduction of infectious organisms into the eye as a result of a perforating wound or ulcer.

external exudative r. Retinitis in which large masses of white and yellow crystals occur beneath the retina due to organization of hemorrhages.

exudative r. Chronic retinitis with elevated areas around the optic disk.

hemorrhagic r. Retinitis with pronounced hemorrhage into the retina. SYN: *apoplectic* **r.**

metastatic r. Acute purulent retinitis resulting from the presence of infective emboli in retinal vessels.

r. pigmentosa A group of hereditary degenerative retinal diseases marked by defective night vision followed by a progressive loss of the field of vision. Rod and cone photoreceptor degeneration is followed by degenerative changes in retinal neurons and the optic blood vessels and nerve head.

TREATMENT: No specific therapy is available, but professional and vocational guidance and genetic counseling can be provided. Family members should be examined to determine whether their vision is affected.

r. of prematurity Retinopathy of prematurity.

r. proliferans Retinitis marked by vascularized masses of connective tissue that project from the retina into the vitreous; the end result of recurrent hemorrhage from the retina into the vitreous.

r. punctata albescens A nonprogressive, degenerative familial disease in which innumerable minute white spots are scattered over the entire retina. There are no pigmentary changes. The disease usually starts early in life.

punctate r. Retinitis marked by numerous white or yellow spots in the fundus of the eye. SEE: *white dot syndrome*.

solar r. Solar retinopathy.

stellate r. Retinitis marked by exudates, hemorrhages, blurring of the optic disk, and formation of a star-shaped figure around the macula.

suppurative r. Retinitis associated with septicemia resulting from pyogenic organisms.

syphilitic r. Retinitis resulting from or associated with syphilis. It may also involve the optic nerve (syphilitic neuroretinitis).

retinoblastoma (rĕt″ĭ-nō-blăs-tō′mă) [L. *retina*, retina, + Gr. *blastos*, germ, + *oma*, tumor] A malignant glioma of the retina, usually unilateral, that occurs in young children and usually is hereditary. One of hundreds of genetic mutations in a tumor regulatory protein (the retinoblastoma protein) may be responsible. The initial diagnostic finding is usually a yellow or white light reflex seen at the pupil (cat's eye reflex). Several treatment options are available depending on the size and extent of the tumor, whether both eyes are involved, and the general health of the patient. Included are enucleation, radiation, scleral plaque irradiation, cryotherapy, photocoagulation, and chemotherapy.

retinochoroid (rĕt″ĭ-nō-kō′royd) [″ + Gr. *chorioeides*, skinlike] Pert. to the retina and choroid. SYN: *chorioretinal*.

retinochoroiditis (rĕt″ĭ-nō-kō-royd-ī′tĭs) [″ + ″ + *itis*, inflammation] Inflammation of the retina and choroid.

r. juxtapapillaris Retinochoroiditis close to the optic nerve.

retinocystoma (rĕt″ĭ-nō-sĭs-tō′mă) [″ + Gr. *kysis*, sac, + *oma*, tumor] Glioma of the retina.

retinodialysis (rĕt″ĭ-nō-dī-ăl′ĭ-sĭs) [″ + Gr. *dialysis*, separation] Detachment of the retina at its periphery. SYN: *disinsertion*.

retinoic acid (ret″ĭn-ō′ĭk) SEE: under *acid*.

retinol (rĕt′ĭ-nŏl) One of the active forms of vitamin A; it is stored in the body primarily in the liver and in adipose tissue. Sources of this 20-carbon alcohol include liver, egg yolk, chicken, whole milk, butter, and fortified breakfast cereal. Vitamin A activity in foods is expressed as retinol equivalents (RE), the resulting amount of retinol after conversion in the body.

⚠ Excessive consumption of retinol supplements, esp. by the elderly, can produce vitamin A toxicity.

retinopathy (ret″ĭn-op′ă-thē) [*retina* + -*pathy*] Any noninflammatory retinal damage or disease. It can cause gradual loss of vision or complete blindness if left untreated. It often results from another, systemic illness (e.g., hypertension or diabetes mellitus). SEE: table.

Common Findings on Funduscopic Examination in Retinopathy

arteriovenous nicking
blot hemorrhages
flame-shaped hemorrhages
focal or generalized arteriolar narrowing
hard exudates
macular edema
microaneurysms
soft exudates ("cotton-wool") spots

albuminuric r. Hypertensive retinopathy.

arteriosclerotic r. Retinopathy accompanying generalized arteriosclerosis and hypertension.

central serous r. ABBR: CSR. Serous detachment under the macula due to leakage of fluid from the choriocapillaris into the subretinal space between the retina and retinal pigment epithelium. It occurs most often in men aged 20 to 40, typically involves one eye, and often resolves spontaneously.

circinate r. A ring of degenerated white exudative area of the retina around the macula. SYN: *circinate retinitis.*

diabetic r. ABBR: DR. Retinal damage marked by microaneurysms, hemorrhage, macular edema or macular ischemia, or retinal exudates in patients with longstanding diabetes mellitus. This common complication of longstanding diabetes may result in blindness. Strict control of blood sugar levels and of high blood pressure reduces the incidence of the disease. Regular ophthalmological screening helps to detect the disease before it causes irreversible visual loss. Treatment includes retinal laser surgery or vitrectomy.

DR is divided into two groups: nonproliferative diabetic retinopathy (NPDR) consisting of blot, dot hemorrhages, exudate, and macular edema; and proliferative diabetic retinopathy (PDR), consisting of abnormal new vessels and fibrotic tissue. Approximately 50% of patients who have had diabetes for more than 15 years will have some form of diabetic retinopathy. SEE: *visual field* for illus.

eclipse r. Solar retinopathy.

hypertensive r. Retinopathy associated with hypertension, toxemia of pregnancy, or glomerulonephritis. Findings on physical examination include a hazy retina, blurred disk margins, distention of retinal arteries, retinal hemorrhages, and white patches in the fundus, esp. surrounding the papilla and at the stellate figure at the macula. SYN: *albuminuric retinitis; albuminuric r.* SEE: *Keith-Wagener-Barker classification.*

r. of prematurity ABBR: ROP. A bilateral disease of the retinal vessels in preterm infants. It is the most prominent cause of blindness among preterm infants. Its cause is unknown despite much research, but oxygen levels and other environmental factors may be factors. The disease is marked by retinal neovascularization in the first weeks of life. Retinal detachment may occur. Cryotherapy or laser photocoagulation can be curative if instituted early in the illness. SYN: *retrolental fibroplasia.*

In treating preterm infants, it is possible to prevent ROP by using only the lowest possible effective oxygen concentration that will not endanger the life of the infant. Monitoring arterial blood oxygen levels is essential in preventing ROP. Too much restriction of oxygen, however, increases the likelihood of hyaline membrane disease and neurological disorders. All preterm infants treated with supplemental oxygen should be examined carefully by an ophthalmologist before discharge from the hospital. Once blindness develops, there is no effective treatment.

solar r. Pathological changes in the retina after looking directly at the sun. This condition is seen frequently following an eclipse of the sun. SYN: *eclipse r.* SEE: *scotoma, eclipse.*

retinopexy (rē-tĭ-nō-pĕk′sē) [″ + Gr. *pexis,* fixation] A procedure involving diathermy, used in the treatment of retinal detachment to create the formation of adhesions between the detached portion and the underlying tissue.

pneumatic r. A treatment for retinal detachment, in which a bubble of gas is instilled into the vitreous. As the bubble attains equilibrium with body gases, it expands and forces the detached area back into place; then, cryotherapy or photocoagulation is used to reattach the retina permanently. SEE: *retinal detachment.*

retinoschisis (rĕt″ĭ-nŏs′kĭ-sĭs) [″ + Gr. *schisis,* a splitting] A splitting of the retina into two layers with cyst formation between the layers.

retinoscope (rĕt′ĭ-nō-skōp) [″ + Gr. *skopein,* to examine] An instrument used in performing retinoscopy.

retinoscopy (ret″ĭn-os′kŏ-pē) [*retina* + *-scopy*] An objective method of determining refractive errors of the eye. The examiner projects light into the eyes and judges error of refraction by the movement of reflected light rays. It differs from a phoropter, which relies on the patient's subjective description of visual clarity when light is focused on the retina. SYN: *skiascopy* (1).

retinosis (rĕt″ĭ-nō′sĭs) [″ + Gr. *osis,* condition] Any degenerative process of the retina not associated with inflammation.

retinotomy (rĕt″ĭn-ŏt′ă-mē) Surgical incision of the retina, e.g., to remove proliferating blood vessels in age-related macular degeneration.

retire **1.** To discontinue formal employment or work at a specific place or task. In the past, in many industries, educational institutions, and public service, retirement was mandated when an employee had attained a specified age. This practice has lost its attractiveness to a large segment of the workforce, esp. among those who enjoy work. SEE: *recreation.* **2.** To go to bed.

retort (rē-tort′, rē′tort″) [L. *retortus,* bent back] A flasklike, long-necked vessel whose neck usually projects to the side, used in distillation.

retract (ri-trakt′) [L. *retractus,* drawn back] To draw back. **retractable** (′ă-bĕl), *adj.*

retractile (rĭ-trăkt′ĭl) [L. *retractilis*] Capable of being drawn back or in.

retraction (ri-trak′shŏn) The act of drawing backward or the condition of being drawn back; shortening.

    clot r. **1.** The shrinking of the clot that forms when blood is allowed to stand, due to the fibrin network formed in the clot. **2.** The platelet-mediated folding of fibrin threads in a formed clot, which diminishes the size of the damaged area.

    dental r. Movement of a tooth posteriorly (deeper into the mouth), e.g., behind the arch formed by the other teeth.

    genital r. Koro.

retraction ring SEE: under *ring.*

retractor (ri-trak′tŏr) **1.** An instrument for holding back the margins of a wound or structures within the wound. **2.** A muscle that draws in any organ or part.

    cheek r. In dentistry, a retractor that encloses the cheek at the angle of the mouth for proper exposure of the operating field.

    Farabeuf r. SEE: *Farabeuf retractor.*

    Hohmann r. SEE: *Hohmann retractor.*

    self-retaining r. A surgical retractor that can be clamped into position to hold tissues away from the operative field without constant use of the hands.

retrain (rē″trān′) To instruct a person in a skill or trade different from his or her previous work. One may learn how to use new tools for a familiar task or to expand one's professional qualifications and employability. **retraining** (″trān′ing), *n.*

retreat (rĭ-trēt′) [ME. *retret,* draw back] A withdrawal (e.g., in psychology) from difficult life situations. This may be direct, as in physical flight, or indirect, as in malingering, illness, abnormal preoccupation, and self-deception.

retrenchment [Fr. *retrenchier,* to cut back] **1.** A budgetary reduction; a cutback in the amount of funds allocated

for a purpose. **2.** A procedure used in plastic surgery to remove excess tissue.

retrieval (rĭ-trē′văl) **1.** In psychology, the process of bringing stored information to the conscious level. **2.** Gathering of an item or items from storage or a repository.

    oocyte r. A procedure to collect eggs contained in the ovarian follicles for use in assisted reproduction.

retro- [L. *retro,* back, backward, behind] Prefix meaning *backward, back, behind.*

retroaction (rĕ″trō-ăk′shŭn) Action in a reverse direction.

retrobuccal (rĕt″rō-bŭk′ăl) [L. *retro,* back, + *bucca,* cheek] Pert. to the back part of the mouth or the area behind the mouth.

retrocecal (rĕt″rō-sē′kăl) [L. *retro,* back, + *caecum,* cecum] Behind or pert. to the area posterior to the cecum.

retrocervical (rĕt″rō-sĕr′vĭ-kăl) [L. *retro,* back, + *cervix,* neck] Posterior to the cervix uteri.

retroclination (re″trō-klī-nā′shŏn) Posterior inclination of an incisor.

retrocolic (rĕt″rō-kŏl′ĭk) [L. *retro,* back, + Gr. *kolon,* colon] Posterior to the colon.

retrocollic spasm SEE: under *spasm.*

retrocollis (re″trō-kol′is) [*retro-* + *collum*] Torticollis with spasms affecting the posterior neck muscles. SYN: *retrocollic spasm.*

retroconduction (rĕt″rō-kŏn-dŭk′shŭn) [″ + ″] Backward conduction, i.e., a reversed flow of ions or electrical impulses, esp. used when speaking of disturbances in cardiac rhythm.

retrocursive (rĕt″rō-kŭr′sĭv) [L. *retro,* back, + *curro,* to run] Stepping or turning backward.

retrodeviation (rĕt″rō-dē″vē-ā′shŭn) [″ + *deviare,* to turn aside] Backward displacement, as of an organ.

retrodisplacement (rĕt″rō-dĭs-plăs′mĕnt) [″ + Fr. *desplacer,* displace] Backward displacement of a part.

retroesophageal (rĕt″rō-ē-sŏf″ă-jē′ăl) [L. *retro,* behind, + Gr. *oisophagos,* gullet] Behind the esophagus.

retrofilling (rĕt″rō-fĭl′ing) The placement of filling material in a root canal through an opening made in the apex of the tooth.

retroflexion (rĕt″rō-flĕk′shŭn) A bending or flexing backward. **retroflexed,** *adj.*

    r. of uterus A condition in which the body of the uterus is bent backward at an angle with the cervix, whose position usually remains unchanged.

retrognathia (rĕt″rō-năth′ē-ă) [L. *retro,* back, + Gr. *gnathos,* jaw] Location of the mandible behind the frontal plane of the maxilla.

retrognathism (rĕt″rō-năth′ĭzm) [″ + Gr. *gnathos,* jaw] The condition of having retrognathia.

retrograde (rĕt′rō-grād) [L. *retro,* backward, + *gradi*, to step] Moving backward; degenerating from a better to a worse state.

retrograde flow The flow of fluid in a direction opposite to that considered normal.

retrograde pyelography A surgical procedure used to visualize the renal pelvis and ureter in which an endoscope is placed through the urethra into the urinary bladder and a catheter is placed into the ureter to instill a contrast medium.

retrography (rĕt″rŏg′ră-fē) [″ + Gr. *graphein*, to write] Mirror writing, a symptom of certain brain diseases. It also may be present in persons with dyslexia.

retrogression (rĕt″rō-grĕsh′ŭn) [L. *retrogressus*, go backward] A going backward, as in the involution, degeneration, or atrophy of a tissue or structure.

retrojection (rĕt″rō-jĕk′shŭn) [″ + *jacio*, throw] Washing out a cavity from within by injection of a fluid.

retrolabyrinthine (rĕt″rō-lăb″ĭ-rĭn′thĭn) [L. *retro*, behind + Gr. *labyrinthos*, a maze] Located behind the labyrinth of the ear.

retrolental (rĕt-rō-lĕn′tăl) Behind the crystalline lens. SYN: *retrolenticular*.

retrolenticular (rĕt″rō-lĕn-tĭk′ū-lăr) Retrolental.

retromammary (rĕt″rō-măm′mă-rē) [″ + *mamma*, breast] Behind the mammary gland.

retromandibular (rĕt″rō-măn-dĭb′ū-lăr) [″ + *mandibulum*, jaw] Behind the lower jaw.

retronasal (rĕt″rō-nā′zăl) [L. *retro*, back, + *nasus*, nose] Pert. to or situated at the back part of the nose.

retro-ocular (rĕt″rō-ŏk′ū-lar) [L. *retro*, behind, + *oculus*, eye] Behind the eye.

retroperitoneal (rĕt″rō-pĕr″ĭ-tō-nē′ăl) [″ + Gr. *peritonaion*, peritoneum] Behind the peritoneum and outside the peritoneal cavity (e.g., the kidneys).

retroperitoneal fibrosis SEE: under *fibrosis*.

retroperitonitis (rĕt″rō-pĕr″ĭ-tō-nī′tĭs) Inflammation behind the peritoneum.

retropharyngeal (rĕt″rō-făr-ĭn′jē-ăl) [L. *retro*, behind, + Gr. *pharynx*, throat] Behind the pharynx.

retropharyngitis (rĕt″rō-făr″ĭn-jī′tĭs) [″ + ″ + *itis*, inflammation] Inflammation of the retropharyngeal tissue.

retropharynx (rĕt″rō-făr′ĭnks) [″ + Gr. *pharynx*, throat] The posterior portion of the pharynx.

retroplacental (rĕt″rō-plă-sĕn′tăl) [″ + *placenta*, a flat cake] Behind the placenta, or between the placenta and the uterine wall.

retroplasia (rĕt″rō-plā′zē-ă) [″ + Gr. *plassein*, to form] The changing of a cell or tissue into a less specialized form.

retroposed (rĕt-rō-pōsd′) [L. *retro*, backward, + *positus*, placed] Displaced backward.

retroposition (rĕt″rō-pō-zĭsh′ŭn) The backward displacement of a tissue or organ.

retropubic (rĕ″trō-pū′bĭk) [″ + ″] Located behind the pubic bone.

retropubic prostatectomy The removal of a diseased prostate gland through an incision made in the lower abdomen just above the pubic symphysis.

retropulsion (rĕt″rō-pŭl′shŭn) [″ + *pulsio*, a thrusting] **1.** The pushing back of any part, as of the fetal head in labor. **2.** A gait disturbance in which patients involuntarily walk backward, seen in some diseases of the central nervous system, including Parkinson's disease. SYN: *retropulsive* **gait**. **3.** Movement of intestinal contents backward (i.e., toward the mouth instead of the anus).

retrorunning (rĕt-rō-rŭn′ēng) The act of running backwards, esp. for conditioning of the hamstring muscle groups for sport-specific training. [Because of the risk of falling, retrorunning regimens should be performed with close supervision when dealing with a nonathletic population.]

retrospective (rĕt-rō-spĕk′tĭv) Looking backward.

retrospective study SEE: under *study*.

retrospectoscope (re″trō-spek′tŏ-skōp″) [Jocular formation fm *retrospect(ive)* + -*scope*] In health care settings, a colloquial term for medical hindsight.

retrospondylolisthesis (rĕt″rō-spŏn″dĭ-lō-lĭs-thē′sĭs) [L. *retro*, behind + Gr. *spondylos*, vertebra, + *olisthesis*, a slipping] The posterior displacement of a vertebra.

retrosternal (rĕt″rō-stĕr′năl) [″ + Gr. *sternon*, chest] Behind the sternum.

retrosternal pulse SEE: under *pulse*.

retrotarsal (rĕt″rō-tăr′săl) [″ + Gr. *tarsos*, a broad, flat surface] Behind the tarsus of the eyelid.

retrouterine (rĕt″rō-ū′tĕr-ĭn) [L. *retro*, backward, + *uterus*, womb] Behind the uterus.

retroversioflexion (rĕt″rō-vĕr″sē-ō-flĕk′shŭn) [″ + *versio*, a turning, + *flexio*, flexion] Retroversion and retroflexion of the uterus.

retroversion (rĕt″rō-vĕr′shŭn) [L. *retro*, back, + *versio*, a turning] A turning, or a state of being turned back; esp., the tipping of an entire organ.

    femoral r. A decrease in the head-neck angle of the femur, causing outward rotation of the shaft of the bone when the person is standing.

    r. of uterus Backward displacement of the uterus with the cervix pointing forward toward the symphysis pubis. Normally the cervix points toward the lower end of the sacrum with the fundus toward the suprapubic region.

retrovirus (re″trō-vī′rŭs) [*retro-* + *virus*] Any of the viruses of the family Retroviridae. Some of these RNA-containing tumor viruses are oncogenic and induce sarcomas, leukemias, lymphomas, and mammary carcinomas in lower animals. These viruses contain reverse transcriptase, an enzyme essential for reverse transcription (i.e., the production of a DNA molecule from an RNA model). **retroviral** (răl), *adj.*

retrude (rĭ-trood′) [L. *re*, back, + *trudere*, to shove] In dentistry, to force backward.

retrusion (rĭ-troo′shŭn) **1.** The process of forcing backward, esp. with reference to the teeth. **2.** A condition in which teeth are retroposed.

Rett syndrome (ret) [Andreas Rett, Austrian neurologist, 1924–1997] A multiple-deficit X-linked developmental disorder marked by mental retardation, impaired language use, breath holding and hyperventilation, seizures, loss of communication skills, tremors of the trunk, repetitive hand movements (hand wringing), difficulties with walking, and abnormally small development of the head. It occurs almost exclusively in girls, after the age of 6 to 18 months, in about one of every 10,000 to 15,000 female children.

return of spontaneous circulation ABBR: ROSC. In cardiopulmonary resuscitation (CPR), the resumption of a normal heart rhythm with a perceptible pulse. ROSC differs from the ultimate goal of CPR, which is the survival of the patient, without injury to the brain, heart, kidneys, lungs, or other organs.

RET-Y (rĕt′wī″) A measure of the size and contents of the reticulocyte. It is used as an early indicator of iron deficiency.

Retzius, Magnus Gustaf (ret′sē-ŭs) Swedish physician and anatomist, 1842–1919, son of Anders Retzius.
    lines of R. Brownish incremental lines seen in microscopic sections of tooth enamel. They appear as concentric lines in transverse sections through the enamel crown.
    stria of R. Benign incremental lines seen periodically in the calcified enamel of teeth.

revaccination (rē″văk-sĭ-nā′shŭn) An inoculation against a disease to sustain a passive immune response (protective antibodies) against a potentially infectious organism.

revascularization (rē′vas″kyŭ-lă-rĭ-zā′shŏn) [*re-* + *vascularization*] Restoration of blood flow to an organ. This may be done surgically or by removing or dissolving thrombi occluding arteries, esp. coronary or renal arteries.
    cerebral r. The surgical restoration of blood flow to the brain, e.g., with an operation to bypass a blockage in the carotid or cerebral arteries.
    hybrid coronary artery r. An invasive treatment for multivessel coronary artery disease in which the patient undergoes both minimally invasive direct coronary artery bypass of the left anterior descending artery and stent placement into the right coronary artery or the circumflex artery.
    percutaneous myocardial r. Transmyocardial **r.**
    transmyocardial r. ABBR: TMR. The use of a laser to bore tiny channels directly through the wall of the heart in an attempt to bring oxygen-rich blood from the left ventricular cavity to areas where the heart muscle is oxygen-deprived, or ischemic. TMR is an alternative to coronary bypass surgery or angioplasty, esp. in patients with complex plaques that would be difficult to reach with standard interventions or in patients who have already undergone many other procedures without effect. SYN: *percutaneous myocardial r.*

reverberation (rĭ″vĕr-bĕr-ā′shŭn) [L. *reverberare*, to cause to rebound] **1.** The process by which closed chains of neurons, when excited by a single impulse, continue to discharge impulses from collaterals of their cells. **2.** The repeated echoing of a sound.

Reverdin needle (rā-vĕr-dan′) [Jacques L. Reverdin, Swiss surgeon, 1842–1929] A needle with an eye at the tip that can be opened and closed by a slide.

reversal (rĭ-vĕr′săl) [L. *reversus*, turned back] **1.** A change or turning in the opposite direction. **2.** In psychology, a change in an instinct or emotion to its opposite, as from love to hate. **3.** Provision of an antidote or antagonist to a drug previously ingested or received by a patient.
    sex r. The changing of an individual's sexual phenotype to that of the opposite sex. SEE: *sexual reassignment.*

reverse anorexia SEE: under *anorexia.*

reverse herbology The study of the interactions between herbal and allopathic medications.

reverse PRN dosing A form of administration of medication in which dosages are given every few hours *or less often.*

reversible (rē-vĕr′sĭ-bl) **1.** Able to change back and forth or from one state to another. **2.** Able to be done and undone. **3.** Able to turn or be turned inside out.

reversible cerebral vasoconstriction syndrome ABBR: RCVS. Any of several forms of a disease, including Call-Fleming syndrome, marked by thunderclap headache and associated with temporary narrowing of arteries within the brain and, often, seizures or strokelike symptoms.

reversible ischemic neurological deficit
ABBR: RIND. A transient stroke resulting from a decrease in cerebral blood flow. Symptoms typically last longer than 24 hr but less than 1 week.

reversion (rĭ-vĕr′zhŭn) **1.** A return to a previously existing condition. **2.** In genetics, the appearance of traits possessed by a remote ancestor. SEE: *atavism.*

revert (rē-vĕrt′) [L. *revertere,* to turn back] To return to an earlier state or condition. SEE: *reversion; revertant.*

revertant (rē-vĕr′tănt) An organism that has reverted to a previous phenotype by mutation.

review, chart A method of quality assurance (and sometimes clinical research) that relies on the systematic analysis of individual patient records. Data may be used to determine the incidence of adverse events, the allocation of resources, the employment of specific therapies, or the degree of compliance with specified standards of care.

review of systems ABBR: ROS. A series of questions concerning each organ system and region of the body, asked of the patient during history taking and physical examination in order to gain an optimal understanding of the patient's presenting illness and medical history.

A sample ROS follows: *General:* The examiner should determine any history of fatigue, travel to other climates or countries, recent weight change, chills, fever, and lifestyle change in the patient. How many persons occupy the patient's dwelling? What is the patient's relationship to the persons with whom he or she lives? Is it a happy home? What are the patient's hobbies and outside interests? How does the patient usually exercise? Does the patient have pets? Any history of military service? Any job-related illnesses? Any sexual partners? Any use of injected drugs? Any recent hospitalizations or illnesses?

Skin: Is the patient experiencing any rash, itching, sunburn, change in the size of moles, vesicles, or hair loss?

Head, face, and neck: Does the patient have headaches, migraine, vertigo, stiffness, pain, or swelling? Has there been trauma to this area?

Eyes: Does the patient wear glasses? When were the eyes last examined for visual acuity and glaucoma? Is the patient experiencing pain, diplopia, scotomata, itch, discharge, redness, or infection?

Ears: Does the patient have acute or chronic hearing loss, pain, discharge, tinnitus, or vertigo? Is there a history of failure to adjust to descent from a high altitude?

Nose: Does the patient have any dryness, crust formation, bleeding, pain, discharge, obstruction, malodor, or sneezing? How acute is the patient's sense of smell?

Mouth and teeth: The patient should be asked about any soreness, ulcers, pain, dryness, infection, hoarseness, bleeding gums, swallowing difficulty, bruxism, or temporomandibular syndrome. What is the condition of the patient's teeth (real or false)?

Breasts: Has the patient had any pain, swelling, tenderness, lumps, bleeding from the nipple, infection, or change in the ability of the nipples to become erect? Has plastic surgery been done, and if so, were implants used?

Respiratory: Has the patient had any cough, pain, wheezing, sputum production (including character of sputum), hemoptysis, or exposure to persons with contagious diseases such as tuberculosis? Is there a history of occupational or other exposure to asbestos, silica, chickens, parrots, or a dusty environment? The presence of dyspnea, cyanosis, tuberculosis, pneumonia, and pleurisy should be determined. If pulmonary function tests were done, the date or dates should be recorded. The extent and duration of all forms of tobacco use should be determined.

Cardiac: The examiner should determine the following: angina, dyspnea, orthopnea, palpitations, heart murmur, heart failure, myocardial infarction, surgical procedures on coronary arteries or heart valves, history of stress tests or angiography, hypertension, rheumatic fever, cardiac arrhythmias, exercise tolerance, history of athletic participation (including jogging and running) and if these are current activities, the dates of electrocardiograms if they were ever taken.

Vascular: Has the patient experienced claudication, cold intolerance (esp. of the extremities), frostbite, phlebitis, or ulcers (esp. of the extremities) due to poor blood supply?

Gastrointestinal: The examiner should assess the patient's appetite, history of recent weight gain or loss, and whether the patient has been following a particular diet for gaining or losing weight. Is the patient a vegetarian? Has he or she had any difficulty in swallowing? Anorexia, nausea, vomiting (including the character of the vomitus), diarrhea and its possible explanation (such as foreign travel or food poisoning), belching, constipation, change in bowel habits, melena, hemorrhoids and history of surgery for this condition, use of laxatives or antacids, jaundice, hepatitis, and other liver disease should be determined.

Renal; urinary and genital tract: The examiner should take a history of kidney or bladder stones and date of last occurrence, dysuria, hematuria, pyuria, nocturia, incontinence, urgency, antibiotics used for urinary tract infections, bed-wetting, sexually transmitted diseases, libido, sexual partners, penile or urethral discharge, and frequency of sexual activity.

Women should be questioned regarding any vulval pruritus, vaginal discharge, vaginal malodor, history of menarche, frequency and duration of menstrual periods, amount of flow, type of menstrual protection used, type or types of contraception and douches used, and the total number of pregnancies, abortions, miscarriages, and normal deliveries. The number, sex, age, and health status of living children, and the cause of death of children who died, should be determined. Vaginal, cervical, and uterine infections; pelvic inflammatory disease; tubal ligation; dilation and curettement; hysterectomy; and dyspareunia should be recorded. Any history of the mother's use of diethylstilbestrol while pregnant with the patient should be determined.

Men should be asked about vasectomy, scrotal pain or swelling, and urinary hesitancy or double voiding.

Musculoskeletal: The examiner should ask about muscle twitches, pain, heat, tenderness, swelling, loss of range of motion or strength, cramps, sprains, strains, trauma, fractures, stiffness, back pain, osteoporosis, and character regarding time of day of onset and duration (esp. with respect to the effect of exercise, back pain, and osteoporosis).

Hematological: The examiner should record history of anemia, bleeding, bruising, hemarthrosis, hemophilia, sickle cell disease or trait, recent blood loss, transfusions received, and blood donation. Did the patient receive a transfusion at a time when blood was not being screened for hepatitis or AIDS? Was the patient ever turned down as a blood donor?

Endocrine: The patient should be questioned about sexual maturation and development, weight change, tolerance to heat or cold (esp. with respect to other persons in the same environment), dryness of hair and skin, hair loss, and voice change. Any change in the rate of beard growth in men, development of facial hair in women, increase in or loss of libido, polyuria, polydipsia, polyphagia, pruritus, diabetes, exophthalmos, goiter, unexplained flushing, and sweating should be noted.

Nervous system: Has the patient experienced any recent change in ability to control muscular activity, or any syncope, stroke (shock), seizures, tremor, coordination, sensory disturbance, falls, pain, change in memory, dizziness, or head trauma?

Emotional and psychological status:

Has there been a history of psychiatric illness, anxiety, depression, overactivity, mania, lassitude, change in sleep pattern, insomnia, hypersomnia, nightmares, sleepwalking, hallucinations, feeling of unreality, paranoia, phobias, obsessions, compulsions, criminal behavior, increase in or loss of libido, or suicidal thoughts? Is the patient satisfied with his or her occupation and with life in general? What is his or her marital and divorce record? Has there been family discord? Does the patient attend religious services? The patient's employment history and any recent job changes, educational history and achievement, and self-image should be assessed.

Révilliod sign (rā-vē-yō′) [Léon Révilliod, Swiss physician, 1835–1919] In hemiplegia, inability of the patient may to blink or close the eye on the paralyzed side without simultaneously closing the other eye. SYN: *orbicular sign.* SEE: *blink; Marcus Gunn syndrome.*

revise (rĕ-vīz′) [L. *revisere,* to look back, revisit] **1.** To update a text, blog, website, or document; to rewrite its content. **2.** In surgery, to reoperate after an earlier surgical procedure has failed.

revised trauma score ABBR: RTS. Pediatric trauma score.

revivification (rē-vĭv″ĭ-fĭ-kā′shŭn) [L. *re,* again, + *vivere,* to live, + *facere,* to make] **1.** An attempt to restore life to those apparently dead; restoration to life or consciousness; also the restoration of life in local parts, as a limb after freezing. **2.** The pairing of surfaces to facilitate healing, as in a wound.

revulsion (rĭ-vŭl′shŭn) **1.** Repugnance, hostility, or extreme distaste for a person or thing. **2.** The act of driving backward, as diverting disease from one part to another by a quick withdrawal of blood from that part—a treatment that has its origins in ancient medical care. **3.** Circulatory changes obtained by sudden and intense reactions to heat and cold. SEE: *counterirritation.*

revulsive (rĭ-vŭl′sĭv) **1.** Causing revulsion. **2.** A counterirritant.

reward **1.** In behavioral science, a positive reinforcement. **2.** Something valuable given to recognize achievement, competence, or performance.

rewarming Restoring a hypothermic patient's body temperature to normal. Techniques used include removing wet clothing; wrapping patients in blankets, hotpacks, or foils; infusing intravenous, nasogastric, or intraperitoneal fluids warmed to about 40°C; increasing the temperature of the patient's blood with extracorporeal bypass machines, or, rarely, immersing the patient in warm water.

Rey Auditory Verbal Learning Test (rā) A neuropsychiatric test used to measure the ability to recall a list of heard words. The test is sometimes used to evaluate the memory of patients with dementia.

Reye syndrome (rī) [Ralph Douglas Kenneth Reye, Australian pathologist, 1912–1977] A syndrome marked by acute encephalopathy and fatty infiltration of the liver and often of the pancreas, heart, kidney, spleen, and lymph nodes. It is seen primarily in children under age 18 after an acute viral infection such as chickenpox or influenza. The mortality rate depends on the severity of the central nervous system involvement but may be as high as 80%. Fortunately, the disease occurs rarely. The cause of the disease is unknown, but association with increased use of aspirin and other salicylates is evident from epidemiological studies. SEE: *Nursing Diagnoses Appendix.*

SYMPTOMS: The patient experiences a viral infection with a brief recovery period, followed in about 1 to 3 days by severe nausea and vomiting, a change in mental status (disorientation, agitation, coma, seizures), and hepatomegaly without jaundice in 40% of cases. The disease should be suspected in any child with acute onset of encephalopathy, nausea and vomiting, or altered liver function, esp. after a recent illness. The severity of the syndrome depends on how badly the brain swells during the illness, reflected in increased intracranial pressure (ICP).

⚠ Aspirin and other salicylates should not be used for any reason in treating children under age 18 with viral infections.

TREATMENT: Supportive care includes intravenous administration of fluids and electrolytes, administration of corticosteroids, and ventilatory assistance. Electrolytes, levels of serum glucose and ammonia, and neurological status should be controlled carefully.

PATIENT CARE: Increased ICP resulting from increased cerebral blood volume results in intracranial hypertension. To decrease intracranial pressure and cerebral edema, fluids are provided at 2/3 maintenance level; an osmotic diuretic such as mannitol along with a loop diuretic such as furosemide may be prescribed. The head of the bed is kept at a 30° angle. Fluid intake should maintain urine output at 1.0 mL/kg/hr, plasma osmolality at 290 mOsm (normal to high), and blood glucose at 150 mg/mL (high), while preventing fluid overload. Proteins are restricted to keep ammonia levels low. Hypoprothrombinemia (resulting from liver injury) is treated with vitamin K or fresh frozen plasma if needed. Temperature

is monitored, and prescribed measures to alleviate hyperthermia are instituted. Precautions against seizure are also instituted. Intake and output are monitored carefully. The patient is observed for evidence of impaired hepatic function, such as signs of bleeding or encephalopathy. All treatments are explained to parents and support is provided to them. The National Reye's Syndrome Foundation provides information and support.

RF *rheumatoid factor.*

RFA *right frontoanterior* fetal position.

R factor SEE: under *factor.*

RFP *right frontoposterior* fetal position.

RFT *right frontotransverse* fetal position.

RH *releasing hormone.* SEE: under *hormone.*

Rh 1. Symbol for the element rhodium. **2.** *Rhesus,* a monkey (*Macaca rhesus*) in which the Rh factor was first identified.

Rhabditis (răb-dī'tĭs) [Gr. *rhabdos,* rod] A genus of small nematode worms, some of which are parasitic.

rhabdo-, rhabd- [Gr. *rhabdos,* rod, wand] Prefixes meaning *rod.*

rhabdoid (răb'doyd) [Gr. *rhabdos,* rod, + *eidos,* form, shape] Resembling a rod.

rhabdomyoblastoma (răb″dō-mī″ō-blăs-tō'mă) Rhabdomyosarcoma.

rhabdomyolysis (rab″dō-mī-ol'ĭ-sĭs, ol'ĭ-sēz″) *pl.* **rhabdomyolyses** [*rhabdo-* + *myo-* + *-lysis*] An acute, sometimes fatal disease in which the by-products of skeletal muscle destruction accumulate in the renal tubules and produce acute renal failure. Rhabdomyolysis may result from crush injuries, the toxic effect of drugs or chemicals on skeletal muscle, extremes of exertion, sepsis, shock, electric shock, and severe hyponatremia. Lipid-lowering drugs such as statins (pravastatin, simvastatin) and/or fibrates (gemfibrozil) are among the commonly prescribed drugs that put patients at risk for rhabdomyolysis. Kidney failure caused by rhabdomyolysis may produce life-threatening hyperkalemia and metabolic acidosis. The diagnosis is made in patients with appropriate histories or exposures who have elevated levels of serum or urine myoglobin or creatine kinase (CK). Management may include the infusion of bicarbonate-containing fluids (to enhance urinary secretion of myoglobin) or hemodialysis. SEE: *reperfusion.*

PATIENT CARE: The goals of treatment are to prevent and treat renal dysfunction, reverse electrolyte abnormalities, and correct the underlying cause. Patients are hydrated aggressively with a goal of achieving urine output between 200 and 300 mL/hr. If urine output does not increase with hydration, loop and osmotic diuretics are prescribed to promote diuresis. Dialysis may be needed for the 10% to 20% of patients with rhabdomyolysis who develop renal failure. Urinary alkalinization (as with sodium bicarbonate) increases myoglobin solubility in the urine and thus its elimination from the body. The patient with rhabdomyolysis should also be monitored closely for electrolyte disturbances (hypocalcemia, hyperkalemia) and dysrhythmias and corrections made as quickly as possible. When localized muscle injuries are present (as after trauma) and compartment syndrome is suspected, direct measurement of compartment pressures is used to diagnose the need for fasciotomy. Bedrest is maintained throughout the acute illness phase. As the patient recovers, physical therapy will help maintain range of motion and prevent other complications of immobilization in hospital.

    traumatic r. SEE: *crush syndrome; reperfusion* (2).

rhabdomyoma (răb″dō-mī-ō′mă) [″ + ″ + *oma,* tumor] A striated muscular tissue tumor. SYN: *myoma striocellulare.*

rhabdomyosarcoma (răb″dō-mī″ō-săr-kō′ mă) [″ + ″ + *sarx,* flesh, + *oma,* tumor] A malignant neoplasm originating in skeletal muscle. SYN: *rhabdomyoblastoma.*

rhabdosarcoma, embryonal (răb″dō-săr-kō′mă) Botryoid sarcoma.

rhabdovirus (răb″dō-vī′rŭs) [″ + L. *virus,* poison] Any of a group of rod-shaped RNA viruses with one important member, the rabies virus, being pathogenic to humans. The virus has a predilection for the tissue of mucus-secreting glands and the central nervous system. All warm-blooded animals are susceptible to infection with these viruses.

rhachialgia (rā″kē-ăl′jē-ă) [Gr. *rhachis,* spine, + *algos,* pain] Pain in the spine.

rhachiocampsis (rā″kē-ō-kămp′sĭs) [″ + *kampsis,* a bending] Curvature of the spine.

rhachioplegia (rā″kē-ō-plē′jē-ă) [″ + *plege,* stroke] Spinal paralysis.

rhachioscoliosis (rā″kē-ō-skō″lē-ō′sĭs) [″ + *skoliosis,* curvature] Curvature of the spine laterally.

rhachis (rā′kĭs) [Gr.] The spinal column.

Rhadinovirus (ră″dĭ-nō-vī′rŭs) [Gr. *rhadinos,* fragile + ″] A genus of herpesviruses that includes human herpes virus 8.

rhagades (răg′ă-dēz) [Gr., tears] Linear fissures appearing in the skin, esp. at the corner of the mouth or anus, causing pain. If due to syphilis, they form a radiating scar on healing.

rhagadiform (ră-găd′ĭ-form) [Gr. *rha-*

gas, tear, + L. *forma,* shape] Fissured; having cracks.

-rhage, -rhagia, -rhagy SEE: *-rrhagia.*

Rh antiserum Human serum that contains antibodies to the Rh factor. SEE: *Rh₀(D) immune globulin.*

Rh blood group SEE: under *blood group.*

-rhea SEE: *-rrhea.*

rhegmatogenous (rĕg″mă-tŏ′jĕ-nus) [Gr. *rhegma,* a breaking, + *gen,* producing, forming] **1.** Caused by or pert. to a tear. **2.** Torn. The term refers almost exclusively to retinal detachment.

rhenium (rē′nē-ŭm) [L. *Rhenus,* Rhine (River) + *-ium* (1)] SYMB: Re. A silvery-white polyvalent transition metal similar to manganese, atomic weight (mass) 186.2, atomic number 75. It is used as a radiopharmaceutical.

rheo- [Gr. *rheos,* stream current] Prefix meaning *current, stream, flow.*

rheobase (rē′ō-bās) [″ + *basis,* base] In unipolar testing with the galvanic current using the negative as the active pole, the minimal voltage required to produce a stimulated response. Also called *threshold of excitation.* SEE: *chronaxie.*

rheobasic (rē″ō-bā′sĭk) Concerning the rheobase.

rheology (rē-ŏl′ō-jē) [″ + *logos,* word, reason] The study of the deformation and flow of materials.

rheophoresis, rheopheresis (rē″ō-fŏr-ē′sĭs) [Gr. *rheos,* current, + *phoresis,* a bearing] Membrane differential filtration.

rheostat (rē′ō-stăt) [″ + *statos,* standing] A device maintaining fixed or variable resistance for controlling the amount of electric current entering a circuit.

rheostosis (rē-ŏs-tō′sĭs) [″ + *osteon,* bone] A hypertrophying and condensing osteitis occurring in streaks, involving the long bones; also known as melorheostosis.

rheotaxis (rē″ō-tăk′sĭs) [″ + *taxis,* arrangement] A reaction to a current of fluid, in which an organism orients itself with the current.

rheumatic (roo-măt′ĭk) [Gr. *rheumatikos*] Pert. to connective tissue disease.

rheumatic disease, functional class Classifications created by the American Rheumatism Association (now the American College of Rheumatology) that define the capacity level at which a patient with rheumatic disease is capable of functioning. Class I is complete functional capacity with ability to carry on all usual duties without handicaps; class II is functional capacity adequate to conduct normal activities despite handicap or discomfort or limited mobility of one or more joints; class III is functional capacity adequate to perform only a few or none of the duties of usual occupations or of self-care; and class IV indicates a patient who is largely or wholly incapacitated and is bedridden or confined to a wheelchair, permitting little or no self-care.

rheumatic fever SEE: under *fever*.

rheumatid (roo′mă-tĭd) A skin lesion associated with rheumatic disease.

rheumatism (roo′mă-tĭzm) [Gr. *rheumatismos,* a suffering from a flux] A general, somewhat archaic term for acute and chronic conditions marked by inflammation, muscle soreness and stiffness, and pain in joints and associated structures. It includes inflammatory arthritis (infectious, rheumatoid, gouty), arthritis due to rheumatic fever or trauma, degenerative joint disease, neurogenic arthropathy, hydroarthrosis, myositis, bursitis, and fibromyalgia. SEE: *arthritis; rheumatic fever.*

    inflammatory r. An old term for any form of arthritis in which there is significant joint inflammation, e.g., gouty, infectious, or rheumatoid arthritis.

    palindromic r. Intermittent migrating joint pain with tenderness, heat, and swelling that lasts from a few hours to as long as a week. The knee is most often involved, but each recurrence often involves a different joint. Between attacks there is no evidence of joint disease. The cause is unknown, and there is no specific treatment.

    soft tissue r. Any of several localized or generalized conditions that cause pain around joints but are not related to or caused by joint disease, e.g., bursitis, tennis elbow, tendinitis, perichondritis, stiff man syndrome, Tietze disease.

rheumatoid (roo′mă-toyd) [Gr. *rheuma,* discharge, + *eidos,* form, shape] Of, or relating to, arthritis or connective tissue disease.

rheumatoid factor SEE: under *factor.*

rheumatologist (roo″mă-tŏl′ō-jĭst) A physician who specializes in rheumatic diseases.

rheumatology (roo″mă-tŏl′ō-jē) The study and treatment of connective tissue and joint diseases.

rhexis (rĕk′sĭs) [Gr., rupture] The rupture of any organ, blood vessel, or tissue.

Rh factor SEE: under *factor.*

Rh gene Any of eight allelic genes that are responsible for the various Rh blood types. They have been designated as R^1, R^2, R^0, R^z, r, r′, r″, and r_y. Genes represented by small r's are responsible for the Rh-negative (Rh⁻) blood type; those by capital R's, for the Rh-positive (Rh⁺) blood type.

rhigosis (rī-gō′sĭs) [Gr., shivering] Perception of cold.

rhinal (rī′năl) Nasal.

rhinalgia (rī-năl′jē-ă) [″ + *algos,* pain] Pain in the nose; nasal neuralgia.

rhinedema (rī″nĕ-dē′mă) [″ + *oidema,* swelling] Edema of the nose.

rhinencephalon (rī″nen″sef″ă-lo″n) [*rhino-* + *encephalon*] The portion of brain concerned with receiving and integrating olfactory impulses. It includes the olfactory bulb, olfactory tract and striae, intermediate olfactory area, pyriform area, paraterminal area, hippocampal formation, fornix, paleopallium, and archipallium. **rhinencephalic** (-sĕ-fal′ik), *adj.*

rhinitis (rī-nī′tĭs) [″ + *itis,* inflammation] Inflammation or irritation of the nasal passages, resulting in runny nose, nasal congestion, and/or postnasal drainage. SEE: *hay fever.*

    acute r. Acute nasal congestion with increased mucus secretion. It is the usual manifestation of the common cold. SEE: *coryza.*

    TREATMENT: General measures include rest, adequate fluids, and a well-balanced diet. Analgesics and antipyretics may be used to make the patient comfortable. Antibiotics are of no value and should not be administered. Antihistamines may relieve early symptoms but do not end or change the course. Inhaled ipratropium lessens secretions. Vasoconstrictors in the form of inhalants, nasal sprays, or drops may give temporary relief. Their use helps prevent the development of middle ear infections by helping to maintain the patency of the eustachian tubes.

    allergic r. Hay fever.

    atrophic r. Chronic inflammation with marked atrophy of the mucous membrane and disturbance in the sense of smell; usually accompanied by ozena. The throat is dry and usually contains crusts. A husky voice or hoarseness is common.

    TREATMENT: The nose should be irrigated using warm alkalinized saline solution twice daily. Surgery is seldom helpful.

    r. caseosa Rhinitis characterized by the accumulation of offensive cheeselike masses in the nose and sinuses and accompanied by a seropurulent discharge.

    chronic hyperplastic r. Chronic inflammation of the nasal mucous membrane accompanied by polypoid formation and underlying sinus pathology. SEE: *sinus.*

    chronic hypertrophic r. Inflammation of the nasal mucous membrane marked by hypertrophy of the mucous membrane of the turbinates and the septum. The symptoms are those of nasal obstruction, postnasal discharge, and recurrent head colds. The treatment is surgical removal of the hypertrophic or mulberry ends of the inferior turbinates and cauterization of the mucosa of the inferior turbinates and septum.

    fibrinous r. Rhinitis marked by the formation of a false membrane in the nasal cavities. SYN: *pseudomembranous* **r**.

hypertrophic r. Rhinitis marked by thickening and swelling of the nasal mucosa.

infectious r. Rhinitis due to infections of the nasal mucosa.

membranous r. Chronic rhinitis accompanied by a fibrinous exudate, as was sometimes seen in patients with diphtheria.

perennial r. Year-round, rather than seasonal, rhinitis.

pseudomembranous r. Fibrinous **r**.

purulent r. Chronic rhinitis accompanied by pus formation.

vasomotor r. Nonallergic rhinitis.

rhino-, rhin- [Gr. *rhis,* stem *rhin-*] Prefixes meaning *nose.* SEE: *naso-*.

rhinoantritis (rī″nō-ăn-trī′tĭs) [″ + *antron,* cavity, + *itis,* inflammation] Inflammation of the nasal cavities and one or both maxillary sinuses (antra).

rhinocanthectomy (rī″nō-kăn-thĕk′tō-mē) [Gr. *rhis,* nose, + *kanthos,* canthus, + *ektome,* excision] Surgical excision of the inner corner of the eye.

rhinocephaly (rī″nō-sĕf′ă-lē) [″ + *kephale,* head] A congenital deformity in which the eyes are fused and the nose is present as a fleshy protuberance above the eyes.

rhinocheiloplasty (rī″nō-kī′lō-plăs″tē) [″ + *cheilos,* lip, + *plastos,* formed] Plastic surgery of the nose and upper lip.

rhinodacryolith (rī″nō-dăk′rē-ō-lĭth) [″ + *dakryon,* tear, + *lithos,* stone] A stone in the nasolacrimal duct.

Rhinoestrus (rī-nĕs′trŭs) A genus of flies belonging to the family Oestridae. Larvae may be deposited in the eye or in the nasal or buccal cavity of mammals.

R. purpureus The Russian gadfly, whose larvae sometimes cause nasomyiasis and ophthalmomyiasis in humans.

rhinogenous (rī-nŏj′ĕn-ŭs) [″ + *gennan,* to produce] Originating in the nose.

rhinokyphosis (rī″nō-kī-fō′sĭs) [″ + *kyphos,* hump, + *osis,* condition] A deformity of the bridge of the nose.

rhinolalia (rī″nō-lā′lē-ă) [″ + *lalia,* speech] A nasal quality of the voice.

r. aperta Rhinolalia caused by undue patency of the posterior nares.

r. clausa Rhinolalia caused by closure of the nasal passages.

rhinolaryngitis (rī″nō-lăr″ĭn-jī′tĭs) [″ + *larynx,* larynx, + *itis,* inflammation] Simultaneous inflammation of the mucosa of the nose and larynx.

rhinolith (rī′nō-lĭth) [″ + *lithos,* stone] A nasal stone.

rhinolithiasis (rī″nō-lĭth-ī′ă-sĭs) The formation of nasal stones.

rhinologist (rī-nŏl′ō-jĭst) [″ + *logos,* word, reason] A specialist in diseases of the nose.

rhinology (rī-nŏl′ō-jē) The science of the nose and its diseases.

rhinomanometry (rī″nō-mă-nŏm′ĕ-trē) The measurement of air flow through and air pressure in the nose.

rhinometer (rī-nŏm′ĕt-ĕr) A device for measuring the nose or its cavities.

rhinomycosis (rī″nō-mī-kō′sĭs) [″ + *mykes,* fungus, + *osis,* condition] Fungi in the mucous membranes and secretions of the nose.

rhinonecrosis (rī″nō-nē-krō′sĭs) [″ + *nekrosis,* state of death] Necrosis of the nasal bones.

rhinopathy (rī-nŏp′ă-thē) [″ + *pathos,* disease] Any nasal disease.

rhinopharyngeal (rī″nō-fă-rĭn′jē-ăl) Pert. to the nasopharynx.

rhinopharyngitis (rī″nō-făr-ĭn-jī′tĭs) [″ + *pharynx,* throat, + *itis,* inflammation] Inflammation of the nasopharynx.

rhinopharyngocele (rī″nō-făr-ĭn′gō-sēl) [″ + ″ + *kele,* tumor, swelling] A nasopharyngeal tumor.

rhinopharyngolith (rī″nō-făr-ĭn′gō-lĭth) [″ + ″ + *lithos,* stone] A stone in the nasopharynx.

rhinopharynx (rī″nō-făr′ĭnks) Nasopharynx.

rhinophonia (rī″nō-fō′nē-ă) Rhinolalia.

rhinophycomycosis (rī″nō-fī″kō-mī-kō′sĭs) [″ + *phykos,* seaweed, + *mykes,* fungus, + *osis,* condition] A fungal infection that may occur in humans or animals. It affects the nasal and paranasal sinuses and may spread to the brain. It is caused by the phycomycete *Entomophthora coronata.*

rhinophyma (rī-nō-fī′mă) [″ + *phyma,* growth] Nodular swelling and congestion of the nose associated with acne rosacea.

rhinoplasty (rī′nō-plăs″tē) [″ + *plastos,* formed] Plastic surgery of the nose.

rhinopneumonitis (rī″nō-nū″mō-nī′tĭs) [Gr. *rhis,* nose, + *pneumon,* lung, + *itis,* inflammation] Inflammation of the nasal and pulmonary mucous membranes.

rhinorrhagia (rī″nō-rā′jē-ă) Epistaxis.

rhinorrhea (rī″nō-rē′ă) [″ + *rhoia,* flow] A thin watery discharge from the nose.

cerebrospinal r. A discharge of spinal fluid from the nose caused by a defect in or trauma to the cribriform plate.

gustatory r. A flow of thin watery material from the nose while one is eating.

rhinosalpingitis (rī″nō-săl″pĭn-jī′tĭs) [″ + *salpinx,* tube, + *itis,* inflammation] Inflammation of the mucosa of the nose and eustachian tube.

rhinoscleroma (rī″nō-sklē-rō′mă) [″ + *skleros,* hard, + *oma,* tumor] A chronic, recurring granulomatous infection of the nasal passages and surrounding structures, sometimes leading to marked deformity of the nasal cavity, nasopharynx, paranasal sinuses, or eyes. The disease is caused by *Klebsiella rhinoscleromatis,* a gram-negative encapsulated bacillus.

TREATMENT: Surgical débridement is combined with prolonged antimicrobial therapy.

SYMPTOMS: The disease presents a hard, nodular growth, which usually begins at the anterior end of the nose and spreads to the lower respiratory tract. There usually is no pain and no tendency to ulceration.

rhinoscope (rī′nō-skōp) [″ + *skopein,* to examine] An instrument for examining the interior of the nose.

rhinoscopy (rī-nŏs′kō-pē) Examination of nasal passages. **rhinoscopic** (rī″nō-skŏp′ĭk), *adj.*

> ***anterior r.*** Examination through the anterior nares.

> ***posterior r.*** Examination through the posterior nares, usually with a small mirror in the nasopharynx.

rhinosporidiosis (rī″nō-spō-rĭd″ē-ō′sĭs) [″ + *sporidion,* little seed, + *osis,* condition] A condition caused by *Rhinosporidium seeberi,* and marked by development of pedunculated polyps on the mucous membranes of the nose, larynx, eyes, penis, vagina, and sometimes skin of various parts of the body. The disease is contracted from cattle and is found in India, Sri Lanka, and other parts of the world.

Rhinosporidium (rī″nō-spō-rĭd′ē-ŭm) A genus of pathogenic Mesomycetozoea closely related to protists and fungi but not classed in either category.

> ***R. seeberi*** The causative agent of rhinosporidiosis.

rhinostenosis (rī″nō-stĕn-ō′sĭs) [″ + *stenos,* narrow, + *osis,* condition] Obstruction of the nasal passages.

rhinotomy (rī-nŏt′ō-mē) [″ + *tome,* incision] Incision of the nose for drainage purposes.

rhinotracheitis (rī″nō-trā″kē-ī′tĭs) [″ + *tracheia,* rough, + *itis,* inflammation] Inflammation of the nasal mucous membranes and the trachea.

rhinovirus (rī″nō-vī′rŭs) One of hundreds of species of picornaviruses that are responsible for upper respiratory infections ("common cold") in humans. Rhinoviruses commonly produce runny nose and congestion, postnasal drainage, cough, malaise, and, in some cases, exacerbations of asthma. The symptoms of rhinoviral infection are treatable, through the use of oxymetazoline nasal spray, pseudoephedrine, or inhaled ipratropium bromide.

Rhipicephalus (rī″pĭ-sĕf′ă-lŭs) [Gr. *rhipis,* fan, + *kephale,* head] A genus of ticks belonging to the family Ixodidae. Several species, esp. *R. sanguineus,* are vectors for the organisms of spotted fever, boutonneuse fever, and other rickettsial diseases.

rhitidosis (rĭt-ĭ-dō′sĭs) Rhytidosis.

rhizo-, rhiz- [Gr. *rhiza,* root] Prefixes meaning *root.*

Rhizobium radiobacter (rī-zō′bē-ŭm rā″dē-ō-băk′tĕr) [″ + ″; ″ + ″] A gram-negative rod that is a rare cause of infection in hospitalized patients, esp. those treated with plastic tubes or catheters. It has long been recognized as a plant pathogen. It has been identified as a human pathogen only in patients with cancers, critical illness, or immunosuppressing illnesses. It was formerly known as *Agrobacterium radiobacter.*

rhizoid (rī′zoyd) [″ + *eidos,* form, shape] 1. Rootlike. 2. A rootlike structure, usually one-celled, occurring in lower forms of plant life. 3. In bacteriology, a colony showing an irregular rootlike system of branching.

rhizome (rī′zōm) [Gr. *rhizoma,* mass of roots] A rootlike stem growing horizontally along or below the ground and sending out roots and shoots.

rhizomelic (rī″zō-mĕl′ĭk) [Gr. *rhiza,* root, + *melos,* limb] Concerning the hip joint and the shoulder joint.

rhizomeningomyelitis (rī″zō-mĕ-nĭn″gō-mī″ĕ-lī′tĭs) Radiculomeningomyelitis.

Rhizopoda (rī-zŏp′ō-dă) [″ + *pous,* foot] A phylum of the kingdom Protista; unicellular amebas with pseudopod locomotion. It includes free-living and pathogenic species such as *Entamoeba histolytica.*

Rhizopus A genus of fungi, a mold that is usually saprophytic, but may be an opportunist; a common cause of mucormycosis.

rhizotomy (rī-zŏt′ō-mē) [″ + *tome,* incision] Surgical section of a nerve root (e.g., the root of a spinal or dental nerve) to relieve pain or reduce spasticity.

> ***anterior r.*** Surgical section of the ventral root of the spinal nerve.

> ***posterior r.*** Surgical section of the dorsal root of the spinal nerve.

Rhodiola rosea (rōd″ē-ō′lă rōz′ē-ă) A succulent plant that grows primarily in cold climates or high altitudes. It is used in alternative and complementary medicine as an adaptogen. SYN: *golden root; hong jing tian.*

rhodium (rōd′ē-ŭm) [*rhodo- + -ium* (1)] SYMB: Rh. A rare silvery-white transition metal, atomic weight 102.905, atomic number 45. It is used in alloys with platinum and as a catalyst.

Rhodnius prolixus (rod′nē-ŭs prō-lĭk′sŭs) The bloodsucking insect of the family Reduviidae that transmits Chagas disease to humans. SEE: *trypanosomiasis.*

rhodo-, rhod- [Gr. *rhodon,* rose] Prefixes meaning *rose, red.*

rhodogenesis (rō″dō-jĕn′ĕ-sĭs) [Gr. *rhodon,* rose, + *genesis,* generation, birth]

Regeneration of rhodopsin that has been bleached by light.

rhodophylaxis (rō″dō-fĭ-lăk′sĭs) [″ + *phylaxis,* protection] The ability of the retinal epithelium to regenerate rhodopsin that has been bleached by light.

rhodopsin (rō-dŏp′sĭn) [″ + *opsis,* vision] The glycoprotein opsin of the rods of the retina; combines with retinal to form a functional photopigment responsive to light. Formerly called visual purple.

Rhodotorula (rō″dō-tŏr′ŭ-lă) [NL] A genus of yeasts that do not ferment carbohydrates. The yeasts are widely distributed in air, dairy products, soil, and water. They have been occasionally identified as a cause of opportunistic infection in compromised hosts.

rhombencephalitis, rhomboencephalitis (rŏmb″ĕn-sĕf-ă-lī′tĭs, rŏm′bō-ĕn-sĕf-ă-lī′tĭs) Brainstem infection, a disease that is most often caused by the bacterium *Listeria moncytogenes* or by West Nile virus, Nipah viruses, or enteroviruses. The infection is often characterized by symptoms such as fever, malaise, headache, nausea, vomiting, altered mental status, ataxia, and strokelike impairment of cranial nerves.

rhombencephalon (rŏm″bĕn-sĕf′ă-lŏn) Hindbrain.

rhomboid (rŏm′boyd) [″ + *eidos,* form, shape] An oblique parallelogram.

rhomboideus (rŏm-boyd′ē-ŭs) [L.] One of two muscles beneath the trapezius muscle. SEE: *muscle* for illus.

rhombomere (rŏm′bō-mēr) Neuromere.

rhonchi (rŏng′kē) Pl. of rhonchus.

rhonchus (rŏng′kŭs) *pl.* **rhonchi** A low-pitched wheezing, snoring, or squeaking sound heard during auscultation of the chest of a person with partial airway obstruction. Mucus or other secretions in the airway, bronchial hyperreactivity, or tumors that occlude respiratory passages can all cause rhonchi.

rhopheocytosis (rō″fē-ō-sī-tō′sĭs) [Gr. *rhophein,* gulp down, + *kytos,* cell, + *osis,* condition] The mechanism by which ferritin is transferred from macrophages in the bone marrow to normoblasts. SEE: *pinocytosis.*

rHu- (ar′hū′) *recombinant human* (proteins or peptides formed by recombinant genetic technologies). Such proteins are produced by inserting a segment of human DNA into the genetic code of other organisms, e.g., bacteria or yeasts.

rhubarb (roo′bärb) [ME. *rubarbe*] An extract made from the roots and rhizome of *Rheum officinale, R. palmatum,* and other species, used as a cathartic and astringent. It is high in oxalic acid. The stems are used as food.

rHuEPO *recombinant human erythropoietin.*

Rhus (roos) [L.] Former name for the genus *Toxicodendron,* which includes poison ivy, poison oak, and poison sumac.

rhyme (rīm) **1.** Correspondence in sound of the ends of words, e.g., *smell, well,* and *foretell.* **2.** A poem in rhyme. **rhyme,** *v.*

rhythm (rith′ĭm) [Gr. *rhythmos,* measured motion] **1.** A measured time or movement; regularity of occurrence of action or function. **2.** In electroencephalography, the regular occurrence of an impulse. **rhythmic** (-mik), *adj.*

 accelerated idioventricular r. ABBR: AIVR. An abnormal ectopic cardiac rhythm originating in the ventricular conducting system. This may occur intermittently after myocardial infarction at a rate of 60 to 100 beats per minute. In this setting it is considered to be an indicator of successful reperfusion of the blocked coronary artery.

 alpha r. In electroencephalography, oscillations in electric potential occurring at a rate of 8½ to 12 per second.

 atrioventricular r. The rhythmic discharges of impulses from the atrioventricular node that occur when the activity of the sinoatrial node is depressed or abolished. SYN: *nodal r.*

 beta r. In electroencephalography, waves ranging in frequency from 15 to 30 per second and of lower voltage than alpha waves. This rhythm is more pronounced in the frontomotor leads.

 bigeminal r. The coupling of extrasystoles with previously normal beats of the heart. SEE: *bigeminal pulse.*

 biological r. The regular occurrence of certain phenomena in living organisms. SEE: *circadian r.; biological clock.*

 cantering r. Gallop.

 cardiac r. The predominant electrical activity of the heart. It may be determined by recording an electrocardiogram or by evaluating tracings made by a cardiac monitor. SEE: *cardiac cycle; electrocardiogram; conduction system of the heart.*

 circadian r. Diverse yet predictable changes in physiological variables, including sleep, appetite, temperature, and hormone secretion, over a 24-hr period. SYN: *diurnal r.*

 coupled r. A rhythm in which every other heartbeat produces no pulse at the wrist.

 delta r. In electroencephalography, slow waves with a frequency of 4 or fewer per second and of relatively high voltage (20 to 200 μV). It may be found over the area of a gross lesion such as a tumor or hemorrhage.

 diurnal r. Circadian **r.**

 ectopic r. A heart rhythm originating outside the sinoatrial node.

 escape r. A heart rhythm that arises from a junctional or ventricular source when impulses from the atria or atrioventricular node are blocked.

gallop r. Gallop.

gamma r. The 50-per-second rhythm seen in the electroencephalogram.

idioventricular r. A cardiac rhythm that arises from pacemakers in ventricular muscle.

junctional r. An electrocardiographic rhythm arising in the atrioventricular junction. It appears as an electrocardiogram as a narrow QRS complex that lacks an upright P wave preceding it.

normal sinus r. The normal heart rhythm whose pacemaker is in the sinoatrial node and whose conduction through the atria, atrioventricular node, and ventricles is unimpaired. The interval between complexes is regular, the ventricular rate is 60 to 100, there are upright P waves in leads I and II, a negative P wave in lead AVR, a P-R interval of 0.12 to 0.20 sec, and one P wave preceding each QRS complex. SYN: *sinus r.*

nyctohemeral r. Day and night rhythm.

shockable r. In emergency cardiac care, any of the following cardiac rhythm disturbances: ventricular fibrillation, pulseless ventricular tachycardia or some poorly tolerated supraventricular tachycardias, e.g., some instances of rapid atrial fibrillation, atrial flutter, or AV nodal re-entrant tachycardia. By contrast, asystole, pulseless electrical activity, heart blocks, and the bradycardias are not shockable. Defibrillation or cardioversion of these latter rhythms may result in injury to the patient.

sinus r. Normal sinus **r.**

theta r. The 4- to 7-per-sec rhythm seen in the electroencephalogram.

ventricular r. 1. The pace and synchrony of ventricular depolarization. 2. An escape rhythm that arises in the ventricles, typically with wide QRS complexes and a rate of 30 to 40 beats per minute.

rhythmicity (rĭth-mĭs′ĭ-tē) The condition of being rhythmic.

rhythm method of birth control A method preventing pregnancy that uses abstinence from sexual relations around the time of ovulation. SEE: *contraception.*

rhytide (rī′tĭd) Wrinkle.

rhytidectomy, rhitidectomy (rĭt″ĭ-dek′tŏ-mē) [Gr. *rhytis,* wrinkle + *-ectomy*] The excision of wrinkles by excision of unwanted skin; a face-lift.

rhytidoplasty (rĭt′ĭ-dō-plăs″tē) [″ + *plassein,* to form] The elimination of facial wrinkles by plastic surgery.

rhytidosis (rĭt″ĭ-dō′sĭs) [″ + *osis,* condition] Wrinkling of the cornea, which occurs when tension in the eyeball is greatly diminished, particularly after the escape of aqueous or vitreous humor; usually a sign of impending death. SYN: *rhitidosis.*

RI *Respiratory index.*

RIA radioimmunoassay.

rib (rĭb) [AS. *ribb*] One of a series of 12 pairs of narrow, curved bones extending laterally and anteriorly from the sides of the thoracic vertebrae and forming a part of the skeletal thorax. With the exception of the vertebral ribs, they are connected to the sternum by costal cartilages. SEE: illus.

bicipital r. An irregular condition resulting from the fusion of two ribs, usually involving the first rib.

cervical r. A supernumerary rib sometimes developing in connection with a cervical vertebra, usually the lowest.

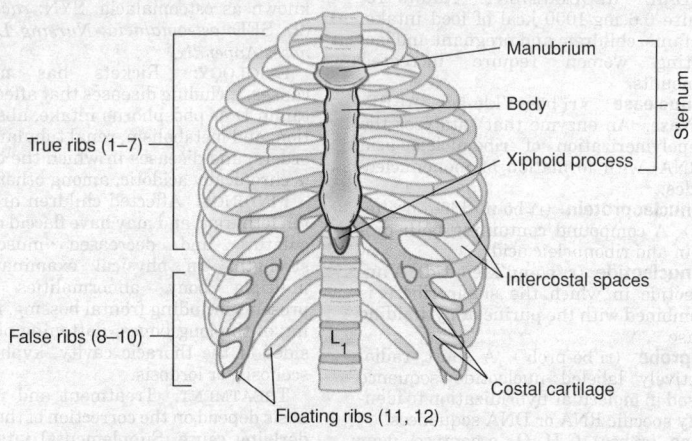

RIB CAGE

Anterior view

Labels: Manubrium, Body, Xiphoid process, Sternum, Intercostal spaces, True ribs (1–7), False ribs (8–10), Floating ribs (11, 12), Costal cartilage, L₁

false r. One of the lower ribs (8, 9, and 10) that do not join the sternum directly. Their cartilage connects to the cartilage of the seventh rib. The variation in the anatomy of the lower ribs may be considerable (i.e., there may be only two false ribs). SYN: *vertebrochondral r.*

lumbar r. A rudimentary rib that develops in relation to a lumbar vertebra.

slipping r. A rib in which the costal cartilage dislocates repeatedly.

sternovertebral r. True rib.

true r. Any of ribs 1–7, which articulate directly with the sternum. SYN: *sternovertebral r.*

vertebral r. Any of ribs 1–7, which articulate directly with the sternum.

vertebrochondral r. False rib.

vertebrocostal r. Any of the three false ribs on each side.

ribbon (rĭb′ŭn) A long, thin, band-shaped structure.

rib cage A colloquial term for thoracic cage.

rib notching An abnormal indentation in the inferior margin of the ribs, seen radiographically. It is characteristically identified in people with coarctation of the aorta.

riboflavin (rī″bō-flā′vĭn) $C_{17}H_{20}N_4O_6$; a water-soluble vitamin of the B complex group. It is an orange-yellow crystalline powder. Symptoms of riboflavin deficiency are photophobia, cheilosis, glossitis, and seborrheic dermatitis, esp. of the face and scalp. SYN: *vitamin B_2*.

FUNCTION: Riboflavin is a constituent of certain flavoproteins that function as coenzymes in cellular oxidation. It is essential for tissue repair.

SOURCES: Riboflavin is found in milk and milk products, leafy green vegetables, liver, beef, fish, and dry yeast. It is also synthesized by bacteria in the body.

DAILY REQUIREMENT: Adults require 0.6 mg/1000 kcal of food intake. Infants, children, and pregnant and lactating women require increased amounts.

ribonuclease (rī″bō-nū′klē-ās) ABBR: RNase. An enzyme that catalyzes the depolymerization of ribonucleic acid (RNA) with formation of mononucleotides.

ribonucleoprotein (rī″bō-nū″klē-ō-prō′tē-ĭn) A compound containing both protein and ribonucleic acid.

ribonucleotide (rī″bō-nū′klē-ō-tīd) A nucleotide in which the sugar ribose is combined with the purine or pyrimidine base.

riboprobe (rī′bŏ-prōb″) A short, radioactively labeled nucleotide sequence used in molecular hybridization to identify specific RNA or DNA sequences.

ribose (rī′bōs) $C_5H_{10}O_5$, a pentose sugar present in ribonucleic acids, riboflavin, and some nucleotides.

ribosome (rī′bō-sōm) A cell organelle made of ribosomal RNA and protein. Ribosomes may exist singly, in clusters called polyribosomes, or on the surface of rough endoplasmic reticulum. In protein synthesis, they are the site of messenger RNA attachment and amino acid assembly in the sequence ordered by the genetic code carried by mRNA.

ribosyl (rī′bō-sĭl) The compound glycosyl, $C_5H_9O_4$, formed from ribose.

ribozyme (rī′bō-zīm) An RNA (ribonucleic acid) molecule that functions as an enzyme (catalyst) and either cleaves (breaks down) other forms of RNA or catalyzes other biochemical reactions occurring within cells. SYN: *catalytic RNA*.

RICE (rīs) Acronym for *r*est, *i*ce, compression, and *e*levation, the elements of management of acute soft tissue injuries.

ricin (rī′sĭn) A white, amorphous, highly toxic protein present in the seed of the castor bean, *Ricinus communis*. It has been used as a biological weapon.

ricinine (rĭs′ĭn-ĕn, -īn) A poisonous alkaloid present in the leaves and seeds of the castor bean plant, *Ricinus communis*.

ricinoleic acid (rĭs″ĕn-ō-lē′ik) SEE: under *acid*.

rickets (rĭk′ĕts) A disease of bone formation in children, most commonly the result of vitamin D deficiency, marked by inadequate mineralization of developing cartilage and newly formed bone, causing abnormalities in the shape, structure, and strength of the skeleton. This condition may be prevented by exposure to ultraviolet light (sunlight or artificial light) and administration of vitamin D in quantities that provide 400 I.U. of vitamin D activity per day. Vitamin D deficiency disease in adults is known as osteomalacia. SYN: *rachitis* (2). SEE: *osteomalacia; Nursing Diagnoses Appendix*.

ETIOLOGY: Rickets has many causes, including diseases that affect vitamin D or phosphorus intake, absorption, and metabolism; renal tubular disorders; and diseases in which the child is chronically acidotic, among others.

FINDINGS: Affected children are often lethargic, and may have flaccid musculature and decreased muscular strength. On physical examination, multiple bony abnormalities are present, including frontal bossing, bowing of the long bones, flattening of the sides of the thoracic cavity, kyphosis, scoliosis, or lordosis.

TREATMENT: Treatment and prognosis depend on the correction of the underlying cause. Supplemental vitamin D therapy is appropriate for some patients.

⚠️ Excessive use of vitamin D (in infants, more than 20,000 I.U. daily; in adults, more than 100,000 I.U. daily) should be avoided because of the risk of hypervitaminosis D.

---

adult r. Osteomalacia.

late r. Rickets that has its onset in older children.

renal r. A disturbance in epiphyseal growth during childhood due to severe chronic renal insufficiency resulting in persistent acidosis. Dwarfism and failure of gonadal development result. The prognosis is poor.

TREATMENT: Renal rickets is treated with a diet low in meat, milk, cheese, and egg yolk. Calcium lactate or calcium gluconate is given in large doses.

vitamin D refractory r. A rare form of rickets that is not caused by vitamin D deficiency and is thus not responsive to vitamin D treatment. It is caused by a defect in renal tubular function that results in excessive loss of phosphorus.

Rickettsia (ri-ket'sē-ă) [Howard T. Ricketts, U.S. pathologist, 1871–1910] A genus of bacteria of the family Rickettsiaceae, order Rickettsiales. They are obligate intracellular parasites and are the causative agents of many diseases. Their vectors are arthropods. SEE: *rickettsial disease; rickettsialpox; rickettsiosis; tick-borne rickettsiosis.*

R. africae The causative agent of African tick bite fever. It is usually found only in sub-Saharan Africa.

R. akari The causative agent of rickettsialpox. The animal reservoir is the house mouse; the vector is a mite.

R. conorii The causative agent of boutonneuse fever found in the Mediterranean, parts of Africa, and India. The animal reservoirs are rodents and dogs; the vectors are ticks of several genera.

R. helvetica Rickettsia japonica.

R. honei The causative agent of a spotted fever that clinically resembles Rocky Mountain spotted fever. It is found only in Australia and neighboring islands.

R. japonica The causative agent of Japanese spotted fever. SYN: **R.** *helvetica.*

R. prowazekii The causative agent of epidemic typhus. It is spread by the human body louse. Unlike most other rickettsias, humans are the primary reservoir for *R. prowazekii,* which was once thought to be a strictly human pathogen. Flying squirrels may be animal reservoirs, and humans acquire infection from their lice or fleas. SYN: *louse-borne typhus.*

R. rickettsii The causative agent of Rocky Mountain spotted fever. The an-

imal reservoirs are rodents and dogs; the vectors are ticks of several genera.

R. slovaca The causative agent of TIBOLA. The species is found in Europe.

R. typhi The agent that causes flea-borne murine (endemic) typhus.

rickettsia (ri-kĕt'sē-ă) *pl.* **rickettsiae** Term applied to any of the bacteria belonging to the family Rickettsiaceae.

rickettsial disease (ri-kĕt'sē-ăl) A disease caused by an organism of the family Rickettsiaceae. The most common types are the spotted-fever group (Rocky Mountain spotted fever and rickettsialpox), epidemic typhus, endemic typhus, Brill's disease, Q fever, scrub typhus, and trench fever.

rickettsialpox (ri-kĕt'sē-ăl-pŏks″) An acute, febrile, self-limited disease caused by *Rickettsia akari.* It is transmitted from the house mouse to humans by a small colorless mite, *Allodermanyssus sanguineus.*

rickettsicidal (ri-kĕt″sĭ-sī'dăl) Lethal to rickettsiae.

rickettsiosis (ri-kĕt″sē-ō'sĭs) Infection with rickettsiae.

rickettsiostatic (ri-kĕt″sē-ō-stăt'ĭk) Preventing or slowing the growth of rickettsiae.

RID *radial immunodiffusion; related identical* **donor**

ridge (rĭj) [ME. *rigge*] An elongated projecting structure or crest.

alveolar r. The bony process of the maxilla or mandible that contains the alveoli or tooth sockets; the alveolar process without teeth present.

basal r. An eminence on the lingual surface of the incisor teeth, esp. the upper ones. It is situated near the gum. SYN: *cingulum* (2).

carotid r. The sharp ridge between the carotid canal and the jugular fossa.

dental r. The raised junction between two planes meeting on the surface of a tooth.

dermal r. One of the ridges on the surface of the fingers that make up the fingerprints; also called *crista cutis.*

epicondylic r. One of two ridges for muscular attachments on the humerus.

external oblique r. An anatomical landmark that is a continuation of the anterior border of the mandibular ramus and extends obliquely to the region of the first molar. It serves as an attachment of the buccinator muscle and appears superior to the mylohyoid ridge on a dental radiograph.

genital r. A ridge that develops on the ventromedial surface of the urogenital ridge and gives rise to the gonads.

gluteal r. A ridge extending obliquely downward from the greater trochanter of the femur for attachment of the gluteus maximus muscle.

interosseous r. A ridge on the fibula

for attachment of the interosseous membrane.

interureteric r. A ridge between the openings of the ureters in the bladder.

mammary r. In mammalian embryos, a ridge extending from the axilla to the groin. The breasts arise from this ridge. In humans, only one breast normally develops on each side, although additional nipples occasionally develop along this ridge line. SYN: *milk line.*

marginal r. Any elevation on the mesial or distal surface or the occlusal surface of a posterior tooth. These ridges resist occlusal loading.

mesonephric r. A ridge that develops on the lateral surface of the urogenital ridge and gives rise to the mesonephros.

mylohyoid r. The line of attachment on the medial aspect of the body of the mandible for the mylohyoid muscle, which forms the floor of the mouth.

superciliary r. Superciliary **arch.**

urogenital r. A ridge on the dorsal wall of the coelom that gives rise to the genital and mesonephric ridges. SYN: *urogenital fold.* SEE: *genital r.; mesonephric r.*

ridge augmentation Localized alveolar ridge augmentation

Riedel, Bernhard M. K. L. (rēd′ĕl) Ger. surgeon, 1846–1916.

R.'s lobe An anomalous tonguelike extension from the right lobe of the liver to the gallbladder.

R.'s struma A form of chronic thyroiditis in which the gland becomes enlarged, hard, and adherent to adjacent tissues. The follicles become atrophic and fibrosis occurs. SYN: *cast iron struma.*

R.'s thyroiditis A rare form of thyroiditis characterized by fibrotic destruction of the thyroid gland. The fibrotic tissue extends beyond the capsule of the gland into the surrounding structures of the neck and may develop sufficiently to compress the trachea. The cause is unknown.

Rieder cell (rē′dĕr) A white blood cell with radially segmented nucleus, found in some T cells in patients with lymphoproliferative disorders.

Riegel pulse (rēg′ĕl) [Franz Riegel, Ger. internist, 1843–1904] A diminution of the pulse in volume during expiration.

Rift Valley virus (rift) [*Rift Valley,* Kenya] SEE: under *virus.*

RIG *rabies immune globulin.*

Riga-Fede disease (rē′gă fā′dā) [Antonio Riga, Italian physician, 1832–1919; Francesco Fede, Italian physician, 1832–1913] Ulceration of the frenum of the tongue with membrane formation. It occurs after abrasion by the lower central incisors.

Riggs disease (rigz) [John M. Riggs, U.S. dentist, 1810–1885] Periodontitis.

right (rīt) [AS. *riht*] ABBR: R; rt. **1.** Pert. to the dextral side of the body (the side away from the heart), which in most persons is the stronger or preferred. SYN: *dexter.* **2.** Legal authority to supervise and control one's own actions or the actions of others.

right-handedness The condition of greater adeptness in using the right hand. This characteristic is found in about 93% of the population. SYN: *dextrality.* SEE: *left-handedness.*

right shift SEE: under *shift.*

right to die The freedom to choose one's own end-of-life care by specifying, for example, whether one would permit or want life-prolonging treatments (e.g., intubation and mechanical ventilation); intravenous or enteral feedings; antibiotics (if infected); narcotic analgesics (if in pain); or medications to hasten death (e.g., in assisted suicide or euthanasia). The moral, ethical, or legal authority to make decisions about many of these issues is a topic of considerable controversy and confusion. Contemporary health care techniques often permit the prolongation of a patient's life, when, in the natural course of biological events, that life might have ended. The ability to postpone death, and the difficulty that health care providers have in predicting when death will occur, has generated many questions about the meaning of care and well-being at the margins of existence. Who should make decisions for patients when they cannot speak for themselves? How should one's wishes be expressed or codified? Who should carry them out if the patient cannot act on his or her own? When must a person's stated wishes be followed precisely, and when should they be factored in with the wishes of loved ones or of those acting on behalf of the patient? Should they ever be ignored or overruled? When does the aid given to a dying person compromise the moral or professional values of others or jeopardize the legal standing of the patient's caregiver? Many of these challenging questions remain unresolved. SEE: *advance directive; assisted suicide; care, end-of-life; euthanasia; suicide.*

rigid (rĭj′ĭd) [L. *rigidus*] Stiff, hard, unyielding.

rigidity (rĭ-jĭd′ĭ-tē) **1.** Tenseness; immovability; stiffness; inability to bend or be bent. **2.** In psychiatry, an excessive resistance to change.

cadaveric r. Rigor mortis.

cerebellar r. Stiffness of the body and extremities resulting from a lesion of the middle lobe of the cerebellum.

clasp-knife r. A condition in which passive flexion of the joint causes increased resistance of the extensors. This gives way abruptly if the pressure to produce flexion is continued.

cogwheel r. The condition that occurs when tremor coexists with rigidity as in Parkinson's syndrome. In this condition, manually manipulated body parts may take on the feel of a cogwheel. This can occur also as an extrapyramidal side effect of antipsychotic drug therapy.

decerebrate r. Sustained contraction of the extensor muscles of the limbs resulting from a lesion in the brainstem between the superior colliculi and the vestibular nuclei.

decorticate r. Decorticate posture.

lead-pipe r. Increased muscular tone in an extremity in which (as opposed to cogwheel rigidity) the affected muscle does not move in a discontinuous or jerking fashion as it is pulled back and forth. SEE: *cogwheel r.*

nuchal r. Inflexibility of the neck movement, esp. forward flexion of the neck. It is a sign of meningeal irritation.

penile r. The ability of the erect penis to resist bending or buckling forces applied to its long axis. The greater its resistance, the more effectively the penis can penetrate during intercourse.

rigid spine syndrome A rare form of muscular dystrophy in which the disease is limited to the paraspinal muscles of the neck and back. Unlike other forms of muscular dystrophy, the weakness and stiffness characteristic of this condition are not progressive.

rigor (rĭg'or) [L. *rigor*, stiffness] **1.** A sudden paroxysmal shaking chill occurring during a febrile illness. Onset of rigors often corresponds to bacteremia. **2.** A state of hardness and stiffness, as in a muscle.

r. mortis The stiffness that occurs in dead bodies. SYN: *cadaveric rigidity.* SEE: *Nysten's law.*

RIGS *Radioimmunoguided surgery.*

rim An edge or border.

alar r. The tissue at the nostrils that constitutes the external nasal valve.

bite r. Occlusion rim.

hypoechoic r. In ultrasonography, a thin border (2 mm or less) around a body part that produces few echoes. The rim is sometimes seen around abscesses, other inflamed structures, structures with many blood vessels at their edges, or the normal fetal heart.

occlusion r. The biting surfaces built on denture bases to make maxillomandibular relation records and to arrange teeth. SYN: *bite r.*

orbital r. The anterior edge of the bony orbit, or eye socket, formed by the maxilla and zygomatic bone inferiorly and the frontal bone superiorly.

rima glottidis (rī'mă) The opening between the vocal folds in the larynx.

rimose (rī'mōs, rī-mōs') [L. *rimosus*] Fissured or marked by cracks.

rimula (rĭm'ū-lă) *pl.* **rimulae** [L.] A minute fissure or slit, esp. of the spinal cord or brain.

RIND (rīnd) *R*eversible *i*schemic *n*eurological *d*eficit, a stroke whose clinical presentation lasts for a short time and then resolves. Despite the short duration of symptoms or signs, images of the brain taken after RIND often reveal infarction.

rind (rīnd) [AS.] A thick or firm outer coating of an organ, plant, or animal.

ring (ring) **1.** A round area, organ, or band around a circular opening. SEE: *annulus.* **2.** In chemistry, a collection of atoms chemically bound in a circle.

abdominal inguinal r. The internal opening of the inguinal canal.

Bandl r. Retraction **r.**

benzene r. The closed ring of six carbon atoms.

biofragmentable anastomosis r. ABBR: BFR; BAR. An absorbable, temporary surgical implant to join resected loops of bowel. The ring is composed of two parts polyglycolic acid (Dexon) and one part barium sulfate. It dissolves about 3 weeks after implantation when major tissue healing has occurred. The ring is easy to use. Postoperative complications may include leakage and, rarely, intestinal stricture.

Cabot r. SEE: *Cabot rings.*

Cannon r. SEE: under *Cannon, Walter B.*

capsular tension r. A ring inserted into the capsule of the eye to maintain its shape or integrity, e.g., to compensate for zonular weakness or defects.

ciliary r. Orbiculus ciliaris.

conjunctival r. A narrow ring at the junction of the edge of the cornea with the conjunctiva. SYN: *anulus conjunctivae.*

constriction r. A stricture of the body of the uterus; a circular area of the uterus that contracts around a part of the fetus.

deep inguinal r. The opening of the inguinal canal deep inside the abdominal wall.

femoral r. The superior aperture of the femoral canal, approx. 1 cm in diameter.

inguinal r. The interior opening of the abdominal inguinal ring and the end of the subcutaneous inguinal ring.

Kayser-Fleischer r. SEE: *Kayser-Fleischer ring.*

lymphoid r. of the pharynx Waldeyer ring.

Müller r. SEE: under *Müller, Johannes P.*

pathologic retraction r. SEE: *retraction r.*

physiologic retraction r. SEE: *retraction r.*

retraction r. A ridge sometimes felt on the uterus above the pubes, marking the line of separation between the upper contractile and lower dilatable segments of the uterus. If the ring is normal, as in a normal delivery, it is called the physiologic retraction ring; if the ring persists, as in prolonged labor, it is called the pathologic retraction ring. SYN: *Bandl contraction ring; Bandl ring.*

Schatzki r. SEE: *Schatzki ring.*

Schwalbe r. SEE: under *Schwalbe, Gustav Albert.*

Soemmering r. SEE: under *Soemmering, Samuel T. von.*

subcutaneous inguinal r. Superficial inguinal **r.**

superficial inguinal r. The opening of the inguinal canal that is just below the skin. SYN: *subcutaneous inguinal* **r.**

teething r. Any relatively soft object on which an infant may chew to relieve discomfort during the eruption of teeth. Teething rings and other teething devices small enough to be inhaled by an infant should never be used.

tonsillar r. The almost complete ring of tonsillar tissue encircling the pharynx. It includes the palatine, lingual, and pharyngeal tonsils.

umbilical r. The opening in the linea alba of the embryo through which the umbilical vessels pass.

vaginal r. **1.** A flexible polymer impregnated with contraceptive hormones which a woman places inside her vagina and leaves in place for 21 or more days. When it is removed, withdrawal bleeding occurs. Side effects can include vaginitis or vaginal irritation. Like other forms of contraception, the ring increases a woman's risk of blood clotting. It should be avoided by smokers. It does not provide protection against sexually transmitted diseases. **2.** A similar device, impregnated with menopausal hormones and used to treat hot flashes, night sweats, and other menopausal symptoms. Like other forms of menopausal hormone replacement, it increases the risk of stroke, heart attack, deep venous thrombosis, breast, and uterine cancers.

vascular r. A congenital abnormality in which an arterial ring encircles the trachea and esophagus. This causes signs of compression of their structures. Surgery may be required to relieve the symptoms.

Ringer, Sydney (ring'ĕr) Brit. physiologist, 1835–1910.

lactated R.'s solution A crystalloid electrolyte sterile solution of specified amounts of calcium chloride, potassium chloride, sodium chloride, and sodium lactate in water for injection. It is used intravenously to replace electrolytes.

R.'s solution A physiologic solution of distilled water containing 8.6 g sodium chloride, 0.3 g potassium chloride, and 0.33 g calcium chloride per liter; for topical (Ringer's irrigation) or intravenous use.

ring removal from swollen finger A technique for the removal of a ring from an injured or swollen finger. One method is described here: One end of a length of string is passed under the ring. The ring is pushed as far from the swollen area toward the hand as possible; the string is wrapped on the side of the swollen area around the finger for about a dozen turns. The end of the string that extends under the ring is grasped. While being held firmly, the string is unwound from the hand side of the ring. This moves the ring toward the free end of the finger. This procedure should be continued until the ring is free. If this technique fails, the ring may have to be cut from the finger with a commercial ring or metal cutter.

ringworm (ring'wŭrm) Any contagious skin infection caused by fungi of the genera *Microsporum* or *Trichophyton*. The hallmark of these conditions is a well-defined red rash, with an elevated, wavy, or worm-shaped border. Ringworm of the scalp is called tinea capitis; of the body, tinea corporis; of the groin, tinea cruris; of the hand, tinea manus; of the beard, tinea barbae; of the nails, tinea unguium; and of the feet, tinea pedis or athlete's foot. SEE: *Nursing Diagnoses Appendix.*

Rinne test (rĭn'nē) [Heinrich Adolf Rinne, Ger. otologist, 1819–1868] The use of a tuning fork to compare bone conduction hearing with air conduction. The vibrating fork is held by its stem on the mastoid process of the ear until the patient no longer hears it. Then it is held close to the external auditory meatus. If the subject still hears the vibrations, air conduction exceeds bone conduction (this is the normal finding). SEE: *Weber test.*

rinse **1.** To wash lightly. **2.** A solution used for irrigation or bathing.

mouth r. A flavored or medicated solution swirled in the mouth, used to treat halitosis, oral infections, aphthous ulcers, stomatitis, or dental biofilm (plaque).

⚠ Some alcoholics may occasionally abuse alcohol-based mouth rinses.

sodium fluoride r. A 0.05% aqueous solution of sodium fluoride also containing coloring and flavoring agents, used as a mouth rinse to help prevent dental caries.

RIPC *Remote ischemic preconditioning.*

ripening **1.** Softening, effacement, and dilation before labor. SEE: *Bishop's score; prostaglandin.* **2.** Maturation of a cataract.

cervical r. SEE: *cervical ripening.*

rippling muscle disease A rare autosomal dominant muscle disease whose symptoms include spontaneous muscle contraction when muscles are stimulated by stretching, percussion, or squeezing. Affected patients are usually recognized during childhood. They may demonstrate weakness of facial muscles, frequent falls, or difficulty walking on their heels or toes as a result of calf muscle weakness.

risk (risk) The probability that a loss or something dangerous or harmful will occur.

    acceptable r. A tolerable level of harm or potential harm.

    additional r. Attributable **fraction**.

    attributable r. Attributable **fraction**.

    material r. A significant potential for harm that a reasonable person would want to consider when making a decision about undergoing a medical or surgical treatment.

    r. for poisoning Accentuated risk of accidental exposure to, or ingestion of, drugs or dangerous products in doses sufficient to cause poisoning. SEE: *Nursing Diagnoses Appendix.*

    population attributable r. The proportion of cases of a disease that result from exposure to a specific risk factor.

    relative r. In epidemiological studies, the relative amount of disease occurring in different populations; the ratio of incidence rate in the exposed group to that in the unexposed group. SEE: *odds ratio.*

    sibling r. The probability that a brother or sister of a person with a disease will also contract the disease contrasted with the probability of the contraction of the disease in an unrelated person.

    r. for trauma Accentuated risk of accidental tissue injury, e.g., wound, burn, or fracture. SEE: *Nursing Diagnoses Appendix.*

    r. for urinary urge incontinence SEE: under *incontinence.*

risk-benefit analysis Examination of the potential positive and negative results of undertaking a specific therapeutic course of action. For example, a man with a slowly growing, localized prostate cancer might want to know whether it is better to undergo surgery (and risk urinary incontinence and erectile dysfunction) or to manage his disease conservatively (and risk the spread of the disease). Factors influencing his decision include:

1 financial cost of the operation;

2 likelihood of disease spread;

3 likelihood of complications with or without the operation;

4 life expectancy;

5 overall state of health; and

6 alternative treatments for his disease.

Risk Evaluation and Mitigation Strategy ABBR: REMS. A plan that addresses the potential hazard of any medical intervention or treatment.

risk factor SEE: under *factor.*

risk for posttrauma syndrome A risk for sustained maladaptive response to a traumatic, overwhelming event. It is a nursing diagnosis accepted at the NANDA 13th Conference (1998).

risk management The methods used by health care organizations to defend their assets against the threats posed by legal liability. It includes identification of health care delivery problems in an institution (as evidenced by previous lawsuits, allegations, and patient or staff complaints); anticipation of problems; and development of standards and guidelines to enhance the quality of care. Several of the most important issues in risk management for health care institutions are listed in the table. SEE: table.

Prominent Issues in Hospital Risk Management

Anesthesia	Intubation errors; medication side effects
Childbirth	Infant trauma or death; delayed responsiveness of staff
Confidentiality	Breaches of privacy
Consent	Failure to disclose risks of and alternatives to treatment
Death	Wrongful or unexpected deaths

risk perception SEE: under *perception.*

risk pool SEE: under *pool.*

risk ratio ABBR: RR. The probability of the occurrence of a disease in a group that has been exposed to some environmental, medicinal, microbial, or toxic influence, relative to its probability in a randomly selected population.

risk-taker An individual who willfully exposes himself or herself to activities that others regard as hazardous.

risorius (rĭ-sŏ′rē-ŭs) [L., laughing] The muscular fibrous band arising over the masseter muscle and inserted into the tissues at the corner of the mouth.

Risperdal Risperidone.

risperidone (rĭs-pĕr′ĭ-dōn″) A benzisoxazole administered orally to manage psychotic disorders. Its therapeutic class is anitipsychotic.

RIST (rĭst) *radioimmunosorbent test.*

ristocetin (rĭs″tō-sē′tĭn) An antibiotic obtained from cultures of *Nocardia lurida.*

risus (rī′sŭs) [L.] Laughter; a laugh.

r. sardonicus A peculiar grin, as seen in tetanus, caused by acute facial spasm.

Ritgen maneuver (rit'gĕn) [A. M. F. von Ritgen, German obstetrician, 1787–1867] A manual method of controlling the delivery of the fetal head. The non-dominant hand exerts pressure against the fetal chin through the perineum. At the same time, the dominant hand exerts pressure against the fetal occiput. The maneuver should be performed slowly and between contractions to avoid perineal lacerations.

Ritter disease (rit'ĕr) [Gottfried Ritter von Rittershain, Ger. physician, 1820–1883] A generalized form of impetigo of the newborn.

ritual (rĭch'ū-ăl) **1.** A customary or prescribed procedure of special, often social or religious, significance. **2.** In psychiatry, any activity performed compulsively to relieve anxiety.

ritualistic surgery SEE: under *surgery*.

rivalry (rī'văl-rē) Competition between two or more individuals, groups, or systems seeking to attain the same goal.

    binocular r. The continuous alternation in the conscious perception of visual stimuli to the two eyes.

    gender r. Competition between the sexes for status and compensation, esp. in business, politics, and sports.

    perceptual r. The conflicting perception of ambiguous sensory data, e.g., of light and dark interlocking images. The viewer sees first the light and then the dark parts of the image as dominant.

    retinal r. Binocular rivalry.

    sibling r. The competition between children for attention and affection from others, esp. their parents.

rivalry strife Alternate sensations of color and shape when the fields of vision of the two eyes cannot combine in one visual image.

Rivermead Motor Assessment (rĭv'ĕr-mēd″) An instrument used to assess the mobility of patients following a stroke. It includes assessments of gross motor function, fine motor function, and postural control.

Rivinus, August (rē-vē'nŭs) August Quirinus Rivinus, Ger. anatomist, 1652–1723.

    duct of R. One of 5 to 15 ducts (the minor sublingual ducts) that drain the posterior portion of the sublingual gland.

    R.'s gland A sublingual gland.

    notch of R. Rivinus incisure.

rivus lacrimalis (rī'vŭs) [L. *rivus,* little stream, + *lacrima,* tear] The pathway under the eyelids through which tears travel from their source in the lacrimal glands to the punctum lacrimale.

riziform (rĭz'ĭ-form) [Fr. *riz,* rice, + L. *forma,* form] Resembling rice grains.

RLE *right lower extremity.*

RLF *retrolental fibroplasia.*

RLL *right lower lobe* of the lung.

RLQ *right lower quadrant* (of abdomen).

RMA *right mentoanterior presentation* (of the fetal face).

RME *rapid maxillary expansion.*

RML *right middle lobe* (of the lung).

RMP *right mentoposterior presentation* (of the fetal face).

RMS *rhabdomyosarcoma.*

RMSF *Rocky Mountain spotted fever.*

RMT *right mentotransverse* (fetal position).

RN *registered nurse; rehabilitation nurse.*

Rn Symbol for the element radon.

RNA [Abbr. of *ribonucleic acid*] A nucleic acid that controls protein synthesis in all living cells and is the sole nucleic acid in certain viruses. It differs from DNA in that its sugar is ribose rather than deoxyribose, and its pyrimidine base is uracil rather than thymine. RNA occurs in several forms that are determined by the number of nucleotides. SEE: *DNA.*

    Messenger RNA (mRNA) carries the code for specific amino acid sequences from the DNA to the cytoplasm for protein synthesis.

    Transfer RNA (tRNA) carries the amino acid groups to the ribosome for protein synthesis.

    Ribosomal RNA (rRNA) exists within the ribosomes and assists in protein synthesis.

    HIV RNA The genetic material of the human immunodeficiency virus (HIV). Its quantity in the bloodstream correlates with the severity and prognosis of the acquired immunodeficiency syndrome. Drug regimens for AIDS, esp. those that use a combination of protease inhibitors and reverse transcriptase inhibitors, aim to decrease the amount of HIV RNA in the blood to undetectable levels.

    snRNA SEE: *snRNA.*

RNAi *RNA interference.*

RNA interference ABBR: RNAi. The blocking of gene expression by disrupting the translation of messenger RNA into proteins. SYN: *posttranscriptional gene silencing.*

RNase *ribonuclease.*

RNC *registered nurse certified.*

ROA *right occipitoanterior* (fetal position).

ROAT *repeat open application test.*

Robertson pupil Argyll Robertson pupil.

robotics (rō-bŏ'tĭks) [Czech robot, robot] **1.** The science and technology of using computerized or automated devices to perform functions that are either too difficult or too repetitive to perform manually. Robotics has numerous applications in health care. Surgeons use automated devices to improve control of their instruments, including scalpels and laparoscopes. Researchers use robots in experiments requiring repetitive tasks (e.g., sample analysis for the presence of minute concentrations of drugs or toxins). **2.** The design, manufacture, and use of robots.

ROC curve *receiver operating curve.*

Rochalimaea (rō″chă-lĭ-mē′ă) Former name for the genus *Bartonella.*

    R. quintana SEE: *Bartonella quintana.*

Rocio (rō′syō) [Brazilian Portuguese] A mosquito-borne viral encephalitis found in Brazil.

rocker board SEE: under *board.*

rocker knife SEE: under *knife.*

rocking A technique in neurodevelopmental rehabilitation for increasing muscle tone in hypotonic patients through vestibular stimulation.

    body r. Rhythmic movements seen esp. in the bored, lonely, cognitively impaired, visually impaired, or disturbed.

Rocky Mountain spotted fever ABBR: RMSF. SEE: under *fever.*

rod (rŏd) [AS. *rodd*, club] **1.** A slender, straight bar. **2.** One of the sensory receptors in the retina that detects light. **3.** A bacterium shaped like a rod, a bacillus.

    enamel r. One of the minute calcium-rich rods or prisms laid down by ameloblasts and forming tooth enamel. SYN: *enamel prism.*

    retinal r. A receptor in the retina that responds to the presence of light. SEE: *retina* for illus.

rodent Any mammal of the Rodentia order, such as mice, rats, and squirrels.

rods and cones The photoreceptor cells of the retina. They are between the pigment epithelium and the bipolar layer of neurons. The rods contain rhodopsin, which is stimulated by light; the cones contain one of three other photopigments, which are stimulated by various wavelengths of visible light (colors). SEE: *cone (2); night vision; rod.*

roentgen (rĕnt′gĕn) [Wilhelm Konrad Roentgen, Ger. physicist, 1845–1923] ABBR: R. A unit for describing the exposure dose of x-rays or gamma rays. One unit can liberate enough electrons and positrons to produce emissions of either charge of one electrostatic unit of electricity per 0.001293 g of air (the weight of 1 cm³ of dry air at 0°C and at 760 mm Hg).

roentgen equivalent (in) man ABBR: rem. A measure of the effect that a specific dose of radiation has on human or mammalian cells. It is expressed numerically as the product of the radiation absorbed dose (rad) and a quality factor (QF) specific for the type of radiation. The SI unit equivalent to the rem is the sievert (Sv). One rem is equal to 0.01 sievert.

roentgenogram (rĕnt-gĕn′ō-grăm, rĕnt′gĕn-ō-grăm″) Radiograph.

roentgenography (rent″gĕn-og′ră-fē) [*roentgen* + *-graphy*] Radiography.

    body section r. Tomography.

    mucosal relief r. An x-ray examination of the intestinal mucosa after ingested barium has been removed and air under slight pressure has been injected. This leaves a light coat of barium on the mucosa and permits x-ray images of the fine detail of the mucosa.

    serial r. Repeated x-ray pictures taken of an area at defined but arbitrary intervals.

roentgenology (rĕnt″gĕn-ŏl′ō-jē) Radiology.

roentgenometer (rĕnt″gĕ-nŏm′ĕ-tĕr) Radiometer.

roentgenotherapy,   **roentgentherapy** (rĕnt″gĕn-ō-thĕr′ăp-ē) Radiotherapy.

Roger disease (rō-zhā′) [Henri L. Roger, Fr. physician, 1809–1891] Ventricular septal defect.

Rogers, Martha (rŏj′ĕrz) A nursing educator, 1914–1994, who developed the Science of Unitary Human Beings. SEE: *Nursing Theory Appendix.*

Rokitansky disease (rō″kĭ-tan′skē) [Karl Freiherr von Rokitansky, Austrian pathologist, 1804–1878] Fulminant hepatitis.

Rolando, Luigi (rō-lan′dō) Italian anatomist and physiologist, 1773–1831.

    R.'s area A motor area in the cerebral cortex, situated in the anterior central convolution in front of the fissure of Rolando in each hemisphere.

    R.'s fissure The furrow between the frontal and parietal lobes of a cerebral hemisphere. SYN: *central fissure; sulcus centralis.*

    R. fracture A comminuted intra-articular fracture of the base of the first metacarpal with distal fragment subluxation. This fracture is similar to a Bennett fracture, but with more comminution.

Rolando fracture SEE: under *Rolando, Luigi.*

role (rōl) [Fr. *rolle*, roll of paper on which a part is written] The characteristic social behavior of an individual in relation to the group.

    gender r. The characteristic lifestyle and behavior pattern of a person with respect to sexual and social conditions associated with being of a particular sex. Usually this behavior represents how the individual feels about his or her own sexual preference; it may not coincide with the true chromosomal and anatomical sexual differentiation of the person.

    sick r. A dependent affect or behavior, or both, associated with physical or mental illness.

role competence The ability to effectively and satisfactorily perform as expected within one's life roles. SEE: *occupational performance*.

role model   One who serves as an example for others by demonstrating the behavior associated with a particular social position or profession.

role performance, ineffective   A change in patterns of behavior and self-expression that do not match the environmental context, norms, and expectations. SEE: *Nursing Diagnoses Appendix*.

role playing   The assignment and acting out of a role in a treatment setting to provide individuals an opportunity to explore the behavior and feelings of others or to see themselves as others see them. It is also used to teach such skills as interviewing, history taking, and doing a physical examination.

role spillover   The impact that immersing oneself in one's occupation may have on other elements of life, such as the ability to participate actively in family affairs or to relax.

Rolfing   (rolf′ing) [Ida P. Rolf, U.S. biochemist, 1897–1979] A therapy consisting of deep manipulation of muscles and fascia to release restricted tissues to restore posture. SYN: *structural integration*.

roll   (rōl) [Fr. *roulle*, scroll fr. L. *rotula*, small wheel] A usually solid, cylindrical structure.

    cotton r.   A cylindrical mass of purified and sterilized cotton used as packing or absorbent material in various dental procedures.

    ilial r.   A sausage-shaped mass in the left iliac fossa. It is due to a collection of feces in or induration of the walls of the sigmoid colon.

    lumbar r.   An air-filled, foam, or gel cushion placed behind the lower back as a support.

    PATIENT CARE: It is used to maintain the normal lordotic curvature of the lumbar spine and thereby to relieve pressure on commonly injured structures such as disks and facet joints.

    scleral r.   SEE: *scleral spur*.

    trochanter r.   A cushion or pillow used to hold the hip of a postoperative patient in neutral position.

roller   (rōl′ĕr) [O.Fr., roll] **1.** A strip of muslin or other cloth rolled up in cylinder form for surgical use. **2.** A roller bandage.

    bandage r.   A device for rolling bandages.

rolling timeframe   In modular education, an approach to learning in which students complete objectives at their own pace and advance to new objectives (and ultimately, to graduation) only after demonstrating mastery of each prerequisite.

roll out   To start or expand, as a new program or an existing initiative.

ROM   (rom) *range of motion; read-only memory; rupture of membranes*.

Roman numeral   (rō′măn) One of the letters used by the ancient Romans for numeration, as distinct from the arabic numerals that we now use. In Roman notation, values are changed either by adding one or more symbols to the initial symbol or by subtracting a symbol to the right of it. For example, V is 5, IV is 4, and VI is 6. Hence, because X is 10, IX is 9 and XI is 11. SEE: Roman numerals in *Latin and Greek Nomenclature Appendix*.

rombergism   (rŏm′bĕrg-ĭzm) The tendency to fall from a standing position when the eyes are closed and the feet are close together. SEE: *Romberg's sign*.

Romberg sign   (rom′bĕrg″) [Moritz Heinrich Romberg, Ger. physician, 1795–1873] The inability to maintain body balance when the eyes are shut and the feet are close together. The sign is positive if the patient sways and falls when the eyes are closed. This is seen in sensory ataxia and following traumatic brain injury.

rongeur   (rŏn-zhŭr′) [Fr., to gnaw] An instrument for removing small amounts of tissue, particularly bone; formerly called *bone nippers*. It is a spring-loaded forceps with a sharp blade that may be either end cutting or side cutting.

Röntgen, Wilhelm Konrad, Roentgen, Wilhelm Konrad   (rent′gĕn, rönt′) German physicist, 1845–1923, who discovered roentgen rays (x-rays) in 1895. He won the Nobel Prize in physics in 1901.

roofer's knee   SEE: under *knee*.

room   (room) An area or space in a building, partitioned off for occupancy or available for specific procedures.

    anechoic r.   A room in which the boundaries are made so that all sound produced in the room is absorbed, i.e., is not reflected.

    birthing r.   A room in which an obstetrical mother may be placed during the first stage of labor. SYN: *labor r.*

    clean r.   A controlled environment facility in which all incoming air passes through a filter capable of removing 99.97% of all particles 0.3 μm and larger. The temperature, pressure, and humidity in the room are controlled. Clean rooms are used in research and in controlling infections, esp. for persons who may not have normally functioning immune systems (e.g., individuals who have been treated with immunosuppressive drugs in preparation for organ transplantation).

    In very rare instances a child is born without the ability to develop an immune system. Such children are kept in a clean room while waiting for specific therapy such as bone marrow transplantation.

delivery r. A room to which an obstetrical patient may be taken for childbirth.

dust-free r. A type of room designed to eliminate or reduce circulating particulate matter, including airborne microorganisms. This kind of room is useful for housing burn patients, removing allergens from the air, providing an environment for transplantation surgery, and preparing drugs and solutions for intravenous use.

labor r. Birthing **r.**

operating r. A room used and equipped for surgical procedures (e.g., in a hospital, surgicenter, or doctor's office).

pharmaceutical clean r. A controlled, typically aseptic environment within a pharmacy in which the concentration of airborne particles is reduced by particle filtration and by air locks or positive pressure ventilation and in which surfaces are easily cleaned or decontaminated. It is used to compound sterile drugs and infusions for dispensing. Operators within the clean room wear gowns, hoods, and masks to avoid shedding cellular debris.

recovery r. An area provided with equipment and nurses needed to care for immediately postoperative patients.

PATIENT CARE: Patients remain there until they regain consciousness, are no longer drowsy and stuporous from the effects of the anesthesia, and have stable vital signs. Patients who are being discharged from a short stay recovery area should also be able to tolerate oral fluids and void without difficulty.

rooming-in The practice of placing an infant in the same hospital room as the mother, beginning immediately after birth.

root (root) **1.** The underground part of a plant. **2.** A bundle of pia-covered axons that emerges from or enters into the brain or spinal cord inside the dura; the central-most end of a peripheral nerve, inside the dura. **3.** A portion of an organ implanted in tissues. SYN: *radix*. **4.** The part of the human tooth covered by cementum; designated by location (mesial, distal, buccal, lingual). **5.** In the coastal regions of the southeastern U.S., esp. among those of Caribbean or African descent, a hex or spell, esp. one that relies on herbal rituals to produce or heal disease.

anterior r. One of the two roots by which a spinal nerve is attached to the spinal cord; contains efferent nerve fibers.

danshen r. **Salvia** miltiorrhiza.

dorsal r. The radix dorsalis or sensory root of each spinal nerve. SYN: *sensory* **r.**

r. of mesentery The origin of the mesentery of the small intestine along the back wall of the abdomen.

motor r. The anterior root of a spinal nerve. SYN: *ventral* **r.**

nail r. The proximal portion of nail covered by the nail fold.

r. of nose The top of the nose where it meets and makes an angle with the base of the forehead between the eyes.

orris r. The powder made from the root of certain species of iris. It is used in making some types of cosmetics. It may be a sensitizer by contact or inhalation.

posterior r. One of the two roots by which a spinal nerve is attached to the spinal cord; contains afferent nerve fibers.

sensory r. Dorsal **r.**

ventral r. Motor **r.**

root cause The source of a problem, that is, the underlying reason that it occurred.

root cause analysis In health care delivery a formal study of a problem used to determine how to avoid or prevent similar problems in the future.

root coverage A general term for one of several periodontal techniques used to treat gingival recession. Dental roots may be covered with tissue grafts, flaps, or tissue regenerative procedures.

root formation The development of tooth roots by Hertwig's root sheath and the epithelial diaphragm. It involves the formation of root dentin with a covering of cementum essential for the attachment of the tooth to the surrounding bony tissues. Root formation or development continues for months or years after the tooth has erupted into the mouth.

root pick A dental instrument for retrieving root fragments resulting from tooth extraction; also called *apical elevator*.

root planing SEE: *planing* (2).

root resorption of teeth Degeneration of tooth roots caused by endocrine imbalance or excessive pressure of orthodontic appliances. Root resorption may be categorized as internal or external. Internal root resorption, sometimes called internal granuloma, is usually a result of pulpal trauma. Affected teeth demonstrate a radiolucent enlargement within the pulp canal on a dental radiograph. External root resorption has a variety of causes, including eruption pressure, localized infection, and forced orthodontic pressure. Radiographs demonstrate roots that appear to be sawed off or shortened.

ETIOLOGY: Traumatic sources of resorption may include pulpal trauma, eruption pressure, localized infection, previous injury, and forced orthodontic pressure; however, resorption has occurred with no identifiable source of trauma.

SYMPTOMS: Patients may be asymptomatic or they may experience localized sensitivity.

TREATMENT: The treatment includes eliminating the trauma, if possible.

rootwork (root′wŏrk″) A traditional form of healing and hexing in the coastal regions of the southeastern U.S., esp. among those of Caribbean or African descent. SEE: *root* (5).

ROP *right occipitoposterior.* In this fetal presentation, the occiput of the fetus is in relationship to the right sacroiliac joint of the mother.

rope ladder A device that helps a person in bed pull up from a supine position to a seated position. It is usually made of two strands of rope with several rigid plastic or wooden rungs strung at intervals. At one end is the first of several rungs that are used to grab and pull oneself up; at the far end the ropes attach to the bed frame at the foot of the bed. SYN: *bed rope ladder.*

Roper-Logan-Tierney Model of Nursing A conceptual model of nursing developed and refined by Nancy Roper, Winifred W. Logan, and Alison J. Tierney. The model focuses on individualized activities of living. The goal of this model of nursing is to provide individualized care.

ropeway (rōp′wā″) A guidewire, esp. one used to cannulate a narrow orifice, such as the sphincter of Oddi.

Rorschach test (ror′shăk) [Hermann Rorschach, Swiss psychiatrist, 1884–1922] A psychological test consisting of 10 different inkblot designs. The subject is asked to interpret each design individually. The test has been used to reveal personality disturbances.

ROS *Reactive oxygen species.* SEE: *oxygen* (2).

rosa (rō′ză) [L.] Rose.

rosacea (rō-zā′sē-ă) [L. *rosaceus,* rosy] A chronic rose-colored eruption, usually localized to the middle of the face (nose, cheeks, forehead, around the eyes, on the chin). There are four types named for the predominant skin finding—telangiectatic (marked by the appearance of spidery blood vessels on affected skin), papulopustular (bumpy/pustular lesions), phymatous (nasal scarring and deformity), and ocular (involving the lids, lashes, or conjunctiva). The condition is common, esp. in persons of Northern European ancestry. It usually is noted first between the ages of 30 and 50. Women are affected more often than men. SYN: *acne rosacea.* SEE: illus.

PATIENT CARE: Rosacea affects approximately 14 million Americans. In many the condition is quite mild; it may be mistaken for a sunburn, mild acne, or age-related changes in complexion.

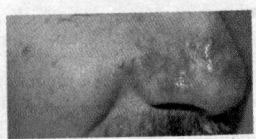

ROSACEA

Treatments vary with the presenting findings. Electrolysis, lasers, and pulse light therapy can be used to treat telangiectases and rhinophyma. Topical medications, such as azelaic acid or metronidazole, are used to treat the papulopustular form of the disease. Oral antibiotics are also used in treatment-resistant disease. Aggravating factors may include ultraviolet light exposure, psychological stress, some foods and beverages, exercise, and skin care products. The health care provider should provide the patient with a list of the most common triggers and printed materials that offer tips for coping with them. Patients with rosacea should avoid irritating the skin of the face during cleansing and should wear a sunscreen that blocks both ultraviolet A and B rays, with a protection factor or 15 or higher on a year-round basis. Sunscreens containing micronized zinc oxide or titanium oxide to absorb photons may be less irritating to sensitive skin. Topical or oral steroids worsen the condition. Actual or feared facial changes affect one's body image and may cause embarrassment, frustration, low self-esteem, anxiety, and depression. Empathic support can be helpful. Individuals who seek organized group support should contact the National Rosacea Society (www.rosacea.org). Telephone: 1-888-NO-BLUSH

    steroid r. Acne caused by systemic or topical use of corticosteroid drugs.

Rosaceae (rō-zās′ē-ē″) [L. *rosa* + *-aceae*] The large family of flowering plants that includes roses. They generate allergic responses in some people.

Rosai-Dorfman disease (rō-sa′ē dorf′măn) ABBR: RDD. A nonmalignant, lymphoproliferative disorder characterized by painless lymph node enlargement, fever, and polyclonal hyperglobulinemia. SYN: *sinus histiocytosis with massive lymphadenopathy.*

rosaniline (rō-zan′ĭ-lĭn, -lĭn″) [L. *rosa,* rose + *aniline*] A basic dye used as the hydrochloride in preparing other dyes. SYN: *fuchsin.*

rosary (rō′ză-rē) Something that resembles a string of beads.

    rachitic r. Palpable areas at the juncture of the ribs with their cartilages. This is seen in conjunction with rickets. SEE: *rachitic beads.*

rose fever SEE: under *fever*.

rose-handler's disease Sporotrichosis.

Rosenbach, Ottomar (rō'zĕn-bok″) Ger. physician, 1851–1907.

    R. sign 1. A fine, rapid tremor of the closed eyelids, seen in hyperthyroidism. **2.** In functional disorders, the inability to obey a command to close the eyes. **3.** The absence of an abdominal skin reflex in intestinal inflammation or hemiplegia.

    R. test An obsolete test for bile in the urine.

roseo- [L. *roseus,* rosy] **1.** Prefix meaning *rose-colored.* **2.** A prefix in chemical terms.

roseola (rō-zē′ō-lă, rō″zē-ō′lă) [L. *roseus,* rosy] A skin condition marked by maculae or red spots of varying sizes on the skin; any rose-colored rash.

    r. idiopathica A macular eruption not associated with any well-defined symptoms.

    r. infantum Exanthem subitum.

roseolovirus (rō″zē-ō′lō-vī″rŭs) [″ + ″] A genus of herpesviruses that infect lymphocytes. Members of the genus include herpesvirus 6 and 7 (HHV-6 and HHV-7).

Rose position (rōz) [Frank A. Rose, Brit. surgeon, 1873–1935] A fully extended position in which the patient's head is allowed to hang over the end of the operating room table to prevent aspiration of blood during surgery on the mouth and lips.

rosette (rō-zĕt′) [Fr., small rose] **1.** A structure that has a rose shape, such as an array of phagocytic cells around an object they are consuming. **2.** A spherical group of fine red vacuoles surrounding the centrosome of a monocyte. **3.** A mature schizont. SYN: *segmenter*.

rosin (rŏz′ĭn) [L. *resina*] A substance distilled from pine trees, sometimes used in adhesives, plastics, or polishes, and occasionally causing allergic contact dermatitis.

Rossolimo reflex (ros″ō-lē′mō) [Gregoriy I. Rossolimo, Russian neurologist, 1860–1928] Plantar flexion of the second to fifth toes in response to percussion of the plantar surface of the toes.

Ross procedure (ros) [Donald Ross, contemporary Brit. cardiac surgeon] Replacement of a diseased aortic valve with the patient's own pulmonary valve. Because the patient's own tissue is used, anticoagulation is not typically needed after the operation. SYN: *pulmonary **autograft**; pulmonary autograft procedure for aortic valve disease*.

Ross River virus (ros) [*Ross River,* Queensland, Australia] SEE: under *virus*.

rostellum (ros-tel′ŭm) *pl.* **rostella** [L. *rostellum,* little beak] A fleshy protrusion on the anterior end of the scolex of a tapeworm, bearing one or more rows of spines or hooks.

rostral (ros′trăl) [L. *rostralis,* pert. to a beak, bill, or a rostrum] **1.** Toward the end of the organism that is nearest the nose. **2.** Resembling a beak.

rostrocaudal (rŏs″trō-kawd′l) [L. *rostrum,* snout, beak (of bird), prow (of ship), speaker's platform + L. *cauda,* tail] In anatomy, along the long (head-to-tail) axis of the body.

rostrum (rŏs′trŭm) *pl.* **rostrums; rostra** [L. *rostrum,* snout, beak (of bird), prow (of ship), speaker's platform] Any hooked or beaked structure.

rosulate (rŏs′ū-lāt) [L. *rosulatus,* like a rose] Shaped like a rosette.

ROT *right occipito transverse* (fetal position).

rot (rŏt) [ME. *roten*] To decay or decompose.

    jungle r. The common term for certain fungal skin diseases that occur in the tropics.

rotameter (rōt′ă-mēt″ĕr, rō-tam′ĕt-) A device that measures the flow of a gas or liquid by rotating as the fluid passes the fins or blades of the device.

Rotarix (rōt′ă-riks″) ABBR: RV1. Human live, oral rotavirus vaccine, monovalent.

rotate (rō-tāt) [L. *rotare,* to turn] To twist or revolve.

RotaTeq (rōt′ă-tek″) ABBR: RV5. Rotavirus vaccine, live, oral pentavalent.

rotation (rō-tā′shŏn) [L. *rotatio,* a turning] The process of turning on an axis.

    external r. Restitution (3).

    fetal r. Twisting of the fetal head as it follows the curves of the birth canal downward.

    injection site r. Administration of parenteral medications such as insulin into a different part of the body each day to avoid local tissue trauma, atrophy, or lipodystrophies.

    PATIENT CARE: Subcutaneous injections of insulin are typically rotated around the abdomen from the right upper quadrant, to the midepigastrium, left upper quadrant, left lower quadrant, hypogastrium, and right lower quadrant before returning to the right upper quadrant. A similar technique is used with low-molecular-weight heparins, colony-stimulating factors, and other drugs.

    optical r. SEE: *optical **activity***.

    tooth r. The repositioning of a tooth by turning it on its long axis to a more normal occlusal position.

rotator (rō-tā′tor) *pl.* **rotatores** A muscle revolving a part on its axis.

rotavirus (rōt′ă-vī″rŭs) [L. *rota,* wheel + *virus*] Any of a group of double-stranded RNA viruses that worldwide are the most common cause of dehydrating diarrhea in children. In the U.S.

during the peak season (October through May), these viruses account for one third of all hospitalizations for diarrhea in children under five. Five hundred or so rotavirus-associated deaths are reported annually, most in children under two. The incubation period of the disease is short (1 to 3 days), and the transmission is the fecal-oral route. The first effective vaccine was withdrawn when its use in infants was associated with intussusception. Two vaccines are available to prevent rotavirus infection: RotaTeq and Rotarix.

Rothmund-Thomson syndrome (rŏth′mŏnd″tŏm′sĭn) ABBR: RTS. A rare autosomal recessive disease in which helicase is formed abnormally. Children affected by RTS have poikiloderma; deformities of bone, nails, and hair; premature aging; and a predisposition to cancer.

Roth spots (roth) [Moritz Roth, Swiss physician and pathologist, 1839–1914] Retinal hemorrhages with pale centers, seen in subacute bacterial endocarditis, severe anemia, and leukemia. It is caused by a systemic infection, esp. acute infective endocarditis.

rotoblation, rotablation, rotoablation (rōt″ŏ-blā′shŏn, rōt″ă-, rōt″ō-a-blā′) [rot(ate) + ablation] Drilling through the core of a plaque obstructing a blood vessel to improve blood flow to the organ supplied by the vessel; rotational atherectomy.

Rotor syndrome (rō-tŏr) A benign form of hyperbilirubinemia transmitted as an autosomal recessive trait, in which there is jaundice, but normal aminotransferase levels and normal hepatic synthesis of albumin and clotting factors.

rototome (rō′tō-tōm) A device for cutting tissue, used in arthroscopic surgery.

rough (rŭf) Not smooth.

roughage (rŭf′ăj) Food fiber that is largely indigestible. SEE: *cellulose; fiber, dietary.*

rouleau (roo-lō′) *pl.* **rouleaux** [Fr., roll] A group of red blood cells that are stuck together, resembling a roll of coins.

rounds (rowndz) A regular gathering of health care professionals, typically at or near a patient's bedside, during which the current status of the patient and planned interventions are reviewed in detail. Specialists or subspecialists may sponsor their own departmental gatherings, e.g., surgical grand rounds, geriatric grand rounds, orthopedic grand rounds, etc.

daily r. Rounds usually conducted in the morning and usually involving a discussion of events that happened during a patient's overnight care. SYN: *morning r.*

grand r. Rounds conducted as part of medical education, used esp. in teaching hospitals, in which all aspects of a patient's condition, management, and problems encountered are presented to faculty members, medical students, and health care workers. This provides an opportunity for all concerned to ask questions and provide comments on the patient's diagnosis, care, and clinical program. The patient is usually, but not always, present during the conference. SYN: *medical grand r.*

hospital r. Ward r.

medical grand r. Grand r.

morning r. Daily r.

ward r. Rounds conducted on inpatients in the unit where the patients reside. SYN: *hospital r.*

roundworm Any member of the phylum Nemathelminthes (Aschelminthes), esp. one belonging to the class Nematoda. SEE: *threadworm.*

routine 1. A regularly performed behavioral sequence. **2.** A standard method of completing a procedure, based on rules or habit. In occupational therapy a customary morning routine might include toileting, bathing, grooming, dressing, eating breakfast, and reading the newspaper.

Roux-en-Y (roo′ĕn-wī′) An anastomosis of the distal divided end of the small bowel to another organ such as the stomach, pancreas, or esophagus. The proximal end is anastomosed to the small bowel below the anastomosis.

Roux-en-y gastric bypass SEE: under *bypass.*

Rovsing sign (rov′sing) [Niels Thorkild Rovsing, Danish surgeon, 1862–1927] Pain referred to McBurney's point on palpation of the left lower abdomen. The sign suggests peritoneal irritation in appendicitis.

Roxicodone Oxycodone.

Roxicodone SR Oxycodone.

Roy, Callista (roy, kă-lĭs′tă) A nursing educator, born 1939, who developed the Roy Adaptation Model of Nursing. SEE: *Nursing Theory Appendix.*

Roy Adaptation Model (roy) A conceptual model of nursing developed by Callista Roy. Individuals and groups are adaptive systems with physiological/physical, self-concept/group identity, role function, and interdependence modes of response to focal, contextual, and residual environmental stimuli. The goal of nursing is promotion of adaptation through increasing, decreasing, maintaining, removing, altering, or changing environmental stimuli. SEE: *Nursing Theory Appendix.*

royal jelly (roi′ĭl) [ME.] A collection of carbohydrates, lipids, minerals, pheromones, and proteins secreted by worker honeybees (*Apis mellifera*). It is used in the hive to nourish larvae, including those that develop into the queen bee.

Its constituents affect blood-forming and immune cells. It is marketed as a nutritional supplement with numerous putative effects on aging and energy.

⚠️ Allergic and anaphylactic reactions to this and other bee products are frequently reported.

RPF *renal plasma flow.*

RPFT *registered pulmonary function technician.*

RPh *registered pharmacist.*

rpm *revolutions per minute.*

RPO *right posterior oblique* position.

RPR *rapid plasma reagin.*

RQ *respiratory quotient.*

-rrhagia, -rhagia, -rhage, -rrhage, -rhagy, -rrhagy [Gr. *-rrhagia,* fr. *rhēgnynai,* to break, burst forth] Suffixes meaning *rupture, profuse fluid discharge.* SEE: *-rrhexis.*

-rrhaphy [Gr. *-rrhaphia,* suture fr. *rhaptein* to sew] Suffix meaning *suture, surgical repair.*

-rrhea, -rhea [Gr. *-rrhoia,* fr. *rhoia,* flow] Suffixes meaning *flow, discharge.* The variant *-rrhoea* is used outside the U.S.

-rrhexis, -rhexis [Gr. *rhēxis,* a breaking, bursting fr. *rhēgnynai,* to break, burst forth] Suffixes meaning *rupture.* SEE: *-rrhagia.*

-rrhoea SEE: *-rrhea.*

rRNA *ribosomal RNA.*

RRT *registered respiratory therapist.*

RSA *right sacroanterior* (fetal position).

RScA *right scapuloanterior* (fetal position).

RScP *right scapuloposterior* (fetal position).

RSI *rapid sequence induction; rapid sequence intubation.*

RSP *right sacroposterior* (fetal position).

RST *right sacrotransverse* (fetal position).

RSV *respiratory syncytial virus; Rous sarcoma virus.*

RSV *Respiratory syncytial virus.*

RT *Radiation therapy; reading test; registered technologist; respiratory therapy.*

RTA *rapid trauma assessment.*

RTS *revised trauma scale.* SEE: under *trauma.*

RTT *Radiation therapy technologist.*

RT(T) *Radiation Therapy Technologist.*

Ru Symbol for the element ruthenium.

RU 486 *Mifepristone.*

rub Friction of one surface moving over another. In auscultation, a roughened surface moving over another causes a characteristic sound.

pericardial r. The scratchy, leathery, or rasping sound heard when inflamed visceral and parietal surfaces move over each other. The sound may be heard when listening to the heart sounds of patients with pericarditis.

pleural friction r. The creaking, grating sounds made when inflamed pleural surfaces move during respiration. It is often heard only during the first day or two of a pleurisy.

rubber dam (rŭ′bĕr) Dam (1).

rubedo (rū-bē-dō) [L. *ruber,* red] Redness of the skin that may be temporary.

rubefacient (roo″bĕ-fā′shĕnt) [L. *rubefaciens,* making red] **1.** Causing redness, esp. of the skin. **2.** An agent that reddens the skin by increasing its blood flow (e.g., rubbing alcohol or capsaicin).

rubella (roo-bel′ă) [L. *rubellus,* reddish] A mild, febrile, highly infectious viral disease formerly common in childhood before development of an effective vaccine. It still occurs among nonimmunized children and young adults, esp. in cities of underdeveloped regions. The virus is transmitted through contact with nasopharygeal secretions, blood, urine, and stool of the infected, and possibly by contact with contaminated clothing, tissues, etc. Humans are the only known host. The disease is contagious from about 10 days before appearance of the rash until about 5 days after its disappearance. SYN: *German* **measles;** *third disease; three-day* **measles.** SEE: *Nursing Diagnoses Appendix.*

SYMPTOMS: A variable 1- to 5-day prodromal period of drowsiness, mild elevation of temperature, slight sore throat, Forschheimer spots (pinpoint reddish areas on the palate), and postauricular, postcervical, and occipital lymphadenopathy commonly precedes the rash and is the hallmark of the disease. The maculopapular rash resembles that of measles or scarlet fever, begins on the forehead and face, spreads downward to the trunk and extremities, and lasts about 3 days, accompanied by fever. The rash appears in only about 50% of infections.

INCUBATION: Infection occurs approx. 14 to 23 days before the advent of symptoms.

COMPLICATIONS: Complications seldom occur in children. Older patients may experience generalized lymphadenopathy and splenomegaly. A transient polyarthritis (of the wrist, finger, knee, toe, and ankle joints) may occur within 5 days of the rash but usually lasts less than 2 weeks. Encephalomyelitis is rare and usually self-limiting. The disease is important because it can produce defects in the developing fetus. Rubella infection during the first trimester of pregnancy is of concern: transplacental transmission to the fetus may result in several types of congenital anomalies. SEE: *congenital r. syndrome.*

PREVENTION: Prophylaxis consists of childhood immunization with a combination measles, mumps, rubella (MMR) vaccine, usually administered between 12 and 15 months of age and repeated at age 4 to 6 years. Preconception care includes updating immunizations at least 3 months before attempting conception (rubella, etc.).

⚠️ Administration of live virus vaccines is contraindicated during pregnancy.

PATIENT CARE: *Injection Site:* For 30 min after receiving the vaccine, the patient is observed for indications of anaphylaxis, and epinephrine 1:10,000 is kept readily available. Warmth should be applied to the injection site for 24 hr following immunization to aid absorption. If swelling persists beyond the initial 24 hr, cold should be applied to promote vasoconstriction and prevent antigenic cyst formation. Acetaminophen (for children) or aspirin (for adults) can be taken for relief of fever.

Confirmed cases of rubella should be reported to local public health officials. Parents need to be taught about respiratory (droplet) isolation and why it is necessary; the need to prevent exposure of pregnant women to rubella must be emphasized.

Children with rubella virus should be made as comfortable as possible, allowed to occupy themselves with books, games, and television. Adolescent or adult patients may have fever and joint pain. If medication is needed for symptomatic relief, adults may use aspirin, but children and adolescents should use acetaminophen to lessen the risk of Reye syndrome.

If a pregnant, unimmunized woman develops rubella in her first trimester, she must be informed of the potential for fetal infection and its serious consequences. Generally speaking, the earlier the infection occurs during the pregnancy, the more severe the damage to the fetus. The combination of cataracts, deafness, and cardiac disease defines congenital rubella syndrome (CRS). Low birth weight, microcephaly, and mental retardation are also common. Appropriate immunoglobulin laboratory studies determine the presence of fetal infection. Counseling is offered regarding the woman's choice for abortion, and the patient is supported in her decision.

Infants born with congenital rubella require contact isolation until they no longer excrete the virus. The duration of the viral excretion is variable, usually several months to a year. Parents are taught that congenital rubella is a lifelong disease, that many related disorders may not appear until later in life, and that cataract and cardiac surgery may be required. Emotional support is offered to parents of an affected child. A referral to social service agencies guides parents to appropriate community resources and organizations. A mental health referral may help them deal with their grief, frustration, and anxiety. Confirmed cases of rubella and congenital rubella syndrome should be reported to the local public health department.

rubella titer A blood test to determine a person's immune status to rubella.

rubella virus vaccine, live SEE: *vaccine, live rubella virus.*

rubeola (roo-bē'ō-lă, roo"bē-ō'lă) [L. *rubeolus,* reddish] **1.** Measles. **2.** Term occasionally applied to an acute infectious disease with mild symptoms and a rose-colored macular eruption.

rubeosis iridis (roo"bē-ō'sĭs ĭ'rĭd-ĭs) [L. *rubeosis iridis,* reddening of the iris] A condition in which new blood vessels form on the anterior surface of the iris. Neovascularization is associated with diabetic retinopathy and central retinal vein occlusion. It can lead to neovascular glaucoma that is difficult to treat.

ruber (roo'bĕr) [L.] Red.

rubescent (roo-bĕs'ĕnt) [L. *rubescere,* to grow red] Growing red; flushing.

rubidium (roo-bid'ē-ŭm) [L. *rubidus,* red + *-ium*] SYMB: Rb. A chemical element, atomic weight (mass) 85.47, atomic number 37. It is used in positron emission tomography (PET scanning).

rubiginous (roo-bĭj'ĭ-nŭs) [L. *rubiginosus*] Rusty.

Rubin, Reva (rū-bĭn) A nursing educator, 1916–1995, who developed the Theory of Clinical Nursing. SEE: *Nursing Theory Appendix.*

rubor (roo'bor) [L.] Discoloration or redness caused by inflammation. It is one of the four classic symptoms of inflammation. The others are calor (heat), dolor (pain), and tumor (swelling).

rubriblast (roo'brĭ-blăst) Pronormoblast.

rubricyte (roo'brĭ-sīt) [L. *ruber,* red, + Gr. *kytos,* cell] A polychromatic normoblast.

rubrospinal (roo"brō-spī'năl) [" + *spina,* thorn] Pert. to a descending tract that consists of a small bundle of nerve fibers in the lateral funiculus of the spinal cord. Fibers arise in the cells of the red nucleus of the midbrain and terminate in the ventral horn of the gray matter.

Rubus idaeus (roo'bŭs i-dē'ŭs) Red raspberry.

rudiment (roo'dĭ-mĕnt) [L. *rudimentum,* beginning] **1.** Something undeveloped. **2.** In biology, a part just beginning to develop. **3.** A structure that never develops fully.

rudimentary (roo"dĭ-mĕn'tă-rē) **1.** Elementary. **2.** Undeveloped; not fully formed.

Ruffini, Angelo (roo-fē'nē) Italian anatomist, 1864–1929.

R. corpuscle One of the encapsulated sensory nerve endings found in the dermis and in subcutaneous tissue, once thought to mediate the sense of warmth, now believed to be a pressure receptor. SYN: *organ of **Ruffini***.

organ of R. *Ruffini* corpuscle.

rufous (roo'fŭs) [L. *rufus*, red] Ruddy; having a ruddy complexion and reddish hair.

ruga (roo'gă) *pl.* **rugae** [L.] A fold or crease, esp. one of the folds of mucous membrane on the internal surface of the stomach. SEE: illus.

palatal r. One of the folds of the mucous membrane of the roof of the mouth. SYN: *palatine* **r.**

palatine r. Palatal **r.**

r. of vagina One of the small ridges on the inner surface of the vagina extending laterally and upward from the columna rugarum (long ridges on the anterior and posterior walls).

rugine (roo-zhēn') **1.** Periosteal elevator. **2.** A raspatory.

rugose, rugous (roo'gōs, -gŭs) [L. *rugosus*, wrinkled] Having many wrinkles or creases; used in describing microbiological colonies.

rugosity (rū-gŏs'ĭ-tē) [L. *rugositas*] **1.** The condition of being folded or wrinkled. **2.** A ridge or wrinkle.

RUL *right upper lobe* (of lung).

rule (rool) [Fr. *riule* fr L. *regula*, ruler, pattern] A guide or principle based on experience or observation.

ABCD prediction r. ABCD **score**.

ABCD r. ABCD **score**.

buccal object r. A dental radiographical technique used to identify the position of an object within a three-dimensional area. A reference radiograph is taken. The projection angle is changed and the resulting radiograph compared with the reference radiograph. If the image remains in the same position, the object is located buccal to the reference object. If the image changes position, the object is lingual to the reference object.

Cieszynski r. SEE: *Cieszynski rule*.

Clark r. SEE: *Clark rule*.

Common R. Any of the U.S. policies designed to protect the rights and interests of citizens who choose to participate in government-funded biomedical research. Those who choose to participate in biomedical research often suffer from life-altering or life-threatening illnesses. As a result they may be more psychologically vulnerable than others and may agree to become investigative subjects because of fear or desperation. The protections provided by the Common Rule are designed to ensure that agencies that perform federally funded human research respect the rights of experimental subjects. Included are the rights of confidentiality and full disclosure (informed consent). Research performed on children or prisoners is given special protections.

convex-concave r., concave-convex rule. A law of joint kinematics that

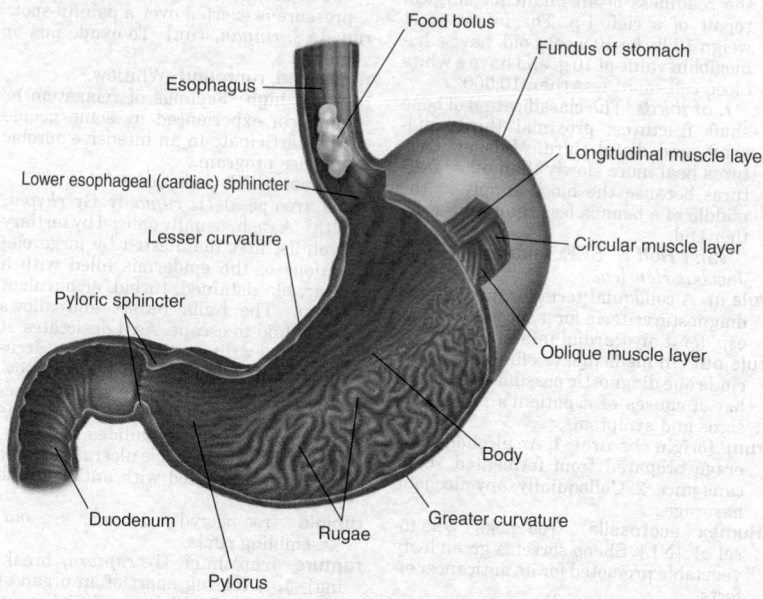

Food bolus
Esophagus
Fundus of stomach
Longitudinal muscle layer
Lower esophageal (cardiac) sphincter
Circular muscle layer
Lesser curvature
Pyloric sphincter
Oblique muscle layer
Body
Duodenum
Rugae
Greater curvature
Pylorus

RUGAE

Rugae of stomach as seen through an endoscope

states that if a convex joint surface moves on a stationary concave surface, the convex joint will slide in the direction opposite that of the angular motion of the bone, and that if a concave joint surface moves on a stationary convex surface, the articular surface will slide in the same direction as the angular motion of the bone.

    Cowling r. SEE: *Cowling rule.*

    decision r. SEE: *decision aid.*

    Durham r. (of criminal responsibility) A legal decision from *Durham v. United States* that limits the culpability of those with psychological or neurological diseases who have committed criminal acts. It states that an unlawful act is not a criminal act if it was committed by someone mentally ill, e.g., psychotic at the time, or was committed by someone with profound neurological disease, e.g., with severe dementia or organic brain injury.

    learned intermediary r. Learned intermediary *doctrine.*

    r. of nines A formula for estimating percentage of body surface areas, particularly helpful in judging the portion of skin that has been burned. For the adult, the head represents 9%; each upper extremity 9%; the back of the trunk 18%, and the front 18%; each lower extremity 18%; and the perineum the remaining 1%. SEE: illus.

    Ottawa ankle r.'s SEE: *Ottawa ankle rules.*

    r. of ten The criteria used to judge the readiness of an infant for surgical repair of a cleft lip. The infant must weigh 10 lb, be 10 weeks old, have a hemoglobin value of 10 g, and have a white blood cell count less than 10,000.

    r. of thirds The classification of bone shaft fractures: proximal third, midshaft, and distal third. Midshaft fractures heal more slowly than other fractures because the blood supply in the middle of a bone is less than that at either end.

    van't Hoff r. SEE: under *van't Hoff, Jacobus Henricus.*

rule in A colloquial term for meeting the diagnostic criteria for a specific disease, esp. for a myocardial infarction.

rule out In medicine, to eliminate or exclude one diagnostic possibility from the list of causes of a patient's presenting signs and symptoms.

rum [origin obscure] **1.** An alcoholic beverage prepared from fermented sugar cane juice. **2.** Colloquially, any alcoholic beverage.

Rumex acetosella (roo′měks ă-sē′tō-sěl′ă) [NL] Sheep sorrel, a green leafy vegetable promoted for its anticancer effects.

rum fits A colloquial phrase for alcohol withdrawal seizures. Most occur during the 7- to 48-hr period following absti-

nence. There may be a single seizure, but most occur in bursts of two to six. These seizures do not represent latent epilepsy.

ruminant (roo″mǐ-nănt) An animal that regurgitates food in order to chew it again. This is called chewing the cud.

rumination (roo″mǐ-nā′shŭn) [L. *ruminatio*] **1.** Regurgitation, esp. with rechewing, of previously swallowed food. This condition may be present in otherwise normal individuals, in emotionally deprived or mentally retarded infants, or in mentally retarded adults. Infants with rumination disorder often have weight loss, malnutrition, and failure to thrive. **2.** In psychiatry, an obsessional preoccupation by a single idea or a set of thoughts, with an inability to dismiss or dislodge them. Also called *merycism.*

Ruminococcus (roo″mǐ-nō-kok′ŭs) A genus of anaerobic gram-positive bacteria found in the intestinal tract of humans and other animals.

rummaging (rŭm′ă-jĭng) [Middle Fr. *arrumer,* to store cargo in the hold of a ship] Searching for lost objects, often in an aimless, repetitive, or fruitless manner. It is a characteristic of some patients affected by dementias and other brain diseases.

rump (rŭmp) [ME. *rumpe*] The posterior end of the back, the gluteal region, or the buttocks.

Rumpel-Leede sign Rumpel-Leede test.

Rumpf symptom (rumpf) [Heinrich Theodor Rumpf, Ger. physician, 1851–1923] A quickening of the pulse when pressure is exerted over a painful spot.

run [AS. *rinnan,* run] To exude pus or mucus.

runaround, runround Whitlow.

runners' high Feelings of relaxation or euphoria experienced by some people who participate in an intensive aerobic exercise program.

run sheet SEE: under *sheet.*

rupia (roo′pē-ă) [L. *rupia,* fr. Gr. *rhypos,* filth] A rash, usually caused by tertiary syphilis, first manifested by large elevations of the epidermis filled with a clear, bloodstained, turbid, or purulent serum. The bulla bursts and allows some fluid to escape. As it desiccates, it is covered with a crust that dries, accumulates new layers, and becomes covered with greenish-brown scales, sometimes to a depth of ½ in (13 mm). It is the thickest of all syphilides and presents the most extensive ulcerations. The condition is treated with antisyphilitic antibiotics.

rupioid (roo′pē-oyd″) [*rupia* + *-oid*] Resembling rupia.

rupture (rŭp′chŭr) [L. *ruptura,* breaking] **1.** A tearing apart of an organ or tissue. **2.** A colloquial term for a hernia. SEE: *hernia.*

    r. of the Achilles tendon Disruption

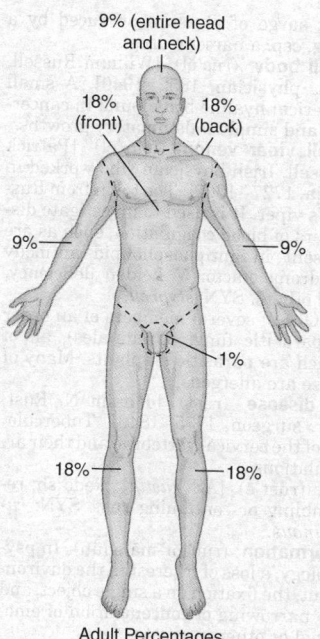

Adult Percentages

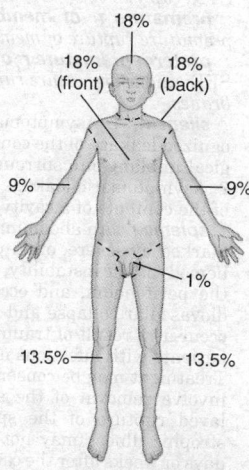

Percentages in a child

RULE OF NINES

of the attachments of the gastrocnemius and soleus muscles to the posterior calcaneus, an injury that typically occurs in middle-aged male athletes participating in basketball or other ball sports, some divers, or patients treated with steroid injections for Achilles tendinitis.

ETIOLOGY: The injury typically occurs during sudden, forceful plantar flexion of the ankle.

SYMPTOMS: After an initial sensation of being struck in the back of the lower limb, the patient typically reports an inability to push up onto his or her tiptoes. The injury is distinguished from others by placing the patient in a prone position with feet extending off the foot of the examining table. The examiner then squeezes the calf muscle and observes the response: if plantar flexion occurs, the tendon is intact; if ankle dorsiflexion results, the tendon is partially intact; if no flexion of any kind occurs, the tendon is ruptured (the Thompson Test).

TREATMENT: Management may involve casting the lower extremity, but usually surgical repair or reinforcement of the damaged tendon is required.

PATIENT CARE: The patient is taught to keep the leg elevated for 48 to 72 hr following the injury, with ice applied intermittently to the joint (or cast) to help control swelling. Nonsteroidal anti-inflammatory drugs (NSAIDs) are provided for pain and inflammation. The patient is fitted for crutches or a walker-frame and instructed in gait training. Rehabilitation exercises consist of flexibility, strengthening, and balance exercises as tolerated. Assisted motion of the ankle reduces the duration of rehabilitation from Achilles tendon rupture, which may in some instances be prolonged or complicated by muscle atrophy or repetitive injury to the tendon.

cap r. Plaque rupture.

cardiac r. A tearing of the heart muscle that may occur after severe chest trauma (or in about 2% of patients who have suffered a myocardial infarction). It typically results in sudden cardiac death or tamponade. SYN: *myocardial r.*

r. of membranes The rupture of the amniotic sac as a normal result of dilation of the cervix uteri in labor. SYN: *amniorrhea.* SEE: *preterm premature rupture of membranes.*

extracapsular r. A leakage or explosion of the contents of a surgical implant beyond the scar tissue that grows to surround it.

myocardial r. Cardiac rupture.

r. of perineum Spontaneous laceration of the perineum during the second stage of labor. The event occurs more commonly in primiparas and may be avoided by having an episiotomy.

plaque r. The separation of a lipid-rich lesion from the wall of a blood vessel. The damage this does to the lining of a blood vessel triggers a cascade of events that result in blood clot formation within the vessel and its eventual obstruction. This is the immediate cause of acute myocardial infarction. SYN: *cap r.*

premature r. of membranes SEE: *premature rupture of membranes.*

preterm premature r. of membranes SEE: under *premature rupture of membranes.*

silent r. **1.** Asymptomatic or unrecognized leakage of the contents of a surgical implant into surrounding tissues. **2.** Asymptomatic leakage or protrusion of the contents of a cavity or structure.

splenic r. An abdominal catastrophe marked by severe, often pleuritic pain, hemodynamic instability, blood loss into the peritoneum, and occasionally cardiovascular collapse and death. It may occur as a result of trauma or rarely in patients with infectious mononucleosis. Treatment may be conservative or may involve removal of the spleen. In delayed rupture of the spleen, a catastrophic illness may not present until days or weeks after the causative injury.

r. of tubes A rupture of a fallopian tube, a surgical emergency in ectopic pregnancy. This may occur without the woman's knowledge of her pregnancy.

r. of the tympanic membrane A disruption of the epithelium that separates the external auditory canal from the middle ear. This can occur as a result of trauma, or more often as a consequence of a middle ear infection.

r. of uterus A rare condition in which the uterine muscles are torn apart by the stresses of unrelieved obstructed labor, the parting of an old cesarean delivery scar, or aggressive induction or augmentation of labor. SEE: *cephalopelvic disproportion; induction of labor; Nursing Diagnoses Appendix.*

RUQ *right upper quadrant* (of abdomen).

rural (roor′ăl) [L. *ruralis,* rustic, country] Pert. to a geographic area (such as a small town or sparsely populated county) where less than 2500 people live.

rush **1.** A strong contraction wave that moves down the small intestine. **2.** The first surge of pleasure produced by a drug, esp. a narcotic drug.

Russell body (rŭs′ĕl) [William Russell, Scot. physician, 1852–1940] A small spherical hyaline body found in cancerous and simple inflammatory growths.

Russell viper venom (rŭs′ĕl) [Patrick Russell, Irish physician who worked in India, 1727–1805] The toxin from Russell's viper. It is used to investigate disorders of blood coagulation, such as are present in antiphospholipid antibody syndrome, factor V Leiden deficiency, and others. SYN: *stypven.*

rust One of several members of an order of parasitic fungi (Uredinales), all of which are parasitic on plants. Many of these are allergens.

Rust disease (rŭst) [Johann N. Rust, Ger. surgeon, 1775–1840] Tuberculosis of the cervical vertebrae and their articulations.

rusty (rŭst′ē) [AS. *rustig*] Reddish; resembling or containing rust. SYN: *rubiginous.*

rut-formation (rŭt′fŏr-mā″shŭn) In psychology, a loss of interest in the environment, the fixation on a single object, and the narrowing of concentration of emotional or other interests.

ruthenium (roo-thē′nē-ŭm) [L. *Ruthenia,* Ukraine + *-ium* (1)] SYMB: Ru. A hard, brittle, transition metal of the platinum group, atomic weight (mass) 101.07, atomic number 44.

rutherford (rŭth′ĕr-fŏrd) [Ernest Rutherford, Brit. physicist, 1871–1937] ABBR: rd. A unit of radioactivity representing 10^6 disintegrations per second.

rutin (roo′tĭn) A flavonoid present in many plants including whole grains and the inner rind of lemons and oranges.

RV *residual volume; right ventricle; rotavirus vaccine.*

RV1 *Rotarix.*

RV5 *fifth right ventricular chest lead* (in electrocardiography); *RotaTeq.*

Rx [℞, abbr. of L. *recipe,* take] **1.** A medical prescription. **2.** In writing prescriptions, "take." SEE: *prescription.*

rye (rī) [AS. *ryge*] A cereal grass that produces a grain used in food and beverage production. When rye grain is infected with a certain fungus, ergot is produced.

S

Σ **1.** The uppercase of the Greek letter sigma. **2.** In statistics, the symbol for *summation* (2). SEE: *σ*.

σ **1.** The lowercase of the Greek letter sigma. **2.** In statistics, the symbol for *standard deviation*. SEE: Σ.

S [L. *signa*, mark] **1.** Symbol for the element sulfur. **2.** In prescription writing, the symbol indicating the instructions to the patient that the pharmacist will place on the dispensed medicine. **3.** *Smooth,* in reference to bacterial colonies. **4.** *Spherical* or *spherical lens*. **5.** *Subject* (pl. Ss); a participant in an experiment. **6.** Symbol for siemens.

s L. *semis,* half; *sinister,* left.

S₃ A ventricular gallop heard after the second heart sound (S_2). It is a sign of heart failure.

S₄ The fourth heart sound, a presystolic gallop (also known as *atrial gallop*), which precedes the first heart sound (S_1). It is abnormal and usually indicative of a stiff (noncompliant) ventricle.

S₁, S₂ Normal first and second heart sounds.

S1, S2, etc. *first sacral nerve, second sacral nerve,* etc.

S-A, SA, S.A. *sinoatrial.*

SAARD *slow-acting antirheumatic drug.*

SABA *short-acting beta agonist.*

Sabiá virus (să-bē-ah′) [*Sabiá,* a village outside São Paulo, Brazil] SEE: under *virus.*

Sabin vaccine (sā′bĭn) [Albert Bruce Sabin, Russian-born U.S. virologist, 1906–1993] SEE: *Live oral poliovirus vaccine.*

Sabouraud dextrose agar (să-boo-rō′) An acidic agar with a high dextrose content. It is used in microbiology to cultivate fungi and yeasts.

sabulous (sab′yŭ-lŭs) [L. *sabulosus,* sandy] Gritty; sandy.

sac (sak) [L. *saccus,* sack, bag] A baglike part of an organ, a cavity or pouch, sometimes containing fluid. SYN: *saccus.* SEE: *cyst.*

   air s. In a mammalian lung, an informal term for *pulmonary alveolus.* SEE: under *alveolus.*

   allantoic s. The expanded end of the allantois, well developed in birds and reptiles.

   alveolar s. Pulmonary **alveolus.**

   amniotic s. The inner fetal membrane that encloses the developing fetus and produces amniotic fluid. SEE: *chorion.*

   chorionic s. The outer fetal membrane that encloses the developing embryo.

   conjunctival s. The cavity, lined with conjunctiva, that lies between the eyelids and the anterior surface of the eye.

   dental s. The mesenchymal tissue surrounding a developing tooth.

   endolymphatic s. The expanded distal end of the endolymphatic duct.

   heart s. The pericardium.

   hernial s. In the peritoneum, a saclike protrusion containing a herniated organ. SEE: *hernia.*

   lacrimal s. The upper dilated portion of the nasolacrimal duct situated in the groove of the lacrimal bone. The upper part is behind the internal tarsal ligament. It is 12 to 15 mm long.

   lesser peritoneal s. Omental **bursa.**

   peritoneal s. The enclosed, transparent mesothelial sac that is squeezed between the abdominal wall and the abdominal viscera.

   vitelline s. Yolk **s.**

   yolk s. In mammals, the embryonic membrane that is the site of formation of the first red blood cells and the cells that will become oogonia or spermatogonia. SYN: *vitelline s.* SEE: *embryo* for illus.

saccade (sa-kod′) [Fr. *saccade,* jerk] A fast, involuntary movement of the eye as it changes from one point of gaze to another. SEE: *nystagmus; vergence.* **saccadic,** *adj.*

saccate (sak′āt″) [L. *saccatus,* baglike] **1.** Encysted. **2.** In bacteriology, making a sac shape, as in a type of liquefaction.

saccharase (sak′ă-rās″) [*saccharo-* + *-ase*] An enzyme such as sucrase that catalyzes the hydrolysis of a disaccharide to monosaccharides.

saccharated (sak′ă-rāt″ĕd) Containing sugar.

saccharide (sak′ă-rīd″) [*saccharo-* + *-ide*] Any of a group of carbohydrates that includes sugars. It includes monosaccharides (single sugars), disaccharides (two sugars, covalently linked), oligosaccharides (a small number of linked sugars), and polysaccharides (multiple covalently linked sugars).

saccharin (săk′ă-rĭn) [*saccharo-* + *-in*] $C_7H_5NO_3S$, a sweet, white, powdered, synthetic product derived from coal tar, 300 to 500 times sweeter than sugar, used as an artificial sweetener.

saccharine (sak′ă-rĭn, -rēn″, -rīn) [*saccharo-* + *-ine*] **1.** Pert. to sugar or saccharin. **2.** Containing or yielding sugar.

3. Excessively sweet or sweet to the point of sickness.

saccharo-, sacchar- [L. *saccharum, saccharon,* fr Gr. *sacchar, saccharon,* sugar] Prefixes meaning *sugar.*

saccharolytic (sak″ă-rō-lit′ik) [*saccharo- + -lytic*] Able to split up sugar.

Saccharomyces (sak″ă-rō-mī′sēz) [*saccharo- +* Gr. *mykēs,* fungus] Yeast (1).

    S. boulardii A species of yeast used as a probiotic to prevent and treat infectious and inflammatory diseases of the intestines.

    S. cerevisiae A yeast used in recombinant DNA technology to manufacture proteins for medical use, e.g., in vaccine components.

saccharum (sak′ă-rŭm) [L. *saccharum,* fr. Gr *saccharon,* sugar] Sugar.

sacciform (sak′sĭ-form″) [*saccus + -form*] Bag-shaped or saclike. SYN: *encysted.*

saccular (sak′yŭ-lăr) Sac-shaped or saclike.

sacculated (sak′yŭ-lāt″ĕd) Consisting of small sacs or saccules.

sacculation (sak″yŭ-lā′shŏn) **1.** Formation into a sac or sacs. **2.** A group of sacs, collectively.

saccule (sak′ūl″) [L. *sacculus,* a little bag] **1.** A small sac. SYN: *sacculus.* **2.** The smaller of two sacs of the vestibular labyrinth in the vestibule of the ear. It communicates with the utricle, cochlear duct, and endolymphatic duct, all of which are filled with endolymph. In its wall is the macula sacculi, a sensory area containing hair cells that respond to gravity or bodily movement. SEE: *labyrinth* for illus.

    laryngeal s. A small diverticulum extending ventrally from the laryngeal ventricle lying between the ventricular fold and the thyroarytenoid muscle.

sachet (sa-shā′) [Fr. *sachet,* little sack] Any material, e.g., paper, foil, or plastic, used to package doses of medication.

SACH foot SEE: under *foot.*

sacral (sak′răl, sā′krăl) [*sacro- + -al*] Pert. to the sacrum.

sacralization (sā″kră-lĭ-zā′shŏn) Fusion of the sacrum and the fifth lumbar vertebra.

sacral nerves The five pairs of spinal nerves, the upper four of which emerge through the posterior sacral foramina, the fifth pair through the sacral hiatus (termination of the sacral canal). All are mixed nerves (motor and sensory).

sacrectomy (sā-krek′tŏ-mē) [*sacro- + -ectomy*] Excision of part of the sacrum.

sacrifice (sak′rĭ-fīs″) [L. *sacrificare,* to make or offer a sacrifice] **1.** To give up or yield something of value. **2.** To experience a loss.

sacro- [L. *(os) sacrum,* sacred (bone)] Prefix meaning *sacrum.*

sacrococcygeal (sā″krō-kok-sij′(ē-)ăl, sak″rō″) [*sacro- + coccygeal*] Pert. to the sacrum and coccyx.

sacrocolpopexy (sā″krō-kol′pŏ-pek″sē, sak″rō-) [*sacro- + colpopexy*] The tethering of a prolapsed uterus or vagina to its proper anatomical position within the pelvis, typically with a support made of surgical mesh.

sacroiliac (sak″rō-il′ē-ak″, sā″krō-) [*sacro- + iliac*] Pert. to the sacrum and ilium.

sacroiliitis (sā″krō-il″ē-īt′ĭs, sak″rō-) [*sacro- +ilio- + -itis*] Inflammation of the sacroiliac joint.

sacrospinalis (sā″krō-spī-nāl′ĭs) [″ + *spina,* thorn] A large muscle group lying on either side of the vertebral column extending from the sacrum to the head. Its two chief components are the iliocostalis and longissimus muscles.

sacrum (sā′krŭm) [L., sacred] The triangular bone situated dorsal and caudal from the two ilia between the fifth lumbar vertebra and the coccyx. It is formed of five united vertebrae and is wedged between the two innominate bones, its articulations forming the sacroiliac joints. It is the base of the vertebral column and, with the coccyx, forms the posterior boundary of the true pelvis. The male sacrum is narrower and more curved than the female sacrum. SYN: *sacral bone.* SEE: illus.

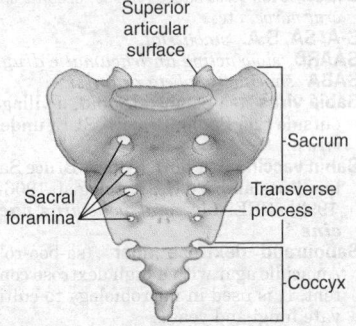

SACRUM AND COCCYX

(ANTERIOR VIEW)

SAD (săd) *seasonal affective disorder; source-to-axis distance.*

saddle A surface or structure that resembles a seat used to ride a horse. The base of artificial dentures is often referred to as a saddle.

    s. area The portion of the buttocks, perineum, and thighs that comes in contact with the seat of the saddle when one rides a horse.

    s. back Lordosis.

S-adenosylmethionine (ă-dĕn″ō-sīl″mĕ-thī′ŭ-nēn″) ABBR: SAM-e. A compound that is synthesized naturally in the central nervous system (CNS) when folate and vitamin B$_{12}$ levels are adequate. SAM-e is involved in the methylation of neurotransmitters, amino acids, proteins, phospholipids, and other neurochemicals. The chemical is used to treat for depression, liver disease, and osteoarthritis. It is an active sulfonium form of methionine that acts as a methyl group donor in various reactions (such as the formation of epinephrine or creatine).

sadism (sā'dĭzm, săd'ĭzm) [Comte Donatien Alphonse François de Sade, Marquis de Sade, 1740–1814] Conscious or unconscious sexual pleasure derived from inflicting mental or physical pain on others. SEE: *algolagnia; masochism*.

sadist (sā'dĭst, săd'ĭst) One who practices sadism.

sadness A normal emotional feeling of dejection or melancholy that one may experience after an unhappy event.

sadomasochism (sā"dō-măs'ĕ-kĭzm, săd"ō-măs'ĕ-kĭzm) Sexual pleasure related to both sadism and masochism.

sadomasochist (sā"dō-măs'ĕ-kĭst) One whose personality includes sadistic and masochistic components.

Saemisch ulcer (sā'mish) [Edwin Theodor Saemisch, Ger. ophthalmologist, 1833–1909] Serpiginous infectious ulcer of the cornea.

safelight (sāf'lĭt) A darkroom device that emits a light of a specified wavelength that causes less fogging of undeveloped film than white light does.

safe period SEE: under *period*.

safe sex, safer sex SEE: under *sex*.

safety (sāf'tē) [ME. *saufte*, safety, health] **1.** A practice that ensures protection from harm or injury. **2.** The condition of being protected. **3.** A device that prevents the unintended discharge of a firearm. **safe** (sāf), *adj*.

safety alert A report issued by a manufacturer of drugs or medical products about the risks associated with those drugs or products. SEE: *black box warning*.

safety net A colloquial term for social or financial support to prevent poor outcomes for indigent people, families, or communities. In health care, the concept includes providing subsidized care for the uninsured, for the very young or the very old, for those with contagious diseases or those who cannot take care of themselves.

safflower oil SEE: under *oil*.

safranin, safranin O A histological stain used in microscopy to highlight cell nuclei by counterstaining them red. It is used for many purposes, including the gram staining of body fluid specimens.

sagittal (săj'ĭ-tăl) [L. *sagittalis*] Arrowlike; in an anteroposterior direction.

sago (sā'gō) [Malay *sagu*] A substance prepared from various palms, consisting principally of starches; used as a demulcent and as a food with little residue.

Saint John's wort An herbal remedy (*Hypericum perforatum*) used to treat mild to moderate depression.

⚠ Caution should be used since this remedy interacts with many other medications.

Saint Vitus' dance Sydenham chorea.

sal (sal) [L. *sal*, salt] Salt or a saltlike substance.

salacious (sĕ-lā'shŭs) [L. *salax*, lustful] Lustful or inciting to lust.

salba (sal'bă) Chia.

Salem sump tube A double-lumen nasogastric tube with an air vent, used to drain gastric or refluxed intestinal secretions or ingested air. The vent protects against damage to the gastric mucosa while facilitating drainage.

salicylate (să-lis'ĭ-lāt") [*salicyl(ic acid)* + *-ate*] Any salt of salicylic acid. Particular salicylates are listed under the first word. SEE: e.g., *magnesium salicylate; methyl salicylate;* **physostigmine** *salicylate*. **salicylated** (-lāt"ĭd), *adj*.

salicylic acid (sal"ĭ-sĭl'ik) SEE: under *acid*.

salicylism (săl'ĭ-sĭl"ĭzm) Intoxication caused by an overdose of salicylic acid or its derivatives.

salicyluric acid (sal"ĭ-sil-ūr'ik) SEE: under *acid*.

salient (sā'lē-ĕnt) [L. *salio*, to spring, jump] Prominent, conspicuous.

saline (sā'lēn", 'līn") [L. *salinus*, pert. to salt] **1.** Pert. to or containing common table salt; salty. **2.** Pert. to or containing a mineral salt that has an aperient or cathartic effect, e.g., epsom salt. **3.** An aqueous solution usually of common table salt and sterile or distilled water. SEE: *normal saline* **solution**; *saline* **solution**. **4.** A mineral salt, e.g., of magnesium, that has as an aperient or cathartic effect. **5.** An aqueous solution of a mineral salt and distilled water, used for its aperient or cathartic effect.

  hypertonic s. An aqueous solution of sodium chloride of greater than 0.85%.

  hypotonic s. An aqueous solution of sodium chloride of less than 0.85%.

saline lock An intravenous portal, usually placed and left in a vein in one of the patient's arms, and used episodically for fluid or medication infusions. Salt water flushes are used to maintain its patency. Saline locks replaced heparin locks in the 1990s because of cost and efficacy and because heparin locks posed a rare but unacceptable risk of heparin-related allergies, esp. heparin-related thrombocytopenia.

salinometer (săl"ĭ-nŏm'ĕ-tĕr) [L. *salinus*, of salt, + *metron*, measure] An instrument for determining the salt content of a solution.

saliva (să-lī′vă) [L. *saliva,* spittle] The fluid secretion of the salivary gland and oral mucous gland that begins the process of digesting food. Saliva moistens food for tasting, chewing, and swallowing; initiates digestion of starches; moistens and lubricates the mouth; and acts as a solvent for excretion of waste products. SYN: *spit* (1); *spittle.*

CHARACTERISTICS: It is normally tasteless, clear, odorless, viscid, and weakly alkaline, being neutralized after being acted on by gastric acid in the stomach. Its specific gravity is 1.002 to 1.006. The amount secreted in 24 hr is estimated to be 1500 ml. The flow varies from 0.2 ml/min from resting glands to 4.0 ml/min with maximum secretion.

COMPOSITION: Saliva is 99.5% water. Inorganic constituents include salts (chlorides, carbonates, phosphates, sulfates) and dissolved gases. Organic constituents include enzymes (amylase and lysozyme), proteins (mucin, albumin, and globulins), small amounts of urea, and unusual waste products, e.g., acetone. Epithelial cells and leukocytes are also present.

DIAGNOSTIC TESTING: Saliva is readily accessible and easy to transport and store and has become useful for clinical laboratory testing. In the year 2000, U.S. Food and Drug Administration–approved diagnostic tests on saliva include assays for antibodies to HIV, estrogen levels, drugs of abuse, and alcohol levels.

    artificial s. An aqueous solution or gel that is useful in treating excessive dryness of the mouth (xerostomia). SYN: *saliva **substitute**.*

saliva ejector A device used during dental procedures to remove saliva.

salivary (săl′ĭ-věr-ē) [L. *salivarius,* slimy] Pert. to, producing, or formed from saliva.

salivary gland SEE: under *gland.*

salivation (săl″ĭ-vā′shŭn) [L. *salivatio,* to spit out] **1.** The act of secreting saliva. **2.** Excessive secretion of saliva. SYN: *ptyalism.*

salivatory (săl′ĭ-vă-tor″ē) Pert. to the secretion of saliva.

Salk vaccine (sok) [Jonas E. Salk, U.S. microbiologist, 1914–1995] Inactivated poliovirus **vaccine**.

Salla disease (săl′a) [Salla, a municipality in Finnish Lapland] A rare form of autosomal recessive mental retardation in which children develop poor muscle tone in the first years of life, ataxia, seizures, and coarsened facial features, among other variably expressed deficits. It is one of the lysosomal storage disorders.

sallow (săl′ō) [AS. *salo*] A sickly yellow color, usually describing complexion or skin color.

salmeterol (săl-mē-těr′al) A long-acting beta-2 agonist used to treat patients with reactive airway disease. Its use is associated with decreased dependence on short-acting beta agonists, decreased nocturnal asthma, and decreased need for steroids in the treatment of asthma.

salmin(e) (săl′mēn, -mĭn) [L. *salmo,* salmon] $C_{30}H_{57}N_{14}O_6$; a toxic protamine obtained from the spermatozoa of salmon. SEE: *protamine; protein.*

Salmonella (săl″mō-něl′ă) [Daniel Elmer Salmon, U.S. veterinarian, 1850–1914] A genus of motile bacilli of the family Enterobacteriaceae. More than 1400 species have been classified. Several species are pathogenic, some producing mild gastroenteritis and others a severe and often fatal food poisoning. Food preparers should cook all foods from animal sources thoroughly, refrigerate leftover cooked foods during storage, and wash hands before and after handling foods. People should avoid ingesting raw eggs in any form and using cracked eggs. SEE: *salmonellosis.*

PATIENT CARE: Patients who have contracted salmonella should drink clear fluids until abdominal pain has subsided. Fluid and electrolyte balance is monitored, hydration is maintained, and supportive therapy is maintained as indicated. Antimicrobial therapy is prescribed based on organism sensitivity. Contact precautions are used if the patient is diapered or incontinent; otherwise, standard precautions suffice, with gloves and gown used when disposing of feces or fecally contaminated objects. Precautions should continue until three consecutive stool cultures are negative for salmonella. Patients whose stool cultures remain positive should be taught correct hand hygiene, should avoid preparing uncooked foods, and should not be employed in any capacity that involves handling food until cultures become negative. All cases of salmonella should be reported to the state health department.

    S. arizonae A species that may infect animals and humans and cause gastroenteritis, urinary tract infection, bacteremia, meningitis, osteomyelitis, and brain abscess.

    S. choleraesuis A species often found to be the cause of septicemia.

    S. enteritidis A species that commonly causes gastrointestinal infections. Approx. 10% to 20% of food poisoning cases are caused by *S. enteritidis.* The organism lives in the ovaries of chickens and contaminates eggs before the shells are formed. The infection is passed to humans when they eat raw eggs (e.g., in homemade ice cream, salad dressings, eggnog) or cooked eggs in which the yolk is still runny. It also lives in the intestinal tracts of animals and may be found in water or meat that is contaminated with feces and is inadequately washed and cooked. Infants, elderly persons, and immunocompromised patients are at greatest risk. SEE: *diarrhea; raw egg; enterocolitis.*

S. paratyphi Any of a group of organisms of *Salmonella,* types A, B, and C, that cause paratyphoid fever.

S. typhi A species causing typhoid fever in humans.

S. typhimurium A species frequently isolated from persons having acute gastroenteritis.

salmonellosis (săl-mō-nĕ-lō′sĭs) Infection with *Salmonella.* In the U.S., the most common infection is acute gastroenteritis caused by *S. enteritidis, S. typhimurium,* or other strains. Typhoid fever, found in developing countries with inadequate sanitation, is caused by *S. typhi.*

SYMPTOMS: Salmonella gastroenteritis is characterized by fever, nausea and vomiting, watery diarrhea, and abdominal cramps 12 to 72 hr after consuming contaminated food or water. The illness usually is self-limiting and lasts from 4 to 7 days.

TREATMENT: Unless severe, salmonella gastroenteritis is treated with fluid replacement and antimotility drugs; antibiotics are not used. For immunocompromised patients, those with severe diarrhea and fever greater than 101°F (38.3°C), and elderly persons or infants, ciprofloxacin or trimethoprim-sulfamethoxazole may be prescribed for 3 to 7 days.

PREVENTION: To reduce the risk of *S. enteritidis* infection, eggs should be kept refrigerated at all times to prevent increased bacterial growth; cracked or dirty eggs should be discarded. Hands and equipment in contact with raw eggs should be washed thoroughly in soap and hot water before other foods are touched. Eggs should be cooked until the yolk is solid and eaten promptly; food containing cooked eggs should not be kept warm for more than 2 hr.

salpingectomy (săl″pĭn-jĕk′tō-mē) [Gr. *salpinx,* tube, + *ektome,* excision] The surgical removal of a fallopian tube.

salpingitis (săl″pĭn-jī′tĭs) [Gr. *salpinx,* tube, + *itis,* inflammation] Inflammation of a fallopian tube, usually as a result of a sexually transmitted infection. The prognosis is affected by the virulence of the organism, degree of in-flammation, and promptness of treatment. The long-term consequences of the infection may include scarring of the fallopian tubes and infertility.

ETIOLOGY: The most common causative organisms are *Neisseria gonorrhoeae* and *Chlamydia trachomatis.* Additional causative organisms include *Staphylococcus aureus, Escherichia coli,* and other aerobic and anaerobic bacilli and cocci. Although common elsewhere, tubercular salpingitis is rare in the U.S.; it is most likely to be present in immunosuppressed women and some immigrant populations. Postpartum salpingitis often results from the upward migration of commensal vaginal streptococci.

SYMPTOMS: Although the disease may be asymptomatic, the patient often presents with signs of an acute pelvic infection. Complaints include unilateral or bilateral pelvic or lower abdominal pain, fever, and chills.

EXAMINATION: If an abscess has formed, bimanual palpation or ultrasonography may reveal a tender adnexal mass.

TREATMENT: Empirical antibiotic therapies may include fluoroquinolones or combination therapies using tetracycline derivatives and cephalosporins. Care must be taken to avoid using fluoroquinolones or tetracyclines in pregnancy. Bedrest and analgesics assist in pain management.

   eustachian s. Eustachitis.

   gonococcal s. Salpingitis due to gonococci.

salpingo-, salping- [Gr. *salpinx,* stem *salping-,* trumpet] Prefixes meaning-*tube* or *salpinx.*

salpingography (săl″pĭng-gŏg′ră-fē) [″ + *graphein,* to write] Radiography of the fallopian tubes after the introduction of a radiopaque contrast medium; used in testing for patency of the tubes in investigating infertility.

salpingo-oophorectomy (săl-pĭng″gō-ō″ŏf-ō-rĕk′tō-mē) [″ + *oon,* egg, + *phoros,* a bearer, + *ektome,* excision] Excision of an ovary and a fallopian tube. SYN: *oophorosalpingectomy; ovariosalpingectomy; salpingo-ovariectomy.*

salpingo-oophoritis (săl-pĭng″ō-ō″ŏf-ō-rī′tĭs) [″ + ″ + ″ + *itis,* inflammation] Inflammation of a fallopian tube and an ovary. SYN: *salpingo-oothecitis.* SEE: *pelvic inflammatory disease; salpingitis.*

salpingoscopy (săl″pĭng-gŏs-kŭ-pē) Microendoscopic examination of the inside of the fallopian tubes, e.g., to diagnose or treat obstruction, adhesions, or other diseases and conditions.

salpingostomy (săl-pĭng-ŏs′tō-mē) The surgical opening of a fallopian tube that has been occluded or for drainage purposes.

salpingotomy (săl″pĭng-gŏt′ă-mē) [″ +

tome, incision] Incision of a fallopian tube.

salpinx (săl′pĭnks) *pl.* **salpinges** [Gr., tube] A fallopian tube or the eustachian tube.

salt (salt) **1. Sodium** chloride. **2.** Pert. to, containing or treated with salt. **3.** To treat with salt or make salty. **4.** Any mineral salt or saline mixture used as an aperient or cathartic, e.g., epsom salts or Glauber salt. **5.** In chemistry, a compound consisting of a positive ion other than hydrogen and a negative ion other than hydroxyl. **6.** A chemical compound resulting from the interaction of an acid and a base.

Salts and water are the inorganic (mineral) constituents of the body. They play specific roles in the functions of cells and are indispensable for life. The principal salts are chlorides, carbonates, bicarbonates, sulfates, and phosphates, combined with sodium, potassium, calcium, or magnesium.

Salts serve the following roles in the body: maintenance of proper osmotic conditions; maintenance of water balance; regulation of blood volume; maintenance of proper acid-base balance; provision for essential constituents of tissue, esp. of bones and teeth; maintenance of normal irritability of muscle and nerve cells; maintenance of conditions for coagulation of the blood; provision for essential components of certain enzyme systems, respiratory pigments and hormones; and regulation of cell membrane and capillary permeability. SEE: *sodium chloride.*

alkaline s. SEE: *hydrogen sulfide in Poisons and Poisoning Appendix.*

aminohippuric acid sodium s. The sodium salt of aminohippuric acid. It is given intravenously to test renal blood flow and the excretory capacity of the renal tubules.

basic s. 1. A salt retaining the ability to react with an acid radical. **2.** A salt of a strong base and a weak acid, which has a pH > 7.0, e.g., sodium acetate.

bath s.s 1. Any of several water-soluble inorganic crystalline compounds, such as Epsom salts (magnesium sulfate), baking soda (sodium bicarbonate), or table salt (sodium chloride), usually colored and scented, and designed to be added to a bath. The salts soften the bathwater and purportedly improve cleaning and enhance the bathing experience. **2.** Methylenedioxypyrovalerone.

bile s. Any of the alkali salts of bile sodium glycocholate and sodium taurocholate.

buffer s. A salt that fixes excess amounts of acid or alkali without a change in hydrogen ion concentration.

double s. Any salt formed from two other salts.

epsom s. Magnesium sulfate.

glow s. Rubbing of the entire body with moist salt for stimulation.

hypochlorite s. A salt of hypochlorous acid used in household bleach and as an oxidizer, deodorant, and disinfectant.

iodized s. A salt containing a trace amount of sodium or potassium iodide in sodium chloride. It is an important source of iodine in the diet. Its use prevents goiter due to iodine deficiency.

neutral s. An ionic compound containing no replaceable hydrogen or hydroxyl ions.

rock s. Sodium chloride in its natural state of rocklike masses in beds or flats.

sea s. A mixture of salts, mainly sodium chloride, obtained by evaporation from sea water.

smelling s. A colloquial term for *aromatic spirits of ammonia.* When the sealed capsule is opened, pungent ammonia gas is released.

substitute s. A chemical, e.g., potassium chloride, with a flavor like that of table salt but with a negligible sodium content. It is used by those whose medical condition requires limited sodium intake.

table s. Sodium chloride.

saltation (săl-tā′shŭn) [L. *saltatio,* leaping] An act of leaping or dancing, as in chorea.

saltatory (săl′tă-tō″rē) Pert. to dancing or leaping.

saltatory conduction The transmission of a nerve impulse along a myelinated nerve fiber. The action potential occurs only at the nodes of Ranvier, making velocity faster than along unmyelinated fibers.

Salter-Harris fracture (săl′tĕr-hăr′ĭs) A classification system to categorize growth plate fractures as one of five types based on the mechanism of injury and the relationship of the fracture line(s) to the epiphyseal plate. The original five types of fractures, since separated by other specialists, were type I—a transverse fracture across the physis; type II—a fracture through the physis and metaphysis but not the epiphysis; type III—a fracture through the physis and epiphysis; type IV—an intra-articular fracture involving the epiphysis, physis, and metaphysis and type V—a compression on the epiphyseal plate. SEE: illus.

salting out A method of separating a specific protein from a mixture of proteins by the addition of a salt (e.g., ammonium sulfate).

salt-losing syndrome The condition of greatly increased sodium loss from the body as a result of renal disease, adrenocortical insufficiency, or gastrointestinal disease.

saltpeter, saltpetre (salt′pĕt′ĕr) [L. *sal petrae,* salt of rock] A common name for potassium nitrate.

Chile s. A common name for sodium

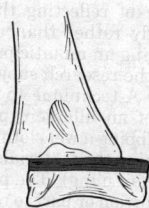

I: Fracture Extends through the physis, separating the two segments; Common in infants

II: Fracture starts though the physis and ends on the shaft, creating a displaced wedge

III: The fracture line extends perpendicularly through the joint surface and then transversely across the physis, resulting in partial displacement of the segment. Growth of the involved physis may be compromised.

IV: Similar to type III fracture, but the transverse line extends across the physis into the shaft. Surgical fixation is often required and physeal growth may be affected

SALTER-HARRIS FRACTURE

V: A crushing injury that compresses the physis. If undetected, avascular necrosis may occur and growth may be inhibited

nitrate, $NaNO_3$; a crystalline powder, saline in taste and soluble in water.

salt poisoning SEE: under *poisoning*.

salubrious (să-lū′brē-ŭs) [L. *salubris*, healthful] Promoting or favorable to health; wholesome.

saluretic Natriuretic.

salutary (săl′ū-tā″rē) [L. *salutaris*, health] Healthful; promoting health; curative.

salvage therapy Treatment that follows the relapse of an illness that had already been treated in standard fashion.

salve (săv) [AS. *sealf*] Ointment.

Salvia (sal′vē-ă) [L. *salvia*, sage (the herb)] A genus of herbs in the mint family

    S. hispanica SEE: *chia*.

    S. miltiorrhiza A species native to China and Japan, valued for its roots as a traditional Chinese herbal remedy. It has been used to treat cardiovascular diseases. Its effectiveness is unproven in humans. It increases the risk of bleeding and should be avoided by patients taking aspirin, warfarin, and other antiplatelet or anticoagulant drugs. SYN: *danshen*.

samaritanism Compassion.

samarium (să-mar′ē-ŭm) [*samarskite*, the mineral in which the element was first found + *-ium*] SYMB: Sm. A rare metallic element of the lanthanide series, atomic weight (mass) 150.35, atomic number 62. Isotopes of samarium are used in nuclear medicine to identify and treat osteoblastic bone metastases and osteogenic sarcoma.

samarium–153 A radiopharmaceutical used to treat bone pain caused by cancer metastases.

Sambucus nigra (sam-bū′kŭs nig′ră, -boo′) [L. *sambucus nigra,* black elderbery] SEE: *elderberry.*

SAM-e *S-adenosylmethionine.*

SAMPLE An acronym to remind the EMS provider the areas to explore in obtaining the patient's medical history. It stands for *symptoms, allergies, medications, pertinent* past medical history, *last* oral intake, and *events* leading up to the incident.

sample (sam′pĕl) **1.** A piece or portion of a whole that demonstrates the characteristics or quality of the whole, e.g., a specimen of blood. **2.** In research, a portion of a population selected to represent the entire population. SEE: *specimen.*

   biased s. In epidemiology or medical research, a sample of a group that does not equally represent the members of the group.

   convenience s. A group of research subjects selected casually, without scrupulously randomizing them, usually because they are easily accessible to the researcher.

   fasting blood s. A laboratory specimen obtained after the patient has abstained from eating for a minimum of 8 hr.

   PATIENT CARE: Fasting samples are used to gauge lipid levels and blood sugar, e.g., in the diagnosis and evaluation of diabetes mellitus or hypercholesterolemia. SYN: *fasting blood draw; fasting blood test.*

   fetal blood s. A small amount of blood drawn from a fetal scalp vein to assess acid-base status. The normal fetal blood pH level is 7.25. Levels between 7.20 and 7.24 reflect a preacidotic state; levels below 7.20 indicate acidosis and fetal jeopardy.

   grab s. In public health and medical statistics, a chaotic set of data from which conclusions are carelessly drawn. Because the sample is not carefully randomized or scientifically selected, the conclusions derived from such sample groups may be inaccurate.

   judgment s. A research cohort whose members are chosen because they share a common set of qualities. Because of the selection criteria used in assembling the group, the judgment sample is not random, and the conclusions drawn from research on such a sample do not have broad applicability to the larger community.

   quota s. A cohort of research subjects selected because a certain percentage of them has a desired characteristic.

   random s. In experimental medicine and epidemiology, an unbiased selection of individuals or items. A random sam-

ple is chosen in research investigations so that study results will have a high probability of reflecting the variables under study rather than unintentionally reflecting an unanticipated characteristic of the research subjects.

   wipe s. A technique to identify the presence of an allergen, pathogen, or toxin by rubbing a wet cloth on a surface and analyzing the materials it picks up.

sampling (sam′pling) The process of selecting a portion or part to represent the whole.

   chorionic villus s. ABBR: CVS. A procedure for obtaining a sample of the chorionic villi. In one method, a catheter is inserted into the cervix and the outer portion of the membranes surrounding the fetus. Microscopic and chemical examination of the sample is useful in prenatal evaluation of the chromosomal, enzymatic, and DNA status of the fetus. CVS may be performed between gestational weeks 8 and 12 in women who are at high-risk for serious fetal chromosomal abnormalities.

   PATIENT CARE: Ultrasonography precedes the CVS in order to identify the location of the fetus and placenta and to avoid injury. Based on ultrasonographic findings, the CVS is performed either through the vagina (with a speculum to visualize the cervix) or through the lower abdominal wall (with a needle). The patient is prepared in either case with sterile cleansing of the area. Her Rh status is determined, and Rh-negative women are given Rh immunoglobulin after CVS. Many women experience cramping or pelvic pressure during the procedure. Potential complications include postprocedure bleeding, infection (chorioamnionitis), fetal injury, or miscarriage, which occurs after roughly 1% to 2% of CVS procedures. After CVS a friend, partner, spouse, or family member should take the patient home. Activities should be limited for about 24 hr. Women affected by symptoms suggestive of complications should return promptly for follow-up care.

   fetal scalp blood s. Obtaining a small amount of blood from the fetal scalp for pH testing. When the monitor recording suggests fetal compromise during labor, the physician or nurse-midwife may elect to perform this procedure. The normal finding for fetal pH is at or above 7.25. Findings between 7.20 and 7.24 indicate a preacidotic state; if the pH is below 7.20, acidosis is present.

   fine-needle capillary s. ABBR: FNC. Obtaining cells from tissue by repeatedly entering the tissue with a small gauge, e.g., 27 g, needle that is not attached to a syringe. The cells obtained in the needle tip are placed on a microscope slide for cytologic analysis. FNC is used, often with fine-needle aspiration biopsy, to evaluate thyroid nodules. SYN: *fine-needle nonaspiration biopsy.*

random s. Randomization.

Samter triad (sam'tĕr) [Max Samter, Ger. immunologist, 1909–1999] Aspirin allergy, asthma, and nasal polyposis.

sanatorium (săn″ă-tō'rē-ŭm) [L. *sanatorius,* healing] Sanitarium.

sand (sănd) [AS.] Fine grains of disintegrated rock.

brain s. Concretion of matter near the base of the pineal gland. SYN: *corpora arenacea.*

sandflies Flies of the order Diptera belonging to the genus *Phlebotomus.* They transmit sandfly fever, Oroya fever, and various types of leishmaniasis.

sandfly fever SEE: under *fever.*

Sandhoff disease (sand'hof″) A rare form of Tay-Sachs disease in which two essential enzymes (hexosaminidase A and B) for metabolizing gangliosides are absent. In Tay-Sachs disease only one enzyme, hexosaminidase A, is absent.

SANE (sān) *Sexual Assault Nurse Examiner.*

sane (sān) [L. *sanus,* healthy] Sound of mind; mentally normal.

Sanfilippo syndrome (san″fĭ-lip'ōz) [S. J. Sanfilippo, contemporary U.S. pediatrician] Mucopolysaccharidosis III.

sanguinarine (săng'gwĭn-ă-rĭn) A benzophenanthridine alkaloid available as an oral rinse and toothpaste. It is used to treat dental plaque and gingivitis.

sanguine (săng'gwĭn) [L. *sanguineus,* bloody] **1.** Optimistic; cheerful. **2.** Plethoric, bloody; marked by abundant and active blood circulation, particularly a ruddy complexion. **3.** Pert. to or consisting of blood.

sanguineous (săng-gwĭn'ē-ŭs) [L. *sanguineus,* bloody] **1.** Bloody; relating to blood. **2.** Having an abundance of blood. SYN: *plethoric.*

sanguinopurulent (săng″gwĭ-nō-pū′rū-lĕnt) [″ + *purulentus,* full of pus] Concerning or containing blood and pus.

sanguis (săng'gwĭs) [L.] Blood.

sanies (sā'nē-ēz) [L., thin, fetid pus] A thin, fetid, greenish discharge from a wound or ulcer, appearing as pus tinged with blood.

saniopurulent (sā″nē-ō-pū′roo-lĕnt) [L. *sanies,* thin, fetid pus, + *purulentus,* full of pus] Having characteristics of sanies and pus; pert. to a fetid, serous, blood-tinged discharge containing pus.

sanitarian (săn″ĭ-tā′rē-ăn) [L. *sanitas,* health] A person who by training and experience is skilled in sanitation and public health.

sanitarium (săn-ĭ-tā′rē-ŭm) [L. *sanitas,* health] An institution for the treatment and recuperation of persons having physical or mental disorders. SYN: *sanatorium.*

sanitary (san'ĭ-ter″ē) [L. *sanitas,* health] **1.** Pert. to or promoting good health. **2.** Clean, free of dirt. **3.** Free of pathogens or toxins.

sanitary napkin A perineal pad, esp. one used for absorbing menstrual fluid. SEE: *menstrual tampon; menstruation.*

sanitation (săn″ĭ-tā′shŭn) [L. *sanitas,* health] The formulation and application of measures to promote and establish conditions favorable to health, esp. public health. SEE: *hygiene.*

sanitize (san'ĭ-tīz″) **1.** To make sanitary. **2.** To inactivate or remove microorganisms from equipment and surfaces. Chemicals, heat, and ionizing radiation can be used. **sanitizer** (-tīz″ĕr), *n.* **sanitization** (săn″ĭt-ĭ-zā′shŏn), *n.*

sanity (săn'ĭ-tē) **1.** Soundness of health or mind; mentally normal. **2.** The ability to think logically or rationally.

SA node Sinoatrial node of the heart.

SaO₂ *oxygen saturation.*

sap (săp) [AS. *saep*] **1.** A fluid essential to the life of plants. **2.** To cause gradual exhaustion or weakness, as to sap one's strength.

cell s. Cytoplasm.

nuclear s. An old term for the contents of a cell's nucleus.

saphena (să-fē'nă) *pl.* **saphenae** [Gr. *saphenes,* manifest] A saphenous vein.

saphenectomy (săf″ĕ-nĕk′tō-mē) [″ + *ektome,* excision] The surgical removal of a saphenous vein.

saphenous (să-fē'nŭs) Pert. to a saphenous vein or nerve.

saphenous nerve A deep branch of the femoral nerve. In the lower leg, it follows the great saphenous vein and supplies the medial side of the leg, ankle, and foot.

saphenous opening SEE: under *opening.*

saphenous vein SEE: under *vein.*

saponification (să-pon″ĭ-fĭ-kā′shŏn) [L. *sapo,* soap + *facere,* to make] **1.** Conversion into soap. It is the hydrolysis or the splitting of fat by an alkali yielding glycerol and three molecules of alkali salt of the fatty acid, the soap. **2.** Hydrolysis of an ester into its corresponding alcohol and acid (free or in the form of a salt).

saponify (să-pŏn′ĭ-fī) To convert into a soap, as when fats are treated with an alkali to produce a free alcohol plus the salt of the fatty acid. Thus, stearin, saponified with sodium hydroxide, yields the alcohol glycerol plus the soap sodium stearate.

saponin (săp'ō-nĭn) [Fr. *saponine,* soap] An unabsorbable glucoside contained in the roots of some plants that forms a lather in an aqueous solution. Saponins cause hemolysis of red blood cells even in high dilutions. When taken orally, they may cause diarrhea and vomiting. Mixtures of saponins are used as laboratory reagents to hemolyze specimens before analysis.

sapro-, sapr- [Gr. *sapros*, rotten] Prefixes meaning *putrid, rotten*.

saprobe (să′prōb) [Gr. *sapros*, putrid, + *bios*, life] Saprophyte. **saprobic,** *adj.*

saprophyte (săp′rō-fīt) [″ + *phyton*, plant] Any organism living on decaying or dead organic matter. Most of the fungi and bacteria are saprophytes. SYN: *saprobe.* SEE: *parasite.* **saprophytic** (-fīt′ĭk), *adj.*

SAPS *secondary antiphospholipid antibody syndrome.*

SAR *specific absorption rate*

Sarcina (săr′sĭ-nă) [L., bundle] A genus of cocci of the family Micrococcaceae. These bacteria are saprophytes and tend to appear in packets of four or eight following binary fission.

sarcina (săr′sĭ-nă) *pl.* **sarcinassarcinae** Any organism of the genus *Sarcina*.

sarco-, sarc- [Gr. *sarx*, stem *sark-*, flesh] Prefixes meaning *flesh* or *muscle*.

sarcocyst (săr′kō-sĭst) [″ + *kystis*, bladder] An elongated tubular body produced by *Sarcocystis*.

Sarcocystis (săr″kō-sĭs′tĭs) [″ + *kystis*, bladder] A genus of sporozoa found in the muscles of higher vertebrates (reptiles, birds, and mammals).

   S. hominis An intracellular protozoan parasite. It was formerly known as *Isospora hominis*.

   S. lindemanni A species infesting the muscles of humans, causing myositis, eosinophilia, and fever.

sarcocystosis (săr″kō-sĭs-tō′sĭs) [″ + ″] Parasitic infection with members of the genus *Sarcocystis*, which causes sarcocysts.

Sarcodina (săr-kō-dī′nă) [″ + *eidos*, form, shape] A subphylum of protozoa that includes the order Amoebida. It is characterized by pseudopod locomotion.

sarcoid (săr′koyd) [″ + *eidos*, form, shape] **1.** Resembling flesh. **2.** A small epithelioid tubercle-like lesion characteristic of sarcoidosis.

   Boeck s. SEE: *Boeck sacroid.*

sarcoidosis (săr″koyd-ō′sĭs) [″ + ″ + *osis*, condition] A chronic multisystem disease of unknown cause, characterized by noncaseating (hard) granulomas and lymphocytic alveolitis. Sarcoidosis occurs most often in the southeastern U.S., is 10 times more common in blacks than whites, and is more common in women than men. SEE: illus.

SYMPTOMS: The lungs are involved in 90% of cases and are the basis for the initial symptoms of fatigue, weight loss, anorexia, night sweats, shortness of breath, and a nonproductive cough. Hilar lymphadenopathy may precede the development of respiratory symptoms from alveolitis. Peripheral lym-

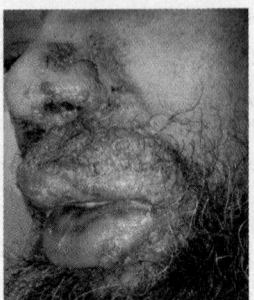

SARCOIDOSIS

phadenopathy, iritis, skin lesions, splenomegaly, hepatomegaly, interstitial nephritis, peritoneal disease, involvement of other visceral organs, and skeletal changes are seen in patients with widespread disease. Immunological abnormalities include T-cell lymphocytopenia, increased blood monocyte count, and anergic reactions to skin tests for common allergens. In approx. 60% to 70% of patients, no permanent damage to the lungs or other organs occurs. Approx. 20% develop residual lung or eye damage, and 10% die of progressive pulmonary fibrosis or associated right-sided heart failure (cor pulmonale).

DIAGNOSIS: Diagnosis is made through clinical, radiographical, and histological findings. Sarcoidosis must be differentiated from other diseases that cause granulomas, e.g., tuberculosis, histoplasmosis, and other fungal infections.

TREATMENT: Sarcoidosis may progress insidiously or rapidly or may remit as the result of treatment with corticosteroids.

sarcolemma (săr″kō-lěm′ă) [″ + *lemma*, husk] The cell membrane of a muscle cell. Transverse tubules penetrate the cytoplasm adjacent to the myofibrils and carry the action potential to the interior of the muscle cell.

sarcoma (săr-kō′mă) *pl.* **sarcomata** [″ + *oma*, tumor] A cancer arising from mesenchymal tissue such as muscle or bone, which may affect the bones, bladder, kidneys, liver, lungs, parotids, and spleen. SEE: *Kaposi sarcoma.*

   botryoid s. A rare malignant connective tissue tumor occurring in the uterus, bladder, vagina, liver, or biliary tree. SYN: *rhabdosarcoma, embryonal.*

   endometrial s. A malignant neoplasm of the endometrial stroma.

   giant cell s. Giant cell **tumor**.

   osteogenic s. A sarcoma composed of bony tissue. It is the most common bony cancer and typically afflicts adolescents. SYN: *osteosarcoma.*

reticulum cell s. A rare form of malignant large cell lymphoma.

spindle cell s. A sarcoma consisting of small and large spindle-shaped cells.

sarcomatoid (sar-kō'mă-toyd) [Gr. *sarx*, flesh, + *oma*, tumor, + *eidos*, form, shape] Resembling a sarcoma.

sarcomatosis (săr″kō-mă-tō'sĭs) [″ + ″ + *osis*, condition] A condition marked by the presence and spread of a sarcoma; sarcomatous degeneration.

sarcomatous (săr-kō'mă-tŭs) Pert. to a sarcoma.

sarcomere (săr'kō-mēr) [″ + *meros*, a part] The unit of contraction of the myofibrils of a muscle cell, made of protein filaments arranged between two Z disks. Thick filaments are made primarily of myosin; thin filaments are made of actin, troponin, tropomyosin, and nebulin. Desmin, myomesin, and titin are stabilizing proteins.

sarcopenia (săr″kō-pēn'ē-ă) Loss of muscular mass and strength, esp. in striated muscles. Sarcopenia commonly occurs with aging as a result of the combined effects of changes in exercise, nutrition, and hormonal activation of muscles (e.g., by growth and steroid hormones).

Sarcophagidae (sar″kō-faj'ĭ-dē) [*sarco-* + *phag-* + *-idea*] The family of flies of the order Diptera that includes the flesh flies. Females deposit their eggs or larvae on the decaying flesh of dead animals. Larvae of two genera, *Sarcophaga* and *Wohlfahrtia*, frequently infest open sores and wounds of humans, giving rise to cutaneous myiasis. SEE: *myiasis*.

sarcoplasm (săr'kō-plăzm) [″ + LL. *plasma*, form, mold] The cytoplasm of muscle cells, esp. striated muscle cells.

sarcoplasmic (săr″kō-plăz'mĭk) Pert. to sarcoplasm.

Sarcoptes (săr-kŏp'tēz) A genus of Acarina that includes the mites that infest humans and animals. *Sarcoptes scabiei* causes scabies in humans. SEE: illus.

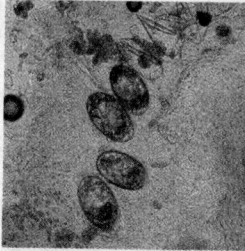

SARCOPTES SCABIEI

sarcosporidiosis (săr″kō-spō-rĭd″ē-ō'sĭs) [″ + ″ + *osis*, condition] Infestation with organisms of the order Sarcosporidia or the condition produced by them.

sarcous (săr'kŭs) [Gr. *sarko*, flesh] Pert. to flesh or muscle.

sarin (săr'ĭn) [An acronym of *Schrader, Ambros, Rüdiger,* and *Van der Linde,* its discoverers] Isopropylmethylphosphonofluoridate; an extremely toxic nerve gas.

SARS (sărz) *severe acute respiratory distress syndrome.*

sarsaparilla (sas″(ă-)pă-ril'ă) A vine (*Smilax officinalis*) that produces a berry used to make root beer. Extracts from the plant contain antioxidants used for many traditional remedies, including treatment of skin diseases such as psoriasis, and sexually transmitted diseases such as syphilis and herpes simplex.

SARS-CoV (sărz'kō-vē') *SARS coronavirus* (the cause of severe acute respiratory distress syndrome).

SART *Sexual Assault Response Team.*

sartorius (săr-tō'rē-ŭs) [L. *sartor,* tailor] A long, ribbon-shaped muscle in the leg that flexes, abducts, laterally rotates the thigh, and flexes the lower leg. This muscle, the longest in the body, enables the crossing of the legs in the tailor's position.

sashimi (să-shī'mē) A traditional Japanese food made of raw fish, usually served as an appetizer. It can occasionally be a source of food-borne toxins or infections. Ingestion of raw fish has been associated with the parasitic infestation anisaikiasis.

sat *saturated.*

satellite (săt'l-īt) [L. *satelles,* attendant] A small structure attached to a larger one, esp. a minute body attached to a chromosome by a slender chromatin filament.

bacterial s. A bacterial colony that grows best when close to a colony of another microorganism. For example, *Haemophilus influenzae* will grow as satellite colonies around the colonies of *Staphylococcus aureus* on blood agar plates.

satellitosis (săt″l-ī-tō'sĭs) [″ + Gr. *osis,* condition] The accumulation of neuroglial cells about neurons of the central nervous system. This condition is seen in certain degenerative and inflammatory conditions.

satiation (sā″shē-ā'shŭn) In nutritional science, a sense of satisfaction or fullness with a meal that keeps a person from wanting to eat any more food.

satiety (sā-tī'ĕt-ē) [L. *satietas,* enough] Being full to satisfaction, esp. with food.

satiety index SEE: under *index.*

saturated (săt'ū-rā″tĕd) [L. *saturare,* to fill] Holding all that can be absorbed, received, or combined, as a solution in which no more of a substance can be dissolved. This term is applied to hydrocarbons in which the maximum number of hydrogen atoms is present and there are no double or triple bonds between the carbon atoms. It is also applied to the hemoglobin-oxygen complex found in red blood cells when no more oxygen can reversibly bind to the hemoglobin.

saturated compound SEE: under *compound*.

saturated hydrocarbon SEE: under *hydrocarbon*.

saturation (săt″ū-rā′shŭn) **1.** The state in which all of a substance that can be dissolved in a solution is dissolved. Adding more of the substance will not increase the concentration. **2.** In organic chemistry, the conversion of all available carbon atom valences so that there are no double or triple bonds between the carbon atoms.

saturation index SEE: under *index*.

saturation time SEE: under *time*.

saturnine (sat′ŭr-nīn″) [L. *Saturnus*, the Roman god; the planet was believed to be made of lead] Pert. to or produced by lead.

saturnism (săt′ŭr-nĭzm) [″ + Gr. *-ismos*, condition] Lead poisoning. SYN: *plumbism*.

saucerization (so″sĕr-ĭ-zā′shŏn) The surgical creation of a shallow area in tissue to remove devitalized tissue and to facilitate drainage. It is used, for example, in biopsies of the skin to remove lesions that extend below the epidermis. **saucerize** (so′sĕr-īz″), *v*.

sauna (so′nă) [Finnish] An enclosure in which a person is exposed to moderate to very high temperatures and often high humidity, produced by water poured on heated stones. A stay in the sauna may be followed by a cool bath or shower. Sauna water is not sterile and may contain harmful microorganisms, including yeasts and molds. Even though the sauna has no proven benefits in preventing illnesses or promoting fitness, the regimen does help to promote relaxation, relieve aches and pains, and loosen stiff joints.

⚠️ Saunas are not advised for those with fever, those who are dehydrated, or those who are unable to sweat. Those who have recently used alcohol or have participated in strenuous exercise should not use a sauna. If soft tissue has been traumatized in the past 24 to 48 hr, the sauna should not be used. Prolonged exposure to the sauna may be dangerous due to induced hyperthermia, dehydration, and renal failure.

savings account, medical A savings account in which deposits may accumulate tax-free and be used as self-financed health insurance to pay incurred or anticipated medical expenses. It is also called a "health-savings account."

saw (so) A cutting instrument with an edge of sharp toothlike projections; used esp. for cutting bone in surgery.

    Gigli s. SEE: *Gigli saw*.

    Stryker s. SEE: under *Stryker, Homer H.*

saw palmetto (pal-met′ō) A low-growing, spreading palm (*Serenoa repens*) native to Florida and the southeastern U.S. coast, whose extract is used to treat benign prostatic hyperplasia. In alternative medicine the synonym *Sabal serrulatum* is used. Research on the clinical effectiveness of saw palmetto is inconclusive.

⚠️ Women of childbearing age, esp. pregnant or breast-feeding women, should avoid saw palmetto.

saxitoxin (săk″sĭ-tŏk′sĭn) A neurotoxin produced by some dinoflagellates and concentrated during feeding by mollusks such as mussels and clams. It causes paralytic shellfish poisoning.

Sb Symbol for the element antimony.

SBE *subacute bacterial endocarditis*.

Sc Symbol for the element scandium.

sc *subcutaneously*.

scab (skăb) [ME. *scabbe*] **1.** The crust of a cutaneous sore, wound, ulcer, or pustule formed by drying of the discharge. **2.** To become covered with a crust.

scabicide (skā′bĭ-sīd) An agent that kills mites, esp. the causative agent of scabies.

scabies (skā′bēz) [L. *scabies*, itch] A contagious infestation of the skin with the itch mite, *Sarcoptes scabiei*. It typically presents as an intensely pruritic rash, composed of scaly papules, insect burrows, and secondarily infected lesions distributed in the webs between the fingers and on the waistline, trunk (esp. the axillae), penis, and arms. It readily spreads in households, among playmates, and between sexual partners. SEE: illus.; Nursing Diagnoses Appendix. **scabietic** (-ĕt′ĭk), *adj*.

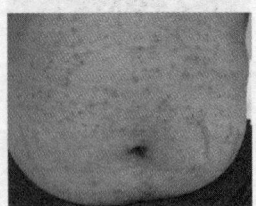

SCABIES

SYMPTOMS: An itchy rash that worsens at night and that involves multiple members of the same household is a common presentation.

DIAGNOSIS: Because the disease is often missed and occasionally overdiagnosed, scrapings from suspect lesions are examined microscopically to confirm the presence of the mite, its eggs, or its excretions.

PATIENT CARE: For children 2 months and older and nonpregnant adults, permethrin 5% cream is applied to the entire body surface. The eyes and mouth are avoided when the cream is being applied. The cream is thoroughly washed off after about 8 to 14 hr. Retreatment is sometimes required if the itch persists for more than a few weeks. Alternatively, nonpregnant patients may be treated with ivermectin given orally. Pregnant women and infants under 2 months of age should be treated with 6% precipitated sulfur in petrolatum daily for 3 days. Infection control in the home includes the washing of all linens, towels, and clothing with hot water and drying them thoroughly.

scaffold (skaf'ōld″) A framework or structural element that holds cells or tissues together.

scala (skā'lă) [L. *scala,* staircase] Any of the three spiral passages of the cochlea of the inner ear.

   s. tympani The duct filled with perilymph that is below the organ of Corti. It extends from the round window to the tip of the cochlea.

   s. vestibuli The duct filled with perilymph that is above the organ of Corti. It extends from the oval window to the tip of the cochlea, where it communicates with the scala tympani through an aperture, the helicotrema.

scalability (skā″lă-bĭ'lĭ-tē) The ability of a health care system to expand to meet increased demands by users. The term is most often applied to the response of electronic health record software to periodic fluctuations in use but is also applied to the ability of health care systems to respond to surges in demand for clinical services.

scald (skŏld) [ME. *scalden,* to burn with hot liquid] **1.** A burn of the skin or flesh caused by moist heat and hot vapors, as steam. **2.** To cause a burn with hot liquid or steam.

   The burn from a scald is deeper than a burn from dry heat. Healing is slower and scar formation greater in scalds. Emergency treatment of a scalded area should include immediate application of cold in the most readily available form, (i.e., ice packs or immersion of the part in very cold water). This should be continued for at least 1 hr.

¹scale (skal) [L. *scala,* staircase] **1.** A graduated or proportioned measure. **2.** A tool that rates people, places, or things in relation to one another.

   absolute s. A scale used for indicating low temperatures based on absolute zero. It is used in thermodynamic calculations of, for example, heat/energy transfer. SYN: *Kelvin scale.* SEE: *absolute temperature; absolute zero.*

   Activities-Specific Balance Confidence S. ABBR: ABC. A 16-item instrument designed to measure a patient's perceived level of confidence in performing common activities of daily living (ADLs) without losing balance and falling. The patient ranks his confidence to complete each item from 0% (no confidence) to 100% (complete confidence).

   ASIA Impairment s. A method of assessing the degree of motor and sensory impairment in spinal cord injured patients. The assessment is based on an examination of the perineum and anus, i.e., on the S4-S5 level of the spinal cord. Grade: A – Complete: No motor or sensory function; Grade B – Incomplete, sensory function is intact, but motor function is absent below and including the S4-S5 level; Grade C – Incomplete, motor function is preserved below the neurological level and more than half of the primary muscles have a muscle grade test of less than 3; Grade D – Incomplete: Motor function is preserved and at least half of the muscles below the S4-S5 level have a muscle grade test of 3 or better; and Grade E – Normal.

   Borg dyspnea s. SEE: *Borg dyspnea scale.*

   Braden s. SEE: *Braden scale.*

   Brazelton Neonatal Assessment S. SEE: *Brazelton Neonatal Assessment Scale.*

   Celsius s. SEE: under *Celsius, Anders.*

   centigrade s. Celsius scale. SEE: under *Celsius, Anders.*

   Clinical Linguistic and Auditory Milestone S. ABBR: CLAMS. An office test used to evaluate language development in children from birth to age 3. SEE: *Denver Developmental Screening Test.*

   s. of contrast The range of densities on a radiograph; the number of tonal grays that are visible.

   Disability Rating S. An instrument to gauge the functional capabilities and progress of a person with moderate to severe brain injury. A person who has no deficits after recovery from brain injury receives a score of 0 (not impaired). A severely impaired person who is unemployable, unable to care for himself, and unable to open his eyes, move, or speak receives the lowest score (29).

   Fahrenheit s. SEE: under *Fahrenheit, Daniel Gabriel.*

   French s. A system to indicate the diameter of catheters and sounds. Each unit on the scale is approximately equivalent to one-third mm; thus a 21 French sound is 7 mm in diameter. The size of the diameter of the catheter increases as the numerical value of French increases.

Geriatric Depression S. ABBR: GDS. A 30-item questionnaire to screen for depression in older adults, e.g., when they first become eligible for Medicare.

Glasgow Coma S. ABBR: GCS. A scale to determine a patient's level of consciousness. It is a rating from 3 to 15 of the patient's ability to open his or her eyes, respond verbally, and move normally. The GCS is used primarily during the examination of patients with trauma or stroke. Repeated examinations can help determine if the patient's brain function is improving or deteriorating. Many EMS systems use the GCS for triage and for determining which patients should be intubated in the field. SEE: table; *coma; Trauma Score.*

Glasgow Outcome S. A scale that assesses current neurological awareness of the environment, and recovery and disability in all types of brain injury. The scale is used in the evaluation of trauma, stupor, or coma, and at prescribed time intervals, such as 3 months, 6 months, and 1 year after injury. The Glasgow group reports the greatest recovery in the 6-month period after injury. The nurse (or other health care practitioner) notes the patient's abilities at a particular time using this practical scale: *Good outcome:* may have minimal disabling sequelae but returns to independent functioning comparable to preinjury level and a full-time job; *Moderate disability:* is capable of independent functioning but not of returning to full-time employment; *Moderate*

Glasgow Coma Scale

Function		Score
Eye opening	spontan-eously	4
	to speech	3
	to pain	2
	none	1
Verbal response	oriented	5
	confused	4
	inappro-priate	3
	incompre-hensible	2
	none	1
Motor response	obeys commands	6
	localizes to pain	5
	withdraws from pain	4
	flexion to pain	3
	extension to pain	2
	none	1

disability: is capable of independent functioning but not of returning to full-time employment; *Severe disability:* depends on others for some aspect of daily living; *Persistive vegetative state:* has no obvious cortical functioning; *Dead.*

Global Assessment of Functioning S. ABBR: GAF scale. A scale that rates a person's social, occupational, and psychological functioning. The scale rates from high functioning, (i.e., highly adapted and integrated to one's environment) to poorly functioning (i.e., self-destructive, homicidal, isolated, or lacking the rudiments of self-care). There is a children's version of the scale, called the Children's Global Assessment of Functioning (CGAF).

Global Assessment of Relational Functioning S. ABBR: GARF scale. A measure of the degree to which a family meets the emotional and functional needs of its members.

hydrogen ion s. A scale used to express the degree of acidity or alkalinity of a solution. The classic pH scale extends from 0.00 (total acidity) to 14 (total alkalinity), the numbers running in inverse order of hydrogen ion (pH) concentration. The pH value is the negative logarithm of the hydrogen ion (pH) concentration of a solution, expressed in moles per liter.

As the hydrogen ion concentration decreases, a change of 1 pH unit means a 10-fold decrease in hydrogen ion concentration. Thus a solution with a pH of 1.0 is 10 times more acid than one with a pH of 2.0 and 100 times more acid than one with a pH of 3.0. A pH of 7.0 indicates neutrality. Very concentrated (>1molar) mineral acids and bases go beyond the classic scale to values < 0.00 and > 14, respectively.

As the hydrogen ion concentration varies in a definite reciprocal manner with the hydroxyl ion (OH^-) concentration, a pH reading above 7.0 indicates alkalinity. In the human body, arterial blood is slightly alkaline, having a normal pH range of 7.35 to 7.45. SEE: *pH.*

Karnofsky S. Karnofsky Index.

Kelvin s. SEE: under *Kelvin, Lord.*

Klein-Bell ADL S. SEE: *Klein-Bell ADL Scale.*

Kurtzke Expanded Disability Status S. SEE: *Kurtzke Expanded Disability Status Scale.*

Morse Falls S. SEE: *Morse Falls Scale.*

Motor Assessment S. An eight-item measurement tool used to assess motor function and physical mobility after a stroke.

Norton s. SEE: *Norton scale.*

Nottingham Extended Activities of Daily Living S. A widely used European scale of a person's activities of daily living that measures mobility and the ability to function in domestic tasks, kitchen tasks, and leisure activities. SEE: *instrumental activities of daily living*.

Oswestry Disability S. Oswestry Disability **Index**.

pain s. An assessment tool used to measure the intensity of a patient's discomfort. SEE: *Numerical Rating Scale; visual analog scale*.

Norton s. SEE: *Norton scale*.

Numerical Rating S., Numeric Rating Scale. ABBR: NRS. A variation of the visual analog scale that uses a scalar numbering system to objectify a patient's pain. Most numeric rating scales use a 10-cm line with tick marks spaced 1 cm apart. The leftmost mark is labeled "0" and has the notation "No Pain." The rightmost mark is labeled "10" and the notation "Worst pain imaginable." The patient is asked to indicate where on the continuum he or she would rate the current intensity of pain.

resource-based relative value s. ABBR: RBRVS. A scale for determining the monetary value of evaluation and management services provided to patients, i.e., services provided to patients by nonsurgeons. The scale is based on the total work required for a given service and on other considerations, including the cost of the physician's practice, the income lost during training, and the relative cost of liability insurance. SEE: *managed care; managed competition*.

Stroke Impact S. An instrument to measure the effect of a stroke on a person's mobility, speech, social activities, manual dexterity, strength, emotions, memory, and daily activities.

visual analog s. An instrument to quantify a subjective experience, such as the intensity of pain. A commonly used visual analog scale is a 10-cm line labeled with "worst pain imaginable" on the right border and "no pain" on the left border. The patient is instructed to make a mark along the line to represent the intensity of pain currently being experienced. The clinician records the distance of the mark in centimeters from the left end of the scale.

Wechsler Adult Intelligence S. SEE: under *Wechsler, David*.

Wechsler Intelligence S. for Children SEE: under *Wechsler, David*.

Zubrod performance s. SEE: *Zubrod performance scale*.

²scale (skal) [Fr. *escale*, husk] **1.** A small dry flake, shed from the upper layers of skin. Some shedding of skin is normal; scale increases in diseases like pityriasis rosea, psoriasis, and tinea pedis and after scratching the skin. SEE: illus. **2.** A film of tartar encrusting the teeth. **3.** To remove a film of tartar from the teeth. **4.** To form a scale on. **5.** To shed scales.

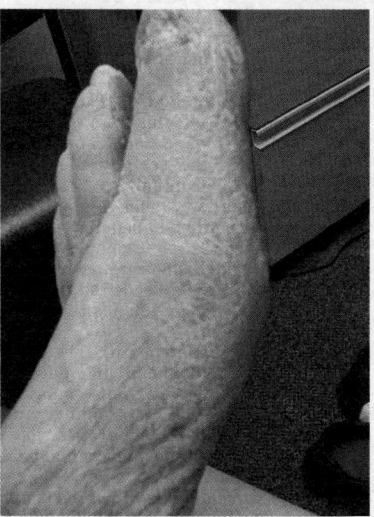

SCALE

³scale (skal) [Old Norse *skál*, bowl] An instrument for weighing.

scalene (skā′lēn″, skā-lēn′) [Gr. *skalēnos*, uneven] **1.** Pert. to a triangle with three unequal sides and angles. **2.** Pert. to a scalenus muscle.

scalenectomy (skā″lĕ-nĕk′tō-mē) [″ + *ektome*, excision] Resection of any of the scalenus muscles.

scalenotomy (skā″lĕ-nŏt′ō-mē) [″ + *tome*, incision] Surgical division of one or more of the scalenus muscles, as in the treatment of thoracic outlet syndrome. SYN: *scaleniotomy*.

scalenus (skā-lē′nŭs) [L., uneven] One of three deeply situated muscles on each side of the neck, extending from the tubercles of the transverse processes of the third through sixth cervical vertebrae to the first or second rib. The three muscles are the scalenus anterior (anticus), medius, and posterior.

scaler (skā′lĕr) [O.Fr. *escale*, husk] **1.** A dental instrument used to remove calculus from teeth. **2.** A device for counting pulses detected by a radiation detector.

magnetostrictive s. An electrically powered device used for calculus and tartar removal as an alternative to ultrasonic scaling or manual curettage. Typical units use a stack of metal strips in the handpiece and move in an elliptical pattern.

sickle s. A manual device used to remove supragingival calculus. The instrument has two parallel cutting edges on the face of the blade that converge to form a point. It is effective but slow and damages enamel more than ultrasonic or magnetostrictive scalers.

sonic s. Ultrasonic **s.**

ultrasonic s. A device that uses high-frequency vibration to remove stains and adherent deposits on the teeth. SYN: *sonic s.*

scaling (skāl'ĭng) [O.Fr. *escale,* husk] The removal of calculus from the teeth.

scall (skawl) [Norse *skalli,* baldhead] Dermatitis of the scalp producing a crusted scabby eruption.

scalloped (skal'ŏpt, skol') Having a boundary or border shaped in a series of connected waves or C-shapes. Some rashes (like the rash of cutaneous T-cell lymphoma) have raised red borders whose outer edge resembles the shape of a scallop shell.

scalp (skălp) [ME., sheath] The hairy integument of the head. In anatomy, this includes the skin, dense subcutaneous tissue, the occipitofrontalis muscle with the galea aponeurotica, loose subaponeurotic tissue, and cranial periosteum.

scalpel (skal'pĕl) [L. *scalpellum,* small surgical knife] A straight or angle-tipped handle for holding a surgical blade. SEE: illus.

harmonic s. ABBR: HS. An ultrasonic dissecting device used in surgery to disrupt, disintegrate, or coagulate tissues, esp. those with a high water or fat content. The device works by cavitating the tissues it contacts. When used laparoscopically, tissues destroyed by the scalpel are removed from the body by aspiration. SYN: *ultrasonic dissector.*

hemostatic s. A scalpel that cuts and cauterizes tissue at the same time.

plasma s. A scalpel that uses argon gas heated to an ionized plasma to divide tissues and cauterize bleeding blood vessels, e.g., during surgery or after trauma. SYN: *plasma* **knife.**

scaly (skā'lē) [O.Fr. *escale,* husk] Pert. to scales or flakes.

scan (skan) [Ult. fr L. *scandere,* to read or measure verse] **1.** An image obtained from a system that compiles information in a sequence pattern, such as computed tomography (CT), ultrasound, or magnetic resonance imaging. **2.** Scintiscan.

bone s. A nuclear medicine scan that uses short half-life radioactively labeled chemicals to make images of bones and bone diseases, such as occult fractures, osteomyelitis, or tumors. This is esp. useful in delineating osteomyelitis and metastases to the bone.

brain s. A procedure for imaging the structure and function of the brain.

CAT s. *computed axial tomography scan,* a colloquial term for computed tomography (CT) scan. SEE: *computed to-mography.*

coronary artery s. ABBR: CAS. A noninvasive diagnostic computed tomography (CT) scan that may identify patients at risk for atherosclerosis and coronary disease episodes by measuring calcium in the coronary arteries.

DEXA s. *dual energy x-ray* **absorptiometry** *.*

gamma s. Any radiologic technique that relies on the detection of gamma particle–emitting radionuclides. Examples of gamma scans are bone scans, gallium scans, and positron emission tomography scans.

HIDA s. An imaging procedure for evaluating diseases of the liver, gallbladder, and bile ducts. Hydroxy-iminodiacetic acid (HIDA), is injected into the bloodstream. Its excretion through the biliary tract is observed with a scintillation counter in a nuclear medicine laboratory. Normally HIDA travels from the bile ducts through the cystic duct and into the gallbladder, then out the common bile duct through the sphincter of Oddi into the duodenum. When the flow of bile is obstructed by disease (e.g., a stone, stricture, or malignancy), the passage of the tracer through the biliary tree is slowed or undetectable. SEE: *cholescintigraphy.*

Meckel s. SEE: under *Meckel, Johann Friedrich (the younger).*

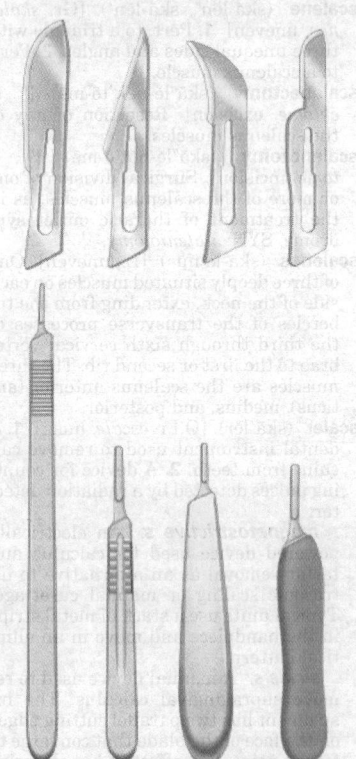

SCALPELS
A. Disposable B. Handles

milk s. A colloquial term for radionuclide reflux imaging. SEE: under *imaging*.

triple rule-out s. CT angiography performed on patients who come to the Emergency Department with chest pain of unknown cause. It is used to determine if a patient with chest pain has an acute coronary syndrome, a pulmonary embolism, or an aortic dissection.

ventilation/perfusion s. ABBR: V/Q scan. An imaging procedure used in the diagnosis of pulmonary embolism. The procedure has two parts: the injection of microscopic spheres into the bloodstream to evaluate perfusion of the lung; and the inhalation of xenon gas to assess pulmonary aeration. Certain patterns of mismatching between ventilation and perfusion of the lung are considered to be diagnostic of pulmonary embolism.

V/Q s. *ventilation/perfusion s.*

scandium (skan′dē-ŭm) [L. *Scandia*, Scandinavia, where the minerals were found containing the element + *-ium* (1)] SYMB: Sc. A rare, soft, lightweight transition metal, atomic weight 44.956, atomic number 21. It is used in health care in alloys, nanomolecules, and some lasers.

scanning (skan′ing) **1.** Recording on an image receptor the emission of radioactive waves from a specific substance injected into the body. **2.** Obtaining different images of a specified anatomical part through a system that compiles information in a sequential pattern, such as computed tomography, ultrasound, or magnetic resonance imaging.

renal s. Scintigraphy to determine renal function, size, and shape. A radioactive substance that concentrates in the kidney is given intravenously. The radiation emitted from the substance as it accumulates in the kidneys is recorded on a suitable photographic film.

scanning laser ophthalmoscope ABBR: SLO. A laser-powered ophthalmoscope for producing images of the choroid or retinal layers of the eye.

scanty (skǎn′tē) [ME. from O. Norse, *skamt*, short] Not abundant; insufficient, as a secretion.

scapha (skā′fä) [NL., skiff] An elongated depression of the ear between the helix and antihelix.

scapho-, scaph- [Gr. *skaphē*, boat] Prefixes meaning *boat-shaped, scaphoid*.

scaphoid (skǎf′oyd) [″ + *eidos*, form, shape] **1.** Boat-shaped, navicular, hollowed. **2.** SEE: under *bone*.

scapula (skǎpū-lä′) [L., shoulder blade] The large, flat, triangular bone that forms the posterior part of the shoulder. It articulates with the clavicle and the humerus. SYN: *shoulder blade*. SEE: illus.; *triceps*.

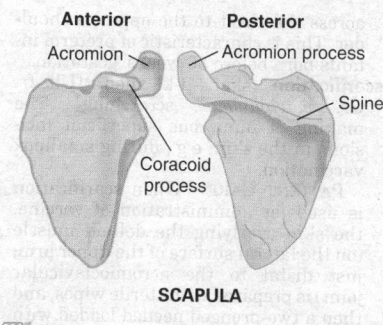

SCAPULA

plane of s. The angle of the scapula in its resting position, normally 30° to 45° forward from the frontal plane toward the sagittal plane. Movement of the humerus in this plane is less restricted than in the frontal or sagittal planes because the capsule is not twisted.

tipped s. A condition in which the inferior angle of the scapula is prominent, usually the result of faulty posture and a tight pectoralis minor muscle. Tipping is a normal motion when a person reaches with the hand behind the back.

winged s. A condition in which the medial border of the scapula is prominent, usually the result of paralysis of the serratus anterior or trapezius muscles. SYN: *angel's wing*.

scapular (skǎp′ū-lăr) Pert. to the shoulder blade.

scapulectomy (skǎp″ū-lĕk′tō-mē) [L. *scapula*, shoulder blade, + Gr. *ektome*, excision] Surgical excision of the scapula.

scapulo-, scapul- [L. *scapula*, shoulder, shoulder blade] Prefixes meaning *shoulder, scapula*.

scapulohumeral (skǎp″ū-lō-hū′mĕr-ăl) [″ + *humerus*, upper arm] Pert. to the scapula and humerus.

scapulothoracic (skǎp″ū-lō-thō-răs′ĭk) [″ + Gr. *thorax*, chest] Pert. to the scapula and thorax.

scapus (skā′pŭs) *pl.* **scapi** [L. *scapus*, stalk] A shaft or stem.

scar (skǎr) [Gr. *eskhara*, scab] A mark left in the skin or an internal organ by the healing of a wound, sore, or injury because of replacement by connective tissue of the injured tissue. Scars may result from wounds that have healed, lesions of diseases, or surgical operations. When it first develops a scar is red or purple. It later takes on the skin color of the patient. SYN: *cicatrix*. SEE: *keloid*.

Scarf sign (skarf) A newborn assessment finding in which the infant's elbow crosses the body midline without resistance as the examiner draws the arm across the chest to the opposite shoulder. This is characteristic of preterm infants born before 30 weeks' gestation.

scarification (skar″ĭ-fĭ-kā′shŏn) [Ult. fr. Gr. *skariphismos*, scratching] The making of numerous superficial incisions in the skin, e.g., during smallpox vaccination.

PATIENT CARE: When scarification is used for administration of vaccine, the skin overlying the deltoid muscle (on the lateral surface of the upper arm, just distal to the acromioclavicular joint) is prepared with sterile wipes, and then a two-pronged needed loaded with an infectious dose of the vaccine is inserted several times under the skin. The penetrated skin is then covered typically with a semi-occlusive dressing. Patients are advised not to disturb the dressing or the underlying lesion while it scabs or forms a scar to avoid spreading the virus to other body parts or other people. Vaccination may result in local discomfort and systemic symptoms such as fever or headache. A few weeks after vaccination, the skin forms a durable scar. This provides evidence that the vaccine has "taken."

scarifier (skăr′ĭ-fī″ĕr) An instrument for making small incisions in the skin. SYN: *scarificator*.

scarlatina (skăr″lă-tē′nă) [L., red] Scarlet **fever**.

   s. anginosa A severe form of scarlatina with extensive necrosis and ulceration of the pharynx and in some cases with peritonsillar abscess.

   s. hemorrhagica Scarlatina with hemorrhage into the skin and mucous membranes.

   s. maligna A fulminant and usually lethal form of scarlatina. **scarlatinal** (-năl), *adj.*

scarlatiniform (skăr-lă-tĭn′ĭ-form) [L. *scarlatina*, red, + *forma*, shape] Resembling scarlatina or its rash.

scarlet fever (skar′lĕt) [L. *scarlatum*] SEE: under *fever*.

scarlet rash A rose-colored rash, specifically that of German measles.

Scarpa, Antonio (skar′pă) Italian anatomist, 1752–1832.

   S. ganglion Vestibular **ganglion**.

SCAT *sheep cell agglutination test*.

scato-, scat- [Gr. *skōr*, stem *skat-*, dung] Prefixes meaning *excrement, fecal matter*. SEE: *sterco-*.

scatology (skă-tŏl′ō-jē) [Gr. *skato-*, dung, + *logos*, word, reason] **1.** Scientific study and analysis of the feces. SYN: *coprology*. **2.** Interest in obscene things, esp. obscene literature.

scatter (skat′ĕr) **1.** The diffusion of electromagnetic radiation when it strikes an object. SEE: *Compton scattering*. **2.** The dispersion or showering of objects from an initial location after energy is applied to them.

   coherent s. An interaction between x-rays and matter in which the incoming photon is absorbed by the atom and leaves with the same energy in a different direction. Less than 5% of the interactions between x-rays and matter in tissue are of this type.

   secondary s. Radiation created when a primary beam of radiation interacts with the patient's body. It is the source of most of the exposure among personnel.

scatter diagram Scattergram.

scattergram (skat′ĕr-gram″) **1.** A graph on which are clustered many data points representing the relation between two variables. **2.** A graph of blood cell populations generated by some types of blood cell analyzers. SYN: *scatter diagram*.

scavenger cell (skav′ĕn-jĕr) SEE: under *cell*.

SCBA *self-contained breathing apparatus*.

SCBU *special care baby unit*.

SCCM *Society of Critical Care Medicine*.

SCD *sequential compression **device***.

Sc.D. *Doctor of Science* (degree).

SCE *saturated calomel electrode*.

Scedosporium (sed″ō-spōr′ē-ŭm) A species of filamentous fungi that grow in soil and are occasionally responsible for fungal infections in humans (e.g., in the lung after inhalation, in skin, or in contaminated wounds). Two pathogenic species are *S. apiospermum* and *S. prolificans*.

scent (sĕnt) Odor.

Schäffer reflex (shăf′ĕr) [Max Schäffer, Ger. neurologist, 1852–1923] Dorsiflexion of the toes and flexion of the foot resulting when the middle portion of the Achilles tendon is pinched.

Schatzki ring (shăts′kē) [Richard Schatzki, U.S. radiologist, 1901–1992] A lower esophageal mucosal ring composed of a thin annular weblike tissue located at the squamocolumnar junction at or near the border of the lower esophageal sphincter. When the diameter of the ring is less than 1.3 cm, dysphagia is present. Treatment involves stretching the ring with dilators.

schedule (skej′ool″) [L. *schedula*, sheet of paper] A timetable, usually written; a plan for action to achieve a certain goal.

   fee s. A list of charges for health care services. Health care providers keep fee schedules in their offices to specify the amount of compensation they want for providing selected services. Managed care organizations and other medical insurance providers publish lists representing the maximum charges they will reimburse for the same services. In many instances, the reimbursement offered by insurers is less than that charged by health care providers. SYN: *fee sheet*.

wear s. The maximum or recommended time that a contact lens may be kept on the eye before it should be removed and cleansed.

Scheie procedure (shī) [Harold G. Scheie, U.S. ophthalmologist, 1909–1990] A treatment for primary open-angle glaucoma consisting of peripheral iridectomy and thermal sclerostomy.

Scheie syndrome (shī) [Harold Glendon Scheie, U.S. ophthalmologist, 1909–1990] Mucopolysaccharidosis IS.

schema (skē′mă) [Gr., shape] A shape, plan, or outline.

schematic (skē-măt′ĭk) [L. *schematicus,* shape, figure] Pert. to a diagram or model; showing part for part in a diagram.

Scheuermann disease (shoy′ĕr-mănz) [Holger W. Scheuermann, Danish physician, 1877–1960] Kyphosis of the spine, first identified in childhood (unlike adult-onset kyphosis, which usually results from osteoporotic compression fracture); sometimes referred to as "round-back". The incidence is about 0.4%, with no gender preference.

SYMPTOMS: About 50% of patients complain of back pain in the affected area; others complain of poor posture or fatigue. There are usually no neurological symptoms unless cord compression occurs.

DIAGNOSIS: The diagnosis is usually made from clinical presentation and the results of a standing x-ray examination of the spine.

TREATMENT: Symptomatic treatment may include nonsteroidal anti-inflammatory drugs, rest, and activity modification. Plaster casts and braces (including the Milwaukee brace) are used to correct the deformity and are usually successful if the child has not stopped growing. Surgery is reserved for those with a significant deformity and those who have stopped growing.

Schick test (shĭk) [Béla Schick, Hungarian-born U.S. pediatrician, 1877–1967] A test formerly used to determine the degree of immunity to diphtheria, in which a dilute toxin was injected intradermally. SEE: *diphtheria*.

Schilder disease (shil′dĕr) [Paul Ferdinand Schilder, Austrian-U.S. neurologist, 1886–1940] A rare variant of multiple sclerosis. It results in brain lesions that may resemble tumors or abscesses during neuroimaging. The disease may respond to treatment with immunosuppressing drugs. SYN: *myelinoclastic diffuse sclerosis*.

Schiller test (shil′ĕr) [Walter Schiller, Austrian-U.S. pathologist, 1887–1960] A test for superficial cancer, esp. of the uterine cervix. The tissue is painted with an iodine solution. Cells lacking glycogen fail to stain, and their presence may indicate a malignant change.

Schilling classification (shil′ing) [Victor Schilling, Ger. hematologist, 1883–1960] Classification of polymorphonuclear neutrophils into four categories according to the number and arrangement of the nuclei in the cells.

Schilling test (shil′ing) [Robert F. Schilling, U.S. hematologist, b. 1919] A test to assess the gastrointestinal absorption of vitamin B_{12} by oral radioactive vitamin B_{12} and injected nonradioactive B_{12}. It is used primarily to diagnose pernicious anemia but can also identify B_{12} malabsorption caused by other agents, including bacterial overgrowth of the gut and pancreatic insufficiency. A person with normal vitamin B_{12} absorption excretes between 8% and 40% of radiolabeled B_{12} in a 24-hr urine collection taken after the injection. Those with decreased B_{12} excretion are retested under several conditions: after receiving intrinsic factor with radiolabeled vitamin B_{12} after receiving antibiotics; and after receiving pancreatic enzymes to distinguish between the possible cause of vitamin malabsorption. SYN: *dicopac test*.

Schiötz tonometer (shē′ĕts) [Hjalamar Schiötz, Norwegian physician, 1850–1927] An instrument for measuring intraocular pressure by the degree of indentation produced by pressure on the cornea.

SCHIP *State Children's Health Insurance Program*.

Schirmer test (shĭr′mĕrz) [Rudolph Schirmer, Ger. ophthalmologist, 1831–1896] The use of an absorbent paper placed in the conjunctival sac as a test for patients with ocular irritation and dry eye, e.g., keratoconjunctivitis sicca. The rate and amount of wetting of the paper provide an estimate of tear production.

schisandra (skĭ-zan′dră) The magnolia vine, a shrub whose berry is used in East Asia as a traditional medicine for a variety of diseases and conditions of the immune system and of the liver.

schisto- [Gr. *schistos,* split, fr. *schizein,* to split] Prefix meaning *split, cleft.*

schistocephalus (skĭs″tō-sĕf′ă-lŭs) [″ + *kephale,* head] A fetus with a cleft head.

schistocyte (skĭs′tō-sīt) [″ + *kytos,* cell] A fragmented red blood cell that appears in the blood in a variety of abnormal shapes, from small triangular forms to round cells with irregular surfaces. Schistocytes are found in patients with hemolytic anemias, severe burns, and several other conditions. SYN: *schizocyte*. SEE: illus.

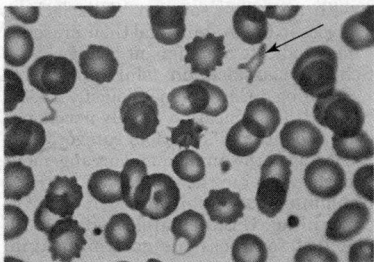

SCHISTOCYTE

In peripheral blood (×600)

schistocytosis (skĭs″tō-sī-tō′sĭs) [″ + ″ + *osis*, condition] Schistocytes in the blood. SYN: *schizocytosis*.

Schistosoma (skĭs″tō-sō′mă) [″ + *soma*, body] A genus of parasitic blood flukes belonging to the family Schistosomatidae, class Trematoda.

   S. haematobium A species common in Africa and southwestern Asia. Adults infest the pelvic veins of the vesical plexus. Eggs work their way through the bladder wall of the host and are discharged in the urine. Urinary schistosomiasis is caused by this organism.

   S. japonicum A species common in many parts of Asia. Adults live principally in branches of the superior mesenteric vein. Eggs work their way through the intestinal wall of the host into the lumen and are discharged with feces. This species also causes Oriental schistosomiasis.

   S. mansoni A species occurring in many parts of Africa and tropical America, including the West Indies. Adults live in branches of the inferior mesenteric veins. Eggs are discharged through either the host's intestine or bladder. This species causes bilharzial dysentery or Manson's intestinal schistosomiasis.

schistosomia (skĭs″tō-sō′mē-ă) [″ + *soma*, body] A deformed fetus with a fissure in the abdomen. The limbs are rudimentary if present.

schistosomiasis (shis″tō-sō-mī′ă-sĭs, skis″) [*schistosome* + *-iasis*] Any of several parasitic diseases due to infestation with flukes of the genus *Schistosoma*. The flukes may colonize the urinary tract, mesenteries, liver, spleen, or biliary tree. Although schistosomiasis rarely is encountered in the U.S., it is endemic throughout Asia, Africa, South America, and some Caribbean islands. An estimated 200 million people are affected worldwide. Infestation occurs by wading or bathing in water contaminated by cercariae. SYN: *bilharziasis; snail fever*.

   TREATMENT: The drug of choice is praziquantel.

schistosomicide (skĭs″tō-sō′mĭ-sī) [″ + ″ + L. *cidus*, killing] A drug or toxin that kills parasites of the genus *Schistosoma*.

schizencephaly (skiz″en″sef′ă-lē) [*schizo-* + *encephalo-*] The presence of one or more clefts running lengthwise through the cerebral hemispheres. This rare disorder results in developmental delays and seizures in affected children.

schizo-, schiz- [Gr. *schizein*, to split] Prefixes meaning *division*.

schizogony (skĭz-ŏg′ō-nē) [″ + *gone*, seed] Asexual reproduction by fission of a cell. Malarial parasites and species of sporozoa (such as *Cryptosporidium*) can reproduce using schizogony. They can also reproduce sexually.

schizoid (skĭz′oyd) [″ + *eidos*, form, shape] **1.** Severely introverted; socially isolated; lacking close personal relationships or the ability to form them. **2.** Resembling schizophrenia.

schizont (skĭz′ŏnt) [″ + *ontos*, being] **1.** A stage appearing in the life cycle of a sporozoan protozoon resulting from multiple division or schizogony. **2.** A stage in the asexual phase of the life cycle of *Plasmodium* organisms found in red blood cells. By schizogony, each gives rise to 12 to 24 or more merozoites. An early schizont is called a *presegmenter;* a mature schizont is called a *rosette* or *segmenter*.

schizonticide (skĭ-zŏn′tĭ-sīd) [″ + ″ + L. *cidus*, killing] Something that destroys schizonts.

schizophrenia (skit″sŏ-frē′nē-ă) [*schizo-* + *-phrenia*] A thought disorder affecting about 0.4% to 1.2% of the population, marked by delusions, hallucinations, and disorganized speech and behavior (the positive symptoms) and by flat affect, social withdrawal, and absence of volition (the negative symptoms). Schizophrenia involves dysfunction in one or more areas such as interpersonal relations, work or education, or self-care. Associated features include inappropriate affect, anhedonia, dysphoric mood, abnormal psychomotor activity, cognitive dysfunction, confusion, lack of insight, and depersonalization. Abnormal neurological findings may show a broad range of dysfunction including slow reaction time, poor coordination, abnormalities in eye tracking, and impaired sensory gating. Some individuals drink excessive amounts of water (water intoxication) and develop abnormalities in urine specific gravity or electrolyte imbalance. Because none of the clinical features are diagnostic, schizophrenia remains a diagnosis of exclusion. It is important to exclude psychoses with known organic causes such as temporal lobe epilepsy, metabolic disturbances, toxic substances, or psychoactive drugs. The onset of schizophrenia typically occurs between the late teens andthe mid-30s; onset before adolescence is rare. Gender differences suggest that women are more likely to have a later onset, more prominent mood symptoms, and a better prognosis. Hospital-based studies show a higher rate of schizophrenia in men; community-based studies suggest an equal sex ratio. SEE: *Nursing Diagnoses Appendix.* **schizophrenic** (-ĭk), *adj.*

ETIOLOGY: The cause of schizophrenia is unknown.

TREATMENT: Medications to control schizophrenia include antipsychotic drugs that act on dopamine receptors in the brain, e.g., chlorpromazine, fluphenazine, haloperidol, clozapine, and risperidone. Each of these may be associated with significant side effects; therefore, drug treatment with any of them requires careful monitoring. Supportive psychotherapy or cognitive behavioral therapy may be helpful for the patient and family.

PROGNOSIS: After initial diagnosis, about one in five patients have well-controlled disease. Eighty percent of those affected suffer frequent relapses that may result in periodic hospitalizations, intensive treatment, or crisis management.

catatonic s. A schizophrenic disorder marked by motor immobility or stupor; excessive, purposeless motor activity; extreme negativism or mutism; echolalia or echopraxia; and peculiar voluntary movements such as posturing.

paranoid s. A schizophrenic disorder characterized by delusions of persecution, grandiosity, jealousy, or hallucinations with persecutory or grandiose content.

residual s. A schizophrenic disorder marked by continuing evidence of flat affect, impoverished or disorganized speech, and eccentric or odd behavior but showing no evidence of delusions, hallucinations, or disorganized speech.

Schmidt syndrome (shmit) [Martin Benno Schmidt, Ger. physician, 1863–1949] A polyglandular autoimmune syndrome that begins at about age 30 and is characterized by primary adrenal insufficiency, autoimmune thyroid disease, and insulin-dependent diabetes mellitus. SYN: *type 2 polyglandular autoimmune syndrome.*

Schmorl disease (shmorl) [Christian G. Schmorl, Ger. pathologist, 1861–1932] Herniation of the nucleus pulposus through a cracked vertebral end plate into the vertebral body. The resulting bone necrosis is detectable on radiograph and is called *Schmorl nodes.*

Schmorl nodes SEE: *Schmorl disease.*

Schnyder crystalline dystrophy (shnīd'ĕr) [Walter F. Schnyder, Swiss ophthalmologist, b. 1892] An autosomal dominant disease of the cornea, characterized by ring-shaped deposits of cholesterol crystals in the anterior corneal stroma. The disease may cause visual impairment.

Schober maneuver (shō'bĕr) A test for flexibility of the lumbar spine, used to determine the presence of ankylosing spondylitis (AS) in patients with low back pain.

PATIENT CARE: The patient is asked to stand erect and a mark is placed on the skin overlying the second sacral vertebra. A second mark is placed on the skin 10 cm above the first. The patient then is asked to bend forward. A repeat measurement of the distance between the two marks should equal or exceed 15 cm. If it does not, the patient may have an inflexible or "bamboo" spine, characteristic of AS.

Schönlein-Henoch purpura (shăn'lĭn-hĕn-ŏk) SEE: *Henoch-Schönlein purpura.*

School Function Assessment ABBR: SFA. A rating scale to measure a student's ability to function effectively alone and with peers in elementary school (kindergarten through 6th grade). The SFA assesses a child's level of participation in various school-related settings, the need for supports, and school-related functional activities. It is used to identify children who qualify for special assistance and to provide guidance for such assistance.

school phobia, school refusal A child's avoidance of school, often through the simulation of physical ailments. It is considered to be a form of separation anxiety rather than truancy.

Schultz reaction (shoolts'ĭs) [Werner Schultz, Ger. physician, 1878–1947] Dale reaction.

Schwalbe, Gustav Albert (shval'bĕ) Ger. anatomist, 1844–1916

S. line S. ring.

S. ring The thickened peripheral margin of the Descemet membrane of the cornea of the eye; it is formed by a circular bundle of connective tissue. SYN: *S. line.*

Schwann, Theodore (shvon) Ger. anatomist and physiologist, 1810–1882.

S. cell Any of the cells that surround and myelinate axons in peripheral nerves. Schwann cells originate in the neural crest and migrate into the embryo along growing axons, separating the axons by leaflets of cytoplasm. Eventually, Schwann cells wrap with myelin those axons that are > 1 μm in diameter; each Schwann cell myelinates only one axon. Schwann cell activity is required for the successful regeneration of peripheral nerves. SEE: *neuron* for illus.

schwannoma (shwŏn-nō'mă) A benign tumor of the neurilemma of a nerve.

schwannosis (shwŏn-nō'sĭs) Hypertrophy of the neurilemma of a nerve.

sci-, scia-, scio- SEE: *skia-*.

sciage (sē-ozh′) [Fr. *sciage*, a sawing] A movement of the hand used in massage resembling that used in sawing.

sciatic (sī-ăt′ĭk) [L. *sciaticus*] **1.** Pert. to the hip or ischium. **2.** Pert. to sciatica. SEE: *sciatica*.

sciatica (sī-ăt′ĭ-kă) [L.] A condition in which pain emanating from the lower back is felt along the distribution of the sciatic nerve in the lower extremity. It typically occurs as a result of lumbar disk disease and is felt in the back of the thigh and sometimes the rest of the leg. In Western countries about 40% to 50% of the population will experience sciatica at some time during their lives. Recovery follows conservative treatment in 3 to 4 weeks in the vast majority of patients. SEE: *meralgia; piriformis syndrome; sciatic nerve; Nursing Diagnoses Appendix*.

ETIOLOGY: The condition may be caused by compression or trauma of the sciatic nerve or its roots, esp. that resulting from a ruptured intervertebral disk or osteoarthrosis of the lumbosacral vertebrae; inflammation of the sciatic nerve resulting from metabolic, toxic, or infectious disorders; or pain referred to the distribution of the sciatic nerve from other sources.

SYMPTOMS: Sciatica, which begins abruptly or gradually, is characterized by a sharp shooting pain running down the back of the thigh. Movement of the limb or lower back generally intensifies the suffering. Pain may be uniformly distributed along the limb, but frequently there are certain spots where it is more intense. Numbness and tingling may be present, and the skin innervated by the nerve may occasionally be hypersensitive to light touch.

DIAGNOSIS: Physical examination of the patient may reveal pain in the lower back during straight leg raising or changes in lower extremity reflexes.

TREATMENT: Although sciatica may be extremely painful and temporarily disabling, in more than 80% of patients it gradually resolves with mild activity restrictions and nonsteroidal anti-inflammatories, narcotic analgesic drugs, or muscle relaxants. Patients whose symptoms do not improve with these therapies should be reevaluated professionally. Occasionally surgery of the lower back, e.g., to remove a herniated disk, is needed although surgery is much less common than in the past.

PATIENT CARE: Patients with sciatica who have had a history of cancer, injecting drugs, have fevers associated with sciatica, or lose control of bowel or bladder function in association with the illness should be evaluated immediately with radiography of the lower back. Elderly patients also may require earlier and closer follow-up care than younger patients. Patients for whom sciatic pain is disabling but in whom objective pathology is not easily demonstrated may benefit from multidisciplinary approaches to their symptoms, e.g., with referrals to chronic pain clinics, chiropractors, physical and occupational therapists, physiatrists, or other specialists.

    extraspinal s. Piriformis syndrome.

sciatic nerve The thickest nerve in the body, the main trunk of the sciatic plexus and carrying axons from spinal segments L4-S3 to the hip and lower extremities. It emerges from the pelvic cavity in the back of the hip through the greater sciatic foramen. The nerve is composed of two side-by-side components, the tibial nerve and the common fibular (peroneal) nerve.

SCID *severe combined immunodeficiency disease.*

science (sī′ĕns) [L. *scientia*, knowledge] The intellectual discipline that uses all available mental and physical resources to better understand, explain, quantitate, and predict normal as well as unusual natural phenomena. The scientific approach involves observation, measurement, the accumulation and analysis of verifiable data, the replication of experimental results.

    applied s. Any project that employs scientific methods to make practical or useful changes to the physical environment, e.g., any form of engineering or technology.

    behavioral s. The science concerned with all aspects of behavior.

    cognitive s. The study of memory, information processing, algorithm use, hypothesis formation, and problem solving in human and computer systems.

    computer s. **1.** The development, configuration, and architecture of computer hardware and software. **2.** The study of computer hardware and software.

    information s. **1.** The study of models and theories common to the fields of electronic, interpersonal, group, organizational, public, and mass communication. **2.** The study of issues related to libraries and the information fields.

    life s. Any of the sciences concerned with living things. These sciences include biology, zoology, medicine, dentistry, surgery, nursing, and psychology.

    occupational s. The science of human activity or occupation. Its goal is to understand how and why people select, organize, perform, and derive meaning from everyday occupations or pursuits.

    soft s. Any science or discipline, e.g.,

sociology or criminology, in which drawing firm conclusions is complicated by numerous variables.

Science Citations Index SEE: under *index*.

Science of Unitary Human Beings A conceptual model of nursing developed by Martha Rogers. The human being and the environment are conceived of as unitary, patterned, open, and pandimensional energy fields. The goal of nursing is to promote human betterment wherever people are. SEE: *homeodynamics; Nursing Theory Appendix.*

scimitar syndrome A rare congenital malformation of the heart and lungs, marked by dextroposition of the heart, a malformed right lung, abnormal connections between the right pulmonary veins and the inferior vena cava, and abnormal pulmonary arterial connections to the right lung.

scintigram (sĭn′tĭ-grăm) The record produced by a scintiscan.

scintigraphy (sĭn-tĭg′ră-fē) The injection and subsequent detection of radioactive isotopes to create images of body parts and identify body functions and diseases.

scintillation (sĭn″tĭ-lā′shŭn) [L. *scintillatio*] **1.** Sparkling; a subjective sensation, as of seeing sparks. **2.** The response of specific crystals to electromagnetic radiation, e.g., the emissions that come from radioactive substances.

scintimammography (sĭn″tĭ-mă-mŏg′rŏ-fē) [scinti(llation) + ″] Mammography enhanced by a radioactive isotope study of healthy and malignant breast tissue. The radioactive tracer is injected into a peripheral vein and is taken up by metabolically active cells. Breast cancer cells are metabolically more active than normal tissues, take up more tracer, and on the image appear brighter than the surrounding healthy cells. Scintimammography can be used to identify breast cancers that are otherwise difficult to visualize and to guide breast biopsies.

scintiphotography (sĭn″tĭ-fō-tŏg′ră-fē) Making images from radioactive emissions, e.g., from radioisotopes injected into the body to determine the health or disease of body structures and functions. SEE: *scintigraphy.*

scintiscan (sĭn′tĭ-skăn) The use of scintiphotography to create a map of scintillations produced when a radioactive substance is introduced into the body. The intensity of the record indicates the differential accumulation of a substance in the various parts of the body.

scintiscanner (sĭn″tĭ-skăn′ĕr) The device used in doing a scintiscan.

scirrho- [Gr. *skirrhos*, hard tumor, fr. *skiros*, hard] Prefix meaning *hard*.

scirrhous (skĭr′rŭs) [L. *scirrhosus*, hard] Hard, like a scirrhus.

scirrhus (skĭr′ŭs) [Gr. *skirrhos*, hard tumor] A hard, cancerous tumor caused by an overgrowth of fibrous tissue.

scission (sĭzh′ŭn) [L. *scindere*, to split] Dividing, cutting, or splitting.

scissors (sĭz′ors) [L. *cisorium*] A cutting instrument composed of two opposed cutting blades with handles, held together by a central pin. This allows the cutting edge to be opened and closed.

scissura (sĭ-sū′ră) *pl.* **scissurae** [L., to split] A fissure or cleft; a splitting.

sclera (sklēr′ă) *pl.* **sclerae** [Gr. *skleros*, hard] The outer layer of the eyeball made of fibrous connective tissue. At the front of the eye, it is visible as the white of the eye and ends at the cornea, which is transparent. **scleral,** *adj.*

blue s. An abnormal thinning of the sclera through which a blue uveal pigment is seen. This may be found in people with disorders of collagen formation such as osteogenesis imperfecta.

sclerectomy (sklĕ-rĕk′tō-mē) [″ + *ektome*, excision] **1.** Excision of a portion of the sclera. SYN: *scleroticectomy.* **2.** Removal of adhesions in chronic otitis media.

scleredema (sklĕr″ĕ-dē′mă) [″ + *oidema*, swelling] Induration of the skin of the upper back and neck, usually occurring in association with type 2 diabetes mellitus, and occasionally in patients after acute streptococcal infections. In diabetic patients it may regress with strict control of blood sugars.

s. adultorum Buschke scleredema.

Buschke s. SEE: *Buschke scleredema.*

s. neonatorum Scleroderma neonatorum.

sclerema (sklĕ-rē′mă) [Gr. *skleros*, hard] Scleroderma.

s. neonatorum Hardening and tightening of the skin and subcutaneous tissue of the newborn. This is a rare disease, sometimes associated with premature birth, neonatal sepsis, and dehydration. SYN: *scleroderma neonatorum.*

scleritis (sklĕ-rī′ĭs) [*sclera* + *-itis*] Any painful inflammatory disease of the sclera of the eye. It may result in degeneration or destruction of the sclera and neighboring tissues and is often associated with systemic inflammatory disease. It occurs much more commonly in the anterior sclera than in the posterior. SYN: *sclerotitis.* SEE: *episcleritis.*

annular s. Inflammation limited to the area surrounding the limbus of the cornea. A complete ring is formed.

anterior s. An inflammation of the sclera, episclera, and conjunctiva. Anterior scleritis may be localized or diffuse.

posterior s. Scleritis limited to the

posterior half of the globe of the eye with loss of vision and ocular pain.

sclero-, sclera-, scler- [Gr. *sklēros,* hard] Prefixes meaning *hard.*

sclerocornea (sklĕ″rō-kor′nē-ă) [″ + L. *corneus,* horny] The sclera and cornea together considered as one coat.

sclerodactylia (sklĕr″ō-dăk-tĭl′ē-ă) [″ + *daktylos,* a finger] Induration of the skin of the fingers and toes. SYN: *acroscleroderma.*

scleroderma (sklĕr″ă-dĕr′mă) [Gr. *skleros,* hard, + *derma,* skin] A chronic manifestation of progressive systemic sclerosis in which the skin is taut, firm, and edematous, limiting movement. SEE: *progressive systemic sclerosis; Nursing Diagnoses Appendix.* **sclerodermatous,** *adj.*

> **circumscribed s.** Localized patches of linear sclerosis of the skin. There is no systemic involvement, and the course of the disease is usually benign.

> **s. neonatorum** Sclerema neonatorum.

sclerogenic (sklĕ″rō-jĕn′ĭk) [″ + *gennan,* to produce] Causing sclerosis or hardening of tissue. SYN: *sclerogenous.*

sclerokeratitis (sklĕr″ō-kĕr-ă-tī′tĭs) [″ + *keras,* horn, + *itis,* inflammation] Cellular infiltration with inflammation of the sclera and cornea. SYN: *sclerokeratosis.*

scleroma (sklē-rō′mă) [″ + *oma,* tumor] An indurated, circumscribed area of granulation tissue in the mucous membrane or skin. SEE: *sclerosis.*

scleromalacia (sklē″rō-mā-lā′sē-ă) [Gr. *skleros,* hard, + *malakia,* softening] A softening of the sclera.

> **s. perforans** A severe form of necrotizing anterior scleritis usually found in patients with an underlying systemic inflammatory illness, e.g., rheumatoid arthritis.

scleromyxedema (sklĕr″ō-mĭk″sē-dē′mă) [″ + *myxa,* mucus, + *oidema,* swelling] A systemic form of papular mucinosis (also known as lichen myxedematosus), in which a scleroderma-like rash is accompanied by lesions of visceral organs and often paraproteinemia.

scleroplasty (sklĕ′rō-plăs″tē) [″ + *plassein,* to form] Plastic surgery of the sclera.

scleroprotein (sklĕ″rō-prō′tē-ĭn) [″ + *protos,* first] A group of proteins noted for their insolubility in most chemicals; found in skeletal tissue, cartilage, hair, and nails and in animal claws and horns.

sclerosant (sklē-rō′sănt) [*sclero-*] Something that produces sclerosis. SYN: *sclerosing solution.*

sclerose (sklē-rōs′) [Gr. *skleros,* hard] To become hardened. **sclerosing, sclerosed,** *adj.*

sclerosis (sklĕ-rō′sĭs) [Gr. *sklērōsis,* hardening] A hardening or induration of an organ or tissue, esp. one due to excessive growth of fibrous tissue. SEE: *arteriosclerosis; cerebrosclerosis.* **sclerotic** (-rot′ik), *adj.*

> **amyotrophic lateral s.** ABBR: ALS. Motor neuron disease. SEE: *Nursing Diagnoses Appendix.*

> **annular s.** Sclerosis in which a hardened substance forms a band about the spinal cord.

> **arterial s.** Arteriosclerosis.

> **arteriolar s.** Sclerosis of the arterioles.

> **diffuse s.** Sclerosis affecting large areas of the brain and spinal cord.

> **hyperplastic s.** Medial **s.**

> **insular s.** Multiple **s.**

> **intimal s.** Atherosclerosis.

> **lateral s.** Sclerosis of the lateral column of the spinal cord. SEE: *motor neuron disease.*

> **lobar s.** Sclerosis of the cerebrum resulting in mental disturbances.

> **medial s.** Sclerosis involving the tunica media of arteries, usually the result of involutional changes accompanying aging. SYN: *hyperplastic s.*

> **multiple s.** ABBR: MS. A chronic disease of the central nervous system (CNS) in which there is destruction of myelin within several regions of the brain and spinal cord at different times. This results in temporary, repetitive, or sustained disruptions in nerve impulse conduction, causing symptoms such as muscular weakness, loss of coordination, numbness, visual disturbances, loss of control of bowel, bladder, and sexual functions. The clinical picture in MS depends upon the extent of demyelination. Multiple sclerosis is a relatively common disorder: more than 400,000 Americans are affected, of whom the majority (about 390,000) are adults. Multiple sclerosis usually begins between ages 20 and 40; women are twice as likely to have the disease as men, and European-Americans are more likely to be affected than African-Americans or Asian-Americans. Four main categories of MS are currently recognized. The *benign* variant is marked by several episodes of nervous system dysfunction, followed by complete recovery. The *primary progressive* variant is marked by rapid loss of neurological functions that do not resolve, causing severe functional impairments that worsen over time. More common than either of these types of MS are the two *relapsing-remitting* variants. In patients with these disorders, neurological deficits develop and then improve either completely or partially. In patients who achieve only partial restoration of neurological function, secondary progression of the disease may result in a gradual accumulation of visual, motor, or

sensory disabilities. SYN: *insular **s.***
SEE: *Nursing Diagnoses Appendix.*

About half of all patients with MS become unable to work within 10 to 15 years of the first onset of symptoms. Within 25 years of the first symptoms, half of these patients cannot walk.

ETIOLOGY: The cause of the disease is unknown although much evidence suggests that T lymphocytes that injure nerve cells and nerve sheaths play an important role, i.e., the disease has an autoimmune basis. Some evidence links MS to hypovitaminosis of vitamin D.

SYMPTOMS: Nearly a quarter of all patients with MS initially develop visual disturbances or blindness. Other consequences of the disease include sudden or progressive weakness in one or more limbs, muscular spasticity, nystagmus, fatigue, tremor, gait instability, recurrent urinary tract infections (caused by bladder dysfunction), incontinence, and alterations in mood, including euphoria, irritability, and depression. SEE: *retrobulbar **neuritis***.

DIAGNOSIS: Diagnosis is usually based on the patient's history. Magnetic resonance imaging may detect areas of the brain and/or spinal cord with demyelination. Lumbar puncture is often performed to assess patients for oligoclonal bands (immunoglobulins released into the cerebrospinal fluid due to inflammation).

TREATMENT: Although there is no known cure for MS, corticosteroids, alpha interferon may be used in specific settings to reduce disability or the frequency of relapses and the progression of disease in patients with some variants of MS. Treatment should be individualized because these therapies are expensive, ineffective in benign or primary progressive disease, and poorly tolerated by some patients. Symptomatic relief (e.g., of spasticity with muscle relaxants, or of bladder dysfunction with anticholinergic drugs) is provided as needed.

PATIENT CARE: The health care professional provides support to patients with MS and their families. The patient is advised to avoid fatigue, overexertion, exposure to extreme heat or cold, and stressful situations, and is encouraged to follow a regular plan of daily activity and exercise based on levels of tolerance. The patient is taught about symptoms that may occur during exacerbations of the disease and the need to adapt the plan of care to changing needs and about the administration of prescribed medications. Physical and occupational therapy help the patient to maintain muscle tone and joint mobility, decrease spasticity, improve balance and coordination, and increase morale. Massages, relaxing baths, yoga, and tai chi may prove helpful. A nutritious, well-balanced diet with adequate roughage and fluids is recommended. Bladder and bowel training programs, self-catheterization, and the use of condom catheters may be required. Independence is encouraged by assisting the patient to develop new methods for activities of daily living (ADL) performance and optimal functioning. Both the patient and family are encouraged to promote safety in the home and the work environment. For support and information, the patient and family should be referred to the National Multiple Sclerosis Society. Telephone: 800-FIGHT-MS; Website: www.nmss.org

myelinoclastic diffuse *s.* Schilder disease.

neural *s.* Sclerosis with chronic inflammation of a nerve trunk with branches.

nuclear *s.* An increase in the refractive index of the crystalline lens, which culminates in the development of nuclear cataracts. Before the cataract fully opacifies, the patient's near vision may improve, a phenomenon known as senopia or *second sight*.

progressive systemic *s.* ABBR: PSS. A chronic disease of unknown cause that occurs four times as frequently in women as in men. It causes sclerosis of the skin and other organs, including the gastrointestinal tract, lungs, heart, and kidneys. The skin is taut, firm, and edematous and is firmly bound to subcutaneous tissue, which often causes limitation of the range of motion. The skin also feels tough and leathery, may itch, and later becomes hyperpigmented. The skin changes usually precede the development of signs of visceral involvement. SEE: *CREST syndrome.* SYN: *systemic **s.***

TREATMENT: There is no specific therapy. General supportive therapy is indicated. Many drugs have been used, including corticosteroids, vasodilators, D-penicillamine, and immunosuppressive agents. Physical therapy will help maintain range of motion and muscular strength but will not influence the course of joint disease.

renal *s.* Nephrosclerosis.

systemic *s.* Progressive systemic **s.**

tuberous *s.* ABBR: TS. An autosomal dominant disorder in which multiple benign tumors appear in the skin, brain, heart, and kidneys of affected children. Infants born with this disease may have facial angiofibromas, astrocytomas of the central nervous system, hamartomas of the retina, and other lesions, producing hydrocephalus, mental retardation, autism, and seizures. SYN: *Bourneville disease; tuberous sclerosis complex.*

vascular s. Atherosclerosis.

venous s. Phlebosclerosis.

sclerostomy (sklĕ-rŏs′tō-mē) [″ + *stoma*, mouth] The surgical formation of an opening in the sclera.

sclerotherapy (sklĕr′ō-thĕr′ă-pē) [″ + *therapeia*, treatment] The injection of irritating chemicals into vascular spaces or body cavities to harden, fill, or destroy them. Sclerotherapy has been used to manage varicose veins, hemorrhoids, esophageal varices, benign hepatic cysts, malignant pleural effusions, and intracranial aneurysms. A common complication of the procedure is injury to neighboring tissues. Common sclerosing agents include absolute ethanol and sodium tetradecyl sulfate.

sclerotica (sklĕ-rŏt′ĭ-kă) [L. *scleroticus*, hard] Sclera.

sclerotic dentin Areas of dentin where the tubules have been filled by mineralization, producing a denser, radiopaque dentin. It is often produced in response to caries, attrition, and abrasion.

sclerotium (sklĕ-rō′shē-ŭm) A hardened mass formed by the growth of certain fungi. The sclerotium formed by ergot on rye is of medical importance because of its toxicity.

sclerotome (sklĕr′ō-tōm) [″ + *tome*, incision] **1.** A knife used in incision of the sclera. **2.** One of a series of segmentally arranged masses of mesenchymal tissue lying on either side of the notochord. They give rise to the vertebrae and ribs.

sclerotomy (sklĕ-rŏt′ō-mē) Surgical incision of the sclera.

anterior s. An incision made at the angle of the anterior chamber of the eye in glaucoma.

posterior s. An incision into the anterior chamber of the eye. It is done during glaucoma surgery as part of a trabeculectomy.

sclerous (sklĕr′ŭs) Hard; indurated. SYN: *sclerosal*.

SCN5A sodium channel A sodium channel found in heart muscle cells. Mutations in this channel produce cardiomyopathy and dysrhythmias, including atrial fibrillation.

scolex (skō′leks″, skō′lĕ-sēz″, skol′ĕ) *pl.* **scoleces, scolices** [Gr. *skolēx*, worm] The headlike segment of a tapeworm, by which it attaches itself to the wall of the intestine. Scolices usually possess hooks, suckers, or bothria (grooves) for attachment.

scoli-, scolio- [Gr. *skolios*, bent, crooked] Prefixes meaning *crooked* or *bent*.

scolices, scoleces (skō′lĭ-sēz″) Plurals of scolex.

scoliometer (skō″lē-ŏm′ĕt-ĕr) [″ + *metron*, measure] A device for measuring curves, esp. the lateral ones of the spine.

scoliosis (skō″lē-ō′sĭs) [Gr. *skoliosis*, crookedness] A lateral curvature of the spine. It usually consists of two curves, the original abnormal curve and a compensatory curve in the opposite direction. Scoliosis may be functional, structural, or idiopathic. Functional or postural scoliosis usually occurs as a result of a discrepancy in leg length and corrects when the patient bends toward the convex side. Structural scoliosis is related to vertebral bone deformities and thus does not correct with posture changes. Idiopathic scoliosis (the most common kind) may be transmitted as an autosomal dominant or multifactorial trait. **scoliotic,** *adj.* SEE: illus.; Nursing Diagnoses Appendix.

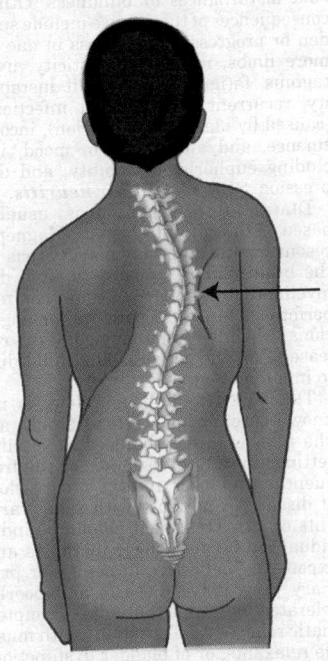

SCOLIOSIS

SYMPTOMS: Scoliosis rarely produces any symptoms until it is well established; then backache, fatigue, and dyspnea from ventilatory compromise may occur. Diagnosis is based on physical examination, anteroposterior and lateral spinal x-rays, and by using the Cobb method to measure the angle of curvature.

TREATMENT: Scoliosis may be treated through the use of a brace to straighten the abnormal spinal curvature or with corrective orthopedic surgery (e.g., the placement of a supportive rod along the spine or spinal fusion).

PATIENT CARE: Muscle strengthening exercises should be done daily when the patient is in and out of the brace. Follow-up assessment and brace adjustment should be done periodically. As the skeleton matures, brace wear is gradually reduced to night-time use only. Surgery is indicated for scoliosis that progresses despite bracing. Postoperative visits are required for several months to monitor correction stability. Provisions are made to assist the adolescent and family to meet the psychosocial needs associated with the illness. The patient and family are taught about treatment management (cast-care, brace-use, traction, electrical stimulation, or surgery), exercises, activity level, skin care, prevention of complications, and breathing exercises. When necessary, preoperative teaching is provided, including preanesthesia breathing exercises, post-operative use of an incentive spirometer, surgical pain management, and prevention of thromboembolic or other complications. Following surgery, all general patient care concerns apply.

Upon discharge, home-health care may be needed, and the school-age child or adolescent will require education in the home until he or she is able to return to school. Activity and activity limitations are explained, and diversional activities suggested. The patient is encouraged to provide self-care as much as possible. Wearing his or her own clothes, washing and styling his or her own hair, and applying make-up help to enhance morale. Educational and support resources are discussed with the patient and family. Pediatricians, pediatric nurse practitioners, school nurses, and other health professionals caring for children should include screening for scoliosis during physical examinations.

cicatricial s. Scoliosis due to fibrous scar tissue contraction resulting from necrosis.

congenital s. Scoliosis present at birth, usually the result of defective embryonic development of the spine.

empyematic s. Scoliosis following empyema and retraction of one side of the chest.

functional s. Scoliosis caused not by actual spinal deformity but by another condition such as unequal leg lengths. The curve reduces when the other condition is ameliorated.

habit s. Scoliosis due to habitually assumed improper posture or position.

inflammatory s. Scoliosis caused by infection or inflammation near the spine, resulting in local muscle spasm.

ischiatic s. Scoliosis due to hip disease.

myopathic s. Scoliosis due to weakening of the spinal muscles.

neuropathic s. Structural scoliosis caused by congenital or acquired neurological disorders.

ocular s. Scoliosis caused by tilting of

the head because of visual defects or extraocular muscle imbalance.

osteopathic s. Scoliosis caused by bony deformity of the spine. SEE: *structural s.*

paralytic s. Scoliosis due to paralysis of muscles.

protective s. An acute side shifting of the lumbar spine, usually away from the side of pathology. The body is attempting to move a nerve root away from a bulging intervertebral disk herniation.

rachitic s. Scoliosis due to rickets.

sciatic s. Scoliosis caused by the patient's assumption of a laterally bent posture to reduce symptoms of sciatica.

static s. Scoliosis due to a difference in the length of the legs.

structural s. An irreversible scoliosis that has a fixed rotation. The vertebral bodies rotate toward the convexity of the curve; the rotation results in a posterior rib hump in the thoracic region on the convex side of the curve. In structural scoliosis, the spine does not straighten when the patient bends.

scombroid (skŏm′broyd) Any fish of the suborder Scombroidea, including mackerel, tuna, bonito, albacore, and skipjack.

scombroid fish poisoning SEE: under *poisoning.*

scoop (skoop) A spoon-shaped surgical instrument.

bone s. A scoop for scraping or removing necrosed bone or the contents of suppurative tracts.

bullet s. A scoop used for dislodging bullets or shrapnel.

ear s. A scoop for removing middle ear granulations.

lithotomy s. A scoop for dislodging encysted stones or debris.

mastoid s. A scoop used in mastoid operations.

renal s. A scoop used for dislodging or removing small stones from the pelvis of a kidney.

-scope [Gr. *skopein,* to look at] Suffix meaning *instrument for viewing or examining.*

scope of practice The extent and limits of the medical interventions that a health care provider may perform.

-scopy [Gr. *skopein,* to look at] Suffix meaning *examination,* esp. with a device or tool.

scorbutic (skor-bū′tĭk) [L. *scorbuticus,* scurvy] Concerning or affected with scurvy.

scorbutus (skor-bū′tŭs) [L., scurvy] Scurvy.

score (skor) **1.** A rating tool or scale to assess the level of health or the severity of an illness. **2.** A rating or grade as compared with a standard of other individuals, esp. in a competitive event. **3.** To mark the skin with lines in order to have landmarks available, as in plastic surgery. **4.** A groove or dividing line in the center of a tablet for facilitating the division of the pill into two parts. Particular scores are listed under the first word. SEE: e.g., *ABCD score; cardiac calcium score; Score for Neonatal Acute Physiology.*

scorecard (skor'kard″) Any method used to evaluate personal or institutional performance, e.g., the compliance of health care professionals with known standards of care, or the satisfaction of patients with their health care experiences.

Score for Neonatal Acute Physiology ABBR: SNAP. A measure of the severity of illness in newborns in neonatal intensive care that assigns risk points to the mean blood pressure, lowest body temperature, ratio of the oxygen saturation to the FIO_2, serum pH, urinary output, presence of multiple seizures, size for gestational age, birth weight, and Apgar scores to gauge the likelihood of morbidity and mortality. A variation of this risk assessment tool is the Score for Neonatal Acute Physiology with Perinatal Extension (SNAPPE).

scoring system A standardized method for evaluating the status of a disease, a laboratory specimen, or a radiologic image. Measurable elements of the object under study are rated according to their severity or stage, and the sum of the scores for each rated element is tallied.

Scorpaenidae (skor″pēn'ĭd-ē) [L. *Scorpaena*, the type genus, fr Gr. *skorpaina* + *-idae*] SEE: *scorpionfish.*

scorpion (skor'pē-ŏn) [Gr. *skorpios*, to cut off] An arthropod of the class Arachnida and order Scorpionida. It varies in length from less than 2 in (5 cm) for the small bark scorpions of Arizona to 8 in (20 cm) for some African scorpions. Most scorpions are nocturnal and reclusive and are most active when the night temperatures remain above 70°F (21°C). The tail of the scorpion contains two venom glands connected to the tip of the stinger.

scorpionfish, scorpion fish (skor'pē-ŏn-fish) Any of the marine fish with spines coated with extremely toxic mucus of the family Scorpaenidae, found in coral reefs worldwide. Those who handle these fish may be stung or even killed by the tissue-destructive enzymes and venoms they release. SEE: *stonefish.*

scoto- [Gr. *skotos*, darkness] Prefix meaning *darkness.*

scotoma (skō-tō'mă) pl. **scotomata** [Gr. *skotoma*, to darken] An island-like blind spot in the visual field.

    absolute s. A scotoma in which there is absolute blindness.

    annular s. A scotoma that encircles

the point of fixation like a ring, not always completely closed but leaving the fixation point intact. SYN: *ring s.*

    arcuate s. An arc-shaped scotoma near the blind spot of the eye. It is caused by a nerve bundle defect on the temporal side of the optic disk.

    central s. A scotoma involving the point of fixation, seen in lesions of the macula.

    centrocecal s. A scotoma that is oval-shaped and includes the fixation point and the blind spot of the eye.

    color s. Color blindness in a limited portion of the visual field.

    eclipse s. A scotoma in the visual field caused by looking directly at a solar eclipse.

    flittering s. Scintillating **s.**

    negative s. A scotoma not perceptible by the patient.

    peripheral s. A scotoma removed from the point of fixation of the vision.

    physiological s. A scotoma caused by an absence of rods and cones where the optic nerve enters the retina.

    positive s. An area in the visual field that is perceived by the patient as a dark spot.

    relative s. A scotoma that causes the perception of an object to be impaired but not completely lost.

    ring s. Annular **s.**

    scintillating s. An irregular scotoma around a luminous patch in the visual field that occurs following mental or physical labor, eyestrain, or during a migraine.

scotometry (skō-tŏm'ĕ-trē) The locating and measurement of scotomata.

scout film In radiology, an x-ray film, esp. of the abdomen, for evaluating the condition of the body before beginning an invasive or potentially hazardous examination.

scr *scruple.*

scrape (skrāp) To remove from the surface with a scalpel or other edged instrument.

scraping (skrā'pĭng) Removal of cells, as from diseased tissue, with an edged instrument for cytologic examination.

scratch (skrăch) [ME. *cracchen*, to scratch] **1.** A mark or superficial injury produced by scraping with the nails on a rough surface. **2.** To make a thin, shallow cut with a sharp instrument. **3.** To rub the skin, esp. with the fingernails, to relieve itching. Scratching temporarily relieves itching by soothing the cutaneous nerves, but in the long run, it may worsen the condition that caused the itching. SEE: *pruritus.*

scratch test Placement of an appropriate dilution of a test material suspected of being an allergen in a lightly scratched area of the skin. If the material is an allergen, a wheal will develop within 15 min. The scratch test is used to detect immunoglobulin E antibody responses, e.g., in patients with a history of allergy to penicillin. SEE: *skin test.*

screen (skrēn) [Fr. *escren*] **1.** To determine the presence of a disease or its characteristics in a broad community or a selected group. **2.** A structure or substance used to protect, guard, or shield from a damaging influence such as x-rays, ultraviolet light, or insects. **3.** A system used to select or reject personnel. **4.** In psychiatry, the blocking of one memory with another.

intensifying s. In radiography, a paired sheet of fluorescent phosphors layered onto a plastic sheet above and below the x-ray film, used to translate into light an incoming image carried by x-ray photons.

tangent s. A simple device used in perimetry to test the central portion of the visual field. SYN: *Bjerrum screen.*

screening (skrēn'ing) **1.** Evaluation of patients for diseases such as cancer, heart disease, or substance abuse before these conditions become clinically obvious. Screening can play an important part in the early diagnosis and management of selected illnesses and in some instances may prolong lives. SYN: *screening test.* **2.** In psychiatry, the initial examination to determine the mental status of a person and the appropriate initial therapy.

cancer s. A program to detect cancer, esp. before it metastasizes and threatens life or health. Common screening tools include the use of colonoscopy (for cancers of the large intestine), mammography (to detect breast cancer), and the Papanicolaou (Pap) test (for cancers of the uterine cervix).

developmental s. Testing preschool children to identify potential problems in growth, learning ability, or social and emotional development. The tests assess cognition, fine and gross motor skills, language use, behavior, and social interaction. Developmental screening is performed at routine well-child checkups and is used to identify conditions such as autism, attention deficit hyperactivity disorder, developmental coordination disorder, disorders of stature, and mental retardation.

health s. SEE: *health risk appraisal.*

high-throughput s. The testing of the biological or pharmacological properties of molecules by immersion in a large number of chemical baths or cellular systems. It is used, e.g., to determine whether any of a group of chemicals has specific therapeutic actions.

newborn s. The testing of infants in the first days of life for serious illnesses (e.g., congenital deafness, cystic fibrosis, hemoglobinopathies, hypothyroidism, and phenylketonuria).

prenatal s. Testing of maternal serum, amniotic fluid, or chorionic villi to evaluate the developing fetus for congenital diseases such as Down syndrome or structural heart defects.

universal newborn hearing s. ABBR: UNHS. A public health effort to identify infants born with impaired hearing at the earliest possible age, e.g., before 6 months). UNHS has been implemented to identify those infants whose hearing loss is more than 40 decibels below the mean, i.e., those infants with the greatest risk of impaired speech acquisition in childhood. Children with profound hearing loss are at risk for poor achievement in school and diminished success in work as adults.

screening test Screening (1).

screw (skroo) A cylindrical fastener with a spiral groove running along its surface, often used in surgeries as an internal fixator (e.g., to attach bones to plates or prostheses).

expansion s. A mechanical device set into a removable or fixed appliance to enlarge the dental arch.

screw-in Implanted; permanently fastened to tissue. Said, for example, of catheter leads used for permanent or semipermanent cardiac pacemaking.

Scribner shunt (skrīb'nĕr) [Belding Scribner, U.S. physician, 1921–2003] A tube, usually made of synthetic material, used to connect an artery to a vein. It is used in patients requiring frequent venipuncture as in hemodialysis. The shunts may develop complications such as infection, thrombosis, and release of septic emboli.

scrobiculate (skrō-bĭk'ū-lāt) [L. *scrobiculus,* little trench] Having shallow depressions; pitted.

scrobiculus (skrō-bĭk'ū-lŭs) [L., little trench] A small groove or pit.

scrofula (skrŏf'ū-lă) [L., breeding sow] A form of extrapulmonary tuberculosis (TB) in which there is infection of the cervical lymph nodes. It is most common in children under age 15 and may be present without obvious disease in the lung. Like other forms of TB, it is treated with antitubercular drugs (e.g., isoniazid, rifampin, pyrazinamide). SEE: *lymphadenitis, tuberculous.*

scrotal thermography SEE: under *thermography.*

scrotum (skrō'tŭm) *pl.* **scrota, scrotums** [L., a bag] The pouch found in most male mammals that contains the testicles and part of the spermatic cord. Constituent parts of the scrotum are skin; a network of nonstriated muscular fibers called dartos; cremasteric, spermatic, and infundibuliform fasciae; cremasteric muscle; and tunica vaginalis. **scrotal** (-tăl), *adj.*

scrubbing [MD. *schrubben*] **1.** Washing the hands, fingernails, and forearms, including the elbows, prior to donning appropriate gowns and gloves to participate in surgery or other sterile procedures. The precise procedure to follow usually is posted in a special area where the washing is done. It typically entails scrubbing with germicidal soap and water, and using a nail brush to remove debris. **2.** Preparing the skin of the patient for surgery with an antiseptic solution.

scrub solution SEE: under *solution*.

scrub typhus SEE: under *typhus*.

scruple (skrū′pĕl) [L. *scrupulus*, small, sharp stone] ABBR: scr. Twenty grains in apothecaries' weight; 1.296 g.

S-CS *strain and counterstrain.*

scuba *self-contained underwater breathing apparatus.*

sculpt (skŭlpt) [Fr. *sculpter*, to carve] To change the form or shape of a material, including a part of the body. In health care, the term is applied to the contouring of both hard and soft tissues, e.g., using by exercise or cosmetic surgery.

Scultetus, Johannes (skul-tāt′ŭs) Latinized form of Schultes (Schultheiss), Johann, Ger. surgeon, 1595–1645.

    S. binder A many-tailed binder or bandage wrapped in a succession of interlocking, overlapping bands and originally used to enclose a splint against a fractured extremity but now used without the splint or impregnated as a supporting bandage of the abdomen or lower extremity. The binder holds dressings in place and supports abdominal muscles postoperatively.

    S. position A position in which the head is low and the body is on an inclined plane.

scum (skŭm) [ME. *scume*] Slimy floating islands of bacteria or impurities on the surface of a culture; an interrupted pellicle of bacterial growth.

scurf (skŭrf) [AS. *scurf*] A branny desquamation of the epidermis, esp. on the scalp. SEE: *dandruff*.

scurvy (skŭr′vē) [L. *scorbutus*] A disease caused by inadequate intake of ascorbic acid (vitamin C), whose symptoms include fatigue; skin, joint, and gum bleeding; impaired wound healing; dry skin; lower extremity edema; follicular hyperkeratosis; and coiling of body hairs. It is rare in Western nations, where it is found primarily among alcoholics, the chronically mentally ill, and the socially isolated. It can be prevented with regular consumption of fruits and vegetables, foodstuffs that provide a rich source of dietary vitamin C. SEE: illus.

    infantile s. A form of scurvy that sometimes follows the prolonged use of condensed milk, sterilized milk, or pro-

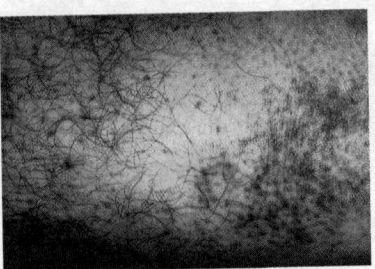

SCURVY

prietary foods that do not contain supplementary vitamin C.

    SYMPTOMS: This condition is characterized by anemia, pseudoparalysis, thickening of the bones from subperiosteal hemorrhage, ecchymoses, nonpitting edema, and a tendency toward fractures of the epiphyses. SYN: *Barlow disease*.

    rebound s. Ascorbic acid deficiency symptoms caused by discontinuation of megadoses of vitamin C.

scute (skūt) [L. *scutum*, shield] A thin plate or scale.

scutum (skū′tŭm) [L., shield] A plate of bone resembling a shield.

scybalous (sĭb′ă-lŭs) [Gr. *skybalon*, dung] Pert. to hard fecal matter.

S.D. **1.** *skin dose.* **2.** *standard deviation.*

SDA **1.** *specific dynamic action.* **2.** *sacrodextra anterior*, the right sacroanterior fetal position.

SDMS *Society of Diagnostic Medical Sonographers.*

SDT *speech detection* **threshold**.

Se Symbol for the element selenium.

S.E. *standard error.*

sea cucumber A cylindrical marine invertebrate of the family Holothuria; some species have tentacles that contain a mild venom. Contact with the organism may produce dermatitis.

seal **1.** To close firmly. **2.** A material such as an adhesive or wax used to make an airtight closure.

    border s. The edge of a denture that contacts the tissues in order to close the area under the denture to entrance by food, air, or liquids.

    posterior palatal s. A seal at the posterior border of a denture.

    velopharyngeal s. A seal between the oral and nasopharyngeal cavities.

sealant A substance applied to prevent leakage into or out of an area.

    dental s. A resin that bonds to the etched enamel of a tooth and forms a protective coating resistant to chemical or physical breakdown. The sealant is placed in the deep pits and fissures to prevent the accumulation of debris and bacteria in cavity-prone areas. Dental sealants are used in addition to fluorides to prevent caries (cavities). Also called *pit and fissure sealant.*

searcher (sĕrch'ĕr) [Fr. *cerchier,* to go around] ²sound.

search strategy (sĕrch) Any method used to identify an object of interest, e.g., to identify journal articles that discuss a topic about which one would like to know more.

seasickness [AS. *sae,* sea, + *seocness,* illness] A form of motion sickness due to the motion of a boat. SEE: *motion sickness.*

seasonal (sēz'ŏn-ăl) Occurring regularly at certain times of the year, e.g., in the summer or winter (but not usually during both). Seasonal allergies follow the predictable pattern of occurring when pollen circulates in the air. Seasonal infections, like influenza, are most common in the winter. **seasonality** (sē″zŏ-nal'ĭt-ē), *n.*

seasonal affective disorder (sēz'ŏn-ăl) ABBR: SAD. A mood disorder characterized by dysphoria or depression in fall and winter, and, sometimes, relative mania or hypomania in the spring and summer. The disorder is more common in women than men, and in younger persons than older ones. SYN: *winter* **depression**.

PATIENT CARE: Treatment consists of phototherapy, esp. during the mornings of the shorter days of the year. Other therapies include antidepressant medications (e.g., bupropion) and psychiatric or psychological counseling (e.g., cognitive behavioral therapy). To increase exposure to natural light, health care professionals should encourage patients to engage in outdoor daytime activities during fall and winter.

seat (sēt) A structure on which another structure rests or is supported.

    basal s. Tissues in the mouth that support a denture.

    bathtub s. **1.** An assistive technology device that helps people with functional limitations to bathe. Some seats have modified features to help people transfer in and out of tubs, pools, or showers. SYN: *bath bench; shower* **s.** **2.** A device for bathing infants.

⚠ Infant drownings have occurred during bathtub seat use.

    elevated toilet s. Raised toilet **s.**

    raised toilet s. A device for raising the height of a toilet to facilitate use by persons with limited strength or movement. SYN: *elevated toilet* **s.**

    rest s. An area on which a denture or restoration rests.

    shower s. Bathtub **s.** (1).

Seating and Mobility Specialist ABBR: SMS. An occupational therapist with specialty certification in providing assistive technology and advice for those needing seating, positioning, or wheeled mobility devices.

seating system Adaptive seating **device**.

sea wasp A common but ambiguous term for several extremely lethal box jellyfish of the class Cubozoa, including *Chironex fleckeri,* of the coastal waters from northern Australia and New Guinea north to the Philippines and Vietnam, and *Carybdea alata Reynaud,* an Australian species also found in the Arabian Sea along the beaches of Pakistan. SEE: *box jellyfish; Cubozoa.*

sebaceous (sē-bā'shŭs) [L. *sebaceus,* made of tallow] Pert. to sebum.

sebaceous gland SEE: under *gland.*

sebo- [L. *sebum,* grease, tallow] Prefix meaning *fat, tallow.*

seborrhea (sĕb-or-ē'ă) [″ + Gr. *rhoia,* flow] A disease of the sebaceous glands marked by an increase in the amount, and often an alteration of the quality, of the fats secreted by the sebaceous glands.

TREATMENT: Mild dandruff, a type of seborrhea, may be treated with a shampoo containing selenium sulfide or sulfur. Severe seborrhea is treated with a lotion or cream containing corticosteroids, rubbed into the affected areas two or three times a day.

    s. capitis Seborrhea of the scalp.

    s. corporis Dermatitis seborrheica.

    s. faciei Seborrhea of the face.

    s. furfuracea Dermatitis seborrheica.

    s. nigricans Seborrhea with pigmented crusts.

    s. oleosa Skin that appears shiny or oily.

    s. sicca Dandruff.

seborrheic (sĕb″ō-rē'ĭk) [L. *sebum,* tallow, + Gr. *rhoia,* flow] Afflicted with or like seborrhea.

sebum (sē'bŭm) [L., tallow] A fatty secretion of the sebaceous glands of the skin. It varies in different parts of the body. Sebum from the ears is called *cerumen;* that from the foreskin is called *smegma.*

    s. palpebrale Lema.

Seckel syndrome (sĕk'ĕl) [H. P. G. Seckel, Ger. Pediatrician, 1900–1960] A rare autosomal recessive disorder characterized by intrauterine growth retardation; dwarfism; facial, skeletal, and dental anomalies; and developmental and neurological deficits.

secondary (sĕk'ŏn-dăr″ē) **1.** Next to or following; second in order. **2.** Produced by a primary cause.

secondary acute respiratory distress syndrome Acute respiratory distress syndrome that results from indirect injury to the lungs, e.g., as a consequence of severe sepsis, pancreatitis, or shock.

SEE: *acute respiratory distress syndrome.*

secondary adrenal insufficiency SEE: under *insufficiency.*

secondary antiphospholipid antibody syndrome ABBR: SAPS. Antiphospholipid antibody syndrome occurring in patients with systemic lupus erythematosus or other rheumatologic syndromes.

secondary nursing care SEE: under *care.*

secondary tumor SEE: under *tumor.*

second cranial nerve The nerve carrying impulses for the sense of sight. It originates in the lateral geniculate body of the thalamus and travels by the optic tract and optic chiasma, where it enters the retina through the optic disk. SYN: *optic nerve.* SEE: *cranial nerve.*

second-hand smoking, secondhand smoking Passive smoking.

second opinion An independent professional review and assessment of a patient made to confirm, add to, or revise the diagnoses and proposed treatments of another medical professional.

secreta (sē-krē′tă) [L.] The products of secretion.

secretagogue (sē-krē′tă-gŏg) [L. *secretum,* secretion, + Gr. *agogos,* leading] **1.** Pert. to the stimulation of secreting organs. **2.** An agent that causes secretion. SYN: *secretogogue.*

secrete (sē-krēt′) [L. *secretio,* separation] **1.** To separate from the blood, a living organism, or a gland. **2.** To form a secretion.

secretin (sē-krē′tĭn) A hormone secreted by the duodenal mucosa that stimulates sodium bicarbonate secretion by the pancreas and bile secretion by the liver. It decreases gastrointestinal peristalsis and motility. SEE: *motilin.*

secretin injection test Cholecystokinin-secretin test.

secretion (sĕ-krē′shŏn) [L. *secretio,* separation] **1.** The making and release of substances by glands. **2.** The substance produced by glandular organs.

   apocrine s. A secretion in which the apical end of a secreting cell is broken off and its contents extruded, as in the mammary gland.

   constituitive s. Secretion of substances (typically proteins) from cells, either continuously or independently of cell-to-cell signaling.

   eccrine s. Secretion of sweat from glands located in the skin, an important means of regulating temperature.

   ectopic hormone s. Ectopic hormone production.

   holocrine s. A secretion in which the entire cell and its contents are extruded as a part of the secretory product, as in sebaceous glands.

   merocrine s. A secretion in which the product is elaborated within cells and

discharged through the cell membrane, the cell itself remaining intact.

   regulated s. The secretion of substances stored in intracellular vesicles after a cell receives a specific stimulus, either from a circulating hormone or from a nerve.

secretoglobin Any of a family of small secreted mammalian proteins (consisting of approx. 70 linked amino acids) of unknown function. They are highly genetically conserved. Many are potent allergens.

secretogogue (sē-krē′tō-gŏg) [L. *secretio,* separation, + Gr. *agogos,* leading] Secretagogue.

secretome (sĕ-krĕt′ōm″) [*secret(ion)* +-*ome*] All of the protein products that a cell or tissue exports.

secretomotor (sē-krē″tō-mō′tor) Something, esp. a nerve, that stimulates secretion.

secretor (si-krēt′ŏr) A person who secretes ABO blood group antigens into mucous secretions such as saliva, gastric juice, or semen. The secretion of such substances is sometimes used for the legal identification of individuals in violent crimes (e.g., rape).

secretory (sē′krĕ-tor″ē) Pert. to or promoting secretion; secreting.

sectio (sĕk′shē-ō) [L., a cutting] A section or cut.

section (sek′shŏn) [L. *sectio,* a cutting] **1.** The act of cutting. **2.** A division or segment of a part. SEE: *plane* for illus. **3.** A surface made by cutting. **4.** In radiology, a slice. SEE: *slice.*

   abdominal s. Laparotomy.

   cesarean s. SEE: *cesarean section.*

   coronal s. Frontal **s.**

   cross s. A section perpendicular to the long axis of an organ.

   frontal s. A section dividing the body into two parts, dorsal and ventral. SYN: *coronal s.*

   frozen s. A thin section of surgically obtained tissue frozen to permit rapid examination of the specimen under the microscope by a pathologist. The specimen is usually obtained intraoperatively, while the patient is still anesthetized. The surgeon's further action (such as to operate, to obtain clear margins, or to close the incision) is influenced by the findings.

   ground s. A section of bone or tooth prepared for histological study by polishing until thin enough for microscope viewing.

   longitudinal s. A section parallel to the long axis of an organ.

   midsagittal s. A section that divides the body into right and left halves.

   paraffin s. A section of a tissue that has been infiltrated with paraffin.

   perineal s. An external incision into the urethra to relieve stricture.

   Pitres s. SEE: *Pitres section.*

sagittal s. A section cut parallel to the median plane of the body.

serial s. Any of several microscopic sections made and arranged in consecutive order.

vaginal s. A surgical incision of the vagina.

sectioning [L. *sectio,* a cutting] The slicing of thin sections of tissue for examination under the microscope. SEE: *microtome.*

ultrathin s. The cutting of sections extraordinarily thin (less than 1 μm thick), esp. for use in electron microscopy.

Section 504 of the Rehabilitation Act of 1973 A U.S. federal statute that prohibits discrimination against or denial of benefits to an individual on the basis of disability by any agency, business, or organization that receives federal support.

Section 508 of the Rehabilitation Act of 1973 A U.S. federal statute that makes it unlawful for a federal agency to deny a person access to electronic or information technology on the basis of disability.

sector (sĕk′tor) [L., cutter] **1.** The area of a circle included between two radii and an arc. **2.** The physical location for a specific activity designated in the incident management system.

rehab s. The location at a multiple-casualty incident, fire, or hazardous materials incident where rescue personnel are sent to be medically monitored, rehydrated, cooled off, or warmed.

staging s. A location within a minute or two's response to the scene of a multiple-casualty incident, hazmat incident, or major fire where emergency vehicles and personnel are assigned to wait till they are needed at the location.

transport s. At a multiple-casualty incident, the place where ambulances or helicopters, or both, are brought in to transport patients to hospitals. At the transport sector, decisions are made regarding where to send patients with specialized problems, and the status of triaged patients is discussed with receiving facilities.

treatment s. The location at a multiple-casualty incident where patients' needs are prioritized and their injuries or illnesses are initially managed before they are taken to a hospital.

triage s. In a multiple-casualty incident, the place where patients are sorted and separated according to the acuity of their illnesses or injuries before they are transported to a treatment sector or hospital.

sectorial (sĕk-tō′rē-ăl) Having cutting edges, as teeth.

secundines (sek′ŭn-dēnz″, -dīnz″, sĕ-kŭn′dinz) [L. *secundinae,* fr. *secundus,* second] Afterbirth.

secure 1. Free from danger, fear, care, or worry. **2.** Under lock and key. **3.** Stable; protected.

S.E.D. *skin erythema dose.*

sedation (si-dā′shŏn) [L. *sedatio,* a calming] **1.** The process of allaying nervous excitement. **2.** The state of being calmed.

conscious s. A minimally depressed level of consciousness during which the patient retains the ability to maintain a patent airway and respond appropriately to physical or verbal commands. This is accomplished by the use of appropriate analgesics and sedatives. This type of sedation is used for several procedures, including changing of wound or burn dressings and endoscopic examinations. SYN: *procedural s.*

⚠️ Conscious sedation must be closely monitored to prevent loss of protective airway reflexes. The health care team must be ready to recognize and respond to complications that require airway management, intubation, and resuscitation. Drugs to reverse the effects of opioids (such as naloxone) and benzodiazepines (such as flumazenil) are used to awaken sedated patients.

deep s. A depressed level of consciousness produced by medications that suppress anxiety, awareness, memory, or pain, in which a patient may not be able to protect his or her own airway, arouse easily, or respond purposefully to verbal commands or physical stimulation.

PATIENT CARE: During deep sedation patients require intensive monitoring of vital signs and neurological status. The patient's airway, breathing, oxygenation, pulse, and blood pressure must be carefully and repeatedly assessed to avoid complications such as anoxic or hypoxic damage to internal organs or cardiorespiratory arrest.

dissociative s. A trancelike state induced by anesthetics in which a patient feels no pain, and has no memory of unpleasant events, but can cooperate with commands and suggestions. In this state the patient has normal airway (protective) reflexes. One drug that produces dissociative sedation is ketamine.

minimal s. The relief of anxiety without any impairment in the ability to breathe, move, or respond to other people.

moderate s. A medically controlled depressed state of consciousness in which patients can maintain an open airway and protective airway reflexes; respond appropriately when stimulated physically or verbally; and spontaneously maintain a stable heart rate and blood pressure.

palliative s. The administration of sedative and hypnotic drugs to dying patients to induce coma and alleviate pain and suffering. It is a technique used in end-of-life care when other measures to achieve comfort for the dying patient have failed. Medications such as barbiturates and opiates are used to tranquilize the patient. The intent is not to hasten death, although ultimately, palliative sedation induces a coma from which the patient will not awaken.

procedural s. Conscious **s.**

sedative (sĕd'ă-tĭv) [L. *sedativus,* calming] **1.** Quieting. **2.** An agent that exerts a soothing or tranquilizing effect. Sedatives may be general, local, or vascular.

sedentary (sĕd'ĕn-tā'rē) [L. *sedentarius*] **1.** Sitting. **2.** Pert. to an inactive occupation or mode of living, i.e., one in which there is minimal physical exertion.

s. lifestyle A lifestyle involving little exercise, even of the least strenuous type. Sedentary living is associated with weight gain, obesity, type 2 diabetes mellitus, and, in many studies, an increased risk of coronary artery disease. SEE: *physical fitness; risk factor.*

sediment (sĕd'ĭ-mĕnt) [L. *sedimentum,* a settling] The substance settling at the bottom of a liquid. SEE: *precipitate.*

urinary s. Substances present in urine (i.e., bacteria, mucus, phosphates, uric acid, calcium oxalate, calcium carbonate, calcium phosphate, magnesium and ammonium phosphate; and more rarely, cystine, tyrosine, xanthine, hippuric acid, hematoidin) that separate and accumulate at the bottom of a container of urine. This process may be accelerated by centrifuging the urine specimen.

sedimentation (sĕd"ĭ-mĕn-tā'shŭn) Formation or depositing of sediment. SEE: *sedimentation rate.*

seed (sēd) [AS. *saed*] **1.** The ripened ovule of a spermatophyte plant usually consisting of the embryo (germ) and a supply of nutrient material enclosed within the seed coat. It is a resting sporophyte. **2.** Semen. **3.** A capsule containing radon or radium in the treatment of cancer. **4.** To introduce microorganisms into a culture medium.

segment (seg'mĕnt) [L. *segmentum,* a portion] **1.** A part or section, esp. a natural one, of an organ or body. **2.** One of the serial divisions of an animal.

anterior s. **1.** In ophthalmology, the ciliary body, cornea, iris and lens of the eye. **2.** In dentistry, the canine and incisor teeth.

bronchopulmonary s. A small subdivision of the lobes of the lung.

P-R s. The line on an electrocardiogram that begins with the end of the P

wave and ends with the beginning of the QRS. It corresponds to the period between the end of atrial depolarization and the onset of ventricular depolarization.

Q-T segment Q-T **interval**.

ST s., S-T segment The line on an electrocardiogram that begins with the end of the QRS complex and ends at the beginning of the T wave. The height of the ST segment is normally equal to that of the P-R interval and the TP interval. ST segment elevation is found in patients with acute myocardial infarction and other conditions. ST segment depression is an indicator of coronary ischemia.

uterine s. One of the two functional divisions of the uterine musculature during labor. During labor the upper uterine segment forcibly contracts, becoming progressively shorter and thicker, exerting traction on the more passive lower segment, and increasing the hydrostatic pressure against the cervix. The combination of forces and traction gradually cause the lower segment to thin, resulting in cervical effacement and dilation. SEE: *physiologic retraction ring.*

segmentation (sĕg"mĕn-tā'shŭn) Cleavage.

segmenter (sĕg'mĕnt"ĕr) A stage in the development of malarial parasites (genus *Plasmodium*) in which the organism undergoes schizogony.

segregation [L. *segregare,* to separate] **1.** Setting apart, separating. **2.** In genetics, the process that takes place in the formation of germ cells (gametogenesis) in which each gamete (egg or sperm) receives only one of each pair of genes.

segregator An instrument composed of two ureteral catheters for securing urine from each kidney separately.

SeHCAT [75]*selenium-labeled artificial bile salt* (a homolog to taurocholate).

seizure (sē'zhŭr) **1.** A convulsion or other clinically detectable event caused by a sudden discharge of electrical activity in the brain. **2.** A sudden attack of pain, disease, or specific symptoms.

absence s. Seizure in which there is a sudden, brief lapse of consciousness, usually for about 2 to 10 sec. The patient (typically a child) shows a blank facial expression that may be accompanied by movements such as repeated eye-blinking or rolling or lip-smacking and minor myoclonus of the upper extremities or neck. There is no convulsion or fall. The patient resumes activity as if the seizure had not occurred. The seizure may be induced by voluntary hyperventilation for 2 to 3 min. This type of attack is characteristic of petit mal epilepsy and may recur repeatedly if it is not recognized and treated. It also may progress to a generalized tonic-clonic seizure.

PATIENT CARE: The time, duration, patient's expression, and any repetitive movements occurring during the seizure are observed and documented, as is the patient's postseizure response. Prescribed medications are administered and evaluated for desired effects and adverse reactions. Support, reassurance, and education regarding the condition as well as drug actions and side effects are provided to the patient and family, and they are encouraged to discuss their feelings and concerns and to ask questions. SEE: *epilepsy*.

    breakthrough s. A seizure that occurs despite the use of therapeutic concentrations of a previously effective antiepileptic drug.

    complex s. A seizure in which the patient suffers a loss of consciousness.

    convulsive s. **1.** A convulsion. **2.** An attack of epilepsy. SEE: *epilepsy*.

    generalized s. A seizure in which abnormal electrical activity occurs in large areas of the brain. Generalized seizures usually result in loss of consciousness.

    grand mal s. SEE: under *epilepsy*.

    jacksonian s. A localized form of epilepsy with spasms confined to one part or one group of muscles. SEE: *epilepsy*.

    nonepileptic s. A seizure often accompanied by loss of consciousness, due to inadequate perfusion of the brain, e.g., during a sudden lowering of blood pressure or, in treated diabetic patients, from hypoglycemia.

    petit mal s. SEE: *epilepsy*.

    psychogenic nonepileptic s. ABBR: PNES. The preferred term for pseudoseizure.

    simple s. A seizure in which there is no loss of consciousness.

    uncinate s. A seizure marked by olfactory and gustatory hallucinations (usually disagreeable), a sense of unreality; and sometimes convulsions and temporary loss of senses of taste and smell. This is associated with lesions of the uncinate gyrus of the temporal lobe of the brain.

seizure trigger Anything that causes seizures to occur. Triggers include consumption of alcohol, withdrawal after heavy alcohol use, fever, lack of sleep, or other physiological or psychological stressors.

SELDI *surface-enhanced laser desorption-ionization.*

Seldinger technique (sel′ding-ĕr) [Sven Ivar Seldinger, Swedish physician, 1921–1998] A method of percutaneous introduction of a catheter into a vessel. The vessel is located and a needle inserted. Once a good blood flow is obtained, a wire is threaded through the needle well into the vessel. The needle is then removed, and the catheter is threaded over the wire into the vessel. The wire helps the insertion of the catheter and guides it into the appropriate vessel. Once the catheter is positioned in the desired intravascular area, the wire is removed. Sterile technique is imperative.

selectin Any of a group of cell surface molecules that influence the attachment and movement of white blood cells to other cells and to the lining of blood vessels, e.g., in inflammatory diseases and conditions.

    P-s. An adhesion receptor molecule for white blood cells that functions during inflammation and tissue repair. Binding with P-selectin glycoprotein ligand 1, it controls the flow of white blood cells and their adhesion to blood vessel walls. It is viewed as a key factor in thrombosis.

selection (sĕ-lek′shŏn) [L. *selectio,* choice] **1.** A choosing or selecting; choice. **2.** In biology, the factors that determine the reproductive ability of a certain genotype.

    adverse s. The enrollment in a health plan of those who are sicker or use more health care services than the general population.

    artificial s. A process by which humans select desirable characteristics in animals and breed them for these phenotypes.

    clonal s. **1.** The process by which T lymphocytes with receptors that react to autoantigens are destroyed in the thymus. **2.** The increase of particular B or T lymphocyte clones after recognition of a specific antigen to which the body has been exposed. SEE: *negative s.; clone.*

    natural s. A theory of evolution proposed by Charles Darwin stating that the genotypes best adapted to their environment have a tendency to survive and reproduce.

    negative s. The process by which immature T lymphocytes (thymocytes) with receptors for autoantigens are destroyed in the thymus. It is part of the mechanism that prevents autoimmune diseases. SEE: *autoimmunity.*

    sexual s. **1.** The choice of the gender of an offspring through methods that increase the likelihood of conceiving either a girl or a boy. **2.** A theory originated to account for differences in secondary sex characteristics between male and female animals (including humans). It assumes that individuals preferentially mate with individuals of the opposite sex that possess identifiably distinct phenotypes.

selection pressure Any change in the environment that encourages particular mutations to succeed. For example, antibiotic use kills susceptible bacteria and allows microorganisms with resistant genes to survive and proliferate.

selective androgen receptor modulator ABBR: SARM. A class of medications that attach to cellular binding sites for male hormones. They maximize anabolic effects but limit side effects. They may be used to treat conditions such as male hypogonadism or age-related bone loss.

selective decontamination of the digestive tract The administration of nonabsorbable antibiotics to reduce the burden of potentially infectious bacteria in the gastrointestinal tract.

It may be used to decrease the incidence of ventilator-associated pneumonia or to rid the gastrointestinal tract of bacteria before surgery.

selective estrogen receptor modulator Estrogen analog.

selective nonoperative management ABBR: SNOM. Nonoperative management.

selective oropharyngeal decontamination ABBR: SOD. SEE: under *decontamination*.

selective progesterone receptor modulator ABBR: SPRM. A class of medications that attach to cellular binding sites for progesterone, and stimulate those sites, block them, or both block and stimulate them. They have several uses in obstetrics and gynecology. Antagonist (blocking) agents like mifepristone can induce abortion. Agonist (receptor-stimulating) drugs may be used to treat uterine fibroids.

selective serotonin reuptake inhibitor SEE: under *inhibitor*.

selenium (sĕ-lē′nē-ŭm) [Gr. *selēnē*, moon + *-ium* (1) (so named because it resembles tellurium)] SYMB: Se. A chemical element resembling sulfur; atomic weight (mass) 78.96, atomic number 34. It is considered an essential trace element in the diet. Toxicity can occur when an excessive amount is ingested, characterized by a sour breath odor, nausea, vomiting, abdominal pain, restlessness, hypersalivation, and muscle spasms.

self 1. In psychology, the sum of mind and body that constitutes the identity of a person. 2. In immunology, an individual's antigenic makeup.

self-acceptance Being realistic about oneself and at the same time comfortable with that personal assessment.

self-antigen (self′ant′ĭ-jen″) Autoantigen.

self-care (self″kar′) 1. A concept in Dorothea Orem's Self-Care Framework and her Theory of Self-Care referring to actions that people initiate and perform on their own behalf in maintaining life, health, and well-being. 2. In rehabilitation, the subset of activities of daily living that includes eating, dressing, grooming, bathing, and toileting. SYN: *personal care*.

   s.-c. deficit Impaired ability to feed, dress, groom or bathe oneself; to use the toilet or maintain personal hygiene on a temporary, permanent, or progressing basis. (Specify level of independence using a standardized functional scale). SEE: *health maintenance, altered; home maintenance management, impaired; Nursing Diagnoses Appendix.*

self-care, readiness for enhanced A pattern of performing activities for oneself that helps to meet health-related goals and can be strengthened. SEE: *Nursing Diagnoses Appendix.*

Self-Care Framework A conceptual model of nursing, also known as the Self-Care Deficit Theory of Nursing and the Self-Care Deficit Nursing Theory, developed by Dorothea Orem. The person is a self-care agent who has a therapeutic self-care demand made up of universal, developmental, and health deviation self-care requisites. The goal of nursing is to help people to meet their therapeutic self-care demands. SEE: *Nursing Theory Appendix.*

self-concept An individual's perception of self in relation to others and the environment. SEE: *self-esteem.*

self-concept, readiness for enhanced A pattern of perceptions or ideas about the self that is sufficient for well-being and can be strengthened. SEE: *Nursing Diagnoses Appendix.*

self-conscious Being aware of oneself, esp. overly aware of appearance and actions, and thus being ill at ease.

self-contained breathing apparatus ABBR: SCBA. A device that provides compressed air for breathing in hazardous breathing environments. It is used, for example, by rescue personnel.

self-contained underwater breathing apparatus ABBR: scuba. A device used by swimmers and divers that enables them to breathe underwater. The mask worn is watertight and is connected to a tank of compressed air. SEE: *bends.*

self-determination theory SEE: under *theory.*

self-differentiation The differentiation of a structure or tissue due to intrinsic factors.

self-digestion Autodigestion.

self-efficacy An aspect of self-perception postulated by Albert Bandura that pertains to one's belief in his or her ability to perform a given task or behavior.

self-esteem One's personal evaluation or view of self, generally thought to influence feelings and behaviors. One's personal successes, expectations, and appraisals of the views others hold toward oneself are thought to influence this personal appraisal. SYN: *self-concept.*

   chronic low s.-e. Long-standing negative feelings about self or capabilities. SEE: *situational low s.-e.; Nursing Diagnoses Appendix.*

   situational low s.-e. Episodic feelings about self or capabilities that develop in response to a loss or change. SEE: *chronic low s.-e.; Nursing Diagnoses Appendix.*

self-examination (self″ĕg-zam″ĭ-nā′shŏn) Inspection and palpation of a body part by the patient to screen for disease. SEE: *breast self-examination; testicular self-examination.*

self-governance **1.** Self-rule; local responsibility for administration and functions of an organization, even though it is part of a larger entity. **2.** A model of health care management in which the power base for decisions of patient care is decentralized. The responsibility and accountability for patient care rest directly with all levels of care providers through self-direction, self-regulation, and self-management. Advisory committees reflecting a cross section of caregivers (new graduates, experienced professionals, faculty, and managers) maintain final decision-making authority within the work setting. SEE: *shared governance.*

self-help (sĕlf′hĕlp″) Action taken by a person to improve his or her life educationally, emotionally, financially, interpersonally, or socially.

self-hypnosis (self″hip-nō′sĭs, -nō′sēz) *pl.* **self-hypnoses** [*self* + *hypnosis*] Self-induced **hypnotism**.

self-insured Having personal financial responsibility for health care costs, as a result of dedicated savings or investments.

self-limited disease A disease that eventually goes away even if untreated.

self-management Active participation by a patient in his or her own health care decisions and interventions. With the education and guidance of professional caregivers, the patient promotes his or her own optimal health or recovery.

self-medication The use of mood-altering substances, such as alcohol or opiates, in an attempt to alleviate depression, anxiety, or other psychiatric disorders.

self-mutilation, risk for A state in which an individual is at high risk to perform a deliberate act upon the self with the intent to injure, not kill, which produces immediate tissue damage to the body. SEE: *Nursing Diagnoses Appendix.*

self-pity A mental defense mechanism involving self-blame, negativism, feelings of rejection, worthlessness, hopelessness, or isolation.

self-retaining retractor (self′ri-tān′ing) SEE: under *retractor.*

self-soothing A deliberate effort to calm oneself. It is an alternative to the use of medications, alcohol, or drugs for man-

aging anxiety and stress, eating disorders, or insomnia.

self-tolerance In immunology, the absence of an immune response to one's own antigens. SEE: *autoimmunity.*

sella turcica (sĕl′ă tŭr′sĭ-kă) [NL., Turkish saddle] On the base of the interior of the skull, a concavity on the superior surface of the body of the sphenoid bone that houses the pituitary gland. Inside the bone under the fossa are sphenoidal air sinuses. SYN: *pituitary **fossa**.*

Sellick maneuver (sel′ik) [Brian A. Sellick, contemporary Brit. anesthetist] The application of digital pressure to the cricoid cartilage in the neck in an unconscious patient to reduce gastric distention and passive regurgitation during positive pressure ventilation, and to improve visualization of the glottic opening during endotracheal intubation.

semantic interference Anything that blocks the acquisition, recall, or retention of words.

semantics (sē-măn′tĭks) [Gr. *semantikos,* significant] The study of the meanings of words.

semen (sē′mĕn) *pl.* **semina** [L. *semen,* seed, semen] A thick, opalescent, viscid secretion discharged from the urethra of the male at the climax of sexual excitement (orgasm). Semen is the mixed product of various glands (prostate and bulbourethral) plus the spermatozoa, which, having been produced in the testicles, are stored in the seminal vesicles.

   Normal values for the seminal fluid ejaculate are as follows: volume, 2 to 5 ml; pH, 7.8 to 8.0; leukocytes, absent or only an occasional one seen per high-power field; sperm count, 60 to 150 million/ml; motility, 80% or more should be motile; morphology, 80% to 90% should be normal.

   frozen s. Semen collected, analyzed and stored at $-196°F$ ($-90°C$) for future use in artificial insemination by clinics specializing in infertility. In artificial insemination the number of successful pregnancies is lower with frozen semen than with fresh.

semenarche (sē′mĕn-ăr″kē) [″ + *arche,* beginning] During puberty, the beginning of the production of semen. SEE: *pubarche; thelarche.*

semi- [L. *semi-,* half] Prefix meaning *half.*

semicircular (sĕm″ē-sŭr′kū-lăr) [″ + *circulus,* a ring] Shaped like a semicircle.

semiconscious (sĕm″ē-kŏn′shŭs) Not fully conscious.

-semide [Fm. *(furo)semide*] A suffix used in pharmacology to designate any loop diuretic similar in chemical structure to that of furosemide.

semiflexion (sĕm″ē-flĕk′shŭn) [″ +

flexio, bending] Halfway between flexion and extension of a limb.

semilunar (sĕm″ē-lū′năr) [L. *semis,* half, + *luna,* moon] Shaped like a crescent.

semimembranous (sĕm″ē-mĕm′bră-nŭs) [″ + L. *membrana,* membrane] Composed partly of a membrane.

seminal (sĕm′ĭ-năl) [L. *seminalis*] Pert. to the semen or seed.

seminal emission Discharge of semen.

semination (sem″ĭ-nā′shŏn) [L. *seminatio,* breeding, propagation] Insemination.

   artificial s. Artificial **insemination**.

seminiferous (sĕm-ĭn-ĭf′ĕr-ŭs) [L. *semen,* seed, + *ferre,* to produce] Producing or conducting semen, as the tubules of the testes.

seminoma (sĕm″ĭ-nō′mă) [″ + Gr. *oma,* tumor] A cancer arising from male germ cells (in the testis) that makes up about half of all testicular malignancies.

   TREATMENT: Seminomas that are confined to the testes are surgically removed. Metastatic disease is treated with surgery (to remove the testis) and radiation and chemotherapy.

semiology (sē″mē-ol′ŏ-jē, sem″ē-) [Gr. *sēmeion,* sign + *-logy*] **1.** Semiotics. **2.** Symptomatology (2).

semiotics (sē″mē-ot′ĭks) [Gr. *sēmeiōtikos,* noticing signs, observant, fr *sēmeion,* sign] The study of signs and systems that convey particular meanings in language and culture. The language can be natural or artificial. The discipline can include gestures, symbols, objects, mannerisms, clothing, and other means for conveying meaning. SYN: *semiology* (1). **semiotic,** *adj.*

semipermeable (sĕm″ē-per′mē-ă-bl) [″ + *per,* through, + *meare,* to pass] Pert. to cell membranes that permit the passage of some materials but not others; selectively permeable.

semipronation (sĕm″ē-prō-nā′shŭn) [″ + *pronus,* prone] **1.** A semiprone position. **2.** The act of assuming a semiprone position.

semiprone (sĕm-ē-prōn′) [″ + *pronus,* prone] In a position on left side and chest, with both thighs flexed on abdomen, the right higher than the left, and left arm back. SYN: *Sims' position.*

semirecumbent (sĕm″ē-rē-kŭm′bĕnt) [″ + *recumbere,* to lie down] Reclining, but not fully recumbent.

semis (sē′mĭs) [L.] ABBR: ss. Half.

semispinalis (sĕm″ē-spī-năl′ĭs) [L.] The deep layer of muscle of the back on either side of the spinal column. It is divided into the following three parts: the semispinalis capitis, semispinalis cervicis, and semispinalis thoracis.

semisupine (sĕm″ē-sū′pīn) [″ + *supinus,* lying on the back] Not completely supine.

semisynthetic (sĕm″ē-sĭn-thĕt′ĭk) [″ +

Gr. *synthetikos,* synthetic] The chemical alteration of a portion of a natural substance.

semitendinosus (sĕm″ē-tĕn″dĭn-ō′sŭs) [L.] The fusiform muscle of the posterior and inner part of the thigh.

semitendinous (sĕm″ē-tĕn′dĭ-nŭs) [L. *semis,* half, + *tendinosus,* tendinous] Of some muscles, partially tendinous.

Semmelweiss, Ignaz Philipp (zĕm′ĕl-vīs″) Hungarian physician, 1818–1865, the discoverer of the mode of transmission of childbed fever (puerperal sepsis) in the 19th century. Semmelweiss is a seminal figure in the history of infection control.

Sen In Thai massage, the streams in which the body's energy flows; they are located in specific areas of the body. Thai massage techniques are designed to balance the Sen.

senescence (sĕ-nes′ĕns) [L. *senescens,* growing old] **1.** The process of growing old. **2.** The period of old age.

   premature s. Aging (typically of cells, but also of whole organisms) that occurs much earlier than is expected under healthy or optimal conditions.

   replicative s. Hayflick limit.

Sengstaken-Blakemore tube (sengz′tă-kĕn-blāk′mor″) [Robert W. Sengstaken, U.S. neurosurgeon, b. 1923; Arthur H. Blakemore, U.S. surgeon, 1897–1970] A three-lumen tube for treating bleeding esophageal varices by directly compressing the bleeding vessels.

senile (sē′nīl, sĕn′īl) [L. *senilis,* old] Pert. to the debility associated with aging.

senility (sē-nĭl′ĭ-tē) [L. *senilis,* old] Mental or physical weakness associated with old age. Many specialists in aging find the term offensive.

   premature s. Onset of senile characteristics before old age (e.g., in Down syndrome).

senior center SEE: under *center.*

senior friendly Easy for senior citizens to use, e.g., certain forms of medication packaging.

Senior-Loken syndrome, Senior-Løken syndrome (sēn′yŏr-lō′kĕn) [Boris Senior, South African pediatrician; Aagot Christie Løken, Norwegian neuropathologist, b. 1911] An autosomal recessive disease characterized by nephronophthisis and progressive degeneration of the retina.

senium (sē′nē-ŭm) [L.] Old age, esp. its debility.

senna (sĕn′ă) [Arabic *sana*] The dried leaves of the plants *Cassia acutifolia* and *C. angustifolia;* used as a cathartic.

sennosides (sĕn′ō-sīdz) Anthraquinone glucosides present in senna that are used as cathartics.

sensate (sĕn-sāt′) Perceived by the senses.

sensate focus An area, such as an erogenous zone, that is particularly sensitive to tactile stimulation.

sensation (sen-sā'shŏn) [L. *sensatio*] An awareness of conditions inside or outside the body resulting from the stimulation of sensory receptors.

   cutaneous **s.** A sensation arising from the receptors of the skin.

   delayed **s.** A sensation not experienced immediately following a stimulus.

   gnostic **s.** One of the more finely developed senses such as touch, tactile discrimination, position sense, and vibration.

   internal **s.** Subjective **s.**

   phantom **s.** Phantom limb pain.

   primary **s.** A sensation that results from a direct stimulus.

   referred **s.** A sensation that seems to arise from one location in the body, even though it originates in another. SYN: *reflex* **s.**

   reflex **s.** Referred **s.**

   somesthetic **s.** Vibration sense; proprioception.

   subjective **s.** A sensation that does not result from any external stimulus and is perceptible only by the subject. SYN: *internal* **s.**

   tactile **s.** A sensation produced through the sense of touch.

sense (sens) [L. *sensus,* a feeling] **1.** To perceive through a sense organ. **2.** The general faculty by which conditions outside or inside the body are perceived. The most important of the senses are sight, hearing, smell, taste, touch and pressure, temperature, weight, resistance and tension (muscle sense), pain, position, proprioception, visceral and sexual sensations, equilibrium, and hunger and thirst. **3.** Any special faculty of sensation connected with a particular organ. **4.** Normal power of understanding. **5.** The ability of an artificial pacemaker to detect an electrically conducted signal produced by the heart, such as a P wave or QRS complex. **6.** In nucleic acid chemistry, the strand of DNA whose nucleotide order codes for messenger RNA.

   color **s.** The ability to distinguish differences in color; one of the three parts of visual function.

   form **s.** The ability to recognize shapes; one of the three parts of visual function.

   kinesthetic **s.** The brain's awareness of the position of muscles, both moving and at rest. The sense may be conscious or unconscious. SYN: *motor* **s.**; *muscular* **s.**

   light **s.** One of the three parts of visual function, the other parts being color sense and form sense. It is tested by visual field examination. SEE: *color* **s.**; *form* **s.**

   motor **s.** Kinesthetic **s.**

   muscular **s.** Kinesthetic **s.**

   posture **s.** Proprioception.

   pressure **s.** The ability to feel various degrees of pressure on the body surface. SYN: *baresthesia.*

   space **s.** The sense by which people recognize objects in space, their relationship, and their dimensions.

   special **s.** The senses of sight, touch, hearing, equilibrium, smell, and taste.

   static **s.** The sense that makes it possible to maintain equilibrium.

   stereognostic **s.** The ability to judge the consistency and shape of objects held in the fingers.

   temperature **s.** The ability to detect differences of temperature. The receptors for heat and cold are free nerve endings in the dermis; sensory impulses may be perceived by the thalamus as a poorly localized temperature sensation. The sensory area of the parietal lobe can localize the sensation much more precisely. Adaptation is fairly rapid unless the temperature is extreme. SYN: *thermal* **s.**; *thermesthesia.*

   thermal **s.** Temperature **s.**

   time **s.** The ability to detect differences in time intervals.

   tone **s.** The ability to distinguish between different tones.

   vibratory **s.** The ability to perceive vibrations transmitted through the skin to deep tissues. It is usually tested by placing a vibrating tuning fork over bony prominences.

   visceral **s.** The subjective perception of the sensations of the internal organs.

sensibility (sĕn"sĭ-bĭl'ĭ-tē) [L. *sensibilitas*] The capacity to receive and respond to stimuli.

   deep **s.** **1.** The sensibility existing after an area of the skin is made anesthetic. **2.** The sensation by which the position of a limb and estimation of difference in weight and tension are apparent.

sensibilization (sĕn"sĭ-bĭl-ĭ-zā'shŭn) **1.** Sensitization. **2.** The induction of susceptibility to or irritation by a foreign substance by injecting it or applying it to the body. SYN: *sensitization.*

sensible (sĕn'sĭ-bl) [L. *sensibilis,* capable of being perceived] **1.** Capable of being perceived by the senses; perceptible. **2.** Having reason. **3.** Measurable.

sensitive (sĕn'sĭ-tĭv) [L. *sensitivus,* of sensation] **1.** Capable of perceiving or feeling a sensation. SYN: *sentient.* **2.** Subject to destructive action of a complement. **3.** Susceptible to suggestions, as a hypnotic. **4.** Abnormally susceptible to a substance, as a drug or foreign protein. SEE: *allergy.*

sensitivity **1.** The susceptibility of a pathogen to treatment with a particular antibiotic. SEE: *sensitivity test, antimicrobial.* **2.** Irritability or excitability to stimulation, e.g., of neurons or people.

3. In assessing the value of a diagnostic test, procedure, or clinical observation, the proportion of people who truly have a specific disease and are so identified by the test. SEE: *specificity, diagnostic.*

sensitivity training SEE: under *training.*

sensitization (sĕn″sĭ-tĭ-zā′shŭn) **1.** The production by B lymphocytes of specific antibodies and by T lymphocytes of specific cellular reactions to a foreign antigen. When the antigen is encountered again, an immune response occurs. The production of antibodies by B lymphocytes or the activation of T lymphocytes when an allergen is first encountered. When the allergen is encountered again, an abnormal immune response occurs. SEE: *hypersensitivity.* **2.** The process of making a person susceptible to a substance by repeated injections of it. SYN: *sensibilization.*

    active s. Sensitization produced by injecting an antigen into a susceptible person.

    autoerythrocyte s. A syndrome characterized by the spontaneous appearance of painful ecchymoses, usually at the site of a bruise. The areas itch and burn. The condition is commonly associated with headache, nausea, vomiting, and occasionally with intracranial, genitourinary, and gastrointestinal bleeding. With few exceptions, the disorder affects women of middle age. The cause is assumed to be autosensitivity to a component of the red blood cell membrane. There is no specific therapy. SYN: *purpura; psychogenic.*

    passive s. Sensitization produced in a healthy person by injecting the person with the serum from a sensitized animal or human.

    protein s. Sensitization as a result of previous injection of a foreign protein into the body.

sensitized (sĕn′sĭ-tīzd) Made susceptible, or immunoreactive, to an antigen.

sensitizer (sĕn′sĭ-tī″zĕr) [L. *sensitivus,* of sensation] In allergy and dermatology, a substance that makes the susceptible individual react to the same or other irritants.

sensitometer (sĕn″sĭ-tŏm′ĕ-tĕr) A calibrated instrument with an optical step wedge and light source that puts a graduated set of densities on a radiographic film; used in quality control monitoring for film processors.

sensitometry (sĕn″sĭ-tŏm′ĕ-trē) In radiography, the use of densities on an exposed and processed film to evaluate, monitor, and maintain processors, intensifying screens, film types, and exposure systems.

sensomobility (sĕn″sō-mō-bĭl′ĕ-tē) [L. *sensus,* a feeling, + *mobilis,* mobile] Movement in response to a stimulus.

sensor (sĕn′sor) **1.** A sense organ. **2.** A device sensitive to electricity, light, heat, pressure, radiation, sound, or other chemical, mechanical, or physical stimuli.

sensorimotor (sĕn″so-rē-mō′tor) [L. *sensus,* a feeling, + *motus,* moving] Both sensory and motor.

sensorineural (sĕn″sō-rē-nū′răl) [″ + *neuralis,* neural] Pert. to a sensory nerve.

sensorium (sĕn-sor′ē-ŭm) *pl.* **sensoriums, sensoria** [L., organ of sensation] **1.** That portion of the brain that functions as a center of sensations. **2.** The sensory apparatus of the body taken as a whole. **3.** Awareness; consciousness. **sensorial** (-sō′rē-ăl), *adj.*

sensory (sĕn′sō-rē) [L. *sensorius*] **1.** Conveying impulses from sense organs to the reflex or higher centers. SYN: *afferent.* **2.** Pert. to sensation.

sensory area Any area of the cerebral cortex in which sensations are perceived.

sensory effect level The concentration of a pollutant or toxin to a level that is detectable and perceived as noxious.

sensory ending A termination of an afferent nerve fiber that upon stimulation gives rise to a sensation. SEE: *receptor, sensory.*

sensory integration Skill and performance required in the development and coordination of sensory input, motor output, and sensory feedback. It includes sensory awareness, visual spatial awareness, body integration, balance, bilateral motor coordination, visuomotor integration, praxis, and other components.

sensory integration disorder ABBR: SID. A general term for a variety of behaviors or characteristics in children, such as a lack of fine motor coordination; clumsiness; and oversensitivity or undersensitivity to touch, noise, smell, taste, or movement. Collectively these characteristics may indicate an inability of the nervous system to integrate and regulate sensory input. However, no definitive diagnostic criteria have been established, and the term is not included in the Diagnostic and Statistical Manual of Mental Disorders (Fourth Edition) (DSM-IV). Examples of SIDs include Asperger syndrome, autism, and attention deficit hyperactivity disorder. SYN: *sensory modulation disorder; sensory processing disorder.*

sensory memory SEE: under *memory.*

sensory modulation disorder Sensory integration disorder.

sensory overload SEE: under *overload.*

sensory/perception, disturbed (specify: visual, auditory, kinesthetic, gustatory, tactile, olfactory) Change in the amount or patterning of incoming stimuli accompanied by a diminished, exaggerated, distorted, or impaired response to such stimuli. SEE: *Nursing Diagnoses Appendix.*

sensory processing disorder Sensory integration disorder.

sensory profile A series of standardized screening questionnaires that help caregivers identify sensory impairments in clients of all ages.

sensory unit A single sensory neuron with its receptors.

sensual (sĕn'shū-ăl) [L. *sensus*, a feeling] Pert. to the gratification of the senses; indulgence of the appetites; not spiritual or intellectual; carnal, worldly.

sensualism (sĕn'shū-ăl-ĭzm) The state of being sensual, in which one's actions are dominated by the emotions.

sensuous (sĕn'shū-ŭs) [L. *sensus*, a feeling] **1.** Pert. to the senses. **2.** Susceptible to influence through the senses.

sentient (sĕn'shē-ĕnt) [L. *sentiens*, perceive] Capable of perceiving sensation. SYN: *sensitive*.

sentiment (sĕn'tĭ-mĕnt) [L. *sentio*, to feel] **1.** Feeling, sensibility; any emotional attitude toward objects or subjects. **2.** Tenderness.

sentinel event (sĕn'tĭn-ĭl) [Fm. Italian *sentinella*, fm. L. *sentire*, to observe] Any occurrence in a professional health care setting that causes serious injury or the risk of serious injury to patients. Most sentinel events occur because of unanticipated errors, e.g., neonatal kidnappings, patient suicides, and wrongsite surgeries.

SEP syringe exchange program.

separation (sep"ă-rā'shŏn) [L. *separatio*, sundering] **1.** The process of disconnecting, disuniting, or severing. **2.** The purification or isolation of a chemical compound from a mixture or solution. SEE: *centrifuge; electrophoresis; iontophoresis.*

   acromioclavicular s. Acromioclavicular **sprain**.

   immunomagnetic s. The detection and/or harvesting of samples containing specific antigens based on their collection by antibodies attached to magnetized beads. The bead-bound antigens can be separated from materials that are not of interest in a magnetic field.

   shoulder s. A colloquial term for an acromioclavicular sprain. SEE: *acromioclavicular* **sprain**.

separator [L. *separator*] **1.** Anything that prevents two substances from mingling. **2.** Any device or instrument used for separating two substances such as cream from milk.

sepsis (sep'sĭs) [Gr. *sēpsis*, putrefaction, decay] A systemic inflammatory response to infection, in which there is fever or hypothermia, tachycardia, tachypnea, and evidence of inadequate blood flow to internal organs. The syndrome is a common cause of death in critically ill patients. Roughly 50% of patients with sepsis die; between 200,000 and 400,000 deaths due to sepsis occur annually in the U.S., making it the 13th leading cause of death. Pathogens may initiate the cascade of inflammatory reactions that constitute sepsis. The number of patients with sepsis has increased significantly in the last 25 years as a result of several factors: the aging of the population; the increased number of patients living with immune-suppressing illnesses (e.g., organ transplants); the increased number of patients living with multiple diseases; and the increased use of invasive or indwelling devices in health care, which serve as portals of entry for infection.

Complications of sepsis include shock, organ failure (e.g., adult respiratory distress syndrome or acute renal failure), disseminated intravascular coagulation, altered mental status, jaundice, metastatic abscess formation, and multiple organ system failure.

ETIOLOGY: Sepsis results from the combined effect of a virulent infection and a powerful host response to the infection (e.g., the body's release of cytokines or chemokines such as tumor necrosis factor, nitric oxide, interleukins, and others). Infections of the lungs, abdomen, and urinary tract are implicated in sepsis more often than are infections at other body sites.

TREATMENT: The primary objectives are resuscitation of the patient, eradication of the underlying cause of infection, support of failing organ systems, and prevention of complications. Resuscitation includes maintaining an open airway; supporting ventilation; providing aggressive fluid support (esp. in the first few hours); maintaining tight control of blood sugars (glucose levels between 80 and 110 mg/dL); providing vasopressor drugs for persistent hypotension; and intensive monitoring. Eradicating the underlying infection involves administering broad-spectrum antibiotics until a precise cause is identified, removing portals of infection or infected prostheses, and draining or débriding abscesses if present. Complications in septic patients are prevented with good supportive care: antithrombotic stockings or pneumatic dressings and sometimes heparin to lessen the risk of venous thrombosis, skin care to prevent decubitus ulcers, enteral nutrition to prevent starvation, and aseptic techniques to limit secondary hospital-acquired infections.

CRITICAL CARE: Invasive hemodynamic monitoring in septic patients typically reveals an elevated cardiac index, decreased systemic vascular resistance, decreased oxygen delivery to tissues, and decreases in mixed venous oxygen saturation. Commonly, laboratory studies in sepsis will reveal leukocytosis (or severe leukopenia), thrombocytopenia, elevated liver enzymes, hypocalcemia, hypoalbuminemia, and increases in the prothrombin time and serum creatinine level.

PATIENT CARE: Specimens of blood and body fluids are collected and cultured. Two or three consecutive blood cultures are obtained while the patient is febrile. The patient's symptoms and vital signs are carefully assessed, and his or her lungs are auscultated for normal and adventitious lung sounds. The patient's urine output is monitored for oliguria, and he or she is observed for any change in mental status. The patient's daily fluid intake and output and body weight also are measured and recorded.

At least one large-bore intravenous catheter is inserted, and prescribed antibiotics are administered. The patient is given information about the therapy and is assessed for desired responses and adverse effects. Antipyretics may be prescribed. Fluid and electrolyte therapy is prescribed to maintain desired balance or correct deficiencies. Oxygen is administered based on SaO_2 readings, tachypnea, and tachycardia. As soon as culture results permit, the patient's antibiotic regimen is revised to use specific drugs to which the offending organism is sensitive. After doses of these drugs are given, serum antibiotic levels (trough and peak) may be monitored to prevent toxicity and ensure effectiveness. The patient is assessed carefully for signs of disseminated intravascular coagulation, adult respiratory distress syndrome, renal failure, heart failure, gastrointestinal ulcers, and hepatic abnormalities, any of which can complicate the clinical picture.

If septic shock occurs, oxygenation and perfusion are vigorously supported. An arterial catheter may be placed to measure blood pressure and provide access for arterial blood gas (ABG) samples. A pulmonary artery catheter may be used to monitor the patient's hemodynamic status. The health care team monitors closely for fluid overload. Nasoendotracheal intubation and mechanical ventilation may be necessary to overcome hypoxia, and ABGs are evaluated to determine FIO_2 and ventilatory volumes. If shock persists after volume expansion, vasopressor and inotropic therapy may sometimes be prescribed to maintain adequate renal and brain perfusion. During vasopressor administration, central pressures and cardiac rate and rhythm are closely monitored. Metabolic (lactic) acidosis may sometimes be corrected with IV bicarbonate therapy. A gram-negative endotoxin vaccine may be prescribed, as may other experimental treatments to block the rapid inflammatory process (corticoste-

roids, opiate antagonists, prostaglandin inhibitors, and calcium channel blockers). The patient's response is assessed, and any adverse reactions are noted.

A quiet, calm milieu and psychological support are provided for the profoundly ill patient. Oral hygiene is provided to prevent stomatitis, sordes, and salivary obstruction, esp. if the patient is permitted nothing by mouth. Nutritional needs are monitored, with consultations with the nutritional therapist to determine the need for enteral or parenteral nutrition. The patient's skin and joint function must be protected by assessing the skin and providing required care, as well as through frequent, careful repositioning, range-of-motion exercises, and correct body alignment, with supportive devices as necessary. The health care team should function as a liaison to family members, offering them emotional support and helping them to understand the patient's illness and the treatment regimen.

puerperal s. Any infection of the genital tract that occurs within 6 weeks after childbirth or abortion. Although once the greatest killer of new mothers, the incidence of postpartum infection has dropped dramatically as a result of aseptic technique during and after childbirth and the use of antibiotic therapy and now occurs in only a small percentage of maternity patients. SYN: _childbed fever; puerperal fever._ SEE: _Nursing Diagnoses Appendix._

SIGNS AND SYMPTOMS: Clinical findings vary with the site and type of infection. _Local_: Infections of perineal lacerations, of an episiotomy, or of the abdominal incision for cesarean delivery exhibit the classic signs of wound infections: redness, edema, ecchymosis, discharge, and interrupted approximation. _Pelvic_: Women whose infections involve the uterus, fallopian tubes, ovaries, or parametrium usually exhibit fever, chills, tachycardia, and abdominal tenderness or pain. Endometritis is accompanied by changes in the character and amount of lochia related to the causative organism; lochia may be scant or profuse, odorless or foul-smelling, colorless or bloody.

ETIOLOGY: The most common causes are group A or B streptococci; coagulase-negative staphylococci, _Clostridium perfringens_, _Bacteroides fragilis_, _Escherichia coli_, and some other gram-negative bacteria. While most of these are a normal part of vaginal flora, they can become pathogenic in the presence of predisposing factors.

RISK FACTORS: Conditions that predispose to postpartum infection include anemia, malnutrition, prolonged and premature rupture of membranes, repeated vaginal examinations during labor, prolonged labor, invasive procedures, surgical interventions (esp. cesarean section), hemorrhage, retained products of conception, and breaks in aseptic technique. Common modes of transmission include upward migration of vaginal bacteria, autoinfection, and contact with infected personnel or contaminated equipment.

DIAGNOSIS: The primary diagnostic criterion is a temperature of 100.4°F (38°C) occurring on any two of the first 10 days after childbirth, exclusive of the first 24 hr. Cultures of any drainage and sensitivity tests identify the causative microbe and the appropriate therapeutic antibiotic.

PATHOLOGY: In minor cases of ulceration, the vaginal tract is covered by a dirty membrane. In streptococcal and staphylococcal infections, the endometrium is smooth and the lymphatics are congested with the invading organisms. As a rule, the uterine cavity is filled with very little lochia. The uterus shows poor involution. If the infection extends farther beyond the uterus, the parametrium or cellular tissues show edema, inflammation, and in some cases purulent infiltration. Extension of the process to the veins produces infectious thrombi, which in turn produce localized abscesses in other parts of the body.

TREATMENT: Treatment includes appropriate antibiotics, incision and drainage if abscess forms, and supportive therapy.

PATIENT CARE: Puerperal infection is prevented by maintaining strict asepsis during the entire labor, delivery, and postpartum period. Hand hygiene is stressed for all care providers. Preventive measures also include good prenatal nutrition; intranatal hemorrhage control; and avoidance of uterine dystocia, prolonged labor (esp. if amniotic fluid is leaking), and traumatic vaginal delivery. Fluid and electrolyte balance is maintained and unusual blood loss replaced.

The health care professional assesses for and reports suspicious clinical findings, and administers prescribed broad-spectrum antibiotics intravenously, changing to specific therapy once cultures have established sensitivity. Analgesics and antiemetics are prescribed and administered as needed. The patient is isolated from the infant while febrile, and other family members are encouraged to nurture the infant. The mother is provided with frequent reassurance about her neonate's status. The patient is given nutritional support, fluid intake and urinary output are measured, and care of the perineum, vaginal secretions, and breasts is provided. Milk is pumped and discarded throughout antibiotic therapy to main-

tain lactation for the woman who wants to breast-feed. If surgery is required, the patient is prepared physically and psychologically for the necessary procedure and the family is given information and emotional support. Postpartum patients should be taught how to maintain good perineal hygiene and keep episiotomy sites clean. Because of early discharge to home and self-care, patients should be advised to report fever that occurs in the week or so following discharge as well as associated chills, headache, malaise, and/or restlessness.

sepsis syndrome Septic **shock**.

septal (sĕp′tăl) Pert. to a septum.

septal myectomy Surgical removal of hypertrophied cardiac muscle from the ventricular septum of patients with obstructive hypertrophic cardiomyopathy whose symptoms of heart failure are not well managed with medication alone.

septate (sĕp′tāt) [L. *saeptum*, a partition] Having a dividing wall.

septectomy (sĕp-tĕk′tō-mē) [″ + Gr. *ektome*, excision] Excision of a septum, esp. the nasal septum or a part of it.

septi- [L. *septem*, seven] Prefix meaning *seven*.

septic (sĕp′tĭk) [Gr. *septikos*, putrefying] **1.** Pert. to sepsis. **2.** Pert. to pathogenic organisms or their toxins.

septicemia (sĕp-tĭ-sē′mē-ă) [″ + *haima*, blood] The presence of pathogenic microorganisms in the blood. SEE: *sepsis; Nursing Diagnoses Appendix.* **septicemic** (-ĭk), *adj.*

septonasal (sĕp-tō-nā′zăl) [L. *saeptum*, a partition, + *nasus*, nose] Pert. to the nasal septum.

septo-optic dysplasia SEE: under *dysplasia.*

septoplasty (sĕp″tō-plăs′tē) [″ + Gr. *plassein*, to form] Plastic surgery of the nasal septum.

septostomy (sep-tos′tŏ-mē) [*septum* + *-stomy*] Surgical formation of an opening in a septum.

amniotic s. Surgical puncturing of the membrane between twins affected by the twin oligohydramnios-polyhydramnios sequence.

balloon atrial s. The surgical enlargement of an opening between the cardiac atria for palliative relief of congestive heart failure in newborns with certain heart defects. A deflated balloon is inserted into a vein, passed through the foramen ovale, and then inflated and pulled vigorously through the atrial septum to enlarge the opening and improve oxygenation of the blood. SYN: *Rashkind procedure.*

surgical atrial s. Septostomy performed with a specialized scalpel or knife to separate fused structures within the hearts of infants born with complex congenital cardiac defects.

septum (sĕp'tŭm) *pl.* **septa** [L. *saeptum,* a partition] A wall dividing two cavities. **septal** (-tăl), *adj.*

   atrial s. Interatrial s.

   atrioventricular s. The septum that separates the right and left atria of the heart from the respective ventricles.

   deviated s. A nasal septum displaced to one side. It sometimes causes impaired air flow through a nostril.

   interatrial s. The myocardial wall between the atria of the heart.

   interdental s. The bony partition across the alveolar process between adjacent teeth that forms part of the tooth sockets.

   intermuscular s. **1.** A connective tissue septum that separates two muscles, esp. one from which muscles may take their origin. **2.** One of two connective tissue septa that separate the muscles of the leg into anterior, posterior, and lateral groups.

   interradicular s. One of the thin bony partitions between the roots of a multirooted tooth that forms part of the walls of the tooth socket.

   interventricular s. The myocardial wall between the ventricles of the heart.

   lingual s. A sheet of connective tissue underlying the midline groove (median sulcus) separating the halves of the tongue.

   mediastinal s. A partition between two parts of an organ or cavity.

   nasal s. The partition that divides the nasal cavity into two nasal fossae. The bony portion is formed by the perpendicular plate of the ethmoid bone and the vomer. The cartilaginous portion is formed by septal and vomeronasal cartilages and medial crura of greater alar cartilages. Both sides of the septum are covered with mucous membranes.

   orbital s. A fibrous sheet extending partially across the anterior opening of the orbit within the eyelids.

   s. pellucidum A thin, translucent, triangular sheet of nervous tissue consisting of two laminae attached to the corpus callosum above and the fornix below. It forms the medial wall and interior boundary of the lateral ventricles of the brain.

   s. primum In the embryonic heart, a septum between the right and left chambers.

   rectovaginal s. The layer of fascia between the rectum and the vagina.

   rectovesical s. The membranous septum between the rectum and the urinary bladder.

   tracheoesophageal s. In the embryo, the partition that develops between the growing laryngotracheal tube (the future larynx, trachea, and lungs) and the developing esophagus.

   ventricular s. Interventricular s.

sequel (sē'kwĕl) [L. *sequela,* sequel] A sequela.

sequela (sē-kwē'lă) *pl.* **sequelae** [L., sequel] A condition following and resulting from a disease.

sequence (sē'kwĕns) [L. *sequentia,* the following, context] **1.** The order or occurrence of a series of related events. **2.** The arrangement of nucleotides in a nucleic acid molecule. **sequential** (sĕ-kwen'chăl), *adj.*

   Goldenhar s. SEE: *Goldenhar sequence.*

   pulse s. In magnetic resonance imaging, a series of radio waves designed to produce proton stimulation necessary to create the image.

   spacer s. The genetic material on a chromosome that separates actively transcribed genes. It may make up the largest part of the genome of some eukaryotic organisms and often consists of tandem repeats of DNA. SYN: *spacer DNA.*

   terminator s. In genetics, a specific series of nucleotides that instructs a cell to stop transcribing a gene.

sequencing (sē'kwĕn-sing) [L. *sequor,* to follow] **1.** The application of particular treatments in a specific order rather than randomly or haphazardly. **2.** The determination of the order of nucleotides in a gene or a genome. SYN: *gene s.; genetic s.*

   deep s. Examination of a nucleic acid genome with such precision that even very rare genetic mutations are identified.

   gene s. Sequencing (2).

   genetic s. Sequencing (2).

sequential (sĕ-kwen'shăl) Occurring in order (i.e., one after another).

sequential therapy (sĕ-kwen'shăl) Any treatment regimen in which the patient is given one treatment followed by another, e.g., two distinct but mutually reinforcing combinations of drugs.

sequester (sē-kwĕs'tĕr) [L. *sequestrare,* to separate] **1.** To isolate. **2.** Sequestrum.

sequestrant (sĕ-kwes'trănt) [L. *sequestrare,* to deposit with a trustee] An agent that promotes or causes sequestration.

   bile acid s. Any of a class of polymeric resins that binds bile acids and prevents these cholesterol-containing compounds from recirculating into the blood from the gastrointestinal tract. Medications from this class are used to treat those with high serum cholesterol levels and to reduce itching in patients with chronic liver diseases.

sequestration (sē"kwĕs-trā'shŏn) [L. *sequestratio,* a deposit with a trustee] **1.** The formation of sequestrum. **2.** The isolation of a patient for treatment or quarantine. **3.** Reduction of hemorrhage of the head or trunk by temporarily stopping the return of blood from the extremities by applying tourniquets to the thighs and arms. **4.** A fragment of nucleus pulposus of the intervertebral disk separating and freely floating in the spinal canal.

    pulmonary s. A nonfunctioning area of the lung that receives its blood supply from the systemic circulation.

sequestrectomy (sē″kwĕs-trĕk′tō-mē) [″ + Gr. *ektome,* excision] Excision of a necrosed piece of bone. SYN: *sequestrotomy.*

sequestrum (sē-kwĕs′trŭm) *pl.* **sequestra** [L., something set aside] A fragment of a necrosed bone that has become separated from the surrounding tissue. It is designated *primary* if the piece is entirely detached, *secondary* if it is still loosely attached, and *tertiary* if it is partially detached but still remaining in place. SYN: *sequester.* **sequestral** (-ăl), *adj.*

serendipity (sĕr″ĕn-dĭp′ĭ-tē) The gift of finding, by chance and insight, valuable or agreeable things not sought for. In medical research, an unexpected reaction or result may produce new insights into some area totally unrelated to that which prompted the investigation.

serglycin (sĕr-glī′sĭn) A proteoglycan found within many cells, esp. in the granule-containing vesicles of blood-forming cells and endothelial cells.

serial (sē′rē-ăl) [L. *series,* row, chain] In numerical order, continuity, or sequence, as in a series.

series (sēr′ēz) [L. *series,* row, chain] **1.** Arrangement of objects in succession or in order. **2.** In electricity, batteries or mode of arranging the parts of a circuit by connecting them successively end to end to form a single path for the current. The parts so arranged are said to be "in series."

    acute abdomen s. A radiological examination that usually includes an erect kidney, ureter, and bladder (KUB) projection, a recumbent KUB projection, and a left lateral decubitus image of the chest. It is used to assess patients with abdominal pain for free air (organ perforation), infection, intestinal obstruction, or stones.

    aliphatic s. Chemical compounds with a structure of an open chain of carbon atoms.

    aromatic s. Any series of organic compounds containing the benzene ring.

    erythrocytic s. The group of immature cells that develop into mature red blood cells.

    fatty s. Aliphatic series, esp. those similar to methane.

    granulocytic s. The immature cells in the bone marrow that develop into mature granular white blood cells. SYN: *leukocytic s.*

    homologous s. In chemistry, compounds that proceed from one to the next by some constant such as a CH_2 group.

    leukocytic s. Granulocytic **s.**

    monocytic s. The immature blood cells that grow in the bone marrow and other blood-forming organs into mature monocytes and macrophages.

    thrombocytic s. The immature blood cells in the bone marrow that develop into megakaryocytes and ultimately form platelets.

    upper GI s. Radiographical and fluoroscopic examinations of the stomach and duodenum after the ingestion of a contrast medium, such as barium sulfate or an iodinized glucose solution.

serine (sĕr′ēn) 2-amino-3-hydroxypropionic acid; an amino acid present in many proteins, including casein, vitellin, and others.

serine protease inhibitor SEE: under *inhibitor.*

sero-, ser- [L. *serum,* whey] Prefixes meaning *serum.*

seroconversion (sēr″ō-kŏn-vĕr′zhŭn) The development of an antibody response to an infection or vaccine, measurable in the serum.

serodiagnosis (sē″rō-dī-ăg-nō′sĭs) [″ + Gr. *dia,* through, + *gnosis,* knowledge] Diagnosis of disease based on tests of serum, esp. immunological tests.

seroepidemiology (sēr″ō-ep″ĭ-dē″mē-ol′ŏ-jē) [*sero-* + *epidemiology*] A study of the distribution of a disease made by taking blood samples from people and checking for disease markers.

serofibrinous (sē″rō-fī′brĭn-ŭs) [″ + *fibra,* fiber] **1.** Composed of both serum and fibrin. **2.** Pert. to a serofibrinous exudate.

seroimmunity (sē″rō-ĭ-mū′nĭ-tē) [″ + *immunitas,* immunity] Immunity produced by the administration of an antiserum.

serological tests for syphilis ABBR: STS. Nonspecific blood tests for syphilis. Two general types are available: (1) Procedures that identify the presence of a nontreponemal antibody against a lipoidal agent that is generated in response to infection with *Treponema pallidum* (i.e., a reagin). These tests include the Wassermann, the Venereal Disease Research Laboratory (VDLR), and the rapid plasma reagin tests. (2) An antibody-specific test, the fluorescent treponemal antibody absorption (FTA-ABS) procedure. Because of a high rate of false-positive findings by the nonspecific antibody tests, diagnosis of syphilitic infection is established by the more accurate FTA test.

serologic test (sĕr″ă-lŏj′ĭk tĕst) Any test done on serum.

serologist (sē-rŏl′ō-jĭst) [″ + Gr. *logos,* word, reason] A person trained in the science of serology.

serology (sē-rol′ō-jē) [″ + Gr. *logos,* word, reason] The scientific study of fluid components of the blood, esp. antigens and antibodies. **serologic, serological** (sēr-ŏ-loj′ĭk, sēr-ŏ-loj′ĭ-kăl), *adj.*

seroma (sĕ-rō′mă) [″ + ″] A mass caused by the accumulation of serum within a tissue or an organ. Seromas may accumulate as a complication of surgery or after other traumatic injuries to soft tissues. SEE: illus.

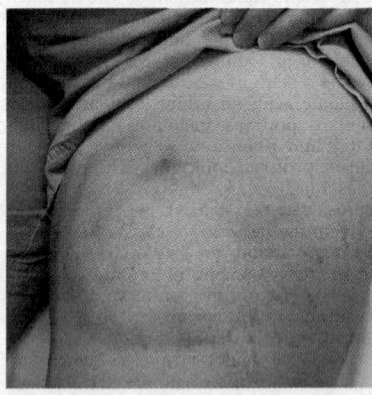

SEROMA

on the front of the thigh

seromucous (sē″rō-mū′kŭs) [″ + *mucus,* mucus] Pert. to a secretion that is part serum and part mucus.

seromuscular (sē″rō-mŭs′kū-lăr) [″ + *muscularis,* muscular] Pert. to the serous and muscular layers of the intestinal wall.

seronegative (sē″rō-nĕg′ă-tĭv) Producing a negative reaction to serological tests.

seropositive (sē″rō-pŏz′ĭ-tĭv) Having a positive reaction to a serological test (i.e., showing the presence of a specific antigen or antibody).

seroprotection (sēr″ō-prō-tĕk′shŭn) An antibody response capable of preventing infection, e.g., after a vaccination or a previous infection with a microorganism.

seropurulent (sē″rō-pū′roo-lĕnt) [″ + *purulentus,* full of pus] Composed of serum and pus, as an exudate.

seroreaction (sē″rō-rē-ăk′shŭn) [″ + ″] **1.** Any reaction taking place in or involving serum. **2.** A reaction to an injection of serum marked by rash, fever, pain, arthralgia, or arthritis.

seroreactivity (sēr″ō-rē″ak″tiv′ĭt-ē) [*sero-* + *reactivity*] The presence of specific

antibodies, e.g., against an infectious microorganism, in the serum of a patient or in blood samples from the population of a community.

serosa (sē-rō′să) [L. *serum,* whey] A serous membrane (e.g., the peritoneum, pleura, and pericardium).

serosanguineous (sē″rō-săn-gwĭn′ē-ŭs) [L. *serum,* whey, + *sanguineus,* bloody] Pert. to serum and blood.

serositis (sē″rō-sī′tĭs) *pl.* **serositides** [″ + Gr. *itis,* inflammation] An inflammation of a serous membrane, such as the pleura, pericardium, or peritoneum. Serositis is one of the cardinal findings in connective tissue diseases like systemic lupus erythematosus.

serosorting (sēr″ō-sort″ing) [*sero-* + *sorting*] Selection of a sexual partner on the basis of shared disease status, e.g., of an HIV-negative partner if one is also HIV-negative. It is a way of limiting the spread of infection and reducing the risks of the partners.

serosurvey (sē″rō-sŭr′vā) [″ + ″] Sampling of blood in a percentage of people living in a community to determine the percentage of those who are resistant or susceptible to a disease, esp. an infectious disease.

serotherapy (sē″rō-thĕr′ă-pē) Passive immunization with antivenins. SYN: *serum therapy.*

serotonergic neuron (sir″ă-tŏ-nĕr′jĭk) SEE: under *neuron.*

serotonin (sir″ō-tō′nĭn) [*sero-* + *tone* + *-in*] $C_{10}H_{12}N_2O$, a vasoconstrictor found in platelets, the gastrointestinal mucosa, mast cells, carcinoid tumors, and the central nervous system. Serotonin through its action on cellular receptors plays important roles in intestinal motility, nausea and vomiting, sleep-wake cycles, obsessive-compulsive behaviors, depression, and eating. SYN: *5-HT; 5-hydroxytryptamine.* SEE: *carcinoid syndrome; selective serotonin reuptake inhibitor.*

serotonin and norepinephrine reuptake inhibitor SEE: under *inhibitor.*

serotonin release assay SEE: under *assay.*

serotonin syndrome The adverse effects of excessive levels of serotonin in the brain, typically caused by exposure to multiple medications that alter the neuronal disposition of serotonin. Common findings are confusion, restlessness, hyperreflexia, agitation, diaphoresis, tremor, and fever.

serotype (sē′rō-tīp) In microbiology, a microorganism determined by the kinds and combination of antigens present on its cell surface.

serous (sēr′ŭs) [L. *serosus*] **1.** Having the nature of serum. **2.** Thin or watery, rather than syrupy, thick, or viscous.

serovar (sēr′ō-văr″) [*serological variation*] Any of the variants within a species defined by variation in serological reactions. SEE: *biovar; morphovar.*

serpiginous (sĕr-pĭj'ĭ-nŭs) [L. *serpere,* to creep] Creeping from one part to another.

serrate (sĕr'āt) [L. *serratus,* toothed] Dentate.

Serratia (se-rā'sh(ē-)ă) [Serafino Serrati, 19th-cent. Italian physicist] A genus of gram-negative bacilli of the family Enterobacteriaceae.

   S. liquefaciens A species that has caused septicemia and other hospital-acquired infections.

   S. marcescens An opportunistic bacterium that causes septicemia and pulmonary disease, esp. in immunocompromised patients, and is found in water, soil, milk, and stools. In the proper environment, the organism will grow on food and produce the red pigment prodigiosin.

serration (sĕr-ā'shŭn) [L. *serratio,* a notching] **1.** A formation with sharp projections like the teeth of a saw. **2.** A single tooth or notch in a serrated edge.

serrefine (sār-fēn') [Fr.] A small wire-spring forceps for compressing bleeding vessels.

serrulate (sĕr'ū-lāt) [L. *serrulatus*] Finely notched or serrated.

Sertoli cell (sĕr-tō'lēz) [Enrico Sertoli, Italian histologist, 1842–1910] One of the supporting elongated cells of the seminiferous tubules of the testes to which spermatids attach to be nourished until they become mature spermatozoa. Sertoli cells produce the hormone inhibin.

sertraline (sĕr'tră-lēn) A selective serotonin reuptake inhibitor and antidepressant, administered orally to manage depression, panic, obsessive-compulsive disorder, and posttraumatic stress disorder. Trade name is Zoloft.

serum (sĕr'ŭm) *pl.* **serums, sera** [L. *serum,* whey] **1.** A pale, watery fluid, esp. the fluid that moistens the surfaces of serous membranes. **2.** The watery portion of the blood after coagulation. It is the fluid found when clotted blood is left standing long enough for the clot to shrink. **3.** Serum obtained from blood that contains antibodies against a specific microorganism. It is used to produce immediate passive immunity. SYN: *immune globulin.*

   antilymphocyte s. ABBR: ALS. An antibody-containing serum used to reduce rejection of transplanted organs and tissues. Its immunosuppressive effects are directed against B and T lymphocytes. SYN: *antilymphocyte globulin.*

   convalescent s. Serum from a person recovering from an infection.

   foreign s. Serum taken from one species and administered to another.

   grouping s. A serum used for determining the blood group to which unknown cells belong. The grouping serums commonly used are human serums from donors and rabbit antiserums prepared commercially.

   immune s. Antiserum.

   polyvalent s. Serum containing antibodies to several antigens.

   pooled s. Serum collected from several donors.

   pregnant mare's s. Serum derived from the blood of pregnant mares. It is a source of hormones, esp. gonadotropins.

serum bank SEE: under *bank.*

serum glutamic-oxaloacetic transaminase ABBR: SGOT. Aspartate aminotransferase.

serum glutamic pyruvic transaminase ABBR: SGPT. Alanine aminotransferase.

serum protein profiling Protein profiling.

serum prothrombin conversion accelerator ABBR: SPCA. Coagulation factor VII, a vitamin-K–dependent serine protease activated in the presence of ionized calcium and Factor III to form thrombin in the coagulation cascade. SYN: *extrinsic **factor**; proconvertin; stable **factor**.* SEE: *blood **coagulation**; coagulation **factor**.*

serum therapy Serotherapy.

serve To deliver a legal document to a person named in it. This is done formally to comply with due process of law.

service Help or assistance (e.g., for persons who are needy, sick, or injured).

service animal SEE: under *animal.*

servomechanism (sŭr"vō-mĕk'ă-nĭzm) In biology and physiology, a self-regulatory control mechanism that operates by negative feedback. For example, when the blood glucose level rises in the normal person, the pancreas responds by releasing insulin, which enables cells to take in and metabolize glucose. The level of other hormones is also regulated by this mechanism.

SES *socioeconomic status.*

sesamoid (sĕs'ă-moyd) [L. *sesamoides*] Resembling a grain of sesame in size or shape.

sesamoiditis (sĕs"ă-moy-dī'tĭs) [" + Gr. *itis,* inflammation] Inflammation of a sesamoid bone.

sesqui- [L. *sesqui-,* one and a half] Prefix meaning *one and a half.*

sessile (sĕs'l) [L. *sessilis,* low] Having no peduncle but attached directly by a broad base.

session (sesh'ŏn) [L. fr. *sedere,* to sit] A formal clinical encounter between a patient and a therapist. In psychology and psychiatry, each visit with a client constitutes a session. A meeting between the parties may have a single objective (e.g., to analyze feelings of loss or grief) or several goals (e.g., to quit smoking *and* increase exercise). Each chiropractic adjustment is a session, as is each whirlpool treatment provided to an injured athlete, or each visit with a speech therapist for a patient with swallowing difficulties.

sestamibi Technetium Tc 99m sestamibi.

set (set) **1.** To fix firmly in place, as to set a bone in reduction of a fracture. **2.** To allow an amalgam or plaster to harden. **3.** In psychology, a group of conditions or attitudes that favor the occurrence of a certain response. **4.** In resistance exercise, a grouping of repetitions of a specific exercise. Particular sets are listed under the first word. SEE: e.g., *Health Plan Employer Data and Information Set; limited data set.*

seton (sē″tŏn) [L. *seta*, bristle] **1.** A thread or threads drawn through a fold of skin to act as a counterirritant or as a guide for instruments. **2.** A suture tied about an anal fistula to maintain drainage while fibrosis gradually obliterates the fistulous tract.

set point SEE: under *point.*

set sensitivity In mechanical ventilation, the inspiratory pressure at which the patient's respiratory effort triggers a breath from the ventilator.

set test A global test of a patient's ability to make categories. It demonstrates motivation, alertness, concentration, short-term memory, and problem solving. The patient is asked to name 10 items in each of four groups: fruits, animals, colors, and towns or cities. Then the patient is asked to categorize, count, name, and remember the items listed. The test is scored by giving one point for each correctly recalled item. A maximum of 40 points is possible. Scoring less than 15 is associated with dementia; more than 25 indicates absence of dementia; and scores between 15 and 24 require further investigation to distinguish between mental changes and cultural, educational, and social factors.

settlement **1.** In health insurance, payment to the policyholder for claims made against the insurance company. **2.** In liability or malpractice litigation, an agreement between disputants that satisfies the needs of both parties.

　　viatical s. The purchase, at a discount, of a life insurance policy from a gravely ill patient. The buyer becomes the beneficiary of the policy; the viator receives a lump sum payment before dying.

setup (sĕt′ŭp) The arrangement of teeth on a trial denture base.

Sever disease (sē′vĕr) [James W. Sever, U.S. orthopedist, 1878–1964] Apophysitis of the calcaneus in adolescent children who are actively engaged in sports. This overuse syndrome is best treated with icing, Achilles tendon stretching, anti-inflammatory medication, and rest from weight bearing. Heel lifts are usually used unless the child has pronated feet, in which case medial heel wedges are indicated.

severe acute respiratory distress syndrome ABBR: SARS. A highly contagious, potentially lethal viral respiratory illness first diagnosed in the People's Republic of China in November 2002, characterized by a fever of higher than 100.4°F (38.0°C), cough, difficulty breathing, or hypoxia. The severe variant of the syndrome is present when a person has a radiograph compatible with pneumonia or autopsy findings consistent with pneumonia. Instances of the disease without pneumonia are considered moderate infections. The disease should be strongly suspected in someone who has had close contact within the last 10 days with a person known to have or suspected of having SARS or in someone who has traveled within the last 10 days to a part of the world where SARS is currently reported. The disease is confirmed by the identification of antibody to the causative virus (SARS coronavirus) or the isolation of SARS coronavirus from the infected person.

severe combined immunodeficiency disease ABBR: SCID. A syndrome marked by gross functional impairment of both humoral and cell-mediated immunity and by susceptibility to fungal, bacterial, and viral infections. Although the disorder may occur sporadically, most commonly it is an X-linked or autosomal recessive trait. If untreated, infants rarely survive beyond their first year. It is important that the disease be recognized early and that patients not be given live viral vaccines or blood transfusions. The immunological defects may be repaired by stem cell transplantation. The optimal donor is an HLA-identical family member of the patient. SYN: *reticular dysgenesis.*

severe congenital neutropenia SEE: under *neutropenia.*

severe cutaneous adverse reaction ABBR: SCAR. Any of several potentially life-threatening rashes resulting from exposure to a drug. Included in this group are acute generalized exanthematous pustulosis, drug reactions with eosinophilia and systemic symptoms, Stevens-Johnson syndrome, and toxic epidermal necrolysis.

Severinghaus electrode (sĕv′ĕ-rĭng-hows″) Carbon dioxide **electrode**.

sewage (soo′ăj) Wastewater discharged from homes or institutions. It may be composed of bodily excretions, the waste water and solid waste of residential and commercial establishments, or the solvents and other toxic wastes of industry. Bodily excretions discharged as sewage are potentially infectious and may be the source of epidemic outbreaks of diarrhea or other contagious illnesses. Other sewage components, esp. toxic oils and solvents, may pollute rivers and beaches, destroying fishing and shellfish beds.

sex (seks) [L. *sexus,* sex] **1.** The characteristics that differentiate males and females in most plants and animals. **2.** Gender.

   chromosomal s. Sex as determined by the presence of the female XX or male XY genotype in somatic cells.

   commercial s. Engaging in sexual practices to earn money or other economic benefits.

   morphological s. The sex of an individual as determined by the form of the external genitalia.

   nuclear s. The genetic sex of an individual determined by the absence or presence of sex chromatin in the body cells, particularly white blood cells.

   oral s. Cunnilingus or fellatio.

   psychological s. The individual's self-image of his or her gender, which may be at variance with the morphological sex.

   safe sex, safer sex The practice of protecting oneself and one's partner(s) as much as possible from sexually transmitted diseases (STDs), including chlamydia, gonorrhea, trichomoniasis, syphilis, herpesviruses, hepatitis viruses, and HIV, or from unwanted pregnancy. Some experts find the term to be unsatisfactory, maintaining that all forms of sexual behavior carry some risk or infection, injury, or pregnancy. Safe or safer sexual practices involve avoiding contact with one's partner's blood or body fluids, e.g., seminal fluid, by wearing condoms during any form of oral, vaginal, or anal intercourse. The risks of transmitting STDs may be further classified as follows: *Safer:* Celibacy; masturbation; dry kissing; masturbation of a partner on healthy, intact skin; oral sex with use of a condom; touching; fantasy. *Possibly Safe:* Condom-protected vaginal or anal intercourse. *Risky:* Wet kissing, oral sex (without a dental dam or latex or plastic barrier or condom), masturbation of a woman without a latex barrier or use of latex gloves, masturbation on open or broken skin, and unprotected sex of any kind.

   ⚠ Alcohol and psychoactive drugs may impair one's judgment regarding the practice of safe sex, resulting in engagement in risky sexual activities. If either partner has evidence of any infection, condoms should always be used even though failure rates for condoms vary from 2% to 12%, depending on the user's

skill and experience. Any person having casual sexual contacts should avoid anal intercourse even with a condom because of the high risk of this type of sexual activity and the low but finite risk of condom failure.

   survival s. Engaging in sexual intercourse to secure basic human needs (food, clothing, or shelter).

sex crime Sexual offense.

sex determination 1. The identification of the gender of an animal or human with an ambiguous physical appearance or ambiguous genitalia. In colloquial speech, this is sometimes called sex testing. **2.** The identification of the gender of a fetus, or, in in vitro fertilization, of a human preimplantation embryo.

sex-determining region Y ABBR: SRY. The gene that determines that gonads will form as testes rather than as ovaries.

sex drive Motivation, both psychological and physiological, for behavior associated with procreation and erotic pleasure.

sex industry Any business whose earnings derive from the exchange of money for sexual favors or the representation of sex in print, photographic media, video, or the Internet. SYN: *sex trade.*

sexing (sĕk'sĭng) Determining the sex of a fetus or embryo.

sexism All of the actions and attitudes that relegate individuals of either sex to a secondary and inferior status in society.

sex-limited The expression of a genetic character or trait in one sex only.

sex-linked SEE: under *characteristic.*

sexology (sĕks-ŏl'ō-jē) [L. *sexus,* sex, + Gr. *logos,* word, reason] The scientific study of sexuality.

sex ratio The ratio of males to females in a given population, usually expressed as the number of males per 100 females. It is used in defining the proportion of births of the two sexes or in the representation by sexual distribution in certain diseases.

sex testing SEE: *sex determination* (1).

sex therapy A form of psychotherapy involving sexual guidance for partners with sexual incompatibilities or sexual dysfunction.

sex trade Sex industry.

sextuplet (sĕks'tŭp-lĕt) [L. *sextus,* six] One of six children born of a single gestation.

sexual (sĕks'ū-ăl) [L. *sexualis*] **1.** Pert. to sex. **2.** Having sex.

sexual adjustment questionnaire ABBR: SAQ. An assessment tool used to measure changes in a person's sexual behavior, thoughts, and feelings during chronic illness.

sexual assault nurse examiner ABBR:

SANE. A forensically trained nurse specialist, often working as part of a sexual assault response team, who ensures that rape victims who come to the Emergency Department are carefully and sensitively screened for evidence of rape and are provided with post-traumatic crisis support.

Sexual Assault Response Team ABBR: SART. A group of health care professionals who have had special preparation in the examination of rape victims. The training includes techniques for collecting, labeling, and storing evidence so it may be used in court proceedings concerning the person accused of rape and in psychological approaches to reduce the emotional trauma to the victim. SEE: *rape*.

sexual dysfunction SEE: under *dysfunction*.

sexual harassment Unsolicited and unwelcome verbal or physical sexually oriented conduct or innuendos. There are two types of sexual harassment: quid pro quo, in which compliance with a harasser's wishes may become a condition of continued employment or advancement; and a hostile work environment in which the unwanted attentions of another person make the workplace a threatening, demeaning, or unsafe environment. A hostile work environment may also be created by offensive conduct that creates an intimidating atmosphere interfering with the work performance of the victim. The victim does not have to be the person harassed.

sexual health The capacity to enjoy and control sexual behavior in accordance with a social and personal ethic; freedom from fear, shame, guilt, false beliefs, and other psychological factors inhibiting sexual response and impairing sexual relationships; and freedom from organic disorder, disease, and deficiencies that interfere with sexual and reproductive functions, as defined by the World Health Organization. Medical studies of human sexual function and activity have provided no evidence that having attained a certain age is, of itself, reason to discontinue participating in and enjoying sexual intercourse. SEE: *sexually transmitted disease*.

sexual intercourse Any sexual union between two or more partners in which at least one partner's genitalia are stimulated. SYN: *coition; coitus; copulation; pareunia*.

sexuality (sĕks-ū-ăl′ĭ-tē) [L. *sexus*, sex] **1.** The state of having sex; the collective characteristics that mark the differences between the male and the female. **2.** The constitution and life of an individual as related to sex; all the dispositions related to intimacy, whether associated with the sex organs or not.

sexuality patterns, ineffective Expressions of concern regarding one's own sexuality. SEE: *Nursing Diagnoses Appendix*.

sexually transmitted disease ABBR: STD. Any disease that may be acquired as a result of sexual intercourse or other intimate contact with an infected individual. A more inclusive term than "venereal disease," STDs include disease caused by bacteria, viruses, protozoa, fungi, and ectoparasites. SEE: table; *Nursing Diagnoses Appendix*.

sexual maturity rating The order and extent of the development of a patient's primary and secondary sexual characteristics as compared with the established norms for chronological age. In both sexes, the changes leading to puberty are the result of major hormonal changes that, although somewhat variable in age of occurrence, proceed in a predictable sequence. Assessing the degree of age-related sexual maturity enables the health care provider to detect abnormalities and to provide anticipatory guidance for the patient and family. An important and easily identified development in a girl is the onset of menstruation. Physical changes in the male such as voice change, facial hair growth, and testicular and penile growth are obvious but occur over a prolonged period.

sexual misconduct Inappropriate sexual contact, speech, or behavior between health care providers and/or their patients.

sexual offense, sex offense Any legally prohibited sexual behavior, including, e.g., exhibitionism, necrophilia, rape, and sexual abuse of a minor. SYN: *sex crime*.

sexual preference The sexual orientation one prefers in choosing his or her sex partners.

sexual stimulant Any drug (e.g., alcohol used in modest amounts) or pheromone that acts as an aphrodisiac for humans or animals.

sex worker, sex trade worker One who engages in sexual activities in exchange for payment. SEE: *prostitution*.

Sézary, Albert (sā″ză-rē′) Fr. dermatologist, 1880–1956.

 S. cell A T lymphocyte that contains an abundance of vacuoles filled with a mucopolysaccharide; present in the blood of patients with cutaneous T-cell lymphoma who develop Sézary syndrome.

 S. syndrome An advanced stage of cutaneous T-cell lymphoma in which there is widespread involvement of the skin and systemic circulation of malignant cells. SEE: *cutaneous T-cell lymphoma*.

SGA *small for gestational age*.

SGIM *Society of General Internal Medicine*.

SGO *Surgeon-General's Office*.

Causative Agents of Sexually Transmitted Diseases

Organism	Associated Diseases
Bacteria	
Klebsiella granulomatis	Donovanosis (granuloma inguinale)
Campylobacter species	Enteritis, proctocolitis
Chlamydia trachomatis	Genital tract infections and Reiter's syndrome
Gardnerella vaginalis	Bacterial (nonspecific) vaginosis
Group B streptococcus	Neonatal sepsis
Haemophilus ducreyi	Chancroid
Mycoplasma hominis	Postpartum fever; meningitis
Neisseria gonorrhoeae	Genital tract infections, disseminated gonococcal infection
Shigella species	Shigellosis; gay bowel syndrome
Treponema pallidum	Syphilis
Ureaplasma urealyticum	Nongonococcal urethritis
Viruses	
Cytomegalovirus	Heterophile-negative infectious mononucleosis, birth defects, protean manifestations in the immunocompromised host
Hepatitis A	Acute hepatitis
Hepatitis B	Acute and chronic hepatitis B, cirrhosis, hepatocellular carcinoma
Hepatitis C	Acute and chronic hepatitis, cirrhosis, hepatocellular carcinoma
Herpes simplex	Genital herpes, aseptic meningitis
Human herpesvirus, type 8	Kaposi's sarcoma, lymphoma
Human immunodeficiency virus types 1 and 2	AIDS (acquired immunodeficiency syndrome)
Human papilloma (70 separate types)	Condyloma acuminata, cervical intraepithelial neoplasia and carcinoma, vulvar carcinoma, penile carcinoma
Human T-lymphotrophic retrovirus, type 1	Human T-cell leukemia or lymphoma
A pox virus	Genital molluscum contagiosum
Protozoa	
Entamoeba histolytica	Amebiasis in people who have oroanal sex
Giardia lamblia	Giardiasis in people who have oroanal sex
Trichomonas vaginalis	Trichomonal vaginitis
Ectoparasites	
Phthirus pubis	Pubic lice infestation
Sarcoptes scabiei	Scabies

NOTE: Many of these diseases can be transmitted by contact that is not sexual.

SGOT *serum glutamic-oxaloacetic transaminase.*

SGPT *serum glutamic pyruvic transaminase.* This liver enzyme is now called alanine aminotransferase.

SH *serum hepatitis.*

shadow [AS. *sceaduwe*] Achromocyte.

shadow-casting A technique to increase the definition of the material being examined by use of electron microscopy. The object is sprayed from an oblique angle with a heavy metal.

shadowing In radiology, loss of the ability to visualize a body structure because of interference by another part.

shaft [AS. *sceaft*] **1.** The principal portion of any cylindrical body. **2.** The diaphysis of a long bone.

  hair s. The keratinized portion of a hair that extends from a hair follicle beyond the surface of the epidermis. SEE: *hair.*

shaken-baby syndrome A syndrome seen in abused infants and children, sometimes referred to as "shaken impact syndrome" because of the accompanying impact injuries to the head. The patient has been subjected to violent, whiplash-type shaking injuries inflicted by an abuser. This may cause coma, convulsions, and increased intracranial pressure, resulting from tearing of the cerebral veins, with consequent bleeding into the subdural space. Retinal hemorrhages and bruises on the arms or trunk where the patient was forcefully grabbed are usually present.

INCIDENCE: About 50,000 cases are reported each year in the U.S. This number probably represents underreporting.

DIAGNOSIS: The presence of retinal hemorrhage, cerebral edema, and subdural hematoma, either singly or in a combination, strongly suggests the diagnosis in the absence of other explanations for the trauma. Radiological imaging is used to identify the specific sites of injury.

PROGNOSIS: The prognosis for affected infants and children is extremely guarded. Only about 15% to 20% of them recover without sequelae, such as vision and hearing impairments, seizure disorders, cerebral palsy, and developmental disorders requiring ongoing medical, educational, and behavioral management. SEE: *battered child syndrome; child abuse*.

⚠ In domestic situations in which a child is abused, it is important to examine other children and infants living in the same home because about 20% of these children will have signs of physical abuse as well. That examination should be done without delay, to prevent further abuse.

shakes (shāks) [AS. *sceacen*] **1.** Shivering caused by a chill, esp. in intermittent fever. **2.** A colloquial term for the state of tremulousness and extreme irritability often seen in chronic alcoholics. SYN: *jitters*.

shake test A quick test to estimate fetal lung maturity. A sample of amniotic fluid is diluted with normal saline, mixed with 95% ethyl alcohol, and shaken for 30 sec. The continued presence of small foamy bubbles in the solution after 15 min confirms the presence of pulmonary surfactant. SYN: *foam stability test; rapid surfactant test*.

shaking **1.** A passive large-amplitude vibratory movement used in massage. **2.** A vibratory technique used in chest physical therapy to facilitate pulmonary drainage.

shaman (shā′mŭn, shŏ′-) [Russ., ascetic] A healer (usually from a tribal or pre-industrial culture) who uses non-Western practices and techniques, including faith healing, spirituality, psychological manipulation, chanting, rituals, magic, and culturally meaningful symbolism to restore health or well-being to the sick. SYN: *medicine man*. SEE: *shamanism*.

shamanism (shā′mŭn-ĭsm, shŏ′-) **1.** Healing by magic and religious rites

practiced by certain peoples of northern Asia who believe good and evil spirits pervade the world and can be influenced only by shamans acting as mediums. **2.** Any similar form of healing, such as that practiced in many tribal cultures. SYN: *aboriginal healing*.

sham therapy Treatment that has no known therapeutic effect. Such treatment may be employed by clinical researchers who are trying to determine whether another intervention will be more effective than doing nothing. Sham therapies are also sometimes used by people engaging in health care fraud.

shank (shăngk) [AS. *sceanca*] **1.** Shin. **2.** The tapered portion of a dental hand instrument between the handle and the blade or nub. It may be straight or angled to provide better access or leverage in its use.

shape (shāp) [AS. *sceapan*] **1.** To mold to a particular form. **2.** Outward form; contour.

shared decision-making Any negotiated agreement between a patient, his or her family, and health care professionals. Successful shared decision-making is dependent on the good will, rationality, and competence of all parties.

shared governance A model of nursing management in which the staff nurse shares responsibility and accountability for patient care with the clinical agency management. Shared governance assumes a participatory style of management and aims to achieve a high quality of patient care and professional nursing practice. Shared governance differs both from self-governance and from the traditional bureaucratic model of nursing management. SEE: *self-governance*.

shared medical appointment A group visit to a health care facility, in which several patients with common medical problems discuss their needs and concerns with one or more health care providers at the same time. SYN: *group medical clinic*.

sharkskin A condition seen in pellagra (nicotinic acid deficiency) in which openings of sebaceous glands become plugged with a dry yellowish material.

sharp end In a health care institution, those personnel and components that work in direct contact with patients.

sharps (shärps) A colloquial term for medical articles that may cause punctures or cuts to those handling them, including all broken medical glassware, syringes, needles, scalpel blades, suture needles, and disposable razors. Potential infectious risks posed by injury with sharps include HIV, hepatitis B, and hepatitis C infections. SEE: *medical waste; red bag waste; Standard and Universal Precautions Appendix*.

shawl sign SEE: under *sign*.

shear (shēr) A frictional force per unit of surface area applied parallel to the planes of any object.

sheath (shēth) **1.** A covering structure of connective tissue, usually of an elongated part, such as the membrane covering a muscle. **2.** An instrument introduced into a vessel during angiographic procedures when multiple catheter changes are anticipated. It facilitates ease of change and decreases morbidity at the puncture site.

PATIENT CARE: The sheath introduced into the femoral artery, the preferred vascular access route for percutaneous coronary intervention, is a 4 to 6 French (1.35 to 2 mm) in size. The sheath remains in place after completion of the procedure and removal of the catheter until anticoagulation is reversed or anticoagulants are below peak action. The sheath is connected to high-pressure tubing and a flushing system; manual or automatic flushing keeps the line patent. A stopcock connected to the system permits drawing of blood samples.

axon s. A myelin sheath or a neurilemma. SEE: *myelin s.*

carotid s. The portion of cervical or pretracheal fascia enclosing the carotid artery, interior jugular vein, and vagus nerve.

crural s. The fascial covering of femoral vessels.

dural s. A fibrous membrane or external investment of the optic nerve.

femoral s. The fascia covering the femoral vessels.

s. of Hertwig SEE: *Hertwig root sheath.*

myelin s. Layers of the cell membrane of Schwann cells (peripheral nervous system) or oligodendrocytes (central nervous system) that wrap nerve fibers, providing electrical insulation and increasing the velocity of impulse transmission. SYN: **Schwann** *sheath.* SEE: *nerve fiber; neuron;* illus.

periarterial lymphoid s. The tissue composed of T lymphocytes that surrounds each arteriole in the spleen. The sheaths are attached to lymphoid follicles containing B cells and make up much of the white pulp. SEE: *spleen.*

pial s. An extension of the pia that closely invests the surface of the optic nerve.

rectus s. A strong fibrous sleeve in which the rectus abdominis and pyramidalis muscles contract. The sheath is formed from the aponeuroses of the abdominal wall muscles as they meet in the linea alba at the abdominal midline.

root s. **1.** One of the layers of a hair follicle derived from the epidermis. It includes the outer root sheath, which is a continuation of the stratum germinativum, and the inner root sheath, which consists of three layers of cells that closely invest the root of the hair. SEE: *hair.* **2.** The epithelial covering that induces root formation in teeth. Also called *Hertwig root sheath.*

tendon s. A dense fibrous sheath that confines a tendon to an osseous groove, converting it into an osteofibrous canal. It is found principally in the wrist and ankle.

shedding [ME. *sheden,* shed] **1.** A colloquial term for the loss of deciduous teeth. **2.** Casting off of the surface layer of the epidermis. **3.** The release of bacteria or viruses from a body surface.

Sheehan syndrome (shē′ăn) [Harold L. Sheehan, Brit. pathologist, 1900–1988] Hypopituitarism due to an infarct of the pituitary after postpartum shock or

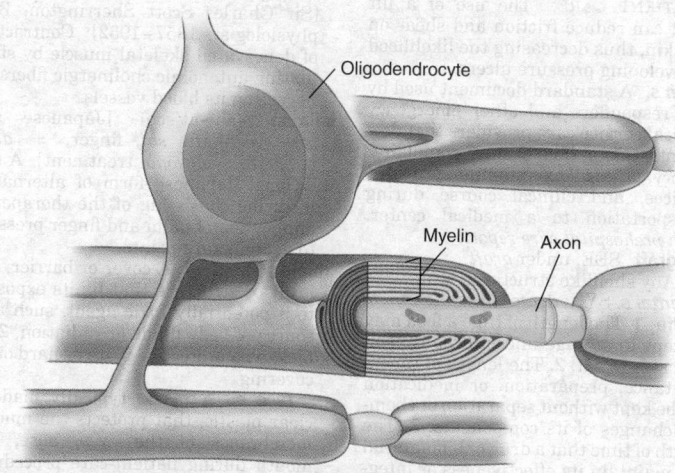

Oligodendrocyte

Myelin   Axon

MYELIN SHEATH

hemorrhage. Damage to the anterior pituitary gland causes partial to complete loss of thyroid, adrenocortical, and gonadal function. SYN: *postpartum pituitary necrosis*.

sheep cell agglutination test ABBR: SCAT. A test for rheumatoid factor in serum. Sheep erythrocytes sensitized with rabbit antisheep erythrocyte immune globulin will be agglutinated if serum containing the rheumatoid factor is added.

sheet (shēt) **1.** A linen or cotton bedcovering. **2.** Something that resembles a sheet (e.g., a sheet of connective tissue).

   beta s. A protein structure in which parallel layers of linked peptides are folded across each other. This structure is characteristic of amyloid proteins.

   draw s. A sheet folded under a patient so that it may be withdrawn without lifting the patient. This is accomplished by turning the patient to the side of the bed to allow one side of the sheet to be removed and replaced with a clean one. The patient is then turned to the other side of the bed. The soiled sheet is removed and replaced with a clean one. In most inpatient facilities, draw sheets have been replaced by paper and plastic pads that resemble disposable diapers.

   face s. A one-page summary of important information about a patient. It includes patient identification, past medical history, medications, allergies, upcoming appointments, insurance status, or other pertinent information.

   fee s. Fee **schedule**.

   flow s. A representation in outline or picture format of a technique or treatment.

   lift s. A sheet folded under a patient over the bottom sheet to assist with moving the patient up in bed.
   PATIENT CARE: The use of a lift sheet can reduce friction and shear on the skin, thus decreasing the likelihood of developing pressure ulcers.

   run s. A standard document used by first responders and other emergency medical service care providers that documents the patient's chief complaint, history, physical examination, provided services, and clinical course during transportation to a medical center. SYN: *prehospital care report*.

sheet graft SEE: under *graft*.

shelf Any shelflike structure.

   dental s. SYN: *dental lamina*.

shelf life 1. The length of time a food may be kept in storage and still be considered safe to eat. **2.** The length of time a substance, preparation, or medication can be kept without separation or chemical changes of its components. **3.** The length of time that a drug or biomaterial will maintain its effectiveness or integrity.

shelf-life extension Preservation of the purity and potency of a therapeutic agent beyond its expected expiration date.

shell (shel) A hard covering, as that for an egg or turtle.

shellac (shĕ-lăk′) A refined resinous substance obtained from plants that contain the secretions of certain insects. It is used in paints, varnishes, dry compounding, and in dentistry.

 Some people may develop contact dermatitis after exposure to shellac.

shellfish (shel′fish″) Any of a group of marine animals that include mollusks and crustaceans. Allergic reactions (urticaria, asthma, angioedema, anaphylaxis) to a wide variety of shellfish are among the most common causes of food allergy in humans.

shell shock SEE: under *shock*.

shelter-in-place,   sheltering-in-place Finding protection from an environmental hazard by sealing oneself in a safe and secure location instead of fleeing or evacuating. One must stay indoors and rely on stored supplies or, if materials must be imported from a contaminated environment, rely on filtration systems that remove toxins, viruses, bacteria, and other potentially dangerous materials until the hazard passes.

Shenton line (shent′ŏnz) [Thomas Shenton, Brit. radiologist, 1872–1955] In radiography, a line determining the relationship of the head of the femur to the acetabulum. The line follows the inferior border of the ramus of the pubic bone and, continuing outward, follows the curve down the medial border of the neck of the femur.

Sherrington phenomenon (shĕr′ing-tŏn) [Sir Charles Scott Sherrington, Brit. physiologist, 1857–1952] Contraction of denervated skeletal muscle by stimulating autonomic cholinergic fibers innervating its blood vessels.

shiatsu (shē-at′soo) [Japanese *shiatsu(ryōhō),* fm *shi,* finger, + *atsu,* pressure + *ryōhō,* treatment] A traditional Japanese form of alternative medicine consisting of the therapeutic application of palm and finger pressure to acupuncture points.

shield (shēld) **1.** A cover or barrier; any layer or structure that limits exposure to a potentially toxic agent, such as a source of body fluids or radiation. **2.** In biology, a protective plate or hard outer covering.

   face s. A mask, typically made of clear plastic, that protects the mucous membranes of the eyes, nose, and mouth during patient-care procedures and activities that carry the risk of generating splashes of blood, body fluids, excretions, or secretions. SEE: *Standard Precautions Appendix*.

gonadal s. A lead covering that is placed over the gonadal area to help protect it during radiation exposure.

nipple s. A cover to protect the sore nipples of a nursing woman.

shift (shift) A change in position or direction.

antigenic s. A major change in the genetic makeup of an organism, usually resulting from gene reassortment or occurring when different species share genetic material. The influenza virus type A is the most common example of an organism that undergoes antigenic shift. This process may create a new pathogen against which there is no immunity in the population, and pandemics can result. SEE: *antigenic* **drift**.

chloride s. The shift of chloride ions from the plasma into the red blood cells upon the addition of carbon dioxide from the tissues, and the reverse movement when carbon dioxide is released in the lungs. It is a mechanism for maintaining constant pH of the blood.

left s. **1.** In hematology, an increase in the number of immature polymorphonuclear leukocytes in the circulating blood. SEE: *Arneth classification of neutrophils*. **2.** In acid-base physiology, a left-shifted oxyhemoglobin dissociation level, indicating an increased affinity of hemoglobin for oxygen. SYN: *s. to the left*.

right s. In hematology, the presence of large numbers of abnormally mature neutrophils in the circulating blood. SYN: *s. to the right*. SEE: *Arneth classification of neutrophils*.

s. to the left Left **s.** **2.** In acid-base physiology, a left-shifted oxyhemoglobin dissociation level, indicating an increased affinity of hemoglobin for oxygen.

s. to the right Right **s.**

shift work SEE: under *work*.

Shiga, Kiyoshi (shē′gă) Japanese bacteriologist, 1871–1957.

S. bacillus *Shigella dysenteriae*.

S. toxin An extremely poisonous compound secreted by enteric bacteria that causes hemorrhagic and necrotic colitis. The toxin was formerly called verotoxin because of its effect on Vero cells.

ETIOLOGY: The toxin acts on the endothelial cells lining the blood vessels. The B subunits of the toxin bind to a component of the cell membrane known as Gb3 and enter the cell. When the protein is inside the cell, the A subunit interacts with the ribosomes to stop protein synthesis. Like the ricin toxin, the A subunit of Shiga toxin is an N-glycosidase that modifies the RNA component of the ribosome to stop protein synthe-

sis, leading to the death of the cell. The breakdown of the endothelial cell lining leads to hemorrhage.

SYMPTOMS: The first sign of shiga toxin activity is usually bloody diarrhea. This is because Shiga toxin is usually taken in with contaminated food or water.

Shigella (shĭ-gĕl′lă) [Kiyoshi Shiga, Japanese physician and bacteriologist, 1871–1951] A genus of gram-negative, non–lactose-fermenting bacilli of the family Enterobacteriaceae. It contains a number of species that cause digestive disturbance ranging from mild diarrhea to a severe and often fatal dysentery. SEE: *bacillary* **dysentery**.

S. boydii A species that causes acute diarrhea in humans.

S. dysenteriae A species that causes severe, epidemic diarrhea.

S. flexneri A species that is a frequent cause of acute diarrhea in humans.

S. sonnei A species that is a frequent cause of bacillary dysentery.

shigellosis (shĭ″gĕl-lō′sĭs) [*Shigella* + *osis*, condition] Infection of the gastrointestinal tract, esp. the distal colon, by *Shigella*. Common symptoms include fever, bloody diarrhea, and abdominal cramps. Because *Shigella* are transmitted from person to person by the fecaloral route, prevention requires thorough handwashing after toileting by toddlers, young children, and adults. The disease may also be contracted by direct oroanal contact and from food or water contaminated by sewage.

shim (shĭm) [Of uncertain origin] In magnetic resonance imaging, a gradient magnetic field that is used to improve the homogeneity of the main magnetic field.

shin (shĭn) [AS. *scinu*, shin] The anterior edge of the tibia, the portion of the leg between the ankle and knee. SYN: *shank*.

saber s. A condition seen in congenital syphilis in which the anterior edge of the tibia is extremely sharp.

shiner (shī′nĕr) A slang term for a black eye, a dark or purplish hue to the skin seen just beneath the eyes. Black eyes may be seen in some people with nasal allergies or after facial injuries.

shingles (shĭng′lz) [L. *cingulus*, a girdle] The colloquial name of the dermatomal rash caused by herpes zoster. SEE: illus.; *herpes zoster*.

shin splints, shinsplints (shin′splints″) Pain in the anterior, posterior, or posterolateral compartment of the tibia. It usually follows strenuous or repetitive exercise and is often related to faulty foot mechanics such as pes planus or pes cavus. The cause may be ischemia of the muscles in the compartment, minute tears in the tissues, or partial avulsion

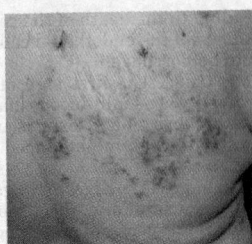

SHINGLES

from the periosteum of the tibial or peroneal muscles. Proper shoes and foot orthotics may help to prevent onset of the condition. A definitive diagnosis is required for proper treatment. Management consists of ice packs, anti-inflammatory medications, decreasing the intensity of exercise, e.g., avoiding hills and hard surfaces when running, and modification of footwear. SYN: *medial tibial stress syndrome*.

shisha (shē'shă) [Persian (Farsi) *shishe*, a bottle] **1.** Water pipe. **2.** A damp blend of fresh tobacco leaves flavored with molasses, honey, mint, cinnamon, etc., traditionally smoked in a water pipe.

shiver (shĭv'ĕr) [ME. *chiveren*] **1.** Involuntary increased muscle activity in response to fear, onset of fever, or exposure to cold. The activity leads to increased heat production. **2.** To tremble or shake.

shock (shok) **1.** A clinical syndrome marked by inadequate perfusion and oxygenation of cells, tissues, and organs, usually due to marginal or markedly lowered blood pressure. SYN: *circulatory **collapse***.

ETIOLOGY: Shock may be caused by dehydration, hemorrhage, sepsis, myocardial infarction, valvular heart disease, cardiac tamponade, adrenal failure, burns, trauma, spinal cord injury, hypoxia, anaphylaxis, poisoning, and other major insults to the body.

SYMPTOMS: Shock results in failure of multiple organ systems, including the brain, heart, kidneys, lungs, skin, and gastrointestinal tract. Common consequences of shock are confusion, agitation, anxiety, or coma; syncope or presyncope; increased work of breathing; respiratory distress; pulmonary edema; decreased urinary output; and/or acute renal failure. Signs of shock include tachycardia, tachypnea, hypotension, and cool, clammy, or cyanotic skin.

TREATMENT: Attempts to restore normal blood pressure and tissue perfusion include fluid resuscitation (in hypovolemic shock); control of hemorrhage (in shock caused by trauma or bleeding); administration of corticosteroids (in adrenal failure); pressor support (in cardiogenic or septic shock); the administration of epinephrine (in anaphylaxis); antibiotic administration with the drainage of infected foci (in sepsis); pericardiocentesis (in cardiac tamponade); transfusion; and oxygenation. Oral or parenterally administered sugars (typically glucose) can treat hypoglycemia caused by insulin, oral hypoglycemic drugs, or insulinomas.

CRITICAL CARE: The shock syndrome is a life-threatening medical emergency and requires very careful therapy and monitoring. If the patient does not respond at once, treatment and monitoring in the best facility available (such as intensive care unit) are essential. It is important that the electrocardiographic, arterial and central venous blood pressures, blood gases, core and skin temperatures, pulse rate, blood volume, blood glucose, hematocrit, cardiac output, urine flow rate, and neurological status be monitored frequently and regularly, e.g., hourly.

PATIENT CARE: Patients at risk for shock include, but are not limited to, those with severe injuries, external or suspected internal hemorrhage, profound fluid loss or sequestration (severe vomiting, diarrhea, burns), allergen exposures, sepsis, impaired left ventricular function, electrical and thermal injuries (including lightning strikes), and diabetes (if receiving supplemental insulin).

One or more large-bore intravenous catheters are inserted, and prescribed fluid therapy is initiated. External monitoring of vital signs is instituted; a pulmonary artery catheter may be placed or impedance cardiography instituted for precise hemodynamic monitoring; and an indwelling urinary catheter is inserted to track urine output hourly. Prescribed oxygen therapy is provided; SaO_2, arterial blood gas levels (ABGs), and ventilatory function are monitored to determine the need for ventilatory support. If occult bleeding is suspected, stools and gastric fluids are tested, and injured tissues and spaces are carefully assessed or imaged. Routine measures are taken to reduce the risk of decubitus ulcers, muscular atrophy, deep venous thrombosis, delirium, and contractures. The patient is maintained in a normothermic environment for comfort. Radiant warmers are useful in preventing hypothermia in patients who cannot be kept clothed or covered during assessment and treatment. The environment is kept as calm and controlled as possible. Procedures and treatments are explained to the patient in a simple, clear, easily understandable manner.

Positioning is based on the type of shock. Hypovolemic shock states respond best to supine positioning or even elevation of the feet and lower legs; cardiac and anaphylactic shock states require head elevation to ease ventilatory effort. Correct body alignment should be maintained, whatever the necessary position. Oral fluids are often withheld to prevent vomiting and aspiration. Oral care and misting are provided frequently to prevent dryness, stomatitis, sordes, and salivary obstructions. The patient's sensorium is closely assessed, and sensory overload is prevented as much as possible. Regular assessments are conducted for acute organ dysfunction, e.g., urine output below 0.5 mL/kg/hr, hypotension, hypoxemia, lactic acidosis, and low platelet count. While providing comfort measures and emotional support, the health care professional acts as a liaison to family members or significant others, providing them with information on the patient's status and the treatment regimen. If shock is irreversible, the family must prepare for the patient's death; family members are encouraged to be with, talk to, and touch the patient, and social work and mental health consultations or spiritual measures may be obtained for the patient and family as determined by their beliefs and desires.

2. An electrical shock, e.g., a discharge of electricity from a cardioverter or defibrillator. SEE: *Nursing Diagnoses Appendix.*

anaphylactic s. Rapidly developing systemic anaphylaxis that produces life-threatening acute airway obstruction followed by vascular collapse within minutes after exposure to an antigen. SEE: *allergy; anaphylaxis.*

ETIOLOGY: The condition is the result of an allergic reaction during which the allergen is absorbed into the blood directly or through the mucosa. The most common agents are bee or wasp venoms, drugs (such as penicillins), and radiographic contrast media. It also can be triggered by severe food allergies (shellfish, peanuts) and by latex exposure. Those with a history of asthma, eczema, or hay fever are at increased risk. Chemical mediators released during the reaction cause constriction of the bronchial smooth muscle, vasodilation, and increased vascular permeability.

SYMPTOMS: Initial symptoms include anxiety, tingling, itching, or warm feelings and skin rash, a metallic taste, swelling of lips and tongue, dyspnea, wheezing, vomiting, abdominal cramps, diarrhea, light-headedness, dizziness, and chest pain. Severe symptoms include acute respiratory distress, hypotension, edema, rash, tachycardia, pale

cool skin, convulsions, and cyanosis. If no treatment is received, unconsciousness and death may result. Tissue swelling can be life-threatening if the larynx is involved, since air flow is obstructed with even minimal swelling.

PREVENTION: A history of past allergic reactions, particularly to bee stings, drugs, blood products, or contrast media, is obtained. The at-risk patient is observed for reaction during and immediately after administration of any of these agents.

PATIENT CARE: At the first sign of life-threatening respiratory distress, an airway is established, the appropriate physician is notified, and oxygen is administered by non–rebreather mask. Venous access is established. Epinephrine is administered, and diphenhydramine and corticosteroids are administered per protocol. Drugs should be administered intravenously if the patient is unconscious or hypotensive, and subcutaneously or intramuscularly if the patient is conscious and normotensive. Airway patency is maintained, and the patient should be observed for early signs of laryngeal edema, e.g., stridor, hoarseness, and dyspnea. Endotracheal intubation or a surgical airway may be necessary. In addition to high-concentration oxygen for all patients in shock, cardiopulmonary resuscitation and defibrillation, as indicated, are initiated if the patient becomes pulseless. The patient is assessed for hypotension and shock; circulatory volume is maintained with prescribed volume expanders, and blood pressure is stabilized with prescribed vasopressors. Blood pressure, central venous pressure, and urinary output are monitored in the hospital setting. Once the initial emergency has subsided, prescribed drugs for long-term management and inhaled bronchodilators for bronchospasm may be considered. The patient is taught to identify and avoid common allergens and to recognize an allergic reaction. Sensitivity testing may be advised to help determine offending allergens. If a patient is unable to avoid exposure to allergens and requires medication, an emergency kit should be kept readily available. Typically, this contains epinephrine in an autoinjector and liquid diphenhydramine. Both patient and family are instructed in its use. The patient with known serious allergies should wear an identifying bracelet or carry a card in his or her wallet. Patients with food allergies should be advised to read labels and to ask about food preparation and content when eating out. Individuals with insect sting allergies should avoid wearing bright-colored clothing, scented cosmetics, hairsprays, or perfumes that attract insects and should use insect repellant and wear closed shoes outdoors.

anesthesia s. Shock due to an overdose of a general anesthetic. The anesthetic should be immediately withheld and oxygen, mechanical ventilation, and vapor drugs should be given.

cardiogenic s. Failure of the heart to pump an adequate supply of blood and oxygen to body tissues. The most common cause of cardiogenic shock is acute myocardial infarction; other causes include failure or stenosis of heart valves (such as aortic or mitral stenosis or regurgitation), cardiomyopathies, pericardial tamponade, and sustained cardiac rhythm disturbances, among others. Cardiogenic shock is often fatal; only about 20% of affected people survive. Its incidence has declined as the care of patients with acute myocardial infarction has incorporated thrombolytic drugs and emergency percutaneous coronary intervention. SEE: *Nursing Diagnoses Appendix.*

PATIENT CARE: The patient is assessed for a history of any cardiac disorder that severely decreases left ventricular function, for anginal pain, dysrhythmias, reduced urinary output, respiratory effort and rate, blood pressure, pulse, dizziness, alterations in mental status, and perfusion of the skin. Signs of poor tissue perfusion include cold, pale, clammy skin; cyanosis; restlessness, mental confusion and obtundation; tachycardia; tachypnea; systolic blood pressure 30 mm Hg below baseline or below 80 mm Hg; and oliguria (urine output below 20 mL/hr). Heart sounds are auscultated for a gallop rhythm and murmurs, the lungs are checked for crackles and wheezes, and neck veins are assessed for distention.

Arterial blood gas values, electrolyte levels, cardiac rhythms, and hemodynamic values (pulmonary artery pressures, wedge pressures, and cardiac output) are monitored intensively. Echocardiography helps to determine left ventricular function and valve abnormalities. Treatment goals include enhancing cardiovascular status by increasing cardiac output, improving myocardial perfusion, and decreasing cardiac workload. Various cardiovascular drugs and mechanical assist techniques are used. Prescribed intravenous fluids are administered via a large-bore intravenous catheter (14 G to 18 G) according to hemodynamic patterns and urine output. Oxygen is administered by face mask or artificial airway to ensure adequate tissue oxygenation. Prescribed inotropic agents and vasopressors are administered and evaluated for desired effects and any adverse reactions.

Some patients will undergo emergent cardiac catheterization, coronary angioplasty, coronary stents, bypass surgery, or placement of intra-aortic balloon pumps, turbine pumps, or temporary or permanent ventricular assist devices. The ICU setting, special procedures, and equipment are explained to the patient and family to reduce their anxiety; a calm environment with as much privacy as possible and frequent rest periods are provided; and frequent family visits are permitted. All invasive sites are assessed for infection and/or hematomas. When the patient's hemodynamic stability is restored, he or she is gradually weaned from supportive mechanical devices and drug therapies. The family must be prepared for the possibility of a fatal outcome and assisted to find effective coping strategies.

compensated s. The early phase of shock in which the body's compensatory mechanisms (such as increased heart rate, vasoconstriction, increased respiratory rate) are able to maintain adequate perfusion to the brain and vital organs. Typically, the patient is normotensive in compensated shock.

cryptic s. Shock without hypotension.

culture s. The emotional trauma of being exposed to the culture, mores, and customs of a culture that is vastly different from the one to which one has been accustomed.

decompensated s. The late phase of shock in which the body's compensatory mechanisms (such as increased heart rate, vasoconstriction, increased respiratory rate) are unable to maintain adequate perfusion to the brain and vital organs. Typically, the patient is hypotensive in decompensated shock.

deferred s. Shock occurring several hours to a day after an injury or illness. SYN: *secondary s.*

distributive s. Shock in which there is a marked decrease in peripheral vascular resistance and consequent hypotension. Examples are septic shock, neurogenic shock, and anaphylactic shock.

electric s. Injury from electricity that varies according to type and strength of current and length and location of contact. Electric shocks range from trivial burns to complete charring and destruction of skin and injury to internal organs, including brain, lungs, kidneys, and heart; and death. Approximately 1000 people are electrocuted accidentally each year in the U.S., and another 4000 are injured. Five percent of admissions to burn centers are related to electrical injury.

Whether or not an electric shock will cause death is influenced by the pathway the current takes through the body, the amount of current, and the skin resistance. Thus, a very small amount of electrical energy applied directly to the heart may be enough to stop it from beating or to trigger ventricular fibrillation.

SYMPTOMS: Burns, loss of consciousness, and/or cardiac arrest are symptoms of electrical injury.

FIRST AID: Rescuers of any electrical shock victim who is unconscious should immediately call for emergency assistance. SEE: *cardiopulmonary resuscitation; electrocution; lightning safety rules*.

TREATMENT: The patient should be freed carefully from the current source by first shutting off the current. Prolonged support in a critical care unit may be needed.

endotoxic s. Septic shock due to release of endotoxins by gram-negative bacteria. Endotoxins are lipopolysaccharides in the cell walls that are released during both reproduction and destruction of the bacteria. They are potent stimulators of inflammation, activating macrophages, B lymphocytes, and cytokines and producing vasodilation, increased capillary permeability, and activation of the complement and coagulation cascades. SEE: *endotoxin; septic* **s.**

hemorrhagic s. Shock due to loss of blood. SEE: *Nursing Diagnoses Appendix.*

hypoglycemic s. Shock produced by extremely low blood sugars (less than 40 mg/dL), usually caused by an injection of an excessive amount of insulin, failure to eat after an insulin injection, or rarely by an insulin-secreting tumor of the pancreas. Insulin-related hypoglycemic shock may be intentionally induced in the treatment of certain psychiatric conditions. SYN: *insulin* **s.** SEE: *hypoglycemia.*

PATIENT CARE: All unconscious patients should be treated for presumptive hypoglycemia with an injection of dextrose (D_{50}). Once the patient is conscious, glucose is given by mouth to attain the desired glucose level. The rescue therapy is followed by a carbohydrate and protein snack to maintain the desired level.

The stabilized patient's immediate history should be reviewed and triggering factors looked for. The patient and family can then be taught ways to avoid such situations in the future or to manage them before hypoglycemia again becomes this serious. If insulin levels need to be adjusted, the patient's preprandial glucose levels for the preceding 24 hr must be reviewed. The patient and family are assisted in processing the event. Their treatment actions are given positive reinforcement, correcting any errors such as inability to recognize early symptoms of insulin shock, overcorrection of insulin deficiency, or use of food products that are absorbed too slowly.

hypovolemic s. Shock occurring when there is an insufficient amount of fluid in the circulatory system. This is usually due to bleeding, diarrhea, or vomiting. SYN: *oligemic* **s.**

insulin s. Hypoglycemic **s.** SEE: *Nursing Diagnoses Appendix.*

irreversible s. Shock of such intensity that even heroic therapy cannot prevent death.

neurogenic s. A form of distributive shock due to decreased peripheral vascular resistance. Damage to either the brain or the spinal cord inhibits transmission of neural stimuli to the arteries and arterioles, which reduces vasomotor tone. The decreased peripheral resistance results in vasodilation and hypotension; cardiac output diminishes due to the altered distribution of blood volume.

obstructive s. Circulatory collapse caused by conditions that block the flow of blood into or out of the heart, such as cardiac tamponade, cardiac tumors, massive pulmonary embolism, or tension pneumothorax. Obstructive shock is characterized by very low cardiac output and increased systemic vascular resistance.

oligemic s. Hypovolemic **s.**

protein s. Shock resulting from parenteral administration of a protein.

psychogenic s. Shock due to emotional stress or to seeing an injury or accident.

refractory s. Shock that does not respond to standard treatments, e.g., with oxygenation and ventilation, fluid resuscitation and the restoration of perfusion, and identification and treatment of infection. It typically requires high doses of vasopressors, e.g., more than 15 mcg/kg/min of dopamine to maintain a blood pressure of 60 mm Hg.

secondary s. Deferred **s.**

septic s. Hypotension and inadequate blood flow to organs resulting from sepsis. The most common organisms are gram-negative and gram-positive bacteria, but fungi and other organisms may also be responsible. SEE: *sepsis.*

ETIOLOGY: Organisms and released endotoxins or exotoxins initiate a systemic inflammatory response. Chemical mediators of inflammation and the cell-mediated immune response (esp. tumor necrosis factor and interleukin 1) cause the physiological changes to septic shock. Initially, vasodilation, increased capillary permeability, and movement of plasma out of blood vessels produce hypovolemia and hypotension. Compensatory vasoconstriction occurs in an effort to maintain blood flow to vital organs. As sepsis progresses, secondary inflammatory mediators are released, increasing vascular endothelial damage.

Selective vasoconstriction produces tissue hypoxia and single or multiple organ dysfunction. Tissue hypoxia is increased by abnormal stimulation of the coagulation and kinin cascades in the capillaries, which produce microthrombi. Within the lung, damage to the capillary endothelium may cause adult respiratory distress syndrome. Septic shock often progresses to multiple organ dysfunction syndrome, which is the most common cause of death in surgical intensive care units.

SYMPTOMS: Confusion and other alterations of consciousness are common symptoms. Other signs include hypotension, fever, tachypnea, tachycardia, decreased urinary output, and cold, clammy skin. Laboratory studies reveal acidosis and, sometimes, renal failure or coagulopathies.

TREATMENT: Empiric therapy with an extended-spectrum penicillin (such as ticarcillin/clavulanate, piperacillin/tazobactam) or third-generation cephalosporin (such as ceftriaxone), plus clindamycin or metronidazole, provide antibiotic coverage until an organism from the primary site of infection is positively identified. Intravenous resuscitation and, if necessary, vasopressors such as dopamine or norepinephrine are used to stabilize blood pressure. Activated drotecogin alfa, a recombinant form of human activated protein, is occasionally effective. Oxygen and other supportive interventions are used to minimize organ damage. Maintaining blood glucose levels between 80 and 110 mg/dL improves chances of survival significantly. Use of corticosteroids is not supported by research.

PATIENT CARE: Intensive care measures are instituted to monitor blood pressure, fluid and electrolyte balance, renal function, and changes in neurological status. Assessment of progressive agitation or confusion should emphasize the possibility of hypoxia. Routine measures to reduce the risk of decubitus ulcers, muscle atrophy, and contractures are needed. Repeated teaching is necessary for family members to understand the severity of the infection, the purpose of interventions, signs of improvement, and the possibility of death.

spinal s. Immediate flaccid paralysis and loss of all sensation and reflex activity below the level of injury in acute transverse spinal cord injury. Arterial hypotension may be present in this condition.

shell s. A term used during World War I to designate a wide variety of psychotic and neurotic disorders associated with the stress of combat. SEE: *posttraumatic stress disorder*.

surgical s. Shock following operations and including traumatic shock. SEE: *traumatic s.*

traumatic s. Shock due to injury or surgery. In the abdomen, it may result from hemorrhage and/or peritonitis secondary to a disrupted or perforated viscus. Additional causes of traumatic shock include the following:

Cerebral injury: Shock from concussion of the brain secondary to cranial contusion or fracture or spontaneous hemorrhage. The shock may be evident immediately or later due to edema or delayed intracranial hemorrhage. *Chemical injury:* Shock due to physiological response to tissue injury, such as fluid mobilization, toxicity of the agent, and reflexes induced by pain due to the effect of chemicals, esp. corrosives. *Crushing injury:* Shock caused by disruption of soft tissue with release of myoglobulins, hemorrhage, and so forth, generally proportional to the extent of the injury. *Fracture (esp. open fracture):* Shock due to blood loss, fat embolism, and the physiological effects of pain. *Heart damage:* Shock caused by myocardial infarction, myocarditis, pericarditis, pericardial tamponade, or direct trauma with ensuing cardiovascular effects. *Inflammation:* Shock caused by severe sepsis, for example, peritonitis due to release of toxins affecting cardiovascular function and significant fluid mobilization. *Intestinal obstruction:* Shock caused by respiratory compromise due to distention, fluid mobilization, release of bacterial toxins, and pain. *Nerve injury:* Shock caused by injury to the area controlling respirations (e.g., high cervical cord injury) or to highly sensitive parts, such as the testicle, solar plexus, eye, and urethra, or secondary to cardiovascular reflexes stimulated by pain. *Operations:* Shock that may occur even after minor operations and paracentesis or catheterization due to rapid escape of fluids resulting in abrupt alteration of intraabdominal pressure dynamics and hemorrhage. *Perforation or rupture of viscera:* Shock resulting from acute pneumothorax, ruptured aneurysm, perforated peptic ulcer, perforation of appendicial abscess or colonic diverticulum, or ectopic pregnancy. *Strangulation:* Shock resulting from strangulated hernia, intussusception, or volvulus. *Thermal injury:* Shock caused by burn, frostbite, or heat exhaustion secondary to fluid mobilization due to the physiological effects of pain. *Torsion of viscera:* Shock caused by torsion of an ovary or a testicle secondary to the physiological effects of pain.

shockable rhythm SEE: under *rhythm*.

shock dose SEE: under *dose*.

shock therapy, shock treatment Electroconvulsive therapy.

shoemaker's cramp SEE: under *cramp*.

Shone anomaly (shōn) [John D. Shone, 20th-cent. Brit. cardiologist] A congenital heart disease characterized by multiple types of obstruction to the outflow of blood from the left ventricle and by mitral valve disease. The anomaly is typically found in children and requires surgical repair. Other features include supravalvular mitral ring, parachute mitral valve, subaortic stenosis, and coarctation.

short-acting beta agonist SEE: under *agonist*.

short bowel syndrome Inadequate absorption of ingested nutrients (esp. vitamin B_{12}, macronutrients, sodium, and magnesium) resulting from a surgical procedure in which a considerable length of the intestinal tract has been removed or bypassed. Aggressive enteral nutrition or creation of an antiperistaltic segment in the remaining intestine may replace the need for partial or total parenteral nutrition in the management of this syndrome. Transplantation of the small intestine would be ideal, but as yet has limited application. SEE: *total parenteral* **nutrition**.

shortening 1. Loss of bone length after a fracture, as a result of malunion or pronounced bony angulation. 2. A decrease in the length of a contracting muscle fiber.

shortness of breath Breathlessness.

shortsightedness (short'sīt'ĕd-nĕs) Myopia.

short stay A brief hospitalization for observation, e.g., after a simple surgery, a biopsy, or a diagnostic study. The time spent in the hospital is typically limited to a few hours.

short-stay unit A ward or clinic used to manage patients requiring a short stay.

short-term Pert. to a brief period of time, usually as long as a day but less than a month. In business and finance, the same period is a year or less.

sho-saiko-to ABBR: SST. A traditional Chinese and Japanese herbal mixture used to treat chronic hepatitis and other illnesses.

shoshin beriberi Shoshin syndrome.

shoshin syndrome (shō'shin") [Japanese *sho*, acute damage + *shin*, heart] Cardiogenic shock resulting from severe, acute thiamine deficiency, e.g. in malnourished alcoholics. SYN: *shoshin beriberi*.

shot A colloquial term for an injection.

shoulder (shōl'dĕr) A part of the shoulder girdle complex, comprising the region of the proximal humerus, clavicle, and scapula. SEE: *scapula*; illus.

   frozen s. Adhesive capsulitis of shoulder.

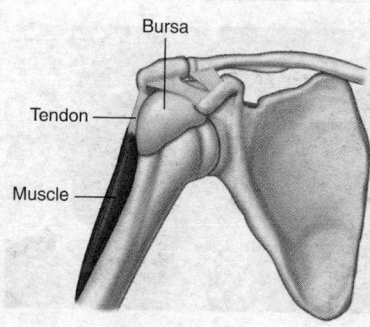

SHOULDER

shoulder blade The scapula.

shoulder girdle syndrome Idiopathic brachial **plexopathy**.

shoulder-hand syndrome Reflex sympathetic **dystrophy**.

show (shō) [AS. *scewian*, to look at] The sanguinoserous discharge from the vagina during the first stage of labor or just preceding menstruation. SYN: *bloody s.*

   bloody s. Show.

show of force The recruitment of large numbers of powerful people to an emotionally escalating situation in an attempt to prevent violent action by an opponent.

shreds (shrĕds) [AS. *screade*] Slender strands of mucus seen in freshly voided urine, indicative of inflammation of the urinary tract or associated organs.

shrink To reduce in size.

shudder [ME. *shuddren*] A temporary convulsive tremor resulting from fright, horror, or aversion.

shunt (shŭnt) [ME. *shunten*, to avoid] 1. To turn away from; to divert. 2. An anomalous passage or one artificially constructed to divert flow from one main route to another. 3. An electric conductor connecting two points in a circuit to form a parallel circuit through which a portion of the current may pass.

   anatomical s. A normal or abnormal direct connection between arterial and venous circulation. An example of a normal anatomical shunt is the bronchial and thebesian vein connection.

   arteriovenous s. An abnormal connection between an artery and the venous system.

   Blalock-Taussig s. SEE: *Blalock-Taussig shunt*.

   cardiovascular s. An abnormal connection between the cavities of the heart or between the systemic and pulmonary vessels.

   dialysis s. An arteriovenous shunt created for use during renal dialysis. SEE: illus.

   left-to-right s. The passage of blood from the left side of the heart to the

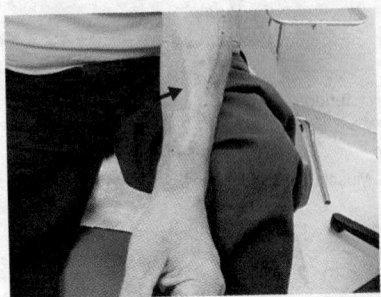

DIALYSIS SHUNT

right side through an abnormal opening (e.g., a septal defect).

    physiological s. The route by which pulmonary blood perfuses unventilated alveoli. This process is caused by an imbalance between ventilation and perfusion.

    pleuroperitoneal s. A conduit connecting the pleural space and the peritoneum, used to drain recurring pleural effusions, such as those that accumulate in patients with certain cancers in the chest. SYN: *Denver shunt*.

    portacaval s. Surgical creation of a connection between the portal vein and the vena cava. SYN: *postcaval s*.

    postcaval s. Portacaval **s**.

    right-to-left s. The movement of blood or other body fluids backward through a shunt. The shunted blood has no opportunity to become oxygenated because of failure to pass through the lungs.

    transjugular intrahepatic portosystemic s. ABBR: TIPS. A shunt inserted through the skin, jugular vein, and liver and then into the portal venous system to manage complications of portal hypertension, such as bleeding caused by esophageal varices or uncontrollable ascites. The shunt decreases pressure within the portal venous circulation (e.g., in patients with cirrhosis), bypassing the liver and allowing portal blood to flow directly into the vena cava. A common complication of the procedure is altered mental status, since blood that was previously detoxified by the liver is directed around it.

shunting A condition in which blood, by going through an abnormal pathway or bypass, does not travel its normal route. It may occur when an arteriovenous fistula forms or in congenital anomalies of the heart in which the blood passes from the right atrium or ventricle directly to the left atrium or ventricle respectively, through a defect in the wall (septum) that normally separates the atria and ventricles. SYN: *blood shunting*.

shuttle (shŭt′l) To transport an object

back and forth; in cell biology or biochemistry, to carry a molecule repeatedly across a cell membrane.

shuttle vector SEE: under *vector*.

shuttle walk test A test of aerobic power or exercise capacity in which a person is made to walk back and forth between two points or around and around a track, often incrementally increasing walking speed with each shuttle completion. The test has been used to assess respiratory function, cardiovascular reserve, fitness for surgery, or geriatric physical fitness. In a typical test, the original shuttle speed is set between 0.6 and 6 km/hr and increased by 0.17 to 0.5 km/hr until the patient becomes fatigued or achieves 12 min of exercise.

Shy-Drager syndrome (shī′drā′gĕr) [George Milton Shy, U.S. neurologist, 1919–1967; G. A. Drager, U.S. physician, 1917–1967] A rare neurodegenerative disease of middle-aged or elderly people marked by chronic orthostatic hypotension, muscular rigidity, slow initiation of body movement, urinary incontinence, bowel dysfunction, erectile dysfunction, episodic loss of consciousness, and cardiac arrhythmias. SYN: *multiple systems atrophy*.

shyness Timidity, esp. in an unfamiliar setting or when encountering strangers. It cannot be classed as abnormal unless it interferes with activities essential to employment or interpersonal relations. SEE: *social phobia*.

SI *Système International;* International System of Measurement. SEE: SI Units Appendix.

Si Symbol for the element silicon.

SIADH *syndrome of inappropriate antidiuretic hormone.*

sialadenitis (sī″ăl-ăd″ĕ-nī′tĭs) [″ + ″ + *itis,* inflammation] Inflammation of a salivary gland. SYN: *sialitis*.

sialadenosis (sī″ăl-ăd″ĕn-ō′sĭs) Painless enlargement of the salivary glands, occurring without findings that suggest salivary gland cancer, infection (sialadenitis), or inflammation. It is most obvious in the parotid glands. Commonly associated conditions include alcoholic cirrhosis, breast-feeding, diabetes mellitus, eating disorders, pregnancy, and malnutrition. SYN: *sialosis*.

sialagogue, sialogogue (sī-ăl′ă-gŏg, sī-ăl′ō-gŏg) [″ + *agogos,* leading] **1.** An agent increasing the flow of saliva. **2.** Pert. to the secretion of saliva. SYN: *ptyalagogue*.

sialic (sī-ăl′ĭk) Pert. to or resembling saliva.

sialitis (sī″ă-līt′tĭs) [″ + *itis,* inflammation] Sialadenitis.

sialo-, sial- [Gr. *sialon,* saliva] Prefixes meaning *saliva.*

sialoadenitis (sī″ă-lō-ăd″ĕ-nī′tĭs) [″ +

aden, gland, + *itis,* inflammation] Si-aladenitis.

sialocele (sī″ă-lō-sēl) [″ + *kele,* tumor, swelling] A cyst or tumor of a salivary gland.

sialogogic (sī″ă-lō-gŏj′ĭk) Producing or promoting a secretion of saliva.

sialogram (sī-ăl′ō-grăm) [″ + *gramma,* something written] A radiograph of the ductal system of a salivary gland. A radiopaque fluid is instilled into the major duct to determine the presence or absence of calcareous deposits or other pathological changes.

sialography (sī″ă-lŏg′ră-fē) [″ + *graphein,* to write] Radiography of the salivary glands and ducts after injection of a radiopaque contrast medium. SYN: *ptyalography; sialoangiography.*

sialolith (sī-al′ō-lith″) [*sialo-* + Gr. *lithos,* stone] Salivary **stone.**

sialolithiasis (sī″ă-lō-lĭ-thī′ă-sĭs) The presence of stones in the salivary ducts. SYN: *salivolithiasis.*

sialorrhea (sī″ă-lō-rē′ă) [″ + *rhoia,* a flow] Ptyalism.

sialosis (sī-ă-lō′sĭs) [″ + *osis,* condition] Sialadenosis.

Siamese twins (sī-ă-mēz′) [After Chang and Eng, conjoined Chinese twins in Siam (Thailand), 1811–1874] SEE: *conjoined* **twin.**

sib (sĭb) [AS. *sibb,* kin] **1.** Sibling. **2.** A blood relative.

Siberian ginseng (sī-bir′ē-ăn) SEE: under *ginseng.*

sibilant (sĭb′ĭ-lănt) [L. *sibilans,* hissing] Hissing or whistling, as a sound heard in certain abnormal lung conditions or in the formation of certain letters in speech, such as the letter "s."

sibling (sĭb′lĭng) [AS. *sibb,* kin, + *-ling,* having the quality of] One of two or more children of the same parents; a brother or sister. SYN: *sib.*

half s. A half brother or sister.

sibship (sĭb′shĭp) Brothers and sisters of a single family.

Sicariidae (sī″kar′ī′ĭ-dē) [*Sicarius,* a genus name + *-idae*] A family of poisonous spiders that includes the brown recluse (*Loxosceles reclusa*) and other *Loxosceles* species.

siccus (sĭk′ŭs) [L.] Dry.

SICK *small indented calcified kidneys.*

sick (sĭk) [AS *seoc,* ill] **1.** Not well. SYN: *ill.* **2.** Mentally ill or disturbed. **3.** Nauseated.

sick building syndrome Symptoms of illness experienced by occupants of or workers in high-rise apartment or office buildings, for which a definite cause has not been established. Many causes have been suggested for the syndrome, including poor indoor air quality, poor lighting, molds, and fungi.

sick call 1. In the military, a scheduled time for those with (relatively) minor illnesses or injuries to visit a clinic. **2.** In jails or prisons, a request by an inmate for health care services. **3.** In home health, a house call or home visit.

sickle cell anemia SEE: under *anemia.*

sickling (sĭk′lĭng) The tendency of red blood cells to change from a biconcave to an arched shape when oxygen tensions are low. The deformity results from the polymerization of abnormal hemoglobin molecules, such as hemoglobin S. Sickled red blood cells clog small blood vessels, producing tissue ischemia or infarction. SEE: *sickle cell anemia.*

sickling test A test that measures the propensity of red blood cells to sickle under conditions of reduced oxygen tension. The test may be performed by adding sodium metabisulfite to a drop of blood and examining the blood smear microscopically. Hemoglobin electrophoresis is an alternative test for sickle cell disease.

sickness (sĭk′nĕs) A state of being unwell. SYN: *illness.*

acute mountain s. ABBR: AMS. Altitude **s.**

African sleeping s. Sleeping **s.** (2).

altitude s. Symptoms such as alterations in consciousness, headache, and shortness of breath that occur on exposure to high altitudes where the oxygen content of ambient air is low, e.g., during aviation or mountaineering. SYN: *acute mountain* **s.***; balloon* **s.**

chronic mountain s. The slow onset of symptoms in people who reside at high altitude for several years. The symptoms include apathy, fatigue, and headache. Laboratory studies often reveal hypoxia and polycythemia. People between ages 40 and 60 are most likely to be affected. The symptoms subside when the person returns to sea level. SYN: *Monge disease.*

car s. Motion **s.**

green s. Chlorosis.

milk s. A disease in humans characterized by weakness, vomiting, and constipation, and caused by ingestion of dairy products or meat from cattle affected with trembles. SYN: *slows; tires.* SEE: *trembles.* SEE: *white* **snakeroot.**

morning s. The nausea and vomiting that affects many women during the first few months of pregnancy. The condition typically starts about 4 to 6 weeks after conception, peaks in incidence and severity between 8 and 11 weeks, and subsides spontaneously between 12 and 16 weeks of gestation. It occurs in 50% to 88% of pregnancies and is the most common complaint in the first trimester. It probably is caused by the high level of human chorionic gonadotropin, low blood sugars related to fasting while asleep, and altered carbohydrate metabolism. SYN: *nausea gravidarum.*

SYMPTOMS: Complaints vary from mild nausea on arising to severe intermittent nausea and vomiting throughout the day. The woman may experience headache, vertigo, and exhaustion, as well. Severe, persistent vomiting with retching between meals should be reported and investigated. SEE: *hyperemesis gravidarum*.

PATIENT CARE: In most cases, dietary management will minimize or eliminate symptoms. The woman is advised to eat dry crackers or toast before rising; to eat something every 2 hr; to drink fluids between meals; and to avoid spicy, greasy, or fried foods and foods with strong odors. Rarely will the patient need antiemetics.

⚠️ The use of any drug during pregnancy should be carefully evaluated before administration to avoid possible damage to the fetus. If vomiting persists, hospitalization with IV fluids and rest are prescribed.

motion s. A syndrome, marked primarily by nausea and/or vomiting, due to a conflict between the true vertical axis and the subjective or perceived vertical axis. Motion sickness is a common illness experienced by car, boat, plane, or space travelers. It is also sometimes felt during motion picture viewing. Susceptibility to motion sickness is greatest between the ages of 2 and 12; it lessens with age but can be provoked in most people if the inciting stimulus is strong enough.

TREATMENT: Antimotion sickness medications include diazepam, diphenhydramine, meclizine, and scopolamine. Some patients with motion sickness benefit by eating small quantities of food when they begin to feel ill. SYN: *car s.*

radiation s. Radiation syndrome.

serum s. An adverse immune response following administration of foreign antigens, esp. antiserum obtained from horses or other animals. Animal serum was formerly used for passive immunization against some infectious diseases but now has very limited use in antitoxins, monoclonal antibodies, and antilymphocyte globulin. Serum sickness can also occur after administration of penicillins and other drugs. Antigen-antibody complexes form and deposit on the walls of small blood vessels, stimulating an inflammatory response that produces a pruritic rash, fever, joint pain and swelling, myalgias, and enlarged lymph nodes 7 to 14 days after exposure. Treatment consists of salicylates (such as aspirin) and antihistamines to minimize inflammation; corticosteroids may be given for severe symptoms. SEE: *Nursing Diagnoses Appendix*.

sleeping s. **1.** Encephalitis lethargica. **2.** Infection with the African trypanosome, *Trypanosoma brucei rhodesiense* or *gambiense*, transmitted by the bite of a tsetse fly. The disease is marked by fever, protracted lethargy, weakness, tremors, and wasting. SYN: *African sleeping s.* SEE: ***Trypanosoma brucei***.

space s. A transient form of motion sickness occurring in space travelers. SEE: *motion s.*

sick sinus syndrome ABBR: SSS. Any of several diseases of the sinoatrial node of the heart in which the node fails to generate impulses appropriately, resulting in long pauses, bradycardia, or bradycardia alternating with tachycardia. It is an occasional cause of palpitations, breathlessness, or loss of consciousness. It is an occasional cause of palpitations, breathlessness, or loss of consciousness. SEE: *Nursing Diagnoses Appendix*.

TREATMENT: A pacemaker should be inserted. Anticoagulant therapy may be required to prevent thromboembolism.

SICU *surgical intensive care unit.*

SID *Society for Investigative Dermatology; sensory integration disorder; source-to-image receptor distance.*

side (sīd) [AS. *side*] **1.** The left or right part of the trunk of the body. **2.** An outer portion considered as facing in a particular direction.

side effect An action or effect of a drug other than that desired. It is commonly an undesirable effect such as nausea, headache, insomnia, rash, confusion, dizziness, or an unwanted drug-drug interaction.

side-lying position A lateral recumbent position in which the individual rests on the right or left side, usually with the knees slightly flexed. This position may be used in persons with mild forms of sleep apnea, in some patients with dysphagia, and in patients predisposed to sacral decubitus ulcers.

side rail A structural support attached to the frame of a bed and intended to prevent a patient from falling.

⚠️ Patients who are confused, intoxicated, or restless have on occasion become trapped in gaps between the bed side rails and the frame and been seriously injured or killed.

SYN: *bed rail.*

sidero-, sider- [Gr. *sidéros*, iron] Prefixes meaning *iron*.

sideroblast (sĭd′ĕr-ō-blăst″) [Gr. *sideros*, iron, + *blastos*, germ] A ferritin-containing normoblast in the bone marrow. Sideroblasts constitute from 20% to 90% of normoblasts in the marrow. The ferritin gives a positive Prussian-blue reaction, indicating the iron is ionized and not bound to the heme protein.

sideropenia (sĭd″ĕr-ō-pē′nē-ă) [″ + *penia*, poverty] Iron deficiency in the blood. **sideropenic**, *adj.*

siderophilin (sīd″ĕ-rō-fĭl′ĭn) [Gr. *sideros*, iron, + *philein*, to love] Any of several iron-binding proteins in the body, e.g., transferrin.

siderophore (sĭd′ĕ-rō-for″) [*sidero-* + *-phore*] **1.** A macrophage that contains hemosiderin. **2.** An iron-binding protein, e.g., one used by disease-causing bacteria to obtain iron stores from the host.

siderosis (sĭd″ĕr-ō′sĭs) [″ + *osis*, condition] **1.** A form of pneumoconiosis resulting from inhalation of dust or fumes containing iron particles. SEE: *hemosiderosis.* **2.** The abnormal deposition or accumulation of iron in the blood or body tissues. **siderotic**, *adj.*

   s. **of the central nervous system** A rare neurological condition marked by bilateral sensorineural hearing loss, often with gait disturbance, cognitive impairment, and myoclonus. Excessive quantities of hemosiderin are found in the leptomeninges and subpial regions of the brain.

   hepatic *s.* Excessive deposition of iron in the liver, found in patients with cirrhosis and hemochromatosis.

   occupational *s.* SYN: *siderosis (1).*

   urinary *s.* Hemosiderin granules in the urine.

sidestream smoke (sīd′strēm″) SEE: under *smoke.*

SIDS *sudden infant death syndrome.*

SIECUS *Sex Information and Education Council of the U.S.*

siemens (sē′mĕnz) A unit of conductance derived from SI units. It is the reciprocal of the resistance in ohms. SYN: *mho.*

sieve (sĭv) A device consisting of a mesh with holes of uniform size. It is used to separate particles above a certain size from solutions or powders.

   molecular *s.* A type of sieve in which the molecular material present in the gel or crystal will adsorb molecules of a certain kind and let others pass.

sievert (sē′vĕrt) [Rolf Maximilian Sievert, Swedish radiologist, 1896–1966] ABBR: Sv. A unit of absorbed radiation energy derived from SI units. One sievert is equal to 1 J/kg or 100 rem.

sig *signa.*

sigh [AS. *sican*] **1.** A deep inspiration followed by a slow audible expiration. **2.** In respiratory and critical care medicine, a mechanically generated breath with a high set tidal volume used to inflate collapsed lung segments and improve ventilation and oxygenation.

sight (sīt) [AS. *sihth*] **1.** The power or faculty of seeing. **2.** Range of sight. **3.** A

thing or view seen. SYN: *vision; visual perception.*

   blind *s.* The ability to see by people who are blind because of a brain lesion rather than because of damage to the eye. Such people are able to reach for and track an object but apparently do not know they can see.

   day *s.* Night **blindness**.

   far *s.* Hyperopia.

   near *s.* Myopia.

   night *s.* Day **blindness**.

sight word acquisition The ability to read a multisyllabic word by recognizing it without breaking it down into its component syllables or sounds.

sigma (sĭg′mă) Σ or σ, the uppercase and lowercase symbols, respectively, for the 18th letter of the Greek alphabet. SEE: Σ; σ.

Sigma Theta Tau (sĭg′mă-thăt′ă-tow′) ABBR: STT. The international honor society of nursing, founded in 1922 by six students and an alumna of the Indiana University Training School. There are 424 chapters in the U.S., Taiwan, Australia, Canada, and Korea. The international headquarters is at Indiana University in Indianapolis.

sigmoid (sĭg′moyd) [Gr. *sigmoeides*] **1.** Shaped like the capital Greek letter sigma, Σ. **2.** Pert. to the sigmoid colon.

sigmoid colon SEE: under *colon.*

sigmoidectomy (sĭg″moyd-ĕk′tō-mē) [″ + *ektome*, excision] Removal of all or part of the sigmoid colon.

sigmoiditis (sĭg″moyd-ī′tĭs) [″ + *itis*, inflammation] Inflammation of the sigmoid colon.

sigmoidoscope (sĭg-moy′dō-skōp) [″ + *skopein*, to examine] A tubular speculum for examination of the sigmoid colon and the rectum.

   flexible *s.* A sigmoidoscope that uses fiberoptics. This permits the tubular extension to flex, enabling the examiner to visualize a greater portion of the colon than would be possible with a rigid sigmoidoscope.

sigmoidoscopy (sĭg″moy-dos′kŏ-pē) [sigmoid + -scopy] Use of a sigmoidoscope to inspect the sigmoid colon. **sigmoidoscopic** (-dŏ-skop′-ĭk), *adj.*

sigmoidostomy (sĭg″moy″dos′tŏ-mē) [sigmoid + -stomy] Creation of a sigmoid colostomy.

sign (sīn) [L. *signum*, a mark, token] **1.** A symbol or abbreviation, esp. one used in pharmacy. **2.** Any objective evidence or manifestation of an illness or disordered function of the body. Signs are apparent to observers, whereas symptoms may be obvious only to the patient. SEE: *symptom.* **3.** To use sign language to communicate.

   [1]Abadie *s.* SEE: [1]*Abadie sign.*

   [2]Abadie *s.* SEE: [2]*Abadie sign.*

   Ahlfeld *s.* SEE: *Ahlfeld sign.*

air bronchogram s. Radiographic appearance of an air-filled bronchus as it passes through an area of increased anatomic density, as in pulmonary edema and pneumonia.

Allis s. SEE: under *Allis, Oscar Huntington.*

Amoss s. SEE: *Amoss sign.*

anterior drawer s. Anterior drawer test.

Auenbrugger s. SEE: *Auenbrugger sign.*

Aufrecht s. SEE: *Aufrecht sign.*

Auspitz s. SEE: *Auspitz sign.*

Babinski s. SEE: under *Babinski, Joseph-François-Felix.*

Battle s. SEE: *Battle sign.*

beaten-silver skull s. The thinned, irregular appearance of the skull, as seen on x-ray examination of children with obstructive hydrocephalus.

Bjerrum s. SEE: under *Bjerrum, Jannik Petersen.*

Beevor s. SEE: *Beevor sign.*

Bloomberg s. Rebound **tenderness**.

Branham s. SEE: *Branham sign.*

Broadbent s. SEE: *Broadbent sign.*

Brudzinski s. SEE: *Brudzinski sign.*

Cardarelli s. SEE: *Cardarelli sign.*

Carnett s. SEE: *Carnett sign.*

Carvallo s. SEE: *Carvallo sign.*

Castell s. SEE: *Castell sign.*

Chadwick s. SEE: *Chadwick sign.*

chandelier s. Intense pelvic and lower abdominal pain brought on by palpation of the cervix. The sign points to the presence of pelvic inflammatory disease.

Chapman s. SEE: *Chapman sign.*

Chvostek s. SEE: *Chvostek sign.*

corona radiata s. Filaments extending outward from a radiographically visualized mass. The presence of such filaments suggests that the mass is growing centrifugally and therefore may be malignant.

Courvoisier s. SEE: under *Courvoisier, Ludwig Georg.*

Cullen s. SEE: *Cullen sign.*

Darier s. SEE: under *Darier, Ferdinand Jean.*

Davidsohn s. SEE: *Davidsohn sign.*

de Musset s. SEE: *Musset sign.*

dimple s. A sign to differentiate dermatofibroma, a benign lesion, from nodular melanoma, which it may mimic. On application of lateral pressure with the thumb and index finger, the dermatofibroma becomes dimpled or indented, whereas melanomas, melanocytic nevi, and normal skin protrude above the initial plane.

Dorendorf s. SEE: *Dorendorf sign.*

drawer s. Drawer test. SEE: *anterior drawer test.*

echo s. Repetition of the closing word of a sentence, a sign of epilepsy or other brain conditions.

Faget s. SEE: *Faget sign.*

fallen lung s. The radiologic appearance of traumatic transection or rupture of the trachea or a main stem bronchus, consisting of a collapsed lung that seems to dangle from the hilum by only its vascular attachments. Pneumothorax, pneumomediastinum, and subcutaneous emphysema are sometimes seen with tracheobronchial tears.

flag s. A peculiar change in hair color in which the hair becomes discolored in a band perpendicular to its long axis. This is seen in kwashiorkor and indicates a period of severe malnutrition.

Frank s. SEE: *Frank sign.*

Friedreich s. SEE: under *Friedreich, Nikolaus.*

Froment s. SEE: *Froment sign.*

Galeazzi s. SEE: *Galeazzi sign.*

Gauss s. SEE: *Gauss sign.*

Goodell s. SEE: *Goodell sign.*

Gottron s. SEE: *Gottron sign.*

Gowers s. SEE: under *Gowers, Sir William Richard.*

Grey Turner s. SEE: *Grey Turner sign.*

Guyon s. SEE: under *Guyon, Felix J.C.*

hair collar s. In the newborn, a ring of long, dark, coarse hair surrounding a midline nodule on the scalp. This may indicate neural tube closure defect.

harlequin s. A benign, transient color change seen in neonates in which one half of the body blanches while the other half becomes redder, with a clear line of demarcation.

Hegar s. SEE: *Hegar sign.*

Hill s. SEE: *Hill sign.*

Hochsinger s. SEE: *Hochsinger sign.*

holster s. Poikiloderma of the upper outer thigh. It is a characteristic finding in patients with dermatomyositis.

Homans s. SEE: *Homans sign.*

Hoover s. SEE: *Hoover sign.*

Jacquemier s. SEE: *Jacquemier sign.*

jersey finger s. Inability to flex the distal interphalangeal joint of a finger as the result of a rupture of the flexor digitorum profundus tendon. The patient is unable to make a fist.

jump s. During physical examination, an involuntary reaction to stimulation of a tender area or trigger point. This may take the form of wincing or sudden jerking of the part being examined, of adjacent areas, or even of the entire body. This sign should not be confused with the startle reaction seen in jumping Frenchmen of Maine.

Kehr s. SEE: *Kehr sign.*

Kernig s. SEE: *Kernig sign.*

Korányi s. SEE: *Korányi sign.*

Kussmaul s. SEE: under *Kussmaul, Adolph.*

Lasègue s. SEE: SEE: *Lasègue sign.*

Lazarus s. SEE: *Lazarus sign.*

lemon s. Scalloping of the frontal

bones of the fetus, a sign in prenatal ultrasonography in which the bones resemble the shape of a lemon. It is indicative of fetal cranial abnormalities found in the second trimester that can be markers for a neural tube defect.

Levine s. SEE: *Levine sign.*

Lhermitte s. SEE: *Lhermitte sign.*

Mannkopf s. SEE: *Mannkopf sign.*

Marie s. SEE: under *Marie, Pierre Marie.*

Markle s. SEE: *Markle sign.*

McBurney s. SEE: under *McBurney, Charles.*

McMurray s. SEE: under *McMurray, Thomas Porter.*

Möbius s. SEE: under *Möbius, Paul Julius.*

Murphy s. SEE: under *Murphy, John Benjamin.*

Musset s. SEE: *Musset sign.*

Myerson s. SEE: *Myerson sign.*

negative s. Minus sign (−) used in subtraction to denote something that is below zero or to indicate a lack.

Nikolsky s. SEE: *Nikolsky sign.*

objective s. In physical diagnosis, a sign that can be seen, heard, measured, or felt by the diagnostician. Finding of such sign(s) can be used to confirm or deny the diagnostician's impressions of the suspected disease. SYN: *physical s.*

obturator s. Pain on inward rotation of the hip, which stretches the obturator internus muscle. The result may be positive in acute appendicitis.

orbicular s., orbicularis sign Révilliod s.

physical s. Objective s.

Pins s. SEE: *Pins sign.*

Popeye s. SEE: under *Popeye sign.*

positive s. of pregnancy Assessment findings present only during pregnancy: fetal heart tones, fetal movements felt by the examiner, and fetal visualization by sonogram.

postural vital s. Measurement of the blood pressure and pulse when a patient is first lying, then sitting, and finally standing. SEE: *orthostatic vital signs determination.*

Potain s. SEE: under *Potain, Pierre Charles Édouard.*

Prehn s. SEE: *Prehn sign.*

presumptive s. of pregnancy Any of the signs and symptoms commonly associated with pregnancy that may be present in other conditions. SEE: *pregnancy.*

probable s. of pregnancy Any of the objective findings that strongly suggest but do not confirm pregnancy. SEE: *pregnancy.*

psoas s. Abdominal pain produced by extension of the hip. The sign indicates a retrocecal or retroperitoneal lesion.

Queckenstedt s. SEE: *Queckenstedt sign.*

raccoon s. Periorbital ecchymosis. It may be present in patients who have a basilar skull fracture.

Raimiste s. Raimiste phenomenon.

Remak s. SEE: *Remak sign.*

Révilliod s. SEE: *Révilliod sign.*

Ripault s. SEE: *Ripault sign.*

Romberg s. SEE: *Romberg sign.*

Rosenbach s. SEE: under *Rosenbach, Ottomar.*

Rovsing s. SEE: *Rovsing sign.*

Scarf s. SEE: *Scarf sign.*

Schamroth s. SEE: *Schamroth sign.*

shawl s. The presence of pigmented skin overlying the neck, upper back, and shoulders. It is a characteristic finding in patients with dermatomyositis.

soft s. Any of a number of signs that, considered collectively, are felt to indicate the presence of damage to the central nervous system. These signs include incoordination, visual motor difficulties, nystagmus, the presence of associated movements, and difficulties with motor control.

solar eclipse s. The appearance of an intussusception on a barium enema when the encircling bowel is seen in line with the ensheathed bowel lumen. The cylindrical ring of the intussusception captures radiographic contrast and resembles the corona seen around the sun during a solar eclipse.

spinnaker sail s. An outline of the thymus of a child by radiolucent lines. It is seen on chest x-ray examinations of children with pneumomediastinum.

steeple s. Narrowing of the column of subglottic air in the trachea, seen on anteroposterior radiographs of the neck in children with croup.

Stellwag s. SEE: *Stellwag sign.*

string s. In gastrointestinal radiology, extreme narrowing of a segment of the terminal ileum (in Crohn disease) or of the pylorus (in congenital pyloric stenosis).

Strümpell s. SEE: under *Strümpell, Adolf G. G. von.*

sunset s. An assessment finding often associated with hydrocephaly in newborns; the newborn's eyes are open with the irises directed downward, resembling the sun setting below the horizon.

Tanyoz s. SEE: *Tanyoz sign.*

theater s. Pain in the anterior knee that is felt after prolonged sitting. It is a symptom sometimes reported by patients with patellofemoral pain syndrome.

thumb s. Protrusion of the thumb across the palm and beyond the clenched fist; seen in Marfan syndrome.

Tinel s. SEE: *Tinel sign.*

Tournay s. SEE: *Tournay sign.*

Trendelenburg s. SEE: *Trendelenburg sign.*

Trousseau s. SEE: under *Trousseau, Armand.*

Uhthoff s. SEE: *Uhthoff sign.*

vital s. The four physical signs concerning functions essential to life: pulse, rate of respiration, blood pressure, and temperature. Some health care professionals consider a patient's level of pain to be a *fifth* vital sign although this is not accepted by all parties. While all health care professionals agree that a patient's experience of pain is a critical feature of his or her adaptation to illness, the traditional vital signs are objectively measurable and verifiable, while the level of pain is considered by many to be experiential or subjective.

von Graefe s. SEE: under *Graefe, Albrecht von.*

Waddell s. SEE: *Waddell sign.*

Walker-Murdoch s. SEE: *Walker-Murdoch sign.*

Westermark s. SEE: *Westermark sign.*

signa (sĭg'nă) [L.] ABBR: S or sig. A term used in writing prescriptions meaning to label the prescription according to the dose, route of administration, and frequency of medication.

signal Any form of communication that provides information. It is usually oral, written, visual, or electronic (i.e., transmitted by radio, telephone, television, laser, or optical fibers).

cellular s. A chemical released by cells and tissues to stimulate metabolic activities within those tissues or in other parts of the body. Neurotransmitters, hormones, peptides, cytokines, arachidonic acid derivatives, and other chemicals are all signaling molecules.

s. void A dark or blank space in a radiographic image of a fluid-filled structure. SEE: *filling **defect***.

signal-to-cut-off ratio ABBR: S/co. A laboratory comparison of some measurable feature of a specimen to the standard set by the laboratory's positive control. For example, in tests for antibodies to hepatitis C antibody, hepatitis C infection is not diagnosed unless a specific S/co is exceeded. Results that fall below the S/co can be found in noninfected patients and are considered to be false positive.

signature (sĭg'nă-tūr) [L. *signatura*, to mark] **1.** The part of a prescription giving instructions to the patient. **2.** The act of writing one's name on a document to certify its validity; the written name on the document.

signer (sī'nĕr) A person who communicates using sign language.

significant (sĭg-nĭf'ĭ-kănt) Important or meaningful.

significant break in coverage Under U.S. law, 63 consecutive days without creditable health insurance coverage.

significant other A person with whom a patient has a close relationship, which may or may not include relatives or a spouse.

signing The use of sign language to communicate.

sign language Representation of words by signs made with the position and movement of the fingers and hand. SEE: *American Sign Language.*

sign-out (sīn'owt″) Handoff.

sildenafil (sĭl-dĕn'ă-fĭl) A phosphodiesterase type 5 inhibitor and anti-impotence agent, administered orally to treat erectile dysfunction.

silencer (sī'lĕn-sĕr) A sequence of base pairs in DNA that prevents the transcription of a gene.

silent Free from noise; mute; still.

silent area Any cortical area in the brain that on stimulation produces no detectable motor activity or sensory phenomenon, and in which a lesion may occur without producing detectable motor or sensory abnormalities.

silent disease A disease that produces no clinically obvious symptoms or signs. Examples include hypertension, many forms of cancer (including small lesions of the breast and prostate cancer), and hearing loss, which may be either not noticed or denied by the individual. Many diseases begin silently, becoming obvious only when they are advanced.

silent rupture SEE: under *rupture.*

silica (sĭl'ĭ-kă) [L. *silex,* flint] SiO_2; silicon dioxide. SEE: *silicon.*

siliceous, silicious (sĭ-lish'ŭs), *adj.*

silicate (sĭl'ĭ-kāt) [L. *silicus,* flintlike] A salt of silicic acid.

silicic (sĭl-ĭs'ĭk) Pert. to silica or silicon.

silicon (sĭl'ĭ-kŏn, -ĭ-kon″) [L. *silex,* flint] SYMB: Si. A nonmetallic chemical element found in the soil, atomic weight 28.086, atomic number 14, specific gravity 2.33. Silicon makes up approx. 25% of the earth's crust, being exceeded only by oxygen. It occurs in trace amounts in skeletal structures (bones and teeth). Silicon is commonly combined with oxygen to form silicon dioxide, SiO_2, which occurs in many forms, both crystalline and amorphous. In a pure state, it forms quartz or rock crystal. It is present in many abrasive materials and is the principal constituent of glass.

silicone (sĭl'ĭ-kōn″) [*silicon* + *-one*] **1.** An organic chemical compound composed of silicon and oxygen in association with other elements such as carbon or halogens. **2.** Any of a group of polymeric organic silicon compounds used in adhesives, lubricants, synthetic rubber, and prostheses.

injectable s. Medical-grade silicone used in the past for breast augmentation, and currently for short-term use in retinal detachment and surgeries of the vitreous or the urethra. The more purified the silicone oils used, the better tolerated and the more biocompatible the implant application. Numerous prostheses are made of silicone, and it is controversially used in breast implants. SEE: *breast implant*.

silicone hydrogel contact lens SEE: under *lens*.

silicosis (sĭl-ĭ-kō′sĭs) [″ + Gr. *osis*, condition] A form of pneumonoconiosis resulting from inhalation of silica (quartz) dust, characterized by the formation of small discrete nodules. In advanced cases, a dense fibrosis and emphysema with impairment of respiratory function may develop.

silicotic (sĭl-ĭ-kŏt′ĭk) **1.** Pert. to silicosis. **2.** One affected with silicosis.

silo-filler's disease (sī′lō-fĭl′ĕrz) A rare respiratory illness produced by exposure to nitrogen oxides released from fermenting organic matter in freshly filled, poorly ventilated farm silos. Silage gases irritate the mouth, nose, pharynx, bronchi, and lungs, interfering with oxygenation and gas exchange. Alveolar damage and hemorrhagic pulmonary edema may result; about 20% of affected persons die of the exposure. Delayed injury to the lungs, esp. emphysema or bronchiolitis obliterans, may occur long after the initial exposure to silage gases.

PREVENTION: No one should enter a silo until 7 to 10 days after it is filled. Good ventilation above the base of a silo should be maintained during the 7- to 10-day period. The area should be fenced in to prevent children or animals from straying into the space surrounding a silo. An exhaust fan should always be activated before a person enters a silo.

TREATMENT: Corticosteroids such as prednisone or methylprednisolone help prevent lung injury in patients exposed to silage gases. SYN: *grain fever*.

silver (sĭl′vĕr) SYMB: Ag. A soft, ductile, malleable metallic element, atomic weight (mass) 107.870, atomic number 47, specific gravity 10.5. Its salts are widely used in medicine for their caustic, astringent, and antiseptic effects. In dentistry, silver is used in prosthetic devices, as an alloy with copper or mercury, as silver solder, and as tapering points to obliterate root canals in the endodontic treatment of teeth. SYN: *argentum*. SEE: *argyria*.

   s. chloride SYMB: AgCl. An insoluble salt of silver.

   colloidal s. 1. Any preparation of silver in which the particles of silver or silver proteinate are suspended in the solution rather than being dissolved in it. **2.** A liquid in which silver particles are suspended. It is marketed as a dietary supplement, but the National Center for Complementary and Alternative Medi-

cine has determined that this product has no safe or effective use.

   s. halide The photosensitive crystals in a radiographic film emulsion that, when exposed to ionizing radiation and developed, form an image.

silver filling SEE: *dental **amalgam***.

silverfish (sĭl′vĕr-fĭsh″) An insect, *Ctenolepisma longicaudata*, whose scales are often found in house dust, are antigenic, and may be a cause of childhood and adult perennial allergies and asthma. This house pest may be controlled with the use of insecticides.

Silybum marianum (sĭ-lē-bŭm′) Milk thistle.

silymarin (sĭ-lē-măr′ĭn) Milk thistle.

simethicone (sī-mĕth′ĭ-kōn) A mixture of liquid demethylpolysiloxanes that because of its antifoaming properties is used to treat intestinal gas.

simian (sim′ē-ăn) [L. *simia*, ape fr. Gr. *simos*, snub-nosed] **1.** Pert. to or resembling apes or monkeys. **2.** An ape or monkey.

simian crease (sim′ē-ăn) [L. *simia*, ape] SEE: under *crease*.

similia similibus curantur (sĭ-mĭl′ē-ă sĭ-mĭl′ĭ-bŭs kū-răn′tūr) [L., likes are cured by likes] The homeopathic doctrine that a drug producing pathological symptoms in those who are well will cure such symptoms in persons with disease.

Simmondsia chinensis (sĭ-mon′zē-ă chĭ-nen′sĭs) SEE: *jojoba*.

Simon position (zē′mon″, sī′mŏn) [Gustav Simon, Ger. surgeon, 1824–1876] An exaggerated lithotomy position in which the hips are somewhat elevated and the thighs are strongly abducted. It is used in operations on the vagina. SYN: *Edebohls position*.

simple (sĭm′pl) [L. *simplex*] **1.** Not complex; not compound. **2.** A medicinal plant.

simple calculated osteoporosis risk estimation ABBR: SCORE. A risk assessment tool for screening women for osteoporosis to determine their need for bone mineral density testing based on their age, race, history of fractures, bone mass, history of rheumatoid arthritis, estrogen use, and body weight.

simple inflammation SEE: under *inflammation*.

Simple Triage and Rapid Treatment ABBR: START. A procedure for quickly classifying injured patients according to the severity of their injuries and for treating those who are most severely injured first.

Simplified Motor Score ABBR: SMS. An assessment tool to gauge the severity of head injuries. It is derived from and works as well as the more detailed Glasgow Coma Scale.

PATIENT CARE: The SMS consists of

evaluating whether a trauma patient obeys commands (the patient scores two points), localizes pain (the patient scores one point), withdraws from pain or is even less responsive (the patient scores no points).

Sims position (simz) [James Marion Sims, U.S. gynecologist, 1813–1883] A semiprone position with the patient on the left side, right knee and thigh drawn well up, the left arm along the patient's back, and the chest inclined forward so that the patient rests on it. It is the position of choice for administering enemas because the sigmoid and descending colon are located on the left side of the body and fluid is readily accepted in this position. It is also used in curettage of the uterus, intrauterine irrigation after labor, flexible sigmoidoscopy, colonoscopy, rectal examination, and postanesthesia recovery.

simul (sī'mŭl, sĭm'ŭl) [L.] At once or at the same time; term used in signature of prescription.

simulation (sĭm-ū-lā'shŭn) [L. *simulatio,* imitation] **1.** Pretense of having a disease; feigning of illness. SEE: *malingerer; Munchausen syndrome*. **2.** The imitation of symptoms of one disease by another. **3.** A replica. **4.** An educational or technological model of an actual situation (such as cardiac arrest) that is used to train new students or to predict or estimate outcomes that may be obtainable in practice.

simulator (sĭm'ū-lā'tor) Any situation or device that imitates or recreates a condition or situation similar to one that might be encountered by a student or trainee. Simulations are used to prepare learners for social, occupational, or educational roles.

   patient s., human patient simulator A mannequin equipped with technologies that make it resemble and respond like a living person, used in health care education for role playing, skill building, and hands-on, active education.

Simulium (sĭ-mū'lē-ŭm) A genus of insects of the order Diptera that includes the black flies (buffalo gnats). The females are blood suckers.

   S. damnosum A species that is the intermediate host of the filarial worm *Onchocerca volvulus*.

   S. venustum A species common in North America.

simultanagnosia (sī"mŭl-tăn"ăg-nō'zē-ă) The failure to perceive simultaneously all the elements of a scene.

simultaneity paradigm (of nursing) (sī"mŭl-tă-nē'ĭt-ē) A nursing theory that views the person as interacting continuously and bidirectionally with the environment, regards health as an evolutionary process, and considers that each society has its own definitions of wellness and illness.

SIMV *synchronized intermittent mandatory ventilation.*

simvastatin (sĭm'vă-stă-tĭn) A 3-hydroxy-3-methylglutaryl-coenzyme A (HMG CoA) reductase inhibitor and lipid-lowering agent. It is administered orally, as an adjunct to dietary therapy, to manage primary hypercholesterolemia and mixed dyslipidemias. Trade name is Zocor.

Sinapis (sĭn-ā'pĭs) [Gr. *sinapi,* mustard] A genus of plants commonly known as mustard plants.

sincipital (sĭn-sĭp'ĭ-tăl) [L. *sinciput,* half a head] Pert. to the sinciput.

sinciput (sĭn'sĭp-ŭt) [L., half a head] **1.** The fore and upper part of the cranium. **2.** The upper half of the skull. SYN: *calvaria.*

sinew (sĭn'ū) [AS. *sinu*] A tendon.

sine wave grating (sīn) [L. *sinus,* curve, fold] A test pattern to assess visual contrast sensitivity.

sing [L., *singulorum*] Of each; used in writing prescriptions.

single (sing'gl) [L. *singulus,* individual, single] **1.** Indivisible. **2.** Unique. **3.** Unmarried. **4.** Lone; alone. **5.** One only.

single-blind, single-blinded (sing'gĕl-blind') Pert. to a method, study, or clinical trial in which only the investigators know what treatment or medication, if any, the subjects receive. A single-blind study attempts to eliminate subjective bias such as the placebo effect from the results. SYN: *single-masked*. SEE: *blind* (2); *double-blind*.

single-masked (sing'gĕl-maskt") Single-blind.

single nucleotide polymorphism SEE: under *polymorphism*.

singleton (sing'gl-tŏn") One of something described, esp. a single infant rather than a twin.

single-use device SEE: under *device*.

Singulair (sing"gū-lăr') SEE: *montelukast.*

singultus (sĭng-gŭl'tŭs) [L.] Hiccup.

sinister (sĭn-ĭs'tĕr) [L.] In anatomy, left; or present on the left side of the body. **sinistrad, sinistral** (sĭn'ĭs-trăd, sĭn'ĭs-trăl), *adj*.

sinistrality (sĭn"ĭs-trăl'ĭ-tē) Left-handedness.

sinistro-, sinistr- [L. *sinister,* stem *sinistr-,* left, on the left side] Prefixes meaning *left.*

sino-, sinu- [L *sinus,* curve, fold] Prefixes meaning *sinus* or *cavity.*

sinoatrial (sĭn"ō-ā'trē-ăl) Pert. to the sinus venosus and atrium.

sinogram (sī'nō-grăm") [L. *sinus,* curve, + Gr. *gramma,* something written] A radiograph of a sinus tract filled with a radiopaque contrast medium to determine the range and course of the tract.

sinonasal (sī"nō-nā'zăl) [*sino-* + *nasal*] Pert. to the nose and nasal sinuses.

sinter (sĭn'tĕr) **1.** The calcium or silica deposits formed from water obtained from mineral springs. **2.** To reduce material to a solid form by heating without melting.

sinuous (sĭn′ū-ŭs) [L. *sinuosus,* winding] Winding; wavy; tortuous.

sinus (sī′nŭs) *pl.* **sinuses,sinus** [L., *sinus,* curve, hollow] **1.** A recess. **2.** A cavity with a narrow opening. **3.** An endothelia-lined, air-filled cavity within a bone. (When lay people speak of "sinuses," they are generally referring to the paranasal sinuses.) **4.** An endothelia-lined channel for venous blood. **5.** A channel leading to an abscess.

   air s Paranasal **s.**

   anal s. Any of the saclike recesses on the inner lining of the anal canal between the anal columns.

   aortic s. Inside the aorta, the pouch behind each of the three leaflets of the aortic valve. The right and left coronary arteries each originate from an orifice in an aortic sinus, leaving one aortic sinus (the noncoronary sinus) as a blind pouch. SYN: *s. of Valsalva.*

   carotid s. The small dilation at the base of the internal carotid artery with baroreceptors in its wall. These receptors respond to changes in arterial blood pressure, and their signals are carried to the hindbrain by the glossopharyngeal nerve (CN IX).

   s. cavernosus Cavernous **s.**

   cavernous s. A 1 cm wide dural sinus extending 2 cm along the medial wall of the base of the middle cranial fossa. The cavernous sinus empties into (a) the transverse sinus via the superior petrosal sinus, (b) the internal jugular vein via the inferior petrosal sinus, (c) the pterygoid plexus via emissary veins, and (d) the facial vein via the superior ophthalmic vein. The right and left cavernous sinuses are interconnected by the anterior and posterior intercavernous sinuses. Tributaries of the cavernous sinus include the superior ophthalmic, superficial middle cerebral, and inferior cerebral veins and the sphenoparietal sinus. SYN: *s. cavernosus.*

   cerebral s. Dural **s.**

   circular s. A set of four interconnected dural sinuses encircling the sella turcica and pituitary gland at the base of the brain. The four sinuses are the right and left cavernous sinuses and the anterior and posterior intercavernous sinuses.

   confluence of the s. The dilated posterior end of the superior sagittal sinus in the skull. This dilation joins one of the transverse sinuses (usually the right), which drains the blood from the superior sagittal sinus toward the internal jugular vein. The other transverse sinus and the occipital sinus also connect to the confluence of the sinuses.)

   coronary s. A large vein on the posterior surface of the heart; it runs in the atrioventricular groove between the left atrium and left ventricle. Most of the blood feeding the heart returns to the right atrium via the coronary sinus. Its direct tributaries include the small, middle, and great cardiac veins.

   cranial venous s. Sinus (3).

   dermal s. A congenital sinus tract connecting the surface of the body with the spinal canal.

   draining s. An abnormal passageway leading from inside the body to the outside. This is usually due to an infectious process.

   dural s. Any of several large endothelia-lined collecting channels into which veins of the brain and inner skull empty and which then empty into the internal jugular vein. These venous sinuses are found between the two layers (periosteal and meningeal) of the dura mater. Their walls have no muscle, and they have no valves to give direction to the blood flow. The venous sinuses in the skull include the superior sagittal, inferior sagittal, straight, transverse, and cavernous sinuses. SYN: *cerebral s.; dural venous s.*

   dural venous s. Dural **s.**

   ethmoid s. Any of the 3 to 18 paranasal sinuses on each side of the skull in and adjacent to the ethmoid bone. The ethmoid sinuses can be categorized as anterior, middle, or posterior, with each group usually draining into a different part of the nasal cavity. Ethmoid sinuses have very thin walls and are interconnected via openings in the septa between the sinuses.

   frontal s. Either of a pair of paranasal sinuses in the frontal bones just above the orbits. These sinuses lie adjacent to each other in the midline, but are usually completely separated by a bony septum. Each frontal sinus drains into the ipsilateral nasal cavity through an opening in the lateral wall along the middle nasal passageway (i.e., middle nasal meatus).

   inferior petrosal s. A dural sinus that drains the cavernous sinus posteriorly into the superior jugular bulb of the internal jugular vein.

   inferior sagittal s. An unpaired midline dural sinus running along the lower, free margin of the falx cerebri (over the top of the corpus callosum). It drains blood from veins in the falx and from the medial surfaces of the hemispheres, and it empties, posteriorly, into the straight sinus.

   intercavernous s. The anterior and the posterior intercavernous sinuses interconnect the right and left cavernous sinuses at the base of the brain. All sinuses are valveless; thus, the cavernous and intercavernous sinuses form a circle (the circular sinus) that envelops the sella turcica.

lactiferous s. Immediately inside the tip of the nipple, the dilated end of any of the 15 to 20 lactiferous ducts, which convey milk from the mammary glands during lactation.

lymph s. Endothelia-lined channels through which lymph flows inside lymph nodes. The walls of lymph sinuses are coated with T and B lymphocytes as well as phagocytic cells, all of which filter the passing lymph. Lymphocytes and macrophages move in and out of the lymph through the sinus walls. SYN: *lymph channel.*

marginal s. **1.** Considered together, the many dilated veins or venous "lakes" that collect blood in the intervillous space of the placenta; the marginal sinus drains into the uterine veins. **2.** A dural sinus along the inside of the rim of the foramen magnum; it drains into the vertebral venous plexus. **3.** A blood-filled sinus in the marginal zone of the spleen. In the passage from the red pulp to the white pulp, some arterial blood flows along (and percolates through) the endothelia-lined walls of the marginal sinus before entering the arterial capillary beds of the white pulp.

mastoid s. An old term for the mastoid antrum.

maxillary s. Either of a pair of paranasal sinuses filling the bodies of the maxillary bones. The maxillary sinuses are large and pyramidal shaped, with average dimensions of 3.5 cm x 2.5 cm x 3.2 cm. The medial floor of the maxillary sinus is immediately above the roots of the first and second upper molars. Each maxillary sinus drains into the ipsilateral nasal cavity through an opening in the lateral wall of the hiatus semilunaris, under the middle nasal concha. SYN: *antrum of Highmore.*

paranasal s. An air cavity in a facial bone, either the frontal, maxillary, sphenoid, or ethmoid bones; most paranasal sinuses occur in pairs. The paranasal sinuses are lined with ciliated epithelium that secretes mucus. The sinuses open into the lateral walls of the nasal cavities via small holes. Healthy paranasal sinuses are radiolucent. SYN: *accessory nasal s.; air s.* SEE: illus.

pericardial s. The oblique or the transverse pericardial sinus, which are spaces between the visceral and parietal layers of the serous pericardium. The oblique sinus runs along the posterior surface of the left atrium between the orifices of the right and the left pulmonary veins. The transverse sinus runs along the posterior surface of the base of the heart between the outflow vessels (the aorta and the pulmonary trunk) in front and the inflow vessels (the pulmonary veins) behind.

petrosal s. The superior or the inferior petrosal sinus.

pilonidal s. Pilonidal **fistula.**

pulmonary s. Either of the pouches within the pulmonic trunk behind each of the three leaflets of the pulmonic valve.

s. rectus Straight **s.**

renal s. The indentation on the medial side of each kidney into which the hilum leads; the renal sinus is largely filled by the renal pelvis.

sagittal s. The superior or the inferior sagittal sinus.

sigmoid s. The continuation of the transverse sinus downward along the wall of the posterior cranial fossa to the jugular canal; there, the sigmoid sinus becomes the superior jugular bulb, the origin of the internal jugular vein.

sphenoid s. Either of a pair of paranasal sinuses in the sphenoid bone just above and behind the nasal cavity. The sphenoid sinuses are located adjacent to the optic chiasm, the pituitary gland, and the internal carotid arteries. Each sphenoid sinus drains through an opening in the sphenoethmoidal recess at the very top of the ipsilateral nasal cavity.

straight s. An unpaired midline du-

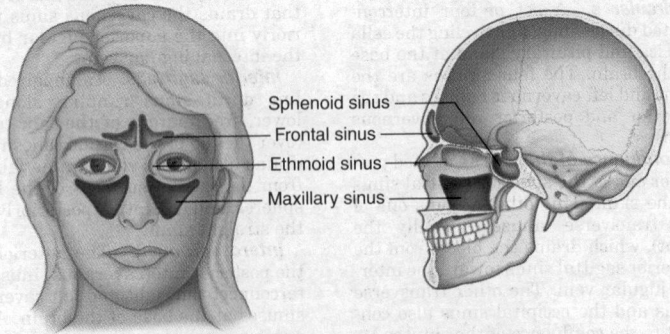

Sphenoid sinus —
Frontal sinus —
Ethmoid sinus —
Maxillary sinus —

PARANASAL SINUS

ral sinus where the falx cerebri and the tentorium cerebelli meet. The straight sinus is the posterior continuation of the inferior sagittal sinus. The straight sinus empties into the transverse sinus contralateral to the one joined by the superior sagittal sinus; nonetheless, the straight sinus often communicates, if only through a small channel, with the confluence of the sinuses. SYN: *s. rectus*.

superior petrosal s. A slender dural sinus that drains the cavernous sinus posteriorly into the transverse sinus.

superior sagittal s. A long unpaired midline channel through the superior margin of the falx cerebri. It begins in the front near the crista galli of the ethmoid bone, and it extends along the entire inner roof of the skull to the internal occipital protuberance in the back. Its posterior end, called the confluence of the sinuses, is dilated and usually joins the right transverse sinus; however, the other transverse sinus and the occipital sinus also communicate with the confluence of the sinuses. Tributaries of the superior sagittal sinus include ascending frontal cerebral veins, superior cerebral veins, diploic veins draining the skull bones, and a number of irregularly shaped venous lacunae. Numerous arachnoid granulations (sites of the return of water and filtrate from the cerebrospinal fluid) protrude into the superior sagittal sinus.

tarsal s. S. tarsi.

s. tarsi A space between the top of the calcaneus bone and the bottom of the tarsal bone. SYN: *tarsal s.*

transverse s. A dural sinus in the lateral edge of the tentorium cerebelli along each lateral upper border of the posterior cranial fossa. One transverse sinus (usually the right) is a continuation of the superior sagittal sinus; the other transverse sinus (typically the smaller of the two) is the continuation of the inferior sagittal sinus, although both transverse sinuses usually have a connection near their origin, in the region of the confluence of sinuses. The transverse sinuses run anteriorly and turn downward to become the sigmoid sinuses at the front edges of the tentorium cerebelli; at this point, the transverse sinuses are joined by the superior petrosal sinuses. Tributaries of the transverse sinuses include inferior cerebral, inferior cerebellar, and diploic veins.

s. tympani A recess in the medial wall of the tympanic cavity beside the promontory and adjacent to the round window. The sinus tympani can be > 3 mm deep.

urogenital s. In the embryo, a space behind the urogenital membrane (a surface structure) and separated from the future rectum by the urorectal septum (an internal structure). The urachus and the mesonephric ducts, i.e., the wolffian ducts, open into the urogenital sinus. The sinus will later give rise to major parts of the urinary bladder, urethra, vagina, and genitourinary tract glands.

s. venosus In the embryo, the portion of the developing heart tube that leads into the cavities destined to form the atria and ventricles. The major embryonic veins (umbilical, vitelline, and common cardinal) all lead into the sinus venosus. Later, the sinus venosus will become the posterior smooth wall of the right atrium, including the openings from the coronary sinus and the venae cava.

venous s. A valveless irregularly shaped venous channel lined by endothelial cells. Large venous sinuses include the coronary sinus of the heart and the dural sinuses inside the skull; small venous sinuses are found inside certain tissues, such as the spleen.

sinus augmentation, sinus lift Oral surgery to replace lost bone in the maxilla (the jaw bone in which the top row of teeth are anchored). It can be used to prepare the maxilla for dental implants, or to repair congenital oral defects.

sinuscope (sī′nŭ-skōp″) [*sinus* + *-scope*] An endoscope used to look inside the structures of the nose, sinuses, and throat.

sinus histiocytosis with massive lymphadenopathy Rosai-Dorfman disease.

sinusitis (sī-nŭs-ī′tĭs) [L. *sinus,* curve, hollow, + Gr. *itis,* inflammation] Inflammation of a sinus, esp. a paranasal sinus. It may be caused by various agents, including viruses, bacteria, or allergy. Predisposing factors include inadequate drainage, which may result from presence of polyps, enlarged turbinates, or a deviated septum; chronic rhinitis; general debility; or dental abscess in maxillary bone.

acute suppurative s. Purulent inflammation with pain over the facial sinuses, often accompanied by fever, chills, and headache.

TREATMENT: Therapy is conservative. Shrinkage in the nasal mucosa is useful to facilitate ventilation and drainage of the sinus. The patient should rest, force fluids, take decongestants, and apply hot packs. If inflammation is due to bacterial infection, antibiotic therapy is indicated.

allergic fungal s. Chronic nasal obstruction with symptoms that include a runny nose and postnasal discharge caused by allergies to soil-based fungi (such as *Curvularia* or *Alternaria*). The condition is occasionally diagnosed in patients with an allergic history and nasal polyposis who have failed treatments for other sinus diseases. Tenacious mucus with a large number of eosinophils is often present.

chronic hyperplastic s. Polyps present in sinuses and nose and underlying osteitis of sinus walls.

TREATMENT: This condition is treated surgically. Conservative surgery involves the removal of polyps and intranasal opening into sinuses for adequate ventilation and drainage. Radical surgery involves the complete removal of sinus mucosa through either the external or the intranasal route.

invasive fungal s. Sinus, ophthalmic, and cerebral invasion by opportunistic fungi. The disease usually occurs in immunosuppressed patients (such as diabetic or neutropenic patients) and is frequently fatal despite aggressive medical and surgical therapies. *Aspergillus, Mucor,* and *Rhizopus* are the most commonly implicated causes.

sinusoid (sī'nŭs-oyd) [" + Gr. *eidos,* form, shape] **1.** Resembling a sinus. **2.** A large, permeable capillary, often lined with macrophages, found in organs such as the liver, spleen, bone marrow, and adrenal glands. Their permeability allows cells or large proteins to easily enter or leave the blood. **sinusoidal,** *adj.*

sinusoidal current Alternating induced electric current, the two strokes of which are equal.

sinusoidal obstruction syndrome ABBR: SOS. A disruption in the normal flow of venous blood from the sinusoids of the liver and the hepatic venules. It occurs primarily after hematopoietic (stem) cell transplantation and is characterized by enlargement of the liver, right upper quadrant pain, jaundice, and massive fluid retention within the peritoneum (ascites) within the first three weeks after transplantation. It was formerly known as *veno-occlusive disease of the liver.*

sinusoidal pattern An abnormal fetal heart rate finding in which the monitor records a consistent rhythmic, uniform, undulating wave. Although the number of beats per minute is within normal limits and the recording shows long-term variability, beat-to-beat variability is absent and no accelerations in heart rate occur with fetal movement.

sinusotomy (sī-nŭs-ŏt'ō-mē) [" + Gr. *tome,* incision] Incision into a sinus.

SiO₂ Silicon dioxide.

sip (sĭp) [ME. *sippen*] **1.** To take a small quantity of liquid or nourishment into the mouth. **2.** A small quantity of liquid, i.e., the amount that can be taken into the mouth with gentle suction.

siphon (sī'fŭn) [Gr. *siphon,* tube] A tube bent at an angle to form two unequal lengths for transferring liquids from one container to another by atmospheric

pressure. One container must be higher than the other for this to work.

siphonage (sī'fŭn-ĭj) Drainage of a body cavity such as the stomach or bladder with a siphon.

Siphonaptera (sī"fō-năp'tĕr-ă) [" + *apteros,* wingless] An order of insects commonly called fleas. They are wingless, undergo complete metamorphosis, and have piercing and sucking mouth parts. The body is compressed laterally, and the legs are adapted for leaping. Fleas feed on the blood of birds and mammals. They transmit the causative organisms of several diseases (bubonic plague, endemic or murine typhus, and tularemia) and are also the intermediate hosts of certain tapeworms. SEE: *flea.*

Sipple syndrome (sip'l) [John H. Sipple, U.S. physician, b. 1930] Multiple endocrine neoplasia, type II.

siRNA *short, interfering ribonucleic acid.*

SIRT (sĭrt) *selective internal **radiation therapy**.*

sirtuin (sĭr'too-ĭn) Any of a class of proteins that are coded by the SIR family of genes. These proteins contribute to chromosome repair and may have a role in extending the life span of cells.

-sis [Gr. *-sis,* a suffix of action] Suffix meaning *action* or *process.* SEE: *-osis.*

sister A term used by the British for *nurse,* esp. a senior or head nurse.

Sister Mary Joseph nodule A hard, periumbilical lymph node sometimes present when pelvic or gastrointestinal tumors have metastasized.

Sistrurus (sis-troor'ŭs) [L. *sistrurus* fr Gr. *seistrouros,* tail shaker] A genus of small poisonous rattlesnakes that includes the pygmy rattlesnakes (*Sistrurus miliarius*).

site (sīt) [L. *situs,* place] Position or location.

active s. The reactive portion of an enzyme, in which the substrate molecules fit and form temporary bonds.

affiliated clinical s. An organization, which may be academic or nonacademic, for-profit or not-for-profit, that contracts with a university, college, or technical school to provide clinical educational opportunities for its students.

antibody combining s. The particular area on an antibody molecule to which part of an antigen links, creating an antigen-antibody reaction. SEE: *antibody; antigen; antigenic determinant.*

antigen binding s. Antigenic determinant.

application s. The part of the body or of an organ where a topical treatment is applied.

binding s. The particular location on a cell surface or chemical to which other chemicals bind or attach.

cleavage s. The location on a polypeptide molecule where peptide bonds are broken down by hydrolysis.

exit s. 1. The location where a missile (e.g., a bullet) leaves the body. **2.** The location on the skin where an implanted device, e.g., a surgical drain, leaves the body. **3.** The location on the skin where applied radiation leaves the body.

implant s. The location in a jaw bone where a dental prosthesis will be or is seated.

insulin injection s. Any of the places on the body suitable for injecting insulin Because insulin is administered at least once daily, it is important to have a plan for selecting the site. The best sites for insulin injection are in the subcutaneous tissue of the abdomen. The arms and legs can also be used, but insulin uptake from these sites is less uniform. It is advisable to map out a number of injection sites in one area, use those, and then use other sites.

port s. The location on the skin where a laparoscope or other device, e.g., subcutaneously implanted medicine reservoir, is inserted into the body. SYN: *puncture s.*

primary s. The tissue of origin of a metastatic tumor.

puncture s. Port s.

receptor s. The particular component of a cell surface that has the ability to react with certain molecules, e.g., proteins or a virus.

splice s. The location on a strand of messenger RNA where the molecule can be cut and reannealed during the regulation of protein synthesis by cells.

site-specific Properties of cellular receptors that vary with their body location or milieu.

site-specific delivery Techniques used to help a therapeutic agent concentrate in the organ where it will have the greatest effect. These include attaching a drug to a monoclonal antibody or administering prodrugs that are converted to active agents only in targeted cells.

sito- [Gr. *sitos,* grain, food] Prefix meaning *grain, food.*

sitosterol (sī-tos′tĕ-rol″) [*sito-* + *sterol*] A cholesterol-like molecule found in plants and a component of plant cell membranes. It differs from cholesterol in the substitution of an ethyl moiety at molecular position 24.

sitosterols (sī-tŏs′tĕr-ŏls) A group of similar organic compounds that occur in plants. Sitosterols contain the steroid nucleus, perhydrocyclopentanophenanthrene. The subgroup beta-sitosterols, which are found in saw palmetto and *Prunus africana,* are used as herbal treatments for benign prostatic hyperplasia and hypercholesterolemia.

situation 1. A set of circumstances. **2.** The physical location of an object in relation to other objects.

situs (sī′tŭs) [L.] A position.

s. inversus The abnormal relation and displacement of viscera to the opposite side of the body.

s. inversus viscerum A less common term for *situs inversus.*

SI units Any of the units specified by the International System of Units adopted by the International Conference of Weights and Measures in 1960 and updated since then. SEE: tables; *International System of Units;* SI Units Appendix.

sixth disease An acute disease of infants, caused by herpesvirus 6. SYN: *exanthem subitum; Zahorsky disease.* SEE: *roseola infantum.*

size-up (sīz′ŭp″) The assessment of the safety of a scene for rescuers and patients before proceeding with the primary patient assessment.

Sjogren-Larsson syndrome (shō′grĕn-lar′sŏn) [Karl Gustaf Torsten Sjögren, Swedish physician, 1896–1974; Tage Konrad Leopold Larsson, Swedish physician, 1905–] A rare autosomal recessive disease that produces abnormal skin and nerve development. It is characterized by learning disabilities, bilateral spasticity, crystalline maculopathy, and congenital ichthyosis.

Sjögren syndrome (shō′grĕn) [Henrik Sjögren, Swedish ophthalmologist, 1899–1986] ABBR: SS. An autoimmune disorder marked by decreased lacrimal and salivary secretions, resulting in dry eyes (keratoconjunctivitis sicca) and dry mouth (xerostomia). In 50% of patients it occurs alone; in the other 50%, it is seen in conjunction with other autoimmune diseases, such as systemic lupus erythematosus, thyroiditis, scleroderma, and esp. rheumatoid arthritis. It occurs primarily in middle-aged women.

In Sjögren syndrome, the lacrimal and salivary glands are destroyed by autoantibodies and T lymphocytes. Approx. 90% of patients have antiribonucleoprotein antibodies in the blood (anti-Ro or anti-La), which are considered

International System of Units (SI Units)

Basic Quantity	Basic Unit	Symbol
Length	meter	m
Mass	kilogram	kg
Time	second	s
Electric current	ampere	A
Thermodynamic temperature	kelvin	K
Luminous intensity	candela	cd
Amount of substance	mole	mol

Prefixes and Their Symbols Used to Designate Decimal Multiples and Submultiples in SI Units

Prefix	Symbol		Factor
tera	T	10^{12}	1 000 000 000 000
giga	G	10^{9}	1 000 000 000
mega	M	10^{6}	1 000 000
kilo	k	10^{3}	1 000
hecto	h	10^{2}	100
deka	da	10^{1}	10
deci	d	10^{-1}	0.1
centi	c	10^{-2}	0.01
milli	m	10^{-3}	0.001
micro	μ	10^{-6}	0.000 001
nano	n	10^{-9}	0.000 000 001
pico	p	10^{-12}	0.000 000 000 001
femto	f	10^{-15}	0.000 000 000 000 001
atto	a	10^{-18}	0.000 000 000 000 000 001

diagnostic markers; approx. 75% also have rheumatoid factor, even if there is no evidence of rheumatoid arthritis. Patients with Sjögren syndrome have a 40% to 60% increased risk of developing non-Hodgkin lymphoma.

SYMPTOMS: The most common signs and symptoms are blurred vision, thick secretions, itching and burning of the eyes, decreased sense of taste, difficulty swallowing, and dry, cracked oral mucous membranes. Enlarged parotid glands, dry nasal membranes, bronchitis and pneumonitis, synovitis, vaginal dryness, superimposed *Candida* infections, and vasculitis also may occur. Patients usually have anemia, leukopenia, and an elevated erythrocyte sedimentation rate.

TREATMENT: Sjögren syndrome can be controlled with symptomatic treatment. Careful oral hygiene, using fluoride toothpaste and mouthwash as well as chlorhexidine rinses, and routine dental examinations are essential to minimize oral infection and tooth decay. Sugarless gum or candies, frequent sips of water, and pilocarpine may help relieve the xerostomia; artificial saliva is not tolerated by most patients. Artificial tears are effective for dry eyes, and glasses are recommended to block the wind when the patient is outside. Clinical manifestations of concurrent autoimmune diseases are treated symptomatically.

SjvO₂ Symbol for *jugular venous oximetry*.

skateboard (skāt′bord″) **1.** A therapeutic device used for upper or lower extremity rehabilitation, consisting of a platform mounted on ball-bearing rollers and typically used to strengthen extremely weak muscles. It assists the patient in making coordinated movements. **2.** A recreational device used by children and adolescents, consisting of a long, narrow platform mounted on wheels. Skateboard use is often associated with high-energy trauma. Common injuries include contusions, lacerations, fractures, and traumatic brain injury.

skatol(e) (skăt′ōl) [Gr. *skatos,* dung] C_9H_9N; beta-methyl indole; a malodorous, solid, heterocyclic nitrogen compound found in feces, formed by protein decomposition in the intestines and giving them their odor.

skein (skān) A continuous, loose coil, as of yarn or thread.

skeletal (skĕl′ĕ-tăl) [Gr. *skeleton,* a dried-up body] Pert. to the skeleton.

skeletal-related event The metastasis of a tumor to bone, and/or its clinical effects.

skeletal survey A radiographic study of the entire skeleton to look for evidence of occult fractures, multiple myeloma, metastatic tumor, or child abuse.

skeletal system The bony framework of the body. SEE: *skeleton*.

skeletal traction SEE: under *traction*.

skeleto-, skelet- [Gr., *skeleto-,* dried up, withered, a mummy] Prefixes meaning *skeleton*.

skeleton (skĕl′ĕt-ŏn) [Gr., a dried-up body] The bony framework of the body consisting of 206 bones: 80 axial or trunk and 126 of the limbs (appendicular). This number does not include teeth or sesamoid bones other than the patella. SEE: illus.; table.

    appendicular s. The bones that make up the shoulder girdle, upper extremities, pelvis, and lower extremities.

    axial s. Bones of the head and trunk.

    cartilaginous s. The part of the skeleton formed by cartilage; in the adult, the cartilage of the ribs and joints. Cartilage is more flexible and resistant to resorption due to pressure than bone.

Skene, Alexander (skēn) Scots-born U.S. gynecologist, 1838–1900.

    S. duct Either of the two slender ducts of the Skene glands that open on

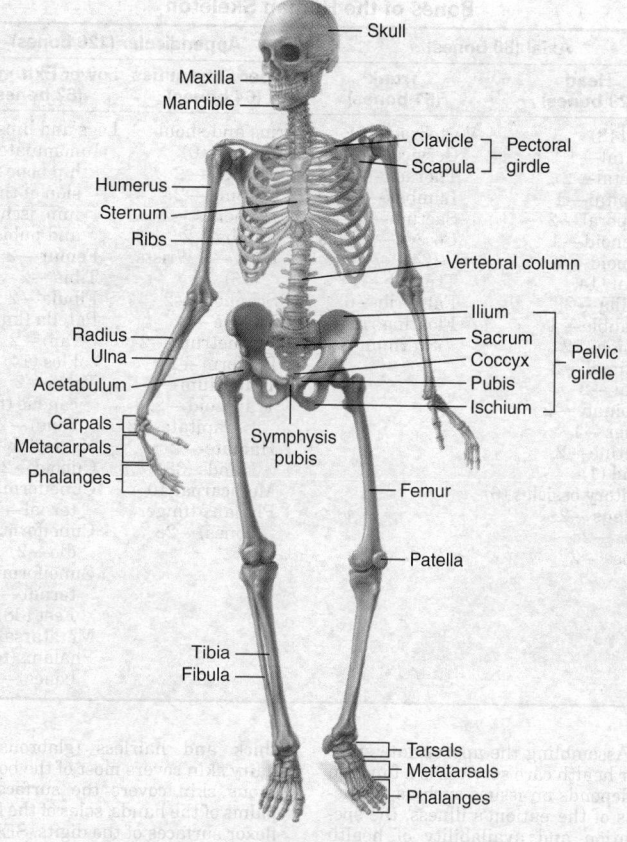

SKELETON

anterior view of the axial (bone colored) and appendicular (blue colored) skeleton

Skull

Maxilla
Mandible

Clavicle ⎤ Pectoral
Scapula ⎦ girdle

Humerus
Sternum
Ribs

Vertebral column

Radius
Ulna
Acetabulum

Ilium
Sacrum
Coccyx
Pubis
Ischium

⎤
⎥ Pelvic
⎥ girdle
⎦

Carpals
Metacarpals
Phalanges

Symphysis
pubis

Femur

Patella

Tibia
Fibula

Tarsals
Metatarsals
Phalanges

either side of the urethral orifice in women. SYN: *paraurethral* **duct**.

S. gland Any of the glands lying just inside of and on the posterior area of the urethra in the female. If the margins of the urethra are drawn apart and the mucous membrane gently everted, the two small openings of the Skene tubules or glands, one on each side of the floor of the urethra, become visible. Trauma frequently causes a gaping of the urethra and ectropion of the mucous membrane. In acute gonorrhea, these glands are almost always infected. SYN: *paraurethral* **gland**.

skew (skū) [Middle English *skewen*, to slip away, escape] **1.** To turn aside, make oblique. **2.** In statistics, to show an asymmetry in a frequency distribution. **3.** Turned aside, asymmetrical, oblique. **4.** A slant or deviation from a straight line. **skewed** (skūd), *adj*.

skew deviation SEE: under *deviation*.

skia-, sci-, scia-, scio- [Gr. *skia*, shade, shadow] Prefixes meaning *shadow*.

skiascopy (skī-ăs′kō-pē) **1.** Retinoscopy. **2.** Fluoroscopy.

skill Proficiency in a specific task.

savant s. Splinter s.

splinter s. A precocious, highly developed behavior or talent that occurs in isolation, i.e., one not associated with other cognitive, manual, social, or verbal skills. Splinter skills are often found in children with autistic spectrum disorders. SYN: *savant s.*

skilled attendant A person formally trained in the care of women during labor and delivery.

skill mix The varied human resources needed to accomplish a clinical task. To provide postoperative care of a cardiac surgery patient, e.g., a surgeon, anesthesiologist, critical care nurses, nursing aides, respiratory therapists, and other personnel must be assembled. A different level of care and a different allocation of health care human resources are needed to provide care to an outpatient with an upper respiratory infec-

Bones of the Human Skeleton

Axial (80 bones)		Appendicular (126 bones)	
Head (29 bones)	Trunk (51 bones)	Upper Extremities (64 bones)	Lower Extremities (62 bones)
Cranial (8)	Vertebrae (26)	Arms and shoulders (10)	Legs and hips (10)
Frontal—1	Cervical—7	Clavicle—2	Innominate or hip bone (fusion of the ilium, ischium, and pubis)—2
Parietal—2	Thoracic—12	Scapula—2	
Occipital—1	Lumbar—5	Humerus—2	
Temporal—2	Sacrum—1	Radius—2	
Sphenoid—1	Coccyx—1 Ribs (24)	Ulna—2 Wrists (16)	Femur—2
Ethmoid—1	True rib—14	Scaphoid—2	Tibia—2
Facial (14)	False rib—6	Lunate—2	Fibula—2
Maxilla—2	Floating rib—4	Triquetrum—2	Patella (kneecap)—2 Ankles (14)
Mandible—1	Sternum (1)	Pisiform—2	
Zygoma—2		Trapezium—2	Talus—2 Calcaneus (heel bone)—2
Lacrimal—2		Trapezoid—2	
Nasal—2		Capitate—2	
Turbinate—2		Hamate—2	Navicular—2
Vomer—1		Hands (38)	Cuboid—2
Palatine—2		Metacarpal 10	Cuneiform, internal—2
Hyoid (1)		Phalanx (finger bones)—28	
Auditory ossicles (6)			Cuneiform, middle—2
Malleus—2			Cuneiform, external—2
Incus—2			Feet (38)
Stapes—2			Metatarsal—10
			Phalanx (toe bones)—28

tion. Assembling the appropriate staffing for health care services is a function that depends on issues such as the demands of the patient's illness, the specialization and availability of health care providers, the institution in which care is provided, and the available financial resources. In military medicine, a broad array of services is provided by medics; patients with similar injuries and illnesses in urban medical centers would likely have access to a wider variety of professionals, each with a more limited set of skills.

skimming In health care, the practice of a for-profit corporation entering the market, attracting the business of patients who can pay, and avoiding treating the indigent.

skin (skin) The organ that forms the outer surface of the body. It shields the body against infection, dehydration, and temperature changes; provides sensory information about the environment; manufactures vitamin D; and excretes salts and small amounts of urea.

Skin consists of two major divisions: the epidermis and the dermis. Depending on its location and local function, skin varies in terms of its thickness, strength, presence of hair, nails, or glands, pigmentation, vascularity, nerve supply, and keratinization. Skin may be classified as thin and hairy or thick and hairless (glabrous). Thin hairy skin covers most of the body. Glabrous skin covers the surface of the palms of the hands, soles of the feet, and flexor surfaces of the digits. SEE: illus.; *hair* for illus; *burn; dermatitis; dermis; eczema; epidermis; rash.*

  alligator s. Severe scaling of the skin with formation of thick plates resembling the hide of an alligator. SEE: *ichthyosis.*

  artificial s. Human skin equivalent.

  bronzed s. Brownish hyperpigmentation of the skin, seen in Addison disease and hemochromatosis, some cases of diabetes mellitus, and cirrhosis.

  deciduous s. Keratolysis.

  elastic s. Ehlers-Danlos syndrome.

  glabrous s. Skin that does not contain hair follicles, such as that over the palms and soles.

  glossy s. Shiny appearance of the skin due to atrophy or injury to nerves.

  hidebound s. Scleroderma.

  loose s. Hypertrophy of the skin.

  parchment s. Atrophy of the skin with stretching.

  photoaged s. Skin changes caused by chronic sun exposure. This condition is prevented by avoiding suntanning and sunburning and has been treated with topical tretinoin and chemical peels. SYN: *photodamaged s.*

  photodamaged s. Photoaged **s.**

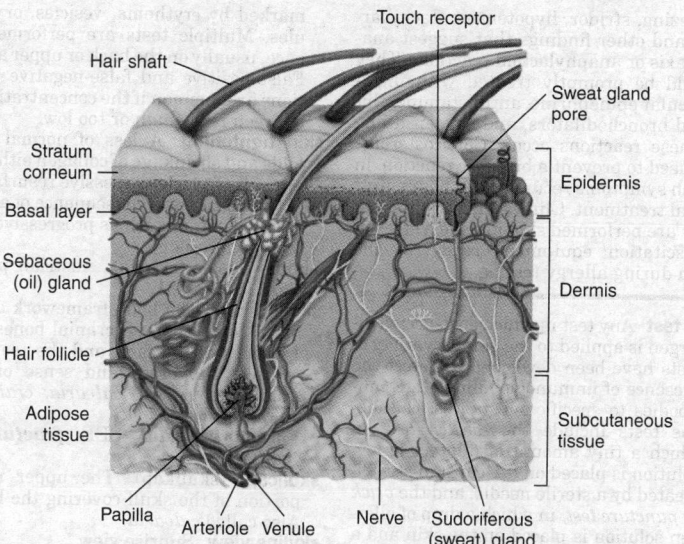

Touch receptor
Hair shaft
Sweat gland pore
Stratum corneum
Basal layer
Epidermis
Sebaceous (oil) gland
Dermis
Hair follicle
Adipose tissue
Subcutaneous tissue
Papilla　Arteriole　Venule　Nerve　Sudoriferous (sweat) gland

STRUCTURE OF THE SKIN AND SUBCUTANEOUS TISSUE

piebald s. Vitiligo.

scarf s. The cuticle, epidermis; the outer layer of the skin.

sun-damaged s. Photoaged **s.**

tissue-engineered s. Human skin equivalent.

true s. Dermis.

skin autofluorescence The abnormal fluorescence of the skin of patients with either diabetes mellitus or excessive oxidative stress when exposed to ultraviolet light. It results from the accumulation of advanced glycosylation end products (AGE) in tissues. AGE accumulation has been linked to cardiovascular diseases, impairments in glucose tolerance, and renal failure.

skin cancer SEE: under *cancer.*

skinfold thickness An anthropometric measurement used to evaluate nutritional status by estimating the amount of subcutaneous fat. Calibrated calipers are used to measure the thickness of a fold of skin at defined body sites that include upper arm or triceps, subscapular region, and upper abdomen.

skin hook (skin) A surgical retractor with one or more sharp, curved pins at its end that holds overlying skin away from an operative field.

skin integrity, impaired A state in which an individual has altered epidermis and/or dermis. SEE: *Nursing Diagnoses Appendix.*

skin integrity, impaired, risk for A state in which an individual's skin is at risk of being adversely altered. SEE: *Nursing Diagnoses Appendix.*

skin marking The application of nontoxic, temporary paints or dyes to the skin to provide landmarks (as in plastic surgery), to permit accurate alignment of wound edges at the time the skin is closed, or to align the treatment beam accurately during radiotherapy. SYN: *surgical marking.*

Skinner box (skĭn′ĕr) [Burrhus Frederic Skinner, U.S. psychologist, 1904–1990] A device used in experimental psychology in programmed learning. It is designed so that an animal that performs a desired behavior is rewarded, for example, by receiving food.

skin popping The subcutaneous injection of illicit drugs, a practice that may result in localized abscesses, limb cellulitis, fasciitis, sepsis, or death. Injection drug users who skin pop may be recognized by the presence of atrophied circular lesions on the skin, usually of the forearms.

skin prep 1. An antimicrobial skin cleanser. 2. Cleaning and draping of the skin before surgical incision or instrumentation. Commonly used preps include gels, solutions, impregnated pads, or sponges.

skin prick test ABBR: SPT. A means of assessing hypersensitivity to an allergen in which a small quantity of a suspected allergen is placed on the end of a needle, which is then used to penetrate the skin. A positive reaction to the test occurs when a wheal rises at the puncture site.

⚠ SPT occasionally triggers life-threatening allergic reactions (anaphylaxis). Patients undergoing allergy testing should be closely monitored for wheezing, stridor, hypotension, tachycardia, and other findings that suggest anaphylaxis or anaphylactoid reactions. They should be promptly treated with intramuscular epinephrine, antihistamines, inhaled bronchodilators, and oxygen if any of these reactions occur. Corticosteroids are used to prevent a biphasic reaction, in which symptoms recur several hours after initial treatment. Clinics where skin prick tests are performed should have a stock of resuscitation equipment ready in the room during allergy testing.

---

skin test   Any test in which a suspected allergen is applied to the skin. A variety of tests have been developed to detect the presence of immunoglobulin E (IgE) antibodies to specific substances. Cutaneous tests include the *scratch test,* in which a tiny amount of dilute allergen solution is placed on a 1-cm skin scratch created by a sterile needle, and the *prick* or *puncture test,* in which a drop of allergen solution is placed on the skin and a needle prick is made in the center of the drop. These tests are performed on the back or arm and are unlikely to produce systemic anaphylaxis. For an intradermal test, approx. 0.01 mL of dilute solution is injected into the skin on the arm using a tuberculin syringe with a 25- to a 27-gauge needle; the patient must be monitored for an anaphylactic reaction.

The appearance of a wheal and flare 15 to 20 min after injection indicates a positive response to cutaneous or intradermal tests; the size of the wheal and intensity of erythema are graded on a scale of 1+ to 4+. Simultaneous tests assess normal skin reactivity. Histamine or another substance known to produce a wheal and flare serves as a positive control; normal saline is usually used for the negative control. Antihistamines inhibit these skin tests and must be discontinued before testing begins.

Delayed hypersensitivity tests are intradermal tests used to assess T cell–mediated responses rather than IgE-mediated responses. They are used to assess for anergy (inability to respond to common antigens) and as the basis for tuberculosis testing with purified protein derivative (PPD). The response is read 24 and 48 hr after the antigen is injected. Positive response is indicated by skin induration greater than 5 mm; a wheal and flare may occur shortly after the injection but fade within 12 hr. Corticosteroid drugs interfere with the test and should be discontinued before testing.

Patch tests are performed to identify allergens producing IgE-mediated contact dermatitis. A dilute solution of suspected allergen is applied using a patch taped to the skin. After 48 hr, the skin is inspected for a positive response

marked by erythema, vesicles, or papules. Multiple tests are performed at once, usually on the back or upper arms. False-positive and false-negative reactions are common if the concentration of allergen is too high or too low.

skin tightening   A loss of normal skin folds and shrinkage of collagen either as a result of overly aggressive resurfacing of the skin or as a consequence of a sclerosing disorder such as progressive systemic sclerosis.

Skoda, Josef   (skō′dă)   Austrian physician, 1805–1881.

skull   (skŭl)   The bony framework of the head, composed of 8 cranial bones, the 14 bones of the face, and the teeth. It protects the brain and sense organs from injury. SYN: *calvaria; cranium.* SEE: illus.; *skeleton.*

    fractured skull   SEE: ***fracture*** *of skull.*

skullcap   (skŭl′kăp)   The upper round portion of the skull covering the brain. Also called *calvaria.*

skyline view   Sunrise view.

Slagle, Eleanor Clarke   (slāg′ĕl)   U.S. social worker, 1871–1942. She was educated in Chicago, worked at Hull House (an early settlement house in that city), and founded the Society for the Promotion of Occupational Therapy (now known as the American Occupational Therapy Association).

slander   (slăn′dĕr)   [L. *scandalum,* cause of offense]   Defaming the character of another through injurious speech. To qualify legally for slander, speech must intentionally impugn the reputation of another and be both malicious and demonstrably false.

slant   A cylinder of solid culture medium that is slanted to increase the surface area of the medium; used in culturing bacteria. SYN: *slope (2).*

slave   **1.** A device that allows body movements to be transferred to an apparatus for lifting, squeezing, and turning laboratory equipment containing radioactive materials. The slave is controlled by the operator from a sufficient distance, and proper shielding is used to prevent the operator from being exposed to radiation or other highly toxic materials. **2.** In robotic surgery, a device that translates the large hand movements of the surgeon (or the surgeon's hand tremors) into the smaller, more precise or more refined movements of the surgical instrument in the operative field.

SLE   *systemic lupus erythematosus.*

sleep   (slēp)   A periodic state of rest accompanied by varying degrees of unconsciousness and relative inactivity. Although sleep is thought of as something that occurs once each 24-hr day, at least half of the world's population has an afternoon nap or siesta as part of their lifelong sleep-wake pattern. The need

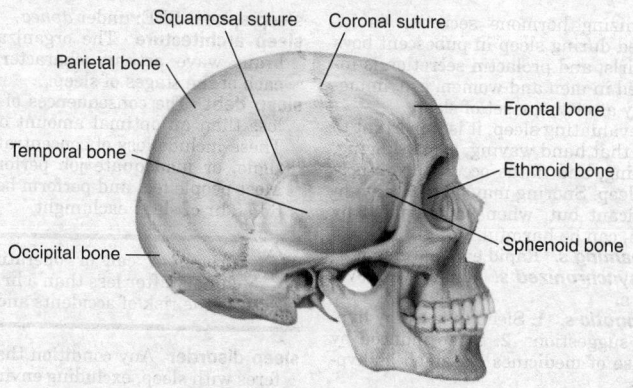

- Squamosal suture
- Coronal suture
- Parietal bone
- Frontal bone
- Temporal bone
- Ethmoid bone
- Occipital bone
- Sphenoid bone

Cranial bones

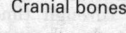

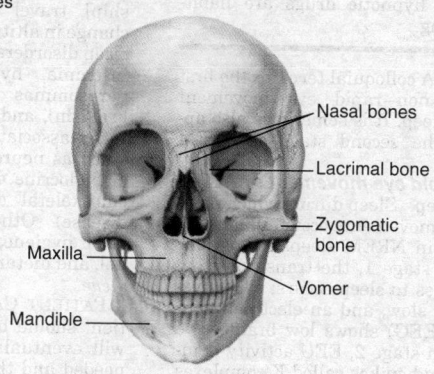

- Nasal bones
- Lacrimal bone
- Zygomatic bone
- Maxilla
- Vomer
- Mandible

BONES OF SKULL

Facial bones

for and value of sleep is obvious; yet there is no explanation of why it provides a daily renewal of a feeling of health and well-being.

The sleep-wake cycle varies in relation to the age and gender of the individual. The newborn may sleep as much as 20 hr each day; a child, 8–14 hr, depending on age; adults, 3–12 hr with a mean of 7–8 hr, which may decrease to 6.5 hr in the elderly. Women over 35 tend to sleep more than men. There is great individual variation in the amount and depth of sleep.

Sleep has two states: non–rapid eye movement (NREM) sleep and rapid eye movement (REM) sleep. NREM sleep and REM sleep alternate during the night; each cycle requires 90–100 min. NREM sleep makes up approx. 75% of the sleep cycle, and REM sleep approx. 25%, with individual variations.

People deprived of sleep for several days or more become irritable, fatigued, unable to concentrate, and usually disoriented. Performance of mental and physical tasks deteriorates. Some peo-

ple experience paranoid thoughts and auditory, visual, and tactile illusions or hallucinations. Deprivation of REM sleep may cause anxiety, overeating, and hypersexuality. The effects of sleep deprivation are reversed when the normal sleep-wake cycle is resumed. SEE: *non–rapid eye movement s.; rapid eye movement s.*

PHYSIOLOGICAL CHANGES DURING SLEEP: The following physiological changes occur during sleep: body temperature falls; secretion of urine decreases; heart rate and respiration become slower and more regular during NREM sleep and then more rapid and less regular during REM sleep. During REM sleep, blood flow to the brain is increased; breathing is more irregular; heart rate and blood pressure vary; cerebral blood flow and metabolic rate increase; and penile erections may occur. There is an increased secretion of growth hormone during the first 2 hr of sleep; surges of adrenocorticotropic hormone (ACTH) and cortisol secretion occur in the last half of the sleep period.

Luteinizing hormone secretion is increased during sleep in pubescent boys and girls, and prolactin secretion is increased in men and women, esp. immediately after the onset of sleep.

In evaluating sleep, it is important to know that hand waving, arm swinging, laughing, and flatus occur during normal sleep. Snoring may be clinically insignificant but, when accompanied by apnea, can be harmful.

    dreaming s.   Rapid eye movement **s.**

    desynchronized s.   Rapid eye movement **s.**

    hypnotic s.   **1.** Sleep induced by hypnotic suggestion. **2.** Sleep induced by the use of medicines classified as hypnotics.

> ⚠ Many hypnotic drugs are habit-forming.

    light s.   A colloquial term for the first stage of non–rapid eye movement (NREM) sleep. It is sometimes also applied to the second stage of NREM sleep.

    non–rapid eye movement s.   ABBR: NREM sleep. Sleep during which non–rapid eye movements occur. Dreams do not occur in NREM sleep. It has four stages: in stage 1, the transition from wakefulness to sleep occurs; eye movements are slow, and an electroencephalogram (EEG) shows low brain wave activity. In stage 2, EEG activity is increased, and spikes called K complexes appear. In stage 3, eye movement ceases; wave frequency is reduced and amplitude increased. In stage 4, the EEG is dominated by large spikes (delta rhythm). Stages 3 and 4 are considered deep sleep. SYN: *synchronized s.* SEE: *rapid eye movement s.; sleep.*

    pathological s.   Excessive or disordered sleep.

    paradoxical s.   A term sometimes used as a synonym for rapid eye movement (REM) sleep. REM sleep is the preferred term.

    rapid eye movement s.   ABBR: REM sleep. Sleep during which rapid eye movements occur. Dreams occur in REM sleep. It follows stage 4 of non–rapid eye movement (NREM) sleep; electroencephalographic activity is similar to that of NREM stage 1; and muscle paralysis normally occurs. SYN: *desynchronized s.; dreaming s.* SEE: *non–rapid eye movement s.; sleep.*

    synchronized s.   Non–rapid eye movement **s.**

sleep, readiness for enhanced   A pattern of natural, periodic suspension of consciousness that provides adequate rest, sustains a desired lifestyle, and can be strengthened. SEE: *Nursing Diagnoses Appendix.*

sleep apnea   SEE: under *apnea.*

sleep architecture   The organization of brain wave activity characteristic of each of the stages of sleep.

sleep debt   The consequences of getting less than an optimal amount of sleep. These include loss of concentration, fatigue, or inadequate job performance. Most people feel and perform best with 6 to 8 hr of sleep each night.

> ⚠ Driving a car or operating machinery after less than 5 hr of sleep increases the risk of accidents and injury.

sleep disorder   Any condition that interferes with sleep, excluding environmental factors (such as noise, excess heat or cold, movement [as on a train, bus, or ship], travel through time zones, or change in altitude). The major classes of sleep disorders are dyssomnias (such as insomnia, hypersomnia, narcolepsy), parasomnias (such as sleepwalking, bruxism), and disruption of sleep patterns associated with medical illness (such as neurological, cerebrovascular, or endocrine disorders, infection, musculoskeletal disorders, or pulmonary disease). Other factors include poor sleep hygiene, effects of drugs or alcohol, and dietary changes. SEE: *sleep hygiene.*

PATIENT CARE: The insomniac patient should be advised that he or she will eventually get as much sleep as needed and that part of the treatment schedule includes not going to bed until he or she feels sleepy. If the patient does not feel sleepy, he or she should stay up and do something pleasurable, such as read, work, or study. Other self-help measures include reduction of tension in one's lifestyle, establishing a regular sleep routine, and avoiding stimulants (such as coffee, tea, or cola) and strenuous exercise before bed. A warm bath just before going to bed relaxes tense muscles. Afternoon naps should be avoided. One should sleep in a quiet, clean, cool, dark environment. A snack or glass of warm milk before going to bed does no harm, but there is no evidence that this practice helps induce sleep.

> ⚠ Some drugs used to treat insomnia are less rapidly biotransformed in older adults than in the young. These drugs have been associated with delirium, increased risk of falls and hip fractures, sleepwalking, motor vehicle accidents, and excessive sedation in older adults.

sleep drunkenness   A condition in which one requires a long period of time to become fully alert after awakening from a deep sleep. During this time the affected person may become ataxic, disoriented, or aggressive. People whose usual awakening sequence includes sleep drunkenness should not attempt to make decisions until they are fully awake and alert.

sleep interruption Sleep **fragmentation**.

sleep maintenance Staying asleep after initially falling asleep. Patients with sleep-maintenance insomnia fall asleep easily but then awaken in the middle of the night and have difficulty resting or sleeping after that.

sleep pattern, disturbed Time-limited disruption of sleep (natural, periodic suspension of consciousness) amount and quality. SEE: *Nursing Diagnoses Appendix*.

sleep-phase syndrome An autosomal dominant condition in which the person sleeps well and for a normal amount of time but not at the usual bedtime hours. Those with delayed sleep-phase syndrome may function best if they go to sleep about the time most people are awakening. Those with advanced sleep-phase syndrome do best when they go to sleep in late afternoon or early evening and arise about midnight. When allowed to sleep at these hours, persons with this condition function normally. SYN: *advanced sleep-phase syndrome*.

sleep state misperception (mĭs″pĕr-sĕp′shŭn) [ME. *mis-*, prefix meaning "wrongly" or showing negation + ″] The subjective sense that one has disordered sleep without objective findings of insomnia, hypersomnia, narcolepsy, sleep apnea, or other sleep disorders.

sleep study A colloquial term for polysomnography. SEE: *polysomnography*.

sleep-wake cycle SEE: under *cycle*.

sleepwalking Autonomic actions performed during sleep. This condition occurs mostly in children, each episode lasting less than 10 min. The eyes are open and the facial expression is blank. The patient appears to awaken, sits on the edge of the bed, and may walk or talk. Activity may cause trauma to the patient and others. The principal aim is to prevent injury by removing objects that could be dangerous, locking doors and windows, and preventing the person from falling down stairs. Night terrors may accompany sleepwalking. There is little or no recollection of the event the next day. Children usually outgrow this condition. SYN: *somnambulism*.

slice (slīs) In radiology, any plane of the body selected for imaging. SYN: *section* (4).

slice culture SEE: under *culture*.

slide **1.** A thin glass plate on which an object is placed for microscopic examination. **2.** A photograph prepared so that it may be used in a film slide pro-

jector. **3.** To move along a smooth surface in continuous contact, as the movement in dentistry of the mandibular teeth toward a centric position with the teeth in contact before closing completely in occlusion.

slimy (slī′mē) [AS. *slim,* smooth] Resembling slime or a viscid substance; regarding a growth, the ability to adhere to a needle so it can be drawn out as a long thread.

sling (sling) A support for an injured upper extremity. SEE: *bandage, triangular* for illus.; *bandage*.

⚠ Prolonged skin-to-skin contact should be avoided while a sling is in use.

    clove-hitch s. A sling made by placing a clove hitch in the center of a roller bandage, fitting it to the hand, and carrying the ends over the shoulder. The sling is tied beside the neck with a square knot, making longer ends. These ends may be carried over and behind the shoulders, brought under each axilla, and tied over the chest.

    counterbalanced s. A rehabilitation device to assist upper extremity motion by suspending the arm by way of an overhead frame and a pulley and weight system. SYN: *suspension s.*

    cravat bandage s. A bandage used for support of the hand or a fractured upper arm. The wrist is laid upon the center of the cravat bandage, the forearm held at a right angle or with the hand elevated above the heart, and the two ends are carried around the neck and tied. SEE: *binder*.

    cravat s. A sling made by placing the center of the cravat under the wrist or forearm with the ends tied around the neck.

    folded cravat s. A lower-arm sling made by placing a broad fold of cloth in position on the chest with one end over the affected shoulder and the other hanging down in front of the chest. The arm is flexed as desired across the sling. The lower end is brought up over the uninjured shoulder and secured with a knot located where it will not press on the affected shoulder.

    infant s. infant **carrier**.

    open s. A sling made by placing the point of a triangular cloth at the tip of the elbow. The ends are brought around at the back of the neck and tied. The point should be brought forward and pinned or tied in a single knot, forming a cup to prevent the elbow from slipping out.

    reversed triangular s. A sling made as follows: a triangular bandage is applied with one end over the injured shoulder, point toward the sound side, the base vertical under the injured elbow. The arm is flexed acutely over the triangle. The lower end is brought upward over the front of the arm and over the sound shoulder. The ends are pulled taut and tied over the sound shoulder. The point is pulled taut over the forearm and fixed to the anterior and posterior layers between the forearm and arm. This sling holds the elbow more acutely flexed (the weight is supported by the elbow).

   simple figure-of-eight roller arm s. A sling made as follows: the arm is flexed on the chest in the desired position, then a bandage is fixed with a single turn toward the uninjured side around the arm and chest, crossing the elbow just above the external epicondyle of the humerus. A second turn is made, overlapping two thirds of the first, and the bandage is brought forward under the tip of the elbow, then upward along the flexed forearm to the root of the neck of the sound side. Then it is brought downward over the scapula, crossing the chest and arm horizontally, overlapping, turning above, and continued as in a progressive figure-of-eight.

   St. John's s. A sling made by applying a triangular bandage with the point downward under the elbow, the upper end over the sound shoulder. The arm is flexed acutely on the chest. The lower end is brought under the affected arm and around the back to knot with the upper end on the sound shoulder. The point is brought up over the elbow and fastened to the base. Support is wholly for the injured shoulder.

   suspension s. Counterbalanced **s.**

   swathe arm s. A sling for support of the arm that is made as follows: the center of a folded cloth band is placed under the acutely flexed elbow. One end of the sling is then carried to the front and upward across the forearm and over the affected shoulder. Then it is brought obliquely across the back to the sound axilla. Next, the other end of the sling is brought around the front of the arm and across the body to the sound axilla, where it is pinned to the first end of the sling and then continued around the back to the part of the sling surrounding the affected elbow, where it is pinned again.

   tension-free transvaginal tape s. Transvaginal tape **s.**

   transvaginal tape s. ABBR: TVT sling. A sling consisting of an adjustable pubourethral mesh inserted through the vagina to hold the urethra and neck of the bladder, used in a surgical procedure to treat urinary stress incontinence in women. It is used to manage conditions such as excessive mobility of the urethrovesical junction, intrinsic sphincter deficiency, or pelvic organ prolapse. SYN: *tension-free transvaginal tape* **s.**

   triangular s. A sling for the arm that is made with suspension from the uninjured side. The triangle is placed on the chest with one end over the sound shoulder, the point under the affected extremity, and the base folded. The injured arm is flexed outside of the triangle. The lower end is carried upward under the axilla of the injured side, back of the shoulder, and tied with the upper end behind the back. The point of the triangle is brought anteriorly and medially around the back of the elbow and fastened to the body of the bandage. This bandage changes the point of carrying and also relieves the clavicle on the injured side of the load. SEE: *triangular* **bandage** for illus.

slip (slip) **1.** To move out of a customary place; to dislocate (e.g., an intervertebral disk). **2.** To slide into or on top of.

slippery elm An herbal remedy used as a demulcent or as a poultice.

SLIT *sublingual* **immunotherapy.**

slit (slit) A narrow opening.

   dorsal s. A surgical procedure to make the foreskin of the penis easily retractable. The foreskin is cut in the dorsal midline but not far enough to extend into the mucous membrane next to the glans.

slit diaphragm SEE: under *diaphragm.*

slope **1.** An inclined plane or surface. **2.** Slant.

   lower ridge s. The slope of the crest of the mandibular residual ridge from the third molar forward as viewed in profile.

SLOS *Smith-Lemli-Opitz syndrome.*

slough (slŭf) [ME. *slughe,* a skin] **1.** Dead matter or necrosed tissue separated from living tissue or an ulceration. **2.** To separate in the form of dead or necrosed parts from living tissue. **3.** To cast off, as dead tissue. SEE: *escharotic.*

sloughing (slŭf'ĭng) The formation of a slough; separation of dead tissue from living.

slow (slō) [AS. *slaw,* dull] **1.** Mentally dull. **2.** Exhibiting retarded speed, as the pulse. **3.** Pert. to a morbid condition or of a fever when it is not acute.

slowing (slō'ing) In neurology, a decrease in the frequency or rate of brain waves as seen on an electroencephalogram. It may result from structural abnormalities of the brain, brain injury, drugs that alter consciousness, drowsiness, seizures, or sleep.

slow-reacting substance of anaphylaxis ABBR: SRS-A. Former name given to leukotrienes C4, D4, and E4, arachidonic acid metabolites that contribute to the pathophysiology of asthma, causing prolonged bronchoconstriction, increased vascular permeability, increased bronchial mucous secretion, and vasoconstriction. SYN: *leukotriene*. SEE: *arachidonic acid; asthma*.

slows (slōz) Milk **sickness**.

SLT *split-liver* **transplantation**.

sludge (slŭjh) Under the Resource Conservation and Recovery Act of 1976, any solid, semisolid, or liquid waste generated from a municipal, commercial, or industrial wastewater treatment plant or air pollution control facility.

SLUDGE **syndrome**   *s(alivation,)* *l(acrimation,) u(rination,) d(efecation, other gastrointestinal symptoms, and) e(mesis)* (a toxicity resulting from drugs or poisons that increase the activity of the parasympathetic nervous system, specifically its cholinergic effects). A prominent cause of SLUDGE syndrome is poisoning by organophosphate pesticides, e.g., malathion.

slump test A test to assess the effects of tension on the neuromeningeal tract (e.g., in nerve root injury, meningeal irritation, meningitis, disk disease, or central nervous system tumors). The patient is directed to sit slumped forward, flexing the entire trunk. The patient's foot is dorsiflexed and the knee is then extended. Inability to extend the knee fully or production of back or leg pain symptoms, or both, are positive signs. If no positive sign is elicited, then the patient actively extends the neck, and knee extension and pain are then reassessed. Variations of this test are used to target injuries to specific spinal nerves.

slurry (slŭr′ē) [ME. *slory*] A thin, watery mixture.

Sly syndrome Mucopolysaccharidosis VII.

Sm Symbol for the element samarium.

SMA *superior mesenteric* **artery**.

small for gestational age ABBR: SGA. **1.** Pert. to an infant whose birth weight is at or below the 10th percentile, as correlated with the number of weeks in utero on the intrauterine growth chart. **2.** Pert. to a fetus that is more than two standard deviations smaller than the mean size of fetuses in its population.

small intestinal bacterial overgrowth ABBR: SIBO. Excessive concentrations of colonic bacteria (exceeding 100,000 microorganisms per milliliter) within the duodenum or jejunum. SIBO may produce abdominal pain, bloating, and diarrhea owing to malabsorption. SYN: *small bowel bacterial overgrowth*.

smallpox (smawl′pŏks) [AS. *smeal*, tiny, + *poc*, pustule] An acute, highly contagious, and frequently fatal viral illness caused by the variola virus. SYN: *variola*. SEE: illus.; *smallpox vaccine*.

SYMPTOMS: Influenza-like symptoms, esp. high fever, chills, headache, backache, and prostration, are com-

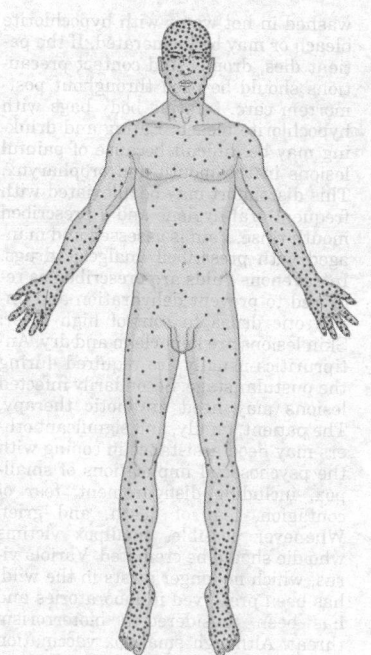

SMALLPOX

Centripetal distribution.

monly the first sign of infection. These symptoms constitute the *preeruptive* stage of smallpox, i.e., the stage that precedes the appearance of the rash. The preeruptive phase lasts about 72 hr and is followed by a maculopapular rash that changes over the next couple of weeks to papules, small blisters, pustules, and then scabs. This *eruptive* phase of the illness usually begins on the mouth, face, and arms and then spreads to other body parts, such as the back and chest.

INCUBATION: The disease typically begins 12 to 14 days after exposure to the virus.

PATIENT CARE: Patients diagnosed with smallpox require airborne precautions with special ventilation and engineering requirements. The patient must be placed in a monitored negative air pressure room that allows 6 to 12 air changes per hour. The room door must remain closed except for entering and exiting. Anyone entering must wear adequate droplet protection. Contact precautions require wearing clean gloves and gown during all patient contact; these barriers must be removed before leaving the room. All contaminated instruments, surfaces, excretions, fluid, or other materials require decontamination with chemicals or heat or incineration. Clothing and bedding should be washed in hot water with hypochlorite bleach or may be incinerated. If the patient dies, droplet and contact precautions should be used throughout postmortem care, treating body bags with hypochlorite bleach. Eating and drinking may be difficult because of painful lesions in the mouth and oropharynx. This discomfort may be alleviated with frequent oral hygiene and a prescribed mouth rinse. Pain is assessed and managed with prescribed analgesic drugs. Intravenous fluids are prescribed as required to prevent dehydration and antipyretic drugs to control high fever. Skin lesions are kept clean and dry. Antipruritics usually are required during the pustular stage. Secondarily infected lesions may need antibiotic therapy. The patient, family, and significant others may need assistance in coping with the psychosocial implications of smallpox, including disfigurement, fear of contagion, fear of death, and grief. Whenever possible, smallpox victims who die should be cremated. Variola virus, which no longer exists in the wild, has been preserved in laboratories and has been considered a bioterrorism threat. Although smallpox vaccination is not required, it has been offered to the military, health department, first responders and key health care workers-because of this threat.

smart card, smartcard (smart kärd) A plastic card, resembling a credit or debit card, that can provide identification, authentication, data storage, and other applications, such as a health insurance card on which the critical details of a person's health history are encoded.

smart pump SEE: under *pump*.

SMBG *self-monitoring of blood glucose.*

smear (smēr) [Old English. *smerian*, to anoint] **1.** In bacteriology, material spread on a surface, as a microscopic slide or a culture medium. **2.** Material obtained from infected matter spread over solid culture media. **3.** Cellular material obtained from a body structure by swabbing, gently scraping, or scratching.

    blood s. A drop of (anticoagulated) whole blood spread thinly on a glass microscope slide so that blood cell types can be examined, counted, and characterized. SYN: *peripheral blood s.*

    Procedure: The slide must be grease free. It is cleaned with alcohol, rinsed in warm water, and wiped clean with a lint-free towel or lens paper.

    A small drop of blood is placed on the slide; the end of another slide (spreader slide) is placed against the first slide at a 45° angle and pulled back against the drop of blood so that the drop spreads between the point of contact of the two slides. Then the spreader slide is pushed forward against the first slide; the blood will form an even, thin smear. The slide is dried by waving it in the air; it should not be heated. The blood smear is covered with Wright stain and allowed to stand 2 min. An equal amount of distilled water or buffer solution is added and mixed uniformly. It is allowed to stand 5 min. The stain is gently washed off and the slide is allowed to dry.

    buccal s. A sample of cells taken from the mucosa lining the cheek for chromosomal or other studies.

    Pap s. Papanicolaou test.

    peripheral blood s. SYN: *blood s.*

smegma (smĕg′mă) [Gr. *smegma*, soap] Secretion of sebaceous glands, specifically, the thick, cheesy, odoriferous secretion found under the labia minora about the clitoris or under the male prepuce. **smegmatic** (-măt′ĭk), *adj.*

smegmolith (smĕg′mō-lĭth) [Gr. *smegma*, soap, + *lithos*, a stone] A calcified mass in the smegma.

smell (smĕl) [ME. *smellen,* to reek] **1.** To perceive by stimulation of the olfactory nerves. The sense of smell is a chemical sense dependent on sensory cells on the surface of the upper part of the nasal septum and the superior nasal concha. These sensory cells live for an average of 30 days and are affected by a variety of factors, including age, nutritional and hormonal states, drugs, and therapeutic radiation. SYN: *olfactory* **perception**. SEE: illus. **2.** The property of something affecting the olfactory organs. In clinical medicine, the smell arising from the patient's body, feces, breath, urine, vagina, or clothing may provide information concerning diagnosis. The smell on a patient's clothing, for example, may be due to a toxic chemical that spilled on the clothes. A patient may attempt to alter or mask the smell of alcohol on the breath by using medicated or flavored lozenges, mouthwashes, sprays, or mints. Even though our sense of smell is relatively weak compared with that of some animals, humans have the capacity to distinguish among as many as 10,000 different odors. The inhaled substance must be volatile (i.e., capable of diffusing in air) for us to perceive it, and the volatile chemical must also be soluble in water. SEE: *odor*.

    Abnormalities in the sense of smell include: *Anosmia:* A loss of the sense of smell. It may be a local and temporary condition resulting from acute and chronic rhinitis, mouth breathing, nasal polyps, dryness of the nasal mucous membrane, pollens, or very offensive odors. It may also result from disease or injury of the olfactory tract, bone disease near the olfactory nerve, disease of the nasal accessory sinuses, meningitis, or tumors or syphilis affecting the olfac-

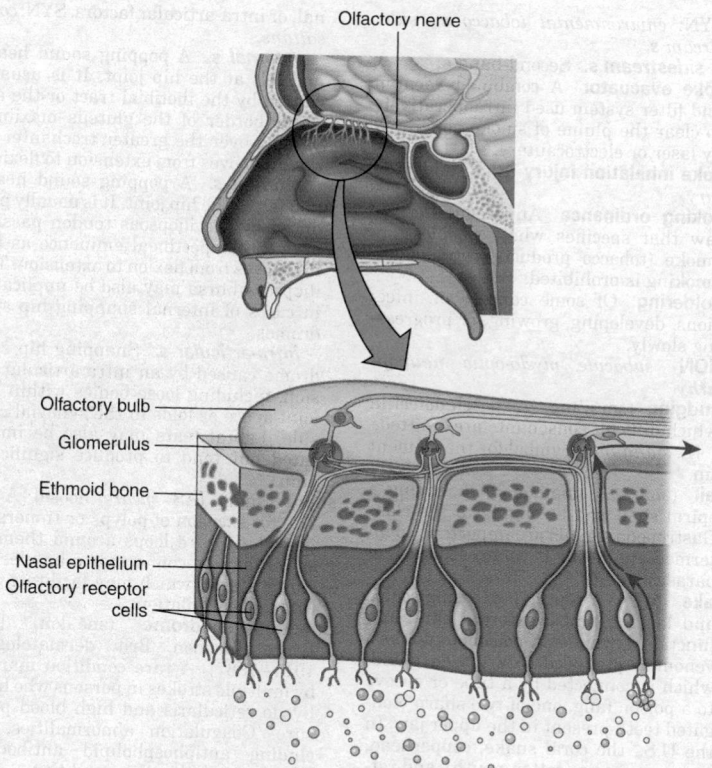

Olfactory nerve

Olfactory bulb
Glomerulus
Ethmoid bone
Nasal epithelium
Olfactory receptor cells

SENSE OF SMELL

tory nerve. It may rarely represent a conversion disorder. Disease of one cranial hemisphere or of one nasal chamber may also account for anosmia. SYN: *anodmia; anosphrasia.*

Hyperosmia: An increased sensitivity to odors.

Kakosmia: The perception of bad odors where none exist; it may be due to head injuries or occur in hallucinations or certain psychoses.

Parosmia: A perverted sense of smell. Odors that are considered agreeable by others are perceived as being offensive, and disagreeable odors are found pleasant. SYN: *parosphresia.*

smile A facial expression that may represent pleasure, amusement, derision, or scorn. The corners of the mouth are turned up in an expression of pleasure or amusement, and the eyes usually appear to be warm and friendly.

Smith fracture (smith) [Robert W. Smith, Irish physician, 1807–1873] A fracture of the distal end of the radius, with anterior displacement of the fragment.

Smith-Lemli-Opitz syndrome (smith′ lem′lē-ō′pits) [David Weyhe Smith, U.S.

pediatrician, 1926–1981; Luc Lemli, Belgian pediatrician, b. 1931; John Marius Opitz, Ger.-born U.S. geneticist, b. 1935] ABBR: SLOS. An autosomal recessive disorder in cholesterol synthesis that results in mental retardation, microcephaly, union of the second and third toes, ambiguous genitalia, weak muscular tone, and other anomalies. SYN: *7-dehydrocholesterol reductase deficiency.*

Smith-Petersen nail (smĭth′pē′tĕr-sĕn) [Marius N. Smith-Petersen, U.S. orthopedic surgeon, 1886–1953] A special nail that on cross-section has three flanges, used for stabilizing fractures of the neck of the femur.

smog [blend of *smoke* and *fog*] Dense fog combined with smoke and other forms of air pollution.

smoke (smōk) Any suspension in the air of particles produced by combustion.

   environmental tobacco s. Second-hand s.

   first-hand s. Mainstream s.

   mainstream s. Smoke released by a burning tobacco product and directly inhaled by the smoker. SYN: *first-hand s.*

   second-hand s. The airborne pollutants released from tobacco smoke into the air, from which they can be inhaled.

SYN: *environmental tobacco* **s.**; *side-stream* **s.**

    sidestream s. Second-hand **s.**

smoke evacuator A combined vacuum and filter system used intraoperatively to clear the plume of smoke generated by laser or electrocautery.

smoke inhalation injury SEE: under *injury*.

smoking ordinance Any regulation or law that specifies where people may smoke (tobacco products), and where smoking is prohibited.

smoldering Of some cancers or infections, developing, growing, or progressing slowly.

SMON *subacute myelo-optic* **neuropathy**.

smudging (smŭj′ĭng) A speech defect in which difficult consonants are omitted.

Sn [L. *stannum*] Symbol for the element tin.

snail (snal) A small mollusk having a spiral shell and belonging to the class Gastropoda. Snails are important as intermediate hosts of many species of parasitic flukes.

snake [ME.] A reptile possessing scales and lacking limbs, external ears, and functional eyelids. In poisonous snakes, venom is produced in a poison gland, which is connected by a tube or groove to a poison fang, one of two sharp elongated teeth present in the upper jaw. In the U.S., the coral snake, copperhead, water moccasin (cottonmouth), and rattlesnake, of which there are 15 species, are poisonous. All except the coral snake belong to the pit viper group, because they possess a sensory pit between the eye and nostril.

    s. bite SEE: under *bite*.

snakeroot (snāk′root″) Any of numerous plants once believed to be useful as a remedy for poisonous snakebites.

    black s. Black cohosh.

    Texas s. SEE: *Aristolochia*.

    Virginia s. SEE: *Aristolochia*.

    white s. A perennial herb (*Eupatorium rugosum Houtt*) that contains the toxin tremetol and was once thought to be useful as a remedy for snakebites. The tremetol causes trembles in animals and milk sickness in humans. SEE: *milk* **sickness**; *trembles*; *tremetol*.

SNAP *Score for Neonatal Acute Physiology*.

snap A sharp cracking sound.

    closing s. The intense first heart sound heard in mitral stenosis.

SNAPPE *Score for Neonatal Acute Physiology with Perinatal Extension*. SEE: *Score for Neonatal Acute Physiology*.

snapping hip A slipping of the soft tissue around the hip joint, producing an palpable snapping sensation or audible snapping sound. Snapping hip syndrome may be caused by internal, external, or intra-articular factors. SYN: *coxa saltans*.

    external s. A popping sound heard and felt at the hip joint. It is usually caused by the iliotibial tract or the anterior border of the gluteus maximus passing over the greater trochanter as the hip moves from extension to flexion.

    internal s. A popping sound heard and felt at the hip joint. It is usually produced by the iliopsoas tendon passing over the iliopectineal eminence as the hip moves from flexion to extension. The iliopsoas bursa may also be implicated in cases of internal snapping hip syndromes.

    intra-articular s. Snapping hip syndrome caused by an intra-articular lesion, including loose bodies within the joint space or folds in the synovial capsule. Labral tears may also be implicated but tend to produce significant pain.

snare (snăr) [AS. *sneare*, noose] A device for excision of polyps or tumors by tightening wire loops around them. A snare may be connected to an electrosurgical unit, which may facilitate cutting and coagulation.

Sneddon syndrome (sne′dŏn) [Ian Bruce Sneddon, Brit. dermatologist, 1915–1987] A rare condition marked by multiple strokes in persons who have livedo reticularis and high blood pressure. Coagulation abnormalities, including antiphospholipid antibodies, are often found in this condition.

sneeze (snēz) [AS. *fneosan*, to pant] **1.** To expel air forcibly through the nose and mouth by spasmodic contraction of muscles of expiration caused by an irritation of nasal mucosa. The sneeze reflex may be produced by a great number of stimuli. Placing a foot on a cold surface will provoke a sneeze in some people, whereas looking at a bright light or sunlight will cause it in others. Firm pressure applied to the middle of the upper lip and just under the nose will sometimes prevent a sneeze that is about to occur. SEE: *photic sneezing; ptarmus*. **2.** The act of sneezing. SEE: *sternutation; sternutatory*.

Snellen, Herman (snel′ĕn) Dutch ophthalmologist, 1834–1908.

    S. chart A chart imprinted with lines of black letters graduating in size from smallest on the bottom to largest on top; used for testing visual acuity.

    S. reflex Congestion of the ear on the same side upon stimulation of the distal end of the divided auriculotemporal nerve. SYN: *auriculocervical nerve reflex*.

    S. test A test for visual acuity in which the patient reads a Snellen chart at a certain distance with one eye, then with the other eye, and then with both eyes.

sniff (snif) **1.** To inhale through the nostrils with the mouth closed. **2.** To smell in short, quick inhalations.

sniffer (snif´ĕr) A colloquial term for any inhaled substance used illicitly to become intoxicated. Examples include benzene, ether, gasoline, and glue.

sniff test 1. Any diagnostic test used to determine if a patient has a deficit in his or her sense of smell **2.** Breath test. **3.** Any diagnostic test in which a patient is asked to inhale through the nostrils forcefully, with the mouth closed **4.** Whiff test.

SNOM *selective nonoperative management.*

snore [AS. *snora*] The noise produced while breathing through the mouth during sleep, caused by air passing through a narrowed upper airway. Most people snore to some extent. Snoring is of no clinical importance to the snorer unless it is prolonged, chronic, and related to other symptoms such as sleep apnea or excessive daytime sleepiness. It may be important to the snorer's partner if the snoring is so loud as to disrupt the partner's sleep. In some cases, the snoring is of such clinical or social importance that plastic or laser surgery to remove redundant tissue in the pharynx is indicated SYN: *stertor.* SEE: *sleep apnea.*

snort (snŏrt) [ME. *snorten*] A slang term for *inhale,* esp. for the inhalation of illicit drugs.

snow, carbon dioxide Carbon dioxide solid therapy.

snowbank A colloquial term for a massive exudate found over the pars plana of the eye in pars planitis.

SNRI *serotonin and norepinephrine reuptake inhibitor.*

snRNA [Abbr. of *small nuclear ribonucleic acids*] Small RNA molecules confined to the cell nucleus. They initiate protein transcription, remove introns from RNA molecules, and add methyl (-CH_3) groups to molecules.

SNS *Society of Neurological Surgeons.*

snuff (snŭf) **1.** A medicinal powder inhaled through the nose. **2.** A powdered form of tobacco inhaled through the nose or placed in the oral cavity. SEE: *smokeless* **tobacco**.

snuffles (snŭf´ls) [D. *snuffelen,* to snuff] Obstructed nasal breathing with discharge from the nasal mucosa, esp. in infants, chiefly in congenital syphilis.

SOAP (sōp) **1.** An acronym for an organized structure for keeping progress notes in the chart. Each entry contains the date, number, and title of the patient's particular problem, followed by the SOAP headings: Subjective findings; Objective findings; Assessment, the documented analysis and conclusions concerning the findings; and Plan for further diagnostic or therapeutic ac-

tion. If the patient has multiple problems, a SOAP entry on the chart is made for each problem. **2.** *Society for Obstetric Anesthesia and Perinatology.*

soap (sōp) A cleansing chemical compound formed by an alkali acting on a fatty acid such as stearic acid to form sodium stearate, $NaC_{18}H_{35}O_2$. Castile soap is made by saponifying olive oil with sodium hydroxide and contains mainly sodium oleate, $NaC_{18}H_{33}O_2$. SEE: *detergent; saponification.*

    antibacterial s. A cleanser chemically altered to increase its ability to kill microorganisms.

SOAPIE An acronym for a charting mnemonic: *S*ubjective, *O*bjective, *A*ssessment, *P*lan, *I*mplementation, *E*valuation.

SOB *short of breath.*

sob [ME. *sobben,* to catch breath] **1.** To weep with convulsive movements of the chest. **2.** A cry or wail resulting from a sudden convulsive inspiration accompanied by spasmodic closure of the glottis. SEE: *sigh.*

social capital (sō´shĭl) [L. *socialis*] Community assets, i.e., interpersonal networks, bonds, and institutions that support communities, maintain their cohesiveness, and help them weather crises.

social class 1. Social standing or position. SYN: *socioeconomic status.* **2.** A group of people with shared culture, privilege, or position.

social distancing Protection of the public health by separating communities so that people who are stricken by a contagious illness cannot pass it on to others who are not. It includes, e.g., having children stay out of school when they are ill; closing workplaces; postponing meetings; and avoiding large social or religious gatherings or sporting events. It is designed to stop the spread of epidemics or pandemics but is not as strict a limitation on social interaction as quarantine.

social engagement Engagement (2)

social functioning The ability of a person to interact easily and successfully with other people.

social influence The impact of peers, family members, educators, or colleagues on a person's thoughts, feelings, and behaviors.

social interaction, impaired The state in which an individual participates in an insufficient or excessive quantity or ineffective quality of social exchange. SEE: *Nursing Diagnoses Appendix.*

social isolation SEE: under *isolation.*

socialization (sō´shă-lĭ-zā´shŭn) The process of adapting an individual to the social customs of society; in the process, he or she becomes an integrated member of the society.

social loafing The tendency of people to

curtail their individual efforts when working in a group or collectively and thus to be less productive than when they work alone.

social network A group of individuals linked by behaviors (e.g., drug abuse), diseases (e.g., a cancer support group), hobbies or lifestyles (e.g., participation in sports or online friendships), family ties, or professions (e.g., nursing).

social referencing The use of nonverbal cues or clues provided by the expressions of others to determine how to perceive and respond to ambiguous social situations.

social relatedness Interpersonal intimacy; empathy; shared subjectivity.

social support Help given to provide feedback, satisfy needs, and validate another's experience. A large body of research suggests that the loss of social support is a cause of physical and psychological disorders. Nursing practice uses social supports such as tangible materials, teaching, and intimate interactions to restore, promote, and care for patients, reinforcing positive experiences.

Society for Assisted Reproductive Technology ABBR: SART. An affiliate of the American Society for Reproductive Medicine consisting of clinics and programs that provide assisted reproductive technology. SART reports annual fertility clinic data to the Centers for Disease Control and Prevention.

Society of Urologic Nurses and Associates ABBR: SUNA. A professional organization of nurses who specialize in the care of patients with diseases of the urinary tract.

socio-, soci- [L. *socius,* allied, sharing, kindred] Prefixes meaning *society, social, sociology, sociological.*

sociobiology (sō″sē-ō-bī-ŏl′ō-jē) [″ + ″] Analysis of social behavior in terms of evolutionary theory. It assumes that animal or human populations evolve and adapt to their environments in different ways (e.g., through individual learning, cultural tradition, or genetic inheritance).

sociocusis, socioacusis (sō″s(h)ē-ŏ-koo′sĭs, sō″s(h)ē-ō-ă-koo′sĭs) Hearing loss that develops over time after repeated exposures to loud noise and not to occupational exposure to noise, physiological changes with age, or disease.

socioeconomic status SEE: under *status.*

sociology (sō-sē-ŏl′ō-jē) [″ + *logos,* word, reason] The study of human social behavior and the origins, institutions, and functions of human groups and societies.

sociomedical (sō″sē-ō-mĕd′ĭ-kăl) Pert. to sociology and medicine, esp. the interrelationships between the two.

sociometry (sō″s(h)ē-om′ĕ-trē) [*socio-* + *-metry*] The measurement of social behaviors. **sociometric** (sō″s(h)ē-ō-me′trĭk), adj.

sociopath (sō′sē-ō-păth) [″ + Gr. *pathos,* disease, suffering] An individual with antisocial personality disorder. SEE: *antisocial* **personality disorder**.

sociopathy (sō″sē-ŏp′ă-thē) [″ + Gr. *pathos,* disease, suffering] The condition of being antisocial.

socket (sŏk′ĕt) [ME. *soket,* a spearhead] **1.** A hollow in a joint or part for another corresponding organ, as a bone socket or an eye socket. SEE: *acetabulum.* **2.** The proximal portion of a prosthesis, into which the stump of an amputated extremity is fitted.

  alveolar s. The bony space occupied by the tooth and periodontal ligament.

  dry s. Localized alveolar **osteitis**.

  tooth s. A dental alveolus of the maxilla or mandible; a cavity that contains the root of a tooth.

socket grafting localized alveolar ridge **augmentation**

soda (sōd′ă) [Italian *soda* via L. *sodanum,* samphire, fr. Arabic *sudā′,* headache (for which samphire was a remedy)] A term loosely applied to various salts of sodium. SEE: *sodium.*

  baking s. Sodium bicarbonate.

  washing s. Sodium carbonate.

sodio- [Fr. *soda* + *-ium*] Prefix meaning *containing sodium.*

sodium (sōd′ē-ŭm) [*soda* + *-ium* (1)] SYMB: Na. An inorganic metallic element, atomic weight (mass) 22.98987, atomic number 11, specific gravity 0.971. Sodium constitutes about 0.15% of body mass. It is the most abundant cation in extracellular fluids, the main contributor to osmotic pressure and hydration, participates in many specialized pumps and receptors on cell membranes, and plays a fundamental part in the electrical activities of the body, e.g., nerve impulse transmission and muscular contraction.

  The normal sodium level in serum is 135 to 145 mmol/L. A decreased level of sodium in the serum is called hyponatremia, an increased level, hypernatremia. These conditions per se are not usually excesses or deficiencies of sodium but rather disturbances in the body's regulation of water, i.e., a change in measured sodium concentrations usually results from water retention or water depletion and not from too little or too much sodium in the body. SYN: *natrium.* SEE: *hypernatremia; hyponatremia.*

  s. acetate $C_2H_3NaO_2$, a chemical compound used to alkalize urine and kidney dialysis solutions. It is also used as a component in many laboratory reagents, e.g., buffers. SYN: *s. ethanoate.*

s. alginate $NaC_6H_7O_6$, a purified carbohydrate product extracted from certain species of seaweed. It is used as a food additive and as a pharmaceutical aid.

s. ascorbate $C_6H_7NaO_6$, the sodium salt of ascorbic acid (vitamin C). It may be used in a sterile solution when parenteral administration of vitamin C is required.

s. benzoate $C_7H_5O_2Na$, a white, odorless powder with sweet taste, used as a food preservative.

s. bicarbonate $NaHCO_3$, a white odorless powder with a salty taste. It is incompatible with acids, acid salts, ammonium chloride, lime water, ephedrine hydrochloride, and iron chloride. It is used to treat acidosis, e.g., in renal failure. It is used orally as an antacid although its effectiveness for this purpose is questionable. Externally, it is used as a mild alkaline wash. It is also used as a component in many laboratory reagents, e.g., buffers, microbiologic media, and control materials. SYN: *baking soda; s. hydrogen carbonate*.

s. carbonate Na_2CO_3, a white crystalline alkaline powder. It is used in industry to manufacture glass, ceramics, soaps, paper, and sodium salts. SYN: *soda ash; washing soda*.

carboxymethylcellulose s. $C_6H_9OCH_2$-COONa, a white powder used as a pharmaceutical aid and a food additive.

s. chloride NaCl, a naturally occurring white crystalline compound; common table salt. It is used in preparation of normal saline solution, as an emetic, and to add flavor to foods. It is incompatible with silver nitrate. In aqueous solution, sodium chloride, a neutral salt, is a strong electrolyte, being almost completely ionized. The sodium and chlorine ions are important in maintaining the proper electrolyte balance in body fluids. The kidneys regulate retention or excretion of sodium chloride in urine; aldosterone directly increases the renal reabsorption of sodium ions. SYN: *salt (1); table salt*.

s. citrate $C_6H_5Na_3O_7$, a white granular powder soluble in water. It is used as an anticoagulant for blood collected for laboratory analysis or used for transfusion.

s. fluoride NaF, a white, poisonous crystalline powder with a salty taste. Minute amounts of sodium fluoride are added to drinking water for fluoridation, in tooth pastes, and in oral rinses (mouth washes) to prevent dental caries (tooth decay). It is also an effective, inexpensive treatment for osteoporosis. SEE: *fluoridation; sodium fluoride **poisoning***.

s. hydrogen carbonate S. bicarbonate.

s. hydroxide NaOH, a whitish solid, soluble in water and making a clear solution. It is an antacid and a caustic. It is used in laundry detergents and in commercial compounds to clean sink traps, toilets, and in the preparation of soap. It is also used as a component in any laboratory reagent that needs pH balancing. SYN: *caustic **soda***.

⚠ It is corrosive. People who handle sodium hydroxide should protect their eyes, mucus membranes, and skin from direct contact.

s. hypochlorite NaOCl, an unstable salt used in solution as an antiseptic, disinfectant, and bleaching agent (household bleach).

s. iodide NaI, a colorless crystalline solid used as an expectorant.

s. lactate $C_3H_5NaO_3$, a sodium salt of inactive lactic acid. it is used intravenously in one-sixth or one-fourth molar solution to control electrolyte disturbances, esp. acidosis.

s. lauryl sulfate $C_{12}H_{25}NaO_4S$, an anionic surface-active agent used as a pharmaceutical acid.

s. monofluoroacetate FCH_2CO_2Na, a toxic pesticide, once banned in the U.S., that inhibits cellular metabolism, esp. in the most metabolically active organs, i.e., the brain and heart. In humans it causes arrhythmias, seizures, coma, and occasionally death. It is used commercially to kill rodents and large animals.

s. monofluorophosphate ABBR: MFP. Na_2PO_3F, a compound used in toothpastes to prevent dental caries (tooth decay)

s. morrhuate, morrhuate sodium The sodium salt of the fatty acids, found in cod liver oil. It is used as a sclerosing agent for the obliteration of varicose veins, including esophageal varices.

s. phosphate P 32 A radiopharmaceutical made with radioactive phosphorus (^{32}P), used in solution to treat polycythemia vera and certain cancers.

s. polyanethol sulfonate ABBR: SPS. A polyanionic detergent and antimicrobial agent used in microbiological assays to enhance recovery of bacteria.

s. salicylate $C_7H_5NaO_3$, a white crystalline substance with a disagreeable, even nauseating, taste, used to reduce pain and temperature. SEE: *acetylsalicylic acid*.

s. sulfate Na_2SO_4, a salt formerly used as a saline cathartic and diuretic, and now used in the manufacture of detergents. The salt grows in the pores of bricks and stones, causing them to crack from the pressure.

s. thiosulfate $Na_2O_3S_2$, a white crystalline substance used externally to remove stains of iodine and intravenously as an antidote for cyanide poisoning.

sodium modeling Titration of sodium concentrations during hemodialysis to relieve the muscle cramping, nausea, vomiting, and blood pressure fluctuations sometimes seen during the procedure.

sodium polyanethol sulfonate SEE: under *sodium*.

sodium restriction Limitation of the intake of sodium chloride (table salt) in the diet. SEE: *low-sodium diet*.

sodomy (sŏd'ŏ-mē) [L. *Sodoma*, Sodom] Anal or oral intercourse.

Soemmering, Samuel T. von (sem'ĕr-ing) Samuel Thomas von Soemmering, Ger. anatomist, 1755–1830.

    S. ring An annular swelling of the periphery of the lens capsule.

SOFAS *Social and Occupational Functioning Assessment Scale.*

soft (sŏft) [AS. *softe*] Not hard, firm, or solid.

soft copy A radiological image visible on a computer screen instead of film.

softcopy, soft copy (sŏft'kŏp″ē) An electronic or digitized document. Softcopy images in radiology are stored digital images that can be manipulated to highlight or enhance image quality and radiologic interpretation. They are often used to assure quality of imaging systems in radiology.

soft drink A nonalcoholic beverage, typically carbonated and sweetened.

softening (sŏf'ĕn-ing) The process of becoming soft. SYN: *malacia*.

    s. of bones Osteomalacia.

    white s. The stage of softening of tissue in which the affected area has become white and anemic.

soft lens associated corneal hypoxia SEE: under *hypoxia*.

soft sign SEE: under *sign*.

soft tissue SEE: under *soft tissue*.

S-OIV *swine-origin influenza virus* SEE: *swine* **influenza**.

sol (sŏl, sōl) [Gr. *sole*, salt water] **1.** The state of a colloid system in which the dispersion medium or solvent forms a continuous phase in which the particles of the solute are dispersed, forming a fluid mass. It is called a hydrosol if the dispersion medium is a liquid and an aerosol if a gas. SEE: *gel*. **2.** Solution.

solace (sŏl'ăs) An object or resource that soothes pain or mental stress. In children a teddy bear or a "security" blanket may provide solace. In later life, one's spouse, a friend, or a hobby may be a source of comfort and security.

Solanaceae (sō″lă-nā'sē-ē″) [L. *solanum*, nightshade + -*aceae*] A family of herbs, shrubs, and trees from which several important drugs such as scopola-

mine and belladonna are derived. Tomatoes and potatoes are members of this family.

solanaceous (sō″lă-nā'shŭs) Pert. to the family Solanaceae.

solanaceous glycoalkaloid (glī″kō-al'kă-loyd″) ABBR: SGA. Any of the steroid chemicals found in plants like potatoes, tomatoes, and eggplants that may prolong the action of some anesthetics and opiates. SGAs inhibit two enzymes, butyrylcholinesterase and acetylcholinesterase, decreasing the metabolization of anesthesia.

solanine (sō'lă-nēn) A poisonous alkaloid found in potatoes, tomatoes, and other members of the nightshade family. SEE: *potato* **poisoning**.

solar (sō'lăr) [L. *solaris*] Pert. to the sun or its rays.

solar eclipse sign SEE: under *sign*.

solarium (sō-lā'rē-ŭm) [L. *solarium*, terrace] **1.** A room or porch exposed to the sun. **2.** A room designed for heliotherapy or for the application of artificial light. **3.** A day or recreational room for patients; often used as a waiting area for family or visitors.

solation (sō-lā'shŭn) In colloidal chemistry, the transformation of a gel into a sol.

solder (sŏd'ĕr) Any fusible alloy usually made of tin and lead but may be mostly silver or gold for use in dentistry. The alloy is applied in a molten state to build up or join metal parts.

    building s. An alloy of silver with large amounts of copper used to increase the height or bulk of contact areas of dental inlays or crowns; also called *sticky solder*.

    gold s. A solder alloy containing a high proportion of gold.

    hard s. A solder that is used in dentistry, has a high fusion point, and is stronger and more tarnish-resistant than softer, low-melting-point solders. This class of solders has increased compressive strength and reduced tensile strength. The increased strength is a result of increased platinum or palladium content within the alloy. This class of alloys is used for appliances that span large distances in the oral cavity.

    soft s. A low-melting-point solder with less strength or tarnishing resistance than hard solder.

soldering (sŏd'ĕr-ĭng) The joining of two pieces of metal by use of a lower-melting-point alloy. When the melted solder cools and solidifies, it joins the parts together. Soldering is used to join many components of dental appliances or orthodontic bands and to add bulk or contours to crowns or inlays.

sole (sōl) [AS. *sole*] **1.** The underpart of the foot. SYN: *planta pedis*. **2.** The portion of a synaptic knob at the termination of a motor nerve fiber that is directly adjacent to the sarcolemma of a muscle fiber.

solenoid (sŏl′lĕ-noyd) A coil of insulated wire in which a magnetic force is created in the long axis of the coil when an electric current flows through the wire. It may be used to activate switches.

Solenopsis (sō-lĕ-nop′sĭs) [Gr. *sōlēn*, pipe, gutter + *-opsis*] A species of small stinging ants, including the fire ants.

S. invicta The red fire ant, introduced into the southern U.S. in the 1930s. Its bite can cause welts or, in some instances, generalized anaphylaxis. SEE: *fire ant bite*.

soleus (sō′lē-ŭs) [L. *solea*, sole of foot] A flat, broad muscle of the calf of the leg.

solid (sŏl′ĭd) [L. *solidus*] **1.** Pert. to a phase of matter in which the atoms or molecules are in fixed positions relative to one other and their primary kinetic energy (motion) is vibration and rotation; not gaseous or liquid. **2.** Such a substance.

solid fuel A combustible substance such as wood, paper, coal, or biomass. Burning these fuels to release heat has been associated with an increase in respiratory diseases and a reduction in childhood growth, esp. when the solid fuels are burned indoors.

solipsism (sŏl′ĭp-sĭzm) [L. *solus*, alone, + *ipse*, self] The theory that the self may know only its feelings and changes and there is then only subjective reality.

solitary (sŏl′ĭ-tăr-ē) [L. *solitarius*, aloneness] Alone; single or existing separately.

solitude Isolation; aloneness.

solo practitioner A physician, dentist, or other practitioner who practices alone rather than with a group or partner.

solubility (sŏl″ū-bĭl′ĭ-tē) [LL. *solubilis*, to loosen, dissolve] The capability of being dissolved.

  aqueous s. The ability of a substance to dissolve in water. The aqueous solubility of a medication determines its ability to be compounded, administered, and absorbed.

soluble (sŏl′yŭ-bĕl) [L. *solubilis*, dissolvable] Able to be dissolved.

solute (sŏl′ūt) [L. *solutus*, to loosen, dissolve] The substance that is dissolved in a solution.

solution (sŏ-loo′shŏn) [L. *solvere*, to loosen, dissolve] **1.** A liquid containing a dissolved substance. **2.** The process by which a solid is homogeneously mixed with a liquid, solid, or gas so that the dissolved substances cannot be distinguished from the resultant fluid. **3.** A mixture formed by dissolution of substances.

  The liquid in which the substances are dissolved is called the *solvent* and the substance dissolved, the *solute*.

  aqueous s. A solution containing water as the solvent.

  balanced s. 1. Isotonic s. **2.** A solution whose concentrations are matched physiologically to the part of the body in which it will be infused or used for irrigation. SEE: *isotonic s.*

  Benedict s. SEE: *Benedict solution*.

  buffer s. A solution of a weak acid and its salt, e.g., carbonic acid, sodium bicarbonate, important in maintaining a constant pH, esp. of the blood.

  Burow s. SEE: *Burow solution*.

  citrate s. A solution, usually combined with dextrose and other agents, to prevent blood clotting. It allows whole blood to be stored until it is needed for transfusion.

  cobra venom s. A sterile physiological salt solution containing minute quantities of cobra venom.

  colloidal s. A solution in which the solute is suspended, not dissolved, such as gelatin or albumin.

  Dakin s. SEE: *Dakin solution*.

  Hartmann s. SEE: *Hartmann solution*.

  heparin lock flush s. A solution of unfractionated heparins formerly used to keep intravenous infusion devices from clotting. Heparin flushes are now seldom used because they are more expensive than saline flushes and pose a risk of heparin-related thrombocytopenia, a potentially life-threatening allergy.

  histidine-tryptophan-ketoglutarate s. ABBR: HTK solution. A preservative to protect a harvested organ before its transplantation into a donor. It is typically infused into the donor organ before the organ is removed from the body and then used to bathe the organ while it is kept in storage at 4° C before implantation into the recipient.

  hyperbaric s. A solution with a specific gravity and osmotic pressure greater than one or greater than the solution to which it is compared. It is important in injecting medicines or anesthetic agents into the spinal fluid in the spinal canal. SEE: *hyperbaric chamber*.

  hypertonic s. A solution having a greater osmotic pressure than that of cells or body fluids; a solution that draws water out of cells, thus inducing plasmolysis.

  hypotonic s. A solution having an osmotic pressure less than that of cells or body fluids; a solution that will cause water to enter cells, thus inducing swelling and possibly lysis.

  iodine s. A solution of iodine or potassium iodide used as a source of iodine.

  irrigating s. Any fluid used to rinse an organ or body cavity. SEE: *irrigation*.

  isobaric s. A solution with a specific

gravity equal to one or equal to the solution with which it is being compared. SEE: *hyperbaric s.*

isohydric s. A solution having the same hydrogen ion concentration or pH as another.

isosmotic s. A solution with the same osmotic pressure as the solution with which it is being compared.

isotonic s. A solution that has a concentration of electrolytes, nonelectrolytes, or both that will exert osmotic pressure equivalent to that of the solution with which it is being compared. Either 0.16 *M* sodium chloride solution (approx. 0.95% salt in water) or 0.3 *M* nonelectrolyte solution is approx. isotonic with human red blood cells. SYN: *balanced s.*

Jessner s. SEE: *Jessner solution.*

lactated Ringer s. SEE: under *Ringer, Sydney.*

Locke-Ringer s. SEE: *Locke solution.*

Lugol s. SEE: *Lugol solution.*

molar s. SYMB: 1 *M.* A solution containing a gram molecular weight or mole of the reagent dissolved in 1 L of solution.

normal s. An obsolete term for a solution in which 1 L contains 1 g equivalent of the solute. This term is discouraged in the SI system.

normal saline s. An isotonic saline solution. SYN: *physiological saline s.* SEE: *isotonic s.*

ophthalmic s. A sterile preparation suitable for instillation in the eye.

oral rehydration s. ABBR: ORS. A solution used to prevent or correct dehydration due to diarrheal illnesses. The World Health Organization recommends that the solution contain 3.5 g sodium chloride; 2.9 g potassium chloride; 2.9 g trisodium citrate; and 1.5 g glucose dissolved in each liter of drinking water.

physiological saline s. Normal saline s.

repair s. Any solution given intravenously to treat an electrolyte or metabolic disturbance.

replacement s. A liquid given to a patient to increase concentrations of specific electrolytes or minerals. It is usually given intravenously, orally, enterally, or interosseously.

Ringer s. SEE: under *Ringer, Sydney.*

saline s. A solution of a salt, usually sodium chloride, and distilled water. A 0.9% solution of sodium chloride is considered isotonic to the body. A normal saline solution consists of 0.85% salt solution, which is necessary to maintain osmotic pressure and the stimulation and regulation of muscular activity.

saturated s. A solution containing all the solute it can dissolve. SEE: *saturation point.*

sclerosing s. Sclerosant.

scrub s. A colloquial term for a skin cleanser for the removal of debris, dirt, microorganisms, oils, and scales from the skin of a patient before incision or instrumentation.

seminormal s. ABBR: 05N or N/2. A solution containing one-half of a gram equivalent weight of reagent in 1 L of solution.

sodium iodide I 125 s. A standardized solution of radioactive iodide, ^{125}I.

standard s. In comparison or analysis, a solution containing a definite amount of a substance.

supersaturated s. A solution in which the saturation point is reached but when it is heated it is possible to dissolve more of the solute. SEE: *saturation point.*

test s. A dissolved reagent used for a specific laboratory purpose.

Tyrode s. SEE: *Tyrode solution.*

volumetric s. A standard solution containing a definite amount of a substance in 1 L of solution; used in volumetric analysis.

solvate (sŏl′vāt) A compound formed by reaction between solvent and solute.

solvation The interaction of solvent molecules with the molecules or ions dissolved in them.

solvent (sŏl′vĕnt) [L. *solvens,* dissolving] **1.** Producing a solution, dissolving. **2.** A liquid holding another substance in solution.

solvent/detergent treated ABBR: SD. Exposed to, soaked in, or washed in chemicals that remove or inactivate lipid-soluble components from solution. Blood products (e.g., coagulation factor concentrates or fresh frozen plasma) are SD-treated to reduce potential contamination of these products by lipid-enveloped viruses (e.g., hepatitis B, hepatitis C, or HIV).

⚠ Reported complications resulting from the use of SD plasma include clotting in some patients (thromboembolism) and bleeding in others.

solvent drag The movement of ions across cell membranes by bulk transport following the movement of water rather than being facilitated by ion channels or cellular pumps.

solvolysis (sŏl-vŏl′ĭ-sĭs) A general term for reactions involving decomposition by hydrolysis, ammonolysis, and sulfolysis.

-som A suffix used in pharmacology to designate any growth hormone derivative.

soma (sō′mă) [Gr. *soma,* body] **1.** The body as distinct from the mind. **2.** All of the body cells except the germ cells. **3.** The body of a cell; the portion containing the nucleus.

soman (sō′măn) Pinacolyl methylphosphonofluoridate; an extremely toxic nerve gas.

somatic (sō-măt′ĭk) [Gr. *soma*, body] **1.** Pert. to nonreproductive cells or tissues. **2.** Pert. to the body. **3.** Pert. to structures of the body wall, such as skeletal muscles (somatic musculature) in contrast to structures associated with the viscera, such as visceral muscles (splanchnic musculature). **4.** Pert. to sensations perceived as originating from superficial or muscular structures of the body rather than sensations seeming to come from the internal organs (the viscera).

somatization (sō″mă-tī-zā′shŭn) The process of expressing a mental condition as a disturbed bodily function.

somatization disorder A condition of recurrent and multiple somatic complaints of several years' duration for which medical attention has been sought but no physical basis for the disorder has been found. The disorder impairs social, occupational, or other forms of functioning. The age of onset is usually before 30. The somatic complaints may be related to virtually any organ system. If these occur in association with a general medical condition, the physical complaints must be in excess of what would be expected from the medical illness. There must be a history of pain related to at least four different sites or functions such as menstruation, sexual intercourse, or urination. There also must be a history of at least two gastrointestinal symptoms other than pain. There must be a history of at least one sexual or reproductive symptom other than pain (e.g., nausea, vomiting, bloating). In women, this may consist of irregular menses, menorrhagia, or vomiting throughout pregnancy. In men, there may be symptoms such as erectile or ejaculatory dysfunction. Both sexes may be affected with hypoactive sexual desire disorder. There must also be a history of at least one symptom, other than pain, that suggests a neurological condition such as impaired coordination or balance, paralysis or localized weakness, difficulty in swallowing or speaking, urinary retention, hallucinations, loss of touch or pain sensation, double vision, blindness, deafness, seizures, amnesia, and loss of consciousness other than fainting. The unexplained symptoms are not intentionally feigned or produced. SEE: *somatoform disorder*.

somato-, somat- [Gr. *sōma*, stem *sōmat-*, body] Prefixes meaning *body*.

somatocrinin (sō″măt-ō-krĭn′ĭn) Growth hormone-releasing hormone.

somatoform disorder (sō-măt′ă-fŏrm″) A psychological disorder in which the physical symptoms suggest a general medical condition and are not explained by another condition such as a medication or another mental disorder. The symptoms must be clinically significant enough to impair function. A variety of conditions are included in this classification, including somatization disorder, conversion disorder, pain disorder, and hypochondriasis. Psychological factors are associated with and precede the condition. Symptoms may include loss of sense of touch, double vision, blindness, deafness, paralysis, and hallucinations. Individuals with conversion symptoms show "la belle indifference" or a relative lack of concern for their symptoms. The symptoms are not intentionally produced or feigned. The diagnosis cannot be established if the condition can be explained by the effects of medication or a neurological or other general medical condition. SYN: *conversion disorder; psychosomatic disease*. SEE: *Nursing Diagnoses Appendix*.

TREATMENT: The patient may benefit from reassurance, esp. when it is provided by a trusted health care professional.

somatogenic (sō″mă-tō-jĕn′ĭk) [″ + *gennan*, to produce] Originating in the body. SEE: *psychogenic*.

somatome (sō′mă-tōm″) [*soma* + *-tome*] A somite.

somatomedin (sō″măt-ō-mē′dĭn) Any of a group of insulin-like growth factors (somatomedin C and somatomedin A) that require growth hormone in order to exert their function of stimulating growth. These proteins are produced in the liver and other tissues.

somatoparaphrenia (sō″mă-tō-par″ă-frē′nē-ă) [*somato-* + *para-* + *-phrenia*] In patients with unilateral brain damage, the delusion that the side of the body opposite the brain injury does not belong to the patient.

somatostatin (sō-măt′ō-stăt″ĭn) A peptide that regulates and inhibits the release of hormones by many different neuroendocrine cells in the brain, pancreas, and gastrointestinal tract. Somatostatin inhibits gastric motility and gastric acid secretion, blocks the exocrine and endocrine function of the pancreas, and inhibits the growth and release of hormones by neuroendocrine tumors. It is also used to treat variceal hemorrhage in patients with cirrhosis and to treat pancreatitis. Octreotide is a synthetic version of somatostatin.

somatotopic (sō″mă-tō-tŏp′ĭk) [″ + *topos*, place] Pert. to the correspondence between a particular part of the body and a particular area of the brain.

somatotroph (sō-măt′ō-trŏf) A cell or adenoma in the pituitary gland that secretes growth hormone.

somatotrophic (sō″mă-tō-trŏf′ĭk) [″ + *tropos*, a turning] **1.** Having selective attraction for or influence on body cells. **2.** Stimulating growth.

somatotropic (sō″mă-tō-trŏp′ĭk) [″ + *trope*, a turn] Influencing the body or body cells.

somatotropin (sō″măt-ō-trō′pĭn) [″ + *tropos*, a turning] Human growth hormone. It increases the rate of cell division and protein synthesis in growing tissues, mobilizes stored fats, and limits glucose production.

> **bovine recombinant s.** A growth hormone made by recombinant methods. Its use in dairy cattle to increase milk production is controversial.

somatotype (sō-măt′ō-tīp) A particular build or type of body, based on physical characteristics. SEE: *ectomorph; endomorph; mesomorph.*

-some, -soma [Gr. *sōma*, body] Suffixes meaning *body.*

somesthetic (sō-mĕs-thĕt′ĭk) Pert. to sensations and sensory structures of the body.

somite (sō′mīt) [Gr. *soma*, body] An embryonic blocklike segment formed on either side of the neural tube and its underlying notochord. Each somite gives rise to a muscle mass supplied by a spinal nerve and each pair gives rise to a vertebra. The ventromedial portion of each somite differentiates into a sclerotome, and the remainder (the dorsolateral portion) becomes a dermomyotome. The sclerotomal cells surround the notochord and the neural tube to form the precursors of the ribs and vertebrae. The dermomyotomes give rise to the dermis and the dorsal muscles.

somnambulism (sŏm-năm′bū-lĭzm) [L. *somnus*, sleep, + *ambulare*, to walk] Sleepwalking.

somni- [L *somnus*, sleep] Prefix meaning *sleep.*

somnogen (som′nŏ-gen″) [*somni- + -gen*] Any agent that induces sleep.

somnolence (sŏm′nŏ-lĕns) [L. *somnolentia*, sleepiness] Prolonged drowsiness or sleepiness. **somnolent,** *adj.*

son-, sono-, soni- [L *sonus*, sound] Prefixes meaning *sound.*

sone (sōn) [L. *sonus*, sound] A unit of loudness; the loudness of a pure tone of 1000 cycles per second, 40 decibels above the listener's threshold of hearing.

sonic (sŏn′ĭk) [L. *sonus*, sound] Pert. to sound.

sonicate (sŏn′ĭ-kāt) [L. *sonus*, sound] To expose to sound waves.

sonication (sŏn″ĭ-kā′shŭn) Exposure to high-frequency sound waves. The technique is used to destroy bacteria, hemolyze blood, and loosen substances adhering to materials such as surgical instruments.

sonogram (sō′nō-grăm) [L. *sonus*, sound, + Gr. *gramma*, something written] The record obtained by use of ultrasonography. SYN: *echogram.*

sonographer (sō-nŏg′ră-fĕr) An individual professionally trained to use ultrasound in the setting of other available clinical information to obtain images of anatomical structures, physiological processes, and disease states for diagnostic purposes. In the U.S., professional societies of sonographers include the Society of Diagnostic Medical Sonographers and the American Society of Echocardiography. Professionally certified sonographers are credentialed by the American Registry of Diagnostic Medical Sonographers.

> **diagnostic medical s.** One who provides patient services for those using diagnostic ultrasound under the supervision of a doctor of medicine or osteopathy.

> **ophthalmic s.** One who is professionally trained to perform diagnostic evaluations of the eye and its diseases, including examinations for ophthalmic foreign bodies, tumors, radiation injuries, inflammatory diseases, and vascular lesions as well as measurements of axial length (e.g., in cataract surgeries and intraocular lens implantation). In the U.S., professionally trained ophthalmic sonographers are certified in their specialty by the American Registry of Diagnostic Medical Sonographers.

sonography (sō-nog′ră-fē) [*sono- + -graphy*] Ultrasonography. **sonographic** (son″ō-graf′ik), *adj.*

sonolucent (son″ō-loo′sĕnt) [*sono- + lucent*] Capable of transmitting sound waves, rather than reflecting them to an ultrasound transducer. It is said of anatomical structures that are fluid-filled rather than solid, such as the gallbladder or urinary bladder. In ultrasonography, these structures appear dark. SYN: *anechoic.*

sonorous (sō-nō′rŭs) [L.] Giving forth a loud and rounded sound.

SOP *standard operating procedure* (as in the performance of a laboratory assay, or in the provision of emergency care.)

sopor (sō′por) [L.] Stupor. **soporose, soporous,** *adj.*

soporific (sō-pō-rĭf′ĭk) [″ + *facere*, to make] **1.** Inducing sleep. **2.** Narcotic; a drug producing sleep. SYN: *somnifacient.*

sorbitol (sor′bĭ-tŏl″) $C_6H_{14}O_6$; a crystalline alcohol present in some berries and fruits. It is used as a sweetening agent and as an excipient in formulating tablets. Ingesting large amounts of sorbitol can produce abdominal cramps, gaseous distention of the intestines, and diarrhea.

sordes (sor′dēz) [L. *sordere*, to be dirty] Crusts or accumulations of food and bacteria on the teeth and about the lips.

PATIENT CARE: The nurse prevents this condition by providing frequent oral hygiene for mouth breathers, patients who cannot drink or are not permitted oral fluids, and debilitated patients. A hydrogen peroxide mouthwash (one part hydrogen peroxide to three parts water) or glycerin applied with a soft brush or sponge-stick may be used to remove crusts. Either treatment should always be followed by rinsing with clear water (mouthwashes are astringent, and glycerin dries the mucous membranes). The nurse encourages oral intake if permitted and positions the patient to discourage mouth breathing. If fluids are restricted, the patient or care provider should use a water mist or spray to moisten membranes.

sore (sor) **1.** Tender; painful. **2.** Any type of tender or painful ulcer or lesion of the skin or mucous membrane.

>**bed s.** Pressure **ulcer**.

>**canker s.** Aphthous **ulcer**.

>**cold s.** A thin-walled blister at the junction of the mucous membranes of the mouth and lips. It is caused by recurrent infection with herpes simplex virus (HSV) in those who have antibodies to HSV. Treatment is recommended only for immunocompromised patients, who are given acyclovir. SEE: *fever* **blister**.

>**Delhi s.** Cutaneous **leishmaniasis**.

>**desert s.** An ulcer of the skin of the arms or legs, sometimes caused by *Corynebacterium diphtheriae* or staphylococci, typically contracted in Australia or Burma.

>**hard s.** A syphilitic chancre; primary lesion of syphilis.

>**jungle s.** Infection of the skin or of poorly tended wounds by *Corynebacterium diphtheriae,* esp. in warm, moist, tropical climates.

>**Oriental s.** Cutaneous **leishmaniasis**.

>**pressure s.** Pressure **ulcer**.

>**primary s.** The initial sore or hard chancre of syphilis.

>**soft s.** Chancroid.

>**tropical s.** Cutaneous **leishmaniasis**.

>**wine s.** A slang term for a superficial infected area of the skin seen in alcoholics with poor personal hygiene. It is erroneously thought to be due to specific action of the wine.

sore throat Inflammation of the tonsils, pharynx, or larynx.

>**herpetic s.t.** Herpetic tonsillitis or pharyngotonsillitis.

>**septic s.t.** Bacterial **pharyngitis**.

>**streptococcal s.t.** Pharyngitis caused by group A beta-hemolytic streptococci. SEE: *scarlet* **fever**.

sorption (sorp′shŭn) [L. *sorbere,* to suck in] The condition of being absorbed.

s.o.s. [L., *si opus sit*] If necessary or required.

Sotos syndrome (sō′tōs) A rare developmental disorder in which cerebral gigantism is associated with scoliosis. Affected children often have behavioral

and psychiatric problems, mental retardation, and seizures.

souffle (soof′fl) [Fr. *souffler,* to puff] A soft blowing sound heard in auscultation; a bruit; an auscultatory murmur.

>**cardiac s.** Cardiac **murmur**.

>**fetal s.** A purring sound heard over the pregnant uterus and having the same rate as the fetal heartbeat. The sound is caused by blood flowing through vessels in the umbilical cord. SYN: *funic* **s.**

>**funic s.** Fetal **s.**

>**placental s.** The loud blowing murmur heard along the side of the uterus, caused by blood entering the dilated arteries of the uterus in the last months of pregnancy and synchronous with the maternal pulse. SYN: *uterine* **s.**

>**splenic s.** The sound heard over the spleen in various diseases.

>**umbilical s.** SEE: *umbilical souffle.*

>**uterine s.** Placental **s.**

¹sound (sownd) [Middle English *soun,* ult. fr. L. *sonus,* sound] **1.** Auditory sensations produced by vibrations; noise. It is measured in decibels (dB), which is the logarithm of the intensity of sound; thus 20 dB represents not twice 10 dB but 10 times as much. Repeated exposure to excessively loud noises, esp. in certain frequencies, will cause permanent injury to the hearing. SEE: *decibel; noise.* **2.** A form of vibrational energy that gives rise to auditory sensations. SEE: *cochlea; ear; organ of Corti.* **4.** Heart sounds. SEE: *diastole; systole.*

>**absent breath s.** The lack of perceptible sounds of airflow during auscultation of the patient's chest.

>ETIOLOGY: Absent breath sounds can be caused by a lack of breathing (apnea) or by lung disorders that block the transmission of the sounds to the surface of the chest, e.g., pneumothorax, pleural effusion.

>**adventitious lung s.** Crackles and wheezes superimposed on the normal breath sounds; indicative of respiratory disease. Most adventitious lung sounds can be divided into continuous (wheezing) and discontinuous (crackles) according to acoustical characteristics.

>**audible s.** Sound containing frequency components between 15 and 15,000 Hz (cycles per second).

>**blowing s.** An organic murmur as of air from an aperture expelled with moderate force.

>**bottle s.** A noise such as fluid in a bottle. SEE: *amphoric.*

>**bowel s.** Any of the normal sounds associated with movement of the intestinal contents through the alimentary tract. Auscultation of the abdomen for bowel sounds are possible indications of valuable diagnostic information. Absent or diminished sounds may indicate paralytic ileus or peritonitis. High-

pitched tinkling sounds are associated with intestinal obstruction.

breath s. Any of the respiratory sounds heard on auscultation of the chest. In a normal chest, they are classified as vesicular, tracheal, and bronchovesicular.

bronchial s. Any of the sounds not heard in the normal lung but occurring in pulmonary disease, indicating infiltration and solidification of the lung. SEE: *bronchial breathing.*

bronchovesicular s. A mixture of bronchial and vesicular sounds.

coarse breath s. A vesicular lung sound that is lower pitched and louder than normal.
ETIOLOGY: Pneumonia, atelectasis, pulmonary edema, and other conditions may cause this type of breath sound.

cracked-pot s. A tympanic resonance heard over air cavities. This percussion sound resembles that made by striking a cracked pot.

diminished breath s. A soft, decreased, or distant vesicular lung sound as heard through a stethoscope.
ETIOLOGY: Diminished breath sounds are common in patients with poor respiratory effort, splinting, emphysema, and other lung conditions.

ejection s. Any noise made during cardiac systole by the valves of the heart or the root of the aorta.

fetal heart s. The sound made by the fetal heart.

friction s. A sound produced by rubbing together two inflamed mucous surfaces.

heart s. The two sounds "lubb" and "dupp" heard when listening to the heart with a stethoscope. They arise from valve closure and muscular structures in the heart and are technically called S_1 and S_2. Third and fourth heart sounds may be present in some heart diseases.

physiological s. A sound perceived when the auditory canals are closed. The sound is produced by the blood flowing through adjacent vessels.

respiratory s. Any sound heard over the lungs, bronchi, or trachea.

split heart s. An abnormal auscultatory finding during a cardiac examination, in which a heart sound that usually has a single component is heard as two distinct noises. It is suggestive of a deep inspiration (which draws more blood than normal into the chest) or a bundle branch block.

succussion s. A splashing sound heard over a cavity with fluid in it.

to-and-fro s. Rasping friction sounds of pericarditis.

tracheal s. A sound normally heard over the trachea or larynx.

tubular s. A sound heard over the trachea or large bronchi.

vesicular s. A normal breath sound heard over the entire lung during breathing.

white s. A sound made up of all audible frequencies.

²**sound** (sownd) [Middle English *sounden,* fr. Fr. *sonder,* to probe] An instrument for introduction into a cavity or canal for exploration. SYN: *searcher.*

urethral s. A device suitable for use in exploring the urethra.

³**sound** (sownd) [Middle English *sund,* Old English *gesund,* healthy] Healthy, not diseased.

sound-conducting apparatus Those parts of the acoustic apparatus that transmit sound.

source (sors) **1.** The initiator of an epidemic disease, e.g., the patient who spreads an illness to others or the origin from which an epidemic spreads, e.g., spoiled food or contaminated water. **2.** A reservoir or storehouse. **3.** In technical and academic writing, the origin of a reference, quotation, or statistic.

Southern blot test An analytical method traditionally used in DNA analysis. After a sample of DNA fragments is separated by agarose gel electrophoresis, the fragments are transferred to a solid cellulose support by blotting. The gel is placed between a concentrated salt solution and absorbent paper. Capillary action draws the fragments onto the solid support. The support is then treated with radiolabeled DNA probes.

Southey tube (sŭth'ē) A very small tube pushed into tissue to help drain edema fluid. It is used in severe congestive heart failure to relieve edema of the legs.

Southwest Oncology Group ABBR: SWOG. A clinical cooperative composed of cancer institutions in the southwestern U.S. that researches the value of innovation in treating and preventing cancer.

sowda (sou'dah) Onchocerciasis; river blindness.

soybean, soy (soy'bēn") [Fm. Dutch or L. fm. Japanese fm. Chinese + bean] A legume (*Glycine max*) used as a source of several nitrogen-rich foods, including beverages, curd (tofu), flour, textured meat substitutes, and oils. Forty percent of raw soybean is protein. The bean can be processed to remove its oils and carbohydrates to isolate soy protein, a foodstuff containing all of the essential amino acids. In the U.S., most of the soybean crop has been genetically modified to make the plant resistant to commercial weed killers. Soy products have multiple health effects related to reducing (or increasing) cancer risk, improving bone health, reducing blood pressure, and impacting human hormone levels, among others.

soybean oil SEE: under *oil*.

sp [L., *spiritus*] *spirit; species*.

spa (spă) [Spa, a Belgium resort town] A mineral spring, esp. one allegedly having healing properties.

space (spās) [L. *spatium*, space] **1.** An area, region, or segment. **2.** A cavity of the body. SYN: *spatium*. **3.** A period or length of time; duration.

   alveolar dead s. The volume of gas in alveoli that are ventilated but not perfused, or ventilated but not fully perfused.

   anatomical dead s. In pulmonary physiology, the area in the trachea, bronchi, and air passages containing air that does not reach the alveoli during inspiration and is not involved in gas exchange. This is termed dead space because the air does not reach the alveoli and is not involved in gas exchange. Normal anatomical dead space is 2.2 mL/kg or 1 mL/lb. SYN: *dead s.* (1). SEE: *physiological dead* **s.**

   circumlental s. The space between the equator of the lens and the ciliary body.

   closest speaking s. The space between the teeth during casual repetition of the sound "s." It is considered the closest relationship of the occlusal surfaces and incisal edges of the mandibular teeth to the maxillary teeth during function and rapid speech.

   dead s. **1.** Anatomical dead **s. 2.** The unobliterated space remaining after closure of a surgical wound. This space favors the accumulation of blood and eventually infection.

   epidural s. The space outside the dura mater of the brain and spinal cord.

   extracellular s. ABBR: EC space. The space between cells. It contains tissue fluid, the water derived from plasma in the adjacent capillaries. The water flows among capillaries, tissue spaces, and cells. SEE: *extracellular fluid*.

   Fontana s. SEE: *Fontana spaces*.

   intercostal s. The interval between ribs, filled by the intercostal muscles.

   interfascial s. Tenon space. SEE: under *Tenon, Jacques R.*

   interglobular s. Czermak spaces.

   interpleural s. Mediastinum.

   interproximal s. The space between the surfaces of adjacent teeth in the dental arch. It is divided into the septal space, gingival to the contact point of the teeth and occupied normally by the interdental papillae of the gingiva, and the embrasure, the space occlusal to the contact point of the teeth.

   interradicular s. The area between the roots of a multirooted tooth, which contains an alveolar bony septum and the periodontal ligament.

   intervillous s. Any area of the maternal side of the placenta where transfer of maternal oxygen, nutrients, and fetal wastes occurs.

   joint s. Joint **cavity**.

   loose s. A distensible lung interstitial tissue surrounding the acinus and terminal bronchioles.

   mechanical dead s. The volume of gas exhaled into a tubing system and rebreathed on the subsequent breath.

   medullary s. The marrow-containing area of cancellous bone.

   palmar s. The midpalmar and thenar spaces of the hand.

   parasinoidal s. Lateral spaces in the dura mater adjacent to the superior sagittal sinus that receive meningeal and diploic veins.

   perforated s. The space pierced by blood vessels at the base of the brain.

   periodontal ligament s. ABBR: PDL space. A radiolucent space that appears on a dental radiograph between the tooth and the adjacent lamina dura. The space is occupied by the periodontal ligament, which lacks the density to be radiopaque.

   periportal s. of Mall SEE: *periportal space of Mall*.

   perivascular s. The spaces within adventitia of larger blood vessels of the brain. They communicate with the subarachnoid space.

   personal s. In psychiatry, an individual's personal area and the surrounding space. This space is important in interpersonal relations and in personal feelings of security and privacy.

   physiological dead s. In the respiratory tract, any nonfunctional alveoli that do not receive air that participates in gas exchange. Possible causes include emphysema, pneumothorax, pneumonia, pulmonary edema, and constriction of bronchioles. SEE: *anatomical dead* **s.**

   plantar s. One of four spaces between the fascial layers of the foot. When the foot is infected, pus may be found there.

   pleural s. The potential space between the visceral and parietal pleura. In some diseases and conditions the space fills with air, blood, lymph, or malignant tumors. Air in the pleural space is called *pneumothorax*. Blood in the space is called *hemothorax*. Lymph accumulations in the pleural space are called *chylothorax*. Malignant tumors that may fill the pleural space include mesothelioma or metastatic lung or breast cancers, among others.

   pneumatic s. Any of the spaces in bone that contain air, esp. those in the paranasal sinuses.

   popliteal s. The space behind the knee joint, containing the popliteal artery and vein and small sciatic and popliteal nerves.

   potential s. A region of the body in which two surface membranes adjoin, separated in health only by a small amount of fluid lubrication. Examples of potential spaces include joint bursae and synovium, and the pericardial, peritoneal, and pleural cavities. These spaces may fill with bacteria, crystals, extracellular fluid, or inflammatory or malignant cells in disease.

prezonular s. The anterior portion of the posterior chamber of the eye.

retroperitoneal s. The potential space outside the parietal peritoneum of the abdominal cavity.

retropharyngeal s. The space behind the pharynx separating prevertebral from visceral fascia. Important as a possible path for the spread of infection from oral cavity trauma downward to visceral organs of the mediastinum.

subarachnoid s. The space between the pia mater and the arachnoid, containing the cerebrospinal fluid.

subumbilical s. The triangular space within the body cavity below the navel.

suprasternal s. Triangular space immediately above the sternum between layers of deep cervical fascia.

Tenon s. SEE: under *Tenon, Jacques R.*

thenar s. A deep fascial space in the hand lying anterior to the adductor pollicis muscle.

tissue s. Any space within tissues not lined with epithelium and containing tissue fluid.

zonular s. A space within the zonule (suspensory ligament of lens). SEE: *dead space.*

space maintainer A device fashioned to keep teeth separated when placed across an edentulous segment of the dental arch. It may consist of bands, bars, springs, or other materials, and is cemented or soldered to orthodontic bands or crowns on the adjacent teeth.

space medicine SEE: under *medicine.*

space-occupying lesion Mass (1).

spacer (spā′sĕr) A specially shaped container that improves the delivery of inhaled aerosols, such as beta₂ agonists, steroids, and other antiasthmatic drugs, to the bronchi and lungs. Spacers form a channel between metered-dose inhalers and the mouth through which medicated mists can be inhaled. They improve the performance of antiasthmatic drugs because without them, a large quantity of inhaled medications end up in the mouth, on the palate, on the buccal mucosa, or on the tongue and fail to reach their intended target in the lower airways.

PATIENT CARE: Spacers improve the delivery of inhaled drugs to any patient who cannot coordinate the use of metered-dose inhalers, and in all patients who used inhaled steroids. They are also recommended for young children, e.g., under the age of 6.

spacer sequence, spacer DNA The genetic material on a chromosome that separates actively transcribed genes. It may make up the largest part of the genome of some eukaryotic organisms and often consists of tandem repeats of DNA.

spallation (spo-lā′shŏn) **1.** The process of breaking into very small parts. The term may be applied to visible structures or to atomic particles. **2.** The release of inert particles into the bloodstream. The splintering of bits of plastic from the pump used in hemodialysis is an example.

span (span) **1.** The distance from one fixed point to another, as the distance, when the hand is fully expanded, from the tip of the thumb to the tip of the little finger. **2.** A length of time. **3.** The duration of a process.

attention s. The duration of sustained concentration on a task or activity. SEE: *attention deficit-hyperactivity disorder; hyperactivity* (3).

digit s. A test of memory and attention. SEE: *digit span test.*

life s. The maximum obtainable age of a member of a species.

memory s. The number of words or objects one can store and recall when asked to do so. SEE: *digit span test.*

sparer (spăr′ĕr) [AS. *sparian,* to refrain] A substance destroyed by catabolism that decreases catabolic action on other substances.

nitrogen s. Protein **s.**

protein s. Carbohydrates and fats, so designated because their presence in the diet prevents tissue proteins from being used as a source of energy.

sparganosis (spăr″gă-nō′sĭs) Infestation with spirometra.

sparing 1. The use of one medicine in place of another, usually to prevent side effects from high doses of the first medicine (e.g., steroid-sparing). **2.** Protective; said of certain surgical operations that preserve vital tissues and their function.

spasm (spazm) [Gr. *spasmos,* convulsion] A sudden, involuntary movement or muscular contraction due to an irritant or trauma. Spasms may be clonic or tonic and involve either visceral muscle or skeletal muscle. When contractions are strong and painful, they are called cramps. The effect of the spasm depends on the part affected: asthma is assumed to be associated with spasm of the muscular coats of smaller bronchi; renal colic to spasm of the muscular coat of the ureter.

TREATMENT: General measures to reduce tension, induce muscle relaxation, and improve circulation are necessary. Specific measures include analgesics, massage, relaxation exercises, heat, cold, or electrotherapy, and, in some cases, gentle therapeutic exercises. Special orthopedic supports or braces are sometimes effective. For vascular spasm, chemical sympathectomy may give relief.

s. of accommodation A spasm of the ciliary muscle, usually due to excessive strain from overuse and common in myopia.

bronchial s. Bronchospasm.

carpal s. Spasm of the muscles of the hand. SEE: *tetany.*

carpopedal s. Spasm of the hands and feet, sometimes seen in hyperventilation syndrome. It is caused by hypocalcemia and commonly occurs during hyperventilation because the lowered carbon dioxide alters the level of ionized calcium. SEE: *hyperventilation tetany.*

choreiform s. Spasmodic movements resembling chorea.

clonic s. Intermittent contractions and relaxation of muscles. SYN: *clonospasm.*

coronary artery s. Intermittent constriction of the large coronary arteries. This may lead to angina pectoris in various conditions and is not necessarily associated with exertion. SEE: *variant angina.*

coronary s. Muscular closure of the coronary arteries, causing angina, ischemia, or myocardial infarction. SEE: *variant angina.*

cynic s. Spasm of the facial muscles causing a grin or snarl like a dog. SYN: *risus sardonicus.*

diffuse s. An esophageal motor disorder characterized by dysphagia, odynophagia, and chest pain.

esophageal s. Intermittent inability to swallow, often associated with intense chest pain, gagging, or breathing difficulty. It can occur after swallowing cold liquids drunk through a straw or in rabies, anxiety, depression, or achalasia. In most patients, it is caused by excessive motor function of the esophageal muscles.

TREATMENT: Nitrates or tricyclic antidepressants are sometimes used to treat the symptoms. Diffuse esophageal spasms can also be treated by surgical division of the esophageal muscles.

facial s. Spasm of the muscles supplied by the facial nerve, affecting one side of the face or the region around the eye. SEE: *cranial nerve; tic.*

habit s. Tic.

hemifacial s. Twitching of facial muscles that usually begins in one eyelid but may spread after many years to half of the face or even to both sides of it. It is usually due to an aneurysm of the vertebral or basilar artery or a tumor of the cerebellopontine angle. In some patients the twitching can be treated with injections of botulinum

toxin if the underlying cause is not treatable.

infantile s. Seizure marked by momentary flexion or extension of the neck, trunk, extremities, or any combination, with onset occurring in the first year of life. Although infantile spasms subside in late infancy, many affected children develop other types of seizures and may be severely retarded.

mobile s. Athetosis.

nictitating s. Clonic spasm of the eyelid with continuous winking.

nodding s. A psychogenic condition in adults, causing nodding of the head from clonic spasms of the sternomastoid muscles. A similar nodding occurs in babies, with the head turning from side to side. SYN: *salaam convulsion.*

pedal s. Spasm of the feet.

retrocollic s. Retrocollis.

saltatory s. A tic of the muscles of the lower extremity, causing convulsive leaping upon attempting to stand. SEE: *jumping Frenchmen of Maine; miryachit; palmus (2); Tourette syndrome.*

tetanic s. A spasm in which contractions occur repeatedly and without interruption.

tonic s. Continued involuntary contractions.

torsion s. A spasm characterized by a turning of a part, esp. the turning of the body at the pelvis.

toxic s. Convulsions due to poison.

vasomotor s. Spasm of smaller arteries.

winking s. Blepharospasm.

spasmogen (spăz′mō-jĕn) [″ + *gennan,* to produce] Something that causes spasms or constrictions, such as in the bronchospasm associated with asthma.

spasmolytic (spăz-mō-lĭt′ĭk) [″ + *lysis,* dissolution] Arresting spasms or that which acts as an antispasmodic.

spasmophilia (spăz-mō-fĭl′ē-ă) [″ + *philein,* to love] Tetany.

spastic (spăs′tĭk) [Gr. *spastikos,* convulsive] 1. Pert. to spasms or convulsions. 2. Produced by spasms. 3. One afflicted with spasms.

spastic colon SEE: under *colon.*

spastic gait SEE: under *gait.*

spastic hemiplegia SEE: under *hemiplegia.*

spasticity (spăs-tĭs′ĭ-tē) A motor disorder characterized by velocity-dependent increased muscle tone, exaggerated tendon jerks, and clonus. Spasticity is the result of an upper motor neuron lesion (i.e., found in the spinal cord or brain rather than in one of the peripheral nerves).

PATIENT CARE: Spasticity can cause abnormal and variable movement patterns and restriction of range of motion. Physical and occupational therapy are used to improve range of motion and use of affected limbs. Medications, such as muscle relaxants (baclofen or diazepam) or botulinum toxin can alleviate spasticity and improve function.

spatial (spā′shăl) Pert. to space. **spatially** (spāsh′ă-lē), *adv.*

spatial discrimination SEE: under *discrimination*.

spatially fractionated radiation SEE: under *radiation*.

spatial resolution SEE: under *resolution*.

spatium (spā′shē-ŭm) *pl.* **spatia** [L.] Space.

spatter (spăt′ĕr) The distribution of droplets into the air or onto solid surfaces, as a result of injuries to blood vessels (blood spatter) or during dental or surgical procedures. In health care, spatter is a potential source of exposure to infectious body fluids. In forensic medicine, the characteristics of spattered fluids are used to reconstruct crime scenes.

spatula (spăch′ū-lă) [L. *spatula*, blade] An instrument for spreading or mixing semisolids. It is usually flat, thin, somewhat flexible, and shaped like a knife without a cutting edge. It may be used in blunt dissection of soft tissues (e.g., brain).

   cervical s. A blade, often made of wood or plastic, with an indented tip adapted to ensure sampling during a Papanicolaou test of the squamous cells of the endocervix of the uterus.

   nasal s. A device for holding mucous flaps in place or to guard against burning from cautery.

spatulate (spăch′ū-lāt) To mix something by use of a spatula. In dentistry, to mix or manipulate certain dental materials with a spatula to achieve a uniform, homogeneous mass.

spay, spaying (spā, spā′ĭng) [Gael. *spoth*, castrate] Surgical removal of ovaries, usually said of animals. SEE: *castration*.

SPCA *Society for the Prevention of Cruelty to Animals*.

spear tackler's spine Injury to the cervical spine resulting from players using their heads as a primary point of impact with their opponents' bodies in contact sports such as football or soccer. This condition is considered an absolute contraindication to participation in contact sports in which high-energy axial loads may be applied to the cervical spine because it markedly heightens the risk of nerve injury or paralysis. Spear tackler's spine is based on four criteria:

   1. developmental stenosis of the cervical vertebral canal;

   2. loss of the normal lordotic cervical curvature;

   3. radiographic evidence of post-traumatic abnormalities of the cervical spine; and

   4. a history of axial loads delivered to the cervical spine.

special care baby unit ABBR: SCBU. A neonatal intensive care unit.

specialist (spĕsh′ăl-ĭst) [L. *specialis*] A dentist, nurse, physician, or other health care professional who has advanced education and training in one clinical area of practice such as internal medicine, pediatrics, surgery, ophthalmology, neurology, maternal and child health, or cardiology. In most specialized areas of health care, there are organizations offering qualifying examinations. When an individual meets all of the criteria of such a board, he or she is called "board certified" in that area.

specialization (spĕsh′ăl-ĭ-zā′shŭn) The limitation of one's practice to a particular branch of medicine, surgery, dentistry, or nursing. This is customarily done after postgraduate training in the area of specialization.

special need (spesh′ăl) Any disability or functional limitation, e.g., attention deficit disorder, autism, blindness, deafness, emotional or psychological disorder, or impaired mobility requiring special assistance.

special needs child A child who is protected by governmental agencies and made ready for adoption after abandonment, abuse, or neglect in his or her home. SYN: *waiting child*.

specialty (spĕsh′ăl-tē) The branch of medicine, surgery, dentistry, or nursing in which a specialist practices.

specialty hospital SEE: under *hospital*.

speciation (spē″sē-ā′shŭn) [L. *species*, a kind] 1. The evolutionary process by which new species of living organisms are formed. 2. The identification of the species of an organism, e.g., of an infectious bacterium.

species (spē′shēz) [L. *species*, a kind] ABBR: sp. In biology, a category of classification for living organisms. This group is just below the genus and is usually capable of interbreeding.

species-specific The characteristics of a species, esp. the immunological nature that differentiates that species from another.

species type The original species that served as the basis for identifying a new genus or subgenus.

specific (spĕ-sif′ĭk) [L. *specificus*, pert. to a kind] 1. Pert. to a remedy that has a curative effect on a particular disease or symptom. 2. Pert. to a species. 3. Pert. to a disease that is always caused by the same organism. 4. Restricted, explicit; not generalized.

specific dynamic action of food Thermic effect of food.

specific gravity ABBR: sp. gr. The mass of a substance compared with the mass of an equal volume of water. For solid and liquid materials, water is used as a standard and considered to have a specific gravity of 1.000. For gases, the weight per unit volume is compared with that of dry air at a specified temperature and usually at atmospheric pressure. SYN: *relative density*.

specificity (spes″ĭ-fis′ĭt-ē) **1.** The state of being specific; having a relation to a definite result or to a particular cause. **2.** The ability of a test to exclude those who are truly free of a disease or condition. It is a test that reports negative when the characteristic looked for is absent.

    antigenic s. The property of mature B and T lymphocytes that enables them to respond to specific foreign antigens entering the body. Antigen specificity requires mature B and T cells that have been previously exposed to the antigen and, therefore, are able to recognize it again and respond by neutralizing or destroying it. The exact process by which B lymphocytes become capable of recognizing and responding to antigens is unknown. Development of antigen specificity by T cells requires macrophage processing of the antigen for recognition.

    diagnostic s. For a diagnostic or screening test, the proportion of people who are truly free of a specific disease and are so identified by the test. SEE: *sensitivity*.

    s. of exercise The design of exercises to stress muscles in a manner similar to the way in which they are to perform. This technique helps the muscle to meet specific demands, including speed and type of contraction, strength and endurance requirements, stabilization, and mobility activities.

specific therapy Administration of a remedy acting directly against the cause of a disease, as penicillin for syphilis or acyclovir for herpes simplex virus. SEE: *nonspecific therapy*.

specific treatment Treatment directed at the cause of a disease.

specimen (spes′ĭ-mĕn) [L. *specimen*, a mark, token] A part of something, intended to show the kind, quality, and other characteristics of the whole. Collected urine, feces, cerebrospinal fluid, sputum, blood, skin, or tissues are all considered to be specimens.

⚠ Persons handling specimens of blood, body fluids, or other excretions should wear protective gloves to limit exposure to infectious agents, such as the hepatitis viruses.

The following information is important in obtaining, containing, and handling biological and forensic samples.

Sterilization of glassware: This is accomplished by the use of hot air or dry heat, boiling water, flowing steam, steam under pressure, certain gases, and germicidal chemicals.

Labels: All containers should be labeled with the names of the patient and attending physician and the room number. Labels should be placed on the container, not on the lid. Request forms, sometimes used as labels, are made up to suit the individual laboratory or hospital. Provision is made for recording necessary data as indicated, including the date the specimen was taken, the circumstances, the substances for which the examination is being performed, and any other information desired.

    SEE: *chain of custody*.

Time: If the required specimen cannot be furnished at once, one should note what is needed and inform the patient, supervisor, and any other caregiver who may attend the patient in one's absence.

Charting: The chart should record all specimens sent to the laboratory, when they were sent, and any other data that seem pertinent such as the appearance of the specimen or unusual occurrences while it was being obtained.

Care of specimen: The specimen should be covered immediately after it is deposited in the container. The label or request form should be checked. One should make sure that the container is intact and in no danger of spilling while in transit. Some types of specimens, e.g., blood, urine, tissues, will need special care with respect to the temperature to be maintained while they are stored or transported and the time allowed before being analyzed. SEE: *sample; Standard and Universal Precautions Appendix*.

specimen label A means of uniquely identifying the source of a clinical specimen sent for laboratory analysis.

    PATIENT CARE: The label should include the full name of the patient, as well as additional identifiers such as the patient's date of birth, the date the laboratory specimen was obtained, the patient care unit, or the last four digits of the patient's social security number. For specimens sent to a blood bank, additional identifiers are required, including the signature or the initials of the person who obtained the specimen.

speckle A grainy distortion (a kind of "noise") in an ultrasonographic image.

spectacles (spĕk′tăk-lz) [L. *spectare*, to see] Glasses.

spectral (spĕk′trăl) [L. *spectrum*, image] Pert. to a spectrum.

spectrin (spĕk′trĭn) An intracellular, calcium-dependent contractile protein that helps maintain the structure and shape of cells, esp. red blood cells.

spectro- [L. *spectrum*, appearance, image] Prefix meaning *spectrum, spectral*.

spectrocolorimeter (spĕk-trō-kŭl-or-ĭm'ĕ-tĕr) [L. *spectrum*, image, + *color*, color, + Gr. *metron*, measure] A device for detecting color blindness by isolating a single spectral color.

spectrofluorometer (spĕk"trō-floo"or-ŏm'ĕ-tĕr) An instrument that measures the degree and frequencies of fluorescence of compounds in chemical reactions or in solution.

spectrograph (spĕk'trō-grăf) ["" + Gr. *graphein*, to write] An instrument designed to photograph spectra on a sensitive photographical plate.

    mass s. A device that separates ions of different masses by employing a magnetic field to deflect them as they travel along a given path.

spectrometer (spĕk-trŏm'ĕ-tĕr) ["" + Gr. *metron*, measure] A spectroscope so constructed that angular deviation of a ray of light produced by a prism or by a diffraction grating thus indicates the wavelength.

spectrometry (spek-trom'ĕ-trē) [*spectro-* + *-metry*] Determination of the wavelength of light rays with a spectrometer.

    mass s. A process that separates and identifies molecules by ionizing them, assessing their ratio of mass to ionic charge, and measuring the electrical current they generate.

    tandem mass s. ABBR: MS/MS. An analytical device that can rapidly assess the biochemical makeup of hundreds of specimens by measuring the mass-to-charge ratio of molecules. SYN: *tandem mass assay.* SEE: *high-performance liquid* **chromatography**; *mass s.*

    PATIENT CARE: It is used in clinical laboratories to screen newborn infants for metabolic disorders such as fatty acid oxidation deficiencies, organic acid disorders, and congenital adrenal hyperplasia.

spectrophotometer (spĕk"trō-fō-tŏm'ĕt-ĕr) ["" + Gr. *photos*, light, + *metron*, measure] An instrument that measures the transmission of a specified light wavelength through a material (e.g., a material in solution). Contrasting the light transmission through a standard solution and the test solution, one can determine a variety of characteristics of the material, esp. its concentration.

spectrophotometric analysis (spek"trō-fōt"ŏ-me'trik) Determination of materials in a substance or mixture by measuring the amount of light they absorb in the infrared, visible, or ultraviolet region of the spectrum.

spectrophotometry (spek"trō-fŏ-tom'ĕ-trē) A measurement of coloring matter in a solution by use of the spectroscope or spectrophotometer. Substances can be measured by controlling the wave-length of light passing through the system and calibrating the response with known materials followed by measurement of the ubknown material. **spectro-photometric** (spek"trō-fōt"ŏ-me'trik), *adj.*

spectropolarimeter (spĕk"trō-pō"lăr-ĭm'ĕ-tĕr) ["" + *polaris,* pole, + *metron,* measure] An instrument for measuring the rotation of light rays of a specific wavelength by passage through a translucent solid.

spectroscope (spĕk'trō-skōp) ["" + Gr. *skopein,* to examine] An instrument for separating radiant energy into its component frequencies or wavelengths by means of a prism or grating to form a spectrum for inspection.

spectroscopic (spĕk"trō-skŏp'ĭk) Pert. to a spectroscope.

spectroscopy (spĕk-trŏs'kō-pē) **1.** The branch of physical science that treats the phenomena observed with the spectroscope, or those principles on which the action is based. **2.** The art of using the spectroscope.

    infrared absorption s. A technique that uses the infrared absorbing properties of molecules to determine their presence in tissues or body fluids. A common clinical application is in the design of oximeters. SEE: *oximeter.*

    nuclear magnetic resonance s. ABBR: NMR spectroscopy. A technique that uses the characteristic absorption of nuclei inside a strong magnetic field to identify and characterize molecules.

spectrum (spek'trŭm) *pl.* **spectra** [L. *spectrum,* image] **1.** The charted band of wavelengths of electromagnetic vibrations obtained by refraction and diffraction of rays of white light. **2.** The range or breadth of a phenomenon; the distribution of values in an array.

    absorption s. The spectrum recorded after light rays have passed through a substance capable of absorbing some of the wavelengths passing through. This spectrum is specific for various chemicals.

    chromatic s. The portion of the spectrum that produces visible light. Wavelengths of about 3900 Å to 7700 Å are visible.

    invisible s. The portion of the spectrum either below the red (infrared) or above the violet (ultraviolet), which is invisible to the eye, the waves being too long or too short to affect the retina. The invisible spectrum includes rays less than 3900 Å in length (ultraviolet, roentgen or x, gamma, and cosmic rays) and those exceeding 7700 Å in length (infrared, high-frequency oscillations used in short- and long-wave diathermy, radio, hertzian, and very long waves). These range in length from 7700 Å to 5,000,000 m.

speech s. The range of sound frequencies produced by the human voice.

visible s. The portion of the spectrum that is detectable by the human eye. The visible spectrum consists of the colors from red to violet with wavelengths of 3900 Å to 7700 Å.

visible electromagnetic s. The complete range of wavelengths of electromagnetic radiation.

spectrum bias Variation in the performance of a diagnostic test due to its application to people of differing ages, genders, nationalities, or specific disease manifestations. A test's sensitivity and specificity may increase or decrease, depending on the population to which it is applied. SYN: *case-mix bias.*

spectrum emission 1. In spectroscopy and fluorometry, the range of wavelengths emitted by a substance. **2.** In the case of atoms, the lines of emission.

speculum (spek′yŭ-lŭm, -lă) *pl.* **specula** [L. *speculum,* a mirror] **1.** An instrument for examination of canals or hollow organs. SEE: illus. **2.** The membrane separating the anterior cornua of lateral ventricles of the brain. SYN: *septum pellucidum.*

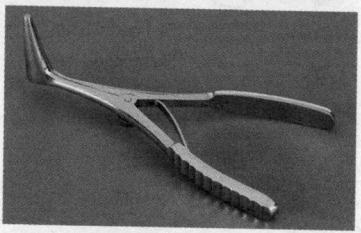

NASAL SPECULUM

bivalve s. A speculum with two opposed blades that can be separated or closed. SEE: *vaginal s.*

duck-bill s. A bivalve speculum with wide blades, used to inspect the vagina and cervix.

ear s. A short, funnel-shaped tube, tubular or bivalve (the former being preferable), used to examine the external auditory canal and eardrum.

eye s. A device for separating the eyelids. Plated steel wire, plain, Luer, Von Graefe, and Steven are the most common types.

Pedersen s. A small vaginal speculum for examining prepubertal patients or others with small vaginal orifices.

vaginal s. A speculum, usually with two opposing portions that, after being inserted, can be pushed apart for examining the vagina and cervix. It should be warmed before use. SEE: illus.

speech (spēch) **1.** The oral expression of one's thoughts. **2.** The utterance of ar-

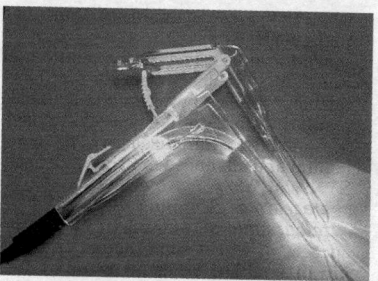

VAGINAL SPECULUM

ticulate words or sounds. **3.** The words spoken for communication.

alaryngeal s. Any of several methods of speech used by patients who have had their larynx removed. These methods include esophageal speech, tracheoesophageal puncture, or speech enhanced by an electrolarynx.

aphonic s. SEE: *aphonia.*

ataxic s. Defective speech due to muscular incoordination, usually the result of cerebellar disorder.

clipped s. Scamping **s.**

cued s. Communicating using both lip reading and manual gestures made near the mouth. It is used to help the hearing impaired to clarify the difference between words that are otherwise easily misinterpreted during speech reading.

echo s. Echolalia.

esophageal s. In those who have had laryngectomies, the modulation by the pharynx, mouth, and tongue of air expelled from the esophagus to produce speech.

explosive s. Sudden, loud speech.

external s. Expression of thought by spoken or written words, and the understanding of spoken or written words of others. SYN: *exophasia.*

inner s. The silent process of thought and production of unuttered words. This function is essential to thinking that is done with words. SYN: *endophasia.*

interjectional s. Speech into which gestures, ejaculatory sounds, and other nonverbal mannerisms are introduced.

mirror s. Speech characterized by reversing the order of syllables of a word.

nasal s. Speech in which air from the oropharynx enters the nasopharynx, usually resulting in abnormal resonance. Emission of air through the nose, weak pressure in articulating consonants, and attempts by the patient to stifle the abnormally spoken air column are also characteristic.

paraphasic s. SEE: *paraphasia.*

scamping s. Speech characterized by omission of consonants or syllables when the person is unable to pronounce them. SYN: *clipped s.*

scanning s. The pronunciation of words in syllables, or slowly and hesitatingly. Pauses between the syllables result in staccato-like speech. It is a symptom of certain diseases of the cerebellum and advanced multiple sclerosis. SYN: *staccato s.*

staccato s. Scanning **s.**

telegraphic s. Nonfluent or halting speech, in which some nouns or verbs are uttered but other elements of normal sentence structure are replaced by pauses or gaps. This type of aphasia is a hallmark of Broca aphasia.

speech abnormality Any disorder, dysfunction, or impairment of speech. Speech abnormalities include expressive and receptive aphasias, dysarthrias, labialism, stammering, stuttering, and word deafness.

speech and language pathologist ABBR: SLP. A health care professional trained to evaluate and treat people who have voice, speech, language, swallowing, or hearing disorders, esp. those that affect their ability to communicate or consume food.

speech delay Any disorder of childhood in the acquisition and use of spoken language. SYN: *expressive language delay.*

speech discrimination SEE: under *discrimination.*

speech disorder Any abnormality that prevents a person from communicating through spoken words. The disorder may develop from brain injury; stroke; muscular paralysis of the organs of speech; structural defects of the mouth, teeth, or tongue; somatization disorders; or cognitive deficits.

speech processor A miniature computer within a cochlear implant that analyzes sounds and converts them into digital signals.

speechreading Lip reading.

speech recognition The ability of a machine or computer to interpret human speech. Also known as voice recognition and speech understanding.

speech spectrum SEE: under *spectrum.*

speech synthesizer An electronic device for producing speech. Activated by a keyboard, it permits persons lacking the ability to speak to communicate.

speech therapist A speech and language pathologist.

speech therapy The study, diagnosis, and treatment of defects and disorders of the voice and of spoken and written communication.

speedball A slang term for a combination of cocaine and heroin taken intravenously.

spend down, spend-down The deliberate depletion of one's financial assets in order to meet the criteria for insurance support from Medicaid.

spent material Any material that has been used in medical care (or other industries) and cannot be reused without reprocessing, reclamation, or decontamination.

sperm (spĕrm) [Gr. *sperma,* seed] **1.** Semen. **2.** Spermatozoa. SEE: illus.

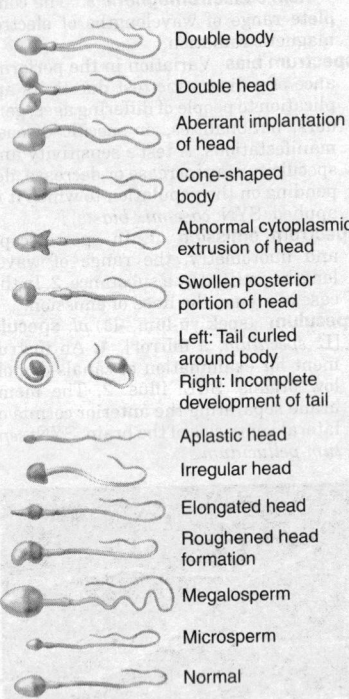

Double body

Double head

Aberrant implantation of head

Cone-shaped body

Abnormal cytoplasmic extrusion of head

Swollen posterior portion of head

Left: Tail curled around body
Right: Incomplete development of tail

Aplastic head

Irregular head

Elongated head

Roughened head formation

Megalosperm

Microsperm

Normal

NORMAL AND ABNORMAL SPERM

sperma (spĕr'mă) [Gr.] **1.** Semen. **2.** Spermatozoa.

sperma-, sperm-, spermi-, spermo- [Gr. *sperma,* seed] Prefixes meaning *seed, semen, sperm.* SEE: *spermato-.*

spermagglutination (spĕr"mă-gloo"tĭnā'shŭn) Agglutination of spermatozoa.

spermatic (spĕr-măt'ĭk) [Gr. *sperma,* seed] Pert. to semen or sperm.

spermatic vein SEE: under *vein.*

spermatid (spĕr'mă-tĭd) A cell arising by division of the secondary spermatocyte to become a spermatozoon. SYN: *spermatoblast.*

spermato-, spermat- [Gr. *sperma,* stem *spermat-,* seed] Prefixes meaning *seed.* SEE: *sperma-.*

spermatocele (spĕr-măt'ō-sēl) [" + *kele,* tumor, swelling] A cystic tumor of the epididymis containing spermatozoa.

spermatocidal (spĕr"mă-tō-sī'dăl) [" + L. *cidus,* kill] Destroying spermatozoa.

spermatocyst (spĕr-măt'ō-sĭst) [" + *kystis,* bladder] **1.** A seminal vesicle.

2. A tumor of the epididymis containing semen. SEE: *spermatocele.*

spermatocyte (spĕr′măt′ō-sīt) [″ + *ky-tos,* cell] A cell originating from a spermatogonium that divides to form spermatids, which become spermatozoa.

    primary s. A cell formed by mitosis of a spermatogonium.

    secondary s. A cell formed by meiosis of a primary spermatocyte. It undergoes a second meiotic division to form two spermatids, each with the haploid number of chromosomes.

spermatogenesis (spĕr″măt-ō-jĕn′ĕ-sĭs) [″ + *genesis,* generation, birth] The formation of mature functional spermatozoa. In the process, undifferentiated spermatogonia become primary spermatocytes, each of which divides to form two secondary spermatocytes. Each of these divides to form two spermatids, which transform into functional motile spermatozoa. In the process, the chromosome number is reduced from the diploid to the haploid number. SEE: illus.; *gametogenesis; maturation; meiosis.*

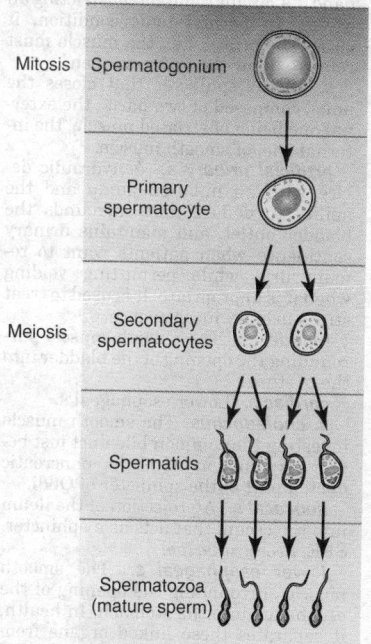

SPERMATOGENESIS

Labels on diagram (left to right, top to bottom):
Mitosis — Spermatogonium
Primary spermatocyte
Meiosis — Secondary spermatocytes
Spermatids
Spermatozoa (mature sperm)

spermatogenic,   **spermatogenous**
(spĕr″mă-tō-jĕn′ĭk,   spĕr″mă-tŏj′ĕ-nŭs) Producing sperm.

spermatogonium (spĕr″măt-ō-gō′nē-ŭm) *pl.* **spermatogonia** [″ + *gone,* generation] A large unspecialized germ cell that in spermatogenesis divides by mi-

tosis to form primary spermatocytes. SEE: *spermatogenesis.*

spermatology (spĕr″mă-tŏl′ō-jē) [″ + *logos,* word, reason] The study of the seminal fluid.

spermatorrhea (spĕr″mă-tō-rē′ă) [″ + *rhoia,* flow] An abnormally frequent involuntary loss of semen without orgasm.

spermatotoxin (spĕr′mă-tō-tŏk′sĭn) [″ + *toxikon,* poison] Spermatoxin.

spermatozoa (spĕr″măt-ō-zō′ă) Pl. of spermatozoon.

spermatozoal (spĕr″mă-tō-zō′ăl) [″ + *zoon,* life] Pert. to spermatozoa.

spermatozoon (spĕr″măt-ō-zō′ŏn) *pl.*
    spermatozoa [″ + *zoon,* life] The mature male sex or germ cell formed within the seminiferous tubules of the testes. The spermatozoon has a broad oval flattened head with a nucleus and a protoplasmic neck or middle piece and tail. It is about 51 μm long and resembles a tadpole. It has the power of self-propulsion by means of a flagellum. It develops after puberty from the spermatids in the testes in enormous quantities. The head pierces the envelope of the ovum and loses its tail when the two cells fuse. This process is called fertilization. SEE: illus.; *sperm* for illus.; *fertilization.*

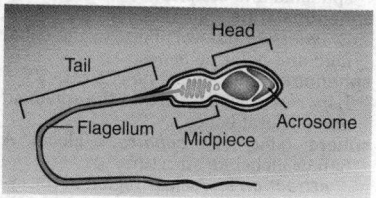

Labels: Head, Tail, Flagellum, Midpiece, Acrosome

SPERMATOZOON

Mature sperm cell

spermic (spĕr′mĭk) Pert. to sperm.

spermicide (spĕr′mĭ-sīd″) An agent that kills spermatozoa. Two spermicides used in contraceptive products are nonoxynol 9 and octoxynol 9.

⚠ The use of spermicides reduces the likelihood of pregnancy during sexual intercourse, but it does not reduce the rate of acquiring sexually transmitted diseases.

SYN: *spermaticide; spermatozoicide.*
spermicidal (spĕr″mĭ-sīd′ăl), *adj.*
spermidine (spĕr′mĭ-dĭn) An amine present in semen.
spermine (spĕr′mĭn) An amine present in semen and other animal tissues.
spermiogenesis (spĕr″mē-ō-jĕn′ĕ-sĭs) The processes involved in the transformation of a spermatid to a functional spermatozoon.

spermiogram (spĕr′mē-ō-grăm) [″ + *gramma*, something written] A record of examining and classifying sperm in a semen sample.

spermosphere (spĕr′mō-sfēr) [″ + *sphaira*, a circle] A mass of spermatids derived from spermatogonia.

sperm penetration assay SEE: under *assay*.

sp. gr. *specific gravity*.

sph *spherical*.

sphacelus (sfăs′ĕl-ŭs) A necrosed mass of tissue. SYN: *gangrene; mortification; necrosis; slough*.

spheno-, sphen- [Gr. *sphēn*, wedge] Prefixes meaning *wedge, sphenoid*.

sphenoid (sfē′noyd) [″ + *eidos*, form] Cuneiform or wedge-shaped.

sphenoidal (sfē-noy′dăl) Pert. to the sphenoid bone.

sphenoiditis (sfē″noy-dī′tĭs) [″ + ″ + *itis*, inflammation] **1.** Inflammation of the sphenoidal sinus. **2.** Necrosis of the sphenoid bone.

sphenoidotomy (sfē″noyd-ŏt′ō-mē) [″ + ″ + *tome*, incision] Incision into the sphenoid bone.

sphenomaxillary (sfē″nō-măk′sĭ-lā-rē) [″ + L. *maxilla*, jawbone] Pert. to the sphenoid bone and the maxilla.

spheno-occipital (sfē″nō-ŏk-sĭp′ĭ-tăl) [″ + L. *occipitalis*, occipital] Pert. to the sphenoid and occipital bones.

sphenopalatine (sfē″nō-păl′ă-tēn) [″ + L. *palatum*, palate] Pert. to the sphenoid and palatine bones.

sphenoparietal (sfē″nō-pă-rī′ĕ-tăl) [″ + L. *paries*, a wall] Pert. to the sphenoid and parietal bones.

sphere (sfēr) [Gr. *sphaira*, a globe] A ball or globelike structure.

  attraction s. A clear region in the cytoplasm close to the nucleus and usually containing a centriole or diplosome (a divided centriole).

  segmentation s. The segmented ovum or morula.

spherical (sfēr′ĭ-kăl) [Gr. *sphairikos*] Pert. to or shaped like a sphere. SYN: *globular*.

spherocylinder (sfē″rō-sĭl′ĭn-dĕr) [Gr. *sphaira*, globe, + *kylindros*, cylinder] A lens with a spherical surface and a cylindrical surface.

spherocyte (sfē′rō-sīt) [″ + *kytos*, cell] An erythrocyte that assumes a spheroid shape, and has no central pallor.

spherocytosis (sfē″rō-sī-tō′sĭs) [″ + ″ + *osis*, condition] A condition in which erythrocytes assume a spheroid shape. It occurs in certain hemolytic anemias.

  hereditary s. An autosomal dominant hemolytic anemia caused by a defect in the red blood cell membrane that makes the cell abnormally fragile and esp. susceptible to changes in the concentration of osmoles in the blood. Affected cells are gradually destroyed in the spleen, resulting in splenic enlarge-

ment, jaundice, and anemia as well as a high incidence of gallstone disease. Surgical removal of the spleen prevents many of this condition's complications but carries with it a risk of postoperative immune suppression.

spheroid (sfē′royd) [″ + *eidos*, form, shape] **1.** A body shaped like a sphere. **2.** Sphere-shaped. **3.** Approx. sphere-shaped.

spheroidal (sfē-roy′dăl) Sphere-shaped.

spheroplast (sfēr′ō-plăst) In bacteriology, the cell and partial cell wall remaining after the organism's cell-wall synthesis has been prevented. Spheroplasts may be formed when synthesis of the cell wall is prevented by the action of certain chemicals, e.g., penicillin, while cells are growing. SEE: *protoplast*.

spherule (sfēr′ūl) [L. *sphaerula*, little globe] **1.** A very small sphere. **2.** A minute granule found in the center of a centromere of a chromosome. **3.** The structures present in tissues infected with *Coccidioides immitis*. These spherules contain up to hundreds of endospores.

sphincter (sfingk′tĕr) [Gr. *sphinktēr*, band] A circular muscle constricting an orifice. In normal tonic condition, it closes the orifice, i.e., the muscle must relax to allow the orifice to open.

  s. ani A sphincter that closes the anus, composed of two parts: the external one being of striated muscle, the internal one, of smooth muscle.

  artificial urinary s. A hydraulic device with an inflation pump and the ability to deflate that surrounds the bladder outlet, and maintains urinary continence when patients want to remain dry, while permitting voiding when it is appropriate. It is used to treat stress urinary incontinence.

  bladder s. The smooth muscle surrounding the opening of the bladder into the urethra.

  cardiac s. Lower esophageal s.

  s. choledochus The smooth muscle investing the common bile duct just before its junction with the pancreatic duct; a part of the sphincter of Oddi.

  ileocecal s. A projection of the ileum into the cecum that acts as a sphincter. SEE: *ileocecal valve*.

  lower esophageal s. The smooth muscle surrounding the opening of the esophagus into the stomach. In health, it separates these linked organs from each other, preventing the reflux of stomach acids into the esophagus. SYN: *cardiac s.*

  s. of Oddi A contracted region at the opening of the common bile duct into the duodenum at the papilla of Vater.

  s. pancreaticus The smooth muscle encircling the pancreatic duct just before it joins the ampulla.

  precapillary s. A smooth muscle cell

found at the beginning of a capillary network. It regulates capillary blood flow. SEE: *artery* for illus.

pyloric s. The thickened circular smooth muscle around the pyloric orifice at the junction of the stomach and duodenum. The sphincter is usually contracted but relaxes at intervals (when gastric pressure exceeds duodenal pressure) to permit acid chyme to enter the duodenum. It then contracts to prevent backup of chyme to the stomach.

upper esophageal s. A sphincter that keeps the opening between the posterior pharynx and the proximal esophagus closed, except during swallowing. It is maintained principally by the cricopharyngeal muscle.

sphincterectomy (sfĭngk″tĕr-ĕk′tō-mē) [″ + *ektome*, excision] **1.** Excision of a sphincter muscle. **2.** Excision of part of the pupillary border of the iris.

sphincteroplasty (sfĭngk′tĕr-ō-plăs″tē) [″ + *plassein*, to form] Surgical repair of a sphincter.

sphincterotome (sfĭngk′tĕr-ō-tōm″) [*sphincter* + *-tome*] A surgical or endoscopic instrument used to incise a sphincter.

sphincterotomy (sfĭngk″tĕr-ŏt′ō-mē) [″ + *tome*, incision] The cutting of a sphincter muscle; done, for example, in eye surgery to enlarge the pupil.

sphingo- [Gr. *sphingein*, to tie tight, bind fast] Prefix used for naming the *sphingomyelins*, e.g., *sphingosine*.

Sphingobacterium (sfĭng″gō-băk-tē′rē-um) A genus of gram-negative bacilli formerly called *Flavobacterium*. It is commonly present in soil and may occasionally cause skin infections and sepsis.

sphingolipid (sfĭng″gō-lip′ĭd) [*sphingo-* + *lipid*] A lipid containing one of several long-chain bases such as sphingosine or dihydrosphingosine or bases of similar chemical structure but containing longer chains. They are a class of fatty molecules primarily found in nervous system tissues or circulating in plasma.

sphingolipidosis (sfĭng″gō-lĭp″ĭ-dō′sĭs) [″ + ″ + *osis*, condition] Any disease marked by a defective metabolism of sphingolipids. These genetic diseases include Sandhoff disease, Fabry disease, Tay-Sachs disease, Kufs disease, Gaucher disease, Krabbe leukodystrophy, Niemann-Pick disease, Batten disease, and Spielmeyer-Vogt disease. They are marked by neurological deterioration, usually beginning a few months after birth and eventually leading to death except in the adult form of Gaucher disease. These diseases can be detected by examining fluid obtained by amniocentesis.

sphingomyelin (sfĭng″gō-mī′ĕ-lĭn) [*sphingo-* + *myelin*] Any of a major group of phosphorus-containing sphingolipids. They are found primarily in nervous tissue and in lipids in the blood. Sphingomyelins are derived from choline phosphate and a ceramide. Deficiencies in sphingomyelin manufacturing are found in many diseases. SEE: *sphingolipidosis.*

sphingosine (sfĭng′gŏ-sēn″, -sĭn) [*sphingo-* + *-ine*] A long-chain base, $C_{18}H_{37}O_2N$, present in sphingolipids. SEE: *dihydrosphingosine; sphingolipid.*

sphygmo- [Gr. *sphygmos*, throbbing, vibration] Prefix meaning *pulse.*

sphygmogram (sfĭg′mō-grăm) [″ + *gramma*, something written] A tracing of the pulse made by using the sphygmograph.

sphygmograph (sfĭg′mō-graf″) [*sphygmo-* + *-graph*] An instrument for recording the strength and pace of the arterial pulse.

sphygmography (sfĭg-mog′ră-fē) [*sphygmo-* + *-graphy*] Recording the arterial pulse with a sphygmograph.

sphygmomanometer (sfĭg′mō-măn-ŏm′ĕt-ĕr) [″ + *manos*, thin, + *metron*, measure] An instrument for determining arterial blood pressure indirectly. The two types are aneroid and mercury. SEE: illus.; *blood pressure.*

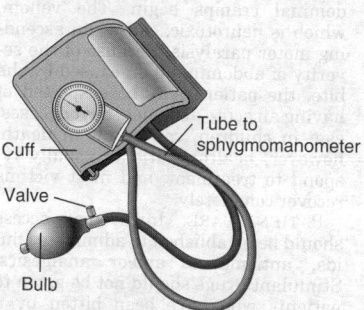

Tube to sphygmomanometer

Cuff

Valve

Bulb

SPHYGMOMANOMETER

sphygmometer (sfĭg-mŏm′ĕt-ĕr) [″ + *metron*, measure] An instrument for measuring the pulse. SYN: *polygraph.*

spica (spī′kă) [L., ear of grain] SEE: *bandage; spica.*

spicular (spĭk′ū-lar) [L. *spiculum*, a dart] Pert. to or resembling a spicule; dartlike.

spicule (spĭk′ūl) A small, needle-shaped structure. SYN: *spiculum.*

bony s. A thin island of developing bone.

cemental s. An excementosis or pointed protuberance extending from the surface cementum of a tooth root.

spiculum (spĭk′ū-lŭm) *pl.* **spicula** [L., a dart] Spicule.

spider (spīd′ĕr) [Old English *spithra*, related to *spin*] **1.** An arachnid, belonging to the order Araneae, class Arachnida, phylum Arthropoda. The body is divided into cephalothorax and abdomen joined by a narrow waist. A spider usually possesses four pairs of legs as well as poison fangs. It often possesses spinnerets. **2.** Anything resembling a spider in appearance.

arterial s. SEE: *spider nevus*.

s. bite SEE: under *bite*.

black widow s. The female of *Latrodectus mactans*. It is native to the southern U.S. but has been reported throughout the country. It prefers to live in woodpiles and other locations where it is well hidden. It is glossy black with a brilliant red spot, usually shaped like an hourglass or two triangles, on the undersurface of the abdomen (Southern black widow), or a row of red, white, or yellow spots down the middle of the abdomen with two crosswise bars (Northern black widow). Its body measures about 1 cm and its leg spread can reach 5 cm.

The bite of a black widow spider initially produces a sensation resembling the prick of a pin and may be mistaken for a flea bite. A numbing pain usually lasts for a short time and then subsides; later the abdominal muscles become rigid and the patient becomes severely diaphoretic. Within 1/2 hr, severe abdominal cramps begin. The venom, which is neurotoxic, causes an ascending motor paralysis. Because of the severity of abdominal pain caused by the bite, the patient may be suspected of having an acute abdomen. Severe cases, esp. in children, can result in death; however, healthy patients usually respond to treatment, and most victims recover completely.

PATIENT CARE: Intravenous access should be established to administer fluids, antiemetics, and/or analgesics. Stimulant drugs should not be given to patients who have been bitten by a black widow spider. Local suction is of little value because the toxin is rapidly absorbed. Symptomatic treatments include intravenous, intramuscular, or oral muscle relaxants, antihistamines, and benzodiazepines. Tetanus prophylaxis should also be administered. Specific antivenins may be used when envenomation has severe neurological consequences.

⚠ Respiratory status must be carefully monitored when morphine or a benzodiazepine is used.

Antivenin generally is used only for very young or very elderly patients experiencing respiratory distress or when severe pain and muscle spasms are not controlled by other measures. Before the administration of antivenin, a skin test is performed to assess for allergic reaction to the horse serum used in making the antivenin. Even if the test is negative, resuscitative medications and equipment should be readily at hand to manage an anaphylactic reaction to the antivenin. In addition to the risk of acute hypersensitivity, delayed serum sickness can occur 7 to 12 days after antivenin administration.

brown recluse s. *Loxosceles reclusa,* 3/8-in (10 mm) long spider native to North America. The venom of the brown recluse spider is toxic and can be lethal. It may produce a large area of necrosis at the site of the bite.

TREATMENT: Dapsone, antivenins, and steroids are often used to treat the envenomation; however, before using dapsone, the patient should be tested for glucose-6-phosphate dehydrogenase deficiency. Tetanus prophylaxis should be administered.

hobo s. A 5-in (45 mm) long brown spider with gray markings found in northwestern North America. Males are more venomous than females. A bite causes erythema, blisters, subsequent necrosis of the skin, and sometimes severe, persistent headaches. Systemic corticosteroid therapy may be helpful. Aplastic anemia, intractable diarrhea, or vomiting may occur and, although rare, may be fatal.

spike 1. The dominant peak in the record of an action potential or electroencephalogram. **2.** The narrow vertical tracing left on an electrocardiogram by the impulse generator of an electronic pacemaker. **3.** A needle used to puncture an object (e.g., a bag of intravenous fluids or a cyst), permitting fluids within the object to flow out. **4.** Any of the structural units that facilitate attachment of viruses to host cell receptors.

spike and wave Electroencephalic evidence of grand mal seizures.

spill (spĭl) [AS. *spillan,* to squander] **1.** To flow out of or release; in medicine, said of a substance that cannot be maintained in the body by one of its organs, esp. the kidneys. In diabetes mellitus, for example, the kidneys spill sugar into the urine. In the nephrotic syndrome, they spill protein. **2.** An overflow.

cellular s. A dissemination of cells through the lymph or the blood resulting in metastasis.

radioactive s. A release of radioactive materials into the environment.

spillway (spĭl′way) The contour of the teeth that allows food to escape from the cusps during mastication.

spina (spī′nă) *pl.* **spinae** [L. *spina,* thorn] **1.** A spinelike protuberance. **2.** The spine.

s. bifida Spina bifida cystica.

s. bifida cystica A congenital defect in the walls of the spinal canal caused by a lack of union between the laminae of the vertebrae during embryonic development. The lumbar portion is the section chiefly affected. It is found in approx. 18 of every 100,000 births. Like other neural tube defects, it can be prevented with folic acid supplementation (800 mg daily) taken by women before and during pregnancy. The consequences of this defect include urinary incontinence, saddle or limb anesthesia, disturbances in gait, and structural changes in the pelvis. SYN: *rachischisis*.

s. bifida occulta A failure of the vertebrae to close without hernial protrusion.

spinal (spī'năl) [L. *spinalis*] Pert. to the spine or spinal cord. SYN: *rachial; rachidial*.

spinal accessory nerve Accessory **nerve**.

spinal cavernous malformation SEE: under *malformation*.

spinal cord Part of the central nervous system, the spinal cord is an ovoid column of nerve tissue 40 to 50 cm long that extends from the medulla to the second lumbar vertebra; it is within the spinal (vertebral) canal, protected by bone, and directly enclosed in the meninges. The center of the cord is gray matter shaped like the letter H; it consists of the cell bodies and dendrites of neurons. The ventral (anterior) horns of the gray matter contain cell bodies of somatic motor neurons; the dorsal (posterior) horns contain cell bodies of interneurons. The white matter is arranged in tracts around the gray matter. It consists of myelinated axons that transmit impulses to and from the brain, or between levels of gray matter in the spinal cord, or that will leave the cord as part of peripheral nerves. The spinal cord is the pathway for sensory impulses to the brain and motor impulses from the brain; it also mediates stretch reflexes and the defecation and urination reflexes. Thirty-one pairs of spinal nerves emerge from the spinal cord and innervate the trunk and limbs. SEE: illus.

spinal cord injury SEE: under *injury*.

spinal curvature Abnormal curvature of the spine, frequently constitutional in children. It may be angular, lateral (scoliosis), or anteroposterior (kyphosis, lordosis).

spinal curvature, lateral Scoliosis.

spinal fusion SEE: under *fusion*.

spinalis (spī-nā'lĭs) [L.] A muscle attached to the spinal process of a vertebra.

spinate (spī'nāt) Having spines or shaped like a thorn.

spindle (spĭn'dl) [AS. *spinel*] **1.** A fusiform-shaped body. **2.** The mitotic spindle, a series of microtubules formed by the centrosomes during cell division; the spindle fibers pull the new sets of chromosomes toward opposite poles of the cell.

enamel s. A tubular hypomineralized structure extending a short distance from the dentinoenamel junction into enamel, seen in ground sections of teeth.

muscle s. A specialized sensory fiber within a muscle that is sensitive to tension and changes in length of the muscle. The central region consists of a nuclear bag with primary or annulospiral receptor endings and several nuclear chains with primary endings and secondary, or flower spray, endings. Each end consists of intrafusal muscle fibers innervated by gamma motor nerves. When these fibers contract, tension on the central bag and chains results in feedback to the muscle fibers outside the muscle spindle, causing them to contract.

neuromuscular s. A complex sensory nerve ending consisting of muscle fibers enclosed within a capsule and supplied by an afferent nerve fiber. It mediates proprioceptive sensations and reflexes.

neurotendinous s. A proprioceptive nerve ending found in a tendon, in muscle septa or sheaths, in muscle tissue, or at the junction of a muscle and tendon. SYN: *Golgi tendon organ*.

sleep s. Electroencephalographic waves with a frequency of 12 or 14 cycles per second that appear during sleep and may participate in sleep maintenance. They become less frequent with aging.

spine (spīn) **1.** A sharp process of bone. **2.** The spinal column, consisting of 33 vertebrae: seven cervical, 12 thoracic, five lumbar, five sacral, and four coccygeal. The bones of the sacrum and coccyx are ankylosed in adult life and counted as one each. SYN: *backbone*.

alar s. The spinous process of the sphenoid bone.

anterior nasal s. The projection formed by the anterior prolongation of the inferior border of the nasal notch of the maxilla.

bamboo s. In ankylosing spondylitis, a spinal column that on a radiograph resembles a bamboo stalk.

bifid s. SEE: *spina bifida cystica; spina bifida occulta*.

fracture of the s. SEE: under *fracture*.

iliac s. One of four spines of the ilium, i.e., the anterior and posterior inferior spines and the anterior and posterior superior spines.

ischial s. The spine of the ischium, a pointed eminence on its posterior border.

mandibular s. The small, tongue-shaped protuberance on the medial as-

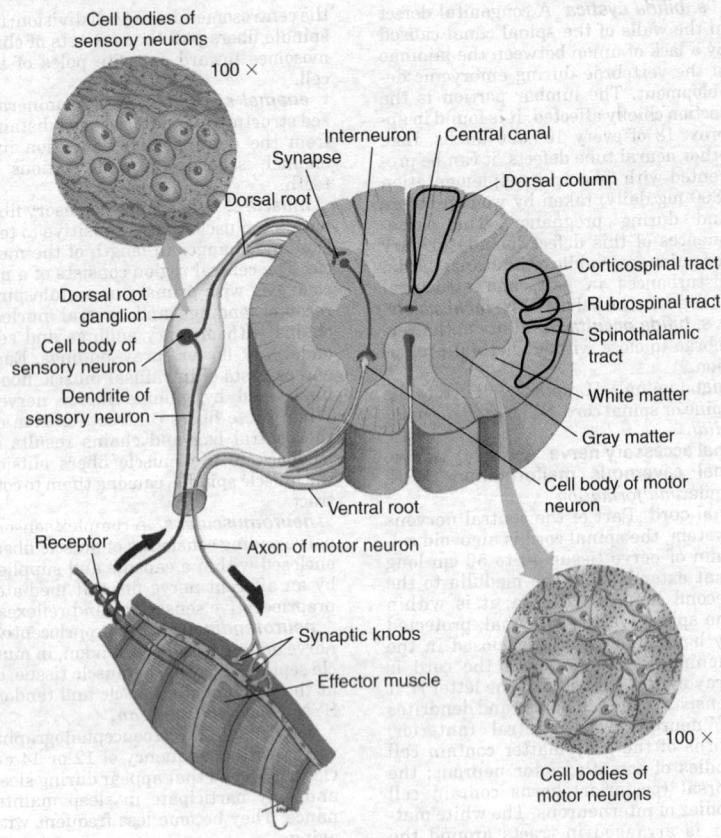

SPINAL CORD

Cross-section with nerve roots on left side and examples of tracts on right side

pect of the mandibular ramus near the mandibular foramen, to which the sphenomandibular ligament is attached.

    pharyngeal s. The point of attachment of the superior pharyngeal constrictor and its fibrous raphe on the inferior surface of the basilar part of the occipital bone.

    posterior nasal s. The spine formed by medial ends of the horizontal processes of the palatine bones at the very back of the hard palate.

    s. of pubis A prominent tubercle on the upper border of the pubis.

    s. of scapula An osseous plate projecting from the posterior surface of the scapula.

    spear tackler's s. SEE: *spear tackler's spine.*

    s. of sphenoid The spinous process of the greater sphenoid wing.

    typhoid s. An acute arthritis due to infection causing spinal ankylosis during or following typhoid fever.

spine arthroplasty device SEE: under *device.*

spinnbarkeit (spĭn'băr-kĭt)   [Ger.] ABBR: SBK. Evaluation of the elasticity of cervical mucus used to determine time of ovulation. The cervical secretion is aspirated and placed on a slide. SBK is measured by pulling upward on the secretion with a forceps. Before ovulation, there is no elasticity. On the day of ovulation, elasticity is good, measuring 12 to 24 cm or more. The day after ovulation, elasticity diminishes. Not all women have clear-cut SBK changes. Therefore, this test is used in conjunction with other signs of ovulation. SEE: *chart, basal temperature; ferning; mittelschmerz; mucorrhea.*

spinobulbar (spī'nō-bŭl'băr)   [" + Gr. *bulbos,* a bulb]   Pert. to the spinal cord and medulla oblongata.

spinocerebellar (spī'nō-sĕr-ĕ-bĕl'ăr)   [" + *cerebellum,* little brain]   Pert. to the spinal cord and cerebellum.

spinoglenoid (spī'nō-glĕn'oyd)   [" + Gr.

glene, socket, + *eidos,* form, shape]
Pert. to the spine of the scapula and the
glenoid cavity.

spinose (spī'nōs) [L. *spina,* thorn] Spinous.

spinotectal (spī"nō-tĕk'tăl) [" + *tectum,* roof] Pert. to the spinal cord and
the tectum, the dorsal portion (corpora
quadrigemina) of the midbrain.

spinous (spī'nŭs) [L. *spina,* thorn] Pert.
to or resembling a spine.

spinous process SEE: under *process.*

spiradenoma (spī"răd-ĕn-ō'mă) [" + "
+ *oma,* tumor] A benign tumor of the
sweat glands. SEE: *spiroma.*

spiral (spī'răl) [L. *spiralis*] Coiling
around a center like the thread of a
screw.

   Curschmann s. SEE: *Curschmann
spirals.*

spirillosis (spī-rĭl-ō'sĭs) [" + Gr. *osis,*
condition] A disease caused by the
presence of spirilla in the blood.

Spirillum (spī-rĭl'ŭm) [L., *spirillum,* little coil] A genus of spiral, motile bacteria of the family Spirillaceae and order Spirochaetales. They are found in
freshwater and saltwater.

   S. minus A species that infects rats
and mice. It causes one form of rat-bite
fever. It was formerly known as *S. minor.*

spirillum (spī-rĭl'ŭm, -rĭl'ă) *pl.* **spirilla**
[L., *spirillum,* little coil] A flagellated
aerobic bacterium with an elongated
spiral shape, of the genus *Spirillum.*
SEE: *bacteria* for illus.

spirit (spĭr'ĭt) [L. *spiritus,* breath] **1.** A
solution of essential or volatile liquid.
2. Any distilled or volatile liquid. **3.** An
alcoholic beverage. **4.** Mood; courage.
5. Soul.

spiritual distress Disruption in the life
principle that pervades a person's entire
being and that integrates and transcends one's biological and psychosocial
nature.

   risk for s.d. At risk for an altered
sense of integration with life and the
universe in which dimensions that tran-
scend and empower the self may be disrupted. SEE: *Nursing Diagnoses Appendix.*

spirituality (spĭr"ĭ-choo-ăl'ĭ-tē) An
awareness of the metaphysical, the religious, or the sublime. In practice, spirituality includes participation in organized religion, contemplation, meditation, prayer, reflection, and activities
fostering self-growth and connections
with others and with nature.

**spiritual well-being, readiness for en-
hanced** Ability to experience and integrate meaning and purpose in life
through connectedness with self, others,
art, music, literature, nature, or a power
greater than oneself. SEE: *Nursing Diagnoses Appendix.*

Spirochaeta (spī"rō-kē'tă) [Gr. *speira,*

coil, + *chaite,* hair] A genus of slender, spiral, motile bacteria of the family
Spirochaetaceae. The species are saprophytes in water and soil.

spirochete (spī'rō-kēt) Any member of
the order Spirochaetales. **spirochetal,**
adj.

spirochetemia (spī"rō-kē-tē'mē-ă) [" +
chaite, hair, + *haima,* blood] Spirochetes in the blood.

spirogram (spī'rō-grăm") [L. *spirare,* to
breathe, + Gr. *gramma,* something
written] A record made by a spirograph
or a spirometer, demonstrating lung
volumes and air flow.

spirograph (spī'rō-grăf) [" + Gr.
graphein, to write] A graphical record
of respiratory movements.

spiroma (spī-rō'mă) [" + *oma,* tumor]
Multiple, benign, cystic epithelioma of
the sweat glands. SEE: *spiradenoma.*

spirometer (spī-rŏm'ĕt-ĕr) [L. *spirare,* to
breathe, + Gr. *metron,* measure] An
apparatus used to measure lung volumes and airflow. The following are typical measurements made on adult patients by using the spirometer:
inspiratory reserve volume: the amount
that a subject can still inhale by special
effort after a normal inspiration; expiratory reserve volume: the volume of air
that can still be exhaled after a normal
exhalation; tidal volume: the volume of
air exhaled or inhaled during normal
breathing; vital capacity: the maximum
volume of air that can be exhaled after
a maximal inhalation; forced vital capacity or forced expiratory volume: the
air that can be exhaled during a maximal exhalation.

spirometra The plerocercoid larvae of
tapeworms, esp. those of the genera *Diphyllobothrium* and *Spirometra.*

spirometry (spī-rŏm'ĕ-trē) [L. *spirare,* to
breathe, + Gr. *metron,* measure]
Measurement of air flow and lung volumes. SEE: *pulmonary function test.*

   incentive s. Spirometry in which visual and vocal stimuli are given to the
patient to produce maximum effort during deep breathing. Incentive spirometry is used most often in postoperative
patients to prevent atelectasis. SEE: illus.

spissated (spĭs'ăt-ĕd) [L. *spissatus*] Inspissated.

spit (spĭt) [AS. *spittan*] **1.** Saliva. **2.** To
expectorate spittle.

spittle (spĭt'tl) [AS. *spatl*] Saliva.

spit tobacco SEE: under *tobacco.*

splanchn-, splanchno- Prefixes meaning
viscera or *splanchnic nerve.*

splanchnic (splăngk'nĭk) [Gr. *splanchni-
kos*] Pert. to the viscera.

splanchnicectomy (splăngk"nē-sĕk'tō-
mē) [Gr. *splanchnos,* viscus, + *ektome,* excision] Resection of the
splanchnic nerves.

splanchnicotomy (splăngk"nĭ-kŏt'ō-mē)

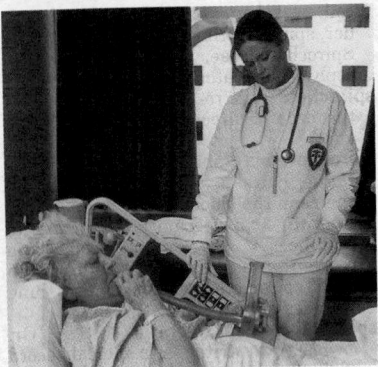

INCENTIVE SPIROMETER

[″ + *tome,* incision] Section of a splanchnic nerve.

splanchnocranium (splăngk″nō-krā′nē-ŭm) [″ + *kranion,* skull] Viscerocranium.

splatter, spatter (splat′ĕr, spat′ĕr) The airborne distribution of particles, e.g., during dental or surgical procedures.

⚠ To avoid exposure to potentially infectious agents or other hazardous particles during procedures in which splatter is anticipated, exposed personnel should wear protective equipment such as goggles, mask or faceshield, gowns, and gloves.

splayfoot (splā′foot) [ME. *splayen,* to spread out, + AS. *fot,* foot] Flatfoot.

spleen (splēn) [Gr. *splen*] A dark red, oval lymphoid organ in the upper left abdominal quadrant posterior and slightly inferior to the stomach; on the inferior side is the hilum, an indentation at which the splenic vessels and nerves enter or exit. The spleen is surrounded by an outer capsule of connective tissue from which strands of connective tissue (trabeculae) extend into the soft pulp (functional tissue), dividing the spleen into compartments.

The white pulp, composed of lymphocytes and follicles, forms sheaths around arterial vessels and collects in larger nodules containing germinal centers. The red pulp contains vascular sinuses and sinusoids with highly permeable walls, and spongelike splenic cords filled with macrophages and dendritic cells. The spleen is part of the mononuclear phagocytic system and its removal (splenectomy), though compensated for by the lymph nodes and liver, decreases immune function and may place the patient at increased risk for infection, esp. from *Streptococcus pneumoniae* and *Haemophilus influenzae*.

FUNCTION: In the embryo, the spleen forms both red and white blood cells; after birth, only lymphocytes are created except in severe anemia, when production of red blood cells may be reactivated. Blood enters via the splenic artery and passes through progressively smaller arterial vessels; foreign antigens are trapped in the white pulp, initiating proliferation of antigen-specific lymphocytes and antibodies. The arterioles terminate in the red pulp, where macrophages remove cell debris, microorganisms, and cells that are old, damaged, abnormal, or coated with antibody.

The vascular capacity of the spleen, 100 mL to 300 mL, is an average of 4% of the total blood, and the spleen may contain 30% of the total platelets. In stressful situations, sympathetic impulses stimulate constriction of the venous sinuses, forcing most of the splenic blood into circulation. If the spleen is enlarged (splenomegaly), its vascular capacity increases dramatically, and increased contact with macrophages may cause anemia, leukopenia, and thrombocytopenia. Removal of the spleen may be necessary in patients with thrombocytopenia. Many disorders cause splenomegaly, including portal hypertension (e.g., in cirrhosis), heart failure, and certain infections. Primary disorders of the spleen, however, are rare. SEE: *lymphatic system* for illus.; *asplenia syndrome; germinal* **center**.

accessory s. Splenic tissue found outside the main bulk of the organ, usually but not always within the peritoneal cavity. If the patient is asymptomatic, the accessory spleen may be found only as an incidental mass on an abdominal scan; alternatively, the condition may exacerbate certain illnesses (e.g., immune thrombocytopenic purpura).

floating s. An enlarged movable spleen that is not protected by the ribs. SYN: *splenectopia*.

sago s. A spleen having the appearance of grains of sago.

wandering s. A dislocated floating spleen.

splenectomy (splē-nek′tŏ-mē) [″ + *ektome,* excision] **1.** Surgical removal of the spleen. **2.** Obliteration of the spleen by trauma or illness, e.g., by infarction resulting from sickle cell anemia.

⚠ Because the spleen removes encapsulated bacteria from the bloodstream, its absence or removal increases the risk of many serious infections. To prevent life-threatening infections, all patients scheduled for splenectomy should be vaccinated against *Haemophilus influenzae, Neisseria meningococcus,* and

Streptococcus pneumoniae about 10 days before surgery.

PATIENT CARE: Preoperatively, the patient is prepared for open abdominal or laparoscopic surgery by agency/surgeon protocol, and postoperative care and concerns are explained. Blood or blood products are transfused to replace deficient blood elements. Symptoms and complications of underlying disorders are also treated.

After splenectomy, the patient should have an intravenous line and receive fluids, medications (including pain relievers), and blood products as prescribed. The patient should be helped to a comfortable position in bed by correctly aligning his or her body alignment. The abdominal assessment should include looking for abrasions or contusions, periumbilical ecchymosis, and abdominal distention, incisional bleeding, or infection or excessive drainage. Increases in the patient's abdominal girth may indicate postoperative blood loss into the abdominal cavity, bowel obstruction, or paralytic ileus. The abdomen should be auscultated for return or bowel sounds, palpated for areas of tenderness, pain, guarding, or rigidity, and percussed for hollow or dull sounds (hollowness indicates gaseous distention; dull sounds suggest intra-abdominal fluid, blood, or solid tissue). Repeat examinations of the patient should occur on a scheduled basis until postoperative stability is ensured. Fevers may suggest peritonitis; decreased urinary output, tachycardia, and hypotension may indicate third-spacing or bleeding. The patient should be assessed for restlessness, agitation, and disorientation and watched for subtle changes that indicate hypoxemia or inadequate organ perfusion. Nasogastric drainage via low or intermittent suction is administered as prescribed. Sequential laboratory studies include white blood cell counts, hemoglobin levels, serum chemistries, coagulation factors, and platelets. Significant changes from prior levels should be noted. Sudden or progressive decompensation of the patient's hemodynamic status may well necessitate reoperation. If a splenectomy patient becomes unstable, breathing should be supported with high-flow oxygen with a non−rebreather mask; and vascular access established and reinforced using a 16- or 18-gauge intravenous catheter; fluids should be administered by bolus to increase blood pressure, decrease heart rate, and increase urine output to 50 to 100 mL/hr. Blood products should be typed and cross-matched. Throughout his the hospitalization, the patient and family will require physical, emotional,

informational, and, in some cases, spiritual support and care. Discharge instructions should be reviewed with the patient, and a printed copy provided for reinforcement. Restrictions may be placed on heavy lifting, stretching, and sports activities for a period of 6 weeks to 6 months. Follow-up appointments should be arranged with the attending physician, surgeon, or primary health care provider as required. Postsplenectomy patients should wear a Medic Alert bracelet or pendant to alert future caregivers of their status.

splenic (splĕn′ĭk) [Gr. *splenikos*] **1.** Pert. to the spleen. **2.** Suffering with chronic disease of the spleen. **3.** Surly, fretful, impatient. SYN: *splenetic*.

splenic sinus Any of the vascular collecting channels that lead into the internal veins of the spleen. The microcirculation in the spleen is quite leaky. Some capillaries empty directly into the splenic sinuses, but others allow blood to percolate through the extracellular red pulp before it drains into the splenic sinuses and thence into the veins.

splenic vein SEE: under *vein*.

splenitis (splē-nī′tĭs) [″ + *itis*, inflammation] Inflammation of the spleen, usually as a result of infection.

ETIOLOGY: Typical causes may include viral (e.g., mononucleosis), bacterial (e.g., bartonellosis, Lyme disease), or fungal (e.g., actinomycoses) infections.

splenium (splē′nē-ŭm) [Gr. *splenion*, bandage] **1.** A compress or bandage. **2.** A structure resembling a bandaged part.

s. corporis callosi The thickened posterior end of the corpus callosum.

splenius (splē′nē-ŭs) A flat muscle on either side of the back of the neck and upper thoracic area. SEE: *muscle* for illus.

spleno-, splen- [Gr. *splēn*, spleen] Prefixes meaning *spleen*.

splenocolic (splē′nō-kŏl′ĭk) [″ + *kolon*, colon] Pert. to the spleen and colon or reference to a fold of peritoneum between the two viscera.

splenocyte (splē′nō-sīt″) [″ + ″] A monocyte found in the spleen or in splenic tissue.

splenomegaly (splē″nō-mē-gā′lē, -mĕg′ă-lē) [″ + *megas*, large] Enlargement of the spleen. Causes include portal hypertension, infections (such as leishmaniasis), autoimmune diseases, and blood disorders (lymphomas, leukemias, and myeloproliferative disorders). It is frequently associated with anemia, leukopenia, and/or thrombocytopenia. Splenomegaly may cause a sense of discomfort in the left upper quadrant of the abdomen, particularly after eating. SEE: *spleen*.

congestive s. Enlargement of the spleen caused by various types of venous congestion: splenic vein obstruction, systemic venous congestion (e.g., due to heart failure), or portal vein hypertension caused by cirrhosis of the liver. Blood flow through the spleen is slowed, increasing red blood cell destruction by macrophages (hypersplenism) and resulting in focal hemorrhages. SEE: *Banti syndrome*.

hemolytic s. Enlarged spleen associated with hemolytic anemia. The increased rigidity of red blood cell membranes results in their increased destruction as they attempt to move from splenic cords into the vascular sinuses. SEE: *spleen*.

splenopancreatic (splē″nō-păn″krē-ăt′ĭk) [″ + *pancreas*, pancreas] Rel. to the spleen and pancreas.

splenopexy (splē′nō-pĕk″sē) [″ + *pexis*, fixation] Artificial fixation of a movable spleen.

splenoportography (splē″nō-por-tŏg′ră-fē) [″ + L. *porta*, gate, + Gr. *graphein*, to write] Radiography of the spleen and portal vein after injection of a radiopaque contrast medium into the spleen.

splenorenal (splē″nō-rē′năl) Pert. to the spleen and kidney.

splenorenal shunt Anastomosis of the splenic vein to the renal vein to enable blood from the portal system to enter the general venous circulation; performed in cases of portal hypertension.

splenorrhaphy (splē-nor′ă-fē) [″ + *rhaphe*, seam, ridge] Suture of a wound of the spleen.

splice (splīs) To take two cut pieces and fasten them together; to link two cut segments of DNA.

spliceosome (splī′sē-ō-sōm) A multipart ribonucleoprotein complex within the nucleus of cells that splices exons and introns from premessenger RNA during the regulation of protein synthesis.

splint (splint) An appliance made of bone, wood, metal, plastics, composites, or plaster of Paris used for the fixation, union, or protection of an injured part of the body. It may be movable or immovable. SEE: illus.

air s. A lightweight splint used for immobilizing fractured or injured extremities. It is usually an inflatable cylinder, open at both ends, that becomes rigid when inflated, thus preventing the part confined in the cylinder from moving. SYN: *blow-up* **s.**; *inflatable* **s.**

⚠️ Because of the tendency for the air cast to straighten out the limb as it is inflated, this device should not be used to immobilize joint dislocations or fractures with gross displacement.

---

airplane s. An appliance usually used on ambulatory patients in the

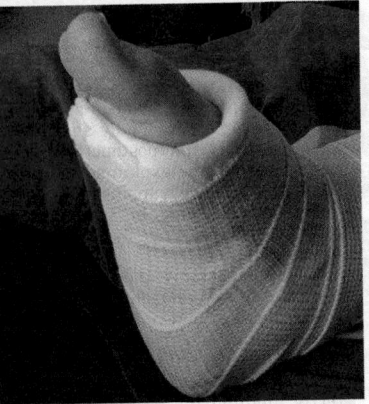

SPLINT

Patient with ankle fracture

treatment of fractures of the humerus. It takes its name from the elevated position in which it holds the arm suspended away from the body.

anchor s. A splint for fracture of the jaw, with metal loops fitting over the teeth and held together by a rod.

Balkan s. A splint used for continuous extension in a fracture of the femur.

banjo traction s. A splint made out of a steel rod bent to resemble the shape of a banjo. It provides anchor points for attachments to the fingers in the treatment of contractures and fractures of the fingers.

Bennett double-ring s. SEE: *Bennett double-ring splint.*

blow-up s. Air **s.**

Bond s. A splint used for fracture of the lower end of the radius.

Bowlby s. SEE: *Bowlby splint.*

box s. A splint used for fracture below the knee.

Cabot s. A splint composed of a metal structure placed posterior to the thigh and leg.

Carter intranasal s. A steel bridge with wings connected by a hinge, used for operation of a depressed nasal bridge.

coaptation s. A small splint adjusted about a fractured part to prevent overriding of the fragments of bones. It is usually covered by a longer splint for fixation of entire section.

cock-up s. A static splint to maintain the wrist in either extension or flexion.

cylinder s. A splint constructed around an injured bone to reduce the potential for flexion contractures.

Denis Browne s. A splint to treat talipes equinovarus (clubfoot), consisting of a curved bar attached to the soles of a pair of high-topped shoes. It is often used in late infancy and applied at bedtime. Its use generally follows casting and manipulation to reduce the deformity.

dorsal blocking s. A splint constructed on the back of the hand to inhibit full extension of one or more of the finger joints and/or the wrist.

Dupuytren s. SEE: under *Dupuytren, Baron Guillaume.*

dynamic s. A splint that assists in movements initiated by the patient. SYN: *functional* **s.**

finger s. A padded strip of malleable metal or plastic used to immobilize a fractured finger. As an alternative, the injured finger is often "buddy taped" to an adjoining finger for support.

flail arm s. ABBR: FAS. An upper-extremity orthotic device to provide support and limited function, consisting of a shoulder-operated harness, a volar supporting structure made of low-temperature thermoplastic material, and a terminal device that allows the arm to grasp or stabilize objects.

functional s. Dynamic **s.**

Gibson walking s. A splint that is a modification of a Thomas splint.

Gordon s. A side splint used for the arm and hand in a Colles fracture.

inflatable s. Air **s.**

interdental s. A rigid or flexible device or compound used to support, protect, or immobilize teeth that have been loosened, replanted, fractured, or subjected to surgical procedures.

Jones nasal s. A splint used for the fracture of nasal bones.

Levis s. A splint of perforated metal extending from below the elbow to the end of the palm, shaped to fit the arm and hand.

mandibular advancement s. A device to maintain an open airway in patients who suffer partial upper airway collapse during sleep. The splint is placed in the mouth at bedtime.

McIntire s. A splint shaped like a double inclined plane, used as a posterior splint for the leg and thigh.

occlusal s. A splint fashioned to cover the incisal and occlusal surfaces of a dental arch to stabilize the teeth, treat bruxism, or facilitate proper occlusal positioning.

opponens s. A splint designed to maintain the thumb in a position to oppose the other fingers.

padded board s. A splint of wood, typically padded on one side and covered with plastic or cloth, to which an injured extremity can be fastened to immobilize it.

permanent fixed s. A nonremovable splint firmly attached to an abutment used to stabilize or immobilize teeth. A fixed bridge may serve as a permanent fixed splint for such support.

resting hand s. Resting pan **s.**

resting pan s. A splint designed to position the fingers and stabilize the hand in a functional position with the fingers held in opposition. SYN: *resting hand* **s.**

static s. Any orthosis that lacks movable parts and is used for positioning, stability, protection, or support.

Stromeyer s. SEE: *Stromeyer splint.*

sugar tong s. A splint commonly used instead of a cast to immobilize a Colles fracture after it has been reduced. The splint permits the affected arm to swell without being compressed within the confines of the cast yet maintain its alignment. Follow-up diagnostic images of the fracture are typically obtained 5 to 7 days after placement of the splint to ensure that adequate reduction of the fracture is maintained.

temporary removable s. Any of a variety of splints used for temporary or intermittent support and stabilization of the teeth.

tenodesis s. A splint fabricated to allow pinch and grasp movements through use of wrist extensors. SYN: *wrist-driven flexor hinge hand* **s.**

Thomas s. SEE: *Thomas splint.*

traction s. A splint that provides continual traction to a midshaft lower extremity fracture.

vacuum s. A negative-pressure splint to immobilize the extremities or torso after an injury. It may be used to safely transport the injured person. The splint consists of a nylon appliance filled with Styrofoam-like beads. The appliance is fitted around the injured body part and air is removed using a vacuum pump. As air is removed, the appliance conforms to the body part without straightening the limb.

⚠️ Distal neurovascular function must be monitored after splint application. If decreased circulation or neurological involvement is noted, the splint must be loosened immediately.

Volkmann s. SEE: *Volkmann, Richard von.*

wrist-driven flexor hinge hand s. Tenodesis **s.**

splinter (splĭn′tĕr) [MD. *splinte,* a wedge] **1.** A fragment from a fractured bone. **2.** A slender, sharp piece of material piercing or embedded in the skin or subcutaneous tissue.

splinter hemorrhage SEE: under *hemorrhage.*

splinting (splĭnt′ĭng) **1.** Fixation of a dislocation or fracture with a splint. Splints are also used to help support weak joints, to assist actively with functional movement, to immobilize to promote healing, and to protect from injury and deformity. **2.** Involuntary tensing of muscles to limit the pain that results from moving them or rubbing them over inflamed, internal body parts.

split (split) [D. *splitten,* to divide] **1.** A longitudinal fissure. **2.** Characterized by a deep fissure.

split-brain surgery SEE: under *surgery.*

split ejaculate In sperm analysis, the separation of the first drops of ejaculated semen from the rest of the ejaculate. The earliest ejaculated fluid contains the highest concentration of spermatozoa. Latter ejaculate contains relatively more seminal fluid.

split foot SEE: under *foot.*

split-mixed insulin dosing (split'mikst') An insulin regimen for diabetic patients in which long- and short-acting insulin doses are given two or more times a day.

PATIENT CARE: A typical regimen divides the total daily dose of insulin by giving two thirds of the daily requirement in the morning and one third in the evening. The morning dose consists of two thirds of a long-acting agent and one third of an immediate or short-acting insulin or insulin analogue. The evening insulin dose is divided equally between long- and rapid-acting insulins. The evening dose is sometimes divided into two separate injections, with the rapid-acting insulin given before the evening meal and the long-acting insulin given at bedtime.

split-thickness (split'thik'nĕss) Pert. to a graft consisting of the epidermis and part of the dermis.

splitting (split'ing) **1.** In chemistry, the breaking up of complex molecules into two or more simpler compounds. **2.** A defense mechanism found in some children and some patients with personality disorders, in which people or things are represented as being either very good (because they support one's desires or behaviors) or very bad (because they are obstructive to those desires or behaviors).

SpO₂ The saturation of arterial blood with oxygen as measured by pulse oximetry, expressed as a percentage. SEE: *oximetry.*

spoken word recognition The ability to hear the speech of others and to recognize the sounds as words rather than as some other auditory stimuli.

spoligotyping (spŏl″ĭ-gō-tīp′ĭng) [Fm. *sp(acer) oligtyping*] The use of the polymerase chain reaction to identify pathogens, such as *Mycobacterium tuberculosis,* in laboratory specimens. It relies on the detection of unique spans of repeated DNA sequences found between the active genes of the pathogen. Culture-based methods of identifying mycobacteria are slow, often taking as long as 4 to 6 weeks to identify microorganisms in sputum or blood. DNA fingerprinting requires considerable tech-

nical expertise. Spoligotyping is simpler, more economical, and a more efficient means of identifying slowly growing microorganisms. SYN: *spacer oligotyping.*

spondee (spon'dē″) [L. *spondeus,* fr Gr. *spondeios,* pert. to or used in a libation, fr *spondē,* libation] A two-syllable word that receives an equal or nearly equal accent on each syllable, e.g., toothbrush, football. Spondaic words are use in audiometry to test for acuity and to establish an auditory baseline **spondaic** (spon-dā″ik), *adj.*

spondylarthritis (spŏn″dĭl-ăr-thrī′tĭs) [″ + *arthron,* joint, + *itis,* inflammation] Inflammation of the joints of the vertebrae; arthritis of the spine. SEE: *spondylitis.*

spondylitic (spŏn″dĭ-lĭt′ĭk) [″ + *itis,* inflammation] **1.** A person with spondylitis. **2.** Pert. to spondylitis.

spondylitis (spon-dĭ-līt′ĭs) [*spondylo- + -itis*] Inflammation of one or more vertebrae.

ankylosing s. ABBR: AS. A chronic, progressive, inflammatory disorder that, unlike other rheumatological diseases, affects men more often than women. It involves primarily the joints between articular processes, costovertebral joints, and sacroiliac joints, and occasionally the iris or the heart valves. Bilateral sclerosis of sacroiliac joints is a diagnostic sign. Those affected have a high incidence of a specific human leukocyte antigen (HLA-B27), which may predispose them to the disease. Changes occurring in joints are similar to those seen in rheumatoid arthritis. Ankylosis may occur, giving rise to a stiff back (poker spine). Nonsteroidal anti-inflammatory drugs and physical therapy are the primary forms of treatment. SYN: *Marie-Strümpell s.; rheumatoid s.; Strümpell disease; Strümpell-Marie disease.*

s. deformans Spondylitis resulting in the outgrowth of bonelike deposits on the vertebrae, which may fuse and cause rigid and distorted spine.

hypertrophic s. Spondylitis in which the bodies of vertebrae hypertrophy. It occurs in most people over 50. Bony changes such as facet degeneration and the formation of bone spurs commonly occur.

Kümmell s. A traumatic spondylitis in which symptoms do not appear until some time after the injury.

Marie-Strümpell s. Ankylosing s.

rheumatoid s. Ankylosing s.

tuberculous s. Pott disease. SEE: under *Pott, John Percivall.*

spondylo-, spondyl- [Gr. *spondylos,* vertebra] Prefixes meaning *vertebra.*

spondylolisthesis (spŏn″dĭ-lō-lis-thē′sĭs) [*spondylo- +* Gr. *olisthesis,* a slipping] Any forward slipping of one vertebra on the one below it. Predisposing factors include spondylolysis, degeneration, elongated pars, elongated pedicles, and birth defects in the spine such as spina bifida. It may occur secondary to fracture of the pars interarticularis. SYN: *spondyloptosis*. SEE: *retrospondylolisthesis*.

spondylolisthetic (spŏn″dĭ-lō-lĭs-thĕt′ĭk) Pert. to spondylolisthesis.

spondylolysis (spŏn″dĭ-lŏl′ĭ-sĭs) [″ + *lysis*, dissolution] The breaking down of a vertebral structure.

spondylopathy (spŏn″dĭl-ŏp′ă-thē) [″ + *pathos*, disease, suffering] Any disorder of the vertebrae.

spondyloptosis (spŏn″dĭ-lō-tō′sĭs) [″ + *ptosis*, a dropping] Spondylolisthesis.

spondylosis (spŏn″dĭ-lō′sĭs) [Gr. *spondylos*, vertebra, + *osis*, condition] Ankylosis of the vertebrae.

   cervical s. Degenerative arthritis, osteoarthritis, of the cervical or lumbar vertebrae and related tissues. It may cause pressure on nerve roots with subsequent pain or paresthesia in the extremities. Cervical spondylosis that can also affect the lumbar spine.

   rhizomelic s. Ankylosis interfering with movements of the hips and shoulders.

sponge (spŭnj) [Gr. *sphongos*, sponge] **1.** An elastic, porous mass forming the internal skeleton of certain marine animals; or a rubber or synthetic substance that resembles a sponge in properties and appearance. SYN: *spongia*. **2.** An absorbent pad made of gauze and cotton used to absorb fluids and blood in surgery or to dress wounds. **3.** Short term for sponge bath. **4.** To moisten, clean, cool, or wipe with a sponge.

   contraceptive s. A sponge impregnated with a spermicide. It is used intravaginally during sexual intercourse as a method of contraception. SEE: illus. SYN: *spermicidal s.* SEE: *contraceptive*.

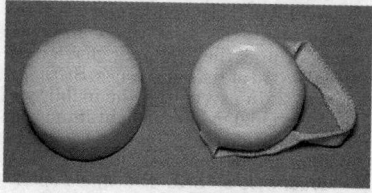

CONTRACEPTIVE SPONGE

   gauze s. A sterile pad made of absorbent material. It is used during surgery and in wound dressing materials.

   gelatin s. A spongy protein derived from animal collagen. It can be used to arrest local bleeding intraoperatively, to embolize blood vessels, or to form a protective coating around recently manipulated tissues.

   spermicidal s. Contraceptive **s.**

spongia (spŏn′jē-ă) [Gr. *sphongos*, sponge] Sponge.

spongiform (spŭn′jĭ-form) [Gr. *sphongos*, sponge, + L. *forma*, shape] Having the appearance or quality of a sponge. SYN: *spongioid*.

spongio-, spongi- [Gr. *spongia*, sponge] Prefixes meaning *sponge*.

spongioblast (spŭn′jē-ō-blăst) [″ + *blastos*, germ] A cell that develops with the embryonic neural tube. It is a precursor of ependymal cells and astrocytes.

spongioblastoma (spŭn″jē-ō-blăs-tō′mă) [″ + ″ + *oma*, tumor] A glioma of the brain derived from spongioblasts.

spongy (spŭn′jē) Resembling a sponge in texture.

sponsor (spon′sŏr) [L. fr. *spondere*, to promise] **1.** A mentor or supporter. **2.** An individual or an organization providing the financial backing for a clinic, hospital, medical mission, professorship, or research study.

spontaneous (spŏn-tā′nē-ŭs) [L.] Occurring unaided or without apparent cause; voluntary.

spontaneous breathing test ABBR: SBT. Temporary cessation of mechanical ventilation while a patient remains intubated with a T-tube in place. An SBT is said to be successful when a patient maintains an oxygen saturation of 88% or more; with an FIO_2 of 50% or less, f/VT (rapid shallow breathing index) < 105, and a positive end-expiratory pressure (PEEP) of 8.0 cm of water or less. When this occurs, the patient may be safely extubated. SYN: *spontaneous breathing trial*.

spontaneous intracranial hypotension SEE: under *hypotension*.

spoon [AS. *spon*, a chip] An instrument consisting of a small bowl on a handle used in scooping out tissues or tumors or in measuring quantities.

sporadic (spŏ-rad′ik) [Gr. *sporadikos*, scattered, strewn] Occurring irregularly, alone, or without linkage to other events.

sporangiophore (spŏ-răn′jē-ō-for) [Gr. *sporos*, seed, + *angeion*, vessel, + *phoros*, a bearer] In microbiology, the supporting stalk for a spore sac of certain fungi.

sporangium (spŏ-răn′jē-ŭm) A sac enclosing spores, seen in certain fungi.

spore (spor) [Gr. *sporos*, seed] **1.** A cell produced by fungi for reproduction. Spores may remain dormant yet viable for months. Cooking destroys spores, but pathogenic spores are usually inhaled rather than ingested. **2.** A resistant cell produced by bacteria to withstand extreme heat or cold or dehydration; such spores may remain viable for decades. Important spore-forming bacteria include the causative agents of tetanus, botulism, and gas gangrene. The spores are heat resistant and can survive an hour of boiling, but they can be destroyed by steam under pressure (i.e., autoclave). **3.** An airborne particle (fungal, bacterial, or derived from mosses or ferns) that may trigger an allergic response when inhaled. **4.** A stage in the life cycle of some parasitic protozoa that contains infective sporozoites.

spore trap A device for sampling ambient air to determine the presence and concentration of circulating aeroallergens.

sporiferous (spor-ĭf′ĕr-ŭs) [″ + L. *ferre*, to bear] Producing spores.

spork (spork) An adapted utensil for persons with limited upper extremity function. The distal end may swivel to allow food to remain level as a result of gravitational force. The bowl end is shaped like a spoon but has modified tines, like a fork.

sporoblast (spor′ō-blăst) [″ + *blastos*, germ] The structure within the oocyst of certain parasitic protozoa (*Eimeria* and *Isospora*) that gives rise to a sporocyst and eventually a spore.

sporocyst (spor′ō-sĭst) [″ + *kystis*, sac] **1.** Any sac containing spores or reproductive cells. **2.** A sac secreted around a sporoblast by certain protozoa before spore production. **3.** A stage in the life cycle of a trematode worm usually found in the tissues of the first intermediate host, a mollusk. It develops from a miracidium and is essentially a germinal sac containing germ cells. It gives rise to daughter sporocysts or rediae.

sporogenesis (spor″ō-jĕn′ĕ-sĭs) [Gr. *sporos*, seed, + *genesis*, generation, birth] The production or formation of spores. SYN: *sporogeny; sporogony*.

sporogenic (spor″ō-jĕn′ĭk) [″ + *gennan*, to produce] Having the ability of developing into spores.

sporogenous (spor-ŏj′ĕ-nŭs) [″ + *gennan*, to produce] Pert. to sporogenesis.

sporogony (spor-ŏg′ō-nē) [″ + *goneia*, generation] Sporogenesis.

sporophore (spor′ō-for) [″ + *phoros*, bearing] The spore-bearing portion of an organism.

sporophyte (spor′ō-fīt) [″ + *phyton*, plant] The spore-bearing stage of a plant exhibiting alternation of generations.

sporoplasm (spor′ō-plăzm) [″ + LL. *plasma*, form, mold] The cytoplasm of spores.

Sporothrix (spor′ō-thriks″) A genus of fungi of the family Moniliaceae (Ophiostomataceae).

    S. schenckii The causative agent of sporotrichosis.

sporotrichosis (spŏ-rah″trĭk-ō′sĭs, spor″ō-trĭk-ō′) [Gr. *sporos*, seed + *trichosis*] A chronic granulomatous infection usually of the skin and superficial lymph node, marked by the formation of abscesses, nodules, and ulcers and caused by the fungus *Sporothrix schenckii*. SYN: *peat moss disease; rose gardener's disease; rose-handler's disease*.

Sporozoa (spor″ō-zō′ă) [″ + *zoon*, animal] A class of parasitic protozoa of the phylum Apicomplexa (apical microlobule complex), kingdom Protista. The mature forms lack a means of self-locomotion. Important genera are *Plasmodium*, *Toxoplasma*, *Cryptosporidium*, *Microsporidia*, and *Isospora*.

sporozoan (spor″ō-zō′ăn) A protozoon belonging to the group formerly called Sporozoa.

sporozoite (spor″ō-zō′īt) [″ + *zoon*, animal] An elongated sickle-shaped cell that develops from a sporoblast within the oocyst in the life cycle of malaria. Upon bursting of the oocyst within a mosquito, sporozoites are released into the body cavity and make their way to the salivary gland. They are introduced into human blood by a mosquito and almost immediately enter liver cells, where they go through two schizogonic divisions and then reenter the bloodstream and infect erythrocytes.

sport [ME. *sporten*, to divert] Mutation.

sports medicine SEE: under *medicine*.

sports vision SEE: under *vision*.

sporulation (spor-ū-lā′shŭn) [L. *sporula*, little spore] **1.** The production of spores, a method of reproduction in fungi, mosses, and ferns. **2.** Bacterial production of spores, resistant forms that can withstand extremes of heat and cold, and dehydration.

spot (spot) **1.** A small surface area differing in appearance from its surroundings. SYN: *macula*. **2.** Randomly collected, as in urine specimen.

    ash-leaf s. White macules found on the trunk and extremities of persons with tuberous sclerosis.

    Bitot s. SEE: *Bitot spots*.

    blind s. 1. Physiological scotoma situated 15° to the outside of the visual fixation point; the point where the optic nerve enters the eye (optic disk), a region devoid of rods and cones. SEE: *scotoma*. **2.** In psychiatry, the inability of an individual to have insight into his or her own personality.

    blue s. Mongolian **s.**

    Brushfield s. SEE: *Brushfield spot*.

    cherry-red s. A red spot occurring on the retina in children with Tay-Sachs disease. SYN: *Tay s.*

    cold s. An area on a nuclear medicine scan in which no radioactive tracer is taken up, indicative of nonfunctioning tissue in a gland or other structure.

    corneal s. Leukoma.

    cotton-wool s. A tiny infarct in the retina, present in hypertension, diabetes mellitus, bacterial endocarditis, and other diseases.

focal s. The area on the x-ray tube target that is bombarded with electrons to produce x-radiation.

Fordyce s. SEE: *Fordyce disease.*

genital s. The area on the nasal mucosa that tends to bleed during menstruation. SEE: *vicarious* **menstruation.**

hematocystic s. Any of the focal red marks seen on esophageal varices. They consist of aneurysms of the wall of the dilated blood vessel. Their presence increases the likelihood that the varix may bleed.

histo s. Scarring of the macula found in those infected with *Histoplasma capsulatum.*

hot s. **1.** An area on the surface of the skin that, when stimulated, experiences a sensation of warmth. **2.** In a nuclear medicine scan, a region of the image that shows an abnormally high concentration of injected isotope. **3.** Any location that has been radioactively contaminated. **4.** In radiation oncology, a tissue region that is exposed to much more radiation than neighboring tissues.

hypnogenic s. Hypnogenic **zone.**

Koplik s. SEE: *Koplik spot.*

liver s. A popular term for a pigmentary skin discoloration, usually in yellow-brown patches. SEE: *Lentigo senilis.*

milk s. A dense area of macrophages in the omentum.

mongolian s. Any of the blue or mulberry-colored spots usually located in the sacral region. It may be present at birth in Asian, American Indian, black, and Southern European infants and usually disappears during childhood. SYN: *blue s.* SEE: illus.

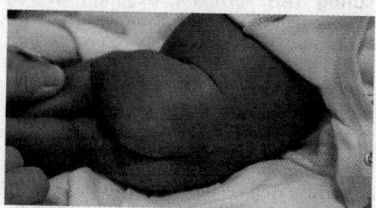

MONGOLIAN SPOTS

rose s. Rose-colored maculae occurring on the abdomen or loins in typhoid fever.

Roth s. SEE: *Roth spots.*

ruby s. Cherry **angioma.**

Soemmering s. SEE: under *Soemmering, Samuel T. von.*

Tardieu s. SEE: *Tardieu spot.*

white s. Light-colored, elevated areas of various sizes occurring on the ventricular surface of the anterior leaflet of the mitral valve in endocarditis.

yellow s. ABBR: y.s. Macula (3).

spot compression SEE: under *compression.*

spotted fever SEE: under *fever.*

spotting The appearance of blood-tinged discharge from the vagina, usually between menstrual periods or at the onset of labor.

spouse **1.** A partner in marriage. **2.** A life partner. **spousal,** *adj.*

spp *species* (plural).

sprain (sprān) [O.Fr. *espraindre,* to wring] Trauma to ligaments that causes pain and disability, depending on the degree of injury to the ligaments. In the most severe sprain, ligaments are completely torn. The ankle joint is the most often sprained. SEE: table; *fracture; strain.*

SYMPTOMS: Pain may be accompanied by heat, discoloration, and localized swelling in the affected area. Moderate to severe sprains are marked by joint laxity, reduced range of motion, and limitation of function. When the sprained ligament is contiguous with the joint capsule (e.g., anterior talofibular ligament, medial collateral ligament), swelling occurs in the acute stage. When the sprain involves other intracapsular or extracapsular ligaments (e.g., calcaneofibular ligament, anterior cruciate ligament), swelling is slight or absent in the acute stage and progressively increases.

DIAGNOSIS: Diagnostic imaging of the joint is often indicated to rule out an avulsion fracture of the ligament's attachment, or other associated fracture

TREATMENT: The affected part should be treated initially with ice or other cooling agents to limit inflammation and hypoxic injury. Circumferential compression, in the form of an elastic wrap, should be applied to the joint and the limb elevated to reduce swelling. Joint range of motion should be restricted to patient tolerance through the use of immobilization devices, crutches, or both. Analgesics and nonsteroidal anti-inflammatory medications may be administered for pain and swelling. In the chronic stage of the injury, massage, intermittent compression, and muscle contractions can be used to reduce swelling.

acromioclavicular s. A sprain to the acromioclavicular and coracoclavicular

Grading System for Sprains

Grade I	Stretching of the ligament without tearing
Grade II	Stretching of the ligament with incomplete tearing
Grade III	Complete tearing of the ligament (also called a rupture)

ligaments, commonly caused by a fall on an outstretched arm or a blow directly to the shoulder. SYN: *acromioclavicular* **separation**; *shoulder* **separation**.

s. of ankle Trauma to the ligaments of the ankle and foot, possibly involving tendon injury, but without an avulsion. Sprains of the lateral ligaments (most commonly the anterior talofibular ligament) account for approx. 90% of all ankle sprains. SEE: *Nursing Diagnoses Appendix*.

TREATMENT: SEE: *sprain* for treatment.

⚠ Ice should not be applied directly to the foot and ankle in patients who are elderly or who have cold allergy or circulatory insufficiency.

s. of back Overstretching of the spinal ligaments, often involving the surrounding muscles and spinal structures. Small fractures of the vertebrae are often associated.

TREATMENT: Treatment includes superficial moist heat and rest. If muscle spasm is present, muscle relaxants, nonsteroidal anti-inflammatory drugs, or both, may be prescribed. After the acute symptoms have subsided, strengthening and flexibility programs are prescribed.

⚠ If back pain develops after acute trauma, or if the patient has a history of cancer, the patient should not be moved until the possibility of a fracture has been ruled out. Persons with a history of back pain and fever or back pain and injection drug use should be evaluated for spinal epidural abscess.

s. of foot Trauma to the ligaments of the foot not involving the ankle.

high ankle s. Syndesmotic ankle **s.**

syndesmotic ankle s. Damage to the ligamentous structures of the distal tibiofibular syndesmotic joint, resulting from dorsiflexion or external rotation of the talus within the ankle mortise, or both, which in turn causes spreading of the joint. The distal tibiofibular syndesmosis is formed by the anterior tibiofibular ligament, the interosseous membrane, and the posterior tibiofibular ligament. SYN: *high ankle s.*

ETIOLOGY: The rate of syndesmotic ankle sprains may be increased when athletes are participating on artificial surfaces, because of the increased friction between the shoe and playing surface.

SYMPTOMS: Patients may describe pain along the fibula, just superior to the lateral malleolus, that worsens during dorsiflexion or external rotation of the talus, or both.

spray [MD. *spraeyen*, to sprinkle]
1. A jet of fine medicated vapor applied to a diseased part or discharged into the air. **2.** A pressurized container. SYN: *atomizer*. **3.** To discharge fluid in a fine stream.

pepper s. A chemical derived from chili peppers (capsaicin) that irritates the eyes, mucous membranes, and bronchi. It is commonly used by law enforcement personnel against individuals to help subdue and apprehend them.

spreader (spred′ĕr) **1.** An instrument for distributing something evenly over a tissue or culture plate. **2.** A bacterial culture that, as it grows, spreads over the surface of the culture medium. **3.** A surgical instrument that divides and holds apart tissues or bones.

bladder-neck s. An instrument used to expose the bladder neck and prostatic cavity during a retropubic prostatectomy.

finger s. An orthotic device, usually made of foam rubber, for holding the thumb and fingers extended while maintaining the normal arches of the hand. SYN: *finger separator*.

root canal s. In dentistry, a pointed instrument of variable diameter and taper, used to apply force to the material used in filling a root canal.

spreading (spred′ing) [AS. *spraedan*, to strew] The extension of a bacterial culture on a growth medium.

spreading factor SEE: under *factor*.

Sprengel deformity (shpreng′ĕl) [Otto Gerhard Karl Sprengel, Ger. surgeon, 1852–1915.] Congenital upward displacement (lack of descent) of the scapula.

spring [AS. *springan*, to jump] **1.** The season of the year that comes after winter and before summer. SYN: *vernal*. **2.** The quick movement of a body to its original position through its elasticity.

spring fever SEE: under *fever*.

sprout [ME. *spruten*] The new, germinated growth from a root, seed, or tuber.

alfalfa s. The initial growth from the germinated seeds of the legume alfalfa, eaten as a source of vegetable protein.

spruce (sproos) Any of the evergreen coniferous trees and shrubs of the genus *Picea* (family Piceaceae), widely found in the Northern Hemisphere. Known side effects of exposure to spruce dusts (e.g., in sawmill workers) include an increased incidence of reactive airways diseases such as asthma. The gum of the spruce is used occasionally in complementary and alternative medicine as an expectorant.

sprue (sproo) **1.** In dentistry, the wax, metal, or plastic used to form the aperture(s) through which molten gold or resin will pass to make a casting; also, the part of the casting that later fills the sprue hole. **2.** A disease of the intestinal tract characterized by malabsorption, weight loss, abdominal distention, bloating, diarrhea, and steatorrhea.

celiac s. Celiac disease.

collagenous s. Infiltration of the small intestine by collagen fibers. Clinically, the disease is similar to severe celiac sprue. It is resistant to treatment with a gluten-free diet and immunosuppressive drugs.

nontropical s. Celiac disease.

tropical s. A disease endemic in Southeast Asia and the Caribbean, marked by diarrhea, nutrient malabsorption, anemia, fatigue, malnutrition, and edema It is similar pathologically to celiac sprue although the involvement of the small intestine is often more extensive. Folate, iron, and vitamin B_{12} deficiencies are common findings. The administration of folic acid and tetracyclines for 6 to 12 months provides effective treatment. SYN: *Hill diarrhea*.

spud (spŭd) [ME. *spudde*, short knife] A short, flattened, spadelike blade to dislodge a foreign substance.

Spumavirus (spū´mă-vī˝rŭs) A genus of retroviruses occasionally transmitted to humans after exposure to the blood or body fluids of infected animals (e.g., apes, cats, or cattle).

spur (spŭr) **1.** A sharp or pointed projection. **2.** A sharp horny outgrowth of the skin.

bone s. Exostosis.

calcaneal s. An exostosis of the heel, often painful and resulting in disability. SYN: *heel s.*

s. cell An erythrocyte with spikes caused by a membrane deformity. Spur cells are often seen in persons with alcoholic cirrhosis and congenital abetalipoproteinemia.

femoral s. A spur sometimes present on the medial and underside of the neck of the femur.

heel s. Calcaneal **s.**

scleral s. Scleral fibers bordered anteriorly by the canal of Schlemm and the trabecular meshwork and posteriorly by the ciliary muscle fibers.

spurious (spū´rē-ŭs) [L. *spurius*] Not true or genuine; adulterated; false.

Spurling maneuver, Spurling test (spŭr´ling) Extending the patient's neck, moving the head to the affected side, and applying an axial load to the cervical spine to determine if symptoms of paresthesia or pain intensify. The maneuver is used in the physical assessment of patients with possible cervical nerve root compression. This test is not performed until the possibility of a cervical spine fracture or dislocation has been ruled out.

sputum (spū´tŭm) *pl.* **sputa** [L.] Mucus expelled from the lung by coughing. It may contain a variety of materials from the respiratory tract, including in some instances cellular debris, mucus, blood, pus, caseous material, and/or microorganisms.

CONDITIONS: A wide variety of illnesses, including typical and atypical pneumonias, tuberculosis, cancers of the lungs or bronchi, reactive airway disease, and occupational diseases of the lungs can be diagnosed with gram staining or culturing of sputum, cytological examination of sputum, or the use of special stains and microscopic techniques.

⚠️ The color or thickness of sputum is not a reliable diagnosis of an illness.

bloody s. Hemoptysis.

currant jelly s. Thick sputum mixed with clotted blood, typically seen in patients with pneumonia caused by *Klebsiella pneumoniae*.

nummular s. Sputum laden with round, coin-shaped solids.

prune juice s. Thin, reddish, bloody sputum.

rusty s. Blood-tinged purulent sputum sometimes seen in patients with pneumococcal pneumonia.

sputum cytology SEE: under *cytology*.

sputum specimen A specimen of mucus from the lungs expectorated through the mouth or obtained via tracheal suctioning with an in-line trap or bronchoscope. Sputum specimens are used to 1. identify the microorganism responsible for lung infections; 2. identify cancer cells shed by lung tumors; 3. aid in the diagnosis and management of occupational lung diseases. SEE: *postural drainage*.

PATIENT CARE: The procedure for coughing up a sputum sample is explained to the patient. The patient should increase fluid intake the evening prior to collection (unless otherwise restricted), brush his or her teeth, remove dentures, and gargle and rinse the mouth with water to remove food particles. These directions may decrease the contamination of the specimen by bacteria in the mouth or the throat. Using the sterile collection container provided, the patient is instructed to take three deep breaths, then force a deep cough and expectorate into a sterile screw-top container. The specimen should be collected in the early morning before ingesting food or drink if possible. The nurse or respiratory therapist examines the specimen to differentiate between sputum and saliva, documents its characteristics (color, viscosity, odor) and volume, and records the date and time the specimen went to the laboratory and the reason the specimen was taken. Five to 10 mL of sputum is typically needed for laboratory analysis. A specimen will be rejected by the laboratory if it contains excessive numbers of epithelial cells from the mouth or throat or if it fails to show adequate numbers of neutrophils on gram staining. If the patient cannot cough up a specimen, the respiratory therapist can use sputum induction techniques such as heated aerosol (nebulization), followed in some instances by postural drainage and percussion. More invasive means of obtaining a sputum specimen are with suction or bronchoscopy. These techniques are used in intubated patients, and in those from whom an uncontaminated specimen is required.

The following procedures should be followed to obtain a specimen by suctioning: the operator should put on sterile gloves, and a face shield, mask, and gown to avoid exposure to airborne pathogens during the procedure; suction equipment, specimen containers, and oxygenating devices should assembled at the bedside; the patient should be hyperoxygenated to an oxygen saturation of 99% to 100% before suctioning; suction is applied for about 10 to 15 sec, and the patient's respiratory and cardiac status are closely monitored for evidence of poor tolerance for the procedure. Sputum may also be collected bronchoscopically, through the inner channel of the bronchoscope. Normal saline is used as an irrigating solution if needed, a technique known as bronchoalveolar lavage (BAL). BAL increases the likelihood of obtaining a diagnostic specimen, although on occasion the fluid used to irrigate the airways may contain local anesthetics, which, becausethey are bacteriostatic, may prevent bacteria from growing in culture. After bronchoscopy, the patient is observed closely for hypoxia and other possible complications, and oral liquids are withheld until the gag reflex has returned and the patient can swallow saliva without difficulty. All sputum specimens should be sent to the laboratory immediately and refrigerated. They should be treated as infective until proven otherwise. Appropriate isolation procedures are used for handling specimens. Common isolates from sputum specimens include *Staphylococcus aureus, Haemophilus influenzae, Streptococcus pneumoniae,* and *Moraxella catarrhalis.*

SQ *subcutaneous.*

squalamine (skwā′lĭ-mēn″) [L. *squalus,* dogfish + ″] An antiangiogenic protein, originally isolated from dog sharks. It has been used to treat the neovascularization of age-related macular degeneration and to limit blood

vessel proliferation needed by a cancer for it to spread and survive.

squalene (skwăl′ēn) An unsaturated carbohydrate present in shark-liver oil and some vegetable oils. It is an intermediate in the biosynthesis of cholesterol.

squam-, squamo- [L. *squama,* scale (of a fish)] Prefixes meaning *scale, squama.*

squama (skwā′mă) *pl.* **squamae** [L.] **1.** A thin plate of bone. **2.** A scale from the epidermis. SYN: *squame.*

squamate (skwā′māt) [L. *squama,* scale] Scaly.

squame (skwām) [L. *squama,* scale] Squama (2).

squamocellular (skwā″mō-sĕl′ū-lăr) [L. *squama,* scale, + *cellula,* little cell] Pert. to or having squamous cells.

squamocolumnar (skwā″mō-kŏ-lŭm′năr) [″ + ″] Pert. to any tissue in which squamous epithelium abuts columnar epithelium.

squamosa (skwā-mō′să) *pl.* **squamosae** [L. scaly] **1.** The squamous part of the temporal bone. **2.** Scaly or platelike.

squamosal (skwā-mō′săl) [L. *squama,* scale] Squamous.

squamous (skwā′mŭs) [L. *squamosus*] Scalelike.

square knot SEE: under *knot.*

squash prep, squash preparation The smearing or compressing of a thin tissue specimen between two slides before microscopic analysis. The specimen is placed flat on the first slide. The second slide is held at a right angle to the first and then dragged along the specimen, distributing it lengthwise along the first slide. The specimen is then fixed with alcohol and stained.

squatting position A position in which the person crouches with legs drawn up closely in front of, or beneath, the body; sitting on one's haunches and heels.

squaw root Blue cohosh.

squeeze-bottle A bottle made of a flexible, semirigid material that can be deformed by applying hand pressure to it. It is used to contain irrigating solutions, esp. those required in ophthalmology.

squeeze test (skwēz) Assessing anterior foot pain by a procedure in which the patient's forefoot is encircled with the examining hand. When applied pressure elicits tenderness, Morton neuroma is often present.

SQUID *superconductive quantum interference* **device***.*

squill (skwĭl) [Gr. *skilla,* a sea onion] An ancient remedy now rarely employed in medical practice, with therapeutic and toxic effects that mimic those of digoxin. It is derived from plants of the lily family.

squint (skwĭnt) [ME. *asquint,* sidelong glance] **1.** Abnormality in which the right and left visual axes do not bear toward an objective point simultaneously. SEE: *strabismus*. **2.** To close the eyes partly, either to block out excess environmental light or to try to improve a refractive error of vision. **3.** To be unable to direct both eyes simultaneously toward a point.

convergent s. Esotropia.

divergent s. Exotropia.

external s. Exotropia.

internal s. Esotropia.

Sr Symbol for the element strontium.

src A family of oncogenes involved in transforming normal cells to cancer cells. Src was the first transforming oncogene discovered. Proteins produced by these genes have tyrosine kinase activity. SEE: *oncogene; transformation*.

SRF *somatotropin-releasing factor.*

sRNA *soluble ribonucleic acid.*

SRS, SRS-A *slow-reacting substance; slow-reacting substance of anaphylaxis.* SEE: *leukotriene.*

SRY *sex-determining region Y.*

SS *saliva sample; Sjögren syndrome; soapsuds; sterile solution.*

ss [L. *semis,* half] **1.** One half; *subjects,* as in ss of an experiment or clinical study. **2.** Single strength.

SSD *source-skin distance.*

SSE *soapsuds enema.*

SSRI *selective serotonin reuptake inhibitor*

SSS *sick sinus syndrome; sterile saline soak.*

ST *sedimentation time.*

stab (stăb) [ME. *stob,* stick] **1.** To pierce with a knife. **2.** A wound produced by piercing with a knife or pointed instrument. **3.** A stab culture.

stabbing (stab'ing) Pert. to an intense pain that feels like a knife stab.

stabile (stā'bīl) [L. *stabilis,* stable] Not moving; fixed.

stability (stă-bil'ĭt-ē) **1.** The condition of remaining unchanged, even in the presence of forces that would normally change the state or condition, e.g., a chemical compound that remains unchanged, or a mature mental state that resists change. **2.** A measure of the ability of an aerosol to remain in suspension. This is determined by the size, type, and concentration of particles, the humidity, and the mobility of the gas in which the particles are transported.

stabilization (stā"bĭl-ī-ză'shŭn) [L. *stabilis,* stable] **1.** The act of making something, such as a body structure, chemical reaction, mood state, or disease process less variable, mobile, or volatile or more rigid. **2.** The fixation of a dental restoration, the mandible, or a tooth so that it will not move, especially under such conditions as chewing, speaking, or swallowing.

dynamic s. An integrated function of neuromuscular systems requiring muscles to contract and fixate the body against fluctuating outside forces, providing postural support with fine adjustments in muscle tension. The term usually pertains to a function of the trunk, shoulder, and hip muscles and includes the lower extremity muscles when they are functioning in a closed chain.

stable (stā'bl) **1.** Firm; steady. **2.** Of an atom or a chemical compound, not subject to spontaneous radioactivity; not readily decomposing. **3.** In psychology, not subject to emotional insecurity or illness.

stable condition A statement that a patient's condition has not changed significantly.

stable disease SEE: under *disease*.

Stachybotrys atra (ā'trā) *Stachybotrys chartarum.*

Stachybotrys chartarum (stăk"ē-bŏ'trĭs kahr-tăr'ŭm) [L] A mold that grows well on wood, plaster, insulation, tobacco products, and sheetrock. Inhalation of spores has been implicated in cases of fatigue, chronic headaches, and respiratory difficulties. SYN: *Stachybotrys atra*.

stachyose (stăk'ē-ōs") A nonabsorbable carbohydrate present in beans. Because the substance is not absorbed or metabolized in the small intestine, it passes into the colon where it is acted on by bacteria to form gas. This may be related to the flatus produced by eating beans.

stack (stăk) [ME. *stak*] **1.** To place objects directly on top of others. **2.** To perform a procedure immediately after a preceding one, without interruption or pause.

stadiometer (stā"dē-ŏm'ă-tĕr) [Gr. stadium + "] A device used to measure body height, esp. of children.

stadium (stā'dē-ŭm) [Gr. *stadion,* alteration] A stage or period in the progress of a disease. SEE: *fastigium*.

staff (stăf) [AS. *staef,* a stick] **1.** An instrument to be introduced into the urethra and bladder as a guide to a surgical knife. **2.** The medical, nursing, and other personnel attached to a hospital.

attending s. The group of physicians and surgeons who have privileges to practice at a hospital.

consulting s. The physicians and surgeons attached to a hospital who may be consulted by members of the attending staff.

house s. A nonspecific term for physicians, esp. interns and residents and other allied health professionals employed as part of the medical care team for a hospital. They are supervised by the permanent hospital staff and receive training to meet the requirements for licensure or certification in their specialty. SEE: *teaching hospital*.

retention of s. Keeping employees on

a stable roster without losses due to attrition, firing, or layoffs.

stage (stāj) [Fr. *estage, étage,* fr L. *staticum,* a standing place] **1.** A period in the course of a disease or in the life history of an organism. **2.** The platform of a microscope on which the slide is placed. **3.** Any of the sequences in a therapeutic plan or protocol.

   algid s. Cold and cyanotic skin that occurs in cholera and some other diseases.

   anal s. In Freudian psychology, the second phase of sexual development, from infancy to childhood, in which the libido is concentrated in the anal region. In order of appearance, the phases of sexual development are oral, anal, phallic, and genital.

   asphyxial s. The preliminary stage of Asiatic cholera.

   cold s. The chill or rigor of a malarial paroxysm.

   eruptive s. **1.** The period in which an exanthem appears. **2.** The middle stage in the pre-eruptive, eruptive, or posteruptive categorization of tooth eruption. It is characterized by root elongation and movement of the tooth mesially and toward the occlusal plane.

   hot s. The febrile stage in a malarial paroxysm.

   s. of invasion The period in which the causative agent is present in the body before the onset of a disease.

   s. of latency The incubation period of an infectious disorder.

   preeruptive s. The stage following an infection (as with measles or chickenpox) before the characteristic rash appears.

   resting s. The stage of a cell between mitotic divisions. The term is inaccurate because the cell is metabolically active and is producing a new set of chromosomes for the next division. SEE: *interphase.*

   sweating s. The third or terminal stage of malaria during which sweating occurs.

stage 0 In situ, or noninvasive. Said of cancers.

staggers (stăg'ĕrz) Vertigo and confusion that occur in decompression illness.

staging The classification of tumors, esp. malignant tumors, by their degree of differentiation, their potential for responding to therapy, and the patient's prognosis.

stagnation (stăg-nā'shŭn) [L. *stagnans,* stagnant] **1.** Cessation of motion. **2.** Stasis.

stain (stān) **1.** A discoloration. **2.** A pigment or dye used in coloring microscopic objects and tissues. **3.** To apply pigment or dye to a tissue or microscopic object or tissue.

   acid s. A chemical used to stain the cytoplasmic or basic components of cells.

   acid-fast s. A stain used in bacteriology, esp. for staining *Mycobacterium tuberculosis, Nocardia,* and other species. A special solution of carbolfuchsin is used, which the organism retains in spite of washing with the decolorizing agent acid alcohol. SEE: *Ziehl-Neelsen method.*

   basic s. A chemical used to add pigment to the nuclear or acidic components of cells.

   calcofluor white s. A fluorescent stain used in microbiology to highlight fungi, including species of *Pneumocystis.*

   contrast s. A stain used to color one part of a tissue or cell, unaffected when another part is stained by another color.

   counter s. SEE: *counterstain.*

   dental s. A discoloration accumulating on the surface of teeth, dentures, or denture base material, most often attributed to the use of tea, coffee, or tobacco. Many stains contain calcium, carbon, copper, iron, nitrogen, oxygen, and sulfur. Stains may be intrinsic or extrinsic. Extrinsic stains of teeth can be removed, e.g,, by brushing, rinsing, or sonication. Intrinsic stains cannot be removed by these methods.

   differential s. In bacteriology, a stain such as Gram stain that enables one to distinguish different types of bacteria.

   double s. A mixture of two contrasting dyes, usually an acid and a basic stain.

   Feulgen s. SEE: *Feulgen stain.*

   Giemsa s. SEE: *Giemsa stain.*

   Gram s. SEE: *Gram stain.*

   hematoxylin-eosin s. A widely used method of staining tissues for microscopic examination. It stains nuclei blue-black and cytoplasm pink.

   intravital s. A nontoxic dye that, when introduced into an organism, selectively stains certain cells or tissues. SYN: *vital s.*

   inversion s. A basic stain that, when under the influence of a mordant, acts as an acid stain.

   Jenner s. SEE: *Jenner stain.*

   Leishman s. SEE: under *Leishman, William Boog.*

   metachromatic s. A stain which causes cells or tissues to take on a color different from the stain itself.

   Movat pentachrome s. SEE: *Movat pentachrome stain.*

   neutral s. A combination of an acid and a basic stain.

   nonspecific s. A dye added to a tissue specimen that binds to tissue indiscriminately, making it more difficult to distinguish one part from the next.

   nuclear s. A basic stain that colors cell nuclei, but does not stain structures in the cytoplasm.

Perls s. SEE: *Perls stain.*

phosphotungstic acid-hematoxylin s. ABBR: PTAH. A histological stain that binds to proteins, used primarily to stain skeletal muscles and mitochondria. It is also used to identify glial cells in the central nervous system and fibrin.

port-wine s. **Nevus** flammeus. SEE: *nevus flammeus* for illus.

special s. A stain that highlights features of a cell or organism that cannot be readily identified with routine histological or microbiological staining techniques.

substantive s. A stain that is directly absorbed by the tissues when they are immersed in the staining solution.

supravital s. Stain that will color living cells or tissues that have been removed from the body.

tumor s. In arteriography, an abnormally dense area in a radiographical image caused by the collection of contrast medium in the vessels. This may be a sign of neoplastic growth.

vital s. Intravital **s.**

Wright s. SEE: *Wright stain.*

stained teeth Deep or superficial discoloration of teeth. A number of conditions cause this (e.g., exposure of the fetus to tetracycline the mother took during pregnancy or mottling caused by exposure to high levels of fluoride in drinking water). The stains may be covered by applying a resin or porcelain laminate veneer over the stain (bonding). The same technique may be used to rebuild or repair chipped or cracked teeth.

staining (stān′ĭng) [O.Fr. *desteindre*] The process of impregnating a substance, esp. a tissue, with pigments so that its components may be visible under a microscope.

staircase phenomenon The effect exhibited by skeletal and heart muscle when subjected to rapidly repeated maximal stimuli following a period of rest. In the resulting series of contractions, each is greater than the preceding one until a state of maximum contraction is reached. SYN: *treppe.*

stalagmometer (stăl-ăg-mŏm′ĕ-tĕr) [Gr. *stalagmos,* dropping, + *metron,* a measure] An instrument for measuring the number of drops in a given amount of fluid.

stalk (stok) An elongated structure usually serving to attach or support an organ or structure.

body s. A bridge of mesoderm that connects the caudal end of the embryo with the chorion. It later forms the structural tissue of the umbilical cord.

optic s. The structure that connects the optic vesicle or cup to the forebrain.

pineal s. Pineal **peduncle.**

yolk s. The duct that connects the embryonic gut to the yolk sac. It disap-

pears during fetal development. SYN: *omphalomesenteric duct; vitelline duct.*

stalking A form of harassment in which one person repeatedly telephones, follows, or writes to another even though these attempts at contact are disruptive, unwanted, or felt to be menacing by the person who is the object of attention.

stamina (stăm′ĭ-nă) [L., thread of the warp, thread of human life] Inherent force, constitutional energy; strength; endurance.

stammering (stăm′ĕr-ĭng) [AS. *stamerian*] Stuttering.

stanch (stŏnch) [Fr. *estanche,* firm] To stop the flow of blood from a wound.

standard [Fr. *estandard,* marking rallying place] That which is established by custom or authority as a model, criterion, or rule.

biological s. The standardization of drugs or biological products (vitamins, hormones, antibiotics) by testing their effects on animals. It is used when chemical analysis is impossible or impracticable.

reasonable patient s. In the giving of informed consent, the amount of information that a rational patient would want before making a choice to pursue or reject a treatment or procedure.

reasonable physician s. In the giving of informed consent, the amount of information that a typical physician would provide to patients before asking that they decide to pursue or reject a treatment.

standard of care **1.** A statement of actions consistent with minimum safe professional conduct under specific conditions, as determined by professional peer organizations. **2.** In forensic medicine, a measure with which the defendant's conduct is compared to determine negligence or malpractice. In negligence law, the degree of care that a reasonable, prudent person should exercise under the same or similar circumstances. SYN: *established customary standard of care.*

standard deviation SEE: under *deviation.*

standard drink In alcohol-related research either one 12 oz serving of beer, 5 oz of wine, or 1.5 oz of distilled spirits.

standard error SEE: under *error.*

standardized (stan′dărd-īzd″) **1.** Brought into conformity with an approved guideline, practice, or unit of measure. **2.** Of an instrument, having its accuracy determined by measuring against a similar device known to be accurate; calibrated.

standardized assessment of concussion instrument, standardized assessment of concussion tool ABBR: SAC. A common battery of neurological, neuropsychological, and physical tests used to index the relative severity of sports-related traumatic brain injury colloquially, a concussion. These results are also an indicator of an athlete's physical readiness to return to competition. The assessment includes tests of orientation, memory, concentration, cognition, and physical exertion.

standardized test A test that has been developed empirically, has adequate norms, definite instructions for administration, and evidence of reliability and validity.

standardized uptake value ABBR: SUV. The amount of radioactive tracer detected by a positron-emission tomographic scan during imaging of a body part. The SUV is equal to the tissue tracer taken up by the tissue of interest, divided by the injected dose of tracer, divided by the body weight of the patient. The SUV is used radiologically to distinguish benign masses from those that are cancerous; to monitor the response of cancerous masses to treatment and/or radiation; and to assess the likelihood that a particular cancer will respond to treatment.

standard patient, standardized patient

standard precautions SEE: *precautions, standard.*

standard survey (of nursing home care) A regularly scheduled, on-site federal investigation of the quality of care provided in a nursing home. The survey assesses compliance with rules promulgated by Medicaid and Medicare.

standard temperature and pressure, dry ABBR: STPD. Gas volume at 0°C, 760 mm Hg total pressure, and partial pressure of water of zero (i.e., dry).

stand-by assistance Help provided to a person who cannot complete an activity of daily living on his own, e.g., the prevention of falls and injuries.

standing orders Orders, rules, regulations, protocols, or procedures prepared by the professional staff of a hospital or clinic and used as guidelines in the preparation and carrying out of medical and surgical procedures.

standstill A cessation of activity.

    atrial s. Cessation of atrial contractions.

    cardiac s. Cessation of contractions of the heart.

    inspiratory s. The temporary cessation of inspiration normally following each inspiration, resulting from stimulation of proprioceptors in the alveoli of the lungs. SEE: *Hering-Breuer reflex.*

    respiratory s. Cessation of respiratory movements.

    ventricular s. Cessation of ventricular contractions.

Stanford-Binet IQ test (stăn'fŭrd-bǐ-nā') [A. Binet, Fr. psychologist, 1857–1911; Stanford University, where the original test was revised by Louis Terman in 1916] A commonly used test of cognitive abilities. It assesses verbal and nonverbal reasoning by subtests that assess a person's language fluency, three-dimensional thought processes, and pattern recognition skills. The test was first used in the late 1800s as an approximate means of classifying and comparing intellectual function in broad groups of people. It has been revised many times since then and is used for a variety of purposes, including the classification of military recruits and the assessment of individuals thought to have subnormal intelligence.

stannic (stăn'ĭk) [L. *stannum,* tin] **1.** Resembling or containing tin. **2.** In chemistry, containing tetravalent tin.

stannous (stăn'ŭs) [L. *stannum,* tin] **1.** Resembling or containing tin. **2.** In chemistry, containing divalent tin.

stannum (stan'ŭm) [L. *stannum,* alloy of silver and lead, tin] SYMB: Sn. Tin.

stanozolol (stăn'ō-zō-lŏl") An anabolic steroid.

stapedectomy (stā"pē-děk'tō-mē) [L. *stapes,* stirrup, + Gr. *ektome,* excision] Excision of the stapes to improve hearing, esp. in cases of otosclerosis. In patients with severely impaired hearing, the stapes is replaced by a prosthesis which is placed in the ear.

    PATIENT CARE: After surgery, the patient is instructed to keep head movements to a minimum and to refrain from blowing the nose or sneezing for at least 1 week, and preferably 2. Subsequently all nose blowing should be done with the mouth open. Dizziness or lightheadedness, bloody drainage from the ear, reduced hearing, and nose bleeding are common initial adverse effects of the surgery. To prevent falls caused by dizziness, the patient is kept at bedrest for the first day after surgery, and then gradually permitted freer ambulation, initially with someone to assist him or her. Bending, suddenly moving the head, lifting heavy weights, and straining during bowel movements should be initially avoided. The patient should not get the operated ear wet for at least 10 days postoperatively. For 30 days after surgery the patient should not fly; climb to high altitudes; dive, scuba, or snorkel (to avoid sudden pressure changes); or be exposed to loud sounds such as those produced by a jet aircraft. Sudden movements of the head should be avoided. Prior to discharge from the hospital, patient and family are taught about caring for the incision and changing the external ear dressing. The patient is warned to avoid contact with anyone with an upper respiratory infection. An appointment is scheduled for follow-up care. SEE: *Nursing Diagnoses Appendix.*

stapedius (stā-pē'dē-ŭs) [L. *stapes,* stirrup] A small muscle of the middle ear inserted in the stapes.

stapes (stā′pēz″, stă-pē′dēz″) *pl.* **stapedes, stapes** [L. *stapes,* stirrup] The auditory ossicle that articulates with the incus. The footplate of the stapes fits into the oval window. SYN: *stirrup; stirrup* **bone.** SEE: *ear.*

staphylo- [Gr. *staphyle,* a bunch of grapes] Prefix meaning the *uvula,* pert. to or resembling a bunch of grapes, or pert. to *Staphylococcus.*

staphylococcal clumping test A coagulation test to identify fibrin-fibrinogen degradation products in patients suspected of having disseminated intravascular coagulation.

staphylococcal food poisoning SEE: under *poisoning.*

staphylococcal scalded skin syndrome Infection and inflammation of the outer layers of skin, predominantly but not exclusively found in children, elderly persons, and immunosuppressed patients. It is caused by exotoxins produced by *Staphylococcus aureus.* Initially, the skin in the affected areas is rough, with a bright red, flat rash; it then becomes wrinkled, and blisters form. The syndrome is treated with antistaphylococcal antibiotics (e.g., nafcillin), and supportive care is provided to minimize the risk of cellulitis or pneumonia. About 2% to 3% of affected patients die of the disease. In survivors, the blisters heal without scarring.

TREATMENT: Beta-lactamase–resistant synthetic penicillin is given. The bullae and denuded skin should be treated symptomatically. Uncomplicated lesions heal without scarring. SYN: *Ritter disease.*

staphylococcemia (stăf″ĭl-ō-kŏk-sē′mē-ă) [″ + ″ + *haima,* blood] The presence of staphylococci in the blood.

Staphylococcus (staf″ĭ-lō-kok′ŭs) [Gr. *staphylē,* a bunch of grapes + *coccus*] A genus of micrococci belonging to the family Staphylococcaceae, order Bacillales. They are gram-positive and when cultured on agar produce white, yellow, or orange colonies. Some species are pathogenic, causing suppurative conditions and elaborating exotoxins destructive to tissues. Some produce enterotoxins and are the cause of a common type of food poisoning.

S. aureus A species that is coagulase positive, often part of resident flora of the skin and the nasal and oral cavities. These bacteria may cause suppurative conditions such as boils, carbuncles, and abscesses, as well as hospital-acquired infections, foreign body (prosthetic) infections, and life-threatening pneumonia or sepsis. Various strains of this species produce toxins, including those that cause food poisoning, staphylococcal scalded skin syndrome, and toxic shock syndrome. Some strains also produce hemolysins and staphylokinase.

methicillin-resistant *S. aureus* ABBR: MRSA. A strain of *S. aureus* resistant to methicillin. MRSA is resistant to all penicillins. Patients with MRSA infections should be isolated; appropriate mask-gown-glove precautions must be used, depending on the site of the infection. MRSA is an important cause of health care associated infections. Handwashing is an essential precaution in caring for patients who harbor this organism. SEE: *isolation; antibiotic* **resistance**.

MRSA is resistant to most antibiotics and is usually acquired in hospitals or nursing homes, spread from patient to patient by contaminated hands, clothing, and equipment. Infection with MRSA can range from pneumonia to flesh-eating diseases. About 0.5% of people in the U.S. have MRSA bacteria on their skin or in their noses and, although not infected, can still spread the bacteria to those at risk. The CDC estimates that 90,000 people die annually in the U.S. from hospital-acquired infections; about 17,000 of these deaths are due to MRSA. Agencies can now reduce and perhaps stop the spread of MRSA infection by following the guidelines of a pilot program of the Pittsburgh, PA, Veterans Affairs Healthcare System.

PATIENT CARE: The Pittsburgh guidelines require that all patients have their noses swabbed for MRSA on admission and discharge. Those with MRSA are isolated from other patients and are cared for in protective isolation. Noninvasive equipment is disinfected after each use with these patients, and strict hand hygiene policies are applied. As a result, there was a drop of more than 70% of MRSA cases in surgical care units. The VA, because of the Pittsburgh results, plans to expand the program to more than 150+ VA hospitals nationwide. The CDC suggests screening high-risk patients (those with weak immune systems, intensive care patients, and patients in nursing homes), rather than recommending universal screening. However, Denmark, Finland, and the Netherlands have essentially eradicated MRSA by using universal screening methods. In addition to screening everyone, agencies may provide MRSA carriers with special soap and antibiotic nasal creams. Additionally, a gene-based MRSA test provides results in hours as opposed to days.

vancomycin-resistant *S. aureus* ABBR: VRSA. A strain of *S. aureus* resistant to vancomycin that may become a serious nosocomial pathogen. Strains with intermediate resistance to vancomycin have caused life-threatening infections. SEE: *Standard Precautions Appendix.*

S. capitis A coagulase-negative *Staphylococcus* species that has been isolated from infections in premature neonates and patients with endocarditis.

S. caprae A coagulase-negative, DNAse-positive *Staphylococcus* species first identified in goats. It can infect humans, e.g., in prosthetic joints and injured bones.

S. epidermidis A coagulase-negative species that is part of the normal flora of the skin. It may colonize, form biofilms on, and infect prosthetic devices and indwelling catheters.

S. haemolyticus A coagulase-negative *Staphylococcus* species that primarily infects premature neonates and patients being treated for cancer or other immune-suppressing conditions. The species can also cause meningitis; infections of the skin, soft tissue, or prosthetic joints; or bacteremia. It is frequently resistant to multiple common antibiotics.

S. hominis A coagulase-negative species frequently recovered from skin. It is not consistently pathogenic for humans.

S. lugdunensis An aggressive coagulase-negative *Staphylococcus* species. It causes infections of soft tissues, the bloodstream, and prostheses.

S. saprophyticus A species that is the second most common cause of urinary tract infection in young, sexually active females. It is a rare cause of pneumonia.

staphylococcus (staf″ĭ-lō-kok′ŭs, -kok′sī″) *pl.* **staphylococci** [Gr. *staphylē*, a bunch of grapes + *coccus*] Any bacterium of the genus *Staphylococcus.* **staphylococcal, staphylococcic** (-kok′ăl, -kok′sik), *adj.* SEE: *Staphylococcus;* illus.

staphylokinase (stăf″ĭ-lō-kī′nās) An exotoxin produced by some strains of *Staphylococcus aureus* that may be used clinically as a thrombolytic drug.

staphylolysin (stăf″ĭ-lŏl′ĭ-sĭn) [″ + *lysis*, dissolution] A hemolysin produced by staphylococci.

staphyloma, staphyloma corneae (stăf″ĭ-lō′mă) [Gr.] Bulging of part of the uvea (choroid, iris, or ciliary body) into a thin, stretched area of sclera. **staphylomatous,** *adj.*

    anterior s. Globular enlargement of the anterior part of the eye. SYN: *keratoglobus.*

    ciliary s. Staphyloma in the region of the ciliary body.

    equatorial s. Staphyloma in the equatorial region of the eye.

    intercalary s. Staphyloma in the region of the union of the sclera with the periphery of the iris.

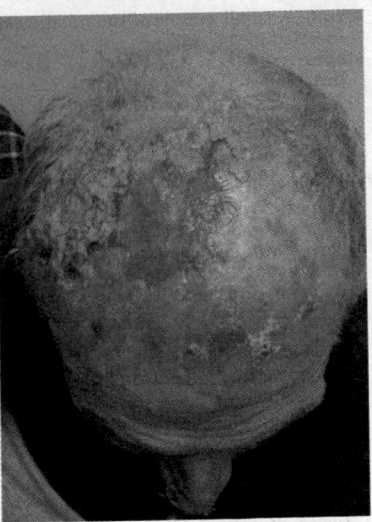

STAPHYLOCOCCUS AUREUS

Scalp infection

    partial s. Staphyloma that extends in one direction, displacing the pupil. The remainder of the cornea is clear.

    posterior s. A bulging of the sclera backward.

    total s. An opaque, protuberant scar found in place of the cornea. It is caused by a perforation of the cornea resulting in poor vision, increased tension, and rupture of thin scar. Treatment involves incision, excision, and ablation.

    uveal s. The protrusion of any portion of the uvea through the sclera.

staple food, staple Any food that supplies a substantial part, at least 25% to 35%, of the caloric requirement and is regularly consumed by a certain population.

stapling (stāp′ling) In surgery, a means of fastening tissues to one another with C-shaped clips. Staples are made of either titanium or an absorbable polymeric material. Stapling can usually be performed more rapidly than suturing. SEE: illus.

    gastric s. The surgical restriction of the gastric cardia. The procedure is used as to treat morbidly obese patients but has many potential side effects, including esophagitis, vitamin deficiencies, and stenosis of the operative site.

star [AS. *steorra*] Aster.

    lens s. A starlike structure developing in the lens of the eye as a result of unequal growth of lens fibers.

starburst (stăr′bŭrst) A visual disturbance in which brilliant flashes are seen around light sources. It is an occasional complication of refractive keratoplasty on the eye.

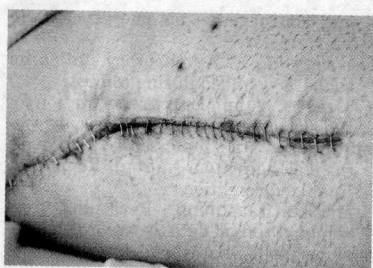

STAPLED INCISION

STAR OF LIFE
Emergency medical care symbol

starch [AS. *stercan*] Plant polysaccharides composed of glucose that are digestible by humans. Staple grains often comprise 50% to 58% of caloric intake. Salivary and pancreatic amylases hydrolyze starches to dextrin and maltose. These in turn are hydrolyzed to glucose, which is absorbed in the bloodstream. Glucose not immediately needed for energy is converted into glycogen and stored in the liver and muscle.
   animal s. Glycogen.
   corn s. Starch obtained from ordinary corn or maize (*Zea mays*). It is used as a dusting powder and an absorbent and is a constituent in many pastes and ointments. It is widely used in industry and as a food.
starch-iodine test A test for the presence of starch. When an iodine solution is applied to a substance or material that contains starch, a dark blue color appears.
stare (stār) [AS. *starian*] To gaze fixedly at anyone or anything.
Stargardt disease (stär′gărt) [Karl Bruno Stargardt, Ger. ophthalmologist, 1875–1927] An autosomal-recessive form of macular degeneration, marked by progressive central visual loss beginning in childhood or adolescence and worsening in middle age. SYN: *fundus flavimaculatus.*
Star of Life symbol The symbol designated by the Department of Transportation (DOT) to represent providers of emergency medical services (EMS). It is displayed on EMS vehicles and outside the emergency departments of hospitals. SEE: illus.

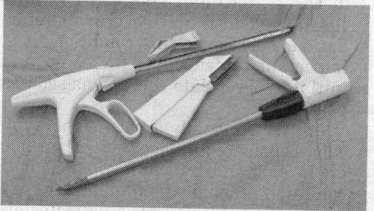

STAPLING DEVICES

Starling, Ernest Henry (star′ling) Brit. physiologist, 1866–1927
   S. law A law that states that the force of blood ejected by the heart is determined primarily by the length of the fibers of its muscular wall (i.e., an increase in diastolic filling lengthens the fibers and increases the force of muscular contraction).
   S. law of intestine A law stating that a stimulus within the intestine (that is, the presence of food) initiates a band of constriction on the proximal side and relaxation on the distal side and results in a peristaltic wave.
starter A pure culture of bacteria or other microorganism used to initiate a particular fermentation, as in the making of cheese.
startle (stär′těl) [ME. *sterten,* stand up stiffly; move quickly] A response to a sudden stimulus marked by jerking body movements and some or all of the following: defensive posture, tremors, sweating, widened pupils, and a temporary increase in pulse and respiratory rates.
starvation (stär-vā′shŭn) [AS. *steorfan,* to die] **1.** The condition of being without food for a long period of time. When everything but air and water is withheld, the sequence of events is as follows: (1) hunger, beginning about 4 hr after the last meal, accompanied by gastric contraction and general restlessness, becoming more acute periodically, esp. at times when meals were customarily taken; (2) utilization of glycogen stored in the liver and muscles; (3) utilization of stored fat; (4) loss of weight; (5) spells of nausea and diminishing acuteness of the sensation of hunger; (6) destruction of body protein. The greatest loss of weight is in the fatty tissues, spleen, and liver. **2.** The condition in which the supply of a specific food is below minimum bodily requirements, such as pro-

tein starvation. SEE: *kwashiorkor*.
3. The condition resulting from failure of the body to digest and absorb essential foodstuffs. SEE: *deficiency disease; diet; dietetics*.

stasis (stā′sĭs, stas′ĭs) [Gr. *stasis*, a standing] Stoppage of the normal flow of fluids, as of the blood or urine, or feces. SYN: *stagnation* (2).

    diffusion s. Stasis with diffusion of lymph or serum.

    intestinal s. Ileus.

    venous s. Stasis of blood caused by venous congestion.

stat (stăt) [L., *statim*] Immediately.

-stat [Gr. *-statēs*, fr, *histanai*, to stand] In pharmacology, a suffix designating an enzyme inhibitor.

state [L. *status*, condition] **1.** A condition. **2.** A mode or condition of being. **3.** Status. Particular states are listed under the first word. SEE: e.g., *dream state; locked-in state; persistent vegetative state*.

State Children's Health Insurance Program ABBR: SCHIP. The former name for Children's Health Insurance Program (CHIP).

state of matter The condition in which matter exists under specified kinetic conditions (e.g. the pressure and temperature). All matter is in one or more states at any time: solid, liquid, gas, or plasma.

static (stăt′ĭk) [Gr. *statikos*, causing to stand] At rest; in equilibrium; not in motion.

static balance SEE: under *balance*.

static equilibrium SEE: under *equilibrium*.

statics (stăt′ĭks) The study of matter at rest and of the forces bringing about equilibrium. SEE: *dynamics*.

statim (stăt′ĭm) [L.] ABBR: stat. Immediately; at once.

statin (stat′ĭn) [*-stat* + *-in*] Any of the drugs of the class known as 3-hydroxy-3-methylglutaryl coenzyme A (HMG CoA) reductase inhibitors. These drugs have powerful lipid-lowering properties. The names of drugs in this class all end in "-statin" (e.g., atorvastatin, pravastatin, rosuvastatin, and simvastatin). Drugs from this class reduce the risk of myocardial infarction and stroke. SYN: *HMG CoA enzyme inhibitor*.

station (stā′shŏn) [L. *statio*, standing, standing still, place, position] **1.** The manner of standing. **2.** A stopping place. **3.** In obstetrics, the relationship in centimeters between the presenting part and the level of the ischial spines. SEE: *forceps*.

    aid s. A temporary or portable health care facility used in the military or at public gatherings or events to assess, stabilize, and triage the sick or the injured.

    base s. A local or regional command

and control center for emergency medical services.

    dressing s. A temporary station for soldiers wounded during combat.

    rest s. A temporary relief station for the sick on a military road or railway.

stationary (stā′shŭn-ĕr-ē) [L. *stationarius*, belonging to a station] Remaining in a fixed condition.

statistical reasoning Reasoning from combinations of data to arrive at conclusions about what is true, false, likely, or improbable.

statistical significance The likelihood that the results of a study are accurate, true, and valid, and unlikely to be the result of randomness or a fluke; numerical meaningfulness.

statistics (stă-tis′tiks) [L. *statisticus*, pert. to a status] The systematic collection, organization, analysis, and interpretation of numerical data pert. to any subject. **statistical** (-tis′tĭ-kăl), *adj*.

    medical s. Statistics pert. to medical sciences, esp. data pert. to human disease.

    morbidity s. Statistics that enumerate the extent, frequency, or severity of disease in a community.

    parametric s. The class of statistics based on the assumption that the samples measured are from normally distributed populations.

    population s. Vital s.

    vital s. Statistics relating to births (natality), deaths (mortality), diseases (morbidity), health, and marriage. Vital statistics for the U.S. are published annually by the National Center for Health Statistics of the Department of Health and Human Services. SYN: *population s.*

statoacoustic (stăt″ō-ă-koo′stĭk) [Gr. *statos*, placed, + *akoustikos*, acoustic] Pert. to balance and hearing.

statoconia (stăt″ō-kō′nē-ă) [″ + *konos*, dust] Otolith.

statokinetic (stăt″ō-kĭn-ĕt′ĭk) [″ + *kinetikos*, moving] Pert. to reactions of the body produced by movement.

statolith (stăt′ō-lĭth) [″ + *lithos*, stone] Otolith.

stature (stăt′ŭr) [L. *statura*] The height of the body in a standing position.

    short s. Body height at a specified age below the level obtained at that age by 70% of the population. A number of diseases, including hormonal, nutritional, and intrauterine growth retardation, may cause this condition. It is important to determine the cause and initiate appropriate therapy as soon as possible.

    tall s. Unusually great height, typically considered to be greater than 200 cm in men and 180 cm in women. This condition is usually familial and may be prevented with estrogens or testosterone, depending on gender of patient.

status (stăt′ŭs, stat′) *pl.* **statuses** [L. *status,* way of standing, posture, status] A state or condition.

s. asthmaticus Persistent and intractable asthma.

s. dysraphicus A condition resulting from imperfect closure of the neural tube of the embryo.

s. epilepticus Continuous seizure activity without a pause for 30 min, i.e., without an intervening period of normal brain function. Status can include two back-to-back seizures without a lucid interval or any seizure lasting more than 5 to 10 min.

estrogen receptor s. The presence or absence of a receptor to the hormone estrogen on breast cancer cells. Tumors that possess receptors either to estrogen alone or to both estrogen and progesterone are more responsive to estrogen-blocking agents such as tamoxifen than are tumors that lack these receptors.

mental s. The functional state of the mind as judged by the individual's behavior, appearance, responsiveness to stimuli of all kinds, speech, memory, and judgment.

s. migrainosus Continuous or daily unilateral, throbbing, and disabling headaches that do not improve with standard therapies for migraine.

s. panicus A panic attack that does not subside, but persists for many hours, days, or weeks without remission.

performance s. A measure of the overall health and functional capability of a patient.

progesterone receptor s. The presence or absence of receptors to the steroid hormone progesterone on breast cancer cells. Tumors that possess receptors to estrogen, to progesterone, or to both are more responsive to hormone-blocking agents, such as tamoxifen, than are tumors that lack these receptors.

socioeconomic s. ABBR: SES. The relative position attained by an individual in a cultural and financial hierarchy. Differences in socioeconomic status are responsible for important disparities in the nutrition, housing, safety, and health of large groups of people. In general, the lower one's SES, the greater one's risk of malnutrition, heart disease, infectious diseases, and early mortality from all causes. Income, education, occupation, vocation, and wealth all contribute to SES.

s. verrucosus The defective development of the cerebral gyri with many small gyri. This gives a warty appearance to the surface of the brain.

statute Any law enacted by a state legislature.

statute of repose Legal protection from prosecution or damages that result from the failure of a project completed in the distant past. A statute of repose protects participants in the project (for example, a heart valve manufacturer for its old, currently obsolete heart valves) for a specified number of years after the valve is no longer made, sold, or used in patient care.

Repose statutes differ from statutes of limitation. A statute of limitations provides protection to the valve manufacturer if an injured patient fails to file a claim of damages some number of months after being injured by the operation to implant it. The statute of repose provides the valve maker with an independent protection that states, in essence, that once a sufficient time has passed, the manufacturer has no ongoing relationship with its old products.

statutes of limitations Federal and state laws that set maximum time limits in which lawsuits can be brought, and actions, claims, or rights can be enforced. No legal action can be brought outside the time allowed by law even if the person or entity has a claim or cause of action. Time limitations vary from state to state.

stay (stā) [ME.] A postponement of an administrative or a judicial ruling.

STD *sexually transmitted disease; skin test dose.*

steady state A dynamic equilibrium in which construction and destruction are balanced. In physiology, the condition in which energy inputs equal expended energy (e.g., in which nutrition equals metabolism).

steal (stēl) The deviation of blood flow from its normal course or rate of flow.

hand ischemic s. Deprivation of blood flow to the radial artery, after an arteriovenous access (i.e., for hemodialysis) has been surgically placed in a patient's arm. If blood flow to the hand is not restored, the limb may become cold, painful, pale, or gangrenous.

intracerebral s. The shunting of blood from ischemic to well-supplied regions of the brain, producing overperfusion of the unaffected tissue and underperfusion of the ischemic tissue.

subclavian s. SEE: *subclavian steal syndrome.*

steam (stēm) [AS. *steam,* vapor] **1.** The invisible vapor into which water is converted at the boiling point. **2.** The mist formed by condensation of water vapor. **3.** Any vaporous exhalation.

steapsin (stē-ăp′sĭn) [Gr. *stear,* fat, + *pepsis,* digestion] Pancreatic lipase.

stearate (stē′ă-rāt) An ester or salt of stearic acid.

stearic acid (stē-ar′ik, stē′ă-rik) SEE: under *acid.*

stearin (stē′ă-rĭn) [Gr. *stear,* fat] A white crystalline solid in animal and vegetable fats; $C_3H_5(CH_3(CH_2)_{16}$

COOH)₃; any of the esters of glycerol and stearic acid, specifically glyceryl tristearate. One of the commonest fats in the body, esp. the solid ones. It breaks down into stearic acid and glycerol.

stearopten(e) (stē″ă-rŏp′tēn) [″ + *ptenos,* volatile] The more solid portion of a volatile oil as distinguished from the more fluid portion or eleoptene. Menthol and thymol are examples.

steatitis (stē″ă-tī′tĭs) [″ + *itis,* inflammation] Inflammation of adipose tissue.

steato- [Gr. *stear,* stem *steat-,* fat, tallow] Prefixes meaning *fat.* SEE: *adipo-; lipo-.*

steatoblepharon (stē″ă-tŏ-blef′ă-ron″) [*steato-* + *blepharo-*] The prolapse of fat from the orbit of the eye below the eyelid. The condition is often associated with dermatochalasis (sagging of eyelid tissues).

steatocystoma multiplex (stē″ă-tō-sĭs-tō′mă) A skin disorder marked by the development of many sebaceous cysts.

steatohepatitis (stē″ăt-ō-hep″ă-tīt′ĭs) [*steato-* + *hepatitis*] Fatty **liver**.

steatoma (stē″ă-tō′mă) [″ + *oma,* tumor] A fatty tumor. SEE: *epidermoid cyst; lipoma.*

steatonecrosis (stē″ă-tō-nē-krō′sĭs) [″ + *nekros,* corpse, + *osis,* condition] Necrosis of fatty tissue.

steatorrhea (stē″ă-tō-rē′ă) [Gr. *steatos,* fat, + *rhoia,* flow] **1.** Increased secretion of fat from the sebaceous glands of the skin. SYN: *seborrhea.* **2.** Fatty stools, as seen in some malabsorption syndromes. Stains, such as Sudan stain, can be used to demonstrate fat in stool. Precise measurements of the quantity of fat in stools can be made with a 72-hr stool collection. During the collection the patient must eat at least 100 g of dietary fat each day. The excretion of more than 7 g/day of fat is abnormal, that is, diagnostic of fat malabsorption. SYN: *fatty stool.*

    s. simplex Excessive secretion of the sebaceous glands of the face.

steatosis (stē″ă-tō′sĭs) [″ + *osis,* condition] **1.** Fatty degeneration. **2.** Disease of the sebaceous glands.

STEC *Shiga toxin-producing E. coli.*

steer (stēr) To direct or guide along a desired course. In education it is to provide guidance to a student; in endoscopy, to push a scope through an organ or toward a lesion.

steerable Capable of being maneuvered, driven, or positioned into a specific anatomical location. Said of medical devices such as those advanced into the body by catheters.

Stegomyia (stĕg″ō-mī′ē-ă) A subgenus of mosquito of the genus *Aedes,* family Culicidae, capable of transmitting many diseases to humans, including dengue, yellow fever, and filariasis.

Steinert disease (stīn′ĕrt) [Hans Gustav Wilhelm Steinert, Ger. physician, 1875–1911] Myotonia dystrophica.

Stein-Leventhal syndrome (stīn-lev′ĕn-thal″) [Irving F. Stein, Sr., U.S. gynecologist, 1887–1976; Michael L. Leventhal, U.S. obstetrician and gynecologist, 1901–1971] Polycystic ovary syndrome.

Steinmann extension (stīn′măn) [Fritz Steinmann, Swiss surgeon, 1872–1932] Traction applied to a limb by applying weight to a pin placed through the bone at right angles to the direction of pull of the traction force.

Steinmann pin A metal rod used for internal fixation of the adjacent sections of a fractured bone.

steinstrasse Tiny fragments of stone that remain in the ureters after lithotripsy, causing obstruction to the flow of urine, persistent pain, or bleeding.

stella (stĕl′ă) [L.] Star.

    s. lentis hyaloidea The posterior pole of the crystalline lens of the eye.

    s. lentis iridica The anterior pole of the crystalline lens of the eye.

stellate (stĕl′āt) [L. *stellatus*] Star-shaped; arranged with parts radiating from a center.

stellectomy (stĕl-lĕk′tō-mē) [″ + *ek-tome,* excision] The surgical removal of the stellate ganglion.

Stellwag sign (stel′wag″, shtel′vok″) [Carl Stellwag von Carion, Austrian oculist, 1823–1904] Widening of the palpebral aperture with absence or lessened frequency of winking, seen in Graves' disease.

stem [AS. *stemn,* tree trunk] **1.** Any stalklike structure. **2.** To derive from or originate in.

stem cell factor SEE: under *factor.*

STEMI *ST-segment elevation myocardial infarction.*

steno-, sten- [Gr. *stenos,* narrow] Prefixes meaning *narrow* or *short.*

stenosis (stĕ-nō′sĭs) [Gr. *stenōsis,* a narrowing] The constriction or narrowing of a passage or orifice. **stenosed, stenotic** (stĕ-nōst′, stĕ-nōzd″, stĕ-not′ik), *adj.*

    ETIOLOGY: Stenosis may result from embryonic maldevelopment, hypertrophy and thickening of a sphincter muscle, inflammatory disorders, or excessive development of fibrous tissue. It may involve almost any tube or duct.

    aortic s. Stenosis of blood flow from the left ventricle to the aorta due to aortic valve disease or obstructions just above or below the valve. The stenosis may be congenital or secondary to diseases of adolescence or adulthood, e.g., rheumatic fever or fibrocalcific degeneration of the valve. It is the most common cardiac valve dysfunction in the

U.S. SYN: *aortostenosis*. SEE: *Nursing Diagnoses Appendix.*

SYMPTOMS: Many patients with mild or moderate aortic stenosis, e.g., with a valve area that is more than 1 cm^2 or a valve gradient that is less than 50 mm Hg, have no symptoms and are unaware of their condition. A heart murmur is usually heard on physical examination of the patient. This murmur is best heard at the right second intercostal space during systole. Palpation of the arteries in severe aortic stenosis may reveal a delayed and weakened pulse, e.g., at the carotids. The heart's apical impulse may be laterally and inferiorly displaced as a result of left ventricular hypertrophy. Alarming symptoms include anginal chest pain, syncope, and dyspnea on exertion. When these occur, surgery to repair or replace the diseased valve are necessary.

PHYSICAL FINDINGS: Transthoracic echocardiography (TTE) diagnoses aortic stenosis and helps to evaluate its severity, determine left ventricular size and function, and detect other valvular disease.

TREATMENT: If the aortic valve area is significantly narrowed, i.e., < 0.8 cm^2, or if the patient has experienced symptoms of heart failure or syncope, percutaneous balloon aortic valvuloplasty or aortic valve replacement may be necessary.

PATIENT CARE: A history of related cardiac disorders is obtained. Cardiopulmonary function is assessed regularly by monitoring vital signs and weight, intake, and output for signs of fluid overload. The patient is monitored for chest pain, which may indicate cardiac ischemia, and the electrocardiogram is evaluated for ischemic changes. Activity tolerance and fatigue are assessed.

After cardiac catheterization, the insertion site is checked according to protocol (often every 15 min for 6 hr) for signs of bleeding; the patient is assessed for chest pain, and vital signs, heart rhythm, and peripheral pulses distal to the insertion site are monitored. Problems are reported to the cardiologist.

Desired outcomes for all aortic valve surgeries include adequate cardiopulmonary tissue perfusion and cardiac output, reduced fatigue with exertion, absence of fluid volume excess, and ability to manage the treatment regimen. Patients with aortic stenosis (with or without surgical repair) require prophylactic antibiotics before invasive procedures (including dental extractions, cleanings) because of the risk they pose for bacteremia and infective endocarditis.

cicatricial s. Stenosis due to a contracted scar.

coronary artery s. A physical obstruction to the flow of blood through the epicardial arteries, usually due to atherosclerotic plaque.

infantile hypertrophic pyloric s. Pyloric **s.**

lumbar spinal s. Stenosis of the spinal canal due to degenerative or traumatic changes at the level of the lumbar vertebrae. This condition causes back pain, often associated with pain that radiates into the legs, esp. when the patient is standing. Sitting often relieves the pain. The diagnosis is performed by spinal imaging, e.g., computed tomography or magnetic resonance imaging scanning. Treatments include physical therapy, braces, analgesic agents, and spinal surgery.

mitral s. ABBR: MS. Stenosis of the mitral valve orifice with obstruction of blood flow from the left atrium to the left ventricle. In most adults, previous bouts of rheumatic carditis are responsible for the lesion. Less often, MS may be present at birth (Lutembacher disease), or it may develop as the mitral valve calcifies during aging.

The abnormality of the valve may predispose patients to infective endocarditis; to left atrial enlargement and atrial arrhythmias; or to left ventricular failure. SEE: *Nursing Diagnoses Appendix.*

pulmonary s. Stenosis of the opening into the pulmonary artery from the right cardiac ventricle.

pyloric s. Stenosis of the pyloric orifice. In infants, excessive thickening of the pyloric sphincter or hypertrophy and hyperplasia of the mucosa and submucosa of the pylorus are usually responsible.

TREATMENT: In infants, treatment may involve open or laparoscopic division of the muscles of the pylorus. Infantile pyloric stenosis is usually diagnosed in the first 6 months of life when babies have trouble with vomiting after eating, sometimes with projectile vomiting and consequent dehydration. The disease occurs in 2 to 3 infants per 1000 births and is more common in boys than girls. In adults, endoscopic stents may be placed to open malignant obstructions. SYN: *infantile hypertrophic pyloric s.*; *pyloristenosis.*

renal artery s. Stenosis in one or both arteries that supply the kidneys; a relatively uncommon cause of hypertension. In young women, the cause is usually fibromuscular dysplasia of one or both arteries. In older people, the cause is usually atherosclerosis.

TREATMENT: Patients may be treated medically with standard antihypertensive drugs, or, in some cases, with renal artery angioplasty or bypass surgery. SEE: illus.

subaortic s. A congenital stenosis of the aortic tract below the aortic valves. SEE: *hypertrophic* **cardiomyopathy**.

tricuspid s. Stenosis of the opening to the tricuspid valve.

Stenotrophomonas maltophilia (stĕn'ō-trō-fō-mōn"as) A gram-negative, motile, strictly anaerobic bacillus of the family Pseudomonadaceae. It may cause pneumonia, meningitis, endocarditis, conjunctivitis, wound infections, and infections related to the use of central venous catheters. Trimethoprim-sulfamethoxazole is used to treat infections with this organism. This species was formerly called *Pseudomonas maltophila* and *Xanthomonas maltophila*. SEE: illus.

Stensen, Niels, Steensen, Niels (stān'sĕn, sten'sĕn) Danish anatomist and geologist, 1638–1686.

S. duct The duct leading from the parotid gland to the oral cavity. SYN: *parotid duct*.

stent (stent) [Charles Thomas Stent, Brit. dentist, 1845–1901] **1.** Originally, a compound used in making dental molds. **2.** Any material or device used to hold tissue in place, to keep open blood vessels, or to provide a support for a graft or anastomosis while healing is taking place.

airway s. A tube or catheter used as a scaffold to keep an airway open. It is used, e.g., to maintain the patency of a trachea or bronchus that has collapsed as a result of compression by neighboring tissues.

bare metal s. A vascular stent made of stainless steel or related materials. It is designed to hold an artery open with

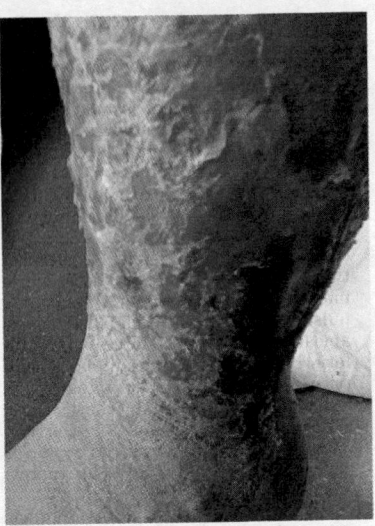

STENOTROPHOMONAS INFECTION OF THE LEG

simple mechanical support. SEE: *drug-eluting s.*

covered s. A stent whose supportive lattice is coated with biocompatible fabric or plastic, e.g., Dacron, polytetrafluoroethylene, or silicone.

drug-eluting s. ABBR: DES. A stent coated with medications that it releases into surrounding intimal cells. It is designed to keep the lumen of an artery from closing both by holding the artery open and by retarding the growth of the vascular endothelium into the stent. SEE: *bare metal s.*

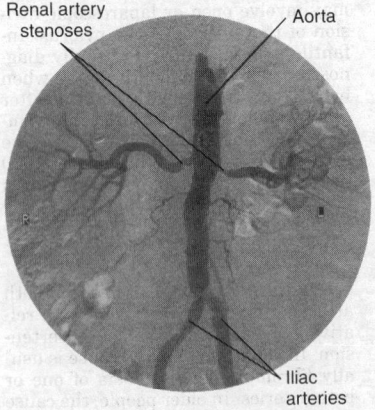
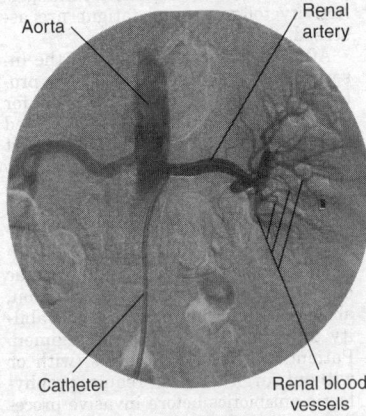

RENAL ARTERY STENOSIS

(A) Renal artery stenosis (before angioplasty); (B) Renal artery stenosis (after angioplasty)
(Courtesy of Arnold Klein, M.D., Northwest Permanente, P.C.)

endoluminal s. A stent placed inside a tubular structure or organ.

endovascular s. A stent placed inside an artery or a vein.

esophageal s. A tube inserted into the esophagus to open a stricture.

intraluminal coronary artery s. A stent made of an inert material, usually metallic, with a self-expanding mesh introduced into the coronary artery. It is used to prevent lumen closure (restenosis) following bypass surgery and to treat acute vessel closure after angioplasty. SEE: illus.

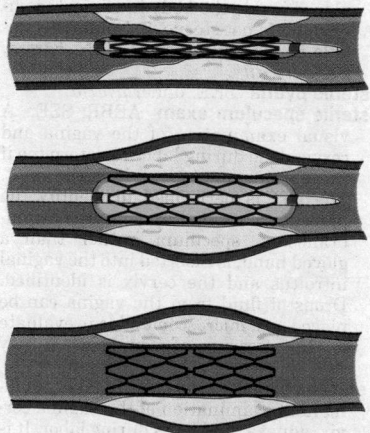

INSERTION OF A CORONARY ARTERY STENT

(A) A balloon catheter with a collapsed stent is advanced to the location of a coronary artery lesion. (B) The balloon is inflated, which expands the stent and compresses the lesion to increase the artery opening. (C) The balloon is then deflated and removed, leaving the expanded stent in place to prevent the artery from closing.

self-expanding s. A stent that opens on its own after it is deployed to the lumen it is intended to occupy, e.g., a blood vessel, tube, or organ.

urologic s. A biologically compatible stent inserted into the ureter or urethra to relieve or prevent urinary tract obstruction. Such stents are commonly placed in the urinary tract after endoureterotomy and endopyelotomy.

step (step) **1.** To move one foot in relation to the other, as in walking. **2.** A series of rests for the foot, used for ascending or descending. **3.** One half of a gait cycle. **4.** A single movement or act within a sequence of behaviors necessary for completing a task.

rate-determining s. The chemical reaction in a series of sequential reactions that takes the longest to occur.

Rönne s. A steplike defect in the visual field.

step-down unit A unit to which stable patients are sent either after being cared for in intensive care units (ICUs) or instead of receiving care in ICUs.

Stephan curve A mathematical model used to determine the impact of ingested foods on the pH of dental plaque and subsequent caries formation. Decalcification of teeth occurs when the pH in the oral cavity is less than 5.5.

DENTAL IMPLICATIONS: To reduce decalcification of tooth surfaces, patients should be encouraged to consume foods that do not result in a drop in plaque pH.

step length When an individual is walking, the distance between the first point of contact of a limb with the ground and the first point of contact of the limb on the opposite side, often but not always the distance from the back of one heel strike to the back of the other.

stepped care SEE: under *care.*

steradian (stē-rā′dē-ăn) The unit of measurement of solid angles. It encloses an area on the surface of a sphere equal to the square of the radius of the sphere.

sterco- [L. *stercus,* stem *stercor-,* dung] Prefix meaning *feces.* SEE: *scato-.*

stercobilin (stĕr″kō-bī′lĭn) [″ + *bilis,* bile] A brown pigment derived from the bile, giving the characteristic color to feces. SEE: *urobilin.*

stercobilinogen (stĕr″kō-bī-lĭn′ō-jĕn) A colorless substance derived from urobilinogen. It is present in the feces and turns brown on oxidation.

stercoraceous (stĕr″kō-rā′shŭs) [L. *stercoraceus*] Pert. to or containing feces.

stereo-, stere- [Gr. *stereos,* solid] [] Prefixes meaning *solid, having three dimensions,* or *firmly established.*

stereoacuity (stĕr″ē-ō-ă-kew′ĭt-ē) The accuracy and sharpness of images acquired with binocular depth perception.

stereochemistry (stĕr″ē-ō-kĕm′ĭs-trē) That branch of chemistry dealing with atoms in their space relationship and the effect of such a relationship on the action and effects of the molecule. **stereochemical,** *adj.*

stereocilia (stĕr″ē-ō-sĭl′ē-ă) *sing.,* **stereocilium** Microvilli on the free surfaces of cells lining the ductus epididymis and ductus deferens, and of the hair cells of the receptors of the inner ear.

stereoencephalotomy (stĕr″ē-ō-ĕn-sĕf″ă-lŏt′ō-mē) [″ + *enkephalos,* brain, + *tome,* incision] Surgical incision by use of stereotaxis during brain surgery.

stereognosis (stĕr″ē-ŏg-nō′sĭs) [″ + *gnosis,* knowledge] The ability to recognize the form of solid objects by touch.

stereogram (stĕr′ē-ō-grăm) [″ + *gramma,* something written] A stereoscopic radiograph.

stereoisomerism (stĕr″ē-ō-ī-sō′mĕr-ĭzm) A condition in which two or more substances may have the same empirical formula but mirror-image structural formulas.

stereology (stĕr″ē-ŏl′ō-jē) [Gr. *stereos,* solid, + *logos,* word, reason] The study of three-dimensional aspects of objects.

stereometry (stĕr″ē-ŏm′ĕ-trē) [″ + *metron,* a measure] The measurement of a solid body or the cubic contents of a hollow body.

stereophotography (stĕr″ē-ō-fō-tŏg′rä-fē) [″ + *phos,* light, + *graphein,* to write] Photography that produces the effect of solidity or depth in the pictures.

stereophotomicrograph (stĕr″ē-ō-fō″tō-mī′krō-grăf) [″ + ″ + *mikros,* tiny, + *graphein,* to write] A photograph showing the solidity or depth of a microscopic subject.

stereopsis (stĕr″ē-op′sis) Stereoscopic vision.

stereoradiography (stĕr″ē-ō-rā″dē-ŏg′rä-fē) [″ + L. *radius,* ray, + Gr. *graphein,* to write] Radiography from two slightly different angles to simulate the distance between the viewer's eyes (usually 4 in.) so that a stereoscopic effect is produced when the radiographs are viewed through a stereoscope.

stereoscope (stĕr′ē-ō-skōp) [″ + *skopein,* to examine] An instrument that creates an impression of solidity or depth of objects seen by combining images of two pictures.

stereoscopic, stereoscopical (stĕr″ē-ō-skop′ĭk, -skop′ĭ-kăl) Pert. to the stereoscope or its use.

stereoscopic digital mammography A means of imaging the breast in which two beams enter the breast from slightly different angles so that a three-dimensional image of the breast can be created. It improves the ability to distinguish structures that are next to each other from those that appear to be adjacent but are actually separated by other tissues.

stereospecific (stĕr″ē-ō-spĕ-sĭf′ĭk) Specific for only one of the possible receptors on a cell.

stereotactic (stĕr″ē-ō-tăk′tĭk) Having precise spatial coordinates; located precisely in three-dimensional space. Stereotactic techniques are used in brain surgery, breast biopsies, and other procedures in which precision is needed in identifying, cutting, or removing tissues.

stereotype **1.** A simplified idea of a person or a concept, often one that is prejudicial to others or lacking in finesse. **2.** A simple movement performed unconsciously.

stereotypy (stĕr-ē-ō-tī′pē) [″ + *typos,* type] The persistent repetition of words, posture, or movement without meaning.

steric, sterical (ster′ik, ster′ĭ-kăl) [*ster(eo)* + *-ic*] Pert. to the spatial arrangement of atoms in a chemical compound. **sterically** (ĭ-k(ă-)lē), *adv.*

sterilant (stĕr′ĭ-lănt) [L. *sterilis,* barren] Any agent used to render objects free of living or potentially infectious organisms.

sterile (stĕr′ĭl) [L. *sterilis,* barren] **1.** Free from living microorganisms, i.e., of bacteria, fungi, protozoa, spores, viruses, and other living organisms. No agent, device, drug, or fluid should be placed inside the body in clinical medicine if it is not sterile. **2.** Not fertile; unable to reproduce young. SYN: *barren.* SEE: *sterility.*

sterile pyuria SEE: under *pyuria.*

sterile speculum exam ABBR: SSE. A visual examination of the vagina and cervix done during labor to determine if there is any amniotic fluid in the vault. The test is performed to identify the presence of premature rupture of membranes. A speculum, rather than a gloved hand, is inserted into the vaginal introitus and the cervix is identified. Drops of fluid from the vagina can be placed on a microscopic slide to evaluate for the presence of ferning when they dry.

sterile vaginal exam ABBR: SVE. A bimanual examination of the vagina, cervix, adnexa, and fetus during labor. It is used to determine the progress of labor, e.g., the position of the fetus, its engagement, and the dilation of the cervix, while minimizing the risk of introducing harmful bacteria.

sterility (stĕr-ĭl′ĭ-tē) [L. *sterilitas,* barrenness] **1.** Freedom from contamination or colonization by living microorganisms. **2.** The inability of the female to become pregnant or for the male to impregnate a female.

When investigating sterility, both partners should be examined. A routine examination for the female includes a study of the vaginal secretions, a bimanual pelvic examination, visualization of the cervix, in some cases, a test for patency of the fallopian tubes, and a record of basal body temperature. A history of pelvic disease in the female is of great importance. The male should have the seminal fluid examined for the number, motility, viability, and normality of the spermatozoa, and occasionally other tests (e.g., of testosterone levels).

TREATMENT: Treatment of sterility depends on the finding and correction of any or all causes of the condition. A high percentage of couples who have an infertility problem during the first year in which they are trying to have a child will, without treatment, produce offspring within 2 to 3 years. SEE: *embryo* *transfer; gamete intrafallopian **transfer**; in vitro **fertilization**.*

absolute s. The inability to produce offspring as a result of anatomical or physiological factors that prevent production of functional germ cells, conception, or the normal development of a zygote.

female s. The inability of a female to conceive. This may result from a failure to produce or transport viable ova or to sustain a pregnancy due to a congenital absence or maldevelopment of the reproductive organs. Sterility also may be secondary to endocrine disorders, infections, trauma, neoplasms, inactivation of the ovaries by irradiation, or surgical excision of the ovaries, tubes, or uterus. SEE: *infertility; gonadal **dysgenesis**.*

male s. The inability of a male either to produce sperm or to produce viable sperm, thereby prohibiting fertilization of the ovum. This may result from congenital factors, such as cryptorchidism or maldevelopment of the testicular ducts or testis, or acquired factors, such as radiation to, or surgical removal of, the testes.

primary s. Sterility resulting from failure of the testis or ovary to produce functional germ cells.

relative s. Sterility due to causes other than a defect of the sex organs.

sterilization (stĕr″ĭ-lĭ-zā′shŏn) [*sterilize*] **1.** Complete removal or destruction of microorganisms in an object. **2.** The act of sterilizing or state of being sterilized. Sterilization can be accomplished by the surgical removal of the testes or ovaries (castration), inactivation by irradiation, or by tying off or removing a portion of the reproductive ducts (ductus deferens or uterine tubes). SEE: *salpingectomy; vasectomy.*

cold s. Immersion of heat-sensitive instruments into microbicidal fluids (such as glutaraldehyde, orthophthalaldehyde, or concentrated hydrogen peroxide) to rid them of bacteria, fungi, mycobacteria, or viruses.

dry heat s. The sterilization of instruments in an oven to raise their surface temperature high enough and long enough to kill any microorganisms.

e-beam s. Electron beam **s.**

electron beam s. Sterilization in which objects are placed into a cloud of electrically charged plasma generated by directing electrons into a container filled with gas, such as helium. SYN: *e-beam **s.***

flash s. Steam-thermal sterilization in which instruments that are difficult to obtain or replace are placed in superheated (270°F, [145°C]) steam for 3 to 10 min.

⚠ The Association of Operating Room Nurses cautions that this procedure should only be used when there is an urgent need for a particular operating instrument that otherwise cannot be met.

fractional s. Sterilization in which heating is done at intervals so that spores can develop into vegetative bacteria and be destroyed. SYN: *intermittent **s.***

gas s. Exposure to gases such as formaldehyde or ethylene oxide (ETO) that destroy microorganisms.

⚠ Because ethylene oxide is toxic if it is inhaled, tools sterilized in ETO must be aerated according to OSHA standards.

hydrogen peroxide gas plasma s. Cold sterilization by concentrated, vaporized hydrogen peroxide. It can be used to decontaminate objects exposed to bacteria, fungi, prions, and viruses.

intermittent s. Fractional **s.**

involuntary s. Any procedure that renders a legally incompetent person permanently infertile. It is performed only under court order, and only when other less drastic means of preventing unwanted procreation have failed.

laparoscopic s. Sterilization by a laparoscope to gain access to the fallopian tubes so they can be banded, clipped, or electrocoagulated.

steam-thermal s. Sterilization by exposure of microorganisms to flowing steam or pressurized steam. There are three types of steam-thermal sterilization: gravity methods, in which ambient air in the sterilization chamber is gradually displaced by steam; prevacuum, in which air in the chamber is mechanically removed; and flash sterilization.

sterilize (stĕr′ĭ-līz) [L. *sterilis,* barren] **1.** To free from microorganisms. **2.** To make incapable of reproduction.

sterilizer (stĕr′ĭ-lī″zĕr) An oven or appliance for sterilizing.

steam s. An autoclave that sterilizes by steam under pressure at temperatures above 100°C.

sternad (stĕr′năd) [Gr. *sternon,* chest] Toward the sternum.

sternebra (stĕr′nē-bră, stĕr′nē-brē) *pl.* **sternebrae** [″ + L. *vertebra,* vertebra] Parts of the sternum during development of the fetus.

sternen (stĕr′nĕn) [Gr. *sternon,* chest] Pert. solely to the sternum and no other structures.

sterno-, stern- [Gr. *sternon,* chest] Prefixes meaning *sternum, breast, breastbone.*

sternoclavicular (stĕr″nō-klă-vĭk′ū-lăr) [″ + L. *clavicula,* little key] Pert. to the sternum and clavicle. SYN: *sternocleidal.*

sternocleidomastoid (stĕr″nō-klī″dō-măs′toyd) [″ + *clavis,* key, + *mas-*

tos, breast, + *eidos,* form, shape] One of two muscles arising from the sternum and inner part of the clavicle.

sternocostal (stĕr″nō-kŏs′tăl) [″ + L. *costa,* rib] Pert. to the sternum and ribs.

sternohyoid (stĕr″nō-hī′oyd) [″ + *hyoeides,* U-shaped] The muscle from the medial end of the clavicle and sternum to the hyoid bone.

sternomastoid (stĕr″nō-măs′toyd) [″ + *mastos,* breast, + *eidos,* form, shape] Pert. to the sternum and mastoid process of the temporal bone.

sternothyroid (stĕr″nō-thī′royd) [″ + *thyreos,* shield, + *eidos,* form, shape] The muscle extending beneath the sternohyoid that depresses the thyroid cartilage.

sternotomy (stĕr-nŏt′ō-mē) [″ + *tome,* incision] The operation of cutting through the sternum. SEE: illus.

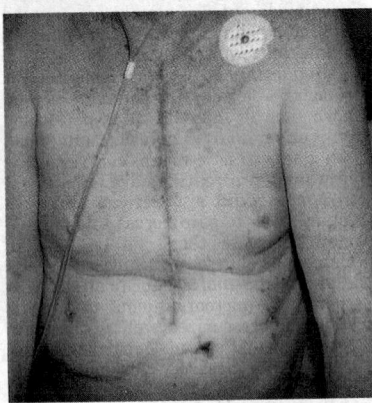

STERNOTOMY

Sternotomy scar that is nearly healed

sternovertebral (stĕr″nō-vĕr′tĕ-brăl) [″ + L. *vertebra,* vertebra] Pert. to the sternum and vertebrae.

sternum (stĕr′nŭm) [L.] The narrow, flat bone in the median line of the thorax in front. It consists of three portions: the manubrium, the body or gladiolus, and the ensiform or xiphoid process. SEE: illus.

    cleft s. A congenital fissure of the sternum.

steroid (stĕr′oyd) **1.** An organic compound containing in its chemical nucleus the perhydrocyclopentanophenanthrene ring. SEE: *steroid **hormone*** for illus.; *perhydrocyclopentanophenanthrene.* **2.** Any of a large group of substances chemically related to sterols, including cholesterol, D vitamins, bile acids, certain hormones, saponins, glucosides of digitalis, and certain carcinogenic substances.

steroid diabetes SEE: under *diabetes.*

steroid hormone SEE: under *hormone.*

steroid hormone therapy Treatment

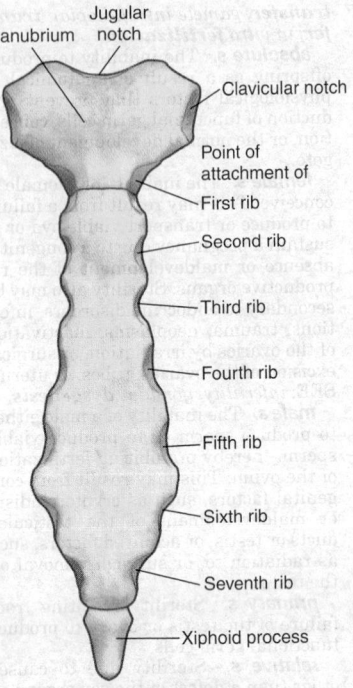

STERNUM

with intravenous, oral, inhaled, or topical adrenal hormones (or their synthetic derivatives), usually to relieve inflammatory diseases (such as asthma or chronic obstructive lung disease; arthritis or colitis; or dermatitis or eczema) or as part of a combined modality treatment for some malignancies. Common side effects of prolonged, high-dose steroid hormone therapy include alterations in the sleep-wake cycle, fluid and sodium retention, muscle weakness, thinning of the skin, cataract formation, diabetes mellitus, osteoporosis, or immune suppression. Few of these effects are likely to occur when steroids are given for 1- or 2-week courses of therapy.

steroidogenesis (stē-roy″dō-jĕn′ē-sĭs) Production of steroids.

steroid withdrawal syndrome The appearance of symptoms of adrenal insufficiency in persons who discontinue the use of corticosteroids after having been treated with them for a prolonged period. In those patients, adrenal function has been suppressed by exogenous hormone and the patient's adrenal glands do not provide an appropriate response when the patient has a serious infection, surgery, or an accident. This failure to respond to stress may be present for as long as a year after discontinuation of corticosteroid therapy. The syndrome may be prevented by gradual rather than abrupt withdrawal of corticosteroid therapy.

sterol (stĕr′ŏl, stēr′ŏl) [Gr. *stereos*, solid, + L. *oleum*, oil] One of a group of substances (such as cholesterol) with a cyclic nucleus and alcohol moiety. They are found free or esterified with fatty acids (cholesterides). They are found in animals (zoosterols) or in plants (phytosterols). They are generally colorless, crystalline compounds, nonsaponifiable and soluble in certain organic solvents.

-sterone [*sterol* + *-one*] Suffix used in biochemistry in naming *steroid hormones*, e.g., *testosterone*.

stertor (stĕr′tor) [NL. *stertor*, to snore] Snoring or snorting; breathing loudly or laboriously. SYN: *stertorous* **respiration**. **stertorous,** *adj.*

stetho-, steth- [Gr. *stēthos*, chest] Prefixes meaning *chest*.

stethoscope (steth′ŏ-skōp″) [*stetho-* + *-scope*] An instrument used to transmit to the examiner's ears sounds produced in the body.

 binaural s. A stethoscope to be used with both ears.

 compound s. A stethoscope in which more than one set is attached to the same fork and chest piece.

 double s. A stethoscope with two earpieces and tubes.

 electronic s. A stethoscope equipped to amplify electronically sounds from the body.

 single s. A stethoscope designed for one ear only.

Stevens-Johnson syndrome (stē′vĕnz-jŏn′sŏn) [Albert M. Stevens, 1884–1945, Frank C. Johnson, 1894–1934, U.S. pediatricians] A systemic skin disease, probably identical to toxic epidermal necrolysis, that produces fevers and lesions of the oral, conjunctival, and vaginal mucous membranes. It is marked by a cutaneous rash that is often widespread and severe. Skin loss may lead to dehydration, infection, or death. SEE: illus.; *erythema multiforme*.

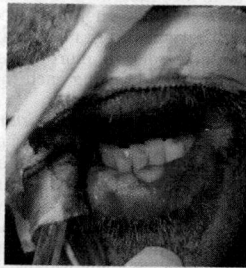

STEVENS-JOHNSON SYNDROME

Stevia (stē′vē-ă) [NL] A genus of shrubs native to South America. A noncaloric

sugar substitute is made from plants of this genus.

STH *somatotropic* **hormone**.

sthenia (sthē′nē-ă) [Gr. *sthenos*, strength] Normal or unusual strength. Opposite of asthenia. **sthenic,** *adj.*

stibophen (stib′ŏ-fen″) $C_{12}H_{16}Na_5O_{16}S_4Sb$, a trivalent tin compound, used in treating schistosomiasis, leishmaniasis, and granuloma inguinale.

stick [Shortening of for *needlestick*] A colloquial term for puncture, esp. the puncturing of the skin or a blood vessel.

STICU *surgical trauma intensive care unit.*

stiff [AS. *stif*] Rigid, firm, inflexible.

stiff man syndrome, stiff person syndrome A rare central nervous system disease characterized by progressive muscular rigidity and spasms. The diagnosis is strongly supported by continuous motor unit activity during electromyography and by the presence of autoantibodies (antiglutamic acid antibody). Treatments include benzodiazepines, for comfort, and immunological therapies such as high-dose corticosteroids, intravenous immunoglobulins, or plasma exchange.

stiff neck Rigidity of neck resulting from spasm of neck muscles. It is a symptom of many disorders. SEE: *torticollis; wryneck.*

stigma (stĭg′mă) *pl.* **stigmatastigmas** [Gr., mark] **1.** A mark or spot on the skin; lesions or sores of the hands and feet that resemble crucifixion wounds. **2.** The spot on the ovarian surface where rupture of a graafian follicle occurs. **3.** A social condition marked by attitudinal devaluing or demeaning of persons who, because of disfigurement or disability, are not viewed as being capable of fulfilling valued social roles.

stigmata (stĭg′mă-tă) Cutaneous evidence of systemic illness.

stigmatic (stĭg-măt′ĭk) [Gr. *stigma*, mark] Pert. to or marked with a stigma.

stilbestrol (stĭl-bĕs′trŏl) Diethylstilbestrol.

stillbirth (stĭl′bĭrth) [AS. *stille*, quiet, + Old Norse *burdhr*, birth] The birth of a dead fetus. In Western nations stillbirths occur in 1 of every 320 pregnancies. Identified risk factors include excess maternal weight, maternal age over 35 years, and smoking during pregnancy.

stillborn, *adj.*

Still disease (stil) [Sir George F. Still, Brit. physician, 1868–1941] Juvenile rheumatoid **arthritis**.

Still murmur A benign, functional midsystolic murmur heard in children. The maximum sound is heard over the left lower sternal border.

-stim In pharmacology, a suffix designating a *hematopoietic colony-stimulating factor*.

stimulant (stĭm′ū-lănt) [L. *stimulans,* goading] Any agent temporarily increasing functional activity. Stimulants may be classified according to the organ upon which they act, as follows: cardiac, bronchial, gastric, cerebral, intestinal, nervous, motor, vasomotor, respiratory, and secretory. Common stimulants include caffeine, low doses of ethanol, methamphetamines, and cocaine.

stimulate (stĭm′ū-lāt) [L. *stimulare,* to goad on] **1.** To increase activity of an organ or structure. **2.** To apply a stimulus.

stimulation (stĭm″yŭ-lā′shŏn) [L *stimulare,* to goad] **1.** An irritating or invigorating action of agents on muscles, nerves, or sensory end organs by which excitation or activity in a part is evoked. **2.** A stimulus.

breast s. In pregnancy, nipple rolling or the application of heat to the breasts to elicit release of endogenous oxytocin and to generate uterine contractions. The procedure also has been used to evaluate placental sufficiency in the third trimester and to increase contractions in patients with ruptured membranes and when contractions are absent, rare, irregular, or of poor quality. SEE: *oxytocin challenge test.*

cognitive s. A treatment for patients with mild dementia, in which patients are exposed to and tasked with mentally challenging exercises to improve their ability to think and interact effectively with their environment and with other people. It is used as an adjunct to medical therapy, often in a recreational setting, to make the activity fun and socially engaging. SYN: *psychostimulation.*

deep brain s. The application of pulsed electrical energy via electrodes to the pars interna of the globus pallidus or the subthalamic nucleus. It is used to treat movement disorders, such as Parkinson disease.

dorsal cord s. The relief of pain with electric stimulation of the posterior spinal cord.

double simultaneous s. In a neurological examination, a test of unilateral neglect. A light touch, audible signal, or visual cue is provided to both sides of the patient at the same time, e.g., both arms, both ears, both the left and right visual fields. Failure to detect one of the stimuli suggests a lesion in the opposite side of the cerebral cortex. Double simultaneous stimulation can also be performed on one side of the body, for instance, by tapping the left arm and left side of the face at the same time. If the distal stimulus is undetected even after

several trials, the patient may have an organic brain syndrome.

electrical s. ABBR: ES. The use of electric current to affect a tissue, e.g., nerve, muscle, or bone. The stimulation of bone, for instance, facilitates and hastens the healing of fractures. SYN: *electrostimulation; electrotherapy.* SEE: *bipolar* (2); *monopolar; transcutaneous electrical nerve s.*

fetal scalp s. An assessment of fetal well-being in which the examiner reaches into the vagina and rubs the scalp of the fetus. The fetal heart rate is monitored for accelerations. If the fetal heart rate does not accelerate appropriately, further testing, such as scalp blood sampling, may be needed.

fetal (vibratory) acoustic s. ABBR: FAST. A noninvasive means of assessing fetal reactivity during labor. It typically is used as an adjunct to nonstress testing. The examiner applies an electronic source of low-frequency sound (such as an electrolarynx) firmly to the mother's abdomen over the fetal head. A reactive test is characterized by fetal heart rate accelerations or other measurable forms of increased fetal activity.

infant s. The use of various techniques to provide neonates and infants identified with or at risk for developmental delay with an environment that has a rich and diverse range of sensations and experiences.

intramuscular s. ABBR: IMS. The insertion of solid needles into sensitive or painful body parts in order to alleviate musculoskeletal, myofascial, or nerve pain. SYN: *dry needling; trigger point dry needling.* SEE: *trigger **point**.*

magnetic cortical s. The induction of painless electrical current within the brain to detect abnormalities in cortical motor neuron function.

neural s. The activation or energizing of a nerve, through an external source.

nipple s. Massaging or suckling the nipple of the breast and surrounding aureola to stimulate uterine contractions or induce labor.

ovarian s. A treatment for female infertility that encourages the ovaries to produce and release more eggs than they normally do during each monthly cycle.

percutaneous electrical nerve s. ABBR: PENS. A treatment for pain in which weak electrical currents are applied to acupuncture needles inserted into trigger points or dermatomes near painful body parts. PENS is sometimes used to treat episodic low back pain and other regional pain syndromes. It may be used as an alternative to transcutaneous electrical nerve stimulation (TENS).

transcranial magnetic s. ABBR:

TMS. The application of pulses from a magnetic coil to induce electrical currents in specific parts of the brain. This treatment has been used in experimental neuroscience to study the activity of different areas of the brain, and in psychiatry as a noninvasive alternative to electroconvulsive therapy.

transcutaneous electrical nerve s. ABBR: TENS. The application of mild electrical stimulation through electrodes placed on the skin over a painful area. It alleviates pain by interfering with transmission of painful stimuli. SEE: illus.

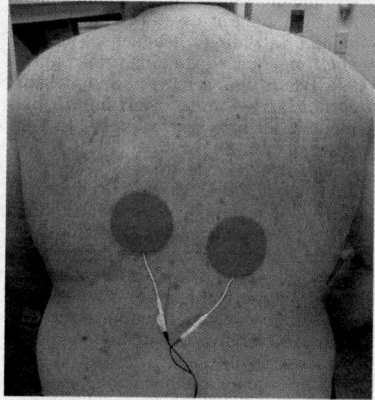

TRANSCUTANEOUS ELECTRICAL NERVE STIMULATION

vagus nerve s. A treatment for seizures and treatment-resistant depression in which a generator sends electrical impulses along the left vagus nerve. The impulse generator is typically inserted under the clavicle on the left side of the chest during a brief surgical procedure. The device is set to generate electrical impulses of appropriate amplitude, frequency, and pulse width to control a patient's symptoms.

stimulator (stĭm″ū-lā′tor) Someone or something that stimulates.

long-acting thyroid s. SEE: *long-acting thyroid stimulator.*

stimulus (stĭm′ū-lŭs) *pl.* **stimuli** [L., a goad] **1.** A change of environment of sufficient intensity to evoke a response in an organism. **2.** An excitant or irritant.

adequate s. 1. Any stimulus capable of evoking a response, i.e., an environmental change possessing a certain intensity, acting for a certain length of time, and occurring at a certain rate. **2.** A stimulus capable of initiating a nerve impulse in a specific type of receptor.

chemical s. A chemical (liquid, gaseous, or solid) that is capable of evoking a response.

conditioned s. A stimulus that gives rise to a conditioned response. SEE: *conditioned reflex.*

electric s. A stimulus resulting from initiation of or cessation of a flow of electrons as from a battery, induction coil, or generator.

homologous s. A stimulus that acts only on specific sensory end organs.

iatrotropic s. Any stimulus or event that makes a person seek or receive medical attention, such as a symptom, a physical finding, or the need for a routine or required health screening examination.

liminal s. Threshold s.

mechanical s. A stimulus produced by a physical change such as contact with objects or changes in pressure.

minimal s. Threshold s.

nociceptive s. A painful and usually injurious stimulus.

subliminal s. A stimulus that is weaker than a threshold stimulus.

thermal s. A stimulus produced by a change in skin temperature, a rise giving sensations of warmth, a fall giving sensations of coldness.

threshold s. The least or weakest stimulus that is capable of initiating a response or giving rise to a sensation. SYN: *liminal s.; minimal s.*

unconditioned s. Any stimulus that elicits an unconditioned response (i.e., a response that occurs by reflex rather than by learning).

sting [AS *stinge*] **1.** A sharp, smarting sensation, as of a wound or astringent. **2.** A puncture wound made by a venomous barb or spine (e.g., of a marine animal or an insect). SEE: *bite.*

SYMPTOMS: Pain at the puncture site is almost universally reported. The patient may also develop local swelling, which at times is massive, and localized itch. Generalized hives, dizziness, a tight feeling in the chest, difficulty breathing, swelling of the lips and tongue, stridor, respiratory failure, hypotension, syncope, or cardiac arrest may also occur. Anaphylactic reactions such as these require prompt effective treatment.

TREATMENT: If the stinger is still present in the skin, it should be carefully removed. Ice should be applied locally to limit inflammation at the site of the sting and systemic distribution of venom. Diphenhydramine (or other antihistamine) should be given by mouth or parenterally; moreover, if signs and symptoms of anaphylaxis exist, epinephrine should be administered. Corticosteroids are given to reduce the risk of delayed allergic responses. Patients who have had large local reactions or systemic reactions to stings should be referred for desensitization (immunotherapy). In this treatment, gradually increasing dilutions of venom are injected subcutaneously over weeks or months until immunological tolerance develops.

PREVENTION: Those with a history of anaphylactic reactions to venom should avoid exposure to the vectors (e.g., ants, bees, snakes, wasps) as much as possible. Protective clothing (e.g., specialized gloves or shoes) may prevent some stings. Cosmetics, perfumes, hair sprays, and bright or white clothing should be avoided to prevent attracting insects. Because foods and odors attract insects, care should be taken when cooking and eating outdoors.

bee s. SEE: *hymenoptera s.*

caterpillar s. Irritating contact with the hairs of a butterfly or moth larva. More than 50 species of larvae possess urticating hairs that contain a toxin. Contact can cause numbness and swelling of the infected area, severe radiating pain, localized swelling, enlarged regional lymph nodes, nausea, and vomiting. Although shock and convulsions may occur, no deaths have been reported. The disease is self-limiting. The larva of the flannel moth, *Megalopyge opercularis,* known as the puss caterpillar or woolly worm, is frequently the cause of this sting, particularly in the southern U.S. The fuzz from these larvae can be transported by wind. Treatment involves local application of moist soaks and administration of antihistamines.

catfish s. A toxic, allergic reaction caused by exposure to the venom contained in venomous glands at the base of catfish fins. The stung part should be immediately immersed in water as hot as the patient can stand for 1 hr or until the pain is controlled. Tetanus prophylaxis should be administered if needed.

hornet s. A sting from a wasp of the family Vespidae. SEE: *hymenoptera s.*

hymenoptera s. Envenomation by a fire ant, bee, hornet, or wasp. The sting from any of these insects may cause localized or, in some sensitized patients, systemic allergic reactions. Stings by venomous insects are one of the most common causes of anaphylaxis found in hospital emergency departments.

scorpion s. Injury resulting from scorpion venom. The stings of most species in the U.S. seldom produce severe toxic reactions, but because of the difficulty of distinguishing one species of scorpion from another, each scorpion sting should be treated as if it had been inflicted by a species capable of delivering a very toxic dose of venom. The stings vary in severity from local tissue reactions consisting of swelling and pain at the puncture site, to systemic reactions that compromise breathing and neuromuscular function. Death may

rarely occur (e.g., in very young children).

TREATMENT: For mild local reactions, cold compresses and antihistamines are sufficient. Severe reactions may need to be treated with airway management, antivenins, and intensive observation in the hospital. For the source of local antivenins, the use of which is controversial, contact the nearest poison control center.

sea anemone s. Contact with the nematocysts or stinging cells of certain species of the flower-like marine coelenterates causing severe dermatitis with chronic ulceration. In some cases, signs and symptoms of a systemic reaction develop, including headache, nausea, vomiting, sneezing, chills, fever, paralysis, delirium, seizures, anaphylaxis, cardiac arrhythmias, heart failure, pulmonary edema, and collapse. In rare cases, it is fatal.

TREATMENT: If there are systemic changes, vigorous therapy is indicated for hypotension. Diazepam is administered for convulsions. An electrocardiogram should be monitored for arrhythmias. Treatment for mild stings is symptomatic; application of vinegar to the sting area may inactivate the irritating secretion. All victims should be observed for 6 to 8 hr after initial therapy for rebound phenomenon.

stingray s. Penetration of the skin by the spine of a stingray and injection of venom.

TREATMENT: The injury should be treated by washing the wound with copious amounts of water; seawater should be used if sterile water is unavailable. The wound, which is very painful, should be cleansed thoroughly, and all foreign material should be removed. The wound site should be soaked in hot water (113°F [45°C]) for 30 to 60 min to inactivate the venom. Surgical débridement may be necessary, and narcotics may be needed for pain. Tetanus prophylaxis may be required, depending on the patient's immunization status. The wound is either packed open or loosely sutured to provide adequate drainage. Failure to treat this sting may result in gas gangrene or tetanus.

wasp s. SEE: *hymenoptera s.*

stinger Burner.

stingray (stĭng'rā) Any of the rays of the family Dasyatidae with wide pectoral fins that resemble wings. Venom glands are located in the spine running along the top of its whiplike tail; severe injuries can be inflicted if this spine penetrates the skin.

S-T interval SEE: under *interval.*

stippling (stĭp'lĭng) [Dutch *stippelen,* to spot] A spotted condition (e.g., in the retina in some diseases of the eye, or in basophilic red blood cells).

gingival s. An orange-peel appearance of healthy gingiva, believed to be due to the enlargement of the underlying connective tissue papillae in response to massage and toothbrushing; the indent lies between the bulging papillae where the epithelia grow downward as rete ridges.

stirrup (stĭr'ŭp) Stapes.

stitch (stich) **1.** A single loop of suture material passed through skin or flesh by a needle, to facilitate healing of a wound. **2.** A local, sharp, or spasmodic pain that often occurs in the side or flank of athletes. The following maneuvers may offer relief: bending forward while tightening the abdomen; breathing deeply and exhaling slowly through pursed lips; tightening the belt or pushing one's fingers into the painful area. It is advisable not to eat for 30 to 90 min before exercising, to warm up before exercising, and to work out at a lower intensity for longer periods.

whip s. Continuous **suture**.

stochastic effect (stŏ-kas'tik, stō-) A phenomenon that occurs purely by chance.

stochastic model (stŏ-kas'tik, stō-) [Gr. *stochastikos*, conjecturing, guessing] SEE: under *model*.

stock (stŏk) [AS. *stocc*, tree trunk] **1.** The original individual, race, or tribe from which others have descended. **2.** A supply or inventory of a drug or medical device.

stockinet (stŏk"ĭ-nĕt') A tubular woven material of uniform size that is open at both ends. It is used to hold bandages in place or to place uniform protection on a leg, finger, arm, or other part of an extremity, or to line a cast. A variant is termed "bias" stockinet and comes in a roll of different widths.

stocking (stŏk'ing) **1.** A snug covering for the foot, ankle, and leg. **2.** An elastic covering for the foot, ankle, and leg that places firm, even pressure on an extremity, useful in managing edema, preventing deep vein thrombosis (DVT) of the leg, and in treating varicose veins. Pneumatic compression devices, which sequentially inflate and deflate, are more effective than simple elasticized stockings. A graduated compression stocking exerts more pressure at the ankle than on the rest of the limb. Its pressure decreases proximally to permit venous return of blood. External compression reduces the cross-sectional area of the limb and increases the velocity of blood flow in both superficial and deep veins. It also improves venous valve function, reduces vein distention, and may have favorable effects on coagulants. In hospitalized patients at low risk for DVT, compression stockings

may be used alone to prevent the formation of blood clots; for those at higher risk, compression stockings usually are used in combination with anticoagulant therapy, such as heparin, low molecular weight heparin, or warfarin. Low-risk patients are those who have had minor surgery (less than 30 min), minor trauma, or minor medical illnesses. SEE: illus.

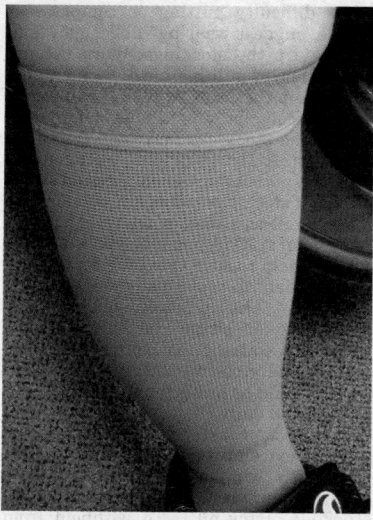

COMPRESSION STOCKING

to manage lymphedema

PATIENT CARE: Health care professionals should consider the following as guiding principles for clinical practice in the use of graduated compression stockings in the management of patients:

1. Apply compression stockings before surgery (when possible).

2. Follow manufacturer's recommendations to ensure correct fit.

3. Document measurements and stocking size at initial use to serve as baseline measures for the patient.

4. Review leg measurements regularly to avoid potential complications related to leg swelling.

5. Be sure the patient's legs and feet are dry before putting on stockings.

6. Remove stockings at least once each shift for skin assessment, hygiene, and care.

7. Provide more than one pair of hose in the correct size to allow for laundering if long-term use is planned.

8. Check stocking periodically during wear to ensure correct placement and to be certain there is no bunching or other restriction that would impede perfusion.

9. Assess neurovascular status regularly during skin care and at other times

using the inspection hole in the foot of the compression stocking.

10. Check patient sitting in a chair to be sure stockings do not compromise perfusion by acting as a tourniquet at the knee.

11. Teach patient and family the reason for using compression stockings, concerns for application and correct fit, care of the skin, and the importance of assessing for leg swelling. If the patient has difficulty putting on compression hose, suggest wearing rubber gloves to help grip the stockings. Warn the patient not to pull too hard, because this could rip the hose. Applying a lubricating silicone lotion to the leg before donning the stockings may help to reduce friction. Assistive devices are available to help with donning compression stockings. If stockings roll or slip down at the top, a roll-on adhesive designed for compression stockings can be applied to the leg to help resolve this problem. Advise the patient to replace stockings every 6 months. The patient should avoid standing or sitting for long periods, wearing constricting clothing (girdles, etc.), and crossing the legs. Legs and feet should be protected from injury and inspected daily.

TED s. Elastic hose worn on the lower extremities to prevent thrombophlebitis, while at prolonged bedrest or during periods of prolonged immobility.

stockpile (stŏk′pīl″) To withhold from immediate use; to maintain in storage for future needs. In many countries stockpiles of food rations, medications, or vaccines are maintained by governmental agencies in anticipation of future public health needs.

stoichiometry (stoy″kē-om′ĕ-trē) [Gr. *stoicheion*, element + *-metry*] The study of the mathematics of chemistry and chemical reactions; chemical accounting and chemical calculations. **stoichiometric** (kē-ŏ-me′trik), *adj.*

stoke (stōk) [Sir George Stokes, Brit. physicist, 1819–1903] A unit of viscosity equal to 10^{-4} m²/sec.

Stokes-Adams syndrome (stōks-ad′ămz) [William Stokes; Robert Adams, Irish physician, 1791–1875] A loss of consciousness caused by a decreased flow of blood to the brain. It may be caused by any transient interference with cardiac output such as incomplete or complete heart block. The patient may be light-headed or become completely unconscious and have brief convulsive body movements. Treatment includes basic and advanced cardiac life support, e.g., rescue breathing, chest compressions, administration of epinephrine, or cardiac pacing, as indicated by the patient's responses. SYN: *Adams-Stokes syndrome.*

PATIENT CARE: The patient's air-way, breathing, apical and radial pulses, blood pressure, and cardiac rhythm are monitored and supported. Emergency treatment (atropine sulfate, external pacing) is provided as necessary according to prescribed protocols. The patient is prepared for cardiac pacemaker implantation; reassurance and support are provided to the patient and family, pacemaker maintenance is taught, and the patient is assisted to return to usual activities.

stoma (stō′mă) *pl.* **stomata, -mas** [Gr., mouth] **1.** A mouth, small opening, or pore. **2.** An artificially created opening between two passages or body cavities or between a cavity or passage and the body's surface. **3.** A minute opening between cells of certain epithelial membranes, esp. peritoneum and pleura.

stomach (stŭm′ăk) [Gr. *stomachos*, mouth, gullet, opening] A muscular, distensible saclike portion of the alimentary tube between the esophagus and duodenum. SEE: illus.

ANATOMY: It is below the diaphragm to the right of the spleen, partly under the liver. It is composed of an upper fundus, a central body, and a distal pylorus. It has two openings: the upper cardiac orifice opens from the esophagus and is surrounded by the lower esophageal (cardiac) sphincter. The lower pyloric orifice opens into the duodenum and is surrounded by the pyloric sphincter. The wall of the stomach has four layers. The outer serous layer (visceral peritoneum) covers almost all of the organ. The muscular layer just beneath it has three layers of smooth muscle: an outer longitudinal layer, a medial circular layer, and an inner oblique layer. The submucosa is made of connective tissue that contains blood vessels. The mucosa is the lining that contains the gastric glands, simple tubular glands of columnar epithelium that secrete gastric juice. Chief cells secrete pepsinogen; parietal cells secrete hydrochloric acid and the intrinsic factor; mucouscells secrete mucus; G cells secrete gastrin.

FUNCTION: The stomach is a reser-

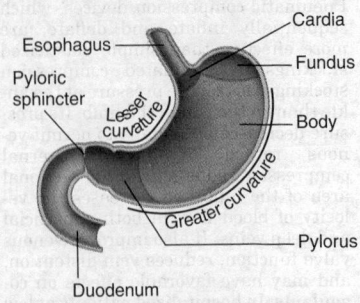

REGIONS OF THE STOMACH

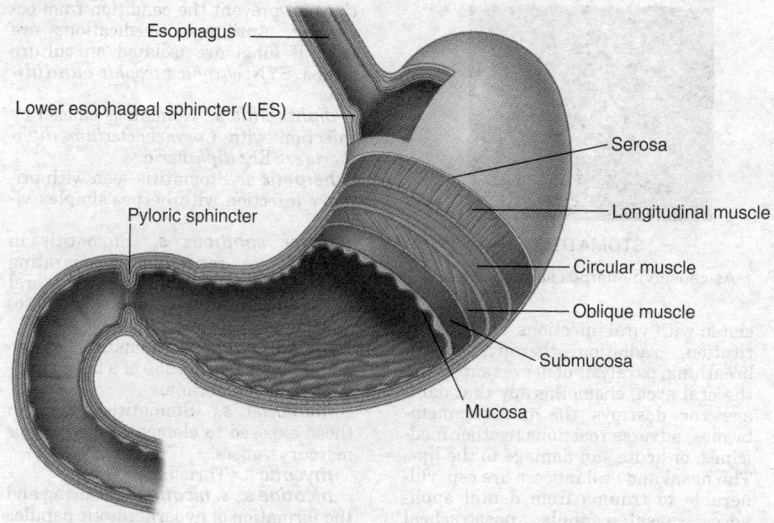

Esophagus

Lower esophageal sphincter (LES)

Serosa

Longitudinal muscle

Pyloric sphincter

Circular muscle

Oblique muscle

Submucosa

Mucosa

MUSCLES OF THE STOMACH WALL

voir that permits digestion to take place gradually; emptying of the stomach is under both hormonal and nervous control. Secretions and motility are increased by parasympathetic impulses (vagus nerves) and decreased by sympathetic impulses. The presence of food stimulates the production of the hormone gastrin, which increases the secretion of gastric juice. Protein digestion begins in the stomach; pepsin digests proteins to peptones. Hydrochloric acid converts pepsinogen to active pepsin and has little effect on unemulsified fats except those of cream. The intrinsic factor in gastric juice combines with vitamin B_{12} (extrinsic factor) to prevent its digestion and promote its absorption in the small intestine. Little absorption takes place in the stomach because digestion has hardly begun, but water and alcohol are absorbed.

bilocular s. Hourglass s.

cascade s. A form of hourglass stomach in which there is a constriction between the cardiac and pyloric portions. The cardiac portion fills first, and then the contents cascade into the pyloric portion.

cow horn s. A high, transversely placed stomach.

foreign bodies in the s. Accidental or intentional ingestion of materials such as coins, nails, bottle tops, marbles, and buttons. In some instances, these should be removed endoscopically (e.g., copper coins).

hourglass s. The division of the stomach (in the form of an hourglass) by a muscular constriction; often associ-

ated with gastric ulcer. SYN: *bilocular s.*

leather-bottle s. A condition of the stomach caused by hypertrophy of the stomach walls or their infiltration with malignant cells. SEE: *linitis plastica.*

thoracic s. A variant of hiatal hernia in which the stomach lies above the diaphragm. This may result from an embryonic anomaly in which the stomach fails to descend, or from a hernia of the diaphragm.

watermelon s. A colloquial term for the pathological changes in the stomach that occur in patients with progressive systemic sclerosis. The disease affects the stomach by causing vascular ectasia in the antrum.

water-trap s. A stomach with the pylorus situated unusually high, causing slow emptying.

stomachal (stŭm'ă-kăl) [Gr. *stomachos,* mouth] Pert. to the stomach.

stomachic (stō-măk'ĭk) **1.** Pert. to the stomach. **2.** A medicine that stimulates the action of the stomach.

stomach intubation SEE: under *intubation.*

stomal (stō'măl) [Gr. *stoma,* mouth] Pert. to a stoma.

stomata Pl. of stoma.

stomatal (stō'mă-tăl) [Gr. *stoma,* mouth] Pert. to stomata.

stomatic (stō-măt'ĭk) Pert. to the mouth.

stomatitis (stō-mă-tīt'ĭs) [*stomato-* + *-itis*] Inflammation of the mouth (including the lips, tongue, and mucous membranes). SEE: illus.; *noma; thrush.*

ETIOLOGY: Stomatitis may be asso-

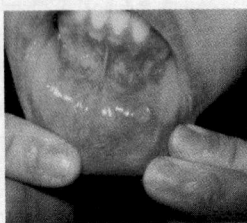

STOMATITIS

As caused by herpes simplex virus

ciated with viral infections, chemical irritation, radiation therapy, mouth breathing, paralysis of nerves supplying the oral area, chemotherapy that damages or destroys the mucous membranes, adverse reactions to other medicines, or acute sun damage to the lips. The nasal and oral mucosa are esp. vulnerable to trauma from dental appliances, nasal cannula, nasotracheal tubes, or catheters administering nutrients. These areas may also be damaged during surgery when an endotracheal tube is in place.

SYMPTOMS: Symptoms include oral pain, esp. when eating or drinking, bad breath, or difficulty in swallowing. Findings include oral ulcers, friability of the mucous membranes, swollen cervical lymph nodes, and sometimes fever.

PATIENT CARE: Treatment depends on the cause but is often symptomatic. The mucous membranes should be kept moist and clear of tenacious secretions. Care of the teeth and gingival tissues should be comprehensive and include flossing. The pain of stomatitis may be alleviated by systemic analgesics or application of anesthetic preparations to painful lesions. It is important for patients with dentures to clean their dentures thoroughly. Dentures should be removed from unconscious or stuporous patient. SEE: *toothbrushing*.

aphthous s. Aphthous **ulcer**.

corrosive s. Stomatitis resulting from intentional or accidental exposure to corrosive substances.

denture s. Stomatitis on the oral mucosa covered by full or partial dentures, most commonly seen on the palate although the inflammation may also be seen overlying the mandible.

PATIENT CARE: Although most patients are asymptomatic (the finding is noticed by dental professionals during oral examination, rather than by the patient), the condition should be treated to prevent progression to more serious oral diseases. Removal of plaque from dentures (as by brushing them carefully), removal of dentures at night, and sanitizing dentures regularly (as with an overnight soak in a chlorhexidine solu-

tion) all prevent the condition from occurring. Antifungal medications are used if fungi are isolated on culture swabs. SYN: *chronic atrophic* **candidiasis**.

diphtheritic s. Stomatitis caused by infection with *Corynebacterium diphtheriae*. SEE: *diphtheria*.

herpetic s. Stomatitis seen with primary infection with herpes simplex virus.

major aphthous s. Stomatitis in which large recurring or migrating painful ulcers appear within the oral cavity (on the gingiva and soft palate) and sometimes on the lips.

membranous s. Stomatitis accompanied by the formation of a false or adventitious membrane.

mercurial s. Stomatitiss seen in those exposed to elemental mercury or mercury vapors.

mycotic s. Thrush.

nicotine s., s. nicotina Fissuring and the formation of hyperkeratotic papules on the palate, usually caused by habitual pipe smoking. It is a form of precancer.

simple s. Stomatitis occurring in patches on the mucous membranes.

traumatic s. Stomatitis resulting from mechanical injury as from ill-fitting dentures, sharp jagged teeth, or biting the cheek.

ulcerative s. Necrotizing ulcerative **gingivitis**.

vesicular s. Aphthous **ulcer**.

Vincent s. Necrotizing ulcerative **gingivitis**.

stomato-, stomat- [Gr. *stoma*, stem *stomat-*, mouth] Prefixes meaning *mouth*.

stomatocyte (stō″mă-tō-sīt″) A swollen erythrocyte with a slitlike area of central pallor that is found in hereditary stomatocytosis.

stomatocytosis, hereditary (stō″mă-tō-sī-tō′sĭs) A disorder of erythrocytes usually inherited as an autosomal dominant. A membrane defect in the red blood cells permits the entry of excess sodium ions and water, causing the cells to swell. Hemolysis and anemia range from mild to severe.

stomatogastric (stō″mă-tō-găs′trĭk) [″ + *gaster*, belly] Pert. to the stomach and mouth.

stomatognathic (stō″mă-tŏg-năth′ĭk) [″ + *gnathos*, jaw] Pert. to the mouth and jaws together.

stomatologist (stō″mă-tŏl′ō-jĭst) [″ + *logos*, word, reason] A specialist in the treatment of diseases of the mouth.

stomatology (stō″mă-tŏl′ō-jē) The science of the mouth and teeth and their diseases.

stomodeum (stō″mō-dē′ŭm) [″ + *hodaios*, a way] An external depression lined with ectoderm and bounded by frontonasal, mandibular, and maxillary processes of the embryo. It forms the anterior portion of the oral cavity. Its floor, the pharyngeal membrane, separates the stomodeum from the foregut. The buccopharyngeal membrane, which forms the floor of the stomodeum, ruptures during the 4th week of gestation, and the gut tube then comes in communication with the amniotic fluid of the amniotic cavity.

-stomy [Gr. *stoma*, mouth] Suffix for a surgical opening in a body part or between body parts.

stone (stōn) **1.** Calculus. **2.** In the U.K., a unit of weight, 14 lb avoirdupois.

dental s. A hemihydrate of gypsum divided into four classes according to the qualities resulting from differing methods of preparation. It is used in dentistry in the preparation of models and study casts.

gray s. A synthetic stone composed of carborundum and rubber used to polish dental restorations.

kidney s. Renal **calculus**.

pulp s. A calcified structure present in the pulp chamber of a tooth. SYN: *denticle* (2).

red s. An abrasive stone with garnet as its main component, used for polishing dental restorations.

salivary s. A calcified stone in the ducts of salivary glands. It usually affects the duct of the submandibular gland. The stone obstructs the flow of saliva, causing severe pain and swelling of the gland, esp. during eating. The treatment is surgical removal of the stone. SYN: *salivary* **calculus**; *sialolith*.

stonefish (stōn'fish″) [From its camouflage coloring] The type species (*Synanceia verrucosa*) of the marine fish family Synanciidae. SEE: *Synanciidae*.

stool (stool) [AS. *stol*, a seat] **1.** Evacuation of the bowels. **2.** Feces.

bilious s. Yellow or yellow-brown discharges in diarrhea.

fatty s. Steatorrhea (2).

pea soup s. Liquid stools characteristic of typhoid.

rice water s. Watery serum stools with detached epithelium, as in cholera.

stool DNA testing Fecal **DNA**.

stool softener A substance that acts as a wetting agent and thus promotes soft, malleable bowel movements. A stool softener is not a laxative.

stopcock (stŏp'kŏk) A valve that regulates the flow of fluid from a container.

stoppage (stŏp'ăj) [AS. *stoppian*] Obstruction of an organ. SEE: *cholestasia*.

storage disease A disorder involving abnormal deposition of a substance in body tissues. SEE: *glycogen storage disease; Wilson disease*.

storage lesion SEE: under *lesion*.

storax (stō'răks) A balsam obtained from the scarred trunk of *Liquidambar*

orientalis. It is a component of tincture of benzoin and has been used as an expectorant.

storiform (stōr'ĭ-form″) Of clusters of cells in a biopsy specimen, shaped like a condensed spiral or whorl.

storm (storm) A sudden outburst or exacerbation of the symptoms of a disease.

cytokine s. The massive release of interleukins, tumor necrosis factor alpha, and other circulating mediators of inflammation during critical illness. These agents may trigger bleeding, clotting, internal organ injury, or shock.

electrical s. Recurring episodes of unstable ventricular tachycardia or ventricular fibrillation within 24 hr of a first life-threatening arrhythmia.

thyroid s. A rare but often life-threatening medical emergency resulting from untreated hyperthyroidism. It is marked by fevers, sweating, restlessness, irritability, tachycardia, hypertension, heart failure, shock, and cardiac arrhythmias, delirium, and coma, among other findings. It may begin when a patient with hyperthyroidism suffers a second illness (such as an infection), after thyroid gland surgery, or after withdrawal from antithyroid drug treatment. SYN: *thyroid* **crisis**; *thyrotoxic* **crisis**.

TREATMENT: Antithyroid medications (such as propylthiouracil) to block sympathetic effects, beta blockers (such as propranolol) to manage tachycardia, high-dose steroids (corticosteroid) to inhibit conversion of T_4 to T_3 and to replace depleted cortisol, and an iodide to block release of thyroid hormone, as well as volume infusions, are needed. Any secondary illness should be aggressively treated as well.

PATIENT CARE: Supplemental oxygen is administered, along with nutrients and vitamins to manage the hypermetabolic state, and sedatives. A calm cool, darkened, and quiet reassuring atmosphere helps to reduce restlessness. Underlying infections are treated with antibiotics. Acetaminophen is given to reduce fevers; anxiolytic drugs are used to reduce psychological distress. Cardiac status, level of consciousness, fluid and electrolyte balance, and blood glucose are monitored closely. After the crisis resolves, adherence to prescribed medications and the close outpatient follow-up may be needed with health care providers. Medical management of hyperthyroidism on an outpatient basis involves adjustment of drug doses, regular follow-up of thyroid function tests, complete blood counts, and prompt evaluation of fevers, sore throat, tachycardias, or other complications. Surgical referral may be needed for the patient requiring thyroidectomy.

stout (stowt) [O.Fr. *estout*, bold] Having a bulky body.

STP *standard temperature and pressure.*

STPD *standard temperature and pressure, dry* (i.e., with all water vapor removed).

Str *Streptococcus.*

strabismus (stră-biz′mŭs) [Gr. *strabismos*, squinting] A disorder of the eye in which optic axes cannot be directed to the same object. This disorder is present in about 4% of children. The squinting eye always deviates to the same extent when the eyes are carried in different directions: *unilateral* when the same eye always deviates; *alternating* when either deviates, the other being fixed; *constant* when the squint remains permanent; *periodic* when the eyes are occasionally free from it. Strabismus can result from reduced visual acuity, unequal ocular muscle tone, or an oculomotor nerve lesion. **strabismal** (măl), *adj.*; **strabismic** (mik), *adj.* SYN: *heterotropia*. SEE: *microstrabismus; squint.*

   accommodative s. Strabismus due to disorder of ocular accommodation. SYN: *bilateral s.*

   alternating s. Strabismus affecting either eye alternately.

   bilateral s. Accommodative **s.**

   concomitant s. Strabismus in which both eyes move freely but retain an unnatural relationship to each other.

   convergent s. Strabismus in which the deviating eye turns inward.

   divergent s. Strabismus in which the deviating eye turns outward.

   horizontal s. Strabismus in which the deviation of the visual axis is in the horizontal plane.

   intermittent s. Strabismus recurring at intervals.

   monocular s. Strabismus in which the same eye habitually deviates.

   monolateral s. Strabismus with the squinting eye always the same.

   nonconcomitant s. Strabismus of an eye that varies in degree with the change in direction in which the eye moves.

   paralytic s. Strabismus due to paralysis of one of the extraocular muscles.

   spastic s. Strabismus due to contraction of an ocular muscle.

   vertical s. Strabismus in which the eye turns upward.

straight back syndrome An abnormally erect position of the spine, associated with pectus excavatum, functional cardiac murmurs, and failed back surgery.

¹strain (strān) **1.** A stock, said of bacteria or protozoa from a specific source and maintained in successive cultures or animal inoculation. **2.** A hereditary streak or tendency.

²strain (strān) [Fr. *estreindere*, to draw tight] **1.** To pass through, as a filter. **2.** To injure by making too strong an effort or by excessive use. **3.** Excessive use of a part of the body so that it is injured. **4.** Trauma to muscles and tendons from violent contraction or excessive or forcible stretch. It may be associated with failure of the synergistic action of muscles. **5.** To make a great effort, as in straining to have a bowel movement. This is done by means of the Valsalva maneuver, which increases intra-abdominal pressure and helps to expel feces. **6.** Force applied per unit area. Tension, compression, or shear stress placed on a tissue leads to distortion of the structure and the release of energy. **7.** Psychological trauma.

   riders′ s. Strain of the adductor longus muscles of the thigh, resulting from strain in riding horseback.

strain and counterstrain ABBR: S-CS. A type of body manipulation used in osteopathy in which trigger points are relaxed, alleviating tissue spasm and inflammation.

strainer (strān′ĕr) **1.** A device for retaining solid pieces while liquid passes through. SYN: *filter.* **2.** In river rescue, a place where water moves through grating, wire mesh, or downed trees.

strait (strāt) [O.Fr. *estreit*, narrow] A constricted or narrow passage.

   s. of pelvis The inferior and superior openings of the true pelvis.

straitjacket A shirt with long sleeves that are tied behind a patient to restrain his or her arms.

⚠ Because patients placed in physical restraints may suffer injury from these restraints, such restraints should be applied to patients only under legally accepted guidelines and protocols.

stramonium (stră-mō′nē-ŭm) [L.] The dried leaves of the toxic anticholinergic plant *Datura stramonium*. SYN: *jimson weed.*

strand (strand) A single thread or fiber, e.g., of nucleic acids in a chromosome.

strangle (străng′gl) [L. *strangulare*, halter] **1.** To choke or suffocate. **2.** To be choked from compression of the trachea.

strangulation (străng″gū-lā′shŭn) [L. *strangulare*, halter] The compression or constriction of a part, as the bowel or throat, causing suspension of breathing or of the passage of contents. Congestion accompanies this condition. **strangulated,** *adj.*

   internal s. The entrapment of a segment of the intestine in an internal hernia or by adhesion, or through a rent or hiatus in the diaphragm, which leads to vascular compromise with ensuing gangrene.

strangury (străng′gū-rē) [Gr. *stranx*, drop, squeezed out, + *ouron*, urine]

Painful and interrupted urination in drops produced by spasmodic muscular contraction of the urethra and bladder.

strap, strapping (străp) [Gr. *strophos,* a cord] **1.** A band, as one of adhesive tape, used to hold dressings in place or to approximate surfaces of a wound. **2.** To bind with strips of adhesive tape.

Strategic National Stockpile (stră-tē′jik) ABBR: SNS. A storehouse of antibiotics, antidotes, and hospital supplies maintained by the U.S. government as a source of backup provisions to protect the public health during disasters or national emergencies. It was established under the auspices of the Centers for Disease Control and Prevention in 2003.

stratification (străt″ĭ-fĭ-kā′shŭn) [L. *stratificare,* to arrange in layers] The classification of objects into a hierarchy; the making of an ordered series of categories.

    risk s. A formal estimate of the probability of a person's succumbing to a disease or benefiting from a treatment for that disease.

stratified (străt′ĭ-fīd) [L. *stratificare,* to arrange in layers] Arranged in layers.

stratified epithelium SEE: under *epithelium.*

stratiform (străt′ĭ-form) [L. *stratum,* layer, + *forma,* shape] Arranged in layers.

stratify (stră′tĭ-fī) [NL. *stratificare*] **1.** To arrange in layers. **2.** To classify into categories, e.g., of risk for a particular illness.

stratum (stră′tŭm, străt′ŭm) *pl.* **strata** [L.] A layer.

    s. basale 1. The innermost or deepest layer of the endometrium. **2. S.** germinativum.

    s. compactum The superficial or outermost layer of the endometrium.

    s. corneum The outermost horny layer of the epidermis.

    s. disjunction The outermost layer of the stratum corneum, which is being shed constantly.

    s. functionale The functional layer of the endometrium.

    s. germinativum The innermost layer of the epidermis; a row of cuboidal cells that divide to replace the rest of the epidermis as it wears away. It is part of the stratum malpighii. SYN: **s.** *basale* (2). SEE: *s. malpighii.*

    s. granulosum A layer of cells containing deeply staining granules of keratohyalin found in the epidermis of the skin between the stratum spinosum and the stratum corneum. SEE: **s.** *malpighii.*

    s. lucidum The translucent layer of the epidermis between the stratum corneum and the stratum granulosum in the palms and soles.

    s. malpighii The inner layer of the epidermis. It includes both the stratum germinativum and stratum spinosum of today's nomenclature.

    s. papillare Papillary **layer**.

    s. reticulare The recticular layer of the corium just beneath the papillary layer.

    s. spinosum The prickle cell layer, so called because of its prominent intercellular attachments. It is part of the stratum malpighii. SEE: **s.** *malpighii.*

    s. spongiosum The middle layer of decidua of the endometrium.

    s. submucosum The layer of smooth muscle fibers of the myometrium lying contiguous with the endometrium.

    s. subserosum The layer of smooth muscle fibers of myometrium that lies immediately under the serous coat.

    s. supravasculare The layer of circular and longitudinal muscle fibers of the myometrium lying between the stratum subserosum and the stratum vasculare.

    s. vasculare The layer of smooth muscle fibers in myometrium lying between the stratum submucosum and the stratum supravasculare.

streak (strēk) A line or stripe. SEE: *stria.*

    angioid s. A linear crack in Bruch membrane radiating outward from the optic nerve. It is associated with pseudoxanthoma elasticum, sickle cell, and Paget disease

    fatty s. Early evidence of atherosclerosis, in which cholesterol, macrophages, and smooth muscle cells accumulate in the intima of arteries. SEE: *atherosclerosis.*

    gonadal s. Ovarian atrophy or aplasia; a finding in persons with Turner syndrome.

    primitive s. In embryology, the initial band of cells from which the embryo begins to develop. These cells are at the caudal end of the embryonic disk. The streak is present at about 15 days after fertilization.

stream (strēm) A steady flow of a liquid.

    cathode s. Negatively charged electrons emitted from a cathode and accelerated in a straight line to interact with an anode. X-ray photons are then produced. SEE: *Bremsstrahlung* **radiation;** *cathode ray.*

strength 1. The maximum force that can be generated by a muscle or muscle group. **2.** The concentration of a solution or substance. **3.** The intensity of light, color, or sound. **4.** The ability to resist deformation, fracture, or abrasion.

    breaking s. The point at which an amount of applied force breaks a material. Also called *tensile strength.*

    compression s. The point at which a

material loses its shape when force is applied. Also called *crushing strength*.

ego s. In psychoanalytic theory, the ability of the ego to maintain its various functions, the prime one of which is to perceive reality and adapt to it.

impact s. The force required to fracture a material.

shear s. The resistance of a material to force applied perpendicular to the plane of the material.

strep throat (strep) Streptococcal **pharyngitis**.

strepto-, strept- [Gr. *streptos,* twisted] Prefixes meaning *twisted, twisted chain.*

Streptobacillus moniliformis (strĕp″tō-bă-sĭl′ŭs mŏ-nĭl″ĭ-fŏr′mĭs) [NL] A gram-negative bacillus present in the mouths of rats, mice, and cats. It is transmitted to humans through bites or by ingestion of milk contaminated by rats. It causes one form of rat-bite fever, marked by prolonged fever, skin rash, and generalized arthritis. The infection may be treated with amoxicillin-clavulanate or doxycycline. SYN: *Haverhill fever.* SEE: *Spirillum minus.*

streptococcal (strĕp″tō-kŏk′ăl) [″ + *kokkos,* berry] Pert. to streptococci.

streptococcal pyrogenic exotoxins The preferred name for those toxic chemicals released by Group A streptococci that were formerly known as erythrogenic toxins. They are responsible for the rash children experience with scarlet fever and for many of the septic manifestations of toxic shock syndrome.

Streptococcus (strĕp″tō-kok′ŭs) [*strepto-* + *coccus*] ABBR: Str. A genus of gram-positive, facultatively anaerobic cocci of the family Streptococcaceae, in which the cells tend to form chains or pairs. Many species are saprophytes, but others are virulent pathogens. They may be classified as alpha (α), beta (β), and gamma (γ) on the basis of their growth on blood agar plates and the hemolysis produced. Alpha-hemolytic streptococci produce partial hemolysis and create a greenish coloration around the colonies. Beta-hemolytic types completely hemolyze blood and form clear zones round colonies; those of the gamma type are nonhemolytic and do not change the color of the medium. Streptococci are also classified into several immunological groups (Lancefield groups) designated by the letters A through H, and K through O. Most human infections are caused by groups A, B, D, F, G, H, K, and O. Approximately 100 types of group A beta-hemolytic streptococci have been identified. SEE: *rheumatic fever; scarlet fever.*

S. agalactiae A group B beta-hemolytic species found in raw milk that is the leading cause of bacterial sepsis and meningitis in newborns and a major cause of endometritis and fever in postpartum women.

Infected infants develop early-onset symptoms in the first 5 days of life, including lethargy, jaundice, respiratory distress, shock, pneumonia, and anorexia. The fatality rate is 50% for very low-birth-weight neonates and 2% to 8% in term infants.

Infected postpartum women develop late-onset symptoms 7 days to several months after giving birth. Symptoms include sepsis, meningitis, seizures, and psychomotor retardation. Neonatal infection may be prevented by detecting colonization by these bacteria in pregnant women and by administering antibiotics prior to birth. SYN: *S., Group B*.

S. anginosus A species that causes abscesses. It was formerly known as *S. milleri*.

S. bovis The former name of a species now known as *S. gallolyticus*.

S. dysgalactiae subsp. equisimilis A species that causes skin infections, such as erysipelas, as well as puerperal sepsis, osteomyelitis, pneumonia, bacteremia, and endocarditis.

S. equisimilis The former name of a species now known as *S. dysgalactiae* subsp. *equisimilis*.

S. faecalis The former name of *Enterococcus faecalis*.

S. gallolyticus A species that causes bloodborne infections, esp. in patients with diseases of the large bowel, e.g. colon cancer.

S., Group B S. agalactiae.

S. iniae A species pathogenic to fish that may cause cellulitis in people who handle affected fish and have skin abrasions.

S. mutans A species that has been implicated in initiation of dental caries and bacterial endocarditis.

S. pneumoniae A species that occurs in pairs with capsules and may be part of the transient flora of the upper respiratory tract. Based on capsular chemistry, more than 80 serological types have been identified. It is the causative agent of certain types of pneumonia, esp. lobar pneumonia, and is associated with other infectious diseases such as meningitis, conjunctivitis, endocarditis, periodontitis, septic arthritis, osteomyelitis, otitis media, septicemia, spontaneous bacterial peritonitis, and, rarely, urinary tract infections. About 40,000 people die of pneumococcal disease each year in the U.S., more than from any other vaccine-preventable illness. SYN: *pneumococcus*.

S. pyogenes Any of the group A beta-hemolytic streptococci causing suppurative infections. These streptococci are the causative agents of scarlet fever, erysipelas, bacterial pharyngitis, puerperal sepsis, and necrotizing fasciitis.

streptococcus (strep″tŏ-kok′ŭs, -kok′sī′) *pl.* **streptococci** [*strepto-* + *coccus*] An organism of the genus *Streptococcus.* SEE: *bacteria* for illus. **streptococcic,** *adj.*

alpha-hemolytic s. Streptococci that, when grown on blood-agar, produce a zone of partial hemolysis around each colony and often impart a greenish appearance to the agar. Included are *S. pneumoniae* and viridans group streptococci.

beta-hemolytic s. group B **s.**

group A s. Beta-hemolytic streptococci (esp. *S. pyogenes*) that produce human diseases, including pharyngitis, cellulitis, erysipelas, impetigo, otitis media, pneumonia, scarlet fever, necrotizing fasciitis, sepsis, sinusitis, and tonsillitis. In addition, group A streptococcus infection may have immunological sequelae such as rheumatic fever and acute glomerulonephritis.

group B s. Streptococci that, when grown on blood-agar, produce complete hemolysis around each colony, indicated by a yellowish zone. Included are *S. pyogenes* and *S. agalactiae.*These streptococci are a leading cause of early-onset neonatal infections and late-onset postpartal infections. In women, this is marked by urinary tract infection, chorioamnionitis, postpartum endometritis, bacteremia, and wound infections complicating cesarean section. Eradication of this organism during labor decreases the chances for neonatal sepsis. Performance of cervical-rectal screening cultures at 35 to 37 weeks' gestation (and intrapartum treatment with penicillin if cultures are positive) prevents the development of neonatal sepsis. SYN: *beta-hemolytic s.*

group D s. Any *Streptococcus* species, including *S. bovis* and *S. equinus,* that is not destroyed by bile or exposure to heat. These strains can be destroyed in a laboratory by a 6.5% concentration of sodium chloride. Many group D streptococci have been reclassified and placed in the genus *Enterococcus* (including *S. faecalis, S. faecium, S. durans,* and *S. avium*). For example *S. faecalis* is now *E. faecalis.* The remaining strains of nonenterococcal group D streptococci include *S. bovis* and *S. equinus.*

nutritionally variant s. ABBR: NVS. The former name for bacteria of the genera *Abiotrophia* or *Granulicatella.*

streptodornase (strĕp″tō-dor′nās) One of the enzymes produced by certain strains of hemolytic streptococci. It is capable of liquefying fibrinous and purulent exudates.

streptogramin (strĕp″tō-grăm′ĭn) Any of a class of antibiotics effective against gram-positive bacteria that bind to the bacterial ribosome and inhibit protein synthesis. An example is the combination antibiotic quinupristin-dalfopristin.

streptolysin (strĕp-tŏl′ĭ-sĭn) An enzyme produced by streptococci that destroys blood cells.

s. O Streptolysin that is inactivated by oxygen.

s. S Streptolysin that is inactivated by heat or acid, but not by oxygen.

Streptomyces (strĕp″tō-mī′sēz) [″ + Gr. *mykes,* mushroom, fungus] A genus of branching, filamentous bacteria of the family Streptomycetaceae. Most species live in the soil, and few are pathogenic. Many produce antibiotics, and some produce immune-suppressing and anticancer drugs. Important species within the genus are *S. coelicolor* and *S. lividans.*

stress (stres) [Fr. *estresse,* narrowness] **1.** Any physical, physiological, or psychological force that disturbs equilibrium **2.** The consequences of forces that disturb equilibrium. **3.** Force applied per unit area. In the physical sciences, stresses include forces that deform or damage materials, such as impact, shear, torsion, compression, and tension. These physical stresses are particularly important in certain branches of health care, e.g., dentistry or orthopedic surgery, and in biotechnology industries, e.g., in the design and use of prostheses, grafts, and perfusion pumps.

Physiological stresses include agents that upset homeostasis, such as infection, injury, disease, internal organ pressures, or psychic strain.

In psychology, stresses include perceptions, emotions, anxieties, and interpersonal, social, or economic events that are considered threatening to one's physical health, personal safety, or well-being. Marital discord; conflicts with others; battle, torture, or abuse; bankruptcy; incarceration; health care crises; and self-doubt are all examples of conditions that increase psychic stresses. The response of an organism or material to stress is known as adaptation. SEE: *adaptation; anxiety; fracture; homeostasis; law of Laplace; relaxation response.*

critical incident s. One's emotional reaction to a catastrophic event such as a mass casualty incident or the death of a patient or coworker. Often such events negatively affect the well-being of health care providers.

oxidative s. The cellular damage caused by oxygen-derived free radical formation. The three most important are superoxide (O_2^-), hydrogen peroxide (H_2O_2), and hydroxyl ions; these are produced during normal metabolic processes as well as in reaction to cell injury. The extent of their damaging potential can be decreased by antioxidants. SEE: *antioxidant; free* **radical***; superoxide; superoxide dismutase.*

prenatal s. Anxiety, tension, depression, or other psychological discomfort experienced by a pregnant woman.

shear s. Shear.

stress incontinence SEE: *stress urinary* **incontinence**.

stress management Any intervention that may help control the physiological changes or psychological discomfort caused by the body's response to stress. There are many methods of stress management, including relaxation techniques (such as yoga, meditation, deep breathing, and progressive muscle relaxation), choosing a lifestyle with meaning and purpose, physical activity, maintenance of a positive attitude and outlook, and prayer.

stressor An agent or condition capable of producing stress.

systemic s. A stressor that produces generalized systemic responses.

topical s. Stress that causes mild inflammation or local damage.

stress overload SEE: under *overload*.

stress platelet Reticulated **platelet**.

stress radiography Strain **radiography**.

stress response protein SEE: under *protein*.

stress test Exercise tolerance test.

abduction s.t. A maneuver to assess whether a patient has suffered a ligamentous injury to the knee. With the patient's hip extended over the edge of the examining table, the examiner externally rotates the patient's lower extremity at the ankle, while providing internal rotation from the lateral border of the thigh. SEE: *valgus* **s.t.**

adenosine s.t. A test for coronary artery disease that uses the drug adenosine as a vasodilator, usually along with radionuclide imaging of the heart or echocardiography. The drug is used in place of physical exercise to demonstrate obstructions in the coronary arteries, e.g., in patients who cannot perform physical exercise or whose exercise testing results have been uninterpretable.

pharmacological s.t. A stress test in which a drug such as dobutamine or another chronotropic or vasodilating drug is used to increase the heart rate during assessments of myocardial perfusion or function.

valgus s.t. A test of ligament laxity, where a passive force is exerted on a joint that, in the presence of ligamentous insufficiency, would cause the medial joint space to open, e.g., medial collateral ligament of the knee and ulnar collateral ligament of the elbow.

varus s.t. A test of ligament laxity, where a passive force is exerted on a joint that, in the presence of ligamentous insufficiency, would cause the lateral joint space to open, e.g., lateral collateral ligament of the knee and radial collateral ligament of the elbow.

stretch (strĕch) [AS. *streccan*, extend] To draw out or extend to full length.

static s. A sustained, low-intensity lengthening of soft tissue (e.g., muscle, tendon, or joint capsule), performed to increase range of motion. The stretch force may be applied continuously for as short as 15 to 30 sec or as long as several hours.

stretcher (strĕch′er) A litter, equipped with wheels, used for transporting patients. SYN: *gurney*.

basket s. A stretcher made of metal or strong synthetic material in which a patient is placed so he or she can be securely extracted by Emergency Medical Services from an accident or otherwise inaccessible site. The stretcher may also be lifted by ropes. SYN: *Stokes stretcher*.

orthopedic s. A metal stretcher that is hinged along its long axis and designed to be split so that it can be placed on both sides of the patient and then reassembled to lift the patient. SYN: *scoop s.*

pole s. A type of stretcher, also known as the Army type, composed of folding cloth or canvas supported by poles.

scoop s. Orthopedic **s.**

spineboard s. A type of stretcher made from a wooden board or strong synthetic material used to secure patients with spinal trauma to prevent movement and possible paralysis; also called a long backboard.

split-frame (scoop) s. A metal stretcher that can be split down the middle, slid under a patient, and reconnected. This device is used for moving patients from narrow spaces but is not designed for spinal immobilization.

Stokes s. Basket **s.**

stretch mark SEE: under *mark*.

stria (strī′ă, strī′ē) *pl.* **striae** [L., *stria*, furrow] A line, stripe, ridge, or thin band that is visible because it contrasts with the surrounding tissue. It may be elevated or of a different color or texture. SEE: *streak*.

s. atrophica A fine pinkish-white or gray line, usually 14 cm long, seen in parts of the body where skin has been stretched. It is commonly seen on thighs, abdomen, and breasts of women who are or have been pregnant; in those whose skin has been stretched by obesity, tumor, or edema; or in people who have taken adrenocortical hormones for a prolonged period. SYN: *stretch mark;* **s.** *gravidarum.* SEE: illus.

striae gravidarum S. atrophica.

s. medullaris A thin axon tract that originates in the septal nuclei, the hy-

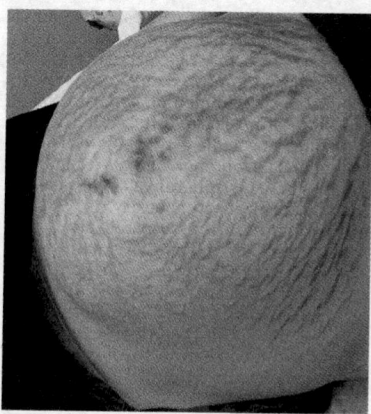

STRIA ATROPHICA

Abdomen of a gravid woman at term

pothalamus, and the anterior thalamic nucleus and synapses in the habenular nuclei of the epithalamus. It is part of the limbic system. SYN: *s. medullaris thalami*. SEE: *limbic system* for illus.

s. medullaris thalami S. medullaris.

olfactory striae Any of three bands of fibers (lateral, intermediate, and medial) that form the roots of the olfactory tract. As it reaches the olfactory areas of the cortex on the undersurface of the brain, the olfactory tract splits into two visible ridges, a large lateral and a small medial stria.

striae of Retzius SEE: under *Retzius, Magnus Gustaf*.

s. terminalis An axon tract that originates in the amygdala and synapses in the hypothalamus. It is a slender, compact tract that curves over the thalamus, arching along the medial surface of the caudate nucleus (below the fornix), and terminates in the anterior hypothalamus. It is part of the limbic system. SEE: *limbic system* for illus.

striatal (strī-ā′tăl) [L. *striatus*, striped] Pert. to the corpus striatum.

striate, striated (strī′āt, strī′ā-tĕd) [L. *striatus*] Striped; marked by streaks or striae.

striate body SEE: under *body*.

striation (strī-ā′shŭn) [L. *striatus*, striped] **1.** The state of being striped or streaked. **2.** Stria.

striatum (strī-ā′tŭm) [L., grooved] The caudate nucleus and the putamen, two large nuclei deep in each cerebral hemisphere that appear distinct but are connected anteriorly and are histologically and functionally a single entity. The striatum and the globus pallidus are the core components of the basal ganglia. SYN: *corpus s.; dorsal s.*

stricture (strik′chŭr) [L. *strictura*, con-traction] A narrowing or constriction of the lumen of a tube, duct, or hollow organ such as the esophagus, ureter, or urethra. Strictures may be congenital or acquired. Acquired strictures may result from infection, trauma, fibrosis due to mechanical or chemical irritation, muscular spasm, or pressure from adjacent structures or tumors. They may be temporary or permanent, depending on the cause.

annular s. Ringlike obstruction of an organ involving the entire circumference of a structure.

anorectal s. A fibrotic narrowing of the anorectal canal.

bridle s. A stricture caused by a band of membrane stretched across a tube, partially occluding it.

cicatricial s. A stricture resulting from a scar or wound.

functional s. A stricture caused by muscular spasm.

impermeable s. A stricture developing within and closing the lumen of a tube or canal so that instruments or substances cannot pass through it.

irritable s. A stricture causing pain when an instrument is passed.

s. of the urethra Partial or complete narrowing of the urethra, occurring most commonly in men. The condition is marked by straining to pass urine, esp. at the commencement of urination. It is caused by spasm of the urethral muscle, congestion of the urethra, and fibrous formation.

strictureplasty (strik′chŭr-plas″tē) [*stricture* + *-plasty*] **1.** A surgical technique for treating or opening a bowel blockage used to spare the intestines from surgical removal, e.g., in managing Crohn's disease. **2.** Surgical release of a stricture.

stride length SEE: under *length*.

strident (strī′dĕnt) Stridulous.

stridor (strī′dŏr, ′dor″) [L., *stridor*, rattling, buzzing] A high-pitched, harsh sound occurring during inspiration, often heard without the use of a stethoscope. It is a sign of upper airway obstruction, which may indicate the presence of a life-threatening condition (e.g., epiglottitis). The lack of stridor should never be interpreted as a sign that the upper airway is patent in the patient with signs of having difficulty breathing.

congenital laryngeal s. Stridor present at birth, resulting from laryngomalacia.

s. dentium The noise from grinding of the teeth. SEE: *bruxism*.

stridulous (strĭd′ū-lŭs) [L. *stridulus*] Making a shrill, grating sound. SYN: *strident*.

string sign SEE: under *sign*.

string test A test formerly used to diagnose intestinal infection with *Giardia* *lamblia,* in which a string is swallowed, then removed, and examined for parasites.

strip (strĭp) [AS. *striepan,* to plunder] **1.** To remove all contents from a hollow organ or tube, esp. by gentle pressure, as to strip the seminal vesicles. **2.** A long slender band of tissue, e.g., one removed surgically for transplantation elsewhere in the body.

stripper A surgical instrument used to remove veins, tendons, or periosteum.

strobila (strō-bī'lă) [Gr. *strobilos,* anything twisted up] The series of proglottids of the adult form of a tapeworm.

stroboscope (strō'bō-skōp) [Gr. *strobos,* whirl, + *skopein,* to examine] A device that produces light intermittently. When the light is shown on moving or vibrating objects, the object appears to be stationary. A photograph taken at the precise time the light is flashed on the object will not be blurred.

stroboscopy The analysis of movements with a periodically flickering light source.

stroke (strōk) [ME.] **1.** A sudden loss of neurological function, caused by vascular injury (loss of blood flow) to an area of the brain. Stroke is both common and deadly: about 700,000 strokes occur in the U.S. each year. Stroke is the third leading cause of death in the U.S. Because of the long-term disability it often produces, stroke is the disease most feared by older Americans. In the U.S., 80% of strokes are caused by cerebral infarction (i.e., blockage of the carotid or intracerebral arteries by clot or atherosclerosis); intracranial hemorrhage and cerebral emboli are responsible for most other strokes. Innovations in the management of stroke (e.g., in prevention, the early use of thrombolytic drugs, vascular ultrasonography, and endarterectomy) have revolutionized the acute and follow-up care of the stroke patient. SYN: *apoplexy; brain **attack**; cerebrovascular accident.* SEE: *carotid **endarterectomy**; intracranial **hemorrhage**; transient ischemic attack;* table.

ETIOLOGY: Risk factors for stroke include advanced age (esp. older than 65

years), atherosclerosis of the aortic arch, atrial fibrillation, carotid artery disease, cigarette use, excessive alcohol use (more than five drinks daily), heart failure, hyperlipidemia, hypertension, a history of myocardial infarction, diabetes mellitus, male gender, close relation of someone who has had a stroke, nonwhite race, peripheral vascular disease, physical inactivity, obesity, using combination hormonal contraception (the pill, ring, patch), being pregnant or immediately postpartum, or a recent transient ischemic attack.

SYMPTOMS: The National Institute of Neurological Disorders and Stroke lists the following as warning signs of stroke: sudden weakness or numbness of the face, arm, or leg; sudden loss of vision, double vision, dimming of vision in one or both eyes; sudden difficulty in speaking or in understanding speech; sudden severe headache; and sudden falling, gait disturbance, or dizziness. The patient who experiences these problems should call 911 immediately. If symptoms disappear in a few minutes, the individual may have experienced a transient ischemic attack (TIA [informally known as a "ministroke" or a "warning stroke"]) and should notify his/her primary care provider immediately for preventive care. In clinical practice, stroke patients often present with more than one stroke symptom (e.g., limb paralysis and aphasia; severe headache and hemibody deficits). It is also important to note that these symptoms are not specific for stroke:sudden dizziness or gait disturbance can occur as a result of intoxication with drugs or alcohol, for example, and sudden severe head pain can result from cluster headache, migraine, and many other disorders.

TREATMENT: Acute ischemic stroke can be treated with recombinant tissue plasminogen activator (rt-PA) if the disease is recognized in the first 90 to 180 min and intracerebral hemorrhage has been excluded with urgent computed tomography (CT) or magnetic resonance imaging (MRI) scanning of the brain. This form of therapy is not without risk; thrombolytic drugs can reduce the potential for long-term disability and death by 20%, but increase the risk of hemorrhage. Hemorrhagic strokes, which have about a 50% mortality, can sometimes be treated by evacuating blood clots from the brain or by repairing intracerebral aneurysms.

⚠ Patients with hemorrhagic stroke should never receive fibrinolytic drugs. Other contraindications to fibrinolysis in stroke include recent or active bleeding or a known propensity for abnormal bleeding; recent lumbar puncture; re-

Stroke and its Causes

Cause of Stroke	Frequency of Occurrence
Emboli from other organs, e.g., heart	about 15%
Cerebrovascular disease	greater than 50%
Trauma	less than 5%
Hypercoagulable states	less than 5%
Unknown	about 25%

cent arterial puncture; recent myocardial infarction; recent surgery or major trauma; seizure at the onset of the stroke; or blood pressure over 185/110 mm Hg that does not improve with simple therapies.

PATIENT CARE: *Acute phase:* The health care team performs a history and physical assessment, including a careful examination of airway, breathing, circulation, and neurological functions. The Glasgow Coma Scale should be used to assess level of consciousness. The severity of a stroke should be assessed with a valid scale, such as the National Institute's of Health Stroke Scale (NIHSS) or other well-publicized assessment tools. Staff provides oxygen by nasal cannula, establishes venous access via two large-bore catheters, and infuses saline intravenously; obtains blood samples for complete blood count, blood glucose, electrolytes, and coagulation studies; and obtains a 12-lead ECG and initiates cardiac monitoring. The stroke team, neurologist, radiologist, and MRI and/or CT technician are alerted. Fever and hyperglycemia are treated aggressively because elevated body temperatures and elevated blood glucose levels havebeen linked to poorer outcomes. Blood pressure is gently controlled to a level less than 180/110 mm Hg: more aggressive pressure control may be hazardous. The patient is positioned in the lateral or semiprone position with the head elevated 15 to 30 degrees to decrease cerebral venous pressure. Neurological status is monitored for signs of deterioration or improvement, and findings are documented on a flow sheet. The National Institute of Neurological Disorders and Stroke (NINDS) suggests the following order of assessment in patients with suspected stroke: level of consciousness, eye movements, visual fields, facial movements, motor function of arms and legs, limb coordination, sensory responses, and language use, including clarity of speech. A history of the incident is obtained, including how and when symptoms started. Past medical history should be reviewed (hypertension, use of anticoagulant drugs, cardiac dysrhythmias). The patient is prepared for prescribed diagnostic studies, including MRI and/or CT, and possibly arteriography.

The patient is oriented frequently and reassured with verbal and tactile contacts. Attention is focused on determining the patient's candidacy for emergent use of thrombolytic therapy. If potential benefits are established, recombinant tissue plasminogen activator (rt-PA) is administered intravenously over 60 min, with 10% of the determined dosage as a bolus in the first 60 sec. Blood pressure is monitored closely once the infusion is started, and any elevation treated aggressively. The patient also is monitored for indications of systemic bleeding (tachycardia, tachypnea, hypotension or acute hypertension, rapid mental status deterioration, severe headache, and nausea and vomiting). When rt-PA administration is complete, the patient is transferred to the neurologic ICU or neurology unit. If clot-busting drugs cannot or should not be administered, monitoring and supportive care is provided. The ability to speak is assessed, and if aphasiais present, a consultation by a speech therapist is obtained. Bladder function is assessed; noninvasive measures are used to encourage voiding in the presence of urinary retention, voiding pattern is determined, and the incontinent patient is kept clean and dry. Use of indwelling catheters is limited because these promote urinary tract infection. Bowel function is assessed, and dietary intervention and stool softeners or laxatives as necessary are used to prevent constipation. Straining at stool or use of enemas is avoided. Fluid and electrolyte balance (intake, output, daily weight, laboratory values) is monitored and maintained. Adequate enteral or parenteral nutrition is provided as appropriate. Nursing measures are instituted to prevent complications of immobility. In consultation with occupational therapists and physical therapists, a program of positioning and mobility is initiated, as appropriate. Examples of activities include repositioning at leastevery 2 hr, maintaining correct body alignment, supporting joints to prevent flexion and rotation contractures, and providing range-of-motion exercises (passive to involved joints, active-assisted or active to uninvolved joints). Irrigation and lubrication prevent oral mucous membranes and eyes (cornea) from drying. Prescribed medical therapy is administered to decrease cerebral edema, and antihypertensives or anticoagulants are given as appropriate for etiology. The patient is observed for seizure activity, and drug therapy and safety precautions are initiated. Most stroke patients are hospitalized for a few days. Patient education about risk modification begins prior to discharge.

Rehabilitative phase: After the acute phase of stroke, rehabilitation goals depend on the severity of the patient's deficit, the age of the patient, the presence of comorbidities and prior functional status, his or her ability to perform activities of daily living independently, and the family and social support systems available. The rehabilitation program consists of various exercises, including neuromuscular retraining, motor learning and motor control, and functional activities that emphasize relearning or retraining in basic skills required for self-care. This may include instruction in the use of adaptive and supportive devices to facilitate independence in daily tasks. The goal of rehabilitation is to achieve an optimal functional outcome that will allow the patient to be discharged to the least restrictive environment. Ideally, the patient will achieve sufficient independence to return tocommunity living, either independently or with family and community support.

All patient efforts should receive positive reinforcement. Patient communication is a priority. Exercises, proper positioning, and supportive devices help to prevent deformities. Quiet rest periods are provided based on the patient's response to activity. The patient should either assist with or perform own personal hygiene and establish independence in other activities of daily living. The rehabilitation team evaluates the patient's ability to feed self and continues to provide enteral feeding as necessary. A bowel and bladder retraining program is initiated, and both patient and family receive instruction in its management. Both patient and family are taught about the therapeutic regimen (activity and rest, diet, and medications), including desired effects and adverse reactions to report. Emotional lability, a consequence of some strokes, is recognized and explained, and assistance is provided to help the patient deal with changes inaffect.

NOTE: The best results are achieved by patients treated in specialized treatment centers with demonstrably low complication rates. All stroke patients are advised to reduce their risk for future stroke by taking prescribed antihypertensive drugs as directed; losing excess weight; exercising regularly; eating a well-balanced diet low in fat, cholesterol, sugar, and salt; stopping smoking; limiting alcohol intake; and maintaining glycemic control. Patient and family are referred to the American Stroke Association or local stroke groups for information and support (http://www.strokeassociation.org).

2. To rub gently in one direction, as in massage. **3.** A gentle movement of the hand across a surface. **4.** In dentistry, a complete simple movement that is often repeated with modifications of position, strength, or speed, perhaps as a part of a continuing activity; e.g., the closing stroke in mastication when the jaw closes and the teeth come together. In scaling or planing the roots of teeth, the scaling instrument is introduced carefully into the subgingival area in what is called an exploratory stroke, perhaps followed by a power stroke designed to break or dislodge encrusted calculus. This is followed by a shaving stroke, intended to smooth or plane the root surface. **5.** A sharp blow.

ischemic s. A stroke caused by diminished blood flow to a particular artery in the brain, e.g., as a result of a clot in the artery or an embolus lodging in the artery. Ischemic stroke is much more common than hemorrhagic stroke.

lacunar s. A pathological change in the brain caused by diminished or no blood flow through one of the brain's small penetrating arteries. When this occurs, there may be no clinically detectable changes in the patient or signs and symptoms of stroke. A group of little strokes may cause progressive dementia.

mini-s. A colloquial and imprecise term for a transient ischemic attack.

paralytic s. A stroke that produces loss of muscular functions.

Stroke Impact Scale SEE: under *¹scale*.

stroking 1. Effleurage. **2.** A technique of slow tactile stimulation over the posterior primary rami, used to inhibit muscle responses and promote relaxation during neuromotor rehabilitation.

stroma (strō′mă) *pl.* **stromata** [Gr., bed covering] **1.** Foundation-supporting tissues of an organ. The opposite of parenchyma. **2.** The membranous lipid-protein framework within a red blood cell to which hemoglobin molecules are attached. **stromal, stromatic,** *adj.*

stromatosis (strō″mă-tō′sĭs) [″ + *osis,* condition] The presence of mesenchymal (structural) tissue infiltrating the uterine endometrium. Contrast with the term adenomyosis.

stromelysin (strō′mă-līs-ĭn) ABBR: MMP-3. Member of the matrix metalloproteinase family of enzymes that plays a major role in the degradation of proteoglycans, gelatin, and other constituents of the extracellular matrix. Two forms of stromelysin have been described, stromelysin-1 and -2. Stromelysin-1 degrades proteoglycans, gelatin, fibronectin, laminin, collagen types III, IV, IX, and X. Stromelysin-2 degrades proteoglycans, fibronectin, laminin, and collagen type IV.

strong (strong) **1.** Potent. **2.** Concentrated. **3.** Biologically or chemically active; said, e.g., of acids, bases, electrolytes, and muscle tissue.

strong dominance SEE: under *dominance.*

Strong Interest Inventory (strong) [Edward K. Strong, U.S. psychologist, b. 1884] ABBR: SII. A psychological test that traditionally measures vocational interests but also identifies personality traits. Previous versions (the original was developed in 1927) were known as the Strong Vocational Interest Bank.

Strongyloides (strŏn″jĭ-loy′dēz) A genus of roundworms that infect humans.

S. stercoralis A roundworm that causes gastrointestinal infections (primarily in persons from developing nations) and opportunistic infections (in immunosuppressed patients). It may occasionally be life threatening. In the U.S., *S. stercoralis* is found mainly in the rural South. The ova hatch in the intestines of the host, and rod-shaped larvae are passed in the stool. In the soil, these may develop into adults and continue their life cycle or may metamorphose into filariform larvae that can infect humans. The filariform larvae enter the skin, pass through the venous system to the lungs, where they migrate upward and are swallowed. A rash or pneumonia may accompany their migration. The larvae mature in the intestine, and ova of the next generation hatch. The rod-shaped larvae may metamorphose into the filariform larvae in the intestine. These may enter the circulation, migrate to the lungs, and begin the cycle again.

Such auto-infection may be sufficient to cause overwhelming systemic infection with fever, severe abdominal pain, shock, and possibly death. Severe reactions are more likely to occur in immunosuppressed patients. The diagnosis is made by finding larvae in the patient's feces. Thiabendazole and mebendazole are the drugs of choice. Repeated courses of treatment may be required.

strongyloidosis (strŏn″jĭ-loy-dō′sĭs) [Gr. *strongylos,* compact, + *osis,* condition] Infestation with organisms of the genus *Strongyloides.*

strongylosis (strŏn″jĭ-lō′sĭs) Infestation with organisms of the genus *Strongylus.*

Strongylus (strŏn′jĭ-lŭs) A genus of nematodes; the several species usually parasitize horses.

strontium (stron′shē-ŭm) [*Strontian,* mining village in Scotland + *-ium*(1)] SYMB: Sr. A dark yellow alkaline earth metal, atomic weight (mass) 87.62, atomic number 38, specific gravity 2.6. Medically it is of interest because its radioactive isotope ^{90}Sr constitutes a radioactive hazard in fallout from atom bombs. The isotope has a half-life of 28 years and is stored in bone when ingested.

Strophanthus (strō-făn′thŭs) [Gr. *strophos,* twisted cord, + *anthos,* flower] A genus of plants yielding a poisonous, white, crystalline glucoside, previously used as a heart stimulant.

structural integration Rolfing.

structure (strŭk′chŭr) [L. *structura,* adjustment, building] The composition and arrangement of the component parts of an organism or a device.

structural (strŭk′chŭ-răl), *adj.*

structured intermittent therapy Treat-ment for a disease in which periods of active drug use are alternated with drug holidays.

struma (stroo′mă) [L. *struma,* a mass, tumor] Goiter.

cast iron s. Riedel struma.

s. lymphomatosa A rare condition involving a diffuse and extensive infiltration of the entire thyroid gland.

s. maligna Carcinoma of the thyroid gland.

s. ovarii A form of ovarian teratoma in which the mass is composed of typical thyroid follicles filled with colloid.

Riedel s. SEE: under *Riedel, Bernhard M. K. L.*

strumectomy (stroo-mĕk′tō-mē) [″ + *ektome,* excision] The removal of a goiter.

Strümpell, Adolf G. G. von (strim′pĕl) Ger. neurologist, 1853–1925.

S. disease Ankylosing **spondylitis**.

S. sign Dorsiflexion of the foot when the thigh is flexed on the abdomen. This sign may be associated with spastic paralysis of the leg.

strut (strŭt) [probably fm. AS. *strutian,* to struggle] A support that stabilizes a structure.

struvite (strū′vīt) Magnesium ammonium phosphate crystals, important in health care because they cause about 15% of all kidney stones. They are formed in the urinary tract in conjunction with some bacterial infections, such as infection with *Proteus mirabilis,* and in some patients with hypercalciuria.

strychnine (strĭk′nīn, -nēn, -nĭn) [Gr. *strychnos,* nightshade] A poisonous alkaloid, used to kill rodents, that may produce nausea and vomiting, symmetrical muscle spasms, fever, muscle breakdown (rhabdomyolysis), and renal failure. It has no therapeutic usefulness but has been used as an experimental tool in neuropharmacology.

s. poisoning SEE: under *poisoning.*

Stryker, Homer H. (strĭk′ĕr) U.S. orthopedic surgeon, 1894–1980.

S. frame A device that supports two rectangular pieces of lightweight but strong material so that one side is on the anterior surface of the patient and the other is on the posterior surface. The patient is sandwiched firmly between the pieces of material. The device may be rotated around the patient's long axis. This permits turning the patient without his or her assistance. After a turn is completed, the uppermost portion of the frame can be moved away from the patient.

S. saw An electric-powered oscillating saw that cuts through bone or dense tissue with minimal damage to the underlying soft tissues.

STS *serological tests for syphilis.*

STU *skin test unit.*

study (stŭd′ē) [L. *studium,* zeal, earnestness, study] **1.** In clinical and surgical medicine, an examination or procedure. **2.** In the medical sciences, an investigation or research project.

action s. In cancer research, an investigation to determine whether a particular lifestyle choice made by patients can be used to prevent cancer.

agent s. In cancer research, an investigation to determine whether a particular intervention or drug can be used to prevent cancer from developing. SYN: *agent prevention s.*

agent prevention s. Agent **s.**

case-control s. In epidemiology and medical research, a technique in which cases are selected on the basis of the dependent variable, i.e., the presence (study group) or absence (control group) of the condition or disease being investigated. Differences in the rates of the factor, trait, exposure, characteristic, or possible cause (independent variables) are then compared between the two groups. For example, a study might involve two groups of patients from the same population—one that has cancer (study group) and one that does not (control group). The smoking rates in these otherwise similar groups could then be compared to see if exposure to cigarettes differed between them. Case control studies are retrospective: they suggest associations between variables but do not prove that one causes the other.

cohort s. In epidemiology, the tabulation and analysis of morbidity or mortality in a cohort, identified at a particular time and followed as the members of the cohort pass through part or all of their life span. SYN: *cohort analysis.*

conversion s. A scientific study of two or more treatments that tries to gauge the effect of switching from one form of therapy to another.

dose-ranging s. An investigation of different selected drug dosages to determine if any is better tolerated or more effective than the others.

electrophysiology s. ABBR: EPS. A procedure to determine the cause of life-threatening cardiac arrhythmias and the effect of treatments to prevent them. EPS is used typically after an episode of sudden death from ventricular tachycardia or ventricular fibrillation, or after symptomatic arrhythmias other than ventricular tachycardia or fibrillation, or in patients at high risk of death from these arrhythmias. Electrodes are placed within the heart and used to stimulate rhythm disturbances; the response of the heart can be studied after administration of antiarrhythmic drug therapy or under other controlled conditions.

first-in-man s. An initial formal analysis in humans of the safety of a new drug or a phase 1 trial of the agent.

mixing s. A test to determine the cause of an elevated prothrombin time, thrombin time, or activated thromboplastin time. The patient's blood is mixed with normal blood. If the abnormal test result is corrected, the patient has a deficiency of a clotting factor. If it is not, an antibody or inhibitor to a clotting factor is present in the patient's serum.

negative s. An investigation in which no benefit of a treatment or no association between a risk factor and an outcome is demonstrated. Such studies may be important in disproving misconceptions about a disease, treatment, or presumed associations between risk factors and outcomes. SYN: *negative* **trial.**

nerve conduction s. ABBR: NCS. An electrodiagnostic test to determine whether the conduction of impulses along specific nerves is normal or pathologically slowed. In the test, an electrical shock is given to a nerve that controls a particular muscle. The time for the muscle to contract and the distance for the electrical stimulus to travel along the nerve are recorded. In patients with neuropathies, the expected velocity of impulse conduction will not be met; slowing will be evident. Patients with cut or injured nerves will show maximal slowing of impulse conduction.

observational s. A research study in which the results are obtained retrospectively or without a control group. Some examples include case reports, chart reviews, and longitudinal studies of large cohorts followed over time. SYN: *observational* **trial.**

open-label s., open label study A clinical trial without a control group, in which both patients and researchers know the identity of the treatment and its dosage.

pilot s. Research that investigates a previously unexamined drug, protocol, or health care technology.

prospective s. A clinical or epidemiological study of patients or subjects that begins with a specific environmental, medical, social event, or intervention and records the consequences of that event in relation to a fixed date or conclusion. Prospective studies in which both the investigators and the research subjects are unaware of treatment assignments are considered among the most meaningful in health care.

retrospective s. A clinical study in which patients or their records are investigated after the patients have experienced the disease, condition, or treatment.

role delineation s. ABBR: RD study. A document that describes those tasks critical for competent job performance by identifying the minimum amount of knowledge and skills required to perform job-related functions. RD study results are often used to develop certification and licensing examinations in the health professions.

stump (stŭmp) The distal portion of an amputated extremity. SYN: *residual **limb***. SEE: illus.

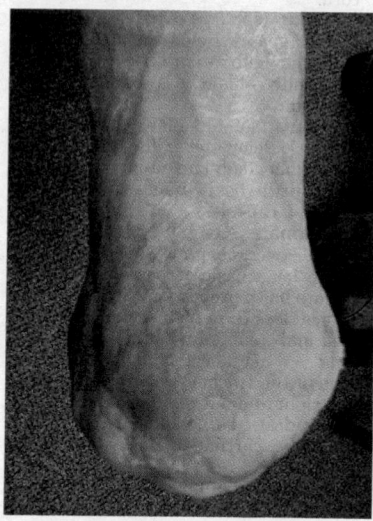

STUMP OF A FOOT

The toes have been removed

stun (stŭn) [Fr. *estoner*, to shake] To render unconscious, e.g. by an electrical shock or trauma to the head.

stunting (stŭnt'ing) A consequence of severe and long-lasting malnutrition in which a child fails to achieve the expected height for his or her age.

It is present when a child is more than 3 standard deviations shorter than an average child of the same age. It is found most often in children whose malnourishment occurs during the first five years of life.

stupe (stūp) [L. *stupa*, tow] A counterirritant for topical use, prepared by adding a small amount of an irritant such as turpentine to a hot liquid.

stupor (stū'por) [L., numbness] A state of altered mental status (decreased responsiveness to one's environment) in which a person is arousable only with vigorous or unpleasant stimulation. **stuporous,** *adj.*

   epileptic s. Postictal confusion or drowsiness that sometimes follows a seizure.

Sturge-Weber syndrome (stŭrj'web'ĕr) [William Sturge, Brit. physician, 1850–1919; Frederick Parkes Weber, Brit. physician, 1863–1962] A phakomatosis marked by port-wine nevi along the distribution of the trigeminal nerve, angiomas of leptomeninges and choroid, intracranial calcifications, mental retardation, seizures, and glaucoma. SYN: *nevoid amentia*.

stuttering (stŭt'ĕr-ĭng) [ME. *stutten*, to stutter] A disruption in the fluency of speech in which affected persons repeat letters or syllables, pause or hesitate abnormally, or fragment words when attempting to speak. The symptoms are exaggerated during times of stress, and may also be worsened by some medications, some strokes, or other diseases and conditions. Stuttering often occurs in more than one family member. SYN: *stammering*.

This condition occurs in approx. 1% to 2% of the school population. Boys are affected three or four times as often as girls. The onset is in two periods: between the ages of 2 and 4 years when speech begins and between 6 and 8 years of age when the need for language increases. It usually resolves spontaneously by adulthood.

Therapies, including relaxation techniques, hypnosis, delayed auditory feedback, and medications such as haloperidol can provide some help.

Educational materials are available from the Stuttering Foundation of America (800-992-9392) and from the American Speech-Language-Hearing Association (800-638-8255).

   acquired s. The sudden appearance of stuttering in a person over age 10 with no previous history of an articulation disorder. It may occur after a stroke, after the administration of certain drugs (e.g., theophylline), as an affectation, or as a reaction to unusually stressful circumstances.

sty, stye (stī) *pl.* **sties, styes** [AS. *stigan*, to rise] A localized inflammatory swelling of one or more of the glands of the eyelid. They are mildly tender, and may discharge some purulent fluid. SEE: *chalazion*.

   SYMPTOMS: General edema of the lid, pain, and localized conjunctivitis mark the condition. As the internal sty progresses, an abscess will form that can be seen through the conjunctiva.

   TREATMENT: Applying warm, moist compresses to the eyelid several times a day for 4 or 5 days usually helps the sty drain. If the sty does not resolve, it can be incised and drained surgically. SYN: *hordeolum*.

   meibomian s. An inflammation of a meibomian gland.

   zeisian s. An inflammation of one of the Zeis' glands.

stylet, stylette (stī-lĕt') [Fr. *stilette*] **1.** A small, sharp-pointed instrument for probing. **2.** A wire used to pass through, stiffen or clear a cannula or catheter.

styliform (stī′lĭ-form) [″ + L. *forma,* form] Long and pointed.

styloglossus (stī-lō-glŏs′ŭs) [Gr. *stylos,* pillar, + *glossa,* tongue] A muscle connecting the tongue and styloid process that raises and retracts the tongue.

stylohyal (stī″lō-hī′ăl) [″ + *hyoeides,* hyoid] Stylohyoid.

stylohyoid (stī-lō-hī′oyd) [″ + *hyoeides,* hyoid] Pert. to the styloid process of the temporal and hyoid bones. SYN: *stylohyal.*

stylohyoideus (stī″lō-hī-oyd′ē-ŭs) A muscle having its origin on the styloid process and its insertion on the hyoid bone. It draws the hyoid bone upward and backward.

styloid (stī′loyd) [″ + *eidos,* form, shape] Resembling a stylus or pointed instrument.

stylomandibular (stī″lō-măn-dĭb′ū-lar) [″ + L. *mandibula,* lower jawbone] Pert. to the styloid process of the temporal bone and mandible.

stylomastoid (stī″lō-măs′toyd) [″ + *mastos,* breast, + *eidos,* form, shape] Concerning to the styloid and mastoid processes of the temporal bone.

stylopharyngeus (stī″lō-făr-ĭn′jē-ŭs) [″ + *pharynx,* throat] The muscle connecting the styloid process and the pharynx that elevates and dilates the pharynx.

stylus (stī′lŭs) [Gr. *stylos,* a pillar] **1.** A probe or slender wire for stiffening or clearing a canal or catheter. **2.** A pointed medicinal preparation in stick form for external application (e.g., silver nitrate). **3.** A pointed writing instrument.

styptic (stĭp′tĭk) [Gr. *styptikos,* contracting] **1.** Contracting a blood vessel; stopping a hemorrhage by astringent action. **2.** Anything that stops a hemorrhage such as alum, ferrous sulfate, or tannic acid. SYN: *astringent; hemostat.*

stypven (stip′ven″) Russell viper venom.

stypven time test A test of coagulation factors that distinguishes between deficiencies of clotting factor VIII and clotting factor X.

styrene (stī′rēn″) C_8H_8, a colorless aromatic liquid hydrocarbon used to make plastics, polymers, rubber, and other materials used in the building industries.

 It is a carcinogen.

SYN: *ethenylbenzene;* **vinyl** *benzene.*

sub- [L. *sub,* under, below] Prefix meaning *under, beneath, in small quantity, less than normal.* SEE: *hypo-.*

subacetate (sŭb-ăs′ĕ-tāt) [″ + *acetum,* vinegar] A basic acetate.

subacid (sŭb-as′id) [*sub-* + *acid*] An imprecise term for *moderately acid.*

subacute (sŭb″ă-kūt′) [″ + *acutus,* sharp] Between acute and chronic, said of the course of a disease or of the healing process that develops at a moderate, rather than a slow or fast pace.

subarachnoid (sŭb″ă-răk′noyd) [″ + Gr. *arachne,* spider, + *eidos,* form, shape] Below or under the arachnoid membrane and above the pia mater of the covering of the brain and spinal cord.

subareolar (sŭb″ă-rē′ō-lăr) [″ + *areola,* a small space] Below the areola.

subatomic (sŭb″ă-tŏm′ĭk) [″ + Gr. *atomos,* indivisible] Less than the size of an atom.

subaxillary (sŭb-ăk′sĭ-lĕr″ē) [″ + *axilla,* armpit] Below the axilla, or armpit.

subcapsular (sŭb-kăp′sū-lăr) [″ + *capsula,* little box] Beneath, below, or within a capsule.

subcarbonate (sŭb″kar′bŏ-nāt″, -năt) [*sub-* + *carbonate*] A nonsystematic name for a basic carbonate. A subcarbonate has a proportion of carbonic acid radical less than the normal carbonate.

subcarinal (sŭb″kă-rī′năl) [*sub-* + *carina* + *-al*] Located just below the carina of the trachea, where it splits into the right and left mainstem bronchi.

subchondral (sŭb″kŏn′drăl) [″ + Gr. *chondros,* cartilage] Below or under a cartilage.

subchorionic (sŭb″kŏr″ē-on′ik) Located beneath the chorion.

subchronic (sŭb″kron′ik) [*sub-* + *chronic*] In human health and disease, of moderate or intermediate duration. The term is imprecise; the period is usually as long as a month but less than 10% of a lifetime.

subclass (sŭb′klăs) In taxonomy, a category between a class and an order.

subclavian (sŭb-klā′vē-ăn) [″ + *clavis,* key] **1.** Under the clavicle or collarbone. **2.** Pert. to the artery or vein that runs beneath the collarbone.

subclavian steal syndrome The clinical consequences of shunting blood from the vertebrobasilar artery, usually on the left side, around an occluded subclavian artery on that side, and into the left arm.

SYMPTOMS: The affected person often experiences numbness or weakness of the arm when he or she tries to use it. In some people, the diversion of blood from the brain into the arm results in signs and symptoms of brainstem ischemia or stroke, such as loss of consciousness. On physical examination, a bruit may be heard over the obstructed subclavian artery, and the blood pressure in the arm on the affected side will be lower than in the unaffected arm.

TREATMENT: The subclavian artery may be surgically bypassed or opened with angioplasty.

subclavian vein SEE: under *vein.*

subclavicular (sŭb″klă-vĭk′ū-lăr) [L. *sub,* under, below, + *clavicula,* little key] Subclavian.

subclavius (sŭb-klā′vē-ŭs) [″ + *clavis,* key] A tiny muscle from the first rib to the undersurface of the clavicle.

subclinical (sŭb-klĭn′ĭ-kăl) [″ + Gr. *klinikos,* pert. to a bed] Pert. to a period before the appearance of typical symptoms of a disease or to a disease or condition that does not present clinical symptoms. Mildly increased or decreased levels of thyroid hormone in the body often present subclinically.

subconjunctival (sŭb″kŏn-jŭnk-tī′văl) [″ + *conjungere,* to join together] Beneath the conjunctiva.

subconsciousness (sŭb-kŏn′shŭs-nĕs) [″ + *conscius,* aware] The condition in which mental processes take place without the individual's being aware of their occurrence. SEE: *subliminal.*

subcortical (sŭb-kor′tĭ-kăl) Pert. to the region beneath the cerebral cortex.

subcranial (sŭb-krā′nē-ăl) [″ + Gr. *kranion,* skull] Beneath or below the cranium.

subcrepitant (sŭb-krĕp′ĭ-tănt) [″ + *crepitare,* to rattle] Partially crepitant or crackling in character; noting a rale.

subculture (sŭb-kŭl′chŭr) [″ + *cultura,* tillage] **1.** To make a culture of bacteria with material derived from another culture. **2.** A relatively cohesive group of individuals living within a society, who, because of shared traditions, customs, socioeconomic status, or genetic heritage, may be predisposed to particular states of health or illness.

subculturing (sŭb-kŭl′chŭr-ĭng) [″ + ″] The growing and replacing of cells in tissue culture for many months.

subcutaneous (sŭb″kū-tā′nē-ŭs) [*sub-* + *subcutaneous*] Beneath the skin.

subcutaneous fat SEE: under *fat.*

subcutaneous interstitial glucose level Blood glucose levels in the interstitial space below the skin. They correlate fairly well with capillary blood glucose levels and can be measured with needle or dialysis-type sensors.

subcuticular (sŭb″kū-tĭk′ū-lăr) [L. *sub,* under, below, + *cuticula,* little skin] Subepidermal.

subcutis (sŭb-kū′tĭs) The layer of connective tissue beneath the skin.

subdeltoid (sŭb-dĕl′toyd) [″ + Gr. *delta,* letter d, + *eidos,* form, shape] Beneath the deltoid muscle.

subdermal (sŭb-dĕr′măl) [″ + Gr. *derma,* skin] Below the skin.

subdiaphragmatic (sŭb″dī″ă-frăg-mat′ik) [*sub-* + *diaphragmatic*] Beneath the diaphragm; subphrenic.

subduct (sŭb-dŭkt′) [″ + *ducere,* to lead] To draw down.

subdural (sŭb-dū′răl) [″ + *durus,* hard] Beneath the dura mater.

subendothelial, **subendothelium** (sŭb″ĕn-dō-thē′lē-ăl, sŭb″ĕn-dō-thē′lē-ŭm) [″ + Gr. *endon,* within, + *thele,* nipple] Beneath the endothelium.

subepidermal (sŭb″ĕp-ĭ-dĕr′măl) [″ + Gr. *epi,* upon, + *derma,* skin] Beneath the epidermis. SYN: *subcuticular.*

subepithelial (sŭb″ĕp-ĭ-thē′lē-ăl) [″ + ″ + *thele,* nipple] Beneath the epithelium.

suberosis (sū″bĕr-ō′sĭs) [L. *suber,* cork, + Gr. *osis,* condition] Pulmonary hypersensitivity reaction in workers exposed to cork. The antigen is present in a mold in the cork.

subfamily (sŭb-făm′ĭ-lē) In taxonomy, the category between a family and a genus.

subfebrile (sŭb-fē′brĭl) [″ + *febris,* fever] Having a mildly increased body temperature, usually considered to be less than 101°F (38.3°C).

subfertility (sŭb″fĕr-tĭl′ĭ-tē) [″ + *fertilis,* fertile] Fertility considered to be less than normal.

subfoveal (sŭb-fō′vē-ăl) [″ + ″] Beneath the fovea of the eye, i.e., beneath the central portion of the macula.

subgenus (sŭb-jē′nŭs) In taxonomy, the category between a genus and a species.

subgingival (sŭb-jĭn′jĭ-văl) [″ + *gingiva,* gum] Beneath the gingiva; pert. to a point or area apical to the margin of the free gingiva, usually within the confines of the gingival sulcus (e.g., subgingival calculus, or the subgingival margin of a restoration).

subglenoid (sŭb-glē′noyd) [″ + Gr. *glene,* socket, + *eidos,* form, shape] Below the glenoid fossa or glenoid cavity.

subglottic (sŭb-glŏt′ĭk) [″ + Gr. *glottis,* back of tongue] Beneath the glottis.

subgranular (sŭb-grăn′ū-lăr) [″ + *granulum,* little grain] Not completely granular.

subgroup (sŭb′groop″) In a research study a selected population of patients who share one or more common traits and thus can be distinguished from the rest of the individuals investigated.

subicular (sŭ-bĭk′ū-lăr) Concerning the uncinate gyrus.

subintimal (sŭb-ĭn′tĭ-măl) [″ + *intima,* innermost] Beneath the intima.

subinvolution (sŭb″in-vŏ-loo′shŏn) [*sub-* + *involution*] Imperfect involution; incomplete return of a part to normal dimensions after physiological hypertrophy.

   s. **of uterus** The lack of involution of the uterus following childbirth, manifested by a large uterus (greater than 100 g) and a continuation of lochia rubra beyond the usual time. It is caused usually by puerperal infection, overdistention of the uterus by multiple pregnancies or polyhydramnios, lack of lactation, malposition of the uterus, and retained secundines. Involution is aided by the certainty that the placenta is intact at the time of delivery and the use of ecbolics to cause uterine contraction.

subjacent (sŭb-jās′ĕnt) [L. *subjacere*, to lie under or near] In anatomy, lying underneath.

subject (sŭb′jekt″ [1., 2., 3.], sŭb-jekt′ [4.]) [L. *subjectus*, brought under (authority), inferior] **1.** A patient undergoing treatment, observation, or investigation; or a healthy person participating in a medical or scientific study. **2.** A body used for dissection. **3.** Susceptible to; prone to experience or suffer. **4.** To submit to a procedure or to the action of another.

subjective (sŭb-jĕk′tĭv) [L. *subjectivus*] Arising from or concerned with the individual; not perceptible to an observer; the opposite of objective.

subjective well-being ABBR: SWB. Wellness.

sublaminar wire (sŭb″lam′ĭ-năr) SEE: under *wire*.

sublesional (sŭb-lē′shŭn-ăl) [L. *sub*, under, below, + *laesio*, wound] Beneath a lesion.

sublethal (sŭb-lē′thăl) [″ + Gr. *lethe*, oblivion] Less than lethal; almost fatal.

sublimate (sŭb′lĭ-māt) [L. *sublimare*, to elevate] **1.** A substance obtained or prepared by sublimation. **2.** To cause a solid or gas to change state without becoming a liquid during transition. For example, ice may evaporate without first becoming a liquid. **3.** An ego defense mechanism by which one converts unwanted aggressive or sexual drives into socially acceptable activities.

sublimation (sŭb″lĭ-mā′shŏn) [L. *sublimatio*] **1.** The altering of the state of a gas or solid without first changing it into a liquid. **2.** A Freudian term pert. to the unconscious mental processes of ego defense whereby unwanted aggressive or sexual drives find an outlet through creative mental work.

sublime (sŭb-līm′) [L. *sublimis*, to the limit] To evaporate a substance directly from the solid into the vapor state and condense it again. For example, metallic iodine on heating does not liquefy but directly forms a violet gas.

subliminal (sŭb-lĭm′ĭn-ăl) [L. *sub*, under, below, + *limen*, threshold] **1.** Below the threshold of sensation; too weak to arouse sensation or muscular contraction. **2.** Beneath consciousness.

sublimis (sŭb-lī′mĭs) [L.] Near the surface.

sublingual (sŭb-lĭng′gwăl) [L. *sub*, under, below, + *lingua*, tongue] Pert. to the area beneath the tongue. SYN: *subglossal*.

subluxation (sŭb″lŭk″-sā′shŏn) [*sub-* + *luxation*] **1.** A partial or incomplete dislocation. **2.** In dentistry, injury to supporting tissues that results in abnormal loosening of teeth without displacement or rotation. When loosely applied to the temporomandibular joint, subluxation refers to the relaxation or stretching of the capsule and ligaments that results in popping noises during movement or partial dislocation of the mandible forward.

radial head s. Nursemaid's **elbow**.

submacular surgery A treatment for wet macular degeneration consisting of surgical removal of subfoveal choroidal neovascularization and the bleeding that accompanies it.

submammary (sŭb-măm′ă-rē) [″ + *mamma*, breast] Below the mammary gland.

submandibular (sŭb″măn-dĭb′ū-lăr) [″ + *mandibula*, lower jawbone] Beneath the mandible or lower jaw.

submarginal (sŭb-măr′jĭn-ăl) [″ + *marginalis*, border] Close to or next to a margin or border of a part. In dentistry, pert. to a deficiency in material or contour at the margin of a restoration in a tooth.

submassive (sŭb″mas′iv) [*sub-* + *massive*] Medical jargon for very severe or injurious but not immediately life-threatening conditions. It is applied to diseases such as liver necrosis (without fulminant hepatic failure) or pulmonary embolism (without unstable hemodynamics).

submaxillary (sŭb-măk′sĭ-lĕr″ē) Below the maxilla or upper jaw.

submembranous (sŭb-mĕm′bră-nŭs) [″ + *membrana*, membrane] Containing partly membranous material.

submental (sŭb-mĕn′tăl) [″ + *mentum*, chin] Under the chin.

submental lipectomy SEE: under *lipectomy*.

submerge (sŭb-mĕrj′) [″ + *mergere*, to immerse] To place under water.

submetacentric (sŭb″mĕt-ă-sĕn′trĭk) [″ + Gr. *meta*, beyond, + *kentron*, center] Pert. to a chromosome in which the centromere is within the two central quarters but not precisely centrally located.

submicron (sŭb-mī′krŏn) [″ + Gr. *mikros*, tiny] A particle smaller than 10^{-5} cm in diameter, visible only with an ultramicroscope. SEE: *micron*.

submicroscopic (sŭb″mī-krŏ-skŏp′ĭk) [″ + ″ + *skopein*, to examine] Too minute to be seen through a microscope.

submucosa (sŭb″mū-kō′să) [L. *sub*, under, below, + *mucosus*, mucus] The layer of connective tissue below the mucosa. It may vary from areolar to quite dense irregular connective tissue and, in addition to the distributing vessels and nerves, may contain fat, mucous glands, or muscle.

submucous resection SEE: under *resection*.

subneural (sŭb-nū′răl) [″ + Gr. *neuron*, nerve] Beneath the neural axis or the central nervous system.

subnormal (sŭb-nor′măl) [″ + *normalis,* accord. to pattern] Less than normal or average.

suboptimal (sŭb-ŏp′tĭ-măl) [″ + *optimus,* best] Less than optimum.

suborbital (sŭb-or′bĭ-tăl) [″ + *orbita,* track] Beneath the orbit.

suborder (sŭb-or′dĕr) In taxonomy, a category between an order and a family.

suboxide (sŭb-ŏk′sīdz) In a series of oxides, one that contains the smallest amount of oxygen.

subpar (sŭb″păr′) [″ + L. *par,* equal] Below accepted standards, said, e.g., of poor performance by an employee or institution.

subpatellar (sŭb″pă-tĕl′ăr) [″ + *patella,* a small pan] Beneath the patella.

subperiosteal (sŭb″pĕr-ē-ŏs′tē-ăl) [″ + ″ + *osteon,* bone] Beneath the periosteum.

subphrenic (sŭb″fren′ik) [*subphrenic* + *phrenic*] Beneath the diaphragm; subdiaphragmatic.

subphylum (sŭb-fī′lŭm) In taxonomy, the category between a phylum and a class.

subpial (sŭb-pī′ăl) [″ + *pia,* soft] Beneath the pia mater.

subplacenta (sŭb″plă-sĕn′tă) [″ + *placenta,* a flat cake] During pregnancy, the endometrium that lines the entire uterine cavity except at the site of the implanted blastocyst. SYN: *decidua parietalis.*

subpleural (sŭb-plū′răl) [″ + Gr. *pleura,* side] Beneath the pleura.

subpoena (sŭ-pē′nă) A court order that requires a person to come to court or appear at a specific time and place to give testimony. Failure to appear can result in punishment by the court.

subpoena duces tecum (sŭ-pē′nă doo′sēz tē′kŭm, soob poy′nă dook′ās tā′koom) A process used in litigation that compels the party having control of documents, items, and materials relevant to issues in a lawsuit to produce them at a designated time and place.

subpubic (sŭb-pū′bĭk) [″ + *pubes,* pubic region] Beneath the pubic arch, as a ligament, or performed beneath the pubic arch.

subretinal (sŭb-rĕt′ĭ-năl) [″ + *rete,* a net] Beneath the retina.

sub-Saharan Africa (sŭb″să-har′ăn) The large region of Africa that lies south of the Sahara desert. Common infections in this region include malaria, meningitis, tuberculosis, HIV, and HIV/AIDS.

subscapular (sŭb-skăp′ū-lăr) [″ + *scapula,* shoulder blade] Below the scapula.

subscleral (sŭb-sklē′răl) [″ + Gr. *skleros,* hard] Beneath the sclera of the eye. SYN: *subsclerotic* (1).

subscriber (sŭb-skrīb′ĕr) Enrollee.

subscription (sŭb-skrĭp′shŭn) [L. *subscriptas,* written under] The part of a prescription that contains directions for compounding ingredients.

subsidence (sŭb-sīd′ĕns) [L. *subsidere,* to sink down] The gradual disappearance of symptoms or manifestations of a disease.

subsistence 1. The minimum amount of something essential for life (e.g., a subsistence diet). 2. Any means of barely supporting life.

subspecies (sŭb′spē-sēz) [L. *sub,* under, below, + *species,* a kind] In taxonomy, subordinate to a species.

substage (sŭb′stāj) [″ + O.Fr. *estage,* position] The part of the microscope below the stage by which attachments are held in place.

substance (sŭb′stăns) [L. *substantia*] 1. Material; matter. 2. Substantia. 3. A chemical or drug. 4. When used in a medicolegal context, a chemical with potential for abuse. A great variety of entities are included: alcohol, nicotine, caffeine, sedatives, hypnotics, anxiolytics, and illicit drugs such as cannabis, heroin, or methamphetamines. Almost any substance may be abused even though its clinical use is approved when used as prescribed.

    anterior perforated s. The portion of the rhinencephalon lying immediately anterior to the optic chiasm. It is perforated by numerous small arteries.

    chromophilic s. A substance found in the cytoplasm of certain cells that stains similar to chromatin with basic dyes. It includes Nissl bodies of neurons and granules in serozymogenic cells.

    colloid s. A jelly-like substance in colloid degeneration.

    ground s. The matrix or intercellular substance in which the cells of an organ or tissue are embedded.

    high threshold s. A substance such as glucose or sodium chloride present in the blood and excreted by the kidney only when its concentration exceeds a certain level.

    ketogenic s. A substance that, in its metabolism, gives rise to ketone bodies.

    low threshold s. A substance such as urea or uric acid that is excreted by the kidney from the blood almost in its entirety. It occurs in the urine in high concentrations.

    Nissl s. SEE: under *Nissl, Franz.*

    posterior perforated s. A triangular area forming the floor of the interpeduncular fossa. It lies immediately behind the corpora mammillaria and contains numerous openings for blood vessels.

    pressor s. A substance that elevates arterial blood pressure.

    reticular s. The skein of threads present in some red blood cells. These are visible only when the cells are appropriately stained.

substance dependence disorder An addictive disorder of compulsive drug use.

It is marked by a cluster of behavioral and physiological symptoms that indicate continual use of the substance despite significant related problems. Patients develop a tolerance for the substance and require progressively greater amounts to elicit the effects desired. In addition, patients experience physical and psychological signs and symptoms of withdrawal if the agent is not used. SEE: *substance **abuse**; substance-induced disorder; substance-related disorder.*

substance P An 11-amino acid peptide that has important functions in the body's response to pain, noxious stimuli, depression, and anxiety. This substance may also be important in eliciting local tissue reactions resembling inflammation. SEE: *neurotransmitter; pain.*

substandard Unable to meet a generally accepted benchmark for quality.

substantia (sŭb-stan′sh(ē-)ă) [L. *substantia*, that which underlies, essence, substance] The material of which any organ or tissue is composed; matter. SYN: *substance.*

    s. gelatinosa The three dorsal-most layers (laminae 1, 2, and 3) of cells in the dorsal horns of the spinal cord.

    s. innominata A region of the brain lying between the globus pallidus of the basal ganglia and the ventral surface of the forebrain.

    s. nigra A slab-shaped basal ganglia nucleus lying along the dorsal surface of the cerebral peduncle in the midbrain tegmentumlocus niger.

    s. propria of the cornea The middle of the five histologic layers of the cornea.

substantivity (sŭb″stăn-tĭv′ĭ-tē) The ability of tissue to absorb an active ingredient and release it slowly over a period of time.

substernal (sŭb-stĕr′năl) [L. *sub*, under, below, + Gr. *sternon*, chest] Situated beneath the sternum.

substituent (sŭb″stĭ′chŭ-ĕnt) One part of a molecule substituted with another atom or group.

substitute (sŭb′stĭ-toot, -tūt) [L. *substitutus*, put in the place of] Something that may be used in place of another.

    blood s. An oxygen-carrying fluid that can be used in place of human blood products for transfusion therapy. Candidate substances that have been investigated for this purpose include polymerized hemoglobin and fluorinated hydrocarbons. SYN: *red blood cell **s**.*

    dairy food s. A food resembling an existing dairy food in taste and appearance but differing in composition from the dairy food for which it is substituted.

    fat s. Fat replacement.

    protein s. A dietary protein source altered to remove an undesirable amino acid that may have adverse effects on a patient unable to metabolize that amino acid. For example, in phenylketonuria, protein substitutes without phenylalanine can be added to the diet to allow normal growth and development of affected children.

    red blood cell s. Blood **s**.

    saliva s. Artificial **saliva**.

substitution (sŭb-stĭ-tū′shŭn) [L. *substitutio*, replacing] **1.** Displacing an atom (or more than one) of an element in a compound by atoms of another element of equal valence. **2.** In psychiatry, the ego defense mechanism of turning from an obstructed desire to one whose gratification is socially acceptable. **3.** The turning from an obstructed form of behavior to a more primitive one, as a substitution neurosis. **4.** The replacement of one substance by another. **5.** Drug substitution.

substitution product A compound formed by an element or a radical replacing another element or radical in a compound.

substitution therapy Replacement therapy.

substitutive (sŭb′stĭ-tū″tĭv) [L. *substitutivus*] Causing a change or substitution of characteristics.

substrate, substratum (sŭb′strāt, sŭb-strā′tŭm) [L. *substratum*, to lie under] **1.** An underlying layer or foundation. **2.** A base, as of a pigment. **3.** The substance acted upon, as by an enzyme. SEE: *enzyme.*

substructure (sŭb′strŭk-chŭr) The underlying structure of supporting material.

subsultus (sŭb-sŭl′tŭs) [L., to leap up] Any tremor, twitching, or spasmodic movement.

subsyndromal (sŭb″sĭn-drō′măl) **1.** Subthreshold. **2.** Having a cluster of symptoms suggesting a particular disease or condition but that do not meet the defined criteria used to make a diagnosis of that disease or condition.

subtarsal (sŭb-tăr′săl) [L. *sub*, under, below, + Gr. *tarsos*, a broad, flat surface] Below the tarsus.

subtentorial (sŭb″tĕn-tōr′ē-ăl) Located beneath the tentorium.

subterminal (sŭb-tĕr′mĭ-năl) [″ + *terminus*, a boundary] Close to the end of an extremity.

subtetanic (sŭb″tē-tăn′ĭk) [″ + Gr. *tetanikos*, suffering from tetanus] Moderately tetanic.

subthalamic (sŭb″thă-lăm′ĭk) [″ + Gr. *thalamos*, inner chamber] Below the thalamus.

subthalamus (sŭb-thăl′ă-mŭs) The portion of the diencephalon lying below the thalamus and above the hypothalamus. SEE: *thalamus.*

subtherapeutic (sŭb″thĕr-ŭ-pūt′ĭk) [″ + ″] **1.** Less than adequately treated. **2.** Taking a drug with a blood level below a desired treatment range. Patients using warfarin for atrial fibrillation, for example, have subtherapeutic anticoagulation when their international normalized ratio (INR) is below 2.0.

subtle (sŭt′ĕl) [L. *subtilis,* fine] **1.** Very fine or delicate. **2.** Very acute. **3.** Mentally acute or crafty. **4.** Causing injury without attracting attention, as subtle poisons or early symptoms of a disease.

subtotal (sŏb′tōt″ĭl, sŏb-tōt′) [″ + L. *totalis,* entire] Pert. to surgical procedures in which a portion of an organ, rather than the complete organ, is removed; partial, limited.

subtraction (sŭb-trak′shŏn) Removal of undesired overlying structures from a radiographical image by superimposing an image taken before the addition of contrast material with one taken after.

subtribe (sŭb′trīb) In taxonomy, the category between a tribe and a genus.

subtype 1. A gene that has a small mutation in its nucleotide sequence. **2.** An organism that carries or expresses an allele with a minor variation that distinguishes it from other members of the species.

subtyping (sŭb′tīp-ĭng) The precise identification of the genetic identity of a microorganism, often using DNA fingerprinting techniques.

subungual (sŭb-ŭng′gwăl) [*sub-* + *ungual*] Situated beneath the nail of a finger or toe.

subungual hematoma A collection of blood under the nail as a result of trauma. This condition may be treated by heating the end of a paper clip and then placing its point against the nail, which permits a small hole to be melted painlessly in the nail and allows the trapped blood to escape.

subunit (sŭb′ū″nĭt) In chemistry, a portion of a compound that represents a smaller part of the molecule than the remainder of the substance. SEE: *beta subunit.*

succedaneous (sŭk″sĕ-dā′nē-ŭs) [L. *succedaneus,* following, substituting] **1.** Pert. to a succedaneum. **2.** Pert. to or acting as a substitute. **3.** A substitute. **4.** SEE: *succedaneous tooth.*

succedaneum (sŭk″sĕ-dā′nē-ŭm) [L. *succedaneus,* following, substituting] **1.** Something that may be used as a substitute. **2.** SEE: *caput succedaneum.*

succimer (sŭk′sĭ-mĕr) An oral drug (2,3-dimercaptosuccinic acid) used to remove lead from the body by chelation. It is used primarily to treat children with acute lead intoxication. Its side effects include gastrointestinal upset, skin rashes, and elevated liver function test results. SEE: *acute lead encephalopathy; acute lead poisoning.*

⚠️ Use of this drug should always be accompanied by identification and removal of the source of the lead exposure.

succinate (sŭk′sĭ-nāt) Any salt of succinic acid.

succinylacetone (sŭk-sĭn″ĭl-ăs′ĭ-tōn″) A potentially toxic by-product of tyrosine metabolism. It accumulates in excessive concentrations in the blood of patients with type 1 tyrosinemia and is responsible for some of the symptoms of the disease.

succus (sŭk′kŭs) *pl.* **succi** [L. *succus,* juice] A juice or fluid secretion.

    s. **entericus** Intestinal **juice.**

succussion (sŭ-kŭsh′ŭn) [L. *succussio,* a shaking] The shaking of a person to detect the presence of fluid in the body cavity by listening for a splashing sound, esp. in the thorax.

suck [AS. *sucan,* to suck] **1.** To draw fluid into the mouth, as from the breast. **2.** To exhaust air from a tube and thus draw fluid from a container. **3.** That which is drawn into the mouth by sucking.

suckle (sŭk′ĕl) To nurse at the breast.

sucralose (soo′krĭ-lōs″) [Fm. *sucr(ose)* + *(ga)l(act)ose*] A sugar substitute manufactured by replacing hydroxyl groups on a sucrose molecule with chloride. It adds a sweet taste to foods without adding calories.

sucrase (sū′krās) [Fr. *sucre,* sugar] A digestive enzyme that splits cane sugar into glucose and fructose, the two being absorbed into the portal circulation. SYN: *invertase.*

sucrose (sū′krōs) [Fr. *sucre,* sugar] A dissacharide, $C_{12}H_{22}O_{11}$, obtained from sugarcane, sugar beet, and other sources. In the intestine, it is hydrolyzed to glucose and fructose by sucrase present in the intestinal juice. The monosaccharides resulting from the digestion of sucrose are absorbed by the small intestine and carried to the liver, where they may be converted to glycogen and stored if they are not needed immediately for energy.

suction [L. *suctio,* sucking] The drawing of fluids or solids from a surface, using negative pressures. SEE: *aspiration.*

    closed s., **closed suctioning** The incorporation of a suction system into a mechanical ventilator that permits airway suctioning without disconnecting patients from the ventilator. Closed suctioning prevents loss of positive end-expiratory pressure and loss of alveolar volume, and decreases contamination of the airway or the ventilator circuit by gases, germs, liquids, or fomites in the intensive care unit.

    endotracheal s. Tracheobronchial suction.

    nasogastric s. The suction of gas, fluid, and solid material from the gastrointestinal tract by use of a tube extending from the suction device to the stomach or intestines via the nasal passage.

    open s. Clearing the airways of a mechanically ventilated patient with a suction catheter inserted into the endotracheal tube after the patient has been disconnected from the ventilator circuit. SEE: *closed* **s.**

tracheobronchial s. Clearing the airways of mucus, pus, or aspirated materials to improve oxygenation and ventilation. SYN: *endotracheal* **s.**

PATIENT CARE: To avoid hypoxia, the patient must be given high-flow oxygen before suctioning. During insertion of the suction tube no negative pressure is used to avoid damaging the fragile lining of the bronchi. Suction is then applied during tubal withdrawal for 15 sec or less. The patient should be in supine position, with head elevated 30 degrees or higher, unless otherwise contradicted. Baseline vital signs and oxygen saturation are assessed, and the patient informed the procedure may initiate coughing. The health care professional performs hand hygiene and puts on clean gloves. The patient is hyperoxygenated for 1 min prior to and after suctioning by increasing the ventilator's fraction of inspired oxygen setting (FIO_2) to 1. The vacuum regulator is adjusted to the desired suction pressure. The catheter is advanced to the carina of the trachea without suctioning to avoid airway injury. The patient with an intact cough reflex will begin to cough. Suctioning begins as the catheter is pulled out of the airway. The patient is checked for desired and adverse effects (such as hypoxia or arrhythmias), and needs are met. Suctioning is repeated as needed to clear secretions (usually no more than two to three passes). When suctioning is complete, the FIO_2 level is returned to the proper setting. Since ventilated patients require frequent oral hygiene, this may be a good time for that to be provided. Gloves are removed, and hand hygiene repeated, and the procedure is documented.

suction channel A passage within an endoscope through which fluids may be injected or removed. During endoscopy it is used to draw blood, feces, mucus, or secretions away from the lens of the scope, so that clinical observations can be made with clarity and tissues can be selected for specimen collection.

suction control chamber SEE: under *chamber.*

suctioning The use of suction to remove debris or body fluids from an airway, body cavity, orifice, or surgical site. SEE: *suction.*

suctorial (sŭk-tō'rē-ăl) [LL. *suctio,* sucking] **1.** Pert. to sucking. **2.** Equipped for sucking.

Sudan (sū-dăn') One of a number of related biological stains for which fats have a special affinity, including Sudan II, Sudan III (G), Sudan IV, and Sudan R.

sudanophil (sū-dăn'ō-fĭl) [*sudan* + Gr. *philein,* to love] A leukocyte that stains readily with Sudan III, indicative of fatty degeneration. **sudanophilic,** *adj.*

sudanophilia (sū-dăn"ō-fĭl'ē-ă) An affinity for Sudan stains.

sudden infant death syndrome ABBR: SIDS. The sudden death of an infant under 1 year old that remains unexplained after a thorough investigation, including a complete autopsy, examination of the death scene, and review of the clinical history. More than 90% of all SIDS deaths occur before the age of 6 months. SIDS is a major contributor to infant mortality in the U.S. and other industrialized nations; about 2500 infants die of SIDS annually in the U.S. SYN: *crib death.*

ETIOLOGY: The causes of SIDS are still not clearly understood. Some evidence has linked SIDS to unrecognized congenital abnormalities of either the central nervous system or the electrical conduction system of the heart; to elevated levels of alpha-fetoprotein; to rare metabolic diseases, occult infections, or unintentional injuries; or, in some cases, child abuse.

RISK FACTORS: Although the cause of SIDS is unknown, some of the identified factors that increase the risk of SIDS include sleeping on the stomach; sharing a bed with an adult; maternal age less than 20 years; tobacco use in the home; living in overcrowded or unsanitary conditions; and lack of prenatal care. Very low-birth-weight babies, nonwhite babies, and male infants have higher rates of SIDS than other babies. More SIDS occurs during the winter months than at other times of year.

PREVENTION: Parents should attempt to remedy those risk factors listed that can be altered or prevented. The prone position for sleep should be avoided. The slogan "Back to Sleep" was devised to remind parents that infants should be positioned on their backs when put to bed. Since the introduction of the "Back to Sleep" campaign, SIDS deaths have declined by about 40%. A firm sleeping surface is recommended. Soft, plush, or bulky items, such as pillows, rolls of bedding, or cushions should not be placed in the infant's sleeping environment. These items could come into close contact with the infant's face, thereby interfering with ventilation or entrapping the infant's head and causing suffocation. Breast-feeding mothers should be advised to avoid alcohol, drugs, and over-the-counter and herbal remedies that could contain substances that would depress the infant's central nervous system. Guidelines from the American Academy of Pediatrics recommend use of a pacifier from age 1 month to help reduce the risk of SIDS by preventing the infant from sleeping too soundly. If the pacifier is rejected, it should not be forced. Use of a pacifier should end by 12 months because continued use increases the risk of ear infections and teeth malalignment. Home monitoring of the infant with apnea monitors or baby-listening devices provide parents with reassurance about the status of their infants, but these tools have not been clearly proven to prevent SIDS. During prenatal checkups, parents should be educated about risk factors for SIDS. Parental smoking should be discouraged, as should smoking by anyone else entering the home. Baby-sitters, day care providers, and others who may be involved in care of the infant should be made aware of the parents' concerns for their infant. Placing in the prone position an infant who is used to sleeping on his back increases the risk for SIDS. SEE: *apnea; apnea alarm mattress.*

PATIENT CARE: Parents can make sure that the crib and bedding they plan to use are safe by accessing the U.S. Consumer Product Safety Commission's guidelines at http://www.cpsc.gov. Loss of an infant because of SIDS usually produces a severe grief and guilt reaction. The family needs expert counseling in the several months after the death. Valuable sources of support and information about SIDS are First Candle/SIDS Alliance (Phone 1-800-221-7437; www.sidsalliance.org) and SIDS Families (www.sidsfamilies.com).

sudden infant death syndrome, risk for Presence of risk factors for sudden death of an infant under 1 year of age. SEE: *Nursing Diagnoses Appendix.*

sudden release test A test to identify anterior shoulder instability. The relocation test for anterior glenohumeral instability is performed. While the patient's glenohumeral joint is externally rotated, the examiner suddenly removes the posteriorly directed stabilizing force. A positive test is marked by the patient's expression of pain and/or apprehension. SYN: *surprise test.* SEE: *relocation test.*

Sudeck disease, Sudeck atrophy (soo′dek″) Reflex sympathetic dystrophy.

SUDEP *sudden unexpected* (or *unexplained) death in epilepsy.*

sudor (sū′dŏr) [L.] Sweat. **sudoral** (sū′dŏr-ăl), *adj.*

sudoresis (sū″dō-rē′sĭs) [L.] Diaphoresis.

sudorific (sū″dor-ĭf′ĭk) [L. *sudorificus*] **1.** Secreting or promoting the secretion of sweat. **2.** An agent that produces sweating. SYN: *diaphoretic.*

sue 1. To initiate legal action. **2.** To make a petition or pleading to the court.

suet (sū′ĕt) [Fr. *sewet*, suet] A hard fat from cattle or sheep kidneys and loins, used as the base of certain ointments and as an emollient.

suffer 1. To experience pain or distress. **2.** To be subjected to injury, loss, or damages.

suffocate (sŭf′ō-kāt) [L. *suffocare*] To impair respiration; to smother, asphyxiate.

suffocation (sŭf″ō-kā′shŭn) Deprivation of air exchange (e.g., by drowning, smothering, or other forms of airway obstruction) that produces an intense sensation of air hunger. SYN: *asphyxiation.* SEE: *asphyxia; resuscitation; unconsciousness.*

   s., risk for Accentuated risk of accidental suffocation (inadequate air available for inhalation). SEE: *Nursing Diagnoses Appendix.*

suffusion (sŭ-fū′zhŏn) [L. *suffusio*, a pouring over] **1.** Extravasation. **2.** A color or liquid spread over or through something, esp. of blood as in conjunctivitis.

sugar (shug′ăr) [Ult. fr. Arabic *sukkar* via L. *succarum*] A sweet-tasting, low-molecular-weight carbohydrate of the monosaccharide or disaccharide groups. Common sugars include fructose, glucose, lactose, maltose, sucrose, and xylose. Oral or parenteral administration of sugars can prevent hypoglycemia caused by insulin or oral hypoglycemic agents.

CLASSIFICATION: Sugars are classified in two ways: the number of atoms of simple sugars yielded on hydrolysis by a molecule of the given sugar and the number of carbon atoms in the molecules of the simple sugars so obtained. Therefore, glucose is a monosaccharide because it cannot be hydrolyzed to a simpler sugar; it is a hexose because it contains six carbon atoms per molecule. Sucrose is a disaccharide because on hydrolysis it yields two molecules, one of glucose and one of fructose. SEE: *carbohydrate.*

   birch s. Xylose.

   blood s. Glucose in the blood, normally 60 to 100 mg/100 mL of blood. It rises after consumption of a meal to variable levels, depending on the content of the meal, the activity level of and medications used by the consumer, and other variables. In diabetes mellitus, fasting blood sugar levels exceed 126 mg/dl. SEE: *glucose.*

   cane s. Sucrose obtained from sugar cane.

   fruit s. Fructose.

   grape s. Glucose.

   invert s. A mixture consisting of one molecule of glucose and one of fructose resulting from the hydrolysis of sucrose.

malt s. Maltose.

milk s. Lactose.

muscle s. Inositol. It is not a true sugar.

simple s. A sugar molecule made of few components (e.g., a monosaccharide or disaccharide).

wood s. Xylose.

sugared beverage, sugar-sweetened beverage, sugary beverage A drink, carbonated or uncarbonated, to which corn syrup, glucose, or other sweetening agents have been added. They are a significant source of calories in the diet, esp. in children, adolescents, and young adults, and contribute to tooth decay.

suggestible (sŭg-jĕs′tĭ-bl) Very susceptible to the opinions of others.

suggestion (sŭg-jĕs′chŭn) [L. *suggestio*] **1.** The imparting of an idea indirectly; the act of implying. **2.** The idea so conveyed. **3.** The psychological process of having an individual adopt or accept an idea without argument or persuasion.

posthypnotic s. A suggestion given during hypnosis that influences the behavior of an individual when awake and alert.

suggestive (sŭg-jes′tĭv) **1.** Pert. to or stimulating suggestion. **2.** Indicative. Said of certain signs, symptoms, or laboratory findings that point toward, but do not completely affirm, a diagnosis.

suggestive therapeutics The practice of treating disease by hypnotic suggestions.

suicide (soo′ĭ-sīd″) [L. *sui*, of oneself + *-cide*] Intentionally causing one's own death. In the U.S., about 35,000 people commit suicide each year; about 325,000 people who attempt suicide receive care in emergency departments. Currently, suicide is the ninth most common cause of death in the U.S.

RISK FACTORS: Although suicide attempts are more frequently made by young women than any other group, successful suicide is most likely to occur when attempted by older men who live alone or young veterans returning from war. These men are most likely to use violent means in their suicide attempts, e.g., shooting themselves, jumping from heights, or hanging. Other risk factors for suicide include having a first-degree relative with a mood disorder; recurrent thoughts or discussion of suicide, esp. if a concrete plan for suicide has been contemplated; the means to commit suicide, esp. a weapon in one's possession; alcoholism; a new diagnosis of a mortal illness; living alone; a recent divorce or job loss; or uncontrolled pain caused by physical illness. Many people who kill themselves have consulted a health care provider in the months or weeks immediately before their death, which suggests that opportunities to intervene in the at-risk population are often missed.

PREVENTION: Health care professionals should be alert to the warning signs of suicide, e.g., statements indicating a desire to die or a prediction that suicide will occur. People contemplating suicide may be depressed, act to get their lives in order, give away possessions, have failing grades or poor work performance, adopt risk-taking behavior, or have a history of alcoholism or drug abuse.

Management of those who are contemplating or have attempted suicide includes removal of lethal means from them and the provision of professional, social, and family support. If the patient is being treated as an outpatient, then he or she should be scheduled for specific future appointments and informed of a telephone number where help or assistance will be immediately available on a 24-hr basis. During a crisis, the patient should not be left alone even for a few minutes. For medicolegal reasons, careful and complete medical records should be kept concerning the plans and actions for management of the patient.

assisted s. ABBR: AS. Providing a patient with the means for ending his or her life (usually a prescription typically provided by a physician for a lethal dose of barbiturates), with the provider knowing that the patient intends to use it to commit suicide. The patient must be physically and mentally capable of committing suicide and is the one who takes the action to end his or her life and must be physically and mentally capable of committing suicide. Whether physicians and other health care professionals should involve themselves in assisted suicide is a topic of active debate. In the U.S. assisted suicide is recognized in the states of Montana, Oregon, and Washington, and its legality has been affirmed by the U.S. Supreme Court. Assisted suicide is legal in Belgium, Colombia, Luxembourg, the Netherlands, and Switzerland. SYN: *physician-assisted s.* SEE: *assisted death; euthanasia.*

physician-assisted s. Assisted **s.**

suicide cluster SEE: under *cluster.*

suicide gene A gene that codes for a protein, usually an enzyme, that makes cells vulnerable to otherwise nontoxic substances or nutrients. Suicide genes can be introduced into cells during gene therapy. The technique is used in cancer therapy to make tumor cells susceptible to treatment with prodrugs, which only become active chemotherapeutic agents when they are metabolized within cells harboring the gene. Suicide gene therapy is also used in graft-versus-host disease to kill the activated donor T cells responsible for the immunological attack on the host.

suicidology (soo″ĭ-sīd-ŏl′ō-jē) [″ + ″ + Gr. *logos,* word, reason] The science of suicide, including its cause, prediction of those susceptible, and prevention.

suit **1.** A lawsuit, legal action, or court proceeding by one party against another for damages or other legal remedies. **2.** An outer garment.

anti-G **s.** A garment designed to produce uniform pressure on the lower extremities and abdomen. Normally the suit is used by aviators to help prevent pooling of blood in the lower half of the body during certain flight maneuvers. The garment has also been used in treating severe forms of postural hypotension. The suit's usefulness in treating shock is questionable.

⚠ This garment is contraindicated in congestive heart failure, cardiogenic shock, and penetrating chest trauma.

sulcate, sulcated (sŭl′kāt, -ĕd) [L. *sulcatus*] Furrowed or grooved.

sulcus (sŭl′kŭs) *pl.* **sulci** [L., groove] A furrow, groove, or fissure, esp. on the surface of the brain.

calcarine **s.** Calcarine **fissure**.

central **s.** The groove that runs down the side of the cerebral hemisphere and separates the parietal and frontal lobes. The central sulcus lies approx. midway along the lateral surface of the cerebral hemisphere, between the frontal and occipital poles of the brain. The gyrus anterior to the central sulcus -- the precentral gyrus -- is the primary motor cortex, and the gyrus posterior to the central sulcus -- the postcentral gyrus -- is the primary sensory cortex. Occasionally, the central sulcus is interrupted and is not a continuous groove from top to bottom. SYN: *s. centralis.*

s. centralis Central **s.**

cingulate **s.** A groove curving transversely along the anterior medial surface of the cerebral hemisphere, which parallels the callosal sulcus, from which it is separated by the cingulate gyrus. The cingulate sulcus forms the lower edge of the medial frontal gyrus and the paracentral lobule.

gingival **s.** The crevice between the free gingiva and the tooth surface. A healthy sulcus produces gingival sulcular fluid (GSF), which helps to remove bacteria from the sulcus. Normal sulcus depth is 0.5–1.5 mm. Inflammation in the sulcus is the first sign of gingivitis. When enlarged by disease, the gingival sulcus deepens and becomes a periodontal pocket.

intraparietal **s.** A groove branching from the postcentral sulcus and running transversely and posteriorly along the lateral surface of the parietal lobe of the brain. It divides the posterior portion of the parietal lobe into two parts, the superior and the inferior parietal lobules.

lateral **s.** Sylvian **fissure**.

median **s.** On the dorsal surface of the tongue, the midline groove that separates the surface into right and left halves.

s. terminalis **1.** A shallow groove along the outside surface of the right atrium of the heart marking the junction of the venae cava and the atrium. The crista terminalis is found at the corresponding location inside the right atrium. **2.** A V-shaped groove on the dorsal surface of the tongue separating the anterior two-thirds of the tongue from the posterior one-third. The anterior (oral) part of the tongue receives different innervation and has different embryological origins from the posterior (pharyngeal) part.

sulfatase (sŭl′fă-tās) An enzyme that hydrolyzes sulfuric acid esters.

sulfate (sŭl′fāt″) [L. *sulphatum*] SO_4^{-2}, a salt or ester of sulfuric acid. Particular sulfates are listed under the first word. SEE: e.g., *amikacin sulfate; dextroamphetamine sulfate; magnesium sulfate.*

sulfatide (sŭl′fă-tīd) Any cerebroside with a sulfate radical esterified to the galactose.

sulfhemoglobin (sŭlf″hēm-ō-glō′bĭn) Sulfmethemoglobin.

sulfhemoglobinemia (sŭlf″hēm-ō-glō″bĭn-ē′mē-ă) A persistent cyanotic condition caused by sulfhemoglobin in the blood.

sulfhydryl (sŭlf-hī′drĭl) The univalent radical, SH, of sulfur and hydrogen.

sulfide (sŭl′fīd) Any compound of sulfur with an element or base.

sulfonamide (sŭl-fŏn′ă-mīd″) Any of a group of compounds consisting of amides of sulfanilic acid derived from their parent compound sulfanilamide. They are characterized by the presence of a $-SO_2NH_2$ moiety in their chemical structure.

⚠ Sulfa drugs may cause allergic reactions, such as rashes, and other adverse reactions, such as nausea and vomiting.

sulfone (sŭl′fōn) An oxidation product of sulfur compound in which the $=SO_2$ is united to two hydrocarbon radicals.

sulfonylurea (sŭl′fū-nil″ūr′ē-ŭ) [*sulfone* + *-yl* + *urea*] One of a class of oral drugs that stimulates the pancreas to produce insulin; used to control high blood sugars in type 2 diabetes mellitus. Members of this group include tolazamide, glyburide, and glipizide.

⚠ Hypoglycemia may occur as a side effect of these medications if they are taken when dietary intake is limited or restricted voluntarily or during illness.

sulforaphane, sulphoraphane (sŭl-fŏr′ă-fān″) [″ + Gr. *phainein,* to show] ABBR: SF. A sulfur-containing compound found in vegetables of the mustard family (Cruciferae). Like other isothiocyanates, it has been shown to prevent cancer in animals.

sulfoxide (sŭl-fŏk′sīd) The divalent radical =SO.

sulfur (sŭl′fŭr) [L. *sulpur, sulphur, sulfur,* brimstone, sulphur] SYMB: S. A pale yellow crystalline element, atomic weight (mass) 32.06, atomic number 16, specific gravity 2.07. It burns with a blue flame, producing sulfur dioxide.

Sulfur is part of some amino acids (cystine, cysteine) and is necessary for the synthesis of proteins such as insulin and keratin. The amount of sulfur (as sulfate) excreted in urine varies with the amount of protein in the diet but more or less parallels the amount of nitrogen excreted, as both are derived from protein catabolism. The S:N ratio is approx. 1:14 (i.e., for each gram of sulfur excreted, 14 g of nitrogen are excreted). The amount of sulfur excreted daily is about 1 g.

DEFICIENCY SYMPTOMS: Sulfur deficiency produces dermatitis and imperfect development of hair and nails. A deficiency of cystine or cysteine proteins in the diet inhibits growth and may be fatal. Tissue oxidation of cystine forms inorganic sulfate if the protein intake is sufficient.

s. (IV) oxide An irritating gas used in industry to manufacture acids and as a bactericide and disinfectant. It is derived from burning fuels that contain sulfur and from volcanic emissions. When absorbed by water on particulates in the atmosphere, the gas is further oxidized (e.g., by light and NO_2) to form sulfuric acid (H_2SO_4). It is a major component of air pollution.

precipitated s. A form of sulfur used in various skin diseases, including scabies. Its keratolytic effect helps to make it effective in those disorders.

sulfurated, sulfureted (sŭl′fū-rā″těd, -rět″ěd) Combined or impregnated with sulfur.

sulfuric acid poisoning SEE: under *poisoning.*

sumac (soo′mak″ shoo′) [Ult. fr Arabic *summāq*] Any of several species of shrub of the genus *Toxicodendron.*

poison s. A shrublike plant, *Toxicodendron vernix,* widely distributed in the U.S. Because it contains the same active substances as poison ivy, the symptoms and treatment of poison sumac dermatitis are the same as for poison ivy dermatitis. SEE: *poison ivy* for illus.

sumatriptan (soo-mă-trĭp′tăn) A drug from the class of 5-hydroxytryptamine antagonists that can be given, either orally or by injection, to treat migraine headaches. Adverse effects include return of the headache and precipitation of angina pectoris in patients with coronary artery disease, among others.

summation (sŭ-mā′shŏn) [L. *summatio,* adding up] **1.** A cumulative action or effect, as of stimuli. An organ will react to two or more weak stimuli as if they were a single strong one. **2.** In mathematics, the process of adding a sequence of numbers, resulting in a sum.

sunburn (sŭn′bŭrn″) Dermatitis due to excessive exposure to the actinic rays of the sun. The rays that produce the characteristic changes in the skin are ultraviolet, between 290 and 320 nm. Some people are more resistant to these rays than others, but the skin will be damaged in anyone who has sufficient exposure.

PREVENTION: Prolonged direct exposure of the skin to sunlight between 10 A.M. and 3 P.M., when ultraviolet rays are strongest, should be avoided to minimize the risk of sunburn and skin cancer. Clothing should be worn to cover the skin or a sun-blocking agent with a sun protective factor (SPF) of 15 or more should be used (to be reapplied each hour if the person is sweating heavily).

⚠ Sunbathing and sunburn are risk factors for skin cancers, including basal cell carcinoma, squamous cell carcinoma, and melanoma.

TREATMENT: Cool, wet dressings may be applied to the burned area if the reaction is moderate. For severe sunburn, lukewarm baths with oatmeal or cornstarch and baking soda should be given. Aspirin or other nonsteroidal anti-inflammatory agents may reduce inflammation and pain.

sundowning (sun′dow-nĭng) Confusion or disorientation that increases in the afternoon or evening. It is a common finding in patients with cognitive disorders (e.g., elderly persons with dementia) and tends to improve when the patient is reassured and reoriented.

sunglasses Eyeglasses that protect the eyes from exposure to visible as well as ultraviolet rays. For optimal eye protection outdoors, wraparound sunglasses or solar shields that block both ultraviolet A and ultraviolet B rays should be worn.

sunrise view An x-ray of the knee in flexion, taken to highlight the patella and its relation to the femoral condyles, e.g., in evaluations of osteoarthritis. SYN: *skyline view.*

sunscreen A substance used as a second line of defense against damage to the skin by ultraviolet rays. It is usually applied as an ointment or cream. SEE: *photosensitivity; ultraviolet* **radiation**.

⚠️ Sunscreens are much less effective in protecting against the damaging effects of the sun than avoiding midday sunlight and wearing protective clothing and headgear—these are the primary defenses against solar injury. Sunscreens should be reapplied after vigorous exercise and swimming. Some sunscreens may cause allergic or contact dermatitis.

sunscreen protective factor index SEE: under *index*.

Sun's soup (sŭnz, soonz) A dietary supplement consisting of a mixture of herbs and vegetables and promoted as a treatment for a variety of cancers. Also known as Selected Vegetables.

sunstroke (sŭn′strōk) [AS. *sunne*, sun, + *strake*, a blow] Heatstroke.

suntan Darkening of the skin caused by exposure to the sun. SEE: *tanning salon; sunburn; sunscreen*.

⚠️ A suntan predisposes exposed skin to basal cell carcinoma, squamous cell carcinoma, melanoma, and premature aging.

super- [L. *super*, over, above] Prefix meaning *above, beyond, superior*. SEE: *hyper-*.

superantigen (soo″pĕr-ăn′tĭ-jĕn) An antigen that binds with class I major histocompatibility antigens and T-cell receptors and causes the simultaneous activation of large numbers of T cells and massive release of cytokines. Such antigens do not have to be processed by macrophages to be recognized by T cells. Exotoxins from bacteria such as staphylococci and group A streptococci act as superantigens. A superantigen known as toxic shock syndrome toxin-I causes toxic shock syndrome.

supercentenarian (soo″pĕr-sen′tĕ-ner′ē-ăn) [*super-* + *centenarian*] **1.** Having lived more than 110 years. **2.** A person who has lived more than 110 years.

superciliary (soo″pĕr-sĭl′ē-ă-rē) [L. *supercilium*, eyebrow] Pert. to or in the region of an eyebrow. SYN: *supraciliary*.

supercilium (soo″pĕr-sĭl′ē-ŭm) *pl.* **supercilia** [L.] **1.** Eyebrow. **2.** A hair of the eyebrow.

superclass (soo′pĕr-klăs) In taxonomy, a category between a phylum and a class.

superego (soo″pĕr-ē′gō) [″ + *ego*, I; later translators of Freud's writings feel the word *uber-ich* should have been translated to over-I or upper-I and not to superego] In Freudian psychoanalytical theory, the portion of the personality associated with ethics, self-criti-

cism, and the moral standard of the community. It is formed in infancy by the individual's adopting as his or her personal standards the values of the significant persons with whom he or she identifies. This helps to form the conscience. The superego functions to protect and to reward when the ego-ideal of behavior or thought is satisfied and to criticize, punish, and evoke a sense of guilt when the reverse is true. In neuroses, symptoms develop when instinctual drives conflict with those dictated by the superego. SEE: *ego*.

supereruption Overeruption.

superfamily (soo″pĕr-făm′ĭ-lē) In taxonomy, a category between an order and a family.

superfecundation (soo″pĕr-fē″kŭn-dā′shŭn) [″ + *fecundare*, to fertilize] Successive fertilization by two or more separate instances of sexual intercourse of two or more ova formed during the same menstrual cycle. Fertilization may be by the same male or by two different males.

superfemale (soo″pĕr-fē′māl) A female having three X chromosomes.

superfetation (soo″pĕr-fē-tā′shŭn) [″ + *fetus*, fetus] The fertilization of two ova in the same uterus at different menstrual periods within a short interval.

superficial (soo″pĕr-fĭsh′ăl) [L. *superficialis*] **1.** Pert. to or situated near the surface (e.g., of the ribs in relation to the lungs). **2.** Not thorough; cursory.

superficial heating The application of heat to the skin and subcutaneous tissues.

superficialis (soo″pĕr-fĭsh-ē-ā′lĭs) [L.] Pert. to a structure such as an artery, vein, or nerve that is close or relatively close to the surface.

superficial muscular aponeurotic system ABBR: SMAS. The nerves, blood vessels, fat, and fibrous tissue that connects the facial skin to its underlying musculature. Operations that rejuvenate the face ("face lifts") often revise or sculpt this tissue to reduce age-related sagging or drooping.

superglue (soo′pĕr-gloo″) An extremely strong adhesive made of cyanoacrylate. It can be used to reapproximate the edges of a wound without sutures.

⚠️ This glue is quite effective in gluing skin to skin. It should not be used near the eyes, mouth, nose, labia, or other sensitive body parts.

SEE: *cyanoacrylate adhesive*.

superinduce (soo″pĕr-ĭn-dūs′) [″ + *in*, into, + *ducere*, to lead] To bring on, over, or above an already existing condition or situation.

superinfection (soo″pĕr-ĭn-fĕk′shŭn) [″ + *infectio*, a putting into] A new infection caused by an organism different from that which caused the initial infection. The microbe responsible is usually resistant to the treatment given for the initial infection.

superior (soo-pē'rē-or) [L. *superus,* upper] **1.** Higher than; situated above something else. **2.** Better than. **3.** One in charge of others.

superiority trial (soo-pēr"ē-or'ĭt-ē) [L. *superior,* above, higher] SEE: under *trial.*

superior vena cava syndrome A partial occlusion of the superior vena cava with resulting interference of venous blood flow from the head and neck to the heart. This emergency condition is typically caused by obstruction of the great vessels, usually by a cancer located in the mediastinum. It is marked by venous engorgement and edema of the head and neck.

supernatant (soo"pĕr-nā'tănt) [" + *natare,* to float] **1.** Floating on a surface, as oil on water. **2.** The clear liquid remaining at the top after a precipitate settles. **3.** The cell-derived fluids containing chemical mediators that develop in a laboratory culture of leukocytes mixed with an antigen or mitogen stimulus. Supernatants can be assessed for the presence of monokines or lymphokines by adding them to other white blood cell cultures and measuring cell proliferation and activity.

supernate (soo'pĕr-nāt) A supernatant fluid.

supernumerary (soo"pĕr-nū'mĕr-ăr"ē) [L. *supernumerarius*] Exceeding the regular number.

supernumerary teeth More than the usual number of teeth. Extra teeth develop in approx. 2% of the population, with almost all of them being maxillary incisors or mesiodens. A cleft palate or other developmental disturbances disrupt the dental lamina and often result in palatal supernumerary teeth.

superolateral (soo"pĕr-ō-lăt'ĕr-ăl) [" + *latus,* side] Above and to the side.

superovulation (soo"pĕr-ŏv"ū-lā'shŭn) [" + *ovulum,* little egg] An increased frequency of ovulation or production of a greater number of ova at one time. This is usually caused by the administration of gonadotropins.

superoxide (soo"pĕr-ŏk'sīd) A highly reactive form of oxygen. Superoxide is produced during the normal catalytic function of certain enzymes, by the oxidation of hemoglobin to methemoglobin, and when ionizing radiation passes through water. It is also produced when granulocytes phagocytize bacteria. Superoxide is destroyed by the enzyme superoxide dismutase, which catalyzes the conversion of two molecules of superoxide anion to one molecule of oxygen and one of hydrogen peroxide. Superoxides play a part in many diseases and con-

ditions, including, e.g., damage to the central nervous system in amyotrophic lateral sclerosis and endothelial damage in hypertension and diabetes mellitus.

superoxide dismutase An enzyme that destroys superoxide. One form of the enzyme contains manganese, and another contains copper and zinc.

superparasitism (soo"pĕr-păr'ă-sī"tĭzm) [" + " + *-ismos,* condition] A condition in which the host is infested or infected with a greater number of parasites than can be supported.

superphosphate (soo"pĕr-fos'fāt) [*super-* + *phosphate*] Acid phosphate.

superpotent (soo"pĕr-pōt'ĕnt) [*super-* + *potent*] Exceptionally strong; characteristic of certain medications.

supersaturate (soo"pĕr-săch'ū-rāt") To add more of a substance to a solution than can be dissolved permanently.

superscription (soo"pĕr-skrĭp'shŭn) [L. *super,* over, above, + *scriptio,* a writing] The beginning of a prescription noted by the sign ℞, signifying (L.) *recipe,* take.

supersensitive (soo"pĕr-sĕn'sĭ-tĭv) [" + *sensitivus,* feeling] Hypersensitive.

supersoft (soo"pĕr-sŏft') [" + AS. *softe,* soft] Exceptionally soft; noting roentgen rays of extremely long wavelength and low penetrating power.

supersonic (soo"pĕr-sŏn'ĭk) [" + *sonus,* sound] **1.** Ultrasonic. **2.** Pert. to speeds greater than that of sound. At sea level, in air at 0°C, the speed of sound is about 331 m, or 1087 ft per second (741 mph). **3.** A sound frequency that is greater than 20,000 cycles per second.

superstructure (soo"pĕr-strŭk'chŭr) The visible portion of a structure, esp. those parts external to the main structure.

supervention (soo"pĕr-vĕn'shŭn) [L. *superventio,* a coming over] The development of an additional condition as a complication to an existing disease.

supervirulent (soo"pĕr-vĭr'ū-lĕnt) [L. *super,* over, above, + *virulentus,* full of poison] More virulent than usual.

supervisor (soo'pĕr-vīz"ĕr) [L. *supervisus,* having looked over] One who directs and evaluates the performance of others. In a health care setting, the supervisor usually has the knowledge and skills to provide the same service as those being directed (e.g., the supervisor of the pharmacy, physical therapy, or maternity nursing).

supervoltage (soo'pĕr-vōl"tĭj) X-rays produced by very high voltage, usually in the megavolt range.

supinate (sū'pĭ-nāt) [L. *supinatus,* bent backward] **1.** To turn the forearm or hand so that the palm faces upward. **2.** To rotate the foot and leg outward.

supination (sū"pĭn-ā'shŭn) [L. *supinatio*] **1.** The turning of the palm or the hand anteriorly or the foot inward and upward. **2.** The act of lying flat upon the back. **3.** The condition of being on the back or having the palm of the hand facing upward or the foot turned inward and upward.

supinator (sū″pĭn-ā′tor) [L.] A muscle producing the motion of supination of the forearm.

supine (soo-pīn′, soo′pīn″) [L. *supinus,* lying on the back] **1.** Lying on the back with the face upward; dorsal. **2.** A position of the hand or foot with the palm or foot facing upward; the opposite of prone.

supine hypotensive syndrome Sudden fall in blood pressure due to diminished venous return caused by compression of the vena cava by the gravid uterus when the pregnant woman rests flat on her back. The low venous return also results in decreased placental perfusion and potentially in fetal hypoxia. SYN: *vena caval syndrome.*

supplement (sŭp′lĕ-ment″) [L. *supplementum,* an addition] **1.** Something added to a food or a diet to increase its nutritional value. SYN: *oral nutritional supplement.* **2.** To add. **supplemental** (sŭp″lĕ-ment′ăl), *adj.*

supplemental feeding SEE: under *feeding.*

supplementation (sŭp″lĕ-men-tā′shŏn) **1.** The addition of a vitamin, mineral, or other nutrient to a food. **2.** The enhancement of the diet with special nutrients.

    preventive s. Nutritional supplementation to preempt diseases such as childhood malnutrition, anemias in chronic diseases, or neural tube defects in pregnancy.

support (sŭ-port′) [L. *supportare,* to carry, convey] **1.** That which assists in keeping something in place. **2.** In dentistry, the abutting teeth, alveolar ridge, and mucosal tissues upon which the denture rests. **3.** In interpersonal relations, active listening, affection, information, praise, and/or other forms of helpful social interaction. Particular supports are listed under the first word. SEE: e.g., *life support; nutritional support; premium support.*

supported employment A program of paid work in regular workplace settings by people with physical, cognitive, developmental, and mental health disorders. Ongoing training is provided by an interdisciplinary team of rehabilitation professionals, employers, and family members.

support hose Elastic stockings that may extend from the toes to the knee or above. These are worn by patients to provide sufficient pressure on the tissues to facilitate venous return and to help to prevent the formation of thrombi in the veins of the legs.

supportive treatment Any of the special

measures employed to supplement specific therapy.

suppository (sŭ-pŏz′ĭ-tō-rē) *pl.* **suppositories** [L. *suppositorium,* something placed underneath] A semisolid substance for introduction into the rectum, vagina, or urethra, where it dissolves. It may be used to stimulate a bowel movement, but often serves as a vehicle for medicines to be absorbed. It is commonly shaped like a cylinder or cone and may be made of soap, glycerinated gelatin, or cocoa butter (oil of theobroma).

    PATIENT CARE: Privacy is provided. The nurse instructs the patient to retain the suppository for about 20 min for effectiveness as a laxative, and for as long as possible (until it dissolves and medication is absorbed) when it is a vehicle, and positions the patient appropriately. The suppository is lubricated and inserted into the appropriate orifice. For neurological rehabilitation, a rectal suppository may be used by the patient after instruction in bowel management. The nurse checks with the patient about effectiveness and notes that in the chart.

suppress (sŭ-pres′) [L. *suppressus,* pressed down, fr. *supprimere,* to press down] **1.** To hold in check or inhibit, e.g., as a suppressive therapy for a chronic infection. **2.** In psychology, to exclude from consciousness. **suppressive** (-pres′iv), *adj.*

suppression (sŭ-presh′ŏn) [L. *suppressio,* a pressing down] **1.** The control, but not complete eradication, of a disease, esp. an infection. In the management of HIV/AIDS, e.g., drug therapies are designed to suppress viral loads to very low levels. **2.** The complete failure of the natural production of a secretion or excretion, as distinguished from retention, in which normal secretion occurs but the discharge is retained within the organ or body. **3.** In Freudian psychoanalysis, the ego defense mechanism of conscious inhibition of an idea or desire, as distinguished from repression, which Freud considered an unconscious process.

    active immune s. The use of agents to block an antigen-specific immune response. An example is the administration of anti-Rh antibodies (Rh₀ immune globulin) to Rh-negative mothers during the 28th week of pregnancy to prevent the formation of maternal antibodies that cause erythroblastosis fetalis in the Rh-positive newborn.

    androgen s. Androgen **deprivation**.

    appetite s. The use of drugs, biofeedback, hypnosis, cognitive therapies, or other means to regulate the desire for food and its consumption.

    fat s. In magnetic resonance imaging, the dampening of bright signals given off by body fat to allow other tissues to become more visible.

lactation s. Inhibition of postpartum production of breast milk, either if the postpartum woman chooses not to breastfeed or when she elects to cease breastfeeding. Recommended actions include avoiding local stimulation of the breasts; wearing a tight-fitting brassiere; applying ice packs; and administering mild over-the-counter analgesics, such as acetaminophen or aspirin, to reduce discomfort. Manual expression of milk is discouraged; although this action may temporarily reduce the discomfort, it also stimulates further milk production. Breast engorgement usually resolves within a few days, and lactation ceases in 1 to 2 weeks.

s. of menses **1.** Amenorrhea after menstruation begins. SEE: _hypothalamic_ **_amenorrhea_**_; pathological hypothalamic amenorrhea._ **2.** Continuous hormonal contraception, used to treat dysmenorrhea, endometriosis, menstrual migraine, occupational demands, personal preferences, or premenstrual dysphoric disorder.

menstrual s. The use of reproductive hormones to lengthen the time between menstrual cycles. This application can lessen the frequency of diseases or conditions that occur perimenstrually.

suppressor T cell SEE: under _cell._

suppurate (sŭp′ū-rāt) [L. _suppurare_] To form or generate pus.

suppuration (sŭp-ū-rā′shŭn) [L. _suppuratio_] **1.** The formation of pus. SEE: _pus._ **2.** Pus.

suppurative (sŭp′ū-rā″tĭv, -ră-tĭv) [L. _suppuratus_] **1.** Pert. to the generation of pus. SEE: _pus; pyogenic._ **2.** An agent that produces pus.

supra- [L.] Prefix meaning _above, beyond,_ or _on the top side._

suprabulge (soo′pră-bŭlj) The part of the crown of a tooth that curves toward the occlusal surface.

supraciliary (soo″pră-sĭl′ē-ĕr″ē) [L. _supra,_ above, on top, beyond, + _cilia,_ eyelid] Superciliary.

supracostal (soo″pră-kŏs′tăl) [″ + _costa,_ rib] Above the ribs.

supradiaphragmatic (soo″pră-dī″ă-frăg-măt′ĭk) [″ + Gr. _dia,_ across, + _phragma,_ wall] Above the diaphragm.

supraduction (soo″pră-dŭk′shŭn) [″ + _ducere,_ to lead] Turning upward of the eye.

supragingival (soo″pră-jĭn′jĭ-văl) Above the gingiva; used in reference to the location of dental restorations, bacterial plaque, or calculus on the tooth. It is often contrasted with subgingival, the gingival margin being the reference point.

supraglenoid (soo″pră-glē′noyd) [″ +

Gr. _glene,_ socket, + _eidos,_ form, shape] Above the glenoid cavity or fossa.

supraglottic airway SEE: under _airway._

supraglottitis (soo″pră-glŏ-tī′ĭs) Epiglottitis.

suprahepatic (soo″pră-hē-păt′ĭk) [″ + Gr. _hepar,_ liver] Located above the liver.

suprahyoid muscles The digastric, geniohyoid, mylohyoid, and stylohyoid muscles.

supralaryngeal airway (soo″pră-lă-rĭn′j(ē-)ăl) SEE: under _airway._

supraliminal (soo″pră-lĭm′ĭ-năl) [L. _supra,_ above, on top, beyond, + _limen,_ threshold] **1.** Above the threshold of consciousness; conscious. **2.** Exceeding the stimulus threshold. SEE: _subliminal._

supramammary (soo″pră-măm′ă-rē) [″ + _mamma,_ breast] Located above the breast.

supramarginal (soo″pră-măr′jĭn-ăl) [″ + _marginalis,_ border] Located above any border.

supramaxillary (soo″pră-măk′sĭ-lĕr-ē) **1.** Pert. to the upper jaw. **2.** Located above the upper jaw.

suprameatal (soo″pră-mē-ā′tăl) [″ + _meatus,_ passage] Above a meatus, esp. the suprameatal spine.

supramental (soo″pră-mĕn′tăl) [L. _supra,_ above, on top, beyond, + _mentum,_ chin] Located above the chin.

supranuclear (soo″pră-nū′klē-ăr) [″ + _nucleus,_ little kernel] Pert. to nerve fibers located above a nucleus in the brain.

supraocclusion (soo″pră-ō-kloo′zhŭn) [″ + _occlusio,_ occlusion] Overeruption.

supraorbital neuralgia Neuralgia of the supraorbital nerve. SYN: _hemicrania_ (1).

supraorbital notch A notch in the superior margin of the orbital arch for transmitting supraorbital vessels and nerve.

suprapatellar (soo″pră-pă-tĕl′ăr) [″ + _patella,_ a small pan] Located above the patella.

supraphysiologic, supraphysiological (soo″pră-fĭz″ē-ō-loj′ik, -loj′ĭ-kăl) Exceeding what is normally found in healthy individuals. The term usually refers to a hormone or medication given in a stronger dose than the amount the body can produce on its own.

suprapubic (soo″pră-pū′bĭk) [″ + NL. _(os) pubis,_ bone of the groin] Located above the pubic arch.

suprapubic aspiration of urine SEE: under _aspiration._

suprarenal (soo″pră-rē′năl) [L. _supra,_ above, on top, beyond, + _ren,_ kidney] **1.** Located above the kidney. **2.** Pert. to the gland above each kidney that secretes glucocorticoids and mineralocorticoids. SEE: _adrenal gland._

suprascapular (soo″pră-skăp′ū-lăr) [″ +

scapula, shoulder blade] Located above the scapula.

suprasellar (soo″pră-sĕl′ăr) [″ + *sella,* saddle] Located above or over the sella turcica.

supraspinous fossa SEE: under *fossa.*

suprasternal (soo″pră-stĕr′năl) [L. *supra,* above, on top, beyond, + Gr. *sternon,* chest] Located above the sternum.

supratentorial (soo″pră-tĕn-tō′rē-ăl) Located above the tentorium.

supratip (soo′pră-tĭp″) The nasal region where the inferior region of the nasal dorsum meets the tip of the nose. Deformities sometimes occur in this area during botched rhinoplasties.

supravaginal (soo″pră-văj′ĭ-năl) [″ + *vagina,* sheath] Located above the vagina or any sheathing membrane.

supraventricular (soo″pră-vĕn-trĭk′ū-lăr) [″ + *ventriculus,* a little belly] Located above the ventricle, esp. the heart ventricles.

sura (sū′ră) [L.] The calf of the leg; the muscular posterior portion of the lower leg.

sural (sū′răl) Pert. to the calf of the leg.

sural neuropathy SEE: under *neuropathy.*

surefooted (shŭr′foot″ĕd) Being able to walk or run without stumbling or falling.

surface (sŭr′făs) [Fr. *sur,* above + Fr. *face,* face] **1.** The exterior boundary of an object. **2.** The external or internal exposed portions of a hollow structure, as the outer or inner surfaces of the cranium or stomach. **3.** The face or faces of a structure such as a bone. **4.** The side of a tooth or the dental arch; usually named for the adjacent tissue or space. The outer or facial surface is called the labial surface of the incisors or canines, and the buccal surface of the premolars and molars. The facial surface may also be called the vestibular surface. The inner surface of each tooth is called the lingual or oral surface. Within the arch, each tooth is said to have a mesial surface, the side toward the midpoint in the front of the dental arch, and a distal surface, the side of the tooth farthest from the midpoint in the front of the dental arch.

bearing s. The region in a joint where opposing structures make contact, rub against each other, and transmit compressive forces.

body s. 1. The exterior of the human body, or one of its parts. **2.** The epidermis. SEE: *body surface area.*

contact s. The surface where two normally adjacent teeth come into contact with each other on the mesial or distal sides. SYN: *proximal s.*

occlusal s. The masticating surface of the premolar and molar teeth.

proximal s. Contact s.

support s. A brace, pillow, or mattress on which part or all of the body rests. Static support surfaces are made or filled with materials such as air, fabric, foam, or gels. Dynamic support surfaces are filled with moving air, beads, or fluid that circulates by electromechanical energy.

surface-enhanced laser desorption-ionization ABBR: SELDI. A technique to separate and image molecules, e.g., DNA or proteins, in biological samples. Molecules are captured on a protein chip, ionized, and imaged. This technique can be used to map the molecules in samples of blood or other bodily fluids.

surfactant (sŭr-fak′tănt) [*surf(ace)-act(ive) a(ge)nt*] A surface-active agent that lowers surface tension (e.g., oils and various forms of detergents). Artificial surfactants may be given endotracheally to relieve respiratory distress.

lung s. Pulmonary s.

modified natural s. A replacement phospholipid from a natural source with some components removed.

pulmonary s. A lipoprotein secreted by type II alveolar cells that decreases the surface tension of the fluid lining the alveoli, permitting expansion. Synthetic lung surfactant is available for treating patients with respiratory distress syndrome. In obstetrics, fetal production of surfactant can be stimulated by administration of a glucocorticoid 24 to 48 hr before an inevitable preterm birth. SYN: *lung s.* SEE: *betamethasone.*

surfer's ear SEE: under *ear.*

surfer's knots Nodules that form on the foot, leg, or chest as a result of trauma from repetitive contact with surfboards.

surge capacity The ability of a community or health care system to respond to sudden increases in demand for services or emergency help, e.g., after a multiple casualty incident.

surgeon (sŭr′jĕn) [Fr. *cirurgien*] A medical practitioner who specializes in surgery.

civil s. A physician certified by the U.S. Bureau of Citizenship and Immigration Services to perform medical examinations on immigrants seeking immigration visas to, or permanent resident status in, the U.S. The examination performed by civil surgeons includes a physical and mental status examination; tests for tuberculosis, syphilis, and HIV and vaccinations for measles, mumps, rubella; poliomyelitis tetanus and diphtheria; pertussis; influenza B; and hepatitis B.

colorectal s. A surgeon specializing in the entire large bowel.

console s. The principal surgeon in robotically assisted surgery (telesurgery), i.e., the one who operates the controls. This surgeon operates from a distant site, does not need to scrub before the procedure, but does require a surgical assistant in the operating room to help with patient or robotic adjustments. SYN: *remote s.*

s. general The chief medical officer in each branch of the armed forces of the U.S. or of the U.S. Public Health Service.

ghost s. Any person, esp. one not designated by the patient or not licensed to practice surgery, who replaces the patient's chosen surgeon in performing an operation, without the patient's consent. Ghosts may include surgical residents or representatives of pharmaceutical or biomedical engineering firms. The use of ghost surgeons is a violation of professional standards and ethics.

remote surgeon Console **s.**

surgery (sŭrj'ĕ-rē) [Fr. *cirurgerie*, ult fr Gr. *cheirurgia*, handwork, surgery] **1.** The branch of medicine dealing with manual and operative procedures to correct deformities and defects, repair injuries, and diagnose and cure certain diseases. **2.** A surgeon's operating room. **3.** Treatment or work performed by a surgeon. SYN: *operation.* SEE: *Nursing Diagnosis Appendix.*

ablative s. Surgery in which a part is removed or destroyed.

aesthetic s. Cosmetic **s.**

ambulatory s. Surgery performed between the time the patient is admitted in the morning and the time the patient is discharged the same day. SYN: *day s.*

antenatal s. Surgery performed on the fetus before delivery. It is performed only at certain medical centers. SEE: *amnioscopy; embryoscopy.*

antimicrobial prophylaxis in s. SEE: *antimicrobial prophylaxis in surgery.*

aseptic s. Surgery performed under sterile conditions.

aural s. Surgery of the ear.

bariatric s. Surgical management of morbid obesity. Common operations are classified either as restrictive (because they decrease the size of the stomach) or malabsorptive (because they limit absorption of nutrients from the gastrointestinal tract), or both restrictive and malabsorptive. They include gastric banding; vertical banded gastroplasty; Roux-en-Y gastric bypass; biliopancreatic diversion or duodenal switch, and long-limb Roux-en-Y gastric bypass. SYN: *weight-loss s.*

PATIENT CARE: This surgery is typically used only for those with a body mass index greater than 40 kg/m^2 or 35 kg/m^2 in the presence of other weight-related health problems, such as hypertension or diabetes mellitus. Complica-

tions include puncture of blood vessels or internal organs, infection, incisional hernia, wound dehiscence, or leakage from surgical sites into the peritoneum. In preparation for surgery the patient should be assessed for other major surgical risks, including heart attack, heart failure, deep vein thrombosis, atelectasis/pneumonia, or respiratory failure after the proposed operation. The patient should be made aware that an intravenous catheter, urinary catheter, and sequential compression stockings will be used to help manage postoperative complications. Incentive spirometry is used to prevent postoperative atelectasis.

Pain and nausea are managed with patient-controlled epidural or intravenous analgesia and antiemetic drugs. Equipment required for obese patients undergoing bariatric surgery includes specially sized litters, operating tables, beds, wheelchairs, blood-pressure cuffs, and gowns. The patient should begin ambulation soon after surgery to help prevent complications of immobility. Adequate staff should be available to assist with transfers and mobilization to prevent patient or staff injuries. Depending on the type of surgery employed, the patient may require vitamin and mineral supplementation after surgery (with B vitamins, calcium, iron, and fat-soluble vitamins). Psychological, nutritional, and physical therapeutic support is critical to optimal outcomes. Instruction at discharge must emphasize diet, hydration, wound care, medications, and prescribed or prohibited activities. Most treated patients have significant, sustainable postoperativeweight loss, with improvement in comorbid conditions such as diabetes mellitus, hypertension, and hyperlipidemia. After massive weight loss some patients may require reconstructive surgery to remove excess abdominal wall fat (panniculectomy).

⚠ The risk for postoperative death associated with bariatric surgery is greatest in patients with heart failure, renal failure, peripheral vascular disease, who are male or over 50 years old, or who undergo open (versus laparoscopic) surgery.

breast conservation s. Removal of a malignant growth from the breast and dissection of axillary lymph nodes without mastectomy. Lumpectomy is an alternative to mastectomy for patients with early stage breast cancer. Its outcomes are equivalent to those of mastectomy when used as part of a treatment plan that includes postoperative radiation therapy to the affected breast.

cardiac s. Surgery on the heart and/

or the proximal great vessels. SEE: *Nursing Diagnoses Appendix.*

cold knife s. Surgery with a simple metal blade or scalpel; conventional surgery.

colorectal s. Surgery on the anus, rectum, or large intestine.

conservative s. Surgery in which as much as possible of a part or structure is retained. It is often an equally effective alternative to radical surgery.

cosmetic s. Surgery performed to revise or change the texture, configuration, or relationship of contiguous structures of a feature of the body. SYN: *aesthetic s.* SEE: *plastic s.*

day s. Ambulatory **s.**

elective s. Surgery that is not necessary for one's health but is performed for another reason, e.g., for cosmetic reasons. SYN: *optional s.*

exploratory s. Surgery performed for diagnosis, e.g. an exploratory laparotomy. Exploratory surgeries may become surgeries in which definitive treatment is rendered when a previously undiagnosed lesion is identified and rectified.

flap s. Surgery in which a flap of tissue or periosteum is raised. An amputation flap is a tissue flap produced to cover the amputation stump.

gamma knife s. Radiosurgery that can destroy an intracranial target by directing gamma radiation at the lesion while trying to spare adjacent healthy tissue. The gamma knife consists of 201 cylindrical gamma ray (cobalt 60) beams designed to intersect at the target lesion, resulting in about 200 times the dose of any single beam aimed at the periphery. The area to be treated is carefully identified with neuroimaging before the gamma knife is used and the proper dose of gamma energy calculated. The procedure takes about 2 to 3 hr, with the patient under mild sedation, given intravenously, and local anesthesia. The gamma knife can be used to treat primary and metastatic brain tumors, trigeminal neuralgia, arteriovenous malformations, and other lesions. Complications include seizures, confusion, paralysis, nausea and vomiting, other radiation reactions, and radiation necrosis of normal brain tissue, but the incidence of side effects is no greater than with other brain irradiation or neurosurgical techniques.

PATIENT CARE: The patient's vital signs and neurological signs must be checked frequently during and after the procedure.

high-risk s. Any operation associated with a 5% or greater likelihood of adverse cardiovascular events. Examples include operations on peripheral arteries, the aorta, or the heart; surgeries that last more than 2 hours; and emergency surgeries, esp. when they are needed by patients with multiple illnesses or age over 75.

IE s. *infarct exclusion* **s.**

image-guided s. The use of real-time computed tomography, magnetic resonance imagery, or ultrasound to place surgical instruments in precise anatomical locations, e.g., during biopsies or tissue resections. Images taken before the operation are compared with those obtained during surgery to improve the localization of tumors or vascular structures, the placement of prosthetic parts, or the identification of moving structures.

infarct exclusion s. ABBR: IE surgery. The surgical repair of damage to the heart muscle due to a heart attack, e.g., repair or patching of post-myocardial infarction ventricular septal defects.

intestinal bypass s. The production of controlled intestinal malabsorption by surgically short-circuiting the small intestine. This surgery is used to treat massive obesity. It is done by anastomosing the proximal jejunum to the distal ileum by bypassing the small intestine between the anastomotic sites. The lengths of jejunum and ileum involved vary by surgeon. Because of long-term metabolic complications (including hepatic injury), this procedure has largely been abandoned in favor of gastric bypass procedures.

laparoscopic s. A form of endoscopic surgery in which a fiberoptic laparoscope is inserted into the body to inspect, resect, or otherwise surgically treat a wide and expanding variety of conditions. Small incisions (ports) are created to insert required instrumentation. In assisted laparoscopic procedures, a smaller-than-standard ancillary incision may be necessary for removal of large specimens or to perform various surgical maneuvers. Laparoscopic surgery may also be used to complement other procedures, e.g., vaginal hysterectomy. Under certain circumstances, e.g., hemorrhage or dense adhesions, laparoscopic procedure cannot be performed. Operating time is longer and equipment is more expensive in laparoscopic surgery than in laparotomy, but the convalescence of patients who have undergone laparoscopic procedures is shorter; and pain, nausea, vomiting, and obstipation are diminished. Common operations performed with a laparoscope include cholecystectomy, appendectomy, colonic surgery, hernia repairs (including hiatal hernias), and many gynecological surgeries. SEE: *laparoscopic laser cholecystectomy.*

laryngeal framework s. Thyroplasty.

limb salvage s. Any operative treatment of an injury to bone or a bony tumor in which the basic integrity of the arm or leg is preserved.

low-risk s. Any operation associated with less than a 1% chance of adverse cardiovascular events. Examples include endoscopies, breast biopsies, skin biopsies, and procedures on the eye, e.g. cataract surgeries.

lung volume reduction s. Surgical removal of emphysematous lung tissue, esp. of inelastic air spaces in the upper lobes of the lungs, to enhance the ability of the rest of the lung to expand and contract. This surgery improves respiratory function for many patients with advanced chronic obstructive lung disease although the long-term benefits of its use are uncertain.

major s. Surgery risking a potential hazard and disruption of physiological function, e.g., entering a body cavity, excision of large tumors, amputation of a large body part, insertion of a prosthesis, and open-heart procedures. All surgeries are potentially dangerous and may involve a risk to life.

manipulative s. Use of manipulation in surgery or bone setting.

maxillofacial s. The branch of dental practice and/or plastic surgery that deals with the diagnosis and the surgical and adjunctive treatment of diseases, injuries, and defects of the mouth and dental structures. SYN: *oral s.*

microfracture s. Surgery to repair joint cartilage in which small holes are drilled into the bones surrounding the joint to stimulate the growth of replacement cartilage. Recovery and rehabilitation from the surgery are protracted.

minor s. A simple operation not involving a major body cavity or structure and usually causing little disruption of the patient's physiological status. As with all surgery, there is risk of injury or death.

mucogingival s. Plastic surgery for correcting diseases of the gingiva and adjacent oral mucosa.

natural orifice s. Natural orifice transluminal endoscopic s.

natural orifice transluminal endoscopic s. ABBR: NOTES. Surgery performed with incisions made through internal organs after an endoscope has been inserted into those organs through the mouth, the vagina, the bladder, or the anus. The surgery produces no external scars because the skin is not cut. For example, a diseased gallbladder is removed through an endoscope inserted through the urinary bladder wall and into the peritoneum or through an incision made in the muscular wall of the stomach. SYN: *natural orifice s.*

oncoplastic s. Surgery to remove malignant tumors from the body and

sculpting the operated tissue to an esthetically pleasing outcome.

one-port umbilical s. ABBR: OPUS. A form of minimally invasive laparoscopic surgery in which a single endoscopic instrument is inserted into the peritoneal cavity through the umbilicus to minimize the visibility of scars on the skin.

open-heart s. Surgery involving direct visualization and surgical procedure of the exposed heart.

optional s. Elective s.

oral s. Maxillofacial s.

orthopedic s. Surgery to prevent and correct musculoskeletal deformities and/or injuries.

palliative s. Surgery to relieve symptoms or improve quality of life, usually in patients with incurable illness.

plastic s. Surgery to repair or restore defective or missing structures, frequently involving the transfer of tissue from one part to another and sometimes including the use of prosthetic materials.

prenatal s. Intrauterine surgical procedures on the fetus. These techniques have been used to repair heart defects and anatomical defects of other organs. SEE: *prenatal diagnosis*.

radical s. Surgery to remove a large amount of damaged or neoplastic tissue and/or adjoining areas of lymphatic drainage to obtain a complete cure. This is in contrast to conservative surgery.

radioguided s. 1. The use of radionuclides, such as isotopes of technetium, to locate lymph nodes or other tissues to excise during an operation. **2.** The use of computed tomography, magnetic resonance imaging, or plain radiography to plan and/or carry out an invasive procedure.

radioimmunoguided s. ABBR: RIGS. The use of tumor-specific, radioactively labeled monoclonal antibodies to detect and stage cancers and distinguish malignant tissue from surrounding normal tissue. This improves the management of surgical tumors.

reconstructive s. Surgery to repair a loss or defect or to restore function.

refractive s. An operation to improve the ability of the eye to focus and thus to eliminate the patient's need for eyeglasses. Examples include keratoplasty and keratomilleusis.

remote s. *Telesurgery.*

ritualistic s. Surgery having no scientific justification, performed in primitive societies without the purpose of treating or preventing disease. Included are alterations of the skin, ears, lips, teeth, genitalia, and head. In some cases, even in advanced societies, surgical procedures without rational justification are considered ritualistic.

scalpel-free s. Surgery that relies on

acoustic, laser, or radioactive energy to divide, destroy or cauterize tissue.

second-look s. Surgery some months after the original operation for cancer to detect possible recurrences. Second-look procedures are also performed on a more immediate basis, e.g., within hours of the initial surgery, when vascular injuries created by the initial operation or condition are suspected. Occasionally an endoscopic second look may be performed instead of an open surgical procedure.

split-brain s. Surgery that disconnects one hemisphere of the brain from the other by cutting the corpus callosum. It is used to treat drug-resistant seizures.

subcutaneous s. Surgery performed through a small opening in the skin.

subtotal s. Surgery in which only a portion of the organ is removed, e.g., subtotal removal of the thyroid gland.

thoracic s. Surgery involving the rib cage and structures contained within the chest. It is used to biopsy or remove masses in the hilum, lung, or mediastinum, to drain abscesses, treat empyema, repair cardiac valves or vessels, or implant devices such as cardioverter/defibrillators in the chest.

PATIENT CARE: *Preoperative:* Preparation involves the usual preoperative teaching, with special emphasis on breathing and coughing, incentive spirometry, incisional splinting, pain evaluation, invasive and noninvasive relief measures that will be available, and basic information about the chest drainage tube and system that will be required in most such surgeries. The health care professional should encourage the patient to voice fears and concerns, allay misapprehensions, and correct misconceptions. *Postoperative care:* All general patient care concerns apply. Vital signs and breath sounds should be monitored. Water-seal chest drainage should be maintained as prescribed and the volume and characteristics of drainage monitored. The health care professional should maintain sterile wound dressings; provide analgesia and comfort to ensure patient cooperation with respiratory toilet,exercises, and rest and activity; provide emotional support and encouragement; and provide instructions to be followed by the patient and family after discharge and follow-up care. As necessary, the respiratory therapist provides mechanical ventilation in the immediate postoperative period and evaluates the patient for weaning from the ventilator.

transsexual s. Surgical therapy for alteration of the anatomical sex of an individual whose psychological gender is not consistent with the anatomical sexual characteristics.

transsphenoidal s. Surgery on the pituitary gland, performed with an incision made through the base of the sphenoid sinus. It is typically performed through the nasal passages or the oral cavity to remove an adenoma of the pituitary gland in patients with acromegaly, prolactinomas, or other pituitary tumors.

video-assisted thoracic s. ABBR: VATS. Surgery for the diagnosis and treatment of many conditions affecting the lung or the pleural space, e.g., biopsies, drainage of empyema, pulmonary resections, Heller procedures.

weight-loss s. Bariatric **s.**

surgical (sŭr'jĭ-kăl) Of the nature of or pert. to surgery.

surgical asepsis The maintenance of strict disinfection procedures or antisepsis and infection control practices during an operation.

surgical count SEE: under *count.*

surgical cutting block Surgical cutting guide.

surgical cutting guide A tool that holds an organ, e.g., a bone, in place during an operation to limit the size of the incision or to rotate the organ and the blade along the same fixed axes. SYN: *surgical cutting block.*

surgical dressing SEE: under *dressing.*

surgical field SEE: under *field.*

surgical margin SEE: under *margin.*

surgical marking Skin marking.

surgical prep A colloquial term for surgical site preparation.

surgical recovery, delayed Extension of the number of postoperative days required to initiate and perform activities that maintain life, health, and well-being. SEE: *Nursing Diagnoses Appendix.*

surgical release SEE: under *release.*

surgical resident SEE: under *resident.*

surgical site preparation The removal of debris, dirt, microorganisms, oils, and scales from the operative site, e.g. skin or mucosa, of a patient about to undergo surgical incision or instrumentation.

surgical technologist A technologist who assists in many operating room functions, including preparing the patient for surgery, ensuring the sterility of the operating room, operating equipment during surgery, and, in some instances, working as a surgical first assistant.

surgical towel A sterile drape used to cover the body during surgery.

surgical ventricular reconstruction SEE: under *reconstruction.*

surname (sŭr'nām) The family name, as distinguished from the individual's first or given name. In some societies, the surname is written first.

surrender (sŭr-ĕn'dĕr) [O.Fr. *surrendre*] Giving up a health care professional license, e.g., at retirement or as a means of resolving a disciplinary action brought forward by a health care supervisory board.

surreptitious (sŭr″ĕp-tish′ŭs) [L. *surrepticius,* concealed, stolen] Evasive, secretive, or stealthy; attempting to avoid detection. **surreptitiously** (-tish′ŭs-lē), *adv.*

surrogate (sŭr′ŏ-găt, -gāt″) [L. *surrogatus,* substituted] **1.** Something or someone replacing another; a substitute. A surrogate may be representative for a person or a marker of a disease. **2.** In psychoanalysis, the representation of one whose identity is concealed from conscious recognition as in a dream; a figure of importance may represent one's loved one.

    sex s. A professional sex partner employed to assist persons with sexual dysfunction.

surrogate mother   SEE: under *mother.*

surveillance (sŭr-vāl′ăns) In health care, the monitoring of a disease, condition, epidemic, risk factor, or physiological function.

    active s. Monitoring the health of a community by a public health agency that requests reports about specific diseases or conditions.

    disease s. In epidemiology and public health, the identification of index patients and their contacts; the detection of outbreaks and epidemics; the determination of the incidence and demographics of an illness; and the policy making that may prevent further spreading of a disease.

    immunological s. The theory that the immune system destroys some malignant cells as they grow in the body. Support for this theory is found in research data that show tumor cells killed by cytotoxic T lymphocytes, natural killer cells, and perhaps, activated macrophages. SEE: *natural killer cell.*

    medical s. Careful, repeated assessment of a person exposed to a pathogen, to see if he or she develops the illness it causes.

    passive s. The monitoring of the health of a community by studying unsolicited reports brought to the attention of public health officials.

    postmarketing s. The review of adverse reactions to drugs and medical technologies that occurs after these agents are released for sale and use. Nurses, pharmacists, physicians, and other practioners participate in this process by recording their observations on the adverse effects of drugs to the Food and Drug Administration, which accumulates these survey data and issues warnings to practitioners when needed.

    sentinel s. Monitoring of the public health by a group of practitioners or institutions that agree to notify a public health agency of all cases of a specific disease or condition.

    syndromic s. Monitoring the health of a community by searching for specific signs or symptoms present in it. It is a public health strategy used to identify disease trends before they become epidemic, e.g., the first signs or symptoms of bioterrorism.

surveillance interval   SEE: under *interval.*

surveillance mammography   Mammography performed for patients who have already been treated for breast cancer. It is used to see if cancer has returned or appeared in a new location.

survey (sŭr′vā″) [Fr. *survieier,* to oversee] **1.** The study of a particular disease or condition, esp. its epidemiological aspects. **2.** In emergency care, the rapid and careful assessment of a patient's respiratory, circulatory, and neurological status. The *primary* survey focuses on the patient's circulation and cardiac rhythm, airway and respiratory effort, and neurological disability. The patient is then undressed or exposed, with environmental protection given to prevent hypothermia. In a *secondary* survey the stabilized patient is examined thoroughly for other conditions that may need prompt care.

surveyor's flexicurve (sŭr-vā′ŏrz) Flexicurve.

survival (sŭr-vī′văl) Continuing to live, e.g., under conditions in which death would be the expected outcome.

    PATIENT CARE: Health care professionals are sometimes asked by patients or their families how long a patient may be expected to live, because he or she has a serious illness or has already reached an advanced age. Even in intensive care units, predicting how long some one may live is difficult. Some illnesses (e.g., widely metastatic breast or lung cancers) leave a patient with weeks or months of life. Some traumas (e.g., gunshot wounds to the brain, heart, or great vessels) confer a survival of hours or less. A patient who is not responding to resuscitative efforts can be expected to live for minutes. For patients who are not at the extremes of illness or injury, several predictive tools can be used to provide crude estimates of survival. The Karnofsky Performance Scale, the Palliative Prognostic Indicator, and the Palliative Performance Scale can be used to gauge survival in grave illnesses. For average members of the population, the Centers for Disease Control and Prevention (National Center for Health Statistics) publishes tables that estimate the life expectancy of Americans based on their current age.

    graft s. Persistent functioning of a transplanted organ or tissue in a recipient of that organ. Survival rates of transplanted organs are influenced by many factors, including the age and health status of both the donor and the recipient of the graft, the immunological match between the donor and the recipient, the preparation of the organ before transplantation, and the use of immunosuppressive drugs. For some organ transplantation, graft survival approximates 90%.

survival analysis An evaluation of how long patients in a clinical trial live. The rate of death is monitored over time. SYN: *time-to-event analysis*.

survival bias The tendency of people who live longer after an illness or injury to receive more medical care. The medical care may not be the cause of the patients' longevity; the care may be an effect of it.

Surviving Sepsis Campaign An international effort to reduce mortality from sepsis. It is a joint undertaking of the European Society of Intensive Care Medicine, the International Sepsis Forum, and the Society of Critical Care Medicine.

survivor (sŭr-vīv′ĕr) An individual who has experienced a serious illness or injury and lived through it (and/or its treatment). In the U.S., for example, in 2005, there were more than 10 million people living after the diagnosis and treatment of cancer.

survivor guilt A grief reaction marked by feelings of depression, loss, or responsibility experienced by those who have survived an event in which others have lost their lives, e.g., a war, genocide, or epidemic illness.

survivorship (sŭr-vī′vŏr-ship″) 1. The condition or state of being a survivor. 2. Living with cancer or long-term illness. 3. In law, the right of a person who survives a partner or joint owner to take over ownership of e.g., an insurance policy after the death of the other joint owner. 4. The likelihood or probability of surviving or living to a certain age. 5. The age one lives or survives to; longevity.

survivorship care SEE: under *care*.

susceptibility (sŭs-sĕp″tĭ-bĭl′ĭ-tē) The degree to which a person is prone to disease or persuasion.

susceptibility factor SEE: under *factor*.

susceptible (sŭ-sĕp′tĭ-bl) [L. *susceptibilis*, capable of receiving] 1. Having little resistance to a disease or foreign protein. 2. Easily impressed or influenced.

sushi (soo′shē) A traditional Japanese food made of raw fish, usually wrapped in a soft rice shell. Some raw fish contain adults or larvae of the nematodes of the family Anisakidae. In order to prevent these organisms from infecting persons who eat raw fish, the U.S. Food and Drug Administration has directed that prior to serving, the fish must be suddenly frozen to −31°F (−34.4°C) or below for 15 hr, or held in a commercial

freezer at −4°F (−20°C) for 24 hr. After that period, the fish may be thawed and served. SEE: *anisakiasis*.

sushi domain An amino acid sequence that creates a specific protein conformation in a polypeptide.

suspended (sŭs-pĕnd′ĕd) [L. *suspendere*, to hang up] 1. Hanging. 2. Temporarily inactive.

suspension (sŭs-pen′shŏn) [L. *suspensio*, a hanging] 1. A condition of temporary cessation, as of any vital process. 2. Treatment using a hanging support to immobilize a body part in a desired position. 3. The state of a solid when its particles are mixed with, but not dissolved in, a fluid or another solid; also a substance in this state. 4. In a clinical trial, the temporary halting of a study while data are analyzed to determine if it is safe to proceed. **suspend**, *v*.

suspensoid (sŭs-pĕn′soyd) [″ + Gr. *eidos*, form, shape] Colloid suspension.

suspensory (sŭs-pĕn′sō-rē) [L. *suspensorius*, hanging] 1. Supporting a part, as a muscle, ligament, or bone. 2. A structure that supports a part. 3. A bandage or sac for supporting or compressing a part, esp. the scrotum.

suspirious (sŭs-pī′rē-ŭs) [L. *suspirare*, to sigh] Breathing with apparent effort; sighing.

sustentacular (sŭs″tĕn-tăk′ū-lăr) [L. *sustentaculum*, support] Supporting; upholding.

sustentacular cell SEE: under *cell*.

sustentaculum (sŭs″tĕn-tăk′ū-lŭm) *pl.* **sustentacula** [L.] A supporting structure.

    s. hepatis A fold of peritoneum upon which rests the right margin of the liver.

    s. tali A process of the calcaneum that supports part of the talus.

¹**Sutton disease** (sŭt′ŏn) [Richard L. Sutton, Sr., U.S. dermatologist, 1878–1952] Halo nevus.

²**Sutton disease** (sŭt′ŏn) [Richard L. Sutton, Jr., U.S. dermatologist, b. 1908] Granuloma fissuratum.

Sutton's law (sŭt′ŏnz) [William "Willie" Sutton, U.S. career criminal and bankrobber, 1901–1980] A method of diagnostic reasoning that states one should look for diseases where they are most likely to be (such as malaria in tropical areas that harbor *Anopheles* mosquitoes; atherosclerosis in patients who are smokers, hypertensives, or diabetics). The law is attributed to Willie Sutton, who, when asked why he robbed banks, said, "Because that's where the money is."

sutura (soo-toor′ă, soo-toor′ē)*pl.* **suturae** [L. *sutura*, a seam] 1. Suture (1). 2. An immovable fibrous or cartilaginous joint. SEE: *synarthrosis*.

sutural (sū′tū-răl) [L. *sutura*, a seam] Pert. to a suture.

suturation (sū″tū-rā′shŭn) The application of sutures; stitching.

suture (soo′chŭr) [L. *sutura*, a seam] **1.** The line of union in an immovable articulation, as those between the skull bones or the articulation itself. SYN: *sutura*. SEE: *raphe; synarthrosis*. **2.** An operation in which soft tissues of the body are united by stitching them together. **3.** The thread, wire, or other material used to stitch parts of the body together. **4.** The seam or line of union formed by surgical stitches. **5.** To unite by stitching.

absorbable surgical s. A sterile strand prepared from collagen derived from healthy mammals or from a synthetic polymer. This type of suture is absorbed and thus does not need to be removed.

apposition s. A suture to accurately approximate the edges off divided tissues.

approximation s. A suture for apposing divided tissues. SEE: *apposition* **s.**

basilar s. The suture between the occipital bone and sphenoid bone that persists until the 16th to 18th year as the anteroposterior growth center of the base of the skull; also called *spheno-occipital synchondrosis*.

bifrontal s. The suture between the frontal and parietal bones.

biparietal s. The suture between the two parietal bones.

buried s. A suture placed so that it is completely covered by skin or other surrounding tissue.

button s. A suture in which the threads are passed through buttons or other prosthetic material on the surface and tied to prevent the suture material from cutting into the skin.

catgut s. A suture material made from the sterilized submucosa of the small intestine of sheep. It is eventually absorbed by body fluids. Treatment with chromium trioxide (chromic catgut) or other chemicals delays the absorption time.

coaptation s. A preliminary suture to approximate wound edges before definitive closure.

cobbler's s. A suture in which the thread has a needle at each end. SYN: *double-armed* **s.**

continuous s. The closure of a wound by means of one continuous thread, usually by transfixing one edge of the wound and then the other alternately from within outward in a variety of techniques. SYN: *running* **s.***; uninterrupted* **s.***; whip* **stitch**.

coronal s. A suture between the frontal and parietal bones. SYN: *frontoparietal* **s.**

cranial s. One of the sutures between the bones of the skull.

dentate s. An osseous suture consisting of long and toothlike processes between the involved bony segments.

double-armed s. Cobbler's **s.**

ethmoidofrontal s. A suture between the ethmoid and frontal bones.

ethmoidolacrimal s. A suture between the ethmoid and lacrimal bones.

false s. A suture of opposing bones in which fibrous union has not occurred.

figure-of-eight s. A suture shaped like the number 8. It is used to repair round or elliptical defects.

frontal s. An occasional suture in the frontal bone from the sagittal suture to the root of the nose. SYN: *mediofrontal* **s.***; metopic* **s.**

frontomalar s. A suture between the frontal and malar bones.

frontomaxillary s. A suture between the frontal bone and superior maxilla.

frontonasal s. A suture between the frontal bones and the nasal bones.

frontotemporal s. A suture between the frontal and temporal bones.

glover's s. Locking **s.**

Halsted s. SEE: under *Halsted, William Stewart.*

harmonic s. A suture in which there is simple apposition of bone.

intermaxillary s. A suture between the superior maxillae.

internasal s. A suture between the nasal bones.

interparietal s. Sagittal **s.**

interrupted s. A suture formed by single stitches inserted separately, the needle usually being passed through one lip of the wound from without inward and through the other from within outward.

lambdoid s. A suture between the parietal bones and the two superior borders of the occipital bone. SYN: *occipital* **s.***; occipitoparietal* **s.**

locking s. A continuous suture in which the needle is passed through the loop of the preceding stitch. SYN: *glover's* **s.**

longitudinal s. Sagittal **s.**

mediofrontal s. Frontal **s.**

metopic s. Frontal **s.**

nasomaxillary s. A suture between the nasal bone and superior maxilla.

nonabsorbable s. A suture made from a material that is not absorbed by the body, such as silk, polymers, cotton, or wire. These sutures ultimately are removed or are placed in tissue deep to the skin where their presence will have minimal long-term consequences.

occipital s. Lambdoid **s.**

occipitomastoid s. A suture between the occipital bone and the mastoid portion of the temporal bone. The occipitomastoid and lambdoid sutures meet at the asterion. SYN: *temporo-occipital* **s.**

occipitoparietal s. Lambdoid **s.**

palatine s. A suture between the palatine bones.

palatine transverse s. A suture between the palatine processes and superior maxilla.

parietal s. Sagittal **s.**

parietomastoid s. A suture between the parietal bone and the mastoid portion of the temporal bone.

petro-occipital s. A suture between the petrous portion of the temporal bone and the occipital bone.

petrosphenoidal s. A suture between the petrous portion of the temporal bone and the ala magna of the sphenoid bone.

purse-string s. A suture entering and exiting around the periphery of a circular opening. Drawing the suture taut closes the opening.

relaxation s. A suture that may be loosened to relieve excessive tension.

relief s. A suture used primarily in abdominal wound closures to bring large margins of the wound close together to relieve tension and to provide protection to the primary wound closure; more commonly called a retention suture. These sutures are made of heavy-grade material and are tied over wound bridges or tubes of latex to avoid injury to the wound.

right-angled s. A suture used in sewing intestine. The needle is passed in the same direction as the long axis of the incision, and the process is repeated on the opposite side of the incision, the suture being continuous.

running s. Continuous **s.**

sagittal s. A suture between the two parietal bones. SYN: *interparietal* **s.**; *longitudinal* **s.**; *parietal* **s.**

serrated s. An articulation by suture in which there is an interlocking of bones by small projections and indentations resembling sawlike teeth.

shotted s. A suture whose ends are passed through a perforated shot that is then compressed tightly over them, instead of tying a knot.

silk s. A suture made of silk. It may be twisted, braided, or floss.

sphenofrontal s. The articulation between the greater wing of the sphenoid bone and the frontal bone.

sphenoparietal s. The articulation between the greater wing of the sphenoid bone and the parietal bone. The pterion of the skull is a region at the posterior end of this suture.

sphenosquamous s. An articulation of the great wing of the sphenoid with the squamous portion of the temporal bone.

sphenotemporal s. A suture between the sphenoid and temporal bones.

squamoparietal s. A suture between the parietal bone and squamous portions of the temporal bone.

squamosphenoidal s. A suture between the squamous portion of the temporal bone and great wing of the sphenoid bone.

squamous s. The junction of the temporal and parietal bones.

subcuticular s. A buried, usually continuous suture in which the needle is passed horizontally under the epidermis into the cutis vera, emerging at the edge of the wound but beneath the skin, then in a similar manner passed through the cutis vera of the opposite side of the wound, and so on until the other angle of the wound is reached.

temporo-occipital s. Occipitomastoid **s.**

temporoparietal s. The suture between the temporal and parietal bones.

tension s. A suture used to reduce the pull on the edges of a wound.

uninterrupted s. Continuous **s.**

vertical mattress s. An interrupted suture in which a deep stitch is taken and the needle inserted upon the same side as that from which it emerged, and passed back through both immediate margins of the wound. The suture is then tied to the free end on the side the needle originally entered. This suture is primarily used in closing the skin.

wire s. A suture of varying gauges of metal (usually stainless steel) that may be used in a wide variety of applications, including wound closure, intestinal repair, and the repair of sternotomies.

Sv *sievert.*

SVE *sterile vaginal exam.*

Svedberg (sved'běrg″) [Theodor Svedberg, Swedish chemist, 1884–1971] ABBR: S. The sedimentation rate of a centrifuged particle, esp. a large molecule such as a protein. One Svedberg equals 10^{-13} s.

Svo₂ *mixed venous oxygen saturation.*

SVV *stroke volume variability.*

swab (swob) **1.** Cotton or gauze on the end of a slender stick, used for cleansing cavities, applying remedies, or obtaining a piece of tissue or secretion for bacteriological examination. **2.** To wipe with a swab.

urethral s. A slender cotton-tipped applicator used to collect a specimen, treat ulcers, or remove secretions. The male urethral swab is a rod about 7 in. (17.8 cm) long.

uterine s. A slender flattened wire, a plain rod, or one with coarse thread on the distal end for absorbing or wiping away discharges.

swaddling (swod'ling) Wrapping an infant in soft materials to restrain reflex body movements and help the child to rest and sleep. It is a traditional practice used in the care of fussy or hyperactive infants, on whom it appears to have a calming effect on reflex motor activity.

⚠️ Swaddled infants may occasionally suffer hyperthermia. In addition, the impact of swaddling on sudden infant death syndrome (SIDS) may depend on the materials used and the position of the infant after his or her movements are restrained.

swaddle (swod′ĕl), v.

swage (swāj) [Fr. souage, decorative border] **1.** To shape metal, esp. around something in order to make a close fit. **2.** Fusing a suture to a needle.

swager (swāj′ĕr) A dental tool or device used to shape silver amalgam or gold by applying pressure from different directions simultaneously.

Swain, Mary Ann Price (swān) A U.S. nursing theorist who, along with Helen Erickson and Evelyn Tomlin, developed and published the grand nursing theory of Modeling and Role Modeling. SEE: *Theory of Modeling and Role Modeling*.

swallow (swăl′ō) [AS. swelgan] To cause or enable the passage of something from the mouth through the throat and esophagus into the stomach by muscular action. SYN: *deglutition*.

swallowing (swăl′ō-ĭng) A complicated act, usually initiated voluntarily but always completed reflexively, whereby food is moved from the mouth through the pharynx and esophagus to the stomach. It occurs in the following three stages. SYN: *deglutition*.

In the *first stage,* food is placed on the surface of the tongue. The tip of the tongue is placed against the hard palate; then elevation of the larynx and backward movement of the tongue forces food through the isthmus of the fauces in the pharynx.

In the *second stage,* the food passes through the pharynx. This involves constriction of the walls of the pharynx, backward bending of the epiglottis, and an upward and forward movement of the larynx and trachea. This may be observed externally with the bobbing of the Adam's apple. Food is kept from entering the nasal cavity by elevation of the soft palate and from entering the larynx by closure of the glottis and backward inclination of the epiglottis. During this stage, respiratory movements are inhibited by reflex.

In the *third stage,* food moves down the esophagus and into the stomach. This movement is accomplished by momentum from the second stage, peristaltic contractions, and gravity. With the body in an upright position, liquids pass rapidly and do not require assistance from the esophagus. However, second-stage momentum and peristaltic contractions are sufficient to allow liquids to be drunk even when the head is lower than the stomach.

Difficulty in swallowing is called dysphagia. SEE: *dysphagia;* illus.

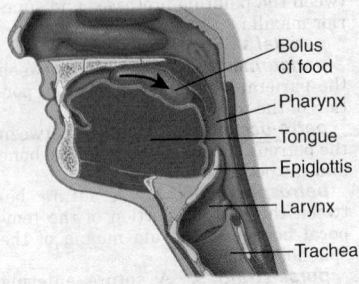

Bolus of food
Pharynx
Tongue
Epiglottis
Larynx
Trachea

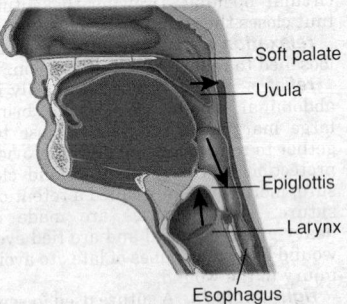

Soft palate
Uvula
Epiglottis
Larynx
Esophagus

SWALLOWING

air s. Voluntary or involuntary swallowing of air. It occurs involuntarily in infants as a result of improper feeding. Adults may swallow air during eating or drinking.

impaired s. Abnormal functioning of the swallowing mechanism associated with deficits in oral, pharyngeal, or esophageal structure or function. SEE: *Nursing Diagnoses Appendix*.

tongue s. SEE: under *tongue-swallowing*.

Swan-Ganz catheter (swon′ganz) [Harold James Swan, Irish-born U.S. cardiologist, 1922–2005; William Ganz, Slovakian-born U.S. cardiologist, 1919–2009] A soft, flexible catheter that is inserted into the pulmonary artery of patients in shock or acute pulmonary edema to determine intracardiac pressures, oxygen saturation, and other hemodynamic parameters.

⚠️ Its use may produce bleeding, vessel rupture, dysrhythmias, and other life-threatening complications.

swan-neck deformity SEE: under *deformity*.

swarming (sworm′ĭng) The spread of bacteria over a culture medium.

sway, postural Forward and backward

movement of the body with motion occurring around the ankle joints when the feet are fixed on the floor. Backward sway is controlled by the anterior tibialis, quadriceps, and abdominal muscles; forward sway is controlled by the gastrocnemius, hamstring, and paraspinal muscles. Patients with lesions of the dorsal and lateral columns of the central nervous system exhibit increased postural sway when they close their eyes and may fall down if they are not supported.

sway-back (swā′băk) A slouched posture in which the pelvis is shifted forward and the thorax posteriorly. Lordosis occurs in the lower lumbar spinal region; a compensating reversal to kyphosis occurs in the upper lumbar and thoracic regions. SEE: illus.

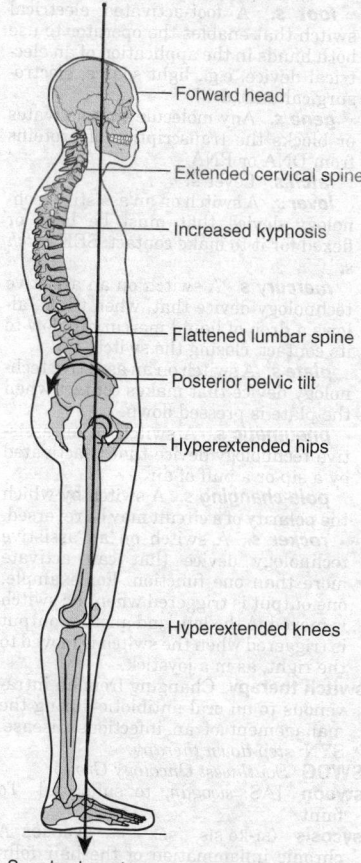

- Forward head
- Extended cervical spine
- Increased kyphosis
- Flattened lumbar spine
- Posterior pelvic tilt
- Hyperextended hips
- Hyperextended knees

Swayback posture

SWAY-BACK

sweat (swĕt) [AS. *sweatan*] **1.** Perspiration. **2.** The condition of perspiring or of being made to perspire freely, as to order a sweat for a patient. **3.** To emit

moisture through the skin's pores. SYN: *perspire*.

It is a colorless, slightly turbid, salty, aqueous fluid, although that from the sweat glands in the axillae, around the anus, and of the ceruminous glands has an oily consistency. It contains urea, fatty substances, and sodium chloride. This salty, watery fluid is difficult to collect without contamination with sebum. Perspiration is controlled by the sympathetic nervous system through true secretory fibers supplying sweat glands.

FUNCTION: Sweat cools the body by evaporation and rids it of what waste may be expressed through the pores of the skin. The daily amount is about a liter; this figure is subject to extreme variation according to physical activity and atmospheric conditions, and in hot conditions may be as much as 10 to 15 L in 24 hr.

bloody s. Hemathidrosis.

colliquative s. Profuse, clammy sweat.

colored s. Chromidrosis.

fetid s. Bromidrosis.

night s. SEE: *night sweat*.

profuse s. Hyperhidrosis.

scanty s. Anhidrosis.

sweating (swĕt′ing) **1.** The act of exuding sweat. **2.** Emitting sweat. **3.** Causing profuse sweat.

excessive s. Hyperhidrosis.

gustatory s. Sweating and flushing over the distribution of the auriculotemporal nerve in response to chewing.

insensible s. Insensible perspiration.

sensible s. The production of moisture on the skin by means of the secretions of the sweat glands.

urinous s. Uridrosis.

sweat lodge Among the indigenous peoples of North America, a tent or hut, traditionally made of arched poles covered in animal hide, used to enclose a steam or vapor bath for healing purposes. SYN: *medicine lodge*.

sweat test A test to diagnose cystic fibrosis in which sweat glands on the skin are stimulated by an electrode after the skin has been wetted with pilocarpine. Elevated levels of chloride in the sweat establish the diagnosis. SYN: *pilocarpine iontophoresis*.

sweep (swēp) To clear debris away, e.g., from the mouth during resuscitation. SEE: *finger sweep*.

sweet [AS. *swete*, sweet] **1.** Pleasing to the taste or smell. **2.** Containing or derived from sugar. **3.** Free from excess of acid, sulfur, or corrosive salts.

sweetener, artificial A chemical compound (e.g., saccharin or aspartame) that tastes sweet but has no available calories. Artificial sweeteners are used in foods and candies as sugar substitutes (e.g., for the overweight or diabetic).

Sweet syndrome (swēt) [R. D. Sweet, contemporary Brit. physician] A febrile illness with raised painful plaques on the limbs, face, and neck; neutrophilic leukocytosis; and dense neutrophilic infiltrates in the skin lesions. It responds promptly to treatment with glucocorticoids. Although the cause is unknown, the condition is often associated with the administration of drugs (such as hydralazine or sulfa drugs) and occasionally is found in persons with connective tissue diseases, hematological malignancies, or inflammatory bowel disease.

swelling (swel'ing) An abnormal transient enlargement, esp. one appearing on the surface of the body. Ice applied to the area helps to limit swelling. SEE: *edema.*

   albuminous s. Cloudy **s.**

   brain s. Brain **edema**.

   Calabar s. A temporary, painless swelling occurring in infestations by the nematode *Loa loa,* and thought to be due to temporary sensitization. SYN: *fugitive s.*

   cloudy s. A degeneration of tissues marked by a cloudy appearance, swelling, and the appearance of tiny albuminoid granules in the cells as observed with a microscope. SYN: *albuminous s.*

   extensive limb s. ABBR: ELS. A large localized tissue reaction in an arm or a leg after the injection of certain vaccines. DTaP (diphtheria, tetanus, and acellular pertussis) vaccination, e.g., results in injection site swelling of muscle and subcutaneous tissue in approx. 2% to 6% of children receiving booster doses of the vaccine. The swelling resolves spontaneously in about 4 days without complications.

   fugitive s. Calabar **s.**

   glassy s. A swelling occurring in amyloid degeneration of tissues. SEE: *amyloid **degeneration**.*

   s. of jaw A swelling in the upper jaw (maxilla) or in the lower jaw (mandible). In the lower jaw, the swelling that may be due to an alveolar abscess, cyst, gumma, sarcoma, or actinomycosis. In the upper jaw, the swelling may be due to an alveolar abscess, parotid tumor, parotitis, carcinoma, sarcoma, necrosis of bone, or disease of antrum.

   white s. A swelling seen in tuberculous arthritis, esp. of the knee.

Swift disease (swift) Acrodynia.

swimmer's ear SEE: under *ear.*

swing bed A hospital bed that can be used either for acute care needs or for skilled nursing as conditions dictate.

swinging flashlight test A test used to detect a relative afferent pupillary defect or Marcus Gunn pupil. Direct light is shone into the normal eye; both pupils

constrict equally due to the consensual response. Light is quickly swung over to the contralateral pupil, which appears to dilate as a result of a relative decrease in the optic nerve fiber function in the affected eye. This response is seen in asymmetrical optic nerve diseases such as glaucoma, optic neuropathy, and optic neuritis.

Swiss ball SEE: under *ball.*

swiss cheese cartilage syndrome Kniest dysplasia.

switch (swich) **1.** A device used to break or open an electrical circuit or to divert a current from one conductor to another. **2.** An assistive technology device used as an input device for a microcomputer. Types of adaptive switches include those activated by the tongue, eyelids, voice, movements of the head and trunk, and gross hand movements.

   foot s. A foot-activated electrical switch that enables the operator to use both hands in the application of an electrical device, e.g., light source, electrosurgical unit, drill.

   gene s. Any molecule that activates or blocks the transcription of proteins from DNA or RNA.

   latch s. Lever **s.**

   lever s. A switch on an assistive technology device that must be bent or flexed for it to make contact. SEE: *latch s.*

   mercury s. A switch on an assistive technology device that, when tilted, allows a drop of liquid mercury to flow to its contact, closing the switch.

   plate s. A switch on an assistive technology device that makes contact when the plate is pressed down.

   pneumatic s. A switch on an assistive technology device that is activated by a sip or a puff of air.

   pole-changing s. A switch by which the polarity of a circuit may be reversed.

   rocker s. A switch on an assistive technology device that can activate more than one function. For example, one output is triggered when the switch is moved to the left, and another output is triggered when the switch is moved to the right, as in a joystick.

switch therapy Changing from an intravenous to an oral antibiotic during the management of an infectious disease. SYN: *step-down therapy.*

SWOG *Southwest Oncology Group.*

swoon [AS. *swogan,* to suffocate] To faint.

sycosis (sī-kō'sĭs, 'sēz") *pl.* **sycoses** A chronic inflammation of the hair follicles.

   SYMPTOMS: The patient has inflammation of hairy areas of the body marked by an aggregation of papules and pustules, each of which is pierced by a hair. The pustules show no disposition to rupture but dry to form yellow-brown crusts. There is itching and burning. If the disease persists, it may lead to extreme destruction of hair follicles and permanent alopecia. The disease is curable with prolonged treatment, and relapses do occur. *Staphylococcus aureus* and *S. epidermidis* entering through hair follicles cause the disease. Trauma and disability are predisposing factors.

s. barbae Sycosis of the beard marked by papules and pustules perforated by hairs and surrounded by infiltrated skin. SYN: *barber's itch; folliculitis barbae*. SEE: illus.

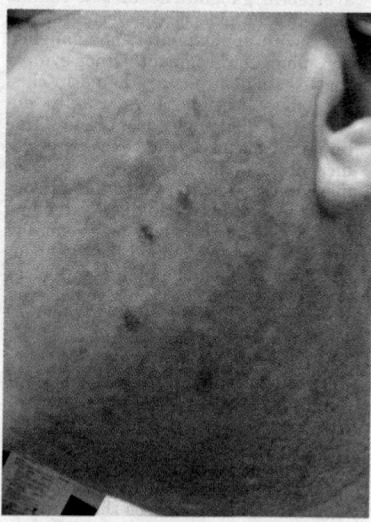

SYCOSIS BARBAE

lupoid s. A pustular lesion of the hair follicles of the beard.

Sydenham chorea (sĭd'ĕn-ămz) [Thomas Sydenham, Brit. physician, 1624–1689] A rare neurological syndrome associated with acute rheumatic fever, marked by involuntary dancing movements of the muscles of the trunk and extremities, anxiety and other psychological symptoms, and, occasionally, cognitive disorders. It is seen infrequently in Western societies because of the prompt and effective treatment of most cases of strep throat.

TREATMENT: Benzodiazepines, such as diazepam or lorazepam, are given to limit the choreiform movements. Penicillin or another appropriate antibiotic is given to eradicate the streptococcal infection causing the rheumatic fever.

PROGNOSIS: Recovery usually occurs within 2 to 3 months. Relapses, esp. in young women, may occur when oral contraceptives are used or during pregnancy. Other complications, such as congestive heart failure or death, may result from the carditis that accompa-

nies rheumatic fever. SYN: *chorea minor*.

syllabus (sĭl'ă-bŭs) [Gr. *syllabos*, table of contents] An abstract of a lecture or outline of a course of study or of a book.

sylvian (sil'vē-ăn) [*Sylvi(us)* + L. adj. suffix *a-anus*] **1.** Pert. to Franciscus Sylvius. "Sylvian" usually refers to the "fissure of Sylvius." SEE: *Sylvius, Franciscus.* **2.** Pert. to Jacobus Sylvius. SEE: *Sylvius, Jacobus.*

Sylvius, Franciscus (sil'vē-ŭs) Franciscus Sylvius, Latinization of François Dubois (Franz de le Boë), Dutch anatomist, 1614–1672.

fissure of S. The deep fissure along the side of the cerebral hemisphere separating the parietal lobe (above) from the temporal lobe (below) of the cerebrum. SYN: *lateral fissure; lateral sulcus; sylvian fissure.*

Sylvius, Jacobus (sil'vē-ŭs) Jacobus Sylvius, Latinization of Jacques Dubois, Fr. anatomist, 1478–1555.

aqueduct of S. A narrow canal from the third to the fourth ventricle. SYN: *aqueductus cerebri; cerebral aqueduct; sylvian aqueduct.*

symbion, symbiont (sĭm'bē-ŏn, -bē-ŏnt) [Gr. *syn,* together, + *bios,* life] An organism that lives with another in a state of symbiosis.

symbiosis (sĭm″bē-ō'sĭs) [Gr.] **1.** The living together in close association of two organisms of different species. If neither organism is harmed, this is called *commensalism;* if the association is beneficial to both, *mutualism;* if one is harmed and the other benefits, *parasitism.* **2.** In psychiatry, a dependent, mutually reinforcing relationship between two persons. In a healthy context, it is characteristic of the infant-mother relationship. In an unhealthy context, it may accentuate shared depression or paranoia.

symbiote (sĭm'bī-ōt) [Gr. *syn,* together, + *bios,* life] An organism symbiotic with another.

symbiotic (sĭm″bī-ŏt'ĭk) Pert. to symbiosis.

symblepharon (sĭm-blĕf'ă-rŏn) [″ + *blepharon,* eyelid] An adhesion between the conjuctivae of the lid and the eyeball, typically caused by burns with acids or bases, surgical trauma, or inadequately treated infections; also caused by Stevens-Johnson syndrome, pemphigoid, and trachoma. The adhesions are surgically lysed to permit free movement and use of the affected eye.

symbol (sĭm'bŏl) [Gr. *symbolon,* a sign] **1.** An object or sign that represents an idea or quality by association, resemblance, or convention. **2.** In psychoanalytical theory, an object used as an unconscious substitute that is not connected consciously with the libido, but into which the libido is concentrated. **3.** A mark or letter representing an atom or an element in chemistry.

phallic s. An object that bears some resemblance to the penis.

symbolia (sĭm-bō'lē-ă) The ability to identify or recognize an object by the sense of touch.

symbolism (sĭm'bŏl-ĭzm) [" + *-ismos*, condition] **1.** The unconscious substitutive expression of subconscious thoughts of sexual significance in terms recognized by the objective consciousness. **2.** An abnormal condition in which everything that occurs is interpreted as a symbol of the patient's own thoughts.

symbolization (sĭm"bŏl-ĭ-zā'shŭn) An unconscious process by which an object or idea comes to represent another object or idea on the basis of similarity or association.

symbrachydactyly (sĭm-brăk"ē-dăk'tĭ-lē) [" + *brachys*, short, + *daktylos*, finger] The webbing of abnormally short fingers.

Syme operation (sīm) [James Syme, Scottish surgeon, 1799–1870] **1.** Amputation of the foot at the ankle joint with removal of the malleoli. **2.** Excision of the tongue. **3.** External urethrotomy.

symmetry (sĭm'ĕt-rē) Correspondence in shape, size, and relative position of parts on opposite sides of a body.

bilateral s. Symmetry of an organism or body whose right and left halves are mirror images of each other or in which a median longitudinal section divides the organism or body into equivalent right and left halves. SYN: *bilateralism*.

radial s. Symmetry of an organism whose parts radiate from a central axis.

sympathectomy, **sympathicectomy** (sĭm"pă-thek'tŏ-mē, sĭm-păth"ĭ-sek'tŏ-mē) [*sympath(etic nervous system)* + *-ectomy*] Excision of a portion of the sympathetic division of the autonomic nervous system, used, e.g., to treat hyperhydrosis (refractory sweating of the palms or feet) or Raynaud's phenomenon. It may include a nerve, plexus, ganglion, or a series of ganglia of the sympathetic trunk.

chemical s. The use of drugs to destroy or temporarily inactivate part of the sympathetic nervous system.

endoscopic transthoracic s. The destruction of sympathetic nerves in the chest by an endoscope directed through the skin of the underarm, behind the lungs, toward the spine. It is used to treat hyperhydrosis.

periarterial s. Removal of the sheath of an artery in which sympathetic nerve fibers are located. It is used in trophic disturbances.

sympathetic (sĭm"pă-thĕt'ĭk) **1.** Pert. to the sympathetic nervous system. **2.** Pert. to or caused by sympathy.

sympathetic nervous system ABBR: SNS. In the autonomic nervous system, those efferent (motor) circuits in which the preganglionic neurons are located in the thoracic and lumbar spinal cord and the main postganglionic neurotransmitter is norepinephrine.

ANATOMY: The primary motor cells of the SNS are found in the intermediolateral column of the thoracic and lumbar segments of the spinal cord. The axons (preganglionic axons) of these neurons exit the spinal ventral roots and synapse on neurons in one or more of the peripheral sympathetic ganglia. Twenty-two sympathetic ganglia (paravertebral ganglia) lie in two chains, one on each side of the vertebral column, with approximately one ganglion per spinal cord segment. Other sympathetic ganglion cells are found in clusters more peripherally, usually entwined in nerve plexuses. Four large unpaired plexuses, the celiac, superior mesenteric, aorticorenal, and inferior mesenteric, are often called the "prevertebral sympathetic ganglia." Extending from these plexuses are many smaller plexuses that are named for the structures they surround and innervate; e.g., cardiac plexuses, the esophageal plexus, the gastric plexus, and theprostatic plexus. SEE: *ganglion; plexus*.

PHYSIOLOGY AND PHARMACOLOGY: Activation of the SNS readies an organism to interact with the outside world. Sympathetic activity dilates pupils, increases heart rate, widens airways, increases circulation to skeletal muscles, decreases circulation to the gastrointestinal tract, and increases the availability of glucose, a direct source of energy. Most of these effects are produced by norepinephrine interacting with adrenergic receptors on effector cells (smooth muscle, cardiac muscle, and secretory cells). The various subtypes of adrenergic receptors are associated with characteristic effects. In general, alpha-1 and alpha-2 adrenergic receptors produce smooth muscle contraction, notably constriction of blood vessels; alpha-2 receptors also produce cardiac muscle relaxation. Beta-1 adrenergic receptors produce cardiac muscle contraction, while beta-2 receptors produce smooth muscle contraction, notably in the airways of the lung. Beta-3 receptors, which are found in adipose-tissue, stimulate lipolysis. Drugs other than norepinephrine and epinephrine (adrenalin) can act on adrenergic receptors, and receptor subtypes differ in their sensitivity to specific drugs. For example, phenylephrine selectively activates and phentolamine selectively blocks alpha adrenergic receptors, while isoproterenol (isoprenaline) selectively activates and propranolol selectively blocks beta adrenergic receptors. The availability of selective drugs allows some autonomic medical symptoms to be targeted selectively. SEE: *autonomic nervous system* for illus. and table; *parasympathetic nervous system*.

sympathetic ophthalmia SEE: under *ophthalmia*.

sympatheticotonia (sĭm″pă-thĕt″ĭ-kō-tō′nē-ă) [″ + *tonos,* act of stretching, tension] A condition marked by excessive tone of the sympathetic nervous system with unusually high blood pressure, fine tremor of the hands, and insomnia; the opposite of vagotonia. It may be present in thyrotoxic patients.

sympathetic plexus One of the plexuses formed at intervals by the sympathetic nerves and ganglia.

sympathiconeuritis (sĭm-păth″ĭ-kō-nū-rī′tĭs) [″ + *neuron,* nerve, + *itis,* inflammation] An inflammation of the sympathetic nerves.

sympathoadrenal (sĭm″păth-ō-ă-drē′năl) [″ + L. *ad,* to, + *ren,* kidney] Pert. to the sympathetic part of the autonomic nervous system and the adrenal medulla.

sympatholytic, sympathicolytic (sĭm″pă-thō-lit′ik, sĭm-păth″ĭ-kō-lit′ik) [*sympath(etic)* + *lytic*] Interfering with, opposing, inhibiting, or destroying impulses from the sympathetic nervous system. SYN: *adrenolytic*.

sympathomimetic (sĭm″pă-thō-mĭ-met′ik) [*sympath(y)* + *mimetic*] Producing effects resembling those resulting from stimulation of the sympathetic nervous system (e.g., the effects following the injection of epinephrine. SYN: *adrenomimetic*.

sympathy (sĭm′pă-thē) [Gr. *sympatheia*] **1.** An association or feeling of closeness between individuals such that something that affects one affects the other. SEE: *empathy*.

symphalangism (sĭm-făl′ăn-jĭzm) [Gr. *syn,* together, + *phalanx,* closely knit row] **1.** An ankylosis of the joints of the fingers or toes. **2.** A web-fingered or web-toed condition.

symphyseal (sĭm-fĭz′ē-ăl) [Gr. *symphysis,* growing together] Pert. to symphysis.

symphysis (sĭm′fĭ-sĭs) *pl.* **symphyses** [Gr., growing together] **1.** A line of fusion between two bones that are separate in early development, as symphysis of the mandible. **2.** A joint in which two bones are connected only by a fibrocartilaginous pad, as the pubic symphysis and the intervertebral disks. SEE: *cartilaginous joint*.

s. of the jaw An anterior, median, vertical ridge on the outer surface of the lower jaw representing a line of union of its halves. SYN: *mandibular symphysis*.

mandibular s. Symphysis of the jaw.

s. pubis The junction of the pubic bones on the midline in front; the bony eminence under the pubic hair.

sympodia (sĭm-pō′dē-ă) [″ + *pous,* foot] A fusion of the lower extremities.

symporter (sim-port′ĕr) A membrane protein that carries two different ions or molecules in the same direction through the membrane, as in the absorption of glucose linked with that of sodium ions in the small intestine. SEE: *antiporter*.

symptom (sim(p)′tŏm) [Gr. *symptōma,* occurrence] Any change in the body or its functions as perceived by the patient. A symptom represents the subjective experience of disease. Symptoms are described by patients in their complaint or history of the present illness. By contrast, signs are the objective findings observed by health care providers during the examination of patients.

Aspects of general symptom analysis include the following: *onset:* date, manner (gradual or sudden), and precipitating factors; *characteristics:* character, location, radiation, severity, timing, aggravating or relieving factors, and associated symptoms; *course since onset:* incidence, progress, and effects of therapy.

alarm s. A symptom that raises the concern that a patient may have a severe illness and requires careful evaluation. For example, in patients with digestive illnesses, findings such as anemia, anorexia, bleeding, dehydration, fever, or weight loss are considered alarm symptoms.

cardinal s. A fundamental symptom of a disease.

constitutional s. A symptom (such as fever, malaise, loss of appetite) caused by or indicating systemic disease. SYN: *general s*.

conversion s. Conversion reaction.

dissociation s. Anesthesia to heat, cold, and pain without loss of tactile sensibility; seen in syringomyelia.

focal s. A symptom caused by a lesion to a specific body part or a particular location in the central or peripheral nervous system. SYN: *local s*.

general s. Constitutional **s.**

indirect s. A symptom occurring secondarily as a result of a disease in another organ system or body part.

irritative voiding s. Painful or unusually sensitive urination, e.g., as a result of urinary tract infection, urinary stones, other foreign bodies, or tumors.

labyrinthine s. A group of symptoms (such as tinnitus, vertigo, or nausea) indicating a disease or lesion of the inner ear.

local s. Focal **s.**

medically unexplained s. ABBR: MUS. A complaint from a patient that has eluded explanation despite assessment by health care practitioners.

negative pathognomonic s. A symptom that never occurs in a certain disease or condition; hence, a symptom whose presence rules out the existence of that disease.

objective s. A symptom apparent to the observer. SEE: *sign (2)*.

passive s. Static **s.**

pathognomonic s. A symptom that is unmistakably associated with a particular disease.

presenting s. The symptom that led the patient to seek medical care.

prodromal s. Prodrome.

rational s. Subjective **s.**

Rumpf s. SEE: *Rumpf symptom.*

signal s. A symptom that is premonitory of an impending condition such as the aura that precedes an attack of epilepsy or migraine.

static s. A symptom pert. to the condition of a single organ or structure without reference to the remainder of the body. SYN: *passive s.*

subjective s. A symptom apparent only to the patient. SYN: *rational s.*

supratentorial s. An informal term for a symptom due to psychological rather than organic causes. The term refers to symptoms with causes originating "above the tentorium cerebelli," i.e., in the brain rather than in the body.

sympathetic s. A symptom for which there is no specific inciting cause and usually occurring at a point more or less remote from the point of disturbance. SEE: *sympathy (1).*

withdrawal s. Any of the symptoms that follow the sudden discontinuation of the use of a substance to which a person has become addicted. SEE: *withdrawal syndrome.*

symptomatic (sĭmp″tō-mătʹĭk) [Gr. *symptomatikos*] Pert. to a symptom.

symptomatic treatment Treatment directed toward constitutional symptoms, such as fever, shock, and pain.

symptomatology (sĭmp″tŏ-mă-tolʹŏ-jē) [*symptom* + *-logy*] **1.** The science of symptoms and indications. **2.** All of the historical features and physical findings that characterize an illness, esp. a seizure disorder, considered as a whole. SYN: *semiology (2).*

symptom complex SEE: under *complex.*

symptom inventory A list of findings or patterns common to particular illnesses or diseases, e.g., psychological illnesses, traumatic injuries, or neoplastic diseases. Symptom inventories are used to assess or screen patients, to assign them to treatment groups, and to randomize groups of individuals by their similarities or differences so that they may be compared in research.

symptom management An approach to palliative care that treats the symptoms rather than the cause of a condition. Its focus includes confusion, dizziness, fa-

tigue, incontinence, nausea, shortness of breath, vomiting, and weakness.

syn-, sym-, sys- [Gr. *syn,* with, together with] Prefixes meaning *joined, together.*

synanthropic (sĭn-ăn-thrŏpʹĭk) [″ + ″] Living in a close association with human beings.

synapse (sĭnʹăps) [Gr. *synapsis,* point of contact] The space between the junction of two neurons in a neural pathway, where the termination of the axon of one neuron comes into close proximity with the cell body or dendrites of another. The electrical impulse traveling along a presynaptic neuron to the end of its axon releases a chemical neurotransmitter that stimulates or inhibits an electrical impulse in the postsynaptic neuron; synaptic transmission is in one direction only. Synapses are susceptible to fatigue, offer a resistance to the passage of impulses, and are markedly susceptible to the effects of oxygen deficiency, anesthetics, and other agents, including therapeutic drugs and toxic chemicals. SYN: *synapsis (1).* SEE: illus.

axodendritic s. The synapse between an axon of one neuron and the dendrites of another.

axosomatic s. The synapse between the axon of one neuron and the cell body of another.

synapsis (sĭn-ăpʹsĭs) [Gr., point of contact] The process of first maturation division in gametogenesis, in which there is conjugation of pairs of homologous chromosomes forming double or bivalent chromosomes. In the resulting meiotic division, the chromosome number is reduced from the diploid to the haploid number. It is at this stage that crossing over occurs.

synaptic (sĭ-năpʹtĭk) Pert. to a synapse or synapsis.

synaptology (sĭn″ăp-tŏlʹō-jē) [″ + *logos,* word, reason] The study of synapses.

synbiotics (sĭn″bīʹot′iks) [*syn-* + *biotics*] Synergistic blends of prebiotics and probiotics used to treat irritable bowel syndrome and inflammatory bowel disease. **synbiotic,** *adj.*

sync, synch (singk) [*sync(hronization)*] In cardiopulmonary resuscitation (CPR), pert. to electrical shocks delivered to a patient during CPR. Synchronized electrical shocks should be used to treat a patient with a tachycardic heart rhythm when that arrhythmia is poorly tolerated, but not immediately life threatening. Fatal arrhythmias, such as ventricular fibrillation or pulseless ventricular tachycardia, should be treated with immediate, unsynchronized defibrillation.

synchondrosis (sĭn″kŏn-drōʹsĭs) [″ + ″ + *osis,* condition] An immovable joint having surfaces between the bones con-

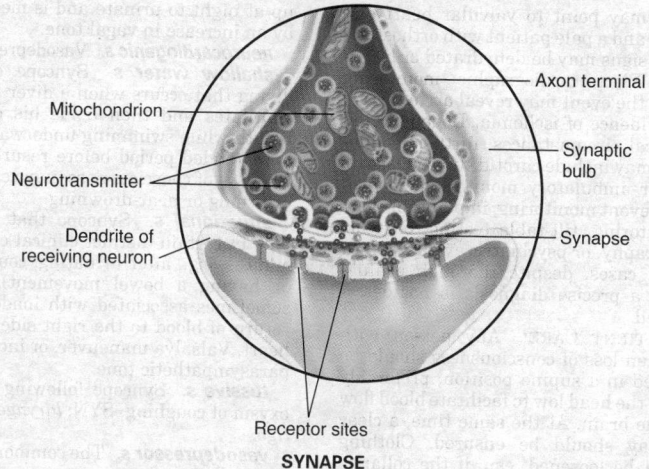

Labels on figure:
- Mitochondrion
- Neurotransmitter
- Dendrite of receiving neuron
- Axon terminal
- Synaptic bulb
- Synapse
- Receptor sites

SYNAPSE

Axon terminal synapse

nected by cartilages. This may be temporary, in which case the cartilage eventually becomes ossified, or permanent. SYN: *symphysis cartilaginosa*.

synchronism Synchrony.

synchronize (sing′krŏ-nīz″) [Gr. *synchronizein*, to be contemporary with] ABBR: SYNC. To coordinate the timing of two or more events or processes. In electrical cardioversion, for example, a shock to the heart is delivered when an R wave is detected on a cardiac monitor. Synchronized shocks are used to treat rhythms such as atrial flutter, atrial fibrillation, or supraventricular tachycardia, in which QRS complexes are recognizable. In these arrhythmias, unsynchronized shocks might induce ventricular fibrillation. **synchronization** (-nĭ-zā′shŏn), *n*.

synchronous communication SEE: under *communication*.

synchrony (sĭng′krŏ-nē) The simultaneous occurrence of separate events. SYN: *synchronism*. **synchronous**, *adj*.

synchrotron (sĭng′kră-trŏn″) A particle accelerator used in medical imaging that accelerates positively or negatively charged particles.

synchysis (sĭn′kĭs-ĭs) [Gr., confound] The fluid state of the vitreous of the eye.

synclinal (sĭn-klī′năl) [Gr. *synklinein*, to lean together] Inclined in the same direction toward a point.

synclitism (sĭn′klĭt-ĭzm) [Gr. *synklinein*, to lean together, + *-ismos*, condition] Parallelism between the planes of the fetal head and those of the maternal pelvis.

synclonus (sĭn′klō-nŭs) [″ + *klonos*, turmoil] **1.** The simultaneous clonic contraction of several muscles. **2.** A disease marked by muscular spasms.

syncope (sĭng′kŏ-pē, sĭn′) [Gr. *synkopē*,

fainting] Transient (and usually sudden) loss of consciousness, accompanied by an inability to maintain an upright posture. Syncope is a common occurrence, accounting for about 1% to 3% of all hospital admissions in the U.S. **syncopal** (-păl), *adj*.

ETIOLOGY: The most frequent causes of syncope are vasovagal (the common fainting spell), cardiogenic (esp. arrhythmogenic, valvular, or ischemic), orthostatic (such as due to dehydration or hemorrhage), and neurogenic, e.g., due to seizures. Many medications (such as sedatives, tranquilizers, excessive doses of insulin), food allergies, hypoglycemia, hyperventilation, massive pulmonary embolism, aortic dissection, atrial myxoma, carotid sinus hypersensitivity, coughing, urination, and psychiatric disease can also result in loss of consciousness.

SYMPTOMS: The patient typically complains of having suffered a sudden and unexpected fall to the ground, with loss of awareness, and then rapid recovery of orientation. Lacerations, abrasions, or other injuries occasionally result from the fall.

DIAGNOSIS: The history may contain useful clues. For example, if the patient stood up just before losing consciousness, an orthostatic cause is likely; if a patient is confused or disoriented for a long time after losing consciousness, seizures are probable; if a young patient passes out while at a wedding or other stressful event, vasovagal syncope is likely. The diabetic patient who becomes agitated and sweaty before passing out should be rapidly assessed and treated for low blood sugar.

The examination of the patient may reveal the cause; e.g., a loud aortic murmur may point to valvular heart disease, and a pale patient with orthostatic vital signs may be dehydrated or bleeding. Electrocardiographic monitoring after the event may reveal arrhythmias or evidence of ischemia. Depending on clinical circumstances, further evaluation may include carotid sinus massage, 24 hr ambulatory monitoring, month-long event monitoring, implantable loop monitoring, tilt-table testing, echocardiography, or psychiatric evaluation. In most cases, despite thorough evaluation, a precise diagnosis is not determined.

PATIENT CARE: Any person with sudden loss of consciousness should be placed in a supine position, preferably with the head low to facilitate blood flow to the brain. At the same time, a clear airway should be ensured. Clothing must be loosened, esp. if the collar is tight.

Fainting (one form of syncope) is usually of short duration and is counteracted by placing the person supine. If recovery from fainting is not prompt and complete, a prompt assessment of airway, breathing, circulation, and cardiac rhythm is needed; assistance should be obtained and the person transported to a hospital. A person who refuses hospital evaluation after recovering from a fainting episode should be encouraged to be examined by a physician as soon as possible.

cardiac s. Syncope of cardiac origin as in Stokes-Adams syndrome, aortic stenosis, tachycardia, bradycardia, or myocardial infarction.

carotid sinus s. Syncope resulting from pressure on, or hypersensitivity of, the carotid sinus. It may result from turning the head to one side or from wearing too tight a collar.

convulsive s. Syncope followed by a seizure. It may be caused by any condition (such as cardiac arrhythmia) that results in inadequate blood flow to the brain.

defecation s. Syncope during or immediately after a bowel movement.

deglutition s. Syncope triggered by swallowing. It is an abnormal reflex in which stimulation of the esophagus elicits vagal motor impulses that cause bradycardia, peripheral vasodilation, and hypotension.

hysterical s. Syncope resulting from a conversion reaction.

laryngeal s. Brief syncope following coughing and tickling in the throat.

local s. Numbness of a part with sudden blanching, as of the fingers. It is a symptom of Raynaud disease or of local asphyxia.

micturition s. Syncope during urination. It usually occurs in men who get up at night to urinate and is mediated by an increase in vagal tone.

neurocardiogenic s. Vasodepressor **s.**

shallow water s. Syncope during diving that occurs when a diver hyperventilates and then holds his or her breath while swimming underwater for an extended period before resurfacing. The loss of consciousness may result in drowning or near-drowning.

situational s. Syncope that occurs only in certain distinct clinical circumstances, e.g., after urinating, coughing, or having a bowel movement). It is sometimes associated with inadequate return of blood to the right side of the heart, Valsalva maneuver, or increased parasympathetic tone.

tussive s. Syncope following a paroxysm of coughing. SYN: *laryngeal vertigo*.

vasodepressor s. The common fainting spell.

SYMPTOMS: The patient, who may have just experienced a stressful or emotionally upsetting event, reports a feeling of wooziness, nausea, and weakness, followed often by a feeling that darkness is closing in on him or her. A ringing in the ears may follow, along with inability to maintain an erect posture. Witnesses may report profuse sweating or a loss of color in the face. During the event, an unusually slow pulse may be present. Several convulsive movements of the body may be noted if blood flow to the brain is inadequate but the loss of consciousness is not accompanied by other signs of seizures, e.g., tongue biting, incontinence, or a prolonged postictal period of confusion.

PATIENT CARE: Placing the patient in a sitting position with the head lowered between the legs or in a horizontal or Trendelenburg position restores blood flow to the brain and promptly aborts the attack. A brief examination should be performed to make sure the affected person can move all extremities and facial muscles and can speak clearly and understand speech. The carotid arteries should be checked for bruits, and the heart for evidence of arrhythmia or heart murmurs. Blood pressure, pulse, and oxygenation, as well as cardiac rhythm, should be monitored. Fluids should be administered by mouth if nausea has resolved, or by vein if the patient cannot take liquids orally and has an intravenous access in place. An electrocardiogram should be obtained or cardiac monitoring ordered if the patient has a history of cardiac disease, is elderly, or has multiple risk factors for cardiac disease or dysrhythmias. A complete blood count, serum electrolytes, bloodurea nitrogen, creatinine, and glucose should be checked. Before the patient is allowed to get up again, vital signs should be checked; if they are normal, the patient should be assisted first to a sitting position and then to a standing position before walking independently. Patients who faint may need specialized follow-up examination, e.g., with a cardiologist, internist, or neurologist. SYN: *vasovagal s.; neurocardiogenic s.*

   vasovagal s. Vasodepressor **s.**

syncretio (sĭn-krē'shē-ō) [L.] The development of adhesions between opposing inflamed surfaces.

syncytial (sĭn-sĭ'shăl) Pert. to a syncytium.

syncytioma (sĭn"sĭt-ē-ō'mă) [*syncytium* + *-oma*] A tumor of the chorion.

   s. benignum A mole.

syncytiotrophoblast (sĭn-sĭt"ē-ō-trō'fōblăst) [" + " + *trophe*, nourishment, + *blastos*, germ] The outer layer of cells covering the chorionic villi of the placenta. These cells are in contact with the maternal blood or decidua.

syncytium (sin-sish'(ē-)ŭm, sin-sish'(ē-)ă) *pl.* **syncytia** [*syn-* + *cyto-* + *-ium* (2)] **1.** A multinucleated mass of protoplasm such as a striated muscle fiber. **2.** A group of cells in which the protoplasm of one cell is continuous with that of adjoining cells such as the mesenchyme cells of the embryo. SEE: *coenocyte.*

syndactylism SEE: *syndactyly.*

syndactyly (sĭn-dăk'tĭ-lē) The fusion, usually congenital, of one or more fingers or toes. SYN: *syndactylism.* **syndactylous** (-lŭs), *adj.*

syndectomy (sĭn-dĕk'tō-mē) [" + *dein*, to bind, + *ektome*, excision] The excision of a circular strip of the conjunctiva around the cornea to relieve pannus. SYN: *peritomy* (1).

syndemic (sĭn"dĕm'ĭk) [*syn-* + analogy with *(en)demic, (epi)demic*] A network of health problems, esp. ones that share common social underpinnings and cause an increased public health burden on a community. An example of a syndemic is the linkage between the ready availability of snack foods, low socioeconomic status, sedentary lifestyle, overeating, obesity, and an increased risk of diabetes mellitus and coronary artery disease.

syndesis (sĭn-dē'sĭs) [" + *desis*, binding] **1.** The condition of being bound together. **2.** Surgical fixation or ankylosis of a joint.

syndesmectomy (sĭn"dĕs-mĕk'tō-mē) [Gr. *syndesmos*, ligament, + *ektome*, excision] The excision of a section of a ligament.

syndesmectopia (sĭn"dĕs-mĕk-tō'pē-ă) [" + *ektopos*, out of place] An abnormal position of a ligament.

syndesmitis (sĭn"dĕs-mī'tĭs) [" + *itis*, inflammation] **1.** An inflammation of a

ligament or ligaments. **2.** An inflammation of the conjunctiva.

syndesmochorial (sĭn"dez"mŏ-kō're-ăl) Pert. to a type of placenta in which there is destruction of the surface layer of the uterine mucosa, thus allowing chorionic villi to come into direct contact with maternal blood vessels.

syndesmography (sĭn-dĕs-mŏg'ră-fē) [Gr. *syndesmos*, ligament, + *graphein*, to write] A treatise on the ligaments.

syndesmology (sĭn"dĕs-mŏl'ō-jē) [" + *logos*, word, reason] The study of the ligaments, joints, their movements, and their disorders.

syndesmoma (sĭn"dĕs-mō'mă) [" + *oma*, tumor] A connective tissue tumor.

syndesmopexy (sĭn-dĕs'mō-pĕk"sē) [" + *pexis*, fixation] Joining of two ligaments or fixation of a ligament in a new place, used in correction of a dislocation.

syndesmophyte (sĭn-dĕs'mō-fīt) [" + *phyton*, plant] **1.** A bony bridge formed between adjacent vertebrae. **2.** A bony outgrowth from a ligament.

syndesmoplasty (sĭn-dĕs'mō-plăs"tē) [" + *plassein*, to form] Plastic surgery on a ligament.

syndesmorrhaphy (sĭn"dĕs-mor'ă-fē) [" + *rhaphe*, seam, ridge] The repair or suture of a ligament.

syndesmosis (sĭn"dĕs-mō'sĭs) *pl.* **syndesmoses** [Gr. *syndesmos*, ligament, + *osis*, condition] An articulation in which the bones are united by ligaments.

syndesmotomy (sĭn"dĕs-mŏt'ō-mē) [" + *tome*, incision] The surgical section of ligaments.

syndrome (sĭn'drōm) [Gr., a running together] A group of symptoms, signs, laboratory findings, and physiological disturbances that are linked by a common anatomical, biochemical, or pathological history. Particular syndromes are listed under the first word. SEE: e.g., *carpal tunnel syndrome; irritable bowel syndrome; toxic shock syndrome.* SYN: *symptom complex.* SEE: *disease; disorder.* **syndromic** (sĭn-drŏm'ĭk), *adj.*

syndrome of inappropriate antidiuretic hormone ABBR: SIADH. A syndrome of increased antidiuretic hormone (ADH) activity in spite of reduced plasma osmolarity. Often first suggested by a relative hyponatremia, it is most commonly associated with disorders of the central nervous system, various tumors, anxiety, pain, pneumonia, and drugs.

syndrome X Metabolic syndrome.

synechia (sĭn-ĕk'ē-ă) *pl.* **synechiae** [Gr. *synecheia*, continuity] An adhesion of parts, esp. adhesion of the iris to the lens and cornea.

   anterior s. An adhesion of the iris to the cornea.

   peripheral anterior s. Adhesion between the iris and periphery of the cornea (PAS); usually near the anterior chamber angle. Can cause glaucoma by blocking the outflow of aqueous. Caused by inflammation

posterior s. An adhesion of the iris to the capsule of the lens.

total s. An adhesion of the entire surface of the iris to the lens.

s. vulvae Fusion of the vulvae, usually congenital.

synechotomy (sĭn″ĕk-ŏt′ō-mē) [″ + tome, incision] The division of a synechia or adhesion.

synechtenterotomy (sĭn″ĕk-tĕn″tĕr-ŏt′ō-mē) [″ + enteron, intestine, + tome, incision] The division of an intestinal adhesion.

synecology (sĭn″ē-kŏl′ō-jē) [Gr. syn, together, + oikos, house, + logos, word, reason] The study of organisms in relationship to their environment in group form.

synencephalocele (sĭn″ĕn-sĕf′ă-lō-sēl″) [″ + enkephalos, brain, + kele, tumor, swelling] An encephalocele with adhesions to adjacent structures.

syneresis (sĭn-ĕr′ĕ-sĭs) [Gr. synairesis, drawing together] The contraction of a gel resulting in its separation from the liquid, as a shrinkage of fibrin when blood clots.

synergetic (sĭn″ĕr-jĕt′ĭk) [Gr. syn, together, + ergon, work] Exhibiting cooperative action, said of certain muscles; working together. SYN: synergic.

synergia (sĭn-ĕr′jē-ă) The association and correlation of the activity of synergetic muscle groups.

synergic (sĭn-ĕr′jĭk) [″ + ergon, work] Pert. to or exhibiting cooperation, as certain muscles. SYN: synergetic.

synergist (sĭn′ĕr-jĭst) 1. A remedy that acts to enhance the action of another. SYN: adjuvant. 2. A muscle or organ functioning in cooperation with another, as the flexor muscles; the opposite of antagonist.

synergistic (sĭn″ĕr-jĭs′tĭk) 1. Pert. to synergy. 2. Acting together.

synergy, synergism (sĭn′ĕr-jē, -jizm) [Gr. synergia] An action of two or more agents, muscles, or organs working with each other, cooperatively.

synergy patterns Primitive movements that dominate reflex and voluntary effort when spasticity is present following a cerebrovascular accident. They interfere with coordinated voluntary movements such as eating, dressing, and walking. Flexion synergy patterns include scapular retraction, shoulder abduction and external rotation, elbow flexion, forearm supination, and wrist and finger flexion in the upper extremity; and hip flexion, abduction and external rotation, knee flexion, and ankle dorsiflexion in the lower extremity. Extension synergy patterns include scapular protraction, shoulder adduction and

internal rotation, elbow extension, forearm pronation, and wrist and finger flexion in the upper extremity; and hip extension, adduction and internal rotation, knee extension, ankle plantar flexion and inversion, and toe flexion in the lower extremity.

synesthesia (sĭn″ĕs-thē′zē-ă) [Gr. syn, together, + aisthesis, sensation] 1. A sensation in one area from a stimulus applied to another part. 2. A subjective sensation of a sense other than the one being stimulated. Hearing a sound may also produce the sensation of smell. SEE: phonism.

s. algica Painful synesthesia.

synesthesialgia (sĭn″ĕs-thē- zē-ăl′jē-ă) [″ + ″ + algos, pain] A painful sensation giving rise to one of different character. SEE: synesthesia.

Syngamus (sĭn′gă-mŭs) A genus of nematodes parasitic in the respiratory tract of birds and mammals. The preferred name for the mammalian parasite is Mammomonogamus. Bird parasites have retained the name Syngamus.

S. laryngeus The former name for Mammomonogamus laryngeus.

syngamy (sĭn′gă-mē) [Gr. syn, together, + gamos, marriage] 1. Sexual reproduction. 2. The final stage of fertilization in which the haploid chromosome sets from the male and female gametes come together following breakdown of the pronuclear membranes to form the zygote. SYN: sexual reproduction.

syngeneic (sĭn-jĕ-nē′ĭk) Pert. to individuals or cells without detectable tissue incompatibility. Strains of mice that are inbred for a great number of generations become syngeneic. Identical twins may be syngeneic.

syngenesis (sĭn-jĕn′ĕ-sĭs) [″ + genesis, generation, birth] Generation from the germ cells derived from both parents, rather than from a single cell from one parent; sexual reproduction.

syngnathia (sĭn-nā′thē-ă) [″ + gnathos, jaw] Congenital adhesions between the jaws.

synizesis (sĭn″ĭ-zē′sĭs) [Gr. synizesis] 1. An occlusion or shutting. 2. A clumping of nuclear chromatin during the prophase of mitosis.

synkaryon (sĭn-kăr′ē-ŏn) [Gr. syn, together, + karyon, kernel] A nucleus resulting from fusion of two pronuclei.

synkinesis (sĭn″kĭ-nē′sĭs) [″ + kinesis, movement] An involuntary movement of one part occurring simultaneously with reflex or voluntary movement of another part.

imitative s. An involuntary movement in a healthy or normal muscle accompanying an attempted movement of a paralyzed muscle on the opposite side.

synnecrosis (sĭn″nĕ-krō′sĭs) [″ + nekrosis, state of death] An association between groups or individuals that causes mutual inhibition or death.

synonym (sĭn'ō-nĭm) [Gr. *synonymon*] ABBR: syn. One of two words that have the same or very similar meaning; an additional or substitute name for the same disease, sign, symptom, or anatomical structure.

synophrys (sĭn-ŏf'rĭs) [Gr. *syn*, together, + *ophrys*, eyebrow] Fusion of the eyebrows above the bridge of the nose.

synophthalmia A congenital anomaly in which the eyes are incompletely separated (i.e., in which there is extreme hypotelorism). SEE: *cyclopia*.

synopsis (sĭn-ŏp'sĭs) [Gr.] A summary; a general review of the whole.

synoptophore (sĭn-ŏp'tō-for) [" + *ops*, sight, + *phoros*, bearing] An apparatus for diagnosis and treatment of strabismus. SYN: *synoptoscope*.

synoptoscope (sĭn-ŏp'tō-skōp) [" + " + *skopein*, to examine] Synoptophore.

synorchidism, synorchism (sĭn-or'kĭd-ĭzm, -kĭzm) [" + *orchis*, testicle, + *-ismos*, condition] The union or partial fusion of the testicles.

synoscheos (sĭn-ŏs'kē-ŏs) [" + *oscheon*, scrotum] An adhesion between the penis and scrotum.

synosteology (sĭn''ŏs-tē-ŏl'ō-jē) [" + " + *logos*, word, reason] The branch of medical science concerned with joints and articulations.

synosteosis (sĭn''ŏs-tē-ō'sĭs) Synostosis.

synosteotomy (sĭn''ŏs-tē-ŏt'ō-mē) [" + *osteon*, bone, + *tome*, incision] Dissection of joints.

synostosis (sĭn''ŏs-tō'sĭs) *pl.* **synostoses** [" + " + *osis*, condition] **1.** Articulation by osseous tissue of adjacent bones. **2.** Union of separate bones by osseous tissue. SYN: *synosteosis*.

synostotic (sĭn''ŏs-tŏt'ĭk) [" + " + *osis*, condition] Pert. to synostosis.

synotia (sĭn-ō'shē-ă) [" + *ous*, ear] The union of, or approximation of, the ears occurring in embryonic development, usually associated with absence or incomplete development of the lower jaw.

synotus (sī-nō'tŭs) [" + *ous*, ear] A fetus with synotia.

synovectomy (sĭn''ō-věk'tō-mē) [L. *synovia*, joint fluid, + Gr. *ektome*, excision] Excision of the synovial membrane.

synovia (sĭn-ō'vē-ă) [L.] Synovial fluid.

synovial (sĭn-ō'vē-ăl) Pert. to synovia.

synovial bursa Bursa.

synovial crypt SEE: under *crypt*.

synovial fluid SEE: under *fluid*.

synovial fold One of the smooth folds of synovial membrane on the inner surface of the joint capsule. SYN: *synovial plica*.

synovial villi Slender avascular processes on the free surface of a synovial

membrane projecting into the joint cavity.

synoviocyte (sĭ-nō'vē-ŏ-sīt″) [*synovium* + *-cyte*] A cell that lines the inner surface of joints and tendon sheaths.

synovioma (sĭn''ō-vē-ō'mă) [L. *synovia*, joint fluid, + Gr. *oma*, tumor] A tumor arising from a synovial membrane.

synoviosarcoma [+ Gr. *sarx*, flesh + *oma*, tumor] A rare malignant tumor that arises from synovial cells, i.e., the cells of the membranes that enclose joints.

synovitis (sĭn''ō-vī'tĭs) [" + Gr. *itis*, inflammation] Inflammation of a synovial membrane. Inflammation may be the result of an aseptic wound, rheumatological diseases, infections, a subcutaneous injury (contusion or sprain), irritation produced by damaged cartilage, overuse, or trauma. SYN: *osteosynovitis*. SEE: *Nursing Diagnoses Appendix*.

SYMPTOMS: The joint is painful, much more so on motion, esp. at night. It is swollen and tense. The condition may fluctuate. In synovitis of the knee, the patella is floated up from the condyles, and it can be readily depressed, to rise again when pressure is taken off. The part is never in full extension, as this increases the pain. Skin, which is very sensitive to pressure only at certain points, is neither thickened nor reddened. After a few days, when pain lessens and swelling diminishes as the effusion and extravasated blood are absorbed, the limb returns to its natural position, and recovery follows.

TREATMENT: The condition is managed symptomatically, restricting or avoiding range of motion that produces pain. Therapeutic treatments include cold, heat, ultrasound, and medications to reduce inflammation. Rehabilitation includes strengthening, flexibility, and neuromuscular regimens.

   chronic s. Synovitis in which an undue amount of fluid remains in the cavity and the membrane itself is edematous. Prolonged inflammation causes thickening of the membrane and articular structures by plastic exudation and the formation of fibrous tissue, which increases joint dysfunction and exacerbates symptoms. The joint is weak but not esp. painful, except on pressure and sometimes not even then. Movements, esp. in extension, are restricted and generally attended by crepitus or creaking. Symptoms are well marked when the patient has an excess accumulation of synovial fluid (the amount of fluid depends on the joint involved and also on the patient's body build). Fluid can be removed with a needle and syringe and sent to the laboratory for analysis.

   dendritic s. Synovitis with villous growths developing in the sac.

   detritic s. Synovitis and proliferation

of the synovial tissues, esp. when occurring around foreign bodies (such as silicone joint prostheses) or loose bodies (such as fragments of cartilage or subchondral bone).

dry s. Synovitis with little or no effusion. SYN: *s. sicca.*

purulent s. Synovitis with purulent effusion within the sac.

serous s. Synovitis with nonpurulent, copious effusion.

s. sicca Dry **s.**

simple s. Synovitis with only slightly turbid, if not clear, effusion.

tendinous s. Inflammation of a tendon sheath. SYN: *vaginal s.*

vaginal s. Tendinous **s.**

vibration s. Synovitis resulting from a vibration wound near a joint.

synovitis acne pustulosis hyperostosis and osteomyelitis syndrome ABBR: SAPHO. Acne-associated **arthritis.**

synovium (sĭn-ō′vē-ŭm) [L. *synovia,* joint fluid] A synovial membrane.

syntactic (sĭn-tăk′tĭk) Pert. to or affecting syntax.

syntaxis (sĭn-tăk′sĭs) [″ + *taxis,* arrangement] A junction between two bones. SYN: *articulation.*

synthase (sĭn′thās) An enzyme that acts as a catalyst for joining two molecules. SYN: *synthetase.*

ATP s. An enzyme that catalyzes the addition of a phosphate group to adenosine diphosphate to produce adenosine triphosphate.

nitric oxide s. ABBR: NOS. An enzyme that synthesizes nitric oxide from arginine; present in the central nervous system, the lining of blood vessels, the heart, joints, some autonomic neurons, and other organs.

synthermal (sĭn-thĕr′măl) [″ + *therme,* heat] Having the same temperature.

synthesis (sĭn′thĕs-ĭs) [Gr.] In chemistry, the union of elements to produce compounds; the process of building up. In general, the process or processes involved in the formation of a complex substance from simpler molecules or compounds, as the synthesis of proteins from amino acids. Synthesis is the opposite of decomposition.

synthesize (sĭn″thĕ-sīz′) To produce by synthesis.

synthetase (sĭn′thĕ-tās) Synthase.

synthetic (sĭn-thĕt′ĭk) [Gr. *synthetikos*] Rel. to or made by synthesis; artificially prepared.

synthorax (sĭn-thō′răks) [Gr. *syn,* together, + *thorax,* chest] Thoracopagus.

Synthroid (sĭn′throid″) SEE: *levothyroxine sodium.*

syntone (sĭn′tōn) [″ + *tonos,* act of stretching, tension] An individual whose personality indicates a stable responsiveness to the environment and its social demands. SEE: *syntonic.*

syntonic (sĭn-tŏn′ĭk) Pert. to a personality characterized by an even temperament, a normal emotional responsiveness to life situations; the opposite of schizoid. SEE: *syntone.*

syntonin (sĭn′tō-nĭn) An acid albumin formed by the action of dilute hydrochloric acid on muscle during gastric digestion.

syntrophism (sĭn′trŏf-ĭzm) [″ + *trophe,* nourishment, + *-ismos,* condition] Stimulation of an organism to grow by mixing with or through the closeness of another strain.

syntrophoblast (sĭn″trō′fō-blast″) [*syn-* + *trophoblast*] The outer syncytial layer of the trophoblast. It comes into an intimate relationship with the uterine endometrium, with which it establishes nutrient relationships. SEE: *trophoblast.*

syntropy (sĭn′trō-pē) [″ + *trope,* a turn] Turning or pointing in the same direction. **syntropic,** *adj.*

synucleinopathy (si-nook″lē-ĭn-op′ă-thē) Any degenerative disease of the central nervous system in which there is an excessive accumulation of alpha-synuclein (a brain protein) in the neurons. The synucleinopathies include Parkinson disease, dementia with Lewy bodies, and multiple system atrophy.

synulosis (sĭn″ū-lō′sĭs) [Gr. *synoulosis*] The formulation of scar tissue. **synulotic,** *adj.*

syphilid(e) (sĭf″ĭl-ĭd) *pl.* **syphilides** [Fr.] A skin eruption caused by secondary syphilis.

syphilis (sĭf′ĭ-lĭs) [*Syphilis,* a shepherd having the disease in a Latin poem] A multistage infection caused by the spirochete *Treponema pallidum.* The disease is typically transmitted sexually, although a small number of congenital infections occur during pregnancy. In the U.S., the incidence of syphilis fluctuates from year to year and decade to decade. In 2009, 13,997 cases were reported in the U.S., a rate of 4.6 per 100,000. **syphilitic** (sĭf″ĭ-lit′ik), *adj.* SYN: *lues.* SEE: illus.; *Standard Precautions Appendix.*

Syphilis is typically passed from person to person by direct contact with skin or mucous membranes. Spirochetes readily penetrate skin and disseminate from the initial site of inoculation to regional lymph nodes, the bloodstream, and multiple other sites, including the central nervous system (CNS). After an incubation period of 10 days to 2 months, a papule appears on the skin that develops into a painless ulcer (chancre) characteristic of the *primary stage* of infection. Chancres and other syphilitic skin lesions are highly infectious. The genitals are the most common site of primary infection and formation of chancres although chancres

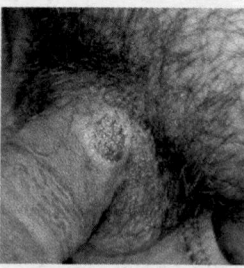

Courtesy of Dr. Henry Foong

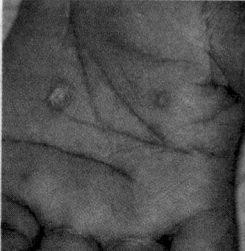

SYPHILIS

Courtesy of Dr. Art. Huntley

may appear on other points of contact, e.g., the lips, mouth, anus, or rectum.

Chancres usually disappear within 3 to 6 weeks even without treatment. Within a few days to several months, the *secondary stage* appears: a widespread body rash, often with systemic symptoms, e.g., fever, headache, generalized lymph node swelling, nausea, vomiting, weight loss, and malaise. Highly infectious, moist, broad, pink or grayish white papules may appear in the perineum (condyloma latum), along with shallow ulcers in the mouth (mucous patches). Hair loss, usually temporary, may also occur, and the nails may become brittle and pitted. If the disease is not eradicated with antibiotics, it establishes latent infection that may cause multiple destructive changes in many organ systems years later.

In the latent (formerly called *tertiary stage*), tissue destruction occurs in the aorta, the CNS, bone, and skin. The consequences include aortic aneurysm, meningitis, sensory and gait disturbances, dementia, and optic atrophy.

SEROLOGICAL TESTS FOR SYPHILIS: The common laboratory tests for syphilis lack optimal sensitivity or specificity. Screening is usually performed with the nontreponemal rapid plasma reagin test (RPR) or the Venereal Disease Research Laboratory test (VDRL); either test may yield inaccurate results. Both tests become reactive about 1 to 2 weeks after initial infection. If either test result is positive, a confirmatory test is done: (1) by identifying the responsible bacterium, *T. pallidum* on dark-field examination of material from a genital lesion; (2) with the microhemagglutination assay for antibody to *T. pallidum* (MHA-TP); or (3) with the fluorescent treponemal antibody absorption test (FHA-ABS). Two-stage testing increases the likelihood of obtaining an accurate diagnosis.

⚠ Those diagnosed with syphilis may have other STDs, esp. HIV infection. Public health experts recommend testing everyone with either of these diseases for the other one and for other STDs (gonorrhea, Chlamydia, or trichomoniasis).

TREATMENT: Intravenous or long-acting intramuscular preparations of penicillin are typically given to patients with syphilis. The duration of treatment varies depending on the stage of the disease and on whether there are comorbid illnesses, e.g., HIV infection, or complications, e.g., evidence of neurosyphilis. Doxycycline or tetracycline may be substituted in nonpregnant patients who are allergic to penicillin although, because of potential bacterial resistance, patients allergic to penicillin should be considered candidates for desensitization. Pregnant patients are not given tetracycline or doxycycline because they discolor primary teeth in the infant.

PATIENT CARE: The patient is taught about the illness and the importance of locating all sexual contacts, treatment, and the need for follow-up care. The patient should avoid sexual contact with anyone until the full course of therapy has been completed, including previous partners who have not received adequate evaluation and treatment, if indicated, for syphilis. Contact precautions are instituted from the time the disease is suspected until 24 hr after initiation of proper antibiotic therapy and whenever draining lesions are present. Standard precautions apply. The patient is informed about safe sex practices and consistent condom use to prevent infection with syphilis and other STDs. Pregnant patients are screened for syphilis to prevent prenatal transmission. Rape victims are tested at the time of the attack and again 1 to 2 weeks later. All cases of syphilis must be reported to local public health authorities by both health care providers and laboratories. SEE: *Standard Precautions Appendix.*

cardiovascular s. Tertiary syphilis involving the heart and great blood vessels, esp. the aorta. Saccular aneurysms of the aorta and aortic insufficiency frequently result.

congenital s. Syphilis transmitted from the mother to the fetus in utero. Transplacental fetal infection may occur if a pregnant woman is not treated by the 18th week of gestation or contracts the disease later in pregnancy. In the U.S. in 2000, 529 cases of congenital syphilis were reported. SYN: *prenatal s.* SEE: *Nursing Diagnoses Appendix.*

endemic s. Chronic, nonvenereal syphilis infection of childhood. It is characterized in its early stages by mucocutaneous or membrane lesions. Later, gummas of bone and skin occur. Penicillin is the treatment of choice.

extragenital s. Syphilis in which the primary chancre is located elsewhere than on genital organs.

latent s. The phase of syphilis during which symptoms are absent and the disease can be diagnosed only by serological tests.

meningovascular s. A form of neurosyphilis in which the meninges and vascular structures of the brain and spinal cord are involved. It may be localized or general. SYN: *meningovascular neurosyphilis.*

prenatal s. Congenital **s.**

serological tests for s. SEE: *serological tests for syphilis.*

tertiary s. The third and most advanced stage of syphilis.

syphilitic (sĭf″ĭ-lit′ik) [*syphilis* + *-itic*] **1.** Pert. to or infected with syphilis. **2.** A person infected with syphilis.

syphilitic macule SEE: under *macule.*

syphiloderm, syphiloderma (sĭf′ĭl-ō-dĕrm″, sĭf″ĭl-ō-dĕr′mă) [″ + Gr. *derma*, skin] A syphilitic cutaneous disorder.

syphiloid (sĭf′ĭ-loyd) [″ + Gr. *eidos*, form, shape] Resembling syphilis.

syphilology (sĭf″ĭl-ŏl′ō-jē) The study of syphilis and its treatment.

syphiloma (sĭf″ĭl-ō′mă) [″ + Gr. *oma*, tumor] A syphilitic tumor; a gumma.

syphilomania (sĭf″ĭl-ō-mā′nē-ă) [″ + Gr. *mania*, madness] Syphilophobia (1).

syphilophobia (sĭf″ĭl-ō-fō′bē-ă) [″ + Gr. *phobos*, fear] **1.** A morbid fear of syphilis. SYN: *syphilomania.* **2.** A delusion of having syphilis. **syphilophobic** (-fō′bĭk), *adj.*

syr (sēr, sĭr) [L., *syrupus*] Syrup.

Syrian rue (sēr′ē-ăn roo) The common name for the plant, *Peganum harmala*, whose seeds are brewed in some cultures to make a tea with hallucinogenic properties. Its seeds contain harmaline alkaloids (harmine, harmaline and tetrahydroharmine) which are members of the class of chemicals known as beta-carboline alkaloids. They increase levels of serotonin in the central and peripheral nervous systems.

syrigmus (sĭr-ĭg′mŭs) [Gr. *syrigmos*, a whistle] An infrequently used synonym for tinnitus.

syringadenoma (sĭr-ĭng″ă-dē-nō′mă) [Gr. *syrinx*, pipe, + *aden*, gland, + *oma*, tumor] Tumor of a sweat gland.

syringe (sĭ-rinj′, sĭr′inj) [Gr. *syrinx*, pipe] **1.** An instrument for injecting fluids into cavities, tissues, or vessels. SEE: illus. **2.** To wash out or introduce fluid with a syringe.

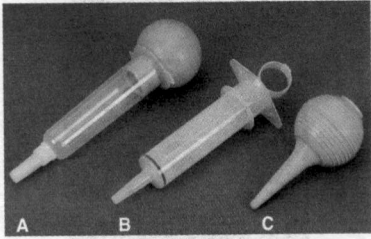

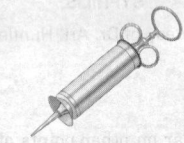

SYRINGES

A. plastic; B. piston; C. rubber bulb; D. metallic.

air s. A syringe on a dental unit that delivers compressed air, water, or both through a fine nozzle to clear or dry an area or to evacuate debris from an operative field.

⚠ Use of high pressure may injure the tissues.

hand s. A hollow rubber bulb that is fitted to a nozzle and delivers air or fluid when squeezed; commonly called a bulb syringe.

hypodermic s. A syringe, fitted with a needle, used to administer drugs subcutaneously.

oral s. A syringe made of plastic or glass. It is not fitted with a needle but is graduated and is used to dispense liquid medication to children. The tip is constructed to prevent its breaking in the child's mouth. An oral syringe may also be used to deliver fluids to impaired patients with an intact swallowing mechanism.

water s. In dentistry, a syringe for delivering water spray to a localized area. The flow, pressure, and temperature are controlled.

syringectomy (sĭr″ĭn-jĕk′tō-mē) [″ + *ektome*, excision] Removal of the walls of a fistula.

syringe exchange program ABBR: SEP. Needle exchange program.

syringocarcinoma (sĭ-rĭng″gō-kăr″sĭ-nō′mă) [″ + *karkinos*, crab, + *oma*, tumor] Carcinoma of a sweat gland.

syringocele (sĭr-ĭn′gō-sēl) [″ + *koilia*, cavity] 1. The central canal of the myelon or spinal cord. 2. A form of meningomyelocele that contains a cavity in the ectopic spinal cord.

syringocystadenoma (sĭr-ĭn″gō-sĭs″tă-dĕ-nō′mă) [″ + *kystis*, bladder, sac, + *aden*, gland, + *oma*, tumor] Adenoma of the sweat glands, characterized by tiny, hard, papular formations.

syringocystoma (sĭr-ĭn″gō-sĭs-tō′mă) [″ + ″ + *oma*, tumor] A cystic tumor arising in ducts of the sweat gland.

syringoencephalomyelia (sĭ-rĭng″gō-ĕn-sĕf″ă-lō-mī-ē′lē-ă) [″ + *enkephalos*, brain, + *myelos*, marrow] A condition of cavities in the brain and spinal cord.

syringoid (sĭr-ĭn′goyd) [Gr. *syrinx*, pipe, + *eidos*, form, shape] Resembling a tube; fistulous.

syringoma (sĭr″ĭn-gō′mă) [″ + *oma*, tumor] A tumor of the sweat glands.

syringomeningocele (sĭr-ĭn″gō-mĕn-ĭn′gō-sēl) [″ + *meninx*, membrane, + *kele*, tumor, swelling] A meningocele similar to a syringomyelocele.

syringomyelia (sĭr-ĭn″gō-mī-ē′lē-ă) [″ + *myelos*, marrow] A disease of the spinal cord characterized by the development of a cyst or cavities with the cord. It usually begins at the site of a congenital malformation of the cerebellum, but sometimes results from spinal cord trauma, tumors, or after spinal cord infection. SYN: *syringomyelus*. SEE: *Nursing Diagnoses Appendix.*

SYMPTOMS: Depending on the location of the syrinx, there may be pain, sensory losses, paralysis, or autonomic dysfunction.

TREATMENT: Some patients are managed conservatively. Sudden enlargement of a cavity may warrant surgery and decompression of the cavity. Persistent pain may necessitate chordotomy or medullary tractotomy for relief.

syringomyelitis (sĭr-ĭn″gō-mī″ĕ-lī′tĭs) [″ + *myelos*, marrow, + *itis*, inflammation] Inflammation coincident with abnormal dilation of the central canal of the spinal cord.

syringomyelocele (sĭr-ĭn″gō-mī″ĕl-ō-sēl) [″ + ″ + *kele*, tumor, swelling] A form of spina bifida in which the cavity of the projecting portion communicates with the central canal of the spinal cord.

syringomyelus (sĭr-ĭn″gō-mī′ĕl-ŭs) Syringomyelia.

syringopontia (sĭr-ĭn″gō-pŏn′shē-ă) [″ +

L. *pons*, bridge] Cavity formation in the pons varolii similar to syringomyelia.

syringotomy (sĭr″ĭn-gŏt′ō-mē) An operation for incision of a fistula.

syrinx (sĭr′ĭnks) [Gr., pipe] 1. A tube or pipe. 2. A pathological cavity (cyst) in the spinal cord or brain. 3. A fistula.

syrup (sĭr′ŭp) [L. *syrupus*] ABBR: syr. A concentrated solution of sugar in water to which specific medicinal substances are usually added. Syrups usually do not represent a very high percentage of the active drug. Some syrups are used principally to give a pleasant odor and taste to solutions.

system (sĭs′tĕm) [L. *systema*, fr. Gr. *systēma*, a composite whole] An organized grouping of structures, such as a group of cells that perform a particular function (e.g., the mononuclear phagocyte system). Particular systems are listed under the first word. SEE: e.g., *circulatory system; International System of Units; metric system.*

systematic (sĭs″tĕ-măt′ĭk) Pert. to a system or organized according to a system.

systematization (sĭs-tĕm″ă-tī-zā′shŭn) The organization of something according to a plan.

Systematized Nomenclature of Medicine ABBR: SNOMED. A systematized collection of medically useful terms published by the American College of Pathologists. The words in the collection are arranged in various fields to permit coding, computerization, sorting, and retrieval of large amounts of information from medical records.

systematized nomenclature of medicine–clinical terms ABBR: SNOMED-CT. A reference terminology optimized for clinical data retrieval and analysis. Concept definition and manipulation are supported through a set of tools with functionality such as

1. acronym resolution, word completion, term completion, spelling correction, display of the authoritative form of the term entered by the user, and decomposition of unrecognized input;

2. automated classification; and

3. conflict management, detection, and resolution.

systemic (sĭs-tĕm′ĭk) 1. Rel. or pert. to a system. 2. Pert. to the blood flow that leaves the left ventricle to deliver oxygen to the body as distinct from the blood flow that leaves the right ventricle to become oxygenated in the lungs.

systemic capillary leak syndrome A rare disease whose hallmarks are episodes of hypotension associated with extravasation of plasma from the systemic circulation.

systemic inflammatory response syndrome ABBR: SIRS. Any severe illness characterized by a heart rate > 90 beats per min, respirations exceeding 20 breaths per minute, a $PaCO_2$ of less than 32 mm Hg, and a white blood count greater than 12,000 cells/mL or less than 4000 cells/mL (or the presence of more than 10% immature (band) white blood cells. SIRS can begin with any serious illness or injury involving inflammation but is most often associated with systemic infection (sepsis) caused by gram-negative bacteria. SEE: *sepsis; septic* **shock**.

ETIOLOGY: Lipopolysaccharide endotoxins released by gram-negative and gram-positive bacteria bind with lymphocytes and endothelial cells, stimulating a cascade of cytokine release, which produces systemic inflammation of blood vessels, tissues, and organs. Shock develops when cytokines cause vasodilation and increased vascular permeability; SIRS is one of the main causes of multiple organ dysfunction syndrome.

TREATMENT: Treatment for SIRS is focused on treating the primary cause. Multiple antibiotic therapy is required in sepsis. Supportive measures include the use of intravenous fluids and pressors, to support blood pressure, and intensive monitoring and optimization of oxygenation, ventilation, blood pressure, cardiac rhythms, serum electrolytes, and renal function.

systemoid (sĭs'tĕ-moyd) [" + *eidos*, form, shape] **1.** Resembling a system. **2.** Pert. to tumors made up of several types of tissues.

Systems Model Neuman systems model.

system testing The evaluation of the function, performance, and suitability of a computing system. Elements of system testing include assessments of usability, final requirements, volume and stress, security and controls, recovery, documentation procedures, and communications ability among separate locations.

systole (sis'tŏ-lē) [Gr. *systolē*, contraction] Contraction of the chambers of the heart. The myocardial fibers shorten, making the chamber smaller and forcing blood out. In the cardiac cycle, atrial systole precedes ventricular systole, which pumps blood into the aorta and pulmonary artery. **systolic,** *adj.* SEE: *diastole; murmur; presystole.*

    anticipated s. A systole that is aborted because it occurs before the ventricle is filled.

    arterial s. The rebound or recoil of the stretched elastic walls of the arteries following ventricular systole.

    atrial s. The contraction of the atria; it occurs before the contraction of the ventricles. About a fourth of the blood that fills the ventricles is squeezed into them during atrial systole. In atrial fibrillation, the atria beat erratically without a defined contraction, and ventricular filling is impaired. Colloquially, atrial systole is called the "atrial kick."

    electrical s. The total duration of the QRST complex in an electrocardiogram; it occurs just before the mechanical systole.

    premature s. Extrasystole.

    ventricular s. Ventricular contraction.

systolic pressure SEE: under *blood pressure.*

systremma (sĭs-trĕm'ă) [Gr. *systremma*, anything twisted together] A cramp in the calf of the leg, the muscles forming a hard knot.

syzygiology (sĭ-zĭj"ē-ŏl'ō-jē) [" + *logos*, word, reason] The study of interdependence or interrelationship of the whole as opposed to that of isolated functions or separate parts. SEE: *holism.*

syzygium (sĭ-zĭj'ē-ŭm) [Gr. *syzygia*, conjunction] Fusion of two parts or structures without loss of identity of the parts. **syzygial,** *adj.*

syzygy (sĭz'ĭ-jē) Fusion of organs, each remaining distinct.

T

12-step program A form of treatment, used initially by those who abuse alcohol or other substances, that relies on social support, interpersonal motivation, abstinence from the addictive substance, and spirituality. Over 200 self-help organizations employ 12-step principles for recovery. These include compulsions for gambling, hoarding of food, and sex. Ancillary groups have also been created, e.g., Al-Anon and Nar-Anon, for friends and family members of alcoholics and addicts. SEE: *Alateen; Alcoholics Anonymous; Al-Anon; Nar-Anon.*

2,4,5-T $C_8H_5Cl_3O_3$, a widely used herbicide and defoliant against broad-leaved plants (weeds). It is contaminated with the carcinogen dioxin during manufacture. It was one of the components of Agent Orange. SYN: *2,4,5-trichlorophenoxyacetic **acid***. SEE: *Agent Orange.*

T *temperature; time; intraocular tension.*

t, T *temporal;* L. *ter,* three times; *tumor*

T₃ *triiodothyronine.*

T₄ *thyroxine.*

t- *therapy related;* resulting from treatment. It is used in hematology to designate a cancer or leukemia that arises after treatment with cytotoxic drugs or radiation therapy, as in "t-AML" (therapy-related acute myeloid leukemia) or "t-MDS" (therapy-related myelodysplastic syndrome).

T₁/₂, t₁/₂ In nuclear medicine, the symbol of half-life of a radioactive substance.

T-1824 Evans blue.

T1, T2, etc. *first thoracic nerve, second thoracic nerve,* etc.

TA *Terminologia Anatomica.*

Ta Symbol for the element tantalum.

tabanid (tăb′ă-nĭd) [L. *tabanus,* horsefly] A member of the dipterous family Tabanidae.

Tabanidae (tă-băn′ĭ-dē) [L. *tabanus,* horsefly] A family of insects belonging to the order Diptera. It includes horseflies, gadflies, deer flies, and mango flies, all bloodsucking insects that attack humans and other warm-blooded animals. These flies are of medical importance because they are vectors of the filarial worm *Loa loa,* tularemia, and other diseases.

Tabanus (tă-bā′nŭs) [L., horsefly] A genus of flies of the family Tabanidae.

tabardillo (tăb″ăr-dē′lyō) [Sp.] An epidemic louse-borne typhus fever occurring in parts of Mexico. SEE: *typhus.*

tabella (tă-bĕl′ă) *pl.* **tabellae** [L., tablet] A medicated mass of material formed into a small disk. SEE: *lozenge; tablet; troche.*

tabes (tā′bēz″) [L. *tabes,* melting, wasting away] A gradual, progressive wasting in any chronic disease.

t. dorsalis A form of neurosyphilis in which the dorsal roots of sensory nerves are damaged by inflammation. It causes problems in coordinating muscles for voluntary movement and ambulation, e.g., a staggering gait, absence of deep tendon reflexes at the ankles, and loss of pain in the lower extremities, interrupted occasionally by flashes of sharp pain (lightning pains). Tabes is frequently seen with the other forms of neurosyphilis, meningitis, and dementia. Physical therapy and teaching are needed to reduce the risk of falls. Penicillin G is the treatment of choice; for those allergic to penicillin, tetracyclines are used. SYN: *locomotor ataxia.* SEE: *syphilis.*

t. ergotica Tabes resulting from the use of ergot.

t. mesenterica Emaciation and malnutrition caused by engorgement and tubercular degeneration of the mesenteric glands.

tabetic (tă-bet′ik) [*tabes*] Pert. to or afflicted with tabes.

tablature (tăb′lă-chŭr) The structure of a cranial bone that consists of outer and inner layers of compact bone, the diploe.

table (tā′bl) [L. *tabula,* board] **1.** A flat-topped structure, as an operating table. **2.** A thin, flat plate, as of bone.

life t. A statistical portrait of the life expectancy of individuals in a population, based on known mortality data for different ages, races, and sexes.

mortality t. A compilation of the death rates of individuals by specific demographic characteristics (e.g., age, race, sex) or specific health status (e.g., accidental death, death during childbirth, or death caused by cancer).

periodic t. A chart with the chemical elements arranged by their atomic numbers. SEE: *periodic law.*

t. of the skull The inner and outer layers of a cranial bone, made of compact bone. These are separated by diploe, spongy bone that contains red bone marrow.

tilt t. A table that can be inclined or tipped over while a person is strapped to it. It is used to study patients with

table 2274 **tachycardia**

loss of consciousness of unknown cause.

water t. The level at which rock or any underground stratum is saturated with water. This overlies an impervious stratum.

tablespoon (tā'bl-spoon) ABBR: Tbs. A rough measure, equal approx. to 15 mL of fluid. To administer a tablespoon of medicine, 15 mL of the substance should be given.

tablet (tăb'lĕt) [Fr. *tablete,* a small table] A small, disklike mass of medicinal powder.

buccal t. A tablet designed to be placed in the mouth and held between the cheek and gum until dissolved and absorbed through the buccal mucosa.

coated t. A type of tablet usually made by enclosing a drug in a protective shell.

compressed t. A tablet made by forcibly compressing powdered medications into the desired shape to decrease their solubility. These tablets may be very hard and not readily soluble.

dispensing t. A tablet that contains a clinically effective large amount of an active drug.

enteric-coated t. A tablet that resists digestion in gastric acid.

fluoride t. A tablet of sodium fluoride for prevention of dental caries and osteoporosis.

hypodermic t. A tablet used to form injectable solutions.

sublingual t. A small, flat, oval tablet placed beneath the tongue to permit direct absorption of the active substance.

t. triturate A tablet made by moistening the medication mixed with a powdered lactose or sucrose and then molding it into shape and allowing the liquid to evaporate. It usually disintegrates readily.

tabletop drill (tā'bĕl-top″) A simulation of an emergency response to a mass casualty in which personnel meet to discuss their ideas but do not physically deploy staff and equipment.

tablet splitting Dividing a pill into two (or more) parts to save money, make a pill easier to swallow, or create a dose that is not marketed by the manufacturer.

⚠ The FDA recommends against this practice because it may produce unequal or nonstandardized medication doses.

taboo, tabu (tă-boo') [Tongan (Polynesian) *tabu, tapu,* inviolable] An act, object, or social custom separated or set aside as being sacred or profane, thus forbidden for general use. SEE: *proscription.*

tabular (tăb'ū-lăr) [L. *tabula,* board]

1. Resembling a table. **2.** Set up in columns, as a tabulation.

tabun (tă'bŭn) Ethyl *N*-dimethylphosphoramidocyanidate; an organophosphate chemical used primarily as a pesticide. It has been used in chemical warfare as a toxic nerve gas.

tache (tŏsh) [Fr., spot] A colored spot or macule on the skin, as a freckle.

tachistoscope (tă-kĭs'tō-skōp) [Gr. *tachistos,* swiftest, + *skopein,* to view] A device used to determine the speed of visual perception. The time of exposure can be adjusted so that the length of time needed for detection of the viewed object can be measured.

tacho- [Gr. *takhos,* speed fr. *takhys,* swift] Prefix meaning *speed.* SEE: *tachy-.*

tachy- [Gr. *takhys,* swift] Prefix meaning *swift, rapid.* SEE: *tacho-.*

tachyarrhythmia (tăk″ē-ă-rĭth'mē-ă) [Gr. *tachys,* swift, + *a,* not, + *rhythmos,* rhythm] Any cardiac rhythm disturbance in which the heart rate exceeds 100 beats per minute (bpm).

tachybrady syndrome Sick sinus syndrome.

tachycardia (tak″ē-kard'ē-ă) [*tachy-* + *-cardia*] An abnormally rapid heart rate, greater than 100 beats per minute (bpm) in adults. SYN: *tachyrhythmia (1).*

atrial t. A rapid regular heart rate arising from an irritable focus in the atria, with a rate of more than 100 bpm but less than 220 bpm.

atrioventricular nodal reentrant t. ABBR: AVNRT. The most common supraventricular tachycardia, resulting from abnormal conduction of electrical impulses through a self-sustaining circuit in the atrioventricular node. It occurs more often in women than in men, often in their twenties. The heart rate is usually between 150 and 250 bpm. SYN: *junctional reciprocating t.* SEE: *re-entry.*

ectopic t. A rapid heartbeat caused by stimuli arising from outside the sinoatrial node.

fetal t. A fetal heart rate faster than 160 bpm that persists throughout one 10-min period.

junctional reciprocating t. Atrioventricular nodal reentrant **t.**

multifocal atrial t. ABBR: MAT. A cardiac arrhythmia sometimes confused with atrial fibrillation, because the heart rate is greater than 100 bpm and the ventricular response is irregular. However, in MAT P waves are clearly visible on the electrocardiogram, and they have at least three distinct shapes. MAT is seen most often in patients with poorly compensated chronic obstructive lung disease. It may resolve with management of the underlying respiratory problem.

narrow complex t. Tachycardia in which the duration of the QRS complex is less than 0.12 seconds. Most narrow complex tachycardias originate from a pacemaker above the ventricles and are therefore supraventricular tachycardias.

nodal t. Tachycardia resulting from a focus in the atrioventricular node. It may be the result of digitalis therapy.

pacemaker-mediated t. A problem of dual-chamber cardiac pacemakers in which tachycardia develops due to improper functioning of the pacemaker. This can be treated by reprogramming the electronic signals to the atrium.

paroxysmal atrial t. A term formerly used for paroxysmal supraventricular tachycardia.

paroxysmal junctional t. Tachycardia due to increased activity of the AV junction. The rate is usually from 120 to 180 bpm.

paroxysmal supraventricular t. ABBR: PSVT. A sporadic arrhythmia with an atrial rate that is usually 160 to 200 bpm. It originates above the bundle of His, and typically appears on the surface electrocardiogram as a rapid, narrow-complex tachycardia. This relatively common arrhythmia may revert to sinus rhythm with rest, sedation, vagal maneuvers, or drug therapy.

paroxysmal ventricular t. Ventricular tachycardia beginning and ending suddenly.

polymorphic ventricular t. Torsade de pointes.

reflex t. Tachycardia resulting from stimuli outside the heart, reflexly accelerating the heart rate or depressing vagal tone.

sinus t. A rapid heart rate (over 100 bpm) originating in the sinoatrial node. It may be caused by fevers, exercise, dehydration, bleeding, caffeine, alcohol, nicotine, stimulant drugs (such as epinephrine, aminophylline), or thyrotoxicosis.
TREATMENT: The underlying cause is addressed.

supraventricular t. ABBR: SVT. A rapid, regular tachycardia in which the pacemaker is found in the sinus node, the atria, or the atrioventricular junction, i.e., above the ventricles. SEE: *paroxysmal supraventricular t.*

ventricular t. ABBR: VT. Three or more consecutive ventricular ectopic complexes (duration greater than 120 msec) occurring at a rate of 100 to 250 bpm. Although nonsustained VT may occasionally be well tolerated, it often arises in hearts that have suffered ischemic damage or cardiomyopathic degeneration and may be a cause of sud-

den death. Nonsustained VT lasts less than 30 sec. Sustained VT lasts more than 30 sec and is much more likely to produce loss of consciousness or other life-threatening symptoms.
TREATMENT: The acute treatment of sustained VT is outlined in advanced life support protocols but may include the administration of lidocaine or other antiarrhythmic drugs, cardioversion, or defibrillation. Chronic, recurring VT may be treated with sotalol, amiodarone, or implantable cardioverter-defibrillators.

wide complex t. ABBR: WCT. An arrhythmia with a sustained rate of more than 100 bpm in which the surface electrocardiogram reveals QRS complexes lasting at least 120 msec. WCT is usually caused by ventricular tachycardia, although it may occasionally result from a supraventricular tachycardia whose conduction through the ventricles produces an abnormally wide QRS complex.

tachycardia-bradycardia syndrome One of several forms of sick sinus syndrome, in which the heart alternately beats very rapidly or very slowly. SEE: *sick sinus syndrome.*

tachycardiac (tăk″ē-kard′ē-ak″) [Gr. *tachys,* swift, + *kardia,* heart] Pert. to or afflicted with tachycardia.

tachygastria (tăk″ē-găs′trē-ă) Increased rate of contractions of the stomach.

tachykinin (tăk″kī′nĭn) [″ + ″] ABBR: TK. Any of a large family of peptides that function as neurotransmitters in the central and peripheral nervous systems. They have extraneuronal activity in other body tissues. Their diverse biological actions are mediated through cellular G proteins.

tachyphylaxis (tăk″ē-fĭ-lăk′sĭs) [″ + *phylaxis,* protection] **1.** Rapid immunization to a toxic dose of a substance by previously injecting tiny doses of the same substance. **2.** Diminishing responsiveness to a drug after routine usage.

tachysterol (tă-kĭs′tĕ-rōl) One of the isomers of ergosterol. It is a compound related to vitamin D.

tachysystole (tak″ĭ-sĭs′tŏ-lē) [*tachy-* + *systole*] An abnormally rapid rate of muscle contraction.

tactical combat casualty care SEE: under *care.*

tactical emergency medical services ABBR: TEMS. Tactical emergency medical support.

tactical medicine SEE: under *medicine.*

tactile (tak′tĭl, tĭl″) [L. *tactilis,* tangible, touchable] Perceptible to the touch. SYN: *tactual.*

tactile defensiveness Any of the behaviors such as avoidance or withdrawal in response to being touched by another person. These defensive reactions are seen most often in children with autism or related disorders.

tactile system That portion of the nervous system concerned with the sensation of touch. It includes sensory nerve endings (Meissner corpuscles, Merkel tactile disks, hair-root endings), afferent nerve fibers, conducting pathways in the cord and brain, and the sensory area of the parietal lobe of the cerebral cortex.

taction (tăk′shŭn) [L. *tactio*] **1.** The sense of touch. **2.** Touching.

tactual (tăk′tū-ăl) [L. *tactus,* touch] Tactile.

tactus (tăk′tŭs) [L.] Touch (1).

taen-, taeni-, taenio-, ten-, teni- [Gr. *tainia,* ribbon, band] Prefixes meaning *tapeworm.*

Taenia (tē′nē-ă) [L. *taenia* fr Gr. *tainia,* tape, ribbon] A genus of parasitic tapeworms belonging to the class Cestoda, phylum Platyhelminthes. They are elongated ribbon-like worms consisting of a scolex, usually with suckers and perhaps hooks, and a chain of segments (proglottids). Adults live as intestinal parasites of vertebrates; larvae parasitize both vertebrates and invertebrates, which are intermediate hosts. SEE: *taeniasis; tapeworm.*

    T. saginata A species whose larvae live in cattle. The adult worm lives in the small intestine of humans, who acquire it by eating insufficiently cooked beef infested with the encysted larval form (cysticercus or bladderworm). Adult worms may reach a length of 15 to 20 ft (4.6 to 6.1 m) or longer. SYN: *beef* **tapeworm**; *unarmed* **tapeworm**. SEE: illus.

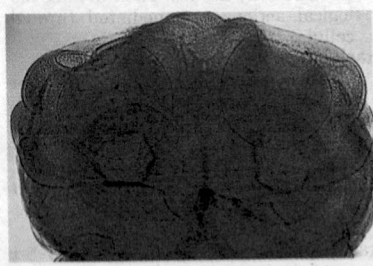

TAENIA SAGINATA

beef tapeworm (orig. mag. ×100)

    T. solium A species whose larvae live in hogs; its scolex possesses a row of hooks about the rostellum. The adult worm lives in the small intestine of humans, who acquire it by eating insufficiently cooked pork. Adult worms may take up residence in the intestine, depriving the host of food. Larval forms of *T. solium* may encyst in the brain, resulting in seizures. In some underdeveloped nations the onset of seizures in adulthood is presumed to be the

result of neurocysticercosis until proved otherwise. The infection is treated with niclosamide or praziquantel. SYN: *armed* **tapeworm**; *pork* **tapeworm**. SEE: illus.

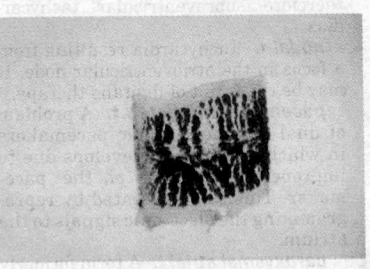

TAENIA SOLIUM

(Orig. mag. ×5)

taenia (tē′nē-ă) [L., tape] **1.** A flat band or strip of soft tissue. **2.** A tapeworm of the genus *Taenia.* SYN: *tenia.*

    t. coli The three bands of smooth muscle into which the longitudinal muscle layer of the colon is gathered. They are taenia mesocolica (mesenteric insertion), taenia libera (opposite mesocolic band), and taenia omentalis (at place of attachment of omentum to transverse colon).

taeniasis (tē-nī′ă-sĭs) [″ + Gr. *-iasis,* condition] Infestation with tapeworms of the genus *Taenia.* SEE: *tapeworm.*

tag (tăg) **1.** A small polyp or growth. **2.** A label or tracer; or the application of a label or tracer.

    hemorrhoidal t. An anal skin tag resulting from uneven postsurgical healing, spontaneous resolution of a previously enlarged external hemorrhoid, secondary to anal skin irritation, or external to an anal fissure. SEE: *sentinel pile.*

    radioactive t. A radioactive isotope that is incorporated into a chemical or organic material to allow its detection in metabolic or chemical processes. SYN: *radiolabel.*

    sentinel t. Sentinel pile.

    skin t. A small outgrowth of skin, usually occurring on the neck, axilla, and groin. SEE: illus.; *acrochordon.*

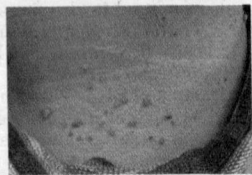

SKIN TAGS

tagging Introduction of a radioactive isotope into a molecule in order to distinguish the molecule from others without that tag. SYN: *labeling*.

Tahyna virus SEE: under *virus*.

tai chi (tī-chē) A traditional Chinese martial art in which a series of slow, controlled movements are made through various postures designed to develop flexibility, balance, strength, relaxation, and mental concentration. Tai chi has been used as a therapeutic exercise by the young and the old, hemophiliacs, people with fibromyalgia, and people recovering from brain injuries.

taijin kyofusho (tī-jēn-kyō-foo-shō) [Jap., literally, fear of interpersonal relationships disorder] ABBR: TKS. A culture-bound syndrome in Japan in which a person becomes fearful that he or she is offensive to others. In the West it is considered a form of social anxiety disorder.

tail (tāl) **1.** The long end of a structure, such as the extremity of the spinal column or the final segments of a polypeptide or nucleic acid. SEE: *cauda*. **2.** An uninterrupted extension of the insurance policy period; also called the *extended reporting endorsement*. SEE: *professional liability insurance*.

taint (tānt) [Fr. *teint,* color, tint] **1.** To spoil or cause putrefaction, as in tainted meat. **2.** To contaminate. **tainted,** *adj*.

Takayasu arteritis (ta″kă-ya′soo) [Michishige Takayasu, Japanese physician, 1872–1938] A rare vasculitis of the aorta and its branches, marked by inflammatory changes in the large arteries. Blood flow through those arteries is limited, esp. to the arms or head of affected persons. The disease, which is found most often in young women of Japanese descent, produces symptoms such as dizziness or arm claudication. Those affected usually have markedly reduced blood pressures or pulses in one or both arms. SYN: *pulseless disease*.

take To be effective, as in administering a vaccine; or to be successful in grafting skin or transplanting an organ.

take-down (tāk′down″) Undoing or reversal of a previous surgical procedure.

talar (tā′lăr) [L. *talaris,* of the ankle] Pert. to the talus, the ankle.

talar tilt test An orthopedic test used to determine the collateral stability of the ankle joint. The amount of laxity in the affected ankle is determined relative to the laxity in the uninvolved limb.

Eversion talar tilt test. The foot and ankle are maintained in the neutral position. The examiner stabilizes the distal lower leg while cupping the calcaneus with the opposite hand. The talus is then rolled outward to eversion.

This test checks the integrity of the deltoid ligament group of the medial ankle, esp. the tibiocalcaneal and tibionavicular ligaments. The mechanical block formed by the lateral malleolus limits the amount of eversion.

Inversion talar tilt test. The foot and ankle are maintained in the neutral position. The examiner stabilizes the distal lower leg while cupping the calcaneus with the opposite hand. The talus is then rolled inward to inversion.

This test checks the integrity of the lateral ligaments, specifically the calcaneofibular, anterior talofibular, and posterior talofibular ligaments (in order of involvement). The anterior talofibular ligament can be isolated through the use of the anterior drawer test.

talc (tălk) [Persian *talk*] $Mg_3Si_4O_{10}(OH)_2$, native hydrous magnesium silicate, a soft, soapy powder used, for example, in pleurodesis. SYN: *talcum*.

⚠ Exposure to talc in the workplace can result in interstitial lung disease. Those who work with talc or other particulates should wear masks that limit respiratory exposure to fine dust particles.

talcosis (tăl-kō′sĭs) [*talc* + *-osis*] Any disease caused by the inhalation or injection of talc. The lungs are often affected.

talcum (tălk′ŭm) [L.] Talc.

talipes (tal′ĭ-pēz″) [*talus* + *pes*] Any of several deformities of the foot, esp. those occurring congenitally. It may also be a nontraumatic deviation of the foot in the direction of one or two of the four lines of movement.

t. arcuatus Talipes in which there is an exaggerated medial arch of the foot. SYN: *pes cavus; t. cavus*.

t. calcaneus Talipes in which the foot is dorsiflexed and the heel alone touches the ground. It causes the patient to walk on the inner side of the heel and often follows infantile paralysis of the calf muscles.

t. cavus T. arcuatus.

t. equinovarus A combination of talipes equinus and talipes valgus. SYN: *clubfoot*.

t. equinus Talipes in which the foot is plantar flexed and the person walks on the toes.

t. percavus Talipes in which there is excessive plantar curvature.

t. valgus Talipes in which the heel and foot are turned outward. SEE: *valgus*.

t. varus Talipes in which the heel is turned inward from the midline of the leg. SEE: *varus*.

talking device Any assistive technology that uses speech-generated software, a telephone terminal device, or other symbols such as braille to read or convey written text to people who are blind or have impaired vision.

tallow (tăl′ō) Fat obtained from suet, the solid fat of certain ruminants.

talocalcaneal (tā″lō-kăl-kā′nē-ăl) [″ + *calcaneus,* heel bone] Pert. to the talus and calcaneus.

talocrural (tā″lō-kroo′răl) [″ + *crus,* leg] Pert. to the talus and leg bones.

talofibular (tā″lō-fĭb′ū-lăr) [″ + *fibula,* pin] Pert. to the talus and fibula.

talon (tăl′ŏn) [L.] The claw of a bird of prey.

     t. noir   Minute black areas on the heels (or less often the toes or hands) caused by repetitive injuries that produce hemorrhage into the skin.

talonid (tăl′ō-nĭd) The crushing part or region of a back (lower molar) tooth.

talus (tā′lŭs) *pl.* **tali** [L., ankle] The ankle bone. It is an irregular, stubby cylinder and articulates with the tibia, fibula, calcaneus, and navicular bone. In front its head has a broad, rounded articular surface that meets the navicular bone. The body of the talus has a saddle-shaped articular surface on the top that meets the distal articular end of the tibia to form the main ankle joint; the outer side of the talus has a broad, convex articular surface that meets the lateral malleolus of the distal end of the fibula. On the bottom of the head and the body of the talus, there are two separate convex articular surfaces that meet the calcaneus (heel) bone. It was formerly called astragalus.

tambour (tăm-boor′) [Fr., drum] A shallow, drum-shaped appliance used in registering information such as changes in rate or intensity of pulse, respiration, or arterial blood pressure.

Tamm-Horsfall mucoprotein (tăm′hors′făl) [Igor Tamm, Russian-born U.S. virologist, 1922–1971; Frank L. Horsfall, Jr., U.S. physician, 1906–1971] A normal mucoprotein in the urine, produced by the ascending limb of the loop of Henle. When this protein is concentrated at low pH, it forms gel, which may protect the kidney from infection by bacteria. SYN: *uromodulin.*

tamoxifen citrate (tă-mŏks′ĭ-fĕn) An antiestrogenic drug used in treating and preventing breast cancer.

tampon (tam′pon″) [Fr. *ta(m)p(i)on,* plug] A roll or pack made of absorbent materials used to stop bleeding, absorb secretions, or obtain specimens from a wound or body cavity.

     menstrual t.   An absorbent material shaped and prepared to provide a hygienic means of absorbing menstrual fluid in the vagina. A cord is attached and remains outside the vagina to facilitate removal. These tampons are made for self-insertion. Washing hands before insertion and after removal as well as changing tampons often guards against toxic shock syndrome. SEE: *menstruation; sanitary napkin.*

     Mikulicz t.   SEE: under *Mikulicz-Radecki, Johann von.*

     nasal t.   A tampon used to compress bleeding blood vessels in the nose.

tamponade, tamponage (tam″pŏ-nād′, tam′pŏ-nŏj) [Fr., *tampon,* rag (used as a) plug] **1.** The act of using a tampon. SYN: *tamponing; tamponment.* **2.** The pathological or intentional compression of a part.

     balloon t.   The application of pressure against a part of the body with an inflatable balloon, typically to stop blood loss. Balloon tamponade has been used to stop bleeding from esophageal varices, ectopic pregnancies, the post-partum uterus, the liver (as after gunshot wounds), damaged blood vessels.

     cardiac t.   A life-threatening condition in which elevated pressures within the pericardium impair the filling of the heart during diastole.

Cardiac tamponade may result from injuries to the heart or great vessels, from cardiac rupture, or from other conditions that produce large pericardial effusions. If fluid accumulates rapidly, as little as 150 mL can impair the filling of the heart. Slow accumulation, as in pericardial effusion associated with cancer, may not produce immediate signs and symptoms because the fibrous wall of the pericardial sac can gradually stretch to accommodate as much as 1 to 2 L of fluid.

ETIOLOGY: Cardiac tamponade may be idiopathic (Dressler syndrome) or may result from any of the following causes: effusion (in cancer, bacterial infections, tuberculosis, and, rarely, acute rheumatic fever); hemorrhage from trauma (as from gunshot or stab wounds of the chest, perforation by catheter during cardiac or central venous catheterization, or after cardiac surgery); hemorrhage from nontraumatic causes (as from rupture of the heart or great vessels, or anticoagulant therapy in a patient with pericarditis); viral, postirradiation, or idiopathic pericarditis; acute myocardial infarction; chronic renal failure; drug reaction (as from procainamide, hydralazine, minoxidil, isoniazid, penicillin, methysergide, or daunorubicin); or connective tissue disorders, e.g., rheumatoid arthritis, systemic lupus erythematosus, rheumatic fever, vasculitis, and scleroderma. Classic signs of tamponade include persistent hypotension despite fluid boluses, muffled heart sounds, distended jugular veins, and paradoxical pulse (a drop in systolic blood pressure of more than 10 mm Hg on inspiration).

DIAGNOSIS: Cardiac tamponade is suggested by chest radiograph (slightly widened mediastinum and enlargement of the cardiac silhouette), ECG (reduced QRS amplitude, electrical alternans of the P wave, QRS complex, and T wave and generalized ST-segment elevation), and pulmonary artery pressure monitoring (increased right atrial pressure, right ventricular diastolic pressure, and central venous pressure). It is definitively diagnosed with echocardiography, or MRI or CT of the chest.

TREATMENT: Pericardiocentesis (needle aspiration of the pericardial cavity) or surgical creation of a pericardial window dramatically improves systemic arterial pressure and cardiac output. In patients with malignant tamponade, a balloon pericardiotomy (a balloon-aided opening in the pericardium) may be made.

PATIENT CARE: The patient is assessed for a history of disorders that can cause tamponade and for symptoms such as chest pain and dyspnea. Oxygen is administered via nonrebreather mask, and intravenous access is established via one or two large-bore catheters for fluid resuscitation. Airway, breathing, circulation, and level of consciousness are closely monitored.

If the patient is unstable, he or she requires arterial blood gas analysis and hemodynamic monitoring and support. Prescribed inotropic drugs and intravenous solutions maintain the patient's blood pressure, and oxygen and ventilatory support are administered as necessary and prescribed.

Pain is assessed, and appropriate analgesia is provided. The patient is prepared for central line insertion, pericardiocentesis, thoracotomy, or other therapies as indicated; brief explanations of procedures and expected sensations are provided; and the patient is reassured to decrease anxiety. The patient is observed for a decrease in central venous pressure and a rise in blood pressure after treatment, which indicate relief of cardiac compression. If the patient is not acutely ill, he or she is educated about the condition, its cause, and its planned treatment, e.g., by surgery to place a pericardial window. The importance of immediately reporting worsening symptoms is stressed. The patient is followed with repeat echocardiography and chest x-rays as deemed necessary. SYN: *pericardial t.*

nasal balloon t. SEE: *nosebleed* for illus.; *epistaxis.*

nasal t. Compression of nasal blood vessels to stop bleeding. SEE: *epistaxis; nosebleed* for illus.

pericardial t. Cardiac **t.** SEE: illus.

tamponing, tamponment (tăm′pŏn-ĭng, tăm-pŏn′mĕnt) Tamponade.

Tanacetum parthenium (tăn′ă-sē′tŭm păr-thĕn′ē-ŭm) SEE: *feverfew.*

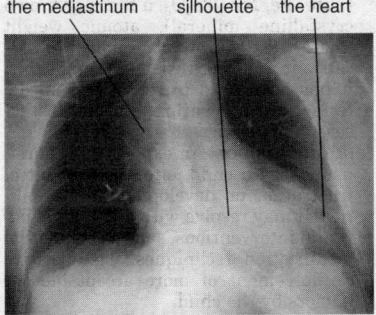

CARDIAC TAMPONADE

Labels: Widening of the mediastinum · Cardiac silhouette · Fluid surrounding the heart

tandem 1. A curved stainless steel tube inserted into the uterine canal during brachytherapy to hold radioactive sources. 2. Any two objects arranged consecutively or working in series with one another.

tandem repeat A short segment of DNA that includes duplicated genetic material.

tang (tăng) 1. A strong taste or flavor. 2. A long, slender projection or prong forming a part of a chisel, file, or knife. 3. In dentistry, an apparatus for joining the rests and retainers to palatal or lingual bars of a denture.

tangential excision (tan-jen′shăl) SEE: under *excision.*

Tannerella (tan″ĕ-rel′ă) A genus of gram-negative, anaerobic, non–spore-forming bacilli (formerly classified as *Bacteroides*).

T. forsythia, Tannerella forsythensis A species found in the periodontal sulcus and associated with periodontitis. SYN: *Bacteroides forsythus.*

tannin (tăn′ĭn) [Fr. *tanin*] 1. An acid found in the bark of certain plants and trees or their products, usually from nutgall. It is found in coffee and to a greater extent in tea. 2. Any of several substances containing tannin.

ACTION/USES: Tannin was formerly used as an astringent, an antidote for various poisons, and a topical hemostatic.

tanning salon A commercial establishment where patrons can expose themselves to ultraviolet light to darken their skin. Because ultraviolet light ages the skin and increases the likelihood of skin cancers, tanning salons are frowned on by dermatologists, cancer specialists, and other health care professionals. SEE: *actinic keratosis; basal cell carcinoma; melanoma; photosensitivity; squamous cell carcinoma.*

tantalum (tant′ă-lŭm) [*Tantalus,* a character in Gr. mythology] SYMB: Ta. A rare metallic element derived from tantalite (Fe, Mn) Ta_2O_6, a black or brown crystalline mineral), atomic weight (mass) 180.947, atomic number 73. Because it is noncorrosive and malleable, it has been used to repair cranial defects, as a wire suture, and in prostheses.

tantrum, temper An explosive outburst, usually by a child, often as a result of frustration or developmental disabilities. It may resolve with a variety of parental interventions, such as behavioral modification techniques, e.g., positive reinforcement of more acceptable behaviors by the child.

¹tap (tap) [Fr. *taper*] **1.** A light blow. **2.** An instrument used for performing a tap. **3.** An instrument used to create an internal thread.

²tap (tap) [Old English *tappian,* to draw off liquid] **1.** To puncture or to empty a cavity of fluid. **2.** Removal or emptying of fluid from a cavity. SEE: *paracentesis; thoracentesis*. **3.** The fluid removed from a cavity.

   spinal t. Lumbar **puncture**.

tape (tāp) **1.** A flexible, narrow strip of linen, cotton, paper, or plastic such as adhesive tape. **2.** To wrap a part with a long bandage made of adhesive or other type of material.

   adhesive t. A fabric, film, or paper, one side of which is coated with an adhesive so that it remains in place when applied to the skin. In general, there are two types of backings for the adhesive material: occlusive and nonocclusive. The former prevents air from going through the backing and the latter does not. The occlusive type increases the possibility of skin irritation, so it is rarely used.

   PATIENT CARE: To prevent skin damage, adhesive tape should be removed by carefully peeling back the tape, following the direction of hair growth while the skin is held taut behind the tape removal edge or alternatively compressing the skin from the tape as it is held on gentle tension. The skin should be checked for irritation. If the adhesive material has irritated the skin, solvents may be used judiciously to assist in removal. Because some patients are allergic to certain adhesive agents, information about this type of allergy should be gathered as part of the history; other varieties of tape may be nonreactive. If the patient is intolerant of all adhesives, alternative bandage applications are used. As an additional measure to prevent skin damage and to increase tape adhesion, tincture of benzoin (or similar) may be applied prior to placing the tape.

taper (tā′pĕr) To decrease in a gradual or progressive fashion the dosage of a medication or the intensity of another form of treatment.

tapetum (tă-pē′tŭm) [L., a carpet] A layer of fibers from the corpus callosum forming the roof and lateral walls of the inferior and posterior horns of the lateral ventricles of the brain. This layer separates the optic radiation from the ventricle and passes to the temporal and occipital lobes.

tapeworm (tāp′wŏrm″) Any of the species of flatworms of the class Cestoda, phylum Platyhelminthes; all are intestinal parasites of humans and other animals. A typical tapeworm consists of a scolex, with hooks and suckers for attachment, and a series of a few to several thousand segments, or proglottids. New proglottids develop at the scolex, so that a worm is actually a linear colony of immature, mature, and gravid proglottids; adult worms range from less than an inch to 50 ft or more, depending on the species. The terminal proglottids, which contain fertilized eggs, break off and pass from the host in the feces. The eggs develop into small, hooked embryos, which, when ingested by the proper intermediate host (usually another vertebrate such as a pig), develop into encysted larvae (cysticerci) in the muscle tissue. Humans acquire tapeworm infestation by eating undercooked meat that contains the cysticerci. SEE: *Diphyllobothrium latum* for illus; *Taenia*.

   Species of medical importance are *Diphyllobothrium latum, Echinococcus granulosus, Hymenolepis nana, Taenia saginata,* and *T. solium*. SEE: *cysticercosis; cysticercus; hydatid; taeniasis*.

   SYMPTOMS: Symptoms are often absent, but abdominal discomfort, bloating, or changes in bowel habits may be present. If tapeworms are very numerous, they may cause intestinal obstruction (but this is rare). Some species of tapeworms may cause severe disease: *Echinococcus* can cause life-threatening cysts in the liver or pericardium; *Taenia solium* can encyst in the brain and cause seizures or strokelike symptoms.

   armed t. Taenia solium.

   beef t. Taenia saginata.

   broad t. Diphyllobothrium latum.

   dog t. 1. Dipylidium caninum. **2. Echinococcus** granulosus.

   dwarf t. Hymenolepis nana.

   fish t. Diphyllobothrium latum.

   heart-shaped t. Diphyllobothrium cordatum

   hydatid t. Echinococcus granulosus.

   mouse t. Hymenolepis nana.

   pork t. Taenia solium.

   rat t. Hymenolepis nana.

   unarmed t. Taenia saginata.

tapotement (tă-pōt′mĕnt) [Fr. *tapoter,*

to drum or tap with the fingers] Percussion (3).

¹tapping (tap′ing) [¹*tap*] Percussion (3).

muscle t. Tapping the skin over the belly of a muscle to recruit more motor units and facilitate contraction. It is usually performed manually over muscles weakened from neurological injury.

²tapping (tap′ing) [²*tap*] The withdrawal of fluid from a body cavity. Examples include paracentesis and thoracentesis.

tar (tar) A dark, viscid mass of complex chemicals obtained by destructive distillation of tobacco, coal, shale, and organic matter, esp. wood from pine and juniper trees.

coal t. A tar produced in the destructive distillation of bituminous coal. It is used as an ingredient in ointments for treating eczema, psoriasis, and other skin diseases.

tarantism (tăr′ăn-tĭzm) [*Taranto*, seaport in southern Italy, + Gr. *-ismos*, condition] A disorder culturally specific to regions of Italy and Northern Africa, marked by stupor, melancholy, and uncontrollable, manic dancing. It is popularly attributed to the bite of the tarantula although some experts believe it to be an example of a mass psychogenic illness. SYN: *tarentism*.

tarantula (tă-răn′tū-lă) A large venomous spider feared by many people; however, its bite is comparable in severity to a bee sting. SEE: *spider **bite***.

Taraxacum officinale (tă-rak′să-kŭm) SEE: *dandelion*.

tardive (tăr′dĭv) [Fr., tardy] Characterized by lateness, esp. pert. to a disease in which the characteristic sign or symptom appears late in the course of the disease. SEE: *tardive **dyskinesia***.

tare (tār) The weight of an empty container. That weight is subtracted from the total weight of the vessel and substance added to it in order to determine the precise weight of the material added to the container.

tared (tărd) A container of known and predetermined tare.

target (tar′gĕt) [Fr. *targette*, small shield] **1.** A structure or organ to which something is directed. **2.** The part of the anode of an x-ray or therapeutic tube in which electrons from the filament or electron gun are focused and x-ray photons are produced. It is usually made of a heavy metal such as tungsten or molybdenum.

tarnish Surface discoloration or reduced luster of metals owing to the effect of corrosive substances or galvanic action. In dental restorations, such action may be enhanced by accumulation of bacterial plaque.

tarsal (tăr′săl) [Gr. *tarsalis*] **1.** Pert. to the tarsus or supporting plate of the eyelid. **2.** Pert. to the ankle or tarsus.

tarsalgia (tăr-săl′jē-ă) [Gr. *tarsos*, a broad, flat surface, + *algos*, pain] Pain in the tarsus or ankle; it may be due to flatfoot, shortening of the Achilles tendon, or other causes.

tarsal tunnel syndrome Neuropathy of the distal portion of the posterior tibial nerve at the ankle caused by chronic pressure on the nerve at the point it passes through the tarsal tunnel. It causes pain in and numbness of the sole of the foot and weakness of the plantar flexion of the toes.

tarsectomy (tar-sĕk′tō-mē) [″ + *ektome*, excision] **1.** Excision of the tarsus or a tarsal bone. **2.** Removal of the tarsal plate of an eyelid.

tarsitis (tăr-sī′tĭs) [″ + *itis*, inflammation] **1.** Inflammation of the tarsus of the foot. **2.** Blepharitis.

tarso-, tars- [Gr. *tarsos*, sole of the foot, ankle, edge of the eyelid] Prefixes meaning *the flat of the foot* or *the edge of the eyelid*.

tarsometatarsal (tăr″sō-mĕt″ă-tăr′săl) [″ + *meta*, between, + *tarsos*, a broad, flat surface] Pert. to the tarsus and the metatarsus.

tarsorrhaphy (tăr-sor′ă-fē) [″ + *rhaphe*, seam, ridge] Blepharorrhaphy.

tarsus (tăr′sŭs) *pl.* **tarsi** [Gr. *tarsos*, a broad, flat surface] **1.** The ankle with its seven bones located between the bones of the lower leg and the metatarsus and forming the proximal portion of the foot. It consists of the calcaneus (os calcis), talus (astragalus), cuboid (os cuboideum), navicular (scaphoid), and first, second, and third cuneiform bones. The talus articulates with the tibia and fibula, the cuboid and cuneiform bones with the metatarsals. SEE: *foot; skeleton;* names of individual bones. **2.** A curved plate of dense white fibrous tissue forming the supporting structure of the eyelid; also called the *tarsal plate*.

tartrate (tăr′trāt) A salt of tartaric acid.

tartrazine (tăr′tră-zēn″) A pyrazole aniline dye widely used to color foods, cosmetics, drugs, and textiles. Its use has been linked to hives and other allergic-type reactions in some individuals.

Tarui disease Phosphofructokinase **deficiency**.

task, cancellation A type of cognitive test that measures attention by determining an individual's ability to select and mark a line through selected target letters or symbols within a larger field of many letters or symbols.

task analysis Division of an activity into components in order to determine the specific abilities needed to perform that activity. Purposeful activities require various levels of cognitive, perceptual (e.g., vision, proprioception), musculoskeletal, and neuromuscular abilities. By understanding the abilities necessary for a task, practitioners are better able to develop a rehabilitation program for patients who cannot do it for themselves.

taste (tāst) [Fr. *taster,* to feel, to taste] **1.** To determine the flavor of a substance by touching it with the tongue. **2.** A chemical sense dependent on the sensory buds concentrated on the surface of the tongue and scattered over the palate, pharynx, larynx, epiglottis, and superior esophagus; the nerves that innervate them; and the smell center (rhinencephalon) in the sylvan fissue of the brain's parietal cortex. The taste buds, when appropriately stimulated, produce one or a combination of the five fundamental taste sensations: sweet, bitter, sour, savory, and salty. The sensation is influenced by the sense of smell. Information from the taste buds is carried to the brainstem by the lingual part of the trigeminal nerve, the chorda tympani and the facial nerve (from the anterior two thirds of the surface of the tongue), the glossopharyngeal nerve (from the posterior third), and the vagus nerve (from the base and pharyngeal areas of the tongue). Loss of taste may be caused by any neurologic condition that interrupts the transmission pathway. Taste abnormalities also occur in normal aging, some infections, trauma, smoking, vitamin or mineral deficiencies, oral disorders, illicit drug use, lack of saliva, or the therapeutic use of cytotoxic drugs. SYN: *gustatory perception*.

The cells of the taste buds undergo continual degeneration and replacement. None survive for more than a few days.

PATIENT CARE: Taste alterations include ageusia (complete loss of tastes); hypogeusia (partial loss of taste); cysgeusia (distorted sense of taste); and cacogeusia (unpleasant or revolting food taste). When designing a nutritional program for people with altered taste, it is important to consider both their personal taste preferences and the availability of foods with enhanced flavors, both of which may optimize nutritional intake. For those with dry mouth from disruption of the salivary glands or from other causes, artificial saliva not only assists in mastication and swallowing but also enhances taste. Young children have difficulty differentiating between an abnormal taste sensation and simple dislike of a taste and often refuse new foods, esp. those with strong odors. Trying the same food at a later time or in a different preparation may elicit a more favorable response.

taste area An area in the cerebral cortex at the lower end of the somesthetic area in the parietal lobe.

taster (tās'tĕr) A person capable of detecting a particular substance by using the taste sense.

TAT *thematic apperception test; turnaround time.*

tattooing (tă-too'ĭng) [Tahitian *tatau*] **1.** Indelible marking of the skin produced by introducing minute amounts of pigments into the skin. Tattooing is usually done to produce a certain design, picture, or name. When it is done commercially, sterile procedures may not be used and hepatitis B or C or HIV may be transmitted to the customer. The technique may also be used to conceal a corneal leukoma, to mask pigmented areas of skin, or to color skin to look like the areola in mammoplasty. **2.** In radiation therapy, the induction of a small amount of indelible pigment under the skin used to designate an area to be treated with radiation.

removal of t. Use of a ruby laser to erase the pigment in an unwanted tattoo. This usually causes no permanent skin changes.

traumatic t. Embedding of fine dirt particles under the superficial layers of the skin after an abrasion of the skin or as a result of forceful deposit of gunpowder granules. This can be prevented by immediate removal of the particles.

tau (tow) **1.** T or τ, the uppercase and lowercase symbols, respectively, for the 19th letter of the Greek alphabet. **2.** A protein associated with microtubules that is found in glial cells of the brains of people affected by neurodegenerative diseases, including Alzheimer disease, Creutzfeldt-Jakob disease, frontotemporal dementia, and some forms of Parkinson disease. In these and related illnesses, high levels of tau can be found in the cerebrospinal fluid.

tauopathy (tow-ŏp'ŭ-thē) [″ + ″] Any neurodegenerative disorder in which abnormal levels of tau protein are found in the brain.

taurine (taw'rĭn) $NH_2CH_2CH_2SO_3H$, a derivative of cysteine. It is present in bile, as taurocholic acid, in combination with bile acid.

taurocholate (taw″rō-kō'lāt) A salt of taurocholic acid.

taurodontism (tor″ŏ-don'tizm) [L *taurus,* Gr. *tauros,* bull + *odont-* + *-ism*] A rare developmental anomaly in which permanent molar teeth have significantly elongated, enlarged pulp chambers. The root furcation is displaced to the apex. SYN: *bull tooth.*

tauto-, taut- [Gr. *tauto-,* the same] Prefixes meaning *identical.*

tautomer (tot'ŏ-mĕr) [*tauto-* + Gr. *meros,* a part] A structural isomer of an organic compound in which a single atom readily moves from one location of the molecule to another and, when conditions are right, back again.

tautomerase (taw-tŏm′ĕr-ās) [″ + ″ + -ase, enzyme] An enzyme that catalyzes tautomeric reactions.

tautomerism (taw-tŏm′ĕr-ĭzm) [″ + ″ + -ismos, condition] A phenomenon in which a chemical may be present in two forms, existing in dynamic equilibrium so that as the amount of one substance is altered, the second is changed into the other form in order to maintain the equilibrium. SEE: *isomerism*.

taxane (tăk′sān) Any of a class of drugs derived from the bark of the yew tree, *Taxus breviflora*. Examples include paclitaxel and docetaxel. Taxanes are used to treat breast, ovarian, and other types of cancer. Side effects include bone marrow suppression, neuropathy, mucositis, and hypersensitivity reactions.

taxis (tăk′sĭs) [Gr., arrangement] **1.** The manual replacement or reduction of a hernia or dislocation. **2.** The response of an organism to its environment; a turning toward (positive taxis) or away from (negative taxis) a particular stimulus. SEE: *chemotaxis*.

Taxol (tăk′sŏl″) A chemotherapeutic drug obtained from the bark of the yew tree, *Taxus brevifolia*. It is used to treat cancers of the breast, ovary, and other organs. Side effects include bone marrow suppression, neuropathy, mucositis, and hypersensitivity reactions.

taxon (tăk′sŏn) [Gr. *taxis*, arrangement] A taxonomic group.

taxonomy (tăks-ŏn′ō-mē) [″ + *nomos*, law] **1.** The laws and principles of classification of living organisms **2.** Classification of learning objectives.

Tay, Warren (tā) Brit. ophthalmologist and pediatrician, 1843–1927.

    T.'s choroiditis A familial condition marked by degeneration of the choroid, esp. in the region about the macula lutea. It occurs in the aged.

Taylor, Euphemia Jane [U.S. nurse, 1878–1957] A pioneer of psychiatric nursing. She graduated from the Johns Hopkins Hospital School of Nursing in 1907 and became Director of Nursing Services at the Henry Phipps Clinic at Johns Hopkins from 1913 to 1919. Due to her efforts, Johns Hopkins was the first general hospital school of nursing to offer a course in psychiatric nursing. She became the Dean of the Yale School of Nursing in 1934 and served in this position until 1944. She was also a leader in the International Council of Nurses until her death.

Taylor brace (tāl′ŏr) [Charles Fayette Taylor, U.S. surgeon, 1827–1899] A brace with two rigid posterior oblique portions and soft straps crossed anteriorly over the chest.

Tay-Sachs disease (tā′săks) [Warren Tay, Brit. physician, 1843–1927; Bernard Sachs, U.S. neurologist, 1858–1944] The most severe (and most com-

mon) of the lipid storage diseases. Tay-Sachs disease is characterized by neurological deterioration in the first year of life. It is caused by a genetic abnormality on chromosome 15, which results in the deficient manufacture of lysosomal beta-hexosaminidase A. As a result of this metabolic error, sphingolipids accumulate in the neural tissues of affected offspring. The illness is especially prominent in families of Eastern European (Ashkenazi) Jews, among whom it is carried by approx. 4 percent of the population. Carriers of the trait can be accurately detected by assay of hexosaminidase A. SEE: *Nursing Diagnoses Appendix; sphingolipidosis*.

    SYMPTOMS: The disease is characterized by normal development until the third to sixth month of life, after which profound regression occurs. Physical findings may include cherry-red spots on the macula and enlargement of the head in the absence of hydrocephalus. Alterations in muscle tone, an abnormal startle response (hyperacusis), blindness, social withdrawal, and mental retardation are common early signs. A vegetative state is nearly universal by the second year of life. Death may occur before age 4.

TB *tuberculosis*.

Tb Symbol for the element terbium.

tb *tubercle bacillus; tuberculosis*.

TBI *total body irradiation; traumatic brain **injury***.

TBP *thyroxine-binding protein*.

Tbs *tablespoon*.

TBSA *total body surface area*.

Tbsp *tablespoon*.

TBW *total body water* (the sum of the mass of water within cells, interstitial tissues, and plasma); *total body weight*.

Tc Symbol for the element technetium.

TCDD $C_{12}H_4Cl_4O_2$, a teratogenetic and carcinogenic dioxin, formerly used as an herbicide and also being a contaminant in Agent Orange. SYN: *2,3,7,8-tetrachlorodibenzo-p-dioxin*. SEE: *dioxin*.

T-cell receptor SEE: under *receptor*.

TCID$_{50}$ *tissue culture infective dose*.

TCR *T-cell receptor*.

Tdap An acronym for tetanus toxoid, reduced diphtheria toxoid, and acellular pertussis (vaccine).

TDD *Telecommunication **device** for the deaf*.

tds L. *ter die sumendum*, to be taken three times a day.

Te Symbol for the element tellurium.

tea (tē) **1.** An infusion of a medicinal plant. **2.** The leaves of the plant *Thea chinensis* or *Camellia sinensis*, from which a beverage is made by steeping the leaves in boiling hot water.

    COMPOSITION: Several pharmacologically active ingredients (caffeine, theophylline) and antioxidants, including polyphenolic compounds, and sufficient fluoride to help prevent tooth decay are present in tea. The caloric content is negligible unless sugar, honey, and/or milk is added prior to consumption. SEE: *caffeine; withdrawal, caffeine.*

⚠️ Tea intake should be limited in those patients with a history of oxalate-containing kidney stones.

black t. Tea made from leaves that have been fermented before they are dried.

green t. Tea made from the leaves of *Camellia sinensis* steamed to prevent fermentation and then rolled and dried. The ingredients of green tea said to influence health are antioxidants called catechins. Green tea is often promoted for the putative prevention of certain types of cancer. Although studies have demonstrated antitumor effects of tea in laboratory animals, studies of the impact of green tea consumption on breast and prostate cancer in humans have failed to show any impact.

herb t., herbal tea Tea made of a variety of plants, e.g., leaves of certain flowers, herbs, barks, and grasses. Some herbs used in these teas have been demonstrated to have pharmacological properties.

t. kombucha SEE: *kombucha tea.*

Paraguay copper t. Tea, also known as yerba maté, made from the leaves and stems of *Ilex paraguayensis*. It is a stimulating drink and contains volatile oil, tannin, and caffeine.

teachable (tēch′ă-bĕl) **1.** Receptive to learning. **2.** Ready to learn.

teachable moment An unplanned experience that gives an educator an opportunity to convey new information or ideas to his or her students.

teach back, teach-back, teachback A method to ensure and improve a patient's understanding of his or her condition, diagnosis, medical regimen, prognosis, or treatment plan.

PATIENT CARE: After the health care provider relays disease-specific information, he or she asks the patient, caregivers, or family members, "Tell me what we've just discussed," or "Explain to me how to take this medication," or "Explain to me how to prepare for surgery," or "Tell me whom to call if problems arise," etc. Providing the opportunity for teaching back is esp. helpful when assisting patients with limited health literacy to adhere to medical plans and retain complicated information, although it may be useful in other clinical encounters, as when patients are anxious, distracted, hurried, or overwhelmed.

team A group of individuals working together to perform a common task.

¹**tear** (tār) [Old English *teran*] **1.** To separate or pull apart by force. **2.** A wound or injury caused by the tearing of a body part. **3.** A third-degree sprain or strain.

bucket handle t. A longitudinal tear, usually beginning in the middle of a meniscus (cartilage) of the knee.

t. of the perineum Laceration of the perineum during delivery. There are four degrees of severity caused by overstretching of the vagina and perineum during delivery. Fetal malposition increases the chance of tears occurring.

A first-degree tear involves superficial tissues of the perineum and vaginal mucosa but does not injure muscular tissue. A second-degree tear involves those tissues included in a first-degree tear and the muscles of the perineum but not the muscles of the anal sphincter. A third-degree tear involves all of the tissues of the second-degree tear and the muscles of the anal sphincter. A fourth-degree tear extends completely through the perineal skin, vaginal mucosa, perineal body, anal sphincter muscles, and the rectal mucosa.

Complications include hemorrhage, infection, cystocele, rectocele, descent of uterus, and occasionally loss of bowel control. Surgery is necessary to treat this condition.

²**tear** (tēr) [Old English *tēar*] A watery substance secreted by the lacrimal glands containing aqueous components as well as secretions of the meibomian glands. The function of tears is to lubricate the surface of the eye. SEE: *Schirmer test.*

artificial t. A solution used to lubricate the conjunctivae.

crocodile t. Tears and excessive saliva produced during eating. This condition is present when nerve fibers of the salivary glands grow abnormally into the lacrimal glands following Bell palsy.

tear break-up test ABBR: TBUT. A test for dry eyes in which fluorescein sodium is applied to the cornea. The amount of time it takes for the first dry spots to appear on the cornea is determined. A TBUT time of less than 10 seconds suggests poor tear film stability.

tear film A liquid consisting of lipids, water, and mucin that coats the outer surface of the eye, lubricating it.

PATIENT CARE: A reduction in the tear film causes a sensation of a dry or gritty eye, such as is seen in Sjögren syndrome, keratoconjunctivitis, sicca, disorders of the lacrimal gland, and other conditions. Keeping eyelids clean, using artificial tears, and withholding medications that may reduce the tear film can prove helpful for some patients. Other treatments may include the wearing of moisture chambers around the eye, and eye lid surgery. Topical lubricants can be used for symptomatic relief.

tease (tēz) [AS. *taesan,* to pluck] To separate a tissue into minute parts with a needle to prepare it for microscopy.

teaspoon (tē'spoon) ABBR: tsp. A household measure equal to approx. 5 mL. Teaspoons used in the home vary from 3 to 6 mL. Because household measures are not accurate, when a teaspoon dose is prescribed or ordered, 5 mL of the substance should be given.

teat (tēt) [ME. *tete,* from AS. *tit,* teat] **1.** The nipple of the mammary gland. SYN: *papilla mammae.* SEE: *breast.* **2.** Any protuberance resembling a nipple.

TECAB [Acronym for *totally endoscopic coronary artery bypass*] A robot-controlled procedure in which the left internal mammary artery is used to bypass the left anterior descending coronary artery without the use of sternotomy. The procedure is a form of minimally invasive coronary artery surgery. In TECAB, several small portholes are made in the chest wall to insert a video camera and robot-controlled and stabilized surgical instruments to improve surgical dexterity and eliminate tremor.

technetium (tek-nē'sh(ē-)ŭm) [Gr. *technētikos,* made, artificial + *-ium* (1)] SYMB: Tc. A synthetic, silvery gray, crystalline chemical element, atomic number 43, average atomic weight (mass) 98.9062. It is a transition metal having a number of isotopes, all of which are radioactive and have various half-lives. Its isotope technetium-99 is used in nuclear medicine for a wide variety of diagnostic tests. SEE: *technetium-99m.*

technetium-99m SYMB: 99mTc. A radioactive isotope of technetium having a half-life of 6 hr, in which the "m" refers to the fact that it is a metastable isotope. 99mTc is used in nuclear medicine for a wide variety of diagnostic tests and imaging studies, e.g., myocardial perfusion scans, bone scans, and V/Q scans.

technetium Tc 99m albumin aggregated injection An injection of technetium-99m that has been aggregated with albumin. It is used intravenously to scan the lungs.

technetium Tc 99m hexamethylpropyleneamine oxime ABBR: HMPAO. A radioactive tracer consisting of technetium-99m linked to hexamethylpropyleneamine oxime. It is used to make nuclear imaging scans of the brain, e.g., in the determination of brain death. Absence of uptake of the molecule by the brain is diagnostic of brain death.

technetium 99m (methoxyisonitrile)

MIBI A radioactive tracer consisting of technetium-99m linked to MIBI. It is used in nuclear medical imaging (e.g., in scintimammography) to identify cancerous breast masses. Other uses of technetium 99m MIBI include cardiac, parathyroid, and thyroid imaging.

technetium Tc 99m methylene diphosphonate A radioactive tracer consisting of technetium-99m linked to methylene diphosphonate. It is used in nuclear medicine to obtain images of bone and bone diseases, e.g., fractures not seen on plain x-rays, malignancies, and osteomyelitis.

technetium Tc 99m RBC A radioactive tracer consisting of technetium-99m linked to red blood cells. It is used in clinical medicine to evaluate occult bleeding, e.g., from the gastrointestinal tract, or the motion of the heart in gated blood pool imaging.red blood cell scan.

technetium Tc 99m sestamibi A radioactive tracer consisting of technetium-99m linked to sestamibi. It is used to image blood flow to the heart muscle, esp. when combined with exercise or pharmacological stress tests. In a heart with normal blood flow, the isotope should be taken up uniformly throughout the heart muscle. Decreased uptake by regions of the heart occurs when coronary artery blood flow to those regions is blocked, e.g., by atherosclerotic plaque. SYN: *sestamibi.*

technetium Tc 99m sulfur colloid A radioactive tracer consisting of technetium-99m linked to sulfur colloid. It is used in nuclear medicine scans to make images of gastric emptying or of the lymph nodes, liver, and spleen.

technical (těk'nĭ-kăl) [Gr. *tekhnikos,* skilled] Pert. to technique or special skill.

technical efficiency The extent to which the most appropriate technologies, e.g., MRI studies, are devoted to the solution of problems, e.g., the diagnosis of diseases of the spinal cord, regardless of their economic costs or sociopolitical impact.

technician (těk-nĭsh'ăn) One who has the knowledge and skill required to carry out specific technical procedures. This person usually has a diploma from a specialized school or an associate degree from college or has received training through preceptorship. Particular technicians are listed under the first word. SEE: e.g., *dental technician; emergency medical technician; respiratory therapy technician.*

technique (tek-nēk') [Gr. *technikos,* pert. to a craft] **1.** A systematic procedure or method by which an involved or scientific task is completed. **2.** The skill in performing details of a procedure or operation. **3.** In radiology, the various technical factors that must be determined to produce a diagnostic radiograph, e.g., kilovoltage, milliamperage, time of exposure, and source-image receptor distance.

Alexander t. SEE: *Alexander technique.*

aseptic t. A method used in surgery to prevent contamination of the wound and operative site. All instruments used are sterilized, and physicians and nurses wear caps, masks, shoe coverings, sterile gowns, and gloves. The technique is adapted at the bedside, e.g., during procedures, and in emergency and treatment rooms. SEE: *Standard Precautions Appendix.*

bisecting angle t. A dental radiographic technique that requires placement of the film as close as possible to the teeth, causing the film to rest against the crown; visualization of a bisector, which bisects the angle formed by the long axis of the teeth and the film; and positioning of the central ray perpendicular to the bisector. The image produced is distorted in a buccolingual direction SYN: *short-cone t.* SEE: *Cieszynski rule.*

compensatory t. 1. The use of modified procedures or assistive devices to enable the successful performance of tasks by persons with a disability. **2.** Any altered pattern of movement in patients with limited mobility in which synergistic muscles are recruited and used to perform movements that would usually be performed by other muscle groups.

crossed finger t. A hazardous method of opening an unconscious patient's mouth by placing the thumb and index finger of a gloved hand on opposite rows of teeth and spreading the jaw open.

depilatory t. Any of several procedures for the temporary removal of hair from the body, including shaving, plucking, chemicals, or hot wax. If chemical depilation is used, care must be taken to avoid skin irritation. The wax treatment involves application of molten wax, which is allowed to cool; then, when the wax is pulled away, the hair comes with it. Permanent depilation is accomplished by electrolysis of each hair follicle. This time-consuming process is done by an electrologist trained in the technique. SEE: *electrolysis; hirsutism.*

enzyme-multiplied immunoassay t. ABBR: EMIT. An enzyme immunoassay based on a mixture of analyte and enzyme substrate such that no immobile phase is necessary. SEE: *enzyme immunoassay; cloned enzyme donor immunoassay.*

forced expiration t. A type of cough that facilitates clearance of bronchial secretions while reducing the risk of bronchiolar collapse. One or two expirations are forced from average to low lung volume with an open glottis. A period of diaphragmatic breathing and relaxation follows.

forced expiratory t. ABBR: FET. The use of sudden exhalations to clear the airways of secretions.

immunomagnetic t. The use of magnetic microspheres to sort, isolate, or identify cells with specific antigenic markers.

long-cone t. Paralleling **t.**

minimal leak t. ABBR: MLT. A method of determining the appropriate cuff inflation volume on endotracheal tubes (ETT). The ETT cuff is inflated until no respiratory sounds are heard. The cuff is then deflated slightly until sounds are heard. Excessive cuff inflation volume may lead to necrosis of the trachea, and excessive leaking may render oxygenation and ventilation ineffective or allow aspiration of large particles from the oral cavity.

Mohs chemosurgery t. SEE: *Mohs chemosurgery technique.*

paralleling t. A dental radiographic technique that requires placement of the film parallel to the teeth and positioning of the central ray perpendicular to the teeth. The orientation of the film, teeth, and central ray produces a radiograph with minimal geometric distortion. SYN: *long-cone t.; right-angle t.*

preclinical t. In dentistry, the use of manikins, mechanical articulator, artificial or extracted teeth, and the dental instruments and materials to study and master the techniques of clinical dentistry.

projective t. Any of several forms of psychological assessment or evaluation. The subject's comments about the results or products of ambiguous activities and tasks that encourage self-expression are evaluated and interpreted to determine indications of his unconscious needs, thoughts, or concerns.

right-angle t. Paralleling **t.**

Seldinger t. SEE: *Seldinger technique.*

short-cone t. Bisecting angle **t.**

sighted guide t. A means of assisting a blind person to navigate unfamiliar situations. A sighted person offers assistance and, if it is accepted, taps the blind person on the hand and offers an arm for support. The sighted person then walks just ahead of and to the side of the blind person to help avoid potential hazards.

techno- [Gr. *tekhnē*, skill, art] Prefix meaning *art, skill.*

technologist (těk″nŏl′ō-jĭst) [Gr. *techne*, art, + *logos*, word, reason] One who specializes in the application of scientific knowledge in solving practical or theoretical problems. The knowledge and skills required for performing these functions are achieved through formal education and a period of supervised clinical practice.

Particular technologists are listed under the first word. SEE: e.g., *cardiovascular technologist; medical technologist; radiation therapy technologist.*

technology (tek-nol'ŏ-jē) [*techno-* + *-logy*] **1.** The practical application of scientific knowledge. **2.** The scientific knowledge used in solving or approaching practical problems and situations. **technologic, technological** (tek″nŏ-loj′ik, i-kăl), *adj.*

 adaptive t. Assistive t.

 assisted reproduction t. ABBR: ART. Any of the techniques to assist infertile women to conceive and give birth. These include hormonal stimulation of ovulation and operative techniques such as in vitro fertilization with embryonic transfer, zygote intrafallopian transfer for women whose infertility results from tubal factors, and gamete intrafallopian transfer for couples whose infertility stems from semen inadequacy. SYN: *assisted reproductive t.*

 assisted reproductive t. Assisted reproduction t.

 assistive t. ABBR: AT. A device or adaptation that enables or assists persons with disabilities to perform everyday tasks of living. Assistive technologies are categorized by rehabilitation personnel as high technology or low technology, with the former including devices that use microprocessors. An example of a high-technology device is an environmental control unit or robotic aid. An example of a low-technology device is a reacher or a tool with a built-up handle. SYN: *adaptive t.; assistive technology device; adaptive device.*

 The Technology Related Assistance for Individuals with Disabilities Act Amendments of 1994 provide for programs that support the development, acquisition, or application of assistive technology devices or equipment to assist persons with activity limitations resulting from functional impairments.

 bar code-enabled point of care t. SEE: *bar code-enabled point of care technology.*

 health information t. ABBR: HIT. The application of information technology to the collection, storage, processing, retrieval, and communication of information relevant to patient care within a health care system.

 information t. ABBR: IT. The use of computers or computer software to collect, store, manipulate, retrieve, exchange, or manage data. SEE: table.

 instructional t. Any tool that helps teachers disseminate and helps students gain exposure to knowledge.

Information Technologies Used in Health Care

The electronic medical record
E-mail communications, e.g., between professionals or to and from patients
Health information systems
Internets; intranets
Pharmacy management, e.g., in drug bar coding; drug advisories, drug formularies
Management systems for reimbursement and quality assurance
Robotics
Telehealth

 wavefront t. A three-dimensional mapping system that measures the irregularities of an optical system, e.g., the human eye or a telescopic lens. It is used in ophthalmology to detect refractive aberrations. Parallel light rays are directed toward the eye. If there are no aberrations, the returning light rays remain parallel. Any deviation indicates a defect that can alter the clarity of a visual image. Visual deficits caused by refractive aberration can be corrected by reshaping of the cornea.

technology-enabled active learning ABBR: TEAL. A means of enhancing the educational experience of students by including computer-assisted interactive media with traditional lectures, group assignments, problem-solving sessions, and readings. SYN: *technology-enabled problem-based learning.*

tectorium (těk-tō′rē-ŭm) *pl.* **tectoria** [L. *tectorium,* a covering] **1.** Any rooflike structure. SEE: *tectum; tegmentum; tegument.* **tectorial,** *adj.* **2.** The membrane that overhangs the receptors for hearing (hair cells) in the organ of Corti.

tectospinal (těk″tō-spī′năl) [L. *tectum,* roof, + *spina,* thorn] From the tectum mesencephali to the spinal cord.

tectospinal tract A nerve tract that passes from the tectum of the midbrain through the medulla to the spinal cord; most of the fibers cross to the other side of the body.

tectum (tek′tŭm) [L. *tectum,* roof] **1.** Any structure serving as, or resembling, a roof. **2.** Lamina quadrigemina.

 t. mesencephali Lamina quadrigemina.

T.E.D. *threshold erythema dose.*

TEE *transesophageal echocardiography.*

teenage Adolescent.

teeth (tēth) Plural of tooth.

teething (tēth′ĭng) [AS. *toth,* tooth] Eruption of the teeth. SEE: *dentition.*

Teff (tef) An effector T cell.

tegmen (těg′měn) *pl.* **tegmina** [L. *teg-*

men, covering] A structure that covers a part. **tegmental,** *adj.*

tegmental nucleus One of several masses of gray matter lying in the tegmentum of the midbrain and upper portion of the pons; it includes the dorsal, pedunculopontile, reticular, and ventral nuclei.

tegmentum (těg-měn′tŭm) [L. *tegmentum,* covering] **1.** A covering, carapace, protective top layer, or integument. SYN: *tegument.* **2.** Inside the brainstem, the layers of cells and axons ventral to the cerebral aqueduct and the fourth ventricle, but dorsal to, (i.e., covering) the substantia nigra and cerebral peduncles in the midbrain, and the pontine nuclei and corticospinal tracts in the hindbrain. Motor nuclei, secondary sensory nuclei, and the brainstem reticular formation are contained in the tegmentum.

tegument (těg′ū-měnt) **1.** Integument. **2.** A covering structure.

tegumental, tegumentary (těg″ū-měn′tǎl, -tǎ-rē) Pert. to the skin or tegument; covering.

teichoic acid (tī-kō′ĭ-k) SEE: under *acid.*

teichopsia (tī-kǒp′sē-ǎ) [Gr. *teichos,* wall, + *opsis,* vision] Zigzag lines bounding a luminous area appearing in the visual field. It causes temporary blindness in that portion of the field of vision. This condition is sometimes associated with migraine headaches or mental or physical strain. SYN: *scintillating scotoma.*

tel-, tele-, telo-, teleo- [Gr. *telos,* end, fulfillment] Prefixes meaning *end, mature, complete.*

tela (tē′lǎ) *pl.* **telae** [L. *tela,* web] Any weblike structure.

telangiectasia, telangiectasis (těl-ăn″jē-ěk-tā′zē-ă, -ěk′tă-sĭs) [Gr. *telos,* end, + *angeion,* vessel, + *ektasis,* dilatation] A vascular lesion formed by dilatation of a group of small blood vessels. It may appear as a birthmark or become apparent in young children. It may also be caused by long-term sun exposure. Although the lesion may occur anywhere on the skin, it is seen most frequently on the face and thighs. **telangiectatic,** *adj.*

   hereditary hemorrhagic t. An autosomal dominant disease marked by thinness of the walls of the blood vessels of the nose, skin, and digestive tract, as well as a tendency to hemorrhage. SYN: *Rendu-Osler-Weber syndrome.*

   spider t. Stellate angioma.

telangiectodes (těl-ăn″jē-ěk-tō′dēz) Tumors that have telangiectasia.

tele-, tel-, telo- [Gr. *tēle,* far off, far away] Prefixes meaning *distant, transmitted over a distance.*

telecanthus (těl″ě-kǎn′thŭs) [Gr. *tele,* distant, + *kanthos,* corner of the eye] Increased distance between the inner canthi of the eyelids.

telecare (tel′ě-kar″) [*tele-* + *care*] The use of communications technologies, together with home measurement and monitoring devices, to evaluate specific health parameters of outpatients and provide them with advice or feedback about their condition. Providers of telecare are known as *telecaregivers.*

teleceptive (těl-ě-sěp′tĭv) [″ + L. *ceptivus,* take] Relating to a teleceptor.

teleconferencing Holding a meeting with people at different geographic locations by means of telecommunication devices. Teleconferencing is accomplished with high-speed telephone connections, satellite links, or desktop computer videoconference software.

telediagnosis (těl″ě-dī″ăg-nō′sĭs) [Gr. *tele,* distant, + *diagignoskein,* to discern] Diagnosis made on the basis of data transmitted electronically to the physician's location.

telediastolic (těl″ě-dī-ă-stǒl′ĭk) [Gr. *telos,* end, + *diastole,* a dilatation] Concerning the last phase of the diastole.

telehealth The use of telecommunications equipment and/or networks to transfer health care information among participants at different locations. Aspects of telehealth include teleradiology (the transmission of radiological images from one site to another), telemedicine (consultation by physicians at a distance), telenursing, and teledermatology.

telekinesis (těl″ě-kĭ-nē′sĭs) [″ + ″] The ability to move objects by pure mental concentration. Claims of telekinetic powers are typical of patients with psychotic illnesses.

telemedicine (tel″ě-med′ĭ-sĭn) [*tele-* + *medicine*] The use of telecommunications equipment to transmit video images, x-rays and other images, electronic medical records, and laboratory results about patients from distant sites. Telemedicine improves access to health care and delivery to facilities that do not have on-site specialists or subspecialists. SYN: *cyber medicine; electronic medicine; wireless medicine.*

telemeter (těl′ě-mē″těr) [″ + *metron,* measure] An electronic device used to transmit information to a distant point.

telemetry (tě-lěm′ě-trē) The transmission of data electronically to a distant location.

telencephalic (těl″ěn-sěf-ǎl′ĭk) [Gr. *telos,* end, + *enkephalos,* brain] Pert. to the endbrain (telencephalon).

telencephalon (těl-ěn-sěf′ǎ-lŏn) [″ + *enkephalos,* brain] The embryonic endbrain or posterior division of the prosencephalon from which the cerebral hemispheres, corpora striata, and rhinencephalon develop.

teleo- [Gr. *tele(i)os,* complete, finished] SEE: *¹tel-.*

teleological (tē″lē-ō-lŏj′ĭ-kăl) Pert. to teleology.

teleology (tĕl-ē-ŏl′ō-jē) [Gr. *teleos,* complete, + *logos,* word, reason] **1.** The belief that everything is directed toward some final purpose. **2.** The doctrine of final causes.

teleomorph (tĕl′ē-ō-mawrf″, tēl′) [″ + G. morphe, form] The sexual state of a fungus (the state in which two fungal nuclei unite and undergo meiosis, forming offspring with new genetic information). Fungi that have teleomorphic states are said to be "perfect" fungi. Fungi that reproduce asexually are said to be "imperfect." **teleomorphic** (tĕl″ē-ō-mawrf′ĭk, tēl″), *adj.* SEE: *anamorph.*

teleonomy (tĕl″ē-ŏn′ō-mē) [″ + *nomos,* law] The concept that, in an organism or animal, the existence of a structure, capability, or function indicates that it had survival value. **teleonomic** (tĕl″ē-ō-nŏm′ĭk), *adj.*

teleoperator (tĕl″ē-ŏp′ĕr-āt″or) A machine or device operated by a person at a distance. Such a machine allows tasks to be done deep in the ocean or on orbiting satellites, and allows radioactive materials to be manipulated without danger of exposure to the radioactivity.

telepathy (tĕ-lĕp′ă-thē) The ability to communicate with others wordlessly, i.e., by broadcasting one's thoughts or by receiving the transmitted thoughts of others. Claims of telepathic powers are typical of patients with psychoses and of some shamans. SYN: *telesthesia* (1).

telephony (tĕ-lĕf′ŏ-nē) Telephone technology, i.e., the electronic transmission of voice, fax, or other information between distant parties using a handheld device containing both a speaker or transmitter and a receiver.

telepresence (tĕl′ĕ-prĕ-zĭns) Virtual attendance rather than physical attendance (i.e., the presence of a person or thing that is brought about by technological means such as telephone, video, or other electronic devices).

teleradiogram (tĕl″ĕ-rā′dē-ō-grăm) [Gr. *tele,* distant, + L. *radius,* ray, + Gr. *gramma,* something written] An x-ray image obtained by teleradiography.

teleradiography (tĕl″ĕ-rā-dē-ŏg′ră-fē) Radiography with the radiation source about 2 m (6½ ft) from the body. Because the rays are virtually parallel at that distance, distortion is minimized. SYN: *teleroentgenography.*

teleradiology (tĕl″ĕ-rā-dē-ŏl′ō-jē) The transmission of an x-ray image to a distant center where it may be interpreted by a radiologist.

teleradium (tĕl″ĕ-rā′dē-ŭm) A radium source distant from the area being treated.

telerehabilitation (tĕl″ĕ-rē″hă-bil″ĭ-tā′shŏn) [*tele-* + *rehabilitation*] The use of internet or telecommunications to provide physical, occupational, or speech therapy to patients in their homes.

teleroentgenogram (tĕl″ĕ-rĕnt-gĕn′ō-grăm) [″ + *roentgen* + Gr. *gramma,* something written] Teleradiogram.

teleroentgenography (tĕl″ĕ-rĕnt″gĕn-ŏg′ră-fē) [″ + ″ + Gr. *graphein,* to write] Teleradiography.

telesurgery (tĕl″ĕ-sŭr′jĕr-ē) [″ + ″] Surgery performed from a remote location, using robotically controlled instruments. Visual, auditory, tactile, and other feedback is provided electronically to the surgeon. SYN: *remote **surgery**.*

telesystolic (tĕl″ĕ-sĭs-tŏl′ĭk) [Gr. *telos,* end, + *systole,* contraction] Pert. to the termination of cardiac systole.

teletherapy (tĕl-ĕ-thĕr′ă-pē) [Gr. *tele,* distant, + *therapeia,* treatment] Cancer treatment in which the radiation source is placed outside the body.

telethonin (tĕl″ĕ-thŏn′ĭn) [Fm *telethon,* after the televised fund-raisers urging donations for muscular dystrophy] A 19kD protein found in the Z disk of striated and cardiac muscle. Mutations in the gene for telethonin result in altered sarcomeres and some forms of muscular dystrophy.

telluric (tĕ-lūr′ĭk) [L. *tellus,* earth] Pert. to the earth.

tellurium (tĕ-loor′ē-ŭm) [L. *tellus,* earth + *-ium* (1)] SYMB: Te. A brittle silvery-white element, atomic weight (mass), 127.60, atomic number 52, specific gravity 6.24. It is used primarily in alloys and as a semiconductor.

telocentric (tĕl″ō-sĕn′trĭk) [Gr. *telos,* end, + *kentron,* center] Location of the centromere in the extreme end of the replicating chromosome so that there is only one arm on the chromosome.

telogen (tĕl′ō-jĕn) [″ + *genesis,* generation, birth] The resting stage of the hair growth cycle. SEE: *anagen; catagen.*

telolecithal (tĕl″ō-lĕs′ĭ-thăl) Pert. to an egg in which the large yolk mass is concentrated at one pole.

telomerase (tĕl″ō-mĕr′ās) An enzyme that helps cells repair the damage that occurs to the end of the DNA molecule during each cycle of cell division. Without such repair, cells eventually age and die. Cancer cells have telomerases that allow infinite repair to the DNA strands, a factor that contributes to their immortality. SEE: *telomere.*

telomere (tĕl′ō-mir′, tēl′) [″ + *meros,* part] A repetitive segment of DNA found on the ends of chromosomes. With each mitotic division, parts of the telomeres of a chromosome are lost. A theory of cellular aging proposes that the telomeres act as a biological clock and that when they are depleted, the cell dies or becomes much less active. **telomeric** (tel″ŏ-mer′ik), *adj.*

telomeric repeat amplification protocol assay (tel″ŏ-mer′ik) SEE: under *assay.*

telophase (těl′ō-fāz) [″ + *phasis,* an appearance] The final phase of mitosis (karyokinesis) during which reconstruction of the daughter nuclei takes place and the cytoplasm of the cell divides, giving rise to two daughter cells.

tempeh (těm′pā) A patty of fermented soybean that is a traditional Indonesian food. The quality of protein in tempeh is close to that of casein.

temper [AS. *temprian,* to mingle] The state of an individual's mood, disposition, or mind (e.g., even-tempered or foul-tempered).

temperament (těm′pĕr-ă-měnt) [L. *temperamentum,* mixture] The combination of intellectual, emotional, ethical, and physical characteristics of a specific individual.

temperance (těm′pĕr-ăns) Moderation in one's thoughts and actions, esp. with respect to use of alcoholic beverages.

temperate (těm′pĕr-ĭt) Moderate; not excessive.

temperature (tem′pĕ(r)-choor″) [L. *temperatura,* proportion] The degree of hotness or coldness of a substance. SEE: illus.

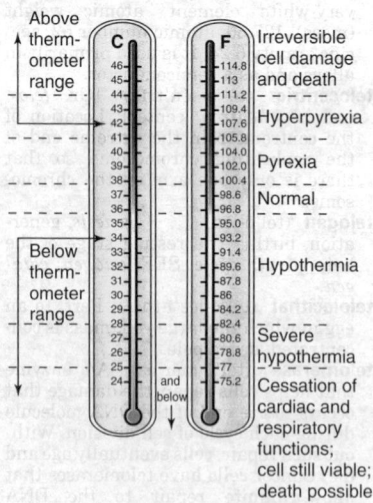

TEMPERATURE REGULATION

Effects of changes in body temperature

absolute t. The temperature measured from absolute zero, which is −273.15°C.

ambient t. The surrounding temperature or that present in the place, site, or location indicated.

axillary t. The temperature obtained by placing a thermometer in the apex of the axilla with the arm pressed closely to the side of the body for the time recommended by the manufacturer of the thermometer. The temperature obtained by this method is usually 0.5° to 1.0°F (0.28° to 0.56°C) lower than oral.

body t. A marker of endocrine, metabolic, or muscle activity; the response of the body to heat or cold in the environment; or the presence of infection, inflammation, among other illnesses; it is one of the vital signs. Body temperature varies with the time of day and the site of measurement. Oral temperature is usually 97.5° to 99.5°F (36° to 38°C). Daily fluctuations in an individual may be 1° or 2°F. Body temperature may be measured by a placing a thermometer in the mouth, the rectum, under the arm, in the bladder, within the chambers of the heart, or in the external auditory canal of the ear. Rectal temperature is usually from 0.5° to 1.0°F (0.28° to 0.56°C) higher than by mouth; axillary temperature is about 0.5°F (0.28°C) lower than by mouth. Oral temperature measurement may be inaccurate if performed just after the patient has ingested cold or hot substances or has been breathing with an open mouth.

Body temperature is regulated by thermoregulatory centers in the hypothalamus that balance heat production and heat loss. Eighty-five percent of body heat is lost through the skin (radiation, conduction, sweating) and the remainder through the lungs and fecal and urinary excretions. Muscular work (including shivering) is a mechanism for raising body temperature. Elevation of temperature above normal is called fever (pyrexia), and subnormal temperature is hypothermia. Other factors that can influence body temperature are age (infants and children have a wider range of body temperature than adults, and elderly have lower body temperatures than others); menstruation cycle in women (the temperature rises in the ovulatory midcycle and remains high until menses); and exercise (temperature rises with moderate to vigorous muscular activity).

core t. The body's temperature in deep internal structures, such as the heart or bladder, as opposed to peripheral parts such as the mouth or axilla. In critical care it is often measured with a thermometer linked to a central venous catheter or pulmonary artery catheter.

critical t. The temperature above which distinct liquid and gas phases do not exist.

inverse t. A condition in which the

body temperature is higher in the morning than in the evening.

maximum t. The temperature above which bacterial growth will not take place.

mean t. The average temperature for a stated period in a given locality.

minimum t. In bacteriology, the temperature below which bacterial growth will not take place.

normal t. The temperature of the body, taken orally, in a healthy individual: normally 97.5° to 99.5°F (36° to 38°C).

optimum t. The temperature at which a procedure is best carried out, such as the culture of a given organism or the action of an enzyme.

oral t. The temperature obtained by placing a thermometer under the patient's tongue with lips closed for 3 min or by electronic thermometer for the length of time noted on the readout or the manufacturer's direction.

PATIENT CARE: It should not be taken for at least 20 min after ingestion of hot or cold liquids. It is not advisable for infants, those who breathe through the mouth, the comatose or obtunded patients, or the critically ill.

rectal t. The temperature obtained by inserting a thermometer into the anal canal to a depth of at least 1½ in (3.8 cm) and holding it in place for 3 to 5 min or, for electronic thermometers, according to the manufacturer's directions. This method should not be used following a rectal operation or if the rectum is diseased. A rectal temperature is more accurate than either oral or axillary temperatures. It averages about 1°F (0.56°C) higher than the oral temperature and approx. 1.5°F (0.84°C) higher than the axillary temperature.

room t. The temperature between 65° and 80°F (18.3° and 26.7°C).

subnormal t. A body temperature below the normal range of 97.5° to 99.5°F (36° to 38°C).

tympanic t. The temperature obtained by placing an electronic probe in the ear canal. Such a reading measures the temperature in the capillary bed of the tympanic membrane and is generally reflective of the core temperature. SEE: *ear thermometry; thermometer, tympanic.*

temperature sense SEE: under *sense.*

template (těm′plāt) A pattern, mold, or form used as a guide in duplicating a molecule, shape, structure, or device.

occlusal t. Bite **plate.**

wax t. SEE: *waxing-up.*

template bleeding time SEE: under *time.*

temple (těm′pl) [O.Fr. from L. *tempora,* pl. of *tempus,* temple] The region of the head in front of the ear and over the zygomatic arch.

tempora (tem′pŏ-ră) [L. *tempora,* loan translation of Gr. *kairia,* the right spot (for striking), the temples] The temples (of the head).

¹temporal (tem′p(ŏ)-răl) [L. *temporalis,* pert. to time, temporary, fr *tempus,* time] Pert. to or limited in time.

²temporal (tem′p(ŏ)-răl) [L. *temporalis,* pert. to the temples, fr *tempora,* temples (of the head)] Pert. to the lateral region or temples of the head.

temporalis (těm″pō-rā′lĭs) [L.] The muscle in the temporal fossa that elevates the mandible.

temporal lobe SEE: under *lobe.*

temporal resolution SEE: under *resolution.*

temporo- [L. *tempula,* fr. *tempus,* stem *temporo-,* time, period of time] Prefix meaning *temple* (of the head).

temporomandibular (těm″pō-rō-mǎn-dĭb′ū-lăr) [″ + *mandibula,* lower jawbone] Pert. to the temporal and mandible bones; esp. important in dentistry because of the articulation of the bones of the temporomandibular joint.

temporomandibular joints The encapsulated, bicondylar, synovial joints between the condyles of the mandible and the temporal bones of the skull.

temporomandibular joint syndrome ABBR: TMJ syndrome. Severe pain in and about the temporomandibular joint, made worse by chewing. The syndrome is marked by limited movement of the joint and clicking sounds during chewing. Tinnitus, pain, and rarely, deafness may be present. Causes include lesions of the temporomandibular joint tissues, malocclusion, overbite, poorly fitting dentures, and tissue changes resulting in pressure on nerves. Treatments may include bite blocks worn at night, nonsteroidal anti-inflammatory drugs, local massage, or joint surgeries. SYN: *Costen's syndrome.*

temporo-occipital (těm″pō-rō-ŏk-sĭp′ĭ-tăl) [″ + *occipitalis,* pert. to the occiput] Pert. to the temporal and occipital bones of the skull or to the temporal and occipital lobes of the brain.

temporoparietal (těm″pō-rō-pă-rī′ě-tăl) [″ + *paries,* wall] Pert. to the temporal and parietal bones.

temporozygomatic (těm″pō-rō-zī″gō-măt′ĭk) [″ + Gr. *zygoma,* cheekbone] Pert. to the temporal and zygomatic bones. SYN: *temporomalar.*

TEMS *tactical emergency medical services; tactical emergency medical support.*

ten-, teni- SEE: *taen-.*

tenacious (tě-nā′shŭs) [L. *tenax*] Adhering to; adhesive; retentive.

tenacity (tě-năs′ĭ-tē) Toughness, stubbornness, obstinacy, durability.

tenaculum (těn-ăk′ū-lŭm) [L., a holder] Sharp, hooklike, pointed instrument with a slender shank for grasping and holding an anatomical part.

tenascin (tĕn'ŭ-sĭn) A large glycoprotein expressed by normal embryonic cells during organogenesis, and by adult cells in inflammation, wound healing, and cancer.

tenascin-C (tĕn-ă'sĭn) A glycoprotein found in the extracellular matrix that influences embryological development, tissue remodeling, and angiogenesis in infectious, inflammatory, and malignant diseases.

tender loving care SEE: under *care*.

tenderness (ten'dĕr-nĕs) [Fr. *tendre* fr L. *tener,* soft, delicate] Sensitivity to pain upon pressure.

> ***jar t.*** Localized pain felt in the right lower quadrant of the abdomen when a patient with appendicitis walks rapidly or drops suddenly from a standing position on the balls of the feet onto the heels. SYN: *jar sign; Markle sign.*

> ***rebound t.*** The production or intensification of pain when pressure that has been applied during palpation, esp. of the abdomen, is suddenly released. SYN: *Blumberg sign.*

tendinitis, tendonitis (ten"dĭ-nīt'ĭs) [*tendo* + *-itis*] Inflammation of a tendon.

> ***calcific t.*** Calcium deposition in a chronically inflamed tendon, esp. a tendon of the shoulder.

> ***rotator cuff t.*** A common cause of shoulder pain, thought to be due to inflammation of the intrinsic tendons of the shoulder, esp. that of the supraspinatus. The onset usually follows injury or overuse during activities involving repeated overhead arm motions, as occurs in certain occupations (construction, painting) and sports (baseball, tennis, swimming).
> ETIOLOGY: People over 40 are particularly susceptible because of decreased vascular supply to the rotator cuff tendons. Those who perform repeated overhead motions are also at risk.
> SYMPTOMS: The patient will describe pain with overhead arm motion; on examination, the extremity may be postured for comfort; muscle strength and tone of the scapular muscles may be decreased.
> TREATMENT: Conservative treatment consists of the use of moist heat and strengthening and range-of-motion exercises; if the patient does not respond to these treatment methods and loss of function is present, corticosteroid injections may be helpful. Surgery to resect the coracoacromial ligament may be indicated in persons who fail other therapies.

tendinopathy, tendonopathy (ten"dĭ-nop'ă-thē) [*tendo* + *-pathy*] Any disease or condition that affects tendon function or structure, esp. chronic tendinitis or tendinosis.

tendinosis (tĕn"dĭ-nō'sĭs) **1.** Degeneration of a tendon from repetitive microtrauma. **2.** Collagen degeneration.

tendinous (tĕn'dĭ-nŭs) [L. *tendinosus*] Pert. to, composed of, or resembling tendons.

tendo [L. *tendo,* stem *tendin-,* tendon] Tendon.

tendon (ten'dŏn) [L. *tendo,* tendon] Fibrous connective tissue serving for the attachment of muscles to bones and other parts. SYN: *sinew; tendo.*

> ***Achilles t.*** SEE: *Achilles tendon.*

> ***calcaneal t.*** Achilles tendon.

> ***central t., central t. of diaphragm*** The central portion of the diaphragm, consisting of a flat aponeurosis into which the muscle fibers of the diaphragm are inserted.

> ***conjoined t.*** A single tendon that is connected to the ends of two different muscles. SYN: *conjoint t.*

> ***conjoint t.*** Conjoined t.

> ***hamstring t.*** Hamstring (1).

> ***t. of Todaro*** A bundle of collagen fibers of variable thickness that connects the wall of the right atrium and the valve of the inferior vena cava.

tendon cell SEE: under *cell.*

tendon suspension Fixation of a tendon. SYN: *tenodesis.*

tendosynovitis (tĕn"dō-sĭn"ō-vī'tĭs) [" + *synovia,* joint fluid, + Gr. *itis,* inflammation] Tenosynovitis.

tendovaginitis (tĕn"dō-văj"ĭn-ī'tĭs) [" + " + Gr. *itis,* inflammation] Tenosynovitis.

Tenebrio (tĕ-nĕb're-ō) A genus of beetles including the species of *T. molitor,* which is an intermediate host of helminth parasites of vertebrates.

tenectomy (tĕ-nĕk'tō-mē) [" + *ektome,* excision] Excision of a lesion of a tendon or tendon sheath.

> ***graduated t.*** Partial division of a tendon.

tenesmus (tĕ-nĕz'mŭs) [Gr. *teinesmos,* a stretching] Spasmodic contraction of anal or bladder sphincter with pain and persistent desire to empty the bowel or bladder, with involuntary ineffectual straining efforts. **tenesmic** (tĕn-ĕz'mĭk), *adj.*

tenia (tē'nē-ă) [L. *taenia,* tape] Taenia.

teniasis (tē-nī'ă-sĭs) [L. *taenia,* tapeworm, + Gr. *-iasis,* a condition] Presence of tapeworms in the body.

tennis elbow A condition marked by pain over the lateral epicondyle of the humerus or the head of the radius. The pain radiates to the outer side of the arm and forearm due to injury or overuse of the extensor carpi radialis brevis or longus muscle, as may occur in playing tennis. The condition is aggravated by resisted wrist extension or forearm supination, or by a stretch force with the wrist flexed, forearm pronated, and elbow extended. Present are weakness of the wrist and difficulty in grasping objects. A reliable diagnostic sign is increased pain when the middle finger or wrist is extended against resistance. SYN: *lateral humeral* **epicondylitis.**

TREATMENT: When elbow soreness is mild, treatment includes resting the arm, using nonsteroidal anti-inflammatory drugs, or applying a wide strap around the forearm, just below the elbow. Injections of a long-acting steroid into the tendon are helpful in about two thirds of patients with slowly resolving symptoms. Physical therapy with an elastic band helps many patients. Patients who do not improve require surgery, e.g., with resection of the extensor carpi radialis brevis or decompression of the posterior interosseous nerve.

tennis toe SEE: under *toe.*

teno- [Irregular formation fr Gr. *tenōn,* stem *tenont-,* tendon] Prefix meaning *tendon.* SEE: *tenont-.*

tenodesis (ten-ŏ-dē′sĭs) [Gr. *tenon,* tendon, + *desis,* a binding] **1.** Surgical fixation of a tendon. Usually a tendon is transferred from its initial point of origin to a new origin in order to restore muscle balance to a joint, to restore lost function, or to increase active power of joint motion. **2.** Flexing of the fingers through tendon action of the extrinsic finger flexor muscles when they are stretched across the wrist joint during wrist extension. This mechanism is used for functional grip in the quadriplegic individual when paralysis is due to loss below the sixth cervical vertebra. SEE: illus.

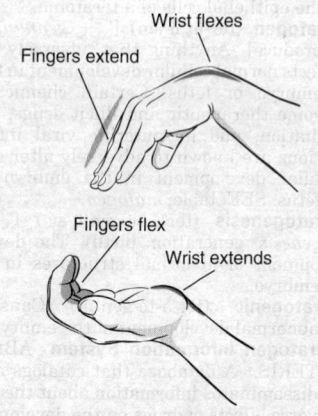

TENODESIS

A. Passive insufficiency of finger extensors occurs when the wrist is flexed, causing the fingers to extend. B. Passive insufficiency of the finger flexors occurs when the wrist is extended, causing the fingers to flex.

tenolysis (tĕn-ŏl′ĭ-sĭs) [″ + *lysis,* dissolution] Tendolysis.

Tenon, Jacques R. (tĕ-nōn′) French surgeon, 1724–1816.

T. capsule A thin connective tissue envelope of the posterior eyeball behind the conjunctiva.

T. space Tissue fluid space between the sclera and the Tenon capsule. SYN: *interfascial space.*

tenonitis (tĕn″ō-nī′tĭs) [″ + *itis,* inflammation] **1.** Inflammation of a tendon. SEE: *tendonitis.* **2.** Inflammation of Tenon capsule.

tenont- [Gr. *tenōn,* stem *tenont-,* tendon] Prefix meaning *tendon.* SEE: *teno-.*

tenoplasty (tĕn′ō-plăs″tē) [″ + *plassein,* to form] Reparative surgery of tendons. SYN: *tendinoplasty; tendoplasty; tenontoplasty.*

Tenormin (tĕn′ĕr-mĭn″) SEE: *atenolol.*

tenorrhaphy (tĕn-or′ă-fē) [″ + *rhaphe,* seam, ridge] Suturing of a tendon.

tenosynovectomy (tĕn″ō-sĭn″ō-vĕk′tō-mē) [″ + *synovia,* joint fluid, + Gr. *ektome,* excision] Excision of a tendon sheath.

tenosynovitis (tĕn″ō-sĭn″ō-vī′tĭs) [″ + ″ + Gr. *itis,* inflammation] An inflammation of a tendon sheath. SYN: *tendosynovitis; tendovaginitis.* SEE: *de Quervain disease.*

t. hyperplastica Painless swelling of extensor tendons over the wrist joint.

de Quervain t. SEE: *de Quervain disease.*

tenotomy (tĕ-nŏt′ō-mē) Surgical section of a tendon. SYN: *tendotomy.*

tenovaginitis (tĕn″ō-văj″ĭn-ī′tĭs) [″ + L. *vagina,* sheath, + Gr. *itis,* inflammation] Inflammation of a tendon sheath. SYN: *tendosynovitis.*

TENS *transcutaneous electrical nerve stimulation.*

tense (tĕns) **1.** Tight, rigid. **2.** Anxious, under mental stress.

tensile strength (tĕn′sĭl) [L. *tensilis,* stretched, tense] The resistance of a structure to stretching or tearing along its longest axis.

Tensilon test (tĕn′sĭ-lŏn″) A test used in the diagnosis of myasthenia gravis (MG). A short-acting anticholinesterase drug, such as edrophonium chloride or neostigmine, is injected, and the patient is observed for improved muscular strength. The patient is also observed after an injection of a placebo (e.g., saline). Improvement with the active drug, but not the placebo, is a strong indication of MG.

tensiometer (tĕn″sē-ŏm′ĕ-tĕr) [L. *tensio,* a stretching, + Gr. *metron,* measure] **1.** A device for determining the surface tension of liquids. **2.** A device used to measure the amount of force a muscle can produce. Also called *cable tensiometer.*

tension (ten′shŏn) [L. *tensio,* a stretching] **1.** The act or process of stretching; the state of being strained or stretched. **2.** Pressure, force. **3.** Expansive force of a gas or vapor. **4.** Mental, emotional, or nervous strain.

    arterial t. Tension resulting from the force exerted by the blood pressure on the walls of arteries.

    arterial oxygen t. ABBR: PaO₂. The partial pressure of oxygen in the plasma of the arterial blood.

    brain tissue oxygen t. ABBR: PbtO2. The oxygen content of the white matter of the brain. It is determined by inserting a small monitor directly into the brain parenchyma. Normal values are >20 mm Hg.

    intraocular t. The pressure of the fluid within the eyeball. SEE: *tonometry; intraocular* ***pressure***.

    intravenous t. Force exerted by the blood pressure on the walls of a vein.

    muscular t. The condition of a muscle in which fibers tend to shorten and thus perform work or liberate heat.

    premenstrual t. Premenstrual dysphoric disorder.

    surface t. The molecular attraction of liquid molecules for one another, resulting in an outer boundary that has a minimal surface area.

    tissue t. The theoretical state of equilibrium between the cells of a tissue.

tensometer (tĕn-sŏm′ĕ-tĕr) [L. *tensio,* a stretching, + Gr. *metron,* measure] A device for testing the tensile strength of materials.

tensor (tĕn′sor) [L., a stretcher] Any muscle that makes a part tense.

tent (tĕnt) [Fr. *tente,* from L. *tenta,* stretched] **1.** A plug of soft material used to maintain or dilate the opening to a sinus, canal, or body cavity. A variety of cylindrically shaped materials may be used. **2.** A portable covering or shelter composed of fabric.

    cool mist t. An enclosure, formerly used for the administration of nebulized medications and mists. It was used in the past to treat asthma, croup, and other respiratory illnesses in children.

    laminaria t. A plug made of *Laminaria digitata* that is placed in the cervical canal of the uterus to dilate it.

    medical t. A portable clinic erected to provide supportive care in outdoor settings, such as war zones, outdoor concerts, or marathon races.

    oxygen t. A tent that in the past was placed over a bed for the continuous administration of oxygen and mist.

    pleural t. In thoracoscopy or thoracic surgery, a mediastinal or subpleural blanket used to reinforce the suture line.

    sponge t. A plug made of compressed sponge that is placed in the cervical canal to dilate it.

tentacle (tĕn′tă-k′l) A slender projection of invertebrates. It is used for prehension, tactile purposes, or feeding.

tentative (tĕn′tă-tĭv) [L. *tentativus,* feel, try] **1.** Pert. to a diagnosis subject to change because of insufficient data. **2.** Indecisive.

tentorial (tĕn-tō′rē-ăl) Pert. to a tentorium.

tentorium (tĕn-tō′rē-ŭm) *pl.* **tentoria** [L., tent] A tentlike structure or part.

    t. cerebelli The process of the dura mater between the cerebrum and cerebellum supporting the occipital lobes.

tenure (tĕn′yĕr) [L. *tenēre,* to hold] **1.** The holding of a property, place, or occupational assignment. **2.** The specification that an employee (typically someone in an academic setting) may hold a position permanently unless he or she behaves with gross negligence.

tepid (tĕp′ĭd) [L. *tepidus,* lukewarm] Slightly warm; lukewarm.

ter- [L., *ter,* thrice] Prefix meaning *three times, threefold.*

tera- In the International System of Units (SI), a prefix signifying 10¹².

teras (tĕr′ăs) *pl.* **terata** [Gr.] A severely deformed fetus.

terato-, terat- [Gr. *teras,* stem *terat-,* monster, marvel, portent] Prefixes meaning *monster.*

teratoblastoma (tĕr″ă-tō-blăs-tō′mă) [Gr. *teratos,* monster, + *blastos,* germ, + *oma,* tumor] A tumor that contains embryonic material but that is not representative of all three germinal layers. SEE: *teratoma.*

teratocarcinoma (tĕr″ă-tō-kăr″sĭ-nō′mă) [″ + *karkinos,* cancer, + *oma,* tumor] A carcinoma that has developed from the epithelial cells of a teratoma.

teratogen (tĕr-ăt′ō-jĕn) [″ + *gennan,* to produce] Anything that adversely affects normal cellular development in the embryo or fetus. Certain chemicals, some therapeutic and illicit drugs, radiation, and intrauterine viral infections are known to adversely alter cellular development in the embryo or fetus. SEE: table; *mutagen.*

teratogenesis (tĕr″ă-tō-gĕn′ĕ-sĭs) [″ + *genesis,* generation, birth] The development of abnormal structures in an embryo.

teratogenic (tĕr″ă-tō-gĕn′ĭk) Causing abnormal development of the embryo.

Teratogen Information System ABBR: TERIS. A database that catalogs and disseminates information about the adverse effects of drugs on the developing fetus.

teratoid (tĕr′ă-toyd) [Gr. *teratos,* monster, + *eidos,* form, shape] Resembling a severely malformed fetus.

teratology (tĕr-ă-tŏl′ō-jē) [″ + *logos,* word, reason] The branch of biology dealing with the study of congenital de-

U.S. FDA Categories for Drugs by Teratogenic or Fetotoxic Potential*

Pregnancy Category	Description	Examples
A	Medications for which no harm has been demonstrated in well-designed studies of pregnant and lactating women.	Folic acid supplementation
B	Medications without known risk when used in human pregnancy or breastfeeding. Studies in laboratory animals have been performed with positive or negative results, but no demonstrable risk in pregnancy is yet known. Individual considerations of risk and benefit guide usage in patients.	Acyclovir, amoxicillin/clavulanate, fluoxetine, glyburide, ranitidine
C	Medications whose use in human pregnancy or breastfeeding has not been adequately studied; risk of usage cannot be excluded but has not been proven. Individual considerations of risk and benefit guide drug usage in patients.	Albuterol, hydrocodone, omeprazole, verapamil
D	Medications known to cause fetal harm when administered during pregnancy or harm to children during breastfeeding. In some specific settings the potential benefits of use may outweigh the risk.	Tetracycline antibiotics
X	Medications judged to be unsafe (contraindicated) in pregnancy. Evidence of risk has accrued from clinical trials or postmarketing surveillance.	Isotretinoin, thalidomide, warfarin

*All medication use during pregnancy should be carefully reviewed with health professionals experienced in reproductive pharmacology and patient care.

formities and abnormal development. **teratologic,** *adj.*

teratoma (tĕr-ă-tō′mă) [″ + *oma,* tumor] A congenital tumor containing one or more of the three primary embryonic germ layers. Hair, teeth, and endodermal elements may be present. SYN: *dermoid cyst.* SEE: *fetus in fetu.*

teratospermia (tĕr″ă-tō-spĕr′mē-ă) [″ + *sperma,* seed] Malformed sperm in semen.

terbium (tĕr′bē-ŭm) [*(Yt)terby,* a village in Sweden + *-ium* (1)] SYMB: Tb. A lanthanide, rare-earth metal, atomic weight (mass) 158.9254, atomic number 65, specific gravity 8.272.

teres (tĕ′rēz) [L., round] Round and smooth; cylindrical; used to describe certain muscles and ligaments.

tergal (tĕr′găl) [L. *tergum,* back] Concerning the back or dorsal surface.

ter in die (tĕr ĭn dē′ă) [L.] ABBR: t.i.d. Three times a day.

term [L. *terminus,* a boundary] **1.** A limit or boundary. **2.** A definite or limited period of duration such as the normal period of pregnancy, approx. nine calendar months or 38 to 42 weeks' gestation.

TERMA An abbreviation for the "total energy released to media," e.g., the amount of radiation to which a cancer is exposed during radiation therapy.

terminal (tĕr′mĭ-năl) [L. *terminalis*] **1.** Pert. to or placed at the end. **2.** Final, last, ultimate. **3.** Fatal.

terminal bars Minute bars of dense intercellular cement that occupy and close spaces between epithelial cells and bind them together.

terminal cancer SEE: under *cancer.*

terminal dribble (drib′ĕl) Postvoid dribbling.

terminal duct lobular unit ABBR: TDLU. The blind ending of the lactiferous duct that contains the lobule and its duct. Most benign and malignant breast lesions arise here.

terminal ganglia Ganglia of the parasympathetic division of the autonomic nervous system that are located in or close to their visceral effectors such as the heart or intestines.

terminal illness SEE: under *illness.*

terminal infection SEE: under *infection.*

terminal weaning The gradual withdrawal of mechanical ventilation from a patient who is not expected to survive without respiratory support.

PATIENT CARE: It is similar to terminal extubation except that the withdrawal of support occurs incrementally, often over a span of several hours or days. At predetermined intervals the ventilatory rate is decreased and/or the fraction of inspired oxygen is decreased. The process continues until the patient is no longer receiving ventilatory support or death has occurred.

The ethical considerations that guide terminal extubation apply equally to terminal weaning. Terminal weaning takes longer than extubation: this gives the patient, his or her family, and professional staff more time to reflect on his or her life and adjust to his or her death.

termination (tĕr″mĭ-nā′shŏn) [L. *terminatio*, fixing of limits] **1.** The distal end of a part. **2.** The cessation of anything.

termination provision A clause in a contract governing insured health care services that specifies those situations under which the contract may be terminated, considered null and void.

Terminologia Anatomica (tĕr″mĭ-nă-lō′jē-ă ăn-ă-tŏm′ĭ-kă) ABBR: TA. The current official nomenclature for human anatomy. It was developed by the Federative Committee on Anatomical Terminology (FCAT) and the 56 Member Associations of the International Federation of Associations of Anatomists (IFAA) and was released in 1998, replacing the Nomina Anatomica, the earlier standard. SEE: *Basle Nomina Anatomica; Nomina Anatomica.*

terminology (tĕr-mĭ-nŏl′ō-jē) [L. *terminus*, a boundary, + Gr. *logos*, word] The vocabulary used in specific arts, sciences, technical endeavors, trades, or professions. SEE: *nomenclature.*

terminus (tĕr′mĭ-nŭs) [L.] An ending; a boundary.

terpene (tĕr′pēn) Any member of the family of hydrocarbons of the formula $C_{10}H_{16}$.

terra (tĕr′ă) [L.] Earth; soil.

terrible triad SEE: under *triad.*

terror [L. *terrere*, to frighten] Great fear.

Terson syndrome Subarachnoid hemorrhage combined with subhyaloid hemorrhage.

tertian (tĕr′shŭn) [L. *tertianus*, the third] Occurring every third day; usually pert. to a form of malarial fever.

tertiary (tĕr′shē-ār-ē) [L. *tertiarius*] Third in order or stage.

tertiary adrenal insufficiency SEE: under *insufficiency.*

tertiary alcohol SEE: under *alcohol.*

tertiary syphilis SEE: under *syphilis.*

tertiary trauma survey A reevaluation of the stabilized trauma patient performed after the initial resuscitation and corrective surgeries for the injuries. It is used to identify additional injuries that may become obvious only after the patient begins rehabilitation.

tesla (tĕs′lă) [Nikola Tesla, Serbian-born U.S. physicist, 1856–1943] ABBR: T. In the SI system, a measure of magnetic strength; 1 tesla equals 1 weber per square meter.

tessellated (tĕs′ĕ-lā″tĕd) [L. *tessella*, a square] Composed of little squares.

test [L. *testum*, earthen vessel] **1.** An examination. **2.** A method to determine the presence or nature of a substance or the presence of a disease. **3.** A chemical reaction. **4.** A reagent or substance used in making a test. Particular tests are listed under the first word. SEE: e.g.,

creatine clearance test; oral glucose tolerance test; tuberculin skin test.

testa (tĕs′tă) [L.] A shell.

testes (tĕs′tēs) [L.] Pl. of testis.

test for lacrimation Schirmer test.

testicle (tes′tĭ-kl) [L. *testiculus*, a little testis] Testis.

testicular (tĕs-tĭk′ū-lăr) Pert. to a testicle.

testicular cancer, germ-cell SEE: under *cancer.*

testicular self-examination A technique that enables a man to detect changes in the size and shape of his testicles and evaluate any tenderness. Each testicle is examined separately and in comparison with the other. The best time to perform the test is just after a warm bath or shower when the scrotal tissue is relaxed. The man places his thumbs on the anterior surface of the testicle, supporting it with the index and middle fingers of both hands. Each testicle is gently rolled between the fingers and thumbs and carefully felt for lumps, hardness, or thickening, esp. as compared with the other testicle. The epididymis is a soft, slightly tender, tube-like body behind the testicle. Abnormal findings should be reported immediately to a health care professional.

testicular sperm aspiration SEE: under *aspiration.*

testicular torsion SEE: under *torsion.*

testis (tĕs′tĭs) *pl.* **testes** [L.] The male gonad; testicle. It is one of two reproductive glands located in the scrotum that produce the male reproductive cells (spermatozoa) and the male hormones testosterone and inhibin. SEE: illus.

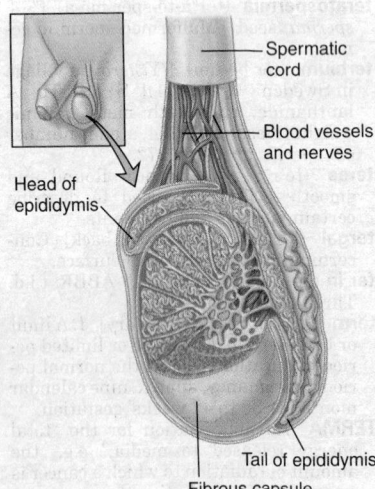

Spermatic cord

Blood vessels and nerves

Head of epididymis

Tail of epididymis

Fibrous capsule

TESTIS

ANATOMY: Each is an ovoid body about 4 cm long and 2 to 2.5 cm in width and thickness, enclosed within a dense inelastic fibrous tunica albuginea. The testis is divided into numerous lobules separated by septa, each lobule containing one to three seminiferous tubules within which the spermatozoa are produced by meiosis. The lobules lead to straight ducts that join a plexus, the rete testis, from which 15 to 20 efferent ducts lead to the epididymis. The epididymis leads to the ductus deferens, through which sperm are conveyed to the urethra. Between the seminiferous tubules are the interstitial cells (cells of Leydig), which secrete testosterone. Within the tubules are sustentacular cells, which secrete inhibin. The testes are suspended from the body by the spermatic cord, a structure that extends from the inguinal ring to the testis and contains the ductus deferens, testicular vessels (spermatic artery, vein, lymph vessels), and nerves.

DISORDERS: Hyperfunction (hypergonadism) may cause early maturity such as large sexual organs with early functional activity and increased growth of hair. Hypofunction (hypogonadism) is indicated by undeveloped testes, absence of body hair, high-pitched voice, sterility, smooth skin, loss of sexual desire, low metabolism, and eunuchoid or eunuch body type.

descent of t. The migration of the testis from the abdominal cavity to the scrotum during fetal development.

displaced t. A testis located abnormally within the inguinal canal or pelvis.

femoral t. An inguinal testis near or superior to the femoral ring.

inverted t. A testis reversed in the scrotum so that the epididymis attaches to the anterior instead of the posterior part of the gland.

perineal t. A testis located in the perineal region outside the scrotum.

undescended t. Cryptorchidism.

test meal A meal usually small and of definite quality and composition, given to aid in chemical analysis of the stomach contents or radiographical examination of the stomach.

testosterone (tes-tos′tĕ-rōn″) [*testis* + *sterone*] A steroid sex hormone that is responsible for the growth and development of masculine characteristics. It directly influences the maturation of male sexual organs, development of sperm within the testes, sexual drive, erectile function of the penis, and male secondary sexual characteristics (facial hair, thickened vocal cords, and pronounced musculature). In addition, it is linked to aggressive and predatory behaviors.

Testosterone is produced in the Leydig cells of the testes and by the metabolic conversion of adrenal androgens (DHEA and DHEA sulfate) in various tissues. It has also been synthesized for replacement therapy in men with sex hormone deficiencies, e.g., men with hypogonadal conditions such as Klinefelter syndrome.

Testosterone adversely affects diseases of the prostate gland by sponsoring the growth of both benign hyperplasia of the gland and carcinomas of the prostate. Both of these conditions may be treated with antiandrogenic therapies. Predatory sexual behaviors also depend on testosterone and can be treated with interventions that block the effects of the hormone.

testotoxicosis (tĕs″tō-tŏk″sĭ-kō′sĭs) [″ + ″] Precocious puberty occurring in boys due to increased secretion of the male hormone, testosterone. Affected boys prematurely develop adult secondary sexual characteristics, increased height and muscle mass, and, in some instances, aggressive behavior.

test-retest reliability SEE: under *reliability*.

test strip Dipstick.

test tube A glass tube closed at one end. It is used in laboratory sciences to hold chemicals and other material.

test-tube baby SEE: under *baby*.

test type Letters or figures of various sizes printed on paper. These are used in testing visual acuity.

tetanic (tĕ-tăn′ĭk) [Gr. *tetanikos*] 1. Pert. to or producing tetanus. 2. Any agent producing tetanic spasms.

tetanization (tĕt″ă-nī-zā′shŭn) [Gr. *tetanos*, stretched] 1. Production of tetanus or tetanic spasms by induction of the disease. 2. Induction of tetanic contractions in a muscle by electrical stimuli.

tetanize (tĕt′ă-nīz) To induce tonic muscular spasms.

tetanolysin (tĕt″ă-nŏl′ĭ-sĭn) A hemolytic component of the toxin produced by *Clostridium tetani*, causative organism of tetanus. It does not cause the clinical signs and symptoms of this disease.

tetanospasmin (tĕt″ă-nō-spăs′mĭn) [″ + *spasmos*, a convulsion] A component of the toxin produced by *Clostridium tetani* that causes tetanus.

tetanus (tĕt′ă-nŭs) [Gr. *tetanos*, stretched] An acute, life-threatening illness caused by the toxin tetanospasmin produced in infected wounds by the bacillus *Clostridium tetani*. The disease is marked by extreme muscular rigidity, violent muscle spasms, and, often, respiratory and autonomic failure. Because of proactive immunization programs in the U.S., the disease affects only 50 patients annually. In nations without effective immunization programs, the disease is very common and usually deadly. SEE: *Clostridium tetani; lockjaw; tetanolysin; tetanospasmin; trismus*.

ETIOLOGY: The responsible bacteria is most likely to proliferate in tetanus-prone wounds (e.g., those contaminated by soil, animal excrement or debris); puncture, avulsion, or bite wounds; burns; frostbite; necrotic tissues; gangrene; injection site infections; umbilical stump infections; or uterine infections. It is less likely to infect shallow wounds with cleanly cut edges. The spores of *C. tetani* germinate in the anaerobic depths of tetanus-prone injuries, producing bacteria that release tetanospasmin. This neurotoxin is carried to the central nervous system, where it blocks impulses that modulate muscle contraction. The incubation period varies from 1 or 2 days to a few months. The shorter the incubation, the more deadly the illness is likely to be.

SYMPTOMS: Unopposed muscular contraction leads to rigidity and spasticity, esp. of the muscles of the jaw, neck, back, abdomen, and esophagus. Lockjaw (trismus) is a hallmark of the disease, as are violent arching of the back muscles (opisthotonus), and a rigid, fixed smile (risus sardonicus). Intense painful muscle spasms may be triggered by noises, bright lights, attempts to swallow or eat, or other stimuli. The patient may also suffer profuse sweating, low-grade fever, and wild fluctuations in pulse, blood pressure, and respirations. Diagnosis usually is based on a history of trauma with no previous tetanus immunization and on the clinical picture presented.

TREATMENT: Early débridement may lessen the burden of toxin-producing bacteria in the wound. Muscle-relaxing drugs, like baclofen and diazepam, and neuromuscular blocking agents, such as vecuronium, reduce muscle spasm. Beta blockers like propranolol decrease the incidence of tachycardias and hypertension. Advanced airway and ventilatory support are best provided in an intensive care unit. Tetanus immune globulin is given to provide passive immunity against circulating tetanus toxin. High doses of penicillin G (or alternatives for the patient with penicillin allergy) are administered intravenously to kill clostridia. Wound debridement and/or surgical exploration may be required to remove the source of the toxin.

PATIENT CARE: The patient is kept in a quiet, dimly lit room, where stimulation is minimized. A patent airway is maintained, oxygen administered to maintain oxygen saturation, and suctioning carried out gently with prehyperventilation and posthyperventilation. Oral feedings are withheld to limit esophageal spasms and the aspiration of nutrients. Intravenous access is established for administration of emer-gency medications, and hydration is provided. Enteral or parenteral nutrition may be needed to meet the patient's increased metabolic needs. A Foley catheter is placed to prevent urinary retention. Cardiac rhythm and vital signs are monitored, and fluid and electrolyte balance managed.

⚠ Recovery from tetanus does not guarantee natural immunity. Therefore, the patient should begin an immunization series before leaving the hospital.

PREVENTION: Initial immunization should begin in infancy. The toxoid should be given in three doses at 4- to 8-week intervals beginning when the infant is 6 to 8 weeks old, and a fourth dose 6 to 12 months thereafter. A fifth dose is usually administered at 4 to 6 years of age before school entry. Tetanus toxoid is commonly given in combination with diphtheria toxoid and acellular pertussis vaccine. Active immunization with adsorbed tetanus toxoid provides protection for at least 10 years. Although it has been the practice to give a tetanus booster every 10 years, current advice is to give a single booster dose at age 50 if the individual received all 5 doses as a child. Tetanus booster vaccination should be given to patients with tetanus-prone wounds who have not received the toxoid in the past 3 years.

artificial t. Tetanus produced by a drug such as strychnine.

ascending t. Tetanus in which muscle spasms occur first in the lower part of the body and then spread upward, finally involving muscles of the head and neck.

cephalic t. A form of tetanus due to a wound of the head, esp. one near the eyebrow. It is marked by trismus, facial paralysis on one side, and pronounced dysphagia. It resembles rabies and is often fatal. SYN: *hydrophobic t.*

chronic t. 1. A latent infection in a healed wound, reactivated on opening the wound. 2. A form of tetanus in which the onset and progress of the disease are slower and more prolonged and the symptoms are less severe.

cryptogenic t. Tetanus in which the site of entry of the organism is not known.

descending t. Tetanus in which muscle spasms occur first in the head and neck and later are manifested in other muscles of the body.

t. dorsalis Tetanus in which the body is bent backward.

extensor t. Tetanus that affects the extensor muscles.

idiopathic t. Tetanus that occurs without any visible lesion.

imitative t. A conversion disorder that simulates tetanus.

t. infantum T. neonatorum.

t. lateralis A form of tetanus in which the body is bent sideways.

local t. Tetanus marked by spasticity of a group of muscles near the wound. Trismus, tonic contraction of jaw muscles, is usually absent.

t. neonatorum Tetanus of very young infants, usually due to infection of the navel caused by using nonsterile technique in ligating the umbilical cord.

t. paradoxus Cephalic tetanus combined with paralysis of the facial or other cranial nerve.

postoperative t. Tetanus that follows an operation as a result of contamination of the surgical incision.

puerperal t. Tetanus that occurs following childbirth.

toxic t. Tetanus produced by overdose of strychnine.

tetanus antitoxin Protective antibody against *Clostridium tetani*, the bacterium that causes tetanus. The antibody develops after inoculation with tetanus toxin or toxoid or infection with *C. tetani*.

tetanus immune globulin SEE: under *globulin*.

tetanus toxoid SEE: under *toxoid*.

tetany (tĕt′ă-nē) [Gr. *tetanos*, stretched] Intermittent tonic muscular spasms that typically involve the arms or legs.

SYMPTOMS: Spasms may be accompanied by numbness, tingling, loss of function, and pain in affected muscle groups.

SIGNS: Characteristic signs include Trousseau sign, Chvostek sign, and the peroneal sign. Prolongation of the isoelectric phase of the S-T segment of the electrocardiogram may be present with tetany that is caused by a low serum calcium level. SEE: *Chvostek sign; hyperventilation; Trousseau sign.*

ETIOLOGY: It may occur in infants, esp. newborns in intensive care and those who have had perinatal asphyxia. Other causative factors include hypocalcemia (e.g., in hypoparathyroidism or after parathyroid surgery), hypomagnesemia, hypokalemia, alkalosis (e.g., in hyperventilation), infection with *Clostridium tetani,* and vitamin D deficiency.

alkalotic t. Tetany resulting from respiratory alkalosis, as in hyperventilation, or from metabolic alkalosis induced by excessive intake of sodium bicarbonate or excessive loss of chlorides by vomiting, gastric lavage, or suction.

duration t. Continuous contraction, esp. in degenerated muscles, in response to a continuous electric current.

hyperventilation t. Tetany caused by continued hyperventilation.

hypocalcemic t. Tetany due to low serum calcium and high serum phosphate levels. This may be due to lack of vitamin D, factors that interfere with calcium absorption such as steatorrhea or infantile diarrhea, or defective renal excretion of phosphorus.

latent t. Tetany that requires mechanical or electrical stimulation of nerves to show characteristic signs of excitability; the opposition of manifest tetany.

manifest t. Tetany in which the characteristic symptoms such as carpopedal spasm, laryngospasm, and convulsions are present; the opposite of latent tetany.

parathyroid t. Tetany resulting from excision of the parathyroid glands or from hyposecretion of the parathyroid glands as a result of disease or disorders of the glands. SEE: *hypoparathyroidism.*

rachitic t. Tetany due to hypocalcemia accompanying vitamin D deficiency.

thyreoprival t. Tetany resulting from removal of the thyroid gland, accompanied by inadvertent removal of the parathyroid glands.

tethering Binding or attachment, e.g., of white blood cells as they migrate through tissues.

tetra-, tetr- [Gr. *tettar-*, four] Prefixes meaning *four.*

tetrabasic (tĕt″ră-bā′sĭk) [Gr. *tetras,* four, + *basis,* base] Having four replaceable hydrogen atoms, said of an acid or acid salt.

tetrabromofluorescein (tĕt″ră-brŏm″ō-flū-or-ĕs′ĭn, -ē-ĭn) A dye, $C_{20}H_8Br_4O_5$, obtained from the action of bromine on fluorescein, used as a stain in microscopy. SYN: *eosin.*

2,3,7,8-tetrachlorodibenzo-p-dioxin (te″tră-klō″rō-dī″ben″zō-pē″dī-ok′sĭn) TCDD.

tetrachlorethylene, tetrachloroethylene, tetrachloroethene (te″tră-klor-eth′ĭ-lēn″, te″tră-klō-rō-eth′ĭ-lēn″, te″tră-klō-rō-eth′ēn″) $Cl_2C=C\text{-}Cl_2$ or C_2Cl_4, a clear, colorless liquid with a characteristic odor, used as a solvent.

tetrachloride (tĕt″ră-klō′rīd) A radical with four atoms of chlorine.

tetracycline (tĕt″ră-sī′klēn) A bacteriostatic antibiotic used, for example, to treat acne, chlamydia, and atypical pneumonia.

⚠ Tetracyclines should not be given to pregnant women or young children, because they damage developing teeth and bones.

tetrad (tĕt′răd) [Gr. *tetras,* four] **1.** A group of four things with something in common. **2.** An element having a valence or combining power of four. **3.** A group of four parts, said of cells produced by division in two planes. **4.** The group of four chromosomes in prophase 1 of mitosis; the pairs of homologous chromosomes, each having two chromatids, that line up together on the spindle fibers. SEE: *meiosis* for illus.

tetraethylpyrophosphate (tĕt-ră-ĕth″ĭl-pī-rō-fŏs′făt) ABBR: TEPP. A powerful cholinesterase inhibitor used as an insecticide. It is poisonous to humans; the antidote is atropine.

tetrahydrocannabinol (te″tră-hī″drō-kan′ă-bĭ-nol″, -kă-nab′ĭ-nol″) [*tetra-* + *hydro-* + *cannabinol,* a cannabinoid] ABBR: THC. $C_{21}H_{30}O_2$, the principal psychoactive component in marijuana and hashish. SEE: *Cannabis sativa; hashish; marijuana.*

tetraiodothyronine (tĕt″ră-ī″ō-dō-thī′rō-nēn) Thyroxine.

tetralogy (te-tral′ŏ-jē) [*tetra-* + *-logy*] The combination of four symptoms or elements.

tetralogy of Fallot (fol-ō′) [Étienne-Louis-Arthur Fallot, Fr. physician, 1850–1911] ABBR: TOF. A congenital malformation of the heart and great vessels marked by a defect in the interventricular septum, pulmonary artery stenosis, dextroposition of the aorta, and right ventricular hypertrophy. The defect can be repaired surgically.

tetramer (te′tră-mĕr) [*tetra-* + *-mer*] A structure such as a molecule or a polymer made of four structural subunits. **tetrameric** (te″tră-mer′ĭk), *adj.* **tetramerous** (tĕ-tram′ĕ-rŭs), *adj.*

tetraparesis (tĕt″ră-păr′ĕ-sĭs) [″ + *parienai,* to let fall] Muscular weakness of all four extremities.

tetrapeptide (tĕt″ră-pĕp′tīd) A peptide that yields four amino acids when it is hydrolyzed.

tetraplegia (tĕt″ră-plē′jē-ă) [″ + *plege,* a stroke] Quadriplegia.

tetraploid (tĕt′ră-ployd) [″ + *ploos,* a fold, + *eidos,* form, shape] **1.** Pert. to tetraploidy, the state of having twice the diploid number of chromosomes. **2.** Having four sets of chromosomes.

tetrasomic (tĕt-ră-sō′mĭk) [″ + *soma,* body] Possessing four instead of the usual pair of chromosomes in an otherwise diploid cell; that is, having a chromosome number of $2n + 2$.

tetravalent (tĕt″ră-vā′lĕnt) Having a valence or combining power of four. SYN: *quadrivalent.*

tetrodotoxin (te″trō-dŏ-tok′sĭn) [L. *Tetrodon,* type genus (of a tropical fish) + *toxin*] $C_{11}H_{17}N_3O_8$, a powerful neurotoxin that blocks the movement of sodium ions through voltage-gated sodium channels in neuronal cell membranes. It prevents depolarization of nerves and the propagation of electrical impulses from one nerve to another.

Most cases of human intoxication result from consumption of the fugu (any of several species of pufferfish of the family Tetraodontidae) prepared as a delicacy. SEE: *blue-ringed octopus.*

tetroxide (tĕ-trŏk′sīd) A chemical compound containing four oxygen atoms.

texting (teks′tĭng) The transmission of written messages electronically, e.g., from one mobile communication device to another.

> ⚠ CAUTION: Because the source of texts cannot be reliably discerned by the receiver, texting is not an acceptable means of transmitting health care information or orders that affect patient care.

SYN: *text messaging.*

text messaging (tekst mes′ă-jing) Texting.

textural (tĕks′tū-răl) [L. *textura,* weaving] Concerning the texture or constitution of a tissue.

texture (tĕks′tūr) [L. *textura*] The organization of a tissue or structure.

textus (tĕks′tŭs) [L.] Tissue.

TFBM *Tissue factor-bearing microparticle.*

Th Symbol for the element thorium.

thalamic (thăl-ăm′ĭk) [Gr. *thalamos,* inner chamber] Pert. to the thalamus.

thalamic pain syndrome Pain affecting one half of the body (alternatively, anesthesia affecting half the body) that results from a stroke or other injury to the thalamus. SYN: *Dejerine-Roussy syndrome.*

thalamo-, thalam- [Gr. *thalamos,* chamber, bed chamber] Prefixes meaning *thalamus.*

thalamocortical (thăl″ăm-ō-kor′tĭ-kăl) [″ + L. *cortex,* rind] Pert. to the thalamus and the cerebral cortex.

thalamotomy (thăl-ă-mŏt′ō-mē) [″ + *tome,* incision] Destruction of a portion of the thalamus, used to treat intractable pain or movement disorders such as Parkinson disease.

thalamus (thăl′ă-mŭs) *pl.* **thalami** [L.] An ovoid collection of nuclei found deep inside the brain and completely surrounded by the cerebral hemisphere. The two thalami make up most of the mass of the diencephalon and each bulges into the lateral wall of the third ventricle. The thalamus filters and modifies most of the information that is being sent from elsewhere to the cerebral cortices: all sensory signals, except olfaction, and most motor programs are processed in the thalamus before they are projected onto the cerebral cortex. At the same time, the cortical layout of information is immediately projected back onto the thalamus and contributes to thalamic filtering and processing.

Stroke damage to the thalamus can produce a range of neurological problems, notably pure sensory deficits, akinesia and intentional disorders, and aphasia. SEE: *thalamic **nucleus***.

thalassemia (thal″ă-sē′mē-ă) [Gr. *thalassa*, sea + *-emia*] Any of a group of hereditary anemias occurring in populations bordering the Mediterranean Sea and in Southeast Asia. Anemia is produced by either a defective production rate of the alpha or beta hemoglobin polypeptide chain or a decreased synthesis of the beta chain. Heterozygotes are usually asymptomatic. The severity in homozygotes varies according to the complexity of the inheritance pattern, but thalassemia may be fatal. SEE: *sickle cell **anemia***.

   t. intermedia A chronic hemolytic anemia caused by deficient alpha chain synthesis. SYN: *hemoglobin H disease*.

   t. major The homozygous form of deficient beta chain synthesis, which presents during childhood. This inherited blood disorder most commonly affects people of Mediterranean, Middle Eastern, Indian, Asian, and Southeast Asian descent. Malaria is endemic in these areas, and the thalassemia trait (carrier status that is generally asymptomatic) may provide protection against malaria. When both parents have the trait and pass it on to a child (25% chance in each pregnancy), the child develops the disorder. The different forms of thalassemia vary in severity, but each affects the body's ability to produce a specific type of hemoglobin. The most severe form is Cooley anemia (beta-thalassemia major), which prevents or greatly reduces the body's ability to produce "adult" hemoglobin (HbA). Clinically thalassemia is characterized by fatigue, splenomegaly, severe anemia, enlargement of the heart, mild jaundice, leg ulcers, and cholelithiasis. When untreated, bone marrow expands as the body attempts to increase blood cell formation, causes thickening of the cranial bones, and increases cheekbone eminences.

   PATIENT CARE: The only cure for Cooley anemia is a bone marrow transplant from a matched sibling. The parents and siblings of a child with thalassemia may undergo human leukocyte antigen testing to identify a potential bone marrow donor. Generally patients under age 15 who have no liver disease and are well chelated have the highest success rates from bone marrow transplant. Without a match, treatment involves transfusions to restore hemoglobin levels and chelation therapy to remove excess transfused iron from the body. Parents are taught to prepare chelation at home for their affected children, select and rotate subcutaneous administration sites, and recognize adverse drug reactions and signs of infection. Complications of chelation therapy include swelling and itching at the site of administration, blurred vision, and high-frequency hearing loss, sometimes accompanied by tinnitus. Young children may develop knock knee (genu valgus) as other metals are removed by the therapy. The child thus requires annual hearing and vision examinations and long-bone x-rays to screen for these problems. When a problem is identified, the drug is discontinued until the adverse reaction resolves and is later restarted at a lower dose. Motivation for this arduous therapy is difficult, and an associated psychosocial problem may be the need for a "holiday" from treatment, esp. among adolescents and young adults. The primary health care provider monitors blood ferritin levels to assess compliance with therapy. Patients and their families require ongoing support and education. SYN: *Cooley anemia*.

   t. minor A mild disease produced by heterozygosity of either the alpha or beta hemoglobin chain. It may be completely asymptomatic. It is usually revealed by chance or as a result of study of the family of a person having thalassemia major. The prognosis is excellent.

thalassotherapy (thă-las″ō-ther′ă-pē) [Gr. *thalassa*, sea + *therapy*] The medical or therapeutic use of seawater or products from the sea. Treatments include living at the seaside, bathing in the sea, taking sea voyages, or consuming or being wrapped in seaweed.

thalidomide (thă-lĭd′ō-mīd) A sedative/hypnotic drug that was removed from the market in 1961 when it was discovered to be the cause of severe birth defects, esp. phocomelia. It has been found to be useful in treating erythema nodosum leprosum, multiple myeloma, Kaposi sarcoma, and several other cancers, and skin and immunological diseases. SEE: *phocomelia*.

 This drug should not be administered to women of childbearing age.

thallium (thal′ē-ŭm) [Gr. *thallos*, a young shoot + *-ium* (1)] SYMB: Tl. A metallic element, atomic weight (mass) 204.37, atomic number 81, specific gravity, 11.85. Its salts may be poisonous in overdose; its radioisotope is used to assess myocardial perfusion and viability.

   t. 201 A radionuclide used to diagnose ischemic heart disease. When injected at the peak of exercise during a graded exercise tolerance test, it circulates to the myocardium. Images of the heart can then be obtained to aid in the diagnosis of impaired coronary blood flow or prior myocardial infarction. SEE: *exercise tolerance test; redistribution.*

t. sulfate A chemical used as a rodenticide. It is also toxic to humans.

thanato-, thanat- [Gr. *thanatos*, death] Prefixes meaning *death.*

thanatognomonic (thăn″ăt-ŏg-nō-mŏn′ĭk) [″ + *gnomonikos*, knowing] Pert. to the approach of death.

thanatology (thăn″ă-tŏl′ō-jē) [Gr. *thanatos*, death, + *logos*, word, reason] The study of death.

thanatophoric dysplasia SEE: under *dysplasia.*

Thayer-Martin medium (thā′ĕr-mär′tĭn) A special medium used for growing the causative organism of gonorrhea, *Neisseria gonorrhoeae.*

theater sign SEE: under *sign.*

thebaine (thē-bā′ĭn) An alkaloid present in opiates and poppy seeds.

theca (thē′kă) *pl.* **thecae** [Gr. *theke*, sheath] A sheath or investing membrane.

thecal (thē′kăl) [Gr. *theke*, sheath] Pert. to a sheath.

theco-, thec-, theci- [Gr. *thēkē*, case, cover] Prefixes meaning *sheath, case, receptacle.*

thecodont (thē′kō-dŏnt) [Gr. *theke*, sheath, + *odous*, tooth] Pert. to teeth that are inserted in sockets.

thecoma (thē-kō′mă) [″ + *oma*, tumor] A spindle-cell tumor of the ovary often occurring during or after menopause. It is usually benign but may present with elevated serum tumor markers, adhesions to neighboring structures, or ascites, all of which may initially suggest prior to its removal that the tumor is malignant.

thel-, thelo- [Gr. *thēlē*, nipple] Prefixes meaning *nipple.*

thelarche (thē-lăr′kē) [″ + *arche*, beginning] The beginning of breast development, a milestone that typically occurs by about age 13 in the U.S. SEE: *pubarche; semenarche.*

Thelazia (thē-lā′zē-ă) [Gr. *thelazo*, to suck] A genus of nematodes that inhabit the conjunctival sac and lacrimal ducts of various species of vertebrates. Occasionally species of *Thelazia* are found in humans.

thelaziasis (thē″lā-zī′ă-sĭs) [″ + *-iasis*, condition] Infestation by worms of the genus *Thelazia.*

thelitis (thē-līt′ĭs) [*thel-* + *-itis*] Mammillitis.

thelium (thē′lē-ŭm) *pl.* **thelia** [L.] **1.** A papilla. **2.** A nipple. **3.** A cellular layer.

thematic apperception test A projective test in which the subject is shown life situations in pictures that could be interpreted in several ways. The subject is asked to provide a story of what the picture represents. The results may provide insights into the subject's personality.

thenal (thē′năl) [Gr. *thenar*, palm] Pert. to the palm or thenar eminence.

thenar (thē′năr) [Gr. *thenar*, palm] **1.** The palm of the hand or sole of the foot. **2.** A fleshy eminence at the base of the thumb. **3.** Concerning the palm.

theobromine (thē-ō-brō′mēn) [Gr. *theos*, god, + *broma*, food] A white powder obtained from *Theobroma cacao*, the plant from which chocolate is obtained. It dilates blood vessels in the heart and peripherally. It is used as a mild stimulant and as a diuretic.

theophylline (thē-of′ĭ-lĭn) [L. *thea*, tea + Gr. *phyllon*, plant + *-ine*] A white crystalline powder used as an oral agent for reactive airway diseases such as asthma. The drug has a narrow therapeutic index, and toxicity to this agent, marked by gastrointestinal upset, tremor, cardiac arrhythmias, and other complications, is common in clinical practice. Other drugs for reactive airway diseases, such as inhaled beta-agonists and inhaled steroids, are often prescribed instead of theophylline to avoid its toxicities. SEE: *aminophylline.*

t. ethylenediamine Aminophylline.

theophylline poisoning SEE: under *poisoning.*

theorem (thē′ō-rĕm) [Gr. *theorema*, principle arrived at by speculation] A proposition that can be proved by use of logic, or by argument, from information previously accepted as being valid.

Bayes t. SEE: *Bayes theorem.*

theory (thē′ō-rē, thēr′ē) [Gr. *theōria*, viewing, spectacle, speculation] A statement that best explains all the available evidence on a given topic. If evidence that contradicts the theory becomes available, the theory must be abandoned or changed to incorporate it. When a theory becomes generally accepted and firmly established, it may be called a doctrine or principle.

activity t. A social theory of aging that asserts that the more active older persons are, the higher their satisfaction and morale. According to this theory, those who age successfully cultivate substitutes for former societal roles that they may have had to relinquish.

t. of aging Any coherent set of concepts that explains the aging process at the cellular, biological, psychological, and sociological levels.

atomic t. **1.** The theory that all matter is composed of atoms. **2.** Any of the theories pert. to the structure, properties, and behavior of the atom.

autoimmune t. of aging The theory that aging occurs because antibodies develop, attack, and destroy the normal cells in the body. According to this theory, a progressive deficiency in immunological tolerance results in the inability to distinguish self from foreign structures.

change t. The use of coaching strategies to encourage people to alter their actions, behaviors, or feelings, esp. from a current dysfunctional state to a desired one.

clonal selection t. of immunity The theory that precursor cell lines for lymphocytes are made up of innumerable clones with identical antigen receptors. The clones capable of reacting with autoantigenic components are eliminated or suppressed in the prenatal period. Those clones not eliminated or suppressed react only with specific foreign antigens that fit their receptors, leading to the proliferation of that lymphocyte cell line. Within the body, there are many different lymphocyte clones, each of which only reacts to one antigen (clonal restriction).

t. of evolution The theory that all living species, including humans, have developed as a result of changes in their genetic material over time. SEE: *natural selection*.

five-elements t., five-element theory A fundamental premise in traditional Chinese medicine and some branches of alternative medicine that holds that illness results from imbalances in the five elements of wood, fire, earth, metal, and water. A similar concept in ancient Western and medieval medicine held that diseases resulted from imbalances in the four elements of earth, air, fire, and water. SEE: *feng shui*.

gate t. The theory that painful stimuli may be prevented from reaching higher levels of the central nervous system by stimulation of larger sensory nerves. This is one of the proposed explanations of the action of acupuncture and of transcutaneous electrical nerve stimulation (TENS) units.

general system t. The theory that all living systems are open systems constantly exchanging information, matter, and energy with the environment. There are three levels of reference for systems: the system level on which one is focusing, (such as a person); the suprasystems level above the focal system, (such as a person's family, community, and culture); and the subsystem, which is below the focal system, (such as the bodily systems and the cell). The theory suggests that the treatment of people is more important than the treatment of illnesses. SEE: *holistic medicine*.

germ t. The theory that infectious diseases are caused by microorganisms.

grand t. A set of abstract ideas that together make a broad statement about human beings, the environment, health, or nursing. A grand theory is broad in scope. It is made up of concepts and propositions that are less abstract and general than the concepts and propositions of a conceptual model but are not as concrete and specific as the concepts and propositions of a middle-range theory. A grand theory sometimes is used in place of a conceptual model as a guide for research or practice. SEE: *Nursing Theory Appendix.*

health belief t. A theory of how and why people choose to make healthy choices in their lives. The theory suggests that people make such decisions intentionally, evaluating their risks for diseases, the likely severity of illnesses, and the potential benefits from taking action, and that they act when they perceive a clear benefit. Other theories about healthy behavior stress physiological or psychological reasons for health-related decisions.

t. of infinitesimals One of Samuel Hahnemann's three "natural laws": that properly diluted substances become more and more powerful as remedies the more dilute they become.

learning t. The theory that learning occurs by application of laws of learning. Learning represents a change in behavior due to practice, education, and experience.

Maslow t. of human motivation SEE: under *Maslow, Abraham H.*

Metchnikoff t. SEE: *Metchnikoff theory.*

middle-range t. A theory comprising limited numbers of variables, each of limited scope. Middle-range theories may be descriptive, explanatory (specifying relationships between two or more concepts), or predictive (envisioning relationships between concepts or effects of certain concepts on others). Examples include the Health Belief Model, the Theory of Maternal Attachment, the Erikson Theory of Psychosocial Development, Watson's Theory of Human Caring, and the Maslow Hierarchy of Needs Theory. Middle-range theories are made up of a limited number of concepts and propositions that are written at a relatively concrete and specific level. Middle-range theories are generated or tested by means of research, and are used as the evidence for practice activities, such as assessment and intervention.

nursing t. A theory that describes, explains, or predicts a phenomenon of interest to nurses and nursing educators.

t. of planned behavior/reasoned action ABBR: TpB. A model used to explain health-seeking behavior that suggests that such behavior depends on personal intention. In this theory an intention to promote health develops from the specific attitudes one holds about the proposed choice, the social pressure one faces (such as peer pressure) if one were to make that choice, and one's sense of empowerment (such as the confidence one holds that one's choice will be faithfully translated into fruitful action).

protection motivation t. ABBR: PMT. A model to explain health-seeking or health-avoidance behavior. It suggests that a person makes health-related choices based on the perception of risks and self-efficacy or of his vulnerability to illness and capacity to take effective action to avoid harm.

t. of psora One of Samuel Hahnemann's three "natural laws": that most chronic diseases result from suppressed itching.

quantum t. The theory that energy can be emitted in discrete quantities (quanta) and that atomic particles can exist only in certain energy states. Quanta are measured by multiplying the frequency of the radiation, v, by Planck's constant, h.

recapitulation t. The theory that during development an individual organism goes through the same progressive stages as did the species in developing from the lower to the higher forms of life; the theory that ontogeny recapitulates phylogeny.

self-determination t. A theory of human motivation and personality that purports to understand and explain human choices in social contexts, as influenced by that person's beliefs, needs, and desire to influence or be affected by his environment.

social learning t. The theory that learning social standards and behavior occurs by observing and imitating others, e.g., family members, peers, or role models. Social learning also includes conforming, learning in context, and modeling. Theories of social learning were developed by the American psychologist, Albert Bandura, who used them, e.g., to explain the impact of media violence on the behavior of children and adolescents.

summation t. The theory that excessive or intense stimulation of nerves will eventually produce a disagreeable sensation, i.e., of pain.

target t. A model used in radiobiology to describe cellular and chromosomal injury caused by radiation. The disruption of some intracellular targets by radiation can produce mutations; the disruption of critical targets is lethal to the cell.

Young-Helmholtz t. SEE: *Young-Helmholtz theory.*

Theory of Adaptation During Childbearing A theory developed by Jacqueline Fawcett that describes the changes in family relationships, functional status, and psychosocial interactions of mothers during pregnancy and the postpartum.

Theory of Clinical Nursing A nursing theory developed by Reva Rubin that focuses on patients' experiences of tension or stress during illness. The goal of nursing is to help patients adjust to, endure through, and usefully integrate health problem situations. SEE: *Nursing Theory Appendix.*

Theory of Culture Care Diversity and Universality A nursing theory developed by Madeleine Leininger that focuses on diversities and universalities in human care. The goal of nursing is to provide culturally congruent care to people. SEE: *Nursing Theory Appendix.*

Theory of Goal Attainment A middle-range nursing theory developed by Imogene King that helps to identify the nature of nurse-client interactions leading to goal attainment. This theory concentrates on working with clients to attain, maintain, and restore health through communication, goal setting, and goal achievement. SEE: *general systems framework; Nursing Theory Appendix.*

Theory of Health as Expanding Consciousness A nursing theory developed by Margaret Newman that proposes that all people in every situation, no matter how disordered and hopeless the situation may seem, are part of a universal process of expanding consciousness. The goal of nursing is the authentic involvement of nurse and patient in a mutual relationship of pattern recognition and augmentation. SEE: *Nursing Theory Appendix.*

Theory of Human Becoming A nursing theory developed by Rosemarie Parse that focuses on the individual's experiences of health. The goal of nursing is to respect and facilitate the quality of life as perceived by the individual and the family. Also known as the Human becoming School of Thought. SEE: *Nursing Theory Appendix.*

Theory of Human Caring A nursing theory developed by Jean Watson that focuses on the transpersonal caring relationship between nurse and patient and the caring actions or interventions used by nurses. The goal of nursing is to help individuals to gain a higher degree of harmony within the mind, body, and soul through the use of 10 clinical caritas processes (initially called carative factors). Use of these processes helps foster a caring relationship between the nurse and the patient. SEE: *Nursing Theory Appendix.*

Theory of Interpersonal Relations A nursing theory developed by Hildegard Peplau that identifies the three phases of the interpersonal process between the nurse and the patient: orientation, working, and termination. In this theory, the goal of nursing is to resolve the patient's perceived health difficulties. SEE: *Nursing Theory Appendix.*

Theory of Modeling and Role Modeling ABBR: MRM. A nursing theory in which the nurse uses the client's assumptions and beliefs on health and disease to plan and implement sound, holistic, and healing interventions. MRM was developed by Helen Cook Erickson, Evelyn Malcolm Tomlin, and Mary Ann Price Swain. SEE: *Nursing Theory Appendix.*

theory of planned behavior/reasoned action SEE: under *theory.*

Theory of Power as Knowing Participation in Change A theory of how influence is wielded and how it impacts personal lives and political systems, developed by Elizabeth A.M. Barrett. It proposes that power is the ability to make choices, the freedom to act on those choices, and the intentional use of choice in creating desired changes.

Theory of the Deliberative Nursing Process A nursing theory developed by Ida Jean Orlando that focuses on how the nurse identifies patients' immediate needs for help. The goal of nursing is to identify and meet patients' immediate needs for help through use of the deliberative nursing process. SEE: *Nursing Theory Appendix.*

Theory of Uncertainty in Illness A nursing theory conceived by Merle Mishel that patients have many questions about the diseases that affect them, the treatments they are offered, the nature of their interactions with health care personnel, and their own emotional and physical responses to care. It suggests that helping patients resolve some of these uncertainties through psychoeducation will diminish knowledge deficits, improve communication between patients and their providers, and enhance the management of symptoms.

Theory of Unpleasant Symptoms A nursing theory conceived by E. R. Lenz proposing that patients perceive illnesses and challenging treatments as clusters of noxious symptoms that both individually and jointly impact their experience of illness, their emotional distress, and their functional abilities. As illness and treatment progress, symptoms change and have varying impacts on each other and on the patient's quality of life.

thèque (tĕk) [Fr., a box] A nest of nevus cells or other cells close to the basal layer of the epidermis.

theragnostics (ther″ăg-nos′tiks) [*therapy* + *diagnostics*] The use of molecular diagnostic techniques, e.g. the identification of the enzymes one person makes that another does not, to guide treatment decisions such as the choice of drugs that will be optimally metabolized by a particular patient.

theranostics Personalized medicine.

therapeutic (thĕr-ă-pū′tĭk) [Gr. *therapeutikos,* treating] **1.** Pert. to results obtained from treatment. **2.** Having medicinal or healing properties. **3.** A healing agent.

therapeutic cloning The use of human embryos as a source of stem cells for the treatment of diseases and medical conditions, e.g., leukemias, Parkinson disease, and spinal cord injury. Therapeutic cloning is banned in the U.S. and is a topic of ethical and religious debate in those countries in which it has been legalized.

therapeutic equivalent SEE: under *equivalent.*

therapeutic humor Humor therapy.

therapeutic misadventure A drug experience that results in an undesired or unintended response to drug therapy. The term includes adverse drug reactions and medication errors. SYN: *medication misadventure.* SEE: *adverse drug reaction; medication* **error**.

therapeutic misconception (mis″kŏn-sep′shŏn) The mistaken impression held by patients enrolled in medical research trials that the research in which they are participating will be beneficial to them personally, i.e., that the investigation gives them their last best hope of a cure.

therapeutic radiology Radiation therapy.

therapeutic ratio The ratio obtained by dividing the effective therapeutic dose by the minimum lethal dose. SYN: *curative* **ratio**.

therapeutic recreation A specialized field within recreation whose specialists plan and direct recreational activities for patients recovering from physical or mental illness or who are attempting to cope with a permanent or temporary disability.

therapeutic regimen management, readiness for enhanced A pattern of regulating and integrating into daily living programs for treatment of illness and its sequelae that are sufficient for meeting health-related goals and can be strengthened. SEE: *Nursing Diagnoses Appendix.*

therapeutic regimen management: ineffective A pattern of regulating and integrating into daily living a program for treatment of illness and the sequelae of illness that is unsatisfactory for meeting specific health goals. SEE: *Nursing Diagnoses Appendix.*

therapeutic regimen management: ineffective family A pattern of regulating and integrating into family processes a program for treatment of illness and the sequelae of illness that is unsatisfactory for meeting specific health needs. SEE: *Nursing Diagnoses Appendix.*

therapeutic relationship The ongoing relationship between a therapist and a client/patient established to support the client's/patient's therapeutic goals. A therapeutic relationship is one of service and is a helpful resource for the client/patient. Characteristics of a healthy therapeutic relationship include personal awareness and insight, trust, respect, safety, authenticity, acceptance, empathy, and collaborative agreement.

therapeutics (thĕr″ă-pū′tĭks) [Gr. *therapeutike,* treatment] That branch of medicine concerned with the application of remedies and the treatment of disease.

therapeutic use of self A health care provider's use of verbal and nonverbal communication, emotional exchange, and other aspects of his or her personality to establish a relationship with the patient that promotes cooperation and healing.

Theraphosidae (thĕr″ă-fŏs′ĭ-dē) The scientific name for the family of mildly venomous, hairy spiders known popularly as tarantulas.

therapist (thĕr′ă-pĭst) [Gr. *therapeia,* treatment] A person skilled in giving therapy, usually in a specific field of health care.

    Particular therapists are listed under the first word. SEE: e.g., *occupational therapist; physical therapist; respiratory therapist.*

therapy (thĕr′ă-pē) [Gr. *therapeia,* treatment] Treatment. Particular therapies are listed under the first word. SEE: e.g., *hormone replacement therapy; occupational therapy; physical therapy.*

Theridiidae (ther″ĭ-dī′ĭ-dē″) [*Theridion,* the type genus + *-idae*] A family of small poisonous spiders that contains the genus *Lactrodectus,* which includes the black widow spider.

therm (thĕrm) [Gr. *thermē,* heat] Any of a several units of heat. SEE: *MET.*

thermal (thĕr′măl) [*therm-* + *-al*] **1.** Pert. to or caused by heat or temperature. SYN: *thermic.* **2.** Aiding the retention of heat.

thermal ablation Destruction of tissue by heating it (as with a microwave or radiofrequency energy) to temperatures at which cells cannot survive.

thermal balloon One of several techniques used to remove the endometrial lining of the uterus. An expandable sac is placed inside the uterus, filled with hot fluid, and pressurized. The hot, pressurized sac destroys the endometrial lining. The technique is used to treat excessive uterine bleeding.

thermal death point SEE: under *point.*

thermal diffusion flowmetry ABBR: TDF. Continuous measurement of regional cerebral blood flow, e.g., in areas of the brain as they are operated upon. It is used to monitor and thus prevent focal brain injury.

thermal spread The dissemination of

heat to neighboring tissues from the tissue to which it has been applied. Thermal spread is a variable that may complicate electrosurgery, laser surgery, or radiofrequency ablation.

thermic (thĕr′mĭk) [*therm-* + *-ic*] Thermal (1).

thermic effect of food ABBR: TEF. The increase in the body's metabolic rate that is produced by the consumption, digestion, metabolism, and storage of food. Foods with relatively low thermic effects include most carbohydrates, since carbohydrates, esp. sugars, cost the body relatively little energy to digest and metabolize. Protein-rich meals have a higher TEF, which is the rationale for low-carbohydrate diets, such as the Atkins and South Beach diets. SYN: *specific dynamic action of food.*

thermistor (thĕr-mĭs′tor) An apparatus for quickly determining very small changes in temperature. Materials that alter their resistance to the flow of electricity as the temperature changes are used in these devices.

thermo-, therm- [Gr. *thermos,* hot; *thermē,* heat] Prefixes meaning *hot, heat.*

thermocautery (thĕr″mō-kaw′tĕr-ē) **1.** Cautery by application of heat. **2.** Cauterizing iron.

thermochemistry (thĕr″mō-kĕm′ĭs-trē) The branch of science concerned with the interrelationship of heat and chemical reactions.

thermocoagulation (thĕr″mō-kō-ăg-ū-lā′shŭn) [″ + L. *coagulatio,* clotting] The use of high-frequency currents to produce coagulation to destroy tissue. SYN: *endocoagulation.*

thermocouple (thĕr′mō-kŭ″pl) [″ + L. *copula,* a bond] Thermopile.

thermocurrent (thĕr″mō-kŭr′ĕnt) An electric current produced by thermoelectric means.

thermocycler (thĕr′mō-sīk″lĕr) A device used to heat and cool clinical and laboratory specimens rapidly. It is used in polymerase chain reaction (PCR) assays.

thermode (thĕr′mōd) A device for heating or cooling a part of the body.

thermodiffusion (thĕr″mō-dĭ-fū′zhŭn) Increased diffusion of a substance as a result of increased heat.

thermodilution (thĕr″mō-dī-lū′shŭn) The use of an injected cold liquid such as sterile saline into the bloodstream and measurement of the temperature change downstream. This technique has been used to determine cardiac output.

thermoduric (thĕr″mō-dūr′ĭk) Pert. to bacteria that thrive best at high temperatures between 40° and 70°C (104° and 158°F).

thermodynamics (thĕr″mō-dī-năm′ĭks) [″ + *dynamis,* power] The branch of physics concerned with laws that govern the production of heat and its conversion into other forms of energy.

thermoelasticity (thĕr″mō-ĭ-lăs-tĭs′-ĭ-tē) The ability of a material (e.g., a component of a prosthesis) to stretch in response to changes in temperature.

thermoelectric (thĕr″mō-ē-lĕk′trĭk) Concerning thermoelectricity.

thermoelectricity (thĕr″mō-ē-lĕk-trĭs′ĭ-tē) Electricity generated by heat.

thermogenesis (thĕr″mō-jĕn′ĕ-sĭs) [″ + *genesis*, generation, birth] The production of heat, esp. in the body.

   dietary t. The heat-producing response to ingesting food. For several hours after eating, the metabolic rate increases. Heat is a by-product of the digestion, absorption, and breakdown of consumed foods, and the synthesis and storage of proteins and fats. Because the calories used in the thermic response are expended, they are not stored as fat.

   nonshivering t. A limited physiological response of the newborn infant to chilling. Hypothermia stimulates sympathetic catabolism of brown fat, which is not coupled with ATP formation, and therefore releases most energy in the form of heat. Brown fat is located mainly in the neck and chest of the infant. SEE: *hypothermia.*

thermograph (thĕr′mō-grăf) [*thermo-* + *-graph*] A device for registering variations of heat.

thermography (thĕr-mog′ră-fē) [*thermo-* + *-graphy*] The detection of the heat in body parts, e.g., blood vessels, muscles and tendons, or skin. Thermography has a wide range of presumptive but unproven uses.

⚠ The FDA has warned that thermography should not be used as a stand-alone screening tool for the diagnosis of diseases.

   scrotal t. Indirect measurement of testicular temperatures used to evaluate patients with male infertility.

thermoinhibitory (thĕr″mō-ĭn-hĭb′ĭ-tor″ē) [″ + L. *inhibere*, to restrain] Arresting or impeding the generation of body heat.

thermolabile (thĕr″mō-lā′bĭl) [*thermo-* +*labile*] Heat-labile.

thermology (thĕr-mŏl′ō-jē) [″ + *logos*, word, reason] The science of heat.

thermoluminescent dosimeter (thĕr″mō-loo-mĭ-nĕs′ĕnt) A monitoring device consisting of a small crystal in a container that can be attached to a patient or to a health care worker. It stores energy when struck by ionizing radiation. When heated, it will emit light proportional to the amount of radiation to which it has been exposed.

thermolysis (thĕr-mŏl′ĭ-sĭs) [″ + *lysis*, dissolution] 1. Loss of body heat, as by

evaporation. 2. Chemical decomposition by heat.

thermolytic (thĕr″mō-lĭt′ĭk) [″ + *lytikos*, dissolving] Promoting thermolysis.

thermometer (thĕr-mom′ĕt-ĕr) [*thermo-* + *-meter*] An instrument for indicating the degree of heat or cold. **thermometric** (thĕr″mŏ-me′trĭk), *adj.* SEE: tables.

   alcohol t. A thermometer containing alcohol.

   Celsius t. SEE: under *Celsius, Anders.*

   centigrade t. Celsius thermometer. SEE: under *Celsius, Anders.*

   clinical t. A thermometer for measuring the body temperature. SEE: *clinical thermometry.*

   differential t. A thermometer recording slight variations of temperature.

   Fahrenheit t. SEE: under *Fahrenheit, Daniel Gabriel.*

   gas t. A thermometer filled with gas, such as air, helium, or oxygen.

   Kelvin t. SEE: under *Kelvin, Lord.*

   mercury t. A thermometer containing mercury for measurement of temperature. Mercury thermometers are seldom employed because they are an important source of heavy metal pollution of rivers, streams, and aquatic life.

   recording t. A device with a suitable sensor that continuously monitors and records temperature.

   rectal t. A thermometer with a round bulb that is inserted into the rectum for determining body temperature.

   self-registering t. A thermometer recording variations of temperature.

   surface t. A thermometer for indicating the temperature of the body's surface. Used, for example, in infant warmers.

Comparative Thermometric Scale

	Celsius*	Fahrenheit
Boiling point of water	100°	212°
	90	194
	80	176
	70	158
	60	140
	50	122
	40	104
Body temperature	37°	98.6°
	30	86
	20	68
	10	50
Freezing point of water	0°	32°
	−10	14
	−20	−4

*Also called *Centigrade.*

Thermometric Equivalents (Celsius and Fahrenheit)

C°	F°	C°	F°	C°	F°	C°	F°
0	32	27	80.6	54	129.2	81	177.8
1	33.8	28	82.4	55	131	82	179.6
2	35.6	29	84.2	56	132.8	83	181.4
3	37.4	30	86.0	57	134.6	84	183.2
4	39.2	31	87.8	58	136.4	85	185
5	41	32	89.6	59	138.2	86	186.8
6	42.8	33	91.4	60	140	87	188.6
7	44.6	34	93.2	61	141.8	88	190.4
8	46.4	35	95	62	143.6	89	192.2
9	48.2	36	96.8	63	145.4	90	194
10	50	37	98.6	64	147.2	91	195.8
11	51.8	38	100.4	65	149	92	197.6
12	53.6	39	102.2	66	150.8	93	199.4
13	55.4	40	104	67	152.6	94	201.2
14	57.2	41	105.8	68	154.4	95	203
15	59	42	107.6	69	156.2	96	204.8
16	60.8	43	109.4	70	158	97	206.6
17	62.6	44	111.2	71	159.8	98	208.4
18	64.4	45	113	72	161.6	99	210.2
19	66.2	46	114.8	73	163.4	100	212
20	68	47	116.6	74	165.2		
21	69.8	48	118.4	75	167		
22	71.6	49	120.2	76	168.8		
23	73.4	50	122	77	170.6		
24	75.2	51	123.8	78	172.4		
25	77	52	125.6	79	174.2		
26	78.8	53	127.4	80	176		

CONVERSION:*Fahrenheit to Celsius:* Subtract 32 and multiply by 5/9. *Celsius to Fahrenheit:* Multiply by 9/5 and add 32.

tympanic t. A thermometer that determines the temperature electronically by measuring it from the tympanic membrane of the ear. SEE: *ear thermometry; temperature, tympanic.*

wet-and-dry-bulb t. Psychrometer.

thermometry (thĕr-mŏm′ĕ-trē) Measurement of temperature.

clinical t. Measurement of the temperature of warm-blooded organisms, esp. humans. The oral temperature of the healthy human body ranges between 96.6° and 100°F (35.9° and 37.8°C). During a 24-hr period, a person's body temperature may vary from 0.5° to 2.0°F (0.28° to 1.1°C). It is highest in late afternoon and lowest during sleep in the early hours of the morning. It is slightly increased by eating, exercising, and external heat, and is reduced about 1.5°F (0.8°C) during sleep. In disease, the temperature of the body deviates several degrees above or below that considered the average in healthy persons.

In acute infections such as meningitis or pneumonia, body temperature sometimes rises as high as 106° to 107°F (41.1° to 41.7°C).

Subnormal temperatures are sometimes seen in exposure, sepsis, or myxedema coma. In general, for every degree of fever, the pulse rises 10 beats per minute.

thermonuclear (thĕr″mō-nū′klē-ăr) Pert. to atomic reactions that result in the fission or fusion of nuclei and the release of large quantities of energy.

thermophile (thĕr′mō-fīl) *pl.* **thermophils** An organism that grows best at elevated temperatures (i.e., 40° to 70°C).

thermopile (thĕr′mō-pīl) [″ + L. *pila,* pile] A thermoelectric battery used in measuring small variations in the degree of heat. It consists of a number of connected dissimilar metallic plates. Under the influence of heat, these plates produce an electric current. SYN: *thermocouple.*

thermoplastic (thĕr″mō-plăs′tĭk) Pert. to or being softened or made malleable by heat.

thermoradiotherapy (thĕr″mō-rā″dē-ō-thĕr′ă-pē) [″ + L. *radius,* ray, + Gr. *therapeia,* treatment] Application of heat to the deep tissues by diathermy. SYN: *thermopenetration.*

thermoreception The ability to detect or sense heat.

thermoreceptor (thĕr″mō-rē-sĕp′tor) [″ + L. *receptor,* a receiver] A sensory receptor that is stimulated by a rise of body temperature.

thermoregulation (thĕr″mō-rĕg″ū-lā′shŭn) Heat regulation.

ineffective t. The state in which the individual's temperature fluctuates between hypothermia and hyperthermia. SEE: *Nursing Diagnoses Appendix.*

thermoregulatory (thĕr″mō-rĕg′ū-lă-tor″ē) Pert. to the regulation of temperature, esp. body temperature.

thermoresistant (thĕr″mō-rē-zĭs′tănt) [″ + L. *resistentia,* resistance] Pert. to an ability to survive in relatively high temperature, characteristic of some types of bacteria.

thermostabile (thĕr″mō-stā′bĭl) [″ + L. *stabilis,* stable] Not changed or destroyed by heat.

thermostat (thĕr′mō-stăt) [″ + *statikos,* standing] An automatic device for regulating the temperature.

thermotaxis (thĕr″mō-tăks′ĭs) [″ + *taxis,* arrangement] **1.** Regulation of bodily temperature. **2.** The movement of certain organisms or cells toward (positive thermotaxis) or away from (negative thermotaxis) heat.

thermotherapy (thĕr″mŏ-ther′ă-pē) [*thermo-* + *therapy*] The therapeutic application of heat to the body or to specific diseased tissues. Heat may be applied superficially with moist hot packs, paraffin bath, fluidotherapy, hot stones, infrared light, and hydrotherapy. Deep-heating agents include ultrasound, diathermy, and lasers.

thermotolerant (thĕr″mō-tŏl′ĕr-ănt) [″ + L. *tolerare,* to tolerate] Able to live normally in high temperature.

theroid (thē′royd) [Gr. *theriodes,* beastlike] Having animal instincts and characteristics.

THI *Transient **hypogammaglobulinemia** of infancy.*

thiaminase (thī-ăm′ĭ-nās) An enzyme that hydrolyzes thiamine.

thiamine hydrochloride (thī′ă-mēn″) [″ + ″] $C_{12}H_{17}ClN_4OS \cdot HCl$; a water-soluble, white crystalline compound that occurs naturally or can be synthesized. It is found in a wide variety of foods including sunflower seeds, pork, whole and enriched grains, legumes, brewers yeast, and fortified baked goods. The daily requirement for adults is 1.2 mg/day for men and 1.1 mg/day for women. SYN: *antiberiberi vitamin; vitamin B_1.*

  FUNCTION: It acts as a coenzyme of carboxylases in the decarboxylation of pyruvic acid and is therefore essential for the liberation of energy and the transfer of pyruvic acid into the Krebs cycle.

  DEFICIENCY SYMPTOMS: Symptoms may include fatigue, muscle tenderness and increased irritability, disturbances of extraocular movement, loss of appetite, or cardiovascular disturbances. Alcoholics are especially prone to develop thiamine deficiency. Prolonged severe deficiency (e.g., during starvation) results in beriberi.

thiamine pyrophosphate (thī′ă-mĭn, -mēn″ pī″rō-fŏs′făt″) An enzyme important in carbohydrate metabolism. It is the active form of thiamine. In people suspected of malnutrition, administering thiamine before the infusion of solutions that contain glucose prevents brain damage (Wernicke-Korsakoff encephalopathy). SYN: *cocarboxylase.*

thiazolidinedione (thī′ă-zō″lĭ-dēn-dī-ŏn) A class of oral hypoglycemic agents that lowers blood sugars by reducing insulin resistance (improving tissue sensitivity to the effects of insulin) in fat and muscle, as well as the liver. A commonly used agent in this class is pioglitazone.

⚠️ Side effects of medications in this class include increased fluid retention, fractures, heart failure, liver injury, and weight gain.

thickened liquids A diet designed to prevent aspiration in patients with dysphagia. Solid particles that make liquids more viscous are added to liquid nutrients to achieve dense but pourable liquids, or liquids that have the consistency of honey or pudding, depending on the patient's needs.

thick filament In a sarcomere, one of the collection of contractile filaments made primarily of myosin, seen microscopically.

thienopyridine (thī″ĕ-nō″pir′ă-dēn″) Any of a group of drugs that block the aggregation of platelets. Drugs in this class are used to prevent arterial clotting and are effective in the prevention of strokes, heart attacks, stent thromboses, and peripheral arterial disease. Examples include prasugrel, ticlopidine, and clopidogrel. Their most common side effect is bleeding. SYN: *adenosine diphosphate **antagonist**; adenosine diphosphate receptor **antagonist**.*

thigh (thī) [AS. *theoh*] The proximal portion of the lower extremity; the portion lying between the hip joint and the knee. SEE: *femur; hip; pectineus; sartorius.*

thigmotaxis (thĭg″mō-tăks′ĭs) [″ + *taxis,* arrangement] The negative or positive response of certain motile cells to touch.

thigmotropism (thĭg-mŏt′rō-pĭzm) [″ + *tropos,* a turning, + *-ismos,* condition] The response of certain motile cells to move toward something that touches them.

thimerosal (thī-mĕr′ō-săl) An organic mercurial antiseptic used topically and as a preservative in pharmaceutical preparations.

⚠️ Children and pregnant women should not be given immune globulin or vaccinations that use thimerosal as a preservative.

thin basement membrane disease Benign familial **hematuria**.

thin client A computer linked to others within a network that does not have its own disc drive and relies heavily for its function on a central server. SEE: *fat client*.

thin filament In a sarcomere, one of the collection of contractile filaments made primarily of actin, seen microscopically.

thinking (thingk′ing) Intellectual activity. Thinking includes the interpretation and ordering of symbols, learning, planning, forming ideas and opinions, organizing information, and problem solving.

    abstract t. The ability to calculate, sort, categorize, conceptualize, draw conclusions, or interpret and condense complex ideas. In clinical medicine, abstract thinking is assessed by asking patients to interpret proverbs. Patients with dementia or other cognitive deficits may fail to do so, as they fail to see the relationships between similar objects and ideas.

    concrete t. Thinking in simple, tangible, real, or nonidealized terms, without drawing relations between objects or concepts.

    critical t. **1.** The ability to interpret argument, evidence, or raw information in a logical and unbiased fashion. **2.** The ability to solve complex problems effectively.

    PATIENT CARE: Critical thinking in clinical settings involves the ability to solve complex problems effectively, using, for example, close observation, communication skills, consensus building, data mining, empathy, experience, logic, mathematics, pattern recognition, and reasoning.

thio-, thi- [Gr. *theion*, sulfur, brimstone] In chemistry, prefixes meaning *sulfur*.

thioamide, thionamide (thī″ō-am′ĭd″) [*thio-* + *amide*] Any drug that inhibits the thyroid gland from making thyroid hormone. Examples include methimazole and propylthiouracil.

thiocyanate (thī″ō-sī′ă-nāt) Any compound containing the radical —SCN.

thioglucosidase (thī″ō-glū-kō′sĭ-dās) An enzyme that catalyzes the hydrolysis of thioglycoside to a thiol and a sugar.

thiopurine (thī″ō-pūr′ēn″) [*thio-* + *purine*] Any sulfur-containing purine used as an antimetabolite to treat a variety of auotimmune, inflammatory, and neoplastic diseases.

thiopurine s-methyltransferase (thī″ō-pūr′ēn″es″meth″ĭl-trans′fĕr-ās″) ABBR: TPMT. An enzyme that metabolizes and inactivates thiopurines (such as the drugs azathioprine and mercaptopurine). People with a genetic deficiency in TPMT have severe bone marrow suppression when they take thiopurines to manage diseases such as rheumatoid arthritis or inflammatory bowel disease.

thiosulfate (thī″ō-sŭl′fāt) Any salt of thiosulfuric acid.

thiourea (thī″ō-ūr-ē′ă) [Gr. *theion*, sulfur, + *ouron*, urine] H_2NCSNH_2; A colorless crystalline compound of urea in which sulfur replaces the oxygen. SYN: *sulfourea*.

third disease Rubella.

third-party payer An entity (other than the patient or the health care provider) that reimburses and manages health care expenses. Third-party payers include insurance companies, governmental agencies, and employers.

third spacing The leakage of fluids normally confined to blood vessels or tissues into potential spaces in the body, e.g., within operative cavities, next to sites of tissue trauma, or within the peritoneum or pleurae. Large volumes of fluid may accumulate in these places but not contribute to hemodynamic stability. A patient who has third-spaces fluid may receive large volumes of intravenous fluid but remain functionally dehydrated.

thirst The sensation resulting from the lack of adequate body water or desire for liquids. Excessive thirst may be an early symptom of diabetes as the kidneys excrete extra water in an effort to decrease circulating glucose levels. Thirst is common following fever, vomiting, diarrhea, bleeding, vigorous exercise, or other causes of hypovolemia or hyperosmolality. In addition, thirst may be associated with the use of diuretics, tricyclic antidepressants, and some antihistamines, among other drugs.

thirteenth step A colloquial term for sexual intercourse between two members of a 12-step recovery program to treat addiction.

thisilyn (this′ĭ-lĭn) A purified extract of milk thistle.

thixotropy (thĭks-ŏt′rō-pē) [Gr. *thixis*, a touching, + *trope*, turning] The property of certain gels in which they liquefy when agitated and revert to a gel on standing.

Thomas, Hugh Owen (tom′ăs) Brit. orthopedic surgeon, 1834–1891.

    T. heel A corrective shoe in which the heel is approx. 12 mm longer and 4 to 6 mm higher on the medial edge. This produces varus of the foot and prevents depression of the head of the talus.

    T. splint A splint originally developed to treat hip-joint disease. It is now used mainly to place traction on the leg in its long axis, in treating fractures of the upper leg. It consists of a proximal ring that fits around the upper leg and to which two long rigid slender steel rods are attached. These extend down to another smaller ring distal to the foot.

T. test A test used to identify hip flexor contractures. Lying supine with the legs off the end of the table, the patient flexes the knee and tries to pull the thigh to the chest. Inability to perform this maneuver or extension of the opposite knee indicates tightness of the iliopsoas or rectus femoris muscle.

Thompson test (tŏmp´sŏn) A test to evaluate the integrity of the Achilles tendon. With the patient lying prone on the examination table, the examiner squeezes the calf while observing for plantar flexion. The result is positive if there is no movement of the foot; this indicates an Achilles tendon rupture. SYN: *Simmonds test.*

Thomsen disease (tom´sĕn) [Asmus Julius Thomsen, Danish physician, 1815–1896] Myotonia congenita.

thoracentesis, thoracocentesis (thō˝răsen-tē´sĭs, ˝ră-kō-) [*thoraco-* + *centesis*] Insertion of a needle through the chest wall and into the pleural space, usually to remove fluid for diagnostic or therapeutic purposes. SYN: *pleurocentesis; thoracocentesis.* SEE: illus.

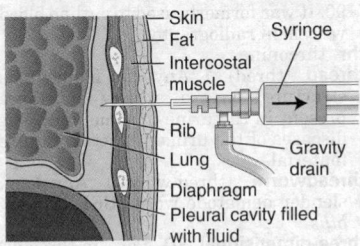

Skin
Fat
Intercostal muscle
Syringe
Rib
Lung
Gravity drain
Diaphragm
Pleural cavity filled with fluid

THORACENTESIS

PATIENT CARE: Before the procedure, the patient is carefully examined, a history is taken, and radiological studies, such as chest x-rays or ultrasonograms, are reviewed. The procedure should be explained to the patient and sensation information provided (stinging with anesthesia instillation). The risks (bleeding, puncture of the lung with subsequent lung collapse, or introduction of infection), as well as the benefits and alternatives to the procedure, should be carefully reviewed. If the patient wishes to proceed, a consent form with the patient's signature must be completed. Allergies to local anesthetics are noted. Baseline vital signs will be obtained and supplemental oxygen administered. Cardiac monitoring is usually performed. A nurse or respiratory therapist may assist the physician and support the patient throughout the procedure. Equipment is assembled for the procedure, and, in most instances, the fluid is identified with ultrasound to avoid injury to the liver, lung, or other tissues. The patient is positioned to make pleural fluid accessible to the examiner.

The patient's skin is prepared per protocol, the area is draped, and local anesthesia is injected subcutaneously. After allowing a short time for this to become effective, the thoracentesis needle is inserted above the rib to avoid damaging intercostal vessels, which run in a neurovascular bundle beneath each rib. The patient is advised not to move, cough, or take a deep breath during the procedure to reduce the risk of injury. When the needle contacts the fluid pocket, fluid can be withdrawn by gravity drainage or with suction. When indicated after removal of the thoracentesis needle or cannula, a larger bore thoracostomy tube may be inserted to provide additional drainage.

During thoracentesis, health care professionals should assess the patient for difficulty in breathing, dizziness, faintness, chest pain, nausea, pallor or cyanosis, weakness, sweating, cough, alterations in vital signs, oxygen saturation levels, or cardiac rhythm. An occlusive dressing should be applied to the puncture site as the needle or cannula is removed, preventing air entry. The fluid obtained is labeled and sent for diagnostic tests (typically Gram stain, cultures, cell count, measurements of fluid chemistries, pH, and, when appropriate, cytology). The amount, color, and character of the fluid is documented, along with the time of the procedure, the exact location of the puncture, and the patient's reaction. After the procedure, a chest x-ray is often obtained to assess results or determine if any injury has occurred, e.g., pneumothorax. The patient should be positioned comfortably. Vital signs are monitored until stable, then as needed. The patient is advised to call for assistance immediately, if difficulty in breathing or pleuritic pain is experienced.

thoracic (thō-răs´ĭk) [Gr. *thorax*, chest] Pert. to the chest or thorax.

thoracic cage The bony structure surrounding the thorax, consisting of the 12 paired ribs, the thoracic vertebrae, and the sternum.

thoracic duct SEE: under *duct.*

thoracic expansion In chest physiotherapy, any technique or exercise that tries to increase inspiratory force and volume.

thoracic gas volume SEE: under *volume.*

thoracic limb SEE: under *limb.*

thoracic outlet compression syndrome, thoracic outlet syndrome ABBR: TOS. A symptom complex caused by the compression of nerves and/or vessels in the neck, such as by the first rib pressing against the clavicle or entrapment of brachial nerves and vessels between the pectoralis minor muscle and the ribs. It is marked by brachial neuritis with or without vascular or vasomotor disturbance in the upper extremities. The practitioner must differentiate TOS from cervical disk lesions, osteoarthritis affecting cervical vertebrae, bursitis, brachial plexus injury, angina, lung cancer, and carpal tunnel syndrome.

thoracic pump SEE: under *pump*.

thoracic surgery SEE: under *surgery*.

thoraco-, thorac-, thoraci- [Gr. *thōrax,* stem, *thōrak-,* breastplate, breast, trunk] Prefixes meaning *chest, chest wall.*

thoracoacromial (thō″ră-kō-ă-krō′mē-ăl) Pert. to the thorax and acromion.

thoracolumbar (thō″răk-ō-lŭm′bar) [″ + L. *lumbus,* loin] Pert. to the thoracic and lumbar parts of the spinal cord; denoting their ganglia and the fibers of the sympathetic nervous system.

thoracoplasty (thō′ră-kō-plas″tē) [*thoraco-* + *-plasty*] Plastic surgery to alter the size and shape of the chest wall. SEE: *empyema*.

thoracoscope (thō-rā′kō-skōp, -răk′ō-skōp) [″ + *skopein,* to examine] An endoscope used to inspect the lungs, pleura, and other chest structures. It is inserted into the pleural space via an incision made through the chest wall.

thoracoscopy (thō″ră-kŏs′kō-pē) A diagnostic examination and/or therapeutic procedure within the pleural cavity with an endoscope.

thoracostomy (thōr″ă-kos′tŏ-mē) [*thoraco-* + *-ostomy*] Incision into the chest wall, usually followed by insertion of a tube between the pleurae and a system for draining fluid from that space. SYN: *chest tube insertion*.

thoracostomy tube (thor″ă-kos′tŏ-mē) [*thoraco-* + *-stomy*] A tube inserted into the pleural space via the chest wall to remove air or fluid present in the space. SYN: *chest tube*.

thoracotomy (thō″răk-ŏt′ō-mē) [″ + *tome,* incision] Surgical incision of the chest wall. SEE: illus.

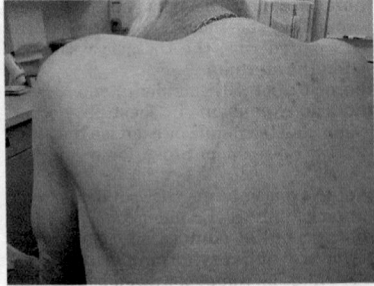

THORACOTOMY SCAR

thorax (thōr′aks″, thor′, thōr′ă-sēz″, thor′) *pl.* **thoracesthoraxes** [L. *thorax,* fr Gr. *thōrax,* breastplate] That part of the body between the base of the neck superiorly and the diaphragm inferiorly. SYN: *chest.* SEE: *rib.*

The surface of the thorax is divided into regions as follows: *Anterior surface:* supraclavicular, above the clavicles; suprasternal, above the sternum; clavicular, over the clavicles; sternal, over the sternum; mammary, the space between the third and sixth ribs on either side; inframammary, below the mammae and above the lower border of the 12th rib on either side. *Posterior surface:* scapular, over the scapulae; interscapular, between the scapulae; infrascapular, below the scapulae. *On sides:* axillary, above the sixth rib.

    barrel-shaped t. A malformed chest rounded like a barrel, seen in advanced pulmonary emphysema.

    bony t. The part of the skeleton that is made up of the thoracic vertebrae, 12 pairs of ribs, and the sternum.

    Peyrot t. SEE: *Peyrot thorax.*

thorium (thō′rē-ŭm, thor′) [*Thor,* a Norse god + *-ium* (1)] SYMB: Th. A radioactive metallic element, atomic weight (mass) 232.04, atomic number 90. It was formerly used to outline blood vessels in radiography.

thr threonine.

thread (thrĕd) **1.** Any thin filamentous structure, e.g., a stringy substance present in the urine in some infectious diseases of the urinary tract. **2.** Suture material.

threadworm (thrĕd′wŭrm″) Any long, slender nematode worm. SEE: *Enterobius.*

three-dimensional, 3D Pert. to three dimensions.

three-dimensional ultrasonography, three-dimensional sonography, three-dimensional ultrasound, 3D ultrasonography, 3D sonography, 3D ultrasound Ultrasonography.

threonine (thrē′ō-nīn) ABBR: thr. $C_4H_9NO_3$ Alpha-amino-beta-hydroxybutyric acid, an essential amino acid.

threshold (thresh′(h)ōld″) **1.** The point at which a psychological or physiological effect begins to be produced. **2.** A measure of the sensitivity of an organ or function that is obtained by finding the lowest value of the appropriate stimulus that will give the response.

    absolute t. The lowest amount or intensity of a stimulus that will give rise to a sensation or a response.

    acoustic reflex t. The decibel level that provokes reflex contraction of the stapedius muscle. Tests that measure the triggering of the acoustic stapedius reflex are used to determine the presence of sensorineural hearing loss.

    anaerobic t. The point at which increased carbon dioxide production and minute ventilation result from increased levels of lactic acid during exercise.

auditory t. The minimum audible sound perceived.

t. of consciousness In psychoanalysis, the point at which a stimulus is just barely perceived.

difference t. Just noticeable difference.

differential t. The lowest limit at which two stimuli can be differentiated from each other.

erythema t. The stage of ultraviolet skin injury in which erythema of the skin due to radiation begins.

ketone t. The level of ketone in the blood above which ketone bodies appear in the urine.

ketosis t. The lower limit at which ketone bodies, on their accumulation in the blood, are excreted by the kidney. At that point, ketone bodies are being produced faster by the liver than the body can oxidize them.

pain t. The minimum level of sensory stimulation that a person will perceive as being unpleasant, noxious, or intolerable.

pressure pain t. ABBR: PPT. The applied mass per area (kg/cm²) that will elicit a complaint of pain in subjects with painful conditions, e.g., fibromyalgia, temperomandibular joint dysfunction, or vulvodynia.

renal t. The concentration at which a substance in the blood normally not excreted by the kidney begins to appear in the urine. The renal threshold for glucose is 160 to 180 mg/dL.

seizure t. The level of neurological stimulation capable of precipitating a seizure.

sensory t. The minimal stimulus for any sensory receptor that will give rise to a sensation.

speech detection t. ABBR: SDT. The lowest level of sound intensity in decibels at which a person identifies a spoken word 50% of the time.

viability t. The body weight or gestational age of an infant below which the ability to survive is doubtful.

threshold limit value ABBR: TLV. The highest concentration of a toxin that an employee can be regularly exposed to at work without adverse health effects.

threshold substance A substance in the blood that, on being filtered through glomeruli of the kidney, is reabsorbed by the tubules up to a certain limit, that being the upper limit of the concentration of the substance in normal plasma. High-threshold substances (such as chlorides or glucose) are entirely or almost entirely reabsorbed. Low-threshold substances (such as phosphates or urea) are reabsorbed in limited quantities. No-threshold substances (such as creatinine sulfate) are excreted entirely.

thrifty Thriving, growing vigorously, and

being healthy, esp. when assessing the health status of animals or plants.

thrill (thrĭl) **1.** An abnormal vibration that is felt on the skin overlying a loud cardiac murmur or an arteriovenous fistula. **2.** A tingling or shivering sensation of tremulous excitement as from pain, pleasure, or horror.

aortic t. A thrill perceived over the aorta or aortic valve.

arterial t. A thrill perceived over an artery.

diastolic t. A thrill perceived over the heart during ventricular diastole.

hydatid t. A thrill felt on palpation of a hydatid cyst.

presystolic t. A thrill sometimes felt over the apex of the heart preceding ventricular contraction.

systolic t. A thrill felt during systole over the precordium. It may be associated with aortic or pulmonary stenosis or an interventricular septal defect.

thrix (thrĭks) Hair.

t. annulata Hair with light and dark segments alternating along the shaft.

-thrix [Gr. *thrix,* stem *trich-,* hair] A suffix meaning *hair.* SEE: *tricho-.*

throat (thrōt) **1.** The pharynx and fauces. **2.** The cavity from the arch of the palate to the glottis and superior opening of the esophagus. **3.** The anterior portion of the neck. **4.** Any narrow orifice.

foreign bodies in t. The presence of foreign objects in the pharynx or throat. Symptoms depend on the location and size of the foreign body and vary from simple discomfort to severe coughing and difficulty in breathing. If the airway is obstructed, suffocation occurs, resulting in unconsciousness and death.

FIRST AID: If complete airway obstruction is present, as evidenced by an inability to speak, breathe, or cough, the Heimlich maneuver should be performed. SEE: *Heimlich maneuver* under Heimlich, Henry Jay.

throb (thrŏb) [ME. *throbben,* of imitative origin] **1.** A beat or pulsation, as of the heart. **2.** To pulsate.

throbbing (thrŏb′ĭng) Pulsation.

thrombasthenia (thrŏm″băs-thē′nē-ă) [Gr. *thrombos,* clot, + *astheneia,* weakness] A bleeding disorder caused by abnormal platelet function characterized by abnormal clot retraction, prolonged bleeding time, and lack of aggregation of the platelets.

thrombectomy (thrŏm-bĕk′tō-mē) [″ + *ektome,* excision] Surgical removal of a thrombus.

thrombi (thrŏm′bī) Pl. of thrombus.

thrombin (thrŏm′bĭn) [Gr. *thrombos,* clot] **1.** An enzyme formed in coagulating blood from prothrombin, which reacts with soluble fibrinogen converting it to fibrin, which forms the basis of a blood clot. SEE: *blood **coagulation**.* **2.** A sterile protein prepared from prothrombin of bovine origin. It is used topically to control capillary oozing during surgical procedures. When used alone, it is not capable of controlling arterial bleeding.

    topical t. A type of fibrin glue that may be applied locally (not injected) to a bleeding wound to stop blood loss.

thrombo-, thromb- [Gr. *thrombos,* lump, curd, blood clot,] Prefixes meaning *blood clot, coagulation, thrombin.*

thromboangiitis (thrŏm″bō-ăn″jē-ī′tĭs) [Gr. *thrombos,* clot, + *angeion,* vessel, + *itis,* inflammation] Inflammation of the intimal layer of a blood vessel, with clot formation. SEE: *thrombosis.*

    t. obliterans Buerger disease. SEE: under *Buerger, Leo.*

thromboarteritis (thrŏm″bō-ăr-tĕ-rī′tĭs) [″ + *arteria,* artery, + *itis,* inflammation] Inflammation of an artery in connection with thrombosis. SYN: *thromboendarteritis.*

thrombocyte (thrŏm′bō-sīt) [″ + *kytos,* cell] Platelet.

thrombocythemia (thrŏm″bō-sī-thē′mē-ă) [″ + ″ + *haima,* blood] Thrombocytosis.

thrombocytopathy (thrŏm″bō-sī-tŏp′ă-thē) [″ + ″ + *pathos,* disease, suffering] Deficient function of platelets.

thrombocytopenia (throm″bō-sīt″ō-pē′nē-ă) [*thrombocyte* + *-penia*] An abnormal decrease in the number of platelets. SYN: *thrombopenia.*

    ETIOLOGY: Acute infections, (such as sepsis), chronic infections (such as HIV), drugs (such as alcohol, heparin, or chemotherapy agents), immune disorders (such as idiopathic thrombocytopenic purpura), leukemia and aplastic anemia, and portal hypertension (such as in cirrhosis) can all cause low platelet counts. Because platelets play a vital role in blood clotting, low levels may increase the risk of bleeding. Platelet counts below 50,000/mm³ increase the risk of hemorrhage with minor trauma; spontaneous bleeding can occur when less than 20,000 are present in a milliliter of blood. Treatment is directed at removing offending drugs or managing the underlying condition.

    PATIENT CARE: The patient is watched for internal hemorrhage (esp. intracranial bleeding) and hematuria, hematemesis, bleeding gums, abdominal distention, melena, prolonged menstruation, epistaxis, ecchymosis, petechiae, or purpura, and is handled carefully, e.g., during blood drawing, to prevent trauma and hemorrhage. Bleeding is controlled by applying pressure to bleeding sites for at least 20 min. If arterial blood collection is necessary for blood gases), a patient care plan should be developed with the physician and the laboratory/blood collection staff to ensure that occult bleeding does not occur. The patient's head should be elevated when lying down. Use of a soft toothbrush or sponge stick helps to prevent injury to oral tissues. Dental flossing is avoided. Normal saline (0.9%) nasal spray or use of a humidifier moistens nasal passages and helps to prevent nosebleeds. An electric razor should be used for shaving. Stools are tested for occult bleeding. Straining at stool and coughing are discouraged; stool softeners are provided as necessary. The patient is advised never to go barefoot and to wear properly fitting shoes and socks.

    During periods of active bleeding, bedrest is maintained. Platelet transfusions are administered as prescribed, and the patient is observed for chills, rigors, fever, or allergic reactions. Acetaminophen and diphenhydramine may prevent or relieve minor transfusion reactions. In patients who have low platelet counts after receiving chemotherapy, the platelet growth factor oprelvekin (Neumega) may be prescribed to reduce the need for platelet transfusions after chemotherapy. Aspirin and other nonsteroidal anti-inflammatory agents should be avoided, as well as herbs such as feverfew, gingko, ginseng, and kava because these substances may inhibit platelet function. Drugs like corticosteroids, immunoglobulin, or gamma globulin may be prescribed to decrease platelet destruction in immune-mediated thrombocytopenia. Folate stimulates bone marrow production of platelets in patients with folate deficiency. When splenectomy is performed to decrease platelet destruction, preoperative and postoperative nursing care is provided as required.

    gestational t. Thrombocytopenia occurring during pregnancy (usually less than 70,000 platelets/mm³). Serious illnesses that cause low platelet counts (such as disseminated intravascular coagulation, HELLP syndrome, idiopathic thrombocytopenic purpura, preeclampsia, systemic lupus erythematosus, or leukemia) should be ruled out. If no illness is present, the condition is usually benign.

    heparin-induced t. Thrombocytopenia caused by an immune reaction to heparin. It may lead to widespread or potentially life-threatening blood clotting rather than bleeding. SEE: *white-clot syndrome.*

⚠️ Patients whose platelet counts drop significantly during exposure to heparin should discontinue the drug immediately.

thrombocytopoiesis (thrŏm″bō-sī″tō-poy-ē′sĭs) [″ + ″ + *poiesis,* production] The formation of platelets.

thrombocytosis (thrŏm″bō-sī-tō′sĭs) [″ + *kytos,* cell] An increase in the number of platelets. SYN: *thrombocythemia.*

thromboelastogram (thrŏm″bō-ē-lăs′tō-grăm) ABBR: TEG. A device used to determine the presence of intravascular fibrinolysis and to monitor the effect of antifibrinolytic therapy on the formation and dissolution of clots.

thromboelastography (throm″bō-ē-las-tog′ră-fē) [*thrombo-* + *elasto-* + *-graphy*] A technique that evaluates the ability of whole blood to coagulate. The technique measures the time it takes for blood to clot, and the firmness or shear strength of the clot. It is used, e.g., to identify the presence of hypercoagulable diseases.

thromboembolic (throm″bō-em-bol′ik) Pert. to or marked by thromboembolism.

thromboembolism (throm″bō-em′bŏ-lizm) [*thrombo-* + *embolism*] The blocking of a blood vessel by a clot (or part of a clot) that has broken off from the place where it formed and traveled to another location. SYN: *embolic **thrombosis**.*

   venous t. ABBR: VTE. A blood clot that forms in a vein and migrates to another location. Typically the clot is a deep venous thrombosis that becomes a pulmonary embolism; it often has serious health consequences.

thromboendarterectomy (thrŏm″bō-ĕnd″ăr-tĕr-ĕk′tō-mē) [″ + *endon,* within, + *arteria,* artery, + *ektome,* excision] Surgical removal of a thrombus from an artery, and removal of the diseased intima of the artery.

thrombogenesis (thrŏm″bō-jĕn′ĕ-sĭs) [″ + *genesis,* generation, birth] The formation of a blood clot.

thrombogenic (thrŏm″bō-jĕn′ĭk) [″ + ″] **1.** Capable of producing a blood clot. **2.** Likely to produce a blood clot.

thrombokinase (throm″bō-kī′nās″) [*thrombo-* + *kinase*] An obsolete term for the Stuart-Prower factor (blood coagulation factor X).

thrombolysis (throm″bol′ĭ-sĭs) [*thrombo-* + *-lysis*] The breaking up of a thrombus. Thrombolytic enzyme therapy is used for lysis of thrombi obstructing coronary arteries in acute myocardial infarction, management of acute massive pulmonary embolism, acute ischemic stroke within 3 hr of symptom onset, after intracranial bleeding has been ruled out, and to lyse deep vein thrombosis via catheter-directed delivery. SYN: *thromboclasis.*

   PATIENT CARE: The health care provider should obtain a complete medical history before administering thrombolytic drugs. Recent surgery, trauma, invasive procedures, uncontrolled hypertension, brain tumors, a history of abnormal bleeding, or pregnancy are all contraindications to their use. In ischemic stroke, the strict time limit for use of thrombolysis is within 3 hr of initial symptoms. Thrombolysis later in the course leads to increased risk of intracranial bleeding and death. The use and administration of thrombolytic drugs should be explained to the patient and family. Each thrombolytic enzyme has specific instructions for reconstitution and dosing, and all are administered intravenously. The drugs should be given through a dedicated IV catheter and line and administered by an infusion controller. Health care professionals should be prepared to initiate anticoagulant and antiplatelet therapy as prescribed during or immediately after thrombolytic treatment to decrease the risk of rethrombosis. The patient's vital signs, heart rhythm, and neurologic status require intensive monitoring during and after therapy. Strict bedrest is required. In patients treated for acute myocardial infarction, reperfusion-induced arrhythmias are treated as prescribed or according to Advanced Cardiac Life Support protocols. Spontaneous bleeding (cerebral, retroperitoneal, GI, and GU) may occur with thrombolysis; the patient should be assessed every 15 min initially, then every 30 min then hourly, then every 4 hr (time span for each varies with the particular drug used). Invasive procedures should be avoided; all puncture sites assessed and reassessed. Patient movement should be restricted, but when necessary, it should be performed gently. Antihistamines or corticosteroids may be used to treat mild allergic responses, but infusion should be stopped if a severe allergic response occurs. Bleeding is the most common adverse effect, occurring internally and at external puncture sites. If uncontrollable bleeding occurs, the infusion should be stopped immediately and the prescriber notified.

   mechanical t. The disruption or removal of a blood clot from a blood vessel with lasers, screws, snares, suction, or ultrasound. It is an alternative (and sometimes an adjunct) to thrombolytic drug therapy in patients who have occluded blood vessels or grafts.

thrombolysis in myocardial infarction ABBR: TIMI. A large series of studies on the use of thrombolytic drugs and percutaneous coronary intervention in patients with acute coronary syndromes. The studies are sponsored by the Thrombolysis in Myocardial Infarction Study Group (TIMI Study Group). Website: www.timi.org

thrombolytic (thrŏm-bō-lĭt′ĭk) Pert. to

or causing the breaking up of a blood clot. SYN: *thromboclastic*.

thrombolytic therapy The use of drugs (e.g., tissue plasminogen activator) that degrade blood clots to treat acute myocardial infarction, pulmonary embolism, or stroke.

thrombomodulin (thrŏm″bō-mō′dū-lĭn) A protein released by the vascular endothelium. Acting in concert with other factors, it helps to prevent formation of intravascular thrombi.

thrombopathy (thrŏm-bŏp′ă-thē) [″ + *pathos*, disease, suffering] A defect in coagulation.

thrombopenia (thrŏm-bō-pē′nē-ă) [″ + *penia*, lack] Thrombocytopenia.

thrombophilia (throm-bō-fĭl′ē-ă) [*thrombo-* + *-philia*] An abnormal tendency to form blood clots.

thrombophlebitis (thrŏm″bō-flĕ-bī′tĭs) [″ + *phleps*, vein, + *itis*, inflammation] Inflammation of a vein in conjunction with the formation of a thrombus. It usually occurs in an extremity, most frequently a leg. SEE: *deep venous thrombosis; phlebitis; Nursing Diagnoses Appendix*.

TREATMENT: Drug therapies include heparins or warfarin.

PATIENT CARE: Prevention includes identifying patients at risk and encouraging leg exercises, use of antiembolic stockings, intermittent pneumatic compression devices, and early ambulation to prevent venous stasis. At-risk patients should be assessed at regular intervals for signs of inflammation, tenderness, aching, and differences in calf circumference measurements. Noninvasive venous ultrasonography provides definitive diagnosis of thrombophlebitis (DVT). It is performed in patients with risk factors for DVT who have a swollen limb and an elevated level of D-dimer in the blood. Anticoagulants are administered as prescribed, the patient is evaluated for signs of bleeding, and coagulation results are monitored to maintain an international normalized ratio (INR) of 2–3. The patient is assessed for signs of pulmonary emboli, dyspnea, tachypnea, hypotension, chest pain, changes of level of consciousness, arterial blood gas abnormalities, and electrocardiogram changes. The patient is prepared for the diagnostic procedures and medical or surgical interventions prescribed.

Patients at greatest risk for thrombophlebitis are those on prolonged bedrest; those with major trauma, congestive heart failure or respiratory failure, obesity, nephrotic syndrome, inflammatory bowel disorders, myeloproliferative disorders, cancer and cancer therapies; pregnancy, recent childbirth, and use of combination hormonal contraceptives or postmenopau-

sal hormone therapy; smoking; varicose veins or previous DVT; central venous catheterization; and people older than 65. At highest risk are those people with multiple risk factors. Patients who are at risk should be taught preventive measures. Long-distance travelers (flying, train, or automobile) should keep well-hydrated (avoiding alcoholic beverages), avoid constrictive clothing, not cross their legs, walk about frequently, and stretch calf muscles while sitting. Properly fitted below-the-knee graduated compression stockings that provide 15 to 30 mm Hg pressure at the ankle can be worn.

   t. migrans Recurring attacks of thrombophlebitis in various sites.

   postpartum iliofemoral t. Thrombophlebitis of the iliofemoral artery that occurs after childbirth.

thromboplastic (thrŏm″bō-plăs′tĭk) [″ + *plassein*, to form] Pert. to or causing blood clot formation.

thromboplastin (throm″bō-plas′tin) [*thrombo-* + *-plast* + *-in*] Coagulation factor III, a lipoprotein found esp. in blood platelets that converts prothrombin to thrombin in the clotting of blood. SYN: *tissue* ***factor***. SEE: *coagulation* ***factor***.

thromboplastinogen (thrŏm″bō-plăs-tĭn′ō-jĕn) Blood clotting factor VIII. SEE: *coagulation factor*.

thrombopoiesis (thrŏm″bō-poy-ē′sĭs) [″ + ″] The formation of platelets.

thrombopoietin (thrŏm″bō-poy-ē′tĭn) ABBR: TPO. A growth factor that acts on the bone marrow to stimulate platelet production as well as the proliferation of other cell lines.

thromboprophylaxis (throm″bō-prō″fĭ-lak′sĭs) [*thrombo-* + *prophylaxis*] Any preventive measure or medication that reduces the likelihood of the formation of blood clots. **thromboprophylactic** (throm″bō-prō″fĭ-lak′tĭk), *adj*.

thrombosed (thrŏm′bōzd) [Gr. *thrombos*, a clot] **1.** Coagulated; clotted. **2.** Pert. to a vessel containing a thrombus.

thrombosis (throm-bō′sĭs) [*thrombo-* + *-osis*] The formation or presence of a blood clot within the vascular system. This is a life-saving process when it occurs during hemorrhage. It is a life-threatening event when it occurs at any other time because the clot can occlude a vessel and stop the blood supply to an organ or a part. The thrombus, if detached, can travel through the bloodstream and occlude a vessel distant from the original site; e.g., a clot in the leg may break off and cause a pulmonary embolus.

ETIOLOGY: Trauma (particularly after an operation and parturition), cardiac and vascular disorders, obesity, hereditary coagulation disorders, age over

65, an excess of erythrocytes and of platelets, an overproduction of fibrinogen, and sepsis are predisposing causes.

SYMPTOMS: *Lungs:* Obstruction of the smaller vessels in the lungs causes an infarct that may be accompanied by sudden pain in the side of the chest, similar to pleurisy; also present are the spitting of blood, a pleural friction rub, and signs of consolidation. *Kidneys:* Blood appears in the urine. *Skin:* Small hemorrhagic spots may appear in the skin. *Spleen:* Pain is felt in the left upper abdomen. *Extremities:* If a large artery in one of the extremities, such as the arm, is suddenly obstructed, the part becomes cold, pale, bluish, and the pulse disappears below the obstructed site. Gangrene of the digits or of the whole limb may ensue. The same symptoms may be present with an embolism.

If the limb is swollen, one should watch for pressure sores. Burning with a hot water bottle or electric pad should be guarded against. Prolonged bedrest may be necessary, depending on the patient's condition.

TREATMENT: Pathological clots are treated with thrombolytic agents (such as streptokinase), antiplatelet drugs (such as heparins or aspirin), anticoagulants (such as warfarin), or platelet glycoprotein receptor antagonists (such as abciximab). When a thrombus or embolus is large and life threatening, surgical removal may be attempted.

cardiac t. Coronary **occlusion**.

catheter-associated t. A thrombosis that forms around a central venous catheter or the electrical leads of a defibrillator or pacemaker.

cerebral sinovenous t. A thrombosis in one of the main veins that carry blood from the brain, such as the superior sagittal sinus, the lateral sinus, or the straight sinus.

coagulation t. Thrombosis due to coagulation of fibrin in a blood vessel.

coronary t. Coronary **occlusion**.

deep vein t., deep venous thrombosis ABBR: DVT. A thrombosis in one or more of the deep veins of the legs (the most common site) or the veins of arms, pelvis, neck, axilla, or chest. The clot may damage the vein or may embolize to other organs, e.g., the heart or lungs. Such emboli are occasionally fatal. SEE: *pulmonary embolism*.

ETIOLOGY: DVT results from one or more of the following conditions: blood stasis, e.g., bedrest; endothelial injury, e.g., after surgery or trauma; hypercoagulability, e.g., factor V Leiden or deficiencies of antithrombin III, protein C, or protein S; congestive heart failure; estrogen use; malignancy; nephrotic syndrome; obesity; pregnancy; thrombocytosis; or many other conditions. DVT is a common occurrence among hospitalized patients, many of whom cannot walk or have one or more of the other risk factors just mentioned.

SYMPTOMS: The patient may report a dull ache or heaviness in the limb, and swelling or redness may be present, but just as often patients have vague symptoms, making clinical diagnosis unreliable.

DIAGNOSIS: Compression ultrasonography is commonly used to diagnose DVT (failure of a vein to compress is evidence of a clot within its walls). Other diagnostic techniques include impedance plethysmography and venography.

TREATMENT: Unfractionated heparin or low molecular weight heparin (LMWH) is given initially, followed by several months of therapy with an oral anticoagulant such as warfarin. The duration of therapy depends on whether the patient has had previous thrombosis and whether, at the end of a specified period of treatment, the patient has an elevated D-dimer level. Patients with increased D-dimers after several months of treatment with anticoagulants are more likely than other patients to have recurrent clots if their anticoagulant regimen is discontinued..

COMPLICATIONS: Pulmonary emboli are common and may compromise oxygenation or result in frank cardiac arrest. Postphlebitic syndrome, a chronic swelling and aching of the affected limb, also occurs often.

PREVENTION: In hospitalized patients and other immobilized persons, early ambulation, pneumatic compression stockings, or low doses of unfractionated heparin, LMWH, or warfarin may be given to reduce the risk of DVT.

effort t. Paget-Schreutter syndrome

embolic t. Thromboembolism.

hepatic vein t. An often fatal thrombotic occlusion of the hepatic veins, marked clinically by hepatomegaly, weight gain, ascites, and abdominal pain. SYN: *Budd-Chiari syndrome*.

infective t. Thrombosis in which there is bacterial infection.

marasmic t. Thrombosis due to wasting diseases.

mural t. Mural **thrombus**.

placental t. Thrombi in the placenta and veins of the uterus.

plate t. Thrombus formed from an accumulation of platelets.

puerperal t. Coagulation in veins following labor.

septic t. An infected blood clot usually found in the heart or the venous sinuses of the brain.

sinus t. Formation of a blood clot in a venous sinus.

stent t. A blood clot that forms inside a device inserted into a blood vessel to keep that vessel open.

PATIENT CARE: Stents are deployed

in completely obstructed or partially blocked arteries to keep blood flowing through them to the organs they supply. When this blood flow stops due to clotting within the stent, the organ may become ischemic and die. To reduce the risk of clotting within a stent, patients use antiplatelet drugs, like aspirin, dipyridamole, or clopidogrel, and medications to lower serum lipid levels. Tobacco cessation, and healthy lifestyle changes (eating lighter, exercising regularly) may also be helpful.

traumatic t. Thrombosis due to a wound or injury of a part.

venous t. Thrombosis of a vein. SEE: *Nursing Diagnoses Appendix.*

thrombospondin (throm″bō-spon′dĭn) ABBR: TSP. A glycoprotein that prevents cell-to-cell adhesion and angiogenesis. Thrombospondin is secreted by some parasites and may enhance their ability to cause disease. It is also found in malignant tumors, where it may block tumor growth and metastasis.

thrombosthenin (thrŏm″bō-sthē′nĭn) [″ + *sthenos*, strength] A contractile protein present in platelets. This protein is active in clot retraction.

thrombotic (thrŏm-bŏt′ĭk) [Gr. *thrombos*, clot] Related to, caused by, or of the nature of a thrombus.

thromboxane A₂ (thrŏm-bŏk′sān) ABBR: TXA₂. An unstable compound synthesized in platelets and other cells from a prostaglandin, PGH₂. It acts to aggregate platelets, is a potent vasoconstrictor, and mediates inflammation. SEE: *eicosanoid; prostaglandin; prostanoids.*

thrombus (throm′bŭs, throm′bī″) *pl.* **thrombi** [Gr. *thrombos*, a clot] A blood clot that adheres to the wall of a blood vessel or organ. It may obstruct the vessel or organ in which it resides, preventing the flow of blood. Anticoagulants are used to prevent and treat this condition.

agonal t. A thrombus formed in the heart just at the time of death.

annular t. A thrombus whose circumference is attached to the walls of a vessel, with an opening still remaining in the center.

antemortem t. A thrombus formed in the heart or large vessels before death.

ball t. A round thrombus in the heart, esp. in the atria.

hyaline t. A thrombus having a glassy appearance, usually occurring in smaller blood vessels.

lateral t. Mural **t.**

mural t. A thrombus forms on the wall of the heart, esp. along an immobile section of the heart damaged by myocardial infarction or cardiomyopathy. Such clots may occasionally embolize, causing stroke or organ damage. SYN: *lateral **t.**; mural thrombosis; parietal **t.***

obstructing t. A thrombus completely occluding the lumen of a vessel.

occluding t. A thrombus that completely closes the vessel.

organized t. A thrombus containing fibrous tissue that may be structured into layers. Tiny blood vessels may course through the clot.

parietal t. Mural **t.**

postmortem t. A thrombus formed in the heart or a large blood vessel after death.

progressive t. Propagated **t.**

propagated t. A thrombus that increases in size. SYN: *progressive **t.***

stratified t. A thrombus composed of layers.

white t. A pale thrombus in any site, made up principally of platelets.

throughput (throo′pŭt″) **1.** In hospital management, the sum of the services provided by a health care institution per unit of time. It includes the number of patients treated, admitted, and discharged; the total number of procedures performed; and the quantity of laboratory or radiological services rendered. It is a measure of institutional volume or capacity and a determinant of productivity. **2.** In the laboratory, the analysis, processing, or testing of multiple samples. Techniques that foster the rapid or simultaneous processing of multiple samples are called *high-throughput.*

throwback (thrō′băk) **1.** To reflect. SEE: *atavism.* **2.** To impair progress.

thrush (thrŭsh) Infection of the mucosa of the mouth caused by *Candida albicans.* In patients with healthy immune systems, it occurs when the balance of normal flora is destroyed during antibiotic therapy or after the use of corticosteroid-based inhalers, which suppress normal white blood cell function in the mouth. It is also common in patients receiving immunosuppressive therapy for organ transplants, in cancer patients, and in those with acquired immunodeficiency syndrome, in whom oral candida infection may be chronic. Occasionally, healthy neonates and persons who wear dentures develop thrush.

Examination reveals white, raised, creamy, easily removable patches on the tongue and other oral mucosal surfaces. The organism is identified by a microscopic examination of scrapings. The infection is treated with a single dose of fluconazole, with clotrimazole lozenges, or with a nystatin oral solution (which must be held in the mouth for 3 min before swallowing) for 14 days; long-term suppressive therapy may be needed for patients with impaired immunity. Dentures should be soaked in an antifungal solution of nystatin. Careful handwashing is essential before doing oral care. SYN: *oropharyngeal **candidiasis**; pseu-*

domembranous **candidiasis**. SEE: *aphtha; candidiasis; stomatitis.*

thrust (thrŭst) **1.** A sudden, forcible forward movement. **2.** In physical medicine, a manipulative technique in which the therapist applies a rapid movement to tear adhesions and increase flexibility of restricted joint capsules.

    abdominal t. Treatment of airway obstruction that consists of inward and upward thrusts of the thumb side of a closed fist in the area between the umbilicus and the xiphoid process. If the patient is conscious, the procedure is performed from behind the person standing; if the patient is unconscious, it can be performed while kneeling beside or straddling the patient and using the heel of the hand rather than a closed fist. SEE: *Heimlich maneuver.*

⚠ This technique is no longer taught for the unconscious patient: the American Heart Association Guidelines replaced it with chest thrusts or CPR compression.

    jaw t. A maneuver for opening the airway of unconscious patients or of patients who cannot control their own airway, by jutting the patient's jaw forward, which in turn moves the tongue away from the back of the throat. This procedure is especially used to open the airway of patients with suspected spinal injury because the cervical spine is not moved during a properly performed jaw thrust.

    subdiaphragmatic abdominal t. Treatment for patients suspected of having a complete airway obstruction. For conscious, standing adults, it consists of upward and inward thrusts of the thumb side of the rescuer's closed fist, coming from behind the victim, in the area between the umbilicus and the xiphoid process. SEE: *Heimlich maneuver.*

    substernal t. A palpable heaving of the chest in the substernal area. This is a physical finding detectable in some persons with right ventricular hypertrophy. SEE: *apical heave.*

    tongue t. The infantile habit of pushing the tongue between the alveolar ridges or incisor teeth during the initial stages of suckling and swallowing. If this habit persists beyond infancy, it may cause anterior open occlusion, jaw deformation, or abnormal tongue function.

Thuja plicata (thoo'jă) [L. *thuja*, fr Gr. *thuia*, cedar] SEE: *Western red cedar.*

thulium (thū'lē-ŭm, thoo') [*Thule*, classical geographical name + *-ium*] SYMB: Tm. A chemical element of the lanthanide series, atomic weight (mass) 168.934, atomic number 69.

thumb (thŭm) The short, thick first finger on the radial side of the hand, having two phalanges and being opposable to the other four digits. SYN: *pollex.* SEE: *hand* for illus.

    gamekeeper's t. An injury to the ulnar collateral ligament of the metacarpophalangeal joint of the thumb. SYN: *skier's t..*

    skier's t. Gamekeeper's thumb.

    tennis t. Calcification and inflammation of the tendon of the flexor pollicis longus muscle owing to repeated irritation and stress while playing tennis.

thumb sign SEE: under *sign.*

thumb sucking The habit of sucking one's thumb. Intermittent thumb sucking is not abnormal, but prolonged and intensive thumb sucking past the time the first permanent teeth erupt at 5 or 6 years of age can lead to a misshapen mouth and displaced teeth. If the habit persists, combined dental and psychological therapy should be instituted.

thump (thŭmp) A punch or blow to the center of the sternum with the fist or a mechanical device.

    chest t. Precordial thump.

    precordial t. A forceful punch delivered to a patient's sternum in an attempt to terminate a lethal cardiac rhythm, such as ventricular fibrillation or ventricular tachycardia.

⚠ This procedure is not routinely used. The critical time it consumes during resuscitation may be better used by starting chest compressions and assigning a second rescuer to obtain an automated external defibrillator.

SYN: *chest t.*

Thunder God vine A toxic plant, *Tripterygium wilfordii,* from which extracts have been obtained that can be used to treat rheumatoid arthritis.

thymectomy (thī-mĕk'tō-mē) [Gr. *thymos,* mind, + *ektome,* excision] Surgical removal of the thymus gland.

-thymia [Gr. *thymos,* spirit, mind] Suffix meaning *a state of the mind.*

thymic (thī'mik) [L. *thymicus*] Pert. to the thymus gland.

thymidine (thī'mĭ-dēn) A nucleoside present in deoxyribonucleotide. It is formed from the condensation product of thymine and deoxyribose.

thymine (thī'mĭn) $C_5N_2H_6O_2$; a pyrimidine base present in DNA (not RNA) where it is paired with adenine.

thymitis (thī-mī'tĭs) [″ + ″] Inflammation of the thymus.

¹thymo-, thym- [Gr. *thymos,* breath, soul, life, temper, anger] Prefixes meaning *soul, spirit, emotion, mind*

²thymo-, thym- [Gr. *thymon, thymos,* thyme, warty growth] Prefixes meaning *thymus.*

thymocyte (thī'mō-sīt) [Gr. *thymos,* mind, + *kytos,* cell] Immature T lymphocytes that reside in the thymus. Less than 1% of the lymphoid stem cells that migrate to the thymus reproduce and develop into T lymphocytes capable of binding with specific antigens.

thymoma (thī-mō'mă) [" + "] A rare neoplasm, usually found in the anterior mediastinum and originating in the epithelial cells of the thymus. It is often associated with myasthenia gravis and autoimmune diseases. Treatments may include surgical removal, radiation therapy, or chemotherapy.

thymopoietin (thī″mō-poy'ĕ-tĭn) A peptide hormone secreted by the thymus that helps thymocytes to mature and respond to specific antigenic stimuli.

thymosin (thī'mō-sĭn) A peptide hormone, produced in cells of the thymus and believed to play a part in T lymphocyte development.

thymulin (thī'mū-lĭn) A peptide hormone, released by the thymus, with immune modulating and analgesic actions.

thymus (thī'mŭs) [Gr. *thymos*] A primary lymphoid organ located in the mediastinal cavity anterior to and above the heart, where it lies over the superior vena cava, aortic arch, and trachea. The thymus comprises two fused lobes, the right larger than the left. The lobes are partially divided into lobules, each of which has an outer cortex packed with immature and developing T lymphocytes (thymocytes) and an inner medulla containing a looser arrangement of mature T lymphocytes. SEE: illus.

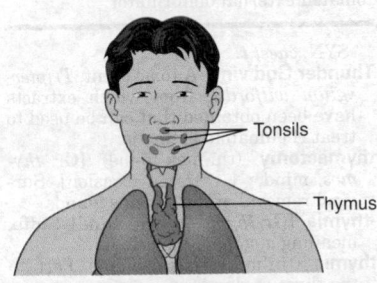

Tonsils

Thymus

THYMUS

The thymus is the primary site for T-lymphocyte differentiation; here, T lymphocytes acquire their range of antigen receptors. During the prenatal period, lymphoid stem cells migrate from the bone marrow to the thymus, filling the cortex of the lobules. Developing thymocytes acquire their characteristic CD surface antigens and their binding receptors. As the thymocytes then move from the cortex into the medulla of the lobules, some are protected but many undergo cell death in a process that culls out those reactive to autoantigens.

Less than 5 % of the thymocytes mature into T cells that pass out of the lobules and migrate to the spleen, lymph nodes, and other lymphoid tissue, where they control cell-mediated immune responses. The thymus produces at least four hormones: thymopoietin, thymulin, thymus humoral factor, and the thymosins.

At birth, the thymus weighs 10-15 g; by puberty, it weighs about 20 g. After this, the cortical regions of the thymus shrink and become replaced by adipose tissue, although the thymus continues to produce hormones and some thymocytes into old age.

PATHOLOGY: Lack of a thymus or thymus hypoplasia is one component of DiGeorge syndrome, which is marked by severe lack of cell-mediated immunity; removal of the thymus of an adult is less catastrophic but leads to a less effective response to new antegens. Thymic hyperplasia results from the growth of lymph follicles containing both B lymphocytes and dendritic cells. It is found in myasthenia gravis and, occasionally, in other autoimmune diseases (e.g., Graves disease, rheumatoid arthritis, and systemic lupus erythematosus). Thymomas involve only the thymic epithelial cells. Other tumors, including those associated with Hodgkin's disease and lymphomas, involve thymocytes.

persistent hyperplastic t. Thymus persisting into adulthood, sometimes hypertrophying.

supernumerary t. Accessory **t.**

thyreo- [Gr. *thyreos,* oblong shield] Prefix meaning *thyroid.*

thyro-, thyr- [Gr. *thyre(os),* oblong shield] Prefixes meaning *thyroid gland.*

thyroarytenoid (thī″rō-ă-rĭt'ĕn-oyd) [" + *arytaina,* ladle, + *eidos,* form, shape] Pert. to the thyroid and arytenoid cartilages.

thyrocalcitonin (thī″rō-kăl″sī-tō'nĭn) Calcitonin.

thyrocardiac (thī″rō-kăr'dē-ăk) [" + *kardia,* heart] **1.** Pert. to the heart and thyroid gland. **2.** A person suffering from thyroid disease complicated by a heart disorder.

thyroepiglottic (thī″rō-ĕp″ĭ-glŏt'ĭk) [" + *epi,* upon, + *glottis,* back of tongue] Pert. to the thyroid and epiglottis.

thyroglobulin (thī″rō-glŏb'ū-lĭn) [" + L. *globulus,* globule] **1.** An iodine-containing glycoprotein secreted by the thyroid gland and stored within its colloid, from which thyroxine and triiodothyronine are derived. **2.** A substance obtained by the fractionation of thyroid glands from the hog, *Sus scrofa.*

thyroglossal (thī″rō-glŏs'săl) [" + *glossa,* tongue] Pert. to the thyroid gland and the tongue.

thyrohyoid (thī″rō-hī'oyd) [" + *hy-*

oeides, U-shaped] Pert. to thyroid cartilage and hyoid bone.

thyroid (thī'royd″) [*thyro-* + *-oid*] **1.** The thyroid gland. **2.** The cleansed, dried, and powdered thyroid gland of animals; thyroid extract. Thyroid extract, because of its unpredictable potency, is used only rarely to treat hypothyroidism and goiter.

   lingual t. A small nodule of ectopic thyroid tissue located on the dorsal tongue, posterior to the circumvallate papillae. It is caused by failure of developing thyroid tissue to migrate from the area of the foramen cecum to its normal location in the neck.

thyroid cartilage SEE: under *cartilage*.

thyroidectomy (thī″royd-ĕk′tō-mē) Excision of the thyroid gland, used typically to treat thyroid cancers, goiters, or Graves disease. SEE: *Nursing Diagnoses Appendix.*

   PATIENT CARE: *Preoperative:* The patient is taught about postoperative care measures and pain management.

   Postoperative: All general patient care concerns apply. Attention to airway compromise due to either hemorrhage or recurrent laryngeal nerve injury is emphasized. The patient is maintained in a semi-Fowler's position, with head and neck well supported to ease incisional tension. A Hemovac, or similar low-suction drain, may be in place for the first 24 to 48 hr. The patient is checked for dysphagia and hoarseness, signs of laryngeal nerve injury, and for bleeding or infection. Evidence of hypocalcemia resulting from unrecognized removal of the parathyroid glands must also be assessed both with postoperative parathyroid hormone levels and with physical assessments for tetany. The patient is watched closely for signs of respiratory distress, and in both the recovery room and the patient care setting, there should be equipment for immediate resuscitation: airway reintubation, tracheostomy tray, or both, as well as various pharmacological agents, e.g., calcium chloride, antithyroid agents, and antihypertensives. Immediate notification of the surgeon for suspected problems is mandatory. Discharge teaching focuses on incisional care and signs of infection to be reported immediately. Regular follow-up care is required to manage hypothyroidism, which develops 2 to 4 weeks after total thyroidectomy, and to assess thyroid size and status following subtotal resection.

   subtotal t. Surgical excision of part of the thyroid gland, as is performed for benign conditions, equivocal or limited forms of low-grade malignancy, and other conditions. The risk of accidental removal of the parathyroid glands is lessened by this procedure.

thyroid function test ABBR: TFT. Any of several tests for evidence of increased or decreased thyroid function, including a clinical physical examination, which is usually reliable, and a variety of reliable laboratory tests. The most common test to assess thyroid function is the measurement of thyroid-stimulating hormone (TSH) with supersensitive assays. Usually, TSH levels are high in hypothyroidism and suppressed in hyperthyroidism, although in patients with pituitary masses this pattern may be reversed. Other thyroid function tests include measurements of free and total thyroxine (T_4) and triiodothyronine (T_3), tests of thyroid-binding globulin levels, antithyroid antibody tests, and thyroid gland radioactive iodine uptake (RAIU) measurement. Many of these test results are more difficult to interpret than are TSH results because their normal ranges may vary with pregnancy, liver disease, nutritional status, and other medical conditions. SEE: *hyperthyroidism; hypothyroidism.*

thyroid gland SEE: under *gland*.

thyroiditis (thī″royd″īt′ĭs) [*thyroid* + *-itis*] Inflammation of the thyroid gland.

   chronic lymphocytic t. Hashimoto thyroiditis.

   giant cell t. Thyroiditis characterized by the presence of giant cells, round-cell infiltration, fibrosis, and destruction of follicles.

   Hashimoto t. SEE: *Hashimoto thyroiditis.*

   postpartum t. A brief alteration in thyroid function occurring in the weeks and months after delivery of a child. Affected women typically become temporarily hyperthyroid and then hypothyroid before returning to normal thyroid function.

   Riedel t. SEE: under *Riedel, Bernhard M. K. L.*

thyroidotomy (thī″royd-ŏt′ō-mē) [″ + ″ + *tome,* incision] Incision of the thyroid gland.

thyroid storm SEE: under *storm*.

thyromegaly (thī″rō-mĕg′ă-lē) [″ + *megas,* large] Enlargement of the thyroid gland.

thyroparathyroidectomy (thī″rō-par″ă-thī″royd″ek′tō-mē) [*thyro-* + *parathyroidectomy*] Surgical removal of the thyroid and parathyroid glands. SEE: *parathyroidectomy; thyroidectomy.*

thyroplasty (thī″rō-plăs′tē) Surgery to alter the configuration of the thyroid cartilage adjacent to the vocal cords. This is done to treat certain types of dysphonia. SYN: *laryngeal framework surgery*.

thyrotomy (thī-rŏt′ō-mē) **1.** The splitting of the thyroid cartilage anteriorly in midline to expose laryngeal structures. **2.** Surgery on the thyroid gland.

thyrotoxic (thī″rō-tŏks′ĭk) [″ + *toxikon,* poison] Pert. to, affected by, or marked by toxic activity of the thyroid gland.

thyrotoxic heart disease A disease due to increased activity of the thyroid gland, marked by cardiac enlargement, atrial fibrillation, and high-output heart failure. SEE: *thyrotoxicosis.*

thyrotoxicosis (thī″rō-tŏks″ĭ-kō′sĭs) [″ + ″ + *osis,* condition] Hyperthyroidism.

thyrotroph (thī′ră-trŏf″) Thyroid hormone producing. The term is usually used to denote cells or adenomas in the pituitary gland that secrete thyroid-stimulating hormone.

thyrotropic (thī″rō-trŏp′ĭk) [″ + *trope,* a turning] Pert. to an affinity for or stimulation of the thyroid gland.

thyrotropin, thyrotrophin (thī″rō′trō′pĭn, thī″rō′trō′fĭn) [*thyro-* + *-tropin*] A hormone secreted by the anterior lobe of the pituitary that stimulates the thyroid gland to secrete thyroxine and triiodothyronine. SYN: *thyroid-stimulating hormone; thyrotropic hormone.*

thyroxine (thī-rŏks′ĭn) [Gr. *thyreos,* shield] ABBR: T_4. One of the principal hormones secreted by the thyroid gland that increases the use of all food types for energy production and increases the rate of protein synthesis in most tissues. It is used to treat hypothyroidism. Chemically, it is 3,5,3′,5′-tetraiodothyronine. SYN: *tetraiodothyronine.* SEE: *thyroid; thyroid function test; triiodothyronine.*

Ti Symbol for the element titanium.

TIA *transient ischemic attack.*

tibia (tĭb′ē-ă) [L., *tibia,* shinbone] The inner and larger bone of the leg between the knee and the ankle; it articulates with the femur above and with the talus below.

   saber-shaped t. A deformity caused by gummatous periostitis (syphilitic) in which the tibia curves outward.

   t. valga Valgus knee.

   t. vara A pathological bowing of the leg (genu varum). Unlike the physiological bowlegs of the infant and toddler, the bowing in tibia vara progressively worsens after the first 2 years of life and is often unilateral. The condition is more common in girls than in boys and more common in blacks than in European Americans. Most cases occur in the first 2 or 3 years of life, but a juvenile form (onset at age 4 to 10 years) and an adolescent form (onset at 11 years or older) are recognized. SYN: *Blount disease.*

   DIAGNOSIS: Diagnosis is based on clinical presentation and x-ray of the leg.

   TREATMENT: In the early stages, simple bracing and splinting may be all

that is necessary. If the disease has gone undetected or untreated, or if it is one of the later-onset forms, surgery may be required.

tibial (tĭb′ē-ăl) [L. *tibialis*] Pert. to the tibia.

tibialis (tĭb″ē-ā′lĭs) [L.] Pert. to the tibia.

tibiofemoral (tĭb″ē-ō-fĕm′or-ăl) [″ + L. *femur,* thigh] Pert. to the tibia and femur.

tibiofibular (tĭb″ē-ō-fĭb′ū-lăr) [″ + L. *fibula,* pin] Pert. to the tibia and fibula.

tibionavicular (tĭb″ē-ō-nă-vĭk′ū-lăr) Pert. to the tibia and navicular bones.

tibiotarsal (tĭb″ē-ō-tăr′săl) [″ + Gr. *tarsos,* broad, flat surface] Pert. to the tibia and tarsus.

TIBOLA *tick-borne lymphadenopathy* (an increase in lymph resulting from infection with *Ricksettsia slovaca,* an intracellular pathogen transmitted to humans by the bite of infected ticks).

tic (tĭk) [Fr.] A spasmodic muscular contraction, most commonly involving the face, mouth, eyes, head, neck, or shoulder muscles. The spasms may be tonic or clonic. The movement appears purposeful, is often repeated, is involuntary, and can be inhibited for a short time only to burst forth with increased severity.

   Children between the ages of 5 and 10 years are esp. likely to develop tics. SEE: *Tourette syndrome.*

   ETIOLOGY: In most cases, the cause is unknown. In some people, the tic is worsened by anxiety and nervous tension.

   convulsive t. Spasm of the facial muscles supplied by the seventh cranial nerve.

   t. douloureux Trigeminal neuralgia. SEE: *Nursing Diagnoses Appendix.*

   facial t. Tic of the facial muscles.

   habit t. Habitual repetition of a grimace or muscular action.

   t. rotatoire Spasmodic torticollis in which the head and neck are forcibly rotated or turned from one side to the other.

   vocal t. Grunts and barking sounds that may be made by those with Tourette syndrome.

tick (tĭk) Any of numerous bloodsucking arthropods of the order Acarida and superfamily Ixodoidea. Ticks transmit many diseases to humans and animals. SEE: *Argasidae; Ixodidae.*

   wood t. **Dermacentor** andersoni.

tick-borne rickettsiosis The spotted-fever group (SFG) of tick-borne rickettsioses. Included are infections caused by the pathogenic organism *Rickettsia rickettsii,* which causes Rocky Mountain spotted fever. There are six other pathogenic SFG rickettsial species, five of which (*R. conorii, R. sibirica, R. japonica, R. australis,* and *R. africae*) are most likely to be transmitted by a tick bite. *R. akari,* which causes rickettsial-pox, is transmitted to humans by mouse mites.

tickle (tĭk'l) [ME. *tikelen*] **1.** A peculiar sensation caused by titillation or touching, esp. in certain areas of the body, resulting in reflex muscular movements, laughter, or other forms of emotional expression. **2.** To arouse such a sensation by touching a surface lightly.

tickling (tĭk'lĭng) Gentle stimulation of a sensitive surface and its reflex effect, such as involuntary laughter. SYN: *titillation.*

t.i.d. L. *ter in die,* three times a day.

tidal (tī'dăl) Periodically rising and falling, increasing and decreasing.

tide (tīd) [Old English *tīd,* time, tide] An alternating rise and fall; a space of time.

    acid t. A temporary increase in the acidity of urine or other body fluid.

    alkaline t. Temporary decrease in acidity of urine following awakening and after meals. The former results from an increased rate of breathing, in which excess carbon dioxide is eliminated; the latter results from an increase of base in the blood following the secretion of HCl into gastric juice.

    fat t. Increased fat in the lymph and blood after a fatty meal.

    red tide Seawater discolored by a dense growth of dinoflagellates in coastal waters. The discolored seawater may be red, green, or brown. The algae that cause the tide produce a variety of poisons that may kill marine vertebrates, accumulate in shellfish, and cause potential health hazards for humans who consume shellfish. Diseases associated with the consumption of shellfish during a red tide include amnesic shellfish poisoning and diarrheal shellfish poisoning. SYN: *harmful algal bloom; toxic algal bloom.*

-tidine A suffix used in pharmacology to designate an H_2 receptor antagonist.

tier (tēr) [Fr. *tire,* rank, sequence] In a health care insurance plan, one of several layers or types of care. Each level provides a different quality and quantity of service. Typically those tiers that provide the greatest number of services are the most expensive.

Tietze syndrome (tēt'sĕ) [Alexander Tietze, Ger. surgeon, 1864–1927] Costochondritis.

tigroid (tī'groyd) [Gr. *tigroeides,* tiger-spotted] Striped, spotted, or marked like a tiger.

tigrolysis (tĭg″rŏl'ĭ-sĭs) Chromatolysis.

tilmus (tĭl'mŭs) [Gr. *tilmos,* a plucking] Carphology.

timbre (tĭm'bĕr, tăm'br) [Fr., a bell to be struck with a hammer] The resonance quality of a sound by which it is distinguished, other than pitch or intensity,

depending on the number and character of the vibrating body's overtones.

time (tīm) The interval between beginning and ending; measured duration.

    activated partial thromboplastin t. ABBR: APTT. A laboratory test to measure the intrinsic pathway of coagulation. In health, the APTT is about 16 to 40 sec, depending on the laboratory methods used. Prolonged PTT may indicate cirrhosis of the liver, disseminated intravascular coagulation, blood clotting factor deficiencies (VIII, IX, X), decreased levels of fibrinogen in the blood, von Willebrand's disease, or the presence of a lupus anticoagulant.

    arise t. In sleep medicine, the time when a person gets out of bed after sleeping as opposed to the time a person becomes alert and awake after sleep.

    association t. SEE: *association test.*

    backup t. In radiography, the time setting selected before an automated exposure, usually 150% of the anticipated total exposure time for projection.

    bleeding t. The time required for blood to stop flowing from a small wound or pinprick. It is assessed using one of several techniques. Depending on the method used, the time may vary from 1 to 3 min (Duke method) or from 1 to 9 min (Ivy method). The Duke method consists of timing the cessation of bleeding after the earlobe has received a standardized puncture. The Ivy method is done in a similar manner following puncture of the skin of the forearm. The validity of this test to predict clinically significant bleeding has been questioned.

    bowel transit t. The length of time it takes for food (or a marker dye) to pass through the gastrointestinal tract, from ingestion to defecation. It is shorter in conditions such as malabsorption and more prolonged in constipation.

    circulation t. The time required for a drop of blood to make the complete circuit of both the systemic and pulmonary systems. Circulation time is determined by injecting a substance into a vein and timing its reappearance in arteries at the injection point. The blood with the contained substance must pass through veins to the heart and through the right atrium and ventricle, through the pulmonary circuit to the lungs, and back through the left atrium and ventricle, and then out through the aorta and arteries to the place of detection. Dyes such as fluorescein and methylene blue and substances such as potassium ferrocyanide and histamine have been used as tracers. Average circulation time is about 1 min.

    Circulation time is reduced in anemia and hyperthyroidism and is increased in hypertension, myxedema, and cardiac failure. Circulation time may also be measured by injecting into a vein a substance that can be tasted when it is transported to the tongue. The normal circulation time from an arm vein to the tongue is 10 to 16 sec. In the aorta, the blood flows at a speed of approx. 30 cm/sec.

clot retraction t. The time required following withdrawal of blood for a clot to completely contract and express the serum entrapped within the fibrin net. The normal time is about 1 hr. Clot retraction depends on the number of platelets in the specimen.

coagulation t. The time required for a small amount of phlebotomized blood to clot. This can be determined by collecting blood in a small test tube and noting elapsed time from the moment blood is shed to the time it coagulates.

cold ischemia t. ABBR: CIT. The time that an organ surgically removed for transplantation remains in a chilled perfusion solution before engraftment.

cycle t. The period between regular events, e.g., inflations of an automated blood pressure monitor.

doubling t. The length of time needed for a malignant tumor cell population to double in size.

door-to-balloon t. The delay between the arrival at a hospital of a patient with an acute myocardial infarction and the opening of the patient's obstructed vessel by percutaneous coronary intervention. The delay should be 90 min or less for optimal outcomes.

dwell t. The length of time a therapeutic substance will be retained in the body.

euglobulin lysis t. A test that determines how rapidly blood clots dissolve. It is used to identify diseases such as disseminated intravascular coagulation, and to monitor the effect of thrombolytic drugs, such as streptokinase and the recombinant enzyme tissue plasminogen activator.

forced expiratory t. ABBR: FET. The time required to forcibly exhale a specified volume of air from the lung.

gestation t. The duration of a normal pregnancy for a species. SEE: *pregnancy* for table.

intestinal transit t. The speed with which consumed food passes through the gut. It is slowed by anticholinergic agents (such as tricyclic antidepressants) and by neuropathic diseases of the stomach or intestines, e.g., diabetes mellitus. Many agents increase intestinal transit, including erythromycin and nonabsorbable laxatives.

into-bed t. In sleep medicine, the time when a person lies down for his or her major sleep time of the day as opposed to other periods of sleep.

kaolin cephalin t. ABBR: KCT, KCCT. A laboratory test to measure the health of the intrinsic pathway of coagulation (the function of clotting factors VII, IX, XI, and XII). When a prolonged kaolin cephalin clotting time does not normalize after the addition of normal plasma, a lupus anticoagulant is present in the blood.

longitudinal relaxation t. T1 t.

lost t. In occupational health, the number of hours, days, or weeks that an employee does not appear for work, as a result of illness, injury, absenteeism, workers' compensation, or unpaid leave.

median lethal t. The time required for half of a population to die after exposure to ionizing radiation.

partial thromboplastin t. The time needed for plasma to clot after the addition of partial thromboplastin. It is used to test for defects of the clotting system.

prothrombin t. ABBR: PT. The time it takes for clotting to occur after thromboplastin and calcium are added to decalcified plasma. The test is used to assess levels of anticoagulation in patients taking warfarin, to determine the cause of unexplained bleeding (as in patients with hemophilia), or to assess the ability of the liver to synthesize blood-clotting proteins. SEE: *international normalized ratio*.

quiet t. 1. The time between measurable events, e.g., in respiratory care, the time between inspiration and expiration. 2. A time of silent reflection, thought, or prayer.

reaction t. The period between application of a stimulus and the response.

recovery t. 1. The time between the end of an anesthetic infusion and the opening of a patient's eyes. 2. The time between the end of an anesthetic infusion and the patient's ability to oxygenate and ventilate without mechanical assistance.

reptilase t. ABBR: RT. A test to identify hypofibrinogenemia or dysfibrinogenemia in plasma.

response t. 1. The delay between the first administration of a medication and the onset of or recovery from its effects. 2. The duration of a reaction.

saturation t. The time required for the arterial blood of a person inhaling pure oxygen to become saturated.

screen t. The number of hours that a person spends each day in front of a computer, or watching movies or television, or playing video games.

setting t. The time required for a material to polymerize or harden, as in dental amalgam, cement, plaster, resin, or stone.

spin lattice relaxation t. T1 t.

spin-spin relaxation t. T2 t.

T1 t. The time it takes for a proton that has been stimulated by radiofrequency (RF) energy to relax back into its usual alignment in tissue. Each tissue in the body has its own distinguishing relaxation time and its own distinctive energy emission after stimulation with RF energy. These physical characteristics of tissues are exploited in magnetic resonance imaging to create pictures of body structures. SYN: *longitudinal relaxation t.; spin lattice relaxation t.*

    T2 t. The time it takes for neighboring, radiofrequency-stimulated protons to relax relative to other protons in tissue (rather than relative to the magnetization provided by a magnetic resonance imaging (MRI) device). The T2 time varies from tissue to tissue. This is exploited in MRI to help generate contrast between adjacent tissues, e.g., between the white matter and grey matter of the brain, or between tissues with high fat content as opposed to those with high water content. SYN: *spin-spin relaxation t.; transverse relaxation t.*

    taipan snake venom t. A test to determine the presence of lupus anticoagulant in a blood specimen. The test relies on the mixing of venom from snakes of the genus *Oxyuranus* with dilute phospholipid and can be used even in patients receiving warfarin anticoagulation.

    template bleeding t. A bedside test to determine the presence of abnormal delays in blood clotting, in which a small cut is made in the skin, and the time it takes for bleeding to stop is measured.

    thermal death t. The time required to kill a bacterium at a certain temperature.

    transverse relaxation t. T2 t.

    turn-around t., turnaround time ABBR: TAT. The time it takes to process an order, carry it out, and report the results, e.g., the time between ordering and reporting laboratory test results.

    PATIENT CARE: In the rushed environment of contemporary hospitals, esp. in emergency departments and intensive care units, TAT can be a problem between physicians and nurses who order lab tests and the laboratorians who complete them and report the results. At the bedside, TAT starts with the ordering of the test. In the lab it begins when the specimen or the order for the test is received; next it is processed; and, finally, the results are reported to the clinician. Decreasing TAT without sacrificing the quality of reported results makes timely modifications in treatment possible; it requires careful planning at the bedside, a rapid system of specimen transport, an easy-to-use order entry system and log, and an efficient laboratory with well-trained professional staff.

time diary Time inventory.

timed up-and-go test ABBR: TUGT. A

test that measures mobility by assessing the time it takes for a person to rise from a chair, walk a measured distance, and turn around. The test is used to assess balance and gait, esp. in the elderly.

timed voiding (tīmd) Bladder training.

time inventory A personal record of how time is used or managed by a patient or client. It provides a detailed outline of daily activities, including the subject's primary and secondary activities, social interaction, and places where daily activities occur. SYN: *time diary*.

time-out (tīm'owt″) **1.** A method of discipline that involves removing a child from social interaction and placing him or her in a restful environment, i.e., a quiet room, for a few minutes because of unacceptable behavior. **2.** In giving informed consent for a procedure, a brief period when the patient is left alone to reflect upon the risks, benefits, and alternatives to the proposed procedure before being asked to decide to accept or reject it.

time pressure The psychological stress that results from having to get things done in less time than is needed or desired. SYN: *time crunch; time squeeze*.

timer (tīm'ĕr) A device for measuring, signaling, recording, or otherwise indicating elapsed time. Various forms of timers are used in radiographic, surgical, and laboratory work.

time-to-event analysis Survival analysis.

time to pregnancy The number of menstrual cycles it takes to fertilize an ovum, either as a result of intercourse or with the use of assisted fertility methods.

time to progression ABBR: TTP. In cancer care, the number of months after the disease is recognized or treated before the patient feels worse or experiences poor health.

time to treatment failure, time-to-treatment failure ABBR: TTF. In cancer care, the number of months after the disease is treated before the cancer spreads and the patient's health worsens.

time use survey An inventory of the activities of a population of interest, used, e.g., to measure economic productivity, health risks, leisure pursuits, and traffic flow.

TIMI *thrombolysis in myocardial infarction.*

timothy grass (tim'ŏ-thē) [*Timothy Hanson*, early 18th-cent. U.S. farmer who cultivated the grass] A common North American grass (*Phleum pratense*). Allergens derived from this grass cause seasonal allergies, esp. during the summer.

tin (tin) SYMB: Sn. A metallic element used in various industries and in making certain tissue stains; atomic weight (mass) 118.69; atomic number 50.

tinct (tĭnkt) *tincture.*

tinction (tĭnk′shŭn) [L. *tingere*, to dye]
1. The process of staining. **2.** A stain.
tinctorial (tĭnk-tō′rē-ăl) [L. *tinctorius*, dyeing] Pert. to staining or color.
tincture (tĭnk′chūr) [L. *tinctura*, a dyeing] An alcoholic extract of vegetable or animal substances. SYN: *tinctura*.
tincture of iodine An obsolete term for a simple alcoholic solution of iodine.
tine (tīn) A sharp, pointed prong.
tinea (tin′ē-ă) [L. *tinea*, bookworm] Any fungal skin disease occurring on various parts of the body. SEE: *dermatomycosis*.
  FINDINGS: There are two types of findings. Superficial findings include scaling, slight itching, reddish or grayish patches, and dry, brittle hair that is easily extracted with the hair shaft. Deep findings include flat, reddish, kerion-like tumors, whose surfaces are studded with dead or broken hairs or by gaping follicular orifices. Nodules may be broken down in the center, discharging pus through dilated follicular openings.
  TREATMENT: Griseofulvin, terbinafine, or ketoconazole is given orally for all types of true trichophyton infections. Local treatment alone is of little benefit in ringworm of the scalp, nails, and, in most cases, the feet. Topical preparations containing fungicidal agents are useful for tinea cruris and tinea pedis.
  Personal hygiene is important in controlling these two common diseases. The use of antiseptic foot baths to control tinea pedis does not prevent spread of the infection from one person to another. Those affected should not let others use their personal items such as clothes, towels, and sports equipment.
  Tinea of the scalp, tinea capitis, is particularly resistant if it is due to *Microsporum audouinii*. It should not be treated topically. Systemic griseofulvin is quite effective.
  t. amiantacea Sticky scaling of the scalp following infection or trauma.
  t. barbae Barber's itch.
  t. capitis A fungal infection of the scalp. It may be due to one of several types of *Microsporum* or to *Trichophyton tonsurans*. SEE: illus.; *kerion*.

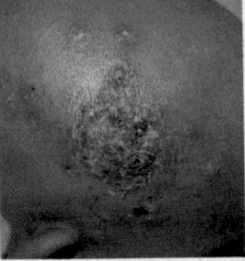

TINEA CAPITIS

t. corporis Tinea of the body. It begins with red, slightly elevated scaly patches that on examination reveal minute vesicles or papules. New patches spring from the periphery while the central portion clears. There is often considerable itching. SEE: illus.

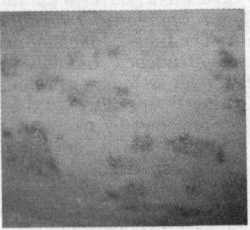

TINEA CORPORIS

t. cruris A fungal skin disease of surfaces of contact in the scrotal, crural, anal, and genital areas. SYN: *dhobie itch; jock itch*. SEE: illus.

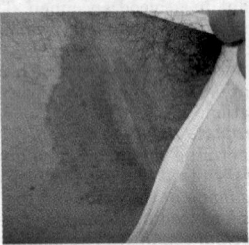

TINEA CRURIS

t. imbricata Chronic tinea caused by *Trichophyton concentricum*. It is present in tropical regions. The annular lesions have scales at their periphery.
t. incognita Tinea corporis that grows rapidly and in unusual patterns after the use of topical steroids.
t. kerion Kerion.
t. nigra An asymptomatic superficial fungal infection that affects the skin of the palms. Caused by *Hortaea werneckii*, it is characterized by deeply pigmented, macular, nonscaly patches. SYN: *pityriasis nigra*.
t. nodosa Sheathlike nodular masses in the hair of the beard and mustache from growth of either *Piedraia hortae*, which causes black piedra, or *Trichosporon beigelii*, which causes white piedra. The masses surround the hairs, which become brittle; hairs may be penetrated by fungus and thus split. SYN: *piedra*.
t. pedis Athlete's **foot**.
t. profunda Majocchi disease.
t. sycosis Barber's **itch** (2).
t. tonsurans Tinea capitis.
t. unguium Onychomycosis.
t. versicolor A fungal infection of the skin producing yellow or fawn-colored

branny patches. A topically applied azole antifungal cream or 2% selenium
sulfide lotion is effective in treating the
causative agent, the fungus *Malassezia
furfur.* SYN: *pityriasis versicolor.* SEE:
illus.

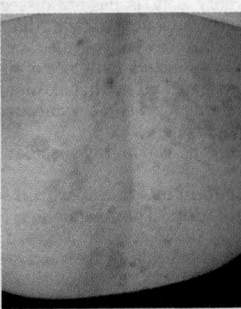

TINEA VERSICOLOR (on back)

Tinel sign (ti-nel') [Jules Tinel, Fr. neurologist, 1879–1952] A tingling sensation on the skin produced by pressing on
or tapping the nerve trunk that has
been damaged or is regenerating after
trauma.

tine test Tuberculin tine test.

Tinetti test (tĭ-net'ē) [Mary Tinetti, contemporary U.S. physician] A measurement of functional ability that incorporates observation of performance of 13
activities with a focus on gait and balance. The activities include sitting, rising from a chair, standing, turning,
reaching up, and bending down. The
rating scale is *normal, adaptive,* or *abnormal* and is often used to assess the
risk of falling.

tingible (tĭn'jĭ-bĕl) [L. *tingere,* to stain]
Capable of being stained by a dye.

tingle (tĭng'gĕl) A prickling or stinging
sensation that may be caused by cold or
nerve injury.

tinnitus (tĭn-ī'tŭs) [L., a jingling] A subjective ringing, buzzing, tinkling, or
hissing sound in the ear. For some patients, this causes only minor irritation;
for others, it is disabling.
    ETIOLOGY: It may be caused by im-
pacted cerumen, myringitis, otitis media,
Ménière disease, otosclerosis, or drug toxicities (esp. salicylates and quinine).

tip (tĭp) [ME.] A point, end, or apex of a
part.

tipping (tĭp'ĭng) Angulation of a structure, such as a tooth about its long axis,
the patella when it moves away from
the frontal plane of the femur, or the
scapula when the inferior angle moves
away from the rib cage.

TIPS *transjugular intrahepatic portosystemic shunt.*

tiqueur (tĭ-kĕr') [Fr.] One afflicted with
a tic.

tire (tīr) **1.** To become fatigued. **2.** To exhaust or fatigue.

tires (tī'ĕrz) **1.** Milk **sickness. 2.** Trembles.

tiring (tīr'ĭng) Fastening wire around
the fragments of a bone.

tissue (tĭsh'oo) [Fr. *tissu,* from L. *texere,*
to weave] A group or collection of similar
cells and their intercellular substance that
perform a particular function. The four
major groups are epithelial, connective,
muscular, and nervous tissues.
    adipose t. Fat.
    areolar t. A form of loose connective
tissue consisting of fibroblasts in a matrix of tissue fluid and collagen and elastin fibers. Many white blood cells are
present. It is found subcutaneously and
beneath the epithelium of all mucous
membranes. SEE: *connective t.* for illus.
    bone t. Osseous **t.**
    bronchus-associated lymphoid t.
ABBR: BALT. Lymph nodules that
contain clusters of T and B lymphocytes
and macrophages within the mucosa of
the bronchial wall; a component of the
mucosal immune system that defends
all mucosal surfaces against pathogens.
SEE: *mucosal immune system.*
    brown adipose t. ABBR: BAT.
Brown **fat.**
    cancellous t. Spongy bone with
many marrow cavities. It is present at
the ends of long bones and in the interior of most flat bones.
    chondroid t. Embryonic cartilage.
    chordal t. Tissue of the notochord or
derived from it. The nucleus pulposus is
derived from the notochord.
    chromaffin t. Chromaffin system.
    connective t. Tissue that supports
and connects other tissues and parts of
the body. Connective tissue has comparatively few cells. Its bulk consists of intercellular substance or matrix, whose
nature gives each type of connective tissue its particular properties. The vascular supply varies: cartilage, none; fibrous, poor; adipose, good; and bone,
abundant. Connective tissue includes
the following types: areolar, adipose, fibrous, elastic, reticular, cartilage, and
bone. Blood may also be considered a
connective tissue.
    elastic t. A form of connective tissue
in which yellow elastic fibers predominate. It is found in certain ligaments,
the walls of blood vessels, esp. the larger
arteries, and around the alveoli of the
lungs.
    embryonic t. Any tissue that arises
from the fertilization of an ovum and
has not become differentiated or specialized.
    endothelial t. Endothelium.
    epithelial t. Epithelium.
    erectile t. Spongy tissue, the spaces
of which fill with blood, causing it to
harden and expand. It is found in the
penis, clitoris, and nipples.
    fatty t. Fat.

fibrous t. Connective tissue consisting principally of collagen fibers. Also called white fibrous or dense connective tissue; may be regular (parallel fibers) or irregular.

gelatiginous t. Tissue from which gelatin may be obtained by treating it with hot water.

glandular t. A group of epithelial cells capable of producing secretions.

granulation t. The newly formed vascular and connective tissue produced in the early stages of wound healing.

hard t. In dentistry, any of the three calcified tissue components of the tooth: enamel, dentin, and cementum.

homologous t. Tissues that are identical in structure.

indifferent t. Tissue composed of undifferentiated cells as in embryonic tissue.

interstitial t. Connective tissue that forms a network with the cellular portions of an organ.

lymphadenoid t. Aggregates of lymphatic tissue found in the spleen and lymph nodes.

lymphoid t. Collections of lymphocytes in all stages of development found in the spleen, thymus, lymph nodes, lymph nodules of the digestive tract (tonsils, Peyer patches), and the respiratory, urinary, and reproductive tracts.

mesenchymal t. The embryonic mesenchyme.

mucosa-associated lymphoid t. ABBR: MALT. Aggregates of T and B lymphocytes found in all mucous membranes, a line of defense against infection. Examples include Peyer patches in the small intestine and lymph nodules in the colon, trachea, and bronchi. MALT contains CD4+ and CD8+ T cells and activated B cells and may occasionally undergo malignant transformation into lymphomas. SEE: *mucosal immune system*.

mucous t. The jellylike connective tissue of the umbilical cord.

muscular t. Muscle.

myeloid t. The bone marrow in which most blood cells are formed.

nerve t. The neurons and neuroglia of the nervous system. SEE: *neuron*.

osseous t. Bone, a connective tissue with a matrix of calcium phosphate and calcium carbonate surrounding osteocytes SYN: *bone t.* SEE: *bone*.

reticular t. A type of connective tissue consisting of delicate fibers forming interlacing networks. Fibers stain selectively with silver stains and are called argyrophil fibers. Reticular tissue supports blood cells in lymph nodes, bone marrow, and the spleen.

sclerous t. Firm connective tissue such as bone and cartilage.

skeletal t. Bone.

soft t. Any noncalcified tissue in the body. This term is especially used in relation to muscles, tendons, ligaments, skin, fat, and other connective tissues that are occasionally the source of pain when they are injured. Unlike bones or joints, which can be fractured or dislocated, soft tissues are bruised or inflamed by trauma. In surgery, soft tissues are dissected. By contrast, components of the (hard) bony skeleton are sawed, chiselled, or drilled. Soft tissues include all types of tissue except bone, i.e., all epithelial, muscle, and nerve tissue, as well as connective tissue excluding bone.

splenic t. The highly vascular splenic pulp.

subcutaneous t. Superficial fascia.

tissue ablation The coagulation, cooking, drying, or destruction of tissues, e.g., with cautery, chemicals, or thermotherapy.

tissue air ratio In radiation therapy, the ratio of the absorbed dose at a given depth to the absorbed dose at the same point in free space.

tissue bank SEE: under *bank*.

tissue engineering The manufacturing of functioning organs for implantation and use inside the body.

tissue expansion, soft A technique used in plastic surgery to expand skin prior to excising an area to achieve a more cosmetic wound closure. One or more expander balloons are inserted under the skin. The balloons are then expanded by progressively increasing the amount of saline solution in them. This is done on a weekly basis for whatever time is required to sufficiently stretch the overlying skin. After the expansion is completed, the plastic surgical procedure is performed. This permits removal of skin without having to cover the area by a skin graft. SEE: *plastic surgery*. *W-plasty; Z-plasty*.

tissue factor SEE: under *factor*.

tissue factor-bearing microparticle (mī″krō-part′ĭ-kĕl) ABBR: TFBM. Any of the pieces of cell membrane released from cancer cells. They stimulate blood clotting and appear to contribute to the hypercoagulable state produced by some malignancies.

tissue filler Any substance used to smooth body contours, eliminate defects in body structure, or improve cosmesis.

tissue integrity, impaired A state in which an individual experiences damage to mucous membrane or corneal, integumentary, or subcutaneous tissue. SEE: *Nursing Diagnoses Appendix*.

tissue perfusion, ineffective (specify type): renal, cerebral, cardiopulmonary, gastrointestinal, peripheral The state in which an individual experiences a decrease in nutrition and oxygenation at the cellular level due to a deficit in capillary blood supply. SEE: *Nursing Diagnoses Appendix*.

tissue plasminogen activator SEE: under *activator*.

tissue processor **1.** A device that prepares tissue samples for sectioning and microscopic examination in the clinical laboratory. **2.** A device that disinfects tissues to use in transplantation or allograft surgery.

tissue reaction The response of living tissues to altered conditions or types of restorative materials, metals or cements.

tissular (tĭsh′ū-lăr) Pert. to living tissues.

titanium (tī-tān′ē-ŭm) [*Titan*, a character in classical myth + *-ium* (1)] SYMB: Ti. A transition metal found in combination with minerals, atomic weight (mass) 47.87, atomic number 22, specific gravity, 4.54. In dentistry, it is used as an alloy chiefly for appliances and implants because of its biological acceptance and resistance to corrosion. It is also widely used in many commercial applications because it is light, strong, and resistant to corrosion.

   t. **dioxide** TiO_2, a chemical used to protect the skin from the sun. It is also used in industrial applications to produce white in paints and plastics.

titer (tīt′ĕr) [F. *titre*, standard] The strength or concentration of a substance or solution.

   agglutination *t.* The highest dilution of a serum that will cause agglutination (clumping) of the antigen being tested.

   antibody *t.* The concentration of a specific antibody in plasma. Antibody titers are used to establish the diagnosis of some infectious diseases: a rising titer indicates a recent exposure to a specific infectious antigen.

titillation (tĭt″ĭl-ā′shŭn) [L. *titillatio*, a tickling] **1.** The act of tickling. **2.** The state of being tickled. **3.** The sensation produced by tickling.

titin (tī′tĭn) An elastic protein in sarcomeres that anchors myosin filaments to the Z disks.

titrate (tī′trāt″) [*titer*] **1.** To measure accurately or to dilute gradually by adding a small volume of a liquid of known concentration to another liquid. **2.** To adjust the dose of a medication a little bit at a time in order to determine the most effective, safe dosage.

titration (tī-trā′shŭn) [Fr. *titre*, a standard] **1.** Estimation of the concentration of a chemical solution by adding known amounts of standard reagents until alteration in color or electrical state occurs. **2.** Determination of the quantity of antibody in an antiserum.

titre (tīt′ĕr) Titer.

titrimetric (tī″trī-mĕt′rĭk) [″ + Gr. *metron*, measure] Pert. to or using titration.

titrimetry (tī-trĭm′ĕ-trē) [*titration* + Gr. *metron*, measure] Analysis by titration.

titubation (tĭt″ū-bā′shŭn) [L. *titubatio*, a staggering] A coarse and backward tremor of the trunk. In patients with cerebellar disease, standing sometimes provokes this tremor.

   lingual *t.* Stuttering.

Tityus (tĭt′ē-ŭs) [L. *Tityus*, fr Gr. *Tityos*, the name of a giant] A genus of scorpions of the family Buthidae found principally in Central and South America.

TIV *totally implantable venous; total intracranial volume; trivalent inactivated virus; type IV.*

TIVA *total intravenous* **anesthesia**.

TJC *The Joint Commission*

Tl Symbol for the element thallium.

TLC *tender loving* **care**; *thin-layer* **chromatography**; *total lung* **capacity**; *triple-lumen catheter.*

TLD *thermoluminescent dosimeter.*

T.L.R. *tonic labyrinthine reflex.*

Tm Symbol for the element thulium.

TMJ *temporomandibular joint.*

TMP *trimethoprim.*

Tn Symbol for normal intraocular tension.

TNF *tumor necrosis factor.*

TNF receptor–associated periodic syndrome ABBR: TRAPS. Familial Hibernian fever.

TNM classification SEE: under *classification.*

TNT *trinitrotoluene.*

toad skin A condition characterized by excessive dryness, wrinkling, and scaling of skin sometimes seen in vitamin deficiencies. SYN: *follicular* **hyperkeratosis**; *phrynoderma.*

toadstool (tōd′stool) Any of various fungi with an umbrella-shaped cap, esp. a poisonous mushroom.

tobacco (tŏ-ba′k′ō) [Sp. *tabaco*] A plant (*Nicotiana tabacum*) whose leaves are cultivated, dried, and adulterated for use in smoking, chewing, and snuffing. The use of tobacco creates more preventable disease and death than the use of any other commercially available product. The tobacco leaf contains nicotine, a highly addictive alkaloid, and numerous other chemicals. During its combustion, it releases hydrocarbons into the oral, digestive, and respiratory tract of the smoker. These substances have been linked to coronary and peripheral arterial disease, emphysema, chronic bronchitis, peptic ulcer disease, and cancers of the lungs, oral cavity, and gastrointestinal tract. SEE: *risk factor; passive smoking.*

   smokeless *t.* Tobacco used in the form of snuff, tobacco powder, or chewing tobacco. These products irritate the oral mucosa and gingiva, and their continued use results in an increased risk of cancer of the mouth, larynx, throat, and esophagus. Smokeless tobacco contains nicotine and is addictive. Its use is greatest among adolescents, esp. males. An estimated 1.4% to 8.8% of adults in the U.S. use smokeless tobacco products. SEE: *snuff* (2).

spit t. SEE: *smokeless t.*

TOBEC *total body electrical conductivity.* One of several means of estimating or measuring body composition.

toco-, toko- [Gr. *tokos,* childbirth, offspring] Prefixes meaning *labor* or *childbirth.*

tocodynamometer, tokodynamometer (tō″kō-dī″nă-mom′ĕt-ĕr) [*toco-* + *dynamometer*] A device for estimating the force of uterine contractions in labor. **tocodynamometry** (-mom′ĕ-trē), *n.*

tocograph (tŏk′ō-grăf) [″ + *graphein,* to write] A device for estimating and recording the force of uterine contractions.

tocography (tō″kŏg′ră-fē) Recording the intensity of uterine contractions.

tocolysis (tō″kō-lī′sĭs) [″ + *lysis,* dissolution] Inhibition of uterine contractions. Drugs used for this include adrenergic agonists, magnesium sulfate, and ethanol.

tocolytic (tō-kō-lĭt′ĭk) [Gr. tokos, childbirth, labor, + -lysis, reduction, relief] **1.** Capable of relieving uterine contraction by reducing the excitability of myometrial muscle. **2.** Any agent that diminishes uterine contractions by reducing myometrial excitability.

tocopherol (tō-kŏf′ĕr-ŏl) [″ + *pherein,* to carry, + L. *oleum,* oil] Generic term for vitamin E (alpha-tocopherol) and a number of chemically related compounds, most of which have the biological activity of vitamin E.

toddler (tŏd′lĕr) **1.** A colloquial term for a child who has begun to walk but whose gait remains clumsy or unsteady. **2.** A child between the ages of 2 and 4 years.

Todd paralysis (tod) [Robert B. Todd, Brit. physician, 1809–1860] Transient, focal neurological deficits, occurring after a seizure, that resemble a stroke but resolve spontaneously.

toe (tō) A digit of the foot. SYN: *digit.* SEE: *foot* for illus.

claw t. Hammertoe.

cock-up t. A toe deformity with dorsiflexion of the metatarsophalangeal joint and flexion of the interphalangeal and distal interphalangeal joints. SEE: *hammertoe.*

mallet t. SEE: *hammertoe.*

Morton t. SEE: *Morton toe.*

pigeon t. Walking with the toes turned inward.

tennis t. Bleeding beneath the toenail resulting from repeated friction with the inside of the shoe. It produces a dark blue or black discoloration of the nail. It is a common problem of athletes who participate in sports that involve repetitive running, jumping, stopping, and starting.

turf t. A hyperextension injury of the first metatarsophalangeal (MTP) joint.

Severe hyperextension also injures the plantar sesamoids and flexor tendons. The injury commonly occurs on artificial surfaces, where the competitors wear light, flexible-soled shoes that allow MTP hyperextension on the firm surface.

webbed t. Toes joined by webs of skin.

toe drop SEE: under *drop.*

toenail (tō′nāl) Unguis. SEE: *nail.*

toe-off (tō′of″) The point in a person's walk (gait) at which the foot rises from the floor.

Toftness radiation detector (tof(t)′nĕs) SEE: under *detector.*

tofu (tō-foo′) Soybean curd. It is a dietary source of proteins, isoflavones, and phytoestrogens.

Togaviridae (tō″gă-vĭr′ĭ-dē) [L. *toga,* coat, + *virus,* poison] A family of RNA viruses that include the genus *Alphavirus.* They cause Western and Eastern equine encephalitis. Other Togaviridae include the rubiviruses (e.g., rubella virus).

toilet (toy′lĕt) [Fr. *toilette,* a little cloth] **1.** The cleansing of a wound. **2.** The maintenance of hygiene esp. of an organ system. For example, pulmonary toiletis the clearance of secretions from the lower airways. **3.** An apparatus for collecting urine, feces, vomit, or other waste products for safe removal and disposal.

toilet training SEE: under *training.*

-toin [Fm. (*hydan*)*toin*] A suffix used in pharmacology to designate an anticonvulsant medication derived from hydantoin.

token economy system Any program using positive reinforcement (operant conditioning) to teach or train desired skills or behaviors.

toko- SEE: *toco-.*

tolerable daily intake (tŏl′ĕr-ŭ-bĭl) [L. *tolerabilis*] ABBR: TDI. That quantity of a chemical contaminant that accidentally enters the food supply and may be consumed daily with no known adverse effects. SEE: *acceptable daily intake.*

tolerable upper limit SEE: under *limit.*

tolerance (tol′ĕ-răns) [L. *tolerantia,* patience] Capacity for enduring a large amount of a substance (such as food, drug, or poison) without an adverse effect and showing a decreased sensitivity to subsequent doses of the same substance.

diabetic glucose t. ABBR: DGT. In an oral glucose tolerance test, having a blood glucose concentration equal to or greater than 200 mg/dL (11.1 mmol/L) two hr after the consumption of 75 g of glucose.

drug t. The progressive decrease in the effectiveness of a drug.

exercise t. The amount of physical

activity that can be done under supervision before exhaustion.

glucose t. The ability of the body to absorb and use glucose. SEE: *oral glucose tolerance test.*

immunological t. The state in which the immune system does not react to the body's own antigens. It is caused by the destruction of lymphocytes that express receptors to autoantigens as they develop. Failure of these mechanisms may result in autoimmune disease.

impaired glucose t. ABBR: IGT. Altered glucose metabolism in which fasting blood sugars are less than 126 mg/dL, and blood sugar levels are over 140 mg/dL but less than 200 mg/dL 2 hr after drinking 75 g of glucose.

⚠ Having either impaired glucose tolerance or impaired fasting glucose predisposes patients to diabetes mellitus, heart attack, stroke, and early death. Patients with abnormal glucose metabolism ought to receive professional dietary counseling. They should also begin a program of regular physical exercise.

oral t. The suppression of autoimmune or allergic responses as a result of eating antigenic material.

pain t. The degree of pain an individual can withstand.

radiation t. The level below which tissue radiation exposure will be least harmful. Some organs are less tolerant to radiation than others.

tissue t. The ability of specific tissues to withstand the effects of ionizing radiation.

tolerance test A test of the ability of the patient or subject to endure the medicine given or exercise taken.

tolerant Capable of enduring or withstanding drugs without experiencing ill effects.

tolerogen (tŏl′ĕr-ă-jĕn) Any substance that causes immunological tolerance; any substance that blocks or prevents an immune response to an antigen. **tolerogenic** (tŏl″ĕr-ă-jĕn′ĭk), *adj.*

tolerogenic (tŏl″ĕr-ō-jĕn′ĭk) Producing immunological tolerance.

toluene (tol′yŭ-ēn″) [*tolu* balsam + *-ene*] A toxic hydrocarbon derived from coal tar. SYN: *methylbenzene.*

toluidine (tŏ-loo′ĭ-dēn″) [*tolu(ene)* + ²-*id* + *-ine*] C_7H_9N; aminotoluene, a derivative of toluene.

-tome [Gr. *-tomos*, cut, cutting, segmented] Suffix meaning *cutting, cutting instrument.*

Tomlin, Evelyn Malcolm (tom′lĭn) A U.S. nursing theorist who, with Helen Erickson and Mary Ann Swain, developed and published the grand nursing theory of Modeling and Role Modeling. SEE: *Nursing Theory Appendix.*

tomo- [Gr. *tomos*, cut, section] Prefix meaning *cut, section, layer.*

tomodensitometry (tō″mō-dĕn-sĭ-tŏm′ĭ-trē) A rarely used synonym for CT scanning.

tomogram (tō′mō-grăm) [Gr. *tome*, incision, + *gramma*, something written] The radiograph obtained during tomography.

tomograph (tō′mō-grăf) [″ + *graphein*, to write] An x-ray tube attached to a Bucky diaphragm by a rigid rod allowing rotation around a fixed point (fulcrum) during the radiographical exposure for tomography.

tomography (tō-mog′ră-fē) [*tomo-* + *-graphy*] A radiographic technique that selects a level in the body and blurs out structures above and below that plane, leaving a clear image of the selected anatomy. This is accomplished by moving the x-ray tube in the opposite direction from the imaging device around a stationary fulcrum defining the plane of interest. Tube movements can be linear, curvilinear, circular, elliptical, figure eight, hypocycloidal, or trispiral. With the exception of renal tomography most tomographic procedures have been replaced by computed tomography (CT). SYN: *body section **radiography**; body section **roentgenography.***

computed axial t. ABBR: CAT. SEE: *computed t.*

computed t. ABBR: CT. A computerized x-ray scanning system that produces a sectional anatomic image. It is achieved by digital processing of x-ray attenuation coefficients from a 360° wedge scan of ionizing radiation. There is considerable use of data from the attenuation coefficients in diagnosis. Computed tomography is colloquially called a *cat scan.*

⚠ CT scans expose patients to radiation on the order of 10 milliSieverts (mSv) per scan. Educational materials about the potential risks and benefits of scanning should be provided to patients to ensure that scans are performed safely and carefully.

computerized axial t. ABBR: CAT. SEE: *computed t.*

electrical impedance t. Cross-sectional body imaging that reconstructs pictures of internal organs based on measurements of their electrical activity as detected by electrodes placed on the surface of the body.

electron-beam t. Ultrafast computed t.

full body computed t. ABBR: FBCT. An examination from head to toe of the body with computed tomographic imaging, promoted as a screening test for cancer and other illnesses.

⚠ The test exposes patients to high levels of radiation, reveals more false positive findings than true positives, and is expensive.

Heidelberg retinal t. ABBR: HRT. A kind of laser scanning system that produces three-dimensional images of the posterior segment of the eye. It is used to diagnose and treat glaucoma.

helical computed t. Computed tomographic (CT) images that are obtained as the CT table moves continuously during a single, held breath. Detailed evaluation of dynamic internal features is feasible with this technique. SYN: *spiral computed t.*

optical coherence t. ABBR: OCT. A radiographical method used to obtain high-resolution cross-sectional images of tissues and their defects, e.g., of the structures of the eye.

panoramic t. Zonography.

positron emission t. ABBR: PET. Reconstruction of brain sections by using positron-emitting radionuclides. By using several different radionuclides, researchers can measure regional cerebral blood flow, blood volume, oxygen uptake, and glucose transport and metabolism, and can locate neurotransmitter receptors. PET has been used with fludeoxyglucose F 18 to identify and localize regional lymph node metastases and to help assess response to therapy.

The images produced by PET are in colors that indicate the degree of metabolism or blood flow. The highest rates appear red, those lower appear yellow, then green, and the lowest rates appear blue. The images in various disease states may then be compared to those of normal subjects. Three- and four-dimensional reconstructions are often achieved through the use of computed tomography (CT) with the same machine. SEE: illus.

quantitative computed t. ABBR: QCT. A method for determining the bone mineral density of a three-dimensional bony specimen, e.g., in the vertebral bodies or the forearms. It is used in the diagnosis of osteopenia and osteoporosis.

single photon emission computed t. ABBR: SPET, SPECT. A medical imaging method for reconstructing sectional images of radiotracer distributions. SEE: *nuclear medicine scanning test; positron emission t.*

spiral computed t. Helical computed t.

ultrafast computed t. Computed tomographic scanning that produces images by rotating the x-ray beam at targets placed around a patient, instead of moving a patient on a gantry through the scanner. The technique minimizes

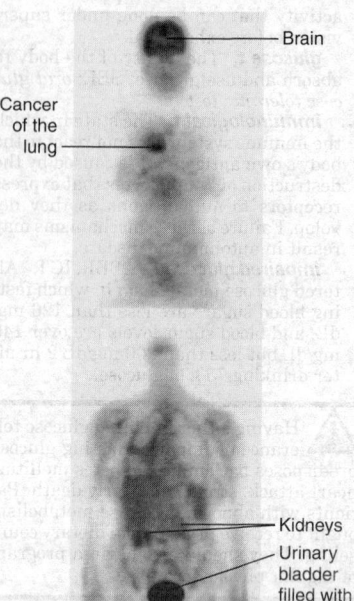

Brain

Cancer of the lung

Kidneys

Urinary bladder filled with contrast

POSITRON EMISSION TOMOGRAPHY

PET scan revealing lung cancer

patient movement artifacts and decreases scanning times to about 50 to 100 msec. It is capable of providing good resolution of vascular structures, such as the aorta and the coronary arteries. SYN: *electron-beam t.*

xenon-enhanced computed t. Computed tomographic scanning that uses the inert gas xenon to improve the visual distinction between healthy and abnormal tissues, esp. to visualize blood flow to different regions of the brain in stroke.

-tomy [Gr. *-tomos,* cut, cutting + *-ia*] Suffix meaning *cutting, incision.*

tone (tōn) [L. *tonus,* a stretching] **1.** That state of a body or any of its organs or parts in which the functions are healthy and normal. In a more restricted sense, the resistance of muscles to passive elongation or stretch. **2.** Normal tension or responsiveness to stimuli, as of arteries or muscles, seen particularly in involuntary muscle (such as the sphincter of the urinary bladder). SYN: *tonicity.* (2). A musical or vocal sound.

muscular t. The state of slight contraction usually present in muscles that contributes to posture and coordination; the ability of a muscle to resist a force for a considerable period without change in length.

pure t. A sound composed of a single frequency. It has no overtones and no harmonics and can be represented graphically by a sinusoidal wave (a wave having the shape of the trigonometric sine curve $y = \sin x$).

tone deafness SEE: under *deafness*.

tongue (tŭng) A freely movable muscular organ that lies partly in the floor of the mouth and partly in the pharynx. It is the organ of taste and contributes also to chewing, swallowing, and speech. SYN: *lingua*. SEE: illus.

ANATOMY: The tongue consists of a body and root and is attached by muscles to the hyoid bone below, the mandible in front, the styloid process behind, and the palate above, and by mucous membrane to the floor of the mouth, the lateral walls of the pharynx, and the epiglottis. A median fold (frenulum linguae) connects the tongue to the floor of the mouth. The surface of the tongue bears numerous papillae of three types: filiform, fungiform, and circumvallate (or vallate). Taste buds are present on the surfaces of many of the papillae, esp. the vallate papillae. Mucous and serous glands (lingual glands) are present; their ducts open on the surface. The lingual tonsils are lymphatic tissue on the base of the tongue. A median fibrous septum extends the entire length of the tongue.

Arteries: The lingual, exterior maxillary, and ascending pharyngeal arteries supply blood to the tongue. *Muscles:* Extrinsic muscles include genioglossus, hypoglossus, and styloglossus; intrinsic muscles consist of four groups: superior, inferior, transverse, and vertical lingualis muscles. The hypoglossal nerves are motor to the tongue; the facial and glossopharyngeal nerves are sensory for taste. *Nerves:* Lingual nerve (containing fibers from trigeminal and facial nerves), glossopharyngeal, vagus, and hypoglossal.

bifid t. A tongue with a cleft at its anterior end. SYN: *cleft t.; forked t.*

black hairy t. Elongation and discoloration (brown, black or white) of the filiform papillae found on the dorsal, middle to posterior third of the tongue. It is associated with alcohol, smoking, toothpaste and mouthwash containing hydrogen peroxide, and liquid antacids.

burning t. Burning mouth syndrome.

cleft t. Bifid **t.**

coated t. A tongue covered with a layer of whitish or yellowish material consisting of desquamated epithelium, bacteria, or food debris. The significance of this is difficult to interpret. It may mean only that the patient slept with his or her mouth open or has not eaten because of loss of appetite. If darkly coated, it may indicate a fungus infection.

dry t. A tongue that is dry and shriveled, usually indicative of dehydration. It may also be the result of mouth breathing.

fern-leaf t. A tongue possessing a prominent central furrow and lateral branches.

filmy t. A tongue possessing symmetrical whitish patches.

fissured t. Scrotal **t.**

forked t. Bifid **t.**

furred t. A coated tongue on which the surface epithelium appears as a coat of white fur. It is seen in nearly all fevers. Unilateral furring may result from disturbed innervation, as in conditions affecting the second and third branches of the fifth nerve. It has been noted in neuralgia of those branches and in fractures of the skull involving the foramen

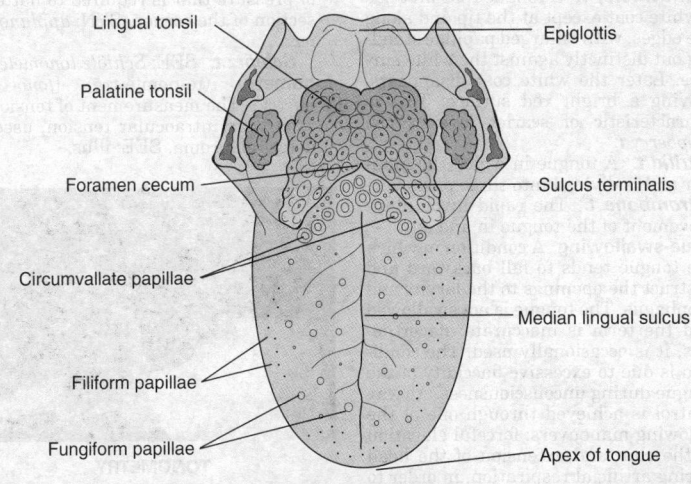

Lingual tonsil — Epiglottis

Palatine tonsil

Foramen cecum — Sulcus terminalis

Circumvallate papillae — Median lingual sulcus

Filiform papillae

Fungiform papillae — Apex of tongue

SURFACE OF TONGUE

rotundum. Yellow fur indicates jaundice.

geographic t. A tongue with white raised areas, normal epithelium, and atrophic regions. This condition is also known as benign migratory glossitis. SEE: illus.

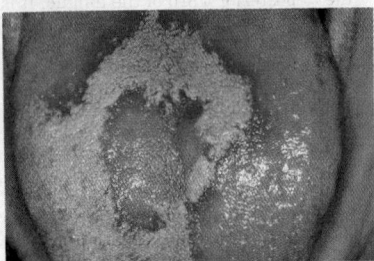

GEOGRAPHIC TONGUE

hairy t. A tongue covered with hairlike papillae entangled with threads produced by the fungi *Aspergillus niger* or *Candida albicans*. This condition is usually seen as the result of antibiotic therapy that inhibits growth of bacteria normally present in the mouth, permitting overgrowth of fungi. SYN: *glossotrichia; lingua nigra.*

parrot t. A dry shriveled tongue seen in typhus.

raspberry t. Strawberry **t.**

scrotal t. A furrowed and rugated tongue, resembling the skin of the scrotum. SYN: *fissured t.*

smoker's t. Leukoplakia.

smooth t. A tongue with atrophic papillae. It is characteristic of many conditions, such as anemia and malnutrition.

split t. A cleft or bifid tongue resulting from developmental arrest.

strawberry t. A tongue that first has a white coat except at the tip and along the edges, with enlarged papillae standing out distinctly against the white surface. Later the white coat disappears, leaving a bright red surface. This is characteristic of scarlet fever. SYN: *raspberry* **t.**

trifid t. A tongue in which the anterior end is divided into three parts.

trombone t. The rapid involuntary movement of the tongue in and out.

tongue-swallowing A condition in which the tongue tends to fall backward and obstruct the openings to the larynx and esophagus. The tongue is not swallowed and the term is inaccurate; nevertheless, it is occasionally used. The condition is due to excessive flaccidity of the tongue during unconsciousness. Airway control is achieved through one of the following maneuvers: forceful elevation of the chin and extension of the head during artificial respiration, in order to open the airway; or insertion of a mechanical airway device, such as an oropharyngeal airway, to push the tongue out of the airway.

⚠️ The rescuer should never place his or her hand inside the victim's mouth to move the tongue.

tongue thrust SEE: under *thrust.*

tongue-tie (tŭng'tī″) Lay term for ankyloglossia, congenital shortness of the frenulum of the tongue. The condition has been shown to have no functional significance, even for speech.

tonic (tŏn'ĭk) [Gr. *tonikos,* from *tonos,* tone] **1.** Pert. to or characterized by tension or contraction, esp. muscular tension. **2.** Restoring tone. **3.** A medicine that increases strength and tone. Tonics are subdivided according to action, such as cardiac or general.

tonicity (tō-nĭs'ĭ-tē) [Gr. *tonos,* act of stretching] **1.** The property of possessing tone, esp. muscular tone. **2.** Tone (2).

tonic receptor SEE: under *receptor.*

tono-, ton- [L. *tonus* fr. Gr. *tonos,* stretching, strain, tension, tone] Prefixes meaning *stretching, tension, tone.*

tonofibril (tŏn'ō-fī″brĭl) Tenofibril.

tonogram (tō'nō-grăm) [″ + *gramma,* something written] The record produced by a tonograph.

tonograph (tō'nō-grăf) [″ + *graphein,* to write] A recording tonometer.

tonography (tō-nŏg'ră-fē) The recording of changes in intraocular pressure.

tonometer (tō-nom'ĕt-ĕr) [*tono-* + *-meter*] An instrument for measuring tension or pressure, esp. intraocular pressure.

applanation t. A device for measuring intraocular pressure (IOP) indirectly. The IOP depends on the amount of pressure that is required to flatten a section of the cornea. SYN: *applanometer.*

Schiötz t. SEE: *Schiötz tonometer.*

tonometry (tō-nom'ĕ-trē) [*tono-* + *-metry*] The measurement of tension of a part, as intraocular tension, used to detect glaucoma. SEE: illus.

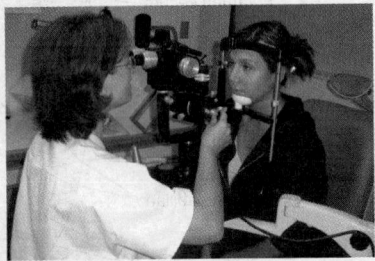

TONOMETRY
Measuring intraocular eye pressure

applanation t. Determining intraocular pressure by measuring the force necessary to flatten the corneal surface.

digital t. Determining intraocular pressure by use of the fingers.

gastric t. Measurement of the partial pressure of carbon dioxide (PCO_2) in the stomach of critically ill patients to determine how well the stomach and other internal organs are perfused with blood and oxygen. Poor gastric perfusion is found in more severe conditions, i.e., those that carry an increased risk of death.

noncontact t. Determining intraocular pressure by measuring the degree of indentation of the cornea produced by a puff of air.

tonoplast (tŏn′ō-plăst) [″ + *plassein,* to form] The membrane surrounding an intracellular vacuole.

tonsil (tŏn′sĭl) [L. *tonsilla,* almond] **1.** A mass of lymphoid tissue in the mucous membranes of the pharynx and base of the tongue. The free surface of each tonsil is covered with stratified squamous epithelium that forms deep indentations, or crypts, extending into the substance of the tonsil. The palatine tonsils, pharyngeal tonsils (adenoids), and lingual tonsils form a ring of immunologically active tissue. **2.** A rounded mass on the inferior surface of the cerebellum lying lateral to the uvula.

INFECTION OF THE TONSILS: Tonsils detect and respond to pathogens entering the body through the mouth and nose. Inflammation of the tonsils (tonsillitis) occurs during upper respiratory infections caused by common viruses. Beta-hemolytic streptococci or, occasionally, *Staphylococcus aureus* infections may occur as primary infections or follow viral infections, most commonly in children and immunocompromised adults. Clinically, the patient will have enlarged, reddened, tender glands, often coated with inflammatory exudate, which may form a pseudomembrane. The tonsils may stay enlarged after multiple infections and are sometimes surgically removed (tonsillectomy). SEE: illus.

Rheumatic fever, an autoimmune inflammatory disease, develops 2 to 3 weeks after streptococcal infections in about 3% of patients; it is believed that antibodies against streptococcal pharyngitis cross-react with antigens in the heart and joints.

cerebellar t. One of a pair of cerebellar lobules on either side of the uvula, projecting from the inferior surface of the cerebellum.

faucial t. Palatine t.

lingual t. A mass of lymphoid tissue located in the root of the tongue.

nasal t. Lymphoid tissue on the nasal septum.

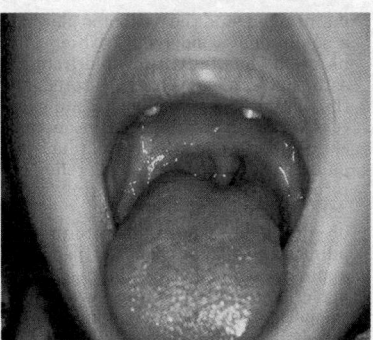

INFLAMED TONSILS
Source: Centers for Disease Control and Prevention

palatine t. Two oval masses of lymphoid tissue that lie in the tonsillar fossa on each side of the oral pharynx between the glossopalatine and pharyngopalatine arches. They are commonly known as the tonsils. SYN: *faucial t.*

pharyngeal t. Lymphoid tissue on the roof of the posterior superior wall of the nasopharynx. It is commonly called adenoids. SEE: *adenoid.*

tonsillar (tŏn′sĭ-lăr) Pert. to a tonsil, esp. the faucial or palatine tonsil.

tonsillar area An area composed of the palatine arch, tonsillar fossa, glossopalatine sulcus, and posterior faucial pillar.

tonsillar crypt SEE: under *crypt.*

tonsillar fossa SEE: under *fossa.*

tonsillar ring SEE: under *ring.*

tonsillectomy (tŏn-sĭl-ĕk′tō-mē) [L. *tonsilla,* almond + Gr. *ektome,* excision] Surgical removal of the tonsils. This procedure is typically performed for children with recurrent infections of the throat or peritonsilar abscess although it may also be used when enlarged tonsils cause obstructive sleep apnea. Whether the procedure is advisable in children with recurrent pharyngeal infections is a matter of debate. Complications of the procedure may include local bleeding, throat pain, injury to the upper airway, and aspiration pneumonia, among others. SEE: *Nursing Diagnoses Appendix.*

PATIENT CARE: *Preoperative:* The anesthetic methods (usually locally injected anesthesia) and expected sensations are explained to the adult patient. For children, the anesthetic methods and hospital routines are explained in simple, nonthreatening language; the child is allowed to try on hospital garb; and the child is shown the operating and recovery rooms, as appropriate to age. Parents are encouraged to remain with the child.

Postoperative: A patent airway is

maintained, and the patient is placed in a semiprone or sidelying position until he or she has fully recovered from anesthesia. Vital signs are monitored, and the patient is assessed for bleeding (excessive swallowing in a semiconscious child), restlessness, tachycardia, and pallor. After the patient's gag reflex has returned, he or she may drink water and nonirritating fluids. Deep breathing and turning help to prevent pulmonary complications. Ice packs are applied and analgesics administered as prescribed. Vocal rest is encouraged and the patient is instructed not to clear the throat or cough, because this may precipitate bleeding. Written discharge instructions covering use of fluids and soft diet and avoidance of overactivity are provided to the patient and family. Within 5 to 10 days postoperatively, a white scab will form in the patient's throat. The patient or family should report any bleeding, ear discomfort, or persistent fever.

tonsillitis (tŏn-sĭl-ī′tĭs) [″ + Gr. *itis,* inflammation] Inflammation of a tonsil, esp. the faucial tonsil. SEE: *Nursing Diagnoses Appendix.*

  acute parenchymatous t. Tonsillitis in which the entire tonsil is affected.

  acute t. Inflammation of the lymphatic tissue of the pharynx, esp. the palatine or faucial tonsils. It may occur sporadically or in epidemic form, and usually is self-limiting.

SYMPTOMS: Throat pain, esp. while swallowing, is the cardinal symptom of tonsillitis; fever and malaise are common. Abrupt-onset headache, nausea and vomiting, and cervical lymphadenopathy are more commonly seen with streptococcal infections. Rhinorrhea, cough, and diarrhea are usually associated with viral infection. The tonsils are usually enlarged and red, but the degree of erythema does not reflect the severity of the pain. An exudate is often, but not always, present on the tonsils. Adolescents should be assessed for infectious mononucleosis, as it is quite common among teenagers and young adults.

ETIOLOGY: Viruses are the most common cause of tonsillitis. Beta-hemolytic streptococci infections may follow viral infections or occur as primary infections, esp. in school-aged children and immunocompromised adults (5% to 20% of cases).

TREATMENT: Viral tonsillitis is treated symptomatically. If group A beta-hemolytic streptococci infection is suspected, a throat culture is taken. Streptococcal tonsillitis must be treated with a 10-day course of oral penicillin or one intramuscular dose of long-acting benzathine penicillin to decrease the risk of rheumatic fever or glomerulone-

phritis. Rheumatic fever develops 2 to 3 weeks after streptococcal infections in about 3% of patients. If chronic tonsillitis occurs, the tonsils may be removed, but this operation is not as common as it was years ago. SEE: *rheumatic fever.*

  follicular t. Inflammation of the follicles on the surface of the tonsil, which become filled with pus.

  ulceromembranous t. Tonsillitis that ulcerates and develops a membranous film.

tonsillolith (tŏn′sĭl-ō-lĭth) [″ + Gr. *lithos,* stone] A stone within a tonsil. SYN: *amygdalolith.*

tonsillotome (tŏn-sĭl′ō-tōm) A surgical instrument used in tonsillectomy.

tonsillotomy (tŏn″sĭl-ŏt′ō-mē) [″ + Gr. *tome,* incision] Incision of the tonsils.

tonus (tō′nŭs) [L., tension] The partial steady contraction of muscle that determines tonicity or firmness; the opposite of clonus. SYN: *tone; tonicity.*

toolkit, tool kit (tool′kit″) **1.** In professional education, a resource, esp. one that helps a professional improve his or her competence, knowledge, or skills. **2.** In computers, software for a specific function, esp. for solving a problem.

tooth (tooth, tēth) *pl.* **teeth** Any of the hard, bony conical structures of the upper and lower jaws used for chewing. A tooth consists of a crown portion above the gum, a root portion embedded in a socket (alveolus) of the jaw bone, and a neck or cervical constricted region between the crown and root. The soft-tissue gingiva covers the neck and root to a variable extent, depending on age and oral hygiene. The major portion of a tooth consists of dentin, which is harder than bone; enamel; and cementum, which is similar to bone. The pulp cavity contains the dental pulp. Each tooth has five surfaces: occlusal, mesial, distal, lingual, and facial or buccal. SEE: illus.; *dentition.*

Everyone has two complete sets of teeth during his life. The 20 primary teeth are the first set of teeth a person develops. They exfoliate by age 14 and are replaced by the 32 permanent teeth. The permanent teeth include the following: incisors, canines (cuspids), premolars (bicuspids), and molars. On average, a child should have 6 teeth at 1 year, 12 teeth at 18 months, 16 teeth at 2 years, and 20 teeth at 12 years. Some children are born with a few erupted teeth; in other children the teeth may not appear until 16 months.

PATIENT CARE: Health care professionals should assess patients' teeth and gums during physical examinations, educate patients about routine dental hygiene (brushing, flossing, gum stimulation, use of oral rinses), and refer them to a dental professional for dental caries, eruption anomalies, or

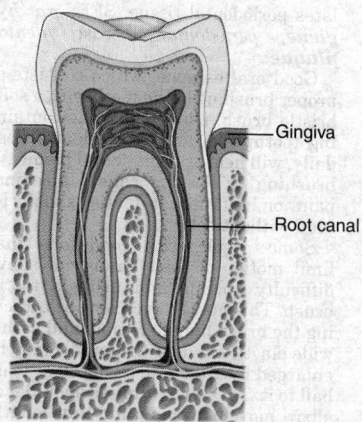

STRUCTURE OF A TOOTH

(longitudinal section)

periodontal problems. SEE: *dental plaque; periodontal disease.*

anterior t. The central and lateral incisors and/or the canines, located adjacent to the midline of the maxilla or mandible.

baby t. Deciduous t.

bicuspid t. A permanent, premolar tooth. There are eight premolars, two in each quadrant (four in each jaw) between the canines and molars. Premolars have two or three cusps on the occlusal surface.

bull t. Taurodontism.

cracked t. A tooth whose enamel and dentin are fractured.

deciduous t. Any of the 20 teeth that make up the primary dentition, which are shed and replaced by the permanent teeth. SYN: *baby t.; milk t.; primary t.* SEE: illus.

hypersensitive t. A tooth sensitive to temperature changes, sweets, or percussion. It may exhibit gingival recession, exposed root dentin, caries, or periodontal disease.

TREATMENT: Popular treatments for hypersensitivity include topical varnishes, sealants, and topical fluoride applications. Other treatments include application of silver nitrate, formalin, glycerin, strontium chloride, potassium nitrate, calcium compounds, sodium citrate, and potassium oxalate.

PATIENT CARE: The patient can reduce sensitivity by a regimen of plaque control, dentifrice with fluoride, self-applied fluoride, and control of diet.

impacted t. A tooth unable to erupt due to crowding by adjacent teeth, malposition of the tooth, or developmental disturbances.

malacotic t. A tooth soft in structure, white in color, and esp. prone to decay.

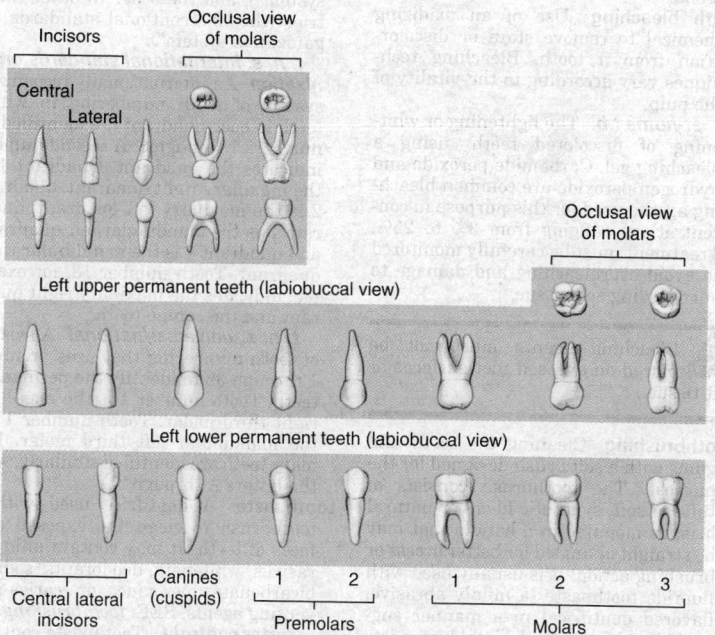

DECIDUOUS TEETH (LEFT SIDE)

milk t. Deciduous **t.**

permanent t. Any of the 32 teeth that develop as the second dentition and replace the deciduous teeth. SYN: *secondary t.* SEE: *deciduous t.* for illus.

primary t. Deciduous **t.**

sclerotic t. A yellowish tooth that is naturally hard and highly resistant to caries.

secondary t. Permanent **t.**

succedaneous t. In dentistry, a permanent tooth that replaces a normally erupted deciduous tooth. It includes the premanent incisors, cuspids, and premolars. The deciduous molars are replaced by the permanent premolars, which are not succedaneous teeth.

wisdom t. Any of the third most-distal molars on each side of both jaws. These four molars may appear as late as the 25th year or may never erupt.

toothache Pain in a tooth or the region about a tooth. The origin of pain in a tooth is physical, chemical, thermal, and bacteriological trauma. Treatment may include restorations, extractions, or topical application of medications, among others. SYN: *dentalgia; odontalgia; odontodynia.*

tooth and nail syndrome A rare autosomal dominantly inherited syndrome characterized by malformed or absent teeth and defects in nail plate development. This syndrome is one of the ectodermal dysplasias. SYN: *Witkop syndrome.*

tooth bleaching Use of an oxidizing chemical to remove stain or discoloration from a tooth. Bleaching techniques vary according to the vitality of the pulp.

at-home t.b. The lightening or whitening of discolored teeth, using a bleaching gel. Carbamide peroxide and hydrogen peroxide are common bleaching agents used for this purpose in concentrations ranging from 3% to 25%. Treatment must be carefully monitored to avoid overbleaching and damage to surrounding soft tissue.

⚠️ Bleaching agents must not be placed on exposed root surfaces or soft tissue.

toothbrushing Cleaning the teeth and gums with a soft brush designed for the purpose. The toothbrush consists of tufts of soft, synthetic fibers or natural bristles mounted in a handle that may be straight or angled for better access or brushing action. It is usually used with fluoride toothpaste (a mildly abrasive, flavored dentifrice) in a manner suggested by dentists and dental hygienists as being suitable for cleaning. The proper use of a toothbrush stimu-

lates periodontal tissue. SEE: *oral hygiene; periodontal disease; dental plaque.*

Good oral hygiene, which consists of proper brushing of the teeth with a soft-bristle brush, using a fluoride-containing toothpaste, and using dental floss daily, will help prevent dental plaque. If brushing or flossing causes bleeding, pain, or irritation, a dentist should be seen without delay.

Some people with conditions that limit motion of their hands may have difficulty holding and using a toothbrush. This may be overcome by attaching the brush handle to the hand with a wide elastic band, or the handle may be enlarged by attaching a rubber or foam ball to it. Those with limited shoulder or elbow movement may find that lengthening the handle by attaching it to a long piece of wood or plastic is beneficial. In addition, an electric toothbrush may be of benefit.

⚠️ If the toothbrush used has hard bristles, or if any toothbrush is used too forcibly, gingival tissue may be eroded and damaged.

tooth numbering system A system used to identify teeth. The American Dental Association recognizes two systems: one used in the U.S. (the "universal/national system"), and the other in other countries (the "international standards organization system").

t. n. s. international standards organization An internationally recognized system of tooth numbering in which teeth in each quadrant are identified by numbers 1 through 8. A second number indicates the quadrant. Quadrant 1 is the maxillary right quadrant; quadrant 2 is the maxillary left quadrant; quadrant 3 is the mandibular left quadrant; and quadrant 4 is the mandibular right quadrant. Tooth number 13, for example, indicates the maxillary right quadrant and the canine tooth.

t. n. s. universal/national A system of tooth numbering that uses numbers 1 through 32 to identify the permanent teeth. Tooth number 1 is the maxillary right third molar. Tooth number 17 is the mandibular left third molar. Primary teeth are identified similarly, with the letters A through T.

toothpaste A dentifrice used with a toothbrush to clean the exposed surfaces of teeth. It may contain mild abrasives, whiteners, deodorants, sodium bicarbonate, peroxide, or caries-preventing agents. SEE: *toothbrushing.*

tartar control t. Toothpaste containing pyrophosphates that act as abrasives to remove plaque from teeth. Some evidence links these toothpastes to irritation of oral tissues.

toothpick Any small tapering sliver of wood or other material used to remove food debris from between the teeth. Early toothpicks were made of gold, carved bone, or ivory.

top-, topo- [Gr. *topos,* place] Prefixes meaning *place, locale.*

topectomy (tō-pĕk′tō-mē) [″ + *ektome,* excision] A form of neurosurgery in which small incisions are made through the thalamofrontal tracts.

tophaceous (tō-fā′shŭs) [L. *tophaceus,* sandy] **1.** Pert. to a tophus. **2.** Sandy or gritty.

tophus (tō′fŭs) *pl.* **tophi** [L., porous stone] A deposit of sodium biurate in tissues near a joint, in the ear, or elsewhere in individuals with gout. SYN: *gouty **pearl**.* SEE: illus.

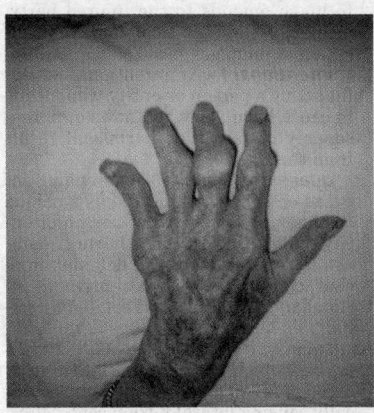

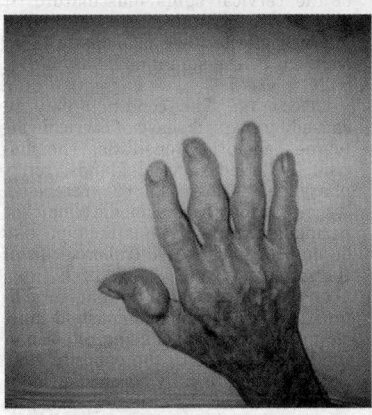

TOPHI
Left and right hands of a patient with multiple deforming gouty tophi

topical (tŏp′ĭ-kăl) [Gr. ″+ ″] Pert. to a definite surface area; local.

topical chemotherapy SEE: under *chemotherapy.*

topical hemostatic agents SEE: under *agent.*

topographical (tŏp″ō-grăf′ĭ-kăl) [″ + ″] Pert. to the description of a region.

topographical disorientation ABBR: TD. A disorder of visuospatial skills in which it is difficult to find one's way from one location to another or to navigate from a starting point to a destination. It is sometimes present in patients who have had a stroke affecting the posterior portions of the brain; it is also common in some dementias, e.g., Alzheimer disease.

topographic memory SEE: under *memory.*

topography (tō-pog′ră-fē) [*top-* + *-graphy*] The physical features of a surface, e.g., of the contours or slope of a body structure.
   corneal t. The use of a camera and a computer to make a three-dimensional map of the cornea of the eye, typically in preparation for surgery. SYN: *videokeratography.*

topoisomerase (tŏp″ō-ī-sŏm′ĕr-ās″, tō″) [″ + ″] One of several enzymes that cleave and rejoin the coiled sugar-phosphate backbone of DNA or RNA.

topology (tō-pŏl′ō-jē) **1.** In obstetrics, the relationship of the presenting fetal part to the pelvic outlet. **2.** In mathematics, the study of the relationships between objects that share a surface or a common border.

toponym (tŏp′ō-nĭm) The name of a region.

toponymy (tō-pŏn′ĭ-mē) [″ + *onoma,* name] Nomenclature of the regions of the body.

Toprol-XL SEE: *metoprolol tartrate.*

TOPV *trivalent oral polio vaccine.* SEE: *poliovirus vaccine, live oral.*

TORCH (torch) An acronym originally from *T*oxoplasmosis, *R*ubella, *C*ytomegalovirus, and *H*erpes simplex. Contemporary usage interprets the O as *Other transplacental infections* (by HIV, hepatitis B, human parvovirus, and syphilis). TORCH infections can attack an embryo or fetus and cause abortion, abnormal fetal development, severe congenital anomalies, mental retardation, and fetal or neonatal death. SEE: *Aicardi-Goutières syndrome.*

torcular herophili (tor′kū-lăr) The confluence of cranial venous sinuses at the internal occipital protuberance of the skull.

toric (tō′rĭk) Pert. to a torus.

toric contact lens (tōr′ik) SEE: under *lens.*

torose, torous (tō′rōs, -rŭs) [L. *torosus,* full of muscle] Knobby or bulging; tubercular.

torpent (tor′pĕnt) [L. *torpens,* numbing] **1.** Medicine that modifies irritation.

2. Not capable of functioning; dormant, apathetic, torpid.

torpid (tor′pĭd) [L. *torpidus,* numb] Not acting vigorously; sluggish.

torpidity (tor-pĭd′ĭ-tē) Sluggishness; inactivity.

torpor (tor′por) [L. *torpor,* numbness] Abnormal inactivity; dormancy; numbness; apathy.

    t. retinae Reduced sensitivity of retina to light stimuli.

torque (tork) [L. *torquere,* to twist] **1.** A force producing rotary motion. **2.** In dentistry, the rotating movement of a handpiece, or the application of force to rotate a tooth around its long axis.

torr (tor) A pressure quantity equivalent to 1/760 of standard atmospheric pressure; for most practical purposes, this equals 1 mm Hg.

torrefaction (tor″ĕ-făk′shŭn) [L. *torrefactio*] Roasting or parching something, esp. a drug, to dry it.

Torre-Muir syndrome Muir-Torre syndrome.

torsade de pointes (tor-sad′dĕ pwont′) A rapid, unstable form of ventricular tachycardia in which the QRS complexes appear to twist, or shift, electrical orientation around the isoelectric line of the electrocardiogram. It often occurs as a life-threatening effect of a medication (such as quinidine, amiodarone, or a tricyclic antidepressant) that prolongs the Q-T interval but may also complicate congenital long QT syndromes. Intravenous magnesium sulfate may be used to treat this arrhythmia. SYN: *polymorphic ventricular tachycardia*.

torsiometer (tor″sē-ŏm′ĕ-tĕr) A device for measuring the rotation of the eyeball around the visual axis (i.e., its anterior-posterior axis).

torsion (tor′shŏn) [L. *torsio,* a twisting] **1.** The act of twisting or the condition of being twisted. **2.** In dentistry, the state of a tooth when rotated around its long axis. **3.** Rotation of the vertical meridians of the eye.

    lung t. A rare injury in which the lung rotates around its pedicle, typically after violent trauma to the chest. The injured lung can usually only be repaired with immediate surgery.

    testicular t. A urological emergency in which the testis is starved of its blood supply as it twists on the spermatic cord. The condition causes unilateral scrotal pain, often accompanied by nausea and vomiting, and typically occurs in young boys or adolescents. A characteristic physical finding is loss of the cremasteric reflex on the affected side. Treatment is a prompt operation to relieve the twisting of the cord. A delay in surgery beyond 6 hr rapidly increases the likelihood that the testicle will be lost.

torsionometer (tor″shŭn-ŏm′ĕ-tĕr) [″ + Gr. *metron,* measure] **1.** A device for measuring the rotation of the vertebral column around the long axis using radiographs of the spine. **2.** A subjective test used in ophthalmology for measuring the rotation of vertical meridians of the eyes.

torsive (tor′sĭv) Twisted, as in a spiral.

torsiversion (tor″sĭ-vĕr′zhŭn) Rotation of a tooth around its long axis.

torso (tor′sō) [It.] The trunk of the body.

torsoclusion (tor″sō-kloo′zhŭn) [″ + L. *occlusio,* to occlude] Malocclusion characterized by rotation of a tooth on its long axis.

tort A wrongful act or injury, committed by an entity or person against another person or another person's property, that may be pursued in civil court by the injured party. The purpose of tort law is to make amends to the injured party, primarily through monetary compensation or damages.

    intentional t. An intentional wrongful act by a person or entity who means to cause harm, or who knows or is reasonably certain that harm will result from the act.

    quasi-intentional t. A wrongful act based on speech committed by a person or entity against another person or entity that causes economic harm or damage to reputation, e.g., a defamation of character or an invasion of privacy.

torticollar (tor″tĭ-kŏl′ăr) Pert. to torticollis.

torticollis (tort″ĭ-kol′ĭs) [L. *tortus,* twisted + L. *collum,* neck] Stiff neck associated with muscle spasm, classically causing lateral flexion contracture of the cervical spine musculature. It may be congenital or acquired. The muscles affected are principally those supplied by the spinal accessory nerve. SYN: *wryneck*.

    ETIOLOGY: The condition may be caused by scars, disease of cervical vertebrae, adenitis, tonsillitis, rheumatism, enlarged cervical glands, retropharyngeal abscess, or cerebellar tumors. It may be spasmodic (clonic) or permanent (tonic). The latter type may be due to Pott disease (tuberculosis of the spine).

    congenital muscular t. Congenital fibrosis of the sternocleidomastoid muscle in the newborn, causing rotation of the infant's head to the opposite side. The condition usually becomes evident in the first 2 weeks of life. Treatments include physical therapy or, in refractory cases, surgical division of the muscle. SYN: *fibromatosis colli*.

    fixed t. An abnormal position of the head owing to organic shortening of the muscles.

    intermittent t. Spasmodic **t.**

ocular t. Torticollis from inequality in sight of the two eyes.

spasmodic t. Torticollis with recurrent but transient contractions of the muscles of the neck and esp. of the sternocleidomastoid. SYN: *intermittent t.* SYN: *cervical* **dystonia**.

TREATMENT: Botulinus toxin has been used to inhibit the spastic contractions of the affected muscles. SEE: *botulinus* **toxin**.

tortipelvis (tor″tĭ-pĕl′vĭs) [″ + *pelvis,* basin] Muscular spasms that distort the spine and hip. SYN: **dystonia** *musculum deformans.*

tort reform In health care, any proposed alteration of state laws imposing liability for torts, esp. for limiting punitive damages in medical malpractice cases.

tortuous (tor′choo-ŭs) [L. *tortuosus,* fr. *torqueo,* to twist] Having many twists or turns.

torture (tor′chŭr) [L. *tortura,* a twisting] Infliction of severe mental or physical pain by various methods, usually for the purpose of coercion.

Torula (tor′ū-lă) The former name of a genus of yeastlike organisms now called *Cryptococcus.*

toruloid (tor′ū-loyd) [L. *torulus,* a little bulge, + Gr. *eidos,* form, shape] Beaded; pert. to an aggregate of colonies like those seen in the budding of yeast.

toruloma (tor-ū-lō′mă) [*Torula,* old name for Cryptococcus, + *oma,* tumor] The nodular lesion of cryptococcosis (torulosis).

Torulopsis glabrata (tor″ū-lŏp′sis glă-brăt′ă) The former name for the fungus now known as *Candida glabrata.*

torulosis (tor-ū-lō′sĭs) Cryptococcosis.

torulus (tor′ū-lŭs) [L. *torulus,* a little elevation] Papilla.

t. tactilis A tactile cutaneous elevation on the palms and soles.

torus (tō′rŭs) *pl.* **tori** [L., swelling] A rounded elevation or swelling.

t. mandibularis An exostosis that develops on the lingual aspect of the body of the mandible.

t. palatinus A benign exostosis located in the midline of the hard palate. Also called *palatine protuberance.*

total body potassium SEE: under *potassium.*

total hip replacement A surgical procedure to treat severe arthritis of the hip. Both the head of the femur and the acetabulum are replaced with synthetic components or augmented by artificial components. SEE: *arthroplasty;* illus.

PATIENT CARE: *Preoperative:* The patient is educated about the procedure, postoperative care, and the expected surgical outcomes. The patient may donate blood before the procedure for use

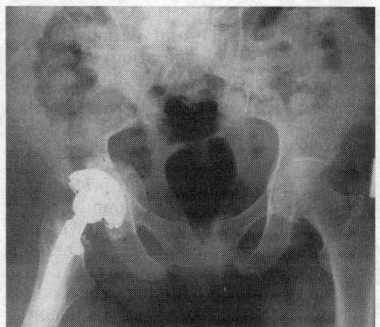

TOTAL HIP REPLACEMENT
(Prosthesis)

if needed, and blood-saving techniques are used during the surgery. The patient is instructed about postoperative limitations, hip abduction methods, use of a trapeze, mobility regimen, gluteal and quadriceps setting, and triceps exercises. The importance of respiratory toilet is explained, and the proper technique for use of incentive spirometry is taught. Prescribed antibiotics and other drugs are administered. Reports of laboratory and radiological studies are reviewed, and the physician is notified of any abnormal findings. The patient is informed about pain evaluation techniques and the availability of analgesics. Epidural or intravenous PCA may be employed. Preoperative preparations are carried out (skin, gastrointestinal tract, urinary bladder, and premedication), and their significance is explained to the patient. The patient should be encouraged to verbalize feelings and concerns.

Postoperative: Dressings and drainage devices are monitored for excessive bleeding, and the area beneath the buttocks is inspected for gravity pooling of drainage. Dressings are replaced or reinforced according to the surgeon's protocol. Vital signs are monitored, and neurovascular status of the affected extremity is checked frequently, comparing it to the unaffected limb. Analgesics are administered as prescribed and required, and the patient is evaluated for response. The patient is repositioned frequently in prescribed positions, and the integrity of all supportive equipment (splints, pillows, traction devices) is maintained during repositioning. The patient should avoid crossing his legs and internal rotation, which enhance the potential for dislocation of the prosthesis and interfere with venous return. Respiratory status is assessed, and incentive spirometry and deep breathing and coughing are encouraged to prevent pulmonary complications. An exercise program and early ambulation (often on the day after the operation) should begin as prescribed by the surgeon (type and extent of weight bearing on affected limb) and in collaboration with the physical therapist. Raised toilet seats and reclining chairs are used to prevent hip flexion. A diet high in protein and vitamin C is provided, wound healing assessed, and skin breakdown prevented. Antithrombotic devices and anticoagulant drugs are given if prescribed, and the patient is assessed for complications like thrombophlebitis, embolism, and dislocation. The patient will usually be transferred to a rehabilitation center or may rehabilitate at home. Teaching on discharge focuses on the exercise regimen and limitations of the patient's activity and the importance of swimming and walking. Outpatient orthopedic follow-up and therapy are arranged as required. The patient should participate in a weight reduction program if necessary.

total joint replacement Surgical removal of a diseased or injured joint and its replacement with an orthosis. SEE: *replacement of knee; total hip replacement; Nursing Diagnoses Appendix.*

total nutrient admixture A comprehensive combination of nutrients given parenterally, including amino acids, carbohydrates, fats, fluids, electrolytes, vitamins, and minerals.

total ossicular replacement Reconstruction of damaged or diseased ossicles in the middle ear with a biologically compatible implant.

totipotent (tō-tĭp′ō-tĕnt) [L. *totus,* all, + *potentia,* power] In embryology, the ability of a cell or group of cells to produce all of the tissues required for development, i.e., the embryonic membranes, the embryo, and finally the fetus.

touch (tŭch) [Fr. *tochier,* to knock, strike, touch] **1.** To perceive by the tactile sense; to feel with the hands, to palpate. **2.** The sense by which pressure on the skin or mucosa is perceived; the tactile sense. SYN: *tactile perception.* **3.** Examination with the hand. SYN: *palpation.*

Various disorders may disturb or impair the tactile sense or the ability to feel normally. There are a number of words and suffixes pert. to sensation and its modifications. A few of the more important ones are as follows: algesia, -algia, anesthesia, dysesthesia, -dynia, esthesia, esthesioneurosis, hyperesthesia, paresthesia, and synesthesia.

after-t. Persistence of the sensation of touch after contact with the stimulus has ceased.

healing t. A form of biofield medicine,

often compared to therapeutic touch, in which hands-on contact with the patient is combined with other spiritual links made between patient and practitioner. SEE: *therapeutic t.*

therapeutic t. The practice of running the hands on or above a patient's body to restore health. It is based on the premise that the human body is a complex system of energy fields, which must be channeled and balanced for optimum health.

vaginal t. Digital examination of the vagina.

vesical t. Digital examination of the bladder.

touch preparation SEE: under *preparation.*

touch up procedure A revision of a minor irregularity that remains after a surgical procedure, esp. after a cosmetic or plastic surgery.

Toupet procedure A surgical treatment for gastroesophageal reflux in which the stomach is partially wrapped around the lower esophagus. The surgery may be performed with a traditional incision or laparoscopically.

de la Tourette, Georges Gilles (toor-et′) Fr. neurologist, 1857–1904.

T. disorder T. syndrome.

T. syndrome A neurological disorder marked by repetitive motor and verbal tics. Those affected blink, jerk, grunt, clear their throats, swing their arms, grasp or clasp others, have obsessive-compulsive behaviors, or use verbal expletives uncontrollably. In some instances, those affected can control the urge to use these mannerisms while in public, but they may express them vigorously when alone. The condition often appears in several family members. It may be caused by a disorder of dopamine uptake in the basal ganglia. Dopamine-blocking drugs such as haloperidol can be used to treat this disorder. SYN: *Gilles de la Tourette syndrome; T. disorder.* SEE: *tic.*

Tournay sign (toor-nā′) [Auguste Tournay, Fr. ophthalmologist, 1878–1969] Dilatation of the pupil of the eye on unusually strong lateral fixation.

tourniquet (toor′ni-kĕt, tur′) [Fr. *tourniquet,* turnstile, turning instrument] Any constrictor used on an extremity to apply pressure over an artery and thereby control bleeding. It is also used to distend veins to facilitate venipuncture or intravenous injections.

Arterial hemorrhage: In emergencies, the tourniquet is applied between the wound and the heart, close to the wound, placing a hard pad over the point of pressure. This should be discontinued as soon as possible and a tight bandage substituted under the loosened tourniquet. SEE: *arterial bleeding* for table.

⚠️ A tourniquet should never be left in place too long. Ordinarily, it should be released from 12 to 18 min after application to determine whether bleeding has ceased. If it has, the tourniquet is left loosely in place so that it may be retightened if necessary. If bleeding has not ceased, it should be retightened at once. In general, a tourniquet should not be used if steady firm pressure over the bleeding site will stop the flow. As an adjunct to surgery on extremities, a pneumatic tourniquet is applied after exsanguinating the limb with an Esmarch or similar bandage. The time a surgical tourniquet is inflated and the pressure to which it is inflated depend upon the age of the patient, body habitus, upper vs. lower extremity, etc., according to established guidelines. The tourniquet is released at appropriate intervals to prevent tissue damage due to ischemia. An additional application utilizes two tourniquets or a double cuff tourniquet for retrograde intravenous nerve block, e.g., Bier block.

---

tourniquet syndrome The enclosing of a body part by an encircling hair or fiber, often accompanied by ischemic strangulation. It most commonly occurs around cylindrical structures, such as fingers, toes, or the penis.

tourniquet test A test used to determine pain thresholds or, alternately, capillary fragility. A blood pressure cuff is inflated sufficiently to occlude venous return. It is kept in place for a set time. The anesthetic effect, or the impact on skin integrity, is subsequently assessed.

Touton cell (toot'ŏn) [Karl Touton, Ger. dermatologist, 1858–1934] A giant multinucleated cell found in lesions of xanthomatosis.

towel clamp SEE: under *clamp*.

towelette (tow"ĕl-ĕt') [ME. *towelle*, towel] A small towel.

toxemia (tok-sē'mē-ă) [*toxi-* + *-emia*] Distribution throughout the body of poisonous products of bacteria growing in a focal or local site, thus producing generalized symptoms.

SYMPTOMS: The condition is marked by fever, diarrhea, vomiting, and symptoms of shock. In tetanus, the nervous system is esp. affected; in diphtheria, nerves and muscles are affected.

t. of pregnancy Former term for pregnancy-induced hypertension. SEE: *eclampsia; preeclampsia; Nursing Diagnoses Appendix.* **toxemic** (-mĭk), *adj.*

toxi-, tox-, toxo- [Gr. *toxon*, bow, bow and arrows] **1.** Prefixes meaning *poison.* **2.** Prefixes meaning *bow-shaped, arched,* or *arrow-shaped.* SEE: *toxico-.*

toxic (tŏks'ĭk) [Gr. *toxikon*, poison] Pert. to, resembling, or caused by poison. SYN: *poisonous.*

toxic algal bloom Red **tide**.

toxicant (tŏks'ĭ-kănt) [L. *toxicans*, poisoning] **1.** Poisonous; toxic. **2.** Any poison.

toxic cloud A mass of airborne toxins, e.g., aerosolized bacterial pathogens chemicals, or fumes released by the burning of a hazardous substance.

toxicemic (tŏks"ĭ-sē'mĭk) Toxemic.

toxicity (tok-sis'ĭt-ē) [*toxic*] The extent, quality, or degree of being poisonous.

contact lens-associated solution t. A mild, generalized punctate staining of the corneal epithelium with fluorescein sodium in patients who wear contact lenses. It can often be remedied by changing the patient's contact lens cleaning solution.

glucose t. **1.** The decrease in insulin secretion and the increase in insulin resistance due to excessively high blood glucose levels. **2.** Damage to arteries, the kidneys, nerves, the retina, and other tissues due to high blood glucose concentrations. SYN: *glucotoxicity.*

neurobehavioral t. Alterations in attention, concentration, coordination, mood, muscle activity, neurological development, or sensation due to exposure to a poisonous chemical, drug, or physical agent.

oxygen t. Tissue damage due to partially reduced forms of oxygen (oxygen radicals or reactive oxygen species.) Those at risk include those exposed to high concentrations of oxygen, esp. when delivered under pressure, e.g., patients receiving mechanical ventilation or hyperbaric oxygen treatment, or scuba divers. Damage to the fragile lipid membranes of the cells that line the lungs may result in progressive respiratory failure, which leads to decreased oxygen tension in the blood.

Prolonged exposure to a high oxygen concentration can cause injuries to tissues other than those in the alveoli of the lungs. In infants, for example, oxygen toxicity contributes to blindness as well as lung disease; in scuba divers, oxygen toxicity may produce neurological injury.

toxico-, toxic- [Gr. *toxikon (pharmakon),* arrow (poison)] Prefixes meaning *poisonous.* SEE: *toxi-.*

Toxicodendron (tok"si-kō-den'dron") [*toxico-* + Gr. *dendron,* tree] A genus of trees and shrubs, formerly called *Rhus,* some species of which, such as poison ivy and poison oak, contain oily resins that produce an allergic contact dermatitis in susceptible people. SEE: *poison ivy, poison sumac.*

toxicoderma (tŏks"ĭ-kō-děr'mă) [" + *derma,* skin] Any skin disease resulting from a poison. SYN: *toxidermitis.*

toxicodynamics (tok"sī-kō-dī-nam'iks) [*toxico-* + *dynamics*] The processes that affect the uptake of, metabolism by, damage to, and disposal of a poison by an organism.

toxicogenic (tŏks″ĭ-kō-jĕn′ĭk) [″ + *gennan*, to produce] Caused by, or producing, a poison.

toxicoid (tŏks′ĭ-koyd) [″ + *eidos*, form, shape] Poisonous.

toxicologist (tŏks″ĭ-kŏl′ō-jĭst) [″ + *logos*, word, reason] A specialist in the field of poisons or toxins.

toxicology (tŏks″ĭ-kŏl′ō-jē) The branch of medical and biological science concerned with toxic substances, their detection, their avoidance, their chemistry and pharmacological actions, and their antidotes and treatment.

toxicopathy (tŏks″ĭ-kŏp′ă-thē) [″ + *pathos*, disease, suffering] Toxicosis.

toxicosis (tok″sĭ-kō′sĭs) [*toxico-* + *-sis*] A disease due to poisoning. SYN: *toxicopathy; toxinosis; toxipathy; toxonosis*.

   endogenous t. A disease attributable to poisons generated within the body. SYN: *autointoxication; autotoxemia*.

   exogenous t. Any toxic condition caused by a poison not generated in the body.

   retention t. Toxicosis from retained products normally excreted shortly after formation.

   T_3 t. Hyperthyroidism caused by excessive levels of triiodothyronine in the blood (rather than excessive levels of T_4).

toxic shock-like syndrome ABBR: TSLS. An infection in which the initial site is skin or soft tissue. This may occur in adults or children and it is readily transmitted from person to person. Typically there is a history of a minor, usually nonpenetrating, local trauma that within the next 1 to 3 days develops into the usual toxic shock syndrome caused by a toxin elaborated by certain strains of *Staphylococcus aureus*. SEE: *toxic shock syndrome*.

toxic shock syndrome ABBR: TSS. A rare disorder similar to septic shock caused by an exotoxin produced by certain strains of *Staphylococcus aureus* and group A streptococci. It was originally described in young women using vaginal tampons but has also been reported in users of contraceptive sponges and diaphragms and after surgical wound packing. A similar syndrome is caused by streptococcal infections. SEE: *Staphylococcus; Nursing Diagnoses Appendix*.

   SYMPTOMS: The diagnosis is made when the following criteria are met: fever of 102°F (38.9°C) or greater; diffuse, macular (flat), erythematous rash, followed in 1 or 2 weeks by peeling of the skin, particularly of the palms and soles; hypotension or orthostatic syncope; and involvement of three or more of the following organ systems: gastrointestinal (vomiting or diarrhea at the onset of illness), muscular (severe myalgia), mucous membrane (vaginal, oropharyngeal, or conjunctival) hyperemia, renal, hepatic, hematological (platelets less than 100,000/mm³), and central nervous system (disorientation or alteration in consciousness without focal neurological signs when fever and hypotension are absent). Results of blood, throat, and cerebrospinal fluid cultures are usually negative. The possibility of Rocky Mountain spotted fever, leptospirosis, or rubeola should be eliminated by blood tests. The disease is fatal in approx. 5% to 15% of cases.

⚠ Anyone who develops these symptoms and signs should seek medical attention immediately. If a tampon is being used, it should be removed at once.

   TREATMENT: Penicillinase-resistant antibiotics such as nafcillin or oxacillin do not affect the initial syndrome but may prevent its recurrence. Supportive care (intravenous fluids, pressor drugs, intensive care) is provided.

toxidermitis (tŏks″ĭ-dĕr-mī′tĭs) [″ + *derma*, skin, + *itis*, inflammation] Toxicoderma.

toxidrome (tŏk′sĭ-drōm) A cluster of symptoms that occurs after patients are exposed to a poisonous agent; a toxic syndrome.

toxigenic (tŏks″ĭ-jĕn′ĭk) [″ + *gennan*, to produce] Producing toxins or poisons.

toxigenicity (tŏks″ĭ-jĕn-ĭs′ĭ-tē) The virulence of a toxin-producing pathogenic organism.

toxin (tok′sĭn) [*tox(ic)* + *-in*] A poisonous substance. SEE: *antitoxin; hazardous material; health hazard; permissible exposure limits; phytotoxin; right-to-know law; toxoid*.

   anthrax t. The three proteins made by the infectious bacterium *Bacillus anthracis* responsible for the deadly effects of anthrax. Anthrax toxin includes protective antigen, which helps lethal and edema factors enter and kill cells by disrupting the cell membrane's normal biochemical functions.

   bacterial t. A poison produced by bacteria that cause cell damage. They include exotoxins, e.g., those secreted by *Staphylococcus aureus* and *Corynebacterium diphtheriae*, and endotoxins. Endotoxins continue to cause damage even after the bacteria are killed. SEE: *bacteria*.

   botulinum t. type A A neuromuscular blocking drug used to paralyze muscles, esp. muscles in spasm. It is also used for cosmetic purposes, e.g., by those desirous of maintaining a fixed facial appearance.

   botulinus t. A neurotoxin that blocks

acetylcholine release, produced by *Clostridium botulinum,* the causative organism for botulism. Seven types of the toxin have been identified.

dermonecrotic t. Any of a group of toxins that can cause necrosis of the skin. Coagulate-positive *Staphylococcus aureus* produces several such toxins. SYN: *exfoliative t.* SEE: *Kawasaki disease; staphylococcal scaled skin syndrome; toxic shock syndrome.*

diphtheria t. The toxin produced by *Corynebacterium diphtheriae.*

dysentery t. The exotoxin of various species of *Shigella.*

erythrogenic t. The former name for the streptococcal pyrogenic exotoxins.

exfoliative t. Dermonecrotic **t.**

iota t. Either of two disease-causing proteins (Ib and Ia) released by the bacterium *Clostridium perfringens.* Ia binds to Ib and gains entry into the host cell cytoplasm. Ib subsequently disrupts the actin cytoskeleton and kills the cell.

plant t. Phytotoxin.

reproductive t. Any chemical or physical agent that destroys or inactivates the ovaries or testes, damages chromosomes, adversely effects reproductive hormones, or has a harmful impact on a developing fetus.

Shiga t. SEE: *Shiga toxin.*

toxin-antitoxin (tŏk'sĭn ăn'tē-tŏk"sĭn) ABBR: T.A.T. An infrequently used mixture of a toxin and an antibody that blocks its effects. It was formerly used in some vaccine formulations.

toxinicide (tŏks-ĭn'ĭs-īd) [″ + *cidus,* kill] Destructive to toxins.

toxinosis (tŏk"sĭ-nō'sĭs) [″ + Gr. *osis,* condition] Toxicosis.

toxipathy (tŏks-ĭp'ă-thē) [″ + Gr. *pathos,* disease, suffering] Toxicosis.

toxocariasis (tŏks"ō-kăr-ī'ă-sĭs) [″ + *kara,* head, + *-iasis,* condition] Infestation with the nematode worms *Toxocara canis* or *T. cati,* which migrate but cannot complete their life cycle in a human host and die after causing tissue damage that ranges from mild to severe. Larvae may be carried to any part of the body where the blood vessel is large enough to accommodate them. They may end up in the brain, retinal vessels, liver, lung, or heart and produce myocarditis, endophthalmitis, epilepsy, or encephalitis. Diagnosis is made by immunological tests and by the presence of larvae in tissue obtained by liver biopsy. It is important that toxocariasis be considered in cases diagnosed as retinoblastoma. SYN: *visceral larva migrans.*

toxoid (tok'soyd″) [*tox(in)* + *-oid*] A toxin chemically modified to retain its antigenicity but no longer poisonous. SYN: *anatoxin.*

alum-precipitated t. Toxoid of diphtheria or tetanus precipitated with alum.

diphtheria t. Diphtheria toxin altered so that it cannot cause disease but is still able to stimulate the production of antibodies for active immunization. It is used in diphtheria-pertussis-tetanus vaccine (DTaP).

tetanus t. Tetanus toxin modified so that its toxicity is greatly reduced but retaining its capacity to promote active immunity. SEE: *toxin.*

toxolecithin (tŏks″ō-lĕs'ĭ-thĭn) [″ + *lekithos,* egg yolk] A compound of lecithin with a toxin such as certain snake venoms.

toxopeptone (tŏks″ō-pĕp'tōn) [″ + *pepton,* digesting] A protein derivative produced by action of a toxin on peptones.

Toxoplasma (tŏks″ō-plăs'mă) A genus of protozoa in the sporozoa group.

T. gondii The causative agent of toxoplasmosis.

toxoplasmin (tŏk″sō-plăs'mĭn) An antigen obtained from mouse peritoneal fluid infected with *Toxoplasma gondii.*

toxoplasmosis (tok-sŏ-plaz″-mō'sĭs) [*Toxoplasma* + *-osis*] Infection with the protozoan *Toxoplasma gondii.* It usually is a recurrence of a mild infection in people with normal immune systems; approx. 30% of the U.S. population have antibodies indicating they have been infected. AIDS patients or those who are receiving immunosuppressive therapy after an organ transplant are esp. susceptible: for them reactivation of dormant organisms may be fatal. Approx. 25% of women infected for the first time during pregnancy pass the infection to the developing fetus.

ETIOLOGY/TRANSMISSION: *T. gondii* is carried by many birds and mammals and is commonly transmitted to humans by inadequate handwashing after handling cat feces or by eating incompletely cooked pork or lamb. Once inside the intestines, the organism may spread via the blood to other organs. It is destroyed by T lymphocytes.

In infected fetuses, toxoplasmosis damages the heart, brain, and lungs. It also causes eye infection (chorioretinitis), which may produce blindness. In AIDS patients, toxoplasmosis is the most common cause of encephalitis; systemic disease also may occur. In immunosuppressed patients, the infection causes reactivation of latent infection in the transplanted organ.

DIAGNOSIS: Toxoplasmosis is diagnosed by clinical presentation, brain biopsy, brain scans, and response to treatment.

SYMPTOMS: In healthy people, primary infection may be indicated only by mild lymphadenopathy. AIDS patients with neurological involvement usually show confusion, weakness, focal neurological deficits, seizures, and decreased levels of consciousness; fever may be present.

TREATMENT: A combination of pyrimethamine, sulfadiazine, and leucovorin (folinic acid) is administered until 2 weeks after symptoms disappear; the latter helps prevent bone marrow depression. Prednisone is added to the regimen for patients with toxoplasma meningitis or chorioretinitis. In AIDS patients, trimethoprim/sulfamethoxazole is used for prophylaxis and sulfadiazine for suppressive therapy after acute infection. Infected pregnant women are treated with spiramycin to prevent placental infections. SEE: *Aicardi-Goutières syndrome*.

TP *triple-P positive parenting program.*

tPA, TPA *tissue plasminogen activator; total parenteral alimentation.*

T-piece T-shaped tubing connected to an endotracheal tube; used to deliver oxygen therapy to an intubated patient who does not require mechanical ventilation. SYN: *T-bar*.

TPI test *Treponema pallidum immobilizing test* (for syphilis).

TPMT *thiopurine s-methyltransferase.*

TPN *triphosphopyridine nucleotide; total parenteral nutrition.*

tr L. *tinctura,* tincture.

trabecula (tră-běk′ū-lă, -lē) *pl.* **trabeculae** [L., a little beam] **1.** A cord of tissue that serves as a supporting structure by forming a septum that extends into an organ from its wall or capsule. **2.** The network of osseous tissue that makes up the cancellous structure of a bone.

    t. carneae Any of the thick muscular tissue bands attached to the inner walls of the ventricles of the heart.

trabecular (tră-běk′ū-lăr) The network of osseous tissue that makes up spongy (cancellous) bone.

trabecular meshwork The fibrous basement membrane in the angle between the iris and the corneal-sclera junction. Aqueous humour exits the anterior chamber of the eye through spaces in the trabecular meshwork and enters the venous sinus of the sclera (the canal of Schlemm).

trabeculate (tră-běk′ū-lāt) Having trabeculae.

trabeculectomy A surgical treatment for glaucoma in which part of the trabecular meshwork is removed to relieve pressure in the anterior chamber of the eye. The opening is made in the sclera (the "white of the eye") under the eyelid. Fluid from the anterior chamber drains in front of the eye instead of being drained through the canal of Schlemm and is absorbed by the conjunctiva.

trabeculoplasty (tră-běk″ū-lō-plăs′tē) Surgical laser procedure done on the trabecular meshwork of the eye to increase the outflow of aqueous in the treatment of glaucoma. SEE: *glaucoma*.

trace (trās) [O.Fr. *tracier*] **1.** A very small quantity. **2.** A visible mark or sign.

trace amine Any of several chemicals synthesized in the body and similar in structure and function to the biogenic amines. Examples include phenylethylamine and tryptamine. Trace amines alter impulse propagation in the brain and influence mood and behavior.

traceback, trace-back (trās′bak″) Identification of the source of an outbreak of disease or of a public health emergency, e.g., in a public health inquiry into the cause of an outbreak of a disease.

trace element SEE: under *element.*

traceforward The anticipation, identification, and planning for the likely effects of a local outbreak of disease or public health emergency.

tracer (trā′sĕr) A radioactive isotope, capable of being incorporated into compounds, that when introduced into the body tags a specific portion of the molecule so that its course may be traced. This is used in absorption and excretion studies, in identification of intermediary products of metabolism, and in determination of distribution of various substances in the body. Radioactive carbon (^{14}C), calcium (^{42}Ca), and iodine (^{131}I) are examples of tracers commonly used. SYN: *tagged atom.* SEE: *label.*

trachea (trā′kē-ă) *pl.* **tracheae** [Gr. *tracheia,* rough] The portion of the respiratory tract that carries air through the neck and upper chest. The trachea runs in the midline of the neck along the front of the esophagus. It is a fibrocartilaginous tube, 9 to 15 cm long, extending from the larynx (at the level of vertebra C6) into the thorax, where, at the level of the sternal angle, it divides into the right and left main (primary) bronchi. The 15 to 20 stacked rings of cartilage composing the skeleton of the trachea are incomplete circles: they are C-shaped with the opening along the back wall of the trachea. The membranes that connect the tracheal rings are elastic, and the whole trachea can bend and stretch. The trachea is lined with a mucosa made of ciliated epithelium that sweeps mucus, trapped dust, and pathogens upward. SYN: *windpipe.* SEE: *bronchi.*

tracheal (trā′kē-ăl) Pert. to the trachea.

tracheal gas insufflation SEE: under *insufflation.*

trachealgia (trā″kē-ăl′jē-ă) [″ + *algos,* pain] Pain in the trachea.

trachealis (trā″kē-ā′lĭs) [L.] A muscle composed of smooth muscle fibers that extends between the ends of the tracheal rings. Its contraction reduces the size of the lumen.

tracheal tickle A maneuver designed to elicit a reflex cough.

tracheal tube Endotracheal tube.

tracheal tugging SEE: under *tugging*.

tracheitis, trachitis (trā″kē-ī′tĭs) [Gr. *tracheia*, rough, + *itis*, inflammation] Inflammation of the trachea, most often caused by infection. It may be acute or chronic and may be associated with bronchitis and laryngitis.

TREATMENT: Patients must be monitored for signs of airway obstruction. Antibiotics are given when bacterial infection is the cause. In children the most common bacterial cause of infection is *Staphylococcus aureus*.

PATIENT CARE: Vital signs are monitored, and the patient is assessed for fever and acute airway obstruction (croupy cough, stridor) due to the presence of inflammation and thick secretions. Humidified oxygen is administered as prescribed, and suctioning is performed as necessary to remove secretions. If airway obstruction results in respiratory failure, emergency endotracheal intubation or tracheostomy is performed. The patient is comforted to reduce anxiety.

trachelectomy (trā″kĕl-ĕk′tō-mē) [″ + *ektome*, excision] Surgical removal of the uterine cervix, e.g., to treat cervical cancer. The procedure is used as an alternative to radical hysterectomy in women of reproductive age who wish to preserve their fertility.

trachelematoma (trā″kĕl-ĕm″ă-tō′mă) [″ + *haima*, blood, + *oma*, tumor] A hematoma situated on the neck.

trachelism, trachelismus (trā′kĕ-lĭzm, trā-kĕ-lĭz′mŭs) [″ + *-ismos*, condition] Backward spasm of the neck, sometimes preceding an epileptic attack.

trachelitis (trā-kĕ-lī′tĭs) [″ + *itis*, inflammation] Inflammation of the mucous membrane of the cervix uteri. SYN: *cervicitis*.

trachelo- [Gr. *trachelos*, neck] Prefix meaning *neck*.

trachelocele (trăk′ĕ-lō-sēl) [″ + *kele*, tumor, swelling] Tracheocele.

trachelocyrtosis (trā″kĕ-lō-sĭr-tō′sĭs) [″ + *kyrtos*, curved, + *osis*, condition] Trachelokyphosis.

trachelodynia (trā″kĕ-lō-dĭn′ē-ă) [″ + *odyne*, pain] Pain in the neck.

trachelokyphosis (trā″kĕl-ō-kī-fō′sĭs) [″ + *kyphosis*, humpback] Excessive anterior curvature of the cervical portion of the spine. SYN: *trachelocyrtosis*.

trachelology (trā″kĕl-ŏl′ō-jē) [″ + *logos*, word, reason] Scientific study of the neck, its diseases, and its injuries.

trachelopexy (trā′kĕl-ō-pĕks″ē) [″ + *pexis*, fixation] Surgical fixation of the cervix uteri to an adjacent part.

trachelorrhaphy (trā″kĕl-or′ă-fē) [″ +

rhaphe, seam, ridge] Suturing of a torn cervix uteri.

tracheloschisis (trā″kĕ-lŏs′kĭ-sĭs) [″ + *schisis*, a splitting] Congenital opening or fissure in the neck.

trachelotomy (trā″kĕl-ŏt′ō-mē) [″ + *tome*, incision] Incision of the cervix of the uterus.

tracheo-, trache- [Gr. *tracheia* (*artēria*), rough (artery)] Prefixes meaning *trachea, windpipe.*

tracheoaerocele (trā″kē-ō-ĕr′ō-sēl) [Gr. *tracheia*, rough, + *aer*, air, + *kele*, tumor, swelling] Hernia or cyst of the trachea containing air.

tracheobronchial (trā″kē-ō-brŏng′kē-ăl) Pert. to the trachea and bronchus.

tracheobronchomegaly (trā″kē-ō-brŏng″kō-mĕg′ă-lē) Congenitally enlarged size of the trachea and bronchi.

tracheobronchoscopy (trā″kē-ō-brŏng-kŏs′kō-pē) [″ + *bronchos*, windpipe, + *skopein*, to examine] Inspection of the trachea and bronchi through a bronchoscope.

tracheocele (trā′kē-ō-sēl) [″ + *kele*, hernia] Protrusion of mucous membrane through the wall of the trachea. SYN: *trachelocele*.

tracheoesophageal (trā″kē-ō-ē-sŏf″ă-jē′ăl) [″ + *oisophagos*, esophagus] Pert. to the trachea and esophagus.

tracheoesophageal puncture SEE: under *puncture*.

tracheolaryngotomy (trā″kē-ō-lăr″ĭn-gŏt′ō-mē) [″ + *larynx*, larynx, + *tome*, incision] Incision into the larynx and trachea.

tracheomalacia (trā″kē-ō-mă-lā′shē-ă) Softening of the tracheal cartilage. It may be caused by pressure of the left pulmonary artery on the trachea or by long-term tracheal intubation.

tracheopathia, tracheopathy (trā″kē-ō-păth′ē-ă, -ŏp′ă-thē) [″ + *pathos*, disease, suffering] A disease of the trachea.

tracheophony (trā″kē-ŏf′ō-nē) [″ + *phone*, a sound] The sound heard over the trachea in auscultation.

tracheoplasty (trā′kē-ō-plăs″tē) [″ + *plassein*, to form] Plastic operation on the trachea.

tracheorrhagia (trā″kē-ō-rā′jē-ă) [Gr. *tracheia*, rough, + *rhegnynai*, to burst forth] Tracheal hemorrhage.

tracheoschisis (trā″kē-ŏs′kĭs-ĭs) [″ + *schisis*, a splitting] A fissure of the trachea.

tracheoscopy (trā″kē-ŏs′kō-pē) [″ + *skopein*, to examine] Inspection of the interior of the trachea by means of reflected light.

tracheostenosis (trā″kē-ō-stĕn-ō′sĭs) [″ + *stenosis*, act of narrowing] Contraction or narrowing of the lumen of the trachea.

tracheostoma (trā″kē-ŏs′tō-mă) Opening into the trachea, via the neck.

tracheostomy (trā″kē-ŏs′tō-mē) [″ + *stoma,* mouth] The surgical opening of the trachea to provide and secure an open airway. This procedure may be performed in emergency situations (e.g., when there is an acute upper airway obstruction) or electively to replace a temporary airway provided by an endotracheal tube that has been in place or is anticipated to remain in place for more than 10 to 12 days. SEE: illus.; *endotracheal tube.*

⚠️ To avoid injury to the structures of the neck, tracheostomy should be performed only by skilled, well-trained health care professionals.

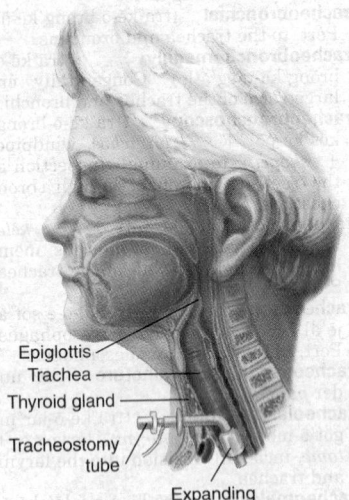

Epiglottis
Trachea
Thyroid gland
Tracheostomy tube
Expanding balloon

TRACHEOSTOMY TUBE IN PLACE

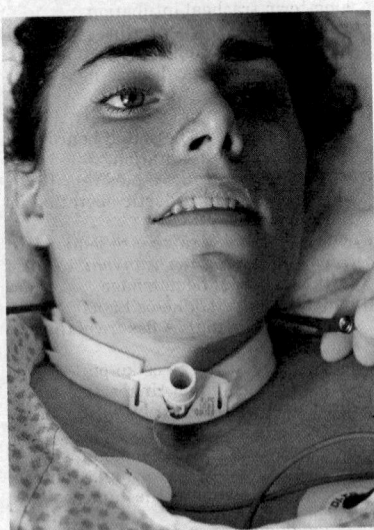

PATIENT WITH TRACHEOSTOMY TUBE

PATIENT CARE: Vital signs are monitored frequently after surgery. Warm, humidified oxygen is administered. The patient is placed in the semi-Fowler position to promote ease of breathing. A restful environment is provided. Communication is established by questions with simple yes and no answers, hand signals, and simple sign language and with use of a slate or an alphabet board for writing. (Written communication requires vision, hand strength, and dexterity and is often difficult or impossible for acutely ill patients.) Later, the patient is taught how to cover the tracheostomy with the cuff deflated to facilitate speech, or is provided with a speaking valve and taught how to use it. Before the patient is able to speak, the nurse should be alert to the patient's unmet needs and assist to prevent increased anxiety. Chest physiotherapy promotes aeration of the lung. Suctioning of secretions with prehyperoxygenation and posthyperoxygenation and tracheostomy care are provided aseptically. Dressing is changed frequently during the first 24 hr postoperatively, and the surgical site is observed for excessive bleeding. Coughing and deep breathing are encouraged at regular intervals. A teaching plan should cover stoma care, which includes cleansing, removing crusts, and filtering air with a suitable filter. The patient and his or her health care team should watch for signs of infection, such as reddening of the skin or drainage of pus from the surgical site. Aspiration is a risk for all tracheostomized patients, but may be reduced when a speaking valve is used. The patient is assessed for signs and symptoms of aspiration, including changes in secretion production, fever, and mental status changes. The patient should not smoke and should avoid secondhand smoke. Activities may be gradually increased to include noncontact sports but should not include swimming. Showering may be permitted if the patient wears a protective plastic bib or uses a hand to cover the stoma. The patient should be reassured that secretions will decrease and that taste and smell will gradually return. If a speaking valve is used, the patient is taught to clean it daily with water and mild, fragrance-free soap, to rinse it thoroughly and allow it to air dry, and to place it in its storage container when not in use. The importance of follow-up care with an ear, nose, and throat specialist is stressed.

mini-t. Placement of a 4 mm (about 1/6th of an inch) cannula through an incision made through the cricothyroid membrane into the trachea. This is done using local anesthesia. This type of tracheostomy is esp. useful in removing sputum retained in the tracheobronchial tree.

tracheostomy button A short tube or cannula placed inside a tracheostomy stoma to keep the tissue open.

tracheostomy care SEE: under *care*.

tracheostomy tube Tracheotomy tube.

tracheotome (trā′kē-ō-tōm) [″ + *tome,* incision] An instrument used to open the trachea.

tracheotomy (trā″kē-ŏt′ō-mē) Incision into the trachea through the skin and soft tissues of the neck. SEE: *tracheostomy.*

tracheotomy tube Any tube inserted into the trachea to gain control of the airway. SYN: *tracheostomy tube.*

trachoma (trā-kō′mă) [Gr., roughness] A chronic, contagious conjunctivitis that is the leading cause of blindness in the world. It is caused by *Chlamydia trachomatis,* which is endemic in Africa, India, and the Middle East and is seen also in the southwestern U.S. The disease is transmitted by flies, clothing, bedding, and hands contaminated by exudate. Over time, the inflammation is followed by scarring, which causes the cornea to become opaque. SYN: *Egyptian ophthalmia; granular conjunctivitis.* SEE: *Standard Precautions Appendix.*

Azithromycin is the drug of choice for treating trachoma, but its expense limits its use in some impoverished nations. Tetracyclines are an alternative.

brawny t. Trachoma with general lymphoid infiltration without granulation of the conjunctiva.

t. deformans Trachoma with scarring.

diffuse t. Trachoma with large granulations.

trachoma body SEE: under *body*.

trachomatous (tră-kō′mă-tŭs) Pert. to trachoma.

trachychromatic (trā″kĭ-krō-mǎt′ĭk) [Gr. *trachys,* rough, + *chroma,* color] Pert. to a nucleus with very deeply staining chromatin.

trachyphonia (trā″kĭ-fō′nē-ă) [″ + *phone,* voice] Roughness or hoarseness of the voice.

tracing (trā′sing) **1.** A graphic record of some event that changes with time such as respiratory movements or electrical activity of the heart or brain. **2.** In dentistry, a graphic display of movements of the mandible.

track (trak) **1.** The path or course of a penetrating injury. **2.** A treatment regimen or protocol.

tract (trakt) [L. *tractus,* extent] **1.** A pathway, course, or channel. **2.** A bundle of parallel axons in the central nervous system that runs along a stereotyped course from a common originating area to a common termination area. **3.** A group of organs or parts that form a continuous pathway.

afferent t. Any axon tract that carries information toward a particular target area.

alimentary t. Digestive **t.**

anterior spinocerebellar t. Ventral spinocerebellar **t.**

ascending t. An axon tract running rostrally in the spinal cord or brain, often a sensory pathway.

biliary t. The organs and ducts through which bile travels on its way to the duodenum. These are the bile canaliculi, right and left hepatic ducts, common hepatic duct, gallbladder, cystic duct, bile duct, and hepatopancreatic ampulla. SEE: *bile ducts; gallbladder; liver.*

central tegmental t. An axon tract connecting the subthalamus and the midbrain reticular formation with the inferior olivary nucleus.

corticobulbar t. An axon tract from the motor cortex that innervates the reticular formation and the cranial nerve nuclei in the hindbrain.

corticohypothalamic t. An axon tract from the frontal, parietal, and occipital cortices that innervates the hypothalamus.

corticospinal t. An axon tract from the motor cortex that travels into the spinal cord, synapsing at all levels. Axons of the corticospinal tract first converge into a bundle in the posterior limb of the internal capsule and continue as a compact bundle through the cerebral peduncle. In the pons, the corticospinal tract separates into several bundles that converge more caudally in the hindbrain as the pyramid. In the caudal hindbrain, the corticospinal tract crosses the midline in the pyramidal decussation and continues down the spinal cord as the lateral corticospinal tract.

cuneocerebellar t. An axon tract originating in the external cuneate nucleus and synapsing in the ipsilateral cerebellum.

descending t. Any axon tract running caudally in the spinal cord or brain, often a motor pathway.

digestive t. The continuous set of tubes that move food from the mouth to the anus. SYN: *alimentary t.*

direct cerebellar t. Dorsal spinocerebellar tract.

dorsal spinocerebellar t. An ipsilateral (uncrossed) axon tract originating throughout Clarke's column in the spinal cord. The tract runs in the lateral funiculus of the spinal cord and terminates in the ipsilateral vermis of the cerebellum. SYN: *direct cerebellar t.*

dorsolateral t. Lissauer tract.

efferent t. Any axon tract that carries information away from a particular target area.

extrapyramidal t. Any of the axon tracts of the extrapyramidal system. SEE: *extrapyramidal system.*

frontopontine t. A tract that passes from the cerebral cortex of the frontal lobe through the internal capsule and cerebral peduncle to the pons. SYN: *Arnold bundle.*

gastrointestinal t. The esophagus, stomach, and intestines.

geniculohypothalamic t. An axon tract originating in the lateral geniculate nucleus of the thalamus and innervating the suprachiasmatic nuclei of the hypothalamus. The suprachiasmatic nuclei contain pacemakers of the circadian rhythm system, and the geniculohypothalamic tract provides visual input that helps to entrain the pacemaker cells.

genital t. In males, the channels by which spermatozoa leave the body. In females, the channels in which the ovum grows and is fertilized and through which the baby leaves the body. SYN: *reproductive t.*

genitourinary t. The genital and urinary tracts together. SYN: *urogenital t.*

habenulo-interpeduncular t. Fasciculus retroflexus.

iliotibial t. A thickened band in the deep fascia along the lateral thigh (the fascia lata) that extends from the tubercle of the iliac crest to the lateral condyle of the tibia. The iliotibial tract is an aponeurosis shared by both the gluteus maximus and tensor fasciae lata muscles, both of which insert into it.

internodal t. In the heart, myocardial tissue in the right atrium that preferentially carries sinoatrial impulses to the left atrium, to the intra-atrial septum, or to the atrioventricular node.

intestinal t. The small and large intestines.

Lissauer t. SEE: *Lissauer tract.*

lower gastrointestinal t. The anus, rectum, colon, cecum, ileum and jejunum.

mammillotegmental t. An axon tract originating in the mammillary body and synapsing in small nuclei near the caudal end of the midbrain tegmentum.

mammillothalamic t. An axon tract originating in the mammillary body and synapsing in the anterior nucleus of the thalamus. The mammillothalamic tract is an integral component of the loop of neural circuits called the limbic system.

medullary reticulospinal t. SEE: *reticulospinal t.*

mesencephalic t. of the trigeminal nerve An axon tract of the unipolar sensory neurons of the trigeminal mesencephalic nucleus. Peripheral processes of these neurons run in the mesencephalic tract to the mandibular nerve (CN V3) and carry proprioceptive information from the face and the teeth. Axons of these neurons run in the mesencephalic tract and innervate a number of central nuclei, including the trigeminal motor nucleus. SYN: *trigeminal mesencephalic t.*

motor t. Any axon tract, usually running caudally in the CNS, that transmits output information.

olfactory t. A white ribbon-like band along the bottom (orbital) surface of each frontal lobe, composed of axons from the mitral cells in olfactory bulb. These axons terminate in the piriform cortex (the primary olfactory cortex) at the base of the cerebral hemisphere.

olivocerebellar t. An axon tract running transversely (as opposed to longitudinally) in the hindbrain from the inferior olivary nucleus to all parts of the cerebellum via the inferior cerebellar peduncle.

optic t. The main bundle of axons from the optic nerves caudal to the optic chiasm. Axons from the temporal half of the retina continue in the ipsilateral optic tract; axons from the nasal half of the retina cross the midline of the brain in the optic chiasm and join the contralateral optic tract. Most optic tract axons synapse in the lateral geniculate nucleus of the thalamus; most of the remaining optic tract axons synapse in the superior colliculus (optic tectum) of the midbrain.

pontine reticulospinal t. SEE: *reticulospinal t.*

pyramidal t. The corticobulbar and corticospinal tracts, which are the major direct outputs of the motor cortex. In cross-sections of the hindbrain, the pyramidal tract has a triangular shape.

reproductive t. Genital **t.**

respiratory t. The respiratory channel from mouth and nose to the alveoli in the lungs.

reticulospinal t. Either of two tracts, the pontine reticulospinal tract or the medullary reticulospinal tract. The pontine reticulospinal tract contains axons originating in the pontine reticular formation; the axons run into the spinal cord along the ventral midline (the medial part of the anterior funiculus). The medullary reticulospinal tract contains axons originating in the medial two thirds of the hindbrain reticular formation; these axons run into the spinal cord in the anterior part of the lateral funiculus.

retinohypothalamic t. The retinal ganglion cell axons from the optic nerves that leave the optic tract at the optic chiasm to innervate the suprachiasmatic nucleus (in the hypothalamus), which contains the pacemaker cells for circadian rhythms.

rubrospinal t. An axon tract originating in the red nucleus of the midbrain. After leaving the red nucleus, axons cross to the contralateral side and descend into the spinal cord, where they terminate in the ventral horns. The red nucleus is innervated by axons from the motor cortices and the cerebellum, and the rubrospinal pathway is an extrapyramidal route to the spinal cord. A major function of rubrospinal axons is to set and adjust the muscle tone in the flexor muscles.

sensory t. Any axon tract, usually traveling rostrally in the CNS, that transmits information related to somatic or visceral sensation.

solitary t. Tractus solitarius.

spinal t. of the trigeminal nerve A tract of somatic sensory axons from the trigeminal nerve that runs caudally from the midpontine level of the brainstem along the spinal nucleus of the trigeminal nerve. The tract carries pain and temperature information from the face, and its axons synapse topographically in the adjacent nucleus. In the transition zone between hindbrain and spinal cord, the spinal tract of the trigeminal nerve disappears into the tract of Lissauer although a few axons of the spinal tract extend as far caudally as spinal cord segment C3-C4. SYN: *trigeminal spinal t.*

spinocerebellar t. The dorsal or the ventral spinocerebellar tract.

spinothalamic t. The lateral or the anterior spinothalamic tract. Both tracts are bundles of axons running rostrally in the ventrolateral quadrant (the ventral half of the lateral funiculus) of the spinal cord, originating from contralateral dorsal horn neurons, and synapsing in the ventral posterolateral nucleus of the thalamus. The lateral spinothalamic tract carries pain and temperature information from the body; the anterior spinothalamic tract (adjacent and dorsal to the lateral tract) carries light touch information.

trigeminal mesencephalic t. Mesencephalic tract of the trigeminal nerve.

trigeminal spinal t. Spinal t. of the trigeminal nerve.

trigeminothalamic t. Trigeminal lemniscus.

upper gastrointestinal t. The esophagus, stomach, and duodenum.

urinary t. The channel followed by urine in the body, from the glomeruli in the kidneys through the ureters, bladder, and urethra.

urogenital t. Genitourinary tract.

uveal t. The vascular and pigmented tissues that constitute the middle layer of the wall of the eye. The tract comprises the iris, ciliary body, and choroid.vascular tunic of the eye.

ventral spinocerebellar t. An axon tract originating in the contralateral dorsal and intermediate horns of the lower spinal cord, from the coccygeal through the lumbar segments. This tract runs in the lateral funiculus of the spinal cord, recrosses the midline, and terminates in the ipsilateral vermis of the cerebellum. SYN: *anterior spinocerebellar t.*

ventricular outflow t. In the heart, the pathway through which blood is normally ejected from the ventricle. For the left ventricle, it includes the walls of the ventricle, the anterior leaflet of the mitral valve, the aortic valve, the ascending aorta, and the arch of the aorta. For the right ventricle, it includes the walls of the ventricle, the pulmonic valve, the pulmonary trunk, and the pulmonary arteries.

vestibulospinal t. An axon tract that conveys balance and equilibrium information to the spinal cord from the vestibular nuclei in the brainstem. The medial vestibulospinal tract is the continuation of the medial longitudinal fasciculus caudally into the spinal cord below the cervical levels; it runs along the medial margin of the ventral quadrant of the cord. The lateral vestibulospinal tract runs caudally in an anterior band in the ventral and ventrolateral quadrant of the spinal cord.

vocal t. The tissues and organs that produce human vocalizations, including lips, tongue, mouth, nasal cavities, pharynx, and larynx.

tractellum (trăk-těl′ŭm) [L.] An anterior flagellum of a protozoan. It propels the cell by traction.

traction (trak′shŏn) [L. *tractio,* a pulling] The process of drawing or pulling. SEE: *Nursing Diagnoses Appendix.*

axis t. Traction in line with the long axis of a course through which a body is to be drawn. SYN: *in-line t.*

Bryant t. SEE: *Bryant traction.*

Buck t. Buck extension.

cervical t. Traction applied to the cervical spine by applying a force to lift the head or a mobilization technique to distract individual joints of the vertebrae. The reaction can be done manually or by a traction device. It is frequently used to relieve pain caused by a herniated disc. SEE: *Crutchfield tongs.*

dynamic t. Use of both tension across an injury and movement to maintain proper alignment and function of an injured body part.

elastic t. Traction exerted by elastic devices such as rubber bands.

external t. Traction applied to any fracture, e.g., compression fractures of the face using metal or plaster headgear for anchorage.

head t. Traction applied to the head as in the treatment of injuries to cervical vertebrae. SEE: *cervical t.*

in-line t. Axis **t.**

intermittent t. The force of traction alternately applied and released at specified intervals.

lumbar t. Traction applied to the lumbar spine usually by applying a force to pull on the pelvis or by using a mobilization technique to distract individual joints of the lumbar vertebrae.

manual t. The application of traction to the joints of the spine or extremities by a therapist trained to know appropriate positions and intensities for the force.

maxillomandibular t. Traction applied to the maxilla and mandible by means of elastic or wire ligatures and interdental wiring or splints.

mechanical t. The use of a device or mechanical linkage (pulleys and weights) to apply a traction force.

skeletal t. Traction applied directly to the bone through surgically applied pins and tongs.

PATIENT CARE: The patient in traction is placed on a firm mattress in the prescribed position. Ropes, weights, and pulleys are assessed daily for wear, chafing, and improper position. Care must be taken to keep the points of insertion of pins and tongs into the skin clean and free of infection. Infection at insertion sites can lead to osteomyelitis. Assessing the area for odor and other signs of infection, cleansing the area, and applying medications and sterile dressings can help prevent osteomyelitis; aseptic technique is used for these procedures. The skin is inspected daily for signs of pressure or friction, and measures are taken to alleviate pressure or friction. Proper traction and postural alignment should be maintained at all times and adjusted as necessary. An exercise regimen is established for the unaffected extremities. Patient complaints should be attended to without delay. Respiratory toilet with incentive spirometry is provided to prevent pulmonary complications. Pain and discomfort are assessed, and analgesics are administered as prescribed. Adequate nutrition and fluid intake promote tissue healing and repair. Dietary and medical management helps prevent constipation and fecal impaction. The affected extremity is assessed daily or more frequently if necessary for complications such as phlebitis and nerve or circulatory impairment, and the lower extremity, for footdrop. Social and diversional activities are promoted. The patient is instructed about the use of a trapeze, exercises, and activity limitations, and discharge plans and follow-up care are provided.

sustained t. The application of a constant traction force up to ½ hr.

weight t. Traction exerted by means of weights.

tractor (trăk'tor) [L., drawer] Any device or instrument for applying traction.

tractotomy (trăk-tŏt'ō-mē) Surgical section of a tract of the central nervous system. It is sometimes used to relieve intractable pain.

tractus (trak'tŭs) *pl.* **tractus** [L. *tractus,* course, region] A tract or path.

t. diagonalis Diagonal **band**.

t. solitarius A thin tract of visceral sensory axons from cranial nerves CN VII, CN IX, and CN X. The tract runs longitudinally, alongside the solitary nucleus in the hindbrain. Axons from the tract, which carries information from mechanoreceptors and chemoreceptors, synapse in the adjacent nucleus. SYN: *fasciculus solitarius; solitary tract*.

tradename The name used to market a formally licensed drug or treatment.

traditional birth attendant A person, esp. one in a developing country, who assists a woman during labor and delivery with skills learned by apprenticeship or personal experience rather than by formal training.

tragacanth (trăg'ă-kănth) [Gr. *tragakantha,* a goat thorn] The dried gummy exudation from the plant *Astragalus gummifer* and related species, grown in Asia. It is used in the form of mucilage, as a greaseless lubricant, and as an application for chapped skin.

tragal (trā'găl) [Gr. *tragos,* goat] Pert. to the tragus.

Trager work (trā'gĕr) [Milton Trager, U.S. physician, d. 1997] A form of massage therapy that involves rhythmic manipulations of the body, combined with mental gymnastics.

tragi (trā'jī) Pl. of tragus.

tragicus (trăj'ĭk-ŭs) [L.] The muscle on the outer surface of the tragus.

tragion (trăj'ē-ŏn) An anthropometric point at the upper margin of the tragus of the ear.

tragomaschalia (trăg"ō-măs-kāl'ē-ă) [Gr. *tragos,* goat, + *maschale,* the armpit] Malodorous perspiration (bromidrosis) of the axilla.

tragophonia, tragophony (trăg"ō-fō'nē-ă, -ŏf'ō-nē) [" + *phone,* voice] A bleating sound heard in auscultation at the level of fluid in hydrothorax. SYN: *egophony*.

tragus (trā'gŭs) *pl.* **tragi** [Gr. *tragos,* goat] A cartilaginous projection in front of the exterior meatus of the ear.

trailing zero SEE: under *zero*.

train (trān) To participate in a program

of instruction to attain competence in a certain occupation.

trainable (trān'ă-bĕl) Having the ability to be instructed and to learn from being taught. In classifying severity of mental retardation or brain damage, it is important to know to what extent individuals may be trainable in various areas such as safety, personal care, or self-feeding.

training (trān'ing) An organized system of instruction.

    aerobic t. Exercise training for aerobic conditioning. The American College of Sports Medicine recommends that healthy people exercise 3 to 5 times a week for 30 to 60 min at a rate of at least 64% of their maximum heart rate.

    athletic t. **1.** The physical and mental training used by athletes to increase their proficiency in sports. **2.** Performing the tasks that an athletic trainer is prepared to do. Athletic training is practiced by athletic trainers, health care professionals who collaborate with physicians to optimize activity and participation of patients and clients. Athletic training encompasses the prevention, diagnosis, and intervention of emergency, acute, and chronic medical conditions involving impairment, functional limitations, and disabilities. SEE: *athletic trainer.*

    autogenic t. A form of self-regulation to promote relaxation, aid stress management, and/or foster well-being using the autonomic nervous system. The practitioner utters or concentrates on a simple phrase (such as "My arms feel heavy and warm") and tries to induce physiological changes, such as increases in blood flow, to the body part on which he or she is concentrating.

    aversive t. Aversion therapy.

    balance t. Training that improves a person's agility and stability of gait and ability to prevent falls. These include stepping over obstacles on a rough or random surface, rapidly shifting direction while walking, developing core muscle strength, and improving ankle strength and lower extremity proprioception.

    bladder t. Training for treatment of stress urinary incontinence in women in which the patient charts the number of urinations, the intervals between urination, and the volume of urine passed. The patient also notes the degree and frequency of incontinence. The intervals between urinations are gradually increased. SYN: *bladder drill; timed voiding.*

    bowel t., bowel retraining A training program for assisting adult patients to reestablish regular bowel habits. Patients with chronic constipation, colostomies, fecal incontinence, or spinal cord injuries affecting the muscles involved in defecation may benefit from bowel training. Assessments include determining the cause and duration of the bowel problem, the normal pattern, the use of enemas, suppositories, or laxatives to promote bowel evacuation, and the patient's mental status and ability to cooperate with the program. Interventions include dietary changes (esp. increased intake of dietary fiber), supervised training to elicit evacuation at convenient times (esp. after meals), biofeedback, Kegel exercises, and psychotherapy.

    PATIENT CARE: The patient is encouraged to increase the dietary intake of fresh fruits and vegetables and whole grains, and to drink 3000 mL of fluid each day. The need to heed normal evacuatory urges is emphasized. Use of laxatives is discouraged, and the actions of stool softeners are explained. The advantages of generating evacuation 30 min after meals to enlist normal peristaltic action are communicated to the patient. Digital anal stimulation or insertion of a suppository, if indicated, is demonstrated.

    endurance t. Physical training for athletic events requiring prolonged effort, such as running a marathon, swimming a long distance, or climbing mountains.

    PATIENT CARE: Patients who participate in endurance sports are likely to lose weight and improve their well-being, and blood glucose and cholesterol levels. It is wise to initiate training slowly, avoid overuse injuries, and gradually increase workload.

⚠️ Patients who have diabetes mellitus, joint disease, a history of smoking or chronic respiratory illnesses, atherosclerotic vascular disease, loss of consciousness or seizures, or complicated medical regimens should consult with health care professionals before beginning endurance training.

    exercise t. The use of repetitive body movements to build endurance, flexibility, or muscular strength.

    habit t. **1.** The development in young children of specific behavior patterns for performing basic activities such as eating, dressing, using the toilet, and sleeping. **2.** An educational tool in which learning of specific tasks is assigned to a structured time of the day, so that the task and the time are associated in the mind of the student. **3.** The treatment is designed to encourage behavioral routines and productive time management.

    in-service t. Clinical education to inform and update staff about important ongoing projects, technologies, and therapeutic agents.

inspiratory muscle t. Training to enhance ventilation by increasing respiratory coordination, endurance, and strength. Examples include breath-holding exercises, breathing against resistance, and incentive spirometry.

interval t. A form of physical training in which periods of high-intensity exercise alternate with periods of lesser exertion or rest and recovery.

mobility t. Training and equipment for people with functional deficits to help them move around safely. For the blind or those with low vision, orientation and mobility (OM) training is used. Orientation is knowing one's location in space; mobility is a plan to get to one's desired location. For the blind or those with impaired vision, OM training also involves the development of sensory awareness and learning to use long canes, guide dogs, or electronic sensing aids.

pelvic floor muscle t. ABBR: PFMT. Repetitive squeezing of the urethral sphincter muscles and elevating the levator ani muscles. It is a treatment for urinary stress incontinence.

resistance t. Repetitive exercises in which the contraction of a muscle is opposed by an applied force or weight. It is used to develop muscle size, strength, and endurance. SYN: *strength* **t.**

sensitivity t. A form of group therapy in which people are given the opportunity to interact verbally, physically, candidly, and honestly to other members of the group. The goals of the therapy are to increase self-awareness, learn constructive ways of dealing with conflicts, establish a better sense of inner direction, and relate to other people with sympathy.

social skills t. The components of rehabilitation programs that focus on the skills necessary for effective interaction with other people.

strength t. Resistance **t.**

stress inoculation t. A treatment for symptoms of post-traumatic stress disorder, in which the patient learns how to identify those cues that revive painful memories and then cope with them using techniques that desensitize him or her to these triggers. Relaxation techniques (such as deep breathing or muscle relaxation) are employed.

toilet t. Teaching a child to control urination and defecation until placed on a toilet. The bowel movements of an infant habitually occur at the same time each day very early in life, but because the child does not have adequate neuromuscular control of bowel and bladder function until the end of the second year, it is not advisable to begin this training until then. Close to that time, placing the child on a small potty chair for a short period several times a day may allow him or her to stay dry. First the diapers are removed while the child is awake, then later removed during naps, and the child is told he or she should be able to stay dry. This schedule may need to be interrupted for several days to a week if the child does not remain dry.

To protect the bed, a rubber sheet should be used during the training period. Training pants or "pull-ups" may help in the transition from passive to active control of toilet habits. There is no difference in ease and timing of training between boys and girls, each taking about 3 to 6 months.

Children who are unsuccessful in remaining dry or controlling their bowels should not be punished. To do so may promote the later development of enuresis or constipation. In any event, it is neither abnormal nor harmful for training to be delayed until well into the third year of life. If not achieved by then, professional evaluation should be undertaken to detect the rare case of genitourinary or gastrointestinal abnormalities that may be contributing to such a delay.

training effect The physiological response of the body to regular repetitive exercise. Beneficial effects include a slower heart rate, lower blood pressure, decreased blood cholesterol levels, increased muscle strength, better oxygen and glucose extraction from the blood, and improvement in mood.

train-of-four ABBR: TOF. A monitoring protocol for counting the number of contractions produced by peripheral nerve stimulators in patients who have received neuromuscular blocking agents (NMBAs) such as Pavulon and vecuronium. When NMBAs are used, staff may be unable to use normal assessment techniques of neurological function.

PATIENT CARE: In TOF, electrodes are placed on the patient's wrist, and the number of thumb twitches is counted. After the NMBA infusion is begun, thumb twitches are measured every 30 min for 2 hr to ensure the appropriate level of paralysis has been reached. The absence of contractions indicates that too much NMBA is being given; 1 to 2 twitches indicate the appropriate level of drug is being administered, and 3 to 4 twitches indicate the need to increase the infusion rate. Once the desired level is reached, response to peripheral nerve stimulation is measured every 4 hr.

Since patients retain sensory nerve function and awareness of their surroundings, analgesics and sedatives are usually administered concurrently. Whether TOF augments clinical assessment of neuromuscular blockade is controversial; it may be more useful with some neuromuscular blocking agents (e.g., vecuronium) than others.

trait (trāt) A distinguishing feature; a characteristic or property of an individual.

    acquired t. A trait that is not inherited; one resulting from the effects of the environment.

    inherited t. A trait due to genes transmitted through germ cells.

    personality t. An enduring pattern of perceiving, communicating, and thinking about oneself, others, and the environment that is exhibited in multiple contexts. SEE: *personality disorder.*

    sickle cell t. The condition of being heterozygous with respect to hemoglobin S, the gene responsible for sickle cell anemia. In people with sickle cell trait, each red blood cell has one copy each of hemoglobin A and hemoglobin S. These cells will not become sickled until extremely low concentrations of oxygen occur. SEE: *hemoglobin S disease.*

trajector (tră-jĕk′tor) [L. *trajectus,* thrown across] A device for determining the approximate location of a bullet in a wound.

TRALI *transfusion-related acute lung injury.*

TRAM *transverse rectus abdominis musculocutaneous reconstruction.*

tramadol (tră′mă-dŏl) A cyclohexanol and centrally acting analgesic, administered orally to treat moderate or moderately severe pain.

trance (trăns) [L. *transitus,* a passing over] A sleeplike state, as in deep hypnosis, in which a person has limited awareness of his surroundings.

    death t. A trance simulating death.

    induced t. A trance caused by some external event such as hypnosis.

tranquilizer (trăn′kwĭ-līz′ĕr) [L. *tranquillus,* calm] A drug that reduces tension, agitation, hyperactivity, and anxiety. The minor tranquilizers include antihistamines (e.g., hydroxyzine), buspirone, and benzodiazepines (e.g., diazepam or alprazolam). Benzodiazepines decrease anxiety, provide sedation but may cause dependence, tolerance, or addiction. The major tranquilizers include neuroleptic drugs such as haloperidol, fluphenazine, or risperidone. They are used to treat psychotic symptoms, such as delusions, hallucinations, and catatonia, and to manage psychotic disorders, such as schizophrenia. Tardive dyskinesia is a notable delayed side effect of many neuroleptic agents.

⚠ Some tranquilizers may injure the developing embryo. Therefore, before prescribing one, one should know whether it is approved for use during pregnancy, esp. early pregnancy.

trans- [L. *trans,* across, through, beyond] Prefix meaning *across, over, beyond, through.*

transabdominal (trăns″ăb-dŏm′ĭ-năl) Through, into, or across the abdomen or abdominal wall.

transacetylation (trăns-ăs″ĕ-tĭl-ā′shŭn) Transfer of an acetyl group ($CH_3CO—$) in a chemical reaction.

transaction The interaction of a person with others, esp. one in which items on an agenda, finances, or ideas are discussed.

transactional analysis Psychotherapy involving role playing in an attempt to understand the relationship between the patient and the therapist and eventually that between the patient and reality.

transamidination (trăns-ăm″ĭ-dĭn-ā′shŭn) The transfer of an amidine group from one amino acid to another.

transaminase (trăns-am′ĭ-nās′) [*trans-* + *amine* + *-ase*] Any of a group of enzymes causing transamination. SYN: *aminotransferase.*

    glutamic-oxaloacetic t. Aspartate **aminotransferase**.

    glutamic-pyruvic t. ABBR: GPT. Alanine **aminotransferase**.

    serum glutamic-pyruvic t. ABBR: SGPT. Alanine **aminotransferase**.

transamination (trăns″ăm-ĭ-nā′shŭn) The transfer of an amino group from one compound to another or the transposition of an amino group within a single compound.

transaortic (trăns″ā-or′tĭk) Done through the aorta, e.g., a surgical procedure.

transatrial (trăns-ā′trē-ăl) Done through the atrium (e.g., a surgical procedure).

transaudient (trăns-aw′dē-ĕnt) [″ + *audire,* to hear] Permeable to sound waves.

transbronchial (trăns-brŏng′kē-ăl) Across the bronchi or the bronchial wall.

transcapillary (trăns″kăp′ĭ-lă-rē) [″ + *capillaris,* relating to hair] Across the endothelial wall of a capillary.

transcatheter arterial chemoembolization (trăns″kath′ĕt-ĕr) ABBR: TACE. A technique for destroying tumors in which a tube is guided into the arterial blood supply of the tumor and drugs, fragments of muscle, or synthetic spheres are introduced to obstruct the artery. It is used to treat liver cancers that cannot be removed surgically.

transcellular (trăns-sĕl′ū-lĕr) [″ + ″] **1.** Passing through cells. **2.** Passing from one cell to another, through adjacent cell membranes.

transcellular fluid SEE: under *fluid.*

transcervical (trăns-sĕr′vĭ-kăl) Done through the cervical os of the uterus.

transcortical (trăns-kor'tĭ-kăl) Joining two parts of the cerebral cortex.

transcortin (trăns-kor'tĭn) A corticosteroid-binding globulin.

transcriptase (trans-krĭp'tās") [*transcript(ion)* + *-ase*] A polymerase enzyme that constructs a messenger RNA molecule that is a complementary copy of the base sequence on a DNA gene. SYN: *RNA polymerase*.

> **reverse t.** An enzyme of retroviruses, including HIV, that catalyzes the construction of double-stranded DNA from the single-stranded RNA of the virus, the reverse of normal transcription.

transcription (trans-krĭp'shŏn) The first step in protein synthesis, in which a messenger RNA (mRNA) molecule is synthesized. This takes place in the nucleus of the cell. The mRNA then travels to the ribosomes in the cytoplasm, the site of protein synthesis. **transcriptional** ('shŏn-ăl), *adj.*

transcriptome (trăns-skrĭp'tōm) All the messenger RNA that can be made from a genome.

transcultural (trăns-kŭl'tū-răl) Pert. to or affecting individuals of different ethnic, racial, or socioeconomic backgrounds. SEE: table.

transcutaneous (trăns"kū-tā'nē-ŭs) Percutaneous.

transcutaneous electrical nerve stimulation SEE: under *stimulation*.

transcutaneous oxygen monitoring Oximetry.

transcytosis (trănz-sī-tō'sĭs) The ferrying of a substance across a cell membrane in coated vesicles.

transdermal infusion system (trănz"dĕrm'ăl) Delivery of medicine through a special gel-like matrix that is applied to the skin. Each application will provide medicine for one or more days. Nitroglycerin, fentanyl, lidocaine, estradiol, testosterone, and scopolamine may be administered through the skin. A transdermal drug patch has three key elements: a backing, the drug, and a liner that is peeled away before application. The absorption, delivery rate, and biodistribution of the drug are not affected by the patient's skin texture, thickness, or color. Drugs are equally well absorbed when applied to arms, thighs, back, or abdomen because various body sites have about the same rate of dermal penetration. When placed on intact skin, a transdermal drug patch creates a concentration gradient between the high concentration of drug in the patch and the low concentration in the skin. The drug then diffuses passively across the outermost skin layer (stratum corneum) into epidermal capillaries. Also called *transdermal drug-delivery system*.

PATIENT CARE: The skin acts as a reservoir for the absorbed drug; therefore simple removal of a patch does not stop release of the drug into the bloodstream. Patients may forget to tell health care providers that they are wearing a patch, or the patch may be overlooked because of its transparency or because the patch is concealed in skin folds. As a result the patient could receive an overdose if a similar drug is administered by another route. Thus, health care professionals should ask specifically about patch use when taking a patient's medication history. Most patches are imprinted with the drug name, dose, and release rate, providing needed information to the care provider. The patient should be taught to keep each patch in its protective wrapper un-

Some Culturally Specific (Folk) Illnesses

Syndrome	Culture	Meaning
Caida de mollera	Latin America	"Sunken fontanel," i.e., dehydration. Thought to be caused by spells or hexes
Latah	S.E. Asia	Obsessive and repetitive use of vulgar language followed by obedient gesturing
Mal de ojo	Latin America	"Evil eye," i.e., a spell put on a child. Causes vomiting, belly pain, dehydration
Piblokto	Eskimo/Inuit	Sudden manic madness, with subsequent amnesia of the event
Root; rootwork	S.E. U.S.	Hexing or healing through sorcery
Tabanka	Trinidad	Depression and/or suicide after abandonment by a wife
Tarantism	Mediterranean	Uncontrollable stupor, melancholy, and manic dancing attributed to the bite of the tarantula
Windigo (witiko)	Native American	Cannabalism as a result of spirit possession
Yonaki	Japanese	A sleep-disorder of childhood, marked by separation anxiety and nocturnal crying
Zar	Northern African/ Middle Eastern	Spirit possession

til ready for use, to inspect it for leakage, and not to use it if it is damaged. If a patch leaks on the skin, the exposed skin should be thoroughly rinsed with water (soap should not be used because it can irritate the drug-exposed skin). The manufacturer's directions for patch application should be followed. Skin that is very hairy, oily, sunburned, scarred, calloused, or damaged; areas that tend to be sweaty; areas prone to friction (e.g., under a bra strap or at the waist line); and bony areas (e.g., the shoulders and hips) should be avoided. Skin should be clean and dry before the patch is applied, and powder, lotion, or residual oil from bath products or sunscreens should be removed by washing with mild soap and water and rinsing thoroughly. The drug name, dose, and delivery rate should be checked before the patch is applied. The patient should then peel off the protective liner and apply the adhesive side of the patch to the skin at the selected site, pressing the patch on firmly so that it adheres well, esp. around the edges. The hands should be washed immediately after applying a patch. Directions for removing a patch should be followed and the patch disposed of according to the manufacturer's instructions. Application sites should be rotated to avoid skin irritation. Depending on the particular drug and the prescribed regimen, a patch may be worn continually or removed for a portion of each day. Transdermal patches are best stored in their original container at room temperature with nothing stacked on top of them so as to protect them from excessive heat or pressure. If the interval between patch changes is lengthy, the patient must develop a system to assist in correctly scheduling the change. If a patient forgets to change a patch at the prescribed interval, he or she should remove the missed patch and apply a new one as soon as the error is discovered. Drug patches are waterproof, and the patient can bathe, shower, or swim while wearing a patch as long as it is not rubbed. If a patch starts to peel because of sweating, immersion in water, or hot, humid weather, it should be replaced, never taped to the skin, or held in place or covered in any way. Patch adhesive can irritate sensitive skin, but the reaction usually subsides when the patch is removed. Localized skin reactions may require treatment with a topical corticosteroid, but they should be reported to the primary care provider to determine the appropriate action.

⚠ 1. Patients should remove a patch before having a magnetic resonance imaging (MRI) scan and replace it afterward with a new patch. The foil backing on many patches can cause MRI-related burns.

2. Patches containing estrogen or nicotine should not be applied to the breasts.

---

transdifferentiation (trănz″dĭf″ĕ-rĕn″shē-ā′shŭn) The conversion of stem cells derived from one tissue into cells normally found in another tissue.

transducer (trans-doo′sĕr, tranz-, -dū′) [L. *traducere, transducere,* to lead across] **1.** A device that converts one form of energy to another. The telephone is an example. It is used in medical electronics to receive the energy produced by sound or pressure and relay it as an electrical impulse to another transducer, which can either convert the energy back into its original form or produce a record of it on a recording device. SYN: *probe.* **2.** In ultrasonography, an electromechanical device that emits high-frequency sounds and receives their echoes.

    pulse-echo t. An ultrasonic transducer that sends out intermittent (pulsed) signals rather than continuous sound waves and receives the echo signal. Pulsed-wave Doppler ultrasound is used to measure blood flow and the depths from which echoes originate.

    continuous wave t. An ultrasonic transducer that sends a constant and continuing signal that is not pulsed.

    transrectal t. A cylindrical ultrasonic transducer inserted into the rectum to evaluate the prostate, rectum, and urinary bladder and to guide prostate biopsy.

    ultrasonic t. A device used in ultrasound that sends and receives the sound wave signal. SEE: *probe; illus.*

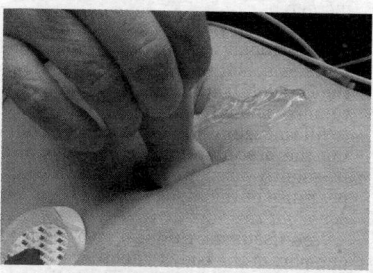

ULTRASONIC TRANSDUCER

ultrasonography of the abdomen

transduction (trăns-dŭk′shŭn) A phenomenon causing genetic recombination in bacteria in which DNA is carried from one bacterium to another by a bacteriophage. SEE: *transformation.*

    protein t. ABBR: PZ. The delivery or insertion of proteins into cells to influence cellular function. It is usually accomplished by linking the protein to a molecule that can penetrate cell membranes.

signal t. Biochemical conversion that is part of a process, such as the docking of hormone to receptor, stimulating cellular production of specific enzymes or other proteins.

transection, transsection (tran-sek′shŏn) [*trans-* + *section*] A cutting made across a long axis; a cross section.

trans fat SEE: under *fat*.

trans-fatty acid SEE: under *acid*.

transfection (trans-fĕk′shŭn) The infection of bacteria by purified phage DNA.

transfer (trans′fĕr) [L. *transferre*, to carry across] The state in which the symptoms of one area are transmitted to a similar area.

autologous fat t. Fat **t.**

bilateral t. The ability to learn a motor skill that one had previously mastered with one limb (usually the dominant hand) with the limb on the opposite side of the body (typically, the nondominant hand).

blastocyst t. An assisted reproduction technique in which a zygote created by in vitro fertilization is incubated in the laboratory to the pre-embryonic stage of the blastocyst before being placed in the uterus.

egg t. The transfer of eggs retrieved from ovarian follicles into the fallopian tubes. SEE: *gamete intrafallopian **t.***

embryo t. Placement of embryos into the uterus through the cervix after in vitro fertilization (IVF) or, in the case of gamete intrafallopian transfer (GIFT), into the fallopian tubes. Fertilization is usually done by placing the sperm and ovum in a special culture tube. SEE: *gamete intrafallopian **t.***; *in vitro fertilization; GIFT; surrogate mother*.

fat t. The implantation of body fat into locations with irregular body contours, e.g., soft tissue defects or hollows that are left behind after the excision of tumors. The implanted body fat is used to fill the volume of tissue removed during the procedure. Fat transfer is also frequently used to rejuvenate the appearance of the aging face. SYN: *autologous fat **t.***

free-tissue t. Surgical relocation of one part of the body to another in order to repair a visible defect. The body part and its supporting blood vessels are sutured into their new location (often a defect created by trauma or by excision of a malignant tumor.

gamete intrafallopian t. ABBR: GIFT. A procedure to help infertile couples conceive. After ovulation is induced, ova are retrieved from a mature follicle via laparoscopy and are transferred along with sperm to the woman's fallopian tube to facilitate fertilization.

SEE: *embryo **t.**; in vitro fertilization; zygote intrafallopian **t.***

gas t. The movement of respiratory gases (carbon dioxide, nitrogen, or oxygen) from the alveoli of the lung to the pulmonary capillaries or from the pulmonary capillaries to the alveoli.

gene t. Removal of a gene from one organism and its insertion into another.

linear energy t. A measure of the rate of energy transfer from ionizing radiation to soft tissue.

magnetization t. In magnetic resonance imaging, a technique that improves imaging of the white matter of the brain.

nuclear t. The removal of DNA from a cell for placement into an egg (e.g., during cloning).

ooplasmic t. Insertion of a donor egg's cytoplasm, along with donor sperm, into the egg of another woman. Ooplasmic transfer is used to treat infertility and results in the development of embryos with two different sources of maternal mitochondrial DNA.

passive t. of antibodies 1. The injection of immunoglobulins from one organism into another. 2. The transfer of protective antibodies from mother to fetus (via the placenta) or from mother to newborn (in breast milk).

somatic cell nuclear t. In cloning, the transfer of genetic material from a differentiated, adult cell into an egg.

zygote intrafallopian t. ABBR: ZIFT. An in vitro fertilization technique in which a woman's ova are surgically removed and mixed with her partner's sperm. The resulting zygotes are placed in her fallopian tube. SEE: *embryo **t.**; in vitro fertilization; GIFT*.

transferase (trăns′fĕr-ās) An enzyme that catalyzes the transfer of atoms or groups of atoms from one chemical compound to another.

gamma glutamyl t. ABBR: GGT. An enzyme present in the liver and biliary tree that is used to diagnose liver, gallbladder, and pancreatic diseases. Elevated levels of GGT are often found in people who use drugs (such as alcohol) that are metabolized by the liver.

transfer board SEE: under *board*.

transference (trans-fĕr′ĕns) [L. *transferre*, to carry across] 1. In psychotherapy, the mental process whereby a person transfers patterns of feelings and behavior that had previously been experienced with important figures such as parents or siblings to another person. Quite often these feelings are shifted to the caregiver.

transfer factor SEE: under *factor*.

transferrin (trăns-fĕr′ĭn) A globulin that binds and transports iron.

transferring (trăns′fĕr-ĭng″) Moving a person with limited function from one location to another. This may be accomplished by the patient or with assistive devices.

transfix (trăns-fĭks') [" + *figere,* to fix] To pierce through or impale with a sharp instrument.

transfixion (trăns-fĭk'shŭn) A maneuver in performing an amputation in which a knife is passed into the soft parts and cutting is from within outward.

transforation (trăns″for-ā'shŭn) [" + *forare,* to pierce] The perforation of the fetal skull at the base in craniotomy.

transforator (trăns′for-ā″tor) An instrument for perforating the fetal skull.

transformant (trans-for′mănt) A cell or organism that has been genetically modified.

transformation (trăns″for-mā'shŭn) [" + *formatio,* a forming] **1.** Change of shape or form. **2.** In oncology, the change of one tissue into another. SEE: *metastasis.* **3.** In bacterial genetics, the acquisition of bacterial DNA fragments by other bacterial cells; antibiotic resistance is often acquired this way.

transformation zone Any area of the body where squamous epithelium meets columnar epithelium. SEE: *squamocolumnar junction.*

transformer (trăns-form′er) [" + *formare,* to form] A stationary induction apparatus to change electrical energy at one voltage and current to electrical energy at another voltage and current through the medium of magnetic energy, without mechanical motion.

    step-down t. A transformer that changes electricity to a lower voltage.

    step-up t. A transformer that changes electricity to a higher voltage.

transfuse (trăns-fūz′) To infuse blood or blood products.

transfusion (trans-fū'zhŏn) [L. *transfusio,* a pouring out] **1.** The collection of blood or a blood component from a donor followed by its infusion into a recipient. In the U.S. more than 12 million blood products are transfused each year. SEE: *intraosseous infusion.* **2.** The injection of saline or other solutions into a vein for a therapeutic purpose.

⚠️ Although the risk of contracting infectious diseases from blood in Europe and North America is very small, transfusions are still associated with considerable hazards. These include the risk of allergic reactions, transfusion reactions, fluid overload, iron overload, hemolysis, alloimmunization, lung injury, and the increased likelihood of dying from a critical illness.

    allogeneic blood t. ABBR: ABT. Transfusion of blood cells from one person to another.

    autologous blood t. **1.** The collection of a patient's own blood before surgery, to be used if the patient needs a transfusion during or after the surgery, to reduce the possibility of needing banked blood, and with it the risk of having a transfusion reaction or contracting a transmissible infection. SEE: *blood doping.*

    PATIENT CARE: The usual blood transfusion checks are performed: the patient's armband name and number are verified by comparing them with those on the chart; the number and blood type of the unit of blood are checked against those of the patient; and the number and blood type of the unit of blood should match that information on all the paperwork.

    blood t. The replacement of blood or one of its components. Effective and safe transfusion therapy requires a thorough understanding of the clinical condition being treated. Most patients require blood components rather than whole blood. SEE: *blood component therapy* for table; *autologous blood t.; exchange t.; transfusion reaction; Standard Precautions Appendix.*

    The following measures should be taken during transfusion therapy: screening donors for transmissible diseases; testing blood for pathogens; ensuring that cross-matched blood products are given to correctly identified patients; intervening promptly in transfusion reactions; avoiding unnecessary transfusions; avoiding volume overload during transfusions; and avoiding hypothermia, electrolyte, and clotting disorders.

    Administration of a single unit may be indicated in young or old surgical patients, in those with coronary disease, and in patients who have an acute blood loss of several units but whose blood pressure, pulse, and oxygen are stabilized by use of one unit.

    The risk of HIV, HBV, or HCV on blood collected and distributed in the U.S. is very low.

    PATIENT CARE: The patient is identified from both the hospital identification band and blood bank band. Two health care professionals (one the administering nurse) verify the patient's ABO and Rh blood type and its compatibility with the unit of blood or packed cells to be administered, as well as the unit's expiration date and time. Outdated blood is not used; it is returned to the blood bank for disposal. The blood or blood product is retrieved from the blood bank refrigerator immediately before administration because blood should not be stored in other than approved refrigerators. Blood cannot be returned to blood bank storage if the unit's temperature exceeds 50°F (10°C), a change that will occur within about 30 min of removal from storage.

Before the transfusion is started, the patient's vital signs (including temperature) are checked and recorded. The blood is inspected visually for clots or discoloration, and the transfusion is administered through an approved line containing a blood filter, preferably piggybacked through physiological saline solution on a Y-type blood administration set. No other intravenous solutions or drugs should be infused with blood (unless specifically prescribed) because of potential incompatibility. In the first 15 min, the blood flow rate is slowed to limit intake to no more than 50 mL. A health care professional remains with the patient during this time and instructs the patient to report any adverse reactions, e.g. back or chest pain, hypotension, fever, increase in temperature of more than 1.8°F (1°C), chills, pain at the infusion site, tachycardia, tachypnea, wheezing, cyanosis, urticaria, or rashes. If any of these occurs, the transfusion is stopped immediately; the vein is kept open with physiological saline solution, and the patient's physician and the blood bank are notified. If incompatibility is suspected, the blood and set are returned to the blood bank; samples of the patient's blood and urine are obtained for laboratory analysis of: hemoglobin in the urine; prothrombin time/international normalized ratio (protime/INR); blood culture; complete blood count; chemistries; and identifying data are recorded from the unit. If no symptoms occur in the first 15 min and vital signs remain stable, the transfusion rate is increased to complete the tranfusion within the prescribed time, or (if necessary) the transfusion is administered as fast as the patient's overall condition permits. Once the transfusion begins, the blood is administered within a maximum of 4 hr to maintain biological effectiveness and limit the risk of bacterial growth. (If the patient's condition does not permit transfusing the prescribed amount within this time frame, arrangements are made to have the blood bank split the unit and properly store the second portion.) The patient's vital signs and response are monitored every 30 min during the transfusion and 30 min afterward; stated precautions are observed, and caregivers monitor for indications of volume overload (distended neck veins, bounding pulse, hypertension, dyspnea). Blood should not be administered through a central line unless an approved in-line warming device is used. A warmer should also be used whenever multiple transfusions place the patient at risk for hypothermia, which can lead to dysrhythmias and cardiac arrest. Pa-

tients planning elective surgery, e.g., hip, knee replacement, hysterectomy. may bank one or two units of their own blood in the weeks before surgery for use if needed. Blood-saving devices are also used in such surgeries, and this blood is returned to the patient before he or she leaves the operating theater.

cadaveric blood t. A transfusion using blood obtained from a cadaver shortly after death.

direct t. The transfer of blood directly from one person to another.

exchange t. The removal of a patient's entire blood volume (as in sickle cell disease, thrombotic thrombocytopenic purpura, hemolytic disease of the newborn) and its replacement with blood donated by others. SYN: *replacement t.*

feto-fetal t. Twin-twin **t.**

granulocyte t. ABBR: GTX. The transfusion of mature granulocytic white blood cells for use in infected patients with severe neutropenia (an absolute neutrophil count < 500 cells/mL). GTX is used primarily to treat patients with refractory infections due to neutropenia caused by cancer chemotherapy or stem cell transplantation.

indirect t. A transfusion of blood from a donor to a suitable storage container and then to the patient.

intrauterine t. The infusion of blood cells into a fetus, to treat prenatal diseases such as erythroblastosis fetalis.

massive t. The replacement of at least half of a person's blood cells in less than a day.

⚠ Common complications include the dilution of coagulation proteins and platelets (increasing the probability of bleeding); a decrease in the plasma calcium concentration (transfused blood is stored in citrate, which binds calcium); metabolic alkalosis (citrate generates bicarbonate); hypothermia (blood is stored cold and must be warmed before it is infused); and alterations in the serum concentration of potassium.

PATIENT CARE: To address complications of massive transfusion in the acutely bleeding patient, the patient's vital signs, complete blood count, serum chemistries, acid/base balance and prothrombin time/partial thromboplastin time (PT/PTT) should be monitored frequently. Coagulation factors, donated plasma, platelets, and electrolytes should be given as indicated by test results.

replacement t. Exchange **t.**

single unit t. The infusion of one unit of packed red blood cells (PRBCs). On average, one unit of PRBCs will increase the hemoglobin level by 1 g/dL.

twin-twin t. A complication of monochorionic multiple pregnancies in which one fetus receives a greater flow of blood than the other from the placenta. It is diagnosed by fetal ultrasonography: one twin's amniotic sac has polyhydramnios (excessive amniotic fluid), while the other twin's sac has oligohydramnios (insufficient amniotic fluid). Death of one or both twins will occur without intervention. Treatments include repeated amniocenteses, laser therapy to prevent the exchange of blood between twins, or intrauterine surgery. SYN: *feto-fetal t.*

transfusion reaction An adverse response to a transfusion caused by the presence of foreign antigens, antibodies, or cytokines. There are three basic types of true transfusion reactions and several other complications of transfusion therapy.

Hemolytic reactions occur when ABO-incompatible blood is given; antibodies or complement (or both), coat blood cells, stimulating hemolysis by macrophages and neutrophils. These reactions occur in less than 1% of all blood transfusions. In acute hemolytic reactions, patients develop fever, chills, nausea, flank pain, hypotension, flushing, and hematuria within 20 min after the transfusion has begun. Delayed reactions develop 3 to 14 days later; the patient presents with fever, jaundice, and a decreased hemoglobin level. In rare cases, disseminated intravascular coagulopathy, respiratory distress syndrome, acute renal tubular necrosis, and/or death may occur.

Allergic reactions occur when patients have been sensitized to foreign antigens on proteins in the blood or plasma. A history of allergies is usually present, indicating the patient has developed immunoglobulin E antibodies to allergens. Patients develop itching and hives. Mild allergic reactions can be prevented or treated with antihistamines; the use of washed red blood cells (RBCs), which have fewer antigens, also reduces the risk of allergic reactions. Very rarely, systemic anaphylaxis occurs, as indicated by severe hypotension, and wheezing.

Febrile reactions are the result of cytokine release by leukocytes while the blood was being stored. Antipyretics are used to treat the transient fever that appears; the use of fresh blood and leukocyte-poor RBC transfusion also reduces the risk of a febrile response.

Other problems associated with blood transfusions include circulatory overload (the most common transfusion reaction). Bacterial, viral, and protozoal infections may occasionally be transmitted by transfusions, and some patients may suffer a graft-versus-host reaction after receiving blood products. The ability to screen blood for antibodies to hepatitis and human immunodeficiency virus has decreased the risk of acquiring these diseases through blood transfusion; however, malaria and bacterial infections can still occasionally be transmitted if the donor is asymptomatic. The acute pulmonary edema caused by circulatory overload can be diagnosed by the crackles, gurgles, and wheezes on auscultation of the chest, severe difficulty in breathing, frothy sputum, decreased oxygen saturation, and abnormal findings on chest x-rays. Immunosuppressed patients may receive irradiated blood to prevent activation of donor leukocytes and graft-versus-host disease.

PATIENT CARE: Hemolytic blood transfusion reactions are prevented by labeling the patient's blood sample for typing and cross-matching; double-checking the patient's name and identification number at the time of transfusion is essential. Antihistamines and antipyretics may be given to patients with a history of multiple blood transfusions, allergies, or a previous febrile transfusion reaction. Patients at risk for circulatory overload are placed in an upright position before the transfusion is started, and the blood is administered very slowly; packed RBCs create less risk than whole blood but also must be transfused over several hours.

All patients receiving blood transfusions should be monitored for an adverse response. Transfusions should be initiated by infusing 50 mL during the first 15 min to detect and prevent severe reactions. The patient is told to report any symptoms experienced during this initial period. Vital signs including temperature are checked. The flow rate is only increased if the initial infusion is completed without complications. Vital signs and clinical responses continue to be monitored at least every 30 min throughout the transfusion. If a reaction occurs, the infusion is stopped immediately, but an intravenous line is kept patent with saline. A description of the patient's signs or symptoms, and the blood container and tubing, are sent to the blood bank; blood and urine samples are sent to the laboratory for analysis. In many hospitals, a specialty transfusion nurse is assigned to supervise transfusions and educate staff about policies, procedures, and guidelines to optimize transfusion safety.

transfusion syndrome, multiple Bleeding that results from the transfusion of multiple units of blood. SEE: *posttransfusion syndrome.*

transfusion-transmitted bacterial infection (trans-fū′zhŏn-trans-mit′ĕd) SEE: under *infection*.

transfusion trigger A colloquial term for the point at which the risks associated with low hematocrit or hemoglobin levels outweigh the risks of adverse reactions associated with a blood transfusion.

PATIENT CARE: The concept of a transfusion trigger is controversial. Some medical authorities recommend transfusions only for patients who are actively compromised by bleeding rather than to adjust for specific levels of hemoglobin or hematocrit. Risks also include those associated with infectious diseases.

transgendered (trans-jen′dĕrd, tranz-) Having a gender identity or gender perception different from one's phenotypic gender.

transgene (trans′jēn″, tranz′) [*trans-* + *gene*] A genetic sequence taken from one organism and inserted into the DNA or RNA of another.

transgenerational (tranz″jĕn-ĕ-rā′shŏn-ăl) [*trans-* + *generational*] Having an effect on several generations of a family. **transgenerationally** (′shŏn-ă-lē), *adv.*

transgenerational design The design of products, workplaces, health care institutions, and residences so as to allow people to use them functionally regardless of the physical or sensory restrictions that they may develop as they age.

transgenic (trans″jen′ik, tranz″) [*trans-* + *-genic*] Pert. to an organism into which hereditary material from another organism has been introduced.

transglutaminase (trans″gloot′ă-mĭ-nās″) [*trans-* + *glutaminase*] Any of a family of enzymes that cross-link proteins or peptides to one another. It is colloquially called *meat glue*.

transient (tran′zē-ĕnt) [L. *transire*, to go by, go across] Not lasting; of brief duration.

transient hypogammaglobulinemia of infancy SEE: under *hypogammaglobulinemia*.

transient hypoglobulinemia (hī″pō-glob″yŭ-lĭn-ēm′ē-ă) Low levels of the immunoglobulin G (IgG) class antibody occurring when an infant is between 5 and 6 months of age. The maternal IgG that has crossed the placenta begins to drop after birth and reaches its lowest level (about 350 mg/dL) at this point. If IgG production is decreased, transient hypogammaglobulinemia develops. Normal blood levels of B cells, IgA, and IgM usually are present, which differentiates this transient disorder from hereditary, X-linked hypogammaglobulinemia. Some infants develop recurrent infections and must be treated with intravenous gamma globulin (IVIG) until IgG production increases.

transient ischemic attack SEE: under *attack*.

transient left ventricular apical ballooning Takotsubo **cardiomyopathy**.

transiliac (trăns-ĭl′ē-ăk) [L. *trans,* across, + *iliacus,* pert. to ilium] Extending between the two ilia.

transilient (trăns-sĭl′ē-ĕnt) Jumping across or passing over as occurs when nerve fibers in the brain link nonadjacent convolutions.

transillumination (trans″ĭ-loo″mĭ-nā′shŏn) [*trans-* + *illumination*] Inspection of a cavity or organ by passing a light through its walls. When pus or a lesion is present, the transmission of light is diminished or absent. Transillumination is used esp. on the breast to identify masses that may be malignant. SYN: *diaphanography; light scanning*.

transischiac (trăns-ĭs′kē-ăk) Across or between the ischia of the pelvis.

transition (trans-ish′ŏn, tranz-) [L. *transitio,* a going across] **1.** Passage from one state or position to another, from one part to another part, or a change in health status, roles, family, abilities, or employment. Transitions often require adaptations within the person, the group, or the environment and define the need for and context of nursing care. **2.** In obstetrics, the final phase of the first stage of labor. Cervical dilation is 8 to 10 cm and strong uterine contractions occur every 1.5 to 2 min and persist for 60 to 90 sec. Accompanying behavioral changes include increasing irritability and anxiety, declining coping abilities, and expressions of a strong desire for the labor to be ended immediately. SYN: *care transition*.

transitional (trăn-zĭsh′ŭn-ăl) Pert. to or marked by change.

transitional year In graduate medical education, a structured educational experience in a general field of study prior to enrollment in a medical or surgical specialty.

transition state In a chemical reaction, the unstable structures and energies of the reactants that result from the weakening of chemical bonds and separation of atoms before they recombine as new compounds.

transition zone of the prostate The central area of the prostate gland. Glandular overgrowth here is responsible for symptoms of bladder obstruction, urinary frequency, and nighttime urination, symptoms of benign prostatic hypertrophy. Relatively fewer cancers start here than at the outer borders of the gland.

transitive movement SEE: under *movement*.

transjugular (trănz-jŭg′ū-lĕr) Through the jugular vein.

transkaryotic (trănz″kăr-ē-ŏt′ĭk) Binding or attachment (e.g., of white blood cells as they migrate through tissues).

translabial (trănz″lā′bē-ĭl) Through or across the labia majora; used for radiological examinations that penetrate the labial and vaginal tissues to examine the uterus, fallopian tubes, and ovaries.

translation (trans-lā′shŏn, tranz-) [L. *translatus,* carried across, transferred (the perfect participle of *transferre*)] **1.** The synthesis of proteins under the direction of ribonucleic acid. **2.** A change from one place to another or a conversion from one form into another.

translator (tranz′lāt″ŏr) [L. *translatus,* carried across, transferred)] **1.** A person or machine that renders from one written work or computer program into another. **2.** Interpreter.

translocation (trăns″lō-kā′shŭn) [″ + *locus,* place] **1.** The alteration of a chromosome by transfer of a portion of it either to another chromosome or to another portion of the same chromosome. The latter is called shift or intrachange. When two chromosomes interchange material, it is called reciprocal translocation. **2.** Movement of bacteria across the intestinal wall to invade the body. **3.** The linear motion of one structure across the parallel surface of another.

translucent (trăns-lū′sĕnt) [″ + *lucens,* shining] Not transparent but permitting passage of light.

transluminal (trănz-lū′mĭ-năl) Within or through the internal bore or cylindrical channel within a blood vessel.

transmethylase (trans″meth′ĭ-lās″) Methyltransferase.

transmethylation (trăns″mĕth-ĭ-lā′shŭn) The process in the metabolism of amino acids in which a methyl group is transferred from one compound to another; for example, the conversion in the body of homocysteine to methionine. In this case, the methyl group is furnished by choline or betaine.

transmigration (trănz″mī-grā′shŭn) [″ + *migrare,* to move from place to place] Wandering across or through, esp. the passage of white blood cells through capillary membranes into the tissues.

   external t. Transfer of an ovum from an ovary to an opposite tube through the pelvic cavity.

   internal t. Transfer of an ovum through the uterus to the opposite oviduct.

transmissible (trăns-mĭs′ă-bl) [L. *transmissio,* a sending across] Capable of transmission, as from animals to humans or from person to person, e.g., an infectious disease.

transmission (trans-mish′ŏn) **1.** The passage of a disease from one person to another. **2.** The passage of genetic material from parent to child.

   airborne t. Transmission of infectious organisms by aerosol or dust par-

ticles. Diseases spread by airborne transmission include varicella-zoster virus and tuberculosis.

   biological t. A condition in which the organism that transmits the causative agent of a disease plays an essential role in the life history of a parasite or germ.

   common vehicle t. Transmission of infectious germs on contaminated objects, substances, or surfaces touched by two or more people.

   direct t. Transmission of infection of one person through contact with another.

   droplet t. Transmission of infectious germs in airborne fluids, e.g., the liquid particles released during coughing or sneezing.

   duplex t. Transmission of impulses through a nerve trunk in both directions by sensory and motor neurons.

   horizontal t. **1.** Transmission of a disease between sexual partners. **2.** The acquisition of an infection by individuals of the same generation. SEE: *vertical t.*

   indirect t. Transmission of an infection from one person to another through an intermediary agent, e.g., air or water, a contaminated surface, or a living disease vector.

   mechanical t. The passive transmission of causative agents of disease, esp. by arthropods. This may be indirect, as when flies pick up organisms from excreta of humans or animals and deposit them on food, or direct, as when they pick up organisms from the body of a diseased individual and directly inoculate them into the body of another individual by bites or through open sores. SEE: *vector.*

   perinatal t. The transmission of an infectious illness from mother to infant during childbirth.

   placental t. The transmission of substances in the mother's blood to the blood of the fetus by way of the placenta.

   synaptic t. The release of a neurotransmitter by a neuron that initiates or inhibits an electrical impulse in the next neuron in the pathway.

   transovarial t. The transmission of causative agents of disease to offspring following invasion of the ovary and infection of eggs; occurs in ticks and mites.

   vertical t. **1.** In certain insects, transovarial transmission of infection from one generation to the next. **2.** In mammals, transmission of infection from the mother's body fluids to the infant either in utero, during delivery, or during the neonatal period (via breast milk).

transmission-based precautions Measures suggested by the Centers for Disease Control and Prevention to reduce the risk of airborne, droplet, and direct-contact transmission of infection in hospitals. SEE: *Standard Precautions Appendix.*

transmission control protocol/internet protocol ABBR: TCP/IP. The standard communication algorithm that governs and facilitates data transmission on the Internet and on many private computing networks.

transmural (trăns-mū′răl) [L. *trans,* across, + *murus,* a wall] Across the wall of an organ or structure, as in transmural myocardial infarction, in which the tissue in the entire thickness of a portion of the cardiac wall dies.

transmutation (trăns″mū-tā′shŭn) [L. *transmutatio,* a changing across] **1.** A mutation. **2.** In physics, the alteration of an element's nucleus, usually by bombarding it with subatomic particles.

transnasal tube (tranz″nā′zăl) [*trans-* + *nasal*] A tube passed through the nose, e.g., into the gastrointestinal tract for feeding, or into the trachea, for ventilation.

transocular (trăns-ŏk′ū-lăr) [″ + *oculus,* eye] Across the eye.

transonance (trăns′ō-năns) [L. *trans,* across + *sonans,* sounding] The transmission of sounds through an organ, as heart sounds through the lungs and chest wall.

transorbital (trăns-or′bĭ-tăl) [″ + *orbita,* track] Passing through the orbit of the eye.

transovarial passage (trăns-ō-vā′rē-ăl) The passage of infectious or toxic agents into the ovary, a process that might invade and infect the oocytes.

transparent (trăns-păr′ĕnt) [″ + *parere,* to appear] **1.** Transmitting light rays so that objects are visible through the substance. **2.** Pervious to radiant energy. **3.** In medical ethics, openly and publicly discussed; available for review by disinterested parties.

transpeptidase (trans-pep′tĭ-dās″) [*trans-* + *peptidase*] An enzyme that catalyzes the transfer of a peptide from one compound to another.

    gamma-glutamyl t. A tissue enzyme whose level is elevated in patients with many conditions that damage the liver, including excessive alcohol consumption or the use of certain drugs, such as phenytoin or barbiturates.

transperitoneal (trăns″pĕr-ĭ-tō-nē′ăl) Across or through the peritoneum.

transphosphorylase (trăns-fŏs-for′ĭ-lās) An enzyme that catalyzes the transfer of a phosphate group from one compound to another.

transphosphorylation (trăns-fŏs″for-ĭ-lā′shŭn) The exchange of phosphate groups from one compound to another.

transpiration (trăns″pī-rā′shŭn) [″ + *spirare,* to breathe] The passage of water or a vapor through a membrane. SEE: *perspiration.*

    cutaneous t. The insensible evaporation of water vapor through the skin.

    pulmonary t. The evaporation of water from the alveolar cells into the air in the lungs.

transpire (trăn-spīr′) To emit vapor through the skin or other tissues. SEE: *perspire.*

transplacental (trăns″plă-sĕn′tăl) Through the placenta, esp. penetration of the placenta by a toxin, chemical, or organism that would affect the fetus.

transplant (trans′plant″) [L. *transplantare,* to remove, transplant] **1.** To transfer tissue or an organ from one part to another (or from one body to another) as in grafting or plastic surgery. **2.** A piece of tissue or organ used in transplantation.

    corneal t. The implantation of a cornea from a healthy donor eye. This is the most common organ transplantation procedure in the U.S. There are two major types of procedures. Lamellar keratoplasty, or split-thickness graft, involves removing a portion of the anterior host cornea and attaching a partial thickness of the donor cornea. Penetrating keratoplasty, or full-thickness graft, involves complete removal of the patient's cornea and replacement with the donor cornea.

    Transmission of donor disease to the recipient is rare, but rabies, Creutzfeldt-Jakob disease, and hepatitis B have been acquired by graft recipients. The technique is more likely to be successful when histocompatibility matching of donor and recipient is as close as possible. The success rate is more than 90% at 1 year. SEE: *keratoplasty.*

    PATIENT CARE: *Preoperative:* The surgical transplant procedure is explained, including duration (1 hr), the need to remain still throughout the procedure, and expected sensations. A preoperative sedative is given.

    Postoperative: Evidence of any sudden, sharp, or excessive pain; bloody, purulent, or clear viscous drainage; or fever must be reported immediately. Prescribed corticosteroid eye drops or topical antibiotics are administered to prevent inflammation and graft rejection, and prescribed analgesics are provided as necessary. A calm, restful environment is provided, and the patient is instructed to lie on the back or on the unaffected side, with the head of the bed flat or slightly elevated according to protocol. Rapid head movements, hard coughing or sneezing, or any other activities that could increase intraocular pressure should be avoided, and the patient should not squint or rub the eyes. Assistance is provided with standing or walking until the patient adjusts to vision changes, and personal items should be within the patient's field of vision.

    Both patient and family are taught to recognize signs of graft rejection (such as inflammation, cloudiness, drainage, and pain at the graft site) and to report such signs immediately. Graft rejection may occur years after surgery; therefore, the graft must be assessed daily for the rest of the patient's life. The patient is encouraged to express his or her anxieties and concerns about graft rejection and is helped to develop effective coping behaviors to deal with these feelings and concerns. Photophobia is a common adverse reaction, but it will gradually decrease as healing progresses; patients are advised to wear dark glasses in bright light. The patient is taught how to correctly instill prescribed eye drops and should wear an eye shield when sleeping.

transplantar (trăns-plăn′tăr) [″ + *planta*, sole] Across the sole of the foot.

transplantation (trans″plan′tā′shŏn) **1.** The grafting of living tissue from its normal position to another site or the transferring of an organ or tissue from one person to another. Organs and tissues successfully transplanted include the heart, lung, kidney, liver, pancreas, cornea, large blood vessels, tendon, cartilage, skin, bone, and bone marrow. Brain tissue has been implanted experimentally to treat Parkinson disease. The matching of histocompatibility antigens that differentiate one person's cells from another's helps prevent rejection of donated tissues. Cyclosporine, tacrolimus, corticosteroids, monoclonal antibodies, and other immunosuppressive agents have been approx. 80% effective in preventing rejection of transplanted organs for 2 or more years. SEE: *autotransplantation; graft; heart t.; organ donation; renal t.; replantation.*

⚠️ Patients who have received organ transplants and who are maintained on immunosuppressant drugs should generally avoid vaccination with live, attenuated organisms unless these vaccinations are specifically approved by their health care providers. Inactive vaccines are usually preferable for these patients.

2. In dentistry, the transfer of a tooth from one alveolus to another.

allogeneic t. Transplantation of material from a donor to another person.

autologous chondrocyte t. Autologous chondrocyte **implantation**.

autologous t. Transplantation of tissue or cells from one location in the body to another site.

autologous bone marrow t. ABBR: ABMT. The harvesting and preservation of a patient's own blood-forming cells, followed by their eventual reintroduction into a patient. The procedure may be used to treat a variety of cancers

and blood disorders. Current practice is to mobilize stem cells into the blood stream with growth factors and then to collect and filter the blood by leukapheresis. In leukapheresis stem cells are identified by a cell surface antigen called CD34. After desirable blood-forming cells with this antigen are removed from the patient's blood, high-dose chemotherapy, monoclonal antibody therapy, or radiation may be used to purge the marrow of diseased cells. Healthy CD34+ cells capable of rebuilding the bone marrow are then returned to the patient and stimulated to reproduce. SYN: *autologous hematopoietic stem cell t.*

autologous hematopoietic stem cell t. Autologous bone marrow **t.**

autoplastic t. Transplantation of tissue from one part to another part of the same body.

bone marrow t. ABBR: BMT. Transplantation of blood-forming stem cells from the bone marrow from one person to another (allogeneic transplantation), or from a person to him or herself (autologous transplantation). It is used in treating aplastic anemia, thalassemia and sickle cell anemia, immunodeficiency disorders, acute leukemia, chronic myelogenous leukemia, non-Hodgkin lymphoma, Hodgkin disease, and testicular cancer, and after radiation therapy, as indicated.

double t. Tandem **t.**

fat t. In cosmetic surgery, the movement of adipose tissue from one body site to another to augment structure, change body contours, or reduce skin wrinkling.

hair t. A surgical procedure for placing plugs of skin containing hair follicles from one body site to another. This time-consuming technique is used to treat baldness.

heart t. Surgical transplantation of the heart from a patient who died of trauma or a disease that left the heart intact and capable of functioning in the recipient. The only absolute contraindications are uncontrollable cancer or infection, irreversible pulmonary vascular disease, or a separate life-threatening disease; in general, however, patients over 65, those with severe renal or liver disease, and those with a history of noncompliance with medical regimens do not receive heart transplants. The major barrier to heart transplantation is the lack of donors; the number of potential recipients is approx. 10 times the number of donors each year.

After receiving a heart transplant, continuous immunosuppression with cyclosporine, corticosteroids, or related drugs is required to prevent rejection of the donated organ. Acute episodes of rejection are treated with monoclonal antibodies (OKT3) or antilymphocyte immune globulin. Clinical signs of rejection (fatigue, dyspnea, hypotension, and extra heart sounds) are nonspecific; therefore biopsies are performed frequently during the first 2 years after surgery. Average patient survival is greater than 75% 1 year after the surgery, and greater than 50% after 10 years. SEE: *rejection* (2).

hematopoietic cell t. ABBR: HCT. Removal of blood-forming cells from one person and their infusion into another. It is used primarily but not exclusively to treat leukemias and lymphomas.

heteroplastic t. Transplantation of a part from one individual to another individual of an unrelated species.

heterotopic t. Transplantation in which the transplant is placed in a different location in the host than it had been in the donor.

homotopic t. Transplantation in which the transplant occupies the same location in the host as it had in the donor.

kidney t. Renal **t.**

liver t. Surgical implantation of a donor liver into a patient with end-stage liver disease. The disease may be caused by alcoholic cirrhosis, chronic cholestatic diseases, chronic or fulminant hepatitis, or toxic liver destruction. Immunosuppressive drugs (such as cyclosporine) must be taken after the procedure to prevent rejection of the grafted organ. With optimal care, about 75% of grafted livers remain functional after 1 yr. Patients with HIV or uncontrolled systemic infections, metastatic cancer, active alcoholism, or other severe cardiac, pulmonary, or neurological illnesses are not candidates for the procedure. In the U.S. about 4000 liver transplants are performed annually.

lung t. Grafting of a donor lung into a recipient with end-stage lung disease, usually caused by pulmonary fibrosis, chronic obstructive lung disease, or pulmonary hypertension. Lung transplantation may be performed as a single-organ operation or as part of a combined heart-lung transplantation, e.g., in congenital heart disease. Immunosuppressive therapy with cyclosporine or tacrolimus, azathioprine, and corticosteroids is necessary to minimize the risk of rejection, which is caused by T lymphocyte activity against the donor tissue. Rejection is diagnosed through the use of bronchial biopsies and pulmonary function tests. Acute rejection, characterized by dyspnea, fever, hypoxemia, rales, and tachypnea, must be differentiated from infection. Chronic rejection, a problem in 25% to 50% of cases, presents as bronchiolitis obliterans and oc-

curs 6 to 14 months after the transplant. Flow rates progressively decrease, with few additional symptoms; bronchodilator therapy is not effective, and giving higher doses of immunosuppressives has mixed success. Sixty percent of lung transplant recipients live 2 years.

renal t. Grafting of a kidney from a living donor or from a cadaver to someone with renal failure. It is used as the definitive form of renal replacement for patients with kidney failure. Tissue typing for human leukocyte antigens (HLAs) as well as ABO blood groups is used to decrease the likelihood of acute or chronic rejection. Family members are often the best-matched donors. In patients with diabetes mellitus, combined renal and pancreatic transplants are sometimes performed with a very high likelihood of success. The high success rate of kidney transplants (85% to 95% at 2 years) is due to immunosuppressive drugs such as corticosteroids, cyclosporine, mycophenolate, and tacrolimus. Because cyclosporine is nephrotoxic, careful monitoring of serum drug levels after transplantation is required. SYN: *kidney t.* SEE: *major histocompatibility complex; suppressive immunotherapy; Nursing Diagnoses Appendix.*

small intestine t. A semi-experimental procedure in which the small intestine is replaced with a donor organ.

split-liver t. ABBR: SLT. Surgical division of a donor liver into two parts, each of which is implanted into a different recipient.

syngeneic t. A specific type of allogeneic transplantation of material between identical twins.

tandem t. The use of sequential bone marrow transplants to treat cancer. An initial autologous transplant is followed by a second, e.g., if remission is not achieved after the first transplant. SYN: *double t.*

t. of the pancreas The implantation of a part of the pancreas (such as cells of the islets of Langerhans) or the entire gland from a donor into a patient whose own pancreas is no longer functioning. In the diabetic patient, pancreas transplantation provides an endogenous source of insulin and may be combined with kidney transplantation. The risks of the surgery and the immunosuppression associated with transplantation must be weighed against the kidney, nerve, and retinal damage associated with uncontrolled diabetes mellitus. Some potential complications of the procedure include infections, blood clotting in the vessels that supply the graft, hypoglycemia, bladder injury, and organ rejection. To prevent rejection, immunosuppressive drugs, such as tacrolimus, mycophenolate mofetil, cyclosporine, and corticosteroids, may be used. Episodes of rejection are treated with the monoclonal antibody OKT3. The 1-year survival rate of combined pancreas-kidney transplants is about 80%, when performed at institutions where the procedure is done frequently. SEE: *diabetes mellitus; rejection.*

transpleural (trăns-ploor'răl) Through the pleura.

transport (trans'port″) [L. *transportare,* to carry across] Movement or transfer of substances. Transport may occur actively, passively, or with the assistance of a carrier.

   active t. The process by which a cell membrane moves molecules against a concentration or electrochemical gradient. This requires metabolic work, i.e., the expenditure of adenosine triphosphate. Potassium, for example, is maintained at high concentrations within cells and low concentrations in extracellular fluid by active transport. Other ions actively transported are sodium, calcium, hydrogen, iron, chloride, iodide, and urate. Several sugars and the amino acids are also actively transported in the small intestine.

   axonal t. The active (energy-dependent) process by which proteins and organelles are moved inside an axon. SYN: *axoplasmic t.*

   carrier-mediated active t. The movement of substances across cell membranes at the expense of adenosine triphosphate.

   protein t. The movement of proteins across cell membranes and into cellular organelles where they participate in specific functions or build the structures of the cell.

transportation of the injured Moving an injured person to a hospital or other treatment center. In serious injuries such as cranial and spinal trauma, airway compromise, and hemorrhage, the patient should be moved by properly trained support personnel with equipment to stabilize vital structures and prevent further injury. In particular, the airway should be secured, ventilation provided, circulation supported, and the spine protected from injury with specially designed appliances. It is crucial that critically injured persons receive care within the first hour of their injury to optimize their chances of survival. Patients with lesser injuries whose vital signs are relatively stable may be transported by ambulance litter, private vehicle, or wheelchair, or by means listed here.

   Carrying in arms: The patient is picked up in both arms, as the carrying of a child.

   One-arm assist: The patient's arm is placed about the neck of the bearer, and the bearer's arm is placed about the pa-tient's waist, thus assisting the patient to walk.

   Chair carry, chair stretcher: Any ordinary firm chair may be used. The patient is seated on the tilted-back chair. One bearer grasps the back of the chair and the other the legs of the chair (either the front or rear, depending on the construction of the chair). Both bearers face in the same direction.

   Fireman's drag: The patient's wrists are crossed and tied with a belt or rope. The bearer kneels alongside the patient, with his or her head under the patient's wrists, and walks on all fours, dragging the patient underneath.

   Fireman's lift: The bearer grasps the patient's left wrist with the right hand. The bearer's head is placed under the patient's left armpit, drawing the patient's body over the bearer's left shoulder. The bearer's left arm should encircle both thighs, then lift the patient. The patient's wrist is transferred to the bearer's left hand, thus leaving one hand free to remove obstacles or to open doors.

   Four-handed basket seat: Each of two bearers grasps own wrist and then grasps the partner's free wrist. The patient sits on this support.

   Pack-strap carry: The patient is supported along the bearer's back. The patient's right arm is brought over the bearer's right shoulder and held by the bearer's left hand. The patient's left arm is brought over the left shoulder and held by the bearer's right hand. The patient is thus carried on the back, with the arms resembling pack straps.

   Piggyback carry: The patient is supported along the bearer's back with the knees raised to the sides of the bearer's torso. This leaves the patient practically in a sitting position astride the bearer's back, with arms around the bearer's neck or trunk.

   Six- or eight-person carry: This is done as the three-person carry, except three or four bearers are on each side of the patient, thus dividing the patient's weight more uniformly.

   Three-handed basket seat: The bearer grasps his or her own wrist; the partner grasps the bearer's wrist and leaves one arm free for supporting the patient.

   Three- or four-person carry: This is the litter-type carry used by emergency squads. Three persons kneel on one side of the patient, place their hands under the patient, and lift up. The head bearer supports the patient's head and shoulders, the center bearer lifts the waist and hips, and the third bearer lifts both the lower extremities. A fourth person, if available, should help steady the patient while he or she is being lifted.

   Two-handed seat: The bearers kneel on either side of the patient. Each passes one arm around the patient's back (under the armpits) and the other arm under the knees and lifts the patient carefully in a sitting position.

Wheelchair, improvised: To make this, the legs of a chair, preferably one with arms, are fastened to parallel boards and skates or casters are attached to the bottom of the boards. A footrest can be made by attaching a broom handle or stick across the parallel boards in front of the chair.

Vehicles: If an ambulance is not available, stretchers can be improvised with ropes and chairs, ladders, or poles. The patient should always be tied to the stretcher during transportation. Several bearers will be necessary to assist entering and leaving the vehicle.

transporter associated with antigen processing ABBR: TAP. An intracellular protein that carries antigens to the endoplasmic reticulum of cells, where the antigens may be transformed for presentation.

transpose (trăns-pōz′) To change places (e.g., moving the insertion of a muscle or ligament to another site).

transposition (trănz″pō-zĭ′shŭn) [L. *trans*, across, + *positio*, a placing] **1.** A transfer of position from one spot to another. SYN: *metathesis*. **2.** Displacement of an organ, esp. a viscus, to the opposite side. **3.** Transplantation of a flap of tissue without severing it entirely from its original position until it has united in the new position.

transposition of the great vessels A fetal deformity of the heart in which the aorta arises from the right ventricle and the pulmonary artery arises from the left ventricle. SEE: *dextroposition of the great vessels.*

transposon (trans-pōz′on″) A genetic unit such as a DNA sequence that is transferred from one cell's genetic material to another. SYN: *movable genetic* **element**.

transpulmonary pressure (trans″pul′mŏ-ner″ē) SEE: under *pressure.*

transpupillary (trans-pū′pĭ-ler″ē) [*trans-* + *pupillary*] Through the pupil of the eye.

transpupillary thermotherapy, transpupillary thermal therapy ABBR: TTT. The use of an infrared laser to elevate the temperature of the retinal pigment epithelium to treat retinal diseases such as melanomas of the choroid, retinoblastoma, or the wet form of macular degeneration.

transradial (trans″rād′ē-ăl, tranz″) [*trans-* + *radial*] **1.** Through, via, or employing the radial artery, as during coronary angiography. **2.** Through, across, or below the radius of the arm, as in a prosthesis below the elbow.

transrectal (trănz-rĕk′tĭl) Into or through the rectum.

transrectal ultrasound SEE: under *ultrasound.*

transrenal DNA (trans″rēn′ăl, tranz″) [*trans-* + *renal*] ABBR: tr-DNA. Short sequences of nucleic acid base pairs, typically less than 180 base pairs in length, that are excreted and detected in the urine. They have been used as a means of diagnosing a variety of malignant and infectious diseases.

trans-retinal (trăns-rĕt′ĭ-năl) The form of retinal created when light strikes the retina. It separates from the opsin of the photopigment (rhodopsin in rods), which is then said to be bleached. The enzyme retinal isomerase converts it back to *cis*-retinal, and the photopigment is again able to respond to light.

transseptal (trăns-sĕp′tăl) [″ + *saeptum*, partition] Across a septum.

transsexual (trăns-sĕks′ū-ăl) [″ + *sexus*, sex] **1.** An individual who has an overwhelming desire to be of the opposite sex. **2.** An individual who has had his or her external sex changed by transsexual surgery.

transsexualism (trăns-sĕks′ū-ă-lĭzm) The condition of being of a certain definite sex (i.e., male or female) but feeling and acting as if a member of the opposite sex. In some instances, the desire to alter this situation leads individuals to seek medical and surgical assistance to alter anatomical characteristics so that their anatomy would more nearly match their feelings about their true sexuality.

transsexual surgery SEE: under *surgery.*

transsphenoidal (trăns″sfē-noy′dăl) Through or across the sphenoid bone.

transsphenoidal surgery (trăn-sfē-noy′dl) Surgery on the pituitary gland performed with an incision made through the base of the sphenoid sinus. Such procedures are typically performed through the nasal passages or the oral cavity and are used to remove a macroadenoma of the pituitary, such as may be found in patients with acromegaly, prolactinomas, or other pituitary tumors.

transstadial (trăn-stā′dē-ăl) Pert. to the passage of an infection from one developmental stage of an organism to another, e.g., from the larval to the nymph stage or from the nymph to the adult. Some important infections transmitted to humans from parasitized arthropods are acquired by the arthropod when it is immature and then are passed transstadially to more mature forms, which subsequently feed on humans.

transthoracic (trăns″thō-răs′ĭk) [″ + Gr. *thorax*, chest] Across the thorax.

transthoracotomy (trăns″thō-ră-kŏt′ō-mē) [″ + Gr. *thorax*, chest, + *tome*, incision] An incision across the thorax.

transthyretin (trănz-thī′rĕt-ĭn) ABBR: TTR. A normal serum prealbumin protein that binds and transports thyroxine (T₄). Mutations in TTR can result in the protein's being deposited as amyloid in various organs.

transtracheal (trans-tra′kē-ăl) Across or through the trachea.

transtracheal jet insufflation SEE: under *insufflation*.

transtympanic neurectomy (trans″tim-pan′ik) [*trans-* + *tympanic*] Surgical interruption of the parasympathetic nerve supply to the parotid and submandibular glands by bilateral sectioning of the tympanic and chorda tympani nerves. The technique is used to treat excessive drooling, esp. in mentally retarded children.

transubstantiation (trăn″sŭb-stăn″shē-ā′shŭn) [″ + *substantia,* substance] Replacement of one tissue for another.

transudate (trans′ū-dāt″) [L. *transudare,* to sweat through, ooze through] Fluid that passes through capillary walls and accumulates in a body cavity as a result either of increased hydrostatic pressure or decreased oncotic pressure. Compared with an exudate, a transudate has fewer cellular components and minimal protein content. It also has a low concentration of lactate dehydrogenase (LDH) and a relatively normal pH.

transudation (trăns-ū-dā′shŭn) Oozing of a fluid through pores or interstices, as of a membrane.

transuranic, transuranium (tranz″ū-ran′ĭk, -rā′nē-ŭm) [*trans-* + *uran(ium)* + *-ic*] Pert. to a chemical element that has an atomic number greater than 92 (the atomic number of uranium). None of the transuranic elements are stable, and they all decay by radioactivity into other elements. Americium, berkelium, and californium are transuranic elements. **transuranic,** *n.*

transureteroureterostomy (trăns″ū-rē′tĕr-ō-ū-rē″tĕr-ŏs′tō-mē) Section of one ureter and joining both ends to the opposite ureter.

transurethral (trăns″ū-rē′thrăl) [″ + Gr. *ourethra,* urethra] Pert. to an operation performed through the urethra.

transurethral laser incision of the prostate SEE: under *incision*.

transurethral needle ablation ABBR: TUNA. The treatment of prostatic hyperplasia with a needle inserted into the penile urethra and directed toward the diseased portion of the gland. The needle is used to destroy prostatic tissue with electromagnetic energy.

transurethral resection of the prostate SEE: under *resection*.

transurethral vaporization of the prostate SEE: under *vaporization*.

transvaginal (trăns-văj′ĭn-ăl) [″ + *va-gina,* sheath] Through the vagina, as for surgical and ultrasonic imaging procedures.

transvaginal tape sling SEE: under *sling*.

transvector (trăns-věk′tor) An animal that transmits a toxin that it does not produce and by which it is itself unaffected, as when a bivalve mollusc, such as the oyster, filters viruses out of the water and transmits them to those who ingest the mollusc.

transvenous (trăns-vē′nŭs) Through a vein.

transversalis (trăns″věr-să′lĭs) [″ + *vertere,* to turn] A structure located at right angles to the long axis of the body.

transversalis fascia A thin membrane forming the peritoneal surface of the transversus muscle and its aponeurosis.

transverse (trăns-věrs′) [L. *transversus*] Lying at right angles to the long axis of the body; crosswise.

transversectomy (trăns″věr-sĕk′tō-mē) [″ + Gr. *ektome,* excision] Excision of a transverse vertebral process.

transverse foramen SEE: under *foramen*.

transverse lie A position of the fetus in utero in which the long axis of the fetus is across the long axis of the mother. SEE: *presentation* for illus.

transverse rectus abdominis musculocutaneous flap reconstruction ABBR: TRAM. A procedure for reconstructing the contours of the breast after mastectomy, in which tissue from the abdomen is mobilized and grafted to the anterior chest wall. Potential complications include infection and necrosis of the graft.

transversion (trans-věr′zhŏn) [*trans-* + *version*] **1.** The eruption of a tooth at an abnormal site. **2.** A mutation in a nucleic acid in which there is a substitution of a purine base by a pyrimidine base (or vice versa).

transversocostal (trăns-věr″sō-kŏs′tăl) Costotransverse.

transversospinalis (trăns-věr″sō-spī-nă′lĭs) [L. *transversus,* turned across, + *spina,* thorn] Semispinalis capitis, semispinalis cervicis.

transversourethralis (trăns-věr″sō-ū″rē-thrā′lĭs) The transverse fibers of the sphincter urethrae muscle.

transversus (trăns-věr′sŭs) [L.] **1.** Any of several small muscles. **2.** Lying across the long axis of a part or organ.

transvestism, transvestitism (trăns-věst′izm, -ĭ-tĭzm) [L. *trans,* across, + *vestitus,* clothed, + Gr. *-ismos,* condition] The desire to dress in the clothes of and be accepted as a member of the opposite sex.

transvestite (trăns-věs′tīt) A person who practices transvestism.

Trantas dots (tran′tăs) [Alexios Trantas, Gr. ophthalmologist, 1867–1960] Chalky concretions of the conjunctiva around the limbus. These are associated with vernal conjunctivitis.

trapeze bar SEE: under *bar*.

trapeziform (tră-pē′zĭ-form) Shaped like a trapezoid.

trapezium (tră-pē′zē-ŭm) [Gr. *trapezion*, a little table] **1.** A four-sided, single-plane geometric figure in which none of the sides are parallel. **2.** The os trapezium, the first bone on the radial side of the distal row of the bones of the wrist. It articulates with the base of the metacarpal bone of the thumb.

trapezius (tră-pē′zē-ŭs) A flat, triangular muscle covering the posterior surface of the neck and shoulder. It raises, retracts, or lowers the scapula, extends the head, and is controlled by the accessory nerves.

trapezoid (trăp′ĕ-zoyd) [Gr. *trapezoeides*, table-shaped] A four-sided figure having two parallel sides and two divergent sides.

trapezoid body A transverse sheet of secondary sensory axons that originate in the cochlear nuclei and that cross the midline just dorsal to the pons in the rostral hindbrain. About half of the cochlear axons remain ipsilateral and ascend toward the inferior colliculus via the lateral lemniscus. Those cochlear axons that cross the cross the midline in the trapezoid body also join the (contralateral) lateral lemniscus and run toward the inferior colliculus.

trapezoid ligament SEE: under *ligament*.

trauma (tro′mă, trow′, ′mă-tă) *pl.* **traumata, traumas** [Gr. *trauma*, a wound] **1.** A physical injury or wound caused by external force or violence. It may be self-inflicted. In the U.S., trauma is the principal cause of death between the ages of 1 and 44. In addition to each death from trauma, there are at least two cases of permanent disability caused by trauma. The principal types of trauma include motor vehicle collisions, military service, falls, burns, gunshot wounds, and drowning. Most deaths occur in the first several hours after the event. **2.** An emotional or psychological shock that may produce disordered feelings or behavior.

    a severity characterization of t. SEE: *a severity characterization of trauma*.

    acoustic t. Injury to hearing by noise, esp. loud noise.

    birth t. **1.** Injury to the fetus during the birthing process. **2.** Otto Rank's term for what he considered the basic source of anxiety in human beings, the birth process. The importance of this concept is controversial.

    blunt cardiac t. Blunt cardiac **injury.**

    blunt t. A wound in which the surface of the skin remains intact, caused by impact or collision with a blunt object, e.g., an automobile fender. SYN: *nonpenetrating wound*.

    head t. Injury to the head, esp. to the scalp and cranium, that may be limited to soft tissue damage or may include the cranial bones and the brain.

    multiple t. Serious injury to two or more regions of the body.

    occlusal t. Any injury to part of the masticatory system as a result of malocclusion or occlusal dysfunction. It may be abrupt in its development in response to a restoration or ill-fitting prosthetic device, or result from years of tooth wear, drift, or faulty oral habits. It may produce adverse periodontal changes, tooth mobility or excessive wear, pain in the temporomandibular joints, or spasms and pain in the muscles of mastication.

    psychic t. A painful emotional experience that may cause anxiety, depression, insomnia, flashbacks, or other psychological symptoms.

    revised t. scale ABBR: RTS. An assessment tool to gauge the severity of a patient's injuries, e.g., after a fall, gunshot wound, or auto accident. It consists of measurements of blood pressure and respiratory rate and the Glasgow Coma Scale. A lower score indicates more severe injuries and a greater likelihood of death.

    toothbrush t. Abrasion or grooving of teeth and gingival injury or recession as a result of improper brushing with a stiff-textured brush.

    vehicular t. A collision involving an auto, truck, van, or motorcycle in which one or more passengers or pedestrians are injured.

trauma center SEE: under *center*.

trauma injury severity score ABBR: TRISS. A calculation of the probability that an injured person will survive serious trauma. It is made on the basis of the patient's age. the type of trauma (blunt versus penetrating), and the injury severity score and revised trauma score.

Trauma Score Numerical grading system that combines the Glasgow Coma Scale and measurements of cardiopulmonary function as a gauge of severity of injury and as a predictor of survival after blunt trauma to the head. Each parameter is given a number (high for normal and low for impaired or absent function). Severity of injury is estimated by summing the numbers. The lowest score is 1, the highest 16. SEE: table.

traumatic (traw-măt′ĭk) [Gr. *traumatikos*] Pert. to or caused by an injury.

traumatism (traw′mă-tĭzm) [Gr. *traumatismos*] A morbid condition of a system owing to an injury or a wound.

traumato-, traumat- [Gr. *trauma*, stem

Revised Trauma Score (RTS)

Glasgow Coma Scale (GCS)	Systolic Blood Pressure (SBP)	Respiratory Rate (RR)	Coded Value
13–15	>89	10–29	4
9–12	76–89	>29	3
6–8	50–75	6–9	2
4–5	1–49	1–5	1
3	0	0	0

$RTS = 0.9368\ GCS_c + 0.7326\ SBP_c + 0.2908\ RR_c$ coded values × revised score coefficient

SOURCE: From Champion, HR, et al: J Trauma 29:623–629, 1989.

traumat-, wound] Prefixes meaning *trauma, wound.*

traumatology (traw-mă-tŏl′ō-jē) [Gr. *trauma*, wound, + *logos*, word, reason] The branch of surgery dealing with wounds and their care.

traumatopathy (traw″mă-tŏp′ă-thē) [″ + *pathos*, disease, suffering] A pathological state caused by trauma.

traumatopnea (traw″mă-tŏp-nē′ă) [″ + *pnoia*, breath] The passage of air in and out of a wound in the chest wall.

travel [ME. *travailen*, to travail, to journey] **1.** To move from place to place, e.g., from one country to another. **2.** The act of moving among different places or countries. Travel to some locations presents health risks, such as deep venous thrombosis, diarrhea, geographically specific infections (e.g., malaria), injury, insomnia, rashes, colds, and influenza.

tray (trā) A flat surface with raised edges.

impression t. In dentistry, a receptacle with raised edges for carrying impression material and supporting it in contact with the surfaces to be recorded until the impression material sets or hardens.

trazodone (trăz′ō-dōn) A triazolopyride and antidepressant. It is administered orally to treat major depression and may be used as an adjunct to psychotherapy. SYN: *Desyrel.*

TRCHII *tanned red cell hemagglutination immunoassay.*

Treacher Collins syndrome (trē′chĕr-kŏl′ĭnz) [Edward Treacher Collins, Brit. ophthalmologist, 1862–1919] Mandibulofacial dysostosis.

treadmill (trĕd′mĭl) A conveyor belt for walking or running in place; the speed of movement and angle of inclination can be varied during tests of cardiopulmonary health and conditioning. SEE: *exercise tolerance test.*

treatment (trēt′mĕnt) [ME. *treten*, to handle] **1.** Medical, surgical, dental, or psychiatric management of a patient. **2.** Any specific procedure used for the cure or the amelioration of a disease or pathological condition. SEE: *therapy.* Particular treatments are listed under the first word. SEE: e.g., *conservative treatment; legally mandated treatment; radiation treatment.*

treatment burden The deterioration in a patient's health that may be caused by exposure to medications, radiation therapy, surgery, or other forms of therapy.

treatment card In dentistry, a specially formatted card or file summarizing a patient's dental care. SEE: *dental chart.*

tree (trē) A structure that resembles a tree.

bronchial t. The right or left primary bronchus with its branches and their terminal arborizations.

decision t. A graphic analysis of the decisions or choices available to a health care manager or provider. The graph includes estimates of the probabilities of all the events that may result from each selection or choice. SEE: *decision analysis.*

tracheobronchial t. The trachea, bronchi, and their branches.

tree nut Any of several nuts, e.g., almonds, cashews, filberts or pecans, that grow on shrubs or trees. They are among the most common sources of food allergy.

Treg (treg) A regulatory T cell.

trehalase (trē-hā′lās) The enzyme that cleaves the bond between glucose molecules in the disaccharide, trehalose.

trehalose (trē-hā′lōs) A disaccharide containing two linked glucose molecules. It is less sweet than sucrose, but can be used as a source of glucose. SYN: *mycose.*

Trematoda (trĕm″ă-tō′dă) [Gr. *trematodes*, pierced] A class of flatworms, commonly called flukes, and belonging to the phylum Platyhelminthes. It includes two orders: Monogenea, which are external or semiexternal parasites having direct development with no asexual multiplication, and Digenea, internal parasites with asexual generation in their life cycle. The Digenea usually require two or more hosts, the hosts alternating. SEE: *fluke.*

trematode (trĕm′ă-tōd) A parasitic flatworm belonging to the class Trematoda. SEE: *cercaria; fluke.*

trematodiasis (trĕm″ă-tō-dī′ă-sĭs) Infestation with a trematode.

tremble (trĕm′bl) [O.Fr. *trembler*] **1.** An involuntary quivering or shaking. **2.** To shiver, quiver, or shake.

trembles (trem′bĕlz) A disease in cattle caused by ingestion of tremetol in plants such as white snakeroot (*Eupatorium urticaefolium*) or rayless goldenrod (*Haplopappus heterophyllus*). Symptoms include weakness, anorexia, nausea and vomiting, and prostration, possibly resulting in death. SYN: *tires*. SEE: *milk sickness; tremetol*.

tremelloid, tremellose (trĕm′ĕ-loyd, -lōs) Jelly-like.

tremolabile (trē″mō-lā′bl) [″ + *labi*, to slip] Of an enzyme, easily destroyed or inactivated by shaking.

tremor (trĕm′or, trē′mor) [L. *tremor*, a shaking] **1.** A quivering, esp. a continuous quivering of a convulsive nature. **2.** An involuntary movement of a part or parts of the body resulting from alternate contractions of opposing muscles. SEE: *subsultus*.

Tremors may be classified as involuntary, static, dynamic, kinetic, or hereditary. Pathological tremors are independent of the will. The trembling may be fine or coarse, rapid or slow, and may appear on movement (intention tremor) or improve when the part is voluntarily exercised. It is often caused by organic disease; trembling may also express an emotion (e.g., fear). All abnormal tremors except palatal and ocular myoclonus disappear during sleep.

   action t. Intention t.

   alcoholic t. The visible tremor exhibited by alcoholics.

   cerebellar t. An intention tremor of 3 to 5 Hz frequency, associated with cerebellar disease.

   coarse t. A tremor in which oscillations are relatively slow.

   continuous t. A tremor that resembles tremors of paralysis agitans.

   enhanced physiological t. An action tremor associated with catecholamine excess (e.g., in association with anxiety, thyrotoxicosis, hypoglycemia, or alcohol withdrawal). It may occur as a side effect of drugs (e.g., epinephrine, caffeine, theophylline, amphetamines, levodopa, tricyclic antidepressants, lithium, and corticosteroids).

   essential t. A benign tremor, usually of the head, chin, outstretched hands, and occasionally the voice, that is to be differentiated from the tremor of Parkinson disease. Unlike Parkinson disease, essential tremor does not cause or presage other neurological complications. Essential tremor, which is made worse by anxiety or action, is usually 8 to 10 cycles per second and that of parkinsonism 4 to 5. Postural tremors occur when the patient tries to hold his hands in a particular position (e.g., when the hands are outstretched). Kinetic trem-

ors occur during purposeful movement (e.g., during finger-to-nose testing). Essential tremor affects 5 to 10 million adults and some children in the U.S. and is probably the most common movement disorder. Its incidence increases with age. In essential tremor, there is usually a family history. The medicines effective in treating parkinsonism have no effect on essential tremor.

PATIENT CARE: Patients with essential tremor often require no treatment other than reassurance. They should avoid stimulants, like caffeine or pseudoephrine, which make trembling worse, and they should rest when tremors are especially prominent. Medications commonly used to treat essential tremor include beta blockers, anticonvulsants, benzodiazepines, and botulinum toxin injections. Tremors that are exceptionally troubling to patients can also be suppressed by thalamic stimulation or surgical excision of the thalamus.

   familial t. A tremor indistinguishable from essential tremor in its clinical manifestation. Unlike essential tremor, it is inherited as an autosomal dominant trait.

   fibrillary t. A tremor caused by consecutive contractions of separate muscular fibrillae rather than of a muscle or muscles.

   fine t. A rapid tremor.

   flapping t. Asterixis.

   forced t. A tremor continuing after voluntary motion has ceased.

   Hunt t. SEE: *Hunt tremor*.

   hysterical t. A fine tremor occurring in hysteria. It may be limited to one extremity or generalized.

   intention t. A tremor exhibited or intensified when attempting coordinated movements. SYN: *action t.*

   intermittent t. A tremor common to paralyzed muscles in hemoplegia when attempting voluntary movement.

   muscular t. Slight oscillating muscular contractions in rhythmical order.

   parkinsonian t. A resting tremor of the fingers and hands, often called a pill-rolling tremor, that is suppressed briefly during voluntary activity. The tremor disappears during all but the lightest phases of sleep.

   physiological t. A tremor occurring in normal individuals. It may be transient and occur in association with excessive physical exertion, excitement, hunger, fatigue, or other causes. SEE: *enhanced physiological t.*

   rest t. A tremor present when the involved part is at rest but absent or diminished when active movements are attempted. SYN: *static t.*

   senile t. A form of benign essential tremor found in individuals older than 60, marked by rapid, alternating movements of the upper extremities that occur at a frequency of about 6 cycles/sec.

static t.   Rest **t.**

volitional t.   Trembling of the limbs or of the body when making a voluntary effort. It is seen in many cerebellar diseases.

tremulous (trĕm'ū-lŭs) [L. *tremulus*] Trembling or shaking.

trench fever   SEE: under *fever*.

trend (trend) [Old English *trendan*, to roll, revolve] The inclination to proceed in a certain direction or at a certain rate; used to describe the prognosis or course of a symptom, disease, or methods of disease management.

pernicious t.   In psychology, an abnormal departure from conventional ideas and social interests.

secular t.   A long-term trend that develops or progresses over many years. The tendency for girls to begin menstruating at younger and younger ages during the twentieth century is an example.

Trendelenburg, Friedrich (tren'dĕl-ĕn-bŭrg") Ger. surgeon, 1844–1924.

T. gait   A sideways lurching of the trunk over the stance leg caused by weakness in the gluteus medius muscle.

T. limp   An abnormal gait in which the patient transfers his or her weight laterally over the femoral head on the weight-bearing side and then shifts the weight back to a central position as the leg on that side is lifted from the ground. It is caused by weak hip adduction.

T. position   A position in which the patient's head is low and the body and legs are on an elevated and inclined plane. This may be accomplished by having the patient lie flat on a bed and then elevating the foot of the bed. In this position, the abdominal organs are pushed up toward the chest by gravity. The foot of the bed may be elevated by resting it on blocks. This position is used in abdominal surgery. It is also usually used in treating shock, but if there is an associated head injury, the head should not be kept lower than the trunk. SYN: *head-down* **position.** SEE: *position* for illus.

reverse T. position   A body position in which the trunk and head are elevated above the pelvis and lower extremities.

T. sign   A pelvic drop on the side of the elevated leg when the patient stands on one leg and lifts the other. It indicates weakness or instability of the gluteus medius muscle on the stance side.

T. test   A test to evaluate the strength of the gluteus medius muscle. The examiner stands behind the patient and observes the pelvis as the patient stands on one leg and then the other. A positive result determines muscle weakness on the standing leg side when the pelvis tilts down on the opposite side.

trepan (trē-păn') [Gr. *trypanon,* a borer] To perforate the skull with a trephine.

trepanation (trĕp"ă-nā'shŭn) [L. *trepanatio*] Surgery using a trepan.

corneal t.   Keratoplasty.

trephination (trĕf"ĭn-ā'shŭn) [Fr. *trephine,* a bore] The process of cutting out a piece of bone with the trephine.

trephine (trē-fīn')   A cylindrical saw for cutting a circular piece of bone out of the skull. **trephine,** *v.*

trephining (trē-fīn'ĭng)   Cutting or extraction of a bone with a trephine.

trephocyte (trĕf'ō-sīt) [Gr. *trephein,* to feed, + *kytos,* cell] Trophocyte.

trepidant (trĕp'ĭ-dănt) [L. *trepidans,* trembling] Pert. to or marked by tremor.

trepidation (trĕp"ĭ-dā'shŭn) [L. *trepidatio,* a trembling] **1.** Fear, anxiety. **2.** Trembling movement, esp. when involuntary.

Treponema (trep"ŏ-nē'mă) [Gr. *trepein,* to turn + *nēma,* thread] A genus of spirochetes of the family Spirochaetaceae. They are parasitic in humans and move by flexing, snapping, and bending. SEE: *bacteria* for illus.

T. carateum   A species that is the causative agent of pinta.

T. denticola   A species that is the causative agent of periodontal disease. Its presence in the oral cavity has been linked to an increased incidence of coronary artery disease.

T. endemicum   A species that is the causative agent of bejel. It often affects the skin, bones, and oral mucous membranes.

T. pallidum   A species that is the causative agent of syphilis. SYN: *Spirochaeta pallida.*

T. pertenue   A species that is the causative agent of yaws (frambesia).

Treponemataceae (trĕp"ō-nē"mă-tā'sē-ē) A family of spiral organisms belonging to the order Spirochaetales; that includes the genera *Borrelia, Leptospira,* and *Treponema.*

treponematosis (trĕp"ō-nē-mă-tō'sĭs) Infection with *Treponema.*

treponeme (trĕp'ō-nēm)   Any organism of the genus *Treponema.*

treponemiasis (trĕp"ō-nē-mī'ă-sĭs) [" + *nema,* thread, + *-iasis,* condition] Infestation with *Treponema.*

treponemicidal (trĕp"ō-nē"mĭ-sī'dăl) [" + " + L. *cidus,* to kill] Destructive to *Treponema.*

treppe (trĕp'ē)   Staircase phenomenon.

tretinoin (trĕt'ĭ-noyn)   All-*trans*-retinoic acid. It is a keratolytic agent used topically in treating acne.

TRH   *thyrotropin-releasing* **hormone.**

tri- [L., Gr. *tri-,* three] Prefix meaning *three.*

triacetate (trī-ăs′ĕ-tāt) Any acetate that contains three acetic acid groups.

triacidic (trī″ă-sĭd′ĭk) Containing three acidic hydrogen ions.

triacylglycerol (trī-ăs″ĭl-glĭs′ă-rŏl″) Triglyceride.

TRIaD (trī′ad″) [An acronym for *t(riangulation)*, *r(everse use dependency, electrical)* *i(nstability of the action potential)*, *a(nd)* *d(ispersion)*] A combination of findings in repolarization of cardiac myocytes. Augmentation of TRIaD is associated with the generation of cardiac arrhythmias.

triad (trī′ad″) [L. *trias*, fr Gr. *trias*, stem *triad-*, group of three] **1.** A group of three things having something in common, e.g., a syndrome. **2.** A trivalent element or radical. SEE: *trivalent.*

   adoption t. The biological parents of a child, the adoptive parents, and the child who is adopted.

   Austrian t. SEE: *Austrian triad.*

   Beck t. SEE: *Beck triad.*

   Bergman t. SEE: *Bergman triad.*

   Carney t. SEE: *Carney triad.*

   catalytic t. The enzymatically active mechanism found in serine proteases, consisting of three amino acids SER-HIS-ASP (serine, histidine, and aspartic acid).

   Charcot t. SEE: under *Charcot, Jean M.*

   Currarino t. SEE: *Currarino triad.*

   Dieulafoy t. SEE: under *Dieulafoy, Georges.*

   female athlete t. A triad consisting of a normal eating habits (eating disorders or disordered eating), amenorrhea, and osteoporosis among young female athletes. It is most common in sports in which low body weight has a beneficial effect on performance or appearance, e.g., gymnastics, running, swimming, and figure skating. Males participating in the same sports or in wrestling may also suffer the health-related effects of excessive training or abnormally restrictive eating. Disordered eating is often the first condition in the triad to appear.

   SYMPTOMS: Signs of the disorder include excessive training, food restriction, ritualized eating habits, and other obsessive behavior, binging and purging, fatigue, anemia, depression, and electrolyte imbalances. Fractures occur because of bone loss, which may not be reversible.

   PATIENT CARE: Screening female high school or younger at-risk athletes for disordered eating and menstrual irregularities is recommended as a first step in preventing development of the disorder. During physical exams required for participation in sports, athletes should be asked about food intake within the past 24 hr, perceived ideal weight, forbidden foods, and use of diet aids. Some women and coaches believe that amenorrhea is a normal consequence of athletic training rather than a sign of injury to the hypothalamic-pituitary axis. A dual-energy x-ray absorptiometry (DEXA) scan or similar study should be considered in athletes with amenorrhea lasting at least 6 months. The patient, dietitian, and primary care provider should agree on a goal weight, after considering the weight requirements for the sport.

   follicular occlusion t. A collective term for three related forms of localized skin abscess: hidradenitis suppurativa, acne conglobata, and dissecting cellulitis of the scalp.

   Garland t. SEE: *Garland triad.*

   Hutchinson t. SEE: under *Hutchinson, Sir Jonathan.*

   lethal t. The combination of acidosis, coagulopathy, and hypothermia in a critically ill patient. It is an indication of very severe illness and has a poor prognosis.

   Samter t. SEE: *Samter triad.*

   terrible t. A colloquial term for a dislocation of the elbow accompanied by fractures of the coronoid process of the ulna and of the radial head. The injury produces an unstable joint.

   Tourette syndrome t. SEE: under *de la Tourette, Georges Gilles.*

triad syndrome Prune belly defect.

triage (trē-äzh′) [Fr., sorting] **1.** The screening and classification of casualties to make optimal use of treatment resources and to maximize the survival and welfare of patients. **2.** Sorting patients and setting priorities for their treatment in urgent care settings, emergency rooms, clinics, hospitals, health maintenance organizations, or in the field.

   PATIENT CARE: To triage a patient the health care professional assesses mental status, airway, breathing, and circulation and makes decisions about treatment priorities. The process is dynamic, e.g., the patient's condition may change and upon reassessment, so may the priority. Common triage categories used in the field during multiple casualty incidents would include: P-1 or red, P-2 or yellow, P-3 or green, and P-0 or deceased.

   Most emergency department triage systems rely on patient surveys, with victims assigned to the following categories based on assessment: emergent (requires stabilization or treatment within minutes to prevent death or further injury), urgent (serious but not life-threatening, should be treated within 2 hr), and nonurgent (minor or stable injury or illness, does not require treatment within 2 hr). In the primary survey of the patient, the Airway, Breathing, Circulation, need for Defibrillation (or neurological Disability) are assessed and the patient is undressed or Exposed. The survey order is remembered with the mnemonic ABCDE. Resuscitation of the patient begins immediately, based on the findings. In the secondary survey, the same elements of care are reviewed, but the emphasis is on assessing the effectiveness of interventions to maintain the airway, support ventilation, control hemorrhage and blood pressure, and restore normal physiology. After stabilization the patient may be admitted to a hospital, or transported to a facility better equipped to manage his or her illness or injuries.

⚠️ Warming measures should be employed to avoid hypothermia caused by "E" (exposure).

---

telephone t. Use of the telephone or other means of communication to assess a patient's health status and to recommend treatment or provide appropriate referrals. It is used, e.g., in emergency departments and the offices of primary care providers to facilitate the outpatient management of common, simple health-related problems.

trial (trī′ăl) In the medical sciences, a test or experiment, as of a drug.

adaptive t. A form of research in which data analyzed as the trial progresses are used to reshape or refocus its design.

clinical t. A study of the effects of a drug administered to human subjects. The goal is to define the clinical efficacy and pharmacological effects of the drug (toxicity, side effects, incompatibilities, interactions). The U.S. government requires strict testing of all new drugs before their approval for use as therapeutic agents.

Clinical trials address a wide variety of health care topics from treatment and diagnosis to prevention of disease. Trial investigators prove or disprove the value or safety of a particular drug or therapy thought to have a positive effect for patients. Clinical trials are therefore experiments, a quest for evidence. They help establish proof of effectiveness, but they do not imply that such proof already exists.

PATIENT CARE: Investigators must employ high ethical standards to ensure that enrollees know how the trial works, the chances of receiving active therapy as opposed to a placebo, the expected outcomes, and what risks and complications the participants may experience. These standards are needed to protect enrollees, esp. those with chronic, poorly controlled, or potentially fatal illnesses from assuming that participation in an experiment guarantees an imminent cure. Participation in the experiment does not guarantee a cure. In many instances trials prove that the intervention tested does not work; in some, that the intervention is hazardous; and, only in a few, that the intervention is as good as doing nothing or as good as the best available contemporary therapy. Even when clinical outcomes are not positive, a trial usually illuminates some elements of pharmacology or pathophysiology that may be used in furthering the understanding of an illness. Many human drug trials, esp. trials of new treatments for cancer, are conducted in four phases, three of them before approval for general use. An increasingly larger number of participants are enrolled for each successive phase

crossover t. A scientific study of a therapeutic agent in which participants are exposed in sequence to the putative cure and subsequently (or previously) to an inactive agent or an agent whose efficacy has been previously established. The participants cross over from one arm of the study to the other and serve as their own control group.

Participants in such trials are usually under the care of a team of physicians and nurses and are closely monitored, often with testing and examinations on a weekly basis. The clinical trial nurse or nurse research specialist has a broad variety of roles, depending on the nature of the investigation. The roles include recruiting and introducing patients to the trial, coordinating their care, gathering data about side effects and tolerance, and, frequently, serving as a principal or collaborative investigator. Trial planning and design, data interpretation and analysis, and assessments of toxicity are all elements of the work. Health insurers and managed care providers may place restrictions on clinical trial coverage. Many states have laws requiring insurers to pay for the routine costs of all or some clinical trials. Patient advocates work with researchers to make sure a clinical trial is relevant, as safe as possible, and accessible to the broadest variety of patients. SYN: *crossover* (2).

equivalence t. A randomized clinical trial in which two distinct agents are compared with each other and sometimes with an inert agent (a placebo) as well. If two agents work equally well, the less expensive, better tolerated, or more easily administered one may be preferred.

negative t. Negative **study**.

noninferiority t. A study to determine if a treatment is no worse than the currently accepted therapy.

observational t. Observational **study**.

parallel t. A research study in which

groups of patients are followed for the same time but are given different treatments; e.g., one group may receive an inactive substance while another is treated with a drug whose effectiveness must be determined. The impact of the drug can thus be compared with the placebo at varying times, such as 4 weeks, 4 months, or 4 years after the study begins.

PEEP decrement t. Sequential decreases in positive end-expiratory pressures (PEEP) until the lowest level of PEEP is achieved that improves lung compliance the most, without reducing the patient's partial pressure of oxygen. PEEP is then adjusted to a value just higher than that value.

phase I t., phase 1 trial A clinical trial to determine the toxicity of a new drug. Such trials test safety and maximum dosage, help researchers discover the best way to administer a treatment (orally or intravenously) and the most appropriate dosage. Phase I trials also help to discover potentially harmful adverse effects of a new treatment. Even though the trial is not designed to show whether the treatment is effective, since an experimental drug is chosen for its promise, the patient may still benefit. Only a small number of patients are included (15 to 25 who have not been helped by other treatments), and there usually is no control group.

phase II t., phase 2 trial A clinical trial to determine the potential effectiveness of a new drug. Generally, if at least 20% of the study subjects respond positively to it, e.g., achieve a 50% reduction in the total size of their measurable tumor, the new therapy will receive further testing. Another crucial statistic is the duration of response. Short-term responses may mean little in terms of survival; long-term responses indicate that the drug is benefiting some patients.

phase III t., phase 3 trial A clinical trial to explore the clinical use of a new drug, esp. relative to other known effective agents (the current standard of care). These trials often include thousands of enrollee patients. By law, all such patients receive real treatment; no placebos are given. But the trial is usually double-blinded, with patients divided randomly into two groups: an experimental group and a control group on standard treatment, with neither patients nor researchers knowing to which group the patient belongs.

phase IV t., phase 4 trial A clinical trial to examine long-term effectiveness and adverse effects that might occur from a treatment after the Food and Drug Administration has approved its use by the public. Such trials, involving thousands or tens of thousands of en-

rollee patients, are either mandated by regulatory authorities or undertaken voluntarily by a pharmaceutical manufacturer once the drug has gone to market. Often it is only in Phase IV trials that especially rare adverse effects emerge. Enrollee patients in a clinical trial should have the approval of their personal oncologist, and they should seek a second opinion (which is covered by insurance) to obtain more input on what trials to consider.

pragmatic t. A trial to evaluate the effectiveness of a treatment investigated under real-world conditions, rather than during the application of stringent exclusion criteria.

randomized controlled t. ABBR: RCT. An experimental study to assess the effects of a particular variable, e.g., a drug or treatment, in which subjects are assigned randomly to an experimental, placebo, or control group. The experimental group receives the drug or procedure; the placebo group's medication is disguised to resemble the drug being investigated. The control group receives nothing. Members of each group are prevented from knowing whether they are receiving active therapy. The researchers gathering the data are also typically blinded to group assignment.

⚠️ Although RCTs are an essential element in proving clinical relationships (such as between the use of a new drug and the safe cure of a disease), most RCTs do not enroll enough patients for a long enough time to detect rare events.

spontaneous breathing t. Spontaneous breathing test.

superiority t. A study that directly compares two treatments to see which of them achieves better results.

triangle (trī′ang-gĕl) [L. *triangulum*] A figure or area formed by three angles and three sides.

anal t. The dorsal triangular region of the perineum from the point at the tip of the coccyx to a line between the two ischial tuberosities. The anal triangle contains the anus.

anterior t. of neck The space bounded by the middle line of the neck, the anterior border of the sternocleidomastoid muscle, and a line running along the lower border of the mandible and continued to the mastoid process of the temporal bone.

cephalic t. The triangle on the anteroposterior plane of the skull formed by lines joining the occiput and forehead and chin, and a line uniting the occiput and the chin.

digastric t. The triangular region of the neck. Its borders are the mandible, stylohyoid muscle, and the anterior belly of the digastric muscle.

facial t. The triangle bounded by the lines uniting the basion and the alveolar and nasal points, and one uniting the nasal and basion.

frontal t. The triangle bounded by the maximum frontal diameter and the lines joining its extremities and the glabella.

Hesselbach t. SEE: under *Hesselbach triangle.*

inferior carotid t. The triangular space bounded by the middle line of the neck, the sternomastoid muscle, and the anterior belly of the omohyoid muscle. SYN: *muscular t.*

lumbocostoabdominal t. The triangle bounded in front by the obliquus abdominis externus, above by the lower border of the serratus posterior inferior and the point of the 12th rib, behind by the outer edge of the erector spinae, and below by the obliquus abdominis internus.

muscular t. Inferior carotid **t.**

mylohyoid t. The triangular space formed by the mylohyoid muscle and the two bellies of the digastric muscle.

occipital t. of the neck The triangle bounded by the sternocleidomastoid, the trapezius, and the omohyoid muscles.

t. of Petit The space above the hip bone between the exterior oblique muscle, the latissimus dorsi, and the interior oblique muscle.

posterior cervical t. The triangular region wrapping around the side of the neck bounded by the upper border of the clavicle, the posterior border of the sternocleidomastoid muscle, and the anterior border of the trapezius muscle.

pubourethral t. A triangular space in the perineum bounded laterally by the ischiocavernous muscle, medially by the bulbocavernous muscle, and posteriorly by the superficial transverse perineus muscle.

submandibular t. The triangular region of the neck, bounded by the inferior border of the mandible, the stylohyoid muscle and the posterior belly of the digastric muscle, and the anterior belly of the digastric muscle; it is one of three triangles included in the anterior triangle of the neck. This was formerly called the submaxillary triangle.

submental t. A superficial region under the chin with its base being the hyoid bone and its right and left walls being the right and left anterior bellies of the digastric muscle. The front wall of the triangle is skin; the back wall is the outer surface of the mylohyoid muscle.

suboccipital t. The triangle bounded by the obliquus inferior and superior muscles on two sides and the rectus capitis posterior major muscle on the third side. The floor contains the posterior arch of the atlas bone and the vertebral artery. It is covered by the semispinalis capitis muscle.

superior carotid t. The space bounded by the anterior belly of the omohyoid muscle, the posterior belly of the digastricus muscle, and the sternomastoid muscle.

suprameatal t. The triangle slightly above and behind the exterior auditory meatus. It is bounded above by the root of the zygoma and anteriorly by the posterior wall of the exterior auditory meatus.

urogenital t. The triangle with its base formed by a line between the two ischial tuberosities and its apex just below the symphysis pubis.

triangulation (trī-ăn″gū-lā′shŭn) In qualitative research, a technique for enhancing the validity of the data gained from investigative research by comparing or synthesizing information gathered from more than one study.

Triatoma (trī-at′ŏ-mă) A genus of blood-sucking insects belonging to the order Hemiptera, family Reduviidae; commonly called conenosed bugs or assassin bugs. It includes the species *T. braziliensis, T. dimidiata, T. infestans, T. protracta, T. recuva,* and *T. rubida.* They are house-infesting pests and some species, esp. *T. infestans,* transmit *Trypanosoma cruzi.*

tribade (trĭb′ăd) A lesbian.

tribasic (trī-bā′sĭk) [Gr. *treis,* three, + L. *basis,* base] Capable of neutralizing or accepting three hydrogen ions.

tribasilar (trī-băs′ĭl-ăr) [″ + L. *basilaris,* base] Having three bases.

tribasilar synostosis A condition resulting from the premature fusion of three skull bones (the occipital, sphenoid, and temporal). This results in arrested cerebral development and cognitive deficits.

tribe (trīb) [L. *tribus,* division of the Roman people] In taxonomy, an occasional subdivision of a family; often equal to or below subfamily and above genus.

tribology (trī-bŏl′ō-jē) The study of the effect of friction on the body, esp. the articulating joints.

triboluminescence (trī″bō-lū″mĭ-nĕs′ĕns) [Gr. *tribein,* to rub, + L. *lumen,* light, + Fr. *escence,* continuing] Luminescence or sparks produced by friction or mechanical force applied to certain chemical crystals.

tribromide (trī-brō′mīd) [Gr. *treis,* three, + *bromos,* stench] A compound having three atoms of bromine in the molecule.

TRIC Acronym for *tr*achoma and *inc*lusion conjunctivitis. SEE: *Chlamydia trachomatis.*

tricarboxylic acid cycle (trī″kar″bok″sil′ik)
SEE: under *cycle.*

TRICARE (trī′kar″) A health insurance plan providing coverage to current and retired members of the U.S. armed forces. Website: www.tricare.mil

triceps (trī′sĕps) [″ + L. *caput,* head] A muscle arising by three heads with a single insertion.

    t. brachii The muscle of the posterior arm with three points of origin (one on the scapula, two on the humerus) and one insertion on the ulna. It extends the forearm and is controlled by the radial nerve. SEE: *arm* for illus.

    t. skin fold The thickness of the skin including subcutaneous fat as measured on the skin over the triceps muscle of the arm. Comparison of the value obtained from a patient to standard values (or the comparison of this value with skin fold measures from other body areas) helps to provide an estimate of body fat. It is used in assessing and documenting both malnutrition and obesity.

    t. surae The muscle group formed by the two heads of the gastrocnemius and the single head of the soleus muscles.

trichalgia (trĭk-ăl′jē-ă) Pain caused by touching or moving the hair.

trichiasis (trĭk-ī′ă-sĭs) [Gr. *thrix,* hair, + *-iasis,* condition] Inversion of eyelashes so that they rub against the cornea, causing a continual irritation of the eyeball. Symptoms are photophobia, lacrimation, and feeling of a foreign body in the eye. The condition is treated by cryotherapy, epilation, electrolysis, and operation, such as correcting the underlying entropion with which this condition is usually associated.

trichilemmoma (trĭk″ĭ-lĕm-ō′mă) A benign tumor of the outer root sheath epithelium of a hair follicle.

Trichina (trĭk-ī′nă) [Gr. *trichinos,* of hair] Trichinella.

trichina (trĭ-kī′nă) *pl.* **trichinae** A larval worm of the genus *Trichinella.*

Trichinella (trĭk″ĭ-nel′ă) A genus of nematode worms belonging to the order Trichurida and the family Trichinellidae. They are parasitic in humans, hogs, rats, and many other mammals.

    T. spiralis The species of *Trichinella* that commonly infests humans, causing trichinosis. Infection occurs when raw or improperly cooked meat, particularly pork and wild game, containing cysts is eaten. Larvae excyst in the duodenum and invade the mucosa of the small intestine, becoming adults in 5 to 7 days. After fertilization, each female deposits 1000 to 2000 larvae, which enter the blood or lymph vessels and circulate to various parts of the body where they encyst, esp. in striated muscle.

trichinellosis (trĭk″ĭ-nĕl-lō′sĭs) [Gr. *trichinos,* of hair, + *osis,* condition] Trichinosis.

trichinosis (trĭk″ĭn-ō′sĭs) [″ + *osis,* condition] Infection by the roundworm parasite *Trichinella spiralis,* resulting from consumption of undercooked pork or wild game containing *T. spiralis* cysts. Gastric juices release the worms from their cysts, which quickly reach sexual maturity. The female roundworms then burrow into the intestinal mucosae of organisms and produce larvae in the gastrointestinal tract that move through the bloodstream and lymphatic system and encyst in striated muscle tissue (chest, diaphragm, arms and legs), where they die. In the U.S. less than 0.5% of pigs are infected, and less than 40 cases of the disease are now reported annually, although it continues to be common throughout the world. SYN: *trichinellosis.* SEE: *Nursing Diagnoses Appendix.*

SYMPTOMS: Anorexia, nausea, vomiting, abdominal cramping, and diarrhea may sometimes be present when the infected meat is eaten (invasion or stage 1). After the larvae penetrate the intestinal mucosa and invade blood and lymph to migrate to the muscles (dissemination or stage 2), patients have fever, muscle pain (most often in the extremities), and periorbital and facial edema. Sometimes patients experience itching and burning of the skin, sweating, and skin lesions. Rarely, signs of encephalitis, myocarditis, and invasion of the diaphragm occur, which can result in death. After encystment (or stage 3), the only symptom may be vague muscular pains, which may persist for weeks.

DIAGNOSIS: Diagnosis is based primarily on the patient's history of ingesting raw or under cooked pork, pork products, or game and the clinical findings. During the invasion stage, stools may contain larvae and mature worms. Laboratory testing reveals an extreme increase in eosinophils circulating in the blood (as high as 15,000/mm³).

TREATMENT: Albendazole is effective during the intestinal stage, and is administered for 14 days after diagnosis. Muscle pains should be relieved by analgesics. Corticosteroids are indicated for allergic reaction, severe inflammation, or central nervous system involvement. Once the larvae have encysted in the muscles, no curative therapy exists. Treatment is generally symptomatic and supportive.

PROGNOSIS: The prognosis depends on the number of worms ingested. The majority of patients recover.

PREVENTION: Pork and wild game should always be cooked to an internal temperature of at least 160°F (71°C) to destroy trichinella; smoking and pickling do not destroy the organism. The meat industry advocates irradiation to ensure roundworm destruction, but this process is controversial.

PATIENT CARE: The caregiver provides support and encourages the patient to report adverse symptoms, because treatment is primarily directed at their relief. The patient should also obtain sufficient rest, bedrest in severe cases to prevent a relapse. Health care professionals should educate the public about the importance of properly cooking and storing meats from all carnivorous animals. Travelers to foreign countries should be advised against eating pork or pork products, as the animals may have been fed raw garbage. All cases of trichinosis should be reported to local public health authorities.

trichinous (trĭk′ĭn-ŭs) [Gr. *trichinos*, of hair] Infested with trichinae.

tricho-, trich- [Gr. *thrix*, stem *trich-*, hair] Prefixes meaning *hair*. SEE: *-thrix*.

trichoanesthesia (trĭk″ō-ăn″ĕs-thē′zē-ă) Loss of sensibility of the hair.

trichobezoar (trĭk″ō-bē′zōr″) [*tricho-* + Arabic *bazahr*, antidote (against poison)] Hairball.

trichocyst (trĭk′ō-sĭst) [″ + *kystis*, bladder] **1.** A cell structure derived from cytoplasm. **2.** In some single-celled organisms, a vesicle equipped with a thread that can be thrust out for the purposes of defense or attack.

Trichodectes (trĭk″ō-dĕk′tēz) [″ + *dektes*, biter] A genus of lice that infests dogs and sheep. Some are the intermediate hosts of tapeworms.

trichoepithelioma (trĭk″ō-ĕp″ĭ-thē-lē-ō″mă) [″ + *epi*, upon, + *thele*, nipple, + *oma*, tumor] A benign skin tumor originating in the hair follicles.

trichoesthesia (trĭk″ō-ĕs-thē′zē-ă) [″ + *aisthesis*, sensation] **1.** The sensation felt when a hair is touched. **2.** A paresthesia causing a sensation of the presence of a hair on a mucous membrane or on the skin.

trichogen (trĭk′ō-jĕn) [″ + *gennan*, to produce] An agent stimulating hair growth.

trichogenous (trĭk-ŏj′ĕn-ŭs) Promoting hair growth.

trichoglossia (trĭk″ō-glŏs′ē-ă) [″ + *glossa*, tongue] A hairy condition of the tongue.

trichohyalin (trĭk″ō-hī′ă-lĭn) [″ + *hyalos*, glass] The hyaline of the hair.

trichoid (trĭk′oyd) [″ + *eidos*, form, shape] Hairlike.

tricholith (trĭk′ō-lĭth) [″ + *lithos*, stone] **1.** A hairy nodule on the hair; seen in piedra. **2.** A calcified intestinal bezoar that contains hair.

trichology (trĭk-ŏl′ō-jē) [″ + *logos*, word, reason] The study of the hair and its care and treatment.

trichoma (trĭk-ō′mă) [Gr., hairiness] **1.** Inversion of one or more eyelashes.

SYN: *entropion*. **2.** Matted, verminous, encrusted hair.

trichomatosis (trĭk″ō-mă-tō′sĭs) [″ + *osis*, condition] Entangled matted hair caused by scalp fungus.

trichomatous (trĭ-kŏm′ă-tŭs) Pert. to or affected with trichoma.

trichome (trī′kōm) [Gr. *trichoma*, a growth of hair] **1.** A hair or other appendage of the skin. **2.** A colony of cyanobacteria in which the cells form chains.

trichomegaly (trĭk″ō-mĕg′ă-lē) [Gr. *trichos*, hair, + *megas*, large] Long, coarse eyebrows.

trichomonacide (trĭk″ō-mō′nă-sīd) Anything that is lethal to trichomonads.

trichomonad (trĭk′ō-mō′nad″) [*tricho-* + *monad* (2)] **1.** Pert. to or resembling the genus *Trichomonas*. **2.** A member of the genus *Trichomonas*. **trichomonal** (-mō′năl), *adj*.

Trichomonas (trĭk″ō′mō′năs) [″ + *monas*, unit] A genus of flagellate parasitic protozoa.

T. hominis A benign trichomonad found in the large intestine.

T. tenax A benign trichomonad that may be present in the mouth.

T. vaginalis A species found in the vagina that produces discharge. *T. vaginalis* is fairly common in women, esp. during pregnancy or following vaginal surgery. It is sometimes found in the male urethra and may be transmitted through sexual intercourse. SEE: illus.; *colpitis macularis*.

TRICHOMONAS VAGINALIS (arrow) AND BACTERIA IN VAGINAL SMEAR (×1000)

SYMPTOMS: *T. vaginalis* causes persistent burning, redness, and itching of the vulvar tissue associated with a profuse vaginal discharge that may be frothy or malodorous or both. Occasionally, infection with *T. vaginalis* is asymptomatic.

TREATMENT: Metronidazole (Flagyl) is taken orally by the woman and her sexual partner. The drug is contraindicated during the first trimester of pregnancy because of potential damage to the developing fetus; clotrimazole vaginal suppositories provide symptomatic relief during the first 12 weeks of gestation.

⚠ Alcohol should not be consumed during metronidazole therapy.

trichomoniasis (trĭk″ō-mō-nī′ă-sĭs) [″ + ″ + -iasis, infection] Infestation with a parasite of the genus *Trichomonas*.

trichomycosis (trĭk″ō-mī-kō′sĭs) [″ + mykes, fungus, + osis, condition] Any disease of the hair caused by a fungus.

  t. axillaris An infection of the axillary region and sometimes pubic hairs caused by *Nocardia tenuis*.

  t. nodosa Piedra.

trichonosis (trĭk-ō-nō′sĭs) [Gr. trichos, hair, + nosos, disease] Any disease of the hair. SYN: *trichopathy*.

trichopathy (trĭk-ŏp′ă-thē) [″ + pathos, disease, suffering] Trichonosis.

trichophagia, trichophagy (trĭk-ō-fā′jē-ă, -ŏf′ă-jē) [″ + phagein, to eat] The habit of eating hair.

trichophobia (trĭk″ō-fō′bē-ă) [″ + phobos, fear] An abnormal dread of hair or of touching it.

trichophytic (trĭk″ō-fĭt′ĭk) [″ + phyton, plant] 1. Pert. to *Trichophyton*. 2. Promoting hair growth.

trichophytic granulosa (trĭk″ō-fĭt′ĭk) Majocchi disease.

trichophytid (trĭ-kŏf′ĭ-tĭd) A skin disorder considered to be an allergic reaction to fungi of the genus *Trichophyton*.

trichophytin (trĭ-kŏf′ĭ-tĭn) An extract prepared from cultures of the fungi of the genus *Trichophyton;* used as an antigen for skin tests and for the treatment of certain trichophytid infections.

trichophytobezoar (trĭk-ō-fī″tō-bē′zor) [″ + phyton, plant, + Arabic bazahr, protecting against poison] A hairball found in the stomach or intestine composed of hair, vegetable fibers, and miscellaneous debris.

Trichophyton (trĭ-kŏf′ĭt-ŏn) A genus of parasitic fungi that lives in or on the skin or its appendages (hair and nails) and is the cause of various dermatomycoses and ringworm infections. Species that produce spores arranged in rows on the outside of the hair are designated ectothrix; if spores are within the hair, endothrix.

  T. mentagrophytes A species, one form of which, called granulare, is parasitic on several mammals including horses, dogs, and rodents and can also affect humans. Another variety, called interdigitale, is associated with tinea pedis.

  T. schoenleinii The causative agent of favus of the scalp. SEE: favus.

  T. tonsurans The most frequent cause of ringworm of the scalp. SEE: tinea capitis.

  T. violaceum The causative agent of

some forms of ringworm of the scalp, beard, or nails.

trichophytosis (trĭk″ō-fī-tō′sĭs) [″ + phyton, plant, + osis, condition] Infestation with *Trichophyton* fungi.

trichoptilosis (trĭk″ŏp-tĭl-ō′sĭs) [″ + ptilon, feather, + osis, condition] 1. The splitting of hairs at their ends, giving them a feather-like appearance. 2. A disease of hair marked by development of nodules along the hair shaft, at which point it splits off.

trichosis (trĭ-kō′sĭs) [″ + osis, condition] Any disease of the hair or its abnormal growth or development in an abnormal place.

Trichosporon (trĭ-kŏs′pō-rŏn) [″ + sporos, a seed] A genus of fungi that causes superficial skin infections in immunocompetent hosts and opportunistic infections (e.g., endocarditis, fungemia, and lung, kidney, and splenic infections) in immunocompromised patients.

  T. beigelii The causative agent of white piedra. SEE: piedra.

trichosporosis (trĭk″ō-spō-rō′sĭs) [″ + ″ + osis, condition] Infestation of the hair with *Trichosporon*.

trichostrongyliasis (trĭk″ō-strŏn-jĭ-lī′ă-sĭs) Infestation with the intestinal parasite *Trichostrongylus*, a rare disease in the U.S.

trichostrongylosis (trĭk″ō-strŏn″jĭ-lō′sĭs) Infestation with *Trichostrongylus*.

Trichostrongylus (trĭk″ō-strŏn′jĭ-lŭs) A genus of nematode worms of the family Trichostrongylidae. These worms are of economic importance because of the damage they cause to domestic animals and birds.

trichotillomania (trĭk″ō-tĭl″ō-mā′nē-ă) [″ + tillein, to pull, + mania, madness] The unnatural and irresistible urge to pull out one's own hair. Clomipramine has been effective in treating this condition.

trichotomous (trī-kŏt′ō-mŭs) [Gr. tricha, threefold, + tome, incision] Divided into three.

trichotomy (trī-kŏt′ō-mē) Division into three parts.

trichotoxin (trĭk″ō-tŏks′ĭn) [Gr. trichos, hair, + toxikon, poison] An antibody or cytotoxin that destroys ciliated epithelial cells.

trichotrophy (trĭ-kŏt′rō-fē) [″ + trophe, nourishment] Nutrition of the hair.

trichroic (trī-krō′ĭk) [Gr. treis, three, + chroa, color] Presenting three different colors when viewed along each of three different axes.

trichroism (trī′krō-ĭzm) [″ + ″ + -ismos, condition] The quality of displaying a different color when viewed along each of three axes. SYN: *trichromatism*.

trichromatic (trī″krō-măt′ĭk) [″ + chroma, color] Pert. to or able to see the three primary colors; denoting normal color vision. SYN: *trichromic*.

trichromatism (trī-krō′mă-tĭzm) Trichroism.

trichromatopsia (trī″krō-mă-tŏp′sē-ă) Normal color vision.

trichromic (trī-krō′mĭk) Pert. to normal color vision or the ability to see the three primary colors. SYN: *trichromatic.*

trichuriasis (trĭk″ū-rī′ă-sĭs) [Gr. *trichos*, hair, + *oura*, tail + *-iasis*, condition] Infestation of worms of the genus *Trichuris* in the colon or in the ileum.

Trichuris (tri-kū′rĭs) A genus of parasitic worms of the phylum Nematoda, the class Adenophorea, and the family Trichuridae.

> **T. trichiura** A species that infests humans when the ova that have undergone incubation in the soil are ingested. The larvae develop into adults, which inhabit the large intestine. Symptoms of infestation include diarrhea and abdominal pain. Rectal prolapse may occur if a great number of worms are present. Mebendazole is the drug of choice; albendazole or ivermectin may be of benefit. SYN: *whipworm.* SEE: illus.

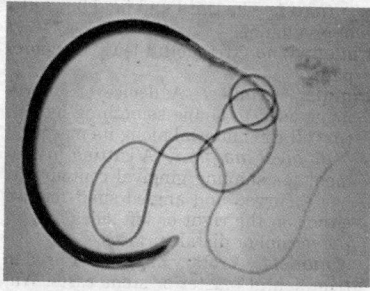

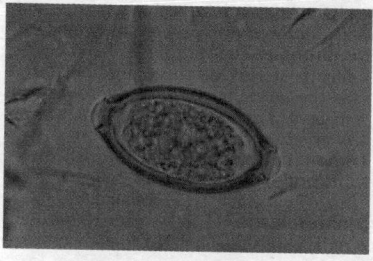

TRICHURIS TRICHIURA

(A) adult female (×4), (B) egg (×500)

tricipital (trī-sĭp′ĭ-tăl) [Gr. *treis*, three, + L. *caput*, head] Three-headed, as the triceps muscle.

trickle (trĭk′ĕl) To let a few drops fall at a time; to allow fluid to flow slowly. Local or topical anesthetics are often applied by trickling them over wounds or mucous membranes.

tricrotic (trī-krŏt′ĭk) [Gr. *trikrotos*, rowed with a triple stroke] Pert. to a pulse in which three accentuated waves or notches occur with each pulse.

tricrotism (trī′krŏt-ĭzm) [″ + *-ismos*, condition] The condition of being tricrotic.

tricuspid (trī-kŭs′pĭd) [Gr. *treis*, three, + L. *cuspis*, point] **1.** Pert. to the tricuspid valve. **2.** Having three points or cusps.

tricuspid area The lower portion of the body of the sternum where sounds of the right atrioventricular orifice are best heard.

tricuspid orifice Right atrioventricular cardiac aperture.

tricuspid tooth A tooth with a crown that has three cusps.

tricuspid valve SEE: under *valve.*

trident, tridentate (trī′dĕnt, trī-dĕn′tāt) [L. *tres, tria,* three, + *dens,* tooth] Having three prongs.

tridermoma (trī″dĕr-mō′mă) [″ + ″ + *oma,* tumor] A teratoid growth containing all three germ layers.

trifid (trī-fĭd) [L. *trifidus,* split thrice] Split into three; having three clefts.

trifocal (trī-fō′kăl) [L. *tri-,* three, + *focus,* hearth] Having three convergence points, as in a trifocal lens. SEE: *bifocal; focus.*

Trifolium pretense (trī-fōl′ē-ŭm prĕ-tĕn′sē) [L., lit. extended trefoil] The scientific name for red clover, an herbal remedy containing phytoestrogens. Despite its estrogenic chemistry it is not an effective treatment for hot flashes occurring in menopause.

trifurcation (trī″fŭr-kā′shŭn) [Gr. *treis,* three, + L. *furca,* fork] **1.** Division into three branches. **2.** In dentistry, the area of root division in a tooth with three roots.

trifurcation involvement The extension of periodontitis or a periodontal pocket into an area where the tooth roots divide.

trigeminal (trī-jĕm′ĭn-ăl) [L. *tres, tria,* three, + *geminus,* twin] Pert. to the trigeminus or fifth cranial nerve.

trigeminy (trī-jĕm′ĭ-nē) Occurring in threes, esp. three pulse beats in rapid succession.

trigenic (trī-jĕn′ĭk) [Gr. *treis,* three, + *gennan,* to produce] In genetics, a condition in which three alleles are present at any particular locus on the chromosome.

trigger (trĭg′ĕr) **1.** Stimulus. **2.** To initiate or start with suddenness. **3.** A chemical that initiates a function or action.

trigger finger SEE: under *finger.*

triggering The initiation of a mechanically generated breath after the detection of a change in airway pressure, after a change in air flow, or after an alteration in the flow wave form.

trigger point SEE: under *point.*

trigger point dry needling ABBR: TrPDN. Intramuscular stimulation.

triglyceride (trī-glĭs′ĕr-īd) Any combinations of glycerol with three of five different fatty acids. These substances, triacylglycerols, are also called neutral fats. In the blood, triglycerides are combined with proteins to form lipoproteins. The liver synthesizes lipoproteins to transport fats to other tissues, where they are a source of energy. Fat in adipose tissue is stored energy. SYN: *triacylglycerol.* SEE: *hyperlipoproteinemia.*

medium-chain t. Triglycerides with 8 to 10 carbon atoms. They are absorbed differently from long chain fatty acids (i.e., via the portal vein through the liver rather than as chylomicrons transported via the lymphatics) and therefore, have been used to treat malabsorption.

trigone (trī′gōn″) [L. fr Gr. *trigōnos,* triangular] A triangular space, esp. one at the base of the bladder, between the two openings of the ureters and the urethra.

trigonal (trĭg′ŏ-năl), *adj.* SYN: **t.** *of bladder.*

t. of bladder Trigone.

carotid t. The triangular area in the neck bounded by the posterior belly of the digastric muscle, the sternocleidomastoid muscle, and the midline of the neck.

collateral t. The angle between the diverging inferior and posterior horns of the lateral ventricle.

habenular t. A depressed triangular area located on the lateral aspect of the posterior portion of the third ventricle. It contains a medial and lateral habenular nucleus.

olfactory t. A small triangular eminence at the root of the olfactory peduncle and anterior to the anterior perforated space of the base of the brain.

trigonectomy (trĭg″gōn-ĕk′tō-mē) [″ + *ektome,* excision] Excision of the base of the bladder.

Trigonella foenum graecum (trĭg″ŏ-nel′ă fē′nŭm grēk′ŭm) SEE: *fenugreek.*

trigonid (trī-gō′nĭd) The first three cusps of a lower molar tooth.

trigonitis (trĭg″ŏ-nī′tĭs) [″ + *itis,* inflammation] Inflammation of the mucous membrane of the trigone of the bladder.

trigonocephalus (trĭg″ō-nō-sĕf′ă-lŭs) A fetus exhibiting trigonocephaly.

trigonocephaly (trī-gō″nō-sĕf′ă-lē) The condition of the head of the fetus being shaped like a triangle.

trihybrid (trī-hī′brĭd) [Gr. *treis,* three, + L. *hybrida,* mongrel] In genetics, the offspring of a cross between two individuals differing in three unit characters.

triiodothyronine (trī″ī-ō″dō-thī′rō-nēn) ABBR: T_3. One of two forms of the principal hormone secreted by the thyroid gland. Chemically it is 3,5,3′-triiodothyronine (liothyronine). SEE: *tetraiodo-thyronine; thyroid gland; thyroid function test; thyroxine.*

trilaminar (trī-lăm′ĭ-năr) Composed of three layers.

trilineage (trī-lin′ē-ăj) [*tri-* + *lineage*] Pert. to or affecting all three types of blood cells (red cells, white cells, and platelets).

trill (trĭl) [It. *trillare,* probably imitative] A tremulous sound, esp. in vocal music.

trilogy (trĭl′ō-jē) A series of three events.

trimanual (trī-măn′ū-ăl) [″ + *manualis,* by hand] Performed with three hands, as an obstetrical maneuver.

trimensual (trī-měn′shū-ăl) [″ + *mensualis,* monthly] Occurring every 3 months.

Trimeresurus (trĭm″ĕ-rĕ-soor′ŭs) [L. *trimerus,* fr Gr. *trimerēs,* having three parts + Gr. *ouros,* tail] A genus of poisonous tropical pit vipers found primarily in East and Southeast Asia.

trimester (trī-měs′tĕr) A 3-month period.

first t. The first 3 months of pregnancy.

second t. The middle 3 months of pregnancy.

third t. The third and final 3 months of pregnancy.

trimethylene (trī-měth′ĭ-lēn) Cyclopropane.

trimmer (trĭm′ĕr) A device or instrument used to shape something by cutting off the material along its margin.

gingival margin t. A cutting instrument for shaping gingival contours. It has a curved and angled shaft for use either on the right or left sides and on the mesial or distal surfaces.

model t. A rotary flat grinder used to trim dental plaster or stone casts. Water keeps the cutting surface clean and obviates any dust problem as the casts are squared into proper study models.

trimorphous (trī-mor′fŭs) [″ + *morphe,* form] 1. Having three different forms as the larva, pupa, and adult of certain insects. 2. Having three different forms of crystals.

Trimox (trī′mŏks″) SEE: *amoxicillin.*

trinitrophenol (trī″nī″trŏ-fē′nōl″) [*tri-* + *nitro-* + *phenol*] Picric acid.

trinitrotoluene (trī″nī-trō-tŏl′ū-ēn) ABBR: TNT. $C_7H_5N_3O_6$, an explosive compound.

triolein (trī-ō′lē-ĕn) Olein.

triorchid, triorchis (trī-or′kĭd, -kĭs) [″ + *orchis,* testicle] A person who has three testicles.

triorchidism (trī-or′kĭd-ĭzm) [″ + ″ + *-ismos,* condition] The condition of having three testicles.

triose (trī′ōs) A monosaccharide having three carbon atoms in its molecule.

trioxsalen (trī-ŏk′să-lĕn) An agent used to promote repigmentation in vitiligo. Trade name is Trisoralen. SEE: *psoralen; vitiligo.*

trip (trĭp) A slang term for hallucinations produced by various drugs, including LSD, mescaline, and some narcotics.

tripara (trĭp'ă-ră) [L. *tres, tria,* three, + *parere,* to bear] [ABBR. Para III.] A woman who has had three pregnancies that have lasted beyond 20 weeks or that have produced an infant of at least 500 g.

Tripedia (trī-pēd'ē-ă) Diphtheria and tetanus toxoids and acellular pertussis vaccine adsorbed. SEE: *DTaP vaccine.*

tripe palm Velvety thickening of the skin of the palms, giving the skin surface the appearance of the villous lining of the intestines. It is usually found in patients with acanthosis nigricans and some internal organ or external (skin) cancers. SYN: *acanthosis palmaris.*

tripeptide (trī-pĕp'tīd) [Gr. *treis,* three, + *pepton,* digested] The product of a combination of three amino acids formed during proteolytic digestion.

triphalangia (trī″fă-lăn'jē-ă) [″ + *phalanx,* closely knit row] A deformity marked by the presence of three phalanges in a thumb or great toe.

triphasic (trī-fā'sĭk) [″ + *phasis,* phase] Of electric currents, consisting of three phases or stages.

triphenylmethane (trī-fĕn″ĭl-mĕth'ān) A coal tar-derived chemical that is the basis of some dyes and stains.

Tripier amputation (trē-pyā') [Léon Tripier, Fr. surgeon, 1842–1891] Amputation of a foot with part of the calcaneus removed.

triple (trĭp'ĕl) [L. *triplus,* threefold] Consisting of three; threefold; treble.

Triple C [Abbr. of *Coricidin Cold and Cough,* a trade name] A colloquial term for an over-the-counter cough medication containing dextromethorphan that, when consumed in large quantities, can cause perceptual alterations and hallucinations. SEE: *dextromethorphan.*

triplegia (trī-plē'jē-ă) [″ + *plege,* stroke] Hemiplegia with paralysis of one limb on the other side of the body.

triple-marker test A test for Down syndrome that assesses maternal serum levels of alpha-fetoprotein, human chorionic gonadotropin, and unconjugated estriol. The test is sometimes used as an alternative to amniocentesis.

triple negative disease Breast cancer in which malignant cells have no detectable estrogen receptors, progesterone receptors, or HER2 receptors. SYN: *triple negative breast cancer.*

Triple-P positive parenting program ABBR: TP. A parental education program, devised in Australia and adopted in many other countries, to help parents intervene nonviolently when their child displays disruptive or hyperactive behavior.

triple rule-out scan SEE: under *scan.*

triplet (trĭp'lĕt) [L. *triplus,* threefold] **1.** One of three children born of a single gestation. SEE: *Hellin law.* **2.** A combination of three of a kind.

triplex (trī'plĕks, trĭp'lĕks) [Gr. *triploos,* triple] Triple; threefold.

triploid (trĭp'loyd) Pert. to triploidy.

triploidy (trĭp'loy-dē) In the human, having three sets of chromosomes.

triplopia (trĭp-lō'pē-ă) [″ + *ope,* vision] A condition in which three images of the same object are seen.

tripod (trī'pŏd) [Gr. *treis,* three, + *pous,* foot] A stand having three supports, usually legs.

tripodia (trī-pō'dē-ă) Having three feet.

tripoding (trī'pŏd-ĭng) The use of three bases for support (e.g., two legs and a cane, or one leg and two crutches).

-tripsy [Gr. *tripsis,* friction, rubbing] Suffix meaning *crushing.*

triptan A class of medications used to treat cluster and migraine headaches. Members of this class act as agonists at 5-hydroxytryptamine (5-HT) receptors in the brain. Each of them has a generic name that ends in *-triptan,* e.g., frovatriptan, naratriptan, rizatriptan, and sumatriptan.

-triptyline A suffix used in pharmacology to designate a cyclic antidepressant.

triquetral (trī-kwē'trăl) [L. *triquetrus*] Triangular.

triquetrum (trī-kwē'trŭm, -tră) *pl.* **triquetra** [L. *triquetrus,* triangular] Triquetral bone. **triquetral** (-trĕl), *adj.*

triradius (trī-rā'dē-ŭs) In classifying fingerprints, the point of convergence of dermal ridges coming from three directions.

trisaccharide (trī-săk'ă-rīd) A carbohydrate that on hydrolysis yields three molecules of simple sugars (monosaccharides).

trismic (trĭz'mĭk) Pert. to trismus.

trismoid (trĭz'moyd) [Gr. *trismos,* grating, + *eidos,* form, shape] Of the nature of trismus.

trismus (trĭz'mŭs) [Gr. *trismos,* grating] Tonic contraction of the muscles of mastication; may occur in mouth infections, encephalitis, inflammation of salivary glands, and tetanus. SYN: *lockjaw.*

trisomic (trī-sōm'ĭk) In genetics, an individual possessing 2n + 1 chromosomes, that is, one set of chromosomes contains an extra (third) chromosome. SEE: *chromosome; karyotype.*

trisomy (trī'sō-mē) In genetics, having three homologous chromosomes per cell instead of two.

   t. **13** A severe developmental disorder in which a third copy of chromosome 13 is present in the cell nucleus. It is often lethal in utero. Children who survive fetal development may have severe facial, scalp, and cranial deformities, and a predisposition to leukemia. SYN: *Patau syndrome.*

t. 18 A severe, usually lethal developmental disorder in which a third copy of chromosome 18 is present in the cell nucleus. Children with trisomy 18 usually do not survive beyond the first year of life. The condition is characterized by cranial, neurological, facial, cardiac, and gastrointestinal malformations. The disease can be sometimes detected during pregnancy with ultrasound or specialized blood tests. SYN: *Edward syndrome.*

t. 21 Down syndrome.

TRISS *trauma injury severity score.*

tristichia (trī-stĭk′ē-ă) [″ + *stichos,* row] The presence of three rows of eyelashes.

trisulfate (trī-sŭl′fāt) A chemical compound containing three sulfate, SO_4, groups.

trisulfide (trī-sŭl′fīd) A chemical compound containing three sulfur atoms.

tritanomalopia (trī″tă-nŏm′ă-lō-pē-ă) [Gr. *tritos,* third, + *anomalos,* irregular, + *ope,* sight] A color vision defect similar to tritanopia but less pronounced. SYN: *tritanomaly.*

tritanomaly (trī″tă-nŏm′ă-lē) Tritanomalopia.

tritanopia (trī″tă-nō′pē-ă) [Gr. *tritos,* third, + *an-,* not, + *ope,* vision] Blue blindness; color blindness in which there is a defect in the perception of blue. SEE: *color blindness.*

tritiate (trĭt′ē-āt) To treat with tritium.

tritiated thymidine (trĭt′ē-āt″ĭd thī′mĭ-dēn″, trĭsh′) ³H-Tdr; a radioactively labeled nucleoside used to measure T lymphocyte proliferation in vitro. Thymidine is essential for DNA synthesis; thus the amount of ³H-Tdr taken up is a general measure of the number of new lymphocytes produced.

tritium (trĭt′ē-ŭm, trĭsh′ē-ŭm) [Gr. *tritos,* third] SYMB: H³. The mass three isotope of hydrogen; triple-weight hydrogen.

triturable (trĭt′ū-ră-bl) [L. *triturare,* to pulverize] Capable of being powdered.

triturate (trĭt′ū-rāt) **1.** To reduce to a fine powder by rubbing. **2.** A finely divided substance made by rubbing.

trituration (trĭt-ū-rā′shŭn) [L. *triturare,* to pulverize] **1.** Reducing to a powder. **2.** A finely ground and easily mixed powder. **3.** The mixing of dental alloy particles with mercury. Trituration may be done either manually in a mortar with a pestle or with a mechanical device. The goal of trituration is to abrade the alloy particles to facilitate the uptake of mercury.

⚠ Mercury compounds are toxic; care should be taken to avoid touching mercury during trituration. Inhaling mercury vapor and mercury particles produced when removing amalgam restorations also should be avoided.

trivalence (trĭv′ă-lĕns) The condition of being trivalent.

trivalent (trī-vā′lĕnt, trĭv′ăl-ĕnt) [Gr. *treis,* three, + L. *valens,* powerful] **1.** Combining with or replacing three hydrogen atoms. **2.** Having three components, e.g., as in a vaccine.

trivalve (trī′vălv) Having three valves.

trivial name A nonsystematic or semisystematic name and qualifying term used to name drugs. These names do not provide assistance in determining biological action or function of the drug. Examples include aspirin, caffeine, and belladonna.

tRNA *transfer RNA.*

trocar (trō′kăr) [Fr. *trois quarts,* three quarters] A sharply pointed surgical instrument contained in a cannula; used for aspiration or removal of fluids from cavities.

trochanter (trō-kan′tĕr) [L. fr. Gr. *tro-chantēr,* head of the femur] Either of the two bony processes below the neck of the femur.

greater t. A thick process at the lateral upper end of the femur projecting upward to the union of the neck and shaft.

lesser t. A conical tuberosity on the medial and posterior surface of the upper end of the femur, at the junction of the shaft and neck.

third t. The gluteal tubercle of the femur when it is unusually prominent.

trochanterplasty (trō-kăn′tĕr-plăs″tē) Plastic surgery of the neck of the femur.

troche, troch (trō′kē, trōk′) [Gr. *trokhiskos,* a small wheel] A solid, discoid, or cylindrical mass consisting chiefly of medicinal powder, sugar, and mucilage. Troches are used by placing them in the mouth and allowing them to remain until, through slow solution or disintegration, their mild medication is released. SYN: *lozenge.*

trochiscus (trō-kĭs′kŭs) [L., Gr. *trochiskos,* a small disk] A medicated tablet or troche.

trochlea (trŏk′lē-ă) *pl.* **trochleae** [Gr. *trokhileia,* system of pulleys] **1.** A structure having the function of a pulley; a ring or hook through which a tendon or muscle projects. **2.** The articular smooth surface of a bone on which glides another bone.

trochlear (trŏk′lē-ăr) **1.** Pert. to a pulley. **2.** Pert. to a trochlea.

trochlearis (trŏk″lē-ā′rĭs) [L.] The superior oblique muscle of the eye.

trochlear nerve The fourth cranial nerve, a small mixed nerve arising from the midbrain. It is both sensory and motor to the superior oblique muscle of the eye. SYN: *fourth cranial nerve.*

trochlea of the elbow A surface on the distal humerus that articulates with the ulna.

trochocardia (trō″kō-kăr′dē-ă) [Gr. *trokhos*, a wheel, + *kardia*, heart] Rotary displacement of the heart on its axis.

trochocephalia, trochocephaly (trō″kō-sē-fā′lē-ă, -sĕf′ă-lē) [″ + *kephale*, head] Roundheadedness, a deformity due to premature union of the frontal and parietal bones.

trochoid (trō′koyd) [Gr. *trokhos*, a wheel, + *eidos*, form, shape] Rotating or revolving, noting an articulation resembling a pivot or pulley. SEE: *joint*, *pivot*.

Troglotrematidae (trŏg″lō-trē-măt′ĭ-dē) A family of flukes that includes *Paragonimus*.

trohoc (trō′hŏk) [*cohort* spelled backwards] A colloquial term for a case control study in which an effect is identified and epidemiologists look retrospectively to find the cause.

Troisier node (trwă-zē-ā′) [Charles E. Troisier, Fr. physician, 1844–1919] Signal **node**.

troland (trō′lănd) A unit of visual stimulation to the retina of the eye. It is equal to the illumination received per square millimeter of the pupil from a source of 1 lux brightness.

Trombicula (trŏm-bĭk′ū-lă) A genus of mites belonging to the Trombiculidae. The larvae, called redbugs or chiggers, cause an irritating dermatitis and rash. Some are vectors of disease.

   T. akamushi A species that transmits the causative agent of scrub typhus.

trombiculiasis (trŏm-bĭk″ū-lī′ă-sĭs) Infestation with Trombiculidae.

Trombiculidae (trŏm-bĭk″ū-lī″dē) A family of mites; only the genus *Trombicula* is of medical significance.

trop-, tropo- [Gr. *tropos*, turn, direction] Prefixes meaning *turn, reaction, change*.

-trope [Gr. *tropos*, turn, direction] Suffix meaning (one that is) *turned inward*.

-troph [Gr. *trophē*, nourishment] Suffix. meaning *nutrient material, food*.

trophedema (trŏf″ĕ-dē′mă) [Gr. *trophe*, nourishment, + *oidema*, a swelling] Permanent, localized edema of a limb or limbs. Repeated low-grade infection may also obstruct the flow of lymph.

Tropheryma whippeli (trō-fĕr′ĭ-mă (h)wĭp-ĕl-ī) A gram-positive, aerobic bacillus that grows in branching filaments. It is the cause of Whipple disease. SEE: *Whipple disease*.

trophic (trŏf′ĭk) [Gr. *trophikos*] Pert. to nourishment, particularly to a type of efferent nerves believed to control the growth and nourishment of the parts they innervate. SEE: *autotrophic*.

-trophic, -trophous [Gr. *trophikos*, pert. to nourishment, fr. *trophē*, food] Suffixes meaning *having the nutritional needs of* (specified by the first element). This suffix is frequently confused with *-tropic*. SEE: *-tropic*.

trophic ulceration of eye A noninfectious ulceration of the corneal epithelium of the eye due to repeated trauma.

trophism (trŏf′ĭzm) Nutrition.

tropho-, troph- [Gr. *trophē*, nourishment] Prefixes meaning *nourishment*.

trophoblast (trō′fō-blast″) [*tropho-* + *-blast*] The outermost layer of the developing blastocyst (blastodermic vesicle). It differentiates into two layers, the cytotrophoblast and syntrophoblast. SEE: *cytotrophoblast; syntrophoblast; fertilization* for illus.

trophoblastic (trō″fō-blast′ĭk), *adj.*

trophoblastic disease ABBR: TD. Any neoplasm of trophoblastic origin. SEE: *chorioadenoma destruens; choriocarcinoma; hydatid mole.*

trophoblastoma (trŏf″ō-blăs-tō′mă) [″ + ″ + *oma*, tumor] A neoplasm due to excessive proliferation of chorionic epithelium. SYN: *chorioepithelioma.*

trophocyte (trŏf′ō-sīt) A cell that nourishes (e.g., Sertoli cells of the testicle, which support developing spermatozoa). SYN: *trephocyte.*

trophoneurosis (trŏf″ō-nū-rō′sĭs) [″ + *neuron*, nerve, + *osis*, condition] Any trophic disorder caused by defective function of the nerves concerned with nutrition of the part.

   disseminated t. Thickening and hardening of the skin. SYN: *sclerema; scleroderma.*

   facial t. Progressive facial atrophy.

   muscular t. Muscular changes in connection with nervous disorders.

trophonucleus (trŏf″ō-nū′klē-ŭs) [″ + *nucleus*, kernel] Protozoan nucleus concerned with vegetative functions in metabolism and not reproduction.

trophopathia (trŏf″ō-păth′ē-ă) [″ + *pathos*, disease, suffering] **1.** Any disorder of nutrition. **2.** A trophic disease.

trophozoite (trŏf″ō-zō′īt) [″ + *zoon*, animal] A sporozoan nourished by its hosts during its growth stage.

-trophy [Gr. *trophē*, nourishment] Suffix meaning *nutrition, nourishment, growth.*

tropia (trō′pē-ă) [Gr. *trope*, turn] Deviation of the eye or eyes away from the visual axis; observed with the eyes open and uncovered. Esotropia indicates inward or nasal deviation; exotropia, outward; hypertropia, upward; hypotropia, downward. SYN: *manifest squint; strabismus.* SEE: *-phoria.*

-tropia Suffix meaning *turning.*

-tropic [Gr. *tropikos*, pert. to a turn, fr. *tropos*, turn] Suffix meaning *turned to, attracted to.* This suffix is frequently confused with *-trophic.* SEE: *-trophic.*

tropical (trŏp′ĭ-kal) [Gr. *tropikos*, turning] Pert. to the tropics.

tropical immersion foot SEE: under *immersion foot*.

tropical lichen SEE: under *lichen*.

-tropin [*trop-* + *-in*] Suffix indicating the stimulating effect of a substance, esp. a hormone, on its target organ.

tropine (trō′pĭn) An alkaloid, $C_8H_{15}NO$, that smells like tobacco. It is present in certain plants.

tropism (trō′pĭzm) [Gr. *trope*, turn, + *-ismos*, condition] The involuntary response of an organism as a bending, turning, or movement toward (positive tropism) or away from (negative tropism) an external stimulus such as light, heat, gravity, or various chemical changes. SEE: *chemotropism; phototropism*.

tropocollagen (trō″pō-kŏl′ă-jĕn) [″ + *collagen*] The basic molecular unit of collagen fibrils, composed of three polypeptide chains.

tropometer (trŏp-ŏm′ĕ-ter) [″ + *metron*, measure] **1.** A device for measuring the rotation of the eyeballs. **2.** An instrument for measuring torsion in long bones.

tropomyosin (trō″pō-mī′ō-sĭn) An inhibitory protein in muscle fibers; it blocks myosin from forming cross-bridges with actin until shifted by troponin-calcium ion interaction.

troponin (trō′pō-nĭn) An inhibitory protein in muscle fibers. The action potential at the sarcolemma causes the sarcoplasmic reticulum to release calcium ions, which bond to troponin and shift tropomyosin away from the myosin-binding sites of actin, permitting contraction. SEE: *muscle* for illus.

    t. I A protein released into the blood by damaged heart muscle (but not skeletal muscle), and therefore a highly sensitive and specific indicator of recent myocardial infarction.

    t. T A protein, found in both skeletal and cardiac muscle, that can be detected in the blood following injury to heart muscle. Assays for it can be used as rapid tests for myocardial infarction (MI). Troponin I (which is released only by heart and not by skeletal muscles) is a more specific marker for MI than troponin T.

Trotter syndrome (trot′ĕr) A unilateral neuralgia in the mandible, tongue, and ear. The causes are mandibular nerve lesions, deafness on the same side due to eustachian tube lesions, and damage to the levator palatini muscle resulting in kinesthesia of the soft palate.

trough (trof) A groove or channel.

    arm t. A concave positioning device attached to a wheelchair armrest that positions the arm and prevents lateral leaning, thus encouraging postural alignment.

    focal t. A three-dimensional area within which structures are accurately reproduced on a panoramic radiograph. Positioning the patient within the focal trough is critical to producing a panoramic radiograph that clearly reproduces oral structures.

    gingival t. Gingival sulcus.

    synaptic t. The depression in a muscle fiber adjacent to the axon terminal of a motor neuron in a myoneural junction.

Trousseau, Armand (troo-sō′) Armand Trousseau, Fr. internist, 1801–1867.

    T. sign A muscular spasm of the hand and wrist from pressure on the nerves and vessels of the upper arm. It is indicative of latent tetany, usually as a result of hypocalcemia.

    T. spots Streaking of the skin with the fingernail, seen in meningitis and other cerebral diseases.

Troyer syndrome (troy′ĕr) [Amish family name in the U.S.] Hereditary spastic **paraplegia**.

troy weight SEE: under *weight*.

trp tryptophan.

true (troo) **1.** Real, genuine, or actual. **2.** Straight.

true rib Any of the seven upper ribs on each side with cartilages articulating directly with the sternum. SEE: *rib*.

truncal (trŭng′kăl) [L. *truncus*, trunk] Rel. to the trunk.

truncate (trŭng′kāt) [L. *truncare*, to cut off] **1.** Having a square end as if it were cut off; lacking an apex. **2.** To shorten by amputation of a part of the entity.

trunk (trŭnk) [L. *truncus*, trunk] **1.** The body exclusive of the head and limbs. SYN: *torso*. **2.** The main stem of a lymphatic vessel, nerve, or blood vessel.

    celiac t. Celiac **artery**.

    pulmonary t. The artery that arises from the base of the right ventricle and bifurcates into the right and left pulmonary arteries.

    sympathetic t. Either of the two long chains of paravertebral sympathetic ganglia, connected by sympathetic axons, and running alongside the entire vertebral column.

TRUS Transrectal **ultrasound**.

trusion (troo′zhŭn) [L. *trudere*, to push; thrust] Malposition of a tooth or teeth.

truss (trŭs) **1.** A restraining device for pushing a hernia, esp. an inguinal or abdominal wall hernia, back into place. A truss is almost always a poor substitute for surgical therapy. **2.** To tie or bind as with a cord or string.

trust In the relations between health care providers and patients, reliance by both parties on the integrity and sincerity of each other, and the patient's confidence in the ability and good will of the care provider. Trust is essential in the relationship between patients and those who provide medical care for them.

truth serum Any of several hypnotic drugs supposedly having the effect of causing a person on questioning to talk freely and without inhibition. In actual practice, serum is not given, but a short-acting barbiturate or benzodiazepine is given intravenously. The reliability of the information obtained is questionable.

trybutyrase (trī-bū'tĕ-rās) An enzyme present in the stomach that digests the short-chain diglycerides of butter. SEE: *digestion*.

try-in (trī'ĭn) The temporary placement of a dental restoration or device to determine its fit and comfortableness.

trypanocide (trī-păn'ŭ-sīd") [Gr. *trypanon*, a borer, + L. *occcidere*, to kill] **1.** Destructive of trypanosomes. **2.** An agent that kills trypanosomes. SYN: *trypanosomicide*. **trypanocidal** (trĭp"ăn-ō-sī'dăl), *adj*.

trypanolysis (trĭp-ăn-ŏl'ĭ-sĭs) [" + *lysis*, dissolution] The dissolution of trypanosomes.

Trypanoplasma (trī"păn-ō-plăz'mă) [" + L. *plasma*, form, mold] A genus of protozoan parasites resembling trypanosomes.

Trypanosoma (tri-păn"ŏ-sō-mă) [Gr. *trypanon*, borer + Gr. *sŏma*, a body] A genus of parasitic flagellate protozoa found in the blood of many vertebrates, including humans. The protozoa are transmitted by insect vectors. The only two species relevant for disease in humans are *T. brucei* and *T. cruzi*. SEE: illus.

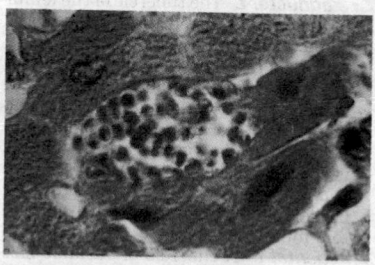

L_____J 20μm

TRYPANOSOMA CRUZI

(Orig. mag. × 1000)

    T. brucei A species with three subspecies: *T. brucei brucei*, *T. brucei gambiense*, and *T. brucei rhodesiense*. The subspecies *T. brucei brucei* causes a wasting disease in cattle called nagana but does not produce disease in humans. The subspecies *T. brucei gambiense* causes African sleeping sickness in western and central Africa. The subspecies *T. brucei rhodesiense*, transmitted by the tsetse fly, causes African sleeping sickness in eastern and southern Africa.

    T. cruzi The causative agent of Amer-

ican trypanosomiasis (Chagas disease). It is transmitted by triatomids (blood-sucking insects of the family Reduviidae).

trypanosome (trī'păn-ō-sōm) Any protozoan belonging to the genus Trypanosoma. **trypanosomal, trypanosomic,** *adj*.

trypanosomiasis (tri-pan"ŏ-sŏ-mī'ă-sĭs) [*Trypanosoma* + *-iasis*] Any of the several diseases occurring in humans and domestic animals caused by a species of *Trypanosoma*.

    African t. Any of several forms of tropical African trypanosomiasis, esp. sleeping sickness. SEE: *sleeping sickness* (2).

    American t. Chagas disease.

    South American trypanosomiasis Chagas disease.

trypanosomicide (trī-păn-ō-sōm'ĭ-sīd") Trypanocide.

trypanosomid (trī-păn'ō-sō-mĭd) A skin eruption in any disease caused by a trypanosome.

trypomastigote (trip"ŏ-mas'ti-gōt") [fr. *tryp(anosome)* + *mastigote*] Any of the circulating forms of the protozoan parasite, *Trypanosomacruzi*. They swim and feed in the blood and may be transmitted from person to person (e.g. in blood transfusions) or from mother to developing fetus across the placenta.

trypsin (trip'sĭn) [Gr. *tripsis*, friction + -IN] A proteolytic enzyme formed in the intestine from trypsinogen. It catalyzes the hydrolysis of peptide bonds in partly digested proteins and some native proteins, the final products being amino acids and various polypeptides. SEE: *chymotrypsin; digestion; enzyme; pancreas*.

tryptic (tik), *adj*.

trypsinogen (trĭp-sĭn'ō-jĕn) [" + *gennan*, to produce] The proenzyme or inactive form of trypsin that is released by the pancreas and converted to trypsin in the intestine.

tryptamine (trĭp'tă-mēn") [*trypt(ophan)* + "] A metabolite of tryptophan that acts as an enhancer of impulse propagation in the brain.

tryptase (trip'tās") An enzyme (specifically a neutral proteinase) produced by mast cells that mediates many allergic phenomena, including anaphylaxis, asthma, conjunctivitis, and rhinitis.

    PATIENT CARE: Elevated serum levels of tryptase are used to confirm the diagnosis of anaphylaxis.

tryptolysis (trĭp-tŏl'ĭ-sĭs) [" + *lysis*, dissolution] The hydrolysis of proteins or their derivatives by trypsin.

tryptone (trĭp'tōn) A peptide produced by the action of trypsin on a protein.

tryptophan (trĭp'tō-făn) ABBR: trp. $C_{11}H_{12}N_2O_2$; An essential amino acid present in high concentrations in animal and fish protein. It is necessary for normal growth and development. Tryptophan is a precursor of serotonin and niacin. In high doses, it may cause nausea, vomiting, and sedation.

tryptophanase (trĭp'tō-făn-ās) An enzyme that catalyzes the splitting of tryptophan into indole, pyruvic acid, and ammonia.

tryptophanuria (trĭp″tō-fă-nū′rē-ă) [*tryptophan* + Gr. *ouron*, urine] The presence of excessive levels of tryptophan in the urine.

TS *test solution; triple strength.*

T/S *thyroid:serum* (thyroid to serum iodine ratio).

T score A measure of bone density in which the mass of a patient's bones is compared with the bone mass of premenopausal women. A T score more than 1 standard deviation (SD) from the norm identifies bone that is osteopenic. A T score more than 2.5 SDs identifies osteoporosis.

TSD *target skin distance.*

tsetse fly (t(s)et′sē, t(s)ēt′) [Tswana (a Bantu language of Southern Africa) *tsètsè*, fly] SEE: under *fly*.

TSH *thyroid-stimulating **hormone**.* SEE: *thyrotropin*.

TSH-RF *thyroid-stimulating hormone-releasing **factor**.*

tsp *teaspoon.*

TSTA *tumor-specific transplantation antigen.*

tsutsugamushi disease (tsoo″tsoo-gă-moo′shĭ, soo″) [Japanese, dangerous bug] Scrub typhus.

TT *transit time* of blood through heart and lungs.

TTE (tē′tē′ē′) *transthoracic echocardiography.*

TTN *transient **tachypnea** of the newborn.*

T3 toxicosis SEE: under *toxicosis*.

T-tube A device inserted into the common bile duct, most often following cholecystectomy and bile duct exploration. It has two main purposes: to allow drainage of bile, and to introduce media, when needed for postoperative biliary imaging (T-tube cholangiogram). On occasion (e.g., in distal duct obstruction due to cancer or when cholangioenterostomy is performed), the tube may be left in for a sustained period.

T.U. *toxic unit; toxin unit.*

tub (tŭb) **1.** A receptacle for bathing. **2.** The use of a cold bath. **3.** To treat by using a cold bath.

tuba (too′bă) [L. *tubus*, tube] Tube.

tubal (tū′băl) [L. *tubus*, tube] Pert. to a tube, esp. the fallopian tube.

tubal factor SEE: under *factor*.

tubal reflux The movement of endometrial, tubal, or uterine tissue into the peritoneal cavity.

tubatorsion (tū″bă-tor′shŭn) [″ + *torsio*, a twisting] The twisting of an oviduct.

tubba, tubboe (tŭb′ă, -ō) Yaws that attacks the palms and soles.

tube (tūb) [L. *tubus*, a tube] A long, hollow, cylindrical structure. Particular tubes are listed under the first word. SEE: e.g., *endotracheal tube; fallopian tube; test tube.*

tubectomy (too-bĕk′tō-mē) Surgical removal of all or part of a tube, esp. the fallopian tube.

tube feeding Enteral tube feeding.

tubeless For a test, accomplished without an endoscope.

tubeless test (tūb′lĕs) A colloquial term for a test of gastrointestinal function that does not rely on the use of an endoscope. Thus there is no direct entrance into or visualization of the GI tract.

tuber (tū′bĕr) *pl.* **tubera** [L., a swelling] A swelling or enlargement.

    t. cinereum A part of the base of the hypothalamus bordered by the mammillary bodies, the optic chiasma, and on either side by the optic tract. It is connected by the infundibulum with the posterior lobe of the pituitary.

tubercle (too′bĕr-kl, tū′) [L. *tuberculum*, a little swelling] **1.** A small rounded elevation or eminence on a bone. **2.** A small nodule, esp. a circumscribed solid elevation of the skin or mucous membrane. **3.** The characteristic lesion resulting from infection by tubercle bacilli. It consists typically of three parts: a central giant cell, a midzone of epithelioid cells, and a peripheral zone of nonspecific structure. SEE: *tuberculosis*.

    adductor t. The tubercle of the femur to which is attached the tendon of the adductor magnus.

    articular t. The tubercle at the base of the zygomatic arch to which is attached the temporomandibular ligament; it is lateral to the articular eminence of the glenoid fossa, with which it is often confused.

    deltoid t. A tubercle on the anterior border of the acromium to which the deltoid muscle attaches.

    dental t. A tubercle of variable size on the crown of a tooth representing a thickened area of enamel or an accessory cusp.

    fibrous t. A fibrous tissue that has replaced a previously inflamed area.

    genital t. The embryonic structure that becomes the clitoris or the penis.

    Gerdy t. SEE: under *Gerdy, Pierre Nicholas.*

    Ghon t. SEE: under *Ghon, Anton.*

    lacrimal t. A small tubercle between the lacrimal crest and the frontal process of the maxilla.

    mental t. A small tubercle on either side of the midline of the chin.

    miliary t. A small tubercle resembling a millet seed, caused by tuberculosis. SEE: *miliary **tuberculosis**.*

Müller tubercle SEE: under *Müller, Johannes P.*

pubic t. A tubercle at the lateral end of the crest of the pubic bone. The inguinal ligament attaches to it.

scalene t. Lisfranc tubercle.

supraglenoid t. A rough, elevated area just above the glenoid cavity of the scapula. The long head of the biceps muscle of the arm attaches to this tubercle.

t. of the upper lip The prominence of the upper part of the vermilion border that represents the distal termination of the philtrum of the upper lip.

tuberculation (tū-bĕr″kū-lā′shŭn) The formation of tubercles.

tuberculid, tuberculide (tū-bĕr′kū-lĭd, -lĭd) [*tuberculum*] A tuberculous cutaneous eruption caused by toxins of tuberculosis. SYN: *tuberculoderma.*

follicular t. A cutaneous eruption characterized by the presence of groups of follicular lesions, esp. on the trunk.

papulonecrotic t. A form of tuberculid characterized by symmetrically distributed bluish papules, esp. on the extremities. These undergo central necrosis and, on healing, leave deep scars.

tuberculin (tū-bĕr′kū-lĭn) [*tuberculum*] A solution of purified protein derivative of *Mycobacterium tuberculosis*. It is injected intradermally to determine whether a person has been infected with tuberculosis. SYN: *purified protein derivative;; tuberculoprotein.* SEE: *tuberculin skin test.*

tuberculin skin test A test to determine the presence of infection with tuberculosis (TB). A solution containing purified protein derivative of TB is injected intradermally into the arm, and the response is read 48 to 72 hr later. A 5-mm induration is considered a positive reaction if the patient has been in close contact with persons infected with TB, is infected with human immunodeficiency virus (HIV), has risk factors for HIV, or has a chest x-ray examination that suggests a history of pulmonary TB. A 10-mm induration is considered positive in people born in nations where TB is endemic, in nursing home patients, in patients with other serious illnesses, and in people of low socioeconomic status. In all other people, a 15-mm induration is considered a positive result. A positive response indicates infection but does not distinguish between active infection and that which has been controlled by the immune system or drugs.

tuberculin tine test A tuberculin test performed with a special disposable instrument that contains multiple sharp points or prongs for piercing the skin. The tines penetrate the skin and introduce the tuberculin applied to them. The test is read in 48 to 72 hr. The tine test has largely been replaced by testing with an intradermal injection of purified protein derivative. SYN: *tine test.*

tuberculitis (tū″bĕr-kū-lī′tĭs) Inflammation of a tubercle.

tuberculocele (tū-bĕr′kū-lō-sēl″) [″ + *kele*, tumor] Tuberculosis of the testis.

tuberculocidal (tū-bĕr″kū-lō-sī′dăl) Anything that destroys *Mycobacterium tuberculosis.*

tuberculoderma (tū-bĕr″kū-lō-dĕr′mă) [″ + Gr. *derma*, skin] Tuberculid.

tuberculoid (tū-bĕr′kū-loyd) [L. *tuberculum*, a little swelling, + Gr. *eidos*, form, shape] Resembling tuberculosis or a tubercle.

tuberculoma (tū-bĕr″kū-lō′mă) [″ + Gr. *oma*, tumor] **1.** A tuberculous abscess. **2.** Any tuberculous neoplasm.

tuberculosis (too-bĕr″kyŭ-lō′sĭs, tū-) [*tubercle* + *-osis*] ABBR: TB. An infectious disease caused by the tubercle bacillus, *Mycobacterium tuberculosis*, and characterized pathologically by inflammatory infiltration, formation of tubercles, caseation, necrosis, abscesses, fibrosis, and calcification. It most commonly affects the respiratory system, but other parts of the body such as the gastrointestinal and genitourinary tracts, bones, joints, nervous system, lymph nodes, and skin may also become infected. Fish, amphibians, birds, and mammals (esp. cattle) are subject to the disease. Three types of the tubercle bacillus exist: human, bovine, and avian. Humans may become infected by any of the three types, but in the U.S. the human type predominates. Infection usually is acquired from contact with an infected person or an infected cow or through drinking contaminated milk. In the U.S., about 10 to 15 million persons have been infected with tuberculosis. In 2005 about 14,000 active cases were reported. In 2009, 11,545 new cases were reported in the U.S. Worldwide, about 2 billion people harbor the infection; about 9 million have active disease, and an estimated 2 million die from TB each year. The percentage of drug-resistant TB cases varies internationally.

Tuberculosis usually affects the lungs, but the disease may spread to other organs, including the gastrointestinal and genitourinary tracts, bones, joints, nervous system, lymph nodes, and skin. Macrophages surround the bacilli in an attempt to engulf them but cannot, producing granulomas with a soft, cheesy (caseous) core. From this state, lesions may heal by fibrosis and calcification and the disease may exist in an arrested or inactive stage. Depending on the person's immune status

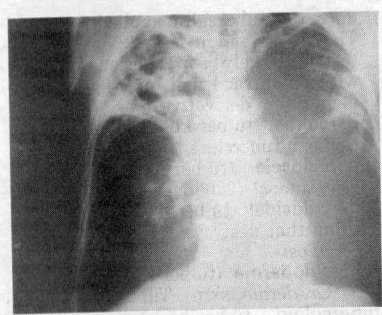

TUBERCULOSIS

anteroposterior x-ray of a patient diagnosed with advanced bilateral pulmonary tuberculosis (SOURCE: Centers for Disease Control and Prevention)

and other factors, the disease may become reactivated as pulmonary TB or disseminated infection. Reactivation or exacerbation of the disease or reinfection gives rise to the chronic progressive form.

The incidence of TB declined steadily from the 1950s to about 1990, when the AIDS epidemic, an increase in the homeless population, an increase in immigrants from areas where TB is endemic, and a decrease in public surveillance caused a resurgence of the disease. Populations at greatest risk for TB include patients with HIV, immigrants from Asia and elsewhere, the urban homeless, alcoholics and other substance abusers, those incar-

cerated in prisons and psychiatric facilities, nursing home residents, patients taking immunosuppressive drugs, and people with chronic respiratory disorders, diabetes mellitus, renal failure, or malnutrition. People from these risk groups should be assessed for TB if they develop pneumonia; all health care workers should be tested annually.

Currently the only vaccine available to prevent tuberculosis is the BCG vaccine. It has limited effectiveness but is used in regions of the world where TB is endemic. SEE: illus.; *immunological therapy; tuberculin skin test; vaccine, BCG; Nursing Diagnoses Appendix.*

INCUBATION PERIOD: Approx. 4 to 12 weeks elapse between the time of infection and the time a demonstrable primary lesion or positive tuberculin skin test (TST) occurs.

SYMPTOMS: Pulmonary TB produces chronic cough, sputum, fevers, sweats, and weight loss. TB may also cause neurological disease (meningitis), bone infections, urinary bleeding, and other symptoms if it spreads to other organs. TB is a major cause of infertility around the world.

DIAGNOSIS: Tests for diagnosing latent infection with tuberculosis include a positive tuberculin skin test (TST) or a blood assay. A presumptive diagnosis of active disease is made by finding acid-fast bacilli in stained smears from sputum or other body fluids. The diagnosis is confirmed by isolating *M. tuberculosis* in cultures or rapid nucleic acid test probes.

TREATMENT: Regimens for TB have

Reported TB Cases, United States, 1982–2010

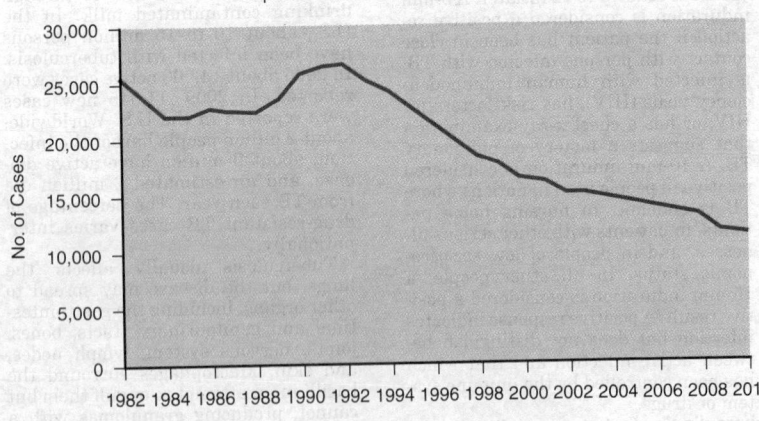

TUBERCULOSIS

Reported tuberculosis cases in the United States, 1982–2010 (adapted from Centers for Disease Control and Prevention)

been developed for patients, depending on their HIV status, the prevalence of multidrug-resistant disease in the community, drug allergies, and drug interactions. Uncomplicated TB in the non–HIV-infected patient is typically treated with a four-drug regimen for 6 months. Regimens change: prescribers should consult published guidelines for current standards of care. Common drugs include isoniazid (INH), rifampin (RIF), ethambutol (EMB), pyrazinamide, ciprofloxacin, and rifapentin. Medications are typically given in combinations rather than alone. A long course of therapy may be prescribed for patients coinfected with HIV/AIDS or for patients with drug-resistant bacilli. Multiply drug-resistant TB (MDR-TB) is tuberculosis resistant to either INH or RIF. Extensively drug-resistant TB (XDR-TB) is resistant to INH or RIF, any fluoroquinolone (e.g., ciprofloxacin), and at least one parenteral TB drug. Both MDR-TB and XDR-TB have very high mortality rates. SEE: *multidrug resistant t.*

⚠️ All patients with HIV should be tested for TB, and all patients with TB should be tested for HIV, because about one fourth of all patients with one disease will be infected with the other.

PATIENT CARE: All patients suspected of or confirmed to have TB should be placed in airborne isolation until they are no longer infectious. Health care professionals and visitors should wear particulate respirators when in the patient's room. Patients should be taught to cough and sneeze into tissues, and to dispose of secretions in a lined bag taped to the side of the bed or in a covered disposal. The patient should wear a mask when outside the isolation room for any reason. Patients should be observed for complications such as hemoptysis, bone or back pain, and bloody urine. The patient and family or other support persons should be taught about the importance of regular follow-up visits, of following and completing the treatment regimen exactly as prescribed, of adverse effects to be reported, and of signs and symptoms of recurring TB. Persons who have been exposed to an infected patient should receive a TB test; chest x-rays and prophylactic INH also may be prescribed.

avian t. A mycobacterial infection of birds caused by species including *Mycobacterium avium.* or *M. genavense.*

bovine t. Tuberculosis of cattle caused by *Mycobacterium bovis.*

endogenous t. Tuberculosis that reactivates after a previous infection.

exogenous t. Tuberculosis originating from a source outside the body.

hematogenous t. The spread of tuberculosis from a primary site to another site via the bloodstream.

latent t. Tuberculosis without active lung disease. It is detected by tuberculin skin testing.

miliary t. Tuberculosis that spreads throughout the body via the bloodstream. It may be fatal.

multidrug-resistant t. ABBR: MDR-TB. Tuberculosis that is resistant to therapy with at least two standard antitubercular drugs (esp. isoniazid and rifampin, the two drugs that have formed the cornerstone of therapy for tuberculosis). MDR-TB must be treated with at least three antitubercular drugs to which the organism is presumed or proven to be sensitive. About 3% of cases of TB are drug resistant.

open t. Tuberculosis in which the tubercle bacilli are present in bodily secretions that leave the body.

tuberculostatic (tū-bĕr″kū-lō-stăt′ĭk) Arresting the growth of the tubercle bacillus.

tuberculotic (tū-bĕr″kū-lŏt′ĭk) Pert. to tuberculosis.

tuberculous (tū-bĕr′kū-lŭs) [L. *tuberculum,* a little swelling] Pert. to or affected with tuberculosis, or conditions marked by infiltration of a specific tubercle, as opposed to the term *tubercular,* referring to a nonspecific tubercle.

tuberculum (tū-bĕr′kū-lŭm) *pl.* **tubercula** [L. *tuberculum,* a little swelling] A small knot or nodule; a tubercle.

tuberosis (tū″bĕr-ō′sĭs) A condition in which nodules develop; a nonspecific term that indicates no specific disease process.

tuberosity (tū-bĕr-ŏs′ĭ-tē) [L. *tuberositas,* tuberosity] **1.** An elevated round process of a bone. **2.** A tubercle or nodule.

ischial t. A palpable prominence on the inferior margin of the ischium that supports a person's weight when sitting.

maxillary t. A rounded eminence on the posteroinferior surface of the maxilla that enlarges with the development and eruption of the third molar. It articulates medially with the palatine bone and laterally with the lateral pterygoid process of the sphenoid. It forms the anterior surface of the pterygopalatine fossa, including a groove for the passage of the maxillary nerve, which is anesthetized in this region for a maxillary or second-division block.

radial t. A bump on the inside (medial) surface of the proximal end of the radius bone onto which the distal tendon of the biceps brachii muscle attaches

tuberous (tū′bĕr-ŭs) Pert. to tubers.

tubes tied A colloquial term for having undergone tubal ligation.

tubi- [L. *tubus,* pipe] Prefix meaning *tube.*

tuboabdominal (tū″bō-ăb-dŏm′ĭn-ăl) [L. *tubus,* tube, + *abdominalis,* pert. to the abdomen] Pert. to the fallopian tubes and the abdomen.

tubo-ovarian (tū″bō-ō-vā′rē-ăn) [″ + L. *ovarium,* ovary] Pert. to the fallopian tube and the ovary.

tubo-ovariotomy (tū″bō-ō-vā-rē-ŏt′ō-mē) [″ + LL. *ovarium,* ovary, + Gr. *tome,* incision] Excision of ovaries and oviducts.

tubo-ovaritis (tū″bō-ō″vă-rī′tĭs) [″ + ″ + Gr. *itis,* inflammation] Inflammation of the ovary and fallopian tube.

tuboperitoneal (tū″bō-pĕr-ĭ-tō-nē′ăl) [″ + Gr. *peritonaion,* peritoneum] Rel. to the fallopian tube and peritoneum.

tuboplasty (too′bō-plas″tē, tū′) [*tubo-* + *-plasty*] **1.** Plastic repair of a tube. **2.** Plastic repair of a fallopian tube or tubes in an attempt to restore patency so that fertilization of the ovum may occur. SYN: *salpingoplasty.*

   *transcervical balloon **t.*** Catheterization and dilation of the fallopian tubes, used to treat infertility in women whose fallopian tubes are occluded proximally. A balloon catheter is inserted through the cervical os of the uterus and into the fallopian tube to the point of occlusion in the tube. The balloon is then expanded by filling it with sterile saline. This dilation of the tube may restore tubal patency. SEE: *balloon **catheter**; infertility.*

tuborrhea (tū-bor-rē′ă) [″ + Gr. *rhoia,* flow] Discharge from the eustachian tube.

tubotorsion (tū″bō-tor′shŭn) The act of twisting a tube.

tubouterine (tū″bō-ū′tĕr-ĭn) [″ + *uterinus,* pert. to the uterus] Rel. to the fallopian tube and the uterus.

tubular (tū′bū-lăr) [L. *tubularis,* like a tube] Pert. to or shaped like a tube or tubule.

tubule (tū′būl) [*tubulus*] A small tube or canal.

   *Bellini **t.*** SEE: under *Bellini, Lorenzo.*

   *collecting **t.*** One of the small ducts that receive urine from several renal tubules, which join together to provide a passage for the urine to larger straight collecting tubules (papillary ducts of Bellini) that open into the pelvis of the kidney. SEE: *kidney* for illus.

   *convoluted **t.** of the kidney* The proximal and distal convoluted tubules of the nephron that, with the loop of Henle and collecting tubule, form the renal tubule through which the glomerular filtrate passes before entering the renal pelvis. SEE: *kidney* for illus.; *nephron.*

   *dentinal **t.*** One of the very small canals in the dentin. These extend from the pulp cavity of the tooth to the enamel and are occupied by odontoblastic processes and occasional nerve filaments.

   *galactophorous **t.*** Lactiferous **t.**

   *Henle **t.*** Henle loop.

   *lactiferous **t.*** One of the lactiferous ducts of the breast. It provides a channel for the milk formed in the lobes of the breast to pass to the nipple.

   *mesonephric **t.*** One of the embryonic tubules that in the female gives rise only to vestigial structures but in the male gives rise to the efferent ducts of the testes.

   *renal **t.*** The part of a nephron through which renal filtrate from the renal corpuscle flows and is changed to urine by reabsorption and secretion. The parts, in order, are the proximal convoluted tubule, the loop of Henle, the distal convoluted tubule, and collecting tubule. SEE: *kidney* for illus; *nephron.*

   *seminiferous **t.*** One of the very small channels of the testes in which spermatozoa develop and through which they leave the testes. These tubules may be either straight or convoluted.

   *transverse **t.*** ABBR: T-tubule. An invagination of the cell membrane of a muscle fiber that carries the action potential to the interior of the cell and the innermost sarcomeres.

tubulin (tū′bū-lĭn) A protein present in the microtubules of cells.

tubulization (too″bū-lĭ-zā′shŭn) A method of repairing severed nerves in which the nerve ends are placed in a tube of absorbable material.

tubuloalveolar (too″bū-lō-ăl-vē′ō-lăr) Consisting of tubes and alveoli, as in a tubuloalveolar salivary gland.

tubulocyst (too′bū-lō-sĭst) The cystic dilatation of a functionless duct or canal.

tubulodermoid (tū″bū-lō-dĕr′moyd) [″ + Gr. *derma,* skin, + *eidos,* form, shape] A dermoid tumor caused by the persistent embryonic tubular structure.

tubulorrhexis (too″bū-lō-rĕk′sĭs) [″ + *rhexis,* a breaking] Focal ruptures of renal tubules.

tubus (too′bŭs) [L.] Tube.

tuft (tŭft) A small clump, cluster, or coiled mass.

   *enamel **t.*** An abnormal structure formed in the development of enamel, consisting of poorly calcified twisted rods.

tugging (tŭg′ing) A dragging or pulling.

   *tracheal **t.*** A slight downward movement of the trachea with each inspiratory effort, resulting from descent of the diaphragm in a person with a low, flat diaphragm. The sign may also be present as a result of the proximity of an aortic aneurysm to the trachea. It should not be confused with the pulsations from a normal vessel beneath the trachea. SYN: *Oliver sign*.

tui na, tui-na, tuina (twā nah) [Chinese *tuī ná,* poke-pinch] A traditional method of Chinese massage in which the body is lifted, squeezed, and pushed to improve circulation and enhance disease resistance.

TUL *tolerable upper **limit**.*

tularemia (tū-lăr-ē′mē-ă) [*Tulare,* part of California where disease was first discovered] An acute plaguelike infectious disease caused by *Francisella tularensis*. It is transmitted to humans by the bite of an infected tick or other bloodsucking insect, by direct contact with infected animals, by eating inadequately cooked meat, or by drinking water that contains the organism. Streptomycin or gentamicin is effective in treating the disease. SYN: *deer fly fever; rabbit fever*.

SYMPTOMS: The incubation period is 2 to 10 days; symptoms include headache, fever, chills, vomiting, and body aches.

tulasi, tulsi (too-lah′sē, tul′ă-, tŭl′ă, tul′sē, tŭl′) [Sanskrit, *tulāsi, tulsi,* incomparable (epithet of the goddess Lakshmi)] SEE: *holy basil*.

tumbu fly (tŭm′boo) SEE: under *fly*.

tumefacient (tū-mĕ-fā′shĕnt) [L. *tumefaciens,* producing swelling] Producing or tending to produce swelling; swollen.

tumefaction (tū″mĕ-făk′shŭn) [L. *tumefactio,* a swelling] Intumescence.

tumentia (tū-mĕn′shē-ă) [L.] Swelling.

    vasomotor t. Irregular swellings in the lower extremities associated with vasomotor disturbances.

tumescence (tū-mĕs′ĕns) **1.** A condition of being swollen or tumid. **2.** A swelling.

tumor (too′mŏr) [L. *tumor,* a swelling] **1.** A swelling or enlargement; one of the four classic signs of inflammation. **2.** An abnormal mass. Growth or proliferation that is independent of neighboring tissues is a hallmark of all tumors, benign and malignant. SYN: *neoplasm*. SEE: *cancer*.

    adenomatoid odontogenic t. Adeno-ameloblastoma.

    brain t. An inexact term for any intracranial mass: neoplastic, cystic, inflammatory (abscess), or syphilitic. SEE: *Nursing Diagnoses Appendix*.

    Neoplastic brain tumors may be benign or malignant. Malignant brain lesions may be primary or secondary, resulting from metastatic spread of other cancers. Primary malignant brain tumors make up from 10% to 30% of adult cancers and about 20% in children, but any of these tumors may occur at any age. Incidence in children is usually greatest before age 12, with astrocytomas, medulloblastomas, ependymomas, and brain stem gliomas being most common. In adults the most common tumors

are gliomas and meningiomas, usually occurring supratentorially. Other malignant tumor types are oligodendrogliomas and acoustic neuromas (Schwannomas). Most malignant brain tumors are metastatic, with 20% to 40% of patients with cancer developing brain metastasis. The cause of primary brain cancers is unknown; however, one known environmental risk is exposure to ionizing radiation. Cell phone use has been implicated in acoustic neuromas. Central nervous system changes occur as the lesions invade and destroy tissue, and, because the tumors compress the brain, cranial nerves, and cerebral blood vessels, the compression causes cerebral edema and increased intracranial pressure (ICP). Most clinical signs are due to the increased ICP, but signs and symptoms may vary due to the type of tumor, its location, and the degree and speed of invasion. Usually the onset of symptoms is insidious, with brain tumors frequently misdiagnosed.

DIAGNOSIS: The patient is evaluated for neurological deficits, such as headache, mental activity changes, behavioral changes, weakness, sensory losses, or disturbances of vision, speech, gait, or balance. The patient is monitored for seizures and increased ICP. Diagnostic tools include skull x-rays, brain scan, CT scan, MRI, cerebral angiography, and EEG. Lumbar puncture demonstrates increased pressure and protein levels, decreased glucose levels, and (sometimes) tumor cells in the cerebrospinal fluid (CSF). Definitive diagnosis is by tissue biopsy performed by stereotactic surgery.

TREATMENT: Treatment includes excision if the tumor is resectable, and size reduction if the tumor is not respectable; relieving cerebral edema, reducing ICP, and managing other symptoms; and preventing further neurological damage. Treatment is determined by the tumor's histology, radiosensitivity, and location. Functional MRI can map the brain function surrounding a tumor to help design a surgical approach that removes the tumor while avoiding damage to areas critical for normal functioning. Surgery, radiation, chemotherapy, and/or decompression for increased ICP with diuretics, corticosteroids, or sometimes ventroatrial or ventroperitoneal CSF shunting. Focused and computerized robotic radiation methods such as the Gamma Knife and Cyberknife permit direct delivery of more radiation to the tumor and less to surrounding normal tissue.

PATIENT CARE: Radiation therapy can cause inflammation; therefore the patient is monitored for increasing ICP. If radiation is to be used after surgery, it will be delayed until the surgical wound has healed. However, even after local healing occurs, radiation can break down the wound; therefore the area of the incision must be assessed for infection and sinus formation. Chemotherapy for malignant brain tumors includes nitrosureas (BCNU, CCNU, procarbazine) to help break down the blood-brain barrier allowing entrance of other chemotherapy agents. Antiemetics are provided before and after chemotherapy to minimize nausea and prevent vomiting. The patient is assessed over the following weeks for bone marrow suppression, is advised to report signs of infection or bleeding, and is to avoid contact with crowds and people with respiratory infections. The oral chemotherapeutic temozolomide (Temodar) crosses the blood-brain barrier and is usually well tolerated by the patient. Intrathecal or intra-arterial administration helps increase drug action. Convection-enhanced delivery systems infuse the antitumor agent directly into the brain, bypassing the blood-brain barrier, to pump drugs slowly through 2 to 4 implanted catheters to where a tumor was removed, to attach to and kill remaining tumor cells, and to shrink a tumor before surgery. A disc-shaped drug wafer can be implanted during surgery to deliver chemotherapy directly to the tumor. MRI spectroscopy reveals the physiology of treated tumors to differentiate dead tissue from an actively growing tumor. The patient must be monitored closely for changes in neurologic status and increases in ICP. A patent airway must be maintained and respiratory changes monitored. The patient's safety must be ensured. Temperature must be monitored closely. Steroids and osmotic diuretics are administered as prescribed. Fluid intake may be restricted to 1500 mL/24 hr. Fluid and electrolyte balance is monitored to prevent dehydration. Stress ulcers may occur; therefore the patient is assessed for abdominal distention, pain, vomiting, and tarry stools. Stools are tested for occult blood. Antacids and anti-histamine-2 agents are administered as prescribed.

For postcraniotomy surgery, all general patient care concerns apply. General neurologic status and ICP remain the assessment priorities. Positioning of the patient after surgery depends on the procedure: after supratentorial craniotomy, the head of the bed should be elevated 30° and the patient positioned on the side to promote venous drainage, reduce cerebral edema, allow drainage of secretions and prevent aspiration. After infratentorial craniotomy, the patient should be kept flat for 48 hr but logrolled side to side every 2 hr to minimize complications from immobility. Because brain tumors and their treatment frequently result in residual disabling neurological deficits, a rehabilitation program should be started early. Physical and occupational therapists help the patient maintain independence and quality of life and provide aids for self-care and mobility. If the patient is aphasic or develops dysphagia, a speech pathologist must be consulted. Depression is common, and psychological consultation for behavioral or drug therapies may be helpful.

Emotional support is provided to the patient and family for treatments, disabilities, changes in lifestyle, and end-of-life issues. The patient and family are referred to resource and support services, e.g., social service, home health care agencies, the American Cancer Society, and other voluntary agencies.

Brenner t. SEE: *Brenner tumor.*

brown t. A benign fibrotic mass found within the bone of patients with unchecked hyperparathyroidism. The tumor appears brown on gross examination because it contains blood and byproducts of the metabolism of hemoglobin.

Buschke-Loewenstein t. A giant condyloma acuminatum, typically found on the genitals or anus, caused by infection with papilloma virus. In men, it is almost always found under the foreskin (it is rarely reported in circumcised men). It may transform into a verrucous carcinoma and cause deep local tissue invasion.

calcifying epithelial odontogenic t. Pindborg tumor.

carotid body t. A benign tumor of the carotid body.

collision t. **1.** A malignant growth made up of two or more different cell types occurring simultaneously in the same location. **2.** A cancerous growth made up of two or more malignancies that have metastasized toward each other.

connective tissue t. Any tumor of connective tissue such as fibroma, lipoma, chondroma, or sarcoma.

Dapaong t. A painful, nodular mass in the large bowel, a result of infection with *Oesophagostomum bifurcum*, a West African worm.

desmoid t. A tumor of fibrous connective tissue. SYN: *desmoma.*

dysembryoplastic neuroepithelial t. ABBR: DNET. A benign mass of misshapen brain cells. DNETs are a relatively rare cause of seizures in children and adolescents.

endocrine-inactive t. A pituitary adenoma that does not secrete a clinically important concentration of hormones. Endocrine-inactive tumors were formerly known as chromophobe adenomas. They are the most commonly detected neoplasms of the pituitary gland.

erectile t. A tumor composed of erectile tissue.

Ewing t. SEE: *Ewing tumor*.

false t. An enlargement due to hemorrhage into tissue or extravasation of fluid into a space, rather than cancer.

fibroid t. Uterine **leiomyoma**.

follicular t. An epidermoid cyst.

functioning t. A tumor that is able to synthesize the same product as the normal tissues from which it arises, esp. an endocrine or nonendocrine tumor that produces hormones.

giant cell t. **1.** A malignant or benign bone tumor that probably arises from connective tissue of the bone marrow. Histologically, it contains a vascular reticulum of stromal cells and multinucleated giant cells. **2.** A yellow giant cell tumor of a tendon sheath. **3.** Epulis. **4.** A chondroblastoma.

giant cell t. of bone A benign or malignant tumor of bone in which the cells are multinucleated and surrounded by cellular spindle cell stroma.

giant cell t. of tendon sheath A localized nodular tenosynovitis.

granulosa cell t. A malignant tumor that arises from the supporting cells (stromal cells) that encircle the ovary. Many of these cells produce estrogen; those that do can cause breast tenderness, endometrial hyperplasia, menorrhagia, or, in children, sexual precocity.

granulosa-theca cell t. An estrogen-secreting tumor of the ovary made up of either granulosa or theca cells.

heterologous t. A tumor in which the tissue differs from that in which it is growing.

homologous t. A tumor in which the tissue resembles that in which it is growing.

Hürthle cell t. SEE: under *Hürthle, Karl W.*

hilus cell t. A rare, steroid-hormone–producing tumor of the ovary. It is an occasional cause of virilization.

islet cell t. A tumor of the islets of Langerhans of the pancreas.

Klatskin t. SEE: under *Klatskin tumor*.

Krukenberg t. SEE: under *Krukenberg, Friedrich Ernst*.

lipoid cell t. of the ovary A masculinizing tumor of the ovary. It may be malignant.

mast cell t. A benign nodular accumulation of mast cells.

melanotic neuroectodermal t. A benign tumor of the jaw, occurring mostly during the first year of life.

mesenchymal mixed t. A tumor composed of tissue that resembles mesenchymal cells.

milk t. A colloquial term for a galactocele. SYN: *galactocele* (1). SEE: *caked breast*.

Pancoast t. SEE: *Pancoast tumor*.

papillary t. A neoplasm composed of or resembling enlarged papillae. SEE: *papilloma*.

phantom t. **1.** An apparent tumor due to muscular contractions or flatus that resolves on reexamination of the patient. **2.** A mass that resembles a tumor in only one view of a chest x-ray film. On other views it either disappears or appears to be an encapsulated fluid collection.

placental site trophoblastic t. ABBR: PSTT. A rare form of gestational trophoblastic disease simulating carcinoma and arising at the attachment of the placenta to the uterine wall.

Pindborg t. SEE: *Pindborg tumor*.

primary t. In a patient with metastatic cancer, the lesion assumed to be the source of the metastases.

primitive neuroectodermal t. ABBR: PNET. Medulloblastoma.

Recklinghausen t. SEE: under *Recklinghausen, Friedrich D. von*.

sand t. Psammoma.

secondary t. A tumor that has formed at a location remote from the original location of the tumor. Generally, a secondary tumor results from the spread of malignant cells through the lymphatic system or bloodstream.

teratoid t. A tumor of embryonic remains from all germinal layers. SEE: *teratoma*.

turban t. Multiple cutaneous cylindromata that cover the scalp like a turban.

uterine t., tumor of the uterus Uterine neoplasia, which may cause sterility or abortion or obstruct labor. Uterine tumors may become infected or twisted on their attachments. SEE: *cancer of uterus; endometrioma; uterine fibroma*.

vascular t. Hemangioma.

Warthin t. SEE: *Warthin tumor*.

Wilms t. SEE: *Wilms tumor*.

tumor ablation Destruction of tumor masses that cannot be treated by chemicals, heat, or other forms of energy.

tumoraffin (tū′mor-ăf-ĭn) [L. *tumor*, a swelling, + *affinis*, related] Having an affinity for tumor cells.

tumor angiogenesis factor SEE: under *factor*.

tumor bed SEE: under *bed*.

tumor burden The sum of cancer cells present in the body.

tumoricidal (too″mor-ĭ-sī′dăl) Lethal to neoplastic cells.

tumorigenesis (too″mor-ĭ-jĕn′ĕ-sĭs) The production of tumors.

tumorigenic (tū″mor-ĭ-jĕn′ĭk) [″ + Gr. *genesis*, generation, birth] Pert. to the formation and development of tumors.

tumorlet A small benign growth (as in the lungs or uterus), usually made of smooth muscle cells.

tumor lysis syndrome Metabolic disarray, often accompanied by acute kidney injury, in patients whose cancers have been rapidly killed (as when lymphoproliferative malignancies are treated with chemotherapy). Each dying malignant cell releases potassium, phosphates, and uric acids into the bloodstream. The effect of cellular destruction produces toxic or potentially fatal concentrations of these chemicals, or severe hypocalcemia. The syndrome may be prevented by making sure certain chemotherapy patients are massively hydrated before treatment and by administering drugs, such as allopurinol or rasburicase, that inhibit or degrade uric acid. Hemodialysis is sometimes required.

tumor marker SEE: under *marker*.

tumor necrosis factor SEE: under *factor*.

tumor necrosis factor receptor–associated periodic syndrome ABBR: TRAPS. A rare, dominantly inherited autoinflammatory disorder marked by bouts of abdominal pain, fever, myalgia and arthralgia, pleurisy, and conjunctivitis. It is caused by a mutation in a cell receptor for tumor necrosis factor. SEE: *tumor necrosis factor*.

tumorous (too′mor-ŭs) Resembling a tumor.

tumor seeding The spread of cancer cells to neighboring tissues, e.g., along the course of a biopsy needle or via a laparoscope.

Tunga (tŭng′gă) [Tupi (language of the Tupi people of Brazil)] A genus of fleas of the family Hectopsyllidae.

    T. penetrans A species common in tropical regions. It infests humans, cats, dogs, rats, pigs, and other animals and produces a severe local inflammation frequently liable to secondary infection. SYN: *chigger flea*; *chigoe* (1). SEE: *chigoe infestation*.

tungiasis (tŭng-gī′ă-sĭs) Infestation of the skin with *Tunga penetrans*.

tungsten (tŭng′stĕn) [Swedish *tung sten*, heavy stone] SYMB: W. A transition metal, atomic weight (mass) 183.84, atomic number 74. SYN: *wolfram*.

tungsten carbide A hard alloy composed of tungsten and carbon. It is used as a metallic alternative to diamond in the manufacture of histological knives and surgical instruments.

tunic (too′nik) [L. *tunica*, a sheath] A layer of tissue.

tunica (too′nĭ-kă) pl. **tunicae** [L. *tunica*, a sheath] A layer or coat of tissue.

    t. adventitia The outermost fibroelastic layer of a blood vessel or other tubular structure. SYN: *t. externa*.

    t. albuginea Albuginea.

    t. externa T. adventitia.

    t. interna SEE: *t. intima*.

    t. intima The lining of a blood vessel composed of an epithelial layer and the basement membrane, a subendothelial connective tissue layer, and usually an internal elastic lamina. SYN: *Bichat tunic*.

    t. media The middle layer in the wall of a blood vessel. The layer is composed of circular or spiraling smooth muscle and some elastic fibers.

    t. mucosa The mucous membrane lining of various structures.

    t. muscularis The smooth muscle layer in the walls of organs such as the bronchi, intestines, and blood vessels.

    t. serosa The membrane lining the walls of the closed body cavities and folded over the organs in those cavities, forming the outermost layer of the wall of these organs. The body cavities are the thoracic, abdominal, and pericardial cavities.

    t. vaginalis The serous membrane surrounding the front and sides of the testicle. It is the thin, flattened remnant of a pouch of peritoneum pulled into the scrotum by the testis as it descends during fetal development.

    t. vasculosa Any vascular layer.

tuning fork A device that vibrates at a specific frequency when it is struck, e.g., 128, 256, or 512 Hz. It is used in simple tests of hearing and vibration sense.

tunnel (tŭn′ĕl) A narrow channel or passageway.

    carpal t. The canal in the wrist bounded by osteofibrous material through which the flexor tendons and the median nerve pass. SYN: *flexor t.* SEE: illus.

    flexor t. Carpal t.

    tarsal t. The osteofibrous canal in the tarsal area bounded by the flexor retinaculum and tarsal bones. The posterior tibial vessels, tibial nerve, and flexor tendons pass through this tunnel.

tunneled (tŭn′ĕld) Placed surgically beneath the skin or into deeper tissues, e.g., into the intestinal wall. A tunneled catheter, e.g., is one that enters a vein through an incision made in the skin near the vein but then is passed through subcutaneous tissues to a second incision distant from the first. Tissue that surrounds the passage through which the catheter passes heals tightly around the catheter, holding it in place.

    Unlike nontunneled catheters, tunneled catheters can remain in place for many months. They are used for intravenous infusions, the administration of chemotherapy, hemodialysis, and blood drawing.

Tuohy needle (too′ē) [Edward B. Tuohy, U.S. anesthesiologist, 1908–1959] A needle with a curved point that is used in epidural anesthesia. The curve reduces the possibility that the point of

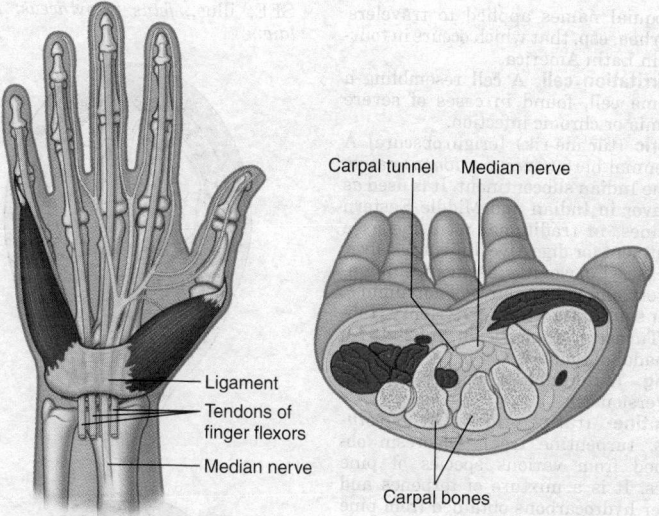

Carpal tunnel   Median nerve

Ligament

Tendons of
finger flexors

Median nerve

Carpal bones

Palm side of hand   **Cross section of wrist**

CARPAL TUNNEL

the needle and the anesthetic will enter
the dura mater.

TUR *tolerable upper limit; transurethral
resection* (of the prostate).

turbid (tŭr′bĭd) [L. *turba,* a tumult]
Cloudy; not clear. SEE: *turbidity.*

turbidimeter (tŭr″bĭ-dim′ĕt-ĕr) [*turbid*
+ *-meter*] An instrument for estimating the degree of turbidity of a fluid.
SEE: *nephelometer.*

turbidimetry (tŭr-bĭ-dim′ĕ-trē) [*turbid*
+ *-metry*] Estimation of the quantity
of suspended particles in a liquid. SEE:
nephelometry.

turbidity (tŭr-bĭd′ĭ-tē) [L. *turbiditas,*
turbidity] Opacity due to the suspension of flaky or granular particles in a
normally clear liquid.

turbinal (tŭr′bĭ-năl) [L. *turbinalis,* fr.
turbo, a child's top] Shaped like an inverted cone.

turbinate (tŭr′bĭ-n-āt) [L. *turbinalis,* fr.
turbo, a child's top] **1.** Shaped like an
inverted cone. **2.** A concha; a scroll-like
bone on the lateral wall of the nasal cavity.

turbinated (tŭr′bĭ-nā″tĕd) [L. *turbo,*
whirl] Top-shaped or cone-shaped.
SEE: *concha.*

turbinectomy (tŭr-bĭn-ĕk′tō-mē) [″ +
Gr. *ektome,* excision] Excision of a turbinated bone.

turbinoplasty (tŭr-bĭn′ō-plăs-tē) Reduction of the size of the nasal turbinates.
The surgery is used occasionally in the
management of snoring and airflow disorders.

turbinotome (tŭr-bĭn′ō-tōm) [″ + Gr.
tome, incision] An instrument for excision of a turbinated bone.

turbinotomy (tŭr-bĭn-ŏt′ō-mē) [″ + Gr.
tome, incision] Surgical incision of a
turbinated bone.

Turcot syndrome (tēr-kōz′) An autosomal recessive syndrome in which multiple colonic polyps are found in conjunction with malignant brain tumors.

turgescence (tŭr-jĕs′ĕns) [L. *turgescens,*
swelling] Swelling or enlargement of a
part.

turgescent (tŭr-jĕs′ĕnt) [L. *turgescens,*
swelling] Swollen; inflated.

turgid (tŭr′jĭd) [L. *turgidus,* swollen]
Swollen; bloated.

turgometer (tŭr-gŏm′ĕ-tĕr) [L. *turgor,*
swelling, + Gr. *metron,* measure] A
device for measuring turgescence.

turgor (tŭr′gor) [L., a swelling] **1.** Normal tension in a cell. **2.** Distention,
swelling.

   skin t. The resistance of the skin to
deformation, esp. to being grasped between the fingers. In a healthy person,
when the skin on the back of the hand
is grasped between the fingers and released, it returns to its normal appearance either immediately or relatively
slowly. The state of hydration of the
skin can determine which of these reactions occurs, but age is the most important factor. As a person ages, the
skin returns much more slowly to its
normal position after having been
pinched between the fingers. The skin
over the forehead or sternum may be
used when assessing turgor in elderly
persons.

   t. vitalis Normal fullness of the capillaries and blood vessels.

turista (tū-rēs′tä) [Sp.] One of the many

colloquial names applied to travelers' diarrhea, esp. that which occurs in tourists in Latin America.

Türk irritation cell A cell resembling a plasma cell, found in cases of severe anemia or chronic infection.

turmeric (tŭr′mĕ-rik) [origin obscure] A perennial herb (*Curcuma longa*) native to the Indian subcontinent. It is used as a flavor in Indian and Middle Eastern cuisines, in traditional medicine as a treatment for digestive difficulties, liver disease, skin wounds, as an anti-inflammatory and is the source of curcumin.

Turner syndrome (tŭrn′ĕr) [Henry Hubert Turner, U.S. physician, 1892–1970] Gonadal dysgenesis.

turning   **1.** Rotating to change position. **2.** Version (2).

turpentine (tŭr′pĕn-tīn) [Gr. *terebinthos*, turpentine tree] Oleoresin obtained from various species of pine trees. It is a mixture of terpenes and other hydrocarbons obtained from pine trees. It was once used in liniments and counterirritants.

TURP syndrome (tŭrp sĭn′drōm″) Hyponatremia that results from bladder irrigation with dilute fluids during and after transurethral resection of the prostate gland.

tussis (tŭs′ĭs) [L.] Cough.

tussive (tŭs′ĭv) [L. *tussis,* cough] Pert. to a cough. SYN: *tussal.*

tutamen (tū-tā′mĕn) *pl.* **tutamina** [L.] Any tissue that has a protective action.

TV *tricuspid valve.*

twelfth cranial nerve The hypoglossal nerve, motor to muscles of the tongue. SEE: *cranial **nerve**; hypoglossal **nerve**.*

Twelve-Item Short-Form Health Survey ABBR: SF-12. An abbreviated version of the Medical Outcomes Study 36-Item Short-Form Health survey. SEE: *Medical Outcomes Study 36-Item Short-Form Health Survey.*

twenty-nail dystrophy SEE: under *dystrophy.*

twig The final branch of a structure such as a nerve or vessel.

twilight sleep A state of partial anesthesia and hypoconsciousness in which pain sense has been greatly reduced by the injection of morphine and scopolamine. The patient responds to pain, but afterward the memory of the pain is dulled or effaced. Although once in common use as a method of analgesia for childbirth and minor surgery, twilight sleep has been replaced by more effective contemporary approaches to pain control.

twilight state A state in which consciousness is disordered, and autonomic dysfunction or dissociation may occur. This may occur in epilepsy.

twin (twin) One of two infants born sharing some common anatomical parts.

SEE: illus.; *fetus papyraceus; Hellin law.*

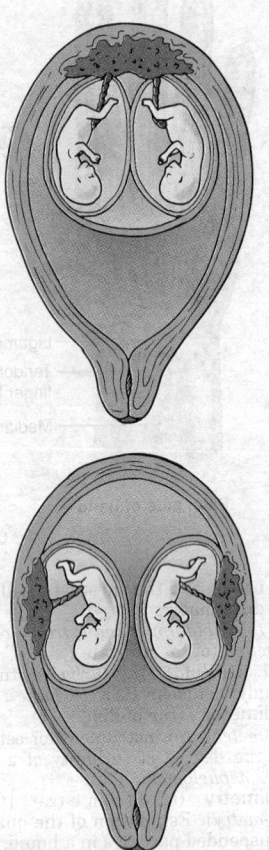

TWINS

A. Monozygotic twins with one placenta, one chorion, and two amnions. B. Dizygotic twins with two placentas, two chorions, and two amnions

INCIDENCE: Per 1000 live births, incidence rates for American whites are 1:88; for American blacks, 1:70. Generally, the rates are higher in blacks and East Indians and lower in Northern Europeans.

RESEARCH ON TWINS: Identical and fraternal twins provide a unique resource for investigating the origin and natural history of various diseases and discovering the different rates of environmental and hereditary factors in causing physical and mental disorders. Esp. important are studies that follow the course of identical twins separated shortly after birth and who then grew up in different social, economic, educational, and environmental conditions. In other research, the second-born twin was found to be at increased risk for an unfavorable outcome (e.g., need for intubation and resuscitation, lower 5-min Apgar score), even when delivered by cesarean section.

biovular t. Dizygotic **t.**

conjoined t. Twins that are united. In some cases, the individuals are joined in a small area and are capable of activity, but the extent of union may be so great that survival is impossible.

dizygotic t. Twins from two separate, fertilized ova. SYN: _biovular **t.**; fraternal **t.**_

enzygotic t. Monozygotic **t.**

fraternal t. Dizygotic **t.**

growth discordant t. The unequal growth of twins while in utero. The smaller twin is at greater risk of having congenital anomalies than is the normal birth-weight twin. SYN: _unequal **t.**_

identical t. Monozygotic **t.**

impacted t. Twins so entwined in utero as to prevent normal delivery.

interlocked t. Twins in which the neck of one becomes interlocked with the head of the other, making vaginal delivery impossible.

monozygotic t. Twins that develop from a single fertilized ovum. Monozygotic twins have the same genetic makeup and, consequently, are of the same gender and strikingly resemble each other physically, physiologically, and mentally. They develop within a common chorionic sac and have a common placenta. Each usually develops its own amnion and umbilical cord. Such twins may result from development of two inner cell masses within a blastocyst, development of two embryonic axes on a single blastoderm, or the division of a single embryonic axis into two centers. SYN: _enzygotic **t.**; identical **t.**; true **t.**; uniovular **t.**_

parasitic t. The smaller of a pair of conjoined twins, when there is a marked disparity in size.

Siamese t.s A culturally insensitive term for conjoined twins. SEE: _conjoined **t.**_

true t. Monozygotic **t.**

unequal t. Growth discordant **t.**

uniovular t. Monozygotic **t.**

vanishing t. Fetal resorption in multiple gestation. SEE: _multiple **gestation.**_

twinge (twĭnj) [AS. _twengan_, to pinch] A sudden keen pain.

twinning (twĭn′ĭng) Delivery of or producing twins.

twinning of teeth A dental anomaly in which two teeth are joined together SYN: _geminism._

Twinrix (twĭn′rĭks) Hepatitis A inactivated, and hepatitis B (recombinant) vaccine.

twitch (twĭch) [ME. _twicchen_] **1.** A single contraction of one muscle fiber in response to one nerve impulse. SEE: _myokymia._ **2.** To jerk convulsively.

twitching (twĭtch′ĭng) Repeated contractions of portions of muscles.

two-point discrimination test A test of cutaneous sensation involving determination of the ability of the patient to detect that the skin is being touched by two pointed objects at once. It is used to determine the degree of sensory loss following disease or trauma affecting the nervous system.

two-way interactive television ABBR: IATV. A means of telecommunication used to link two geographically distant sites via real-time audio and visual media.

TXA$_2$ _thromboxane A$_2$._

tylectomy (tī-lĕk′tō-mē) [Gr. _tylos_, knot, + _ektome_, excision] Lumpectomy.

tylion (tĭl′ē-ŏn) [Gr. _tyleion_, knot] The point at the middle of the anterior edge of the optic groove.

tyloma (tī-lō′mă) [Gr. _tylos_, knot, + _oma_, tumor] A callus.

tylosis (tī-lō′sĭs) [" + _osis_, condition] Formation of a callus.

tympanal (tĭm′păn-ăl) [Gr. _tympanon_, drum] Tympanic (1).

tympanectomy (tĭm″păn-ĕk′tō-mē) [" + _ektome_, excision] Excision of the tympanic membrane.

tympanic (tĭm-păn′ĭk) [Gr. _tympanon_, drum] **1.** Pert. to the tympanum. SYN: _tympanal._ **2.** Resonant. SYN: _tympanitic (2)._

tympanites (tĭm-păn-ī′tēz) [Gr., distention] Distention of the abdomen or intestines due to the presence of gas. SYN: _meteorism; tympanism; tympanosis._

tympanitic (tĭm-păn-ĭt′ĭk) **1.** Pert. to or characterized by tympanites. **2.** Tympanic (2).

tympanitis (tĭm-păn-ī′tĭs) [Gr. _tympanon_, drum, + _itis_, inflammation] Otitis media.

tympano-, tympan- [L. fr. Gr. _tympanon_, drum] Prefixes meaning _tympanic membrane_ or _eardrum_. SEE: _myringo-._

tympanocentesis (tĭm″pă-nō-sĕn-tē′sĭs) Drainage of fluid from the middle ear by using a small gauge needle to puncture the tympanic membrane. The fluid is cultured to determine the identity of any microbes that may be present.

tympanoeustachian (tĭm″pă-nō-ū-stā′kē-ăn) Pert. to the tympanic cavity and eustachian tube.

tympanography (tĭm″pă-nŏg′ră-fē) Radiographic examination of the eustachian tubes and middle ear after introduction of a contrast medium.

tympanohyal (tĭm″pă-nō-hī′ăl) Pert. to the tympanic cavity and hyoid arch.

tympanomalleal (tĭm″pă-nō-măl′ē-ăl) Pert. to the tympanic membrane and malleus.

tympanomandibular (tĭm″pă-nō-măn-dĭb'ū-lăr) Pert. to the middle ear and mandible.

tympanomastoiditis (tĭm"păn-ō-măs"toy-dī'tĭs) [" + *mastos*, breast, + *eidos*, form, shape, + *itis*, inflammation] Inflammation of the tympanum and mastoid cells.

tympanometry (tĭm"pă-nŏm'ĕ-trē) A procedure for objective evaluation of the mobility and patency of the eardrum and for detection of middle-ear disorders and patency of the eustachian tubes. SEE: *audiometry*.

tympanoplasty (tĭm"păn-ō-plăs'tē) [" + *plassein*, to form] Any of several surgical procedures to cure a chronic inflammatory process in the middle ear or to restore function to the sound-transmitting mechanism of the middle ear. SEE: *Nursing Diagnoses Appendix*.

tympanosclerosis (tĭm"pă-nō-sklĕ-rō'sĭs) Infiltration by hard fibrous tissue around the ossicles of the middle ear.

tympanosis (tĭm-pă-nō'sĭs) [" + *osis*, condition] Tympanites.

tympanostomy (tĭm"pă-nŏs'tō-mē) Myringotomy.

tympanostomy tube A tube placed through the tympanic membrane of the ear to allow ventilation of the middle ear as part of the treatment of otitis media with effusion. SYN: *grommet*. SEE: *otitis media with effusion*.

tympanotemporal (tĭm"pă-nō-tĕm'pō-răl) Pert. to the tympanic cavity and area of the temporal bone.

tympanotomy (tĭm"păn-ŏt'ō-mē) [" + *tome*, incision] Incision of the tympanic membrane. SYN: *myringotomy*.

tympanous (tĭm'păn-ŭs) [Gr. *tympanon*, a drum] Marked by abdominal distention with gas.

tympanum (tĭm'păn-ŭm) [L.; Gr. *tympanon*] The middle ear or tympanic cavity. SYN: *cavum tympani*; . SEE: *middle ear*.

tympany (tĭm'pă-nē) **1.** Abdominal distention with gas. **2.** Tympanic resonance on percussion. It is a clear hollow note like that of a drum. It indicates a pathological condition of the lung or of a cavity.

Tyndall effect [John Tyndall, Irish physicist, 1820–1893] The scattering of light as it passes through a colloid filled with particles. It is seen, for example, in a slit lamp examination of an eye with an inflamed anterior chamber.

type (tīp) [Gr. *typos*, mark] The general character of a person, disease, or substance.

   asthenic t. Having a thin, flat, long-chested body build with poor muscular development.

   athletic t. Having broad shoulders, a deep chest, flat abdomen, thick neck, and powerful muscular development.

   blood t. Blood group.

   body t. Classification of the human body according to muscle and fat distribution. SEE: *ectomorph; endomorph; mesomorph; somatotype*.

   phage t. Distinguishing subgroups of bacteria by the type of bacteriophage associated with that specific bacterium.

   pyknic t. Having a rounded body, large chest, thick shoulders, broad head, thick neck, and usually short stature.

Type D personality SEE: under *personality*.

TYPHIM VI (tī'fĭm) Typhoid VI polysaccharide vaccine.

typhlectasis (tĭf-lĕk'tă-sĭs) [Gr. *typhlon*, cecum, + *ektasis*, dilatation] Cecal distention.

typhlectomy (tĭf-lĕk'tō-mē) [" + *ektome*, excision] Excision of the cecum. SYN: *cecectomy*.

typhlenteritis (tĭf"lĕn-tĕr-ī'tĭs) [" + *enteron*, intestine, + *itis*, inflammation] Inflammation of the cecum. SYN: *typhlitis*.

typhlitis (tĭf-lī'tĭs) [" + *itis*, inflammation] Cecitis.

typhlodicliditis (tĭf"lō-dĭk-lĭ-dī'tĭs) [" + *diklis*, door, + *itis*, inflammation] Inflammation of the ileocecal valve.

typhloenteritis (tĭf"lō-ĕn-tĕr-ī'tĭs) [" + *enteron*, intestine, + *itis*, inflammation] Cecitis.

typhlon (tĭf'lŏn) [Gr.] Cecum.

typho- [Gr. *typhos*, vapor, smoke] Prefix meaning *fever, typhoid*.

typhoid (tī'foyd) [Gr. *typhos*, fever, + *eidos*, form, shape] Pert. to or resembling typhus.

typhoidal (tī-foy'dăl) Pert. to or resembling typhoid.

typhoid fever SEE: under *fever*.

typholysin (tī-fŏl'ĭ-sĭn) [" + *lysis*, dissolution] A lysin destructive to typhoid bacilli.

typhomalarial (tī"fō-mă-lā'rē-ăl) [" + It. *malaria*, bad air] Having symptoms of both typhoid and malarial fevers.

typhous (tī'fŭs) [Gr. *typhos*, fever] Pert. to typhus fever.

typhus (tī'fŭs) [Gr. *typhos*, fever] Any of several rickettsial infections transmitted to humans by lice, fleas, or mites. The causative microbe invades the lining of blood vessels and smooth muscle cells, causing widespread vasculitis. The most common causes of typhus are *Rickettsia prowazekii, R. typhi*, and *Orientia tsutsugamushi. R. prowazekii* causes the epidemic typhus found in crowded conditions with poor sanitation, e.g., refugee camps. SEE: *Nursing Diagnoses Appendix*.

   SYMPTOMS: The disease may be mild, marked only by a flat rash that spreads out from the trunk and petechiae or by flulike symptoms. In more severe cases, patients have fever, skin necrosis, and gangrene on the tips of the fingers, toes, earlobes, and penis as a result of thrombus formation in blood vessels; focal inflammation and thrombosis in organs throughout the body, including the brain, produce organ-specific signs. Rickettsial infections are diagnosed by identifying the organism through immunofluorescent staining.

TREATMENT: Typhus is treated with doxycycline for 7 days. SEE: *Standard Precautions Appendix.*

COMPLICATIONS: Bronchopneumonia occurs more frequently than lobar pneumonia. Hypostatic congestion of the lungs, nephritis, and parotid abscess also may occur.

PROGNOSIS: The prognosis is variable. Mortality may be quite high in epidemic typhus and almost nonexistent in murine typhus. Broad-spectrum antibiotics are life-saving if given early enough.

endemic t. Murine t.

epidemic t. An infectious disease caused by *Rickettsia prowazekii* and transmitted by the human body louse (*Pediculus humanus corporis*).

flea-borne t. Murine t.

louse-borne t. Rickettsia prowazekii.

Mexican t. A louse-borne epidemic typhus present in certain portions of Mexico.

mite-borne t. Scrub t.

murine t. A disease caused by *Rickettsia typhi* and occurring in nature as a mild infection of rats and transmitted from rat to rat by the rat-louse or flea. Humans may acquire it by being bitten by infected rat fleas or ingesting food contaminated by rat urine or flea feces. SYN: *endemic t.; flea-borne t.*

Queensland tick t. ABBR: QTT. A febrile illness causing a spotted fever and transmitted to humans by the bite of *Ixodes* ticks infected with *Rickettsia australis.* The disease is found principally in eastern coastal Australia and is similar to Rocky Mountain Spotted Fever in the U.S.

recrudescent t. The recurrence of epidemic typhus after the initial attack.

scrub t. An acute febrile illness, occasionally complicated by pneumonia, meningoencephalitis, respiratory distress syndrome, or septic shock caused by *Orientia tsutsugamushi.* Generally limited to Asian and Pacific nations, the disease is transmitted to humans by the bites of infected mites and chiggers. It can be treated with tetracyclines or azithromycin. The mortality rate in untreated patients is about 1% to 4%. SYN: *mite-borne t.; tsutsugamushi disease.*

typical (tĭp′ĭ-kăl) [Gr. *typikos,* pert. to type] Pert. to or conforming to a type, condition, or group.

typing (tīp′ĭng) Identification of type (e.g., of a specimen of genetic material through the detection of its specific nucleic acid sequences).

bacteriophage t. Determination of the subdivision of a bacterial species by a type-specific bacteriophage.

blood t. The method used to determine the antigens present on a person's blood cells.

tissue t. The determination of the human leukocyte antigens present on a cell or organ. Tissue typing is an essential element in matching proposed donors and recipients for organ transplantation. SEE: *transplantation.*

typo-, typ- [Gr. *typos,* a blow, print, imprint] Prefixes meaning *type.*

typodont (tī′pō-dŏnt) A replica of the natural dentition and alveolar mucosa used in training dental professionals.

typoscope (tī′pō-skōp) [Gr. *typos,* type, + *skopein,* to examine] A reading aid device for patients with amblyopia or cataract.

typus (tī′pŭs) [L.] Type.

tyr *tyrosine.*

tyramine (tī′ră-mēn) An intermediate product in the conversion of tyrosine to epinephrine. Tyramine is found in most cheeses and in beer, broad bean pods, yeast, wine, and chicken liver.

⚠️ When persons taking certain monoamine oxidase inhibitors eat these foods, they may experience severe hypertension, headache, palpitation, neck pain, and perhaps intracranial hemorrhage.

tyrannism (tĭr′ăn-ĭzm) [Gr. *tyrannos,* tyrant, + *-ismos,* condition] Sadism.

Tyrode solution (tī′rōd″) [Maurice Vejux Tyrode, U.S. pharmacologist, 1878–1930] A modified Ringer's solution containing, in addition, a small amount of magnesium chloride and acid and sodium phosphates.

tyrogenous (tī-rŏj′ĕn-ŭs) [Gr. *tyros,* cheese, + *gennan,* to produce] Having origin in or produced by cheese.

Tyroglyphus (tī-rŏg′lĭ-fŭs) [Gr. *tyros,* cheese, + *glyphein,* to carve] A genus of sarcoptoid mites commonly known as cheese mites. They infest cheese and dried vegetable food products and occasionally infest humans, causing pruritus. This genus includes species that cause grocer's itch, vanillism, and copra itch.

tyroid (tī′royd) [Gr. *tyros,* cheese + *-oid*] Caseous; cheesy.

tyromatosis (tī″rō-mă-tō′sĭs) [Gr. *tyros,* cheese + *-oma* + *-osis*] Caseation (1).

tyrosinase (tī-rō′sĭn-ās) [Gr. *tyros,* cheese] An enzyme that acts on tyrosine to produce melanin. It is used as a tumor marker for malignant melanoma, since almost all melanomas express the enzyme.

tyrosine (tī″rō-sĭn) ABBR: tyr. $C_9H_{11}NO_3$; an amino acid present in many proteins, esp. casein. It serves as a precursor of epinephrine, thyroxine, and melanin. Two vitamins (ascorbic acid and folic acid) are essential for its metabolism.

tyrosinemia (tī″rō-sĭ-nē′mē-ă) A disease of tyrosine metabolism caused by a deficiency of the enzyme tyrosine aminotransferase. In addition to an accumulation of tyrosine in the blood, mental retardation, keratitis, and dermatitis are present. Treatment consists of controlling phenylalanine and tyrosine intake.

tyrosinosis (tī″rō-sĭn-ō′sĭs) [″ + osis, condition] A condition resulting from faulty metabolism of tyrosine, whereby its oxidation products appear in the urine.

tyrosinuria (tī″rō-sĭn-ū′rē-ă) [″ + ouron, urine] Tyrosine in the urine.

tyrosis (tī-rō′sĭs) [″ + osis, condition] 1. Curdling of milk. 2. Vomiting of cheesy substance by infants. 3. Caseation (1).

tyrosyluria (tī″rō-sĭl-ū′rē-ă) Increased tyrosine-derived products in the urine.

tyvelose (tī′vĕl-ōs) A carbohydrate, 3-6-dideoxy-D-mannose, derived from certain strains of Salmonella and Trichinella.

Tzanck cell A degenerated cell from the keratin layer of the skin, disconnected from adjacent cells. It is seen in pemphigus.

Tzanck test (tsănk) [Arnault Tzanck, Fr. dermatolologist, 1886–1954] The examination of cells scraped from the lower surface of a vesicle to determine the underlying disease (e.g., infection with a herpesvirus).

tzetze (sĕt′sē) Tsetse **fly**.

U **1.** *unit.* **2.** Symbol for the element uranium.

235U Isotope of uranium with atomic weight 235.

U-100 *one hundred units of insulin per mL of solution.* A common concentration of commercially available insulins. Similarly, U-500 signifies that 500 units of insulin are present in 1 mL of solution.

UA *Unstable **angina**.*

UAO *upper airway obstruction.*

ubiquinol (ū-bĭk′wĭ-nŏl) Coenzyme QH₂, the reduced form of ubiquinone.

ubiquinone (ū-bik′wĭ-nōn″, ū″bi-kwi-nōn′) [*ubi(quitous)* + *quinone*] A lipid-soluble quinone present in virtually all cells. It is a vitamin-like substance that can be synthesized from tyrosine in a multistep process, collects reducing equivalents during intracellular respiration, is a coenzyme for several mitochondrial enzymes involved in production of adenosine triphosphate, and is converted to its reduced form, ubiquinol, while involved in this process. Ubiquinone is widely used in Europe and Asia as a health food supplement for congestive heart failure and other disorders, although confirmation of its effectiveness is uncertain. SYN: *coenzyme Q10.*

ubiquitin (ū-bĭk′wĭ-tĭn) An intracellular protein that helps to destroy misfolded proteins. It is also important in promoting the functions of proteins that make up ribosomes.

UBT *urea breath test.*

UBW *Usual body weight.*

UCD *Urea cycle disorder.*

UDP *uridine diphosphate.*

UDS *Unscheduled DNA synthesis.*

UHDRS *Unified Huntington Disease Rating Scale.*

Uhthoff sign (oot′hof″) [Wilhelm Uhthoff, Ger. ophthalmologist, 1853–1927] In patients with multiple sclerosis, the transient decrease in vision, double vision, or nystagmus when body temperature rises.

UI *Urinary **incontinence**.*

ulcer (ŭl′sĕr) [L. *ulcus*, sore, ulcer] A lesion of the skin or mucous membranes marked by inflammation, necrosis, and sloughing of damaged tissues. A wide variety of insults may produce ulcers, including trauma, caustic chemicals, intense heat or cold, arterial or venous stasis, cancers, drugs (such as nonsteroidal anti-inflammatory drugs [NSAIDs]), and infectious agents such as *Herpes simplex* or *Helicobacter pylori*.

   amputating u. An ulcer that destroys tissue to the bone by encircling the part.

   aphthous u. An ulcer of the oral mucosa, usually less than 0.5 cm in diameter. If it persists for longer than 2 weeks, it should be biopsied to rule out cancer. SYN: *aphthous stomatitis; canker sore.* SEE: illus.

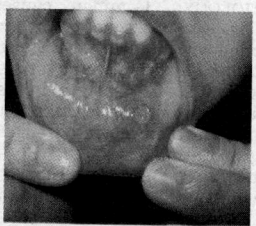

APHTHOUS ULCER

   ETIOLOGY: Aphthous ulcers are found in stomatitis, Behçet syndrome, Crohn disease, acquired immunodeficiency syndrome, and some cancers.
   TREATMENT: For patients with oral ulcers, application of a topical anesthetic or a protective paste provides symptomatic relief and makes it possible to eat without pain.

   arterial u. Ischemic **u.**

   Buruli u. An infection of the skin and underlying tissues with *Mycobacterium ulcerans*. The infection, common in the tropics and subtropics, develops slowly from a painless or minimally painful nodule on the skin into underlying bone, which it gradually destroys. The spread of the disease may be prevented with bacille Calmette-Guérin (BCG) vaccine.

   Cameron u. SEE: *Cameron ulcer.*

   chronic leg u. Any long-standing, slowly healing ulcer of a lower extremity, esp. one caused by occlusive disease of the arteries or veins or by varicose veins.

   Curling u. SEE: *Curling ulcer.*

   Cushing u. SEE: under *Cushing, Harvey.*

   decubitus u. Pressure **u.**

   denture u. An ulcer of the oral mucosa caused by irritation from wearing dentures.

   PATIENT CARE: To prevent irritation and ulceration of the mucous membranes of the mouth, denture wearers should clean dentures daily and remove them while sleeping. Poorly fitting dentures should be reconstructed or padded by a denturist.

diabetic foot u. Diabetic foot **infection**.

duodenal u. An open sore on the mucosa of the first portion of the duodenum, most often the result of infection with *Helicobacter pylori*. It is the most common form of peptic ulcer. SEE: *peptic u.*

follicular u. A tiny ulcer originating in a lymph follicle and affecting a mucous membrane.

fungal u. 1. An ulcer in which the granulations protrude above the edges of the wound and bleed easily. **2.** An ulcer caused by a fungus.

gastric u. An ulcer of the gastric mucosa.

ETIOLOGY: Common causes are NSAIDs, use of alcohol or tobacco, and infection with *H. pylori*. SEE: *peptic u.*

Hunner u. Interstitial **cystitis**.

indolent u. A nearly painless ulcer usually found on the leg, characterized by an indurated, elevated edge and a nongranulating base.

ischemic u. An ulcer caused by diminished blood flow through an artery, esp. one that nourishes a finger or toe. These ulcers are usually found in patients with peripheral vascular disease. They may result in loss of digits as a result of gangrene. SYN: *arterial u.*

Marjolin u. SEE: *Marjolin ulcer.*

Meleney u. SEE: under *Meleney ulcer.*

Mooren u. SEE: *Mooren ulcer.*

peptic u. An ulcer in the lining of the duodenum, the lower end of the esophagus, or the stomach (usually along the lesser curvature). Peptic ulcer disease is a common illness, affecting about 10% of men and 5% of women during their lifetimes. SEE: *Curling ulcer; Helicobacter pylori; stress u.; Zollinger-Ellison syndrome; Nursing Diagnoses Appendix.*

ETIOLOGY: Common causes of peptic ulcer are factors that increase gastric acid production or impair mucosal barrier protection, e.g., salicylates and NSAIDs, smoking, *H. pylori* infection of the upper gastrointestinal tract, pathological hypersecretory disorders, consumption of alcohol and coffee, and severe physiological stress. Ulcers occur in men and women and occur most frequently in patients over age 65, with about 1.6 million cases diagnosed annually in the U.S. The relationship between peptic ulcer and emotional stress is not completely understood.

SYMPTOMS: Patients with peptic ulcers may be asymptomatic or have gnawing epigastric pain, esp. in the middle of the night or when no food has been eaten for several hours. At times, heartburn, nausea, vomiting, hematemesis, melena, or unexplained weight loss may signify peptic disease. Food in-

take often relieves the discomfort. Peptic ulcers that perforate the upper gastrointestinal tract may penetrate the pancreas, causing symptoms of pancreatitis (severe back pain) and chemical peritonitis followed by bacterial peritonitis or an acute abdomen as irritating gastrointestinal (GI) contents and bacteria enter the abdominal cavity. Bacterial peritonitis can lead to sepsis, shock, and death.

DIAGNOSIS: Endoscopy (esophagogastroduodenoscopy) provides the single best test to diagnose peptic ulcers because it allows direct visualization of the mucosa and permits carbon-13 urea breath testing, cytological studies, and biopsy to diagnose *H. pylori* and rule out cancer. During endoscopy, tissue can be excised, vessels ligated, or sclerosants injected. Barium swallow or upper GI x-ray series may also be used to provide images for diagnosis or follow-up and may be the initial test for patients whose symptoms are not severe.

TREATMENT: *H. pylori* causes most peptic ulcers in the duodenum; antibiotics (clarithromycin and amoxicillin) are prescribed to treat *H. pylori*, and antisecretory (proton pump inhibitor) drugs like lansoprazole or omeprazole should be given to all patients with duodenal ulcers. Bismuth or other coating agents may be used as a barrier to protect the duodenal mucosa. Peptic ulceration of the stomach may be treated with the same medications if biopsies and breath tests reveal *H. pylori*. When patients have ulcers caused by the use of NSAIDs or tobacco, withholding these agents and treating with an H_2 blocker, e.g., ranitidine, provides an effective cure. The prostaglandin analogue misoprostol may also be used to suppress or prevent peptic ulcer caused by use of NSAIDs. GI bleeding is managed initially with passage of a nasogastric tube and iced saline lavage, possibly with norepinephrine added. Gastroscopy then allows visualization of the bleeding site and laser or cautery coagulation. When conservative medical treatment is ineffective, vagotomy and pyloroplasty may be used to reduce hydrochloric acid secretion and enlarge the pylorus to enhance gastric emptying. More extreme surgical therapy (including subtotal gastric resection) may be needed in rare instances of uncontrollable hemorrhage or perforation occurring as a result of peptic ulcer disease.

PATIENT CARE: The ambulatory patient is educated about agents that increase the risk for peptic ulceration and given specific instructions to avoid them. Instruction should include the importance of adhering to prescription drug therapies, adverse reactions to H_2-

receptor antagonists and omeprazole (dizziness, fatigue, rash, diarrhea), and the need for follow-up examination and care.

For the hospitalized patient with ulcer-related bleeding, careful monitoring of vital signs, fluid balance, hemoglobin levels, and blood losses may enhance early recognition of worsening disease. Intravenous (IV) access is established, and IV opiates are administered as prescribed for pain control. The patient is kept nil per os (NPO). Electrolytes and fluids are replaced as needed. Endoscopic or other diagnostic and treatment procedures are explained to the patient, and the effects of prescribed therapies or transfusions are carefully assessed. All patient care concerns apply after major surgery. The patient is assessed for possible complications: hemorrhage, shock, malabsorption problems (iron, folate, or vitamin B_{12} deficiency anemias), and dumping syndrome. To avoid these problems, the patient is advised to drink fluids between meals rather than with meals, eat 4 to 6 small, high-protein, low-carbohydrate meals daily, and lie down after eating. Before and after discharge, health care professionals should help the patient to develop coping mechanisms to relieve anxiety. Patients are taught to recognize signs and symptoms of disease recurrence (e.g., coffee-ground emesis, the passage of black or tarry stools, or epigastric pain). Patients who use antacids and have a history of cardiac disease or whose sodium intake is restricted for any reason are warned to take only those antacids that have low amounts of sodium. The need for ongoing medical care is stressed.

perforating u. An ulcer that erodes through an organ, e.g., the stomach or duodenum.

phagedenic u. Tropical **u.**

pressure u. Damage to the skin or underlying structures from compression of tissue and inadequate perfusion. Pressure ulcers typically occur in patients who are bedridden or chair bound. Patients with sensory and mobility deficits (such as patients with spinal cord injury, stroke, or coma); malnourished patients; patients with peripheral vascular disease; hospitalized elderly patients; and nursing home residents are all at risk. Some evidence also suggests that incontinence is a risk factor. SYN: *bed **sore**; decubitus **u.**; pressure **sore***. SEE: *Norton scale* for table.

The most common sites of skin breakdown are over bony prominences (the sacrum and the trochanters, the heels, the lateral malleoli and also the shoulder blades, ischial tuberosities, occiput, ear lobes, elbows, and iliac crests). The combination of pressure, shearing

forces, friction, and moisture leads to tissue injury and occasionally necrosis. If the ulcer is not treated vigorously, it will progress from a simple red patch of skin to erosion into the subcutaneous tissues, eventually extending to muscle or bone. Deep ulcers often become infected with bacteria and develop gangrene. SEE: illus.

TREATMENT AND PREVENTION: The most important principle is to prevent the initial skin damage that promotes ulceration. In patients at risk, aggressive nursing practices, such as frequent turning of immobile patients and the application of skin protection to bony body parts, are frequently effective. Gel flotation pads, alternating pressure mattresses, convoluted foam mattresses and sheepskins or imitation sheepskins may be employed. Specialized air-fluid beds, waterbeds, or beds with polystyrene beads provide expensive but effective prophylaxis. If the patient develops an ulcer, topical treatments with occlusive hydrocolloid dressings, polyurethane films, absorbable gelatin sponges, collagen dressings, wound-filter dressings, water-vapor permeable dressings, and antibiotic ointments aid the healing of partial-thickness sores. Deeper lesions may need surgical débridement. Skin-damaging agents such as harsh alkaline soaps, alcohol-based products, tincture of benzoin, hexachlorophene, and petroleum gauze should be avoided. Consultation with a wound care specialist is advantageous.

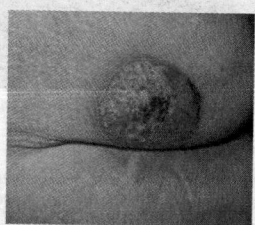

PRESSURE UCLER

PATIENT CARE: The skin is thoroughly cleansed, rinsed, and dried, and emollients are gently applied by minimizing the force and friction used, esp. over bony prominences. Patients who are not able to position themselves are repositioned every 1–2 hr to prevent tissue hypoxia resulting from compression. A turning sheet or pad is used to turn patients with minimal skin friction. Care providers should avoid elevating the head of the bed higher than 30° (except for short periods) to reduce shearing forces on the skin and subcutaneous tissues overlying the sacrum. Range-of-motion exercises are provided, early ambulation is encouraged, and nutritious high-protein meals are offered.

Low-pressure mattresses and special beds are kept in proper working order. Doughnut-type cushions should not be used because they decrease blood flow to tissues resting in the center of the doughnut.

Ulcers are cleansed and débrided, and other therapeutic measures are instituted according to institutional protocol or prescription. Consultation with a nutritionist may be needed to assess and optimize the patient's nutritional status, and to provide high-protein meals with added vitamin C to promote healing, protein and calorie-rich supplements, or enteral feedings. Weak or debilitated patients should be assisted to eat, with care taken to prevent swallowing difficulties.

rodent u. A basal cell carcinoma that has caused extensive local invasion and tissue destruction, esp. on the face. The usual sites are the outer angle of the eye, near the side and on the tip of the nose, and at the hairline. SYN: *Jacob u.* SEE: illus.

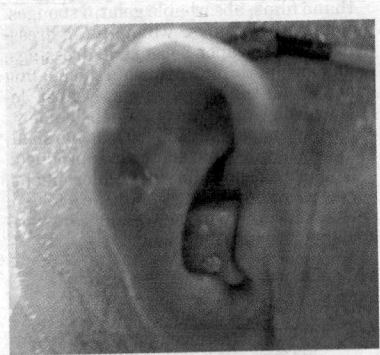

RODENT ULCER

On the ear

Saemisch u. SEE: *Saemisch ulcer*.

serpiginous u. A creeping ulcer that heals in one part and extends to another. SEE: *Mooren ulcer*.

shield u. A corneal ulcer found in some patients with vernal conjunctivitis. The ulcer is sometimes associated with corneal plaques that may permanently impair vision.

stercoral u. A rarely occurring ulcer of the colon caused by pressure from impacted feces. Perforation through the walls of the colon may cause peritonitis, sepsis, and sometimes death.

stress u. Multiple small, shallow ulcers that form in the mucosa of the stomach or, occasionally, in the duodenum in response to extreme physiological stressors. SEE: *Curling ulcer; Cushing ulcer* under Cushing, Harvey; *peptic u.*

traumatic u. An ulcer due to injury of the oral mucosa. Its causes include biting, denture irritation, toothbrush injury, and sharp edges of teeth or restorations.

trophic u. An ulcer caused by the failure to supply nutrients to a part.

tropical u. **1.** An indolent ulcer, usually of a lower extremity, that occurs in those living in hot, humid areas. The cause may or may not be known; it may be caused by a combination of bacterial, environmental, and nutritional factors. SYN: *phagedenic u.* **2.** The tropical sore caused by leishmaniasis.

varicose u. An ulcer, esp. of the lower extremity, associated with varicose veins.

venereal u. An ulcer caused by a sexually transmitted disease, i.e., chancre or chancroid.

venous stasis u. A poorly and slowly healing ulcer, usually located on the lower extremity above the medial malleolus. Typically it is edematous, pigmented, and scarred. The skin is extremely fragile and easily injured. In the U.S. about 3.5% of people over 65 have venous stasis ulcers. Women are three times more likely than men to be affected. SEE: illus.

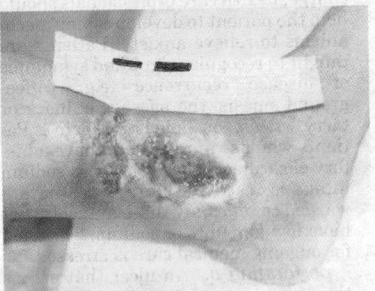

VENOUS STASIS ULCER

On lateral malleolus

PATIENT CARE: Assessment includes a detailed medical and surgical history and physical examination. When the lower extremities are examined, characteristic markers of venous ulceration include ankle flare (distention of small veins on the medial aspect of the foot due to chronic venous hypertension); dermatitis; pigmentation changes on the skin surface, usually appearing as brown discolorations affecting the medial part of the leg; woody induration of the leg; and varicosities. The health care professional should examine the leg for lesions superior to the medial malleolus and should carefully measure the size, shape, and margins of wounds; drainage or exudates; surrounding skin; and pain or tenderness. The patient should be advised to elevate the legs 7 in (18 cm) above the heart for 2 to 4 hr during the day and at night. Compression devices (such as graduated pressure stockings, Unna boot) are used to help reduce edema, improve venous blood flow, and aid healing. Before applying any compression device or wrap, the health care professional should measure the patient's leg circumference at the wound and the wound size of the ulcer. The wound should be cleansed regularly, and aggressive debridement employed as needed. Wounds with light to moderate drainage benefit from a moisture-retentive dressing (such as hydrocolloid, transparent film, some foams), whereas wounds with moderate to heavy drainage do better with an absorbent dressing (such as foams, alginates, special absorptive dressings). Underlying problems such as obesity, deep venous thrombosis, diabetes, and cardiovascular disease must be assessed and managed as part of the wound care protocol.

ulcera (ŭl′sĕr-ă) Pl. of ulcus.

ulcerate (ŭl′sĕ-rāt″) [L. *ulcerare,* to form ulcers] To produce or become affected with an ulcer. **ulcerated** (ŭl′sĕ-rāt″ĕd), *adj.*

ulceration (ŭl″sĕr-ā′shŭn) A suppurative or non-healing lesion on a surface such as skin, cornea, or mucous membrane.

ulcerative (ŭl′sĕr-ā-tĭv) [L. *ulcerare,* to form ulcers] Pert. to or causing ulceration.

ulcerogangrenous (ŭl″sĕr-ō-găng′grĕ-nŭs) Rel. to an ulcer that contains gangrenous tissue.

ulceromembranous (ŭl″sĕr-ō-mĕm′brăn-ŭs) [″ + *membrana,* membrane] Pert. to ulceration and formation of a fibrous pseudomembrane.

ulcerous (ŭl′sĕr-ŭs) Pert. to or affected with an ulcer.

ulcus (ŭl′kŭs) *pl.* **ulcera** [L.] Ulcer.

ulegyria (ū″lē-jī′rē-ă) [Gr. *oule,* scar, + *gyros,* ring] A condition in which gyri of the cerebral cortex are abnormal due to scar tissue from injuries, usually occurring in early development.

ulitis (ū-lī′tĭs) Gingivitis.

Ulmus fulva (ŭl′mŭs fŭl′vă) [L., lit. "tawny elm"] The scientific name for slippery elm. Also known as *Ulmus rubra.*

ulna (ŭl′nă) [L., elbow] The larger bone of the forearm, between the wrist and the elbow, on the side opposite that of the thumb. It articulates with the head of the radius and humerus proximally, and with the radius and carpals distally.

ulnad (ŭl′năd) [″ + *ad,* to] In the direction of the ulna.

ulnar (ŭl′năr) [L. *ulna,* elbow] Rel. to the ulna, or to the nerve or artery named from it.

ulnar drift SEE: under *drift.*

ulnaris (ŭl-nā′rĭs) **1.** Ulnar. **2.** Concerning the ulna.

ultimate (ŭl′tĭm-ĭt) [L. *ultimus,* last] Final or last.

ultimobranchial body (ŭl″tĭ-mō-brăng′kē-ăl) SEE: under *body.*

ultra- [L. *ultra,* on the far side (of), beyond] Prefix meaning *beyond, extremely, excessively.*

ultrabrachycephalic (ŭl″tră-brăk″ĭ-sĕ-făl′ĭk) [L. *ultra,* beyond, + Gr. *brachys,* short, + *kephale,* head] Having a cephalic index of 90 or more.

ultracentrifugation (ŭl″tră-sen″trĭ-fyŭ-gā′shŏn) Treatment or preparation of substances by use of the ultracentrifuge.

   analytical u. Ultracentrifugation to determine molecular mass, structure, and size.

   preparative u. Ultracentrifugation to purify mixed solutions of proteins. It separates them based on their densities or their sedimentation coefficients.

ultracentrifuge (ŭl″tră-sen′trĭ-fūj″) [*ultra-* + *centrifuge*] A high-speed centrifuge capable of producing centrifugal forces more than 100,000 times gravity. It is used in the study of homogeneous mixtures of high molecular mass such as plasma lipoproteins, viruses, and other substances present in body fluids.

ultraclean (ŭl′tră-klēn) [*ultra-* + *clean*] Purified to a very high level by filtration or some other mechanism. For example, purified air used to ventilate an operating room is known as *ultraclean air,* and the room so purified is known as an *ultraclean room.* Other situations in which the purification is at a lower level are known as *clean,* e.g., *clean air; clean room.*

ultradian (ŭl-trā′dē-ăn) [″ + *dies,* day] Concerning biological rhythms that occur less frequently than every 24 hr.

ultrafilter (ŭl-tră-fĭl′tĕr) A filter by which colloidal particles may be separated from their dispersion medium or from crystalloids.

ultrafiltration (ŭl″tră-fĭl-tră′shŭn) [″ + *filtrum,* a filter] Filtration of a colloidal substance in which the dispersed particles, but not the liquid, are held back.

Ultram Tramadol.

ultramicrotome (ŭl″tră-mī′krō-tōm) A microtome that makes extremely thin slices of tissue.

ultrarapid (ŭl″tră-ră′pĭd) [L. *ultra-,* beyond, + *rapidus,* seizing, rapid] Exceptionally fast; said of, e.g., centrifuges, some chemical reactions, and some forms of tissue fixation or freezing.

ultrasonic (ŭl-tră-sŏn′ĭk) [″ + *sonus,* sound] Pert. to sounds of frequencies above approx. 20,000 cycles/sec, which are inaudible to the human ear. SEE: *supersonic; ultrasonography; ultrasound.*

ultrasonic cleaning The use of ultrasonic

energy to sterilize objects, including medical and surgical instruments.

ultrasonic dissector Harmonic scalpel.

ultrasonics (ŭl-tră-sŏn′ĭks) The division of acoustics that studies inaudible sounds, i.e., those with frequencies greater than 20,000 cycles/sec (20,000 Hz or 20 kHz). Biological effects may result, depending on the intensity of the beams. Heating effects are produced by beams of low intensity, paralytic effects by those of moderate intensity, and lethal effects by those of high intensity. The lethal action of ultrasonics is primarily the result, either directly or indirectly, of cavitation of tissues. Ultrasonics is used clinically for therapeutic and diagnostic purposes; diagnostic ultrasound uses transducers that emit in the range from 2-15 MHz. In dentistry, instruments producing 29 kHz are used in periodontal surgery, curettage, and root planing. SEE: *ultrasound.*

ultrasonogram (ŭl″tră-sŏn′ō-grăm) The image produced by use of ultrasonography.

ultrasonography (ŭl″tră-sŏ-nog′ră-fē) [*ultra-* + *sonography*] The use of ultrasound to produce an image or photograph of an organ or tissue. SYN: *sonography.*
ultrasonographic (son″ŏ-graf′ik), *adj.*

   arterial duplex u. A diagnostic procedure that helps to identify areas within arteries where blood flow is blocked or reduced. SEE: *LEAS.*

   Doppler u. The shift in frequency produced when an ultrasound wave is echoed from something in motion. The use of the Doppler effect permits measuring the velocity of that which is being studied, e.g., blood flow in a vessel. SEE: illus.

   endobronchial u. ABBR: EBUS. The fitting of a bronchoscope with an ultrasound transducer to identify masses adjacent to the bronchi. EBUS has been used to improve the diagnostic yield of transbronchial lung biopsies and needle aspiration in patients suspected of having lung cancer and sarcoidosis.

   four-dimensional u. An ultrasonic technique, often used during pregnancy, providing images of the fetus in three dimensions and in real time. The technique is called four dimensional because there are three spatial variables plus time.

   gray-scale u. Sonographic B-mode scanning that permits echoes to be displayed in shades of gray according to their amplitudes.

   pelvic u. Transvaginal u.

   three-dimensional u., three-dimensional ultrasound, 3D ultrasonography, 3D ultrasound An ultrasonic technique, often used during pregnancy, providing images of the fetus in three dimensions.

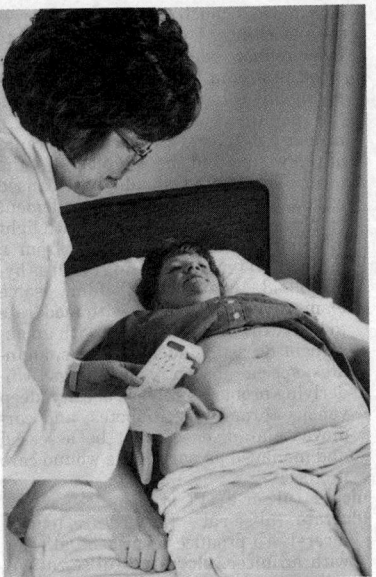

DOPPLER ULTRASONOGRAPHY
Doppler probe used on abdomen

   transrectal u. of the prostate The use of an ultrasonic detection device placed in the rectum in order to guide biopsy of the prostate.

   transvaginal u. An ultrasonic examination of the uterus, fallopian tubes, endometrium, and, in pregnant patients, the fetus, by placing a transducer inside the vagina.

PATIENT CARE: It may be used to diagnose ectopic pregnancy, determine multiple pregnancies, locate the placenta, identify ovarian cysts and pelvic cancers, and visualize tubo-ovarian abscesses. The patient prepares for the ultrasound by removing her clothing from the waist down and dressing in a clean gown. She is helped into a supine position on an examination table, and her knees are placed in approx. 90° of flexion with her feet supported in stirrups. The ultrasound transducer is covered with a condom or sterile glove coated with a lubricant gel. The patient is told that the probe will be inserted into her vagina, and that the gel may feel cold and slippery. The probe is then directed toward the internal organs, from which sound wave (echo) images are obtained, usually painlessly and without ionizing radiation exposure. SYN: *endovaginal ultrasound; pelvic u.*

ultrasound (ŭl′tră-sownd″) [*ultra-* + *sound*] Inaudible sound in the frequency range of approx. 20,000 to 10 billion (10^9) cycles/sec. Ultrasound has velocities that differ in density and elasticity from one kind of tissue to the next. This property permits the use of ultrasound in outlining the shape of various tissues and organs in the body. In obstetrics, for example, identifying the size and position of the fetus, placenta, and umbilical cord enables estimation of gestational age, detects some fetal anomalies and fetal death, and facilitates other diagnostic procedures, e.g., amniocentesis. In physical therapy, the thermal effects of ultrasound are used to treat musculoskeletal injuries by warming tissue, increasing tissue extensibility, and improving local blood flow. Ultrasound is used to facilitate movement of certain medications, e.g., pain relievers, into tissue (phonophoresis). Ultrasound is also used with electric current for muscular stimulation. The diagnostic and therapeutic uses of ultrasound require special equipment. SEE: illus; *phonophoresis; sonographer; ultrasonography.*

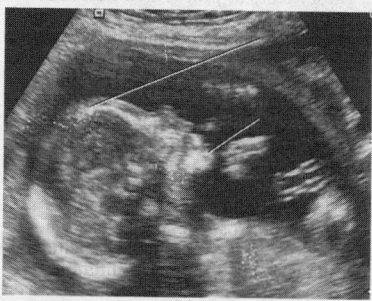

FETAL ULTRASOUND IMAGE

A-mode u. In ultrasonography a display in which imaging data are represented as echo amplitudes (on the y-axis) and time (on the x-axis), similar to the way electromagnetic waves are represented on an oscilloscope. SYN: *A-mode; A-mode (amplitude modulation) display.*

B-mode u. In ultrasonography, a display that uses dots of differing intensities to represent echoes received from tissues that more strongly or weakly reflect sound waves. SYN: *B-scan.*

continuous wave u. A form of ultrasound used in echocardiography in which a dual crystal transducer continuously generates and receives an ultrasound signal. It is used to measure blood velocities, e.g., across heart valves. A serious shortcoming of continuous wave ultrasound is its inability to identify depth accurately.

continuous wave Doppler u. Doppler ultrasonography that uses spectral Doppler in a constant series of echoes both originating and being received by

the same transducer. It is used to study obstruction of blood flow through vessels.

duplex Doppler u. Doppler ultrasonography that uses a transducer with two functions: pulsed-wave Doppler and B-mode imaging.

endobronchial u. ABBR: EBUS. The use of ultrasonic transducers carried within a bronchoscope to evaluate tissues in or adjacent to the trachea and bronchi. EBUS can be used to identify solid masses to be biopsied. It helps distinguish solid masses, which may be malignant, from blood vessels such as the aorta or pulmonary arteries, which should not be penetrated with a biopsy needle.

endorectal u. ABBR: ERUS. **1.** An imaging technique in which an ultrasound transducer is placed inside the rectum and used to evaluate the depth of colon and prostate cancers and the extent to which they have spread to neighboring lymph nodes. **2.** Transrectal **u.**

endovaginal u. Transvaginal **ultrasonography**.

high-intensity focused u. ABBR: HIFU. A noninvasive form of thermotherapy in which ultrasonic energy is used to generate heat for therapeutic purposes within the body. HIFU has been used to cauterize internal blood vessels that are bleeding, to cavitate or coagulate growths or solid malignancies, e.g., breast, liver, pancreatic, or prostate cancers. The ultrasound transducer is placed on the skin and the energy from the transducer is directed at radiographically localized tissue depths and volumes.

interventional u. The use of ultrasonography as a guide for local injections or for the placement of catheters, needles, or probes into body cavities or tumors. Interventional ultrasound is used to treat hepatocellular carcinoma, prostate cancer, and other solid tumors.

intravascular u. ABBR: IVUS. In ultrasonography, a technique for imaging intimal tissue proliferation and blood vessel blockages.

keepsake fetal u. A colloquialism for a three-dimensional image of an unborn child visualized in the womb with ultrasonography treated as a memento. The image is kept by expectant parents as part of a scrapbook of pregnancy and anticipated childbirth.

M-mode u. An ultrasonic display mode in which the motion of structures is seen on the vertical axis of the display, used, e.g., to show the movement of the heart's valves and walls during diastole and systole. SYN: *motion-mode display; time-motion mode **u.***

pelvic u. Examination of the pelvis with an ultrasonic transducer placed inside the vagina. It is used in assessment of diseases or conditions affecting the cervix, uterus, fallopian tubes, or ovaries. SYN: *endovaginal u.*

pulsed-wave Doppler u. SEE: *pulse-echo transducer.*

quantitative u. ABBR: QUS. Measurement of the density of a body tissue, e.g., bone, by determining how rapidly sound travels through the tissue and how different sonic wavelengths are absorbed. QUS is used to diagnose osteopenia and osteoporosis.

real-time u. A sonographic procedure that provides rapid, multiple images of an anatomical structure in the form of motion.

time-motion mode u. M-mode **u.**

transrectal u. ABBR: TRUS. Imaging of the prostate gland and periprostatic tissues with an ultrasound transducer inserted into the anus and directed toward the anterior rectum. It is used to identify malignant tumors, guide biopsies, and provide assessments of tumor staging. SYN: *endorectal u.* (2).

ultrasound-assisted lipectomy SEE: under *lipectomy.*

ultrastructure (ŭl′tră-strŭk″chŭr) The fine structure of tissues. It is visible only by use of electron microscopy.

ultratrace element SEE: under *element.*

ultraviolet (ŭl″tră-vī′ō-lĕt) [″ + *viola,* violet] Beyond the visible spectrum at its violet end, said of rays between the violet rays and x-rays. SEE: *infrared ray.*

ultraviolet therapy Treatment with ultraviolet radiation. SEE: *heliotherapy; phototherapy.*

ululation (ŭl″ū-lā′shŭn) [L. *ululare,* to howl] Howling; wailing.

umani (oo-măn′ē) The sense of taste triggered by glutamates, such as monosodium glutamate (MSG). It has been proposed as a fifth taste sensation, in addition to the traditionally recognized tastes (bitter, salty, sour, sweet).

umbilical (ŭm-bĭl′ĭ-kăl) [L. *umbilicus,* navel] Pert. to the umbilicus.

umbilical cord SEE: under *cord.*

umbilical cord blood SEE: under *cord blood.*

umbilical souffle A hissing sound said to arise from the umbilical cord.

umbilical vesicle SEE: under *vesicle.*

umbilicate (ŭm-bĭl′ĭ-kāt) [L. *umbilicatus,* dimpled] Dimpled, pitted, or shaped like a navel. Said of the appearance of certain rashes, such as molluscum contagiosum. **umbilicated,** *adj.*

umbilication (ŭm-bĭl-ĭ-kā′shŭn) [L. *umbilicatus,* dimpled] 1. A depression resembling a navel. 2. Formation at the apex of a pustule or vesicle of a pit or depression.

umbilicus (ŭm-bĭ-lī′kŭs, -bĭl′ĭ-kŭs) pl. **umbilici** [L., a pit] A depressed point in the middle of the abdomen; the scar

that marks the former attachment of the umbilical cord to the fetus.

umbo (ŭm′bō) [L., boss of a shield] The projecting center of a round surface.

u. of tympanic membrane The central depressed portion of the concavity on the lateral surface of the tympanic membrane. It marks the point where the malleus is attached to the inner surface.

umbra (ŭm′bră) [L., shade, shadow] The edge of the radiographic image proper.

umbrella filter SEE: under *filter.*

UMP *uridine monophosphate.*

¹ **un-** [Rel. to L. *in-,* not, and Gr. *a-, an-*] Prefix meaning *not.*

² **un-** [Rel. to Lat. *ante,* before, and Gr. *anti,* opposite, in place of] Prefix expressing the reversal of an action or of removal.

unbiased (ŭn-bī′ĭst) 1. Neutral; impartial; uninfluenced. 2. Scientifically randomized.

unbundling Separately billing for laboratory tests or procedures that are normally linked in order to extract more money from a payer (such as Medicare). This practice is illegal in the U.S.

uncal (ŭng′kăl) Concerning the uncus of the brain.

uncal herniation Transtentorial *herniation.*

Uncaria (ŭng″kar′ē-ă) [L. *uncus,* hook] A genus of tropical Asian woody vines.

U. guianensis U. tomentosa.

U. tomentosa A species used medicinally for its extracts, which include alkaloids used as an anti-inflammatory for arthritis and also for their effects on thinking, concentration, and sedation. It has also been promoted as a treatment for AIDS but without scientific validation. SYN: *cat's claw; U. guianensis.*

uncertainty (ŭn″sĕrt′ăn-tē) The state of being uncertain; feelings of doubt, ambiguity.

unciform, unciforme (ŭn′sĭ-form) [L. *uncus,* hook, + *forma,* shape] Uncinate.

uncinariasis (ŭn″sĭn-ă-rī′ă-sĭs) The condition of being infested with hookworms (i.e., worms of the genus *Uncinaria*).

uncinate (ŭn′sĭn-āt) [L. *uncinatus,* hooked] Hook-shaped; hooked. SYN: *unciform.*

uncinate bundle of Russell [James S. Risien Russell, Brit. physician, 1863–1939] Fibers that arise in the fastigial superior cerebellar peduncle and pass inferiorly to the vestibular nuclei and reticular formation by which impulses are carried to muscles, esp. those of the neck and body.

uncinate seizure SEE: under *seizure.*

uncoating (ŭn-kōt′ĭng) The release of viral nucleic acids from the capsid that covers them. Uncoating of viruses can be complete or incomplete and can occur before a virus enters the cell or after it penetrates a cell membrane.

uncombable hair syndrome A rare disorder, typically identified in childhood, in which hair grows in unruly bundles, sometimes called a "spun glass arrangement." The hair is dry, shiny, or blond, and easily broken. Cross-sectioning often reveals a triangular or grooved shaft. The condition is often associated with other birth defects. SYN: *spun glass hair syndrome*. SEE: *pili trianguli et canaliculi*.

uncomplemented (ŭn-kŏm′plē-mĕnt″ĕd) Not joined or associated with complement and thus inactive.

unconcern Profound uninterest or nonchalance out of proportion to societal norms. It is a characteristic of some brain diseases, including certain forms of brain injury, dementias, intoxications, and strokes.

unconscious (ŭn-kŏn′shŭs) [AS. *un*, not, + L. *conscius*, aware] **1.** Lacking in awareness of the environment; insensible. SEE: *unconsciousness*. **2.** In Freudian psychiatry, that part of the mind that consists of unrecognized feelings and drives.

unconsciousness (ŭn-kŏn′shŭs-nĕs) [AS. *un*, not, + L. *conscius*, aware] The state of being partly or completely unaware of external stimuli. Unconsciousness occurs normally in sleep, and pathologically, in such conditions as syncope (fainting), shock, unperfused cardiac dysrhythmias, and intoxications. SEE: *coma; Glasgow Coma Scale; Nursing Diagnoses Appendix*.

uncontrolled area (ŭn″kŏn-trōld′) For radiation protection purposes, an area occupied by the general public.

unction (ŭnk′shŭn) [L. *unctio*, ointment] **1.** The application of an ointment. **2.** Ointment.

uncus (ŭn′kŭs) [L. *uncus*, hook] **1.** A structure that is hook-shaped. **2.** On the surface of the brain, the bulge at the front-most inner end of the parahippocampal gyrus along the medial edge of the temporal lobe. SYN: *uncinate gyrus*.

undeclared (ŭn′dĕ-klard′) Not revealed or communicated; unannounced; unadvertised.

undeclared ingredient An active component (typically of a fraudulent over-the-counter supplement or other product) that is not revealed to purchasers.

underachiever A person whose achievements are less than what is predicted to be possible, based on his or her aptitudes, intelligence, and socioeconomic status.

underactive Functioning at less than full efficiency or productivity; said, for example, of glands such as the thyroid or the adrenals.

underage drinking The consumption of

alcohol under a legally specified age, usually before one's 21st birthday.

underbite (ŭn″dĕr-bīt′) A condition in which the lower incisors pass in front of the upper incisors when the mouth is closed.

undercorrection (ŭn″dĕr-kŏ-rĕk′shŭn) In refractive eye surgeries such as LASIK, too small a change in shape of the cornea that results in inadequate focusing of light rays (failure of light to fall onto the retina).

undercut (ŭn′dĕr-kŭt) A condition of having overhanging tissue as could be the case in preparing a dental cavity for restoration. Undercutting helps to keep the filling material in place.

underdose (ŭn′dĕr-dōs″) **1.** To give a dose too small to effect a clinically relevant response. **2.** A dose too small to effect a clinically relevant response.
underdosing (-dōs″ing), *n.*

undernutrition (ŭn″dĕr-noo-trish′ŏn, -nū-) **1.** Inadequate nutrition from any cause.

SYMPTOMS: The condition is marked by loss of body weight that begins with loss of glycogen, then loss of body fat, and finally loss of protein. Vitamin, mineral, and micronutrient deficiencies are also usually present. SEE: *malnutrition*.

2. Reduced caloric consumption with adequate intake of all micronutrients. **3.** In pediatrics, a synonym for failure to thrive. SEE: *failure to thrive*.

understaging (ŭn′dĕr-stāj″ing) Underestimation of the severity of a patient's illness, esp. an illness such as metastatic cancer. It can occur, for example, as a result of errors in pathological evaluation.

undertoe (ŭn′dĕr-tō) [″ + *ta*, toe] The displacement of the great toe underneath the others.

underuse (ŭn′dĕr-ūs″) Failure to employ readily available forms of care for patients. SYN: *underutilization*.

underutilization (ŭn″dĕr-ūt″ĭl-ĭ-zā′shŏn) Underuse.

undervaccination (ŭn″dĕr-vak″sĭ-nā′shŏn) Selective, partial, or delayed vaccination.

underweight (ŭn′dĕr-wāt″) Body weight for height that is 15% to 20% below healthy weight; a body mass index below 18.5 kg/m^2. By this standard, which is the one promoted both by the World Health Organization and the National Heart, Lung, and Blood Institute, a person who stands 5′7″ tall is underweight if he or she weighs less than 120 lb.

In children, underweight can be defined as having a weight-for-height that is less than the 5th percentile for one's age.

undetectable (ŭn″di-tek′tă-bĕl) Not found with contemporary laboratory testing; unmeasurable. The term applies to chemicals, contaminants, pathogens, or toxins in samples of air, blood, other fluids, or tissues.

undifferentiated connective tissue disease ABBR: UCTD. A connective tissue disease that does not fully meet the criteria for any of the well-defined rheumatological conditions such as rheumatoid arthritis, Sjögren's syndrome, or systemic lupus erythematosus. Signs and symptoms of connective tissue disease must be present for several years. These may include polyarticular arthritis, Raynaud's phenomenon, pleuritis, or pericarditis. The patient with UCTD will also have a positive antinuclear antibody test as well as other autoantibodies. Diagnostic difficulties in UCTD may be found in people who have evidence of mixed connective tissue disease or overlap syndrome.

undifferentiation (ŭn-dĭf″ĕr-ĕn-shē-ā′shŭn) [AS. *un*, not, + L. *differens*, bearing apart] An alteration in cell character to a more embryonic type or toward a malignant state. SYN: *anaplasia*.

undulant (ŭn′dyŭ-lănt, ′jŭ-) [L. *undulare*, to rise in waves] Rising and falling like waves, or moving like them.

undulate (ŭn′dū-lāt) [L. *undulatio*, wavy] Wavy; having a wavy border with shallow sinuses, said of bacterial colonies.

undulation (ŭn-dū-lā′shŭn) A continuous wavelike motion or pulsation.

unfractionated (ŭn″frak′shŏ-nāt″ĕd) For a chemical mixture or compound, not separated; not arranged, crystallized, selected, or sorted out; undistilled.

ung [L.] *unguentum*, ointment.

ungual (ŭng′gwăl) [L. *unguis*, nail] Pert. to or resembling the nails.

ungual tuberosity The spatula-shaped extremity of the terminal phalanx that supports the nails of fingers and toes.

unguent, unguentum (ŭng′gwĕnt) [L. *unguentum*, ointment] Ointment.

ungui- [L. *unguis*, nail, claw] Prefix meaning *nail*.

unguis (ŭng′gwĭs) *pl.* **ungues** [L., nail] **1.** A fingernail or toenail. SYN: *onyx*. **2.** The lacrimal bone. **3.** A white prominence on the floor of the posterior horn of the lateral ventricle. SYN: *hippocampus minor*.

    u. incarnatus An ingrowing nail, esp. a toenail.

ungulate (ŭng′gyŭ-lāt″) [L. *ungulatus*, having claws or hooves] **1.** Having or resembling hooves. **2.** Pert. to hoofed mammals such as cattle, deer, elephants, horses, and swine, now classified among several taxonomic orders. **3.** An ungulate mammal.

uni- [L. *unus*, one] Prefix meaning *one*. SEE: *mono-*.

uniarticular (ū″nē-ăr-tĭk′ū-lăr) [L. *unus*,

one, + *articulus*, joint] Pert. to a single joint.

uniaxial (ū″nē-ăk′sē-ăl) [″ + *axis*, axis] Having a single axis.

unicameral (ū″nĭ-kăm′ĕr-ăl) [″ + *camera*, vault] Having a single cavity.

unicellular (ū″nĭ-sĕl′ū-lăr) [″ + *cellula*, a little box] Having only one cell.

unicorn, unicornous (ū′nĭ-korn, ū-nĭ-kor′nŭs) [″ + *cornu*, horn] Having a single cornu or horn. Women with a unicornous uterus are at higher risk for repeated pregnancy loss.

unicuspid (ū″nĭ-kŭs′pĭd) Having a single cusp.

Unified Huntington Disease Rating Scale ABBR: UHDRS. A systematic means of assessing the progression over time of symptoms of Huntington disease. It includes the degree of behavioral disturbance and of degenerative chorea and dystonia, and the functional capacity exhibited by the patient.

Unified Parkinson disease rating scale ABBR: UPDRS. An instrument that rates the severity of Parkinson disease. It consists of 42 items and measures the effects of the disease on a patient's activities of daily living, behavior, mentation, mood, movement, and the complications he or she may experience from treatment.

unifocal (ū″ni-fō′kăl) [*uni-* + *focal*] Having a single origin, location, or shape.

uniform Having the identical shape or form of other objects of the same class.

uniglandular (ū″nĭ-glăn′dū-lăr) Concerning or having one gland.

unilaminar (ū″nĭ-lăm′ĭ-năr) Having a single layer.

unilateral (ū″nĭ-lăt′ĕr-ăl) [″ + *latus*, side] Affecting or occurring on only one side. SEE: *contralateral; homolateral; ipsilateral*.

unilateral neglect Impairment in sensory and motor response, mental representation, and spatial attention of the body and the corresponding environment characterized by inattention to one side and overattention to the opposite side. Left side neglect is more severe and persistent than ride-side neglect. SEE: *Nursing Diagnoses Appendix*.

unilobar (ū″nĭ-lō′băr) Having a single lobe.

unilocular (ū″nĭ-lŏk′ū-lăr) [″ + *loculus*, a small space] Having only one cavity.

uninsured (ŭn″in-shoord′) Not indemnified by either a private or publicly funded health insurance plan. In 2011, approximately 50 million Americans were uninsured.

uninuclear (ū″n-nū′klē-ăr) [″ + *nucleus*, a kernel] Having only one nucleus.

uninucleated (ū″nĭ-nū′le-āt″ĕd) Having a single nucleus.

uniocular (ū″nē-ŏk′ū-lăr) [″ + *oculus*, eye] Pert. to or having only one eye.

union (ūn′yŭn) [L. *unio*] **1.** The act of joining two or more things into one part, or the state of being so united. **2.** Growing together of severed or broken parts, as of bones or the edges of a wound. SEE: *healing*.

secondary u. 1. A healing by second intention with adhesion of granulating surfaces. SEE: *healing*. **2.** Operative correction of nonunion of a fracture.

uniovular (ū″nē-ŏv′ū-lăr) [″ + *ovum*, egg] Monozygotic, as in the case of twins that develop from a single ovum.

uniparous (ū-nĭp′ă-rŭs) [″ + *parere*, to bring forth, to bear] **1.** Giving birth to one offspring at a time. **2.** Having produced one child weighing at least 500 g or having a pregnancy lasting 20 weeks, regardless of the fetus's viability.

unipolar (ū″nĭ-pō′lăr) [″ + *polus*, pole] **1.** Having or pert. to one pole. **2.** Having a single process, as a unipolar neuron.

unipotent, unipotential (ū-nĭp′ō-tĕnt, ū″nĭ-pō-tĕn′shăl) In cell biology, committed to a single, differentiated structure and a single mode of functioning.

unique (ū-nēk′) [Fr. *unique*, fr L. *unicus*, one (and) only, sole] **1.** Being the only one; sole. **2.** Singularly distinctive; unparalleled. **3.** An individual visit with a health care provider for which fees may be charged or to which administrative costs may be assigned.

Unique Physician Identification Number ABBR: UPIN. A six-digit code, consisting of numbers and letters, assigned in the U.S. to all health care providers who take care of Medicare patients. It allows the Centers for Medicare and Medicaid Services to collect information about a provider's billing practices and to assess his or her utilization of medical services.

uniseptate (ū″nē-sĕp′tāt) Having only one septum.

unisex (ū′nĭ-sĕks″) **1.** Lack of gender distinction by external appearance, esp. with respect to hairstyle or clothing. **2.** Suitable for use by either sex.

UNIT *Universal Nonverbal Intelligence Test.*

unit (ū′nĭt) [From *unity*] ABBR: u, U. **1.** One of anything. **2.** A determined amount adopted as a standard of measurement. Particular units are listed under the first word. SEE: e.g., *British thermal unit; dental unit; SI units*

unitary (ū′nĭ-tĕr-ē) Rel. to a single unit.

unit of capacity The capacity of a condenser that gives a difference of potential of 1 volt when charged with 1 coulomb. SYN: *curie; farad*.

United Network for Organ Sharing ABBR: UNOS. An organization established in 1984 to facilitate donation of organs for possible transplantation. Website: www.unos.org. SEE: *organ donation*.

United States Adopted Names ABBR: USAN. A dictionary of nonproprietary names, brand names, code designations, and Chemical Abstracts Service registry numbers for drugs published by the U.S. Pharmacopeial Convention, Inc. The purpose is to have nonproprietary names assigned to new drugs in accordance with established principles. SEE: *USAN and the USP Dictionary of Drug Names.*

United States Pharmacopeia ABBR: USP, US Phar. The official pharmacopeia of the United States, issued every 5 years, but with periodic supplements, prepared under the supervision of a national committee of pharmacists, pharmacologists, physicians, chemists, biologists, and other scientific and allied personnel. The USP was adopted as standard in 1906. Beginning with the United States Pharmacopeia XIX, 1975, the National Formulary has been included in that publication. SEE: *National Formulary; United States Pharmacopeial Convention, Inc.*

United States Pharmacopeial Convention, Inc. ABBR: USP. A nonprofit corporation that owns the trademark and copyright to the United States Pharmacopeia–National Formulary (USP-NF). SEE: *National Formulary; United States Pharmacopeia.*

United States Psychiatric Rehabilitation Association ABBR: USPRA. An organization of rehabilitation professionals and agencies that helps people with psychological and psychiatric diagnoses live functional, healthy, and satisfying lives in their communities.

United States Public Health Service ABBR: USPHS. An agency of the U.S. Department of Health and Human Services (HHS). It assesses health care needs and promotes national and international health. Included within the USPHS are the Centers for Disease Control and Prevention (CDC); Food and Drug Administration (FDA); Alcohol, Drug Abuse and Mental Health Administration; Agency for Toxic Substances and Disease Registry; and various USPHS regional offices.

unit of force An arbitrary measure of a certain amount of force. For example, a *dyne* is the amount of force acting continuously on a mass of 1 g that will accelerate the mass 1 cm/sec.

univalence (ū″nĭ-vā′lĕns) The condition of having only one valence.

univalent (ū″nĭ-vā′lĕnt, ū-nĭv′ă-lĕnt) [″ + *valens*, to be powerful] Possessing the power of combining or replacing one atom of hydrogen. SYN: *monovalent.*

universal (ū″nĭ-vĕr′săl) [L. *universalis*, combined into one] Applicable to or commonly found in every condition, situation, or member of a population.

universal coverage A health insurance

plan that reimburses all citizens for all or part of their health care costs. It may insure all health-related services or specific ("safety-net") services only, or it may be tiered, providing different services depending on the amount of funding the insured person chooses to contribute to the plan. SYN: *universal health insurance coverage.*

universal cuff A device fitted around the palm of the hand to permit attachment of self-care tools when normal grasp is absent. SYN: *palmar cuff.*

universal design The design of places and objects to enable access and use by all persons, to the greatest extent possible, without adaptation or modification.

universal health insurance coverage Universal coverage.

Universal Nonverbal Intelligence Test ABBR: UNIT. A psychometric test designed to assess general intelligence without testing a subject's understanding of language.

universal precautions Guidelines designed to protect workers with occupational exposure to bloodborne pathogens (such as HIV and hepatitis B virus). These "universal blood and body fluid precautions" (e.g., gloves, masks, and gowns), originally recommended by the Centers for Disease Control and Prevention in 1985, were mandated by the OSHA Bloodborne Pathogens Standard in 1991 for workers in all U.S. health care settings. SEE: *Standard Precautions Appendix.*

universal recipient A person belonging to blood type AB, Rh positive, whose serum will not agglutinate the cells of the other ABO blood types. The recipient's blood must be tested by cross-matching before transfusion to exclude minor antigenic mismatches.

unknowns (ŭn″nŏnz′) In hypnotherapy those feelings, ideas, or images that are unfamiliar to a person and therefore potentially frightening, hazardous, or uncomfortable.

unlicensed assistive personnel (pĕr-sŏn-nĕl′) ABBR: UAP. Unlicensed health care personnel who work under the direction of a registered nurse. In addition to delivering direct patient care, they may take blood samples, provide respiratory treatments, or keep track of medical records. Some UAPs are multiskilled. Each state regulates UAP practice independently.

unload (ŭn″lōd′) To remove weight or stress from a weight-bearing organ, as by the use of a cane or crutches to reduce the physical stresses on an injured leg.

unlocking Mobilizing or freeing, e.g., a joint and its associated muscles.

unmask (ŭn″mask′) To reveal or make evident a disguised clinical condition, e.g., by treating a different condition

that made it difficult to perceive the first condition.

Unna (paste) boot A bootlike dressing of the lower extremity made of layers of gauze and Unna paste. It is used in treating chronic ulcers of the leg. SEE: illus.

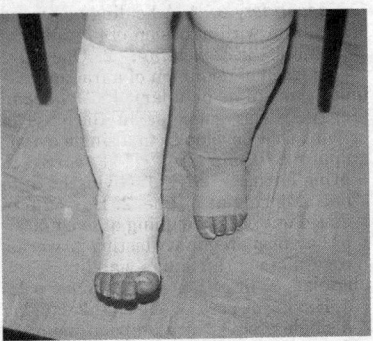

UNNA BOOT

Boot uncovered on right leg; covered with cohesive bandage on left leg

Unna paste (un′ă) [Paul G. Unna, Ger. dermatologist, 1850–1929] A mixture of 15% zinc oxide in a glycogelatin base.

unobtrusive (ŭn″ŏb-troo′siv) Tending to blend in rather than stand out; barely perceptible; subtle. **unobtrusiveness** (′siv-nĕs), *n.*

unorthodox 1. Unconventional. Not in conformity with generally accepted standards of care. 2. Bizarre. Unscientific. Irrational.

UNOS *United Network for Organ Sharing.*

unrelated (ŭn″rĕ-lāt′ĕd) In organ transplantation, pert. to a donor who has no connection by blood to the recipient but shares many human leukocyte antigen (HLA) markers.

unresectable (ŭn″rĕ-sek′tă-bl) [*'un-* + *resectable*] Unable to be removed surgically; said of certain large or complex tumors that have surrounded or invaded vital organs to such an extent that they cannot be removed completely.

unsaturated (ŭn-săt′ū-rāt″ĕd) [AS. *un*, not, + L. *saturare*, to fill] 1. Capable of dissolving or absorbing to a greater degree. 2. Not combined to the greatest possible extent.

unsaturated compound SEE: under *compound.*

unscheduled DNA synthesis ABBR: UDS. The ability of a cell to repair and replace large sections of damaged genetic code, e.g., after exposure to a carcinogen.

unsealed source radiation Radioactive nuclides that are given to patients orally or by intravenous injection, e.g., iodine-131, given as a treatment for thyroid gland ablation.

unsex (ŭn-sĕks′) [″ + L. *sexus,* sex] **1.** To castrate; to spay or excise the ovaries or testes. **2.** To deprive of sexual character.

unsponsored (ŭn″spon′sŏrd) Having no (health) insurance; uninsured.

unstriated (ŭn-strī′āt-ĕd) [″ + *striatus,* striped] Unstriped, as smooth muscle fibers.

UOP *Urinary output.*

up and go test A timed test of lower-extremity mobility. It measures the time required to rise from a chair, walk 10 ft, turn, and return to the sitting position. Performance on this test is affected by abnormal gaits that increase the risk of falling.

upcode (ŭp′kōd″) To assign a higher billing code to a patient visit than is justified by common practice or law.

UPDRS *Unified Parkinson Disease Rating Scale.*

upjo (ŭp′jō″) A commonly used acronym for *ureteropelvic junction obstruction.* The ureteropelvic junction is the last segment of the ureter, through which urine normally passes into the bladder. It is a common location for kidney stones to lodge and obstruct the flow of urine when they pass from the renal pelvis down the ureter.

upper (ŭp′ĕr) **1.** In anatomy, a synonym for *proximal, central,* or *superior,* e.g., upper gastrointestinal tract, upper motor neuron. **2.** In toxicology, a colloquial term for a stimulant drug, such as an amphetamine.

upper airway cough syndrome ABBR: UACS. The formal term for *postnasal drip syndrome.* SEE: *postnasal drip syndrome.*

upper airway obstruction SEE: under *obstruction.*

upper airway resistance syndrome ABBR: UARS. A type of sleep-disordered breathing, caused by increased airflow obstruction, in which a person awakens multiple times and then suffers daytime drowsiness or fatigue.

upper gastrointestinal tract SEE: under *tract.*

upper GI *upper gastrointestinal.*

upper motor neuron lesion SEE: under *lesion.*

upper respiratory infection SEE: under *infection.*

upregulate (ŭp-rĕg′yŭ-lāt) **1.** To increase the responsiveness of a cell or organ to a stimulus. **2.** To increase the number of receptors on a cell membrane.

upstream (ŭp′strēm″) In descriptions of genetic material, codons or base pairs that are on the 5′ side of a specific gene.

uptake (ŭp′tāk) The absorption of nutrients, chemicals (including radioactive materials), and medicines by tissues or by an entire organism.

urachal (ū′ră-kăl) [Gr. *ourachos,* fetal urinary canal] Rel. to the urachus.

uracil (ū′ră-sĭl) $C_4H_4N_2O_2$; a pyrimidine base found in RNA (not DNA) which, if paired, pairs with adenine.

uranium (ū-rā′nē-ŭm) [*Uranus* (the planet) + *-ium* (1)] SYMB: U. A radioactive metallic element, the parent of radium and other radioelements, atomic weight, 238.029, atomic number 92. Uranium ore contains the isotopes ^{238}U, ^{235}U, and ^{234}U.

   depleted u. The metal remaining after the most active radioisotope (^{235}U) has been extracted from uranium. It is a heavy metal, used in munitions, e.g., in armor-piercing weapons.

   It is estimated that, worldwide, more than 1 million tons of depleted uranium are stored. About 95% of the depleted uranium produced until now is stored as uranium hexafluoride, $(D)UF_6$. The long-term storage of $(D)UF_6$ presents environmental, health, and safety risks because of its chemical instability. When UF_6 is exposed to moist air, it reacts with the water in the air to produce UO_2F_2 (uranyl fluoride) and HF (hydrogen fluoride), which are both highly soluble and toxic. SEE: *enriched u.*

   enriched u. Uranium with a higher concentration of the radioisotope ^{235}U than is found in natural uranium ore. The isotope ^{235}U is used to manufacture nuclear fuel rods (for electrical power generation) and nuclear weapons. SEE: *depleted u.*

uranous A common oxidation state of uranium (U^{+4} or U (IV)) with a quadruple positive charge.

uranyl (ū′ră-nĭl) The bivalent uranium radical UO^{2+}. It forms salts with many acids. An example is uranyl nitrate, $UO_2 (NO_3)_2$.

urase (ū′rās) Urease.

urate (ū′rāt) [Gr. *ouron,* urine] The combination of uric acid with a base; a salt of uric acid.

urbanicity (ŭr″bă-nis′ĭt-ē) The qualities that characterize a geographic area as a city. Characteristics include population density, industrialization, communication media, health care, educational infrastructure, social networks, and concentration of technology and services.

urban legend (ŭr′băn) [L. *urbanus*] Myth (2). Urban legends about health care are widely disseminated by patients and practitioners. One favorite is the internet prank that states that dihydrogen monoxide is a deadly toxin widely consumed by human beings. Its chemical formula is H_2O.

   Most urban legends are not humorous or malicious pranks but are based on misunderstandings or unrecognized errors in reasoning, e.g., the common but false belief that emergency rooms are busiest during certain phases of the moon.

urea (ū-rē′ă) [Gr. *ouron*, urine] The diamide of carbonic acid, a crystalline solid having the formula CH_4N_2O; found in blood, lymph, and urine.

It is formed in the liver from ammonia derived from the deamination of amino acids.

Urea is the chief nitrogenous constituent of urine and, along with carbon dioxide, the final product of protein metabolism in the body. In normal conditions, urea represents 80% to 90% of the total urinary nitrogen. It is odorless and colorless, appears as white prismatic crystals, and forms salts with acids. The amount of urea excreted varies directly with the amount of protein in the diet. Its excretion is increased in fever, diabetes, or increased activity of the adrenal gland, and is decreased in kidney failure.

urea balance test A test of kidney function performed by measuring intake and output of urea.

urea cycle SEE: under *cycle*.

urea cycle disorder ABBR: UCD. Any of six inherited disorders in which an enzyme in the urea cycle is missing or nonfunctional, resulting in the accumulation of excess ammonia in the bloodstream. Lethargy, failure to thrive, nausea and vomiting, encephalopathy, and coma are common symptoms, esp. in newborns.

urea frost White flaky deposits of urea seen on the skin in patients with advanced uremia.

ureagenetic (ū-rē″ă-jĕn-ĕt′ĭk) [″ + *genesis*, generation, birth] Pert. to or producing urea.

urea nitrogen The nitrogen of urea (as distinguished from nitrogen in blood proteins).

Ureaplasma urealyticum (ū-rē″ă-plăs′mă) A mycoplasma that is usually sexually transmitted. It may cause inflammation of the reproductive or urinary tracts in males and females. It has been implicated in a wide variety of infections in babies with low birth weight.

urea-reduction ratio The relative decrease (or clearance) of blood urea nitrogen during hemodialysis. The ratio is a measure of the adequacy of renal replacement. The failure to achieve an adequate ratio leads to increased morbidity and mortality among patients with renal failure.

urease (ū′rē-ās) [Gr. *ouron*, urine] **1.** An enzyme that accelerates the hydrolysis of urea into carbon dioxide and ammonia. It is used in determining the amount of urea in blood or in urine. **2.** An enzyme used by certain microorganisms to facilitate their existence in otherwise inhospitable body locations.

uremia (ū-rē′mē-ă) [*uro-* + *-emia*] Intoxication caused by the body's accumulation of metabolic by-products normally excreted by healthy kidneys. SEE: *azotemia; uremic* **coma**. **uremic** (′mĭk), *adj.*

ETIOLOGY: Although nitrogen-containing waste products have long been considered the principal cause of uremia, other metabolic waste products (such as glycosylated wastes and by-products of abnormal oxidation) may actually be the most important toxins responsible for uremia.

SYMPTOMS: Symptoms include nausea, vomiting, anorexia, headache, dizziness, coma, or convulsions.

TREATMENT: Dialysis removes many soluble waste products that accumulate in renal failure and helps improve some conditions associated with uremia. Other uremic conditions can be alleviated with a protein-restricted diet, careful management of acid-base balance, and calcium and folate supplementation.

extrarenal u. Prerenal **u.**

prerenal u. Uremia resulting not from primary renal disease but from such conditions as disturbances in circulation, fluid balance, or metabolism arising in other parts of the body. SYN: *extrarenal u.*

ureogenesis (ūr″ē-ō-jĕn′ĕ-sĭs) [″ + *genesis*, generation, birth] Formation of urea.

ureotelic (ū″rē-ō-tĕl′ĭk) [*urea* + Gr. *telikos*, belonging to the completion] Concerning animals that excrete amino nitrogen in the form of urea. Included in this group are mammals. SEE: *urea cycle; uricotelic.*

uresis (ū-rē′sĭs) [Gr. *ouresis*] Urination.

ureter (ū′rĕ-ter, ū-rē′tĕr) [Gr. *oureter*] The tube that carries urine from the kidney to the bladder. It originates in the pelvis of the kidney and terminates in the posterior base of the bladder. Each kidney has one ureter measuring from 28 to 34 cm long, the right being slightly shorter than the left. The diameter varies from 1 mm to 1 cm. The wall consists of three layers: the mucosal, muscular, and fibrous layers. SEE: *kidney; urethra.*

ureteralgia (ū″rē-tĕr-ăl′jē-ă) [″ + *algos*, pain] Pain in the ureter.

ureterectasis (ū-rē″tĕr-ĕk′tă-sĭs) [″ + *ektasis*, dilatation] Dilatation of the ureter.

ureterectomy (ū-rē″tĕr-ĕk′tō-mē) [″ + *ektome*, excision] Excision of a ureter.

ureteritis (ū-rē″tĕr-ī′tĭs) [″ + *itis*, inflammation] Inflammation of the ureters.

uretero- [Gr. *oureter*, fr. *ourein*, to urinate] Prefix meaning *ureter*. SEE: *urethro-*.

ureterocele (ū-rē′tĕr-ō-sēl) [″ + *kele*,

tumor, swelling] Cystlike dilatation of the ureter near its opening into the bladder; usually a result of congenital stenosis of the ureteral orifice.

ureterography (ū-rē″tĕr-ŏg′ră-fē) [″ + graphein, to write] Radiography of the ureter after injection of a radiopaque substance into it.

ureterohydronephrosis (ū-rē″tĕr-ō-hī″drō-nĕ-frō′sĭs) [″ + hydor, water, + nephros, kidney, + osis, condition] Dilatation of the ureter and the pelvis of the kidney resulting from a mechanical or inflammatory obstruction in the urinary tract.

ureteroileostomy (ū-rē″tĕr-ō-ĭl″ē-ŏs′tō-mē) [″ + ileum, ileum, + stoma, mouth] Surgical anastomosis of a ureter to an isolated segment of the ileum. The ileum is connected to an abdominal stoma so that urine leaves the body via that opening.

ureterolithiasis (ū-rē″tĕr-ō-lĭth-ī′ăs-ĭs) [″ + ″ + iasis, condition] Development of a stone in the ureter.

ureterolithotomy (ū-rē″tĕr-ō-lĭth-ŏt′ō-mē) [″ + ″ + tome, incision] Surgical incision for removal of a stone from the ureter.

ureterolysis (ū-rē″tĕr-ŏl′ĭ-sĭs) [″ + lysis, dissolution] **1.** Rupture of a ureter. **2.** Paralysis of the ureter. **3.** The process of loosening adhesions around the ureter.

ureteroneocystostomy (ū-rē″tĕr-ō-nē″ō-sĭs-tŏs′tō-mē) [″ + neos, new, + kystis, bladder, + stoma, mouth] Surgical formation of a new passage between a ureter and the bladder.

ureteropelvic (ū-rēt′ĕ-rō-pel′vik) [uretero- + pelvic] Pert. to the anatomical transition zone where urine leaves the pelvis of the kidney (renal pelvis) and enters the ureter. Kidney stones often lodge in this location as they leave the renal pelvis.

ureteroplasty (ū-rē′tĕr-ō-plăs″tē) [″ + plassein, to form] Plastic surgery of the ureter.

ureteropyelostomy (ū-rē″tĕr-ō-pī′ĕ-lŏs′tō-mē) [″ + ″ + stoma, mouth] Ureteroneopyelostomy.

ureteroscope (ū-rē′tĕr-ō-skōp″) A rigid or flexible endoscope used to examine and treat diseases of the urinary bladder or ureters. Ureteroscopes are inserted into the urethra and advanced upward toward the kidneys. They can be used to biopsy suspicious lesions or remove urinary stones lodged in the ureters.

ureterosigmoidostomy (ū-rē″tĕr-ō-sĭg-moyd-ŏs′tō-mē) [″ + sigma, letter S, + eidos, shape, + stoma, mouth] Surgical implantation of the ureter into the sigmoid colon.

ureterostomy (ū-rē″tĕr-ŏs′tō-mē) [″ + stoma, mouth] The formation of a permanent fistula for drainage of a ureter.

cutaneous u. Surgical implantation of the ureter into the skin. This allows urine to drain via the ureter to the outside of the body by going through the stoma.

ureterotomy (ū-rē″tĕr-ŏt′ō-mē) [″ + tome, incision] Incision or surgery of the ureter.

ureteroureterostomy (ū-rē″tĕr-ō-ū-rē″tĕr-ŏs′tō-mē) [″ + ″ + stoma, mouth] **1.** The formation of a connection from one ureter to the other. **2.** The re-establishment of a passage between the ends of a divided ureter.

ureterovaginal (ū-rē″tĕr-ō-văj′ĭ-năl) [″ + L. vagina, sheath] Relating to a ureter and the vagina, denoting a fistula connecting them.

ureterovesical (ū-rē′tĕr-ō-vĕs″ĭ-kl) Relating to the entry point of the ureter into the urinary bladder. Kidney stones frequently lodge at this location.

urethra (ū-rē′thră) [Gr. ourethra] The tube for the discharge of urine extending from the bladder to the outside. In females, its orifice lies in the vestibule between the vagina and clitoris; in males, the urethra passes through the prostate gland and the penis, opening at the tip of the glans penis. In males, it serves as the passage for semen as well as urine. Its lining, the mucosa, is thrown into folds and contains the openings of the urethral glands. Surrounding the mucosa is a lamina propria containing many elastic fibers and blood vessels, outside of which is an indefinite muscular layer. SEE: penis; illus.

urethral (ū-rē′thrăl), adj.

urethrectomy (ūr″ē-threk′tō-mē) [urethro- + -ectomy] Surgical excision of the urethra or a portion of the urethra.

urethrism, urethrismus (ū′rē-thrĭzm, ū″rē-thrĭz′mŭs) [″ + -ismos, condition] Irritability or spasm of the urethra.

urethritis (ūr″ē-thrīt′ĭs) [urethra + -itis] Inflammation of the urethra.

anterior u. Inflammation of that portion of the urethra anterior to the anterior layer of the triangular ligament.

gonococcal u. Urethritis caused by Neisseria gonorrhoeae.

nongonococcal u. ABBR: NGU. Urethral inflammation caused by organisms other than Neisseria gonorrhoeae. NGU is the most common sexually transmitted disease in men; it accounts for 4 to 6 million physician visits annually. The symptoms usually include painful urination and a urethral discharge. The two organisms most frequently associated with NGU are Chlamydia trachomatis and Ureaplasma urealyticum. Other causes include herpes simplex virus, Trichomonas vaginalis, Haemophilus influenzae, Gardnerella vaginalis, and Clostridium difficile.

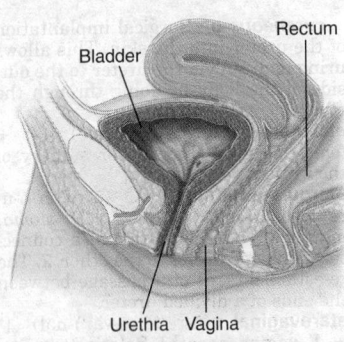

Rectum

Bladder

Urethra   Vagina

FEMALE URETHRA

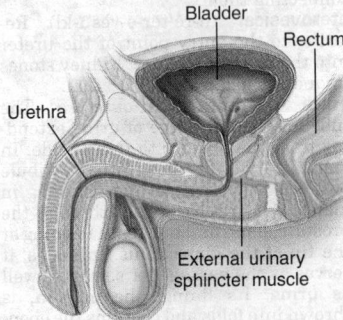

Bladder

Rectum

Urethra

External urinary
sphincter muscle

MALE URETHRA

TREATMENT: NGU due to *C. tracho-matis* or *U. urealyticum* is treated with doxycycline or azithromycin. Appropriate antibiotics are used for other causative organisms.

     nonspecific u. ABBR: NSU. Nongonococcal urethritis.

     posterior u. Inflammation of membranous and prostatic portions of the urethra.

     specific u. Urethritis due to a specific organism, usually gonococcus.

urethro-, urethr- [L. *urethra,* fr. Gr. *ourēthra,* fr. *ourein,* to urinate] [Gr. *ourethra*] Prefixes meaning *urethra.* SEE: *uretero-.*

urethrobulbar (ū-rē″thrō-bŭl′băr) Concerning the urethra and the bulbar penis.

urethrocele (ū-rē′thrō-sēl) [″ + *kele,* tumor, swelling] **1.** Pouchlike protrusion of the urethral wall in the female. **2.** Thickening of connective tissue around the urethra in the female.

urethrography (ū-rē-thrŏg′ră-fē) [″ + *graphein,* to write] Radiography of the urethra after it has been filled with contrast medium.

     voiding u. Radiographic examination of the urethra during urination af-

ter the introduction of a contrast medium.

urethropexy (ū-rē′thrō-pĕks-ē) [″ + Gr. *pexis,* fixation] Surgical fixation of the urethra.

urethroplasty (ū-rē′thrō-plăs″tē) [″ + *plassein,* to mold] Reparative surgery of the urethra.

urethrorectal (ū-rē″thrō-rĕk′tăl) [Gr. *ourethra,* urethra, + L. *rectus,* straight] Pert. to the urethra and rectum.

urethroscopy (ū-rē-thrŏs′kō-pē) An examination of the mucous membrane of the urethra with a urethroscope.

urethrostomy (ū-rē-thrŏs′tō-mē) [″ + *stoma,* mouth] The formation of a permanent fistula opening into the urethra by perineal section and fixation of the membranous urethra in the perineum.

urethrotome (ū-rē′thrō-tōm) [″ + *tome,* incision] An instrument for incision of a urethral stricture.

urethrotomy (ū-rē-thrŏt′ō-mē) Incision of a urethral stricture.

urge **1.** A strong desire; a force or a motive that impels action. **2.** The need to urinate or defecate.

urgency (ŭr′jĕn-sē) [*urgent*] A sudden, almost uncontrollable need to urinate.

urgent (ŭr′jĕnt) [L. *urgere,* to push forward, drive] Requiring a rapid response or intervention; pressing.

urgi-center (ŭr′jĭ-sent″ĕr) [*urge(nt)* + *center*] Emergi-center.

Urginea (ŭr-jin′ē-ă) Squill.

URI *upper respiratory infection.*

-uria [Gr. *ouron,* urine + *-ia*] Suffix meaning *presence (of something) in the urine, condition of the urine.*

uric (ū′rĭk) [Gr. *ourikos,* urine] Of or pert. to urine.

uric acid SEE: under *acid.*

uricase (ū′rĭ-kās″, -kāz″) [*uric* + *-ase*] An enzyme present in the liver and kidneys of most mammals, but not humans. This enzyme is capable of oxidizing uric acid into allantoin and carbon dioxide. SYN: *urate* **oxidase.**

uricosuria (ū″rĭ-kō-sū′rē-ă) [″ + *ouron,* urine] The excessive excretion of uric acid in the urine.

uricosuric (ū″rĭ-kō-sū′rĭk) Potentiating the excretion of uric acid in the urine.

uricosuric agent SEE: under *agent.*

uricotelic (ū″rĭ-kō-tĕl′ĭk) [″ + *telikos,* belonging to the completion] Concerning animals that excrete amino nitrogen in the form of uric acid. Included in this group are birds and reptiles. SEE: *urea cycle; ureotelic.*

uridine (ūr′ĭ-dīn) A nucleoside that is one of the four main riboside components of ribonucleic acid. It consists of uracil and D-ribose.

     u. diphosphate A uridine-containing nucleotide important in certain metabolic reactions, in which it transports sugars such as glucose and galactose.

urinal (ū′rĭn-ăl) [L. *urina,* urine] **1.** A container into which one urinates. **2.** A toilet or bathroom fixture for receiving urine and flushing it away.

   condom u. Condom catheter.

urinalysis (ū″rĭ-năl′ĭ-sĭs) [″ + Gr. *ana,* apart, + *lysis,* a loosening] Analysis of the urine. SEE: *urine.*

   COLLECTION OF URINE: For a routine urinalysis, a voided specimen of urine in a clean container is usually sufficient. For culture, either a clean-catch or a catheterized specimen is required. For a clean-catch specimen, the individual cleanses the perineum or glans penis with soap and water or an antiseptic solution such as benzalkonium chloride before voiding. A midstream specimen of urine is then collected in a sterilized container. A catheterized specimen is obtained by passing a catheter into the bladder, using sterile technique. SEE: *suprapubic catheter.*

   NOTE: A urine specimen may be obtained to test for excretion of drugs of abuse. In such cases, care must be taken to ensure that appropriate consent is obtained, that the specimen was produced by the individual, and that there was no opportunity for the specimen to be diluted.

urinary (ū′rĭ-nār″ē) [L. *urina,* urine] Pert. to, secreting, or containing urine.

urinary bladder SEE: under *bladder.*

urinary calculus SEE: under *calculus.*

urinary director appliance SEE: under *appliance.*

urinary diversion The surgical redirection of urine flow. SEE: *Nursing Diagnoses Appendix.*

urinary elimination, impaired Dysfunction in urine elimination. SEE: *Nursing Diagnoses Appendix.*

urinary elimination, readiness for enhanced A pattern of urinary functions that is sufficient for meeting eliminatory needs and can be strengthened. SEE: *Nursing Diagnoses Appendix.*

urinary incontinence SEE: under *incontinence.*

urinary retention The state in which the individual experiences incomplete emptying of the bladder. High urethral pressure inhibits voiding until increased abdominal pressure causes urine to be involuntarily lost, or high urethral pressure inhibits complete emptying of the bladder.

   PATIENT CARE: Ultrasound can be used to measure residual urine after voiding (i.e., to determine postvoid residual urinary retention). Other uses of bladder ultrasound include: identifying an obstruction in an indwelling catheter (indicated by a significant urine volume when the bladder should be almost empty), or the presence of bladder distension and the need for urinary catheterization.

Health care professionals should use standard precautions when a bladder scanner is employed. The procedure, which is painless, should be explained to the patient and appropriate privacy (screening and draping) provided. The probe (also known as the "transducer") should then be cleansed with a disinfectant. The health care provider then gently palpates the patient's pubic symphysis and places ultrasound gel or a bladder scan gel pad midline on the patient's abdomen about 1 to 1½ in (2.5 to 4 cm) above it. The probe is then placed on the gel with its directional icon toward the patient's head and aimed toward the bladder. Pointing the probe slightly downward toward the coccyx provides an accurate view of the bladder for most patients. The scan button should then be pressed and released. The orientation of the probe is readjusted until the bladder image is centered. The volume of urine in the bladder is calculated by software, and the measurement is displayed. A volume greater than 200 mL is abnormal. The gel should be wiped from the patient's skin or the gel pad discarded, and the patient made comfortable.

The health care provider should document any patient concerns that led to the scanning, the urine volume indicated, the patient's response to the scan, any follow-up treatment, and whether the patient's primary health care provider was contacted. SEE: illus.; Nursing Diagnoses Appendix.

urinary system The organ system that includes the kidneys, ureters, bladder, and urethra. The kidneys form urine from blood plasma by filtration, reabsorption, and secretion. The formation of urine includes the excretion of waste products, but the kidneys also regulate the water and mineral content and the acid-base balance of the blood and all other body fluids. The other organs of the system are concerned with the elimination of urine after it has been formed.

urinary tract infection SEE: under *infection.*

urinate (ū′rĭ-nāt) [L. *urinare,* to discharge urine] To pass urine from the bladder. SYN: *micturate.*

urination (ū″rĭ-nā′shŭn) [L. *urinatio,* a discharging of urine] The release of urine from the body. SYN: *micturition; uresis.*

   DIFFERENTIAL DIAGNOSIS: Increased frequency is seen in polydipsia; polyuria; diabetes mellitus and diabetes insipidus; irritation of the bladder, urethra, or urinary meatus; diseases of the spinal cord; enlarged prostate in males; pregnancy in females; beer drinking; interstitial nephritis; use of medications (e.g., diuretics); and phimosis. Decreased frequency occurs after dehydra-

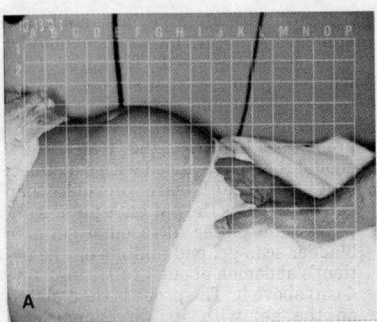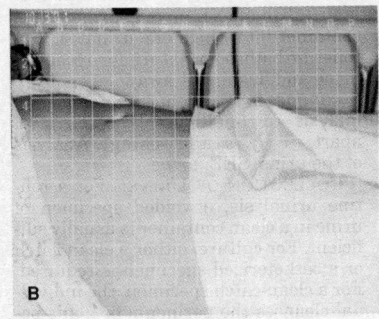

URINARY RETENTION

(A) Massive distention of the bladder by two liters of urine. (B) After catheterization of the bladder.

tion, sweating, diarrhea, or bleeding; and in anuria, oliguria, uremia, and anticholinergic drug use. SEE: *urine*.

urine (ūr′ĭn) [Fr. *urine*, fr L. *urina*, urine] The fluid and dissolved solutes (including salts and nitrogen-containing waste products) that are eliminated from the body by the kidneys. SEE: tables.

    COMPOSITION: Urine consists of approx. 95% water and 5% solids. Solids amount to 30 to 70 g/L and include the following (values are in grams per 24 hr unless otherwise noted): *Organic substances:* urea (10 to 30), uric acid (0.8 to 1.0), creatine (10 to 40 mg/24 hr in men and 10 to 270 mg/24 hr in women), creatinine (15 to 25 mg/kg of body weight per day), ammonia (0.5 to 1.3). *Inorganic substances:* chlorides (110 to 250 nmol/L depending on chloride intake), calcium (0.1 to 0.2), magnesium (3 to 5 nmol/24 hr), phosphorus (0.4 to 1.3). *Osmolarity:* 0.1 to 2.5 mOsm/L.

    In addition to the foregoing, many other substances may be present depending on the diet and state of health of the individual. Among component substances indicating pathological states are abnormal amounts of albumin, glucose, ketone bodies, blood, pus, casts, and bacteria. SEE: illus.

    double-voided u. A urine sample voided within 30 min after the patient has emptied the bladder.

    fractional u. A collection of urine taken during a few specified hours or from a specified quantity rather than from the entire amount voided during a day. SYN: *block u.*

    residual u. Urine left in the bladder after urination, an abnormal occurrence that may accompany enlargement of the prostate or the use of drugs, e.g., antihistamines or anticholinergics, that prevent complete voiding of urine. SYN: *postvoid residual*.

urine cytology Microscopic examination of a urinary specimen for cancer cells.

urino-, urin- [L. *urina*, urine] Prefixes meaning *urine*. SEE: *uro-*.

urinoma (ū″rĭ-nō′mă) [″ + Gr. *oma*, mass] A cyst containing urine.

urinometer (ū″rĭ-nŏm′ĕ-tĕr) [″ + Gr. *metron*, measure] A device, a form of hydrometer, for determining the specific gravity of urine. SEE: *hydrometer*.

urinose, urinous (ū′rĭ-nōs, ū′rĭ-nŭs) [L. *urina*, urine] Having the characteristics of or containing urine.

URL *uniform resource locator* (the unique address of a page on the Internet); *upper reference limit* (of a test).

uro-, ur- [Gr. *ouron*, urine] Prefixes meaning *urine*. SEE: *urino-*.

urobilin (ū″rō-bī′lĭn) [″ + L. *bilis*, bile] A brown pigment formed by the oxidation of urobilinogen, a decomposition product of bilirubin. Urobilin may be formed from the urobilinogen in stools or in urine after exposure to air.

urobilinuria (ū″rō-bī″lĭn-ū′rē-ă) [″ + ″ + Gr. *ouron*, urine] Excess of urobilin in the urine.

urochrome (ū′rō-krōm) [″ + *chroma*, color] The pigment that gives urine its characteristic color. It is derived from urobilin.

urocortin (ūr″ō-kŏr′tĭn) Any of a family of neuropeptides functionally related to corticotropin-releasing hormone that decreases appetite, delays gastric emptying, and decreases distal colonic motility

urodynamics (ū″rō-dī-năm′ĭks) The study of the holding or storage of urine in the bladder, the facility with which it empties, and the rate of movement of urine out of the bladder during micturition.

uroflow (ūr′ŏ-flō″) [*uro-* + *flow*] The volume of urine voided in a specified period. Low flow rates associated with high bladder pressures occur in bladder outlet obstruction.

uroflowmeter (ū″rō-flō′mē″tĕr) A device for recording urine flow; used to quan-

Significance of Changes in Urine

QUANTITY

Normal	Abnormal	Significance
1000–3000 mL/day		Varies with fluid intake, food consumed, exercise, temperature, kidney function
	High (polyuria >3000 mL/day)	Diabetes insipidus, diabetes mellitus, water intoxication, chronic nephritis, diuretic use
	Low (oliguria)	Dehydration, hemorrhage, diarrhea, vomiting, urinary obstruction, or many intrinsic kidney diseases
	None (anuria)	Same as oliguria

COLOR

Normal	Abnormal	Significance
Yellow to amber		Depends on concentration of urochrome pigment
	Pale	Dilute urine, diuretic effect
	Milky	Fat globules, pus, crystals
	Red	Drugs, blood or muscle pigments
	Green	Bile pigment (jaundiced patient)
	Brown-black	Toxins, hemorrhage, drugs, metabolites

HEMATURIA (blood in urine)

Normal	Abnormal	Significance
0–2 RBC/high-powered field (hpf)		Normal (physiological) filtration
	3 or more RBCs/hpf	Extrarenal: urinary tract infections, cancers, or stones. Renal: infections, trauma, malignancies, glomerulopathies, polycystic kidneys

PYURIA (leukocytes in urine)

Normal	Abnormal	Significance
0–9 leukocytes per hpf		
	10 or more leukocytes/hpf	Urinary tract infection, urethritis, vaginitis, urethral syndrome, pyelonephritis, and others

PROTEINURIA

Normal	Abnormal	Significance
10–150 mg/day		
	30–300 mg/day of albumin	Indicative of initial glomerular leakage in diabetes mellitus or hypertension (microalbuminuria)
	>300 mg/day	Macroalbuminuria. Indicative of progressive kidney failure. Injury to glomeruli or tubulointerstitium of kidney.
	>3500 mg/day	Nephrotic range proteinuria. Evaluation may include kidney biopsy.

Table continued on following page

Significance of Changes in Urine (Continued)

SPECIFIC GRAVITY

Normal	Abnormal	Significance
1.010–1.025		Varies with hydration
	1.010 (Low)	Excessive fluid intake, impaired kidney concentrating ability
	>1.025 (High)	Dehydration, hemorrhage, salt-wasting, diabetes mellitus, and others

ACIDITY

Normal	Abnormal	Significance
Acid (slight)		Diet of acid-forming foods (meats, eggs, prunes, wheat) overbalances the base-forming foods (vegetables and fruits)
	High acidity	Acidosis, diabetes mellitus, many pathological disorders (fevers, starvation)
	Alkaline	Vegetarian diet changes urea into ammonium carbonate; infection or ingestion of alkaline compounds

titate obstruction to urine flowing from the bladder.

uroflowmetry (ū″rō-flō′mĕ-trē) Timed measurement of the rate of urination. Uroflowmetry is used to diagnose conditions that result in slow urinary output, e.g., bladder outlet obstruction resulting from enlargement of the prostate gland. The maximal volume of urinary flow over time is called the Qmax. A Qmax of less than 10 mL of urine/second is an indication of significantly reduced urinary output.

urogastrone (ū″rō-găs′trōn) [″ + *gaster,* belly] A polypeptide present in urine that has an inhibitory effect on gastric secretion.

urogenital (ū″rō-jĕn′ĭ-tăl) [″ + L. *genitalia,* genitals] Pert. to the urinary and reproductive organs.

urogenital atrophy SEE: under *atrophy.*

urogenital system Genitourinary system.

urogenous (ū-rŏj′ĕn-ŭs) [″ + *gennan,* to produce] **1.** Producing urine. **2.** Originating in urine.

urogram (ū′rō-grăm) [″ + *gramma,* something written] A radiograph of the urinary tract.

urography (ū-rŏg′ră-fē) [Gr. *ouron,* urine, + *graphein,* to write] Radiography of the urinary tract after the introduction of a contrast medium.

　　ascending u. Urography in which the radiopaque contrast agent is injected into the bladder during cystoscopy. SYN: *cystoscopic u.; retrograde u.*

　　cystoscopic u. Ascending **u.**

　　descending u. Urography in which an injected contrast agent is excreted by the kidney and studied by x-ray examination during excretion. SYN: *excretory u.; intravenous u.*

　　excretory u. Descending **u.**

　　intravenous u. Descending **u.**

　　retrograde u. Ascending **u.**

Common Disorders of Urination

Anuria	Complete (or nearly complete) absence of urination
Diversion	Drainage of urine through a surgically constructed passage (e.g., a ureterostomy or ileal conduit)
Dysuria	Painful or difficult urination (e.g., in urethritis, urethral stricture, urinary tract infection, prostatic hyperplasia, or bladder atony)
Enuresis	Involuntary discharge of urine, esp. by children at night (bedwetting)
Incontinence	Loss of control over urination from any cause (e.g., from involuntary relaxation of urinary sphincter muscles or overflow from a full or paralyzed bladder)
Nocturia	Excessive urination at night
Oliguria	Decreased urinary output (usually less than 500 mL/day), often associated with dehydration, shock, hemorrhage, acute renal failure, or other conditions in which renal perfusion or renal output are impaired
Polyuria	Increased urinary output (usually more than 3000 mL/day), such as occurs in diabetes mellitus, diabetes insipidus, and diuresis

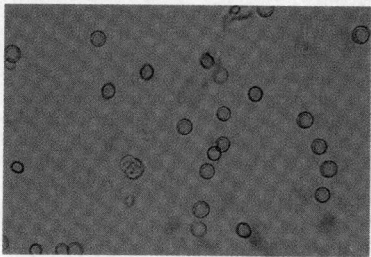

URINE

Red blood cells and one white blood cell
(×400)

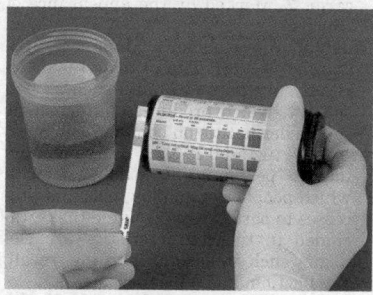

URINE TESTING KIT

Commercial testing kits contain a reagent for
a specific substance. A chemical reaction
with the urine causes a color change that
you interpret using a color chart

urogynecologist (ŭr″ō-gīn″ĕ-kol′ŏ-jĭst)
[*uro-* + *gynecologist*] A gynecologist
who specializes in the care of women
with urinary problems, such as stress
urinary incontinence, overactive bladder, or pelvic organ prolapse.

urokinetic (ū″rō-kĭ-nĕt′ĭk) [″ + *kinesis,*
movement] Resulting reflexly from
stimulation of the urinary organs.

urolith (ŭr′ŏ-lĭth″) [*uro-* + Gr. *lithos,*
stone] Renal **calculus. urolithic** (ŭr″ō-
lĭth′ĭk), *adj.*

urolithiasis (ū″rō-lĭ-thī′ă-sĭs) [″ + ″ +
-iasis, condition] The formation of kidney stones. SEE: *Nursing Diagnoses Appendix.*

urological (ū-rō-lŏj′ĭk-ăl) [″ + *logos,*
word, reason] Pert. to urology.

urologist (ū-rŏl′ō-jĭst) A physician who
specializes in the practice of urology.

urology (ū-rŏl′ō-jē) [″ + *logos,* word,
reason] The branch of medicine concerned with the urinary tract in both
sexes and the male genital tract.

uromedulin, human (ū″rō-mĕd′ū-lĭn)
The most abundant protein of renal origin in normal urine. This glycoprotein
is the same protein termed Tamm-Horsfall mucoprotein. SEE: *mucoprotein,
Tamm-Horsfall.*

uromelanin (ū-rō-mĕl′ăn-ĭn) [″ + *melas,* black] A black pigment occurring in
urine resulting from the decomposition
of urochrome.

uromodulin (ŭr″ō-moj′yŭ-lĭn) Tamm-
Horsfall mucoprotein.

uropathogen (ū″rō-păth′ō-jĕn) [″ + *pathos,* disease, suffering, + *gennan,* to
produce] A microorganism capable of
causing disease of the urinary tract.

uropathy (ū-rŏp′ă-thē) Any disease affecting the urinary tract.

   obstructive u. Any disease that
blocks the flow of urine (e.g., prostatic
hyperplasia).

uropepsin (ū″rō-pĕp′sĭn) The end product of pepsin metabolism. It is excreted
in the urine.

uroporphyria (ū″rō-por-fīr′ē-ă) Porphyria in which an excess amount of
uroporphyrin is excreted in the urine.

uroporphyrin (ū″rō-por′fĭ-rĭn) A red pigment present in the urine and feces in
cases of porphyria; may also be present
in the urine of persons taking certain
drugs.

uroporphyrinogen (ū″rō-por″fĭ-rĭn′ō-jĕn)
Any one of several porphyrins that are
the precursors of uroporphyrins.

   u. I An abnormal isomer of a precursor of protoporphyrin, which accumulates in one form of porphyria. It causes
the urine to be red, the teeth to fluoresce
brightly in ultraviolet light, and the
skin to be abnormally sensitive to sunlight. This is observed in congenital
erythropoietic porphyria.

uroscopy (ū-rŏs′kō-pē) [″ + *skopein,* to
examine] **1.** Examination of the urine.
2. Diagnosis by examination of the
urine.

urothelium (ū″rō-thēl′ē-ŭm) The endothelium that lines the urinary tract, extending from the renal calyces, through
the ureters, to the urinary bladder. **urothelial** (ū″rō-thē′lē-ăl), *adj.*

urtica (ŭr-tī′kă) *pl.* **urticae** [L., nettle]
Wheal.

Urtica dioica (dī-ō′ĭ-kă, dē-) The scientific name for the stinging nettle, an
herb used to treat allergic conditions
such as allergic rhinitis. Exposure to the
herb can cause a rash. Extracts made
from it are promoted for their diuretic
effects.

urticant (ŭr′tĭ-kănt) That which causes
hives.

urticaria (ŭrt″ĭ-kar′ē-ă) [L. *urtica,* nettle]
An allergic reaction marked by multiple
discrete swellings on the skin (wheals)
that are intensely itchy and last up to
24 hr. The wheals appear primarily on
the chest, back, extremities, face, or
scalp. SYN: *hives.* SEE: illus.; *allergy;
angioedema.*

   ETIOLOGY: Urticaria is caused by vasodilation and increased permeability of
capillaries of the skin due to the release
by mast cells of vasoactive mediators.

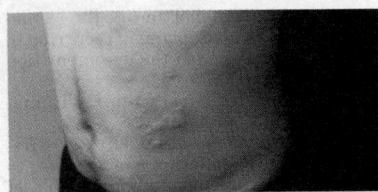

URTICARIA

The mast cell degranulation is due to an immunoglobulin E–mediated reaction to allergens (e.g., foods, drugs, or drug additives), heat, cold, and, rarely, infections or emotions. Urticaria is a primary sign of local and systemic anaphylactic reactions. It affects people of all ages but is most common between the ages of 20 and 40. Angioedema is frequently associated with urticaria.

TREATMENT: Drugs that block histamine-1 (H_1) receptors (antihistamines) are the primary treatment for urticaria. The use of both H_1 and H_2 receptor blockers has been recommended but has not been proven more effective. Patients should avoid identified allergens. Doxepin, calcium channel blockers, or immunosuppresive drugs may be needed for symptoms that are not well controlled with antihistamines. Known triggers of urticaria should be avoided.

aquagenic u. Urticaria caused by exposure of the skin to water.

u. bullosa Eruption of temporary vesicles with infusion of fluid under the epidermis.

cholinergic u. Urticaria that develops after exposure to high ambient temperatures (e.g., after exercise, a warm shower or bath, or during a fever). The hives that develop are typically small (1 to 3 mm) and are often surrounded by erythema. SYN: *generalized heat u.*

chronic u. Urticaria that occurs frequently for 6 weeks or more. It is often associated with angioedema and/or autoimmune disease.

cold u. Cold-induced urticaria that may progress to angioedema.

u. factitia Urticaria following slight irritation of the skin.

generalized heat u. Cholinergic urticaria.

giant u. Angioedema.

u. medicamentosa Urticaria caused by an allergic reaction to a drug (e.g., a sulfa drug).

papular u. Urticaria in which the wheal is followed by a lingering papule and considerable itching. It is most commonly observed in debilitated children. SYN: *prurigo simplex.*

physical u. Urticaria due to the direct effects of physical forces on the skin. Cold temperature (cold urticaria), pressure (pressure urticaria), ultraviolet radiation (solar urticaria), and scratching (dermographism) are some causes of physical urticaria.

u. pigmentosa Urticaria characterized by persistent, pigmented maculopapular lesions that urticate when stroked (Darier's sign). It typically occurs in childhood. Biopsy reveals infiltration by mast cells.

pressure u. Urticaria produced by pressure perpendicular to the surface of the skin. The persistent red swelling appears after a delay of 1 to 4 hr.

solar u. Urticaria occurring in certain people after exposure to sunlight.

urticate (ŭr′tĭ-kāt) **1.** To produce urticaria. **2.** Marked by the appearance of wheals.

urushiol (ū-roo′shē-ol″) [Japanese *urushi,* lac + *-ol*] The principal toxic irritant substance of plants such as poison ivy, which produces characteristic severe dermatitis on contact.

usability (ūz″ă-bil′ĭt-ē) A design characteristic pertaining to the ease with which people can employ tools and processes to perform goal-related tasks. Included in the characteristics are elements such as ease of learning, recall, satisfaction, and efficiency.

USACHPPM *U.S. Army Center for Health Promotion and Preventive Medicine.*

USAEC *United States Atomic Energy Commission.*

USAN *United States Adopted Names* (for drugs).

USAN and the USP Dictionary of Drug Names A dictionary of nonproprietary names, brand names, code designations, and Chemical Abstracts Service registry numbers for drugs. SEE: *United States Adopted Names.*

USCOM [Acronym for *u(ltra)s(onic) c(ardiac) o(utput) m(onitor)*] A noninvasive device that measures cardiac output.

USDA *United States Department of Agriculture.*

USDA organic A USDA designation for food that specifies that 95% of its components are organic.

usenet A world-wide collection of user-submitted notes or messages on various subjects that are posted to servers on the Internet.

Usher syndrome (ŭsh′ĕr) [Charles Howard Usher, Brit. ophthalmologist, 1865–1942] An autosomal recessive disorder marked by a combination of congenital sensorineural deafness and retinitis pigmentosa that results in a gradual loss of vision. One variant of the syndrome also interferes with normal balance. SEE: *retinitis pigmentosa.*

USP, US Phar *United States Pharmacopeia; United States Pharmacopeial Convention, Inc.*

USPHS *United States Public Health Service.*

USP-NF *United States Pharmacopeia–National Formulary.*

USPRA *United States Psychiatric Rehabilitation Association.*

USPSTF *United States Preventive Services Task Force.*

Ustilago (ŭs-tĭl-ā'gō) A mold parasite of plants, commonly called smut, which renders grains unfit to eat.

uta (ū'tă) American leishmaniasis.

Utah Elbow (ū'tah) A myoelectric prosthesis that uses an electrode and microprocessors to control both the elbow and the terminal device. The system is also designed to permit a natural elbow swing during walking.

uterine (ūt'ĕ-rīn", -rĭn) [L. *uterinus*] Pert. to the uterus.

uterine artery Doppler velocimetry SEE: *Doppler echocardiography.*

uterine factor (ūt'ĕ-rīn", -rĭn) SEE: under *factor.*

uterine tube Fallopian tube.

utero-, uter- [L. *uterus,* uterus] Prefixes meaning *uterus, uterine.* SEE: *hystero-; metro-.*

uteroabdominal (ū"tĕr-ō-ăb-dŏm'ĭ-năl) [L. *uterus,* womb, + *abdomen,* belly] Pert. to both the uterus and abdomen.

uterocervical (ū"tĕr-ō-sĕr'vĭ-kăl) [" + *cervix,* neck] Rel. to the uterus and cervix.

uteroovarian (ū"tĕr-ō-ō-vā'rē-ăn) [" + LL. *ovarium,* ovary] Rel. to the uterus and ovary.

uteropexia, uteropexy (ū"tĕr-ō-pĕks'ē-ă, ū'tĕr-ō-pĕks"ē) [" + Gr. *pexis,* fixation] Fixation of the uterus to the abdominal wall.

uteroplacental (ū"tĕr-ō-plă-sĕn'tăl) [" + *placenta,* a flat cake] Rel. to the placenta and uterus.

uterosacral (ū"tĕr-ō-sā'krăl) [" + *sacralis,* pert. to the sacrum] Rel. to the uterus and sacrum.

uterotomy (ū-tĕr-ŏt'ō-mē) Incision of the uterus.

uterotubal (ū"tĕr-ō-tū'băl) [" + *tuba,* tube] Relating to the uterus and oviducts.

uterovaginal (ū"tĕr-ō-văj'ĭ-năl) [" + *vagina,* sheath] Rel. to the uterus and vagina.

uterus (ūt'ĕ-rŭs) [L. *uterus,* womb] The reproductive organ for containing and nourishing the embryo and fetus from the time the fertilized egg is implanted to when the fetus is born. SYN: *womb.* SEE: illus.; *genitalia, female* for illus.

ANATOMY: The uterus is a muscular, hollow, pear-shaped organ situated in the midpelvis between the sacrum and the pubic symphysis. Before child-bearing, it is about 3 in. (7.5 cm) long, 2 in. (5 cm) wide, and 1 in. (2.5 cm) thick. Its upper surface is covered by the perimetrium, and it is supported by the pel-

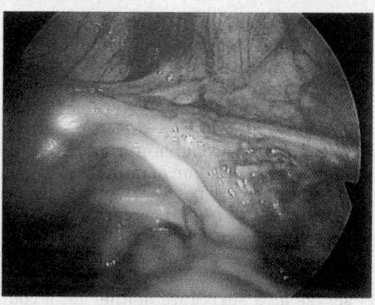

UTERUS

Uterus and its ligaments seen laparoscopically (×1/3)

vic diaphragm supplemented by the two broad ligaments, two round ligaments, and two uterosacral ligaments. It is usually tilted forward over the top of the urinary bladder. The upper portion of the uterus, between the openings of the fallopian tubes, is the fundus; the large central portion is the body; and the narrow lower end is the cervix, which projects into the vagina. The cavity of the uterus is widest in the fundus. The canal of the cervix is narrow, opens into the uterine cavity at the internal os, and into the vagina at the external os.

The wall of the uterus consists of the outer perimetrium, middle myometrium, and inner endometrium. The uterine and ovarian arteries supply blood to the uterus.

POSITIONS: *Anteflexion:* The uterus bends forward. *Anteversion:* The fundus is displaced forward toward the pubis, while the cervix is tilted up toward the sacrum. *Retroflexion:* The uterus bends backward at the junction of the body and the cervix. *Retroversion:* The uterus inclines backward with retention of the normal curve; this position is the opposite of anteversion. SEE: *hysterectomy; pregnancy.*

u. acollis A uterus without a cervix.

u. arcuatus A uterus with a depressed arched fundus.

u. bicornis A uterus in which the fundus is divided into two parts.

u. biforis A uterus in which the external os is divided into two parts by a septum.

u. bilocularis A uterus in which the cavity is divided into two parts by a partition.

bipartite u. A uterus in which the body is partially divided by a median septum.

u. cordiformis A heart-shaped uterus.

Couvelaire u. SEE: *Couvelaire uterus.*

u. didelphys Double uterus.

double u. A congenital anomaly in

which abnormalities in the formation of the müllerian ducts result in a duplication of the uterus, a uterus with a divided cavity, or sometimes, two copies of the cervix or vagina. SYN: *dimetria; u. didelphys.*

u. duplex A double uterus resulting from failure of union of müllerian ducts.

fetal u. A uterus that is retarded in development and possesses an extremely long cervical canal.

gravid u. A pregnant uterus.

host u. The uterus of a woman who serves as a surrogate mother for a couple who wants their fertilized egg carried to term.

pubescent u. An adult uterus that resembles that of a prepubertal female.

u. unicornis A uterus possessing only one lateral half and usually having only one uterine tube. About 20% to 30% of women who have this structural abnormality also experience repeated spontaneous abortion during early pregnancy.

UTI *Urinary tract infection.*

utilitarianism (ū″til′ĭ-ter′ē-ă-ni″zĕm) The moral philosophy that holds that an action is ethical according to its utility or usefulness in enhancing the welfare, safety, happiness, or pleasure of the community at large. This doctrine is popularly summarized as *an action is ethical if it generates the greatest good for the greatest number of people.*

act u. The moral theory that the best action is the one that enhances the general welfare more than any other available or known alternative. An action is judged in terms of the goodness of its consequences with no consideration of the rules of action.

rule u. The moral theory that an action that follows a demonstrably proven ethical formula will necessarily be a good act. The ethical rule is judged to be correct by the amount of good it effects when it is followed.

utilization (ūt″ĭl-ĭ-zā′shŏn) [L. *utilis,* usable] In health care, the consumption of services or supplies, such as the number of office visits a person makes per year with a health care provider, the number of prescription drugs taken, or the number of days a person is hospitalized.

utilization behavior The compulsive or thoughtless use of any found object even though its use is not appropriate for the context in which it was found. Finding a toothbrush in a grocery store and automatically using it to brush one's teeth in public is an example.

utilization review Evaluation of the necessity, quality, effectiveness, or efficiency of medical services, procedures, and facilities. In regard to a hospital, the review includes appropriateness of admission, services ordered and pro-

vided, length of stay, and discharge practices.

utricle (ū′trĭk′l) [L. *utriculus,* a little bag] **1.** A small sac. **2.** The larger of two sacs of the vestibular labyrinth in the vestibule of the inner ear. It communicates with the semicircular ducts, the saccule, and the endolymphatic duct, all of which are filled with endolymph. In its wall is the macula utriculi, a sensory area with hair cells that respond to movement of otoliths as the position of the head changes.

prostatic u. A small blind pouch of the urethra extending into the substance of the prostate gland. It is a remnant of the embryonic müllerian duct. The ejaculatory duct opens into or at the opening of the prostatic utricle.

utricular (ū-trĭk′ū-lăr) [L. *utriculus,* a little bag] **1.** Pert. to the utricle. **2.** Like a bladder.

utriculitis (ū-trĭk-ū-lī′tĭs) [″ + Gr. *itis,* inflammation] Inflammation of the utricle, that of either the vestibule or the prostate.

uva-ursi (ū′vă-ŭr′sē) An evergreen perennial shrub, *Arctostaphylos uva-ursi* (family Ericaceae)—commonly known as bearberry—whose dried leaves are used as a urinary antiseptic and diuretic. There have been few clinical trials on its effectiveness.

uvea (ū′vē-ă) [L. *uvea, uva,* grape] The highly vascular middle layer of the eyeball, immediately beneath the sclera. It consists of the iris, ciliary body, and choroid, and forms the pigmented layer. **uveal** (ū′vē-ăl), *adj.*

uveitic (ū-vē-ĭt′ĭk) [″ + Gr. *itis,* inflammation] Marked by or pert. to uveitis.

uveitis (ū-vē-ī′tĭs) A nonspecific term for any intraocular inflammatory disorder. The uveal tract structures—iris, ciliary body, and choroid—are usually involved, but other nonuveal parts of the eye, including the retina and cornea, may be involved.

Uveitis that is not associated with known infections or that is associated with diseases of unknown cause is termed endogenous uveitis. This is thought to be due to an autoimmune phenomenon.

TREATMENT: Corticosteroids and other immunosuppressive agents, including cyclosporine, are used in treating some causes of uveitis, but their use may make some types of uveitus worse.

Short-acting cycloplegic agents such as hematropine, scopolamine, or cyclopentolate are used during therapy to prevent inflammatory adhesions (posterior synechiae) between the iris and lens.

diffuse u. Panuveitis.

intermediate u. Pars planitis.

sympathetic u. Severe, bilateral uveitis that starts as inflammation of the uveal tract of one eye resulting from a puncture wound. The injured eye is termed the "exciting eye." SEE: *sympathetic ophthalmia*.

TREATMENT: High-dose corticosteroids are often effective.

uveitis-glaucoma-hyphema syndrome
ABBR: UGH. A rare complication of cataract surgery with intraocular lens implantation in which patients experience brief episodes of visual loss affecting a single eye, typically months or years after cataract surgery.

uveoplasty (ū′vē-ō-plăs″tē) [″ + Gr. *plassein*, to form] Reparative operation of the uvea.

uvula (ū′vyŭ-lă) [L. *uvula*, a little grape] **1.** The free edge of the soft palate that hangs at the back of the throat above the root of the tongue. It is made of muscle, connective tissue, and mucous membrane. **2.** Any small projection. **uvular** (ū′vyŭ-lăr), *adj*.

u. fissa A cleft uvula.

u. vermis A small triangular elevation on the vermis of the cerebellum of the brain.

u. vesicae A median projection of mucous membrane of the urinary bladder located immediately anterior to the orifice of the urethra.

uvulectomy (ū″vū-lĕk′tō-mē) [″ + Gr. *ektome*, excision] Surgical removal of the uvula.

uvulitis (ū″vū-lī′tĭs) [″ + Gr. *itis*, inflammation] Inflammation of the uvula.

uvulopalatopharyngoplasty (ū″vū-lō-păl″ă-tō-fă-rĭn″gō-plăs′tē) ABBR: UPPP. Plastic surgery of the oropharynx in which redundant soft palate, uvula, pillars, fauces, and sometimes posterior pharyngeal wall mucosa are removed. The procedure may be done by using laser therapy. It is usually done to correct intractable snoring or sleep apnea. SEE: *sleep disorder; snore*.

U wave SEE: *wave*.

V **1.** *Vibrio; vision; visual acuity.* **2.** Symbol for the element vanadium.

V̇ **1.** Symbol for gas flow. **2.** Symbol for ventilation.

v L. *vena,* vein; *volt.*

VA *vertebral* **artery***; Veterans Administration.*

vacate (vă′kāt) [L. *vacare,* to be empty] In law, to overturn a ruling or judgment.

vaccina (văk-sī′nă) Vaccinia.

vaccinal (văk′sĭn-ăl) Pert. to vaccine or to vaccination.

vaccinate (văk′sĭn-āt) [L. *vaccinus,* pert. to cows] To inoculate with vaccine to produce immunity against disease.

vaccination (vak″sĭ-nā′shŏn) [*vaccinate*] **1.** Inoculation with any vaccine or toxoid to establish resistance to a specific infectious disease. SEE: *immunization.* **2.** A scar left on the skin by inoculation of a vaccine.

   antitumor v. The injection of tumor-associated antigens (e.g., from melanomas or other solid tumors) into cancer patients in order to raise a long-lasting and effective immune response against the tumor. The tumor antigen is often presented to the vaccinee in the presence of dendritic cells in order to improve the presentation of the antigen and heighten the immune response. SYN: *antitumor vaccine; tumor vaccine.*

   catch-up v. The immunization of unvaccinated children at the most convenient times (e.g., on the first day of school) rather than at the optimal time for antibody production. Because many children miss vaccines at regularly scheduled times, catch-up immunization offers unvaccinated children, their families, and the communities in which they live a second opportunity for disease prevention and control. SYN: *catch-up immunization.*

   mass v. The use of vaccines during an outbreak of a communicable disease in an attempt to prevent an epidemic. In the U.S. mass vaccinations are sometimes carried out in schools and hospitals during meningitis or hepatitis epidemics.

vaccine (vak-sēn′, vak′sēn″) [L. (*variola*) *vaccina,* cow(pox)] **1.** An infectious liquid derived from cowpox lesions and used to prevent and attenuate smallpox in humans. SEE: *Jenner, Edward.* **2.** Any suspension containing antigenic molecules derived from a microorganism, given to stimulate an immune response to an infectious disease. Vaccines may be made from weakened or killed microorganisms; inactivated toxins; toxoids derived from microorganisms; or immunologically active surface markers extracted or copied from microorganisms. They can be given intramuscularly, subcutaneously, intradermally, orally, or intranasally; as single agents; or in combinations. SEE: *Recommended Immunization Schedules Appendix.*

   The ideal vaccine should be effective, well tolerated, easy and inexpensive to manufacture, and easy to administer and store. In practice, side effects from vaccines (such as fevers, muscle aches, and pain at the injection site) are common but generally mild. Adverse reactions to vaccines that should be reported include anaphylaxis, shock, seizures, active infection, and death. SEE: *immunization.*

⚠️ Because vaccines may cause side effects, all those who receive them should carefully review federally mandated Vaccine Information Sheets before they are immunized.

---

   adsorbed anthrax v. A cell-free, aluminum-hydroxide-adsorbed vaccine, administered to raise protective antibodies against *Bacillus anthracis. B. anthracis* has been used in biological warfare.

   antitumor v. Antitumor **vaccination.**

   autogenous v. Bacterial vaccine prepared from lesions of the individual to be inoculated. SYN: *homologous v.*

   bacterial v. A suspension of killed or attenuated bacteria; used for injection into the body to produce active immunity to the same organism.

   BCG v. Bacille Calmette-Guérin vaccine, a preparation of a dried, living but attenuated culture of *Mycobacterium bovis.* In areas with a high incidence of tuberculosis (TB), it is used to provide passive immunity to infants against disseminated TB or TB meningitis, and it affords some protection against leprosy. It is not effective prevention against pulmonary infection with TB, nor can it be used in pregnant women or in the immunosuppressed. It also produces hypersensitivity to TB skin tests, making them unreliable for several years. The vaccine can be used in cancer chemotherapy, e.g., to treat multiple myeloma and cancer of the colon, or as a bladder wash in patients with carcinoma of the bladder. SEE: *bacille Calmette-Guérin*.

cholera v. A vaccine prepared from killed or inactivated *Vibrio cholerae*.

dendritic cell v. An anticancer vaccine made by extracting dendritic (antigen-presenting) cells from a patient with cancer, stimulating those cells to reproduce themselves, and then exposing them to antigens taken from the patient's cancer. The antigenically exposed dendritic cells are then injected back into the patient.

diphtheria v. A vaccination against *Corynebacterium diphtheriae*. SEE: *DTaP v.*

DNA v. A vaccine made by genetic engineering in which the gene that codes for an antigen is inserted into a bacterial plasmid and then injected into the host. Once inside the host, it uses the nuclear machinery of the host cell to manufacture and express the antigen. Unlike other vaccines, DNA vaccines may have the potential to induce cellular as well as humoral immune responses.

DPT v. An obsolete combination of diphtheria and tetanus toxoids and killed pertussis bacilli. It is no longer given in pediatric immunizations because of the superiority of DTaP, a vaccine that contains only acellular pertussis.

DTaP v. A preparation of diphtheria and tetanus toxoids and acellular pertussis proteins. It is used to immunize children against all three infections or adults at high risk of complications of infection with pertussis.

edible v. A genetically manipulated food containing organisms or related antigens that may provide active immunity against infection. Edible vaccines against many microorganisms are being developed, with the goal of using them to vaccinate children in nonindustrialized countries where there are obstacles to the use of traditional injectable vaccines.

Haemophilus influenzae type b v. ABBR: HIB. A vaccine created by combining purified polysaccharide antigen from the *Haemophilus influenzae* bacteria and a carrier protein. It reduces the risks of childhood epiglottitis, meningitis, and other diseases caused by *H. influenzae*.

hepatitis B v. A vaccine prepared from hepatitis B protein antigen produced by genetically engineered yeast. The vaccine prevents acute infection with hepatitis B, the chronic carrier state of hepatitis B infection. In developing nations where hepatitis B infection is endemic, it has been shown to decrease the incidence of hepatocellular carcinoma resulting from hepatitis B infection. The World Health Organization recommends that the vaccine be given to all infants and adolescents, all health care workers, all patients receiving hemodialysis, all incarcerated prisoners, men who have sex with men, and those who inject drugs.

hepatitis B virus vaccine A recombinant vaccine used to vaccinate children and others at high risk for coming in contact with either hepatitis B carriers or blood or fluids from such people. It contains noninfectious hepatitis B surface antigen (HBsAg), which stimulates the production of antibodies and provides active immunity. Included in the high-risk group are health care workers, hemodialysis patients, police officers and other public safety workers, people with other forms of chronic hepatitis, intravenous drug users, family members and sexual partners of those infected with hepatitis B virus, and people who travel extensively abroad. SEE: *hepatitis B immune globulin*.

heterogeneous v. A vaccine made from some source other than the patient's own tissues or cells; the opposite of autogenous vaccine.

heterologous v. A vaccine derived from an organism different from the organism against which the vaccine is used.

homologous v. Autogenous **v.**

HPV v. A vaccine that protects against several types of human papillomavirus infection, specifically those associated with genital warts and cervical cancer.

human diploid cell rabies v. ABBR: HDCV. An inactivated virus vaccine prepared from fixed rabies virus grown in human diploid cell tissue culture.

inactivated poliovirus v., poliovirus vaccine, inactivated An injectable vaccine made from three types of inactivated polioviruses. Developed by Jonas E. Salk, it was the first successful vaccine against poliomyelitis and is now the only polio vaccine administered in the U.S. SYN: *Salk vaccine*.

Infants should be given three doses, the first at 2 months of age, followed by two more doses at 8-week intervals. A fourth dose should be given at age 18 months unless poliomyelitis is endemic in the area, in which case the fourth dose is given 6 to 12 months after the third. Additional doses are recommended before beginning school and then every 5 years until age 18.

influenza virus v. A polyvalent vaccine containing either inactivated or live attenuated antigenic variants of the influenza virus (types A and B either individually or combined) for annual usage. It prevents epidemic disease and the morbidity and mortality caused by influenza virus, esp. in the aged and the chronically ill. The vaccine is reformulated each year to match the strains of influenza present in the population.

killed v. A vaccine prepared from dead microorganisms. This type of vaccine is used to prevent disease caused by highly virulent microbes.

live attenuated influenza v. ABBR: LAIV. A live virus vaccine made with influenza viruses adapted to replicate in the nose, sinuses, and pharynx but not in the lower respiratory tract. LAIV is typically administered by nasal inhalation rather than by intramuscular injection.

live attenuated measles (rubeola) virus v. A vaccine prepared from live strains of the measles virus. It is the preferred form except in patients who have lymphoma; active tuberculosis; sensitivity to eggs; leukemia, or other generalized malignancy; or are undergoing radiation therapy; prolonged treatment with drugs that suppress the immune response, i.e., corticosteroids or antimetabolites; administration of gamma globulin, blood, or plasma. Those persons should be given immune globulin immediately following exposure.

live measles and mumps virus v. A standardized vaccine containing attenuated measles and mumps viruses.

live measles and rubella virus v. A standardized vaccine containing attenuated measles and rubella viruses.

live measles, mumps, and rubella virus v. ABBR: MMR vaccine. A standardized vaccine containing attenuated measles, mumps, and rubella viruses.

live measles virus v. A standardized attenuated virus vaccine for use in immunizing against measles.

live oral poliovirus v., poliovirus vaccine, live oral A vaccine prepared from three types of live attenuated polioviruses. In 1999, an advisory panel to the CDC recommended that its routine use be discontinued. Because it contains a live, although weakened virus, it had been causing 8 to 10 cases of polio each year in the U.S. This risk was deemed no longer acceptable since by that date polio epidemics had been eliminated in the U.S. Therefore, since 1999 the live oral poliovirus vaccine has not been recommended or routinely given in the U.S. Instead only the inactivated poliovirus vaccine is approved and given in the U.S. Recommendations outside the U.S., where polio outbreaks still occur, include the use of live oral polio vaccines. SYN: *Sabin v.*

live rubella virus v. An attenuated virus vaccine used to prevent rubella (German measles). All nonpregnant susceptible women of childbearing age should be provided with this vaccine to prevent fetal infection and the congenital rubella syndrome, i.e., possible fetal death, prematurity, impaired hearing, cataract, mental retardation, and other serious conditions. SEE: *rubella.*

⚠️ Women of child-bearing age who receive vaccination are advised to use effective birth control measures for at least 3 months after immunization. Before administering the RA27/3 rubella vaccine, a history of allergies, esp. to neomycin, and of reactions to previous vaccinations should be obtained, and the primary care provider made aware of any problems. Those who are immunocompromised should not receive this vaccine, which is more immunogenic than previous preparations.

Lyme disease v. A vaccine that uses as an antigen either the outer surface protein (OspA) of *Borrelia burgdorferi* or the decorin protein of the same microbe. Lyme vaccine is available in the U.S. for veterinary use only.

meningococcal v. Any of the vaccines prepared from bacterial polysaccharides from certain types of meningococci. Meningococcal polysaccharide vaccines A, C, Y, and W135 are available for preventing diseases caused by those serogroups. A vaccine for meningococcal serogroup B is not available.

PATIENT CARE: All adolescents should initially receive meningococcal vaccine at age 11 or 12 and a booster at age 16. Patients with complement deficiencies, HIV, or asplenia should received two doses two months apart, beginning as early as age 2. SEE: *acute meningococcal* **meningitis**.

mumps virus., mumps virus vaccine live A live attenuated vaccine used to prevent mumps. Its use should be governed by the same restrictions listed for live attenuated measles virus vaccine.

peptide v. A vaccine that stimulates antibody production against specific amino acid sequences, e.g., those expressed on the surface of pathogens or cancer cells.

pertussis v. A vaccine against *Bordetella pertussis*. SEE: *DTaP v.*

plague v. A vaccine made either from a crude fraction of killed plague bacilli, *Yersinia pestis,* or synthetically from recombinant proteins. It is rarely used, except in a laboratory or for field workers in areas where plague is endemic.

pneumococcal conjugate v. A pneumococcal vaccine used for active immunization of infants and toddlers. SEE: *PCV7, PCV13.*

pneumococcal 7-valent conjugate v. ABBR: PCV7. A pneumococcal vaccine used for active immunization of infants and toddlers. The vaccine contains antigens from 7 capsular serotypes of *Streptococcus pneumoniae* and is used to immunize children against pneumococcal diseases, such as otitis media, pneumonia, and meningitis.

polyvalent v. A vaccine produced from cultures of a number of strains of the same species.

polyvalent pneumococcal v. A vaccine that contains 23 of the known 83 pneumococcal capsular polysaccharides, and induces immunity against *Streptococcus pneumoniae,* which causes ear, sinus, lung, blood, and meningeal infections. This vaccine is used to prevent pneumococcal disease in alcoholics; and in those who have sickle cell diseases; asplenia; chronic heart, lung, liver, or kidney disease; diabetes mellitus; immunological illnesses; and in those over 65.

PATIENT CARE: The value of vaccination is continually rising, as *S. pneumoniae* becomes more and more resistant to antibiotics. The vaccine should not be coadministered in the same syringe as other vaccines. Common adverse reactions include pain at the site of injection and sometimes a low-grade fever.

rabies v. A vaccine prepared from killed rabies virus used for pre-exposure immunization for persons at high occupational risk. Following a bite by a rabid animal, both the vaccine and rabies immune globulin, containing preformed antibodies, are given. SEE: *human diploid cell rabies v.; rabies.*

reassortant v. A vaccine made by combining antigens from several viruses or from several strains of the same virus.

Sabin v. Live oral poliovirus **v.** SEE: *poliomyelitis.*

Salk v. SEE: *inactivated poliovirus v.*

sensitized v. A vaccine prepared from bacteria treated with their specific immune serum.

smallpox v. A vaccine used to provide immunity against smallpox. The vaccine is made from live vaccinia virus (not from the smallpox virus). Similarities between the two viruses make the vaccine about 95% effective in preventing smallpox in those exposed to the virus. Smallpox vaccine was not used for many years because smallpox had been eradicated worldwide. However, concerns over the use of smallpox as a biological weapon have resulted in vaccination of persons at high risk, e.g., public health workers, health care response teams, members of the armed services. The general public is not vaccinated. The CDC recommends that persons who could be exposed to the monkeypox virus should also be vaccinated against smallpox.

tetanus v. A vaccine against *Clostridium tetani.* SEE: *DTaP v.*

tumor v. Antitumor **vaccination**.

typhoid v. One of two forms of vaccine against typhoid fever. Attenuated live virus is used for an oral vaccine taken in four doses by adults and children over age 6; it provides protection for 5 years. This vaccine should not be given to people taking antimicrobial drugs or to those with AIDS. A parenteral type of the vaccine, made from the capsular polysaccharide of *Salmonella typhi,* given to children at least 6 months old, requires two doses 4 weeks apart, is effective 55% to 75% of the time, and lasts 3 years.

typhus v. A sterile suspension of the killed rickettsial organism of a strain or strains of epidemic typhus rickettsiae.

varicella (chickenpox) v. A chickenpox vaccine prepared from attenuated virus. SEE: *chickenpox; herpes zoster.*

yellow fever v. A vaccine made from a live attenuated strain of yellow fever that protects against this tropical, mosquito-borne, viral hemorrhagic fever.

vaccine adverse event reporting system ABBR: VAERS. A national surveillance system for monitoring undesirable reactions to administered vaccines.

vaccine buffer stock Buffer stock.

vaccine extraimmunization (ek″strā-im″yŭ-nĭ-zā-shŏn) Admistration of excessive or repetitive doses of vaccines to children or adults, usually because of incomplete or inaccurate record keeping.

vaccine refusal Unwillingness to allow oneself or a family member to be immunized against a preventable contagious disease, such as measles, mumps, rubella, or chickenpox. It occurs most often in people who fear adverse effects from vaccination, in people who have religious or philosophical objections to vaccination, and in people who have had allergies to a component of a vaccine.

vaccine safety datalink project ABBR: VSD. A collaboration between the CDC and several major managed care organizations and health insurers to assess the effects of vaccinations on public health. The VSD has studied the effects of vaccination on autism, hair loss, thrombocytopenia, and neurological development in children. Website:http://www.cdc.gov/vaccinesafety/Activities/VSD.html

vaccine therapy Injection of infectious organisms, particles, or antigens to produce active immunization against a disease. SYN: *opsonic therapy.*

vaccinia (vak-sin′ē-ă) [*vaccine* + *-ia*] ABBR: VV. A contagious disease of cattle, produced in humans by inoculation with cowpox virus to confer immunity against smallpox. Papules form about the third day after vaccination, changing to umbilicated vesicles about the fifth day, and at the end of the first week becoming umbilicated pustules surrounded by red areolae. They dry and form scabs, which fall off about the second week, leaving a white pitted depression. SYN: *cowpox; vaccina.* SEE: *vaccination; varicella; variola.*

   v. necrosum Spreading necrosis at the site of a smallpox vaccination; may be accompanied by similar necrotic areas elsewhere on the body. SYN: *progressive v.*

   progressive v. v. necrosum.

vaccinia immune globulin An immune globulin containing vaccinia-specific antibodies. It is used for dermal complications of vaccination for smallpox (i.e., severe eczema vaccinatum and progressive vaccinia). An intravenous formulation (IV-VIG) is now being produced and tested.

vacciniform (văk-sĭn′ĭ-form) [L. *vaccinus,* pert. to cows, + *forma,* shape] Pert. to vaccinia or cowpox.

Vaccinium macrocarpon (văk-sĭn′ē-ŭm măk″rō-kăr′pŭn) [L., blueberry + Gr. *makros,* long + *karpos,* fruit] The scientific name for cranberry.

vaccinogenous (văk″sĭn-ŏj′ĕn-ŭs) [L. *vaccinus,* pert. to cows, + Gr. *gennan,* to produce] Producing vaccine or pert. to its production.

vaccinosis (văk-sĭn-ō′sĭs) Chronic illness, discomfort, or malaise that results from immunization.

vaccinostyle (văk-sĭn′ō-stīl) A pointed stylus used in vaccination.

vacuolar (văk′ū-ō-lăr) [L. *vacuum,* empty] Pert. to or possessing vacuoles.

vacuolated (văk′ū-ō-lāt″ĕd) Pert. to or possessing vacuoles.

vacuolation (văk″ū-ō-lā′shŭn) Formation of vacuoles. SYN: *vacuolization.*

vacuole (văk′ū-ōl) [L. *vacuum,* empty] A membrane-bound cell organelle, which may contain water, secretions, enzymes, or the remains of ingested material.

   autophagic v. A vacuole that contains recognizable fragments of the ribosomes or mitochondria.

   contractile v. A cavity filled with fluid in the cytoplasm of a protozoan. The cavity is emptied by sudden contraction of its walls.

   heterophagous v. A vacuole that contains substances that come from outside the cell.

   plasmocrine v. A vacuole present in the cytoplasm of a secretory cell that is filled with crystalloid material.

   rhagiocrine v. A vacuole present in the cytoplasm of a secretory cell that is filled with colloid material.

vacuolization (văk″ū-ō-lĭ-zā′shŭn) [L. *vacuum,* empty] Vacuolation.

vacuum (văk′ū-ŭm) [L., empty] A space exhausted of its air content.

vacuum aspiration SEE: under *aspiration.*

vacuum-assisted wound closure ABBR: wound VAC. A treatment for surgical wounds consisting of a pump that applies negative pressure to a wound space via tubing inserted into the wound; the pump is secured in place with a disposable sponge covered by a vapor-permeable dressing. SYN: *negative pressure wound therapy.* SEE: illus.

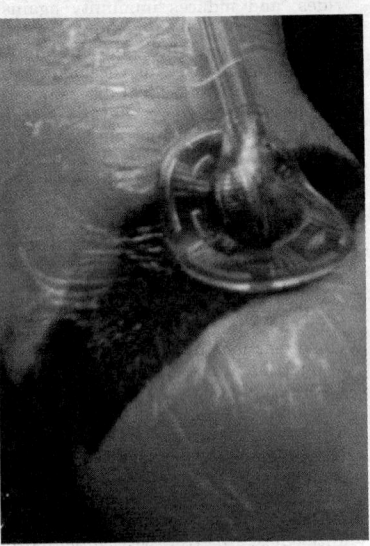

VACUUM-ASSISTED WOUND CLOSURE

vacuum extractor A device for applying traction to the fetus during delivery by using a suction cup attached to the fetal head. Its use may be hazardous except in the hands of experts.

vacuum phenomenon In radiographic studies, the appearance of gas within a joint space or bone, e.g., in a degenerated intravertebral disk.

vacuum tube A vessel of insulating material (usually glass) that is sealed and has a vacuum sufficiently high to permit the free flow of electrons between the electrodes that extend into the tube from the outside. In England, it is called a vacuum valve.

vagabond's disease Discoloration of the skin caused by exposure and scratching owing to the presence of lice. SEE: *pediculosis corporis.*

vagal (vā′găl) [L. *vagus,* wandering] Pert. to the vagus nerve.

vagal attack SEE: under *attack.*

vagal maneuver Any physical action that increases parasympathetic tone and decreases the conduction of the electrical impulses of the heart. Vagal maneuvers may be used as first-line interventions in the evaluation or management of supraventricular tachycardias. Examples include bearing down or straining; massaging the carotid sinus; coughing; gagging; or immersing the face or neck in ice water. SEE: *Valsalva maneuver*.

vagi (vā′gī) Pl. of vagus.

vagina (vă-jī′nă) *pl.* **vaginae, vaginas** [L., sheath] A musculomembranous tube that forms the passageway between the cervix uteri and the vulva. SEE: illus.

ANATOMY: In the uppermost part, the cervix divides the vagina into four small vaulted cavities, called fornices: two lateral, the anterior, and the posterior. The bladder and urethra are adjacent to the anterior wall of the vagina, and the rectum is behind the posterior wall. The cavity of the vagina is a potential space; the walls are usually in contact with each other. Close to the cervix uteri the walls form a horizontal crescent shape, at the midpoint an H shape, and close to the vulva the shape of a vertical slit. The vaginal mucosa is stratified squamous epithelium that is very resistant to bacterial colonization. This lining is in folds called rugae, and the connective tissue external to it also permits stretching. The blood supply of the vagina is furnished from the inferior vesical, inferior hemorrhoidal, and uterine arteries. Except for the area close to the entrance, the vaginal tissue and mucosa contain few, if any, sensory nerve endings. The vagina is a passage for the insertion of the penis, for the reception of semen, and for the discharge of the menstrual flow. It also serves as the birth canal.

artificial v. A vagina constructed by plastic surgery for a patient whose vagina was removed for treatment of carcinoma or one who has congenital absence of the vagina.

bulb of v. The small erectile body on each side of the vestibule of the vagina. SEE: *vestibule of vagina*.

foreign bodies in v. Objects that enter the vagina accidentally or are inserted deliberately. A great variety of foreign bodies may be present in the vagina, esp. in children. Foreign bodies in adults include vaginal tampons, pessaries, and contraceptive diaphragms. The treatment is to remove the foreign body. Antibiotic therapy is not usually necessary.

septate v. A congenital condition in which the vagina is divided longitudinally into two parts. This division may be partial or complete.

vaginal (văj′ĭn-ăl) [L. *vagina*, sheath] Pert. to the vagina or to any enveloping sheath.

vaginal birth after previous cesarean ABBR: VBAC. Vaginal childbirth after cesarean delivery of a previous pregnancy. The risk of uterine rupture is 1% to 2%.

vaginal intraepithelial neoplasia SEE: under *neoplasia*.

vaginalitis (văj-ĭn-ăl-ī′tĭs) [″ + Gr. *itis*, inflammation] Inflammation of the tunica vaginalis testis.

vaginal lubricant A fluid, usually a water-soluble ointment or cream, used to reduce vaginal dryness or sexual friction. As a lubricant, petroleum jelly is of little or no value. Estrogen-containing vaginal creams reduce friction-associated discomfort related to postmenopausal atrophy. A natural and effective lubricant is human saliva.

vaginal rejuvenation Labioplasty (2).

vaginal vibrator A device used for erotic stimulation. It is usually applied to the clitoris or intravaginally.

vaginapexy (văj′ĭn-ă-pĕk′sē) [″ + Gr. *pexis*, fixation] Repair of a relaxed and prolapsed vagina. SYN: *colpopexy*.

vaginate (văj′ĭn-āt) [L. *vaginatus*] Forming or enclosed in a sheath.

vaginectomy (văj-ĭn-ĕk′tō-mē) [L. *vagina*, sheath, + Gr. *ektome*, excision] **1.** Vaginalectomy. **2.** Excision of the vagina or a part of it.

vaginismus (văj″ĭn-ĭz′mŭs) [L.] Painful spasm of the vagina from contraction of

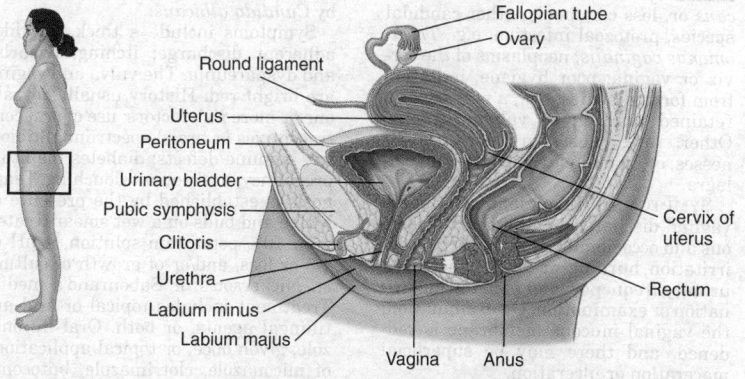

Round ligament
Uterus
Peritoneum
Urinary bladder
Pubic symphysis
Clitoris
Urethra
Labium minus
Labium majus
Fallopian tube
Ovary
Cervix of uterus
Rectum
Vagina
Anus

VAGINA AND OTHER FEMALE ORGANS

the outer third of the muscles surrounding it, a condition that may interfere with coitus. SEE: *Nursing Diagnoses Appendix.*

Severe vaginismus may prevent intercourse. It origin may be physical or psychological. Diagnosis is based on pelvic examination (to rule out vaginal infections or structural anomalies) and sexual history, including childhood experiences and familial attitudes and current sexual practices and responses.

PATIENT CARE: Patients with vaginismus need factual information and emotional support. Information about sexual concerns, practices, and responses should be geared specifically to the problem or question posed by the patient. Correcting myths and misinformation and teaching the woman about the range of normal sexual responses can be helpful. Treatments include pelvic relaxation exercises, sex therapy, counseling and cognitive behavioral therapy, and instrumental dilator therapy. Addressing the patient's emotional concerns provides psychological support. The woman should be helped to attain security and comfort in her own sexual responses. Additional suggestions for patients may include advice about extending foreplay to increase vaginal relaxation and lubrication.

vaginitis (vaj″ĭ-nīt′ĭs) [*vagina* + *-itis*] **1.** Inflammation of a sheath. **2.** Inflammation of the vagina. SYN: *colpitis.* SEE: *sexually transmitted disease; Nursing Diagnoses Appendix; vulvovaginitis.*

ETIOLOGY: Inflammation of the vagina may be caused by overgrowth or invasion of organisms such as gonococci, Chlamydiae, *Gardnerella vaginalis,* staphylococci, streptococci, spirochetes; viruses such as herpes; irritation from chemicals in douching, hygiene sprays, detergents, menstrual products, or toilet tissue; fungal infection (candidiasis) caused by overgrowth of *Candida albicans* or, less commonly, other candidal species; protozoal infection, e.g., *Trichomonas vaginalis;* neoplasms of the cervix or vagina; poor hygiene; irritation from foreign bodies, e.g., a pessary or a retained tampon; or vulvar atrophy. Other, rare, causes are parasitic illnesses, or, in malnourished women, pellagra.

SYMPTOMS: The patient experiences vaginal discharge, sometimes malodorous and occasionally stained with blood; irritation, burning, or itching; increased urinary frequency; and pain during urination or examination. On examination, the vaginal mucous membrane is reddened, and there may be superficial maceration or ulceration.

TREATMENT: Specific therapy is given as indicated for the underlying cause. Improved perineal hygiene is emphasized by instructing in the proper method of cleaning the anus after a bowel movement, the proper use of menstrual protection materials, and the necessity of drying the vulva following urination.

PREVENTION: In addition to being taught improved perineal hygiene, patients should be encouraged to wear all-cotton underpants or panties with a cotton crotch area, not to wear underwear to bed, and to avoid tight-fitting pants or panty hose that promote moisture and growth of organisms .

PATIENT CARE: During examination of the patient, aseptic techniques are used to collect specimens. The health care provider supports the patient throughout the procedures, explaining each procedure and warning the patient of possible discomfort. The patient should be advised that persistent or recurrent candidiasis indicates a need for assessment for pregnancy or diabetes mellitus. If vaginitis is due to a sexually transmitted disease, the sexual partner should receive treatment with the patient to prevent reinfection. Certain sexually transmitted vaginal infections must be reported to local or state public health officials with the patient's known sexual contacts.

v. adhaesiva Inflammation of the vagina causing adhesions between its walls.

atrophic v. Postmenopausal thinning and dryness of the vaginal epithelium related to decreased estrogen levels. SYN: *postmenopausal v.; senile v.; urogenital atrophy.*

Symptoms include burning and pain during intercourse. Estrogen replacement therapy, hormone replacement therapy, or application of topical estrogen restores the integrity of the vaginal epithelium and supporting tissues and relieves symptoms.

candidal v. A yeast infection caused by *Candida albicans.*

Symptoms include a thick, curdlike adherent discharge; itching; dysuria; and dyspareunia. The vulva and vagina are bright red. History usually reveals one or more risk factors: use of oral contraceptives or broad-spectrum antibiotics; immune defects; diabetes mellitus; pregnancy; or frequent douching. Diagnosis is established by the presence of hyphe and buds on a wet smear treated with 10% potassium solution, a pH of 4.5 or less, and/or of growth of culture on Nickerson's or Sabouraud's media. Treatment includes topical or oral antifungal agents, or both. Oral fluconazole, given once, or topical applications of miconazole, clotrimazole, butoconazole, or terconazole, given 3 to 7 days, promptly relieve symptoms. Recurrence of symptoms after treatment is often due to presence of candida species other than *C. albicans,* presence of a mixed infection, or reinfection. Either use of a different agent or a longer course of treatment (14 to 21 days) is indicated, as well as testing for hyperglycemia. SYN: *moniliasis.*

chlamydial v. The most common sexually transmitted vaginal infection in the U.S., caused by an obligate intracellular parasite, *Chlamydia trachomatis.* Chlamydial infection is also a major cause of pelvic inflammatory disease, tubal occlusion, infertility, ectopic pregnancy, nongonococcal urethritis, and ophthalmia neonatorum. Asymptomatic chlamydial infection has been implicated in the development of preterm labor and birth in high-risk women. Patients may be asymptomatic or have a thin or purulent vaginal discharge, dysuria, and/or lower abdominal pain. Diagnosis is established by testing for specific monoclonal antibodies. Doxycycline is the drug of choice, except during pregnancy (it damages fetal bone and tooth formation). During pregnancy the infection is treated with erythromycin or azithromycin. SEE: *Chlamydia.*

emphysematous v. A rare, benign vaginitis with gas-bubble formation in the vaginal wall.

granular v. Vaginitis with cellular infiltration and enlargement of papillae.

nonspecific v. A rare vaginitis in which no particular factor or etiological agent is identifiable; a contact-related allergic response may be involved. The inflammation usually resolves spontaneously. Treatments include topical creams and ointments. SEE: *bacterial vaginosis.*

DIAGNOSIS: The diagnosis is established when clinical symptoms of vaginitis are present, but no organisms are found in laboratory specimens.

postmenopausal v. Atrophic **v.**

v. testis Inflammation of the tunica vaginalis of the testis.

Trichomonas vaginalis v. Vaginitis caused by flagellate protozoa that infect the vagina, urethra, and Skene ducts. Although the individual inflammatory response can include severe vulvar irritation and burning, dysuria, dyspareunia, and profuse, thin, frothy, yellow-green to gray discharge, nearly 50% of infected women are asymptomatic. Sixty percent of the sexual partners of infected women share the infection. On inspection, the vulva may appear reddened and edematous. About 10% of infected women exhibit characteristic "strawberry patches" in the upper vagina and upper cervix. Diagnosis is based on seeing the highly motile organism with three to five flagella in a saline

wet smear. Oral metronidazole is the organism-specific treatment. SEE: *Trichomonas.*

vagino-, vagin- [L. *vagina,* sheath] Prefixes meaning *vagina.*

vaginoabdominal (văj″ĭn-ō-ăb-dŏm′ĭn-ăl) [L. *vagina,* sheath, + *abdominalis,* abdominal] Pert. to the vagina and abdomen.

vaginocele (văj-ĭn-ō-sēl) [″ + Gr. *kele,* tumor, swelling] Vaginal hernia. SYN: *colpocele.*

vaginodynia (văj″ĭn-ō-dĭn′ē-ă) [″ + Gr. *odyne,* pain] Pain in the vagina.

vaginogenic (văj″ĭn-ō-jĕn′ĭk) [″ + Gr. *gennan,* to produce] Developed from or originating in the vagina.

vaginogram (văj′ĭn-ō-grăm) [″ + gramma, something written] A radiograph of the vagina.

vaginography (văj-ĭn-ŏg′ră-fē) [″ + Gr. *graphein,* to write] Radiography of the vagina. This technique is useful in diagnosing ureterovaginal fistula.

vaginolabial (văj″ĭn-ō-lā′bē-ăl) [″ + *labium,* lip] Pert. to the vagina and labia.

vaginomycosis (văj″ĭn-ō-mī-kō′sĭs) [″ + Gr. *mykes,* fungus, + *osis,* condition] A fungus infection (mycosis) of the vagina.

vaginopathy (văj″ĭ-nŏp′ă-thē) [″ + Gr. *pathos,* disease, suffering] Any disease of the vagina.

vaginoperineal (văj″ĭn-ō-pĕr-ĭ-nē′ăl) [″ + Gr. *perinaion,* perineum] Pert. to the vagina and perineum.

vaginoperineoplasty (văj″ĭn-ō-pĕr″ĭ-nē′ō-plăs″tē) Plastic surgery involving the vagina and perineum.

vaginoperineorrhaphy (văj″ĭn-ō-pĕr″ĭ-nē-or′ăf-ē) [″ + ″ + *rhaphe,* seam, ridge] Repair of a laceration involving both the perineum and vagina. SYN: *colpoperineorrhaphy.*

vaginoperineotomy (văj″ĭn-ō-pĕr″ĭn-ē-ŏt′ō-mē) [″ + ″ + *tome,* incision] Surgical incision of the vagina and perineum; usually done to facilitate childbirth. SEE: *episiotomy.*

vaginoperitoneal (văj″ĭn-ō-pĕr″ĭ-tō-nē′ăl) Rel. to the vagina and peritoneum.

vaginoplasty (vă-jī′nō-plăs″tē) [″ + Gr. *plassein,* to form] Plastic surgery on the vagina.

vaginoscope (văj′ĭn-ō-skōp) [″ + Gr. *skopein,* to examine] An instrument for inspection of the vagina. This may be a speculum or an optical instrument.

vaginoscopy (văj″ĭn-ŏs′kō-pē) Visual examination of the vagina.

vaginosis (vaj″ĭ-nō′sĭs) [*vagina* + *-osis*] An abnormality or disease of the vagina.

bacterial v. ABBR: BV. Infection of the vagina by *Gardnerella vaginalis.* BV, formerly called *Gardnerella vaginitis,* is the most common form of vaginitis in the U.S. It is characterized by vaginal discharge with the absence of lactobacilli and an overgrowth of anaerobic bacteria. Causes include new or multiple sexual partners, douching, and, possibly, cigarette smoking. It is unknown why the bacterial shift occurs; and, although sexual activity may play a role, women who have never had sexual intercourse are also affected.

Diagnosis is confirmed by characteristic fishy odor produced when the vaginal discharge is mixed with 10% potassium hydroxide. A wet smear reveals vaginal epithelial cells that are heavily stippled with bacteria (clue cells). The pH of the discharge is always greater than 5.5. Treatment is with metronidazole, tinidazole, or clindamycin, antibiotics that in pill, cream, or gel form are effective against anaerobes but maintain lactobacilli. Asymptomatic bacterial vaginosis during pregnancy has been implicated in causing preterm labor. Treatment during pregnancy to reduce preterm delivery is controversial and is not recommended during the first trimester. SYN: *Gardnerella vaginalis vaginitis.* SEE: *nonspecific* **vaginitis.**

vaginotomy (văj″ĭ-nŏt′ō-mē) [″ + Gr. *tome,* incision] Incision of the vagina.

vaginovesical (văj″ĭ-nō-vĕs′ĭ-kăl) [″ + *vesica,* bladder] Pert. to the vagina and bladder.

vaginovulvar (văj″ĭn-ō-vŭl′văr) [″ + *vulva,* covering] Vulvovaginal.

vagitis (vă-jī′tĭs) [L. *vagus,* wandering, + Gr. *itis,* inflammation] Inflammation of the vagal nerve.

vagolysis (vā-gŏl′ĭ-sĭs) [L. *vagus,* wandering, + Gr. *lysis,* dissolution] Surgical destruction of the vagus nerve.

vagolytic (vā″gō-lĭt′ĭk) **1.** Pert. to vagolysis. **2.** An agent that prevents function of the vagus nerve.

vagomimetic (vā″gō-mĭ-mĕt′ĭk) [″ + Gr. *mimetikos,* imitating] Resembling action caused by stimulation of the vagus nerve.

vagotomy (vā-gŏt′ō-mē) [″ + Gr. *tome,* incision] Section of the vagus nerve.
   medical v. Administration of drugs to prevent function of the vagus nerve.

vagotonia (vā″gō-tō′nē-ă) [″ + Gr. *tonos,* tension] Hyperirritability of the parasympathetic nervous system. SEE: *sympatheticotonia.* **vagotonic,** *adj.*

vagotropic (vā″gō-trŏp′ĭk) [″ + Gr. *tropos,* a turning] Acting on the vagus nerve.

vagotropism (vā-gŏt′rō-pĭzm) [″ + ″ + *-ismos,* condition] Affinity for the vagus nerve, as a drug.

vagovagal (vā″gō-vā′găl) Pert. to reflex activity mediated entirely through the vagus nerve (i.e., via efferent and afferent impulses transmitted through the vagus nerve).

vagrant (vā′grănt) [L. *vagrans*] **1.** Wandering from place to place without a fixed home. **2.** A homeless person who wanders from place to place.

vagus nerve stimulation SEE: under *stimulation.*

VAIN *vaginal intraepithelial neoplasia.*

val *valine.*

valence, valency (vā′lĕns, vā′lĕn-sē) [L. *valentia,* power, strength] **1.** The property of an atom or group of atoms causing them to combine in definite proportion with other atoms or groups of atoms. Valency may be as high as 8 and is determined by the number of electrons in the outer orbit (energy level) of the atom. **2.** The degree of the combining power or replacing power of an atom or group of atoms, the hydrogen atom being the unit of comparison. The number indicates how many atoms of hydrogen can unite with one atom of another element.

valerian (vă-lēr′ē-an) [Fr *Valeria,* the name of a Roman province, where the plant was common] A perennial herb, *Valeriana officinalis,* used as a sedative and sleep aid. The drug acts by inhibiting the breakdown of gamma-aminobutyric acid in the brain. It may interact with other sedatives and hypnotics such as alcohol and barbituates. Its effectiveness is limited.

valgus (val′gŭs) [L. *valgus, valga, valgum* bent, bent outward, bowleg(ged)] Bent or turned outward, used esp. of deformities in which the most distal anatomical part is angled outward and away from the midline of the body. The classical Latin adjective *valgus, valga, valgum* means "bowleg" or "bowlegged" and applies to the appearance of the defect. The modern medical Latin adjective applies to the cause of the defect; thus a "valgus knee" is caused by the *outward bending* of the tibia and fibula (away from the center of the body), resulting in "genu valgum," or "knock-knee." SEE: illus.; *varus.*

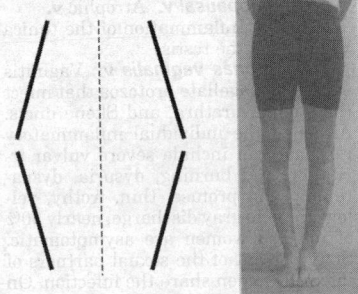

BOWLEG

In medical usage, referred to as "varus knee" or "genu varum."

valid (văl′ĭd) [L. *validus,* strong] Producing the desired effect; correct.

validate (văl'ĭ-dāt) To ensure that the item in question is valid and correct.

validation, consensual The process of testing thoughts, emotions, and behaviors with other human beings. The desired outcome is acknowledgment of similar viewpoints and feelings.

validation group In research, a group of subjects who are enrolled to determine whether the findings obtained from a previous cohort apply to a different cohort and are generally applicable.

validation therapy A communication technique used for patients with moderate to late dementia in which the caregiver makes statements to the patient that demonstrate respect for the patient's feelings and beliefs. This method helps prevent argumentative and agitated behavior. In some cases, the caregiver may need to agree with the patient's statements, even though they are not true or real. It is used when reality orientation is not successful.

validity (vă-lid'ĭt-ē) [L. *validitas,* bodily) strength] **1.** The degree to which data or results of a study are correct or true. **2.** The extent to which a situation as observed reflects the true situation.

concurrent v The degree to which two measuring devices or methods agree with each other; the degree to which an unproven measurement instrument matches the results obtained by an instrument known to provide accurate results.

construct v. The degree to which a measurement accurately counts the objects it is intended to evaluate; the fitness of a test to its target or to the theory that it is intended to illuminate. For instance, a researcher wants to determine how important spirituality is to survival in patients with cancer. He or she may design a test to measure spirituality. As a first approximation he or she decides to measure the number of times per month that her subjects attend religious services and to correlate that number with months of survival after the diagnosis of cancer. If the researcher finds that people who report themselves as attending church frequently do not survive cancer more than those who rarely attend church, there are at least two possible explanations for the findings: 1. Spirituality is unrelated to cancer survival; or, 2. the test of spirituality did not have construct validity, i.e., the number of times a month that a person attends church may prove to be an inaccurate measure of religious faith.

face v. The degree to which a measurement is logical, reasonable, or acceptable and therefore, assumed to be true; plausibility.

predictive v. The degree to which a test measurement of current variables accurately forecasts future results or outcomes.

valine (văl'ēn, vā'lēn) ABBR: val. A branched-chain amino acid, $C_5H_{11}NO_2$, derived from digestion of proteins. It is essential in the diet, esp. for normal growth in infants.

valinemia (văl'ĭ-nē'mē-ă) An increased concentration of valine in the blood, usually caused by a deficiency of the enzyme valine transaminase.

vallate (văl'āt) [L. *vallatus,* walled] Having a rim around a depression.

vallecula (văl-lĕk'ū-lă) [L., a depression] A depression or crevice.

v. cerebelli A deep fissure on the inferior surface of the cerebellum.

v. epiglottica A depression lying lateral to the median epiglottic fold and separating it from the pharyngoepiglottic fold.

v. ovata A depression in the liver in which rests the gallbladder.

vallum unguis (văl'ŭm ŭng'gwĭs) The fold of skin overlapping the nail.

Valsalva, Antonio M. (val"sal'vă) Antonio Maria Valsalva, Italian anatomist, 1666–1723.

V. maculopathy Macular bleeding due to a sudden increase in abdominal or chest pressure. It causes sudden central visual loss that often resolves spontaneously.

V. maneuver An attempt to forcibly exhale with the glottis, nose, and mouth closed. This maneuver causes increased intrathoracic pressure, slowing of the pulse, decreased return of blood to the heart, and increased venous pressure. If the eustachian tubes are not obstructed, the pressure on the tympanic membranes also will be increased. When this maneuver is done with just the glottis closed, only intrathoracic pressure will increase. This maneuver may be helpful in converting supraventricular tachycardias to normal sinus rhythm or in clearing ears that have become blocked during a descent from a high altitude. SEE: *Müller maneuver; Toynbee maneuver.*

valsartan (văl-săr'tăn) An angiotensin II receptor antagonist and hypertensive, administered orally to manage hypertension. SYN: *Diovan.*

value (văl'ū) [ME. from L. *valere,* to be of value] **1.** The amount of a specific substance or the magnitude of an entity. **2.** Something that is cherished or held dear.

value-based insurance design ABBR: VBID. A health insurance plan that charges patients less for those services that are deemed to be the most helpful to them and more for services that are elective or of relatively low value, i.e., provide little health benefit.

valve (valv) [L. *valva,* leaf of a folding door] Any of various membranous structures in a hollow organ or passage that temporarily close to permit the flow of fluid in one direction only.

aortic v. ABBR: AoV. The valve at the junction of the left ventricle and the ascending aorta. It is composed of three segments (semilunar cusps) and prevents regurgitation. SEE: *cardiac v.* for illus.

bicuspid v. Mitral **v.**

Bjork-Shiley heart v. A synthetic artificial heart valve that is no longer commercially available but remains implanted in thousands of patients. The valve has been known to fracture at its struts during use, which results in death in the majority of cases.

cardiac v. Any of the four valves that prevent the backflow of blood as it passes into, through, and out of the heart. In order of the entry of the venous blood into the right atrium, they are the tricuspid, pulmonary, mitral, and aortic. SEE: illus.

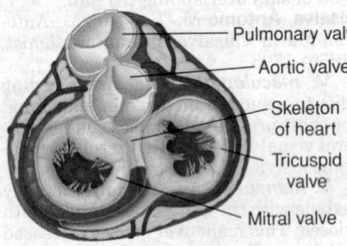

Pulmonary valve

Aortic valve

Skeleton of heart

Tricuspid valve

Mitral valve

Ventricles relaxed

CARDIAC VALVES

with ventricles relapsed

Carpentier-Edwards v. SEE: *Carpentier-Edwards valve.*

check v. A valve that permits fluids or gases to flow in just one direction. Check valves are used in infusion sets to prohibit backflow of fluids during intravenous therapy.

eustachian v. The valve at the entrance of the inferior vena cava.

external nasal v. The outermost opening of the nose (the alar rim).

flutter V. A one-way valve used in chest tube drainage systems that allows fluids or gases to flow out of the chest, but does not let them reenter the body SYN: *Heimlich flutter valve; Heimlich valve.*

Houston v. SEE: *Houston valve.*

ileocecal v. A projection of two membranous folds of the ileum of the small intestine into the cecum of the colon. It prevents backup of fecal material into the small intestine. SYN: *valvula coli.*

inspiratory impedance threshold v. SEE: *inspiratory impedance threshold v.*

internal nasal v. Nasal **v.**

left atrioventricular v. Mitral **v.**

mitral v. The valve that closes the orifice between the left cardiac atrium and the left ventricle during ventricular systole. SYN: *bicuspid v.; left atrioventricular v.*

nasal v. The site of greatest obstruction to airflow through the nasal passages. It extends from the bony cave near the piriform aperture into part of the cartilaginous vestibule of the nose. SYN: *internal nasal v.*

pop-off v. A safety valve that releases gas into the atmosphere from a ventilator circuit when the pressure in the circuit exceeds a known, safe level.

prosthetic heart v. A substitute valve used to replace a diseased valve. There are two main types of prostheses: those made from biological tissues, e.g., the heart valves of animals, esp. pigs, and those made from biocompatible materials, e.g., metals or polymers. Biocompatible mechanical valves may be constructed in a variety of ways, e.g., from a ball that moves up and down in a cage; with bileaflet valves that close in the midline; or with a single leaflet (which tilts to open and close). SEE: illus.

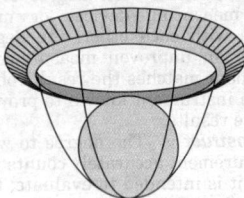

Caged ball valve

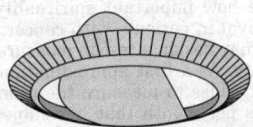

Monoleaflet

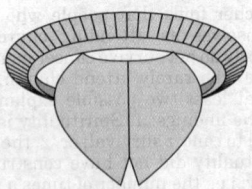

Bileaflet

TYPES OF MECHANICAL HEART VALVES

A. caged ball valve; B. monoleaflet. C. bileaflet

pulmonary v. The valve at the junction of the right ventricle and pulmonary artery. It is composed of three semilunar cusps and prevents regurgitation of blood from the pulmonary artery back into the right ventricle. SEE: *cardiac v.* for illus.

pyloric v. The prominent circular membranous fold at the pyloric orifice of the stomach. SYN: *valvula pylori.*

reducing v. A device to reduce the pressure of gas that has been compressed in a cylinder.

right atrioventricular v. Tricuspid **v.**

semilunar v. The type of valve separating the heart and aorta and the heart and pulmonary artery. SEE: *cardiac v.* for illus.

tricuspid v. ABBR: TV. The valve that closes the orifice between the right cardiac atrium and right ventricle during ventricular systole. SYN: *right atrioventricular v.; valvula tricuspidalis.* SEE: *cardiac v.* for illus.

valvectomy (văl-věk′tŏ-mē) Surgical excision of a valve, esp. a heart valve. SEE: *valvuloplasty.*

valved holding chamber SEE: under *chamber.*

valvotomy (văl-vŏt′ō-mē) [″ + Gr. *tome,* incision] Valvulotomy.

mitral balloon v. Expansion of a balloon in the orifice of a mitral valve as a means of treating mitral stenosis, instead of mitral valve replacement or commissurotomy. SYN: *valvuloplasty.*

valvula (văl′vū-lă) *pl.* **valvulae** [L., a small fold] A valve, specifically a small valve.

v. coli Ileocecal valve.

valvulae (văl′vū-lē) Pl. of valvula.

valvular (văl′vū-lăr) [L. *valvula,* a small fold] Pert. to or having one or more valves.

valvulitis (văl″vū-lī′tĭs) [″ + Gr. *itis,* inflammation] Inflammation of a valve, esp. a cardiac valve.

valvuloplasty (văl′vū-lō-plăs″tē) Plastic or restorative surgery on a valve, esp. a cardiac valve.

percutaneous balloon v. The percutaneous insertion of one or more balloons across a stenotic heart valve. Inflating the balloons decreases the constriction. This technique has been used to treat mitral and/or pulmonic stenosis.

valvulotome (văl′vū-lō-tōm) [″ + Gr. *tome,* incision] An instrument for incising a valve.

valvulotomy (văl″vū-lŏt′ō-mē) The process of cutting through a valve. SYN: *valvotomy.*

vanadium (vă-nād′ē-ŭm) [*Vanadis,* a Norse goddess + *-ium* (1)] SYMB: V. A light gray transition metal, atomic weight (mass), 50.941, atomic number 23.

van Buren disease (van būr′ĕn) [William Holme van Buren, U.S. surgeon, 1819–1883] Induration of the corpora cavernosa of the penis. SYN: *Peyronie disease.*

Vandellia cirrhosa (văn-děl′ē-ă sĭ-rō′să) [NL] A slender parasitic catfish indigenous to the Amazon. It attaches itself to the gills of other spiny fishes and extracts blood for food. It occasionally swims into and inserts itself in the urethra or rectum of human bathers, from whom it must be surgically removed. This nearly transparent vertebrate is also known as the "toothpick fish," "vampire fish," "carnero," or "candiru urethra."

van der Hoeve syndrome (van′děr-hoov″ĕ) [Jan van der Hoeve, Dutch ophthalmologist, 1878–1952] Conductive deafness caused by otosclerosis-like changes in the temporal bone. Blue sclerae and osteogenesis imperfecta are also present.

van der Waals forces (văn′děr-wŏlz) [Johannes D. van der Waals, Dutch physicist, 1837–1923] The definite but weak forces of attraction between the nuclei of atoms of compounds. These forces do not result from ionic attraction, hydrogen bonding, or sharing of electrons, but rather from the motion of electrons in atoms and molecules.

vanilla (vă-nĭl′ă) [Sp. *vainilla,* little sheath] Any one of a group of tropical orchids. The cured seed pods of *Vanilla planifolia* contain an aromatic substance, also called vanilla, that is used for flavoring.

vanillin (vă-nĭl′ĭn) A crystalline compound found in vanilla pods or produced synthetically; used for flavoring foods and in pharmaceuticals.

vanillism (vă-nĭl′ĭzm) Irritation of the skin, mucous membranes, and conjunctiva sometimes experienced by workers handling raw vanilla. It is caused by a mite.

vanillylmandelic acid, vanilmandelic acid (van″ĭ-lil″man-dē′lik, van″ĭl-man-dē′lik) SEE: under *acid.*

van't Hoff, Jacobus Henricus (vant-hof′) Dutch physical chemist, 1852–1911

van't Hoff law The osmotic pressure of a solution is equal to the product of its temperature, the ideal gas constant, and its solute concentration.

van't Hoff rule 1. The rule that the speed of chemical reactions is doubled, at least, for each 10°C rise in temperature. The rule is an approximation that works best when temperatures approximate those under which the reaction normally occurs. 2. Any substance in a dilute solution exerts an osmotic pressure that is equivalent to the pressure of an equal volume of gas in solution. 3. A technique used to predict the greatest number of mirror-image versions of a molecule that can rotate plane polarized light.

vapocoolant (vă″pō-kool′ănt) [″ + *cool-*

ant] A volatile liquid that evaporates on contact with the skin, causing a local refrigerant effect and providing local anesthesia for injections, intravenous insertions, and other procedures.

vapor (vā′por) [L., steam] **1.** The gaseous state of any substance. **2.** A medicinal substance for administration by inhalation.

vaporization (vā″pŏ-rĭ-zā′shŏn) [*vapor*] **1.** The conversion of a liquid or solid into vapor. **2.** The therapeutic use of a vapor.

   laser v. The resection of tissue by converting it to gas with laser energy.

   transurethral v. of the prostate ABBR: TUVP. A treatment for prostatic hyperplasia in which a laser is used to vaporize hypertrophic prostatic tissue.

vaporize (vā′por-īz) To change a material to a vapor form.

vaporizer (vā′por-ī″zer) A device for converting liquids into a vapor spray.

vaporous (vā′por-ŭs) [L. *vapor*, steam] Pert. to or producing vapors.

vapor-treated Exposed to steam in order to clean, decontaminate, or sterilize. Clotting factors are steam-treated to remove potentially infectious agents such as pathogenic viruses.

VAQTA (văk′tă) Hepatitis A vaccine, inactivated.

Vaquez disease (vă-kez′) [Louis Henri Vaquez, Fr. physician, 1860–1936] Polycythemia vera.

variability (var″ē-ă-bil′ĭt-ē) [*variable*] The ability or tendency to change.

   baseline v. Fluctuations in the fetal heart rate, recorded by the electronic monitor, that reflect the status of the fetal autonomic nervous system. Absence of short-term variability (beat-to-beat changes) is a sign of fetal compromise. Long-term variability (wavelike undulations) occurs normally three to five times per minute. Increased long-term variability is common during fetal sleep but may reflect prematurity, congenital abnormalities such as anencephaly, or fetal response to drugs.

   genetic v. **1.** The range of minor alterations present in a genome, such as the number of diverse alleles of a specific gene that are found as a result of small mutations in the DNA of a species. **2.** The expression of those diverse genes in living organisms and their impact on health or disease.

   heart rate v. ABBR: HRV. Spontaneous fluctuations above and below the mean heart rate. A reduced HRV is associated with an increased incidence of total mortality and cardiac events in post-myocardial infarction patients, as well as in apparently healthy individuals, esp. older persons.

variable (vā′rē-ă-b'l) [L. *variare*, to vary] **1.** Any changing, measurable thing. In statistics, it is often possible to measure and graph the relationship of one variable to another (e.g., height and weight in the growing child). **2.** Changing in form, structure, behavior, or physiology.

   binary v. Dichotomous **v.**

   dependent v. In epidemiology and research design, the condition or disease under study or the response part of a dose-response curve. In a study measuring smoking and heart disease, for example, heart disease would be the dependent variable.

   dichotomous v. A variable that alternates between just two values, e.g., dead or alive; male or female; positive or negative. SYN: *binary v.*

   independent v. In epidemiology and research, the agent that incites a response; the stimulus (e.g., the dose part of a dose-response curve). In the smoking and heart disease study cited in the entry called *dependent variable,* smoking would be the independent variable.

variance (văr′ē-ăns) [L. *variare*, to vary] A statistical index of the degree to which measurements in a data set are different from each other or deviate from the mean; the square of the standard deviation.

variant (văr′ē-ănt) That which is different from the characteristics of the other organisms or entities in a particular classification, esp. a disease, species, or physical appearance.

variate (vā′rē-āt) Variable (2).

variation (vā″rē-ā′shŭn) A difference between individuals of a certain species or class.

   continuous v. Variation in which the difference between successive groups or individuals is quite small.

   meristic v. Variation in number as opposed to kind.

varication (văr″ĭ-kā′shŭn) **1.** Formation of a varix. **2.** The condition of a varicosity.

variced (văr′ĭ-sĕd) Pert. to a varix.

varicella (văr″ĭ-sĕl′ă) [L., a tiny spot] An acute infectious disease, usually seen in children under age 15, caused by varicella-zoster virus. Its hallmark is a rash, described clinically as having a "dewdrop on a rose petal" pattern, scattered in clusters ("crops") over the trunk, face, scalp, upper extremities, and sometimes the thighs. It is transmitted mainly by respiratory droplets that contain infectious particles; direct contact with a lesion and contaminated equipment also can spread the virus. Reactivation of the virus in adults causes shingles. SYN: *chickenpox*. SEE: illus; *herpes zoster; varicella-zoster immune globulin.*

   SYMPTOMS: After an incubation period of 2 to 3 weeks (usually 13 to 17 days), patients develop fever, malaise, anorexia, and lymphadenopathy, fol-

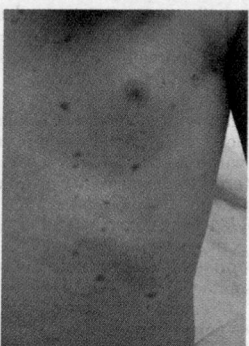

VARICELLA (CHICKENPOX)

of newborns (esp. those who are premature) to varicella; healthy adults who are susceptible to varicella and who have been exposed; pregnant women who have no history of having had varicella and who have had significant exposure. The use of VZIg in pregnant women will not prevent fetal infection or congenital varicella syndrome. Live attenuated vaccine is now available for general use.

⚠ Because severe illness and death have resulted from varicella in children being treated with corticosteroids, these children should avoid exposure to varicella.

lowed by the appearance of an extremely pruritic rash that starts flat and, over time, becomes a small blister on a red base, and then eventually forms crusted scabs. All three stages of the rash may be present on the body at one time. Varicella may be transmitted to others until all lesions are crusted over.

Occasionally, when chickenpox occurs in adults or immunosuppressed children, it is complicated by superimposed bacterial pneumonia, encephalitis, or thrombocytopenia. Immunization with varicella vaccine provided during infancy is designed to prevent these complications.

ETIOLOGY: Chickenpox may strike people of any age who have not been previously been exposed to the virus. Epidemics are most frequent in winter and spring in temperate climates.

DIFFERENTIAL DIAGNOSIS: Impetigo, dermatitis herpetiformis, herpes zoster, and furunculosis occasionally must be distinguished from varicella although usually the difference is obvious.

COMPLICATIONS: Secondary infections may occur, caused by scratching, which may result in abscess formation; at times, development of erysipelas or even septicemia may result. Occasionally, lesions in the vicinity of the larynx may cause edema of the glottis and threaten the life of the patient. Encephalitis is a rare complication. Varicella may be fatal in children with leukemia or children who are taking adrenocorticosteroids.

PREVENTION: Administration of varicella-zoster immune globulin (VZIg) within 72 hr of exposure will prevent clinical varicella in susceptible, healthy children. The following conditions should alert one to the possible need for use of VZIg: immunocompromised children; newborns of mothers who develop varicella in the period 5 days before to 48 hr after delivery; postnatal exposure

TREATMENT: Otherwise healthy affected children are treated with diphenhydramine or hydroxyzine to reduce itch and acetaminophen to reduce fever. Children at increased risk for complications and immunosuppressed adults are given varicella-zoster immune globulin as prophylaxis after exposure. If varicella infection develops in immunosuppressed persons or pregnant women in the third trimester, intravenous acyclovir is administered. Immunization with varicella vaccination is recommended for those children who have not had chickenpox and have not previously received the immunization. SEE: *Standard Precautions Appendix.*

v. gangrenosa Varicella in which necrosis occurs around the vesicles, resulting in gangrenous ulceration.

varicella-zoster immune globulin ABBR: VZIg. An immune globulin obtained from the blood of healthy persons found to have high antibody titers to varicella-zoster. SEE: *varicella.*

varicelliform (văr″ĭ-sĕl′ĭ-form) Resembling varicella. SYN: *varicelloid.*

varicelloid (văr″ĭ-sĕl′oyd) [″ + Gr. *eidos,* form, shape] Varicelliform.

varices (văr′ĭ-sēz) [L.] Pl. of varix.

variciform (văr-ĭs′ĭ-form) [L. *varix,* twisted vein, + *forma,* shape] Varicose.

varicoblepharon (văr″ĭ-kō-blĕf′ă-rŏn) [″ + Gr. *blepharon,* eyelid] Varicose tumor of the eyelid.

varicocele (văr′ĭ-kō-sēl) [″ + Gr. *kele,* tumor, swelling] Enlargement of the veins of the spermatic cord, commonly occurring above the left testicle. Varicoceles, present in more than 10% of males, are usually identified during adolescence. Male infertility has been linked to varicoceles, but a definitive causal relation has not been established. SYN: *varicole.*

SYMPTOMS: There is a dull ache along the cord and a slight dragging sensation in the groin. On examination, the vessels on the affected side of the scrotum are full, feel like a bundle of worms, and are sometimes purplish.

TREATMENT: Most varicoceles are asymptomatic and are followed conservatively. When they cause intolerable symptoms, or when they are found during the evaluation of men with infertility, they may be surgically repaired. However, there is no firm evidence that varicocele repair improves male fertility.

ovarian v. Varicosity of the veins of the ovarian or pampiniform plexus of the broad ligament.

utero-ovarian v. Varicosity of the veins of the ovarian (pampiniform) plexus and the uterine plexus of the broad ligament.

varicocelectomy (văr″ĭ-kō-sē-lĕk′tō-mē) [L. *varix*, twisted vein, + Gr. *kele*, tumor, swelling, + *ektome*, excision] Excision of a portion of the scrotal sac with ligation of the dilated veins to relieve varicocele.

varicocele embolization SEE: under *embolization.*

varicography (văr″ĭ-kŏg′ră-fē) [″ + Gr. *graphein*, to write] Radiography of varicose veins after the injection of a contrast medium.

varicoid (văr′ĭ-koyd) [″ + Gr. *eidos*, form, shape] Resembling a varix.

varicole (văr′ĭ-kōl) Varicocele.

varicomphalus (văr″ĭ-kŏm′fă-lŭs) [″ + Gr. *omphalos*, navel] Varicose tumor of the navel.

varicophlebitis (văr″ĭ-kō-flē-bī′tĭs) [″ + Gr. *phleps*, vein, + *itis*, inflammation] Phlebitis combined with varicose veins.

varicose (văr′ĭ-kōs) [L. *varicosus*, full of dilated veins] Pert. to varices; distended, swollen, knotted veins. SYN: *variciform.*

varicose vein SEE: under *vein.*

varicosis (văr″ĭ-kō′sĭs) [L.] A varicose condition of veins.

varicosity (văr″ĭ-kŏs′ĭ-tē) [L. *varix*, twisted vein] **1.** The condition of being varicose. **2.** Varix (1).

varicotomy (văr″ĭ-kŏt′ō-mē) [″ + Gr. *tome*, incision] Excision of a varicose vein.

varicula (văr-ĭk′ū-lă) [L., a tiny dilated vein] A small varix, esp. of the conjunctiva.

variety (vă-rī′ĕ-tē) [L., *varietas*, variety] The classification of individuals in a subpopulation of a species.

variola (vă-rī′ō-lă) [L., pustule] Smallpox. **variolar** (-lăr), *adj.*

   v. major Smallpox with its full-blown, classic symptoms. SYN: *v. vera.*

   v. minor A mild form of smallpox with sparse rash and low-grade fever. SYN: *alastrim; amaas.*

   v. vera Variola major.

VARIVAX (văr′ĭ-văks) Varicella virus vaccine live.

varix (var′iks, var′ĭ-sēz″) *pl.* **varices** [L., twisted or dilated vein] **1.** A tortuous dilatation of a vein. SEE: *varicose vein.* **2.** Less commonly, dilatation of an artery or lymph vessel.

   aneurysmal v. A direct communication between an artery and a varicose vein without an intervening sac.

   arterial v. A varicosity or dilation of an artery.

   chyle v. A varix of a lymphatic vessel that conveys chyle.

   esophageal v. A tortuous dilatation of an esophageal vein, esp. in the distal portion. It results from any condition that causes portal hypertension, typically cirrhosis of the liver. SEE: *Müller maneuver; Nursing Diagnoses Appendix;* illus.

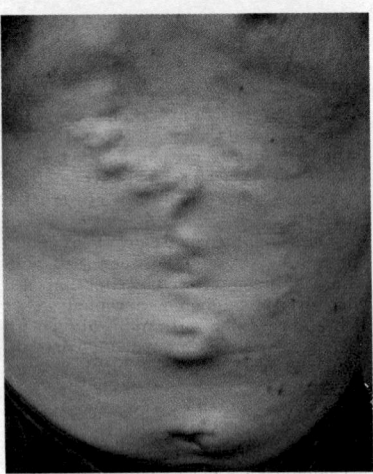

ESOPHAGEAL VARIX IN A PATIENT WITH CIRRHOSIS OF THE LIVER

Courtesy of John Roberts, MD

SYMPTOMS: If an esophageal varix bursts, massive hemorrhage occurs, and the patient may die within minutes.

TREATMENT: Medical treatment includes administration of a beta blocker, such as nadolol, with a nitrate, such as isosorbide, to lower portal pressures and decrease the likelihood of variceal bleeding. Invasive therapies include the injection of sclerosing agents or rubber banding of the dilated vein.

PATIENT CARE: Bleeding esophageal varices constitute a medical emergency, requiring immediate treatment to control hemorrhage and prevent hypovolemic shock. The patient's vital signs, oxygen saturation, arterial blood gas, electrolyte and fluid volume balance, and level of consciousness are closely monitored. Intravenous access must be established promptly and fluid resuscitation, followed by transfusion and the administration of plasma are critical to early stabilization of the patient. Medical therapies also include the use of vasoconstricting drugs, such as vasopression. Endoscopy is used to identify the site of the ruptured vessels which may then be treated with sclerotherapy, ligation, or banding.

Surgical procedures to prevent rebleeding include portocaval or mesocaval shunts, portosystemic anastomosis, splenorenal shunting or liver transplantation. All procedures are explained, sensation messages provided, and reassurance and emotional support offered.

lymphaticus v. Dilatation of a lymphatic vessel.

turbinal v. Permanent dilatation of veins of turbinate bodies.

varnish (văr′nĭsh) A solution of gums and resins in a solvent. When these are applied to a surface, the solvent evaporates and leaves a hard, more or less flexible film. In dentistry, varnishes are used to protect sensitive tooth areas such as the pulp. SYN: *cavity v.*

cavity v. Varnish.

varus (vā′rŭs) [L, *varus, vara, varum*, bent, bent inward, knock-knee(d)] Bent or turned inward, used esp. of deformities in which the most distal anatomical part is turned inward and toward the midline of the body. The classical Latin adjective *varus, vara, varum* means "knock-knee" or "knock-kneed" and applies to the appearance of the defect. The modern medical Latin adjective applies to the cause of the defect; thus a "varus knee" is caused by the *inward bending* of the tibia and fibula (towards the center of the body), resulting in *"genu varum,"* or "bowleg." SEE: illus.; *valgus*.

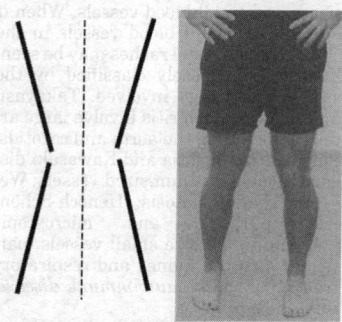

KNOCK-KNEE

In medical usage, referred to as "valgus knee" or "genu valgum."

vas (vas, vā′ză) *pl.* **vasa** [L. *vas,* vessel] A vessel or duct.

v. aberrans 1. A narrow tube varying in length from 1½ to 14 in (3.8 to 35.6 cm), occasionally found connected with the lower part of the canal of the epididymis or with the commencement of the vas deferens. 2. A vestige of the bile ducts sometimes found in the liver.

v. afferens An afferent vessel of a lymph node.

v. deferens The secretory duct of the testis, a continuation of the epididymis. This slim, muscular tube, approx. 18 in (45.7 cm) long, transports the sperm from each testis to the ejaculatory duct, which empties into the prostatic urethra. SYN: *ductus deferens.* SEE: illus.; *genitalia* for illus.

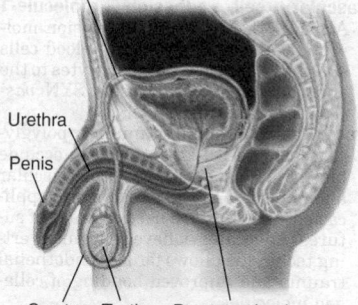

Vas deferens

Urethra

Penis

Scrotum Testis Prostate gland

VAS DEFERENS AND OTHER MALE ORGANS

v. prominens Blood vessel on the cochlea's accessory spiral ligament.

v. spirale A large blood vessel beneath the tunnel of Corti in the basilar membrane.

vasa (vā′ză) [L. *vas,* vessel] Pl. of vas.

v. brevia Branches of the splenic artery going to the greater curvature of the stomach. SYN: *short gastric arteries.*

v. efferentia The secretory ducts of the testis to the head of the epididymis.

v. nervorum The blood vessels supplying nerves.

v. previa, vasa praevia The blood vessels of the umbilical cord presenting before the fetus.

v. recta 1. Tubules that become straight before entering the mediastinum testis. 2. Capillary branches of the renal efferent arterioles, parallel to the loops of Henle.

v. vasorum Minute blood vessels that are distributed to the walls of the larger veins and arteries.

vasal (vā′săl) [L. *vas,* vessel] Pert. to a vas or vessel.

vasalgia (vă-săl′jē-ă) Pain in a vessel of any kind.

vascular (văs′kū-lăr) [L. *vasculum,* a small vessel] Pert. to or composed of blood vessels.

vascular access A portal of entry into the circulation, e.g., by a dialysis catheter. SEE: table.

vascular brachytherapy SEE: under *brachytherapy.*

Methods of Accessing the Vasculature

Intraosseously (through the cortex of a bone, esp. a bone in the leg)

Intravenously (peripherally or centrally)

Via surgically implanted ports (e.g., for the frequent or long-term administration of antibiotics, blood products, or cancer chemotherapy.)

By venous cutdown

vascular cell adhesion molecule-1 ABBR: VCAM-1. A cell adhesion molecule that helps bind white blood cells such as lymphocytes or monocytes to the endothelium of blood vessels. SYN: *vascular cell adhesion protein*.

vascular clip A small titanium or polyglycolic acid vessel clamp used to occlude blood vessels or to perform vascular anastomoses. In the anastomotic application, the clips are used in place of sutures. Advocates believe that this everting technique allows for less endothelial trauma and improved bonding of collagen molecules.

vascular disrupting agent SEE: under *agent*.

vascular endothelium The simple squamous epithelial tissue lining the blood vessels. It is a semipermeable barrier between the blood and the vascular smooth muscle, produces vasodilator chemicals, and may inhibit vasoconstrictor substances. Damage to the endothelium leads to increased production of prostaglandins and stimulates blood clotting.

vascularity (văs″kū-lăr′ĭ-tē) The state of being vascular.

vascularization (văs″kū-lăr-ĭ-zā′shŭn) [L. *vasculum*, a small vessel] The development of new blood vessels in a structure.

vascularize (văs′kū-lăr″īz) [L. *vasculum*, a small vessel] To become vascular by development of new blood vessels.

vascular parkinsonism Parkinson disease produced by small strokes that affect the basal ganglia, not by neuronal loss in these regions of the brain. Compared with patients who have classical Parkinson disease, people with vascular parkinsonism tend to be older and are more likely to have lower body rigidity, difficulty walking, and disturbances of balance. Upper body tremor is relatively infrequent. A history of atherosclerotic vascular disease, diabetes mellitus, high blood pressure, or hyperlipidemia is common in vascular parkinsonism. Efforts to prevent vascular parkinsonism focus on the treatment of these predispositions.

vascular stiffening The loss of arterial elasticity that occurs in patients with diabetes mellitus, hypertension, and aging.

vascular system The blood vessels: the arteries, capillaries, and veins. The vessels carry blood to and from the heart and contribute to the regulation of blood pressure. Exchange of materials between the blood and tissues takes place in capillary networks. Pulmonary and systemic circulation are included. Moreover, the lymphatic system, which returns a significant amount of tissue fluid to the venous circulation, is usually considered a part of the vascular system.

vascular technologist A technologist who obtains ultrasonic or radiographic images of blood vessels.

vasculature (văs′kū-lă-tūr″) The arrangement of blood vessels in the body or any part of it, including their relationship and functions.

vasculitis (vas″kyŭ-līt′ĭs, -lit′ĭ-dēz″) *pl.* **vasculitides** [L. *vasculum*, small vessel + *-itis*] Inflammation of blood vessels. SYN: *angiitis*.

It is usually caused by deposition of antigen-antibody immune complexes or other immune-mediated events. Vasculitis due to immune complexes is seen in patients with systemic lupus erythematosus, rheumatoid arthritis, hepatitis B and C, serum sickness, and drug reactions. Vasculitis found in patients with inflammatory bowel disease, Wegener granulomatosis, graft rejection, polyarthritis nodosa, and temporal arteritis involves other immune-mediated processes. Vasculitis often affects the renal glomeruli, joints, cerebral vessels, testes, or respiratory system.

Vasculitis can affect large, medium-sized, and small blood vessels. When it is found in small blood vessels in the skin, characteristic rashes may be seen. Vasculitis is loosely classified by the size of the vessel involved. Takayasu and giant cell arteritis involve large arteries, including the aorta and carotids. Polyarteritis nodosa and Kawasaki disease involve medium-sized vessels; Wegener granulomatosis, Henoch-Schönlein purpura, and microscopic polyangiitis involve small vessels, particularly in the kidney and respiratory tract. SEE: illus; *autoimmune disease; immune complex*.

SYMPTOMS: Although fever, pain, and malaise are common, the inflammatory changes of the blood vessels are seen primarily through the signs and symptoms associated with the organ or tissues involved. Vasculitis in superficial vessels may present as painful nodules. Inflammation of the glomerular capillaries of the kidney in small vessel vasculitis may produce glomerulonephritis and decreased renal function. When blood vessels of the respiratory tract are involved, pneumonitis, sinusitis, and ulceration of the nasopharynx may result. Involvement of vessels in the heart leads to coronary artery disease and aneurysms.

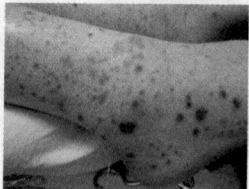

VASCULITIS

TREATMENT: Immunosuppressive therapy (with drugs such as cyclophosphamide and prednisone, or monoclonal antibodies such as rituximab) is used to treat most forms of autoimmune-mediated vasculitis.

livedoid v. Vasculitis with bloodclotting that affects small blood vessels in the skin, esp. near the feet and ankles. The cause in most cases is unknown, but it may be associated with diseases such as antiphospholipid antibody syndrome, systemic lupus erythematosus or scleroderma.

rejection v. Vasculitis that occurs when antigen-antibody complexes are deposited on the walls of small blood vessels in transplanted organs. Although the transplant rejection process is dominated by T-cell–mediated activities, antibodies also may form against the histocompatibility antigens on the transplanted organ and compromise its viability. SEE: *major histocompatibility complex.*

rheumatoid v. A relatively rare complication of severe rheumatoid arthritis, characterized by blood vessel inflammation, esp. in the skin, eyes (the sclera), and nerves. It can produce deep dermal ulcers, localized skin infarction, ischemia or necrosis of the fingertips, scleritis, and inflammation of multiple nerves (mononeuritis multiplex).

vasculogenesis (văs″kū-lō-jĕn′ĕ-sĭs) [″ + Gr. *genesis,* generation, birth] Development of the vascular system.

vasculomotor (văs″kū-lō-mō′tor) Vasomotor.

vasculopathy (vas″kyŭ-lop′ă-thē) [L. *vasculum,* small vessel + *-pathy*] Any disease affecting blood vessels.

idiopathic polypoidal choroidal v. Hemorrhage from the choroidal blood vessels near the macula of the retina. It produces acute, painless, unilateral visual loss.

transplant v. Obstruction to blood flow through the vessels of a transplanted organ. On pathological examination of involved vessels, the intima is globally thickened, and infiltrated by fibroblasts, mononuclear cells, and smooth muscle cells. It is one cause of transplant failure.

vasectomy (văs-ĕk′tō-mē) [L. *vas,* vessel, + Gr. *ektome,* excision] Removal of all or a segment of the vas deferens. Bilateral vasectomy is the most successful method of male contraception. The procedure prevents sperm (which are manufactured in the testicles) from being expelled in the male ejaculate. It is usually carried out as an outpatient or same day procedure under local or light intravenous anesthesia. SEE: illus.

NOTE: Persons who have had this surgical procedure ejaculate in a normal manner but the ejaculate contains semen, produced independently in the seminal vesicles, without sperm.

PATIENT CARE: Postoperatively, the patient applies cold packs to the surgical site, to limit swelling, pain, and inflammation. Activities are limited, and sexual activity is avoided for a week. An athletic supporter or tightly fitting underwear are worn to support the scrotum and limit pain. The procedure is considered successful when two consecutive sperm samples are shown to be free of sperm, typically 8 to 12 weeks postoperatively. Men choose vasectomy only when they want to become permanently sterile. Nonetheless, the procedure can be reversed, although vasectomy reversal is a more complicated operation than the initial severing of the tubes.

⚠ Patients should be advised that vasectomy does not prevent sexually transmitted diseases.

vasectomy reversal Surgery to rejoin the previously severed vas deferens. Although this procedure may be successful, the chance of success varies in published reports.

vasiform (văs′ĭ-form) [″ + *forma,* shape] Resembling a tubular structure or vas.

vasitis (vă-sī′tĭs) Inflammation of the ductus deferens of the testicle.

vaso-, vas-, vasi- [L. *vas,* vessel] Prefixes meaning *channel, vessel, blood vessel.*

vasoactive (văs″ō-ăk′tĭv) Affecting blood vessels.

vasoactive intestinal polypeptide ABBR: VIP. A peptide present in the mucosa of the gastrointestinal tract. One of its principal actions is to inhibit gastric acid secretion. Vasoactive intestinal polypeptide is also present in nerve fibers of the female genital tract.

vasoconstriction (văs″ō-kŏn-strĭk′shŭn) A decrease in the diameter of blood vessels, which decreases blood flow and raises blood pressure.

hypoxic pulmonary v. Narrowing of

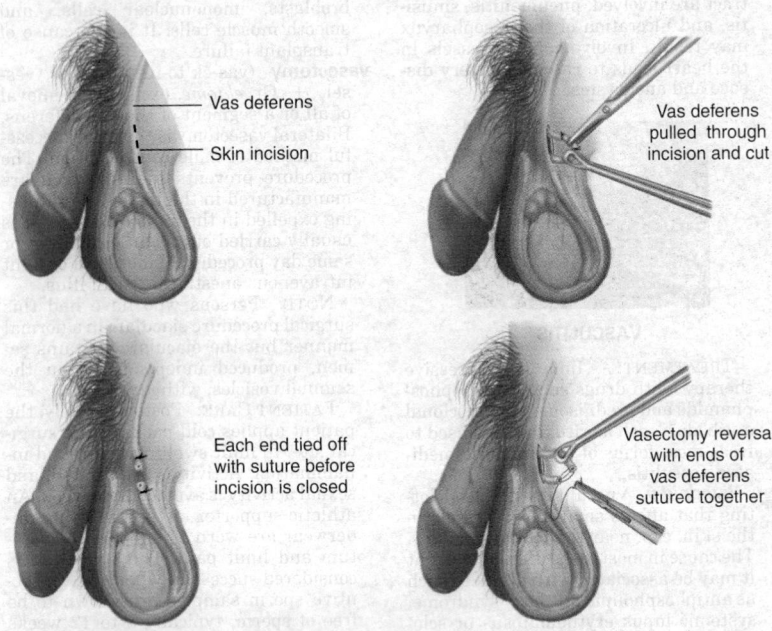

- Vas deferens
- Skin incision

Vas deferens pulled through incision and cut

Each end tied off with suture before incision is closed

Vasectomy reversal with ends of vas deferens sutured together

VASECTOMY AND ITS REVERSAL

the small arterioles in the alveoli in response to hypoxia.

vasoconstrictive (văs″ō-kŏn-strĭk′tĭv) [″ + *constrictus*, bound] Causing constriction of the blood vessels.

vasoconstrictor (văs″ō-kŏn-strĭk′tor) [″ + *constrictor*, a binder] **1.** Causing constriction of the blood vessels. **2.** That which constricts or narrows the caliber of blood vessels, as a drug or a nerve.

vasodepression (văs″ō-dē-prĕsh′ŭn) [″ + *depressio*, a pressing down] Vasomotor depression or collapse.

vasodepressor (văs″ō-dē-prĕs′or) [″ + *depressor*, that which presses down] **1.** Having a depressing influence on the circulation, lowering blood pressure by dilatation of blood vessels. **2.** An agent that decreases circulation.

vasodilatation (văs″ō-dĭl-ă-tā′shŭn) [″ + *dilatare*, to enlarge] Dilatation of blood vessels, esp. small arteries and arterioles.

  antidromic v. Vasodilatation resulting from stimulation of the dorsal root of a spinal nerve.

  reflex v. Blood vessel dilation caused by stimulation of its dilator nerves or inhibition of its constrictor substance or nerves. This can be done by stimulating the sensory reflex arc.

vasodilation (văs″ō-dī-lā′shŭn) An increase in the diameter of blood vessels, which increases blood flow and lowers blood pressure.

vasodilative (văs″ō-dī′lā-tĭv) Causing dilation of blood vessels.

vasodilator (văs″ō-dī-lā′tor) [″ + *dilatare*, to enlarge] **1.** Causing relaxation of blood vessels. **2.** A nerve or drug that dilates blood vessels.

vasoepididymostomy (văs″ō-ĕp″ĭ-dĭd-ĭ-mŏs′tō-mē) [″ + Gr. *epi*, upon, + *didymos*, testicle, + *stoma*, mouth] The formation of a passage between the vas deferens and the epididymis.

vasography (văs-ŏg′ră-fē) [″ + Gr. *graphein*, to write] Radiography of the blood vessels, usually after the injection of a contrast medium.

vasohypertonic (văs″ō-hī″pĕr-tŏn′ĭk) [″ + Gr. *hyper*, over, above, excessive, + *tonikos*, pert. to tension] Vasoconstrictor.

vasohypotonic (văs″ō-hī″pō-tŏn′ĭk) [″ + Gr. *hypo*, under, beneath, below, + *tonikos*, pert. to tension] Vasodilator.

vasoinhibitor (văs″ō-ĭn-hĭb′ĭ-tor) [″ + *inhibere*, to restrain] An agent that decreases the action of vasomotor nerves.

vasoinhibitory (văs″ō-ĭn-hĭb′ĭ-tor-ē) Restricting vasomotor activity.

vasoligation (văs″ō-lĭ-gā′shŭn) [″ + *ligare*, to bind] Ligation of a vessel, specifically the vas deferens.

vasomotion (văs″ō-mō′shŭn) [″ + *motio*, movement] Change in caliber of a blood vessel.

vasomotor (vā″zō-mōt′or) [*vaso-* + *motor*] Pert. to the nerves that innervate the smooth muscle in the walls of arteries and veins and thereby alter or preserve vascular tone. Sympathetic impulses to all arteries and veins maintain normal constriction. More impulses per second cause vasoconstriction; fewer impulses per second, vasodilation. If a stressful stimulus, such as hemorrhage, causes increased vasomotor nerve activity, vasoconstriction results, which limits blood loss and maintains blood pressure. SEE: *vasoconstrictor; vasodilator.*

vasomotor epilepsy SEE: under *epilepsy.*

vasomotor spasm SEE: under *spasm.*

vasomotor system The part of the nervous system that controls the size of the blood vessels.

vasoneuropathy (văs″ō-nū-rŏp′ă-thē) Disease due to the combined effect of the vascular and nervous systems.

vaso-orchidostomy (văs″ō-or″kĭd-ŏs′tō-mē) [″ + Gr. *orchis,* testicle, + *stoma,* mouth] Surgical connection of the epididymis to the severed end of the vas deferens.

vasopeptidase inhibitor (vă″zō-pep′tĭ-dās″) SEE: under *inhibitor.*

vasopressin receptor antagonist SEE: under *antagonist.*

vasopressor (văs″ō-prĕs′or) **1.** Causing contraction of the smooth muscle of arteries and arterioles. This increases resistance to the flow of blood and thus elevates blood pressure. **2.** An agent that stimulates contraction of smooth muscle of arteries and arterioles.

vasopuncture (văs′ō-pŭnk″chūr) [″ + *punctura,* prick] Puncture of the vas deferens.

vasoreflex (văs″ō-rē′flĕx) A reflex that alters the caliber of blood vessels.

vasorrhaphy (văs-or′ă-fē) [″ + Gr. *rhaphe,* seam, ridge] Surgical suture of the vas deferens.

vasosection (văs″ō-sĕk′shŭn) [″ + *sectio,* a cutting] Surgical division of the vasa deferentia.

vasosensory (văs″ō-sĕn′sō-rē) [″ + *sensorius,* pert. to sensation] Pert. to sensation in the blood vessels.

vasospasm (văs′ō-spăzm) [″ + Gr. *spasmos,* a convulsion] Spasm of a blood vessel. SYN: *angiohypotonia; angiospasm; vasoconstriction.* **vasospastic,** *adj.*

vasostimulant (văs″ō-stĭm′ū-lănt) [L. *vas,* vessel, + *stimulans,* goading] Exciting vasomotor action.

vasostomy (vă-sŏs′tō-mē) [″ + Gr. *stoma,* mouth] Surgery to make an opening into the vas deferens.

Vasotec (vā′zō-tĕk″) SEE: *enalapril.*

vasotomy (văs-ŏt′ō-mē) [″ + Gr. *tome,* incision] Incision of the vas deferens.

vasotonia (văs″ō-tō′nē-ă) [″ + Gr. *tonos,* act of stretching, tension] The tone of blood vessels.

vasotrophic (văs″ō-trŏf′ĭk) [″ + Gr. *trophe,* nourishment] Pert. to the nutrition of blood vessels.

vasotropic (văs″ō-trŏp′ĭk) Affecting blood vessels.

vasovasostomy (văs″ō-vă-sŏs′tō-mē) [″ + *vas,* vessel, + *stoma,* mouth] The rejoining of the previously severed ductus deferens of the testicle; the revision of a vasectomy.

vasovesiculectomy (văs″o-vĕ-sĭk″ū-lĕk′tō-mē) [″ + *vesicula,* tiny sac, + Gr. *ektome,* excision] Excision of the vas deferens and seminal vesicles.

vasovesiculitis (văs″ō-vĕ-sĭk″ū-lī′tĭs) [″ + *vesicula,* a tiny bladder, + Gr. *itis,* inflammation] Inflammation of the vas deferens and seminal vesicles.

vastus (văs′tŭs) [L., vast] **1.** Great, large, extensive. **2.** One of three muscles of the anterior thigh.

Vata In Ayurvedic medicine, the dosha made up of the elements of space and air. Vata is responsible for space, movement, breathing, natural urges, and sensory functions, and is associated with an astringent taste. People who have a Vata constitution often have dry skin and a slender frame.

Vater, Abraham (fot′ĕr) Ger. botanist and anatomist, 1684–1751.

    V. ampulla Papilla of **Vater.**

    V. corpuscles Pacinian corpuscles.

    papilla of V. The duodenal end of the drainage systems of the pancreatic and common bile ducts. SYN: *duodenal papilla; hepatopancreatic ampulla; Vater ampulla.*

VATS *video-assisted thoracic **surgery*** (used to treat conditions such as empyema, or loculations in the pleural space).

vault (vawlt) A part or structure resembling a dome or arched roof.

VBAC *vaginal birth after previous cesarean.*

VC *vital capacity.*

VCAM-1 *vascular cell adhesion molecule-1.*

VD *venereal disease.*

VDH *valvular disease of the heart.*

VDRL *Venereal Disease Research Laboratories.*

vection (vĕk′shŭn) [L. *vectio,* a carrying] **1.** Transfer of disease agents by a vector from the sick to the well. **2.** Illusion of self-motion. This may be produced experimentally by having the subject seated within a drum that rotates while the subject remains stationary.

vector (vek′tŏr) [L. *vector,* a carrier] **1.** A quantity that is completely specified by magnitude, direction, and sense, which can be represented by a straight line of appropriate length and direction. **2.** A carrier, usually an insect or other arthropod, that transmits the causative organisms of disease from infected to noninfected individuals. **3.** An agent such as a retrovirus that is used to introduce genetic material into the nucleus of a diseased cell in an attempt to cure a genetic illness or a malignancy.

biological v. An animal vector in which the disease-causing organism multiplies or develops prior to becoming infective for a susceptible person.

mechanical v. A vector in or upon which growth and development of the infective agent do not occur.

shuttle v. A short DNA segment, such as may be found in a bacteriophage or a plasmid, that carries DNA between organisms of two different species.

vectorcardiogram (věk″tor-kăr′dē-ō-grăm) [″ + Gr. *kardia*, heart, + *gramma*, something written] A graphic record of the direction and magnitude of the electrical forces of the heart's action by means of a continuous series of vector loops. Analysis of the configuration of these loops permits certain statements to be made about the state of health or diseased condition of the heart. At any moment the electrical activity of the heart can be represented as an electrical vector with a specific direction and magnitude. This is called the instantaneous cardiac vector. A series of these vectors may be established for the entire cardiac cycle. By joining the tips of these vectors with a continuous line, the vectorcardiogram loop is formed. The configuration so obtained may be projected on the frontal plane or viewed as a three-dimensional loop. Three vectorcardiogram loops are formed during each cardiac cycle: one for the electrical activity of the atrium; one for ventricular depolarization; one for ventricular repolarization.

spatial v. Depiction of the vectorcardiogram in three planes (frontal, sagittal, and horizontal).

vectorcardiography (věk″tor-kăr″dē-ŏg′ră-fē) Analysis of the direction and magnitude of the electrical forces of the heart's action by a continuous series of loops (vectors) that represent the cardiac cycle.

vectorial (věk-tō′rē-ăl) [L. *vector*, a carrier] Pert. to a vector.

vedic medicine [Sanskrit *veda*, knowledge, science] SEE: under *medicine*.

VEE *Venezuelan equine encephalitis.*

veer (vēr) [Fr. *virer*, to turn] In neurology, to exhibit ataxia.

vegan (věj′ăn) A vegetarian who omits all animal protein from the diet.

veganism (věj′ă-nĭzm) A form of vegetarianism in which no forms of animal protein are consumed. The diet is devoid of meat, fish, poultry, eggs and dairy products.

vegetable (věj′ě-tă-bl) **1.** Pert. to, of the nature of, or derived from plants. **2.** A herbaceous plant, esp. one cultivated for food. **3.** The edible part or parts of plants

that are used as food, including the leaves, stems, seeds and seed pods, flowers, roots, tubers, and fruits.

Vegetables are important sources of minerals and vitamins; provide bulk, which stimulates intestinal motility; and are sources of energy. Caloric value is indirectly proportional to water content. Copper is estimated at 1.2 mg/kg for leafy vegetables, and 0.7 mg/kg for nonleafy ones.

Plant and vegetable proteins individually do not contain the complete complement of essential amino acids. By combining vegetables, it is possible to obtain an adequate and balanced mixture of essential amino acids. For example, corn is low in lysine but has an adequate amount of tryptophan; beans are adequate in lysine but low in tryptophan. Although neither is a sufficient source of protein alone, in combination, they are an adequate protein source. Similarly rice and beans serve to complement the deficiencies in the other and together are a complete source of protein.

All starches in vegetables must be changed to sugars before they can be absorbed. Dry heat changes starch to dextrin; heat and acid or an enzyme change dextrin to dextrose. In germinating grain, starch is changed to dextrin and dextrose. Fermented dextrose produces alcohol and carbon dioxide.

cruciferous v. A family of vegetables (including broccoli, brussels sprouts, cabbage, and cauliflower) named for their cross-shaped flowers. People who eat a diet rich in these vegetables are found to have a decreased incidence of cardiovascular diseases, strokes, and cancer, among other illnesses.

vegetal (věj′ě-tăl) **1.** Pert. to plants. **2.** Tropic or nutritional, esp. with reference to that part of an ovum which contains the yolk. SEE: *vegetal pole*.

vegetarian (vej-ě-ter′ē-ăn) [from *vegetable*, coined 1847 by the Vegetarian Society] A person who does not eat animal flesh or, in some instances, any animal by-products. Different approaches result in individual variation in whether fish, eggs, and/or dairy foods are accepted dietary components. Vegetarians must carefully plan their meals to ensure that they have an adequate diet. **vegetarian,** *adj.* **vegetarianism** (′ē-ă-nĭzm), *n.*

vegetate (věj′ě-tāt) [LL. *vegetare,* to grow] **1.** To grow luxuriantly with the production of fleshy or warty outgrowths such as a polyp. **2.** To lead a passive existence mentally or physically, or both; to do little more than eat and maintain autonomic body functions.

vegetation (věj-ě-tā′shŭn) A morbid luxurious outgrowth on any part, esp. wartlike projections made up of collections of fibrin in which are enmeshed white and red blood cells; sometimes seen on denuded areas of the endocardium covering the valves of the heart.

adenoid v. Fungus-like masses of lymphoid tissue in the nasopharynx.

vegetative (věj'ě-tā″tĭv) **1.** Having the power to grow, as plants. **2.** Functioning involuntarily. **3.** Quiescent, passive, denoting a stage of development.

vegetative function Any of the nonconscious body processes needed to keep the body alive.

vegetative state Persistent vegetative state.

VEGF *vascular endothelial growth factor.*

vehicle (vē'ĭ-kl) [L. *vehiculum,* that which carries] **1.** An inert agent that carries the active ingredient in a medicine (e.g., a syrup in liquid preparations). **2.** Any object that carries another (e.g., a work surface may be a vehicle that transmits germs from one person to another; a patch applied to the skin may be a vehicle that permits drug delivery to the body).

vehicular trauma (vē-hik'yŭ-lăr) SEE: under *trauma.*

veil (vāl) [L. *velum,* a covering] **1.** Any veil-like structure. **2.** A piece of the amniotic sac occasionally covering the face of a newborn infant. SYN: *caul.* **3.** Slight alteration in the voice in order to disguise it.

Veillonella (vā″lō-něl′ă) A genus of gram-negative, anaerobic diplococci that inhabit the oral cavity and gastrointestinal tract. Although Veillonella species rarely cause human disease, occasional episodes of bone or blood-borne infection have been reported.

vein (vān) [L. *vena,* vein] A vessel carrying blood toward the heart. Most veins originate in capillaries and drain into increasingly larger veins until their blood is delivered to the right atrium of the heart. Portal veins also originate in capillaries, but their branches decrease in size to pass through another set of capillaries before joining more typical veins on their way toward the heart. For all veins, the precursor veins that empty into a secondary vein are called tributaries of the secondary vein. SEE: illus.; *circulation; vena.*

anterior tibial v. A vein that drains blood from the lower leg and foot and that merges with the posterior tibial vein to form the popliteal vein in the popliteal fossa.

axillary v. The continuation of the basilic vein in the upper arm; it accompanies the axillary artery and becomes the subclavian vein at the lateral border of the first rib. Tributaries of the axillary vein include the brachial, the cephalic, and the subscapular veins.

azygos v. A vein running along the back wall of the thorax on the right side of the thoracic aorta; at the level of the fourth thoracic vertebra, the azygos vein curves forward, over the top of the hilum (root) of the right lung, and empties its blood into the superior vena cava. The azygos vein receives blood from the back wall of the trunk via the hemiazygos, accessory azygos, right superior intercostal, right intercostal, mediastinal, pericardial, right subcostal, and right ascending lumbar veins. The patterns and interconnections of the azygos, hemiazygos, and accessory azygos veins are variable.

basilic v. A superficial vein running along the lateral side of the upper limb. It begins in the dorsal veins of the hand, continues along the dorsal (posterior) medial side of the anterior forearm where it angles medially, and then passes over ventral (anterior) medial side of the elbow; in the antecubital fossa, it is joined by the median cubital vein, a branch of the cephalic vein. Approx. one third of the way up the medial surface of the arm, the basilic vein dives, alongside the medial edge of the biceps brachii muscle, to run alongside the brachial artery; when the brachial artery becomes the axillary artery, the basilic vein becomes the axillary vein. It is usually chosen for intravenous injection or withdrawal of blood.

brachial v. Either of a pair of veins that accompany the brachial artery into the upper arm (as venae comitantes) and then empty into the axillary vein.

brachiocephalic v. The brachiocephalic vein is formed by the merger of the subclavian and internal jugular veins in the root of the neck. The right brachiocephalic vein is about 2.5 cm long and the left is about 6 cm long. The right and the left brachiocephalic veins join, behind the junction of the right border of the sternum and the right first costal cartilage, to form the superior vena cava. Tributaries of both brachiocephalic veins include the vertebral, internal mammary, and inferior thyroid veins; the left brachiocephalic vein also receives the left superior intercostal, thymic, and pericardial veins.

cardiac v. Any of the veins that run along the surface of the heart parallel to the coronary arteries, drain the heart muscle, and empty into the coronary sinus or the right atrium. SEE: *coronary artery* for illus.

cardinal v. Along with the umbilical and the vitelline veins, the cardinal veins form one of the three venous systems of the early embryo. The cardinal veins return blood to the heart from the body of the embryo, and they are the precursors of the major thoracic veins, including the subclavian, brachioce-

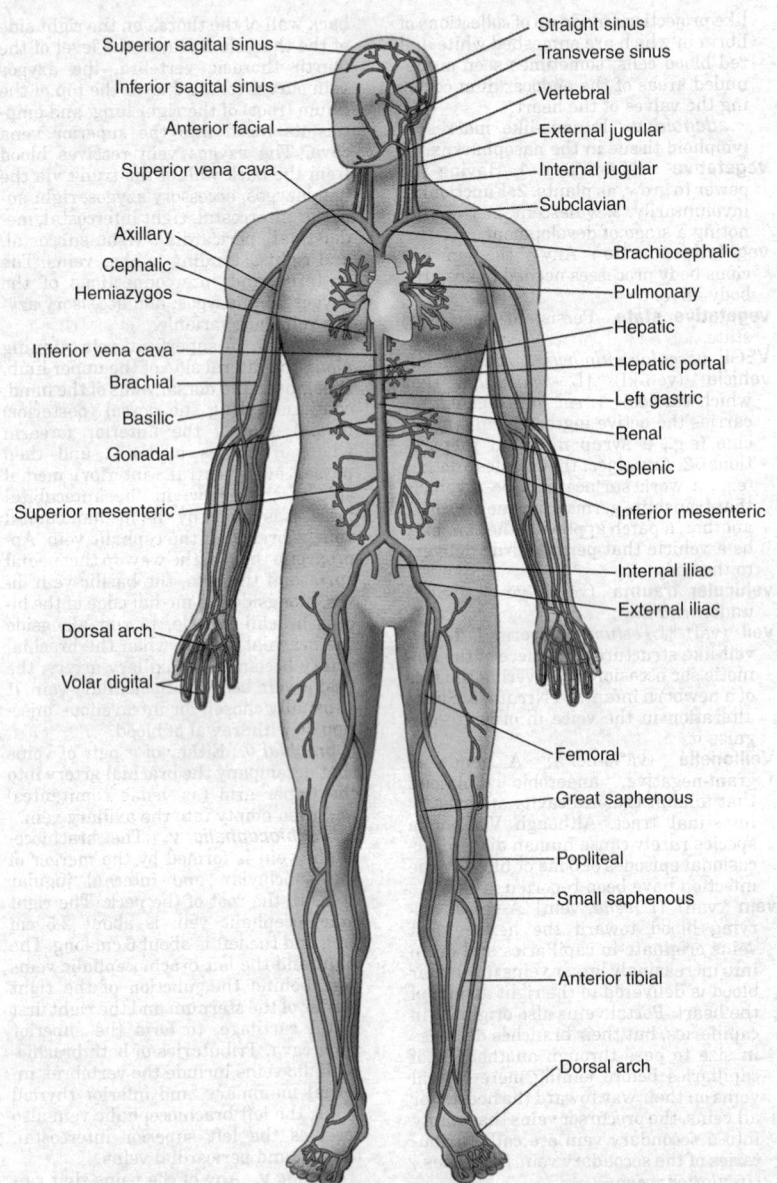

Straight sinus
Transverse sinus
Vertebral
External jugular
Internal jugular
Subclavian
Brachiocephalic
Pulmonary
Hepatic
Hepatic portal
Left gastric
Renal
Splenic
Inferior mesenteric
Internal iliac
External iliac
Femoral
Great saphenous
Popliteal
Small saphenous
Anterior tibial
Dorsal arch

Superior sagital sinus
Inferior sagital sinus
Anterior facial
Superior vena cava
Axillary
Cephalic
Hemiazygos
Inferior vena cava
Brachial
Basilic
Gonadal
Superior mesenteric
Dorsal arch
Volar digital

SYSTEMIC VEINS

phalic, azygos, internal jugular veins, and the superior vena cava.

    cephalic v. A superficial vein of the upper limb, it forms over the "anatomical snuff box", behind the base of the thumb, and runs medially onto the anterior (ventral) surface of the forearm. It runs up the lateral side of the anterior (ventral) surface of the forearm, it crosses in front of the elbow, and contin-

ues up the arm along the biceps brachii and deltoid muscles. Below the clavicle, the cephalic vein dives into the intra-clavicular fossa to empty into the axillary vein. In the antecubital fossa, a large branch, the median cubital vein, runs laterally and joins the basilic vein.

    cerebral v. Any of the veins draining the brain. Cerebral veins differ from veins outside the skull in that (1) cere-

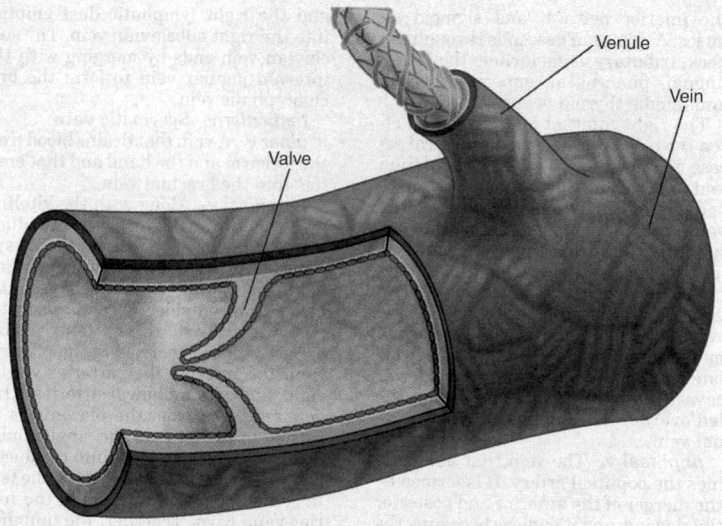

STRUCTURE OF A VEIN AND VENULE

bral veins do not run with cerebral arteries; (2) cerebral veins do not have valves; and (3) walls of cerebral veins contain no muscle.

The venous circulation of the brain begins with venules that run from inside the brain to the surface where they bend 90° and run along the surface inside the pia mater. Anastomosing venous plexuses collect in the pia to form the cerebral veins, which eventually cross the subarachnoid space and empty into dural sinuses. The dural sinuses interconnect and eventually empty into the internal jugular veins. SEE: *dural sinus.*

common iliac v. The vein accompanying the common iliac artery; it is formed by the union of the external and internal iliac veins, and it ends by merging with the opposite common iliac vein to form the inferior vena cava. The right iliac vein is shorter than the left. Tributaries of the common iliac vein include the iliolumbar, lateral sacral, and median sacral veins.

external iliac v. The continuation of the femoral vein proximal to the inguinal ligament; it accompanies the external iliac artery, and it joins the internal iliac vein to form the common iliac vein. Tributaries of the external iliac vein include the inferior epigastric, deep circumflex iliac, and pubic veins.

external jugular v. A vein that drains blood from the scalp and face; it arises from the merger of the posterior facial and posterior auricular veins behind the angle of the mandible. The external jugular vein runs superficially down the neck, crossing the sternocleidomastoid

muscle, to drain into the subclavian vein. Tributaries of the external jugular vein include the posterior external jugular, transverse cervical, suprascapular, and anterior jugular veins.

great cardiac v. A large vein on the anterior surface of the heart; it runs in the anterior interventricular groove alongside the left anterior descending artery. It drains the same area of the heart that is supplied by the artery, and it also receives blood from the left marginal vein. The great cardiac vein follows the coronary sulcus to the left to empty into the coronary sinus on the posterior surface of the heart.

great saphenous v. Long saphenous **v.**

greater saphenous v. Long saphenous **v.**

innominate v. Brachiocephalic **v.**

internal iliac v. The vein that accompanies the internal iliac artery; it merges with the external iliac vein to form the common iliac vein. Tributaries of the internal iliac vein include the gluteal, internal pudendal, obturator, lateral sacral, anterior sacral, middle rectal, vesical, uterine, and vaginal veins.

internal jugular v. A large vein in the neck, it drains the skull, brain, and parts of the face and neck. It originates in the jugular foramen at the base of the skull and descends vertically (behind the sternocleidomastoid muscle) in the carotid sheath. At its base, the internal jugular vein merges with the subclavian vein behind the clavicle to form the brachiocephalic vein.

The internal jugular vein is forms in the base of the skull by the merger of the inferior petrosal and sigmoid sinuses. As the vein descends through the neck, tributary veins include the facial, lingual, pharyngeal, superior thyroid, and middle thyroid veins.

The right internal jugular vein is often the blood vessel used for medical access to the central venous circulation and to the right side of the heart.

ovarian v. In females, any of the veins that accompany the ovarian artery and that drain the ovary and Fallopian tube. Outside the broad ligament, the ovarian veins collect into two veins on each side of the body. These veins accompany the ovarian artery and merge into a single vein; the right ovarian vein then empties into the inferior cava (below the renal vein), while the left ovarian vein empties into the left renal vein.

popliteal v. The vein that accompanies the popliteal artery. It is formed by the merger of the anterior and posterior tibial veins, and it ends by becoming the femoral vein at the distal opening of the adductor canal. The short saphenous vein is a major tributary of the popliteal vein.

posterior tibial v. A deep vein in the lower limb that accompanies the posterior tibial artery; the vein drains the region supplied by the artery. The posterior tibial vein merges with the anterior tibial vein to form the popliteal vein in the popliteal fossa behind the knee.

pulmonary v. Any of the four veins (two from each lung) that return newly-oxygenated blood to the left atrium of the heart. Pulmonary veins have no valves.

radial v. A vein that drains blood from the forearm and the hand and then empties into the brachial vein.

renal v. A large vein that drains blood from the kidney and empties into the inferior vena cava; the renal veins lie on top of (anterior to) the renal arteries. To reach the vena cava, the left renal vein passes over the aorta and is three times as long as the right renal vein. Tributaries of the left renal vein include the left testicular or ovarian vein and the left adrenal vein.

small saphenous v. Short saphenous v.

splenic v. A large vein that drains the spleen and empties into the portal vein. Tributaries of the splenic vein include the short gastric, left gastroepiploic, and pancreatic veins.

subclavian v. A large vein draining the arm and shoulder; it is the continuation of the axillary vein, beginning at the outer border of the first rib. Tributaries of the subclavian vein include the external jugular, dorsal scapular, and anterior jugular veins; the thoracic duct empties into the left subclavian vein, and the right lymphatic duct empties into the right subclavian vein. The subclavian vein ends by merging with the internal jugular vein to form the brachiocephalic vein.

testicular v. Spermatic **vein.**

ulnar v. A vein that drains blood from the forearm and the hand and that empties into the brachial vein.

umbilical v. Along with the vitelline and the cardinal veins, the umbilical vein forms one of the three venous systems of the early embryo. The umbilical vein is a conduit for getting oxygenated blood from outside the embryo to the embryonic heart. In the fetus, deoxygenated blood is carried to the placenta from the internal iliac arteries via the right and left umbilical arteries. Oxygenated blood from the placenta is returned to the fetus in the single umbilical vein, which empties into the ductus venosus, a shunt that bypasses the fetal liver and connects directly to the inferior vena cava. Together, the umbilical vein and the umbilical arteries are the main contents of the umbilical cord.

varicose v. A dilated vein. This condition may occur in almost any part of the body but is most common in the lower extremities and in the esophagus. SEE: *Nursing Diagnoses Appendix.*

ETIOLOGY: The development of varicose veins of the legs is promoted and aggravated by pregnancy, obesity, genetics, chronic constipation, straining at stool, and occupations requiring prolonged standing. Esophageal varices are caused by portal hypertension that accompanies cirrhosis of the liver or mechanical obstruction and occlusion of hepatic veins.

SYMPTOMS: Most varicose veins of the legs are asymptomatic, although they may be cosmetically undesirable. Esophageal varices and hemorrhoidal varices may bleed profusely. SEE: illus.

TREATMENT: In hemorrhage, elevation of the extremity and firm, gentle pressure over the wound will stop the bleeding. The patient should not be permitted to walk until the acute condition is controlled. Sclerotherapy, rubber band ligation, or octreotide may be used to control bleeding caused by hemorrhage from esophageal varices.

PATIENT CARE: The patient with lower extremity varicosities is taught to avoid anything that impedes venous return, such as wearing garters and tight girdles, crossing the legs at the knees, and prolonged sitting. After the legs have been elevated for 10 to 15 min, support hose are applied. The patient should not sit in a chair for longer than 1 hr at a time. Walking is encouraged for at least 5 min every hour. The patient should elevate the legs whenever possible, but no less than twice a day for

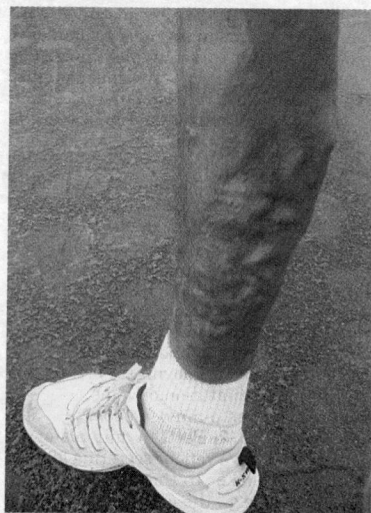

VARICOSE VEINS IN LEG

30 min each time, and should avoid prolonged standing. Exercise, esp. walking, is encouraged to promote the muscular contraction that moves blood through the veins and minimizes venous stasis. Signs of thrombophlebitis, a complication of varicose veins, include heat and local pain. If surgery is performed, elastic stockings or antithrombus devices are applied postoperatively, and the foot of the bed is elevated above the level of the heart. Analgesics are prescribed and administered as needed. Circulatory assessment (color and temperature of toes, pedal pulses) is carried out according to protocol or the surgeon's orders. The patient is watched for complications such as bleeding, infection, and neurosensory problems. Overweight patients must lose weight.

    vitelline v. Along with the umbilical and the cardinal veins, the vitelline veins form one of the three venous systems of the early embryo. The vitelline veins return blood from the yolk sac. These veins are the precursors of many of the gut veins, including the portal system, and are focal structures in the developing liver.

velamentous (věl″ă-měn′tŭs) Expanding like a veil, or sheet.

velar (vē′lăr) [L. *velum,* a veil] Pert. to a velum or veil-like structure.

vellus (věl′ŭs) [L., fleece] The fine hair present on the body after the lanugo hair of the newborn is gone.

velopharyngeal (věl″ō-fă-rǐn′jē-ăl) [L. *velum,* veil, + Gr. *pharynx,* throat] Pert. to the soft palate and the pharynx.

Velpeau, Alfred (vel-pō′) Alfred-Ar-

mand-Louis-Marie Velpeau, Fr. anatomist and surgeon, 1795–1867.

    V. bandage A special immobilizing roller bandage that incorporates the shoulder, forearm, and arm.

    V. deformity A deformity seen in the fracture of Colles, in which the lower fragment is displaced backward.

velum (vē′lŭm) [L., veil] Any veil-like structure.

vena (vē′nă) *pl.* **venae** [L.] A vein.

    vena cava The inferior vena cava or the superior vena cava, the principal venous return trunks to the heart.

    inferior v. cava The large vein that returns blood to the right atrium from the regions of the body below the diaphragm.

    superior v. cava The large unpaired vein that returns blood to the right atrium from the upper body; it is formed by the merger of the right and left brachiocephalic veins, and its main tributary is the azygos vein.

vena caval syndrome Supine hypotensive syndrome.

venacavography (vē″nă-kā-vŏg′ră-fē) Radiography of the vena cava during the injection of a contrast medium.

venation (vē-nā′shŭn) The distribution of veins to an organ or structure.

vendor (věn′dĕr) [L. *vendor,* seller] Any person or company that designs, develops, sells, and/or supports goods or services to or for another party.

venectasia (vē″něk-tā′zē-ă) [L. *vena,* a vein, + Gr. *ektasis,* dilation] Dilation of a vein. SYN: *phlebectasia.*

venectomy (vē-něk′tō-mē) [″ + Gr. *ektome,* excision] Phlebectomy.

veneer (vě-nēr′) In dentistry, a manmade material, such as porcelain, that can be bonded to the surface of a tooth. It is used for cosmetic reasons.

venepuncture (věn′ē-pŭnk″chūr) [L. *vena,* vein, + *punctura,* a point] Venipuncture.

venereal (vē-nē′rē-ăl) [L. *venereus*] Pert. to or resulting from sexual intercourse.

venereal disease A term formerly used to describe any illness transmitted by intimate sexual contact. SEE: *Nursing Diagnoses Appendix.*

venereologist (vě-nēr″ē-ŏl′ō-jĭst) [″ + Gr. *logos,* word, reason] A doctor who specializes in the treatment of sexually transmitted diseases.

venereology (vē-nēr″ē-ŏl′ō-jē) The scientific study and treatment of sexually transmitted diseases.

venesection (věn″ē-sěk′shŭn) [L. *vena,* vein, + *sectio,* a cutting] Surgical opening of a vein for withdrawal of blood. SYN: *phlebotomy.*

venin, venene (ven′ĭn, ve″nēn′) [*ven(om)* + *-in*] [L. *venenum,* poison] Any of the toxic substances in snake venom.

venipuncture (věn″ĭ-pŭnk″chūr) [L. *vena,* vein, + *punctura,* a point] Puncture of a vein, typically to obtain a specimen of blood. The pain of venipuncture may be diminished by several methods, including application of cold to the area just prior to the puncture; injection of sterile, normal saline intracutaneously to produce blanching of the site; and use of a local anesthetic to produce a wheal at the site. SEE: *intravenous infusion;* illus.

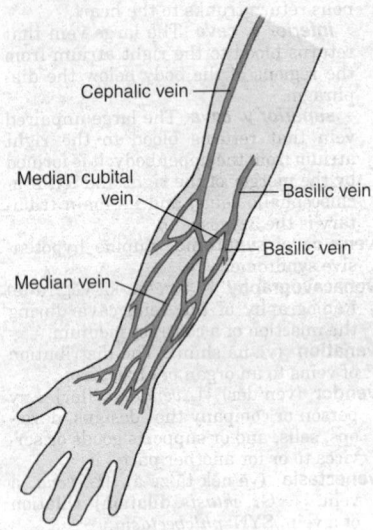

Cephalic vein

Median cubital vein

Basilic vein

Basilic vein

Median vein

VENIPUNCTURE

Antecubital area of arm showing proper veins for venipuncture

venisuture (věn′ĭ-sū″chūr) [″ + *sutura,* a seam] Suture of a vein. SYN: *phleborrhaphy.*

venlafaxine (věn-lă-făk′sēn″) An antidepressant that works by inhibiting serotonin and norepinephrine reuptake, thereby improving mood.

veno-, ven-, veni- [L. *vena,* vein] Prefixes meaning *vein* or the *vena cava.*

venocavogram (vē″nō-kav′ŏ-gram″) [*vena cava* + *-gram*] A radiological image of the vena cava, usually obtained to look for obstructing blood clots.

venoclysis (vē-nŏk′lĭ-sĭs) [″ + Gr. *klysis,* a washing] The continuous injection of medicinal or nutrient fluid intravenously.

venofibrosis (vē″nō-fĭ-brō′sĭs) Phlebosclerosis.

venogram (vē′nō-grăm) [″ + Gr. *gramma,* something written] 1. A radiograph of the veins. SYN: *phlebogram.* 2. A tracing of the venous pulse.

venography (vē-nŏg′ră-fē) [″ + Gr. *graphein,* to write] 1. A radiographic procedure to visualize veins filled with a contrast medium; most commonly used to detect thrombophlebitis. 2. The making of a tracing of the venous pulse.

venom (věn′ŏm) [Fr. *venim* fr. L. *venenum,* poison] A poison secreted by some animals, e.g., insects, spiders, or snakes, and transmitted by bites or stings.

 snake v. The poisonous secretion of the labial glands of certain snakes. Venoms contain proteins, chiefly toxins and enzymes, which are responsible for their toxicity. They are classified as neurocytolysins, hemolysins, hemocoagulins, proteolysins, and cytolysins on the basis of the effects produced.

venomotor (vē″nō-mō′tor) [L. *vena,* vein, + *motus,* moving] Pert. to constriction or dilatation of veins.

venomous (věn′ŏ-mŭs) [*venom* + *-ous*] 1. Poisonous. 2. Pert. to animals or insects that have venom-secreting glands.

venomous snake In the U.S., any of the pit vipers, e.g., the copperhead, cottonmouth (water moccasin), and rattlesnake, of the family Crotalidae, and, in the southern U.S., the coral snakes (genus *Micrurus*), esp. *M. fulvius* and *M. euryxanthus.* Venomous snakes have a worldwide distribution. Specific names of snakes in the general vocabulary are listed under the first word. SEE: e.g., *cobra; copperhead; daboia.*

veno-occlusive (vē″nō-ŏ-kloo′sĭv) Pert. to the obstruction of veins.

veno-occlusive disease The former name for the disease now called *sinusoidal obstruction syndrome.* SEE: *sinusoidal obstruction syndrome.*

venoperitoneostomy (vē″nō-pěr″ĭ-tō″nē-ŏs′tō-mē) [L. *vena,* vein, + Gr. *peritonaion,* peritoneum, + *stoma,* mouth] A one-way valve shunt that connects the peritoneum with the internal jugular or subclavian vein, permitting the escape of ascitic fluid into the venous circulation. SEE: *LeVeen shunt.*

venosclerosis (vē″nō-sklě-rō′sĭs) [″ + Gr. *sklerosis,* to harden] Sclerosis of the veins. SYN: *phlebosclerosis.*

venosity (vē-nŏs′ĭ-tē) [L. *vena,* vein] 1. A condition in which there is an excess of venous blood in a part, causing venous congestion. 2. Deficient aeration of venous blood.

venospasm (vē′nō-spăzm) [″ + Gr. *spasmos,* a convulsion] Contraction of a vein, which may follow infusion of a cold or irritating substance into the vein.

venostasis (vē″nō-stā′sĭs) [″ + Gr. *stasis,* standing still] The trapping of blood in an extremity by compression of veins, a method sometimes employed for reducing the amount of blood being returned to the heart.

venostat (vē′nō-stăt) [″ + Gr. *statikos,* standing] An appliance for performing venous compression.

venotomy (vē-nŏt′ō-mē) [″ + Gr. *tome*, incision] Incision of a vein.

venous (vē′nŭs) [L. *vena*, vein] Pert. to the veins or blood passing through them.

venous admixture A mixture of venous and arterial blood.

venous blood Blood circulating in veins. In systemic veins it is dark and poorly oxygenated; in the pulmonary veins it is fully oxygenated.

venous cutdown Surgical incision in a vein to place a catheter to permit intravenous administration of fluids or drugs. It is used in patients with vascular collapse when gaining percutaneous access to the circulation is difficult; however, this procedure is usually tried only when subclavian, jugular, or femoral access cannot be established.

venous hum A murmur heard on auscultation over the larger veins of the neck.

venous hyperemia SEE: under *hyperemia*.

venous hypertension SEE: under *hypertension*.

venous port, venous access port Part of a venous access device consisting of a subcutaneously implanted port through which medications are injected. Leading from the port is a catheter that is inserted in the cephalic, jugular, or subclavian vein. The catheter extends into the superior vena cava. The port has a self-sealing septum through which a needle is inserted to have access for administering medications, such as cancer chemotherapy agents, and for drawing blood samples. The septum of the port is made to withstand from 1,000 to 2,000 punctures depending on the size needle used. Sterile technique is used each time a needle enters the port. The port permits unrestricted patient activity. Each time it is used care must be taken to be certain the line is open and that the catheter in the vein has remained in the proper position. SEE: illus.

PATIENT CARE: Venous access ports are useful for patients requiring intermittent intravenous (IV) therapy such as chemotherapy or antibiotics, parenteral nutrition, blood products, or IV fluids, and/or intermittent blood sampling. The port may be implanted for 3 months to several years. It consists of a self-sealing silicone rubber septum (resembling the head of a stethoscope and measuring 7 to 10 mm in diameter) covering a metal or plastic reservoir and a silicone catheter connecting the reservoir to a central vein. Ports may have one or two lumens. The dual-lumen port has two noncommunicating reservoirs with their own catheters in a single port body. The most common site for port implantation is in the anterior chest below the clavicle, although other sites such as the upper arm are options. Once the site

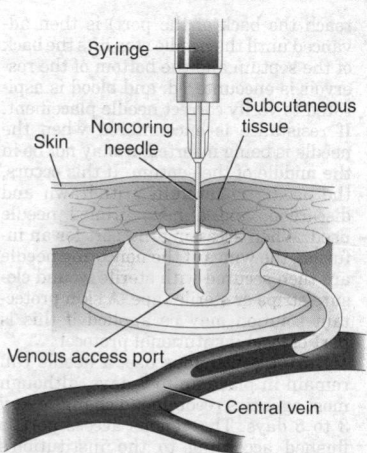

IMPLANTABLE VENOUS ACCESS PORT

heals (5 to 7 days), the skin covering the device protects the patient from infection. Ports also may be open-ended (requiring flushing with a heparinized saline solution to prevent clotting, or valved (with no flushing needed between uses). The patient should be aware of which type device has been implanted, or should carry a wallet card identifying the device. When a port is not in active use the patient can participate in normal activities.

Sterile technique should be used when accessing a port. A topical anesthetic spray or cream should be applied, if the port has been recently implanted, or if the patient requests analgesia to prevent or reduce discomfort. The patient is positioned, so the site is easily viewed. The septum is palpated (unless newly implanted), and assessed for signs and symptoms of infection, such as redness, swelling, pain, and local warmth. Any infection should be documented, the patient's primary health care provider notified, and the site not accessed. For access, the port septum should be localized and stabilized using the nondominant hand, stretching the skin taut with the thumb and first two fingers. Patient anxiety about the procedure can be eased by speaking reassuringly to the patient throughout, explaining what is being done and the rationale for each action. The site is then prepared following agency procedure. The primed, noncoring needle (20 gauge is appropriate for most injections and infusions) is then held perpendicular to the septum with the dominant hand and inserted at a point between the thumb and fingers. Minimal resistance should be noted as the skin and port septum are punctured. The needle (which should be just long enough to reach the back of the port) is then advanced until the needle stop hits the back of the septum and the bottom of the reservoir is encountered, and blood is aspirated to verify correct needle placement. If resistance is encountered when the needle is being inserted, it may not be in the middle of the septum. If this occurs, the needle is carefully withdrawn and discarded, and a new, primed needle used. When accessing the port for an infusion, the wings of the noncoring needle are then secured with sterile wound closure strips or sterile tape. A skin protectant solution may be applied if this is part of local institutional protocol.

During continuous use, a needle can remain in place up to 7 days, although most agencies recommend change every 3 to 5 days. The venous access port is flushed according to the institution's protocol, prior to being deaccessed. Following administration of prescribed therapy, the port is deaccessed. Hands are washed and nonsterile gloves are donned. Any dressing and tape are removed, and the skin held taut over the port with thumb and first two fingers. Maintaining light pressure on the port body, the needle is pulled straight out in a smooth movement, avoiding side-to-side movements that could damage the septum. A small amount of capillary bleeding may occur at the needle site, which is then covered with an adhesive bandage as desired. Documentation should include needle size, prescribed infusions or bolus dosings, needle and dressing changes and dates, patient tolerance of therapy(ies), complications, blood draws, and any changes in the patient's physical assessment.

venous return The amount of blood returning to the atria of the heart.

venous sinus A large-capacity vessel that carries venous blood. Important venous sinuses are those of the dura mater draining the brain and those of the spleen.

venovenostomy (vē″nō-vē-nŏs′tō-mē) [″ + ″ + Gr. *stoma,* mouth] The formation of an anastomosis of a vein joined to a vein.

vent (vĕnt) [O.Fr. *fente,* slit] An opening in any cavity, esp. one for excretion.

venter (vĕn′tĕr) [L., belly] **1.** A belly-shaped part. **2.** The cavity of the abdomen. **3.** The wide swelling part or belly of a muscle.

ventilation (vent″ĭ-lā′shŏn) [*ventilatio,* an airing] **1.** The movement of air into and out of the lungs. **2.** Circulation of fresh air in a room and withdrawal of foul air. **3.** In physiology, the amount of air inhaled per day. This can be estimated by spirometry, multiplying the tidal air by the number of respirations per day. An average figure is 10,000 L. This must not be confused with the total

amount of oxygen consumed, which is on the average only 360 L/day. These volumes are more than doubled during hard physical labor.

adaptive support v. ABBR: ASV. A type of mechanical ventilation in which the minute ventilation is not allowed to fall below a set threshold (e.g., in adults, below 100 mL/kg/min), but the inspiratory pressure, inspiratory time, and tidal volume are all adjusted by the ventilator to the patient's needs.

airway pressure release v. A type of mechanical ventilation in which patients breathe spontaneously at any phase of the ventilator's duty cycle at high continuous positive airway pressures (CPAP). Periodically, the level of CPAP is lowered to eliminate waste gases from the circuit.

alveolar v. The movement of air into and out of the alveoli. It is a function of the size of the tidal volume, the rate of ventilation, and the amount of dead space present in the respiratory system. It is determined by subtracting the dead space volume from the tidal volume and multiplying the result by the respiratory rate.

assist-control v. A type of mechanical ventilation with a minimum frequency of respirations determined by ventilator settings. It also permits the patient to initiate ventilation at the same tidal volume or pressure as set on the ventilator.

asynchronous v. In emergency cardiac or critical care, the administration of artificial breaths to a patient that are timed independently of chest compressions.

continuous positive-pressure v. A type of mechanically assisted pulmonary ventilation. A device administers air or oxygen to the lungs under a continuous pressure that never returns to zero.

differential lung v. The use of different ventilatory strategies in each lung in a patient with focal lung disease, e.g., a patient undergoing surgery to remove a tumor in one lobe of a lung but not another, or a patient with more severe COPD on one side of the chest than another. This technique requires a double-lumen endotracheal tube.

dual control v. Mechanical ventilation initiated by either a change in airway pressures or by a change in gas flowing through the ventilator circuit. Dual control is asserted when pressure limited breaths are delivered and the pressure changes from breath to breath to meet a desired delivered tidal volume. It improves the coordination between the patient's respiratory efforts and machine-generated breaths.

high-frequency jet v. A type of ventilation that continuously ventilates at

100 to 150 cycles/min. It is used in respiratory failure to provide continuous ventilation without the side effects of positive-pressure ventilation.

high-frequency oscillatory v. ABBR: HFOV. Pulmonary ventilation with multiple rapid breaths given at small tidal volumes. It limits the stretching and collapse of the alveoli that occur in conventional mechanical ventilation.

high-frequency percussive v. Mechanical ventilation that decreases peak and end-expiratory pressure by delivering hundreds of shallow (low tidal volume) breaths per minute. It is a time-cycled, pressure-limited mode of ventilation.

intermittent mandatory v. ABBR: IMV. Machine ventilation that delivers pressurized breaths at intervals while allowing for spontaneous breathing.

intermittent positive-pressure v. A mechanical method of assisting pulmonary ventilation, using a device that inflates the lungs under positive pressure. Exhalation is usually passive. SYN: *intermittent positive-pressure breathing*.

inverse ratio v. ABBR: IRV. Mechanical ventilation in which the normal temporal relationship between inspiration and expiration is reversed (the inspiration time is longer than the expiratory time). It is sometimes used in severely hypoxemic patients who have not responded to other ventilatory maneuvers. Because it is uncomfortable for patients, paralysis and sedation are needed.

liquid v. A ventilatory technique used to treat both premature infants with surfactant-deficient lungs and adults with acute respiratory distress syndrome.

mandatory minute v. Ventilatory support that provides mechanical breaths when the patient's spontaneous breathing does not achieve the preset mechanical ventilatory rate.

maximum sustainable v. The normal maximum breathing pattern that can be maintained for 15 min (usually approx. 60% of maximum voluntary ventilation).

maximum voluntary v. The maximum amount of gas that can be ventilated into and out of the lungs in a voluntary effort in a given time, measured in liters per minute.

mechanical v. Any form of artificially supplied ventilation.

minute v. ABBR: MV. The volume of air inhaled and exhaled in 60 sec. SEE: *minute volume*.

noninvasive v. The use of airway support administered through a face (nasal) mask instead of an endotracheal tube. Inhaled gases are given with positive end-expiratory pressure often with pressure support or with assist control

ventilation at a set tidal volume and rate. Numerous studies have shown this technique to be as effective as, and better tolerated than, intubation and mechanical ventilation in patients with exacerbations of chronic obstructive pulmonary disease. SEE: illus.

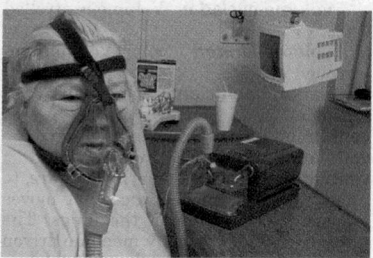

NONINVASIVE POSITIVE PRESSURE VENTILATION

positive-pressure mechanical v. Mechanical ventilatory support that applies positive pressure to the airway. The objectives include improving pulmonary gas exchange, relieving acute respiratory acidosis, relieving respiratory distress, preventing and reversing atelectasis, improving pulmonary compliance, preventing further lung injury, and avoiding complications. Positive-pressure ventilation can be life saving, but complications such as toxic effects of oxygen, laryngeal injury, tracheal stenosis, alveolar injury, barotrauma, pneumonia, and psychological problems may occur. SEE: *positive end-expiratory pressure*.

pressure support v. A type of assisted ventilation that supplements a spontaneous breath. The patient controls the frequency and the duration and flow of inspiration from the ventilator.

protective v. A type of mechanical ventilation in which tidal volumes are set to avoid overstretching the alveoli, and pressures at the end of an inhaled breath are set to avoid alveolar collapse.

pulmonary v. The inspiration and expiration of air from the lungs.

reduced v. Respiratory depression.

synchronized intermittent mandatory v. ABBR: SIMV. Periodic assisted ventilation with positive pressure initiated by the patient and coordinated with spontaneous patient breaths. SEE: *intermittent mandatory v.*

transtracheal catheter v. An emergency procedure in which a catheter is placed percutaneously through the cricothyroid membrane and attached to a high-pressure, high-flow jet ventilator. This form of ventilation is used for patients with an upper airway obstruction who cannot be intubated.

volume-controlled v. A form of mechanical ventilation in which the peak inspiratory flow rate, fraction of inspired oxygen, positive end-expiratory pressure, respiratory rate, and tidal volume are preset and delivered to the patient. SYN: *volume-cycled v.; volume-limited v.*

volume-cycled v. Volume-controlled v.

volume-limited v. Volume-controlled v.

ventilation coefficient SEE: under *coefficient.*

ventilation index SEE: under *index.*

ventilation tube SEE: *grommet.*

ventilator (vent'ĭ-lāt"ŏr) [L. *ventilare,* to fan] A mechanical device that moves gases into and out of the lungs. The mechanism is typically machine driven and automated.

automatic transport v. ABBR: ATV. A portable battery- or gas-powered ventilator that can be used while transporting patients between locations. The ATV is designed for short-term use and often has separate volume and rate controls.

ventilator bundle SEE: under *bundle.*

ventilator dependent Dependent upon mechanical life support because of inability to breathe effectively. A ventilator is used when a patient cannot breathe well enough to maintain normal levels of oxygen and carbon dioxide in the blood. SYN: *respirator dependent.*

ventilator graphics Visual representations of airway pressures or airway flows as they vary over time.

ventilatory weaning response, dysfunctional ABBR: DVWR. A state in which a patient cannot adjust to lowered levels of mechanical ventilator support, which interrupts and prolongs the weaning process. SEE: *Nursing Diagnoses Appendix.*

Ventolin (věn'tǐ-lǐn) SEE: *albuterol.*

ventouse (věn-toos') [Fr.] A glass or glass-shaped vessel used in cupping.

ventouse delivery SEE: under *delivery.*

ventrad (věn'trǎd) [L. *venter,* belly, + *ad,* to] Toward the ventral aspect.

ventral (věn'trǎl) [L. *ventralis,* pert. to the belly] **1.** Pert. to the venter (belly). **2.** Toward the belly of the organism.

ventralis (věn-trā'lĭs) [L.] Anterior, or closer to the front.

ventricle (věn'trǐ-kl) [L. *ventriculus,* a little belly] **1.** A small cavity. **2.** One of the four, interconnected, ependyma-lined cavities inside the brain in which cerebrospinal fluid is generated continuously. SEE: illus.

fifth v. An unofficial name for the space between the two laminae of the septum pellucidum inside the brain.

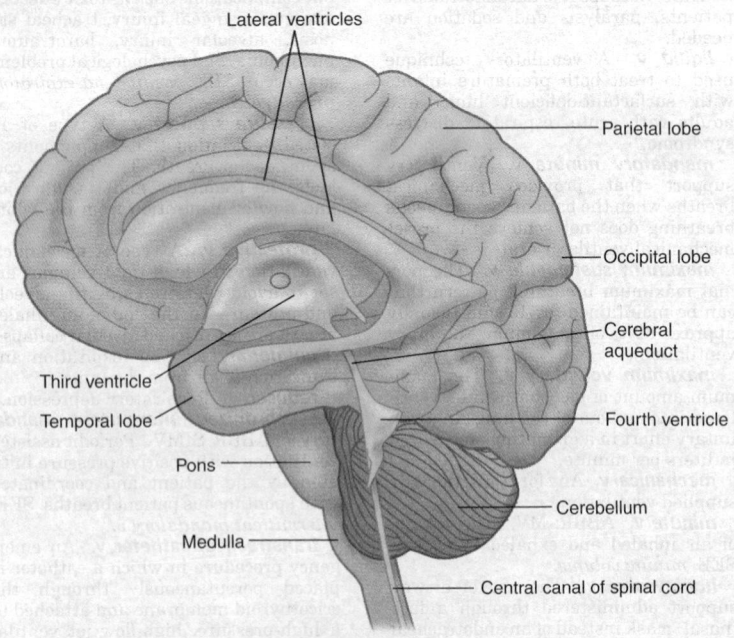

Lateral ventricles

Parietal lobe

Occipital lobe

Cerebral aqueduct

Third ventricle

Temporal lobe

Fourth ventricle

Pons

Cerebellum

Medulla

Central canal of spinal cord

VENTRICLES OF THE BRAIN
Left lateral view

fourth v. The most caudal of the cerebrospinal fluid (CSF)-filled cavities inside the brain. The fourth ventricle extends beneath the cerebellum in the roof of the hindbrain from the caudal end of the cerebral aqueduct to the central canal of the medulla (above the middle of the olivary nuclei). The choroid plexus inside the fourth ventricle adds CSF to the fluid draining through the cerebral aqueduct from the third ventricle. CSF flows out of the fourth ventricle into the subarachnoid space surrounding the brain and spinal cord, exiting through three small openings: the median aperture (foramen of Magendie) and the two lateral apertures (foramina of Luschka).

laryngeal v. Inside the larynx, the disk-shaped space below the vestibular folds and above the vocal folds.

lateral v. One of the two mirror-image, cerebrospinal fluid (CSF)-filled cavities inside the cerebral hemispheres of the brain. Each lateral ventricle is C-shaped and runs parallel to the caudate nucleus and the fornix, from deep inside the frontal lobe to far into the temporal lobe; a tapering branch, the posterior horn, of each lateral ventricle extends deep into the occipital lobe. CSF from the intraventricular choroid plexus continually exits each lateral ventricle into the single third ventricle through an interventricular foramen (foramen of Monroe).

left v. The muscular chamber of the heart that receives blood from the left atrium and that pumps it into the systemic circulation via the aorta.

v. of Morgagni Laryngeal ventricle.

right v. The muscular chamber of the heart that receives blood from the right atrium and that pumps it into the lungs via the pulmonary trunk.

terminal ventricle Ventriculus terminalis

third v. The thin, disk-shaped cavity in the midline of the brain between the left and right thalami that is filled with cerebrospinal fluid (CSF). The lamina terminalis forms the front wall of the third ventricle, the fornices overlie the third ventricle, and the pineal body hangs outside the back top (dorsocaudal) corner. An extension of the third ventricle continues below the thalami and separates the walls of the left and right hypothalami. CSF flows through the two interventricular foramina into the rostral end of the third ventricle from the lateral ventricles. Along with CSF added by the choroid plexus of the third ventricle, CSF flows out of the third ventricle through the narrow cerebral aqueduct and into the fourth ventricle. SYN: .

ventricular (vĕn-trĭk′ū-lăr) [L. *ventriculus,* a little belly] Pert. to a ventricle.

ventricular assist device SEE: under *device.*

ventricular assist pumping Use of a device to temporarily replace the pumping action of a diseased or nonfunctioning heart. SEE: *intra-aortic balloon counterpulsation.*

ventricular compliance SEE: under *compliance.*

ventricular remodeling Reshaping of heart muscle in response to injuries such as myocardial infarction, overload (hypertension), or valvular heart disease such as aortic stenosis or mitral regurgitation. Cardiac hypertrophy, fibrosis, and myocyte death are all potential consequences.

ventricular septal defect SEE: under *defect.*

ventriculitis (vĕn-trĭk″ū-lī′tĭs) [″ + Gr. *itis,* inflammation] Inflammation of a ventricle.

ventriculoatriostomy (vĕn-trĭk″ū-lō-ā″trē-ŏs′tō-mē) [″ + *atrium,* corridor, + Gr. *stoma,* mouth] Plastic surgery for the relief of hydrocephalus. Subcutaneous catheters are placed to connect a cerebral ventricle to the right atrium via the jugular vein. The catheters contain one-way valves so that cerebrospinal fluid can flow into the catheters, but blood may not flow back into the cerebral ventricle.

ventriculocisternostomy (vĕn-trĭk″ū-lō-sĭs″tĕr-nŏs′tō-mē) [″ + *cisterna,* box, chest, + Gr. *stoma,* mouth] Plastic surgery to create an opening between the ventricles of the brain and the cisterna magna.

ventriculocordectomy (vĕn-trĭk″ū-lō-kor-dĕk′tō-mē) [″ + Gr. *khorde,* cord, + *ektome,* excision] Surgery for the relief of laryngeal stenosis. The ventricular floor is removed, but the buccal processes are left in place.

ventriculogram (ven-trĭk′yŭ-lŏ-gram″) [*ventriculus* + *-gram*] **1.** A radiograph of the cerebral ventricles. **2.** An image of the cardiac ventricles, used to estimate ejection fraction and assess wall motion.

ventriculography (vĕn-trĭk″ū-lŏg′ră-fē) [″ + Gr. *graphein,* to write] **1.** An obsolete technique for visualizing the brain radiographically, that relied on the injection of air into the cerebrospinal fluid. It has been replaced by CT and MRI scans of the brain. **2.** Visualization of ventricles of the heart by radiograph after injection of a contrast material.

ventriculometry (vĕn-trĭk″ū-lŏm′ĕ-trē) [″ + Gr. *metron,* measure] The measurement of the intraventricular cerebral pressure.

ventriculoperitoneal Pert. to the peritoneum and the ventricles of the brain.

ventriculoperitoneal shunt ABBR: VPS. A shunt connecting the ventricles of the brain to the peritoneum, used to treat hydrocephalus.

ventriculopuncture (věn-trĭk′ū-lō-pŭnk″tūr) [″ + *punctura,* a point] The use of a needle to puncture a lateral ventricle of the brain.

ventriculoscopy (věn-trĭk″ū-lŏs′kō-pē) [″ + Gr. *skopein,* to examine] Examination of the ventricles of the brain with an endoscope.

ventriculostomy (věn-trĭk″ū-lŏs′tō-mē) [″ + Gr. *stoma,* mouth] Plastic surgery to establish communication between the floor of the third ventricle of the brain and the cisterna interpeduncularis. This is done to treat hydrocephalus.

ventriculotomy (věn-trĭk″ū-lŏt′ō-mē) [″ + Gr. *tome,* incision] Surgical incision of a ventricle.

ventriculus (věn-trĭk′ū-lŭs) [L., a little belly] **1.** Ventricle. **2.** Stomach. **3.** A ventricle of the brain or heart.

   v. terminalis A small, ependymalined cavity normally found in the tail end of the conus medullaris of the human spinal cord. terminal ventricle.

ventro-, ventr-, ventri- [L. *venter,* stem *ventr-,* womb, belly] Prefixes meaning *abdomen* or *ventral* (anterior).

ventrodorsal (věn″trō-dor′săl) [″ + *dorsum,* back] In a direction from the front to the back.

ventrofixation (věn″trō-fĭks-ā′shŭn) [″ + *fixatio,* to fix] The suture of a displaced viscus to the abdominal wall.

ventrolateral (věn″trō-lăt′ĕr-ăl) [″ + *latus,* side] Both ventral and lateral.

ventromedial (věn″trō-mē′dē-ăl) [″ + *medianus,* median] Both ventral and medial.

ventroscopy (věn-trŏs′kō-pē) [L. *venter,* belly, + Gr. *skopein,* to examine] Examination of the abdominal cavity by illumination. SYN: *celioscopy.*

ventrosuspension (věn″trō-sŭs-pěn′shŭn) [″ + *suspensio,* a hanging] The fixation of a displaced uterus to the abdominal wall.

ventrotomy (věn-trŏt′ō-mē) [″ + Gr. *tome,* incision] Incision into the abdominal cavity. SYN: *celiotomy; laparotomy.*

Venturi mask (ven-toor′ē) [Giovanni Battista Venturi, Italian scientist, 1746–1822] A mask for administering a controlled concentration of oxygen to a patient. These devices are better known as air entrainment masks rather than Venturi masks because they do not actually work by the principle discovered by G.B. Venturi.

venturimeter (věn″tūr-ĭm′ĕ-tĕr) A device for measuring the flow of fluids through vessels.

venula (věn′ū-lă) [L., little vein] Venule.

venule (věn′ūl) [L., *venula,* little vein] A tiny vein continuous with a capillary. SYN: *venula.* SEE: *vein* for illus.

Venus, crown of (vē′nŭs) A papular eruption around the hairline on the forehead caused by secondary syphilis.

verapamil (věr-ăp′ă-mĭl) A calcium channel blocker, administered orally or intravenously to manage hypertension, angina pectoris, variant angina, and supraventricular arrhythmias. It is sometimes given to prevent migraines. Its therapeutic classes are antianginal, antiarrhythmic, antihypertensive, and vascular headache suppressant. SYN: *Covera-HS; Verelan.*

verbal fluency task Any test in which a patient is asked to name or list as many items in a category as he or she can in a limited period of time, usually 60 seconds. Common tasks include naming all the animals or plants one can think of or saying as many words as one can think of that begin with a particular letter of the alphabet. The tests are used to assess memory and concentration. SYN: *controlled word association; verbal fluency test.*

verbal fluency test Verbal fluency task.

verbigeration (věr-bĭj″ĕr-ā′shŭn) [L. *verbigerare,* to chatter] Repetition of words that are either meaningless or have no significance.

verdigris (věr″dĭ-grĭs) [O.Fr. *vert de Grece,* green of Greece] **1.** A mixture of basic copper acetates. **2.** The green-gray deposit of copper carbonate on copper and bronze vessels.

verdohemoglobin (věr″dō-hēm′ō-glōb″ĭn) A greenish pigment occurring as an intermediate product in the formation of bilirubin from hemoglobin.

Verelan Verapamil.

verge (věrj) An edge or margin.

   anal v. The transitional area between the smooth perianal area and the hairy skin.

vergence (věr′jĕns) [L. *vergere,* to bend] A turning of one eye with reference to the other; may be horizontal (convergence or divergence) or vertical (intravergence or supravergence). SEE: *-phoria.*

verify (věr′ĭ-fī″) [L. *verificare,* to establish the truth] To confirm the accuracy of a report, a laboratory test, or an evaluation.

vermicidal (věr″mĭ-sī′dăl) [L. *vermis,* worm, + *cidus,* kill] Destroying parasitic worms in the intestines.

vermicide (věr′mĭ-sīd) **1.** Destroying worms. **2.** An agent that will kill intestinal worms.

vermicular (věr-mĭk′ū-lăr) [L. *vermicularis*] Resembling a worm.

vermiculation (věr-mĭk″ū-lā′shŭn) [L. *vermiculare,* to wriggle] A wormlike motion, as in the intestines. SEE: *peristalsis.*

vermicule (věr′mĭ-kūl) [L. *vermiculus,* a small worm] **1.** A small worm. **2.** Having a wormlike shape.

vermiculose, vermiculous (vĕr-mĭk′ŭ-lōs, vĕr-mĭk′ū-lŭs) [L. *vermicularis,* wormlike] **1.** Infested with worms or larvae. **2.** Wormlike.

vermiform (vĕr′mĭ-form) [L. *vermis,* worm, + *forma,* shape] Shaped like a worm.

vermiform appendix SEE: under *appendix.*

vermifugal (vĕr-mĭf′ū-găl) [″ + *fugare,* to put to flight] Expelling worms from the intestines.

vermifuge (vĕr′mĭ-fūj) Anthelmintic.

vermilionectomy (vĕr-mĭl″yŏn-ĕk′tō-mē) [″ + Gr. *ektome,* excision] Surgical removal of the vermilion border of the lip.

vermin (vĕr′mĭn) [L. *vermis,* worm] Animals such as mice, rats, roaches, lice, and bedbugs that despoil food, infest dwellings, or spread disease.

verminal (vĕr′mĭ-năl) Pert. to or caused by worms.

vermination (vĕr″mĭn-ā′shŭn) Vermin or worm infestation.

verminosis (vĕr″mĭn-ō′sĭs) [″ + Gr. *osis,* condition] Infestation with vermin.

vermis (vĕr′mĭs) [L. worm] **1.** A worm. **2.** Vermis cerebelli.

   v. cerebelli The median connecting lobe of the cerebellum.

vernal (vĕr′năl) [L. *vernalis,* pert. to spring] Pert. to or happening in the spring.

Vernet syndrome (ver-nā′) [Maurice Vernet, Fr. physician, 1887–1974] Paralysis of the glossopharyngeal, vagus, and spinal accessory nerves on the opposite side of a lesion involving the jugular foramen. It may occur, e.g., after a fracture of the occipital condyle.

vernix (vĕr′niks) [L. *vernix,* varnish] Varnish.

   v. caseosa A protective sebaceous deposit covering the fetus during intrauterine life, consisting of exfoliations of the outer skin layer, lanugo, and secretions of the sebaceous glands. It helps the neonate conserve body heat. It is most abundant in the creases and flexor surfaces. It is not necessary to remove this after the fetus is delivered. SEE: *sebum.*

verometer (vĕr-ŏm′ĭ-tĕr) [Fm. O. Fr. *veer* + ″] A device that measures the ability of a lens to bend light rays into focus.

verotoxin (vĕr-ō-tŏks′ĭn) A heat-labile toxin produced by some types of *Escherichia coli.*

verruca (vĕr-roo′kă) *pl.* **verrucae** [L., wart] Wart.

   v. acuminata A pointed, reddish, moist wart about the genitals and the anus. It develops near mucocutaneous junctures, forming pointed, tufted, or pedunculated pinkish or purplish projections of varying lengths and consistency. Venereal warts should be treated

with topically applied podophyllum resin. SYN: *condyloma; genital wart; venereal wart.*

   v. digitata A form of verruca seen on the face and scalp, possibly serving as a starting point of cutaneous horns. Several filiform projections with horny caps are formed, closely grouped on a comparatively narrow base that in turn may be separated from the skin surface by a slightly contracted neck.

   v. filiformis A small threadlike growth on the neck and eyelids covered with smooth and apparently normal epidermis.

   v. gyri hippocampi One of the small wartlike protuberances on the convex surface of the gyrus hippocampi.

   v. plana A flat or slightly raised wart.

   v. plantaris Plantar wart.

   v. vulgaris The common wart, usually found on the backs of the hands and fingers; however, it may occur on any area of the skin.

verruciform (vĕ-roo′sĭ-form) [L. *verruca,* wart, + *forma,* shape] Wartlike.

verrucose, verrucous (vĕr′roo-kōs, vĕr-roo′kŭs) [L. *verrucosus,* wartlike] Wartlike, with raised portions.

verrucosis (vĕr″oo-kō′sĭs) [L. *verruca,* wart, + Gr. *osis,* condition] The condition of having multiple warts.

verruga peruana (vĕ-roo′gă pĕr-wăn′ă) [Sp., Peruvian wart] A clinical form of bartonellosis. It is marked by a chronic, benign cutaneous eruption consisting of raised, reddish-purple nodules on the skin and mucous membranes. SEE: *bartonellosis.*

versicolor (vĕr′sĭ-kŏl″or) [L., of changing colors] **1.** Having many shades or colors. **2.** Changeable in color. SEE: *tinea versicolor.*

version (vĕr′zhŏn) [L. *versio,* a turning] **1.** Altering the position of the fetus in the uterus. It may occur naturally or may be done mechanically by the physician to facilitate delivery. SEE: *conversion.* **2.** Deflection of an organ such as the uterus from its normal position.

   bipolar v. Cephalic **v.**

   cephalic v. Turning of the fetus so that the head presents. This may be done by internal and/or external manipulation. SYN: *bimanual v.; bipolar v.; external cephalic v.; fetal v.*

   combined v. Mechanical version by combined internal and external manipulation.

   external v. Improving the presentation of an unengaged fetus by placing one's hands on the mother's abdomen and pushing, turning, or rotating the fetus.

   external cephalic v. Cephalic **v.**

   internal v. Podalic **v.**

   pelvic v. Turning a fetus from a transverse lie to a vertex (head down) presentation.

podalic v. Using two hands (one inside the uterus and one on the abdominal wall) to change a twin fetus from a breech to a vertex presentation. SYN: *internal v.*

spontaneous v. Unassisted conversion of fetal presentation by uterine muscular contractions.

vertebra (věr′tě-brǎ) *pl.* **vertebrae** [L.] Any of the 33 bony segments of the spinal column: 7 cervical, 12 thoracic, 5 lumbar, 5 sacral, and 4 coccygeal vertebrae. In adults, the five sacral vertebrae fuse to form a single bone, the sacrum; four rudimentary coccygeal vertebrae fuse to form the coccyx.

A typical vertebra consists of a ventral body and a dorsal or neural arch. In the thoracic region, the body bears on each side two costal pits for reception of the head of the rib. The arch that encloses the vertebral foramen is formed of two roots or pedicles and two laminae. The arch bears seven processes: a dorsal spinous process, two lateral transverse processes, and four articular processes (two superior and two inferior). A deep concavity, the inferior vertebral notch, on the inferior border of the arch provides a passageway for a spinal nerve. The successive vertebral foramina form the vertebral, or spinal, canal that encloses the spinal cord.

The bodies of successive vertebrae articulate with one another and are separated by intervertebral disks, disks of fibrous cartilage enclosing a central mass, the nucleus pulposus. The inferior articular processes articulate with the superior articular processes of the next succeeding vertebra in the caudal direction. Several ligaments (supraspinous, interspinous, anterior and posterior longitudinal, and the ligamenta flava) hold the vertebrae in position, yet permit a limited degree of movement. Motions of the vertebral column include forward bending (flexion), backward bending (extension), side bending (lateral flexion), and rotation. Lateral flexion and rotation motions are coupled so that whenever the vertebrae bend to the side, they also rotate and vice versa. SEE: *sacrum* for illus.

basilar v. The lowest of the lumbar vertebrae.

cervical v. One of the seven vertebrae of the neck.

coccygeal v. One of the rudimentary vertebrae of the coccyx.

fixed v. The sacral and coccygeal vertebrae that fuse to form the sacrum and coccyx.

lumbar v. One of the five vertebrae between the thoracic vertebrae and the sacrum.

odontoid v. Axis (2).

v. prominens The seventh cervical vertebra.

sacral v. One of the five fused vertebrae forming the sacrum. SEE: *sacrum* for illus.

thoracic v. One of the 12 vertebrae that connect the ribs and form part of the posterior wall of the thorax. SEE: *spinal column* for illus.

vertebral (věr′tě-brǎl) [L. *vertebra,* vertebra] Pert. to a vertebra or the vertebral column.

vertebral body SEE: under *body.*

Vertebrata (věr″tě-brā′tǎ) A subphylum of the phylum Chordata characterized by possession of a segmented backbone or spinal column. It includes the classes Agnatha (cyclostomes), Chondrichthyes (cartilaginous fishes), Osteichthyes (bony fishes), Amphibia, Reptilia, Aves, and Mammalia. Members of this subphylum possess an axial notochord at some period of their existence.

vertebrate (věr′tě-brāt) [L. *vertebra,* vertebra] Having or resembling a vertebral column.

vertebrated (věr′tě-brāt″ěd) Composed of jointed segments.

vertebrectomy (ver″tě-brek′tǒ-mē) [*vertebra* + *-ectomy*] Surgical removal of all or a part of a back bone.

vertebro-, vertebr- [L. vertebra, vertebra, (spinal) joint] Prefixes indicating *vertebra.*

vertebroarterial (věr″tě-brō-ǎr-tē′rē-ǎl) [″ + Gr. *arteria,* artery] Pert. to the vertebral artery.

vertebrobasilar (věr″tě-brō-bǎs′ǐ-lǎr) [″ + *basilaris,* basilar] Pert. to the vertebral and basilar arteries.

vertebrocostal (věr″tě-brō-kǒs′tǎl) [″ + *costa,* rib] Costovertebral.

vertebroplasty (ver′tē-brō-plǎs-tē) Plastic surgical repair of a vertebra.

vertebrosternal (věr″tě-brō-stěr′nǎl) [″ + Gr. *sternon,* chest] Pert. to a vertebra and the sternum.

vertex (věr′těks) [L., summit] The top of the head. SYN: *crown.*

vertical (věr′tǐ-kǎl) [L. *verticalis,* summit] **1.** Pert. to or situated at the vertex. **2.** Perpendicular to the plane of the horizon of the earth; upright.

vertical-banded gastroplasty A bariatric surgical procedure that restricts the passage of food into the stomach, increasing the feeling of satiety after a meal.

verticalis (věr″tǐ-kā′lǐs) [L.] Vertical, indicating any plane that passes through the body parallel to the long axis of the body.

verticality (věr″tǐ-kǎl′ǐ-tē) The ability to perceive accurately the vertical position in the absence of environmental cues. Deficits in vertical perception may result in a tendency for patients to fall.

verticillate (věr-tǐs′ǐl-āt, -tǐs-ǐl′āt) [L.

verticillus, a little whirl] Arranged like the spokes of a wheel or a whorl.

vertiginous (vĕr-tĭj'ĭ-nŭs) [L. *vertiginosus,* one suffering from dizziness] Pert. to or afflicted with vertigo.

vertigo (vĕr'tĭ-gō, vĕr-tī'gō) [L. *vertigo,* a turning round] The sensation of moving around in space (subjective vertigo) or of having objects move about the person (objective vertigo). Vertigo is sometimes inaccurately used as a synonym for dizziness, lightheadedness, or giddiness. It may be caused by a variety of entities, including middle ear disease; toxic conditions such as those caused by salicylates, alcohol, or streptomycin; sunstroke; postural hypotension; or toxemia due to food poisoning or infectious diseases. SEE: *vection* (2).

PATIENT CARE: Assessment should include whether the patient experiences a sense of turning or whirling and its direction; whether it is intermittent and the time of day it occurs; whether it is associated with drugs, turning over in bed, occupation, or menses; whether it is associated with nausea and vomiting or with nystagmus and migraine. Safety measures, such as the use of siderails in bed, are instituted. The patient should ambulate gradually after a slow, assisted move from a sitting position. The call bell should be available at all times; tissues, water, and other supplies should be within easy reach; and furniture and other obstacles should be removed from the path of ambulation. The patient who has undergone ear surgery and experiences severe vertigo should be confined to bed for several days and then begin to gradually increase activity.

   alternobaric v. Vertigo associated with a sudden decrease in the pressure to which the inner ear is exposed. This could occur when a scuba diver ascends quickly or when an aircraft ascends quickly. SEE: *bends.*

   auditory v. Vertigo due to disease of the ear.

   benign paroxysmal positional v. ABBR: BPPV. A disorder of the inner ear (labyrinth) characterized by intermittent attacks of vertigo triggered by positional changes of the head. Each episode of vertigo may last from less than a minute to a few minutes, with varying degrees of symptom severity. Episodes may recur for weeks intermittently over a period of years.

   SYMPTOMS: A sudden change in head position (such as turning over from one side to another in bed) brings on symptoms that may include dizziness or vertigo, lightheadedness, imbalance, and nausea. Dropping the head back when lying down, rolling over in bed, and getting out of bed are common problematic motions. BPPV may be called

"top shelf" vertigo because its sufferers often feel dizzy and unsteady when tipping their heads back to look up. Stationary beauty parlor hairdryers may bring on symptoms. Symptoms of vertigo are often accompanied by nystagmus.

   PATIENT CARE: Motion sickness medications (e.g., the antihistamine meclizine) may be prescribed to control associated nausea. Several physical maneuvers (habituation or Brand-Daroff exercises) taught to the patient provide effective relief of symptoms. SYN: *canalithiasis.* SEE: *canalith repositioning maneuver.*

   central v. Vertigo caused by disease of the central nervous system.

   cerebral v. Vertigo due to brain disease.

   epidemic v. Vertigo that may occur in epidemic form. It is believed to be due to vestibular neuronitis.

   epileptic v. Vertigo accompanying or following an epileptic attack.

   essential v. Vertigo from an unknown cause.

   gastric v. Vertigo associated with a gastric disturbance.

   horizontal v. Vertigo that occurs while the patient is supine.

   hysterical v. Vertigo accompanying hysteria.

   labyrinthine v. An out-of-date term for Ménière disease.

   laryngeal v. Fainting that occurs while coughing vigorously.

   objective v. Vertigo in which stationary objects appear to be moving.

   ocular v. Vertigo caused by disease of the eye.

   organic v. Vertigo due to a brain lesion.

   peripheral v. Vertigo due to disturbances in the peripheral areas of the central nervous system.

   positional v. Vertigo that occurs when the head is tilted toward a specific axis. SYN: *postural v.* SEE: *benign paroxysmal v.; Brandt-Daroff maneuvers; canalith repositioning maneuver.*

   postural v. Positional **v.**

   rotary v. Subjective **v.**

   subjective v. Vertigo in which the patient has the sensation of turning or rotating. SYN: *rotary v.*

   toxic v. Vertigo caused by the presence of a toxin in the body.

   vertical v. Vertigo produced by standing or by looking up or down.

   vestibular v. Vertigo due to disease or malfunction of the vestibular apparatus.

verumontanitis (vĕr″ū-mŏn″tăn-ī'tĭs) [L. *veru,* spit, dart, + *montanus,* mountainous, + Gr. *itis,* inflammation] Inflammation of the verumontanum. SYN: *colliculitis.*

verumontanum (vĕr″ū-mŏn-tā'nŭm) [L.

veru, spit, dart, + *montanus*, mountainous] An elevation on the floor of the prostatic portion of the urethra where the seminal ducts enter.

Vesalius, Andreas (vi-săl'ē-ŭs) Latinized form of Andreas van Wesel (Vesal), Flemish anatomist, 1514–1564.

vein of V. The small emissary vein from the cavernous sinus passing through the foramen of Vesalius and conveying blood to the pterygoid plexus.

vesica (vĕ-sī'kă) [L.] A bladder.

vesical (vĕs'ĭ-kăl) Pert. to or shaped like a bladder.

vesical reflex SEE: under *reflex*.

vesicant (vĕs'ĭ-kănt) [L. *vesicare*, to blister] **1.** Blistering; causing or forming blisters. **2.** An agent used to produce blisters. It is much less severe in its effects than are escharotics. **3.** A blistering gas used in chemical warfare. SYN: *vesicatory*. SEE: *gas, vesicant*.

vesication (vĕs'ĭ-kā'shŭn) **1.** The process of blistering. **2.** A blister.

vesicatory (vĕs'ĭ-kă-tor''ē) Vesicant.

vesicle (ves'ĭ-kĕl) [L. *vesicula*, a little bladder] A small blister-like elevation on the skin containing serous fluid. Vesicles may vary in diameter from a few millimeters to a centimeter. They may be round, transparent, opaque, or dark elevations of the skin, sometimes containing seropurulent or bloody fluid. In sudamina, they result from sweat that cannot escape from the skin; in herpes, they are mounted on an inflammatory base, having no tendency to rupture but associated with burning pain. In herpes zoster, they follow dermatomes. In dermatitis venenata, they result from contact with poison ivy or oak and are accompanied by great itching. They are also seen in dermatitis herpetiformis or multiformis. In impetigo contagiosa, they occur, esp. in children, in discrete form, flat and umbilicated, filled with straw-colored fluid, with no tendency to break. They dry up, forming yellow crusts with little itching. They are also seen in vesicular eczema, molluscum contagiosum, miliaria (prickly heat or heat rash), chickenpox, smallpox, and scabies. SEE: *herpes; miliaria*.

brain v. One of the five embryonic subdivisions of the brain.

compound v. Multilocular **v.**

optic v. A hollow outgrowth from the lateral aspects of the embryonic brain. The retinae and optic nerves develop from these paired vesicles.

seminal v. One of two saccular glands below the urinary bladder in males. The duct from each joins the vas deferens on its own side to form the ejaculatory duct. The seminal vesicle produces an alkaline, fructose-rich secretion that enhances sperm motility and nourishes the sperm.

synaptic v. A membranous sac located within the presynaptic membrane of an axon terminal and containing a neurotransmitter.

transfer v. An intracellular vesicle that carries proteins from one organelle to another; e.g., from the endoplasmic reticulum to the Golgi apparatus.

vesico- [L. *vesica*, bladder] Prefix meaning *bladder, vesicle*.

vesicocele (vĕs'ĭ-kō-sēl'') [L. *vesica*, bladder, + Gr. *kele*, tumor, swelling] Hernia of the bladder into the vagina. SYN: *cystocele*.

vesicoclysis (vĕs''ĭ-kŏk'lĭ-sĭs) ['' + Gr. *klysis*, a washing] Injection of fluid into the bladder.

vesicofixation (vĕs''ĭ-kō-fĭks-ā'shŭn) [L. *vesica*, bladder, + *fixatio*, a fixing] Attachment of the uterus to the bladder or the bladder to the abdominal wall.

vesicoprostatic (vĕs''ĭ-kō-prŏs-tăt'ĭk) ['' + Gr. *prostates*, prostate] Pert. to the bladder and prostate.

vesicopustule (vĕs'ĭ-kō-pŭs'tūl) ['' + *pustula*, blister] A vesicle in which pus has developed.

vesicostomy (vĕs''ĭ-kŏs'tō-mē) ['' + Gr. *stoma*, mouth] Surgical production of an opening into the bladder.

vesicotomy (vĕs''ĭ-kŏt'ō-mē) ['' + Gr. *tome*, incision] Incision of the bladder.

vesicoureteral (vĕs''ĭ-kō-ū-rē'tĕr-ăl) ['' + Gr. *oureter*, ureter] Pert. to the urinary bladder and a ureter.

vesicouterine (vĕs''ĭ-kō-ū'tĕr-ĭn) ['' + *uterinus*, pert. to the womb] Pert. to the urinary bladder and uterus.

vesicula (vĕ-sĭk'ū-lă) *pl.* **vesiculae** [L.] A small bladder or vesicle.

vesicular (vĕ-sĭk'ū-lăr) Pert. to vesicles or small blisters.

vesicular eczema SEE: under *eczema*.

vesiculated (vĕ-sĭk'ū-lāt''ĕd) Having vesicles present.

vesiculation (vĕ-sĭk''ū-lā'shŭn) [L. *vesicula*, a tiny bladder] The formation of vesicles or the state of having or forming them.

vesiculectomy (vĕ-sĭk''ū-lĕk'tō-mē) ['' + Gr. *ektome*, excision] Partial or complete excision of a vesicle, particularly a seminal vesicle.

vesiculitis (vĕ-sĭk''ū-lī'tĭs) ['' + Gr. *itis*, inflammation] Inflammation of a vesicle, particularly the seminal vesicle.

vesiculo-, vesicul- [L. *vesicula*, little bladder, vesicle] Prefixes meaning *vesicle*.

vesiculogram (vĕ-sĭk'ū-lō-grăm) ['' + Gr. *gramma*, something written] A radiograph of the seminal vesicles.

vesiculography (vĕ-sĭk''ū-lŏg'ră-fē) ['' + Gr. *graphein*, to write] Radiography of the seminal vesicles after the injection of a contrast medium. This procedure has been replaced by ultrasound imaging.

vesiculopapular (vĕ-sĭk''ū-lō-pă-pŭl''ū-lăr) ['' + *papula*, pimple] Pert. to vesicles and papules.

vesiculopustular (vĕ-sĭk″ū-lō-pŭs′tū-lăr) [″ + *pustula,* blister] Pert. to vesicles and pustules.

vesiculotomy (vĕ-sĭk″ū-lŏt′ō-mē) [″ + Gr. *tome,* incision] Surgical incision into a vesicle, as a seminal vesicle.

vesiculotubular (vĕ-sĭk″ū-lō-tū′bū-lăr) [″ + *tubularis,* like a tube] Pert. to sounds from auscultation of the chest that have both vesicular and tubular qualities.

Vespidae (vĕs′pĭ-dē) [L. *vespa,* wasp] A family of wasps, including paper wasps, hornets, and yellow jackets.

Vespula vulgaris (vĕs′pūl-ă vūl-gār′ĭs) [NL., common (little) wasp] The scientific name for the yellow jacket. The yellow jacket is a black-and-yellow-striped stinging wasp whose venom, abbreviated *Ves v* by the World Health Organization, may cause anaphylaxis in susceptible individuals.

vessel (vĕs′ĕl) [Fr. *vessel* fr. L. *vascellum,* a little vessel] A tube, duct, or canal to convey the fluids of the body. SYN: *vas.*

   blood v. Any of the vessels carrying blood (arteries, veins, and capillaries).

   collateral v. A vessel parallel to the vessel from which it arose.

   conception v. ABBR: CV. In acupuncture, a meridian that runs down the midline of the body from the chin to the perineum.

   conduit v. One of the large blood vessels that conducts fluid from the heart to the systemic circulation. The elasticity of these vessels is an important factor in the development of hypertension.

   governor v. ABBR: GV. One of the meridians used in acupuncture and shiatsu. It runs along the center of the back of the body.

   great v. One of the large blood vessels entering and leaving the heart.

   lacteal v. SEE: *lacteal.*

   lymphatic v. SEE: *lymphatic.*

   mixing v. An animal infected by more than one influenza virus at a time and in which the genes of the virus may assort themselves in novel, potentially hazardous combinations.

   nutrient v. One of the vessels supplying specific areas such as the interior of bones.

vestibular bulb One of the two sacculated collections of veins, lying on either side of the vagina beneath the bulbocavernosus muscle, connected anteriorly by the pars intermedia, and through this strip of cavernous tissue communicating with the erectile tissue of the clitoris. The vestibular bulbs are the homologues of the male corpus spongiosum. Injury during labor may give rise to troublesome bleeding. SEE: *Bartholin gland; vagina; vestibule of vagina.*

vestibular nerve A main division of the acoustic or eighth cranial nerve; arises

in the vestibular ganglion and is concerned with equilibrium.

vestibule (vĕs′tĭ-būl″) A space, chamber, or cavity forming the entryway to another cavity. **vestibular** (ves-tib′yŭ-lăr), *adj.*

   buccal v. The part of the oral vestibule bounded by the teeth, gingiva, and alveolar processes and laterally by the cheek.

   laryngeal v. The portion of the larynx above the vocal cords.

   oral v. The thin space between the teeth and gums, and the lips and cheeks.

   nasal v. The anterior part of the nostrils, containing the vibrissae.

   vaginal v. An almond-shaped space between the lines of attachment of the labia minora. The clitoris is situated at the superior angle; the inferior boundary is the fourchette. The vestibule is approx. 4 to 5 cm long and 2 cm in greatest width when the labia minora are separated. Four major structures open into the vestibule: the urethra anteriorly, the vagina into the midportion, and the two secretory ducts of the glands of Bartholin laterally. The mucous membrane is stratified squamous epithelium. SEE: *Bartholin gland; vagina; vestibular bulb.*

vestibulodynia (ves-tib″yŭ-lō-din′ē-ă) [*vestibule* + *-odynia*] Vulvodynia.

vestibuloplasty (vĕs-tĭb′ū-lō-plăs″tē) [″ + Gr. *plassein,* to mold] Plastic surgery of the vestibule of the mouth.

vestibulotomy (vĕs-tĭb″ū-lŏt′ō-mē) [″ + Gr. *tome,* incision] Surgical incision into the vestibule of the inner ear.

vestibulum (vĕs-tĭb′ū-lŭm) *pl.* **vestibula** [L.] Vestibule.

vestige (vĕs′tĭj) [L. *vestigium,* footstep] A small degenerate or incompletely developed structure that has been more fully developed in the embryo or in a previous stage of the species.

vestigial (vĕs-tĭj′ē-ăl) Pert. to a vestige. SYN: *rudimentary.*

vestigium (vĕs-tĭj′ē-ŭm) *pl.* **vestigia** [L., a footstep] Vestige.

veterinarian (vĕt″ĕr-ĭ-nār′ē-ăn) One who is trained and licensed to practice veterinary medicine and surgery.

veterinary (vĕt′ĕr-ĭ-nār″ē) **1.** Pert. to animals, their diseases, and their treatment. **2.** A veterinarian.

VF *ventricular **fibrillation**;* vocal ***fremitus.***

V factor SEE: under *factor.*

V.H. *viral hepatitis.*

via (vē′ă, vī′ă) *pl.* **viae** [L.] Any passage in the body such as nasal, intestinal, or vaginal.

viability (vī″ă-bĭl′ĭ-tē) [L. *vita,* life, + *habilis,* fit] The capacity for living, growing, developing, or surviving. It is used, for example, in reference to a premature fetus once it reaches a certain size or gestational age, or in determining the likelihood that an injured limb or transplanted organ will survive or flourish. **viable,** *adj.*

Viagra SEE: *sildenafil.*

vial (vī′ăl) [Gr. *phiale,* a drinking cup] A small glass bottle for medicines or chemicals.

   multiple-dose v. A container that holds more than one dose of a medication.

⚠️ Contamination of multiple-dose vials may occur when health care providers fail to follow standard precautions or sterile procedures. Multiple-dose vials should be stored at temperatures specified by the manufacturer or pharmacist and be discarded when or if contamination is suspected or after the expiration date on the vial.

   single-dose v. A container that holds enough medication for one patient's immediate needs. Single-dose vials should not be reused or refilled.

viator (vī′ă-tŏr) An individual, usually one with a terminal illness, who sells rights to his or her insurance policy in exchange for an antemortem benefit collection.

vibex (vī′běks) *pl.* **vibices** [L. *vibix,* mark of a blow] A narrow linear mark of hemorrhage into the skin.

vibration (vī-brā′shŭn) **1.** A to-and-fro movement. SYN: *oscillation.* **2.** A form of massage that involves shaking, quivering, trembling, swinging, rocking, or back-and-forth movements. It is most commonly applied with the fingers, a full hand, or an appliance. Chest-wall vibration is a component of pulmonary hygiene; it improves respiratory function in patients with chronic obstructive pulmonary disease, and can be used as an adjunctive treatment for pneumonia when it is used with postural drainage.

vibrative (vīb′ră-tĭv) **1.** Vibratory. **2.** Pert. to sound produced by vibration of parts of the respiratory tract as air passes through.

vibrator (vī′brāt″ŏr) [L. *vibrator,* a shaker] A device that produces rapid to-and-fro movements in the body or one of its parts. In health care, vibrators are used in hearing aids and middle ear implants; in pulmonary hygiene to assist in clearing secretions or to stimulate diaphragmatic movement; in patients with sexual dysfunction (such as patients with spinal cord injuries affecting orgasm, or other orgasmic difficulties); or in the relief of muscle spasm in some patients with neurological deficits.

   whole body v. Exposure of the entire body to vibration as would occur in occupations such as truck and tractor drivers, jackhammer operators, helicopter pilots, and construction workers using various vibration-producing tools. Such exposure may produce diseases of the peripheral nerves, prostatitis, and back disorders.

vibratory (vī′brā-tō″rē) [L. *vibrator,* a shaker] Having a vibrating or oscillatory movement.

vibratory sense SEE: under *sense.*

Vibrio (vib′rē-ō) A genus of curved, motile, gram-negative bacilli, several of which may be pathogenic for humans.

   V. cholerae The causative agent of cholera.

   V. mimicus A species that is a recognized cause of gastroenteritis (nausea, vomiting, watery diarrhea) in people who consume raw seafood and shellfish.

   V. parahaemolyticus A marine vibrio, a common cause of gastroenteritis involving raw or poorly cooked seafood.

   V. vulnificus A marine vibrio that may cause fulminant gangrene if it contaminates wounds or may cause fatal septicemia if ingested by those with impaired gastric, liver, kidney, or immune function. The usual source in such cases is raw shellfish.

vibrio (vib′rē-ō) *pl.* **vibriones** An organism of the genus *Vibrio.* SEE: *bacteria* for illus.

vibriocidal (vĭb″rē-ō-sī′dăl) Destructive to vibrio organisms.

vibrion (vē″brē-ŏn′) [Fr.] A vibrio.

vibriosis (vĭb″rē-ō′sĭs) Infection with bacteria of the genus *Vibrio.*

vibrissae (vī-brĭs′ē) *sing.,* **vibrissa** [L. *vibrissa,* that which shakes] Stiff hairs within the nostrils at the anterior nares.

vibromassage (vī″brō-mă-sazh′) A massage in which a mechanical vibrator is used. It is used in rehabilitation, e.g., in desensitizing surgical incisions or reducing excessive scarring.

vibrometer (vī-brŏm′ĕt-ĕr) [L. *vibrare,* to shake, + Gr. *metron,* measure] A device used to measure the vibratory sensation threshold. It is particularly useful in judging the progression or remission of peripheral neuropathy.

vibrotactile (vī″brō-tăk′tĭl) [″ + ″] Pert. to the sense of touch that perceives vibrations.

vibrotactile aid SEE: under *aid.*

vicarious (vī-kā′rē-ŭs) [L. *vicarius,* change, alternation] Acting as a substitute; pert. to assumption of the function of one organ by another.

vicarious learning Learning through indirect experience.

Vicodin (vī′kŭ-dĭn) SEE: *hydrocodone bitartrate.*

Vicq d'Azyr tract (vik-dă-zēr′) [Felix Vicq d'Azyr, Fr. anatomist, 1748–1794] A large myelinated bundle arising in mammillary nuclei and terminating in the anterior thalamic nuclei of the brain.

vidarabine (vī-dăr′ă-bēn) An antiviral

agent effective against the herpes simplex and herpes zoster–varicella viruses.

video-assisted Facilitated by live televised images; used for certain surgical techniques.

video clip A brief, recorded, viewable file linked to a website or an electronic message used to educate students or to relay visual information, e.g., from real-time ultrasonography or angiography, from one user to another.

video display terminal ABBR: VDT. A terminal used in information processing (computer terminal) and entertainment (TV picture tube) that produces an image on a screen (target) by bombarding it with electrons. This causes the fluorescent material that coats the screen to emit light. The effects on workers involved with the use of VDTs have been investigated with respect to a variety of factors. There is no evidence that reproductive or visual health is impaired by working with VDTs. Those who work with VDTs may experience musculoskeletal difficulties if the workplaces are poorly designed. This may be due to the screen being positioned in a way that promotes poor posture, or the chair being of improper design. SEE: *ergonomics.*

video electroencephalography ABBR: V-EEG. The simultaneous use of digital video recording and 16-channel electroencephalography. It is used as a diagnostic aid in refractory epilepsy and may help confirm a diagnosis of psychogenic seizures.

videofluoroscopy (vid′ē-ō-floo(-ŏ)r″os′kŏ-pē″) [*video* + *fluoroscopy*] A videotaped dynamic x-ray of the functioning of an organ, esp. in the gastrointestinal tract.

videognosis (vĭd″ē-ŏg-nō′sĭs) [L. *videre,* to see, + Gr. *gnosis,* knowledge] Diagnosis using data and radiographic images transmitted by the use of television.

videokeratography, video keratography (vid′ē-ō-ker″ă-tog′ră-fē) Corneal **topography.**

video microscopy SEE: under *microscopy.*

video-stroboscope A closed-circuit television recording technique used to obtain images while the field is illuminated by use of a stroboscope. Using this provides sequential views of objects in motion.

vidian artery (vĭd′ē-ăn) SEE: under *artery.*

vidian nerve SEE: under *nerve.*

view (vū) [Fr. *veue,* sight fr L. *viduta,* seen] A body part as seen in an x-ray image.

PATIENT CARE: A radiographic view is described from the viewer's perspective, i.e., a PA (posteroanterior) projection is an AP (anteroposterior) view.

view box A device made of lights placed behind a translucent screen and used to provide backlighting for a radiographic image. It helps clinicians see the brightness, contrast, and details of an image. Also known as an illuminator.

vigil (vĭj′ĭl) [L., awake] Insomnia, wakefulness.

coma v. A delirious, drowsy state in which the patient is partially conscious and occasionally responsive to stimuli. SEE: *vigilambulism.*

vigilambulism (vĭj″ĭl-ăm′bū-lĭzm) [″ + *ambulare,* to walk, + Gr. *-ismos,* condition] Automatism that occurs while the person is awake; resembles somnambulism.

vigilance (vĭj′ĭ-lăns) [L. *vigilantia,* wastefulness] The condition of being attentive, alert, and watchful.

vignetting (vĭn-yĕt′ĭng) In radiology, a loss in brightness and focus toward the periphery of the output phosphor during image intensification.

vigor (vĭg′or) [L.] Active force or strength of body or mind.

Villaret syndrome (vē-la-rā′) [Maurice Villaret, Fr. neurologist, 1877–1946] Ipsilateral paralysis of the 9th, 10th, 11th, 12th, and sometimes the 7th cranial nerves and the cervical sympathetic fibers. It is caused by a lesion in the posterior retroparotid space. The signs and symptoms include paralysis and anesthesia of the pharyngeal area with difficulty swallowing; loss of taste sensation in the posterior third of the tongue; paralysis of the vocal cords and the sternocleidomastoid and trapezius muscles; and Horner's syndrome.

villi (vĭl′ī) [L.] Pl. of villus.

villoma (vĭ-lō′mă) [L. *villus,* tuft of hair, + Gr. *oma,* tumor] A villous tumor.

villose, villous (vĭl′ōs, vĭl′ŭs) [L. *villus,* tuft of hair] Pert. to or furnished with villi or with fine hairlike extensions.

villositis (vĭl″ōs-ī′tĭs) [″ + Gr. *itis,* inflammation] Inflammation of the placental villi.

villosity (vĭ-lŏs′ĭ-tē) The condition of being covered with villi.

villus (vĭl′ŭs) *pl.* **villi** [L., tuft of hair] A small fold or projection of some mucous membranes.

arachnoid v. Arachnoid granulation.

chorionic v. One of the tiny vascular projections of the chorionic surface that become vascular and help to form the placenta. SEE: *embryo* for illus.; *chorion.*

intestinal v. One of the multiple, minute projections of the intestinal mucosa into the lumen of the small intestine. These projections increase the surface area for absorption of water and nutrients; each contains a capillary network and a lacteal. SEE: illus.

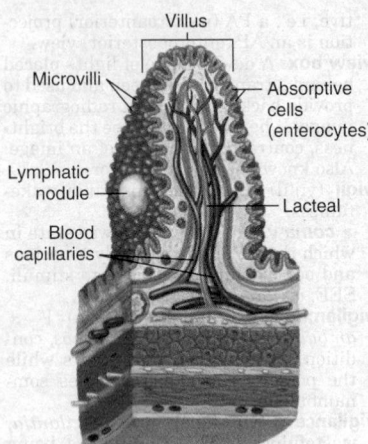

VILLI OF SMALL INTESTINE

villusectomy (vĭl″ŭs-ĕk′tō-mē) [″ + Gr. *ektome*, excision] Surgical removal of a synovial villus.

VIN *vulvar intraepithelial neoplasia.*

Vinca (vĭn′kă) A genus of herbs including periwinkles, from which vincristine and vinblastine are obtained.

Vincent angina (vin′sĕnt) [Fr. physician, 1862–1950] Necrotizing ulcerative **gingivitis**.

vinclozolin A fungicide used in agriculture, esp. for the protection of vegetables and fruits (e.g., grapevines in vineyards). It is an antiandrogen, (an agent that opposes the action of male hormones).

vinculum (vĭn′kū-lŭm) *pl.* **vincula** [L., to bind, tie] A uniting band or bundle. SYN: *frenulum; frenum; ligament.*

    v. tendinum **1.** Slender tendinous filaments connecting the phalanges with the flexor tendons. **2.** The ringlike ligament of the ankle or wrist.

vinegar (vĭn′ĕ-găr) [ME. *vinegre,* from Fr. *vin,* wine, + *aigre,* sour] An impure solution containing 4% to 6% acetic acid. It is the product of fermentation of weak alcoholic solutions such as apple cider. SEE: *condiment.*

vinyl (vī′nĭl) The univalent hydrocarbon molecule, $CH_2{=}CH{-}$.

    v. benzene, vinylbenzene Styrene.

    v. chloride $CH_2{=}CHCl$, a vinyl radical attached to a chlorine atom. It is used commercially to make pipes, tubing, and plastic resin. Some people exposed to vinyl chloride develop hepatic angiosarcoma.

    v. cyanide $CH_3{=}CHCN$, a toxic liquid compound used in making plastics. SYN: *acrylonitrile.*

    v. polysiloxane In dentistry, an impression material used to make molded copies of teeth and gums. SYN: *polyvinylsiloxane.*

vinylbenzene (vī′nĭl-ben′zēn″, -ben-zēn′) Styrene.

violaceous (vī″ĕ-lā′shŭs) [L. *violaceus,* violet] Having a purple discoloration, esp. of the skin.

violate (vī′ĕ-lāt″) [L. *violare,* to injure] To harm or injure a person, esp. to rape a female.

violence (vī′ŏ-lĕns) [L. *violentia,* ferocity, vehemence] The use of force or physical compulsion to abuse or damage a person, place, or thing.

    domestic v. Abuse or neglect occurring within families. Domestic violence includes child abuse, spouse abuse, elder abuse, sexual abuse, marital rape, and lapses in household firearm safety.

    intimate partner v. Physical, sexual, or verbal abuse of a spouse or sexual partner.

    PATIENT CARE: Every patient should be screened for intimate partner violence during each health care encounter. Health care settings should have a well-tested screening tool available for caregivers, as well as signs in each waiting room and restroom identifying resources for the abused, such as telephone hotlines and regional shelters. If a patient screens positive for abuse, more complete assessment tools are useful to ascertain the degree of risk that is present. It is important for health care professionals to have a concrete intervention plan in place to protect vulnerable patients.

    perinatal v. Abuse or assault of women just before or after childbirth.

    risk for v., directed at others Behavior in which an individual demonstrates that he or she can be physically, emotionally, or sexually harmful to others. SEE: *Nursing Diagnoses Appendix.*

    risk for v., directed at self Behavior in which a person demonstrates that he can be physically, emotionally, or sexually harmful to himself. SEE: *Nursing Diagnoses Appendix.*

violet (vī′ō-lĕt) [ME. *violett,* from L. *viola,* violet] One of the colors of the visible spectrum; similar to purple.

    gentian v. $C_{25}H_{30}ClN_3$; a dye derived from coal tar that is widely used as a stain in histology, cytology, and bacteriology. It has also been used therapeutically as a topical anti-infective. Its chemical name is hexamethylpararosaniline chloride.

viosterol (vī-ŏs′tĕr-ōl) A solution of irradiated ergosterol in vegetable oil. SYN: *calciferol.*

viper (vī′pĕr) [L. *vipera,* snake or serpent] Any venomous snake of the family Viperidae. SEE: *Viperidae.*

    pit v. Any viper of the subfamily Crotalinae, found in Asia and the Americas. SEE: *crotaline.*

Viperidae (vī-per′ĭ-dē) [L. *vipera,* snake or serpent + *-idea*] The scientific name for a family of venomous snakes found nearly worldwide, having long, hinged fangs allowing deep penetration and injection of venom. The family includes the European viper, gaboon viper, puff adder, Russel viper, and saw-scaled viper.

VIPoma (vī-pō′mă) [*vasoactive intestinal polypeptide* + *oma,* tumor] A rare form of neuroendocrine tumor that causes watery diarrhea, hypokalemia, and achlorhydria as a result of the release of vasoactive intestinal peptide.

-vir [Fm. *vir(us)* or *vir(al)*] Suffix used in pharmacology to designate an *antiviral agent.*

viral (vī′răl) Pert. to or caused by a virus.

viral breakthrough The ability of a virus, such as hepatitis C or HIV, to mutate into a drug-resistant form during treatment with antiviral drugs. The mutation becomes evident when concentrations of the virus reappear in the plasma of treated patients after initially becoming undetectable.

viral coat Capsid.

viral interference The inhibition of the multiplication of one type of virus by the presence of another virus in the same cell. SEE: *interferon.*

viral load SEE: under *load.*

viral set point SEE: under *point.*

viral transport medium SEE: under *medium.*

Virchow node (fir′kō) Sentinel **node**

viremia (vī″rēm′ē-ă) The presence of viruses in the blood.

vires (vī′rēs) Pl. of vis.

virgin (vĕr′jĭn) [L. *virgo,* a maiden] **1.** A woman or man who has not had sexual intercourse. **2.** Uncontaminated; fresh; new.

virginal (vĕr′jĭn-ăl) [L. *virgo,* a maiden] Pert. to a virgin or to virginity.

virginity (vĕr-jĭn′ĭt-ē) [L. *virginitas,* maidenhood] The state of being a virgin; not having experienced sexual intercourse.

virile (vĭr′ĭl) [L. *virilis,* masculine] Masculine.

virilism (vĭr′ĭl-ĭzm) [″ + Gr. *-ismos,* condition] The presence or development of male secondary characteristics in a woman.

virility (vĭr-ĭl′ĭ-tē) [L. *virilitas,* masculinity] **1.** The state of possessing masculine qualities. **2.** Sexual potency in the male.

virilization (vĭr″ĭ-lĭ-zā′shŭn) The production of masculine secondary sex characteristics in a woman. These include deepening of the voice, development of male-type baldness, clitoral enlargement, and increased growth of facial and body hair. Virilization may be caused by one of several endocrine diseases that lead to excess production of testosterone, or by the woman's taking anabolic steroids, e.g., to attempt to en-

hance muscular development. SYN: *virilescence.*

virion (vī′rē-ŏn, vī′rē-ŏn) A complete virus particle; a unit of genetic material, the genome, surrounded by a protective protein coat, the capsid. Sometimes the capsid is surrounded by a lipid envelope. SYN: *particle* (4). SEE: *capsid.*

viroid (vī′royd) A small, naked, infectious molecule of RNA. Viroids differ from viruses by the absence of a dormant phase and by genomes that are much smaller than those of known viruses.

virologic, virological (vī″rŏ-loj′ĭk, vī″rŏ-loj′i-kăl) Pert. to virology. **virologically** (vī″rŏ-loj′i-k(ă-)lē), *adv.*

virology (vī-rŏl′ō-jē) [L. *virus,* poison, + Gr. *logos,* word, reason] The study of viruses and viral diseases.

viropexis (vī″rō-pĕk′sĭs) [″ + Gr. *pexis,* fixation] The fixation of a virus particle to a cell. This leads to the inclusion of the virus inside the cell.

virotherapy (vī″rō-thĕr′ă-pē) The use of viruses to infect and kill rapidly replicating cells, esp. cancer cells. Oncolytic viruses used in virotherapy include some adenoviruses, influenza virus, mumps virus, Newcastle virus, and poliovirus.

virotoxin A poisonous substance (usually a protein) released by a virus that destroys or alters the metabolic integrity of cells.

virtual (vĭr′choo-ăl) [L. *virtualis,* (being) in essence or effect] **1.** Having actual authority or real power without official acknowledgement or title. **2.** In computer technology, made, conducted, or simulated by software on a computer, computer network, or online. **virtuality** (vĭr″choo-al′ĭt-ē), *n.* **virtually** (-ă-lē), *adv.*

virtual colonoscopy SEE: under *colonoscopy.*

virucide, viricide (vī′rŭ-sīd″) [*virus* + -*cide*] An agent that destroys or inactivates a virus, esp. a chemical substance used on living tissue. **virucidal** (vī″rŭ-sīd′ăl), *adj.*

virulence (vir′yŭ-lĕns) [L. *virulentia,* stench] **1.** The relative power of an agent or a microorganism to cause harm or disease. Properties that influence the virulence of an organism include 1. the strength of its adhesion molecules, which link it to the target cell; 2. its ability to secrete enzymes or exotoxins that damage target cells, or endotoxins that interfere with the body's normal regulatory systems; and 3. its ability to inhibit or evade the actions of white blood cells and their chemical mediators. SEE: *immunocompetence; immunocompromised.* **2.** The property of being virulent; venomousness, as of a disease. SEE: *attenuation.*

virulent (vĭr′ū-lĕnt) [L. *virulentus,* poison] **1.** Very poisonous. **2.** Infectious;

able to overcome the host's defensive mechanism.

viruliferous (vĭr-yŭ-lĭf′ér-ŭs) [*virul(ence)* + ″] Colonized or infected by a virus and able to transmit that virus to another organism.

viruria (vĭr-ūr′ē-ă) [″ + Gr. *ouron,* urine] The presence of viruses in the urine.

virus (vī′rŭs) [L. *virus,* poison] A pathogen composed of nucleic acid within a protein shell, which can grow and reproduce only after infecting a host cell. More than 400 types of viruses that cause a great variety of illness are known. All of them can attach to cell membranes, enter the cytoplasm, take over cellular functions, reproduce their parts, and assemble themselves into mature forms capable of infecting other cells.

Some of the most virulent diseases are caused by viruses, e.g., the hemorrhagic fever caused by Ebola virus. Viruses are also responsible for the common cold, childhood exanthems (such as chickenpox, measles, rubella), latent infections (such as herpes simplex), some cancers or lymphomas (such as Epstein-Barr virus), and diseases of all organ systems.

Although viral architecture is very complex, every virus contains at least a genome and a capsid. Most animal viruses are also surrounded by a lipid envelope, a bilayered membrane analogous to a cell membrane. The envelope may be parasitized from host cells. Its chemical components are phospholipids and glycoproteins. The lipid envelope is frequently dotted with spikes.

Viruses with lipid envelopes have a greater ability to adhere to cell membranes and to avoid destruction by the immune system. Both the capsid and envelope are antigenic. Frequent mutations change some viral antigens so that the lymphocytes are unable to create an antibody that can neutralize the original antigen and its replacement. The common influenza viruses have antigens that mutate or combine readily, requiring new vaccines with each mutation. The body's primary immune defenses against viruses are cytotoxic T lymphocytes, interferons, and, to some extent, immunoglobulins; destruction of the virus often requires destruction of the host cell.

When viruses enter a cell, they may immediately trigger a disease process or remain quiescent for years. They damage the host cell by blocking its normal protein synthesis and using its metabolic machinery for their own reproduction. New viruses are then released either by destroying their host cell or by forming small buds that break off and infect other cells. SEE: illus.; table.

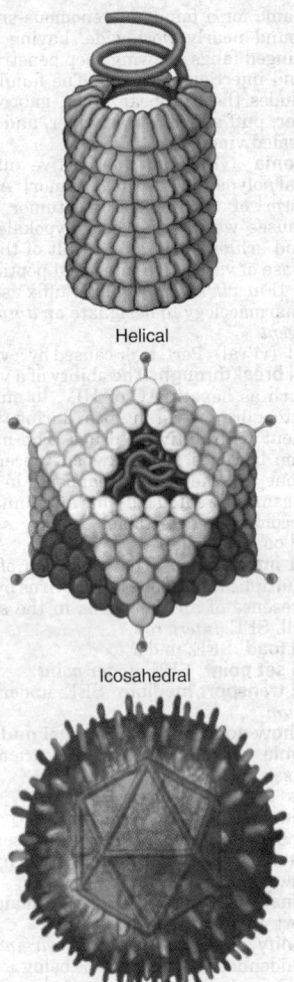

Helical

Icosahedral

Spherical

VIRAL SHAPES

CLASSIFICATION: The 400 known viruses are classified in several ways: by genome core (RNA or DNA), host (animals, plants, or bacteria), method of reproduction (such as retrovirus), mode of transmission (such as enterovirus), and disease produced (such as hepatitis virus).

TREATMENT: Antiviral drugs include such agents as acyclovir (for herpes simplex); oseltamivir and zanamivir (for influenza A); interferons (for chronic hepatitis B and C); ribavirin (for respiratory syncytial virus and chronic hepatitis C); and lamivudine (for HIV).

attenuated v. A virus with reduced

Common Viral Characteristics

Characteristics	Examples
Genetic material	
RNA	HIV, hepatitis A, polio, measles, mumps, rhinovirus, influenza
DNA	Herpesviruses, hepatitis B, adenoviruses, human papilloma viruses, cytomegalovirus
Hosts	
Humans	Measles, mumps, rubella, varicella-zoster, poliovirus
Humans and animals	Rabies, influenza, hantavirus, encephalitis virus
Plants	Tobacco mosaic virus, cowpea mosaic virus
Bacteria	Phages
Envelope	
Present	Herpesviruses, rabies, HIV
Absent	Rotavirus, Norwalk virus, adenovirus
Respiratory	Influenza, parainfluenza, hantavirus
Teratogenic	Varicella-zoster virus, cytomegalovirus, rubella
Neurological and fatal	Rabies
Paralytic encephalitic	Polio, many encephalitis viruses
Fulminant	Yellow fever, hantavirus, Ebola-Marburg
Latent	Herpesviruses
Cancer causing	Human T-cell lymphotrophic virus, hepatitis viruses, papillomavirus

pathogenicity as a result of treatment or repeated passage through hosts.

B v. Cercopithecine **herpesvirus** 1.

bacterial v. Bacteriophage.

Banna v. ABBR: BAV. The type species of the genus Seadornavirus (family Reoviridae), isolated in Asia. It is transmitted to humans by the mosquito or tick bite and is implicated in some cases of encephalitis.

Barmah Forest v. A virus transmitted by mosquito bite that causes rash, fever, joint pain, and stiffness. It is found mostly in Australia and neighboring islands.

cercopithecine v. 1 Cercopithecine **herpesvirus** 1.

cowpea mosaic v. A plant virus used in vaccine development to deliver antigens from pathogens and tumors. Because the virus does not infect animals, it is considered a safe vehicle for antigen display in humans and other species.

coxsackie v. SEE: *coxsackievirus.*

cytomegalic v. ABBR: CMV. Cytomegalovirus.

deer tick v. A Flavivirus that is a cause of meningoencephalitis. It is transmitted to humans by the bite of infected ticks and causes disease similar to that caused by Powassan virus.

defective v. A virus particle that, because of a lack of certain essential factors, is unable to replicate. Sometimes this can be overcome by the presence of a helper virus that provides the missing factor(s).

delta hepatitis v. ABBR: HDV. SEE: *hepatitis D.*

DNA v. A virus such as the papilloma virus and the herpesviruses whose genome is deoxyribonucleic acid (DNA).

EB v. Epstein-Barr virus.

enteric v. Enterovirus.

enteric cytopathogenic human orphan v. ABBR: echovirus. An orphan virus that was accidentally discovered in human feces and is not known to be associated with a disease. Initially, 33 echovirus serotypes were designated, but numbers 10 and 28 have been reclassified. Various serotypes have been associated with aseptic meningitis, encephalitis, acute upper respiratory infection, enteritis, pleurodynia, and myocarditis.

enteric orphan v. SEE: *enteric cytopathogenic human orphan v.*

Epstein-Barr v. SEE: *Epstein-Barr virus.*

fixed v. A rabies virus stabilized and modified but only partially attenuated by serial passage through rabbits.

foamy v. Spumavirus.

GB v. type C Hepatitis G **v.**

Guanarito v. An arenavirus from the Tacaribe virus group that chronically infects rodents. It is the cause of sporadic outbreaks of Venezuelan hemorrhagic fever.

helper v. A virus that permits a defective virus present in the same cell to replicate. SEE: *defective v.*

hepatitis G v. An RNA Flavivirus found in blood in about 2% of blood donors that may be transmitted by injection, drug abuse, sexual contact, transfusions, and childbirth (from mother to infant). It is remotely related to hepatitis C virus. It causes chronic viremia but does not seem to cause hepatitis or liver damage. SYN: *GB v. type C.*

herpes simplex v. ABBR: HSV-1, HSV-2. Either of two human DNA viruses (HSV-1 and -2) that cause repeated painful vesicular eruptions on the genitals and other mucosal surfaces and on the skin. After initial contact with the skin or mucous membranes, the virus migrates along nerve fibers to sensory ganglia, where it establishes a latent infection. Under a variety of stimuli, such as sexual contact, exposure to ultraviolet light, febrile illnesses, or emotional stress, it may reappear, traveling back to the site of initial contact although the vast majority of herpes simplex infections are neither recognized nor symptomatic. The rash caused by the infection has a red base, on which small blisters cluster. Herpetic rashes on the mouth or nose are called *cold sores* or *fever blisters*. SYN: *herpesvirus hominis*. SEE: *Nursing Diagnoses Appendix*.

In immunosuppressed patients, the virus can cause a widely disseminated rash. Some infections with HSV may involve the brain and meninges; these typically cause fevers, headaches, altered mental status, seizures, or coma, requiring parenteral therapy with antiviral drugs. In newborns, infection involving the internal organs also may occur. Experienced ophthalmologists should manage ocular infection with HSVs. Health care providers are at risk for herpetic whitlow (finger infections) from contact with infected mucous membranes if gloves and meticulous hand hygiene are not used.

TREATMENT: Acyclovir and related drugs, e.g., famciclovir, valacyclovir, may be used to treat outbreaks of HSV-1 and HSV-2 and are also effective in preventing recurrences of disease.

PATIENT CARE: Standard precautions prevent spread of the virus. Prescribed antiviral agents and analgesics are administered; their use is explained to the patient, with instruction given about adverse effects to report.

The patient with HSV-1 is instructed to avoid skin-to-skin contact with uninfected individuals when lesions are present or prodromal symptoms are felt. To decrease the discomfort from oral lesions, the patient is advised to use a soft toothbrush or sponge stick, a saline- or bicarbonate-based (not alcohol-based) mouthwash, and oral anesthetics such as viscous lidocaine if necessary. He or she should eat soft foods. Use of lip balm with sunscreen reduces reactivation of oral lesions.

The patient with genital herpes should wash the hands carefully after bathroom use. He or she also should avoid sexual intercourse during the active stage of the disease and should practice safe sex. A pregnant woman must be advised of the potential risk to the infant during vaginal delivery and the use of cesarean delivery if she has an HSV outbreak when labor begins and her membranes have not ruptured. The patient with genital herpes may experience feelings of powerlessness. He requires assistance to identify coping mechanisms, strengths, and support resources; should be encouraged to voice feelings about perceived changes in sexuality and behavior; and should be provided with current information about the disease and treatment options. A referral is made for additional counseling as appropriate.

⚠ Caregivers with active oral or cutaneous lesions should avoid providing patient care.

herpes v. SEE: *herpesvirus*.

human immunodeficiency v. ABBR: HIV. A retrovirus of the subfamily lentivirus that causes acquired immunodeficiency syndrome (AIDS). The most common type of HIV is HIV-1, identified in 1984. HIV-2, first discovered in West Africa in 1986, causes a loss of immune function and the subsequent development of opportunistic infections identical to those associated with HIV-1 infections. The two types developed from separate strains of simian immunodeficiency virus. In the U.S., the number of those infected with HIV-2 is very small, but blood donations are screened for both types of HIV. SEE: illus.; *acquired immunodeficiency syndrome*.

human papilloma v. SEE: under *papillomavirus*.

human T-cell lymphotropic v. type I ABBR: HTLV-I. A virus associated with adult T-cell leukemia.

human T-cell lymphotropic v. type II ABBR: HTLV-II. A virus associated with hairy cell leukemia.

human T-cell lymphotropic v. type III ABBR: HTLV-III. The former name for *human immunodeficiency virus* (HIV).

influenza v. An RNA virus that infects the respiratory tract of humans (as well as birds, pigs, dogs, and horses), causing influenza. It is a roughly spherical virus. It is composed of eight segments, including a nucleoprotein (which folds its nucleic acids and helps them to be transcribed), a hemagglutinin (which helps it to enter cells), a neuraminidase (which helps it to bud out of infected cells), several transcriptases (which make copies of the viral RNA), a matrix protein (which supports the outer membrane), and several nonstructural proteins. The virus mutates frequently and causes annual disease outbreaks, some of which (pandemics) affect millions of people. It can be treated with antiviral drugs and prevented with annual vac-

Normal Immune System

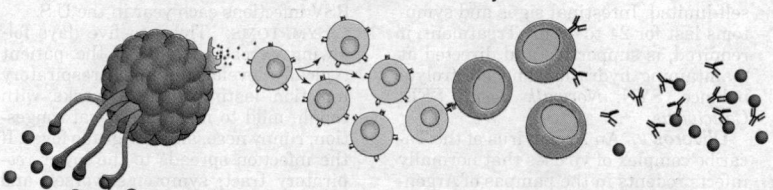

| Phagocyte digests virus | T4 cells multiply to attack virus | T4 cells trigger B cells to produce antibodies | Antibodies label viruses for phagocytosis |

Immune System with HIV

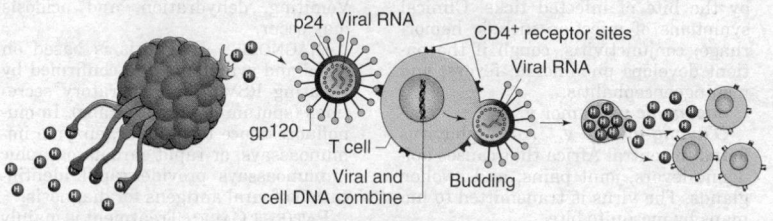

| HIV cannot be destroyed by phagocyte | HIV is unharmed | HIV makes viral DNA in host cell | HIV virus leaves host cell to attack other T4 cells |

EFFECT OF HIV ON IMMUNE SYSTEM

HIV contains several proteins: gp 120 protein around it and viral RNA and p24 protein inside. The gp 120 proteins attach to CD4+ receptors of T lymphocytes; HIV enters the cell and makes viral DNA; the enslaved host cell produces new viruses that bud, which destroy the host cell's membrane, causing cellular death and allowing the virus to leave to attack other CD4+ lymphocyte cells.

cinations that target its frequently evolving antigens.influenza.

JC v. A DNA papovavirus that causes progressive multifocal leukoencephalopathy in immunosuppressed patients. It is carried asymptomatically by a large percentage of the population.

Junin v. An Arenavirus that chronically infects rodents. It is the cause of sporadic outbreaks of Argentine hemorrhagic fever, a potentially lethal infection usually found in South America.

Kunjin v. A group B Flavivirus that is one of the causative agents of encephalitis in Australia.

Kyasanur Forest v. A single-stranded RNA virus transmitted to humans by tick bite. It causes a two-stage illness: fever followed by a brief remission, and then meningoencephalitis, hemorrhagic pneumonia, and hepatic and splenic disruption.

Langat v. ABBR: LGT. A tick-borne Flavivirus, responsible for encephalitis, primarily in mice. It causes mild disease in humans. Its genetic similarity to other tick-borne encephalitis viruses makes it a candidate for the development of encephalitis vaccines.

latent v. A virus that has the ability to infect the host, initially causing little or no evidence of illness but persisting for the lifetime of the infected host; later on, a specific triggering mechanism may cause the virus to produce a clinically apparent disease. This occurs with herpes simplex virus, which remains latent in sensory ganglia and is reactivated by trauma to the skin supplied by the distal sensory nerves associated with these ganglia. After reactivation, the virus may cause localized or generalized lesions in the affected area and the central nervous system.

lytic v. Any virus that, after infecting a cell, lyses it.

masked v. A virus that ordinarily occurs in the host in a noninfective state but is activated and demonstrated by indirect methods.

neurotropic v. A virus that reproduces in nerve tissue.

Nipah v. ABBR: NiV. A member of the family of paramyxoviruses that can cause outbreaks of encephalitis and respiratory disease in humans. It is transmitted to humans from infected swine, e.g., in slaughterhouses.

Norwalk v. ABBR: NLV. A Calicivirus that is the causative organism in over half of the reported cases of epidemic viral gastroenteropathy. It commonly causes nausea, vomiting, and diarrhea. The incubation period ranges from 18 to 72 hr. Outbreaks are usually self-limited. Intestinal signs and symptoms last for 24 to 48 hr. Treatment, if required, is supportive and directed at maintaining hydration and electrolyte balance. SYN: *Norwalk agent.* SEE: *Calicivirus.*

Oliveros v. An Arenavirus of the Tacaribe complex of viruses that normally infects rodents in the pampas of Argentina. It may cause a fatal hemorrhagic fever in humans.

Omsk hemorrhagic fever v. A single-stranded RNA virus in the Flavivirus genus. It can be transmitted to people by the bite of infected ticks. Clinical symptoms of infection include hemorrhage, conjunctivitis, cough if the patient develops pneumonia, fevers, and meningoencephalitis.

oncogenic v. Tumor **v.**

O'nyong-nyong v. An Alphavirus found in central Africa that causes epidemic fevers, joint pains, and swollen glands. The virus is transmitted to humans by mosquito bite.

orphan v. One of several viruses that initially were not thought to be associated with human illness. This group includes the enteroviruses and rhinoviruses.

parainfluenza v. One of a group of viruses that affects infants and young children. It causes respiratory infections that may be mild or may progress to pneumonia. Most infections are so mild as to be clinically inapparent.

Puumala v. ABBR: PUUV. A member of the Hantavirus family and the causative agent of nephropathia epidemica.

Powassan v. A rare Flavivirus, transmitted by tick bite, which occasionally causes encephalitis.

pox v. Poxvirus.

Rauscher leukemia v. SEE: *Rauscher leukemia virus.*

reassortant v. A virus whose genetic material has been recombined or reshuffled so that it contains new nucleic acid sequences, new antigenic structures, and new combinations of protein products.

respiratory syncytial v. ABBR: RSV. A single-stranded RNA virus that is an important cause of upper and lower respiratory tract disease in infants, children, and the older population. When limited to the upper respiratory tract, RSV causes symptoms of the common cold. In the lower respiratory tract, it causes bronchiolitis, pneumonia, or respiratory distress and can be life-threatening. Respiratory syncytial virus is the most common cause of lower respiratory infections in infants and children under age 2. It is spread by physical contact, usually with infected nasal or oral secretions. In the U.S., its season begins in the fall and peaks in winter. About 90,000

young children are hospitalized with RSV infections each year in the U.S.

SYMPTOMS: Three to five days following exposure to RSV, the patient typically develops an upper respiratory infection lasting 1 to 2 weeks with cough, mild to moderate nasal congestion, runny nose, and low-grade fever. If the infection spreads to the lower respiratory tract, symptoms worsen and may include wheezing and difficulty breathing. Infants and children with RSV pneumonia exhibit retractions; rapid grunting respirations, poor oxygenation, and respiratory distress. Vomiting, dehydration, and acidosis may occur.

DIAGNOSIS: Diagnosis is based on signs and symptoms and confirmed by isolating RSV from respiratory secretions (sputum or throat swabs). Immunofluorescence techniques, enzyme immunoassays, or rapid chromatographic immunoassays provide rapid identification of viral antigens for diagnosis.

PATIENT CARE: Treatment is mainly supportive. Antibiotics are not effective. Acetaminophen or ibuprofen are given for pain or fever. Oxygen is administered if the patient's oxygen saturation SpO_2 falls below 92%. Bronchodilators, such as albuterol and epinephrine, are used to treat wheezing. In patients with severe RSV infections, noninvasive positive-pressure ventilation or intubation and mechanic ventilation are required. Intravenous fluids are administered as prescribed if the patient cannot take enough fluid orally. Nasopharyngeal suction may be needed to clear congestion (by bulb syringe for infants).

Strict adherence to infection control measures is important in preventing an outbreak in any facility. This includes using meticulous hand hygiene (the most important step in preventing RSV spread) before donning gloves for patient care, after removing gloves, and if any potentially contaminated surfaces have been touched. Standard and contact precautions should be observed for all patients with known or suspected RSV (gown, mask and eye protection for direct contact with respiratory secretions or droplets). Protective coverings should be removed in this order: gloves (followed by hand hygiene), goggles or face shield, gown, and finally mask or respirator, discarding them in an infectious waste container in the patient's room. The patient with RSV should be in a private room and dedicated equipment should be used in patient care, with terminal equipment disinfection by the appropriate agency facility. Room assignments should be arranged to avoid cross-contamination whenever possible. Individuals with symptoms of respiratory infection should be prevented from caring for or visiting pediatric, immunocompromised, or cardiac patients.

The administration of high doses of respiratory syncytial virus immune globulin is an effective means of preventing lower respiratory tract infection in infants and young children at high risk for contracting this disease. Palivizumab, a monoclonal antibody given intramuscularly, can prevent RSV disease in high-risk infants and children.

Rift Valley v. A Phlebovirus that causes sporadic epidemics of hemorrhagic fever among humans and animals in Africa. It is transmitted by the bite of infected mosquitoes.

RNA v. A virus such as the HIV, influenza virus, and polio virus whose genome is ribonucleic acid (RNA).

Ross River v. An Alphavirus transmitted by mosquito bite that causes fevers, rash, and epidemic arthritis in multiple joints. It is typically found in Australia and neighboring islands.

Sabiá v. An arenavirus that causes Brazilian hemorrhagic fever. The reservoir for the virus is unknown. Ribavirin, which is effective against Lassa fever, may be effective against Brazilian hemorrhagic fever.

sandfly fever v. Toscana **v.**

simian immunodeficiency v. A family of HIV-like retroviruses that primarily infects African green monkeys, in whom it produces an HIV/AIDS-like suppression of immunity.

Sindbis v. An Alphavirus typically found in South Africa or Oceania that is disseminated to humans by mosquitoes of the genus *Culex*. It can cause a transient febrile illness accompanied by a diffuse maculopapular rash and muscle and joint pains.

slow v. A virus that replicates and causes disease indolently. SEE: *slow virus infection*.

street v. A rabies virus obtained from an infected animal rather than from a laboratory strain.

SV 40 v. Simian virus 40, a member of the Papovirus family. The virus produces sarcomas after subcutaneous inoculation into newborn hamsters.

Tacaribe complex v. A group of viruses, originally identified in South America, that cause hemorrhagic fever in humans. They are members of the Arenavirus family and are typically found in rodents. One member of this group is the Sabiá virus.

Tahyna v. ABBR: TAH. A European arbovirus of the Bunyaviridae family. It is transmitted to humans by mosquito bite and causes fevers, respiratory illnesses, encephalitis, and meningitis.

Toscana v. A Bunyavirus transmitted by insect bite, esp. the bite of the sandfly (*Phlebotomus papatasi*). The virus is endemic in Sicily, Cyprus, and elsewhere in the Mediterranean and may cause encephalitis, aseptic meningitis, or septicemia. SYN: *sandfly fever v.*

transfusion-transmissible v. ABBR: TTV. A single-stranded DNA virus, found in recipients of blood transfusions, that colonizes in the liver. It is not known whether the virus causes liver disease, e.g., chronic hepatitis, or benignly colonizes the liver.

tanapox v. A double-stranded DNA poxvirus that occasionally infects humans, causing a pustular, nodular rash, fever, headache, and other symptoms. It is related to other orthopoxviruses (which cause smallpox, monkeypox, and vaccinia).

tumor v. A virus that causes malignant neoplasms. Viruses suspected of causing tumors in humans include Epstein-Barr virus (associated with Burkitt lymphoma), hepatitis B virus (associated with hepatocellular carcinoma), papilloma virus (associated with carcinoma of the cervix), and human herpesvirus 8 (associated with Kaposi sarcoma). SYN: *oncogenic v.*

vaccinia v. A double-stranded DNA virus, the causative agent of cowpox and a member of the Orthopoxvirus genus. Vaccines against smallpox are derived from live cultures of vaccinia virus. SEE: *Orthopoxvirus.*

varicella-zoster v. The herpesvirus that causes chickenpox and shingles. SYN: *human herpesvirus 3.*

West Nile v. A Flavivirus that primarily infects birds but can be transmitted by mosquito bite to humans and other animals. Since West Nile virus was identified in the U.S. in 1999, it has produced a nationwide epidemic of encephalitis. Although infection is usually asymptomatic, signs and symptoms that are more likely to be observed in the very young, the very old, or the very sick include fever, headache, stiff neck, fatigue, loss of appetite, nausea or vomiting, muscle pain, aches, and weakness. Infection is occasionally fatal. Those over age 50 are at greatest risk for serious complications and death.

In 2009, 45 states in the U.S. reported having human cases of West Nile fever. There were 720 reported cases of this viral infection in the U.S. in 2009 and 32 fatalities. Infected patients sometimes suffer long-term consequences of infection, including fatigue and malaise, difficulty concentrating or thinking, or movement disorders. The disease is sometimes spread from patient to patient by blood transfusion or organ transplantation.

PATIENT CARE: Disease transmission can be prevented with mosquito control and mosquito avoidance measures. Health care professionals should advise patients and families to limit time out of doors, esp. at dusk and dawn, to wear protective clothing (long sleeves, long pants, and socks), to place mosquito netting over infant carriers or strollers, and to apply an FDA-approved insect repellant (e.g., DEET, picaridin, or oil of lemon eucalyptus). Mosquito breeding grounds should be eliminated: standing water should be removed from flower pots, bird baths, pool covers, rain gutters, and discarded tires. Window and door screens should be installed and kept in good repair to prevent mosquitoes from entering homes. SEE: illus.

VECTOR OF WEST NILE VIRUS

The Culex mosquito, vector of West Nile virus

virusemia (vī″rŭs-ēm′ē-ă) [″ + Gr. *haima*, blood] Viremia.

virus shedding, viral shedding The release of a virus from the host.

virustatic (vīr″ŭ-stăt′ĭk) [″ + Gr. *statikos*, bringing to a standstill] Stopping the growth of viruses.

vis (vĭs) *pl.* **vires** [L., strength] Force, strength, energy, power.

VISA, VRSA (vē′să) *Vancomycin-Intermediate/Resistant Staphylococcus aureus.*

viscera (vĭs′ĕr-ă) *sing.,* **viscus** [L.] Internal organs enclosed within a cavity, esp. the abdominal organs.

visceral (vĭs′ĕr-ăl) [L. *viscera*, body organs] Pert. to viscera.

visceral fat SEE: under *fat.*

visceral malposition The appearance of an internal organ in the wrong location within the body, e.g., on the wrong side of the body.

viscero-, viscer-, visceri- [L. *viscera*, body organs] Prefixes meaning *viscera.*

viscerocranium (vĭs″ĕ-rō-krā′nē-ŭm) [*viscero-* + *cranium*] That portion of the skull derived from the pharyngeal arches. The viscerocranium comprises the bones of the face. SEE: *neurocranium.*

viscerogenic (vĭs″ĕr-ō-jĕn′ĭk) [″ + Gr.

gennan, to produce] Originating in the viscera.

visceromegaly (vĭs″ĕr-ō-mĕg′ă-lē) [″ + Gr. *megalos,* great] Generalized enlargement of the abdominal visceral organs.

visceroptosis (vĭs″ĕr-ŏp-tō′sĭs) [″ + Gr. *ptosis,* a dropping] Downward displacement of a viscus.

viscerosensory (vĭs″ĕr-ō-sĕn′sō-rē) [″ + *sensorius,* sensory] Pert. to sensations aroused by stimulation of visceroreceptors.

viscerotropic (vĭs″ĕr-ō-trŏp′ĭk) [″ + Gr. *tropos,* a turn] Primarily affecting the viscera.

viscerovisceral reaction (vĭs″ĕr-ō-vĭs′ĕr-ăl) A reaction taking place in the viscera as a result of stimulation of visceral receptors. Such reactions are usually below the level of consciousness.

viscid (vĭs′ĭd) [L. *viscidus,* clammy, sticky] Adhering, glutinous, sticky.

viscoelasticity (vĭs″kō-ē″lăs-tĭs′ĭ-tē) The property of being viscous and elastic.

viscosimeter (vĭs″kŏ-sim′ĕt-ĕr) [L. *viscosus,* viscous + *-meter*] A device for measuring the viscosity of a fluid, esp. of blood.

viscosimetry (vĭs″kō-sĭm′ĕ-trē) Measurement of the viscosity of a substance.

viscosity (vĭs″kŏs′ĭ-tē) [L. *viscosus,* viscous] 1. The state of being sticky or gummy. 2. Resistance offered by a fluid to change of form or relative position of its particles due to attraction of molecules to each other.

specific v. The internal friction of a fluid, measured by comparing the rate of flow of the liquid through a tube with that of some standard liquid, or by measuring the resistance to rotating paddles.

viscous (vĭs′kŭs) Sticky, gummy, gelatinous, with high viscosity.

Viscum album (vĭs′kŭm al′bŭm) [L. *viscum album,* white mistletoe] SEE: *mistletoe.*

viscus (vĭs′kŭs) *pl.* **viscera** [L., body organ] Any internal organ enclosed within a cavity such as the thorax or abdomen.

visibility (vĭz″ĭ-bĭl′ĭ-tē) [L. *visibilitas*] The quality of being visible.

visible (vĭz′ĭ-bl) [L. *visibilis*] Capable of being seen.

visile (vĭz′ĭl) [L. *visum,* seeing] 1. Pert. to vision. 2. Readily recalling what is seen, more than that which is audible or motile.

vision (vizh′ŏn) [L. *visio,* a seeing] 1. The act of seeing external objects. SYN: *sight; visual function.* SEE: *reading machine for the blind.* 2. The sense by which light, color, form, and contrast are apprehended. 3. An imaginary sight.

achromatic v. Complete color blindness.

artificial v. An experimental technique to make it possible for some blind people to see as a result of electrical stimulation of the retina or the connection of digital video cameras to the visual cortex of the brain.

binocular v. The visual sensation produced when the images perceived by each eye are fused to appear as one.

central v. Vision resulting from light falling on the fovea centralis.

day v. A condition in which one sees better during the day than at night, found in peripheral lesions of the retina such as retinitis pigmentosa. SYN: *photopic v.*

dichromatic v. A form of defective color vision in which only two of the primary colors are perceived.

double v. Diplopia.

functional v. The processing and use of visual information in the performance of visually related tasks, e.g., reading, driving, or recognizing individuals at a distance or in a crowd.

half v. Hemianopia.

indirect v. Peripheral **v.**

intermediate v. Visual foci that lie 18–84 in (45.7 cm–2.13 m) from the eye. Objects commonly viewed within this range include computer displays and other objects on tabletops and desks.

low v. A significant loss of vision that cannot be corrected medically, surgically, or with eyeglasses.

monocular v. Vision using only one eye.

multiple v. Polyopia.

night n. The ability to see at night or in light of low intensity. It results from dark adaptation in which the pupil dilates, rhodopsin increases, and the intensity threshold of the retina is lowered. Any decrease in the oxygen content of the blood is accompanied by some loss of night vision. Thus, smoking cigarettes or being in an atmosphere with decreased oxygen content decreases night vision. SEE: *scotopic v.*

no v. Complete blindness. SEE: *low v.*

oscillating v. Oscillopsia.

peripheral v. Vision resulting from rays falling on the retina outside of the macular field. SYN: *indirect v.*

phantom v. An experience of visual sensations following surgical removal of an eye; usually a transient condition.

photopic v. Day vision.

scotopic v. Vision at low light levels, primarily as a function of the rods. SEE: *night v.*

sports v. The use of eye safety procedures, ophthalmology, optometry, and visual training to protect or enhance athletic performance.

stereoscopic v. Vision in which things have the appearance of solidity and relief, as though seen in three dimensions. Binocular vision produces this effect. SYN: *stereopsis.*

tunnel v. **1.** Visual acuity limited to the central visual field, e.g., two to three degrees of visual radius. SYN: *peripheral vision loss.* **2.** An inability to appreciate the full scope of an issue.

v. without sight The ability of the blind who are also unable to perceive visual stimuli, including bright light, to respond to light.

vision correction Any means of improving the visual acuity of the eye, e.g., with surgery or with visual appliances such as contact lenses or eyeglasses.

vision therapy Orthoptics.

visit An encounter between a patient and a health professional that requires either the patient to travel from his or her home to the professional's usual place of practice (office visit) or vice versa (home visit).

visitability (vĭz″ĭt-ă-bĭl′ĭ-tē) Ease of accessibility to a residence, esp. those features that help disabled people to enter, move around in, and use the toilet in a newly designed home. Architectural features include having at least one entrance without a step, 32-in wide passages from one room to another, and an easily accessible bathroom on the first floor.

Visiting Nurse Association A voluntary health agency that provides nursing services in the home, including health supervision, education and counseling, and maintenance of the medical regimen. Nurses and other personnel such as home health aides who are specifically trained for tasks of personal bedside care provide the services offered by the agency. These agencies originated in the visiting or district nurse service provided to the poor in their homes by voluntary agencies such as the New York City Mission, which existed in the 1870s. The first visiting nurse associations were established in Buffalo, Boston, and Philadelphia between 1886 and 1887.

VistA-Office Electronic Health Record ABBR: VOE. Electronic medical record software developed by the U.S. Veterans Administration and marketed to private medical practices beginning in 2005.

visual (vĭzh′ū-ăl) [L. *visio,* a seeing] **1.** Pert. to vision. **2.** One whose learning and memorizing processes are largely of a visual nature.

visual acuity SEE: under *acuity.*

visual angle SEE: under *angle.*

visual cone SEE: under *cone.*

visual-constructional apraxia SEE: under *apraxia.*

visual evoked response SEE: under *response.*

visual field SEE: under *field*.

visual function SEE: under *function*.

visual inspection with acetic acid ABBR: VIA. Inspection of the surface of the uterine cervix after 5% acetic acid has been applied to it. VIA is a test sometimes used to determine whether the cervix is infected with human papilloma virus or whether irregularities seen on the cervix may be cancerous or precancerous.

visualization (vĭzh″ū-ăl-ĭ-zā′shŭn) Viewing or sensing a picture of an object, esp. the picture of a body structure as obtained by radiographic study.

visualize (vĭzh′ū-ăl-īz) **1.** To make visible. **2.** To imagine or picture something in one's mind.

visual object agnosia SEE: under *agnosia*.

visual point SEE: under *point*.

visual threat The sudden presentation of a visual stimulus to a patient, typically a gesture that rapidly approaches the patient's eyes, e.g., the examiner's fast-moving hand. The normal neurological response to a visual threat is to blink the eyelids or flinch.

visuognosis (vĭzh″ū-ŏg-nō′sĭs) [″ + Gr. *gnosis*, knowledge] The recognition and appreciation of what is seen.

visuosensory (vĭzh″ū-ō-sĕn′sō-rē) [L. *visio*, a seeing, + *sensorius*, sensory] Pert. to the recognition of visual impressions.

visuospatial (vĭzh″ū-ō-spā′shăl) Pert. to the ability to discern spatial relationships from visual presentations.

vita glass (vīt′ă) SEE: under *glass*.

vital (vī′tăl) [L. *vitalis*, pert. to life] **1.** Pert. to or characteristic of life. **2.** Contributing to or essential for life.

vitality (vī-tăl′ĭ-tē) **1.** Animation, action. **2.** The state of being alive.

vitalometer (vī″tă-lŏm′ĕ-tĕr) A diagnostic device that measures the response of a nerve in the pulp of a tooth to an electrical stimulus. SYN: *pulp tester*.

vital statistics SEE: under *statistics*.

vitamer (vī′tă-mĕr) Any of a number of compounds that have specific vitamin activity.

vitamin (vī′tă-mĭn) [L. *vita*, life, + *amine*] An accessory but vital nutrient that serves as a coenzyme or cofactor in an essential metabolic process. Small quantities of the substance assist biological reactions such as oxidation and reduction, or the synthesis of nucleic acids, hemoglobin, clotting factors, or collagen. Vitamin deficiencies produce well-recognized syndromes (e.g., scurvy [vitamin C deficiency], or beriberi [thiamine deficiency]). Unlike proteins, carbohydrates, fats, and organic salts, vitamins are not energy sources or components of body structures. Instead, they are agents that hasten or facilitate

biochemical processes involving these other organic molecules. SEE: *dietary reference intakes; mineral*.

Only vitamins A, D, and K are made within the body. The rest must be consumed in the diet. Vitamin A is formed from its precursor, carotene; vitamin D is formed by the action of ultraviolet light on the skin; and vitamin K is formed by the symbiotic action of bacteria within the intestines.

A common classification system distinguishes fat-soluble vitamins (A, D, E, and K) from water-soluble vitamins (B and C). Fat-soluble vitamins are poorly assimilated in diseases that interfere with the digestion of fat, such as steatorrhea, but accumulate in organs like the liver when taken in excess. Water-soluble vitamins are readily lost from the body in urine and sweat and are more likely to be lacking from the body than overabundant. SEE: *Vitamins Appendix*.

One's need for vitamins increases in conditions that deplete their stores from the body, such as pregnancy and lactation, alcoholism, and febrile illnesses. Some drugs block the action of specific vitamins, or create illnesses that can be prevented with vitamin supplementation. In patients taking isoniazid for tuberculosis, for example, vitamin supplementation with pyridoxine is needed to prevent peripheral neuropathy.

SYMPTOMS: Refer to the *Vitamins Appendix* for signs and symptoms of vitamin deficiency.

vitamin A A fat-soluble vitamin formed within the body from alpha, beta, and gamma carotene, the yellow pigments of plants. It is essential for normal growth and development, normal function and integrity of epithelial tissues, formation of visual pigment, and normal tooth and bone development. It is stored in the liver. The recommended daily requirement for adults is 1,000 mcg. Retinol is the form of vitamin A found in mammals. One retinol equivalent (RE) is equal to 6 mcg of beta-carotene. Excessive intake of vitamin A may cause acute or chronic effects and may increase risk of developing cancer in smokers. SYN: *retinol*. SEE: *hypervitaminosis; Vitamins Appendix*.

SOURCES: Butterfat, egg yolks, and cod liver oil are rich sources. The vitamin is found also in liver, green leafy and yellow vegetables, prunes, pineapples, oranges, limes, and cantaloupes.

STABILITY: This vitamin resists boiling for some time if not exposed to oxidation. It is quite stable with brief exposure to heat but not with continued high temperatures (above 212°F [100°C]).

DEFICIENCY DISORDERS: A deficiency of vitamin A causes interference with growth, reduced resistance to infections, and interference with nutrition of the cornea, conjunctiva, trachea, hair follicles, and renal pelvis. Thus these tissues have an increased susceptibility to infections. Vitamin A deficiency also interferes with the ability of the eyes to adapt to darkness (night blindness) and impairs visual acuity. Children with vitamin A deficiency experience impaired growth and development. SEE: *Bitot spots.*

vitamin A₁ A form of vitamin A found in fish liver oils.

vitamin A₂ A compound found in the livers of freshwater fish; similar in properties to vitamin A but with different ultraviolet absorption spectra.

Vitamin B₃ Niacin.

Vitamin B₉ Folic acid.

vitamin B₁ Thiamine hydrochloride.

vitamin B₂ Riboflavin. SEE: *Vitamins Appendix.*

vitamin B₄ Adenine.

vitamin B₅ Pantothenic acid.

vitamin B₆ Pyridoxine; found in rice, bran, and yeast. Excess doses (2 to 5 g/day for months) have caused impairment of central nervous system function. SEE: *Vitamins Appendix.*

vitamin B₇ Biotin.

vitamin B₈ Inositol.

vitamin B₁₀ ABBR: PABA. Para aminobenzoic acid.

vitamin B₁₁ Choline.

vitamin B₁₂ A red crystalline substance, a cobamide, extracted from the liver, that is essential for the formation of red blood cells. Its deficiency results in pernicious anemia. It is used for prophylaxis and treatment of these and other diseases in which there is defective red cell formation. The recommended adult daily requirement is 2 μg/day. The terms vitamin B₁₂ and cyanocobalamin are used interchangeably as the generic term for all of the cobamides active in humans. SYN: *cyanocobalamin.* SEE: *Vitamins Appendix.*

vitamin B₁₇ Laetrile.

vitamin B complex A group of water-soluble vitamins isolated from liver, yeast, and other sources. Only grain-made yeast preserves its potency if dried. Among vitamins included are thiamine (B₁), riboflavin (B₂), niacin (nicotinic acid), pyridoxine (B₆), biotin, folic acid, and cyanocobalamin (B₁₂).

SOURCES: *Thiamine:* Whole grains, wheat embryo, brewer's yeast, legumes, nuts, egg yolk, fruits, and vegetables. *Riboflavin:* Brewer's yeast, liver, meat, esp. pork and fish, poultry, eggs, milk, and green vegetables. *Nicotinic acid:* Brewer's yeast, liver, meat, poultry, and green vegetables. *Pyridoxine:* Rice, bran, and yeast. *Folic acid:* Leafy green vegetables, organ meats, lean beef and veal, and wheat cereals. *General:* Fortified cereals, breads and baked goods are good sources of these.

ACTION/USES: The B vitamins affect growth, stimulate appetite, lactation, and the gastrointestinal, neurological, and endocrine systems; aid in prevention of marasmus; stimulate appetite; are important in metabolism of carbohydrates, including sugar; and stimulate biliary action.

Vitamin B₁, thiamine, affects growth and nutrition and carbohydrate metabolism. B₂, riboflavin, affects growth and cellular metabolism. Nicotinic acid prevents pellagra. Pyridoxine is used by patients taking the antitubercular drug, isoniazid, to prevent peripheral neuropathy.

NOTE: Prolonged use of antibiotics may destroy intestinal flora that produce some of the B vitamins. Vitamin supplementation may be required to prevent deficiencies.

STABILITY: B vitamins are stable during normal cooking, although they may be destroyed by excessive heating for 2 to 4 hr. Baking soda destroys thiamine. Riboflavin and nicotinic acid are more stable than thiamine and are not destroyed by heat or oxidation.

DEFICIENCY DISORDERS: Deficiency causes beriberi, pellagra, digestive disturbances, enlargement of the liver, disturbance of the thyroid, degeneration of sex glands, and disturbance of the nervous system. It also induces edema; affects the heart, liver, spleen, and kidneys; enlarges the adrenals; and causes dysfunction of the pituitary and salivary glands.

vitamin C $C_6H_8O_6$, a vitamin that occurs naturally in fresh fruits, esp. citrus, and vegetables. It is necessary for formation of collagen in connective tissues and in maintenance of integrity of intercellular cement in many tissues, esp. capillary walls. Vitamin C is used as a dietary supplement and in the prevention and treatment of scurvy. Scurvy develops after approx. 3 months of ascorbic acid deficiency in the diet. High daily doses (1 to 5 g/day) of vitamin C are purported to prevent or treat the common cold, but this has not been established. Continual consumption of high doses can cause kidney stones. SYN: *antiscorbutic vitamin; ascorbic acid.* SEE: *Vitamins Appendix.*

NOTE: The recommended adult daily allowance is 60 mg. Smoking causes an increased need of vitamin C. Excess doses of vitamin C for an extended period can interfere with absorption of vitamin B₁₂, cause uricosuria, and promote formation of oxalate kidney stones.

SOURCES: Vitamin C is found in raw cabbage, young carrots, orange juice, lettuce, celery, onions, tomatoes, radishes, and green peppers. Citrus fruits and rutabagas are esp. rich in this vitamin. Strawberries are about as rich a source as tomatoes. Apples, pears, apricots, plums, peaches, and pineapples also contain vitamin C.

STABILITY: The vitamin is destroyed easily by heat in the presence of oxygen, as in open-kettle boiling. It is less affected by heat in an acid medium; otherwise, it is stable.

DEFICIENCY DISORDERS: Vitamin C deficiency causes scurvy, imperfect prenatal skeletal formation, defective teeth, pyorrhea, anorexia, and anemia. It also leads to undernutrition injury to bone, cells, and blood vessels.

vitamin D Any of a group of fat-soluble vitamins having antirachitic activity. The group includes D_2 (calciferol), D_3 (irradiated 7-dehydrocholesterol), D_4 (irradiated 22-dihydroergosterol), and D_5 (irradiated dehydrositosterol). The D vitamins are essential for the metabolism of calcium and phosphorus and therefore are necessary for the normal development of bones and teeth. The recommended daily allowance is 10 μg. The stability of this vitamin is not affected by oxidation, heat (unless over 212°F [100°C]), or long cooking. A deficiency of vitamin D causes imperfect skeletal formation, rickets and other bone diseases, and caries. SEE: *Vitamins Appendix.*

SOURCES: Butterfat, cod liver oil, salmon and cod livers, and egg yolk contain vitamin D. Ergosterol in the skin, when activated by sunlight or ultraviolet radiation, has the potency of vitamin D.

ACTION/USES: Vitamin D is used to treat and prevent infantile rickets, spasmophilia (infantile tetany), and softening of bone. Vitamin D is also important in normal growth and mineralization of skeleton and teeth.

Prolonged excessive doses of vitamin D (100,000 IU daily) cause hypercalcemia with anorexia, nausea, vomiting, polyuria, polydipsia, weakness, anxiety, pruritus, and altered renal function.

vitamin D analogue SEE: under *analogue.*

vitamin E A vitamin that consists of eight components: four tocopherols (of which alpha tocopherol is the most common constituent) and four tocotrienols. Vitamin E is an antioxidant found in many common foods. Deficiencies of the vitamin in the general population are rare. SEE: *Vitamins Appendix.*

⚠️ 1. Doses of vitamin E in excess of 100 mg/kg/day in low birth weight neonates have been implicated in the development of necrotizing enterocolitis and sepsis. 2. Vitamin E supplementation in adults that exceeds 400 International Units/day increases mortality.

vitamin H Biotin.

vitamin K An antihemorrhagic factor whose activity is associated with compounds derived from naphthoquinone. Vitamin K is fat soluble and is found in broccoli, collards, beet greens, (most green vegetables); vitamin K_2 is found in fishmeal. Vitamin K_3 is synthesized as menadione sodium bisulfite. Vitamin K is necessary for synthesis of clotting factors VII, IX, X, and prothrombin by the liver. Its deficiency prolongs blood-clotting time and causes bleeding. Its roles in bone metabolism include the conversion of osteocalcin to its active form and matrix Gla-protein (MGP) function in bones, teeth, and cartilage. Within the kidney, vitamin K inhibits the formation of calcium oxalate stones. It appears to have a role in normal retinal signaling. In the newborn, the colon is sterile until food is ingested and bacteria colonize the site. Because this bacterial source of vitamin K is not immediately available, an intramuscular injection of 1 mg of water-soluble vitamin K_1 (phytonadione) is recommended for all newborns.

Large doses may cause hemolysis in those with glucose-6-phosphate dehydrogenase deficiency and in some healthy people. Large doses in the newborn may lead to anemia and kernicterus. The recommended adult daily allowance is 65 μg for women and 80 μg for men. SEE: *Vitamins Appendix.*

ACTION/USES: Vitamin K helps to eliminate prolonged bleeding in operations and in the biliary tract of jaundiced patients. Bile salts are necessary for its absorption.

vitamin K epoxide reductase An enzyme that is a coagulation factor. It inhibits the activation of vitamin K–dependent clotting factors in the bloodstream and alters a person's sensitivity to warfarin.

vitamin loss SEE: under *loss.*

vitamin supplement A vitamin tablet or capsule containing one or more vitamins. Some supplements may contain more than a dozen vitamins and an even greater number of minerals. In general, healthy adult men and healthy nonpregnant, nonlactating women consuming a normal, varied diet do not need vitamin supplements.

The difficulties of those who take vitamin supplements are: 1. People who take the supplements are usually already consuming an adequate diet. 2. The vitamins chosen are often not the ones inadequate in their diet. 3. The dose may be many times greater than the daily needs. SEE: *Food Guide Pyramid; vitamin C.*

vitellary (vĭt'ĕl-ā-rē) [L. *vitellus,* yolk of an egg] Vitelline.

vitellin (vī-tĕl'ĭn) A protein that can be extracted from egg yolk and contains lecithin. SEE: *nucleoprotein; ovovitellin.*

vitelline (vī-tĕl'ēn) Pert. to the yolk of an egg or the ovum.

vitelline duct Yolk stalk.

vitellolutein (vī"tĕl-ō-lū'tē-ĭn) [L. *vitellus,* yolk, + *luteus,* yellow] A yellow pigment present in lutein.

vitellorubin (vī"tĕl-ō-rū'bĭn) [" + *ruber,* red] A red pigment present in lutein.

vitellose (vī-tĕl'ōs) A proteose present in vitellin.

vitellus (vī-tĕl'ŭs) [L.] The yolk of an ovum, esp. the yolk of a hen's egg.

Vitex agnus-castus (vī'teks" ag'nŭs kast'ŭs) [L., lit. chaste-lamb chaste tree] SEE: *chaste tree berry.*

vitiation (vĭsh"ē-ā'shŭn) [L. *vitiare,* to corrupt] Injury, contamination, impairment of use or efficiency.

vitiligines (vĭt"ĭ-lĭj'ĭ-nēz) Depigmented areas of skin. SEE: *vitiligo.*

vitiliginous (vĭt"ĭ-lĭj'ĭ-nŭs) Pert. to vitiligo.

vitiligo (vĭt-ĭl-ī'gō) [L.] A skin disorder characterized by the localized loss of melanocytes, with patchy loss of skin pigment. The depigmented areas, which appear most commonly on the hands, face, and genital region, are flat and pale and surrounded by normal pigmentation. Vitiligo affects all ages and races but is most noticeable in people with dark skin. The cause is unknown but may be an autoimmune process because autoantibodies to melanocytes have been identified and vitiligo often occurs with autoimmune diseases. SYN: *leukoderma; piebald skin.* SEE: illus.

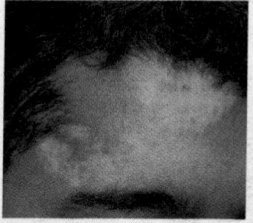

VITILIGO

TREATMENT: Oral and topical synthetic trioxsalen and a natural psoralen, methoxsalen, are used with exposure to long-wave ultraviolet light, but the efficacy is doubtful. The lesions may be masked by use of cosmetic preparations. Vitiliginous areas should be protected from sunburn by applying a 5% aminobenzoic acid solution or gel to the

affected areas. The use of 5% fluorouracil cream applied under an occlusive dressing to the depigmented areas may cause erosion of the dermis and, after re-epithelialization, pigment may reappear.

   v. capitis Vitiligo of the scalp with depigmentation of the hairs of the affected area.

   perinevic v. Vitiligo surrounding a nevus.

vitium (vĭsh'ē-ŭm) *pl.* **vitia** [L., fault] A fault, defect, or vice.

vitrectomy (vĭ-trĕk'tō-mē) [L. *vitreus,* glassy, + Gr. *ektome,* excision] The surgical removal of the vitreous of the eye. The removed vitreous is replaced, usually with gas or liquid. This process is used to treat epiretinal membranes, macular pucker, macular hole, and other disorders of the retina or the vitreous.

   enzymatic v. Pharmacological vitrectomy.

   pharmacological v. A method of vitrectomy in which enzymes are used to liquefy the vitreous and weaken its attachment to the limiting membrane of the retina. SYN: *enzymatic v.*

vitreodentin (vĭt"rē-ō-dĕn'tĭn) A particularly hard and brittle form of dentin.

vitreomacular traction syndrome (vi"trē-ō-mak'yŭ-lär) [*vitre(ous)* + *macular*] ABBR: VTS. Chronic tugging on the macula after a partial posterior detachment of the vitreous. It is a cause of unilateral visual blurring.

vitreoretinal (vĭt"rē-ō-rĕt'ĭ-năl) Pert. to the vitreous and the retina.

vitreous (vĭt'rē-ŭs) [L. *vitreus,* glassy] **1.** Glassy. **2.** The transparent, colorless, semisolid mass composed of collagen fibrils and hyaluronic acid. It fills the posterior cavity of the eye between the lens and the retina. SYN: *vitreous body; vitreous humor.*

vitreous body SEE: under *body.*

vitreous face Condensation of the anterior surface of the vitreous behind the lens and the posterior surface of the vitreous attached to the internal limiting membrane of the retina. SEE: *hyaloid membrane.*

vitrescence (vĭ-trĕs'ĕns) Becoming hard and transparent like glass.

vitreum (vĭt'rē-ŭm) Vitreous body.

vitrification (vī"trĭ-fĭ-kā'shŏn) [L. *vitrum,* glass] **1.** The conversion of a silicate material into a smooth, viscous substance by heat. The silicate material hardens on cooling and possesses a smooth, glossy surface. In dentistry, it is related to the extensive use of ceramics, cements, and porcelains. These vary by the additive components that determine their density and refractive qualities. **2.** A technique to preserve fertility in which oocytes that have been removed from an ovary are treated with a cryopreservative (which prevents damage from cold temperatures) and then are cooled very rapidly to very low temperatures. The oocytes may be restored to body temperature at a later date, fertilized, and implanted into the uterus.

vitriol (vĭt′rē-ōl) [L. *vitriolum*] A sulfate of any of various metals.

vitronectin (vī″trō-nĕk′tĭn) An adhesive glycoprotein found in the blood and the extracellular matrix. It contributes to blood clotting, cell growth and differentiation, the ability of tumors to metastasize, and normal wound healing. SYN: *complement S protein*.

vitropression (vĭt″rō-prĕsh′ŭn) [L. *vitrum*, glass, + *pressio*, a squeezing] A method of temporarily eliminating redness of the skin caused by hyperemia by pressure with a glass slide on the skin for the purpose of studying any lesions or discolorations.

vivi- [L. *vivus*, alive, living] Prefix meaning *alive*.

vivification (vĭv″ĭ-fĭ-kā′shŭn) [″ + *facere*, to make] 1. Trimming of the surface layer of a wound to aid the union of tissues. 2. Transformation of protein through assimilation into the living matter of cellular organisms.

viviparity (vĭv″ĭ-păr′ĭ-tē) The ability to produce living young rather than producing young by laying an egg that hatches.

viviparous (vĭv-ĭp′ăr-ŭs) [″ + *parere*, to bring forth, to bear] Developing young within the body, the young being expelled and born alive; the opposite of oviparous.

vivisect (vĭv′ĭ-sĕkt) [L. *vivus*, alive, + *sectio*, a cutting] To dissect a living animal for experimental purposes.

vivisection (vĭv″ĭ-sĕk′shŭn) [″ + *sectio*, a cutting] Cutting of or operation on a living animal for physiological investigation and the study of disease.

vivisectionist (vĭv″ĭ-sĕk′shŭn-ĭst) One who practices or believes in vivisection. SEE: *antivivisection*.

vivisector (vĭv-ĭs-ĕk′tor) [″ + *sector*, a cutting] One who practices vivisection.

Vivotif (vīv′ō-tĭf) Typhoid vaccine, live, oral Ty21a.

VLBW *very low birth* **weight**.

VLDL *very low-density* **lipoprotein**.

VMA *vanillylmandelic* **acid**.

V$_{max}$ *maximum velocity*.

VNA *Visiting Nurse Association*.

V-neck sign The presence of pigmented skin beneath the chin (on the upper chest) in a patient without a significant history of sun exposure. It is a characteristic finding in patients with dermatomyositis.

VO$_2$ *oxygen consumption*.

vocal (vō′kăl) [L. *vocalis*, talking] Pert. to the voice.

vocal abuse SEE: under *abuse*.

vocal apparatus The organs, including the pharynx, larynx, teeth, tongue, and lips, that produce sounds and speech.

vocal cord Either of two thin, reedlike folds of tissue within the larynx that vibrate as air passes between them, producing sounds that are the basis of speech.

    false v.c. Ventricular **fold** of the larynx.

    true v.c. Vocal fold. SEE: illus.

vocal cord dysfunction SEE: under *dysfunction*.

vocal cords, false The ventricular folds of the larynx.

vocal cords, true Vocal folds.

vocal folds The true vocal cords; the inferior pair of folds within the larynx; each contains a vocal ligament. They form the edges of the rima glottidis and are involved in the production of sound. SYN: *vocal cords, true*.

vocal ligament SEE: under *ligament*.

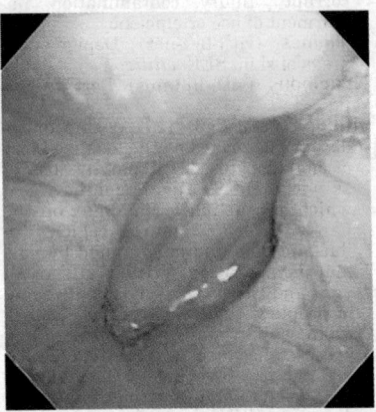

Vocal cords (closed, seen endoscopically)

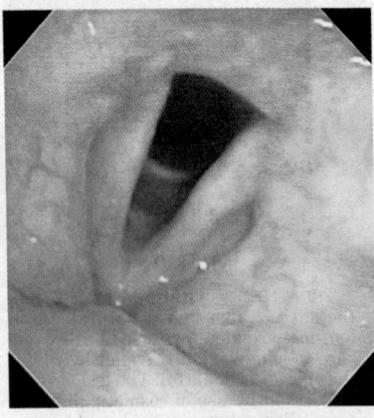

VOCAL CORDS

Vocal cords (open, seen endoscopically)

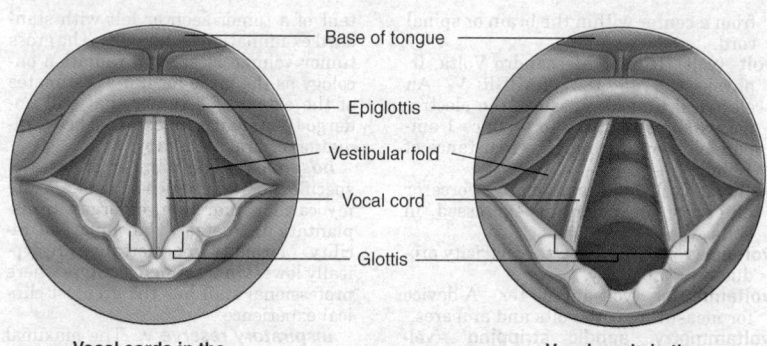

Vocal cords in the closed position

Vocal cords in the open position

VOCAL CORDS AND GLOTTIS

vocal signs The indication of disease by changes in the voice.

vocal tract SEE: under *tract*.

vocational guidance SEE: under *guidance*.

voces (vō′sēz) [L.] Pl. of vox.

voice (voys) [Fr. *voice*, fr. L. *vox*] A sound uttered by human beings produced by vibration of the vocal cords.

    amphoric v. Cavernous **v.**

    cavernous v. A hollow voice sound heard during auscultation of the chest, indicating a pulmonary cavity. SEE: *amphoric v.*

    eunuchoid v. The characteristic high-pitched voice of a male in whom the normal sexual development has not occurred or in a male who was castrated before puberty.

voice break The sudden interruption of speech or a sudden decrease in vocal amplitude. It is a sign of laryngeal spasm.

voiceprint (voys′prĭnt) A graph of the characteristics of an individual's speech pattern. Voiceprints, like fingerprints, can be used to distinguish one person from another and are useful in forensic medicine and in identifying the voices of criminal suspects.

voices (voys′ĕz) In psychiatry, verbal-auditory hallucinations expressed as being heard by the patient.

void (voyd) [O.Fr. *voider*, to empty] **1.** To evacuate the bowels or bladder. **2.** An empty space, e.g., one seen in radiographical evaluation of arteries or veins.

voiding (voyd′ing) An evacuation of the bowels or bladder

    prompted v. Reminding patients, esp. those with cognitive impairments, to urinate at specified times in order to avoid episodic incontinence.

    scheduled v. Urinating at prescribed times during the day, e.g., every 2 hr.

voir dire (vwar dēr) [Fr. *voir dire*, to say the truth] A preliminary interview of a prospective juror to determine his or her impartiality or suitability for jury service or as a case witness.

vol% *volume percent.*

vol *volume.*

vola (vō′lă) [L. *vola*, hollow of the hand, palm (of the hand); sole (of the foot)] The palm of the hand or sole of the foot. The preferred Latin terms for the palm of the hand and the sole of the foot are *palma* and *planta*, respectively. **volar** (vō′lăr), *adj.*

volatile (vŏl′ă-tĭl) [L. *volatilis*, flying] Easily vaporized or evaporated. Examples of volatile liquids are ether (boiling point, 34.5°C) and ethyl chloride (boiling point, 12.2°C).

volatilization (vŏl″ă-tĭl-ī-zā′shŭn) Conversion of a solid or liquid into a vapor.

volatilize (vŏl′ă-tĭl-īz) To vaporize a liquid or solid.

volition (vō-lĭsh′ŭn) [L. *volitio*, will] The act or power of willing or choosing.

volitional (vō-lĭsh′ŭn-ăl) Pert. to volition.

Volkmann, Richard von (folk′măn) Ger. surgeon, 1830–1889.

    V. contracture Degeneration, contracture, fibrosis, and atrophy of a muscle resulting from injury to its blood supply; usually seen in the hand. SYN: *ischemic paralysis.*

    V. deformity Congenital tibiotarsal dislocation.

    V. splint A splint used for fracture of the lower extremity consisting of a footpiece and two lateral supports.

Volkmann canal (folk′măn) [Alfred Wilhelm Volkmann, Ger. physiologist, 1800–1877] Any of the small canals found in bone through which blood vessels pass from the periosteum. They connect with the blood vessels of haversian canals or the marrow cavity.

volley (vŏl′ē) [L. *volare*, to fly] The simultaneous or nearly simultaneous discharge of a number of nerve impulses from a center within the brain or spinal cord.

volt (vōlt) [Count Alessandro Volta, It. physicist, 1745–1827] ABBR: V. An electrical unit of pressure, the electromotive force required to produce 1 ampere of current through a resistance of 1 ohm.

voltage (vōl'tĭj) Electromotive force or difference in potential expressed in volts.

voltaic (vŏl-tā'ĭk) Pert. to electricity produced by a battery.

voltammeter (vōlt-ăm'mē-tĕr) A device for measuring both volts and amperes.

voltammetry, anodic stripping (vōltăm'ĭ-trē) ABBR: ASV. An analytical technique used to assay blood lead content.

voltampere (vōlt-ăm'pēr) The value obtained by multiplying volts times amperes.

voltmeter (vŏlt'mē"tĕr) A device for measuring voltage, esp. for determining the voltage between two points of an electrical circuit.

volubility (vŏl"ū-bĭl'ĭ-tē) [L. *volubilitas*, flow of discourse] Excessive speech.

volume (vol'yŭm, ūm") [L. *volumen*, roll of sheets] The space occupied by a substance, usually a gas or liquid. Liquid volume is expressed in liters or milliliters; gas volume in cubic centimeters.

clinical target v. ABBR: CTV. In radiation therapy, the grossly detectable tumor volume plus any microscopic tumor that extends outward from the grossly involved margins. The objective in radiation oncology is to treat the visible tumor and the surrounding margins adequately to destroy as many malignant cells as possible.

closing v. The amount of gas remaining in the lung when the small airways close during a maximum expiratory effort. It is increased in patients with small airway disease.

compressed v. The portion of the mechanically delivered tidal volume that is not delivered to the patient owing to expansion of the ventilator circuit with pressure. Tubing with a high compliance increases the compressed volume, esp. when the tidal volume is delivered under high pressure.

expiratory reserve v. The maximal amount of air that can be forced from the lungs after normal expiration.

forced expiratory v. ABBR: FEV. The volume of air that can be expired after a full inspiration. The expiration is done as quickly as possible and the volume measured at precise times with the abbreviation and number, e.g. FEV½, FEV 1, FEV 2, and FEV 3 sec. This provides valuable information concerning the ability to expel air from the lungs.

gross tumor v. The demonstrable ex-

tent of a tumor seen or felt with standard examination techniques. The gross tumor volume is used in radiation oncology as the basis for initial estimates of the extent of a tumor that will undergo treatment with external beam radiation or brachytherapy.

hospital v. The number of cases of specific conditions (such as stroke, acute myocardial infarction, or organ transplantation) treated at an inpatient facility. Morbidity and mortality are typically lowest in treatment centers where professional staff has the greatest clinical experience.

inspiratory reserve v. The maximal amount of air that can be inhaled after a normal inspiration.

mean corpuscular v. ABBR: MCV. The mean volume of an average erythrocyte. Normal values range from 82 to 92 cubic microns.

minute v. The volume of gas expired or inspired per minute in quiet breathing, usually measured as expired ventilation.

packed cell v. Hematocrit.

plasma v. The total quantity of plasma in the body. It decreases with dehydration and increases with greater salt and water intake and during early pregnancy. Plasma volume can be measured with injected fluorescent-labeled albumin.

residual v. ABBR: RV. The volume of air remaining in the lungs after maximal expiration. This air is essential for continuous gas exchange.

stroke v. The amount of blood ejected by the left ventricle at each heartbeat. The amount varies with age, sex, and exercise but averages 60 to 80 mL.

thoracic gas v. ABBR: VTG. The volume of gas contained within the chest during body plethysmography when the mouth shutter is closed. This measurement is a rough estimate of the functional residual capacity of the lung.

tidal v. The volume of air inspired and expired in a normal breath.

volume controller Buret (2).

volume depletion Loss of body fluids, e.g., by bleeding, sweating, urinating, or vomiting. Excessive loss of body fluids without replenishment results in dehydration, hypotension, and kidney failure.

volume expander Any solution used as an intravenous infusion to increase blood pressure by treating relative or absolute dehydration. Such expanders include isotonic or balanced solutions, solutions containing crystalloids, (such as lactated Ringer solution), dextrans, and blood components.

volume overload SEE: under *overload*.

volume percent ABBR: vol%. The number of cubic centimeters (milliliters) of a substance (usually oxygen or carbon dioxide) contained in 100 mL of another substance (e.g., blood).

volume rendering The imaging of the surface elements, internal geometry, and components of a three-dimensional structure.

volumetric (vŏl″ū-mĕt′rĭk) [L. *volumen,* a volume, + Gr. *metron,* measure] Pert. to measurement of volume.

volumetric analysis Quantitative analysis performed by the measurement of the volume of solutions or liquids.

volumetric brain imaging SEE: under *imaging.*

volumetric capnography SEE: under *capnography.*

voluntary (vol″ŭn-ter″ē) [L. *voluntarius,* willing, voluntary, fr *voluntas,* will] Pert. to or under control of the will. **voluntarily** (vol″ŭn-ter′ĭ-lē), *adj.*

voluntary health agency Any nonprofit, nongovernmental agency, governed by lay or professional people and organized on a national, state, or local level, whose primary purpose is health related. This term applies to agencies supported mainly by voluntary public contributions. These agencies are usually engaged in programs of service, education, and research related to a particular disability or group of diseases and disabilities; for example, the American Heart Association, American Cancer Society, National Lung Institute, and their state and local affiliates. The term can also be applied to such agencies as nonprofit hospitals, visiting nurse associations, and other local service organizations that have both lay and professional governing boards and are supported by both voluntary contributions and charges and fees for service provided.

volunteer (vol″ŭn-tēr′) [Fr. *voluntaire,* fr L. *voluntarius,* willing, voluntary] **1.** One who works without pay on behalf of a cause or an institution. **2.** One who freely participates in a research study, without expectation of payment, recognition, or reward. Healthy volunteers often participate in research as control subjects.

voluptuous (vō-lŭp′tū-ŭs) [L. *voluptas,* pleasure] **1.** Pert. to, arising from, or provoking, consciously or otherwise, sensual desire, usually applied to the female sex. **2.** Given to sensualism.

volute (vō-lūt′) [L. *volutus,* rolled] Convolute.

volutrauma (vŏl′ū-traw″mă) [L. *volumen,* scroll, something rolled, + Gr. *trauma,* wound] A lung injury caused by excessively high tidal volumes during the use of mechanical ventilation.

volvulosis (vŏl″vū-lō′sĭs) Onchocerciasis.

volvulus (vŏl′vū-lŭs) [L. *volvere,* to roll] A twisting of the bowel on itself, causing obstruction. A prolapsed mesentery is the predisposing cause. This usually occurs at the sigmoid and ileocecal areas of the intestines.

vomer (vō′mĕr) [L., plowshare] The plow-shaped bone that forms the lower and posterior portion of the nasal septum, articulating with the ethmoid, the sphenoid, the two palatine bones, and the two maxillae.

vomerine (vō′mĕr-ĭn) Pert. to the vomer.

vomeronasal (vō″mĕr-ō-nā′săl) Pert. to the vomer and nasal bones.

vomeronasal organ Organ of Jacobson.

vomica (vom′ĭ-kă) *pl.* **vomicae** [L., ulcer] **1.** An obsolete term for a cavity in the lungs, as from suppuration. **2.** An obsolete term for sudden and profuse expectoration of putrid purulent matter.

vomicose (vŏm′ĭ-kōs) Marked by many ulcers; ulcerous; purulent.

vomit (vom′ĭt) [L. *vomitare,* to vomit] **1.** Material ejected from the stomach through the mouth. **2.** To eject stomach contents through the mouth. SYN: *vomitus.* SEE: *melena; nausea.*

PHYSIOLOGY: The act is usually a reflex involving the coordinated activity of both voluntary and involuntary muscles. A certain position is assumed, the glottis is closed, the diaphragm and abdominal muscles contract, and the cardiac sphincter of the stomach relaxes while antiperistaltic waves course over the duodenum, stomach, and esophagus.

    bilious v. Bile forced back into the stomach and ejected with vomited matter.

    black v. Vomit containing blood acted on by gastric digestion; seen in digestion conditions where blood collects in the stomach.

    coffee-ground v. Vomit having the appearance and consistency of coffee grounds because of blood mixed with gastric contents. It can occur in any condition associated with hemorrhage into the stomach.

    fecal v. Feces in vomitus. This occurs in strangulated hernia or intestinal obstruction preventing normal bowel movements.

vomiting (vom′ĭt-ĭng) Ejection through the mouth of the contents of the gastrointestinal tract. Vomiting, along with diarrhea and hemorrhage, is an important potential cause of dehydration. It may result from toxins, drugs (such as those given for cancer chemotherapy), uremia, and fevers; cerebral tumors; meningitis; diseases of the stomach such as ulcer, cancer, dysmotility, or dyspepsia; hormonal changes in early pregnancy, reflux from pressure of the gravid uterus in pregnancy, uterine or ovarian disease, irritation of the fauces, intestinal parasites, biliary colic; intestinal obstruction; motion sickness; and neurological disorders such as migraine. Vomiting may also be psychogenic in origin. Esophageal vomiting may result from reflux or obstruction. SYN: *emesis*. SEE: table; *bulimia; hyperemesis gravidarum.*

TREATMENT: Antiemetic medicines may be administered orally, rectally, intramuscularly, or intravenously. Fluids may be given by mouth if the patient will accept them. If vomiting continues, and dehydration or acid-base imbalances occurs, intravenous fluids and electrolytes must be used to replace those lost in the vomit.

PATIENT CARE: Causative factors such as drugs, food, diseases, and psychological factors are assessed and treated if possible. Frequency, amount, time, and characteristics of the vomit are assessed. The patient is positioned to protect the airway and prevent aspiration; in the hospital, suction equipment is provided for the patient's safety. Food and fluids are withheld for several hours, and oral care is offered. For the pre-operative patient, restriction of foods and fluids for approx. 8 hr before surgery helps prevent postoperative vomiting. Comfort measures, e.g., a cool cloth applied to the face, are instituted. Vital signs, skin turgor, and urine output are monitored for evidence of dehydration. The health care giver promotes a calm environment and provides distraction.

anticipatory v. Vomiting that precedes a feared event, such as chemotherapy.

cyclic v. Periodic, recurring attacks of vomiting typically occurring in patients with a family history of migraine headaches. Such vomiting causes metabolic alkalosis as a result of chloride loss.

PATIENT CARE: The patient's symptoms are assessed and documented, vital signs monitored, fluid and electrolyte balance maintained, and prescribed medications administered to relieve

headache, nausea, and vomiting. A calm, stress-free environment is provided.

dry v. Nausea and retching without vomit.

epidemic v. Sudden unexplained attacks of gastroenteritis characterized by nausea, vomiting, and sometimes diarrhea. Although not proven, the symptoms are believed to be due to a virus. Treatment is symptomatic.

induced v. Vomiting induced by administration of certain emetics, e.g., syrup of ipecac or amorphine, or by physical stimulation of the posterior pharynx.

⚠️ Vomiting should never be induced after patients ingest caustic chemicals or in patients who cannot protect their airways.

pernicious v. Hyperemesis gravidarum.

projectile v. Ejection of vomit with great force.

psychogenic v. Occasional or persistent vomiting associated with severe emotional stress or brought on by the anticipation of stress.

stercoraceous v. Vomiting of fecal matter.

vomitus (vŏm′ĭ-tŭs) Vomit.

von Gierke disease SEE: *Gierke disease.*

von Graefe sign SEE: under *Graefe, Albrecht von.*

von Hippel-Lindau syndrome Hippel disease.

von Recklinghausen SEE: under *Recklinghausen, Friedrich D. von.*

von Willebrand disease SEE: *Willebrand disease.*

voodoo (voo′doo″) [Louisiana Fr. *voudou*, ult. fr a West African language, e.g., Fon or Ewe *vodŭ*, spirit, deity, demon] **1.** A religion that combines elements of Roman Catholicism with traditional African religion, magic, ritual, and witchcraft, primarily practiced in

Causes of Vomiting

Cause	Example
Gastrointestinal diseases	Esophageal obstruction, gastric distention, peptic ulcer disease, gastroparesis, cholecystitis, cholelithiasis, pancreatitis, intestinal obstruction, ileus
Metabolic illnesses	Hyponatremia, hypokalemia, hypercalcemia, adrenal insufficiency, uremia, ketoacidosis
Intoxications	Acetaminophen, arsenic, mercury, methanol, opiates, mescaline, food poisoning
Drug side effects	Antidepressants, digitalis, erythromycin, theophyllines, many chemotherapeutic drugs for the treatment of cancer (e.g., cisplatin)
Intracranial illnesses	Migraine, meningitis, intracranial hemorrhage
Febrile illnesses	Strep throat (esp. in children), pyelonephritis
Pregnancy	Hyperemesis gravidarum

the coastal regions of the southeastern U.S. and the Caribbean Islands, esp. Haiti. **2.** One who practices this religion. **3.** A charm or fetish used in this religion. **4.** A colloquial, disparaging term for nonsensical, simplistic, irrational, or superstitious activities or practices, e.g., "voodoo economics" or "voodoo science."

voracious (vō-rā′shŭs) [L. *vorare,* to devour] Having an insatiable or ravenous appetite.

vortex (vor′tĕks) *pl.* **vortices** [L., a whirlpool] A structure having a spiral or whorled appearance.

    coccygeal v. The region over the coccyx where lanugo hairs of the embryo come to a point.

    v. of heart The region at the apex of the heart where muscle fibers of the ventricles make a tight spiral and turn inward.

    v. lentis Spiral patterns on the surface of the lens owing to a concentric pattern of fiber growth.

vortices (vor′tĭ-sēz) [L.] Pl. of vortex.

    v. pilorum Hair whorls as in arrangement of hairs on the scalp.

vorticose (vor′tĭk-ōs) [L. *vortices,* whirlpools] Whirling or having a whorled arrangement.

vox (vŏks) *pl.* **voces** [L.] Voice.

voxel (vok′sĕl) [By analogy with *pixel*] A *vo*lume *el*ement, an individually representable volume of tissue detected by a digital radiographical imaging device, represented on the final image by a picture element (pixel).

voyeur (vwah-yĕr′, voy-ĕr′) [Fr., one who sees] One who derives sexual plea-

sure from watching naked people or the sexual activity of others.

voyeurism (voy′yĕr-ĭzm) The experiencing of sexual gratification by watching naked people or the sexual activity of others.

V/Q mismatch In ventilation/perfusion (V/Q) scanning, a region of the lung that ventilates normally but does not receive normal blood flow. SYN: *mismatch.*

VR *right vision; ventilation **rate**; vocal **resonance.***

VRE *vancomycin-resistant enterococci.*

VRSA *vancomycin-resistant **Staphylococcus** aureus.*

VS *vesicular sound; vital signs; volumetric solution.*

VSD *ventricular septal defect.*

VSG *variable surface **glycoprotein**.*

V$_T$ *tidal volume.*

VTE *venous **thromboembolism***

vulgaris (vŭl-gā′rĭs) [L.] Ordinary, common.

vulnerable (vŭl′nĕr-ă-bl) [L. *vulnerare,* to wound] Easily injured or wounded.

vulnerary (vŭl′nĕr-ār″ē) **1.** Pert. to wounds. **2.** An agent, esp. a folk remedy or herb, used to promote wound healing.

vulsella, vulsellum (vŭl-sĕl′ă, vŭl-sĕl′ŭm) [L. *vulsella,* tweezers] A forceps with a hook on each blade.

vulva (vŭl′vă, vŭl′vĕ″, ′vĕ″) *pl.* **vulvae** [L. *vulva,* covering] That portion of the female external genitalia lying posterior to the mons veneris, consisting of the labia majora, labia minora, clitoris, vestibule of the vagina, vaginal opening, Bartholin glands. SEE: illus. **vulval, vulvar** (vŭl′văl, vŭl′văr), *adj.*

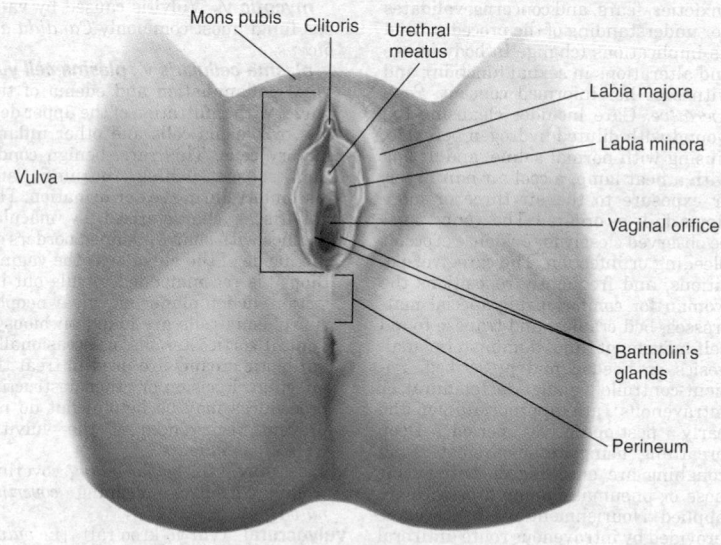

VULVA
Inferior view of the perineum

vulvar leukoplakia Lichen sclerosis et atrophicus.

vulvar vestibulitis syndrome Severe pain felt on pressing or touching the vestibule of the vagina or on attempted vaginal entry. Findings of localized erythema are limited to the mucosa of the vestibule. Although the cause is unknown, the syndrome often develops in women who have intractable moniliasis or who are receiving long-term antibiotic therapy. No therapy, including vestibulectomy, has been 100% effective. SEE: *vulvodynia*.

vulvectomy (vŭl-vĕk′tō-mē) [″ + Gr. *ektome,* excision] Excision of the vulva, used to manage cancers of the vulva. Surgical approaches depend on the extent of the disease. They range from simple vulvar excision (for small, confined lesions with no lymph node involvement) to radical vulvectomy with bilateral superficial and deep inguinal node dissection. If metastasis is extensive, resection may include the urethra, vagina, and rectum. Plastic surgery, including pelvic area reconstruction via a mucocutaneous graft may be carried out at a later date. SEE: *vulvar cancer*.

PATIENT CARE: The caregiver provides emotional support, encourages questions, and answers them. *Preoperative:* Care includes skin preparation, teaching about postoperative care (pain management, pulmonary hygiene, and venous stasis prevention) administration of prophylactic medications to prevent infection, and insertion of an indwelling catheter. The nurse encourages the woman to express her anxieties, fears, and concerns; validates her understanding of the procedure and its implications (change in body image and alterations in sexual function); and witnesses her informed consent. *Postoperative:* Care includes cleansing the wound with diluted hydrogen peroxide, rinsing with normal saline, and drying with a heat lamp, a cool-air hair dryer, or exposure to the air three or more times daily as ordered. The wound must be observed closely for evidence of occult bleeding or infection. The caregiver positions, and frequently repositions the woman for comfort using special mattresses, bed cradles, and trapeze to aid self-movement and administers analgesics as needed and prescribed. Patient-controlled analgesia (epidural or intravenous) are appropriate for the early post-operative period. Deep breathing using an inspirometer and coughing are encouraged. Antiembolic hose or pneumatic pump dressings are applied. Nourishment and hydration is provided by intravenous route until oral fluid and solids are tolerated. Antidiarrheal drugs are administered as needed. Wounds are cleansed to prevent infec-

tion. Stool softeners and a low-residue diet may be appropriate as the patient progresses. Depending on the extent of the procedure, home health care is arranged. Discharge teaching emphasizes care of the wound and catheter. The patient is advised to report bleeding, purulent discharge, or intolerable pain to the primary caregiver. After a simple vulvectomy, sexual intercourse may resume when the wound has healed (about 6 to 8 wk after surgery). Adjuvant postoperative treatments may include chemotherapy with or without radiation therapy. Irradiation may be used for palliative care if advanced age, poor health, extensive metastasis, or patient preference rules out surgical treatment.

vulvitis (vŭl-vīt′ĭs) [*vulva* + *-it is*] Inflammation of the vulva.

   acute nongonorrheal v. Vulvitis resulting from chafing of the opposed lips of the vulva, nonvenereal infection, or accumulation of sebaceous matter around the clitoris.

   desquamative v. Erosion or scarring of the vulva as a result of immunological or blistering conditions, such as contact dermatitis, lichen planus, lupus, or squamous cell carcinoma.

   follicular v. Inflammation of the hair follicles of the vulva.

   gangrenous v. Necrosis and sloughing of areas of the vulva, often a complication of infectious diseases such as diphtheria, scarlatina, herpes genitalis, or typhoid fever.

   leukoplakic v. Lichen sclerosis et atrophicus.

   mycotic v. Vulvitis caused by various fungi, most commonly *Candida albicans.*

   plasma cellularis v., plasma cell vulvitis Inflammation and edema of the vulva, with infiltration of the upper dermis by plasma cells and other inflammatory cells. This rare, benign condition causes itching, burning, and discomfort during sex or urination. The vulvitis is characterized by macular patches with sharply defined borders on the inside of the vulva near the vagina. Biopsy is recommended to rule out infection, lichen planus or vulvar neoplasia (plasma cells are found on biopsy). Topical corticosteroids or, occasionally, antibiotic creams are used to treat the infection. Excision or other destructive procedures may be helpful but do not prevent recurrences of the vulvitis. SYN: *Zoon vulvitis.*

vulvo-, vulv- [L. *volva, vulva,* covering, womb] Prefixes meaning *covering, vulva.*

vulvocrural (vŭl″vō-kroo′răl) [L. *vulva,* covering, + *cruralis,* pert. to the leg] Pert. to the vulva and thigh.

vulvodynia (vŭl″vō-din′ē-ă) [*vulvo-* +

-odynia] Nonspecific vulvar pain of unknown cause. Common complaints include sporadic pain, dyspareunia, and pruritus. A provisional diagnosis is based on the patient's symptoms, and an absence of any other vulvovaginal or systemic pathology. Palliative treatment is individualized; some women report relief of symptoms with an oxalate-restricted diet. SYN: *vestibulodynia*. SEE: *vaginitis; candidal vulvar **pruritus**; vulvar vestibulitis syndrome*.

The Vulvar Pain Foundation provides information and support for women with vulvodynia. Address: P.O. Box 4177, Graham, NC 27253; Telephone: 336-226-0704; Website: www.vulvarpainfoundation.org/. Other support groups may be found on the Internet.

PATIENT CARE: The health care professional encourages the woman to express her feelings and concerns. Careful review of the woman's history focuses on identifying coexisting disorders, and noting those factors or events that preceded the symptoms and those that increase or decrease symptoms. Instruction for the patient's palliative self-care emphasizes personal hygiene, including care of the vulva (e.g., avoiding tight clothing, wearing 100% cotton underwear, using tampons and pads correctly); using hypoallergenic detergents; avoiding chemical irritants; reducing stress; identifying and treating infections; and offering local topical anesthetics. Other treatments include physical therapy, trigger point injections, sexual counseling, cognitive behavioral therapy, biofeedback, and some pain-relieving antidepressants or anticonvulsants. Most treatments are often partly effective, and some women have refractory symptoms.

vulvopathy (vŭl-vŏp′ă-thē) [″ + Gr. *pa-thos,* disease, suffering] Any disorder of the vulva.

vulvovaginal (vŭl″vō-văj′ĭ-năl) [″ + *vagina,* a sheath] Pert. to the vulva and vagina. SYN: *vaginovulvar*.

vulvovaginal gland SEE: under *gland*.

vulvovaginitis (vŭl″vō-văj″ĭ-nī′tĭs) [″ + ″ + Gr. *itis,* inflammation] Simultaneous inflammation of the vulva and vagina, or of the vulvovaginal glands. The condition may be due to chemical irritation produced by materials present in medications, tight-fitting or nonabsorbent underclothes, inadequate perineal hygiene, allergic conditions, or infectious agents such as bacteria, yeasts, viruses, and parasites.

    diabetic v. Mycotic vulvar infection commonly occurring in diabetes mellitus.

VURD syndrome A combination of urinary tract abnormalities consisting of posterior urethral valves, unilateral urinary reflux, and dysplasia of the affected kidney. This condition typically occurs in male infants.

vv *veins.*

v/v *volume of dissolved substance per volume of solvent.*

VW *vessel wall.*

v/w *volume of a substance per unit of weight (mass) of another component.*

VX A toxic nerve gas, O-ethyl-[S]-[2-diisopropylaminoethyl]-methylphosphonothiolate, that might cause severe damage to public health if it were used in an act of biological terrorism.

V-Y-plasty A technique used in plastic surgery to repair a skin defect or to lengthen a scar as to release tension. A V-shaped incision is made, and the tissue at the apex of the V is placed on tension and advanced to create a straight limb of Y-shaped defect. The edges of the new wound are then sutured so that a Y-shaped scar is now produced.

W **1.** Symbol for the element tungsten (wolfram). **2.** *watt.*

w *week; wife; with.*

Waardenburg syndrome (var′dĕn-bŭrg″) [Petrus Johannes Waardenburg, Dutch ophthalmologist, 1886–1979] One of several related autosomal disorders that may produce skin, neurological, ophthalmic, and auditory deficits.

Wada test (wod′ä) [Juhn Atsushi Wada, Japanese-born Canadian neurosurgeon, b. 1924] A test to identify which side of the brain is used for what purposes, e.g., primarily language and memory. The test is employed before neurosurgery to prevent injury to essential parts of the brain. A dose of a barbiturate is injected into an internal carotid artery. After that side of the brain is sedated, the patient is asked to speak and to identify cards imprinted with pictures or words. After the first hemisphere of the brain recovers from sedation, the patient is asked to recall those objects or words that were shown. The test is then repeated on the opposite hemisphere.

Waddell signs (wad′ĕl, wa-del′) [Gordon Waddell, Scottish orthopedic surgeon] Any of a group of clinical tests occasionally used to identify patients whose back pain is not organic, i.e., more likely to be of psychological origin. The signs were once thought to discriminate patients who were malingering or seeking disability from those who had disk disease or back strain. The signs have not proved to be sensitive or specific when studied carefully.

wafer (wā′fĕr) A thin envelope or disk used to enclose a medication or to separate two structures from one another.

wafer implant SEE: under *implant.*

WAGR syndrome An acronym for a rare cluster of conditions and illnesses in childhood, including Wilms tumor of the kidney, aniridia, gonadoblastoma, and mental retardation. Children affected by this sporadically occurring disease have mutations of chromosome 11 and at least two of the four listed conditions.

waist (wāst) The small part of the human trunk between the thorax and hips.

waist circumference A gauge of abdominal obesity, obtained by measuring the abdomen at the level of the superior iliac crest with a tape measure. Among non-Asian American males, a waist circumference greater than 40 in (102 cm) increases the risk of diabetes mellitus, hypertension, hyperlipidemia, and heart disease. A circumference greater than 35 in (88 cm) conveys similar risks

for non-Asian American women. Americans of Asian ancestry have a lower risk of obesity than African Americans, European Americans, and Hispanics. Among Asians risks rise for men with a waist line that measures 36 in (91 cm) and for women when the waist exceeds 32 in (81 cm). SEE: *waist-to-hip ratio.*

PATIENT CARE: To measure an individual's waist, have the patient face away from the care provider with hands placed on the top of the hipbones or iliac crests. This spot should them be marked on each hip, using a felt-tip pen or skin marker. A measuring tape is then placed around the patient at the level of the iliac crests. It should be parallel to the floor and snug but not tight enough to dent the skin. The patient then exhales normally, and the measurement is taken and recorded. Weight loss should be encouraged when waist circumferences exceed guidelines, or when the body mass index is greater than 25 kg/m², using dietary modification and exercise. Physical activity should consist of more than 35 min of moderate-intensity aerobic exercise daily (unless contraindicated). Brisk walking is a good choice for most individuals, although any form of exercise that a patient finds enjoyable should be encouraged.

waist-to-hip ratio The measured circumference of the waist divided by the measured circumference of the hip. It has been used as one of several means of estimating abdominal body fat. Other anthropometrics that are similarly used are the "waist circumference," the "waist-to-height ratio," and the "body mass index." Although each of these measurements, if abnormal, has been statistically linked to increased risks for cardiovascular disease, they vary in their specificity and usefulness in people of differing ages and ethnicities.

waiting child Special needs child.

waiting list A form of health care rationing that is used esp. in the distribution of scarce resources, such as organs for transplantation.

waived test Any relatively simple laboratory test (such as a fecal occult blood test) that is permitted under the Clinical Laboratory Improvement Amendments (CLIA) of the U.S. Food and Drug Administration to be performed without special laboratory certification, inspection, or proficiency testing.

waiver **1.** An exemption from some aspect of a federal health care statute that gives a facility the right to deliver care in a manner that varies from published standards. **2.** The voluntary surrender of some legal right or privilege.

wakeful (wāk'fŭl) [AS. *wacian,* to be awake, + *full,* complete] **1.** Not able to sleep; sleepless. **2.** Alert.

Wald, Lillian (wald) U.S. nurse, 1867–1940, who founded the Henry Street Settlement in New York City, one of the world's first visiting nurse associations and one of the first settlement houses in a U.S. city..

Wald cycle (wald) [George Wald, U.S. biochemist (Nobel Laureate), 1906–1997] The transformations involved in the breakdown or resynthesis of rhodopsin.

Waldenström disease (val'dĕn-strām″) [Johann Henning Waldenström, Swedish surgeon, 1877–1972] Osteochondritis deformans juvenilis. SEE: *Waldenström's macroglobulinemia.*

Waldeyer-Hartz, Heinrich W. G. von, (val'di″ĕr-harts′) Ger. anatomist, 1836–1921.

    W. ring Lymphoid ring of the pharynx.

wale A welt; a raised ridge on the skin or on the epithelial lining of an organ.

walk 1. A method of locomotion of upright bipeds such as humans. **2.** The particular way an individual moves. SEE: *gait.*

walker (wok'ĕr) A device used to assist a person in walking, esp. a person prone to falling. It consists of a stable platform made of lightweight tubing that may be adjusted to a height that permits it to be grasped by the hands and used as support while taking a step. The walker is then moved forward and another step is taken. SEE: *crutch.*

Walker-Murdoch sign (wok'ĕr-mŭr'dok″) A test to evaluate the presence of arachnodactyly, in which the wrist is encircled by the opposite hand. Marfan's syndrome is suggested when the thumb of the surrounding hand overlaps the opposing pinky.

walking [AS. *wealcan,* to roll] The act of moving on foot; advancing by steps.

    impaired w. Limitation of independent movement within the environment on foot. SEE: *locomotion; Nursing Diagnoses Appendix.*

walking system A complex device that enables patients with spinal injuries resulting in paralysis of the legs to walk. The device uses computer-controlled electrical stimulation to muscles so that walking may be accomplished. Each of these devices is made esp. for each patient, and their use is experimental.

walking wounded In military medicine, an ambulatory case.

Walk Test A group of performance-based tests that measure the distance a patient walks in a defined time, e.g., 2 min, 6 min, and 12 min. Walk tests measure the functional level of patients suffering from a wide range of cardiac, respiratory, neurological, and musculoskeletal conditions.

wall [AS. *weall*] The limiting or surrounding substance or material of a vessel, cavity, or structure, such as an artery, vein, chest, or bladder. In dentistry, it may refer to specific boundaries of a cavity preparation or its location within the tooth, for example, cavity walls: buccal, lingual, mesial, distal, pulpal, coronal, axial, cervical, facial, incisal, gingival, or enamel.

    cell w. A wall made of cellulose and other materials that encloses a plant cell in a rigid framework. Plant cells have both cell membranes and cell walls. Plant cell walls cannot be digested by humans. SEE: *cellulose.*

Wallenberg syndrome (vol'ĕn-bĕrg) [Adolf Wallenberg, Ger. physician, 1862–1949] A syndrome resulting from occlusion of the posteroinferior cerebellar artery or one of its branches supplying the lower portion of the brainstem. Dysphagia, muscular weakness or paralysis, impairment of pain and temperature senses, and cerebellar dysfunction are characteristic. SYN: *lateral medullary infarct; lateral medullary syndrome.*

wallerian degeneration (wal-ir'ē-ăn) SEE: under *degeneration.*

walleye (wăl'ī) [ME. *wawil-eghed*] **1.** An eye in which the iris is light-colored or white. **2.** Leukoma or dense opacity of the cornea. **3.** A squint in which both visual axes diverge. SYN: *strabismus, divergent.*

Walsh, Mary B. A U.S. nurse-educator and author who, with Helen Yura, published the first comprehensive text on nursing process in 1967. SEE: *nursing process; Nursing Theory Appendix.*

wandering (wăn'dĕr-ĭng) [AS. *wandrian*] Moving about; not fixed.

wandering [specify sporadic or continual] Locomotion (with dementia or brain injury) characterized by its frequency and persistence: course appears to be meandering, aimless, or repetitive; frequently incongruent with boundaries, limits, or obstacles; impaired navigational ability. SEE: *Nursing Diagnoses Appendix.*

Wangiella (wăng″gē-ĕl'ă) [NL.] A genus of fungi that live in soil and rotting vegetation and have brown septate hyphae. The only known species in the genus is *W. dermatiditis.* The fungus primarily produces skin infections, although occasionally it can cause severe pneumonias or infections of the eye or brain, esp. in those with immunosuppressive diseases or conditions.

warble (wor'bĕl) The maggot (larva) of any of the flies of the genus *Hypoderma* (the warble fly). Larvae of the genus *Cuterebra* can infest the skin of humans and other animals, causing myiasis. SEE: *Cuterebra; Hypoderma; myiasis.*

Warburg, Otto H. (wor'bürg) Ger. biochemist, 1883–1970.

    W. apparatus A capillary manometer used for determining oxygen consumption and carbon dioxide production of small bits of cellular tissue. It is widely used in metabolism studies.

ward (ward) A large room in a hospital for the care of several patients.

    accident w. A ward reserved for the care of traumatic injuries.

    psychiatric w. A ward in a general hospital for mentally ill patients.

warfarin (wor'fă-rĭn) [Abbrev. of Wisconsin Alumni Research Foundation] $C_{19}H_{16}O_4$, a synthetic coumarin anticoagulant, originally developed as a rodenticide. It is popularly but inaccurately called a *blood thinner.*

    w. potassium $C_{19}H_{15}KO_4$, the potassium salt of warfarin, used as an anticoagulant.

    w. sodium $C_{19}H_{15}NaO_4$, the sodium salt of potassium, used to treat or prevent thrombi and embolisms. Coumadin is one of its trade names.

warfarin resistance syndrome A rare, autosomal dominant condition in which anomalies in the vitamin K receptor site interfere with or neutralize the effects of warfarin. Families with such anomalies have great difficulty achieving anticoagulation with warfarin.

warm-up (warm'ŭp″) Light or preliminary exercise, muscle stretching, or play movements performed to prepare oneself mentally and physiologically for more vigorous exercise. How much these preparations contribute to the prevention of injury is uncertain. **warm up,** *v.*

wart (wort) A circumscribed cutaneous elevation resulting from hypertrophy of the papillae and epidermis. SEE: illus.

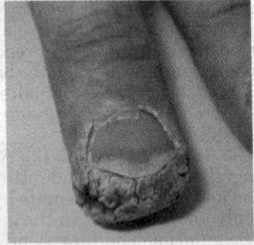

COMMON WARTS

    common w. Verruca vulgaris.

    genital w. A wart of the genitalia, caused by strains of human papillomavirus (HPV) some of which are transmitted by sexual contact. In women they may be associated with cancer of the cervix and vulva. An estimated 1 million

new cases of genital warts occur each year in the U.S., making genital warts the most common sexually transmitted illness. They commonly occur with other genital infections, and grow rapidly in the presence of heavy perspiration, poor hygiene, or the hormonal changes related to pregnancy. SYN: *venereal w.* SEE: illus.

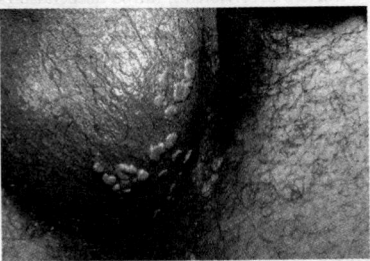

GENITAL WARTS

TREATMENT: A variety of therapies, including topically applied chemicals such as podophyllin (10% to 25% in compound tincture of benzoine), trichloroacetic acid, or dichloroacetic acid usually remove small warts; other treatments include CO_2 laser therapy, cryosurgery, electrocautery, 5-fluorouracil, imiquimod, and recombinant interferon alfa-2a. Nevertheless, there is no completely safe and effective therapy available for genital warts.

PATIENT CARE: A history is obtained for unprotected sexual contact with a partner with known infection, a new partner, or multiple partners. Standard precautions are used to examine the patient, to collect a specimen, or to perform associated procedures. The health care professional inspects the genitalia for warts growing on the moist genital surfaces, such as the subpreputial sac, the urethral meatus, and less commonly, the penile shaft or scrotum in male patients and the vulva and vaginal and cervical wall in female patients. Multiple warts have a cauliflower-like appearance. The patient usually reports no other symptoms, as the warts are generally painless, but a few complain of itching and pain. Diagnosis usually is made by visual inspection, but darkfield examination of wart cell scrapings may be used to differentiate HPV warts from those associated with second-stage syphilis. Biopsy is indicated if cancer is suspected. A nonthreatening, nonjudgmental atmosphere is provided to encourage the patient to verbalize feelings about perceived changes in sexual behavior and body image. Sexual abstinence or condom use during intercourse is recommended until healing is complete. The patient must inform sexual partners about the risk for genital warts and the need for evaluation. The patient should be tested for human immunodeficiency virus and for other sexually transmitted diseases. Genital warts can recur and the virus can mutate, causing warts of a different strain. The patient should report for weekly treatment until all warts are removed and then schedule a checkup for 3 months after all warts have disappeared. If podophyllin is applied, the patient is taught to remove it with soap and water 4 to 6 hrs after the application. Female patients should have a Papanicolaou test on a schedule recommended by their health care providers.

   plantar w. A wart on a pressure-bearing area, esp. the sole of the foot. SYN: *verruca plantaris*. SEE: illus.

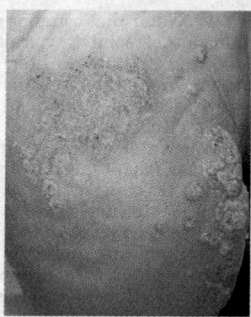

PLANTAR WART

   seborrheic w. Seborrheic keratosis.
   venereal w. Genital wart.
Wartenberg neurological pinwheel (wart′ĕn-bĕrg″) [Robert Wartenberg, Russian-born U.S. neurologist, 1886–1956] Pinwheel.
Warthin tumor (war′thin) [Aldred Warthin, U.S. pathologist, 1866–1931] A common benign tumor of the parotid gland. SYN: *papillary cystadenoma lymphomatosum*.
wash (wash) **1.** The act of cleaning, esp. a part or all of the body. **2.** A medicinal preparation used in cleaning or coating.
   bladder w. Filling the urinary bladder with liquid and then collecting the liquid after voiding to analyze it for abnormal cells or disease markers.
   eye w. A solution used to rinse the eyes. SYN: *collyrium*.
washout (wăsh′owt″) The lowering of the concentration of a substance from a solution, or from the human body, by withholding the substance and allowing it to be lost, metabolized, or excreted.
washout, nitrogen The removal of nitrogen from the body by breathing either 100% oxygen or a combination of oxygen and helium. Used to measure total lung capacity.
wasp [AS. *waesp*] Term sometimes applied to all insects belonging to the sub-

order Apocrita, order Hymenoptera (except the Formicidae or ants), but more generally restricted to the superfamilies Scolioidea, Vespoidea, and Specoidea. Members have the base of the abdomen constricted, and females have a piercing ovipositor, which in many species is modified into a sting. Many are social, living in large colonies. Common representatives are yellow jackets and hornets.
waste (wāst) [L. *vastus*, empty, desolate] **1.** Cachexia. **2.** Loss by breaking down of bodily tissue. **3.** Excreted material no longer useful to an organism.
   hazardous w. In health care, any blood, tissues, or human remains; cytotoxic drugs; infectious materials; radioactive isotopes; discarded surgical materials such as needles or sponges; or toxic substances.
   PATIENT CARE: These materials must be clearly labeled and securely stored before disposal, to prevent them from endangering public health.
   medical w. Infectious or physically dangerous medical or biological waste. Included are discarded blood and blood products; waste from the pathology department, including body parts, tissues, or fluids discarded during surgery or at autopsy; contaminated animal carcasses; animal body parts and bedding; sharps; discarded preparations made from genetically altered living organisms and their products. SEE: *sharps; Standard Precautions Appendix.*
   nuclear w. Any radioactive material produced as an unwanted byproduct of the extraction, conversion, enrichment, fabrication, or use of radionuclides in nuclear reactors.
   red bag w. Medical refuse, including potentially infectious materials and other hazardous products, that is placed in special containers to prevent them from contaminating the environment or spreading disease. SEE: *Standard Precautions Appendix.*
   solid w. Garbage, rubbish, trash, refuse, or sludge, as well as other discarded materials produced by agricultural, community, industrial, home, medical, mining, or municipal processes. Efforts to limit the environmental impact of solid waste, from the point of production through recovery processes to disposal and recycling, are known as solid waste management.
waste product Any of the metabolic byproducts that would be harmful if allowed to accumulate and are removed from the body by elimination. Carbon dioxide is exhaled from the lungs; undigested food and bile pigments are eliminated by the colon. The kidneys form urine and excrete nitrogenous wastes (such as urea and creatinine)

and excess amounts of minerals (such as sodium chloride).

wastewater (wăst'wat"ĕr) Water that has been released from homes, hospitals, or industry after it has been used or altered. It may contains significant concentrations of environmental pollutants.

wasting (wāst'ĭng) [L. *vastare*, to devastate] Enfeebling; causing loss of strength or size; emaciating. SEE: *marasmus.*

watchful waiting (wach'fŭl) A strategy that includes frequent observation of a patient's condition rather than immediate intervention with drugs or surgery.

water (wat'ĕr) H_2O, hydrogen combined with oxygen, forming a clear, tasteless, odorless fluid.

Water freezes at 32°F (0°C) and boils at 212°F (100°C). It is the principal chemical constituent of the body, composing approx. 65% of the body weight of an adult male and 55% of the adult female. It is distributed within the intracellular fluid and outside the cells in the extracellular fluid. Water is indispensable for metabolic activities within cells, being the medium in which chemical reactions usually take place. Outside of cells, it is the principal transporting agent of the body. The following properties of water are important to living organisms: it is an almost universal solvent; it is a medium in which acids, bases, and salts ionize, and the concentrations of these substances (electrolytes) are regulated by the body; it possesses a high specific heat and has a high latent heat of vaporization (important in regulating a constant body temperature); it possesses a high surface tension; and it is an important reacting agent and essential in all hydrolytic reactions.

Water is the principal constituent of all body fluids (blood, lymph, tissue fluid), secretions (saliva, gastric juice, bile, sweat), and excretory fluid (urine). Intake of water is determined principally by the sense of thirst. Excessive intake may lead to water intoxication; excessive loss to dehydration. Humans can survive for only a short time without water intake. The exact length of survival time varies with ambient temperature, moisture in available food, and amount of physical activity.

    ammonia w. Ammonium hydroxide.

    boiled rice w. The water remaining after rice has been cooked in it and removed; formerly used as an oral rehydration agent, esp. for children with diarrhea. Oral rehydration solutions are a better source of fluids and electrolytes and have replaced the use of boiled rice water for rehydration.

    bound w. Intracellular water at-

tached to organic molecules. It is not available for metabolic processes.

    w. of crystallization Water of hydration.

    deionized w. Water that has been passed through a substance that removes cations and anions present as contaminants. As ionic purity increases, so does the electrical resistance of the water.

⚠ Deionization is not synonymous with sterilization. It does not remove bacterial, fungal, or viral pathogens from water.

    distilled w. Water purified by distillation. It is used in preparing pharmaceuticals.

    fresh w. Water that contains a specified amount of solute, typically less than 1000 mg of solute per liter.

    gray w. Wastewater that has been used in kitchens, laundries, sinks, showers, and tubs, but not toilets.

    hard w. Water that contains dissolved salts of magnesium or calcium.

    heavy w. D_2O; an isotopic variety of water, esp. deuterium oxide, in which hydrogen has been displaced by its isotope, deuterium. Its properties differ from ordinary water in that heavy water has a higher freezing and boiling point and does not support life.

    w. of hydration Water within the crystalline structure of an ionic compound that can be removed by heating or other means, leaving a pure salt. SYN: *w. of crystallization.*

    w. for injection Distilled, sterilized water for parenteral use.

    mineral w. Water that contains sufficient inorganic salts to cause it to have therapeutic properties.

    potable w. Water suitable for drinking. Drinking water should be free of disease-causing organisms and should contain only trace amounts of organic and/or inorganic chemicals.

    purified w. Water that is filtered to be free of biological or chemical contaminants or is obtained by distillation or deionization.

    pyrogen-free w. Water free of fever-producing proteins (bacteria and their metabolic products). SEE: *w. for injection.*

    soft w. Water that contains very little, if any, dissolved salts of magnesium or calcium.

waterborne (wă'tĕr-bŏrn") Carried in water, esp. drinking water, surface water, lakes, rivers, or recreational swimming pools.

waterborne disease Any disease transmitted by consuming or bathing in water. Common disease-causing agents that contaminate water include *Cryp-*

tosporidium, Cyclospora, some hepatitis viruses, *Escherichia coli* 0157:H7, and metallic toxins.

Information on waterborne contamination can be obtained from the Environmental Protection Agency's Safe Drinking Water Hotline: www.epa.gov/watrhome, 1-800-426-4791

waterbug (wat'ĕr-bŭg″) **1.** American **cockroach. 2.** Oriental **cockroach.**

water cure Hydrotherapy.

waterfowl (wot'ĕr-fowl″) Ducks, geese, and swans. They are vectors of diseases such as avian influenza.

Waterhouse-Friderichsen syndrome (wăt'ĕr-hows-frĭd'ĕ-rĭk-sĕn) [Rupert Waterhouse, Brit. physician, 1873–1958; Carl Friderichsen, Danish physician, 1886–1979] Acute adrenal failure due to hemorrhage into the adrenal gland caused by meningococcal infection. SEE: *adrenal gland; meningitis, acute meningococcal.*

watermelon stomach (wat'ĕr-mel'ŏn) SEE: under *stomach.*

water moccasin Cottonmouth.

water pipe A pipe for smoking, with a bowl mounted on a container of water that cools the smoke, and used to smoke marijuana, tobacco, or another substance. SYN: *hookah; narghile; shisha* (1).

waters The common term for the amniotic fluid surrounding the fetus.

water seal chamber SEE: under *chamber.*

watershed A tissue that receives minimal blood flow because of its position at the smallest branches of an artery. This tissue may infarct when blood pressures drop, e.g., when patients are in shock and the distant reaches of small blood vessels do not receive an adequate supply of blood.

Waters projection (wat'ĕrz) Maxillary sinus radiograph.

water syringe SEE: under *syringe.*

watery diarrhea, hypokalemia, hypochlorhydria syndrome ABBR: WDHA. A rare syndrome characterized by the passage of loose stools, a low serum potassium level, and an elevated gastric pH. It is caused by excessive pancreatic secretion of vasoactive intestinal peptide (VIP). SYN: *pancreatic cholera.*

Watson, Margaret Jean Harman (wăt'sŏn) A nursing educator, born 1940, who developed the Theory of Human Caring. SEE: *Nursing Theory Appendix.*

Watson-Schwartz test (wŏt'sŏn-shwärts) [Cecil J. Watson, U.S. physician, 1901–1983; Samuel Schwartz, U.S. physician, b. 1916] A test used in acute porphyria to differentiate porphobilinogen from urobilinogen.

Watsu Treatment performed in a pool of water at body temperature (98°F). The practitioner performs a series of stretches and pressure-point massage on the client to strengthen muscles and increase flexibility.

watt [James Watt, Scottish engineer, 1736–1819] ABBR: W. A unit of electrical power. One watt is the power produced by 1 ampere of current flowing with a force or pressure (i.e., electromotive force) of 1 volt. In SI units, 1 W equals 1 J/sec. In other units, 1 W equals 1 newton m/sec. This is also equal to 0.7376 ft-lb/sec. SEE: *electromotive force.*

wattage (wŏt'ĭj) The electrical power produced or consumed by an electrical device, expressed in watts.

wave (wāv) **1.** A disturbance, usually orderly and predictable, observed as a moving ridge with a definable frequency and amplitude. **2.** An undulating or vibrating motion. **3.** An oscillation seen in the recording of an electrocardiogram, electroencephalogram, or other graphic record of physiological activity.

a w. **1.** A venous neck wave produced by atrial contraction. **2.** A component of right atrial and pulmonary artery wedge pressure tracings produced by atrial contraction. The a wave just precedes the first heart sound. It is absent in atrial fibrillation and is larger in atrioventricular dissociation and in conditions causing dilation of the right atrium.

alpha w. An electroencephalographic deflection often generated by cells in the visual cortex of the brain. SEE: *alpha rhythm.*

beta w. An electroencephalographic deflection. Its frequency is between 18 and 30 Hz. SEE: *beta rhythm.*

blast w. A shock wave produced by a blast or explosion. The wave front consists of air under very high pressure that can cause great damage to people, objects, and structures.

brain w. The fluctuation, usually rhythmic, of electrical impulses produced by the brain. SEE: *electroencephalography.*

c w. A component of right atrial and pulmonary capillary wedge pressure waves. It reflects the closing of the tricuspid valve at the beginning of ventricular systole. An abnormal configuration is seen in increased right heart pressure and with abnormalities of the tricuspid valve.

delta w. An abnormal deflection seen on the electrocardiogram in patients with pre-excitation syndromes, such as Wolff-Parkinson-White syndrome. It occurs at the beginning of the QRS complex and is classically described as causing the complex to have a "slurred upstroke."

dicrotic w. A positive wave following the dicrotic notch.

electromagnetic w. A wave-form

produced by simultaneous oscillation of electric and magnetic fields perpendicular to each other. The direction of propagation of the wave is perpendicular to the oscillations. The following waves, in order of increasing frequency and decreasing wavelength, are electromagnetic: radio, television, microwave, infrared, visible light, ultraviolet, x-rays, and gamma rays. SEE: *electromagnetic spectrum* for table.

excitation w. The wave of irritability originating in the sinoatrial node that sweeps over the conducting tissue of the heart and induces contraction of the atria and ventricles.

F w. Flutter waves in atrial fibrillation, detectable on the electrocardiogram at 250 to 350 per minute.

f w. A fibrillatory wave seen as the wavy base line on the electrocardiogram tracing of atrial fibrillation. These waves are caused by multiple ectopic foci in the atria.

J w. An upwardly curving deflection of the J point of the electrocardiogram, found in patients whose body temperature is less than 32°C. This finding is one cardiac effect of hypothermia. The J wave has a particular shape; viewed from above, its surface is convex. SYN: *Osborne w.*

light w. An electromagnetic wave that stimulates the retina or other optical sensors.

Mayer w. SEE: *Mayer wave*.

Osborne w. J wave.

P w. SEE: *electrocardiogram*.

postdicrotic w. A recoil or second wave (not always present) in a blood pressure tracing.

pulse w. The pressure wave originated by the systolic discharge of blood into the aorta. It is not due to the passage of the ejected blood but is the result of the impact being transmitted through the arterial walls. The velocity in the aorta may be as high as 500 cm/sec and as low as 0.07 cm/sec in capillaries. The speed of transmission varies with the nature of the arterial wall, increasing with age as the arteries become less resilient. Thus in arteriosclerosis, the velocity is increased over normal.

Q w. A downward or negative wave of an electrocardiogram following the P wave. It is usually not prominent and may be absent without significance. New Q waves are present on the electrocardiogram after patients suffer myocardial infarction. SEE: *electrocardiogram*.

R w. SEE: *electrocardiogram*.

radio w. An electromagnetic wave between the frequencies of 10^{11} and 10^4 Hz.

S w. SEE: *electrocardiogram*.

shock w. 1. A compression wave produced by a shock such as an earthquake or explosion that is characterized by a sudden change in air pressure, density, and velocity. **2.** An electromagnetic or sonic shock wave focused at a specific target (e.g., within the body). **3.** A sudden disruption. SEE: *extracorporeal shock wave lithotripsy; shock w.*

sound w. A vibration of a vibrating medium that, on stimulating sensory receptors of the cochlea, is capable of giving rise to a sensation of sound. In dry air, the velocity is 1087 ft (331.6 m)/sec at 0°C; in water, it is approx. four times faster than in air.

T w. The portion of the electrical activity of the heart that reflects repolarization of the ventricles. SEE: *electrocardiogram; interval, Q-T*.

theta w. A brain wave present in the electroencephalogram. It has a frequency of about 4 to 7 Hz.

U w. In the electrocardiogram, a low-amplitude deflection that follows the T wave. It is exaggerated in hypokalemia and with digitalis use, and negative in ventricular hypertrophy. SEE: *QRST complex; electrocardiogram*.

ultrashort w. An arbitrary designation of radio waves of a wavelength of less than 1 m.

ultrasonic w. A sound wave of greater frequency than 20 kHz. These waves do not produce sound audible to the human ear.

waveform The shape or the representation of a signal, e.g., in cardiology, the shape of the electrical shock used in cardioversion or defibrillation.

biphasic w. A waveform used by some defibrillators that discharges energy in two phases (first positive, then negative). The shock applied by a biphasic defibrillator uses 30-40% less peak current at the same applied energy level than a monophasic defibrillator and is both less injurious to the heart and more likely to terminate ventricular fibrillation.

damped sinusoidal w. A defibrillation waveform that rises sharply to a peak voltage and then returns gradually to zero.

monophasic w. A waveform used by some defibrillators that delivers a single shock of positive energy to the myocardium.

truncated exponential w. A defibrillation waveform that rises sharply to a peak voltage and then is abruptly cut off and returns to zero.

wavelength (wāv'lĕngth) The distance between the beginning and end of a single wave cycle, usually measured from the top of one wave to the top of the next one.

wave scheduling A method for assigning appointments for patients that brings several patients in to see their health care professionals at the same time e.g., at the beginning of each hour instead of every 15 or 20 min during the hour.

wax [AS. *weax*] **1.** A substance obtained from bees (beeswax), plants, or petroleum (paraffin). It is solid at room temperature. In medicine, a purified form, white wax, is used in making ointments and to stop bleeding from bones during surgery. In dentistry, it is used, e.g., to create fixed appliances or dentures. **2.** Any substance with the consistency of beeswax. **3.** Earwax. SYN: *cerumen*.

   bone w. A polymer used to fill defects in damaged body parts and to control bleeding from injured bone, e.g., in orthopedic surgery. Its use is occasionally associated with side effects, including the formation of foreign-body reactions or the development of infections.

   casting w. A mixture of several waxes that can be carved or formed into shapes to be cast in metal.

waxing-up In dentistry, the shaping of wax around the contours of a trial denture or cast restoration.

wax pattern A molded or carved pattern in wax used extensively in dentistry and jewelry-making whereby casts are made using the lost wax technique.

waxy (wăks'ē) [AS. *weax*, wax] Resembling or pert. to wax.

WBC *white blood cell; white blood count.*

weak (wēk) [Old Norse *veikr*, flexible] **1.** Lacking physical strength or vigor; infirm, esp. as compared with what would be the normal or usual for that individual. **2.** Dilute, as in a weak solution, or weak tea. **3.** Biologically or chemically active; said, e.g., of acids, bases, electrolytes, muscles, or toxins.

weak dominance SEE: under *dominance*.

weakness (wēk'nĕs) **1.** Fatigue; lack of strength; lack of energy. **2.** Any structural or functional deficiency.

   positional w. The apparent weakness of a muscle when tested in a shortened range of motion. This is a normal phenomenon of the length-tension curve of a muscle. To differentiate positional weakness from general muscle weakness and assess strength accurately, the muscle must be tested throughout its entire range of motion.

   PATIENT CARE: The patient should be positioned carefully when testing for muscle force production.

   stretch w. A form of positional weakness in which the apparent weakness of a muscle results from prolonged positioning in a lengthened position, thus shifting the muscle length-tension curve to the right. This phenomenon is observed when the force production of the lengthened muscle is limited when it is tested in a relatively short position.

   PATIENT CARE: Care must be taken in positioning when testing for muscle

force production. To assess strength accurately, muscles should be tested in their functional or ideal positions or throughout the entire range of motion.

wean (wēn) **1.** To accustom an infant to discontinuation of breast milk by substitution of other nourishment.

   PATIENT CARE: When weaning an infant is abrupt or sudden, some women may feel guilt about the end of a special relationship with their infants and experience remorse or grief. The nurse can assist by suggesting alternative ways the mother can nurture her infant. The nurse can also assist the mother with engorgement by instructing her to wear a supporting bra and to pump the breasts lightly to relieve some of the pressure but not to empty them. Ice packs and mild analgesics may be taken to relieve discomfort.

   2. The gradual discontinuation of a therapy. SEE: *weaning from ventilator support.*

weaning from ventilator support The act of gradually removing persons with reversible forms of respiratory failure who are receiving mechanical ventilation from that support. This may be done by alternating full ventilatory support with increasingly long periods of unassisted breathing. The timing and frequency of the weaning periods should be individualized to each patient. Usually by the time the patient can tolerate 2 hr of spontaneous breathing, ventilatory support may be discontinued.

   PATIENT CARE: Weaning from mechanical ventilation is done only in the stable patient in whom the acute precipitating event has been corrected. The respiratory therapist should review current arterial blood gas reports, breathing pattern, vital signs, and vital capacity before each attempt at weaning. The procedure should be described to the patient and he or she should be told what to expect and what his or her role in weaning will be. The nurse, physician, and respiratory therapist should reassure the patient that he or she will not be endangered by weaning trials or left alone during these periods. The nurse and respiratory therapist should also provide positive reinforcement regarding the patient's progress and the anticipated successful termination of support. Patient status and response to the procedure should be continuously evaluated.

weaning readiness screen SEE: under *screen*.

weanling (wēn'lĭng) A young child or infant recently changed from breast to formula feeding.

weaponize (wĕ'pŏn-īz) To convert a bacterial culture or some other substance into an agent that can be used to injure or kill.

wear and care regimen Wear and care practice.

wear pattern The location of tooth erosion as determined by the characteristics of the facets of the teeth.

wear period SEE: under *period*.

web (web) A thin tissue or membrane extending across a space.

    esophageal w. A group of thin membranous structures that include mucosal and submucosal coats across the esophagus. They may be congenital or may follow trauma, inflammation, or ulceration of the esophagus. SEE: *Plummer-Vinson syndrome*.

    terminal w. A microscopic weblike network that is beneath the microvilli of intestinal absorption cells, and beneath the stereocilia of the hair cells of the inner ear.

web-based (web'bāst') Founded on, or depending on the Internet. Said, for example, of certain forms of education and knowledge dissemination.

webbed [AS. *webb*, a fabric] Having a membrane or tissue connecting adjacent structures, as the toes of a duck's feet.

Weber, Ernst Heinrich (web'ĕr) Ger. anatomist and physiologist, 1795–1878.

    W's law The increase in stimulus necessary to produce the smallest perceptible increase in sensation bears a constant ratio to the strength of the stimulus already acting.

Weber, Moritz I. (vā'bĕr) Ger. anatomist, 1795–1875.

Weber-Christian disease (web'ĕr-krĭs'chĕn) [Fredrick Parkes Weber, Brit. physician, 1863–1962; Henry A. Christian, U.S. physician, 1876–1951] Relapsing, febrile, nodular, nonsuppurative panniculitis, a generalized disorder of fat metabolism characterized by recurring episodes of fever and the development of crops of subcutaneous fatty nodules.

Weber syndrome (web'ĕr) [Sir Hermann David Weber, Brit. physician, 1823–1918] Paralysis of the oculomotor nerve on one side with contralateral spastic hemiplegia. It is caused by a lesion of the crus cerebri.

Weber test [Friedrich Eugen Weber, Ger. otologist, 1823–1891] A test for unilateral deafness. A vibrating tuning fork held against the midline of the top of the head is perceived as being so located by those with equal hearing ability in the ears; to persons with unilateral conductive-type deafness, the sound will be perceived as being more pronounced on the diseased side; in persons with unilateral nerve-type deafness, the sound will be perceived as being louder in the good ear. SEE: *hearing*.

webinar (web'ĭ-nar') [(*World Wide*) *Web* (*based sem*)*inar*] An interactive lecture, meeting, presentation, or educational forum broadcast from one location to people using networked computers at remote locations.

Wechsler, David (weks'lĕr) Romanian-born U.S. psychologist, 1896–1981.

    W. Adult Intelligence Scale ABBR: WAIS. A commonly used intelligence test to evaluate cognitive function in people over 16. It consists of seven verbal and seven nonverbal (performance) subsections. It assesses vocabulary, verbal comprehension, verbal reasoning, short-term memory, arithmetic skills, problem solving, visual perception, logic, and visual-motor coordination.

    W. Intelligence Scale for Children ABBR: WISC. A widely used intelligence test for children between 5 and 16. The test is often used by professional testers or licensed psychologists to diagnose learning disorders. It consists of two scales: one assesses language skills, the other visual and motor skills.

wedge (wej) **1.** A solid object with a broad base and two sides arising from the base to intersect each other and to form an acute angle opposite the base. **2.** In radiography, a filter placed in the primary x-ray beam to vary the intensity. **3.** Lift (2).

    step w. A quality control device consisting of increasing thicknesses of absorber through which radiographs are taken to determine the amounts of radiation reaching the film.

wedging 1. Suffocation that results from compression of the chest between two firm surfaces. It is an occasional cause of sudden infant death syndrome, e.g., when an infant becomes lodged between a sleeping partner and a wall or mattress. It can also occur in adults, e.g., when they are trapped in collapsing buildings or between massive structures. **2.** The squeezing or entrapment of any anatomical structure between two others. **3.** The obstruction of blood flow through a vessel by a catheter placed into its lumen.

WEE *western equine encephalomyelitis.*

WeeFIM The Functional Independence Measure adapted for children aged 6 months to 7 years. SEE: *Functional Independence Measure*.

weeping [AS. *wepan*, to lament] **1.** Shedding tears. **2.** Moist, dripping.

    bloody w. Hemorrhage from the conjunctiva.

weeverfish (wē'vĕr-fĭsh") [O.Fr. *wivre*, serpent + "] Any of several species of poisonous, bottom-dwelling fish of shallow salt waters, with dorsal and opercular spines that are used to inject a toxin into skin and soft tissue.

Wegener granulomatosis, Wegener syndrome (veg'ĕn-ĕr) [Frederich Wegener, Ger. pathologist, 1843–1917] A systemic necrotizing vasculitis marked by pneumonitis and glomerulonephritis; small and medium-sized blood vessels throughout the body may be affected. The average age of onset is 40, and the disease affects men more often than women.

ETIOLOGY: The precise etiology is unknown. Autoantibodies have been identified in the blood of approx. 90% of patients. Granulomas may be present in the lung, upper respiratory tract, and small arteries and veins. Localized or diffuse inflammatory patches are seen in the glomerular capillaries of the kidney.

SYMPTOMS: Chronic pneumonitis and glomerulonephritis are the most prominent signs; ulcerations of the nasopharyngeal mucosa also are common. Other signs and symptoms include muscle and joint pain, skin rashes, fever, and neuropathy.

TREATMENT: Suppressive immunotherapeutic drugs such as cyclophosphamide and corticosteroids are used to control the disease. Trimethoprim-sulfamethoxazole may prevent relapses. There is a 1-year, 80% mortality rate in untreated patients; when treatment is effective, patients can live normal lifespans. Those with diffuse glomerular damage may develop chronic renal failure. SEE: *granuloma*.

Weigert, Carl (vī′gĕrt) Ger. pathologist, 1845–1904.

    W. elastic fiber stain **Weigert** elastic stain.

    W. elastic stain A histological stain used to identify elastin in tissue samples. SYN: ***Weigert*** *elastic fiber stain*.

weighing, underwater Hydrodensitometry.

weight (wāt) The gravitational force exerted on an object, usually by the earth. The unit of weight is the newton (1 newton equals 0.225 lb). The difference between weight and mass is that the weight of an object varies with the force of gravity, but the mass remains the same. For example, an object weighs less on the moon than on earth because the force of gravity is less on the moon; but the mass of the object is the same in both places. SEE: *mass (3)*.

Many diseases cause alterations of body weight (BW). BW decreases in Addison's disease, AIDS, cancer, chronic diarrhea, chronic infections, untreated type I diabetes mellitus, anorexia, prolonged lactation, marasmus, obstruction of the pylorus or thoracic duct, starvation, tuberculosis, and peptic ulcer.

Normal weight depends on the frame of the individual. SEE: table.

    apothecaries′ w. SEE: *apothecaries′ weights and measures*.

    atomic w. ABBR: at. wt. The weight of an atom of an element compared with that of ¹⁄₁₂ the weight of carbon-12. The term is widely used, but the correct term is *atomic mass*.

    avoirdupois w. SEE: *avoirdupois measure*.

    birth w. The weight of a newborn. The normal weight of a newborn is between 5.5 lb (2.5 kg) and 10 lb (4.5 kg) and is directly related to the gestational age at which the infant was born. Birth weight is an important index of maturation and chance for survival. Weight of less than 2.5 kg is known as low birth weight (LBW) and is associated with an increased chance of death in the perinatal period. Medical advances have increased the chance of survival of newborns of 2.0 kg or more. SEE: *large for gestational age; small for gestational age*. SEE: *low birth weight*.

    dosing w. The body weight used for calculating the appropriate dosage of a medication for those whose weight exceeds the usual average range. Weight-based dosing is used to correct for different drug distributions and pharmacodynamics in overweight or obese patients.

⚠ Obese patients metabolize fat-soluble medications differently from lean patients, and the differences may result in clinically important undermedication or overmedication. One formula used to calculate a safe weight-based dosage for obese patients depends on the total body weight (TBW) and ideal body weight (IBW) as follows: dosing weight = (0.3)(TBW−IBW) + IBW.

    drained w. The weight of food solids that remain after the liquids in which they have been prepared are removed.

    dry w. The body weight of a person after ideal hemodialysis, i.e., of a patient in renal failure who has neither edema nor high blood pressure.

    equivalent w. An obsolete term for the weight of a chemical element that is equivalent to and will replace a hydrogen atom (1.008 g) in a chemical reaction.

    extremely low birth w. ABBR: ELBW. A birth weight of less than 1000 g (2.2 lb).

    gram molecular w. Gram molecular **mass**.

    ideal body w. ABBR: IBW. The weight in pounds or kilograms a person should weigh, based on height and frame, to achieve and maintain optimal health. Several tables, such as the Metropolitan Life Height and Weight Table, show ideal body weights for men and women of varying heights. These references may be used to help set goals for patients who are underweight or overweight. SEE: *weight* for table.

    low birth w. ABBR: LBW. Abnor-

1983 Metropolitan Height and Weight Tables for Men and Women According to Frame, Ages 25 to 59

Men					Women				
Height (in shoes)*		Weight in Pounds (in indoor clothing)†			Height (in shoes)*		Weight in Pounds (in indoor clothing)†		
Ft.	In.	Small Frame	Medium Frame	Large Frame	Ft.	In.	Small Frame	Medium Frame	Large Frame
5	2	128–134	131–141	138–150	4	10	102–111	109–121	118–131
5	3	130–136	133–143	140–153	4	11	103–113	111–123	120–134
5	4	132–138	135–145	142–156	5	0	104–115	113–126	122–137
5	5	134–140	137–148	144–160	5	1	106–118	115–129	125–140
5	6	136–142	139–151	146–164	5	2	108–121	118–132	128–143
5	7	138–145	142–154	149–168	5	3	111–124	121–135	131–147
5	8	140–148	145–157	152–172	5	4	114–127	124–138	134–151
5	9	142–151	148–160	155–176	5	5	117–130	127–141	137–155
5	10	144–154	151–163	158–180	5	6	120–133	130–144	140–159
5	11	146–157	154–166	161–184	5	7	123–136	133–147	143–163
6	0	149–160	157–170	164–188	5	8	126–139	136–150	146–167
6	1	152–164	160–174	168–192	5	9	129–142	139–153	149–170
6	2	155–168	164–178	172–197	5	10	132–145	142–156	152–173
6	3	158–172	167–182	176–202	5	11	135–148	145–159	155–176
6	4	162–176	171–187	181–207	6	0	138–151	148–162	158–179

SOURCE OF BASIC DATA: Build Study, 1979, Society of Actuaries and Association of Life Insurance Medical Directors of America, 1980. Copyright 1983 Metropolitan Life Insurance Company. Reprinted Courtesy of Metropolitan Life Insurance Company, *Statistical Bulletin*. Copyright 1983 Metropolitan Life Insurance Company.

* Shoes with 1-in. heels.

† Indoor clothing weighing 5 lb for men and 3 lb for women.

mally low weight of a newborn, usually less than 2500 g. Its causes include: preterm delivery of less than 37 weeks, multiple gestation, an abnormal uterus or cervix, congenital (genetic) anomalies in the fetus, maternal smoking or illicit drug use, placental malformation or malfunction, inadequate maternal nutrition, or a variety of other socioeconomic problems. Early, regular prenatal care and control of chronic and acute health problems help reduce risk. A series of ultrasounds can monitor fetal development. Early delivery is necessary if the fetus does not show signs of improvement. Incomplete maturation of the newborn's lungs is the most common cause of morbidity and mortality in LBW infants. Surfactants and a variety of neonatal technological supports decrease burden of this disease. Nursing/perinatal considerations include maintaining normal body temperature; diagnosis and treatment of hypoglycemia; maintenance of fluid, electrolyte, and nutritional status; and careful monitoring of newborn intake and output. Respiratory distress may be present, requiring oxygen and ventilation. Many preterm infants also have hyperbilirubinemia and are treated with phototherapy.

molecular w. ABBR: mol. wt.; MW. The weight of a molecule attained by totaling the atomic weight (mass) of its constituent atoms. SEE: *atomic w.*

set point w. The concept that body weight is controlled by the central nervous system and set at a certain value. The value is more or less stable until something occurs to alter it, e.g., when a disturbance of hypothalamic function interferes with the satiety and feeding centers.

troy w. A system of weighing gold, silver, precious metals, and jewels in which 5760 gr equal 1 lb (1gr equals 0.0648 g). SEE: *Weights and Measures Appendix.*

usual body w. ABBR: UBW. Body weight value used to compare a person's current weight with his or her own baseline weight. The UBW may be a more realistic goal than the ideal body weight for some individuals. SEE: *ideal body w.*

very low birth w. ABBR: VLBW. A body weight at delivery of less than 1500 g (but more than 500 g). Newborns that are this small make up about 1% of all births in the U.S. but account for about 60% of deaths in the first month of life.

w. in volume ABBR: w/v. The amount by weight (mass) of a solid substance dissolved in a measured quantity of liquid. Percent w/v expresses the number of grams of an ingredient in 100 mL of solution.

w. in weight ABBR: w/w. The amount by weight of a solid substance dissolved in a known amount (by weight) of liquid. Percent w/w expresses the number of grams of one ingredient in 100 g of solution.

weight bearing Supporting some or all of the mass of the body on bones, muscles, and tendons, e.g. those that have been recently injured and are now being rehabilitated.

weight cycling Rapid increases and decreases in body weight. It is colloquially called a *yo-yo diet.*

weighting (wāt′ĭng) **1.** In radiation therapy that uses two opposing fields, the use of a higher dose for one of the fields. **2.** In statistical or numerical analysis, the placing of emphasis on a variable or the gauging of the impact of a variable among a group of potential influences on an outcome.

weightlessness The condition of not being acted on by the force of gravity. It is present when astronauts travel in areas so distant from the earth, moon, or planets that the force of gravity is virtually absent.

weight-loss surgery SEE: under *surgery.*

weights and measures SEE: *Weights and Measures Appendix.*

weight velocity The increase in body weight of a child over a specified period of time (e.g., a month or a year).

Weil disease (vīl) [Adolf Weil, Ger. physician, 1848–1916] Leptospirosis caused by any one of several serotypes of *Leptospira interrogans* such as *L. icterohemorrhagica* in rats, *L. pomona* in swine, or *L. canicola* in dogs. All of these may be pathogenic for humans.

ETIOLOGY: The infection is caused by contact with infected rat urine or feces.

SYMPTOMS: Symptoms include muscular pains, fever, jaundice, and enlargement of the liver and spleen.

TREATMENT: Penicillins or tetracyclines are curative.

PREVENTION: Doxycycline may be used to prevent infection in those exposed to the spirochetes.

Weil-Felix reaction, Weil-Felix test (vīl-fā′lĭks) [Edmund Weil, Austrian bacteriologist, 1880–1922; Arthur Felix, Ger. bacteriologist, 1887–1956] The agglutination of certain *Proteus* organisms caused by the development of *Proteus* antibodies in certain rickettsial diseases.

Welch bacillus (welsh) [William Henry Welch, U.S. pathologist, 1850–1934] *Clostridium perfringens,* the causative organism of gas gangrene. SEE: *gas gangrene.*

weld (wĕld) [variant of *well,* to boil] To fuse or join two objects with heat.

well-being committee (wĕl′bē″ĭng) An administrative body convened by a health care facility to review instances of inappropriate behavior by staff. The committee may also assist in the rehabilitation of impaired practitioners.

Wellbutrin SR (wĕl′bū-trĭn″) SEE: *bupropion.*

Wellens syndrome (wel′ĕn) [Hein J.J. Wellens, contemporary Dutch cardiologist] The electrocardiographic (ECG) signs of impending occlusion of the left main or left anterior descending coronary artery. ECG shows an inverted symmetrical T wave with little or no associated change of the ST segment or R wave. Inversion appears principally in the V leads. The finding identifies patients who are at risk for an extensive myocardial infarction.

wellness (wel′nĕs) Good health, as well as its appreciation and enjoyment, esp. when actively pursued, e.g., by moderate diet and exercise. Wellness is more than a lack of disease symptoms; it is often considered to be a state of mental and physical balance and fitness. SYN: *subjective well-being.*

Wells syndrome Eosinophilic **cellulitis**.

welt [ME. *welte*] An elevation on the skin produced by a lash, blow, or allergic stimulus. The skin is unbroken and the mark is reversible.

wen (wĕn) [AS.] A cyst resulting from the retention of secretion in a sebaceous gland. One or more rounded or oval elevations, varying in size from a few millimeters to about 10 cm, appear slowly on the scalp, face, or back. They are painless, rather soft, and contain a yellow-white caseous mass. The sac and contents should be carefully dissected to prevent its recurrence. SYN: *sebaceous cyst; steatoma.* SEE: *Fordyce disease.*

Wenckebach, Karel F. (veng′kĕ-bok″) Dutch internist, 1864–1940.

W. period A form of incomplete heart block in which, as detected by electrocardiography, there is progressive lengthening of the P-R interval until there is no ventricular response; and then the cycle of increasing P-R intervals begins again. SYN: **Wenckebach** *phenomenon.*

W. phenomenon Wenckebach period.

Werdnig-Hoffmann disease (vĕrd′nĭg-hof′măn) [Guido Werdnig, Austrian neurologist, 1844–1919; Johann Hoffmann, Ger. neurologist, 1857–1919] Spinal muscular atrophy.

Werdnig-Hoffmann paralysis Infantile muscular atrophy, considered by some to be identical with amyotonia congenita.

Werdnig-Hoffmann syndrome Werdnig-Hoffmann paralysis.

Werlhof disease (verl′hof″) [Paul G. Werlhof, Ger. physician, 1699–1767] Idiopathic thrombocytopenic purpura.

Wermer syndrome (wĕrm′ĕr) [Paul

Wermer, U.S. internist, 1898–1975] Multiple endocrine neoplasia, type I.

Werner syndrome (věrn′ěr) [C. W. O. Werner, Ger. physician, 1879-1936] An autosomal recessive disease in which adults age at an accelerated pace. SEE: *progeria*.

Wernicke, Carl (ver′nĭk-ĕ) Ger. neurologist, 1848–1905.

W. aphasia An injury to the Wernicke's area in the temporal lobe of the dominant hemisphere of the brain, resulting in an inability to comprehend the spoken or written word. Visual and auditory pathways are unaffected, but patients are unable to differentiate between words or interpret their meaning. Although patients speak fluently, they are unable to function socially because their ability to communicate effectively is impaired by paraphasia. They also may be unable to repeat spoken words. If the condition is due to a stroke, the aphasia may improve with time. The disorder is often caused by impairment of blood flow through the lower division of the left middle cerebral artery. SEE: *speech, paraphasic*.

W. area An area in the dominant hemisphere of the brain that recalls, recognizes, and interprets words and other sounds in the process of using language. SYN: *Wernicke center*.

W. center Wernicke's area.

W. encephalopathy Encephalopathy associated with thiamine (vitamin B1) deficiency; usually associated with chronic alcoholism or other causes of severe malnutrition. SYN: *Wernicke's syndrome*.

W.'s syndrome Wernicke's encephalopathy.

Westermark sign (wes′tĕr-mark″) An abnormal x-ray finding in pulmonary embolism. It consists of diminished vascular markings distal to the clot in combination with unusually prominent vessels proximal to it.

Western blot test A technique for analyzing protein antigens. Initially, the antigens are separated by electrophoresis on a gel and transferred to a solid membrane by blotting. The membrane is incubated with antibodies, and then the bound antibodies are detected by enzymatic or radioactive methods. This method is used to detect small amounts of antibodies.

Western Ontario McMaster Osteoarthritis Index ABBR: WOMAC. A self-administered assessment test of hip or knee pain, disability, and joint stiffness in osteoarthritis patients.

Western red cedar An evergreen tree (*Thuja plicata*) that flourishes in the rainforests of the northwestern U.S. and western Canada. Bark dust shed by the tree is a common source of occupational asthma and rhinitis.

West Nile virus SEE: under *virus*.

Westphal-Edinger nucleus SEE: *Edinger-Westphal nucleus*.

West syndrome (west) [W. J. West, Brit. physician, 1794–1848] A form of epilepsy occurring in the first 12 months of life and characterized by myoclonic jerking, EEG hypsarrhythmia, and abnormal brain and behavioral development. It often results from an underlying lesion in the brain (e.g., as in tuberous sclerosis). Most children who survive to the age of 5 have less than normal intelligence, and many have persisting seizures.

wet (wet) **1.** Soaked with moisture, usually water. **2.** A colloquial term for edematous or overhydrated.

wet brain An increased amount of cerebrospinal fluid with edema of the meninges; may be associated with alcoholism.

wet cup SEE: under *cup*.

wet dream Nocturnal emission.

wet nurse SEE: under *nurse*.

wet nurse phenomenon The production of milk in response to repeated stimulation of the nipples in unpregnant women who have previously been pregnant.

wet pack SEE: under *pack*.

wetting (wet′ing) Involuntary release of urine; urinary incontinence. SEE: *enuresis; nocturia*.

Wetzel grid (wĕt′sĕl) [Norman C. Wetzel, U.S. pediatrician, 1897–1984] A graph for use in evaluating growth and development in children aged 5 to 18 years.

Wharton jelly The gelatinous intercellular material of the umbilical cord; it consists of collagen, mucin, and hyaluronic acid. It is rich in hyaluronic acid, and in primitive stem cells. SYN: *umbilical cord matrix*.

wheal (hwēl) A more or less round and temporary elevation of the skin, white in the center with a pale-red periphery, accompanied by itching. It is seen in urticaria, insect bites, anaphylaxis, and angioneurotic edema. SYN: *pomphus*.

wheal and flare reaction The response within 10 to 15 min to an antigen injected into the skin. The injected skin elevates and blanches, and becomes surrounded by a red rim of inflamed tissue.

wheat (hwēt) [AS. *hwaete*] Any of various cereal grasses, widely cultivated for its edible grain used in making flour. Wheat preparations and pastas include macaroni, vermicelli, and noodles, which are made from flour and water, molded, dried, and slightly baked. They are easy to digest.

STRUCTURE: Wheat is composed of the husk or outer coat, which is removed before grinding; bran coats, which are removed in making white flour and contain the mineral substances; gluten, which contains the fat and protein; and starch, the center of the kernel. Refined wheat products do not include the bran and germ, which contain B complex vitamins, phosphorus, and iron.

Individuals who are gluten intolerant, e.g., persons with celiac sprue, cannot digest the protein gluten found in wheat.

wheat germ The embryonic portion of the wheat seed or kernel. It contains vitamin E, thiamine, riboflavin, and other micronutrients.

wheat grass A chlorophyll-rich grass whose extracted juice is promoted as a treatment for anemia, ulcerative colitis, and other ailments.

Wheatstone bridge (hwēt′stōn″) [Sir Charles Wheatstone, Brit. scientist and inventor, 1802–1875] An electric circuit with two branches, each containing two resistors. These branches are joined to complete the circuit. If the resistance in three resistors is known, the resistance of the fourth, unknown, one can be calculated.

wheel ((h)wēl) A disk attached through its middle to an axle that rotates. In dentistry, small wheels are attached to a handpiece or lathe, and used for polishing and shaping teeth, restorations, and appliances.

    carborundum w. A cutting wheel containing silicon carbide, in variable grit sizes.

    diamond w. In dentistry, a wheel that contains diamond powder or chips.

    medicine w. A symbol used by Native Americans to represent wholeness and balance. The medicine wheel consists of a circle with four quadrants representing spiritual, mental, physical, and emotional planes of existence. SEE: illus.

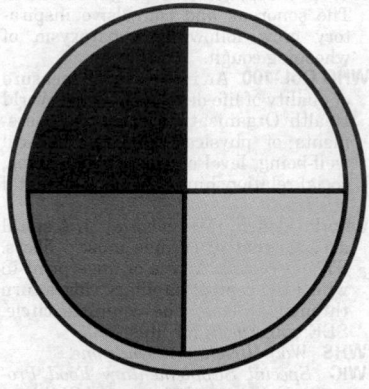

MEDICINE WHEEL

    polishing w. In dentistry, a wheel made of soft material suitable for polishing teeth or restorations.

    pregnancy w. A round calculator, similar to a slide rule in its construction, that uses the first day of the last menstrual period of a pregnant woman to identify the expected date that her baby will be born.

wheelchair ((h)wēl′char″) A type of mobility device for personal transport. Traditional wheelchairs have a seating area set between two large wheels, with two smaller wheels at the front. These can be self-propelled through handrims or pushed by another person. Advances in wheelchair design have provided alternatives that accommodate obstacles and rough terrain. Lightweight, collapsible models exist, as well as models designed for racing and sports. Powered wheelchairs and scooters, driven by electric motors, can be controlled through electronic switches and enable mobility by persons with muscle weakness or paralysis.

wheelchair lift A device that provides safe vertical transport for a person in a wheelchair to enable him or her to access public conveyances such as city buses or public facilities.

wheeze (hwēz) [ME. *whesen*] A continuous musical sound heard predominantly during expiration that is caused by narrowing of the lumen of a respiratory passageway. Often noted only by the use of a stethoscope, it occurs in asthma, croup, hay fever, mitral stenosis, and bronchitis. It may result from asthma, tumors, foreign body airway obstructions, bronchial spasm, pulmonary infections, emphysema and other chronic obstructive lung diseases, or pulmonary edema.

wheezing The production of whistling sounds during difficult breathing such as occurs in asthma, coryza, croup, and other respiratory disorders. SEE: *wheeze*.

whey The watery material separated from the curd of milk that has coagulated.

whiff test A colloquial term for a test used to detect bacterial vaginosis. The discharge from the vaginal area is swabbed, placed on a slide, and 10% KOH (potassium hydroxide) is added. The presence of a fishy odor is indicative of bacterial vaginosis. SYN: *sniff test (4)*.

whiplash injury SEE: under *injury*.

Whipple disease (hwip′ĕl) [George Hoyt Whipple, U.S. pathologist, 1878–1976] An infectious disease with gastrointestinal and systemic features caused by the organism *Trophermya whippeli*. This rare disease resembles idiopathic steatorrhea. SYN: *intestinal lipodystrophy*.

    TREATMENT: Intensive antibiotic therapy with procaine penicillin followed by maintenance therapy with tetracycline yields good results.

Whipple procedure ((h)wip′ĕl) [Allen

Whipple, U.S. surgeon, 1881–1961]
Pancreaticoduodenectomy.

whipworm (wĭp′wŭrm) *Trichuris trichiura.*

whisper (hwĭs′pĕr) [AS. *hwisprian*]
1. Speech with a low, soft voice; a low, sibilant sound. **2.** To utter in a low sound.

   cavernous w. Direct transmission of a whisper through a cavity in auscultation.

whispered voice test A bedside estimate of hearing impairment in which the examiner stands 2 ft from one of the patient's ears and whispers a number followed by a letter. An approximate 30 dB hearing loss is suggested by inability to hear paired numbers and letters, esp. if the patient fails to detect several pairs of them. A patient who performs poorly on the test should be referred for formal testing by an audiologist.

whispering disease An informal term for ovarian cancer. This cancer is so called because its presenting symptoms are subtle or easily misdiagnosed.

whistle (hwĭs′ĕl) **1.** A sound produced by pursing one's lips and blowing. **2.** A tubular device driven by wind that produces a loud and usually shrill sound.

whistleblower ((h)wis′ĕl-blō″ĕr) One who reports illegal, improper, unethical, or unprofessional behavior to authorities. The person divulging the information is usually an employee of the institution where the alleged activities occurred. Protection afforded to whistleblowers varies, depending on the nature of the misconduct that is alleged and the jurisdiction of the place where the event occurred.

whistling face syndrome Freeman-Sheldon syndrome.

white (hwīt) In vision, the achromatic color of maximum lightness that reflects all rays of the spectrum.

white cell Leukocyte.

white-clot syndrome Widespread blood clotting, usually in several veins and arteries at once, that is associated with thrombocytopenia. Caused by an adverse immune reaction to heparin, the condition is often life threatening. SEE: *heparin-induced* **thrombocytopenia**.

white dot syndrome Any of a group of inflammatory diseases of the choroid and retina that manifest with visual loss. On inspection of the ocular fundus, well-demarcated whitish lesions are seen.

white of egg The albumin of an egg.

white of eye The part of the sclera visible around the iris.

white gangrene SEE: under *gangrene.*

whitehead (hwīt′hĕd) A closed comedo containing pale, dried sebum. SEE: *blackhead; comedo.*

white leg Phlegmasia alba dolens.

whitepox (hwīt′pŏks) Variola minor.

whites Slang for leukorrhea.

white softening SEE: under *softening.*

Whitmore-Jewett staging system (hwit′mor″joo′ĭt) [Hugh Jewett, U.S. urologist, 1903–1990] A method of staging prostate cancer. The cancer either is confined entirely to the prostate gland or has spread to regional lymph nodes or, in the worse case, has spread to distant tissues such as bones.

whitlow (hwĭt′lō) [ME. *whitflawe,* white flow] Suppurative inflammation at the end of a finger or toe. It may be deep seated, involving the bone and its periosteum, or superficial, affecting parts of the nail. SYN: *felon; panaris; paronychia; runaround.*

   herpetic w. Whitlow due to herpes simplex virus. It is painful and accompanied by lymphadenopathy. Herpetic whitlow occurs commonly in health care workers as a result of exposure to viral shedding from patients with herpetic lesions on the skin.

WHO *World Health Organization.*

whole body counter An instrument that detects the radiation present in the entire body.

whole body CT scanning Head-to-toe computed tomographic screening of patients who are brought to the Emergency Department with multiple injuries. It is used to identify occult but clinically significant trauma or injuries for which treatment might otherwise be delayed or unrecognized. SYN: *full body CT scanning.*

whole bowel irrigation SEE: under *irrigation.*

whole grain An entire kernel of grain, consisting of the bran, the endosperm, and the germ.

wholism (hō′lizm) [By clang association or as a pun with *holism*] Holism.

whoop (hoop) [AS. *hwopan,* to threaten] The sonorous and convulsive inspiratory crow following a paroxysm of whooping cough.

WHO QoL-100 An international measure of quality of life developed by the World Health Organization based on assessments of physical and psychological well-being, level of independent living, social relationships, and environmental quality.

whorl (hwŭrl) [ME. *whorle*] **1.** A spiral arrangement of cardiac muscle fibers. SYN: *vortex.* **2.** A type of fingerprint in which the central papillary ridges turn through at least one complete circle. SEE: *fingerprint* for illus.

WHS *Wolf-Hirschhorn syndrome.*

WIC *Special Supplementary Food Program for Women, Infants, and Children.*

wick (wĭk) Any material that absorbs liquids. Wicks are used in wounds and cavities to drain accumulated fluids.

Wickham striae (wik′ăm) [L. F. Wickham, Fr. dermatologist, 1861–1913]

Lines that are demonstrable on the buccal mucosa in patients with lichen planus.

Widal reaction, Widal test (vē-dal′) [Georges Fernand Isidore Widal, Fr. physician, 1862–1929] An agglutination test for typhoid fever.

wide range achievement test ABBR: WRAT. A brief test that measures the ability of children to read, spell, and make arithmetic calculations.

wig A covering for the head to simulate hair if the individual is bald or partially bald. Wigs may be made of hair or synthetic fibers such as acrylic. Wigs are esp. beneficial for use by patients who have lost their hair due to exposure to certain types of cytotoxic agents used in cancer chemotherapy.

wild (wīld) Occurring in nature; uncultivated or undomesticated by humans.

wild cherry The dried bark of *Prunus serotina,* used principally in the form of syrup as a flavored vehicle for cough medicine.

wildcrafting (wīld′kraft″ing) The collection of herbal remedies from natural sites rather than the cultivation and harvesting of the same plants on farms.

wild-type (wīld′tīp″) Pert. to the genotype or phenotype that predominates in a species in nature.

wild type, *n.*

will [AS.] **1.** The mental faculty used in choosing or deciding on an act or thought. **2.** The power of controlling one's actions or emotions.

will call prescription management Any system that organizes and safeguards prescribed pharmaceuticals until they are ready for pickup or retrieval by the patient to whom they have been prescribed.

Willebrand disease, von Willebrand disease (vil′ĕ-brant″) [Erik Adolph von Willebrand, Finnish physician, 1870–1949] ABBR: vWD. A congenital autosomal dominant bleeding disorder caused by a deficiency of von Willebrand factor (a protein that helps platelets stick to injured blood vessels during the formation of blood clots. Inadequate amounts of the protein result in easy bruising or bleeding. Common symptoms of the disorder are frequent bleeding from the gums after brushing the teeth, frequent or prolonged nosebleeds, heavy menstrual periods, or heavy bleeding after childbirth or surgery.

The disease is the most common inherited bleeding disorder. Unlike hemophilia A and B, which are X-linked, it affects both genders. Despite its high prevalence in the population (about 3% of Americans are affected), vWD is often undiagnosed because many affected people have only mild episodes of bleeding. vWD can be diagnosed by the demonstration of low levels of von Willebrand factor in the blood; by a prolonged bleeding time; or by factor VIII deficiency (one function of von Willebrand factor is to carry clotting factor VIII in plasma). Treatments for heavy bleeding episodes (or for necessary surgeries) may include the administration of clotting factors containing von Willebrand factor or factor VIII or synthetic vasopressin.

Williams-Beuren syndrome (wil′yămz-būr′ĕn) [J.C.P. Williams; A.J. Beuren, Ger. cardiologist, 1919–1984] Williams syndrome.

Williamsia (wĭl-yăm′zē-ă) A genus of mycolic acid containing actinomycetes. Most members of the genus are thought to be nonpathogenic bacteria found in a variety of natural environments. They have rarely been identified in culture specimens as a cause of human disease.

Williams syndrome (wil′yămz) [J.C.P. Williams, 20th-cent. New Zealand cardiologist] ABBR: WS. A rare congenital disorder caused by a deletion of part of chromosome 7 characterized by impaired growth, heart disease, hypercalcemia, mental retardation, sensitivity to loud sounds, and "elfin" facial features, among other anomalies. Some children with WS are described as excessively sociable, hyperactive, and musically talented, but these behavioral markers are not universally present. SYN: *Williams-Beuren syndrome.*

Willis, Thomas (wil′is) Brit. anatomist, 1621–1675.

circle of W. An arterial anastomosis that encircles the optic chiasm and hypophysis, from which the principal arteries supplying the brain are derived. It receives blood from the two internal carotid arteries and the basilar artery formed by union of the two vertebral arteries. SEE: illus.

W. cord One of the cords crossing the superior longitudinal sinus transversely.

willow bark (wil′ō) The bark of many species of the genus *Salix,* the willow tree. This bark is the source of salicylic acid, the active principle in aspirin.

Wilms tumor (vilmz) [Max Wilms, Ger. surgeon, 1867–1918] A rapidly developing tumor of the kidney that usually occurs in children. It is the most common renal tumor of childhood. It is associated with chromosomal deletions, esp. from chromosomes 11 and 16. In the past, the mortality from this type of cancer was extremely high; however, newer approaches to therapy have been very effective in controlling the tumor in about 90% of patients. SYN: *embryonal carcinosarcoma; nephroblastoma.* SEE: *Nursing Diagnoses Appendix.*

Wilson disease (wil′sŏn) [Samuel Alexander Kinnier Wilson, Brit. internist, 1877–1937] A hereditary syndrome

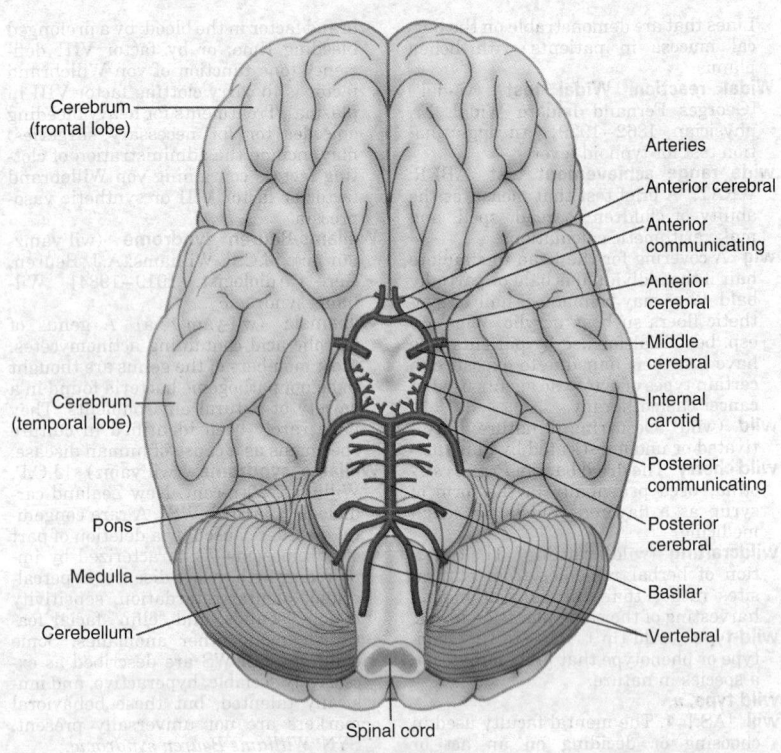

Cerebrum
(frontal lobe)

Arteries

Anterior cerebral

Anterior
communicating

Anterior
cerebral

Middle
cerebral

Internal
carotid

Cerebrum
(temporal lobe)

Posterior
communicating

Posterior
cerebral

Pons

Medulla

Basilar

Cerebellum

Vertebral

Spinal cord

CIRCLE OF WILLIS

Inferior view of brain

transmitted as an autosomal recessive trait in which a decrease of ceruloplasmin permits accumulation of copper in various organs (brain, liver, kidney, and cornea) associated with increased intestinal absorption of copper. A pigmented ring (Kayser-Fleischer ring) at the outer margin of the cornea is pathognomonic. This syndrome is characterized by degenerative changes in the brain, cirrhosis of the liver, hemolysis, splenomegaly, tremor, muscular rigidity, involuntary movements, spastic contractures, psychic disturbances, dysphagia, and progressive weakness and emaciation. SYN: *hepatolenticular degeneration; Westphal-Strümpell pseudosclerosis.*

TREATMENT: The untreated disease is fatal. The goal is to prevent further copper accumulation in tissues by avoiding foods high in copper such as organ meats, shellfish, nuts, dried legumes, chocolate, and whole cereals. Reduction of the copper in the tissues is achieved by giving the copper binder, D-penicillamine, orally until the serum copper level returns to normal. Carefully controlled doses of this therapy will probably be required for the pa-

tient's entire lifetime. Blood cell counts and hemoglobin should be monitored every 2 weeks during the first 6 weeks of treatment. Nonsteroidal anti-inflammatory drugs or systemic corticosteroids may help to relieve symptoms.

⚠ The copper binder, D-penicillamine, may cause pyridoxine and iron deficiency.

Wilson-Mikity syndrome (wĭl′sĭn-mĭk′ĭtē) [Miriam G. Wilson, U.S. pediatrician, b. 1922; Victor G. Mikity, U.S. radiologist, b. 1919] A so-called pulmonary dysmaturity syndrome seen in premature infants. The symptoms are insidious onset of dyspnea, tachypnea, and cyanosis in the first month of life. Radiographs of the lungs reveal evidence of emphysema that develops into multicysts. Therapy is directed at the pulmonary insufficiency and cardiac failure. The death rate is about 25%.

windburn Erythema and irritation of the skin caused by exposure to wind. Simultaneous exposure to the sun, moisture, wind, and cold may cause a severe dermatitis.

windchill The cooling effect wind has on exposed human skin. The effect is intensified if the skin is moist or wet.

windchill factor SEE: under *factor*.

windigo, witigo (win′dĭ-gō″, wit′ĭ-gō″) [Ojibwa, Cree] A culture-bound illness, found only in indigenous cultures of Northern Canada, in which people practice cannibalism believing they have been possessed by malevolent spirits. The disease is considered by Western psychiatrists to be a form of depression accompanied by agitation.

window (win′dō″) [Old Norse *vindauga*, wind-eye] **1.** An aperture for the admission of light or air or both. **2.** A small aperture into a cavity, esp. that of the inner ear. SYN: *fenestra*. **3.** A period after acute infection when neither the cause of the infection nor antibodies against it can be detected in blood or body fluids.

   aortic w. In radiology, in a left anterior oblique or lateral view of the chest, a clear area bounded by the aortic arch, the bifurcation of the trachea, and the pericardial border.

   beryllium w. Part of a radiographic tube, made of beryllium, through which x-ray photons pass to the outside when a low-energy beam is required.

   cochlear w. Round **w.**

   w. level ABBR: WL. In digital imaging, including computed tomography, the center of the range of gray scale in the image.

   oval w. The opening from the middle ear cavity to the inner ear, over which the plate of the stapes fits; it transmits vibrations for hearing.

   pericardial w. A surgically constructed drainage portal through the pericardium into the peritoneum, used for the relief of pericardial effusions or tamponade.

   radiation w. A translucent lead glass window in a radiographic control booth.

   radiographic w. A thinner area on the glass envelope of an x-ray tube from which x-rays are emitted toward the patient.

   round w. A membrane-covered opening below the oval window. Vibrations in the inner ear cause the membrane to bulge outward, decreasing the pressure in the cochlea and preventing damage to the hair cells. SYN: *cochlear w.*

   vestibular w. Oval **w.**

   w. width ABBR: WW. In digital imaging, the number of shades of gray in an image.

windowing Cutting a hole in a structure, such as a plaster cast or the pericardium, to relieve pressure, permit drainage, or allow access to an underlying structure.

windpipe (wĭnd′pīp) Trachea.

wine (wīn) [L. *vinum*, wine] **1.** Fermented juice of any fruit, usually made from grapes and containing 10% to 15% alcohol. Taken in moderation (1 or 2 glasses a night) it is part of the Mediterranean diet.

   red w. An alcoholic beverage made from pressed grapes, which contains polyphenolic antioxidants. Consumption of red wine, not in excess of 1 to 2 glasses per day, is associated with reduced risk of coronary artery disease.

wine sore SEE: under *sore*.

wing [Old Danish *wingae*] A structure resembling the wing of a bird. SEE: *ala*.

wink (wingk) The brief, voluntary closure of one eye.

winking Wink.

   jaw w. SEE: *jaw winking*.

winter cherry (wint′ĕr) A medicinal herb (*Physalis alkekengi*) that is a member of the nightshade family and native to Eurasia. Its berries are toxic in large doses. It is used in alternative and complementary medicine as an anxiolytic and antidepressant. SYN: *Indian ginseng*.

wintergreen oil SEE: under *oil*.

winter itch SEE: under *itch*.

wipe (wīp) **1.** To rub with a fabric, e.g., for cleansing, sampling, or sterilizing a surface. **2.** A piece of cloth or paper impregnated with an antiseptic or disinfectant.

wire (wīr) **1.** Metal drawn out into threads of varying thickness. **2.** To join fracture fragments together with wire.

   arch w. In orthodontics, a cable, usually of metal, used to apply tension to the teeth.

   guide w. A wire used to enter tight spaces (e.g., obstructed valves or channels) within the body.

   Kirschner w. SEE: *Kirschner wire*.

   Luque w.s SEE: *Luque wires*.

   pacing w. A pacemaker electrode.

   separating w. In dentistry, a brass wire used to separate teeth before banding them.

   sublaminar w. A metal thread used to attach corrective devices to the spinal column during neurosurgery.

wired Slang for tense and anxious, esp. when the condition is caused by the effect of a psychoactive drug.

wire localization SEE: under *localization*.

wiring (wīr′ĭng) Fastening bone fragments together with wire.

   circumferential w. A method of treating a fractured mandible by passing wires around the bone and a splint in the oral cavity.

   continuous loop w. The forming of wire loops on both mandibular and maxillary teeth to provide attachment sites for rubber bands. These are used in treating fractures of the mandible. SYN: *Stout's w.*

   craniofacial suspension w. Wiring using bones not contiguous with the oral cavity for attachment of wires that lead from those bones to the fractured jaw segments.

Gilmer w. SEE: *Gilmer wiring*.

Ivy loop w. SEE: *Ivy loop wiring*.

perialveolar w. The use of wires to fix a splint to the mandible. The wires are passed through the alveolar process from the buccal plate to the palate.

pyriform w. Wiring using the nasal bones to stabilize a fracture of the jaw. The wires are passed through the pyriform aperture of the nasal bone and then to the segment.

silver w. Abnormal reflections of light seen on the ophthalmoscopic examination of the retina of persons with long-standing, uncontrolled hypertension.

Stout's w. Continuous loop wiring.

Wirsung, Johann Georg (vir′zung) Ger. anatomist, 1600–1643.

duct of W. Pancreatic **duct**.

Wisconsin Card Sorting Test (wĭs-kŏn′sĭn) ABBR: WCST. A neuropsychiatric test in which subjects are asked to group a series of symbols by their form and color. The test and its adaptations are used to assess disorders that affect the frontal lobes of the brain, e.g., schizophrenia.

Wiskott-Aldrich syndrome (vis′kŏt-ăl′drĭch) [Alfred Wiskott, Ger. pediatrician, 1898–1978; Robert A. Aldrich, U.S. pediatrician, 1917–1998] An X-linked immune deficiency syndrome whose hallmarks are decreased resistance to infection, eczema, and thrombocytopenia. The number of T lymphocytes in the blood and lymph nodes declines, blood levels of immunoglobulin M class antibodies are reduced, and the response to many antigens is inadequate. Bone marrow transplantation (technically, "hematopoietic stem cell transplantation) and stem-cell gene therapy are potentially curative treatments.

witch hazel (wich′ hā′zĕl) A flowering shrub, *Hamamelis virginiana*, of eastern North America, whose bark yields an astringent extract used as an herbal remedy.

Withania somnifera (wĭ-thān′ē-ă som-nif′ĕ-ră) SEE: *ashwagandha*.

withdrawal (with-dro′ăl) Cessation of administration of a drug, esp. a narcotic or alcohol to which the individual has become either physiologically or psychologically addicted. Withdrawal symptoms vary with the type of drug used. Neonates may exhibit withdrawal symptoms from drugs or alcohol ingested by the mother during pregnancy. SEE: *drug addiction*.

alcohol w. Alcohol withdrawal syndrome.

caffeine w. SEE: *caffeine; caffeine withdrawal* **headache**; *coffee; tea*.

withdrawal bleeding SEE: *bleeding*.

withdrawal of care, withdrawal from care 1. The discontinuation of life-sustaining therapies, e.g., mechanical ventilation, from a patient who is expected to die without this support. **2.** The legal termination of a relationship between a patient and caregivers.

withdrawal syndrome Irritability, autonomic hyperactivity, hallucinations, or other phenomena resulting from the withdrawal of alcohol, stimulants, or some opiates.

withhold [with-hōld′] In health insurance, to pay an amount of money only if certain services are used according to the rules of the health plan. Withholding is typically used as a financial incentive for providers and patients to limit their use of costly or elective services.

withholding life support Removal of or no further administration of medical intervention during end-of-life care, with the expectation that the patient will die as a result.

witkop (wĭt′kŏp) [Afrikaans, white scalp] Matted crusts in the hair producing a scalplike structure; seen in South African natives.

witness A person having knowledge or information about a particular subject or event.

expert w. A qualified person who assists a judge and jury in understanding technical aspects of a lawsuit, such as breaches of the standard of care and damages or injuries sustained. SEE: table.

fact w. A person who has knowledge of circumstances surrounding the events of the alleged incident in a complaint or petition for damages. SYN: *material w.*

material w. Fact **w.**

Witzel jejunostomy (vĭt′zl) [Friedrich O. Witzel, Ger. surgeon, 1865–1925] A jejunostomy created by inserting a rubber or silicone catheter into the jejunum and bringing it to the skin surface. Medication and feedings can be administered on a long-term basis. SEE: *jejunostomy*.

witzelsucht (vĭt′sĕl-zookt) A condition produced by frontal lobe lesions characterized by self-amusement from poor jokes and puns. SEE: *moria*.

primary affective w. A peculiar variety of witzelsucht characterized by teutonization of nomenclature.

WNL *within normal limits*.

Wobe-Mugos E A mixture of enzymes, including chymotrypsin and trypsin (obtained from cow and pig pancreas) and papain (from papaya) used as anti-inflammatory and anticancer treatments, esp. in the treatment of multiple myeloma.

Wohlfahrtia (vōl-fart′ē-ă) [Peter Wohlfahrtia, Ger. author, 1675–1726] A genus of flies parasitic in animal tissue, belonging to the family Sarcophagidae, order Diptera. SEE: *Sarcophagidae*.

W. magnifica A species found in southeast Europe. The larvae may occur in human and animal wounds.

Ethical Requirements for Expert Witnesses

Requirement	Rationale
Experts should testify only about those aspects of care for which they have direct knowledge, specific educational background, and clinical experience	Limits the likelihood that generalists will provide testimony outside their areas of specialization or expertise
The testimony should be based on a complete review of all the facts of a case	Decreases the chances that the medical record will be misinterpreted as a result of bias or incomplete study
The testimony must be scientifically up-to-date and its conclusions must be verifiable using evidence-based scholarship	Prevents the witness from relying on subjective impressions, ideas, or personal experiences
The payment that the witness receives must not be contingent on securing a victorious outcome at trial	Limits the motivation to alter testimony purely for financial gain

W. vigil A species found in Canada and the northern United States.

Wolbachia (wŏl-bak′ē-ă) A genus of bacteria that live only inside the cells of host insects. They have been associated with the blindness caused by *Onchocerca volvulus* and other microfiliarial infections.

wolffian body (wool′fē-ăn) SEE: under *body*.

wolffian cyst SEE: under *cyst*.

wolffian duct SEE: under *duct*.

Wolff law (volf) [Julius Wolff, Ger. anatomist and surgeon, 1835–1902] A law that states that bones structurally adapt to the specific forces acting on them.

Wolff-Parkinson-White syndrome (wŏlf′păr′kĭn-sŏn-wīt′) [Louis Wolff, U.S. cardiologist, 1898–1972; Sir John Parkinson, Brit. physician, 1885–1976; Paul Dudley White, U.S. cardiologist, 1886–1973] ABBR: WPW. A disease manifested by occasional episodes of potentially life-threatening tachycardia, in which there is an abnormal electrical pathway in the heart connecting the atria to the ventricles.
ETIOLOGY: In some families, the disease is transmitted as an autosomal dominant trait.
DIAGNOSIS: In electrocardiography, the P-R interval is less than 0.12 sec and the QRS complex is widened as a result of an initial electrical deflection, called the delta wave.
TREATMENT: Ablation of the abnormal accessory pathway cures about 92% of patients. SEE: *pre-excitation, ventricular*.

wolfram (wool′frăm) [Ger. *Wolfram*, tungsten] SYMB: W. Tungsten.

wolfsbane (wŏlfs′bān) Common name for several species of *Aconitum*, a genus of highly toxic, hardy perennials. Also called *monkshood*. SEE: *aconite*.

WOMAC Western Ontario McMaster Osteoarthritis Index.

woman An adult human female.

womb (woom) [AS. *wamb*] Uterus.

Women's Health Initiative ABBR: WHI. A 15-year study of the most common causes of death and disability in postmenopausal women. Website: http://www.nhlbi.nih.gov/whi/background.htm.

Wood's rays (wŭdz) [Robert Williams Wood, U.S. physicist, 1868–1955] Ultraviolet rays; used to detect fluorescent materials in the skin and hair in certain disease states such as tinea capitis. The terms Wood's light and Wood's lamp have become synonymous with Wood's rays, even though these are misnomers.

woodruff A low-growing, hardy perennial herb (*Galium odoratum* or *Asperula odorata*) used in alternative medicine to treat nervousness, insomnia, and cardiac irregularity. Liver damage has been reported in some patients after long-term use.

wool fat SEE: under *fat*.

woolly hair syndrome A rare congenital disorder in which infants are born with wiry or unusually curly hair; sometimes associated with abnormal heart development; sometimes found only on hair that grows on nevi.

word blindness SEE: under *blindness*.

Word catheter SEE: under *catheter*.

word deafness SEE: under *deafness*.

word salad The use of words indiscriminantly and haphazardly, that is, without logical structure or meaning. It is a finding in uncontrolled mania and schizophrenia.

work (wŏrk) **1.** A force moving a resistance. The amount of work done is the mathematical product of the force in the direction of movement, times the distance the object is moved in that direction. NOTE: If the object is not moved, then no work is done even though energy is expended. The SI unit of work is the joule (J). The dimensionally equivalent newton-meter (N·m) is sometimes used instead to signify work in physics. SEE: *calorie; erg*. **2.** The job, occupation, or task one performs as a means of providing a livelihood. **3.** The effort employed to explore interpersonal or psychological issues.

w. of breathing ABBR: WOB. The amount of effort used to expand the lungs. It is determined by lung and thoracic compliance, airway resistance, and the use of accessory muscles for inspiration or forced expiration. It is measured in joules/L, joules/min and sometimes kg/m/min. The measurement of the WOB is analogous to the typical description of work in physics (work = force x distance). In respiratory physiology, work = pressure x volume.

crown w. A colloquial term for a dental crown.

shift w. A staffing arrangement in which some employees work during the day and others in the evening or at night. Shift work is a common method of scheduling used in many industries to maximize productivity over a 24-hr day and in health care, where patients' needs may arise at any time of the day or night. A great number of persons work regularly at night, either on a permanent or rotating schedule. In most of these workers, adaptation to the altered work schedule is imperfect; sleep disturbances and other medical and psychosocial problems have often been found in shift workers. Among other problems, many night-time or rotating shift workers often have family obligations during the day, which compromise their ability to obtain adequate rest before or after work.

social w. Provision of social services (in fields such as child welfare, criminal justice, hospital-based medicine, or mental health) and the promotion of social welfare by a professionally trained person. Social work often involves advocacy and aid for individuals who are poor, elderly, homeless, unemployed, or discriminated against in society because of gender, race, or other biases.

Trager w. SEE: *Trager work*.

workaholic A colloquial term for a person addicted to occupational or productive pursuits who has difficulty relaxing or enjoying familial, social, or leisure activities.

workaround (wŭrk'ă-rownd") A temporary, improvised solution to a problem that may relieve the obstacle but circumvents rather than repairs it.

work capacity evaluation ABBR: WCE. A comprehensive assessment of functional status based on simulated physical demands of a job. Typically, a comprehensive work capacity evaluation includes timed, performance-based demonstrations of standing, sitting, walking, kneeling, crawling, pushing, pulling, lifting, reaching, carrying, balance, flexibility, dexterity, hand strength, and coordination. SEE: *functional assessment*.

worker role interview A semi-structured interview used by occupational therapists to identify environmental and psychosocial factors that influence a person's ability to return to work.

workflow The processes involved in completing a job, including such functions as the organization of human or other resources; the design of tasks; the development of procedures (and their implementation), followed by feedback, oversight, and quality improvement.

work hardening SEE: under *hardening:*

working memory SEE: under *memory*.

working through The combined efforts of a patient and mental health practitioner to understand the basis of behaviors, feelings, symptoms, or thoughts.

work-life balance SEE: under *balance*.

workout In athletics, a practice, conditioning, or training session.

workup (wŏrk'ŭp") The process of obtaining all of the necessary data for diagnosing and treating a patient. It should be done in an orderly manner so that essential elements will not be overlooked. Included are retrieval of all previous medical and dental records, the patient's family and personal medical history, social and occupational history, physical examination, laboratory studies, x-ray examinations, and indicated diagnostic surgical procedures. The patient's workup is an ongoing process wherein all hospital personnel involved cooperate in attempting to determine the correct diagnosis and effective therapy. SEE: *charting; problem-oriented medical record*.

sepsis w. A colloquial term for the evaluation of a patient, esp. a neonate, with a fever, for laboratory evidence of severe infection. Common tests for febrile neonates include a complete blood count; blood cultures, cerebrospinal fluid, urine, and stool samples; and chest x-ray. Most neonates with a fever are given immediate treatment with broad-spectrum antibiotics pending the results of cultures.

World Federation of Occupational Therapists ABBR: WFOT. An international organization that promotes educational standards for occupational therapists and serves as an advocate for occupational therapy and for those professionals affiliated with its member associations.

World Health Organization ABBR: WHO. The United Nations agency concerned with international public health, specifically the detection, monitoring, prevention, and eradication of diseases. Its headquarters are located in Geneva, Switzerland. Its website is: www.who.int/en/

worm (wŏrm) **1.** An elongated invertebrate belonging to one of the following phyla: Platyhelminthes (flatworms); Nemathelminthes or Aschelminthes (roundworms or threadworms); Acanthocephala (spinyheaded worms); and Annelida (Annulata) (segmented worms). SYN: *helminth.* **2.** Any small, limbless, creeping animal. **3.** The median portion of the cerebellum. **4.** Any wormlike structure.

   bladder w. Cysticercus.

   guinea w. A nematode worm (*Dracunculus medinensis*) that is a parasite affecting subcutaneous tissues of humans and animals, found in tropical Africa and South Asia. The worm causes infection when its larvae are drunk in unfiltered or unsanitary water. The larvae enter the body through the stomach or duodenum, migrate through internal organs, and become adults. After mating, the adult female burrows to the subcutaneous tissue, often of the leg. The worm has been eradicated in Asia. SEE: *Medina w.*

   herring w. Anisakis simplex.

   nodular w. The common name of worms of the genus *Oesophagostomum.*

   proboscis w. Acanthocephala.

   spiny-headed w. Acanthocephala.

   thorny-headed w. Acanthocephala.

wormian bone (wor′mē-ăn) SEE: under *bone.*

wormwood (wĕrm′wood) A toxic substance, absinthium, obtained from *Artemisia absinthium.* It was used in certain alcoholic beverages (absinthe), but because of its toxicity such use is prohibited in most countries.

worried well Persons who are healthy, but who, because of their anxiety or an imagined illness, frequent medical care facilities seeking reassurance concerning their health.

wound (woond) A break in the continuity of body structures caused by violence, trauma, or surgery to tissues. In treating the nonsurgically created wound, tetanus prophylaxis must be considered. If not previously immunized, the patient should be given tetanus immune globulin.

   PATIENT CARE: Successful wound assessment relies on a thorough, organized approach. This assessment includes the wound's location, size, depth, undermining, drainage, wound edges, base, and surrounding tissues. Include an assessment for any redness, swelling, tenderness, and gangrene/necrosis. The assessment includes the patient's vital signs and measures used, which improve the wound healing. The assessment includes the patient's vital signs and measures taken to improve the wound healing. Multiple diagnostic modalities (such as radiographic studies) may be employed to further delineate the extent of the injury.

   abdominal w. A traumatic injury or surgical incision which may be superficial or extend to intraperitoneal or extraperitoneal organs or tissues. In cases of abdominal trauma, a careful examination (often including peritoneal lavage, ultrasonography, or computed tomographic scanning of the abdomen) is necessary to determine the precise nature of the injury and the proper course of treatment. Superficial injuries may require no more than ordinary local care; immediate laparotomy may be needed, however, when major bleeding or organ damage has occurred. Intravenous fluids, blood components, antibiotics, and tetanus prophylaxis are given when necessary. Major abdominal trauma may be overlooked in comatose or otherwise critically injured patients when there is no obvious abdominal injury. SEE: *abdomen.*

   bullet w. A penetrating wound caused by a missile discharged from a firearm. The extent of injury depends on the wound site and the speed and character of the bullet. SEE: *Nursing Diagnoses Appendix; gunshot w.*

   TREATMENT: Tetanus booster injection or tetanus immune globulin and antibiotics, if indicated, should be given. An appropriate bandage should be applied. Emergency surgery may be necessary. Complications, including hemorrhage and shock, should be treated.

   contused w. A bruise in which the skin is not broken. It may be caused by a blunt instrument. Injury of the tissues under the skin, leaving the skin unbroken, traumatizes the soft tissue. Ruptured blood vessels underneath the skin cause discoloration. If extravasated blood becomes encapsulated, it is termed hematoma; if it is diffuse, ecchymosis. SEE: *ecchymosis; hematoma.*

   TREATMENT: Cold compresses, pressure, and rest, along with elevation of the injured area, will help prevent or reduce swelling. When the acute stage is over (within 24 to 48 hr), continued rest, heat, and elevation are prescribed. Aseptic drainage may be indicated.

   crushing w., crush wound Crush injury.

   fishhook w. An injury caused by a fishhook becoming embedded in soft tissue. Deeply embedded fishhooks are difficult to remove. One should push the hook through, then cut off the barb with an instrument, and pull the remainder of the fishhook out by the route of entry. Antitetanus treatment should be given as indicated. Because these injuries often become infected, prophylactic use of a broad-spectrum antibiotic is indicated.

   gunshot w. ABBR: GSW. A penetrating injury from a bullet shot from a gun. At very close range, the wound may have gunpowder deposits and the skin burn marks. GSWs can crush, penetrate, stretch, cavitate, or fracture body structures. The severity of the wound may depend on the structures damaged, the velocity and caliber of the bullet, and the underlying health of the victim. SEE: *bullet w.*

knuckle w. Any injury to the metacarpal bones, esp. one that results from a fist fight. These wounds commonly include fractures and penetrating injuries contaminated with oral or periodontal bacteria. SYN: *knuckle tooth w.*

knuckle tooth w. Knuckle w.

nonpenetrating w. Blunt **trauma**.

open w. A contusion in which the skin is also broken, such as a gunshot, incised, or lacerated wound. SEE: illus.

penetrating w. A wound in which the skin is broken and the agent causing the wound enters subcutaneous tissue or a deeply lying structure or cavity.

perforating w. Any wound that has breached the body wall or internal organs. The perforation may be partial or complete.

puncture w. A wound made by a sharp-pointed instrument such as a dagger, ice pick, or needle. A puncture wound usually is collapsed, which provides ideal conditions for infection. The placement of a drain, antitetanus therapy or prophylaxis, and gas gangrene prophylaxis may be required. This will depend on the nature of the instrument that caused the injury.

subcutaneous w. A wound, such as contusion, that is unaccompanied by a break in the skin.

sucking chest w. A wound that penetrates the thorax and draws air into the pleural cavity, usually resulting in an expanding pneumothorax.

tunnel w. A wound having a small entrance and exit of uniform diameter.

wound ballistics The study of the effects on the body produced by penetrating projectiles.

wound bed SEE: under *bed*.

wound care SEE: under *care*.

wound disruption Dehiscence (1).

wound healing SEE: *healing; inflammation*.

wound VAC *Vacuum-assisted wound closure.*

W-plasty A technique used in plastic surgery to prevent contractures in straight-line scars. Either side of the wound edge is cut in the form of connected W's, and the edges are sutured together in a zigzag fashion. SEE: *tissue expansion, soft; Z-plasty.*

wrap (rap) **1.** A covering, esp. one that is wound tightly around an object, as an elastic wrap or a compression wrap. **2.** To wind a covering around an object.

compression w. An elastic bandage used to prevent or reduce the formation of edema. The wrap is applied starting distally; it uses overlapping spirals to progress proximally. Greater pressure is applied distally than proximally, creating a compression gradient that encourages venous and lymphatic return. SEE: illus.

Wright maneuver (rīt) A physical finding in patients with thoracic outlet compression syndrome affecting the supply of blood to the arm. The radial pulse is palpated while the shoulder is abducted and externally rotated (without altering the normal resting position

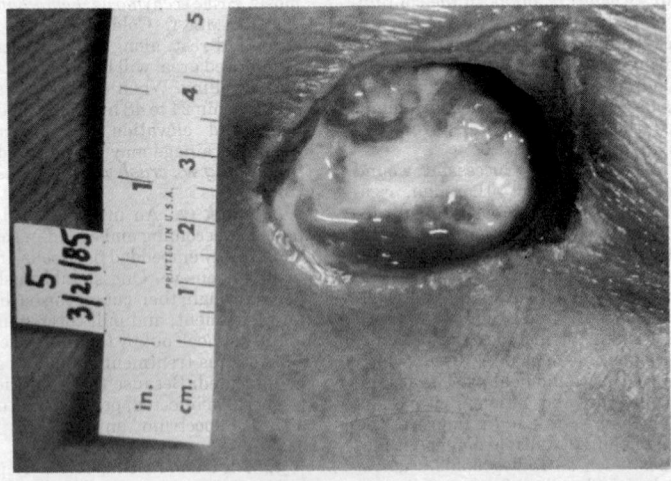

OPEN WOUND

An open cavitary wound

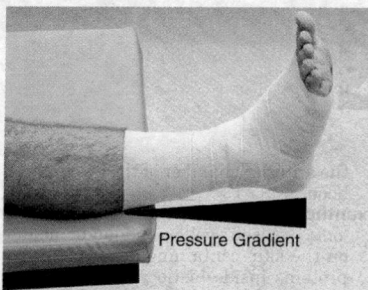

COMPRESSION WRAP

of the head or neck). A reduction in the pulse with reproduction of the patient's shoulder or arm symptoms is suggestive of obstruction of the subclavian or axillary artery.

Wright stain (rīt) [James H. Wright, U.S. pathologist, 1871–1928] A combination of eosin and methylene blue used in staining blood cells to reveal malarial parasites and to differentiate white blood cells.

wrinkle (ring′kl) [AS. *gewrinclian*, to wind] **1.** A crevice, furrow, or ridge in the skin. **2.** To make creases or furrows, as in the skin by habitual frowning.

wrinkle test A test of sensibility following complete transection of or damage to peripheral nerves based on the characteristic sympathetic response of skin following extended immersion in water. SEE: *nerve*.

Wrisberg ganglion (riz′bĕrg″, vris′berk″) [Heinrich August Wrisberg, Ger. anatomist, 1739–1808] Cardiac ganglia.

wrist (rĭst) [AS] The joint or region between the hand and the forearm. SEE: *hand* for illus.; *skeleton*.

wristband (rist′band″) **1.** A unique patient identification device secured around a patient's limb.

⚠ To avoid patient misidentification, a wristband should include the patient's last and first name; date of birth; hospital assignment; attending physician; allergies; primary language; and, depending on the circumstances, other unique identifiers, e.g., last four digits of Social Security number, or time of birth (for newborns). Wristbands should be comfortable, tamperproof, waterproof, and difficult to alter.

2. A device secured around a patient's limb and used to identify specific patient needs, such as the patient's allergies, risk of falling, or code status.

wrist-driven hand orthosis SEE: under *orthosis*.

wrist-driven wrist-hand orthosis SEE: under *orthosis*.

wrist drop SEE: under *drop*.

wrist unit A component of an upper-extremity prosthesis that attaches the terminal device to the forearm section and provides for pronation or supination.

writing (rīt′ing) The act of forming characters, letters, symbols, or words in order to communicate ideas.
    mirror w. SEE: *mirror writing*.

writing therapy Writing a journal or diary to explore and record one's feelings and thus to make progress toward desired psychological goals.

written action plan SEE: under *plan*.

written treatment agreement A formal contract or plan established by a health care provider and a patient, specifying the manner in which certain forms of care will be delivered. Written treatment agreements are used most often in managing prescriptions for narcotic pain relievers. SEE: *drug contract*.

wrongful birth, wrongful life The idea that conception would have been prevented or pregnancy would have been interrupted if the parents had been adequately informed of the possibility that the mother would give birth to a physically or mentally challenged child.

wryneck (rī′nĕk) Torticollis.

wt *weight*.

Wuchereria (voo″kĕr-ē′rē-ă) [Otto Wucherer, Ger. physician, 1820–1873] A genus of filarial worms of the class Nematoda, commonly found in the tropics.
    W. bancrofti A parasitic worm that is the causative agent of elephantiasis. Adults of the species live in human lymph nodes and ducts. Females give birth to sheathed microfilariae, which remain in internal organs during the day but at night are in circulating blood, where they are sucked up by night-biting mosquitoes, in which they continue their development, becoming infective larvae in about 2 weeks. They are then passed on to humans when the mosquito bites. SYN: *Filaria bancrofti*.
    W. malayi A species occurring in Southeast Asia and largely responsible for lymphangitis and elephantiasis in that region. It closely resembles *W. bancrofti*.

wuchereriasis (voo″kĕr-ē-rī′ă-sĭs) Elephantiasis.

Wunderlich syndrome (wŭn′dĕr-lich, voon′dĕr-likh) [Carl R. A. Wunderlich, Ger. physician, 1815–1877] Sudden, severe atraumatic bleeding into a kidney, with hematoma formation.

w/v *weight (mass) in volume*.

w/w *weight in weight* (either the weight [mass] of one substance in the weight [mass] of another, or the weight [mass] of a substance relative to the total weight [mass] of a mixture).

wye (wī) [Pronunciation of the letter *y*] A three-way connector or three-branched device, shaped like the letter *y*.

Wymox (wī′mŏks″) SEE: *amoxicillin*.

X Symbol for Kienböck unit of x-ray dose; symbol for xanthine.

Xalatan Latanoprost.

Xanax (zan′aks″) Alprazolam.

xanthelasma (zan″thĕ-laz′mă) [*xantho-* + Gr. *elasma,* (metal) plate] A xanthoma on the eyelids, esp. near the inner canthus. SEE: illus.

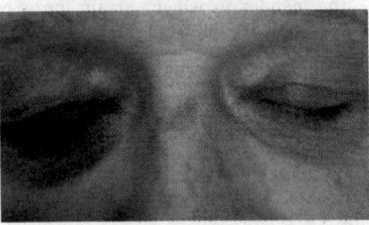

XANTHELASMA

xanthene (zan′thēn″) [*xantho-* + *-ene*] $O=(C_6H_4)_2=CH_2$, a crystalline compound, from which various dyes are formed, including rhodamine and fluorescein.

xanthic (zan′thik) [*xantho-* + *-ic*] **1.** Yellow. **2.** Pert. to xanthine.

xanthine oxidase ABBR: XO. An enzyme of the oxidoreductase class that contains iron and molybdenum and catalyzes hypoxanthine to xanthin.

xanthinuria (zan″thin-ūr′ē-ă) [*xanthine* + *-uria*] The excretion of large amounts of xanthine in the urine. SYN: *xanthuria.*

xantho-, xanth- [Gr. *xanthos,* yellow, yellowish] Prefixes meaning *yellow.*

xanthochromia (zan″thŏ-krō′mē-ă) [*xantho-* + *chrom-* + *-ia*] Yellowish discoloration resembling jaundice, as of the skin in patches or of the cerebrospinal fluid. **xanthochromic** (zan″thŏ-krō′mik), *adj.*

xanthogranuloma (zan″thŏ-gran″yŭ-lō′mă) [*xantho-* + *granuloma*] A tumor having characteristics of both an infectious granuloma and a xanthoma.

juvenile x. A skin disease that may be present at birth or develop in the first months of life. Firm, dome-shaped yellow, pink, or orange papules, ranging from a few millimeters to 4 cm in diameter, are usually present on the scalp, face, and upper trunk. Biopsy of these lesions reveals lipid-filled histiocytes, inflammatory cells, and Touton cells. The lesions regress spontaneously during the first years of life. Juvenile xanthogranuloma of the iris is one of the most common causes of bleeding into

the anterior chamber of the eye in childhood.

xanthoma (zan-thō′mă) [*xantho-* + *-oma*] A soft, yellow plaque or nodule on the skin containing deposits of lipoproteins inside histiocytes. Xanthomas are esp. likely to be found on the skin of patients with hyperlipidemia.

x. disseminatum The presence of xanthomata throughout the body, esp. on the face, in tendon sheaths, and in mucous membranes. SEE: *Hand-Schüller-Christian disease.*

x. tuberosum A form of xanthoma that may appear on the neck, shoulders, trunk, or extremities, consisting of small elastic and yellowish nodules.

xanthomatosis (zan″thō″mă-tō′sĭs) [*xanthoma* + *-osis*] A deposition of lipid in tissues, usually accompanied by hyperlipemia. Cholesterol may accumulate in tumor nodules (xanthoma) or in individual cells, esp. histiocytes and reticuloendothelial cells.

xanthomatous (zn-thō′măt-ŭs) [*xanthoma* + *-ous*] Pert. to a xanthoma or to xanthomatosis.

xanthophyll (zan′thŏ-fil″) [*xantho-* + Gr. *phyllon,* leaf] A yellow pigment derived from carotene. It is present in some plants and egg yolk.

xanthopsia (zan-thop′sē-ă) [*xantho-* + *-opsia*] A condition in which objects appear to be yellow.

xanthous (zan′thŭs) [*xantho-* + *-ous*] Yellow or yellowish.

xanthurenic acid (zanth″yŭ-ren′ĭk) SEE: under *acid.*

x-disease Aflatoxicosis.

XDR-TB *extensively drug-resistant tuberculosis.*

Xe Symbol for the element xenon.

XELOX *Xeloda (capecitabine), oxaliplatin* (chemotherapeutic agents to treat colorectal cancer).

xeno-, xen- [Gr. *xenos,* stranger, guest, host] Prefixes meaning *strange, foreign, alien.*

xenobiotic (zen″ō-bī-ot′ik, zēn″) [*xeno-* + *biotic* (2)] An antibiotic not produced by the body and foreign to it.

xenodiagnosis (zen″ō-dī′ăg-nō′sĭs, zēn″) [*xeno-* + *diagnosis*] The diagnosis of parasitic infection in humans or animals using an intermediate host such as an insect as a culture tool. Uninfected insects are allowed to feed on the infected person. A few days or weeks later, the insects are tested for the presence of infection, e.g., Chagas disease or leishmaniasis.

xenogeneic (zen″ŏ-jĕ-nē′ik, zēn″) [*xeno-* + *(iso)geneic*] In tissue grafting, obtained from a different species.

xenogenous (zĕ-noj′ĕ-nŭs) [*xeno-* + *-genous*] **1.** Caused by a foreign body. **2.** Originating in the host, as a toxin resulting from stimuli applied to cells of the host.

xenograft (zen′ŏ-graft″, zēn″) [*xeno-* + *graft*] Xenotransplant.

xenon (zē′non″, zen′on″) [Gr. *xenon*, strange] SYMB: Xe. A chemical element, one of the noble gases, atomic weight (mass) 131.29, atomic number 54. Xenon is analgesic and hypnotic and can be used as an (expensive) anesthetic agent. It has no teratogenic effects, does not suppress cardiac function, and has a short recovery time. SEE: *noble* ***gas***.
    PATIENT CARE: Radioactive isotopes of xenon, including Xe^{133} and Xe^{127}, are used in ventilation/perfusion (V/Q) lung scans to diagnose pulmonary embolism. The xenon gas is the ventilation agent in the study, i.e., the agent that highlights how well gases move in and out of lung tissues. An isotope of technetium is used to demonstrate pulmonary blood flow.

xenophobia (zen″ŏ-fō′bē-ă, zēn″) [*xeno-* + *-phobia*] Abnormal fear or dislike of strangers.

Xenopsylla (zen″op-sil′ă) [*xeno-* + Gr. *psylla*, flea] A genus of fleas belonging to the family Pulicidae, order Siphonaptera. Members of the genus sometimes transmit tapeworms to human beings.
    X. cheopis A species that infests rats; other hosts include humans. This species is a vector for a number of pathogens including *Hymenolepis nana* (the dwarf tapeworm); *Salmonella* organisms; the causative organisms of bubonic and sylvatic plague and endemic typhus. SYN: *rat* ***flea***.

xenotransplant (zen″ŏ-trans′plant″) [*xeno-* + *transplant*] A surgical transplant of tissue from an individual of one species to an individual of a different species. **xenotransplant,** *v.* **xenotransplantation** (zen″ŏ-trans″plan″tā′shŏn), *n.* SYN: *heterograft; heterotransplant; xenograft.* SEE: *autograft; graft; isograft.*

xenotropic (zen″ŏ-trop′ik, zēn″, -trō′pik) [*xeno-* + *-tropic*] Of some viruses, capable of growing in a species that differs from their normal host

xero-, xer- [Gr. *xēros,* dry] Prefixes meaning *dry*.

xerocyte (zer′ŏ-sīt″) [*xero-* + *-cyte*] An erythrocyte that is dehydrated and appears to have "puddled" at one end, seeming half dark and half light. This type of cell is found in hereditary xerocytosis. SEE: illus.; *hereditary xerocytosis.*

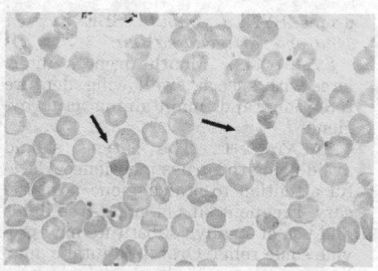

XEROCYTES

xeroderma (zer″ŏ-dĕr′mă) [*xero-* + *derma*] Roughness and dryness of the skin; mild ichthyosis.
    x. pigmentosum A rare, progressive, autosomal recessive degenerative disease characterized by severe photosensitivity developing in the first years of life. There is rapid onset of erythema, bullae, pigmented macules, hypochromic spots, and telangiectasia. The skin becomes atrophic, dry, and wrinkled. A variety of benign and malignant growths appear early in life. The condition is treated symptomatically; sunlight is avoided. SYN: *Kaposi disease; melanosis lenticularis.*

xerography (zĕ-rog′ră-fē) [*xero-* + *-graphy*] Xeroradiography.

xerophthalmia (zer-of-thal′mē-ă) [*xero-* + *ophthalmia*] Conjunctival dryness with keratinization of the epithelium following chronic conjunctivitis or a disease caused by vitamin A deficiency. SYN: *xeroma; xerophthalmus.* SEE: *Schirmer test.*

xerosis (zĕ-rō′sĭs) [*xero-* + *-sis*] Abnormal dryness of the skin, mucous membranes, or conjunctiva. SEE: illus. **xerotic,** *adj.*

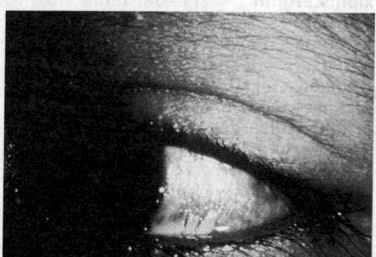

CONJUNCTIVAL XEROSIS
SOURCE: Centers for Disease Control and Prevention

xerostomia (zer″ŏ-stō′mē-ă) [*xero-* + *stoma* + *-ia*] Decreased production or lack of saliva. This condition may be due to the action of drugs such as diuretics, antihistamines, and anticholinergics; dehydration; anxiety; radiation therapy to the head or neck; or Sjögren syndrome. SYN: *dry mouth*. SEE: *Sjögren syndrome; artificial saliva*.

SYMPTOMS: Mouth dryness interferes with speech, swallowing, denture retention, and maintaining oral hygiene.

TREATMENT: The patient should avoid using the drugs mentioned. Careful attention to oral hygiene is necessary. Frequent sips of sugar-free fluids and use of a saliva substitute may provide some relief. Oral fluid intake ameliorates dry mouth due to dehydration. Pilocarpine may increase saliva production.

XGP   *xanthogranulomatous* **pyelonephritis**.

-ximab [from the shape of the Gr. letter chi (X) in *chimera* as if it were a Latin "X" + *m(onoclonal) a(nti)b(ody)*] A suffix for *chimeric monoclonal antibody*. Antibodies made from -ximabs usually elicit a neutralizing antibody response in a patient who receives them. SEE: *-zumab*.

X inactivation The silencing of the genes on one of a woman's paired X chromosomes, allowing the other chromosome's genes to be expressed phenotypically. The process is not universal but affects 75% or more of the genes on the chromosome. Genes that are found near the short end of the chromosome are more likely than the rest to be expressed phenotypically, i.e., to escape inactivation.

xiong-gui-tiao-xue-yin   (shung-gwei-tyow-shwe-yin) [Chinese] An herbal medicine used primarily in Japanese kampo for diseases and conditions associated with lactation or postpartum depression. SYN: *kyuki-chouketsu-in*.

xiphi-, xiphi-, xipho-, [Gr. *xiphos*, sword] Prefixes meaning *sword-shaped, xiphoid*.

xiphisternum   (zī″fĭ-stĕr′nŭm,   zĭf″ĭ-) [*xiphi-* + *sternum*t] Xiphoid process.

xiphoid (zī′foyd″, zif′oyd″) [*xiphi-* + *-oid*] Sword-shaped. SYN: *ensiform*.

X-linked (eks′lingkt″) Transmitted by genes found only on the X chromosome.

X-linked disorder A disease caused by genes located on the X chromosome. SEE: *choroideremia; hemophilia*.

X^m The X chromosome that a child receives from his or her mother.

X^p The X chromosome that a daughter receives from her father.

x-radiation SEE: under *radiation*.

x-ray (eks′rā″) [Translation of Ger. *X-Strahl*, "X" standing for *unknown*,

coined by Wilhelm Roentgen.] **1.** Electromagnetic radiation having a wavelength between 0.1 and 100 angstrom units. **2.** A colloquial term for an image of a part of the body made with electromagnetic radiation. The formal term is *radiograph*.

x-ray photon An uncharged particle of energy, moving in waves produced by the interaction of high-speed electrons with a target (commonly tungsten). These particles vary from those of lower energy (1 to 0.1 A.U.), used in diagnostic imaging, to those of higher energy (0.1 to 10^{-4} A.U.), used in therapy. SYN: *roentgen ray*.

XRT   *radiation therapy*.

XX-Male syndrome A congenital cause of male infertility in which individuals are born with male external genitalia (and gonads that are testicular rather than ovarian), while having a 46-XX karyotype (the karyotype that is usually associated with the human female). Most XX-males have a gene that determines male sexual characteristics appended to the end of one of their X chromosomes.

xylene (zī′lēn″) [Gr. *xylon*, wood, timber + *-ene*] A mixture of isomeric dimethylbenzenes used in making lacquers and rubber cement. SYN: *xylol*.

xylenol (zī′lĕ-nol″, -nōl″) [*xylene* + *-ol*] Any of six dimethylphenols found in the pine-type coal tar disinfectants.

xylitol (zī′lĭ-tol″, -tōl″) [Ger. *Xylit*, fr. Ger. *Xyl(ose)*, xylose + Ger. *-it*, -ite + *-ol*] A five-carbon sugar alcohol that has a sweet taste and chemical properties similar to those of sucrose. It may be used in place of sucrose as a sweetener. The use of xylitol in the diet might reduce tooth decay in children. SEE: *wood sugar*.

xylol (zī′lol″, -lōl″) [Gr. *xylon*, wood, timber + *-ol*] Xylene.

xylose (zī′lōs) [Gr. *xylon*, wood, timber + *²-ose*] A colorless crystalline sugar. It is obtained from tree sap but is also found in fruits and vegetables; it is used as a sucrose substitute in diabetic diets. SYN: *birch sugar; wood sugar*.

xylulose (zīl′yŭ-lōs″) [Gr. *xylon*, wood, timber + *(cell)ulose*] A pentose sugar present in nature as L-xylulose. It appears in the urine in essential pentosuria and in the form of D-xylulose.

xylyl (zī′lil) [Gr. *xylon*, wood, timber + *-yl*] $CH_3C_6H_4CH_2$—, a radical formed by the removal of a hydrogen atom from xylene.

Y Symbol for the element yttrium.

yage (ya'hā) [Sp. *yagé,* fr. a S. American Indian language] **1.** A tropical South American vine, *Banisteriopsis caapi,* whose bark is boiled to make a tea with hallucinogenic properties. **2.** The popular name of the tea made from the vine of the same name.

yard (yard) A measure of 3 ft or 36 in.; equal to 0.9144 m. SEE: *Weights and Measures Appendix.*

yawn (yan) To open the mouth involuntarily and take a deep breath, a movement mediated by neurotransmitters in the hypothalamus. It is often accompanied by stretching. and is associated with drowsiness, boredom, anxiety, or fatigue. **yawning** (yan'ing), *n.*

yaws (yaz) [From Carib *yaya,* sore] An infectious nonvenereal disease caused by a spirochete, *Treponema pertenue,* and mainly found in humid, equatorial regions. The disease is marked by fevers, joint pains, and caseating eruptions on the hands, feet, face, and external genitals. The infection is rarely, if ever, fatal but can be disfiguring and disabling. It is treated with penicillin. SYN: *bouba; frambesia; parangi; pian.*

Yb Symbol for the element ytterbium.

Y-connector 1. A glass or plastic connector that divides one incoming line into two outgoing ones. **2.** A glass or plastic connector that joins two incoming lines into one outgoing line.

years of life lost The number of years a person might have lived if the accident or disease that killed him had not occurred.

yeast (yēst) **1.** Any of several unicellular fungi of the genera *Saccharomyces* or *Candida,* which reproduce by budding. They are capable of fermenting carbohydrates. Yeasts, esp. *C. albicans* may cause systemic infections as well as vaginitis and oral thrush. Yeast infections are frequently present in patients with malignant lymphomas, poorly controlled diabetes mellitus, AIDS, or other conditions that compromise immune systems. SYN: *Saccharomyces.* SEE: illus.; *Candida; candidiasis; fungi.* **2.** A commercial product composed of meal impregnated with living fungi, used, for example, in fermenting beer and ale and baking bread.

brewer's y. Yeast obtained during the brewing of beer. It is a rich source of folic acid and chromium.

dried y. Dried yeast cells from strains of *Saccharomyces cerevisiae.* It

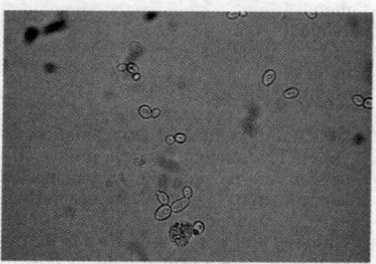

BUDDING YEAST

(×400)

is used as a source of proteins and vitamins, esp. B complex.

yellow (yel'ō) One of the primary colors resembling that of a ripe lemon.

yellow fever SEE: under *fever.*

yellow nail syndrome A condition marked by slowing of nail growth, yellowish discoloration, bilateral lymphedema, and recurrent pleural or pericardial effusions. It is typically found in those with underlying autoimmune, lymphatic, or malignant diseases.

Yergason test (yĕr'gă-sŏnz) [Robert Mosley Yergason, 20th-cent. U.S. physician] A test to identify subluxation of the long head of the biceps brachii muscle from the bicipital groove caused by disruption of the transverse humeral ligament. The patient is seated, the glenohumeral joint is in the anatomical position, the elbow flexed to 90°, and the forearm supinated to assume the "palm up" position. The evaluator resists the patient as the shoulder is externally rotated and the elbow flexed. A positive test result is marked by a "snapping" sensation as the long head of the biceps brachii subluxates from the bicipital groove, indicating a tear of the transverse humeral ligament.

Yersinia (yĕr-sin'ē-ă) [Alexandre Emil Jean Yersin, Swiss bacteriologist who worked in Paris, 1863–1943] A genus of gram-negative coccobacilli of the family Enterobacteriaceae; several are human pathogens.

Y. enterocolitica A species that causes acute mesenteric lymphadenitis and enterocolitis. The disease may progress to a septicemic form in children, and mortality may be as high as 50%. Therapy with trimethoprim-sulfamethoxazole, aminoglycosides, tetracycline, third-generation cephalosporin, or quinolones is effective.

Y. pestis The species that causes bubonic and pneumonic plague. SEE: *plague*.

Y. pseudotuberculosis A species that causes pseudotuberculosis in humans.

yersiniosis (yĕr-sin″ē-ō′sīs) [*Yersinia* + *-osis*] Infection with *Yersinia* organisms.

yin-yang (yin-yang) [Chinese *yīn*, moon, the dark, passive, female principle + *yáng*, sun, the bright, active, male principle] The ancient Chinese philosophical concept of complementary opposites that alternately give rise to each other, such as light and dark. In traditional Chinese philosophy and medicine, the goal is to have a proper balance of such forces. SEE: illus.

YIN-YANG

-yl [Gr. *hylē*, wood, matter, substance] Suffix in chemistry used in naming *radicals*, e.g., *acyl*.

-ylene [*-yl* + *-ene*] Suffix in chemistry used in naming a divalent hydrocarbon radical or an unsaturated hydrocarbon.

Y-linked (wī′lingkt″) Transmitted by genes found only on the Y chromosome.

YMSM *young men having sex with men*.

yocto- [Fm. *octo-*, representing the eighth power of a thousandth] ABBR: y. In the International System of Units (SI), a prefix signifying 10^{-24}.

yoga (yō′gă) [Sanskrit *yoga*, yoking, union] A system of traditional Hindu beliefs, rituals, and activities that aims to provide spiritual enlightenment and self-knowledge. In the Western world, the term has been associated primarily with physical postures (asanas) and coordinated, diaphragmatic breathing. Many practitioners of complementary medicine use yoga to treat chronic musculoskeletal pain, anxiety, insomnia, and other conditions.

Hatha y. A branch of yoga popular in the West that relies on breathing techniques and the use of body postures to attain fitness, relaxation, and enlightenment.

yogurt, yoghurt (yō′gŭrt) [Turkish *yogurt*] A form of curdled milk created by culturing milk with *Lactobacillus bulgaricus*. Yogurt is a source of calcium and protein that may be better tolerated than milk by those with lactase deficiency. Yogurt with live bacterial cultures is probiotic and may be useful for replenishing intestinal flora eradicated by antibiotics. SEE: *milk*.

yoke (yōk) A tissue connecting two structures.

yolk (yōk) The contents of the ovum; sometimes only the nutritive portion. SYN: *vitellus*. SEE: *zona pellucida*.

yotta- [Fm. *octo-*, representing the eighth power of a thousand] In the International System of Units (SI), a prefix signifying 10^{24}.

young-old (yŭng′ōld″) Between 65 and 75 years old.

youth (ūth) The period between childhood and maturity.

youth friendly User friendly (acceptable or appealing) to young people between the ages of 10 and 24. The term is used for elements of health care that are accessible to and comfortable for preteens, adolescents, and young adults.

y.s. *yellow spot*.

ytterbium (i-tĕr′bē-ŭm) [*Ytterby*, a village and quarry near Stockholm, Sweden, where first discovered in 1878 + *-ium* (1)] SYMB: Yb. A rare lanthanide element, atomic weight (mass) 173.04, atomic number 70. It is used in screens in radiography.

yttrium (i′trē-ŭm) [*Ytterby*, a village and quarry near Stockholm, Sweden, where first discovered in 1787 + *-ium* (1)] SYMB: Y. A transition metal, atomic weight (mass) 88.905, atomic number 39.

Yura, Helen (ūr′ă) A U.S. nurse-educator and author who published the first comprehensive text on the nursing process with Mary B. Walsh. SEE: *nursing process; Nursing Theory Appendix*.

yushi (ū′shē) [Japanese] Minamata disease.

Z

Z **1.** *Zuckung,* (Ger., contraction). **2.** Symbol for atomic number

z zero; zone.

zafirlukast (ză-fir′loo-kast″, za″fir-loo′kast) A leukotriene inhibitor used to treat asthma.

Zahn line (zon) [Frederick W. Zahn, Ger. pathologist, 1845–1904] One of the transverse whitish marks on the free surface of a thrombus made by the edges of layered platelets.

Zahorsky disease (ză-hor′skē) Sixth disease.

Zantac (zan′tak″) Ranitidine.

zar (zar) A culture-bound illness specific to Northern Africa and the Middle East in which people are possessed by evil spirits. The disease has characteristics reminiscent of the Western illness known as dissociative identity disorder.

Zavanelli maneuver (zav″ă-nel′ē) [William Angelo Zavanelli, U.S. obstetrician and gynecologist, b. 1926] In obstetrics, the manual return of the head of a partially born fetus with intractable shoulder dystocia to the vagina. This is followed by cesarean section.

Z-79 Committee of the American National Standards Institute A committee that develops standards for anesthetic and ventilatory equipment. The label "Z-79" signifies that a device meets the established standard.

Z disk SEE: under *disk.*

ZDV *zidovudine.*

zea (zē′ă) [Gr. *zeia,* (coarse) wheat, spelt] Maize or corn.

zeaxanthin (zē″ă-zan′thĭn) [*Zea,* the genus name for corn (maize) + *xantho-* + *-in*] A pigmented antioxidant (a member of the carotenoid family) that is found in broccoli, corn, leafy green vegetables, and squash. Consumption of zeaxanthin-rich foods has been associated with a decreased risk of age-related macular degeneration.

zein (zē′ĭn) [*Zea,* the genus name for corn (maize) + *-in*] A protein obtained from maize. It is deficient in tryptophan and lysine.

zeisian (zī′sē-ăn) Pert. to something originally described by Eduard Zeis.

zeitgeber (tsīt′gă″bĕr, zīt′) [Ger. *Zeitgeber,* timekeeper] Any of the mechanisms in nature that keep internal biological clocks synchronized (entrained) with the environment. Zeitgebers can be physical, involving light or temperature, e.g., sunrise, sunset, or social, involving regular activities, e.g., consistent mealtimes.

zeitgeist (tsīt′gīst″) [Ger. *Zeitgeist,* spirit of the time] The spirit of the people, or trend of thought at a particular time.

zelotypia (zē″lō-tip′ē-ă) [Gr. *zēlos,* eager rivalry + *typo-* + *-ia*] **1.** Morbid or monomaniacal zeal in the interest of any project or cause. **2.** Insane jealousy.

Zenker, Friedrich Albert von (tseng′kĕr, zeng′) Ger. pathologist, 1825–1898.

   Z. degeneration A glassy or waxy hyaline degeneration of skeletal muscles in acute infectious diseases, esp. in typhoid. SYN: *zenkerism.*

   Z. diverticulum Herniation of the mucous membrane of the esophagus through a defect in the wall of the esophagus. It is usually located in the posterior hypopharyngeal wall. Small diverticula are asymptomatic. Large diverticula trap food and may cause esophageal obstruction, dysphagia, or the regurgitation of food. Treatment is by surgery or endoscopy.

   Z. fluid A tissue fixative consisting of mercuric chloride, potassium dichromate, glacial acetic acid, and water. It is used to examine cells, esp. nuclei, in detail.

zenkerism (zeng′kĕr-ĭzm) Zenker degeneration. SEE: under *Zenker, Friedrich Albert von.*

zeolite (zē′ō-līt″) [Gr. *zein,* to boil + *-lite*] A mineral containing aluminum and silica used to adsorb liquids and stop bleeding.

zepto- [Fm L. *septem,* seven, representing the seventh power of a thousandth] In the International System of Units (SI), a prefix signifying 10^{-21}.

zero (zēr′ō) [It *zero,* ult. fr. Arabic *sifr,* empty, zero, cipher] ABBR: z. SYMB: 0. **1.** A number that is neither positive nor negative; a number that has no value; nothing. **2.** The point from which the graduation figures of a scale commence.

   On the Celsius scale, e.g., zero (0°) is the temperature of melting ice. SEE: *thermometer.*

   absolute z. The temperature at which all molecular motion (translational, vibrational, rotational) ceases. It is the lowest possible temperature, −273.15°C or −459.6°F; equal to 0° Kelvin.

   leading z. A zero that precedes a decimal point, e.g., as in "levothyroxine 0.05 mg p.o. daily." Leading zeros should always be employed when writing prescriptions for doses of drugs that are fractions of a unit. In the example above, an alternative method of writing the drug dose without decimals is "levothyroxine 50 μg p.o. daily."

   limes z. SYMB: L0. The greatest amount of toxin that, when mixed with one unit of antitoxin and injected into a guinea pig weighing 250 g, will cause no local edema.

   trailing z. A zero that follows a decimal point, e.g., "lisinopril 5.0 grams orally twice a day." Trailing zeros appear on the Joint Commission on the Accreditation of Hospitals (JCAHO) "Do not use" list.

   ⚠ The use of a zero after a decimal point may result in the administration of a drug at ten times its prescribed dose if the decimal point is illegible or not seen.

zero population growth ABBR: ZPG. The demographic equilibrium in which in a given period the population neither increases nor decreases, i.e., the death and birth rates are equal.

zero-sum game A game in which the sum of the wins is equal to the sum of the losses. In such a game, every victory by one party results in equivalent losses by other participants.

Zestril (zes'tril) SEE: *lisinopril.*

zeta-chain associated protein kinase 70kDa deficiency SEE: under *deficiency.*

zetta- [Fm. L. *septem,* seven, representing the seventh power of a thousand] In the International System of Units (SI), a prefix signifying 10^{21}.

Ziehl-Neelsen method (zēl-nēl'sĕn) [Franz Ziehl, Ger. bacteriologist, 1857–1926; Friedrich Karl Adolf Neelsen, Ger. pathologist, 1854–1894] A method for staining *Mycobacterium tuberculosis.* A solution of carbolfuchsin is applied, then the organism retains after rinsing with acid alcohol

ZIFT *zygote intrafallopian transfer.*

zinc (zink) [Ger. *Zink*] SYMB: Zn. A bluish-white, crystalline metallic element, atomic weight (mass) 65.37, atomic number 30, specific gravity 7.13, boiling point 906°C. It is found as a carbonate and silicate (calamine) and as a sulfide (blende). Dietary sources are red meat, esp. beef, lamb, and liver; eggs; seafood; and, to a lesser extent, grain products.

   FUNCTION: Zinc is an essential dietary element for animals, including humans. It is involved in most metabolic pathways. The recommended dietary intake is 12 to 15 mg of zinc daily for adults, 19 mg daily during the first 6 months of pregnancy, and 5 mg daily for infants.

   DEFICIENCY SYMPTOMS: Loss of appetite, growth retardation, hypogonadism and dwarfism, skin changes, im-

munological abnormalities, altered rate of wound healing, and impaired taste characterize this condition. Zinc deficiency during pregnancy may lead to developmental disorders in the child.

   z. acetate $Zn(O_2CCH_3)_2$, white, pearly crystals used as an astringent, antiseptic, contraceptive, and copper-binding compound.

   z. cadmium sulfide A fluorescent material used in radiographic imaging intensification screens.

   z. finger A small protein that can be constructed to bind to specific DNA sequences within genes.

   z. oxide and eugenol Two substances that react together to produce a relatively hard mass, used in dentistry for impression material, cavity liners, sealants, temporary restorations, and cementing layers.

   z. salt A bluish-white metal used to make various containers and to galvanize iron to prevent rust. The most commonly used compounds are zinc oxide as a pigment for paints and ointments. The salts also are used as a wood preservative, in soldering, in medicine to neutralize tissue, and in dilute solutions as an astringent and emetic.

   z. stearate $Zn(C_{18}H_{35}O_2)_2$, a very fine smooth powder used as a nonirritating antiseptic and astringent for burns and abrasions.

   zinc sulfate $ZnSO_4$, an astringent used in a 0.25% solution for temporary relief of minor eye irritation.

   z. undecylenate $C_{22}H_{38}O_4Zn$, a fine white powder used as a topical antifungal.

zinc deficiency syndrome Acrodermatitis enteropathica.

zinciferous (zing-kif'ĕr-ŭs, zin-sif') [*zinc* + *-ferous*] Containing zinc.

zinc protoporphyrin A biochemical marker of iron deficiency. It is only moderately effective in diagnosing the disease.

Zinn, Johann (zin, tsin) Johann Gottfried Zinn, Ger. anatomist and botanist, 1727–1759.

   annulus of Z. A ring of fibrous tissue behind the eye that surrounds the optic nerve and the ophthalmic artery and vein. It consists of the origins of five of the extraocular muscles: the superior oblique, and the inferior, lateral, medial, and superior rectus muscles.

   tendon of Z. The portion of the fibrous ring (annulus tendineus communis) from which the inferior rectus muscle of the eye originates.

   zonule of Z. Ciliary zonule.

zipper pull A device allowing people with limited function to fasten zippers on clothing, esp. those in back.

zirconium (zĭr-kō'nē-ŭm) [*zircon* + *-ium* (1)] SYMB: Zr. A transition metal found only in combination with other elements, atomic weight (mass) 91.22, atomic number 40. It is used in corrosion-resistant alloys and as a white pigment in dental porcelain and other ceramics.

Zithromax (zith′rō-maks″) SEE: *azithromycin.*

Z line SEE: under *line.*

Zn Symbol for the element zinc.

zoacanthosis (zō″ă-kan-thō′sĭs) [*zoo-* + *acanthosis*] Dermatitis due to foreign bodies such as bristles, hairs, or stingers from animals.

zoanthropy (zō-an′thrŏ-pē) [*zoo-* + Gr. *anthrōpos,* human being] The delusion that one is an animal.

Zocor (zō′kor″) Simvastatin.

-zolamide A suffix used in pharmacology to designate an inhibitor.

Zollinger-Ellison syndrome (zol′ing-ĕr-el′ĭ-sŏn) [Robert M. Zollinger, 1903–1992; Edwin H. Ellison, 1918–1970, U.S. surgeons] A condition caused by neuroendocrine tumors, usually of the pancreas, which secrete excess amounts of gastrin. This stimulates the stomach to secrete great amounts of hydrochloric acid and pepsin, which in turn leads to peptic ulceration of the stomach and small intestine. About 60% of the tumors are malignant. Hyperacidity produced by the tumor can be treated with proton-pump inhibitors (such as omeprazole). Surgical removal of the tumor (called gastrinoma) may be curative.

Zoloft (zō′loft″) Sertraline.

zolpidem (zŏl′pĭ-dem″) An imidazopyridine used to treat insomnia. Its therapeutic class is sedatives/hypnotics.

zona (zō′nă) *pl.* **zonae** [L. *zona,* belt, girdle, zone fr. Gr. *zōnē*] **1.** A band, girdle, layer, or zone. **2.** Herpes zoster.

  z. fasciculata The middle layer of the adrenal cortex. It secretes glucocorticoids, mainly cortisol.

  z. glomerulosa The outer layer of the adrenal cortex. It secretes mineralocorticoids, mainly aldosterone.

  z. incerta A thin nucleus in the brain located below the thalamus and above the subthalamic nucleus. It is the object of certain deep brain stimulation procedures to treat central motor disorders, such as Parkinson's disease.

  z. intermedia Lateral horn.

  z. pellucida The inner, solid, thick, membranous envelope of the ovum. It is pierced by many radiating canals, giving it a striated appearance. SYN: *z. radiata; z. striata; vitelline membrane.*

  z. radiata Z. pellucida.

  z. reticularis The inner layer of the adrenal cortex. It secretes very small amounts of androgens and estrogens.

  z. striata Z. pellucida.

zonal (zōn′ăl) [*zone* + *-al*] Pert. to a zone.

zonary (zōn′ă-rē) [*zone*] Pert. to a zone.

zone (zōn) [L. *zona,* fr. Gr. *zōnē,* a girdle] ABBR: z. **1.** An area or belt. **2.** A lobe of an organ or a gland.

  border z. The partially damaged part of an organ that is found between tissue that is severely injured by an infarct and nearby tissue that is still well supplied with blood, oxygen, and nutrients.

  cell-free z. In dentistry, an area below the odontoblastic layer of the dental pulp that has relatively few cells. SYN: *z. of Weil.*

  cell-rich z. The area of increased cell frequency between the cell-free zone and the central pulp of the tooth.

  chemoreceptor trigger z. ABBR: CTZ. A zone in the medulla that is sensitive to certain chemical stimuli. Stimulation of this zone may produce nausea.

  ciliary z. The peripheral annular sector of the anterior surface of the iris of the eye. The ciliary zone is separated from the inner, more narrow annulus, the pupillary zone, of the iris by a wavy boundary, the collarette. These regions are used in automated iris recognition technology.

  cold z. In a hazardous materials incident, an unexposed area where rescue personnel wait for assignments and the command post is located, which is safe from any potential contamination.

  comfort z. The range of temperature, humidity, and, when applicable, solar radiation and wind in which an individual doing work at a specified rate and in a certain specified garment is comfortable.

  epileptogenic z. Any area of the brain that after stimulation produces an epileptic seizure.

  erogenous z. An area of the body that may produce erotic sensations when stimulated. These areas include, but are not limited to, the breasts, lips, genital and anal regions, buttocks, and sometimes the special senses that cause sexual excitation, such as the sense of smell or taste.

  H z. H **band.**

  hot z. In a hazardous materials incident or biohazard laboratory, the area where the hazardous materials are located. This area cannot be entered without protective equipment, special permission, and specialized training.

  hypnogenic z. Any area of the body that, when pressed on, induces hypnosis. SYN: *hypnogenic* **spot.**

  Looser z.s SEE: *Looser zones.*

  lung z. A hypothetical region of the lung defined by the relationship between the degree of alveolar ventilation and pulmonary blood flow (perfusion). Three lung zones have been identified: I, ventilation exceeds perfusion; II, ventilation and perfusion are equal; and III, perfusion exceeds ventilation. Zone I is found in the upper lung field, where gravity impedes perfusion, and zone III in the inferior portion of the lung, where gravity assists perfusion.

peripheral z. ABBR: PZ. The lateral border of the prostate gland. Most prostate cancers begin here. SYN: *peripheral z. of the prostate.*

peripheral z. of the prostate Peripheral **z.**

pupillary z. The innermost of two annular areas visible on the anterior surface of the iris. SEE: *ciliary z.*

z. of stasis The area of skin beneath the coagulated surface of a burn in which blood flow is diminished and tissue fluid collects. This region of a burn may become necrotic if it becomes infected or fails to receive adequate blood flow.

transition z. **1.** Tissue that includes two or more cell types linking two distinct regions of an organ. **2.** Squamocolumnar **junction**.

transitional z. The area of the lens of the eye where the epithelial capsule cells change into lens fibers.

trigger z. Trigger **point**.

warm z. In a hazardous materials incident, the area between the hot zone and the cold zone, where decontamination occurs. Only specialized personnel who are appropriately dressed are permitted in this location.

z. of Weil Cell-free **z.**

zone of stasis SEE: under *zone.*

zoning (zōn'ing) The occurrence of a stronger fixation of complement in a lesser amount of suspected serum; a phenomenon occasionally observed in diagnosing syphilis by the complement-fixation method.

zonography (zō-nog'ră-fē) [*zone* + *-graphy*] A type of tomography, using a tomographic angle less than 10°, that produces an image of a larger thickness of tissue. This technique is used for kidneys or structures lacking inherent contrast.

zonula (zōn'yŭ-lă) [L. *zonula*, little girdle] A small zone. SYN: *zonule.*

z. adherens The portion of the junctional complex between columnar epithelial cells below the zonula occludens where there is an intercellular space of about 200 angstrom units and the cellular membranes are supported by filamentous material.

z. ciliaris Ciliary **zonule**.

z. occludens Tight **junction**.

zonular (zōn'ū-lăr) Pert. to a zonula.

zonular space SEE: under *space.*

zonule (zōn'ūl″) [*zonula*] **1.** A small band or area. SYN: *zonula.* **2.** The ciliary zonule.

ciliary z. The suspensory ligament of the crystalline lens. SYN: *zonula ciliaris; z. of Zinn.*

z. of Zinn SEE: under *Zinn, Johann.*

zonulitis (zōn″yŭ-līt'ĭs) [*zonula* + *-itis*] Inflammation of the ciliary zonule.

zonulolysis (zōn″yŭ-lol'ĭ-sĭs, -lī'sĭs) [*zonule* + *-lysis*] The use of enzymes to dissolve the zonula ciliaris of the eye. SYN: *zonulysis.*

zonulotomy (zōn″yŭ-lot'ŏ-mē) [*zonule* + *-tomy*] Surgical incision of the ciliary zonule.

zonulysis (zōn″yŭ-lī'sĭs) [*zonule* + *-lysis*] Zonulolysis.

zoo- [Gr. *zōion*, animal] Prefix meaning *animal, animal life.*

zoobiology (zō″ŏ-bī-ol'ŏ-jē) [*zoo-* + *biology*n] The biology of animals.

zoochemistry (zō″ŏ-kem'ĭ-strē) [*zoo-* + *chemistry*] Biochemistry of animals.

zoogeography (zō″ō-jē-ŏg'ră-fē) The study of the distribution of animals on the earth.

zooglea (zō″ō-glē'ă) [″ + *gloios*, sticky] A stage in development of certain organisms in which colonies of microbes are embedded in a gelatinous matrix.

zooid (zō'oyd) [″ + *eidos*, form, shape] **1.** Resembling an animal. **2.** A form resembling an animal; an organism produced by fission. **3.** An animal cell that can move or exist independently.

zoolagnia (zō″ō-lăg'nē-ă) [″ + *lagneia*, lust] Sexual desire for animals.

zoologist (zō-ŏl'ō-jĭst) [″ + *logos*, word, reason] A biologist who specializes in the study of animal life.

zoology (zō-ŏl'ō-jē) The science of animal life.

zoom (zoom) To magnify ("zoom in") or shrink ("zoom out") an image in order to highlight some of its smaller features or some of the environment in which the imaged object is situated.

zoomania (zō″ō-mā'nē-ă) [Gr. *zoon*, animal, + *mania*, madness] A morbid and excessive affection for animals.

Zoomastigophora (zō″ō-măs″tĭ-gŏ'fŏ-ră) A class of unicellular organisms within the phylum Sarcomastigophora. These organisms usually have one or more flagella, which may be absent in some species. It includes free-living and parasitic species such as *Giardia lamblia.*

Zoon balanitis (zoon, zōn) [Johannes Jacobus Zoon, Dutch dermatologist, b. 1902] Infiltration of the skin of the penis by plasma cells; typically found in older men who are not circumcised. It causes a palpable, visible plaque. SYN: *balanitis circumscripta plasmacellularis; plasma cell balanitis.*

zoonosis (zō-ō-nō'sĭs) *pl.* **zoonoses** [″ + *nosos*, disease] An infection common in animal populations that occasionally infects humans. More than 250 organisms are known to cause zoonotic infections, of which 30 to 40 are spread from pets and animals used by the blind and deaf. The immunosuppressed and those who work with animals are esp. at risk of developing zoonoses.

zoonotic (-nŏt′ĭk), *adj.*

Zoon vulvitis Plasmacellularis vulvitis.

zooparasite (zō″ō-păr′ă-sīt) [″ + *para,* beside, + *sitos,* food] An animal parasite.

zoopathology (zō″ō-păth-ŏl′ō-jē) [″ + *pathos,* disease, + *logos,* word, reason] The science of the diseases of animals.

zoophile (zō′ō-fīl) [″ + *philein,* to love] **1.** One who likes animals. **2.** An antivivisectionist.

zoophilia (zō″ō-fīl′ē-ă) The preference for obtaining sexual gratification by having intercourse or other sexual activity with animals.

zoophilism (zō-ŏf′ĭl-ĭzm) [″ + ″ + *-ismos,* condition] An abnormal love of animals.

zoophyte (zō′ō-fīt) [″ + *phyton,* plant] An animal that appears plantlike; any of numerous invertebrate animals resembling plants in appearance or mode of growth.

zooplankton (zō″ō-plănk′tŏn) [″ + *planktos,* wandering] A small animal organism present in natural waters. SEE: *phytoplankton.*

zoopsychology (zō″ō-sī-kŏl′ō-jē) Animal psychology.

zoosadism (zō″ō-sā′dĭzm) Mistreatment of animals.

zoospore (zō′ō-spor) [″ + *sporos,* seed] A motile asexual spore that moves by means of one or more flagella.

zootechnics (zō″ō-tĕk′nĭks) [Gr. *zoon,* animal, + *techne,* art] The complete care, management, and breeding of domestic animals.

zootic (zō-ŏt′ĭk) Pert. to animals.

Zostavax (zō′stă-văks″) [From *zo(ster)* + *vacc(ine)*] Varicella-zoster virus vaccine.

zoster (zŏs′tĕr) [Gr. *zoster,* girdle] Herpes zoster.

    z. auricularis Herpes zoster of the ear.

    z. ophthalmicus SEE: under *herpes zoster ophthalmicus.*

    z. sine herpete Cutaneous pain of dermatomal distribution, suggestive of herpes zoster but without the typical rash of shingles. That the pain is caused by a reactivation of herpes zoster may be confirmed by antibody titer or polymerase chain reaction tests.

zosteroid (zŏs′tĕr-oyd) [″ + *eidos,* form, shape] Resembling herpes zoster.

ZPG *zero population growth.*

Z-plasty (z-plăs′tē) The use of a Z-shaped incision in plastic surgery to relieve tension in scar tissue. The area under tension is lengthened at the expense of the surrounding elastic tissue. SEE: illus.; *tissue expansion, soft; W-plasty.*

Zr Symbol for the element zirconium.

Z-track (z-trăk′) An injection technique in which the surface (skin and subcutaneous) tissues are pulled and held to one side before insertion of the needle

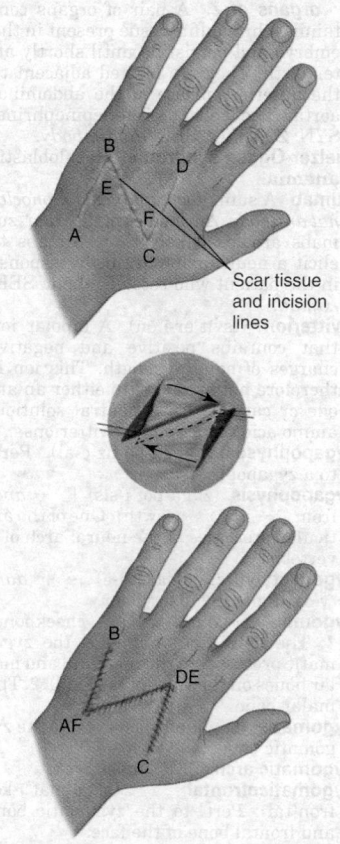

Scar tissue and incision lines

Z-PLASTY METHOD OF CORRECTING A DEFORMING SCAR

deep into the muscle in the identified site. The medication is injected slowly, followed by a 10-sec delay; then the needle is removed, and the tissues are quickly permitted to resume their normal position. This provides a Z-shaped track, which makes it difficult for the injected irritating drug to seep back into subcutaneous tissues.

Zubrod performance scale (zoo′brod″) [Charles Gordon Zubrod, U.S. oncologist, 1914–1999] A rating scale measuring the ability of a cancer patient to carry out the activities of daily living. The ranges are a score of 0 (fully active, unrestricted by disease) to 1 (able to carry out light work), 2 (ambulatory but resting for as much as 50% of the day), 3 (resting in bed or a chair for more than half the day), 4 (confined to bed at all times) and 5 (patient has died).

Zuckerkandl, Emil (tsuk′ĕr-kon″dĕl) Austro-Hungarian anatomist, 1849–1910.

    Z. bodies Organs of **Z.**

organs of Z. A pair of organs containing chromaffin tissue present in the embryo and persisting until shortly after birth. They are located adjacent to the anterior surface of the abdominal aorta. The cells secrete epinephrine. SYN: *Z. bodies*. SEE: *aortic body*.

Zuelzer-Ogden syndrome Megaloblastic anemia.

-zumab A suffix for *humanized monoclonal antibody*. Antibodies made from -zumabs are less likely than -ximabs to elicit a neutralizing antibody response in the patient who receives them. SEE: *-ximab*.

zwitterion (tsvĭt'ĕr-ī″ŏn) A dipolar ion that contains positive and negative charges of equal strength. This ion is therefore not attracted to either an anode or cathode. In a neutral solution, amino acids function as zwitterions.

zygapophyseal (zī″gă-pō-fiz′ē-ăl) Pert. to a zygapophysis.

zygapophysis (zī″gă-pŏf′ĭ-sĭs) [″ + *apo*, from, + *physis*, growth] One of the articular processes of the neural arch of a vertebra.

zygodactyly (zī″gō-dăk′tĭl-ē) [″ + *daktylos*, digit] Syndactylism.

zygoma (zi-gō′mà) [Gr., cheekbone] 1. The long arch that joins the zygomatic processes of the temporal and malar bones on the sides of the skull. 2. The malar bone.

zygomatic (zī″gō-măt′ĭk) Pert. to the zygomatic bone.

zygomatic arch SEE: under *arch*.

zygomaticofrontal (zī″gō-măt″ĭ-kō-frŏn′tăl) Pert. to the zygomatic bone and frontal bone of the face.

zygomaticum (zī″gō-măt′ĭ-kŭm) [L.] Zygomatic bone.

zygomaticus (zī″gō-măt′ĭk-ŭs) [L.] A muscle that draws the upper lip upward and outward.

Zygomycetes (zī″gō-mī-sēt′ēz) In one system of taxonomy, a class of the true fungi that includes those which cause mucormycosis and entomophthoramycosis. This class is equivalent to the phylum Zygomycotina in another system of taxonomy.

zygomycosis (zī″gō-mī-kō′sĭs) Any of the fungal infections caused by various species of the class Zygomycetes (or phylum Zygomycotina), including those involved in mucormycosis and entomophthoramycosis.

Zygomycotina (zī″gō-mī″kō-tēn′ă) [NL.] In one system of taxonomy, a phylum of the true fungi. It is synonymous with the class Zygomycetes in another system of taxonomy.

zygosis (zī-gō′sĭs) [Gr. *zygosis*, a balancing] The sexual union of two unicellular animals.

zygosity (zī-gŏs′ĭ-tē) [Gr. *zygon*, yoke] The composition or characteristics of a zygote.

zygospore (zī′gō-spor) A spore formed by fusion of morphologically identical structures. SYN: *zygosperm*.

zygote (zī′gŏt) [Gr. *zygotos*, yoked] The cell produced by the union of two gametes; the fertilized ovum.

zygote intrafallopian transfer SEE: under *transfer*.

zygotene (zī′gō-tēn) [Gr. *zygotos*, yoked] The second stage of the prophase of the first meiotic division. During this stage, the homologous chromosomes pair side by side. SEE: *cell division*.

zygotic (zī-gŏt′ĭk) Pert. to a zygote.

zygotomere (zī-gō′tō-mēr) [″ + *meros*, part] Sporoblast.

zym-, zymo- [Gr. *zymē*, leaven] Prefixes meaning *fermentation* or *enzyme*.

zymase (zī′mās) [Gr. *zyme*, leaven, + *-ase*, enzyme] Any of a group of enzymes that, in the presence of oxygen, convert certain carbohydrates into carbon dioxide and water or, in the absence of oxygen, into alcohol and carbon dioxide or lactic acid. It is found in yeast, bacteria, and higher plants and animals. SEE: *fermenting enzyme*.

-zyme [Gr. *zymē*, leaven] Suffix meaning *enzyme*.

zymogen (zī′mō-jĕn) [″ + *gennan*, to produce] A protein that becomes an enzyme. It exists in an inactive form antecedent to the active enzyme. **zymogenic**, *adj*. SYN: *proenzyme*. SEE: *pepsinogen; trypsinogen*.

zymogenous (zī-mŏj′ĕ-nŭs) Zymogenic.

zymogram (zī′mō-grăm) An electrophoretic graph of the separation of the enzymes in a solution.

zymohexase (zī″mō-hĕk′sās) The enzyme involved in splitting fructose 1,6-diphosphate into dihydroxyacetone phosphate and phosphoglyceric aldehyde.

zymologist (zī-mŏl′ō-jĭst) One who specializes in the study of enzymes.

zymology (zī-mŏl′ō-jē) The science of fermentation.

zymolysis (zī-mŏl′ĭ-sĭs) [Gr. *zyme*, leaven, + *lysis*, dissolution] The changes produced by an enzyme; the action of enzymes.

zymolyte (zī′mō-līt″) Substrate.

zymolytic (zī″mō-lĭt′ĭk) [″ + *lytikos*, dissolved] Causing a reaction catalyzed by an enzyme.

zymoprotein (zī″mō-prō′tē-ĭn) Any protein that also functions as an enzyme.

zymosan (zī′mō-săn) An anticomplement obtained from the walls of yeast cells.

zymose (zī′mōs) Invertase.

zymosterol (zī-mŏs′tĕr-ŏl) A sterol obtained from yeast.

zymotic (zī-mŏt′ĭk) Pert. to or produced by fermentation.

Zyprexa (zī-prĕk′sŭ) SEE: *olanzapine*.

Zyrtec Cetirizine.

Z.Z.'Z." Symbol for increasing strengths of contraction.

Appendices

Table of Contents

Index to Appendices

APPENDIX 1
Nutrition

Appendix 1-1 Explanation of Dietary Reference Values

AI, Adequate Intake The amount of a specific nutrient needed to achieve a specific indication, e.g., to maintain bone mass.

DRI, Dietary Reference Intake A nutrient recommendation index based on the parameters specified in the Average Intake, Estimated Average Requirement, Recommended Dietary Allowance and Upper Intake values.

DRV, Daily Reference Value Standards for nutrient intake set for both macronutrient and micronutrient dietary components that lack a Recommended Dietary Allowance. The Dietary Reference Value for some nutrients represents their Upper Limit.

DV, Daily Value A dietary reference term that encompasses the Dietary Reference Value and Reference Daily Intake. It is used to calculate the labeled percent of each nutrient that a serving of the product provides.

EAR, Estimated Average Requirement The estimated intake of a nutrient that meets the nutritional needs of 50% of the individuals within a given age-gender cohort.

ESADDI, Estimated Safe and Adequate Daily Intake The amount of a nutrient calculated to meet the needs of half of the individuals in that age group.

RDA, Recommended Dietary Allowance The amount of a specific dietary component, as established by the National Academy of Sciences, required to meet the needs of 97% of the individuals in a given age-gender cohort. $RDA = EAR + 2SD_{EAR}$

RDI, Reference Daily Intake The nutrient intake standard established by the U.S. Food and Drug Administration as a food label reference for macronutrients and micronutrients.

RNI, Recommended Nutrient Intake The Canadian nutrient intake standard.

US RDA, U.S. Recommended Daily Allowance A nutritional standard formerly promulgated by the FDA and now replaced by the Recommended Dietary Allowance.

UL, Tolerable Upper Intake Level The highest intake per day that is likely to produce no adverse health risks.

Appendix 1-2 Recommended Daily Dietary Allowances [a]

Category	Age (yr) or Condition	Weight (kg)	Weight (lb)	Height (cm)	Height (in.)	Protein (g)	Vitamin A (μg RE)[c]	Vitamin E (mg α-TE)[d]	Vitamin K (μg)	Vitamin C (mg)	Iron (mg)	Zinc (mg)	Iodine (μg)	Selenium (μg)
Infants	0.0–0.5	6	13	60	24	9.1	400	4	2.0	40	0.27	2	110	15
	0.5–1.0	9	20	71	28	13.5	500	5	2.5	50	11	3	130	20
Children	1–3	13	29	90	35	13	300	6	30	15	7	3	90	20
	4–8	20	44	112	44	19	400	7	35	25	10	5	90	30
Male	9–13	45	99	157	62	34	600	11	60	45	8	8	120	40
	14–18	66	145	176	69	52	900	15	75	75	11	11	150	55
	19–30	72	160	177	70	56	900	15	120	90	8	11	150	55
	31–50	79	174	176	70	56	900	15	120	90	8	11	150	55
	51+	77	170	173	68	56	900	15	120	90	8	11	150	55
Female	9–13	46	101	157	62	34	600	11	60	45	8	8	120	40
	14–18	55	120	163	64	46	700	15	75	65	15	9	150	55
	19–30	58	128	164	65	46	700	15	90	75	18	8	150	55
	31–50	63	138	163	64	46	700	15	90	75	18	8	150	55
	51+	65	143	160	63	46	700	15	90	75	8	8	150	55
Pregnant	19–30					71	770	15	90	85	27	11	220	60
	31–50					71	1300	19	90	120	9	12	290	70
Lactating						71	1300	19	90	120	9	12	290	70

[a] The allowances, expressed as average daily intakes over time, are intended to provide for individual variations among most normal persons living in the United States under usual environmental stresses. Diets should be based on a variety of common foods in order to provide other nutrients for which human requirements have been less well defined.

[b] Weights and heights of reference adults are actual medians for the U.S. population of the designated age, as reported by NHANES II [second National Health and Nutrition Examination Survey]. The median weights and heights of those under 19 years of age were taken from Hamill et al. [Physical Growth: National Center for Health Statistics percentiles. Am J Clin Nutr 32:607, 1979]. The use of these figures does not imply that the height-to-weight ratios are ideal.

[c] Retinol equivalents. 1 RE = 1 μg retinol or 6 μg beta-carotene.

[d] Alpha-tocopherol equivalents. 1 mg d-alpha tocopherol = 1 alpha- TE.

SOURCE: From National Research Council. Dietary Reference Intakes: Applications in Dietary Assessment, Copyright 2000 and Dietary Reference Intakes: Applications in Dietary Planning, Copyright 2003 by the National Academy of Sciences. Courtesy of the National Academy Press Washington, DC. www.nap.edu

Appendix 1–3 Dietary Reference Intakes: Recommended Intakes for Individuals

Life Stage Group	Calcium (mg/day)	Phosphorus (mg/day)	Magnesium (mg/day)	Vitamin D (μm/day)ᵃ,ᵇ	Fluoride (mg/day)	Thiamine (mg/day)	Riboflavin (mg/day)	Niacin (mg/day)ᶜ	Vitamin B_6 (mg/day)	Folate (μg/day)ᵈ	Vitamin B_{12} (μg/day)	Pantothenic Acid (mg/day)	Biotin (μg/day)	Choline (mg/day)ᵉ
Infants														
0–6 mo	210*	100*	30*	5*	0.01*	0.2*	0.3*	2*	0.1*	65*	0.4*	1.7*	5*	125
7–12 mo	270*	275*	75*	5*	0.5*	0.3*	0.4*	4*	0.3*	80*	0.5*	1.8*	6*	150
Children														
1–3 years	500*	460	80	5*	0.7*	0.5	0.5	6	0.5	150	0.9	2	8	200
4–8 years	800*	500	130	5*	1*	0.6	0.6	8	0.6	200	1.2	3	12	250
Males														
9–13 years	1,300*	1,250	240	5*	2*	0.9	0.9	12	1.0	300	1.8	4	20	375
14–18 years	1,300*	1,250	410	5*	3*	1.2	1.3	16	1.3	400	2.4	5	25	550
19–30 years	1,000*	700	400	5*	4*	1.2	1.3	16	1.3	400	2.4	5	30	550
31–50 years	1,000*	700	420	5*	4*	1.2	1.3	16	1.3	400	2.4	5	30	550
51–70 years	1,200*	700	420	10*	4*	1.2	1.3	16	1.7	400	2.4ᶠ	5	30	550
>70 years	1,200*	700	420	15*	4*	1.2	1.3	16	1.7	400	2.4ᶠ	5	30	550
Females														
9–13 years	1,300*	1,250	240	5*	2*	0.9	0.9	12	1.0	300	1.8	4	20	375
14–18 years	1,300*	1,250	360	5*	3*	1.0	1.0	14	1.2	400ᵍ	2.4	5	25	400
19–30 years	1,000*	700	310	5*	3*	1.1	1.1	14	1.3	400ᵍ	2.4	5	30	425
31–50 years	1,000*	700	320	5*	3*	1.1	1.1	14	1.3	400ᵍ	2.4	5	30	425
51–70 years	1,200*	700	320	10*	3*	1.1	1.1	14	1.5	400	2.4ᶠ	5	30	425
>70 years	1,200*	700	320	15*	3*	1.1	1.1	14	1.5	400	2.4ᶠ	5	30	425
Pregnancy														
≤18 years	1,300*	1,250	400	5*	3*	1.4	1.4	18	1.9	600ʰ	2.6	6	30	450
19–30 years	1,000*	700	350	5*	3*	1.4	1.4	18	1.9	600ʰ	2.6	6	30	450
31–50 years	1,000*	700	360	5*	3*	1.4	1.4	18	1.9	600ʰ	2.6	6	30	450

Lactation													
≤18 years	1,300*	700	360	5*	3*	1.4	1.6	17	2.0	500	2.8	7	35	550
19–30 years	1,000*	700	310	5*	3*	1.4	1.6	17	2.0	500	2.8	7	35	550
31–50 years	1,000*	700	320	5*	3*	1.4	1.6	17	2.0	500	2.8	7	35	550

[a] As cholecalciferol. 1 μg cholecalciferol = 40 IU vitamin D.

[b] In the absence of adequate exposure to sunlight.

[c] As niacin equivalents (NE). 1 mg of niacin = 60 mg of tryptophan; 0–6 months = preformed niacin (not NE).

[d] As dietary folate equivalents (DFE). 1 DFE = 1 μg food folate = 0.6 μg of folic acid from fortified food or as a supplement consumed with food = 0.5 μg of a supplement taken on an empty stomach.

[e] Although AIs have been set for choline, there are few data to assess whether a dietary supply of choline is needed at all stages of the life cycle, and it may be that the choline requirement can be met by endogenous synthesis at some of these stages.

[f] Because 10 to 30% of older people may malabsorb food-bound B_{12}, it is advisable for those older than 50 years to meet their RDA mainly by consuming foods fortified with B_{12} or a supplement containing B_{12}.

[g] In view of evidence linking folate intake with neural tube defects in the fetus, it is recommended that all women capable of becoming pregnant consume 400 μg from supplements or fortified foods in addition to intake of food folate from a varied diet.

[h] It is assumed that women will continue consuming 400 μg from supplements or fortified food until their pregnancy is confirmed and they enter prenatal care, which ordinarily occurs after the end of the periconceptional period—the critical time for formation of the neural tube.

This table presents Recommended Dietary Allowances (RDAs) in bold type and Adequate Intakes (AIs) in ordinary type followed by an asterisk (*). RDAs and AIs may both be used as goals for individual intake. RDAs are set to meet the needs of almost all (97 to 98%) individuals in a group. For healthy breastfed infants, the AI is the mean intake. The AI for other life-stage and gender groups is believed to cover needs of all individuals in the group.

Appendix 1–4 Dietary Reference Intakes: Tolerable Upper Intake Levels (UL^a) for Certain Nutrients and Food Components

Life-Stage Group	Calcium (g/day)	Phosphorus (g/day)	Magnesium (mg/day)^b	Vitamin D (μg/day)	Fluoride (mg/day)	Niacin (mg/day)^c	Vitamin B$_6$ (mg/day)	Folate (μg/day)	Choline (g/day)
0–6 mo	ND^d	ND	ND	25	0.7	ND	ND	ND	ND
7–12 mo	ND	ND	ND	25	0.9	ND	ND	ND	ND
1–3 years	2.5	3	65	50	1.3	10	30	300	1.0
4–8 years	2.5	3	110	50	2.2	15	40	400	1.0
9–13 years	2.5	4	350	50	10	20	60	600	2.0
14–18 years	2.5	4	350	50	10	30	80	800	3.0
19–70 years	2.5	4	350	50	10	35	100	1,000	3.5
> 70 years	2.5	3	350	50	10	35	100	1,000	3.5
Pregnancy									
≤18 years	2.5	3.5	350	50	10	30	80	800	3.0
19–50 years	2.5	3.5	350	50	10	35	100	1,000	3.5
Lactation									
≤ 18 years	2.5	4	350	50	10	30	80	800	3.0
19–50 years	2.5	4	350	50	10	35	100	1,000	3.5

^{a}UL = The maximum level of daily nutrient intake that is likely to pose no risk of adverse effects. Unless otherwise specified, the UL represents total intake from food, water, and supplements. Due to lack of suitable data, ULs could not be established for thiamine, riboflavin, vitamin B$_{12}$, pantothenic acid, and biotin. In the absence of ULs, extra caution may be warranted in consuming levels above recommended intakes.

^{b}The UL for magnesium represents intake from a pharmacological agent only and does not include intake from food and water.

^{c}The ULs for niacin and folate apply to synthetic forms obtained from supplements, fortified foods, or a combination of the two.

^{d}ND: Not determinable due to lack of data of adverse effects in this age group and concern with regard to lack of ability to handle excess amounts. Source of intake should be from food only to prevent high levels of intake.

Appendix 1–5 **Choose MyPlate**

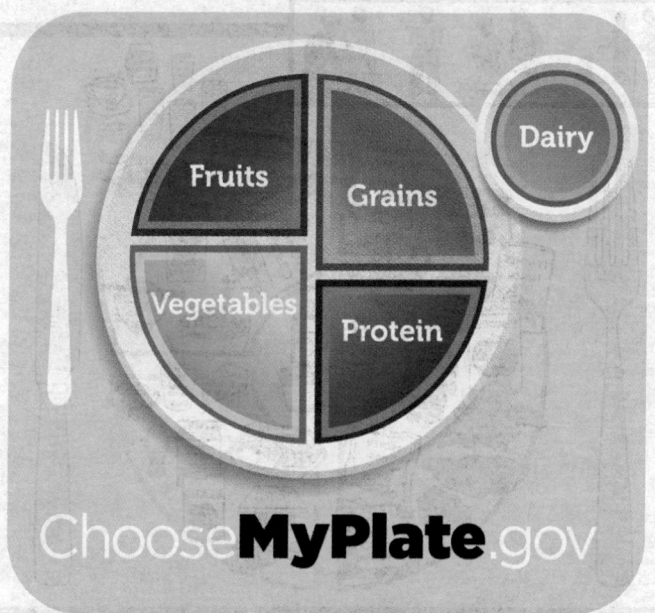

MyPlate for Older Adults

2011© TUFTS UNIVERSITY

Vegetables	Fruits	Grains	Dairy	Protein Foods
Eat more red, orange, and dark-green veggies like tomatoes, sweet potatoes, and broccoli in main dishes. Add beans or peas to salads (kidney or chickpeas), soups (split peas or lentils), and side dishes (pinto or baked beans), or serve as a main dish. Fresh, frozen, and canned vegetables all count. Choose "reduced sodium" or "no-salt-added" canned veggies.	Use fruits as snacks, salads, and desserts. At breakfast, top your cereal with bananas or strawberries; add blueberries to pancakes. Buy fruits that are dried, frozen, and canned (in water or 100% juice), as well as fresh fruits. Select 100% fruit juice when choosing juices.	Substitute whole-grain choices for refined-grain breads, bagels, rolls, breakfast cereals, crackers, rice, and pasta. Check the ingredients list on product labels for the words "whole" or "whole grain" before the grain ingredient name. Choose products that name a whole grain first on the ingredients list.	Choose skim (fat-free) or 1% (low-fat) milk. They have the same amount of calcium and other essential nutrients as whole milk, but less fat and calories. Top fruit salads and baked potatoes with low-fat yogurt. If you are lactose intolerant, try lactose-free milk or fortified soymilk (soy beverage).	Eat a variety of foods from the protein food group each week, such as seafood, beans and peas, and nuts as well as lean meats, poultry, and eggs. Twice a week, make seafood the protein on your plate. Choose lean meats and ground beef that are at least 90% lean. Trim or drain fat from meat and remove skin from poultry to cut fat and calories.

For a 2,000-calorie daily food plan, you need the amounts below from each food group.
To find amounts personalized for you, go to Choose**MyPlate**.gov.

Eat 2½ cups every day	Eat 2 cups every day	Eat 6 ounces every day	Get 3 cups every day	Eat 5½ ounces every day
What counts as a cup? 1 cup of raw or cooked vegetables or vegetable juice; 2 cups of leafy salad greens	**What counts as a cup?** 1 cup of raw or cooked fruit or 100% fruit juice; ½ cup dried fruit	**What counts as an ounce?** 1 slice of bread; ½ cup of cooked rice, cereal, or pasta; 1 ounce of ready-to-eat cereal	**What counts as a cup?** 1 cup of milk, yogurt, or fortified soymilk; 1½ ounces natural or 2 ounces processed cheese	**What counts as an ounce?** 1 ounce of lean meat, poultry, or fish; 1 egg; 1 Tbsp peanut butter; ½ ounce nuts or seeds; ¼ cup beans or peas

MyPlate for Older Adults

Food Group	MyPlate for Older Adults Food Action Plans	Examples of Good Choices (Each food quantity equals one serving)	Suggested amounts for men and women over age 50:
Fruits and Vegetables	Make fruits and vegetables one half of your plate: Concepts: Fresh whole fruits and vegetables are encouraged. If you cannot get to the market, keep frozen, dried or canned fruits/vegetables on hand. Deep-colored fruits and vegetables have higher amounts of vitamins, minerals and fiber.	Fruits: Berries: $\frac{1}{2}$ cup strawberries, Melons: $\frac{1}{2}$ cup diced cantaloupe Mixed fruit: 4-oz. container 100% fruit juices: $\frac{1}{2}$ cup juice (orange, mango, grape, grapefruit. Vegetables: Raw, dark, leafy greens: Spinach, romaine, watercress, 1 cup raw greens is equivalent to $\frac{1}{2}$ cup of vegetables. Carrots: 1 medium carrot or 6 baby carrots = $\frac{1}{2}$ cup Sweet Potato: $\frac{1}{2}$ cup cooked and sliced, or masked = $\frac{1}{2}$ cup Tomato juice: $\frac{1}{2}$ cup One half of an acorn squash = $\frac{3}{4}$ cup Corn: 1 small ear (about 6" long) = $\frac{1}{2}$ cup.	Fruits: Women: $1\frac{1}{2}$ cups Men: 2 cups Vegetables: Women: 2 cups Men: $2\frac{1}{2}$ cups
Grains	Make at least one half of your grains whole. Choose whole, enriched, and fortified grains and cereals such as brown rice and 100% whole wheat bread. Grains are a good source of dietary fiber, thiamin, riboflavin, niacin, folate, iron, magnesium and selenium.	Brown rice: 1 oz. counts as $\frac{1}{2}$ cup equivalent whole grain 1 large bagel = 4-oz. equivalents Oatmeal = $\frac{1}{2}$ cup counts as 1-oz. equivalent whole grains. 1 small whole grain or refined grain muffin = 1-oz. equivalents 1 cup cooked pasta = 2-oz. equivalents.	Women: 3-oz. equivalents Men: 3-oz. equivalents
Protein Foods	Choose a variety of protein foods, esp. those that are lean or low in fat. Foods in this group provide important nutrients vital for immune function, bone, muscle, and cartilage as well as for enzyme reactions and blood formation. Choosing wisely from this group includes minimizing foods high in saturated fat and cholesterol and including beans and nuts.	1 small steak (eye of round, filet) = $3\frac{1}{2}$ to 4-oz. equivalents 1 soy or bean burger patty = 2-oz. equivalents. 1 cup lentil or other bean soups = 2-oz. equivalents 1 oz. of nuts (e.g., almonds) = 2-oz. equivalents 1 whole egg = 1-oz. equivalents 1 can tuna fish = 3- to 4- oz. equivalents.	Women: 5-oz. equivalents Men: $5\frac{1}{2}$-oz. equivalents
Dairy	Switch to fat-free or low-fat (1%) milk Most dairy group choices should be low fat or fat free. Those who are sensitive to lactose should choose dairy items treated with enzyme preparations added to milk to lower the lactose content.	These food examples count as a cup of dairy food: $1\frac{1}{2}$ oz. hard cheese 1 cup fluid whole, low-fat, skim milk or yogurt 1 cup calcium-fortified soy milk $1\frac{1}{2}$ cup ice cream	Women: 3 cups Men: 3 cups

MyPlate for Older Adults (Continued)

Food Group	MyPlate for Older Adults Food Action Plans	Examples of Good Choices (Each food quantity equals one serving)	Suggested Amounts for men and women over age 50:
Oils	Some foods contain enough oil sufficient for the daily suggested amount. These foods include nuts, fish, cooking oil, and salad dressings.	Some oil equivalents (1 tablespoon [Tbs]) = 3 teaspoons [tsp]): Margarine 4 olives = $\frac{1}{2}$ tsp oil Avocado = $\frac{1}{2}$ medium = 3 tsp Peanuts = 1 oz = 3 tsp	Women: 5 tsp Men: 6 tsp

Pay Special Attention to:
Fluid. Drink 8 eight-ounce glasses every day whether you feel thirsty or not. Do not count in those 8 daily glasses alcoholic beverages or fluids that contain caffeine.
Fiber. Dietary fiber may help to relieve constipation.
Supplements. It is difficult for people over 70 to get enough calcium, vitamin B_{12}, and vitamin D in their diets. They should take supplements of these three nutrients regularly.

SOURCE: Lichtenstein, A., Rasmussen, H.M. MyPlate for Older Adults, release date November 2, 2011. Jean Mayer, USDA Human Nutrition Research Center on Aging, Copyright Tufts University. Printed with permission of the authors. Rasmussen, H.M. Eating guidelines for older adults: Food group portion advice for this age group: U.S. Department of Agriculture, ChooseMyPlate.gov Website. Washington, DC. Accessed June 21, 2012.

Appendix 1–6 Vitamins *

Vitamin	Chief Functions	Results of Deficiency or Overdose	Characteristics	Good Sources
VITAMIN A Retinol (animal sources) Carotene Beta-carotene (plant sources)	Maintains epithelial membranes; functions in resisting infection; needed to form rhodopsin; prevents night blindness; ensures proper bone growth; facilitates RNA transcription.	*Deficiency:* Increased susceptibility to infection; abnormal function of gastrointestinal, genitourinary, and respiratory tracts; skin dries, shrivels, thickens; sometimes pustule formation; xerophthalmia (a characteristic eye disease). *Overdose:* Bleeding disorders; bone decalcification; immune system stimulation; fatigue; nausea; diarrhea; dry skin; brittle nails; jaundice.	Fat soluble; stable during cooking; destroyed by heat and oxygen together; marked capacity for storage in the liver.	Liver; dark green leafy vegetables, esp. escarole, kale, and parsley; yellow-orange fruits, esp. carrots, apricots, and cantaloupe; butter or fortified margarine; milk and dairy products; meats, fish, and poultry.
VITAMIN B₁ Thiamine	Involved in carbohydrate metabolism; essential for normal nervous tissue function; acts as a coenzyme for cellular energy production.	*Deficiency:* Weakness; wasting; mental confusion; peripheral paralysis; edema; beriberi.	Water soluble; stable during most cooking; destroyed by alkali or sulfites; not stored in the body. Deficiency often accompanies alcoholism.	Brewer's yeast; pork; soy milk; liver; milk; enriched or whole-grain cereals; beans; nuts.
VITAMIN B₂ Riboflavin	Acts as a coenzyme in cellular oxidation; essential to normal growth; participates in light adaptation; vital to protein metabolism; associated with functions of niacin and vitamin B₆.	*Deficiency:* Cheilosis; glossitis; dermatitis around mouth and nose; corneal reddening; hypersensitivity to light.	Water soluble; alcohol soluble; stable during most cooking; destroyed by alkali; unstable in light.	Milk and dairy products; collard greens; broccoli; whole-grain or enriched breads and cereals; liver; meat, fish, and poultry; eggs; legumes.
VITAMIN B₆ Pyridoxine Pyridoxal Pyridoxamine	Used in hemoglobin synthesis; essential for metabolism of tryptophan to niacin; needed for utilization of other amino acids.	*Deficiency:* Anemias; depressed immunity; dermatitis around mouth and nose; neuritis; anorexia; nausea; vomiting.	Water soluble; alcohol soluble; inactivated by heat, sunlight, or air.	Meats; liver; cereal grains; bananas; nuts.

*See App. 1-2 for recommended daily allowances.

Vitamins (Continued)

Vitamin	Chief Functions	Result of Deficiency or Overdose	Characteristics	Good Sources
VITAMIN B$_{12}$ Cyanocobalamin Hydroxycobalamin	Needed for myelin synthesis; essential for proper red blood cell development; associated with folate metabolism.	*Deficiency:* Pernicious anemia; neurological disorders.	Water soluble; alcohol soluble; unstable in hot alkaline or acid solutions.	Synthesized by gastrointestinal flora; meat; yeast; milk; eggs.
VITAMIN C Ascorbic acid	Acts as an antioxidant; essential to formation of collagen; facilitates iron absorption; facilitates conversion of cholesterol to bile acids; essential to synthesis of serotonin.	*Deficiency:* Joint tenderness; lowered resistance to infections; susceptibility to dental caries, pyorrhea, and bleeding gums; delayed wound healing; bruising; anemia; hemorrhaging; scurvy. *Overdose:* Nausea; diarrhea; hemolytic anemia; gout; kidney stones.	Water soluble; destroyed by light; heat hastens the process; lost in cooking when water is discarded; cooking loss is increased in iron or copper utensils. Stored in the body to a limited extent.	Citrus fruit; strawberries; green peppers; mustard greens; cauliflower.
VITAMIN D Calciferol Ergocalciferol Cholecalciferol Calcitriol Antirachitic factor	Promotes gastrointestinal absorption of calcium and phosphorus; promotes bone and tooth mineralization; promotes renal calcium absorption; antirachitic.	*Deficiency:* Interferes with utilization of calcium and phosphorus in bone and tooth formation; irritability; weakness; rickets in young children; osteomalacia in adults. *Overdose:* Irritability; kidney stone formation; calcification of soft tissues.	Fat soluble; soluble in organic solvents; relatively stable when refrigerated; stored in liver; often associated with vitamin A.	Formed in the skin by sunlight exposure; fortified milk and dairy products; egg yolks; liver; fatty fish, esp. salmon, tuna, herring, and sardines; oysters.
VITAMIN E Alpha-tocopherol Beta-tocopherol Gamma-tocopherol	Prevents oxidative damage of lipids and cell membranes; promotes red blood cell stability.	*Deficiency:* Immune system suppression; red blood cell hemolysis.	Fat soluble; destroyed by heat; destroyed by oxidation.	Vegetable oils, esp. soybean and corn; wheat germ.

FOLATE Folacin Folic acid	Needed for normal hematopoiesis; important coenzyme for nucleic acid synthesis; facilitates fetal development for neural tube closure; functions interrelated with those of vitamin B_{12}.	*Deficiency:* Note: Neural tube defects including spina bifida and anencephalus are associated with maternal deficiency; alcohol interferes with absorption; diarrhea; glossitis; macrocytic anemia. *Overdose:* Masking of $vitamin_{12}$ deficiency, which may lead to nerve damage.	Slightly water soluble; destroyed by heat at low pH; loss in food stored at room temperature.	Liver; green leafy vegetables; legumes; beets; broccoli; cauliflower; citrus fruits; sweet potatoes.
VITAMIN K Phylloquinone (plant form) Menaquinone (bacterial form)	Regulates blood coagulation; regulates blood Ca^{++} levels.	*Deficiency:* Hemorrhagic disease; malabsorption of fat can cause deficiency. *Overdose:* Kernicterus.	Fat soluble; stable to heat.	Produced by gastrointestinal flora; green leafy vegetables esp. broccoli; cauliflower; liver.
NIACIN Nicotinic acid Nicotinamide	Facilitates glycolysis, tissue respiration, fat synthesis, and cellular energy production.	*Deficiency:* Dermatitis; edema; diarrhea; irritability; mental confusion. *Overdose:* Flushed skin; intestinal irritation; liver damage.	Soluble in hot water and alcohol; stable during cooking; not destroyed by light, air, or alkali.	Milk; eggs; meat; legumes; whole-grain or enriched breads and cereals.Note: Also formed in the body from dietary tryptophan (amino acid).

Appendix 1–7 FDA-Approved Dietary Health Claims

Health Claim	Requirements	Sample Claim
Calcium and osteoporosis Low calcium intake is one risk factor for osteoporosis. Lifelong adequate intake of calcium helps maintain bone health by increasing, as much as genetically possible, the amount of bone formed in the teens and early adult life and by helping to slow the rate of bone loss that occurs later in life.	Food or supplement must be "high" in calcium and must not contain more phosphorus than calcium. Claims must cite other risk factors; state the need for regular exercise and a healthful diet; explain that adequate calcium early in life helps reduce fracture risk later by increasing, as much as genetically possible, a person's peak bone mass; and must indicate that those at greatest risk of developing osteoporosis later in life are white and Asian teenage and young adult women who are in their bone-forming years. Claims for products with more than 400 mg of calcium per day must state that a daily intake over 2,000 mg offers no added known benefit to bone health.	*Regular exercise and a healthy diet with enough calcium help teen and young adult white and Asian women maintain good bone health and may reduce their high risk of osteoporosis later in life.*
Dietary fat and cancer Diets high in fat increase the risk of some types of cancer, such as cancers of the breast, colon, and prostate. Although scientists do not know how total fat intake affects cancer development, low-fat diets reduce the risk. Experts recommend that Americans consume 30% or less of daily calories as fat. Typical U.S. intakes are 37%.	Foods must meet criteria for "low fat." Fish and game meats must meet criteria for "extra lean." Claims may not mention specific types of fats and must use "total fat" or "fat" and "some types of cancer" or "some cancers" in discussing the nutrient-disease link.	*Development of cancer depends on many factors. A diet low in total fat may reduce the risk of some cancers.*

Dietary saturated fat and cholesterol and risk of coronary heart disease
Diets high in saturated fat and cholesterol increase total and low-density (bad) blood cholesterol levels and the risk of coronary heart disease. Diets low in saturated fat and cholesterol decrease the risk. Guidelines recommend that American diets contain less than 10% of calories from saturated fat and less than 300 mg cholesterol daily. The average American adult diet has 13% saturated fat and 300 to 400 mg cholesterol a day.

Foods must meet criteria for "low saturated fat," "low cholesterol," and "low fat." Fish and game meats must meet criteria for "extra lean." Claims must use "saturated fat and cholesterol" and "coronary heart disease" or "heart disease" in discussing the nutrient-disease link.

Although many factors affect heart disease, diets low in saturated fat and cholesterol may reduce the risk of this disease.

Dietary soluble fiber, such as that found in whole oats and psyllium seed husk, and coronary heart disease When included in a diet low in saturated fat and cholesterol, soluble fiber may affect blood lipid levels, such as cholesterol, and thus lower the risk of heart disease. However, because soluble dietary fibers constitute a family of very heterogeneous substances that vary greatly in their effect on the risk of heart disease, the FDA has determined that sources of soluble fiber for this health claim must be considered case by case. To date, the FDA has reviewed and authorized two sources of soluble fiber eligible for this claim: whole oats and psyllium seed husk.

Foods must meet criteria for "low saturated fat," "low cholesterol," and "low fat." Foods that contain whole oats must contain at least 0.75 g of soluble fiber per serving. Foods that contain psyllium seed husk must contain at least 1.7 g of soluble fiber per serving. The claim must specify the daily dietary intake of the soluble fiber source necessary to reduce the risk of heart disease and the contribution one serving of the product makes toward that intake level. Soluble fiber content must be stated in the nutrition label. Claims must use "soluble fiber" qualified by the name of the eligible source of soluble fiber and "heart disease" or "coronary heart disease" in discussing the nutrient-disease link. Because of the potential hazard of choking, foods containing dry or incompletely hydrated psyllium seed husk must carry a label statement telling consumers to drink adequate amounts of fluid, unless the manufacturer shows that a viscous adhesive mass is not formed when the food is exposed to fluid.

Diets low in saturated fat and cholesterol that include 3 g of soluble fiber from whole oats per day may reduce the risk of heart disease. One serving of this whole-oats product provides [number] grams of this soluble fiber.

FDA-Approved Dietary Health Claims (Continued)

Health Claim	Requirements	Sample Claim
Fiber-containing grain products, fruits, and vegetables and cancer Diets low in fat and rich in fiber-containing grain products, fruits, and vegetables may reduce the risk of some types of cancer. The exact role of total dietary fiber, fiber components, and other nutrients and substances in these foods is not fully understood.	Foods must meet criteria for "low fat" and, without fortification, be a "good source" of dietary fiber. Claims must not specify types of fiber and must use "fiber," "dietary fiber," or "total dietary fiber" and "some types of cancer" or "some cancers" in discussing the nutrient-disease link.	*Low-fat diets rich in fiber-containing grain products, fruits, and vegetables may reduce the risk of some types of cancer, a disease associated with many factors.*
Fruits, vegetables, and grain products that contain fiber, particularly soluble fiber, and risk of coronary heart disease Diets low in saturated fat and cholesterol and rich in fruits, vegetables, and grain products that contain fiber, particularly soluble fiber, may reduce the risk of coronary heart disease. (It is impossible to adequately distinguish the effects of fiber, including soluble fiber, from those of other food components.)	Foods must meet criteria for "low saturated fat," "low fat," and "low cholesterol." They must contain, without fortification, at least 0.6 g of soluble fiber per reference amount, and the soluble fiber content must be listed. Claims must use "fiber," "dietary fiber," "some types of dietary fiber," "some dietary fibers," or "some fibers" and "coronary heart disease" or "heart disease" in discussing the nutrient-disease link. The term "soluble fiber" may be added.	*Diets low in saturated fat and cholesterol and rich in fruits, vegetables, and grain products that contain some types of dietary fiber, particularly soluble fiber, may reduce the risk of heart disease, a disease associated with many factors.*

Folate and neural tube birth defects Defects of the neural tube occur within the first six weeks after conception, often before the pregnancy is known. The U.S. Public Health Service recommends that all women of childbearing age in the United States consume 0.4 mg (400 μg) of folic acid daily to reduce their risk of having a baby affected with spina bifida or other neural tube defects.

Foods must meet or exceed criteria for "good source" of folate, i.e., at least 40 μg of folic acid per serving (at least 10% of the Daily Value). A serving of food cannot contain more than 100% of the Daily Value for vitamin A and vitamin D because of their potential risk to fetuses. Claims must use "folate," "folic acid," or "folacin" and "neural tube defects," "birth defects such as spina bifida or anencephaly," "birth defects of the brain or spinal cord, anencephaly," or spina bifida, "spina bifida and anencephaly, birth defects of the brain or spinal cord," "birth defects of the brain and spinal cord," or "brain or spinal cord birth defects" in discussing the nutrient-disease link. Folic acid content must be listed on the Nutrition Facts panel.

Healthful diets with adequate folate may reduce a woman's risk of having a child with a brain or spinal cord birth defect.

Fruits and vegetables and cancer Diets low in fat and rich in fruits and vegetables may reduce the risk of some cancers. Fruits and vegetables are low-fat foods and may contain fiber or vitamin A (as beta-carotene) and vitamin C. (The effects of these vitamins cannot be adequately distinguished from those of other fruit or vegetable components.)

Foods must meet criteria for "low fat" and, without fortification, be a "good source" of fiber, vitamin A, or vitamin C. Claims must characterize fruits and vegetables as foods that are low in fat and may contain dietary fiber, vitamin A, or vitamin C; characterize the food itself as a "good source" of one or more of these nutrients, which must be listed; refrain from specifying types of fatty acids; and use "total fat" or "fat," "some types of cancer" or "some cancers," and "fiber," "dietary fiber," or "total dietary fiber" in discussing the nutrient-disease link.

Low-fat diets rich in fruits and vegetables (foods that are low in fat and may contain dietary fiber, vitamin A, or vitamin C) may reduce the risk of some types of cancer, a disease associated with many factors. Broccoli is high in vitamins A and C, and it is a good source of dietary fiber.

FDA-Approved Dietary Health Claims (Continued)

Health Claim	Requirements	Sample Claim
Sodium and hypertension (high blood pressure) Hypertension is a risk factor for coronary heart disease and stroke deaths. The most common source of sodium is table salt. Diets low in sodium may help lower blood pressure and related risks in many people. Guidelines recommend daily sodium intakes of not more than 2,400 mg. Typical U.S. intakes are 3,000 to 6,000 mg.	Foods must meet criteria for "low sodium." Claims must use "sodium" and "high blood pressure" in discussing the nutrient-disease link.	*Diets low in sodium may reduce the risk of high blood pressure, a disease associated with many factors.*
Dietary sugar alcohol and dental caries (cavities) Eating foods high in sugar and starches between meals may promote tooth decay. Sugarless candies made with certain sugar alcohols do not.	Foods must meet the criteria for "sugar free." The sugar alcohol must be xylitol, sorbitol, mannitol, maltitol, isomalt, lactitol, hydrogenated starch hydrolysates, hydrogenated glucose syrups, erythritol, or a combination of these. When the food contains a fermentable carbohydrate, e.g., sugar or flour, the food must not lower plaque pH in the mouth below 5.7 while it is being eaten or up to 30 minutes afterwards. Claims must use "sugar alcohol," "sugar alcohols," or the name(s) of the sugar alcohol present and "dental caries" or "tooth decay" in discussing the nutrient-disease link. Claims must state that the sugar alcohol present "does not promote," "may reduce the risk of," "is useful in not promoting," or "is expressly for not promoting" dental caries.	Full claim: *Frequent between-meal consumption of foods high in sugars and starches promotes tooth decay. The sugar alcohols in this food do not promote tooth decay. On small packages only: Does not promote tooth decay.*

Appendix 1–8 FDA-Approved Terminology for Food Labels

cholesterol-free A food for which a serving meets all of the five following requirements: contains less than 2 mg of cholesterol; contains 5 g or less of total fat; is 20% or less total fat on a dry weight basis; has 2 g or less saturated fatty acids; and is 6% or less saturated fatty acids on a dry weight basis.

extra lean Description of the fat content of meat, poultry, seafood, or game meat that contains less than 5 g fat, less than 2 g saturated fat, and less than 95 mg cholesterol per serving and per 100 g.

free A food or product that contains no amount of or physiologically inconsequential amounts of fat, saturated fat, cholesterol, sodium, sugar, or calories.

good source One serving of a food or product that contains 10% to 19% of the Daily Value for a particular nutrient.

healthy A food low in fat and saturated fat with limited amounts of cholesterol and sodium. Additionally, single-item foods must contain 10% or more of vitamin A, vitamin C, iron, protein, or fiber while not exceeding 360 mg sodium; meal-type products must provide 10% of 2 or 3 of these nutrients as well as not exceeding 480 mg of sodium per serving.

high A product that contains 20% or more of the Daily Value for a particular nutrient.

lean Description of the fat content of meat, poultry, seafood, or game meat that contains less than 10 g fat, less than 4.5 g saturated fat, and less than 95 mg cholesterol per serving and per 100 g.

less A food containing 25% less of a nutrient or of calories than the reference food.

light 1. A nutritionally altered product that contains either $\frac{1}{3}$ fewer calories or half the fat of the reference food. If the caloric content of the reference food is derived 50% or more from fat, then the reduction must reduce the fat by 50%. **2.** A reduction by 50% in the sodium content of a low-calorie, low-fat food.

low A food or product that can be consumed in large amounts without exceeding the Daily Value for the referenced nutrient.

low cholesterol A food for which a serving meets all of the six following requirements: contains 20 mg or less of cholesterol; contains 0.2 mg or less total fat on a dry weight basis; contains 5 g or less of total fat per serving; is 20% or less total fat on a dry weight basis; contains 2 g or less saturated fatty acids per serving; and is 6% or less saturated fatty acids on a dry weight basis.

more One serving of a food that contains at least 10% more of the Daily Value of a nutrient than the reference food. This 10% rule also applies to the claims of fortified, enriched, added, extra, and plus, specifically where the food has been altered to attain the increase in nutrient content.

SOURCE: The Food and Drug Administration's Final Rule on Food Labeling: Definitions of the terms Cholesterol-Free and Low Cholesterol were published in the July 19, 1990 Federal Register.

APPENDIX 2
Complementary and Alternative Medicine

Appendix 2–1 Herbal Medicines and Their Uses

Common Name	Uses	Adverse Reactions and Contraindications	Interactions	Route/Commonly Used Doses
aloe	**External:** Use on burns/sunburns, wounds, skin irritation; used as anti-infective agent, moisturizer. **Internal:** Used as laxative and for general healing.	Contact dermatitis, intestinal contractions. Avoid oral use in various GI conditions (i.e., obstruction, inflammation), ulcers, abdominal pain, menstruation, kidney conditions.	May increase risk associated with cardiac glycosides. Use with other K+-wasting drugs may add to hypokalemic effect of aloe.	**PO:** *Capsules* — 50–200 mg daily; *gel* — 30 ml t.i.d.; *tincture (1:10, 50% alcohol)* — 15–60 drops. **Top:** Aloe gel can be applied liberally to affected area 3–5 times daily.
anise	Common cold, cough/bronchitis, fevers, liver and gallbladder complaints, loss of appetite.	Occasional allergic reactions (skin, respiratory, and GI). Avoid if allergy to anise exists.	Excessive doses may interfere with anticoagulants, MAO inhibitors, and hormone therapy.	**PO:** *Dried fruit* — 0.5–1 g; *essential oil* — 50–200 mL; *tea* — 3 times daily. **Top:** Typical strength is 2 g of flower heads in 100 mL of water. For poultice, dilute tincture 3–10 times with water. For mouthwash, dilute tincture 10 times with water.
arnica	**External:** Used after injuries (bruises, dislocations, contusions, muscular and joint problems). Inflammation caused by insect bites.	Prolonged use on broken skin may cause edematous dermatitis with pustular formations. Eczema (long-term use). Use of higher concentrations may cause toxic skin reactions with vesicle formation and necrosis. Avoid use on broken skin; avoid if allergy to arnica and plants in Asteraceae family exists.	None known.	
black cohosh	Premenstrual symptoms, perimenopausal and postmenopausal symptoms such as hot flashes, depression, mood swings, profuse sweating, and sleep disorders. Dysmenorrhea. Rheumatism.	GI discomfort (occasionally). Avoid during pregnancy and lactation.	None known.	**PO:** *Dried root* — 20 g in 34 oz water 3 times daily; *liquid extract (1:1, 90% alcohol)* — 0.3–2 mL. Do not use for more than 6 mo.

	Uses	Side Effects/Precautions	Interactions	Dosage
brewer's yeast	Common cold, cough/bronchitis, dyspepsia, eczema, acne, fevers, inflammation (oral, pharyngeal), loss of appetite, prevention of infections.	Allergic skin reactions may occur. Migraine headaches may be triggered in susceptible patients. GI gas may result from large doses. Avoid during pregnancy and lactation.	Concurrent use with MAO inhibitors can cause an increase in BP.	PO: 6 g of brewer's yeast daily.
camphor	**External:** Pain relief for warts, cold sores, hemorrhoids, muscular aches. Antipruritic. Inflammatory conditions of the respiratory tract. **Internal:** Circulatory regulation disorders, catarrhal diseases of the respiratory tract (internal use is unsafe and should be avoided).	Skin irritation (local effect), contact dermatitis may occasionally occur following application of oily salves with camphor. Avoid during pregnancy and lactation. Avoid if GI conditions (infectious, inflammatory) exist.	None known.	**Top:** 0.1–3% 3–4 times daily for cold sores, antipruritic agent, hemorrhoids. **Inhaln:** 1 tbsp of camphor solution per quart of water in a hot steam vaporizer or bowl up to 3 times daily.
chamomile	**External:** Inflammation of skin and mucous membranes, bacterial skin diseases including oral cavity and gums. Respiratory tract inflammation and irritation. Anogenital inflammation. **Internal:** GI spasms and inflammatory conditions.	Contact dermatitis, severe hypersensitivity reactions, anaphylaxis, vomiting. Avoid during pregnancy and lactation.	None known.	**PO:** *Dried flower heads*— 2–8 g 3 times daily; *tea*— 1 cup of tea 3–4 times daily. Tea is made by steeping 3 g of flower heads in 150 mL of boiling water for 10 min. *Liquid extract*— 1–4 mL 3 times daily.
comfrey	**External:** Bruises and sprains.	No adverse reactions known. Avoid during pregnancy and lactation. Do not use on broken or abraded skin.	None known.	**Top:** 5–20% comfrey ointment. Use should be limited to 10 days.
dill	Dyspepsia, fever, colds, cough, bronchitis, digestive aid.	Contact dermatitis. No contraindications known.	None known.	**PO:** *Dill seeds*— 3 g; *dill oil*— 100–300 mg/day.

Herbal Medicines and Their Uses (Continued)

Common Name	Uses	Adverse Reactions and Contraindications	Interactions	Route/Commonly Used Doses
echinacea	Bacterial and viral infections. Prevention and treatment of colds, coughs, flu, and bronchitis. Fevers. Wounds and burns. Inflammation of the mouth and pharynx. Urinary tract infections. Vaginal candidiasis.	Tingling sensation on tongue, nausea, vomiting, allergic reaction, fever. Avoid if multiple sclerosis, leukoses, collagenoses, AIDS, or tuberculosis is present; avoid if hypersensitivity and cross-sensitivity exist in patients allergic to sunflower seeds and the daisy family, including ragweed; avoid during pregnancy and lactation.	May possibly interfere with immunosuppressant agents because of its immunostimulant activity.	**PO:** *Fluid extract*— 1–2 mL t.i.d.; *solid form (6.5:1)*— 150–300 mg t.i.d. Should not be used for more than 8 weeks at a time.
eucalyptus	Cough/bronchitis, rheumatism, catarrhs of the respiratory tract.	Nausea, vomiting, and diarrhea may occur after ingestion of eucalyptus (rare). Avoid if severe liver disease, GI tract and bile duct inflammation, hypotension, kidney inflammation are present.	Induction of liver enzymes, which may increase the metabolism of other drugs.	**PO:** *Eucalyptus oil*— 300–600 mg/day. **Top:** *Eucalyptus oil (5–20%) in vegetable oil or semisolid preparations*, used for local application by diluting 30 mL of oil in 500 mL of lukewarm water.
fennel	Dyspepsias, catarrhs of the respiratory tract.	Allergic reactions (skin and respiratory tract) have been reported. Avoid during pregnancy and lactation.	None known.	**PO:** *Dried fruit/seed*— 5–7 g/day; *tea*— 1 cup daily. Tea is made by steeping 1–2 g of ground seed/fruit in 150 mL boiling water for 10 min and then straining.
feverfew	Prophylaxis of migraine headaches, fever, arthritis. Toothaches and as an antiseptic.	Dizziness, heartburn, indigestion, inflammation (lips, mouth, tongue), light-headedness, mouth ulceration, and weight gain. Allergic contact dermatitis (reported with many species of feverfew). Avoid during pregnancy and lactation.	May inhibit platelet activity (avoid use with warfarin or other anticoagulants).	**PO:** 50–125 mg of freeze-dried leaf per day with food. 50–100 mg feverfew extract daily (standardized to 0.2–0.35% parthenolide).

garlic	**Internal:** Reduction of BP and serum cholesterol level. **External:** Dermal fungal infections including tinea corporis, cruris, and pedis.	GI irritation (rare), allergic reactions, alters intestinal flora. No contraindications known when used in normal amounts.	Decreases platelet aggregation (may affect warfarin and other anticoagulant therapy).	**PO:** One clove of fresh garlic 1–2 times daily.
ginger	Prevention and treatment of nausea and vomiting associated with motion sickness, loss of appetite, pregnancy, surgery, and chemotherapy. Prevention of postoperative nausea and vomiting. May be used for dyspepsia, flatulence, relief of joint pain in rheumatoid arthritis, cramping, and diarrhea. Migraine headache. Tonic (toning/strengthening agent) in gout, gas, respiratory infections, anti-inflammatory, stimulant (tones the gut, increases saliva and gastric juices, acts as anticoagulant, decreases blood cholesterol).	Minor heartburn, dermatitis. Avoid during pregnancy and lactation (if using amounts larger than those typically found in food); avoid if gallstones exist. Use cautiously in patients with increased risk of bleeding or diabetes.	**Natural Product–Drug:** may theoretically increase risk of bleeding when used with anticoagulants and antiplatelet agents. **Natural Product–Natural Product:** may theoretically increase risk of bleeding when used with other herbs that have anticoagulant or antiplatelet activities.	**PO:** 1000 mg ginger taken 3–60 min before travel for motion sickness or before surgery. *Chemotherapy-induced nausea*—2–4 g/day. *Migraine headache*—500 mg at onset then 500 mg every 4 hr up to 1.5–2 g/day for 3–4 days. *Osteoarthritis*—170 mg tid or 255 mg bid of ginger extract.
ginkgo	Symptomatic relief of organic brain dysfunction (dementia syndromes, short-term memory deficits, inability to concentrate, depression), intermittent claudication, vertigo and tinnitus of vascular origin.	Dizziness, headache, upset stomach, allergic skin reaction, palpitations. Avoid if hypersensitivity exists; avoid during pregnancy and lactation.	**Natural Product–Drug:** theoretically may potentiate effects of antiplatelet agents and MAO inhibitors. **Natural Product–Natural Product:** may increase risk of bleeding when used with other herbs with antiplatelet effects (some include angelica, arnica, chamomile, feverfew, garlic, ginger, and licorice).	**PO:** *native dry extract*— 120–240 mg in 2 or 3 doses for organic brain syndromes; 120–160 mg in 2 or 3 doses for intermittent claudication, vertigo, and tinnitus.

Herbal Medicines and Their Uses (Continued)

Common Name	Uses	Adverse Reactions and Contraindications	Interactions	Route/Commonly Used Doses
ginseng	Improving physical and mental stamina, general tonic to energize during times of fatigue and inability to concentrate, sedative, sleep aid, antidepressant, diabetes. Enhanced sexual performance/aphrodisiac. Increased longevity. Adjunctive treatment of cancer. Increased immune response. Increased appetite.	Depression, dizziness, headaches, insomnia, hypertension, tachycardia, amenorrhea, vaginal bleeding, skin eruptions, estrogen-like effects, mastalgia, Stevens-Johnson syndrome. Avoid during pregnancy and lactation; avoid if manic-depressive disorders or psychosis exists.	**Natural Product–Food:** may potentiate effects of caffeine in coffee or tea. **Natural Product–Drug:** may decrease anticoagulant activity of warfarin. Avoid concomitant use with warfarin, heparin, aspirin, and NSAIDs. May interfere with phenelzine treatment and cause headache, tremulousness, and manic episodes. May potentiate the toxic effects of corticosteroids. **Natural Product–Natural Product:** may increase risk of bleeding when used with herbs that have antiplatelet or anticoagulant activities.	**PO:** *capsule*— 200–600 mg/day; *root powder*— 0.6–3 g 1–3 times daily.
glucosamine	Osteoarthritis. Temporomandibular joint (TMJ) arthritis. Glaucoma.	Nausea, heartburn, diarrhea, constipation, headache, drowsiness, skin reactions.	May antagonize the effects of antidiabetics. May induce resistance to some chemotherapy drugs.	500 mg 3 times daily.
goldenseal	Infections of the mucous membranes (bacterial and fungal), conjunctivitis, and GI infections associated with diarrhea, cirrhosis, gallbladder inflammation, and cancer. Topically used to treat eczema, acne, itching.	CNS stimulant, hallucinations, occasionally delirium, nausea, vomiting, constipation, ulceration (vaginal use), may affect production of B vitamins in colon. Avoid during pregnancy and lactation; avoid if hypertension exists.	**Natural Product–Drug:** may interfere with antacids, sucralfate, H_2 antagonists, antihypertensive agents and anticoagulants. May have additive effects when used concurrently with other drugs with sedative properties. **Natural Product–Natural Product:** concurrent use with herbs that have sedative properties may potentiate sedative effects.	**PO:** *dried root and rhizone*— 0.5–1 g t.i.d.; *liquid extract*— (1:1 in 60% ethanol)— 0.3–1 mL t.i.d.; *tincture*— (1:10 in 60% ethanol)— 2–4 mL t.i.d. **Top:** used as mouthwash 3–4 times daily.

| hawthorne | Hypertension, mild to moderate HF, angina, spasmolytic, sedative. | Agitation, dizziness, headache, sedation (high dose), sleeplessness, hypotension (high dose), palpitations, nausea. Avoid during pregnancy. | **Natural Product–Drug:** increases vitamin C utilization in body, may inhibit metabolism of ACE inhibitor, potentiates effect of cardiac glycosides, concurrent use with other coronary vasodilators (theophylline, caffeine, epinephrine) may potentiate vasodilatory effects, may have additive CNS depressant effect when used with other CNS depressants. **Natural Product–Natural Product:** additive effect with other cardiac glycoside–containing herbs (digitalis leaf, black hellebore, oleander leaf). | **PO:** *Hawthorne fluid extract (1:1 in 25% alcohol)*— 0.5–1 mL t.i.d.; *hawthorn fruit tincture (1:5 in 45% alcohol)*— 1–2 mL t.i.d.; *dried hawthorn berries*— 300–1000 mg t.i.d. |
| kava-kava | Anxiety, stress, restlessness, insomnia, mild muscle aches and pains. Menstrual cramps and PMS. | Dizziness, headache, sedation, sensory disturbances, pupil dilation, visual accommodation disorders, gastrointestinal complaints, allergic skin reactions, yellow discoloration of skin, pellagroid dermopathy, weight loss, ataxia, muscle weakness. Avoid during pregnancy and lactation; avoid if endogenous depression exists. Do not give to children under 12 yr of age. | **Natural Product–Drug:** additive effect when used with alprazolam. Potentiates effect of CNS depressants (ethanol, barbiturates, benzodiazepines), has decreased the effectiveness of levodopa in a few cases. May have additive effects with antiplatelet agents and MAO inhibitors. **Natural Product–Natural Product:** May have additive sedative effects when used with other herbs with sedative properties. | **PO:** *dried kava root extract*— 100 mg 3 times daily for anti-anxiety; *kavalactones*— 180–210 mg for insomnia. |

Herbal Medicines and Their Uses (Continued)

Common Name	Uses	Adverse Reactions and Contraindications	Interactions	Route/Commonly Used Doses
ma-huang	Asthma, hay fever, colds, weight-loss aid.	Increased BP and heart rate and cardiac arrhythmias, insomnia, motor restlessness, headaches, nausea, vomiting, anxiety. Avoid during pregnancy and lactation. Avoid if heart disease, hypertension, diabetes, hyperthyroidism, or BPH is present.	Potentiates sympathomimetic effects of antihypertensives, antidepressants, MAO inhibitors, and caffeine.	PO: *Ephedra* — 15–30 mg of 2–3 times daily; *crude herb* — 500–1000 mg 2–3 times daily.
milk thistle	Cirrhosis, chronic hepatitis, gallstones, psoriasis, liver cleansing and detoxification, treatment of liver toxicity due to *Amanita* mushroom poisoning (European IV formulation) and chemicals. Dyspepsia (in combination with other herbs). Diabetes.	Mild laxative, mild allergic reaction. Avoid during pregnancy and lactation.	None known.	PO: *Extract (70%)* — 200–400; *dried fruit/seed* — 12–15 g/day; *tea* — 3–4 times daily 30 min before meals. Tea is prepared by steeping and 3–5 g of crushed fruit/seed in 150 mL of boiling water for 10 min and then straining.
mugwort	GI ailments (colic, diarrhea, constipation), worm infestations, persistent vomiting, hysteria, epilepsy, menstrual problems and irregular periods; as a sedative.	Allergic reactions. Avoid during pregnancy and lactation.	None known.	PO: *Tincture* — 5 ml 30 min before bedtime or 1–4 mL up to 3 times daily.
nettle	Urinary tract infections, kidney and bladder stones. Supportive treatment for rheumatic ailments.	Allergic reactions (rare). Avoid during pregnancy and lactation.	None known.	PO: *Tea* — 1 cup up to 3 times daily with adequate fluid intake. Tea is made by steeping 1.5–5 g of nettle in 150 mL of boiling water for 10 min and then straining. *Dried extract (7:1)* — 770 mg twice daily; *liquid extract (1:1, 25% alcohol)* — 3–4 mL 3 times daily. **Top:** *Tincture (1:10)* for external use.

	Uses	Drug Interactions	Side Effects/Contraindications	Dosage
oak bark	External: Inflammatory skin disease. Internal: diarrhea (nonspecific, acute), mild inflammation of oral and pharyngeal regions and genital and anal areas.	May reduce or inhibit the absorption of alkaloids and other alkaline drugs.	GI disturbances, kidney damage, liver necrosis. Avoid during pregnancy and lactation. Avoid oak bark baths if weeping eczema, large areas of skin damage, febrile or infectious disease, cardiac insufficiency is present.	**PO:** For diarrhea, 1 cup of tea up to 3 times daily for 3–4 days. Tea is made by steeping 1 g coarsely ground bark in 150 mL of boiling water and then straining. **Top:** For rinses, compresses, gargles, use 20 g bark in 1 liter of water. For baths, use 5 g bark in 1 liter of water and add to bath water. Topical use should be limited to 2–3 week. Use not recommended because of toxicity.
pennyroyal	External: Skin diseases. Internal: Digestive disorders, liver and gallbladder disorders, gout, colds, and increased urinary frequency.	None known.	Abortifacient in high doses. Hepatotoxicity (use not recommended because of hepatotoxicity). Avoid during pregnancy and lactation.	
peppermint	Colds, coughs, inflammation of mouth and pharynx, GI cramps and as an antiflatulent and antipyretic agent. The oil is used topically for myalgias, toothaches, pruritus, urticaria and as an antiinfective agent.	Gastric acid–blocking drugs.	Heartburn when taken orally. Allergic reactions (headache and flushing). External use may cause skin irritation and contact dermatitis. In small children and babies, the oil may cause bronchial spasms and collapse when applied to their facial, nasal, or chest areas. Avoid during pregnancy and lactation. Avoid use of oil on infants/small children. Avoid if hypersensitivity to peppermint exists. Avoid if bile duct obstruction, severe liver disease, or gallbladder inflammation is present.	**PO:** *Peppermint oil* — 0.2–0.4 mL 3 times daily in diluted preparation; *capsules* — 1–2 capsules 3 times daily (0.2 mL/capsule). **Top:** 5–20% peppermint oil in oily preparations, 5–10% in aqueous/ethanol preparations, 1–5% in nasal preparations. To apply, rub small amount on affected skin areas. **Inhaln:** 3–4 drops of oil placed in hot water and inhaled. Inhalation contraindicated in children.

Herbal Medicines and Their Uses (Continued)

Common Name	Uses	Adverse Reactions and Contraindications	Interactions	Route/Commonly Used Doses
psyllium	Constipation, diarrhea, lowering serum cholesterol	Flatulence, abdominal distention, esophageal/bowel obstruction if not taken with water/fluid. Allergic reactions. Avoid if fecal impaction, GI tract obstruction or narrowing is present.	Interferes with absorption of other drugs taken simultaneously.	PO: 3.5 g 1–3 times daily of the seed husk taken with adequate fluids.
Saint John's wort	Management of mild to moderate depression. Externally used for inflammation of the skin, blunt injuries, wounds, and burns. Other uses are for capillary strengthening, decreasing uterine bleeding, and reducing tumor size.	Dizziness, restlessness, sleep disturbances, fatigue, hypertension, GI side effects, abdominal pain, bloating, constipation, dry mouth, feeling of fullness, flatulence, nausea, vomiting, allergic skin reactions, phototoxicity, photodermatitis. Avoid during pregnancy and lactation. Do not give to children.	Concurrent use with alcohol or other antidepressants may increase the risk of adverse reactions. Concurrent use with indinavir may significantly reduce blood concentrations of indinavir.	PO: *hypericum extract* — 300 mg 3 times daily for depression. Top: *hypericin* — 0.2–1 mg daily.
saw palmetto	Urination problems in BPH, irritable bladder.	Headaches, stomach problems (rare). Avoid during pregnancy and lactation; avoid if breast cancer exists.	Oral contraceptives and hormone therapy (possible).	PO: *Whole berry* — 1–2 g of dried berry daily; *tea* — 1 cup of tea 3 times daily. Tea is made by steeping 0.5–1 g of dried berry in 150 ml of boiling water for 10 min and then straining. *Saw palmetto extracts with 80–90% fatty acids* — 160 mg twice daily or 320 mg once daily.

spruce	Colds, cough, bronchitis, fevers, inflammation of the mouth and pharynx.	May worsen bronchial spasms. Avoid during pregnancy and lactation. Avoid if asthma or whooping cough exists. Avoid baths with spruce if extensive skin damage, acute skin diseases, fevers, infectious diseases, or cardiac insufficiency is present.	None known.	**PO:** *Fresh shoots* — 5–6 g/per day. *Essential oil* — given as 4 drops in water or with sugar 3 times daily. **Top:** 200–300 g of shoots boiled in 1 liter of water; steep for 5 min, strain, and add to full bath. **Inhal:** Inhale 2 g of oil in hot water several times daily.
uva-ursi	Urinary tract infections.	Nausea, vomiting, GI upset, hepatotoxicity, high toxic doses (30–100 g of uva-ursi) can cause death. Avoid during pregnancy and lactation. Avoid if kidney disorders or GI irritable disorders exist. Do not give to children.	Use with urine-acidifying drugs may reduce the efficacy of uva-ursi.	**PO:** 1 cup of tea up to 4 times daily. Tea is made by steeping 3 g of dried leaf in 150 mL cold water for 12–24 hr and then straining. This herb should not be used for more than 1 week at a time, no more than 5 times a year.
valerian	Restlessness, sleeping disorders due to nervous conditions. Anxiety.	Morning drowsiness, headaches, excitability, insomnia. Avoid during pregnancy and lactation.	Use with alcohol and other sedatives may potentiate sedative effects.	**PO:** *Extract (0.8% valeric acid)* — 150–300 mg 30 min before bedtime. *Tea* — 1 cup 1–3 times daily. Tea is made by steeping 2–3 g of root in 150 mL of boiling water for 5–10 min and then straining.
woodruff	Nervousness, sleeplessness, hysteria, cardiac irregularity.	Headache, stupor (high doses). Liver damage (reversible) may occur with long-term use in susceptible patients. Avoid during pregnancy and lactation.	None known.	**PO:** 1 cup of tea once a day, shortly before bedtime. Tea is made with 2 teaspoonfuls (1.8 g) in one glass of water.

BPH: benign prostatic hyperplasia; Inhaln: Inhalation; PO: by mouth; PSA: prostate-specific antigen; Top: topical.

* NOTE : Instruct patient to consult health care professional before taking any prescription or OTC medications concurrently with any of these herbal products. The purity, safety, and effectiveness of many herbal remedies remain untested and unproven.

SOURCE: Vallerand, AH; Sanoski, CA: with Deglin, JH: Davis's Drug Guide for Nurses, 13th edition, F.A. Davis, Philadelphia, 2012.

Appendix 2–2 **Forms of Herbal Preparations**

bath A form of hydrotherapy. Immerse the full body in a bath with 500 ml or 1 pint of infusion or decoction. The full-strength herbal infusion or decoction is used for foot or hand baths.

capsule or pill Powdered herbs may be enclosed in gelatin capsules or pressed into a hard pill. The powder can also be rolled into a pill with bread or cream cheese. This is one of the most common ways herbs are supplied and used.

compress A clean cloth is soaked in an herbal infusion or decoction and applied over injured or inflamed areas. Also called a fomentation.

crude herb The fresh or dried herb in an unprocessed form. Measurements are expressed by weight.

decoction An aqueous preparation of hard and woody herbs, which are made soluble by simmering in almost boiling water for 30 minutes or more. If the active ingredients are volatile oils, it is important to cover the pan to prevent vaporization. The decoction is then strained while hot and either stored or consumed as needed.

essential oils Volatile oils, usually mixtures of a variety of odoriferous organic compounds of plants.

extract Concentrated form of natural products obtained by treating crude herb with solvent and then discarding the solvent to result in a fluid extract, solid extract, powdered extract, or tincture. Strength is expressed as the ratio of the concentration of the crude herb to the extract (e.g., 5:1 means five parts crude herb is concentrated in 1 part extract, and 1:2 means one part of extract is comparable to 0.5 parts herb).

fluid extract Concentrated tinctures with a strength of one part solvent to one part herb.

fomentation A clean cloth is soaked in an herbal infusion or decoction and applied over injured or inflamed areas.

infusion The preferred method used for soft plant parts such as leaves, flowers, or green stems, an infusion is prepared just like making a tea. In the case of volatile oils or heat-sensitive ingredients, soaking in water or milk for 6 to 12 hours in a sealed earthenware pot makes a cold infusion.

liniment Usually a mixture of herbs and alcohol or vinegar to be applied topically over muscles and ligaments.

lozenge Dissolvable tablet often used for upper respiratory and throat problems. It is made by combining a powdered herb with sugar and viscous jelly obtained from either an edible gum or mucilaginous plant.

ointment An herb or mixture of herbs in a semi-solid mixture such as petroleum jelly. This is applied externally for injuries or inflammation. If made with volatile oils, it can even be used as a respiratory anticatarrhal. Also known as a salve.

powdered extract A solid extract which has been dried to a powder.

poultice A raw or mashed herb applied directly to the body or wrapped in cheesecloth or other clean cloth. It is used either hot or cold for bruises, inflammation, spasm, and pain.

salve An herb or mixture of herbs in a semi-solid mixture such as petroleum jelly. This is applied externally for injuries or inflammation. If made with volatile oils, it can even be used as a respiratory anticatarrhal.

tincture An alcohol-based preparation. Alcohol is a better solvent than water for many plant ingredients, so mixing herbs in alcohol such as vodka or wine with a specific water/alcohol ratio is a common method of extraction. The mixture is soaked for about 2 weeks. Then the herbs are strained out and the liquid is saved in a dark, well-stoppered bottle. Tinctures are much stronger volume-for-volume than infusions or decoctions. Strengths are typically 1:5 to 1:10.

tea Made by steeping herbs in hot water (The same as an *Infusion*). Place 1 tsp dried herb or 2 to 3 tsp fresh herb into 1 cup (250 ml) hot or boiling water. Steep for 5 to 15 minutes. For larger quantities, use 1 oz (30 g) of herb in 1 pint (500 ml) of hot water. Bruise or powder seeds before making an infusion or tea. The shelf life of these bioactive fluids is short, even in the refrigerator. Discard them after 8 to 12 hours.

SOURCE: Sierpina, VS: Integrative Health Care: Complementary and Alternative Therapies for the Whole Person, F.A. Davis, Philadelphia, 2001.

Appendix 2–3 Premises of Mind-Body Medicine

Mind and body are simply two aspects of a whole individual. The mind is no less medically real and significant than the body.

Every person has self-healing abilities.

Each person is unique, and must be responded to as such. To be most effective, the treatment program must be individualized for each person.

Each person is an integration of physical, psychological, intellectual, and spiritual aspects. All aspects are equally important. All must be addressed in the approach to health.

Patients' healing abilities are strongly affected by their expectations and beliefs. The expectations, attitudes, beliefs, and words of practitioners strongly influence the expectations of their patients.

Mainline medicine does not have a monopoly on the search for health.

Patients need to be actively involved in their own healing and in the decision making concerning their treatments.

SOURCE: Modified from Mind-Body Medicine: A Clinician's Guide to Psychoneuroimmunology, Watkins, A, p. 99, 1997, by permission of the publisher Churchill Livingstone, and Sierpina, VS: Integrative Health Care: Complementary and Alternative Therapies for the Whole Person, F.A. Davis, Philadelphia, 2001.

Appendix 2–4 Websites for Complementary and Alternative Medicine

This list of Web sites, though not exhaustive, is intended to provide general sources of useful information on complementary and alternative medical therapies. Many of these Web sites provide links to information on specific therapies and medical conditions. Inclusion of a Web site on this list does not imply endorsement of the information contained on that site.

Alternative Health News Online
www.altmedicine.com

Alternative Link, LLC (information on billing codes)
www.alternativelink.com/ali/home/

Alternative Medicine Homepage, Falk Library of the Health Sciences, University of Pittsburgh
www.pitt.edu/cbw/altm.html

American Association of Naturopathic Physicians
www.naturopathic.org

American Chiropractic Association
www.amerchiro.org

American Holistic Medical Association
www.holisticmedicine.org

American Osteopathic Association
www.am-osteo-assn.org

The Ardell Wellness Report
www.yourhealth.com

Ask Dr. Weil
www.drweil.com

Biotecnoquimica (Venezuela–Spanish language)
www.biotecnoquimica.com

Children's Hospital, Boston: Center for Holistic Pediatric Education and Research (CHPER)
www.childrenshospital.org/holistic

Choices for Health
www.choicesforhealth.com/professional.html

Duke's Phytochemical and Ethnobotanical Database
www.ars-grin.gov/duke

Fetzer Institute (a nonprofit organization promoting the study of the spiritual elements of life)
http://www.fetzer.org

Healthfinder
www.healthfinder.com

HerbalGram (American Botanical Council)
www.herbalgram.org

HerbMed
www.herbmed.org

Holistic Medicine Interest Group (Oregon Health Sciences University)
www.ohsu.edu/ohmig/index.html

Longwood Herbal Task Force
www.mcp.edu/herbal

McMaster University (Hamilton, Ontario) Alternative Medicine Health Care Information Resources
http://hsl.mcmaster.ca/tomflem/altmed.html

Medical College of Wisconsin: Alternative Medicine Resources
www.intmed.mcw.edu/gimcme/altmed.html

MEDLINE (U.S. National Library of Medicine)
www.nlm.nih.gov

National Council for Reliable Health Information (NCRHI)
www.ncahf.org

National Institutes of Health, National Center for CAM
nccam.nih.gov

Natural Healthline
www.naturalhealthvillage.com

Nurse Healers–Professional Associates International
www.therapeutic-touch.org

Office of Dietary Supplements (National Institutes of Health): The International Bibliographic Information on Dietary Supplements (IBIDS)
odp.od.nih.gov/ods/databases/ibids.html

Quackwatch
www.quackwatch.com

Tufts University Nutrition Navigator
www.navigator.tufts.edu

University of Texas Medical Board's Alternative and Integrative Healthcare Program
atc.utmb.edu/altmed

University of Washington Medicinal Herb Garden
www.nnlm.nlm.nih.gov/pnr/uwmhg

WebMD Self-Care Advisor
www.mywebmd.com

WholeHealthMD
www.wholehealthmd.com

APPENDIX 3
Normal Reference Laboratory Values

BLOOD, PLASMA, OR SERUM VALUES

Determination	Reference Range		Minimal mL Required *	Note
	Conventional	SI		
Acetoacetate plus acetone	Negative		1-B	Use unhemolyzed serum
Aldolase	1.3–8.2 U/L	22–137 nmol · sec⁻¹/L	2-S	Collect in heparinized tube; deliver *immediately* packed in ice
Ammonia	12–55 μmol/L	12–55 μmol/L	2-B	liver *immediately* packed in ice
Amylase	4–25 units/mL	4–25 arb. unit	1-S	
Ascorbic acid	0.4–1.5 mg/100 mL	23–85 μmol/L	7-B	Collect in heparinized tube before any food is given
Bilirubin	Direct: up to 0.4 mg/100 mL	Up to 7 μmol/L	1-S	any food is given
	Total: up to 1.0 mg/100 mL	Up to 17 μmol/L		
Blood volume	8.5–9.0% of body weight in kg	80–85 mL/kg		
CA-125	<20 U/mL	<20 kU/L		
Calcium	8.5–10.5 mg/100 mL (slightly higher in children)	2.1–2.6 mmol/L	1-S	Collect in plain red top tube
Carbamazepine	4.0–12.0 μg/mL	17–51 μmol/L	1-S	
Carbon dioxide content	24–30 mEq/L	24–30 mmol/L	3-B	Fill tube to top
Carbon monoxide	<5% of total hemoglobin		0.5	Fill tube to top
Carcinoembryonic antigen	0.0–2.5 ng/mL	0.0–2.5 μg/L	3-S	Collect in plain red top tube
Carotenoids	0.8–4.0 μg/mL	1.5–7.4 μmol/L		Vitamin A may be done on same specimen
Ceruloplasmin	27–37 mg/100 mL	1.8–2.5 μmol/L	2-S	
Chloramphenicol	10–20 μg/mL	31–62 μmol/L	0.2-S	
Chloride	100–106 mEq/L	100–106 mmol/L	1-S	
CK isoenzymes	5% MB or less		0.2-S	
Copper	Total: 100–200 μg/100 mL	16–31 μmol/L	1-S	
C reactive protein	0–1.0 mg/dl	0–10 mg/L	0.5	Collect in serum separator tube or heparinized plasma

BLOOD, PLASMA, OR SERUM VALUES (Continued)

Determination	Reference Range		Minimal mL Required*	Note
	Conventional	SI		
Creatine kinase (CK)	Female: 10–79 U/L	$167-1317$ nmol · sec^{-1}/L	1-S	
	Male: 17–148 U/L	$283-2467$ nmol · sec^{-1}/L		
Creatinine	0.6–1.5 mg/100 mL	$53-133$ μmol/L	1-S	Collect in oxalate and refrigerate
Ethanol	0 mg/100 mL	0 mmol/L	2-B	Collect with oxalate-fluoride mixture
Glucose	Fasting: 70–110 mg/100 mL	$3.9-5.6$ mmol/L	1-P	
Iron	50–150 μg/100 mL (higher in males)	$9.0-26.9$ μmol/L	1-S	
Iron-binding capacity	250–410 μg/100 mL	$44.8-73.4$ μmol/L	1-S	Collect with oxalate-fluoride mixture; deliver immediately packed in ice
Lactic acid	0.6–1.8 mEq/L	$0.6-1.8$ mmol/L	2-B	
Lactic dehydrogenase	45–90 U/L	$750-1500$ nmol · sec^{-1}/L	1-S	Unsuitable if hemolyzed
Lead	50 μg/100 mL or less	Up to 2.4 μmol/L	2-B	Collect with oxalate-fluoride mixture
Lipase	2 units/mL or less	Up to 2 arb. unit	1-S	
Lipids				
Cholesterol	<200 mg/dl	<5.18 mmol/L	1-S	Fasting
Triglycerides	40–150 mg/100 mL	$0.4-1.5$ g/L	1-S	Fasting
Lipoprotein electrophoresis (LEP)			2-S	Fasting, do not freeze serum
Lithium	0.6–1.2 mEq/L	$0.6-1.2$ nmol/L	1-S	
Magnesium	1.5–2.0 mEq/L	$0.8-1.3$ mmol/L	1-S	
5' Nucleotidase	1–11 U/L	$17-183$ nmol · sec^{-1}/L	1-S	
Osmolality	280–296 mOsm/kg water	$280-296$ mmol/kg	1-S	
Oxygen saturation (arterial)	96–100%	$0.96-1.00$	3-B	Deliver in sealed heparinized syringe packed in ice
PCO$_2$	35–45 mm Hg	$4.7-6.0$ kPa	2-B	Collect and deliver in sealed heparinized syringe
pH	7.35–7.45	Same	2-B	Collect without stasis in sealed heparinized syringe; deliver packed in ice

PO_2	75–100 mm Hg (dependent on age) while breathing room air Above 500 mm Hg while on 100% O_2	10.0–13.3 kPa	2-B	
Phenobarbital	15–50 µg/mL	65–215 µmol/L	1-S	
Phenytoin (Dilantin)	10–20 µg/mL	20–80 µmol/L	1-S	
Phosphatase (acid)	Male–Total: 0.13–0.63 sigma U/mL	36–175 nmol · sec⁻¹/L	1-S	Must always be drawn just before analysis or stored as frozen serum; avoid hemolysis
	Female–Total: 0.01–0.56 sigma Prostatic: 0–0.05 Fishman-Lerner U/100 mL	2.8–156 nmol · sec⁻¹/L		
Phosphatase (alkaline)	13–39 U/L, infants and adolescents up to 104 U/L	217–650 nmol · sec⁻¹/L, up to 1.26 µmol/L	1-S	
Phosphorus (inorganic)	3.0–4.5 mg/100 mL (infants in first year up to 6.0 mg/100 mL)	1.0–1.5 mmol/L	1-S	
Potassium	3.5–5.0 mEq/L	3.5–5.0 mmol/L	1-S	Serum must be separated promptly from cells
Primidone (Mysoline)	4–12 µg/mL	18–55 µmol/L	1-S	
Procainamide	4–10 µg/mL	17–42 µmol/L	1-S	
Prostate-specific antigen	<4.0 ng/mL	<4.0 µ/L	2	Serum separator or EDTA plasma
Protein: Total	6.0–8.4 g/100 mL	60–84 g/L	1-S	
Albumin	3.5–5.0 g/100 mL	35–50 g/L	1-S	Globulin equals total protein minus albumin
Globulin	2.3–3.5 g/100 mL	23–35 g/L		Quantitation by densitometry
Electrophoresis	(% of total protein)		1-S	
Albumin	52–68			
Globulin:				
Alpha₁	4.2–7.2			
Alpha₂	6.8–12			
Beta	9.3–15			
Gamma	13–23			
Pyruvic acid	0–0.11 mEq/L	0–0.11 mmol/L	2-B	Collect with oxalate fluoride. Deliver immediately packed in ice
Quinidine	1.2–4.0 µg/mL	3.7–12.3 µmol/L	1-S	
Salicylate:	0		2-P	
Therapeutic	20–25 mg/100 mL;	1.4–1.8 mmol/L		

BLOOD, PLASMA, OR SERUM VALUES (Continued)

Determination	Reference Range		Minimal mL Required*	Note
	Conventional	SI		
Sodium	25–30 mg/100 mL to age 10 yr 3 hr post dose	1.8–2.2 mmol/L	1-S	
Sulfonamide	135–145 mEq/L	135–145 mmol/L	2-P	
Transaminase, aspartate amino-transferase	5–15 mg/100 mL		1-S	
	7–27 U/L	117–450 nmol · sec⁻¹/L		
Transaminase, alanine amino-transferase	1–21 U/L	17–350 nmol · sec⁻¹/L	1-S	
Troponin-I	0–0.5 ng/mL	0–0.5 μg/L	0.6	Collect in light green top tube
Troponin-I	0–0.5 ng/mL		0.6	Collect in light green top tube
Urea nitrogen (BUN)	8–25 mg/100 mL	2.9–8.9 mmol/L	1-S	
Uric acid	3.0–7.0 mg/100 mL	0.18–0.42 mmol/L	1-S	
Vitamin A	0.15–0.6 μg/mL	0.5–2.1 μmol/L	3-S	

URINE VALUES

Determination	Reference Range		Minimal mL Required*	Note
	Conventional	SI		
Acetone plus acetoacetate (quantitative)	0	0 mg/L	2 mL	
Amylase	24–76 units/mL	24–76 arb. unit	24-hr specimen	
Calcium	300 mg/day or less	7.5 mmol/day or less	24-hr specimen	Collect in special bottle with 10 mL of concentrated HCl
Catecholamines	Epinephrine: under 20 μg/day	<109 nmol/day	24-hr specimen	Should be collected with 10 mL of concentrated HCl (pH should be between 2.0 and 3.0)
	Norepinephrine: under 100 μg/day	<590 nmol/day	1st morning void	
Chorionic gonadotropin	0	0 arb. unit	24-hr specimen	
Copper	0–100 μg/day	0–1.6 μmol/day	24-hr specimen	
Coproporphyrin	50–250 μg/day	80–380 nmol/day	24-hr specimen	Collect with 5 g of sodium carbonate
Creatine	Children under 80 lb (36 kg): 0–75 μg/day	0–115 nmol/day	24-hr specimen	Also order creatinine
	Under 100 mg/day or less than 6% of creatinine. In pregnancy: up to 12%. In children under 1 yr: may equal creatinine. In older children: up to 30% of creatinine.			
Creatinine	15–25 mg/kg of body weight/day	0.13–0.22 mmol · kg⁻¹/day	24-hr specimen	
Cystine or cysteine	0	0	10 mL	Qualitative
Hemoglobin and myoglobin	0		Freshly voided sample	Chemical examination with benzidine
5–Hydroxyindoleacetic acid	2–9 mg/day (women lower than men)	10–45 μmol/day	24-hr specimen	
Lead	0.08μg/mL or 120 μg/day or less	0.39 μmol/L or less	24-hr specimen	Collect with 10 mL of concentrated HCl

URINE VALUES (Continued)

Determination	Reference Range		Minimal mL Required*	Note
	Conventional	SI		
Phosphorus (inorganic)	Varies with intake; average, 1 g/day	32 mmol/day	24-hr specimen 10 mL	Collect with 10 mL of concentrated HCl
Porphobilinogen	0	0	24-hr specimen	Use freshly voided urine
Protein: Quantitative	<150 mg/24 hr	<0.15 g/day		
Steroids: 17–Ketosteroids (per day)	Age Male Female 10 1–4 mg 1–4 mg 20 6–21 4–16 30 8–26 4–14 50 5–18 3–9 70 2–10 1–7	3–14 µmol 3–14 µmol 21–73 14–56 28–90 14–49 17–62 10–31 7–35 3–24	24-hr specimen	Not valid if patient is receiving meprobamate
17–Hydroxysteroids	3–8 mg/day (women lower than men)	8–22 µmol/day as tetrahydrocortisol	24-hr specimen	Keep cold; chlorpromazine and related drugs interfere with assay
Sugar: Quantitative glucose	0	0 mmol/L	24-hr or other timed specimen	
Urobilinogen	Up to 1.0 Ehrlich U	To 1.0 arb. unit	2-hr sample (1–3 P.M.)	
Uroporphyrin	0–30 µg/day	<36 nmol/day	Coproporphyrin	
Vanillylmandelic acid (VMA)	Up to 9 mg/24 hr	Up to 45 µmol/day	24-hr specimen	Collect as for catecholamines

SPECIAL ENDOCRINE TESTS

Steroid Hormones

Determination	Reference Range		Minimal mL Required*	Note
	Conventional	SI		
Aldosterone	Excretion:		5/day	Keep specimen cold
	5–19 µg/24 hr	14–53 nmol/day		
	Supine:		3-S, P	Fasting, at rest, 210-mEq sodium diet
	48±29 pg/mL	133±80 pmol/L		
	Upright (2 hr):			Upright, 2 hr, 210-mEq sodium diet
	65± 23 pg/mL	180±64 pmol/L		
	Supine:			Fasting, at rest, 110-mEq sodium diet
	107±45 pg/mL	279±125 pmol/L		
	Upright (2 hr):			Upright, 2 hr, 110-mEq sodium diet
	239±123 pg/mL	663±341 pmol/L		
	Supine:			Fasting, at rest, 10-mEq sodium diet
	175±75 pg/mL	485±208 pmol/L		
	Upright (2 hr):			Upright, 2 hr, 10–mEq sodium diet
	532±228 pg/mL	1476±632 pmol/L		
Cortisol	8 A.M. :		1-P	Fasting
	5–25 µg/100 mL	0.14–0.69 µmol/L		
	8 P.M. :		1-P	At rest
	Below 10 µg/100 mL	0–0.28 µmol/L		
	4-hr ACTH test:		1-P	20 U ACTH, IV per 4 hr
	30–45 µg/100 mL	0.83–1.24 µmol/L		
	Overnight suppression test:		1-P	8 A.M. sample after 0.5 mg dexamethasone by mouth at midnight
	Below 5 µg/100 mL	0.14 nmol/L		
	Excretion:		2/day	Keep specimen cold
	20–70 µg/24 hr	55–193 nmol/day		
Dehydroepiandrosterone (DHEA)	Male		2-S, P	
	0.5–5.5 ng/mL	1.7–19 nmol/L		

SPECIAL ENDOCRINE TESTS (Continued)
Steroid Hormones

Determination	Reference Range		Minimal mL Required*	Note
	Conventional	SI		
Dehydroepiandrosterone sulfate (DHEA–S)	Female			
	1.4–8.0 ng/mL	4.9–28 nmol/L		Adult
	0.3–4.5 ng/mL	1.0–15.6 nmol/L	2-S, P	Postmenopausal
	Male			
	151–446 μg/100 mL	3.9–11.4 μgmol/L		Adult
	Female			
	84–433 μg/100 mL	2.2–11.1 μmol/L	1-P	Postmenopausal
	1.7–177 μg/100 mL	0.04–4.5 μmol/L		
11–Deoxycortisol	Responsive			8 A.M. sample, preceded by 4.5 g of metyrapone by mouth per 24 hr or by single dose of 2.5 g by mouth at midnight
	Over 7.5 μg/100 mL	>0.22 μmol/L	5-S, P	
		<184 pmol/L		
Estradiol	Male: <50 pg/mL	84–1325 pmol/L		Adult
	Female: 23–361 pg/mL	<110 pmol/L		Postmenopausal
	<30 pg/mL	<73 pmol/L		Prepubertal
	<20 pg/mL	3.2 nmol/L	5-S, P	
	Male: <1.0 ng/mL			
Progesterone	Female			
	0.2–0.6 ng/mL	0.6–1.9 nmol/L		Follicular phase
	0.3–3.5 ng/mL	0.95–11 nmol/L		Midcycle peak
	6.5–32.2 ng/mL	21–102 nmol/L		Postovulatory
Testosterone	Adult male:		1-P	A.M. sample
	300–1100 ng/100 mL	10.4–38.1 nmol/L		
	Adolescent male:			
	Over 100 ng/100 mL	>3.5 nmol/L		
	Female			
	25–90 ng/100 mL	0.87–3.12 nmol/L	2-P	A.M. sample
Unbound testosterone	Adult male:			
	3.06–24.0 ng/100 mL	106–832 pmol/L		
	Adult female:			
	0.09–1.28 ng/100 mL	3.1–44.4 pmol/L		

Polypeptide Hormones

Determination	Reference Range		Minimal mL Required*	Note
	Conventional	SI		
Adrenocorticotropin (ACTH)	15–70 pg/mL	3.3–15.4 pmol/L	5-P	Place specimen on ice and send promptly to laboratory. Use EDTA tube only.
Alpha subunit	<0.5–2.5 ng/mL	<0.4–2.0 nmol/L	2-S	Adult male or female
	<0.5–5.0 ng/mL	<0.4–4.0 nmol/L		Postmenopausal female
Calcitonin	Male: 0–14 pg/mL	0–4.1 pmol/L	5-S	Test done only on known or suspected cases of medullary carcinoma of the thyroid
	Female: 0–28 pg/mL	0–8.2 pmol/L		
	>100 pg/mL in medullary carcinoma	>29.3 pmol/L		
Follicle-stimulating hormone (FSH)	Male 3–18 mIU/mL	3–18 arb. unit	5-S, P	Same sample may be used for LH
	Female: 4.6–22.4 mIU/mL	4.6–22.4 arb. unit		Pre- or postovulatory
	13–41 mIU/mL	13–41 arb. unit		Midcycle peak
	30–170 mIU/mL	30–170 arb. unit		Postmenopausal
Growth hormone	Below 5 ng/mL	<233 pmol/L	1-S	Fasting, at rest
	Children: Over 10 ng/mL	>465 pmol/L		After exercise
	Male: Below 5 ng/mL	<233 pmol/L		
	Female: Up to 30 ng/mL	0–1395 pmol/L		After glucose load
	Male: Below 5 ng/mL	<233 pmol/L		
	Female: Below 5 ng/mL	<233 pmol/L		
Insulin	6–26 μU/mL	43–187 pmol/L	1-S	Fasting
	Below 20 μU/mL	<144 pmol/L		During hypoglycemia
	Up to 150 μU/mL	0–1078 pmol/L		After glucose load
Luteinizing hormone (LH)	Male: 3–18 mIU/mL	3–18 arb. unit	5-S, P	Same sample may be used for FSH
	Female:			
	2.4–34.5 mIU/mL	2.4–34.5 arb. unit		Pre- or postovulatory
	43–187 mIU/mL	43–187 arb. unit		Midcycle peak
	30–150 mIU/mL	30–150 arb. unit		Postmenopausal
Parathyroid hormone	<25 pg/mL	<2.94 pmol/L	5-P	Keep blood on ice, or plasma frozen, if it is to be sent any distance; A.M. sample
Prolactin	2–15 ng/mL	0.08–6.0 nmol/L	2-S	

SPECIAL ENDOCRINE TESTS (Continued)
Polypeptide Hormones

Determination	Reference Range		Minimal mL Required*	Note
	Conventional	SI		
Renin activity	Supine:		4-P	EDTA tubes, on ice, normal diet
	1.1±0.8 ng/mL/hr	0.9±0.6 nmol/L/hr		
	Upright:			
	1.9±1.7 ng/mL/hr	1.5±1.3 nmol/L/hr		Low-sodium diet,
	Supine:			
	2.7±1.8 ng/mL/hr	2.1±1.4 nmol/L/hr		
	Upright:			
	6.6±2.5 ng/mL/hr	5.1±1.9 nmol/L/hr		Low-sodium diet
	Diuretics:			
	10.0±3.7 ng/mL/hr	7.7±2.9 nmol/L/hr		
Somatomedin C (Sm–C, IGF–1)	0.08–2.8 U/mL	0.08–2.8 arb. unit	2-P	EDTA plasma prepubertal
	0.9–5.9 U/mL	0.9–5.9 arb. unit		During puberty
	0.34–1.9 U/mL	0.34–1.9 arb. unit		Adult males
	0.45–2.2 U/mL	0.45–2.2 arb. unit		Adult females

Thyroid Hormones

Determination	Reference Range		Minimal mL Required*	Note
	Conventional	SI		
Thyroid-stimulating hormone (TSH)	0.5–5.0 μU/mL	0.5–5.0 arb. unit	2-S	
Thyroxine-binding globulin capacity	15–25 μg T$_4$/100 mL	193–322 nmol/L	2-S	
Total triiodothyronine (T$_3$)	75–195 ng/100 mL	1.16–3.00 nmol/L	2-S	
Reverse triiodothyronine (rT$_3$)	13–53 ng/mL	0.2–0.8 nmol/L	2-S	
Total thyroxine by RIA (T$_4$)	4–12 μg/100 mL	52–154 nmol/L	1-S	
T$_3$ resin uptake	25–35%	0.25–0.35	2-S	
Free thyroxine index (FT$_4$ I)	1–4		2-S	

VITAMIN D DERIVATIVES

Determination	Reference Range		Minimal mL Required *	Note
	Conventional	SI		
1,25-Dihydroxy–vitamin D	26–65 pg/mL	62–155 pmol/L	1-S	
25-Hydroxy–vitamin D	8–55 ng/mL	19.4–137 nmol/L	1-S	

HEMATOLOGIC VALUES

Determination	Reference Range		Minimal mL Required *	Note
	Conventional	SI		
Coagulation factors				
Factor I (fibrinogen)	0.15–0.35 g/100 mL	4.0–10.0 μmol/L	4.5-P	Collect in Vacutainer containing sodium citrate
Factor II (prothrombin)	60–140%	0.60–1.40	4.5-P	Collect in plastic tubes with 3.8% sodium citrate
Factor V (accelerator globulin)	60–140%	0.60–1.40	4.5-P	Collect as in factor II
Factor VII–X (proconvertin-Stuart)	70–130%	0.70–1.30	4.5-P	Collect as in factor II
Factor X (Stuart factor)	70–130%	0.70–1.30	4.5-P	Collect as in factor II
Factor VIII (antihemophilic globulin)	50–200%	0.50–2.0	4.5-P	Collect as in factor II
Factor IX (plasma thromboplastic cofactor)	60–140%	0.60–1.40	4.5-P	Collect as in factor II
Factor XI (plasma thromboplastic anteecedent)	60–140%	0.60–1.40	4.5-P	Collect as in factor II
Factor XII (Hageman factor)	60–140%	0.60–1.40	4.5-P	Collect as in factor II
Coagulation screening tests:				
Bleeding time (Simplate)	3–9.5 min	180–570 sec		
D-dimer	<500 ng/mL	<500 μg/L	4.5 mL	Collect in 3.8% sodium citrate
Prothrombin time	Less than 2-sec deviation from control	Less than 2-sec deviation from control	4.5-P	Collect in Vacutainer containing 3.8% sodium citrate

HEMATOLOGIC VALUES (Continued)

Determination	Reference Range		Minimal mL Required*	Note
	Conventional	SI		
International Normalized Ratio (INR)	1.0	1.0	4.5 mL	Collect in 3.8% sodium citrate
Partial thromboplastin time (activated)	25–38 sec	25–38 sec	4.5-P	Collect in Vacutainer containing 3.8% sodium citrate
Whole-blood clot lysis	No clot lysis in 24 hr	0/day	2.0-whole blood	Collect in sterile tube and incubate at 37°C
Fibrinolytic studies:				
Euglobin lysis	No lysis in 2 hr	0/2 hr	4.5-P	Collect as in factor II
Fibrinogen split products	Negative reaction at >1:4 dilution	0 (at 1:4 dilution)	4.5-S	Collect in special tube containing thrombin and epsilon aminocaproic acid
Thrombin time	Control ±5 sec	Control ± 5 sec	4.5-P	Collect as in factor II
"Complete" blood count:				
Hematocrit	Male: 45–52% Female: 37–48%	Male: 0.45–0.52 Female: 0.37–0.48	1-B	Use EDTA as anticoagulant; the seven listed tests are performed automatically on the Ortho ELT 800, which directly determines cell counts, hemoglobin (as the cyanmethemoglobin derivative), and MCV and computes hematocrit, MCH, and MCHC
Hemoglobin	Male: 13–18 g/100 mL Female: 12–16 g/100 mL	Male: 8.1–11.2 mmol/L Female: 7.4–9.9 mmol/L		
Leukocyte count	4,300–10,800/mm³	4.3–10.8 × 10⁹/L		
Erythrocyte count	4.2–5.9 million/mm³	4.2–5.9 × 10¹²/L		
Mean corpuscular volume (MCV)	86–98 μm³/cell	86–98 fl		
Mean corpuscular hemoglobin (MCH)	27–32 pg/RBC	1.7–2.0 pg/cell		
Mean corpuscular hemoglobin concentration (MCHC)	32–36%	0.32–0.36		

Test	Value (conventional)	Value (SI)	Specimen	Note
Erythrocyte sedimentation rate	Male: 1–13 mm/hr Female: 1–20 mm/hr	Male: 1–13 mm/hr Female: 1–20 mm/hr	5-B	Use EDTA as anticoagulant
Erythrocyte enzymes Glucose-6-phosphate dehydrogenase	5–15 U/g Hb	5–15 U/g	9-B	Use special anticoagulant (ACD solution)
Pyruvate kinase	13–17 U/g Hb	13–17 U/g	8-B	Use special anticoagulant (ACD solution)
Ferritin (serum) Iron deficiency	0–12 ng/mL 13–20 Borderline	0–4.8 nmol/L 5.2–8 nmol/L Borderline		
Iron excess	>400 ng/L	>160 nmol/L		
Folic acid Normal	>3.3 ng/mL	>7.3 nmol/L	1-S	
Borderline	2.5–3.2 ng/mL	5.75–7.39 nmol/L	1-S	
Haptoglobin	40–336 mg/100 mL	0.4–3.36 g/L	1-S	
Hemoglobin studies: Electrophoresis for abnormal hemoglobin			5-B	Collect with anticoagulant
Electrophoresis for: A$_2$ hemoglobin	3.0%	0.015–0.035	5-B	Use oxalate as anticoagulant
Borderline	0.3–3.5%	0.03–0.035		
Hemoglobin F (fetal hemoglobin)	Less than 2%	<0.02	5-B	Collect with anticoagulant
Hemoglobin, met- and sulf-	0	0	5-B	Use heparin as anticoagulant
Serum hemoglobin	2–3 mg/100 mL	1.2–1.9 µmol/L	2-S	Use heparin as anticoagulant
Thermolabile hemoglobin	0	0	1-B	Any anticoagulant
Lupus anticoagulant	0	0	4.5-P	Collect as in factor II
LE (lupus erythematosus) preparation: Method I	0	0	5-B	Use heparin as anticoagulant
Method II	0	0	5-B	Use defibrinated blood
Leukocyte alkaline phosphatase:			20-Isolated blood leukocytes Smear-B	Special handling of blood necessary
Qualitative method	Males: 33–188 U Females (off contraceptive pill): 30–160 U	33–188 U 30–160 U		

HEMATOLOGIC VALUES (Continued)

Determination	Reference Range		Minimal mL Required*	Note
	Conventional	SI		
Muramidase	Serum, 3–7 μg/mL	3–7 mg/L	1-S	
	Urine, 0–2 μg/mL	0–2 μg/L	1-U	
Osmotic fragility of erythrocytes	Increased if hemolysis occurs in over 0.5% NaCl; decreased if hemolysis is incomplete in 0.3% NaCl		5-B	Use heparin as anticoagulant
Peroxide hemolysis	Less than 10%	0.10	6-B	Use EDTA as anticoagulant
Platelet count	150,000–350,000/mm³	150–350 x 10⁹/L	0.5-B	Use EDTA as anticoagulant; counts are performed on Clay Adams Ultraflow; when counts are low, results are confirmed by hand counting
Platelet function tests:				
Clot retraction	50–100%/2 hr	0.50–1.00/2 hr	4.5-P	Collect as in factor II
Platelet aggregation	Full response to ADP, epinephrine, and collagen	1.0	18-P	Collect as in factor II
Platelet factor 3	33–57 sec	33–57 sec	4.5-P	Collect as in factor II
Reticulocyte count	0.5–2.5% red cells	0.005–0.025	0.1-B	
Vitamin B₁₂	205–876 pg/mL	150–674 pmol/L	12-S	
Borderline	140–204 pg/mL	102.6–149 pmol/L		

CEREBROSPINAL FLUID VALUES

Determination	Reference Range		Minimal mL Required*	Note
	Conventional	SI		
Bilirubin	0	0	2	
Cell count	0–5 mononuclear cells		0.5	
Chloride	120–130 mEq/L	120–130 mmol/L	0.5	
Colloidal gold	0000000000–0001222111	Same	0.1	

Determination	Conventional	SI	Minimal mL Required*	Note
Albumin	Mean: 29.5 mg/100 mL ±2 SD: 11–48 mg/100 mL	0.295 g/L ±2 SD: 0.11–0.48	2.5	
IgG	Mean: 4.3 mg/100 mL ±2 SD: 0–8.6 mg/100 mL	0.043 g/L ±2 SD: –0.086		
Glucose	50–75 mg/100 mL	2.8–4.2 mmol/L	0.5	
Pressure (initial)	70–180 mm of water	70–180 arb. unit		
Protein:				
Lumbar	15–45 mg/100 mL	0.15–0.45 g/L	1	
Cisternal	15–25 mg/100 mL	0.15–0.25 g/L	1	
Ventricular	5–15 mg/100 mL	0.05–0.15 g/L	1	

MISCELLANEOUS VALUES

Determination	Reference Range		Minimal mL Required*	Note
	Conventional	SI		
Carcinoembryonic antigen (CEA)	0–2.5 ng/mL	0–2.5 µg/L	20-P	Must be sent on ice
Chylous fluid			1-S	Use fresh specimen
Digitoxin	17±6 ng/mL	22±7.8 nmol/L	1-S	Medication with digitoxin or digitalis
Digoxin	1.2±0.4 ng/mL	1.54±0.5 nmol/L	1-S	Medication with digoxin 0.25 mg per day
	1.5±0.4 ng/mL	1.92±0.5 nmol/L	1-S	Medication with digoxin 0.5 mg per day
Duodenal drainage				
pH (urine)	5–7	5–7		pH should be in proper range with minimal amount of gastric juice
Gastric analysis	Basal:			
	Females: 2.0±1.8 mEq/hr	0.6±0.5 µmol/sec		
	Males: 3.0±2.0 mEq/hr	0.8±0.6 µmol/sec		
	Maximal (after histalog or gastrin)			
	Females: 16±5 mEq/hr	4.4±1.4 µmol/sec		
	Males: 23±5 mEq/hr	6.4±1.4 µmol/sec		

MISCELLANEOUS VALUES (Continued)

Determination	Reference Range		Minimal mL Required*	Note
	Conventional	SI		
Gastrin-I	0–200 pg/mL	0–95 pmol/L	4-P	Heparinized sample
Immunologic tests:				
Alpha-fetoprotein	Undetectable in normal adults		2-S	
Alpha-1-antitrypsin	85–213 mg/100 mL	0.85–2.13 g/L	10-B	Fasting sample preferred
Rheumatoid factor	<60 IU/mL		10 mL clotted blood	Send to laboratory promptly
Antinuclear antibodies	Negative at a 1:8 dilution of serum		2-S	
Anti-DNA antibodies	Negative at a 1:10 dilution of serum		2-S	
Antibodies to Sm and RNP (ENA)	None detected		10 mL clotted blood	
Antibodies to SS-A (Ro) and SS-B (La)	None detected		10 mL clotted blood	
Autoantibodies to:				
Thyroid colloid and microsomal antigens	Negative at a 1:10 dilution of serum		2-S	Low titers in some elderly normal women
Gastric parietal cells	Negative at a 1:20 dilution of serum		2-S	
Smooth muscle	Negative at a 1:20 dilution of serum		2-S	
Mitochondria	Negative at a 1:20 dilution of serum		2-S	
Interstitial cells of the testes	Negative at a 1:10 dilution of serum		2-S	
Skeletal muscle	Negative at a 1:60 dilution of serum		2-S	
Adrenal gland	Negative at a 1:10 dilution of serum		2-S	
Bence Jones Protein	No Bence Jones protein detected in a 50-fold concentrate of urine		50-U	
Complement, total hemolytic	150–250 U/mL		10-B	Must be sent on ice

Test	Conventional value	SI value	Specimen	Comments
Cryoprecipitable proteins	None detected			
C3	Range, 83–177 mg/100 mL	0.83–1.77 g/L	10-S	Collect and transport at 37°C
C4	Range, 15–45 mg/100 mL	0.15–0.45 g/L	2-S	
Factor B	12–30 mg/100 mL		2-S	5 mL clotted blood
C1 esterase inhibitor	13.2–24 mg/100 mL		5 mL clotted blood	5 mL clotted blood
Hemoglobin A_{1c}	3.8–6.4%	0.038–0.064	5-P	Send EDTA tube on ice promptly to laboratory
Hypersensitivity pneumonitis screen	No antibodies to those antigens assayed		5 mL clotted blood	
Immunoglobulins:				
IgG	639–1349 mg/100 mL	6.39–13.49 g/L	2-S	
IgA	70–312 mg/100 mL	0.7–3.12 g/L	2-S	
IgM	86–352 mg/100 mL	0.86–3.52 g/L	2-S	
Viscosity	1.4–1.8 relative viscosity units		10-B	Expressed as the relative viscosity of serum compared with water
Iontophoresis	Children: 0–40 mEq sodium/L; Adults 0–60 mEq sodium/L	Children: 0–40 mmol/L; Adults 0–60 mmol/L	1-S	Value given in terms of sodium
Propranolol (includes bioactive 4-OH metabolite)	100–300 ng/mL	386–1158 nmol/L		Obtain blood sample 4 hr after last dose of beta-blocking agent
Stool fat	Less than 5 g in 24 hr or less than 4.0% of measured fat intake in 3-day period	<5 g/day	24-hr or 3-day specimen	
Stool nitrogen	Less than 2 g/day or 10% of urinary nitrogen	<2 g/day	24-hr or 3-day specimen	
Synovial fluid: Glucose	Not less than 20 mg/100 mL lower than simultaneously drawn blood sugar	Blood glucose	mL of fresh fluid	
D-Xylose absorption	5–8 g/5 hr in urine; 40 mg per 100 mL in blood 2 hr after ingestion of 25 g of D-Xylose	33–53 mmol/day; 2.7 mmol/L	5-U; 5-B	Collect with oxalate–fluoride mixture; For directions see Benson et al.: N Engl J Med 256:335, 1957

* Abbreviations used: SI, Système International d'Unités; P, plasma; S, serum; B, blood; and U, urine.
SOURCE: Adapted from Scully, Robert E. (ed): Case Records of the Massachusetts General Hospital, New England Journal of Medicine, vol. 314, pp. 39–49, January 2, 1986, with permission, and other sources. Copyright 1986 Massachusetts Medical Society. All rights reserved.

APPENDIX 4
Prefixes, Suffixes, and Combining Forms

a-, an-. Without; away from; not.

ab-, abs-. From; away from; absent.

abdomin-, abdomino-. Abdomen.

abort-, aborto-. To miscarry.

abs-. SEE: *ab-*.

acanth-, acantho-. Thorn; spine.

acous-, acoust-, acousto-. Hearing.

acro-. Extremity; top; extreme point.

actin-, actino-. Ray; some form of radiation.

ad-. Adherence; increase; toward.

-ad. Toward; in the direction of.

aden-, adeno-. Gland.

adip-, adipo-. Fat.

adren-, adreno-. Adrenal glands.

adrenal-, adrenalo-. Adrenal glands.

-aemia. Blood.

aer-, aero-. Air or gas.

-aesthesia, aesthesio-. SEE: *-esthesia*.

af-. Toward.

-agogue. An agent that promotes the expulsion of a specific substance.

-agra. Sudden severe pain.

-al. 1. Relating to, e.g., abdominal, intestinal. **2.** In chemistry, an aldehyde.

albumin-, albumino-. Albumin.

-algesia, -algia. Suffering; pain.

algi-. Pain.

all-. SEE: *allo-*.

allo-, all-. Other.

amb-, ambi-. Both; on both sides; around; about.

amph-, amphi-, ampho-. Both; on both sides; on all sides; double; around; about.

an-. SEE: *a-*.

ana-, an-. Up; against; back.

andro-. Man; male; masculine.

angi-, angio-. Blood or lymph vessels.

aniso-. Unequal; asymmetrical; dissimilar.

ankyl-, ankylo-. Crooked; bent; fusion or growing together of parts.

ante-. Before.

antero-. Anterior; front; before.

anthropo-. Human beings; human life.

ant-, anti-. Against.

antr-, antro-. Antrum.

apo-. From; derived from; separated from; opposed.

arch-, arche-, archi-. First; principal; beginning; original.

arteri-, arterio-. Artery.

arthr-, arthro-. Joint.

-ase. Enzyme.

-asis, -esis, -iasis, -isis, -sis. Condition; pathological state.

astro-. Star; star-shaped.

atelo-. Imperfect; incomplete.

ather-, athero-. Fatty plaque.

atmo-. Steam; vapor.

atreto-. Absence of an opening.

aut-, auto-. Self.

axio-. Axis; the long axis of a tooth.

axo-. Axis; axon.

azot-, azoto-. Nitrogenous compounds.

bacteri-, bacterio-. Bacteria; bacterium.

balan-, balano-. Glans clitoridis; glans penis.

bar-, baro-. Weight; pressure.

basi-, basio-. Base; foundation.

bi-, bis-. Two; double; twice.

bili-. Bile.

bio-. Life.

bis-. SEE: *bi-*.

blast-, -blast. Germ; bud; embryonic state of development.

blenn-, blenno-. Mucus.

blephar-, blepharo-. Eyelid.

brachio-. Arm.

brachy-. Short.

brady-. Slow.

brom-, bromo-. Bromine.

bronch-, bronchi-, broncho-. Airway.

bronchiol-, bronchiolo-. Bronchiole.

cac-, caci-, caco-. Bad; ill.

calc-, calco-. Calcium.

calcan-, calcaneo-. Calcaneum (heel bone).

carcin-, carcino-. Cancer.

cardi-, cardio-. Heart.

carpo-. Carpus.

cary-, caryo-. SEE: *kary-*.

cat-, cata-, cath-, kat-, kata-. Down; downward; destructive; against; according to.

cath-. SEE: *cat-*.

cel-, celo-. 1. Tumor; hernia. **2.** Cavity.

-cele. Tumor; swelling; hernia.

cent-. Hundred.

cephal-, cephalo-. Head.

cerebell-, cerebello-. Cerebellum.

cervic-, cervico-. Neck; the neck of an organ.

cheil-, cheilo-. SEE: *chil-*.

chem-, chemo-. Chemical; drug.

chil-, chilo-. Lip; lips.

chir-, chiro-. Hand.

chlor-, chloro-. Green.

chol-, chole-. Bile; gall.

cholangi-, cholangio-. Bile vessel.

cholecyst-, cholecysto-. Gallbladder.

choledoch-, choledocho-. Bile duct.

chondr-, chondro-. Cartilage.

chrom-, chromo-. Color.

-cide. Causing death.

cine-. Movement.

circum-. Around.

clavicul-, claviculo-. Clavicle.

-cle, -cule. Little, e.g., molecule, corpuscle.

cleid-, cleido-. Clavicle.

co-, com-, con-. Together.

colp-, colpo-. SEE: *kolp-*.

contra-. Against; opposite.

crani-, cranio-. Skull; cranium.

cry-, cryo-. Cold.

-cusia, -cusis. Hearing.

cyan-, cyano-. Blue.

cycl-, cyclo-. Circular; cyclical; ciliary body of the eye.

cyst-, cysto-, -cyst. Cyst; urinary bladder.

cyt-, cyto-, -cyte. Cell.

dacry-. Tears.

dactyl-, dactylo-. Finger; toe.

de-. From; down; not.

dec-, deca-. Ten.

deci-. One tenth.

demi-. Half.

dent-, denti-, dento-. Teeth.

derm-, derma-, dermato-, dermo-. Skin.

deuter-, deutero-, deuto-. Second; secondary.

dextro-. Right.

di-. 1. Double; twice; two. 2. Apart from.

dia-. Through; between; asunder.

dipla-, diplo-. Double; twin.

dips-, dipso-. Thirst.

dis-. 1. Double; twice. 2. Negative; apart; absence of.

dors-, dorsi-, dorso-. Back.

duoden-, duodeno-. Duodenum.

-dynia. Pain.

dys-. Difficult; bad; painful.

-eal. Pertaining to.

ec-, ecto-. Out; on the outside.

-ectomy. Excision.

ectro-. Congenital absence of a part.

ef-, es-, ex-, exo-. Out.

electr-, electro-. Electricity.

embol-, embolo-. Plug.

-emesis. Vomiting.

-emia. Blood.

en-. In; into.

enantio-. Opposite.

end-, endo-. Within.

ent-, ento-. Within; inside.

enter-, entero-. Intestine.

ep-, epi-. Upon; over; at; in addition to; after.

episi-, episio-. Vulva.

erythr-, erythro-. Red.

eschar-, escharo-. Scab.

-esis. SEE: -*asis*.

esophag-, esophago-. Esophagus.

-esthesia. Sensation.

etio-. Causation.

eu-. Well; good; healthy; normal.

eury-. Broad.

ex-. Out; away from; completely.

exo-. Out; outside of; without.

extra-. Outside of; in addition; beyond.

-facient. Causing; making happen.

femor-, femoro-. Thigh.

-ferous. Producing.

ferri-, ferro-. Iron.

fibro-. Fibers; fibrous tissues.

fluo-. Flow.

fluor-, fluoro-. Luminous; fluorescence.

fore-. Before; in front of.

-form. Form.

-fuge. To expel; to drive away; fleeing.

galact-, galacto-. Milk.

gam-, gamo-. Marriage; sexual union.

gaster-, gastero-, gastr-, gastro-. Stomach.

gen-. Producing; forming.

-gen, -gene, -genesis, -genetic, -genic. Producing; forming.

glauc-, glauco-. Gray.

genito-. Organs of reproduction.

gero-. Old age.

giga-. Billion.

gingiv-, gingivo-. Gums (of the mouth).

-globin. Protein.

gloss-, glosso-. Tongue.

gluc-, gluco-, glyc-, glyco-. Sugar; glycerol or similar substance.

gnath-, gnatho-. Jaw; cheek.

-gog, -gogue. Make flow.

gon-, gono-. Semen; seed; genitals; offspring.

-gram. A tracing; a mark.

-graph. Instrument for drawing or recording.

-graphy. Writing; record.

-gravida. Pregnant.

gyn, gyne-, gyneco-, gyno-. Woman; female.

gyro-. Circle; spiral; ring.

hem-, hema-, hemato-, hemo-. Blood.

hemi-. Half.

hepat-, hepato-. Liver.

heredo-. Heredity.

heter-, hetero-. Other; different.

hex-, hexa-. Six.

histo-. Tissue.

hol-, holo-. Complete; entire; homogeneous.

homeo-. Likeness; resemblance; constant, unchanging state.

homo-. Same; likeness.

hydra-, hydro-, hydr-. Water.

hyo-. Hyoid bone.

hyp-, hyph-, hypo-. Less than; below or under; beneath; deficient.

hyper-. Above; excessive; beyond.

hypno-. Sleep; hypnosis.

hyster-, hystero-. Uterus.

-ia. Condition, esp. an abnormal state.

-iasis. SEE: *asis*.

-iatric. Medicine; medical profession; physicians.

-ic. Pertaining to; relating to.

ichthyo-. Fish.

-id. Secondary skin eruption distant from primary infection site.

ideo-. Mental images.

idio-. Individual; distinct.

ileo-. Ileum.

ilio-. Ilium; flank.

im-. SEE: *in-*. Used before b,m, or p.

immun-, immuno-. Immune; immunity.

in-. In; inside; within; intensive action; negative.

infra-. Below; under; beneath; inferior to; after.

inter-. Between; in the midst.

intra-, intro-. Within; in; into.

ipsi-. Same; self.

irid-, irido-. Iris.

ischio-. Ischium.

-isis. SEE: -*asis*.

-ism. Condition; theory.

iso-. Equal.

-ite. 1. Of the nature of. 2. In chemistry, a salt of an acid with the termination -*ous*.

-itis. Inflammation of.

-ize. To treat by special method.

jejuno-. Jejunum.

juxta-. Close proximity.

kary-, karyo-, cary-, caryo-. Nucleus; nut.

kat-, kata-. SEE: *cat-*.

kera-, kerato-. Horny substance; cornea.

ket-, keto-. Ketone bodies (acids and acetones).

kilo-. Thousand.

kinesi-, kino-, -kinesis. Movement.

klepto-. To steal.

kolp-, kolpo-, colp-, colpo-. Vagina.

kypho-. Humped.

kysth-, kystho-. Vagina.

lab-, labi-. Lip.

lact-. Milk.

laparo-. Flank; abdominal wall.

laryng-, laryngo-. Larynx.

latero-. Side.

leio-. Smooth.

lepido-. Flakes; scales.

-lepsy. Seizure.

lepto-. Thin; fine; slight; delicate.

leuk-, leuko-, leuc-. White; white blood cell.

linguo-. Tongue.

lip-, lipo-. Fat.

-lite, -lith, lith-, litho-. Stone; calculus.

-logia, -logy. Science of; study of.

lord-, lordo-. Curve; swayback.

lumbo-. Loins.

lyo-. Loosen; dissolve.

-lysis. 1. Loosen; dissolve. **2.** In medicine, reduction of; relief from.

macr-, macro-. Large; long.

mal-. Ill; bad; poor.

mamm-, mammo-. Breast.

-mania. Frenzy; madness.

mast-, masto-. Breast.

meat-, meato-. Opening; meatus.

med-, medi-, medio-. Middle.

medull-, medullo-. Soft inner part; medulla.

mega-, megal-, megalo-. Large; of great size.

-megalia, -megaly. Enlargement of a body part.

meio-, mio-. Less; smaller.

melan-, melano-. Black.

mening-, meningo-. Meninges.

menta-, mento-. Mind.

mes-, meso-. 1. Middle. **2.** In anatomy, the mesentery. **3.** In medicine, secondary; partial.

mesio-. Toward the middle.

meta-. 1. Change; transformation; next in a series. **2.** In chemistry, the 1,3 position of benzene derivatives.

metacarp-, metacarpo-. Metacarpus (bones of the hand).

-meter. Measure.

metr-, metra-, metro-. Uterus.

micr-, micro-. Small.

mio-. SEE: *meio-*.

mon-, mono-. Single; one.

muc-, muci-, muco-, myxa-, myxo-. Mucus.

multi-. Many; much.

musculo-, my-, myo-. Muscle.

my-, myo-. SEE: *musculo-*.

myc-, myco-. Fungus.

myel-, myelo-. Spinal cord; bone marrow.

myring-, myringo-. Tympanic membrane, eardrum.

myx-, myxo-. SEE: *muc-*.

nano-. 1. One billionth. **2.** Dwarfism (nanism).

narco-. Numbness; stupor.

naso-. Nose.

necr-, necro-. Death; necrosis.

neo-. New; recent.

nephr-, nephra-, nephro-. Kidney.

neur-, neuri-, neuro-. Nerve; nervous system.

nitr-, nitro-. Nitrogen.

non-. No.

normo-. Normal; usual.

noso-. Disease.

noto-. The back.

nucleo-. Nucleus.

nyct-, nycto-. Night; darkness.

ob-. Against.

occipit-, occipito-. Occiput.

octa-, octo-. Eight.

oculo-. Eye.

-ode, -oid. Form; shape; resemblance.

odont-, odonto-. Tooth; teeth.

-odynia, odyno-. Pain.

-oid. SEE: *-ode*.

oleo-. Oil.

olig-, oligo-. Few; small.

-ology. Science of; study of.

-oma. Tumor.

omo-. Shoulder.

omphal-, omphalo-. Navel.

onco-. Tumor; swelling; mass.

onych-, onycho-. Fingernails; toenails.

oo-, ovi-, ovo-. Egg; ovum.

oophor-, oophoro-, oophoron-. Ovary.

ophthalm-, ophthalmo-. Eye.

-opia. Vision.

opisth-, opistho-. Backward.

-opsy. View of.

optico-, opto-. Eye; vision.

orchi-, orchid-, orchido-. Testicle.

-orexia. Appetite.

oro-. Mouth.

orth-, ortho-. Straight; correct; normal; in proper order.

os-. Mouth; bone.

oscheo-. Scrotum.

-ose. 1. Carbohydrate. **2.** Primary alteration of a protein.

-osis. Condition; status, process; abnormal increase.

osmo-. 1. Odor; smell. **2.** Impulse. **3.** Osmosis.

oste-, osteo-. Bone.

-ostomosis, -ostomy, -stomosis, -stomy. A created mouth or outlet.

ot-, oto-. Ear.

-otomy. Cutting.

-ous. 1. Possessing; full of. **2.** Pertaining to.

ovi-, ovo-. SEE: *oo-*.

ox-. Oxygen.

oxy-. 1. Sharp; keen; acute; acid; pungent. **2.** Oxygen in a compound. **3.** Hydroxyl group.

pach-, pachy-. Thick.

-pagus. Twins joined at a specific site, e.g., craniopagus.

pali-, palin-. Recurrence; repetition.

pan-. All; entire.

pant-, panto-. All or the whole of something.

papulo-. Pimple; papule.

para-, -para. 1. Prefix: near; alongside of; departure from normal. **2.** Suffix: Bearing offspring.

patell-, patello-. Patella; kneecap.

path-, patho-, -path, -pathic, -pathy. Disease; suffering.

ped-, pedi-, pedo-. Foot.

pedia-. Child.

pedicul-, pediculo-. Louse.

-penia. Decrease from normal; deficiency.

pent-, penta-. Five.

-pepsia. Digestion.

per-. Throughout; through; utterly; intense.

peri-. Around; about.

perineo-. Perineum.

peritoneo-. Peritoneum.

pero-. Deformed.

petro-. 1. Stone. **2.** The petrous portion of the temporal bone.

-pexy. Fixation, usually surgical.

phaco-. Lens of the eye.

phag-, phago-. Eating; ingestion; devouring.

phalang-, phalango-. Phalanges (bones of fingers and toes).

phall-. Penis.

pharmaco-. Drug; medicine.

pharyng-, pharyngo-. Pharynx.

-phasia. Speech.

-phil, -philia, -philic. Love for; tendency toward; craving for.

phlebo-. Vein.

-phobia. Abnormal fear or aversion.

phono-. Sound; voice.

-phoresis. Transmission.

-phoria. In ophthalmology, a turning with reference to the visual axis.

photo-. Light.

phren-, phreno-, -phrenia. 1. Mind. **2.** Diaphragm.

-phylaxis. Protection.

physico-. Physical; natural.

physio-. Pertaining to nature.

physo-. Air; gas.

phyt-, phyto-. Plant; something that grows.

pico-. One trillionth.

picr-, picro-. Bitter.

-piesis. Pressure.

pimel-, pimelo-. Fat.

plagio-. Slanting; oblique.

-plakia. Plaque.

-plasia. Growth; cellular proliferation.

plasm-, -plasm. 1. Prefix: Living substance or tissue. **2.** Suffix: To mold.

-plastic. 1. Molded. **2.** Restoration of lost or badly formed features.

platy-. Broad.

-plegia. Paralysis; stroke.

pleur-, pleuro-. Pleura; side; rib.

-ploid. Chromosome pairs of a specific number.

plur-, pluri-. Several; more.

pneo-. Breath; breathing.

pneum-, pneuma-, pneumato-. Air; gas; respiration.

pneumo-, pneumono-. Air; lung.

pod-, podo-. Foot.

poikil-, poikilo-. Varied, irregular.

-poiesis, -poietic. Production; formation.

polio-. Gray matter of the nervous system.

poly-. Much; many.

post-. After.

postero-. Posterior; behind; toward the back.

-praxis. 1. Act; activity. **2.** Practice; use.

pre-. Before; in front of.

presby-. Old age.

pro-. Before; in behalf of.

proct-, procto-. Anus; rectum.

proso-. Forward, anterior.

prostat-, prostato-. Prostate gland.

proto-. 1. First. **2.** In chemistry, the lowest of a series of compounds with the same elements.

pseud-, pseudo-. False.

psych-, psycho-. Mind; mental processes.

psychro-. Cold.

-ptosis. Prolapse, downward displacement.

pubio-, pubo-. Pubic bone or region.

pulmo-. Lung.

py-, pyo-. Pus.

pycn-, pycno-, pykn-, pykno-. Dense; thick; compact; frequent.

pyelo-. Pelvis.

pyg-, pygo-. Buttocks.

pykn-, pykno-. SEE: *pycn-*.

pyle-. Orifice, esp. of the portal vein.

pyloro-. Gatekeeper, i.e., the pylorus.

pyreto-. Fever.

pyro-. Heat; fire.

quadr-, quadri-. Four.

quinqu-. Five.

rachi-, rachio-. Spine.

radio-. 1. Radiant energy; a radioactive substance. **2.** In chemistry, a radioactive isotope.

re-. Back; again.

recto-. Straight; rectum.

ren-, reno-. Kidney.

reticulo-. Reticulum.

retro-. Backward; back; behind.

rhabdo-. Rod.

rheo-, -(r)rhea. Current; stream; to flow; to discharge.

rhino-. Nose.

rhizo-. Root.

rhodo-. Red.

roseo-. Rose-colored.

-(r)rhage, -(r)rhagia. Rupture; profuse fluid discharge.

-(r)rhaphy. A suturing or stitching.

-(r)rhexis. Rupture of a specific body part.

sacchar-, saccharo-. Sugar.

sacro-. Sacrum.

salping-, salpingo-. Auditory tube; fallopian tube.

sapro-. Putrid; rotten.

sarco-. Flesh.

scapho-. Boat-shaped; scaphoid.

scapulo-. Shoulder.

scato-. Dung; fecal matter.

schisto-. Split; cleft.
schizo-. Division.
scirrho-. Hard; hard tumor or scirrhus.
sclero-. 1. Hard. 2. Relating to the sclera.
-sclerosis. Dryness; hardness.
-scope. Instrument for viewing or examining (includes other methods of examination).
-scopy. Examination.
scoto-. Darkness.
sebo-. Fatty substance.
semi-. Half.
septi-. Seven.
sero-. Serum.
sesqui-. One and one half.
sial-, sialo-. Saliva.
sidero-. Iron; steel.
-sis. SEE: *-asis.*
sitio-, sito-. Bread; made from grain; food.
skeleto-. Skeleton.
skia-. Shadow.
sodio-. Sodium.
somat-, somato-. Body.
spectro-. Appearance; image; form; spectrum.
sperma-, spermat-, spermato-. Sperm; spermatozoa.
spheno-. Wedge; sphenoid bone.
sphygmo-. Pulse.
spir-, spiro-. Breathe.
spleno-. Spleen.
spondyl-, spondylo-. Vertebra.
spongio-. Spongelike.
staphylo-. Uvula; bunch of grapes; *Staphylococcus.*
steato-. Fat.
steno-. Narrow; short.
sterco-. Feces.
stere-, stereo-. Three-dimensional.
sterno-. Sternum.
stetho-. Chest.
stomato-. Mouth.
-stomosis, -stomy. SEE: *-ostomosis.*
strepto-. Twisted.
sub-. Under; beneath; in small quantity; less than normal.
super-. Above; beyond; superior.
supra-. Above; beyond; on top.
syn-, sym-. With; together with; along; beside.
tachy-. Swift; rapid.
taen-, taeni-, ten-, teni-. Tapeworm.
tarso-. 1. Flat of the foot. 2. Edge of the eyelid.
tauto-. Same.
techno-. Art; skill.
tel-, tele-. 1. End. 2. Distant.
teleo-. Perfect; complete.
temporo-. Temples of the head.
ten-, teni-. SEE: *taen-.*
tendo-, teno-. Tendon.

ter-. Three.
tera-. One trillionth.
terato-. Severely malformed fetus.
tetra-. Four.
thalamo-. Chamber; part of the brain where a nerve originates; thalamus.
thanato-. Death.
theco-. Sheath; case; receptacle.
thermo-. Hot; heat.
thio-. Sulfur.
thorac-, thoraci-, thoraco-. Chest; chest wall.
thrombo-. Blood clot; thrombus.
thymo-. 1. Thymus. 2. Soul; emotions.
thy-, thyro-. Thyroid gland; oblong; shield.
thyroid-, thyroido-. Thyroid gland.
toco-. Childbirth.
-tome. Cutting instrument.
tomo-. Section; layer.
-tomy. Cutting operation; excision.
ton-, tono-. Tension.
top-, topo-. Place; locale.
tox-, toxi-, toxico-, toxo-, -toxic. Toxin; poison; toxic.
trachelo-. Neck.
tracheo-. Trachea; windpipe.
trans-. Across; over; beyond; through.
traumato-. Trauma.
tri-. Three.
trich-, trichi-, tricho-. Hair.
troph-, tropho-, -trophic. Nourishment.
-tropin. Stimulation of a target organ by a substance, esp. a hormone.
tubo-. Tube.
tympan-, tympano-. Eardrum; tympanum.
typhlo-. 1. Cecum. 2. Blindness.
typho-. Fever; typhoid.
ulo-. Scar; scarring.
ultra-. Beyond; excess.
uni-. One.
uretero-. Ureter.
urethro-. Urethra.
-uria. Urine.
urin-, urino-, uro-. Urine.
uter-, utero-. Uterus.
vagin-, vagino-. Vagina.
varic-, varico-. Dilated vein.
vaso-. Vessel, e.g., blood vessel.
veno-. Vein.
ventro-, ventr-, ventri-. Abdomen; anterior surface of the body.
vertebro-. Vertebra; vertebrae.
vesico-. Bladder; vesicle.
viscero-. Viscera.
vitr-, vitro-, vitre-, vitreo-. 1. Vitreous body (of the eye). 2. Glassy.
vulvo-. 1. Vulva. 2. Covering.
xanth-. Yellow.
xeno-. Strange; foreign.
xero-. Dry.
xiph-, xiphi-, xipho-. Xiphoid cartilage.
zoo-. Animal; animal life.

APPENDIX 5
Medical Abbreviations

A	accommodation; acetum; angström unit; anode; anterior	ALP	alkaline phosphatase
a	artery	ALS	amyotrophic lateral sclerosis
ā	before	ALT	alanine aminotransferase
A₂	aortic second sound	alt. dieb.	every other day
aa	of each; arteries	alt. hor.	every other hour
AAA	abdominal aortic aneurysm	alt. noc.	every other night
		AM	morning
abd	abdominal/abdomen	Am	mixed astigmatism
ABG	arterial blood gas	a.m.a.	against medical advice
ABI	ankle-brachial index	AMI	acute myocardial infarction
ABO	three basic blood groups	AML	acute myelogenous (myeloblastic) leukemia
AC	adrenal cortex; air conduction; alternating current; axiocervical	AMLS	Advanced Medical Life Support
a.c., ac	before a meal	amp	ampule; amputation
acc.	accommodation	ANA	antinuclear antibody
A/CA	accommodative/ convergence accommodation ratio	anat	anatomy or anatomic
		ANNA	anti-neuronal nuclear antibody
ACE	angiotensin-converting enzyme	ANP	atrial natriuretic peptide
ACh	acetylcholine	ant.	anterior
AChE	acetylcholinesterase	anti-CCP	anticyclic citrullinated peptide
AChR	acetylcholine receptor	Ao.	aorta
ACLS	advanced cardiac life support	A-P	anterior-posterior
ACTH	adrenocorticotropic hormone	A&P	auscultation and percussion
AD	advance directive	ap	before dinner
ad	to; up to	APAP	acetaminophen
ADH	antidiuretic hormone	aPTT	activated partial thromboplastin
ADHD	attention deficit-hyperactivity disorder	AQ, aq	water
ADL, ADLs	activities of daily living	aq. dest.	distilled water
ad lib.	freely; as desired	aq. frig.	cold water
admov.	apply	ARC	AIDS-related complex
ad sat.	to saturation	ARDS	acute respiratory distress syndrome
AED	antiepileptic drug	ARMD	age-related macular degeneration
AF	atrial fibrillation		
AFB	acid-fast bacillus	AS	ankylosing spondylitis; aortic stenosis; auris sinistra (left ear)
AFP	alpha-fetoprotein		
A/G; A-G ratio	albumin/globulin ratio		
Ag	silver; antigen	As.	astigmatism
AGC	atypical glandular cells	ASA	acetylsalicylic acid
AgNO₃	silver nitrate	ASC	atypical squamous cells
ah	hypermetropic astigmatism	asc.	ascending
		ASCA	anti-Saccharomyces cerevisiae antibody
AHF	antihemophilic factor		
AI	aortic incompetence; aortic insufficiency	ASC-US	atypical squamous cells of undetermined significance
AICD	automatic implantable cardiac defibrillator	ASCVD	atherosclerotic cardiovascular disease
AIDS	acquired immunodeficiency syndrome	ASD	atrial septal defect
AK	above the knee	AsH	hypermetropic astigmatism
Al	aluminum		
Alb	albumin	AsM	myopic astigmatism
ALL	acute lymphocytic leukemia	AST	aspartate aminotransferase

Ast	astigmatism	CABG	coronary artery bypass graft
ATCC	American Type Culture Collection	CaCO₃	calcium carbonate
at. wt.	atomic weight	CAD	coronary artery disease
Au	gold	CAH	chronic active hepatitis
A-V; AV; A/V	arteriovenous; atrioventricular	Cal	large calorie
		CAP	let (the patient) take
av.	avoirdupois	cap.	capsule
AVM	arteriovenous malformation	C&S	culture and sensitivity
		cath	catheter
AVP	arginine vasopressin	CBC	complete blood count
B	boron; bacillus	CBI	continuous bladder irrigation
Ba	barium		
BAC	blood alcohol concentration	CBRNE	chemical, biological, radiological, nuclear, and explosive agents
BBB	blood-brain barrier; bundle branch block		
		CBT	cognitive behavioral therapy
BBT	basal body temperature		
BCG	bacille Calmette-Guérin	CC	chief complaint
BCLS	basic cardiac life support	cc	cubic centimeter
		CCl₄	carbon tetrachloride
BCP	birth control pills	CCU	coronary care unit; critical care unit
BD	Buerger disease		
BE	barium enema	CD4	T-helper cells
Be	beryllium	CD8	cytotoxic cells
BHS	beta-hemolytic streptococci	CDC	Centers for Disease Control and Prevention
Bi	bismuth		
b.	bone	CEA	carcinoembryonic antigen
bib.	drink		
b.i.d., bid	twice a day	CF	cystic fibrosis; Christmas factor
b.i.n.	twice a night		
bipap	bilevel positive airway pressure	CFTR	cystic fibrosis transmembrane regulator
BK	below the knee		
BLS	basic life support	cg	centigram
BM	bowel movement	CHD	congenital heart disease; coronary heart disease
BMI	body mass index		
BMR	basal metabolic rate		
BMS	bone marrow suppression	ChE	cholinesterase
		CHF	congestive heart failure
BMT	bone marrow transplantation	CI	cardiac index
		Ci	curie
BNP	brain natriuretic peptide	CIN	cervical intraepithelial neoplasia
bol.	pill	CIS	carcinoma in situ
BP	blood pressure	CK	creatine kinase
B.P.	British Pharmacopeia	CK-MB	serum creatine kinase, myocardial-bound
BPH	benign prostatic hyperplasia		
		Cl	chlorine
bpm	beats per minute	CLL	chronic lymphocytic leukemia
BRM	biologic response modifier		
		cm	centimeter
BROW	barley, rye, oats, and wheat	c.m.s.	to be taken tomorrow morning
BSA	body surface area	CMT	certified medication technician
BSE	breast self-examination	CMV	cytomegalovirus
BUN	blood urea nitrogen	c.n.	tomorrow night
BW	birth weight; body weight	CNS	central nervous system
		c.n.s.	to be taken tomorrow night
Bx	biopsy		
C	Calorie (kilocalorie); Celsius	CO	carbon monoxide; cardiac output
c	calorie (small calorie)	CO₂	carbon dioxide
c̄	with	Co	cobalt
CA	coronary artery	c/o	complains of
ca.	about; approximately; cancer	COLD	chronic obstructive lung disease

comp.	compound; compounded of	D and C	dilatation and curettage
COMT	catechol-O-methyltransferase	dB	decibel
		DBP	diastolic blood pressure
COPD	chronic obstructive pulmonary disease	DC	direct current; doctor of chiropractic
COX-2	cyclooxygenase 2 inhibitors	dc	discontinue
		Derm	dermatology
CP	cerebral palsy; cleft palate	det.	let it be given
		DEXA	dual-energy x-ray absorptiometry
CPAP	continuous positive airway pressure	DFV	Doppler flow velocimetry
CPC	clinicopathologic conference	DHT	dihydrotestosterone
		DI	diabetes insipidus
CPD	cephalopelvic disproportion	DIC	disseminated intravascular coagulation
CPHSS	Cincinnati Prehospital Stroke Scale	dieb. alt.	every other day
CPK	creatine phosphokinase	dieb. tert.	every third day
CPM	continuous passive motion	dil.	dilute; diluted
		dim.	halved
CPR	cardiopulmonary resuscitation	DISIDA (scan)	diisopropyl iminodiacetic acid (cholescintigraphy)
CR	conditioned reflex; controlled release; crown-rump length	DJD	degenerative joint disease
CREST	calcinosis, Raynaud phenomenon, esophageal dysfunction, sclerodactyly, telangiectasia (cluster of features of systemic sclerosis scleroderma)	DKA	diabetic ketoacidosis
		dL	deciliter
		DM	diabetes mellitus
		DMARD	disease-modulating antirheumatic drug
		DNA	deoxyribonucleic acid
		DNH	do not hospitalize
CRP	c. reactive protein	DNR	do not resuscitate
CRS-R	Conners Rating Scales–Revised	DOA	dead on arrival
		DOB	date of birth
CS	cardiogenic shock; cesarean section; culture and sensitivity	DOE	dyspnea on exertion
		DPat	diphtheria-acellular pertussis tetanus (vaccine)
CSF	cerebrospinal fluid; colony-stimulating factor	DPT	diphtheria-pertussis-tetanus (vaccine)
		dr.	dram
CSH	combat support hospital	DRE	digital rectal examination
CT	computed/computerized tomography	DRG	diagnosis-related group
Cu	copper	DSM-IV-TR	*Diagnostic and Statistical Manual of Mental Disorders, 4th Edition, Text Revision*
CV	cardiovascular		
CVA	cardiovascular accident; cerebrovascular accident; costovertebral angle	DTR	deep tendon reflex(es)
		DTs	delirium tremens
		dur. dolor	while pain lasts
CVC	central venous catheter	DVT	deep vein thrombosis
CVP	central venous pressure	Dx	diagnosis
CVRB	critical value read back	D5W	dextrose 5% in water
CVS	chorionic villi sampling	DWI	driving while intoxicated
CXR	chest x-ray		
D	diopter; dose	E	eye; *Escherichia*
D5/0.9 NaCl	5% dextrose and normal saline solution (0.9% NaCl)	EBV	Epstein-Barr virus
		ECF	extended care facility; extracellular fluid
D5/½/NS	5% dextrose and half-normal saline solution (0.45% NaCl)	ECG	electrocardiogram, electrocardiograph
		ECHO	echocardiography
D5W	5% dextrose in water	ECMO	extracorporeal membrane oxygenation
d	density; right		
/d	per day		

ECT	electroconvulsive therapy	fl.	flexor
ED	emergency department; effective dose; erythema dose; erectile dysfunction	Fld	fluid
		FP	family practice; family practitioner
		FSH	follicle-stimulating hormone
EDD	estimated date of delivery (formerly EDC: estimated date of confinement)	FTT	failure to thrive
		FUO	fever of unknown origin
		G, g, gm	gram
		GABA	gamma-aminobutyric acid
EEG	electroencephalogram		
EENT	eye, ear, nose, and throat	GABA$_B$	gamma-aminobutyric acid type B
EF	ejection fraction	*GABRB3*	GABA$_A$ receptor gene
EGD	esophagogastro-duodenoscopy	garg	gargle
		GB	gallbladder; Guillain-Barré
EIA	enzyme immunosorbent assay	GC	gonococcus or gonorrheal
EKG	electrocardiogram; electrocardiograph	GDM	gestational diabetes mellitus
ELISA	enzyme-linked immunosorbent assay	GDS	Geriatric Depression Scale
elix.	elixir	GERD	gastroesophageal reflux disease
Em	emmetropia		
EMA-IgA	immunoglobulin A antiendomysial	GFR	glomerular filtration rate
EMG	electromyogram, electromyography	GGT	gamma-glutamyl transferase
EMS	emergency medical service	GH	growth hormone
		GI	gastrointestinal
Endo	endocrine	GnRH	gonadotropin-releasing hormone
ENT	ear, nose, and throat		
EOM	extraocular muscles	GP	general practitioner
EP	extrapyramidal	G6PD	glucose-6-phosphate dehydrogenase
EPS	extrapyramidal symptoms		
		gr	grain
ER	Emergency Room, extended-release	grad	by degrees
ERCP	endoscopic retrograde cholangiopancrea-tography	GRAS	generally recognized as safe
		GSW	gunshot wound
ESR	erythrocyte sedimentation rate	GTT	glucose tolerance test
		Gtt, gtt	drops
ESRD	end-stage renal disease	GU	genitourinary
EST	electroshock therapy	guttat.	drop by drop
ESWL	extracorporeal shock wave lithotripsy	GVHD	graft-versus-host disease
ET-1	endothelin-1	GYN	gynecology
ETOH, EtOH	ethyl alcohol	H	hydrogen
ext.	extensor; external	H$^+$	hydrogen ion
F	Fahrenheit	h, hr	hour
f	female	H&H	hematocrit and hemoglobin
FA	fatty acid		
F and E	fluid and electrolyte	H1N1	hemagglutinin type 1 and neuraminidase type 1
FAP	familial adenomatous polyposis		
FBS	fasting blood sugar	H$_2$	histamine 2
FD	fatal dose; focal distance	HAART	highly active antiretroviral therapy
FDA	(U.S.) Food and Drug Administration	HAV	hepatitis A virus
		HBV	hepatitis B virus
Fe	iron	HCG	human chorionic gonadotropin
FEV	forced expiratory volume		
		HCP	health care professional
FFP	fresh frozen plasma	HCT, Hct	hematocrit
FHT	fetal heart tone	HCV	hepatitis C virus
FISH	fluorescence in situ hybridization	HD	hearing distance
		HDL	high-density lipoprotein

HDV	hepatitis D	IDDM	insulin-dependent diabetes mellitus
HEENT	head, eye, ear, nose, and throat	IDM	infants of diabetic mothers
HELLP	hemolysis, elevated liver enzymes, low platelets	IED	improvised explosive device
HEPA	high–efficiency particulate air	Ig	immunoglobulin
HER2	human EGF (epidermal growth factor) receptor 2	IgE	immunoglobulin E
		IgG	immunoglobulin G
		IL-1	interleukin 1
		IL-8	interleukin 8
HEV	hepatitis E	IM	intramuscular
HF	heart failure	in d.	daily
Hg	mercury	INF	interferon
hgb	hemoglobin	inf.	inferior
HGSIL	high-grade squamous intraepithelial lesion	inj.	injection
		INR	international normalized ratio
Hib	*Haemophilus influenzae* type B	instill.	instillation
		int.	internal
HIDA	hepatobiliary iminodiacetic acid (cholescintigraphy)	IOP	intraocular pressure
		IPPB	intermittent positive pressure breathing
HIV	human immunodeficiency virus	IQ	intelligence quotient
		IRV	inspiratory reserve volume
HLA	human leukocyteantigen	I.U.*	international unit
h/o	history of	IUCD	intrauterine contraceptive device
HOB	head of bed		
H₂O	water	IUD	intrauterine device
H₂O₂	hydrogen peroxide	IUFD	intrauterine fetal death
hor. decub.	bedtime	IV	intravenous
hor. som., h.s.	bedtime	IVP	intravenous pyelogram
HPI	history of present illness	J	joule
		JNC 7	*The Seventh Report of the Joint National Committee on Prevention, Detection, Evaluation, and Treatment of High Blood Pressure*
HPV	human papillomavirus		
HR	heart rate		
HRT	hormone replacement therapy		
HSIL	high-grade squamous intraepithelial lesion		
HSV	herpes simplex virus	JRA	juvenile rheumatoid arthritis
HTLV-III	human T lymphotropic virus type III		
		jt.	joint
HTN	hypertension	K	potassium
hx, Hx	history	kg	kilogram
Hy	hyperopia	KI	potassium iodine
Hz	hertz (cycles per second)	KOH	potassium hydroxide
		KS	Kaposi sarcoma
I	iodine	KUB	kidney, ureter, and bladder
¹³¹I	radioactive isotope of iodine (atomic weight 131)		
		kv	kilovolt
		KVO	keep vein open
¹³²I	radioactive isotope of iodine (atomic weight 132)	L	liter
		L&D	labor and delivery
		lab	laboratory
I&O	intake and output	lat	lateral
IBW	ideal body weight	lb	pound
IC	inspiratory capacity	LBW	low birth weight
ICD	implantable cardioverter defibrillator	LD₅₀	lethal dose, median
		LDH	lactate dehydrogenase
		LDL	low-density lipoprotein
ICP	intracranial pressure	LE	lower extremity; lupus erythematosus
ICS	intercostal space		
ICSH	interstitial cell-stimulating hormone	LEEP	loop electrosurgical excision procedure
ICU	intensive care unit	LFT	liver function test
Id.	the same	LGA	large for gestational age

LH	luteinizing hormone	MM	mucous membrane; multiple myeloma
Li	lithium		
lig	ligament	mm	millimeter
liq.	liquid; fluid	mm Hg	millimeters of mercury
LLE	left lower extremity	mMol	millimole
LLL	left lower lobe	MMR	measles-mumps-rubella (vaccine)
LLQ	left lower quadrant		
lmp	last menstrual period	MMSE	Mini-Mental Status Examination
LOC	level/loss of consciousness		
		Mn	manganese
LP	lumbar puncture	mol wt	molecular weight
LR	lactated Ringer (solution)	mor. dict.	as directed
		mor. sol.	as accustomed
LSIL	low-grade squamous epithelial lesion	MPC	maximum permitted concentration
LTD	lowest tolerated dose	MPN	most probable number
LUE	left upper extremity	mr	milliroentgen
LUL	left upper lobe	MRA	magnetic resonance angiography
LUQ	left upper quadrant		
LV	left ventricle	MRgFUS	MR-guided focused ultrasound surgery
LVAD	left ventricular assist device		
		MRI	magnetic resonance imaging
LVH	left ventricular hypertrophy		
		MS	mitral stenosis; multiple sclerosis
M	master; medicine; molar; thousand; muscle		
		MV	mitral valve
		mV	millivolt
m	male; meter; minim; mole; meta; muscle	MVA	motor vehicle accident
		MW	molecular weight
MA	mental age	My	myopia
MAO-B	monoamine oxidase-B	N	nitrogen
man. prim.	first thing in the morning	n	nerve
		N/A	not applicable
MAP	mean arterial pressure	Na	sodium
MAT	Miller Analogies Test	NAA	nucleic acid amplification
MBD	minimal brain dysfunction		
		NAD	no acute distress
mc; mCi	millicurie	n.b.	note well
mcg	microgram	nCi	nanocurie
MCH	mean corpuscular hemoglobin	NDC	National Drug Code
		NG, ng	nasogastric
MCHC	mean corpuscular hemoglobin concentration	NGT	nasogastric tube
		NH_3	ammonia
		Ni	nickel
MCV	mean corpuscular volume	NICU	neonatal intensive care unit
MD	muscular dystrophy	NIDDM	noninsulin-dependent diabetes mellitus
MDI	metered-dose inhaler		
MED	minimum effective dose	NIH	National Institutes of Health
med	medial		
MELD	Model for End-Stage Liver Disease	NK	natural killer
		NKA	no known allergies
μEq	microequivalent	NMDA	N-methyl D-aspartate
mEq	milliequivalent	NMJ	neuromuscular junction
mEq/L	milliequivalent per liter	NMS	neuroleptic malignant syndrome
ME ratio	myeloid/erythroid ratio		
MG	myasthenia gravis	nn	nerves
Mg	magnesium	noct.	in the night
$MgSO_4$	magnesium sulfate	noct. maneq.	night and morning
μg	microgram	non rep; n.r.	do not repeat
mg	milligram	NPN	nonprotein nitrogen
MI	myocardial infarction	NPO; n.p.o.	nothing by mouth
MID	minimum infective dose	NRC	normal retinal correspondence
mist.	a mixture		
ml	milliliter	NS	normal saline
MLD	minimum lethal dose	NSAID	nonsteroidal anti-inflammatory drug
MLF	medial longitudinal fasciculus		
		NSR	normal sinus rhythm

N&V, N/V	nausea and vomiting		PD	interpupillary distance; Parkinson disease; peritoneal dialysis
O	pint			
O$_2$	oxygen		pd	prism diopter; pupillary distance
OB	obstetrics			
OC	oral contraceptive			
OCD	obsessive-compulsive disorder		PDA	patent ductus arteriosus
O.D.	right eye		PDR	*Physicians' Desk Reference*
ol.	oil			
om. mane vel noc.	every morning or night		PE	physical examination; pulmonary embolism
omn. hor.	every hour		PEEP	positive end expiratory pressure
omn. noct.	every night		PEFR	peak expiratory flow rate
OmPC	outer membrane porin C		PEG	percutaneous endoscopic gastrostomy
OOB	out of bed			
OPD	outpatient department			
OR	operating room		per	through or by
ORIF	open reduction with/ and internal fixation		PERRLA	pupils equal, regular, react to light and accommodation
O.S.	left eye			
OSHA	Occupational Safety and Health Administration		PET	positron emission tomography
OT	occupational therapy		PFP, P4P	pay for performance
OTC	over-the-counter		PFT	pulmonary function test
OU	each eye		pH	hydrogen ion concentration
oz	ounce			
P, p	melting point		Pharm; Phar.	pharmacy
p̄	after		PI	present illness; previous illness
P$_2$	pulmonic second sound			
P-A; PA; pa	placenta abruption; posteroanterior; pulmonary artery		PICC	peripherally inserted central catheter
PABA	para-aminobenzoic acid (vitamin B10)		PID	pelvic inflammatory disease
Paco$_2$	partial pressure of carbon dioxide in alveolar gas		PIH	pregnancy-induced hypertension
			pil.	pill
PACU	postanesthesia care unit		PIP	proximal interphalangeal
PAD	peripheral arterial disease		PIPDA (scan)	99mTc-para-isopropylacetanilido-iminodiaacetic acid (cholescintigraphy)
PALS	pediatric advanced life support			
P-ANCA	perinuclear antineutrophil cytoplasmic antibody		PKU	phenylketonuria
			PM	afternoon/evening
			PMH	past medical history
PAO$_2$	alveolar oxygen partial pressure		PMI	point of maximal impulse
Pap, Pap test	Papanicolaou smear		PMN	polymorphonuclear neutrophil leukocytes
part. vic	in divided doses			
Pb	lead		PMS	premenstrual syndrome
PBI	protein-bound iodine		PND	paroxysmal nocturnal dyspnea
p.c.	after meals			
PCA	patient-controlled analgesia		PNH	paroxysmal nocturnal hemoglobinuria
Pco$_2$	carbon dioxide pressure		PNS	peripheral nervous system
PCOS	polycystic ovarian syndrome		PO; p.o.	orally
PCP	*Pneumocystis carinii* pneumonia; primary care physician; primary care provider		POLST	physician orders for life-sustaining therapy
			post.	posterior
			PP	placenta previa
PCR	polymerase chain reaction		PPD	purified protein derivative (TB test)
			ppm	parts per million
PCWP	pulmonary capillary wedge pressure		p.r.	through the rectum

PRBCs	packed red blood cells	RQ	respiratory quotient
p.r.n.	as needed	RR	recovery room;
pro time/PT	prothrombin time		respiratory rate
PSA	prostate-specific antigen	RSV	respiratory syncytial virus
PSV	prostate-specific antigen	RT	radiation therapy; respiratory therapy
PT	prothrombin time; physical therapy	R/T	related to
		RUE	right upper extremity
Pt	platinum; patient	RUL	right upper lobe
pt	pint	RUQ	right upper quadrant
PTT	partial thromboplastin time	S	mark
		$\bar{s}$	without
Pu	plutonium	S.	sacral
PUBS	percutaneous umbilical blood sampling	S-A; S/A; SA	sinoatrial
PUVA	psoralen ultraviolet A	SAD	seasonal affective disorder
p.v.	through the vagina	SARS	severe acute respiratory syndrome
PVC	premature ventricular contraction	SB	small bowel
PVR	peripheral vascular resistance	Sb	antimony
		SBP	systolic blood pressure
q	every	SC, sc, s.c.	subcutaneous(ly)
q.d.*	every day	SCI	spinal cord injury
QFT-G	QuantiFERON-TB Gold	S.D.	standard deviation
q.h.	every hour	SDAT	senile dementia of the Alzheimer type
q.2h.	every 2 hours		
q.3h.	every 3 hours	S.E.	standard error
q.4h.	every 4 hours	Se	selenium
q.i.d.*	four times a day	Sed rate	sedimentation rate
q.l.	as much as wanted	semih.	half an hour
qns	quantity not sufficient	SERM	selective estrogen receptor modulator
q.o.d.*	every other day		
q.p.	as much as desired	SGA	small for gestational age
q.s.	as much as needed		
qt	quart	SI	international system of units
q.v.	as much as you please	Si	silicon
RA	rheumatoid arthritis	SIADH	syndrome of inappropriate diuretic hormone
Ra	radium		
rad	radiation absorbed dose		
RAI	radioactive iodine	SIDS	sudden infant death syndrome
RAIU	radioactive iodine uptake		
RBC	red blood cell; red blood count	Sig.	write on label
		SJS	Stevens-Johnson syndrome
RD	Raynaud disease		
RDA	recommended daily/dietary allowance	SLE	systemic lupus erythematosus
RDS	respiratory distress syndrome	SLP	speech-language pathology
RE	right eye	Sn	tin
Re	rhenium	SNF	skilled nursing facility
REM	rapid eye movement	SNRI	serotonin and norepinephrine reuptake inhibitor
RF	rheumatoid factor		
RFT	renal function test		
Rh	rhesus factor; rhodium	SNS	sympathetic nervous system
RHD	rheumatic heart disease		
RLE	right lower extremity	SOB	shortness of breath
RLL	right lower lobe	sol	solution, dissolved
RLQ	right lower quadrant	s.o.s.	if necessary
RML	right middle lobe of lung	S/P	no change after
		SPECT	single-photon emission computed tomography
Rn	radon		
RNA	ribonucleic acid		
R/O	rule out	sp gr	specific gravity
ROM	range of motion	SPF	skin protection factor
ROS	review of systems	sph	spherical
RPM	revolutions per minute	spt.	spirit

s.q.	subcutaneous(ly)	TN	trigeminal nerve
Sr	strontium	TNF	tumor necrosis factor
ss	a half	TNF-I	tumor necrosis factor
SSRI	selective serotonin		inhibitor
	reuptake inhibitor	TNF-α	tumor necrosis factor
SSS	sick sinus syndrome		alpha
st.	let it/them stand	TNM	tumor-node-metastasis
Staph	*Staphylococcus*	TNT	trinitrotoluene
stat.	immediately	TNTM	too numerous to
STD	sexually transmitted		mention
	disease	top.	topically
Strep	*Streptococcus*	TORB	telephone order read
STS	serologic test for		back
	syphilis	TPI	*Treponema pallidum*
STU	skin test unit		immobilization test
sup.	superior		for syphilis
supf.	superficial	TPN	total parenteral
SV	stroke volume;		nutrition
	supraventricular	TPO	thyroid peroxidase
SVC	superior vena cava	TPR	temperature, pulse, and
Sx	symptoms		respiration
syr.	syrup	tr, tinct.	tincture
T	temperature	TRAP criteria	tremor, rigidity,
T₃	triiodothyronine		akinesia or postural
T₄	tetraiodothyronine;		instablity
	thyroxine		bradykinesia, and
T6	thoracic nerve pair 6		postural instability
TA	toxin-antitoxin	Treg	regulatory T cell
Ta	tantalum	trit.	triturate, grind
T&A	tonsillectomy and	TSD	time since death
	adenoidectomy	TSE	testicular self-
TAH	total abdominal		examination
	hysterectomy	TSH	thyroid-stimulating
TAT	thematic apperception		hormone
	test	tTG	antitransglutaminase
T.A.T.	toxin-antitoxin	TUMA	transurethral
TB	tuberculin; tuberculosis;		microwave antenna
	tubercle bacillus	TUR	transurethral resection
Tb	terbium	TURP	transurethral resection
t.d.s.	to be taken three times		of the prostate
	daily	Tx	treatment
Te	tellurium; tetanus	U	uranium; unit*
TEE	transesophageal	UA	urinalysis
	echocardiogram	UC	ulcerative colitis
TEN	toxic epidermal	UE	upper extremity
	necrolysis	UHF	ultrahigh frequency
TENS	transcutaneous	ult. praes.	the last ordered
	electrical nerve	Umb; umb	umbilicus
	stimulation	ung.	ointment
TG	thyroglobulin	URI	upper respiratory
Th	thorium		infection
THR	total hip replacement	US	ultrasonic, ultrasound
TIA	transient ischemic	USAN	United States Adopted
	attack		Name
TIBC	total iron-binding	USP	United States
	capacity		Pharmacopeia
t.i.d.	three times a day	ut. dict.	as directed
t.i.n.	three times a night	UTI	urinary tract infection
tinct., tr	tincture	UV	ultraviolet
TKR	total knee replacement	v	vein
Tl	thallium	VA	visual acuity
TLC, tlc	tender loving care; thin	VC	vital capacity
	layer	VD	venereal disease
	chromatography; total	VDRL	Venereal Disease
	lung capacity		Research
TM	tympanic membrane		Laboratories
TMJ	temporomandibular	VF	ventricular fibrillation
	joint	Vf	field of vision

VLBW	very low birth weight	WAIS	Wechsler Adult Intelligence Scale
VLDL	very low density lipoprotein	WAP	written action plan
VMA	vanillylmandelic acid	WBC	white blood cell; white blood count
VOE	VistA-Office Electronic Health Record	WDWN	well-developed, well-nourished
vol.	volume	WF/BF	white female/black female
vol %	volume percent	WH	well–hydrated
VORB	verbal order read back	WM/BM	white male/black male
V/Q	ventilation/perfusion	WN	well-nourished
VS	volumetric solution; vesicular sound; vital signs	WNL	within normal limits
		wt.	weight
VSD	ventricular septal defect	w/v.	weight in volume
		x	multiplied by
VT	ventricular tachycardia	y	yocto-
vv	veins	yo	years old
VZIG	varicella zoster immune globulin	yr	year
		Z	atomic number
W	tungsten	Zn	zinc
w	watt		

---

* To avoid errors in the administration of medications and infusions, spell out the word instead of using the indicated abbreviation. For example, use "international unit" instead of "I.U."; "every day" instead of "q.d."; "every other day" instead of "q.o.d."; and "unit" instead of "U."

APPENDIX 6
Symbols

GENERAL SYMBOLS

℥	Ounce	−	Minus; deficiency; alkaline reaction; negative
○	Pint	±	Plus or minus; either positive or negative; indefinite
℔	Pound		
℞	Recipe (L. take)		
M	Misce (L. mix)	#	Number; following a number, pounds
aa	Of each		
A, Å, AU	angström unit	÷	Divided by
C-1, C-2, etc.	Complement	×	Multiplied by; magnification
c, c̄	cum (L. with)	/	Divided by
Δ	Change; heat	=	Equals
E_0	Electroaffinity	≈	Approximately equal
F_1	First filial generation	>	Greater than; from which is derived
F_2	Second filial generation		
mμ	Millimicron, nanometer	<	Less than; derived from
μg	Microgram	≮	Not less than
mEq	Milliequivalent	≯	Not greater than
mg	Milligram	≤	Equal to or less than
mg%	Milligrams percent; milligrams per 100 ml	≥	Equal to or greater than
		≠	Not equal to
n	Subscripted n indicates the number of the molecules can vary from two to greater	√	Root; square root; radical
		²√	Square root
		³√	Cube root
		∞	Infinity
QO_2	Oxygen consumption	:	Ratio; "is to"
m-	Meta-	::	Equality between ratios, "as"
o-	Ortho-	∴	Therefore
p-	Para-	°	Degree
p̄	After	%	Percent
PO_2	Partial pressure of oxygen	π	3.1416 (ratio of circumference of a circle to its diameter)
PCO_2	Partial pressure of carbon dioxide	□, ♂	Male
		○, ♀	Female
s̄	Without	⇄	Denotes a reversible reaction
s̄s̄, ss	[L. semis]. One half	↑	Increase
μm	Micrometer	↓	Decrease
μ	Micron (former term for micrometer)		
μμ	Micromicron		
+	Plus; excess; acid reaction; positive		

SPECIAL SYMBOLS USED IN TABER'S

  Caution/Safety note

  Provided on Taber's*Plus*

APPENDIX 7
Units of Measurement (Including SI Units)

Appendix 7–1 Scientific Notation

Sometimes it is necessary to use very large and very small numbers. These can best be indicated and handled in calculations by use of scientific notation, which is to say by use of exponents. Use of scientific notation requires writing the number so that it is the result of multiplying some whole number power of 10 by a number between 1 and 10. Examples are:

$$1234 = 1.234 \times 10^3$$

$$0.01234 = 1.234 \times \frac{1}{100} = 1.234 \times 10^{-2}$$

$$0.001234 = 1.234 \times \frac{1}{1000} = 1.234 \times 10^{-3}$$

To convert a number to its equivalent in scientific notation:

Place the decimal point to the right of the first non-zero digit. This will now be a number between 1 and 9.

Multiply this number by a power of 10, the exponent of which is equal to the number of places the decimal point was moved. The exponent is positive if the decimal point was moved to the left, and negative if it was moved to the right. For example:

$$\frac{1,234,000.0 \times 0.000072}{6000.0} = \frac{1.234 \times 10^6 \times 7.2 \times 10^{-5}}{6.0 \times 10^3}$$

Now, by simply adding or subtracting the exponents of ten, and remembering that moving an exponent from the denominator of the fraction to the numerator changes its sign,

$$= \frac{1.234 \times 10^6 \times 10^{-5} \times 10^{-3} \times 7.2}{6} = \frac{1.234 \times 10^{-2} \times 7.2}{6}$$

Now, dividing by 6,

$$= 1.234 \times 10^{-2} \times 1.2 = 1.4808 \times 10^{-2} = \frac{1.4808}{100} = 0.014808$$

The last operation changed 1.4808×10^{-2} into the final value, 0.014808, which is not expressed in scientific notation.

Appendix 7–2 SI Units (Système International d'Unités or International System of Units)

This system includes two types of units important in clinical medicine. The *base units* are shown in the first table, derived units in the second table, and derived units with special names in the third table.

SI BASE UNITS

Quantity	Name	Symbol
Length	meter	m
Mass	kilogram	kg
Time	second	s
Electric current	ampere	A
Temperature	kelvin	K
Luminous intensity	candela	cd
Amount of a substance	mole	mol

SOME SI DERIVED UNITS

Quantity	Name of Derived Unit	Symbol
Area	square meter	m^2
Volume	cubic meter	m^3
Speed, velocity	meter per second	m/s
Acceleration	meter per second squared	m/s^2
Mass density	kilogram per cubic meter	kg/m^3
Concentration of a substance	mole per cubic meter	mol/m^3
Specific volume	cubic meter per kilogram	m^3/kg
Luminescence	candela per square meter	cd/m^2
Body mass index	kilogram per meter squared	kg/m^2

SI DERIVED UNITS WITH SPECIAL NAMES

Quantity	Name	Symbol	Expressed in Terms of Other Units
Frequency	hertz	Hz	s^{-1}
Force	newton	N	$kg \cdot m \cdot s^{-2}$ or $kg \cdot m/s^2$
Pressure	pascal	Pa	$N \cdot m^{-2}$ or N/m^2
Energy, work, amount of heat	joule	J	$kg \cdot m^2 \cdot s^{-2}$ or $N \cdot m$
Power	watt	W	$J \cdot s$ or J/s
Quantity of electricity	coulomb	C	$A \cdot s$
Electromotive force	volt	V	W/A
Capacitance	farad	F	C/V
Electrical resistance	ohm	Ω	V/a
Conductance	siemens	S	A/V
Inductance	henry	H	$W\phi/A$
Illuminance	lux	lx	ln/m^2
Absorbed (radiation) dose	gray	Gy	J/kg
Dose equivalent (radiation)	sievert	Sv	J/kg
Activity (radiation)	becquerel	Bq	s^{-1}

PREFIXES AND MULTIPLES USED IN SI

Prefix	Symbol	Power	Multiple or Portion of a Multiple
tera	T	10^{12}	1,000,000,000,000.
giga	G	10^9	1,000,000,000.
mega	M	10^6	1,000,000.
kilo	k	10^3	1,000.
hecto	h	10^2	100.
deca	da	10^1	10.
unity			1
deci	d	10^{-1}	0.1
centi	c	10^{-2}	0.01
milli	m	10^{-3}	0.001
micro	μ	10^{-6}	0.000001
nano	n	10^{-9}	0.000000001
pico	p	10^{-12}	0.000000000001
femto	f	10^{-15}	0.000000000000001
atto	a	10^{-18}	0.000000000000000001

Appendix 7–3 Metric System

MASSES

Mass		Grams
1 Kilogram	=	1000.0
1 Hectogram	=	100.0
1 Decagram (Dekagram)	=	10.0

Table continued on following page

MASSES (Continued)

Mass		Grams
1 gram	=	1.0
1 decigram	=	0.1
1 centigram	=	0.01
1 milligram	=	0.001
1 microgram	=	10^{-6}
1 nanogram	=	10^{-9}
1 picogram	=	10^{-12}
1 femtogram	=	10^{-15}
1 attogram	=	10^{-18}

Arabic numbers are used with masses and measures, as 10 g, or 3 ml. Portions of masses and measures are usually expressed decimally, e.g., 10^{-1} indicates 0.1; $10^{-6} = 0.000001$. Appendix 7–1: Scientific Notation Appendix.

Appendix 7–4 Weights and Measures

Arabic numerals are used with masses and measures, as 10 g, or 3 mL. Portions of masses and measures are usually expressed decimally. For practical purposes, 1 cm^3 (cubic centimeter) is equivalent to 1 mL (milliliter) and 1 drop (gtt.) of water is equivalent to a minim (m).

LENGTH

Millimeters (mm)	Centimeters (cm)	Inches (in)	Feet (ft)	Yards (yd)	Meters (m)
1.0	0.1	0.03937	0.00328	0.0011	0.001
10.0	1.0	0.3937	0.03281	0.0109	0.01
25.4	2.54	1.0	0.0833	0.0278	0.0254
304.8	30.48	12.0	1.0	0.333	0.3048
914.40	91.44	36.0	3.0	1.0	0.9144
1000.0	100.0	39.37	3.2808	1.0936	1.0

1 μm = 1 micrometer = 0.001 millimeter. 1 mm = 100 μm.
1 km = 1 kilometer = 1000 meters = 0.62137 statute mile.
1 statute mile = 5280 feet = 1.609 kilometers.
1 nautical mile = 6076.042 feet = 1852.276 meters.

VOLUME (FLUID)

Milliliters (mL)	Cubic Inches (in^3)	U.S. Fluid Quarts (qt)	Liters (L)
1.0	0.061	0.00106	0.001
3.697	0.226	0.00391	0.00369
16.3866	1.0	0.0173	0.01639
29.573	1.8047	0.03125	0.02957
946.332	57.75	1.0	0.9463
1000.0	61.025	1.0567	1.0

1 gallon = 4 quarts = 8 pints = 3.785 liters.
1 pint = 473.16 mL.

WEIGHT

Grains (gr)	Grams (g)	Apothecaries' Ounces (f℥)	Kilograms (kg)
1.0	0.0648	0.00208	0.000065
15.432	1.0	0.03215	0.001
480.0	31.1	1.0	0.0311
7000.0	453.5924	14.583	0.45359
15432.358	1000.0	32.15	1.0

1 microgram (μg) = 0.001 milligram.
1 mg = 1 milligram = 0.001 g; 1000 mg = 1 g.

CIRCULAR MEASURE

60 seconds = 1 minute   60 minutes = 1 degree
90 degrees = 1 quadrant   4 quadrants = 360 degrees = circle

LIQUID MEASURE

16 ounces = 1 pint	4 quarts = 1 gallon	1 quart = 946.35 milliliters
1000 milliliters = 1 liter	31.5 gallons = 1 barrel (U.S.)	1 liter = 1.0566 quart
4 gills = 1 pint	2 pints = 1 quart	

A U.S. gallon is equal to 0.8327 British gallon; therefore, a British gallon is equal to
1.201 U.S. gallons. 1 liter is equal to 1.0567 quarts.

LINEAR MEASURE

1 inch = 2.54 centimeters	40 rods = 1 furlong	8 furlongs = 1 statute mile
12 inches = 1 foot	3 feet = 1 yard	5.5 yards = 1 rod
1 statute mile =	3 statute miles =	1 nautical mile =
5280 feet	1 statute league	6076.042 feet

HOUSEHOLD MEASURES AND WEIGHTS*

Approximate Equivalents: 60 gtt. = 1 teaspoonful
= 5 ml = 60 minims = $\frac{1}{8}$ ounce

1 teaspoon = $\frac{1}{8}$ fl oz	16 teaspoons (liquid) = 1 cup
3 teaspoons = 1 tablespoon	12 tablespoons (dry) = 1 cup
1 tablespoon = $\frac{1}{2}$ fl oz	1 cup = 8 fl oz

1 tumbler or glass = 8 fl oz; $\frac{1}{2}$ pint

---

* Household measures are not precise. For instance, a household tsp will hold from 3 to 5 ml
of liquid. Therefore, household equivalents should not be substituted for medication prescribed by the physician.
NOTE: Traditionally, the word "weights" is used in these tables, but "masses" is the correct
term.

Appendix 7–5 **Conversion Rules and Factors**

To convert units of one system into the other, multiply the number of units in column
I by the equivalent factor opposite that unit in column II.

WEIGHT

1 gram	=	0.03527 avoirdupois ounce
1 gram	=	0.03215 apothecaries' ounce
1 kilogram	=	35.274 avoirdupois ounces
1 kilogram	=	32.151 apothecaries' ounces
1 kilogram	=	2.2046 avoirdupois pounds
1 grain	=	64.7989 milligrams
1 grain	=	0.0648 gram
1 avoirdupois ounce	=	28.3495 grams
1 apothecaries' ounce	=	31.1035 grams
1 avoirdupois pound	=	453.5924 grams

VOLUME (AIR OR GAS)

1 cubic centimeter (cm³)	=	0.06102 cubic inch
1 cubic meter (m³)	=	35.314 cubic feet
1 cubic meter	=	1.3079 cubic yard
1 cubic inch (in³)	=	16.3872 cubic centimeters
1 cubic foot (ft³)	=	0.02832 cubic meter

CAPACITY (FLUID OR LIQUID)

1 liter	=	2.1134 pints
1 liter	=	1.0567 quart
1 liter	=	0.2642 gallon
1 fluid dram	=	3.697 milliliters
1 fluid ounce	=	29.573 milliliters
1 pint	=	473.1765 milliliters
1 quart	=	946.353 milliliters
1 gallon	=	3.785 liters

TIME

1 millisecond = one thousandth (0.001) of a second   1 minute = 1/60 of an hour
1 second = 1/60 of a minute   1 hour = 1/24 of a day

TEMPERATURE

Given a temperature on the Fahrenheit scale, to convert it to degrees Celsius, subtract 32 and multiply by 5/9. Given a temperature on the Celsius scale, to convert it to degrees Fahrenheit, multiply by 9/5 and add 32. Degrees Celsius are equivalent to degrees Centigrade. SEE: *thermometer, Celsius* for table.

PRESSURE

TO OBTAIN	MULTIPLY	BY
lb/sq in	atmospheres	14.696
lb/sq in	in of water	0.03609
lb/sq in	ft of water	0.4335
lb/sq in	in of mercury	0.4912
lb/sq in	kg/sq meter	0.00142
lb/sq in	kg/sq cm	14.22
lb/sq in	cm of mercury	0.1934
lb/sq ft	atmospheres	2116.8
lb/sq ft	in of water	5.204
lb/sq ft	ft of water	62.48
lb/sq ft	in of mercury	70.727
lb/sq ft	cm of mercury	27.845
lb/sq ft	kg/sq meter	0.20482
lb/cu in	g/mL	0.03613
lb/cu ft	lb/cu in	1728.0
lb/cu ft	gm/mL	62.428
lb/U.S. gal	gm/L	8.345
in of water	in of mercury	13.60
in of water	cm of mercury	5.3543
ft of water	atmospheres	33.95
ft of water	lb/sq in	2.307
ft of water	kg/sq meter	0.00328
ft of water	in of mercury	1.133
ft of water	cm of mercury	0.4461
atmospheres	ft of water	0.02947
atmospheres	in of mercury	0.03342
atmospheres	kg/sq cm	0.9678
bars	atmospheres	1.0133
in of mercury	atmospheres	29.921
in of mercury	lb/sq in	2.036
mm of mercury	atmospheres	760.0
g/mL	lb/cu in	27.68
g/sq cm	kg/sq meter	0.1
kg/sq meter	lb/sq in	703.1
kg/sq meter	in of water	25.40
kg/sq meter	in of mercury	345.32
kg/sq meter	cm of mercury	135.95
kg/sq meter	atmospheres	10332.0
kg/sq cm	atmospheres	1.0332

FLOW RATE

TO OBTAIN	MULTIPLY	BY
cu ft/hr	cc/min	0.00212
cu ft/hr	L/min	2.12
L/min	cu ft/hr	0.472

PARTS PER MILLION

Conversion of parts per million (ppm) to percent:
1 ppm = 0.0001%, 10 ppm = 0.001%, 100 ppm = 0.01%, 1000 ppm = 0.1%,
10,000 ppm = 1%, etc.

ENERGY

1 foot pound = 1.35582 joule
1 joule = 0.2389 Calorie (kilocalorie)
1 Calorie (kilocalorie) = 1000 calories = 4184 joules
A large Calorie, or kilocalorie, is always written with a capital C.

pH

The pH scale is simply a series of numbers stating where a given solution would stand in a series of solutions arranged according to acidity or alkalinity. At one extreme (high pH) lies a highly alkaline solution; at the other extreme (low pH) is an acid solution containing 3.65 g of hydrogen chloride per liter of water. Halfway between lies purified water, which is neutral. All other solutions can be arranged on this scale, and their acidity or alkalinity can be stated by giving the numbers that indicate their relative positions. If the pH of a certain solution is 5.3, it falls between gastric juice and urine on the above scale, is moderately acid, and will turn litmus red.

Tenth-normal HCl	−1.00	⎫ Litmus is red in
Gastric juice	1.4	⎬ this acid range
Urine	* 6.0	⎭
Water	7.00	—Neutral
Blood	7.35–7.45	⎫ Litmus is blue in
Bile	* 7.5	⎪ this alkaline
Pancreatic juice	8.5	⎬ range.
Tenth-normal NaOH	13.00	⎭

* These body fluids vary rather widely in pH; typical figures have been used for simplicity. Urine samples obtained from healthy individuals may have pH readings anywhere between 4.7 and 8.0.

APPENDIX 8
Medical Emergencies

Appendix 8–1 Poisons and Poisoning

Substance	Pathology	Symptoms	Emergency Measures	Comments
Acetaminophen	Production of toxic intermediate metabolite that cannot be detoxified due to glutathione depletion.	Phase 1 (0–24 hr): Sometimes asymptomatic—anorexia, nausea, vomiting. Phase 2 (24–48 hr): GI symptoms resolve; hepatotoxicity is subclinical, but liver function tests and coagulation tests are abnormal. If liver damage is significant, patient may progress to phase 3. Phase 3 (48–96 hr): Problems due to severe hepatic compromise—bleeding disorders, hypoglycemia, hepatic encephalopathy. Phase 4 (>96 hr): Recovery period. Laboratory values return to normal and symptoms resolve.	Administer activated charcoal. Toxicity is unlikely at a dose <140 mg/kg. For significant serum levels of acetaminophen, acetylcysteine can be administered orally in a loading dose followed by a maintenance regimen.	Patients with toxic levels of acetaminophen 4 hr after ingestion require hospitalization for observation and supportive measures. Hepatic failure can occur several days after the ingestion, and renal complications or failure can also develop. Most patients recover fully without further sequelae. In some instances, hepatic failure may require transplantation. Check acetaminophen levels routinely in patients with any oral overdose.
Acids Acetic Hydrochloric Nitric Phosphoric Sulfuric Any other strong acid	Immediate destruction and necrosis with eschar formation of mucous membranes and tissues on contact.	Burning pain on contact with mucous membranes of the mouth and throat, dysphagia, abdominal pain, nausea, hematemesis, thirst, esophageal or gastric perforation, shock, death.	Establishment of airway patency, aggressive volume resuscitation, radiographic evaluation of damage, irrigation of exposed tissues. Surgical intervention may be required.	Permanent damage to the esophagus and stomach can result in chronic dysphagia and stricture formation.

Alkalis	Irreversible destruction and liquefactive tissue necrosis that penetrates beyond surface contact with alkali.	Immediate burning and blistering of tissue on contact; severe pain of mouth, esophagus, and chest; esophageal or gastric perforation; pancreatitis; hematemesis; shock; death.	Establishment of airway patency, aggressive volume resuscitation, radiographic evaluation of damage, irrigation of exposed tissues. Surgical intervention may be required.	Permanent damage to the esophagus and stomach can result in chronic dysphagia, stricture formation, and necrosis of tissue.
Ammonia and ammonium hydroxide	Tissue destruction due to alkaline injury on contact with mucous membranes. Degree of destruction depends on alkalinity of product and amount and length of exposure.	Burning of mouth and throat, chest pain, esophageal and gastric damage, hematemesis. Inhalation of gas can cause coughing, bronchospasm, and pulmonary edema.	Airway protection if needed, supplemental humidified oxygen and bronchodilators for inhalation exposures; moderate amounts of water or milk to dilute ingestion, analgesics for pain. Additional procedures may be required to assess extent of tissue injury.	Most significant damage is seen with intentional massive ingestions or occupational exposures to concentrated strengths of ammonia. Most accidental exposures to household strength products resolve without residual damage.
Amphetamines and amphetamine-like agents	Excessive stimulation of the CNS and of peripheral alpha and beta receptor sites.	Excitement, restlessness, tremors, hyperactive reflexes, nausea, vomiting, diarrhea, palpitations, arrhythmias, hypertension, hyperthermia, dehydration, mydriasis, agitation, seizures, coma, death.	Supportive care including airway maintenance and cardiac monitoring; administration of activated charcoal and a cathartic; cooling measures for hyperthermia; benzodiazepines for seizures; vasodilators and beta-adrenergic blockers.	Toxicity can occur with slightly higher than therapeutic doses. Tolerance can readily develop with repeated use.
Antidepressants: selective serotonin reuptake inhibitors (SSRI) Fluoxetine Paroxetine Sertraline Bupropion Fluvoxamine	CNS depression, excessive stimulation of serotonin receptors.	Serotonin syndrome: hypomania, confusion, myoclonus, diaphoresis, hyperreflexia, tremor, hyperthermia, agitation, restlessness, insomnia, nausea, vomiting, drowsiness, ataxia, seizures, coma.	Maintenance of airway, breathing, and circulation; oral administration of activated charcoal to adsorb ingested drug from the gastrointestinal tract. Cooling measures for febrile patients, e.g., those with serotonin excess.	SSRIs are less likely than tricyclic antidepressants to cause airway compromise, cardiac dysrhythmias, coma, ICU admission, or death. Drugs (such as alcohol or sedatives) that are coingested with SSRIs may pose additional health risks.

Poisons and Poisoning (Continued)

Substance	Pathology	Symptoms	Emergency Measures	Comments
Antidepressants: cyclic Amitriptyline Amoxapine Clomipramine Desipramine Doxepin Imipramine Nortriptyline Protriptyline	Toxic cardiovascular and CNS effects secondary to anticholinergic activity, inhibited reuptake of neurotransmitters, peripheral alpha-adrenergic blockade, alteration of cardiac cells resulting in conduction disturbances.	Confusion, dizziness, altered mental status (lethargy to coma), hypotension, tachycardia, hyperthermia, mydriasis, dry mucous membranes, prolonged QRS complex, cardiac dysrhythmias, seizures.	Cardiac monitoring; assessment of width of QRS complex on the 12-lead ECG; gastric decontamination with activated charcoal; alkalinization of the urine with bicarbonate-containing solutions.	Patients with wide QRS complexes (>0.12s) or cardiac dysrhythmias are monitored in the CCU or ICU.
Antihistamines: sedating (major classes) Alkylamines Ethanolamines Ethylenediamines Phenothiazines Piperazines	Excessive central and peripheral anticholinergic effects.	Lethargy, agitation, confusion, miosis, tachycardia, hyperthermia, decreased GI motility, hypotension, respiratory depression, ataxia, stupor, seizures, dysrhythmias, coma, circulatory collapse, death.	Maintenance of airway, breathing, circulation, and fluids for hypotension; gastric decontamination by activated charcoal. If patient is sedated, intubate the airway. Give IV physostigmine for anticholinergic toxicity, benzodiazepines for seizures.	Most ingestions are complex to manage because many antihistamines are commercially available in combination with various analgesics and decongestants. With early intervention, most overdoses have excellent outcomes without consequences.
Arsenic and arsenic salts	Disruption of enzymatic reactions that are essential for cellular metabolism; possible phosphate replacement or interaction with sulfhydryl groups.	Nausea, vomiting, hemorrhagic gastritis, severe watery diarrhea, dehydration, pulmonary edema, hypotension, delirium, encephalopathy, arrhythmias, convulsions, shock, death. Symptoms may have delayed onset.	Support of the patient's airway and breathing, and aggressive fluid replacement to support the circulation; activated charcoal or gastric lavage for larger ingestions, dimercaprol (BAL) 3–5 mg/kg IM every 4–6 hr for symptomatic patients.	Toxicity depends on the type of arsenic, amount involved, and route of exposure. Systemic toxicity can result from percutaneous absorption. Arsenic is a carcinogen.

Aspirin —SEE: *salicylates*

Agent	Mechanism	Signs and Symptoms	Treatment	Comments
Atropine and anticholinergic agents	Acetylcholine blockade at muscarinic receptor sites; affects exocrine glands and cardiac tissue.	Dry mouth and burning pain in throat, thirst, blurred vision, mydriasis, dry, hot, flushed skin, hyperpyrexia, tachycardia, palpitations, restlessness, excitement, confusion, convulsions, delirium; rarely, death.	Airway maintenance and ventilation assistance, gastric lavage, activated charcoal and cathartic, diazepam for sedation and control of convulsions, physostigmine 0.5–1 mg IV for life-threatening atropine toxicity, cooling measures for hyperthermia.	Classes of drugs that possess anticholinergic activity include antihistamines, antipsychotics, antispasmodics, cyclic antidepressants, and skeletal muscle relaxants. Atropine in ophthalmic preparations may be toxic to infants/young children. Severity of toxicity depends on the agent ingested.
Barbiturates Amobarbital Aprobarbital Butabarbital Mephobarbital Methohexital Pentobarbital Phenobarbital Secobarbital Talbutal Thiopental	Depressed neuronal activity of the brain, hypotension caused by depression of central sympathetic tone, inhibition of cardiac contractility.	Drowsiness, confusion, ataxia, vertigo, slurred speech, shallow respiration and pulse, headache, stupor, hypotension, areflexia, cyanosis, hypothermia, cardiovascular collapse, respiratory arrest, death.	Airway maintenance and ventilation assistance, treatment of hypotension, activated charcoal and cathartic, alkalinization of urine to enhance phenobarbital elimination, hemoperfusion for severe toxicity.	
Benzene Xylene Toluene	Irritation of mucous membranes and airway caused by agents and their metabolites, CNS depression, myocardial effects resulting in conduction disturbances.	Burning sensation of mouth and stomach, nausea, vomiting, chest pain, cough, headache, pneumonitis (if inhaled), vertigo, ataxia, confusion, stupor, ventricular dysrhythmias, convulsions, coma, respiratory failure, death.	Airway maintenance and ventilation assistance, activated charcoal and cathartic, therapy for arrhythmias and seizures. Gastric lavage within 30 min is useful for larger ingestions.	Chronic exposure can result in permanent renal damage, bone marrow suppression, and neuropsychological damage.

Poisons and Poisoning (Continued)

Substance	Pathology	Symptoms	Emergency Measures	Comments
Benzodiazepines Alprazolam Chlordiazepoxide Clonazepam Clorazepate Diazepam Estazolam Flurazepam Lorazepam Midazolam Oxazepam Prazepam Quazepam Temazepam Triazolam	Generalized CNS depressant effects caused by enhanced activity of gamma-aminobutyric acid, an inhibitory neurotransmitter.	Confusion, dizziness, somnolence, ataxia, hypotension, coma, respiratory depression, cardiovascular depression.	Airway maintenance and ventilation assistance, if necessary; administration of activated charcoal. For ingestions by patients with no history of chronic use, flumazenil (a benzodiazepine antagonist) can be administered as a specific antidote. Flumazenil should be avoided in chronic users – it may trigger seizures.	Generally considered safe, even in high doses. Fatalities are rare and usually due to coingestions with other CNS depressants.
Boric acid and borate salts	Exact mechanism of toxicity unknown.	Headache, nausea, vomiting (vomitus may be blue green), fever, oliguria or anuria, diarrhea, stomach pain, lethargy, restlessness, distinctive erythroderma, tremor, convulsions, renal and hepatic injury or failure, cyanosis, coma, shock with vascular collapse, death.	Airway maintenance and ventilatory assistance. Treat convulsions with benzodiazepines. Activated charcoal is not effective. Hemodialysis may sometimes be needed for large ingestions, e.g., more than 12 g.	Reports of toxicity from boric acid ingestions and exposures has declined in recent years due to decreased use as an irrigant and antiseptic agent.

Botulinum toxin	Potent neurotoxicity produced by *Clostridium botulinum*; prevents release of acetylcholine by irreversibly binding to cholinergic nerve terminals.	Nausea, vomiting, occasional diarrhea, dysphagia, diplopia, loss of visual acuity and pupillary reflexes, profuse sweating, rapid and weak pulse, death usually caused by respiratory failure. Symptoms may present up to a week after ingestion.	Airway maintenance and ventilatory assistance, as needed. Trivalent botulinum antitoxin may be administered in severe overdoses to bind free toxin, although its use often causes hypersensitivity reactions.	Even with excellent supportive care, recovery may take months to years. Common long-term sequelae include dysgeusia, dry mouth, dyspepsia, constipation, tachycardia, arthralgias, and fatigue. Botulinum antitoxin is available from the local health department.
Cadmium salts or fumes	Diverse multisystemic toxicities that are not clearly understood.	Nausea, vomiting, diarrhea, abdominal cramps, salivation, gastritis, headache, vertigo, exhaustion, collapse, acute renal failure, chemical pneumonitis with pulmonary edema on inhalation, death.	Gastric lavage and catharsis, with chelating agents such as EDTA, may be useful in some acute exposures. Inhalation may require ventilatory support.	Long-term effects vary with duration and severity of exposure. Renal function may be affected. Chronic exposures have resulted in osteomalacia, emphysema, and increased risk of lung or prostate cancer.
Calcium channel blockers Myocardial and vascular effects Bepridil Diltiazem Verapamil Primarily vascular effects Amlodipine Felodipine Isradipine Nicardipine Nifedipine	Prevention of calcium entry into cells, resulting in decreased myocardium contractility, blockade of AV and SA nodes, and peripheral vasodilation.	Nausea, vomiting, dizziness, headache, confusion, stupor, hyperglycemia, hypotension, bradycardia, metabolic acidosis, cardiac conduction disturbances, seizures, coma, death.	Maintenance of airway, breathing, and circulation; fluids and vasopressors for hypotension; multiple-dose activated charcoal; calcium chloride or calcium gluconate for hypotension and bradydysrhythmias, atropine or isoproterenol for bradycardia.	Intentional overdoses of calcium channel blockers are life threatening and often fatal despite aggressive management.

Poisons and Poisoning (Continued)

Substance	Pathology	Symptoms	Emergency Measures	Comments
Camphor	CNS stimulant with toxic effects; underlying mechanism is not known.	Burning of mouth and throat, nausea, vomiting, headache, CNS hyperactivity followed by CNS depression, vertigo, liver function abnormalities, delirium, tremor, convulsions, apnea, coma, death from respiratory arrest secondary to status epilepticus.	Airway maintenance, gastric lavage with copious amounts of fluid, activated charcoal and cathartic, benzodiazepines for seizures.	Fatalities have been reported with 1- or 2-g doses; however, most exposures can be effectively managed and resolved without residual complications.
Carbon monoxide	Hemoglobin binding preventing delivery of oxygen to cells; has significantly greater affinity for hemoglobin than oxygen.	Mild headache, dyspnea with moderate exertion, irritability, fatigue, nausea, vomiting, confusion, ataxia, syncope, convulsions, death from respiratory arrest.	100% oxygen by face mask or endotracheal tube, IV fluids, cardiac monitoring, hyperbaric oxygen for significant exposures.	Residual effects can include dementia, psychosis, paralysis, peripheral neuropathy, and parkinsonism. Consider CO toxicity in persons with significant smoke inhalation burns.
Carbon tetrachloride	Metabolites cause renal and hepatic toxicity; potent CNS depressant effects.	Nausea, vomiting, abdominal pain, headache, confusion, drowsiness, coma, renal and hepatic failure. Death is caused by respiratory arrest, circulatory collapse, or ventricular fibrillation.	Airway maintenance and ventilation assistance, gastric lavage, activated charcoal and cathartic, acetylcysteine to decrease effects of intermediate metabolite.	Toxicity from inhalation can be severe; small ingestions (<10 mL) can be fatal.
Chlorate salts	Potent oxidative properties that destroy red blood cells; toxicity to kidneys are due to direct effects and hemolysis.	Abdominal pain, nausea, vomiting, diarrhea, methemoglobinemia, intravascular hemolysis, delirium, coagulopathy, coma, convulsions, cyanosis, renal failure, death.	Activated charcoal and methylene blue for mild toxicities, hemodialysis to remove toxin. Sodium thiosulfate IV has been used to inactivate the chlorate ion, with inconsistent results.	In some instances, exchange transfusions have been advocated to reverse effects of poisoning.

Agent	Mechanism	Signs and Symptoms	Treatment	Comments
Chlorinated compounds Chlorine Chlorine gas Sodium hypochlorite	Corrosive effect on contact with mucous membranes.	Immediate burning of mouth and throat, coughing, choking, bronchospasm, chest and abdominal pain, stridor, pulmonary edema, esophageal burns.	For inhalation, humidified supplemental oxygen and bronchodilators; for dilute ingestions, water or milk; for concentrated ingestions, gastric lavage and endoscopic evaluation.	Esophageal damage can result in stricture formation.
Chlorinated hydrocarbon pesticides Aldrin Chlordane DDT (chlorophenothane) Dieldrin Heptachlor Lindane Thiodan Toxaphene	Direct toxicity to neuronal axons, interfering with transmission; affects myocardium stability resulting in arrhythmias.	Vomiting, headache, fatigue, tremors, ataxia, weakness, confusion, seizures, respiratory depression, arrhythmias, coma. In agents other than DDT, seizure may be first sign of toxicity.	Maintenance of airway, breathing, circulation; activated charcoal and cathartic; lavage for large ingestions; multiple-dose activated charcoal and cholestyramine to enhance removal; appropriate therapy for seizures and arrhythmias.	These agents can be absorbed transdermally and by inhalation. Toxicity and outcomes vary.
Cocaine	CNS stimulation and inhibition of neuronal uptake of catecholamines, depressed conduction, and myocardial contractility.	Anxiety, agitation, delirium, hypertension, tachycardia, hyperthermia, diaphoresis, tremor, mydriasis, flushing, seizures, ECG abnormalities, stroke, areflexia, coma, death.	Airway maintenance and ventilatory assistance, cardiac monitoring, activated charcoal for ingestion, benzodiazepines, cooling measures.	Overdose can result from inhalation, injection, or absorption of the drug from the gastrointestinal tract ("body packing").
Copper salts	Mucous membrane irritation, multisystemic toxicities with salts. Elemental copper is poorly absorbed and causes little toxicity.	Pain in mouth, esophagus, and stomach; abdominal pain; vomiting, gastroenteritis; shock; hepatic and renal injury; hemolysis; seizures; coma; death.	Fluid replacement and pressors, whole-bowel irrigation; dimercaprol and penicillamine for large ingestions.	Long-term copper exposures have resulted in liver fibrosis, cirrhosis, and renal dysfunction.

Poisons and Poisoning (Continued)

Substance	Pathology	Symptoms	Emergency Measures	Comments
Cyanide	Nonspecific inhibition of enzyme systems; binds to cytochrome oxidase of cells, blocking oxygen use.	Nausea, vomiting, abdominal pain, almond odor of breath, headache, dyspnea, agitation, confusion, syncope, convulsions, lethargy, coma, cardiovascular collapse, death. Onset of symptoms is abrupt.	Oxygen and assisted ventilation, if needed; gastric lavage, activated charcoal, and cathartic; inhalation of amyl nitrite pearls until antidote is available. Antidote kit contains amyl and sodium nitrites and sodium thiosulfate. The administration of vitamin B_{12} may be helpful.	Oxygen and assisted ventilation, if needed; activated charcoal by mouth. Antidotes include a vitamin B_{12} analogue, hydroxocobalamin.
Digoxin and digitalis	Excessive excitability and automaticity of myocardium resulting in conduction disturbances and dysrhythmias; AV block.	Anorexia, nausea, vomiting, diarrhea, headache, fatigue, weakness, drowsiness, electrolyte disturbances, confusion, delirium, visual disturbances, dysrhythmias, bradycardia, AV block, death from ventricular fibrillation.	Cardiac monitoring, activated charcoal, digoxin-specific antibody fragments (Fab) for severe toxicity, lidocaine or phenytoin for ventricular irritability. Correct electrolyte abnormalities, such as hypokalemia, immediately.	Most poisonings result from ingestion of prescribed digoxin, esp. in patients with renal failure, hypokalemia, or advanced age.
Dinitrophenol and pentachlorophenol	Uncoupling of oxidative phosphorylation in mitochondria, hypermetabolic state and lactic acid production. Dinitrophenol oxidizes hemoglobin to methemoglobin.	Fatigue, thirst, nausea, vomiting, abdominal pain, sweating, flushing, restlessness, excitement, hyperthermia, tachycardia, hyperpnea, metabolic acidosis, cyanosis, seizures, coma, death from respiratory or circulatory failure.	Maintenance of airway, breathing, circulation; activated charcoal by mouth; methylene blue IV; fluid replacement; benzodiazepines; cooling measures.	Ingestion of 1–3 g of these agents can be lethal. Many accidental transdermal poisonings have been reported.

Ergotamines or ergot alkaloids	Central sympatholytic effects: serotonin release and interference with neuronal uptake. Peripherally, may act as a partial alpha-adrenergic agonist or an antagonist at adrenergic, dopaminergic, and tryptaminergic receptors.	Nausea, vomiting, dizziness, diarrhea, headache, thirst, weak pulse, tingling and numbness of extremities, dyspnea, hallucinations, blood pressure changes, hemorrhagic vesiculations, paresthesias, peripheral ischemia, convulsions, loss of consciousness, gangrene.	Protect the airway, and provide ventilatory assistance as needed. Give multiple doses of activated charcoal to enhance drug elimination. Provide benzodiazepines to control seizures. Use nitroglycerin, heparin, or thrombolytics for organ ischemia.	Outcome is based on route and amount of ingestion.
Ethanol	CNS depression; effects can be additive when combined with other CNS depressants.	Impaired motor coordination, slurred speech, inebriation, ataxia, peripheral vasodilation, rapid pulse, nausea, vomiting, drowsiness, stupor, coma, hypotension, tachycardia, hypothermia, death from respiratory or circulatory failure.	Provide intravenous fluids, esp. with dextrose, to prevent hypoglycemia. Give parenteral thiamine. Provide other supportive measures, including airway control and ventilation, external warming, and prophylaxis against alcohol withdrawal symptoms as indicated.	Ethanol is often coingested with other toxic substances in suicide attempts; emergency treatment may vary depending on other substances ingested.
Ethylene glycol	Metabolism to oxalic, glyoxylic, and glycolic acids; conversion to lactate, increasing the lactic acid level; calcium oxalate crystal formation and deposition in tissues; metabolite toxicity to kidneys, CNS, and lungs.	Nausea, vomiting, excitability, hypotension, abdominal cramps, weakness, metabolic acidosis, ataxia, vertigo, arrhythmias, stupor, coma, death from respiratory or renal failure with uremia.	Maintain airway, breathing, and circulation. Provide ethanol, folic acid, 4-methylpyrazole, pyridoxine, and thiamine. Hemodialysis will remove ethylene glycol from the blood in cases of severe toxicity.	Outcomes vary; in general, comatose patients have a poor prognosis.
Fluoride salts	Direct metabolic and cytotoxic effects; multiple adverse effects from calcium and magnesium binding.	Salivation, thirst, nausea, abdominal pain, vomiting, diarrhea, muscle weakness, hypocalcemia, hyperkalemia, tetanic contractions, death due to vascular collapse and shock.	Maintenance of airway, breathing, circulation; cardiac monitoring; calcium salts; for severe toxicity, IV calcium chloride; therapy for electrolyte disturbances.	Degree of toxicity depends on salt solubility and the amount of elemental fluoride ingested. Pediatric toxicities are often caused by fluorinated toothpaste ingestions.

Poisons and Poisoning (Continued)

Substance	Pathology	Symptoms	Emergency Measures	Comments
Hydrogen sulfide gas	Inhibition of oxidative phosphorylation enzymes, potent inhibition of cytochrome oxidase. Exposure results in cellular hypoxia.	Irritated mucous membranes, conjunctivitis, headache, nausea, vomiting, weakness, bradycardia, hypotension, dyspnea, rapid loss of consciousness with larger exposure, pulmonary edema, cyanosis, convulsions, coma, death due to cardiac or respiratory arrest.	High-flow oxygen, advanced cardiac life support as indicated, sodium nitrite, blood pressure monitoring, hyperbaric oxygen if available. Methemoglobin level should be recorded 30 min after sodium nitrate infusion.	If patient is immediately removed from the exposure, recovery may be rapid and complete. More severe exposures have resulted in permanent neurological changes and myocardial ischemia.
Ipecac syrup or fluid extract	Cardiac and neuromuscular toxicity with systemic absorption; toxicities are seen with chronic and prolonged use.	Vomiting, diarrhea, lethargy, irritability, hypothermia, hypotonia, dehydration, gastritis, seizures, cardiac toxicity, neuromuscular toxicity, shock, death.	Activated charcoal may be given if the patient is not vomiting. Supportive care includes fluid replacement, correction of electrolyte abnormalities, cardiac monitoring, and therapy for dysrhythmias.	Chronic exposures are reported in patients with eating disorders; cases of toxicity secondary to Munchausen syndrome by proxy have also been documented.
Iron salts	Several mechanisms: direct corrosive effects on GI mucosa, hepatocellular toxicity, cardiovascular compromise, metabolic acidosis. Neurological manifestations are caused by hypoperfusion, metabolic acidosis, and hepatic compromise.	Nausea, vomiting, severe gastroenteritis, hematemesis, diarrhea, tachycardia, hypotension, lethargy, cyanosis, convulsions, coma, shock, or death.	Use gastric lavage or whole-bowel irrigation to remove tablets from the gastrointestinal tract. Intravenous deferoxamine is used as an iron-chelating agent.	Patients with systemic complications require hospital admission, constant monitoring, and supportive care until resolution. Late complications (2–8 wk) include GI stricture and obstruction. Toxicity is unlikely at a dose <20 mg/kg.

Isopropanol Isopropyl alcohol Rubbing alcohol	Potent CNS depressant metabolized to acetone; may contribute to CNS depression.	Nausea, vomiting, abdominal pain, hypotension, ataxia, areflexia, inebriation, muscle weakness, ketonemia, ketonuria, respiratory depression, hemorrhagic tracheobronchitis, myocardial depression, coma, death.	Maintain airway and provide ventilatory support when neurological depression is present. Do not induce emesis. Irrigate the GI tract after recent ingestions. Use hemodialysis for near-fatal overdoses.	A majority of cases resolve without consequences.
Lead and lead salts	Heavy metal interaction with sulfhydryl groups and interference with action of numerous enzymes, interference with heme production and survival of red blood cells. Chronic exposure can cause irreversible CNS and developmental effects.	Abdominal pain, vomiting, lethargy, behavioral changes, ataxia, arthralgias, abdominal or renal colic, anemia, acute encephalopathy, seizures, coma, death.	Use whole-bowel irrigation to empty the GI tract shortly after oral ingestions. Chelating agents that remove lead from the blood include Calcium Disodium Versenate, dimercaprol and related compounds, and D-penicillamine. Seizures are treated with benzodiazepines.	Chronic exposure to lead can produce renal and neuropsychiatric effects, esp. in children. Blood lead levels and erythrocyte protoporphyrin levels are used to gauge the effect of treatment.
Lithium	Lithium often produces cellular disturbances in the central nervous system, kidneys, and gastrointestinal tract. This is probably due to its effects on cell membrane ion transport, as well as its effects on cAMP.	Nausea, vomiting, diarrhea, fine resting tremor, lethargy, confusion, tremors, ataxia, ECG abnormalities, profound weakness, muscle fasciculations, hyperreflexia, clonus, stupor, seizures, acute renal failure, coma, death.	Maintain the airway and provide assisted ventilation to patients who are comatose or difficult to arouse. For acute ingestions use gastric lavage or whole bowel irrigation. Activated charcoal is ineffective because it does not bind to metals. Hemodialysis is used to clear lithium from the body in life-threatening intoxications.	Chronic or acute-on-chronic overdoses are more life threatening than acute poisonings. Chronic exposure permits intracellular accumulation. In acute poisonings, most lithium remains in the extracellular fluid for many hours, causing toxicity.

Poisons and Poisoning (Continued)

Substance	Pathology	Symptoms	Emergency Measures	Comments
Mercuric salts	Reaction with carboxyl, sulfhydryl, phosphoryl, and amide groups; interference with enzyme and cellular functions; toxicity involving multiple organ systems.	Burning of mouth and throat, thirst, abdominal pain, nausea, corrosive gastroenteritis, hematemesis, diarrhea, dehydration, shock, acute tubular necrosis. Neurological symptoms such as tremor, irritability and other personality changes, and depression are common.	The patient should be treated with oxygen and the gastrointestinal tract decontaminated, e.g., with whole-bowel irrigation). Chelating agents such as dimercaprol, dimercaptosuccinic acid, or D-penicillamine, should be given to bind and remove mercury from the body.	Doses of 1–4 g of mercuric chloride can be fatal. Chronic poisonings have resulted in neurological abnormalities, renal dysfunction, and gastrointestinal symptoms.
Methanol	Metabolism to formaldehyde and formic acid.	Latent period (24–72 hr) before development of symptoms, dizziness, inebriation, blurred vision, headache, nausea, vomiting, abdominal pain, delirium, visual disturbances that may progress to blindness, weak and rapid pulse, shallow respirations, cyanosis, coma, metabolic acidosis, respiratory failure, death.	Activated charcoal for recent ingestion, ethanol IV or orally to inhibit toxic metabolites, hemodialysis in severe cases, aggressive management of metabolic acidosis. Folic acid and 4-methylpyrazole can be used as antidotes.	Visual impairment, optic atrophy, and blindness are due to effects of formic acid on the optic nerve.
Mushrooms containing cyclopeptides *Amanita phalloides* (death cap) *Amanita tennifolia* *Amanita virosa* (destroying angels) *Galerina autumnalis* *Galerina marginata* *Galerina venenata* *Lepiota helveola* *Lepiota josserandii*	Cytotoxicity of cyclopeptides (phallotoxins, amatoxins, virotoxins), cellular insult causing hepatic, renal, GI, and CNS damage.	Phase 1 (6–12 hr): Nausea, abdominal pain, vomiting, watery diarrhea, thirst. Phase 2 (12–24 hr): Symptomatic improvement, elevated hepatic enzymes. Phase 3 (1–6 days): Restlessness, delirium, hallucinations, hematuria, gastroenteritis, pancreatitis, hypoglycemia, shock, acute renal failure, jaundice, hepatic coma, death.	Activated charcoal; fluid and electrolyte resuscitation; hepatic transplantation in fulminant hepatic failure.	Cyclopeptide-containing mushrooms are responsible for most mushroom fatalities in North America. Toxic cyclopeptides are heat stable, insoluble in water, and not affected by drying.

Mushrooms containing muscarine *Amanita muscaria* (fly agaric) *Amanita panterina* (panther) *Clitocybe dealbata* (sweater) *Clitocybe dilatata* *Clitocybe illudens* Most *Inocybe* species	Peripheral cholinergic effect due to muscarine; stimulation of autonomic nervous system.	Lacrimation, diaphoresis, salivation, abdominal cramps, vomiting, loss of bowel and bladder control	Gastric decontamination with activated charcoal may adsorb recently ingested mushroom toxins from the GI tract. Patients with fulminant hepatic failure will need intensive care and possible referral for liver transplantation.	Identification of ingested mushroom may help guide therapy if uneaten mushroom samples are available for analysis. Patients afflicted with fulminant liver failure have a high risk of death if a donor liver is not available.
Naphthalene	Metabolism to numerous by-products including alpha-napthol, a potent hemolytic agent.	Fever, nausea, vomiting, abdominal pain, diarrhea, lethargy, seizures, hemolysis, pallor, jaundice, cyanosis.	Activated charcoal; IV hydration and urinary alkalinization; transfusions for hemolysis.	Hemolysis is acute and severe in patients with glucose-6-phosphate dehydrogenase deficiency. Naphthalene is used in mothballs and toilet bowl cleaners, but less toxic agents are available.
Nicotine	Binding to cholinergic nicotine receptors; toxicity due to sympathetic and parasympathetic stimulation followed by ganglionic and neuromuscular blockade.	Nausea, vomiting, abdominal pain, headache, salivation, diarrhea, hyperpnea, diaphoresis, tachycardia, hypertension, pallor, agitation, tremor, ataxia, confusion, dysrhythmias, hypotension, shock, muscle paralysis, coma, death.	Maintenance of airway, breathing, circulation; activated charcoal; thorough washing of exposed skin; therapy for seizures, hypertension, hypotension, and arrhythmias.	Because most commercial sources of nicotine are not concentrated, a majority of exposures cause mild toxicity and resolve without complications.
Nitroglycerines, nitrates, nitrites	Vasodilation causing hypotension. Nitrites are potent oxidizing agents that cause methemoglobinemia.	Headache, hypotension, syncope, skin flushing, nausea, methemoglobinemia, cyanosis, symptoms of cardiac ischemia or cerebrovascular disease, seizures secondary to hypotension.	Activated charcoal; administration of intravenous fluids, anticonvulsant medication, hemodialysis, or therapies for GI bleeding (if needed).	Most cases can be managed successfully with early, aggressive interventions. Drugs for erectile dysfunction should not be taken by patients being treated with nitrates.

Poisons and Poisoning (Continued)

Substance	Pathology	Symptoms	Emergency Measures	Comments
Nonsteroidal anti-inflammatory agents Ibuprofen Ketoprofen Naproxen and many others	Inhibition of prostacyclin and prostaglandin E_2 production resulting in acute renal failure.	Nausea, vomiting, gastrointestinal distress and bleeding, tinnitus, metabolic acidosis, CNS depression, respiratory depression, mild hepatic toxicity, acute renal failure, seizures.	Activated charcoal for recent ingestions; intravenous fluids: administration of gastric protectants, e.g., proton pump inhibitors or H_2 receptor antagonists.	Baseline renal and hepatic function should be assessed. Most toxic exposures to this class of agents are successfully treated and resolve fully without residual sequelae.
Opioids and Opiates Codeine Dilaudid Fentanyl Heroin Morphine Methadone Oxycodone Oxycontin and other synthetic opioids	Excessive stimulation of CNS opiate receptors causing sedation and respiratory failure.	Drowsiness, nausea, dysphoria, bradypnea, miosis, hypothermia, respiratory depression, hypotension, bradycardia, weak pulse, coma, apnea, death.	The airway should be secured and ventilatory assistance provided to comatose or apneic patients. Naloxone, naltrexone, or nalmefene can be given as an antidote. Activated charcoal may adsorb recently ingested pills.	Antidotes are useful in reversing effects of the opiates, but administration may precipitate severe withdrawal symptoms. The effects of naloxone are short-term. The drug may need to be given repeatedly or by intravenous infusion to prevent repeated episodes of respiratory depression or coma.
Oxalic acid and oxalate salts	Corrosion of tissues on contact; precipitation with calcium to form insoluble deposits throughout organs, causing systemic damage.	Irritation of mouth and esophagus, vomiting, weakness, shock, tetany, convulsions, cardiac arrest, death. Inhalation can cause pneumonitis and pulmonary edema.	Calcium chloride, calcium gluconate, or calcium carbonate to precipitate oxalate; flushing and lavage with copious amounts of water; IV calcium chloride or calcium gluconate for symptomatic hypocalcemia; maintenance of high urine output; therapy for seizures and arrhythmias.	Ingestions of 5–15 g of oxalic acid have resulted in death.

Parathion and other organophosphates	Acetylcholinesterase inhibition, resulting in excessive acetylcholine stimulation of muscarinic and nicotinic receptors.	Nausea, vomiting, diarrhea, abdominal pain, tremor, muscle fasciculations, excessive salivation and sweating, dehydration, bradycardia, weakness, shock, death usually caused by respiratory paralysis.	Maintain airway and clear secretions. Provide assistance with ventilation. Decontaminate exposed skin and remove soaked clothing. Decontaminate the GI tract. Use atropine and/or pralidoxime for anticholinergic crises. Give diazepam or related drugs for seizures, and standard antiarrhythmic protocols for ventricular rhythm disturbances.	Toxicity depends on the relative toxicity of the organophosphate and the quantity involved.
Phenol	Corrosive injury to skin, eyes, and respiratory tract; protein denaturation and coagulation necrosis.	Vomiting, diarrhea, gastrointestinal injury, agitation, confusion, seizures, hypotension, shock, coma, respiratory failure, death.	Multiple-dose activated charcoal and cathartic; washing of exposed areas; benzodiazepines for seizures. Low molecular weight polyethylene glycol has been used for gastric decontamination and topical exposures. If corrosion has occurred, tube passage may cause rupture.	Corrosive burns of the skin and mucous membranes and GI perforation can occur. Esophageal stricture and renal failure rarely occur.
Phenothiazines and neuroleptics	Prominent cardiovascular and CNS effects; toxicity due to inhibitory effects of dopaminergic, cholinergic, alpha-adrenergic, histaminic, and serotonergic receptors.	Sedation, somnolence, stupor, dry mouth, tachycardia, labile blood pressure, hypothermia or hyperthermia, dysrhythmias, extrapyramidal symptoms, coma, NMS, seizures, cardiac arrest, death, akathisias.	Maintain airway and provide ventilatory and circulatory support if necessary. Decontaminate the GI tract. Follow standard ACLS protocols for managing cardiac rhythm disturbances. Give diphenhydramine or benztropine for dystonias. Bromocriptine, benzodiazepines, and/or dantrolene may be helpful in NMS.	Although death from neuroleptic overdose is rare, NMS may be fatal in 20% or more of affected patients.

Poisons and Poisoning (Continued)

Substance	Pathology	Symptoms	Emergency Measures	Comments
Phosphorus and phosphides	Local irritation and tissue burns; direct toxic effect to myocardium and vessels; hepatic, renal, and GI damage due to latent systemic toxicity.	Painful burns to mucous membranes and skin on contact, nausea, vomitus and diarrhea with garlicky odor, jaundice, metabolic derangements, dysrhythmias, coma, shock, seizures, hepatic or renal failure, cardiac arrest. Inhalation can cause pneumonitis and pulmonary edema.	Maintenance of airway, breathing, circulation; endoscopy to assess GI burns; cautious gastric lavage with hydrogen peroxide or potassium permanganate, followed by activated charcoal and mineral oil cathartic; fluid replacement and correction of electrolyte imbalance.	After acute effects from ingestion, a symptom-free period of a few weeks may be followed by a stage of systemic toxicity involving the liver, kidneys, heart, CNS, and GI tract.
Salicylates Aspirin Salicylate salts	Effect on multiple organ systems, uncoupling of oxidative phosphorylation, and interference with the Krebs cycle. Effects are due to stimulation of respiratory center, intracellular uncoupling of oxidative phosphorylation, and alteration of platelet function.	Nausea, vomiting, agitation, hyperthermia, lethargy, hyperglycemia or hypoglycemia, hyperpnea, tachypnea, tinnitus, hemorrhagic gastritis, delirium, stupor, acid-base disturbances, electrolyte imbalance, cerebral edema, convulsions, cardiovascular collapse.	Maintenance of airway, breathing, circulation; lavage; activated charcoal; urinary alkalinization; correction of acid-base and fluid-electrolyte abnormalities; hemodialysis for severe toxicity or deteriorating condition.	The prognosis of patients suffering from an acute toxic ingestion can be assessed on the basis of serum levels obtained within 6 hr of ingestion.
Strychnine	Competitive antagonism of glycine at postsynaptic spinal cord motor neuron.	Muscle twitching, extensor spasm, opisthotonos, trismus or facial grimacing, seizures, medullary paralysis, death. Symptoms occur within 20 min.	Activated charcoal; dark and quiet environment; benzodiazepines or neuromuscular blockade; mechanical ventilation.	Poisonings are rare since commercial use in rodenticides has decreased. Most exposures result in death. The approximate fatal dose for a child is 15 mg; for an adult, 5–10 mg/kg.

	Mechanism	Clinical features	Treatment
Thallium salts	Combination with mitochondrial sulfhydryl groups, interference with oxidative phosphorylation.	Nausea, vomiting, abdominal pain, hematemesis, bloody diarrhea, headache, alopecia, hematuria, proteinuria, elevated hepatic enzymes, lethargy, tremors, ataxia, delirium, seizures, coma, death.	Activated charcoal; fluids and electrolytes intravenously; benzodiazepines for seizures. Hemoperfusion and hemodialysis may be moderately successful. Alopecia and Mee's sign, single white transverse lines on the nails 2–3 weeks postexposure, are common diagnostic features. Longterm neurological impairment can occur.
Theophylline —SEE: *xanthine derivatives*			
Xanthine derivatives Aminophylline Caffeine Theophylline	Antagonism of adenosine activity and release of catecholamines; in high doses, phosphodiesterase inhibition. Toxic effects are secondary to smooth muscle relaxation, peripheral vasodilation, myocardial stimulation, and CNS excitation.	Nausea, protracted vomiting, hypotension, respiratory alkalosis, metabolic acidosis, hypokalemia, tachycardia, hypercalcemia, ventricular dysrhythmias, seizures, death due to cardiovascular collapse.	Activated charcoal. For deteriorating conditions, charcoal hemoperfusion. Treat seizures with benzodiazepines or barbiturates, and cardiac rhythm disturbances with standard ACLS protocols. Monitor theophylline levels several times a day. Eliminate drugs that increase theophylline levels, such as erythromycins or related antibiotics, cimetidine, estrogens, or allopurinol. Consider the use of safer drugs, such as levalbuterol or other inhaled medications.
Warfarin and related anticoagulant compounds	Inhibition of vitamin K 2,3-epoxide reductase and quinone reductase activity (these are necessary to activate vitamin K, which is essential in coagulation).	Fatigue, hematuria, nosebleeds, ecchymoses, GI hemorrhage, hypotension, intracranial hemorrhage, hemorrhagic shock, death (rare).	Decontaminate the GI tract (for recent ingestions only). Hold warfarin if the protime is slightly elevated and no bleeding is present. Give vitamin K for markedly prolonged protimes with INR greater than 6–9 or fresh frozen plasma for life-threatening bleeding. Most accidental ingestions resolve without further sequelae. Intentional ingestions or delay in seeking treatment may result in severe coagulopathy. Bleeding patients require hospitalization, frequent monitoring of blood pressure, pulse, hemoglobin levels and the prothrombin time/INR. Cauterization of bleeding lesions may be needed.

AV = atrioventricular; BAL = British anti-lewisite; CNS = central nervous system; ECG = electrocardiogram; EDTA = ethylenediaminetetra-acetic acid; GI = gastrointestinal; NMS = neuroleptic malignant syndrome; PT = prothrombin time; SA = sinoatrial.

Appendix 8-2 Emergency Situations

Medical Emergency	Underlying Causes	Findings	Treatment
Acute myocardial infarction (MI, AMI) Acute coronary syndromes (ACS)	Most heart attacks are caused by the rupture of a plaque in the wall of the coronary artery that results in the blockage of blood flow and the death of myocardial tissue. Risk factors often present include tobacco use, hypertension, hypercholesterolemia, diabetes mellitus, obesity, physical inactivity, or family history of heart disease. Men and postmenopausal women are at greater risk than premenopausal women. Modification of risk factors lowers the risk for disease.	Patients often complain of tightness, heaviness, pressure, pain, or burning in the chest. The symptoms may radiate into the neck, jaw, shoulders, back, or arms. Shortness of breath, nausea and vomiting, or sweating often accompany the chest pain or pressure. Some patients (esp. older individuals, women, or diabetics) may report difficulty breathing, nausea and vomiting, or loss of consciousness as their only symptoms. A 12-lead ECG may show evidence of an MI, although a large percentage of patients may have a nondiagnostic ECG initially. Abnormal levels of cardiac enzymes, e.g., troponins, creatinine kinase, usually appear in the blood about 8 hr after chest pain begins.	Supplemental oxygen, aspirin, other antiplatelet drugs, anticoagulants, beta blockers, and narcotics like morphine should be used acutely to alleviate pain, improve oxygenation and blood flow, and reduce stress. Cardiac monitoring, oximetry, and automatic blood pressure monitors are used to identify changes in heart rhythm, hemodynamics, and breathing. A 12-lead ECG should be completed within 10 min of the patient's presentation to the hospital, and preferably while the patient is in transit to the hospital. If an ST segment elevation MI is identified, patients should be triaged to percutaneous coronary intervention (PCI) in the first 90 min or, if PCI is not available, to fibrinolytic therapy within 30 min (unless contraindicated). Other treatments depend on the presentation, e.g., the patient in shock may be treated with pressors; a patient with acute pulmonary edema may need diuretics, etc. Nonsteroidal anti-inflammatory drugs (esp. those that are COX-2 selective) should be discontinued. The patient in full cardiac arrest is treated with advanced life support protocols.

Airway obstruction	Complete or partial obstruction of the oropharynx or nasopharynx, larynx, or trachea, with impairment of gas exchange, caused by foreign bodies, anatomical abnormalities, allergic reactions, infection, or trauma.	Signs of respiratory distress, including a rapid respiratory rate, wheezing, stridor, or labored breath are usually present. The patient usually appears agitated. Cyanosis of the fingers or lips may be present when there is inadequate oxygen in the blood. Loss of consciousness may occur if airway obstruction is not effectively relieved.	Foreign body airway obstruction is treated using the Heimlich maneuver in adults and back blows and chest thrusts in infants and children. Endotracheal intubation or cricothyroidotomy, along with mechanical ventilation, may be life-saving interventions.
Angina pectoris	Inadequate supply of oxygen to the myocardium when oxygen demand exceeds supply. Unstable angina, marked by more frequent attacks, pain with less exertion or at rest, reduced response to nitroglycerin, or more severe episodes may indicate a progression in the patient's coronary artery disease and a higher risk for MI. Stable angina is discomfort typical of the patient's usual pattern.	Similar to MI. Chest discomfort typically resolves in less than 15 min, and improves with nitroglycerin and rest. There may be evidence of ischemia on a 12-lead ECG. Cardiac enzymes usually do not show evidence of acute MI on initial testing.	Oxygen, nitroglycerin, and aspirin are given initially, and the patient's response is noted. Beta blockers, to slow heart rate and lower blood pressure, are used unless there is evidence of heart block, heart failure, or active wheezing. Morphine is used for refractory pain and breathlessness. Heparins are used for pain that does not resolve with initial treatments. Persistent symptoms, ECG changes, or elevated cardiac enzymes suggest an acute coronary syndrome and may require further treatments (see above under Acute Myocardial Infarction). The patient with new or unstable angina is usually admitted to the hospital for further studies and stabilization.

Emergency Situations (Continued)

Medical Emergency	Underlying Causes	Findings	Treatment
Arterial bleeding	Trauma to blood vessels; surgery; erosion of arteries by ulcers, infection, or cancer.	Blood that spurts out in pulsatile fashion from a vessel is characteristic of bleeding from an artery. (Blood that oozes from a vessel continuously is characteristic of bleeding from a vein.)	Arterial bleeding from a vessel in an arm or leg can often be controlled with pressure applied directly over the bleeding vessel or just proximal to it. Arterial ligation may be performed surgically if direct pressure does not limit blood loss. Arterial bleeding from peptic ulcers is typically controlled with the injection of sclerosing agents during endoscopy or with electrocoagulation or coaptation. Bleeding from other internal vessels may also be controlled endoscopically, e.g., bleeding from bronchial arteries during bronchoscopy. In some instances, blood flow through internal arteries can be stopped with therapeutic embolization.
Asthma	Episodic bronchospasm, caused by exposure to allergens (such as pollens), smoke, pollutants, cold air, exercise, or other triggers of airway inflammation.	Difficulty breathing, wheezing, and chest tightness. Patients are often able to identify the triggering event. They may report that their inhalers are not providing adequate relief. Physical findings include tachypnea, tachycardia, and labored breathing, often with a prolonged expiratory phase and wheezing. Cyanosis of the fingers or the lips suggests inadequate oxygenation. Patients may be agitated, frightened, or, in severe attacks, lethargic or comatose.	Supplemental oxygen should be supplied, and the patient should be given inhaled bronchodilators, e.g. beta-2-agonists, such as albuterol. Oral or intravenous steroids are used to reduce airway inflammation. Epinephrine may be injected subcutaneously in severe asthma; antibiotics are used when there is evidence or suspicion of a bacterial infection. Helium-oxygen mixtures may be given for the patient to inhale. Severe asthma may result in respiratory failure and the need for ventilatory support, e.g., noninvasive ventilation or tracheal intubation.

Chronic Obstructive Pulmonary Disease (COPD), exacerbation of	An acute or gradual worsening of pulmonary function in patients with chronic lung disease, typically brought on by a viral or bacterial infection, or by congestive heart failure, allergies, pulmonary emboli, or the rupture of an emphysematous bleb at the margins of the lung.	Patients typically report increased shortness of breath, cough, sputum production, and fevers, and appear to labor more than usual to breathe. Tachypnea, tachycardia, and hypoxemia or carbon dioxide retention are often present. Breath sounds may be distant, or wheezing may be present.	Oxygen is supplied, and the patient is carefully monitored clinically. Continuous oximetry should be used, and arterial blood gases checked when there is clinical suspicion of impending respiratory failure. Bronchodilators (such as albuterol and ipratropium) are given by inhalation. Corticosteroids are used to reduce airway inflammation. Antibiotics are used when there is evidence or suspicion of a bacterial infection. Severe exacerbations may result in respiratory failure and the need for ventilatory support, e.g., noninvasive ventilation or tracheal intubation.
Cold-induced soft tissue injury (frostnip, chilblain, frostbite)	*Frostnip:* superficial, reversible injury caused by ice crystal formation on the surface of the skin. *Chilblain:* superficial injury caused by exposure to cold, humid air. Tissue does not freeze. *Frostbite:* destruction of tissue by freezing. The extent of tissue loss reflects the duration of cold exposure and the magnitude of temperature depression.	*Frostnip:* usually, paresthesias, pain, and numbness. *Chilblain:* redness, itching, numbness, burning, and pain. *Frostbite:* similar to chilblain. Frostbitten skin may be waxy and white or mottled and cyanotic. The frozen part will have no sensation. Surrounding tissue may be painful and tender. As the tissue thaws its appearance changes. In partial-thickness frostbite the skin becomes red and warm. Blisters containing clear fluid may appear. In full-thickness frostbite the blisters contain a bloody fluid. There is no sensation in full-thickness frostbite.	Initial treatment involves removing the patient from the cold environment. Concomitant hypothermia is a hazard. The frozen parts should not be rewarmed if there is danger of refreezing. Rapid rewarming should be performed by soaking the injured part in warm water (42°C). Rubbing or other manipulation of frozen tissue may worsen the injury. Further treatment may be needed for more serious injuries.

Emergency Situations (Continued)

Medical Emergency	Underlying Causes	Findings	Treatment
Congestive heart failure (CHF)	An impairment in the ability of the heart to move blood into the systemic circulation, either because of damage to heart muscle, e.g., after a heart attack, failure of the heart muscle to relax properly, pericardial restriction, valvular heart disease, or other causes.	Most patients are winded with exertion, and some are short of breath at rest. Many cannot lie flat in bed at night because the supine position makes them breathless. Lower extremity and sacral swelling are common physical findings, along with ascites, liver enlargement, and elevated jugular veins. Crackles or wheezes may be heard in the lung bases or throughout the lungs in left ventricular CHF. The patient is often hypoxemic. Chest x-rays may show an enlarged heart with fluffy infiltrates near the hila.	Oxygen, potent diuretics, morphine sulfate, nitroglycerin, nesiritide, and ACE inhibitors may be used to manage CHF or acute pulmonary edema as long as the patient is not hypotensive. Noninvasive positive pressure ventilation, or intubation and mechanical ventilation may be needed to support respiration. Hypotensive patients may be treated with dobutamine, combinations of dopamine and nitroprusside, or other drugs and interventions.
Fractures and Dislocations	Most fractures and dislocations are caused by significant trauma, e.g., automobile collisions, falls, or sports injuries. Fractures that occur without a powerful mechanism of injury are termed "pathological." They may occur in patients with underlying malignancies that have spread to bone or in patients with osteoporosis.	Limb fractures or joint dislocations are often clinically obvious. The affected limbs are usually swollen, visibly deformed or rotated, and exquisitely painful to gentle touch or any movement. Patients with rib fractures may complain of pain on breathing or coughing. The injured chest wall is tender and may be bruised. Patients with fractures of the vertebral bodies (or patients suspected of having vertebral fractures) often complain of neck, thoracic, or lumbar pain after a fall or automobile accident. X-rays of the affected bones confirm the diagnosis.	Primary treatment includes immobilization (splinting) of any affected bones or joints until diagnostic x-rays can be obtained. Analgesics are given as required, and cold packs or ice are applied to limit pain and inflammation. Limb fractures or dislocations are sometimes amenable to immediate treatment with closed reduction, although operative reductions and placement of fasteners may be needed to obtain optimal healing. Patients suspected of having vertebral fractures should be placed in firm cervical collars or restrained on spinal boards until examination and x-rays clearly demonstrate that the spine is stable.

Gastrointestinal (GI) bleeding	Upper gastrointestinal bleeding often results from esophagitis, esophageal tears, gastritis, peptic ulcer disease, esophageal varices, or vascular malformations. Lower GI bleeding typically is caused by hemorrhoids, anal fissures, diverticula, vascular malformations, or cancers.	The rapidly bleeding patient may present in shock, i.e., dizzy on arising, hypotensive, tachycardic, cool, clammy, diaphoretic, and confused. Bleeding from the upper GI tract often reveals itself when the patient vomits bright red blood or digested blood that resembles coffee grounds. Occasionally, bleeding from the upper GI tract is so vigorous that it causes the loss of bright red blood from the rectum. Usually, however, this is a finding in lower GI bleeding. Digested blood that is expelled in the feces is typically black and tarry (melenic).	Patients with significant blood loss are treated immediately with intravenous fluids. Blood is obtained for typing and cross-matching, and transfusions are given when indicated. Upper GI bleeding resulting from peptic ulcer disease, esophagitis, or gastritis may respond to treatment with IV or oral proton pump inhibitors. The loss of bright red blood from the upper GI tract should be promptly evaluated with esophagogastroduodenoscopy (EGD). Patients with a bleeding ulcer vessel or esophageal varices may be treated with endoscopic therapies to cauterize or band bleeding vessels or with medical therapies including agents such as octreotide. Patients suspected of having lower GI blood loss are evaluated with colonoscopy, e.g., to identify arteriovenous malformations, cancers, diverticula, or ulcerative colitis.
Hyperglycemia	Elevated blood glucose levels are usually caused by impairments in glucose metabolism (type 1 or type 2 diabetes mellitus, gestational diabetes mellitus, or drugs or infections that temporarily predispose patients to high blood glucose levels). In diabetics sudden elevations of blood glucose are typically caused by failure to maintain a careful dietary and medical regimen, taking medications such as corticosteroids, or serious illnesses, e.g., infections, heart attack, stroke.	Patients often report thirst, frequent urination, increased appetite, and increased consumption of fluids. Those who become dehydrated may be dizzy when they get up from a bed or chair. Blood chemistries typically reveal a blood glucose of more than 200 mg/dl, and glucose is present in the urine.	Fluids are administered by mouth (if possible) and intravenously. Insulin or oral hypoglycemic agents are given.

Emergency Situations (Continued)

Medical Emergency	Underlying Causes	Findings	Treatment
Hyperthermia (heat cramps, heat exhaustion, heatstroke)	Inability of the body to cope with heat stress resulting from excessive heat production or decreased heat loss. *Heat cramps:* muscle cramps and fatigue accompanied by water and mild salt depletion. *Heat exhaustion:* serious dehydration with water and electrolyte depletion. Patients maintain thermoregulatory control. Heat exhaustion may progress to *heatstroke*, characterized by thermoregulatory failure and profound dehydration.	The person with heat cramps complains of painful muscle spasms. There is a history of recent exertion in a hot environment. The patient has been sweating profusely with inadequate or hypotonic fluid replacement. The patient with heat exhaustion has also been sweating in a hot environment. Symptoms include thirst, weakness, fatigue, vomiting, and anorexia. The skin is cool and clammy. Body temperature may be normal or subnormal. The heatstroke victim will have an altered mental status and will be tachycardic, hypotensive, hyperthermic, and tachypneic. Signs of dehydration will be present.	First aid begins with removal of the patient from the hot environment. Heat cramp victims are treated with an oral or intravenous fluid and electrolyte solution. Heat exhaustion is treated by intravenous fluids. Patients with severe dehydration may require more than 4 L of IV fluid. Patients with heatstroke require rapid cooling. Many techniques are available, but evaporation with water is practical and effective. The patient may be sprayed with water and fanned until the core temperature is about 38.5°C. Cooling beyond this may cause overshoot hypothermia. IV fluid resuscitation as for heat exhaustion is also needed.
Hypoglycemia	The most frequent causes are an excessive dose of insulin or an oral hypoglycemic agent, or inadequate food intake by a diabetic patient treated with those drugs, e.g., during an illness that causes anorexia, nausea, or vomiting. Low blood sugars deprive the brain and other organs of the glucose they need for normal metabolism.	Mental status may vary from confused to agitated to unconscious. The patient is often sweaty, tremulous, and tachycardic. Occasionally, hypoglycemia may mimic strokes or seizures.	Mild hypoglycemia usually responds to a snack. Glucose or dextrose should be given immediately—intravenously if the patient is unable to safely eat, orally if the patient is conscious and sufficiently oriented. One mg of glucagon, administered by intramuscular injection, is an alternative. Blood sugar levels should be tested with a glucometer. Hospitalization may be necessary if the patient has taken an overdose of long-acting insulin or an oral antihyperglycemic agent.

Hypothermia

Core temperature less than 35°C (95°F), caused by decreased heat production, increased heat loss, or impaired temperature regulation. Exposure to cold or wet conditions, sepsis, or profound hypothyroidism may be predisposing conditions. Central nervous system, cardiovascular, and respiratory systems are impaired when the temperature is below 35°C.

Lethargy, confusion, and fatigue in mild cases. Heart rate and respiratory rate may be increased. As hypothermia worsens, the patient stops shivering. Heart rate, blood pressure, and respirations slow. The patient eventually loses consciousness. Respirations and pulses may be difficult to detect.

Cold or wet clothing should be removed. The patient should be rewarmed. Warm blankets, warm oxygen, and warm IV fluids may be used. An accurate core temperature must be recorded, if possible. Temperatures less than 32°C may require more aggressive rewarming techniques, such as gastric lavage, peritoneal lavage, hemodialysis, or cardiopulmonary bypass. If pulses are absent, cardiopulmonary resuscitation is indicated.

Seizure

An abnormal electrical discharge by central nervous system neurons that produces autonomic, behavioral, motor, or sensory abnormalities. Seizures may result from structural diseases of the brain, e.g., arteriovenous malformations, strokes, trauma, or tumors, from metabolic disorders, e.g., severe electrolyte disorders, low blood sugars, renal failure, or hypoxia, or from drugs (or drug or alcohol withdrawal).

During a generalized motor seizure, the patient is unconscious and has repetitive back-and-forth movements of the upper and lower extremities. Patients may bite the tongue, lose control of the bowels or bladder, or injure themselves when they fall. After the seizure, there is usually a period of gradual and progressive return to normal consciousness, which may take 30 to 60 min. Some patients may have a brief period of focal paralysis after the event.

During the seizure, the patient should be guarded against injury. This may involve helping the patient to the floor and moving furniture out of the way. Supplemental oxygen should be given. Objects should not be inserted into the patient's mouth—an obstructed airway may result. Medications such as lorazepam, diazepam, fosphenytoin, or phenobarbital may be used to abort the seizure. Most seizure patients will require some investigation into the cause of the seizure. In patients with a history of prior seizures, this may include checking blood levels of anticonvulsant medications. Patients with first-time seizures may need a more extensive evaluation, including a CT scan, an EEG, MRI, blood work, and a lumbar puncture.

Emergency Situations (Continued)

Medical Emergency	Underlying Causes	Findings	Treatment
Stroke (cerebrovascular accident)	Inadequate blood flow to an area of the brain causing tissue death. In thrombotic stroke, blood vessels narrowed by atherosclerosis limit delivery of oxygenated blood to the brain or a portion of it. In embolic stroke, clots travel from other areas of the body to block cerebral vessels. Hemorrhagic stroke results from bleeding caused by hypertension or rupture of cerebral aneurysms.	Patients often present with weakness or numbness on one side of the body or the face; with speech disturbances; or with confusion, clumsiness, difficulty walking, loss of consciousness, or coma.	Oxygen is administered and cardiac monitoring is begun. A computed tomographic (CT) scan of the brain is used to rule out a hemorrhage as a cause of new neurological deficits. Tissue plasminogen activator (a thrombolytic, or "clot-busting" drug) may be given to patients who present in the first 4.5 hr of nonhemorrhagic stroke.
Suicidal ideation	Major depression; alcohol abuse; dysphoria; adjustment disorders; borderline personality disorders; psychotic disorders; poor social situations and recent stressful events. Older men living alone are most likely to use lethal means to harm or kill themselves. Younger persons are most likely to come to an emergency department in distress.	Patients may report feelings of hopelessness, misery, anxiety or tension, or may feel that life has lost its meaning or joy. People who have taken medications in an attempt to overdose may have signs and symptoms related to the ingested drug(s) and may need inpatient stabilization. Consult Appendix 9–1.	Hospitalization is indicated for patients who are intoxicated by drug or alcohol overdose or who have a concrete plan to take their own lives. Outpatient therapy may be appropriate for people without the means to use potentially lethal drugs or devices to jeopardize their health and safety. Antidepressant medications, counseling, alcohol and drug rehabilitation, therapies, and psychiatric consultation are used individually or in combination for selected suicidal patients.

| Thermal burns | First- and second-degree burns: partial-thickness injuries involving only the epidermis or the epidermis and dermis. *Third-degree burns:* full-thickness injuries involving the deeper tissues. Burns impair the skin's ability to prevent heat and water loss. Burned skin is not an effective barrier to injection. Severity depends on the character and temperature of the agent, the duration of exposure, and the type of skin injured. | *First-degree burns:* red and painful. *Second-degree burns:* red, painful, and blistered. These burns heal without scarring. *Third-degree burns:* may be white or charred. The subcutaneous nerves have been destroyed; thus there is no pain. Surrounding areas are painful. Full-thickness burns heal poorly, leaving a scar. | The first step is to stop the burning process. Oxygen should be administered if there has been smoke inhalation. Jewelry and clothing should be removed in anticipation of swelling. Sterile sheets or dressings should be applied to the burned areas. |
| Transient ischemic attack (TIA) | See *Stroke* . | Symptoms and signs are similar to those of a stroke, but usually last less than 1 or 2 hr. | Patients with TIAs are treated with antiplatelet therapies, such as aspirin or clopidogrel, and are evaluated with electrocardiographic monitoring, e.g., to rule out atrial fibrillation, CT scans of the head (to rule out small strokes), and carotid ultrasonography (to determine whether the patient has a surgically correctable stenosis of the carotid arteries). |

APPENDIX 9
Standard Precautions

Appendix 9–1 Healthcare-Associated Infections

INTRODUCTION

Healthcare-associated infections (HAI) are infections caused by a wide variety of common and unusual bacteria, fungi, and viruses during the course of receiving medical care.

Medical advances have brought lifesaving care to patients in need, yet many of those advances come with a risk of HAI. These infections related to medical care can be devastating and even deadly. As our ability to prevent HAIs grows, these infections are increasingly unacceptable.

Recent successes in HAI elimination have been very encouraging. Reductions have been demonstrated for other HAIs as well, but much more remains to be done.

Wherever patient care is provided, adherence to infection prevention guidelines is needed to ensure that all care is safe care. This includes traditional hospital settings as well as outpatient surgery centers, long-term care facilities, rehabilitation centers, and community clinics. The information on this website is intended to inform patients and healthcare personnel and help move healthcare systems toward elimination of HAIs.

DISEASES AND ORGANISMS IN HEALTHCARE SETTINGS

The following are pathogens associated with healthcare-associated infections (HAI): *Acinetobacter; Burkholderia cepacia; Clostridium difficile; Clostridium sordellii;* Enterobacteriaceae (carbapenem-resistance); Hepatitis; Human Immunodeficiency Virus (HIV); Influenza; *Klebsiella;* Methicillin-resistant *Staphylococcus aureus; Mycobacterium abscessus;* Norovirus; *Staphylococcus aureus;* Tuberculosis (TB); Vancomycin-intermediate *Staphylococcus aureus* and Vancomycin-resistant *Staphylococcus aureus;* Vancomycin-resistant Enterococci (VRE).

The pathogens and/or diseases are covered in the vocabulary section of *Taber's* under the following terms (main entries or subentries), respectively: *Acinetobacter; Burkholderia cepacia; Clostridium difficile; Clostridium sordellii;* Enterobacteriaceae; Hepatitis; Human Immunodeficiency Virus; Influenza; *Klebsiella* and its subentries; *Staphylococcus aureus,* methicillin-resistant; *Mycobacterium* and its subentries; Norovirus; *Staphylococcus aureus;* Tuberculosis; *Staphylococcus aureus,* vancomycin-resistant; *Enterococcus,* vancomycin-resistant

---

SOURCE: Adapted from http://www.cdc.gov/hai. Retrieved July 5, 2012.

Appendix 9–2 Bloodborne Pathogens

What Are Bloodborne Pathogens?

Bloodborne pathogens are infectious microorganisms in human blood that can cause disease in humans. These pathogens include, but are not limited to, hepatitis B (HBV), hepatitis C (HCV) and human immunodeficiency virus (HIV). Needlesticks and other sharps-related injuries may expose workers to bloodborne pathogens. Workers in many occupations, including first aid team members, housekeeping personnel in some industries, nurses and other healthcare personnel may be at risk of exposure to bloodborne pathogens.

What Can Be Done to Control Exposure to Bloodborne Pathogens?

In order to reduce or eliminate the hazards of occupational exposure to bloodborne pathogens, an employer must implement an exposure control plan for the worksite with details on employee protection measures. The plan must also describe how an employer will use a combination of engineering and work practice controls, ensure the use of personal protective clothing and equipment, provide training , medical surveillance, hepatitis B vaccinations, and signs and labels, among other provisions. Engineering controls are the primary means of eliminating or minimizing employee exposure and include the use of safer medical devices, such as needleless devices, shielded needle devices, and plastic capillary tubes.

How Can OSHA Help?

OSHA has developed this webpage (see footnote below) to provide workers and employers useful, up-to-date information on bloodborne pathogens. For other valuable worker protection information, such as Workers' Rights, Employer Responsibilities and other services OSHA offers, read OSHA's Workers page (www.osha.gov/workers.html).

SOURCE: Adapted from http://www.osha.gov/SLTC/bloodbornepathogens. Retrieved July 5, 2012.

Nursing Appendix

Table of Contents

APPENDIX N1
Conceptual Models and Theories of Nursing

Jacqueline Fawcett, PhD, FAAN

Appendix N1-1 The Forerunners

FLORENCE NIGHTINGALE'S NOTES ON NURSING

Overview

Nightingale maintained that *every* woman is a nurse because every woman, at one time or another in her life, has charge of the personal health of someone. Nightingale equated knowledge of nursing with knowledge of sanitation. The focus of nursing knowledge was how to keep the body free from disease or in such a condition that it could recover from disease. According to Nightingale, nursing ought to signify the proper use of fresh air, light, warmth, cleanliness, quiet, and the proper selection and administration of diet—all at the least expense of vital power to the patient. That is, she maintained that the purpose of nursing was to put patients in the best condition for nature to act upon them.

Implications for Nursing Practice

Nursing practice encompasses care of both well and sick people. Nursing actions focus on both patients and their environments. Thirteen "hints" provided the boundaries of nursing practice:

1. **Ventilation and warming**—the nurse must be concerned first with keeping the air that patients breathe as pure as the external air, without chilling them.
2. **Health of houses**—attention to pure air, pure water, efficient drainage, cleanliness, and light will secure the health of houses.
3. **Petty management**—all the results of good nursing may be negated by one defect: not knowing how to manage what you do when you are there and what shall be done when you are not there.
4. **Noise**—unnecessary noise, or noise that creates an expectation in the mind, is that which hurts patients. Anything that wakes patients suddenly out of their sleep will invariably put them into a state of greater excitement and do them more serious and lasting mischief than any continuous noise, however loud.
5. **Variety**—the nerves of the sick suffer from seeing the same walls, the same ceiling, the same surroundings during a long confinement to one or two rooms. The majority of cheerful cases are to be found among those patients who are not confined to one room, whatever their suffering, and the majority of depressed cases will be seen among those subjected to a long monotony of objects about them.
6. **Taking food**—the nurse should be conscious of patients' diets and remember how much food each patient has had and ought to have each day.
7. **What food?**—to watch for the opinions the patient's stomach gives, rather than to read "analyses of foods," is the business of all those who have to decide what the patient should eat.
8. **Bed and bedding**—the patient should have a clean bed every 12 hours. The bed should be narrow, so that the patient does not feel "out of humanity's reach." The bed should not be so high that the patient cannot easily get in and out of it. The bed should be in the lightest spot in the room, preferably near a window. Pillows should be used to support the back below the breathing apparatus, to allow shoulders room to fall back, and to support the head without throwing it forward.
9. **Light**—with the sick, second only to their need of fresh air is their need of light. Light, especially direct sunlight, has a purifying effect upon the air of a room.
10. **Cleanliness of rooms and walls**—the greater part of nursing consists in preserving cleanliness. The inside air can be kept clean only by excessive care to rid rooms and their furnishings of the organic matter and dust with which they become saturated. Without cleanliness, you cannot have all the effects of ventilation; without ventilation, you can have no thorough cleanliness.
11. **Personal cleanliness**—nurses should always remember that if they allow patients to remain unwashed or to remain in clothing saturated with perspiration or other excretion, they are interfering injuriously with the natural processes of health just as much as if they were to give their patients a dose of slow poison.

12. **Chattering hopes and advices**—there is scarcely a greater worry which invalids have to endure than the incurable hopes of their friends. All friends, visitors, and attendants of the sick should avoid the practice of attempting to cheer the sick by making light of their danger and by exaggerating their probabilities of recovery.
13. **Observation of the sick**—the most important practical lesson nurses can learn is what to observe, how to observe, which symptoms indicate improvement, which indicate the reverse, which are important, which are not, and which are the evidence of neglect and what kind of neglect.

Implications for Nursing Education

Nightingale's primary contribution to nursing education was her belief that nursing schools should be administratively and economically independent from hospitals, even though the training could take place in the hospital. The purpose of nursing education was to teach the theoretical and practical knowledge underlying physician's orders. Knowledge of the 13 "hints" for nursing practice was considered an essential part of the training of every nurse.

Reference

Nightingale, F. (1859). *Notes on nursing: What it is, and what it is not.* London: Harrison and Sons. [Commemorative edition printed by J. B. Lippincott Company, Philadelphia, 1992]

VIRGINIA HENDERSON'S DEFINITION OF NURSING

Overview

The unique function of the nurse is to help individuals, sick or well, to perform those activities contributing to health or its recovery (or to peaceful death) that they would perform unaided if they had the necessary strength, will, or knowledge, and to do this in such a way as to help them gain independence as soon as possible.

Implications for Nursing Practice

The practice of nursing requires nurses to know and understand patients by putting themselves in the place of the patients. Nurses should not take at face value everything that patients say, but rather should interact with patients to ascertain their true feelings. *Basic nursing care* involves helping the patient perform the following activities unaided:

1. Breathe normally.
2. Eat and drink adequately.
3. Eliminate body wastes.
4. Move and maintain desirable postures.
5. Sleep and rest.
6. Select suitable clothes and dress and undress.
7. Maintain body temperature within normal range by adjusting clothing and modifying the environment.
8. Keep the body clean and well groomed and protect the integument.
9. Avoid dangers in the environment and avoid injuring others.
10. Communicate with others in expressing emotions, needs, fears, or opinions.
11. Worship according to one's faith.
12. Work in such a way that there is a sense of accomplishment.
13. Play or participate in various forms of recreation.
14. Learn, discover, or satisfy the curiosity that leads to normal development and health and use the available health facilities.

Implications for Nursing Education

Henderson's definition of nursing identifies an area of health and human welfare in which the nurse is an expert and independent practitioner. This kind of nursing requires a liberal education within a college or university, with grounding in the physical, biological, and social sciences and ability to use analytic processes. The professional aspects of the curriculum should focus on the nurse's major function of supplementing patients when they need strength, will, or knowledge in performing daily activities or in carrying out prescribed therapy, with emphasis on the individualization of patient care.

Reference

Henderson, V. (1966). *The nature of nursing. A definition and its implications for practice, research, and education.* New York: Macmillan.

Appendix N1-2 **Conceptual Models**

A conceptual model is defined as a set of relatively abstract and general concepts that address the phenomena of central interest to a discipline, the propositions that broadly describe those concepts, and the propositions that state relatively abstract and general relations between two or more of the concepts. Conceptual models of nursing, which also are referred to as conceptual frameworks, conceptual systems, and paradigms, provide distinctive frames of reference for thinking about human beings, their environments, their health, and nursing.

DOROTHY JOHNSON'S BEHAVIORAL SYSTEM MODEL

Overview

Focus is on the person as a behavioral system, made up of all the patterned, repetitive, and purposeful ways of behavior that characterize life. Seven subsystems carry out specialized tasks or functions needed to maintain the integrity of the whole behavioral system and to manage its relationship to the environment:

1. **Attachment or affiliative**—function is the security needed for survival as well as social inclusion, intimacy, and formation and maintenance of social bonds.
2. **Dependency**—function is the succoring behavior that calls for a response of nurturance as well as approval, attention or recognition, and physical assistance.
3. **Ingestive subsystem**—function is appetite satisfaction in terms of when, how, what, how much, and under what conditions the individual eats, all of which is governed by social and psychological considerations as well as biological requirements for food and fluids.
4. **Eliminative**—function is elimination in terms of when, how, and under what conditions the individual eliminates wastes.
5. **Sexual**—functions are procreation and gratification, with regard to behaviors dependent upon the individual's biological sex and gender role identity, including but not limited to courting and mating.
6. **Aggressive**—function is protection and preservation of self and society.
7. **Achievement**—function is mastery or control of some aspect of self or environment, with regard to intellectual, physical, creative, mechanical, social, and care-taking (of children, partner, home) skills.

The *structure* of each subsystem includes four elements:

1. **Drive or goal**—the motivation for behavior.
2. **Set**—the individual's predisposition to act in certain ways to fulfill the function of the subsystem.
3. **Choice**—the individual's total behavioral repertoire for fulfilling subsystem functions, which encompasses the scope of action alternatives from which the person can choose.
4. **Action**—the individual's actual behavior in a situation. Action is the only structural element that can be observed directly; all other elements must be inferred from the individual's actual behavior and from the consequences of that behavior.

The three *functional requirements* are needed by each subsystem to fulfill its functions:

1. **Protection** from noxious influences with which the system cannot cope.
2. **Nurturance** through the input of appropriate supplies from the environment.
3. **Stimulation** to enhance growth and prevent stagnation.

Implications for Nursing Practice

Nursing practice is directed toward restoration, maintenance, or attainment of behavioral system balance and dynamic stability at the highest possible level for the individual. Johnson's practice methodology, which is called the Nursing Diagnostic and Treatment Process, encompasses four steps:

1. **Determination of the existence of a problem** The nurse obtains past and present family and individual behavioral system histories by means of interviews, structured and unstructured observations, and objective methodologies. The nurse obtains data about the nature of behavioral system functioning in terms of the efficiency and effectiveness with which the client's goals are obtained. The nurse obtains data to determine the degree to which the behavior is purposeful, orderly, and

predictable. The nurse interviews the client and family to determine the condition of the subsystem structural components and uses the obtained data to: make inferences about drive strength, direction, and value; make inferences about the solidity and specificity of the set; make inferences about the range of behavior patterns available to the client; make inferences about the usual behavior in a given situation. The nurse assesses and compares the client's behavior with the following indices for behavioral system balance and stability: the behavior is succeeding to achieve the consequences sought; effective motor, expressive, or social skills are evident; the behavior is purposeful; the behavior is orderly; the behavior is predictable; the amount of energy expended to achieve desired goals is acceptable; the behavior reflects appropriate choices; the client is sufficiently satisfied with the behavior; the nurse makes inferences about the organization, interaction, and integration of the subsystems.

2. **Diagnostic classification of problems** *Internal Subsystem Problems* are present when: functional requirements are not met; inconsistency or disharmony among the structural components of subsystems is evident; the behavior is inappropriate in the ambient culture. *Intersystem Problems* are present when: the entire behavioral system is dominated by one or two subsystems; a conflict exists between two or more subsystems.

3. **Management of nursing problems** The general goals of action are to: restore, maintain, or attain the client's behavioral system balance and stability; help the client to achieve a more optimum level of balance and functioning when this is possible and desired. The nurse determines what nursing is to accomplish on behalf of the behavioral system by determining who makes the judgment regarding the acceptable level of behavioral system balance and stability. The nurse identifies the value system of the nursing profession as well as his or her own explicit value system.

   The nurse negotiates with the client to select a type of treatment: The nurse temporarily *Imposes External Regulatory or Control Mechanisms* by: setting limits for behavior by either permissive or inhibitory means; inhibiting ineffective behavioral responses; assisting the client to acquire new responses; reinforcing appropriate behaviors. The nurse *Repairs Damaged Structural Components* in the desirable direction by: reducing drive strength by changing attitudes; redirecting goals by changing attitudes; altering set by instruction or counseling; adding choices by teaching new skills. The nurse *Fulfills Functional Requirements* of the subsystems by: protecting the client from overwhelming noxious influences; supplying adequate nurturance through an appropriate input of essential supplies; providing stimulation to enhance growth and to inhibit stagnation. The nurse negotiates the treatment modality with the client by: establishing a contract with the client; helping the client to understand the meaning of the nursing diagnosis and the proposed treatment. If the diagnosis and/or proposed treatment is rejected, the nurse continues to negotiate with the client until agreement is reached.

4. **Evaluation of behavioral system balance and stability** The nurse compares the client's behavior after treatment to indices of behavioral system balance and stability.

Implications for Nursing Education

Education for nursing practice requires a thorough grounding in the natural and social sciences, with emphasis on the genetic, neurological, and endocrine bases of behavior; psychological and social mechanisms for the regulation and control of behavior; social learning theories; and motivational structures and processes. The professional aspects of the curriculum focus on study of the behavioral system as a whole and as a composite of subsystems; pathophysiology; the clinical sciences of nursing and medicine; and the health care system.

References

Johnson, D. E. (1980). The behavioral system model for nursing. In J. P. Riehl & C. Roy, *Conceptual models for nursing practice* (2nd ed., pp. 207–216). New York: Appleton-Century-Crofts.

Johnson, D. E. (1990). The behavioral system model for nursing. In M. E. Parker (Ed.), *Nursing theories in practice* (pp. 23–32). New York: National League for Nursing.

Holaday, B. (2010). Dorothy E. Johnson: Behavioral system model. In M.R. Alligood & A. Marriner Tomey, *Nursing Theorists and Their Work* (7th ed., pp. 366-390). St. Louis: Mosby Elsevier.

IMOGENE KING'S CONCEPTUAL SYSTEM
Overview

Focus is on the continuing ability of individuals to meet their basic needs so that they may function in their socially defined roles, and on individuals' interactions within three open, dynamic, interacting systems.

1. **Personal systems** are individuals, who are regarded as rational, sentient, social beings. Concepts related to the personal system are:

   Perception— a process of organizing, interpreting, and transforming information from sense data and memory that gives meaning to one's experience, represents one's image of reality, and influences one's behavior.

   Self— a composite of thoughts and feelings that constitute a person's awareness of individual existence, of who and what he or she is.

   Growth and development— cellular, molecular, and behavioral changes in human beings that are a function of genetic endowment, meaningful and satisfying experiences, and an environment conducive to helping individuals move toward maturity.

   Body image—a person's perceptions of his or her body.

   Time—the duration between the occurrence of one event and the occurrence of another event.

   Space—the physical area called territory that exists in all directions.

   Learning—gaining knowledge.

2. **Interpersonal systems** are composed of two, three, or more individuals interacting in a given situation. The concepts associated with this system are:

   Interactions—the acts of two or more persons in mutual presence; a sequence of verbal and nonverbal behaviors that are goal directed.

   Communication—the vehicle by which human relations are developed and maintained; encompasses intrapersonal, interpersonal, verbal, and nonverbal communication.

   Transaction—a process of interaction in which human beings communicate with the environment to achieve goals that are valued; goal-directed human behaviors.

   Role—a set of behaviors expected of a person occupying a position in a social system.

   Stress—a dynamic state whereby a human being interacts with the environment to maintain balance for growth, development, and performance, involving an exchange of energy and information between the person and the environment for regulation and control of stressors.

   Coping—a way of dealing with stress.

3. **Social systems** are organized boundary systems of social roles, behaviors, and practices developed to maintain values and the mechanisms to regulate the practices and roles. The concepts related to social systems are:

   Organization—composed of human beings with prescribed roles and positions who use resources to accomplish personal and organizational goals.

   Authority—a transactional process characterized by active, reciprocal relations in which members' values, backgrounds, and perceptions play a role in defining, validating, and accepting the authority of individuals within an organization.

   Power—the process whereby one or more persons influence other persons in a situation.

   Status—the position of an individual in a group or a group in relation to other groups in an organization.

   Decision making—a dynamic and systematic process by which goal-directed choice of perceived alternatives is made and acted upon by individuals or groups to answer a question and attain a goal.

   Control—being in charge.

Implications for Nursing Practice

Nursing practice is directed toward helping individuals maintain their health so they can function in their roles. King's practice methodology, which is the essence of the Theory of Goal Attainment, is called the Interaction-Transaction Process.

1. **Assessment phase**

   Perception The nurse and the client meet in some nursing situation and perceive each other. Accuracy of perception will depend upon verifying the nurse's inferences with the client. The nurse can use the Goal-Oriented Nursing Record (GONR) throughout the assessment phase.

   Judgment The nurse and the client make mental judgments about the other.

   Action The nurse and the client take some mental action.

   Reaction The nurse and the client mentally react to each one's perceptions of the other.

2. **Disturbance** is the *diagnosis phase* of the interaction-transaction process. The nurse and the client communicate and interact, and the nurse identifies the client's concerns, problems, and disturbances in health. The nurse conducts a nursing history to determine the client's activities of daily living, using the Criterion-Referenced Measure of Goal Attainment Tool (CRMGAT); roles; environmental stressors; per-

ceptions; and values, learning needs, and goals. The nurse records the data from the nursing history on the GONR, the medical history and physical examination data, results of laboratory tests and x-ray examination, and information gathered from other health professionals and the client's family members on the GONR. The nurse also records diagnoses on the GONR.

3. **Planning phase**

   Mutual Goal Setting The nurse and the client interact purposefully to set mutually agreed on goals. The nurse interacts with family members if the client cannot verbally participate in goal setting. Mutual goal setting is based on the nurse's assessment of the client's concerns, problems, and disturbances in health; the nurse's and client's perceptions of the interference; and the nurse's sharing of information with the client and his or her family to help the client attain the goals identified. The nurse records the goals on the GONR.

   Exploration of Means to Achieve Goals The nurse and the client interact purposefully to explore the means to achieve the mutually set goals.

   Agreement on Means to Achieve Goals The nurse and the client interact purposefully to agree on the means to achieve the mutually set goals. The nurse records the nursing orders with regard to the means to achieve goals on the GONR.

4. **Transaction** is the *implementation phase* of the interaction-transaction process. Transaction refers to the valuational components of the interaction. The nurse and the client carry out the measures agreed upon to achieve the mutually set goals. The nurse can use the GONR flow sheet and progress notes to record the implementation of measures used to achieve goals.

5. **Attainment of goals** is the *evaluation phase* of the interaction-transaction process. The nurse and the client identify the outcome of the interaction-transaction process. The outcome is expressed in terms of the client's state of health, or ability to function in social roles. The nurse and the client make a decision with regard to whether the goal was attained and, if necessary, determine why the goal was not attained. The nurse can use the CRMGAT to record the outcome and the GONR to record the discharge summary.

Implications for Nursing Education

King's Conceptual System and the theory of goal attainment lead to a focus on the dynamic interaction of the nurse-client dyad. This focus, in turn, leads to emphasis on nursing student behavior as well as client behavior. The concepts related to the personal, interpersonal, and social systems serve as the theoretical content for nursing courses in associate degree, baccalaureate, and master's nursing programs. The theoretical knowledge is used by students in learning experiences involving concrete nursing situations.

References

King, I. M. (1981). *A theory for nursing. Systems, concepts, process.* New York: Wiley. [Reissued 1990. Albany, NY: Delmar.]

King, I. M. (1986). *Curriculum and instruction in nursing.* Norwalk, CT: Appleton-Century-Crofts.

King, I.M. (1992). King's theory of goal attainment. *Nursing Science Quarterly*, 5, 19–26.

King, I.M. (2006). Part One: Imogene M. King's theory of goal attainment. In M.E. Parker, *Nursing theories and nursing practice* (2nd ed., pp. 235-243). Philadelphia: F.A. Davis.

MYRA LEVINE'S CONSERVATION MODEL

Overview

Focus is on conservation of the person's wholeness. Adaptation is the process by which people maintain their wholeness or integrity as they respond to environmental challenges and become congruent with the environment. Sources of challenges are:

1. **Perceptual environment**—encompasses that part of the environment to which individuals respond with their sense organs.

2. **Operational environment**—includes those aspects of the environment that are not directly perceived, such as radiation, odorless and colorless pollutants, and microorganisms.

3. **Conceptual environment**—the environment of language, ideas, symbols, concepts, and invention.

Individuals respond to the environmental challenges by means of four integrated processes:

1. *Fight-or-flight mechanism*
2. *Inflammatory-immune* response

3. *Stress* response
4. *Perceptual awareness*— includes the basic orienting, haptic, auditory, visual, and taste-smell systems.

Implications for Nursing Practice

Nursing practice is directed toward promoting wholeness for all people, well or sick. Patients are partners or participants in nursing care and are temporarily dependent on the nurse. The nurse's goal is to end the dependence as quickly as possible. Levine's practice methodology is a nursing process directed toward conservation, which is defined as "keeping together," and consists of three steps:

1. **Trophicognosis**—formulation of a nursing care judgment arrived at by the scientific method. The nurse observes and collects data that will influence nursing practice rather than medical practice. The nurse uses appropriate assessment tools derived from the Conservation Model and data to establish an objective and scientific rationale for nursing practice. The nurse fully understands his or her role in medical and paramedical prescriptions and the basis for the prescribed medical regimen. The nurse consults with the physician to share information and clarify nursing decisions. The nurse understands the basis for the prescribed paramedical regimen and determines the nursing processes required by medical and paramedical treatment. The nurse assesses the patient's *Conservation of Energy* by determining his or her ability to perform necessary activities without producing excessive fatigue. The nurse assesses the patient's *Conservation of Structural Integrity* by determining his or her physical functioning. The nurse assesses the patient's *Conservation of Personal Integrity* by determining his or her moral and ethical values and life experiences. The nurse assesses the patient's *Conservation of Social Integrity* by taking the patient's family members, friends, and conceptual environment into account. The nurse understands the basis for implementation of the nursing care plan, including principles of nursing science, and how to adapt nursing techniques to the unique cluster of needs demonstrated in the individual patient. The nurse identifies the provocative facts within the data collected, that is, the data that provoke attention on the basis of knowledge of the situation. The provocative facts provide the basis for an hypothesis, or trophicognosis.
2. **Intervention/Action**—test of the hypothesis. The nurse implements the nursing care plan within the structure of administrative policy, availability of equipment, and established standards of nursing. The nurse accurately records and transmits evaluation of the patient's response to implementation of the nursing care plan and identifies the general type of nursing intervention required:
    Therapeutic— when nursing intervention influences adaptation favorably or toward renewed social well-being.
    Supportive— when nursing intervention cannot alter the course of the adaptation and can only maintain the status quo or fail to halt a downward course.
    Intervention is structured according to four conservation principles:
    Principle of conservation of energy— balancing the patient's energy output and energy input to avoid excessive fatigue.
    Principle of conservation of structural integrity— focusing attention on healing by maintaining or restoring the structure of the body through prevention of physical breakdown and promotion of healing.
    Principle of conservation of personal integrity— maintaining or restoring the individual patient's sense of identity, self-worth and acknowledgment of uniqueness.
    Principle of conservation of social integrity— acknowledging patients as social beings and helping them to preserve their places in family, community, and society.
3. **Evaluation of Intervention/Action**—the nurse's evaluation of the effects of the intervention/action. The nurse evaluates the effects of intervention and revises the trophicognosis as necessary. An indicator of the success of nursing interventions is the patient's organismic response.

Implications for Nursing Education

Education focuses on understanding both the person and the environment, with emphasis placed on processes by which the person adapts to environmental challenges. Theoretical and clinical knowledge related to the four conservation principles provides the structure for nursing courses. Students are prepared for the practice of holistic nursing and for lifelong learning.

References

Levine, M. E. (1973). *Introduction to clinical nursing* (2nd ed.). Philadelphia: F. A. Davis.

Levine M. E. (1996). The conservation principles: A retrospective. *Nursing Science Quarterly, 9,* 38–41.

Schaefer, K. M., & Pond, J. B. (Eds.). (1991). *Levine's conservation model: A framework for nursing practice.* Philadelphia: F. A. Davis.

Schaefer, K.M. (2010). Myra Estrin Levine: The conservation model. In M.R. Alligood & A. Marriner Tomey, *Nursing theorists and their work* (7th ed., pp. 225-241). St. Louis: Mosby Elsevier

BETTY NEUMAN'S SYSTEMS MODEL

Overview

Focus is on the wellness of the client system in relation to environmental stress and reactions to stress. The client system, which can be an individual, a family or other group, or a community, is a composite of five interrelated variables:

1. **Physiological variables**—bodily structure and function.
2. **Psychological variables**—mental processes and relationships.
3. **Sociocultural variables**—social and cultural functions.
4. **Developmental variables**—developmental processes of life.
5. **Spiritual variables**—aspects of spirituality on a continuum from complete unawareness or denial to a consciously developed high level of spiritual understanding.

The client system is depicted as a central core, which is a basic structure of survival factors common to the species, surrounded by three types of concentric rings:

1. **Flexible line of defense**—the outermost ring; a protective buffer for the client's normal or stable state that prevents invasion of stressors and keeps the client system free from stressor reactions or symptomatology.
2. **Normal line of defense**—lies between the flexible line of defense and the lines of resistance; represents the client system's normal or usual wellness state.
3. **Lines of resistance**—the innermost concentric rings; involuntarily activated when a stressor invades the normal line of defense. They attempt to stabilize the client system and foster a return to the normal line of defense. If they are effective, the system can reconstitute; if ineffective, death may ensue.

Environment is defined as "all internal and external factors or influences surrounding the client system":

1. **Internal environment**—"all forces or interactive influences internal to or contained solely within the boundaries of the defined client system"; the source of *intrapersonal stressors.*
2. **External environment**—all forces or interactive influences external to or existing outside the defined client system; the source of *interpersonal and extrapersonal stressors.*
3. **Created environment**—subconsciously developed by the client as a symbolic expression of system wholeness. It supersedes and encompasses the internal and external environments, and functions as a subjective safety mechanism that may block the true reality of the environment and the health experience.

Implications for Nursing Practice

Nursing practice is directed toward facilitating optimal wellness through retention, attainment, or maintenance of client system stability. Neuman's practice methodology is the Neuman Systems Model Nursing Process Format, which encompasses three steps:

1. **Nursing diagnosis** —formulated on the basis of assessment of the variables and lines of defense and resistance making up the client system.
2. **Nursing goals**—negotiated with the client for desired prescriptive changes to correct variances from wellness.
3. **Nursing outcomes** The nurse implements nursing interventions through the use of one or more of the three prevention-as-intervention modalities.
   Primary Prevention as Intervention— nursing actions to retain system stability are implemented by: preventing stressor invasion; providing resources to retain or strengthen existing client/client system strengths; supporting positive coping and functioning; desensitizing existing or possible noxious stressors; motivating the client/client system toward wellness; coordinating and integrating interdisciplinary theories and epidemiological input; educating or reeducating the client/client system; using stress as a positive intervention strategy.
   Secondary Prevention as Intervention— nursing actions to attain system stability are implemented by: protecting the client/client system's basic structure;

mobilizing and optimizing the client/client system's internal and external resources to attain stability and energy conservation; facilitating purposeful manipulation of stressors and reactions to stressors; motivating, educating, and involving the client/client system in mutual establishment of health care goals; facilitating appropriate treatment and intervention measures; supporting positive factors toward wellness; promoting advocacy by coordination and integration; providing primary preventive intervention as required.

Tertiary Prevention as Intervention— nursing actions to maintain system stability are implemented by: attaining and maintaining the highest possible level of client/client system wellness and stability during reconstitution; educating, reeducating, and/or reorienting the client/client system as needed; supporting the client/client system toward appropriate goals; coordinating and integrating health services resources; providing primary and/or secondary preventive intervention as required. The nurse evaluates the outcome goals by: confirming attainment of outcome goals with the client/client system; reformulating goals as necessary with the client/client system. The nurse and client/client system set intermediate and long-range goals for subsequent nursing action that are structured in relation to short-term goal outcomes. The nurse uses the Neuman Systems Model Assessment and Intervention Tool, the Neuman Systems Model Nursing Diagnosis Taxonomy, and any other relevant clinical tools to guide collection of data and facilitate documentation of nursing diagnoses, nursing goals, and nursing outcomes.

Implications for Nursing Education

The model is an appropriate curriculum guide for all levels of nursing education. The components of the model serve as curriculum content, including the five variable areas (physiological, psychological, sociocultural, developmental, spiritual), the three categories of stressors (intrapersonal, interpersonal, extrapersonal), and the three prevention-as-intervention modalities (primary, secondary, tertiary).

References

Lowry, L. (Ed.). (1998). *The Neuman systems model and nursing education: Teaching strategies and outcomes.* Indianapolis: Sigma Theta Tau International Center for Nursing Press.

Neuman, B., & Fawcett, J. (Eds.). (2011). *The Neuman systems model* (5th ed.). Upper Saddle River, NJ: Pearson..

Aylward, P.D. (2006). Betty Neuman: The Neuman systems model and global applications. In M.E. Parker, *Nursing theories and nursing practice* (2nd ed., pp. 281-294). Philadelphia: F.A. Davis.

DOROTHEA OREM'S SELF-CARE FRAMEWORK

Overview

Focus is on patients' deliberate actions to meet their own and dependent others' therapeutic self-care demands and nurses' deliberate actions to implement nursing systems designed to assist individuals and multiperson units who have limitations in their abilities to provide continuing and therapeutic self-care or care of dependent others. The concepts of Orem's conceptual model are:

1. **Self-care**—behavior directed by individuals to themselves or their environments to regulate factors that affect their own development and functioning in the interests of life, health, or well-being.
2. **Self-care agency**—a complex capability of maturing and mature individuals to determine the presence and characteristics of specific requirements for regulating their own functioning and development, make judgments and decisions about what to do, and perform care measures to meet specific self-care requisites. The person's ability to perform self-care is influenced by 10 *power components:*
    Ability to maintain attention and exercise requisite vigilance with respect to self as self-care agent and internal and external conditions and factors significant for self-care.
    Controlled use of available physical energy that is sufficient for the initiation and continuation of self-care operations.
    Ability to control the position of the body and its parts in the execution of the movements required for the initiation and completion of self-care operations.
    Ability to reason within a self-care frame of reference.
    Motivation (i.e., goal orientations for self-care that are in accord with its characteristics and its meaning for life, health, and well-being).
    Ability to make decisions about care of self and to operationalize these decisions.

Ability to acquire technical knowledge about self-care from authoritative sources, to retain it, and to operationalize it.

A repertoire of cognitive, perceptual, manipulative, communication, and interpersonal skills adapted to the performance of self-care operations.

Ability to order discrete self-care actions or action systems into relationships with prior and subsequent actions toward the final achievement of regulatory goals of self-care.

Ability to consistently perform self-care operations, integrating them with relevant aspects of personal, family, and community living.

The person's ability to perform self-care as well as the kind and amount of self-care required are influenced by 10 internal and external factors called *basic conditioning factors:*

Age

Gender

Developmental state

Health state

Sociocultural orientation

Health care system factors; for example, medical diagnostic and treatment modalities

Family system factors

Patterns of living including activities regularly engaged in

Environmental factors

Resource availability and adequacy

The person's ability to perform self-care also is influenced by 10 *self-care agency power components:*

Ability to maintain attention and exercise requisite vigilance with respect to self as self-care agent and internal and external conditions and factors significant for self-care.

Controlled use of available physical energy that is sufficient for the initiation and continuation of self-care operations.

Ability to control the position of the body and its parts in the execution of the movements required for the initiation and completion of self-care operations.

Ability to reason within a self-care frame of reference.

Motivation (i.e., goal orientations for self-care that are in accord with its characteristics and its meaning for life, health, and well-being).

Ability to make decisions about care of self and to operationalize these decisions.

Ability to acquire technical knowledge about self-care from authoritative sources, to retain it, and to operationalize it.

A repertoire of cognitive, perceptual, manipulative, communication, and interpersonal skills adapted to the performance of self-care operations.

Ability to order discrete self-care actions or action systems into relationships with prior and subsequent actions toward the final achievement of regulatory goals of self-care.

Ability to consistently perform self-care operations, integrating them with relevant aspects of personal, family, and community living.

3. **Therapeutic self-care demand**—the action demand on individuals to meet three types of self-care requisites:

Universal self-care requisites— actions that need to be performed to maintain life processes, the integrity of human structure and function, and general well-being.

Developmental self-care requisites— actions that need to be performed in relation to human developmental processes, conditions, and events and in relation to events that may adversely affect development.

Health deviation self-care requisites— actions that need to be performed in relation to genetic and constitutional defects, human structural and functional deviations and their effects, and medical diagnostic and treatment measures prescribed or performed by physicians.

4. **Self-care deficit**—the relationship of inadequacy between self-care agency and the therapeutic self-care demand.

5. **Nursing agency**—a complex property or attribute that enables nurses to know and help others to know their therapeutic self-care demands, meet their therapeutic self-care demands, and regulate the exercise or development of their self-care agency.

Nursing agency is influenced by 8 *nursing agency power components:*

Valid and reliable knowledge of all three areas of nursing operation (social, interpersonal, professional-technologic).

Intellectual and practical skills specific to the three areas [of nursing operation].

situations.

Sustaining motives.

Willingness to provide nursing.

Ability to unify different action sequences toward result achievement.

Consistency in performance of nursing operations.

Making adjustments in [nursing operations] because of prevailing or emerging conditions.

Ability to manage self as the essential professional operative element in nursing practice situations.

6. **Nursing system**—a series of coordinated deliberate practical actions performed by nurses and patients directed toward meeting the patient's therapeutic self-care demand and protecting and regulating the exercise or development of the patient's self-care agency.

Implications for Nursing Practice

Nursing practice is directed toward helping people to meet their own and their dependent others' therapeutic self-care demands. Orem's practice methodology encompasses the Professional-Technologic Operations of Nursing Practice:

1. **Case Management Operations**—The nurse uses a case management approach to control, direct, and check each of the nursing diagnostic, prescriptive, regulatory, and control operations. The nurse maintains an overview of the interrelationships between the social, interpersonal, and professional-technologic systems of nursing. The nursing history and other appropriate tools are used for collection and documentation of information and measurement of the quality of nursing. The nurse records appropriate information in the patient's chart and records progress notes as appropriate.

2. **Diagnostic Operations**—The nurse identifies the unit of service for nursing practice as an individual, an individual member of a multiperson unit, or a multiperson unit. The nurse determines why the person needs nursing in collaboration with the patient or family and with continued review of decisions by the patient or family. The nurse collects demographic data about the patient and information about the nature and boundaries of the patient's health care situation and nursing's jurisdiction within those boundaries. The nurse calculates the person's present and future therapeutic self-care demand and determines the person's self-care agency or dependent-care agency. The nurse identifies the influence of power components and basic conditioning factors on the exercise and operability of self-care or dependent-care agency.

The nurse determines whether the person should be helped to refrain from self-care actions or dependent-care actions for therapeutic purposes and whether the person should be helped to protect already developed self-care or dependent-care capabilities for therapeutic purposes. The nurse determines the person's potential for self-care or dependent-care agency in the future by: identifying the person's ability to increase or deepen self-care or dependent-care knowledge; identifying the person's ability to learn techniques of care; identifying the person's willingness to engage in self-care or dependent-care; identifying the person's ability to effectively and consistently incorporate essential self-care or dependent-care measures into daily living.

The nurse calculates the self-care deficit or dependent-care deficit by: determining the qualitative or quantitative inadequacy of self-care agency or dependent-care agency in relation to the calculated therapeutic self-care demand; determining the nature of and reasons for the existence of the self-care deficit or dependent-care deficit; specifying the extent of the self-care deficit or dependent-care deficit as complete or partial.

The nurse states the nursing diagnosis for the individual or a multiperson unit within the context of four levels:

Level 1: Focuses on health and well-being, with emphasis on the relationship of self-care and self-care management to the overall life situation.

Level 2: Deals with the relationship between the therapeutic self-care demand and self-care agency.

Level 3: Expresses the relationship of the action demand by particular self-care requisites to particular self-care operations as influenced by the power components.

Level 4: Expresses the influence of the basic conditioning factors on the therapeutic self-care demand and self-care agency.

3. **Prescriptive Operations**—The nurse specifies the means to be used and all measures needed to meet the therapeutic self-care demand, in collaboration with the patient or family. The nurse specifies the roles to be played by the nurse(s), patient, and dependent-care agent(s) in meeting the therapeutic self-care demand and in regulating the patient's exercise or development of self- or dependent-care agency, in collaboration with the patient or family.

4. **Regulatory Operations: Design of Nursing Systems for Performance of Regulatory Operations**—The nurse designs a *nursing system*, which is a series of

coordinated deliberate practical actions performed by the nurse and the patient directed toward meeting the patient's therapeutic self-care demand and protecting and regulating the exercise or development of the patient's self- or dependent-care agency, in collaboration with the patient or family.

The nursing system includes one or more *methods of helping,* which are sequential series of actions that will overcome or compensate for the health-associated limitations of patients to regulate their own or their dependents' functioning and development.

The selection of the appropriate nursing system is based on the answer to the question of who can or should perform self-care actions, and the determination of the patient's role (no role, some role) in the production and management of self-care. The *wholly compensatory nursing system* is selected when the patient cannot or should not perform any self-care actions, and thus the nurse must perform them. The *partly compensatory nursing system* is selected when the patient can perform some, but not all, self-care actions. The *supportive-educative nursing system* is selected when the patient can and should perform all self-care actions. A single patient may require one or a sequential combination of the three types of nursing systems. All three nursing systems are most appropriately used with individuals. Multiperson units usually require combinations of the partly compensatory and supportive-educative nursing systems, although it is possible that such multiperson units as families or residence groups would need wholly compensatory nursing systems under some circumstances.

Wholly compensatory nursing system— The nurse accomplishes the patient's therapeutic self-care, compensates for the patient's inability to engage in self-care, and supports and protects the patient. The nurse selects wholly compensatory nursing system subtype 1 for persons unable to engage in any form of deliberate action, including persons who are unable to control their position and movement in space; are unresponsive to stimuli or responsive to internal and external stimuli only through hearing and feeling; are unable to monitor the environment and convey information to others because of loss of motor ability.

The nurse selects the following *method of helping* : Acting for or doing for the patient.

The nurse selects *wholly compensatory nursing system subtype* 2 for persons who are aware and who may be able to make observations, judgments, and decisions about self-care and other matters but cannot or should not perform actions requiring ambulation and manipulative movements.

The nurse selects one or more of the following *methods of helping:* providing a developmental environment; acting for or doing for the patient; supporting the patient psychologically; guiding the patient; teaching the patient.

The nurse selects *wholly compensatory nursing system subtype 3* for persons who are unable to attend to themselves and make reasoned judgments and decisions about self-care and other matters but who can be ambulatory and may be able to perform some measures of self-care with continuous guidance and supervision.

The nurse selects one or more of the following *methods of helping:* providing a developmental environment; guiding the patient; providing support for the patient; acting for or doing for the patient.

Partly compensatory nursing system— The nurse performs some self-care measures for the patient, compensates for self-care limitations of the patient, assists the patient as required, and regulates the patient's self-care agency; the patient performs some self-care measures, regulates self-care agency, and accepts care and assistance from the nurse.

When the nurse selects *partly compensatory nursing system subtype 1* , the patient performs universal measures of self-care and the nurse performs medically prescribed measures and some universal self-care measures. The nurse selects one or more of the following *methods of helping: acting for or doing for the patient; guiding the patient; supporting the patient; providing a developmental environment; teaching the patient.*

When the nurse selects *partly compensatory nursing system subtype 2* , the patient learns to perform some new care measures. The nurse selects one or more of the following *methods of helping:* acting for or doing for the patient; guiding the patient; supporting the patient; providing a developmental environment; teaching the patient.

Supportive-educative nursing system— The nurse regulates the exercise and development of the patient's self-care agency or dependent-care agency; the patient accomplishes self-care or dependent-care and regulates the exercise and development of self-care agency or dependent-care agency.

The nurse selects *supportive-educative nursing system subtype 1* if the patient can perform care measures, and the appropriate methods of helping are guiding the patient and supporting the patient. The nurse selects *supportive-educative nursing system subtype 2* if the patient can perform care measures and the appropriate method of helping is teaching the patient. The nurse selects *supportive-educative nursing system subtype 3* if the patient can perform care measures and the appropriate method of helping is providing a developmental environment. The nurse selects *supportive-educative nursing system subtype 4* if the patient is competent in self-care and the appropriate method of helping is guiding the patient periodically.

5. **Regulatory Operations: Planning for Regulatory Operations**—The nurse specifies what is needed to produce the nursing system(s) selected for the patient.

6. **Regulatory Operations: Production of Regulatory Care**—Nursing systems are produced by means of the actions of nurses and patients during nurse-patient encounters. The nurse produces and manages the designated nursing system(s) and method(s) of helping for as long as the patient's self-care deficit or dependent-care deficit exists. The nurse provides the following direct nursing care operations:

> Performs and regulates self-care or dependent-care tasks for patients or assists patients with their performance of self- or dependent-care tasks.
>
> Coordinates self- or dependent-care task performance so that a unified system of care is produced and coordinated with other components of health care.
>
> Helps patients, their families, and others bring about systems of daily living for patients that support the accomplishment of self-care or dependent-care and are, at the same time, satisfying in relation to patients' interests, talents, and goals.
>
> Guides, directs, and supports patients in their exercise of, or in the withholding of the exercise of, their self-care agency or dependent-care agency.
>
> Stimulates patients' interests in self-care or dependent-care by raising questions and promoting discussions of care problems and issues when conditions permit.
>
> Is available to patients at times when questions are likely to arise.
>
> Supports and guides patients in learning activities and provides cues for learning as well as instructional sessions.
>
> Supports and guides patients as they experience illness or disability and the effects of medical care measures and as they experience the need to engage in new measures of self-care or change their ways of meeting ongoing self-care requisites.

The nurse carries out the following decision-making operations regarding the continuation of or need for changes in direct nursing care:

> Monitors and assists patients to monitor themselves to determine if self-care or dependent-care measures were performed and to determine the effects of self-care or dependent-care, the results of efforts to regulate the exercise or development of self-care agency or dependent-care agency, and the sufficiency and efficiency of nursing action directed to these ends.
>
> Makes judgments about the sufficiency and efficiency of self-care or dependent-care, the regulation of the exercise or development of self-care agency or dependent-care, and nursing assistance.
>
> Makes judgments about the meaning of the results derived from nurses' performance when monitoring patients and judging outcomes of self-care or dependent-care for the well-being of patients. Makes or recommends adjustments in the nursing care system through changes in nurse and patient roles.

7. **Control Operations**—The nurse performs control operations concurrently with or separate from the production of regulatory care. The nurse makes observations and evaluates the nursing system to determine whether:

> The nursing system that was designed is actually produced.
>
> There is a fit between the current prescription for nursing and the nursing system that is being produced.
>
> Regulation of the patient's functioning is being achieved through performance of care measures to meet the patient's therapeutic self-care demand.
>
> Exercise of the patient's self-care agency or dependent-care agency is being properly regulated.
>
> Developmental change is in process and is adequate.
>
> The patient is adjusting to any declining powers to engage in self-care or dependent-care.

Implications for Nursing Education

The Self-Care Framework provides a body of knowledge that can be used for curriculum development. The focus of both undergraduate and graduate nursing curricula is on components of self-care, self-care agency, self-care deficits, nursing agency, and nursing systems. Education for clinical skills emphasizes the methods of helping.

Reference

Orem, D. E. (2001). *Nursing: Concepts of practice* (6th ed.). St. Louis: Mosby.

Orem, D.E. (2006). Part One: Dorothea E. Orem's self-care deficit nursing theory. In M.E. Parker, *Nursing theories and nursing practice* (2nd ed., pp. 141-149). Philadelphia: F.A. Davis

MARTHA ROGERS' SCIENCE OF UNITARY HUMAN BEINGS

Overview

Focus is on unitary, irreducible human beings and their environments. The four basic concepts are:

1. **Energy fields**—irreducible, indivisible, pandimensional unitary human beings and environments that are identified by pattern and manifesting characteristics that are specific to the whole and cannot be predicted from knowledge of the parts. Human and environmental energy fields are integral with each other.
2. **Openness**—a characteristic of human and environmental energy fields; energy fields are continuously and completely open.
3. **Pattern**—the distinguishing characteristic of an energy field. Pattern is perceived as a single wave that gives identity to the field. Each human field pattern is unique and is integral with its own unique environmental field pattern. Pattern is an abstraction that cannot be seen; what are seen or experienced are manifestations of field pattern.
4. **Pandimensionality**—a nonlinear domain without spatial or temporal attributes.

The three principles of homeodynamics, which describe the nature of human and environmental energy fields, are:

1. **Resonancy**—asserts that human and environmental fields are identified by wave patterns that manifest continuous change from lower to higher frequencies.
2. **Helicy**—asserts that human and environmental field patterns are continuous, innovative, and unpredictable, and are characterized by increasing diversity.
3. **Integrality**—emphasizes the continuous mutual human field and environmental field process.

Implications for Nursing Practice

Nursing practice is directed toward promoting the health and well-being of all persons, wherever they are. Rogers' practice methodology, which is called the Health Patterning Practice Method, encompasses the following phases:

1. **Pattern Manifestation Knowing and Appreciation—Assessment**—The continuous process of apprehending and identifying manifestations of the human energy field and environmental energy field patterns that relate to current health events. The nurse uses one or more Science of Unitary Human Beings–based research instruments or clinical tools to guide application and documentation of the practice methodology. The nurse acts with pandimensional authenticity, that is, with a demeanor of genuineness, trustworthiness, and knowledgeable caring. The nurse focuses on the client as a unified whole (a unitary human being) and participates in individualized nursing by looking at each client and determining the range of behaviors that are normal for him or her. The nurse always takes diversity among clients into account, for that diversity has distinct implications for what will be done and how it will be done. The nurse comes to know human energy field pattern and environmental energy field pattern through manifestations of that pattern in the form of the client's experiences, perceptions, and expressions. The nurse attends to expressions of experiences and perceptions in such forms as the client's verbal responses, responses to questionnaires, and personal ways of living and relating. The nurse collects such relevant pattern information as the client's sensations, thoughts, feelings, awareness, imagination, memory, introspective insights, intuitive apprehensions, recurring themes and issues that pervade the client's life, metaphors, visualizations, images, nutrition, work and play, exercise, substance use, sleep/wake cycles, safety, decelerated/accelerated field rhythms, space-time shifts, interpersonal networks, and professional health care access and use.
2. **Voluntary Mutual Patterning**—The continuous process whereby the nurse, with the client, patterns the environmental energy field to promote harmony related to the health events. The nurse facilitates the client's actualization of potentials for health and well-being. The nurse has no investment in the client's changing in a particular way. The nurse does not attempt to change anyone to conform to arbitrary health ideals. Rather, the nurse enhances the client's efforts to actualize health potentials from his or her point of view. The nurse helps to create an environment where

healing conditions are optimal and invites the client to heal him- or herself as the nurse and the client participate in various health patterning modalities. The nurse uses many different modes of health patterning, including such noninvasive modalities as therapeutic touch; imagery; meditation; relaxation; balancing activity and rest; unconditional love; attitudes of hope, humor, and upbeat moods; the use of sound, color, and motion; health education; wellness counseling; nutrition counseling; meaningful presence; meaningful dialogue; affirmations (expressions of intentionality); bibliotherapy; journal keeping; esthetic experiences of art, poetry, and nature; collaborative advocacy; and computer-based virtual reality. The nurse recognizes that both noninvasive modalities and technology are simply tools used to apply knowledge in practice.

3. **Pattern Manifestation Knowing and Appreciation —Evaluation**—The nurse evaluates voluntary mutual patterning by means of pattern manifestation knowing. The nurse monitors and collects additional pattern information as it unfolds during voluntary mutual patterning and considers the pattern information within the context of continually emerging health patterning goals affirmed by the client.

Implications for Nursing Education

Education for nursing practice requires a commitment to lifelong learning. Education for professional nursing occurs at the baccalaureate, masters, and doctoral levels in college and university settings. The purpose of professional nursing educational programs is to provide the knowledge and tools necessary for nursing practice. The liberal arts and sciences are a predominant component of the curriculum. The principles of resonancy, helicy, and integrality represent the major integrating concepts of the nursing courses.

References

Barret, E. A. M. (1998). A Rogerian practice methodology for health patterning. *Nursing Science Quarterly* , 11, 136–138.

Cowling, W. R. III. (1997). Pattern appreciation: The unitary science/practice of reaching for essence. In M. Madrid (Ed.), *Patterns of Rogerian knowing* (pp. 129–142). New York: National League for Nursing Press.

Madrid, M., & Barrett, E. A. M. (Eds.). (1994). *Rogers' scientific art of nursing practice.* New York: National League for Nursing.

Malinski, V.M. (2006). Part One: Martha E. Rogers' science of unitary human beings. In M.E. Parker, *Nursing theories and nursing practice* (2nd ed., pp. 160-167). Philadelphia: F.A. Davis.

Rogers, M. E. (1990). Nursing: Science of unitary, irreducible, human beings: Update 1990. In E. A. M. Barrett (Ed.), *Visions of Rogers' science-based nursing* (pp. 5–11). New York: National League for Nursing.

Rogers, M. E. (1992). Nursing science and the space age. *Nursing Science Quarterly,* 5, 27–34.

CALLISTA ROY'S ADAPTATION MODEL

Overview

Focuses on the responses of the human adaptive system, which can be an individual or a group, to a constantly changing environment. Adaptation is the central feature of the model. Problems in adaptation arise when the adaptive system is unable to cope with or respond to constantly changing stimuli from the internal and external environments in a manner that maintains the integrity of the system. Environmental stimuli are categorized as:

1. **Focal**—the stimuli most immediately confronting the person.
2. **Contextual**—the contributing factors in the situation.
3. **Residual**—other unknown factors that may influence the situation. When the factors making up residual stimuli become known, they are considered focal or contextual stimuli.

Adaptation occurs through two types of innate or acquired coping mechanisms used to respond to changing environmental stimuli:

1. **Regulator coping subsystem**—for individuals; receives input from the external environment and from changes in the individual's internal state and processes the changes through neural-chemical-endocrine channels to produce responses.
2. **Cognator coping subsystem**—for individuals; also receives input from external and internal stimuli that involve psychological, social, physical, and physiological factors, including regulator subsystem outputs. These stimuli then are processed

through cognitive/emotive pathways, including perceptual/information processing, learning, judgment, and emotion.

3. **Stabilizer subsystem control process**—for groups; involves the established structures, values, and daily activities used by a group to accomplish its primary purpose and contribute to common purposes of society.

4. **Innovator Subsystem control process**—pertains to humans in groups; involves the structures and processes necessary for change and growth in human social systems.

Responses take place in four modes for individuals and groups:

1. **Physiological/physical mode**

   Physiological mode—for individuals; concerned with basic needs requisite to maintaining the physical and physiological integrity of the individual human system. It encompasses oxygenation; nutrition; elimination; activity and rest; protection; senses; fluid, electrolyte, and acid-base balance; neurologic function; and endocrine function. The basic underlying need is physiologic integrity.

   Physical mode—for groups; pertains to the manner in which the collective human adaptive system manifests adaptation relative to basic operating resources, that is, participants, physical facilities, and fiscal resources. The basic underlying need is resource adequacy, or wholeness achieved by adapting to change in physical resource needs.

2. **Self-concept/group identity mode**

   Self-concept mode—for the individual; addresses the composite of beliefs and feelings that a person holds about him- or herself at a given time. The basic underlying need is psychic and spiritual integrity, the need to know who one is so that one can be or exist with a sense of unity, meaning, and purposefulness in the universe. The Physical Self refers to the individual's appraisal of his or her own physical being, including physical attributes, functioning, sexuality, health and illness states, and appearance; includes the components of body sensation and body image. The Personal Self refers to the individual's appraisal of his or her own characteristics, expectations, values, and worth, including self-consistency, self-ideal, and the moral-ethical-spiritual self.

   Group identity mode—for groups; addresses shared relations, goals, and values, which create a social milieu and culture, a group self-image, and coresponsibility for goal achievement. Identity integrity is the underlying need, which implies the honesty, soundness, and completeness of the group members' identification with the group and involves the process of sharing identity and goals. This mode encompasses Interpersonal Relationships, Group Self-Image, Social Milieu, and Group Culture.

3. **Role function mode**—for the individual, focuses on the roles that the individual occupies in society. The basic underlying need is social integrity, the need to know who one is in relation to others so that one can act. For the group, focuses on the action components associated with group infrastructure that are designed to contribute to the accomplishment of the group's mission, or the tasks or functions associated with the group. The basic underlying need is role clarity, the need to understand and commit to fulfill expected tasks, so that the group can achieve common goals.

4. **Interdependence mode**—behavior pertaining to interdependent relationships of individuals and groups. The basic underlying need is relational integrity, the feeling of security in nurturing relationships. For the individual, focuses on interactions related to the giving and receiving of love, respect, and value, and encompasses Affectional Adequacy, Developmental Adequacy, Resource Adequacy, Significant Others, and Support Systems. For the group, pertains to the social context in which the group operates including both private and public contacts both within the group and with those outside the group, and encompasses Affectional Adequacy, Developmental Adequacy, Resource Adequacy, Context, Infrastructure, and Resources.

The four modes are interrelated. Responses in any one mode may have an effect on or act as a stimulus in one or all of the other modes. Responses in each mode are judged as either:

1. **Adaptive**—promote the goals of human adaptive system, including survival, growth, reproduction, and mastery.

2. **Ineffective**—those that do not contribute to the goals of the human adaptive system.

Implications for Nursing Practice

Nursing practice is directed toward promoting adaptation in each of the four response modes, thereby contributing to the person's health, quality of life, and dying with dignity. Roy's practice methodology is the Roy Adaptation Model Nursing Process, which encompasses six steps:

1. **Assessment of behavior**—The nurse systematically gathers data about the behavior of the human adaptive system and judges the current state of adaptation in each adaptive mode.

    The nurse uses one or more of the Roy Adaptation Model–based research instruments or clinical tools to guide application and documentation of the practice methodology and systematically gathers data about observable and nonobservable behaviors for each aspect of the four adaptive modes, focusing on the individual or the group of interest. The nurse gathers behavioral data by means of observation, objective measurement, and purposeful interviews.

    The nurse, in collaboration with the human adaptive system of interest, makes a tentative judgment about behaviors in each adaptive mode. Behaviors are tentatively judged as adaptive or ineffective responses, using the criteria of the human adaptive system's individualized goals and comparison of the behaviors with norms signifying adaptation. If norms are not available, the nurse considers adaptation difficulty as pronounced regulator activity with cognator ineffectiveness for individuals, or pronounced stabilizer activity with innovator ineffectiveness for groups. The nurse sets priorities for further assessment, taking the goals of adaptation into account.

    The first priority is behaviors that threaten the survival of the individual, family, group, or community. The second priority is behaviors that affect the growth of the individual, family, group, or community. The third priority is behaviors that affect the continuation of the human race or of society. The fourth priority is behaviors that affect the attainment of full potential for the individual or group.

2. **Assessment of stimuli**—The nurse recognizes that stimuli must be amenable to independent nurse functions. Consequently, factors such as medical diagnoses and medical treatments are not considered stimuli because those factors cannot be independently managed by nurses.

    The nurse identifies the internal and external focal and contextual stimuli that are influencing the behaviors of particular interest. The nurse recognizes that residual stimuli typically are present and attempts to confirm the presence of those stimuli by asking the human adaptive system about other stimuli and/or by recourse to theoretical or experiential knowledge. When residual stimuli finally are identified, they are classified as contextual or focal stimuli. The nurse identifies the internal stimulus of the adaptation level, and determines whether it reflects integrated, compensatory, or compromised life processes.

    In situations where all behaviors are judged as adaptive responses, assessment of stimuli focuses on identifying potential threats to adaptation. The nurse identifies stimuli by means of observation, objective measurement, and purposeful interviews.

    The nurse validates perceptions and thoughts about relevant stimuli with the human adaptive system of interest, using Orlando's deliberative nursing process:

    The nurse shares perceptions and thoughts about relevant stimuli with the human adaptive system.

    The nurse asks if those are the relevant stimuli.

    The human adaptive system confirms or does not confirm the identified stimuli as relevant.

    If the stimuli are not confirmed as relevant, the nurse and the human adaptive system discuss their perceptions of the situation until agreement about relevant stimuli is reached.

3. **Nursing diagnosis**—The nurse uses a process of judgment to make a statement conveying the adaptation status of the human adaptive system of interest. The nursing diagnosis is a statement that identifies the behaviors of interest together with the most relevant influencing stimuli. The nurse uses one of three different approaches to state the nursing diagnosis:

    Behaviors are stated within each adaptive mode and with their most relevant influencing stimuli.

    A summary label for behaviors in each adaptive mode with relevant stimuli is used.

    A label that summarizes a behavioral pattern across adaptive modes that is affected by the same stimuli is used.

    The nurse may link the Roy Adaptation Model–based nursing diagnosis with a relevant diagnosis from the taxonomy of the North American Nursing Diagnosis Association (NANDA). The nurse assigns a priority to each nursing diagnosis—the first priority is behaviors that threaten the survival of the individual, family, group, or community; the second priority is behaviors that affect the growth of the individual, family, group, or community; the third priority is behaviors that affect the continuation of the human race or of society; the fourth priority is behaviors that affect the attainment of full potential for the individual or group.

4. **Goal setting**—The nurse articulates a clear statement of the behavioral outcomes in response to nursing provided to the human adaptive system. The nurse actively involves the human adaptive system in the formation of behavioral goals if possible. The nurse states goals as specific short-term and long-term behavioral outcomes of nursing intervention. The goal statement designates the behavior of interest, the way in which the behavior will change, and the time frame for attainment of the goal. Goals may be stated for ineffective behaviors that are to be changed to adaptive behaviors and also for adaptive behaviors that should be maintained or enhanced.

5. **Nursing intervention**—The nurse selects and implements nursing approaches that have a high probability of changing stimuli or strengthening adaptive processes. Nursing intervention is the management of stimuli. The nurse manages the focal stimulus first if possible, and then manages the contextual stimuli. The nurse uses the McDonald and Harms nursing judgment method, in collaboration with the human adaptive system, to select a nursing intervention:

> Alternative approaches to management of stimuli are listed, along with the consequences of management of each stimulus.
>
> The probability (high, moderate, low) for each consequence is determined.
>
> The value of the outcomes of each approach is designated as desirable or undesirable.

The options are shared with the human adaptive system. The nursing intervention with the highest probability of reaching the valued goal is selected. The nurse determines and implements the steps that will manage the stimulus appropriately.

6. **Evaluation**—The nurse judges the effectiveness of nursing interventions in relation to the behaviors of the human adaptive system. The nurse systematically reassesses observable and nonobservable behaviors for each aspect of the four adaptive modes. The nurse gathers the behavioral data by means of observation, objective measurement, and purposeful interviews. The nurse uses the following criteria to judge the effectiveness of nursing intervention:

> The goal was attained.
>
> The human adaptive system manifests behavior stated in the goals.
>
> The human adaptive system demonstrates a positive response to the stimuli that frees energy for responses to other stimuli.

If the criteria for nursing intervention effectiveness are met, and if there is no threat that the behavior will become ineffective again, then that behavior may be deleted from nursing concern. If, however, the criteria are not met, the nurse must determine what went wrong. Possibilities are:

> The goals were unrealistic or unacceptable to the human adaptive system.
>
> The assessment data were inaccurate or incomplete.
>
> The selected nursing intervention approaches were not implemented properly.

The nurse then returns to Assessment of Behaviors to closely examine behaviors that continue to be ineffective and to try to further understand the situation. The end result of the Roy Adaptation Model Nursing Process is an update of the nursing care plan.

Implications for Nursing Education

The model is an appropriate curriculum guide for diploma, associate degree, baccalaureate degree, and master's degree nursing education programs. Curriculum content is based on the components of the conceptual model. The vertical strands of the curriculum focus on theory and practice. The theory strand encompasses content on the adapting person, health/illness, and stress/disruption. The practice strand emphasizes nursing management of environmental stimuli. The horizontal strands include the nursing process and student adaptation and leadership.

Reference

Roy, C. (2009). *The Roy adaptation model* (3rd ed.). Upper Saddle River, NJ: Pearson.

Roy, C., & Zhan, L. (2006). Sister Callista Roy's adaptation model and its applications. In M.E. Parker, *Nursing theories and nursing practice* (2nd ed., pp. 268-280). Philadelphia: F.A. Davis.

Appendix N1-3 Nursing Theories

A theory is defined as one or more relatively concrete and specific concepts that are derived from a conceptual model, the propositions that narrowly describe those concepts, and the propositions that state relatively concrete and specific relations between two or more of the concepts. Grand theories are rather broad in scope. They are made up of concepts and propositions that are less abstract and general than the concepts and propositions of a conceptual model but are not as concrete and specific as the concepts and propositions of a middle-range theory. Middle-range theories are narrower in scope than grand theories. They are made up of a limited number of concepts and propositions that are written at a relatively concrete and specific level.

HELEN ERICKSON, EVELYN TOMLIN, AND MARY ANN SWAIN'S THEORY OF MODELING AND ROLE MODELING

Overview

A grand theory or paradigm for the practice of professional nursing that focuses on the processes by which the nurse seeks to understand the client's unique model of the world and by which the nurse understands that unique model within the context of scientific theories and plans nursing interventions that promote health. The two major concepts of the theory are:

1. **Modeling**—an act that represents the process the nurse uses to develop an image and understand the client's world from the client's perspective. Modeling encompasses the art and science of nursing. The art of modeling is the development of a mirror image of the situation from the client's perspective, which requires communication skills that help the nurse to enter into the foreign world of the client. The science of modeling is the scientific aggregation and analysis of data collected about the client's model of the world.
2. **Role Modeling**—occurs only after modeling has been accomplished. It involves the facilitation of the individual in attaining, maintaining, or promoting health through purposeful interventions, which are planned on the basis of the analysis and synthesis of data about the client's model of the world. Role modeling also encompasses the art and science of nursing. The art of role modeling occurs when the nurse plans and implements unique interventions with respect to a theoretical base for the practice of nursing. Role modeling is the essence of nurturance, the basis for the predictive and prescriptive component of nursing practice. It requires an unconditional acceptance of the client as the client is while gently encouraging and facilitating growth and development at the client's own pace and within the client's own model of the world.

Implications for Nursing Practice

The nursing process is an ongoing, interactive exchange of information, feelings, and behavior between nurses and clients. The nurse's goal is to nurture and support the client's self-care. Nursing practice is directed toward collection of data primarily from clients but also from families, nurses, and other health care providers. Data collection is organized into four categories:

1. **Description of the situation, including:** *Overview of the situation*—an overview of the client's situation from the client's perspective;
   Etiology—identification of relevant etiological factors, including stressors and destressors;
   Therapeutic needs—identification of possible therapeutic interventions
2. **Immediate and long-term expectations**—development of an understanding of the client's personal orientation regarding present and future expectations.
3. **Resource potential**—available internal and external resources.
   External—determination of the nature of the external support system, from the social network, support system, and health care system.
   Internal—determination of the client's strengths, virtues, and currently available internal resources, including adaptive potential, feeling states, and psychological status.
4. **Current and future goals and life tasks**—determination of the client's current developmental status, so as to understand his or her personal model and to use appropriate communication skills.

Data collection is followed by aggregation, analysis, and synthesis of the data. Nursing diagnoses are derived from the analysis and synthesis of the data. Nursing interventions that are acceptable within the client's model of the world are then developed. The goals of nursing intervention and their associated aims are:

1. **Goal:** Develop a trusting and functional nurse-client relationship. *Aim:* Build trust.
2. **Goal:** Facilitate a futuristic and positive self-projection. *Aim:* Promote the client's positive orientation.
3. **Goal:** Promote affiliated individuation with the minimum possible degree of ambivalence. *Aim:* Promote client's control.
4. **Goal:** Promote a dynamic, adaptive, and holistic health state. *Aim:* Affirm and promote the client's strengths.

5. **Goal:** Promote and nurture coping mechanisms that satisfy basic needs and permit growth-need satisfaction. *Aim:* Set mutual goals that are health-directed.

Implications for Nursing Education

Education of professional nursing practice requires consideration of seven factors that are required for implementation of the modeling and role modeling theory. These factors are:

Have confidence in nursing.
Establish a belief system.
Promote adherence.
Develop a language.
Give and get collegial support.
Be willing to take risks.
Believe in yourself.

Reference

Erickson, H.C., Tomlin, E.M., & Swain, M.A.P. (1983).*Modeling and role modeling: A theory and paradigm for nursing.* Englewood Cliffs, NJ: Prentice Hall.

MADELEINE LEININGER'S THEORY OF CULTURE CARE DIVERSITY AND UNIVERSALITY

Overview

A grand theory focusing on the discovery of human care diversities and universalities and ways to provide culturally congruent care to people. The concepts of the theory are:

1. **Care**—abstract and concrete phenomena related to assisting, supporting, or enabling experiences or behaviors toward or for others with evident or anticipated needs to ameliorate or improve a human condition or lifeway.
2. **Caring**—the actions and activities directed toward assisting, supporting, or enabling another individual or group with evident or anticipated needs to ameliorate or improve a human condition or lifeway or to face death.
3. **Culture**—the learned, shared, and transmitted values, beliefs, norms, and lifeways of a particular group that guide thinking, decisions, and actions in patterned ways; encompasses several cultural and social structure dimensions: technological factors, religious and philosophical factors, kinship and social factors, political and legal factors, economic factors, educational factors, and cultural values and lifeways.
4. **Language**—word usages, symbols, and meanings about care.
5. **Ethnohistory**—past facts, events, instances, experiences of individuals, groups, cultures, and institutions that are primarily people centered (ethno) and which describe, explain, and interpret human lifeways within particular cultural contexts and over short or long periods of time.
6. **Environmental context**—the totality of an event, situation, or particular experiences that give meaning to human expressions, interpretations, and social interactions in particular physical, ecological, sociopolitical, and/or cultural settings.
7. **Health**—a state of well-being that is culturally defined, valued, and practiced, and which reflects the ability of individuals (or groups) to perform their daily role activities in culturally expressed, beneficial, and patterned lifeways.
8. **Worldview**—the way people tend to look out on the world or their universe to form a picture of or a value stance about their life or the world around them.
9. **Cultural care**—the subjectively and objectively transmitted values, beliefs, and patterned lifeways that assist, support, or enable another individual or group to maintain well-being and health, to improve his or her human condition and lifeway, to deal with illness, handicaps, or death. The two dimensions are:
   Cultural care diversity— the variabilities and/or differences in meanings, patterns, values, lifeways, or symbols of care within or between collectivities that are related to assistive, supportive, or enabling human care expressions.
   Cultural care universality— the common, similar, or dominant uniform care meanings, patterns, values, lifeways, or symbols that are manifest among many cultures and reflect assistive, supportive, facilitative, or enabling ways to help people.
10. **Care systems**—the values, norms, and structural features of an organization designed for serving people's health needs, concerns, or conditions. The two types of care systems are:
    Generic (emic) lay care system— traditional or local indigenous health care or cure practices that have special meanings and uses to heal or assist people,

which are generally offered in familiar home or community environmental contexts with their local practitioners.

Professional (etic) health care system— professional care or cure services offered by diverse health personnel who have been prepared through formal professional programs of study in special educational institutions.

11. **Culturally congruent care**— culturally based care knowledge, acts, and decisions used in sensitive and knowledgeable ways to appropriately and meaningfully fit the cultural values, beliefs, and lifeways of clients for their health and well being, or to prevent illness, disabilities, or death. The three modes of culturally congruent care are:

Culture care preservation and/or maintenance refers to assistive, supportive, facilitative, or enabling professional act or decisions that help cultures to retain, preserve, or maintain beneficial care beliefs and values or to face handicaps and death.

Culture care accommodation and/or negotiation refers to assistive, accommodating, facilitative, or enabling creative provider care actions or decisions that help cultures to adapt to or negotiate with others for culturally congruent, safe, and effective care for their health, well being, or to deal with illness or dying.

Culture care repatterning and/or restructuring refers to assistive, supportive, facilitative, or enabling professional actions and mutual decisions that would help people to reorder, change, modify, or restructure their life ways and institutions for better (or beneficial) health care patterns, practices, or outcomes

12. **Cultural and social structure factors**— Factors that influence expressions and meanings of care, including gender and class differences in religion or spirituality, kinship or social ties, politics, legal issues, education, economics, technology, philosophy of life, and cultural beliefs and values.

Implications for Nursing Practice

Nursing practice is directed toward improving and providing culturally congruent care to people. A practice methodology for the Theory of Culture Care Diversity and Universality is as follows:

Goals of Nursing Practice are: to improve and to provide culturally congruent care to people that is beneficial, will fit with, and be useful to the client, family, or culture group healthy lifeways; to provide culturally congruent nursing care in order to improve or offer a different kind of nursing care service to people of diverse or similar cultures.

Clients include individuals, families, subcultures, groups, communities, and institutions.

Culturalogical Assessment The nurse maintains a holistic or total view of the client's world by using the Sunrise Model and Enablers to guide assessment of cultural beliefs, values, and lifeways.

The nurse is aware that the client may belong to a subculture or special group that maintains its own values and beliefs that differ from the values and beliefs of the dominant culture. The nurse shows a genuine interest in the client and learns from and maintains respect for the client. The nurse asks open-ended questions and maintains the role of an active listener, learner, and reflector. The nurse shares professional knowledge only if the client asks about such knowledge.

The nurse begins the assessment with such questions as: What would you like to share with me today about your experiences or beliefs, to help you keep well? Are there some special ideas or ways you would like nurses to care for you? The nurse gives attention to clients' gender differences, communication modes, special language terms, interpersonal relationships, and use of space and foods.

Nursing Judgments, Decisions, and Actions [Nursing practice requires the coparticipation of nurses and clients working together to identify, plan, implement, and evaluate the appropriate mode(s) of culturally congruent care. Nursing decisions and actions encompass assisting, accommodating, supporting, facilitating, and enabling. Nurse and client select one or more mode of culturally congruent care.

Culture Care Preservation and/or Maintenance— used when professional decisions and actions are needed to help clients of a designated culture to retain, preserve, or maintain care beliefs

Culture Care Accommodation and/or Negotiation— used when professional decisions and actions are needed to help clients of a designated culture adapt to or negotiate with others for care.

Culture Care Repatterning and/or Restructuring— used when professional decisions and actions are needed to help clients of a designated culture to reorder, change, modify, or restructure their life ways and institutions.

Clinical Protocols Specific nursing practices or clinical protocols are derived from the findings of research guided by the Theory of Culture Care Diversity and Universality. The research findings are used to develop protocols for cultural-congruent care that blends with the particular cultural values, beliefs, and lifeways of the client, and is assessed to be beneficial, satisfying, and meaningful to the client.

Implications for Nursing Education

Professional nursing care, learned in formal educational programs, builds upon the generic care given by naturalistic lay and folk care givers. The curriculum emphasizes transcultural nursing knowledge, with formal study about different cultures in the world, as well as culture-universal and culture-specific health care needs of people and nursing care practices. Transcultural nurse generalists are prepared at the baccalaureate level for the general use of transcultural nursing concepts, principles, and practices. Transcultural nurse specialists, who are prepared at the doctoral level, have in-depth understanding of a few cultures and can function as field practitioners, teachers, researchers, or consultants. Certification is awarded by the Transcultural Nursing Society to nurses who have educational preparation in transcultural nursing or the equivalent and who demonstrate basic clinical competence in transcultural nursing.

Reference

Leininger, M.M., & McFarland, M.R. (2006). *Culture care diversity and universality: A worldwide nursing theory* (2nd ed.). Boston: Jones and Bartlett.

MARGARET NEWMAN'S THEORY OF HEALTH AS EXPANDING CONSCIOUSNESS
Overview

A grand theory focusing on health as the expansion of consciousness, with emphasis on the idea that every person in every situation, no matter how disordered and hopeless the situation may seem, is part of the universal process of expanding consciousness. The concepts of the theory are:

1. **Consciousness**—the informational capacity of human beings, that is, the ability of humans to interact with their environments. Consciousness encompasses interconnected cognitive and affective awareness, physiochemical maintenance including the nervous and endocrine systems, growth processes, the immune system, and the genetic code. Consciousness can be seen in the quantity and quality of the interaction between human beings and their environments. The process of life is toward higher levels of consciousness; sometimes this process is smooth, pleasant, harmonious; other times it is difficult and disharmonious, as in disease.

2. **Pattern**—a fundamental attribute of all there is and reveals unity in diversity; information that depicts the whole, understanding of the meaning of all the relationships at once; relatedness; self-organizing over time, such that it becomes more highly organized with more information. Pattern identifies particular people and is an identification of the wholeness of the person. Pattern is manifested as exchanging (interchanging matter and energy between person and environment and transforming energy from one form to another); communicating (interchanging information from one system to another); relating (connecting with other persons and the environment); valuing (assigning worth); choosing (selecting of one or more alternatives); moving (rhythmic alternating between activity and rest); perceiving (receiving and interpreting information); feeling (sensing physical and intuitive awareness); and knowing (personal recognition of self and world). Pattern encompasses three dimensions—Movement-Space-Time, Rhythm, and Diversity.

   Movement-Space-Time —movement is the natural condition of life, an essential property of matter and a means of communicating; when movement ceases, it is an indication that life has gone out of the organism; movement is the means whereby one perceives reality and becomes aware of self; movement is a means whereby space and time become a reality. Space encompasses personal space, inner space, and life space as dimensions of space relevant to the individual, and territoriality, shared space, and distancing as dimensions relevant to the family. Time is a function of movement; the amount of time perceived to be passing (subjective time); clock time (objective time). Time and space have a complementary relationship.

   Rhythm —basic to movement; the rhythm of movement is an integrating experience.

   Diversity —seen in the parts.

Implications for Nursing Practice

Nursing practice is directed toward facilitating pattern recognition by connecting with the client in an authentic way, and assisting the client to discover new rules for a higher level of organization or consciousness. Newman's Research as Praxis Protocol is a research/practice methodology. The phenomenon of interest is the process of expanding consciousness.

The Interview The meeting of the nurse and the study participant/client occurs when there is a mutual attraction via congruent patterns, i.e., interpenetration of the two fields. The nurse and study participant/client enter into a partnership, with the mutual goal of participating in an authentic relationship, trusting that in the process of its unfolding, both will emerge at a higher level of consciousness.

Transcription The nurse listens carefully to and transcribes the tape of the interview soon after the interview is completed. The nurse is sensitive to the relevance of the data and may omit comments made by the study participant/client that do not directly relate to his or her life pattern, with an appropriate note to the place on the tape where such comments occurred, in case those comments seem important later.

Development of the Narrative: Pattern Recognition The nurse selects the statements deemed most important to the study participant/client and arranges the key segments of the data in chronological order to highlight the most significant events and persons. The data remain the same except in the order of presentation. Natural breaks where a pattern shift occurs are noted and form the basis of the sequential patterns. Recognition of the pattern of the whole, made up of segments of the study participant/client's relationships over time, will emerge for the nurse. The nurse then transmutes the narrative into a simple diagram of the sequential pattern configurations.

Diagram: Pattern Recognition The nurse then transmutes the narrative into a simple diagram of the sequential pattern configurations.

Follow-Up: Pattern Recognition The nurse conducts a second interview with the study participant/client to share the diagram or other visual portrayal of the pattern. The nurse does not interpret the diagram. Rather, it is used simply to illustrate the study participant/ client's story in graphic form, which tends to accentuate the contrasts and repetitions in relationships over time. The mutual viewing of the graphic form is an opportunity for the study participant/client to confirm and clarify or revise the story being portrayed. The mutual viewing also is an opportunity for the nurse to clarify any aspect of the story about which he or she has any doubt.

The nature of the pattern of person-environment interaction will begin to emerge in terms of energy flow (e.g., blocked, diffuse, disorganized, repetitive, or whatever descriptors and metaphors come to mind to describe the pattern). The study participant/client may express signs that pattern recognition is occurring (or already has occurred in the interval following the first interview) as the nurse and study participant/client reflect together on the study participant/client's life pattern. Sometimes, no signs of pattern recognition emerge, and if so, that characterizes the pattern for that person. It is not to be forced.

Application of Theory of Health as Expanding Consciousness The nurse undertakes more intense analysis of the data in light of the Theory of Health as Expanding Consciousness after the interviews are completed. The nurse evaluates the nature of the sequential patterns of interaction in terms of quality and complexity and interprets the patterns according to the study participant/client's position on Young's spectrum of consciousness. The sequential patterns represent presentational construing or relationships. Any similarities of pattern among a group of study participants/clients having a similar experience may be designated by themes and stated in propositional form.

Implications for Nursing Education

Education for nursing should be the professional doctoral degree, the Doctor of Nursing (ND), which requires a strong arts and sciences background as pre-professional education. Students and practicing nurses who plan to use the Theory of Health as Expanding Consciousness have to be prepared for personal transformation in the way that they view the world and nursing.

Reference

Newman, M. A. (1994). *Health as expanding consciousness* (2nd ed.). New York: National League for Nursing.

Brown, J.W. (2010). Margaret A. Newman: Health as expanding consciousness. In A. Marriner Tomey & M.R. Alligood, *Nursing theorists and their work* (7th ed., pp. 480-502). St. Louis: Mosby Elsevier.

Picard, C., & Jones, D. (Eds.). (2005). *Giving voice to what we know: Margaret Newman's theory of health as expanding consciousness in practice, research, and education.* Sudbury, MA: Jones and Bartlett.

IDA JEAN ORLANDO'S THEORY OF THE DELIBERATIVE NURSING PROCESS OVERVIEW

Overview

A middle-range predictive theory focusing on an interpersonal process that is directed toward facilitating identification of the nature of the patient's distress and his or her immediate needs for help. The concepts of the theory are:

1. **Patient's behavior**—behavior observed by the nurse in an immediate nurse-patient situation. The two dimensions are:

   Need for help— a requirement of the patient that, if supplied, relieves or diminishes immediate distress or improves immediate sense of adequacy or well-being.

   Improvement— an increase in patients' mental and physical health, their well-being, and their sense of adequacy. The need for help and improvement can be expressed in both nonverbal and verbal forms. Visual manifestations of nonverbal behavior include such motor activities as eating, walking, twitching, and trembling, as well as such physiological forms as urinating, defecating, temperature and blood pressure readings, respiratory rate, and skin color. Vocal forms of nonverbal behavior—nonverbal behavior that is heard—include crying, moaning, laughing, coughing, sneezing, sighing, yelling, screaming, groaning, and singing. Verbal behavior refers to what a patient says, including complaints, requests, questions, refusals, demands, and comments or statements.

2. **Nurse's reaction**—the nurse's nonobservable response to the patient's behavior. The three dimensions are:

   Perception— physical stimulation of any one of the five senses by the patient's behavior.

   Thought— an idea that occurs in the nurse's mind.

   Feeling— a state of mind inclining the nurse toward or against a perception, thought, or action; occurs in response to the nurse's perceptions and thoughts.

3. **Nurse's activity**—the observable actions taken by nurses in response to their reactions, including instructions, suggestions, directions, explanations, information, requests, and questions directed toward the patient; making decisions for the patient; handling the patient's body; administering medications or treatments; and changing the patient's immediate environment. The two dimensions of nurse's activity are:

   Automatic nursing process— actions decided on by the nurse for reasons other than the patient's immediate need.

   Deliberative nursing process (process discipline)—a specific set of nurse behaviors or actions directed toward the patient's behavior that ascertain or meet the patient's immediate needs for help.

Implications for Nursing Practice

Nursing practice is directed toward identifying and meeting the patient's immediate needs for help through use of Orlando's Practice Methodology.

Observations encompass any and all information pertaining to a patient that the nurse acquires while on duty.

Direct Observations are the nurse's reaction to the patient's behavior. Direct observations are any perception, thought, or feeling the nurse has from his or her own experience of the patient's behavior at any or several moments in time.

Indirect Observations consist of any information that is derived from a source other than the patient. This information pertains to, but is not directly derived from, the patient.

Actions are carried out with or for the patient

Nurse's Activity: Deliberative Nursing Process — The process used to share and validate the nurse's direct and indirect observations is the Deliberative Nursing Process. Clinical protocols contain the specific requirements for the Deliberative Nursing Process. The nurse may express and explore any aspect of his or her reaction to the patient's behavior—perception, thought, or feeling. If exploration of one aspect of the nurse's reaction does not result in identification of the patient's need for help, then another aspect of the reaction can be explored. If exploration of all aspects of the nurse's reaction does not yield a verbal response from the patient, then the nurse may use negative expressions to demonstrate continued interest in the patient's behavior and to give the patient permission to respond with his or her own negative reaction. Examples of negative expressions by the nurse are: Is it that you don't think I'll understand? Am I wrong? It looked like that procedure was very painful, and you didn't say a word about it.

Direct Help — The nurse meets the patient's need directly when the patient is unable to meet his or her own need and when the activity is confined to the nurse-patient contact

Indirect Help — The nurse meets the patient's need indirectly when the activity extends to arranging the services of a person, agency, or resource that the patient cannot contact by himself or herself.

Reporting The nurse receives reports about the patient's behavior from other nurses, and from other health professionals. The nurse reports his or her observations of the patient's behavior to other nurses and other health professionals.

Recording The nurse records the nursing process, including: the nurse's perception of or about the patient; the nurse's thought and/or feeling about the perception; what the nurse said and/or did to, with, or for the patient.

Implications for Nursing Education

Students should be trained in the use of the deliberative nursing process for all person-to-person contacts. The purpose of training is to change the nurse's activity from personal and automatic to disciplined and professional. Training is facilitated by use of process recordings that include perceptions of or about the patient, thoughts and/or feelings about the perception, and what was said and/or done to, with, or for the patient. The process discipline can be successfully taught in 6 to 12 weeks.

References

Orlando, I. J. (1961). *The dynamic nurse-patient relationship: Function, process and principles.* New York: G. P. Putnam's Sons. [Reprinted 1990, New York: National League for Nursing]

Orlando, I. J. (1972). *The discipline and teaching of nursing process: An evaluative study.* New York: G. P. Putnam's Sons.

ROSEMARIE PARSE'S THEORY OF HUMAN BECOMING
Overview

A grand theory focusing on human experiences of participation with the universe in the cocreation of health. The concepts of the theory are:

1. **Human becoming**—a unitary construct referring to the human being's living health.
2. **Meaning**—the linguistic and imagined content of something and the interpretation that one gives to something.
3. **Rhythmicity**—the cadent, paradoxical patterning of the human-universe mutual process.
4. **Transcendence**—reaching beyond with possibles—the hopes and dreams envisioned in multidimensional experiences [and] powering the originating of transforming.
5. **Imaging**—reflective/prereflective coming to know the explicit/tacit all-at-once.
6. **Valuing**—confirming/not confirming cherished beliefs in light of a personal world view.
7. **Languaging**—signifying valued images through speaking/being silent and moving/being still.
8. **Revealing/Concealing**—disclosing/not disclosing all-at-once.
9. **Enabling/Limiting**—living the opportunities/restrictions present in all choosings all-at-once.
10. **Connecting/Separating**—being with and apart from others, ideas, objects, and situations all-at-once.
11. **Powering**—the pushing/resisting process of affirming/not affirming being in light of nonbeing.
12. **Originating**—inventing new ways of conforming/nonconforming in the certainty/uncertainty of living.
13. **Transforming**—shifting the view of the familiar/unfamiliar, the changing of change in coconstituting anew in a deliberate way.

The three major principles of the theory of human becoming are:

1. **Structuring meaning is the imaging and valuing of languaging**
   Imaging: explicit-tacit; reflective-prereflective.
   Valuing: confirming-not confirming.
   Languaging: speaking-being silent; moving-being still.

2. **Configuring rhythmical patterns of relating is the revealing-concealing and enabling-limiting of connecting-separating**
   Revealing-concealing; disclosing-not disclosing.
3. **Cotranscending with possibles is the powering and originating of transforming**
   Powering: pushing-resisting; affirming-not affirming; being-nonbeing
   Originating: Certainty-uncertainty; conforming-not conforming
   Transforming: Familiar-unfamiliar

Implications for Nursing Practice

Nursing practice is directed toward respecting the quality of life as perceived by the person and the family. The practice methodology is as follows:

Principle 1: Structuring meaning *Illuminating Meaning:* explicating what was, is, and will be. *Explicating:* making clear what is appearing now through languaging.

Principle 2: Cocreating rhythmical patterns. *Synchronizing rhythms:* dwelling with the pitch, yaw, and roll of the human-universe process. *Dwelling with:* immersing with the flow of connecting/separating.

Principle 3: Cotranscending with possibles.*Moving beyond:* propelling with envisioned possibles of transforming.

Contexts of nursing Nurse-person situations and nurse-group situations. Participants include children and adults. Locations include homes, shelters, health care centers, parish halls, all departments of hospitals and clinics, rehabilitation centers, offices, and other milieus where nurses are with people.

Goal of discipline of nursing is quality of life from the person's, family's, and community's perspective.

Goal of the human becoming nurse is to be truly present with people as they enhance their quality of lives.

True presence is a special way of "being with" in which the nurse is attentive to moment-to-moment changes in meaning as she or he bears witness to the person's or group's own living of value priorities.

Coming-to-be Present is an all-at-once gentling down and lifting up. True presence begins in the coming-to-be-present moments of preparation and attention. Preparation involves: an emptying to be available to bear witness to the other or others; being flexible, not fixed but gracefully present from one's center; dwelling with the universe at the moment, considering the attentive presence about to be. Attention involves focusing on the moment at hand for immersion.

Face-to-face discussions — Nurse and person engage in dialogue. Conversation may be through discussion in general or through interpretations of stories, films, drawings, photographs, music, metaphors, poetry, rhythmic movements, and other expressions.

Silent immersion — A process of the quiet that does not refrain from sending and receiving messages. A chosen way of becoming in the human-universe process lived in the rhythm of speaking–being silent, moving–being still as valued images incarnate meaning. True presence without words.

Lingering presence — Recalling a moment through a lingering presence that arises after an immediate engagement. A reflective-prereflective "abiding with" attended to through glimpses of the other person, idea, object, or situation.

Ways of Changing Health Patterns in True Presence *Creative Imagining Picturing* by seeing, hearing, and feeling, what a situation might be like if lived in a different way.

Affirming Personal Becoming Uncovering preferred personal health patterns by critically thinking about how or who one is.

Glimpsing the paradoxical Changing one's view of a situation by recognizing incongruities in that situation.

Implications for Nursing Education

Course content flows from the three principles of the theory. Clinical courses emphasize the knowledge and skills requisite to the application of the practice methodology. Graduate education builds on baccalaureate education and prepares specialists who concentrate on creating and testing concepts of the theory of human becoming.

References

Parse, R. R. (1992). Human becoming: Parse's theory of nursing. *Nursing Science Quarterly, 5,* 35–42.

Parse, R. R. (Ed.). (1995). *Illuminations: The human becoming theory in practice and research.* New York: National League for Nursing.

Parse, R. R. (1998). *The human becoming school of thought: A perspective for nurses and other health care professionals.* Thousand Oaks, CA: Sage.

Parse, R.R. (2006). Part One: Rosemarie Rizzo Parse's human becoming school of thought. In M.E. Parker, *Nursing theories and nursing practice* (2nd ed., pp. 187-194). Philadelphia: F.A. Davis.

Parse, R.R. (2007). The humanbecoming school of thought in 2050. *Nursing Science Quarterly,* 20, 308-311.

NOLA PENDER'S HEALTH PROMOTION MODEL

Overview

A middle-range theory focusing on the relation of individual characteristics and experiences, behavior-specific, cognitions and affect, commitment to a plan of action, and competing demands and preferences as to health-promoting behavior. The concepts of the theory are as follows:

1. **Individual characteristics and experiences** —prior related behavior and inherited and acquired characteristics that influence beliefs, affect, and performance of health-promoting behavior.

   Prior related behavior—a behavior, enacted in the past, that is the same as or similar to the health-promoting behavior of interest.

   Personal factors—inherited and acquired biological, psychological, and sociocultural characteristics.

   Personal biological factors—encompass characteristics such as age, gender, body mass index, pubertal status, menopausal status, aerobic capacity, strength, agility, and balance.

   Personal psychological factors—encompass characteristics such as self-esteem, self-motivation, personal competence, perceived health status, and definition of health.

   Personal sociocultural factors—encompass characteristics such as race, ethnicity, acculturation, education, and socioeconomic status.

2. **Behavior-specific cognitions and affect**—factors that act as motivators for commitment to a plan of action and performance of health-promoting behavior and that are modifiable through nursing actions.

   Perceived benefits of action —perception of anticipated positive outcomes that will occur as a result of performing a health-promoting behavior. There is a positive relation between perceived benefits of action and commitment to a plan of action.

   Perceived barriers to action—perception of anticipated, imagined, or real blocks and personal costs of performing a health-promoting behavior; a constraint on commitment to a plan of action.

   Perceived self-efficacy—perception of personal capability to organize and execute a health-promoting behavior; the higher the perceived self-efficacy, the lower the perceived barriers to action and the higher the likelihood of commitment to a plan of action and actual performance of a health-promoting behavior.

   Activity-related affect—subjective positive or negative feelings that occur before, during, or following performance of a health-promoting behavior. There is a reciprocal positive relation between affect toward a behavior and perceived self-efficacy, such that the more positive the affect, the greater the perceived self-efficacy and vice versa. There is a positive relation between affect toward a behavior and commitment to a plan of action and performance of a health-promoting behavior.

   Interpersonal influences—cognitions about the behaviors, beliefs, or attitudes of significant others, including family, peers, and health care providers. Commitment to a plan of action and performance of health-promoting behavior is more like to occur when significant others model the behavior, expect the behavior to occur, and provide assistance and support to enable the behavior. The cognitions include:

   Norms that reflect expectations of significant others;

   Social support, including instrumental and emotional encouragement;

   Modeling, which refers to vicarious learning through observing others who are performing a health-promoting behavior.

   Situational influences—personal perceptions and cognitions of a particular external environmental situation that can facilitate or impede performance of health-promoting behavior, including perceptions of options available, demand characteristics, and aesthetic environmental features.

3. **Commitment to a plan of action**—intention to perform a health-promoting behavior and identification of a planned strategy that leads to performance of the behavior. There is a positive relation between commitment to a plan of action and maintenance of performance of a health-promoting behavior over time.

4. **Immediate competing demands and preferences**—competing demands are alternative behaviors over which individuals have low control due to environmental contingencies, such as work or family care responsibilities; competing preferences are alternative behaviors over which individuals exert relatively high control, such as choice of a particular food for a snack or meal. Commitment to a plan of action is less likely to result in the desired health-promoting behavior when competing demands require immediate attention or when competing preferences are more attractive.

5. **Health-promoting behavior**—action outcome directed toward attaining positive health outcomes.

Implications for Nursing Practice

Nursing practice is directed toward modification of cognitions, affect, and the interpersonal and physical environment to create incentives for health actions for people of all ages.

Implications for Nursing Education

Education for nursing practice focuses on promotion of health and prevention of illness and disease prevention. Health education strategies are emphasized.

Reference

Pender, N.J., Murdaugh, C.L., & Parsons, M.A. (2006). *Health promotion in nursing practice* (5th ed.). Upper Saddle River, NJ: Prentice Hall.

HILDEGARD PEPLAU'S THEORY OF INTERPERSONAL RELATIONS

Overview

A middle-range descriptive theory focusing on the phases of the interpersonal process that occurs when an ill person and a nurse come together to resolve a difficulty felt in relation to health. The one concept of the theory is nurse-patient relationship, which is an interpersonal process made up of four components—two persons, the professional expertise of the nurse, and the client's problem or need for which expert nursing services are sought, and which has three discernible phases; one phase has two subphases:

1. **Orientation**—the phase in which the nurse first identifies himself or herself by name and professional status and states the purpose, nature, and time available for the patient; the phase during which the nurse conveys professional interest and receptivity to the patient, begins to know the patient as a person, obtains essential information about the patient's health condition, and sets the tone for further interactions.

2. **Working**—the phase in which the major course occurs. The two subphases are:
   Identification—the subphase during which the patient learns how to make use of the nurse-patient relationship.
   Exploitation—the subphase during which the patient makes full use of available professional services.

3. **Termination**—the phase in which the work accomplished is summarized and closure occurs.

Implications for Nursing Practice

Nursing practice is directed toward promoting favorable changes in patients, which is accomplished through the nurse-patient relationship. Within that relationship, the nurse's major function is to study the interpersonal relations between the patient/client and others. Peplau's clinical methodology, which can be used for both nursing practice and nursing research, is as follows:

Observation—Purpose is the identification, clarification, and verification of impressions about the interactive drama, of the pushes and pulls in the relationship between nurse and patient, as they occur.

Participant Observation — Nurse's Behavior includes observation of the nurse's words, voice tones, body language, and other gestural messages. Patient's Behavior includes observation of the patient's words, voice tones, body language, and other gestural messages

Interpersonal phenomena include observation of what goes on between the patient and the nurse.

Reframing empathic linkages occurs when the nurse's and/or the patient's ability to feel in self the emotions experienced by the other person in the same situation is converted to verbal communications by the nurse asking: What are you feeling right now?

Communication aims are the selection of symbols or concepts that convey both the reference, or meaning in the mind of the individual, and referent, the object or actions symbolized in the concept; and the wish to struggle toward the development of common understanding for words between two or more people.

Interpersonal techniques are verbal interventions used by nurses during nurse-patient relationships aimed at accomplishing problem resolution and competence development in patients.

Principle of clarity — Words and sentences used to communicate are clarifying events when they occur within the frame of reference of common experiences of both or all participants, or when their meaning is established or made understandable as a result of joint and sustained effort of all parties concerned. Clarity in communication is promoted when the nurse and the patient discuss their preconceptions about the meaning of words and work toward a common understanding. Clarity is achieved when the meaning of a word to the patient is expressed and talked over and a new view is expanded in awareness.

Principle of continuity — Continuity in communication occurs when language is used as a tool for the promotion of coherence or connections of ideas expressed and leads to discrimination of relationships or connections among ideas and the feelings, events, or themes conveyed in those ideas. Continuity is promoted when the nurse is able to pick up threads of conversation that the patient offers in the course of a conversation and over a longer period such as a week, and when he or she aids the patient to focus and to expand these threads.

Recording is the written record of the communication between nurse and patient, that is, the data collected through participant observation and reframing of empathic linkages. The aim is to capture the exact wording of the interaction between the nurse and the patient.

Data analysis focuses on testing the nurse's hypotheses, which are formulated from first impressions or hunches about the patient.

Phases of the nurse-patient relationship — Identify the phase of nurse-patient relationship in which communication occurred
:

Roles: Identify the roles taken by the nurse and the patient in each phase of the nurse-patient relationship.

Relations: Identify the connections, linkages, ties, and bonds that go on or went on between a patient and others, including family, friends, staff, or the nurse. Analyze the relations to identify their nature, origin, function, and mode.

Pattern integrations: Identify the patterns of the interpersonal relation between two or more people which together link or bind them and which enable the people to transform energy into patterns of action that bring satisfaction or security in the face of a recurring problem. Determine the type of pattern integration: complementary—the behavior of one person fits with and thereby complements the behavior of the other person; mutual—the same or similar behaviors are used by both persons; alternating—different behaviors used by two persons alternate between the two persons; antagonistic—the behaviors of the two persons do not fit but the relationship continues.

Implications for Nursing Education

Nursing is an educative instrument, a maturing force, that aims to promote forward movement of personality in the direction of creative, constructive, productive, personal, and community living. The task of each school of nursing is the fullest development of the nurse as a person who is aware of how he or she functions in a situation and as a person who wants to nurse patients in a helpful way.

References

Peplau, H. E. (1952). *Interpersonal relations in nursing.* New York: G. P. Putnam's Sons. [Reprinted 1991. New York: Springer]

Peplau, H. E. (1992). Interpersonal relations: A theoretical framework for application in nursing practice. *Nursing Science Quarterly, 5,* 13–18.

Peplau, H. E. (1997). Peplau's theory of interpersonal relations. *Nursing Science Quarterly, 10,* 162–167.

Peden, A.R. (2006). Hildegard E. Peplau's process of practice-based theory development and its applications. In M.E. Parker, *Nursing theories and nursing practice* (2nd ed., pp. 58-69). Philadelphia: F.A. Davis.

REVA RUBIN'S THEORY OF CLINICAL NURSING

Overview

A grand theory focusing on patients as persons undergoing subjectively involved experiences of varying degrees of tension or stress in a health problem situation. The major concepts are the situation of the patient and nursing care. Statements related to the patient situation and nursing care are:

1. Nursing care is dependent on the best estimate available of the situation of the patient.
2. Nursing care exists in a one-to-one relationship with the patient.
3. The relationship of nursing care to the situation of the patient is an ever-changing process of interaction.
4. The situation of the patient is expressed as a fraction or ratio that reflects the level or intensity of nursing care required.

> If the situation for the patient is relatively insignificant, one that the patient can cope with quite well, then nursing care probably need not go beyond careful assessment.
> If the situation for the patient is overwhelming, nursing care may have to encompass a whole series of activities to reduce the effects of the situation or reinforce the capacities of the patient in coping with the situation.

5. Situations within the sphere of proper nursing concern are fluid.

Implications for Nursing Practice

Nursing practice is directed toward helping the patient adjust to, endure through, and usefully integrate the health problem situation in its many ramifications through the phenomenon of *situational fluidity,* which characterizes nursing care in terms of:

1. **Time** —nursing operates within the immediate present; patient needs and behavior have an immediacy if not an urgency.
2. **Definition or diagnostic sets** —nursing diagnoses are based on the definition of capacities and limitations of the persons who are patients in relation to the situations in which they find themselves.
3. **Actions** —nursing actions are primarily directed toward helping the patient realign observations and expectations into a better "fit" with each other; nursing conveys a message to patients about themselves in their immediate situations.

Implications for Nursing Education

Education for nursing practice and nursing research emphasizes learning the naturalistic method of observation of patients in action, involved in a natural situation and setting. The learners typically are graduate students in nursing. The nurse-observer is viewed as an identifiable and functional part of the setting, as well as a helpful adjunct in the situation. The student is trained to observe while providing nursing care for the patient in a particular situation and to then record the entire nurse-patient interaction. The recorded observation serves as a database for evaluation of the quality and adequacy of nursing care as well as for generation of new theories.

References

Rubin, R. (1968). A theory of clinical nursing. *Nursing Research, 17,* 210–212.
Rubin, R. (1984). *Maternal identity and the maternal experience.* New York: Springer.

JEAN WATSON'S THEORY OF HUMAN CARING

Overview

A middle-range explanatory theory focusing on the human component of caring and the moment-to-moment encounters between the one who is caring and the one who is being cared for, especially the caring activities performed by nurses as they interact with others. The concepts of the theory are:

1. **Transpersonal caring relationship**—human-to-human connectedness, whereby each person is touched by the human center of the other; a special kind of relationship involving a high regard for the whole person and his or her being-in-the world. The concept transpersonal caring relationship encompasses three dimensions:

> *Self*— transpersonal-mindbodyspirit oneness, an embodied self, and an embodied spirit.
> *Phenomenal field*— the totality of human experience, one's being-in-the-world.
> *Intersubjectivity*— refers to an intersubjective human-to-human relationship in which the person of the nurse affects and is affected by the person of the other, both of whom are fully present in the moment and feel a union with the other.

2. **Caring occasion/caring moment**—The coming together of nurse and other(s), which involves action and choice both by the nurse and the other. The moment of coming together in a caring occasion presents them with the opportunity to decide how to be in the relationship—what to do with the moment.

3. **Caring (healing) consciousness**—A holographic dynamic that is manifest within a field of consciousness, and which exists through time and space and is dominant over physical illness.

4. **Clinical Caritas Processes**—those aspects of nursing that actually potentiate therapeutic healing processes for both the one caring and the one being cared for. The 10 carative factors are:

> Practice of loving kindness and equanimity within the context of caring consciousness
>
> Being authentically present and enabling and sustaining the deep belief system and subjective life world of self and one-being-cared-for
>
> Cultivation of one's own spiritual practices and transpersonal self, going beyond ego self, opening to others with sensitivity and compassion
>
> Developing and sustaining a helping-trusting, authentic caring relationship
>
> Being present to, and supportive of, the expression of positive and negative feelings as a connection with deeper spirit of self and the one-being-cared-for
>
> Creative use of self and all ways of knowing as part of the caring process; to engage in artistry of caring-healing practices
>
> Engaging in genuine teaching-learning experience that attends to unity of being and meaning, attempting to stay within others' frames of reference
>
> Creating healing environments at all levels (physical as well as non-physical, subtle environment of energy and consciousness, whereby wholeness, beauty, comfort, dignity, and peace are potentiated)
>
> Assisting with basic needs, with an intentional caring consciousness, administering "human care essentials," which potentiate alignment of mind-body-spirit, wholeness, and unity of being in all aspects of care, tending to both embodied spirit and evolving spiritual emergence
>
> Opening and attending to spiritual-mysterious, and existential dimensions of one's own life-death; soul care for self and the one-being-cared-for

Implications for Nursing Practice

Nursing practice is directed toward helping persons gain a higher degree of harmony within the mind, body, and soul, which generates self-knowledge, self-reverence, self-healing, and self-care processes while increasing diversity, which is pursued through use of the 10clinical caritas processes.

Requirements for a Transpersonal Caring Relationship: The nurse considers the person to be valid and whole, regardless of illness or disease, and makes a moral commitment and directs intentionality and consciousness to the protection, enhancement, and potentiation of humanity, wholeness, and healing, such that a person creates or co-creates his or her own meaning for existence, healing, wholeness, and caring.

The nurse orients intent, will, and consciousness toward affirming the subjective/ intersubjective significance of the person; a search to sustain mind-body-spirit unity and I/Thou versus I/It relationships.

The nurse has the ability to realize, accurately detect, and connect with the inner condition (spirit) of another.

The nurse recognizes that actions, words, behaviors, cognition, body language, feelings, intuition, thought, senses, and the energy field gestalt all contribute to the interconnection.

The nurse has the ability to assess and realize another's condition of being in the world and to feel a union with the other. This ability is translated via movements, gestures, facial expressions, procedures, information, touch, sound, verbal expressions, and other scientific, aesthetic, and human means of communication into nursing art acts wherein the nurse responds to, attends to, or reflects the condition of the other. Drawn from the ontological caring consciousness stance and basic competencies of the nurse, this ability expands and translates into advanced caring healing modalities, nursing arts, advanced nursing therapeutics, and healing arts.

The nurse understands that the caring healing modalities potentiate harmony, wholeness, and comfort and produce inner healing by releasing some of the disharmony and blocked energy that interfere with the natural healing processes. Transpersonal caring-healing modalities include intentional conscious use of auditory modalities (music, sounds of nature, wind, sea, chimes, chants, familiar sounds), visual modalities (light, color, form, texture, works of art), olfactory modalities (aromatherapy, breathwork, breathing fresh air, inhalation-exhalation), tactile modalities (acupressure, body therapy, caring touch, foot reflexology, shiatsu, therapeutic massage), gustatory modalities (foods in one's diet), mental-cognitive modalities (importance of mind and imagination through story), kinesthetic modalities (basic skin care, deep massage and other body work, movement, dance, yoga, Tai Chi, applied kinesiology, chiropractic), caring consciousness modalities (physical presence, psychological presence, therapeutic presence).

The nurse understands that his or her own life history and previous experiences, including opportunities, studies, consciousness of having lived through or experienced human feelings and various human conditions, or of having imagined others' feelings in various circumstances, are valuable contributors to the transpersonal caring relationship.

Authentic Presencing The nurse is authentically present as self and other in a reflective mutuality of being and becoming and centers consciousness and intentionality on caring, healing, and wholeness, rather than on disease, problems, illness, complications, and technocures.

The nurse attempts to stay within the other's frame of reference, join in a mutual search for meaning and wholeness of being, and potentiate comfort measures, pain control, a sense of well being, or spiritual transcendence of suffering.

Implications for Nursing Education

Professional nursing education should be at the postbaccalaureate level of the Doctorate of Nursing (N.D.). The nature of human life is the subject matter of nursing. The curriculum acknowledges caring as a moral ideal and incorporates philosophical theories of human caring, health, and healing. Core areas of content are the humanities, social-biomedical science, and human caring content and process. Courses should use art, music, literature, poetry, drama, and movement to facilitate understanding of responses to health and illness as well as to new caring-healing modalities.

References

Watson, J. (1985). *Nursing: Human science and human care. A theory of nursing.* Norwalk, CT: Appleton-Century-Crofts. [Reprinted 1988. New York: National League for Nursing]

Watson, J. (2008). *Nursing: The philosophy and science of caring* (rev. ed.). Boulder, CO: University Press of Colorado

Watson, J (1997). The theory of human caring: Retrospective and prospective. *Nursing Science Quarterly, 10,* 49–52.

Watson, J. (2006). Part One: Jean Watson's theory of human caring. In M.E. Parker, *Nursing theories and nursing practice* (2nd ed., pp. 295-302). Philadelphia: F.A. Davis.

SOURCE: Adapted from overviews written by Jacqueline Fawcett for the videotape and CD-ROM series, *The Nurse Theorists: Portraits of Excellence,* produced by Studio Three, Samuel Merritt College of Nursing, Oakland, CA, and funded by the Helene Fuld Health Trust (1987–1990); and from Fawcett, J. (2005). Contemporary nursing knowledge: *Analysis and evaluation of nursing models and theories.* (2nd ed.). Philadelphia: F.A. Davis.

APPENDIX N-2
Nursing Interventions Classification System
Intervention Labels and Definitions

Abuse Protection Support—Identification of high-risk dependent relationships and actions to prevent further infliction of physical or emotional harm

Abuse Protection Support: Child—Identification of high-risk, dependent child relationships and actions to prevent possible or further infliction of physical, sexual, or emotional harm or neglect of basic necessities of life

Abuse Protection Support: Domestic Partner—Identification of high-risk, dependent domestic relationships and actions to prevent possible or further infliction of physical, sexual, or emotional harm or exploitation of a domestic partner

Abuse Protection Support: Elder—Identification of high-risk, dependent elder relationships and actions to prevent possible or further infliction of physical, sexual, or emotional harm; neglect of basic necessities of life; or exploitation

Abuse Protection Support: Religious—Identification of high-risk, controlling religious relationships and actions to prevent infliction of physical, sexual, or emotional harm and/or exploitation

Acid-Base Management—Promotion of acid-base balance and prevention of complications resulting from acid-base imbalance

Acid-Base Management: Metabolic Acidosis—Promotion of acid-base balance and prevention of complications resulting from serum HCO_3 levels lower than desired

Acid-Base Management: Metabolic Alkalosis—Promotion of acid-base balance and prevention of complications resulting from serum HCO_3 levels higher than desired

Acid-Base Management: Respiratory Acidosis—Promotion of acid-base balance and prevention of complications resulting from serum PCO_2 levels higher than desired

Acid-Base Management: Respiratory Alkalosis—Promotion of acid-base balance and prevention of complications resulting from serum PCO_2 levels lower than desired

Acid-Base Monitoring—Collection and analysis of patient data to regulate acid-base balance

Active Listening—Attending closely to and attaching significance to a patient's verbal and nonverbal messages

Activity Therapy—Prescription of and assistance with specific physical, cognitive, social, and spiritual activities to increase the range, frequency, or duration of an individual's (or group's) activity

Acupressure—Application of firm, sustained pressure to special points on the body to decrease pain, produce relaxation, and prevent or reduce nausea

Admission Care—Facilitating entry of a patient into a health care facility

Airway Insertion and Stabilization—Insertion or assisting with insertion and stabilization of an artificial airway

Airway Management—Facilitation of patency of air passages

Airway Suctioning—Removal of airway secretions by inserting a suction catheter into the patient's oral airway and/or trachea

Allergy Management—Identification, treatment, and prevention of allergic responses to food, medications, insect bites, contrast material, blood, or other substances

Amnioinfusion—Infusion of fluid into the uterus during labor to relieve umbilical cord compression or to dilute meconium-stained fluid

Amputation Care—Promotion of physical and psychological healing before and after amputation of a body part

Analgesic Administration—Use of pharmacologic agents to reduce or eliminate pain

Analgesic Administration: Intraspinal—Administration of pharmacologic agents into the epidural or intrathecal space to reduce or eliminate pain

Anaphylaxis Management—Promotion of adequate ventilation and tissue perfusion for an individual with a severe allergic (antigen-antibody) reaction

Anesthesia Administration—Preparation for and administration of anesthetic agents and monitoring of patient responsiveness during administration

Anger Control Assistance—Facilitation of the expression of anger in an adaptive nonviolent manner

Animal-Assisted Therapy—Purposeful use of animals to provide affection, attention, diversion, and relaxation

Anticipatory Guidance—Preparation of patient for an anticipated developmental and/or situational crisis

Anxiety Reduction—Minimizing apprehension, dread, foreboding, or uneasiness related to an unidentified source of anticipated danger

Area Restriction—Limitation of patient mobility to a specified area for purposes of safety or behavior management

Aroma therapy—Administration of essential oils through massage, topical ointments or lotions, baths, inhalation, douches, or compresses (hot or cold) to calm and soothe, provide pain relief, enhance relaxation and comfort

Art Therapy—Facilitation of communication through drawings or other art forms

Artificial Airway Management—Maintenance of endotracheal and tracheostomy tubes and preventing complications associated with their use

Aspiration Precautions—Prevention or minimization of risk factors in the patient at risk for aspiration

Assertiveness Training—Assistance with the effective expression of feelings, needs, and ideas while respecting the rights of others

Asthma Management—Identification, treatment, and prevention of reactions to inflammation/constriction in airway passages

Attachment Promotion—Facilitation of the development of the parent-infant relationship

Autogenic Training—Assisting with self-suggestions about feelings of heaviness and warmth for the purpose of inducing relaxation

Autotransfusion—Collecting and reinfusing blood which has been lost intraoperatively or postoperatively from clean wounds

Bathing—Cleaning of the body for the purposes of relaxation, cleanliness, and healing

Bed Rest Care—Promotion of comfort and safety and prevention of complications for a patient unable to get out of bed

Bedside Laboratory Testing—Performance of laboratory tests at the bedside or point of care

Behavior Management—Helping a patient to manage negative behavior

Behavior Management: Overactivity/Inattention—Provision of a therapeutic milieu which safely accommodates the patient's attention deficit and/or overactivity while promoting optimal function

Behavior Management: Self-Harm—Assisting the patient to decrease or eliminate self-mutilating or self-abusive behaviors

Behavior Management: Sexual—Delineation and prevention of socially unacceptable sexual behaviors

Behavior Modification—Promotion of a behavior change

Behavior Modification: Social Skills—Assisting the patient to develop or improve interpersonal social skills

Bibliotherapy—Use of literature to enhance the expression of feelings and the gaining of insight

Biofeedback—Assisting the patient to modify a body function using feedback from instrumentation

Bioterrorism Preparedness—Preparing for an effective response to bioterrorism events or disaster

Birthing—Delivery of a baby

Bladder Irrigation—Instillation of a solution into the bladder to provide cleansing or medication

Bleeding Precautions—Reduction of stimuli that may induce bleeding or hemorrhage in at-risk patients

Bleeding Reduction—Limitation of the loss of blood volume during an episode of bleeding

Bleeding Reduction: Antepartum Uterus—Limitation of the amount of blood loss from the pregnant uterus during third trimester of pregnancy

Bleeding Reduction: Gastrointestinal—Limitation of the amount of blood loss from the upper and lower gastrointestinal tract and related complications

Bleeding Reduction: Nasal—Limitation of the amount of blood loss from the nasal cavity

Bleeding Reduction: Postpartum Uterus—Limitation of the amount of blood loss from the postpartum uterus

Bleeding Reduction: Wound—Limitation of the blood loss from a wound that may be a result of trauma, incisions, or placement of a tube or catheter

Blood Products Administration—Administration of blood or blood products and monitoring of patient's response

Body Image Enhancement—Improving a patient's conscious and unconscious perceptions and attitudes toward his/her body

Body Mechanics Promotion—Facilitating the use of posture and movement in daily activities to prevent fatigue and musculoskeletal strain or injury

Bottle Feeding—Preparation and administration of fluids to an infant via a bottle

Bowel Incontinence Care—Promotion of bowel continence and maintenance of perianal skin integrity

Bowel Incontinence Care: Encopresis—Promotion of bowel continence in children

Bowel Irrigation—Instillation of a substance into the lower gastrointestinal tract

Bowel Management—Establishment and maintenance of a regular pattern of bowel elimination

Bowel Training—Assisting the patient to train the bowel to evacuate at specific intervals

Breast Examination—Inspection and palpation of the breasts and related areas

Breastfeeding Assistance—Preparing a new mother to breastfeed her infant

Calming Technique—Reducing anxiety in patient experiencing acute distress

Capillary Blood Sample—Obtaining and arteriovenous sample from peripheral body site, such as the heel, finger, or other transcutaneous site

Cardiac Care—Limitation of complications resulting from an imbalance between myocardial oxygen supply and demand for a patient with symptoms of impaired cardiac function

Cardiac Care: Acute—Limitation of complications for a patient recently experiencing an episode of an imbalance between myocardial oxygen supply and demand resulting in impaired cardiac function

Cardiac Care: Rehabilitative—Promotion of maximum functional activity level for a patient who has suffered an episode of impaired cardiac function which resulted from an imbalance between myocardial oxygen supply and demand

Cardiac Precautions—Prevention of an acute episode of impaired cardiac function by minimizing myocardial oxygen consumption or increasing myocardial oxygen supply

Caregiver Support—Provision of the necessary information, advocacy, and support to facilitate primary patient care by someone other than a health care professional

Case Management—Coordinating care and advocating for specified individuals and patient populations across settings to reduce cost, reduce resource use, improve quality of health care, and achieve desired outcomes

Cast Care: Maintenance—Care of a cast after the drying period

Cast Care: Wet—Care of a new cast during the drying period

Cerebral Edema Management—Limitation of secondary cerebral injury resulting from swelling of brain tissue

Cerebral Perfusion Promotion—Promotion of adequate perfusion and limitation of complications for a patient experiencing or at risk for inadequate cerebral perfusion

Cesarean Section Care—Preparation and support of patient delivering a baby by cesarean section

Chemical Restraint—Administration, monitoring, and discontinuation of psychotropic agents used to control an individual's extreme behavior

Chemotherapy Management—Assisting the patient and family to understand the action and minimize side effects of antineoplastic agents

Chest Physiotherapy—Assisting the patient to move airway secretions from peripheral airways to more central airways for expectoration and/or suctioning

Childbirth Preparation—Providing information and support to facilitate childbirth and to enhance the ability of an individual to develop and perform the role of parent

Circulatory Care: Arterial Insufficiency—Promotion of arterial circulation

Circulatory Care: Mechanical Assist Device—Temporary support of the circulation through the use of mechanical devices or pumps

Circulatory Care: Venous Insufficiency—Promotion of venous circulation

Circulatory Precautions—Protection of a localized area with limited perfusion

Circumcision Care—Preprocedural and postprocedural support to males undergoing circumcision

Code Management—Coordination of emergency measures to sustain life

Cognitive Restructuring—Challenging a patient to alter distorted thought patterns and view self and the world more realistically

Cognitive Stimulation—Promotion of awareness and comprehension of surroundings by utilization of planned stimuli

Communicable Disease Management—Working with a community to decrease and manage the incidence and prevalence of contagious diseases in a specific population

Communication Enhancement: Hearing Deficit—Assistance in accepting and learning alternate methods for living with diminished hearing

Communication Enhancement: Speech Deficit—Assistance in accepting and learning alternate methods for living with impaired speech

Communication Enhancement: Visual Deficit—Assistance in accepting and learning alternate methods for living with diminished vision

Community Disaster Preparedness—Preparing for an effective response to a large-scale disaster

Community Health Development—Facilitating members of a community to identify a community's health concerns, mobilize resources, and implement solutions

Complex Relationship Building—Establishing a therapeutic relationship with a patient who has difficulty interacting with others

Conflict Mediation—Facilitation of constructive dialogue between opposing parties with a goal of resolving disputes in a mutually acceptable manner

Constipation/Impaction Management—Prevention and alleviation of constipation/impaction

Consultation—Using expert knowledge to work with those who seek help in problem-solving to enable individuals, families, groups, or agencies to achieve identified goals

Contact Lens Care—Prevention of eye injury and lens damage by proper use of contact lenses

Controlled Substance Checking—Promoting appropriate use and maintaining security of controlled substances

Coping Enhancement—Assisting a patient to adapt to perceived stressors, changes, or threats which interfere with meeting life demands and roles

Cost Containment—Management and facilitation of efficient and effective use of resources

Cough Enhancement—Promotion of deep inhalation by the patient with subsequent generation of high intrathoracic pressures and compression of underlying lung parenchyma for the forceful expulsion of air

Counseling—Use of an interactive helping process focusing on the needs, problems, or feelings of the patient and significant others to enhance or support coping, problem-solving, and interpersonal relationships

Crisis Intervention—Use of short-term counseling to help the patient cope with a crisis and resume a state of functioning comparable to or better than the pre-crisis state

Critical Path Development—Constructing and using a timed sequence of patient care activities to enhance desired patient outcomes in a cost-efficient manner

Culture Brokerage—The deliberate use of culturally competent strategies to bridge or mediate between the patient's culture and the biomedical health care system

Cutaneous Stimulation—Stimulation of the skin and underlying tissues for the purpose of decreasing undesirable signs and symptoms such as pain, muscle spasm, or inflammation

Decision-Making Support—Providing information and support for a patient who is making a decision regarding health care

Delegation—Transfer of responsibility for the performance of patient care while retaining accountability for the outcome

Delirium Management—Provision of a safe and therapeutic environment for the patient who is experiencing an acute confusional state

Delusion Management—Promoting the comfort, safety, and reality orientation of a patient experiencing false, fixed beliefs that have little or no basis in reality

Dementia Management—Provision of a modified environment for the patient who is experiencing a chronic confusional state

Dementia Management: Bathing—Reduction of aggressive behavior during cleaning of the body

Deposition/Testimony—Provision of recorded sworn testimony for legal proceedings based upon knowledge of the case

Developmental Care—Structuring the environment and providing care in response to the behavioral cues and states of the preterm infant

Developmental Enhancement: Adolescent—Facilitating optimal physical, cognitive, social, and emotional growth of individuals during the transition from childhood to adulthood

Developmental Enhancement: Child—Facilitating or teaching parents/caregivers to facilitate the optimal gross motor, fine motor, language, cognitive, social, and emotional growth of preschool and school-aged children

Dialysis Access Maintenance—Preservation of vascular (arterial-venous) access sites

Diarrhea Management—Prevention and alleviation of diarrhea

Diet Staging—Instituting required diet restrictions with subsequent progression of diet as tolerated

Discharge Planning—Preparation for moving a patient from one level of care to another within or outside the current health care agency

Distraction—Purposeful focusing of attention away from undesirable sensations

Documentation—Recording of pertinent patient data in a clinical record

Dressing—Choosing, putting on, and removing clothes for a person who cannot do this for self

Dying Care—Promotion of physical comfort and psychological peace in the final phase of life

Dysreflexia Management—Prevention and elimination of stimuli which cause hyperactive reflexes and inappropriate autonomic responses in a patient with a cervical or high thoracic cord lesion

Dysrhythmia Management—Preventing, recognizing, and facilitating treatment of abnormal cardiac rhythms

Ear Care—Prevention or minimization of threats to ear or hearing

Eating Disorders Management—Prevention and treatment of severe diet restriction and overexercising or binging and purging of food and fluids

Electroconvulsive Therapy (ECT) Management—Assisting with the safe and efficient provision of electroconvulsive therapy in the treatment of psychiatric illness

Electrolyte Management—Promotion of electrolyte balance and prevention of complications resulting from abnormal or undesired serum electrolyte levels

Electrolyte Management: Hypercalcemia—Promotion of calcium balance and prevention of complications resulting from serum calcium levels higher than desired

Electrolyte Management: Hyperkalemia—Promotion of potassium balance and prevention of complications resulting from serum potassium levels higher than desired

Electrolyte Management: Hypermagnesemia—Promotion of magnesium balance and prevention of complications resulting from serum magnesium levels higher than desired

Electrolyte Management: Hypernatremia—Promotion of sodium balance and prevention of complications resulting from serum sodium levels higher than desired

Electrolyte Management: Hyperphosphatemia—Promotion of phosphate balance and prevention of complications resulting from serum phosphate levels higher than desired

Electrolyte Management: Hypocalcemia—Promotion of calcium balance and prevention of complications resulting from serum calcium levels lower than desired

Electrolyte Management: Hypokalemia—Promotion of potassium balance and prevention of complications resulting from serum potassium levels lower than desired

Electrolyte Management: Hypomagnesemia—Promotion of magnesium balance and prevention of complications resulting from serum magnesium levels lower than desired

Electrolyte Management: Hyponatremia—Promotion of sodium balance and prevention of complications resulting from serum sodium levels lower than desired

Electrolyte Management: Hypophosphatemia—Promotion of phosphate balance and prevention of complications resulting from serum phosphate levels lower than desired

Electrolyte Monitoring—Collection and analysis of patient data to regulate electrolyte balance

Electronic Fetal Monitoring: Antepartum—Electronic evaluation of fetal heart rate response to movement, external stimuli, or uterine contractions during antepartal testing

Electronic Fetal Monitoring: Intrapartum—Electronic evaluation of fetal heart rate response to uterine contractions during intrapartal care

Elopement Precautions—Minimizing the risk of a patient leaving a treatment setting without authorization when departure presents a threat to the safety of patient or others

Embolus Care: Peripheral—Limitation of complications for a patient experiencing, or at risk for, occlusion of peripheral circulation

Embolus Care: Pulmonary—Limitation of complications for a patient experiencing, or at risk for, occlusion of pulmonary circulation

Embolus Precautions—Reduction of the risk of an embolus in a patient with thrombi or at risk for developing thrombus formation

Emergency Care—Providing life-saving measures in life-threatening situations

Emergency Cart Checking—Systematic review of the contents of an emergency cart at established time intervals

Emotional Support—Provision of reassurance, acceptance, and encouragement during times of stress

Endotracheal Extubation—Purposeful removal of the endotracheal tube from the nasopharyngeal or oropharyngeal airway

Energy Management—Regulating energy use to treat or prevent fatigue and optimize function

Enteral Tube Feeding—Delivering nutrients and water through a gastrointestinal tube

Environmental Management—Manipulation of the patient's surroundings for therapeutic benefit, sensory appeal, and psychological well-being

Environmental Management: Attachment Process—Manipulation of the patient's surroundings to facilitate the development of the parent-infant relationship

Environmental Management: Comfort—Manipulation of the patient's surroundings for promotion of optimal comfort

Environmental Management: Community—Monitoring and influencing the direction of the physical, social, cultural, economic, and political conditions that affect the health of groups and communities

Environmental Management: Home Preparation—Preparing the home for safe and effective delivery of care

Environmental Management: Safety—Monitoring and manipulation of the physical environment to promote safety

Environmental Management: Violence Prevention—Monitoring and manipulation of the physical environment to decrease the potential for violent behavior directed toward self, others, or environment

Environmental Management: Worker Safety—Monitoring and manipulating of the worksite environment to promote safety and health of workers

Environmental Risk Protection—Preventing and detecting disease and injury in populations at risk from environmental hazards

Examination Assistance—Providing assistance to the patient and another health care provider during a procedure or exam

Exercise Promotion—Facilitation of regular physical activity to maintain or advance to a higher level of fitness and health

Exercise Promotion: Strength Training—Facilitating regular resistive muscle training to maintain or increase muscle strength

Exercise Promotion: Stretching—Facilitation of systematic slow-stretch-hold muscle exercises to induce relaxation, prepare muscles/joints for more vigorous exercise, or to increase or maintain body flexibility

Exercise Therapy: Ambulation—Promotion and assistance with walking to maintain or restore autonomic and voluntary body functions during treatment and recovery from illness or injury

Exercise Therapy: Balance—Use of specific activities, postures, and movements to maintain, enhance, or restore balance

Exercise Therapy: Joint Mobility—Use of active or passive body movement to maintain or restore joint flexibility

Exercise Therapy: Muscle Control—Use of specific activity or exercise protocols to enhance or restore controlled body movement

Eye Care—Prevention or minimization of threats to eye or visual integrity

Fall Prevention—Instituting special precautions with patient at risk for injury from falling

Family Integrity Promotion—Promotion of family cohesion and unity

Family Integrity Promotion: Childbearing Family—Facilitation of the growth of individuals or families who are adding an infant to the family unit

Family Involvement Promotion—Facilitating family participation in the emotional and physical care of the patient

Family Mobilization—Utilization of family strengths to influence patient's health in a positive direction

Family Planning: Contraception—Facilitation of pregnancy prevention by providing information about the physiology of reproduction and methods to control conception

Family Planning: Infertility—Management, education, and support of the patient and significant other undergoing evaluation and treatment for infertility

Family Planning: Unplanned Pregnancy—Facilitation of decision-making regarding pregnancy outcome

Family Presence Facilitation—Facilitation of the family's presence in support of an individual undergoing resuscitation and/or invasive procedures

Family Process Maintenance—Minimization of family process disruption effects

Family Support—Promotion of family values, interests, and goals

Family Therapy—Assisting family members to move their family toward a more productive way of living

Feeding—Providing nutritional intake for patient who is unable to feed self

Fertility Preservation—Providing information, counseling, and treatment that facilitate reproductive health and the ability to conceive

Fever Treatment—Management of a patient with hyperpyrexia caused by nonenvironmental factors

Financial Resource Assistance—Assisting an individual/family to secure and manage finances to meet health care needs

Fire-Setting Precautions—Prevention of fire-setting behaviors

First Aid—Providing initial care of a minor injury

Fiscal Resource Management—Procuring and directing the use of financial resources to ensure the development and continuation of programs and services

Flatulence Reduction—Prevention of flatus formation and facilitation of passage of excessive gas

Fluid Management—Promotion of fluid balance and prevention of complications resulting from abnormal or undesired fluid levels

Fluid Monitoring—Collection and analysis of patient data to regulate fluid balance

Fluid Resuscitation—Administering prescribed intravenous fluids rapidly

Fluid/Electrolyte Management—Regulation and prevention of complications from altered fluid and/or electrolyte levels

Foot Care—Cleansing and inspecting the feet for the purposes of relaxation, cleanliness, and healthy skin

Forgiveness Facilitation—Assisting an individual to forgive and/or experience forgiveness in relationship with self, others, and higher power

Gastrointestinal Intubation—Insertion of a tube into the gastrointestinal tract

Genetic Counseling—Use of an interactive helping process focusing on assisting an individual, family, or group, manifesting or at risk for developing or transmitting a birth defect or genetic condition, to cope

Grief Work Facilitation—Assistance with the resolution of a significant loss

Grief Work Facilitation: Perinatal Death—Assistance with the resolution of a perinatal loss

Guilt Work Facilitation—Helping another to cope with painful feelings of responsibility, actual or perceived

Hair Care—Promotion of neat, clean, attractive hair

Hallucination Management—Promoting the safety, comfort, and reality orientation of a patient experiencing hallucinations

Health Care Information Exchange—Providing patient care information to other health professionals

Health Education—Developing and providing instruction and learning experiences to facilitate voluntary adaptation of behavior conducive to health in individuals, families, groups, or communities

Health Policy Monitoring—Surveillance and influence of government and organization regulations, rules, and standards that affect nursing systems and practices to ensure quality care of patients

Health Screening—Detecting health risks or problems by means of history, examination, and other procedures

Health System Guidance—Facilitating a patient's location and use of appropriate health services

Heat Exposure Treatment—Management of patient overcome by heat due to excessive environmental heat exposure

Heat/Cold Application—Stimulation of the skin and underlying tissues with heat or cold for the purpose of decreasing pain, muscle spasms, or inflammation

Hemodialysis Therapy—Management of extracorporeal passage of the patient's blood through a dialyzer

Hemodynamic Regulation—Optimization of heart rate, preload, afterload, and contractility

Hemofiltration Therapy—Cleansing of acutely ill patient's blood via a hemofilter controlled by the patient's hydrostatic pressure

Hemorrhage Control—Reduction or elimination of rapid and excessive blood loss

High-Risk Pregnancy Care—Identification and management of a high-risk pregnancy to promote healthy outcomes for mother and baby

Home Maintenance Assistance—Helping the patient/family to maintain the home as a clean, safe, and pleasant place to live

Hope Instillation—Facilitation of the development of a positive outlook in a given situation

Hormone Replacement Therapy—Facilitation of safe and effective use of hormone replacement therapy

Humor—Facilitating the patient to perceive, appreciate, and express what is funny, amusing, or ludicrous in order to establish relationships, relieve tension, release anger, facilitate learning, or cope with painful feelings

Hyperglycemia Management—Preventing and treating above normal blood glucose levels

Hypervolemia Management—Reduction in extracellular and/or intracellular fluid volume and prevention of complications in a patient who is fluid overloaded

Hypnosis—Assisting a patient to induce an altered state of consciousness to create an acute awareness and a directed focus experience

Hypoglycemia Management—Preventing and treating low blood glucose levels

Hypothermia Treatment—Rewarming and surveillance of a patient whose core body temperature is below 35°C

Hypovolemia Management—Expansion of intravascular fluid volume in a patient who is volume depleted

Immunization/Vaccination Management—Monitoring immunization status, facilitating access to immunizations, and providing immunizations to prevent communicable disease

Impulse Control Training—Assisting the patient to mediate impulsive behavior through application of problem-solving strategies to social and interpersonal situations

Incident Reporting—Written and verbal reporting of any event in the process of patient care that is inconsistent with desired patient outcomes or routine operations of the health care facility

Incision Site Care—Cleansing, monitoring, and promotion of healing in a wound that is closed with sutures, clips, or staples

Infant Care—Provision of developmentally appropriate family-centered care to the child under 1 year of age

Infection Control—Minimizing the acquisition and transmission of infectious agents

Infection Control: Intraoperative—Preventing nosocomial infection in the operating room

Infection Protection—Prevention and early detection of infection in a patient at risk

Insurance Authorization—Assisting the patient and provider to secure payment for health services or equipment from a third party

Intracranial Pressure (ICP) Monitoring—Measurement and interpretation of patient data to regulate intracranial pressure

Intrapartal Care—Monitoring and management of stages one and two of the birth process

Intrapartal Care: High-Risk Delivery—Assisting vaginal birth of multiple or malpositioned fetuses

Intravenous (IV) Insertion—Insertion of a needle into a peripheral vein for the purpose of administering fluids, blood, or medications

Intravenous (IV) Therapy—Administration and monitoring of intravenous fluids and medications

Invasive Hemodynamic Monitoring—Measurement and interpretation of invasive hemodynamic parameters to determine cardiovascular function and regulate therapy as appropriate

Kangaroo Care—Promoting closeness between parent and physiologically stable preterm infant by preparing the parent and providing the environment for skin-to-skin contact

Labor Induction—Initiation or augmentation of labor by mechanical or pharmacological methods

Labor Suppression—Controlling uterine contractions prior to 37 weeks of gestation to prevent preterm birth

Laboratory Data Interpretation—Critical analysis of patient laboratory data in order to assist with clinical decision-making

Lactation Counseling—Use of an interactive helping process to assist in maintenance of successful breastfeeding

Lactation Suppression—Facilitating the cessation of milk production and minimizing breast engorgement after giving birth

Laser Precautions—Limiting the risk of injury to the patient related to use of a laser

Latex Precautions—Reducing the risk of systemic reaction to latex

Learning Facilitation—Promoting the ability to process and comprehend information

Learning Readiness Enhancement—Improving the ability and willingness to receive information

Leech Therapy—Application of medicinal leeches to help drain replanted or transplanted tissue engorged with venous blood

Limit Setting—Establishing the parameters of desirable and acceptable patient behavior

Lower Extremity Monitoring—Collection, analysis, and use of patient data to categorize risk and prevent injury to the lower extremities

Malignant Hyperthermia Precautions—Prevention or reduction of hypermetabolic response to pharmacological agents used during surgery

Mechanical Ventilation—Use of an artificial device to assist a patient to breathe

Mechanical Ventilatory Weaning—Assisting the patient to breathe without the aid of a mechanical ventilator

Medication Administration—Preparing, giving, and evaluating the effectiveness of prescription and nonprescription drugs

Medication Administration: Ear—Preparing and instilling otic medications

Medication Administration: Enteral—Delivering medications through a tube inserted into the gastrointestinal system

Medication Administration: Eye—Preparing and instilling ophthalmic medications

Medication Administration: Inhalation—Preparing and administering inhaled medications

Medication Administration: Interpleural—Administration of medication through an interpleural catheter for reduction of pain

Medication Administration: Intradermal—Preparing and giving medications via the intradermal route

Medication Administration: Intramuscular (IM)—Preparing and giving medications via the intramuscular route

Medication Administration: Intraosseous—Insertion of a needle through the bone cortex into the medullary cavity for the purpose of short-term, emergency administration of fluid, blood, or medication

Medication Administration: Intraspinal—Administration and monitoring of medication via an established epidural or intrathecal route

Medication Administration: Intravenous (IV)—Preparing and giving medications via the intravenous route

Medication Administration: Nasal—Preparing and giving medications via nasal passages

Medication Administration: Oral—Preparing and giving medications by mouth

Medication Administration: Rectal—Preparing and inserting rectal suppositories

Medication Administration: Skin—Preparing and applying medications to the skin

Medication Administration: Subcutaneous—Preparing and giving medications via the subcutaneous route

Medication Administration: Vaginal—Preparing and inserting vaginal medications

Medication Administration: Ventricular Reservoir—Administration and monitoring of medication through an indwelling catheter into the lateral ventricle of the brain

Medication Management—Facilitation of safe and effective use of prescription and over-the-counter drugs

Medication Prescribing—Prescribing medication for a health problem

Meditation Facilitation—Facilitating a person to alter his/her level of awareness by focusing specifically on an image or thought

Memory Training—Facilitation of memory

Milieu Therapy—Use of people, resources, and events in the patient's immediate environment to promote optimal psychosocial functioning

Mood Management—Providing for safety, stabilization, recovery, and maintenance of a patient who is experiencing dysfunctionally depressed mood or elevated mood

Multidisciplinary Care Conference—Planning and evaluating patient care with health professionals from other disciplines

Music Therapy—Using music to help achieve a specific change in behavior, feeling, or physiology

Mutual Goal Setting—Collaborating with patient to identify and prioritize care goals, then developing a plan for achieving those goals

Nail Care—Promotion of clean, neat, attractive nails and prevention of skin lesions related to improper care of nails

Nausea Management—Prevention and alleviation of nausea

Neurologic Monitoring—Collection and analysis of patient data to prevent or minimize neurological complications

Newborn Care—Management of neonate during the transition to extrauterine life and subsequent period of stabilization

Newborn Monitoring—Measurement and interpretation of physiologic status of the neonate the first 24 hours after delivery

Nonnutritive Sucking—Provision of sucking opportunities for the infant

Normalization Promotion—Assisting parents and other family members of children with chronic illnesses or disabilities in providing normal life experiences for their children and families

Nutrition Management—Assisting with or providing a balanced dietary intake of foods and fluids

Nutrition Therapy—Administration of food and fluids to support metabolic processes of a patient who is malnourished or at high risk for becoming malnourished

Nutritional Counseling—Use of an interactive helping process focusing on the need for diet modification

Nutritional Monitoring—Collection and analysis of patient data to prevent or minimize malnourishment

Oral Health Maintenance—Maintenance and promotion of oral hygiene and dental health for the patient at risk for developing oral or dental lesions

Oral Health Promotion—Promotion of oral hygiene and dental care for a patient with normal oral and dental health

Oral Health Restoration—Promotion of healing for a patient who has an oral mucosa or dental lesion

Order Transcription—Transferring information from order sheets to the nursing patient care planning and documentation system

Organ Procurement—Guiding families through the donation process to ensure timely retrieval of vital organs and tissue for transplant

Ostomy Care—Maintenance of elimination through a stoma and care of surrounding tissue

Oxygen Therapy—Administration of oxygen and monitoring of its effectiveness

Pain Management—Alleviation of pain or a reduction in pain to a level of comfort that is acceptable to the patient

Parent Education: Adolescent—Assisting parents to understand and help their adolescent children

Parent Education: Childrearing Family—Assisting parents to understand and promote the physical, psychological, and social growth and development of their toddler, preschool, or school-aged child/children

Parent Education: Infant—Instruction on nurturing and physical care needed during the first year of life

Parenting Promotion—Providing parenting information, support and coordination of comprehensive services to high-risk families

Pass Facilitation—Arranging a leave for a patient from a health care facility

Patient Contracting—Negotiating an agreement with an individual that reinforces a specific behavior change

Patient-Controlled Analgesia (PCA) Assistance—Facilitating patient control of analgesic administration and regulation

Patient Rights Protection—Protection of health care rights of a patient, especially a minor, incapacitated, or incompetent patient unable to make decisions

Peer Review—Systematic evaluation of a peer's performance compared with professional standards of practice

Pelvic Muscle Exercise—Strengthening and training the levator ani and urogenital muscles through voluntary, repetitive contraction to decrease stress, urge, or mixed types of urinary incontinence

Perineal Care—Maintenance of perineal skin integrity and relief of perineal discomfort

Peripheral Sensation Management—Prevention or minimization of injury or discomfort in the patient with altered sensation

Peripherally Inserted Central (PIC) Catheter Care—Insertion and maintenance of a peripherally inserted central catheter, either midline or centrally located

Peritoneal Dialysis Therapy—Administration and monitoring of dialysis solution into and out of the peritoneal cavity

Pessary Management—Placement and monitoring of a vaginal device for treating stress urinary incontinence, uterine retroversion, genital prolapse, or incompetent cervix

Phlebotomy: Arterial Blood Sample—Obtaining a blood sample from an uncannulated artery to assess oxygen and carbon dioxide levels and acid-base balance

Phlebotomy: Blood Unit Acquisition—Procuring blood and blood products from donors

Phlebotomy: Cannulated Vessel—Aspirating a blood sample through an indwelling vascular catheter for laboratory tests

Phlebotomy: Venous Blood Sample—Removal of a sample of venous blood from an uncannulated vein

Phototherapy: Mood/Sleep Regulation—Administration of doses of bright light in order to elevate mood and/or normalize the body's internal clock

Phototherapy: Neonate—Use of light therapy to reduce bilirubin levels in newborn infants

Physical Restraint—Application, monitoring, and removal of mechanical restraining devices or manual restraints which are used to limit physical mobility of a patient

Physician Support—Collaborating with physicians to provide quality patient care

Pneumatic Tourniquet Precautions—Applying a pneumatic tourniquet while minimizing the potential for patient injury from use of the device

Positioning—Deliberative placement of the patient or a body part to promote physiological and/or psychological well-being

Positioning: Intraoperative—Moving the patient or body part to promote surgical exposure while reducing the risk of discomfort and complications

Positioning: Neurologic—Achievement of optimal, appropriate body alignment for the patient experiencing or at risk for spinal cord injury or vertebrae irritability

Positioning: Wheelchair—Placement of a patient in a properly selected wheelchair to enhance comfort, promote skin integrity, and foster independence

Postanesthesia Care—Monitoring and management of the patient who has recently undergone general or regional anesthesia

Postmortem Care—Providing physical care of the body of an expired patient and support for the family viewing the body

Postpartal Care—Monitoring and management of the patient who has recently given birth

Preceptor: Employee—Assisting and supporting a new or transferred employee through a planned orientation to a specific clinical area

Preceptor: Student—Assisting and supporting learning experiences for a student

Preconception Counseling—Screening and providing information and support to individuals of childbearing age before pregnancy to promote health and reduce risks

Pregnancy Termination Care—Management of the physical and psychological needs of the woman undergoing a spontaneous or elective abortion

Premenstrual Syndrome (PMS) Management—Alleviation/attenuation of physical and/or behavioral symptoms occurring during the luteal phase of the menstrual cycle

Prenatal Care—Monitoring and management of patient during pregnancy to prevent complications of pregnancy and promote a healthy outcome for both mother and infant

Preoperative Coordination—Facilitating preadmission diagnostic testing and preparation of the surgical patient

Preparatory Sensory Information—Describing in concrete and objective terms the typical sensory experiences and events associated with an upcoming stressful health care procedure/treatment

Presence—Being with another, both physically and psychologically, during times of need

Pressure Management—Minimizing pressure to body parts

Pressure Ulcer Care—Facilitation of healing in pressure ulcers

Pressure Ulcer Prevention—Prevention of pressure ulcers for an individual at high risk for developing them

Product Evaluation—Determining the effectiveness of new products or equipment

Program Development—Planning, implementing, and evaluating a coordinated set of activities designed to enhance wellness, or to prevent, reduce, or eliminate one or more health problems for a group or community

Progressive Muscle Relaxation—Facilitating the tensing and releasing of successive muscle groups while attending to the resulting differences in sensation

Prompted Voiding—Promotion of urinary continence through the use of timed verbal toileting reminders and positive social feedback for successful toileting

Prosthesis Care—Care of a removable appliance worn by a patient and the prevention of complications associated with its use

Pruritus Management—Preventing and treating itching

Quality Monitoring—Systematic collection and analysis of an organization's quality indicators for the purpose of improving patient care

Radiation Therapy Management—Assisting the patient to understand and minimize the side effects of radiation treatments

Rape-Trauma Treatment—Provision of emotional and physical support immediately following a reported rape

Reality Orientation—Promotion of patient's awareness of personal identity, time, and environment

Recreation Therapy—Purposeful use of recreation to promote relaxation and enhancement of social skills

Rectal Prolapse Management—Prevention and/or manual reduction of rectal prolapse

Referral—Arrangement for services by another care provider or agency

Religious Addiction Prevention—Prevention of a self-imposed controlling religious lifestyle

Religious Ritual Enhancement—Facilitating participation in religious practices

Relocation Stress Reduction—Assisting the individual to prepare for and cope with movement from one equipment to another

Reminiscence Therapy—Using the recall of past events, feelings, and thoughts to facilitate pleasure, quality of life, or adaptation to present circumstances

Reproductive Technology Management—Assisting a patient through the steps of complex infertility treatment

Research Data Collection—Collecting research data

Resiliency Promotion—Assisting individuals, families, and communities in development, use, and strengthening of protective factors to be used in coping with environmental and societal stressors

Respiratory Monitoring—Collection and analysis of patient data to ensure airway patency and adequate gas exchange

Respite Care—Provision of short-term care to provide relief for family caregiver

Resuscitation—Administering emergency measures to sustain life

Resuscitation: Fetus—Administering emergency measures to improve placental perfusion or correct fetal acid-base status

Resuscitation: Neonate—Administering emergency measures to support newborn adaptation to extrauterine life

Risk Identification—Analysis of potential risk factors, determination of health risks, and prioritization of risk reduction strategies for an individual or group

Risk Identification: Childbearing Family—Identification of an individual or family likely to experience difficulties in parenting and prioritization of strategies to prevent parenting problems

Risk Identification: Genetic—Identification and analysis of potential genetic risk factors in an individual, family, or group

Role Enhancement—Assisting a patient, significant other, and/or family to improve relationships by clarifying and supplementing specific role behaviors

Seclusion—Solitary containment in a fully protective environment with close surveillance by nursing staff for purposes of safety or behavior management

Security Enhancement—Intensifying a patient's sense of physical and psychological safety

Sedation Management—Administration of sedatives, monitoring of the patient's response, and provision of necessary physiological support during a diagnostic or therapeutic procedure

Seizure Management—Care of a patient during a seizure and the postictal state

Seizure Precautions—Prevention or minimization of potential injuries sustained by a patient with a known seizure disorder

Self-Awareness Enhancement—Assisting a patient to explore and understand his/her thoughts, feelings, motivations, and behaviors

Self-Care Assistance—Assisting another to perform activities of daily living

Self-Care Assistance: Bathing/Hygiene—Assisting patient to perform personal hygiene

Self-Care Assistance: Dressing/Grooming—Assisting patient with clothes and makeup

Self-Care Assistance: Feeding—Assisting a person to eat

Self-Care Assistance (IADL)—Assisting and instructing a person to perform instrumental activities of daily living (IADL) needed to function in the home or community

Self-Care Assistance: Toileting—Assisting another with elimination

Self-Care Assistance: Transfer—Assisting a person to change body location

Self-Esteem Enhancement—Assisting a patient to increase his/her personal judgment of self-worth

Self-Hypnosis Facilitation—Teaching and monitoring the use of self-initiated hypnotic state for therapeutic benefit

Self-Modification Assistance—Reinforcement of self-directed change initiated by the patient to achieve personally important goals

Self-Responsibility Facilitation—Encouraging a patient to assume more responsibility for own behavior

Sexual Counseling—Use of an interactive helping process focusing on the need to make adjustments in sexual practice or to enhance coping with a sexual event/disorder

Shift Report—Exchanging essential patient care information with other nursing staff at change of shift

Shock Management—Facilitation of the delivery of oxygen and nutrients to systemic tissue with removal of cellular waste products in a patient with severely altered tissue perfusion

Shock Management: Cardiac—Promotion of adequate tissue perfusion for a patient with severely compromised pumping function of the heart

Shock Management: Vasogenic—Promotion of adequate tissue perfusion for a patient with severe loss of vascular tone

Shock Management: Volume—Promotion of adequate tissue perfusion for a patient with severely compromised intravascular volume

Shock Prevention—Detecting and treating a patient at risk for impending shock

Sibling Support—Assisting a sibling to cope with a brother's or sister's illness/chronic condition/disability

Simple Guided Imagery—Purposeful use of imagination to achieve relaxation and/or direct attention away from undesirable sensations

Simple Massage—Stimulation of the skin and underlying tissues with varying degrees of hand pressure to decrease pain, produce relaxation, and/or improve circulation

Simple Relaxation Therapy—Use of techniques to encourage and elicit relaxation for the purpose of decreasing undesirable signs and symptoms such as pain, muscle tension, or anxiety

Skin Care: Donor Site—Prevention of wound complications and promotion of healing at the donor site

Skin Care: Graft Site—Prevention of wound complications and promotion of graft site healing

Skin Care: Topical Treatments—Application of topical substances or manipulation of devices to promote skin integrity and minimize skin breakdown

Skin Surveillance—Collection and analysis of patient data to maintain skin and mucous membrane integrity

Sleep Enhancement—Facilitation of regular sleep/wake cycles

Smoking Cessation Assistance—Helping another to stop smoking

Socialization Enhancement—Facilitation of another person's ability to interact with others

Specimen Management—Obtaining, preparing, and preserving a specimen for a laboratory test

Spiritual Growth Facilitation—Facilitation of growth in patient's capacity to identify, connect with, and call upon the source of meaning, purpose, comfort, strength, and hope in his/her life

Spiritual Support—Assisting the patient to feel balance and connection with a greater power

Splinting—Stabilization, immobilization, and/or protection of an injured body part with a supportive appliance

Sports-Injury Prevention: Youth—Reduce the risk of sport-related injury in young athletes

Staff Development—Developing, maintaining, and monitoring competence of staff

Staff Supervision—Facilitating the delivery of high-quality patient care by others

Subarachnoid Hemorrhage Precautions—Reduction of internal and external stimuli or stressors to minimize risk of rebleeding prior to aneurysm surgery

Substance Use Prevention—Prevention of an alcoholic or drug use lifestyle

Substance Use Treatment—Supportive care of patient/family members with physical and psychosocial problems associated with the use of alcohol or drugs

Substance Use Treatment: Alcohol Withdrawal—Care of the patient experiencing sudden cessation of alcohol consumption

Substance Use Treatment: Drug Withdrawal—Care of a patient experiencing drug detoxification

Substance Use Treatment: Overdose—Monitoring, treatment, and emotional support of a patient who has ingested prescription or over-the-counter drugs beyond the therapeutic range

Suicide Prevention—Reducing risk of self-inflicted harm with intent to end life

Supply Management—Ensuring acquisition and maintenance of appropriate items for providing patient care

Support Group—Use of a group environment to provide emotional support and health-related information for members

Support System Enhancement—Facilitation of support to patient by family, friends, and community

Surgical Assistance—Assisting the surgeon/dentist with operative procedures and care of the surgical patient

Surgical Precautions—Minimizing the potential for iatrogenic injury to the patient related to a surgical procedure

Surgical Preparation—Providing care to a patient immediately prior to surgery and verification of required procedures/tests and documentation in the clinical record

Surveillance—Purposeful and ongoing acquisition, interpretation, and synthesis of patient data for clinical decision-making

Surveillance: Community—Purposeful and ongoing acquisition, interpretation, and synthesis of data for decision-making in the community

Surveillance: Late Pregnancy—Purposeful and ongoing acquisition, interpretation, and synthesis of maternal-fetal data for treatment, observation, or admission

Surveillance: Remote Electronic—Purposeful and ongoing acquisition of patient data via electronic modalities (telephone, video, conferencing, e-mail) from distant locations as well as interpretation and synthesis of patient data for clinical decision-making with individuals or populations

Surveillance: Safety—Purposeful and ongoing collection and analysis of information about the patient and the environment for use in promoting and maintaining patient safety

Sustenance Support—Helping a needy individual/family to locate food, clothing, or shelter

Suturing—Approximating edges of a wound using sterile suture material and a needle

Swallowing Therapy—Facilitating swallowing and preventing complications of impaired swallowing

Teaching: Disease Process—Assisting the patient to understand information related to a specific disease process

Teaching: Foot Care—Preparing a patient at risk and/or significant other to provide preventive foot care

Teaching: Group—Development, implementation, and evaluation of a patient-teaching program for a group of individuals experiencing the same health condition

Teaching: Individual—Planning, implementation, and evaluation of a teaching program designed to address a patient's particular needs

Teaching: Infant Nutrition—Instruction on nutrition and feeding practices during the first year of life

Teaching: Infant Safety—Instruction on safety during first year of life

Teaching: Infant Stimulation—Teaching parents and caregivers to provide developmentally appropriate sensory activities to promote development and movement during the first year of life

Teaching: Preoperative—Assisting a patient to understand and mentally prepare for surgery and the postoperative recovery period

Teaching: Prescribed Activity/Exercise—Preparing a patient to achieve and/or maintain a prescribed level of activity

Teaching: Prescribed Diet—Preparing a patient to correctly follow a prescribed diet

Teaching: Prescribed Medication—Preparing a patient to safely take prescribed medications and monitor for their effects

Teaching: Procedure/Treatment—Preparing a patient to understand and mentally prepare for a prescribed procedure or treatment

Teaching: Psychomotor Skill—Preparing a patient to perform a psychomotor skill

Teaching: Safe Sex—Providing instruction concerning sexual protection during sexual activity

Teaching: Sexuality—Assisting individuals to understand physical and psychosocial dimensions of sexual growth and development

Teaching: Toddler Nutrition—Instruction on nutrition and feeding practices during the second and third years of life

Teaching: Toddler Safety—Instruction on safety during the second and third years of life

Teaching: Toilet Training—Instruction on determining the child's readiness and strategies to assist the child to learn independent toileting skills

Technology Management—Use of technical equipment and devices to monitor patient condition or sustain life

Telephone Consultation—Eliciting patient's concerns, listening, and providing support, information, or teaching in response to patient's stated concerns, over the telephone

Telephone Follow-up—Providing results of testing or evaluating patient's response and determining potential for problems as a result of previous treatment, examination, or testing, over the telephone

Temperature Regulation—Attaining and/or maintaining body temperature within a normal range

Temperature Regulation: Intraoperative—Attaining and/or maintaining desired intraoperative body temperature

Temporary Pacemaker Management—Temporary support of cardiac pumping through the insertion and use of temporary pacemakers

Therapeutic Play—Purposeful and directive use of toys and other materials to assist children in communicating their perception and knowledge of their world and to help in gaining mastery of their environment

Therapeutic Touch—Attuning to the universal healing field, seeking to act as an instrument for healing influence, and using the natural sensitivity of the hands to gently focus and direct the intervention process

Therapy Group—Application of psychotherapeutic techniques to a group, including the utilization of interactions between members of the group

Total Parenteral Nutrition (TPN) Administration—Preparation and delivery of nutrients intravenously and monitoring of patient responsiveness

Touch—Providing comfort and communication through purposeful tactile contact

Traction/Immobilization Care—Management of a patient who has traction and/or a stabilizing device to immobilize and stabilize a body part

Transcutaneous Electrical Nerve Stimulation (TENS)—Stimulation of skin and underlying tissues with controlled, low-voltage electrical vibration via electrodes

Transport—Moving a patient from one location to another

Trauma Therapy: Child—Use of an interactive helping process to resolve a trauma experienced by a child

Triage: Disaster—Establishing priorities of patient care for urgent treatment while allocating scarce resources

Triage: Emergency Center—Establishing priorities and initiating treatment for patients in an emergency center

Triage: Telephone—Determining the nature and urgency of a problem(s) and providing directions for the level of care required, over the telephone

Truth Telling—Use of whole truth, partial truth, or decision delay to promote the patient's self-determination and well-being

Tube Care—Management of a patient with an external drainage device exiting the body

Tube Care: Chest—Management of a patient with an external water-seal drainage device exiting the chest cavity

Tube Care: Gastrointestinal—Management of a patient with a gastrointestinal tube

Tube Care: Umbilical Line—Management of a newborn with an umbilical catheter

Tube Care: Urinary—Management of a patient with urinary drainage equipment

Tube Care: Ventriculostomy/Lumbar Drain—Management of a patient with an external cerebrospinal fluid drainage system

Ultrasonography: Limited Obstetric—Performance of ultrasound exams to determine ovarian, uterine, or fetal status

Unilateral Neglect Management—Protecting and safely reintegrating the affected part of the body while helping the patient adapt to disturbed perceptual abilities

Urinary Bladder Training—Improving bladder function for those with urge incontinence by increasing the bladder's ability to hold urine and the patient's ability to suppress urination

Urinary Catheterization—Insertion of a catheter into the bladder for temporary or permanent drainage of urine

Urinary Catheterization: Intermittent—Regular periodic use of a catheter to empty the bladder

Urinary Elimination Management—Maintenance of an optimum urinary elimination pattern

Urinary Habit Training—Establishing a predictable pattern of bladder emptying to prevent incontinence for persons with limited cognitive ability who have urge, stress, or functional incontinence

Urinary Incontinence Care—Assistance in promoting continence and maintaining perineal skin integrity

Urinary Incontinence Care: Enuresis—Promotion of urinary continence in children

Urinary Retention Care—Assistance in relieving bladder distention

Values Clarification—Assisting another to clarify her/his own values in order to facilitate effective decision-making

Vehicle Safety Promotion—Assisting individuals, families, and communities to increase awareness of measures to reduce unintentional injuries in motorized and non-motorized vehicles

Venous Access Devices (VAD) Maintenance—Management of the patient with prolonged venous access via tunneled and non-tunneled (percutaneous) catheters, and implanted ports

Ventilation Assistance—Promotion of an optimal spontaneous breathing pattern that maximizes oxygen and carbon dioxide exchange in the lungs

Visitation Facilitation—Promoting beneficial visits by family and friends

Vital Signs Monitoring—Collection and analysis of cardiovascular, respiratory, and body temperature data to determine and prevent complications

Vomiting Management—Prevention and alleviation of vomiting

Weight Gain Assistance—Facilitating gain of body weight

Weight Management—Facilitating maintenance of optimal body weight and percent body fat

Weight Reduction Assistance—Facilitating loss of weight and/or body fat

Wound Care—Prevention of wound complications and promotion of wound healing

Wound Care: Closed Drainage—Maintenance of a pressure drainage system at the wound site

Wound Irrigation—Flushing of an open wound to cleanse and remove debris and excessive drainage

---

SOURCE: Dochterman, J McCloskey and Bulecheck, GM: Nursing Interventions Classification, ed. 5, Mosby (Elsevier), St. Louis, 2007, with permission.

APPENDIX N-3
Nursing Outcomes Classification System
Outcome Labels and Definitions

Abuse Cessation—Evidence that the victim is no longer exploited

Abuse Protection—Protection of self or dependent others from abuse

Abuse Recovery: Emotional—Extent of healing of psychological injuries due to abuse

Abuse Recovery: Financial—Extent of control of monetary and legal matters following financial exploitation

Abuse Recovery: Physical—Extent of healing of physical injuries due to abuse

Abuse Recovery: Sexual—Extent of healing of physical and psychological injuries due to sexual abuse or exploitation

Abuse Recovery Status—Extent of healing following physical or psychological abuse that may include sexual or financial exploitation

Abusive Behavior Self-Restraint—Self-restraint of abuse and neglectful behaviors towards others

Acceptance: Health Status—Reconciliation significant change in health circumstances

Activity Tolerance—Psychological response to energy-consuming movements with daily activities

Adaptation to Physical Disability—Adaptive response to a significant functional challenge due to a physical disability

Adherence Behavior—Self-initiated actions to promote wellness, recovery, and rehabilitation

Aggression Self-Control—Self-restraint of assaultive, combative, or destructive behavior toward others

Allergic Response: Localized—Severity of localized hypersensitive immune response to a specific environmental (exogenous) antigen

Allergic Response: Systemic—Severity of systemic hypersensitive immune response to a specific environmental (exogenous) antigen

Ambulation—Ability to walk from place to place independently with or without assistive device

Ambulation: Wheelchair—Ability to move from place to place in a wheelchair

Anxiety Self-Control—Personal actions to eliminate or reduce feelings of apprehension, tension, or uneasiness from an unidentifiable source

Anxiety Level—Severity of manifested apprehension, tension, or uneasiness arising from an unidentifiable source

Appetite—Desire to eat when ill or receiving treatment

Aspiration Prevention—Personal actions to prevent the passage of fluid and solid particles into the lung

Asthma Self-Management—Personal actions to reverse inflammatory condition resulting in bronchial constriction of the airways

Balance—Ability to maintain body equilibrium

Blood Coagulation—Extent to which blood clots within normal period of time

Blood Glucose Level—Extent to which plasma glucose levels in plasma and urine are maintained in normal range

Blood Loss Severity—Severity of internal or external bleeding/hemorrhage

Blood Transfusion Reaction—Severity of complications with blood transfusions reaction

Body Image—Perception of own appearance and body functions

Body Mechanics Performance—Personal actions to maintain proper body alignment and to prevent muscular skeletal strain

Body Positioning: Self-Initiated—Ability to change own body position independently with or without assistive device

Bone Healing—Extent of regeneration of cells and tissues following bone injury

Bowel Continence—Control of passage of stool from the bowel

Bowel Elimination—Formation and evacuation of stool

Breastfeeding Establishment: Infant—Infant attachment to and sucking from the mother's breast for nourishment during the first 3 weeks of breastfeeding

Breastfeeding Establishment: Maternal—Maternal establishment of proper attachment of an infant to and sucking from the breast for nourishment during the first 3 weeks of breastfeeding

Breastfeeding Maintenance—Continuation of breastfeeding for nourishment of an infant/toddler

Breastfeeding Weaning—Progressive discontinuation of breastfeeding

Cardiac Disease Self-Management—Personal actions to manage heart disease and prevent disease progression

Cardiac Pump Effectiveness—Adequacy of blood volume ejected from the left ventricle to support systemic perfusion pressure

Caregiver Adaptation to Patient Institutionalization—Adaptive response of family caregiver when the care recipient is moved to an institution

Caregiver Emotional Health—Emotional well-being of a family care provider while caring for a family member

Caregiver Home Care Readiness— Extent of preparedness of a caregiver to assume responsibility for the health care of a family member in the home

Caregiver Lifestyle Disruption— Severity of disturbances in the lifestyle of a family member due to caregiving

Caregiver-Patient Relationship— Positive interactions and connections between the caregiver and care recipient

Caregiver Performance: Direct Care— Provision by family care provider of appropriate personal and health care for a family member

Caregiver Performance: Indirect Care— Arrangement and oversight by family care provider of appropriate care for a family member

Caregiver Physical Health— Physical well-being of a family care provider while caring for a family member

Caregiver Stressors— Severity of biopsychosocial pressure on a family care provider caring for another over an extended period of time

Caregiver Well-Being— Extent of positive perception of primary care provider's health status and life circumstances

Caregiving Endurance Potential— Factors that promote family care provider continuance over an extended period of time

Child Adaptation to Hospitalization— Adaptive response of a child from 3 years through 17 years of age to hospitalization

Child Development: 1 month- Milestones of physical, cognitive, and psychoscial progression by 1 month of age

Child Development: 2 months— Milestones of physical, cognitive, and psychosocial progression by 2 months of age

Child Development: 4 months— Milestones of physical, cognitive, and psychosocial progression by 4 months of age

Child Development: 6 months— Milestones of physical, cognitive, and psychosocial progression by 6 months of age

Child Development: 12 months— Milestones of physical, cognitive, and psychosocial progression by 12 months of age

Child Development: 2 years— Milestones of physical, cognitive, and psychosocial progression by 2 years of age

Child Development: 3 years— Milestones of physical, cognitive, and psychosocial progression by 3 years of age

Child Development: 4 years— Milestones of physical, cognitive, and psychosocial progression by 4 years of age

Child Development: Preschool— Milestones of physical, cognitive, and psychosocial progression from 3 years through 5 years of age

Child Development: Middle Childhood— Milestones of physical, cognitive, and psychosocial progression from 6 years through 11 years of age

Child Development: Adolescence— Milestones of physical, cognitive, and psychosocial progression from 12 years through 17 years of age

Circulation Status— Unobstructed, unidirectional blood flow at an appropriate pressure through large vessels of the systemic and pulmonary circuits

Client Satisfaction: Access to Care Resources— Extent of positive perception of access to nursing staff, supplies, and equipment needed for care

Client Satisfaction: Caring— Extent of positive perception of nursing staff's concern for the client

Client Satisfaction: Communication— Extent of positive perception of information exchanged between client and nursing staff

Client Satisfaction: Continuity of Care— Extent of positive perception of coordination of cares as the patient moves from one care setting to another

Client Satisfaction: Cultural Needs Fulfillment— Extent of positive perception of integration of cultural beliefs, values, and social structures into nursing care

Client Satisfaction: Functional Assistance— Extent of positive perception of nursing assistance to achieve mobility and self-care as independently as health conditions permit

Client Satisfaction: Physical Care— Extent of positive perception of nursing care to maintain body functions and cleanliness

Client Satisfaction: Physical Environment— Extent of positive perception of living environment, treatment environment, equipment and supplies in acute or long term care settings

Client Satisfaction: Protection of Rights— Extent of positive perception of protection of a client's legal and moral rights provided by nursing staff

Client Satisfaction: Psychological Care— Extent of positive perception of nursing assistance to perform emotional and mental activities as independently as health condition permits

Client Satisfaction: Safety— Extent of positive perception of procedures, information, and nursing care to prevent harm or injury

Client Satisfaction: Symptom Control— Extent of positive perception of nursing care to relieve symptoms of illness

Client Satisfaction: Teaching— Extent of positive perception of instruction provided by nursing staff to improve knowledge, understanding, and participation in care

Client Satisfaction: Technical Aspects of Care— Extent of positive perception of nursing staff's knowledge and expertise used in providing care

Cognition— Ability to execute complex mental processes

Cognitive Orientation—Ability to identify person, place, and time accurately

Comfort Level—Extent of positive perception of physical and psychological ease

Comfortable Death—Physical and psychological ease with the impending end of life

Communication—Reception, interpretation, and expression of spoken, written, and nonverbal messages

Communication: Expressive—Expression of meaningful verbal and/or nonverbal messages

Communication: Receptive—Reception and interpretation of verbal and/or nonverbal messages

Community Competence—Capacity of a community to collectively problem solve to achieve community goals

Community Disaster Readiness—Community preparedness to respond to a natural or man-made calamitous event

Community Health Status—The general state of well-being of a community or population

Community Health Status: Immunity—Resistance of community members to the invasion and spread of an infectious agent that could threaten public health

Community Risk Control: Chronic Disease—Community actions to reduce the risk of chronic diseases and related complications

Community Risk Control: Communicable Disease—Community actions to eliminate or reduce the spread of infectious agents (bacteria, fungi, parasites, and viruses) that threaten public health

Community Risk Control: Lead Exposure—Community actions to reduce lead exposure and poisoning

Community Risk Control: Violence—Community actions to eliminate or reduce intentional violent acts resulting in serious physical or psychological harm

Community Violence Level—Incidence of violent acts compared with local, state or national values

Compliance Behavior—Personal actions to promote wellness, recovery, and rehabilitation based on professional advice

Concentration—Ability to focus on a specific stimulus

Coordinated Movement—Ability of muscles to work together voluntarily for purposeful movement

Coping—Personal actions to manage stressors that tax an individual's resources

Decision Making—Ability to make judgements and choose between two or more alternatives

Depression Self-Control—Personal actions to minimize melancholy and maintain interest in life events

Depression Level—Severity of melancholic mood and loss of interest in life events

Diabetes Self-Management—Personal actions to manage diabetes mellitus and prevent disease progression

Dignified Life Closure—Personal actions to maintain control during approaching end of life

Discharge Readiness: Independent Living—Readiness of a patient to relocate from a health care institution to living independently

Discharge Readiness: Supported Living—Readiness of a patient to relocate from a health care institution to a lower level of supported living

Distorted Thought Self-Control—Self-restraint or disruption in perception, thought processes, and thought content

Electrolyte Acid/Base Balance—Balance of the electrolytes and non-electrolytes in the intracellular and extracellular compartments of the body

Endurance—Capacity to sustain activity

Energy Conservation—Personal actions to manage energy for initiating and sustaining activity

Falls Occurrence—Number of falls in the past (define period of time)

Fall Prevention Behavior—Personal or family caregiver actions to minimize risk factors that might precipitate falls in the personal environment

Family Coping—Family actions to manage stressors that tax family resources

Family Functioning—Capacity of the family system to meet the needs of its members during developmental transitions

Family Health Status—Overall health and social competence of family unit

Family Integrity—Family members' behaviors that collectively demonstrate cohesion, strength, and emotional bonding

Family Normalization—Capacity of the family system to maintain routines and develop strategies for optimal functioning when a member has a chronic illness or disability

Family Participation in Professional Care—Family involvement in decision-making, delivery, and evaluation of care provided by health care personnel

Family Physical Environment—Physical arrangements in the home that provide safety and stimulation to family members

Family Resiliency—Capacity of the family system to successfully adapt and function competently following significant adversity or crises

Family Social Climate—Supportive milieu as characterized by family member relationships and goals

Family Support During Treatment—Family presence and emotional support for an individual undergoing treatment

Fear Self-Control—Personal actions to eliminate or reduce disabling feelings of apprehension, tension, or uneasiness from an identifiable source

Fear Level—Severity of manifested apprehension, tension, or uneasiness arising from an identifiable source

Fear Level: Child—Severity of manifested apprehension, tension, or uneasiness arising from an identifiable source in a child from 1 year through 17 years of age

Fetal Status: Antepartum—Extent to which fetal signs are within normal limits from conception to the onset of labor

Fetal Status: Intrapartum—Extent to which fetal signs are within normal limits from onset of labor to delivery

Fluid Balance—Water balance in the intracellular and extracellular compartments of the body

Fluid Overload Severity—Severity of excess fluids in the intracellular and extracellular compartments of the body

Grief Resolution—Adjustment to actual or impending loss

Growth—Normal increase in bone size and body weight during growth years

Health Beliefs—Personal convictions that influence health behaviors

Health Beliefs: Perceived Ability to Perform—Personal conviction that one can carry out a given health behavior

Health Beliefs: Perceived Control—Personal conviction that one can influence a health outcome

Health Beliefs: Perceived Resources—Personal conviction that one has adequate means to carry out a health behavior

Health Beliefs: Perceived Threat—Personal conviction that threatening health problem is serious and has potential negative consequences for lifestyle

Health Orientation—Personal commitment to health behaviors as lifestyle priorities

Health Promoting Behavior—Personal actions to sustain or increase wellness

Health Seeking Behavior—Personal actions to promote optimal wellness, recovery, and rehabilitation

Hearing Compensation Behavior—Personal Actions to identify, monitor, and compensate for hearing loss

Hemodialysis Access—Functionality of a dialysis access site

Hope—Otimism that is personally satisfying and life-supporting

Hydration—Adequate water in the intracellular and extracellular compartments of the body

Hyperactivity Level—Severity of patterns of inattention or impulsivity in a child from 1 year through 17 years of age

Identity—Distinguishes between self and non-self and characterizes one's essence

Immobility Consequences: Physiological—Severity of compromise in physiological functioning due to impaired physical mobility

Immobility Consequences: Psycho-Cognitive—Severity of compromise in psycho-cognitive functioning due to impaired physical mobility

Immune Hypersensitivity Response—Severity of inappropriate immune responses

Immune Status—Natural and acquired appropriately targeted resistance to internal and external antigens

Immunization Behavior—Personal actions to obtain immunization to prevent a communicable disease

Impulse Self-Control—Self-restraint of compulsive or impulsive behaviors

Infection Severity: Newborn Severity of infection and associated symptoms during the first 28 days of life

Infection Severity—Severity of infection and associated symptoms

Information Processing—Ability to acquire, organize, and use information

Joint Movement: Ankle—Active range of motion of the ankle with self-initiated movement

Joint Movement: Elbow—Active range of motion of the elbow with self-initiated movement

Joint Movement: Fingers—Active range of motion of the fingers with self-initiated movement

Joint Movement: Hip—Active range of motion of the hip with self-initiated movement

Joint Movement: Knee—Active range of motion of the knee with self-initiated movement

Joint Movement: Neck—Active range of motion of the neck with self-initiated movement

Joint Movement: Passive—Joint movement with assistance

Joint Movement: Shoulder—Active range of motion of the shoulder with self-initiated movement

Joint Movement: Spine—Active range of motion of the spine with self-initiated movement

Joint Movement: Wrist—Active range of motion of the wrist with self-initiated movement

Kidney Function—Filtration of blood and elimination of metabolic waste products through the formation of urine

Knowledge: Body Mechanics—Extent of understanding conveyed about proper body alignment, balance and coordinated movement

Knowledge: Breastfeeding—Extent of understanding conveyed about lactation and nourishment of infant through breastfeeding

Knowledge: Cardiac Disease Management Extent of understanding conveyed about heart disease and the prevention of complications

Knowledge: Child Physical Safety—Extent of understanding conveyed about safely caring for a child from 1 year through 17 years of age

Knowledge: Conception Prevention—Extent of understanding conveyed about prevention of unintended pregnancy

Knowledge: Diabetes Management—Extent of understanding conveyed about diabetes mellitus and the prevention of complications

Knowledge: Diet—Extent of understanding conveyed about recommended diet

Knowledge: Disease Process—Extent of understanding conveyed about a specific disease process

Knowledge: Energy Conservation—Extent of understanding conveyed about energy conservation techniques

Knowledge: Fall Prevention—Extent of understanding conveyed about prevention of falls

Knowledge: Fertility Promotion—Extent of understanding conveyed about fertility testing and the conditions that affect conception

Knowledge: Health Behavior—Extent of understanding conveyed about the promotion and protection of health

Knowledge: Health Promotion—Extent of understanding conveyed about information needed to obtain and maintain optimal health

Knowledge: Health Resources—Extent of understanding conveyed about relevant health care resources

Knowledge: Illness Care—Extent of understanding conveyed about illness-related information needed to achieve and maintain optimal health

Knowledge: Infant Care—Extent of understanding conveyed about caring for a baby from birth to 1st birthday

Knowledge: Infection Control—Extent of understanding conveyed about prevention and control of infection

Knowledge: Labor and Delivery—Extent of understanding conveyed about labor and vaginal delivery

Knowledge: Medication—Extent of understanding conveyed about the safe use of medication

Knowledge: Ostomy Care—Extent of understanding conveyed about maintenance of an ostomy for elimination

Knowledge: Parenting—Extent of understanding about provision of a nurturing and constructive environment for a child from 1 year through 17 years of age

Knowledge: Personal Safety—Extent of understanding conveyed about preventing unintentional injuries

Knowledge: Postpartum Maternal Health—Extent of understanding conveyed about maternal health following delivery

Knowledge: Preconception Maternal Health—Extent of understanding conveyed about maternal health prior to conception to ensure a healthy pregnancy

Knowledge: Pregnancy—Extent of understanding conveyed about promotion of a healthy pregnancy and prevention of complications

Knowledge: Prescribed Activity—Extent of understanding conveyed about prescribed activity and exercise

Knowledge: Sexual Functioning—Extent of understanding conveyed about sexual development and responsible sexual practices

Knowledge: Substance Use Control—Extent of understanding conveyed about controlling the use of drugs, tobacco, or alcohol

Knowledge: Treatment Procedure(s)—Extent of understanding conveyed about procedure(s) required as part of a treatment regimen

Knowledge: Treatment Regimen—Extent of understanding conveyed about a specific treatment regimen

Leisure Participation—Use of relaxing, interesting, and enjoyable activities to promote well-being

Loneliness Severity—Severity of emotional, social, or existential isolation response

Maternal Status: Antepartum—Extent to which maternal well-being is within normal limits from conception to the onset of labor

Maternal Status: Intrapartum—Extent to which maternal well-being is within normal limits from onset of labor to delivery

Maternal Status: Postpartum—Extent to which maternal well-being is within normal limits from delivery of placenta to completion of involution

Mechanical Ventilation Response: Adult—Alveolar exchange and tissue perfusion are supported by mechanical ventilation

Mechanical Ventilation Weaning Response: Adult—Respiratory and psychological adjustment to progressive removal of mechanical ventilation

Medication Response—Therapeutic and adverse effects of prescribed medication

Memory—Ability to cognitively retrieve and report previously stored information

Mobility—Ability to move purposefully in own environment independently with or without assistive device

Mood Equilibrium—Appropriate adjustment of prevailing emotional tone in response to circumstances

Motivation—Inner urge that moves or prompts an individual to positive action(s)

Nausea & Vomiting Control—Personal actions to control nausea, retching, and vomiting symptoms

Nausea & Vomiting Disruptive Effects—Severity of observed or reported disruptive effects of nausea, retching, and vomiting on daily functioning

Nausea & Vomiting Severity—Severity of nausea, retching, and vomiting symptoms

Neglect Cessation—Evidence that the victim is no longer receiving substandard care

Neglect Recovery—Extent of healing following the cessation of substandard care

Neurological Status—Ability of the peripheral and central nervous system to receive, process, and respond to internal and external stimuli

Neurological Status: Autonomic—Ability of the autonomic nervous system to coordinate visceral and homeostatic function

Neurological Status: Central Motor Control—Ability of the central nervous system to coordinate skeletal muscle activity for body movement

Neurological Status: Consciousness—Arousal, orientation, and attention to the environment

Neurological Status: Cranial Sensory/ Motor Function—Ability of the cranial nerves to convey sensory and motor impulses

Neurological Status: Spinal Sensory/ Motor Function—Ability of the spinal nerves to convey sensory and motor impulses

Newborn Adaptation—Adaptive response to the extrauterine environment by a physiologically mature newborn during the first 28 days

Nutritional Status—Extent to which nutrients are available to meet metabolic needs

Nutritional Status: Biochemical Measures—Body fluid components and chemical indices of nutritional status

Nutritional Status: Energy—Extent to which nutrients and oxygen provide cellular energy

Nutritional Status: Food and Fluid Intake—Amount of food and fluid taken into the body over a 24-hour period

Nutritional Status: Nutrient Intake—Adequacy of usual pattern of nutrient intake

Oral Hygiene—Condition of the mouth, teeth, gums, and tongue

Ostomy Self-Care—Personal actions to maintain ostomy for elimination

Pain: Adverse Psychological Response—Severity of observed or reported adverse cognitive and emotional responses to physical pain

Pain Control—Personal actions to control pain

Pain: Disruptive Effects—Severity of observed or reported disruptive effects of chronic pain on daily functioning

Pain Level—Severity of observed or reported pain

Parent-Infant Attachment—Parent and infant behaviors that demonstrate an enduring affectionate bond

Parenting Performance—Parental actions taken to provide a child a nurturing and constructive physical, emotional, and social environment

Parenting: Adolescent Physical Safety—Parental actions to avoid physical injury in an adolescent from 12 years through 17 years of age

Parenting: Early/Middle Childhood Physical Safety—Parental actions to avoid physical injury of a child from 3 years through 11 years of age

Parenting: Infant/Toddler Physical Safety—Parental actions to avoid physical injury to a child from birth through 2 years of age

Parenting: Pyschosocial Safety—Parental actions to protect a child from social contacts that might cause harm or injury

Participation in Health Care Decisions—Personal involvement in selecting and evaluating health care options to achieve desired outcome

Personal Autonomy—Personal actions of a competent individual to exercise governance in life decisions

Personal Health Status—Overall physical, psychological, social, and spiritual functioning of an adult 18 years or older

Personal Safety Behavior—Personal actions of an adult to control behaviors that can cause physical injury

Personal Well-Being—An individual's expressed satisfaction with health status

Physical Aging—Normal physical changes that occur with the natural aging process

Physical Fitness—Performance of physical activities with vigor

Physical Injury Severity—Severity of injuries from accidents and trauma

Physical Maturation: Female—Normal physical changes in the female that occur with the transition from childhood to adulthood

Physical Maturation: Male—Normal physical changes in the male that occur with the transition from childhood to adulthood

Play Participation—Use of activities by a child from 1 year through 11 years of age to promote enjoyment, entertainment, and development

Post Procedure Recovery Status—Extent to which an individual returns to baseline function following a procedure(s) requiring anesthesia or sedation

Prenatal Health Behavior—Personal actions to promote a healthy pregnancy and a healthy newborn

Preterm Infant Organization—Extrauterine integration of physiologic and behavioral function by the infant born 24 to 37 (term) weeks of gestation

Psychomotor Energy—Personal drive and energy to maintain activities of daily living, nutrition, and personal safety

Psychosocial Adjustment: Life Change—Adaptive psychosocial response of an individual to a significant life change

Quality of Life—Extent of positive perception of current life circumstances

Respiratory Status: Airway Patency—Open, clear tracheobronchial passages for air exchange

Respiratory Status: Gas Exchange— Alveolar exchange of CO_2 or O_2 to maintain arterial blood gas concentrations

Respiratory Status: Ventilation— Movement of air in and out of the lungs

Rest—Quantity and pattern of diminished activity for mental and physical rejuvenation

Risk Control—Personal actions to prevent, eliminate, or reduce modifiable health threats

Risk Control: Alcohol Use—Personal actions to prevent, eliminate, or reduce alcohol use that poses a threat to health

Risk Control: Cancer—Personal actions to detect or reduce the threat of cancer

Risk Control: Cardiovascular Health—Personal actions to eliminate or reduce threats to cardiovascular health

Risk Control: Drug Use—Personal actions to prevent, eliminate, or reduce drug use that poses a threat to health

Risk Control: Hearing Impairment— Personal actions to prevent, eliminate, or reduce threats to hearing function

Risk Control: Sexually Transmitted Diseases (STDs)—Personal actions to prevent, eliminate, or reduce behaviors associated with sexually transmitted disease

Risk Control: Tobacco Use—Personal actions to prevent, eliminate, or reduce tobacco use

Risk Control: Unintended Pregnancy—Personal actions to prevent or reduce the possibility of unintended pregnancy

Risk Control: Visual Impairment— Personal actions to prevent, eliminate, or reduce the threats to visual function

Risk Detection—Personal actions to identify personal health threats

Role Performance—Congruence of an individual's role behavior with role expectations

Safe Home Environment—Physical arrangements to minimize environmental factors that might cause physical harm or injury in the home

Seizure Control—Personal actions to reduce or minimize the occurrence of seizure episodes

Self-Care Status—Ability to perform basic personal care activities and household tasks

Self-Care: Activities of Daily Living (ADLs)—Ability to perform the most basic physical tasks and personal care activities independently with or without assistive device

Self-Care: Bathing—Ability to cleanse own body independently with or without assistive device

Self-Care: Dressing—Ability to dress oneself independently with or without assistive device

Self-Care: Eating—Ability to prepare and ingest food and fluid independently with or without assistive device

Self-Care: Hygiene—Ability to maintain own personal cleanliness and kept appearance independently with or without assistive device

Self-Care: Instrumental Activities of Daily Living (IADLs)—Ability to perform activities needed to function in the home or community independently with or without assistive device

Self-Care: Non-Parenteral Medication—Ability to administer oral and topical medications to meet therapeutic goals independently with or without assistive device

Self-Care: Oral Hygiene—Ability to care for own mouth and teeth independently with or without assistive device

Self-Care: Parenteral Medication— Ability to administer parenteral medications to meet therapeutic goals independently with or without assistive device

Self-Care: Toileting—Ability to toilet self independently with or without assistive device

Self-Direction of Care—Care recipient actions taken to direct others who assist with or perform physical tasks and personal health care

Self-Esteem—Personal judgment of self-worth

Self-Mutilation Restraint—Personal actions to refrain from intentional self-inflicted injury (non-lethal)

Sensory Function Status—Extent to which an individual correctly perceives skin stimulation, sounds, proprioception, taste and smell, and visual images

Sensory Function: Cutaneous—Extent to which stimulation of the skin is correctly sensed

Sensory Function: Hearing—Extent to which sounds are correctly sensed

Sensory Function: Proprioception— Extent to which the position and movement of the head and body are correctly sensed

Sensory Function: Taste and Smell— Extent to which chemicals inhaled or dissolved in saliva are correctly sensed

Sensory Function: Vision—Extent to which visual images are correctly sensed

Sexual Functioning—Integration of physical, socioemotional, and intellectual aspects of sexual expression and performance

Sexual Identity—Acknowledgment and acceptance of own sexual identity

Skeletal Function—Ability of the bones to support the body and facilitate movement

Sleep—Natural periodic suspension of consciousness during which the body is restored

Social Interaction Skills—Personal behaviors that promote effective relationships

Social Involvement—Social interactions with persons, groups, or organizations

Social Support—Perceived availability and actual provision of reliable assistance from others

Spiritual Health—Connectedness with self, others, higher power, all life, nature, and the universe that transcends and empowers the self

Stress Level—Severity of manifested physical or mental tension resulting form factors that alter an existing equilibrium

Student Health Status—Physical, cognitive/emotional, and social status of school age children that contribute to school attendance, participation in school activities, and ability to learn

Substance Addiction Consequences—Severity of change in health status and social functioning due to substance addiction

Suffering Severity—Severity of anguish associated with a distressing symptom, injury, or loss that has potential long-term effects

Suicide Self-Restraint—Personal actions to refrain from gestures and attempts at killing self

Swallowing Status—Safe passage of fluids and/or solids from the mouth to the stomach

Swallowing Status: Esophageal Phase—Safe passage of fluids and/or solids from the pharynx to the stomach

Swallowing Status: Oral Phase—Preparation, containment, and posterior movement of fluids and/or solids in the mouth

Swallowing Status: Pharyngeal Phase—Safe passage of fluids and/or solids from the mouth to the esophagus

Symptom Control—Personal actions to minimize perceived adverse changes in physical and emotional functioning

Symptom Severity—Severity of perceived adverse changes in physical, emotional, and social functioning

Symptom Severity: Perimenopause—Severity of symptoms caused by declining hormonal levels

Symptom Severity: Premenstrual Syndrome (PMS)—Severity of symptoms caused by cyclic hormonal fluctuations

Systemic Toxin Clearance: Dialysis—Clearance of toxins from the body with peritoneal or hemodialysis

Thermoregulation—Balance among heat production, heat gain, and heat loss

Thermoregulation: Newborn—Balance among heat production, heat gain, and heat loss during the first 28 days of life

Tissue Integrity: Skin and Mucous Membranes—Structural intactness and normal physiological function of skin and mucous membranes

Tissue Perfusion: Abdominal Organs—Adequacy of blood flow through the small vessels of the abdominal viscera to maintain organ function

Tissue Perfusion: Cardiac—Adequacy of blood flow through the coronary vasculature to maintain heart function

Tissue Perfusion: Cerebral—Adequacy of blood flow through the cerebral vasculature to maintain brain function

Tissue Perfusion: Peripheral—Adequacy of blood flow through the small vessels of the extremities to maintain tissue function

Tissue Perfusion: Pulmonary—Adequacy of blood flow through pulmonary vasculature to perfuse alveoli/capillary unit

Transfer Performance—Ability to change body location independently with or without assistive device

Treatment Behavior: Illness or Injury—Personal actions to palliate or eliminate pathology

Urinary Continence—Control of the elimination of urine from the bladder

Urinary Elimination—Collection and discharge or urine

Vision Compensation Behavior—Personal actions to compensate for visual impairment

Vital Signs—Extent to which temperature, pulse, respiration, and blood pressure are within normal range

Weight: Body Mass—Extent to which body weight, muscle, and fat are congruent to height, frame, gender, and age

Weight Control—Personal actions to achieve and maintain optimum body weight

Will to Live—Desire, determination, and effort to survive

Wound Healing: Primary Intention—Extent of regeneration of cells and tissues following intentional closure

Wound Healing: Secondary Intention—Extent of regeneration of cells and tissues in an open wound

SOURCE: Moorhead, S, Johnson, M, and Maas, M: Nursing Outcomes Classification, ed 4, Mosby, St. Louis, 2007 , with permission.

APPENDIX N-4

Nursing Diagnoses*

Quick View of Contents

Appendices N4–1 and N4–2   Organize all approved NANDA nursing diagnoses by two nursing models: Gordon's Functional Health Patterns and Doenges and Moorhouse's Diagnostic Divisions. The use of a nursing model as a framework helps to organize the data needed to identify and validate nursing diagnoses.

Appendix N4–3   Lists the most recently approved NANDA nursing diagnoses (2012–2014) for quick reference.

Appendix N4–4   Provides a guide to choosing appropriate nursing diagnoses by alphabetically listing almost 300 diseases/disorders with their commonly associated nursing diagnoses. Each of the listed diseases/disorders has been cross-referenced from its position in the body of the dictionary. The nursing diagnoses are written in the form of patient problem statements, also known as PES format (Problem, Etiology, Signs/Symptoms). The phrases "may be related to" and "possibly evidenced by" in the patient problem statements serve to help one individualize the care for the specific patient situations. A "risk for" diagnosis is not evidenced by signs and symptoms, as the problem has not occurred and nursing interventions are directed at prevention. Because the patient's health status is perpetual and ongoing, other nursing diagnoses may be appropriate based on changing patient situations. To identify other applicable nursing diagnoses, check Appendix N4–1, then turn to Appendix N4–5 to test and validate your choices.

Appendix N4–5   Details the NANDA-approved diagnoses through 2012–2014 in alphabetical order with their associated etiology [Related/Risk Factors] and signs and symptoms [Defining Characteristics]. This specific focus on assessment data/evaluation criteria helps you complete the validation process.

---

*Nursing Diagnoses—Definitions & Classifications 2012–2014. Copyright © NANDA International, 2012. Used by arrangement with Wiley-Blackwell Publishing, a company of John Wiley & Sons, Inc.

Appendix N4-1 Gordon's Functional Health Patterns

HEALTH PERCEPTION—HEALTH MANAGEMENT PATTERN
Bleeding, risk for
Contamination
Contamination, risk for
Energy Field, disturbed
Falls, risk for
Health, deficient community
Health Behavior, risk-prone
Health Maintenance, ineffective (specify)
Health Management, ineffective [self]
Health Management, readiness for enhanced [self]
Health Management Deficit
Health Management Deficit, risk for (specify area)
Immunization Status, readiness for enhanced
Infection, risk for (specify type/area)
Injury (trauma), risk for
Noncompliance (specify area)
Noncompliance, risk for (specify area)
Perioperative—Positioning Injury, risk for
Poisoning, risk for
Protection, ineffective (specify)
Suffocation, risk for
Therapeutic Regimen: ineffective management
Therapeutic Regimen: family, ineffective management
Therapeutic Regimen Management, risk for ineffective
Therapeutic Regimen Management, ineffective community
Thermal Injury, risk for
Vascular Trauma, risk for

NUTRITIONAL—METABOLIC PATTERN
Adverse Reaction to Iodinated Contrast Media, risk for
Allergy Response, risk for
Aspiration, risk for
Blood Glucose Level, risk for unstable
Body Temperature, imbalanced, risk for
Breastfeeding, effective
Breastfeeding, ineffective
Breastfeeding, interrupted
Breast Milk, insufficient
Dentition, impaired
Dry Eye, risk for
Electrolyte Imbalance, risk for
Failure to thrive, adult
Fluid Balance, readiness for enhanced
Fluid Volume, risk for deficient
Fluid Volume Deficient [active loss]
Fluid Volume Excess
Fluid Volume Imbalance, risk for
Hyperthermia
Hypothermia
Infant Feeding Pattern, ineffective
Jaundice, neonatal
Jaundice, risk for neonatal
Latex Allergy Response
Latex Allergy Response, risk for
Liver Function, risk for impaired
Nausea
Nutrition: imbalanced, less than body requirements or Nutritional Deficit (specify type)
Nutrition: imbalanced, more than body requirements or Exogenous Obesity
Nutrition: imbalanced, risk for more than body requirements or Risk for Obesity
Nutrition: readiness for enhanced
Oral Mucous Membrane, impaired (specify impairment)
Pressure Ulcer (specify stage)
Skin Integrity, impaired
Skin Integrity, impaired, risk for or Risk for Skin Breakdown
Swallowing, impaired (uncompensated)
Thermoregulation, ineffective
Tissue Integrity, impaired (specify type)

ELIMINATION PATTERN
Bowel Incontinence
Constipation
Constipation, perceived
Constipation, risk for
Constipation Pattern, intermittent
Diarrhea
Gastrointestinal Motility, dysfunctional
Gastrointestinal Motility, risk for dysfunctional
Incontinence, functional urinary
Incontinence, overflow urinary
Incontinence, reflex urinary
Incontinence, risk for urge urinary
Incontinence, stress urinary
Incontinence, total urinary
Incontinence, urge urinary
Urinary Elimination, impaired
Urinary Elimination, readiness for enhanced
Urinary Retention [acute/chronic]

ACTIVITY—EXERCISE PATTERN
Activity Intolerance [specify level]
Activity Intolerance, risk for
Adaptive Capacity, decreased, intracranial
Airway Clearance, ineffective
Autonomic Dysreflexia
Autonomic Dysreflexia, risk for
Breathing Pattern, ineffective
Cardiac Output, decreased
Development, risk for delayed
Developmental Delay: Self Care Skills (specify level)
Disorganized Infant Behavior
Disuse Syndrome, risk for
Diversional Activity, deficient
Dysfunctional Ventilatory Weaning Response

Fatigue
Gas Exchange, impaired
Gastrointestinal Perfusion, risk for ineffective
Growth and Development, delayed
Growth, risk for disproportionate
Home Maintenance, impaired
Infant Behavior, readiness for enhanced organized
Infant Behavior, risk for disorganized
Joint Contractures, risk for
Lifestyle, sedentary
Mobility, Bed, impaired
Mobility, Wheelchair, impaired
Peripheral Neurovascular Dysfunction, risk for
Physical Mobility, impaired (specify level)
Renal Perfusion, ineffective
Self-Care Deficit, bathing-hygiene (specify level)
Self-Care Deficit, dressing-grooming (specify level)
Self-Care Deficit, feeding (specify level)
Self-Care, readiness for enhanced
Self-Care Deficit, toileting (specify level)
Self-Care Deficit, total (specify level)
Self-Neglect
Shock, risk for
Sudden Infant Death Syndrome, risk for
Surgical Recovery, delayed
Tissue Perfusion, ineffective peripheral

Tissue Perfusion, risk for decreased cardiac
Tissue Perfusion, risk for ineffective cerebral
Tissue Perfusion, risk for ineffective peripheral
Transfer ability, impaired (specify level)
Ventilation, impaired spontaneous
Walking, impaired (specify level)
Wandering
Wheelchair Transfer Ability, impaired

SLEEP—REST PATTERN
Insomnia
Sleep, readiness for enhanced
Sleep Deprivation
Sleep Onset, delayed
Sleep Pattern, interrupted
Sleep Pattern Reversal

COGNITIVE—PERCEPTUAL PATTERN

Activity (Task) Planning, ineffective
Activity (Task) Planning, risk for ineffective
Attention-Concentration Deficit
Cognitive Impairment, risk for
Comfort, impaired

Comfort, readiness for enhanced
Confusion, acute
Confusion, risk for acute
Confusion, chronic
Decisional Conflict (specify)
Decision-Making, readiness for enhanced
Deficient Knowledge [learning need] (specify level)
Environmental Interpretation Syndrome, impaired
Knowledge, readiness for enhanced
Memory, impaired
Memory Loss, uncompensated
Pain, acute (specify level/location)
Pain, chronic (specify level/location)
Self-Management, ineffective pain (acute/chronic)
Sensory Deprivation
Sensory Loss, uncompensated (specify type/degree)
Sensory Overload
Thought Processes, disturbed
Unilateral Neglect

SELF-PERCEPTION—SELF-CONCEPT PATTERN
Anxiety
Anxiety, anticipatory (mild, moderate, severe)
Anxiety, Death
Anxiety, mild
Anxiety, moderate
Anxiety, severe (panic)
Body Image, disturbed
Depression, reactive (specify focus)
Fear (Specify Focus)
Hope, readiness for enhanced
Hopelessness
Human Dignity, risk for compromised
Impulse Control, ineffective
Loneliness, risk for
Personal Identity, disturbed
Personal Identity, disturbed risk for
Power, readiness for enhanced
Powerlessness (Severe, Moderate, Low)
Powerlessness, risk for
Self-Concept, readiness for enhanced
Self-Esteem, chronic low
Self-Esteem, risk for chronic low
Self-Esteem, situational low
Self-Esteem, situational low, risk for
Violence, risk for self-directed

ROLE—RELATIONSHIP PATTERN
Attachment, risk for impaired
Attachment, weak parent-infant
Caregiver Role Strain
Caregiver Role Strain, risk for
Communication, impaired, verbal
Communication, readiness for enhanced
Conflict, unresolved independence-dependence
Developmental Delay: Communication Skills (specify type)

Developmental Delay: Social Skills (specify)
Family Process, dysfunctional
Family processes, interrupted (specify)
Family processes, readiness for enhanced
Grieving
Grieving, anticipatory
Grieving, complicated
Grieving, risk for complicated
Grieving, dysfunctional
Parental Role Conflict
Parenting, impaired (specify)
Parenting, readiness for enhanced
Parenting, risk for impaired (specify)
Relationship, ineffective
Relationship, readiness for enhanced
Relationship, risk for ineffective
Relocation Stress Syndrome
Relocation Stress Syndrome, risk for
Role Performance, ineffective (specify)
Separation, parent-infant
Social Interaction, impaired
Social Isolation or Social Rejection
Social Isolation
Sorrow, Chronic
Violence, Other-Directed, risk for

SEXUALITY—REPRODUCTIVE PATTERN
Childbearing Process, ineffective
Childbearing Process, readiness for enhanced
Childbearing Process, risk for ineffective
Maternal-Fetal Dyad, risk for disturbed
Rape Trauma Syndrome [specify]

Rape Trauma Syndrome: Compound Reaction
Rape Trauma Syndrome: Silent Reaction
Sexual Dysfunction
Sexuality Pattern, ineffective

COPING—STRESS TOLERANCE PATTERN
Community Coping, ineffective
Coping, avoidance
Coping, defensive
Coping, enhanced, readiness for
Coping, ineffective (specify)
Coping, readiness for enhanced community
Denial, ineffective or Denial
Family Coping, readiness for enhanced
Post-Trauma Syndrome
Post-Trauma Syndrome, risk for
Resilience, impaired (individual)
Resilience, readiness for enhanced
Resilience, risk for compromised
Self-mutilation
Self-mutilation, risk for
Stress Overload
Suicide, risk for
Support System Deficit

VALUE—BELIEF PATTERN
Moral Distress
Religiosity, impaired
Religiosity, readiness for enhanced
Religiosity, risk for impaired
Spiritual Distress
Spiritual Distress, risk for
Spiritual Well-Being, readiness for enhanced

Note: Information appearing in parentheses has been added to clarify and facilitate the use of nursing diagnoses.
SOURCE: Adapted from Gordon, M: Manual of Nursing Diagnosis, ed. 10, St. Louis, MO, Mosby/Elsevier Science, 2002, with permission.

Appendix N4–2 Doenges and Moorhouse's Diagnostic Divisions

ACTIVITY/REST
Activity Intolerance
Activity Intolerance, risk for
Activity Planning, ineffective
Activity Planning, ineffective, risk for
Disuse Syndrome, risk for
Diversional Activity, deficient
Fatigue
Insomnia
Lifestyle, sedentary
Mobility, impaired Bed
Mobility, impaired Wheelchair
Sleep, readiness for enhanced
Sleep Deprivation
Transfer ability, impaired
Walking, impaired

CIRCULATION
Autonomic Dysreflexia
Autonomic Dysreflexia, risk for
Bleeding, risk for
Cardiac Output, decreased
Gastrointestinal Perfusion, risk for
Intracranial Adpative Capacity, Decreased
Renal Perfusion, risk for Ineffective
Shock, risk for
Tissue Perfusion, Ineffective Peripheral
Tissue Perfusion, risk for Ineffective Peripheral
Tissue Perfusion, risk for Decreased Cardiac

Tissue Perfusion, risk for Ineffective
Cerebral

EGO INTEGRITY
Anxiety [specify level]
Anxiety, death
Behavior, risk-prone health
Body Image, disturbed
Conflict, decisional
Coping, defensive
Coping, ineffective
Coping, readiness for enhanced
Decision Making, readiness for enhanced
Denial, ineffective
Dignity, risk for compromised human
Distress, moral
Energy Field, disturbed
Fear
Grieving
Grieving, complicated
Grieving, risk for complicated
Health Behavior, risk-prone
Hope, readiness for enhanced
Hopelessness
Impulse Control, ineffective
Personal Identity, disturbed
Post-Trauma Syndrome
Post-Trauma Syndrome, risk for
Power, readiness for enhanced
Powerlessness
Powerlessness, risk for
Rape-Trauma Syndrome
Relationship, ineffective
Relationship, risk for ineffective
Relationship, readiness for enhanced
Religiosity, impaired
Religiosity, readiness for enhanced
Religiosity, risk for impaired
Relocation Stress Syndrome
Relocation Stress Syndrome, risk for
Resilience, impaired individual
Resilience, readiness for enhanced
Resilience, risk for compromised
Self-Concept, readiness for enhanced
Self-Esteem, chronic low
Self-Esteem, situational low
Self-Esteem, risk for situational low
Sorrow, Chronic
Spiritual Distress
Spiritual Distress, risk for
Spiritual Well-Being, readiness for
enhanced

ELIMINATION
Bowel Incontinence
Constipation
Constipation, perceived
Constipation, risk for
Diarrhea
Motility, dysfunctional gastrointestinal
Motility, risk for dysfunctional
gastrointestinal
Urinary Elimination, impaired
Urinary Elimination, readiness for
enhanced
Urinary Incontinence, functional
Urinary Incontinence, overflow

Urinary Incontinence, reflex
Urinary Incontinence, risk for urge
Urinary Incontinence, stress
Urinary Incontinence, urge
Urinary Retention [acute/chronic]

FOOD/FLUID
Blood Glucose LEvel, risk for
unstable
Breastfeeding, readiness for
enhanced
Breastfeeding, ineffective
Breastfeeding, interrupted
Breast Milk, insufficient
Dentition, impaired
Electrolyte Imbalance, risk for
Failure to Thrive, Adult
Fluid Balance, readiness for enhanced
[Fluid Volume, deficient (hyper/
hypotonic)]
Fluid Volume, deficient [isotonic]
Fluid Volume, excess
Fluid Volume, risk for deficient
Fluid volume, risk for imbalanced
Infant Feeding Pattern, ineffective
Liver Function, risk for impaired
Nausea
Nutrition: less than body
requirements, imbalanced
Nutrition: more than body
requirements, imbalanced
Nutrition: risk for more than body
requirements, imbalanced
Nutrition, readiness for enhanced
Oral Mucous Membrane, impaired
Swallowing, impaired

HYGIENE
Self-Care, readiness for enhanced
Self-Care Deficit, bathing
Self-Care Deficit, dressing
Self-Care Deficit, feeding
Self-Care Deficit, toileting
Self Neglect

NEUROSENSORY
Confusion, acute
Confusion, chronic
Confusion, risk for acute
Infant Behavior, disorganized
Infant Behavior, readiness for
enhanced organized
Infant Behavior, risk for disorganized
Memory, impaired
Neglect, unilateral
Peripheral Neurovascular Dysfunction,
risk for
Sensory/Perception, disturbed (specify:
visual, auditory, kinesthetic,
gustatory, tactile, olfactory)
Stress Overload

PAIN/DISCOMFORT
Comfort, impaired
Comfort, readiness for enhanced
Pain, acute
Pain, chronic

RESPIRATION
Airway Clearance, ineffective
Aspiration, risk for
Breathing Pattern, ineffective
Gas Exchange, impaired
Ventilation, impaired spontaneous
Ventilatory Weaning Response,
  dysfunctional

SAFETY
Adverse Reaction to Iodinated
  Contrast Media, risk for
Allergy Response, risk for
Allergy Response, latex
Allergy Response, risk for latex
Body Temperature, risk for imbalanced
Childbearing Process, readiness for
  enhanced
Contamination
Contamination, risk for
Dry Eye, risk for
Environmental Interpretation
  Syndrome, impaired
Falls, risk for
Health Maintenance, ineffective
Home Maintenance, impaired
Hyperthermia
Hypothermia
Immunization status, readiness for
  enhanced
Infection, risk for
Injury, risk for
Neonatal Jaundice
Maternal/Fetal Dyad, risk for
  disturbed
Mobility, impaired physical
Poisoning, risk for
Protection, ineffective
Self-Mutilation
Self-Mutilation, risk for
Skin Integrity, impaired
Skin Integrity, impaired, risk for
Sudden Infant Death Syndrome, risk
  for
Suffocation, risk for
Suicide, risk for
Surgical Recovery, delayed
Thermal Injury, risk for
Thermoregulation, ineffective
Tissue Integrity, impaired
Trauma, risk for
Trauma, risk for vascular
Violence, risk for other-directed
Violence, risk for self-directed

Wandering [specify sporadic or
  continual]

SEXUALITY
Childbearing Process, ineffective
Childbearing Process, readiness for
  enhanced
Childbearing Process, risk for
  ineffective
Sexual Dysfunction
Sexuality Pattern, ineffective

SOCIAL INTERACTION
Attachment, risk for impaired parent/
  child
Caregiver Role Strain
Caregiver Role Strain, risk for
Communication, impaired, verbal
Communication, readiness for
  enhanced
Conflict, parental role
Coping, compromised family
Coping, disabled family
Coping, ineffective community
Coping, readiness for enhanced
  community
Coping, readiness for enhanced family
Family Processes, dysfunctional
Family Processes, interrupted
Family Processes, readiness for
  enhanced
Loneliness, risk for
Parenting, impaired
Parenting, readiness for enhanced
Parenting, risk for impaired
Role Performance, ineffective
Social Interaction, impaired
Social Isolation

TEACHING/LEARNING
Development, risk for delayed
Growth, risk for disproportionate
Growth and Development, delayed
Health, deficient community
Knowledge, deficient (specify)
Knowledge (specify), readiness for
  enhanced
Self-Health Management, ineffective
Self-Health Management, readiness for
  enhanced
Therapeutic Regimen Management,
  ineffective family
Therapeutic Regimen Management,
  readiness for enhanced

SOURCE: Adapted from Doenges, M. E., Moorhouse, M. F., and Geissler-Murr, A.
C.: Nurse's Pocket Guide: Diagnoses, Prioritized Interventions, and Rationales, ed.
13, F. A. Davis, Philadelphia, 2012, with permission.

Appendix N4–3 Additional Nursing Diagnoses Approved Through 2012–2014

Activity Planning, Risk for Ineffective

Adverse Reaction to Iodinated Contrast Media, Risk for

Allergy Response, Risk for

Breast Milk, Insufficient

Childbearing Process, Ineffective

Childbearing Process, Risk for Ineffective

Dry Eye, Risk for

Health, Deficient Community

Impulse Control, Ineffective

Jaundice, Risk for Neonatal

Personal Identity, Disturbed Risk for

Relationship, Ineffective

Relationship, Risk for Ineffective

Self-Esteem, Risk for Chronic Low

Thermal Injury, Risk for

Tissue Perfusion, Risk for Ineffective Peripheral

SOURCE: NURSING DIAGNOSES – Definitions & Classifications 2012–2014, Copyright © NANDA International, 2012. Used by arrangement with Wiley–Blackwell Publishing, a company of John Wiley & Sons, Inc.

Appendix N4–4 Nursing Diagnoses Grouped by Diseases/Disorders

abdominal perineal resection

(also refer to *surgery, general*)

disturbed Body Image may be related to presence of surgical wounds possibly evidenced by verbalizations of feelings or perceptions, fear of reaction by others, preoccupation with change.

risk for Constipation: risk factors may include decreased physical activity, slowed gastric motility, abdominal muscle weakness, insufficient fluid intake, change in usual foods and/or eating pattern.

risk for Sexual Dysfunction: risk factors may include altered body structure or function (radical resection/treatment procedures), vulnerability, psychological concern about response of significant other(s), and disruption of sexual response pattern (e.g., erection difficulty).

abortion, elective termination

risk for decisional Conflict: risk factors may include unclear personal values/beliefs, lack of experience or interference with decision making, information from divergent sources, deficient support system.

deficient Knowledge [Learning Need] regarding reproduction, contraception, self-care, Rh factor may be related to lack of exposure/recall or misinterpretation of information possibly evidenced by request for information, statement reflecting misconception, inaccurate follow-through of instructions, development of preventable complications.

risk for Moral Distress: risk factors may include perception of moral/ethical implications of therapeutic procedure, time constraints for decision making.

Anxiety may be related to situational or maturational crises, unmet needs, unconscious conflict about essential values or beliefs, possibly evidenced by increased tension, apprehension, fear of unspecific consequences, sympathetic stimulation, focus on self.

acute Pain/impaired Comfort may be related to aftereffects of procedure, drug effect, possibly evidenced by verbal report, distraction behaviors, changes in muscle tone, changes in vital signs

risk for [maternal] injury risk factors may include surgical procedure, effects of anesthesia and medications.

abortion, spontaneous termination

risk for Bleeding risk factors may include pregnancy-related complications.

risk for Spiritual Distress risk factors may include challenged beliefs/values, blame for loss directed at self or God.

deficient Knowledge [Learning Need] regarding cause of abortion, self-care, contraception/future pregnancy may be related to lack of familiarity with new self or healthcare needs, sources for support, possibly evidenced by requests for information and statement of concern or misconceptions, development of preventable complications.

Grieving related to perinatal loss, possibly evidenced by crying, expressions of sorrow, or changes in eating habits or sleep patterns.

risk for ineffective Sexuality Pattern: risk factors may include increasing fear of pregnancy and/or repeat loss, impaired relationship with significant other(s), self-doubt regarding own femininity.

abruptio placentae

risk for Shock risk factors may include hypotension, hypovolemia.

Fear related to threat of death (perceived or actual) to fetus/self, possibly evidenced by verbalization apprehension, increased tension, sympathetic stimulation.

acute Pain may be related to collection of blood between uterine wall and placenta, uterine contractions, possibly evidenced by verbal reports, abdominal guarding, muscle tension, or alterations in vital signs.

risk for disturbed Maternal-Fetal Dyad risk factors may include complication of pregnancy, compromised oxygen transport

abscess, brain (acute)

acute Pain may be related to inflammation, edema of tissues, possibly evidenced by reports of headache, restlessness, irritability, and moaning.

risk for Hyperthermia: risk factors may include illness [inflammatory process], hypermetabolic state and dehydration.

acute Confusion may be related to delirium [cerebral edema/altered perfusion, fever], possibly evidenced by fluctuation in cognition/level of consciousness, increased agitation/restlessness, hallucinations.

risk for Suffocation/Trauma: risk factors may include disease process [seizure activity]. cognitive difficulties.

abscess, skin/tissue

impaired Skin/Tissue Integrity may be related to immunological deficit, infection, possibly evidenced by disruption of skin, destruction of skin layers or tissues, invasion of body structures

risk for Infection [spread] risk factors may include broken skin, traumatized tissues, chronic disease, malnutrition, insufficient knowledge.

abuse, physical
(also refer to *battered child syndrome*)

risk for Trauma: risk factors may include vulnerable client, recipient of verbal threats, history of physical abuse.

Powerlessness may be related to interpersonal interactions, lifestyle of helplessness as evidenced by verbal expressions of having no control, reluctance to express true feelings, apathy, passivity.

chronic low Self-Esteem may be related to continual negative evaluation of self/capabilities, personal vulnerability, willingness to tolerate possible life-threatening domestic violence as evidenced by self-negative verbalization, evaluates self as unable to deal with events, rationalizes away/rejects positive feedback.

abuse, psychological

ineffective Coping may be related to situational or maturational crisis, overwhelming threat to self, personal vulnerability, inadequate support systems, possibly evidenced by verbalized concern about ability to deal with current situation, chronic worry, anxiety, depression, poor self-esteem, inability to problem-solve, high illness rate, destructive behavior toward self or others.

Powerlessness may be related to abusive relationship, lifestyle of helplessness as evidenced by verbal expressions of having no control, reluctance to express true feelings, apathy, passivity.

Sexual Dysfunction may be related to ineffectual or absent role model, vulnerability, psychological abuse (harmful relationship) possibly evidenced by reported difficulties, inability to achieve desired satisfaction, conflicts involving values, seeking confirmation of desirability.

achalasia (cardiospasm)

impaired Swallowing may be related to neuromuscular impairment, possibly evidenced by observed difficulty in swallowing or regurgitation.

imbalanced Nutrition: less than body requirements may be related to inability and/or reluctance to ingest adequate nutrients to meet metabolic demands and nutritional needs, possibly evidenced by reported or observed inadequate intake, weight loss, and pale conjunctiva and mucous membranes.

acute Pain may be related to spasm of the lower esophageal sphincter, possibly evidenced by reports of substernal pressure, recurrent heartburn, or gastric fullness (gas pains).

Anxiety [specify level]/Fear may be related to recurrent pain, choking sensation, altered health status, possibly evidenced by verbalizations of distress, apprehension, restlessness, or insomnia.

risk for Aspiration risk factors may include regurgitation or spillover of esophageal contents.

deficient Knowledge [Learning Need] regarding condition, prognosis, self-care, and treatment needs may be related to lack of familiarity with pathology and treatment of condition, possibly evidenced by requests for information, statement of concern, or development of preventable complications.

acidosis, metabolic
Refer to *diabetic ketoacidosis.*

acidosis, respiratory
(also refer to underlying cause/condition)
impaired Gas Exchange may be related to ventilation perfusion imbalance (decreased oxygen-carrying capacity of blood, altered oxygen supply, alveolar-capillary membrane changes) possibly evidenced by dyspnea with exertion, tachypnea, changes in mentation, irritability, tachycardia, hypoxia, hypercapnia.

acne
impaired Skin Integrity may be related to secretions, infectious process as evidenced by disruptions of skin surface.

disturbed Body Image may be related to change in visual appearance as evidenced by fear of rejection of others, focus on past appearance, negative feelings about body, change in social involvement.

situational low Self-Esteem may be related to adolescence, negative perception of appearance as evidenced by self-negating verbalizations, expressions of helplessness.

acoustic neuroma
[disturbed auditory Sensory Perception] may be related to altered sensory reception (compression of eight cranial nerve), possibly evidenced by unilateral sensorieural hearing loss, tinnitus.

risk for Falls risk factors may include hearing difficulties, dizziness, sense of unsteadiness.

acromegaly
chronic Pain may be related to soft tissue swelling, joint degeneration, peripheral nerve compression possibly evidenced by verbal reports, altered ability to continue previous activities, changes in sleep pattern, fatigue.

disturbed Body Image may be related to biophysical illness or changes, possibly evidenced by verbalization of feelings, concerns, fear of rejection or of reaction of others, negative comments about body, actual change in structure or appearance, change in social involvement.

risk for Sexual Dysfunction risk factors may include altered body structure, changes in libido.

acute respiratory distress syndrome (ARDS)
ineffective Airway Clearance may be related to loss of ciliary action, increased amount and viscosity of secretions, and increased airway resistance, possibly evidenced by presence of dyspnea, changes in depth/rate of respiration, use of accessory muscles for breathing, wheezes/crackles, cough with or without sputum production.

impaired Gas Exchange may be related to changes in pulmonary capillary permeability with edema formation, alveolar hypoventilation and collapse, with intrapulmonary shunting; possibly evidenced by tachypnea, use of accessory muscles, cyanosis, hypoxia per arterial blood gases (ABGs)/oximetry; anxiety and changes in mentation.

risk for deficient Fluid Volume: risk factors may include active loss from diuretic use and restricted intake.

risk for decreased Cardiac Output: risk factors may include alteration in preload (hypovolemia, vascular pooling, diuretic therapy, and increased intrathoracic pressure/use of ventilator/positive end-expiratory pressure, PEEP).

Anxiety [specify level]/Fear may be related to physiologic factors (effects of hypoxemia); situational crisis, change in health status/threat of death; possibly evidenced by increased tension, apprehension, restlessness, focus on self, and sympathetic stimulation.

risk for barotrauma Injury: risk factors may include increased airway pressure associated with mechanical ventilation (PEEP).

ADD
Refer to *Attention Deficit Disorder*

addiction
Refer to *Substance dependence/abuse rehabilitation*

Addison's disease

deficient [hypotonic] Fluid Volume may be related to vomiting, diarrhea, increased renal losses, possibly evidenced by delayed capillary refill, poor skin turgor, dry mucous membranes, report of thirst.

risk for Electrolyte Imbalance risk factors may include vomiting, diarrhea, endocrine dysfunction.

decreased Cardiac Output may be related to hypovolemia and altered electrical conduction (dysrhythmias) and/or diminished cardiac muscle mass, possibly evidenced by alterations in vital signs, changes in mentation, and irregular pulse or pulse deficit.

Fatigue may be related to decreased metabolic energy production, altered body chemistry (fluid, electrolyte, and glucose imbalance), possibly evidenced by unremitting overwhelming lack of energy, inability to maintain usual routines, decreased performance, impaired ability to concentrate, lethargy, and disinterest in surroundings.

disturbed Body Image may be related to changes in skin pigmentation and mucous membranes, loss of axillary/pubic hair, possibly evidenced by verbalization of negative feelings about body and decreased social involvement.

risk for impaired physical Mobility: risk factors may include neuromuscular impairment (muscle wasting/weakness) and dizziness/syncope.

imbalanced Nutrition: less than body requirements may be related to glucocorticoid deficiency; abnormal fat, protein, and carbohydrate metabolism; nausea, vomiting, anorexia, possibly evidenced by weight loss, muscle wasting, abdominal cramps, diarrhea, and severe hypoglycemia.

risk for impaired Home Maintenance: risk factors may include effects of disease process, impaired cognitive functioning, and inadequate support systems.

adenoidectomy

Anxiety [specify level]/Fear may be related to separation from supportive others, unfamiliar surroundings, and perceived threat of injury/abandonment, possibly evidenced by crying, apprehension, trembling, and sympathetic stimulation (pupil dilation, increased heart rate).

risk for ineffective Airway Clearance: risk factors may include sedation, collection of secretions/blood in oropharynx, and vomiting.

risk for deficient Fluid Volume : risk factors may include operative trauma to highly vascular site/hemorrhage.

acute Pain may be related to physical trauma to oronasopharynx, presence of packing, possibly evidenced by restlessness, crying, and facial mask of pain.

adjustment disorder

moderate to severe Anxiety may be related to situational/maturational crisis, threat to self-concept, unmet needs, fear of failure, dysfunctional family system, fixation in earlier level of development possibly evidenced by overexcitement/restlessness, increased tension, insomnia, feelings of inadequacy, focus on self, difficulty concentrating, continuous attention-seeking behaviors, numerous physical complaints.

risk for self/other-directed Violence: risk factors may include depressed mood, hopelessness, powerlessness, inability to tolerate frustration, rage reactions, unmet needs, negative role modeling, substance use/abuse, history of suicide attempt.

ineffective Coping may be related to situational/maturational crisis, dysfunctional family system, negative role modeling, unmet dependency needs, retarded ego development possibly evidenced by inability to problem-solve, chronic worry, depressed/anxious mood, manipulation of others, destructive behaviors, increased dependency, refusal to follow rules.

complicated Grieving may be related to real or perceived loss of any concept of value to individual, bereavement overload/cumulative grief, thwarted grieving response, feelings of guilt generated by ambivalent relationship with the lost concept/person possibly eviden¬ced by difficulty in expressing/denial of loss, excessive/inappropriately expressed anger, labile affect, developmental regression, changes in concentration/pursuit of tasks.

adoption/loss of child custody

risk for Complicated Grieving risk factors may include actual loss of child, expectations for future of child and self, thwarted grieving response to loss.

risk for Powerlessness risk factors may include perceived lack of options, no input into decision process, no control over outcome.

adrenal crisis, acute

(also refer to *Addison's disease*; *shock*)

deficient [hypotonic] Fluid Volume may be related to failure of regulatory mechanism (damage to/suppression of adrenal gland), inability to concentrate urine possibly evidenced by decreased venous filling/pulse volume and pressure, hypotension, dry mucous membranes, changes in mentation, decreased serum sodium.

acute pain may be related to effects of disease process/metabolic imbalances, decreased tissue perfusion, possibly evidenced by reports of severe pain in abdomen, lower back, or legs.

impaired physical Mobility may be related to neuromuscular impairment, decreased muscle strength/control possibly evidenced by generalized weakness, inability to perform desired activities/movements.

risk for Hyperthermia: risk factors may include presence of illness/infectious process, dehydration.

risk for ineffective Protection: risk factors may include hormone deficiency, drug therapy, nutritional/metabolic deficiencies.

adrenalectomy

ineffective Tissue Perfusion (specify) may be related to hypovolemia and vascular pooling (vasodilation), possibly evidenced by diminished pulse, pallor/cyanosis, hypotension, and changes in mentation.

risk for Infection: risk factors may include inadequate primary defenses (incision, traumatized tissues), suppressed inflammatory response, invasive procedures.

deficient Knowledge [Learning Need] regarding condition, prognosis, self-care and treatment needs may be related to unfamiliarity with long-term therapy requirements, possibly evidenced by request for information and statement of concern/misconceptions.

adrenal insufficiency
Refer to *Addison's disease*

adult respiratory distress syndrome (ARDS)
Refer to *acute respiratory distress syndrome.*

affective disorder
Refer to *bipolar disorder*; *depressive disorders, major.*

affective disorder, seasonal
(also refer to *depressive disorders, major*)

intermittent ineffective Coping may be related to situational crisis (fall/winter season), disturbance in pattern of tension release, and inadequate resources available possibly evidenced by verbalizations of inability to cope, changes in sleep pattern (too little or too much), reports of lack of energy/fatigue, lack of resolution of problem, behavioral changes (irritability, discouragement).

risk for imbalanced Nutrition: more/less than body requirements: risk factors may include eating in response to internal cues other than hunger, alteration in usual coping patterns, change in usual activity level, decreased appetite, lack of energy/interest to prepare food.

agoraphobia
Also refer to *phobia*

Anxiety [panic] may be related to contact with feared situation (public place, crowds), possibly evidenced by tachycardia, chest pain, dyspnea, gastrointestinal distress, faintness, sense of impending doom.

agranulocytosis

risk for Infection risk factors may include suppressed inflammatory response.

risk for impaired Oral Mucous Membrane: risk factors may include infection.

risk for imbalanced Nutrition: less than body requirements: risk factors may include ingest food or fluids (lesions of oral cavity).

AIDS (acquired immunodeficiency syndrome)
(also refer to *HIV infection*)

risk for Infection, [progression to sepsis/onset of new opportunistic infection]: risk factors may include depressed immune system, use of antimicrobial agents, inadequate primary defenses; broken skin, traumatized tissue; malnutrition, and chronic disease processes.

risk for deficient Fluid Volume: risk factors may include excessive losses: copious diarrhea, profuse sweating, vomiting, hypermetabolic state or fever; and restricted intake (nausea, anorexia; lethargy).

acute/chronic Pain may be related to tissue inflammation/destruction: infections, internal/external cutaneous lesions, rectal excoriation, malignancies, necrosis, peripheral neuropathies, myalgias, and arthralgias, possibly evidenced by verbal reports, self-focusing/narrowed focus, alteration in muscle tone, paresthesias, paralysis, guarding behaviors, changes in vital signs (acute), autonomic responses, and restlessness.

risk for ineffective Breathing Pattern/impaired Gas Exchange risk factors may include muscular impairment—wasting of respiratory musculature, decreased energy, fatigue, respiratory muscle fatigue; retained secretions—tracheobronchial obstruction; pain

imbalanced Nutrition: less than body requirements may be related to altered ability to ingest, digest, and/or absorb nutrients (nausea/vomiting, hyperactive gag reflex, intestinal disturbances); increased metabolic activity/nutritional needs (fever, infection), possibly evidenced by weight loss, decreased subcutaneous fat/muscle mass; lack of interest in food/aversion to eating, altered taste sensation; abdominal cramping, hyperactive bowel sounds, diarrhea, sore and inflamed buccal cavity.

Fatigue may be related to decreased metabolic energy production, increased energy requirements (hypermetabolic state), overwhelming psychological/emotional demands; altered body chemistry (side effects of medication, chemotherapy), possibly evidenced by unremitting/overwhelming lack of energy, inability to maintain usual routines, decreased performance; impaired ability to concentrate, lethargy/restlessness, and disinterest in surroundings.

ineffective Protection may be related to chronic disease affecting immune and neurological systems, inadequate nutrition, drug therapies, possibly evidenced by deficient immunity, impaired healing, neurosensory alterations, maladaptive stress response, fatigue, anorexia, disorientation.

Social Isolation may be related to alteration in physical appearance/mental status, state of wellness, perceptions of unacceptable social behavior or values, phobic fear of others (transmission of disease); possibly evidenced by expressed feelings of aloneness/rejection, absence of supportive significant other(s) (SOs), and withdrawal from usual activities.

chronic Confusion may be related to physiological changes (hypoxemia, central nervous system [CNS] infection by HIV, brain malignancies, and/or disseminated systemic opportunistic infection), altered drug metabolism or excretion, accumulation of toxic elements (renal failure, severe electrolyte imbalance, hepatic insufficiency), possibly evidenced by clinical evidence of organic impairment, altered response to stimuli, memory deficit, and altered personality.

AIDS dementia
(also refer to *Dementia, presenile/senile*)
impaired Environmental Interpretation Syndrome may be related to dementia, depression, possibly evidenced by consistent disorientation, inability to follow simple directions, loss of social functioning from memory decline.

ineffective Protection may be related to immune disorder inadequate nutrition, drug therapies, possibly evidenced by deficient immunity, impaired healing, neurosensory alterations, maladaptive stress response, fatigue, anorexia, disorientation.

alcohol abuse/withdrawal
Refer to *Drug overdose, acute [depressants]*; *Delirium tremens*; *Substance dependency/abuse rehabilitation*.

alcohol intoxication, acute
(also refer to *Delirium tremens*)
acute Confusion may be related to substance abuse, hypoxemia possibly evidenced by hallucinations, exaggerated emotional response, fluctuation in cognition/level of consciousness, increased agitation.

risk for ineffective Breathing Pattern risk factors may include hypoventilation syndrome, neuromuscular dysfunction, fatigue.

risk for Aspiration: risk factors may include reduced level of consciousness, depressed cough/gag reflexes, delayed gastric emptying

aldosteronism, primary
Fluid Volume, deficient [isotonic] may be related to increased urinary losses, possibly evidenced by dry mucous membranes, poor skin turgor, dilute urine, excessive thirst, weight loss.

impaired physical Mobility may be related to neuromuscular impairment, decreased muscle strength, and pain, possibly evidenced by limited range of motion, slowed movement, limited ability to perform gross/fine motor skills

risk for decreased Cardiac Output : risk factors may include hypovolemia and altered heart rhythm.

alkalosis, respiratory
(also refer to underlying cause/condition)
impaired Gas Exchange may be related to ventilation perfusion imbalance (decreased oxygen-carrying capacity of blood, altered oxygen-supply, alveolar-capillary membrane changes) possibly evidenced by dyspnea, tachypnea, changes in mentation, tachycardia, hypoxia, hypocapnia.

allergy, latex
Refer to *latex allergy*.

alopecia
disturbed Body Image may be related to effects of illness or therapy, or aging process, change in appearance, possibly evidenced by verbalization of feelings, concerns, fear of rejection or reaction of others, focus on past appearance, preoccupation with change, feelings of helplessness.

Alzheimer's disease
(also refer to *dementia, presenile/senile*)
risk for Injury/Trauma: risk factors may include inability to recognize/identify danger in environment, disorientation, confusion, impaired judgment, weakness, muscular incoordination, balancing difficulties, and altered perception.
chronic Confusion related to physiological changes (neuronal degeneration); possibly evidenced by inaccurate interpretation of/response to stimuli, progressive/long-standing cognitive impairment, short-term memory deficit, impaired socialization, altered personality, and clinical evidence of organic impairment.
disturbed Sensory Perception (specify) may be related to altered sensory reception, transmission, and/or integration (neurologic disease/deficit), socially restricted environment (homebound/institutionalized), sleep deprivation possibly evidenced by changes in usual response to stimuli, change in problem-solving abilities, exaggerated emotional responses (anxiety, paranoia, hallucinations), inability to tell position of body parts, diminished/altered sense of taste.
Sleep Deprivation may be related to sensory impairment, changes in activity patterns, psychological stress (neurological impairment), possibly evidenced by wakefulness, disorientation (day/night reversal), increased aimless wandering, inability to identify need or time for sleeping, changes in behavior, lethargy; dark circles under eyes, and frequent yawning.
ineffective Health Maintenance may be related to deterioration affecting ability in all areas including coordination/communication, cognitive impairment; ineffective coping, possibly evidenced by reported or observed inability to take responsibility for meeting basic health practices, lack of equipment/financial or other resources, and impairment of personal support system.
risk for Stress Overload: risk factors may include inadequate resources, chronic illness, physical demands, threats of violence.
Compromised family Coping/Caregiver Role Strain may be related to family disorganization, role changes, family/caregiver isolation, long-term illness/complexity and amount of homecare needs exhausting supportive/financial capabilities of family member(s), lack of respite; possibly evidenced by verbalizations of frustrations in dealing with day-to-day care, reports of conflict, feelings of depression, expressed anger/guilt directed toward client, and withdrawal from interaction with client/social contacts.
risk for Relocation Stress Syndrome: risk factors may include little or no preparation for transfer to a new setting, changes in daily routine, sensory impairment, physical deterioration, separation from support systems.

amputation
risk for ineffective peripheral Tissue Perfusion: risk factors may include reduced arterial/venous blood flow; tissue edema, hematoma formation; hypovolemia.
acute Pain may be related to tissue and nerve trauma, psychological impact of loss of body part, possibly evidenced by reports of incisional/phantom pain, guarding/protective behavior, narrowed/self-focus, and autonomic responses.
impaired physical Mobility may be related to loss of limb (primarily lower extremity), altered sense of balance, pain/discomfort, possibly evidenced by reluctance to attempt movement, impaired coordination; decreased muscle strength, control, and mass.
situational low Self-Esteem may be related to loss of a body part, change in functional abilities, possibly evidenced by verbalization of feelings of powerlessness, grief, preoccupation with loss, negative feelings about body, focus on past strength, function, or appearance; change in usual patterns of responsibility or physical capacity to resume role, fear of rejection or reaction by others, and unwillingness to look at or touch residual limb.

amyotrophic lateral sclerosis (ALS)
impaired physical Mobility may be related to muscle wasting/weakness, possibly evidenced by impaired coordination, limited range of motion, and impaired purposeful movement.
ineffective Breathing Pattern/impaired spontaneous Ventilation may be related to neuromuscular impairment, decreased energy, fatigue, tracheobronchial obstruction, possibly evidenced by shortness of breath, fremitus, respiratory depth changes, and reduced vital capacity.
impaired Swallowing may be related to muscle wasting and fatigue, possibly evidenced by recurrent coughing/choking and signs of aspiration.
Powerlessness [specify level] may be related to chronic/debilitating nature of illness, lack of control over outcome, possibly evidenced by expressions of frustration about inability to care for self and depression over physical deterioration.
Grieving may be related to perceived potential loss of self/physiopsychosocial well-being, possibly evidenced by sorrow, choked feelings, expression of distress, changes in eating habits/sleeping patterns, and altered communication patterns/libido.

impaired verbal Communication may be related to physical barrier (neuromuscular impairment), possibly evidenced by impaired articulation, inability to speak in sentences, and use of nonverbal cues (changes in facial expression).

risk for Caregiver Role Strain: risk factors may include illness severity of care receiver, complexity and amount of home-care needs, duration of caregiving required, caregiver is spouse, family/caregiver isolation, lack of respite/recreation for caregiver.

anaphylaxis
(also refer to *shock*)

ineffective Airway Clearance may be related to airway spasm (bronchial), laryngeal edema possibly evidenced by diminished/adventitious breath sounds, cough ineffective or absent, difficulty vocalizing, wide-eyed.

decreased Cardiac Ouput may be related to decreased preload–increased capillary permeability (third spacing) and vasodilation possibly evidenced by tachycardia/palpitations, changes in blood pressure (BP), anxiety, restlessness.

anemia

Activity Intolerance may be related to imbalance between oxygen supply (delivery) and demand, possibly evidenced by reports of fatigue and weakness, abnormal heart rate or blood pressure (BP) response, decreased exercise/activity level, and exertional discomfort or dyspnea.

imbalanced Nutrition: less than body requirements may be related to failure to ingest/ inability to digest food or absorb nutrients necessary for formation of normal red blood cells (RBCs); possibly evidenced by weight loss/weight below normal for age, height, body build; decreased triceps skinfold measurement, changes in gums/oral mucous membranes; decreased tolerance for activity, weakness, and loss of muscle tone.

deficient Knowledge [Learning Need] regarding condition, prognosis, self-care and treatment needs may be related to inadequate understanding or misinterpretation of dietary/physiologic needs, possibly evidenced by inadequate dietary intake, request for information, and development of preventable complications.

Anemia, iron-deficiency
also refer to *anemia*

fatigue may be related to anemia, malnutrition, possibly evidenced by feeling tired, inability to maintain usual routines or level of physical activity.

risk for deficient Fluid Volume risk factors may include active or chronic blood loss.

risk for impaired Oral Mucous Membrane risk factors may include dehydration, malnutrition, vitamin deficiency.

anemia, sickle cell

impaired Gas Exchange may be related to decreased oxygen-carrying capacity of blood, reduced RBC life span, abnormal RBC structure, increased blood viscosity, predisposition to bacterial pneumonia/pulmonary infarcts, possibly evidenced by dyspnea, use of accessory muscles, cyanosis/signs of hypoxia, tachycardia, changes in mentation, and restlessness.

ineffective Tissue Perfusion: (specify) may be related to stasis, vaso-occlusive nature of sickling, inflammatory response, atrioventricular (AV) shunts in pulmonary and peripheral circulation, myocardial damage (small infarcts, iron deposits, fibrosis), possibly evidenced by signs and symptoms dependent on system involved, for example: renal: decreased specific gravity and pale urine in face of dehydration; cerebral: paralysis and visual disturbances; peripheral: distal ischemia, tissue infarctions, ulcerations, bone pain; cardiopulmonary: angina, palpitations.

acute/chronic Pain may be related to intravascular sickling with localized vascular stasis, occlusion, infarction/necrosis and deprivation of oxygen and nutrients, accumulation of noxious metabolites, possibly evidenced by reports of localized, generalized, or migratory joint and/or abdominal/back pain; guarding and distraction behaviors (moaning, crying, restlessness), facial grimacing, narrowed focus, and autonomic responses.

deficient Knowledge [Learning Need] regarding disease process, genetic factors, prognosis, self-care and treatment needs may be related to lack of exposure/recall, misinterpretation of information, unfamiliarity with resources, possibly evidenced by questions, statement of concern/misconceptions, exacerbation of condition, inadequate follow-through of therapy instructions, and development of preventable complications.

risk for Sedentary Lifestyle risk factors may include lack of interest or motivation, lack of resources, lack of training or knowledge of specific exercise needs, safety concerns or fear of injury.

delayed Growth and Development may be related to effects of physical condition, possibly evidenced by altered physical growth and delay/difficulty performing skills typical of age group.

risk for sedentary Lifestyle: risk factors may include lack of interest/motivation, resources; lack of training or knowledge of specific exercise needs, safety concerns/fear of injury.

compromised family Coping may be related to chronic nature of disease/disability, family disorganization, presence of other crises/situations impacting significant person/ parent, lifestyle restrictions, possibly evidenced by significant person/parent expressing preoccupation with own reaction and displaying protective behavior disproportionate to patient's ability or need for autonomy.

aneurysm, ventricular

decreased cardiac ouput may be related to altered stroke volume, changes in heart rate or rhythm, possible evidenced by dyspnea, adventitious breath sounds, S_3/S_4 heart sounds, changes in hemodynamic measurements, dysrhythmias.

ineffective Tissue Perfusion (specify) may be related to decreased arterial blood flow, possibly evidenced by blood pressure changes, diminished pulses, edema, dyspnea, dysrthythmias, altered mental status, decreased renal function.

activity intolerance may be related to imbalance between oxygen supply and demand, possibly evidenced by weakness, fatigue, abnormal heart rate/blood pressure response to activity, electrocardiogram changes (dysrthythmias, ischemia).

angina pectoris

acute Pain may be related to decreased myocardial blood flow, increased cardiac work-load/oxygen consumption, possibly evidenced by verbal reports, narrowed focus, distraction behaviors (restlessness, moaning), and autonomic responses (diaphoresis, changes in vital signs).

decreased Cardiac Output may be related to inotropic changes (transient/prolonged myocardial ischemia, effects of medications), alterations in rate/rhythm and electrical conduction, possibly evidenced by changes in hemodynamic readings, dyspnea, restlessness, decreased tolerance for activity, fatigue, diminished peripheral pulses, cool/pale skin, changes in mental status, and continued chest pain.

Anxiety [specify level] may be related to situational crises, change in health status and/or threat of death, negative self-talk possibly evidenced by verbalized apprehension, facial tension, extraneous movements, and focus on self.

Activity Intolerance may be related to imbalance between oxygen supply and demand, possibly evidenced by exertional dyspnea, abnormal pulse/BP response to activity, and electrocardiogram (ECG) changes.

deficient Knowledge [Learning Need] regarding condition, prognosis, self-care and treatment needs may be related to lack of exposure, inaccurate/misinterpretation of information, possibly evidenced by questions, request for information, statement of concern, and inaccurate follow-through of instructions.

risk for sedentary Lifestyle: risk factors may include lack of training or knowledge of specific exercise needs, safety concerns/fear of myocardial injury.

risk for risk-prone health Behavior: risk factors may include condition requiring long-term therapy/change in lifestyle, multiple stressors, assault to self-concept, and altered locus of control.

anorexia nervosa

imbalanced Nutrition: less than body requirements may be related to psychological restrictions of food intake and/or excessive activity, self-induced vomiting, laxative abuse, possibly evidenced by weight loss, poor skin turgor/muscle tone, denial of hunger, unusual hoarding or handling of food, amenorrhea, electrolyte imbalance, cardiac irregularities, hypotension.

risk for deficient Fluid Volume: risk factors may include inadequate intake of food and liquids, chronic/excessive laxative or diuretic use, self-induced vomiting.

disturbed Thought Processes may be related to severe malnutrition/electrolyte imbalance, psychological conflicts; possibly evidenced by impaired ability to make decisions, problem-solve, nonreality-based verbalizations, ideas of reference, altered sleep patterns, altered attention span/distractibility; perceptual disturbances with failure to recognize hunger, fatigue, anxiety, and depression.

disturbed Body Image/chronic low Self-Esteem may be related to perceptual developmental changes, possibly evidenced by verbalized perceptions reflecting altered view of body appearance, refusal to verify actual change.

chronic low Self-Esteem may be related to lack of approval, repeated negative reinforcement, perceived lack of respect from others possibly evidenced by reports feelings of shame or guilt; overly conforming, dependent on may be related to issues of control in family, situational or maturational crises, history of inadequate coping methods possibly evidenced by enmeshed family, dissonance among family members, focus on "identified patient," family developmental tasks not being met, family members acting as enablers, ill-defined family rules, functions, or roles.

impaired Parenting may be related to issues of control in family, situational or maturational crises, history of inadequate coping methods possibly evidenced by enmeshed family, dissonance among family members, focus on "identified patient", family developmental tasks not being met, family members acting as enablers, ill-defined family rules, functions, or roles.

antisocial personality disorder

risk for other-directed Violence: risk factors may include contempt for authority/rights of others, inability to tolerate frustration, need for immediate gratification, easy agitation, vulnerable self-concept, inability to verbalize feelings, use of maladjusted coping mechanisms, history of substance abuse.

ineffective Coping may be related to very low tolerance for external stress, lack of experience of internal anxiety (e.g., guilt, shame), personal vulnerability, unmet expectations, multiple life changes, possibly evidenced by choice of aggression and manipulation to handle problems or conflicts, inappropriate use of defense mechanisms (e.g., denial, projection), chronic worry, anxiety, destructive behaviors, high rate of accidents.

chronic low Self-Esteem may be related to lack of positive and/or repeated negative feedback, unmet dependency needs, retarded ego development, dysfunctional family system, possibly evidenced by acting-out behaviors (e.g., substance abuse, sexual promiscuity, feelings of inadequacy, nonparticipation in therapy).

compromised/disabled family Coping may be related to family disorganization or role changes, highly ambivalent family relationships, client providing little support in turn for the primary person(s), history of abuse or neglect in the home, possibly evidenced by expressions of concern or complaints, preoccupation of primary person with own reactions to situation, display of protective behaviors disproportionate to client's abilities, or need for autonomy.

impaired Social Interaction may be related to inadequate personal resources (shallow feelings), immature interests, underdeveloped conscience, unaccepted social values, possibly evidenced by difficulty meeting expectations of others, lack of belief that rules pertain to self, sense of emptiness or inadequacy covered by expressions of self-conceit, arrogance, or contempt; behavior unaccepted by dominant cultural group.

anxiety disorder, generalized

Anxiety [specify level]/Powerlessness may be related to real or perceived threat to physical integrity or self-concept (may or may not be able to identify the threat), unconscious conflict about essential values/beliefs and goals of life, unmet needs, negative self-talk, possibly evidenced by sympathetic stimulation, extraneous movements (foot shuffling, hand/arm fidgeting, rocking movements, restlessness), persistent feelings of apprehension and uneasiness, a general anxious feeling that patient has difficulty alleviating, poor eye contact, focus on self, impaired functioning, free-floating anxiety, and nonparticipation in decision making.

ineffective Coping may be related to level of anxiety being experienced by the patient, personal vulnerability; unmet expectations/unrealistic perceptions, inadequate coping methods and/or support systems possibly evidenced by verbalization of inability to cope/problem-solve, excessive compulsive behaviors (e.g., smoking, drinking), and emotional/muscle tension, alteration in societal participation, high rate of accidents.

Insomnia may be related to stress, repetitive thoughts, possibly evidenced by reports of difficulty in falling/staying asleep, dissatisfaction with sleep, nonrestorative sleep, lack of energy.

risk for compromised family Coping: risk factors may include inadequate/incorrect information or understanding by a primary person, temporary family disorganization and role changes, prolonged disability that exhausts the supportive capacity of significant other(s).

impaired Social Interaction/Social Isolation may be related to low self-concept, inadequate personal resources, misinterpretation of internal/external stimuli, hypervigilance possibly evidenced by discomfort in social situations, withdrawal from or reported change in pattern of interactions, dysfunctional interactions; expressed feelings of difference from others; sad, dull affect.

anxiety disorders

[severe/panic] Anxiety may be related to situational or maturational crisis, internal transmission and contagion, threat to physical integrity or self-concept, unmet needs, dysfunctional family system, independence conflicts evidenced by somatic complaints, nightmares, excessive psychomotor activity, refusal to attend school, persistent worry or fear of catastrophic doom to family or self.

ineffective Coping may be related to situational or maturational crisis, multiple life changes or losses, personal vulnerability, lack of self-confidence possibly evidenced by inability, to problem-solve, persistent or overwhelming fears, inability to meet role expectations, social inhibition, panic attacks.

impaired Social Interaction may be related to excessive self-consciousness, inability to interact with unfamiliar people, altered thought processes possibly evidenced by verbalized or observed discomfort in social situations, inability to receive or communicate a satisfying sense of belonging, caring, or interest; use of unsuccessful social interaction behaviors

risk for Self-Mutilation/self-directed Violence risk factors may include panic states, dysfunctional family, history of self-destructive behaviors, emotional disturbance, increasing motor activity

compromised/disabled family Coping may be related to situational or developmental crisis (e.g., divorce, addition to the family), unrealistic parental expectations, frequent disruptions in living arrangements, high-risk family situations (neglect or abuse, substance abuse), possibly evidenced by SO reports of frustration with clinging behaviors, emotional lability, harsh or punitive response to tyrannical behaviors, disproportionate protective behavior

Aortic aneurysm, abdominal (AAA)
risk for ineffective Renal Perfusion risk for ineffective Renal Perfusion: risk factors may include hypertension, hypovolemia, hypoxia.

risk for Infection risk factors may include turbulent blood flow through arteriosclerotic lesion.

acute Pain may be related to physical agent [vascular enlargement-dissection or rupture], possibly evidenced by verbal/coded reports, guarding behavior, facial mask, change in vital signs.

aortic aneurysm repair, abdominal
(also refer to *Surgery, general*)
Anxiety related to change in health status, threat of death, surgical intervention, possibly evidenced by expressed concerns, apprehension, increased tension, changes in vital signs.

risk for Bleeding risk factors may include aneurysm, treatment-related side effects—surgery, failure of vascular repair.

risk for ineffective renal/peripheral Tissue Perfusion: risk factors may include hypertension, treatment-related side effects—surgery, hypovolemia, hypoxia.

aortic stenosis
decreased Cardiac Output may be related to altered contractility, altered preload or afterload possibly evidenced by fatigue, dyspnea, changes in vital signs, jugular vein distension, increased CVP/PAWP, and syncope.

risk for impaired Gas Exchange: risk factors may include alveolar-capillary membrane change.

risk for acute Pain: risk factors may include physical agent [episodic ischemia of myocardial tissues and stretching of left atrium].

Activity Intolerance may be related to imbalance between oxygen supply and demand (decreased/fixed cardiac output), possibly evidenced by exertional dyspnea, reported fatigue/weakness, and abnormal blood pressure or ECG changes/dysrhythmias in response to activity.

aplastic anemia
(also refer to *anemia*)
risk for ineffective Protection: risk factors may include abnormal blood profile (leukopenia, thrombocytopenia), drug therapies (antineoplastics, antibiotics, NSAIDs [nonsteroidal anti-inflammatory drugs], anticonvulsants).

Fatigue may be related to anemia, disease states, malnutrition possibly evidenced by verbalization of overwhelming lack of energy, inability to maintain usual routines/level of physical activity, tired, compromised libido, lethargy, increase in physical complaints.

appendicitis
acute Pain may be related to physical agent [distention of intestinal tissues/inflammation], possibly evidenced by verbal reports, guarding behavior, narrowed focus, and diaphoresis, changes in vital signs.

risk for deficient Fluid Volume: risk factors may include excessive losses through normal routes (vomiting), deviations affecting intake of fluids nausea, anorexia), and factors influencing fluid needs (hypermetabolic state).

risk for Infection: risk factors may include tissue destruction [release of pathogenic organisms into peritoneal cavity]

arrhythmia, cardiac
Refer to *dysrhythmia, cardiac*.

Arterial occlusive disease, peripheral
ineffective peripheral Tissue Perfusion may be related to deficient knowledge of disease process [PAD], hypertension, smoking, sedentary lifestyle,possibly evidenced by altered skin characteristics, diminished pulses, claudication, delayed peripheral wound healing

risk for impaired Walking risk factors may include limited endurance, pain.

risk for impaired Skin/Tissue integrity risk factors may include altered circulation or sensation.

arthritis, juvenile rheumatoid
(also refer to *arthritis, rheumatoid*)
risk for delayed Development: risk factors may include chronic illness, effects of required therapy.

risk for Social Isolation: risk factors may include delay in accomplishing developmental task, altered state of wellness, and alterations in physical appearance.

arthritis, rheumatoid

acute/chronic Pain may be related to accumulation of fluid/inflammatory process, degeneration of joint, and deformity, possibly evidenced by verbal reports, narrowed focus, guarding/protective behaviors, and physical and social withdrawal.

impaired physical Mobility/Walking may be related to musculoskeletal deformity, pain/discomfort, decreased muscle strength, possibly evidenced by limited range of motion, impaired coordination, reluctance to attempt movement, and decreased muscle strength/control and mass.

Self-Care Deficit [specify] may be related to musculoskeletal impairment, decreased strength/endurance and range of motion, pain on movement, possibly evidenced by inability to manage activities of daily living (ADLs).

disturbed Body Image/ineffective Role Performance may be related to change in body structure/function, impaired mobility/ability to perform usual tasks, focus on past strength/function/appearance, possibly evidenced by negative self-talk, feeling of helplessness, change in lifestyle/physical abilities, dependence on others for assistance, decreased social involvement.

arthritis, septic

acute Pain may be related to joint inflammation, possibly evidenced by verbal or coded reports, guarding behaviors, restlessness, narrowed focus.

impaired physical Mobility may be related to joint stiffness, pain or discomfort, reluctance to initiate movement, possibly evidenced by limited range of motion, slowed movement.

Self-Care Deficity [specify] may be related to musculoskeletal impairment, pain or discomfort, decreased strength, impaired coordination, possibly evidenced by inability to perform desired ADLs.

risk for Infection [spread]: risk factors may include presence of infectious process, chronic disease states, invasive procedures.

arthroplasty

risk for Infection: risk factors may include breach of primary defenses (surgical incision), stasis of body fluids at operative site, and altered inflammatory response.

risk for Bleeding: risk factors may include surgical procedure, trauma to vascular area.

impaired physical Mobility may be related to decreased strength, pain, musculoskeletal changes, possibly evidenced by impaired coordination and reluctance to attempt movement.

acute Pain may be related to tissue trauma, local edema, possibly evidenced by verbal reports, narrowed focus, guarded movement, and diaphoresis, changes in vital signs.

arthroscopy, knee

deficient Knowledge [Learning Need] regarding procedure/outcomes and self-care needs may be related to unfamiliarity with information/resources, misinterpretations, possibly evidenced by questions and requests for information, misconceptions.

risk for impaired Walking: risk factors may include joint stiffness, discomfort, prescribed movement restrictions, use of assistive devices/crutches for ambulation.

Asperger's disorder

impaired Social Interaction may be related to skill deficit about ways to enhance mutuality, communication barriers (poor pragmatic language skills), compulsions, repetitive motor mannerisms, possibly evidenced by observed discomfort in social situations, dysfunctional interactions with others, inability to receive or communicate satisfying sense of belonging.

risk for Delayed Development risk factors may include behavior disorders, lack of eye contact, doesn't pick up on social cues, trouble with sensory integration.

impaired Parenting may be related to developmental delay of child, deficient knowledge of child development, lack of social supports.

risk for Injury risk factors may include rituals, repetitive motor mannerisms, poor coordination, vulnerability to manipulation of peers.

asthma

(also refer to *emphysema*)

ineffective Airway Clearance may be related to increased production/retained pulmonary secretions, bronchospasm, decreased energy/fatigue, possibly evidenced by wheezing, difficulty breathing, changes in depth/rate of respirations, use of accessory muscles, and persistent ineffective cough with or without sputum production.

impaired Gas Exchange may be related to altered delivery of inspired oxygen/air trapping, possibly evidenced by dyspnea, restlessness, reduced tolerance for activity, cyanosis, and changes in ABGs and vital signs.

Anxiety [specify level] may be related to perceived threat of death, possibly evidenced by apprehension, fearful expression, and extraneous movements.

Activity Intolerance may be related to imbalance between oxygen supply and demand, possibly evidenced by fatigue and exertional dyspnea.

risk for Contamination: risk factors may include presence of atmospheric pollutants, environmental contaminants in the home (e.g., smoking/secondhand tobacco smoke).

athlete's foot

impaired Skin Integrity may be related to fungal invasion, humidity, secretions, possibly evidenced by disruption of skin surface, reports of painful itching.

risk for Infection [spread]: risk factors may include multiple breaks in skin, exposure to moist and warm environment.

atrial fibrillation

Activity Intolerance may be related to imbalance between oxygen supply and demand possibly evidenced by dyspnea, dizziness, presyncope or syncopal episodes.

risk for ineffective cerebral Tissue Perfusion: risk factors may include arterial fibrillation, embolism, thrombolytic therapy (microemboli).

attention deficit disorder (ADD)

ineffective Coping may be related to situational/maturational crisis, retarded ego development, low self-concept possibly evidenced by easy distraction by extraneous stimuli, shifting between uncompleted activities.

chronic low Self-Esteem may be related to retarded ego development, lack of positive/repeated negative feedback, negative role models possibly evidenced by lack of eye contact, derogatory self comments, hesitance to try new tasks, inadequate level of confidence.

deficient Knowledge regarding condition, prognosis, therapy may be related to misinformation/misinterpretations, unfamiliarity with resources possibly evidenced by verbalization of problems/misconceptions, poor school performance, unrealistic expectations of medication regimen.

autistic disorder

impaired Social Interaction may be related to abnormal response to sensory input/inadequate sensory stimulation, organic brain dysfunction; delayed development of secure attachment/trust, lack of intuitive skills to comprehend and accurately respond to social cues, disturbance in self-concept, possibly evidenced by lack of responsiveness to others, lack of eye contact or facial responsiveness, treating persons as objects, lack of awareness of feelings in others, indifference/aversion to comfort, affection, or physical contact; failure to develop cooperative social play and peer friendships in childhood.

impaired verbal Communication may be related to inability to trust others, withdrawal into self, organic brain dysfunction, abnormal interpretation/response to and/or inadequate sensory stimulation, possibly evidenced by lack of interactive communication mode, no use of gestures or spoken language, absent or abnormal nonverbal communication; lack of eye contact or facial expression; peculiar patterns of speech (form, content, or speech production), and impaired ability to initiate or sustain conversation despite adequate speech.

risk for Self-Mutilation: risk factors may include organic brain dysfunction, inability to trust others, disturbance in self-concept, inadequate sensory stimulation or abnormal response to sensory input (sensory overload); history of physical, emotional, or sexual abuse; and response to demands of therapy, realization of severity of condition.

disturbed Personal Identity may be related to organic brain dysfunction, lack of development of trust, maternal deprivation, fixation at presymbiotic phase of development, possibly evidenced by lack of awareness of the feelings or existence of others, increased anxiety resulting from physical contact with others, absent or impaired imitation of others, repeating what others say, persistent preoccupation with parts of objects, obsessive attachment to objects, marked distress over changes in environment; autoerotic/ritualistic behaviors, self-touching, rocking, swaying.

compromised/disabled family Coping may be related to family members unable to express feelings; excessive guilt, anger, or blaming among family members regarding child's condition; ambivalent or dissonant family relationships, prolonged coping with problem exhausting supportive ability of family members, possibly evidenced by denial of existence or severity of disturbed behaviors, preoccupation with personal emotional reaction to situation, rationalization that problem will be outgrown, attempts to intervene with child are achieving increasingly ineffective results, family withdraws from or becomes overly protective of child.

battered child syndrome

risk for Trauma: risk factors may include dependent position in relationship(s), vulnerability (e.g., congenital problems/chronic illness), history of previous abuse/neglect, lack/nonuse of support systems by caregiver(s).

interrupted Family Processes/impaired Parenting may be related to poor role model/identity, unrealistic expectations, presence of stressors, and lack of support, possibly evidenced by verbalization of negative feelings, inappropriate caretaking behaviors, and evidence of physical/psychological trauma to child.

chronic low Self-Esteem may be related to deprivation and negative feedback of family members, personal vulnerability, feelings of abandonment, possibly evidenced by lack of eye contact, withdrawal from social contacts, discounting own needs, nonassertive/ passive, indecisive, or overly conforming behaviors.

Post-Trauma Syndrome may be related to sustained/recurrent physical or emotional abuse; possibly evidenced by acting-out behavior, development of phobias, poor impulse control, and emotional numbness.

ineffective Coping may be related to situational or maturational crisis, overwhelming threat to self, personal vulnerability, inadequate support systems, possibly evidenced by verbalized concern about ability to deal with current situation, chronic worry, anxiety, depression, poor self-esteem, inability to problem-solve, high illness rate, destructive behavior toward self/others.

benign prostatic hyperplasia

[acute/chronic] Urinary Retention/overflow Urinary Incontinence may be related to mechanical obstruction (enlarged prostate), decompensation of detrusor musculature, inability of bladder to contract adequately, possibly evidenced by frequency, hesitancy, inability to empty bladder completely, incontinence or dribbling, nocturia, bladder distention, residual urine.

acute Pain may be related to mucosal irritation, bladder distention, colic, urinary infection, and radiation therapy, possibly evidenced by verbal reports (bladder or rectal spasm), narrowed focus, altered muscle tone, grimacing, distraction behaviors, restlessness, and changes in vital signs.

risk for deficient Fluid Volume/Electrolyte Imbalance: risk factors may include postobstructive diuresis, renal or endocrine dysfunction.

Fear/Anxiety [specify level] may be related to change in health status (possibility of surgical procedure, malignancy); embarrassment or loss of dignity associated with genital exposure before, during, and after treatment, and concern about sexual ability, possibly evidenced by increased tension, apprehension, worry, expressed concerns regarding perceived changes, and fear of unspecific consequences.

bipolar disorder

risk for other-directed Violence: risk factors may include irritability, impulsive behavior; delusional thinking; angry response when ideas are refuted or wishes denied; manic excitement, with possible indicators of threatening body language/verbalizations, increased motor activity, overt and aggressive acts; and hostility.

imbalanced Nutrition: less than body requirements may be related to inadequate intake in relation to metabolic expenditures, possibly evidenced by body weight 20% or more below ideal weight, observed inadequate intake, inattention to mealtimes, and distraction from task of eating; laboratory evidence of nutritional deficits/imbalances.

risk for Poisoning [lithium toxicity]: risk factors may include narrow therapeutic range of drug, patient's ability (or lack of) to follow through with medication regimen and monitoring, and denial of need for information/therapy.

Insomnia may be related to psychological stress, lack of recognition of fatigue/need to sleep, hyperactivity, possibly evidenced by denial of need to sleep, interrupted nighttime sleep, one or more nights without sleep, changes in behavior and performance, increasing irritability/restlessness, and dark circles under eyes.

disturbed Sensory/Perception (specify) [overload] may be related to decrease in sensory threshold, endogenous chemical alteration, psychological stress, sleep deprivation, possibly evidenced by increased distractibility and agitation, anxiety, disorientation, poor concentration, auditory/visual hallucination, bizarre thinking, and motor incoordination.

interrupted Family Processes may be related to situational crises (illness, economics, change in roles); euphoric mood and grandiose ideas/actions of patient, manipulative behavior and limit-testing, patient's refusal to accept responsibility for own actions, possibly evidenced by statements of difficulty coping with situation, lack of adaptation to change or not dealing constructively with illness; ineffective family decision-making process, failure to send and to receive clear messages, and inappropriate boundary maintenance.

bone cancer

acute Pain may be related to bone destruction, pressure on nerves, possibly evidenced by verbal or coded report, protective behavior, changes in vital signs.

risk for Trauma: risk factors may include increased bone fragility, general weakness, balancing difficulties.

bone marrow transplantation

risk for Injury: risk factors may include immune dysfunction or suppression, abnormal blood profile, action of donor T cells.

deficient Diversional Activity may be related to hospitalization or length of treatment, restriction of visitors, limitation of activities, possibly evidenced by expressions of boredom, restlessness, withdrawal, and requests for something to do.

risk for imbalanced Nutrition: less than body requirements: risk factors may include increased metabolic needs for healing, altered ability to ingest nutrients—nausea, vomiting, anorexia, taste changes, oral lesions.

borderline personality disorder

risk for self/other-directed Violence/Self-Mutilation: risk factors may include use of projection as a major defense mechanism, pervasive problems with negative transference, feelings of guilt/need to "punish" self, distorted sense of self, inability to cope with increased psychological or physiological tension in a healthy manner.

Anxiety [severe to panic] may be related to unconscious conflicts (experience of extreme stress), perceived threat to self-concept, un-met needs, possibly evidenced by easy frustration and feelings of hurt, abuse of alcohol/other drugs, transient psychotic symptoms and performance of self-mutilating acts.

chronic low Self-Esteem/ disturbed personal Identity may be related to lack of positive feedback, un-met dependency needs, retarded ego development/fixation at an earlier level of development, possibly evidenced by difficulty identifying self or defining self-boundaries, feelings of depersonalization, extreme mood changes, lack of tolerance of rejection or being alone, unhappiness with self, striking out at others, performance of ritualistic self-damaging acts, and belief that punishing self is necessary.

Social Isolation may be related to immature interests, unaccepted social behavior, inadequate personal resources, and inability to engage in satisfying personal relationships, possibly evidenced by alternating clinging and distancing behaviors, difficulty meeting expectations of others, experiencing feelings of difference from others, expressing interests inappropriate to developmental age, and exhibiting behavior unaccepted by dominant cultural group.

botulism (food-borne)

deficient Fluid Volume [isotonic] may be related to active losses—vomiting, diarrhea; decreased intake—nausea, dysphagia, possibly evidenced by reports of thirst; dry skin/mucous membranes, decreased BP and urine output, change in mental state, increased hematocrit (Hct).

impaired physical Mobility may be related to neuromuscular impairment possibly evidenced by limited ability to perform gross/fine motor skills.

Anxiety [specify level]/Fear may be related to threat of death, interpersonal transmission possibly evidenced by expressed concerns, apprehension, awareness of physiological symptoms, focus on self.

risk for impaired spontaneous Ventilation: risk factors may include neuromuscular impairment, presence of infectious process.

Contamination may be related to lack of proper precautions in food storage/preparation as evidenced by gastrointestinal and neurological effects of exposure to biological agent

brain tumor

acute Pain may be related to pressure on brain tissues, possibly evidenced by reports of headache, facial mask of pain, narrowed focus, and autonomic responses (changes in vital signs).

disturbed Thought Processes may be related to altered circulation to and/or destruction of brain tissue, possibly evidenced by memory loss, personality changes, impaired ability to make decisions/conceptualize, and inaccurate interpretation of environment.

disturbed Sensory/Perception (specify) may be related to altered sensory reception/integration, possibly evidenced by changes in sensory acuity, change in behavior pattern, poor concentration/problem-solving abilities, disorientation.

risk for deficient Fluid Volume: risk factors may include recurrent vomiting from irritation of vagal center in medulla, and decreased intake.

Self-Care Deficit [specify] may be related to sensory/neuromuscular impairment interfering with ability to perform tasks, possibly evidenced by unkempt/disheveled appearance, body odor, and verbalization/observation of inability to perform activities of daily living.

breast cancer

(also refer to *cancer*)

Anxiety [specify level] may be related to change in health status, threat of death, stress, interpersonal transmission possibly evidenced by expressed concerns, apprehension, uncertainty, focus on self, diminished productivity.

deficient Knowledge [Learning Need] regarding diagnosis, prognosis, and treatment options may be related to lack of exposure/unfamiliarity with information resources, information misinterpretation, cognitive limitation/anxiety possibly evidenced by verbalizations, statements of misconceptions, inappropriate behaviors.

risk for disturbed Body Image: risk factors may include significance of body part with regard to sexual perceptions.

risk for ineffective Sexual Dysfunction: risk factors may include health-related changes, medical treatments, concern about relationship with significant other.

bronchitis

ineffective Airway Clearance may be related to excessive, thickened mucous secretions, possibly evidenced by presence of rhonchi, tachypnea, and ineffective cough.

Activity Intolerance [specific level] may be related to imbalance between oxygen supply and demand, possibly evidenced by reports of fatigue, dyspnea, and abnormal vital sign response to activity.

acute Pain may be related to localized inflammation, persistent cough, aching associated with fever, possibly evidenced by reports of discomfort, distraction behavior, and facial mask of pain.

bronchopneumonia

(also refer to *bronchitis*)

ineffective Airway Clearance may be related to tracheal bronchial inflammation, edema formation, increased sputum production, pleuritic pain, decreased energy, fatigue, possibly evidenced by changes in rate/depth of respirations, abnormal breath sounds, use of accessory muscles, dyspnea, cyanosis, effective/ineffective cough—with or without sputum production.

impaired Gas Exchange may be related to inflammatory process, collection of secretions affecting oxygen exchange across alveolar membrane, and hypoventilation, possibly evidenced by restlessness/changes in mentation, dyspnea, tachycardia, pallor, cyanosis, and ABGs/oximetry evidence of hypoxia.

risk for Infection [spread]: risk factors may include decreased ciliary action, stasis of secretions, presence of existing infection.

bulimia nervosa

(also refer to *anorexia nervosa*)

impaired Dentition may be related to dietary habits, poor oral hygiene, chronic vomiting possibly evidenced by erosion of tooth enamel, multiple caries, abraded teeth.

impaired Oral Mucous Membrane may be related to malnutrition or vitamin deficiency; poor oral hygiene; chronic vomiting possibly evidenced by sore, inflamed buccal mucosa; swollen salivary glands; ulcerations of mucosa; reports of constant sore mouth/throat.

risk for deficient Fluid Volume/Bleeding: risk factors may include consistent self-induced vomiting, chronic or excessive laxative or diuretic use, esophageal erosion or tear (Mallory-Weiss syndrome).

deficient Knowledge [Learning Need] regarding condition, prognosis, complication, treatment may be related to lack of exposure to/unfamiliarity with information about condition, learned maladaptive coping skills possibly evidenced by verbalization of misconception of relationship of current situation and behaviors, distortion of body image, binging and purging behaviors, verbalized need for information/desire to change behaviors.

burn (dependent on type, degree, and severity of the injury)

risk for deficient Fluid Volume/Bleeding: risk factors may include loss of fluids through wounds, capillary damage and evaporation, hypermetabolic state, insufficient intake, hemorrhagic losses.

risk for ineffective Airway Clearance: risk factors may include mucosal edema and loss of ciliary action (smoke inhalation), direct upper airway injury by flame, steam, chemicals.

risk for Infection: risk factors may include loss of protective dermal barrier, traumatized/necrotic tissue, decreased hemoglobin, suppressed inflammatory response, environmental exposure/invasive procedures.

acute/chronic Pain may be related to destruction of/trauma to tissue and nerves, edema formation, and manipulation of impaired tissues, possibly evidenced by verbal reports, narrowed focus, distraction and guarding behaviors, facial mask of pain, and autonomic responses (changes in vital signs).

risk for imbalanced Nutrition: less than body requirements: risk factors may include hypermetabolic state in response to burn injury/stress, inadequate intake, protein catabolism.

Post-Trauma Syndrome may be related to life-threatening event, possibly evidenced by re-experiencing the event, repetitive dreams/nightmares, psychic/emotional numbness, and sleep disturbance.

ineffective Protection may be related to extremes of age, inadequate nutrition, anemia, impaired immune system, possibly evidenced by impaired healing, deficient immunity, fatigue, anorexia.

deficient Diversional Activity may be related to long-term hospitalization, frequent lengthy treatments, and physical limitations, possibly evidenced by expressions of boredom, restlessness, withdrawal, and requests for something to do.

risk for delayed Development: risk factors may include effects of physical disability, separation from significant other(s), and environmental deficiencies.

bursitis
acute/chronic Pain may be related to inflammation of affected joint, possibly evidenced by verbal reports, guarding behavior, and narrowed focus.
impaired physical Mobility may be related to inflammation and swelling of joint, and pain, possibly evidenced by diminished range of motion, reluctance to attempt movement, and imposed restriction of movement by medical treatment.

calculi, urinary
acute Pain may be related to increased frequency/force of ureteral contractions, tissue distention/trauma and edema formation, cellular ischemia possibly evidenced by reports of sudden, severe, colicky pains; guarding and distraction behaviors, self focus, and autonomic responses.
impaired Urinary Elimination may be related to stimulation of the bladder by calculi, renal or ureteral irritation, mechanical obstruction of urinary flow, edema, inflammation possibly evidenced by urgency and frequency; oliguria (retention); hematuria.
risk for deficient Fluid Volume: risk factors may include stimulation of renal-intestinal reflexes causing nausea, vomiting, and diarrhea; changes in urinary output, postoperative diuresis; and decreased intake.
risk for Infection: risk factors may include stasis of urine.
deficient Knowledge [Learning Need] regarding condition, prognosis, self-care and treatment needs may be related to lack of exposure/recall and information misinterpretation, possibly evidenced by requests for information, statements of concern, and recurrence/development of preventable complications.

cancer
(also refer to *chemotherapy*)
Fear/death Anxiety may be related to situational crises, threat to/change in health/socioeconomic status, role functioning, interaction patterns; threat of death, separation from family, interpersonal transmission of feelings, possibly evidenced by expressed concerns, feelings of inadequacy/helplessness, insomnia; increased tension, restlessness, focus on self, sympathetic stimulation.
Grieving may be related to potential loss of physiologic well-being (body part/function), perceived separation from significant other(s)/lifestyle (death), possibly evidenced by anger, sadness, withdrawal, choked feelings, changes in eating/sleep patterns, activity level, libido, and communication patterns.
acute/chronic Pain may be related to the disease process (compression of nerve tissue, infiltration of nerves or their vascular supply, obstruction of a nerve pathway, inflammation), or side effects of therapeutic agents, possibly evidenced by verbal reports, self-focusing/narrowed focus, alteration in muscle tone, facial mask of pain, distraction/guarding behaviors, autonomic responses, and restlessness.
Fatigue may be related to decreased metabolic energy production, increased energy requirements (hypermetabolic state), overwhelming psychological/emotional demands, and altered body chemistry (side effects of medications, chemotherapy), possibly evidenced by unremitting/overwhelming lack of energy, inability to maintain usual routines, decreased performance, impaired ability to concentrate, lethargy/listlessness, and disinterest in surroundings.
impaired Home Maintenance may be related to debilitation, lack of resources, and/or inadequate support systems, possibly evidenced by verbalization of problem, request for assistance, and lack of necessary equipment or aids.
risk for interrupted Family Processes: risk factors may include situational or transitional crises—long-term illness, change in roles or economic status; developmental—anticipated loss of a family member.
readiness for enhanced family Coping possibly evidenced by verbalizations of impact of crisis on own values, priorities, goals, or relationships.

candidiasis
impaired Skin/Tissue Integrity may be related to infectious lesions, possibly evidenced by disruption of skin surfaces and mucous membranes.
acute Pain/impaired Comfort may be related to exposure of irritated skin and mucous membranes to excretions (urine, feces), possibly evidenced by verbal or coded reports, restlessness, guarding behaviors.
risk for Sexual Dysfunction: risk factors include presence of infectious process and vaginal discomfort.

cardiac catheterization
Anxiety [specify level] may be related to threat to or change in health status, stress, family heredity possibly evidenced by expressed concerns, apprehension, uncertainty, focus on self.

risk for decreased Cardiac Output: risk factors may include altered heart rate and rhythm (vasovagal response, ventricular dysrhythmias), decreased myocardial contractility (ischemia).

risk for decreased cardiac Tissue Perfusion (specify):: risk factors may include coronary artery spasm, hypovolemia, hypoxia, [thrombosis, emboli]

risk for impaired Gas Exchange: risk factors may include alveolar-capillary membrane changes (atelectasis), intestinal edema, inadequate function or premature discontinuation of chest tubes, and diminished oxygen-carrying capacity of the blood.

risk for Adverse Reaction to Iodinated Contrast Media: risk factors may include underlying disease—heart disease, concurrent use of medications (e.g., beta-blockers, metformin), history of allergies.

cardiac surgery

risk for decreased Cardiac Output: risk factors may include decreased preload (hypovolemia), depressed myocardial contractility, changes in SVR (afterload), and alterations in electrical conduction (dysrhythmias).

risk for Bleeding/deficient Fluid Volume [isotonic]: risk factors may include intraoperative bleeding with inadequate blood replacement; bleeding related to insufficient heparin reversal, fibrinolysis, or platelet destruction; or volume depletion effects of intraoperative or postoperative diuretic therapy.

risk for impaired Gas Exchange: risk factors may include alveolar-capillary membrane changes (atelectasis), intestinal edema, inadequate function or premature discontinuation of chest tubes, and diminished O2-carrying capacity of the blood.

acute Pain,/[Discomfort] may be related to tissue inflammation or trauma, edema formation, intraoperative nerve trauma, and myocardial ischemia, possibly evidenced by reports of incisional discomfort, pain in chest and donor site; paresthesia or pain in hand, arm, shoulder; anxiety, restlessness, irritability; distraction behaviors; and changes in heart rate and BP

impaired Skin/Tissue Integrity related to mechanical trauma (surgical incisions, puncture wounds) and edema evidenced by disruption of skin surface and tissues.

cardiomyopathy

decreased Cardiac Output may be related to altered contractility, possibly evidenced by dyspnea, fatigue, chest pain, dizziness, syncope

Activity Intolerance may be related to imbalance between oxygen supply and demand, possibly evidenced by weakness, fatigue, dyspnea, abnormal heart rate and BP response to activity, ECG changes.

ineffective Role Performance may be related to changes in physical health, stress, demands of job/life, possibly evidenced by change in usual patterns of responsibility, role strain, change in capacity to resume role.

Carotid endarterectomy

risk for ineffective cerebral TiIssue Perfusion: risk factors may include carotid stenosis, embolism, thrombolytic therapy.

carpal tunnel syndrome

acute/chronic Pain may be related to pressure on median nerve, possibly evidenced by verbal reports, reluctance to use affected extremity, guarding behaviors, expressed fear of reinjury, altered ability to continue previous activities.

impaired physical Mobility may be related to neuromuscular impairment and pain, possibly evidenced by decreased hand strength, weakness, limited range of motion, and reluctance to attempt movement.

risk for Peripheral Neurovascular Dysfunction: risks include mechanical compression (e.g., brace, repetitive tasks/motions), immobilization.

deficient Knowledge [Learning Need] regarding condition, prognosis and treatment/ safety needs may be related to lack of exposure/recall, information misinterpretation, possibly evidenced by questions, statements of concern, request for information, inaccurate follow-through of instructions/development of preventable complications.

casts

(also refer to *fractures*)

risk for Peripheral Neurovascular Dysfunction: risk factors may include presence of fracture(s), mechanical compression (cast), tissue trauma, immobilization, vascular obstruction.

risk for impaired Skin Integrity: risk factors may include pressure of cast, moisture/ debris under cast, objects inserted under cast to relieve itching, and/or altered sensation/circulation.

Self-Care Deficit [specify] may be related to impaired ability to perform self-care tasks, possibly evidenced by statements of need for assistance and observed difficulty in performing activities of daily living.

cataract

disturbed visual Sensory/Perception may be related to altered sensory reception/status of sense organs, and therapeutically restricted environment (surgical procedure, patching), possibly evidenced by diminished acuity, visual distortions, and change in usual response to stimuli.

risk for Trauma: risk factors may include poor vision, reduced hand/eye coordination.

Anxiety [specify level]/Fear may be related to alteration in visual acuity, threat of permanent loss of vision/independence, possibly evidenced by expressed concerns, apprehension, and feelings of uncertainty.

deficient Knowledge [Learning Need] regarding ways of coping with altered abilities, therapy choices, lifestyle changes may be related to lack of exposure/recall, misinterpretation, or cognitive limitations, possibly evidenced by requests for information, statement of concern, inaccurate follow-through of instructions/development of preventable complications.

cat scratch disease

acute Pain may be related to effects of circulating toxins (fever, headache, and lymphadenitis), possibly evidenced by verbal reports, guarding behavior, and autonomic response (changes in vital signs).

Hyperthermia may be related to inflammatory process, possibly evidenced by increased body temperature, flushed warm skin, tachypnea, and tachycardia.

celiac disease

imbalanced Nutrition: less than body requirements may be related to inability to absorb nutrients (mucosal damage, loss of villi, proliferation of crypt cells, shortened transit time through gastrointestinal tract), possibly evidenced by weight loss, abdominal distention, steatorrhea, evidence of anemia, vitamin deficiencies.

Diarrhea may be related to irritation, malabsorption, possibly evidenced by abdominal pain, hyperactive bowel sounds, at least three loose stools per day.

risk for deficient Fluid Volume risk factors may include mild to massive steatorrhea, diarrhea.

Cellulitis

risk for Infection [abscess, bacteremia]: risk factors may inlcude broken skin, chronic disease, presence of pathogens, insufficient knowledge to avoid exposure to pathogens.

acute Pain/impaired Comfort may be related to inflammatory process, circulating toxins possibly evidenced by reports of localized pain or headache, guarding behaviors, restlessness, changes in vital signs.

impaired Tissue Integrity may be related to trauma, inflammation and/or invasion of tissues by infectious bacterial agent, or altered circulation; possibly evidenced by redness, warmth, edema, tenderness or pain under the surface of skin, or deep in tissues.

cerebrovascular accident (CVA)

ineffective cerebral Tissue Perfusion may be related to interruption of blood flow (occlusive disorder, hemorrhage, cerebral vasospasm/edema), possibly evidenced by altered level of consciousness, changes in vital signs, changes in motor/sensory responses, restlessness, memory loss; sensory, language, intellectual, and emotional deficits.

impaired physical Mobility may be related to neuromuscular involvement (weakness, paresthesia, flaccid/hypotonic paralysis, spastic paralysis), perceptual/cognitive impairment, possibly evidenced by inability to purposefully move involved body parts/limited range of motion; impaired coordination, and/or decreased muscle strength/control.

impaired verbal [and/or written] Communication may be related to impaired cerebral circulation, neuromuscular impairment, loss of facial/oral muscle tone and control; generalized weakness/fatigue, possibly evidenced by impaired articulation, does not/cannot speak (dysarthria); inability to modulate speech, find and/or name words, identify objects and/or inability to comprehend written/spoken language; inability to produce written communication.

Self-Care Deficit [specify] may be related to neuromuscular impairment, decreased strength/endurance, loss of muscle control/coordination, perceptual/cognitive impairment, pain/discomfort, and depression, possibly evidenced by stated/observed inability to perform ADLs, requests for assistance, disheveled appearance, and incontinence.

risk for impaired Swallowing: risk factors may include muscle paralysis and perceptual impairment.

risk for unilateral Neglect: risk factors may include sensory loss of part of visual field with perceptual loss of corresponding body segment.

impaired Home Maintenance may be related to condition of individual family member, insufficient finances/family organization or planning, unfamiliarity with resources, and inadequate support systems, possibly evidenced by members expressing difficulty in managing home in a comfortable manner/requesting assistance with home maintenance, disorderly surroundings, and overtaxed family members.

situational low Self-Esteem/disturbed Body Image may be related to functional impairment, loss, focus on past function/strength, and cognitive or perceptual changes, possibly evidenced by actual change in function, self-negating verbalizations, reports perceptions reflecting altered view of body function

Grieving may be related to loss of processes of body [neuromuscular impairments], loss of job/role function, status/independence, possibly evidenced by psychological distress, despair, anger, disorganization.

cesarean birth

deficient Knowledge [Learning Need] regarding surgical procedure and expectation, postoperative routines and therapy, and self-care needs may be related to lack of information/misinterpretation, possibly evidenced by statements of concern, questions, and misconceptions.

risk for deficient Fluid Volume/Bleeding:: risk factors may include restrictions of oral intake, blood loss; pregnancy-related complications.

risk for impaired Attachment: risk factors may include separation, existing health conditions of mother or infant, lack of privacy.

cesarean birth, postpartal

(also refer to *postpartal period*)

risk for impaired parent/infant Attachment: risk factors may include developmental transition/gain of a family member, situational crisis (e.g., surgical intervention, physical complications interfering with initial acquaintance/interaction, negative self-appraisal).

acute Pain/[Discomfort] may be related to surgical trauma, effects of anesthesia, hormonal effects, bladder/abdominal distention possibly evidenced by verbal reports (e.g., incisional pain, cramping/afterpains, spinal headache), guarding/distraction behaviors, irritability, facial mask of pain.

risk for situational low Self-Esteem: risk factors may include perceived "failure" at life event, maturational transition, perceived loss of control in unplanned delivery.

risk for Injury: risk factors may include biochemical or regulatory functions (e.g., orthostatic hypotension, development of PIH or eclampsia), effects of anesthesia, thromboembolism, abnormal blood profile (anemia/excessive blood loss, rubella sensitivity, Rh incompatibility), tissue trauma.

risk for Infection: risk factors may include tissue trauma/broken skin, decreased Hb, invasive procedures and/or increased environmental exposure, prolongs rupture of amniotic membranes, malnutrition.

Self-Care Deficit (specify) may be related to effects of anesthesia, decreased strength and endurance, physical discomfort possibly evidenced by verbalization of inability to perform desired ADL(s).

cesarean birth, unplanned

(also refer to *cesarean birth, postpartal*)

deficient Knowledge [Learning Need] regarding underlying procedure, pathophysiology, and self-care needs may be related to incomplete/inadequate information, possibly evidenced by request for information, verbalization of concerns/misconceptions and inappropriate/exaggerated behavior.

Anxiety [specify level] may be related to actual/perceived threat to mother/fetus, emotional threat to self-esteem, un-met needs/expectations, and interpersonal transmission, possibly evidenced by increased tension, apprehension, feelings of inadequacy, sympathetic stimulation, and narrowed focus, restlessness.

Powerlessness may be related to interpersonal interaction, perception of illness-related regimen, lifestyle of helplessness possibly evidenced by verbalization of lack of control, lack of participation in care or decision making, passivity.

risk for disturbed Maternal-Fetal Dyad:: risk factors may include compromised oxygen transport, complication of pregnancy.

risk for acute Pain: risk factors may include increased/prolonged contractions, psychological reaction.

risk for Infection: risk factors may include invasive procedures, rupture of amniotic membranes, break in skin, decreased hemoglobin, exposure to pathogens.

chemotherapy

(also refer to *cancer*)

risk for deficient Fluid volume: risk factors may include gastrointestinal losses (vomiting), interference with adequate intake (stomatitis/anorexia), losses through abnormal routes (indwelling tubes, wounds, fistulas), and hypermetabolic state.

imbalanced Nutrition: less than body requirements may be related to inability to ingest adequate nutrients (nausea, stomatitis, and fatigue), hypermetabolic state, possibly evidenced by weight loss (wasting), aversion to eating, reported altered taste sensation, sore, inflamed buccal cavity; diarrhea and/or constipation.

impaired Oral Mucous Membrane may be related to side effects of therapeutic agents/radiation, dehydration, and malnutrition, possibly evidenced by ulcerations, leukoplakia, decreased salivation, and reports of pain.

disturbed Body Image may be related to anatomical/structural changes; loss of hair and weight, possibly evidenced by negative feelings about body, preoccupation with change, feelings of helplessness/hopelessness, and change in social environment.

ineffective Protection may be related to inadequate nutrition, drug therapy/radiation, abnormal blood profile, disease state (cancer), possibly evidenced by impaired healing, deficient immunity, anorexia, fatigue.

readiness for enhanced Hope possibly evidenced by expressed desire to enhance belief in possibilities/sense of meaning to life.

cholecystectomy

acute Pain may be related to interruption in skin/tissue layers with mechanical closure (sutures/staples) and invasive procedures (including T-tube/nasogastric (NG) tube), possibly evidenced by verbal reports, guarding/distraction behaviors, and autonomic responses (changes in vital signs).

ineffective Breathing Pattern may be related to decreased lung expansion (pain and muscle weakness), decreased energy/fatigue, ineffective cough, possibly evidenced by fremitus, tachypnea, and decreased respiratory depth/vital capacity.

risk for deficient Fluid Volume: risk factors may include vomiting/NG aspiration, medically restricted intake, altered coagulation.

cholelithiasis

acute Pain may be related to inflammation and distortion of tissues, ductal spasm, possibly evidenced by verbal reports, guarding/distraction behaviors, and autonomic responses (changes in vital signs).

imbalanced Nutrition: less than body requirements may be related to inability to ingest/absorb adequate nutrients (food intolerance/pain, nausea/vomiting, anorexia), possibly evidenced by aversion to food/decreased intake and weight loss.

deficient Knowledge [Learning Need] regarding pathophysiology, therapy choices, and self-care needs may be related to lack of information, misinterpretation, possibly evidenced by verbalization of concerns, questions, and recurrence of condition.

chronic obstructive lung disease

ineffective Airway Clearance may be related to bronchospasm, increased production of tenacious secretions, retained secretions, and decreased energy/fatigue, possibly evidenced by presence of wheezes, crackles, tachypnea, dyspnea, changes in depth of respirations, use of accessory muscles, cough (persistent), and chest x-ray findings.

impaired Gas Exchange may be related to altered oxygen delivery (obstruction of airways by secretions/bronchospasm, air-trapping) and alveoli destruction, possibly evidenced by dyspnea, restlessness, confusion, abnormal ABG values, and reduced tolerance for activity.

Activity Intolerance may be related to imbalance between oxygen supply and demand, and generalized weakness, possibly evidenced by verbal reports of fatigue, exertional dyspnea, and abnormal vital sign response.

imbalanced Nutrition: less than body requirements may be related to inability to ingest adequate nutrients (dyspnea, fatigue, medication side effects, sputum production, anorexia), possibly evidenced by weight loss, reported altered taste sensation, decreased muscle mass/subcutaneous fat, poor muscle tone, and aversion to eating/lack of interest in food.

risk for Infection: risk factors may include decreased ciliary action, stasis of secretions, and debilitated state/malnutrition.

circumcision

deficient Knowledge [Learning Need] regarding surgical procedure, prognosis, and treatment may be related to lack of exposure, misinterpretation, unfamiliarity with information resources, possibly evidenced by request for information, verbalization of concern/misconceptions, inaccurate follow-through of instructions.

acute Pain may be related to trauma to/edema of tender tissues, possibly evidenced by crying, changes in sleep pattern, refusal to eat

impaired Urinary Elimination may be related to tissue injury or inflammation or development of urethral fistula, possibly evidenced by edema, difficulty voiding.

risk for Bleeding risk factors may include decreased clotting factors immediately after birth, previously undiagnosed problems with bleeding or clotting.

risk for Infection: risk factors may include immature immune system, invasive procedure, tissue trauma, environmental exposure.

cirrhosis

(also refer to *Substance dependence/abuse rehabilitation*; *hepatitis, acute viral*)

risk for impaired Liver Function: risk factors may include viral infection, alcohol abuse.

imbalanced Nutrition: less than body requirements may be related to inability to ingest/absorb nutrients (anorexia, nausea, indigestion, early satiety), abnormal bowel function, impaired storage of vitamins, possibly evidenced by aversion to eating, observed lack of intake, muscle wasting, weight loss, and imbalances in nutritional studies.

excess Fluid Volume may be related to compromised regulatory mechanism (e.g., syndrome of inappropriate antidiuretic hormone [SIADH], decreased plasma proteins/malnutrition) and excess sodium/fluid intake, possibly evidenced by generalized or abdominal edema, weight gain, dyspnea, BP changes, positive hepatojugular reflex, change in mentation, altered electrolytes, changes in urine specific gravity, and pleural effusion.

risk for impaired Skin Integrity: risk factors may include altered circulation/metabolic state, poor skin turgor, skeletal prominence, and presence of edema/ascites, accumulation of bile salts in skin.

risk for Bleeding: risk factors may include abnormal blood profile, altered clotting factors—decreased production of prothrombin, fibrinogen, and factors VIII, IX, and X; impaired vitamin K absorption; release of thromboplastin, portal hypertension, development of esophageal varices.

risk for acute Confusion: risk factors may include alcohol abuse, increased serum ammonia level, and inability of liver to detoxify certain enzymes/drugs.

Self-Esteem (specify)]/disturbed Body Image may be related to biophysical changes, altered physical appearance, uncertainty of prognosis, changes in role function, personal vulnerability, self-destructive behavior (alcohol-induced disease), possibly evidenced by verbalization of changes in lifestyle, fear of rejection/reaction of others, negative feelings about body or abilities, and feelings of helplessness, hopelessness, powerlessness.

risk for ineffective Protection: risk factors may include abnormal blood profile (altered clotting factors), portal hypertension/development of esophageal varices.

cocaine hydrochloride poisoning, acute
(also refer to *substance dependence/abuse rehabilitation*)

ineffective Breathing Pattern may be related to pharmacological effects on respiratory center of the brain, possibly evidenced by tachypnea, altered depth of respiration, shortness of breath, and abnormal ABGs.

risk for decreased Cardiac Output: risk factors may include drug effect on myocardium (degree dependent on drug purity/quality used), alterations in electrical rate/rhythm/conduction, preexisting myocardiopathy.

risk for impaired Liver Function: risk factors may include cocaine abuse

imbalanced Nutrition: less than body requirements may be related to anorexia, insufficient/inappropriate use of financial resources, possibly evidenced by reported inadequate intake, weight loss/less than normal weight gain; lack of interest in food, poor muscle tone, signs/laboratory evidence of vitamin deficiencies.

risk for Infection: risk factors may include injection techniques, impurities of drugs; localized trauma/nasal septum damage, malnutrition, altered immune state.

ineffective Coping may be related to personal vulnerability, negative role modeling, inadequate support systems; ineffective/inadequate coping skills with substitution of drug, possibly evidenced by use of harmful substance, despite evidence of undesirable consequences.

disturbed Sensory/Perception (specify) may be related to exogenous chemical, altered sensory reception/transmission/integration (hallucination), altered status of sense organs, possibly evidenced by responding to internal stimuli from hallucinatory experiences, bizarre thinking, anxiety/panic changes in sensory acuity (sense of smell/taste).

coccidioidomycosis (San Joaquin/Valley Fever)
acute Pain may be related to inflammation, possibly evidenced by verbal reports, distraction behaviors, and narrowed focus.

Fatigue may be related to decreased energy production; states of discomfort, possibly evidenced by reports of overwhelming lack of energy, inability to maintain usual routine, emotional lability/irritability, impaired ability to concentrate, and decreased endurance/libido.

deficient Knowledge [Learning Need] regarding nature/course of disease, therapy and self-care needs may be related to lack of information, possibly evidenced by statements of concern and questions.

colitis, ulcerative
Diarrhea may be related to inflammation or malabsorption of the bowel, presence of toxins and/or segmental narrowing of the lumen, possibly evidenced by increased bowel sounds/peristalsis, urgency, frequent/watery stools (acute phase), changes in stool color, and abdominal pain/cramping.

acute/chronic Pain may be related to inflammation of the intestines/hyperperistalsis and anal/rectal irritation, possibly evidenced by verbal reports, guarding/distraction behaviors.

risk for deficient Fluid Volume: risk factors may include continued gastrointestinal losses (diarrhea, vomiting, capillary plasma loss), altered intake, hypermetabolic state.

imbalanced Nutrition: less than body requirements may be related to altered intake/absorption of nutrients (medically restricted intake, fear that eating may cause diarrhea) and hypermetabolic state, possibly evidenced by weight loss, decreased subcutaneous fat/muscle mass, poor muscle tone, hyperactive bowel sounds, steatorrhea, pale conjunctiva and mucous membranes, and aversion to eating.

ineffective Coping may be related to chronic nature and indefinite outcome of disease, multiple stressors (repeated over time), personal vulnerability, severe pain, inadequate sleep, lack of/ineffective support systems, possibly evidenced by verbalization of inability to cope, discouragement, anxiety; preoccupation with physical self, chronic worry, emotional tension; depression, and recurrent exacerbation of symptoms.

risk for Powerlessness: risk factors may include unresolved dependency conflicts, feelings of insecurity/resentment, repression of anger and aggressive feelings, lacking a sense of control in stressful situations, sacrificing own wishes for others, and retreat from aggression or frustration.

colostomy

risk for impaired Skin Integrity: risk factors may include absence of sphincter at stoma and chemical irritation from caustic bowel contents, reaction to product/removal of adhesive, and improperly fitting appliance.

risk for Diarrhea/Constipation: risk factors may include interruption/alteration of normal bowel function (placement of ostomy), changes in dietary/fluid intake, and effects of medication.

deficient Knowledge [Learning Need] regarding changes in physiologic function and self-care/treatment needs may be related to lack of exposure/recall, information misinterpretation, possibly evidenced by questions, statement of concern, and inaccurate follow-through of instruction/development of preventable complications.

disturbed Body Image may be related to biophysical changes (presence of stoma; loss of control of bowel elimination) and psychosocial factors (altered body structure, disease process/associated treatment regimen, e.g., cancer, colitis), possibly evidenced by verbalization of change in perception of self, negative feelings about body, fear of rejection/reaction of others, not touching/looking at stoma, and refusal to participate in care.

impaired Social Interaction may be related to fear of embarrassing situation secondary to altered bowel control with loss of contents, odor, possibly evidenced by reduced participation and verbalized/observed discomfort in social situations.

risk for Sexual Dysfunction: risk factors may include altered body structure/function, radical resection/treatment procedures, vulnerability/psychological concern about response of significant other(s), and disruption of sexual response pattern (e.g., erection difficulty).

coma

risk for Suffocation: risk factors may include cognitive impairment/loss of protective reflexes and purposeful movement.

risk for deficient Fluid Volume/imbalanced Nutrition: less than body requirements: risk factors may include inability to ingest food or fluids, increased needs—hypermetabolic state.

[total] Self-Care Deficit may be related to cognitive impairment and absence of purposeful activity, evidenced by inability to perform ADLs.

risk for ineffective cerebral Tissue Perfusion: risk factors may include head trauma, substance abuse, embolism, cerebral aneurysm, brain tumor/neoplasm.

risk for Infection: risk factors may include may include stasis of body fluids (oral, pulmonary, urinary), invasive procedures, and nutritional deficits.

coma, diabetic
Refer to *diabetic ketoacidosis*.

complex regional brain syndrome

acute/chronic Pain may be related to continued nerve stimulation, possibly evidenced by verbal reports, distraction or guarding behaviors, narrowed focus, changes in sleep patterns, and altered ability to continue previous activities.

ineffective peripheral Tissue Perfusion may be related to reduction of arterial blood flow (arteriole vasoconstriction), possibly evidenced by extremity pain, altered skin characteristics, diminished pulses, and edema.

[disturbed tactile Sensory Perception] may be related to altered sensory reception (neurological deficit, pain), possibly evidenced by change in usual response to stimuli, abnormal sensitivity of touch, physiological anxiety, and irritability.

risk for ineffective Role Performance: risk factors may include situational crisis, chronic disability, debilitating pain.

risk for compromised family Coping: risk factors may include temporary family disorganization and role changes and prolonged disability that exhausts the supportive capacity of Significant others

concussion of the brain

acute Pain may be related to trauma to/edema of cerebral tissue, possibly evidenced by reports of headache, guarding/distraction behaviors, and narrowed focus.

risk for deficient Fluid Volume: risk factors may include vomiting, decreased intake, and hypermetabolic state (fever).

risk for impaired Memory: risk factors may include neurological disturbances.

deficient Knowledge [Learning Need] regarding condition, treatment/safety needs, and potential complications may be related to lack of recall, misinterpretation, cognitive limitation, possibly evidenced by questions/statement of concerns, development of preventable complications.

conduct disorder (childhood, adolescence)

risk for self/other-directed Violence: risk factors may include retarded ego development, antisocial character, poor impulse control, dysfunctional family system, loss of significant relationships, history of suicidal/acting-out behaviors.

defensive Coping may be related to inadequate coping strategies, maturational crisis, multiple life changes/losses, lack of control of impulsive actions, and personal vulnerability, possibly evidenced by inappropriate use of defense mechanisms, inability to meet role expectations, poor self-esteem, failure to assume responsibility for own actions, hypersensitivity to slight or criticism, and excessive smoking/drinking/drug use.

ineffective Impulse Control may be related to chronic low self-esteem, anger, disorder of development, mood, personality possibly evidenced by acting without thinking, irritability, temper outbursts.

chronic low Self-Esteem may be related to life choices perpetuating failure, personal vulnerability, possibly evidenced by self-negating verbalizations, anger, rejection of positive feedback, frequent lack of success in life events.

compromised/disabled family Coping may be related to excessive guilt, anger, or blaming among family members regarding child's behavior; parental inconsistencies; disagreements regarding discipline, limit setting, and approaches; and exhaustion of parental resources (prolonged coping with disruptive child), possibly evidenced by unrealistic parental expectations, rejection or overprotection of child; and exaggerated expressions of anger, disappointment, or despair regarding child's behavior or ability to improve or change.

impaired Social Interaction may be related to retarded ego development, developmental state (adolescence), lack of social skills, low self-concept, dysfunctional family system, and neurological impairment, possibly evidenced by dysfunctional interaction with others (difficulty waiting turn in games or group situations, not seeming to listen to what is being said), difficulty playing quietly and maintaining attention to task or play activity, often shifting from one activity to another and interrupting or intruding on others.

Conn's syndrome

Refer to *aldosteronism, primary*.

constipation

Constipation may be related to weak abdominal musculature, gastrointestinal obstructive lesions, pain on defecation, diagnostic procedures, pregnancy, possibly evidenced by change in character/frequency of stools, feeling of abdominal/rectal fullness or pressure, changes in bowel sounds, abdominal distention.

impaired Comfort may be related to abdominal fullness or pressure, straining to defecate, and trauma to delicate tissues, possibly evidenced by verbal reports, reluctance to defecate, and distraction behaviors.

deficient Knowledge [Learning Need] regarding dietary needs, bowel function, and medication effect may be related to lack of information/misconceptions, possibly evidenced by development of problem and verbalization of concerns or questions.

coronary artery bypass surgery

risk for decreased Cardiac Output: risk factors may include decreased myocardial contractility, diminished circulating volume (preload), alterations in electrical conduction, and increased SVR (afterload).

acute Pain may be related to direct chest tissue/bone trauma, invasive tubes/lines, donor site incision, tissue inflammation/edema formation, intraoperative nerve trauma, possibly evidenced by verbal reports, autonomic responses (changes in vital signs), and distraction behaviors/ (restlessness), irritability.

disturbed Sensory/Perception (specify) may be related to restricted environment (postoperative/acute), sleep deprivation, effects of medications, continuous environmental sounds/activities, and psychological stress of procedure, possibly evidenced by disorientation, alterations in behavior, exaggerated emotional responses, and visual/auditory distortions.

ineffective Role Performance may be related to situational crises (dependt role)/recuperative process, uncertainty about future, possibly evidenced by delay/alteration in physical capacity to resume role, change in usual role or responsibility change in self/others' perception of role.

Crohn's disease

(also refer to *colitis, ulcerative*)

imbalanced Nutrition: less than body requirements may be related to intestinal pain after eating; and decreased transit time through bowel, possibly evidenced by weight loss, aversion to eating, and observed lack of intake.

Diarrhea may be related to inflammation of small intestines, presence of toxins, particularly dietary intake, possibly evidenced by hyperactive bowel sounds, cramping, and frequent loose liquid stools.

deficient Knowledge [Learning Need] regarding condition, nutritional needs, and prevention of recurrence may be related to insufficient information/misinterpretation, unfamiliarity with resources, possibly evidenced by statements of concern/questions, inaccurate follow-through of instructions, and development of preventable complications/exacerbation of condition.

croup

ineffective Airway Clearance may be related to presence of thick, tenacious mucus and swelling/spasms of the epiglottis, possibly evidenced by harsh/brassy cough, tachypnea, use of accessory breathing muscles, and presence of wheezes.

deficient Fluid Volume [isotonic] may be related to decreased ability/aversion to swallowing, presence of fever, and increased respiratory losses, possibly evidenced by dry mucous membranes, poor skin turgor, and scanty/concentrated urine.

croup, membranous
(also refer to *croup*)

risk for Suffocation: risk factors may include inflammation of larynx with formation of false membrane.

Anxiety [specify level]/Fear may be related to change in environment, perceived threat to self (difficulty breathing), and transmission of anxiety of adults, possibly evidenced by restlessness, facial tension, glancing about, and sympathetic stimulation.

Cushing's syndrome

risk for excess Fluid Volume: risk factors may include compromised regulatory mechanism (fluid/sodium retention).

risk for Infection: risk factors may include immunosuppressed inflammatory response, skin and capillary fragility, and negative nitrogen balance.

imbalanced Nutrition: less than body requirements may be related to inability to utilize nutrients (disturbance of carbohydrate metabolism), possibly evidenced by decreased muscle mass and increased resistance to insulin.

Self-Care Deficit [specify] may be related to muscle wasting, generalized weakness, fatigue, and demineralization of bones, possibly evidenced by statements of/observed inability to complete or perform ADLs.

disturbed Body Image may be related to change in structure/appearance (effects of disease process, drug therapy), possibly evidenced by negative feelings about body, feelings of helplessness, and changes in social involvement.

Sexual Dysfunction may be related to loss of libido, impotence, and cessation of menses, possibly evidenced by verbalization of concerns and/or dissatisfaction with and alteration in relationship with significant other.

risk for Trauma [fractures]: risk factors may include increased protein breakdown, negative protein balance, demineralization of bones.

cystic fibrosis

ineffective Airway Clearance may be related to excessive production of thick mucus and decreased ciliary action, possibly evidenced by abnormal breath sounds, ineffective cough, cyanosis, and altered respiratory rate/depth.

risk for Infection: risk factors may include stasis of respiratory secretions and development of atelectasis.

imbalanced Nutrition: less than body requirements may be related to impaired digestive process and absorption of nutrients, possibly evidenced by failure to gain weight, muscle wasting, and retarded physical growth.

deficient Knowledge [Learning Need] regarding pathophysiology of condition, medical management, and available community resources may be related to insufficient information/misconceptions, possibly evidenced by statements of concern, questions; inaccurate follow-through of instructions, development of preventable complications.

compromised family Coping may be related to chronic nature of disease and disability, inadequate/incorrect information or understanding by a primary person, and possibly evidenced by significant person attempting assistive or supportive behaviors with less than satisfactory results, protective behavior disproportionate to patient's abilities or need for autonomy.

cystitis

acute Pain may be related to inflammation and bladder spasms, possibly evidenced by verbal reports, distraction behaviors, and narrowed focus.

impaired Urinary Elimination may be related to inflammation/irritation of bladder, possibly evidenced by frequency, nocturia, and dysuria.

deficient Knowledge [Learning Need] regarding condition, treatment, and prevention of recurrence may be related to inadequate information/misconceptions, possibly evidenced by statements of concern and questions; recurrent infections.

cytomegalic inclusion disease
Refer to *herpes*.

cytomegalovirus (CMV) infection
risk for disturbed visual Sensory Perception: risk factors may include inflammation of the retina.
risk for fetal Infection: risk factors may include transplacental exposure, contact with blood/body fluids.

deep vein thrombosis (DVT)
Refer to *thrombophlebitis*.

dehiscence (abdominal)
impaired Skin Integrity may be related to altered circulation, altered nutritional state (obesity/malnutrition), and physical stress on incision, possibly evidenced by poor/delayed wound healing and disruption of skin surface/wound closure.
risk for Infection: risk factors may include inadequate primary defenses (separation of incision, traumatized intestines, environmental exposure).
risk for impaired Tissue Integrity: risk factors may include exposure of abdominal contents to external environment.
Fear/[severe] Anxiety may be related to crises, perceived threat of death, possibly evidenced by fearfulness, restless behaviors, and sympathetic stimulation.
deficient Knowledge [Learning Need] regarding condition/prognosis and treatment needs may be related to lack of information/recall and misinterpretation of information, possibly evidenced by development of preventable complication, requests for information, and statement of concern.

dehydration
deficient Fluid volume [specify] may be related to etiology as defined by specific situation, possibly evidenced by dry mucous membranes, poor skin turgor, decreased pulse volume/pressure, and thirst.
risk for impaired Oral Mucous Membrane: risk factors may include dehydration and decreased salivation.
deficient Knowledge [Learning Need] regarding fluid needs may be related to lack of information/misinterpretation, possibly evidenced by questions, statement of concern, and inadequate follow-through of instructions/development of preventable complications.

delirium tremens (acute alcohol withdrawal)
Anxiety [severe/panic]/Fear may be related to cessation of alcohol intake/physiological withdrawal, threat to self-concept, perceived threat of death, possibly evidenced by increased tension, apprehension, fear of unspecified consequences; identifies object of fear.
disturbed Sensory/Perception (specify) may be related to exogenous (alcohol consumption/sudden cessation)/endogenous (electrolyte imbalance, elevated ammonia and blood urea nitrogen—BUN) chemical alterations, sleep deprivation, and psychological stress, possibly evidenced by disorientation, restlessness, irritability, exaggerated emotional responses, bizarre thinking and visual and auditory distortions/hallucinations.
risk for decreased Cardiac Output: risk factors may include direct effect of alcohol on heart muscle, altered SVR, presence of dysrhythmias.
risk for Trauma: risk factors may include alterations in balance, reduced muscle coordination, cognitive impairment, and involuntary clonic/tonic muscle activity.
imbalanced Nutrition: less than body requirements may be related to poor dietary intake, effects of alcohol on organs involved in digestion, interference with absorption/metabolism of nutrients and amino acids, possibly evidenced by reports of inadequate food intake, altered taste sensation, lack of interest in food, debilitated state, decreased subcutaneous fat/muscle mass, signs of mineral/electrolyte deficiency, including abnormal laboratory findings.

delivery, precipitous/out of hospital
(also refer to *labor, precipitous*; *labor stages I–II*)
risk for deficient Fluid Volume: risk factors may include presence of nausea/vomiting, lack of intake, excessive vascular loss.
risk for Infection: risk factors may include broken/traumatized tissue, increased environmental exposure, rupture of amniotic membranes.
risk for fetal Injury: risk factors may include rapid descent/pressure changes, compromised circulation, environmental exposure.

delusional disorder
risk for self/other-directed Violence: risk factors may include perceived threats of danger, increased feelings of anxiety, acting out in an irrational manner.
[severe] Anxiety may be related to inability to trust possibly evidenced by rigid delusional system, frightened of other people and own hostility.

Powerlessness may be related to lifestyle of helplessness, feelings of inadequacy, interpersonal interaction possibly evidenced by verbal expressions of no control/influence over situation(s), use of paranoid delusions, aggressive behavior to compensate for lack of control.

impaired Social Interaction may be related to mistrust of others/delusional thinking, lack of knowledge/skills to enhance mutuality possibly evidenced by discomfort in social situations, difficulty in establishing relationships with others, expression of feelings of rejection, no sense of belonging.

dementia, presenile/senile
(also refer to *Alzheimer's disease*)
impaired Memory may be related to neurological disturbances, possibly evidenced by observed experiences of forgetting, inability to determine if a behavior was performed, inability to perform previously learned skills, inability to recall factual information or recent/past events.

Fear may be related to decreases in functional abilities, public disclosure of disabilities, further mental/physical deterioration possibly evidenced by social isolation, apprehension, irritability, defensiveness, suspiciousness, aggressive behavior.

Self-Care Deficit [specify] may be related to cognitive decline, physical limitations, frustration over loss of independence, depression, possibly evidenced by impaired ability to perform ADLs.

risk for Trauma: risk factors may include changes in muscle coordination/balance, impaired judgment, seizure activity.

risk for sedentary Lifestyle: risk factors may include lack of interest/motivation, resources; lack of training or knowledge of specific exercise needs, safety concerns/fear of injury.

risk for Caregiver Role Strain: risk factors may include illness severity of care receiver, duration of caregiving required, care receiver exhibiting deviant/bizarre behavior; family/caregiver isolation, lack of respite/recreation, spouse is caregiver.

Grieving may be related to awareness of something "being wrong," predisposition for anxiety and feelings of inadequacy, family perception of potential loss of loved one, possibly evidenced by expressions of distress, anger at potential loss, choked feelings, crying, alteration in activity level, communication patterns, eating habits, and sleep patterns.

depressant abuse
(also refer to *Drug Overdose, acute [depressants]*)
ineffective Denial may be related to weak underdeveloped ego, unmet self-needs possibly evidenced by inability to admit impact of condition on life, minimizes symptoms/problem, refuses healthcare attention.

ineffective Coping may be related to weak ego possibly evidenced by abuse of chemical agents, lack of goal-directed behavior, inadequate problem solving, destructive behavior toward self.

imbalanced Nutrition: less than body requirements may be related to use of substance in place of nutritional food possibly evidenced by loss of weight, pale conjunctiva and mucous membranes, electrolyte imbalances, anemias.

risk for Injury: risk factors may include changes in sleep, decreased concentration, loss of inhibitions.

depression, postpartum
risk for impaired Attachmen t: risk factors may include anxiety associated with the parent role, inability to meet personal needs, perceived guilt regarding relationship with infant.

Fatigue maybe related to stress, sleep deprivation, depression as evidenced by reports overwhelming lack of energy, inability to maintain usual routines, increase in physical complaints.

situational low Self-Esteem may be related to developmental changes, disturbed body image, possibly evidenced by evaluation of self as unable to deal with situation, self-negating verbalizations, reports helplessness.

depressive disorders, major depression, dysthymia
risk for self-directed Violence: risk factors may include depressed mood and feeling of worthlessness and hopelessness.

[moderate to severe] Anxiety may be related to stress, unconscious conflict about essential values or goals of life, unmet needs, threat to self-concept, interpersonal transmission or contagion, possibly evidenced by feelings of inadequacy, sleep disturbances, fatigue, difficulty concentrating, diminished productivity/ability to problem-solve, ruminatio

Insomnia may be related to biochemical alterations (decreased serotonin), unresolved fears and anxieties, and inactivity, possibly evidenced by difficulty in falling/remaining asleep, early morning awakening/awakening later than desired, reports of not feeling rested, and physical signs (e.g., dark circles under eyes, excessive yawning); hypersomnia (using sleep as an escape).

Social Isolation/ impaired Social Interaction may be related to alterations in mental status/thought processes (depressed mood), inadequate personal resources, decreased energy/inertia, difficulty engaging in satisfying personal relationships, feelings of worthlessness/low self-concept, inadequacy in or absence of significant purpose in life, and knowledge/skill deficit about social interactions, possibly evidenced by decreased involvement with others, expressed feelings of difference from others, remaining in home/room/bed, refusing invitations/suggestions of social involvement, and dysfunctional interaction with peers, family, and/or others.

interrupted Family Processes may be related to situational crises of illness of family member with change in roles/responsibilities, developmental crises (e.g., loss of family member/relationship), possibly evidenced by statements of difficulty coping with situation, family system not meeting needs of its members, difficulty accepting or receiving help appropriately, ineffective family decision-making process, and failure to send and to receive clear messages.

risk for impaired Religiosity: risk factors may include ineffective support/coping, lack of social interaction, depression.

risk for Injury [effects of electroconvulsive therapy (ECT)]: risk factors may include effects of therapy on the cardiovascular, respiratory, musculoskeletal, and nervous systems; and pharmacological effects of anesthesia.

dermatitis seborrheic
impaired Skin Integrity may be related to chronic inflammatory condition of the skin, possibly evidenced by disruption of skin surface with dry or moist scales, yellowish crusts, erythema, and fissures.

diabetes, gestational
also refer to *diabetes mellitus*
risk for unstable blood Glucose: risk factors may include pregnancy, dietary intake, lack of diabetes management, inadequate blood glucose monitoring.

risk for disturbed Maternal-Fetal Dyad: risk factors may include impaired glucose metabolism, compromised oxygen transport—changes in circulation; treatment-related side effects.

deficient Knowledge [Learning Need] regarding diabetic condition, prognosis, and treatment needs may be related to lack of resources or exposure to information, misinformation, possibly evidenced by questions, statements of misconceptions, inaccurate follow-through of instructions, development of preventable complications.

diabetes mellitus
deficient Knowledge [Learning Need] regarding disease process/treatment and individual care needs may be related to unfamiliarity with information/lack of recall, misinterpretation, possibly evidenced by requests for information, statements of concern/misconceptions, inadequate follow-through of instructions, and development of preventable complications.

risk for unstable blood Glucose: risk factors may include lack of adherence to diabetes management, medication management, inadequate blood glucose monitoring, physical activity level, health status, stress, rapid growth periods.

imbalanced Nutrition: less than body requirements may be related to inability to utilize nutrients (imbalance between intake and utilization of glucose) to meet metabolic needs, possibly evidenced by change in weight, muscle weakness, increased thirst/urination, and hyperglycemia.

risk-prone health Behavior may be related to inadequate comprehension, multiple stressors, as evidenced by minimizes health status change, failure to achieve optimal sense of cont

risk for Infection: risk factors may include decreased leukocytic function, circulatory changes, and delayed healing.

risk for disturbed Sensory/Perception (specify): risk factors may include endogenous chemical alteration (glucose/insulin and/or electrolyte imbalance).

compromised family Coping may be related to inadequate or incorrect information or understanding by primary person(s), other situational/developmental crises or situations the significant person(s) may be facing, lifelong condition requiring behavioral changes impacting family, possibly evidenced by family expressions of confusion about what to do, verbalizations that they are having difficulty coping with situation; family does not meet physical/emotional needs of its members; Significant other(s) preoccupied with personal reaction (e.g., guilt, fear), display protective behavior disproportionate (too little/too much) to client's abilities or need for autonomy.

diabetic ketoacidosis
deficient Fluid Volume [specify] may be related to hyperosmolar urinary losses, gastric losses, and inadequate intake, possibly evidenced by increased urinary output/dilute

urine, reports of weakness, thirst; sudden weight loss, hypotension, tachycardia, delayed capillary refill, dry mucous membranes, poor skin turgor.

unstable Blood Glucose: may be related to medication management, lack of diabetes management, inadequate blood glucose monitoring, presence of infection, possibly evidenced by elevated serum glucose level, presence of ketones in urine, nausea, weight loss, blurred vision, irritability.

Fatigue may be related to decreased metabolic energy production, altered body chemistry (insufficient insulin), increased energy demands (hypermetabolic state/infection), possibly evidenced by overwhelming lack of energy, inability to maintain usual routines, decreased performance, impaired ability to concentrate, listlessness.

risk for Infection: risk factors may include high glucose levels, decreased leukocyte function, stasis of body fluids, invasive procedures, alteration in circulation/perfusion.

dialysis, general
(also refer to *dialysis, peritoneal*; *hemodialysis*)

imbalanced Nutrition: less than body requirements may be related to inadequate ingestion of nutrients (dietary restrictions, anorexia, nausea/vomiting, stomatitis), loss of peptides and amino acids (building blocks for proteins) during procedure, possibly evidenced by reported inadequate intake, aversion to eating, altered taste sensation, poor muscle tone/weakness, sore/inflamed buccal cavity, pale conjunctiva/mucous membranes.

Grieving may be related to actual or perceived loss, chronic and/or fatal illness, and thwarted grieving response to a loss, possibly evidenced by verbal expression of distress/unresolved issues, denial of loss; altered eating habits, sleep and dream patterns, activity levels, libido; crying, labile affect; feelings of sorrow, guilt, and anger.

disturbed Body Image/situational low Self-Esteem may be related to situational crisis and chronic illness with changes in usual roles/body image, possibly evidenced by verbalization of changes in lifestyle, focus on past function, negative feelings about body, feelings of helplessness/powerlessness, extension of body boundary to incorporate environmental objects (e.g., dialysis setup), change in social involvement, overdependence on others for care, not taking responsibility for self-care/lack of followthrough, and self-destructive behavior.

Self-Care Deficit [specify] may be related to perceptual/cognitive impairment (accumulated toxins); intolerance to activity, decreased strength and endurance; pain/discomfort, possibly evidenced by reported inability to perform ADLs, disheveled/unkempt appearance, strong body odor.

Powerlessness may be related to illness-related regimen and health care environment, possibly evidenced by verbal expression of having no control, depression over physical deterioration, nonparticipation in care, anger, and passivity.

compromised/ disabled family Coping may be related to inadequate or incorrect information or understanding by a primary person, temporary family disorganization and role changes, patient providing little support in turn for the primary person, and prolonged disease/disability progression that exhausts the supportive capacity of significant persons, possibly evidenced by expressions of concern or reports about response of significant other(s)/family to patient's health problem, preoccupation of significant other(s) with own personal reactions, display of intolerance/rejection, and protective behavior disproportionate (too little or too much) to patient's abilities or need for autonomy.

dialysis, peritoneal
(also refer to *dialysis, general*)

risk for excess Fluid Volume: risk factors may include inadequate osmotic gradient of dialysate, fluid retention (dialysate drainage problems/inappropriate osmotic gradient of solution, bowel distention), excessive PO/IV intake.

risk for Trauma: risk factors may include improper placement during insertion or manipulation of catheter.

acute Pain/impaired Comfort may be related to catheter irritation, improper catheter placement, presence of edema, abdominal distention, inflammation or infection, rapid infusion or infusion of cold or acidic dialysate, possibly evidenced by verbal reports, guarding or distraction behaviors, and self-focus

risk for Infection [peritoneal]: risk factors may include contamination of catheter/infusion system, skin contaminants, sterile peritonitis (response to composition of dialysate).

risk for ineffective Breathing Pattern: risk factors may include increased abdominal pressure restricting diaphragmatic excursion, rapid infusion of dialysate, pain or discomfort, inflammatory process—atelectasis/pneumonia.

diarrhea
deficient Knowledge [Learning Need] regarding causative/contributing factors and therapeutic needs may be related to lack of information/misconceptions, possibly evi-

denced by statements of concern, questions, and development of preventable complications.

risk for deficient Fluid Volume: risk factors may include excessive losses through gastrointestinal tract, altered intake.

acute Pain may be related to abdominal cramping and irritation/excoriation of skin, possibly evidenced by verbal reports, facial grimacing, and autonomic responses.

impaired Skin Integrity may be related to effects of excretions on delicate tissues, possibly evidenced by reports of discomfort and disruption of skin surface/destruction of skin layers.

digitalis toxicity

decreased Cardiac Output may be related to altered myocardial contractility/electrical conduction, properties of digitalis (long half-life and narrow therapeutic range), concurrent medications, age/general health status and electrolyte/acid-base balance, possibly evidenced by changes in rate/rhythm/conduction (development/worsening of dysrhythmias), changes in mentation, worsening of heart failure, elevated serum drug levels.

risk for imbalanced Fluid Volume: risk factors may include excessive losses from vomiting/diarrhea, decreased intake/nausea, decreased plasma proteins, malnutrition, continued use of diuretics; excess sodium/fluid retention.

deficient Knowledge [Learning Need] regarding condition/therapy and self-care needs may be related to information misinterpretation and lack of recall, possibly evidenced by inaccurate follow-through of instructions and development of preventable complications.

dilation and curettage (D and C)
(also refer to *abortion, spontaneous*)

deficient Knowledge [Learning Need] regarding surgical procedure, possible postprocedural complications, and therapeutic needs may be related to lack of exposure/unfamiliarity with information, possibly evidenced by requests for information and statements of concern/misconceptions.

dilation of cervix, premature
(also refer to *labor, preterm*)

Anxiety [specify level] may be related to situational crisis, threat of death/fetal loss possibly evidenced by increased tension, apprehension, feelings of inadequacy, sympathic stimulation, and repetitive questioning.

risk for disturebed Maternal-Fetal Dyad: rrisk factors may include surgical intervention, use of tocolytic drugs.

risk for fetal Injury: risk factors may include premature delivery, surgical procedure.

Grieving may be related to perceived potential fetal loss possibly evidenced by expression of distress, guilt, anger, choked feelings

dislocation/subluxation of joint

acute Pain may be related to lack of continuity of bone/joint, muscle spasms, edema, possibly evidenced by verbal or coded reports, guarded or protective behaviors, narrowed focus, changes in vital signs.

risk for Injury: risk factors may include nerve impingement, improper fitting of splint device.

impaired physical Mobility may be related to immobilization device, activity restrictions, pain, edema, decreased muscle strength, possibly evidenced by limited range of motion, limited ability to perform motor skills, gait changes.

disseminated intravascular coagulation (DIC)

risk for deficient Fluid Volume: risk factors may include failure of regulatory mechanism (coagulation process) and active loss/hemorrhage.

ineffective Tissue Perfusion (specify) may be related to alteration of arterial/venous flow (microemboli throughout circulatory system and hypovolemia), possibly evidenced by changes in respiratory rate and depth, changes in mentation, decreased urinary output, and development of acral cyanosis/focal gangrene.

Anxiety [specify level]/Fear may be related to sudden change in health status/threat of death, interpersonal transmission/contagion, possibly evidenced by sympathetic stimulation, restlessness, focus on self, and apprehension.

risk for impaired Gas Exchange: risk factors may include reduced oxygen-carrying capacity, development of acidosis, fibrin deposition in microcirculation, and ischemic damage of lung parenchyma.

acute Pain may be related to bleeding into joints/muscles, with hematoma formation, and ischemic tissues with areas of acral cyanosis/focal gangrene, possibly evidenced by verbal reports, narrowed focus, alteration in muscle tone, guarding/distraction behaviors, restlessness, autonomic responses.

dissociative disorders

Anxiety [severe/panic]/Fear may be related to maladaptation of ineffective coping continuing from early life, unconscious conflict(s), threat to self-concept, un-met needs, or phobic stimulus, possibly evidenced by maladaptive response to stress (e.g., dissociating self/fragmentation of the personality), increased tension, feelings of inadequacy, and focus on self, projection of personal perceptions onto the environment.

risk for at self/other-directed Violence: risk factors may include dissociative state/conflicting personalities, depressed mood, panic states, and suicidal/homicidal behaviors.

disturbed Personal Identity may be related to psychological conflicts (dissociative state), childhood trauma/abuse, threat to physical integrity/self-concept, and underdeveloped ego, possibly evidenced by alteration in perception or experience of self, loss of one's own sense of reality/the external world, poorly differentiated ego boundaries, confusion about sense of self, purpose or direction in life; memory loss, presence of more than one personality within the individual.

compromised family Coping may be related to multiple stressors repeated over time, prolonged progression of disorder that exhausts the supportive capacity of significant person(s), family disorganization and role changes, high-risk family situation possibly evidenced by family/significant other(s) describing inadequate understanding or knowledge that interferes with assistive or supportive behaviors; relationship and marital conflict.

diverticulitis

acute Pain may be related to inflammation of intestinal mucosa, abdominal cramping, and presence of fever/chills, possibly evidenced by verbal reports, guarding/distraction behaviors, autonomic responses, and narrowed focus.

Diarrhea/Constipation may be related to altered structure/function and presence of inflammation, possibly evidenced by signs and symptoms dependent on specific problem (e.g., increase/decrease in frequency of stools and change in consistency).

deficient Knowledge [Learning Need] regarding disease process, potential complications, therapeutic and self-care needs may be related to lack of information/misconceptions, possibly evidenced by statements of concern, request for information, and development of preventable complications.

risk for Powerlessness: risk factors may include chronic nature of disease process with recurrent episodes despite cooperation with medical regimen.

Down syndrome

(also refer to *mental retardation*)

delayed Growth and Development may be related to effects of physical/mental disability, possibly evidenced by altered physical growth; delay/inability in performing skills and self-care/self-control activities appropriate for age.

risk for Trauma: risk factors may include cognitive difficulties and poor muscle tone/coordination, weakness.

imbalanced Nutrition: less than body requirements may be related to poor muscle tone and protruding tongue, possibly evidenced by weak and ineffective sucking/swallowing and observed lack of adequate intake with weight loss/failure to gain.

interrupted Family Processes may be related to situational/maturational crisis requiring incorporation of new skills into family dynamics, possibly evidenced by confusion about what to do, verbalized difficulty coping with situation, unexamined family myths.

risk for complicated Grieving: risk factors may include loss of "the perfect child," chronic condition requiring long-term care, and unresolved feelings.

risk for impaired Attachment: risk factors may include ill infant/child who is unable to effectively initiate parental contact due to altered behavioral organization, inability of parents to meet personal needs.

risk for Social Isolation: risk factors may include withdrawal from usual social interactions and activities, assumption of total child care, and becoming overindulgent/overprotective.

drug overdose, acute (depressants)

(also refer to *substance dependence/abuse rehabilitation*)

ineffective Breathing Pattern/impaired Gas Exchange may be related to neuromuscular impairment/CNS depression, decreased lung expansion, possibly evidenced by changes in respirations, cyanosis, and abnormal ABGs.

risk for Trauma/Suffocation/Poisoning: risk factors may include CNS depression/agitation, hypersensitivity to the drug(s), psychological stress.

risk for self/other-directed Violence: risk factors may include suicidal behaviors, toxic reactions to drug(s).

risk for Infection: risk factors may include drug injection techniques, impurities in injected drugs, localized trauma; malnutrition, altered immune state.

drug withdrawal

[disturbed Sensory Perception (specify)] may be related to biochemical imbalance, altered sensory integration possibly evidenced by sensory distortions, poor concentration, irritability, hallucinations

risk for Injury: risk factors may include CNS agitation (depressants).

risk for Suicide: risk factors may include alcohol or other substance abuse, legal or disciplinary problems, depressed mood (stimulants).

acute Pain/impaired Comfort may be related to biochemical changes associated with cessation of drug use possibly evidenced by reports of muscle aches, fever, diaphoresis, rhinorrhea, lacrimation, malaise.

Self-Care Deficit (specify) may be related to perceptual or cognitive impairment, therapeutic management (restraints) possibly evidenced by inability to meet own physical needs.

Insomnia may be related to cessation of substance use, fatigue possibly evidenced by reports of insomnia/hypersomnia, decreased ability to function, increased irritability.

Fatigue may be related to altered body chemistry (drug withdrawal), sleep deprivation, malnutrition, poor physical condition possibly evidenced by verbal reports of overwhelming lack of energy, inability to maintain usual level of physical activity, inability to restore energy after sleep, compromised concentration.

Duchenne's muscular dystrophy
Refer to *Muscular dystrophy (Duchenne's)*.

dysmenorrhea

acute Pain may be related to exaggerated uterine contractility, possibly evidenced by verbal reports, guarding/distraction behaviors, narrowed focus, and autonomic responses (changes in vital signs).

risk for Activity Intolerance: risk factors may include severity of pain and presence of secondary symptoms (nausea, vomiting, syncope, chills), depression.

ineffective Coping may be related to chronic, recurrent nature of problem; anticipatory anxiety, and inadequate coping methods, possibly evidenced by muscular tension, headaches, general irritability, chronic depression, and verbalization of inability to cope, report of poor self-concept.

dysrhythmia, cardiac

risk for decreased Cardiac Output: risk factors may include altered electrical conduction and reduced myocardial contractility.

deficient Knowledge [Learning Need] regarding medical condition/therapy needs may be related to lack of information/misinterpretation and unfamiliarity with information resources, possibly evidenced by questions, statement of misconception, failure to improve on previous regimen, and development of preventable complications.

risk for Poisoning [digitalis toxicity]: risk factors may include limited range of therapeutic effectiveness, lack of education/proper precautions, reduced vision/cognitive limitations.

eclampsia
also refer to *pregnancy-induced hypertension*.

Anxiety [specify]/Fear may be related to situational crisis, threat of change in health status or death (self/fetus), separation from support system, interpersonal contagion possibly evidenced by expressed concerns, apprehension, increased tension, decreased self-assurance, difficulty concentrating.

risk for maternal Injury risk factors may include tissue edema, hypoxia, tonic-clonic convulsions, abnormal blood profile and/or clotting factors.

impaired physical Mobility may be related to prescribed bedrest, discomfort, anxiety possibly evidenced by difficulty turning, postural instability.

risk for Self-Care Deficit (specify): risk factors may include weakness, discomfort, physical restrictions.

ectopic pregnancy (tubal)
(also refer to *abortion, spontaneous termination*)

acute Pain may be related to distention/rupture of fallopian tube, possibly evidenced by reports, guarding/distraction behaviors, facial mask of pain, and autonomic responses (diaphoresis, changes in vital signs).

risk for Bleeding/deficient Fluid Volume [isotonic]: risk factors may include pregnancy-related complications, hemorrhagic losses and decreased or restricted intake.

Anxiety [specify level]/Fear may be related to threat of death and possible loss of ability to conceive, possibly evidenced by increased tension, apprehension, sympathetic stimulation, restlessness, and focus on self.

eczema (dermatitis)
Pain [Discomfort] may be related to cutaneous inflammation and irritation, possibly evidenced by verbal reports, irritability, and scratching.

risk for Infection: risk factors may include broken skin and tissue trauma.
Social Isolation may be related to alterations in physical appearance, possibly evidenced by expressed feelings of rejection and decreased interaction with peers.

edema, pulmonary
excess Fluid Volume may be related to decreased cardiac functioning, excessive fluid/sodium intake, possibly evidenced by dyspnea, presence of crackles (rales), pulmonary congestion on x-ray, restlessness, anxiety, and increased central venous pressure (CVP)/pulmonary pressures.
impaired Gas Exchange may be related to altered blood flow and decreased alveolar/capillary exchange (fluid collection/shifts into interstitial space/alveoli), possibly evidenced by hypoxia, restlessness, and confusion.
Anxiety [specify level]/Fear may be related to perceived threat of death (inability to breathe), possibly evidenced by responses ranging from apprehension to panic state, restlessness, and focus on self.

electroconvulsive therapy
decisional Conflict may be related to lack of relevant or multiple and divergent sources of information, mistrust of regimen or healthcare personnel, sense of powerlessness, support system deficit.
risk for Injury risk factors may include effects of therapeutic procedure, and pharmacological effects of anesthesia.
acute Confusion may be related to central nervous system effects of electric shock, medications, and anesthesia, possibly evidenced by fluctuation in cognition, agitation.
impaired Memory may be related to neurological disturbance, possibly evidenced by reported or observed experiences of forgetting, difficulty recalling recent events or factual information.

emphysema
impaired Gas Exchange may be related to alveolar capillary membrane changes/destruction, possibly evidenced by dyspnea, restlessness, changes in mentation, abnormal ABG values.
ineffective Airway Clearance may be related to increased production/retained tenacious secretions, decreased energy level, and muscle wasting, possibly evidenced by abnormal breath sounds (rhonchi), ineffective cough, changes in rate/depth of respirations, and dyspnea.
Activity Intolerance may be related to imbalance between oxygen supply and demand, possibly evidenced by reports of fatigue/weakness, exertional dyspnea, and abnormal vital sign response to activity.
imbalanced Nutrition: less than body requirements may be related to inability to ingest food (shortness of breath, anorexia, generalized weakness, medication side effects), possibly evidenced by lack of interest in food, reported altered taste, loss of muscle mass and tone, fatigue, and weight loss.
risk for Infection: risk factors may include inadequate primary defenses (stasis of body fluids, decreased ciliary action), chronic disease process, and malnutrition.
Powerlessness may be related to illness-related regimen and health care environment, possibly evidenced by verbal expression of having no control, depression over physical deterioration, nonparticipation in therapeutic regimen; anger, and passivity.

encephalitis
risk for ineffective cerebral Tissue Perfusion: risk factors may include cerebral edema altering/interrupting cerebral arterial/venous blood flow, hypovolemia, exchange problems at cellular level (acidosis).
Hyperthermia may be related to increased metabolic rate, illness, and dehydration, possibly evidenced by increased body temperature, flushed/warm skin, and increased pulse and respiratory rates.
acute Pain may be related to inflammation/irritation of the brain and cerebral edema, possibly evidenced by verbal reports of headache, photophobia, distraction behaviors, restlessness, and autonomic response (changes in vital signs).
risk for Trauma/Suffocation: risk factors may include restlessness, clonic/tonic activity, altered sensorium, cognitive impairment; generalized weakness, ataxia, vertigo.

endocarditis
risk for decreased Cardiac Output: risk factors may include inflammation of lining of heart and structural change in valve leaflets.
Anxiety [specify level] may be related to change in health status and threat of death, possibly evidenced by apprehension, expressed concerns, and focus on self.
acute Pain may be related to generalized inflammatory process and effects of embolic phenomena, possibly evidenced by reports, narrowed focus, distraction behaviors, and autonomic responses (changes in vital signs).
risk for Activity Intolerance: risk factors may include imbalance between oxygen supply and demand, debilitating condition.

risk for ineffective Tissue Perfusion (specify): risk factors may include embolic interruption of arterial flow (embolization of thrombi/valvular vegetations).

endometriosis

acute/chronic Pain may be related to pressure of concealed bleeding/formation of adhesions, possibly evidenced by verbal reports (pain between/with menstruation), guarding/distraction behaviors, and narrowed focus.

Sexual Dysfunction may be related to pain secondary to presence of adhesions, possibly evidenced by verbalization of problem, and altered relationship with partner.

deficient Knowledge [Learning Need] regarding pathophysiology of condition and therapy needs may be related to lack of information/misinterpretations, possibly evidenced by statements of concern and misconceptions.

enteral feeding

imbalanced Nutrition: less than body requirements may be related to conditions that interfere with nutrient intake or increase nutrient need or metabolic demand—cancer and associated treatments, anorexia, surgical procedures, dysphagia, or decreased level of consciousness, possibly evidenced by body weight 10% or more under ideal, decreased subcutaneous fat or muscle mass, poor muscle tone, changes in gastric motility and stool characteristics.

risk for Infection: risk factors may include invasive procedure with surgical placement of feeding tube, malnutrition, chronic disease, improper preparation, handling or contamination of the feeding solution.

risk for Aspiration: risk factors may include presence of feeding tube, bolus tube feedings, increased intragastric pressure, delayed gastric emptying, medication administration.

risk for imbalanced Fluid Volume: risk factors may include active loss or failure of regulatory mechanisms specific to underlying disease process or trauma, inability to obtain or ingest fluids.

Fatigue may be related to decreased metabolic energy production, increased energy requirements—hypermetabolic state, healing process; altered body chemistry—medications, chemotherapy, possibly evidenced by overwhelming lack of energy, inability to maintain usual routines/accomplish routine tasks, lethargy, impaired ability to concentrate

enteritis

Refer to *colitis, ulcerative*; *Crohn's disease*.

epididymitis

acute Pain may be related to inflammation, edema formation, and tension on the spermatic cord, possibly evidenced by verbal reports, guarding/distraction behaviors (restlessness), and autonomic responses (changes in vital signs).

risk for Infection [spread]: risk factors may include presence of inflammation/infectious process, insufficient knowledge to avoid spread of infection.

deficient Knowledge [Learning Need] regarding pathophysiology, outcome, and self-care needs may be related to lack of information/misinterpretations, possibly evidenced by statements of concern, misconceptions, and questions.

epilepsy

Refer to *seizure disorder*.

erectile dysfunction

Sexual Dysfunction may be related to altered body function possibly evidenced by reports of disruption of sexual response pattern, inability to achieve desired satisfaction.

situational low Self-Esteem may be related to functional impairment; rejection of other(s).

failure to thrive, infant/child

imbalanced Nutrition: less than body requirements, may be related to inability to ingest/digest/absorb nutrients (defects in organ function/metabolism, genetic factors), physical deprivation/psychosocial factors), possibly evidenced by lack of appropriate weight gain/weight loss, poor muscle tone, pale conjunctiva, and laboratory tests reflecting nutritional deficiency.

delayed Growth and Development may be related to inadequate caretaking (physical/emotional neglect or abuse); indifference, inconsistent responsiveness, multiple caretakers; environmental and stimulation deficiencies, possibly evidenced by altered physical growth, flat affect, listlessness, decreased response; delay or difficulty in performing skills or self-control activities appropriate for age group.

risk for impaired Parenting: risk factors may include lack of knowledge, inadequate bonding, unrealistic expectations for self/infant, and lack of appropriate response of child to relationship.

deficient Knowledge [Learning Need] regarding pathophysiology of condition, nutritional needs, growth/development expectations, and parenting skills may be related to lack of information/misinformation or misinterpretation, possibly evidenced by verbalization of concerns, questions, misconceptions; and development of preventable complications.

fatigue syndrome, chronic
Fatigue may be related to disease state, inadequate sleep, possibly evidenced by verbalization of unremitting/overwhelming lack of energy, inability to maintain usual routines, listless, compromised concentration.
chronic Pain may be related to chronic physical disability possibly evidenced by verbal reports of headache, sore throat, arthralgias, abdominal pain, muscle aches; altered ability to continue previous activities, changes in sleep pattern.
Self-Care Deficit [specify] may be related to tiredness, pain/discomfort possibly evidenced by reports of inability to perform desired ADLs.
risk for ineffective Role Performance: risk factors may include health alterations, stress.

femoral popliteal bypass
also refer to *surgery, general*
risk for ineffective peripheral Tissue Perfusion: risk factors may include interruption of arterial blood flow, hypovolemia.
risk for Peripheral Neurovascular Dysfunction: risk factors may include vascular obstruction, immobilization, mechanical compression, dressings
impaired Walking may be related to surgical incisions, dressings, possibly evidenced by inability to walk desired distance, climb stairs, negotiate inclines.

fetal alcohol syndrome
risk for Injury [CNS damage]: risk factors may include external chemical factors (alcohol intake by mother), placental insufficiency, fetal drug withdrawal in utero/postpartum and prematurity.
disorganized Infant Behavior may be related to prematurity, environmental overstimulation, lack of containment/boundaries, possibly evidenced by change from baseline physiological measures; tremors, startles, twitches, hyperextension of arms/legs, deficient self-regulatory behaviors, deficient response to visual/auditory stimuli.
risk for impaired Parenting: risk factors may include mental and/or physical illness, inability of mother to assume the overwhelming task of unselfish giving and nurturing, presence of stressors (financial/legal problems), lack of available or ineffective role model, interruption of bonding process, lack of appropriate response of child to relationship.
ineffective [maternal Coping may be related to personal vulnerability, low self-esteem, inadequate coping skills, and multiple stressors (repeated over period of time), possibly evidenced by inability to meet basic needs/fulfill role expectations/problem solve, and excessive use of drug(s).
dysfunctional Family Processes may be related to lack of or insufficient support from others, mother's drug problem and treatment status, together with poor coping skills, lack of family stability, overinvolvement of parents with children and multigenerational addictive behaviors, possibly evidenced by abandonment, rejection, neglectful relationships with family members, and decisions and actions by family that are detrimental.

fetal demise
Grieving may be related to death of fetus/infant (wanted or unwanted), possibly evidenced by verbal expression of distress, anger, loss; crying; alteration in eating habits or sleep pattern.
situational low Self-Esteem may be related to perceived "failure" at a life event, possibly evidenced by negative self-appraisal in response to life event in a person with a previous positive self-evaluation, verbalization of negative feelings about the self (helplessness, uselessness), difficulty making decisions.
risk for Spiritual Distress: risk factors may include loss of loved one, low self-esteem, poor relationships, challenged belief and value system (birth is supposed to be the beginning of life, not of death) and intense suffering.

fibromyalgia syndrome, primary
acute/chronic Pain may be related to idiopathic diffuse condition possibly evidenced by reports of achy pain in fibrous tissues (muscles, tendons, ligaments), muscle stiffness or spasm, disturbed sleep, guarding behaviors, fear of reinjury or exacerbation, restlessness, irritability, self-focusing, reduced interaction with others
Fatigue may be related to disease state, stress, anxiety, depression, sleep deprivation possibly evidenced by verbalization of overwhelming lack of energy, inability to maintain usual routines or desired level of physical activity, tired, feelings of guilt for not keeping up with responsibilities, increase in physical complaints, listless
risk for Hopelessness: risk factors may include chronic debilitating physical condition, prolonged activity restriction (possibly self-induced) creating isolation, lack of specific therapeutic cure, prolonged stress.

fractures
(also refer to *casts*; *traction*)
risk for Trauma [additional injury]: risk factors may include loss of skeletal integrity/
  movement of skeletal fragments, use of traction apparatus, and so on.
acute Pain may be related to muscle spasms, movement of bone fragments, tissue
  trauma/edema, traction/immobility device, stress and anxiety, possibly evidenced by
  verbal reports, distraction behaviors, self-focusing/narrowed focus, facial mask of
  pain, guarding/protective behavior, alteration in muscle tone, and autonomic responses (changes in vital signs).
,risk for Peripheral Neurovascular Dysfunction: risk factors may include reduction/in-
  terruption of blood flow (direct vascular injury, tissue trauma, excessive edema,
  thrombus formation, hypovolemia).
impaired physical Mobility may be related to neuromuscular/skeletal impairment, pain/
  discomfort, restrictive therapies (bedrest, extremity immobilization), and psychological immobility, possibly evidenced by inability to purposefully move within the physical environment, imposed restrictions, reluctance to attempt movement, limited
  range of motion, and decreased muscle strength/control.
risk for impaired Gas Exchange: risk factors may include altered blood flow, blood/fat
  emboli, alveolar/capillary membrane changes (interstitial/pulmonary edema, congestion).
deficient Knowledge [Learning Need] regarding healing process, therapy requirements,
  potential complications, and self-care needs may be related to lack of exposure, misinterpretation of information, possibly evidenced by statements of concern, questions,
  and misconceptions.

frostbite
impaired Tissue Integrity may be related to altered circulation and thermal injury,
  possibly evidenced by damaged/destroyed tissue.
acute Pain may be related to diminished circulation with tissue ischemia/necrosis and
  edema formation, possibly evidenced by reports, guarding/distraction behaviors, narrowed focus, and autonomic responses (changes in vital signs).
risk for Infection: risk factors may include traumatized tissue/tissue destruction, altered
  circulation, and compromised immune response in affected area.

gallstones
Refer to *cholelithiasis*.

gangrene, dry
ineffective peripheral Tissue Perfusion may be related to interruption in arterial flow,
  possibly evidenced by cool skin temperature, change in color (black), atrophy of affected part, and presence of pain.
acute Pain may be related to tissue hypoxia and necrotic process, possibly evidenced by
  reports, guarding/distraction behaviors, narrowed focus, and autonomic responses
  (changes in vital signs).

gas, lung irritant
ineffective Airway Clearance may be related to irritation/inflammation of airway, possibly evidenced by marked cough, abnormal breath sounds (wheezes), dyspnea, and
  tachypnea.
risk for impaired Gas Exchange: risk factors may include irritation/inflammation of
  alveolar membrane (dependent on type of agent and length of exposure).
Anxiety [specify level] may be related to change in health status and threat of death,
  possibly evidenced by verbalizations, increased tension, apprehension, and sympathetic stimulation.

gastritis, acute
acute Pain may be related to irritation/inflammation of gastric mucosa, possibly evidenced by verbal reports, guarding/distraction behaviors, and autonomic responses
  (changes in vital signs).
risk for deficient Fluid Volume [isotonic]: risk factors may include excessive losses
  through vomiting and diarrhea, continued bleeding, reluctance to ingest/restrictions
  of oral intake.

gastritis, chronic
risk for imbalanced Nutrition: less than body requirements: risk factors may include
  inability to ingest adequate nutrients (prolonged nausea/vomiting, anorexia, epigastric pain).
deficient Knowledge [Learning Need] regarding pathophysiology, psychological factors,
  therapy needs, and potential complications may be related to lack of information/
  misinterpretation, possibly evidenced by verbalization of concerns, questions, misconceptions, and continuation of problem.

gastroenteritis
also refer to *enteritis*; *gastritis, chronic*.

Diarrhea may be related to toxins, contaminants, travel, infectious process, parasites possibly evidenced by at least three loose, liquid stools/day, hyperactive bowel sounds, abdominal pain.

risk for deficient Fluid Volume: risk factors may include excessive losses (diarrhea, vomiting), hypermetabolic state (infection), decreased intake (nausea, anorexia), extremes of age or weight.

gastroesophageal reflux disease (GERD)

acute/chronic Pain may be related to acidic irritation of mucosa, muscle spasm, recurrent vomiting possibly evidenced by reports of heartburn, distraction behaviors.

impaired Swallowing may be related to GERD, esophageal defects, achalasia possibly evidenced by reports of heartburn or epigastric pain, "something stuck" when swallowing, food refusal or volume limiting, nighttime coughing or awakening.

risk for imbalanced Nutrition: less than body requirements risk factors may include limiting intake, recurrent vomiting.

risk for Insomnia: risk factors may include nighttime heartburn, regurgitation of stomach contents.

risk for Aspiration: risk factors may include incompetent lower esophageal sphincter, regurgitation of gastric acid.

gender identity disorder (For individuals experiencing persistent and marked distress regarding uncertainty about issues relating to personal identity, e.g., sexual orientation and behavior.)

Anxiety [specify level] may be related to unconscious/conscious conflicts about essential values/beliefs (ego-dystonic gender identification), threat to self-concept, un-met needs, possibly evidenced by increased tension, helplessness, hopelessness, feelings of inadequacy, uncertainty, insomnia, focus on self, and impaired daily functioning.

ineffective Role Performance/disturbed personal Identity may be related to crisis in development in which person has difficulty knowing/accepting to which sex he or she belongs or is attracted, sense of discomfort and inappropriateness about anatomic sex characteristics, possibly evidenced by confusion about sense of self, purpose or direction in life, sexual identification/preference, verbalization of desire to be/insistence that person is the opposite sex, change in self-perception of role, and conflict in roles.

ineffective Sexuality Pattern may be related to ineffective or absent role models and conflict with sexual orientation and/or preferences, lack of/impaired relationship with significant other, possibly evidenced by verbalizations of discomfort with sexual orientation/role and lack of information about human sexuality.

risk for compromised/disabled family Coping: risk factors may include inadequate/incorrect information or understanding, significant other unable to perceive or to act effectively in regard to patient's needs, temporary family disorganization and role changes, and patient providing little support in turn for primary person.

readiness for enhanced family Coping possibly evidenced by family member's attempts to describe growth or impact of crisis on own values, priorities, goals, or relationships, family member is moving in direction of health-promoting and enriching lifestyle that supports client's search for self and choosing experiences that optimize wellness.

genetic disorder

Anxiety may be related to presence of specific risk factors (e.g., exposure to teratogens), situational crisis, threat to self-concept, conscious or unconscious conflict about essential values and life goals possibly evidenced by increased tension, apprehension, uncertainty, feelings of inadequacy, expressed concerns.

deficient Knowledge [Learning Need] regarding purpose/process of genetic counseling may be related to lack of awareness of ramifications of diagnosis, process necessary for analyzing available options, and information misinterpretation possibly evidenced by verbalization of concerns, statement of misconceptions, request for information.

risk for interrupted Family Processes: risk factors may include situational crisis, individual/family vulnerability, difficulty reaching agreement regarding options.

Spiritual Distress may be related to intense inner conflict about the outcome, normal grieving for the loss of the perfect child, anger that is often directed at God/greater power, religious beliefs/moral convictions possibly evidenced by verbalization of inner conflict about beliefs, questioning of the moral and ethical implications of therapeutic choices, viewing situation as punishment, anger, hostility, and crying.

risk for complicated Grieving: risk factors may include preloss psychological symptoms, predisposition for anxiety and feelings of inadequacy, frequency of major life events.

glaucoma

disturbed visual Sensory/Perception, may be related to altered sensory reception and altered status of sense organ (increased intraocular pressure/atrophy of optic nerve head), possibly evidenced by progressive loss of visual field.

Anxiety [specify level] may be related to change in health status, presence of pain, possibility/reality of loss of vision, un-met needs, and negative self-talk, possibly evidenced by apprehension, uncertainty, and expressed concern regarding changes in life event.

glomerulonephritis

excess Fluid Volume may be related to failure of regulatory mechanism (inflammation of glomerular membrane inhibiting filtration), possibly evidenced by weight gain, edema/anasarca, intake greater than output, and blood pressure changes.

acute Pain may be related to effects of circulating toxins and edema/distention of renal capsule, possibly evidenced by verbal reports, guarding/distraction behaviors, and autonomic responses (changes in vital signs).

imbalanced Nutrition: less than body requirements may be related to anorexia and dietary restrictions, possibly evidenced by aversion to eating, reported altered taste, weight loss, and decreased intake.

deficient Diversional Activity may be related to treatment modality/restrictions, fatigue, and malaise, possibly evidenced by statements of boredom, restlessness, and irritability.

risk for disproportionate Growth: risk factors may include infection, malnutrition, chronic illness.

goiter

disturbed Body Image may be related to visible swelling in neck possibly evidenced by verbalization of feelings, fear of reaction of others, actual change in structure, change in social involvement.

Anxiety may be related to change in health status/progressive growth of mass, perceived threat of death.

risk for imbalanced Nutrition: less than body requirements: risk factors may include decreased ability to ingest/difficulty swallowing.

risk for ineffective Airway Clearance: risk factors may include tracheal compression/obstruction.

gonorrhea
(also refer to *sexually transmitted disease—STD*)

risk for Infection [dissemination/bacteremia]: risk factors may include presence of infectious process in highly vascular area and lack of recognition of disease process.

acute Pain may be related to irritation/inflammation of mucosa and effects of circulating toxins, possibly evidenced by verbal reports of genital or pharyngeal irritation, perineal/pelvic pain, guarding/distraction behaviors.

deficient Knowledge [Learning Need] regarding disease cause/transmission, therapy, and self-care needs may be related to lack of information/misinterpretation, denial of exposure, possibly evidenced by statements of concern, questions, misconceptions, and inaccurate follow-through of instructions/development of preventable complications.

gout

acute Pain may be related to inflammation of joint(s), possibly evidenced by verbal reports, guarding/distraction behaviors, and autonomic responses (changes in vital signs).

impaired physical Mobility may be related to joint pain/edema, possibly evidenced by reluctance to attempt movement, limited range of motion, and therapeutic restriction of movement.

deficient Knowledge [Learning Need] regarding cause, treatment, and prevention of condition may be related to lack of information/misinterpretation, possibly evidenced by statements of concern, questions, misconceptions, and inaccurate follow-through of instructions.

Guillain-Barré syndrome (acute polyneuritis)

risk for ineffective Breathing Pattern/Airway Clearance: risk factors may include weakness/paralysis of respiratory muscles, impaired gag/swallow reflexes, decreased energy/fatigue.

disturbed Sensory/Perception: (specify) may be related to altered sensory reception/transmission/integration (altered status of sense organs, sleep deprivation), therapeutically restricted environment, endogenous chemical alterations (electrolyte imbalance, hypoxia), and psychological stress, possibly evidenced by reported or observed change in usual response to stimuli, altered communication patterns, and measured change in sensory acuity and motor coordination.

impaired physical Mobility may be related to neuromuscular impairment, pain/discomfort, possibly evidenced by impaired coordination, partial/complete paralysis, decreased muscle strength/control.

Anxiety [specify level]/Fear may be related to situational crisis, change in health status/threat of death, possibly evidenced by increased tension, restlessness, helplessness, apprehension, uncertainty, fearfulness, focus on self, and sympathetic stimulation.

risk for Disuse Syndrome: risk factors include paralysis and pain.

hallucinogen abuse
Also refer to *Substance dependence/abuse rehabilitation*
Anxiety/Fear may be related to situational crisis, threat to or change in health status, perceived threat of death, inexperience or unfamiliarity with effects of drug possibly evidenced by assumptions of "losing my mind or control," apprehension, preoccupation with feelings of impending doom, sympathetic stimulation.
Self-Neglect may be related to substance use, executive processing ability, possibly evidenced by inadequate personal/environmental hygiene, nonadherence to health activities.
Self-Care Deficit (specify) may be related to perceptual or cognitive impairment, therapeutic management (restraints) possibly evidenced by inability to meet own physical needs.

hay fever
impaired Comfort may be related to irritation or inflammation of upper airway mucous membranes and conjunctiva, possibly evidenced by verbal reports, irritability, and restlessness.
deficient Knowledge [Learning Need] regarding underlying cause, appropriate therapy, and required lifestyle changes may be related to lack of information, possibly evidenced by statements of concern, questions, and misconceptions.

heart failure, chronic
decreased Cardiac Output may be related to altered myocardial contractility/inotropic changes; alterations in rate, rhythm, and electrical conduction; and structural changes (valvular defects, ventricular aneurysm), possibly evidenced by tachycardia/dysrhythmias, changes in blood pressure, extra heart sounds, decreased urine output, diminished peripheral pulses, cool/ashen skin, orthopnea, crackles; dependent/generalized edema and chest pain.
excess Fluid Volume may be related to reduced glomerular filtration rate/increased ADH production, and sodium/water retention, possibly evidenced by orthopnea and abnormal breath sounds, S_3 heart sound, jugular vein distention, positive hepatojugular reflex, weight gain, hypertension, oliguria, generalized edema.
risk for impaired Gas Exchange: risk factors may include alveolar capillary membrane changes (fluid collection/shifts into interstitial space/alveoli).
Activity Intolerance may be related to imbalance between oxygen supply/demand, generalized weakness, and prolonged bedrest/sedentary lifestyle, possibly evidenced by reported/observed weakness, fatigue; changes in vital signs, presence of dysrhythmias; dyspnea, pallor, and diaphoresis.
risk for impaired Skin Integrity: risk factors may include prolonged chair or bedrest, edema, vascular pooling, decreased tissue perfusion.
deficient Knowledge [Learning Need] regarding cardiac function/disease process, therapy and self-care needs may be related to lack of information/misinterpretation, possibly evidenced by questions, statements of concern/misconceptions; development of preventable complications or exacerbations of condition.

heatstroke
Hyperthermia may be related to prolonged exposure to hot environment/vigorous activity with failure of regulating mechanism of the body, possibly evidenced by high body temperature (greater than 105°F/40.6°C), flushed/hot skin, tachycardia, and seizure activity.
decreased Cardiac Output may be related to functional stress of hypermetabolic state, altered circulating volume/venous return, and direct myocardial damage secondary to hyperthermia, possibly evidenced by decreased peripheral pulses, dysrhythmias/tachycardia, and changes in mentation.

hemodialysis
(also refer to *dialysis, general*)
risk for Injury, [loss of vascular access]: risk factors may include clotting/thrombosis, infection, disconnection/hemorrhage.
risk for deficient Fluid Volume/Bleeding: risk factors may include excessive fluid losses or shifts via ultrafiltration, fluid restrictions, altered coagulation, disconnection of shun
risk for excess Fluid volume: risk factors may include rapid or excessive fluid intake—IV, blood, plasma expanders, saline given to support BP during procedure
ineffective Protection may be related to chronic disease state, drug therapy, abnormal blood profile, inadequate nutrition, possibly evidenced by altered clotting, impaired healing, deficient immunity, fatigue, anorexia.

hemophilia
risk for deficient Fluid Volume [isotonic]: risk factors may include impaired coagulation/hemorrhagic losses.

risk for acute/chronic Pain: risk factors may include nerve compression from hematomas, nerve damage or hemorrhage into joint space.

risk for impaired physical Mobility: risk factors may include joint hemorrhage, swelling, degenerative changes, and muscle atrophy.

ineffective Protection may be related to abnormal blood profile, possibly evidenced by altered clotting.

compromised family Coping may be related to prolonged nature of condition that exhausts the supportive capacity of significant person(s), possibly evidenced by protective behaviors disproportionate to patient's abilities/need for autonomy.

hemorrhoidectomy

acute Pain may be related to edema/swelling and tissue trauma, possibly evidenced by verbal reports, guarding/distraction behaviors, focus on self, and autonomic responses (changes in vital signs).

risk for Urinary Retention: risk factors may include perineal trauma, edema/swelling, and pain.

deficient Knowledge [Learning Need] regarding therapeutic treatment and potential complications may be related to lack of information/misconceptions, possibly evidenced by statements of concern and questions.

hemorrhoids

acute Pain may be related to inflammation and edema of prolapsed varices, possibly evidenced by verbal reports, and guarding/distraction behaviors.

Constipation may be related to pain on defecation and reluctance to defecate, possibly evidenced by frequency, less than usual pattern and hard, formed stools.

hemothorax

(also refer to *pneumothorax*)

risk for Trauma/Suffocation: risk factors may include concurrent disease/injury process, dependence on external device (chest drainage system), and lack of safety education/precautions.

Anxiety [specify level] may be related to change in health status and threat of death, possibly evidenced by increased tension, restlessness, expressed concern, sympathetic stimulation, and focus on self.

hepatitis, acute viral

impaired Liver Function related to viral infection as evidenced by jaundice, hepatic enlargement, abdominal pain, marked elevations in serum liver function tests.

Fatigue may be related to decreased metabolic energy production and altered body chemistry, possibly evidenced by reports of lack of energy/inability to maintain usual routines, decreased performance, and increased physical complaints.

imbalanced Nutrition: less than body requirements may be related to inability to ingest adequate nutrients (nausea, vomiting, anorexia); hypermetabolic state, altered absorption and metabolism, possibly evidenced by aversion to eating/lack of interest in food, altered taste sensation, observed lack of intake, and weight loss.

acute Pain/ impaired Comfort may be related to inflammation and swelling of the liver, arthralgias, urticarial eruptions, and pruritus, possibly evidenced by verbal reports, guarding or distraction behaviors, focus on self, and changes in vital signs.

risk for Infection: risk factors may include inadequate secondary defenses and immunosuppression, malnutrition, insufficient knowledge to avoid exposure to pathogens/spread to others.

risk for impaired Tissue Integrity: risk factors may include bile salt accumulation in the tissues.

risk for impaired Home Management: risk factors may include debilitating effects of disease process and inadequate support systems (family, financial, role model).

deficient Knowledge [Learning Need] regarding disease process/transmission, treatment needs, and future expectations may be related to lack of information/recall, misinterpretation, unfamiliarity with resources, possibly evidenced by questions, statements of concerns/misconceptions, inaccurate follow-through of instructions, and development of preventable complications.

hernia, hiatal

chronic Pain may be related to regurgitation of acidic gastric contents, possibly evidenced by verbal reports, facial grimacing, and focus on self.

deficient Knowledge [Learning Need] regarding pathophysiology, prevention of complications and self-care needs may be related to lack of information/misconceptions, possibly evidenced by statements of concern, questions, and recurrence of condition.

herniation of nucleus pulposus (ruptured intervertebral disk)

acute/chronic Pain may be related to nerve compression/irritation and muscle spasms, possibly evidenced by verbal reports, guarding/distraction behaviors, preoccupation with pain, self/narrowed focus, and autonomic responses (changes in vital signs when pain is acute), altered muscle tone/function, changes in eating/sleeping patterns and libido, physical/social withdrawal.

impaired physical Mobility may be related to pain (muscle spasms), therapeutic restrictions (e.g., bedrest, traction/braces), muscular impairment, and depression, possibly evidenced by reports of pain on movement, reluctance to attempt/difficulty with purposeful movement, decreased muscle strength, impaired coordination, and limited range of motion.

deficient Diversional Activity may be related to length of recuperation period and therapy restrictions, physical limitations, pain and depression, possibly evidenced by statements of boredom, disinterest, "nothing to do," and restlessness, irritability, withdrawal.

heroin withdrawal
acute Pain/ Impaired Comfort may be related to cessation of drug, muscle tremors/twitching, possibly evidenced by reports of muscle aches, hot or cold flashes, diaphoresis, lacrimation, rhinorrhea, drug cravings.

severe Anxiety may be related to CNS hyperactivity possibly evidenced by apprehension, pervasive anxious feelings, jittery, restlessness, weakness, insomnia, anorexia.

risk for ineffective Self-Health Management: risk factors may include protracted withdrawal, economic difficulties, family or social support deficits, perceived barriers or benefits.

herpes, herpes simplex
acute Pain may be related to presence of localized inflammation and open lesions, possibly evidenced by verbal reports, distraction behaviors, and restlessness.

risk for [secondary] Infection: risk factors may include broken/traumatized tissue, altered immune response, and untreated infection/treatment failure.

risk for ineffective Sexuality Patterns: risk factors may include lack of knowledge, values conflict, and/or fear of transmitting the disease.

herpes zoster (shingles)
acute Pain may be related to inflammation/local lesions along sensory nerve(s), possibly evidenced by verbal reports, guarding/distraction behaviors, narrowed focus, and autonomic responses (changes in vital signs).

deficient Knowledge [Learning Need] regarding pathophysiology, therapeutic needs, and potential complications may be related to lack of information/misinterpretation, possibly evidenced by statements of concern, questions, and misconceptions.

high altitude pulmonary edema (HAPE)
(also refer to *mountain sickness, acute*)
impaired Gas Exchange may be related to ventilation perfusion imbalance, alveolar-capillary membrane changes, altered oxygen supply possibly evidenced by dyspnea, confusion, cyanosis, tachycardia, abnormal ABGs.

excess Fluid Volume may be related to compromised regulatory mechanism possibly evidenced by shortness of breath, anxiety, edema, abnormal breath sounds, pulmonary congestion.

HIV Infection
(also refer to *AIDS*)
risk-prone Health Behavior may be related to life-threatening, stigmatizing condition or disease, assault to self-esteem, altered locus of control, inadequate support systems, possibly evidenced by verbalization of nonacceptance or denial of diagnosis, failure to take action that prevents health problems.

deficient Knowledge [Learning Need] regarding disease, prognosis, and treatment needs may be related to lack of exposure or recall, information misinterpretation, unfamiliarity with information resources, or cognitive limitation, possibly evidenced by statement of misconception, request for information, inappropriate or exaggerated behaviors (hostile, agitated, hysterical, apathetic), inaccurate follow-through of instructions, or development of preventable complications.

risk for ineffective Self-Health Management: risk factors may include complexity of healthcare system and access to care, economic difficulties; complexity of therapeutic regimen—confusing or difficult dosing schedule, duration of regimen; mistrust of regimen and/or healthcare personnel—client and provider interactions; health beliefs or cultural influences, perceived seriousness, susceptibility, or benefits of therapy; decisional conflicts, powerlessness.

risk for complicated Grieving: risk factors may include preloss psychological symptoms, predisposition for anxiety and feelings of inadequacy, frequency of major life events.

Hodgkin's disease
(also refer to *cancer*; *chemotherapy*)
Anxiety [specify level]/Fear may be related to threat to self-concept and threat of death, possibly evidenced by apprehension, insomnia, focus on self, and increased tension.

deficient Knowledge [Learning Need] regarding diagnosis, pathophysiology, treatment, and prognosis may be related to lack of information/misinterpretation, possibly evidenced by statements of concern, questions, and misconceptions.

acute Pain/ impaired Comfort may be related to manifestations of inflammatory response (fever, chills, night sweats) and pruritus, possibly evidenced by verbal reports, distraction behaviors, and focus on self.

risk for ineffective Breathing Pattern/Airway Clearance: risk factors may include tracheobronchial obstruction (enlarged mediastinal nodes and/or airway edema).

hospice/end of life care

acute/chronic Pain may be related to biological, physical, psychological agent possibly evidenced by verbal/coded report, changes in appetite/eating, sleep pattern; protective behavior, restlessness, irritability.

Activity Intolerance/Fatigue may be related to generalized weakness, bedrest/immobility, pain, imbalance between oxygen supply and demand possibly evidenced by inability to maintain usual routine, verbalized lack of desire/interest in activity, decreased performance, lethargy.

Grieving/death Anxiety may be related to anticipated loss of physiological well-being, change in body function, perceived threat of death or dying process, possibly evidenced by changes in communication pattern, denial of potential loss; choked feelings, anger, fear of loss of physical or mental abilities; negative death images or unpleasant thoughts about any event related to death or dying; anticipated pain related to dying; powerlessness over issues related to dying, worrying about impact of one's own death on SO(s), being the cause of other's grief and suffering, concerns of overworking the caregiver as terminal illness incapacitates.

compromised/disabled family Coping/Caregiver Role Strain may be related to prolonged disease/disability progression, temporary family disorganization and role changes, unrealistic expectations, inadequate or incorrect information or understanding by primary person, possibly evidenced by client expressing despair about family reactions or lack of involvement, history of poor relationship between caregiver and care receiver; altered caregiver health status; SO attempting assistive or supportive behaviors with less than satisfactory results, apprehension about future regarding caregiver's ability to provide care; SO describing preoccupation about personal reactions; displaying intolerance, abandonment, rejection; family behaviors that are detrimental to well-being

risk for Spiritual Distress: risk factors may include physical or psychological stress, energy-consuming anxiety; situational losses; blocks to self-love, low self-esteem, inability to forgive.

risk for moral Distress: risk factors may include conflict among decision makers, cultural conflicts, end-of-life decisions, loss of autonomy, physical distance of decision makers.

hydrocephalus

ineffective cerebral Tissue Perfusion may be related to decreased arterial/venous blood flow (compression of brain tissue), possibly evidenced by changes in mentation, restlessness, irritability, reports of headache, pupillary changes, and changes in vital signs.

disturbed visual Sensory/Perception may be related to pressure on sensory/motor nerves, possibly evidenced by reports of double vision, development of strabismus, nystagmus, pupillary changes, and optic atrophy.

risk for impaired physical Mobility: risk factors may include neuromuscular impairment, decreased muscle strength, and impaired coordination.

risk for decreased Adaptive Intracranial Capacity: risk factors may include brain injury, changes in perfusion pressure/intracranial pressure.

risk for Infection: risk factors may include invasive procedure/presence of shunt.

deficient Knowledge [Learning Need] regarding condition, prognosis, and long-term therapy needs/medical follow-up may be related to lack of information/misperceptions, possibly evidenced by questions, statements of concern, request for information, and inaccurate follow-through of instruction/development of preventable complications.

hyperactivity disorder

ineffective Impulse Control may be related to compunction, possibly evidenced by acting without thinking, temper outbursts.

defensive Coping may be related to mild neurological deficits, dysfunctional family system, abuse/neglect possibly evidenced by denial of obvious problems, projection of blame/responsibility, grandiosity, difficulty in reality testing perceptions.

impaired Social Interaction may be related to retarded ego development, negative role models, neurological impairment possibly evidenced by discomfort in social situations, interrupts/intrudes on others, difficulty waiting turn in games/group activities, difficulty maintaining attention to task.

disabled family Coping may be related to excessive guilt, anger, or blaming among family members, parental inconsistencies, disagreements regarding discipline/limit-setting/approaches, exhaustion of parental expectations possibly evidenced by unrealistic parental expectations, rejection or overprotection of child, exaggerated expression of feelings, despair regarding child's behavior.

hyperbilirubinemia

risk for Injury [CNS involvement]: risk factors may include prematurity, hemolytic disease, asphyxia, acidosis, hyponatremia, and hypoglycemia.

risk for Injury [effects of treatment]: risk factors may include physical properties of phototherapy and effects on body regulatory mechanisms, invasive procedure (exchange transfusion), abnormal blood profile, chemical imbalances.

deficient Knowledge [Learning Need] regarding condition, prognosis, treatment/safety needs may be related to lack of exposure/recall and information misinterpretation, possibly evidenced by questions, statement of concern, and inaccurate follow-through of instructions/development of preventable complications.

hyperemesis gravidarum

deficient Fluid Volume [isotonic] may be related to excessive gastric losses and reduced intake, possibly evidenced by dry mucous membranes, decreased/concentrated urine, decreased pulse volume and pressure, thirst, and hemoconcentration.

risk for Electrolyte Imbalance: risk factors may include vomiting, dehydration.

imbalanced Nutrition: less than body requirements may be related to inability to ingest/digest/absorb nutrients (prolonged vomiting), possibly evidenced by reported inadequate food intake, lack of interest in food/aversion to eating, and weight loss.

risk for ineffective Coping: risk factors may include situational/maturational crisis (pregnancy, change in health status, projected role changes, concern about outcome).

hypertension

deficient Knowledge [Learning Need] regarding condition, therapeutic regimen, and potential complications may be related to lack of information/recall, misinterpretation, cognitive limitations, and/or denial of diagnosis, possibly evidenced by statements of concern/questions, and misconceptions, inaccurate follow-through of instructions, and lack of BP control.

risk-prone health Behavior may be related to condition requiring change in lifestyle, altered locus of control, and absence of feelings/denial of illness, possibly evidenced by verbalization of nonacceptance of health status change and lack of movement toward independence.

risk for Activity Intolerance: risk factors may include generalized weakness, imbalance between oxygen supply and demand.

risk for Sexual Dysfunction : risk factors may include side effects of medication.

risk for decreased Cardiac Output: risk factors may include increased afterload (vasoconstriction), fluid shifts/hypovolemia, myocardial ischemia, ventricular hypertrophy/rigidity.

acute Pain may be related to increased cerebrovascular pressure, possibly evidenced by verbal reports (throbbing pain located in suboccipital region, present on awakening and disappearing spontaneously after being up and about), reluctance to move head, avoidance of bright lights and noise, or increased muscle tension.

hypertension, pulmonary
Refer to *pulmonary hypertension*.

hyperthyroidism
(also refer to *thyrotoxicosis*)

Fatigue may be related to hypermetabolic imbalance with increased energy requirements, irritability of CNS, and altered body chemistry, possibly evidenced by verbalization of overwhelming lack of energy to maintain usual routine, decreased performance, emotional lability/irritability, and impaired ability to concentrate.

Anxiety [specify level] may be related to increased stimulation of the CNS (hypermetabolic state, pseudocatecholamine effect of thyroid hormones), possibly evidenced by increased feelings of apprehension, overexcited/distressed, irritability/emotional lability, shakiness, restless movements, or tremors.

risk for imbalanced Nutrition: less than body requirements: risk factors may include inability to ingest adequate nutrients for hypermetabolic rate/constant activity, impaired absorption of nutrients (vomiting/diarrhea), hyperglycemia/ relative insulin insufficiency.

risk for impaired Tissue Integrity: risk factors may include altered protective mechanisms of eye related to periorbital edema, reduced ability to blink, eye discomfort/dryness, and development of corneal abrasion/ulceration.

hypoglycemia

acute Confusion may be related to inadequate glucose for cellular brain function and effects of endogenous hormone activity, possibly evidenced by increased restlessness, misperceptions, fluctuation in cognition/level of consciousness.

risk for unstable blood Glucose: risk factors may include dietary intake, lack of adherence to diabetes management, inadequate blood glucose monitoring, medication management.

deficient Knowledge [Learning Need] regarding pathophysiology of condition and therapy/self-care needs may be related to lack of information/recall, misinterpretations, possibly evidenced by development of hypoglycemia and statements of questions/misconceptions.

hypoparathyroidism (acute)

risk for Injury: risk factors may include neuromuscular excitability/tetany and formation of renal stones.

acute Pain may be related to recurrent muscle spasms and alteration in reflexes, possibly evidenced by verbal reports, distraction behaviors, and narrowed focus.

risk for ineffective Airway Clearance: risk factors may include spasm of the laryngeal muscles.

Anxiety [specify level] may be related to threat to, or change in, health status, physiological responses.

hypothermia (systemic)

(also refer to *frostbite*)

Hypothermia may be related to exposure to cold environment, inadequate clothing, age extremes (very young/elderly), damage to hypothalamus, consumption of alcohol/medications causing vasodilation, possibly evidenced by reduction in body temperature below normal range, shivering, cool skin, pallor.

deficient Knowledge [Learning Need] regarding risk factors, treatment needs, and prognosis may be related to lack of information/recall, misinterpretation, possibly evidenced by statements of concerns/misconceptions, occurrence of problem, and development of complications.

hypothyroidism

(also refer to *myxedema*)

impaired physical Mobility may be related to weakness, fatigue, muscle aches, altered reflexes, and mucin deposits in joints and interstitial spaces, possibly evidenced by decreased muscle strength/control and impaired coordination.

Fatigue may be related to decreased metabolic energy production, possibly evidenced by verbalization of unremitting/overwhelming lack of energy, inability to maintain usual routines, impaired ability to concentrate, decreased libido, irritability, listlessness, decreased performance, increase in physical complaints.

disturbed Sensory/Perception (specify) may be related to mucin deposits and nerve compression, possibly evidenced by paresthesias of hands and feet or decreased hearing.

Constipation may be related to decreased peristalsis/physical activity, possibly evidenced by frequency less than usual pattern, decreased bowel sounds, hard dry stools, and development of fecal impaction.

hysterectomy

acute Pain may be related to tissue trauma/abdominal incision, edema/hematoma formation, possibly evidenced by verbal reports, guarding/distraction behaviors, and autonomic responses (changes in vital signs).

impaired Urinary Elimination /[acute] Urinary Retention: risk factors may include mechanical trauma, surgical manipulation, presence of localized edema/hematoma, or nerve trauma with temporary bladder atony.

risk for Sexual Dysfunction: risk factors may include concerns regarding altered body function/structure, perceived changes in femininity, changes in hormone levels, loss of libido, and changes in sexual response pattern.

risk for complicated Grieving risk factors may include preloss psychological symptoms, predisposition for anxiety and feelings of inadequacy, frequency of major life events.

ileocolitis

Refer to *Crohn's disease*.

ileostomy

Refer to *colostomy*.

ileus

acute Pain may be related to distention/edema and ischemia of intestinal tissue, possibly evidenced by verbal reports, guarding/distraction behaviors, narrowed focus, and autonomic responses (changes in vital signs).

Diarrhea/Constipation may be related to presence of obstruction/changes in peristalsis, possibly evidenced by changes in frequency and consistency or absence of stool, alterations in bowel sounds, presence of pain, and cramping.

risk for deficient Fluid Volume: risk factors may include increased intestinal losses (vomiting and diarrhea) and decreased intake.

impetigo

impaired Skin Integrity may be related to presence of infectious process and pruritus, possibly evidenced by open/crusted lesions.

acute Pain may be related to inflammation and pruritus, possibly evidenced by verbal reports, distraction behaviors, and self-focusing.

risk for [secondary] Infection: risk factors may include broken skin, traumatized tissue, altered immune response, and virulence/contagious nature of causative organism.

risk for Infection [transmission]: risk factors may include virulent nature of causative organism, insufficient knowledge to prevent infection of others.

infection, prenatal
(also refer to AIDS)

risk for maternal/fetal Infection: risk factors may include inadequate primary defenses (e.g., broken skin, stasis of body fluids), inadequate secondary defenses (e.g., decreased hemoglobin, immunosuppression), inadequate acquired immunity, environmental exposure, malnutrition, rupture of amniotic membranes.

deficient Knowledge regarding treatment/prevention, prognosis of condition may be related to lack of exposure to information and/or unfamiliarity with resources, misinterpretation possibly evidenced by verbalization of problem, inaccurate follow-through of instructions, development of preventable complications/continuation of infectious process.

impaired Comfort may be related to body response to infective agent, properties of infection (e.g., skin or tissue irritation, development of lesions), possibly evidenced by verbal reports, restlessness, withdrawal from social contacts.

infection, wound

risk for Infection [sepsis]: risk factors may include presence of infection, broken skin, traumatized tissues, chronic disease (e.g., diabetes, anemia), stasis of body fluids, invasive procedures, altered immune response.

impaired Skin/Tissue Integrity may be related to altered circulation, presence of infection, wound drainage, nutritional deficit, possibly evidenced by delayed healing, damaged tissues, invasion of body structures.

risk for delayed Surgical Recovery: risk factors may include presence of infection, activity restrictions or limitations, nutritional deficiencies.

inflammatory bowel disease
Refer to *colitis, ulcerative*; *Crohn's disease*

infertility

situational low Self-Esteem may be related to functional impairment (inability to conceive), unrealistic self-expectations, sense of failure possibly evidenced by self-negating verbalizations, expressions of helplessness, perceived inability to deal with situation.

chronic Sorrow may be related to perceived physical disability (inability to conceive) possibly evidenced by expressions of anger, disappointment, emptiness, self-blame, helplessness, sadness, feelings interfering with client's ability to achieve maximum well-being.

risk for Spiritual Distress: risk factors may include energy-consuming anxiety, low self-esteem, deteriorating relationship with SO, viewing situation as deserved or punishment for past behaviors.

influenza

Pain [Discomfort] may be related to inflammation and effects of circulating toxins, possibly evidenced by verbal reports, distraction behaviors, and narrowed focus.

risk for deficient Fluid Volume: risk factors may include excessive gastric losses, hypermetabolic state, and altered intake.

Hyperthermia may be related to effects of circulating toxins and dehydration, possibly evidenced by increased body temperature, warm/flushed skin, and tachycardia.

risk for ineffective Breathing: risk factors may include response to infectious process, decreased energy/fatigue.

insulin shock
Refer to *hypoglycemia*.

intestinal obstruction
Refer to *ileus*.

irritable bowel syndrome

acute Pain may be related to abnormally strong intestinal contractions, increased sensitivity of intestine to distention, hypersensitivity to hormones gastrin and cholecystokinin, skin/tissue irritation/perirectal excoriation possibly evidenced by verbal reports, guarding behavior, expressive behavior (restlessness, moaning, irritability).

Constipation may be related to motor abnormalities of longitudinal muscles/changes in frequency and amplitude of contractions, dietary restrictions, stress possibly evidenced by change in bowel pattern/decreased frequency, sensation of incomplete evacuation, abdominal pain/distention.

Diarrhea may be related to motor abnormalities of longitudinal muscles/changes in frequency and amplitude of contractions possibly evidenced by precipitous passing of liquid stool on rising or immediately after eating, rectal urgency/incontinence, bloating.

Kawasaki disease

Hyperthermia may be related to increased metabolic rate and dehydration, possibly evidenced by increased body temperature greater than normal range, flushed skin, increased respiratory rate, and tachycardia.

acute Pain may be related to inflammation and edema/swelling of tissues, possibly evidenced by verbal reports, restlessness, guarding behaviors, and narrowed focus.

impaired Skin Integrity may be related to inflammatory process, altered circulation, and edema formation, possibly evidenced by disruption of skin surface including macular rash and desquamation.

impaired Oral Mucous Membranes may be related to inflammatory process, dehydration, and mouth breathing, possibly evidenced by pain, hyperemia, and fissures of lips.

risk for decreased Cardiac Output: risk factors may include structural changes/inflammation of coronary arteries and alterations in rate/rhythm or conduction.

kidney stone(s)
Refer to *calculi, urinary*.

labor, induced/augmented

deficient Knowledge [Learning Need] regarding procedure, treatment needs, and possible outcomes may be related to lack of exposure/recall, information misinterpretation, and unfamiliarity with information resources, possibly evidenced by questions, statements of concern/misconception, and exaggerated behaviors.

risk for maternal Injury: risk factors may include adverse effects/response to therapeutic interventions.

risk for impaired fetal Gas Exchange: risk factors may include altered placental perfusion/cord prolapse.

acute Pain may be related to altered characteristics of chemically stimulated contractions, psychological concerns, possibly evidenced by verbal reports, increased muscle tone, distraction/guarding behaviors, and narrowed focus.

labor, precipitous

Anxiety [specify level] may be related to situational crisis, threat to self/fetus, interpersonal transmission possibly evidenced by increased tension; scared, fearful, restless/jittery; sympathetic stimulation.

risk for impaired Skin/Tissue Integrity: risk factors may include rapid progress of labor, lack of necessary equipment.

acute Pain may be related to occurrence of rapid, strong muscle contractions; psychological issues possibly evidenced by verbalizations of inability to use learned pain-management techniques, sympathetic stimulation, distraction behaviors (e.g., moaning, restlessness).

labor, preterm

Activity Intolerance may be related to muscle/cellular hypersensitivity, possibly evidenced by continued uterine contractions/irritability.

risk for Poisoning: risk factors may include dose-related toxic/side effects of tocolytics.

risk for fetal Injury: risk factors may include delivery of premature/immature infant.

Anxiety [specify level] may be related to situational crisis, perceived or actual threats to self/fetus and inadequate time to prepare for labor, possibly evidenced by increased tension, restlessness, expressions of concern, and autonomic responses (changes in vital signs).

deficient Knowledge [Learning Need] regarding preterm labor treatment needs and prognosis may be related to lack of information and misinterpretation, possibly evidenced by questions, statements of concern, misconceptions, inaccurate follow-through of instruction, and development of preventable complications.

labor, stage I (active phase)

acute Pain/[Discomfort] may be related to contraction-related hypoxia, dilation of tissues, and pressure on adjacent structures, combined with stimulation of both parasympathetic and sympathetic nerve endings, possibly evidenced by verbal reports, guarding/distraction behaviors (restlessness), muscle tension, and narrowed focus.

impaired Urinary Elimination may be related to altered intake/dehydration, fluid shifts, hormonal changes, hemorrhage, severe intrapartal hypertension, mechanical compression of bladder, and effects of regional anesthesia, possibly evidenced by changes in amount/frequency of voiding, urinary retention, slowed progression of labor, and reduced sensation.

risk for ineffective Coping, [Individual/Couple]: risk factors may include situational crises, personal vulnerability, use of ineffective coping mechanisms, inadequate support systems, and pain.

labor, stage II (expulsion)

acute Pain may be related to strong uterine contractions, tissue stretching/dilation, and compression of nerves by presenting part of the fetus, and bladder distention, possibly evidenced by verbalizations, facial grimacing, guarding/distraction behaviors (restlessness), narrowed focus, and autonomic responses (diaphoresis).

Cardiac Output [fluctuation] may be related to changes in SVR, fluctuations in venous return (repeated/prolonged Valsalva's maneuvers, effects of anesthesia/medications, dorsal recumbent position occluding the inferior vena cava and partially obstructing the aorta, possibly evidenced by decreased venous return, changes in vital signs (BP, pulse), urinary output, or fetal bradycardia.

risk for impaired fetal Gas Exchange: risk factors may include mechanical compression of head/cord, maternal position/prolonged labor affecting placental perfusion, and effects of maternal anesthesia, hyperventilation.

risk for impaired Skin/Tissue Integrity: risk factors may include untoward stretching/lacerations of delicate tissues (precipitous labor, hypertonic contractile pattern, adolescence, large fetus) and application of forceps.

risk for Fatigue: risk factors may include pregnancy, stress, anxiety, sleep deprivation, increased physical exertion, anemia, humidity/temperature, lights.

laminectomy, cervical

also refer to *laminectomy, lumbar*

risk for Perioperative-Positioning Injury: risk factors may include immobilization, muscle weakness, obesity, advanced age.

risk for ineffective Airway Clearance: risk factors may include retained secretions, pain, muscle weakness

risk for impaired Swallowing: risk factors may incluse operative edema, pain, neuromuscular impairment.

laminectomy, lumbar (lumbar)

ineffective Tissue Perfusion (specify): may be related to diminished/interrupted blood flow (dressing, edema/hematoma formation), hypovolemia, possibly evidenced by paresthesia, numbness; decreased range of motion, muscle strength.

risk for [spinal] Trauma: risk factors may include temporary weakness of spinal column, balancing difficulties, changes in muscle tone/coordination.

acute Pain may be related to traumatized tissues, localized inflammation, and edema, possibly evidenced by altered muscle tone, verbal reports, and distraction/guarding behaviors, autonomic changes.

impaired physical Mobility may be related to imposed therapeutic restrictions, neuromuscular impairment, and pain, possibly evidenced by limited range of motion, decreased muscle strength/control, impaired coordination, and reluctance to attempt movement.

risk for [acute] Urinary Retention: risk factors may include pain and swelling in operative area and reduced mobility/restrictions of position.

laryngectomy

(also refer to *cancer; chemotherapy*)

ineffective Airway Clearance may be related to partial/total removal of the glottis, temporary or permanent change to neck breathing, edema formation, and copious/thick secretions, possibly evidenced by dyspnea/difficulty breathing, changes in rate/depth of respiration, use of accessory respiratory muscles, weak/ineffective cough, abnormal breath sounds, and cyanosis.

impaired Skin/Tissue Integrity may be related to surgical removal of tissues/grafting, effects of radiation or chemotherapeutic agents, altered circulation/reduced blood supply, compromised nutritional status, edema formation, and pooling/continuous drainage of secretions, possibly evidenced by disruption of skin/tissue surface and destruction of skin/tissue layers.

impaired Oral Mucous Membrane may be related to dehydration/absence of oral intake, poor/inadequate oral hygiene, pathological condition (oral cancer), mechanical trauma (oral surgery), decreased saliva production, difficulty swallowing and pooling/drooling of secretions, and nutritional deficits, possibly evidenced by xerostomia (dry mouth), oral discomfort, thick/mucoid saliva, decreased saliva production, dry and crusted/coated tongue, inflamed lips, absent teeth/gums, poor dental health, and halitosis.

impaired verbal Communication may be related to anatomic deficit (removal of vocal cords), physical barrier (tracheostomy tube), and required voice rest, possibly evidenced by inability to speak, change in vocal characteristics, and impaired articulation.

risk for Aspiration: risk factors include impaired swallowing, facial/neck surgery, presence of tracheostomy/feeding tube.

laryngitis
Refer to *croup*.

latex allergy
latex Allergy Response may be related to no immune mechanism response possibly evidenced by contact dermatitis – erythema, blisters; delayed hypersensitivity – eczema, irritation; hypersensitivity – generalized edema, wheezing/bronchospasm, hypotension, cardiac arrest.

Anxiety [specify level]/Fear may be related to threat of death possibly evidenced by expressed concerns, hypervigilance, restlessness, focus on self.

risk for risk-prone health Behavior: risk factors may include health status requiring change in occupation.

lead poisoning, acute
(also refer to *lead poisoning, chronic*)
Contamination may be related to flaking/peeling paint (young children), improperly lead-glazed ceramic pottery, unprotected contact with lead (e.g., battery manufacture/recycling, bronzing, soldering/welding), imported herbal products/medicinals possibly evidenced by abdominal cramping, headache, irritability, decreased attentiveness, constipation, tremors.

risk for Trauma: risk factors may include loss of coordination, altered level of consciousness, clonic or tonic muscle activity, neurologic damage.

risk for deficient Fluid Volume: risk factors may include excessive vomiting, diarrhea, or decreased intake.

deficient Knowledge [Learning Need] regarding sources of lead and prevention of poisoning may be related to lack of information/misinterpretation, possibly evidenced by statements of concern, questions, and misconceptions.

lead poisoning, chronic
(also refer to *lead poisoning, acute*)
Contamination may be related to flaking/peeling paint (young children), improperly lead-glazed ceramic pottery, unprotected contact with lead (e.g., battery manufacture/recycling, bronzing, soldering/welding), imported herbal products/medicinals possibly evidenced by chronic abdominal pain, headache, personality changes, cognitive deficits, seizures, neuropathy.

imbalanced Nutrition: less than body requirements may be related to decreased intake (chemically induced changes in the gastrointestinal tract), possibly evidenced by anorexia, abdominal discomfort, reported metallic taste, and weight loss.

chronic Pain may be related to deposition of lead in soft tissues and bone, possibly evidenced by verbal reports, distraction behaviors, and focus on self.

risk for delayed Development/disproportionate Growth: risk factors may include lead poisoning.

leukemia, acute
(also refer to *chemotherapy*)
risk for Infection: risk factors may include inadequate secondary defenses (alterations in mature white blood cells, increased number of immature lymphocytes, immunosuppression and bone marrow suppression), invasive procedures, and malnutrition.

Anxiety [specify level]/Fear may be related to change in health status, threat of death, and situational crisis, possibly evidenced by sympathetic stimulation, apprehension, feelings of helplessness, focus on self, and insomnia.

Activity Intolerance [specify level] may be related to reduced energy stores, increased metabolic rate, imbalance between oxygen supply and demand, or therapeutic restrictions (bedrest)/effect of drug therapy, possibly evidenced by generalized weakness, reports of fatigue and exertional dyspnea; abnormal heart rate or BP response.

acute Pain may be related to physical agents (infiltration of tissues/organs/CNS, expanding bone marrow) and chemical agents (antileukemic treatments), possibly evidenced by verbal reports (abdominal discomfort, arthralgia, bone pain, headache); distraction behaviors, narrowed focus, and autonomic responses (changes in vital signs).

risk for deficient Fluid Volume/Bleeding: risk factors may include excessive losses (vomiting, diarrhea, coagulopathy), decreased intake (nausea, anorexia), increased fluid need (hypermetabolic state/fever), predisposition for kidney stone formation, tumor lysis syndrome.

leukemia, chronic
(also refer to *chemotherapy*)
risk for Infection: risk factors may include inadequate secondary defenses (alterations in mature WBCs, increased number of immature lymphocytes, immunosuppression, and bone marrow suppression), invasive procedures, and risk factors may include malnutrition.
ineffective Protection may be related to abnormal blood profiles, drug therapy—cytotoxic agents, steroids; radiation treatments possibly evidenced by deficient immunity, impaired healing, altered clotting, weakness.
Fatigue may be related to disease state, anemia possibly evidenced by verbalizations, inability to maintain usual routines, listlessness
imbalanced Nutrition: less than body requirements may be related to inability to ingest nutrients possibly evidenced by lack of interest in food, anorexia, weight loss, abdominal fullness, pain.

long-term care
(also refer to condition requiring/contributing to need to facility placement.)
Anxiety [specify level]/Fear may be related to change in health status, role functioning, interaction patterns, socioeconomic status, environment; unmet needs, recent life changes, and loss of friends/Significant other(s), possibly evidenced by apprehension, restlessness, insomnia, repetitive questioning, pacing, purposeless activity, expressed concern regarding changes in life events, and focus on self.
Grieving may be related to perceived/actual or potential loss of physiopsychosocial well-being, personal possessions and significant other(s); as well as cultural beliefs about aging/debilitation, possibly evidenced by denial of feelings, depression, sorrow, guilt; alterations in activity level, sleep patterns, eating habits, and libido.
risk for Poisoning [drug toxicity]: risk factors may include effects of aging (reduced metabolism, impaired circulation, precarious physiological balance, presence of multiple diseases/organ involvement) and use of multiple prescribed/OTC drugs.
impaired Memory may be related to neurological disturbances, hypoxia, fluid imbalance possibly evidenced by inability to recall events/factual information, reports experience of forgetting.
Insomnia may be related to internal factors (illness, psychological stress, inactivity) and external factors (environmental changes, facility routines), possibly evidenced by reports of difficulty in falling asleep/not feeling rested, interrupted sleep/awakening earlier than desired; change in behavior/performance, increasing irritability, and listlessness.
risk for Sexual Dysfunction: risk factors may include biopsychosocial alteration of sexuality, interference in psychological/physical well-being, self-image, and lack of privacy/Significant other(s).
risk for Relocation Stress Syndrome: risk factors may include temporary or permanent move that may be voluntary or involuntary, lack of predeparture counseling, multiple losses, feeling of powerlessness, lack of or inappropriate use of support system, changes in psychosocial or physical health status.
risk for impaired Religiosity: risk factors may include life transition, ineffective support or coping, lack of social interaction, depression.

lupus erythematosus, systemic (SLE)
Fatigue may be related to inadequate energy production/increased energy requirements (chronic inflammation), overwhelming psychological or emotional demands, states of discomfort, and altered body chemistry (including effects of drug therapy), possibly evidenced by reports of unremitting and overwhelming lack of energy/inability to maintain usual routines, decreased performance, lethargy, and decreased libido.
acute Pain may be related to widespread inflammatory process affecting connective tissues, blood vessels, serosal surfaces, and mucous membranes, possibly evidenced by verbal reports, guarding/distraction behaviors, self-focusing, and autonomic responses (changes in vital signs).
impaired Skin/Tissue integrity may be related to chronic inflammation, edema formation, and altered circulation, possibly evidenced by presence of skin rash/lesions, ulcerations of mucous membranes, and photosensitivity.
disturbed Body Image may be related to presence of chronic condition with rash, lesions, ulcers, purpura, mottled erythema of hands, alopecia, loss of strength, and altered body function, possibly evidenced by hiding body parts, negative feelings about body, feelings of helplessness, and change in social involvement.

Lyme disease
acute/chronic Pain may be related to systemic effects of toxins, presence of rash, urticaria, and joint swelling/inflammation, possibly evidenced by verbal reports, guarding behavior, autonomic responses, and narrowed focus.

Fatigue may be related to increased energy requirements, altered body chemistry, and states of discomfort evidenced by reports of overwhelming lack of energy/inability to maintain usual routines, decreased performance, lethargy, and malaise.

risk for decreased Cardiac Output risk factors may include alteration in rate/rhythm/ conduction.

macular degeneration

disturbed visual Sensory Perception may be related to altered sensory reception possibly evidenced by reported/measured change in sensory acuity, change in usual response to stimuli.

Anxiety [specify level]/Fear may be related to situational crisis, threat to or change in health status and role function possibly evidenced by expressed concerns, apprehension, feelings of inadequacy, diminished productivity, impaired attention.

risk for impaired Home Maintenance: risk factors may include impaired cognitive functioning, inadequate support systems.

risk for impaired Social Interaction: risk factors may include limited physical mobility, environmental barriers.

Mallory-Weiss syndrome

risk for deficient Fluid Volume: risk factors may include excessive vascular losses, presence of vomiting, and reduced intake.

deficient Knowledge [Learning Need] regarding causes, treatment, and prevention of condition may be related to lack of information/misinterpretation, possibly evidenced by statements of concern, questions, and recurrence of problem.

mastectomy

impaired Skin/Tissue Integrity may be related to surgical removal of skin/tissue, altered circulation, drainage, presence of edema, changes in skin elasticity/sensation, and tissue destruction (radiation), possibly evidenced by disruption of skin surface and destruction of skin layers/subcutaneous tissues.

impaired physical Mobility may be related to neuromuscular impairment, pain, and edema formation, possibly evidenced by reluctance to attempt movement, limited range of motion, and decreased muscle mass/strength.

bathing/dressing Self-Care deficit may be related to temporary loss/altered action of one or both arms, possibly evidenced by statements of inability to perform/complete self-care tasks.

disturbed Body Image//situational low Self-Esteem may be related to loss of body part denoting femininity, fear of rejection or reaction of others, behaviors inconsistent with self-value system possibly evidenced by not looking at or touching area, self-negating verbalizations, preoccupation with loss, and change in social involvement or relationship.

risk for complicated Grieving: risk factors may include preloss psychological symptoms, predisposition for anxiety and feelings of inadequacy, frequency of major life events.

mastitis

acute Pain may be related to erythema and edema of breast tissues, possibly evidenced by verbal reports, guarding/distraction behaviors, self-focusing, autonomic responses (changes in vital signs).

risk for Infection [spread/abscess formation]: risk factors may include traumatized tissues, stasis of fluids, and insufficient knowledge to prevent complications.

deficient Knowledge [Learning Need] regarding pathophysiology, treatment, and prevention may be related to lack of information/misinterpretation, possibly evidenced by statements of concern, questions, and misconceptions.

risk for ineffective Breastfeeding: risk factors may include inability to feed on affected side/interruption in breastfeeding.

mastoidectomy

risk for Infection [spread]: risk factors may include preexisting infection, surgical trauma, and stasis of body fluids in close proximity to brain.

acute Pain may be related to inflammation, tissue trauma, and edema formation, possibly evidenced by verbal reports, distraction behaviors, restlessness, self-focusing, and autonomic responses (changes in vital signs).

disturbed auditory Sensory Perception may be related to presence of surgical packing, edema, and surgical disturbance of middle ear structures, possibly evidenced by reported/tested hearing loss in affected ear.

measles

acute Pain may be related to inflammation of mucous membranes, conjunctiva, and presence of extensive skin rash with pruritus, possibly evidenced by verbal reports, distraction behaviors, self-focusing, and autonomic responses (changes in vital signs).

Hyperthermia may be related to presence of viral toxins and inflammatory response, possibly evidenced by increased body temperature, flushed/warm skin, and tachycardia.

risk for [secondary] Infection: risk factors may include altered immune response and traumatized dermal tissues.

deficient Knowledge [Learning Need] regarding condition, transmission, and possible complications may be related to lack of information/misinterpretation, possibly evidenced by statements of concern, questions, misconceptions, and development of preventable complications.

melanoma, malignant
Refer to *cancer; chemotherapy*.

meningitis, acute meningococcal
risk for Infection [spread]: risk factors may include hematogenous dissemination of pathogen, stasis of body fluids, suppressed inflammatory response (medication-induced), and exposure of others to pathogens.

risk for ineffective cerebral Tissue Perfusion: risk factors may include cerebral edema altering/interrupting cerebral arterial/venous blood flow, hypovolemia, exchange problems at cellular level (acidosis).

Hyperthermia may be related to infectious process (increased metabolic rate) and dehydration, possibly evidenced by increased body temperature, warm/flushed skin, and tachycardia.

acute Pain may be related to inflammation/irritation of the meninges with spasm of extensor muscles (neck, shoulders, and back), possibly evidenced by verbal reports, guarding/distraction behaviors, narrowed focus, and autonomic responses (changes in vital signs).

risk for Trauma/Suffocation: risk factors may include alterations in level of consciousness, possible development of clonic/tonic muscle activity (seizures), and generalized weakness/prostration, ataxia, vertigo.

meniscectomy
impaired Walking may be related to pain, joint instability, and imposed medical restrictions of movement, possibly evidenced by impaired ability to move about environment as needed/desired.

deficient Knowledge [Learning Need] regarding postoperative expectations, prevention of complications, and self-care needs may be related to lack of information, possibly evidenced by statements of concern, questions, and misconceptions.

menopause
ineffective Thermoregulation may be related to fluctuation of hormonal levels possibly evidenced by skin flushed/warm to touch, diaphoresis, night sweats; cold hands/feet.

Fatigue may be related to change in body chemistry, lack of sleep, depression possibly evidenced by reports of lack of energy, tired, inability to maintain usual routines, decreased performance.

risk for ineffective Sexuality Pattern: risk factors may include perceived altered body function, changes in physical response, myths/inaccurate information, impaired relationship with significant other.

risk for stress Urinary Incontinence risk factors may include degenerative changes in pelvic muscles and structural support.

readiness for enhanced Self-Health Management: possibly evidenced by expressed desire for management of life cycle changes, increased control of health practice.

mental delay (formerly mental retardation)
(also refer to *Down syndrome*)
impaired verbal Communication may be related to developmental delay/impairment of cognitive and motor abilities, possibly evidenced by impaired articulation, difficulty with phonation, and inability to modulate speech/find appropriate words (dependent on degree of retardation).

risk for Self-Care Deficit [specify]: risk factors may include impaired cognitive ability and motor skills.

risk for imbalanced Nutrition: risk for more than body requirements: risk factors may include decreased metabolic rate coupled with impaired cognitive development, dysfunctional eating patterns, and sedentary activity level.

risk for sedentary Lifestyle: risk factors may include lack of interest/motivation, resources; lack of training or knowledge of specific exercise needs, safety concerns/fear of injury.

impaired Social Interaction may be related to impaired thought processes, communication barriers, and knowledge/skill deficit about ways to enhance mutuality, possibly evidenced by dysfunctional interactions with peers, family, and/or significant other(s), and verbalized/observed discomfort in social situation.

compromised family Coping may be related to chronic nature of condition and degree of disability that exhausts supportive capacity of significant other(s), other situational or developmental crises or situations the significant other(s) may be facing, unrealistic expectations of significant other(s), possibly evidenced by preoccupation of significant other with personal reaction, significant other withdraws or enters into limited interaction with individual, protective behavior disproportionate (too much or too little) to patient's abilities or need for autonomy.

impaired Home Maintenance may be related to impaired cognitive functioning, insufficient finances/family organization or planning, lack of knowledge, and inadequate support systems, possibly evidenced by requests for assistance, expression of difficulty in maintaining home, disorderly surroundings, and overtaxed family members.

risk for Sexual Dysfunction : risk factors may include biopsychosocial alteration of sexuality, ineffectual/absent role models, misinformation/lack of knowledge, lack of significant other(s), and lack of appropriate behavior control.

Metabolic syndrome

risk for unstable Blood Glucose Level: risk factors may include dietary intake, weight gain, physical activity level.

sedentary Lifestyle may be related to deficient knowledge of health benefits of physical exercise, lack of interest/motivation or resources; possibly evidenced by verbalized preference for activities low in physical activity, choice of a daily routine lacking physical exercise.

compromised family Coping may be related to chronic nature of condition and degree of disability that exhausts supportive capacity of SO(s), other situational or developmental crises or situations SO(s) may be facing, unrealistic expectations of SO(s), possibly evidenced by preoccupation of SO with personal reaction, SO(s) withdraw(s) or enter(s) into limited interaction with individual, protective behavior disproportionate (too much or too little) to client's abilities or need for autonomy.

impaired Home Maintenance may be related to impaired cognitive functioning, insufficient finances and family organization or planning, lack of knowledge, and inadequate support systems, possibly evidenced by requests for assistance, expression of difficulty in maintaining home, disorderly surroundings, and overtaxed family members.

risk for ineffective tissue Perfusion (specify): risk factors may include arterial plaque formation (elevated triglycerides, low levels of HDL), prothrombotic state, proinflammatory state.

miscarriage
Refer to *abortion, spontaneous termination*.

mitral stenosis

Activity Intolerance may be related to imbalance between oxygen supply and demand, possibly evidenced by reports of fatigue, weakness, exertional dyspnea, and tachycardia.

impaired Gas Exchange may be related to altered blood flow, possibly evidenced by restlessness, hypoxia, and cyanosis (orthopnea/paroxysmal nocturnal dyspnea).

decreased Cardiac Output may be related to impeded blood flow as evidenced by jugular vein distention, peripheral/dependent edema, orthopnea/paroxysmal nocturnal dyspnea.

deficient Knowledge [Learning Need] regarding pathophysiology, therapeutic needs, and potential complications may be related to lack of information/recall, misinterpretation, possibly evidenced by statements of concern, questions, inaccurate follow-through of instructions, and development of preventable complications.

mononucleosis, infectious

Fatigue may be related to decreased energy production, states of discomfort, and increased energy requirements (inflammatory process), possibly evidenced by reports of overwhelming lack of energy, inability to maintain usual routines, lethargy, and malaise.

acute Pain/[Discomfort] may be related to inflammation of lymphoid and organ tissues, irritation of oropharyngeal mucous membranes, and effects of circulating toxins, possibly evidenced by verbal reports, distraction behaviors, and self-focusing.

Hyperthermia may be related to inflammatory process, possibly evidenced by increased body temperature, warm/flushed skin, and tachycardia.

deficient Knowledge [Learning Need] regarding disease transmission, self-care needs, medical therapy, and potential complications may be related to lack of information/misinterpretation, possibly evidenced by statements of concern, misconceptions, and inaccurate follow-through of instructions.

mood disorders
Refer to *depressive disorders*.

mountain sickness, acute (AMS)
acute Pain may be related to reduced oxygen tension possibly evidenced by reports of headache.

Fatigue may be related to stress, increased physical exertion, sleep deprivation possibly evidenced by overwhelming lack of energy, inability to restore energy even after sleep, compromised concentration, decreased performance.

risk for deficient Fluid Volume: risk factors may include increased water loss (e.g., over-breathing dry air), exertion, altered fluid intake (nausea).

multiple personality
Refer to *dissociative disorders*.

multiple sclerosis
Fatigue may be related to decreased energy production/increased energy requirements to perform activities, psychological/emotional demands, pain/discomfort, medication side effects, possibly evidenced by verbalization of overwhelming lack of energy, inability to maintain usual routine, decreased performance, impaired ability to concentrate, increase in physical complaints.

disturbed visual, kinesthetic, tactile Sensory Perception may be related to delayed/interrupted neuronal transmission, possibly evidenced by impaired vision, diplopia, disturbance of vibratory or position sense, paresthesias, numbness, and blunting of sensation.

impaired physical Mobility may be related to neuromuscular impairment, discomfort/pain, sensoriperceptual impairments, decreased muscle strength, control and/or mass, deconditioning, as evidenced by limited ability to perform motor skills, limited range of motion, gait changes/postural instability.

Powerlessness/Hopelessness may be related to illness-related regimen and lifestyle of helplessness, possibly evidenced by verbal expressions of having no control or influence over the situation, depression over physical deterioration that occurs despite patient compliance with regimen, nonparticipation in care or decision making when opportunities are provided, passivity, decreased verbalization/affect.

impaired Home Maintenance may be related to effects of debilitating disease, impaired cognitive and/or emotional functioning, insufficient finances, and inadequate support systems, possibly evidenced by reported difficulty, observed disorderly surroundings, and poor hygienic conditions.

compromised/disabled family Coping may be related to situational crises/temporary family disorganization and role changes, patient providing little support in turn for significant other(s), prolonged disease/disability progression that exhausts the supportive capacity of significant other(s), feelings of guilt, anxiety, hostility, despair, and highly ambivalent family relationships, possibly evidenced by client expressing/confirming concern or report about significant other(s)' response to client's illness, significant other(s) preoccupied with own personal reactions, intolerance, abandonment, neglectful care of the patient, and distortion of reality regarding client's illness.

mumps
acute Pain may be related to presence of inflammation, circulating toxins, and enlargement of salivary glands, possibly evidenced by verbal reports, guarding/distraction behaviors, self-focusing, and autonomic responses (changes in vital signs).

Hyperthermia may be related to inflammatory process (increased metabolic rate), and dehydration, possibly evidenced by increased body temperature, warm/flushed skin, and tachycardia.

risk for deficient Fluid Volume: risk factors may include hypermetabolic state and painful swallowing with decreased intake.

muscular dystrophy (Duchenne's)
impaired physical Mobility may be related to musculoskeletal impairment/weakness, possibly evidenced by decreased muscle strength, control, and mass; limited range of motion; and impaired coordination.

delayed Growth and Development may be related to effects of physical disability, possibly evidenced by altered physical growth and altered ability to perform self-care/self-control activities appropriate to age.

risk for imbalanced Nutrition: more than body requirements: risk factors may include sedentary lifestyle and dysfunctional eating patterns.

compromised family Coping may be related to situational crisis/emotional conflicts around issues about hereditary nature of condition and prolonged disease/disability that exhausts supportive capacity of family members, possibly evidenced by preoccupation with personal reactions regarding disability and displaying protective behavior disproportionate (too little/too much) to client's abilities/need for autonomy.

myasthenia gravis
ineffective Breathing Pattern/Airway Clearance may be related to neuromuscular weakness and decreased energy/fatigue, possibly evidenced by dyspnea, changes in rate/depth of respiration, ineffective cough, and adventitious breath sounds.

impaired verbal Communication may be related to neuromuscular weakness, fatigue, and physical barrier (intubation), possibly evidenced by facial weakness, impaired articulation, hoarseness, and inability to speak.

impaired Swallowing may be related to neuromuscular impairment of laryngeal/pharyngeal muscles and muscular fatigue, possibly evidenced by reported/observed difficulty swallowing, coughing/choking, and evidence of aspiration.

Anxiety [specify level]/Fear may be related to situational crisis, threat to self-concept, change in health/socioeconomic status or role function, separation from support systems, lack of knowledge, and inability to communicate, possibly evidenced by expressed concerns, increased tension, restlessness, apprehension, sympathetic stimulation, crying, focus on self, uncooperative behavior, withdrawal, anger, and noncommunication.

deficient Knowledge [Learning Need] regarding drug therapy, potential for crisis (myasthenic or cholinergic) and self-care management may be related to inadequate information/misinterpretation, possibly evidenced by statements of concern, questions, and misconceptions; development of preventable complications.

impaired physical Mobility may be related to neuromuscular impairment, possibly evidenced by reports of progressive fatigability with repetitive/prolonged muscle use, impaired coordination, and decreased muscle strength/control.

disturbed visual Sensory Perception may be related to neuromuscular impairment, possibly evidenced by visual distortions (diplopia) and motor incoordination.

myeloma, multiple
(also refer to *cancer*)

acute/chronic Pain may be related to destruction of tissues/bone, side effects of therapy possibly evidenced by verbal or coded reports, guarding/protective behaviors, changes in appetite/weight, sleep; reduced interaction with others.

impaired physical Mobility may be related to loss of integrity of bone structure, pain, deconditioning, depressed mood possibly evidenced by verbalizations, limited range of motion, slowed movement, gait changes.

risk for ineffective Protection: risk factors may include presence of cancer, drug therapies, radiation treatments, inadequate nutrition.

myocardial infarction
(also refer to *myocarditis*)

acute Pain may be related to ischemia of myocardial tissue, possibly evidenced by verbal reports, guarding/distraction behaviors (restlessness), facial mask of pain, self-focusing, and autonomic responses (diaphoresis, changes in vital signs).

Anxiety [specify level]/Fear may be related to threat of death, threat of change of health status/role functioning and lifestyle, interpersonal transmission/contagion, possibly evidenced by increased tension, fearful attitude, apprehension, expressed concerns/uncertainty, restlessness, sympathetic stimulation, and somatic complaints.

risk for decreased Cardiac Output: risk factors may include changes in rate and electrical conduction, reduced preload, increased systemic vascular resistance, and altered muscle contractility/depressant effects of some medications, infarcted/dyskinetic muscle, structural defects.

risk for sedentary Lifestyle: risk factors may include lack of resources; lack of training or knowledge of specific exercise needs, safety concerns/fear of injury.

myocarditis
(also refer to *myocardial infarction*)

Activity Intolerance may be related to imbalance in oxygen supply and demand (myocardial inflammation/damage), cardiac depressant effects of certain drugs, and enforced bedrest, possibly evidenced by reports of fatigue, exertional dyspnea, tachycardia/palpitations in response to activity, ECG changes/dysrhythmias, and generalized weakness.

risk for decreased Cardiac Output: risk factors may include degeneration of cardiac muscle.

deficient Knowledge [Learning Need] regarding pathophysiology of condition/outcomes, treatment, and self-care needs/lifestyle changes may be related to lack of information/misinterpretation, possibly evidenced by statements of concern, misconceptions, inaccurate follow-through of instructions, and development of preventable complications.

myringotomy
Refer to *mastoidectomy*.

myxedema
(also refer to *hypothyroidism*)

disturbed Body Image may be related to change in structure/function (loss of hair/thickening of skin, mask-like facial expression, enlarged tongue, menstrual and reproductive disturbances), possibly evidenced by negative feelings about body, feelings of helplessness, and change in social involvement.

imbalanced Nutrition: more than body requirements may be related to decreased metabolic rate and activity level, possibly evidenced by weight gain greater than ideal for height and frame.

risk for decreased Cardiac Output: risk factors may include altered electrical conduction and myocardial contractility.

narcolepsy

Insomnia may be related to medical condition, possibly evidenced by hypersomnia, reports of unsatisfying nighttime sleep, vivid visual or auditory illusions or hallucinations at onset of sleep, sleep interrupted by vivid or frightening dreams.

risk for Trauma risk factors may include sudden loss of muscle tone, momentary paralysis (cataplexy), sudden inappropriate sleep episodes.

risk for chronic low Self-Esteem risk factors may include negative evaluation of self, personal vulnerability, chronic physical condition, impaired work or social performance, problems with social relationships, reduced quality of life.

necrotizing cellulitis, fasciitis

Hyperthermia may be related to inflammatory process, response to circulatory toxins, possibly evidenced by body temperature above normal range; flushed, warm skin; tachycardia, altered mental status.

impaired Tissue Integrity may be related to inflammation, edema, ischemia, possibly evidenced by damaged or destroyed tissue, dermal gangrene.

neglect/abuse

Refer to *battered child syndrome*.

neonatal, normal newborn

risk for impaired Gas Exchange: risk factors may include prenatal or intrapartal stressors, excess production of mucus, or cold stress.

risk for Hypothermia: risk factors may include large body surface in relation to mass, limited amounts of insulating subcutaneous fat, nonrenewable sources of brown fat and few white fat stores, thin epidermis with close proximity of blood vessels to the skin, inability to shiver, and movement from a warm uterine environment to a much cooler environment

risk for impaired Attachment: risk factors may include developmental transition (gain of a family member), anxiety associated with the parent role, lack of privacy (healthcare interventions, intrusive family/visitors).

risk for imbalanced Nutrition: less than body requirements: risk factors may include rapid metabolic rate, high caloric requirement, increased insensible water losses through pulmonary and cutaneous routes, fatigue, and a potential for inadequate or depleted glucose stores.

risk for Infection: risk factors may include inadequate secondary defenses (inadequate acquired immunity, e.g., deficiency of neutrophils and specific immunoglobulins) and inadequate primary defenses (e.g., environmental exposure, broken skin, traumatized tissues, decreased ciliary action).

neonatal, premature newborn

impaired Gas Exchange may be related to alveolar-capillary membrane changes (inadequate surfactant levels), altered blood flow (immaturity of pulmonary arteriole musculature), altered oxygen supply (immaturity of central nervous system and neuromuscular system, tracheobronchial obstruction), altered oxygen-carrying capacity of blood (anemia), and cold stress, possibly evidenced by respiratory difficulties, inadequate oxygenation of tissues, and acidemia.

ineffective Breathing Pattern/Infant Feeding Pattern may be related to immaturity of the respiratory center, poor positioning, drug-related depression, metabolic imbalances, or decreased energy/fatigue, possibly evidenced by dyspnea, tachypnea, periods of apnea, nasal flaring/use of accessory muscles, cyanosis, abnormal ABGs, and tachycardia.

risk for ineffective Thermoregulation: risk factors may include immature CNS development (temperature regulation center), decreased ratio of body mass to surface area, decreased subcutaneous fat, limited brown fat stores, inability to shiver or sweat, poor metabolic reserves, muted response to hypothermia, and frequent medical/nursing manipulations and interventions.

risk for deficient Fluid Volume: risk factors may include extremes of age and weight, excessive fluid losses (thin skin, lack of insulating fat, increased environmental temperature, immature kidney/failure to concentrate urine).

risk for disorganized Infant Behavior: risk factors may include prematurity (immature central nervous system, hypoxia), lack of containment/boundaries, pain, or overstimulation, separation from parents.

nephrectomy
acute Pain may be related to surgical tissue trauma with mechanical closure (suture), possibly evidenced by verbal reports, guarding/distraction behaviors, self-focusing, and autonomic responses (changes in vital signs).
risk for deficient Fluid Volume: risk factors may include excessive vascular losses and restricted intake.
ineffective Breathing Pattern may be related to incisional pain with decreased lung expansion, possibly evidenced by tachypnea, fremitus, changes in respiratory depth/chest expansion, and changes in ABGs.
Constipation may be related to reduced dietary intake, decreased mobility, gastrointestinal obstruction (paralytic ileus), and incisional pain with defecation, possibly evidenced by decreased bowel sounds, reduced frequency/amount of stool, and hard/formed stool.

nephrolithiasis
Refer to *calculi, urinary*.

nephrotic syndrome
excess Fluid Volume may be related to compromised regulatory mechanism with changes in hydrostatic/oncotic vascular pressure and increased activation of the renin-angiotensin-aldosterone system, possibly evidenced by edema/anasarca, effusions/ascites, weight gain, intake greater than output, and blood pressure changes.
imbalanced Nutrition: less than body requirements may be related to excessive protein losses and inability to ingest adequate nutrients (anorexia), possibly evidenced by weight loss/muscle wasting (may be difficult to assess due to edema), lack of interest in food, and observed inadequate intake.
risk for Infection: risk factors may include chronic disease and steroidal suppression of inflammatory responses.
risk for impaired Skin Integrity: risk factors may include presence of edema and activity restrictions.

neuralgia, trigeminal
acute Pain may be related to neuromuscular impairment with sudden violent muscle spasm, possibly evidenced by verbal reports, guarding/distraction behaviors, self-focusing, and autonomic responses (changes in vital signs).
deficient Knowledge [Learning Need] regarding control of recurrent episodes, medical therapies, and self-care needs may be related to lack of information/recall and misinterpretation, possibly evidenced by statements of concern, questions, and exacerbation of condition.

neuritis
acute/chronic Pain may be related to nerve damage usually associated with a degenerative process, possibly evidenced by verbal reports, guarding/distraction behaviors, self-focusing, and autonomic responses (changes in vital signs).
deficient Knowledge [Learning Need] regarding underlying causative factors, treatment, and prevention may be related to lack of information/misinterpretation, possibly evidenced by statements of concern, questions, and misconceptions.

nicotine withdrawal
readiness for enhanced Self-Health Management possibly evidenced by expressed concerns, desire to seek higher level of wellness.
risk for imbalanced Nutrition: more than body requirements: risk factors may include return of appetite, normalization of basal metabolic rate, reating in response to internal cues.
risk for ineffective Self-Health Management: risk factors may include economic difficulties, lack of support systems, continued environmental exposure.

nonketotic hyperglycemic-hyperosmolar coma
deficient Fluid Volume may be related to excessive renal losses, inadequate oral intake, extremes of age, presence of infection possibly evidenced by sudden weight loss, dry skin and mucous membranes, poor skin turgor, hypotension, increased pulse, fever, change in mental status (confusion to coma).
imbalanced Nutrition: less than body requirements may be related to decreased preload (hypovolemia), altered heart rhythm (hyper- or hypokalemia) possibly evidenced by decreased hemodynamic pressures (e.g., CVP), ECG changes, dysrhythmias.
decreased Cardiac Output may be related to inadequate utilization of nutrients (insulin deficiency), decreased oral intake, hypermetabolic state, possibly evidenced by recent weight loss, imbalance between glucose and insulin levels.
risk for Trauma: risk factors may include weakness, cognitive limitations or altered consciousness, loss of large- or small-muscle coordination (risk for seizure activity).

obesity
imbalanced Nutrition: more than body requirements may be related to food intake that
exceeds body needs, psychosocial factors, socioeconomic status, possibly evidenced by
weight of 20% or more over optimum body weight, excess body fat by skinfold/other
measurements, reported/observed dysfunctional eating patterns, intake more than
body requirements.
sedentary Lifestyle may be related to lack of interest/motivation, resources; lack of training or knowledge of specific exercise needs, safety concerns/fear of injury, possibly
evidenced by demonstration of physical deconditioning, choice of a daily routine lacking physical exercise.
Activity Intolerance may be related to imbalance between oxygen supply and demand,
and sedentary lifestyle, possibly evidenced by fatigue or weakness, exertional discomfort, and abnormal heart rate or BP response.
risk for Sleep Deprivation: risk factors may include inadequate daytime activity, discomfort, sleep apnea.
disturbed Body Image/chronic low Self-Esteem may be related to view of self in contrast
with societal values, family/subculture encouragement of overeating; control, sex, and
love issues; possibly evidenced by negative feelings about body, fear of rejection/re-
action of others, feelings of hopelessness/powerlessness, and lack of follow-through
with treatment plan.
impaired Social Interaction may be related to self-concept disturbance, absence of or
ineffective supportive Significant others(s), limited mobility, possibly evidenced by
reluctance to participate in social gatherings, verbalized or observed discomfort in
social situations, dysfunctional interactions with others, feelings of rejection.

obsessive-compulsive disorder
[severe] Anxiety may be related to earlier life conflicts possibly evidenced by repetitive
actions, recurring thoughts, decreased social and role functioning.
risk for impaired Skin/Tissue Integrity risk factors may include repetitive behaviors
related to cleansing (e.g., hand washing, brushing teeth, showering).
risk for ineffective Role Performance: risk factors may include psychological stress,
health-illness problems.

opioid abuse
Refer to *depressant abuse.*

organic brain syndrome
Refer to *Alzheimer's disease.*

osteoarthritis (degenerative joint disease)
Refer to *arthritis, rheumatoid.* (Although this is a degenerative process versus the
inflammatory process of rheumatoid arthritis, nursing concerns are the same.)

osteomyelitis
acute Pain may be related to inflammation and tissue necrosis, possibly evidenced by
verbal reports, guarding/distraction behaviors, self-focus, and autonomic responses
(changes in vital signs).
Hyperthermia may be related to increased metabolic rate and infectious process, possibly evidenced by increased body temperature and warm/flushed skin.
ineffective [bone] Tissue Perfusion may be related to inflammatory reaction with thrombosis of vessels, destruction of tissue, edema, and abscess formation, possibly evidenced by bone necrosis, continuation of infectious process, and delayed healing.
risk for impaired Walking: risk factors may include inflammation and tissue necrosis,
pain, joint instability.
deficient Knowledge [Learning Need] regarding pathophysiology of condition, long-term
therapy needs, activity restriction, and prevention of complications may be related to
lack of information/misinterpretation, possibly evidenced by statements of concern,
questions and misconceptions, and inaccurate follow-through of instructions.

osteoporosis
risk for Trauma: risk factors may include loss of bone density/integrity, increasing risk
of fracture with minimal or no stress.
acute/chronic Pain may be related to vertebral compression on spinal nerve/muscles/
ligaments, spontaneous fractures, possibly evidenced by verbal reports, guarding/dis-
traction behaviors, self-focus, and changes in sleep pattern.
impaired physical Mobility may be related to pain and musculoskeletal impairment,
possibly evidenced by limited range of motion, reluctance to attempt movement/ex-
pressed fear of reinjury, and imposed restrictions/limitations.

palsy, cerebral (spastic hemiplegia)
impaired physical Mobility may be related to muscular weakness/hypertonicity, increased deep tendon reflexes, tendency to contractures, and underdevelopment of af-

fected limbs, possibly evidenced by decreased muscle strength, control, mass, limited range of motion, and impaired coordination.

compromised family Coping may be related to permanent nature of condition, situational crisis, emotional conflicts/temporary family disorganization, and incomplete information/understanding of client's needs, possibly evidenced by verbalized anxiety/guilt regarding client's disability, inadequate understanding and knowledge base, and displaying protective behaviors disproportionate (too little/too much) to client's abilities or need for autonomy.

delayed Growth and Development may be related to effects of physical disability, possibly evidenced by altered physical growth, delay or difficulty in performing skills (motor, social, expressive), and altered ability to perform self-care/self-control activities appropriate to age.

pancreatitis

acute Pain may be related to obstruction of pancreatic/biliary ducts, chemical contamination of peritoneal surfaces by pancreatic exudate/autodigestion, extension of inflammation to the retroperitoneal nerve plexus, possibly evidenced by verbal reports, guarding/distraction behaviors, self-focusing, grimacing, autonomic responses (changes in vital signs), and alteration in muscle tone.

risk for deficient Fluid Volume/Bleeding: risk factors may include excessive gastric losses (vomiting, nasogastric suctioning), increase in size of vascular bed (vasodilation, effects of kinins), third-space fluid transudation, ascites formation, alteration of clotting process, hemorrhage.

risk for unstable Blood Glucose Level: risk factors may include decreased insulin production, increased glucagon release, physical health status, stress.

imbalanced Nutrition: less than body requirements may be related to vomiting, decreased oral intake as well as altered ability to digest nutrients (loss of digestive enzymes/insulin), possibly evidenced by reported inadequate food intake, aversion to eating, reported altered taste sensation, weight loss, and reduced muscle mass.

risk for Infection: risk factors may include inadequate primary defenses (stasis of body fluids, altered peristalsis, change in pH secretions), immunosuppression, nutritional deficiencies, tissue destruction, and chronic disease.

panic disorder

Fear may be related to unfounded morbid dread of a seemingly harmless object/situation, possibly evidenced by physiological symptoms, mental/cognitive behaviors indicative of panic, withdrawal from/total avoidance of situations placing client in contact with feared object.

[severe to panic] Anxiety may be related to unidentified stressors, limitations placed on ritualistic behavior, possibly evidenced by episodes of immobilizing apprehension, behaviors indicative of panic, expressed feelings of terror or inability to cope.

paranoid personality disorder

risk for other/self-directed Violence: risk factors may include perceived threats of danger, paranoid delusions, and increased feelings of anxiety.

[severe] Anxiety may be related to inability to trust (has not mastered tasks of trust versus mistrust), possibly evidenced by rigid delusional system (serves to provide relief from stress that justifies the delusion), frightened of other people and own hostility.

Powerlessness may be related to feelings of inadequacy, lifestyle of helplessness, maladaptive interpersonal interactions (e.g., misuse of power, force; abusive relationships), sense of severely impaired self-concept, and belief that individual has no control over situation(s), possibly evidenced by paranoid delusions, use of aggressive behavior to compensate, and expressions of recognition of damage paranoia has caused self and others.

[disturbed Sensory Perception (specify)] may be related to psychological stress, possibly evidenced by change in behavior pattern/usual response to stimul

compromised family Coping may be related to temporary or sustained family disorganization/role changes, prolonged progression of condition that exhausts the supportive capacity of significant other(s), possibly evidenced by family system not meeting physical/emotional/spiritual needs of its members, inability to express or to accept wide range of feelings, inappropriate boundary maintenance; significant other(s) describes preoccupation with personal reactions.

paraplegia

(also refer to *quadriplegia*)

impaired Transfer Ability may be related to loss of muscle function/control, injury to upper extremity joints (overuse).

disturbed kinesthetic/tactile Sensory Perception may be related to neurological deficit with loss of sensory reception and transmission, psychological stress, possibly evidenced by reported/measured change in sensory acuity and loss of usual response to stimuli.

reflex Urinary Incontinence/impaired Urinary Elimination may be related to loss of nerve conduction above the level of the reflex arc, possibly evidenced by lack of awareness of bladder filling/fullness, absence of urge to void, and uninhibited bladder contraction, urinary tract infections, kidney stone formation.

situational low Self-Esteem may be related to situational crisis, loss of body functions, change in physical abilities, perceived loss of self/identity, possibly evidenced by negative feelings about body or self, feelings of helplessness, powerlessness, delay in taking responsibility for self-care or participation in therapy, and change in social involvement.

Sexual Dysfunction may be related to loss of sensation, altered function, and vulnerability, possibly evidenced by seeking of confirmation of desirability, verbalization of concern, and alteration in relationship with significant other, and change in interest in self/others.

parathyroidectomy

acute Pain may be related to presence of surgical incision and effects of calcium imbalance (bone pain, tetany), possibly evidenced by verbal reports, guarding/distraction behaviors, self-focus, and autonomic responses (changes in vital signs).

risk for excess Fluid Volume: risk factors may include preoperative renal involvement, stress-induced release of ADH, and changing calcium/electrolyte levels.

risk for ineffective Airway Clearance: risk factors may include edema formation and laryngeal nerve damage.

deficient Knowledge [Learning Need] regarding postoperative care/complications and long-term needs may be related to lack of information/recall, misinterpretation, possibly evidenced by statements of concern, questions, and misconceptions.

parenteral feeding

imbalanced Nutrition: less than body requirements may be related to conditions that interfere with nutrient intake or increase nutrient need or metabolic demand—cancer and associated treatments, anorexia, surgical procedures, dysphagia, or decreased level of consciousness, possibly evidenced by body weight 10% or more under ideal, decreased subcutaneous fat or muscle mass, poor muscle tone.

risk for Infection

risk for Injury [multifactor]: risk factors may include catheter-related complications (air emboli, septic thrombophlebitis).

risk for imbalanced Fluid Volume: risk factors may include active loss or failure of regulatory mechanisms specific to underlying disease process or trauma, complications of therapy—high glucose solutions/hyperglycemia—hyperosmolar nonketotic coma and severe dehydration; inability to obtain or ingest fluids.

Fatigue may be related to decreased metabolic energy production, increased energy requirements—hypermetabolic state, healing process; altered body chemistry—medications, chemotherapy; possibly evidenced by overwhelming lack of energy, inability to maintain usual routines/accomplish routine tasks, lethargy, impaired ability to concentrate.

Parkinson's disease

impaired Walking may be related to neuromuscular impairment (muscle weakness, tremors, bradykinesia) and musculoskeletal impairment (joint rigidity), possibly evidenced by inability to move about the environment as desired, increased occurrence of falls.

impaired Swallowing may be related to neuromuscular impairment/muscle weakness, possibly evidenced by reported/observed difficulty in swallowing, drooling, evidence of aspiration (choking, coughing).

impaired verbal Communication may be related to muscle weakness and incoordination, possibly evidenced by impaired articulation, difficulty with phonation, and changes in rhythm and intonation.

risk for Stress Overload: risk factors may include inadequate resources, chronic illness, physical demands.

Caregiver Role Strain may be related to illness, severity of care receiver, psychological/cognitive problems in care receiver, caregiver is spouse, duration of caregiving required, lack of respite/recreation for caregiver, possibly evidenced by feeling stressed, depressed, worried; lack of resources/support, family conflict.

pelvic inflammatory disease

risk for Infection [spread]: risk factors may include presence of infectious process in highly vascular pelvic structures, delay in seeking treatment.

acute Pain may be related to inflammation, edema, and congestion of reproductive/pelvic tissues, possibly evidenced by verbal reports, guarding/distraction behaviors, self-focus, and autonomic responses (changes in vital signs).

Hyperthermia may be related to inflammatory process/hypermetabolic state, possibly evidenced by increased body temperature, warm/flushed skin, and tachycardia.

risk for situational low Self-Esteem: risk factors may include perceived stigma of physical condition (infection of reproductive system).

deficient Knowledge [Learning Need] regarding cause/complications of condition, therapy needs, and transmission of disease to others may be related to lack of information/misinterpretation, possibly evidenced by statements of concern, questions, misconceptions, and development of preventable complications.

periarteritis nodosa
Refer to *polyarteritis (nodosa)*.

pericarditis
acute Pain may be related to inflammation and presence of effusion, possibly evidenced by verbal reports of pain affected by movement/position, guarding/distraction behaviors, self-focus, and autonomic responses (changes in vital signs).

Activity Intolerance may be related to imbalance between oxygen supply and demand (restriction of cardiac filling/ventricular contraction, reduced cardiac output), possibly evidenced by reports of weakness/fatigue, exertional dyspnea, abnormal heart rate or blood pressure response, and signs of congestive heart failure.

risk for decreased Cardiac Output: risk factors may include accumulation of fluid (effusion), restricted cardiac filling/contractility.

Anxiety [specify level] may be related to change in health status and perceived threat of death, possibly evidenced by increased tension, apprehension, restlessness, and expressed concerns.

perinatal loss/death of child
Grieving may be related to death of fetus/infant possibly evidenced by verbal expressions of distress, anger, loss, guilt; crying, change in eating habits/sleep.

situational low Self-Esteem may be related to perceived failure at a life event, inability to meet personal expectations possibly evidenced by negative self-appraisal in response to situation/personal actions, expressions of helplessness/hopelessness, evaluation of self as unable to deal with situation.

risk for ineffective Role Performance: risk factors may include stress, family conflict, inadequate support system.

risk for interrupted Family Processes: risk factors may include situational crisis, developmental transition [loss of child], family roles shift.

risk for Spiritual Distress: risk factors may include blame for loss directed at self/God, intense suffering, alienation from other/support systems.

peripheral arterial occlusive disease
refer to *arterial occlusive disease*

peripheral vascular disease (atherosclerosis)
ineffective peripheral Tissue Perfusion may be related to reduction or interruption of arterial/venous blood flow, possibly evidenced by changes in skin temperature/color, lack of hair growth, blood pressure/pulse changes in extremity, presence of bruits, and reports of claudication.

Activity Intolerance may be related to imbalance between oxygen supply and demand, possibly evidenced by reports of muscle fatigue/weakness and exertional discomfort (claudication).

risk for impaired Skin/Tissue Integrity: risk factors may include altered circulation with decreased sensation and impaired healing.

peritonitis
risk for Infection [spread/septicemia]: risk factors may include inadequate primary defenses (broken skin, traumatized tissue, altered peristalsis), inadequate secondary defenses (immunosuppression), and invasive procedures.

deficient Fluid Volume [mixed] may be related to fluid shifts from extracellular, intravascular, and interstitial compartments into intestines and/or peritoneal space, excessive gastric losses (vomiting, diarrhea, nasogastric suction), hypermetabolic state, and restricted intake, possibly evidenced by dry mucous membranes, poor skin turgor, delayed capillary refill, weak peripheral pulses, diminished urinary output, dark/concentrated urine, hypotension, and tachycardia.

acute Pain may be related to chemical irritation of parietal peritoneum, trauma to tissues, accumulation of fluid in abdominal/peritoneal cavity, possibly evidenced by verbal reports, muscle guarding/rebound tenderness, distraction behaviors, facial mask of pain, self-focus, autonomic responses (changes in vital signs).

risk for imbalanced Nutrition: less than body requirements: risk factors may include nausea/vomiting, intestinal dysfunction, metabolic abnormalities, or increased metabolic needs.

pheochromocytoma
Anxiety [specify level] may be related to excessive physiological (hormonal) stimulation of the sympathetic nervous system, situational crises, threat to/change in health

status, possibly evidenced by apprehension, shakiness, restlessness, focus on self, fearfulness, diaphoresis, and sense of impending doom.

deficient Fluid Volume [mixed] may be related to excessive gastric losses (vomiting/ diarrhea), hypermetabolic state, diaphoresis, and hyperosmolar diuresis, possibly evidenced by hemoconcentration, dry mucous membranes, poor skin turgor, thirst, and weight loss.

decreased Cardiac Output/ineffective Tissue Perfusion (specify) may be related to altered preload/decreased blood volume, altered systemic vascular resistance, and increased sympathetic activity (excessive secretion of catecholamines), possibly evidenced by cool/clammy skin, change in blood pressure (hypertension/postural hypotension), visual disturbances, severe headache, and angina.

deficient Knowledge [Learning Need] regarding pathophysiology of condition, outcome, preoperative and postoperative care needs may be related to lack of information/recall, possibly evidenced by statements of concern, questions, and misconceptions.

phlebitis
Refer to *thrombophlebitis*.

phobia
(also refer to *anxiety disorder, generalized*)
Fear may be related to learned irrational response to natural or innate origins (phobic stimulus), unfounded morbid dread of a seemingly harmless object/situation, possibly evidenced by sympathetic stimulation and reactions ranging from apprehension to panic, withdrawal from/total avoidance of situations that place individual in contact with feared object.

impaired Social Interaction may be related to intense fear of encountering feared object/ activity or situation and anticipated loss of control, possibly evidenced by reported change of style/pattern of interaction, discomfort in social situations, and avoidance of phobic stimulus.

placenta previa
risk for deficient Fluid Volume: risk factors may include excessive vascular losses (vessel damage and inadequate vasoconstriction).

impaired fetal Gas Exchange may be related to altered blood flow, altered carrying capacity of blood (maternal anemia), and decreased surface area of gas exchange at site of placental attachment, possibly evidenced by changes in fetal heart rate/activity and release of meconium.

Fear may be related to threat of death (perceived or actual) to self or fetus, possibly evidenced by verbalization of specific concerns, increased tension, sympathetic stimulation.

risk for deficient Diversional Activity: risk factors may include imposed activity restrictions/bedrest.

pleurisy
acute Pain may be related to inflammation/irritation of the parietal pleura, possibly evidenced by verbal reports, guarding/distraction behaviors, self-focus, and autonomic responses (changes in vital signs).

ineffective Breathing Pattern may be related to pain on inspiration, possibly evidenced by decreased respiratory depth, tachypnea, and dyspnea.

risk for Infection, [pneumonia]: risk factors may include stasis of pulmonary secretions, decreased lung expansion, and ineffective cough.

pneumonia
Refer to *bronchitis; bronchopneumonia*.

pneumothorax
(also refer to *hemothorax*)
ineffective Breathing Pattern may be related to decreased lung expansion (fluid/air accumulation), musculoskeletal impairment, pain, inflammatory process, possibly evidenced by dyspnea, tachypnea, altered chest excursion, respiratory depth changes, use of accessory muscles/nasal flaring, cough, cyanosis, and abnormal ABGs.

risk for decreased Cardiac Output: risk factors may include compression/displacement of cardiac structures.

acute Pain may be related to irritation of nerve endings within pleural space by foreign object (chest tube), possibly evidenced by verbal reports, guarding/distraction behaviors, self-focus, and autonomic responses (changes in vital signs).

polyarteritis (nodosa)
ineffective Tissue Perfusion (specify) may be related to reduction/interruption of blood flow, possibly evidenced by organ tissue infarctions, changes in organ function, and development of organic psychosis.

Hyperthermia may be related to widespread inflammatory process, possibly evidenced by increased body temperature and warm/flushed skin.

acute Pain may be related to inflammation, tissue ischemia, and necrosis of affected area, possibly evidenced by verbal reports, guarding/distraction behaviors, self-focus, and autonomic responses (changes in vital signs).

Grieving may be related to perceived loss of self, possibly evidenced by expressions of sorrow and anger, altered sleep and/or eating patterns, and changes in activity level or libido.

polycythemia vera

Activity Intolerance may be related to imbalance between oxygen supply and demand, possibly evidenced by reports of fatigue/weakness.

ineffective Tissue Perfusion (specify) may be related to reduction/interruption of arterial/venous blood flow (insufficiency, thrombosis, or hemorrhage), possibly evidenced by pain in affected area, impaired mental ability, visual disturbances, and color changes of skin/mucous membranes.

polyradiculitis

Refer to *Guillain-Barré syndrome*.

postoperative recovery period

ineffective Breathing Pattern may be related to neuromuscular and perceptual/cognitive impairment, decreased lung expansion/energy, and tracheobronchial obstruction, possibly evidenced by changes in respiratory rate and depth, reduced vital capacity, apnea, cyanosis, and noisy respirations.

risk for imbalanced Body Temperature: risk factors may include exposure to cool environment, effect of medications/anesthetic agents, extremes of age/weight, and dehydration.

risk for acute Confusion: risk factors may include pharmaceutical agents—anesthesia, pain.

risk for deficient Fluid Volume: risk factors may include restriction of oral intake, loss of fluid through abnormal routes (indwelling tubes, drains), normal routes (vomiting, loss of vascular integrity, changes in clotting ability), and extremes of age and weight.

acute Pain may be related to disruption of skin, tissue, and muscle integrity, musculoskeletal/bone trauma, and presence of tubes and drains, possibly evidenced by verbal reports, alteration in muscle tone, facial mask of pain, distraction/guarding behaviors, narrowed focus, and autonomic responses.

impaired Skin/Tissue Integrity may be related to mechanical interruption of skin/tissues, altered circulation, effects of medication, accumulation of drainage, and altered metabolic state, possibly evidenced by disruption of skin surface/layers and tissues.

risk for Infection: risk factors may include broken skin, traumatized tissues, stasis of body fluids, presence of pathogens/contaminants, environmental exposure, and invasive procedures.

postpartal period

readiness for enhanced Family Processes possibly evidenced by expressing willingness to enhance family dynamics..

risk for deficient Fluid Volume: risk factors may include excessive blood loss during delivery, reduced intake/inadequate replacement, nausea/vomiting, increased urine output, and insensible losses.

acute Pain/impaired Comfort may be related to tissue trauma and edema, muscle contractions, bladder fullness, and physical or psychological exhaustion, possibly evidenced by reports of cramping (afterpains), self-focusing, alteration in muscle tone, distraction behaviors, and changes in vital signs.

impaired Urinary Elimination may be related to hormonal effects (fluid shifts/continued elevation in renal plasma flow), mechanical trauma/tissue edema, and effects of medication/anesthesia, possibly evidenced by frequency, dysuria, urgency, incontinence, or retention.

Constipation may be related to decreased muscle tone associated with diastasis recti, prenatal effects of progesterone, dehydration, excess analgesia or anesthesia, pain (hemorrhoids, episiotomy, or perineal tenderness), prelabor diarrhea, and lack of intake, possibly evidenced by frequency less than usual pattern, hard-formed stool, straining at stool, decreased bowel sounds, and abdominal distention.

Insomnia may be related to pain/discomfort, intense exhilaration/excitement, anxiety, exhausting process of labor/delivery, and needs/demands of family members, possibly evidenced by verbal reports of difficulty in falling asleep or staying asleep/dissatisfaction with sleep, lack of energy, nonrestorative sleep.

risk for impaired Attachment/Parenting: risk factors may include lack of support between or from SO(s), ineffective or no role model, anxiety associated with the parental role, unrealistic expectations, presence of stressors (e.g., financial, housing, employment).

postpartum psychosis

ineffective Coping may be related to situational/maturational crisis, inadequate level of confidence in ability to cope, inadequate level of perception of control, possibly evidenced by inability to meet basic needs, inability to problem-solve, sleep pattern disturbance, poor concentration.

risk for other-directed Violence risk factors may include mood swings, increased anxiety, despondency, hopelessness, psychotic symptomatology.

post-traumatic stress disorder

Post-Trauma Syndrome related to having experienced a traumatic life event, possibly evidenced by re-experiencing the event, somatic reactions, psychic/emotional numbness, altered lifestyle, impaired sleep, self-destructive behaviors, difficulty with interpersonal relationships, development of phobia, poor impulse control/irritability, and explosiveness.

risk for other-directed Violence: risk factors may include a startle reaction, an intrusive memory causing a sudden acting-out of a feeling as if the event were occurring; use of alcohol/other drugs to ward off painful effects and produce psychic numbing, breaking through the rage that has been walled off, response to intense anxiety or panic state, and loss of control.

ineffective Coping may be related to personal vulnerability, inadequate support systems, unrealistic perceptions, un-met expectations, overwhelming threat to self, and multiple stressors repeated over period of time, possibly evidenced by verbalization of inability to cope or difficulty asking for help, muscular tension/headaches, chronic worry, and emotional tension.

complicated Grieving may be related to actual/perceived object loss (loss of self as seen before the traumatic incident occurred as well as other losses incurred in/after the incident), loss of physiopsychosocial well-being, thwarted grieving response to a loss, and lack of resolution of previous grieving responses, possibly evidenced by verbal expression of distress at loss, anger, sadness, labile affect, alterations in eating habits, sleep/dream patterns, libido; reliving of past experiences, expression of guilt, and alterations in concentration.

interrupted Family Processes may be related to situational crisis, failure to master developmental transitions, possibly evidenced by expressions of confusion about what to do and that family is having difficulty coping, family system not meeting physical/emotional/spiritual needs of its members, not adapting to change or dealing with traumatic experience constructively, and ineffective family decision-making process.

pregnancy 1st trimester (prenatal period)

risk for imbalanced Nutrition: less than body requirements: risk factors may include changes in appetite, insufficient intake (nausea/vomiting, inadequate financial resources and nutritional knowledge); meeting increased metabolic demands (increased thyroid activity associated with the growth of fetal and maternal tissues).

impaired Comfort may be related to hormonal influences, physical changes, possibly evidenced by verbal reports (nausea, breast changes, leg cramps, hemorrhoids, nasal stuffiness), alteration in muscle tone, inability to relax

risk for disturbed Maternal-Fetal Dyad: risk factors may include environmental and hereditary factors and problems of maternal well-being that directly affect the developing fetus, e.g., malnutrition, substance use.

[maximally compensated] Cardiac Output may be related to increased fluid volume/maximal cardiac effort and hormonal effects of progesterone and relaxin (that place the patient at risk for hypertension and/or circulatory failure), and changes in peripheral resistance (afterload), possibly evidenced by variations in blood pressure and pulse, syncopal episodes, or presence of pathological edema.

readiness for enhanced family Coping possibly evidenced by movement toward health-promoting and enriching lifestyle, choosing experiences that optimize pregnancy experience and wellness.

risk for Constipation: risk factors may include changes in dietary/fluid intake, smooth muscle relaxation, decreased peristalsis, and effects of medications (e.g., iron).

Fatigue/Insomnia may be related to increased carbohydrate metabolism, altered body chemistry, increased energy requirements to perform activities of daily living, discomfort, anxiety, inactivity, possibly evidenced by reports of overwhelming lack of energy/inability to maintain usual routines, difficulty falling asleep/dissatisfaction with sleep, decreased quality of life.

risk for ineffective Role Performance: risk factors may include maturational crisis, developmental level, history of maladaptive coping, or absence of support systems.

deficient Knowledge [Learning Need] regarding normal physiological/psychological changes and self-care needs may be related to lack of information/recall and misinterpretation of normal physiological/psychological changes and their impact on the client/family, possibly evidenced by questions, statements of concern, misconceptions, and inaccurate follow-through of instructions/development of preventable complications.

pregnancy 2nd trimester (prenatal period)
also refer to *pregnancy, 1st trimester*
risk for disturbed Body Image: risk factors may include perception of biophysical changes, response of others.
ineffective Breathing Pattern may be related to impingement of the diaphragm by enlarging uterus, possibly evidenced by reports of shortness of breath, dyspnea, and changes in respiratory depth.
risk for [decompensated] Cardiac Output: risk factors may include increased circulatory demand, changes in preload (decreased venous return) and afterload (increased peripheral vascular resistance), and ventricular hypertrophy.
risk for excess Fluid Volume: risk factors may include changes in regulatory mechanisms, sodium and water retention.
Sexual Dysfunction may be related to conflict regarding changes in sexual desire and expectations, fear of physical injury to woman or fetus, possibly evidenced by reported difficulties, limitations, or changes in sexual behaviors or activities.

pregnancy 3rd trimester (prenatal period)
also refer to *pregnancy, 1st and 2nd trimesters*
deficient Knowledge [Learning Need] regarding preparation for labor and delivery, infant care may be related to lack of exposure or experience, misinterpretations of information, possibly evidenced by request for information, statement of concerns, misconceptions.
impaired Urinary Elimination may be related to uterine enlargement, increased abdominal pressure, fluctuation of renal blood flow, and glomerular filtration rate (GFR), possibly evidenced by urinary frequency, urgency, dependent edema.
risk for ineffective Coping/compromised family Coping: risk factors may include situational or maturational crisis, personal vulnerability, unrealistic perceptions, absent or insufficient support systems.
risk for disturbed Maternal-Fetal Dyad: risk factors may include presence of hypertension, infection, substance use or abuse, altered immune system, abnormal blood profile, tissue hypoxia, premature rupture of membranes.

pregnancy, adolescent
(also refer to *pregnancy, prenatal period*)
interrupted Family Processes may be related to situational/developmental transition (economic, change in roles/gain of a family member), possibly evidenced by family expressing confusion about what to do, unable to meet physical/emotional/spiritual needs of the members, family inability to adapt to change or to deal with traumatic experience constructively, does not demonstrate respect for individuality and autonomy of its members, ineffective family decision-making process, and inappropriate boundary maintenance.
Social Isolation may be related to alterations in physical appearance, perceived unacceptable social behavior, restricted social sphere, stage of adolescence, and interference with accomplishing developmental tasks, possibly evidenced by expressions of feelings of aloneness/rejection/difference from others, uncommunicative, withdrawn, no eye contact, seeking to be alone, unacceptable behavior, and absence of supportive significant other(s).
disturbed Body Image/situational/chronic low Self-Esteem may be related to situational/maturational crisis, biophysical changes, and fear of failure at life events, absence of support systems, possibly evidenced by self-negating verbalizations, expressions of shame/guilt, fear of rejection/reaction of others, hypersensitivity to criticism, and lack of follow-through/nonparticipation in prenatal care.
deficient Knowledge [Learning Need] regarding pregnancy, developmental/individual needs, future expectations may be related to lack of exposure, information misinterpretation, unfamiliarity with information resources, lack of interest in learning, possibly evidenced by questions, statements of concern/misconception, sense of vulnerability/denial of reality, inaccurate follow-through of instruction, and development of preventable complications.
risk for impaired Parenting: may be related to chronological age/developmental stage, un-met social/emotional/maturational needs of parenting figures, unrealistic expectation of self/infant/partner, ineffective role model/social support, lack of role identity, and presence of stressors (e.g., financial, social).

pregnancy, high-risk
Anxiety [specify level] may be related to situational crisis, threat of maternal/fetal death (perceived or actual), interpersonal transmission/contagion possibly evidenced by increased tension, apprehension, feelings of inadequacy, somatic complaints, difficulty sleeping

deficient Knowledge [Learning Need] regarding high-risk situation/preterm labor may be related to lack of exposure to/misinterpretation of information, unfamiliarity with individual risks and own role in risk prevention/management possibly evidenced by request for information, statement of concerns/misconceptions, inaccurate follow-through of instructions.

risk of maternal injury: risk factors may include pre-existing medical conditions, complications of pregnancy.

risk for Activity Intolerance: risk factors may include presence of circulatory/respiratory problems, uterine irritability.

risk for Ineffective Therapeutic Regimen Management: risk factors may include client value system, health beliefs/cultural influences, issues of control, presence of anxiety, complexity of therapeutic regimen, economic difficulties, perceived susceptibility.

pregnancy-induced hypertension (pre-eclampsia)

deficient Fluid Volume [isotonic] may be related to a plasma protein loss, decreasing plasma colloid osmotic pressure allowing fluid shifts out of vascular compartment, possibly evidenced by edema formation, sudden weight gain, hemoconcentration, nausea/vomiting, epigastric pain, headaches, visual changes, decreased urine output.

decreased Cardiac Output may be related to hypovolemia/decreased venous return, increased SVR, possibly evidenced by variations in blood pressure/hemodynamic readings, edema, shortness of breath, change in mental status.

risk for disturbed Maternal-Fetal Dyad: risk factors may include vasospasm of spiral arteries and relative hypovolemia.

deficient Knowledge [Learning Need] regarding pathophysiology of condition, therapy, self-care/nutritional needs, and potential complications may be related to lack of information/recall, misinterpretation, possibly evidenced by statements of concern, questions, misconceptions, inaccurate follow-through of instructions/development of preventable complications.

premenstrual dysphoric disorder (PDD)

chronic/acute Pain may be related to cyclic changes in female hormones affecting other systems (e.g., vascular congestion/spasms), vitamin deficiency, fluid retention, possibly evidenced by increased tension, apprehension, jitteriness, verbal reports, distraction behaviors, somatic complaints, self-focusing, physical and social withdrawal.

excess Fluid Volume may be related to abnormal alterations of hormonal levels, possibly evidenced by edema formation, weight gain, and periodic changes in emotional status/irritability.

Anxiety [moderate to panic] may be related to cyclic changes in female hormones affecting other systems, possibly evidenced by feelings of inability to cope or loss of control, depersonalization, increased tension, apprehension, jitteriness, somatic complaints, and impaired functioning

ineffective Coping may be related to personal vulnerability, threat to self-concept, multiple stressors, possibly evidenced by reports inability to cope, inadequate problem-solving, sleep pattern disturbance.

deficient Knowledge [Learning Need] regarding pathophysiology of condition and self-care/treatment needs may be related to lack of information/misinterpretation, possibly evidenced by statements of concern, questions, misconceptions, and continuation of condition, exacerbating symptoms.

premenstrual tension syndrome (PMS)
refer to *premenstrual dysphoric disorder*

pressure ulcer or sore
(also refer to *ulcer, decubitus*)

ineffective peripheral Tissue Perfusion may be related to reduced/interrupted blood flow, possibly evidenced by presence of inflamed, necrotic lesion.

deficient Knowledge [Learning Need] regarding cause/prevention of condition and potential complications may be related to lack of information/misinterpretation, possibly evidenced by statements of concern, questions, misconceptions, and inaccurate follow-through of instructions.

preterm labor
Refer to *labor, preterm.*

prostatectomy

impaired Urinary Elimination may be related to mechanical obstruction (blood clots, edema, trauma, surgical procedure, pressure/irritation of catheter/balloon), and loss of bladder tone, possibly evidenced by dysuria, frequency, dribbling, incontinence, retention, bladder fullness, suprapubic discomfort.

risk for Bleeding/deficient Fluid Volume: risk factors may include trauma to highly vascular area with excessive vascular losses, restricted intake, postobstructive diuresis.

acute Pain may be related to irritation of bladder mucosa and tissue trauma/edema, possibly evidenced by verbal reports (bladder spasms), distraction behaviors, self-focus, and autonomic responses (changes in vital signs).

disturbed Body Image may be related to perceived threat of altered body/sexual function, possibly evidenced by preoccupation with change/loss, negative feelings about body, and statements of concern regarding functioning.

risk for Sexual Dysfunction: risk factors may include situational crisis (incontinence, leakage of urine after catheter removal, involvement of genital area), and threat to self-concept/change in health status.

pruritus

impaired Comfort/acute Pain may be related to cutaneous hyperesthesia and inflammation, possibly evidenced by verbal reports, distraction behaviors, and self-focus.

risk for impaired Skin Integrity: risk factors may include mechanical trauma (scratching) and development of vesicles/bullae that may rupture.

psoriasis

impaired Skin Integrity may be related to increased epidermal cell proliferation and absence of normal protective skin layers, possibly evidenced by scaling papules and plaques.

disturbed Body Image may be related to cosmetically unsightly skin lesions, possibly evidenced by hiding affected body part, negative feelings about body, feelings of helplessness, and change in social involvement.

pulmonary edema

impaired Gas Exchange may be related to alveolar-capillary membrane changes (fluid collection or shifts into interstitial space or alveoli) possibly evidenced by dyspnea, restlessness, irritability, abnormal rate/depth of respirations, lethargy, confusion.

[moderate to severe] Anxiety may be related to change in health status, threat of death, interpersonal transmission possibly evidenced by expressed concerns, distressed, apprehension, extraneous movement.

risk for impaired spontaneous Ventilation risk factors may include respiratory muscle fatigue, problems with secretion management

pulmonary embolus

ineffective Breathing Pattern may be related to tracheobronchial obstruction (inflammation, copious secretions, or active bleeding), decreased lung expansion, inflammatory process, possibly evidenced by changes in depth and/or rate of respiration, dyspnea/use of accessory muscles, altered chest excursion, abnormal breath sounds (crackles, wheezes), and cough (with or without sputum production).

impaired Gas Exchange may be related to ventilation-perfusion imbalance, alveolar-capillary membrane changes (atelectasis, airway or alveolar collapse, pulmonary edema or effusion, excessive secretions or active bleeding), possibly evidenced by profound dyspnea, restlessness, apprehension, somnolence, cyanosis, and changes in ABGs or pulse oximetry (hypoxemia and hypercapnia)

Fear/Anxiety [specify level] may be related to severe dyspnea/inability to breathe normally, perceived threat of death, threat to/change in health status, physiological response to hypoxemia/acidosis, and concern regarding unknown outcome of situation, possibly evidenced by restlessness, irritability, withdrawal or attack behavior, sympathetic stimulation (cardiovascular excitation, pupil dilation, sweating, vomiting, diarrhea), crying, voice quivering, and impending sense of doom.

pulmonary hypertension

impaired Gas Exchange may be related to changes in alveolar membrane, increased pulmonary vascular resistance possibly evidenced by dyspnea, irritability, decreased mental acuity, somnolence, abnormal ABGs.

decreased Cardiac Output may be related to increased pulmonary vascular resistance, decreased blood return to left side of heart possibly evidenced by increased heart rate, dyspnea, fatigue.

Activity Intolerance may be related to imbalance between oxygen supply and demand, possibly evidenced by reports of weakness/fatigue, abnormal vital signs with activity.

Anxiety may be related to change in health status, stress, threat to self-concept possibly evidenced by expressed concerns, uncertainty, anxious, awareness of physiological symptoms, diminished productivity/ability to problem-solve.

purpura, idiopathic thrombocytopenic

ineffective Protection may be related to abnormal blood profile, drug therapy (corticosteroids or immunosuppressive agents), possibly evidenced by altered clotting, fatigue, deficient immunity.

Activity Intolerance may be related to decreased oxygen-carrying capacity/imbalance between oxygen supply and demand, possibly evidenced by reports of fatigue/weakness.

deficient Knowledge [Learning Need] regarding therapy choices, outcomes, and self-care needs may be related to lack of information/misinterpretation, possibly evidenced by statements of concern, questions, and misconceptions.

pyelonephritis

acute Pain may be related to acute inflammation of renal tissues, possibly evidenced by verbal reports, guarding/distraction behaviors, self-focus, and autonomic responses (changes in vital signs).

Hyperthermia may be related to inflammatory process/increased metabolic rate, possibly evidenced by increase in body temperature, warm/flushed skin, tachycardia, and chills.

impaired Urinary Elimination may be related to inflammation/irritation of bladder mucosa, possibly evidenced by dysuria, urgency, and frequency.

deficient Knowledge [Learning Need] regarding therapy needs and prevention may be related to lack of information/misinterpretation, possibly evidenced by statements of concern, questions, misconceptions, and recurrence of condition.

quadriplegia
(also refer to *paraplegia*)

ineffective Breathing Pattern may be related to neuromuscular impairment (diaphragm and intercostal muscle function), reflex abdominal spasms, gastric distention, possibly evidenced by decreased respiratory depth, dyspnea, cyanosis, and abnormal ABGs.

risk for Trauma [additional spinal injury]: risk factors may include temporary weakness/instability of spinal column.

Grieving may be related to perceived loss of self, anticipated alterations in lifestyle and expectations, and limitation of future options/choices, possibly evidenced by expressions of distress, anger, sorrow; choked feelings; and changes in eating habits, sleep, and communication patterns.

total Self-Care Deficit related to neuromuscular impairment, evidenced by inability to perform self-care tasks.

bowel Incontinence/Constipation may be related to disruption of nerve innervation, perceptual impairment, changes in dietary and fluid intake, change in activity level, side effects of medication possibly evidenced by inability to evacuate bowel voluntarily; increased abdominal pressure or distention; dry, hard-formed stool; change in bowel sounds.

impaired bed/wheelchair Mobility may be related to loss of muscle function/control. may be related to loss of muscle function and control possibly evidenced by inability to reposition self, impaired ability to operate wheelchair.

risk for Autonomic Dysreflexia: risk factors may include altered nerve function (spinal cord injury at T6 or above), bladder/bowel/skin stimulation (tactile, pain, thermal).

impaired Home Maintenance may be related to permanent effects of injury, inadequate/absent support systems and finances, and lack of familiarity with resources, possibly evidenced by expressions of difficulties, requests for information and assistance, outstanding debts/financial crisis, and lack of necessary aides and equipment.

rape

deficient Knowledge [Learning Need] regarding required medical/legal procedures, prophylactic treatment for individual concerns (STDs, pregnancy), community resources/supports may be related to lack of information, possibly evidenced by statements of concern, questions, misconceptions, and exacerbation of symptoms.

Rape-Trauma Syndrome (acute phase) related to actual or attempted sexual penetration without consent, possibly evidenced by wide range of emotional reactions, including anxiety, fear, anger, embarrassment, and multisystem physical complaints.

risk for impaired Tissue Integrity: risk factors may include forceful sexual penetration and trauma to fragile tissues.

ineffective Coping may be related to personal vulnerability, un-met expectations, unrealistic perceptions, inadequate support systems/coping methods, multiple stressors repeated over time, overwhelming threat to self, possibly evidenced by verbalizations of inability to cope or difficulty asking for help, muscular tension/headaches, emotional tension, chronic worry.

Sexual Dysfunction may be related to biopsychosocial alteration of sexuality (stress of post-trauma response), vulnerability, loss of sexual desire, impaired relationship with significant other, possibly evidenced by alteration in achieving sexual satisfaction, change in interest in self/others, preoccupation with self.

Raynaud's phenomenon

acute/chronic Pain may be related to vasospasm/altered perfusion of affected tissues and ischemia/destruction of tissues, possibly evidenced by verbal reports, guarding of affected parts, guarding of affected parts, self-focusing, and restlessness.

ineffective peripheral Tissue Perfusion may be related to periodic reduction of arterial blood flow to affected areas, possibly evidenced by pallor, cyanosis, coolness, numbness, paresthesia, slow healing of lesions.

deficient Knowledge [Learning Need] regarding pathophysiology of the condition, potential for complications, therapy/self-care needs may be related to lack of information/misinterpretation, possibly evidenced by statements of concern, questions, and misconceptions; development of preventable complications.

regional enteritis
Refer to *Crohn's disease*.

renal failure, acute
excess Fluid Volume may be related to compromised regulatory mechanisms (decreased kidney function), possibly evidenced by weight gain, edema/anasarca, intake greater than output, venous congestion, changes in BP/CVP, and altered electrolyte levels.
imbalanced Nutrition: less than body requirements may be related to inability to ingest/digest adequate nutrients (anorexia, nausea/vomiting, ulcerations of oral mucosa, and increased metabolic needs) in addition to therapeutic dietary restrictions, possibly evidenced by lack of interest in food/aversion to eating, observed inadequate intake, weight loss, loss of muscle mass.
risk for Infection: risk factors may include depression of immunological defenses, invasive procedures/devices, and changes in dietary intake/malnutrition.
risk for acute Confusion: risk factors may include accumulation of toxic waste products and altered cerebral perfusion

renal failure, chronic
risk for decreased Cardiac Output: risk factors may include fluid imbalances affecting circulating volume, myocardial workload, systemic vascular resistance; alterations in rate, rhythm, cardiac conduction—electrolyte imbalances, hypoxia; accumulation of toxins—urea; soft-tissue calcification—deposits of calcium phosphate.
risk for Bleeding: risk factors may include abnormal blood profile—suppressed erythropoietin production or secretion, decreased RBC production and survival, altered clotting factors; increased capillary fragility.
risk for acute Confusion: risk factors may include electrolyte imbalance, increased blood urea nitrogen/creatinine, azotemia
risk for impaired Skin Integrity: risk factors may include altered metabolic state and circulation (anemia with tissue ischemia), altered sensation (peripheral neuropathy), decreased skin turgor, reduced activity or immobility, accumulation of toxins in the skin.
risk for impaired Oral Mucous Membrane: risk factors may include decreased or lack of salivation, fluid restrictions, chemical irritation, conversion of urea in saliva to ammonia.

renal transplantation
risk for excess Fluid Volume: risk factors may include compromised regulatory mechanism (implantation of new kidney requiring adjustment period for optimal functioning).
disturbed Body Image may be related to failure and subsequent replacement of body part and medication-induced changes in appearance, possibly evidenced by preoccupation with loss/change, negative feelings about body, and focus on past strength/function.
Fear may be related to potential for transplant rejection/failure and threat of death, possibly evidenced by increased tension, apprehension, concentration on source, and verbalizations of concern.
risk for Infection: risk factors may include broken skin/traumatized tissue, stasis of body fluids, immunosuppression, invasive procedures, nutritional deficits, and chronic disease.
risk for ineffective Coping/compromised family Coping: risk factors may include situational crises, family disorganization and role changes, prolonged disease exhausting supportive capacity of significant others/family, therapeutic restrictions/long-term therapy needs.

respiratory distress syndrome, acute
ineffective Airway Clearance may be related to loss of ciliary action, increased amount and viscosity of secretions, and increased airway resistance, possibly evidenced by presence of dyspnea, changes in depth and rate of respiration, use of accessory muscles for breathing, wheezes and crackles, cough with or without sputum production
impaired Gas Exchange may be related to changes in pulmonary capillary permeability with edema formation, alveolar hypoventilation and collapse, with intrapulmonary shunting, possibly evidenced by tachypnea, use of accessory muscles, cyanosis, hypoxia per ABGs or oximetry, anxiety, and changes in mentation.
risk for deficient Fluid Volume risk factors may include active loss from diuretic use and restricted intake.

risk for decreased Cardiac Output: risk factors may include alteration in preload (hypovolemia, vascular pooling, diuretic therapy, and increased intrathoracic pressure, use of ventilator and positive end-expiratory pressure [PEEP]).

Anxiety [specify level]/Fear may be related to physiological factors (effects of hypoxemia), situational crisis, change in health status and threat of death possibly evidenced by increased tension, apprehension, restlessness, focus on self, and sympathetic stimulation.

risk for [barotrauma] Injury: risk factors may include increased airway pressure associated with mechanical ventilation (PEEP).

respiratory distress syndrome, premature infant
(also refer to *neonatal, premature newborn*)

impaired Gas Exchange may be related to alveolar-capillary membrane changes (inadequate surfactant levels), altered oxygen supply (tracheobronchial obstruction, atelectasis), altered blood flow (immaturity of pulmonary arteriole musculature), altered oxygen-carrying capacity of blood (anemia), and cold stress, possibly evidenced by tachypnea, use of accessory muscles—retractions, expiratory grunting, pallor, or cyanosis, abnormal ABGs, and tachycardia.

impaired spontaneous Ventilation may be related to respiratory muscle fatigue and metabolic factors, possibly evidenced by dyspnea, increased metabolic rate, restlessness, use of accessory muscles, and abnormal ABGs.

risk for Infection: risk factors may include inadequate primary defenses (decreased ciliary action, stasis of body fluids, traumatized tissues), inadequate secondary defenses (deficiency of neutrophils and specific immunoglobulins), invasive procedures, and malnutrition (absence of nutrient stores, increased metabolic demands).

risk for ineffective Gastrointestinal Perfusion: risk factors may include persistent fetal circulation and exchange problems.

isk for impaired Attachment r: risk factors may include premature or ill infant who is unable to effectively initiate parental contact (altered behavioral organization), separation, physical barriers, anxiety associated with the parental role and demands of infant.

respiratory syncytial virus (RSV)

impaired Gas Exchange may be related to inflammatin of airways, ventilation perfusion imbalance, apnea, possibly evidenced by dyspnea, abnormal arterial blood gases/hypoxia

ineffective Airway Clearance may be related to infection, retained secretions, exudate in the alveoli, possibly evidenced by dyspnea, adventitious breath sounds, ineffective cough

risk for deficient Fluid Volume.: risk factors may include increased insensible losses (fever, diaphoresis), decreased oral intake

retinal detachment

disturbed visual Sensory Perception related to decreased sensory reception, possibly evidenced by visual distortions, decreased visual field, and changes in visual acuity.

deficient Knowledge [Learning Need] regarding therapy, prognosis, and self-care needs may be related to lack of information/misconceptions, possibly evidenced by statements of concern and questions.

risk for impaired Home Maintenance: risk factors may include visual limitations, activity restrictions.

Reye's syndrome

deficient Fluid Volume [isotonic] may be related to failure of regulatory mechanism (diabetes insipidus), excessive gastric losses (pernicious vomiting), and altered intake, possibly evidenced by increased/dilute urine output, sudden weight loss, decreased venous filling, dry mucous membranes, decreased skin turgor, hypotension, and tachycardia.

ineffective cerebral Tissue Perfusion may be related to diminished arterial/venous blood flow and hypovolemia, possibly evidenced by memory loss, altered consciousness, and restlessness/agitation.

risk for Trauma: risk factors may include generalized weakness, reduced coordination, and cognitive deficits.

ineffective Breathing Pattern may be related to decreased energy and fatigue, cognitive impairment, tracheobronchial obstruction, and inflammatory process (aspiration pneumonia), possibly evidenced by tachypnea, abnormal ABGs, cough, and use of accessory muscles.

rheumatic fever

acute Pain may be related to migratory inflammation of joints, possibly evidenced by verbal reports, guarding/distraction behaviors, self-focus, and autonomic responses (changes in vital signs).

Hyperthermia may be related to inflammatory process/hypermetabolic state, possibly evidenced by increased body temperature, warm/flushed skin, and tachycardia.

Activity Intolerance may be related to generalized weakness, joint pain, and medical restrictions/bedrest, possibly evidenced by reports of fatigue, exertional discomfort, and abnormal heart rate in response to activity.

risk for decreased Cardiac Output: risk factors may include cardiac inflammation/enlargement and altered contractility.

rickets (osteomalacia)

delayed Growth and Development may be related to dietary deficiencies/indiscretions, malabsorption syndrome, and lack of exposure to sunlight, possibly evidenced by altered physical growth and delay or difficulty in performing motor skills typical for age.

deficient Knowledge [Learning Need] regarding cause, pathophysiology, therapy needs and prevention may be related to lack of information, possibly evidenced by statements of concern, questions, misconceptions, and inaccurate follow-through of instructions.

ringworm, tinea

(also refer to *athlete's foot*)

impaired Skin Integrity may be related to fungal infection of the dermis, possibly evidenced by disruption of skin surfaces/presence of lesions.

deficient Knowledge [Learning Need] regarding infectious nature, therapy, and self-care needs may be related to lack of information/misinformation, possibly evidenced by statements of concern, questions, and recurrence/spread.

rubella

acute Pain/impaired Comfort may be related to inflammatory effects of viral infection and presence of desquamating rash, possibly evidenced by verbal reports, distraction behaviors/restlessness.

deficient Knowledge [Learning Need] regarding contagious nature, possible complications, and self-care needs may be related to lack of information/misinterpretations, possibly evidenced by statements of concern, questions, and inaccurate follow-through of instructions.

scabies

impaired Skin Integrity may be related to presence of invasive parasite and development of pruritus, possibly evidenced by disruption of skin surface and inflammation.

deficient Knowledge [Learning Need] regarding communicable nature, possible complications, therapy, and self-care needs may be related to lack of information/misinterpretation, possibly evidenced by questions and statements of concern about spread to others.

scarlet fever

Hyperthermia may be related to effects of circulating toxins, possibly evidenced by increased body temperature, warm/flushed skin, and tachycardia.

acute Pain/impaired Comfort may be related to inflammation of mucous membranes and effects of circulating toxins (malaise, fever), possibly evidenced by verbal reports, distraction behaviors, guarding (decreased swallowing), and self-focus.

risk for deficient Fluid Volume: risk factors may include hypermetabolic state (hyperthermia) and reduced intake.

schizophrenia (schizophrenic disorders)

[disturbed Sensory Perception (specify)] may be related to biochemical/electrolyte imbalance, psychological stress, possibly evidenced by disorientation to space/time, hallucinations, change in behavior pattern.

impaired Verbal Communication may be related to altered perceptions, alteration in self-concept, psychological barriers, e.g., psychosis possibly evidenced by inappropriate verbalizations, difficulty in comprehending usual communication pattern, difficulty in use of facial expressions

Social Isolation may be related to alterations in mental status, mistrust of others/delusional thinking, unacceptable social behaviors, inadequate personal resources, and inability to engage in satisfying personal relationships, possibly evidenced by difficulty in establishing relationships with others; dull affect, uncommunicative/withdrawn behavior, seeking to be alone, inadequate/absent significant purpose in life, and expression of feelings of rejection.

ineffective Health Maintenance/impaired Home Maintenance may be related to impaired cognitive/emotional functioning, altered ability to make deliberate and thoughtful judgments, altered communication, and lack/inappropriate use of material resources, possibly evidenced by inability to take responsibility for meeting basic health practices in any or all functional areas and demonstrated lack of adaptive behaviors to internal or external environmental changes, disorderly surroundings, accumulation of dirt/unwashed clothes, repeated hygienic disorders.

risk for self/other-directed Violence: risk factors may include disturbances of thinking/ feeling (depression, paranoia, suicidal ideation), lack of development of trust and appropriate interpersonal relationships, catatonic/manic excitement, toxic reactions to drugs (alcohol).

ineffective Coping may be related to personal vulnerability, inadequate support system(s), unrealistic perceptions, inadequate coping methods, and disintegration of thought processes, possibly evidenced by impaired judgment/cognition and perception, diminished problem-solving/decision-making capacities, poor self-concept, chronic anxiety, depression, inability to perform role expectations, and alteration in social participation.

interrupted Family Processes/ disabled family Coping may be related to ambivalent family system/relationships, changes of roles, and difficulty of family member in coping effectively with patient's maladaptive behaviors, possibly evidenced by deterioration in family functioning, ineffective family decision-making process, difficulty relating to each other, client's expression of despair at family's lack of reaction/ involvement, neglectful relationships with patient, extreme distortion regarding patient's health problem, including denial about its existence/severity or prolonged overconcern.

Self-Care Deficit [specify] may be related to perceptual and cognitive impairment, immobility (withdrawal/isolation and decreased psychomotor activity), and side effects of psychotropic medications, possibly evidenced by inability or difficulty in areas of feeding self, keeping body clean, dressing appropriately, toileting self, and/or changes in bowel/bladder elimination.

sciatica

acute/chronic Pain may be related to peripheral nerve root compression, possibly evidenced by verbal reports, guarding/distraction behaviors, and self-focus.

impaired physical Mobility may be related to neurological pain and muscular involvement, possibly evidenced by reluctance to attempt movement and decreased muscle strength/mass.

scleroderma

(also refer to *lupus erythematosus, systemic—SLE*)

impaired physical Mobility may be related to musculoskeletal impairment and associated pain, possibly evidenced by decreased strength, decreased range of motion, and reluctance to attempt movement.

ineffective Tissue Perfusion, (specify) may be related to reduced arterial blood flow (arteriolar vasoconstriction), possibly evidenced by changes in skin temperature/color, ulcer formation, and changes in organ function (cardiopulmonary, gastrointestinal, renal).

imbalanced Nutrition: less than body requirements may be related to inability to ingest/ digest/absorb adequate nutrients (sclerosis of the tissues rendering mouth immobile, decreased peristalsis of esophagus/small intestines, atrophy of smooth muscle of colon), possibly evidenced by weight loss, decreased intake/food and reported/observed difficulty swallowing.

risk-prone health Behavior may be related to disability requiring change in lifestyle, inadequate support systems, assault to self-concept, and altered locus of control, possibly evidenced by verbalization of nonacceptance of health status change and lack of movement toward independence/future-oriented thinking.

disturbed Body Image may be related to skin changes with induration, atrophy, and fibrosis, loss of hair, and skin and muscle contractures, possibly evidenced by verbalization of negative feelings about body, focus on past strength/function or appearance, fear of rejection/reaction by others, hiding body part, and change in social involvement.

scoliosis

disturbed Body Image may be related to altered body structure, use of therapeutic device(s), and activity restrictions, possibly evidenced by negative feelings about body, change in social involvement, and preoccupation with situation or refusal to acknowledge problem.

deficient Knowledge [Learning Need] regarding pathophysiology of condition, therapy needs and possible outcomes may be related to lack of information/misinterpretation, possibly evidenced by statements of concern, questions, misconceptions, and inaccurate follow-through of instructions.

risk-prone health Behavior may be related to lack of comprehension of long-term consequences of behavior, possibly evidenced by failure to adhere to treatment regimen/ keep appointments and evidence of failure to improve.

seizure disorder

deficient Knowledge [Learning Need] regarding condition and medication control may be related to lack of information/misinterpretations, scarce financial resources, possibly evidenced by questions, statements of concern/misconceptions, incorrect use of anticonvulsant medication, recurrent episodes/uncontrolled seizures.

chronic low Self-Esteem/disturbed personal Identity may be related to perceived neurological functional change/weakness, perception of being out of control, stigma associated with condition, possibly evidenced by negative feelings about "brain"/self, change in social involvement, feelings of helplessness, and preoccupation with perceived change or loss.

impaired Social Interaction may be related to unpredictable nature of condition and self-concept disturbance, possibly evidenced by decreased self-assurance, verbalization of concern, discomfort in social situations, inability to receive/communicate a satisfying sense of belonging/caring, and withdrawal from social contacts/activities.

risk for Trauma/Suffocation: risk factors may include weakness, balancing difficulties, cognitive limitations/altered consciousness, loss of large or small-muscle coordination (during seizure).

sepsis

also refer to *sepsis, puerperal*

risk for deficient Fluid Volume: risk factors may include marked increase in vascular compartment, massive vasodilation, capillary permeability, vascular shifts to interstitial space, and reduced intake.

risk for decreased Cardiac Output: risk factors may include decreased preload—venous return and circulating volume; altered afterload—increased systemic vascular resistance; negative inotropic effects of hypoxia, complement activation, and lysosomal hydrolase.

risk for impaired Gas Exchange: risk factors may include effects of endotoxins on the respiratory center in the medulla—hyperventilation and respiratory alkalosis; hypoventilation; changes in vascular resistance, alveolar-capillary membrane changes—increased capillary permeability leading to pulmonary congestion; interference with oxygen delivery and utilization in the tissues—endotoxin-induced damage to the cells and capillaries

risk for Shock: risk factors may include infection/sepsis, hypovolemia—fluid shifts/third spacing; hypotension, hypoxemia.

sepsis, puerperal

(also refer to *sepsis*)

risk for Infection [spread/septic shock]: risk factors may include presence of infection, broken skin, and/or traumatized tissues, rupture of amniotic membranes, high vascularity of involved area, stasis of body fluids, invasive procedures, and/or increased environmental exposure, chronic disease (e.g., diabetes, anemia, malnutrition), altered immune response, and untoward effect of medications (e.g., opportunistic/secondary infection).

Hyperthermia may be related to inflammatory process/hypermetabolic state, possibly evidenced by increase in body temperature, warm/flushed skin, and tachycardia.

risk for impaired Attachment: risk factors may include interruption in bonding process, physical illness, perceived threat to own survival.

risk for ineffective peripheral Tissue Perfusion: risk factors may include interruption/reduction of blood flow (presence of infectious thrombi).

serum sickness

acute Pain may be related to inflammation of the joints and skin eruptions, possibly evidenced by verbal reports, guarding/distraction behaviors, and self-focus.

deficient Knowledge [Learning Need] regarding nature of condition, treatment needs, potential complications, and prevention of recurrence may be related to lack of information/misinterpretation, possibly evidenced by statements of concern, questions, misconceptions, and inaccurate follow-through of instructions.

sexually transmitted disease (STD)

risk for Infection [transmission]: risk factors may include contagious nature of infecting agent and insufficient knowledge to avoid exposure to/transmission of pathogens.

impaired Skin/Tissue Integrity may be related to invasion of/irritation by pathogenic organism(s), possibly evidenced by disruptions of skin/tissue and inflammation of mucous membranes.

deficient Knowledge [Learning Need] regarding condition, prognosis/complications, therapy needs, and transmission may be related to lack of information/misinterpretation, lack of interest in learning, possibly evidenced by statements of concern, questions, misconceptions, inaccurate follow-through of instructions, and development of preventable complications.

shock
(also refer to *shock, cardiogenic*; *shock, hemorrhagic/hypovolemic*)
ineffective Tissue Perfusion (specify) may be related to changes in circulating volume and/or vascular tone, possibly evidenced by changes in skin color/temperature and pulse pressure, reduced blood pressure, changes in mentation, and decreased urinary output.
Anxiety [specify level] may be related to change in health status and threat of death, possibly evidenced by increased tension, apprehension, sympathetic stimulation, restlessness, and expressions of concern.

shock, cardiogenic
(also refer to *shock*)
decreased Cardiac Output may be related to structural damage, decreased myocardial contractility, and presence of dysrhythmias, possibly evidenced by ECG changes, variations in hemodynamic readings, jugular vein distention, cold/clammy skin, diminished peripheral pulses, and decreased urinary output.
risk for impaired Gas Exchange: risk factors may include ventilation perfusion imbalance, alveolar-capillary membrane changes.

shock, hemorrhagic/hypovolemic
(also refer to *shock*)
deficient Fluid Volume [isotonic] may be related to excessive vascular loss, inadequate intake/replacement, possibly evidenced by hypotension, tachycardia, decreased pulse volume and pressure, change in mentation, and decreased/concentrated urine.

shock, septic
Refer to *sepsis*.

sick sinus syndrome
(also refer to *dysrhythmia, cardiac*)
decreased Cardiac Output may be related to alterations in rate, rhythm, and electrical conduction, possibly evidenced by ECG evidence of dysrhythmias, reports of palpitations/weakness, changes in mentation/consciousness, and syncope.
risk for Trauma: risk factors may include changes in cerebral perfusion with altered consciousness/loss of balance.

smallpox
risk of Infection [spread]: risk factors may include contagious nature of organism, inadequate acquired immunity, presence of chronic disease, immunosuppression.
deficient Fluid Volume may be related to hypermetabolic state, decreased intake (pharyngeal lesions, nausea), increased losses (vomiting), fluid shifts from vascular bed possibly evidenced by reports of thirst, decreased blood pressure, venous filling and urinary output; dry mucous membranes, decreased skin turgor, change in mental state, elevated Hct.
impaired Tissue Integrity may be related to immunological deficit possibly evidenced by disruption of skin surface, cornea, mucous membranes.
Anxiety [specify level]/Fear may be related to threat of death, interpersonal transmission/contagion, separation from support system possibly evidenced by expressed concerns, apprehension, restlessness, focus on self.
interrupted Family Processes may be related to temporary family disorganization, situational crisis, change in health status of family member possibly evidenced by changes in satisfaction with family, stress-reduction behaviors, mutual support; expression of isolation from community resources.
ineffective community Coping may be related to human-made disaster (bioterrorism), inadequate resources for problem-solving possibly evidenced by deficits of community participation, high illness rate, excessive community conflicts, expressed vulnerability/powerlessness.

snow blindness
disturbed visual Sensory Perception may be related to altered status of sense organ (irritation of the conjunctiva, hyperemia), possibly evidenced by intolerance to light (photophobia) and decreased/loss of visual acuity.
acute Pain may be related to irritation/vascular congestion of the conjunctiva, possibly evidenced by verbal reports, guarding/distraction behaviors, and self-focus.
Anxiety [specify level] may be related to situational crisis and threat to/change in health status, possibly evidenced by increased tension, apprehension, uncertainty, worry, restlessness, and focus on self.

somatoform disorders
ineffective Coping may be related to severe level of anxiety that is repressed, personal vulnerability, un-met dependency needs, fixation in earlier level of development, retarded ego development, and inadequate coping skills, possibly evidenced by verbal-

ized inability to cope/problem-solve, high illness rate, multiple somatic complaints of several years' duration, decreased functioning in social/occupational settings, narcissistic tendencies with total focus on self/physical symptoms, demanding behaviors, history of "doctor shopping" and refusal to attend therapeutic activities.

chronic Pain may be related to severe level of repressed anxiety, low self-concept, unmet dependency needs, history of self or loved one having experienced a serious illness, possibly evidenced by verbal reports of severe/prolonged pain, guarded movement/protective behaviors, facial mask of pain, fear of reinjury, altered ability to continue previous activities, social withdrawal, demands for therapy/medication.

disturbed Sensory Perception (specify) may be related to psychological stress (narrowed perceptual fields, expression of stress as physical problems/deficits, poor quality of sleep, presence of chronic pain, possibly evidenced by reported change in voluntary motor or sensory function (paralysis, anosmia, aphonia, deafness, blindness, loss of touch or pain sensation), *la belle indifférence* (lack of concern over functional loss).

impaired Social Interaction may be related to inability to engage in satisfying personal relationships, preoccupation with self and physical symptoms, altered state of wellness, chronic pain, and rejection by others, possibly evidenced by preoccupation with own thoughts, sad/dull affect, absence of supportive significant other(s), uncommunicative/withdrawn behavior, lack of eye contact, and seeking to be alone.

spinal cord injury (SCI)
Refer to paraplegia; quadriplegia.

sprain of ankle or foot
acute Pain may be related to trauma to/swelling in joint, possibly evidenced by verbal reports, guarding/distraction behaviors, self-focusing, and autonomic responses (changes in vital signs).

impaired Walking may be related to musculoskeletal injury, pain, and therapeutic restrictions, possibly evidenced by reluctance to attempt movement, inability to move about environment easily.

stapedectomy
risk for Trauma: risk factors may include increased middle-ear pressure with displacement of prosthesis and balancing difficulties/dizziness.

risk for Infection: risk factors may include surgically traumatized tissue, invasive procedures, and environmental exposure to upper respiratory infections.

acute Pain may be related to surgical trauma, edema formation, and presence of packing, possibly evidenced by verbal reports, guarding/distraction behaviors, and self-focus.

stimulant abuse
imbalanced Nutrition: less than body requirements may be related to anorexia, insufficient or inappropriate use of financial resources, possibly evidenced by reported inadequate intake, weight loss or less than normal weight gain; lack of interest in food, poor muscle tone, signs or laboratory evidence of vitamin deficiencies

risk for Infection: risk factors may include injection techniques, impurities of drugs; localized trauma or nasal septum damage, malnutrition, altered immune state.

Insomnia may be related to CNS sensory alterations, psychological stress possibly evidenced by constant alertness, racing thoughts preventing rest, denial of need to sleep, reported inability to stay awake, initial insomnia then hypersomnia.

Fear/Anxiety [specify] may be related to paranoid delusions associated with stimulant use possibly evidenced by feelings or beliefs that others are conspiring against or are about to attack or kill client.

[disturbed Sensory Perception (specify)] may be related to exogenous chemical, altered sensory reception, transmission, or integration (hallucination), altered status of sense organs, possibly evidenced by responding to internal stimuli from hallucinatory experiences, bizarre thinking, anxiety or panic changes in sensory acuity (sense of smell/taste).

substance dependence/abuse rehabilitation (following acute detoxification)
ineffective Denial/Coping may be related to threat of unpleasant reality, lack of emotional support from others, overwhelming stress, possibly evidenced by lack of acceptance that drug use is causing the present situation, delay in seeking or refusal of healthcare attention to the detriment of health, use of manipulation to avoid responsibility for self, projection of blame or responsibility for problems.

ineffective Coping may be related to personal vulnerability, negative role modeling, inadequate support systems, previous ineffective or inadequate coping skills with substitution of drug(s), possibly evidenced by impaired adaptive behavior and problem-solving skills, decreased ability to handle stress of illness or hospitalization, financial affairs in disarray, employment or school difficulties—losing time on job or not maintaining steady employment, poor work or school performances, on-the-job injuries; verbalization of inability to cope or ask for help.

Powerlessness may be related to substance addiction with/without periods of abstinence, episodic compulsive indulgence, attempts at recovery, and lifestyle of helplessness, possibly evidenced by ineffective recovery attempts, statements of inability to stop behavior/requests for help, continuous/constant thinking about drug and/or obtaining drug, alteration in personal/occupational and social life.

imbalanced Nutrition: less than body requirements may be related to insufficient dietary intake to meet metabolic needs for psychological/physiological/economic reasons, possibly evidenced by weight less than normal for height/body build, decreased subcutaneous fat/muscle mass, reported altered taste sensation, lack of interest in food, poor muscle tone, sore/inflamed buccal cavity, laboratory evidence of protein/vitamin deficiencies.

Sexual Dysfunction may be related to altered body function (neurological damage and debilitating effects of drug use), changes in appearance, possibly evidenced by progressive interference with sexual functioning, a significant degree of testicular atrophy, gynecomastia, impotence/decreased sperm counts in men; and loss of body hair, thin/soft skin, spider angiomas, and amenorrhea/increase in miscarriages in women.

dysfunctional Family Processes may be related to abuse and history of alcoholism or drug use, inadequate coping skills, lack of problem-solving skills, genetic predisposition or biochemical influences, possibly evidenced by feelings of anger, frustration, or responsibility for alcoholic's behavior; suppressed rage, shame, embarrassment, repressed emotions, guilt, vulnerability, disturbed family dynamics or deterioration in family relationships, family denial or rationalization, closed communication systems, triangulating family relationships, manipulation, blaming, enabling to maintain substance use, inability to accept or receive help.

risk for fetal Injury: risk factors may include drug/alcohol use, exposure to teratogens.

deficient Knowledge [Learning Need] regarding condition, effects on pregnancy, prognosis, treatment needs may be related to lack or misinterpretation of information, lack of recall, cognitive limitations, interference with learning, possibly evidenced by statements of concern, questions, misconceptions, inaccurate follow-through of instructions, development of preventable complications, continued use in spite of complications.

surgery, general
(also refer to *postoperative recovery period*)

deficient Knowledge [Learning Need] regarding surgical procedure/expectation, postoperative routines/therapy, and self-care needs may be related to lack of information/misinterpretation, possibly evidenced by statements of concern, questions, and misconceptions.

Anxiety [specify level]/Fear may be related to situational crisis, unfamiliarity with environment, change in health status/ threat of death and separation from usual support systems, possibly evidenced by increased tension, apprehension, decreased self-assurance, fear of unspecific consequences, focus on self, sympathetic stimulation, and restlessness.

risk for perioperative-positioning Injury: risk factors may include disorientation, immobilization, muscle weakness, obesity/edema.

risk for Injury risk factors may include wrong client, procedure, site, implants, equipment or materials; interactive conditions between individual and environment; external environment—physical design, structure of environment, exposure to equipment, instrumentation, positioning, use of pharmaceutical agents; internal environment—tissue hypoxia, abnormal blood profile or altered clotting factors, broken skin.

risk for Infection: risk factors may include broken skin, traumatized tissues, stasis of body fluids; presence of pathogens or contaminants, environmental exposure, invasive procedures.

risk for imbalanced Body Temperature: risk factors may include exposure to cool environment, use of medications, anesthetic agents; extremes of age, weight; dehydration.

ineffective Breathing Pattern may be related to chemically induced muscular relaxation, perception or cognitive impairment, decreased lung expansion, energy; tracheobronchial obstruction

risk for deficient Fluid Volume: risk factors may include preoperative fluid deprivation, nausea, blood loss, and excessive gastrointestinal losses (vomiting or gastric suction), extremes of age and weight.

synovitis (knee)

acute Pain may be related to inflammation of synovial membrane of the joint with effusion, possibly evidenced by verbal reports, guarding/distraction behaviors, self-focus, and autonomic responses (changes in vital signs).

impaired Walking may be related to pain and decreased strength of joint, possibly evidenced by reluctance to attempt movement, inability to move about environment as desired.

syphilis, congenital
(also refer to *sexually transmitted disease—STD*)
acute Pain may be related to inflammatory process, edema formation, and development of skin lesions, possibly evidenced by irritability/crying that may be increased with movement of extremities and autonomic responses (changes in vital signs).
impaired Skin/Tissue Integrity may be related to exposure to pathogens during vaginal delivery, possibly evidenced by disruption of skin surfaces and rhinitis.
delayed Growth and Development may be related to effect of infectious process, possibly evidenced by altered physical growth and delay or difficulty performing skills typical of age group.
deficient Knowledge [Learning Need] regarding pathophysiology of condition, transmissibility, therapy needs, expected outcomes, and potential complications may be related to caretaker/parental lack of information, misinterpretation, possibly evidenced by statements of concern, questions, and misconceptions.

syringomyelia
disturbed Sensory Perception (specify) may be related to altered sensory perception (neurological lesion), possibly evidenced by change in usual response to stimuli and motor incoordination.
Anxiety [specify level]/Fear may be related to change in health status, threat of change in role functioning and socioeconomic status, and threat to self-concept, possibly evidenced by increased tension, apprehension, uncertainty, focus on self, and expressed concerns.
impaired physical Mobility may be related to neuromuscular and sensory impairment, possibly evidenced by decreased muscle strength, control, and mass and impaired coordination.
Self-Care Deficit [specify] may be related to neuromuscular and sensory impairments, possibly evidenced by statement of inability to perform care tasks.

Tay-Sachs disease
delayed Growth and Development may be related to effects of physical condition, possibly evidenced by altered physical growth, loss of/failure to acquire skills typical of age, flat affect, and decreased responses.
disturbed visual Sensory Perception may be related to neurological deterioration of optic nerve, possibly evidenced by loss of visual acuity.
[family] Grieving may be related to expected eventual loss of infant/child, possibly evidenced by expressions of distress, denial, guilt, anger, and sorrow; choked feelings; changes in sleep/eating habits; and altered libido.
[family] Powerlessness may be related to absence of therapeutic interventions for progressive/fatal disease, possibly evidenced by verbal expressions of having no control over situation/outcome and depression over physical/mental deterioration.
risk for Spiritual Distress: risk factors may include challenged belief and value system by presence of fatal condition with racial/religious connotations and intense suffering.
compromised family Coping may be related to situational crisis, temporary preoccupation with managing emotional conflicts and personal suffering, family disorganization, and prolonged/progressive disease, possibly evidenced by preoccupation with personal reactions, expressed concern about reactions of other family members, inadequate support of one another, and altered communication patterns.

thrombophlebitis
ineffective peripheral Tissue Perfusion may be related to interruption of venous blood flow, venous stasis, possibly evidenced by changes in skin color/temperature over affected area, development of edema, pain, diminished peripheral pulses, slow capillary refill.
acute Pain/[discomfort] may be related to vascular inflammation/irritation and edema formation (accumulation of lactic acid), possibly evidenced by verbal reports, guarding/distraction behaviors, and self-focus.
risk for impaired physical Mobility: risk factors may include pain and discomfort and restrictive therapies/safety precautions.
deficient Knowledge [Learning Need] regarding pathophysiology of condition, therapy/self-care needs, and risk of embolization may be related to lack of information/misinterpretation, possibly evidenced by statements of concern, questions, inaccurate follow-through of instructions, and development of preventable complications.

thrombosis, venous
Refer to *thrombophlebitis*.

thrush
impaired Oral Mucous Membrane may be related to presence of infection as evidenced by white patches/plaques, oral discomfort, mucosal irritation, bleeding.

thyroidectomy
(also refer to *hyperthyroidism*; *hypoparathyroidism*; *hypothyroidism*)
risk for ineffective Airway Clearance: risk factors may include hematoma/edema formation with tracheal obstruction, laryngeal spasms.
impaired verbal Communication may be related to tissue edema, pain/discomfort, and vocal cord injury/laryngeal nerve damage, possibly evidenced by impaired articulation, does not/cannot speak, and use of nonverbal cues/gestures.
risk for Injury [tetany]: risk factors may include chemical imbalance/excessive CNS stimulation.
risk for head/neck Trauma: risk factors may include loss of muscle control/support and position of suture line.
acute Pain may be related to presence of surgical incision/manipulation of tissues/muscles, postoperative edema, possibly evidenced by verbal reports, guarding/distraction behaviors, narrowed focus, and autonomic responses (changes in vital signs).

thyrotoxicosis
(also refer to *hyperthyroidism*)
risk for decreased Cardiac Output: risk factors may include uncontrolled hypermetabolic state increasing cardiac workload, changes in venous return and SVR; and alterations in rate, rhythm, and electrical conduction.
Anxiety [specify level] may be related to physiological factors/CNS stimulation (hypermetabolic state and pseudocatecholamine effect of thyroid hormones), possibly evidenced by increased feelings of apprehension, shakiness, loss of control, panic, changes in cognition, distortion of environmental stimuli, extraneous movements, restlessness, and tremors.
deficient Knowledge [Learning Need] regarding condition, treatment needs, and potential for complications/crisis situation may be related to lack of information/recall, misinterpretation, possibly evidenced by statements of concern, questions, misconceptions; and inaccurate follow-through of instructions.

TIA (Transient ischemic attack)
ineffective cerebral Tissue Perfusion may be related to interruption of blood flow (e.g., vasospasm) possibly evidenced by altered mental status, behavioral changes, language deficit, change in motor/sensory response.
Anxiety/Fear may be related to change in health status, threat to self-concept, situational crisis, interpersonal contagion possibly evidenced by expressed concerns, apprehension, restlessness, irritability.
risk for ineffective Denial: risk factors may include change in health status requiring change in lifestyle, fear of consequences, lack of motivation

tic douloureux
Refer to *neuralgia, trigeminal*.

tonsillectomy
Also refer to *adenoidectomy*.
acute Pain may be related to physical trauma to oronasopharynx, presence of packing, possibly evidenced by restlessness, crying, and facial mask of pain.
Anxiety [specify level]/Fear may be related to separation from supportive others, unfamiliar surroundings, and perceived threat of injury or abandonment, possibly evidenced by crying, apprehension, trembling, and sympathetic stimulation (pupil dilation, increased heart rate).
risk for ineffective Airway Clearance: risk factors may include sedation, collection of secretions and blood in oropharynx, and vomiting.
risk for deficient Fluid Volume: risk factors may include operative trauma to highly vascular site, hemorrhage.

tonsillitis
acute Pain may be related to inflammation of tonsils and effects of circulating toxins, possibly evidenced by verbal reports, guarding/distraction behaviors, reluctance/refusal to swallow, self-focus, and autonomic responses (changes in vital signs).
Hyperthermia may be related to presence of inflammatory process/hypermetabolic state and dehydration, possibly evidenced by increased body temperature, warm/flushed skin, and tachycardia.
deficient Knowledge [Learning Need] regardless cause/transmission, treatment needs, and potential complications may be related to lack of information/misinterpretation, possibly evidenced by statements of concern, questions, inaccurate follow-through of instructions, and recurrence of condition.

total joint replacement
risk for Infection: risk factors may include inadequate primary defenses (broken skin, exposure of joint), inadequate secondary defenses/immunosuppression (long-term cor-

ticosteroid use), invasive procedures/surgical manipulation, implantation of foreign body, and decreased mobility.

impaired physical Mobility may be related to pain and discomfort, musculoskeletal impairment, and surgery/restrictive therapies, possibly evidenced by reluctance to attempt movement, difficulty purposefully moving within the physical environment, reports of pain/discomfort on movement, limited range of motion, and decreased muscle strength/control.

risk for ineffective peripheral Tissue Perfusion: risk factors may include reduced arterial/venous blood flow, direct trauma to blood vessels, tissue edema, improper location/dislocation of prosthesis, and hypovolemia.

acute Pain may be related to physical agents (traumatized tissues/surgical intervention, degeneration of joints, muscle spasms), and psychological factors (anxiety, advanced age), possibly evidenced by verbal reports, guarding/distraction behaviors, self-focus, and autonomic responses (changes in vital signs).

risk for Constipation: risk factors may include insufficient physical activity, decreased mobility, weakness, insufficient fiber or fluid intake, dehydration, poor eating habits, decreased gastrointestinal motility, effects of medications—anesthesia, opiate analgesics; environmental changes, inadequate toileting.

toxemia of pregnancy
Refer to *pregnancy-induced hypertension.*

toxic shock syndrome
Hyperthermia may be related to inflammatory process/hypermetabolic state and dehydration, possibly evidenced by increased body temperature, warm/flushed skin, and tachycardia.

deficient Fluid Volume [isotonic] may be related to increased gastric losses (diarrhea, vomiting), fever/hypermetabolic state, and decreased intake, possibly evidenced by dry mucous membranes, increased pulse, hypotension, delayed venous filling, decreased/concentrated urine, and hemoconcentration.

acute Pain may be related to inflammatory process, effects of circulating toxins, and skin disruptions, possibly evidenced by verbal reports, guarding/distraction behaviors, self-focus, and autonomic responses (changes in vital signs).

impaired Skin/Tissue Integrity may be related to effects of circulating toxins and dehydration, possibly evidenced by development of desquamating rash, hyperemia, and inflammation of mucous membranes.

traction
(also refer to *casts*; *fractures*)
acute Pain may be related to direct trauma to tissue/bone, muscle spasms, movement of bone fragments, edema, injury to soft tissue, traction/immobility device, anxiety, possibly evidenced by verbal reports, guarding/distraction behaviors, self-focus, alteration in muscle tone, and autonomic responses (changes in vital signs).

impaired physical Mobility may be related to neuromuscular/skeletal impairment, pain, psychological immobility, and therapeutic restrictions of movement, possibly evidenced by limited range of motion, inability to move purposefully in environment, reluctance to attempt movement, and decreased muscle strength/control.

risk for Infection: risk factors may include invasive procedures (including insertion of foreign body through skin/bone), presence of traumatized tissue, and reduced activity with stasis of body fluids.

deficient Diversional Activity may be related to length of hospitalization/therapeutic intervention and environmental lack of usual activity, possibly evidenced by statements of boredom, restlessness, and irritability.

transfusion reaction, blood
(also refer to *anaphylaxis*)
risk for imbalanced Body Temperature : risk factors may include infusion of cold blood products, systemic response to toxins.

Anxiety [specify level] may be related to change in health status and threat of death, exposure to toxins possibly evidenced by increased tension, apprehension, sympathetic stimulation, restlessness, and expressions of concern.

risk for impaired Skin Integrity: risk factors may include immunological response.

transplantation recipient
Anxiety/Fear may be related to unconscious conflict about essential values/beliefs, situational crisis, threat of death (organ rejection), unfamiliarity with environmental experience, possibly evidenced by reports apprehension/increased tension, uncertainty, worried, insomnia, increased vital signs.

risk for Infection: risk factors may include medically chronic disease, induced immunosuppression, suppressed inflammatory response, invasive procedures, broken skin/traumatized tissues.

ineffective Coping/compromised family coping may be related to situational crisis, high degree of threat, uncertainty, family disorganization or role changes, prolonged diasesa exhausting supportive capicity of family/SO, possibly evidenced by reports of inability to cope, sleep pattern disturbance, fatigue, poor concentration, protective behaviors disproportionate to client's needs, SO describes preoccupation with personal reaction.

risk for ineffective Protection: risk factors may include drug therapies, compromised immune system, effects of debilitating disease.

readiness for enhanced Self-Health Management possibly evidenced by expressed desire to manage treatment/prevent sequelae, no unexpected acceleration of illness symptoms.

risk for ineffective Self-Health Management: risk factors may include complexity of therapeutic regimen and healthcare system, economic difficulties, family patterns of healthcare.

traumatic brain injury

ineffective cerebral Tissue Perfusion may be related to interruption of blood flow—hemorrhage, hematoma, cerebral edema (localized or generalized response to injury, metabolic alterations, drug or alcohol overdose), decreased systemic BP—hypovolemia, cardiac dysrhythmias; hypoxia, possibly evidenced by altered level of consciousness, memory loss, changes in motor or sensory responses, restlessness, changes in vital signs.

risk for decreased Intracranial Adaptive Capacity: risk factors may include brain injuries, systemic hypotension with intracranial hypertension.

risk for ineffective Breathing Pattern: risk factors may include neuromuscular dysfunction—injury to respiratory center of brain; perception or cognitive impairment, tracheobronchial obstruction.

[disturbed Sensory Perception (specify)] may be related to altered sensory reception, transmission and/or integration—neurological trauma or deficit, possibly evidenced by disorientation to time, place, person; change in usual response to stimuli, motor incoordination, altered communication patterns, visual or auditory distortions, altered thought processes or bizarre thinking, exaggerated emotional responses, change in behavior pattern.

risk for Infection risk factors may include traumatized tissues, broken skin, invasive procedures, decreased ciliary action, stasis of body fluids, nutritional deficits, suppressed inflammatory response—steroid use; altered integrity of closed system—cerebrospinal fluid leak.

risk for imbalanced Nutrition: less than body requirements: risk factors may include altered ability to ingest nutrients—decreased level of consciousness; weakness of muscles for chewing or swallowing, hypermetabolic state.

impaired physical Mobility may be related to perceptual or cognitive impairment, decreased strength and endurance, restrictive therapies or safety precautions possibly evidenced by inability to purposefully move within physical environment—bed mobility, transfer, ambulation; impaired coordination, limited range of motion, decreased muscle strength or control.

risk for impaired Memory/chronic Confusion: risk factors may include head injury, neurological disturbances.

interrupted Family Processes may be related to situational transition and crisis, uncertainty about ultimate outcome, expectations possibly evidenced by difficulty adapting to change or dealing with traumatic experience constructively, family not meeting needs of all members, difficulty accepting or receiving help appropriately, inability to express or to accept feelings of members.

Self-Care Deficit (specify) may be related to neuromuscular or musculoskeletal impairment, weakness, pain, perceptual or cognitive impairment possibly evidenced by inability to perform desired or appropriate ADLs.

trichinosis

acute Pain may be related to parasitic invasion of muscle tissues, edema of upper eyelids, small localized hemorrhages, and development of urticaria, possibly evidenced by verbal reports, guarding/distraction behaviors (restlessness), and autonomic responses (changes in vital signs).

deficient Fluid Volume [isotonic] may be related to hypermetabolic state (fever, diaphoresis); excessive gastric losses (vomiting, diarrhea); and decreased intake/difficulty swallowing, possibly evidenced by dry mucous membranes, decreased skin turgor, hypotension, decreased venous filling, decreased/concentrated urine, and hemoconcentration.

ineffective Breathing Pattern may be related to myositis of the diaphragm and intercostal muscles, possibly evidenced by resulting changes in respiratory depth, tachypnea, dyspnea, and abnormal ABGs.

deficient Knowledge [Learning Need] regarding cause/prevention of condition, therapy needs, and possible complications may be related to lack of information, misinterpretation, possibly evidenced by statements of concern, questions, and misconceptions.

tuberculosis (pulmonary)

risk for Infection [spread/reactivation]: risk factors may include inadequate primary defenses (decreased ciliary action/stasis of secretions, tissue destruction/extension of infection), lowered resistance/suppressed inflammatory response, malnutrition, environmental exposure, insufficient knowledge to avoid exposure to pathogens, or inadequate therapeutic intervention.

ineffective Airway Clearance may be related to thick, viscous, or bloody secretions; fatigue/poor cough effort, and tracheal/pharyngeal edema, possibly evidenced by abnormal respiratory rate, rhythm, and depth; adventitious breath sounds (rhonchi, wheezes), stridor, and dyspnea.

risk for impaired Gas Exchange: risk factors may include decrease in effective lung surface, atelectasis, destruction of alveolar-capillary membrane, bronchial edema; thick, viscous secretions.

Activity Intolerance may be related to imbalance between oxygen supply and demand, possibly evidenced by reports of fatigue, weakness, and exertional dyspnea.

imbalanced Nutrition: less than body requirements may be related to inability to ingest adequate nutrients (anorexia, effects of drug therapy, fatigue, insufficient financial resources), possibly evidenced by weight loss, reported lack of interest in food/altered taste sensation, and poor muscle tone.

risk for ineffective Self–Health Management: risk factors may include complexity of therapeutic regimen, economic difficulties, family patterns of healthcare, perceived seriousness or benefits (especially during remission), side effects of therapy.

tympanoplasty
Refer to *stapedectomy*.

typhus (tick-borne/Rocky Mountain spotted fever)

Hyperthermia may be related to generalized inflammatory process (vasculitis), possibly evidenced by increased body temperature, warm/flushed skin, and tachycardia.

acute Pain may be related to generalized vasculitis and edema formation, possibly evidenced by verbal reports, guarding/distraction behaviors, self-focus, and autonomic responses (changes in vital signs).

Tissue Perfusion, ineffective (specify) may be related to reduction/interruption of blood flow (generalized vasculitis/thrombi formation), possibly evidenced by reports of headache/abdominal pain, changes in mentation, and areas of peripheral ulceration/necrosis.

ulcer, decubitus

impaired Skin/Tissue Integrity may be related to altered circulation, nutritional deficit, fluid imbalance, impaired physical mobility, irritation of body excretions/secretions, and sensory impairments, evidenced by tissue damage/destruction.

acute Pain may be related to destruction of protective skin layers and exposure of nerves, possibly evidenced by verbal reports, distraction behaviors, and self-focus.

risk for Infection: risk factors may include broken/traumatized tissue, increased environmental exposure, and nutritional deficits.

ulcer, peptic (acute)

Fear/Anxiety [specify level] may be related to change in health status and threat of death, possibly evidenced by increased tension, restlessness, irritability, fearfulness, trembling, tachycardia, diaphoresis, lack of eye contact, focus on self, verbalization of concerns, withdrawal, and panic or attack behavior.

acute Pain may be related to caustic irritation/destruction of gastric tissues, possibly evidenced by verbal reports, distraction behaviors, self-focus, and autonomic responses (changes in vital signs).

deficient Knowledge [Learning Need] regarding condition, therapy/self-care needs, and potential complications may be related to lack of information/recall, misinterpretation, possibly evidenced by statements of concern, questions, misconceptions; inaccurate follow-through of instructions, and development of preventable complications/recurrence of condition.

ulcer, venous stasis

impaired Skin/Tissue Integrity may be related to altered venous circulation, edema formation, inflammation, decreased sensation possibly evidenced by destruction of skin layers, invasion of body structures.

ineffective peripheral Tissue Perfusion may be related to interruption of venous flow— small-vessel vasoconstrictive reflex, possibly evidenced by skin discoloration, edema formation, altered sensation, delayed healing.

unconsciousness
Refer to *coma*

urinary diversion
risk for impaired Skin Integrity: risk factors may include absence of sphincter at stoma, character/flow of urine from stoma, reaction to product/chemicals, and improperly fitting appliance or removal of adhesive.
disturbed Body Image related factors may include biophysical factors (presence of stoma, loss of control of urine flow), and psychosocial factors (altered body structure, disease process/associated treatment regimen, such as cancer), possibly evidenced by verbalization of change in body image, fear of rejection/reaction of others, negative feelings about body, not touching/looking at stoma, refusal to participate in care.
acute Pain may be related to physical factors (disruption of skin/tissues, presence of incisions/drains), biological factors (activity of disease process, such as cancer, trauma), and psychological factors (fear, anxiety), possibly evidenced by verbal reports, self-focusing, guarding/distraction behaviors, restlessness, and autonomic responses (changes in vital signs).
impaired Urinary Elimination may be related to surgical diversion, tissue trauma, and postoperative edema, possibly evidenced by loss of continence, changes in amount and character of urine, and urinary retention.

urolithiasis
Refer to *calculi, urinary*.

uterine bleeding, dysfunctional
Anxiety [specify level] may be related to perceived change in health status and unknown etiology, possibly evidenced by apprehension, uncertainty, fear of unspecified consequences, expressed concerns, and focus on self.
Activity Intolerance may be related to imbalance between oxygen supply and demand/decreased oxygen-carrying capacity of blood (anemia), possibly evidenced by reports of fatigue/weakness.

uterus, rupture of, in pregnancy
deficient Fluid Volume [isotonic] may be related to excessive vascular losses, possibly evidenced by hypotension, increased pulse rate, decreased venous filling, and decreased urine output.
decreased Cardiac Output may be related to decreased preload (hypovolemia), possibly evidenced by cold/clammy skin, decreased peripheral pulses, variations in hemodynamic readings, tachycardia, and cyanosis.
acute Pain may be related to tissue trauma and irritation of accumulating blood, possibly evidenced by verbal reports, guarding/distraction behaviors, self-focus, and autonomic responses (changes in vital signs).
Anxiety [specify level] may be related to threat of death of self/fetus, interpersonal contagion, physiological response (release of catecholamines), possibly evidenced by fearful/scared affect, sympathetic stimulation, stated fear of unspecified consequences, and expressed concerns.

vaginismus
acute Pain may be related to muscle spasm and hyperesthesia of the nerve supply to vaginal mucous membrane, possibly evidenced by verbal reports, distraction behaviors, and self-focus.
Sexual Dysfunction may be related to physical and/or psychological alteration in function (severe spasms of vaginal muscles), possibly evidenced by verbalization of problem, inability to achieve desired satisfaction, and alteration in relationship with significant other.

vaginitis
impaired Tissue Integrity may be related to irritation/inflammation and mechanical trauma (scratching) of sensitive tissues, possibly evidenced by damaged/destroyed tissue, presence of lesions.
acute Pain may be related to localized inflammation and tissue trauma, possibly evidenced by verbal reports, distraction behaviors, and self-focus.
deficient Knowledge [Learning Need] regarding hygienic/therapy needs and sexual behaviors/transmission of organisms may be related to lack of information/misinterpretation, possibly evidenced by statements of concern, questions, and misconceptions.

varices, esophageal
(also refer to *ulcer, peptic [acute]*)
risk for Bleeding/deficient Fluid Volume [isotonic]: risk factors may include presence of varices, reduced intake, and gastric losses (vomiting), vascular loss..
Anxiety [specify level]/Fear may be related to change in health status and threat of death, possibly evidenced by increased tension/apprehension, sympathetic stimulation, restlessness, focus on self, and expressed concerns.

varicose veins
chronic Pain may be related to venous insufficiency and stasis, possibly evidenced by verbal reports.
disturbed Body Image may be related to change in structure (presence of enlarged, discolored, tortuous superficial leg veins), possibly evidenced by hiding affected parts and negative feelings about body.
risk for impaired Skin/Tissue Integrity: risk factors may include altered circulation/venous stasis and edema formation.

venereal disease
Refer to *sexually transmitted disease—STD*.

ventricular fibrillation
decreased Cardiac Output may be related to altered electrical conduction and reduced myocardial contractility possibly evidenced by absence of measurable cardiac output, loss of consciousness, no palpable pulses.

ventricular tachycardia
risk for decreased Cardiac Output : risk factors may include altered electrical conduction and reduced myocardial contractility.

West Nile fever
Hyperthermia may be related to infectious process possibly evidenced by elevated body temperature, skin flushed/warm to touch, tachycardia, increased respiratory rate.
acute Pain may be related to infectious process/circulating toxins possibly evidenced by reports of headache, myalgia, eye pain, abdominal discomfort.
risk for deficient Fluid Volume: risk factors may include hypermetabolic state, decreased intake anorexia, nausea, losses from normal routes (vomiting, diarrhea).
risk for impaired Skin Integrity: risk factors may include hyperthermia, decreased fluid intake, alterations in skin turgor, bedrest, circulating toxins

Wilms' tumor
(also refer to *cancer; chemotherapy*)
Anxiety [specify level]/Fear may be related to change in environment and interaction patterns with family members and threat of death with family transmission and contagion of concerns, possibly evidenced by fearful/scared affect, distress, crying, insomnia, and sympathetic stimulation.
risk for Injury: risk factors may include nature of tumor (vascular, mushy with very thin covering) with increased danger of metastasis when manipulated.
interrupted Family Processes may be related to situational crisis of life-threatening illness, possibly evidenced by a family system that has difficulty meeting physical, emotional, and spiritual needs of its members, and inability to deal with traumatic experience effectively.
deficient Diversional Activity may be related to environmental lack of age-appropriate activity (including activity restrictions) and length of hospitalization/treatment, possibly evidenced by restlessness, crying, lethargy, and acting-out behavior.

wound, gunshot (depends on site and speed/character of bullet)
risk for deficient Fluid Volume: risk factors may include excessive vascular losses, altered intake/restrictions.
acute Pain may be related to destruction of tissue (including organ and musculoskeletal), surgical repair, and therapeutic interventions, possibly evidenced by verbal reports, guarding/distraction behaviors, self-focus, and autonomic responses (changes in vital signs).
Tissue Integrity, impaired may be related to mechanical factors (yaw of projectile and muzzle blast), possibly evidenced by damaged or destroyed tissue.
risk for Infection: risk factors may include tissue destruction and increased environmental exposure, invasive procedures, and decreased hemoglobin.
Post-Trauma Syndrome, risk for: risk factors may include nature of incident (catastrophic accident, assault, suicide attempt) and possibly injury/death of other(s) involved.

Note: Information appearing in brackets has been added to clarify and facilitate the use of nursing diagnoses.

Appendix N4-5 Nursing Diagnoses Through 2012-2014 in Alphabetical Order

Information appearing in brackets has been added by the authors to clarify and facilitate the use of nursing diagnoses.

A "RISK FOR" diagnosis is *not* evidenced by signs and symptoms, because the problem has not yet occurred, and nursing interventions are directed at prevention. Therefore, *risk* factors that are present are noted instead.

New nursing diagnoses for 2012-2014 appear in Appendix N4-3.

ACTIVITY INTOLERANCE [SPECIFY LEVEL]

Diagnostic Division: Activity / Rest

Definition: Insufficient physiological or psychological energy to endure or complete required or desired daily activities.

RELATED FACTORS
Generalized weakness; Sedentary lifestyle; Bed rest; Immobility; Imbalance between oxygen supply and demand; [Anemia]; [Cognitive deficits, extreme stress; depression]; [Pain, dysrhythmias, vertigo]

DEFINING CHARACTERISTICS

Subjective
Report of fatigue or weakness; Exertional discomfort or dyspnea; [Verbalizes no desire and/or lack of interest in activity]

Objective
Abnormal heart rate or blood pressure response to activity; Electrocardiographic changes reflecting arrhythmias or ischemia; [Pallor, cyanosis]

ACTIVITY INTOLERANCE, RISK FOR

Diagnostic Division: Activity / Rest

Definition: At risk for experiencing insufficient physiologic or psychological energy to endure or complete required or desired daily activities.

RISK FACTORS
History of previous activity intolerance; Presence of circulatory/respiratory problems; [Dysrhythmias]; Deconditioned status; [Aging]; Inexperience with an activity; [Diagnosis of progressive disease state/debilitating condition, anemia, extensive surgical procedures]; [Verbalized reluctance/inability to perform expected activity]

ACTIVITY PLANNING, INEFFECTIVE

Diagnostic Division: Activity / Rest

Definition: Inability to prepare for a set of actions fixed in time and under certain conditions.

RELATED FACTORS
Unrealistic perception of events [or] personal competence; Lack of family/friend support; Compromised ability to process information; Defensive flight behavior when faced with proposed solution; Hedonism [motivated by pleasure and/or pain]

DEFINING CHARACTERISTICS

Subjective
Reports fear/worries toward a task to be undertaken; Excessive anxieties toward a task to be undertaken

Objective
Failure pattern of behavior; Lack of plan, resources, sequential organization; History of procrastination; Unmet goals for chosen activity

ACTIVITY PLANNING, RISK FOR INEFFECTIVE

Diagnostic Division: Activity / Rest

Definition: At risk for an inability to prepare for a set of actions fixed in time and under certain conditions

RISK FACTORS
Compromised ability to process information; Defensive flight behavior when faced with proposed solution; Hedonism; History of procrastination; Ineffective/insufficient support systems; Unrealistic perception of events/personal competence

ADVERSE REACTION TO IODINATED CONTRAST MEDIA, RISK FOR

Diagnostic Division: Safety

Definition: At risk for any noxious or unintended reaction associated with the use of iodinated contrast media that can occur within seven (7) days after contrast agent injection

RISK FACTORS
Anxiety; Concurrent use of medications (e.g., beta-blockers, interleukin-2, metformin, nephrotoxic medications); Dehydration; Extremes of age; Fragile veins (e.g., prior or actual chemotherapy treatment or radiation in the limb to be injected, multiple attempts to obtain intravenous access, indwelling intravenous lines in place for more than 24 hours, previous axillary lymph node dissection in the limb to be injected, distal intravenous access sites: hand, wrist, foot, ankle); Generalized debilitation; History of allergies/previous adverse effect from iodinated contrast media; Physical and chemical properties of the contrast media (e.g., iodine concentration, viscosity, high osmolality, ion toxicity); Unconsciousness; Underlying disease (e.g., heart disease, pulmonary disease, blood dyscrasias, endocrine disease, renal disease, pheochromocytoma, autoimmune disease)

AIRWAY CLEARANCE, INEFFECTIVE

Diagnostic Division: Respiration

Definition: Inability to clear secretions or obstructions from the respiratory tract to maintain a clear airway.

RELATED FACTORS
Environmental
Smoking; Second-hand smoke; Smoke inhalation

Obstructed Airway
Retained secretions; Secretions in the bronchi; Exudate in the alveoli; Excessive mucus; Airway spasm; Foreign body in airway; Presence of artificial airway

Physiological
Chronic obstructive pulmonary disease (COPD); Asthma; Allergic airways; Hyperplasia of the bronchial walls; Neuromuscular dysfunction; Infection

DEFINING CHARACTERISTICS

Subjective
Dyspnea

Objective
Diminished/adventitious breath sounds [rales, crackles, rhonchi, wheezes]; Ineffective/absent cough; Excessive sputum; Changes in respiratory rate and rhythm; Difficulty vocalizing; Wide-eyed; Restlessness; Orthopnea; Cyanosis

ALLERGY RESPONSE; RISK FOR

Diagnostic Division: Safety

Definition: Risk of an exaggerated immune response or reaction to substances

RISK FACTORS
Chemical products (e.g., bleach, cosmetics); Dander; Environmental substances (e.g., mold, dust, pollen); Foods (e.g., peanuts, shellfish, mushrooms); Insect stings; Pharmaceutical agents (e.g., penicillins); Repeated exposure to environmental substances

ANXIETY [MILD, MODERATE, SEVERE, PANIC]

Diagnostic Division: Ego / Integrity

Definition: Vague uneasy feeling of discomfort or dread accompanied by an autonomic response (the source often nonspecific or unknown to the individual); a feeling of apprehension caused by anticipation of danger. It is an alerting signal that warns of impending danger and enables the individual to take measures to deal with threat

RELATED FACTORS

Unconscious conflict about essential [beliefs]/goals/values of life; Situational/maturational crises; Stress; Familial association/heredity; Interpersonal transmission/contagion; Threat to self-concept [perceived or actual]; [Unconscious conflict]; Threat of death [perceived or actual]; Threat to or change in health status [progressive/debilitating disease, terminal illness], interaction patterns, role function/status, environment [safety], economic status; Unmet needs; Exposure to toxins; Substance abuse; [Positive or negative self-talk]; [Physiological factors, e.g., hyperthyroidism, pheochromocytoma, drug therapy including steroids]

DEFINING CHARACTERISTICS

Subjective
Behavioral
Reports concerns due to change in life events; Insomnia

Affective
Regretful; Rattled; Distressed; Apprehensive; Uncertainty; Fear; Feelings of inadequacy; Jittery; Worried; Painful/persistent increased helplessness; [Sense of impending doom]; [Hopelessness]

Cognitive
Fear of unspecified consequences; Awareness of physiologic symptoms

Physiological
Shakiness
Sympathetic: Dry mouth; Heart pounding; Weakness; Respiratory difficulties; Anorexia; Diarrhea
Parasympathetic: Tingling in extremities; Nausea; Abdominal pain; Diarrhea; Urinary hesitancy/frequency; Faintness; Fatigue; Sleep disturbance; [Chest, back, neck pain]

Objective
Behavioral
Poor eye contact; Glancing about; Scanning; Vigilance; Extraneous movement [e.g., foot shuffling, hand/arm movements, rocking motion]; Fidgeting; Restlessness; Diminished productivity; [Crying/tearfulness]; [Pacing/purposeless activity]; [Immobility]

Affective
IIncreased wariness; Focus on self; Irritability; Overexcited; Anguish

Physiological
Voice quivering; Trembling/hand tremors; Increased tension; Facial tension; Increased perspiration
Sympathetic: Cardiovascular excitation; Facial flushing; Superficial vasoconstriction; Increased pulse/respiration; Increased blood pressure; Twitching; Pupil dilation; Increased reflexes
Parasympathetic: Urinary urgency; Decreased blood pressure/pulse

Cognitive
Preoccupation; Impaired attention; Difficulty concentrating; Forgetfulness; Diminished ability to problem-solve; Diminished ability to learn; Rumination; Tendency to blame others; Blocking of thought; Confusion; Decreased perceptual field

---

ASPIRATION, RISK FOR

Diagnostic Division: Respiration

Definition: At risk for entry of gastrointestinal secretions, oropharyngeal secretions, [or exogenous food] or solids or fluids into the tracheobronchial passages [due to dysfunction or absence of normal protective mechanisms].

RISK FACTORS

Reduced level of consciousness [sedation/anesthesia]; Depressed cough/gag reflex; Impaired swallowing [inability of the epiglottis and true vocal cords to close off traches]; Facial/oral/neck surgery or trauma; Wired jaws; [Congenital malformations]; Situations hindering elevation of upper body [weakness, paralysis]; Incompetent lower esophageal sphincter [hiatal hernia or other esophageal disease affecting stomach valve function]; Delayed gastric emptying; Decreased gastrointestinal motility; Increased intragastric pressure; Increased gastric residual; Presence of tracheostomy or endotracheal (ET) tube; [Inadequate or over-inflation of tracheostomy/ET tube cuff]; [Presence of] gastrointestinal tubes; Tube feedings; Treatment-related side effects (e.g., pharmaceutical agents)

ATTACHMENT, RISK FOR IMPAIRED

Diagnostic Division: Social Interaction

Definition: At risk for disruption of the interactive process between parent/significant other and child that fosters the development of a protective and nurturing reciprocal relationship.

RISK FACTORS
Inability of parent(s) to meet personal needs; Disorganized infant behavior; Parental conflict resulting from disorganized infant behavior; Anxiety associated with the parent role; [Parents who themselves experienced altered attachment]; Premature infant; Ill child who is unable to initiate parental contact; Parent-child separation; Physical barriers; Lack of privacy; Substance abuse; [Difficult pregnancy and/or birth (actual or perceived)]; [Uncertainty of paternity; conception as a result of rape/sexual abuse]

AUTONOMIC DYSREFLEXIA

Diagnostic Division: Circulation

Definition: Life-threatening, uninhibited sympathetic response of the nervous system to a noxious stimulus after a spinal cord injury (SCI) at T7 or above.

RELATED FACTORS
Bladder/bowel distension; [Catheter insertion, obstruction, irrigation]; Skin irritation; Deficient patient/caregiver knowledge; [Sexual excitation, menstruation, pregnancy, labor/delivery]; [Environmental temperature extremes]

DEFINING CHARACTERISTICS

Subjective
Headache (a diffuse pain in different portions of the head and not confined to any nerve distribution area); Paresthesia; Chilling; Blurred vision; Chest pain; Metallic taste in mouth; Nasal congestion

Objective
Paroxysmal hypertension (sudden periodic elevated blood pressure in which systolic pressure >140 mm Hg and diastolic >90 mm Hg); Bradycardia or tachycardia (heart rate <60 or >100 beats per minute, respectively); Diaphoresis (above the injury); Red splotches on skin (above the injury); Pallor (below the injury); Horner's syndrome [contraction of the pupil, partial ptosis of the eyelid, enophthalmos and sometimes loss of sweating over the affected side of the face]; Conjunctival congestion; Pilomotor reflex [gooseflesh formation when skin is cooled]

AUTONOMIC DYSREFLEXIA, RISK FOR

Diagnostic Division: Circulation

Definition: At risk for life threatening, uninhibited response of the sympathetic nervous system, postspinal shock, in an individual with a spinal cord injury [SCI] or lesion at T6 or above (has been demonstrated in clients with injuries at T7 and T8)

RISK FACTORS
An injury at T6 or above AND at least one of the following noxious stimuli.

Cardiopulmonary Stimuli
Deep vein thrombosis; Pulmonary emboli

Musculoskeletal—Integumentary Stimuli
Cutaneous stimulations (e.g., pressure ulcer, ingrown toenail, dressings, burns, rash); Sunburns; Wounds; Pressure over bony prominences/genitalia; Range-of-motion exercises; Spasms; Fractures; Heterotopic bone

Gastrointestinal Stimuli
Constipation; Difficult passage of feces; Fecal impaction; Bowel distension; Hemorrhoids; Digital stimulation; Suppositories; Enemas; Gastrointestinal system pathology; Esophageal reflux; Gastric ulcers; Gallstones

Urologic Stimuli
Bladder distention/spasm; Detrusor sphincter dyssynergia; Instrumentation; Surgery; Urinary tract infection; Cystitis; Urethritis; Epididymitis; Calculi; Catheterization

Regulatory Stimuli
Temperature fluctuations; Extreme environmental temperatures

Situational Stimuli
Positioning; Surgical [/diagnostic]procedure; Constrictive clothing (e.g., straps, stockings, shoes); Reactions to pharmaceutical agents(e.g., decongestants, sympathomimetics, vasoconstrictors); Narcotic/opiate withdrawal

Neurological Stimuli
Painful/irritating stimuli below the level of injury;

Reproductive [and Sexuality] Stimuli
Sexual intercourse; Ejaculation; [Vibrator overstimulation; Scrotal compression]; Menstruation; Pregnancy; Labor and delivery; Ovarian cyst

---

BEHAVIOR, DISORGANIZED INFANT

Diagnostic Division: Neurosensory

Definition: Disintegrated physiological and neurobehavioral responses of infant to the environment.

RELATED FACTORS
Prenatal
Congenital/genetic disorders; Teratogenic exposure; [Exposure to drugs/substances]

Postnatal
Oral/motor problems; Feeding intolerance; Malnutrition; Invasive procedures; Pain

Individual
Low postconceptual age; Immature neurological system; Prematurity; Illness; [Infection]; [Hypoxia/birth asphyxia]

Environmental
Physical environment inappropriateness; Sensory inappropriateness/overstimulation/deprivation; Lack of containment within environment

Caregiver
Cue misreading; Deficient knowledge regarding behavioral cues; Environmental stimulation contribution

DEFINING CHARACTERISTICS
Objective
Regulatory Problems
Inability to inhibit startle; Irritability

State-Organization System
Active-awake (fussy, worried gaze); Quiet-awake (staring, gaze aversion); Diffuse sleep; State-oscillation; Irritable crying

Attention-Interaction System
Abnormal response to sensory stimuli (e.g., difficult to soothe, unable to sustain alert status)

Motor System
Finger splaying; Fisting; Hands to face; Hyperextension of extremities; Tremors; Startles; Twitches; Jittery; Uncoordinated movement; Changes to motor tone; Altered primitive reflexes

Physiological
Bradycardia; Tachycardia; Arrhythmias; Skin color changes; "Time-out signals" (e.g., gaze, grasp, hiccough, cough, sneeze, sigh, slack jaw, open mouth, tongue thrust); Feeding intolerances; Desaturation

---

BEHAVIOR, READINESS FOR ENHANCED ORGANIZED INFANT

Diagnostic Division: Neurosensory

Definition: A pattern of modulation of the physiological and behavioral systems of functioning (i.e., autonomic, motor, state, organizational, self-regulatory, and attentional-interactional systems) in an infant that is sufficient for well-being and can be strengthened.

DEFINING CHARACTERISTICS
Objective
Stable physiological measures; Definite sleep-wake states; Use of some self-regulatory behaviors; Response to stimuli (e.g., visual, auditory)

BEHAVIOR, RISK FOR DISORGANIZED INFANT

Diagnostic Division: Neurosensory

Definition: At risk for alteration in integrating and modulation of the physiological and behavioral systems of functioning (i.e., autonomic, motor, state-organization, self-regulatory, and attentional-interactional systems).

RISK FACTORS

Pain; Oral/motor problems; Environmental overstimulation; Lack of containment within environment; Invasive/painful procedures; Prematurity; [immaturity of the central nervous system; generic problems that alter neurologic and/or physiologic functioning conditions resulting in hypoxia and/or birth asphyxia]; [Malnutrition; infection; drug addiction]; [Environmental events or conditions such as separation from parent, exposure to loud noise, excessive handling, bright lights]

BLEEDING, RISK FOR

Diagnostic Division: Circulation

Definition: At risk for a decrease in blood volume that may compromise health.

RISK FACTORS

Aneurysm, trauma, history of falls; Gastrointestinal disorders (e.g., gastric ulcer disease, polyps, varices); Impaired liver function (e.g., cirrhosis, hepatitis); Pregnancy-related complications (e.g., placenta previa, molar pregnancy, placenta abruptio [placental abruption]); Postpartum complications (e.g., uterine atony, retained placenta); Inherent coagulopathies (e.g., thrombocytopenia, [hereditary hemorrhagic telangiectasia—HTT]); Treatment-related side effects (e.g., surgery, medications, administration of platelet-deficient blood products, chemotherapy); Circumcision; Deficient knowledge; Disseminated intravascular coagulopathy

BLOOD GLUCOSE LEVEL, RISK FOR UNSTABLE

Diagnostic Division: Food / Fluid

Definition: At risk for variation of blood glucose/sugar levels from the normal range that may compromise health

RISK FACTORS

Deficient knowledge of diabetes management (e.g., action plan); Developmental level; Dietary intake; Inadequate blood glucose monitoring; Lack of acceptance of diagnosis; Lack of adherence to diabetes management plan (e.g., adhering to action plan); Lack of diabetes management (e.g., action plan); Medication management; Mental health status; Physical activity level; Physical health status; Pregnancy; Rapid growth periods; Stress; Weight gain; Weight loss

BODY IMAGE, DISTURBED

Diagnostic Division: Perception / Cognition

Definition: Confusion [and/or dissatisfaction] in mental picture of one's physical self.

RELATED FACTORS

Biophysical; Illness; Trauma; Injury; Surgery; [Mutilation, pregnancy]; Treatment regimen[change caused by biochemical agents (drugs), dependence on machine]; Psychosocial; Cultural; Spiritual; Cognitive; Perceptual; Developmental changes; [Maturational changes]; [Significance of body part or functioning with regard to age, sex, developmental level, or basic human needs]

DEFINING CHARACTERISTICS

Behaviors of acknowledgement/avoidance/monitoring of one's body; Nonverbal response to actual/perceived change in body (e.g., appearance, structure, function); Reports feelings that reflect an altered view of one's body (e.g., appearance, structure, function); Reports perceptions that reflect an altered view of one's body in appearance

Subjective

Focus on past strength/function/appearance; Reports negative feelings about body (e.g., feelings of helplessness, hopelessness, or powerlessness); [Depersonalization/grandiosity]; Preoccupation with change/loss; Refusal to verify actual change; Emphasis on remaining strengths; Heightened achievement; Personalization of body part/loss by name; Depersonalization of part or loss by use of impersonal pronouns; Reports change in lifestyle; Reports fear of reaction by others

Objective
Missing body part; Actual change in structure/function; Not looking at/not touching body part; Trauma to nonfunctioning part; Change in ability to estimate spatial relationship of body to environment; Extension of body boundary to incorporate environmental objects; Intentional/unintentional hiding/ overexposing body part; Change in social involvement; [Aggression; low frustration tolerance level]; Behaviors of acknowledging one's body; Behaviors of monitoring one's body

---

BODY TEMPERATURE, RISK FOR IMBALANCED

Diagnostic Division: Safety

Definition: At risk for failure to maintain body temperature within normal range.

RISK FACTORS
Extremes of age/weight; Exposure to extremes of environmental temperature; Inappropriate clothing for environmental temperature; Dehydration; Inactivity; Vigorous activity; Pharmaceutical agents causing vasoconstriction/vasodilation; Sedation; [Use or overdose of certain drugs or exposure to anesthesia]; Illness/trauma affecting temperature regulation [e.g., infections, systemic or localized; neoplasms, tumors; collagen/vascular disease]; Altered metabolic rate

---

BREASTFEEDING, EFFECTIVE

Diagnostic Division: Food / Fluid

Definition: Mother-infant dyad/family exhibits adequate proficiency and satisfaction with breastfeeding process.

RELATED FACTORS
Basic breastfeeding knowledge; Normal [maternal] breast structure; Normal infant oral structure; Infant gestational age greater than 34 weeks; Support sources [available]; Maternal confidence

DEFINING CHARACTERISTICS

Subjective
Maternal verbalization of satisfaction with the breastfeeding process

Objective
Mother able to position infant at breast to promote a successful latch-on response; Infant is content after feedings; Regular and sustained sucking at the breast (8 to 10 times/ 24 hours); Appropriate infant weight patterns for age; Effective mother/infant communication pattern (infant cues, maternal interpretation and response); Signs and/or symptoms of oxytocin release (let-down or milk ejection reflex); Adequate infant elimination patterns for age; [soft stools; more than 6 wet diapers per day of unconcentrated urine]; Eagerness of infant to nurse [breastfeed]

BREASTFEEDING, INEFFECTIVE

Diagnostic Division: Role Relationships

Definition: Dissatisfaction or difficulty a mother, infant, or child experiences with the breastfeeding process.

RELATED FACTORS
Prematurity; Infant anomaly; Poor infant sucking reflex; Infant receiving [numerous or repeated] supplemental feedings with artificial nipple; Maternal anxiety/ambivalence; Deficient knowledge; Previous history of breastfeeding failure; Interrupted breastfeeding; Nonsupportive partner/family; Maternal breast anomaly; Previous breast surgery; [Maternal physical discomfort during feeding]

DEFINING CHARACTERISTICS

Subjective
Unsatisfactory breastfeeding process; Persistence of sore nipples beyond the first week of breastfeeding; Insufficient emptying of each breast per feeding; Inadequate/perceived inadequate milk supply

Objective
Observable signs of inadequate infant intake [decrease in number of wet diapers, inappropriate weight loss/inadequate gain]; Insufficient opportunity for suckling at the

breast; Infant inability [failure] to latch onto maternal breast correctly; Infant arch-ing/crying at the breast; Infant resisting latching on; Infant exhibiting fussiness/cry-ing within the first hour after breastfeeding; Infant unresponsive to other comfort measures; No observable signs of oxytocin release; Lack of infant weight gain; Sus-tained infant weight loss; Unsustained suckling at the breast

BREASTFEEDING, INTERRUPTED

Diagnostic Division: Role Relationships

Definition: Break in the continuity of the breastfeeding process as a result of inability or inadvisability to put a baby to breast for feeding.

RELATED FACTORS
Maternal/infant illness; Infant prematurity; Maternal employment; Contraindications to breastfeeding [e.g., certain pharmaceutical agents]; Need to abruptly wean infant

DEFINING CHARACTERISTICS

Subjective
Infant receives no nourishment at the breast for some or all feedings; Maternal desire to provide breast milk for child's nutritional needs; Deficient knowledge about ex-pression/storage of breast milk; Maternal desire to maintain breastfeeding for child's nutritional needs

Objective
Mother-child separation

BREASTFEEDING, READINESS FOR ENHANCED

Diagnostic Division: Role Relationships

Definition: A pattern of proficiency and satisfaction of the mother-infant dyad that is sufficient to support the breastfeeding process and can be strengthened

DEFINING CHARACTERISTICS

Subjective
Eagerness of infant to nurse; Infant content after feeding; Mother able to position infant at breast to promote a successful latching-on response; Mother reports satisfaction with the breastfeeding process

Objective
Adequate infant elimination patterns for age; Appropriate infant weight pattern for age; Effective mother-infant communication patterns; Regular suckling/swallowing at the breast; Signs/Symptoms of oxytocin release are present; Sustained sucking/swallow-ing at the breast

BREAST MILK, INSUFFICIENT

Diagnostic Division: Food / Fluid

Definition: Low production of maternal breast milk

RELATED FACTORS
INFANT: Ineffective latching on and/or sucking; Insufficient opportunity to suckle; Re-jection of breast; Short sucking time
MOTHER: Alcohol intake; Fluid volume depletion (e.g., dehydration, hemorrhage); Mal-nutrition; Medication side effects (e.g., contraceptives, diuretics); Pregnancy; Tobacco Smoking

DEFINING CHARACTERISTICS

Subjective
INFANT: Does not seem satisfied after sucking time; Refuses to suck; Wants to suck very frequently

Objective
INFANT: Constipation; Frequent crying; Long breastfeeding time; Voids small amounts of concentrated urine (less than four to six times a day); Weight gain is lower than 500 g in a month (comparing two measures)
MOTHER: Milk production does not progress; No milk appears when mother's nipple is pressed; Volume of expressed breast milk is less than prescribed volume

BREATHING PATTERN, INEFFECTIVE

Diagnostic Division: Activity/Rest

Definition: Inspiration and/or expiration that does not provide adequate ventilation.

RELATED FACTORS

Neuromuscular dysfunction; Spinal cord injury; Neurological immaturity; Musculo-skeletal impairment; Bony/chest wall deformity; Anxiety [/panic attack]; Pain; Fatigue; [Deconditioning]; Respiratory muscle fatigue; Neurological damage; Body position; Obesity; Hyperventilation; Hypoventilation syndrome; [alteration of patient's normal $O_2 : CO_2$ ratio (e.g., O_2 therapy in COPD)]

DEFINING CHARACTERISTICS

Subjective
[Feeling breathless]

Objective
Dyspnea; Orthopnea; Bradypnea; Tachypnea; Alterations in depth of breathing; Prolonged expiration phases; Pursed-lip breathing; Decreased minute ventilation/vital capacity; Decreased inspiratory/expiratory pressure; Use of accessory muscles to breathe; Assumption of three-point position; Altered chest excursion, [paradoxical breathing patterns]; Nasal flaring; [Grunting]; Increased anterior-posterior diameter

CARDIAC OUTPUT, DECREASED

Diagnostic Division: Activity/Rest

Definition: Inadequate blood pumped by the heart to meet the metabolic demands of the body.

NOTE: In a hypermetabolic state, although cardiac output may be within normal range, it may still be inadequate to meet the needs of the body's tissues. Cardiac output and tissue perfusion are interrelated, although there are differences. When cardiac output is decreased, tissue perfusion problems will develop; however, tissue perfusion problems can exist without decreased cardiac output.

RELATED FACTORS

Altered heart rate/rhythm [conduction]; Altered stroke volume: Altered preload [e.g., decreased venous return]; Altered afterload [e.g., altered systemic vascular resistance]; Altered contractility [e.g., ventricular-septal rupture, ventricular aneurysm, papillary muscle rupture, valvular disease]

DEFINING CHARACTERISTICS

Subjective
Altered Heart Rate/Rhythm
: Palpitations

Altered Preload
Fatigue

Altered Afterload
[Feeling breathless]

Altered Contractility
Orthopnea/paroxysmal nocturnal dyspnea [PND]

Behavioral/Emotional
Anxiety

Objective
Altered Heart Rate/Rhythm
[Dys]arrhythmias (tachycardia, bradycardia); EKG [ECG] changes

Altered Preload
Jugular vein distention (JVD); Edema; Weight gain; Increased/decreased central venous pressure (CVP); Increased/decreased pulmonary artery wedge pressure (PAWP); Murmurs

Altered Afterload
Dyspnea; Clammy skin; Skin [and mucous membrane] color changes [cyanosis, pallor]; Prolonged capillary refill; Decreased peripheral pulses; Variations in blood pressure readings; Increased/decreased systemic vascular resistance (SVR); Increased/decreased pulmonary vascular resistance (PVR); Oliguria; [Anuria]

Altered Contractility

Crackles; Cough; Decreased cardiac output/cardiac index; Decreased ejection fraction; Decreased stroke volume index (SVI)/left ventricular stroke work index (LVSWI); S3 or S4 sounds [gallop rhythm]

Behavioral/Emotional

Restlessness

CAREGIVER ROLE STRAIN

Diagnostic Division: Role Relationships

Definition: Difficulty in performing family/significant other caregiver role.

RELATED FACTORS
Care Receiver Health Status

Illness severity/chronicity; Unpredictability of illness course; Instability of care receiver's health; Increasing care needs; Dependency; Problem behaviors; Psychological or cognitive problems; Addiction; Codependency; Substance Abuse

Caregiving Activities

Discharge of family members to home with significant care needs [e.g., premature birth/congenital defect, frail elder post stroke]; Unpredictability of care situation; 24-hour care responsibilities; Amount/complexity of activities; Ongoing changes in activities; Years of caregiving

Caregiver Health Status

Physical problems; Psychological/cognitive problems; Inability to fulfill one's own/others' expectations; Unrealistic expectations of self; Marginal coping patterns; Substance abuse; Co-dependency

Socioeconomic

Competing role commitments; Alienation/isolation from others; Insufficient recreation

Caregiver–Care Receiver Relationship

Unrealistic expectations of caregiver by care receiver; History of poor relationship; Mental status of elder inhibiting conversation; Presence of abuse/ violence

Family Processes

History of marginal family coping/family dysfunction

Resources

Inadequate physical environment for providing care (e.g., housing, temperature, safety); Inadequate equipment for providing care; Inadequate transportation; Insufficient finances; Inexperience with caregiving; Insufficient time; Physical energy; Emotional strength; Lack of support; Lack of caregiver privacy; Deficient knowledge about community resources; Difficulty accessing community resources; Inadequate community resources (e.g., respite services, recreational resources); Difficulty accessing formal assistance/support; Inadequate informal assistance/support; Caregiver is not developmentally ready for caregiver role

DEFINING CHARACTERISTICS
Subjective
Caregiving Activities

Apprehension about: Possible institutionalization of care receiver; The future regarding care receiver's health/ caregiver's ability to provide care; Care receiver's care if caregiver was unable to provide care

Caregiver Health Status—physical

Gastrointestinal upset; Weight change; Fatigue; Headaches; Rash; Hypertension; Cardiovascular disease; Diabetes

Caregiver Health Status—emotional

Reports feeling depressed; Anger; Stress; Frustration; Increased nervousness; Disturbed sleep pattern; Lack of time to meet personal needs

Caregiver Health Status—socioeconomic

Changes in leisure activities; Refuses career advancement

Caregiver–Care Receiver Relationship

Reports difficulty watching care receiver go through the illness; Reports grief/uncertainty regarding changed relationship with care receiver

Family Processes

Reports concerns about family members

Objective
Caregiving Activities
Difficulty performing/completing required tasks; Preoccupation with care routine; Dysfunctional change in caregiving activities

Caregiver Health Status—emotional
Impatience; Increased emotional lability; Somatization; Ineffective coping; Sleep deprivation

Caregiver Health status—socioeconomic
Low work productivity; Withdraws from social life

Family Processes
Family conflict

NOTE: [Authors' note: The presence of this problem may encompass other numerous problems/high-risk concerns such as deficient Diversional Activity, Insomnia, Fatigue, Anxiety, ineffective Coping, compromised/disabled family Coping, decisional Conflict, ineffective Denial, Grieving, Hopelessness, Powerlessness, Spiritual Distress, ineffective Health Maintenance, impaired Home Maintenance, ineffective Sexuality Pattern, readiness for enhanced family Coping, interrupted Family Processes, Social Isolation. Careful attention to data gathering will identify and clarify the client's specific needs, which can then be coordinated under this single diagnostic label]

CAREGIVER ROLE STRAIN, RISK FOR

Diagnostic Division: Role Relationships

Definition: Caregiver is vulnerable for felt difficulty in performing the family caregiver role.

RISK FACTORS
Illness severity of the care receiver; Psychological/cognitive problems in care receiver; Co-dependency; Discharge of family member with significant home care needs; Premature birth; Congenital defect; Unpredictable illness course; Instability in the care receiver's health; Duration of caregiving required; Inexperience with caregiving; Complexity/amount of caregiving tasks; Caregiver's competing role commitments; Caregiver health impairment; Caregiver is female/spouse; Caregiver not developmentally ready for caregiver role [e.g., a young adult needing to provide care for middle-aged parent]; Developmental delay of the care receiver/caregiver; Presence of situational stressors that normally affect families (e.g., significant loss, disaster or crisis, economic vulnerability, major life events [such as birth, hospitalization, leaving home, returning home, marriage, divorce, change in employment, retirement, death]); Inadequate physical environment for providing care (e.g., housing, transportation, community services, equipment); Family/caregiver isolation; Lack of respite/recreation for caregiver; Marginal family adaptation; Family dysfunction before the caregiving situation; Marginal caregiver's coping patterns; Past history of poor relationship between caregiver and care receiver; Care receiver exhibits deviant/bizarre behavior; Presence of abuse/violence; Substance abuse

---

CHILDBEARING PROCESS, INEFFECTIVE

Diagnostic Division: Sexuality

Definition: Pregnancy and childbirth process and care of the newborn that does not match the environmental context, norms, and expectations

RELATED FACTORS
Deficient knowledge (e.g., of labor and delivery, newborn care); Domestic violence; Inconsistent prenatal health visits; Lack of: Appropriate role models for parenthood, Cognitive readiness for parenthood, Maternal Confidence, Prenatal health visits, A realistic birth plan, Sufficient support systems; Maternal powerlessness/psychological distress; Suboptimal maternal nutrition; Substance abuse; Unplanned/unwanted pregnancy; Unsafe environment

DEFINING CHARACTERISTICS
During Pregnancy
Subjective
Does not: Access support systems appropriately, Report appropriate physical preparations, Report appropriate prenatal lifestyle (e.g., nutrition, elimination, sleep, bodily movement, exercise, personal hygiene), Report availability of support systems, Report managing unpleasant symptoms of pregnancy, Report realistic birth plan, Seek nec-

essary knowledge (e.g., of labor and delivery, newborn care); Failure to prepare necessary newborn care items

Objective
Inconsistent/lack of prenatal health visits; Lack of respect for unborn baby
During Labor and Delivery
Subjective
Does not: Access support systems appropriately, Demonstrate attachment behavior to the newborn baby, Report availability of support systems, Report lifestyle (e.g., diet, elimination, sleep, bodily movement, personal hygiene) that is appropriate for the stage of labor, Respond appropriately to onset of labor

Objective
Lacks proactivity during labor and delivery
After Birth
Subjective
Does not: Access support systems appropriately, Demonstrate appropriate: baby feeding techniques/breast care/attachment behavior to the baby/basic baby care techniques, Provide safe environment for the baby, Report appropriate postpartum lifestyle (e.g., diet, elimination, sleep, bodily movement, exercise, personal hygiene), Report availability of support systems

---

CHILDBEARING PROCESS, READINESS FOR ENHANCED

Diagnostic Division: Sexuality

Definition: A pattern for preparing for and maintaining a healthy pregnancy, childbirth process, and care of newborn that is sufficient for ensuring well-being and can be strengthened.

DEFINING CHARACTERISTICS
During Pregnancy

Subjective
Reports appropriate prenatal lifestyle (e.g., nutrition, elimination, sleep, bodily movement, exercise, personal hygiene), a realistic birth plan, appropriate physical preparations, availability of support systems; Reports managing unpleasant symptoms in pregnancy; Seeks necessary knowledge (e.g., of labor and delivery, newborn care)

Objective
Attends regular prenatal health visits; Demonstrates respect for unborn baby; Prepares necessary newborn care items
During Labor and Delivery

Subjective
Reports lifestyle (e.g., diet, elimination, sleep, bodily movement, exercise, personal hygiene) that is appropriate for the stage of labor

Objective
Responds appropriately to onset of labor; Is proactive during labor and delivery, uses relaxation techniques appropriate for stage of labor, utilizes support systems appropriately; Demonstrates attachment behavior to the newborn baby
After Birth

Subjective
Reports appropriate postpartum lifestyle (e.g., diet, elimination, sleep, bodily movement, exercise, personal hygiene)

Objective
Demonstrates attachment behavior to the baby, basic baby care techniques, appropriate baby feeding techniques; Provides safe environment for the baby; Utilizes support system appropriately; Demonstrates appropriate breast care

---

CHILDBEARING PROCESS, RISK FOR INEFFECTIVE

Diagnostic Division: Sexuality

Definition: Risk for a pregnancy and childbirth process and care of the newborn that does not match the environmental context, norms, and expectations

RISK FACTORS
Deficient knowledge (e.g., of labor and delivery, newborn care); Domestic violence; Inconsistent prenatal health visits; Lack of: Appropriate role models for parenthood, Cognitive readiness for parenthood, Maternal confidence, Prenatal health visits, A

realistic birth plan, Sufficient support systems; Maternal powerlessness/psychological distress; Suboptimal maternal nutrition; Substance abuse; Unwanted/unplanned pregnancy

COMFORT, IMPAIRED

Diagnostic Division: Pain / Discomfort

Definition: Perceived lack of ease, relief, and transcendence in physical, psychospiritual, environmental, cultural, and social dimensions.

RELATED FACTORS
Illness-related symptoms; Insufficient resources (e.g., financial, social support); Lack of environmental/situational control; Lack of privacy; Noxious environmental stimuli; Treatment-related side effects (e.g., medication, radiation)

DEFINING CHARACTERISTICS

Subjective
Reports: distressing symptoms, lack of contentment/ease in situation, hunger, itching, being uncomfortable, cold, hot; Disturbed sleep pattern, inability to relax; Anxiety, fear

Objective
Restlessness, irritability, moaning, crying; Sighing

COMFORT, READINESS FOR ENHANCED

Diagnostic Division: Pain / Discomfort

Definition: A pattern of ease, relief and transcendence in physical, psychospiritual, environmental, and/or social dimensions that is sufficient for well-being and can be strengthened.

DEFINING CHARACTERISTICS

Subjective
Expresses desire to enhance: comfort/feeling of contentment; Relaxation; Resolution of complaints

Objective
[Appears relaxed/calm]; [Participates in comfort measures of choice]

COMMUNICATION, READINESS FOR ENHANCED

Diagnostic Division: Perception / Cognition

Definition: A pattern of exchanging information and ideas with others that is sufficient for meeting one's needs and life's goals, and can be strengthened.

DEFINING CHARACTERISTICS

Subjective
Expresses willingness to enhance communication; Expresses thoughts/feelings; Expresses satisfaction with ability to share information/ideas with others

Objective
Able to speak or write a language; Forms words, phrases, and sentences; Uses and interprets nonverbal cues appropriately

CONFLICT, PARENTAL ROLE

Diagnostic Division: Social Interaction

Definition: Parent experience of role confusion and conflict in response to crisis.

RELATED FACTORS
Separation from child due to chronic illness [/disability]; Intimidation with invasive modalities (e.g., intubation)/restrictive modalities (e.g., isolation); Specialized care centers; Home care of a child with special needs [e.g., apnea monitoring, hyperalimentation]; Change in marital status; [Conflicts of the role of the single parent]; Interruptions of family life due to home care regimen (e.g., treatments, caregivers, lack of respite)

DEFINING CHARACTERISTICS

Subjective

Parent(s) express(es) concerns/feeling of inadequacy to provide for child's needs (e.g., physical and emotional); Parent(s) express(es) concerns about changes in parental role; Parent(s) express(es) concern about family (e.g., functioning, communication, health); Express(es) concern about perceived loss of control over decisions relating to their child; Verbalize(s) feelings of frustration/ guilt; Anxiety; Fear; [Verbalizes concern about role conflict of wanting to date while having responsibility of child care]

Objective

Demonstrates disruption in caretaking routines; Reluctant to participate in usual caretaking activities even with encouragement and support

---

CONFUSION, ACUTE

Diagnostic Division: Perception / Cognition

> **Definition:** Abrupt onset of reversible disturbances of consciousness, attention, cognition, and perception that develop over a short period of time

RELATED FACTORS

Substance abuse; [Medication reaction/interaction; Anesthesia/surgery; Metabolic imbalances]; Fluctuation in sleep-wake cycle; Over 60 years of age; Delirium [including febrile epilepticum— following or instead of an epileptic attack; toxic and traumatic]; Dementia; [Exacerbation of a chronic illness, hypoxemia]; [Severe pain]

NOTE: Although no time frame is presented to aid in differentiating acute from chronic confusion, the definition of chronic confusion identifies an irreversible state. Therefore, our belief is that acute confusion is potentially reversible.

DEFINING CHARACTERISTICS

Subjective

Hallucinations [Visual/auditory]; [Exaggerated emotional responses]

Objective

Fluctuation in cognition/level of consciousness; Fluctuation in psychomotor activity, [tremors, body movement]; Increased agitation/restlessness; Misperceptions; [Inappropriate responses]; Lack of motivation to initiate/follow through with goal-directed/ purposeful behavior

---

CONFUSION, CHRONIC

Diagnostic Division: Perception / Cognition

> **Definition:** Irreversible, longstanding, and/or progressive deterioration of intellect and personality characterized by decreased ability to interpret environmental stimuli and decreased capacity for intellectual thought processes, and manifested by disturbances of memory, orientation, and behavior.

RELATED FACTORS

Alzheimer's disease [dementia of Alzheimer's type]; Korsakoff's psychosis; Multi-infarct dementia; Cerebral vascular attack; Head injury

DEFINING CHARACTERISTICS
Objective

Clinical evidence of organic impairment; Altered interpretation/response to stimuli; Progressive/longstanding cognitive impairment; No change in level of consciousness; Impaired socialization; Impaired short-term/long-term memory; Altered personality

---

CONFUSION, RISK FOR ACUTE

Diagnostic Division: Perception / Cognition

> **Definition:** At risk for reversible disturbances of consciousness, attention, cognition, and perception that develop over a short period of time.

RISK FACTORS

Substance abuse; Pharmaceutical agents: anesthesia. Anticholinergics, diphenhydramine, opioids, psychoactive drugs, multiple medications; Metabolic abnormalities: decreased hemoglobin, electrolyte imbalances, dehydration, increased BUN/creatinine, azotemia, malnutrition; Infection; Urinary retention; Pain; Fluctuation in sleep-wake cycle; Decreased mobility; Decreased restraints; History of stroke; Impaired cognition; Dementia; Sensory deprivation; Over 60 years of age; Male gender.

CONSTIPATION

Diagnostic Division: Elimination

Definition: Decrease in normal frequency of defecation accompanied by difficult or incomplete passage of stool and/or passage of excessively hard, dry stool.

RELATED FACTORS
Functional
Irregular defecation habits; Inadequate toileting (e.g., timeliness, positioning for defecation, privacy); Insufficient physical activity; Abdominal muscle weakness; Recent environmental changes; Habitual denial/ignoring of urge to defecate

Psychological
Emotional stress; Depression; Mental confusion

Pharmacological
Antilipemic agents; Laxative abuse; Calcium carbonate; Aluminum-containing antacids; Nonsteroidal anti-inflammatory agents; Opiates; Anticholinergics; Diuretics; Iron salts; Phenothiazines; Sedatives; Bismuth salts; Sympathomimetics; Anticonvulsants; Antidepressants; Calcium channel blockers

Mechanical
Hemorrhoids; Pregnancy; Obesity; Rectal abscess/ulcer/prolapse; Rectal anal fissures/strictures; Rectocele; Prostate enlargement; Postsurgical obstruction; Neurological impairment; Hirschsprung's disease; Tumors; Electrolyte imbalance

Physiological
Poor eating habits; Change in usual foods/eating patterns; Insufficient fiber/fluid intake; Dehydration; Inadequate dentition/oral hygiene; Decreased motility of gastrointestinal tract

DEFINING CHARACTERISTICS
Subjective
Change in bowel pattern; Unable to pass stool; Decreased volume/frequency of stool; Increased abdominal pressure; Feeling of rectal fullness/pressure; Abdominal pain; Pain with defecation; Nausea; Vomiting; Headache; Indigestion; Generalized fatigue

Objective
Hard, formed stool; Straining with defecation; Hypoactive/ hyperactive bowel sounds; Borborygmi; Distended abdomen; Abdominal tenderness with/without palpable muscle resistance; Palpable abdominal/rectal mass; Percussed abdominal dullness; Presence of soft paste-like stool in rectum; Oozing liquid stool; Bright red blood with stool; Severe flatus; Anorexia; Atypical presentations in older adults (e.g., change in mental status, urinary incontinence, unexplained falls, elevated body temperature)

CONSTIPATION, PERCEIVED

Diagnostic Division: Elimination

Definition: Self-diagnosis of constipation combined with abuse of laxatives, enemas, and/or suppositories to ensure a daily bowel movement.

RELATED FACTORS
Cultural/family health beliefs; Faulty appraisal, [long-term expectations/habits]; Impaired thought processes

DEFINING CHARACTERISTICS
Subjective
Expectation of a daily bowel movement; Expectation of passage of stool at the same time every day; Overuse of laxatives/enemas/suppositories

CONSTIPATION, RISK FOR

Diagnostic Division: Elimination

Definition: At risk for a decrease in normal frequency of defecation accompanied by difficult or incomplete passage of stool and/or passage of excessively hard, dry stool

RISK FACTORS
Functional
Irregular defecation habits; Inadequate toileting (e.g., timeliness, positioning for defecation, privacy); Insufficient physical activity; Abdominal muscle weakness; Recent environmental changes; Habitual denial/ignoring of urge to defecate

Psychological
Emotional stress; Depression; Mental confusion

Physiological
Change in usual foods/eating patterns; Insufficient fiber/fluid intake; Dehydration; Poor eating habits; Inadequate dentition or oral hygiene; Decreased motility of gastrointestinal tract

Pharmacological
Phenothiazines; Nonsteroidal anti-inflammatory agents; Sedatives; Aluminum-containing antacids; Laxative abuse; Bismuth salts; Iron salts; Anticholinergics; Antidepressants; Anticonvulsants; Antilipemic agents; Calcium channel blockers; Calcium carbonate; Diuretics; Sympathomimetics; Opiates

Mechanical
Hemorrhoids; Pregnancy; Obesity; Rectal abscess/ulcer; Rectal anal stricture/fissures; Rectal prolapse; Rectocele; Prostate enlargement; Postsurgical obstruction; Neurological impairment; Hirschsprung's disease; Tumors; Electrolyte imbalance

---

CONTAMINATION

Diagnostic Division: Safety

Definition: Exposure to environmental contaminants in doses sufficient to cause adverse health effects.

RELATED FACTORS
External
Chemical contamination of food/water; Presence of atmospheric pollutants; Inadequate municipal services (trash removal, sewage treatment facilities); Geographic area (living in area where high level of contaminants exist); Playing in outdoor areas where environmental contaminants are used; Personal/household hygiene practices; Economically disadvantaged (increases potential for multiple exposure, lack of access to healthcare, and poor diet); Use of environmental contaminants in the home (e.g., pesticides, chemicals, environmental tobacco smoke); Lack of breakdown of contaminants once indoors (breakdown is inhibited without sun and rain exposure); Flooring surface (carpeted surfaces hold contaminant residue more than hard floor surfaces); Flaking, peeling paint/plaster in presence of young children; Paint, lacquer, etc. in poorly ventilated areas/without effective protection; Inappropriate use/lack of protective clothing; Unprotected contact with heavy metals or chemicals (e.g., arsenic, chromium, lead); Exposure to radiation (occupation in radiology, employment in nuclear industries and electrical generating plants, living near nuclear industries and/or electrical generating plants); Exposure to disaster (natural or man-made); exposure to bioterrorism; Exposure through ingestion of radioactive material (e.g., food/water contamination)

Internal
Age (children less than 5 years, older adults); Gestational age during exposure; Developmental characteristics of children; Female gender; Pregnancy; Nutritional factors (e.g., obesity, vitamin and mineral deficiencies); Pre-existing disease states; Smoking; Concomitant exposures; Previous exposures

DEFINING CHARACTERISTICS
(Defining characteristics are dependent on the causative agent. Agents cause a variety of individual organ responses as well as systemic responses.)

Pesticides
Major categories of pesticides: Insecticides, herbicides, fungicides, antimicrobials, rodenticides); (Major pesticides: organophosphates, carbamates, organochlorines, pyrethrum, arsenic, glycophosphates, bipyridyls, chlorophenoxy compounds) Dermatological/gastrointestinal/neurological/pulmonary/renal effects of pesticide exposure

Chemicals
(Major chemical agents: petroleum based agents, anticholinesterase Type I agents act on proximal tracheobronchial portion of the respiratory tract; Type II agents act on alveoli; Type III agents produce systemic effects); Dermatological/ gastrointestinal/ immunological/neurological/pulmonary/renal effects of chemical exposure

Biologics
[Toxins from living organisms (bacteria, viruses, fungi)] Dermatological/gastrointestinal/neurological/pulmonary/renal effects of exposure to biologics (toxins from living organisms (bacteria, viruses, fungi)

Pollution
(Major locations: Air, water, soil); (Major agents: Asbestos, radon, tobacco [smoke], heavy metal, lead, noise, exhaust fumes); Neurological/pulmonary effects of pollution exposure

Waste
(Categories of waste: trash, raw sewage, industrial waste); Dermatological/gastrointestinal/hepatic/pulmonary effects of waste exposure

Radiation
(Categories: Internal—ingestion of radioactive material (e.g., food/water contamination), External exposure through direct contact with radioactive material); Immunological/genetic/neurological/oncological effects of radiation exposure

---

CONTAMINATION, RISK FOR

Diagnostic Division: Safety

Definition: At risk for exposure to environmental contaminants in doses sufficient to cause adverse health effects

RISK FACTORS
External
Chemical contamination of food/water; Presence of atmospheric pollutants; Inadequate municipal services (trash removal, sewage treatment facilities); Geographic area (living in area where high level of contaminants exist); Playing in outdoor areas where environmental contaminants are used; Personal/household hygiene practices; Economically disadvantaged (increases potential for multiple exposure, lack of access to healthcare, and poor diet); Use of environmental contaminants in the home (e.g., pesticides, chemicals, environmental tobacco smoke); Lack of breakdown of contaminants once indoors (breakdown is inhibited without sun and rain exposure); Flooring surface (carpeted surfaces hold contaminant residue more than hard floor surfaces); Flaking, peeling paint/plaster in presence of young children; Paint, lacquer, etc. in poorly ventilated areas/without effective protection; Inappropriate use/lack of protective clothing; Unprotected contact with heavy metals or chemicals (e.g., arsenic, chromium, lead); Exposure to radiation (occupation in radiography, employment in nuclear industries and electrical generating plants, living near nuclear industries and/or electrical generating plants); Exposure to disaster (natural or man-made); exposure to bioterrorism

Internal
Age (children less than 5 years, older adults); Gestational age during exposure; Developmental characteristics of children; Female gender; Pregnancy; Nutritional factors (e.g., obesity, vitamin and mineral deficiencies); Pre-existing disease states; Smoking; Concomitant exposure; Previous exposures

---

COPING, COMPROMISED FAMILY

Diagnostic Division: Social Interaction

Definition: Usually supportive primary person (family member, significant other, or close friend) provides insufficient, ineffective, or compromised support, comfort, assistance, or encouragement that may be needed by the client to manage or master adaptive tasks related to his or her health challenge

RELATED FACTORS
Coexisting situations affecting the significant person; Situational/developmental crises the significant person may be facing; Prolonged disease [/disability progression] that exhausts the supportive capacity of significant people; Exhaustion of supportive capacity of significant people; Incorrect understanding of information by a primary person; Lack of reciprocal support; Little support provided by client, in turn, for primary person; Inadequate information available to a primary person; Inadequate understanding of information by a primary person; Incorrect information obtained by a primary person; Temporary preoccupation by a significant person; Temporary family disorganization/role changes; [Lack of mutual decision-making skills]; [Diverse coalitions of family members]

DEFINING CHARACTERISTICS

Subjective

Client expresses a complaint/concern about significant other's response to health problem; Significant other expresses an inadequate understanding/knowledge base, which interferes with effective supportive behaviors; Significant other describes preoccupation with personal reaction (e.g., fear, anticipatory grief, guilt, anxiety) to client's need

Objective

Significant person attempts assistive/supportive behaviors with unsatisfactory results; Significant other displays protective behavior disproportionate to the client's abilities/need for autonomy; Significant other enters into limited personal communication with client; Significant other withdraws from client; [Significant other displays sudden outbursts of emotions/emotional lability or interferes with necessary nursing/medical interventions]

COPING, DEFENSIVE

Diagnostic Division: Ego / Integrity

Definition: Repeated projection of falsely positive self-evaluation based on a self-protective pattern that defends against underlying perceived threats to positive self-regard.

RELATED FACTORS

Conflict between self-perception and value system, uncertainty; Fear of failure, humiliation, or repercussions; low level of self-confidence; Low level of confidence in others, deficient support system; Unrealistic expectations of self; Lack of resilience

DEFINING CHARACTERISTICS

Subjective

Denial of obvious problems/weaknesses; Projection of blame/responsibility; Hypersensitivity to slight/criticism; Grandiosity; Rationalization of failures; [Refuses/rejects assistance]

Objective

Superior attitude toward others; Difficulty establishing/maintaining relationships [avoidance of intimacy]; Hostile laughter; Ridicule of others; [aggressive behavior]; Difficulty in perception of reality testing, reality distortion; Lack of follow-through or participation in treatment/therapy; [Attention-seeking behavior]

COPING, DISABLED FAMILY

Diagnostic Division: Social Interaction

Definition: Behavior of a primary person (family member, significant other, or close friend) that disables his or her capacities and the client's capacities to effectively address tasks essential to either person's adaptation to the health challenge.

RELATED FACTORS

Significant person with chronically unexpressed feelings (e.g., guilt, anxiety, hostility, despair); Dissonant coping styles for dealing with adaptive tasks by the significant person and client/among significant people; Highly ambivalent family relationships; Arbitrary handling of a family's resistance to treatment [that tends to solidify defensiveness as it fails to deal adequately with underlying anxiety]; [High-risk family situations, such as single or adolescent parent, abusive relationship, substance abuse, acute/chronic disabilities, member with terminal illness]

DEFINING CHARACTERISTICS

Subjective

[Expresses despair regarding family reactions/lack of involvement]

Objective

Psychosomaticism; Intolerance; Rejection; Abandonment; Desertion; Agitation; Aggression; Hostility; Depression; Carrying on usual routines without regard for client's needs; Disregarding client's needs; Neglectful care of the client in regard to basic human needs/illness treatment; Neglectful relationships with other family members; Family behaviors that are detrimental to well-being; Distortion of reality regarding the client's health problem; Impaired restructuring of a meaningful life for self; Impaired individualization; Prolonged overconcern for client; Taking on illness signs of client; Client's development of dependence

COPING, INEFFECTIVE

Diagnostic Division: Ego / Integrity

Definition: Inability to form a valid appraisal of the stressors, inadequate choices of practiced responses, and/or inability to use available resources.

RELATED FACTORS
Situational/maturational crisis; High degree of threat; Inadequate opportunity to prepare for stressor; Disturbance in pattern of appraisal of threat; Inadequate level of confidence in ability to cope; Inadequate level of perception of control; Uncertainty; Inadequate resources available; Inadequate social support created by characteristics of relationships; Disturbance in pattern of tension release; Inability to conserve adaptive energies; Gender differences in coping strategies; [Work overload; No vacations; Too many deadlines]; [Impairment of nervous system; Cognitive/sensory/perceptual impairment; Memory loss]; [Severe/chronic pain]

DEFINING CHARACTERISTICS
Subjective
Reports inability to cope or inability to ask for help; Sleep pattern disturbance; Fatigue; Substance abuse; [Reports of muscular/emotional tension]; [Lack of appetite]

Objective
Lack of goal-directed behavior/resolution of problem, including inability to attend to and difficulty with organizing information; [Lack of assertive behavior]; Use of forms of coping that impede adaptive behavior [including inappropriate use of defense mechanisms, verbal manipulation]; Inadequate problem-solving; Inability to meet role expectations/basic needs [e.g., skipping meals, little/no exercise]; Decreased use of social support; Poor concentration; Change in usual communication patterns; High illness rate [e.g., high blood pressure, ulcers, irritable bowel, frequent headaches/neckaches]; Risk-taking; Destructive behavior toward others/self [including overeating, excessive smoking/drinking, overuse of prescribed/OTC medications, illicit drug use]; [Behavioral changes, e.g., impatience, frustration, irritability, discouragement]

COPING, INEFFECTIVE COMMUNITY

Diagnostic Division: Social Interaction

Definition: Pattern of community activities for adaptation and problem-solving that is unsatisfactory for meeting the demands or needs of the community. [Community is defined as "a group of people with a common identity or perspective, occupying space during a given period of time, and functioning through a social system to meet its needs within a larger social environment."]

RELATED FACTORS
Deficits in community social support services and resources; Inadequate resources for problem-solving; Ineffective or nonexistent community systems (e.g., lack of emergency medical system, transportation system, or disaster planning systems); Natural or man-made disasters

DEFINING CHARACTERISTICS
Subjective
Community does not meet its own expectations; Reports of community vulnerability; Reports of community powerlessness; Stressors perceived as excessive

Objective
Deficits in community participation; Excessive community conflicts; High illness rates; Increased social problems (e.g., homicides, vandalism, arson, terrorism, robbery, infanticide, abuse, divorce, unemployment, poverty, militancy, mental illness)

COPING, READINESS FOR ENHANCED

Diagnostic Division: Ego / Integrity

Definition: A pattern of cognitive and behavioral efforts to manage demands that is sufficient for well-being and can be strengthened.

RELATED FACTORS
To be developed

DEFINING CHARACTERISTICS

Subjective
Defines stressors as manageable; Seeks social support/knowledge of new strategies; Acknowledges power; Aware of possible environmental changes

Objective
Uses a broad range of problem-oriented/ emotion-oriented strategies; Uses spiritual resources

---

COPING, READINESS FOR ENHANCED COMMUNITY

Diagnostic Division: Social Interaction

Definition: A pattern of community activities for adaptation and problem-solving that is sufficient for meeting the demands or needs of the community for the management of current and future problems/stressors and can be strengthened

DEFINING CHARACTERISTICS

Subjective
Agreement that community is responsible for stress management

Objective
Active planning by community for predicted stressors; Active problem- solving by community when faced with issues; Positive communication among community members; Positive communication between community/aggregates and larger community; Programs available for recreation/ relaxation; Resources sufficient for managing stressors

---

COPING, READINESS FOR ENHANCED FAMILY

Diagnostic Division: Social Interaction

Definition: A pattern of management of adaptive tasks by primary person (family member, significant other, or close friend) involved with the client's health challenge that is sufficient for health and growth, in regard to self and in relation to the client, and can be strengthened.

DEFINING CHARACTERISTICS

Subjective
Significant person attempts to describe growth impact of crisis [on his or her own values, priorities, goals, or relationships]; Individual expresses interest in making contact with others who have experienced a similar situation

Objective
Significant person moves in direction of health promotion/enriching lifestyle; Chooses experiences that optimize wellness

---

DEATH ANXIETY

Diagnostic Division: Ego / Integrity

Definition: Vague uneasy feeling of discomfort or dread generated by perceptions of a real or imagined threat to one's existence

RELATED FACTORS
Anticipating: pain/suffering/adverse consequences of general anesthesia/impact of death on others; Confronting the reality of terminal disease; Experiencing dying process; Perceived proximity of death; Discussions on the topic of death; Observations related to death; Near-death experience; Uncertainty of prognosis; Nonacceptance of own mortality; Uncertainty about: the existence of a higher power/life after death/an encounter with a higher power

DEFINING CHARACTERISTICS

Subjective
Reports fear of: developing a terminal illness/the process of dying/prolonged dying/loss of mental [/physical] abilities when dying/pain or suffering relating to dying/premature death
Reports: negative thoughts related to death and dying; Feeling powerlessness over dying; Deep sadness; Worrying about: The impact of one's own death on significant others; [about meeting one's creator or feeling doubt about the existence of God or highr being]; Concerns of overworking the caregiver

DEATH SYNDROME, RISK FOR SUDDEN INFANT

Diagnostic Division: Safety

Definition: Presence of risk factors for sudden death of and infant under 1 year of age [Sudden Infant Death Syndrome (SIDS) is the sudden death of an infant under 1 year of age, which remains unexplained after a thorough case investigation, including performance of a complete autopsy, examination of the death scene, and review of the clinical history. SIDS is a subset of Sudden Unexpected Death in Infancy (SUDI) that is the sudden and unexpected death of an infant due to natural or unnatural causes.]

RISK FACTORS
Modifiable
Delayed/lack of prenatal care; Infants placed to sleep in the prone/side-lying position; Soft underlayment (loose articles in the sleep environment); Infant overheating/overwrapping; Prenatal/postnatal smoke exposure

Potentially Modifiable
Young maternal age; Low birth weight; Prematurity

Nonmodifiable
Male gender; Ethnicity (e.g., African American, Native American); Seasonality of SIDS deaths (higher in winter and fall months); Infant age of 2 to 4 months

RELATED FACTORS
To be developed

DECISIONAL CONFLICT (Specify)

Diagnostic Division: Ego Integrity

Definition: Uncertainty about course of action to be taken when choice among competing actions involves risk, loss, or challenge to values and beliefs.

RELATED FACTORS
Unclear personal values/beliefs; Perceived threat to value system; Lack of experience/ interference with decision making; Lack of relevant information; Multiple/divergent sources of information; Moral obligations require performing/not performing actions; Moral principles/rules/values support mutually inconsistent courses of action; Support system deficit; [Age, developmental state]; [Family system; Sociocultural factors]; [Cognitive/ emotional/behavioral level of functioning]

DEFINING CHARACTERISTICS
Subjective
Verbalizes: Uncertainty about choices; Undesired consequences of alternative actions being considered; Feeling of distress while attempting a decision; Questioning moral principles/rules/values or personal values/beliefs while attempting a decision

Objective
Vacillation among alternative choices; Delayed decision making; Self-focusing; Physical signs of distress or tension (increased heart rate; increased muscle tension; restlessness; etc.)

DECISION-MAKING, READINESS FOR ENHANCED

Diagnostic Division: Cognitive – Perceptual Pattern

Definition: A pattern of choosing courses of action that is sufficient for meeting short— and long-term health-related goals and can be strengthened.

RELATED FACTORS
To be developed

DEFINING CHARACTERISTICS
Subjective
Expresses desire to enhance: Decision making; Congruency of decisions with personal values and goals; Congruency of decisions with sociocultural values and goals; Risk-benefit analysis of decisions; Understanding of choices for decision making; Understanding of the meaning of choices; Use of reliable evidence for decisions

DENIAL, INEFFECTIVE

Diagnostic Division: Ego / Integrity

Definition: Conscious or unconscious attempt to disavow the knowledge or meaning of an event to reduce anxiety and/or fear, leading to the detriment of health.

RELATED FACTORS
Anxiety; Threat of inadequacy in dealing with strong emotions; Lack of control of life situation; Fear of loss of autonomy; Overwhelming stress; Lack of competency in using effective coping mechanisms; Threat of unpleasant reality; Fear of separation/death; Lack of emotional support from others

DEFINING CHARACTERISTICS
Subjective
Minimizes symptoms; Displaces source of symptoms to other organs; Unable to admit impact of disease on life pattern; Displaces fear of impact of the condition; Does not admit fear of death or invalidism; Refuses healthcare attention

Objective
Delays seeking healthcare attention; Does not perceive personal relevance of symptoms or danger; Unable to admit impact of disease on life pattern; Makes dismissive gestures/comments when speaking of distressing events; Displays inappropriate affect; Uses self-treatment

DENTITION, IMPAIRED

Diagnostic Division: Food / Fluid

Definition: Disruption in tooth development/eruption patterns or structural integrity of individual teeth.

RELATED FACTORS
Dietary habits; Nutritional deficits; Selected prescription medications; Chronic use of tobacco/coffee/tea/red wine; Ineffective oral hygiene; Sensitivity to heat or cold; Chronic vomiting; Deficient knowledge regarding dental health; Excessive use of abrasive cleaning agents/intake of fluorides; Barriers to self-care; Lack of access to professional care; Economically disadvantaged; Genetic predisposition; Bruxism; [Traumatic injury/surgical intervention]

DEFINING CHARACTERISTICS
Subjective
Toothache

Objective
Halitosis; Tooth enamel discoloration; Erosion of enamel; Excessive plaque; Worn down/abraded teeth; Crown/root caries; Tooth fracture(s); Loose teeth; Missing teeth; Absent teeth; Premature loss of primary teeth; Incomplete eruption for age (may be primary or permanent teeth); Excessive calculus; Malocclusion/tooth misalignment; Asymmetrical facial expression

DEVELOPMENT, RISK FOR DELAYED

Diagnostic Division: Teaching / Learning

Definition: At risk for delay of 25% or more in one or more of the areas of social or self-regulatory behavior, or in cognitive, language, gross or fine motor skills.

RISK FACTORS
Prenatal
Maternal age <15 or >35 years; Unplanned/unwanted pregnancy; Lack of/late/inadequate prenatal care; Inadequate nutrition; Economically disadvantaged; Illiteracy; Genetic/ endocrine disorders; Infections; Substance abuse

Individual
Prematurity; Congenital/genetic disorders; Vision/hearing impairment; Frequent otitis media; Inadequate nutrition; Failure to thrive; Chronic illness; Brain damage (e.g., hemorrhage in postnatal period, shaken baby, abuse, accident); Seizures; Positive drug screen(s); Substance abuse; Lead poisoning; Foster/adopted child; Behavior disorders; Technology-dependent; Natural disasters; Treatment-related side effects (e.g., chemotherapy, radiation therapy, pharmaceutical agents)

Environmental
Economically disadvantaged; Violence

Caregiver
Learning disabilities; Severe learning disability; Abuse; Mental illness

DIARRHEA

Diagnostic Division: Elimination

Definition: Passage of loose, unformed stools.

RELATED FACTORS
Psychological
High stress levels and anxiety

Situational
Laxative/alcohol abuse; toxins; contaminants; Adverse effects of pharmaceutical agents; Radiation; Tube feedings; Travel

Physiological
Inflammation; Irritation; Infectious processes; Parasites; Malabsorption

DEFINING CHARACTERISTICS

Subjective
Abdominal pain; Urgency; cramping

Objective
Hyperactive bowel sounds; At least 3 loose or liquid stools per day

DIGNITY, RISK FOR COMPROMISED HUMAN

Diagnostic Division: Ego Integrity

Definition: At risk for perceived loss of respect and honor.

RISK FACTORS
Loss of control of body functions; exposure of the body; Perceived humiliation/invasion of privacy; Disclosure of confidential information; Stigmatizing label; Use of undefined medical terms; Perceived dehumanizing treatment/intrusion by clinicians; Inadequate participation in decision making; Cultural incongruity

MORAL DISTRESS

Diagnostic Division: Ego Integrity

Definition: Response to the inability to carry out one's chosen ethical/moral decision/action.

RELATED FACTORS
Conflict among decision-makers, [e.g., patient/family, health care providers, insurance payers, regulatory agencies]; Conflicting information guiding moral/ethical decision-making; Cultural conflicts; Treatment decisions; End of life decisions; Loss of autonomy; Time constraints for decision-making; Physical distance of decision maker

DEFINING CHARACTERISTICS

Subjective
Expresses anguish (e.g., powerlessness, guilt, frustration, anxiety, self-doubt, fear) over difficulty acting on one's moral choice

DISUSE SYNDROME, RISK FOR

Diagnostic Division: Activity / Rest

Definition: At risk for deterioration of body systems as the result of prescribed or unavoidable musculoskeletal inactivity.

NOTE: NANDA identifies complications from immobility can include pressure ulcer, constipation, stasis of pulmonary secretions, thrombosis, urinary tract infection/retention, decreased strength/endurance, orthostatic hypotension, decreased range of joint motion, disorientation, body image disturbance, and powerlessness.

RISK FACTORS
Severe pain, [chronic pain]; Paralysis [other neuromuscular impairment]; Mechanical or prescribed immobilization; Altered level of consciousness [chronic physical or mental illness]

DIVERSIONAL ACTIVITY, DEFICIENT

Diagnostic Division: Activity / Rest

> **Definition:** Decreased stimulation from (or interest or engagement in) recreational or leisure activities.

NOTE: Internal/external factors that may or may not be beyond the individual's control.

RELATED FACTORS
Environmental lack of diversional activity [e.g., long-term hospitalization; frequent, lengthy treatments, home-bound]; [Physical/ developmental limitations]; [Bedridden]; [Fatigue; [Pain]; [Situational crisis]; [Lack of resources]; [Psychological condition/depression]

DEFINING CHARACTERISTICS

Subjective
Reports feeling bored(e.g., wish there was something to do, to read, etc.); Usual hobbies cannot be undertaken in the current settingl [home or other care setting]; [Changes in abilities/physical limitations]

Objective
[Flat affect; disinterest, inattentiveness]; [Lethargy]; [Withdrawal]; [Restlessness]; [Crying]; [Hostility]; [Overeating or lack of interest in eating]; [Weight loss or gain]

DRY EYE, RISK FOR

Diagnostic Division: Safety

> **Definition:** At risk for eye discomfort or damage to the cornea and conjunctiva due to reduced quantity or quality of tears to moisten the eye

RISK FACTORS
Aging; Autoimmune diseases (rheumatoid arthritis, diabetes mellitus, thyroid disease, gout, osteoporosis, etc.); Contact lenses; Environmental factors (air-conditioning, excessive wind, sunlight exposure, air pollution, low humidity); Female gender; History of allergy; Hormones; Lifestyle (e.g., smoking, caffeine use, prolonged reading); Mechanical ventilation therapy; Neurological lesions with sensory or motor reflex loss (lagophthalmos, lack of spontaneous blink reflex due to decreased consciousness and other medical conditions); Oscular surface damage; Place of living; Treatment-related side effects (e.g., pharmaceutical agents such as angiotensin-converting enzyme inhibitors, antihistamines, diuretics, steroid, antidepressants, tranquilizers, analgesics, sedatives, neuromuscular blockage agents; surgical operations); Vitamin A deficiency

ELECTROLYTE IMBALANCE, RISK FOR

Diagnostic Division: Food / Fluid

> **Definition:** At risk for change in serum electrolyte levels that may compromise health.

RISK FACTORS
Deficient fluid volume; Diarrhea; Vomiting; Endocrine dysfunction; Excess fluid volume; Renal dysfunction; Impaired regulatory mechanisms (e.g., diabetes insipidus, syndrome of inappropriate secretion of antidiuretic hormone); Treatment-related side effects (e.g., medications, drains)

ENERGY FIELD, DISTURBED

Diagnostic Division: Activity / Rest

> **Definition:** Disruption of the flow of energy [aura] surrounding a person's being that results in disharmony of the body, mind, and/or spirit.

RELATED FACTORS
Slowing or blocking of energy flow secondary to:

Pathophysiological factors
Illness; Pregnancy; Injury

Treatment related factors:
Immbolility; Labor and delivery; Perioperative experience; Chemotherapy

Situational factors
Pain; Fear; Anxiety; Grieving

Maturational factors
Age-related developmental difficulties/crisis

DEFINING CHARACTERISTICS
Objective
Perceptions of changes in patterns of energy flow, such as: Movement (wave/spike/tingling/dense/flowing); Sounds (tone/words); Temperature change (warmth/coolness); Visual changes (image/color); Disruption of the field (deficient, hole, spike, bulge, obstruction, congestion, diminished flow in energy field)

ENVIRONMENTAL INTERPRETATION SYNDROME, IMPAIRED

Diagnostic Division: Perception / Cognition

Definition: Consistent lack of orientation to person, place, time, or circumstances over more than 3 to 6 months, necessitating a protective environment.

RELATED FACTORS
Dementia [e.g., Alzheimer's disease, multi-infarct, Pick's disease, AIDS dementia]; Huntington's disease; Depression

DEFINING CHARACTERISTICS

Subjective
[Loss of occupation or social function from memory decline]

Objective
Consistent disorientation; Chronic confusional states; Inability to follow simple directions; Inability to reason/concentrate; Slow in responding to questions; Loss of occupation/social functioning

---

FAILURE TO THRIVE, ADULT

Diagnostic Division: Food / Fluid

Definition: A progressive functional deterioration of a physical and cognitive nature. The individual's ability to live with multisystem diseases, cope with ensuing problems, and manage his or her care is remarkably diminished.

RELATED FACTORS
Depression; [Major disease/degenerative condition]; [Aging process]

DEFINING CHARACTERISTICS

Subjective
Reports loss of interest in pleasurable outlets; Altered mood state; Reports desire for death

Objective
Inadequate nutritional intake; Consumption of minimal to no food at most meals (i.e., consumes less than 75% of normal requirements); Anorexia; Unintentional weight loss (e.g., 5% in 1 month, 10% in 6 months); Physical decline (e.g., fatigue, dehydration, incontinence of bowel and bladder); Cognitive decline: demonstrated difficulty responding to environmental stimuli; demonstrated difficulty with reasoning, decision-making, judgment, memory, concentration, decreased perception; Apathy; Decreased participation in activities of daily living [ADLs]; Self-care deficit; Neglect of home environment/financial responsibilities; Decreased social skills/social withdrawal; Frequent exacerbations of chronic health problems

---

FALLS, RISK FOR

Diagnostic Division: Safety

Definition: At risk for increased susceptibility to falling that may cause physical harm.

RISK FACTORS

Adults:
History of falls; Wheelchair use; Use of assistive devices (e.g., walker, cane); Age 65 or over; Lives alone; Lower limb prosthesis

Physiological:
Acute illness; Postoperative conditions; Visual/hearing difficulties; Arthritis; Orthostatic hypotension; Faintness when turning/extending neck; Sleeplessness; Anemia; Vascular disease; Neoplasms (i.e., fatigue/limited mobility); Urinary urgency; Incontinence; Diarrhea; Postprandial blood sugar changes; [Hypoglycemia]; Impaired physical mobility; Foot problems; Decreased lower extremity strength; Impaired balance; Difficulty with gait; Proprioceptive deficits [e.g., unilateral neglect]; Neuropathy

Cognitive:
Diminished mental status [e.g., confusion, delirium, dementia, impaired reality testing]

Medications:
Antihypertensive agents; Angiotensin—converting enzyme inhibitors; Diuretics; Tricyclic antidepressants; Antianxiety agents; Hypnotics; Tranquilizers; Narcotics/opiates; Alcohol use

Environment:
Restraints; Weather conditions (e.g., wet floors/ice); Cluttered environment; Throw rugs; Lacks antislip material in bath/shower; Unfamiliar, dimly lit room

Children
Age 2 or younger; Male gender when <1 year of age; Lack of: gate on stairs; window guards; automobile restraints; Unattended infant on elevated surface (e.g., bed, changing table); Bed located near window; Lack of parental supervision

---

FAMILY PROCESSES, DYSFUNCTIONAL

Diagnostic Division: Role/Relationships

Definition: Psychosocial, spiritual, and physiological functions of the family unit are chronically disorganized, which leads to conflict, denial of problems, resistance to change, ineffective problem-solving, and a series of self-perpetuating crises

RELATED FACTORS
Substance abuse; Family history of substance abuse/resistance to treatment; Inadequate coping skills; Addictive personality; Lack of problem-solving skills; Biochemical influences; Genetic predisposition to substance abuse

DEFINING CHARACTERISTICS

Subjective
Feelings
Anxiety; Tension; Distress; Chronic low self-esteem; Worthlessness; Lingering resentment; Anger; Suppressed rage; Frustration; Shame; Embarrassment; Hurt; Unhappiness; Guilt; Emotional isolation; Loneliness; Powerlessness; Insecurity; Hopelessness; Rejection; Responsibility for substance abuser's behavior; Vulnerability; Mistrust; Depression; Hostility; Fear; Confusion; Dissatisfaction; Loss; Being different from other people; Emotional control by others; Being unloved; Lack of identity; Abandonment; Confuses love and pity; Moodiness; Failure; Reports feeling misunderstood

Roles and Relationships
Family denial; Deterioration in family relationships; Disturbed family dynamics; Ineffective spouse communication; Marital problems; Intimacy dysfunction; Altered role function; Disrupted family roles/rituals; Inconsistent parenting; Low perception of parental support; Chronic family problems; Lack of skills necessary for relationships; Lack of cohesiveness; Pattern of rejection; Economic problems; Neglected obligations

Objective
Feelings
Repressed emotions

Roles and Relationships
Closed communication systems; Triangulating family relationships; Reduced ability of family members to relate to each other for mutual growth and maturation; Family does not demonstrate respect for individuality/ autonomy of its members

Behaviors
Substance abuse; Nicotine addiction; Enabling maintenance of substance use pattern (e.g., alcohol); Inadequate understanding/deficient knowledge of/about substance

abuse; Family special occasions are substance-use centered; Rationalization/denial of problems; Refusal to get help; Inability to accept/receive help appropriately; Inappropriate expression of anger; Blaming; Criticizing; Verbal abuse of children/spouse/parent; Lying; Broken promises; Lack of reliability; Manipulation; Dependency; Inability to express/accept a wide range of feelings; Difficulty with intimate relationships; Diminished physical contact; Harsh self-judgment; Difficulty having fun; Self-blaming; Social isolation; Seeking approval/affirmation; Impaired/contradictory/paradoxical/controlling communication; Power struggles; Ineffective problem-solving skills; Orientation toward tension relief rather than achievement of goals; Agitation; Escalating conflict; Chaos; Disturbances in concentration; Disturbances in academic performance in children; Failure to accomplish developmental tasks; Difficulty with life cycle transitions; Inability to meet emotional/security/spiritual needs of its members; Inability to adapt to change; Immaturity; Stress-related physical illnesses; Inability to deal constructively with traumatic experiences; Complicated grieving; Conflict avoidance

FAMILY PROCESSES, INTERRUPTED

Diagnostic Division: Role Relationships

Definition: A change in family relationships and/or functioning.

RELATED FACTORS
Situational transition/crises; Developmental transition/ crises [e.g., loss or gain of a family member, adolescence, leaving home for college]; Shift in health status of a family member; Shift in family roles; Power shift of family members; Modification in family finances/social status; Interaction with community

DEFINING CHARACTERISTICS
Subjective
Changes in: Power alliances; Satisfaction with family; Expressions of conflict within family; Effectiveness in completing assigned tasks; Stress-reduction behaviors; Expressions of conflict with/isolation from community resources; Somatic complaints; [Family expresses confusion about what to do; verbalizes they are having difficulty responding to change]

Objective
Changes in: Assigned tasks; Participation in problem solving/decision making; Communication patterns; Mutual support; Availability for emotional support/affective responsiveness; Intimacy; Patterns; Rituals

FAMILY PROCESSES, READINESS FOR ENHANCED

Diagnostic Division: Role Relationships

Definition: A pattern of family functioning that is sufficient to support the well-being of family members and can be strengthened

RELATED FACTORS
To be developed

DEFINING CHARACTERISTICS
Subjective
Expresses willingness to enhance family dynamics; Communication is adequate; Relationships are generally positive; Interdependent with community; Family tasks are accomplished; Energy level of family supports activities of daily living; Family adapts to change

Objective
Family functioning meets needs of family members; Activities support the safety/growth of family members; Family roles are appropriate/flexible for developmental stages; Respect for family members is evident; Boundaries of family members are maintained; Family resilience is evident; Balance exists between autonomy and cohesiveness

FATIGUE

Diagnostic Division: Activity / Rest

Definition: An overwhelming sustained sense of exhaustion and decreased capacity for physical and mental work at the usual level.

RELATED FACTORS

Psychological
Stress; anxiety; reports boring lifestyle; depression

Environmental
Noise; lights; humidity; temperature

Situational
Occupation; negative life events

Physiological
Increased physical exertion; sleep deprivation; Pregnancy; disease states; malnutrition; anemia; Poor physical condition; [Altered body chemistry (e.g., medications, drug withdrawal, chemotherapy)]

DEFINING CHARACTERISTICS

Subjective
Reports an unremitting/overwhelming lack of energy; Inability to maintain usual routines/level of physical activity; Perceived need for additional energy to accomplish routine tasks; Increase in rest requirements; Reports feeling tired; Inability to restore energy even after sleep; Feelings of guilt for not keeping up with responsibilities; Compromised libido; Increase in physical complaints

Objective
Lethargic; Listless; Drowsy; Lack of energy; Compromised concentration; Disinterest in surroundings; Introspection; Decreased performance; [Accident-prone]

FEAR

Diagnostic Division: Ego/Integrity

Definition: Response to perceived threat [real or imagined] that is consciously recognized as a danger

RELATED FACTORS
Innate origin (e.g., sudden noise, height, pain, loss of physical support); Innate releasers (neurotransmitters); Phobic stimulus; Learned response (e.g., conditioning, modeling from or identification with others); Unfamiliarity with environmental experience(s); Separation from support system in potentially stressful situation (e.g., hospitalization, hospital procedures [/treatments]); Language barrier; Sensory impairment

DEFINING CHARACTERISTICS

Subjective
Reports: Apprehension; Excitement; Being scared; Alarm; Panic; Terror; Dread; Decreased self-assurance; Increased tension; Jitteriness

Cognitive
Identifies object of fear; Stimulus believed to be a threat

Physiological
Anorexia; Nausea; Fatigue; Dry mouth; [Palpitations]

Objective
Cognitive
Diminished productivity/learning ability/problem-solving ability

Behaviors
Increased alertness; Avoidance behaviors[/flight]; Attack behaviors; Impulsiveness; Narrowed focus on the source of the fear

Physiological
Increased pulse; Vomiting; Diarrhea; Muscle tightness; Increased respiratory rate; Dyspnea; Increased systolic blood pressure; Pallor; Increased perspiration; Pupil dilation

---

FEEDING PATTERN, INEFFECTIVE INFANT

Diagnostic Division: Food/Fluid

Definition: Impaired ability of an infant to suck or coordinate the suck/swallow response resulting in inadequate oral nutrition for metabolic needs

RELATED FACTORS
Anatomical abnormality; Neurological decay; Neurological impairment; Oral hypersensitivity; Prematurity; Prolonged nil by mouth (NPO) status

DEFINING CHARACTERISTICS

Subjective
Inability to coordinate sucking, swallowing, and breathing; Inability to initiate an effective suck; Inability to sustain an effective suck

FLUID BALANCE, READINESS FOR ENHANCED

Diagnostic Division: Food / Fluid

> **Definition:** A pattern of equilibrium between the fluid volume and chemical composition of body fluids that is sufficient for meeting physical needs and can be strengthened

DEFINING CHARACTERISTICS

Subjective
Expresses willingness to enhance fluid balance; No excessive thirst

Objective
Stable weight; No evidence of edema; Moist mucous membranes; Intake adequate for daily needs; Straw-colored urine; Specific gravity within normal limits; Urine output appropriate for intake; Good tissue turgor; Risk for deficient fluid volume

[FLUID VOLUME, DEFICIENT (HYPER/HYPOTONIC)]

Diagnostic Division: Food / Fluid

> **Definition:** Decreased intravascular, interstitial, and/or intracellular fluid. This refers to dehydration with changes in sodium.

NOTE: NANDA has restricted Fluid Volume deficit to address only isotonic dehydration. For patient needs related to dehydration associated with alterations in sodium, the authors have provided this second diagnostic category

RELATED FACTORS

Hypertonic dehydration: uncontrolled diabetes mellitus/insipidus, HHNC, increased intake of hypertonic fluids/IV therapy, inability to respond to thirst reflex/inadequate free water supplementation (high-osmolarity enteral feeding formulas), renal insufficiency/failure); [Hypotonic dehydration: chronic illness/malnutrition, excessive use of hypotonic IV solutions (e.g., D5W), renal insufficiency]

DEFINING CHARACTERISTICS

Subjective
[Fatigue]; [Nervousness]; [Exhaustion]; [Thirst]

Objective
[Increased urine output, dilute urine (initially)]; [Decreased output/oliguria]; [Weight loss]; [Decreased venous filling]; [Hypotension (postural)]; [Increased pulse rate]; [Decreased pulse volume/pressure]; [Decreased skin turgor]; [Dry skin/mucous membranes]; [Increased body temperature]; [Change in mental status (e.g., confusion)]; [Hemoconcentration]; [Altered serum sodium]

FLUID VOLUME, DEFICIENT [ISOTONIC]

Diagnostic Division: Food / Fluid

> **Definition:** Decreased intravascular, interstitial and/or intracellular fluid. This refers to dehydration, water loss alone without change in sodium.

NOTE: This diagnosis has been structured to address isotonic dehydration (hypovolemia) when fluids and electrolytes are lost in even amounts and excluding states in which changes in sodium occur. For client needs related to dehydration associated with alterations in sodium, refer to [deficient Fluid Volume: hyper/hypotonic]

RELATED FACTORS

Active fluid volume loss [e.g., hemorrhage, gastric intubation, diarrhea, wounds; abdominal cancer; burns, fistulas, ascites (third spacing); use of hyperosmotic radiopaque contrast agents]; Failure of regulatory mechanisms [e.g., fever/thermoregulatory response, renal tubule damage]; [Impaired access/intake/absorption of fluids]

DEFINING CHARACTERISTICS

Subjective
Thirst; Weakness

Objective

Decreased urine output; Increased urine concentration; Decreased venous filling; Decreased pulse volume/pressure; Sudden weight loss (except in third spacing); Decreased BP; Increased pulse rate; Increased body temperature; Decreased skin/tongue turgor; Dry skin/mucous membranes; Change in mental status; Elevated hematocrit

FLUID VOLUME EXCESS

Diagnostic Division: Food/Fluid

Definition: Increased isotonic fluid retention.

RELATED FACTORS

Compromised regulatory mechanism [e.g., syndrome of inappropriate antidiuretic hormone (SIADH), or decreased plasma proteins as found in conditions such as malnutrition, draining fistulas, burns, organ failure]; Excess fluid intake; Excess sodium intake; [Drug therapies such as chlorpropamide, tolbutamide, vincristine, triptylines, carbamazepine]

DEFINING CHARACTERISTICS

Subjective

Anxiety; [Difficulty breathing]

Objective

Edema; Anasarca; Weight gain over short period of time; Intake exceeds output; Oliguria; Specific gravity changes; Adventitious breath sounds [rales or crackles]; Changes in respiratory pattern; Dyspnea; Orthopnea; Pulmonary congestion; Pleural effusion; Pulmonary artery pressure changes; BP changes; Increased central venous pressure; Jugular vein distension; Positive hepatojugular reflex; S_3 heart sound; Change in mental status; Restlessness; Decreased Hb/Hct; Electrolyte imbalance; Azotemia

FLUID VOLUME , RISK FOR DEFICIENT

Diagnostic Division: Foood/Fluid

Definition: At risk for experiencing decreased intravascular, interstitial, and/or intracellular fluid. This refers to a risk of dehydration, water loss alone without change in sodium.

RISK FACTORS

Extremes of age/weight; Loss of fluid through abnormal routes (e.g., indwelling tubes); Factors influencing fluid needs (e.g., hypermetabolic state); Excessive losses through normal routes (e.g., diarrhea); Deviations affecting access/intake/absorption of fluids; Active fluid volume loss; Deficient knowledge; Failure of regulatory mechanisms; Pharmaceutical agents (e.g., diuretics)

FLUID VOLUME, RISK FOR IMBALANCED

Diagnostic Division: Food/Fluid

Definition: At risk for a decrease, increase, or rapid shift from one to the other of intravascular, interstitial, and/or intracellular fluid that may compromise health. This refers to body fluid loss, gain, or both.

RISK FACTORS

Abdominal surgery, intestinal obstruction; Pancreatitis, ascites; Burns, sepsis, Traumatic injury (e.g., fractured hip); Receiving apheresis

GAS EXCHANGE, IMPAIRED

Diagnostic Division: Respiration

Definition: Excess or deficit in oxygenation and/or carbon dioxide elimination at the alveolar-capillary membrane [This may be an entity of its own but also may be an end result of other pathology with an interrelatedness between airway clearance and/or breathing pattern problems.]

RELATED FACTORS

Ventilation-perfusion imbalance [as in altered blood flow (e.g., pulmonary embolus, increased vascular resistance), vasospasm, heart failure, hypovolemic shock]; Alveolar-capillary membrane changes [e.g., acute adult respiratory distress syndrome); chronic conditions such as restrictive/obstructive lung disease, pneumoconiosis, respiratory depressant drugs, brain injury, asbestosis/silicosis]; [Altered oxygen supply (e.g., altitude sickness)]; [Altered oxygen-carrying capacity of blood (e.g., sickle cell/other anemia, carbon monoxide poisoning)]

DEFINING CHARACTERISTICS

Subjective
Dyspnea; Visual disturbances; Headache upon awakening; [sense of impending doom]

Objective
Confusion; [Decreased mental acuity]; Restlessness; Irritability; [Agitation]; Somnolence; [Lethargy]; Abnormal ABGs/arterial pH; Hypoxia; Hypoxemia; Hypercapnia; Decreased carbon dioxide; Cyanosis (in neonates only); Abnormal skin color (e.g., pale, dusky); Abnormal breathing (e.g., rate, rhythm, depth); Nasal flaring; Tachycardia; [Dysrhythmias]; Diaphoresis; [Polycythemia]

GASTROINTESTINAL MOTILITY, DYSFUNCTIONAL

Diagnostic Division: Elimination

Definition: Increased, decreased, ineffective, or lack of peristaltic activity within the gastrointestinal system.

RELATED FACTORS
Aging, prematurity; Surgery; Malnutrition, Enteral feedings; Pharmaceutical agents (e.g., narcotics/opiates, laxatives, antibiotics, anesthesia); Food intolerance (e.g., gluten, lactose); Ingestion of contaminants (e.g., food, water); Sedentary lifestyle, immobility; Anxiety

DEFINING CHARACTERISTICS

Subjective
Absence of flatus; Abdominal cramping, pain; Diarrhea, Difficulty passing stool; Nausea, regurgitation

Objective
Change in bowel sounds (e.g., absent, hypoactive, hyperactive); Abdominal distension; Accelerated gastric emptying, diarrhea; Increased gastric residual, bile-colored gastric residual; Dry stool, hard stool; Vomiting

GASTROINTESTINAL MOTILITY, RISK FOR DYSFUNCTIONAL

Diagnostic Division: Elimination

Definition: At risk for increased, decreased, ineffective, or lack of peristaltic activity within the gastrointestinal system.

RISK FACTORS
Aging, Abdominal surgery, decreased gastrointestinal circulation; Food intolerance (e.g., gluten, lactose), change in food or water, unsanitary food preparation; Pharmaceutical agents (e.g., antibiotics, laxatives, , narcotics/opiates, proton pump inhibitors); Gastrointestinal reflux disease (GERD); Diabetes mellitus; Infection (e.g., bacterial, parasitic, viral); Sedentary lifestyle, immobility; Stress, anxiety; Prematurity

GASTROINTESTINAL PERFUSION, RISK FOR INEFFECTIVE

Diagnostic Division: Activity / Rest

Definition: At risk for decrease in gastrointestinal circulation that may compromise health.

RISK FACTORS
Acute gastrointestinal hemorrhage; [hypovolemia]; Trauma, abdominal compartment syndrome; Vascular disease e.g., peripheral vascular disease, aortoiliac occlusive disease), abdominal aortic aneurysm; Poor left ventricular performance, hemodynamic instability; Coagulopathy (e.g. sickle cell anemia, disseminated intravascular coagulation), abnormal partial thromboplastin time, abnormal prothrombin time; [emboli]; Gastrointestinal disease (e.g., duodenal or gastric ulcer, ischemic colitis, ischemic pancreatitis), gastric paresis; gastroesophageal varices; Liver dysfunction, renal failure, diabetes mellitus, stroke; Smoking, Treatment-related side effects (e.g., cardiopulmonary bypass, pharmaceutical agents, anesthesia, gastric surgery); Age >60 years, female gender; Anemia; Myocardial infarction

GLUCOSE, RISK FOR UNSTABLE BLOOD

Diagnostic Division: Food / Fluid

Definition: Risk for variation of blood glucose/sugar levels from the normal range.

RISK FACTORS

Lack of acceptance of diagnosis; deficient knowledge of diabetes management (e.g., action plan); Lack of diabetes management/adherence to diabetes management (e.g., action plan); Inadequate blood glucose monitoring; Medication management; Dietary intake; Weight gain/loss; Rapid growth periods; Pregnancy; Physical health status/ activity level; Stress; Mental health status; Developmental level

GRIEVING

Diagnostic Division: Ego / Integrity

Definition: A normal complex process that includes emotional, physical, spiritual, social, and intellectual responses and behaviors by which individuals, families, and communities incorporate an actual, anticipated, or perceived loss into their daily lives

RELATED FACTORS

Anticipatory loss of a significant other/significant object (e.g., possession, job, status, home, parts & processes of body); Death of a significant other; Loss of a significant object (e.g., possession, job, status, home, parts and processes of body)

DEFINING CHARACTERISTICS

Subjective

Anger; Pain; Suffering; Despair; Blame; Alteration in: activity level, dream patterns; Making meaning of the loss; Personal growth; Experiencing relief; Disturbed sleep pattern

Objective

Detachment; Disorganization; Psychological distress; Panic behavior; Maintaining the connection to the deceased; Alterations in immune/neuroendocrine function

GRIEVING, COMPLICATED

Diagnostic Division: Ego / Integrity

Definition: A disorder that occurs after the death of a significant other [/object], in which the experience of distress accompanying bereavement fails to follow normative expectations and manifests in functional impairment

RELATED FACTORS

Death of a significant other; Emotional instability; Lack of social support; [Loss of significant object (e.g., possessions, job, status, home, ideals, parts and processes of the body—amputation, paralysis, chronic/terminal illness]

DEFINING CHARACTERISTICS

Subjective

Reports: Anxiety; Lack of acceptance of the death; Persistant painful memories; Distressful feelings about the deceased; Self-blame; Reports feelings of: Anger; Mistrust; Disbelief; Detachment from others; Reports feeling: Dazed; Empty; Stunned; In shock; Decreased sense of wellbeing; Fatigue; Low levels of intimacy; Depression; Yearning

Objective

Decreased functioning in life roles; Persistant emotional distress; Separation/traumatic distress; Preoccupation with thoughts of the deceased; Longing/searching for the deceased; Self-blame; Experiencing somatic symptoms of the deceased; Rumination; Grief avoidance

GRIEVING, RISK FOR COMPLICATED

Diagnostic Division: Ego / Integrity

Definition: At risk for a disorder that occurs after the death of a significant other, in which the experience of distress accompanying bereavement fails to follow normative expectations and manifests in functional impairment.

RISK FACTORS

Death of a significant other; Emotional instability; Lack of social support; [Loss of significant object (e.g., possessions, job, status, home, parts & processes of body)]

GROWTH, RISK FOR DISPROPORTIONATE

Diagnostic Division: Teaching / Learning

Definition: At risk for growth above the 97th percentile or below the 3rd percentile for age, crossing two percentile channels

RISK FACTORS
Prenatal
Maternal nutrition; Maternal infection; Multiple gestation; Substance abuse; Teratogen exposure; Congenital/genetic disorders [e.g., dysfunction of endocrine gland, tumors]

Individual
Prematurity; Malnutrition; Caregiver's/individual maladaptive feeding behaviors; Insatiable appetite; Anorexia; [Impaired metabolism, greater-than-normal energy requirements]; Infection; Chronic illness [e.g., chronic inflammatory diseases]; Substance [use]/abuse [including anabolic steroids]

Environmental
Deprivation; Economically disadvantaged; Violence; Natural disasters; Teratogen; Lead poisoning

Caregiver
Abuse; Mental illness, Severe learning disability; Learning difficulties (mental handicap)

GROWTH AND DEVELOPMENT, DELAYED

Diagnostic Division: Teaching / Learning

Definition: Deviations from age—group norms.

RELATED FACTORS
Inadequate caretaking; [Physical/emotional neglect or abuse]; Indifference; Inconsistent responsiveness; Multiple caretakers; Separation from significant others; Environmental/stimulation deficiencies; Effects of physical disability [handicapping condition]; Prescribed dependence [insufficient expectations for self-care]; [Physical/emotional illness (chronic, traumatic), e.g., chronic inflammatory disease, pituitary tumors, impaired nutrition/metabolism, greater-than-normal energy requirements; prolonged/painful treatments; prolonged/repeated hospitalizations]; [Sexual abuse]; [Substance use/abuse]

DEFINING CHARACTERISTICS
Subjective
Inability to perform self-care or self-control activities appropriate for age

Objective
Delay/difficulty in performing skills typical of age group; [Loss of previously acquired skills, precocious/accelerated skill attainment]; Altered physical growth; Flat affect, listlessness, decreased response time; [Sleep disturbances, negative mood/response]

HEALTH, DEFICIENT COMMUNITY

Diagnostic Division: Teaching / Learning

Definition: Presence of one or more health problems or factors that deter wellness or increase the risk of health problems experienced by an aggregate

RELATED FACTORS
Lack of access to public healthcare providers; Lack of community experts; Limited resources; Program has inadequate community support; Program has inadequate consumer satisfaction; Program has inadequate evaluation plan; Program has inadequate outcome data; Program partly addresses health problem

DEFINING CHARACTERISTICS
Subjective
No program available to enhance wellness for an aggregate or population; No program available to prevent one or more health problems for an aggregate or population; No program available to reduce one or more health problems for an aggregate or population; No program available to eliminate one or more health problems for an aggregate or population

Objective
Incidence of risks relating to hospitalization, physiological states, and/or psychological states experienced by aggregates or populations; Incidence of health problems experienced by aggregates or populations

HEALTH BEHAVIOR, RISK-PRONE

Diagnostic Division: Ego Integrity

   Definition: Impaired ability to modify lifestyle/behaviors in a manner that improves health status.

RELATED FACTORS
Inadequate comprehension; Low self-efficacy; Multiple stressors; Smoking, excessive alcohol; Inadequate social support; Low socioeconomic status; Negative attitudes toward health care

DEFINING CHARACTERISTICS
Subjective
Minimizes health status change; Failure to achieve optimal sense of control

Objective
Failure to take actions that prevents health problems; Demonstrates nonacceptance of health status change

HEALTH MAINTENANCE, INEFFECTIVE

Diagnostic Division: Safety

   Definition: Inability to identify, manage, and/or seek out help to maintain health.

NOTE: This diagnosis contains components of other nursing diagnoses. We recommend subsuming health maintenance interventions under the "basic" nursing diagnosis when a single causative factor is identified (e.g., deficient Knowledge; Communication, impaired verbal; Thought Processes, disturbed; Individual/Family Coping, ineffective; Growth and Development, delayed).

RELATED FACTORS
Deficient communication skills [written, verbal, gestural]; Unachieved developmental tasks; Inability to make appropriate judgments; Perceptual/cognitive impairment; Diminished/lack of gross motor skills; Diminished/lack of fine motor skills; Ineffective individual/family coping; Complicated grieving; Spiritual distress; Insufficient resources (e.g., equipment, finances); [Lack of psychosocial supports]

DEFINING CHARACTERISTICS
Subjective
Lack of expressed interest in improving health behaviors; [Reported compulsive behaviors]

Objective
Demonstrated lack of knowledge about basic health practices; Inability to take the responsibility for meeting basic health practices; History of lack of health-seeking behavior; Demonstrated lack of adaptive behaviors to environmental changes; Impairment of personal support systems; [Observed compulsive behaviors]

HEALTH MANAGEMENT, INEFFECTIVE SELF

Diagnostic Division: Teaching / Learning

   Definition: A pattern of regulating and integrating into daily living a program for treatment of illness and the sequelae of illness that is unsatisfactory for meeting specific health goals.

RELATED FACTORS
Complexity of health care system or therapeutic regimen; Decisional conflicts; Economic difficulties; Excessive demands made (e.g., individual or family); Family conflict; Family patterns of health care; Inadequate number of cues to action; Knowledge deficit; Regimen; Perceived seriousness, susceptibility, barriers, or benefits; Powerlessness; Social support deficits

DEFINING CHARACTERISTICS
Subjective
Verbalizes desire to manage the illness; Verbalizes difficulty with prescribed regimens

Objective

Failure to include treatment regimens in daily routines/take action to reduce risk factors; Makes choices in daily living ineffective for meeting the health goals; [Unexpected acceleration of illness symptoms]

HOME MAINTENANCE, IMPAIRED

Diagnostic Division: Activity / Rest

> **Definition:** Inability to independently maintain a safe growth-promoting immediate environment.

RELATED FACTORS

Disease; Injury; Illness; Insufficient family organization/ planning; Insufficient finances; Impaired functioning; Lack of role modeling; Unfamiliarity with neighborhood resources; Deficient knowledge; Inadequate support systems

DEFINING CHARACTERISTICS

Subjective

Household members report difficulty in maintaining their home in a comfortable [safe] fashion; Household members request assistance with home maintenance; Household members report outstanding debts/financial crises

Objective

Disorderly/unclean surroundings; Offensive odors; Inappropriate household temperature; Presence of vermin; Repeated unhygienic disorders/infections; Lack of necessary equipment; Unavailable cooking equipment; Insufficient/lack of clothes/linen; Overtaxed family members

---

HOPE, READINESS FOR ENHANCED

Diagnostic Division: Ego / Integrity

> **Definition:** A pattern of expectations and desires for mobilizing energy on one's own behalf that is sufficient for well-being and can be strengthened.

DEFINING CHARACTERISTICS

Subjective

Expresses desire to enhance: Hope; Belief in possibilities; Congruency of expectations with desires; Ability to set achievable goals; Problem-solving to meet goals; Expresses desire to enhance: Sense of meaning to life; Interconnectedness with others; Spirituality

---

HOPELESSNESS

Diagnostic Division: Self-perception

> **Definition:** Subjective state in which an individual sees limited or no alternatives or personal choices available and is unable to mobilize energy on own behalf.

RELATED FACTORS

Prolonged activity restriction, social isolation; Failing or deteriorating physiological condition; Long-term stress; abandonment; Lost belief in spiritual power/transcendent values [/God]

DEFINING CHARACTERISTICS

Subjective

Verbal cues (despondent content, "I can't," sighing); [Believes things will not change/ problems will always be there]

Objective

Passivity; Decreased verbalization; Decreased affect; Decreased appetite; Decreased response to stimuli; [Depressed cognitive functions, problems with decisions, thought processes; regression]; Lack of initiative/involvement in care; Sleep pattern disturbance; Turning away from speaker; Shrugging in response to speaker; [Withdrawal from environs]; [Closing eyes]; [Lack of involvement/interest in significant others]; [Angry outbursts]; [Substance abuse]

HUMAN DIGNITY, RISK FOR COMPROMISED

Diagnostic Division: Self-Perception

Definition: At risk for perceived loss of respect and honor

RISK FACTORS

Cultural incongruity; Disclosure of confidential information; Exposure of the body; Inadequate participation in decision-making; Loss of control of body functions; Perceived dehumanizing treatment; Perceived humiliation; Perceived intrusion by clinicians; Perceived invasion of privacy; Stigmatizing label; Use of undefined medical terms

HYPERTHERMIA

Diagnostic Division: Safety

Definition: Body temperature is elevated above normal range.

RELATED FACTORS

Exposure to hot environment; Inappropriate clothing; Vigorous activity; Dehydration; Decreased perspiration; Pharmaceutical agents; Anesthesia; Increased metabolic rate; Illness; Trauma

DEFINING CHARACTERISTICS

Subjective
[Headache]

Objective
Increase in body temperature above normal range; Flushed skin; Skin warm to touch; Tachycardia; [Unstable BP]; Tachypnea; Convulsions; [Muscle rigidity/fasciculations]; [Confusion]

HYPOTHERMIA

Diagnostic Division: Safety

Definition: Body temperature is below normal range.

RELATED FACTORS

Exposure to cool environment [prolonged exposure, e.g., homeless, immersion in cold water/near-drowning]; induced hypothermia/cardiopulmonary bypass]; Inadequate clothing; Evaporation from skin in cool environment; Decreased ability to shiver; Aging [or very young]; [Debilitating] illness; Trauma; Damage to hypothalamus; Malnutrition; Decreased metabolic rate; Inactivity; Consumption of alcohol; Pharmaceutical agents; [Drug overdose]

DEFINING CHARACTERISTICS
Objective

Body temperature below normal range; Shivering; Piloerection; Cool skin; Pallor; Slow capillary refill; Cyanotic nail beds; Hypertension; Tachycardia; [Core temperature 95°F/35°C: increased respirations, poor judgment, shivering]; [Core temperature 95° to 93.2°F/35° to 34°C: bradycardia or tachycardia, myocardial irritability/dysrhythmias, muscle rigidity, shivering, lethargic/confused, decreased coordination]; [Core temperature 93.2° to 86°F/34° to 30°C: hypoventilation, bradycardia, generalized rigidity, metabolic acidosis, coma]; [Core temperature 86°F/30°C: no apparent vital signs, heart rate unresponsive to drug therapy, comatose, cyanotic, dilated pupils, apneic, areflexic, no shivering (appears dead)]

IMMUNIZATION STATUS, READINESS FOR ENHANCED

Diagnostic Division: Safety

Definition: A pattern of conforming to local, national, and/or international standards of immunization to prevent infectious disease(s) that is sufficient to protect a person, family or community and can be strengthened.

DEFINING CHARACTERISTICS

Subjective
Expresses desire to enhance: Knowledge of immunization standards; Immunization status; Identification of providers of immunizations; Record-keeping of immuniza-

tions; Identification of possible problems associated with immunizations; Behavior to prevent infectious diseases

---

IMPULSE CONTROL, INEFFECTIVE

Diagnostic Division: Perception / Cognition

Definition: A pattern of performing rapid, unplanned reactions to internal or external stimuli without regard for the negative consequences of these reactions to the impulsive individual or to others

RELATED FACTORS
Anger; Chronic low self-esteem; Co-dependency; Compunction; Delusion; Denial; Disorder of cognition/development/mood/personality; Disturbed body image; Economically disadvantaged; Environment that might cause frustration/irritation; Fatigue; Hopelessness; Ineffective coping; Insomnia; Organic brain disorders; Smoker; Social isolation; Stress vulnerability; Substance abuse; Suicidal feeling; Unpleasant physical symptoms

DEFINING CHARACTERISTICS

Subjective
Asking personal questions of others; Inability to save money or regulate finances; Sharing personal details inappropriately

Objective
Acting without thinking; Irritability; Pathological gambling; Sensation seeking; Sexual promiscuity; Temper outbursts; Too familiar with strangers; Violence

---

INCONTINENCE, BOWEL

Diagnostic Division: Elimination

Definition: Change in normal bowel habits characterized by involuntary passage of stool.

RELATED FACTORS
Toileting self-care deficit; Environmental factors (e.g., inaccessible bathroom); Impaired cognition; Immobility; Dietary habits; Medications; Laxative abuse; Stress; Colorectal lesions; Impaired reservoir capacity; Incomplete emptying of bowel; Impaction; Chronic diarrhea; General decline in muscle tone; Abnormally high abdominal/intestinal pressure; Rectal sphincter abnormality; Loss of rectal sphincter control; Lower/upper motor nerve damage

DEFINING CHARACTERISTICS

Subjective
Recognizes rectal fullness but reports inability to expel formed stool; Urgency; Inability to delay defecation; Self-report of inability to recognize rectal fullness

Objective
Constant dribbling of soft stool; Fecal staining of clothing/bedding; Fecal odor; Red perianal skin; Inability to recognize/inattention to urge to defecate

---

INCONTINENCE, FUNCTIONAL URINARY

Diagnostic Division: Elimination

Definition: Inability of a usually continent person to reach the toilet in time to avoid unintentional loss of urine

RELATED FACTORS
Altered environmental factors [e.g., poor lighting or inability to locate bathroom]; Impaired cognition; Impaired vision; Neuromuscular limitations; Psychological factors; Weakened supporting pelvic structures; [Reluctance to request assistance/use bedpan]; [Increased urine production]

DEFINING CHARACTERISTICS

Subjective
Senses need to void; [voiding in large amounts]

Objective
Amount of time required to reach toilet exceeds length of time between sensing the urge to void and uncontrolled voiding; Loss of urine before reaching toilet; May be incontinent only in the early morning; Able to completely empty bladder

INCONTINENCE, OVERFLOW URINARY

Diagnostic Division: Elimination

Definition: Involuntary loss of urine associated with overdistension of the bladder

RELATED FACTORS
Bladder outlet obstruction; Detrusor external sphincter dyssynergia; Detrusor hypocontractility; Fecal impaction; Severe pelvic prolapse; Side effects of anticholinergic medications; Side effects of calcium channel blockers; Side effects of decongestant medications; Urethral obstruction

DEFINING CHARACTERISTICS

Subjective
Reports involuntary leakage of small volumes of urine; Nocturia

Objective
Bladder distension; High post-void residual volume; Observed involuntary leakage of small volumes of urine

INCONTINENCE, REFLEX URINARY

Diagnostic Division: Elimination

Definition: Involuntary loss of urine at somewhat predictable intervals when a specific bladder volume is reached

RELATED FACTORS
Neurological impairment above level of pontine/sacral micturition center; Tissue damage (e.g., due to radiation cystitis, inflammatory bladder conditions, radical pelvic surgery)

DEFINING CHARACTERISTICS

Subjective
Inability to voluntarily inhibit/initiate voiding; No sensation of bladder fullness/urge to void/voiding; Sensation of urgency without voluntary inhibition of bladder contraction; Sensations associated with full bladder (e.g., sweating, restlessness, abdominal discomfort)

Objective
Incomplete emptying with [brain] lesion above pontine micturition center; Incomplete emptying with [spinal cord] lesion above sacral micturition center; Predictable pattern of voiding

INCONTINENCE, STRESS URINARY

Diagnostic Division: Elimination

Definition: Sudden leakage of urine with activities that increase intra-abdominal pressure

RELATED FACTORS
Degenerative changes in pelvic muscles; High intra-abdominal pressure [e.g., obesity, gravid uterus]; Intrinsic urethral sphincter deficiency; Weak pelvic muscles

DEFINING CHARACTERISTICS

Subjective
Reports involuntary leakage of small amounts of urine in the absence of detrusor contraction/an overdistensed bladder; Reports involuntary leakage of small amounts of urine on extertion [e.g., lifting, impact aerobics]/with coughing, laughing, and/or sneezing

Objective
Observed involuntary leakage of small amounts of urine in the absence of detrusor contaction/an overdistensed bladder; Observed involuntary leakage of small amounts of urine on extertion [e.g., lifting, impact aerobics]/with coughing, laughing, and/or sneezing

INCONTINENCE, URGE URINARY

Diagnostic Division: Elimination

Definition: Involuntary passage of urine occurring soon after a strong sense of urgency to void

RELATED FACTORS

Alcohol intake; Atrophic urethritis/vaginitis; Bladder infection; Caffeine intake; Decreased bladder capacity [e.g., history of pelvic inflammatory disease (PID), abdominal surgeries, indwelling urinary catheter]; Detrusor hyperactivity with impaired bladder contractility; Diuretic use; Fecal impaction; [Increased fluids]

DEFINING CHARACTERISTICS

Subjective

Reports inability to reach toilet in time to avoid urine loss; Reports involuntary loss of urine with bladder contractions/spasms; Reports urinary urgency

Objective

Observed inability to reach toilet in time to avoid urine loss

INCONTINENCE, RISK FOR URGE URINARY

Diagnostic Division: Elimination

Definition: At risk for involuntary passage of urine occurring soon after a strong sensation of urgency to void

RISK FACTORS

Atrophic urethritis/vaginitis; Effects of alcohol, caffeine, and/or pharmaceutical agents; Detrusor hyperactivity with impaired bladder contractility; Fecal impaction; Impaired bladder contractility; Ineffective toileting habits; Involuntary sphincter relaxation; Small bladder capacity

INFANT FEEDING PATTERN, INEFFECTIVE

Diagnostic Division: Food/Fluid

Definition: Impaired ability to suck or coordinate the suck-swallow response, resulting in inadequate oral nutrition for metabolic needs.

RELATED FACTORS

Prematurity; Neurological impairment/delay; Oral hypersensitivity; Prolonged NPO; Anatomic abnormality

DEFINING CHARACTERISTICS

Subjective

[Caregiver reports infant is unable to initiate or sustain an effective suck]

Objective

Inability to initiate/sustain an effective suck; Inability to coordinate sucking, swallowing, and breathing

INFECTION, RISK FOR

Diagnostic Division: Safety

Definition: At risk for being invaded by pathogenic organisms.

RISK FACTORS

Inadequate primary defenses (broken skin (e.g., intravenous catheter placement, invasive procedures), traumatized tissue (e.g., trauma, tissue destruction), decrease in ciliary action, stasis of body fluids, change in pH of secretions, altered peristalsis, premature/prolonged rupture of amniotic membranes, smoking); Inadequate secondary defenses (e.g., decreased hemoglobin, leukopenia, suppressed inflammatory response, immunosuppression (e.g., inadequate acquired immunity; pharmaceutical agents including immunosuppressants, steroids, monoclonal antibodies, immunomodulators)); Increased environmental exposure to pathogens (outbreaks); Invasive procedures; Chronic disease (diabetes mellitus, obesity); Malnutrition; Deficient knowledge to avoid exposure to pathogens

INJURY, RISK FOR

Diagnostic Division: Safety

Definition: At risk of injury as a result of environmental conditions interacting with the individual's adaptive and defensive resources.

NOTE: The potential for injury differs from individual to individual, and situation to situation. It is our belief that the environment is not safe, and there is no way to list everything that might present a danger to someone. Rather, we believe nurses have the responsibility to educate people throughout their life cycles to live safely in their environment.

RISK FACTORS
Internal
Physical (e.g., broken skin, altered mobility); Tissue hypoxia; Malnutrition; Abnormal blood profile (e.g., leukocytosis/leukopenia, altered clotting factors, thrombocytopenia, sickle cell, thalassemia, decreased hemoglobin); Biochemical dysfunction; Sensory dysfunction; Integrative/effector dysfunction; Immune/autoimmune dysfunction; Developmental age (physiological, psychosocial); Psychological (affective, orientation)

External
Biological (e.g., immunization level of community, microorganism); Chemical (e.g., pollutants, poisons, drugs, pharmaceutical agents, alcohol, nicotine, preservatives, cosmetics, dyes); Nutritional (e.g., vitamins, food types); Physical (e.g., design, structure, and arrangement of community, building, and/or equipment), Mode of transport; Human (e.g., nosocomial agents, staffing patterns; cognitive, affective, and psychomotor factors)

INJURY, RISK FOR PERIOPERATIVE POSITIONING

Diagnostic Division: Safety

> **Definition:** At risk for injury as a result of the environmental conditions found in the perioperative setting.

RISK FACTORS
Disorientation; sensory/perceptual disturbances due to anesthesia; Immobilization; Muscle weakness; [Pre-existing musculoskeletal conditions]; Obesity; Emaciation; Edema; [Elderly]

INSOMNIA

Diagnostic Division: Activity / Rest

> **Definition:** A disruption in amount and quality of sleep that impairs functioning.

RELATED FACTORS
Intake of stimulants/alcohol; Pharmaceutical agents; Gender-related hormonal shifts; Stress (e.g., ruminative pre-sleep pattern); Depression; Fear; Anxiety; Grief; Impairment of normal sleep pattern (e.g., travel, shift work); Inadequate sleep hygiene (current); Activity pattern (e.g., timing, amount); Physical discomfort (e.g., pain, shortness of breath, cough, gastroesophageal reflux, nausea, incontinence/urgency); Environmental factors (e.g., ambient noise, daylight/darkness exposure, ambient temperature/humidity, unfamiliar setting); Frequent daytime naps; Interrupted sleep; Parental responsibilities

DEFINING CHARACTERISTICS
Subjective
Patient reports: Difficulty falling/staying asleep; Waking up too early; Dissatisfaction with sleep (current); Nonrestorative sleep; Sleep disturbances that produce next-day consequences; Lack of energy; Difficulty concentrating; Changes in mood; Decreased health status/quality of life; Increased accidents

Objective
Observed lack of energy; Observed changes in affect; Increased work/school absenteeism

INTRACRANIAL ADAPTIVE CAPACITY, DECREASED

Diagnostic Division: Circulation

> **Definition:** Intracranial fluid dynamic mechanisms that normally compensate for increases in intracranial volumes are compromised, resulting in repeated disproportionate increases in intracranial pressure (ICP) in response to a variety of noxious and non-noxious stimuli.

RELATED FACTORS
Brain injuries; Sustained increase in ICP of 10 to 15 mmHg; Decreased cerebral perfusion pressure ≤to 50 to 60 mm Hg; Systemic hypotension with intracranial hypertension

DEFINING CHARACTERISTICS
Objective
Repeated increases in ICP of >10 mmHg for more than 5 minutes following any of a variety of external stimuli; Disproportionate increase in ICP following stimulus; Elevated P2 ICP waveform; Volume-pressure response test variation (volume-pressure ratio 2, pressure-volume index < 10); Baseline ICP greater than or equal to 10 mm Hg; Wide amplitude ICP waveform; [Altered level of consciousness—coma]; [Changes in vital signs, cardiac rhythm]

JAUNDICE, NEONATAL

Diagnostic Division: Safety

Definition: The yellow-orange tint of the neonate's skin and mucous membranes that occurs after 24 hours of life as a result of unconjugated bilirubin in the circulation.

RELATED FACTORS
Neonate age 1 to 7 days; Feeding pattern not well established; Abnormal weight loss (>7% – 8% in breastfeeding newborn; 15% in term infant); Stool (meconium) passage delayed; Infant experiences difficulty making the transition to extrauterine life

DEFINING CHARACTERISTICS
Objective
Yellow-orange skin, yellow sclera; Yellow mucous membranes; Abnormal skin bruising; Abnormal blood profile (e.g., hemolysis; total serum bilirubin >2 mg/dL; inherited disorder; total serum bilirubin in the high-risk range on age in hour-specific nomogram)

JAUNDICE, RISK FOR NEONATAL

Diagnostic Division: Safety

Definition: At risk for the yellow-orange tint of the neonate's skin and mucous membranes that occurs after 24 hours of life as a result of unconjugated bilirubin in the circulation

RISK FACTORS
Abnormal weight loss (>7–8% in breastfeeding newborn, 15% in term infant); Feeding pattern not well established; Infant experiences difficulty making the transition to extrauterine life; Neonate aged 1–7 days; Prematurity; Stool (meconium) passage delayed

KNOWLEDGE, DEFICIENT [LEARNING NEED] (SPECIFY)

Diagnostic Division: Perception / Cognition

Definition: Absence or deficiency of cognitive information related to a specific topic. [Lack of specific information necessary for patient/significant other(s) to make informed choices regarding condition/lifestyle changes.]

RELATED FACTORS
Lack of exposure; Information misinterpretation; Unfamiliarity with information resources; Lack of recall; Cognitive limitation; Lack of interest in learning; [Request for no information]; [Inaccurate/incomplete information presented]

DEFINING CHARACTERISTICS

Subjective
Reports the problem; [Request for information]; [Statements reflecting misconceptions]
Objective
Inaccurate follow-through of instruction; Inaccurate performance of test; Exaggerated/inappropriate behaviors (e.g., hysterical, hostile, agitated, apathetic); [Development of preventable complication]

KNOWLEDGE (SPECIFY), READINESS FOR ENHANCED

Diagnostic Division: Perception / Cognition

Definition: A pattern of cognitive information related to a specific topic, or its acquisition, that is sufficient for meeting health-related goals and can be strengthened

RELATED FACTORS
To be developed

DEFINING CHARACTERISTICS

Subjective
Expresses an interest in learning; Explains knowledge of the topic; Describes previous experiences pertaining to the topic

Objective
Behaviors congruent with expressed knowledge

LATEX ALLERGY RESPONSE

Diagnostic Division: Safety

Definition: A hypersensitive reaction to natural latex rubber products

RELATED FACTORS
Hypersensitivity to natural latex rubber protein

DEFINING CHARACTERISTICS
Life-threatening reactions occurring in the first hour after exposure to latex protein
Bronchospasm; Cardiac arrest; Contact urticaria progressing to generalized symptoms; Dyspnea; Edema of the lips/throat/tongue/uvula; Hypotension; Respiratory arrest; Syncope; Tightness in chest; Wheezing

Orofacial Characteristics
Edema of eyelids/the sclerae; Erythema of the eyes; Facial erythema/itching; Itching of the eyes; Nasal congestion/erythema; Nasal/oral itching; Rhinorrhea; Tearing of the eyes

Gastrointestinal Characteristics
Abdominal pain; Nausea

Generalized Characteristics
Flushing; Generalized discomfort/edema; Increasing complaint of total body warmth; Restlessness

Type IV reactions occurring 1 hour or more after exposure to latex protein
Discomfort reaction to additives such as thiurams and carbamates; Eczema; Irritation; Redness

LATEX ALLERGY RESPONSE, RISK FOR

Diagnostic Division: Safety

Definition: Risk of hypersensitivity to natural latex rubber products that may compromise health.

RISK FACTORS
History of reactions to latex; Allergies to bananas, avocados, tropical fruits, kiwi, chestnuts, poinsettia plants; History of allergies and asthma; Professions with daily exposure to latex; Multiple surgical procedures, especially beginning in infancy

LIFESTYLE, SEDENTARY

Diagnostic Division: Activity / Rest

Definition: Reports a habit of life that is characterized by a low physical activity level

RELATED FACTORS
Lack of interest/motivation/resources (time, money, companionship, facilities); Lack of training for accomplishment of physical exercise; Deficient knowledge of the health benefits of physical exercise

DEFINING CHARACTERISTICS

Subjective
Reports preference for activities low in physical activity

Objective
Chooses a daily routine lacking physical exercise; Demonstrates physical deconditioning

LIVER FUNCTION, RISK FOR IMPAIRED

Diagnostic Division: Food / Fluid

Definition: At risk fora decrease in liver function that may compromise health.

RISK FACTORS
Viral infection (e.g., hepatitis A, hepatitis B, hepatitis C, Esptein-Barr); HIV co-infection; Hepatotoxic medications (e.g., acetaminophen, statins); Substance abuse (e.g., alcohol, cocaine)

LONELINESS, RISK FOR

Diagnostic Division: Self-Perception

Definition: At risk for experiencing discomfort associated with a desire or need for more contact with others.

RISK FACTORS
Affectional deprivation; Physical isolation; Cathectic deprivation; Social isolation; [Problems of attachment for children]; [Chaotic family relationships]

MATERNAL/FETAL DYAD, RISK FOR DISTURBED

Diagnostic Division: Sexuality

Definition: At risk for disruption of the symbiotic maternal-fetal dyad as a result of comorbid or pregnancy-related conditions

RISK FACTORS
Complications of pregnancy (e.g., premature rupture of membranes, placenta previa or abruption, late prenatal care, multiple gestation); Compromised O_2 transport (e.g., anemia, cardiac disease, asthma, hypertension, seizures, premature labor , hemorrhage; [sickle-cell anemia]); Impaired glucose metabolism (e.g., diabetes, steroid use); Physical abuse; Substance abuse (e.g., tobacco, alcohol, drugs); Treatment-related side effects (e.g., pharmaceutical agents, surgery)

MEMORY, IMPAIRED

Diagnostic Division: Perception / Cognition

Definition: Inability to remember or recall bits of information or behavioral skills [Impaired memory may be attributed to physiopathological or situational causes that are either temporary or permanent.]

RELATED FACTORS
Hypoxia; Anemia; Fluid and electrolyte imbalance; Decreased cardiac output; Neurological disturbances [e.g., brain injury/concussion]; Excessive environmental disturbances; [Manic state, fugue, traumatic event]; [Substance use/abuse]; [Effects of medications]; [Age]

DEFINING CHARACTERISTICS

Subjective
Reports experience of forgetting; Inability to recall recent or past events/factual information [/familiar persons, places, items]

Objective
Inability to recall if a behavior was performed; Inability to learn/retain new skills/information; Inability to perform a previously learned skill; Forgets to perform a behavior at a scheduled time

MOBILITY, IMPAIRED BED

Diagnostic Division: Activity / Rest

Definition: Limitation of independent movement from one bed position to another.

RELATED FACTORS
Neuromuscular/musculosketal impairment; Insufficient muscle strength; Deconditioning; Obesity; Environmental consraints (i.e., bed size/type, treatment equipment, restraints); Pain; Sedating pharmaceutical agents; Deficient knowledge; Cognitive impairment

DEFINING CHARACTERISTICS

Subjective
[Reported difficulty performing activities]

Objective
Impaired ability to: Turn from side to side; Move from supine to sitting or sitting to supine; Reposition self in bed; Move from supine to prone or prone to supine; Move from supine to long-sitting or long-sitting to supine

---

MOBILITY, IMPAIRED PHYSICAL

Diagnostic Division: Activity / Rest

Definition: Limitation in independent, purposeful physical movement of the body or of one or more extremities.

RELATED FACTORS
Sedentary lifestyle; Activity intolerance; Disuse; Deconditioning; Decreased endurance; Limited cardiovascular endurance; Decreased muscle strength/control/mass; Joint stiffness; Contractures; Loss of integrity of bone structures; Pain/discomfort; Neuromuscular/musculoskeletal impairment; Sensoriperceptual/cognitive impairment; Developmental delay; Depressive mood state; Anxiety; Malnutrition; Altered cellular metabolism; Body mass index above 75th age-appropriate percentile; Deficient knowledge regarding value of physical activity; Cultural beliefs regarding age-appropriate activity; Lack of environmental supports (e.g., physical or social); Prescribed movement restrictions; Pharmaceutical agents; Reluctance to initiate movement

NOTE: Specify level of independence using a standardized functional scale.

DEFINING CHARACTERISTICS

Subjective
[Report of pain/discomfort on movement]; [Unwillingness to move]

Objective
Limited range of motion; Limited ability to perform gross fine/motor skills; Difficulty turning; Slowed movement; Uncoordinated/jerky movements; Movement-induced tremor; Decreased [slower] reaction time; Postural instability; Gait changes; Engages in substitutions for movement (e.g., increased attention to other's activity, controlling behavior, focus on preillness disability/activity)

MOBILITY, IMPAIRED WHEELCHAIR

Diagnostic Division: Activity / Rest

Definition: Limitation of independent operation of wheelchair within environment.

RELATED FACTORS
Neuromuscular/musculosketal impairments (e.g., contractures); Insufficient muscle strength; Limited endurance; Deconditioning; Obesity; Impaired vision; Pain; Depressed mood; Cognitive impairment; Deficient knowledge; Environmental constraints (e.g., stairs, inclines, uneven surfaces, unsafe obstacles, distances, lack of assistive devices or persons, wheelchair type)

DEFINING CHARACTERISTICS
Objective
Impaired ability to operate manual wheelchair on: a decline, an incline, curbs, even/uneven surface; Impaired ability to operate power wheelchair on: a decline, an incline, curbs, even/uneven surface

---

NAUSEA

Diagnostic Division: Food / Fluid

Definition: A subjective phenomenon of an unpleasant feeling in the back of the throat and stomach that may or may not result in vomiting.

RELATED FACTORS
Treatment
Gastric irritation; Gastric distension; Pharmaceutical agents [e.g., analgesics—aspirin/nonsterodial anti-inflammatory drugs/opioids, anesthesia, antivirals for HIV, steroids, antibiotics, chemotherapeutic agents]; [Radiation therapy/exposure]

Biophysical

Biochemical disorders (e.g., uremia, diabetic ketoacidosis); Localized tumors (e.g., acoustic neuroma, primary or secondary brain tumors, bone metastases at base of skull); Intra-abdominal tumors; Toxins (e.g., tumor-produced peptides, abnormal metabolites due to cancer); Esophageal/pancreatic disease; Liver/splenetic capsule stretch; Gastric distension [e.g., delayed gastric emptying, pyloric intestinal obstruction, external compression of the stomach, other organ enlargement that slows stomach functioning (squashed stomach syndrome)]; Gastric irritation [e.g., pharyngeal and/or peritoneal inflammation]; Motion sickness; Meniere's disease; Labyrinthitis; Increased intracranial pressure; Meningitis; Pain; Pregnancy

Situational

Noxious odors/taste; Unpleasant visual stimulation; Pain; Psychological factors; Anxiety; Fear

DEFINING CHARACTERISTICS

Subjective

Reports nausea ["sick to stomach"]; Reports sour taste in mouth

Objective

Aversion toward food; Increased salivation; Increased swallowing; Gagging sensation

---

NONCOMPLIANCE [ADHERENCE, INEFFECTIVE] (SPECIFY)

Diagnostic Division: Teaching / Learning

Definition: Behavior of person and/or caregiver that fails to coincide with a health-promoting or therapeutic plan agreed on by the person (and/or family and/or community) and healthcare professional. In the presence of an agreed upon health-promoting, or therapeutic plan, the person's or caregiver's behavior is fully or partially nonadherent and may lead to clinically ineffective or partially ineffective outcomes.

NOTE: When the plan of care is reviewed with the client/significant other, use of the term noncompliance may create a negative response and sense of conflict between healthcare providers and client. Labeling the client noncompliant may also lead to problems with third-party reimbursement. Where possible, use of the Nursing Diagnosis: ineffective Therapeutic Regimen Management is recommended.]

RELATED FACTORS

Health Care Plan

Duration; Cost; Intensity; Complexity; Financial flexibility of plan

Individual factors

Personal/developmental abilities; Skill relevant to the regimen behavior; Deficient knowledge related to the regimen behavior; Motivational forces; Individual's value system; Health beliefs; Cultural influences; Spiritual values; Significant others; [Altered thought processes such as depression, paranoia]; [Difficulty changing behavior, as in addictions]; [Denial]; [Issues of secondary gain]

Health System

Individual health coverage; Credibility of provider; Difficulty in client-provider relationship; Provider continuity/regular follow-up; Provider reimbursement; Communication/teaching skills of the provider; Access/ convenience of care; Satisfaction with care

Network

Involvement of members in health plan; Social value regarding plan; Perceived beliefs of significant others

DEFINING CHARACTERISTICS

Subjective

[Does not perceive illness/risk to be serious, does not believe in efficacy of therapy, unwilling to follow treatment regimen or accept side effects/limitations

Objective

Behavior indicative of failure to adhere; Objective tests provide evidence of failure to adhere (e.g., physiological measures, detection of physiologic markers); Failure to progress; Evidence of development of complications/exacerbation of symptoms; Failure to keep appointments; [Inability to set or attain mutual goals]

NUTRITION: LESS THAN BODY REQUIREMENTS, IMBALANCED

Diagnostic Division: Food / Fluid

Definition: Intake of nutrients insufficient to meet metabolic needs.

RELATED FACTORS
Inability to ingest/digest food; Inability to absorb nutrients; Insufficient finances; Biological/psychological factors; [Increased metabolic demands, e.g., burns]; [Lack of information, misinformation, misconceptions]

DEFINING CHARACTERISTICS

Subjective
Reports food intake less than RDA (recommended daily allowance); Lack of food; Lack of interest in food; Aversion to eating; Reports altered taste sensation; Perceived inability to ingest food; Satiety immediately after ingesting food; Abdominal pain/cramping; Lack of information, misinformation, misconceptions

Objective
Body weight 20% or more below ideal weight range[for height and frame]; [Decreased subcutaneous fat/muscle mass]; Loss of weight with adequate food intake; Hyperactive bowel sounds; Diarrhea; Steatorrhea; Weakness of muscles required for swallowing or mastication; Poor muscle tone; Sore buccal cavity; Pale mucous membranes; Capillary fragility; Excessive loss of hair [or increased growth of hair on body (lanugo)]; [Cessation of menses]; [Abnormal laboratory studies (e.g., decreased albumin, total proteins; iron deficiency; electrolyte imbalances)]

NUTRITION: MORE THAN BODY REQUIREMENTS, IMBALANCED

Diagnostic Division: Food / Fluid

Definition: Intake of nutrients that exceeds metabolic needs.

RELATED FACTORS
Excessive intake in relationship to metabolic need; Excessive intake in relation to physical activity (caloric expenditure)

NOTE: Underlying cause is often complex and may be difficult to diagnose/treat

DEFINING CHARACTERISTICS

Subjective
Dysfunctional eating patterns (e.g., pairing food with other activities); Eating in response to external cues (e.g., time of day, social situation); Concentrating food intake at end of day; Eating in response to internal cues other than hunger (e.g., anxiety); Sedentary lifestyle

Objective
Weight 20% over ideal for height and frame [obese]; Triceps skinfold > than 15 mm in men and 25 mm in women [Percentage of body fat greater than 22% for trim women and 15% for trim men]

NUTRITION: READINESS FOR ENHANCED

Diagnostic Division: Food / Fluid

Definition: A pattern of nutrient intake that is sufficient for meeting metabolic needs and can be strengthened

DEFINING CHARACTERISTICS

Subjective
Expresses knowledge of healthy food and fluid choices/willingness to enhance nutrition; Eats regularly; Attitude toward eating/drinking is congruent with health goals

Objective
Consumes adequate food/fluid; Follows an appropriate standard for intake (e.g., the food pyramid or American Diabetic Association guidelines); Safe preparation/storage of food/fluids

---

NUTRITION: RISK FOR MORE THAN BODY REQUIREMENTS, IMBALANCED

Diagnostic Division: Food / Fluid

Definition: At risk for an intake of nutrients that exceeds metabolic needs.

RISK FACTORS
Dysfunctional eating patterns; Pairing food with other activities; Eating in response to external cues other than hunger (e.g., time of day, social situation); Eating in response

to internal cues other than hunger (such as anxiety); Concentrating food intake at the end of day; Parental obesity; Rapid transition across growth percentiles in children; Reports use of solid food as major food source before 5 months of age; Higher baseline weight at beginning of each pregnancy; Observed use of food as reward/comfort measure; [Frequent/repeated dieting]; [Alteration in usual activity patterns/sedentary lifestyle]; [Majority of foods consumed are concentrated, high-calorie/fat sources]; [Lower socioeconomic status]

ORAL MUCOUS MEMBRANE, IMPAIRED

Diagnostic Division: Food/Fluid

Definition: Disruption of the lips and/or soft tissue of the oral cavity.

RELATED FACTORS
Dehydration; Nil by mouth (NPO) for more than 24 hours; Malnutrition; Decreased salivation; Treatment—related side effects (e.g., chemotherapy, pharmaceutical agents, radiation therapy); Diminished hormone levels (women); Mouth breathing; Deficient knowledge of appropriate oral hygiene; Ineffective oral hygiene; Barriers to oral self-care/professional care; Mechanical factors (e.g., ill-fitting dentures; braces; tubes [Endotrachial, nasogastric], surgery in oral cavity); Loss of supportive structures; Trauma; Cleft lip or palate; Chemical irritants (e.g., alcohol, tobacco, acidic foods, drugs, regular use of inhalers or other noxious agents); Immunosuppression; Immunocompromised; Decreased platelets; Infection; Stress; Depression

DEFINING CHARACTERISTICS

Subjective
Xerostomia [dry mouth]; Oral pain/discomfort; Reports bad taste in mouth; Diminished taste; Difficulty eating/swallowing

Objective
Coated tongue; Smooth atrophic tongue; Geographic tongue; Gingival/mucosal pallor; Stomatitis; Hyperemia; Gingival hyperplasia; Macroplasia; Vesicles; Nodules; Papules; White patches/plaques; Spongy patches; White, curd-like exudate; Oral lesions/ulcers; Fissures; Bleeding; Cheilitis; Desquamation; Mucosal denudation; Purulent drainage/exudates; Presence of pathogens; Enlarged tonsils; Edema; Halitosis; Gingival recession, pocketing deeper than 4 mm; [Carious teeth]; Red or bluish masses (e.g., hemangiomas); Difficult speech

OTHER-DIRECTED VIOLENCE, [ACTUAL]/RISK FOR

Diagnostic Division: Safety

Definition: At risk for behaviors in which an individual demonstrates that he or she can be physically, emotionally, and/or sexually harmful to others.

RISK FACTORS
History of: Other—directed violence (e.g., hitting, kicking, scratching, biting or spitting, throwing objects at someone; attempted rape, rape, sexual molestation; urinating/defecating on a person); Threats of violence (e.g., verbal threats against property/person, social threats, cursing, threatening notes/letters, threatening gestures, sexual threats); Violent antisocial behavior (e.g., stealing, insistent borrowing, insistent demands for privileges, insistent interruption of meetings; refusal to eat/take medication, ignoring instructions); Indirect violence, (e.g., tearing off clothes, urinating/defecating on floor, stamping feet, temper tantrum; running in corridors, yelling, writing on walls, ripping objects off walls, throwing objects, breaking a window, slamming doors; sexual advances); Substance abuse; History of witnessing family violence; Neurological impairment (e.g., positive EEG, computed tomography, or magnetic resonance imaging scan, neurological findings; head trauma; seizure disorders, [temporal lobe epilepsy]); Cognitive impairment (e.g., learning disabilities, attention deficit disorder, decreased intellectual functioning); [Organic brain syndrome]; Pathological intoxication, [toxic reaction to medication]; Psychotic symptomatology (e.g., auditory, visual, command hallucinations; paranoid delusions; loose, rambling, or illogical thought processes); [Panic states]; [Rage reactions]; [Catatonic/manic excitement]; Cruelty to animals; Firesetting; Motor vehicle offenses (e.g., frequent traffic violations, use of motor vehicle to release anger); Suicidal behavior; Impulsivity; Availability of weapon(s); Body language (e.g., rigid posture, clenching of fists and jaw, hyperactivity, pacing, breathlessness, threatening stances); [Hormonal imbalance (e.g., premenstrual syndrome—PMS, postpartal depression/psychosis)]; Prenatal/perinatal complications; [Expressed intent/desire to harm others directly or indirectly]; [Almost

continuous thoughts of violence]; Cruelty to animals; Firesetting; History of childhood abuse; Motor vehicle offenses (e.g., frequent traffic violations, use of a motor vehicle to release anger)

PAIN, ACUTE

Diagnostic Division: Pain / Discomfort

Definition: Unpleasant sensory and emotional experience arising from actual or potential tissue damage or described in terms of such damage (International Association for the Study of Pain); sudden or slow onset of any intensity from mild to severe with an anticipated or predictable end and a duration of less than 6 months.

RELATED FACTORS
Injury agents (biological, chemical, physical, psychological)

DEFINING CHARACTERISTICS

Subjective
Coded report (e.g., use of pain scale); [may be less from patients under 40, men, and some cultural groups]; Changes in appetite; [Pain unrelieved and/or increased beyond tolerance]

Objective
Observed evidence of pain; Guarding behavior; Protective gestures; Positioning to avoid pain; Facial mask (e.g., eyes lack luster, beaten look, fixed or scattered movement, grimace); Sleep pattern disturbance; Expressive behavior (e.g., restlessness, moaning, crying, vigilance, irritability, sighing); Distraction behavior (e.g., pacing, seeking out other people and/or activities, repetitive activities); Diaphoresis; Changes in blood pressure/heart rate/respiratory rate; Pupillary dilation; Self-focus; Narrowed focus (altered time perception, impaired thought processes, reduced interaction with people and environment)

PAIN, CHRONIC

Diagnostic Division: Pain / Comfort

Definition: An unpleasant sensory and emotional experience arising from actual or potential tissue damage or described in terms of such damage (International Association for the Study of Pain); sudden or slow onset of any intensity from mild to severe, constant or recurring without an anticipated or predictable end and with a duration of greater than 6 months.

NOTE: [Pain is a signal that something is wrong. Chronic pain can be recurrent and periodically disabling (e.g., migraine headaches) or may be unremitting. Although chronic pain syndrome includes various learned behaviors, psychologic factors become the primary contribution to impairment. It is a complex entity, combining elements from other nursing diagnoses (e.g., Powerlessness; deficient Diversional Activity; interrupted Family Processes; Self-care Deficit, and risk for Disuse Syndrome).]

RELATED FACTORS
Chronic physical/psychosocial disability

DEFINING CHARACTERISTICS

Subjective
Coded report (e.g., use of pain scale); Fear of reinjury; Altered ability to continue previous activities; Changes in sleep patterns; Fatigue; Anorexia; [Preoccupation with pain]; [Desperately seeks alternative solutions/therapies for relief/control of pain]

Objective
Observed protective behavior; Guarding behavior; Irritability; Restlessness; Facial mask (e.g., eyes lack luster, beaten look, fixed or scattered movement, grimace); Self-focusing; Reduced interaction with people; Depression; Atrophy of involved muscle group; Sympathetic mediated responses (temperature, cold, changes of body position, hypersensitivity)

PARENTING, READINESS FOR ENHANCED

Diagnostic Division: Role Relationships

Definition: A pattern of providing an environment for children or other dependent person(s) that is sufficient to nurture growth and development and can be strengthened

DEFINING CHARACTERISTICS

Subjective
Expresses willingness to enhance parenting; Children or other dependent person(s) express(es) satisfaction with home environment

Objective
Emotional support of children [/dependent person(s)]; Evidence of attachment; Needs of children [/dependent person(s)] are met (e.g., physical and emotional); Exhibits realistic expectations of children [/dependent person(s)]

PARENTING, IMPAIRED

Diagnostic Division: Role Relationships

Definition: Inability of the primary caretaker to create, maintain, or regain an environment that promotes the optimum growth and development of the child.

RELATED FACTORS
Infant or Child
Premature birth; Multiple births; Not desired gender; Illness; Separation from parent; Difficult temperament; Temperamental conflicts with parental expectations; Handicapping condition; Developmental delay; Altered perceptual abilities; Attention deficit hyperactivity disorder

Knowledge
Deficient knowledge about child development/health maintenance, parenting skills; Inability to respond to infant cues; Unrealistic expectations [for self, infant, partner]; Lack of education; Limited cognitive functioning; Lack of cognitive readiness for parenthood; Poor communication skills; Preference for physical punishment

Physiological
Physical illness

Psychological
Young parental age; Lack of prenatal care; Difficult birthing process; High number of/ closely spaced pregnancies; Sleep disruption/ deprivation; Depression; History of substance abuse; Disability; History of mental illness

Social
Presence of stress (e.g., financial, legal, recent crisis, cultural move [e.g., from another country/cultural group within same country]); Job problems; Unemployment; Financial difficulties; Relocations; Poor home environment; Situational/chronic low self-esteem; Lack of family cohesiveness; Marital conflict; Change in family unit; Inadequate child-care arrangements; Role strain; Single parents; Lack of/or poor parental role model; Lack of valuing of parenthood; Inability to put child's needs before own; Unplanned or unwanted pregnancy; Lack of resources; Lack of transportation; Poor problem-solving skills; Maladaptive coping strategies; Lack of social support networks; Social isolation; History of being abusive/being abused; Legal difficulties; Mother/father of child not involved; Economically disadvantaged

DEFINING CHARACTERISTICS
Subjective
Parental
Statements of inability to meet child's needs; Reports inability to control child; Negative statements about child; Reports frustration/role inadequacy

Objective
Infant or Child
Frequent accidents/illness; Failure to thrive; Poor academic performance/cognitive development; Poor social competence; Behavioral disorders; Incidence of trauma (e.g., physical and psychological)/abuse; Lack of attachment; Lack of separation anxiety; Runaway

Parental
Maternal-child interaction deficit; Little cuddling; Inadequate attachment; Inadequate child health maintenance; Unsafe home environment; Inappropriate child care arrangements; Inappropriate stimulation (e.g., visual, tactile, auditory); Inappropriate caretaking skills; Inconsistent care/behavior management; Inflexibility in meeting needs of child; Frequently punitive; Rejection of/hostility to child; Child abuse/neglect; Abandonment; Paternal-child interaction deficit

PARENTING, RISK FOR IMPAIRED

Diagnostic Division: Role Relationships

Definition: At risk for inability of the primary caretaker to create, maintain, or regain an environment that promotes the optimum growth and development of the child.

RISK FACTORS
Infant or Child
Altered perceptual abilities; Attention-deficit hyperactivity disorder; Difficult temperament; Temperamental conflicts with parental expectation; Premature birth; Multiple births; Not gender desired; Illness; Prolonged separation from parent; Handicapping condition/developmental delay

Knowledge
Unrealistic expectation of child; Deficient knowledge about child development/health maintenance, parenting skills; Low educational level; Lack of cognitive readiness for parenthood; Low cognitive functioning; Poor communication skills; Inability to respond to infant cues; Preference for physical punishment

Physiological
Physical illness

Psychological
Young parental age; Closely spaced pregnancies; High number of pregnancies; Difficult birthing process; Sleep disruption/deprivation; Depression; History of substance abuse; Disability; History of mental illness

Social
Stress; Unemployment; Financial difficulties; Poor home environment; Relocation [including cultural move (e.g., from another country/cultural group within same country)]; Situational/chronic low self-esteem; Lack of family cohesiveness; Marital conflict; Change in family unit; Inadequate child care arrangements; Role strain; Single parent; Father/mother of child not involved; Parent-child separation; Poor/lack of parental role model; Lack of valuing of parenthood; Unplanned/unwanted pregnancy; Late/lack of prenatal care; Lack of resources/access to resources; Lack of transportation; Poor problem-solving skills; Maladaptive coping strategies; Lack of social support network; Social isolation; History of being abused/ being abusive; Legal difficulties; Economically disadvantaged; Job problems

PERIOPERATIVE POSITIONING INJURY, RISK FOR

Diagnostic Division: Safety

Definition: At risk for inadvertent anatomical and physical changes as a result of posture or equipment used during an invasive/surgical procedure

RISK FACTORS
Disorientation; Edema; Emaciation; Immobilization; Muscle weakness; Obesity; Sensory/perceptual disturbances due to anesthesia

PERIPHERAL NEUROVASCULAR DYSFUNCTION, RISK FOR

Diagnostic Division: Neurosensory

Definition: At risk for disruption in the circulation, sensation, or motion of an extremity.

RISK FACTORS
Fractures; Trauma; Burns; Vascular obstruction; Mechanical compression (e.g., tourniquet, cane, cast, brace, dressing, restraint); Orthopedic surgery; Immobilization

PERSONAL IDENTITY, DISTURBED

Diagnostic Division: Self-Perception

Definition: Inability to maintain an integrated and complete perception of self.

RELATED FACTORS
Chronic/situational low self-esteem; dysfunctional family processes; Situational crises, stages of growth or development, social role change; Ingestion or Inhalation of toxic chemicals, use of psychoactive pharmaceutical agents; Cultural discontinuity, dis-

crimination or perceived prejudice; Manic states, multiple personality disorder, psychiatric disorders (e.g., pyschoses, depression, dissociative disorder), organic brain syndromes; Cult indoctrination

DEFINING CHARACTERISTICS

Subjective
Disturbed body image, delusional description of self; Reports fluctuating feelings about self; feelings of strangeness, emptiness; Uncertainty about goals, cultural or ideological values (e.g., beliefs, religion, moral questions); Gender confusion; Unable to distinguish between inner and outer stimuli

Objective
Contradictory personal traits; Ineffective relationships; Ineffective coping or role performance

---

PERSONAL IDENTITY, RISK FOR DISTURBED

Diagnostic Division: Self-Perception

Definition: Risk for the inability to maintain an integrated and complete perception of self

RISK FACTORS
Chronic/situational low self-esteem; Cult indoctrination; Cultural discontinuity; Discrimination; Dysfunctional family processes; Ingestion/inhalation of toxic chemicals; Manic states; Multiple personality disorder; Organic brain syndromes; Perceived prejudice; Psychiatric disorders (e.g., psychoses, depression, dissociative disorder); Situational crises; Social role change; Stages of development/growth; Use of psychoactive pharmaceutical agents

---

POISONING, RISK FOR

Diagnostic Division: Safety

Definition: At risk for accidental exposure to, or ingestion of, drugs or dangerous products in sufficient doses that may compromise health [/or the adverse effects of prescribed medication/drug use].

RISK FACTORS
Internal
Reduced vision; Deficient knowledge regarding pharmaceutical agents/poisoning prevention; Lack of proper precaution; [Unsafe habits]; [Disregard for safety measures]; [Lack of supervision]; Reports occupational is setting without adequate safeguards; Cognitive/emotional difficulties; [Age, e.g., young child, elderly person]; [Chronic disease state/disability]; [Cultural or religious beliefs/practices]

External
Large supplies of pharmaceutical agents in house; Pharmaceutical agents stored in unlocked cabinets accessible to children/ confused individuals; Availability of illicit drugs potentially contaminated by poisonous additives; Dangerous products placed within reach of children/confused individuals; [Therapeutic margin of safety of specific drugs (e.g., therapeutic versus toxic level, half-life, method of uptake and degrada-tion in body, adequacy of organ function)]; [Use of multiple herbal supplements or megadosing]

POST-TRAUMA SYNDROME [SPECIFY STAGE]

Diagnostic Division: Ego / Integrity

Definition: Sustained maladaptive response to a traumatic, overwhelming event.

RELATED FACTORS
Events outside the range of usual human experience; Serious threat to self/loved ones; Serious injury to self/loved ones; Serious accidents (e.g., industrial, motor vehicle); Abuse (physical and psychological); Criminal victimization; Witnessing mutilation/ violent death; Tragic occurrence involving multiple deaths; Disasters; Sudden destruction of one's home/community; Epidemics; Wars; Being held prisoner of war; Torture

DEFINING CHARACTERISTICS

Subjective
Intrusive thoughts/dreams; Nightmares; Flashbacks; Palpitations; Headaches; [Loss of interest in usual activities]; [Loss of feeling of intimacy/sexuality]; Hopelessness;

Shame; [Excessive verbalization of the traumatic event]; [Verbalization of survival guilt/guilt about behavior required for survival]; Anxiety; Guilt; Fear; Grieving; Reports feeling numb; Depression; Difficulty concentrating; Gastric irritability; [Changes in appetite/sleep pattern]; [Chronic fatigue/easy fatigability]

Objective
Hypervigilance; Exaggerated startle response; Irritability; Neurosensory irritability; Denial; Repression; Avoidance; Alienation; Detachment; Psychogenic amnesia; Altered mood states; Aggression;° [Poor impulse control/explosiveness]; Rage; Anger□nic attacks; Horror; Substance abuse; Compulsive behavior; Enuresis (in children); [Difficulty with interpersonal relationships]; [Dependence on others]; [Work/school failure]

[Stages: Acute subtype: Begins within 6 months and does not last longer than 6 months; Chronic subtype: Lasts longer than 6 months; Delayed subtype: Period of latency of 6 months or longer before onset of symptoms]

POST-TRAUMA SYNDROME, RISK FOR

Diagnostic Division: Ego / Integrity

Definition: At risk for sustained maladaptive response to a traumatic, overwhelming event.

RISK FACTORS
Occupation (e.g., police, fire, rescue, corrections, emergency room staff, mental health worker, [responder family members]); Perception of event; Exaggerated sense of responsibility; Diminished ego strength; Survivor's role in the event; Inadequate social support; Unsupportive environment; Displacement from home; Duration of the event

POWER, READINESS FOR ENHANCED

Diagnostic Division: Ego Integrity

Definition: A pattern of participating knowingly in change that is sufficient for well-being and can be strengthened.

DEFINING CHARACTERISTICS

Subjective
Expresses readiness to enhance: Power; Knowledge for participation in change; Awareness of possible changes to be made; Identification of choices that can be made for change; Expresses readiness to enhance: Freedom to perform actions for change; Involvement in creating change; Participation in choices for daily living and health

POWERLESSNESS [SPECIFY LEVEL]

Diagnostic Division: Ego / Integrity

Definition: The lived experience of lack of control over a situation, including a perception that one's actions do not significantly affect an outcome

RELATED FACTORS
Institutional environment [e.g., loss of privacy, personal possessions, control over therapies]; Unsatisfying interpersonal interactions [e.g., misuse of power, force; abusive relationships]; Illness-related regimens [e.g., chronic/debilitating conditions]

DEFINING CHARACTERISTICS

Subjective
Reports: Alienation, Doubt regarding role performance, Frustration over inability to perform previous activities, Lack of control, Shame

Objective
Dependence on others; Depression over physical deterioration; Nonparticipation in care

POWERLESSNESS, RISK FOR

Diagnostic Division: Ego / Integrity

Definition: At risk for the lived experience of lack of control over a situation, including a perception that one's actions do not significantly affect an outcome

RISK FACTORS
Anxiety; Caregiving; Chronic/situational low self-esteem; Deficient knowledge; Economically disadvantaged; Illness; Ineffective coping patterns; Lack of social support; Pain; Progressive debilitating disease; Social marginalization; Stigmatized condition/disease; Unpredictable course of illness

PROTECTION, INEFFECTIVE

Diagnostic Division: Safety

Definition: Decrease in the ability to guard self from internal or external threats such as illness or injury.

RELATED FACTORS
Extremes of age; Inadequate nutrition; Substance abuse; Abnormal blood profiles (e.g., leukopenia, thrombocytopenia, anemia, coagulation); Pharmaceutical agents (e.g., antineoplastic, corticosteroid, immune, anticoagulant, thrombolytic); Treatment—related side effects (e.g., surgery, radiation); Cancer; Immune disorders

DEFINING CHARACTERISTICS

Subjective
Neurosensory alterations; Chilling; Itching; Insomnia; Fatigue; Weakness; Anorexia

Objective
Deficient immunity; Impaired healing; Altered clotting; Maladaptive stress response; Perspiring [inappropriate]; Dyspnea; Cough; Restlessness; Immobility; Disorientation; Pressure ulcers

RAPE-TRAUMA SYNDROME

Diagnostic Division: Ego / Integrity

Definition: Sustained maladaptive response to a forced, violent sexual penetration against the victim's will and consent. [Rape is not a sexual crime, but a crime of violence and identified as sexual assault. Although attacks are most often directed toward women, men also may be victims.]

NOTE: This syndrome includes the following three subcomponents: Rape-Trauma, Compound reaction, and Silent reaction

RELATED FACTORS
Rape [actual/attempted forced sexual penetration

DEFINING CHARACTERISTICS

Subjective
Embarrassment; Humiliation; Shame; Guilt; Self-blame; Chronic self-esteem; Helplessness; Powerlessness; Shock; Fear; Anxiety; Anger; Revenge; Nightmares; Disturbed sleep pattern; Change in relationships; Sexual dysfunction

Objective
Physical trauma [e.g., bruising, tissue irritation]; Muscle tension/spasms; Confusion; Disorganization; Impaired decision-making; Agitation; Hyperalertness; Aggression; Mood swings; Vulnerability; Dependence; Depression; Substance abuse; Suicide attempts; Denial; Phobias; Paranoia; Dissociative disorders

RELATIONSHIP, INEFFECTIVE

Diagnostic Division: Ego / Integrity

Definition: A pattern of mutual partnership that is insufficient to provide for each other's needs

RELATED FACTORS
Cognitive changes in one partner; Developmental crises; History of domestic violence; Incarceration of one partner; Poor communication skills; Stressful life events; Substance abuse; Unrealistic expectations

DEFINING CHARACTERISTICS

Subjective
Does not identify partner as a key person; Does not meet developmental goals appropriate for family life-cycle stage; Reports dissatisfaction with: Complementary rela-

tionship between partners, Fulfilling emotional/physical needs between partners, Sharing of idea/information between partners

Objective

Inability to communicate in a satisfying manner between partners; No demonstration of: Mutual respect between partners, Mutual support in daily activities between partners, Understanding of partner's insufficient (physical, social, psychological) functioning, Well-balanced autonomy/collaboration between partners

RELATIONSHIP, READINESS FOR ENHANCED

Diagnostic Division: Ego / Integrity

Definition: A pattern of mutual partnership that is sufficient to provide for each other's needs and can be strengthened.

DEFINING CHARACTERISTICS

Subjective

Reports: Desire to enhance communication between partners; Satisfaction with sharing of information and ideas between partners; Satisfaction with fulfilling physical and emotional needs by one's partner; Satisfaction with complementary relationship between partners; Identifies each other as a key person

Objective

Demonstrates: Mutual respect between partners; Well-balanced autonomy and collaboration between partners; Mutual support in daily activities between partners; Understanding of partner's insufficient (physical, social, psychological) function; Meets developmental goals appropriate for family life cycle stage

RELATIONSHIP, RISK FOR INEFFECTIVE

Diagnostic Division: Ego / Integrity

Definition: Risk for a pattern of mutual partnership that is insufficient to provide for each other's needs

RISK FACTORS

Cognitive changes in one partner; Developmental crises; History of domestic violence; Incarceration of one partner; Poor communication skills; Stressful life events; Substance abuse; Unrealistic expectations

RELIGIOSITY, IMPAIRED

Diagnostic Division: Ego Integrity

Definition: Impaired ability to exercise reliance on beliefs and/or participate in rituals of a particular faith tradition.

NOTE: [NANDA] recognizes that the term 'religiosity" may be culture specific; however, the term is useful in the U.S. and is well-supported in the U.S. literature.

RELATED FACTORS

Developmental and Situational

Life transitons; Aging; End-stage life crises

Physical

Illness; Pain

Psychological Factors

Ineffective support/coping; Anxiety; Fear of death; Personal crisis [/disaster]; Lack of security; Use of religion to manipulate

Sociocultural

Cultural/environmental barriers to practicing religion; Lack of social integration; Lack of sociocultural interaction

Spiritual

Spiritual crises; Suffering

DEFINING CHARACTERISTICS

Subjective

Reports emotional distress because of separation from faith community; Reports a need to reconnect with previous belief patterns/customs; Questions religious belief patterns/customs; Difficulty adhering to prescribed religious beliefs and rituals (e.g., religious ceremonies, dietary regulations, clothing, prayer, worship/religious services, private religious behaviors/reading religious materials/media, holiday observances, meetings with religious leaders)

RELIGIOSITY, READINESS FOR ENHANCED

Diagnostic Division: Ego / Integrity

Definition: A pattern of reliance on religious beliefs and/or participation in rituals of a particular faith tradition that is sufficient for well-being and can be strengthened.

RELATED FACTORS
To be developed

DEFINING CHARACTERISTICS

Subjective
Expresses desire to strengthen religious belief patterns/customs that have provided comfort/religion in the past; Requests assistance to increase participation in prescribed religious beliefs (e.g., religious ceremonies, dietary regulations/rituals, clothing, prayer, worship/religious services, private religious behaviors, reading religious materials/media, holiday observances); Requests assistance to expand religious options; Requests religious experiences/materials; Requests meeting with religious leaders/facilitators; Requests forgiveness/ reconciliation; Questions/rejects belief patterns/customs that are harmful

RELIGIOSITY, RISK FOR IMPAIRED

Diagnostic Division: Ego Integrity

Definition: At risk for an impaired ability to exercise reliance on religious beliefs and/or participate in rituals of a particular faith tradition.

NOTE: [NANDA] recognizes that the term 'religiosity" may be culture specific; however, the term is useful in the U.S. and is well-supported in the U.S. literature.

RISK FACTORS
Developmental
Life transitions

Environmental
Lack of transportation; Barriers to practicing religion

Physical
Illness; Hospitalization; Pain

Psychological
Ineffective coping/caregiving; Ineffective support; Depression; Lack of security

Sociocultural
Lack of social interaction; Social isolation; Cultural barrier to practicing religion

Spiritual
Suffering

RELOCATION STRESS SYNDROME

Diagnostic Division: Ego / Integrity

Definition: Physiological and/or psychosocial disturbance following transfer from one environment to another.

RELATED FACTORS
Losses; Reports feelings of powerlessness; Lack of adequate support system; Lack of predeparture counseling; Unpredictability of experience; Isolation; Language barrier; Impaired psychosocial health; Passive coping; Decreased health status; Move from one environment to another

DEFINING CHARACTERISTICS

Subjective
Anxiety (e.g., separation); Anger; Insecurity; Worry; Fear; Loneliness; Depression; Reports unwillingness to move; Concern over relocation; Sleep pattern disturbance

Objective
Increased [frequency of] verbalization of needs; Pessimism; Frustration; Increased physical symptoms/illness; Withdrawal; Aloneness; Alienation; [Hostile behavior/outbursts]; Loss of identity; Loss of self-worth; Situational/chronic low self-esteem; Dependency; [Increased confusion]; [Cognitive impairment]

RELOCATION STRESS SYNDROME, RISK FOR

Diagnostic Division: Ego/Integrity

Definition: At risk for physiological and/or psychosocial disturbance following transfer from one environment to another.

RISK FACTORS
Move from one environment to another; Moderate-to-high degree of environmental change [e.g., physical, ethnic, cultural]; Lack of adequate support system; Lack of predeparture counseling; Passive coping; Reports powerlessness; Losses; Moderate mental competence; Unpredictability of experiences; Decreased health status

RENAL PERFUSION, RISK FOR INEFFECTIVE

Diagnostic Division: Activity/Rest

Definition: At risk for a decrease in blood circulation to the kidney that may compromise health.

RISK FACTORS
Hypovolemia; [interuption of blood flow], vascular embolism, vasculitis; Hypertension, malignant hypertension; Renal disease (polycystic kidney), polynephritis , exposure to nephrotoxins, bilateral cortical necrosis; Diabetes mellitus, malignancy; Cardiac surgery, cardiopulmonary bypass; Hypoxemia, hypoxia, metabolic acidosis; Multitrauma, abdominal compartment syndrome, burns, infection (e.g., sepsis, localized infection), systemic inflammatory response syndrome; Treatment-related side effects (e.g., pharmaceutical agents, surgery); Advanced age; Female gender; Glomerulonephritis; Interstitial nephritis; Renal artery stenosis; Smoking, substance abuse

RESILIENCE, IMPAIRED INDIVIDUAL

Diagnostic Division: Ego/Integrity

Definition: Decreased ability to sustain a pattern of positive responses to an adverse situation or crisis.

RELATED FACTORS
Demographics that increase chance of maladjustment, large family size, minority status, poverty, gender; Vulnerability factors which encompass indices that exacerbate the negative effects of the risk condition, substance abuse; poor impulse control, Neighborhood violence; Low intelligence, low maternal education; Inconsistent parenting, parental mental illness; Psychological disorders, violence

DEFINING CHARACTERISTICS

Subjective
Depression, guilt, isolation or social isolation, low self-esteem, shame; Lower perceived health status; Renewed elevation of distress; Decreased interest in academic activities, vocational activities

Objective
Using maladaptive coping skills (i.e., drug use, violence, etc.)

RESILIENCE, READINESS FOR ENHANCED

Diagnostic Division: Ego/Integrity

Definition: A pattern of positive responses to an adverse situation or crisis that is sufficient for optimizing human potential and can be strengthened

DEFINING CHARACTERISTICS

Subjective
Presence of a crisis; Reports an enhanced sense of control/self-esteem, takes responsibilities for actions; Expressed desire to enhance resilience; Sets goals, makes progress

toward goals; Identifies available resources or support systems; Involvement in activities

Objective
Demonstrates positive outlook; Enhances personal coping skills, use of effective communication skills, effective use of conflict management strategies; Increases positive relationships with others; Access to resources; Safe environment is maintained

RESILIENCE, RISK FOR COMPROMISED

Diagnostic Division: Ego / Integrity

Definition: At risk for decreased ability to sustain a pattern of positive responses to an adverse situation or crisis.

RISK FACTORS
Chronicity of existing crises; Multiple coexisting adverse situations; Presence of an additional new crisis (e.g., unplanned pregnancy, death of a spouse or family member, loss of job, illness, loss of housing)

ROLE CONFLICT, PARENTAL

Diagnostic Division: Social Interaction

Definition: Parental experience of role confusion and conflict in response to crisis

RELATED FACTORS
Change in marital status; Home care of a child with special needs; Interruptions of family life sue to home care regimen (e.g., treatment, caregivers, lack of respite); Intimidation by invasive modalities (e.g., intubation)/restrictive modalities (e.g., isolation); Parent-child separation due to chronic illness; Specialized care center

DEFINING CHARACTERISTICS

Subjective
Demonstrates disruption in caretaking routines; Reports concern about: Changes in parental role, Family (e.g., functioning, communication, health), Perceived loss of control over decisions relating to child; Reports feelings of frustration/guilt/inadequacy to provide for child's needs (e.g., physical, emotional)

Objective
Anxiety; Fear; Reluctant to participate in usual caretaking activities

ROLE PERFORMANCE, INEFFECTIVE

Diagnostic Division: Social Interaction

Definition: Patterns of behavior and self-expression that do not match the environmental context, norms, and expectations.

NOTE: [There is a typology of roles: sociopersonal (friendship, family, marital, parenting, community), home management, intimacy (sexuality, relationship building), leisure/exercise/recreation, self-management, socialization (developmental transitions), community contributor, and religious.]

RELATED FACTORS
Knowledge
Inadequate/lack of role model; Inadequate role preparation (e.g., role transition, skill, rehearsal, validation); Lack of education; [Developmental transitions]; Unrealistic role expectations

Physiological
Body image alteration; Cognitive deficits; Neurological defects; Physical illness; Mental illness; Depression; Chronic/situational low self-esteem; Fatigue; Pain; Substance abuse; Physical illness

Social
Inadequate role socialization [e.g., role model, expectations, responsibilities]; Young age; Developmental level; Lack of resources; Economically disadvantaged; Stress; Conflict; Job schedule demands; Domestic violence; Inadequate support system; Lack of rewards; Inappropriate linkage with the healthcare system

DEFINING CHARACTERISTICS

Subjective

Altered role perceptions; Change in self-/other's perception of role; Change in usual patterns of responsibility/capacity to resume; Inadequate opportunities for role enactment; Role dissatisfaction; Role overload; Role denial; Discrimination [by others]; Powerlessness

Objective

Deficient knowledge; Inadequate adaptation to change; Inappropriate developmental expectations; Inadequate confidence; Inadequate motivation; Inadequate self-management; Inadequate external support for role enactment; Ineffective coping/role performance; Role strain; Role conflict/ confusion; Role ambivalence; [Failure to assume role]; Uncertainty; Anxiety; Depression; Pessimism; Domestic violence; Harassment; System conflict

---

SELF-CARE, READINESS FOR ENHANCED

Diagnostic Division: Activity / Rest

Definition: A pattern of performing activities for oneself that helps to meet health-related goals and can be strengthened.

DEFINING CHARACTERISTICS

Subjective

Expresses desire to enhance independence in maintaining: life/health/personal development/well-being; Expresses desire to enhance: Self-care; Knowledge of strategies for self-care; Responsibility for self-care

NOTE: Note: Based on the definition and defining characteristics of this ND, the focus appears to be broader than simply meeting routine basic ADLs and addresses independence in maintaining overall health, personal development, and general well-being.

SELF-CARE, DEFICIT, BATHING

Diagnostic Division: Hygiene

Definition: Impaired ability to perform or complete bathing activities for self (Specify level of independence using a standardized functional scale)

NOTE: Self-Care also may be expanded to include the practices used by the client to promote health, the individual responsibility for self, a way of thinking. Refer to Nursing Diagnoses impaired Home Maintenance, ineffective Health Maintenance

RELATED FACTORS

Weakness; Decreased motivation; Neuromuscular/musculoskeletal impairment; Environmental barriers; Severe anxiety; Pain; Perceptual/cognitive impairment; [Mechanical restrictions such as cast, splint, traction, ventilator]; Inability to perceive body part/spatial relationship [bathing/hygiene]

DEFINING CHARACTERISTICS
Objective

Inability to: access bathroom, dry body, get bath supplies, obtain water source, regulate bath water, and/or wash body

---

SELF-CARE, DEFICIT, DRESSING

Diagnostic Division: Activity / Rest

Definition: Impaired ability to perform or complete dressing activities for self

NOTE: Specify level of independence using a standardized functional scale.

RELATED FACTORS

Cognitive/perceptual impairment; Musculoskeletal/neuromuscular impairment; Decreased motivation; Discomfort; Environmental barriers; Fatigue; Pain; Severe anxiety; Weakness

DEFINING CHARACTERISTICS
Objective

Impaired ability to: fasten/obtain clothing, put on/take off necessary items of clothing, put on/take off shoes/socks; Inability to: choose clothing, maintain appearance at a satisfactory level, pick up clothing, put clothing on lower/upper body, put on shoes/sock, remove clothes/shoes/socks, use assistive devices, use zippers

SELF-CARE, DEFICIT, FEEDING

Diagnostic Division: Activity/Rest

Definition: Impaired ability to perform or complete self-feeding activities

NOTE: Specify level of independence using a standardized functional scale.

RELATED FACTORS
Cognitive/perceptual impairment; Neuromuscular/musculoskeletal impairment; Decreased motivation; Discomfort; Environmental barriers; Fatigue; Pain; Severe anxiety; Weakness

DEFINING CHARACTERISTICS
Objective
Inability to: Bring food from a receptacle to the mouth, Chew food, Complete a meal, Get food onto utensil, Handle utensils, Ingest food in a socially acceptable manner, Ingest food safely, Ingest sufficient food, Manipulate food in the mouth, Open containers, Pick up cup or glass, Prepare food for ingestion, Swallow food, Use assistive device

SELF-CARE, DEFICIT, TOILETING

Diagnostic Division: Activity/Rest

Definition: Impaired ability to perform or complete toileting activities for self

NOTE: Specify level of independence using a standardized functional scale.

RELATED FACTORS
Cognitive/perceptual impairment; Musculoskeletal/neuromuscular impairment; Decreased motivation; Environmental barriers; Fatigue; Impaired mobility status/transfer ability; Pain; Severe anxiety; Weakness

DEFINING CHARACTERISTICS
Objective
Inability to: Carry out proper toilet hygiene, Flush/get to toilet or commode, Manipulate clothing for toileting, Rise from/sit on toilet or commode

SELF-CONCEPT, READINESS FOR ENHANCED

Diagnostic Division: Self-Perception

Definition: A pattern of perceptions or ideas about the self that is sufficient for well-being and can be strengthened

DEFINING CHARACTERISTICS

Subjective
Expresses willingness to enhance self-concept; Accepts strengths/limitations; Expresses confidence in abilities; Expresses satisfaction with thoughts about self/sense of worthiness; Expresses satisfaction with body image/personal identity/role performance

Objective
Actions are congruent with verbal expression

SELF-DIRECTED VIOLENCE, [ACTUAL]/RISK FOR

Diagnostic Division: Safety

Definition: At risk for behaviors in which an individual demonstrates that he or she can be physically, emotionally, and/or sexually harmful to self.

RISK FACTORS
Age 15–19, 45 or older; Marital status (single, widowed, divorced); Employment problems (e.g., unemployed, recent job loss/failure); Occupation (executive, administrator/owner of business, professional, semiskilled worker); Conflictual interpersonal relationships; Family background (e.g., chaotic or conflictual, history of suicide); Sexual orientation (bisexual [active], homosexual [inactive]); Physical health problems (e.g., hypochondriasis, chronic or terminal illness); Mental health problems (e.g., severe

depression, [bi-polar disorder], psychosis, severe personality disorder, alcoholism or drug abuse); Emotional problems (e.g., hopelessness, [lifting of depressed mood], despair, increased anxiety, panic, anger, hostility); History of multiple suicide attempts; Suicidal ideation; Suicidal plan; Lack of personal resources (e.g., poor achievement, poor insight, affect unavailable and poorly controlled); Lack of social resources (e.g., poor rapport, socially isolated, unresponsive family); Verbal cues (e.g., talking about death, "better off without me," asking questions about lethal dosages of drugs); Behavioral cues (e.g., writing forlorn love notes, directing angry messages at a significant other who has rejected the person, giving away personal items, taking out a large life insurance policy); Engagement in autoerotic sexual acts

SELF-ESTEEM, CHRONIC LOW

Diagnostic Division: Self-Perception

Definition: Longstanding negative self-evaluating/feelings about self or self-capabilities.

RELATED FACTORS

Repeated negative reinforcement, failures; Lack of affection, approval, or membership in group; Perceived lack of belonging or respect from others; Perceived discrepancy between self and cultural or spiritual norms; Traumatic event or situation; Ineffective adaptation to loss; Psychiatric disorder

DEFINING CHARACTERISTICS

Subjective

Reports feelings of shame or guilt; Evaluation of self as unable to deal with events; Rejects positive or exaggerates negative feedback about self

Objective

Hesitant to try new things or /situations; Frequent lack of success in life events; Overly conforming; Dependent on others' opinions; Lack of eye contact; Nonassertive behavior; Passive; Indecisive behavior; Excessively seeks reassurance

SELF-ESTEEM, SITUATIONAL LOW

Diagnostic Division: Self-Perception

Definition: Development of a negative perception of self-worth in response to a current situation (specify).

RELATED FACTORS

Developmental changes [e.g., maturational transitions, adolescence, aging]; Functional impairments; Disturbed body image; Loss [e.g., loss of health status, body part, independent functioning; memory deficit/cognitive impairment]; Social role changes; Failures/rejections; Lack of recognition [/rewards]; [Feelings of abandonment by SO]; Behavior inconsistent with values

DEFINING CHARACTERISTICS

Subjective

Reports current situational challenge to self-worth; Reports helplessness/uselessness; Evaluation of self as unable to deal with situations or events

Objective

Self-negating verbalizations; Indecisive/nonassertive behavior

SELF-ESTEEM, RISK FOR CHRONIC LOW

Diagnostic Division: Self-Perception

Definition: At risk for longstanding negative self-evaluating/feelings about self or self-capabilities

RISK FACTORS

Ineffective adaptation to loss; Lack of affection/membership in a group; Perceived discrepancy between self and cultural/spiritual norms; Perceived lack of belonging; Perceived lack of respect from others; Psychiatric disorder; Repeated failures; Repeated negative reinforcement; Traumatic event; Traumatic situation

SELF-ESTEEM, RISK FOR SITUATIONAL LOW

Diagnostic Division: Self-Perception

Definition: At risk for developing a negative perception of self-worth in response to a current situation. (specify situation)

RISK FACTORS

Developmental changes; Disturbed body image; Functional impairment; Loss [e.g., loss of health status, body part, independent functioning, memory deficit/cognitive impairment]; Social role changes; Unrealistic self-expectations; History of learned helplessness; History of neglect/abuse/ abandonment; Behavior inconsistent with values; Lack of recognition [/rewards]; Failures; Rejections; Decreased control over environment; Physical illness

SELF-HEALTH MANAGEMENT, INEFFECTIVE

Diagnostic Division: Safety

Definition: Pattern of regulating and integrating into daily living a therapeutic regimen for the treatment of illness and its sequelae that is unsatisfactory for meeting specific health goals

RELATED FACTORS

Complexity of healthcare system; Complexity of therapeutic regimen; Decisional conflicts; Deficient knowledge; Economic difficulties; Excessive demands made (e.g./ individual, family); Family conflict; Family patterns of healthcare; Inadequate number of cues to action; Perceived barriers, benefits, seriousness, and/or susceptibility; Powerlessness; Regimen; Social support deficit

DEFINING CHARACTERISTICS

Subjective

Failure to include treatment regimens in daily living; Failure to take action to reduce risk factors; Ineffective choices in daily living for meeting health goals

Objective

Reports desire to manage the illness; Reports difficulty with prescribed regimens

SELF-HEALTH MANAGEMENT, READINESS FOR ENHANCED

Diagnostic Division: Safety

Definition: A pattern of regulating and integrating into daily living a therapeutic regimen for the treatment of illness and its sequelae that is sufficient for meeting health-related goals and can be strengthened

DEFINING CHARACTERISTICS

Subjective

Choices of daily living are appropriate for meeting goals (e.g., treatment, prevention); Describes reduction of risk factors; Expresses desire to manage the illness (e.g., treatment, prevention of sequelae)

Objective

Expresses little difficulty with prescribed regimens; No unexpected acceleration of illness symptoms

SELF-MUTILATION

Diagnostic Division: Safety

Definition: Deliberate self-injurious behavior causing tissue damage with the intent of causing nonfatal injury to attain relief of tension.

RELATED FACTORS

Adolescence; Peers who self-mutilate; Isolation from peers; Dissociation; Depersonalization; Psychotic state (e.g., command hallucinations); Character disorder; Borderline personality disorders; Developmentally delayed/autistic individual; History of self-directed violence; History of inability to plan solutions/see long-term consequences; Childhood illness/surgery; Childhood sexual abuse; Battered child; Disturbed/unstable body image; Eating disorders; Ineffective coping; Perfectionism; Reports negative feelings (e.g., depression, rejection, self-hatred, separation anxiety, guilt, depersonalization); Low/unstable self-esteem; Poor communication between parent and adolescent; Lack of family confidant; Feels threatened with loss of significant relationship [e.g., loss of parent/parental relationship]; Disturbed interpersonal relationships; Use of manipulation to obtain nurturing relationship with others; Family substance abuse/divorce; Violence between parental figures; Family history of self-destructive behaviors; Living in nontraditional setting (e.g., foster, group, or institutional care); Incarceration; Inability to express tension verbally; Mounting tension that is intolerable; Need for quick reduction of stress; Irresistible urge to cut self; Impulsivity; Labile behavior; Sexual identity crisis; Substance abuse; Irresistible urge for self-directed violence; Emotional disorder

DEFINING CHARACTERISTICS

Subjective
Self-inflicted burns (e.g., eraser, cigarette); Ingestion/inhalation of harmful substances/objects

Objective
Cuts/scratches on body; Picking at wounds; Biting; Abrading; Severing; Insertion of object(s) into body orifice(s); Hitting; Constricting a body part

---

SELF-MUTILATION, RISK FOR

Diagnostic Division: Safety

Definition: At risk for deliberate self-injurious behavior causing tissue damage with the intent of causing nonfatal injury to attain relief of tension.

RISK FACTORS
Adolescence; Peers who self-mutilate; Isolation from peers; Dissociation; Depersonalization; Psychotic state (e.g., command hallucinations); Character disorders; Borderline personality disorders; Developmentally delayed/autistic individuals; History of self-directed violence; History of inability to plan solutions/see long-term consequences; Childhood illness/surgery; Childhood sexual abuse; Battered child; Disturbed body image; Eating disorders; Inadequate coping; Loss of control over problem-solving situations; Perfectionism; Reports negative feelings (e.g., depression, rejection, self-hatred, separation anxiety, guilt); Low/unstable self-esteem; Feels threatened with loss of significant relationship [e.g., loss of parent/parental relationship]; Loss of siginificant relationship(s); Disturbed interpersonal relationships; Use of manipulation to obtain nurturing relationship with others; Family substance abuse/divorce; Violence between parental figures; Family history of self-destructive behaviors; Living in nontraditional settings (e.g., foster, group, or institutional care); Incarceration; Inability to express tension verbally; Mounting tension that is intolerable; Need for quick reduction of stress; Irresistible urge for self-directed violence; Impulsivity; Sexual identity crisis; Substance abuse; Emotional disorder; Inadequate coping

---

SELF-NEGLECT

Diagnostic Division: Activity / Rest

Definition: A constellation of culturally framed behaviors involving one or more self-care activities in which there is a failure to maintain a socially accepted standard of health and well-being.

RELATED FACTORS
Major life stressor, depression; Obsessive-compulsive disorder, schizotypal or paranoid personality disorders; Frontal lobe dysfunction and executive processing ability, cognitive impairment (e.g., dementia), Capgras syndrome; Functional impairment, learning disability; Lifestyle choice, substance abuse, malingering; Maintaining control, fear of institutionalization

DEFINING CHARACTERISTICS
Objective
Inadequate personal or environmental hygiene; Nonadherence to health activities

---

SEXUAL DYSFUNCTION

Diagnostic Division: Sexuality

Definition: The state in which an individual experiences a change in sexual function during the sexual response phases of desire, excitation, and/or orgasm, which is viewed as unsatisfying, unrewarding, or inadequate.

RELATED FACTORS

Ineffectual/ absent role models; Lack of significant other; Lack of privacy; Misinformation or deficient knowledge; Vulnerability; Physical abuse; Psychosocial abuse (e.g., harmful relationships); Altered body function/structure (e.g., pregnancy, recent childbirth, drugs, surgery, anomalies, disease process, trauma, [paraplegia/quadriplegia], radiation, [effects of aging]); Biopsychosocial alteration of sexuality; Values conflict

DEFINING CHARACTERISTICS

Subjective

Verbalization of problem [e.g., loss of sexual desire, premature ejaculation, dyspareunia, vaginismus]; Actual/perceived limitations imposed by disease/therapy; Perceived deficiency of sexual desire; Perceived alteration in sexual excitation; Alterations in achieving sexual satisfaction; Inability to achieve desired satisfaction; Alterations in achieving perceived sex role; Seeking confirmation of desirability [concern about body image]; Change of interest in self/others

---

SEXUALITY PATTERN, INEFFECTIVE

Diagnostic Division: Sexuality

Definition: Expressions of concern regarding one's own sexuality.

RELATED FACTORS

Knowledge/skill deficit about alternative responses to health-related transitions, altered body function or structure, illness, or medical treatment; Lack of privacy; Impaired relationship with a significant other; Lack of significant other; Ineffective/absent role models; Conflicts with sexual orientation or variant preferences; Fear of pregnancy/acquiring a sexually transmitted disease

DEFINING CHARACTERISTICS

Subjective

Reports: Difficulties with sexual behaviors/activities; Changes in sexual behaviors/activities; Limitations in sexual behaviors/activities; Alteration in relationship with significant other; Alteration in achieving perceived sex role; Values conflict; [Expressions of feeling alienated, lonely, loss, powerless, angry]

SHOCK, RISK FOR

Diagnostic Division: Circulation

Definition: At risk for an inadequate blood flow to the body's tissues, which may lead to life-threatening cellular dysfunction

RISK FACTORS

Hypotension; Hypovolemia; Hypoxemia, hypoxia; Infection, sepsis, systemic inflammatory response syndrome

---

SKIN INTEGRITY, IMPAIRED

Diagnostic Division: Safety

Definition: Altered epidermis and/or dermis.

RELATED FACTORS

External

Hyperthermia; Hypothermia; Chemical substance; Radiation; Pharmaceutical agents; Physical immobilization; Humidity; Moisture; [Excretions/secretions]; Mechanical factors (e.g., shearing forces, pressure, restraint); [Trauma/injury]; [Surgery]; Extremes of age

Internal

Imbalanced nutritional state (e.g., obesity, emaciation); Impaired metabolic state; Changes in fluid status; Skeletal prominence; Changes in turgor (change in elasticity); [Presence of edema]; Impaired circulation/sensation; Changes in pigmentation; Developmental factors; Immunological deficit; [Psychogenic factors e.g., obsessive compulsive behaviors]

DEFINING CHARACTERISTICS

Subjective

[Reports of itching, pain, numbness of affected/surrounding area]

Objective
Disruption of skin surface [epidermis]; Destruction of skin layers [dermis]; Invasion of body structures

SKIN INTEGRITY, RISK FOR IMPAIRED

Diagnostic Division: Safety

Definition: At risk for alteration in epidermis and/or dermis.

NOTE: Risk should be determined by the use of a standardized risk assessment tool [e.g., Braden, Norton, or similar scale].

RISK FACTORS
External
Chemical substance; Radiation; Hypothermia; Hyperthermia; Physical immobilization; Humidity; Moisture; Excretions; Secretions; Mechanical factors (e.g., shearing forces, pressure, restraint); Extremes of age

Internal
Imbalanced nutritional state (e.g., obesity, emaciation); Impaired metabolic state; [Presence of edema]; Skeletal prominence; Changes in skin turgor [/elasticity]; Impaired circulation/sensation; Changes in pigmentation; Developmental factors; Immunological factors; Medications; Psychogenetic factors

SLEEP, READINESS FOR ENHANCED

Diagnostic Division: Activity / Rest

Definition: A pattern of natural, periodic suspension of consciousness that provides adequate rest, sustains a desired lifestyle, and can be strengthened

DEFINING CHARACTERISTICS

Subjective
Expresses willingness to enhance sleep; Reports being rested after sleep; Follows sleep routines that promote sleep habits

Objective
Amount of sleep and REM sleep is congruent with developmental needs; Occasional use of pharmaceutical agents to induce sleep

SLEEP DEPRIVATION

Diagnostic Division: Activity / Rest

Definition: Prolonged periods of time without sleep (sustained natural, periodic suspension of relative consciousness).

RELATED FACTORS

Sustained environmental stimulation; Sustained uncomfortable sleep environment; Inadequate daytime activity; Sustained circadian asynchrony; Aging-related sleep stage shifts; Nonsleep-inducing parenting practices; Sustained inadequate sleep hygiene; Prolonged use of pharmacological agents or dietary antisoporifics; Prolonged discomfort (e.g., physical, psychological); Periodic limb movement (e.g., restless leg syndrome, nocturnal myoclonus); Sleep-related enuresis/painful erections; Nightmares; Sleep walking; Sleep terror; Sleep apnea; Sundowner's syndrome; Dementia; Idiopathic central nervous system hypersomnolence; Narcolepsy; Familial sleep paralysis

DEFINING CHARACTERISTICS

Subjective
Daytime drowsiness; Decreased ability to function; Malaise; Lethargy; Fatigue; Anxiety; Perceptual disorders (e.g., disturbed body sensation, delusions, feeling afloat); Heightened pain sensitivity

Objective
Restlessness; Irritability; Inability to concentrate; Slowed reaction; Listlessness; Apathy; Fleeting nystagmus; Hand tremors; Acute confusion; Transient paranoia; Agitation; Combativeness; Hallucinations

SLEEP PATTERN, DISTURBED

Diagnostic Division: Activity / Rest

Definition: Time-limited interruptions of sleep amount and quality due to external factors.

RELATED FACTORS

Ambient temperature, humidity; Lighting; Noise; Noxious odors; Physical restraint; Change in daylight-darkness exposure; Caregiving responsibilities; Lack of sleep privacy or control; Sleep partner; Unfamiliar sleep furnishings; Interruptions (e.g., for therapeutics, monitoring, lab tests)

DEFINING CHARACTERISTICS

Subjective

Dissatisfaction with sleep; Reports: being awakened, no difficulty falling asleep, and/or not feeling well rested

Objective

Change in normal sleep pattern; Decreased ability to function

SOCIAL INTERACTION, IMPAIRED

Diagnostic Division: Social Interaction

Definition: Insufficient or excessive quantity or ineffective quality of social exchange.

RELATED FACTORS

Deficit about ways to enhance mutuality (e.g., knowledge, skills); Communication barriers [including head injury, stroke, other neurological conditions affecting ability to communicate]; Self-concept disturbance; Absence of significant others; Limited physical mobility [e.g., neuromuscular disease]; Therapeutic isolation; Sociocultural dissonance; Environmental barriers; Disturbed thought processes

DEFINING CHARACTERISTICS

Subjective

Discomfort in social situations; Inability to receive/communicate a satisfying sense of social engagement (e.g., belonging, caring, interest, or shared history); Family reports changes in interaction (e.g., style, pattern)

Objective

Use of unsuccessful social interaction behaviors; Dysfunctional interaction with others

SOCIAL ISOLATION

Diagnostic Division: Social Interaction

Definition: Aloneness experienced by the individual and perceived as imposed by others and as a negative or threatening state.

RELATED FACTORS

Factors contributing to the absence of satisfying personal relationships (e.g., delay in accomplishing developmental tasks); Immature interests; Alterations in physical appearance; Altered state of wellness; Alterations in mental status; Unaccepted social behavior/values; Inadequate personal resources; Inability to engage in satisfying personal relationships; [Traumatic incidents or events causing physical and/or emotional pain]

DEFINING CHARACTERISTICS

Subjective

Reports feelings of aloneness imposed by others; Reports feelings of rejection; Insecurity in public; Inability to meet expectations of others; Reports inadequate purpose in life; Developmentally inappropriate interests; Experiences feelings of differences from others; Reports values unacceptable to the dominant cultural group

Objective

Absence of supportive significant other(s) [family, friends, group]; Sad/dull affect; Uncommunicative; Withdrawn; No eye contact; Evidence of handicap (e.g., physical, mental); Illness; Developmentally inappropriate behaviors; Repetitive meaningless actions; Seeks to be alone; Preoccupation with own thoughts; Shows behavior unaccepted by dominant cultural group; Exists in a subculture; Projects hostility

SORROW, CHRONIC

Diagnostic Division: Ego/Integrity

Definition: A cyclical, recurring and potentially progressive pattern of pervasive sadness experienced (by a parent,caregiver, individual with chronic illness or disability) in response to continual loss, throughout the trajectory of an illness or disability.

RELATED FACTORS
Death of a loved one; Experiences chronic illness/ disability (e.g., physical or mental); Crises in management of the illness/disability; Crises related to developmental stages; Missed opportunities/milestones; Unending caregiving

DEFINING CHARACTERISTICS
Subjective
Reports negative feelings (e.g., anger, being misunderstood, confusion, depression, disappointment, emptiness, fear, frustration, guilt, self-blame, helplessness, hopelessness, loneliness, low self-esteem, recurring loss, being overwhelmed); Reports feelings of sadness (e.g., periodic, recurrent); Reports feelings that interfere with ability to reach highest level of personal/social well-being

SPIRITUAL DISTRESS

Diagnostic Division: Ego Integrity

Definition: Impaired ability to experience and integrate meaning and purpose in life through connectedness with self, others, art, music, literature, nature, and/or a power greater than oneself.

RELATED FACTORS
Active dying; Loneliness; Social alienation; Self-alienation; Sociocultural deprivation; Anxiety; Pain; Life change; Chronic illness [of self or others]; Death; [Challenged belief/ value system (e.g., moral/ethical implications of therapy]

DEFINING CHARACTERISTICS

Subjective
Connections to Self
Expresses lack of: Hope; Meaning/purpose in life; Serenity (e.g., peace); Love; Acceptance; Self-forgiveness; Courage; [Expresses:] Anger; Guilt

Connections with Others
Refuses interactions with significant other(s)/spiritual leaders; Verbalizes being separated from support system; Expresses alienation

Connections with Art, Music, Literature, Nature
Inability to express previous state of creativity (e.g., singing/listening to music/writing); Disinterest in nature/reading spiritual literature

Connections with Power Greater Than Self
Sudden changes in spiritual practices; Inability to pray/participate in religious activities; Inability to experience the transcendent; Expresses feeling abandoned; Expresses hopelessness/suffering/having anger toward power greater than self; Requests to see a spiritual leader

Objective
Connections to Self
Ineffective coping

Connections with Power Greater Than Self
Inability for introspection

SPIRITUAL DISTRESS, RISK FOR

Diagnostic Division: Ego Integrity

Definition: At risk for an impaired ability to experience and integrate meaning and purpose in life through connectedness with self, others, art, music, literature, nature, and/or a power greater than oneself

RISK FACTORS
Physical
Physical/chronic illness; Substance abuse

Psychosocial
Stress; Anxiety; Depression; Low self-esteem; Poor relationships; Blocks to experiencing love; Inability to forgive; Loss; Separated support systems; Racial/cultural conflict; Change in religious rituals/spiritual practices

Developmental
Life changes

Environmental
Environmental changes; Natural disasters

SPIRITUAL WELL-BEING, READINESS FOR ENHANCED

Diagnostic Division: Ego Integrity

Definition: A pattern of experiencing and integrating meaning and purpose in life through connectedness with self, others, art, music, literature, nature, and/or a power greater than oneself that is sufficient for well-being and can be strengthened

DEFINING CHARACTERISTICS
Connections to Self

Subjective
Expresses desire for enhanced: Acceptance; Coping; Courage; Self-forgiveness; Hope; Joy; Love; Meaning/purpose in life; Satisfying philosophy of life; Surrender; Expresses desire for enhanced serenity (e.g., peace); Meditation

Connections with Others

Subjective
Requests interactions with significant others/spiritual leaders; Requests forgiveness of others

Connections with Powers Greater than Self
Participates in religious activities; Prays; Expresses reverence/awe; Reports mystical experiences

Objective
Connections with Others
Provides service to others
Connections with Art, Music, Literature, and Nature

Objective
Displays creative energy (e.g., writing, poetry, singing); Listens to music; Reads spiritual literature; Spends time outdoors

---

SPONTANEOUS VENTILATION, IMPAIRED

Diagnostic Division: Activity / Rest

Definition: Decreased energy reserves resulting in an inability to maintain independent breathing that is adequate to support life.

RELATED FACTORS
Metabolic factors; [hypermetabolic state (e.g., infection), nutritional deficits/depletion of energy stores]; Respiratory muscle fatigue; [Airway size/resistance; problems with secretion management]

DEFINING CHARACTERISTICS

Subjective
Reports apprehension; [Difficulty breathing]

Objective
Dyspnea; Increased metabolic rate; Increased heart rate; Increased restlessness; Decreased cooperation; Increased use of accessory muscles; Decreased tidal volume; Decreased P O_2; Decreased Sa O_2; Increased P CO_2

STRESS OVERLOAD

Diagnostic Division: Ego / Integrity

Definition: Excessive amounts and types of demands that require action.

RELATED FACTORS
Inadequate resources (e.g., financial, social, education/knowledge level); Intense, repeated stressors (e.g., family violence, chronic illness, terminal illness); Multiple co-

existing stressors (e.g., environmental threats/demands; physical threats/demands; social threats/demands)

DEFINING CHARACTERISTICS

Subjective
Reports difficulty in functioning/problems with decision making; Reports a feeling of pressure/tension/increased feelings of impatience/anger; Reports negative impact from stress (e.g., physical symptoms, psychological distress, feeling of being sick or of going to get sick); Reports excessive situational stress (e.g., rates stress level as a seven or above on a 10-point scale

Objective
Demonstrates increased feelings of impatience/anger

SUDDEN INFANT DEATH SYNDROME, RISK FOR

Diagnostic Division: Safety

Definition: At risk for sudden death of an infant under 1 year of age

RISK FACTORS
Modifiable
Delayed/lack of prenatal care; Infant overheating/overwrapping; Infant placed in prone/side—lying position to sleep; Postnatal/prenatal infant smoke exposure; Soft underlayment (loose articles in the sleep environment)

Potentially Modifiable
Low birth weight; Prematurity; Young maternal age

Nonmodifiable
Ethnicity (e.g., African-American or Native American); Infant age 2–4 months; Male gender; Seasonality of sudden infant death syndrome deaths (e.g., winter and fall months)

SUFFOCATION, RISK FOR

Diagnostic Division: Safety

Definition: At risk of accidental suffocation (inadequate air available for inhalation).

RISK FACTORS
Internal
Reduced olfactory sensation; Reduced motor abilities; Deficient knowledge regarding safety situations/precautions; Cognitive/emotional difficulties [e.g., altered consciousness/mentation]; Disease/injury process

External
Pillow/propped bottle in an infant's crib; Hanging a pacifier around infant's neck; Playing with plastic bags; Inserting small objects into airway; Leaving children unattended in water; Discarding refrigerators without removed doors; Vehicle warming in closed garage [/faulty exhaust system]; Fuel-burning heaters not vented to outside; Household gas leaks; Smoking in bed; Low-strung clothesline; Eating large mouthfuls [or pieces] of food

---

SUICIDE, RISK FOR

Diagnostic Division: Safety

Definition: At risk for self-inflicted, life-threatening injury.

RISK FACTORS
Behavioral
History of prior suicide attempt; Buying a gun; Stockpiling medicines; Making/changing a will; Giving away possessions; Sudden euphoric recovery from major depression; Impulsiveness; Marked changes in behavior/ attitude/school performance

Demographic
Age (e.g., elderly people, young adult males, adolescents); Race (e.g., Caucasian, Native American); Male gender; Divorced; Widowed

Physical
Physical/terminal illness; Chronic pain

Psychological:
Family history of suicide; Childhood abuse; Substance abuse; Psychiatric illness/disorder (e.g., depression, schizophrenia, bipolar disorder); Guilt; Homosexual youth

Situational
Living alone; Retired; Economically disadvantaged; Relocation; Institutionalization; Loss of autonomy/independence; Presence of gun in home; Adolescents living in nontraditional settings (e.g., juvenile detention center, prison, half-way house, group home)

Social
Loss of important relationship; Disrupted family life; Poor support systems; Social isolation; Grieving; Loneliness; Hopelessness; Helplessness; Legal/disciplinary problems; Cluster suicides

Verbal
Threats of killing oneself; States desire to die [/end it all]

SURGICAL RECOVERY, DELAYED

Diagnostic Division: Pain / Discomfort

Definition: Extension of the number of postoperative days required to initiate and perform activities that maintain life, health, and well-being.

RELATED FACTORS
Extensive/prolonged surgical procedure; Pain; Obesity; Preoperative expectations; Postoperative surgical site care

DEFINING CHARACTERISTICS
Subjective
Perception that more time is needed to recover; Report of pain/discomfort; Fatigue; Loss of appetite with or without nausea; Postpones resumption of work/employment activities

Objective
Evidence of interrupted healing of surgical area (e.g., red, indurated, draining, immobilized); Difficulty in moving about; Requires help to complete self-care

---

SWALLOWING, IMPAIRED

Diagnostic Division: Food / Fluid

Definition: Abnormal functioning of the swallowing mechanism associated with deficits in oral, pharyngeal, or esophageal structure or function.

RELATED FACTORS
Congenital Deficits
Upper airway anomalies; Mechanical obstruction (e.g., edema, tracheostomy tube, tumor); History of tube feeding; Neuromuscular impairment (e.g., decreased or absent gag reflex, decreased strength or excursion of muscles involved in mastication, perceptual impairment, facial paralysis); Conditions with significant hypotonia; Respiratory disorders; Congenital heart disease; Behavioral feeding problems; Self-injurious behavior; Failure to thrive; Protein-energy malnutrition

Neurological Problems
Nasal/nasopharyngeal cavity defects; Upper airway anomalies; Oropharynx/ laryngeal abnormalities; Tracheal/laryngeal/ esophageal defects; Gastroesophageal reflux disease; Achalasia; Traumas; Acquired anatomic defects; Cranial nerve involvement; Traumatic head injury; Prematurity; Developmental delay; Cerebral palsy

DEFINING CHARACTERISTICS
Subjective
Esophageal Phase Impairment
Complaints [reports] of "something stuck"; Odynophagia; Food refusal; Volume limiting; Heartburn; Epigastric pain; Nighttime coughing/awakening

Objective
Oral Phase Impairment
Weak suck resulting in inefficient nippling; Slow bolus formation; Lack of tongue action to form bolus; Premature entry of bolus; Incomplete lip closure; Food pushed out of/ falls from mouth; Lack of chewing; Coughing/choking/gagging before a swallow; Piecemeal deglutition; Abnormality in oral phase of swallow study; Inability to clear oral

cavity; Pooling in lateral sulci; Nasal reflux; Sialorrhea or drooling; Long meals with little consumption

Pharyngeal Phase Impairment

Food refusal; Altered head positions; Delayed/multiple swallows; Inadequate laryngeal elevation; Abnormality in pharyngeal phase by swallow study; Choking; Coughing; Gagging; Nasal reflux; Gurgly voice quality; Unexplained fevers; Recurrent pulmonary infections

Esophageal Phase Impairment

Observed evidence of difficulty in swallowing (e.g., stasis of food in oral cavity, coughing/choking); Abnormality in esophageal phase by swallow study; Hyperextension of head (e.g., arching during or after meals); Repetitive swallowing; Bruxism; Unexplained irritability surrounding mealtimes; Acidic-smelling breath; Regurgitation of gastric contents (wet burps); Vomitus on pillow; Vomiting; Hematemesis

---

THERAPEUTIC REGIMEN MANAGEMENT, INEFFECTIVE FAMILY

Diagnostic Division: Teaching/Learning

Definition: A pattern of regulating and integrating into family processes a program for treatment of illness and its sequelae that is unsatisfactory for meeting specific health goals.

RELATED FACTORS

Complexity of healthcare system/therapeutic regimen; Decisional conflicts; Economic difficulties; Excessive demands; Family conflict

DEFINING CHARACTERISTICS

Subjective

Reports difficulty with prescribed regimen; Reports desire to manage the illness

Objective

Inappropriate family activities for meeting health goals; Acceleration of illness symptoms of a family member; Failure to take action to reduce risk factors; Lack of attention to illness

---

THERAPEUTIC REGIMEN MANAGEMENT: READINESS FOR ENHANCED

Diagnostic Division: Teaching/Learning

Definition: A pattern of regulating and integrating into daily living programs for treatment of illness and its sequelae that are sufficient for meeting health-related goals and can be strengthened.

DEFINING CHARACTERISTICS

Subjective

Expresses desire to manage the illness (e.g., treatment, prevention); Expresses little difficulty with prescribed regimens; Describes reduction of risk factors

Objective

Choices of daily living are appropriate for meeting goals (e.g., treatment, prevention); No unexpected acceleration of illness symptoms

---

THERMAL INJURY, RISK FOR

Diagnostic Division: Safety

Definition: At risk for damage to skin and mucous membranes due to extreme temperatures

RISK FACTORS

Cognitive impairment (e.g., dementia, psychoses); Developmental level (infants, aged); Exposure to extreme temperatures; Fatigue; Inadequate supervision; Inattentiveness; Intoxication (alcohol, drug); Lack of knowledge (patient, caregiver); Lack of protective clothing (e.g., flame-retardant sleepwear, gloves, ear covering); Neuromuscular impairment (e.g., stroke, amyotrophic lateral sclerosis, multiple sclerosis); Neuropathy; Smoking; Treatment-related side effects (e.g., pharmaceutical agents); Unsafe environment

THERMOREGULATION, INEFFECTIVE

Diagnostic Division: Safety

Definition: Temperature fluctuation between hypothermia and hyperthermia.

RELATED FACTORS
Trauma [e.g., intracranial surgery, or head injury]; Illness [e.g., cerebral edema, CVA]; Extremes of age [e.g., loss/absence of brown adipose tissue]; Fluctuating environmental temperature; [Changes in hypothalamic tissue causing alterations in emission of thermosensitive cells and regulation of heat loss/production]; [Changes in metabolic rate/activity]; [Changes in level/action of thyroxine and catecholamines]; [Chemical reactions in contracting muscles]

DEFINING CHARACTERISTICS
Objective
Fluctuations in body temperature above and below the normal range; Tachycardia; Reduction in body temperature below normal range; Moderate pallor; Mild shivering; Piloerection; Cyanotic nail beds; Slow capillary refill; Hypertension; Skim warm/cool to touch; Flushed skin; Increased respiratory rate; Seizures; Increase in body temperature above normal range

TISSUE INTEGRITY, IMPAIRED

Diagnostic Division: Safety

Definition: Damage to mucous membrane, corneal, integumentary, or subcutaneous tissues.

RELATED FACTORS
Altered circulation; Nutritional factors (e.g., deficit or excess); [Metabolic/endocrine dysfunction]; Deficient/excess fluid volume; Deficient knowledge; Impaired physical mobility; Chemical irritants [e.g., body excretions, secretions, medications]; Radiation; Temperature extremes; Mechanical factors (e.g., pressure, shear, friction); [Surgery]; [Infection]

DEFINING CHARACTERISTICS
Objective
Damaged tissue (e.g., cornea, mucous membrane, integumentary, subcutaneous); Destroyed tissue

TISSUE PERFUSION, INEFFECTIVE PERIPHERAL

Diagnostic Division: Activity / Rest

Definition: Decrease in blood circulation to the periphery that may compromise health.

RELATED FACTORS
Deficient Knowledge of aggravating factors (e.g., smoking, sedentary lifestyle, trauma, obesity, salt intake, immobility); Deficient knowledge of disease process (e.g., diabetes, hyperlipidemia, [peripheral artery disease, chronic venous insufficiency]); Hypertension; Sedentary lifestyle; Smoking; Diabetes mellitus

DEFINING CHARACTERISTICS
Subjective
Extremity pain, claudication; Parasthesia; [altered sensations]

Objective
Diminished or absent pulses; [diminished arterial pulsations; bruits; blood pressure changes in extremities]; Altered skin characteristics (color, elasticity, hair, moisture, nails, sensation, temperature); Skin color pale on elevation, color does not return to leg on lowering it; [skin erythema or dependent rubor with chronic dryness, scaling, flaking]; [Varicosities, spider veins]; Edema; Altered motor function; Delayed peripheral wound healing; [ulcerations]; Ankle-brachial index < 0.90; Blood pressure changes in extremities; Capillary refill time > 3 seconds; Shorter total distances achieved in the six-minute walk test; Shorter pain free distances achieved in the six-minute walk test

TISSUE PERFUSION, RISK FOR DECREASED CARDIAC

Diagnostic Division: Activity / Rest

Definition: At risk for a decrease in cardiac (coronary) circulation that may compromise health.

RISK FACTORS
Coronary artery spasm, cardiac surgery, cardiac tamponade; Deficient knowledge of modifiable risk factors (e.g., smoking, sedentary lifestyle, obesity), hypertension, hyperlipidemia; Birth control pills; Substance abuse; Elevated C-reactive protein, hypoxemia, hypoxia; Family history of coronary artery disease; Diabetes mellitus; Hypovolemia

TISSUE PERFUSION, RISK FOR INEFFECTIVE CEREBRAL

Diagnostic Division: Activity / Rest

Definition: At risk for a decrease in cerebral tissue circulation that may compromise health.

RISK FACTORS
Head trauma, cerebral aneurysm, brain tumor, neoplasm of the brain; Carotid stenosis, aortic atherosclerosis, arterial dissection; Atrial fibrillation, sick sinus syndrome, atrial myxoma, left atrial appendage thrombosis; Recent myocardial infarction, akinetic left ventricular segment, dilated cardiomyopathy, mitral stenosis, mechanical prosthetic valve, infective endocarditis, embolism; Coagulopathy (e.g., sickle cell anemia; disseminated intravascular coagulation), abnormal partial thromboplastin time; abnormal prothrombin time; Hypertension, hypercholesterolemia; Substance abuse; Thrombolytic therapy; Treatment-related side effects (cardiopulmonary bypass, pharmaceutical agents)

TISSUE PERFUSION, RISK FOR INEFFECTIVE PERIPHERAL

Diagnostic Division: Activity / Rest

Definition: At risk for a decrease in blood circulation to the periphery that may compromise health.

RISK FACTORS
Age>60 years; Deficient knowledge of aggravating factors (e.g., smoking, sedentary lifestyle, trauma, obesity, salt intake, immobility); Deficient knowledge of disease process (e.g., diabetes, hyperlipidemia); Diabetes mellitus; Endovascular procedures; Hypertension; Sedentary Lifestyle; Smoking

TRANSFER ABILITY, IMPAIRED

Diagnostic Division: Activity / Rest

Definition: Limitation of independent movement between two nearby surfaces.

NOTE: Specify level of independence using a standardized functinal scale

RELATED FACTORS
Insufficient muscle strength; Deconditioning; Neuromuscular impairment; Musculoskeletal impairment (e.g., contractures); Impaired balance; Pain; Obesity; Impaired vision; Deficient knowledge; Cognitive impairment; Environment constraints (e.g., bed height, inadequate space, wheelchair type, treatment equipment, restraints)

DEFINING CHARACTERISTICS
Inability to transfer from: Bed to chair/chair to bed; Bed to standing/standing to bed; Chair to standing/standing to chair; Chair to floor/floor to chair; Standing to floor/floor to standing; Chair to car/car to chair; Inability to transfer: On/off a toilet or commode; In/out of tub or shower; Between uneven levels

TRAUMA, RISK FOR

Diagnostic Division: Safety

Definition: At risk of accidental tissue injury (e.g., wound, burn, fracture).

RISK FACTORS
Internal
Weakness; Balancing difficulties; Reduced muscle coordination; Reduced hand-eye coordination; Poor vision; Reduced sensation; Deficient knowledge regarding safety procedures/precautions; Economically disadvantaged; Cognitive/emotional difficulties; History of previous trauma

External [includes but is not limited to:]
Slippery floors (e.g., wet or highly waxed; Unanchored electic wires; Lacks antislip material in bath/shower; Use of unsteady ladders/chairs; Obstructed passageways; Entering unlighted rooms; Inadequate stair rails; Lack of gate at top of stairs; High beds; Inappropriate call-for-aid mechanisms for bed-bound client; Unsafe window protection in homes with young children; Pot handles facing toward front of stove; Bathing in very hot water (e.g., unsupervised bathing of young children); Potential igniting gas leaks; Delayed lighting of gas appliances; Wearing flowing clothing around open flames; Flammable children's clothing/toys; Smoking in bed/near oxygen; Grease waste collected on stoves; Children playing with dangerous objects; Accessibility of guns; Playing with explosives; Experimenting with chemicals; Inadequately stored combustibles (e.g., matches, oily rags)/ corrosives (e.g., lye); Contact with corrosives; Overloaded fuse boxes; Faulty electrical plugs; Frayed wires; Defective appliances; Overloaded electrical outlets; Exposure to dangerous machinery; Contact with rapidly moving machinery; Struggling with restraints; Contact with intense cold; Lack of protection from heat source; Overexposure to radiation; Large icicles hanging from the roof; Use of cracked dishware; Knives stored uncovered; High-crime neighborhood; Driving a mechanically unsafe vehicle; Driving at excessive speeds; Driving without necessary visual aids; Driving while intoxicated; Children riding in the front seat in car; Nonuse/misuse of seat restraints; Unsafe road/walkways; Physical proximity to vehicle pathways (e.g., direways, lanes, railroad tracks); Misuse [/nonuse] of necessary headgear [e.g., for bicycles, motorcycles, skateboarding, skiing]

UNILATERAL NEGLECT

Diagnostic Division: Perception / Cognition

Definition: Impairment in sensory and motor response, mental representation, and spatial attention of the body, and the corresponding environment, characterized by inattention to one side and overattention to the opposite side. Left-side neglect is more severe and persistent than right-side neglect.

RELATED FACTORS
Brain injury from: Cerebrovascular problems; Neurological illness; Trauma; Tumor; Left hemiplegia from cerebrovascular accident (CVA) of the right hemisphere; Hemianopsia

DEFINING CHARACTERISTICS

Subjective
[Reports feeling that part does not belong to own self]

Objective
Marked deviation of the eyes/head/trunk (as if drawn magnetically) to the non-neglected side to stimuli and activities on that side; Failure to move eyes/head/limbs/trunk in the neglected hemisphere despite being aware of a stimulus in that space; Failure to notice people approaching from the neglected side; Displacement of sounds to the non-neglected side; Appears unaware of positioning of neglected limb; Lack of safety precautions with regard to the neglected side; Failure to: eat food from portion of the plate on the neglected side; dress/groom neglected side; Difficulty remembering details of internally represented familiar scenes that are on the neglected side; Use of only vertical half of page when writing; Failure to cancel lines on the half of the page on the neglected side; Substitution of letters to form alternative words that are similar to the original in length when reading; Distortion/omission of drawing on the half of the page on the neglected side; Perseveration of visual motor tasks on non-neglected side; Transfer of pain sensation to the non-neglected side

URINARY ELIMINATION, IMPAIRED

Diagnostic Division: Elimination

Definition: Dysfunction in urine elimination.

RELATED FACTORS

Multiple causality; Sensory motor impairment; Anatomical obstruction; UTI; [Mechanical trauma; [Fluid/volume states]; [Psychogenic factors]; [Surgical diversion]

DEFINING CHARACTERISTICS

Subjective

Frequency; Urgency; Hesitancy; Dysuria; Nocturia; [Enuresis]

Objective

Incontinence; Retention

URINARY ELIMINATION, READINESS FOR ENHANCED

Diagnostic Division: Elimination

Definition: A pattern of urinary functions that is sufficient for meeting eliminatory needs and can be strengthened

DEFINING CHARACTERISTICS

Subjective

Expresses willingness to enhance urinary elimination; Positions self for emptying of bladder

Objective

Urine is straw colored/odorless; Amount of output/specific gravity is within normal limits; Fluid intake is adequate for daily needs

URINARY RETENTION [ACUTE/CHRONIC]

Diagnostic Division: Elimination

Definition: Incomplete emptying of the bladder.

RELATED FACTORS

High urethral pressure; Inhibition of reflex arc; Strong sphincter; Blockage [e.g., benign prostatic hypertrophy—BPH, perineal swelling]; [Habituation of reflex arc]; [Infections]; [Neurological diseases/trauma]; [Use of medications with side effect of retention (e.g., atropine, belladonna, psychotropics, antihistamines, opiates)]

DEFINING CHARACTERISTICS

Subjective

Sensation of bladder fullness; Dribbling; Dysuria

Objective

Bladder distension; Small, frequent voiding or absence of urine output; Residual urine [150 ml or more]; Overflow incontinence; [Reduced stream]

VASCULAR TRAUMA, RISK FOR

Diagnostic Division: Safety

Definition: At risk for damage to a vein and its surrounding tissues related to the presence of a catheter and/or infused solutions.

RISK FACTORS

Insertion site, impaired ability to visualize the insertion site; Catheter type, catheter width; Nature of solution (e.g., concentration, chemical irritant, temperature, pH), infusion rate, length of insertion time; Inadequate catheter fixation

VENTILATORY WEANING RESPONSE, DYSFUNCTIONAL (DVWR)

Diagnostic Division: Activity / Rest

Definition: Inability to adjust to lowered levels of mechanical ventilator support that interrupts and prolongs the weaning process.

RELATED FACTORS
Physiological

Ineffective airway clearance; Sleep pattern disturbance; Inadequate nutrition; Uncontrolled pain; [Muscle weakness/fatigue]; [Inability to control respiratory muscles]; [Immobility]

Psychological
Deficient knowledge of the weaning process; Perceived inefficacy about the ability to wean; Decreased motivation; Decreased self-esteem; Anxiety; Fear; Insufficient trust in healthcare providers; Hopelessness; Powerlessness; [Unprepared for weaning attempt]

Situational
Uncontrolled episodic energy demands; Inappropriate pacing of diminished ventilator support; Inadequate social support; Adverse environment (e.g., noisy, active environment, negative events in the room, low nurse:patient ratio; unfamiliar nursing staff, [extended nurse absence from bedside]); History of ventilator dependence > 4 days; History of multiple unsuccessful weaning attempts

DEFINING CHARACTERISTICS
Responds to lowered levels of mechanical ventilator support with:

Mild DVWR

Subjective
Reports feelings of increased need for oxygen; Breathing discomfort; Fatigue; Warmth; Queries about possible machine malfunction

Objective
Restlessness; Slight increase of respiratory rate from baseline; Increased concentration on breathing

Moderate DVWR

Subjective
Reports apprehension

Objective
Slight increase from baseline blood pressure (<20 mm Hg); Slight increase from baseline heart rate (<20 beats/min); Baseline increase in respiratory rate (<5 breaths/min); Minimal respiratory accessory muscle use; Decreased air entry on auscultation; Hypervigilance to activities; Wide-eyed look; Inability to respond to coaching/cooperate; Diaphoresis; Color changes; Pale; Slight cyanosis

Severe DVWR

Objective
Agitation; Decreased level of consciousness; Deterioration in arterial blood gases [ABGs] from current baseline; Increase from baseline BP (>20 mm Hg); Increase from baseline heart rate (>20 beats/min); Respiratory rate increases significantly from baseline; Full respiratory accessory muscle use; Shallow/gasping breaths; Paradoxical abdominal breathing; Adventitious breath sounds; Audible airway secretions; Asynchronized breathing with the ventilator; Profuse diaphoresis; Cyanosis

---

VERBAL COMMUNICATION, IMPAIRED

Diagnostic Division: Perception / Cognition

Definition: Decreased, delayed, or absent ability to receive, process, transmit, and/or use a system of symbols.

RELATED FACTORS
Decreased circulation to brain; Brain tumor; Anatomic defect (e.g., cleft palate, alteration of the neurovascular visual system, auditory system, or phonatory apparatus); Differences related to developmental age; Physical barrier (tracheostomy, intubation); Physiological conditions [e.g., dyspnea]; Alteration of central nervous system (CNS); Weakened musculoskeletal system; Psychological barriers (e.g., psychosis, lack of stimuli); Emotional conditions [depression, panic, anger]; Stress; Environmental barriers; Cultural differences; Lack of information; Treatment-related side effects (e.g., pharmaceutical agents); Alteration in self-concept; Chronic/situational low self-esteem; Altered perceptions; Absence of Significant others.

DEFINING CHARACTERISTICS

Subjective
[Reports of difficulty expressing self]

Objective
Inability to speak language of caregiver; Speaks/verbalizes with difficulty; Stuttering; Slurring; Does not/cannot speak; Willful refusal to speak; Difficulty forming words/sentences (e.g., aphonia, dyslalia, dysarthria); Difficulty expressing thoughts verbally (e.g., aphasia, dysphasia, apraxia, dyslexia); Inappropriate verbalization, [incessant, loose association of ideas, flight of ideas]; Difficulty in comprehending/maintaining

usual communication pattern; Absence of eye contact; Difficulty in selective attending; Partial/total visual deficit; Inability/difficulty in use of facial/body expressions; Disorientation to person/space/time; Dyspnea; [Inability to modulate speech]; [Message inappropriate to content]; [Use of nonverbal cues (e.g., pleading eyes, gestures, turning away)]; [Frustration; Anger; Hostility]

WALKING, IMPAIRED

Diagnostic Division: Activity / Rest

Definition: Limitation of independent movement within the environment on foot.

NOTE: Specify level of independence using a standardized functional scale

RELATED FACTORS
Insufficient muscle strength; Neuromuscular impairment; Musculoskeletal impairment (e.g., contractures); Limited endurance; Deconditioning; Fear of falling; Impaired balance; Impaired vision; Pain; Obesity; Depressed mood; Cognitive impairment; Lack of knowledge; Environmental constraints (e.g., stairs, inclines, uneven surfaces, unsafe obstacles, distances, lack of assistive devices or person, restraints)

DEFINING CHARACTERISTICS
Impaired ability to: Walk required distances; Walk on an incline/decline; Walk on uneven surfaces; Navigate curbs; Climb stairs

WANDERING [Specify sporadic or continual]

Diagnostic Division: Activity / Rest

Definition: Meandering, aimless, or repetitive locomotion that exposes the individual to harm; frequently incongruent with boundaries, limits, or obstacles.

RELATED FACTORS
Cognitive impairment (e.g., memory and recall deficits, disorientation, poor visuoconstructive or visuospatial ability, language defects); Sedation; Cortical atrophy; Premorbid behavior (e.g., outgoing, sociable personality; premorbid dementia); Separation from familiar environment; Overstimulating environment; Emotional state (e.g., frustration, anxiety, boredom, depression, agitation); Physiological state or need (e.g., hunger, thirst, pain, urination, constipation); Time of day

DEFINING CHARACTERISTICS
Objective
Frequent/continuous movement from place to place, often revisiting the same destinations; Persistent locomotion in search of something; Scanning/ searching behaviors; Haphazard locomotion; Fretful locomotion/pacing; Long periods of locomotion without an apparent destination; Locomotion into unauthorized or private spaces; Trespassing; Locomotion resulting in unintended leaving of a premises; Inability to locate significant landmarks in a familiar setting; Getting lost; Locomotion that cannot be easily dissuaded; Shadowing a caregiver's locomotion; Hyperactivity; Periods of locomotion interspersed with periods of nonlocomotion (e.g., sitting, standing, sleeping)